ANNUAL STATEMENT STUDIES

FINANCIAL RATIO BENCHMARKS

2014
2015

RMA
Annual Statement Studies®
Copyright, Ordering, Licensing, and Use of Data

To **obtain permission** to copy, quote, reproduce, replicate, disseminate, or distribute the Statement Studies® data/material please fax or e-mail a brief letter stating who you are and how you intend to use the Statement Studies® data to: Statement Studies Information Products at fax number 215-446-4100 or via e-mail to studies@rmahq.org. Depending on the requested use, RMA may require a license agreement and royalty fee. A **License Agreement is required** if you wish to use or incorporate any portion of the data, in whole or in part in other products that will in turn be sold to others, such as in software oriented or derived products, scholarly publications, or training materials.

To **purchase** a copy, or additional copies, of the Statement Studies® data in book or online format, contact RMA's Customer Relations at 1-800-677-7621. Regional data presented in the same fashion as you see in this book is only available in eStatement Studies.

If you have a **question regarding the data** please reference the detailed explanatory notes provided in the Introduction section of the enclosed product. If you are unable to find the answer to your question please contact us by e-mail at: studies@rmahq.org. Be sure to include your detailed question along with your telephone number, fax number, and e-mail address.

The Risk Management Association
1801 Market Street, Suite 300
Philadelphia, PA 19103

ISBN# 978-1-57070-334-8

TABLE OF CONTENTS

Information on Copyright, Ordering, Licensing, and use of Data 2
List of Participating Institutions 5
Introduction to Statement Studies and Organization of Content 7
Definition of Ratios 10
Explanation of Noncontractor Balance Sheet and Income Data 19
Explanation of Contractor—Percentage-of-Completion Basis of Accounting 20
IDP Sample Report 23
NAICS Codes Appearing in the Statement Studies 27
Full Descriptions of Industries Appearing in the Statement Studies 33

	Description Index	Data Set Begins On
Agriculture, Forestry, Fishing and Hunting	33	95
Mining	34	157
Utilities	35	173
Construction—General Industries Format*	36	187
Manufacturing	39	249
Wholesale Trade	57	759
Retail Trade	62	901
Transportation and Warehousing	66	1023
Information	69	1099
Finance and Insurance	71	1139
Real Estate and Rental and Leasing	72	1193
Professional, Scientific and Technical Services	74	1235
Management of Companies and Enterprises	78	1319
Administrative and Support and Waste Management and Remediation Services	78	1325
Educational Services	81	1389
Health Care and Social Assistance	82	1411
Arts, Entertainment and Recreation	86	1489
Accommodation and Food Services	87	1529
Other Services (Except Public Administration)	88	1553
Public Administration	91	1627
Construction—Percentage of Completion Basis of Accounting*	92	1653

Supplemental Information:

Construction Financial Management Association Data 1673
Text—Key Word Index of Industries Appearing in the Statement Studies 1677
RMA's Credit & Lending Dictionary 1685

*General Industries Format means that a valid construction NAICS was assigned to the subject companies contained in the sample; however, the financial statements were prepared using a general or traditional manufacturing or service industries presentation of results versus using a percentage-of-completion method of accounting. Industries found in the percentage-of-completion presentation follow the presentation used by RMA in the past.

About RMA

Founded in 1914, The Risk Management Association is a not-for-profit, member-driven professional association whose sole purpose is to advance the use of sound risk principles in the financial services industry. RMA promotes an enterprise approach to risk management that focuses on credit risk, market risk, and operational risk.

Headquartered in Philadelphia, Pennsylvania, RMA has 2,500 institutional members that include banks of all sizes as well as nonbank financial institutions. They are represented in the association by 16,000 risk management professionals who are chapter members in financial centers throughout North America, Europe, and Asia/Pacific. Visit RMA on the Web at www.rmahq.org.

RMA ACKNOWLEDGES AND THANKS THE FOLLOWING INSTITUTIONS, CONTRIBUTORS TO THE 2014 STATEMENT STUDIES DATA SUBMISSION PROGRAM.

Alabama

BBVA Compass
Regions Bank

Arkansas

Simmons First National Bank

California

Bank of Agriculture & Commerce
Bank of Stockton
Bank of the West
Citizens Business Bank
First Banks Inc.
Grandpoint Bank
Pacific Enterprise Bank
Wells Fargo Bank N.A.
Westamerica Bank

Colorado

CoBank
Sunflower Bank N.A.

Connecticut

Chelsea Groton Bank
Dime Bank
The Milford Bank

Florida

Bank of Tampa
CenterState Bank
Seacoast National Bank

Georgia

Georgia Bank & Trust
SunTrust Banks
United Community Bank

Hawaii

American Savings Bank
Central Pacific Bank
Finance Factors Ltd.
First Hawaiian Bank

Illinois

Alpine Bank & Trust Co.
National Republic Bank Chicago
Old National Bank
The Northern Trust Company
TCF National Bank

Indiana

1st Source Bank
First Federal Savings Bank Evansville
Home Building Savings Bank
Lake City Bank
Old National Bank
STAR Financial Bank

Iowa

American Trust & Saving Bank
Farmers State Bank - Marion
Heartland Financial USA, Inc.
MidWestOne Bank
Peoples Trust & Savings Bank
Security National Bank

Kansas

Carson Bank
Emprise Bank
Fidelity Bank
INTRUST Bank, N.A.
Sunflower Bank N.A.

Kentucky

Community Trust Bank Inc.
Old National Bank

Louisiana

Whitney Bank

Maine

Gorham Savings Bank
Kennebunk Savings
Norway Savings Bank
The First NA

Maryland

Country First Bank
First United Bank & Trust
Frederick County Bank
New Windsor State Bank
OBA Bank
Sandy Spring Bank
Susquehanna Bank Inc.
The Bank of Glen Burnie
The Columbia Bank

Massachusetts

BankFive
Bristol County Savings Bank
Eastern Bank
Enterprise Bank & Trust Co.
North Middlesex Savings Bank
PeoplesBank
The Lowell Five Cent Savings Bank

Michigan

Citizens National Bank of Cheboygan
Commercial Bank
Mercantile Bank of Michigan
Talmer Bank & Trust
TCF National Bank
The State Bank

Minnesota

AgriBank FCB
AgStar Financial Services
American Bank of Saint Paul
Anchor Bank
Beacon Bank
Citizens Independent Bank
Community Bank Corporation
Fidelity Bank
First Minnetonka City Bank
KleinBank
North Star Bank
Roundbank
Stearns Bank N.A.
TCF National Bank
US Bank N.A.

Mississippi

Hancock Bank
The Peoples Bank
Trustmark National Bank

Missouri

Armed Forces Bank
Cass Commercial Bank
Commerce Bank N.A.
First Banks Inc.
Hawthorn Bank
Pulaski Bank
Royal Banks of Missouri
Sunflower Bank N.A.

Montana

First Interstate Bancsystem
First National Bank of North Platte
First National Bank of Omaha

New Hampshire

Connecticut River Bank N.A.
Fulton Bank of New Jersey
Peapack-Gladstone Bank
Sun National Bank
TD BankNorth N.A.

New York

Canandaigua National Bank & Trust
CIT Group
Community Bank N.A.
Elmira Savings Bank
M & T Bank
NBT Bank N.A.
Pioneer Bank
Steuben Trust Company
The Adirondack Trust Company
The Adirondack Trust Company
Tioga State Bank
Tompkins Trust Co.

North Carolina

Bank of America
BB&T
First Citizens Bank & Trust Co.
HomeTrust Bank

North Dakota

Bell State Bank & Trust

Ohio

FirstMerit Bank N.A.
Huntington National Bank
KeyCorp
Liberty Savings Bank FSB
WesBanco Bank Inc.

Oregon

Columbia State Bank
Pacific Continental Bank
People's Bank of Commerce
Umpqua Bank

Pennsylvania

AmeriServ Financial Bank
Bryn Mawr Trust
CNB Bank
Community Bank
DNB First
Dollar Bank FSB
Ephrata National Bank
First Columbia Bank & Trust Co.
First Commonwealth Bank
First National Bank of Pennsylvania
Firstrust Bank
Fulton Bank
Lafayette Ambassador Bank
Luzerne Bank
National Penn Bank
New Tripoli Bank
Orrstown Bank
PeoplesBank a Codorus Valley Company
PNC Bank
QNB Bank
S&T Bank
Santander Bank N.A.
Somerset Trust Company
Washington Financial Bank
WesBanco Bank Inc.
Woodlands Bank
York Traditions Bank

Rhode Island

Citizens Financial Group
Coastway Community Bank
Washington Trust Company

South Carolina

Greer State Bank
Harbor National Bank

South Dakota

First Interstate Bancsystem
First National Bank in Sioux Falls
First National Bank of Omaha
First PREMIER Bank

Tennessee

First Farmers and Merchants Bank
First Tennessee Bank
Paragon Bank

Texas

Amarillo National Bank
American Bank of Texas
Comerica Bank
Extraco Banks N.A.
First State Bank Central Texas
Frost Bank
Independent Bank
Southside Bank
Southwest Bank

Utah

Zions Bancorporation

Vermont

Community National Bank
Merchants Bank
The Bank of Bennington

Virginia

Capital One
First Community Bank
Monarch Bank
United Bank
Virginia National Bank

Washington

Banner Bank
Columbia State Bank
Heritage Bank formerly Whidbey Island Bank
Northwest Farm Credit Services
Security State Bank
Washington Federal
Washington Trust Bank

West Virginia

United Bank
WesBanco Bank Inc.

Wisconsin

Associated Bank National Association
Bank of Sun Prairie
First National Bank and Trust Company
Foundations Bank
Horicon Bank
TCF National Bank
The Business Bank

Wyoming

First Interstate Bancsystem

Introduction to *Annual Statement Studies: Financial Ratio Benchmarks, 2014-2015* and General Organization of Content

The notes below will explain the presentation of *Annual Statement Studies: Financial Ratio Benchmarks,* describe how the book is organized, and answer most of your questions.

- **The Quality You Expect from RMA:** RMA is the most respected source of objective, unbiased information on issues of importance to credit risk professionals. For over 95 years, RMA's *Annual Statement Studies*® has been the industry standard for comparison financial data. Material contained in today's *Annual Statement Studies* was first published in the March 1919 issue of the *Federal Reserve Bulletin.* In the days before computers, the *Annual Statement Studies* data was recorded in pencil on yellow ledger paper! Today, it features data for over 778 industries derived directly from more than 276,000 statements of financial institutions' borrowers and prospects.

- **Data That Comes Straight from Original Sources:** The more than 276,000 statements used to produce the composites presented here come directly from RMA member institutions and represent the financials from their commercial customers and prospects. RMA does not know the names of the individual entities. In fact, to ensure confidentiality, company names are removed before the data is even delivered to RMA. The raw data making up each composite is not available to any third party.

- **Data Presented in Common Size:** *Annual Statement Studies: Financial Ratio Benchmarks* contains composite financial data. Balance sheet and income statement information is shown in common size format, with each item a percentage of total assets and sales. RMA computes common size statements for each individual statement in an industry group, then aggregates and averages all the figures. In some cases, because of computer rounding, the figures to the right of the decimal point do not balance exactly with the totals shown. A minus sign beside the value indicates credits and losses.

- **Includes the Most Widely Used Ratios:** Nineteen of the most widely used ratios in the financial services industry accompany the balance sheet information, including various types of liquidity, coverage, leverage, and operating ratios.

- **Organized by the NAICS for Ease of Use:** This edition is organized according to the North American Industry Classification System (NAICS), a product of the U.S. Office of Management and Budget. At the top of each page of data, you will find the NAICS. Please note, in the revised 2012 catalog some industries were merged to create its new 2012 NAICS. In these instances, RMA recalculated aggregate historical reporting. For detailed 2012 and 2007 NAICS mapping, please visit the RMA site or: http://www.census.gov/eos/www/naics/

- **Twenty Sections Outline Major Types of Businesses:** To provide further delineation, the book is divided into 20 sections outlining major lines of businesses. If you know the NAICS number you are looking for, use the NAICS-page guide provided in the front of this book. In general, the book is arranged in ascending NAICS numerical order. For your convenience, full descriptions of each NAICS are presented in this book. In addition, you will find a text-based index near the end of the book.

- **If You Do Not Know the NAICS Code You Are Looking for...** If you do not know the precise industry NAICS you are looking for, contact the Census Bureau at 1-888-75NAICS or naics@census.gov. Describe the activity of the establishment for which you need an industry code and you will receive a reply. Another source to help you assign the correct NAICS industry name and number can be found at www.census.gov/epcd/www/naics.html.

- **Can't Find the Industry You Want?** There are a number of reasons you may not find the industry you are looking for (i.e., you know you need industry xxxxxx but it is not in the product). Many times we have information on an industry, but it is not published because the sample size was too small or there were significant questions concerning the data. (For an industry to be displayed in the *Annual Statement Studies: Financial Ratio Benchmarks,* there must be at least 30 valid statements submitted to RMA.) In other instances, we simply do not have the data. Generally, most of what we receive is published.

- **Composite Data Not Shown?** When there are fewer than 10 financial statements in a particular asset or sales size category, the composite data is not shown because a sample this small is not considered representative and could be misleading. However, all the data for that industry is shown in the All Sizes column. The total number of statements for each size category is shown in bold print at the top of each column. In addition, the number of statements used in a ratio array will differ from the number of statements in a sample because certain elements of data may not be present in all financial statements. In these cases, the number of statements used is shown in parentheses to the left of the array.

- **Presentation of the Data on Each Page-Spread:** For all non-contracting spread statements, the data for a particular industry appears on both the left and right pages. The heading Current Data Sorted by Assets is in the five columns on the left side. The center section of the double-page presentation contains the Comparative Historical Data, with the All Sizes column for the current year shown under the heading 4/1/13-3/31/14. Comparable data from past editions of the *Annual Statement Studies: Financial Ratio Benchmarks* also appears in this section. Current Data Sorted by Sales is displayed in the five columns to the far right.

- **Companies with Less than $250 Million in Total Assets:** In our presentation, we used companies having less than $250 million in total assets—except in the case of contractors who use the percentage-of-completion method of accounting. *The section for contractors using the percentage-of-completion method of accounting contains data only sorted by revenue.* There is no upper limit placed on revenue size for any industry. Its information is found on only one page.

- **Page Headers:** The information shown at the top of each page includes the following: 1) the identity of the industry group; 2) its North American Industry Classification (NAICS) code; 3) a breakdown by size categories of the types of financial statements reported; 4) the number of statements in each category; 5) the dates of the statements used; and 6) the size categories. For instance, 16 (4/1-9/30/13) means that 16 statements with fiscal dates between April 1 and September 30, 2013 make up part of the sample.

- **Page Footers:** At the bottom of each page, we have included the sum of the sales (or revenues) and total assets for all the financial statements in each size category. This data allows recasting of the common size statements into dollar amounts. To do this, divide the number at the bottom of the page by the number of statements in that size category. Then multiply the result by the percentages in the common size statement.
  Please note: The dollar amounts will be an approximation because RMA computes the balance sheet and income statement percentages for each individual statement in an industry group, then aggregates and averages all the figures.

- **Our Thanks to CFMA:** RMA appreciates the cooperation of the Construction Financial Management Association in permitting us to reproduce excerpts from its *Construction Industry Annual Financial Survey*. This data complements the RMA contractor industry data. For more details on this data, please visit www.cfma.org.

- **Recommended for Use as General Guidelines:** RMA recommends you use *Annual Statement Studies: Financial Ratio Benchmarks* data only as general guidelines and not as absolute industry norms. There are several reasons why the data may not be fully representative of a given industry:

  1. **Data Not Random**—The financial statements used in the *Annual Statement Studies: Financial Ratio Benchmarks* are not selected by any random or statistically reliable method. RMA member banks voluntarily submit the raw data they have available each year with no limitation on company size.

  2. **Categorized by Primary Product Only**—Many companies have varied product lines; however, the *Annual Statement Studies: Financial Ratio Benchmarks* categorizes them by their primary product NAICS number only.

3. **Small Samples**—Some of the industry samples are small in relation to the total number of firms for a given industry. A relatively small sample can increase the chances that some composites do not fully represent an industry.

4. **Extreme Statements**—An extreme or outlier statement can occasionally be present in a sample, causing a disproportionate influence on the industry composite. This is particularly true in a relatively small sample.

5. **Operational Differences**—Companies within the same industry may differ in their method of operations, which in turn can directly influence their financial statements. Since they are included in the sample, these statements can significantly affect the composite calculations.

6. **Additional Considerations**—There are other considerations that can result in variations among different companies engaged in the same general line of business. These include different labor markets, geographical location, different accounting methods, quality of products handled, sources and methods of financing, and terms of sale.

For these reasons, RMA does not recommend using the *Annual Statement Studies: Financial Ratio Benchmarks* figures as absolute norms for a given industry. Rather, you should use the figures only as general guidelines and as a supplement to the other methods of financial analysis. RMA makes no claim regarding how representative the figures printed in this book are.

DEFINITION OF RATIOS

Introduction

On each data page, below the common-size balance sheet and income statement information, you will find a series of ratios computed from the financial statement data.

Here is how these figures are calculated for any given ratio:

1. The ratio is computed for each financial statement in the sample.
2. These values are arrayed (listed) in an order from the strongest to the weakest. In interpreting ratios, the "strongest" or "best" value is not always the largest numerical value, nor is the "weakest" always the lowest numerical value. (For certain ratios, there may be differing opinions as to what constitutes a strong or a weak value. RMA follows general banking guidelines consistent with sound credit practice to resolve this problem.)
3. The array of values is divided into four groups of equal size. The description of each ratio appearing in the *Statement Studies* provides details regarding the arraying of the values.

What Are Quartiles?

Each ratio has three points, or "cut-off values," that divide an array of values into four equal-sized groups called quartiles, as shown below. The quartiles include the upper quartile, upper-middle quartile, lower-middle quartile, and the lower quartile. The upper quartile is the cut-off value where one-quarter of the array of ratios falls between it and the strongest ratio. The median is the midpoint—that is, the middle cut-off value where half of the array falls above it and half below it. The lower quartile is the point where one-quarter of the array falls between it and the weakest ratio. In many cases, the average of two values is used to arrive at the quartile value. You will find the median and quartile values on all *Statement Studies* data pages in the order indicated in the chart below.

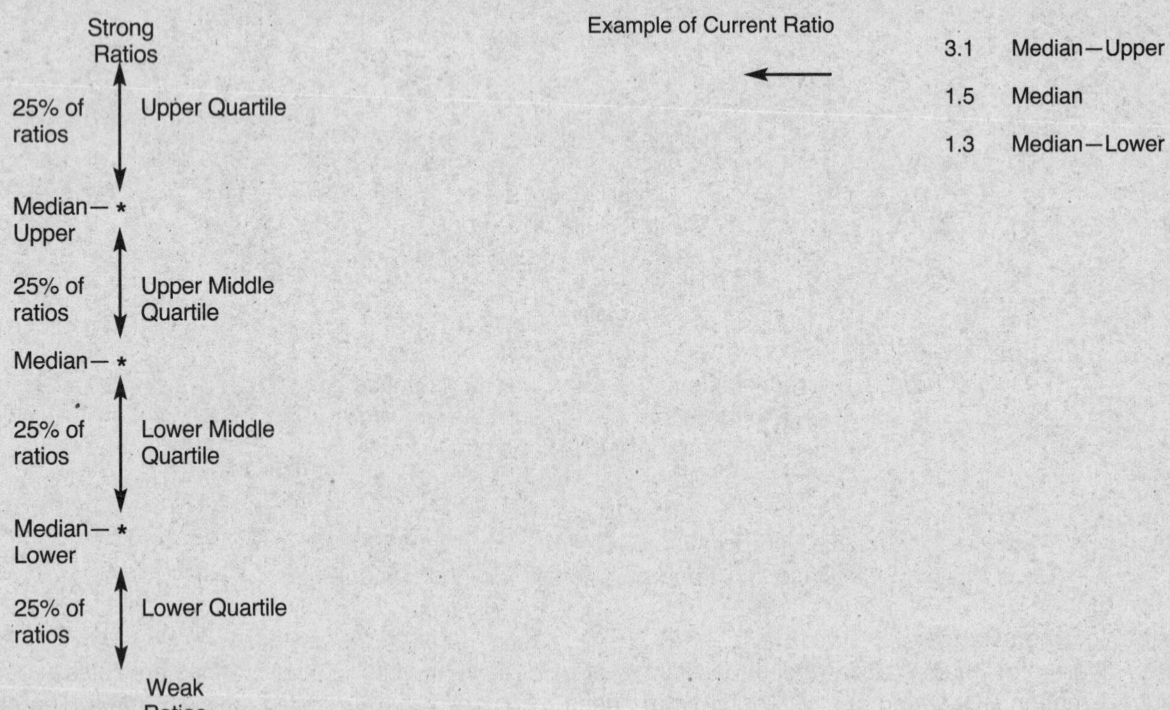

Why Use Medians/Quartiles Instead of the Average?

There are several reasons medians and quartiles are used instead of an average. Medians and quartiles eliminate the influence an "outlier" (an extremely high or low value compared to the rest of the values). They also more accurately reflect the ranges of ratio values than a straight averaging method would.

It is important to understand that the spread (range) between the upper and lower quartiles represents the middle 50% of all the companies in a sample. Therefore, ratio values greater than the upper quartile or less than the lower quartile may begin to approach "unusual" values.

Non-Conventional Values:

For some ratio values, you will occasionally see an entry that is other than a conventional number. These entries are defined as follows:

(1) UND—This stands for "undefined," the result of the denominator in a ratio calculation approaching zero.

(2) NM—This may occasionally appear as a quartile or median for the ratios sales/working capital, debt/worth, and fixed/worth. It stands for "no meaning" in cases where the dispersion is so small that any interpretation is meaningless.

(3) 999.8—When a ratio value equals 1,000 or more, it also becomes an "unusual" value and is given the "999.8" designation. This is considered to be a close enough approximation to the actual unusually large value.

Linear versus Nonlinear Ratios:

An array that is ordered in ascending sequence or in descending sequence is linear. An array that deviates from true ascending or true descending when its values change from positive to negative (low to high positive, followed by high to low negative) is non-linear.

A specific example of a nonlinear ratio would be the Sales/Working Capital ratio. In other words, when the Sales/Working Capital ratio is positive, then the top quartile would be represented by the *lowest positive* ratio. However, if the ratio is negative, the top quartile will be represented by the *highest negative* ratio! In a nonlinear array such as this, the median could be either positive or negative because it is whatever the middle value is in the particular array of numbers.

Nonlinear Ratios

Sales/Working Capital
Fixed/Worth
Debt/Worth

Linear Ratios

Current Ratio
Quick Ratio
Sales Receivables
Days' Receivables
Cost of Sales/Inventory
Days' Inventory
Cost of Sales/Payables
Days' Payables
EBIT/Interest
Net Profit + Deprec, Depletion, Amort/Current Maturities Long-Term Debt
% Profits Before Taxes/Tangible Net Worth
% Profits Before Taxes/Total Assets
Sales/Net Fixed Assets
Sales/Total Assets
% Depreciation, Depletion, Amortization/Sales
% Officers', Directors', Owners' Compensation/Sales

Important Notes on Ratios:

Turnover Ratios—For certain ratios (sales/receivables, cost of sales/inventory, cost of sales/payables) you will see two numbers, one in **BOLD** and one in regular type. These ratios are generally called turnover ratios. The number in **BOLD** represents **the number of days** and the number in regular type is the **number of times**. Please see the definition of sales/receivables on the following pages for a more complete description of the two types of calculations and what each means.

Inventory Presentations—**Inventory presentations** are based on fiscal year-end point-in-time balances, not averages. In addition, our data capture does not permit us to know what method of inventory accounting (LIFO or FIFO, for instance) was used.

The following ratios contained in the *Statement Studies* are grouped into five principal categories: liquidity, coverage, leverage, operating, and specific expense items.

LIQUIDITY RATIOS

Liquidity is a measure of the quality and adequacy of current assets to meet current obligations as they come due. In other words, can a firm quickly convert its assets to cash—without a loss in value—in order to meet its immediate and short-term obligations? For firms such as utilities that can readily and accurately predict their cash inflows, liquidity is not nearly as critical as it is for firms like airlines or manufacturing businesses that can have wide fluctuations in demand and revenue streams. These ratios provide a level of comfort to lenders in case of liquidation.

1. Current Ratio

How to Calculate: Divide total current assets by total current liabilities.

$$\frac{\text{Total Current Assets}}{\text{Total Current Liabilities}}$$

How to Interpret: This ratio is a rough indication of a firm's ability to service its current obligations. Generally, the higher the current ratio, the greater the "cushion" between current obligations and a firm's ability to pay them. While a stronger ratio shows that the numbers for current assets exceed those for current liabilities, the composition and quality of current assets are critical factors in the analysis of an individual firm's liquidity.

The ratio values are arrayed from the highest positive to the lowest positive.

2. Quick Ratio

How to Calculate: Add cash and equivalents to trade receivables. Then, divide by total current liabilities.

$$\frac{\text{Cash \& Equivalents + Trade Receivables (net)}}{\text{Total Current Liabilities}}$$

How to Interpret: Also known as the "acid test" ratio, this is a stricter, more conservative measure of liquidity than the current ratio. This ratio reflects the degree to which a company's current liabilities are covered by its most liquid current assets, the kind of assets that can be converted quickly to cash and at amounts close to book value. Inventory and other less liquid current assets are removed from the calculation. Generally, if the ratio produces a value that's less than 1 to 1, it implies a "dependency" on inventory or other "less" current assets to liquidate short-term debt.

The ratio values are arrayed from the highest positive to the lowest positive.

3. Sales/Receivables

How to Calculate: Divide net sales by trade receivables.

$$\frac{\text{Net Sales}}{\text{Trade Receivables (net)}}$$

Please note—In the contractor section, both accounts receivable-progress billings and accounts receivable-current retention are included in the receivables figure used in calculating the revenues/receivables and receivables/payables ratios.

How to Interpret: This ratio measures the number of times trade receivables turn over during the year. The higher the turnover of receivables, the shorter the time between sale and cash collection.

> For example, a company with sales of $720,000 and receivables of $120,000 would have a sales/receivables ratio of 6.0. This means receivables turn over six times a year. If a company's receivables appear to be turning more slowly than the rest of the industry, further research is needed and the quality of the receivables should be examined closely.

Cautions—A problem with this ratio is that it compares one day's receivables, shown at statement date, to total annual sales and does not take into consideration seasonal fluctuations. An additional problem in interpretation may arise when there is a large proportion of cash sales to total sales.

When the receivables figure is zero, the quotient will be undefined (UND) and represents the best possible ratio. The ratio values are therefore arrayed starting with undefined (UND) and then from the numerically highest value to the numerically lowest value. The only time a zero will appear in the array is when the sales figure is low and the quotient rounds off to zero. By definition, this ratio cannot be negative.

4. Days' Receivables

The sales/receivables ratio will have a figure printed in bold type directly to the left of the array. This figure is the days' receivables.

How to Calculate the Days' Receivables: Divide the sales/receivables ratio into 365 (the number of days in one year).

$$\frac{365}{\text{Sales/Receivable ratio}}$$

How to Interpret the Days' Receivables: This figure expresses the average number of days that receivables are outstanding. Generally, the greater the number of days outstanding, the greater the probability of delinquencies in accounts receivable. A comparison of a company's daily receivables may indicate the extent of a company's control over credit and collections.

Please note—You should take into consideration the terms offered by a company to its customers because these may differ from terms within the industry.

> For example, using the sales/receivable ratio calculated above, 365 ÷ 6 = 61 (i.e., the average receivable is collected in 61 days).

5. Cost of Sales/Inventory

How to Calculate: Divide cost of sales by inventory.

$$\frac{\text{Cost of Sales}}{\text{Inventory}}$$

How to Interpret: This ratio measures the number of times inventory is turned over during the year.

High Inventory Turnover—On the positive side, high inventory turnover can indicate greater liquidity or superior merchandising. Conversely, it can indicate a shortage of needed inventory for sales.

Low Inventory Turnover—Low inventory turnover can indicate poor liquidity, possible overstocking, or obsolescence. On the positive side, it could indicate a planned inventory buildup in the case of material shortages.

Cautions—A problem with this ratio is that it compares one day's inventory to cost of goods sold and does not take seasonal fluctuations into account. When the inventory figure is zero, the quotient will be undefined (UND) and represents the best possible ratio. The ratio values are arrayed starting with undefined (UND) and then from the numerically highest value to the numerically lowest value. The only time a zero will appear in the array is when the figure for cost of sales is very low and the quotient rounds off to zero.

Please note—For service industries, the cost of sales is included in operating expenses. In addition, please note that the data collection process does not differentiate the method of inventory valuation.

6. Days' Inventory

The days' inventory is the figure printed in bold directly to the left of the cost of sales/inventory ratio.

How to Calculate the Days' Inventory: Divide the cost of sales/inventory ratio into 365 (the number of days in one year).

$$\frac{365}{\text{Cost of Sales/Inventory ratio}}$$

How to Interpret: Dividing the inventory turnover ratio into 365 days yields the average length of time units are in inventory.

7. Cost of Sales/Payables

How to Calculate: Divide cost of sales by trade payables.

$$\frac{\text{Cost of Sales}}{\text{Trade Payables}}$$

Please note—In the contractor section, both accounts payable-trade and accounts payable-retention are included in the payables figure used in calculating the cost of revenues/payables and receivables/payables ratios.

How to Interpret: This ratio measures the number of times trade payables turn over during the year. The higher the turnover of payables, the shorter the time between purchase and payment. If a company's payables appear to be turning more slowly than the industry, then the company may be experiencing cash shortages, disputing invoices with suppliers, enjoying extended terms, or deliberately expanding its trade credit. The ratio comparison of company to industry suggests the existence of these or other possible causes. If a firm buys on 30-day terms, it is reasonable to expect this ratio to turn over in approximately 30 days.

Cautions—A problem with this ratio is that it compares one day's payables to cost of goods sold and does not take seasonal fluctuations into account. When the payables figure is zero, the quotient will be undefined (UND) and represents the best possible ratio. The ratio values are arrayed starting with undefined (UND) and then from the numerically highest to the numerically lowest value. The only time a zero will appear in the array is when the figure for cost of sales is very low and the quotient rounds off to zero.

8. Days' Payables

The days' payables is the figure printed in bold type directly to the left of the cost of sales/payables ratio.

How to Calculate the Days' Payables: Divide the cost of sales/payables ratio into 365 (the number of days in one year).

$$\frac{365}{\text{Cost of Sales/Payables ratio}}$$

How to Interpret: Division of the payables turnover ratio into 365 days yields the average length of time trade debt is outstanding.

9. Sales/Working Capital

How to Calculate: Divide net sales by net working capital (current assets less current liabilities equals net working capital).

$$\frac{\text{Net Sales}}{\text{Net Working Capital}}$$

How to Interpret: Because it reflects the ability to finance current operations, working capital is a measure of the margin of protection for current creditors. When you relate the level of sales resulting from operations to the underlying working capital, you can measure how efficiently working capital is being used.

Low ratio (close to zero)—A low ratio may indicate an inefficient use of working capital.

High ratio (high positive or high negative)—A very high ratio often signifies overtrading, which is a vulnerable position for creditors.

Please note—sales/working capital ratio is a nonlinear array. In other words, an array that is NOT ordered from highest positive to highest negative as is the case for linear arrays. The ratio values are arrayed from the lowest positive to the highest positive, to undefined (UND), and then from the highest negative to the lowest negative. If working capital is zero, the quotient is undefined (UND).

If the sales/working capital ratio is positive, then the top quartile would be represented by the *lowest positive* ratio. However, if the ratio is negative, the top quartile will be represented by the *highest negative* ratio! In a nonlinear array such as the sales/working capital ratio, the median could be either positive or negative because it is whatever the middle value is in the particular array of numbers.

Cautions—When analyzing this ratio, you need to focus on working capital, not on the sales figure. Although sales cannot be negative, working capital can be. If you have a large, positive working capital number, the ratio will be small *and* positive—which is good. Because negative working capital is bad, if you have a large, negative working capital number, the sales/working capital ratio will be small *and* negative—which is NOT good. Therefore, the lowest positive ratio is the best and the lowest negative ratio is the worst. If working capital is a small negative number, the ratio will be large, which is the best of the negatives.

COVERAGE RATIOS

Coverage ratios measure a firm's ability to service its debt. In other words, how well does the flow of a company's funds cover its short-term financial obligations? In contrast to liquidity ratios that focus on the possibility of liquidation, coverage ratios seek to provide lenders a comfort level based on the belief the firm will remain a viable enterprise.

1. Earnings Before Interest and Taxes (EBIT)/Interest

How to Calculate: Divide earnings (profit) before annual interest expense and taxes by annual interest expense.

$$\frac{\text{Earnings Before Interest \& Taxes}}{\text{Annual Interest Expense}}$$

How to Interpret: This ratio measures a firm's ability to meet interest payments. A high ratio may indicate that a borrower can easily meet the interest obligations of a loan. This ratio also indicates a firm's capacity to take on additional debt.

Please note—Only statements reporting annual interest expense were used in the calculation of this ratio. The ratio values are arrayed from the highest positive to the lowest positive and then from the lowest negative to the highest negative.

2. Net Profit + Depreciation, Depletion, Amortization/Current Maturities Long-Term Debt

How to Calculate: Add net profit to depreciation, depletion, and amortization expenses. Then, divide by the current portion of long-term debt.

$$\frac{\text{Net Profit + Depreciation, Depletion, Amortization Expenses}}{\text{Current Portion of Long-Term Debt}}$$

How to Interpret: This ratio reflects how well cash flow from operations covers current maturities. Because cash flow is the primary source of debt retirement, the ratio measures a firm's ability to service principal repayment and take on additional debt. Even though it is a mistake to believe all cash flow is available for debt service, this ratio is still a valid measure of the ability to service long-term debt.

Please note—Only data for corporations with the following items was used:

(1) Profit or loss after taxes (positive, negative, or zero).

(2) A positive figure for depreciation/depletion/amortization expenses.

(3) A positive figure for current maturities of long-term debt.

Ratio values are arrayed from the highest to the lowest positive and then from the lowest to the highest negative.

LEVERAGE RATIOS

How much protection do a company's assets provide for the debt held by its creditors? Highly leveraged firms are companies with heavy debt in relation to their net worth. These firms are more vulnerable to business downturns than those with lower debt-to-worth positions. While leverage ratios help measure this vulnerability, keep in mind that these ratios vary greatly depending on the requirements of particular industry groups.

1. Fixed/Worth

How to Calculate: Divide fixed assets (net of accumulated depreciation) by tangible net worth (net worth minus intangibles).

$$\frac{\text{Net Fixed Assets}}{\text{Tangible Net Worth}}$$

How to Interpret: This ratio measures the extent to which owner's equity (capital) has been invested in plant and equipment (fixed assets). A lower ratio indicates a proportionately smaller investment in fixed assets in relation to net worth and a better "cushion" for creditors in case of liquidation. Similarly, a higher ratio would indicate the opposite situation. The presence of a substantial number of fixed assets that are leased—and not appearing on the balance sheet—may result in a deceptively lower ratio.

Fixed assets may be zero, in which case the quotient is zero. If tangible net worth is zero, the quotient is undefined (UND). If tangible net worth is negative, the quotient is negative.

Please note—Like the sales/working capital ratio discussed above, this fixed/worth ratio is a nonlinear array. In other words, it is an array that is NOT ordered from highest positive to highest negative as a linear array would be. The ratio values are arrayed from the lowest positive to the highest positive, to undefined (UND), and then from the highest negative to the lowest negative.

If the Fixed/Worth ratio is positive, then the top quartile would be represented by the *lowest positive* ratio. However, if the ratio is negative, the top quartile will be represented by the *highest negative* ratio! In a nonlinear array such as this, the median could be either positive or negative because it is whatever the middle value is in the particular array of numbers.

2. Debt/Worth

How to Calculate: Divide total liabilities by tangible net worth.

$$\frac{\text{Total Liabilities}}{\text{Tangible Net Worth}}$$

How to Interpret: This ratio expresses the relationship between capital contributed by creditors and that contributed by owners. Basically, it shows how much protection the owners are providing creditors. The higher the ratio, the greater the risk being assumed by creditors. A lower ratio generally indicates greater long-term financial safety. Unlike a highly leveraged firm, a firm with a low debt/worth ratio usually has greater flexibility to borrow in the future.

Tangible net worth may be zero, in which case the ratio is undefined (UND). Tangible net worth may also be negative, which results in the quotient being negative. The ratio values are arrayed from the lowest to highest positive, to undefined, and then from the highest to lowest negative.

Please note—Like the sales/working capital ratio discussed above, this debt/worth ratio is a nonlinear array. In other words, it is an array that is NOT ordered from highest positive to highest negative as a linear array would be. The ratio values are arrayed from the lowest positive to the highest positive, to undefined (UND), and then from the highest negative to the lowest negative.

If the debt/worth ratio is positive, then the top quartile would be represented by the *lowest positive ratio*. However, if the ratio is negative, the top quartile will be represented by the *highest negative ratio*! In a nonlinear array such as this, the median could be either positive or negative because it is whatever the middle value is in the particular array of numbers.

OPERATING RATIOS

Operating ratios are designed to assist in the evaluation of management performance.

1. % Profits Before Taxes/Tangible Net Worth

How to Calculate: Divide profit before taxes by tangible net worth. Then, multiply by 100.

$$\frac{\text{Profit Before Taxes}}{\text{Tangible Net Worth}} \times 100$$

How to Interpret: This ratio expresses the rate of return on tangible capital employed. While it can serve as an indicator of management performance, you should always use it in conjunction with other ratios. Normally associated with effective management, a high return could actually point to an undercapitalized firm. Conversely, a low return that's usually viewed as an indicator of inefficient management performance could actually reflect a highly capitalized, conservatively operated business.

This ratio has been multiplied by 100 because it is shown as a percentage.

Profit before taxes may be zero, in which case the ratio is zero. Profits before taxes may be negative, resulting in negative quotients. Firms with negative tangible net worth have been omitted from the ratio arrays. Negative ratios will therefore only result in the case of negative profit before taxes. If the tangible net worth is zero, the quotient is undefined (UND). If there are fewer than 10 ratios for a particular size class, the result is not shown. The ratio values are arrayed starting with undefined (UND), then from the highest to the lowest positive values, and finally from the lowest to the highest negative values.

2. % Profits Before Taxes/Total Assets

How to Calculate: Divide profit before taxes by total assets and multiply by 100.

$$\frac{\text{Profit Before Taxes}}{\text{Total Assets}} \times 100$$

How to Interpret: This ratio expresses the pre-tax return on total assets and measures the effectiveness of management in employing the resources available to it. If a specific ratio varies considerably from the ranges found in this book, the analyst will need to examine the makeup of the assets and take a closer look at the earnings figure. A heavily depreciated plant and a large amount of intangible assets or unusual income or expense items will cause distortions of this ratio.

This ratio has been multiplied by 100 since it is shown as a percentage. If profit before taxes is zero, the quotient is zero. If profit before taxes is negative, the quotient is negative. These ratio values are arrayed from the highest to the lowest positive and then from the lowest to the highest negative.

3. Sales/Net Fixed Assets

How to Calculate: Divide net sales by net fixed assets (net of accumulated depreciation).

$$\frac{\text{Net Sales}}{\text{Net Fixed Assets}}$$

How to Interpret: This ratio is a measure of the productive use of a firm's fixed assets. Largely depreciated fixed assets or a labor-intensive operation may cause a distortion of this ratio.

This ratio is a measure of the productive use of a firm's fixed assets. Largely depreciated fixed assets or a labor-intensive operation may cause a distortion of this ratio.

They are arrayed from undefined (UND) and then from the highest to the lowest positive values.

4. Sales/Total Assets

How to Calculate: Divide net sales by total assets.

$$\frac{\text{Net Sales}}{\text{Total Assets}}$$

How to Interpret: This ratio is a general measure of a firm's ability to generate sales in relation to total assets. It should be used only to compare firms within specific industry groups and in conjunction with other operating ratios to determine the effective employment of assets.

The only time a zero will appear in the array will be when the net sales figure is low and the quotient rounds off to zero. The ratio values cannot be negative. They are arrayed from the highest to the lowest positive values.

EXPENSE TO SALES RATIOS

The following two ratios relate specific expense items to net sales and express this relationship as a percentage. Comparisons are convenient because the item, net sales, is used as a constant. Variations in these ratios are most pronounced between capital- and labor-intensive industries.

1. % Depreciation, Depletion, Amortization/Sales

How to Calculate: Divide annual depreciation, amortization, and depletion expenses by net sales and multiply by 100.

$$\frac{\text{Depreciation, Amortization, Depletion Expenses}}{\text{Net Sales}} \times 100$$

2. % Officers', Directors', Owners' Compensation/Sales

How to Calculate: Divide annual officers', directors', owners' compensation by net sales and multiply by 100. Include total salaries, bonuses, commissions, and other monetary remuneration to all officers, directors, and/or owners of the firm during the year covered by the statement. This includes drawings of partners and proprietors.

$$\frac{\text{Officers', Directors', Owners' Compensation}}{\text{Net Sales}} \times 100$$

Only statements showing a positive figure for each of the expense categories shown above were used. The ratios are arrayed from the lowest to highest positive values.

Explanation of Noncontractor Balance Sheet and Income Data

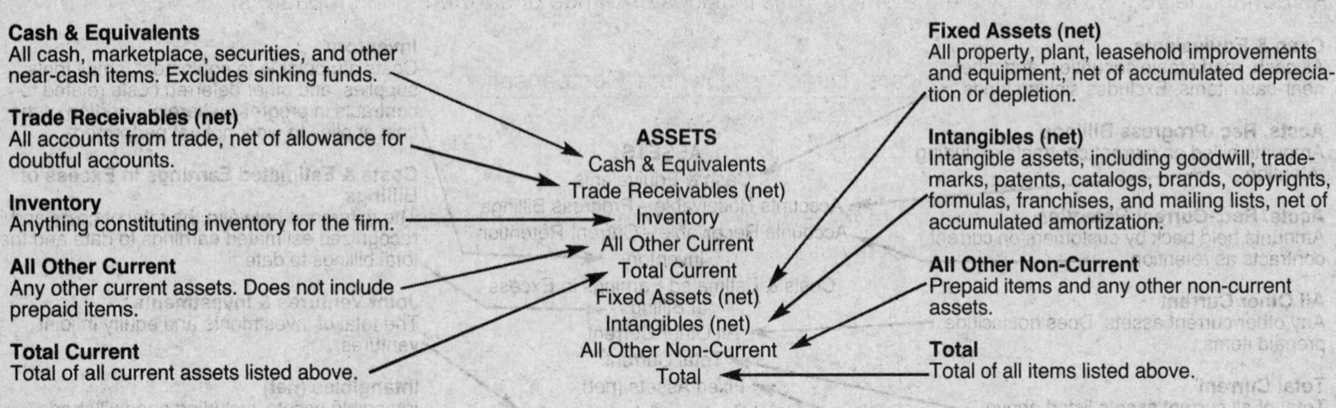

Cash & Equivalents
All cash, marketplace, securities, and other near-cash items. Excludes sinking funds.
Trade Receivables (net)
All accounts from trade, net of allowance for doubtful accounts.
Inventory
Anything constituting inventory for the firm.
All Other Current
Any other current assets. Does not include prepaid items.
Total Current
Total of all current assets listed above.
ASSETS
Cash & Equivalents
Trade Receivables (net)
Inventory
All Other Current
Total Current
Fixed Assets (net)
Intangibles (net)
All Other Non-Current
Total
Fixed Assets (net)
All property, plant, leasehold improvements and equipment, net of accumulated depreciation or depletion.
Intangibles (net)
Intangible assets, including goodwill, trademarks, patents, catalogs, brands, copyrights, formulas, franchises, and mailing lists, net of accumulated amortization.
All Other Non-Current
Prepaid items and any other non-current assets.
Total
Total of all items listed above.

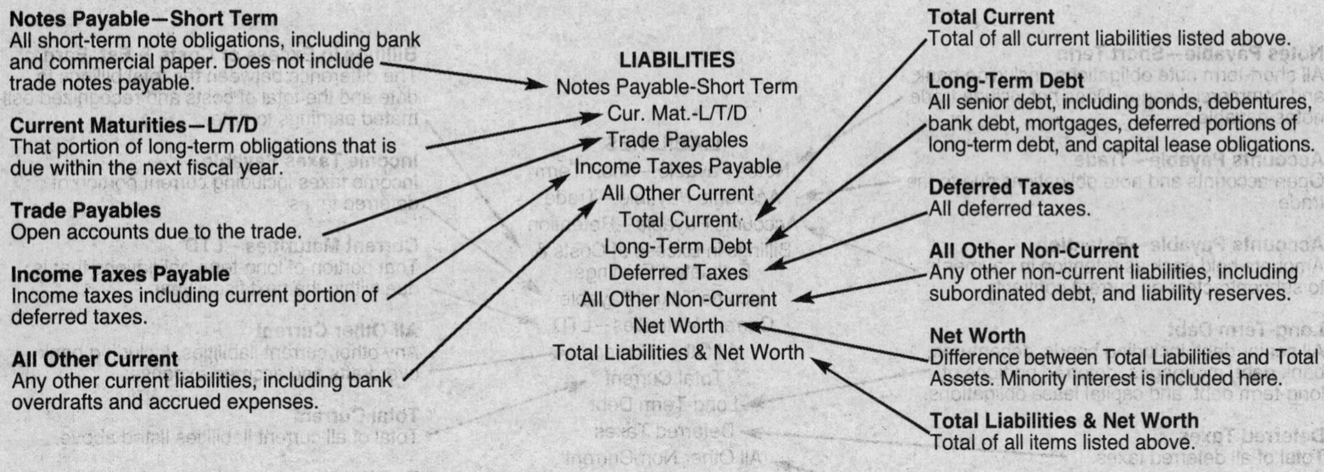

Notes Payable—Short Term
All short-term note obligations, including bank and commercial paper. Does not include trade notes payable.
Current Maturities—L/T/D
That portion of long-term obligations that is due within the next fiscal year.
Trade Payables
Open accounts due to the trade.
Income Taxes Payable
Income taxes including current portion of deferred taxes.
All Other Current
Any other current liabilities, including bank overdrafts and accrued expenses.
LIABILITIES
Notes Payable-Short Term
Cur. Mat.-L/T/D
Trade Payables
Income Taxes Payable
All Other Current
Total Current
Long-Term Debt
Deferred Taxes
All Other Non-Current
Net Worth
Total Liabilities & Net Worth
Total Current
Total of all current liabilities listed above.
Long-Term Debt
All senior debt, including bonds, debentures, bank debt, mortgages, deferred portions of long-term debt, and capital lease obligations.
Deferred Taxes
All deferred taxes.
All Other Non-Current
Any other non-current liabilities, including subordinated debt, and liability reserves.
Net Worth
Difference between Total Liabilities and Total Assets. Minority interest is included here.
Total Liabilities & Net Worth
Total of all items listed above.

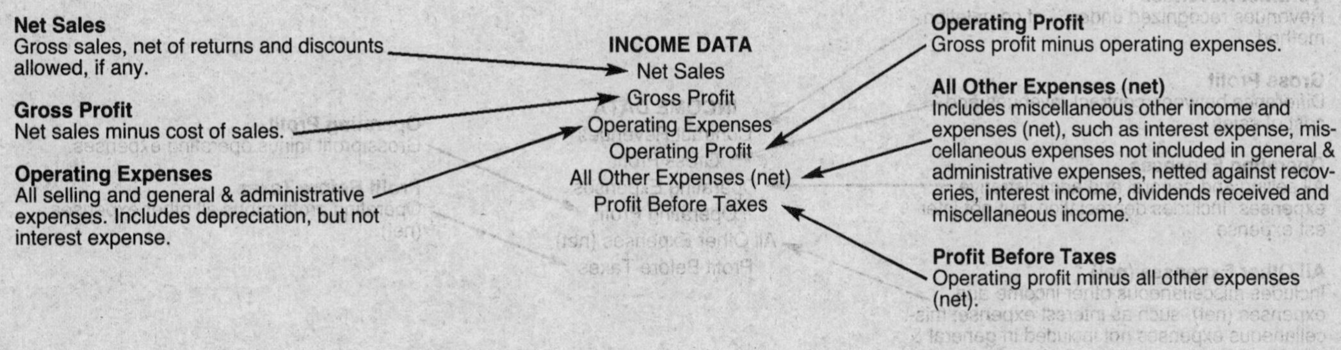

Net Sales
Gross sales, net of returns and discounts allowed, if any.
Gross Profit
Net sales minus cost of sales.
Operating Expenses
All selling and general & administrative expenses. Includes depreciation, but not interest expense.
INCOME DATA
Net Sales
Gross Profit
Operating Expenses
Operating Profit
All Other Expenses (net)
Profit Before Taxes
Operating Profit
Gross profit minus operating expenses.
All Other Expenses (net)
Includes miscellaneous other income and expenses (net), such as interest expense, miscellaneous expenses not included in general & administrative expenses, netted against recoveries, interest income, dividends received and miscellaneous income.
Profit Before Taxes
Operating profit minus all other expenses (net).

Explanation of Contractor Percentage-of-Completion Basis of Accounting Balance Sheet and Income Data

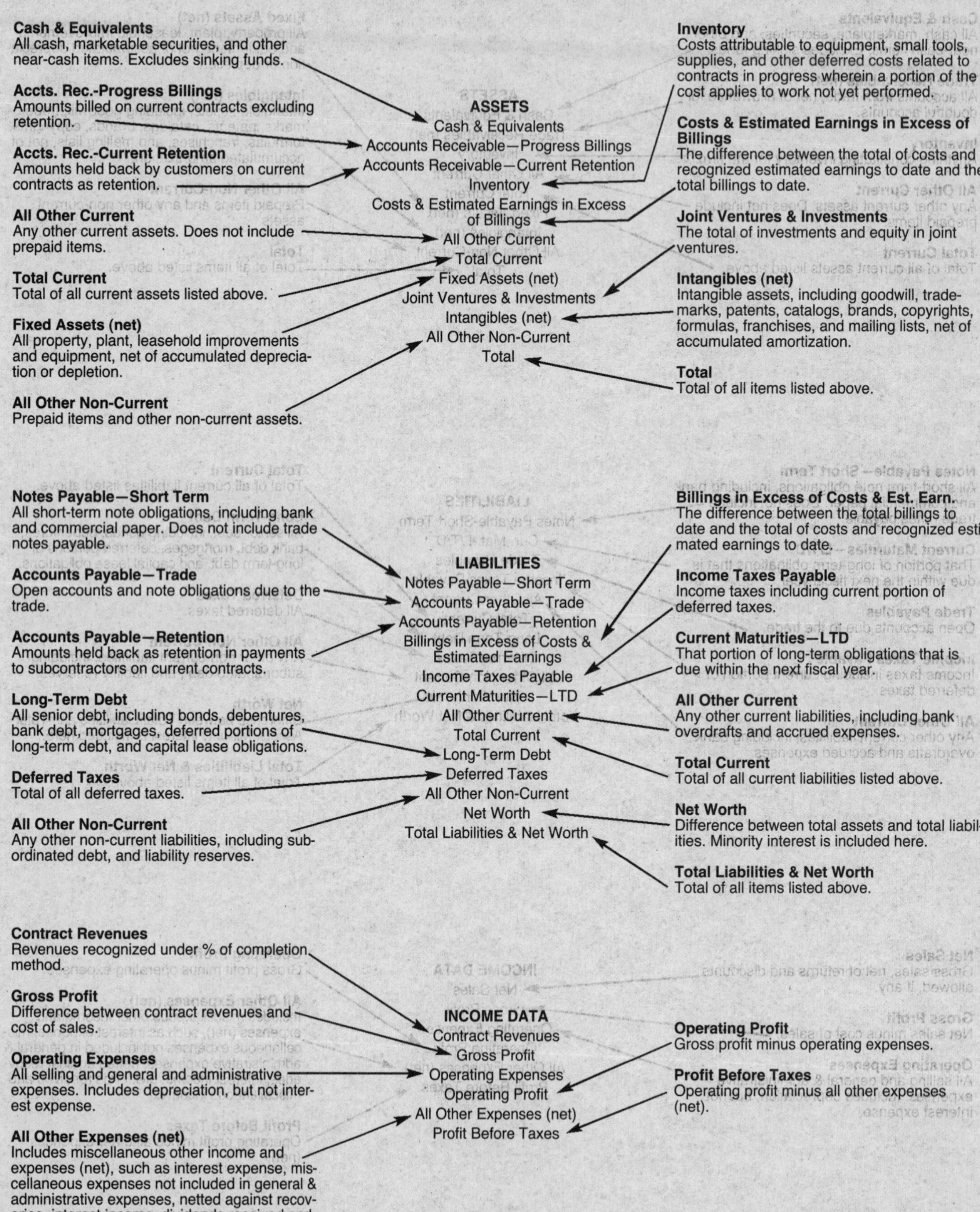
Cash & Equivalents
All cash, marketable securities, and other near-cash items. Excludes sinking funds.
Accts. Rec.-Progress Billings
Amounts billed on current contracts excluding retention.
Accts. Rec.-Current Retention
Amounts held back by customers on current contracts as retention.
All Other Current
Any other current assets. Does not include prepaid items.
Total Current
Total of all current assets listed above.
Fixed Assets (net)
All property, plant, leasehold improvements and equipment, net of accumulated depreciation or depletion.
All Other Non-Current
Prepaid items and other non-current assets.
ASSETS
Cash & Equivalents
Accounts Receivable—Progress Billings
Accounts Receivable—Current Retention
Inventory
Costs & Estimated Earnings in Excess of Billings
All Other Current
Total Current
Fixed Assets (net)
Joint Ventures & Investments
Intangibles (net)
All Other Non-Current
Total
Inventory
Costs attributable to equipment, small tools, supplies, and other deferred costs related to contracts in progress wherein a portion of the cost applies to work not yet performed.
Costs & Estimated Earnings in Excess of Billings
The difference between the total of costs and recognized estimated earnings to date and the total billings to date.
Joint Ventures & Investments
The total of investments and equity in joint ventures.
Intangibles (net)
Intangible assets, including goodwill, trademarks, patents, catalogs, brands, copyrights, formulas, franchises, and mailing lists, net of accumulated amortization.
Total
Total of all items listed above.
Notes Payable—Short Term
All short-term note obligations, including bank and commercial paper. Does not include trade notes payable.
Accounts Payable—Trade
Open accounts and note obligations due to the trade.
Accounts Payable—Retention
Amounts held back as retention in payments to subcontractors on current contracts.
Long-Term Debt
All senior debt, including bonds, debentures, bank debt, mortgages, deferred portions of long-term debt, and capital lease obligations.
Deferred Taxes
Total of all deferred taxes.
All Other Non-Current
Any other non-current liabilities, including subordinated debt, and liability reserves.
LIABILITIES
Notes Payable—Short Term
Accounts Payable—Trade
Accounts Payable—Retention
Billings in Excess of Costs & Estimated Earnings
Income Taxes Payable
Current Maturities—LTD
All Other Current
Total Current
Long-Term Debt
Deferred Taxes
All Other Non-Current
Net Worth
Total Liabilities & Net Worth
Billings in Excess of Costs & Est. Earn.
The difference between the total billings to date and the total of costs and recognized estimated earnings to date.
Income Taxes Payable
Income taxes including current portion of deferred taxes.
Current Maturities—LTD
That portion of long-term obligations that is due within the next fiscal year.
All Other Current
Any other current liabilities, including bank overdrafts and accrued expenses.
Total Current
Total of all current liabilities listed above.
Net Worth
Difference between total assets and total liabilities. Minority interest is included here.
Total Liabilities & Net Worth
Total of all items listed above.
Contract Revenues
Revenues recognized under % of completion method.
Gross Profit
Difference between contract revenues and cost of sales.
Operating Expenses
All selling and general and administrative expenses. Includes depreciation, but not interest expense.
All Other Expenses (net)
Includes miscellaneous other income and expenses (net), such as interest expense, miscellaneous expenses not included in general & administrative expenses, netted against recoveries, interest income, dividends received and miscellaneous income.
INCOME DATA
Contract Revenues
Gross Profit
Operating Expenses
Operating Profit
All Other Expenses (net)
Profit Before Taxes
Operating Profit
Gross profit minus operating expenses.
Profit Before Taxes
Operating profit minus all other expenses (net).

For further analysis, please refer to *Industry Default Probabilities and Cash Flow Measures*

If you think *Financial Ratio Benchmarks* is a valuable resource, wait until you see its companion study. Now in its thirteenth year and bigger than ever, *Industry Default Probabilities and Cash Flow Measures* is a major expansion of our *Annual Statement Studies.* It brings together the power of Moody's Analytics RiskCalc™ Plus for private companies and the *Statement Studies* database to provide distribution statistics on one-year and five-year probability of default estimates by industry. The new benchmarks add substantial value to the critical analysis of cash flow for private companies.

The latest edition of *Industry Default Probabilities and Cash Flow Measures* includes many new industries, stronger statements, five years of historical data sorted by assets and sales. In short, it is more like our traditional *Statement Studies*.

Industry Default Probabilities and Cash Flow Measures includes:

- Probability of default estimates on a percentage scale, mapped to a "dot" EDF bond rating scale.
- Cash flow measures on a common-size percentage scale. Ratios include:
  - Cash from Trading
  - Cash after Operations
  - Net Cash after Operations
  - Cash after Debt Amortization
  - Debt Service P&I Coverage
  - Interest Coverage (Operating Cash)
- Change in position, normalized, year over year, for eight financial statement line items. Ratios include:
  - Change in Inventory
  - Total Current Assets (TCA)
  - Total Assets (TA)
  - Retained Earnings (RE)
  - Net Sales (NS)
  - Cost of Goods Sold (CGS)
  - Profit before Interest & Taxes (PBIT)
  - Depreciation/Depletion/Amortization (DDA)
- Trend data available for the past five years.
- Other ratios.
  - Sustainable Growth Rate
  - Funded Debt/EBITDA
- Data arrayed by asset and sales size.

Please see the next page for a copy of a sample report. Please see the inside front cover for more information, or upgrade now to eStatement Studies online database by calling 1-800-677-7621.

INDUSTRY DEFAULT PROBABILITIES AND CASH FLOW MEASURES SAMPLE REPORT

AGRICULTURE—Soybean Farming NAICS 111110

Current Data Sorted by Assets							Comparative Historical Data	
						Type of Statement		
	1	2	2	3	2	Unqualified	2	10
	1	3	3		1	Reviewed	12	2
1	3	6				Compiled	1	8
8	11	6				Tax Returns	4	22
7	9	14	7		2	Other	7	25
	16 (4/1-9/30/12)		76 (10/1/12-3/31/13)				4/1/08-3/31/09	4/1/09-3/31/10
0-500M	500M-2MM	2-10MM	10-50MM	50-100MM	100-250MM		ALL	ALL
16	25	31	12	3	5	**NUMBER OF STATEMENTS**	26	67
%	%	%	%	%	%	**ASSETS**	%	%
21.0	15.2	4.9	9.9			Cash & Equivalents	13.6	14.5
8.3	14.9	19.8	13.3			Trade Receivables (net)	24.5	12.0
6.8	10.6	17.7	9.5			Inventory	12.4	14.5
2.5	4.0	4.2	1.9			All Other Current	7.6	3.8
38.5	44.7	46.7	34.5			Total Current	58.0	44.7
50.5	49.0	44.9	48.0			Fixed Assets (net)	34.8	41.5
.5	.3	3.1	15.1			Intangibles (net)	2.7	6.5
10.5	6.0	5.4	2.4			All Other Non-Current	4.5	7.3
100.0	100.0	100.0	100.0			Total	100.0	100.0
						LIABILITIES		
95.5	14.7	9.9	3.1			Notes Payable-Short Term	4.4	14.2
5.9	6.5	3.7	3.2			Cur. Mat.-L.T.D.	3.1	4.1
3.4	7.4	11.2	5.4			Trade Payables	13.0	7.2
.0	.0	.7	.0			Income Taxes Payable	.1	.1
4.7	6.0	10.0	5.3			All Other Current	10.3	7.0
109.5	34.5	35.5	17.1			Total Current	31.0	32.6
38.9	33.3	28.7	41.6			Long-Term Debt	18.7	37.7
.0	.4	.1	1.4			Deferred Taxes	.4	.4
1.4	7.3	3.6	4.8			All Other Non-Current	7.0	2.5
-49.8	24.5	32.2	35.1			Net Worth	42.9	26.8
100.0	100.0	100.0	100.0			Total Liabilties & Net Worth	100.0	100.0
						INCOME DATA		
100.0	100.0	100.0	100.0			Net Sales	100.0	100.0
						Gross Profit		
91.1	91.1	83.8	92.8			Operating Expenses	95.1	85.9
8.9	8.9	16.2	7.2			Operating Profit	4.9	14.1
4.3	2.3	4.7	7.4			All Other Expenses (net)	3.2	6.6
4.6	6.6	11.6	-.1			Profit Before Taxes	1.7	7.6
						RATIOS		
2.0	2.9	2.0	2.4				5.2	2.8
.1	1.5	1.3	2.1			Current	1.6	1.5
.1	.4	.8	1.4				1.1	.8
1.4	2.5	1.0	2.1				2.1	1.6
.1	.9	.6	1.4			Quick	.9	.9
.0	.0	.3	.7				.5	.2
0 UND	0 UND	0 UND	13 27.8				8 46.7	0 UND
0 UND	1 376.0	27 13.5	49 7.5			Sales/Receivables	45 8.0	4 96.2
0 UND	23 16.2	54 6.8	62 5.9				63 5.8	37 9.8
						Cost of Sales/Inventory		
						Cost of Sales/Payables		
7.7	9.4	2.5	4.4				3.8	6.8
-3.6	28.1	13.2	8.4			Sales/Working Capital	10.5	12.3
-1.5	-9.8	-13.9	22.8				94.0	-24.9
7.3	14.4	13.7	23.3				8.8	8.9
(12) 1.9	(23) 3.6	(26) 6.7	(11) 3.6			EBIT/Interest	(20) 4.2	(47) 3.8
-7.3	-.2	2.7	.2				.6	1.2
						Net Profit + Depr., Dep., Amort./Cur. Mat. L/T/D		
.5	.4	.4	1.0				.1	.2
NM	1.9	1.5	1.7			Fixed/Worth	.8	1.2
-.9	NM	25.3	NM				1.4	9.9
1.3	.6	.6	.7				.6	.6
NM	2.2	2.7	1.5			Debt/Worth	1.2	2.1
-2.3	NM	26.6	NM				3.9	29.7
	109.2	78.7					35.0	36.5
	(19) 14.6	(25) 23.3				% Profit Before Taxes/Tangible Net Worth	(25) 19.1	(51) 12.0
	-3.6	7.4					-2.0	4.3
47.8	33.3	15.6	18.5				13.8	14.9
8.6	6.2	7.2	4.6			% Profit Before Taxes/Total Assets	7.0	5.2
-4.8	-1.3	3.1	-1.1				-2.4	.3
33.4	45.7	15.5	13.1				44.8	31.1
7.8	6.1	3.2	3.8			Sales/Net Fixed Assets	11.0	5.8
2.7	1.6	.7	.4				1.5	1.0
4.9	4.2	1.8	2.1				2.5	3.2
2.5	2.1	1.3	1.3			Sales/Total Assets	2.0	1.8
1.5	1.0	.4	.2				.9	.5
1.0	1.0	1.4	1.4				.7	1.1
(11) 2.5	(18) 4.0	(23) 5.2	(10) 2.9			% Depr., Dep., Amort./Sales	(23) 2.3	(54) 4.2
12.9	11.8	10.6	15.0				8.9	12.5
								2.6
						% Officers', Directors' Owners' Comp/Sales		(21) 5.1
								11.4
12420M	95761M	215791M	542153M	351149M	1313305M	Net Sales ($)	685004M	751059M
4674M	29970M	151398M	319492M	184530M	833900M	Total Assets ($)	596750M	462939M

M = $ thousand MM = $ million

See Pages 9 through 22 for Explanation of Ratios and Data

AGRICULTURE—Soybean Farming NAICS 111110

Comparative Historical Data				Current Data Sorted by Sales					
			Type of Statement						
5	16	10	Unqualified		2		1	2	5
6	10	8	Reviewed				1	3	4
6	13	10	Compiled	1	1	3	1	3	1
15	27	25	Tax Returns	12	10	3			
28	44	39	Other	8	10	4	6	4	7
4/1/10-3/31/11 ALL	**4/1/11-3/31/12 ALL**	**4/1/12-3/31/13 ALL**		**16 (4/1-9/30/12)**			**76 (10/1/12-3/31/13)**		
				0-1MM	**1-3MM**	**3-5MM**	**5-10MM**	**10-25MM**	**25MM & OVER**
60	110	92	**NUMBER OF STATEMENTS**	21	23	10	9	12	17
%	%	%	**ASSETS**	%	%	%	%	%	%
9.7	14.6	11.7	Cash & Equivalents	14.2	11.7	16.3		10.1	10.0
12.6	11.9	14.8	Trade Receivables (net)	1.5	9.7	18.4		28.1	18.5
16.2	9.0	13.3	Inventory	4.0	14.8	2.5		19.3	17.8
4.5	2.5	4.2	All Other Current	2.3	3.8	6.0		5.5	6.8
43.0	37.9	44.0	Total Current	22.0	39.9	43.2		63.0	53.2
43.0	46.8	46.6	Fixed Assets (net)	66.2	54.2	43.0		28.7	34.1
5.5	3.7	3.2	Intangibles (net)	.5	.0	7.7		4.3	8.5
8.5	11.7	6.2	All Other Non-Current	11.3	5.9	6.0		4.0	4.2
100.0	100.0	100.0	Total	100.0	100.0	100.0		100.0	100.0
			LIABILITIES						
10.0	15.3	24.7	Notes Payable-Short Term	73.3	16.5	5.4		9.0	6.0
5.2	5.8	5.4	Cur. Mat.-L.T.D.	2.8	8.7	4.1		4.9	7.3
8.7	6.8	8.0	Trade Payables	.3	3.5	21.8		11.2	10.2
.4	.1	.4	Income Taxes Payable	.0	.0	.0		1.3	1.1
7.6	9.2	7.7	All Other Current	2.7	2.7	4.6		19.3	10.0
32.0	37.1	46.2	Total Current	79.1	31.4	35.8		45.7	34.6
24.7	35.9	31.3	Long-Term Debt	22.2	53.4	37.9		10.2	23.8
.8	.2	.3	Deferred Taxes	.0	.0	.9		.0	1.2
3.3	9.6	4.7	All Other Non-Current	.7	4.6	5.1		1.8	6.3
39.3	17.3	17.5	Net Worth	-2.0	10.6	20.3		42.3	34.1
100.0	100.0	100.0	Total Liabilties & Net Worth	100.0	100.0	100.0		100.0	100.0
			INCOME DATA						
100.0	100.0	100.0	Net Sales	100.0	100.0	100.0		100.0	100.0
			Gross Profit						
86.7	85.0	88.7	Operating Expenses	82.5	89.3	86.7		93.7	90.2
13.3	15.0	11.3	Operating Profit	17.5	10.7	13.3		6.3	9.8
3.6	6.2	4.1	All Other Expenses (net)	10.0	4.5	.6		-.1	1.6
9.7	8.8	7.2	Profit Before Taxes	7.6	6.2	12.8		6.5	8.2
			RATIOS						
2.4	2.4	2.3		2.0	2.5	3.9		2.3	2.3
1.3	1.1	1.3	Current	.2	1.8	1.0		1.4	1.6
.6	.4	.6		.1	.6	.3		1.0	1.2
1.3	1.7	1.7		1.4	1.6	3.4		1.8	1.7
.6	.6	.7	Quick	.2	.3	.9		.7	.8
.2	.2	.2		.0	.0	.2		.5	.5
0 UND	**0** UND	**0** UND		**0** UND	**0** UND	**0** UND		**29** 12.6	**10** 35.4
18 20.5	**4** 81.2	**13** 28.8	Sales/Receivables	**0** UND	**0** UND	**21** 17.2		**35** 10.4	**37** 9.9
48 7.7	**36** 10.0	**43** 8.5		**0** UND	**22** 16.5	**42** 8.6		**56** 6.5	**50** 7.3
			Cost of Sales/Inventory						
			Cost of Sales/Payables						
5.2	5.7	5.5		5.9	3.0	6.7		5.0	7.8
17.2	46.8	16.5	Sales/Working Capital	-4.3	11.5	NM		13.6	13.0
-10.6	-7.9	-10.9		-1.6	-38.9	-9.3		NM	27.3
10.5	13.0	13.3		4.0	12.2			27.6	30.4
(51) 5.5	(76) 3.2	(79) 3.6	EBIT/Interest	(14) 1.9	(19) 3.1			11.6	(16) 6.2
1.7	1.2	1.2		-2.6	-.8			6.0	3.3
7.8	22.8	5.1							
(13) 3.9	(10) 5.1	(10) 3.2	Net Profit + Depr., Dep., Amort./Cur. Mat. L/T/D						
1.9	2.4	.5							
.5	.3	.5		1.1	.8	.2		.3	.4
1.1	1.4	1.5	Fixed/Worth	1.9	1.7	NM		1.0	.9
2.9	NM	NM		-5.2	20.7	-1.7		1.7	2.0
.7	.6	.7		.6	.5	.6		.7	.8
1.9	2.4	2.2	Debt/Worth	1.1	5.7	NM		1.4	1.9
3.8	NM	NM		-8.9	35.8	-4.4		4.8	4.3
43.4	44.4	68.3		55.0	74.1			111.4	53.8
(53) 20.8	(83) 17.0	(69) 14.6	% Profit Before Taxes/Tangible Net Worth	(14) 4.7	(19) 23.3			(11) 29.2	(14) 23.0
2.4	2.4	2.9		-2.6	-10.0			13.0	7.0
14.8	14.2	17.7		13.2	16.4	45.4		20.9	18.3
6.3	5.2	6.6	% Profit Before Taxes/Total Assets	4.0	6.3	15.5		12.6	9.5
1.2	.8	1.2		-1.1	-4.3	4.8		4.5	5.7
17.7	27.8	19.7		10.9	8.4	56.1		19.8	19.3
5.5	4.7	4.7	Sales/Net Fixed Assets	.5	2.7	7.2		9.2	8.8
.9	.8	1.2		.1	1.1	3.5		3.3	3.2
2.4	3.1	2.9		2.0	2.6	3.9		3.3	3.2
1.6	1.6	1.6	Sales/Total Assets	.3	1.1	2.2		1.8	2.1
.4	.4	.8		.1	.5	1.2		1.4	1.3
1.3	1.3	1.4		2.4	1.4			1.4	.6
(47) 2.8	(79) 4.0	(68) 2.8	% Depr., Dep., Amort./Sales	(16) 12.6	(18) 7.6			(11) 1.9	(14) 1.5
8.3	15.0	10.6		22.7	13.6			2.7	3.4
	1.1	3.6							
	(28) 2.8	(16) 7.1	% Officers', Directors' Owners' Comp/Sales						
	6.8	9.7							
1491565M	**2722989M**	**2530579M**	Net Sales ($)	**9870M**	**38149M**	**38926M**	**58731M**	**165297M**	**2219606M**
1095325M	**1700125M**	**1523964M**	Total Assets ($)	**37922M**	**55209M**	**22187M**	**67911M**	**102101M**	**1238634M**

M = $ thousand MM = $ million

See Pages 9 through 22 for Explanation of Ratios and Data

NAICS CODES APPEARING IN THE STATEMENT STUDIES

NAICS Codes	Page
111110	96-97
111140	98-99
111150	100-101
111199	102-103
111211	104-105
111219	106-107
111310	108-109
111331	110-111
111332	112-113
111335	114-115
111411	116-117
111421	118-119
111910	120-121
111920	122-123
111998	124-125
112111	126-127
112112	128-129
112120	130-131
112210	132-133
112310	134-135
112920	136-137
113110	138-139
113310	140-141
114111	142-143
114112	144-145
115111	146-147
115112	148-149
115114	150-151
115116	152-153
115210	154-155
211111	158-159
212111	160-161
212312	162-163
212319	164-165
212321	166-167
213111	168-169
213112	170-171
221111	174-175
221118	176-177
221122	178-179
221210	180-181
221310	182-183
221320	184-185
236115	188-189, 1654
236116	190-191
236117	192-193, 1655
236118	194-195, 1656
236210	196-197, 1657
236220	198-199, 1658
237110	200-201, 1659
237120	202-203
237130	204-205
237210	206-207, 1660
237310	208-209, 1661
237990	210-211, 1662
238110	212-213, 1663
238120	214-215, 1664
238130	216-217
238140	218-219
238150	220-221, 1665
238160	222-223, 1666
238190	224-225
238210	226-227, 1667
238220	228-229, 1668
238290	230-231
238310	232-233, 1669
238320	234-235, 1670
238330	236-237
238340	238-239
238350	240-241
238390	242-243
238910	244-245, 1671
238990	246-247, 1672
311119	250-251
311211	252-253
311352	254-255
311411	256-257
311412	258-259
311421	260-261
311423	262-263
311511	264-265
311513	266-267
311520	268-269
311611	270-271
311612	272-273
311615	274-275
311710	276-277
311811	278-279
311812	280-281
311821	282-283
311911	284-285
311919	286-287
311920	288-289
311930	290-291
311941	292-293
311942	294-295
311991	296-297
311999	298-299
312111	300-301
312112	302-303
312120	304-305
312130	306-307
313110	308-309
313210	310-311
313230	312-313
313310	314-315
313320	316-317
314110	318-319
314120	320-321
314910	322-323
314999	324-325
315210	326-327
315220	328-329
315240	330-331
315280	332-333
315990	334-335
316110	336-337
316210	338-339
321113	340-341
321114	342-343
321211	344-345
321214	346-347
321911	348-349
321912	350-351
321918	352-353
321920	354-355
321991	356-357
321992	358-359
321999	360-361
322121	362-363
322211	364-365
322212	366-367
322219	368-369
322220	370-371
322230	372-373
322291	374-375
322299	376-377
323111	378-379
323113	380-381
323117	382-383
323120	384-385
324110	386-387
324121	388-389
324191	390-391
324199	392-393
325180	394-395
325193	396-397
325199	398-399
325211	400-401
325311	402-403
325314	404-405
325320	406-407
325411	408-409
325412	410-411
325510	412-413
325520	414-415
325611	416-417
325612	418-419
325620	420-421
325910	422-423
325991	424-425
325998	426-427

NAICS CODES APPEARING IN THE STATEMENT STUDIES

NAICS Codes	Page
326111	428-429
326112	430-431
326113	432-433
326121	434-435
326122	436-437
326130	438-439
326140	440-441
326150	442-443
326160	444-445
326191	446-447
326199	448-449
326212	450-451
326220	452-453
326291	454-455
326299	456-457
327120	458-459
327211	460-461
327215	462-463
327320	464-465
327331	466-467
327332	468-469
327390	470-471
327910	472-473
327991	474-475
327999	476-477
331110	478-479
331210	480-481
331221	482-483
331222	484-485
331318	486-487
331420	488-489
331491	490-491
331492	492-493
331511	494-495
331513	496-497
331523	498-499
331524	500-501
332111	502-503
332117	504-505
332119	506-507
332216	508-509
332311	510-511
332312	512-513
332313	514-515
332321	516-517
332322	518-519
332323	520-521
332439	522-523
332510	524-525
332613	526-527
332618	528-529
332710	530-531
332721	532-533
332722	534-535
332811	536-537
332812	538-539
332813	540-541
332911	542-543
332912	544-545
332913	546-547
332919	548-549
332991	550-551
332994	552-553
332996	554-555
332999	556-557
333111	558-559
333112	560-561
333120	562-563
333131	564-565
333132	566-567
333241	568-569
333243	570-571
333244	572-573
333249	574-575
333314	576-577
333318	578-579
333413	580-581
333414	582-583
333415	584-585
333511	586-587
333514	588-589
333515	590-591
333517	592-593
333519	594-595
333612	596-597
333613	598-599
333911	600-601
333912	602-603
333922	604-605
333923	606-607
333924	608-609
333992	610-611
333993	612-613
333994	614-615
333999	616-617
334111	618-619
334118	620-621
334210	622-623
334220	624-625
334290	626-627
334310	628-629
334412	630-631
334413	632-633
334416	634-635
334417	636-637
334418	638-639
334419	640-641
334510	642-643
334511	644-645
334512	646-647
334513	648-649
334514	650-651
334515	652-653
334516	654-655
334519	656-657
335121	658-659
335122	660-661
335129	662-663
335311	664-665
335312	666-667
335313	668-669
335314	670-671
335911	672-673
335931	674-675
335999	676-677
336111	678-679
336211	680-681
336212	682-683
336214	684-685
336310	686-687
336320	688-689
336350	690-691
336360	692-693
336370	694-695
336390	696-697
336411	698-699
336412	700-701
336413	702-703
336510	704-705
336611	706-707
336612	708-709
336991	710-711
336999	712-713
337110	714-715
337121	716-717
337122	718-719
337127	720-721
337211	722-723
337212	724-725
337214	726-727
337215	728-729
337910	730-731
337920	732-733
339112	734-735
339113	736-737
339114	738-739
339115	740-741
339116	742-743
339910	744-745
339920	746-747
339930	748-749
339950	750-751

NAICS CODES APPEARING IN THE STATEMENT STUDIES

NAICS Codes	Page
339991	752-753
339992	754-755
339999	756-757
423110	760-761
423120	762-763
423130	764-765
423140	766-767
423210	768-769
423220	770-771
423310	772-773
423320	774-775
423330	776-777
423390	778-779
423410	780-781
423420	782-783
423430	784-785
423440	786-787
423450	788-789
423460	790-791
423490	792-793
423510	794-795
423520	796-797
423610	798-799
423620	800-801
423690	802-803
423710	804-805
423720	806-807
423730	808-809
423740	810-811
423810	812-813
423820	814-815
423830	816-817
423840	818-819
423850	820-821
423860	822-823
423910	824-825
423920	826-827
423930	828-829
423940	830-831
423990	832-833
424110	834-835
424120	836-837
424130	838-839
424210	840-841
424310	842-843
424320	844-845
424330	846-847
424340	848-849
424410	850-851
424420	852-853
424430	854-855
424440	856-857
424450	858-859
424460	860-861
424470	862-863
424480	864-865
424490	866-867
424510	868-869
424590	870-871
424610	872-873
424690	874-875
424710	876-877
424720	878-879
424810	880-881
424820	882-883
424910	884-885
424920	886-887
424930	888-889
424940	890-891
424950	892-893
424990	894-895
425110	896-897
425120	898-899
441110	902-903
441120	904-905
441210	906-907
441222	908-909
441228	910-911
441310	912-913
441320	914-915
442110	916-917
442210	918-919
442299	920-921
443141	922-923
443142	924-925
444110	926-927
444120	928-929
444130	930-931
444190	932-933
444210	934-935
444220	936-937
445110	938-939
445120	940-941
445210	942-943
445230	944-945
445291	946-947
445292	948-949
445299	950-951
445310	952-953
446110	954-955
446120	956-957
446130	958-959
446191	960-961
446199	962-963
447110	964-965
447190	966-967
448110	968-969
448120	970-971
448140	972-973
448150	974-975
448190	976-977
448210	978-979
448310	980-981
451110	982-983
451120	984-985
451140	986-987
451211	988-989
452111	990-991
452990	992-993
453110	994-995
453210	996-997
453220	998-999
453310	1000-1001
453910	1002-1003
453920	1004-1005
453930	1006-1007
453991	1008-1009
453998	1010-1011
454111	1012-1013
454113	1014-1015
454210	1016-1017
454310	1018-1019
454390	1020-1021
481111	1024-1025
481211	1026-1027
481219	1028-1029
482111	1030-1031
483111	1032-1033
483113	1034-1035
483211	1036-1037
484110	1038-1039
484121	1040-1041
484122	1042-1043
484210	1044-1045
484220	1046-1047
484230	1048-1049
485310	1050-1051
485320	1052-1053
485410	1054-1055
485510	1056-1057
485991	1058-1059
485999	1060-1061
487210	1062-1063
488119	1064-1065
488190	1066-1067
488210	1068-1069
488310	1070-1071
488320	1072-1073
488330	1074-1075
488390	1076-1077
488410	1078-1079
488490	1080-1081

NAICS CODES APPEARING IN THE STATEMENT STUDIES

NAICS Codes	Page	NAICS Codes	Page	NAICS Codes	Page
488510	1082-1083	531120	1196-1197	541890	1306-1307
488991	1084-1085	531130	1198-1199	541910	1308-1309
488999	1086-1087	531190	1200-1201	541921	1310-1311
492110	1088-1089	531210	1202-1203	541922	1312-1313
493110	1090-1091	531311	1204-1205	541940	1314-1315
493120	1092-1093	531312	1206-1207	541990	1316-1317
493130	1094-1095	531390	1208-1209	551112	1320-1321
493190	1096-1097	532111	1210-1211	551114	1322-1323
511110	1100-1101	532112	1212-1213	561110	1326-1327
511120	1102-1103	532120	1214-1215	561210	1328-1329
511130	1104-1105	532210	1216-1217	561311	1330-1331
511199	1106-1107	532291	1218-1219	561320	1332-1333
511210	1108-1109	532299	1220-1221	561330	1334-1335
512110	1110-1111	532310	1222-1223	561422	1336-1337
512131	1112-1113	532411	1224-1225	561439	1338-1339
512191	1114-1115	532412	1226-1227	561440	1340-1341
512199	1116-1117	532420	1228-1229	561499	1342-1343
515112	1118-1119	532490	1230-1231	561510	1344-1345
515120	1120-1121	533110	1232-1233	561520	1346-1347
515210	1122-1123	541110	1236-1237	561599	1348-1349
517110	1124-1125	541191	1238-1239	561612	1350-1351
517210	1126-1127	541199	1240-1241	561621	1352-1353
517911	1128-1129	541211	1242-1243	561710	1354-1355
517919	1130-1131	541213	1244-1245	561720	1356-1357
518210	1132-1133	541214	1246-1247	561730	1358-1359
519130	1134-1135	541219	1248-1249	561740	1360-1361
519190	1136-1137	541310	1250-1251	561790	1362-1363
522220	1140-1141	541320	1252-1253	561910	1364-1365
522291	1142-1143	541330	1254-1255	561920	1366-1367
522292	1144-1145	541370	1256-1257	561990	1368-1369
522298	1146-1147	541380	1258-1259	562111	1370-1371
522310	1148-1149	541410	1260-1261	562119	1372-1373
522320	1150-1151	541430	1262-1263	562211	1374-1375
522390	1152-1153	541490	1264-1265	562212	1376-1377
523110	1154-1155	541511	1266-1267	562219	1378-1379
523120	1156-1157	541512	1268-1269	562910	1380-1381
523130	1158-1159	541513	1270-1271	562920	1382-1383
523910	1160-1161	541519	1272-1273	562991	1384-1385
523920	1162-1163	541611	1274-1275	562998	1386-1387
523930	1164-1165	541612	1276-1277	611110	1390-1391
523991	1166-1167	541613	1278-1279	611210	1392-1393
523999	1168-1169	541614	1280-1281	611310	1394-1395
524113	1170-1171	541618	1282-1283	611430	1396-1397
524114	1172-1173	541620	1284-1285	611511	1398-1399
524126	1174-1175	541690	1286-1287	611519	1400-1401
524127	1176-1177	541711	1288-1289	611610	1402-1403
524128	1178-1179	541712	1290-1291	611620	1404-1405
524210	1180-1181	541720	1292-1293	611699	1406-1407
524291	1182-1183	541810	1294-1295	611710	1408-1409
524292	1184-1185	541820	1296-1297	621111	1412-1413
524298	1186-1187	541840	1298-1299	621112	1414-1415
525910	1188-1189	541850	1300-1301	621210	1416-1417
525990	1190-1191	541860	1302-1303	621310	1418-1419
531110	1194-1195	541870	1304-1305	621320	1420-1421

NAICS CODES APPEARING IN THE STATEMENT STUDIES

NAICS Codes	Page
621330	1422-1423
621340	1424-1425
621391	1426-1427
621399	1428-1429
621410	1430-1431
621420	1432-1433
621492	1434-1435
621493	1436-1437
621498	1438-1439
621511	1440-1441
621512	1442-1443
621610	1444-1445
621910	1446-1447
621991	1448-1449
621999	1450-1451
622110	1452-1453, 1454-1455
622210	1456-1457
622310	1458-1459
623110	1460-1461
623210	1462-1463
623220	1464-1465
623311	1466-1467
623312	1468-1469
623990	1470-1471
624110	1472-1473
624120	1474-1475
624190	1476-1477
624210	1478-1479
624221	1480-1481
624229	1482-1483
624310	1484-1485
624410	1486-1487
711110	1490-1491
711130	1492-1493
711211	1494-1495
711212	1496-1497
711310	1498-1499
711320	1500-1501
711410	1502-1503
712110	1504-1505
712130	1506-1507
713110	1508-1509
713120	1510-1511
713210	1512-1513
713290	1514-1515
713910	1516-1517
713920	1518-1519
713930	1520-1521
713940	1522-1523
713950	1524-1525
713990	1526-1527
721110	1530-1531
721120	1532-1533
721211	1534-1535
721214	1536-1537
721310	1538-1539
722310	1540-1541
722320	1542-1543
722410	1544-1545
722511	1546-1547
722513	1548-1549
722515	1550-1551
811111	1554-1555
811118	1556-1557
811121	1558-1559
811122	1560-1561
811191	1562-1563
811192	1564-1565
811198	1566-1567
811212	1568-1569
811219	1570-1571
811310	1572-1573
811412	1574-1575
811490	1576-1577
812112	1578-1579
812199	1580-1581
812210	1582-1583
812220	1584-1585
812310	1586-1587
812320	1588-1589
812331	1590-1591
812332	1592-1593
812910	1594-1595
812930	1596-1597
812990	1598-1599
813110	1600-1601
813211	1602-1603
813212	1604-1605
813219	1606-1607
813311	1608-1609
813312	1610-1611
813319	1612-1613
813410	1614-1615
813910	1616-1617
813920	1618-1619
813930	1620-1621
813990	1622-1623
814110	1624-1625
921110	1628-1629
921120	1630-1631
921130	1632-1633
921140	1634-1635
921190	1636-1637
922160	1638-1639
923110	1640-1641
923120	1642-1643
924110	1644-1645
925110	1646-1647
925120	1648-1649
926110	1650-1651

DESCRIPTION OF INDUSTRIES INCLUDED IN THE STATEMENT STUDIES

AGRICULTURE, FORESTRY, FISHING AND HUNTING

NAICS #		Page
111110	**Soybean Farming.** This industry comprises establishments primarily engaged in growing soybeans and/or producing soybean seeds.	96-97
111140	**Wheat Farming.** This industry comprises establishments primarily engaged in growing wheat and/or producing wheat seeds.	98-99
111150	**Corn Farming.** This industry comprises establishments primarily engaged in growing corn (except sweet corn) and/or producing corn seeds.	100-101
111199	**All Other Grain Farming.** This U.S. industry comprises establishments primarily engaged in growing grains and/or producing grain(s) seeds (except wheat, corn, rice, and oilseed(s) and grain(s) combinations).	102-103
111211	**Potato Farming.** This U.S. industry comprises establishments primarily engaged in growing potatoes and/or producing seed potatoes (except sweet potatoes).	104-105
111219	**Other Vegetable (except Potato) and Melon Farming.** This U.S. industry comprises establishments primarily engaged in one or more of the following: (1) growing melons and/or vegetables (except potatoes; dry peas; dry beans; field, silage, or seed corn; and sugar beets); (2) producing vegetable and/or melon seeds; and (3) growing vegetable and/or melon bedding plants.	106-107
111310	**Orange Groves.** This industry comprises establishments primarily engaged in growing oranges.	108-109
111331	**Apple Orchards.** This U.S. industry comprises establishments primarily engaged in growing apples.	110-111
111332	**Grape Vineyards.** This U.S. industry comprises establishments primarily engaged in growing grapes and/or growing grapes to sun dry into raisins.	112-113
111335	**Tree Nut Farming.** This U.S. industry comprises establishments primarily engaged in growing tree nuts.	114-115
111411	**Mushroom Production.** This U.S. industry comprises establishments primarily engaged in growing mushrooms under cover in mines underground, or in other controlled environments.	116-117
111421	**Nursery and Tree Production.** This U.S. industry comprises establishments primarily engaged in (1) growing nursery products, nursery stock, shrubbery, bulbs, fruit stock, sod, and so forth, under cover or in open fields and/or (2) growing short rotation woody trees with a growth and harvest cycle of 10 years or less for pulp or tree stock.	118-119
111910	**Tobacco Farming.** This industry comprises establishments primarily engaged in growing tobacco.	120-121
111920	**Cotton Farming.** This industry comprises establishments primarily engaged in growing cotton.	122-123
111998	**All Other Miscellaneous Crop Farming.** This U.S. industry comprises establishments primarily engaged in one of the following: (1) growing crops (except oilseeds and/or grains; vegetables and/or melons; fruits and/or tree nuts; greenhouse, nursery and/or floriculture products; tobacco; cotton; sugarcane; hay; sugar beets; or peanuts); (2) growing a combination of crops (except a combination of oilseed(s) and grain(s); and a combination of fruit(s) and tree nut(s)) with no one crop or family of crop(s) accounting for one-half of the establishment's agricultural production (i.e., value of crops for market); or (3) gathering tea or maple sap.	124-125
112111	**Beef Cattle Ranching and Farming.** This U.S. industry comprises establishments primarily engaged in raising cattle (including cattle for dairy herd replacements).	126-127
112112	**Cattle Feedlots.** This U.S. industry comprises establishments primarily engaged in feeding cattle for fattening.	128-129
112120	**Dairy Cattle and Milk Production.** This industry comprises establishments primarily engaged in milking dairy cattle.	130-131

NAICS # **Page**

112210 Hog and Pig Farming. This industry comprises establishments primarily engaged in raising hogs and pigs. These establishments may include farming activities, such as breeding, farrowing, and the raising of weanling pigs, feeder pigs, or market size hogs. 132-133

112310 Chicken Egg Production. This industry comprises establishments primarily engaged in raising chickens for egg production. The eggs produced may be for use as table eggs or hatching eggs. 134-135

112920 Horses and Other Equine Production. This industry comprises establishments primarily engaged in raising horses, mules, donkeys and other equines. 136-137

113110 Timber Tract Operations. This industry comprises establishments primarily engaged in the operation of timber tracts for the purpose of selling standing timber. 138-139

113310 Logging. This industry comprises establishments primarily engaged in one or more of the following: (1) cutting timber; (2) cutting and transporting timber; and (3) producing wood chips in the field. 140-141

114111 Finfish Fishing. This U.S. industry comprises establishments primarily engaged in the commercial catching or taking of finfish (e.g., bluefish, salmon, trout, tuna) from their natural habitat. 142-143

114112 Shellfish Fishing. This U.S. industry comprises establishments primarily engaged in the commercial catching or taking of shellfish (e.g., clams, crabs, lobsters, mussels, oysters, sea urchins, shrimp) from their natural habitat. 144-145

115111 Cotton Ginning. This U.S. industry comprises establishments primarily engaged in ginning cotton. 146-147

115112 Soil Preparation, Planting, and Cultivating. This U.S. industry comprises establishments primarily engaged in performing a soil preparation activity or crop production service, such as plowing, fertilizing, seed bed preparation, planting, cultivating, and crop protecting services. 148-149

115114 Postharvest Crop Activities (except Cotton Ginning). This U.S. industry comprises establishments primarily engaged in performing services on crops, subsequent to their harvest, with the intent of preparing them for market or further processing. These establishments provide postharvest activities, such as crop cleaning, sun drying, shelling, fumigating, curing, sorting, grading, packing, and cooling. 150-151

115116 Farm Management Services. This U.S. industry comprises establishments primarily engaged in providing farm management services on a contract or fee basis usually to citrus groves, orchards, or vineyards. These establishments always provide management and may arrange or contract for the partial or the complete operations of the farm establishment(s) it manages. Operational activities may include cultivating, harvesting, and/or other specialized agricultural support activities. 152-153

115210 Support Activities for Animal Production. This industry comprises establishments primarily engaged in performing support activities related to raising livestock (e.g., cattle, goats, hogs, horses, poultry, sheep). These establishments may perform one or more of the following: (1) breeding services for animals, including companion animals (e.g., cats, dogs, pet birds); (2) pedigree record services; (3) boarding horses; (4) dairy herd improvement activities; (5) livestock spraying; and (6) sheep dipping and shearing. 154-155

MINING

211111 Crude Petroleum and Natural Gas Extraction. This U.S. industry comprises establishments primarily engaged in (1) the exploration, development and/or the production of petroleum or natural gas from wells in which the hydrocarbons will initially flow or can be produced using normal pumping techniques or (2) the production of crude petroleum from surface shales or tar sands or from reservoirs in which the hydrocarbons are semisolids. Establishments in this industry operate oil and gas wells on their own account or for others on a contract or fee basis. 158-159

UTILITIES

NAICS # **Page**

212111 **Bituminous Coal and Lignite Surface Mining.** This U.S. industry comprises establishments primarily engaged in one or more of the following: (1) surface mining of bituminous coal and lignite; (2) developing bituminous coal and lignite surface mine sites; (3) surface mining and beneficiating (e.g., cleaning. washing, screening, and sizing coal) of bituminous coal; or (4) beneficiating (e.g., cleaning, washing, screening, and sizing coal), but not mining, bituminous coal. 160-161

212312 **Crushed and Broken Limestone Mining and Quarrying.** This U.S. industry comprises (1) establishments primarily engaged in developing the mine site, mining or quarrying crushed and broken limestone (including related rocks, such as dolomite, cement rock, marl, travertine, and calcareous tufa); and (2) preparation plants primarily engaged in beneficiating limestone (e.g., grinding or pulverizing). 162-163

212319 **Other Crushed and Broken Stone Mining and Quarrying.** This U.S. industry comprises: (1) establishments primarily engaged in developing the mine site and/or mining or quarrying crushed and broken stone (except limestone and granite); (2) preparation plants primarily engaged in beneficiating (e.g., grinding and pulverizing) stone (except limestone and granite); and (3) establishments primarily engaged in mining or quarrying bituminous limestone and bituminous sandstone. 164-165

212321 **Construction Sand and Gravel Mining.** This U.S. industry comprises establishments primarily engaged in one or more of the following: (1) operating commercial grade (i.e., construction) sand and gravel pits; (2) dredging for commercial grade sand and gravel; and (3) washing, screening, or otherwise preparing commercial grade sand and gravel. 166-167

213111 **Drilling Oil and Gas Wells.** This U.S. industry comprises establishments primarily engaged in drilling oil and gas wells for others on a contract or fee basis. This industry includes contractors that specialize in spudding in, drilling in, redrilling, and directional drilling. 168-169

213112 **Support Activities for Oil and Gas Operations.** This U.S. industry comprises establishments primarily engaged in performing support activities on a contract or fee basis for oil and gas operations (except site preparation and related construction activities). Services included are exploration (except geophysical surveying and mapping); excavating slush pits and cellars, well surveying; running, cutting, and pulling casings, tubes, and rods; cementing wells, shooting wells; perforating well casings; acidizing and chemically treating wells; and cleaning out, bailing, and swabbing wells. 170-171

UTILITIES

221111 **Hydroelectric Power Generation.** This U.S. industry comprises establishments primarily engaged in operating hydroelectric power generation facilities. These facilities use water power to drive a turbine and produce electric energy. The electric energy produced in these establishment is provided to electric power transmission systems or to electric power distribution systems. 174-175

221118 **Other Electric Power Generation.** This U.S. industry comprises establishments primarily engaged in operating electric power generation facilities (except hydroelectric, fossil fuel, nuclear, solar, wind, geothermal, biomass). These facilities convert other forms of energy, such as tidal power, into electric energy. The electric energy produced in these establishments is provided to electric power transmission systems or to electric power distribution systems. . . 176-177

221122 **Electric Power Distribution.** This U.S. industry comprises electric power establishments primarily engaged in either (1) operating electric power distribution systems (i.e., consisting of lines, poles, meters, and wiring) or (2) operating as electric power brokers or agents that arrange the sale of electricity via power distribution systems operated by others. 178-179

221210 **Natural Gas Distribution.** This industry comprises: (1) establishments primarily engaged in operating gas distribution systems (e.g., mains, meters); (2) establishments known as gas marketers that buy gas from the well and sell it to a distribution system; (3) establishments known as gas brokers or agents that arrange the sale of gas over gas distribution systems operated by others; and (4) establishments primarily engaged in transmitting and distributing gas to final consumers. 180-181

NAICS #		Page
221310	**Water Supply and Irrigation Systems.** This industry comprises establishments primarily engaged in operating water treatment plants and/or operating water supply systems. The water supply system may include pumping stations, aqueducts, and/or distribution mains. The water may be used for drinking, irrigation, or other uses.	182-183
221320	**Sewage Treatment Facilities.** This industry comprises establishments primarily engaged in operating sewer systems or sewage treatment facilities that collect, treat, and dispose of waste.	184-185

CONSTRUCTION—GENERAL

NAICS #		Page
236115	**New Single-Family Housing Construction (except For-Sale Builders).** This U.S. industry comprises general contractor establishments primarily respon-sible for the entire construction of new single-family housing, such as single-family detached houses and town houses or row houses where each housing unit (1) is separated from its neighbors by a ground-to-roof wall and (2) has no housing units constructed above or below. This industry includes general contractors responsible for the on-site assembly of modular and prefabricated houses. Single-family housing design-build firms and single-family construction management firms acting as general contractors are included in this industry.	188-189
236116	**New Multifamily Housing Construction (except For-Sale Builders).** This U.S. industry comprises general contractor establishments responsible for the construction of new multifamily residential housing units (e.g., high-rise, garden, and town house apartments and condominiums where each unit is not separated from its neighbors by a ground-to-roof wall). Multifamily design-build firms and multifamily housing construction management firms acting as general contractors are included in this industry.	190-191
236117	**New Housing For-Sale Builders.** This U.S. industry comprises operative builders primarily responsible for the entire construction of new houses and other residential buildings, single-family and multifamily, on their own account for sale. Operative builders are also known as speculative or merchant builders.	192-193
236118	**Residential Remodelers.** This U.S. industry comprises establishments primarily responsible for the remodeling construction (including additions, alterations, reconstruction, maintenance and repair work) of houses and other residential buildings, single-family and multifamily. Included in this industry are remodeling general contractors, operative remodelers, remodeling design-build firms, and remodeling project construction management firms.	194-195
236210	**Industrial Building Construction.** This industry comprises establishments primarily responsible for the construction (including new work, additions, alterations, maintenance, and repairs) of industrial buildings (except warehouses). The construction of selected additional structures, whose production processes are similar to those for industrial buildings (e.g., incinerators, cement plants, blast furnaces, and similar nonbuilding structures), is included in this industry. Included in this industry are industrial building general contractors, industrial building operative builders, industrial building design-build firms, and industrial building construction management firms.	196-197
236220	**Commercial and Institutional Building Construction.** This industry comprises establishments primarily responsible for the construction (including new work, additions, alterations, maintenance, and repairs) of commercial and institutional buildings and related structures, such as stadiums, grain elevators, and indoor swimming pools. This industry includes establishments responsible for the on-site assembly of modular or prefabricated commercial and institutional buildings. Included in this industry are commercial and institutional building general contractors, commercial and institutional building operative builders, commercial and institutional building design-build firms, and commercial and institutional building project construction management firms.	198-199
237110	**Water and Sewer Line and Related Structures Construction.** This industry comprises establishments primarily engaged in the construction of water and sewer lines, mains, pumping stations, treatment plants and storage tanks. The work performed may include new work, reconstruction, rehabilitation, and repairs. Specialty trade contractors are included in this group if they are engaged in activities primarily related to water and sewer line and related structures construction. All structures (including buildings) that are integral parts of water and sewer networks (e.g., storage tanks, pumping stations, water treatment plants, and sewage treatment plants) are included in this industry.	200-201

CONSTRUCTION-GENERAL

NAICS # **Page**

237120 **Oil and Gas Pipeline and Related Structures Construction.** This industry comprises establishments primarily engaged in the construction of oil and gas lines, mains, refineries, and storage tanks. The work performed may include new work, reconstruction, rehabilitation, and repairs. Specialty trade contractors are included in this group if they are engaged in activities primarily related to oil and gas pipeline and related structures construction. All structures (including buildings) that are integral parts of oil and gas networks (e.g., storage tanks, pumping stations, and refineries) are included in this industry. 202-203

237130 **Power and Communication Line and Related Structures Construction.** This industry comprises establishments primarily engaged in the construction of power lines and towers, power plants, and radio, television, and telecommunications transmitting/receiving towers. The work performed may include new work, reconstruction, rehabilitation, and repairs. Specialty trade contractors are included in this group if they are engaged in activities primarily related to power and communication line and related structures construction. All structures (including buildings) that are integral parts of power and communication networks (e.g., transmitting towers, substations, and power plants) are included. 204-205

237210 **Land Subdivision.** This industry comprises establishments primarily engaged in servicing land and subdividing real property into lots, for subsequent sale to builders. Servicing of land may include excavation work for the installation of roads and utility lines. The extent of work may vary from project to project. Land subdivision precedes building activity and the subsequent building is often residential, but may also be commercial tracts and industrial parks. These establishments may do all the work themselves or subcontract the work to others. Establishments that perform only the legal subdivision of land are not included in this industry. 206-207

237310 **Highway, Street, and Bridge Construction.** This industry comprises establishments primarily engaged in the construction of highways (including elevated), streets, roads, airport runways, public sidewalks, or bridges. The work performed may include new work, reconstruction, rehabilitation, and repairs. Specialty trade contractors are included in this group if they are engaged in activities primarily related to highway, street, and bridge construction (e.g., installing guardrails on highways). 208-209

237990 **Other Heavy and Civil Engineering Construction.** This industry comprises establishments primarily engaged in heavy and engineering construction projects (excluding highway, street, bridge, and distribution line construction). The work performed may include new work, reconstruction, rehabilitation, and repairs. Specialty trade contractors are included in this group if they are engaged in activities primarily related to engineering construction projects (excluding highway, street, bridge, distribution line, oil and gas structure, and utilities building and structure construction). Construction projects involving water resources (e.g., dredging and land drainage), development of marine facilities, and projects involving open space improvement (e.g., parks and trails) are included in this industry. 210-211

238110 **Poured Concrete Foundation and Structure Contractors.** This industry comprises establishments primarily engaged in pouring and finishing concrete foundations and structural elements. This industry also includes establishments performing grout and shotcrete work. The work performed may include new work, additions, alterations, maintenance, and repairs. . . . 212-213

238120 **Structural Steel and Precast Concrete Contractors.** This industry comprises establishments primarily engaged in: (1) erecting and assembling structural parts made from steel or precast concrete (e.g., steel beams, structural steel components, and similar products of precast concrete); and/or (2) assembling and installing other steel construction products (e.g., steel rods, bars, rebar, mesh, and cages) to reinforce poured-in-place concrete. The work performed may include new work, additions, alterations, maintenance, and repairs. 214-215

238130 **Framing Contractors.** This industry comprises establishments primarily engaged in structural framing and sheathing using materials other than structural steel or concrete. The work performed may include new work, additions, alterations, maintenance, and repairs. 216-217

238140 **Masonry Contractors.** This industry comprises establishments primarily engaged in masonry work, stone setting, brick laying, and other stone work. The work performed may include new work, additions, alterations, maintenance, and repairs. 218-219

238150 **Glass and Glazing Contractors.** This industry comprises establishments primarily engaged in installing glass panes in prepared openings (i.e., glazing work) and other glass work for buildings. The work performed may include new work, additions, alterations, maintenance, and repairs. 220-221

CONSTRUCTION-GENERAL

NAICS #		Page
238160	**Roofing Contractors.** This industry comprises establishments primarily engaged in roofing. This industry also includes establishments treating roofs (i.e., spraying, painting, or coating) and installing skylights. The work performed may include new work, additions, alterations, maintenance, and repairs.	222-223
238190	**Other Foundation, Structure, and Building Exterior Contractors.** This industry comprises establishments primarily engaged in building foundation and structure trades work (except poured concrete, structural steel, precast concrete, framing, masonry, glass and glazing, roofing, and siding). The work performed may include new work, additions, alterations, maintenance, and repairs.	224-225
238210	**Electrical Contractors and Other Wiring Installation Contractors.** This industry comprises establishments primarily engaged in installing and servicing electrical wiring and equipment. Electrical contractors included in this industry may include both the parts and labor when performing work. Electrical contractors may perform new work, additions, alterations, maintenance, and repairs.	226-227
238220	**Plumbing, Heating, and Air-Conditioning Contractors.** This industry comprises establishments primarily engaged in installing and servicing plumbing, heating, and air-conditioning equipment. Contractors in this industry may provide both parts and labor when performing work. The work performed may include new work, additions, alterations, maintenance, and repairs.	228-229
238290	**Other Building Equipment Contractors.** This industry comprises establishments primarily engaged in installing or servicing building equipment (except electrical; plumbing; heating, cooling, or ventilation equipment). The repair and maintenance of miscellaneous building equipment is included in this industry. The work performed may include new work, additions, alterations, maintenance, and repairs.	230-231
238310	**Drywall and Insulation Contractors.** This industry comprises establishments primarily engaged in drywall, plaster work, and building insulation work. Plaster work includes applying plain or ornamental plaster, and installation of lath to receive plaster. The work performed may include new work, additions, alterations, maintenance, and repairs.	232-233
238320	**Painting and Wall Covering Contractors.** This industry comprises establishments primarily engaged in interior or exterior painting or interior wall covering. The work performed may include new work, additions, alterations, maintenance, and repairs.	234-235
238330	**Flooring Contractors.** This industry comprises establishments primarily engaged in the installation of resilient floor tile, carpeting, linoleum, and hard wood flooring. The work performed may include new work, additions, alterations, maintenance, and repairs.	236-237
238340	**Tile and Terrazzo Contractors.** This industry comprises establishments primarily engaged in setting and installing ceramic tile, stone (interior only), and mosaic and/or mixing marble particles and cement to make terrazzo at the job site. The work performed may include new work, additions, alterations, maintenance, and repairs.	238-239
238350	**Finish Carpentry Contractors.** This industry comprises establishments primarily engaged in finish carpentry work. The work performed may include new work, additions, alterations, maintenance, and repairs.	240-241
238390	**Other Building Finishing Contractors.** This industry comprises establishments primarily engaged in building finishing trade work (except drywall, plaster and insulation work; painting and wall covering work; flooring work; tile and terrazzo work; and finish carpentry work). The work performed may include new work, additions, alterations, or maintenance and repairs.	242-243
238910	**Site Preparation Contractors.** This industry comprises establishments primarily engaged in site preparation activities, such as excavating and grading, demolition of buildings and other structures, septic system installation, and house moving. Earth moving and land clearing for all types of sites (e.g., building, nonbuilding, mining) is included in this industry. Establishments primarily engaged in construction equipment rental with operator (except cranes) are also included.	244-245
238990	**All Other Specialty Trade Contractors.** This industry comprises establishments primarily engaged in specialized trades (except foundation, structure, and building exterior contractors; building equipment contractors; building finishing contractors; and site preparation contractors). The specialty trade work performed includes new work, additions, alterations, maintenance, and repairs.	246-247

MANUFACTURING

311119 **Other Animal Food Manufacturing.** This U.S. industry comprises establishments primarily engaged in manufacturing animal food (except dog and cat) from ingredients, such as grains, oilseed mill products, and meat products. 250-251

311211 **Flour Milling.** This U.S. industry comprises establishments primarily engaged in (1) milling flour or meal from grains (except rice) or vegetables and/or (2) milling flour and preparing flour mixes or doughs. 252-253

311352 **Confectionery Manufacturing from Purchased Chocolate.** This U.S. industry comprises establishments primarily engaged in manufacturing chocolate confectioneries from chocolate produced elsewhere. Included in this industry are establishments primarily engaged in retailing chocolate confectionery products not for immediate consumption made on the premises from chocolate made elsewhere. 254-255

311411 **Frozen Fruit, Juice, and Vegetable Manufacturing.** This U.S. industry comprises establishments primarily engaged in manufacturing frozen fruits; frozen vegetables; and frozen fruit juices, ades, drinks, cocktail mixes and concentrates. 256-257

311412 **Frozen Specialty Food Manufacturing.** This U.S. industry comprises establishments primarily engaged in manufacturing frozen specialty foods (except seafood), such as frozen dinners, entrees, and side dishes; frozen pizza; frozen whipped topping; and frozen waffles, pancakes, and french toast. 258-259

311421 **Fruit and Vegetable Canning.** This U.S. industry comprises establishments primarily engaged in manufacturing canned, pickled, and brined fruits and vegetables. 260-261

311423 **Dried and Dehydrated Food Manufacturing.** This U.S. industry comprises establishments primarily engaged in (1) drying (including freeze-dried) and/or dehydrating fruits, vegetables, and soup mixes and bouillon and/or (2) drying and/or dehydrating ingredients and packaging them with other purchased ingredients, such as rice and dry pasta. 262-263

311511 **Fluid Milk Manufacturing.** This U.S. industry comprises establishments primarily engaged in (1) manufacturing processed milk products, such as pasteurized milk or cream and sour cream and/or (2) manufacturing fluid milk dairy substitutes from soybeans and other nondairy substances. 264-265

311513 **Cheese Manufacturing.** This U.S. industry comprises establishments primarily engaged in (1) manufacturing cheese products (except cottage cheese) from raw milk and/or processed milk products and/or (2) manufacturing cheese substitutes from soybean and other nondairy substances. 266-267

311520 **Ice Cream and Frozen Dessert Manufacturing.** This industry comprises establishments primarily engaged in manufacturing ice cream, frozen yogurts, frozen ices, sherbets, frozen tofu, and other frozen desserts (except bakery products). 268-269

311611 **Animal (except Poultry) Slaughtering.** This U.S. industry comprises establishments primarily engaged in slaughtering animals (except poultry and small game). Establishments that slaughter and prepare meats are included in this industry. 270-271

311612 **Meat Processed from Carcasses.** This U.S. industry comprises establishments primarily engaged in processing or preserving meat and meat byproducts (except poultry and small game) from purchased meats. This industry includes establishments primarily engaged in assembly cutting and packing of meats (i.e., boxed meats) from purchased meats. 272-273

311615 **Poultry Processing.** This U.S. industry comprises establishments primarily engaged in (1) slaughtering poultry and small game and/or (2) preparing processed poultry and small game meat and meat byproducts. 274-275

311710 **Seafood Product Preparation and Packaging.** This industry comprises establishments primarily engaged in one or more of the following: (1) canning seafood (including soup); (2) smoking, salting, and drying seafood; (3) eviscerating fresh fish by removing heads, fins, scales, bones, and entrails; (4) shucking and packing fresh shellfish; (5) processing marine fats and oils; and (6) freezing seafood. Establishments known as "floating factory ships" that are engaged in the gathering and processing of seafood into canned seafood products are included in this industry. 276-277

MANUFACTURING

NAICS #		Page
311811	**Retail Bakeries.** This U.S. industry comprises establishments primarily engaged in retailing bread and other bakery products not for immediate consumption made on the premises from flour, not from prepared dough.	278-279
311812	**Commercial Bakeries.** This U.S. industry comprises establishments primarily engaged in manufacturing fresh and frozen bread and bread-type rolls and other fresh bakery (except cookies and crackers) products.	280-281
311821	**Cookie and Cracker Manufacturing.** This U.S. industry comprises establishments primarily engaged in manufacturing cookies, crackers, and other products, such as ice cream cones.	282-283
311911	**Roasted Nuts and Peanut Butter Manufacturing.** This U.S. industry comprises establishments primarily engaged in one or more of the following: (1) salting, roasting, drying, cooking, or canning nuts; (2) processing grains or seeds into snacks; and (3) manufacturing peanut butter.	284-285
311919	**Other Snack Food Manufacturing.** This U.S. industry comprises establishments primarily engaged in manufacturing snack foods (except roasted nuts and peanut butter).	286-287
311920	**Coffee and Tea Manufacturing.** This industry comprises establishments primarily engaged in one or more of the following: (1) roasting coffee; (2) manufacturing coffee and tea concentrates (including instant and freeze-dried); (3) blending tea; (4) manufacturing herbal tea; and (5) manufacturing coffee extracts, flavorings, and syrups.	288-289
311930	**Flavoring Syrup and Concentrate Manufacturing.** This industry comprises establishments primarily engaged in manufacturing flavoring syrup drink concentrates and related products for soda fountain use or for the manufacture of soft drinks.	290-291
311941	**Mayonnaise, Dressing, and Other Prepared Sauce Manufacturing.** This U.S. industry comprises establishments primarily engaged in manufacturing mayonnaise, salad dressing, vinegar, mustard, horseradish, soy sauce, tarter sauce, Worcestershire sauce, and other prepared sauces (except tomato-based and gravy).	292-293
311942	**Spice and Extract Manufacturing.** This U.S. industry comprises establishments primarily engaged in (1) manufacturing spices, table salt, seasonings, flavoring extracts (except coffee and meat), and natural food colorings and/or (2) manufacturing dry mix food preparations, such as salad dressing mixes, gravy and sauce mixes, frosting mixes, and other dry mix preparations.	294-295
311991	**Perishable Prepared Food Manufacturing.** This U.S. industry comprises establishments primarily engaged in manufacturing perishable prepared foods, such as salads, sandwiches, prepared meals, fresh pizza, fresh pasta, and peeled or cut vegetables.	296-297
311999	**All Other Miscellaneous Food Manufacturing.** This U.S. industry comprises establishments primarily engaged in manufacturing food (except animal food; grain and oilseed milling; sugar and confectionery products; preserved fruits, vegetables, and specialties; dairy products; meat products; seafood products; bakeries and tortillas; snack foods; coffee and tea; flavoring syrups and concentrates; seasonings and dressings; and perishable prepared food). Included in this industry are establishments primarily engaged in mixing purchased dried and/or dehydrated ingredients including those mixing purchased dried and/ or dehydrated ingredients for soup mixes and bouillon.	298-299
312111	**Soft Drink Manufacturing.** This U.S. industry comprises establishments primarily engaged in manufacturing soft drinks and artificially carbonated waters.	300-301
312112	**Bottled Water Manufacturing.** This U.S. industry comprises establishments primarily engaged in purifying and bottling water (including naturally carbonated).	302-303
312120	**Breweries.** This industry comprises establishments primarily engaged in brewing beer, ale, malt liquors, and nonalcoholic beer.	304-305
312130	**Wineries.** This industry comprises establishments primarily engaged in one or more of the following: (1) growing grapes and manufacturing wine and brandies; (2) manufacturing wine and brandies from grapes and other fruits grown elsewhere; and (3) blending wines and brandies.	306-307
313110	**Fiber, Yarn, and Thread Mills.** This industry comprises establishments primarily engaged in one or more of the following: (1) spinning yarn; (2) manufacturing thread of any fiber; (3) texturizing, throwing, twisting, and winding purchased yarn or manmade fiber filaments; and (4) producing hemp yarn and further processing into rope or bags.	308-309

MANUFACTURING

NAICS #		Page
313210	**Broadwoven Fabric Mills.** This industry comprises establishments primarily engaged in weaving broadwoven fabrics and felts (except tire fabrics and rugs). Establishments in this industry may weave only, weave and finish, or weave, finish, and further fabricate fabric products. . .	310-311
313230	**Nonwoven Fabric Mills.** This industry comprises establishments primarily engaged in manufacturing nonwoven fabrics and felts. Processes used include bonding and/or interlocking fibers by mechanical, chemical, thermal, or solvent means, or by combinations thereof.	312-313
313310	**Textile and Fabric Finishing Mills.** This industry comprises (1) establishments primarily engaged in finishing of textiles, fabrics, and apparel, and (2) establishments of converters who buy fabric goods in the grey, have them finished on contract, and sell at wholesale. Finishing operations include: bleaching, dyeing, printing (e.g., roller, screen, flock, plisse), stonewashing, and other mechanical finishing, such as preshrinking, shrinking, sponging, calendering, mercerizing, and napping; as well as cleaning, scouring, and the preparation of natural fibers and raw stock. . .	314-315
313320	**Fabric Coating Mills.** This industry comprises establishments primarily engaged in coating, laminating, varnishing, waxing, and rubberizing textiles and apparel.	316-317
314110	**Carpet and Rug Mills.** This industry comprises establishments primarily engaged in (1) manufacturing woven, tufted, and other carpets and rugs, such as art squares, floor mattings, needlepunch carpeting, and door mats and mattings, from textile materials or from twisted paper, grasses, reeds, sisal, jute, or rags and/or (2) finishing carpets and rugs.	318-319
314120	**Curtain and Linen Mills.** This industry comprises establishments primarily engaged in manufacturing household textile products, such as curtains, draperies, linens, bedspreads, sheets, tablecloths, towels, and shower curtains, from purchased materials. The household textile products may be made on a stock or custom basis for sale to individual retail customers. . . .	320-321
314910	**Textile Bag and Canvas Mills.** This industry comprises establishments primarily engaged in manufacturing textile bags or other canvas and canvas-like products, such as awnings, sails, tarpaulins, and tents from purchased textile fabrics or yarns.	322-323
314999	**All Other Miscellaneous Textile Product Mills.** This U.S. industry comprises establishments primarily engaged in manufacturing textile products (except carpets and rugs; curtains and linens; textile bags and canvas products; rope, cordage, and twine; and tire cords and tire fabrics) from purchased materials.	324-325
315210	**Cut and Sew Apparel Contractors.** This industry comprises establishments commonly referred to as contractors primarily engaged in (1) cutting materials owned by others for apparel and accessories and/or (2) sewing materials owned by others for apparel and accessories.	326-327
315220	**Men's and Boys' Cut and Sew Apparel Manufacturing.** This industry comprises establishments primarily engaged in manufacturing men's and boys' cut and sew apparel from purchased fabric. Men's and boys' clothing jobbers, who perform entrepreneurial functions involved in apparel manufacture, including buying raw materials, designing and preparing samples, arranging for apparel to be made from their materials, and marketing finished apparel, are included.	328-329
315240	**Women's, Girls', and Infants' Cut and Sew Apparel Manufacturing.** This industry comprises establishments primarily engaged in manufacturing women's, girls', and infants' apparel from purchased fabric. Women's, girls', and infants' clothing jobbers, who perform entrepreneurial functions involved in apparel manufacture, including buying raw materials, designing and preparing samples, arranging for apparel to be made from their materials, and marketing finished apparel, are included.	330-331
315280	**Other Cut and Sew Apparel Manufacturing.** This industry comprises establishments primarily engaged in manufacturing cut and sew apparel from purchased fabric (except men's, boys', women's, girls', and infants' apparel). Clothing jobbers for these products, who perform entrepreneurial functions involved in apparel manufacture, including buying raw materials, designing and preparing samples, arranging for apparel to be made from their materials, and marketing finished apparel, are included. Examples of products made by these establishments are fur or leather apparel, sheep-lined clothing, team athletic uniforms, band uniforms, academic caps and gowns, clerical vestments, and costumes.	332-333

MANUFACTURING

NAICS #		Page
315990	**Apparel Accessories and Other Apparel Manufacturing.** This industry comprises establishments primarily engaged in manufacturing apparel and accessories (except apparel knitting mills, cut and sew apparel contractors, men's and boys' cut and sew apparel, women's and girls' cut and sew apparel, and other cut and sew apparel). Jobbers, who perform entrepreneurial functions involved in apparel accessories manufacture, including buying raw materials, designing and preparing samples, arranging for apparel accessories to be made from their materials, and marketing finished apparel accessories, are included. Examples of products made by these establishments are belts, caps, gloves (except medical, sporting, safety), hats, and neckties. . .	334-335
316110	**Leather and Hide Tanning and Finishing.** This industry comprises establishments primarily engaged in one or more of the following: (1) tanning, currying, and finishing hides and skins; (2) having others process hides and skins on a contract basis; and (3) dyeing or dressing furs. . .	336-337
316210	**Footwear Manufacturing.** This industry comprises establishments primarily engaged in manufacturing footwear (except orthopedic extension footwear).	338-339
321113	**Sawmills.** This U.S. industry comprises establishments primarily engaged in sawing dimension lumber, boards, beams, timbers, poles, ties, shingles, shakes, siding, and wood chips from logs or bolts. Sawmills may plane the rough lumber that they make with a planing machine to achieve smoothness and uniformity of size.	340-341
321114	**Wood Preservation.** This U.S. industry comprises establishments primarily engaged in (1) treating wood sawed, planed, or shaped in other establishments with creosote or other preservatives, such as chromated copper arsenate, to prevent decay and to protect against fire and insects and/or (2) sawing round wood poles, pilings, and posts and treating them with preservatives.	342-343
321211	**Hardwood Veneer and Plywood Manufacturing.** This U.S. industry comprises establishments primarily engaged in manufacturing hardwood veneer and/or hardwood plywood.	344-345
321214	**Truss Manufacturing.** This U.S. industry comprises establishments primarily engaged in manufacturing laminated or fabricated wood roof and floor trusses.	346-347
321911	**Wood Window and Door Manufacturing.** This U.S. industry comprises establishments primarily engaged in manufacturing window and door units, sash, window and door frames, and doors from wood or wood clad with metal or plastics.	348-349
321912	**Cut Stock, Resawing Lumber, and Planing.** This U.S. industry comprises establishments primarily engaged in one or more of the following: (1) manufacturing dimension lumber from purchased lumber; (2) manufacturing dimension stock (i.e., shapes) or cut stock; (3) resawing the output of sawmills; and (4) planing purchased lumber. These establishments generally use woodworking machinery, such as jointers, planers, lathes, and routers to shape wood.	350-351
321918	**Other Millwork (including Flooring).** This U.S. industry comprises establishments primarily engaged in manufacturing millwork (except wood windows, wood doors, and cut stock). . . .	352-353
321920	**Wood Container and Pallet Manufacturing.** This industry comprises establishments primarily engaged in manufacturing wood pallets, wood box shook, wood boxes, other wood containers, and wood parts for pallets and containers.	354-355
321991	**Manufactured Home (Mobile Home) Manufacturing.** This U.S. industry comprises establishments primarily engaged in making manufactured homes (i.e., mobile homes) and nonresidential mobile buildings. Manufactured homes are designed to accept permanent water, sewer, and utility connections and although equipped with wheels, they are not intended for regular highway movement.	356-357
321992	**Prefabricated Wood Building Manufacturing.** This U.S. industry comprises establishments primarily engaged in manufacturing prefabricated wood buildings and wood sections and panels for prefabricated wood buildings.	358-359
321999	**All Other Miscellaneous Wood Product Manufacturing.** This U.S. industry comprises establishments primarily engaged in manufacturing wood products (except establishments operating sawmills and preservation facilities; establishments manufacturing veneer, engineered wood products, millwork, wood containers, pallets, and wood container parts; and establishments making manufactured homes (i.e., mobile homes) and prefabricated buildings and components).	360-361

MANUFACTURING

NAICS #		Page
322121	**Paper (except Newsprint) Mills.** This U.S. industry comprises establishments primarily engaged in manufacturing paper (except newsprint and uncoated groundwood paper) from pulp. These establishments may manufacture or purchase pulp. In addition, the establishments may also convert the paper they make.	362-363
322211	**Corrugated and Solid Fiber Box Manufacturing.** This U.S. industry comprises establishments primarily engaged in laminating purchased paper or paperboard into corrugated or solid fiber boxes and related products, such as pads, partitions, pallets, and corrugated paper without manufacturing paperboard. These boxes are generally used for shipping.	364-365
322212	**Folding Paperboard Box Manufacturing.** This U.S. industry comprises establishments primarily engaged in converting paperboard (except corrugated) into folding paperboard boxes without manufacturing paper and paperboard.	366-367
322219	**Other Paperboard Container Manufacturing.** This U.S. industry comprises establishments primarily engaged in converting paperboard into paperboard containers, (except corrugated, solid fiber, and folding paperboard boxes) without manufacturing paperboard.	368-369
322220	**Paper Bag and Coated and Treated Paper Manufacturing.** This industry comprises establishments primarily engaged in one or more of the following: (1) cutting and coating paper and paperboard; (2) cutting and laminating paper, paperboard, and other flexible materials (except plastics film to plastics film); (3) manufacturing bags, multiwall bags, sacks of paper, metal foil, coated paper, laminates, or coated combinations of paper and foil with plastics film; (4) manufacturing laminated aluminum and other converted metal foils from purchased foils; and (5) surface coating paper or paperboard.	370-371
322230	**Stationery Product Manufacturing.** This industry comprises establishments primarily engaged in converting paper or paperboard into products used for writing, filing, art work, and similar applications.	372-373
322291	**Sanitary Paper Product Manufacturing.** This U.S. industry comprises establishments primarily engaged in converting purchased sanitary paper stock or wadding into sanitary paper products, such as facial tissues and handkerchiefs, table napkins, toilet paper, towels, disposable diapers, sanitary napkins, and tampons.	374-375
322299	**All Other Converted Paper Product Manufacturing.** This U.S. industry comprises establishments primarily engaged in converting paper or paperboard into products (except containers, bags, coated and treated paper, stationery products, and sanitary paper products) or converting pulp into pulp products, such as egg cartons, food trays, and other food containers from molded pulp.	376-377
323111	**Commercial Printing (except Screen and Books).** This U.S. industry comprises establishments primarily engaged in gravure printing without publishing (except books, grey goods, and manifold business forms). This industry includes establishments engaged in gravure printing on purchased stock materials, such as stationery, letterhead, invitations, labels, and similar items, on a job order basis.	378-379
323113	**Commercial Screen Printing.** This U.S. industry comprises establishments primarily engaged in screen printing without publishing (except books, grey goods, and manifold business forms). This industry includes establishments engaged in screen printing on purchased stock materials, such as stationery, invitations, labels, and similar items, on a job order basis. Establishments primarily engaged in printing on apparel and textile products, such as T-shirts, caps, jackets, towels, and napkins, are included in this industry.	380-381
323117	**Books Printing.** This U.S. industry comprises establishments primarily engaged in printing or printing and binding books and pamphlets without publishing.	382-383
323120	**Support Activities for Printing.** This industry comprises establishments primarily engaged in performing prepress and postpress services in support of printing activities. Prepress services may include such things as platemaking, typesetting, tradebinding and sample mounting. Postpress services include such things as book or paper bronzing, die-cutting, edging, embossing, folding, gilding, gluing, and indexing. This industry comprises establishments primarily engaged in performing prepress and postpress services in support of printing activities. Prepress services may include such things as platemaking, typesetting, tradebinding and sample mounting. Postpress services include such things as book or paper bronzing, die-cutting, edging, embossing, folding, gilding, gluing, and indexing.	384-385

MANUFACTURING

NAICS #		Page
324110	**Petroleum Refineries.** This industry comprises establishments primarily engaged in refining crude petroleum into refined petroleum. Petroleum refining involves one or more of the following activities: (1) fractionation; (2) straight distillation of crude oil; and (3) cracking.	386-387
324121	**Asphalt Paving Mixture and Block Manufacturing.** This U.S. industry comprises establishments primarily engaged in manufacturing asphalt and tar paving mixtures and blocks from purchased asphaltic materials.	388-389
324191	**Petroleum Lubricating Oil and Grease Manufacturing.** This U.S. industry comprises establishments primarily engaged in blending or compounding refined petroleum to make lubricating oils and greases and/or rerefining used petroleum lubricating oils.	390-391
324199	**All Other Petroleum and Coal Products Manufacturing.** This U.S. industry comprises establishments primarily engaged in manufacturing petroleum products (except asphalt paving, roofing, and saturated materials and lubricating oils and greases) from refined petroleum and coal products made in coke ovens not integrated with a steel mill.	392-393
325180	**Other Basic Inorganic Chemical Manufacturing.** This industry comprises establishments primarily engaged in manufacturing basic inorganic chemicals (except industrial gases and synthetic dyes and pigments). This industry comprises establishments primarily engaged in manufacturing basic inorganic chemicals (except industrial gases and synthetic dyes and pigments).	394-395
325193	**Ethyl Alcohol Manufacturing.** This U.S. industry comprises establishments primarily engaged in manufacturing nonpotable ethyl alcohol.	396-397
325199	**All Other Basic Organic Chemical Manufacturing.** This U.S. industry comprises establishments primarily engaged in manufacturing basic organic chemical products (except aromatic petrochemicals, industrial gases, synthetic organic dyes and pigments, gum and wood chemicals, cyclic crudes and intermediates, and ethyl alcohol).	398-399
325211	**Plastics Material and Resin Manufacturing.** This U.S. industry comprises establishments primarily engaged in (1) manufacturing resins, plastics materials, and nonvulcanizable thermoplastic elastomers and mixing and blending resins on a custom basis and/or (2) manufacturing noncustomized synthetic resins.	400-401
325311	**Nitrogenous Fertilizer Manufacturing.** This U.S. industry comprises establishments primarily engaged in one or more of the following: (1) manufacturing nitrogenous fertilizer materials and mixing ingredients into fertilizers; (2) manufacturing fertilizers from sewage or animal waste; and (3) manufacturing nitrogenous materials and mixing them into fertilizers.	402-403
325314	**Fertilizer (Mixing Only) Manufacturing.** This U.S. industry comprises establishments primarily engaged in mixing ingredients made elsewhere into fertilizers.	404-405
325320	**Pesticide and Other Agricultural Chemical Manufacturing.** This industry comprises establishments primarily engaged in the formulation and preparation of agricultural and household pest control chemicals (except fertilizers).	406-407
325411	**Medicinal and Botanical Manufacturing.** This U.S. industry comprises establishments primarily engaged in (1) manufacturing uncompounded medicinal chemicals and their derivatives (i.e., generally for use by pharmaceutical preparation manufacturers) and/or (2) grading, grinding, and milling uncompounded botanicals.	408-409
325412	**Pharmaceutical Preparation Manufacturing.** This U.S. industry comprises establishments primarily engaged in manufacturing in-vivo diagnostic substances and pharmaceutical preparations (except biological) intended for internal and external consumption in dose forms, such as ampoules, tablets, capsules, vials, ointments, powders, solutions, and suspensions.	410-411
325510	**Paint and Coating Manufacturing.** This industry comprises establishments primarily engaged in (1) mixing pigments, solvents, and binders into paints and other coatings, such as stains, varnishes, lacquers, enamels, shellacs, and water repellant coatings for concrete and masonry, and/or (2) manufacturing allied paint products, such as putties, paint and varnish removers, paint brush cleaners, and frit.	412-413
325520	**Adhesive Manufacturing.** This industry comprises establishments primarily engaged in manufacturing adhesives, glues, and caulking compounds.	414-415
325611	**Soap and Other Detergent Manufacturing.** This U.S. industry comprises establishments primarily engaged in manufacturing and packaging soaps and other detergents, such as laundry detergents; dishwashing detergents; toothpaste gels, and tooth powders; and natural glycerin.	416-417

MANUFACTURING

NAICS #		Page
325612	**Polish and Other Sanitation Good Manufacturing.** This U.S. industry comprises establishments primarily engaged in manufacturing and packaging polishes and specialty cleaning preparations.	418-419
325620	**Toilet Preparation Manufacturing.** This industry comprises establishments primarily engaged in preparing, blending, compounding, and packaging toilet preparations, such as perfumes, shaving preparations, hair preparations, face creams, lotions (including sunscreens), and other cosmetic preparations.	420-421
325910	**Printing Ink Manufacturing.** This industry comprises establishments primarily engaged in manufacturing printing and inkjet inks and inkjet cartridges.	422-423
325991	**Custom Compounding of Purchased Resins.** This industry comprises establishments primarily engaged in (1) custom mixing and blending plastics resins made elsewhere or (2) reformulating plastics resins from recycled plastics products.	424-425
325998	**All Other Miscellaneous Chemical Product and Preparation Manufacturing.** This U.S. industry comprises establishments primarily engaged in manufacturing chemical products (except basic chemicals, resins, synthetic rubber; cellulosic and noncellulosic fiber and filaments; pesticides, fertilizers, and other agricultural chemicals; pharmaceuticals and medicines; paints, coatings and adhesives; soap, cleaning compounds, and toilet preparations; printing inks; explosives; custom compounding of purchased resins; and photographic films, papers, plates, and chemicals).	426-427
326111	**Plastics Bag and Pouch Manufacturing.** This U.S. industry comprises establishments primarily engaged in (1) converting plastics resins into plastics bags or (2) forming, coating or laminating plastics film and sheet into single wall or multiwall plastics bags. Establishments in this industry may print on the bags they manufacture.	428-429
326112	**Plastics Packaging Film and Sheet (including Laminated) Manufacturing.** This U.S. industry comprises establishments primarily engaged in converting plastics resins into plastics packaging (flexible) film and packaging sheet.	430-431
326113	**Unlaminated Plastics Film and Sheet (except Packaging) Manufacturing.** This U.S. industry comprises establishments primarily engaged in converting plastics resins into plastics film and unlaminated sheet (except packaging).	432-433
326121	**Unlaminated Plastics Profile Shape Manufacturing.** This U.S. industry comprises establishments primarily engaged in converting plastics resins into nonrigid plastics profile shapes (except film, sheet and bags), such as rod, tube, and sausage casings.	434-435
326122	**Plastics Pipe and Pipe Fitting Manufacturing.** This U.S. industry comprises establishments primarily engaged in converting plastics resins into rigid plastics pipes and pipe fittings.	436-437
326130	**Laminated Plastics Plate, Sheet (except Packaging), and Shape Manufacturing.** This industry comprises establishments primarily engaged in laminating plastics profile shapes such as plate, sheet (except packaging), and rod. The lamination process generally involves bonding or impregnating profiles with plastics resins and compressing them under heat.	438-439
326140	**Polystyrene Foam Product Manufacturing.** This industry comprises establishments primarily engaged in manufacturing polystyrene foam products.	440-441
326150	**Urethane and Other Foam Product (except Polystyrene) Manufacturing.** This industry comprises establishments primarily engaged in manufacturing plastics foam products (except polystyrene).	442-443
326160	**Plastics Bottle Manufacturing.** This industry comprises establishments primarily engaged in manufacturing plastics bottles.	444-445
326191	**Plastics Plumbing Fixture Manufacturing.** This U.S. industry comprises establishments primarily engaged in manufacturing plastics or fiberglass plumbing fixtures. Examples of products made by these establishments are plastics or fiberglass bathtubs, hot tubs, portable toilets, and shower stalls.	446-447
326199	**All Other Plastics Product Manufacturing.** This U.S. industry comprises establishments primarily engaged in manufacturing plastics products (except film, sheet, bags, profile shapes, pipes, pipe fittings, laminates, foam products, bottles, plumbing fixtures, and resilient floor coverings).	448-449
326212	**Tire Retreading.** This U.S. industry comprises establishments primarily engaged in retreading, or rebuilding tires.	450-451

MANUFACTURING

NAICS #		Page
326220	**Rubber and Plastics Hoses and Belting Manufacturing.** This industry comprises establishments primarily engaged in manufacturing rubber hose and/or plastics (reinforced) hose and belting from natural and synthetic rubber and/or plastics resins. Establishments manufacturing garden hoses from purchased hose are included in this industry.	452-453
326291	**Rubber Product Manufacturing for Mechanical Use.** This U.S. industry comprises establishments primarily engaged in molding, extruding or lathe-cutting rubber to manufacture rubber goods (except tubing) for mechanical applications. Products of this industry are generally parts for motor vehicles, machinery, and equipment.	454-455
326299	**All Other Rubber Product Manufacturing.** This U.S. industry comprises establishments primarily engaged in manufacturing rubber products (except tires; hoses and belting; and molded, extruded, and lathecut rubber goods for mechanical applications) from natural and synthetic rubber.	456-457
327120	**Clay Building Material and Refractories Manufacturing.** This industry comprises establishments primarily engaged in shaping, molding, baking, burning, or hardening clay refractories, nonclay refractories, ceramic tile, structural clay tile, brick, and other structural clay building materials. A refractory is a material that will retain its shape and chemical identity when subjected to high temperatures and is used in applications that require extreme resistance to heat, such as furnace linings.	458-459
327211	**Flat Glass Manufacturing.** This U.S. industry comprises establishments primarily engaged in (1) manufacturing flat glass by melting silica sand or cullet or (2) manufacturing both flat glass and laminated glass by melting silica sand or cullet.	460-461
327215	**Glass Product Manufacturing Made of Purchased Glass.** This U.S. industry comprises establishments primarily engaged in coating, laminating, tempering, or shaping purchased glass.	462-463
327320	**Ready-Mix Concrete Manufacturing.** This industry comprises establishments, such as batch plants or mix plants, primarily engaged in manufacturing concrete delivered to a purchaser in a plastic and unhardened state. Ready-mix concrete manufacturing establishments may mine, quarry, or purchase sand and gravel.	464-465
327331	**Concrete Block and Brick Manufacturing.** This U.S. industry comprises establishments primarily engaged in manufacturing concrete block and brick.	466-467
327332	**Concrete Pipe Manufacturing.** This U.S. industry comprises establishments primarily engaged in manufacturing concrete pipe.	468-469
327390	**Other Concrete Product Manufacturing.** This industry comprises establishments primarily engaged in manufacturing concrete products (except block, brick, and pipe).	470-471
327910	**Abrasive Product Manufacturing.** This industry comprises establishments primarily engaged in manufacturing abrasive grinding wheels of natural or synthetic materials, abrasive-coated products, and other abrasive products.	472-473
327991	**Cut Stone and Stone Product Manufacturing.** This U.S. industry comprises establishments primarily engaged in cutting, shaping, and finishing granite, marble, limestone, slate, and other stone for building and miscellaneous uses. Stone product manufacturing establishments may mine, quarry, or purchase stone.	474-475
327999	**All Other Miscellaneous Nonmetallic Mineral Product Manufacturing.** This U.S. industry comprises establishments primarily engaged in manufacturing nonmetallic mineral products (except pottery, ceramics, and plumbing fixtures; clay building materials and refractories; glass and glass products; cement; readymix concrete; concrete products; lime; gypsum products; abrasive products; cut stone and stone products; ground and treated minerals and earth; and mineral wool).	476-477
331110	**Iron and Steel Mills and Ferroalloy Manufacturing.** This industry comprises establishments primarily engaged in one or more of the following: (1) direct reduction of iron ore; (2) manufacturing pig iron in molten or solid form; (3) converting pig iron into steel; (4) making steel; (5) making steel and manufacturing shapes (e.g., bar, plate, rod, sheet, strip, wire); (6) making steel and forming pipe and tube; and (7) manufacturing electrometallurgical ferroalloys. Ferroalloys add critical elements, such as silicon and manganese for carbon steel and chromium, vanadium, tungsten, titanium, and molybdenum for low- and high-alloy metals. Ferroalloys include iron-rich alloys and more pure forms of elements added during the steel manufacturing process that alter or improve the characteristics of the metal being made.	478-479

MANUFACTURING

NAICS #		Page
331210	**Iron and Steel Pipe and Tube Manufacturing from Purchased Steel.** This industry comprises establishments primarily engaged in manufacturing welded, riveted, or seamless pipe and tube from purchased iron or steel.	480-481
331221	**Rolled Steel Shape Manufacturing.** This U.S. industry comprises establishments primarily engaged in rolling or drawing shapes (except wire), such as plate, sheet, strip, rod, and bar, from purchased steel.	482-483
331222	**Steel Wire Drawing.** This U.S. industry comprises establishments primarily engaged in drawing wire from purchased steel.	484-485
331318	**Other Aluminum Rolling, Drawing, and Extruding.** This U.S. industry comprises establishments primarily engaged in (1) rolling, drawing, or extruding shapes (except flat rolled sheet, plate, foil, and welded tube) from purchased aluminum and/or (2) recovering aluminum from scrap and rolling, drawing, or extruding shapes (except flat rolled sheet, plate, foil, and welded tube) in integrated mills.	486-487
331420	**Copper Rolling, Drawing, Extruding, and Alloying.** This industry comprises establishments primarily engaged in one or more of the following: (1) recovering copper or copper alloys from scraps; (2) alloying purchased copper; (3) rolling, drawing, or extruding shapes, (e.g., bar, plate, sheet, strip, tube, wire) from purchased copper; and (4) recovering copper or copper alloys from scrap and rolling, drawing, or extruding shapes (e.g., bar, plate, sheet, strip, tube, wire).	488-489
331491	**Nonferrous Metal (except Copper and Aluminum) Rolling, Drawing, and Extruding.** This U.S. industry comprises establishments primarily engaged in (1) rolling, drawing, or extruding shapes (e.g., bar, plate, sheet, strip, tube) from purchased nonferrous metals) and/or (2) recovering nonferrous metals from scrap and rolling, drawing, and/or extruding shapes (e.g., bar, plate, sheet, strip, tube) in integrated mills.	490-491
331492	**Secondary Smelting, Refining, and Alloying of Nonferrous Metal (except Copper and Aluminum).** This U.S. industry comprises establishments primarily engaged in (1) alloying purchased nonferrous metals and/or (2) recovering nonferrous metals from scrap. Establishments in this industry make primary forms (e.g., bar, billet, bloom, cake, ingot, slab, slug, wire) using smelting or refining processes.	492-493
331511	**Iron Foundries.** This U.S. industry comprises establishments primarily engaged in pouring molten pig iron or iron alloys into molds to manufacture castings, (e.g., cast iron manhole covers, cast iron pipe, cast iron skillets). Establishments in this industry purchase iron made in other establishments.	494-495
331513	**Steel Foundries (except Investment).** This U.S. industry comprises establishments primarily engaged in manufacturing steel castings (except steel investment castings). Establishments in this industry purchase steel made in other establishments.	496-497
331523	**Nonferrous Metal Die-Casting Foundries.** This U.S. industry comprises establishments primarily engaged in introducing molten nonferrous metal, under high pressure, into molds or dies to make nonferrous metal die-castings. Establishments in this industry purchase nonferrous metals made in other establishments.	498-499
331524	**Aluminum Foundries (except Die-Casting).** This U.S. industry comprises establishments primarily engaged in pouring molten aluminum into molds to manufacture aluminum castings. Establishments in this industry purchase aluminum made in other establishments.	500-501
332111	**Iron and Steel Forging.** This U.S. industry comprises establishments primarily engaged in manufacturing iron and steel forgings from purchased iron and steel by hammering mill shapes. Establishments making iron and steel forgings and further manufacturing (e.g., machining, assembling) a specific manufactured product are classified in the industry of the finished product. Iron and steel forging establishments may perform surface finishing operations, such as cleaning and deburring, on the forgings they manufacture.	502-503
332117	**Powder Metallurgy Part Manufacturing.** This U.S. industry comprises establishments primarily engaged in manufacturing powder metallurgy products by compacting them in a shaped die and sintering. Establishments in this industry generally make a wide range of parts on a job or order basis.	504-505

MANUFACTURING

NAICS #		Page
332119	**Metal Crown, Closure, and Other Metal Stamping (except Automotive).** This U.S. industry comprises establishments primarily engaged in (1) stamping metal crowns and closures, such as bottle caps and home canning lids and rings; and/or (2) manufacturing other unfinished metal stampings and spinning unfinished metal products (except automotive and coins). Establishments making metal stampings and metal spun products and further manufacturing (e.g. machining, assembling) a specific product are classified in the industry of the finished product. Metal stamping and metal spun products establishments may perform surface finishing operations, such as cleaning and deburring, on the products they manufacture.	506-507
332216	**Saw Blade and Handtool Manufacturing.** This U.S. industry comprises establishments primarily engaged in (1) manufacturing saw blades, all types (including those for power sawing machines) and/or (2) manufacturing nonpowered hand and edge tools.	508-509
332311	**Prefabricated Metal Building and Component Manufacturing.** This U.S. industry comprises establishments primarily engaged in manufacturing prefabricated metal buildings, panels, and sections.	510-511
332312	**Fabricated Structural Metal Manufacturing.** This U.S. industry comprises establishments primarily engaged in fabricating structural metal products, such as concrete reinforcing bars and fabricated bar joists.	512-513
332313	**Plate Work Manufacturing.** This industry comprises establishments primarily engaged in manufacturing fabricated metal plate work by cutting, punching, bending, shaping, and welding purchased metal plate.	514-515
332321	**Metal Window and Door Manufacturing.** This U.S. industry comprises establishments primarily engaged in manufacturing metal framed windows (i.e., typically using purchased glass) and metal doors.	516-517
332322	**Sheet Metal Work Manufacturing.** This U.S. industry comprises establishments primarily engaged in manufacturing sheet metal work (except stampings).	518-519
332323	**Ornamental and Architectural Metal Work Manufacturing.** This U.S. industry comprises establishments primarily engaged in manufacturing ornamental and architectural metal work, such as staircases, metal open steel flooring, fire escapes, railings, and scaffolding.	520-521
332439	**Other Metal Container Manufacturing.** This U.S. industry comprises establishments primarily engaged in manufacturing metal (light gauge) containers (except cans).	522-523
332510	**Hardware Manufacturing.** This industry comprises establishments primarily engaged in manufacturing metal hardware, such as metal hinges, metal handles, keys, and locks (except coin-operated time locks).	524-525
332613	**Spring Manufacturing.** This U.S. industry comprises establishments primarily engaged in manufacturing springs from purchased wire, strip, or rod.	526-527
332618	**Other Fabricated Wire Product Manufacturing.** This U.S.industry comprises establishments primarily engaged in manufacturing fabricated wire products (except springs) made from purchased wire.	528-529
332710	**Machine Shops.** This industry comprises establishments known as machine shops primarily engaged in machining metal parts on a job or order basis. Generally machine shop jobs are low volume using machine tools, such as lathes (including computer numerically controlled); automatic screw machines; and machines for boring, grinding, and milling.	530-531
332721	**Precision Turned Product Manufacturing.** This U.S. industry comprises establishments known as precision turned manufacturers primarily engaged in machining precision products of all materials on a job or order basis. Generally precision turned product jobs are large volume using machines, such as automatic screw machines, rotary transfer machines, computer numerically controlled (CNC) lathes, or turning centers.	532-533
332722	**Bolt, Nut, Screw, Rivet, and Washer Manufacturing.** This U.S. industry comprises establishments primarily engaged in manufacturing metal bolts, nuts, screws, rivets, and washers, and other industrial fasteners using machines, such as headers, threaders, and nut forming machines.	534-535
332811	**Metal Heat Treating.** This U.S. industry comprises establishments primarily engaged in heat treating, such as annealing, tempering, and brazing, metals and metal products for the trade.	536-537

MANUFACTURING

NAICS #		Page
332812	**Metal Coating, Engraving (except Jewelry and Silverware), and Allied Services to Manufacturers.** This U.S. industry comprises establishments primarily engaged in one or more of the following: (1) enameling, lacquering, and varnishingmetals and metal products; (2) hot dip galvanizing metals and metal products; (3) engraving, chasing, or etching metals and metal products (except jewelry; personal goods carried on or about the person, such as compacts and cigarette cases; preciousmetal products (except precious plated flatware and other plated ware); and printing plates); (4) powder coatingmetals and metal products; and (5) providing other metal surfacing services for the trade.	538-539
332813	**Electroplating, Plating, Polishing, Anodizing, and Coloring.** This U.S. industry comprises establishments primarily engaged in electroplating, plating, anodizing, coloring, buffing, polishing, cleaning, and sandblasting metals and metal products for the trade.	540-541
332911	**Industrial Valve Manufacturing.** This U.S. industry comprises establishments primarily engaged in manufacturing industrial valves and valves for water works and municipal water systems.	542-543
332912	**Fluid Power Valve and Hose Fitting Manufacturing.** This U.S. industry comprises establishments primarily engaged in manufacturing fluid power valves and hose fittings.	544-545
332913	**Plumbing Fixture Fitting and Trim Manufacturing.** This U.S. industry comprises establishments primarily engaged in manufacturing metal and plastics plumbing fixture fittings and trim, such as faucets, flush valves, and shower heads.	546-547
332919	**Other Metal Valve and Pipe Fitting Manufacturing.** This U.S. industry comprises establishments primarily engaged in manufacturing metal valves (except industrial valves, fluid power valves, fluid power hose fittings, and plumbing fixture fittings and trim).	548-549
332991	**Ball and Roller Bearing Manufacturing.** This U.S. industry comprises establishments primarily engaged in manufacturing ball and roller bearings of all materials.	550-551
332994	**Small Arms, Ordnance, and Ordnance Accessories Manufacturing.** This U.S. industry comprises establishments primarily engaged in manufacturing small firearms that are carried and fired by the individual.	552-553
332996	**Fabricated Pipe and Pipe Fitting Manufacturing.** This U.S. industry comprises establishments primarily engaged in fabricating, such as cutting, threading and bending metal pipes and pipe fittings made from purchased metal pipe.	554-555
332999	**All Other Miscellaneous Fabricated Metal Product Manufacturing.** This U.S. industry comprises establishments primarily engaged in manufacturing fabricated metal products (except forgings and stampings, cutlery and handtools, architectural and structural metals, boilers, tanks, shipping containers, hardware, spring and wire products, machine shop products, turned products, screws, nuts and bolts, metal valves, ball and roller bearings, ammunition, small arms and other ordnances, fabricated pipes and pipe fittings, industrial patterns, and enameled iron and metal sanitary ware).	556-557
333111	**Farm Machinery and Equipment Manufacturing.** This U.S. industry comprises establishments primarily engaged in manufacturing agricultural and farm machinery and equipment, and other turf and grounds care equipment, including planting, harvesting, and grass mowing equipment (except lawn and garden-type).	558-559
333112	**Lawn and Garden Tractor and Home Lawn and Garden Equipment Manufacturing.** This U.S. industry comprises establishments primarily engaged in manufacturing powered lawnmowers, lawn and garden tractors, and other home lawn and garden equipment, such as tillers, shredders, and yard vacuums and blowers.	560-561
333120	**Construction Machinery Manufacturing.** This industry comprises establishments primarily engaged in manufacturing construction machinery, surface mining machinery, and logging equipment.	562-563
333131	**Mining Machinery and Equipment Manufacturing.** This U.S. industry comprises establishments primarily engaged in (1) manufacturing underground mining machinery and equipment, such as coal breakers, mining cars, core drills, coal cutters, rock drills and (2) manufacturing mineral beneficiating machinery and equipment used in surface or underground mines.	564-565

MANUFACTURING

NAICS #		Page
333132	**Oil and Gas Field Machinery and Equipment Manufacturing.** This U.S. industry comprises establishments primarily engaged in (1) manufacturing oil and gas field machinery and equipment, such as oil and gas field drilling machinery and equipment; oil and gas field production machinery and equipment; and oil and gas field derricks and (2) manufacturing water well drilling machinery.	566-567
333241	**Food Product Machinery Manufacturing.** This U.S. industry comprises establishments primarily engaged in manufacturing food and beverage manufacturing-type machinery and equipment, such as dairy product plant machinery and equipment (e.g., homogenizers, pasteurizers, ice cream freezers), bakery machinery and equipment (e.g., dough mixers, bake ovens, pastry rolling machines), meat and poultry processing and preparation machinery, and other commercial food products machinery (e.g., slicers, choppers, and mixers).	568-569
333243	**Sawmill, Woodworking, and Paper Machinery Manufacturing.** This U.S. industry comprises establishments primarily engaged in (1) manufacturing sawmill and woodworking machinery (except handheld), such as circular and band sawing equipment, planning machinery, and sanding machinery and/or (2) manufacturing paper industry machinery for making paper and paper products, such as pulp making machinery, paper and paperboard making machinery, and paper and paperboard converting machinery.	570-571
333244	**Printing Machinery and Equipment Manufacturing.** This U.S. industry comprises establishments primarily engaged in manufacturing printing and bookbinding machinery and equipment, such as printing presses, typesetting machinery, and bindery machinery.	572-573
333249	**Other Industrial Machinery Manufacturing.** This U.S. industry comprises establishments primarily engaged in manufacturing industrial machinery (except agricultural and farm-type; construction and mining machinery; food manufacturing-type machinery; semiconductor making machinery; sawmill, woodworking, and paper making machinery; and printing machinery and equipment).	574-575
333314	**Optical Instrument and Lens Manufacturing.** This U.S. industry comprises establishments primarily engaged in one or more of the following: (1) manufacturing optical instruments and lens, such as binoculars, microscopes (except electron, proton), telescopes, prisms, and lenses (except ophthalmic); (2) coating or polishing lenses (except ophthalmic); and (3) mounting lenses (except ophthalmic).	576-577
333318	**Other Commercial and Service Industry Machinery Manufacturing.** This U.S. industry comprises establishments primarily engaged in manufacturing commercial and service industry equipment (except optical instruments and lenses, and photographic and photocopying equipment).	578-579
333413	**Industrial and Commercial Fan and Blower and Air Purification Equipment Manufacturing.** This U.S. industry comprises establishments primarily engaged in (1) manufacturing stationary air purification equipment, such as industrial dust and fume collection equipment, electrostatic precipitation equipment, warm air furnace filters, air washers, and other dust collection equipment and/or (2) manufacturing attic fans and industrial and commercial fans and blowers, such as commercial exhaust fans and commercial ventilating fans.	580-581
333414	**Heating Equipment (except Warm Air Furnaces) Manufacturing.** This U.S. industry comprises establishments primarily engaged in manufacturing heating equipment (except electric and warm air furnaces), such as heating boilers, heating stoves, floor and wall furnaces, and wall and baseboard heating units.	582-583
333415	**Air-Conditioning and Warm Air Heating Equipment and Commercial and Industrial Refrigeration Equipment Manufacturing.** This U.S. industry comprises establishments primarily engaged in (1) manufacturing air-conditioning (except motor vehicle) and warm air furnace equipment and/or (2) manufacturing commercial and industrial refrigeration and freezer equipment.	584-585
333511	**Industrial Mold Manufacturing.** This U.S. industry comprises establishments primarily engaged in manufacturing industrial molds for casting metals or forming other materials, such as plastics, glass, or rubber.	586-587
333514	**Special Die and Tool, Die Set, Jig, and Fixture Manufacturing.** This U.S. industry comprises establishments, known as tool and die shops, primarily engaged in manufacturing special tools and fixtures, such as cutting dies and jigs.	588-589

MANUFACTURING

NAICS #		Page
333515	**Cutting Tool and Machine Tool Accessory Manufacturing.** This U.S. industry comprises establishments primarily engaged in manufacturing accessories and attachments for metal cutting and metal forming machine tools.	590-591
333517	**Machine Tool Manufacturing.** This U.S. industry comprises establishments primarily engaged in (1) manufacturing metal cutting machine tools (except handtools) and/or (2) manufacturing metal forming machine tools (except handtools), such as punching, sheering, bending, forming, pressing, forging and die-casting machines.	592-593
333519	**Rolling Mill and Other Metalworking Machinery Manufacturing.** This U.S. industry comprises establishments primarily engaged in manufacturing rolling mill machinery and equipment and/or other metal working machinery (except industrial molds; special dies and tools, die sets, jigs, and fixtures; cutting tools and machine tool accessories; and machine tools).	594-595
333612	**Speed Changer, Industrial High-Speed Drive, and Gear Manufacturing.** This U.S. industry comprises establishments primarily engaged in manufacturing gears, speed changers, and industrial high-speed drives (except hydrostatic).	596-597
333613	**Mechanical Power Transmission Equipment Manufacturing.** This U.S. industry comprises establishments primarily engaged in manufacturing mechanical power transmission equipment (except motor vehicle and aircraft), such as plain bearings, clutches (except motor vehicle and electromagnetic industrial control), couplings, joints, and drive chains.	598-599
333911	**Pump and Pumping Equipment Manufacturing.** This U.S. industry comprises establishments primarily engaged in manufacturing general purpose pumps and pumping equipment (except fluid power pumps and motors), such as reciprocating pumps, turbine pumps, centrifugal pumps, rotary pumps, diaphragm pumps, domestic water system pumps, oil well and oil field pumps and sump pumps.	600-601
333912	**Air and Gas Compressor Manufacturing.** This U.S. industry comprises establishments primarily engaged in manufacturing general purpose air and gas compressors, such as reciprocating compressors, centrifugal compressors, vacuum pumps (except laboratory), and nonagricultural spraying and dusting compressors and spray gun units.	602-603
333922	**Conveyor and Conveying Equipment Manufacturing.** This U.S. industry comprises establishments primarily engaged in manufacturing conveyors and conveying equipment, such as gravity conveyors, trolley conveyors, tow conveyors, pneumatic tube conveyors, carousel conveyors, farm conveyors, and belt conveyors.	604-605
333923	**Overhead Traveling Crane, Hoist, and Monorail System Manufacturing.** This U.S. industry comprises establishments primarily engaged in manufacturing overhead traveling cranes, hoists, and monorail systems.	606-607
333924	**Industrial Truck, Tractor, Trailer, and Stacker Machinery Manufacturing.** This U.S. industry comprises establishments primarily engaged in manufacturing industrial trucks, tractors, trailers, and stackers (i.e., truck-type), such as forklifts, pallet loaders and unloaders, and portable loading docks.	608-609
333992	**Welding and Soldering Equipment Manufacturing.** This U.S. industry comprises establishments primarily engaged in manufacturing welding and soldering equipment and accessories (except transformers), such as arc, resistance, gas, plasma, laser, electron beam, and ultrasonic welding equipment; welding electrodes; coated or cored welding wire; and soldering equipment (except handheld).	610-611
333993	**Packaging Machinery Manufacturing.** This U.S. industry comprises establishments primarily engaged in manufacturing packaging machinery, such as wrapping, bottling, canning, and labeling machinery.	612-613
333994	**Industrial Process Furnace and Oven Manufacturing.** This U.S. Industry comprises establishments primarily engaged in manufacturing industrial process furnaces, ovens, induction and dielectric heating equipment, and kilns (except cement, chemical, wood).	614-615
333999	**All Other Miscellaneous General Purpose Machinery Manufacturing.** This U.S. industry comprises establishments primarily engaged in manufacturing general purpose machinery (except ventilating, heating, air-conditioning, and commercial refrigeration equipment; metal working machinery; engines, turbines, and power transmission equipment; pumps and compressors; material handling equipment; power-driven handtools; welding and soldering equipment; packaging machinery; industrial process furnaces and ovens; fluid power cylinders and actuators; fluid power pumps and motors; and scales and balances).	616-617

MANUFACTURING

NAICS # **Page**

334111 **Electronic Computer Manufacturing.** This U.S. industry comprises establishments primarily engaged in manufacturing and/or assembling electronic computers, such as mainframes, personal computers, workstations, laptops, and computer servers. Computers can be analog, digital, or hybrid. Digital computers, the most common type, are devices that do all of the following: (1) store the processing program or programs and the data immediately necessary for the execution of the program; (2) can be freely programmed in accordance with the requirements of the user; (3) perform arithmetical computations specified by the user; and (4) execute, without human intervention, a processing program that requires the computer to modify its execution by logical decision during the processing run. Analog computers are capable of simulating mathematical models and contain at least analog, control, and programming elements. The manufacture of computers includes the assembly or integration of processors, coprocessors, memory, storage, and input/output devices into a user-programmable final product. . . . 618-619

334118 **Computer Terminal and Other Computer Peripheral Equipment Manufacturing.** This U.S. industry comprises establishments primarily engaged in manufacturing computer terminals and other computer peripheral equipment (except storage devices). 620-621

334210 **Telephone Apparatus Manufacturing.** This industry comprises establishments primarily engaged in manufacturing wire telephone and data communications equipment. These products may be standalone or board-level components of a larger system. Examples of products made by these establishments are central office switching equipment, cordless telephones (except cellular), PBX equipment, telephones, telephone answering machines, LAN modems, multi-user modems, and other data communications equipment, such as bridges, routers, and gateways. 622-623

334220 **Radio and Television Broadcasting and Wireless Communications Equipment Manufacturing.** This industry comprises establishments primarily engaged in manufacturing radio and television broadcast and wireless communications equipment. Examples of products made by these establishments are: transmitting and receiving antennas, cable television equipment, GPS equipment, pagers, cellular phones, mobile communications equipment, and radio and television studio and broadcasting equipment. 624-625

334290 **Other Communications Equipment Manufacturing.** This industry comprises establishments primarily engaged in manufacturing communications equipment (except telephone apparatus, and radio and television broadcast, and wireless communications equipment). 626-627

334310 **Audio and Video Equipment Manufacturing.** This industry comprises establishments primarily engaged in manufacturing electronic audio and video equipment for home entertainment, motor vehicle, public address and musical instrument amplifications. Examples of products made by these establishments are video cassette recorders, televisions, stereo equipment, speaker systems, household-type video cameras, jukeboxes, and amplifiers for musical instruments and public address systems. 628-629

334412 **Bare Printed Circuit Board Manufacturing.** This U.S. industry comprises establishments primarily engaged in manufacturing bare (i.e., rigid or flexible) printed circuit boards without mounted electronic components. These establishments print, perforate, plate, screen, etch, or photoprint interconnecting pathways for electric current on laminates. 630-631

334413 **Semiconductor and Related Device Manufacturing.** This U.S. industry comprises establishments primarily engaged in manufacturing semiconductors and related solid state devices. . . 632-633

334416 **Capacitor, Resistor, Coil, Transformer, and Other Inductor Manufacturing.** This U.S. industry comprises establishments primarily engaged in manufacturing electronic inductors, such as coils and transformers. 634-635

334417 **Electronic Connector Manufacturing.** This U.S. industry comprises establishments primarily engaged in manufacturing electronic connectors, such as coaxial, cylindrical, rack and panel, pin and sleeve, printed circuit and fiber optic. 636-637

334418 **Printed Circuit Assembly (Electronic Assembly) Manufacturing.** This U.S. industry comprises establishments primarily engaged in loading components onto printed circuit boards or who manufacture and ship loaded printed circuit boards. Also known as printed circuit assemblies, electronics assemblies, or modules, these products are printed circuit boards that have some or all of the semiconductor and electronic components inserted or mounted and are inputs to a wide variety of electronic systems and devices. 638-639

MANUFACTURING

NAICS # **Page**

334419 **Other Electronic Component Manufacturing.** This U.S. industry comprises establishments primarily engaged in manufacturing electronic components (except electron tubes; bare printed circuit boards; semiconductors and related devices; electronic capacitors; electronic resistors; coils, transformers and other inductors; connectors; and loaded printed circuit boards). 640-641

334510 **Electromedical and Electrotherapeutic Apparatus Manufacturing.** This U.S. industry comprises establishments primarily engaged in manufacturing electromedical and electrotherapeutic apparatus, such as magnetic resonance imaging equipment, medical ultrasound equipment, pacemakers, hearing aids, electrocardiographs, and electromedical endoscopic equipment. 642-643

334511 **Search, Detection, Navigation, Guidance, Aeronautical, and Nautical System and Instrument Manufacturing.** This U.S. industry comprises establishments primarily engaged in manufacturing search, detection, navigation, guidance, aeronautical, and nautical systems and instruments. 644-645

334512 **Automatic Environmental Control Manufacturing for Residential, Commercial, and Appliance Use.** This U.S. industry comprises establishments primarily engaged in manufacturing automatic controls and regulators for applications, such as heating, air-conditioning, refrigeration and appliances. 646-647

334513 **Instruments and Related Products Manufacturing for Measuring, Displaying, and Controlling Industrial Process Variables.** This U.S. industry comprises establishments primarily engaged in manufacturing instruments and related devices for measuring, displaying, indicating, recording, transmitting, and controlling industrial process variables. These instruments measure, display or control (monitor, analyze, and so forth) industrial process variables, such as temperature, humidity, pressure, vacuum, combustion, flow, level, viscosity, density, acidity, concentration, and rotation. 648-649

334514 **Totalizing Fluid Meter and Counting Device Manufacturing.** This U.S. industry comprises establishments primarily engaged in manufacturing totalizing (i.e., registering) fluid meters and counting devices. 650-651

334515 **Instrument Manufacturing for Measuring and Testing Electricity and Electrical Signals.** This U.S. industry comprises establishments primarily engaged in manufacturing instruments for measuring and testing the characteristics of electricity and electrical signals. 652-653

334516 **Analytical Laboratory Instrument Manufacturing.** Instruments and instrumentation systems for laboratory analysis of the chemical or physical composition or concentration of samples of solid, fluid, gaseous, or composite material. 654-655

334519 **Other Measuring and Controlling Device Manufacturing.** This U.S. industry comprises establishments primarily engaged in manufacturing measuring and controlling devices (except search, detection, navigation, guidance, aeronautical, and nautical instruments and systems; automatic environmental controls for residential, commercial, and appliance use; instruments for measurement, display, and control of industrial process variables; totalizing fluid meters and counting devices; instruments for measuring and testing electricity and electrical signals; analytical laboratory instruments; watches, clocks, and parts; irradiation equipment; and electromedical and electrotherapeutic apparatus). 656-657

335121 **Residential Electric Lighting Fixture Manufacturing.** This U.S. industry comprises establishments primarily engaged in manufacturing fixed or portable residential electric lighting fixtures and lamp shades of metal, paper, or textiles. Residential electric lighting fixtures include those for use both inside and outside the residence. 658-659

335122 **Commercial, Industrial, and Institutional Electric Lighting Fixture Manufacturing.** This U.S. industry comprises establishments primarily engaged in manufacturing commercial, industrial, and institutional electric lighting fixtures. 660-661

335129 **Other Lighting Equipment Manufacturing.** This U.S. industry comprises establishments primarily engaged in manufacturing electric lighting fixtures (except residential, commercial, industrial, institutional, and vehicular electric lighting fixtures) and nonelectric lighting equipment. 662-663

335311 **Power, Distribution, and Specialty Transformer Manufacturing.** This U.S. industry comprises establishments primarily engaged in manufacturing power, distribution, and specialty transformers (except electronic components). Industrial-type and consumer-type transformers in this industry vary (e.g., step up or step down) voltage but do not convert alternating to direct or direct to alternating current. 664-665

MANUFACTURING

NAICS #		Page
335312	**Motor and Generator Manufacturing.** This U.S. industry comprises establishments primarily engaged in manufacturing electric motors (except internal combustion engine starting motors), power generators (except battery charging alternators for internal combustion engines), and motor generator sets (except turbine generator set units). This industry includes establishments rewinding armatures on a factory basis.	666-667
335313	**Switchgear and Switchboard Apparatus Manufacturing.** This U.S. industry comprises establishments primarily engaged in manufacturing switchgear and switchboard apparatus.	668-669
335314	**Relay and Industrial Control Manufacturing.** This U.S. industry comprises establishments primarily engaged in manufacturing relays, motor starters and controllers, and other industrial controls and control accessories.	670-671
335911	**Storage Battery Manufacturing.** This U.S. industry comprises establishments primarily engaged in manufacturing storage batteries.	672-673
335931	**Current-Carrying Wiring Device Manufacturing.** This U.S. industry comprises establishments primarily engaged in manufacturing current-carrying wiring devices.	674-675
335999	**All Other Miscellaneous Electrical Equipment and Component Manufacturing.** This U.S. industry comprises establishments primarily engaged in manufacturing industrial and commercial electric apparatus and other equipment (except lighting equipment, household appliances, transformers, motors, generators, switchgear, relays, industrial controls, batteries, communication and energy wire and cable, wiring devices, and carbon and graphite products). This industry includes power converters (i.e., AC to DC and DC to AC), power supplies, surge suppressors, and similar equipment for industrial-type and consumer-type equipment.	676-677
336111	**Automobile Manufacturing.** This U.S. industry comprises establishments primarily engaged in (1) manufacturing complete automobiles (i.e., body and chassis or unibody) or (2) manufacturing automobile chassis only.	678-679
336211	**Motor Vehicle Body Manufacturing.** This U.S. industry comprises establishments primarily engaged in manufacturing truck and bus bodies and cabs and automobile bodies. The products made may be sold separately or may be assembled on purchased chassis and sold as complete vehicles.	680-681
336212	**Truck Trailer Manufacturing.** This U.S. industry comprises establishments primarily engaged in manufacturing truck trailers, truck trailer chassis, cargo container chassis, detachable trailer bodies, and detachable trailer chassis for sale separately.	682-683
336214	**Travel Trailer and Camper Manufacturing.** This U.S. industry comprises establishments primarily engaged in one or more of the following: (1) manufacturing travel trailers and campers designed to attach to motor vehicles; (2) manufacturing pickup coaches (i.e., campers) and caps (i.e., covers) for mounting on pickup trucks; and (3) manufacturing automobile, utility and light-truck trailers. Travel trailers do not have their own motor but are designed to be towed by a motor unit, such as an automobile or a light truck.	684-685
336310	**Motor Vehicle Gasoline Engine and Engine Parts Manufacturing.** This industry comprises establishments primarily engaged in (1) manufacturing and/or rebuilding motor vehicle gasoline engines and engine parts and/or (2) manufacturing and/or rebuilding carburetors, pistons, piston rings, and engine valves, whether or not for vehicular use.	686-687
336320	**Motor Vehicle Electrical and Electronic Equipment Manufacturing.** This industry comprises establishments primarily engaged in manufacturing and/or rebuilding electrical and electronic equipment for motor vehicles and internal combustion engines. The products made can be used for all types of transportation equipment (i.e., aircraft, automobiles, trucks, trains, ships) or stationary internal combustion engine applications.	688-689
336350	**Motor Vehicle Transmission and Power Train Parts Manufacturing.** This industry comprises establishments primarily engaged in manufacturing and/or rebuilding motor vehicle transmissions and power train parts.	690-691
336360	**Motor Vehicle Seating and Interior Trim Manufacturing.** This industry comprises establishments primarily engaged in manufacturing motor vehicle seating, seats, seat frames, seat belts, and interior trimmings.	692-693
336370	**Motor Vehicle Metal Stamping.** This industry comprises establishments primarily engaged in manufacturing motor vehicle stampings, such as fenders, tops, body parts, trim, and molding.	694-695

MANUFACTURING

NAICS #		Page
336390	**Other Motor Vehicle Parts Manufacturing.** This industry comprises establishments primarily engaged in manufacturing and/or rebuilding motor vehicle parts and accessories (except motor vehicle gasoline engines and engine parts, motor vehicle electrical and electronic equipment, motor vehicle steering and suspension components, motor vehicle brake systems, motor vehicle transmissions and power train parts, motor vehicle seating and interior trim, and motor vehicle stampings).	696-697
336411	**Aircraft Manufacturing.** This U.S. industry comprises establishments primarily engaged in one or more of the following: (1) manufacturing or assembling complete aircraft; (2) developing and making aircraft prototypes; (3) aircraft conversion (i.e., major modifications to systems); and (4) complete aircraft overhaul and rebuilding (i.e., periodic restoration of aircraft to original design specifications).	698-699
336412	**Aircraft Engine and Engine Parts Manufacturing.** This U.S. industry comprises establishments primarily engaged in one or more of the following: (1) manufacturing aircraft engines and engine parts; (2) developing and making prototypes of aircraft engines and engine parts; (3) aircraft propulsion system conversion (i.e., major modifications to systems); and (4) aircraft propulsion systems overhaul and rebuilding (i.e., periodic restoration of aircraft propulsion system to original design specifications).	700-701
336413	**Other Aircraft Parts and Auxiliary Equipment Manufacturing.** This U.S. industry comprises establishment primarily engaged in (1) manufacturing aircraft parts or auxiliary equipment (except engines and aircraft fluid power subassemblies) and/or (2) developing and making prototypes of aircraft parts and auxiliary equipment. Auxiliary equipment includes such items as crop dusting apparatus, armament racks, inflight refueling equipment, and external fuel tanks.	702-703
336510	**Railroad Rolling Stock Manufacturing.** This industry comprises establishments primarily engaged in one or more of the following: (1) manufacturing and/or rebuilding locomotives, locomotive frames and parts; (2) manufacturing railroad, street, and rapid transit cars and car equipment for operation on rails for freight and passenger service; and (3) manufacturing rail layers, ballast distributors, rail tamping equipment and other railway track maintenance equipment.	704-705
336611	**Ship Building and Repairing.** This U.S. industry comprises establishments primarily engaged in operating a shipyard. Shipyards are fixed facilities with drydocks and fabrication equipment capable of building a ship, defined as watercraft typically suitable or intended for other than personal or recreational use. Activities of shipyards include the construction of ships, their repair, conversion and alteration, the production of prefabricated ship and barge sections, and specialized services, such as ship scaling.	706-707
336612	**Boat Building.** This U.S. industry comprises establishments primarily engaged in building boats. Boats are defined as watercraft not built in shipyards and typically of the type suitable or intended for personal use.	708-709
336991	**Motorcycle, Bicycle, and Parts Manufacturing.** This U.S. industry comprises establishments primarily engaged in manufacturing motorcycles, bicycles, tricycles and similar equipment, and parts.	710-711
336999	**All Other Transportation Equipment Manufacturing.** This U.S. industry comprises establishments primarily engaged in manufacturing transportation equipment (except motor vehicles, motor vehicle parts, boats, ships, railroad rolling stock, aerospace products, motorcycles, bicycles, armored vehicles and tanks).	712-713
337110	**Wood Kitchen Cabinet and Countertop Manufacturing.** This industry comprises establishments primarily engaged in manufacturing wood or plastics laminated on wood kitchen cabinets, bathroom vanities, and countertops (except freestanding). The cabinets and counters may be made on a stock or custom basis.	714-715
337121	**Upholstered Household Furniture Manufacturing.** This U.S. industry comprises establishments primarily engaged in manufacturing upholstered household-type furniture. The furniture may be made on a stock or custom basis.	716-717
337122	**Nonupholstered Wood Household Furniture Manufacturing.** This U.S. industry comprises establishments primarily engaged in manufacturing nonupholstered wood household-type furniture and freestanding cabinets (except television, radio, and sewing machine cabinets). The furniture may be made on a stock or custom basis and may be assembled or unassembled (i.e., knockdown).	718-719

MANUFACTURING

NAICS #		Page
337127	**Institutional Furniture Manufacturing.** This U.S. industry comprises establishments primarily engaged in manufacturing institutional-type furniture (e.g., library, school, theater, and church furniture). The furniture may be made on a stock or custom basis and may be assembled or unassembled (i.e., knockdown).	720-721
337211	**Wood Office Furniture Manufacturing.** This U.S. industry comprises establishments primarily engaged in manufacturing wood office-type furniture. The furniture may be made on a stock or custom basis and may be assembled or unassembled (i.e., knockdown).	722-723
337212	**Custom Architectural Woodwork and Millwork Manufacturing.** This U.S. industry comprises establishments primarily engaged in manufacturing custom designed interiors consisting of architectural woodwork and fixtures utilizing wood, wood products, and plastics laminates. All of the industry output is made to individual order on a job shop basis and requires skilled craftsmen as a labor input. A job might include custom manufacturing of display fixtures, gondolas, wall shelving units, entrance and window architectural detail, sales and reception counters, wall paneling, and matching furniture.	724-725
337214	**Office Furniture (except Wood) Manufacturing.** This U.S. industry comprises establishments primarily engaged in manufacturing nonwood office-type furniture. The furniture may be made on a stock or custom basis and may be assembled or unassembled (i.e., knockdown).	726-727
337215	**Showcase, Partition, Shelving, and Locker Manufacturing.** This U.S. industry comprises establishments primarily engaged in manufacturing wood and nonwood office and store fixtures, shelving, lockers, frames, partitions, and related fabricated products of wood and nonwood materials, including plastics laminated fixture tops. The products are made on a stock basis and may be assembled or unassembled (i.e., knockdown). Establishments exclusively making furniture parts (e.g., frames) are included in this industry.	728-729
337910	**Mattress Manufacturing.** This industry comprises establishments primarily engaged in manufacturing innerspring, box spring, and noninnerspring mattresses, including mattresses for waterbeds.	730-731
337920	**Blind and Shade Manufacturing.** This industry comprises establishments primarily engaged in manufacturing one or more of the following: venetian blinds, other window blinds, shades; curtain and drapery rods, poles; and/or curtain and drapery fixtures. The blinds and shades may be made on a stock or custom basis and may be made of any material.	732-733
339112	**Surgical and Medical Instrument Manufacturing.** This U.S. industry comprises establishments primarily engaged in manufacturing medical, surgical, ophthalmic, and veterinary instruments and apparatus (except electrotherapeutic, electromedical and irradiation apparatus). Examples of products made by these establishments are syringes, hypodermic needles, anesthesia apparatus, blood transfusion equipment, catheters, surgical clamps, and medical thermometers.	734-735
339113	**Surgical Appliance and Supplies Manufacturing.** This U.S. industry comprises establishments primarily engaged in manufacturing surgical appliances and supplies. Examples of products made by these establishments are orthopedic devices, prosthetic appliances, surgical dressings, crutches, surgical sutures, and personal industrial safety devices (except protective eyewear).	736-737
339114	**Dental Equipment and Supplies Manufacturing.** This U.S. industry comprises establishments primarily engaged in manufacturing dental equipment and supplies used by dental laboratories and offices of dentists, such as dental chairs, dental instrument delivery systems, dental hand instruments, and dental impression material and dental cements.	738-739
339115	**Ophthalmic Goods Manufacturing.** This U.S. industry comprises establishments primarily engaged in manufacturing ophthalmic goods. Examples of products made by these establishments are prescription eyeglasses (except manufactured in a retail setting), contact lenses, sunglasses, eyeglass frames, and reading glasses made to standard powers, and protective eyewear.	740-741
339116	**Dental Laboratories.** This U.S. industry comprises establishments primarily engaged in manufacturing dentures, crowns, bridges, and orthodontic appliances customized for individual application.	742-743

WHOLESALE

NAICS #		Page
339910	**Jewelry and Silverware Manufacturing.** This industry comprises establishments primarily engaged in one or more of the following: (1) manufacturing, engraving, chasing, or etching jewelry; (2) manufacturing, engraving, chasing, or etching metal personal goods (i.e., small articles carried on or about the person, such as compacts or cigarette cases); (3) manufacturing, engraving, chasing, or etching precious metal solid, precious metal clad, or pewter flatware and other hollowware; (4) stamping coins; (5) manufacturing unassembled jewelry parts and stock shop products, such as sheet, wire, and tubing; (6) cutting, slabbing, tumbling, carving, engraving, polishing, or faceting precious or semiprecious stones and gems; (7) recutting, repolishing, and setting gem stones; and (8) drilling, sawing, and peeling cultured and costume pearls. This industry includes establishments primarily engaged in manufacturing precious solid, precious clad, and precious plated jewelry and personal goods.	744-745
339920	**Sporting and Athletic Goods Manufacturing.** This industry comprises establishments primarily engaged in manufacturing sporting and athletic goods (except apparel and footwear).	746-747
339930	**Doll, Toy, and Game Manufacturing.** This industry comprises establishments primarily engaged in manufacturing dolls, such as complete dolls, doll parts, doll clothes, action figures, toys, games (including electronic), hobby kits, and children's vehicles (except metal bicycles and tricycles).	748-749
339950	**Sign Manufacturing.** This industry comprises establishments primarily engaged in manufacturing signs and related displays of all materials (except printing paper and paperboard signs, notices, displays).	750-751
339991	**Gasket, Packing, and Sealing Device Manufacturing.** This U.S. industry comprises establishments primarily engaged in manufacturing gaskets, packing, and sealing devices of all materials.	752-753
339992	**Musical Instrument Manufacturing.** This U.S. industry comprises establishments primarily engaged in manufacturing musical instruments (except toys).	754-755
339999	**All Other Miscellaneous Manufacturing.** This U.S. industry comprises establishments primarily engaged in miscellaneous manufacturing (except medical equipment and supplies, jewelry and flatware, sporting and athletic goods, dolls, toys, games, office supplies (except paper), musical instruments, fasteners, buttons, needles, pins, brooms, brushes, mops, and burial caskets).	756-757

WHOLESALE TRADE

NAICS #		Page
423110	**Automobile and Other Motor Vehicle Merchant Wholesalers.** This industry comprises establishments primarily engaged in the merchant wholesale distribution of new and used passenger automobiles, trucks, trailers, and other motor vehicles, such as motorcycles, motor homes, and snowmobiles.	760-761
423120	**Motor Vehicle Supplies and New Parts Merchant Wholesalers.** This industry comprises establishments primarily engaged in the merchant wholesale distribution of motor vehicle supplies, accessories, tools, and equipment; and new motor vehicle parts (except new tires and tubes).	762-763
423130	**Tire and Tube Merchant Wholesalers.** This industry comprises establishments primarily engaged in the merchant wholesale distribution of new and/or used tires and tubes for passenger and commercial vehicles.	764-765
423140	**Motor Vehicle Parts (Used) Merchant Wholesalers.** This industry comprises establishments primarily engaged in the merchant wholesale distribution of used motor vehicle parts (except used tires and tubes) and establishments primarily engaged in dismantling motor vehicles for the purpose of selling the parts.	766-767
423210	**Furniture Merchant Wholesalers.** This industry comprises establishments primarily engaged in the merchant wholesale distribution of furniture (except hospital beds, medical furniture, and drafting tables).	768-769
423220	**Home Furnishing Merchant Wholesalers.** This industry comprises establishments primarily engaged in the merchant wholesale distribution of home furnishings and/or housewares.	770-771
423310	**Lumber, Plywood, Millwork, and Wood Panel Merchant Wholesalers.** This industry comprises establishments primarily engaged in the merchant wholesale distribution of lumber; plywood; reconstituted wood fiber products; wood fencing; doors and windows and their frames (all materials); wood roofing and siding; and/or other wood or metal millwork.	772-773

WHOLESALE

NAICS # — **Page**

423320 **Brick, Stone, and Related Construction Material Merchant Wholesalers.** This industry comprises establishments primarily engaged in the merchant wholesale distribution of stone, cement, lime, construction sand, and gravel; brick; asphalt and concrete mixtures; and/or concrete, stone, and structural clay products. 774-775

423330 **Roofing, Siding, and Insulation Material Merchant Wholesalers.** This industry comprises establishments primarily engaged in the merchant wholesale distribution of nonwood roofing and nonwood siding and insulation materials. 776-777

423390 **Other Construction Material Merchant Wholesalers.** This industry comprises (1) establishments primarily engaged in the merchant wholesale distribution of manufactured homes (i.e., mobile homes) and/or prefabricated buildings and (2) establishments primarily engaged in the merchant wholesale distribution of construction materials (except lumber, plywood, millwork, wood panels, brick, stone, roofing, siding, electrical and wiring supplies, and insulation materials). 778-779

423410 **Photographic Equipment and Supplies Merchant Wholesalers.** This industry comprises establishments primarily engaged in the merchant wholesale distribution of photographic equipment and supplies (except office equipment). 780-781

423420 **Office Equipment Merchant Wholesalers.** This industry comprises establishments primarily engaged in the merchant wholesale distribution of office machines and related equipment (except computers and computer peripheral equipment). 782-783

423430 **Computer and Computer Peripheral Equipment and Software Merchant Wholesalers.** This industry comprises establishments primarily engaged in the merchant wholesale distribution of computers, computer peripheral equipment, loaded computer boards, and/or computer software. 784-785

423440 **Other Commercial Equipment Merchant Wholesalers.** This industry comprises establishments primarily engaged in the merchant wholesale distribution of commercial and related machines and equipment (except photographic equipment and supplies; office equipment; and computers and computer peripheral equipment and software) generally used in restaurants and stores. 786-787

423450 **Medical, Dental, and Hospital Equipment and Supplies Merchant Wholesalers.** This industry comprises establishments primarily engaged in the merchant wholesale distribution of professional medical equipment, instruments, and supplies (except ophthalmic equipment and instruments and goods used by ophthalmologists, optometrists, and opticians). 788-789

423460 **Ophthalmic Goods Merchant Wholesalers.** This industry comprises establishments primarily engaged in the merchant wholesale distribution of professional equipment, instruments, and/or goods sold, prescribed, or used by ophthalmologists, optometrists, and opticians. . . . 790-791

423490 **Other Professional Equipment and Supplies Merchant Wholesalers.** This industry comprises establishments primarily engaged in the merchant wholesale distribution of professional equipment and supplies (except ophthalmic goods and medical, dental, and hospital equipment and supplies). 792-793

423510 **Metal Service Centers and Other Metal Merchant Wholesalers.** This industry comprises establishments primarily engaged in the merchant wholesale distribution of products of the primary metals industries. Service centers maintain inventory and may perform functions, such as sawing, shearing, bending, leveling, cleaning, or edging, on a custom basis as part of sales transactions. 794-795

423520 **Coal and Other Mineral and Ore Merchant Wholesalers.** This industry comprises establishments primarily engaged in the merchant wholesale distribution of coal, coke, metal ores, and/or nonmetallic minerals (except precious and semiprecious stones and minerals used in construction, such as sand and gravel). 796-797

423610 **Electrical Apparatus and Equipment, Wiring Supplies, and Related Equipment Merchant Wholesalers.** This industry comprises establishments primarily engaged in the merchant wholesale distribution of electrical construction materials; wiring supplies; electric light fixtures; light bulbs; and/or electrical power equipment for the generation, transmission, distribution, or control of electric energy. 798-799

WHOLESALE

NAICS #		Page
423620	**Household Appliances, Electric Housewares, and Consumer Electronics Merchant Wholesalers.** This industry comprises establishments primarily engaged in the merchant wholesale distribution of household-type electrical appliances, room air-conditioners, gas and electric clothes dryers, and/or household-type audio or video equipment.	800-801
423690	**Other Electronic Parts and Equipment Merchant Wholesalers.** This industry comprises establishments primarily engaged in the merchant wholesale distribution of electronic parts and equipment (except electrical apparatus and equipment, wiring supplies and construction material; and electrical appliances, television and radio sets).	802-803
423710	**Hardware Merchant Wholesalers.** This industry comprises establishments primarily engaged in the merchant wholesale distribution of hardware, knives, or handtools.	804-805
423720	**Plumbing and Heating Equipment and Supplies (Hydronics) Merchant Wholesalers.** This industry comprises establishments primarily engaged in the merchant wholesale distribution of plumbing equipment, hydronic heating equipment, house-hold- type gas appliances (except gas clothes dryers), and/or supplies.	806-807
423730	**Warm Air Heating and Air-Conditioning Equipment and Supplies Merchant Wholesalers.** This industry comprises establishments primarily engaged in the merchant wholesale distribution of warm air heating and air-conditioning equipment and supplies.	808-809
423740	**Refrigeration Equipment and Supplies Merchant Wholesalers.** This industry comprises establishments primarily engaged in the merchant wholesale distribution of refrigeration equipment (except household-type refrigerators, freezers, and air-conditioners).	810-811
423810	**Construction and Mining (except Oil Well) Machinery and Equipment Merchant Wholesalers.** This industry comprises establishments primarily engaged in the merchant wholesale distribution of specialized machinery, equipment, and related parts generally used in construction, mining (except oil well) and logging activities.	812-813
423820	**Farm and Garden Machinery and Equipment Merchant Wholesalers.** This industry comprises establishments primarily engaged in the merchant wholesale distribution of specialized machinery, equipment, and related parts generally used in agricultural, farm, and lawn and garden activities.	814-815
423830	**Industrial Machinery and Equipment Merchant Wholesalers.** This industry comprises establishments primarily engaged in the merchant wholesale distribution of specialized machinery, equipment, and related parts generally used in manufacturing, oil well, and warehousing activities.	816-817
423840	**Industrial Supplies Merchant Wholesalers.** This industry comprises establishments primarily engaged in the merchant wholesale distribution of supplies for machinery and equipment generally used in manufacturing, oil well, and warehousing activities.	818-819
423850	**Service Establishment Equipment and Supplies Merchant Wholesalers.** This industry comprises establishments primarily engaged in the merchant wholesale distribution of specialized equipment and supplies of the type used by service establishments (except specialized equipment and supplies used in offices, stores, hotels, restaurants, schools, health and medical facilities, photographic facilities, and specialized equipment used in transportation and construction activities).	820-821
423860	**Transportation Equipment and Supplies (except Motor Vehicle) Merchant Wholesalers.** This industry comprises establishments primarily engaged in the merchant wholesale distribution of transportation equipment and supplies (except marine pleasure craft and motor vehicles).	822-823
423910	**Sporting and Recreational Goods and Supplies Merchant Wholesalers.** This industry comprises establishments primarily engaged in the merchant wholesale distribution of sporting goods and accessories; billiard and pool supplies; sporting firearms and ammunition; and/or marine pleasure craft, equipment, and supplies.	824-825
423920	**Toy and Hobby Goods and Supplies Merchant Wholesalers.** This industry comprises establishments primarily engaged in the merchant wholesale distribution of games, toys, fireworks, playing cards, hobby goods and supplies, and/or related goods.	826-827
423930	**Recyclable Material Merchant Wholesalers.** This industry comprises establishments primarily engaged in the merchant wholesale distribution of automotive scrap, industrial scrap, and other recyclable materials. Included in this industry are auto wreckers primarily engaged in dismantling motor vehicles for the purpose of wholesaling scrap.	828-829

WHOLESALE

NAICS #		Page
423940	**Jewelry, Watch, Precious Stone, and Precious Metal Merchant Wholesalers.** This industry comprises establishments primarily engaged in the merchant wholesale distribution of jewelry, precious and semiprecious stones, precious metals and metal flatware, costume jewelry, watches, clocks, silverware, and/or jewelers' findings.	830-831
423990	**Other Miscellaneous Durable Goods Merchant Wholesalers.** This industry comprises establishments primarily engaged in the merchant wholesale distribution of durable goods (except motor vehicle and motor vehicle parts and supplies; furniture and home furnishings; lumber and other construction materials; professional and commercial equipment and supplies; metals and minerals (except petroleum); electrical goods; hardware, and plumbing and heating equipment and supplies; machinery, equipment and supplies; sporting and recreational goods and supplies; toy and hobby goods and supplies; recyclable materials; and jewelry, watches, precious stones and precious metals).	832-833
424110	**Printing and Writing Paper Merchant Wholesalers.** This industry comprises establishments primarily engaged in the merchant wholesale distribution of bulk printing and/or writing paper generally on rolls for further processing.	834-835
424120	**Stationery and Office Supplies Merchant Wholesalers.** This industry comprises establishments primarily engaged in the merchant wholesale distribution of stationery, office supplies and/or gift wrap.	836-837
424130	**Industrial and Personal Service Paper Merchant Wholesalers.** This industry comprises establishments primarily engaged in the merchant wholesale distribution of kraft wrapping and other coarse paper, paperboard, converted paper (except stationery and office supplies), and/or related disposable plastics products.	838-839
424210	**Drugs and Druggists' Sundries Merchant Wholesalers.** This industry comprises establishments primarily engaged in the merchant wholesale distribution of biological and medical products; botanical drugs and herbs; and pharmaceutical products intended for internal and external consumption in such forms as ampoules, tablets, capsules, vials, ointments, powders, solutions, and suspensions.	840-841
424310	**Piece Goods, Notions, and Other Dry Goods Merchant Wholesalers.** This industry comprises establishments primarily engaged in the merchant wholesale distribution of piece goods, fabrics, knitting yarns (except industrial), thread and other notions, and/or hair accessories.	842-843
424320	**Men's and Boys' Clothing and Furnishings Merchant Wholesalers.** This industry comprises establishments primarily engaged in the merchant wholesale distribution of men's and/or boys' clothing and furnishings.	844-845
424330	**Women's, Children's, and Infants' Clothing and Accessories Merchant Wholesalers.** This industry comprises establishments primarily engaged in the merchant wholesale distribution of (1) women's, children's, infants', and/or unisex clothing and accessories and/or (2) fur clothing.	846-847
424340	**Footwear Merchant Wholesalers.** This industry comprises establishments primarily engaged in the merchant wholesale distribution of footwear (including athletic) of leather, rubber, and other materials.	848-849
424410	**General Line Grocery Merchant Wholesalers.** This industry comprises establishments primarily engaged in the merchant wholesale distribution of a general line (wide range) of groceries.	850-851
424420	**Packaged Frozen Food Merchant Wholesalers.** This industry comprises establishments primarily engaged in the merchant wholesale distribution of packaged frozen foods (except dairy products).	852-853
424430	**Dairy Product (except Dried or Canned) Merchant Wholesalers.** This industry comprises establishments primarily engaged in the merchant wholesale distribution of dairy products (except dried or canned).	854-855
424440	**Poultry and Poultry Product Merchant Wholesalers.** This industry comprises establishments primarily engaged in the merchant wholesale distribution of poultry and/or poultry products (except canned and packaged frozen).	856-857
424450	**Confectionery Merchant Wholesalers.** This industry comprises establishments primarily engaged in the merchant wholesale distribution of confectioneries; salted or roasted nuts; popcorn; potato, corn, and similar chips; and/or fountain fruits and syrups.	858-859

WHOLESALE

NAICS # **Page**

424460 **Fish and Seafood Merchant Wholesalers.** This industry comprises establishments primarily engaged in the merchant wholesale distribution of fish and seafood (except canned or packaged frozen). 860-861

424470 **Meat and Meat Product Merchant Wholesalers.** This industry comprises establishments primarily engaged in the merchant wholesale distribution of meats and meat products (except canned and packaged frozen) and/or lard. 862-863

424480 **Fresh Fruit and Vegetable Merchant Wholesalers.** This industry comprises establishments primarily engaged in the merchant wholesale distribution of fresh fruits and vegetables. 864-865

424490 **Other Grocery and Related Products Merchant Wholesalers.** This industry comprises establishments primarily engaged in the merchant wholesale distribution of groceries and related products (except a general line of groceries; packaged frozen food; dairy products (except dried and canned); poultry products (except canned); confectioneries; fish and seafood (except canned); meat products (except canned); and fresh fruits and vegetables). Included in this industry are establishments primarily engaged in the bottling and merchant wholesale distribution of spring and mineral waters processed by others. 866-867

424510 **Grain and Field Bean Merchant Wholesalers.** This industry comprises establishments primarily engaged in the merchant wholesale distribution of grains, such as corn, wheat, oats, barley, and unpolished rice; dry beans; and soybeans and other inedible beans. Included in this industry are establishments primarily engaged in operating country or terminal grain elevators primarily for the purpose of wholesaling. 868-869

424590 **Other Farm Product Raw Material Merchant Wholesalers.** This industry comprises establishments primarily engaged in the merchant wholesale distribution of farm products (except grain and field beans, livestock, raw milk, live poultry, and fresh fruits and vegetables). 870-871

424610 **Plastics Materials and Basic Forms and Shapes Merchant Wholesalers.** This industry comprises establishments primarily engaged in the merchant wholesale distribution of plastics materials and resins, and unsupported plastics film, sheet, sheeting, rod, tube, and other basic forms and shapes. 872-873

424690 **Other Chemical and Allied Products Merchant Wholesalers.** This industry comprises establishments primarily engaged in the merchant wholesale distribution of chemicals and allied products (except agricultural and medicinal chemicals, paints and varnishes, fireworks, and plastics materials and basic forms and shapes). 874-875

424710 **Petroleum Bulk Stations and Terminals.** This industry comprises establishments with bulk liquid storage facilities primar-ily engaged in the merchant wholesale distribution of crude petroleum and petroleum products, including liquefied petroleum gas. 876-877

424720 **Petroleum and Petroleum Products Merchant Wholesalers (except Bulk Stations and Terminals).** This industry comprises establishments primarily engaged in the merchant wholesale distribution of petroleum and petroleum products (except from bulk liquid storage facilities). 878-879

424810 **Beer and Ale Merchant Wholesalers.** This industry comprises establishments primarily engaged in the merchant wholesale distribution of beer, ale, porter, and other fermented malt beverages. 880-881

424820 **Wine and Distilled Alcoholic Beverage Merchant Wholesalers.** This industry comprises establishments primarily engaged in the merchant wholesale distribution of wine, distilled alcoholic beverages, and/or neutral spirits and ethyl alcohol used in blended wines and distilled liquors. 882-883

424910 **Farm Supplies Merchant Wholesalers.** This industry comprises establishments primarily engaged in the merchant wholesale distribution of farm supplies, such as animal feeds, fertilizers, agricultural chemicals, pesticides, plant seeds, and plant bulbs. 884-885

424920 **Book, Periodical, and Newspaper Merchant Wholesalers.** This industry comprises establishments primarily engaged in the merchant wholesale distribution of books, periodicals, and newspapers. 886-887

424930 **Flower, Nursery Stock, and Florists' Supplies Merchant Wholesalers.** This industry comprises establishments primarily engaged in the merchant wholesale distribution of flowers, florists' supplies, and/or nursery stock (except plant seeds and plant bulbs). 888-889

NAICS #		Page
424940	**Tobacco and Tobacco Product Merchant Wholesalers.** This industry comprises establishments primarily engaged in the merchant wholesale distribution of tobacco products, such as cigarettes, snuff, cigars, and pipe tobacco.	890-891
424950	**Paint, Varnish, and Supplies Merchant Wholesalers.** This industry comprises establishments primarily engaged in the merchant wholesale distribution of paints, varnishes, and similar coatings; pigments; wallpaper; and supplies, such as paint brushes and rollers.	892-893
424990	**Other Miscellaneous Nondurable Goods Merchant Wholesalers.** This industry comprises establishments primarily engaged in the merchant wholesale distribution of nondurable goods (except printing and writing paper; stationery and office supplies; industrial and personal service paper; drugs and druggists' sundries; apparel, piece goods, and notions; grocery and related products; farm product raw materials; chemical and allied products; petroleum and petroleum products; beer, wine, and distilled alcoholic beverages; farm supplies; books, periodicals and newspapers; flower, nursery stock and florists' supplies; tobacco and tobacco products; and paint, varnishes, wallpaper, and supplies).	894-895
425110	**Business to Business Electronic Markets.** This industry comprises business-to-business electronic markets bringing together buyers and sellers of goods using the Internet or other electronic means and generally receiving a commission or fee for the service. Business-to-business electronic markets for durable and nondurable goods are included in this industry.	896-897
425120	**Wholesale Trade Agents and Brokers.** This industry comprises wholesale trade agents and brokers acting on behalf of buyers or sellers in the wholesale distribution of goods. Agents and brokers do not take title to the goods being sold but rather receive a commission or fee for their service. Agents and brokers for all durable and nondurable goods are included in this industry.	898-899

RETAIL TRADE

NAICS #		Page
441110	**New Car Dealers.** This industry comprises establishments primarily engaged in retailing new automobiles and light trucks, such as sport utility vehicles, and passenger and cargo vans, or retailing these new vehicles in combination with activities, such as repair services, retailing used cars, and selling replacement parts and accessories.	902-903
441120	**Used Car Dealers.** This industry comprises establishments primarily engaged in retailing used automobiles and light trucks, such as sport utility vehicles, and passenger and cargo vans.	904-905
441210	**Recreational Vehicle Dealers.** This industry comprises establishments primarily engaged in retailing new and/ or used recreational vehicles commonly referred to as RVs or retailing these new vehicles in combination with activities, such as repair services and selling replacement parts and accessories.	906-907
441222	**Boat Dealers.** This U.S. industry comprises establishments primarily engaged in (1) retailing new and/or used boats or retailing new boats in combination with activities, such as repair services and selling replacement parts and accessories, and/or (2) retailing new and/or used outboard motors, boat trailers, marine supplies, parts, and accessories.	908-909
441228	**Motorcycle, ATV, and All Other Motor Vehicle Dealers.** This U.S. industry comprises establishments primarily engaged in retailing new and/or used motorcycles, motor scooters, motorbikes, mopeds, off-road all-terrain vehicles, personal watercraft, utility trailers, and other motor vehicles (except automobiles, light trucks, recreational vehicles, and boats) or retailing these new vehicles in combination with activities such as repair services and selling replacement parts and accessories.	910-911
441310	**Automotive Parts and Accessories Stores.** This industry comprises one or more of the following: (1) establishments known as automotive supply stores primarily engaged in retailing new, used, and/or rebuilt automotive parts and accessories; (2) automotive supply stores that are primarily engaged in both retailing automotive parts and accessories and repairing automobiles; and (3) establishments primarily engaged in retailing and installing automo-tive accessories.	912-913
441320	**Tire Dealers.** This industry comprises establishments primarily engaged in retailing new and/or used tires and tubes or retailing new tires in combination with automotive repair services.	914-915

RETAIL

NAICS #		Page
442110	**Furniture Stores.** This industry comprises establishments primarily engaged in retailing new furniture, such as household furniture (e.g., baby furniture box springs and mattresses) and outdoor furniture; office furniture (except those sold in combination with office supplies and equipment); and/or furniture sold in combination with major appliances, home electronics, home furnishings, or floor coverings.	916-917
442210	**Floor Covering Stores.** This industry comprises establishments primarily engaged in retailing new floor coverings, such as rugs and carpets, vinyl floor coverings, and floor tile (except ceramic or wood only); or retailing new floor coverings in combination with installation and repair services.	918-919
442299	**All Other Home Furnishings Stores.** This U.S. industry comprises establishments primarily engaged in retailing new home furnishings (except floor coverings, furniture, and window treatments).	920-921
443141	**Household Appliance Stores.** This U.S. industry comprises establishments known as appliance stores primarily engaged in retailing an array of new household appliances, such as refrigerators, dishwashers, ovens, irons, coffeemakers, hair dryers, electric razors, room air-conditioners, microwave ovens, sewing machines, and vacuum cleaners, or retailing new appliances in combination with appliance repair services.	922-923
443142	**Electronics Stores.** This U.S. industry comprises: (1) establishments known as consumer electronics stores primarily engaged in retailing a general line of new consumer-type electronic products such as televisions, computers, and cameras; (2) establishments specializing in retailing a single line of consumer-type electronic products; (3) establishments primarily engaged in retailing these new electronic products in combination with repair and support services; (4) establishments primarily engaged in retailing new prepackaged computer software; and/or (5) establishments primarily engaged in retailing prerecorded audio and video media, such as CDs, DVDs, and tapes.	924-925
444110	**Home Centers.** This industry comprises establishments known as home centers primarily engaged in retailing a general line of new home repair and improvement materials and supplies, such as lumber, plumbing goods, electrical goods, tools, housewares, hardware, and lawn and garden supplies, with no one merchandise line predominating. The merchandise lines are normally arranged in separate departments.	926-927
444120	**Paint and Wallpaper Stores.** This industry comprises establishments known as paint and wallpaper stores primarily engaged in retailing paint, wallpaper, and related supplies.	928-929
444130	**Hardware Stores.** This industry comprises establishments known as hardware stores primarily engaged in retailing a general line of new hardware items, such as tools and builders' hardware.	930-931
444190	**Other Building Material Dealers.** This industry comprises establishments (except those known as home centers, paint and wallpaper stores, and hardware stores) primarily engaged in retailing specialized lines of new building materials, such as lumber, fencing, glass, doors, plumbing fixtures and supplies, electrical supplies, prefabricated buildings and kits, and kitchen and bath cabinets and countertops to be installed.	932-933
444210	**Outdoor Power Equipment Stores.** This industry comprises establishments primarily engaged in retailing new outdoor power equipment or new outdoor power equipment in combination with activities, such as repair services and selling replacement parts.	934-935
444220	**Nursery, Garden Center, and Farm Supply Stores.** This industry comprises establishments primarily engaged in retailing nursery and garden products, such as trees, shrubs, plants, seeds, bulbs, and sod, that are predominantly grown elsewhere. These establishments may sell a limited amount of a product they grow themselves.	936-937
445110	**Supermarkets and Other Grocery (except Convenience) Stores.** This industry comprises establishments generally known as supermarkets and grocery stores primarily engaged in retailing a general line of food, such as canned and frozen foods; fresh fruits and vegetables; and fresh and prepared meats, fish, and poultry. Included in this industry are delicatessen-type establishments primarily engaged in retailing a general line of food.	938-939
445120	**Convenience Stores.** This industry comprises establishments known as convenience stores or food marts (except those with fuel pumps) primarily engaged in retailing a limited line of goods that generally includes milk, bread, soda, and snacks.	940-941

RETAIL

NAICS #		Page
445210	**Meat Markets.** This industry comprises establishments primarily engaged in retailing fresh, frozen, or cured meats and poultry. Delicatessen-type establishments primarily engaged in retailing fresh meat are included in this industry.	942-943
445230	**Fruit and Vegetable Markets.** This industry comprises establishments primarily engaged in retailing fresh fruits and vegetables.	944-945
445291	**Baked Goods Stores.** This U.S. industry comprises establishments primarily engaged in retailing baked goods not for immediate consumption and not made on the premises.	946-947
445292	**Confectionery and Nut Stores.** This U.S. industry comprises establishments primarily engaged in retailing candy and other confections, nuts, and popcorn not for immediate consumption and not made on the premises.	948-949
445299	**All Other Specialty Food Stores.** This U.S. industry comprises establishments primarily engaged in retailing miscellaneous specialty foods (except meat, fish, seafood, fruit and vegetables, confections, nuts, popcorn, and baked goods) not for immediate consumption and not made on the premises.	950-951
445310	**Beer, Wine, and Liquor Stores.** This industry comprises establishments primarily engaged in retailing packaged alcoholic beverages, such as ale, beer, wine, and liquor.	952-953
446110	**Pharmacies and Drug Stores.** This industry comprises establishments known as pharmacies and drug stores engaged in retailing prescription or nonprescription drugs and medicines.	954-955
446120	**Cosmetics, Beauty Supplies, and Perfume Stores.** This industry comprises establishments known as cosmetic or perfume stores or beauty supply shops primarily engaged in retailing cosmetics, perfumes, toiletries, and personal grooming products.	956-957
446130	**Optical Goods Stores.** This industry comprises establishments primarily engaged in one or more of the following: (1) retailing and fitting prescription eyeglasses and contact lenses; (2) retailing prescription eyeglasses in combination with the grinding of lenses to order on the premises; and (3) selling nonprescription eyeglasses.	958-959
446191	**Food (Health) Supplement Stores.** This U.S. industry comprises establishments primarily engaged in retailing food supplement products, such as vitamins, nutrition supplements, and body enhancing supplements.	960-961
446199	**All Other Health and Personal Care Stores.** This U.S. industry comprises establishments primarily engaged in retailing specialized lines of health and personal care merchandise (except drugs, medicines, optical goods, cosmetics, beauty supplies, perfume, and food supplement products).	962-963
447110	**Gasoline Stations with Convenience Stores.** This industry comprises establishments engaged in retailing automotive fuels (e.g., diesel fuel, gasohol, gasoline) in combination with convenience store or food mart items. These establishments can either be in a convenience store (i.e., food mart) setting or a gasoline station setting. These establishments may also provide automotive repair services.	964-965
447190	**Other Gasoline Stations.** This industry comprises establishments known as gasoline stations (except those with convenience stores) primarily engaged in one of the following: (1) retailing automotive fuels (e.g., diesel fuel, gasohol, gasoline) or (2) retailing these fuels in combination with activities, such as providing repair services; selling automotive oils, replacement parts, and accessories; and/or providing food services.	966-967
448110	**Men's Clothing Stores.** This industry comprises establishments primarily engaged in retailing a general line of new men's and boys' clothing. These establishments may provide basic alterations, such as hemming, taking in or letting out seams, or lengthening or shortening sleeves.	968-969
448120	**Women's Clothing Stores.** This industry comprises establishments primarily engaged in retailing a general line of new women's, misses'; and juniors' clothing, including maternity wear.	970-971
448140	**Family Clothing Stores.** This industry comprises establishments primarily engaged in retailing a general line of new clothing for men, women, and children, without specializing in sales for an individual gender or age group. These establishments may provide basic alterations, such as hemming, taking in or letting out seams, or lengthening or shortening sleeves.	972-973
448150	**Clothing Accessories Stores.** This industry comprises establishments primarily engaged in retailing single or combination lines of new clothing accessories, such as hats and caps, costume jewelry, gloves, handbags, ties, wigs, toupees, and belts.	974-975

RETAIL

NAICS #		Page
448190	**Other Clothing Stores.** This industry comprises establishments primarily engaged in retailing specialized lines of new clothing (except general lines of men's, women's, children's, infants', and family clothing). These establishments may provide basic alterations, such as hemming, taking in or letting out seams, or lengthening or shortening sleeves.	976-977
448210	**Shoe Stores.** This industry comprises establishments primarily engaged in retailing all types of new footwear (except hosiery and specialty sports footwear, such as golf shoes, bowling shoes, and spiked shoes). Establishments primarily engaged in retailing new tennis shoes or sneakers are included in this industry.	978-979
448310	**Jewelry Stores.** This industry comprises establishments primarily engaged in retailing one or more of the following items: (1) new jewelry (except costume jewelry); (2) new sterling and plated silverware; and (3) new watches and clocks. Also included are establishments retailing these new products in combination with lapidary work and/or repair services.	980-981
451110	**Sporting Goods Stores.** This industry comprises establishments primarily engaged in retailing new sporting goods, such as bicycles and bicycle parts; camping equipment; exercise and fitness equipment; athletic uniforms; specialty sports footwear; and sporting goods, equipment, and accessories.	982-983
451120	**Hobby, Toy, and Game Stores.** This industry comprises establishments primarily engaged in retailing new toys, games, and hobby and craft supplies (except needlecraft).	984-985
451140	**Musical Instrument and Supplies Stores.** This industry comprises establishments primarily engaged in retailing new musical instruments, sheet music, and related supplies; or retailing these new products in combination with musical instrument repair, rental, or music instruction.	986-987
451211	**Book Stores.** This U.S. industry comprises establishments primarily engaged in retailing new books.	988-989
452111	**Department Stores (except Discount Department Stores).** This U.S. industry comprises establishments known as department stores that have separate departments for various merchandise lines, such as apparel, jewelry, home furnishings, and linens, each with separate cash registers and sales associates. Department stores in this industry generally do not have central customer checkout and cash register facilities.	990-991
452990	**All Other General Merchandise Stores.** This industry comprises establishments primarily engaged in retailing new goods in general merchandise stores (except department stores, warehouse clubs, super-stores, and supercenters). These establishments retail a general line of new merchandise, such as apparel, automotive parts, dry goods, hardware, groceries, housewares or home furnishings, and other lines in limited amounts, with none of the lines predominating.	992-993
453110	**Florists.** This industry comprises establishments known as florists primarily engaged in retailing cut flowers, floral arrangements, and potted plants purchased from others. These establishments usually prepare the arrangements they sell.	994-995
453210	**Office Supplies and Stationery Stores.** This industry comprises establishments primarily engaged in one or more of the following: (1) retailing new stationery, school supplies, and office supplies; (2) selling a combination of new office equipment, furniture, and supplies; and (3) selling new office equipment, furniture, and supplies in combination with selling new computers.	996-997
453220	**Gift, Novelty, and Souvenir Stores.** This industry comprises establishments primarily engaged in retailing new gifts, novelty merchandise, souvenirs, greeting cards, seasonal and holiday decorations, and curios.	998-999
453310	**Used Merchandise Stores.** This industry comprises establishments primarily engaged in retailing used merchandise, antiques, and secondhand goods (except motor vehicles, such as automobiles, RVs, motorcycles, and boats; motor vehicle parts; tires; and mobile homes).	1000-1001
453910	**Pet and Pet Supplies Stores.** This industry comprises establishments primarily engaged in retailing pets, pet foods, and pet supplies.	1002-1003
453920	**Art Dealers.** This industry comprises establishments primarily engaged in retailing original and limited edition art works. Included in this industry are establishments primarily engaged in displaying works of art for retail sale in art galleries.	1004-1005

NAICS # Page

453930 **Manufactured (Mobile) Home Dealers.** This industry comprises establishments primarily engaged in retailing new and/ or used manufactured homes (i.e., mobile homes), parts, and equipment. 1006-1007

453991 **Tobacco Stores.** This U.S. industry comprises establishments primarily engaged in retailing cigarettes, cigars, tobacco, pipes, and other smokers' supplies. 1008-1009

453998 **All Other Miscellaneous Store Retailers (except Tobacco Stores).** This U.S. industry comprises establishments primarily engaged in retailing specialized lines of merchandise (except motor vehicle and parts dealers; furniture and home furnishings stores; electronic and appliance stores; building material and garden equipment and supplies dealers; food and beverage stores; health and personal care stores; gasoline stations; clothing and clothing accessories stores; sporting goods, hobby, book and music stores; general merchandise stores; florists; office supplies, stationery and gift stores; used merchandise stores; pet and pet supplies stores; art dealers; manufactured home (i.e., mobile homes) dealers; and tobacco stores). This industry also includes establishments primarily engaged in retailing a general line of new and used merchandise on an auction basis. 1010-1011

454111 **Electronic Shopping.** This U.S. Industry comprises establishments engaged in retailing all types of merchandise using the Internet. 1012-1013

454113 **Mail-Order Houses.** This U.S. industry comprises establishments primarily engaged in retailing all types of merchandise using mail catalogs or television to generate clients and display merchandise. Included in this industry are establishments primarily engaged in retailing from catalog showrooms of mail-order houses as well as establishments providing a combination of Internet and mail-order sales. 1014-1015

454210 **Vending Machine Operators.** This industry comprises establishments primarily engaged in retailing merchandise through vending machines that they service. 1016-1017

454310 **Fuel Dealers.** This industry comprises establishments primarily engaged in retailing heating oil, liquefied petroleum (LP) gas, and other fuels via direct selling. 1018-1019

454390 **Other Direct Selling Establishments.** This industry comprises establishments primarily engaged in retailing merchan-dise (except food for immediate consumption and fuel) via direct sale to the customer by means, such as in-house sales (i.e., party plan merchandising), truck or wagon sales, and portable stalls (i.e., street vendors). 1020-1021

TRANSPORTATION AND WAREHOUSING

481111 **Scheduled Passenger Air Transportation.** This U.S. industry comprises establishments primarily engaged in providing air transportation of passengers or passengers and freight over regular routes and on regular schedules. Establishments in this industry operate flights even if partially loaded. Scheduled air passenger carriers including commuter and helicopter carriers (except scenic and sightseeing) are included in this industry. 1024-1025

481211 **Nonscheduled Chartered Passenger Air Transportation.** This U.S. industry comprises establishments primarily engaged in providing air transportation of passengers or passengers and cargo with no regular routes and regular schedules. 1026-1027

481219 **Other Nonscheduled Air Transportation.** This U.S. industry comprises establishments primarily engaged in providing air transportation with no regular routes and regular schedules (except nonscheduled chartered passenger and/or cargo air transportation). These establishments provide a variety of specialty air transportation or flying services based on individual customer needs using general purpose aircraft. 1028-1029

482111 **Line-Haul Railroads.** This U.S. industry comprises establishments known as line-haul railroads primarily engaged in operating railroads for the transport of passengers and/or cargo over a long distance within a rail network. These establishments provide for the intercity movement of trains between the terminals and stations on main and branch lines of a line-haul rail network (except for local switching services). 1030-1031

483111 **Deep Sea Freight Transportation.** This U.S. industry comprises establishments primarily engaged in providing deep sea transportation of cargo to or from foreign ports. 1032-1033

TRANSPORTATION

NAICS #		Page
483113	**Coastal and Great Lakes Freight Transportation.** This U.S. industry comprises establishments primarily engaged in providing water transportation of cargo in coastal waters, on the Great Lakes System, or deep seas between ports of the United States, Puerto Rico, and United States island possessions or protectorates. Marine transportation establishments using the facilities of the St. Lawrence Seaway Authority Commission are considered to be using the Great Lakes Water Transportation System. Establishments primarily engaged in providing coastal and/or Great Lakes barge transportation services are included in this industry.	1034-1035
483211	**Inland Water Freight Transportation.** This U.S. industry comprises establishments primarily engaged in providing inland water transportation of cargo on lakes, rivers, or intracoastal waterways (except on the Great Lakes System).	1036-1037
484110	**General Freight Trucking, Local.** This industry comprises establishments primarily engaged in providing local general freight trucking. General freight establishments handle a wide variety of commodities, generally palletized and transported in a container or van trailer. Local general freight trucking establishments usually provide trucking within a metropolitan area which may cross state lines. Generally the trips are same-day return.	1038-1039
484121	**General Freight Trucking, Long-Distance, Truckload.** This U.S. industry comprises establishments primarily engaged in providing long-distance general freight truckload (TL) trucking. These long-distance general freight truckload carrier establishments provide full truck movement of freight from origin to destination. The shipment of freight on a truck is characterized as a full single load not combined with other shipments.	1040-1041
484122	**General Freight Trucking, Long-Distance, Less Than Truckload.** This U.S. industry comprises establishments primarily engaged in providing long-distance, general freight, less than truckload (LTL) trucking. LTL carriage is characterized as multiple shipments combined onto a single truck for multiple deliveries within a network. These establishments are generally characterized by the following network activities: local pickup, local sorting and terminal operations, line-haul, destination sorting and terminal operations, and local delivery.	1042-1043
484210	**Used Household and Office Goods Moving.** This industry comprises establishments primarily engaged in providing local or long-distance trucking of used household, used institutional, or used commercial furniture and equipment. Incidental packing and storage activities are often provided by these establishments.	1044-1045
484220	**Specialized Freight (except Used Goods) Trucking, Local.** This industry comprises establishments primarily engaged in providing local, specialized trucking. Local trucking establishments provide trucking within a metropolitan area that may cross state lines. Generally the trips are same-day return.	1046-1047
484230	**Specialized Freight (except Used Goods) Trucking, Long-Distance.** This industry comprises establishments primarily engaged in providing long-distance specialized trucking. These establishments provide trucking between metropolitan areas that may cross North American country borders.	1048-1049
485310	**Taxi Service.** This industry comprises establishments primarily engaged in providing passenger transportation by automobile or van, not operated over regular routes and on regular schedules. Establishments of taxicab owner/operators, taxicab fleet operators, or taxicab organizations are included in this industry.	1050-1051
485320	**Limousine Service.** This industry comprises establishments primarily engaged in providing an array of specialty and luxury passenger transportation services via limousine or luxury sedans generally on a reserved basis. These establishments do not operate over regular routes and on regular schedules.	1052-1053
485410	**School and Employee Bus Transportation.** This industry comprises establishments primarily engaged in providing buses and other motor vehicles to transport pupils to and from school or employees to and from work.	1054-1055
485510	**Charter Bus Industry.** This industry comprises establishments primarily engaged in providing buses for charter. These establishments provide bus services to meet customers' road transportation needs and generally do not operate over fixed routes and on regular schedules.	1056-1057
485991	**Special Needs Transportation.** This U.S. industry comprises establishments primarily engaged in providing special needs transportation (except to and from school or work) to the infirm, elderly, or handicapped. These establishments may use specially equipped vehicles to provide passenger transportation.	1058-1059

TRANSPORTATION

NAICS # **Page**

485999 **All Other Transit and Ground Passenger Transportation.** This U.S. industry comprises establishments primarily engaged in providing ground passenger transportation (except urban transit systems; interurban and rural bus transportation, taxi and/or limousine services (except shuttle services), school and employee bus transportation, charter bus services, and special needs transportation). Establishments primarily engaged in operating shuttle services and vanpools are included in this industry. Shuttle services establishments generally provide travel on regular routes and on regular schedules between hotels, airports, or other destination points. . . . 1060-1061

487210 **Scenic and Sightseeing Transportation, Water.** This industry comprises establishments primarily engaged in providing scenic and sightseeing transportation on water. The services provided are usually local and involve same-day return to place of origin. 1062-1063

488119 **Other Airport Operations.** This U.S. industry comprises establishments primarily engaged in (1) operating international, national, or civil airports, or public flying fields or (2) supporting airport operations, such as rental of hangar space, and providing baggage handling and/or cargo handling services. 1064-1065

488190 **Other Support Activities for Air Transportation.** This industry comprises establishments primarily engaged in providing specialized services for air transportation (except air traffic control and other airport operations). 1066-1067

488210 **Support Activities for Rail Transportation.** This industry comprises establishments primarily engaged in providing specialized services for railroad transportation including servicing, routine repairing (except factory conversion, overhaul or rebuilding of rolling stock), and maintaining rail cars; loading and unloading rail cars; and operating independent terminals. 1068-1069

488310 **Port and Harbor Operations.** This industry comprises establishments primarily engaged in operating ports, harbors (including docking and pier facilities), or canals. 1070-1071

488320 **Marine Cargo Handling.** This industry comprises establishments primarily engaged in providing stevedoring and other marine cargo handling services (except warehousing). 1072-1073

488330 **Navigational Services to Shipping.** This industry comprises establishments primarily engaged in providing navigational services to shipping. Marine salvage establishments are included in this industry. 1074-1075

488390 **Other Support Activities for Water Transportation.** This industry comprises establishments primarily engaged in providing services to water transportation (except port and harbor operations; marine cargo handling services; and navigational services to shipping). 1076-1077

488410 **Motor Vehicle Towing.** This industry comprises establishments primarily engaged in towing light or heavy motor vehicles, both local and long distance. These establishments may provide incidental services, such as storage and emergency road repair services. 1078-1079

488490 **Other Support Activities for Road Transportation.** This industry comprises establishments primarily engaged in providing services (except motor vehicle towing) to road network users. . . 1080-1081

488510 **Freight Transportation Arrangement.** This industry comprises establishments primarily engaged in arranging transportation of freight between shippers and carriers. These establishments are usually known as freight forwarders, marine shipping agents, or customs brokers and offer a combination of services spanning transportation modes. 1082-1083

488991 **Packing and Crating.** This U.S. industry comprises establishments primarily engaged in packing, crating, and otherwise preparing goods for transportation. 1084-1085

488999 **All Other Support Activities for Transportation.** This U.S. industry comprises establishments primarily engaged in providing support activities to transportation (except for air transportation; rail transportation; water transportation; road transportation; freight transportation arrangement; and packing and crating). 1086-1087

492110 **Couriers and Express Delivery Services.** This industry comprises establishments primarily engaged in providing air, surface, or combined courier delivery services of parcels generally between metropolitan areas or urban centers. The establishments of this industry form a network including courier local pick-up and delivery to serve their customers' needs. 1088-1089

493110 **General Warehousing and Storage.** This industry comprises establishments primarily engaged in operating merchandise warehousing and storage facilities. These establishments generally handle goods in containers, such as boxes, barrels, and/or drums, using equipment, such as forklifts, pallets, and racks. They are not specialized in handling bulk products of any particular type, size, or quantity of goods or products. 1090-1091

NAICS # Page

493120 **Refrigerated Warehousing and Storage.** This industry comprises establishments primarily engaged in operating refrigerated warehousing and storage facilities. Establishments primarily engaged in the storage of furs for the trade are included in this industry. The services provided by these establishments include blast freezing, tempering, and modified atmosphere storage services. 1092-1093

493130 **Farm Product Warehousing and Storage.** This industry comprises establishments primarily engaged in operating bulk farm product warehousing and storage facilities (except refrigerated). Grain elevators primarily engaged in storage are included in this industry. 1094-1095

493190 **Other Warehousing and Storage.** This industry comprises establishments primarily engaged in operating warehousing and storage facilities (except general merchandise, refrigerated, and farm product warehousing and storage). 1096-1097

INFORMATION

511110 **Newspaper Publishers.** This industry comprises establishments known as newspaper publishers. Establishments in this industry carry out operations necessary for producing and distributing newspapers, including gathering news; writing news columns, feature stories, and editorials; and selling and preparing advertisements. These establishments may publish newspapers in print or electronic form. 1100-1101

511120 **Periodical Publishers.** This industry comprises establishments known either as magazine publishers or periodical publishers. These establishments carry out the operations necessary for producing and distributing magazines and other periodicals, such as gathering, writing, and editing articles, and selling and preparing advertisements. These establishments may publish magazines and other periodicals in print or electronic form. 1102-1103

511130 **Book Publishers.** This industry comprises establishments known as book publishers. Establishments in this industry carry out design, editing, and marketing activities necessary for producing and distributing books. These establishments may publish books in print, electronic, or audio form. 1104-1105

511199 **All Other Publishers.** This U.S. industry comprises establishments generally known as publishers (except newspaper, magazine, book, directory, database, music, and greeting card publishers). These establishments may publish works in print or electronic form. 1106-1107

511210 **Software Publishers.** This industry comprises establishments primarily engaged in computer software publishing or publishing and reproduction. Establishments in this industry carry out operations necessary for producing and distributing computer software, such as designing, providing documentation, assisting in installation, and providing support services to software purchasers. These establishments may design, develop, and publish, or publish only. 1108-1109

512110 **Motion Picture and Video Production.** This industry comprises establishments primarily engaged in producing, or producing and distributing motion pictures, videos, television programs, or television commercials. 1110-1111

512131 **Motion Picture Theaters (except Drive-Ins).** This U.S. industry comprises establishments primarily engaged in operating motion picture theaters (except drive-ins) and/or exhibiting motion pictures or videos at film festivals, and so forth. 1112-1113

512191 **Teleproduction and Other Postproduction Services.** This U.S. industry comprises establishments primarily engaged in providing specialized motion picture or video postproduction services, such as editing, film/tape transfers, subtitling, credits, closed captioning, and animation and special effects. 1114-1115

512199 **Other Motion Picture and Video Industries.** This U.S. industry comprises establishments primarily engaged in providing motion picture and video services (except motion picture and video production, distribution, exhibition, and teleproduction and other postproduction services). 1116-1117

515112 **Radio Stations.** This U.S. industry comprises establishments primarily engaged in broadcasting aural programs by radio to the public. Programming may originate in their own studio, from an affiliated network, or from external sources. 1118-1119

INFORMATION

NAICS # **Page**

515120 **Television Broadcasting.** This industry comprises establishments primarily engaged in broadcasting images together with sound. These establishments operate television broadcasting studios and facilities for the programming and transmission of programs to the public. These establishments also produce or transmit visual programming to affiliated broadcast television stations, which in turn broadcast the programs to the public on a predetermined schedule. Programming may originate in their own studio, from an affiliated network, or from external sources. 1120-1121

515210 **Cable and Other Subscription Programming.** This industry comprises establishments primarily engaged in operating studios and facilities for the broadcasting of programs on a subscription or fee basis. The broadcast programming is typically narrowcast in nature (e.g., limited format, such as news, sports, education, or youth-oriented). These establishments produce programming in their own facilities or acquire programming from external sources. The programming material is usually delivered to a third party, such as cable systems or direct-to-home satellite systems, for transmission to viewers. 1122-1123

517110 **Wired Telecommunications Carriers.** This industry comprises establishments engaged in (1) operating and maintaining switching and transmission facilities to provide point-to-point communications via landlines, microwave, or a combination of landlines and satellite linkups or (2) furnishing telegraph and other non-vocal communications using their own facilities. 1124-1125

517210 **Wireless Telecommunications Carriers (except Satellite).** This industry comprises establishments engaged in operating and maintaining switching and transmission facilities to provide communications via the airwaves. Establishments in this industry have spectrum licenses and provide services using that spectrum, such as cellular phone services, paging services, wireless Internet access, and wireless video services. 1126-1127

517911 **Telecommunications Resellers.** This U.S. industry comprises establishments engaged in purchasing access and network capacity from owners and operators of telecommunications networks and reselling wired and wireless telecommunications services (except satellite) to businesses and households. Establishments in this industry resell telecommunications; they do not operate transmission facilities and infrastructure. Mobile virtual network operators (MVNOs) are included in this industry. 1128-1129

517919 **All Other Telecommunications.** This U.S. industry comprises establishments primarily engaged in providing specialized telecommunications services, such as satellite tracking, communications telemetry, and radar station operation. This industry also includes establishments primarily engaged in providing satellite terminal stations and associated facilities connected with one or more terrestrial systems and capable of transmitting telecommunications to, and receiving telecommunications from, satellite systems. Establishments providing Internet services or voice over Internet protocol (VoIP) services via client-supplied telecommunications connections are also included in this industry. 1130-1131

518210 **Data Processing, Hosting, and Related Services.** This industry comprises establishments primarily engaged in providing infra-structure for hosting or data processing services. These establishments may provide specialized hosting activities, such as Web hosting, streaming services or application hosting, provide application service provisioning, or may provide general time-share mainframe facilities to clients. Data processing establishments provide complete processing and specialized reports from data supplied by clients or provide automated data processing and data entry services. 1132-1133

519130 **Internet Publishing and Broadcasting and Web Search Portals.** This industry comprises establishments primarily engaged in 1) publishing and/or broadcasting content on the Internet exclusively or 2) operating Web sites that use a search engine to generate and maintain extensive databases of Internet addresses and content in an easily searchable format (and known as Web search portals). The publishing and broadcasting establishments in this industry do not provide traditional (non-Internet) versions of the content that they publish or broadcast. They provide textual, audio, and/or video content of general or specific interest on the Internet exclusively. Establishments known as Web search portals often provide additional Internet services, such as e-mail, connections to other web sites, auctions, news, and other limited content, and serve as a home base for Internet users. 1134-1135

519190 **All Other Information Services.** This industry comprises establishments primarily engaged in providing other information services (except news syndicates, libraries, archives, Internet publishing and broadcasting, and Web search portals). 1136-1137

NAICS # Page

FINANCE AND INSURANCE

522220 **Sales Financing.** This industry comprises establishments primarily engaged in sales financing or sales financing in combination with leasing. Sales financing establishments are primarily engaged in lending money for the purpose of providing collateralized goods through a contractual installment sales agreement, either directly from or through arrangements with dealers. . . . 1140-1141

522291 **Consumer Lending.** This U.S. industry comprises establishments primarily engaged in making unsecured cash loans to consumers. . . . 1142-1143

522292 **Real Estate Credit.** This U.S. industry comprises establishments primarily engaged in lending funds with real estate as collateral. . . . 1144-1145

522298 **All Other Nondepository Credit Intermediation.** This U.S. industry comprises establishments primarily engaged in providing nondepository credit (except credit card issuing, sales financing, consumer lending, real estate credit, international trade financing, and secondary market financing). . . . 1146-1147

522310 **Mortgage and Nonmortgage Loan Brokers.** This industry comprises establishments primarily engaged in arranging loans by bringing borrowers and lenders together on a commission or fee basis. . . . 1148-1149

522320 **Financial Transactions Processing, Reserve, and Clearinghouse Activities.** This industry comprises establishments primarily engaged in providing one or more of the following: (1) financial transaction processing (except central bank); (2) reserve and liquidity services (except central bank); and/or (3) check or other financial instrument clearinghouse services (except central bank). . . . 1150-1151

522390 **Other Activities Related to Credit Intermediation.** This industry comprises establishments primarily engaged in facilitating credit intermediation (except mortgage and loan brokerage; and financial transactions processing, reserve, and clearinghouse activities). . . . 1152-1153

523110 **Investment Banking and Securities Dealing.** This industry comprises establishments primarily engaged in underwriting, originating, and/or maintaining markets for issues of securities. Investment bankers act as principals (i.e., investors who buy or sell on their own account) in firm commitment transactions or act as agents in best effort and standby commitments. This industry also includes establishments acting as principals in buying or selling securities generally on a spread basis, such as securities dealers or stock option dealers. . . . 1154-1155

523120 **Securities Brokerage.** This industry comprises establishments primarily engaged in acting as agents (i.e., brokers) between buyers and sellers in buying or selling securities on a commission or transaction fee basis. . . . 1156-1157

523130 **Commodity Contracts Dealing.** This industry comprises establishments primarily engaged in acting as principals (i.e., investors who buy or sell for their own account) in buying or selling spot or futures commodity contracts or options, such as precious metals, foreign currency, oil, or agricultural products, generally on a spread basis. . . . 1158-1159

523910 **Miscellaneous Intermediation.** This industry comprises establishments primarily engaged in acting as principals (except investment bankers, securities dealers, and commodity contracts dealers) in buying or selling of financial contracts generally on a spread basis. Principals are investors that buy or sell for their own account. . . . 1160-1161

523920 **Portfolio Management.** This industry comprises establishments primarily engaged in managing the portfolio assets (i.e., funds) of others on a fee or commission basis. Establishments in this industry have the authority to make investment decisions, and they derive fees based on the size and/or overall performance of the portfolio. . . . 1162-1163

523930 **Investment Advice.** This industry comprises establishments primarily engaged in providing customized investment advice to clients on a fee basis, but do not have the authority to execute trades. Primary activities performed by establishments in this industry are providing financial planning advice and investment counseling to meet the goals and needs of specific clients. . . 1164-1165

523991 **Trust, Fiduciary, and Custody Activities.** This U.S. industry comprises establishments primarily engaged in providing trust, fiduciary, and custody services to others, as instructed, on a fee or contract basis, such as bank trust offices and escrow agencies (except real estate). . . . 1166-1167

REAL ESTATE

NAICS # **Page**

523999 **Miscellaneous Financial Investment Activities:** This U.S. industry comprises establishments primarily engaged in acting as agents and/or brokers (except securities brokerages and commodity contracts brokerages) in buying or selling financial contracts and those providing financial investment services (except securities and commodity exchanges; portfolio management; investment advice; and trust, fiduciary, and custody services) on a fee or commission basis. . . 1168-1169

524113 **Direct Life Insurance Carriers.** This U.S. industry comprises establishments primarily engaged in initially underwriting (i.e., assuming the risk and assigning premiums) annuities and life insurance policies, disability income insurance policies, and accidental death and dismemberment insurance policies. 1170-1171

524114 **Direct Health and Medical Insurance Carriers.** This U.S. industry comprises establishments primarily engaged in initially underwriting (i.e., assuming the risk and assigning premiums) health and medical insurance policies. Group hospitalization plans and HMO establishments (except those providing health care services) that provide health and medical insurance policies without providing health care services are included in this industry. 1172-1173

524126 **Direct Property and Casualty Insurance Carriers.** This U.S. industry comprises establishments primarily engaged in initially underwriting (i.e., assuming the risk and assigning premiums) insurance policies that protect policyholders against losses that may occur as a result of property damage or liability. 1174-1175

524127 **Direct Title Insurance Carriers.** This U.S. industry comprises establishments primarily engaged in initially underwriting (i.e., assuming the risk and assigning premiums) insurance policies to protect the owners of real estate or real estate creditors against loss sustained by reason of any title defect to real property. 1176-1177

524128 **Other Direct Insurance (except Life, Health, and Medical) Carriers.** This U.S. industry comprises establishments primarily engaged in initially underwriting (e.g., assuming the risk, assigning premiums) insurance policies (except life, disability income, accidental death and dismemberment, health and medical, property and casualty, and title insurance policies). 1178-1179

524210 **Insurance Agencies and Brokerages.** This industry comprises establishments primarily engaged in acting as agents (i.e., brokers) in selling annuities and insurance policies. 1180-1181

524291 **Claims Adjusting.** This industry comprises establishments primarily engaged in investigating, appraising, and settling insurance claims. 1182-1183

524292 **Third Party Administration of Insurance and Pension Funds.** This U.S. industry comprises establishments primarily engaged in providing third party administration services of insurance and pension funds, such as claims processing and other administrative services to insurance carriers, employee-benefit plans, and self-insurance funds. 1184-1185

524298 **All Other Insurance Related Activities.** This U.S. industry comprises establishments primarily engaged in providing insurance services on a contract or fee basis (except insurance agencies and brokerages, claims adjusting, and third party administration). Insurance advisory services and insurance ratemaking services are included in this industry. 1186-1187

525910 **Open-End Investment Funds.** This industry comprises legal entities (i.e., open-end investment funds) organized to pool assets that consist of securities or other financial instruments. Shares in these pools are offered to the public in an initial offering with additional shares offered continuously and perpetually and redeemed at a specific price determined by the net asset value. 1188-1189

525990 **Other Financial Vehicles.** This industry comprises legal entities (i.e., funds (except insurance and employee benefit funds; open-end investment funds; trusts, estates, and agency accounts; and Real Estate Investment Trusts (REITs)). 1190-1191

REAL ESTATE AND RENTAL AND LEASING

531110 **Lessors of Residential Buildings and Dwellings.** This industry comprises establishments primarily engaged in acting as lessors of buildings used as residences or dwellings, such as single-family homes, apartment buildings, and town homes. Included in this industry are owner-lessors and establishments renting real estate and then acting as lessors in subleasing it to others. The establishments in this industry may manage the property themselves or have another establishment manage it for them. 1194-1195

REAL ESTATE

NAICS # **Page**

531120 **Lessors of Nonresidential Buildings (except Miniwarehouses).** This industry comprises establishments primarily engaged in acting as lessors of buildings (except miniwarehouses and self-storage units) that are not used as residences or dwellings. Included in this industry are: (1) owner-lessors of nonresidential buildings; (2) establishments renting real estate and then acting as lessors in subleasing it to others; and (3) establishments providing full service office space, whether on a lease or service contract basis. The establishments in this industry may manage the property themselves or have another establishment manage it for them. 1196-1197

531130 **Lessors of Miniwarehouses and Self-Storage Units.** This industry comprises establishments primarily engaged in renting or leasing space for self-storage. These establishments provide secure space (i.e., rooms, compartments, lockers, containers, or outdoor space) where clients can store and retrieve their goods. 1198-1199

531190 **Lessors of Other Real Estate Property.** This industry comprises establishments primarily engaged in acting as lessors of real estate (except buildings), such as manufactured home (i.e., mobile home) sites, vacant lots, and grazing land. 1200-1201

531210 **Offices of Real Estate Agents and Brokers.** This industry comprises establishments primarily engaged in acting as agents and/or brokers in one or more of the following: (1) selling real estate for others; (2) buying real estate for others; and (3) renting real estate for others. 1202-1203

531311 **Residential Property Managers.** This U.S. industry comprises establishments primarily engaged in managing residential real estate for others. 1204-1205

531312 **Nonresidential Property Managers.** This U.S. industry comprises establishments primarily engaged in managing nonresidential real estate for others. 1206-1207

531390 **Other Activities Related to Real Estate.** This industry comprises establishments primarily engaged in performing real estate related services (except lessors of real estate, offices of real estate agents and brokers, real estate property managers, and offices of real estate appraisers). 1208-1209

532111 **Passenger Car Rental.** This industry comprises establishments primarily engaged in renting passenger cars without drivers, generally for short periods of time. 1210-1211

532112 **Passenger Car Leasing.** This industry comprises establishments primarily engaged in leasing passenger cars without drivers, generally for long periods of time. 1212-1213

532120 **Truck, Utility Trailer, and RV (Recreational Vehicle) Rental and Leasing.** This industry comprises establishments primarily engaged in renting or leasing, without drivers, one or more of the following: trucks, truck tractors or buses: semitrailers, utility trailers, or RVs (recreational vehicles). 1214-1215

532210 **Consumer Electronics and Appliances Rental.** This industry comprises establishments primarily engaged in renting consumer electronics equipment and appliances, such as televisions, stereos, and refrigerators. Included in this industry are appliance rental centers. 1216-1217

532291 **Home Health Equipment Rental.** This U.S. industry comprises establishments primarily engaged in renting hometype health and invalid equipment, such as wheel chairs, hospital beds, oxygen tanks, walkers, and crutches. 1218-1219

532299 **All Other Consumer Goods Rental.** This U.S. industry comprises establishments primarily engaged in renting consumer goods and products (except consumer electronics and appliances; formal wear and costumes; prerecorded video tapes and discs for home electronic equipment; home health furniture and equipment; and recreational goods). Included in this industry are furniture rental centers and party rental supply centers. 1220-1221

532310 **General Rental Centers.** This industry comprises establishments primarily engaged in renting a range of consumer, commercial, and industrial equipment. Establishments in this industry typically operate from conveniently located facilities where they maintain inventories of goods and equipment that they rent for short periods of time. The type of equipment that establishments in this industry provide often includes, but is not limited to: audio visual equipment, contractors' and builders' tools and equipment, home repair tools, lawn and garden equipment, moving equipment and supplies, and party and banquet equipment and supplies. . . . 1222-1223

532411 **Commercial Air, Rail, and Water Transportation Equipment Rental and Leasing.** This U.S. industry comprises establishments primarily engaged in renting or leasing off-highway transportation equipment without operators, such as aircraft, railroad cars, steamships, or tugboats. . . . 1224-1225

PROFESSIONAL SERVICES

NAICS # Page

532412 **Construction, Mining, and Forestry Machinery and Equipment Rental and Leasing.** This U.S. industry comprises establishments primarily engaged in renting or leasing heavy equipment without operators that may be used for construction, mining, or forestry, such as bulldozers, earthmoving equipment, well-drilling machinery and equipment, or cranes. 1226-1227

532420 **Office Machinery and Equipment Rental and Leasing.** This industry comprises establishments primarily engaged in renting or leasing office machinery and equipment, such as computers, office furniture, duplicating machines (i.e., copiers), or facsimile machines. 1228-1229

532490 **Other Commercial and Industrial Machinery and Equipment Rental and Leasing.** This industry comprises establishments primarily engaged in renting or leasing nonconsumer-type machinery and equipment (except heavy construction, transportation, mining, and forestry machinery and equipment without operators; and office machinery and equipment). Establishments in this industry rent or lease products, such as manufacturing equipment; metalworking, telecommunications, motion picture, or theatrical machinery and equipment; institutional (i.e., public building) furniture, such as furniture for schools, theaters, or buildings; or agricultural equipment without operators. 1230-1231

533110 **Lessors of Nonfinancial Intangible Assets (except Copyrighted Works).** This industry comprises establishments primarily engaged in assigning rights to assets, such as patents, trademarks, brand names, and/or franchise agreements for which a royalty payment or licensing fee is paid to the asset holder. 1232-1233

PROFESSIONAL, SCIENTIFIC, AND TECHNICAL SERVICES

541110 **Offices of Lawyers.** This industry comprises offices of legal practitioners known as lawyers or attorneys (i.e., counselors-at-law) primarily engaged in the practice of law. Estab-lishments in this industry may provide expertise in a range or in specific areas of law, such as criminal law, corporate law, family and estate law, patent law, real estate law, or tax law. 1236-1237

541191 **Title Abstract and Settlement Offices.** This U.S. industry comprises establishments (except offices of lawyers and attorneys) primarily engaged in one or more of the following activities: (1) researching public land records to gather information relating to real estate titles; (2) preparing documents necessary for the transfer of the title, financing, and settlement; (3) conducting final real estate settlements and closings; and (4) filing legal and other documents relating to the sale of real estate. Real estate settlement offices, title abstract companies, and title search companies are included in this industry. 1238-1239

541199 **All Other Legal Services.** This U.S. industry comprises establishments of legal practitioners (except offices of lawyers and attorneys, settlement offices, and title abstract offices). These establishments are primarily engaged in providing specialized legal or paralegal services. . . 1240-1241

541211 **Offices of Certified Public Accountants.** This U.S. industry comprises establishments of accountants that are certified to audit the accounting records of public and private organizations and to attest to compliance with generally accepted accounting practices. Offices of certified public accountants (CPAs) may provide one or more of the following accounting services: (1) auditing financial statements; (2) designing accounting systems; (3) preparing financial statements; (4) developing budgets; and (5) providing advice on matters related to accounting. These establishments may also provide related services, such as bookkeeping, tax return preparation, and payroll processing. 1242-1243

541213 **Tax Preparation Services.** This U.S. industry comprises establishments (except offices of CPAs) engaged in providing tax return preparation services without also providing accounting, bookkeeping, billing, or payroll processing services. Basic knowledge of tax law and filing requirements is required. 1244-1245

541214 **Payroll Services.** This U.S. industry comprises establishments (except offices of CPAs) engaged in the following without also providing accounting, bookkeeping, or billing services: (1) collecting information on hours worked, pay rates, deductions, and other payroll- related data from their clients and (2) using that information to generate paychecks, payroll reports, and tax filings. These establishments may use data processing and tabulating techniques as part of providing their services. 1246-1247

PROFESSIONAL SERVICES

NAICS # **Page**

541219 **Other Accounting Services.** This U.S. industry comprises establishments (except offices of CPAs) engaged in providing accounting services (except tax return preparation services only or payroll services only). These establishments may also provide tax return preparation or payroll services. Accountant (except CPA) offices, bookkeeper offices, and billing offices are included in this industry. 1248-1249

541310 **Architectural Services.** This industry comprises establishments primarily engaged in planning and designing residential, institutional, leisure, commercial, and industrial buildings and structures by applying knowledge of design, construction procedures, zoning regulations, building codes, and building materials. 1250-1251

541320 **Landscape Architectural Services.** This industry comprises establishments primarily engaged in planning and designing the development of land areas for projects, such as parks and other recreational areas; airports; highways; hospitals; schools; land subdivisions; and commercial, industrial, and residential areas, by applying knowledge of land characteristics, location of buildings and structures, use of land areas, and design of landscape projects. 1252-1253

541330 **Engineering Services.** This industry comprises establishments primarily engaged in applying physical laws and principles of engineering in the design, development, and utilization of machines, materials, instruments, structures, processes, and systems. The assignments undertaken by these establishments may involve any of the following activities: provision of advice, preparation of feasibility studies, preparation of preliminary and final plans and designs, provision of technical services during the construction or installation phase, inspection and evaluation of engineering projects, and related services. 1254-1255

541370 **Surveying and Mapping (except Geophysical) Services.** This industry comprises establishments primarily engaged in performing surveying and mapping services of the surface of the earth, including the sea floor. These services may include surveying and mapping of areas above or below the surface of the earth, such as the creation of view easements or segregating rights in parcels of land by creating underground utility easements. 1256-1257

541380 **Testing Laboratories.** This industry comprises establishments primarily engaged in performing physical, chemical, and other analytical testing services, such as acoustics or vibration testing, assaying, biological testing (except medical and veterinary), calibration testing, electrical and electronic testing, geotechnical testing, mechanical testing, nondestructive testing, or thermal testing. The testing may occur in a laboratory or on-site. 1258-1259

541410 **Interior Design Services.** This industry comprises establishments primarily engaged in planning, designing and administering projects in interior spaces to meet the physical and aesthetic needs of people using them, taking into consideration building codes, health and safety regulations, traffic patterns and floor planning, mechanical and electrical needs, and interior fittings and furniture. Interior designers and interior design consultants work in areas, such as hospitality design, health care design, institutional design, commercial and corporate design, and residential design. This industry also includes interior decorating consultants engaged exclusively in providing aesthetic services associated with interior spaces. 1260-1261

541430 **Graphic Design Services.** This industry comprises establishments primarily engaged in planning, designing, and managing the production of visual communication in order to convey specific messages or concepts, clarify complex information, or project visual identi-ties. These services can include the design of printed materials, packaging, advertising, signage systems, and corporate identification (logos). This industry also includes commercial artists engaged exclusively in generating drawings and illustrations requiring technical accuracy or interpretative skills. 1262-1263

541490 **Other Specialized Design Services.** This industry comprises establishments primarily engaged in providing professional design services (except architectural, landscape architecture, engineering, interior, industrial, graphic, and computer system design). 1264-1265

541511 **Custom Computer Programming Services.** This U.S. industry comprises establishments primarily engaged in writing, modifying, testing, and supporting software to meet the needs of a particular customer. 1266-1267

541512 **Computer Systems Design Services.** This U.S. industry comprises establishments primarily engaged in planning and designing computer systems that integrate computer hardware, software, and communication technologies. The hardware and software components of the system may be provided by this establishment or company as part of integrated services or may be provided by third parties or vendors. These establishments often install the system and train and support users of the system. 1268-1269

PROFESSIONAL SERVICES

NAICS #		Page
541513	**Computer Facilities Management Services.** This U.S. industry comprises establishments primarily engaged in providing onsite management and operation of clients' computer systems and/or data processing facilities. Establishments providing computer systems or data processing facilities support services are included in this industry.	1270-1271
541519	**Other Computer Related Services.** This U.S. industry comprises establishments primarily engaged in providing computer related services (except custom programming, systems integration design, and facilities management services). Establishments providing computer disaster recovery services or software installation services are included in this industry.	1272-1273
541611	**Administrative Management and General Management Consulting Services.** This U.S. industry comprises establishments primarily engaged in providing operating advice and assistance to businesses and other organizations on administrative management issues, such as financial planning and budgeting, equity and asset management, records management, office planning, strategic and organizational planning, site selection, new business startup, and business process improvement. This industry also includes establishments of general management consultants that provide a full range of administrative; human resource; marketing; process, physical distribution, and logistics; or other management consulting services to clients.	1274-1275
541612	**Human Resources Consulting Services.** This U.S. industry comprises establishments primarily engaged in providing advice and assistance to businesses and other organizations in one or more of the following areas: (1) human resource and personnel policies, practices, and procedures; (2) employee benefits planning, communication, and administration; (3) compensation systems planning; (4) wage and salary administration; and (5) executive search and recruitment.	1276-1277
541613	**Marketing Consulting Services.** This U.S. industry comprises establishments primarily engaged in providing operating advice and assistance to businesses and other organizations on marketing issues, such as developing marketing objectives and policies, sales forecasting, new product developing and pricing, licensing and franchise planning, and marketing planning and strategy.	1278-1279
541614	**Process, Physical Distribution, and Logistics Consulting Services.** This U.S. industry comprises establishments primarily engaged in providing operating advice and assistance to businesses and other organizations in areas, such as: (1) manufacturing operations improvement; (2) productivity improvement; (3) production planning and control; (4) quality assurance and quality control; (5) inventory management; (6) distribution networks; (7) warehouse use, operations, and utilization; (8) transportation and shipment of goods and materials; and (9) materials management and handling.	1280-1281
541618	**Other Management Consulting Services.** This U.S. industry comprises establishments primarily engaged in providing management consulting services (except administrative and general management consulting; human resources consulting; marketing consulting; or process, physical distribution, and logistics consulting). Establishments providing telecommunications or utilities management consulting services are included in this industry.	1282-1283
541620	**Environmental Consulting Services.** This industry comprises establishments primarily engaged in providing advice and assistance to businesses and other organizations on environmental issues, such as the control of environmental contamination from pollutants, toxic substances, and hazardous materials. These establishments identify problems (e.g. inspect buildings for hazardous materials), measure and evaluate risks, and recommend solutions. They employ a multidisciplined staff of scientists, engineers, and other technicians with expertise in areas, such as air and water quality, asbestos contamination, remediation, and environmental law. Establishments providing sanitation or site remediation consulting services are included in this industry.	1284-1285
541690	**Other Scientific and Technical Consulting Services.** This industry comprises establishments primarily engaged in providing advice and assistance to businesses and other organizations on scientific and technical issues (except environmental).	1286-1287
541711	**Research and Development in Biotechnology.** This U.S. industry comprises establishments primarily engaged in conducting biotechnology research and experimental development. Biotechnology research and experimental development involves the study of the use of microorganisms and cellular and bio-molecular processes to develop or alter living or non-living materials. This research and development in biotechnology may result in development of new biotechnology processes or in prototypes of new or genetically altered products that may be reproduced, utilized, or implemented by various industries.	1288-1289

PROFESSIONAL SERVICES

NAICS # **Page**

541712 **Research and Development in the Physical, Engineering, and Life Sciences (except Biotechnology).** This U.S. Industry comprises establishments primarily engaged in conducting research and experimental development (except biotechnology research and experimental development) in the physical, engineering, and life sciences, such as agriculture, electronics, environmental, biology, botany, computers, chemistry, food, fisheries, forests, geology, health, mathematics, medicine, oceanography, pharmacy, physics, veterinary and other allied subjects. . . . 1290-1291

541720 **Research and Development in the Social Sciences and Humanities.** This industry comprises establishments primarily engaged in conducting research and analyses in cognitive development, sociology, psychology, language, behavior, economic, and other social science and humanities research. 1292-1293

541810 **Advertising Agencies.** This industry comprises establishments primarily engaged in creating advertising campaigns and placing such advertising in periodicals, newspapers, radio and television, or other media. These establishments are organized to provide a full range of services (i.e., through in-house capabilities or subcontracting), including advice, creative services, account management, production of advertising material, media planning, and buying (i.e., placing advertising). 1294-1295

541820 **Public Relations Agencies.** This industry comprises establishments primarily engaged in designing and implementing public relations campaigns. These campaigns are designed to promote the interests and image of their clients. Establishments providing lobbying, political consulting, or public relations consulting are included in this industry. 1296-1297

541840 **Media Representatives.** This industry comprises establishments of independent representatives primarily engaged in selling media time or space for media owners. 1298-1299

541850 **Outdoor Advertising.** This industry comprises establishments primarily engaged in creating and designing public display advertising, campaign materials, such as printed, painted, or electronic displays, and/or placing such displays on indoor or outdoor billboards and panels, or on or within transit vehicles or facilities, shopping malls, retail (in-store) displays, and other display structures or sites. 1300-1301

541860 **Direct Mail Advertising.** This industry comprises establishments primarily engaged in (1) creating and designing advertising campaigns for the purpose of distributing advertising materials (e.g., coupons, flyers, samples) or specialties (e.g., key chains, magnets, pens with customized messages imprinted) by mail or other direct distribution; and/ or (2) preparing advertising materials or specialties for mailing or other direct distribution. These establishments may also compile, maintain, sell, and rent mailing lists. 1302-1303

541870 **Advertising Material Distribution Services.** This industry comprises establishments primarily engaged in the direct distribution or delivery of advertisements (e.g., circulars, coupons, handbills) or samples. Establishments in this industry use methods, such as delivering advertisements or samples door-to-door, placing flyers or coupons on car windshields in parking lots, or handing out samples in retail stores. 1304-1305

541890 **Other Services Related to Advertising.** This industry comprises establishments primarily engaged in providing advertising services (except advertising agency services, public relations agency services, media buying agency services, media representative services, display advertising services, direct mail advertising services, advertising material distribution services, and marketing consulting services). 1306-1307

541910 **Marketing Research and Public Opinion Polling.** This industry comprises establishments primarily engaged in systematically gathering, recording, tabulating, and presenting marketing and public opinion data. 1308-1309

541921 **Photography Studios, Portrait.** This U.S. industry comprises establishments known as portrait studios primarily engaged in providing still, video, or digital portrait photography services. . . 1310-1311

541922 **Commercial Photography.** This U.S. industry comprises establishments primarily engaged in providing commercial photography services, generally for advertising agencies, publishers, and other business and industrial users. 1312-1313

541940 **Veterinary Services.** This industry comprises establishments of licensed veterinary practitioners primarily engaged in the practice of veterinary medicine, dentistry, or surgery for animals; and establishments primarily engaged in providing testing services for licensed veterinary practitioners. 1314-1315

NAICS # Page

541990 **All Other Professional, Scientific, and Technical Services.** This industry comprises establishments primarily engaged in the provision of professional, scientific, or technical services (except legal services; accounting, tax preparation, bookkeeping, and related services; architectural, engineering, and related services; specialized design services; computer systems design and related services; management, scientific, and technical consulting services; scientific research and development services; advertising and related services; market research and public opinion polling; photographic services; translation and interpretation services; and veterinary services). 1316-1317

MANAGEMENT OF COMPANIES AND ENTERPRISES

551112 **Offices of Other Holding Companies.** This U.S. industry comprises legal entities known as holding companies (except bank holding) primarily engaged in holding the securities of (or other equity interests in) companies and enterprises for the purpose of owning a controlling interest or influencing the management decisions of these firms. The holding companies in this industry do not administer, oversee, and manage other establishments of the company or enterprise whose securities they hold. 1320-1321

551114 **Corporate, Subsidiary, and Regional Managing Offices.** This U.S. industry comprises establishments (except government establishments) primarily engaged in administering, overseeing, and managing other establishments of the company or enterprise. These establishments normally undertake the strategic or organizational planning and decisionmaking role of the company or enterprise. Establishments in this industry may hold the securities of the company or enterprise. 1322-1323

ADMINISTRATIVE AND SUPPORT AND WASTE MANAGEMENT AND REMEDIATION SERVICES

561110 **Office Administrative Services.** This industry comprises establishments primarily engaged in providing a range of day-to-day office administrative services, such as financial planning; billing and recordkeeping; personnel; and physical distribution and logistics for others on a contract or fee basis. These establishments do not provide operating staff to carry out the complete operations of a business. 1326-1327

561210 **Facilities Support Services.** This industry comprises establishments primarily engaged in providing operating staff to perform a combination of support services within a client's facilities. Establishments in this industry typically provide a combination of services, such as janitorial; maintenance; trash disposal; guard and security; mail routing; reception; laundry; and related services to support operations within facilities. These establishments provide operating staff to carry out these support activities; but, are not involved with or responsible for the core business or activities of the client. Establishments providing facilities (except computer and/or data processing) operation support services and establishments operating correctional facilities (i.e., jails) on a contract or fee basis are included in this industry. 1328-1329

561311 **Employment Placement Agencies.** This U.S. industry comprises establishments primarily engaged in listing employment vacancies and in referring or placing applicants for employment. The individuals referred or placed are not employees of the employment agencies. 1330-1331

561320 **Temporary Help Services.** This industry comprises establishments primarily engaged in supplying workers to clients' businesses for limited periods of time to supplement the working force of the client. The individuals provided are employees of the temporary help service establishment. However, these establishments do not provide direct supervision of their employees at the clients' work sites. 1332-1333

ADMIN & WASTE MANAGEMENT SERVICES

NAICS #		Page
561330	**Professional Employer Organizations.** This industry comprises establishments primarily engaged in providing human resources and human resource management services to client businesses. Establishments in this industry operate in a coemployment relationship with client businesses or organizations and are specialized in performing a wide range of human resource and personnel management duties, such as payroll, payroll tax, benefits administration, workers' compensation, unemployment, and human resource administration. Professional employer organizations (PEOs) are responsible for payroll, including withholding and remitting employment-related taxes, for some or all of the employees of their clients, and also serve as the employer of those employees for benefits and related purposes.	1334-1335
561422	**Telemarketing Bureaus and Other Contact Centers.** This U.S. industry comprises establishments primarily engaged in providing telemarketing services on a contract or fee basis for others, such as: (1) promoting clients' products or services by telephone, (2) taking orders for clients by telephone, and (3) soliciting contributions or providing information for clients by telephone. These establishments never own the product or provide the services they are representing and generally can originate and/or receive calls for others.	1336-1337
561439	**Other Business Service Centers (including Copy Shops).** This U.S. industry comprises (1) establishments generally known as copy centers or shops primarily engaged in providing photocopying, duplicating, blueprinting, and other document copying services, without also providing printing services (e.g., offset printing, quick printing, digital printing, prepress services) and (2) establishments (except private mail centers) engaged in providing a range of office support services (except printing services), such as document copying services, facsimile services, word processing services, on-site PC rental services, and office product sales.	1338-1339
561440	**Collection Agencies.** This industry comprises establishments primarily engaged in collecting payments for claims and remitting payments collected to their clients.	1340-1341
561499	**All Other Business Support Services.** This U.S. industry comprises establishments primarily engaged in providing business support services (except secretarial and other document preparation services; telephone answering and telemarketing services; private mail services or document copying services conducted as separate activities or in conjunction with other office support services; monetary debt collection services; credit reporting services; repossession services; and court reporting and stenotype recording services).	1342-1343
561510	**Travel Agencies.** This industry comprises establishments primarily engaged in acting as agents in selling travel, tour, and accommodation services to the general public and commercial clients.	1344-1345
561520	**Tour Operators.** This industry comprises establishments primarily engaged in arranging and assembling tours. The tours are sold through travel agencies or tour operators. Travel or wholesale tour operators are included in this industry.	1346-1347
561599	**All Other Travel Arrangement and Reservation Services.** This U.S. industry comprises establishments (except travel agencies, tour operators, and convention and visitors bureaus) primarily engaged in providing travel arrangement and reservation services.	1348-1349
561612	**Security Guards and Patrol Services.** This U.S. industry comprises establishments primarily engaged in providing guard and patrol services, such as bodyguard, guard dog, and parking security services.	1350-1351
561621	**Security Systems Services (except Locksmiths).** This U.S. industry comprises establishments primarily engaged in (1) selling security alarm systems, such as burglar and fire alarms, along with installation, repair, or monitoring services or (2) remote monitoring of electronic security alarm systems.	1352-1353
561710	**Exterminating and Pest Control Services.** This industry comprises establishments primarily engaged in exterminating and controlling birds, mosquitoes, rodents, termites, and other insects and pests (except for crop production and forestry production). Establishments providing fumigation services are included in this industry.	1354-1355
561720	**Janitorial Services.** This industry comprises establishments primarily engaged in cleaning building interiors, interiors of transportation equipment (e.g., aircraft, rail cars, ships), and/ or windows.	1356-1357

ADMIN & WASTE MANAGEMENT SERVICES

NAICS #		Page
561730	**Landscaping Services.** This industry comprises (1) establishments primarily engaged in providing landscape care and maintenance services and/or installing trees, shrubs, plants, lawns, or gardens and (2) establishments primarily engaged in providing these services along with the design of landscape plans and/or the construction (i.e., installation) of walkways, retaining walls, decks, fences, ponds, and similar structures.	1358-1359
561740	**Carpet and Upholstery Cleaning Services.** This industry comprises establishments primarily engaged in cleaning and dyeing used rugs, carpets, and upholstery.	1360-1361
561790	**Other Services to Buildings and Dwellings.** This industry comprises establishments primarily engaged in providing services to buildings and dwellings (except exterminating and pest control; janitorial; landscaping care and maintenance; and carpet and upholstery cleaning).	1362-1363
561910	**Packaging and Labeling Services.** This industry comprises establishments primarily engaged in packaging client-owned materials. The services may include labeling and/or imprinting the package.	1364-1365
561920	**Convention and Trade Show Organizers.** This industry comprises establishments primarily engaged in organizing, promoting, and/or managing events, such as business and trade shows, conventions, conferences, and meetings (whether or not they manage and provide the staff to operate the facilities in which these events take place).	1366-1367
561990	**All Other Support Services.** This industry comprises establishments primarily engaged in providing day-to-day business and other organizational support services (except office administrative services, facilities support services, employment services, business support services, travel arrangement and reservation services, security and investigation services, services to buildings and other structures, packaging and labeling services, and convention and trade show organizing services).	1368-1369
562111	**Solid Waste Collection.** This U.S. industry comprises establishments primarily engaged in one or more of the following: (1) collecting and/or hauling nonhazardous solid waste (i.e., garbage) within a local area; (2) operating nonhazardous solid waste transfer stations; and (3) collecting and/or hauling mixed recyclable materials within a local area.	1370-1371
562119	**Other Waste Collection.** This U.S. industry comprises establishments primarily engaged in collecting and/or hauling waste (except nonhazardous solid waste and hazardous waste) within a local area. Establishments engaged in brush or rubble removal services are included in this industry.	1372-1373
562211	**Hazardous Waste Treatment and Disposal.** This U.S. industry comprises establishments primarily engaged in (1) operating treatment and/or disposal facilities for hazardous waste or (2) the combined activity of collecting and/or hauling of hazardous waste materials within a local area and operating treatment or disposal facilities for hazardous waste.	1374-1375
562212	**Solid Waste Landfill.** This U.S. industry comprises establishments primarily engaged in (1) operating landfills for the disposal of nonhazardous solid waste or (2) the combined activity of collecting and/or hauling nonhazardous waste materials within a local area and operating landfills for the disposal of nonhazardous solid waste.	1376-1377
562219	**Other Nonhazardous Waste Treatment and Disposal.** This U.S. industry comprises establishments primarily engaged in (1) operating nonhazardous waste treatment and disposal facilities (except landfills, combustors, incinerators and sewer systems or sewage treatment facilities) or (2) the combined activity of collecting and/or hauling of nonhazardous waste materials within a local area and operating waste treatment or disposal facilities (except landfills, combustors, incinerators and sewer systems, or sewage treatment facilities). Compost dumps are included in this industry.	1378-1379
562910	**Remediation Services.** This industry comprises establishments primarily engaged in one or more of the following: (1) remediation and cleanup of contaminated buildings, mine sites, soil or ground water; (2) integrated mine reclamation activities, including demolition, soil remediation, waste water treatment, hazardous material removal, contouring land and revegitation; and (3) asbestos, lead paint and other toxic material abatement.	1380-1381
562920	**Materials Recovery Facilities.** This industry comprises establishments primarily engaged in (1) operating facilities for separating and sorting recyclable materials from nonhazardous waste streams (i.e., garbage) and/or (2) operating facilities where commingled recyclable materials, such as paper, plastics, used beverage cans, and metals are sorted into distinct categories.	1382-1383

EDUCATION

NAICS # **Page**

562991 **Septic Tank and Related Services.** This U.S. industry comprises establishments primarily engaged in (1) pumping (i.e., cleaning) septic tanks and cesspools and/or (2) renting and/or servicing portable toilets. 1384-1385

562998 **All Other Miscellaneous Waste Management Services.** This U.S. industry comprises establishments primarily engaged in providing waste management services (except waste collection, waste treatment and disposal, remediation, operation of materials recovery facilities, septic tank pumping and related services, and waste management consulting services). 1386-1387

EDUCATIONAL SERVICES

611110 **Elementary and Secondary Schools.** This industry comprises establishments primarily engaged in furnishing academic courses and associated course work that comprise a basic preparatory education. A basic preparatory education ordinarily constitutes kindergarten through 12th grade. This industry includes school boards and school districts. 1390-1391

611210 **Junior Colleges.** This industry comprises establishments primarily engaged in furnishing academic, or academic and technical, courses and granting associate degrees, certificates, or diplomas below the baccalaureate level. The requirement for admission to an associate or equivalent degree program is at least a high school diploma or equivalent general academic training. Instruction may be provided in diverse settings, such as the establishment's or client's training facilities, educational institutions, the workplace, or the home, and through correspondence, television, Internet, or other means. 1392-1393

611310 **Colleges, Universities, and Professional Schools.** This industry comprises establishments primarily engaged in furnishing academic courses and granting degrees at baccalaureate or graduate levels. The requirement for admission is at least a high school diploma or equivalent general academic training. Instruction may be provided in diverse settings, such as the establishment's or client's training facilities, educational institutions, the workplace, or the home, and through correspondence, television, Internet, or other means. 1394-1395

611430 **Professional and Management Development Training.** This industry comprises establishments primarily engaged in offering an array of short duration courses and seminars for management and professional development. Training for career development may be provided directly to individuals or through employers' training programs; and courses may be customized or modified to meet the special needs of customers. Instruction may be provided in diverse settings, such as the establishment's or client's training facilities, educational institutions, the workplace, or the home, and through correspondence, television, Internet, or other means. . . 1396-1397

611511 **Cosmetology and Barber Schools.** This U.S. industry comprises establishments primarily engaged in offering training in barbering, hair styling, or the cosmetic arts, such as makeup or skin care. These schools provide job-specific certification. 1398-1399

611519 **Other Technical and Trade Schools.** This U.S. industry comprises establishments primarily engaged in offering job or career vocational or technical courses (except cosmetology and barber training, aviation and flight training, and apprenticeship training). The curriculums offered by these schools are highly structured and specialized and lead to job-specific certification. 1400-1401

611610 **Fine Arts Schools.** This industry comprises establishments primarily engaged in offering instruction in the arts, including dance, art, drama, and music. 1402-1403

611620 **Sports and Recreation Instruction.** This industry comprises establishments, such as camps and schools, primarily engaged in offering instruction in athletic activities to groups of individuals. Overnight and day sports instruction camps are included in this industry. 1404-1405

611699 **All Other Miscellaneous Schools and Instruction.** This U.S. industry comprises establishments primarily engaged in offering instruction (except business, computer, management, technical, trade, fine arts, athletic, language instruction, tutoring, and automobile driving instruction). Also excluded from this industry are academic schools, colleges, and universities. 1406-1407

611710 **Educational Support Services.** This industry comprises establishments primarily engaged in providing noninstructional services that support educational processes or systems. 1408-1409

NAICS # **Page**

HEALTH CARE AND SOCIAL ASSISTANCE

621111 Offices of Physicians (except Mental Health Specialists). This U.S. industry comprises establishments of health practitioners having the degree of M.D. (Doctor of medicine) or D.O. (Doctor of osteopathy) primarily engaged in the independent practice of general or specialized medicine (except psychiatry or psychoanalysis) or surgery. These practitioners operate private or group practices in their own offices (e.g., centers, clinics) or in the facilities of others, such as hospitals or HMO medical centers. 1412-1413

621112 Offices of Physicians, Mental Health Specialists. This U.S. industry comprises establishments of health practitioners having the degree of M.D. (Doctor of medicine) or D.O. (Doctor of osteopathy) primarily engaged in the independent practice of psychiatry or psychoanalysis. These practitioners operate private or group practices in their own offices (e.g., centers, clinics) or in the facilities of others, such as hospitals or HMO medical centers. 1414-1415

621210 Offices of Dentists. This industry comprises establishments of health practitioners having the degree of D.M.D. (Doctor of dental medicine), D.D.S. (Doctor of dental surgery), or D.D.Sc. (Doctor of dental science) primarily engaged in the independent practice of general or specialized dentistry or dental surgery. These practitioners operate private or group practices in their own offices (e.g., centers, clinics) or in the facilities of others, such as hospitals or HMO medical centers. They can provide either comprehensive preventive, cosmetic, or emergency care, or specialize in a single field of dentistry. 1416-1417

621310 Offices of Chiropractors. This industry comprises establishments of health practitioners having the degree of D.C. (Doctor of chiropractic) primarily engaged in the independent practice of chiropractic. These practitioners provide diagnostic and therapeutic treatment of neuromusculoskeletal and related disorders through the manipulation and adjustment of the spinal column and extremities, and operate private or group practices in their own offices (e.g., centers, clinics) or in the facilities of others, such as hospitals or HMO medical centers. 1418-1419

621320 Offices of Optometrists. This industry comprises establishments of health practitioners having the degree of O.D. (Doctor of optometry) primarily engaged in the independent practice of optometry. These practitioners provide eye examinations to determine visual acuity or the presence of vision problems and to prescribe eyeglasses, contact lenses, and eye exercises. They operate private or group practices in their own offices (e.g., centers, clinics) or in the facilities of others, such as hospitals or HMO medical centers, and may also provide the same service as opticians, such as selling and fitting prescription eyeglasses and contact lenses. . . 1420-1421

621330 Offices of Mental Health Practitioners (except Physicians). This industry comprises establishments of independent mental health practitioners (except physicians) primarily engaged in (1) the diagnosis and treatment of mental, emotional, and behavioral disorders and/or (2) the diagnosis and treatment of individual or group social dysfunction brought about by such causes as mental illness, alcohol and substance abuse, physical and emotional trauma, or stress. These practitioners operate private or group practices in their own offices (e.g., centers, clinics) or in the facilities of others, such as hospitals or HMO medical centers. 1422-1423

621340 Offices of Physical, Occupational and Speech Therapists, and Audiologists. This industry comprises establishments of independent health practitioners primarily engaged in one of the following: (1) administering medically prescribed physical therapy treatment for patients suffering from injuries or muscle, nerve, joint, and bone disease; (2) planning and administering educational, recreational, and social activities designed to help patients or individuals with disabilities, regain physical or mental functioning or to adapt to their disabilities; and (3) diagnosing and treating speech, language, or hearing problems. These practitioners operate private or group practices in their own offices (e.g., centers, clinics) or in the facilities of others, such as hospitals or HMO medical centers. 1424-1425

621391 Offices of Podiatrists. This U.S. industry comprises establishments of health practitioners having the degree of D.P. (Doctor of podiatry) primarily engaged in the independent practice of podiatry. These practitioners diagnose and treat diseases and deformities of the foot and operate private or group practices in their own offices (e.g., centers, clinics) or in the facilities of others, such as hospitals or HMO medical centers. 1426-1427

HEALTH CARE

NAICS # **Page**

621399 **Offices of All Other Miscellaneous Health Practitioners.** except physicians; dentists; chiropractors; optometrists; mental health specialists; physical, occupational, and speech therapists; audiologists; and podiatrists). These practitioners operate private or group practices in their own offices (e.g., centers, clinics) or in the facilities of others, such as hospitals or HMO medical centers. 1428-1429

621410 **Family Planning Centers.** This industry comprises establishments with medical staff primarily engaged in providing a range of family planning services on an outpatient basis, such as contraceptive services, genetic and prenatal counseling, voluntary sterilization, and therapeutic and medically indicated termination of pregnancy. 1430-1431

621420 **Outpatient Mental Health and Substance Abuse Centers.** This industry comprises establishments with medical staff primarily engaged in providing outpatient services related to the diagnosis and treatment of mental health disorders and alcohol and other substance abuse. These establishments generally treat patients who do not require inpatient treatment. They may provide a counseling staff and information regarding a wide range of mental health and substance abuse issues and/or refer patients to more extensive treatment programs, if necessary. 1432-1433

621492 **Kidney Dialysis Centers.** This U.S. industry comprises establishments with medical staff primarily engaged in providing outpatient kidney or renal dialysis services. 1434-1435

621493 **Freestanding Ambulatory Surgical and Emergency Centers.** This U.S. industry comprises establishments with physicians and other medical staff primarily engaged in (1) providing surgical services (e.g., orthoscopic and cataract surgery) on an outpatient basis or (2) providing emergency care services (e.g., setting broken bones, treating lacerations, or tending to patients suffering injuries as a result of accidents, trauma, or medical conditions necessitating immediate medical care) on an outpatient basis. Outpatient surgical establishments have specialized facilities, such as operating and recovery rooms, and specialized equipment, such as anesthetic or X-ray equipment. 1436-1437

621498 **All Other Outpatient Care Centers.** This U.S. industry comprises establishments with medical staff primarily engaged in providing general or specialized outpatient care (except family planning centers, outpatient mental health and substance abuse centers, HMO medical centers, kidney dialysis centers, and freestanding ambulatory surgical and emergency centers). Centers or clinics of health practitioners with different degrees from more than one industry practicing within the same establishment (i.e., Doctor of medicine and Doctor of dental medicine) are included in this industry. 1438-1439

621511 **Medical Laboratories.** This U.S. industry comprises establishments known as medical laboratories primarily engaged in providing analytic or diagnostic services, including body fluid analysis, generally to the medical profession or to the patient on referral from a health practitioner. 1440-1441

621512 **Diagnostic Imaging Centers.** This U.S. industry comprises establishments known as diagnostic imaging centers primarily engaged in producing images of the patient generally on referral from a health practitioner. 1442-1443

621610 **Home Health Care Services.** This industry comprises establishments primarily engaged in providing skilled nursing services in the home, along with a range of the following: personal care services; homemaker and companion services; physical therapy; medical social services; medications; medical equipment and supplies; counseling; 24-hour home care; occupation and vocational therapy; dietary and nutritional services; speech therapy; audiology; and high-tech care, such as intravenous therapy. 1444-1445

621910 **Ambulance Services.** This industry comprises establishments primarily engaged in providing transportation of patients by ground or air, along with medical care. These services are often provided during a medical emergency but are not restricted to emergencies. The vehicles are equipped with lifesaving equipment operated by medically trained personnel. 1446-1447

621991 **Blood and Organ Banks.** This U.S. industry comprises establishments primarily engaged in collecting, storing, and distributing blood and blood products and storing and distributing body organs. 1448-1449

621999 **All Other Miscellaneous Ambulatory Health Care Services.** This U.S. industry comprises establishments primarily engaged in providing ambulatory health care services (except offices of physicians, dentists, and other health practitioners; outpatient care centers; medical and diagnostic laboratories; home health care providers; ambulances; and blood and organ banks). . . . 1450-1451

HEALTH CARE

NAICS # **Page**

622110 **General Medical and Surgical Hospitals.** This industry comprises establishments known and licensed as general medical and surgical hospitals primarily engaged in providing diagnostic and medical treatment (both surgical and nonsurgical) to inpatients with any of a wide variety of medical conditions. These establishments maintain inpatient beds and provide patients with food services that meet their nutritional requirements. These hospitals have an organized staff of physicians and other medical staff to provide patient care services. These establishments usually provide other services, such as outpatient services, anatomical pathology services, diagnostic X-ray services, clinical labora-tory services, operating room services for a variety of procedures, and phar-macy services. 1452-1453

622110 **General Medical and Surgical Hospitals (Non-Profit).** This industry comprises establishments known and licensed as general medical and surgical hospitals primarily engaged in providing diagnostic and medical treatment (both surgical and nonsurgical) to inpatients with any of a wide variety of medical conditions. These establishments maintain inpatient beds and provide patients with food services that meet their nutritional requirements. These hospitals have an organized staff of physicians and other medical staff to provide patient care services. These establishments usually provide other services, such as outpatient services, anatomical pathology services, diagnostic X-ray services, clinical laboratory services, operating room services for a variety of procedures, and pharmacy services. 1454-1455

622210 **Psychiatric and Substance Abuse Hospitals.** This industry comprises establishments known and licensed as psychiatric and substance abuse hospitals primarily engaged in providing diagnostic, medical treatment, and monitoring services for inpatients who suffer from mental illness or substance abuse disorders. The treatment often requires an extended stay in the hospital. These establishments maintain inpatient beds and provide patients with food services that meet their nutritional requirements. They have an organized staff of physicians and other medical staff to provide patient care services. Psychiatric, psychological, and social work services are available at the facility. These hospitals usually provide other services, such as outpatient services, clinical laboratory services, diagnostic X-ray services, and electroencephalograph services. 1456-1457

622310 **Specialty (except Psychiatric and Substance Abuse) Hospitals.** This industry consists of establishments known and licensed as specialty hospi-tals primarily engaged in providing diagnostic and medical treatment to inpatients with a specific type of disease or medical condition (except psychiatric or substance abuse). Hospitals providing long-term care for the chronically ill and hospitals providing rehabilitation, restorative, and adjustive services to physically challenged or disabled people are included in this industry. These establishments maintain inpatient beds and provide patients with food services that meet their nutritional requirements. They have an organized staff of physicians and other medical staff to provide patient care services. These hospitals may provide other services, such as outpatient services, diagnostic X-ray services, clinical laboratory services, operating room services, physical therapy services, educational and vocational services, and psychological and social work services. 1458-1459

623110 **Nursing Care Facilities (Skilled Nursing Facilities).** This industry comprises establishments primarily engaged in providing inpatient nursing and rehabilitative services. The care is generally provided for an extended period of time to individuals requiring nursing care. These establishments have a permanent core staff of registered or licensed practical nurses who, along with other staff, provide nursing and continuous personal care services. 1460-1461

623210 **Residential Intellectual and Developmental Disability Facilities.** This industry comprises establishments (e.g. group homes, hospitals, intermediate care facilities) primarily engaged in providing residential care services for persons diagnosed with mental retardation. These facilities may provide some health care, though the focus is on room, board, protective supervision, and counseling. 1462-1463

623220 **Residential Mental Health and Substance Abuse Facilities.** This industry comprises establishments primarily engaged in providing residential care and treatment for patients with mental health and substance abuse illnesses. These establishments provide room, board, supervision, and counseling services. Although medical services may be available at these establishments, they are incidental to the counseling, mental rehabilitation, and support services offered. These establishments generally provide a wide range of social services in addition to counseling. . . . 1464-1465

HEALTH CARE

NAICS # **Page**

623311 **Continuing Care Retirement Communities.** This U.S. industry comprises establishments primarily engaged in providing a range of residential and personal care services with on-site nursing care facilities for (1) the elderly and other persons who are unable to fully care for themselves and/or (2) the elderly and other persons who do not desire to live independently. Individuals live in a variety of residential settings with meals, housekeeping, social, leisure, and other services available to assist residents in daily living. Assistedliving facilities with on-site nursing care facilities are included in this industry. 1466-1467

623312 **Assisted Living Facilities for the Elderly.** This U.S. industry comprises establishments primarily engaged in providing residential and personal care services (i.e., without on-site nursing care facilities) for (1) the elderly or other persons who are unable to fully care for themselves and/or (2) the elderly or other persons who do not desire to live independently. The care typically includes room, board, supervision, and assistance in daily living, such as housekeeping services. 1468-1469

623990 **Other Residential Care Facilities.** This industry comprises establishments primarily engaged in providing residential care (except residential mental retardation facilities, residential health and substance abuse facilities, continuing care retirement communities, and homes for the elderly). These establishments also provide supervision and personal care services. 1470-1471

624110 **Child and Youth Services.** This industry comprises establishments primarily engaged in providing nonresidential social assistance services for children and youth. These establishments provide for the welfare of children in such areas as adoption and foster care, drug prevention, life skills training, and positive social development. 1472-1473

624120 **Services for the Elderly and Persons with Disabilities.** This industry comprises establishments primarily engaged in providing nonresidential social assistance services to improve the quality of life for the elderly, persons diagnosed with mental retardation, or persons with disabilities. These establishments provide for the welfare of these individuals in such areas as day care, nonmedical home care or homemaker services, social activities, group support, and companionship. 1474-1475

624190 **Other Individual and Family Services.** This industry comprises establishments primarily engaged in providing nonresidential individual and family social assistance services (except those specifically directed toward children, the elderly, persons diagnosed with mental retardation, or persons with disabilities). 1476-1477

624210 **Community Food Services.** This industry comprises establishments primarily engaged in the collection, preparation, and delivery of food for the needy. Establishments in this industry may also distribute clothing and blankets to the poor. These establishments may prepare and deliver meals to persons who by reason of age, disability, or illness are unable to prepare meals for themselves; collect and distribute salvageable or donated food; or prepare and provide meals at fixed or mobile locations. Food banks, meal delivery programs, and soup kitchens are included in this industry. 1478-1479

624221 **Temporary Shelters.** This U.S. industry comprises establishments primarily engaged in providing (1) short term emergency shelter for victims of domestic violence, sexual assault, or child abuse and/or (2) temporary residential shelter for homeless individuals or families, runaway youth, and patients and families caught in medical crises. These establishments may operate their own shelters or may subsidize housing using existing homes, apartments, hotels, or motels. 1480-1481

624229 **Other Community Housing Services.** This U.S. industry comprises establishments primarily engaged in providing one or more of the following community housing services: (1) transitional housing to low-income individuals and families; (2) volunteer construction or repair of lowcost housing, in partnership with the homeowner who may assist in the construction or repair work; and (3) the repair of homes for elderly or disabled homeowners. These establishments may subsidize housing using existing homes, apartments, hotels, or motels or may require a low-cost mortgage or sweat equity. These establishments may also provide low-income families with furniture and household supplies. 1482-1483

ENTERTAINMENT

NAICS # Page

624310 **Vocational Rehabilitation Services.** This industry comprises (1) establishments primarily engaged in providing vocational rehabilitation or habilitation services, such as job counseling, job training, and work experience, to unemployed and underemployed persons, persons with disabilities, and persons who have a job market disadvantage because of lack of education, job skill, or experience and (2) establishments primarily engaged in providing training and employment to persons with disabilities. Vocational rehabilitation job training facilities (except schools) and sheltered workshops (i.e., work experience centers) are included in this industry. 1484-1485

624410 **Child Day Care Services.** This industry comprises establishments primarily engaged in providing day care of infants or children. These establishments generally care for preschool children, but may care for older children when they are not in school and may also offer prekindergarten educational programs. 1486-1487

ARTS, ENTERTAINMENT, AND RECREATION

711110 **Theater Companies and Dinner Theaters.** This industry comprises (1) companies, groups, or theaters primarily engaged in producing the following live theatrical presentations: musicals; operas; plays; and comedy, improvisational, mime, and puppet shows and (2) establishments, commonly known as dinner theaters, engaged in producing live theatrical productions and in providing food and beverages for consumption on the premises. Theater groups or companies may or may not operate their own theater or other facility for staging their shows. 1490-1491

711130 **Musical Groups and Artists.** This industry comprises (1) groups primarily engaged in producing live musical entertainment (except theatrical musical or opera productions) and (2) independent (i.e., freelance) artists primarily engaged in providing live musical entertainment. Musical groups and artists may perform in front of a live audience or in a studio, and may or may not operate their own facilities for staging their shows. 1492-1493

711211 **Sports Teams and Clubs.** This U.S. industry comprises professional or semiprofessional sports teams or clubs primarily engaged in participating in live sporting events, such as baseball, basketball, football, hockey, soccer, and jai alai games, before a paying audience. These establishments may or may not operate their own arena, stadium, or other facility for presenting these events. 1494-1495

711212 **Racetracks.** This U.S. industry comprises establishments primarily engaged in operating racetracks. These establishments may also present and /or promote the events, such as auto, dog, and horse races, held in these facilities. 1496-1497

711310 **Promoters of Performing Arts, Sports, and Similar Events with Facilities.** This industry comprises establishments primarily engaged in (1) organizing, promoting, and/or managing live performing arts productions, sports events, and similar events, such as state fairs, county fairs, agricultural fairs, concerts, and festivals, held in facilities that they manage and operate and/or (2) managing and providing the staff to operate arenas, stadiums, theaters, or other related facilities for rent to other promoters. 1498-1499

711320 **Promoters of Performing Arts, Sports, and Similar Events without Facilities.** This industry comprises promoters primarily engaged in organizing, promoting, and/or managing live performing arts productions, sports events, and similar events, such as state fairs, county fairs, agricultural fairs, concerts, and festivals, in facilities that are managed and operated by others. Theatrical (except motion picture) booking agencies are included in this industry. 1500-1501

711410 **Agents and Managers for Artists, Athletes, Entertainers, and Other Public Figures.** This industry comprises establishments of agents and managers primarily engaged in representing and/or managing creative and performing artists, sports figures, entertainers, and other public figures. The representation and management includes activities, such as representing clients in contract negotiations; managing or organizing client's financial affairs; and generally promoting the careers of their clients. 1502-1503

712110 **Museums.** This industry comprises establishments primarily engaged in the preservation and exhibition of objects of historical, cultural, and/or educational value. 1504-1505

712130 **Zoos and Botanical Gardens.** This industry comprises establishments primarily engaged in the preservation and exhibition of live plant and animal life displays. 1506-1507

RESTAURANT/LODGING

NAICS # **Page**

713110 **Amusement and Theme Parks.** This industry comprises establishments, known as amusement or theme parks, primarily engaged in operating a variety of attractions, such as mechanical rides, water rides, games, shows, theme exhibits, refreshment stands, and picnic grounds. These establishments may lease space to others on a concession basis. 1508-1509

713120 **Amusement Arcades.** This industry comprises establishments primarily engaged in operating amusement (except gambling, billiard, or pool) arcades and parlors. 1510-1511

713210 **Casinos (except Casino Hotels).** This industry comprises establishments primarily engaged in operating gambling facilities that offer table wagering games along with other gambling activities, such as slot machines and sports betting. These establishments often provide food and beverage services. Included in this industry are floating casinos (i.e., gambling cruises, riverboat casinos). 1512-1513

713290 **Other Gambling Industries.** This industry comprises establishments primarily engaged in operating gambling facilities (except casinos or casino hotels) or providing gambling services. . . . 1514-1515

713910 **Golf Courses and Country Clubs.** This industry comprises (1) establishments primarily engaged in operating golf courses (except miniature) and (2) establishments primarily engaged in operating golf courses, along with dining facilities and other recreational facilities that are known as country clubs. These establishments often provide food and beverage services, equipment rental services, and golf instruction services. 1516-1517

713920 **Skiing Facilities.** This industry comprises establishments primarily engaged in (1) operating downhill, cross-country, or related skiing areas and/or (2) operating equipment, such as ski lifts and tows. These establishments often provide food and beverage services, equipment rental services, and ski instruction services. Four season resorts without accommodations are included in this industry. 1518-1519

713930 **Marinas.** This industry comprises establishments, commonly known as marinas, engaged in operating docking and/or storage facilities for pleasure craft owners, with or without one or more related activities, such as retailing fuel and marine supplies; and repairing, maintaining, or renting pleasure boats. 1520-1521

713940 **Fitness and Recreational Sports Centers.** This industry comprises establishments primarily engaged in operating fitness and recreational sports facilities featuring exercise and other active physical fitness conditioning or recreational sports activities, such as swimming, skating, or racquet sports. 1522-1523

713950 **Bowling Centers.** This industry comprises establishments engaged in operating bowling centers. These establishments often provide food and beverage services. 1524-1525

713990 **All Other Amusement and Recreation Industries.** This industry comprises establishments (except amusement parks and arcades; gambling industries; golf courses and country clubs; skiing facilities; marinas; fitness and recreational sports centers; and bowling centers) primarily engaged in providing recreational and amusement services. 1526-1527

ACCOMMODATION AND FOOD SERVICES

721110 **Hotels (except Casino Hotels) and Motels.** This industry comprises establishments primarily engaged in providing short-term lodging in facilities known as hotels, motor hotels, resort hotels, and motels. The establishments in this industry may offer food and beverage services, recreational services, conference rooms and convention services, laundry services, parking, and other services. 1530-1531

721120 **Casino Hotels.** This industry comprises establishments primarily engaged in providing short-term lodging in hotel facilities with a casino on the premises. The casino on premises includes table wagering games and may include other gambling activities, such as slot machines and sports betting. These establishments generally offer a range of services and amenities, such as food and beverage services, entertainment, valet parking, swimming pools, and conference and convention facilities. 1532-1533

721211 **RV (Recreational Vehicle) Parks and Campgrounds.** This U.S. industry comprises establishments primarily engaged in operating sites to accommodate campers and their equipment, including tents, tent trailers, travel trailers, and RVs (recreational vehicles). These establishments may provide access to facilities, such as washrooms, laundry rooms, recreation halls and playgrounds, stores, and snack bars. 1534-1535

OTHER SERVICES

NAICS #		Page
721214	**Recreational and Vacation Camps (except Campgrounds).** This U.S. industry comprises establishments primarily engaged in operating overnight recreational camps, such as children's camps, family vacation camps, hunting and fishing camps, and outdoor adventure retreats that offer trail riding, white-water rafting, hiking, and similar activities. These establishments provide accommodation facilities, such as cabins and fixed campsites, and other amenities, such as food services, recreational facilities and equipment, and organized recreational activities.	1536-1537
721310	**Rooming and Boarding Houses.** This industry comprises establishments primarily engaged in operating rooming and boarding houses and similar facilities, such as fraternity houses, sorority houses, off-campus dormitories, residential clubs, and workers' camps. These establishments provide temporary or longer-term accommodations which, for the period of occupancy, may serve as a principal residence. These establishments also may provide complementary services, such as housekeeping, meals, and laundry services.	1538-1539
722310	**Food Service Contractors.** This industry comprises establishments primarily engaged in providing food services at institutional, governmental, commercial, or industrial locations of others based on contractual arrangements with these type of organizations for a specified period of time. The establishments of this industry provide food services for the convenience of the contracting organization or the contracting organization's customers. The contractual arrangement of these establishments with contracting organizations may vary from type of facility operated (e.g., cafeteria, restaurant, fast-food eating place), revenue sharing, cost structure, to providing personnel. Management staff is always provided by the food service contractors.	1540-1541
722320	**Caterers.** This industry comprises establishments primarily engaged in providing single event-based food services. These establishments generally have equipment and vehicles to transport meals and snacks to events and/or prepare food at an off-premise site. Banquet halls with catering staff are included in this industry. Examples of events catered by establishments of this industry are graduation parties, wedding receptions, business or retirement luncheons, and trade shows.	1542-1543
722410	**Drinking Places (Alcoholic Beverages).** This industry comprises establishments known as bars, taverns, nightclubs, or drinking places primarily engaged in preparing and serving alcoholic beverages for immediate consumption. These establishments may also provide limited food services.	1544-1545
722511	**Full-Service Restaurants.** This U.S. industry comprises establishments primarily engaged in providing food services to patrons who order and are served while seated (i.e., waiter/waitress service) and pay after eating. These establishments may provide this type of food service to patrons in combination with selling alcoholic beverages, providing carryout services, or presenting live nontheatrical entertainment.	1546-1547
722513	**Limited-Service Restaurants.** This U.S. industry comprises establishments primarily engaged in providing food services (except snack and nonalcoholic beverage bars) where patrons generally order or select items and pay before eating. Food and drink may be consumed on premises, taken out, or delivered to the customer's location. Some establishments in this industry may provide these food services in combination with selling alcoholic beverages.	1548-1549
722515	**Snack and Nonalcoholic Beverage Bars.** This U.S. industry comprises establishments primarily engaged in (1) preparing and/or serving a specialty snack, such as ice cream, frozen yogurt, cookies, or popcorn or (2) serving nonalcoholic beverages, such as coffee, juices, or sodas for consumption on or near the premises. These establishments may carry and sell a combination of snack, nonalcoholic beverage, and other related products (e.g., coffee beans, mugs, coffee makers) but generally promote and sell a unique snack or nonalcoholic beverage.	1550-1551

OTHER SERVICES (EXCEPT PUBLIC ADMINISTRATION)

811111	**General Automotive Repair.** This U.S. industry comprises establishments primarily engaged in providing (1) a wide range of mechanical and electrical repair and maintenance services for automotive vehicles, such as passenger cars, trucks, and vans, and all trailers or (2) engine repair and replacement.	1554-1555
811118	**Other Automotive Mechanical and Electrical Repair and Maintenance.** This U.S. industry comprises establishments primarily engaged in providing specialized mechanical or electrical repair and maintenance services (except engine repair and replacement, exhaust systems repair, and transmission repair) for automotive vehicles, such as passenger cars, trucks, and vans, and all trailers.	1556-1557

OTHER SERVICES

NAICS # **Page**

811121 **Automotive Body, Paint, and Interior Repair and Maintenance.** This U.S. industry comprises establishments primarily engaged in repairing or customizing automotive vehicles, such as passenger cars, trucks, and vans, and all trailer bodies and interiors; and/or painting automotive vehicles and trailer bodies. 1558-1559

811122 **Automotive Glass Replacement Shops.** This U.S. industry comprises establishments primarily engaged in replacing, repairing, and/or tinting automotive vehicle, such as passenger car, truck, and van, glass. 1560-1561

811191 **Automotive Oil Change and Lubrication Shops.** This U.S. industry comprises establishments primarily engaged in changing motor oil and lubricating the chassis of automotive vehicles, such as passenger cars, trucks, and vans. 1562-1563

811192 **Car Washes.** This U.S. industry comprises establishments primarily engaged in cleaning, washing, and/or waxing automotive vehicles, such as passenger cars, trucks, and vans, and trailers. 1564-1565

811198 **All Other Automotive Repair and Maintenance.** This U.S. industry comprises establishments primarily engaged in providing automotive repair and maintenance services (except mechanical and electrical repair and maintenance; body, paint, interior, and glass repair; motor oil change and lubrication; and car washing) for automotive vehicles, such as passenger cars, trucks, and vans, and all trailers. 1566-1567

811212 **Computer and Office Machine Repair and Maintenance.** This U.S. industry comprises establishments primarily engaged in repairing and maintaining computers and office machines without retailing new computers and office machines, such as photocopying machines; and computer terminals, storage devices, printers; and CD-ROM drives. 1568-1569

811219 **Other Electronic and Precision Equipment Repair and Maintenance.** This U.S. industry comprises establishments primarily engaged in repairing and maintaining (without retailing) electronic and precision equipment (except consumer electronics, computers and office machines, and communications equipment). Establishments in this industry repair and maintain equipment, such as medical diagnostic imaging equipment, measuring and surveying instruments, laboratory instruments, and radar and sonar equipment. 1570-1571

811310 **Commercial and Industrial Machinery and Equipment (except Automotive and Electronic) Repair and Maintenance.** This industry comprises establishments primarily engaged in the repair and maintenance of commercial and industrial machinery and equipment. Establishments in this industry either sharpen/install commercial and industrial machinery blades and saws or provide welding (e.g., automotive, general) repair services; or repair agricultural and other heavy and industrial machinery and equipment (e.g., forklifts and other materials handling equipment, machine tools, commercial refrigeration equipment, construction equipment, and mining machinery). 1572-1573

811412 **Appliance Repair and Maintenance.** This U.S. industry comprises establishments primarily engaged in repairing and servicing household appliances without retailing new appliances, such as refrigerators, stoves, washing machines, clothes dryers, and room air-conditioners. . . 1574-1575

811490 **Other Personal and Household Goods Repair and Maintenance.** This industry comprises establishments primarily engaged in repairing and servicing personal or household-type goods without retailing new personal and household-type goods (except home and garden equipment, appliances, furniture, and footwear and leather goods). Establishments in this industry repair items, such as garments; watches; jewelry; musical instruments; bicycles and motorcycles; motorboats, canoes, sailboats, and other recreational boats. 1576-1577

812112 **Beauty Salons.** This U.S. industry comprises establishments (except those known as barber shops or men's hair stylist shops) primarily engaged in one or more of the following: (1) cutting, trimming, shampooing, weaving, coloring, waving, or styling hair; (2) providing facials; and (3) applying makeup (except permanent makeup). 1578-1579

812199 **Other Personal Care Services.** This U.S. industry comprises establishments primarily engaged in providing personal care services (except hair, nail, facial, nonpermanent makeup, or nonmedical diet and weight reducing services). 1580-1581

812210 **Funeral Homes and Funeral Services.** This industry comprises establishments primarily engaged in preparing the dead for burial or interment and conducting funerals (i.e., providing facilities for wakes, arranging transportation for the dead, selling caskets and related merchandise). Funeral homes combined with crematories are included in this industry. 1582-1583

OTHER SERVICES

NAICS #		Page
812220	**Cemeteries and Crematories.** This industry comprises establishments primarily engaged in operating sites or structures reserved for the interment of human or animal remains and/or cremating the dead.	1584-1585
812310	**Coin-Operated Laundries and Drycleaners.** This industry comprises (1) establishments primarily engaged in operating facili-ties with coin-operated or similar self-service laundry and drycleaning equipment for customer use on the premises and (2) establishments primarily engaged in supplying and servicing coin-operated or similar self-service laundry and drycleaning equipment for customer use in places of business operated by others, such as apartments and dormitories.	1586-1587
812320	**Drycleaning and Laundry Services (except Coin-Operated).** This industry comprises establishments primarily engaged in one or more of the following: (1) providing drycleaning services (except coin-operated); (2) providing laundering services (except linen and uniform supply or coin-operated); (3) providing dropoff and pickup sites for laundries and/or drycleaners; and (4) providing specialty cleaning services for specific types of garments and other textile items (except carpets and upholstery), such as fur, leather, or suede garments; wedding gowns; hats; draperies; and pillows. These establishments may provide all, a combination of, or none of the cleaning services on the premises.	1588-1589
812331	**Linen Supply.** This U.S. industry comprises establishments primarily engaged in supplying, on a rental or contract basis, laundered items, such as table and bed linens; towels; diapers; and uniforms, gowns, or coats of the type used by doctors, nurses, barbers, beauticians, and waitresses.	1590-1591
812332	**Industrial Launderers.** This U.S. industry comprises establishments primarily engaged in supplying, on a rental or contract basis, laundered industrial work uniforms and related work clothing, such as protective apparel (flame and heat resistant) and clean room apparel; dust control items, such as treated mops, rugs, mats, dust tool covers, cloths, and shop or wiping towels.	1592-1593
812910	**Pet Care (except Veterinary) Services.** This industry comprises establishments primarily engaged in providing pet care services (except veterinary), such as boarding, grooming, sitting, and training pets.	1594-1595
812930	**Parking Lots and Garages.** This industry comprises establishments primarily engaged in providing parking space for motor vehicles, usually on an hourly, daily, or monthly basis and/or valet parking services.	1596-1597
812990	**All Other Personal Services.** This industry comprises establishments primarily engaged in providing personal services (except personal care services, death care services, drycleaning and laundry services, pet care services, photofinishing services, or parking space and/or valet parking services).	1598-1599
813110	**Religious Organizations.** This industry comprises (1) establishments primarily engaged in operating reli-gious organizations, such as churches, religious temples, and monasteries and/or (2) establishments primarily engaged in administering an organized religion or promoting religious activities.	1600-1601
813211	**Grantmaking Foundations.** This U.S. industry comprises establishments known as grantmaking foundations or charitable trusts. Establishments in this industry award grants from trust funds based on a competitive selection process or the preferences of the foundation managers and grantors; or fund a single entity, such as a museum or university.	1602-1603
813212	**Voluntary Health Organizations.** This U.S. industry comprises establishments primarily engaged in raising funds for health related research, such as disease (e.g., heart, cancer, diabetes) prevention, health education, and patient services.	1604-1605
813219	**Other Grantmaking and Giving Services.** This U.S. industry comprises establishments (except voluntary health organizations) primarily engaged in raising funds for a wide range of social welfare activities, such as educational, scientific, cultural, and health.	1606-1607

PUBLIC ADMINISTRATION

NAICS #		Page
813311	**Human Rights Organizations.** This U.S. industry comprises establishments primarily engaged in promoting causes associated with human rights either for a broad or specific constituency. Establishments in this industry address issues, such as protecting and promoting the broad constitutional rights and civil liberties of individuals and those suffering from neglect, abuse, or exploitation; promoting the interests of specific groups, such as children, women, senior citizens, or persons with disabilities; improving relations between racial, ethnic, and cultural groups; and promoting voter education and registration. These organizations may solicit contributions and offer memberships to support these causes.	1608-1609
813312	**Environment, Conservation and Wildlife Organizations.** This U.S. industry comprises establishments primarily engaged in promoting the preservation and protection of the environment and wildlife. Establishments in this industry address issues, such as clean air and water; global warming; conserving and developing natural resources, including land, plant, water, and energy resources; and protecting and preserving wildlife and endangered species. These organizations may solicit contributions and offer memberships to support these causes.	1610-1611
813319	**Other Social Advocacy Organizations.** This U.S. industry comprises establishments primarily engaged in social advocacy (except human rights and environmental protection, conservation, and wildlife preservation). Establishments in this industry address issues, such as peace and international understanding; community action (excluding civic organizations); or advancing social causes, such as firearms safety, drunk driving prevention, drug abuse awareness. These organizations may solicit contributions and offer memberships to support these causes.	1612-1613
813410	**Civic and Social Organizations.** This industry comprises establishments primarily engaged in promoting the civic and social interests of their members. Establishments in this industry may operate bars and restaurants for their members.	1614-1615
813910	**Business Associations.** This industry comprises establishments primarily engaged in promoting the business interests of their members. These establishments may conduct research on new products and services; develop market statistics; sponsor quality and certification standards; lobby public officials; or publish newsletters, books, or periodicals for distribution to their members.	1616-1617
813920	**Professional Organizations.** This industry comprises establishments primarily engaged in promoting the professional interests of their members and the profession as a whole. These establishments may conduct research; develop statistics; sponsor quality and certi-fication standards; lobby public officials; or publish newsletters, books, or periodicals for distribution to their members.	1618-1619
813930	**Labor Unions and Similar Labor Organizations.** This industry comprises establishments primarily engaged in promoting the interests of organized labor and union employees.	1620-1621
813990	**Other Similar Organizations (except Business, Professional, Labor, and Political Organizations).** This industry comprises establishments (except religious organizations, social advocacy organizations, civic and social organizations, business associations, professional organizations, labor unions, and political organizations) primarily engaged in promoting the interest of their members.	1622-1623
814110	**Private Households.** This industry comprises private households primarily engaged in employing workers on or about the premises in activities primarily concerned with the operation of the household. These private households may employ individuals, such as cooks, maids, nannies, and butlers, and outside workers, such as gardeners, caretakers, and other maintenance workers.	1624-1625

PUBLIC ADMINISTRATION

921110	**Executive Offices.** This industry comprises government establishments serving as offices of chief executives and their advisory committees and commissions. This industry includes offices of the president, governors, and mayors, in addition to executive advisory commissions.	1628-1629
921120	**Legislative Bodies.** This industry comprises government establishments serving as legislative bodies and their advisory committees and commissions. Included in this industry are legislative bodies, such as Congress, state legislatures, and advisory and study legislative commissions.	1630-1631

NAICS # Page

921130 **Public Finance Activities.** This industry comprises government establishments primarily engaged in public finance, taxation and monetary policy. Included are financial administration activities, such as monetary policy; tax administration and collection; custody and disbursement of funds; debt and investment administration; auditing activities; and government employee retirement trust fund administration. 1632-1633

921140 **Executive and Legislative Offices, Combined.** This industry comprises government establishments serving as councils and boards of commissioners or supervisors and such bodies where the chief executive (e.g., county executive or city mayor) is a member of the legislative body (e.g., county or city council) itself. 1634-1635

921190 **Other General Government Support.** This industry comprises government establishments primarily engaged in providing general support for government. Such support services include personnel services, election boards, and other general government support establishments that are not classified elsewhere in public administration. 1636-1637

922160 **Fire Protection.** This industry comprises government establishments primarily engaged in fire fighting and other related fire protection activities. Government establishments providing combined fire protection and ambulance or rescue services are classified in this industry. . . 1638-1639

923110 **Administration of Education Programs.** This industry comprises government establishments primarily engaged in the central coordination, planning, supervision and administration of funds, policies, intergovernmental activities, statistical reports and data collection, and centralized programs for educational administration. Government scholarship programs are included in this industry. 1640-1641

923120 **Administration of Public Health Programs.** This industry comprises government establishments primarily engaged in the planning, administration, and coordination of public health programs and services, including environmental health activities, mental health, categorical health programs, health statistics, and immunization services. Government establishments primarily engaged in conducting public health-related inspections are included in this industry. 1642-1643

924110 **Administration of Air and Water Resource and Solid Waste Management Programs.** This industry comprises government establishments primarily engaged in one or more of the following: (1) the administration, regulation, and enforcement of air and water resource programs; (2) the administration and regulation of solid waste management programs; (3) the administration and regulation of water and air pollution control and prevention programs; (4) the administration and regulation of flood control programs; (5) the administration and regulation of drainage development and water resource consumption programs; (6) the administration and regulation of toxic waste removal and cleanup programs; and (7) coordination of these activities at intergovernmental levels. 1644-1645

925110 **Administration of Housing Programs.** This industry comprises government establishments primarily engaged in the administration and planning of housing programs. 1646-1647

925120 **Administration of Urban Planning and Community and Rural Development.** This industry comprises government establishments primarily engaged in the administration and planning of the development of urban and rural areas. Included in this industry are government zoning boards and commissions. 1648-1649

926110 **Administration of General Economic Programs.** This industry comprises government establishments primarily engaged in the administration, promotion and development of economic resources, including business, industry, and tourism. Included in this industry are government establishments responsible for the development of general statistical data and analyses and promotion of the general economic well-being of the governed area. 1650-1651

CONSTRUCTION—PERCENTAGE OF COMPLETION

236115 **New Single-Family Housing Construction (except For-Sale Builders).** This U.S. industry comprises general contractor establishments primarily responsible for the entire construction of new single-family housing, such as single-family detached houses and town houses or row houses where each housing unit (1) is separated from its neighbors by a ground-to-roof wall and (2) has no housing units constructed above or below. This industry includes general contractors respon-sible for the on-site assembly of modular and prefabricated houses. Single-family housing design-build firms and single-family construction management firms acting as general contractors are included in this industry. 1654

CONSTRUCTION-% OF COMPLETION

NAICS # Page

236117 **New Housing For-Sale Builders.** This U.S. industry comprises operative builders primarily responsible for the entire construction of new houses and other residential buildings, single-family and multifamily, on their own account for sale. Operative builders are also known as speculative or merchant builders. 1655

236118 **Residential Remodelers.** This U.S. industry comprises establishments primarily responsible for the remodeling construction (including additions, alterations, reconstruction, maintenance and repair work) of houses and other residential buildings, single-family and multifamily. Included in this industry are remodeling general contractors, operative remodelers, remodeling design-build firms, and remodeling project construction management firms. 1656

236210 **Industrial Building Construction.** This industry comprises establishments primarily responsible for the construction (including new work, additions, alterations, maintenance, and repairs) of industrial buildings (except warehouses). The construction of selected additional structures, whose production processes are similar to those for industrial buildings (e.g., incinerators, cement plants, blast furnaces, and similar nonbuilding structures), is included in this industry. Included in this industry are industrial building general contractors, industrial building operative builders, industrial building design-build firms, and industrial building construction management firms. 1657

236220 **Commercial and Institutional Building Construction.** This industry comprises establishments primarily responsible for the construction (including new work, additions, alterations, maintenance, and repairs) of commercial and institutional buildings and related structures, such as stadiums, grain elevators, and indoor swimming pools. This industry includes establishments responsible for the on-site assembly of modular or prefabricated commercial and institutional buildings. Included in this industry are commercial and institutional building general contractors, commercial and institutional building operative builders, commercial and institutional building design-build firms, and commercial and institutional building project construction management firms. 1658

237110 **Water and Sewer Line and Related Structures Construction.** This industry comprises establishments primarily engaged in the construction of water and sewer lines, mains, pumping stations, treatment plants and storage tanks. The work performed may include new work, reconstruction, rehabilitation, and repairs. Specialty trade contractors are included in this group if they are engaged in activities primarily related to water and sewer line and related structures construction. All structures (including buildings) that are integral parts of water and sewer networks (e.g., storage tanks, pumping stations, water treatment plants, and sewage treatment plants) are included in this industry. 1659

237210 **Land Subdivision.** This industry comprises establishments primarily engaged in servicing land and subdividing real property into lots, for subsequent sale to builders. Servicing of land may include excavation work for the installation of roads and utility lines. The extent of work may vary from project to project. Land subdivision precedes building activity and the subsequent building is often residential, but may also be commercial tracts and industrial parks. These establishments may do all the work themselves or subcontract the work to others. Establishments that perform only the legal subdivision of land are not included in this industry. 1660

237310 **Highway, Street, and Bridge Construction.** This industry comprises establishments primarily engaged in the construction of highways (including elevated), streets, roads, airport runways, public sidewalks, or bridges. The work performed may include new work, reconstruction, rehabilitation, and repairs. Specialty trade contractors are included in this group if they are engaged in activities primarily related to highway, street, and bridge construction (e.g., installing guardrails on highways). 1661

237990 **Other Heavy and Civil Engineering Construction.** This industry comprises establishments primarily engaged in heavy and engineering construction projects (excluding highway, street, bridge, and distribution line construction). The work performed may include new work, reconstruction, rehabilitation, and repairs. Specialty trade contractors are included in this group if they are engaged in activities primarily related to engineering construction projects (excluding highway, street, bridge, distribution line, oil and gas structure, and utilities building and structure construction). Construction projects involving water resources (e.g., dredging and land drainage), development of marine facilities, and projects involving open space improvement (e.g., parks and trails) are included in this industry. 1662

CONSTRUCTION-% OF COMPLETION

NAICS #		Page
238110	**Poured Concrete Foundation and Structure Contractors.** This industry comprises establishments primarily engaged in pouring and finishing concrete foundations and structural elements. This industry also includes establishments performing grout and shotcrete work. The work performed may include new work, additions, alterations, maintenance, and repairs.	1663
238120	**Structural Steel and Precast Concrete Contractors.** This industry comprises establishments primarily engaged in: (1) erecting and assembling structural parts made from steel or precast concrete (e.g., steel beams, structural steel components, and similar products of precast concrete); and/or (2) assembling and installing other steel construction products (e.g., steel rods, bars, rebar, mesh, and cages) to reinforce poured-in-place concrete. The work performed may include new work, additions, alterations, maintenance, and repairs.	1664
238150	**Glass and Glazing Contractors.** This industry comprises establishments primarily engaged in installing glass panes in prepared openings (i.e., glazing work) and other glass work for buildings. The work performed may include new work, additions, alterations, maintenance, and repairs.	1665
238160	**Roofing Contractors.** This industry comprises establishments primarily engaged in roofing. This industry also includes establishments treating roofs (i.e., spraying, painting, or coating) and installing skylights. The work performed may include new work, additions, alterations, maintenance, and repairs.	1666
238210	**Electrical Contractors and Other Wiring Installation Contractors.** This industry comprises establishments primarily engaged in installing and servicing electrical wiring and equipment. Electrical contractors included in this industry may include both the parts and labor when performing work. Electrical contractors may perform new work, additions, alterations, maintenance, and repairs.	1667
238220	**Plumbing, Heating, and Air-Conditioning Contractors.** This industry comprises establishments primarily engaged in installing and servicing plumbing, heating, and air-conditioning equipment. Contractors in this industry may provide both parts and labor when performing work. The work performed may include new work, additions, alterations, maintenance, and repairs.	1668
238310	**Drywall and Insulation Contractors.** This industry comprises establishments primarily engaged in drywall, plaster work, and building insulation work. Plaster work includes applying plain or ornamental plaster, and installation of lath to receive plaster. The work performed may include new work, additions, alterations, maintenance, and repairs.	1669
238320	**Painting and Wall Covering Contractors.** This industry comprises establishments primarily engaged in interior or exterior painting or interior wall covering. The work performed may include new work, additions, alterations, maintenance, and repairs.	1670
238910	**Site Preparation Contractors.** This industry comprises establishments primarily engaged in site preparation activities, such as excavating and grading, demolition of buildings and other structures, septic system installation, and house moving. Earth moving and land clearing for all types of sites (e.g., building, nonbuilding, mining) is included in this industry. Establishments primarily engaged in construction equipment rental with operator (except cranes) are also included.	1671
238990	**All Other Specialty Trade Contractors.** This industry comprises establishments primarily engaged in specialized trades (except foundation, structure, and building exterior contractors; building equipment contractors; building finishing contractors; and site preparation contractors). The specialty trade work performed includes new work, additions, alterations, maintenance, and repairs.	1672

AGRICULTURE, FORESTRY, FISHING AND HUNTING

Current Data Sorted by Assets							Comparative Historical Data	
						Type of Statement		
	1	4	6	1	3	Unqualified	10	5
		1	4			Reviewed	2	6
	4	1				Compiled	8	6
10	12	7	2			Tax Returns	22	15
6	16	15	6	1		Other	25	28
	9 (4/1-9/30/13)		91 (10/1/13-3/31/14)				4/1/09-3/31/10	4/1/10-3/31/11
0-500M	500M-2MM	2-10MM	10-50MM	50-100MM	100-250MM		ALL	ALL
16	33	28	18	2	3	NUMBER OF STATEMENTS	67	60
%	%	%	%	%	%	**ASSETS**	%	%
17.3	11.4	13.2	8.3			Cash & Equivalents	14.5	9.7
16.8	21.1	16.8	15.4			Trade Receivables (net)	12.0	12.6
8.0	16.5	10.0	21.4			Inventory	14.5	16.2
1.1	4.9	2.0	2.2			All Other Current	3.8	4.5
43.3	53.8	41.9	47.4			Total Current	44.7	43.0
39.0	37.1	50.7	41.1			Fixed Assets (net)	41.5	43.0
4.4	1.0	4.1	7.5			Intangibles (net)	6.5	5.5
13.3	8.1	3.2	4.1			All Other Non-Current	7.3	8.5
100.0	100.0	100.0	100.0			Total	100.0	100.0
						LIABILITIES		
50.7	13.9	6.8	7.0			Notes Payable-Short Term	14.2	10.0
11.5	2.6	1.7	3.6			Cur. Mat.-L.T.D.	4.1	5.2
8.0	15.5	9.1	9.8			Trade Payables	7.2	8.7
.0	.0	.7	.2			Income Taxes Payable	.1	.4
20.7	8.6	8.6	5.6			All Other Current	7.0	7.6
90.8	40.6	26.9	26.2			Total Current	32.6	32.0
28.2	31.1	35.6	21.6			Long-Term Debt	37.7	24.7
.0	.0	.3	.5			Deferred Taxes	.4	.8
6.1	2.2	3.4	9.0			All Other Non-Current	2.5	3.3
-25.1	26.2	33.9	42.7			Net Worth	26.8	39.3
100.0	100.0	100.0	100.0			Total Liabilties & Net Worth	100.0	100.0
						INCOME DATA		
100.0	100.0	100.0	100.0			Net Sales	100.0	100.0
						Gross Profit		
89.2	89.0	77.3	87.0			Operating Expenses	85.9	86.7
10.8	11.0	22.7	13.0			Operating Profit	14.1	13.3
1.3	1.6	8.2	5.4			All Other Expenses (net)	6.6	3.6
9.5	9.4	14.5	7.6			Profit Before Taxes	7.6	9.7
						RATIOS		
1.8	2.3	3.1	2.6				2.8	2.4
.9	1.6	1.6	2.2			Current	1.5	1.3
.1	1.0	1.0	1.1				.8	.6
1.4	1.9	2.4	2.0				1.6	1.3
.5	1.1	1.2	.7			Quick	.9	.6
.0	.3	.6	.3				.2	.2
0 UND	**0** UND	**0** UND	**7** 53.3				**0** UND	**0** UND
0 UND	**18** 20.6	**20** 18.0	**44** 8.3			Sales/Receivables	**4** 96.2	**18** 20.5
36 10.2	**43** 8.4	**56** 6.5	**56** 6.5				**37** 9.8	**48** 7.7
						Cost of Sales/Inventory		
						Cost of Sales/Payables		
16.8	6.3	3.8	3.5				6.8	5.2
NM	19.6	9.4	7.0			Sales/Working Capital	12.3	17.2
-2.3	NM	223.7	NM				-24.9	-10.6
21.1	17.9	7.5	24.0				8.9	10.5
(12) 14.2	(28) 5.8	(18) 4.9	(16) 9.5			EBIT/Interest	(47) 3.8	(51) 5.5
-.3	2.4	1.6	3.1				1.2	1.7
								7.8
						Net Profit + Depr., Dep., Amort./Cur. Mat. L/T/D		(13) 3.9
								1.9
.1	.2	.3	.4				.2	.5
NM	.8	1.2	1.3			Fixed/Worth	1.2	1.1
-.7	3.0	19.8	3.4				9.9	2.9
.9	.8	.6	.8				.6	.7
NM	2.4	1.4	1.4			Debt/Worth	2.1	1.9
-2.6	10.6	19.2	4.9				29.7	3.8
	99.5	48.9	56.3				36.5	43.4
	(29) 52.3	(23) 13.7	(17) 32.3			% Profit Before Taxes/Tangible Net Worth	(51) 12.0	(53) 20.8
	11.0	5.8	7.1				4.3	2.4
71.3	27.8	14.5	22.2				14.9	14.8
31.0	8.2	6.8	7.0			% Profit Before Taxes/Total Assets	5.2	6.3
.0	3.9	2.5	2.4				.3	1.2
117.5	59.3	17.7	13.5				31.1	17.7
18.4	11.6	1.8	4.0			Sales/Net Fixed Assets	5.8	5.5
3.9	3.1	.3	.5				1.0	.9
7.5	3.6	1.7	2.3				3.2	2.4
3.7	2.7	.8	1.4			Sales/Total Assets	1.8	1.6
2.6	2.0	.2	.3				.5	.4
.8	.5	.7	1.1				1.1	1.3
(11) 3.1	(22) 2.0	(19) 5.8	(16) 3.2			% Depr., Dep., Amort./Sales	(54) 4.2	(47) 2.8
7.4	8.4	10.7	11.4				12.5	8.3
	2.0						2.6	
	(17) 3.3					% Officers', Directors' Owners' Comp/Sales	(21) 5.1	
	6.6						11.4	
19379M	**119800M**	**185725M**	**1119638M**	**48346M**	**456827M**	Net Sales ($)	**751059M**	**1491565M**
4419M	**36982M**	**129930M**	**455015M**	**137412M**	**490812M**	Total Assets ($)	**462939M**	**1095325M**

M = $ thousand MM = $ million

See Pages 9 through 22 for Explanation of Ratios and Data

Comparative Historical Data | Current Data Sorted by Sales

			Type of Statement						
16	10	15	Unqualified		1		2	3	9
10	8	5	Reviewed			2		1	2
13	10	5	Compiled	1		2	1	1	
27	25	31	Tax Returns	6	18	5	1	1	
44	39	44	Other	9	14	10	4	2	5
4/1/11-3/31/12	4/1/12-3/31/13	4/1/13-3/31/14			9 (4/1-9/30/13)		91 (10/1/13-3/31/14)		
ALL	ALL	ALL		0-1MM	1-3MM	3-5MM	5-10MM	10-25MM	25MM & OVER
110	92	100	**NUMBER OF STATEMENTS**	16	33	19	8	8	16
%	%	%	**ASSETS**	%	%	%	%	%	%
14.6	11.7	11.8	Cash & Equivalents	7.6	13.3	9.0			10.5
11.9	14.8	18.5	Trade Receivables (net)	6.3	15.5	22.3			20.8
9.0	13.3	13.9	Inventory	5.2	11.3	23.7			19.8
2.5	4.2	2.9	All Other Current	1.7	4.5	1.7			2.8
37.9	44.0	47.1	Total Current	20.7	44.5	56.6			53.8
46.8	46.6	41.5	Fixed Assets (net)	68.6	43.7	33.2			29.7
3.7	3.2	4.2	Intangibles (net)	6.2	3.2	1.1			9.2
11.7	6.2	7.3	All Other Non-Current	4.5	8.5	9.1			7.3
100.0	100.0	100.0	Total	100.0	100.0	100.0			100.0
			LIABILITIES						
15.3	24.7	16.9	Notes Payable-Short Term	12.7	29.8	16.6			6.3
5.8	5.4	3.9	Cur. Mat.-L.T.D.	3.2	6.4	1.1			3.6
6.8	8.0	11.0	Trade Payables	.6	9.8	12.9			11.6
.1	.4	.2	Income Taxes Payable	.0	.0	.0			.3
9.2	7.7	9.9	All Other Current	11.0	11.7	4.3			10.6
37.1	46.2	41.9	Total Current	27.5	57.7	34.9			32.4
35.9	31.3	29.6	Long-Term Debt	48.4	32.4	29.7			16.1
.2	.3	.3	Deferred Taxes	.0	.0	.0			1.2
9.6	4.7	4.4	All Other Non-Current	1.6	4.6	1.5			8.3
17.3	17.5	23.9	Net Worth	22.6	5.2	33.8			42.0
100.0	100.0	100.0	Total Liabilties & Net Worth	100.0	100.0	100.0			100.0
			INCOME DATA						
100.0	100.0	100.0	Net Sales	100.0	100.0	100.0			100.0
			Gross Profit						
85.0	88.7	84.9	Operating Expenses	61.7	87.8	87.5			91.4
15.0	11.3	15.1	Operating Profit	38.3	12.2	12.5			8.6
6.2	4.1	4.3	All Other Expenses (net)	13.6	3.2	3.0			1.0
8.8	7.2	10.9	Profit Before Taxes	24.7	8.9	9.5			7.6
			RATIOS						
2.4	2.3	2.5		2.5	2.5	3.4			2.5
1.1	1.3	1.5	Current	1.8	1.3	2.1			1.7
.4	.6	.9		.3	.8	1.0			1.2
1.7	1.7	1.8		2.1	1.7	2.2			1.8
.6	.7	.8	Quick	.6	.8	1.1			.7
.2	.2	.3		.3	.1	.3			.5
0 UND	**0** UND	**0** UND		**0** UND	**0** UND	**0** 999.8			**11** 33.3
4 81.2	**13** 28.8	**20** 18.2	Sales/Receivables	**0** UND	**1** 392.5	**16** 23.2			**36** 10.0
36 10.0	**43** 8.5	**49** 7.5		**24** 15.5	**36** 10.0	**70** 5.2			**53** 6.9
			Cost of Sales/Inventory						
			Cost of Sales/Payables						
5.7	5.5	5.3		3.9	5.4	1.9			5.4
46.8	16.5	18.4	Sales/Working Capital	13.0	21.2	9.6			15.2
-7.9	-10.9	-59.6		-5.9	-23.9	-96.6			31.6
13.0	13.3	20.0		10.0	19.8	19.6			23.5
(76) 3.2	(79) 3.6	(76) 6.0	EBIT/Interest	(11) 5.3	(24) 3.2	(13) 6.2			(14) 9.4
1.2	1.2	1.9		1.7	.3	2.0			3.5
22.8	5.1	10.5							
(10) 5.1	(10) 3.2	(14) 3.0	Net Profit + Depr., Dep., Amort./Cur. Mat. L/T/D						
2.4	.5	1.7							
.3	.5	.3		.8	.4	.0			.3
1.4	1.5	1.1	Fixed/Worth	2.3	1.2	.8			.7
NM	NM	8.9		NM	-4.8	2.9			2.0
.6	.7	.7		.8	.6	.6			1.0
2.4	2.2	1.8	Debt/Worth	1.6	3.5	1.4			1.5
NM	NM	15.7		NM	-8.1	11.5			3.1
44.4	68.3	80.1		51.2	99.6	59.7			59.8
(83) 17.0	(69) 14.6	(81) 32.3	% Profit Before Taxes/Tangible Net Worth	(12) 17.7	(24) 47.0	(16) 18.4			(15) 39.7
2.4	2.9	9.9		10.4	5.2	4.5			11.7
14.2	17.7	23.8		21.2	47.5	17.1			23.2
5.2	6.6	8.2	% Profit Before Taxes/Total Assets	5.9	7.4	6.9			13.1
.8	1.2	2.6		1.7	.4	2.5			4.2
27.8	19.7	35.1		4.5	45.8	105.1			13.8
4.7	4.7	6.0	Sales/Net Fixed Assets	1.1	5.6	18.7			8.3
.8	1.2	1.8		.1	1.4	2.0			3.3
3.1	2.9	3.5		1.9	3.7	3.6			3.6
1.6	1.6	2.0	Sales/Total Assets	.3	2.3	2.4			2.0
.4	.8	.7		.1	.7	1.0			1.3
1.3	1.4	.9		1.0	.9	.4			1.1
(79) 4.0	(68) 2.8	(71) 3.1	% Depr., Dep., Amort./Sales	(11) 7.8	(22) 4.4	(10) 5.9			(15) 1.6
15.0	10.6	8.7		12.7	9.0	15.8			5.7
1.1	3.6	1.9			1.9				
(28) 2.8	(16) 7.1	(33) 3.3	% Officers', Directors' Owners' Comp/Sales		(16) 2.6				
6.8	9.7	6.6			5.7				
2722989M	**2530579M**	**1949715M**	Net Sales ($)	**8827M**	**60970M**	**74620M**	**47194M**	**123435M**	**1634669M**
1700125M	**1523964M**	**1254570M**	Total Assets ($)	**32460M**	**70859M**	**163698M**	**59840M**	**47110M**	**880603M**

M = $ thousand MM = $ million

See Pages 9 through 22 for Explanation of Ratios and Data

Current Data Sorted by Assets							Comparative Historical Data	
						Type of Statement		
	1	2	4	1		Unqualified	21	12
	1	3	1			Reviewed	16	17
1	1	4	1			Compiled	17	8
2	1	4				Tax Returns	22	21
3	2	11	10	2	1	Other	51	35
13 (4/1-9/30/13)			43 (10/1/13-3/31/14)				4/1/09-3/31/10	4/1/10-3/31/11
0-500M	500M-2MM	2-10MM	10-50MM	50-100MM	100-250MM		ALL	ALL
6	6	24	16	3	1	NUMBER OF STATEMENTS	127	93
%	%	%	%	%	%	**ASSETS**	%	%
		9.5	7.0			Cash & Equivalents	13.8	9.9
		15.6	16.0			Trade Receivables (net)	14.5	15.2
		17.8	16.1			Inventory	10.3	13.8
		1.8	4.3			All Other Current	4.8	5.3
		44.7	43.4			Total Current	43.4	44.2
		46.5	42.9			Fixed Assets (net)	46.4	45.3
		4.4	6.3			Intangibles (net)	3.6	3.9
		4.4	7.4			All Other Non-Current	6.6	6.5
		100.0	100.0			Total	100.0	100.0
						LIABILITIES		
		10.5	7.5			Notes Payable-Short Term	12.9	14.6
		4.5	2.8			Cur. Mat.-L.T.D.	4.0	5.0
		9.3	10.3			Trade Payables	9.3	9.2
		.0	.3			Income Taxes Payable	.3	.3
		9.6	12.5			All Other Current	13.2	11.2
		33.9	33.3			Total Current	39.6	40.2
		17.5	19.4			Long-Term Debt	32.6	21.0
		.1	.2			Deferred Taxes	.4	.7
		5.2	9.0			All Other Non-Current	3.8	5.0
		43.1	38.1			Net Worth	23.7	33.1
		100.0	100.0			Total Liabilties & Net Worth	100.0	100.0
						INCOME DATA		
		100.0	100.0			Net Sales	100.0	100.0
						Gross Profit		
		91.6	92.9			Operating Expenses	89.6	88.3
		8.4	7.1			Operating Profit	10.4	11.7
		3.0	.3			All Other Expenses (net)	3.5	4.7
		5.5	6.8			Profit Before Taxes	6.9	7.0
						RATIOS		
		3.6	3.1				2.6	2.0
		1.3	1.4			Current	1.3	1.1
		.6	1.0				.7	.6
		1.0	2.2				1.9	1.3
		.3	.7			Quick	.8	.6
		.1	.3				.2	.2
		0 UND	**14** 26.4				**0** UND	**0** UND
		9 42.9	**22** 16.6			Sales/Receivables	**19** 19.2	**15** 23.9
		38 9.5	**62** 5.9				**44** 8.4	**53** 6.8
						Cost of Sales/Inventory		
						Cost of Sales/Payables		
		3.0	6.8				4.9	6.4
		21.6	14.8			Sales/Working Capital	16.5	35.8
		-6.9	NM				-16.2	-8.2
		10.1	10.1				9.8	15.2
		(20) 2.5	3.5			EBIT/Interest	(109) 2.6	(80) 3.7
		1.0	.8				.5	1.2
							2.3	13.4
						Net Profit + Depr., Dep., Amort./Cur. Mat. L/T/D	(18) 1.5	(11) 1.9
							1.0	.8
		.5	.6				.4	.6
		1.2	1.9			Fixed/Worth	1.2	1.3
		2.6	NM				5.4	7.3
		.5	.8				.6	.6
		1.0	2.2			Debt/Worth	2.0	2.1
		5.8	NM				15.2	31.6
		36.0	43.1				32.3	37.8
		(21) 12.7	(12) 11.5			% Profit Before Taxes/Tangible Net Worth	(101) 8.7	(74) 13.3
		-.7	4.2				-1.1	1.0
		18.0	13.1				12.0	13.6
		3.1	6.0			% Profit Before Taxes/Total Assets	2.3	4.2
		-.3	-.4				-.7	.0
		11.2	45.2				20.8	23.1
		3.6	4.1			Sales/Net Fixed Assets	3.7	3.6
		.9	1.3				.8	.7
		3.1	2.9				2.7	3.0
		1.3	1.4			Sales/Total Assets	1.4	1.3
		.6	.8				.5	.5
		1.6	.5				1.9	1.0
		(21) 6.8	(13) 1.6			% Depr., Dep., Amort./Sales	(99) 5.1	(75) 4.0
		16.4	6.6				12.1	13.7
							1.6	1.1
						% Officers', Directors' Owners' Comp/Sales	(37) 3.9	(25) 3.4
							7.1	6.3
6853M	24921M	196140M	916076M	396314M	152553M	Net Sales ($)	3637165M	3779093M
1423M	8280M	114230M	440097M	231405M	230653M	Total Assets ($)	1792627M	2107477M

M = $ thousand MM = $ million

See Pages 9 through 22 for Explanation of Ratios and Data

Comparative Historical Data				Current Data Sorted by Sales					
			Type of Statement						
13	8	8	Unqualified		1	1	2		4
11	10	5	Reviewed			1	2		2
8	3	7	Compiled	1	3	1	1	1	
17	7	7	Tax Returns	4	2		1		
38	22	29	Other	1	6	2	3	8	9
					13 (4/1-9/30/13)		43 (10/1/13-3/31/14)		
4/1/11-3/31/12 ALL	4/1/12-3/31/13 ALL	4/1/13-3/31/14 ALL		0-1MM	1-3MM	3-5MM	5-10MM	10-25MM	25MM & OVER
87	50	56	**NUMBER OF STATEMENTS**	6	12	5	9	9	15
%	%	%	**ASSETS**	%	%	%	%	%	%
12.1	11.4	12.1	Cash & Equivalents		13.5				3.5
15.0	18.9	17.8	Trade Receivables (net)		17.2				25.1
13.4	13.1	15.0	Inventory		13.3				25.7
3.5	3.0	3.9	All Other Current		1.4				4.9
44.0	46.4	48.8	Total Current		45.4				59.2
42.3	41.5	41.4	Fixed Assets (net)		43.7				27.5
6.0	5.1	4.1	Intangibles (net)		.0				6.9
7.7	7.0	5.7	All Other Non-Current		11.0				6.4
100.0	100.0	100.0	Total		100.0				100.0
			LIABILITIES						
10.6	10.9	14.2	Notes Payable-Short Term		23.6				12.4
7.6	4.6	3.9	Cur. Mat.-L.T.D.		3.7				3.6
11.1	18.2	11.6	Trade Payables		10.0				15.9
.2	.0	.1	Income Taxes Payable		.0				.3
5.3	10.0	9.9	All Other Current		7.7				14.9
34.8	43.7	39.7	Total Current		45.0				47.1
25.6	25.0	17.8	Long-Term Debt		14.6				17.2
.5	.2	.2	Deferred Taxes		.0				.6
6.0	14.1	6.5	All Other Non-Current		4.5				11.2
33.2	17.0	35.9	Net Worth		35.9				23.9
100.0	100.0	100.0	Total Liabilties & Net Worth		100.0				100.0
			INCOME DATA						
100.0	100.0	100.0	Net Sales		100.0				100.0
			Gross Profit						
87.4	87.9	91.7	Operating Expenses		96.4				95.0
12.6	12.1	8.3	Operating Profit		3.6				5.0
4.8	5.7	2.8	All Other Expenses (net)		2.9				1.3
7.8	6.4	5.5	Profit Before Taxes		.7				3.8
			RATIOS						
3.1	2.3	3.7			4.8				1.6
1.3	1.4	1.4	Current		1.9				1.4
.7	.4	.6			.5				1.0
1.9	1.7	1.7			1.6				1.0
.7	.7	.5	Quick		.3				.5
.3	.2	.2			.1				.2
0 UND	0 UND	0 UND			0 UND				20 18.0
12 29.2	23 15.6	20 18.6	Sales/Receivables		0 UND				26 14.3
49 7.4	55 6.6	49 7.5			43 8.5				65 5.6
			Cost of Sales/Inventory						
			Cost of Sales/Payables						
5.3	5.6	3.7			2.1				9.8
14.4	11.8	16.2	Sales/Working Capital		3.4				15.9
-23.9	-5.6	-11.0			NM				247.4
8.2	14.1	10.6							6.6
(67) 3.4	(43) 2.7	(46) 3.2	EBIT/Interest						3.5
1.6	-.2	1.1							1.2
4.4									
(13) 1.7			Net Profit + Depr., Dep., Amort./Cur. Mat. L/T/D						
-.1									
.4	.4	.4			.2				.6
1.0	1.1	1.1	Fixed/Worth		1.0				2.2
22.3	8.7	2.8			2.4				-11.6
.5	.8	.5			.3				1.6
1.9	1.9	1.8	Debt/Worth		.7				6.3
68.0	14.4	14.9			3.7				-26.7
45.1	35.1	36.0			14.0				50.4
(66) 17.8	(39) 4.9	(45) 12.7	% Profit Before Taxes/Tangible Net Worth		(10) 3.0				(11) 16.8
1.6	-2.7	1.6			.8				7.7
14.3	13.7	14.8			12.2				10.1
6.3	3.8	3.7	% Profit Before Taxes/Total Assets		2.0				5.4
1.0	-1.7	-.1			.3				.7
28.1	25.7	26.0			25.9				54.9
6.8	7.1	4.5	Sales/Net Fixed Assets		1.9				11.8
.8	.7	1.3			.6				2.9
3.2	3.5	3.2			2.2				3.2
1.2	1.5	1.4	Sales/Total Assets		.8				2.2
.4	.4	.7			.4				1.0
1.0	.6	.8			.7				.4
(71) 3.8	(39) 2.3	(45) 3.9	% Depr., Dep., Amort./Sales		(10) 10.1				(14) 1.0
10.9	9.3	12.3			18.9				4.7
.5	1.0	.5							
(19) 3.9	(10) 4.7	(10) 1.2	% Officers', Directors' Owners' Comp/Sales						
5.8	10.8	4.0							
2974334M	1917954M	1692857M	Net Sales ($)	2320M	22617M	17486M	69654M	139038M	1441742M
1900192M	1029883M	1026088M	Total Assets ($)	10205M	32419M	28633M	122493M	61490M	770848M

M = $ thousand MM = $ million

See Pages 9 through 22 for Explanation of Ratios and Data

Current Data Sorted by Assets							Comparative Historical Data	
						Type of Statement		
	1	2	2			Unqualified	4	5
		2	3	1	2	Reviewed	7	7
		5	2			Compiled	8	9
2	5	12	1	1		Tax Returns	27	31
2	6	15	4		2	Other	15	18
8 (4/1-9/30/13)		62 (10/1/13-3/31/14)					4/1/09-3/31/10	4/1/10-3/31/11
0-500M	**500M-2MM**	**2-10MM**	**10-50MM**	**50-100MM**	**100-250MM**		ALL	ALL
4	12	36	12	2	4	**NUMBER OF STATEMENTS**	61	70
%	%	%	%	%	%	**ASSETS**	%	%
	20.6	5.4	5.1			Cash & Equivalents	8.9	8.6
	3.8	7.7	7.2			Trade Receivables (net)	7.0	5.9
	13.2	18.2	14.8			Inventory	15.8	18.8
	3.8	5.4	8.4			All Other Current	5.2	4.9
	41.4	36.6	35.6			Total Current	37.0	38.2
	51.9	57.2	54.8			Fixed Assets (net)	51.1	51.6
	.6	1.4	1.5			Intangibles (net)	1.2	1.9
	6.1	4.8	8.1			All Other Non-Current	10.7	8.2
	100.0	100.0	100.0			Total	100.0	100.0
						LIABILITIES		
	25.3	13.8	11.8			Notes Payable-Short Term	21.7	28.5
	11.8	3.3	4.8			Cur. Mat.-L.T.D.	4.3	5.5
	9.5	2.3	2.9			Trade Payables	4.5	3.9
	.1	.0	.0			Income Taxes Payable	.1	.0
	7.5	5.5	4.0			All Other Current	4.4	4.3
	54.2	24.9	23.5			Total Current	34.9	42.3
	22.8	16.6	20.8			Long-Term Debt	26.6	29.3
	.0	.1	.0			Deferred Taxes	.6	.6
	3.9	2.2	.5			All Other Non-Current	2.7	2.6
	19.1	56.1	55.2			Net Worth	35.2	25.2
	100.0	100.0	100.0			Total Liabilities & Net Worth	100.0	100.0
						INCOME DATA		
	100.0	100.0	100.0			Net Sales	100.0	100.0
						Gross Profit		
	88.1	86.9	85.5			Operating Expenses	88.7	89.2
	11.9	13.1	14.5			Operating Profit	11.3	10.8
	.0	1.9	1.7			All Other Expenses (net)	5.0	3.9
	11.9	11.2	12.8			Profit Before Taxes	6.3	6.9
						RATIOS		
	1.8	3.8	4.6				1.8	2.2
	.7	1.6	1.7			Current	1.1	1.3
	.5	.9	1.0				.4	.4
	.8	1.0	1.1				.8	.9
	.5	.5	.3			Quick	.3	.2
	.2	.2	.0				.0	.0
	0 UND	0 UND	0 UND				0 UND	0 UND
	0 UND	14 25.4	6 59.1			Sales/Receivables	0 UND	0 UND
	13 29.0	44 8.3	26 13.8				31 11.9	28 12.8
						Cost of Sales/Inventory		
						Cost of Sales/Payables		
	17.3	2.0	1.4				5.6	3.3
	-9.4	6.6	7.0			Sales/Working Capital	20.6	8.9
	-3.7	-22.1	-110.5				-4.0	-3.6
	31.9	10.0	33.9				7.0	9.4
	(10) 6.1	(29) 4.0	5.4			EBIT/Interest	(54) 2.9	(62) 3.8
	1.8	1.0	1.5				1.0	.9
						Net Profit + Depr., Dep., Amort./Cur. Mat. L/T/D		
	.8	.8	.5				.6	.6
	1.5	1.0	1.2			Fixed/Worth	1.3	1.2
	3.5	1.6	2.2				3.4	23.6
	1.1	.3	.3				.6	.5
	2.6	.6	.5			Debt/Worth	1.7	1.9
	18.3	2.2	3.1				5.6	289.4
	77.2	22.5	14.6				26.8	30.9
	(10) 26.8	6.1	(11) 11.9			% Profit Before Taxes/Tangible Net Worth	(52) 11.2	(54) 12.2
	6.3	.3	3.1				.8	1.5
	24.2	9.2	9.9				10.8	11.6
	11.3	2.1	4.6			% Profit Before Taxes/Total Assets	4.1	5.2
	2.6	.2	.8				.1	.1
	83.3	2.1	1.8				6.6	8.8
	2.2	1.0	1.2			Sales/Net Fixed Assets	1.9	1.7
	1.1	.5	.4				.4	.6
	2.4	1.0	.8				2.2	1.7
	1.3	.6	.6			Sales/Total Assets	.8	.7
	.7	.3	.2				.3	.5
		6.2	3.1				2.7	3.6
		(31) 11.1	(11) 8.5			% Depr., Dep., Amort./Sales	(54) 6.8	(59) 7.7
		17.3	15.3				16.4	17.6
		.9					.7	.3
		(11) 1.6				% Officers', Directors' Owners' Comp/Sales	(16) 2.1	(16) 1.5
		2.1					3.7	3.7
1941M	25488M	151132M	174766M	379708M	409566M	Net Sales ($)	694681M	633061M
546M	14479M	180725M	215608M	143686M	595854M	Total Assets ($)	580585M	757356M

M = $ thousand MM = $ million

See Pages 9 through 22 for Explanation of Ratios and Data

Comparative Historical Data				Current Data Sorted by Sales					
			Type of Statement						
3	3	5	Unqualified	1	1		1	1	1
6	9	8	Reviewed			2	1	3	2
9	11	7	Compiled		1	2	2	2	
24	24	21	Tax Returns	7	4	4	4	1	1
22	29	29	Other	7	14	2	4	1	1
4/1/11-3/31/12 ALL	**4/1/12-3/31/13 ALL**	**4/1/13-3/31/14 ALL**		**8 (4/1-9/30/13)**			**62 (10/1/13-3/31/14)**		
				0-1MM	**1-3MM**	**3-5MM**	**5-10MM**	**10-25MM**	**25MM & OVER**
64	76	70	**NUMBER OF STATEMENTS**	15	20	10	12	8	5
%	%	%	**ASSETS**	%	%	%	%	%	%
5.1	4.9	9.1	Cash & Equivalents	10.5	8.1	7.4	13.6		
7.3	9.6	6.3	Trade Receivables (net)	3.6	5.8	5.9	8.1		
17.8	17.6	16.1	Inventory	12.7	13.7	22.8	19.9		
5.6	6.1	5.0	All Other Current	2.3	5.1	4.6	7.2		
35.8	38.2	36.5	Total Current	29.1	32.8	40.6	48.7		
56.8	53.2	56.0	Fixed Assets (net)	60.9	59.8	47.4	46.7		
.8	3.2	1.2	Intangibles (net)	2.0	.4	2.1	.0		
6.6	5.4	6.3	All Other Non-Current	8.0	7.0	9.9	4.6		
100.0	100.0	100.0	Total	100.0	100.0	100.0	100.0		
			LIABILITIES						
19.9	14.7	19.8	Notes Payable-Short Term	10.0	24.3	11.9	31.9		
3.3	4.8	4.8	Cur. Mat.-L.T.D.	2.5	9.1	3.5	2.4		
5.6	5.4	3.4	Trade Payables	1.8	4.4	3.3	1.8		
.1	.0	.1	Income Taxes Payable	.1	.0	.0	.0		
6.4	6.1	5.4	All Other Current	2.6	1.1	16.0	.6		
35.4	31.0	33.5	Total Current	17.0	38.9	34.8	36.7		
27.2	25.8	19.3	Long-Term Debt	25.5	22.5	11.3	11.2		
.6	.5	.1	Deferred Taxes	.0	.0	.2	.0		
2.6	3.2	2.0	All Other Non-Current	4.5	.9	1.7	.0		
34.2	39.4	45.2	Net Worth	53.0	37.7	51.9	52.0		
100.0	100.0	100.0	Total Liabilties & Net Worth	100.0	100.0	100.0	100.0		
			INCOME DATA						
100.0	100.0	100.0	Net Sales	100.0	100.0	100.0	100.0		
			Gross Profit						
90.2	87.0	87.1	Operating Expenses	86.4	91.0	79.7	84.9		
9.8	13.0	12.9	Operating Profit	13.6	9.0	20.3	15.1		
3.3	2.5	1.7	All Other Expenses (net)	2.8	1.5	1.6	.1		
6.6	10.5	11.1	Profit Before Taxes	10.7	7.5	18.7	15.0		
			RATIOS						
2.0	2.0	2.9		3.9	2.3	2.0	6.2		
1.4	1.2	1.3	Current	2.1	1.2	1.2	2.3		
.6	.7	.8		.9	.7	.8	.8		
.9	.9	1.0		2.8	.9	.7	2.5		
.3	(75) .3	.5	Quick	.9	.6	.5	.4		
.1	.1	.1		.3	.1	.0	.1		
0 UND	**0** UND	**0** UND		**0** UND	**0** UND	**0** UND	**0** UND		
3 128.0	**0** UND	**8** 44.8	Sales/Receivables	**5** 81.1	**12** 29.8	**3** 113.5	**2** 153.8		
38 9.6	**60** 6.1	**23** 15.9		**22** 16.5	**22** 16.9	**43** 8.4	**59** 6.2		
			Cost of Sales/Inventory						
			Cost of Sales/Payables						
3.5	3.5	2.6		1.7	3.7	2.6	1.4		
11.1	11.4	11.7	Sales/Working Capital	6.0	12.9	29.8	2.8		
-7.4	-11.7	-14.6		-15.8	-6.0	NM	-39.5		
6.3	13.5	13.5			9.3		47.4		
(53) 3.2	(65) 3.8	(56) 4.0	EBIT/Interest		(17) 3.3		(11) 7.7		
1.0	1.3	1.5			1.1		1.6		
			Net Profit + Depr., Dep., Amort./Cur. Mat. L/T/D						
.8	.7	.8		.8	.9	.3	.5		
1.2	1.2	1.1	Fixed/Worth	.9	1.0	.9	.8		
2.8	2.3	2.1		1.9	2.1	1.2	1.5		
.4	.4	.4		.3	.5	.4	.2		
1.8	1.2	.9	Debt/Worth	.7	1.0	.8	.5		
4.4	4.3	3.4		3.1	3.2	3.7	1.9		
23.7	30.9	24.4		6.1	22.3	51.5	22.3		
(55) 8.8	(68) 11.8	(65) 7.5	% Profit Before Taxes/Tangible Net Worth	(14) 1.3	(18) 9.4	17.7	(10) 13.6		
.7	1.9	1.1		-11.1	.3	3.2	7.3		
10.9	14.7	14.9		5.9	11.7	16.8	19.7		
4.1	4.8	4.6	% Profit Before Taxes/Total Assets	1.0	4.4	6.1	9.5		
.3	.6	.5		-2.7	-.1	2.0	3.0		
3.4	4.3	3.4		1.0	1.7	17.5	5.6		
1.0	1.5	1.1	Sales/Net Fixed Assets	.6	1.1	1.0	1.7		
.4	.5	.5		.3	.5	.6	1.2		
1.2	1.3	1.5		.7	1.4	1.4	1.6		
.8	.8	.6	Sales/Total Assets	.4	.6	.6	.8		
.3	.3	.3		.2	.4	.4	.5		
3.6	2.6	4.7		4.9	8.2		5.3		
(55) 7.9	(66) 7.1	(55) 9.0	% Depr., Dep., Amort./Sales	(12) 11.3	(16) 11.7		(10) 8.3		
16.1	12.3	16.5		23.4	16.8		16.4		
1.8	1.2	.9							
(22) 4.5	(19) 1.7	(17) 1.6	% Officers', Directors' Owners' Comp/Sales						
8.9	4.5	2.8							
539827M	**1049520M**	**1142601M**	Net Sales ($)	**8848M**	**39365M**	**38570M**	**86322M**	**145310M**	**824186M**
701172M	**1406996M**	**1150898M**	Total Assets ($)	**37455M**	**74316M**	**94569M**	**119227M**	**338732M**	**486599M**

M = $ thousand MM = $ million

See Pages 9 through 22 for Explanation of Ratios and Data

Current Data Sorted by Assets							Comparative Historical Data	
Type of Statement								
Unqualified			2	3	2	1	17	10
Reviewed		1	4	3			12	8
Compiled		2	6	1			19	19
Tax Returns	8	11	21	5			35	36
Other	2	7	7	8	1		23	37
	13 (4/1-9/30/13)			82 (10/1/13-3/31/14)			4/1/09-3/31/10	4/1/10-3/31/11
	0-500M	500M-2MM	2-10MM	10-50MM	50-100MM	100-250MM	ALL	ALL
NUMBER OF STATEMENTS	10	21	40	20	3	1	106	110
ASSETS	%	%	%	%	%	%	%	%
Cash & Equivalents	41.9	10.2	3.9	4.7			9.9	7.0
Trade Receivables (net)	.0	1.6	4.5	14.0			11.1	11.0
Inventory	.0	17.9	13.9	18.0			19.1	19.7
All Other Current	.9	14.1	5.8	4.3			3.8	5.3
Total Current	42.8	43.9	28.1	41.0			43.9	43.0
Fixed Assets (net)	48.7	44.7	59.5	49.0			43.8	49.0
Intangibles (net)	.0	3.5	1.9	5.0			1.2	1.3
All Other Non-Current	8.5	7.9	10.4	5.1			11.0	6.8
Total	100.0	100.0	100.0	100.0			100.0	100.0
LIABILITIES								
Notes Payable-Short Term	8.4	29.9	20.7	14.3			21.1	18.3
Cur. Mat.-L.T.D.	8.4	9.4	4.0	1.9			8.6	3.8
Trade Payables	.0	5.4	4.2	12.2			6.7	6.9
Income Taxes Payable	.0	.5	.0	.1			.2	.2
All Other Current	1.4	7.6	2.7	3.2			8.0	4.5
Total Current	18.2	52.7	31.7	31.7			44.5	33.6
Long-Term Debt	41.3	24.5	37.1	20.6			24.9	26.0
Deferred Taxes	.0	.5	.1	1.4			.3	.3
All Other Non-Current	.4	8.0	3.4	3.9			1.8	9.5
Net Worth	40.1	14.4	27.7	42.4			28.5	30.7
Total Liabilties & Net Worth	100.0	100.0	100.0	100.0			100.0	100.0
INCOME DATA								
Net Sales	100.0	100.0	100.0	100.0			100.0	100.0
Gross Profit								
Operating Expenses	87.1	90.1	90.0	86.0			90.7	88.4
Operating Profit	12.9	9.9	10.0	14.0			9.3	11.6
All Other Expenses (net)	1.9	1.1	1.2	2.4			1.9	4.3
Profit Before Taxes	11.0	8.8	8.7	11.7			7.4	7.3
RATIOS								
Current	22.0	1.7	1.9	2.4			1.8	2.3
	1.8	1.2	1.0	1.4			1.2	1.4
	1.1	.5	.2	1.1			.8	1.0
Quick	21.4	1.1	.5	1.4			1.0	1.0
	1.8	.3	.2	.6			.4	.4
	1.1	.0	.0	.2			.1	.1
Sales/Receivables	0 UND	0 UND	0 UND	3 105.0			0 UND	0 UND
	0 UND	0 UND	1 312.0	33 11.1			9 40.2	5 80.6
	0 UND	7 53.7	27 13.3	72 5.1			35 10.4	36 10.1
Cost of Sales/Inventory								
Cost of Sales/Payables								
Sales/Working Capital	4.0	9.9	3.7	3.5			4.3	3.4
	13.5	118.9	534.1	14.2			20.4	13.7
	NM	-7.8	-2.9	52.8			-28.6	288.1
EBIT/Interest		12.6	9.0	11.2			7.1	8.6
		(18) 9.0	(39) 3.3	4.4			(95) 2.8	(93) 4.4
		2.8	1.7	1.5			1.3	1.6
Net Profit + Depr., Dep., Amort./Cur. Mat. L/T/D							6.3	7.2
							(13) 3.9	(15) 3.4
							2.2	1.9
Fixed/Worth	.4	.4	.8	.9			.6	.7
	.9	1.0	1.4	1.3			1.1	1.2
	2.7	6.1	16.3	2.5			3.1	2.8
Debt/Worth	.3	.4	.6	.6			.8	.6
	1.3	1.8	1.7	1.7			2.0	1.8
	5.7	NM	17.6	6.3			7.5	6.2
% Profit Before Taxes/Tangible Net Worth		67.3	30.5	32.6			34.2	43.6
		(16) 21.9	(32) 11.7	(19) 14.0			(89) 12.9	(94) 15.9
		2.4	2.9	2.0			2.4	3.4
% Profit Before Taxes/Total Assets	18.0	25.9	8.3	9.5			13.7	11.1
	9.2	10.5	3.9	5.2			4.6	4.4
	-5.5	.6	1.0	.7			.9	1.4
Sales/Net Fixed Assets	19.9	30.8	5.3	11.3			13.0	9.2
	3.9	2.4	.9	1.7			3.1	2.0
	.7	1.2	.5	.2			.8	.7
Sales/Total Assets	3.1	2.6	1.5	2.4			2.7	2.2
	1.6	1.5	.7	.5			1.2	.9
	.4	.7	.3	.2			.5	.4
% Depr., Dep., Amort./Sales		1.0	4.2	.9			1.3	2.4
		(13) 8.6	(33) 15.0	(19) 9.5			(89) 4.2	(90) 6.9
		17.4	21.9	14.9			13.0	13.1
% Officers', Directors' Owners' Comp/Sales			.7				1.4	1.0
			(11) 1.8				(37) 3.7	(27) 2.7
			3.9				5.8	4.3
Net Sales ($)	27194M	50822M	252417M	795717M	443739M	689592M	4342060M	1664563M
Total Assets ($)	2830M	22363M	193852M	439461M	215319M	220121M	2187837M	1295142M

M = $ thousand MM = $ million

See Pages 9 through 22 for Explanation of Ratios and Data

Comparative Historical Data | **Current Data Sorted by Sales**

4/1/11-3/31/12 ALL	4/1/12-3/31/13 ALL	4/1/13-3/31/14 ALL	Type of Statement	0-1MM	1-3MM	3-5MM	5-10MM	10-25MM	25MM & OVER
10	8	8	Unqualified					2	6
12	13	8	Reviewed		1			3	4
21	13	9	Compiled		3	3	2		1
40	41	45	Tax Returns	13	22	3	6	1	
26	32	25	Other	5	6	5	4	1	4
				13 (4/1-9/30/13)		82 (10/1/13-3/31/14)			
109	107	95	**NUMBER OF STATEMENTS**	18	32	11	12	7	15
%	%	%	**ASSETS**	%	%	%	%	%	%
9.1	6.0	9.4	Cash & Equivalents	16.8	8.7	6.2	1.1		7.5
7.1	9.2	5.9	Trade Receivables (net)	.2	2.0	4.2	3.3		23.1
19.6	14.1	15.1	Inventory	4.0	8.4	24.0	17.4		29.2
5.7	5.1	6.8	All Other Current	.6	8.8	6.9	7.0		7.6
41.6	34.4	37.2	Total Current	21.6	27.9	41.3	28.7		67.4
45.2	53.0	51.5	Fixed Assets (net)	65.6	57.5	52.1	60.5		23.8
2.5	1.2	3.1	Intangibles (net)	3.5	4.1	4.8	.1		3.2
10.7	11.4	8.2	All Other Non-Current	9.3	10.4	1.8	10.7		5.6
100.0	100.0	100.0	Total	100.0	100.0	100.0	100.0		100.0
			LIABILITIES						
15.7	12.5	20.3	Notes Payable-Short Term	7.1	19.8	35.9	30.6		20.7
4.0	6.7	5.1	Cur. Mat.-L.T.D.	7.3	7.2	4.7	2.6		1.5
7.1	6.6	6.2	Trade Payables	1.3	2.0	3.6	6.3		21.2
.1	.3	.1	Income Taxes Payable	.0	.3	.0	.0		.2
4.3	4.4	3.9	All Other Current	.6	3.1	4.8	.4		5.9
31.2	30.6	35.7	Total Current	16.4	32.4	49.1	39.9		49.5
23.7	32.6	30.1	Long-Term Debt	35.7	19.5	36.0	62.8		10.0
.3	.3	.4	Deferred Taxes	.0	.3	2.6	.0		.2
4.7	4.7	4.1	All Other Non-Current	.6	.7	1.9	2.7		10.4
40.1	31.9	29.7	Net Worth	47.3	47.1	10.5	-5.4		29.9
100.0	100.0	100.0	Total Liabilities & Net Worth	100.0	100.0	100.0	100.0		100.0
			INCOME DATA						
100.0	100.0	100.0	Net Sales	100.0	100.0	100.0	100.0		100.0
			Gross Profit						
88.1	85.0	89.2	Operating Expenses	80.8	87.4	91.1	89.5		98.0
11.9	15.0	10.8	Operating Profit	19.2	12.6	8.9	10.5		2.0
2.6	2.8	1.5	All Other Expenses (net)	2.2	1.6	1.4	2.1		-.3
9.4	12.2	9.3	Profit Before Taxes	17.0	11.0	7.4	8.4		2.3
			RATIOS						
2.3	2.3	2.1		2.3	2.0	2.1	2.4		1.9
1.4	1.2	1.2	Current	1.2	1.1	1.4	1.3		1.4
1.0	.4	.5		.6	.3	.2	.3		1.1
1.3	.9	1.2		2.2	.6	.8	.7		1.1
.5	.3	.4	Quick	1.0	.2	.2	.1		.6
.1	.1	.1		.3	.0	.0	.0		.3
0 UND	0 UND	0 UND		0 UND	0 UND	0 UND	0 UND		12 29.9
1 260.6	3 133.0	0 999.8	Sales/Receivables	0 UND	0 UND	10 38.1	4 93.9		21 17.6
26 13.8	31 11.7	28 13.0		0 UND	14 25.3	21 17.6	54 6.7		33 11.0
			Cost of Sales/Inventory						
			Cost of Sales/Payables						
3.2	3.4	4.2		3.9	3.0	3.3	2.7		10.9
14.0	24.4	28.8	Sales/Working Capital	17.8	43.4	19.4	510.3		28.8
372.3	-7.2	-7.8		-9.9	-4.4	-4.4	-4.0		54.6
11.2	10.4	10.3		9.3	12.9	6.9	6.4		25.2
(96) 3.8	(98) 4.4	(90) 4.2	EBIT/Interest	(16) 5.7	(30) 6.0	(10) 2.8	3.2		5.6
1.8	1.6	1.5		.1	1.7	1.3	1.0		2.3
9.2	11.2								
(10) 4.4	(11) 10.1		Net Profit + Depr., Dep., Amort./Cur. Mat. L/T/D						
1.9	2.2								
.6	.7	.7		.8	.6	.4	1.0		.3
1.1	1.3	1.2	Fixed/Worth	1.1	1.2	2.6	2.4		.8
2.4	4.7	3.8		2.8	2.4	-2.5	-1.2		2.0
.6	.5	.6		.3	.4	1.4	.7		1.7
1.3	1.8	1.7	Debt/Worth	.8	.7	2.0	7.3		2.5
4.0	8.9	7.8		4.5	3.2	-3.6	-2.7		7.3
34.0	33.2	34.9		28.9	41.4				51.2
(98) 15.6	(87) 14.6	(80) 13.8	% Profit Before Taxes/Tangible Net Worth	(16) 8.2	(29) 5.8				22.2
2.4	2.0	2.2		-2.4	2.4				7.8
12.7	12.4	11.4		11.9	14.1	11.8	7.7		13.8
5.3	5.5	4.8	% Profit Before Taxes/Total Assets	6.3	3.9	7.6	5.3		4.7
1.1	1.0	.8		-1.3	1.0	.4	-1.2		2.4
14.5	9.8	11.4		1.4	3.7	37.3	3.7		41.2
2.9	2.0	1.5	Sales/Net Fixed Assets	.9	1.0	2.3	1.9		12.2
.8	.6	.7		.3	.5	.5	.5		7.8
2.5	2.3	2.2		.8	1.4	2.2	1.6		7.8
1.0	.9	.9	Sales/Total Assets	.5	.6	.9	1.1		3.1
.5	.4	.4		.2	.2	.4	.3		1.5
1.2	3.5	1.1		12.7	8.0				.4
(89) 6.6	(89) 8.3	(75) 11.4	% Depr., Dep., Amort./Sales	(13) 18.2	(26) 16.2				.9
13.7	14.2	20.6		43.8	24.0				1.6
1.5	.8	.8							
(33) 3.1	(29) 2.9	(18) 2.8	% Officers', Directors' Owners' Comp/Sales						
5.3	6.1	5.3							
3367715M	2621727M	2259481M	Net Sales ($)	7587M	54598M	42677M	87039M	111170M	1956410M
1819733M	1774762M	1093946M	Total Assets ($)	23677M	137388M	91020M	149239M	34517M	658105M

M = $ thousand MM = $ million

See Pages 9 through 22 for Explanation of Ratios and Data

	Current Data Sorted by Assets						Comparative Historical Data	
Type of Statement								
Unqualified					1		8	7
Reviewed			5	8	6	1	13	17
Compiled		2	5	5	2	2	12	21
Tax Returns	1	8	4	2			23	12
Other			7	6	1	1	15	15
	9 (4/1-9/30/13)		58 (10/1/13-3/31/14)				4/1/09-3/31/10	4/1/10-3/31/11
	0-500M	500M-2MM	2-10MM	10-50MM	50-100MM	100-250MM	ALL	ALL
NUMBER OF STATEMENTS	1	10	21	21	10	4	71	72
ASSETS	%	%	%	%	%	%	%	%
Cash & Equivalents		7.8	7.3	2.9	1.4		8.1	6.2
Trade Receivables (net)		7.5	13.5	14.2	15.5		11.3	11.9
Inventory		.0	15.5	22.4	25.8		13.3	15.5
All Other Current		.1	4.3	2.9	5.0		5.9	6.4
Total Current		15.4	40.6	42.4	47.6		38.7	40.0
Fixed Assets (net)		71.5	51.3	41.1	38.3		48.6	48.3
Intangibles (net)		.7	.8	.9	3.7		2.1	1.9
All Other Non-Current		12.4	7.3	15.7	10.4		10.6	9.8
Total		100.0	100.0	100.0	100.0		100.0	100.0
LIABILITIES								
Notes Payable-Short Term		73.4	24.4	14.4	18.3		21.4	20.2
Cur. Mat.-L.T.D.		6.5	3.5	2.9	3.3		6.5	3.6
Trade Payables		.4	14.3	8.4	5.1		5.8	5.8
Income Taxes Payable		.0	.3	1.0	.1		.4	1.0
All Other Current		1.7	2.7	6.5	2.3		6.1	5.0
Total Current		82.0	45.2	33.3	29.1		40.2	35.6
Long-Term Debt		35.4	23.8	29.0	25.1		31.6	29.7
Deferred Taxes		.0	.9	.0	.2		.3	.5
All Other Non-Current		.0	2.3	4.0	.4		3.2	1.6
Net Worth		-17.5	27.8	33.8	45.3		24.7	32.7
Total Liabilties & Net Worth		100.0	100.0	100.0	100.0		100.0	100.0
INCOME DATA								
Net Sales		100.0	100.0	100.0	100.0		100.0	100.0
Gross Profit								
Operating Expenses		94.5	90.0	90.9	90.2		90.9	90.4
Operating Profit		5.5	10.0	9.1	9.8		9.1	9.6
All Other Expenses (net)		1.3	2.5	1.8	.2		2.4	1.3
Profit Before Taxes		4.2	7.4	7.4	9.6		6.6	8.3
RATIOS								
		1.1	1.4	1.6	2.1		2.3	2.2
Current		.4	1.1	1.2	1.4		1.2	1.3
		.0	.8	.8	1.3		.7	.8
		.9	1.2	.8	.9		1.5	1.1
Quick		.4	(20) .4	.4	.6		.5	.4
		.0	.1	.2	.3		.1	.2
		0 UND	0 UND	9 41.1	30 12.0		0 UND	0 UND
Sales/Receivables		0 UND	14 26.1	31 11.6	49 7.4		21 17.6	28 13.0
		0 UND	38 9.5	58 6.3	101 3.6		58 6.3	58 6.3
Cost of Sales/Inventory								
Cost of Sales/Payables								
		NM	11.4	4.0	3.2		3.5	3.5
Sales/Working Capital		-26.6	66.8	11.0	3.8		14.9	13.2
		-1.7	-15.2	-23.9	8.6		-6.3	-13.6
			7.7	7.8	9.8		9.3	7.2
EBIT/Interest			(19) 2.7	(19) 3.8	3.7		(64) 3.3	(65) 2.8
			1.0	2.5	2.5		.7	1.1
							5.8	7.0
Net Profit + Depr., Dep., Amort./Cur. Mat. L/T/D							(16) 3.1	(12) 2.7
							.0	.6
		2.1	.6	.7	.5		.7	.7
Fixed/Worth		NM	1.8	1.5	1.0		1.9	1.3
		-1.0	9.0	2.4	1.8		4.7	2.7
		2.6	.9	1.4	.6		1.1	.9
Debt/Worth		NM	2.1	2.1	1.5		2.7	1.5
		-2.7	12.8	4.9	3.1		9.3	4.5
			20.4	38.9	26.3		40.8	29.3
% Profit Before Taxes/Tangible Net Worth			(17) 6.0	17.2	19.3		(60) 15.1	(66) 10.8
			1.0	5.9	8.6		-2.9	.9
		30.4	11.5	9.8	10.0		11.4	10.6
% Profit Before Taxes/Total Assets		6.0	3.3	4.9	6.2		5.9	4.9
		-.1	.3	3.1	3.7		-1.1	.4
		7.4	8.8	9.8	4.2		4.1	4.3
Sales/Net Fixed Assets		4.0	2.4	2.1	2.6		2.2	2.0
		3.2	.9	1.3	1.0		1.1	.7
		4.3	2.7	1.6	1.2		1.8	2.0
Sales/Total Assets		3.0	1.1	.7	.7		1.0	.7
		2.2	.6	.6	.4		.5	.5
		3.9	1.6	3.6	3.4		3.1	3.3
% Depr., Dep., Amort./Sales		7.4	(18) 4.5	(19) 6.0	5.1		(65) 5.6	(66) 5.9
		10.4	10.1	7.3	6.9		9.3	10.1
							1.1	.9
% Officers', Directors' Owners' Comp/Sales							(19) 2.1	(17) 1.7
							5.4	4.5
Net Sales ($)	1183M	46398M	226892M	884276M	537640M	394607M	1696471M	1604983M
Total Assets ($)	55M	13492M	119382M	493646M	658797M	519291M	1509619M	1920070M

M = $ thousand MM = $ million

See Pages 9 through 22 for Explanation of Ratios and Data

Comparative Historical Data / Current Data Sorted by Sales

4/1/11-3/31/12 ALL	4/1/12-3/31/13 ALL	4/1/13-3/31/14 ALL		0-1MM	1-3MM	3-5MM	5-10MM	10-25MM	25MM & OVER
			Type of Statement						
5	3	1	Unqualified						1
9	20	20	Reviewed			1	5	3	11
18	13	16	Compiled	2	1	2	3	4	4
14	15	15	Tax Returns	1	5	2	3	3	1
17	17	15	Other	1	1	2		6	5
				9 (4/1-9/30/13)			58 (10/1/13-3/31/14)		
63	68	67	**NUMBER OF STATEMENTS**	4	7	7	11	16	22
%	%	%	**ASSETS**	%	%	%	%	%	%
5.5	6.3	6.1	Cash & Equivalents				2.9	7.5	4.0
13.8	11.9	12.5	Trade Receivables (net)				9.9	14.4	18.8
16.5	16.9	16.5	Inventory				19.1	16.2	20.9
6.0	6.2	4.2	All Other Current				2.2	2.1	6.9
41.8	41.3	39.4	Total Current				34.1	40.1	50.6
48.7	47.3	48.1	Fixed Assets (net)				53.0	48.0	37.7
1.7	1.6	1.2	Intangibles (net)				1.0	1.3	2.3
7.8	9.8	11.3	All Other Non-Current				11.9	10.6	9.5
100.0	100.0	100.0	Total				100.0	100.0	100.0
			LIABILITIES						
18.5	17.4	28.1	Notes Payable-Short Term				36.2	20.1	21.0
2.8	4.6	3.7	Cur. Mat.-L.T.D.				4.5	2.1	3.1
8.2	8.3	8.3	Trade Payables				8.1	9.1	13.5
1.3	.2	.4	Income Taxes Payable				.5	.0	1.0
7.1	4.6	3.5	All Other Current				1.3	4.3	5.2
37.8	35.1	43.9	Total Current				50.6	35.7	43.8
28.7	23.5	27.1	Long-Term Debt				22.3	22.2	23.3
.1	.1	.3	Deferred Taxes				.1	.0	.1
6.1	3.9	2.0	All Other Non-Current				4.4	1.2	2.7
27.3	37.5	26.6	Net Worth				22.7	41.0	30.1
100.0	100.0	100.0	Total Liabilties & Net Worth				100.0	100.0	100.0
			INCOME DATA						
100.0	100.0	100.0	Net Sales				100.0	100.0	100.0
			Gross Profit						
87.7	92.9	90.9	Operating Expenses				99.2	93.7	92.9
12.3	7.1	9.1	Operating Profit				.8	6.3	7.1
1.7	1.6	1.5	All Other Expenses (net)				.9	.4	.5
10.7	5.5	7.6	Profit Before Taxes				-.1	5.9	6.6
			RATIOS						
1.9	1.9	1.5	Current				1.6	1.5	1.6
1.3	1.3	1.2					1.0	1.3	1.3
.9	.9	.8					.7	.8	1.1
.9	1.0	.8	Quick				.7	1.1	.8
.4	.4	(66) .4					.5	.5	.5
.1	.2	.2					.1	.1	.3
0 UND	**0** UND	**0** UND	Sales/Receivables				**0** UND	**0** UND	**29** 12.8
26 14.3	**27** 13.3	**23** 15.6					**17** 22.0	**27** 13.5	**36** 10.2
68 5.4	**48** 7.6	**53** 6.9					**65** 5.6	**46** 7.9	**79** 4.6
			Cost of Sales/Inventory						
			Cost of Sales/Payables						
4.4	4.8	4.0	Sales/Working Capital				4.6	3.8	3.8
10.2	12.3	21.9					-649.6	26.4	8.7
-83.5	-41.8	-26.7					-41.2	-36.3	49.1
9.5	7.5	9.3	EBIT/Interest				7.0	5.6	11.7
(58) 5.5	(62) 2.9	(61) 3.8					(10) 2.8	(13) 2.7	4.1
3.0	1.0	2.2					-1.4	2.1	2.9
8.9		3.7	Net Profit + Depr., Dep., Amort./Cur. Mat. L/T/D						
(11) 4.4		(11) 2.4							
2.4		.7							
.5	.6	.7	Fixed/Worth				.8	.5	.5
1.1	1.2	1.5					1.5	1.1	1.2
3.8	2.4	2.5					-45.4	1.8	2.3
.8	.7	1.1	Debt/Worth				.4	.6	1.2
1.3	1.5	2.1					1.9	1.6	2.4
4.2	4.9	6.9					-60.1	3.4	4.4
31.2	29.1	28.1	% Profit Before Taxes/Tangible Net Worth					19.7	34.8
(55) 20.7	(63) 14.1	(58) 15.3						(15) 10.5	(21) 22.9
8.7	2.4	5.4						4.7	8.3
12.6	11.2	11.7	% Profit Before Taxes/Total Assets				11.3	6.3	12.6
8.9	3.7	5.1					4.0	3.5	6.2
2.4	.3	1.7					-2.2	2.3	3.7
6.2	6.7	6.8	Sales/Net Fixed Assets				5.1	11.9	7.0
2.6	2.7	3.0					3.9	2.3	3.8
.9	1.3	1.2					1.4	1.4	1.2
2.5	2.1	2.4	Sales/Total Assets				2.9	2.8	2.2
.8	1.0	1.0					1.1	1.2	.9
.5	.6	.6					1.0	.7	.6
3.7	2.5	3.1	% Depr., Dep., Amort./Sales				4.0	2.9	1.8
(54) 5.6	(60) 5.4	(60) 5.7					6.0	(14) 5.9	(20) 4.0
9.0	8.0	9.4					10.1	8.0	5.8
1.3	1.0	1.2	% Officers', Directors' Owners' Comp/Sales						
(20) 2.1	(19) 2.0	(22) 2.8							
3.2	3.8	5.1							
2062209M	2905680M	2090996M	Net Sales ($)	2803M	15613M	26885M	82755M	272871M	1690069M
2010783M	2306711M	1804663M	Total Assets ($)	21130M	14274M	41717M	88171M	297793M	1341578M

M = $ thousand MM = $ million

See Pages 9 through 22 for Explanation of Ratios and Data

Current Data Sorted by Assets							Comparative Historical Data	
						Type of Statement		
			4	2	4	Unqualified	18	13
		3	9	3		Reviewed	19	13
2		10	1	1		Compiled	21	14
5	9	2	2			Tax Returns	19	18
2	3	8	14	5	5	Other	41	46
	23 (4/1-9/30/13)		71 (10/1/13-3/31/14)				4/1/09-3/31/10	4/1/10-3/31/11
0-500M	500M-2MM	2-10MM	10-50MM	50-100MM	100-250MM		ALL	ALL
9	12	23	30	11	9	NUMBER OF STATEMENTS	118	104
%	%	%	%	%	%	**ASSETS**	%	%
	15.3	12.7	10.8	4.9		Cash & Equivalents	9.7	9.8
	11.0	19.7	15.2	11.7		Trade Receivables (net)	17.0	17.7
	2.7	8.2	12.9	16.0		Inventory	13.2	12.6
	8.5	2.4	7.6	14.9		All Other Current	5.8	5.6
	37.5	42.9	46.5	47.5		Total Current	45.6	45.8
	53.5	43.2	37.6	34.3		Fixed Assets (net)	40.5	38.1
	.1	6.0	4.4	4.0		Intangibles (net)	1.4	1.6
	8.9	7.8	11.5	14.2		All Other Non-Current	12.5	14.5
	100.0	100.0	100.0	100.0		Total	100.0	100.0
						LIABILITIES		
	23.5	9.8	6.5	3.9		Notes Payable-Short Term	13.8	14.3
	15.9	4.6	3.8	1.1		Cur. Mat.-L.T.D.	3.0	3.9
	4.0	11.9	10.4	6.2		Trade Payables	10.3	10.8
	.0	.3	.2	.1		Income Taxes Payable	.3	.5
	9.3	5.9	5.2	8.3		All Other Current	16.4	9.3
	52.7	32.5	26.1	19.7		Total Current	43.7	38.7
	44.2	22.1	18.5	13.9		Long-Term Debt	26.4	21.6
	.0	1.6	1.1	.0		Deferred Taxes	1.0	.8
	2.1	4.2	6.5	.9		All Other Non-Current	8.6	10.4
	1.0	39.7	47.7	65.4		Net Worth	20.3	28.4
	100.0	100.0	100.0	100.0		Total Liabilties & Net Worth	100.0	100.0
						INCOME DATA		
	100.0	100.0	100.0	100.0		Net Sales	100.0	100.0
						Gross Profit		
	91.8	90.7	90.7	88.4		Operating Expenses	93.8	93.9
	8.2	9.3	9.3	11.6		Operating Profit	6.2	6.1
	11.9	2.2	4.4	1.0		All Other Expenses (net)	1.7	.5
	-3.7	7.1	4.9	10.6		Profit Before Taxes	4.5	5.6
						RATIOS		
	2.2	2.7	4.6	4.7			2.6	2.5
	.6	1.2	2.3	2.9		Current	1.5	1.6
	.1	.7	1.1	1.7			.8	.8
	1.5	2.6	2.5	2.0			1.6	1.5
	.5	.8	1.2	1.2		Quick	.7	.9
	.1	.5	.6	.9			.3	.4
	0 UND	**2** 196.0	**15** 23.9	**22** 16.9			**1** 426.3	**4** 99.4
	0 UND	**27** 13.5	**31** 11.7	**29** 12.8		Sales/Receivables	**28** 13.1	**30** 12.2
	5 76.3	**55** 6.6	**54** 6.8	**36** 10.0			**49** 7.4	**51** 7.1
						Cost of Sales/Inventory		
						Cost of Sales/Payables		
	9.2	7.4	3.5	2.9			5.0	5.5
	-33.1	57.0	8.6	4.8		Sales/Working Capital	13.6	12.5
	-8.0	-19.9	67.4	7.3			-25.2	-43.0
	23.3	16.8	33.6				9.6	10.2
	(10) 2.0	(21) 5.2	(25) 11.6			EBIT/Interest	(102) 3.6	(97) 5.1
	-.4	1.9	.8				.5	.9
		7.6					11.6	11.1
		(11) 2.5				Net Profit + Depr., Dep., Amort./Cur. Mat. L/T/D	(27) 3.6	(26) 2.8
		1.6					1.5	.8
	.3	.4	.4	.2			.5	.4
	6.4	1.9	.8	.6		Fixed/Worth	1.1	.9
	NM	2.8	2.7	.7			NM	2.4
	.7	.5	.4	.2			.6	.5
	40.7	2.1	1.3	.6		Debt/Worth	1.9	1.5
	-38.2	6.3	5.0	1.2			NM	6.1
		45.7	37.6	27.6			33.2	36.6
		(21) 22.0	(26) 19.9	20.2		% Profit Before Taxes/Tangible Net Worth	(89) 12.9	(88) 16.0
		6.2	3.4	9.6			2.3	2.4
	20.7	19.9	19.9	16.2			15.3	13.4
	1.1	7.6	8.7	12.4		% Profit Before Taxes/Total Assets	4.7	7.5
	-7.2	2.4	.1	4.3			-.4	.1
	24.4	15.8	9.0	9.7			14.4	13.6
	9.6	7.5	3.7	5.9		Sales/Net Fixed Assets	4.9	5.6
	3.3	1.8	2.4	1.2			2.4	2.4
	6.7	3.8	1.9	2.5			3.3	3.3
	3.1	1.8	1.4	1.5		Sales/Total Assets	1.7	1.7
	1.7	1.0	1.1	.4			1.1	1.1
		.7	1.8	1.9			1.2	1.5
		(21) 3.9	(28) 3.2	2.4		% Depr., Dep., Amort./Sales	(104) 2.4	(89) 3.1
		6.5	5.3	3.1			5.2	4.7
							1.5	1.0
						% Officers', Directors' Owners' Comp/Sales	(38) 1.9	(24) 1.5
							3.8	4.3
19327M	**46135M**	**236482M**	**1191602M**	**1023100M**	**1588563M**	Net Sales ($)	**4996250M**	**3335279M**
2513M	**11589M**	**103647M**	**771874M**	**694059M**	**1458869M**	Total Assets ($)	**3235705M**	**2233915M**

M = $ thousand MM = $ million

See Pages 9 through 22 for Explanation of Ratios and Data

Comparative Historical Data				Current Data Sorted by Sales					
			Type of Statement						
13	7	10	Unqualified					1	9
14	13	15	Reviewed			1	2	2	10
23	21	14	Compiled	2	1	2	3	6	
23	16	18	Tax Returns	2	7	2	5		2
42	49	37	Other	1	3	3	4	7	19
					23 (4/1-9/30/13)		71 (10/1/13-3/31/14)		
4/1/11-3/31/12 ALL	**4/1/12-3/31/13 ALL**	**4/1/13-3/31/14 ALL**		**0-1MM**	**1-3MM**	**3-5MM**	**5-10MM**	**10-25MM**	**25MM & OVER**
115	106	94	**NUMBER OF STATEMENTS**	5	11	8	14	16	40
%	%	%	**ASSETS**	%	%	%	%	%	%
11.2	7.8	12.8	Cash & Equivalents		19.5		15.8	13.0	9.2
17.4	14.9	14.2	Trade Receivables (net)		4.1		17.2	15.4	16.8
14.4	13.8	10.7	Inventory		2.5		9.5	9.6	15.8
4.9	7.8	7.7	All Other Current		17.3		3.7	11.3	7.2
48.0	44.3	45.5	Total Current		43.4		46.2	49.3	49.0
38.9	39.1	41.0	Fixed Assets (net)		54.6		46.2	30.2	37.8
3.5	3.6	4.0	Intangibles (net)		.0		3.8	10.4	3.8
9.6	13.0	9.5	All Other Non-Current		1.9		3.8	10.1	9.4
100.0	100.0	100.0	Total		100.0		100.0	100.0	100.0
			LIABILITIES						
16.5	18.3	9.6	Notes Payable-Short Term		12.7		8.9	9.7	5.0
3.5	3.2	4.9	Cur. Mat.-L.T.D.		9.8		10.9	3.3	2.8
10.2	10.1	8.6	Trade Payables		4.6		10.2	13.4	9.8
.1	.3	.3	Income Taxes Payable		.0		.4	.0	.5
6.3	7.6	7.4	All Other Current		7.7		7.0	8.2	7.1
36.7	39.5	30.7	Total Current		34.8		37.3	34.6	25.2
22.5	22.5	21.3	Long-Term Debt		23.3		16.3	18.9	14.9
.4	.7	.9	Deferred Taxes		.0		1.8	.0	1.2
8.1	8.7	4.8	All Other Non-Current		10.9		2.2	4.3	4.9
32.3	28.6	42.2	Net Worth		31.0		42.6	42.3	53.8
100.0	100.0	100.0	Total Liabilties & Net Worth		100.0		100.0	100.0	100.0
			INCOME DATA						
100.0	100.0	100.0	Net Sales		100.0		100.0	100.0	100.0
			Gross Profit						
95.2	96.1	91.2	Operating Expenses		96.0		95.8	90.9	92.7
4.8	3.9	8.8	Operating Profit		4.0		4.2	9.1	7.3
.6	1.4	3.6	All Other Expenses (net)		.5		.6	1.7	.0
4.2	2.5	5.2	Profit Before Taxes		3.6		3.6	7.4	7.3
			RATIOS						
3.7	2.8	4.4			8.7		2.2	2.5	4.4
1.5	1.3	1.6	Current		1.3		1.2	1.3	2.3
.9	.7	1.0			.5		.8	.9	1.3
2.3	1.4	2.4			4.8		1.8	2.3	2.2
.8 (105)	.7	1.0	Quick		.6		.7	.8	1.2
.3	.2	.5			.2		.3	.3	.7
3 126.2	0 999.8	2 217.2			0 UND		0 UND	8 48.5	20 18.7
26 13.8	26 14.3	25 14.8	Sales/Receivables		0 UND		26 14.3	19 19.0	30 12.3
50 7.3	50 7.3	44 8.3			4 100.4		36 10.0	56 6.5	51 7.2
			Cost of Sales/Inventory						
			Cost of Sales/Payables						
4.5	4.8	4.0			23.8		7.8	4.2	3.6
11.2	15.4	10.6	Sales/Working Capital		163.6		66.3	12.7	7.3
-80.0	-18.5	298.9			-14.9		-44.4	NM	18.7
19.0	13.9	19.1			11.0		19.4	18.5	29.8
(106) 5.9	(95) 3.3	(82) 9.1	EBIT/Interest		4.7		(13) 5.2	(14) 9.0	(35) 10.4
.9	-.4	1.7			.3		2.2	2.3	2.2
8.3	4.8	8.8							11.0
(28) 2.1	(23) 2.5	(29) 4.1	Net Profit + Depr., Dep., Amort./Cur. Mat. L/T/D						(18) 6.0
-.8	1.5	1.6							2.5
.4	.4	.3			.3		.7	.2	.5
.7	.8	.8	Fixed/Worth		.9		2.0	.9	.7
2.2	3.8	2.6			48.2		3.2	2.1	1.2
.5	.6	.4			.1		.5	.6	.4
1.3	1.3	1.3	Debt/Worth		.8		1.9	1.8	.7
4.8	8.0	5.0			108.5		7.6	6.5	1.7
29.9	29.4	35.3					82.9	44.8	35.2
(97) 14.5	(86) 10.4	(83) 20.8	% Profit Before Taxes/Tangible Net Worth				20.4	(13) 20.8	(38) 20.7
3.0	-4.0	5.9					5.6	5.6	9.4
17.9	11.6	19.4			35.3		17.1	20.1	18.0
6.5	3.9	8.7	% Profit Before Taxes/Total Assets		10.6		7.0	6.7	10.6
1.0	-3.8	1.2			-1.7		1.2	1.9	2.3
13.2	9.5	13.2			23.7		22.7	13.2	9.3
6.1	5.4	5.9	Sales/Net Fixed Assets		8.5		8.3	6.0	4.9
2.4	2.5	2.7			5.9		2.6	3.3	2.4
3.2	2.7	3.6			11.3		6.7	3.8	2.3
1.8	1.6	1.7	Sales/Total Assets		5.7		2.6	1.3	1.6
1.1	1.0	1.1			3.3		1.4	.6	1.2
1.4	1.5	1.5					1.1	.8	1.6
(97) 2.7	(91) 2.9	(84) 2.8	% Depr., Dep., Amort./Sales				(13) 3.9	2.3	(38) 2.4
5.1	4.8	4.8					5.8	4.6	3.6
1.2	1.1	1.0							1.0
(30) 3.1	(30) 1.7	(24) 1.5	% Officers', Directors' Owners' Comp/Sales						(10) 1.5
6.4	3.1	2.6							2.5
3707485M	3570228M	4105209M	Net Sales ($)	1802M	23245M	30695M	100917M	260376M	3688174M
2411281M	2586095M	3042551M	Total Assets ($)	15298M	4845M	59773M	49092M	304782M	2608761M

M = $ thousand MM = $ million

See Pages 9 through 22 for Explanation of Ratios and Data

Current Data Sorted by Assets							Comparative Historical Data	
						Type of Statement		
			3		2	Unqualified	13	14
			2			Reviewed	6	5
		3				Compiled	13	21
7	4	5	2			Tax Returns	16	29
	5	6	2		3	Other	19	9
13 (4/1-9/30/13)			31 (10/1/13-3/31/14)				4/1/09-3/31/10	4/1/10-3/31/11
0-500M	**500M-2MM**	**2-10MM**	**10-50MM**	**50-100MM**	**100-250MM**		**ALL**	**ALL**
7	9	14	9		5	**NUMBER OF STATEMENTS**	67	78
%	%	%	%	%	%	**ASSETS**	%	%
		12.2		DATA NOT AVAILABLE		Cash & Equivalents	13.8	9.2
		6.4				Trade Receivables (net)	9.3	7.0
		5.3				Inventory	7.9	6.7
		7.0				All Other Current	6.9	3.7
		30.8				Total Current	37.9	26.6
		51.2				Fixed Assets (net)	46.2	53.1
		.2				Intangibles (net)	1.1	1.4
		17.8				All Other Non-Current	14.7	18.9
		100.0				Total	100.0	100.0
						LIABILITIES		
		12.3				Notes Payable-Short Term	11.9	13.0
		2.3				Cur. Mat.-L.T.D.	4.1	4.8
		2.8				Trade Payables	8.0	3.7
		.0				Income Taxes Payable	.0	.0
		6.5				All Other Current	8.1	10.2
		23.9				Total Current	32.0	31.7
		41.2				Long-Term Debt	29.8	34.9
		.0				Deferred Taxes	.8	.8
		8.7				All Other Non-Current	3.6	6.2
		26.2				Net Worth	33.7	26.4
		100.0				Total Liabilities & Net Worth	100.0	100.0
						INCOME DATA		
		100.0				Net Sales	100.0	100.0
						Gross Profit		
		95.7				Operating Expenses	91.1	91.1
		4.3				Operating Profit	8.9	8.9
		2.6				All Other Expenses (net)	4.7	5.2
		1.8				Profit Before Taxes	4.2	3.7
						RATIOS		
		3.7					2.6	1.9
		1.0				Current	1.2	1.0
		.6					.6	.2
		2.6					1.7	1.3
		.5				Quick	.7	.5
		.0					.2	.1
		0 UND					0 UND	0 UND
		4 102.1				Sales/Receivables	2 151.2	0 UND
		13 28.2					41 9.0	33 11.2
						Cost of Sales/Inventory		
						Cost of Sales/Payables		
		4.2					2.6	6.0
		NM				Sales/Working Capital	19.4	NM
		-5.3					-13.9	-3.9
		6.5					10.9	8.0
		(13) 4.4				EBIT/Interest	(59) 2.6	(68) 2.1
		.4					.5	.0
								12.1
						Net Profit + Depr., Dep., Amort./Cur. Mat. L/T/D		(14) 3.0
								1.5
		.5					.4	.7
		1.8				Fixed/Worth	1.1	1.4
		-5.2					4.4	17.2
		.1					.4	.5
		2.0				Debt/Worth	1.5	1.5
		-7.9					11.6	34.6
							40.6	36.2
						% Profit Before Taxes/Tangible Net Worth	(52) 5.9	(61) 6.4
							-1.8	-2.5
		8.6					10.8	7.2
		4.8				% Profit Before Taxes/Total Assets	3.2	2.6
		-3.8					-1.5	-2.7
		4.7					14.6	3.2
		1.6				Sales/Net Fixed Assets	1.8	1.2
		.5					.8	.6
		1.4					1.6	1.3
		.8				Sales/Total Assets	.8	.6
		.3					.4	.3
		1.2					1.9	3.0
		(11) 5.0				% Depr., Dep., Amort./Sales	(53) 5.0	(73) 5.6
		9.1					9.5	10.3
								1.2
						% Officers', Directors' Owners' Comp/Sales		(10) 2.3
								7.5
13336M	15434M	99385M	158647M		478930M	Net Sales ($)	1632191M	1757725M
1689M	9047M	82228M	209670M		742245M	Total Assets ($)	2443328M	2245555M

M = $ thousand MM = $ million

See Pages 9 through 22 for Explanation of Ratios and Data

Comparative Historical Data				Current Data Sorted by Sales					
			Type of Statement						
15	7	5	Unqualified				1		4
5	4	2	Reviewed				2		
11	10	3	Compiled		1	1	1		
16	13	18	Tax Returns	4	5		6	2	1
12	15	16	Other	5	4	1	2	1	3
4/1/11-3/31/12 ALL	4/1/12-3/31/13 ALL	4/1/13-3/31/14 ALL		13 (4/1-9/30/13)			31 (10/1/13-3/31/14)		
				0-1MM	**1-3MM**	**3-5MM**	**5-10MM**	**10-25MM**	**25MM & OVER**
59	49	44	**NUMBER OF STATEMENTS**	9	10	2	12	3	8
%	%	%	**ASSETS**	%	%	%	%	%	%
12.4	8.9	15.9	Cash & Equivalents		15.0		26.5		
6.7	6.1	5.6	Trade Receivables (net)		5.8		3.8		
6.3	5.5	7.7	Inventory		13.8		2.3		
5.5	5.9	8.0	All Other Current		9.7		6.0		
30.9	26.4	37.2	Total Current		44.3		38.6		
55.2	57.4	51.0	Fixed Assets (net)		48.3		49.1		
2.2	1.2	1.1	Intangibles (net)		.2		3.3		
11.7	15.0	10.7	All Other Non-Current		7.2		9.0		
100.0	100.0	100.0	Total		100.0		100.0		
			LIABILITIES						
9.4	11.5	21.0	Notes Payable-Short Term		46.7		13.6		
6.4	3.3	3.0	Cur. Mat.-L.T.D.		1.3		2.9		
4.3	2.4	3.5	Trade Payables		5.1		1.1		
.1	.2	.1	Income Taxes Payable		.0		.1		
18.9	5.4	4.1	All Other Current		3.3		5.3		
39.0	22.9	31.8	Total Current		56.3		23.0		
29.0	41.5	36.2	Long-Term Debt		61.9		40.0		
.4	.4	.1	Deferred Taxes		.0		.1		
3.0	1.3	5.6	All Other Non-Current		5.3		.0		
28.6	33.9	26.3	Net Worth		-23.6		36.9		
100.0	100.0	100.0	Total Liabilties & Net Worth		100.0		100.0		
			INCOME DATA						
100.0	100.0	100.0	Net Sales		100.0		100.0		
			Gross Profit						
93.4	79.6	88.6	Operating Expenses		91.1		86.6		
6.6	20.4	11.4	Operating Profit		8.9		13.4		
2.6	2.6	2.2	All Other Expenses (net)		6.0		1.6		
4.1	17.9	9.2	Profit Before Taxes		2.9		11.7		
			RATIOS						
2.5	3.9	8.9			61.3		20.6		
1.2	1.0	1.8	Current		2.6		1.9		
.3	.5	.7			.2		.8		
1.4	3.0	5.0			16.5		19.9		
.5	.6	.7	Quick		1.2		1.7		
.1	.3	.2			.1		.3		
0 UND	0 UND	0 UND			0 UND		0 UND		
2 200.7	0 UND	3 138.2	Sales/Receivables		0 UND		0 UND		
26 14.2	36 10.0	16 23.4			4 83.7		11 33.1		
			Cost of Sales/Inventory						
			Cost of Sales/Payables						
4.8	3.0	2.1			1.5		1.9		
46.9	449.8	18.1	Sales/Working Capital		4.8		23.3		
-7.6	-8.5	-8.6			-6.4		-19.1		
8.2	13.6	7.0					6.1		
(50) 2.4	(41) 4.6	(37) 3.8	EBIT/Interest				(11) 3.8		
.2	1.5	1.1					.9		
			Net Profit + Depr., Dep., Amort./Cur. Mat. L/T/D						
.7	.6	.5			.5		.5		
1.4	1.2	1.0	Fixed/Worth		2.8		1.1		
20.3	-10.6	11.6			-.8		NM		
.5	.2	.3			.0		.3		
1.7	1.1	1.0	Debt/Worth		16.6		.9		
20.8	-28.9	26.5			-2.3		NM		
32.3	61.8	28.6							
(46) 10.4	(36) 11.2	(34) 10.7	% Profit Before Taxes/Tangible Net Worth						
.5	4.2	-1.2							
13.3	19.6	13.3			23.0		17.2		
4.1	4.9	6.1	% Profit Before Taxes/Total Assets		.9		4.3		
-.8	1.5	-1.6			-6.1		.7		
4.3	3.9	11.3			30.4		3.8		
1.3	1.1	1.1	Sales/Net Fixed Assets		5.3		1.1		
.6	.7	.6			.7		.6		
1.4	1.2	2.3			3.7		1.3		
.8	.7	.7	Sales/Total Assets		1.1		.8		
.4	.5	.4			.4		.3		
2.5	2.6	1.2					3.6		
(50) 6.0	(39) 7.2	(33) 4.3	% Depr., Dep., Amort./Sales				(11) 4.6		
12.8	9.6	8.5					7.5		
	1.0	.9							
	(10) 2.9	(16) 2.7	% Officers', Directors' Owners' Comp/Sales						
	14.9	5.3							
1120507M	639748M	765732M	Net Sales ($)	4021M	15459M	7840M	79451M	42625M	616336M
1433425M	1095900M	1044879M	Total Assets ($)	12847M	26015M	3059M	157644M	51122M	794192M

M = $ thousand MM = $ million

See Pages 9 through 22 for Explanation of Ratios and Data

Current Data Sorted by Assets							Comparative Historical Data	
						Type of Statement		
	1		2	1	1	Unqualified	2	4
1	2	6	5	4	1	Reviewed	3	8
		4	3	2		Compiled	9	12
4	3	3				Tax Returns	7	7
1		1	4			Other	6	9
9 (4/1-9/30/13)			40 (10/1/13-3/31/14)				4/1/09-3/31/10 ALL	4/1/10-3/31/11 ALL
0-500M	500M-2MM	2-10MM	10-50MM	50-100MM	100-250MM			
6	6	14	14	7	2	**NUMBER OF STATEMENTS**	27	40
%	%	%	%	%	%	**ASSETS**	%	%
		4.2	8.2			Cash & Equivalents	7.7	8.3
		12.7	8.3			Trade Receivables (net)	10.4	9.5
		13.9	21.1			Inventory	18.0	15.6
		4.4	2.8			All Other Current	2.8	3.8
		35.1	40.4			Total Current	38.9	37.2
		52.8	54.6			Fixed Assets (net)	55.1	52.6
		.1	.5			Intangibles (net)	.9	.8
		12.0	4.5			All Other Non-Current	5.2	9.4
		100.0	100.0			Total	100.0	100.0
						LIABILITIES		
		11.7	15.6			Notes Payable-Short Term	19.9	11.3
		1.8	2.5			Cur. Mat.-L.T.D.	2.9	5.5
		1.4	1.0			Trade Payables	4.4	5.1
		.0	.4			Income Taxes Payable	.0	.1
		6.3	8.1			All Other Current	5.4	3.9
		21.2	27.6			Total Current	32.7	25.8
		17.7	27.1			Long-Term Debt	29.1	32.6
		.0	1.9			Deferred Taxes	.8	1.2
		20.1	7.6			All Other Non-Current	9.6	7.2
		41.0	35.8			Net Worth	27.8	33.2
		100.0	100.0			Total Liabilties & Net Worth	100.0	100.0
						INCOME DATA		
		100.0	100.0			Net Sales	100.0	100.0
						Gross Profit		
		83.9	80.4			Operating Expenses	95.4	87.1
		16.1	19.6			Operating Profit	4.6	12.9
		3.3	10.8			All Other Expenses (net)	2.0	4.3
		12.8	8.8			Profit Before Taxes	2.7	8.6
						RATIOS		
		4.7	3.6				1.6	2.1
		2.1	2.1			Current	1.2	1.2
		1.2	1.2				.7	.9
		2.2	1.1				1.1	.9
		.9	.8			Quick	.5	.7
		.2	.2				.2	.3
		0 UND	**0** UND				**0** 999.8	**0** UND
		3 108.6	**41** 8.9			Sales/Receivables	**27** 13.6	**32** 11.3
		126 2.9	**91** 4.0				**52** 7.1	**64** 5.7
						Cost of Sales/Inventory		
						Cost of Sales/Payables		
		1.5	1.8				5.0	3.5
		5.1	3.5			Sales/Working Capital	25.5	17.8
		NM	NM				-12.3	-87.4
		38.3	16.9				5.6	6.9
		(13) 4.4	(13) 7.2			EBIT/Interest	(25) 2.3	(37) 2.7
		1.3	1.3				.6	1.2
						Net Profit + Depr., Dep., Amort./Cur. Mat. L/T/D		
		.7	.9				.8	.8
		.9	1.2			Fixed/Worth	1.6	1.7
		NM	4.8				4.2	2.7
		.4	.8				.8	.7
		1.2	1.3			Debt/Worth	2.2	2.0
		NM	4.9				4.8	5.3
		105.5	24.4				28.0	26.9
		(11) 32.3	(12) 20.8			% Profit Before Taxes/Tangible Net Worth	(22) 12.8	(38) 16.9
		4.9	2.3				.8	-.8
		20.3	13.5				12.6	11.8
		7.0	6.4			% Profit Before Taxes/Total Assets	3.2	5.0
		1.5	-.9				-1.7	-.3
		5.3	1.9				3.8	4.5
		2.1	1.2			Sales/Net Fixed Assets	2.0	1.5
		.7	.9				1.2	.8
		1.7	.8				2.1	1.7
		.9	.7			Sales/Total Assets	.9	.7
		.4	.5				.7	.5
			4.8				4.1	2.9
			(12) 5.8			% Depr., Dep., Amort./Sales	(25) 5.8	(33) 6.1
			9.2				7.6	8.9
						% Officers', Directors' Owners' Comp/Sales		
3111M	12818M	71016M	294361M	329225M	224102M	Net Sales ($)	446648M	951941M
1448M	8626M	61998M	407676M	539872M	361277M	Total Assets ($)	461559M	1353560M

M = $ thousand MM = $ million

See Pages 9 through 22 for Explanation of Ratios and Data

Comparative Historical Data / Current Data Sorted by Sales

4/1/11-3/31/12 ALL	4/1/12-3/31/13 ALL	4/1/13-3/31/14 ALL	Type of Statement	0-1MM	1-3MM	3-5MM	5-10MM	10-25MM	25MM & OVER
3	4	5	Unqualified			1		1	3
9	10	19	Reviewed	3	3	3	1	3	6
12	7	9	Compiled	1		1	1	1	5
3	8	10	Tax Returns	4	3	1	2		
8	6	6	Other	2			3	1	
				9 (4/1-9/30/13)			40 (10/1/13-3/31/14)		
35	35	49	NUMBER OF STATEMENTS	10	6	6	7	6	14
%	%	%	**ASSETS**	%	%	%	%	%	%
10.7	10.0	8.9	Cash & Equivalents	18.0					9.9
8.2	8.8	9.3	Trade Receivables (net)	10.6					10.4
18.3	15.5	16.0	Inventory	4.0					16.0
4.8	4.5	3.5	All Other Current	.4					3.6
42.0	38.7	37.7	Total Current	33.0					39.9
45.2	47.8	52.3	Fixed Assets (net)	53.9					49.1
1.8	1.4	1.3	Intangibles (net)	.4					2.7
11.0	12.1	8.7	All Other Non-Current	13.2					8.2
100.0	100.0	100.0	Total	100.0					100.0
			LIABILITIES						
9.4	16.2	10.2	Notes Payable-Short Term	11.0					8.2
2.8	2.9	2.6	Cur. Mat.-L.T.D.	2.7					2.6
5.2	2.7	2.6	Trade Payables	1.1					3.4
.3	.2	.2	Income Taxes Payable	.0					.3
10.0	7.7	8.8	All Other Current	12.5					8.4
27.8	29.7	24.4	Total Current	27.3					22.9
28.0	25.5	25.5	Long-Term Debt	25.3					22.3
.9	.8	1.0	Deferred Taxes	.0					2.9
3.1	2.9	8.8	All Other Non-Current	15.8					2.4
40.2	41.1	40.4	Net Worth	31.6					49.6
100.0	100.0	100.0	Total Liabilities & Net Worth	100.0					100.0
			INCOME DATA						
100.0	100.0	100.0	Net Sales	100.0					100.0
			Gross Profit						
86.5	83.6	84.6	Operating Expenses	88.2					79.9
13.5	16.4	15.4	Operating Profit	11.8					20.1
2.0	1.8	4.8	All Other Expenses (net)	12.1					4.6
11.5	14.6	10.6	Profit Before Taxes	-.3					15.5
			RATIOS						
11.1	3.2	4.4		5.3					2.7
1.4	1.4	1.8	Current	3.4					1.8
1.1	1.1	1.3		.5					1.3
2.7	1.1	1.7		5.1					1.3
.7	.7	.9	Quick	2.0					1.0
.2	.2	.3		.4					.7
0 UND	0 UND	0 UND		0 UND					15 24.2
3 125.6	17 21.2	30 12.0	Sales/Receivables	0 UND					51 7.2
54 6.7	76 4.8	85 4.3		101 3.6					70 5.2
			Cost of Sales/Inventory						
			Cost of Sales/Payables						
1.9	3.4	2.3		2.1					3.2
5.3	6.5	4.6	Sales/Working Capital	5.6					3.7
167.2	55.4	37.7		-3.5					5.9
7.7	12.0	13.6							10.2
(29) 2.7	(31) 6.2	(40) 7.1	EBIT/Interest						7.7
1.0	4.0	1.5							5.3
	6.7								
	(10) 4.3		Net Profit + Depr., Dep., Amort./Cur. Mat. L/T/D						
	1.8								
.6	.6	.7		.4					.9
1.2	1.0	1.2	Fixed/Worth	1.1					1.2
4.6	1.7	3.5		NM					1.4
.4	.7	.6		.5					.8
1.8	1.3	1.3	Debt/Worth	3.6					1.1
8.9	3.5	4.7		-9.2					1.6
29.8	52.2	32.4							25.0
(27) 14.2	(32) 27.6	(42) 22.0	% Profit Before Taxes/Tangible Net Worth						20.8
3.6	16.0	5.9							18.5
14.8	17.1	13.7		14.8					13.4
5.8	7.9	7.6	% Profit Before Taxes/Total Assets	-1.4					10.3
.2	5.2	.4		-8.1					6.5
3.6	3.5	3.7		UND					1.8
1.6	2.1	1.4	Sales/Net Fixed Assets	1.5					1.2
1.3	1.1	.9		.5					1.1
1.2	1.1	1.2		1.4					.8
.7	.8	.7	Sales/Total Assets	.5					.7
.6	.6	.5		.4					.6
3.0	3.6	3.9							4.9
(32) 5.2	(32) 5.9	(36) 5.7	% Depr., Dep., Amort./Sales						5.4
8.0	7.6	9.7							8.7
			% Officers', Directors' Owners' Comp/Sales						
578249M	895697M	934633M	Net Sales ($)	5890M	11153M	21601M	52911M	106188M	736890M
863735M	1313726M	1380897M	Total Assets ($)	23424M	17334M	28568M	61196M	145934M	1104441M

M = $ thousand MM = $ million

See Pages 9 through 22 for Explanation of Ratios and Data

Current Data Sorted by Assets							Comparative Historical Data	
						Type of Statement		
			2		1	Unqualified	3	6
			7	1	2	Reviewed	15	15
	3	4	3			Compiled	18	13
1	4	4	1			Tax Returns	29	22
2	9	22	9	5	3	Other	48	45
	6 (4/1-9/30/13)		77 (10/1/13-3/31/14)				4/1/09-3/31/10	4/1/10-3/31/11
0-500M	500M-2MM	2-10MM	10-50MM	50-100MM	100-250MM		ALL	ALL
3	16	30	22	6	6	NUMBER OF STATEMENTS	113	101
%	%	%	%	%	%	**ASSETS**	%	%
	13.3	6.9	3.9			Cash & Equivalents	8.7	8.8
	5.9	16.2	14.5			Trade Receivables (net)	7.7	10.7
	2.4	7.2	9.9			Inventory	9.3	8.7
	1.1	3.3	4.8			All Other Current	6.3	4.6
	22.7	33.6	33.1			Total Current	32.1	32.8
	69.0	60.3	55.6			Fixed Assets (net)	57.7	58.5
	3.7	1.1	1.1			Intangibles (net)	1.6	1.3
	4.7	5.0	10.1			All Other Non-Current	8.7	7.3
	100.0	100.0	100.0			Total	100.0	100.0
						LIABILITIES		
	5.7	6.1	6.2			Notes Payable-Short Term	13.8	16.1
	1.4	3.5	1.7			Cur. Mat.-L.T.D.	2.9	4.8
	.7	2.5	3.5			Trade Payables	3.0	3.7
	.0	.2	.0			Income Taxes Payable	.1	.1
	7.2	3.7	3.5			All Other Current	4.0	3.4
	14.9	16.0	14.9			Total Current	23.8	28.2
	49.1	34.5	26.1			Long-Term Debt	44.7	47.5
	.0	.6	.9			Deferred Taxes	.3	.1
	2.9	6.2	6.3			All Other Non-Current	6.7	7.1
	33.0	42.7	51.9			Net Worth	24.5	17.1
	100.0	100.0	100.0			Total Liabilities & Net Worth	100.0	100.0
						INCOME DATA		
	100.0	100.0	100.0			Net Sales	100.0	100.0
						Gross Profit		
	67.5	79.0	77.7			Operating Expenses	83.5	82.4
	32.5	21.0	22.3			Operating Profit	16.5	17.6
	10.2	8.6	6.0			All Other Expenses (net)	8.0	8.1
	22.2	12.4	16.2			Profit Before Taxes	8.6	9.5
						RATIOS		
	10.6	6.6	6.0				5.2	5.3
	2.5	1.8	2.2			Current	1.9	1.8
	.5	.9	1.2				.8	.7
	9.7	2.7	3.1				2.7	3.4
	2.3	1.3	.8			Quick	.7	.8
	.5	.3	.3				.1	.2
	0 UND	**0** UND	**5** 70.7				**0** UND	**0** UND
	0 UND	**56** 6.5	**31** 11.6			Sales/Receivables	**9** 42.5	**20** 18.3
	79 4.6	**166** 2.2	**126** 2.9				**73** 5.0	**95** 3.8
						Cost of Sales/Inventory		
						Cost of Sales/Payables		
	2.2	2.0	2.0				1.9	1.6
	4.9	2.9	4.8			Sales/Working Capital	5.8	6.8
	-34.4	-17.6	18.2				-11.6	-13.6
	36.3	12.4	26.0				9.5	8.5
	(11) 10.6	(22) 4.6	(19) 5.3			EBIT/Interest	(89) 3.3	(85) 3.5
	4.6	2.0	.9				1.0	1.3
							9.7	4.6
						Net Profit + Depr., Dep., Amort./Cur. Mat. L/T/D	(17) 3.4	(13) 3.4
							1.8	1.6
	.9	.8	.8				.7	.7
	2.1	1.6	1.1			Fixed/Worth	1.5	1.7
	8.1	3.8	2.3				41.7	-17.5
	.5	.5	.2				.5	.6
	1.8	1.5	.8			Debt/Worth	1.7	1.9
	11.8	6.2	1.9				NM	-21.3
	94.5	53.4	31.9				30.0	25.6
	(14) 40.1	(28) 22.4	(21) 16.8			% Profit Before Taxes/Tangible Net Worth	(85) 9.6	(73) 11.0
	19.2	.7	-1.0				-.2	1.7
	28.6	19.2	14.3				11.1	11.5
	16.6	4.1	10.0			% Profit Before Taxes/Total Assets	3.6	5.2
	1.9	.3	-.5				-.5	-.2
	2.3	2.0	2.0				2.6	2.3
	.8	.8	1.0			Sales/Net Fixed Assets	.9	.9
	.5	.3	.4				.4	.4
	1.2	.8	.7				1.1	.9
	.5	.5	.5			Sales/Total Assets	.6	.6
	.3	.2	.3				.3	.3
		3.3	4.3				3.5	3.9
		(21) 7.1	6.7			% Depr., Dep., Amort./Sales	(93) 6.7	(90) 8.3
		10.4	8.5				11.6	15.6
							1.7	1.5
						% Officers', Directors' Owners' Comp/Sales	(23) 4.9	(16) 3.5
							8.7	8.8
3852M	19107M	82846M	327070M	160986M	949914M	Net Sales ($)	1223504M	1176009M
829M	20999M	131914M	529815M	399980M	823377M	Total Assets ($)	1634792M	1769898M

M = $ thousand MM = $ million

See Pages 9 through 22 for Explanation of Ratios and Data

Comparative Historical Data				Current Data Sorted by Sales					
			Type of Statement						
7	2	3	Unqualified					1	2
16	17	10	Reviewed			2	1	4	3
11	10	10	Compiled	2	3	2	2		1
30	11	10	Tax Returns	3	4	1	2		
51	47	50	Other	16	11	6	4	8	5
4/1/11-3/31/12 ALL	**4/1/12-3/31/13 ALL**	**4/1/13-3/31/14 ALL**		**6 (4/1-9/30/13)**			**77 (10/1/13-3/31/14)**		
				0-1MM	**1-3MM**	**3-5MM**	**5-10MM**	**10-25MM**	**25MM & OVER**
115	87	83	**NUMBER OF STATEMENTS**	21	18	11	9	13	11
%	%	%	**ASSETS**	%	%	%	%	%	%
9.8	10.9	9.6	Cash & Equivalents	14.1	6.1	11.7		8.3	9.2
12.2	10.7	13.1	Trade Receivables (net)	6.6	10.3	25.1		11.7	12.5
7.6	9.5	7.0	Inventory	3.5	4.9	8.6		4.8	18.7
6.0	8.1	4.3	All Other Current	1.0	.8	15.1		4.0	6.2
35.7	39.3	34.0	Total Current	25.3	22.1	60.6		28.9	46.6
55.2	51.2	56.5	Fixed Assets (net)	71.5	67.2	32.0		54.2	41.5
1.1	2.2	2.0	Intangibles (net)	.7	1.3	.2		1.4	4.8
8.0	7.3	7.5	All Other Non-Current	2.5	9.4	7.2		15.6	7.2
100.0	100.0	100.0	Total	100.0	100.0	100.0		100.0	100.0
			LIABILITIES						
12.2	10.5	7.6	Notes Payable-Short Term	4.0	5.8	20.8		4.4	11.4
3.4	3.4	2.2	Cur. Mat.-L.T.D.	1.5	4.1	1.9		2.1	.8
3.0	3.2	3.2	Trade Payables	1.0	1.4	2.6		1.3	12.8
.2	.0	.1	Income Taxes Payable	.0	.3	.0		.0	.0
4.3	5.7	4.2	All Other Current	4.0	6.1	4.4		2.2	5.1
23.1	22.9	17.3	Total Current	10.5	17.7	29.7		10.1	30.1
45.2	31.2	31.2	Long-Term Debt	51.5	31.5	16.7		27.5	12.1
.1	.0	.5	Deferred Taxes	.1	.4	.0		.8	.1
6.7	7.9	4.8	All Other Non-Current	3.7	5.6	4.2		1.9	8.7
25.0	37.9	46.2	Net Worth	34.3	44.8	49.4		59.8	49.0
100.0	100.0	100.0	Total Liabilties & Net Worth	100.0	100.0	100.0		100.0	100.0
			INCOME DATA						
100.0	100.0	100.0	Net Sales	100.0	100.0	100.0		100.0	100.0
			Gross Profit						
83.7	77.5	75.7	Operating Expenses	67.4	81.6	73.7		74.8	80.5
16.3	22.5	24.3	Operating Profit	32.6	18.4	26.3		25.2	19.5
8.5	4.6	6.8	All Other Expenses (net)	19.2	4.8	.9		2.2	.9
7.8	18.0	17.5	Profit Before Taxes	13.4	13.6	25.3		23.0	18.6
			RATIOS						
4.8	10.0	7.4		7.9	11.3	23.8		11.7	3.8
1.8	2.7	2.2	Current	1.8	1.2	4.6		2.5	1.8
.8	1.1	1.1		.4	.2	1.4		1.9	1.1
2.6	6.2	6.0		7.1	4.2	6.6		6.6	1.6
1.0	1.2	1.5	Quick	1.5	.6	2.1		2.5	.5
.3	.2	.4		.4	.2	.8		1.3	.2
0 UND	0 UND	0 UND		0 UND	0 UND	24 15.5		9 39.3	6 66.2
19 19.0	22 16.8	31 11.9	Sales/Receivables	8 46.6	4 90.3	76 4.8		20 17.9	36 10.2
104 3.5	81 4.5	135 2.7		130 2.8	140 2.6	281 1.3		166 2.2	55 6.6
			Cost of Sales/Inventory						
			Cost of Sales/Payables						
1.7	1.6	2.0		1.3	2.1	1.2		1.6	2.4
6.2	4.0	3.1	Sales/Working Capital	3.7	11.9	2.0		3.0	5.9
-22.8	36.1	52.7		-6.5	-25.6	2.5		24.9	52.7
9.1	17.4	19.7		7.1	39.1			19.7	24.8
(89) 2.9	(70) 5.0	(65) 5.6	EBIT/Interest	(11) 5.0	(14) 4.0			(12) 10.3	(10) 6.1
1.5	1.4	2.1		.1	1.3			5.9	.8
12.9	29.8	13.4							
(15) 2.4	(12) 8.5	(15) 3.7	Net Profit + Depr., Dep., Amort./Cur. Mat. L/T/D						
1.0	5.9	1.8							
.7	.5	.8		.9	.9	.5		.5	.7
1.5	1.1	1.2	Fixed/Worth	2.1	2.1	.7		1.0	.8
51.8	4.3	3.3		8.9	3.8	1.1		1.5	1.3
.5	.2	.3		.3	.4	.1		.2	.3
1.6	1.2	1.1	Debt/Worth	1.6	1.6	.8		.6	.8
-27.3	5.1	4.5		13.6	5.9	3.2		1.7	3.0
26.3	50.0	47.7		74.9	43.7	65.8		38.1	
(85) 11.6	(73) 18.3	(76) 19.7	% Profit Before Taxes/Tangible Net Worth	(19) 3.7	(16) 30.2	(10) 34.9		12.8	
1.3	6.0	3.1		-.8	2.4	7.3		7.7	
11.6	19.5	18.9		15.6	30.2	19.9		13.6	19.1
4.4	9.4	9.6	% Profit Before Taxes/Total Assets	1.3	4.1	17.2		10.0	11.5
.0	1.4	1.1		-.5	.2	5.1		6.0	.7
3.3	3.9	2.5		.8	1.5	4.2		1.6	5.6
1.2	1.2	1.1	Sales/Net Fixed Assets	.3	.8	1.8		1.1	2.7
.4	.6	.4		.1	.3	1.1		.5	1.3
1.1	1.0	.9		.5	.8	.9		.6	1.7
.6	.6	.5	Sales/Total Assets	.3	.5	.6		.4	1.1
.3	.3	.3		.1	.2	.4		.3	.8
3.3	2.9	3.4		6.5	6.7			4.8	1.7
(92) 7.1	(75) 6.5	(61) 6.6	% Depr., Dep., Amort./Sales	(11) 9.2	(11) 8.3			(11) 5.1	(10) 3.3
14.3	11.6	8.4		18.2	14.1			8.4	5.6
1.5									
(11) 3.2			% Officers', Directors' Owners' Comp/Sales						
5.0									
1484295M	**903689M**	**1543775M**	Net Sales ($)	**10076M**	**31143M**	**40864M**	**59576M**	**219284M**	**1182832M**
1940268M	**1361846M**	**1906914M**	Total Assets ($)	**59243M**	**80451M**	**89452M**	**82375M**	**577638M**	**1017755M**

M = $ thousand MM = $ million

See Pages 9 through 22 for Explanation of Ratios and Data

Current Data Sorted by Assets / Comparative Historical Data

0-500M	500M-2MM	2-10MM	10-50MM	50-100MM	100-250MM	Type of Statement	4/1/09-3/31/10 ALL	4/1/10-3/31/11 ALL
				1		Unqualified	4	4
		1	3	2		Reviewed	7	14
1	3	7	2	1		Compiled	10	9
1	3	5				Tax Returns	10	11
	5	16	9			Other	24	20
	8 (4/1-9/30/13)		52 (10/1/13-3/31/14)					
2	11	29	14	4		NUMBER OF STATEMENTS	55	58
%	%	%	%	%	%	**ASSETS**	%	%
	28.1	8.0	2.8		DATA NOT AVAILABLE	Cash & Equivalents	7.3	9.2
	15.1	22.6	19.4			Trade Receivables (net)	15.9	15.1
	8.0	9.6	9.0			Inventory	11.8	11.5
	.6	4.4	5.8			All Other Current	5.3	5.4
	51.8	44.5	37.0			Total Current	40.3	41.1
	42.6	47.4	57.3			Fixed Assets (net)	48.7	49.0
	.1	1.3	.1			Intangibles (net)	.7	.7
	5.5	6.9	5.6			All Other Non-Current	10.2	9.3
	100.0	100.0	100.0			Total	100.0	100.0
						LIABILITIES		
	31.3	10.4	9.3			Notes Payable-Short Term	18.3	18.1
	5.6	1.9	3.2			Cur. Mat.-L.T.D.	3.5	5.7
	10.2	8.7	4.5			Trade Payables	6.3	6.6
	.0	.0	.1			Income Taxes Payable	.2	.1
	3.4	3.9	6.6			All Other Current	6.4	7.5
	50.5	24.9	23.6			Total Current	34.7	38.0
	21.8	30.5	28.8			Long-Term Debt	33.4	30.0
	.0	.0	.5			Deferred Taxes	.3	.5
	7.2	6.8	2.6			All Other Non-Current	5.7	4.7
	20.5	37.8	44.5			Net Worth	25.9	26.7
	100.0	100.0	100.0			Total Liabilties & Net Worth	100.0	100.0
						INCOME DATA		
	100.0	100.0	100.0			Net Sales	100.0	100.0
						Gross Profit		
	86.0	71.3	73.6			Operating Expenses	88.7	83.7
	14.0	28.7	26.4			Operating Profit	11.3	16.3
	3.1	5.7	5.2			All Other Expenses (net)	3.9	2.9
	10.9	23.1	21.2			Profit Before Taxes	7.4	13.4
						RATIOS		
	5.4	8.2	3.0				2.6	4.7
	1.3	3.1	2.0			Current	1.3	1.2
	.2	.9	1.2				.7	.6
	5.4	6.5	2.2				1.8	2.4
	.8	2.1	1.6			Quick	.7	.6
	.2	.5	.6				.2	.2
	0 UND	**0** UND	**0** UND				**0** UND	**0** UND
	2 156.9	**81** 4.5	**70** 5.2			Sales/Receivables	**29** 12.6	**24** 15.4
	49 7.4	**182** 2.0	**203** 1.8				**95** 3.8	**162** 2.3
						Cost of Sales/Inventory		
						Cost of Sales/Payables		
	2.9	1.4	1.6				3.6	2.0
	28.4	3.1	5.0			Sales/Working Capital	8.9	14.4
	-5.4	NM	NM				-21.8	-10.3
		24.6	10.4				5.9	10.8
		(27) 7.5	(13) 4.8			EBIT/Interest	(50) 2.6	(54) 3.9
		3.6	1.1				.8	1.3
							3.9	23.2
						Net Profit + Depr., Dep., Amort./Cur. Mat. L/T/D	(15) 2.9	(12) 2.4
							1.5	1.4
	.1	.5	.7				1.0	.6
	2.0	.9	1.2			Fixed/Worth	1.2	1.3
	-1.1	10.7	2.1				3.6	3.3
	.5	.5	.7				1.2	.7
	1.4	.9	1.1			Debt/Worth	2.3	2.0
	-6.4	11.6	2.1				9.0	8.3
		48.5	35.6				35.0	42.3
		(23) 16.0	(13) 14.5			% Profit Before Taxes/Tangible Net Worth	(46) 7.4	(50) 16.2
		4.3	.1				.3	4.6
	20.7	31.1	17.8				11.5	18.3
	12.4	6.4	7.5			% Profit Before Taxes/Total Assets	3.8	5.0
	-14.0	2.1	.0				-.5	1.1
	22.2	5.5	2.4				5.3	7.1
	6.2	2.2	.7			Sales/Net Fixed Assets	2.0	1.7
	2.1	.6	.2				.7	.8
	3.0	1.2	.7				2.0	2.0
	1.9	.7	.4			Sales/Total Assets	.7	.8
	1.1	.4	.2				.4	.4
		2.7	2.5				2.6	2.6
		(19) 5.6	(11) 4.1			% Depr., Dep., Amort./Sales	(44) 9.2	(40) 6.6
		9.4	12.8				13.7	12.2
								2.2
						% Officers', Directors' Owners' Comp/Sales		(12) 5.2
								9.1
7281M	30732M	109350M	373968M	118463M		Net Sales ($)	789742M	1032899M
609M	13659M	137380M	275931M	295756M		Total Assets ($)	712848M	990039M

M = $ thousand MM = $ million

See Pages 9 through 22 for Explanation of Ratios and Data

Comparative Historical Data				Current Data Sorted by Sales					
			Type of Statement						
4	3	1	Unqualified					1	
9	9	6	Reviewed			2	2		2
16	19	14	Compiled	4	2	2	5	1	
19	8	9	Tax Returns		3	4	2		
25	33	30	Other	1	13	4	7	3	2
				8 (4/1-9/30/13)			52 (10/1/13-3/31/14)		
4/1/11-3/31/12 ALL	**4/1/12-3/31/13 ALL**	**4/1/13-3/31/14 ALL**		**0-1MM**	**1-3MM**	**3-5MM**	**5-10MM**	**10-25MM**	**25MM & OVER**
73	72	60	**NUMBER OF STATEMENTS**	5	18	12	16	5	4
%	%	%	**ASSETS**	%	%	%	%	%	%
7.7	7.7	10.5	Cash & Equivalents		14.1	15.1	9.7		
12.5	19.4	19.5	Trade Receivables (net)		19.4	12.4	27.1		
7.4	9.7	8.5	Inventory		9.7	6.9	10.5		
6.1	4.4	4.3	All Other Current		2.5	1.8	6.7		
33.6	41.2	42.8	Total Current		45.6	36.2	54.1		
51.9	50.7	49.7	Fixed Assets (net)		45.9	49.9	41.4		
1.6	1.3	1.0	Intangibles (net)		.7	3.7	.1		
12.8	6.7	6.5	All Other Non-Current		7.7	10.1	4.4		
100.0	100.0	100.0	Total		100.0	100.0	100.0		
			LIABILITIES						
19.1	15.8	17.6	Notes Payable-Short Term		11.4	29.6	21.2		
2.7	5.1	3.1	Cur. Mat.-L.T.D.		3.3	3.1	2.8		
3.4	2.8	7.3	Trade Payables		3.9	9.9	12.2		
.2	.0	.0	Income Taxes Payable		.0	.0	.1		
6.5	7.5	4.5	All Other Current		6.1	1.1	2.6		
32.0	31.1	32.5	Total Current		24.7	43.7	38.8		
36.0	32.7	26.4	Long-Term Debt		24.8	38.2	26.0		
.4	.1	.1	Deferred Taxes		.0	.0	.0		
3.1	7.2	5.6	All Other Non-Current		5.3	9.7	5.6		
28.6	28.9	35.4	Net Worth		45.2	8.4	29.6		
100.0	100.0	100.0	Total Liabilties & Net Worth		100.0	100.0	100.0		
			INCOME DATA						
100.0	100.0	100.0	Net Sales		100.0	100.0	100.0		
			Gross Profit						
77.5	77.4	74.9	Operating Expenses		69.7	82.8	79.3		
22.5	22.6	25.1	Operating Profit		30.3	17.2	20.7		
4.5	5.0	4.3	All Other Expenses (net)		3.4	3.4	1.2		
17.9	17.5	20.9	Profit Before Taxes		26.9	13.8	19.5		
			RATIOS						
5.7	3.1	5.3			13.7	12.3	4.1		
1.3	1.6	2.2	Current		5.0	2.4	2.1		
.5	.9	.8			1.0	.1	1.3		
2.5	2.6	4.8			9.5	10.8	3.2		
.8	1.2	1.7	Quick		3.6	2.1	1.6		
.1	.4	.4			.6	.1	1.0		
0 UND	**0** UND	**0** UND			**0** UND	**0** UND	**0** UND		
31 11.6	**79** 4.6	**53** 6.9	Sales/Receivables		**83** 4.4	**6** 63.8	**76** 4.8		
182 2.0	**281** 1.3	**192** 1.9			**192** 1.9	**159** 2.3	**215** 1.7		
			Cost of Sales/Inventory						
			Cost of Sales/Payables						
1.8	1.8	1.5			1.5	1.6	1.6		
10.9	10.1	4.8	Sales/Working Capital		2.9	5.0	3.3		
-4.0	-35.7	-21.9			NM	-5.9	12.1		
12.3	15.3	23.3			30.6	22.8	40.8		
(62) 5.2	(63) 4.0	(53) 7.8	EBIT/Interest		8.7	(10) 5.0	(15) 7.8		
1.7	1.3	1.9			1.0	1.5	4.4		
10.4	9.6								
(16) 5.6	(11) 4.5		Net Profit + Depr., Dep., Amort./Cur. Mat. L/T/D						
2.5	2.7								
.7	.7	.5			.3	.4	.4		
1.4	1.5	1.1	Fixed/Worth		1.0	2.1	1.1		
23.8	20.1	7.9			1.6	-1.9	NM		
.7	.6	.5			.4	.3	.4		
2.0	1.5	.9	Debt/Worth		.9	3.7	1.1		
39.7	34.0	10.7			5.4	-4.3	NM		
56.9	37.3	40.3			47.3		52.1		
(58) 26.2	(56) 16.6	(49) 14.9	% Profit Before Taxes/Tangible Net Worth		(16) 16.6		(12) 23.8		
4.2	1.6	3.8			3.7		6.8		
22.9	21.0	21.1			30.0	47.7	36.4		
7.5	6.4	7.6	% Profit Before Taxes/Total Assets		8.4	4.5	11.0		
.6	.1	1.7			.0	-.1	3.9		
2.2	5.2	5.8			6.9	12.1	5.6		
1.2	1.4	2.0	Sales/Net Fixed Assets		1.3	4.3	2.7		
.7	.5	.6			.6	.7	1.1		
1.0	1.3	1.5			.9	5.4	1.6		
.6	.6	.7	Sales/Total Assets		.5	1.1	.8		
.3	.3	.4			.4	.5	.6		
3.1	2.4	2.7			.2		2.9		
(60) 6.4	(60) 5.6	(41) 6.3	% Depr., Dep., Amort./Sales		(10) 4.1		(12) 4.2		
9.8	12.6	11.4			9.6		7.8		
1.6	2.7								
(14) 2.2	(10) 4.2		% Officers', Directors' Owners' Comp/Sales						
4.8	5.7								
759183M	794166M	639794M	Net Sales ($)	2448M	35201M	44222M	99911M	71353M	386659M
1343736M	1136782M	723335M	Total Assets ($)	17711M	86000M	71955M	127291M	174287M	246091M

M = $ thousand MM = $ million

See Pages 9 through 22 for Explanation of Ratios and Data

Current Data Sorted by Assets							Comparative Historical Data	
						Type of Statement		
		1				Unqualified	2	4
		3	3			Reviewed	7	11
	3	6	1			Compiled	25	18
	2	1				Tax Returns	4	6
	3	1	4			Other	13	13
	5 (4/1-9/30/13)		23 (10/1/13-3/31/14)				4/1/09-3/31/10	4/1/10-3/31/11
0-500M	500M-2MM	2-10MM	10-50MM	50-100MM	100-250MM		ALL	ALL
	8	12	8			**NUMBER OF STATEMENTS**	51	52
%	%	%	%	%	%	**ASSETS**	%	%
DATA NOT AVAILABLE		4.8		DATA NOT AVAILABLE	DATA NOT AVAILABLE	Cash & Equivalents	3.9	5.4
		28.6				Trade Receivables (net)	18.3	18.4
		23.8				Inventory	16.3	17.2
		.3				All Other Current	1.2	1.9
		57.5				Total Current	39.7	42.9
		33.6				Fixed Assets (net)	50.5	48.1
		1.8				Intangibles (net)	1.5	.8
		7.1				All Other Non-Current	8.4	8.2
		100.0				Total	100.0	100.0
						LIABILITIES		
		4.8				Notes Payable-Short Term	14.3	8.9
		8.8				Cur. Mat.-L.T.D.	4.8	4.0
		16.5				Trade Payables	14.3	19.4
		.0				Income Taxes Payable	.4	.0
		8.9				All Other Current	6.1	4.9
		38.9				Total Current	39.9	37.2
		16.6				Long-Term Debt	43.2	35.6
		.3				Deferred Taxes	.9	.2
		.0				All Other Non-Current	1.6	2.2
		44.2				Net Worth	14.4	24.7
		100.0				Total Liabilities & Net Worth	100.0	100.0
						INCOME DATA		
		100.0				Net Sales	100.0	100.0
						Gross Profit		
		95.0				Operating Expenses	93.9	94.1
		5.0				Operating Profit	6.1	5.9
		.4				All Other Expenses (net)	4.0	3.1
		4.6				Profit Before Taxes	2.1	2.8
						RATIOS		
		2.1					1.9	2.0
		1.6				Current	.9	1.2
		1.1					.5	.7
		1.2					1.0	1.2
		1.0				Quick	.5	.6
		.5					.2	.3
		21 17.1					**0** UND	**6** 60.1
		25 14.7				Sales/Receivables	**25** 14.8	**25** 14.8
		39 9.3					**42** 8.8	**34** 10.8
						Cost of Sales/Inventory		
						Cost of Sales/Payables		
		10.6					11.4	11.0
		20.7				Sales/Working Capital	-247.5	46.8
		758.4					-14.9	-18.1
		36.6					7.3	6.3
		(11) 8.5				EBIT/Interest	(48) 2.2	(45) 2.8
		2.3					.4	.8
						Net Profit + Depr., Dep., Amort./Cur. Mat. L/T/D		
		.4					1.0	.6
		.6				Fixed/Worth	3.2	1.6
		1.1					-6.0	7.1
		.7					1.7	1.0
		1.1				Debt/Worth	4.6	2.6
		1.7					-26.9	8.7
		37.1					33.3	42.3
		(11) 18.1				% Profit Before Taxes/Tangible Net Worth	(35) 16.1	(43) 21.5
		12.3					-6.2	2.5
		15.7					10.7	10.2
		7.9				% Profit Before Taxes/Total Assets	3.3	5.0
		5.4					-2.1	-1.1
		29.4					14.4	14.1
		11.0				Sales/Net Fixed Assets	3.8	5.4
		7.2					1.9	2.3
		4.4					4.1	3.7
		3.5				Sales/Total Assets	2.2	2.2
		2.4					1.0	1.2
							1.7	1.8
						% Depr., Dep., Amort./Sales	(50) 2.9	(45) 2.6
							6.7	6.2
							1.0	1.1
						% Officers', Directors' Owners' Comp/Sales	(19) 1.3	(22) 1.5
							2.4	2.7
	38591M	219382M	235250M			Net Sales ($)	997478M	1271029M
	8257M	61477M	129020M			Total Assets ($)	602912M	714783M

M = $ thousand MM = $ million

See Pages 9 through 22 for Explanation of Ratios and Data

Comparative Historical Data				Current Data Sorted by Sales					
			Type of Statement						
1	2	1	Unqualified					1	
5	8	6	Reviewed			1		2	3
9	9	10	Compiled		1		3	4	2
3	4	3	Tax Returns	1	1			1	
18	10	8	Other	1		1	1	5	
4/1/11-3/31/12	4/1/12-3/31/13	4/1/13-3/31/14		5 (4/1-9/30/13)			23 (10/1/13-3/31/14)		
ALL	ALL	ALL		0-1MM	1-3MM	3-5MM	5-10MM	10-25MM	25MM & OVER
36	33	28	**NUMBER OF STATEMENTS**	2	2	2	4	13	5
%	%	%	**ASSETS**	%	%	%	%	%	%
6.6	7.0	7.5	Cash & Equivalents					2.2	
17.9	22.1	19.6	Trade Receivables (net)					22.0	
18.4	22.0	18.2	Inventory					21.3	
1.6	1.7	1.0	All Other Current					.4	
44.5	52.8	46.3	Total Current					45.9	
44.3	39.8	43.5	Fixed Assets (net)					45.9	
3.0	1.7	4.3	Intangibles (net)					1.0	
8.1	5.7	6.0	All Other Non-Current					7.2	
100.0	100.0	100.0	Total					100.0	
			LIABILITIES						
8.4	9.6	3.8	Notes Payable-Short Term					3.7	
3.1	4.4	5.1	Cur. Mat.-L.T.D.					4.3	
20.7	11.9	13.3	Trade Payables					15.8	
.4	.0	.0	Income Taxes Payable					.0	
8.0	4.9	9.3	All Other Current					9.6	
40.6	30.8	31.6	Total Current					33.4	
27.9	24.9	25.3	Long-Term Debt					25.2	
.1	.5	.1	Deferred Taxes					.3	
2.2	5.5	5.3	All Other Non-Current					.9	
29.2	38.3	37.7	Net Worth					40.2	
100.0	100.0	100.0	Total Liabilties & Net Worth					100.0	
			INCOME DATA						
100.0	100.0	100.0	Net Sales					100.0	
			Gross Profit						
91.7	95.2	92.5	Operating Expenses					96.5	
8.3	4.8	7.5	Operating Profit					3.5	
4.4	1.9	1.5	All Other Expenses (net)					1.1	
4.0	2.9	5.9	Profit Before Taxes					2.4	
			RATIOS						
1.6	3.1	2.9						3.1	
1.2	1.7	1.8	Current					1.6	
.5	1.2	.9						.8	
1.0	1.5	1.6						1.1	
(35) .7	.9	1.0	Quick					.9	
.3	.4	.5						.4	
13 28.7	**15** 24.3	**12** 30.8						**18** 19.8	
26 13.8	**27** 13.5	**22** 16.4	Sales/Receivables					**21** 17.4	
34 10.8	**36** 10.0	**29** 12.5						**25** 14.7	
			Cost of Sales/Inventory						
			Cost of Sales/Payables						
15.7	8.1	7.2						6.1	
42.0	15.6	18.6	Sales/Working Capital					20.5	
-9.6	49.7	NM						NM	
7.1	12.0	19.4						15.1	
(31) 3.4	(30) 3.6	(24) 6.5	EBIT/Interest					(12) 2.2	
1.3	1.1	1.0						.1	
			Net Profit + Depr., Dep., Amort./Cur. Mat. L/T/D						
.6	.3	.5						.5	
1.2	1.1	1.0	Fixed/Worth					1.0	
7.6	1.9	2.0						3.7	
1.2	1.0	.7						.8	
2.0	1.9	1.1	Debt/Worth					1.0	
9.8	3.7	3.4						4.4	
30.9	35.6	35.6						17.4	
(30) 19.4	(31) 17.5	(25) 17.4	% Profit Before Taxes/Tangible Net Worth					(11) -1.8	
9.7	2.7	-.5						-3.0	
9.4	11.0	13.6						8.9	
5.4	5.1	6.5	% Profit Before Taxes/Total Assets					1.7	
.6	1.0	.8						-1.3	
15.3	17.5	14.9						12.3	
6.2	7.4	7.9	Sales/Net Fixed Assets					7.1	
2.7	2.9	2.9						2.9	
3.7	4.1	4.5						4.3	
2.7	2.9	3.3	Sales/Total Assets					2.5	
1.2	1.6	1.7						1.7	
1.2	1.5	1.2						1.2	
(28) 2.5	(27) 2.4	(24) 2.2	% Depr., Dep., Amort./Sales					(11) 2.5	
6.9	4.2	4.4						4.9	
.8	.9	.8							
(13) 1.4	(12) 2.0	(11) 1.3	% Officers', Directors' Owners' Comp/Sales						
2.2	4.8	2.3							
846545M	810015M	493223M	Net Sales ($)	477M	4169M	8353M	29963M	225578M	224683M
424103M	400761M	198754M	Total Assets ($)	1998M	3258M	3296M	7248M	109096M	73858M

M = $ thousand MM = $ million

See Pages 9 through 22 for Explanation of Ratios and Data

Current Data Sorted by Assets | **Comparative Historical Data**

0-500M	500M-2MM	2-10MM	10-50MM	50-100MM	100-250MM	Type of Statement	4/1/09-3/31/10 ALL	4/1/10-3/31/11 ALL
		2	3	5	4	Unqualified	27	19
		10	14	2	1	Reviewed	33	28
4	2	23	5		1	Compiled	44	32
10	11	6	1			Tax Returns	23	27
7	10	18	20	4	2	Other	65	71
45 (4/1-9/30/13)			120 (10/1/13-3/31/14)					
21	23	59	43	11	8	**NUMBER OF STATEMENTS**	192	177
%	%	%	%	%	%	**ASSETS**	%	%
11.3	7.9	5.4	4.3	4.8		Cash & Equivalents	5.2	6.3
9.6	16.3	13.2	9.8	7.6		Trade Receivables (net)	11.2	12.7
31.6	25.8	38.6	41.9	41.5		Inventory	33.3	30.5
4.2	.5	3.1	1.4	.7		All Other Current	2.8	3.4
56.7	50.5	60.3	57.4	54.6		Total Current	52.5	53.0
33.5	37.4	31.2	35.0	32.3		Fixed Assets (net)	37.4	36.7
4.8	2.9	3.8	2.7	5.5		Intangibles (net)	3.1	3.4
5.1	9.2	4.8	5.0	7.6		All Other Non-Current	7.0	7.0
100.0	100.0	100.0	100.0	100.0		Total	100.0	100.0
						LIABILITIES		
29.6	11.1	12.6	15.3	16.8		Notes Payable-Short Term	19.1	17.3
2.4	1.8	2.9	4.6	2.8		Cur. Mat.-L.T.D.	3.8	3.9
6.6	8.1	9.6	9.1	6.3		Trade Payables	10.2	9.9
.1	1.0	.6	2.0	2.5		Income Taxes Payable	1.1	1.1
11.9	6.5	5.1	6.4	3.1		All Other Current	7.7	5.8
50.6	28.4	30.9	37.3	31.5		Total Current	41.9	38.0
35.3	26.9	26.0	19.2	28.6		Long-Term Debt	27.6	24.0
.0	.7	.5	2.8	2.5		Deferred Taxes	.9	1.0
6.3	26.3	5.2	3.0	.9		All Other Non-Current	5.9	5.6
7.8	17.7	37.4	37.6	36.6		Net Worth	23.8	31.4
100.0	100.0	100.0	100.0	100.0		Total Liabilties & Net Worth	100.0	100.0
						INCOME DATA		
100.0	100.0	100.0	100.0	100.0		Net Sales	100.0	100.0
45.0	52.5	34.6	39.7	33.0		Gross Profit	40.0	41.1
41.7	48.0	31.4	33.2	27.0		Operating Expenses	37.7	38.1
3.3	4.6	3.2	6.5	6.1		Operating Profit	2.4	3.0
1.1	4.8	.4	2.2	2.3		All Other Expenses (net)	3.2	2.0
2.2	-.2	2.8	4.2	3.7		Profit Before Taxes	-.8	1.0
						RATIOS		
4.0	3.9	4.6	2.6	2.5			2.4	2.8
2.3	2.1	2.2	1.5	1.8		Current	1.4	1.5
.9	.5	1.3	1.2	1.4			.8	1.0
2.0	2.0	1.7	.6	.5			.8	.9
(20) .8	.6	.5	.3	.3		Quick	.4	.5
.2	.2	.3	.2	.1			.1	.1
0 UND	**0** UND	**12** 31.0	**15** 24.0	**11** 33.3			**8** 47.5	**6** 61.7
4 100.9	**11** 33.9	**26** 14.3	**26** 13.9	**32** 11.5		Sales/Receivables	**21** 17.7	**22** 16.4
18 20.2	**36** 10.2	**42** 8.7	**52** 7.0	**40** 9.2			**47** 7.7	**46** 7.9
0 UND	**0** UND	**45** 8.2	**99** 3.7	**72** 5.1			**28** 13.1	**14** 25.7
38 9.7	**54** 6.7	**140** 2.6	**203** 1.8	**281** 1.3		Cost of Sales/Inventory	**107** 3.4	**82** 4.5
118 3.1	**130** 2.8	**365** 1.0	**406** .9	**608** .6			**297** 1.2	**252** 1.4
0 UND	**0** UND	**5** 76.1	**21** 17.2	**15** 23.6			**4** 86.9	**6** 61.8
3 127.6	**24** 15.1	**22** 16.4	**45** 8.1	**41** 8.8		Cost of Sales/Payables	**28** 13.0	**24** 15.1
18 20.4	**41** 8.9	**63** 5.8	**65** 5.6	**54** 6.7			**68** 5.4	**55** 6.7
10.3	5.0	2.4	3.8	1.2			3.3	4.1
24.1	10.4	5.9	6.3	3.7		Sales/Working Capital	10.7	10.9
NM	-35.6	14.9	11.4	18.0			-22.4	-149.8
7.4	11.0	6.0	6.2	3.4			5.3	5.2
(18) 4.0	(21) 4.5	(53) 2.2	(42) 3.2	2.2		EBIT/Interest	(176) 1.6	(164) 1.9
-.8	-1.7	1.2	1.3	1.4			-.8	-.1
		3.9	3.5				4.4	4.3
		(14) 1.7	(17) 1.5			Net Profit + Depr., Dep., Amort./Cur. Mat. L/T/D	(54) 2.4	(35) 1.7
		1.1	.8				1.4	.5
.2	.2	.3	.5	.5			.4	.4
1.4	3.3	.8	1.1	.7		Fixed/Worth	1.3	1.0
-6.1	-3.9	1.7	1.5	1.6			5.2	3.0
.8	.6	.4	.9	1.3			.9	.7
5.0	3.3	1.5	1.9	1.7		Debt/Worth	2.3	1.8
-9.5	-8.4	5.1	2.7	2.1			8.9	5.5
101.1	65.9	25.9	19.2	10.9			29.9	27.5
(15) 11.7	(15) 6.8	(53) 6.9	(40) 9.4	(10) 8.2		% Profit Before Taxes/Tangible Net Worth	(159) 7.0	(150) 7.5
-7.8	-17.5	.7	1.0	.0			-7.9	-5.1
29.4	24.9	6.5	7.8	4.3			8.7	8.9
11.2	4.7	2.4	2.9	3.2		% Profit Before Taxes/Total Assets	1.9	2.9
-3.4	-8.0	.4	.5	.9			-3.9	-2.0
80.4	20.7	12.2	7.5	4.0			10.0	13.4
11.3	9.9	6.7	4.1	3.6		Sales/Net Fixed Assets	4.4	5.3
5.0	4.3	3.2	1.6	1.7			2.1	2.2
6.7	3.8	2.3	1.9	1.2			2.6	2.8
3.7	2.2	1.6	1.0	.7		Sales/Total Assets	1.2	1.4
2.3	1.3	.8	.6	.6			.8	.8
.9	1.3	1.6	1.7	2.0			1.9	1.8
(14) 2.3	(14) 2.7	(54) 2.6	(42) 2.7	3.0		% Depr., Dep., Amort./Sales	(173) 3.5	(150) 3.4
4.0	5.6	4.7	3.4	4.2			5.5	5.1
3.2	3.5	1.5					2.1	2.2
(13) 5.1	(12) 6.3	(19) 3.4				% Officers', Directors' Owners' Comp/Sales	(56) 3.1	(62) 4.2
12.5	10.4	7.2					8.4	8.4
33697M	62156M	488055M	1121910M	678309M	1672133M	Net Sales ($)	4705062M	3607806M
6506M	23653M	296639M	931376M	754252M	1276092M	Total Assets ($)	4689088M	3346617M

M = $ thousand MM = $ million

See Pages 9 through 22 for Explanation of Ratios and Data

Comparative Historical Data				Current Data Sorted by Sales					
			Type of Statement						
21	16	14	Unqualified				1	4	9
25	27	27	Reviewed		2		6	9	10
36	34	35	Compiled	1	6	5	14	6	3
25	33	28	Tax Returns	5	14	1	6	1	1
75	77	61	Other	7	12	6	10	11	15
				45 (4/1-9/30/13)			120 (10/1/13-3/31/14)		
4/1/11-3/31/12 ALL	**4/1/12-3/31/13 ALL**	**4/1/13-3/31/14 ALL**		**0-1MM**	**1-3MM**	**3-5MM**	**5-10MM**	**10-25MM**	**25MM & OVER**
182	187	165	**NUMBER OF STATEMENTS**	13	34	12	37	31	38
%	%	%	**ASSETS**	%	%	%	%	%	%
6.5	7.7	6.1	Cash & Equivalents	5.6	5.7	2.2	10.5	5.9	3.6
12.2	11.2	11.8	Trade Receivables (net)	5.2	12.6	10.7	13.3	11.7	12.4
31.7	32.6	36.5	Inventory	32.3	41.8	33.1	31.9	37.9	37.4
3.7	2.2	2.2	All Other Current	.6	3.1	1.9	3.8	1.6	.9
54.2	53.7	56.5	Total Current	43.7	63.2	47.9	59.5	57.1	54.3
34.6	36.7	33.7	Fixed Assets (net)	37.8	29.2	40.2	30.6	36.0	35.5
3.5	2.8	3.7	Intangibles (net)	6.9	2.8	1.7	4.2	3.0	4.0
7.7	6.8	6.1	All Other Non-Current	11.7	4.8	10.2	5.7	4.0	6.3
100.0	100.0	100.0	Total	100.0	100.0	100.0	100.0	100.0	100.0
			LIABILITIES						
19.7	17.8	16.3	Notes Payable-Short Term	27.7	14.0	10.9	12.5	17.0	19.5
3.4	3.1	3.2	Cur. Mat.-L.T.D.	3.2	1.1	4.0	2.1	4.5	4.7
10.5	9.7	8.6	Trade Payables	3.2	7.4	8.8	7.8	11.7	9.7
.7	.8	1.1	Income Taxes Payable	.1	.5	1.4	.7	1.8	1.6
9.4	7.9	6.5	All Other Current	15.5	7.5	3.1	3.5	5.4	7.4
43.7	39.4	35.7	Total Current	49.7	30.5	28.2	26.7	40.3	42.9
23.2	29.2	25.6	Long-Term Debt	45.5	20.0	29.5	20.2	37.3	18.2
1.3	1.1	1.2	Deferred Taxes	.0	.8	.9	.4	1.5	2.6
6.7	6.7	7.8	All Other Non-Current	4.8	13.7	8.0	10.0	2.7	5.6
25.2	23.6	29.7	Net Worth	.1	35.0	33.4	42.7	18.2	30.6
100.0	100.0	100.0	Total Liabilties & Net Worth	100.0	100.0	100.0	100.0	100.0	100.0
			INCOME DATA						
100.0	100.0	100.0	Net Sales	100.0	100.0	100.0	100.0	100.0	100.0
42.8	43.5	39.7	Gross Profit	59.8	45.9	24.0	39.2	34.4	37.1
40.0	38.5	35.1	Operating Expenses	60.7	39.5	23.5	32.5	28.6	34.0
2.8	5.0	4.6	Operating Profit	-1.0	6.4	.5	6.7	5.9	3.1
1.3	1.5	1.7	All Other Expenses (net)	2.8	.8	1.9	2.1	1.8	1.7
1.5	3.5	2.9	Profit Before Taxes	-3.7	5.6	-1.4	4.6	4.0	1.4
			RATIOS						
2.7	3.0	3.2	Current	3.6	6.5	4.7	4.8	2.2	2.4
1.4	1.5	1.8		1.4	2.7	2.3	2.6	1.5	1.4
.9	1.0	1.2		.8	1.2	1.6	1.4	1.2	1.2
1.0	1.0	1.0	Quick	1.0	2.0	.7	1.9	.9	.7
.4	.4	(164) .5		.8	(33) .5	.4	.6	.3	.3
.2	.2	.2		.1	.2	.2	.4	.2	.2
7 49.2	**5** 67.5	**9** 39.3	Sales/Receivables	**0** UND	**1** 329.5	**7** 53.8	**11** 31.9	**14** 26.9	**12** 29.4
23 15.6	**20** 18.1	**24** 15.1		**4** 100.9	**17** 21.6	**23** 15.8	**26** 13.9	**25** 14.7	**29** 12.8
47 7.8	**39** 9.3	**38** 9.5		**25** 14.4	**36** 10.2	**63** 5.8	**59** 6.2	**36** 10.2	**41** 9.0
16 23.1	**22** 16.9	**44** 8.3	Cost of Sales/Inventory	**0** UND	**16** 23.5	**39** 9.3	**27** 13.7	**66** 5.5	**72** 5.1
101 3.6	**122** 3.0	**135** 2.7		**78** 4.7	**94** 3.9	**174** 2.1	**94** 3.9	**174** 2.1	**146** 2.5
332 1.1	**304** 1.2	**304** 1.2		**228** 1.6	**365** 1.0	**228** 1.6	**304** 1.2	**332** 1.1	**365** 1.0
9 40.6	**4** 89.8	**5** 73.8	Cost of Sales/Payables	**0** UND	**0** UND	**0** 765.4	**5** 77.4	**19** 19.3	**15** 24.7
29 12.4	**26** 13.8	**27** 13.7		**5** 68.6	**18** 20.6	**8** 44.0	**20** 18.0	**46** 8.0	**37** 9.8
69 5.3	**61** 6.0	**55** 6.6		**28** 13.2	**50** 7.3	**46** 8.0	**42** 8.6	**66** 5.5	**57** 6.4
3.2	3.7	3.8	Sales/Working Capital	4.7	4.3	2.2	2.4	4.0	5.0
11.1	9.5	7.4		24.0	6.8	3.6	5.4	8.1	10.0
-35.3	185.1	21.5		-47.2	29.6	21.1	15.4	14.1	23.2
5.9	5.9	6.3	EBIT/Interest	5.3	9.9	7.8	12.2	3.4	5.3
(169) 2.0	(177) 2.6	(153) 2.8		-.1	(27) 4.1	1.2	(35) 3.1	(30) 1.8	(36) 3.4
-.4	.9	1.0		-2.2	1.2	-12.4	1.4	1.4	1.1
3.1	4.0	3.5	Net Profit + Depr., Dep., Amort./Cur. Mat. L/T/D				3.7		2.2
(35) 1.3	(43) 2.0	(37) 1.6					(11) 2.1		(12) 1.2
.5	.9	1.0					1.3		.7
.4	.4	.4	Fixed/Worth	1.1	.1	.3	.3	.5	.7
1.1	1.2	1.1		5.7	.5	1.2	.6	1.2	1.0
4.1	3.0	3.1		-6.1	4.7	4.1	1.9	2.3	1.9
1.0	.9	.7	Debt/Worth	3.2	.4	.2	.4	1.2	1.1
2.1	1.9	1.8		18.2	1.2	1.6	.8	2.1	1.9
6.6	5.8	6.2		-9.5	8.7	11.0	4.0	4.8	3.9
23.1	25.2	25.4	% Profit Before Taxes/Tangible Net Worth		65.9	9.8	28.8	21.5	22.9
(150) 6.6	(159) 7.1	(140) 8.1			(27) 11.3	(10) .3	(33) 6.9	(27) 13.5	(34) 10.0
-1.6	.4	.6			1.7	-18.5	1.0	2.1	2.4
8.9	8.0	9.3	% Profit Before Taxes/Total Assets	23.1	26.0	3.0	12.2	6.3	6.7
2.2	3.3	3.2		-2.1	4.9	.4	2.9	3.0	3.5
-3.1	-.1	.1		-11.0	.2	-8.6	.4	1.4	.5
10.9	11.7	11.7	Sales/Net Fixed Assets	23.8	24.2	10.5	15.5	11.3	8.4
5.1	5.0	5.7		6.1	7.7	3.6	6.7	4.1	4.7
2.4	2.6	2.7		2.7	3.9	1.8	2.8	1.7	3.2
2.5	2.6	2.6	Sales/Total Assets	3.0	3.6	2.1	2.5	2.2	2.2
1.4	1.4	1.5		1.8	2.1	1.1	1.7	1.1	1.3
.8	.8	.8		.6	.7	.6	.7	.8	.9
1.8	1.6	1.6	% Depr., Dep., Amort./Sales		1.1	1.0	1.6	2.0	1.5
(153) 3.3	(162) 2.9	(141) 2.8			(24) 1.9	(11) 2.3	(31) 2.8	(30) 3.1	(36) 2.7
5.0	4.7	4.1			2.9	8.1	3.9	4.2	4.1
2.9	2.2	2.5	% Officers', Directors' Owners' Comp/Sales		2.9		2.1		
(58) 5.6	(69) 3.8	(49) 4.5			(18) 5.3		(10) 4.6		
9.2	6.5	8.2			10.7		6.0		
3822699M	4001579M	4056260M	Net Sales ($)	8399M	66709M	45053M	266221M	477820M	3192058M
3509022M	3355799M	3288518M	Total Assets ($)	7046M	69177M	55658M	242905M	508842M	2404890M

M = $ thousand MM = $ million

See Pages 9 through 22 for Explanation of Ratios and Data

Current Data Sorted by Assets | **Comparative Historical Data**

						Type of Statement		
					1	Unqualified		
						Reviewed	3	3
1		1				Compiled	1	
4	7	3				Tax Returns	10	2
1	3	2	4			Other		6
	4 (4/1-9/30/13)		23 (10/1/13-3/31/14)				4/1/09-3/31/10	4/1/10-3/31/11
0-500M	**500M-2MM**	**2-10MM**	**10-50MM**	**50-100MM**	**100-250MM**		**ALL**	**ALL**
6	10	6	4		1	**NUMBER OF STATEMENTS**	14	11
%	%	%	%	%	%	**ASSETS**	%	%
	13.2			DATA NOT AVAILABLE		Cash & Equivalents	12.3	3.3
	.6					Trade Receivables (net)	10.1	12.0
	6.9					Inventory	11.1	14.5
	.5					All Other Current	11.8	3.7
	21.1					Total Current	45.3	33.5
	64.2					Fixed Assets (net)	45.5	46.8
	.0					Intangibles (net)	4.9	.1
	14.6					All Other Non-Current	4.3	19.6
	100.0					Total	100.0	100.0
						LIABILITIES		
	26.7					Notes Payable-Short Term	20.2	15.6
	10.5					Cur. Mat.-L.T.D.	5.3	2.1
	1.6					Trade Payables	.8	2.1
	.0					Income Taxes Payable	1.7	2.4
	2.0					All Other Current	5.9	12.4
	40.7					Total Current	33.9	34.6
	62.8					Long-Term Debt	31.8	20.0
	.0					Deferred Taxes	.2	.2
	.2					All Other Non-Current	5.3	3.0
	-3.7					Net Worth	28.8	42.2
	100.0					Total Liabilities & Net Worth	100.0	100.0
						INCOME DATA		
	100.0					Net Sales	100.0	100.0
						Gross Profit		
	82.1					Operating Expenses	92.1	79.6
	17.9					Operating Profit	7.9	20.4
	.6					All Other Expenses (net)	1.3	3.0
	17.3					Profit Before Taxes	6.7	17.4
						RATIOS		
	1.0						3.0	1.6
	.4					Current	1.5	.9
	.1						.5	.3
	.6						2.4	.5
	.2					Quick	.4	.2
	.1						.1	.1
	0 UND						0 UND	0 UND
	0 UND					Sales/Receivables	0 UND	13 27.9
	0 UND						28 13.0	33 10.9
						Cost of Sales/Inventory		
						Cost of Sales/Payables		
	NM						3.0	4.0
	-70.0					Sales/Working Capital	25.3	-32.1
	-5.3						-27.8	-4.8
	33.2						6.0	5.0
	8.5					EBIT/Interest	(13) 2.3	(10) 2.0
	3.0						.1	1.1
						Net Profit + Depr., Dep., Amort./Cur. Mat. L/T/D		
	.9						.4	.5
	NM					Fixed/Worth	1.8	.8
	-1.8						-10.8	2.7
	1.0						1.1	.6
	NM					Debt/Worth	3.9	1.4
	-3.0						-13.2	3.6
							22.2	27.0
						% Profit Before Taxes/Tangible Net Worth	(10) 9.1	7.0
							1.8	3.8
	62.2						12.3	7.9
	32.3					% Profit Before Taxes/Total Assets	2.4	3.6
	8.0						-1.0	1.4
	7.2						44.8	5.3
	4.6					Sales/Net Fixed Assets	4.4	1.9
	3.2						1.6	.4
	4.1						3.8	1.5
	2.5					Sales/Total Assets	1.6	.5
	1.9						.9	.3
							3.9	
						% Depr., Dep., Amort./Sales	(12) 5.5	
							8.8	
						% Officers', Directors' Owners' Comp/Sales		
11364M	35363M	15256M	176142M		226332M	Net Sales ($)	95535M	153213M
1829M	9759M	25557M	106832M		197949M	Total Assets ($)	78063M	130818M

M = $ thousand MM = $ million

See Pages 9 through 22 for Explanation of Ratios and Data

Comparative Historical Data				Current Data Sorted by Sales					
			Type of Statement						
1		1	Unqualified						1
3			Reviewed						
4	2	2	Compiled			1	1		
16	17	14	Tax Returns	4	6	2	2		
9	13	10	Other	2	3	1	1	1	2
4/1/11-3/31/12 ALL	**4/1/12-3/31/13 ALL**	**4/1/13-3/31/14 ALL**		**4 (4/1-9/30/13)**			**23 (10/1/13-3/31/14)**		
				0-1MM	**1-3MM**	**3-5MM**	**5-10MM**	**10-25MM**	**25MM & OVER**
33	32	27	**NUMBER OF STATEMENTS**	6	9	4	4	1	3
%	%	%	**ASSETS**	%	%	%	%	%	%
14.7	15.0	13.3	Cash & Equivalents						
8.8	3.7	3.9	Trade Receivables (net)						
8.2	7.2	10.2	Inventory						
2.7	.7	.9	All Other Current						
34.3	26.5	28.3	Total Current						
49.8	53.5	51.6	Fixed Assets (net)						
.4	.2	1.2	Intangibles (net)						
15.5	19.7	18.9	All Other Non-Current						
100.0	100.0	100.0	Total						
			LIABILITIES						
16.1	30.2	15.1	Notes Payable-Short Term						
13.6	13.9	6.8	Cur. Mat.-L.T.D.						
4.6	.4	2.5	Trade Payables						
.0	.0	.3	Income Taxes Payable						
17.1	7.1	11.5	All Other Current						
51.4	51.6	36.1	Total Current						
36.3	49.8	44.9	Long-Term Debt						
.0	.0	.1	Deferred Taxes						
.0	2.1	1.5	All Other Non-Current						
12.3	-3.4	17.4	Net Worth						
100.0	100.0	100.0	Total Liabilties & Net Worth						
			INCOME DATA						
100.0	100.0	100.0	Net Sales						
			Gross Profit						
90.0	82.4	79.2	Operating Expenses						
10.0	17.6	20.8	Operating Profit						
5.3	3.9	3.1	All Other Expenses (net)						
4.8	13.7	17.7	Profit Before Taxes						
			RATIOS						
1.5	1.4	1.3							
.9	.8	.6	Current						
.1	.1	.1							
1.2	1.3	.7							
.5	.3	.3	Quick						
.1	.1	.1							
0 UND	**0** UND	**0** UND							
0 UND	**0** UND	**0** UND	Sales/Receivables						
29 12.6	**4** 97.2	**8** 45.6							
			Cost of Sales/Inventory						
			Cost of Sales/Payables						
20.6	11.2	13.2							
-141.2	-85.8	-79.0	Sales/Working Capital						
-2.5	-4.7	-7.9							
8.0	11.4	34.3							
(27) 3.3	(29) 3.6	(25) 16.2	EBIT/Interest						
.6	1.4	2.9							
			Net Profit + Depr., Dep., Amort./Cur. Mat. L/T/D						
.7	1.1	.4							
2.4	2.5	1.2	Fixed/Worth						
-9.3	-1.1	-2.5							
.9	1.1	.3							
5.6	3.7	4.1	Debt/Worth						
-12.4	-4.4	-7.1							
62.0	53.1	68.6							
(22) 16.8	(21) 19.1	(18) 26.6	% Profit Before Taxes/Tangible Net Worth						
-1.1	8.2	15.3							
12.8	39.0	46.0							
4.3	6.4	20.2	% Profit Before Taxes/Total Assets						
-3.6	1.6	3.2							
27.2	13.3	16.7							
4.8	3.9	5.2	Sales/Net Fixed Assets						
.7	1.4	2.5							
4.6	3.0	4.1							
1.4	1.7	2.0	Sales/Total Assets						
.6	.7	.7							
3.3	3.3	1.6							
(26) 5.2	(20) 6.5	(16) 4.6	% Depr., Dep., Amort./Sales						
13.4	15.1	12.1							
	1.5								
	(14) 3.3		% Officers', Directors' Owners' Comp/Sales						
	5.4								
446502M	**218955M**	**464457M**	Net Sales ($)	**3269M**	**17303M**	**15419M**	**33359M**	**13268M**	**381839M**
275644M	**156936M**	**341926M**	Total Assets ($)	**11796M**	**11152M**	**5296M**	**21700M**	**19339M**	**272643M**

M = $ thousand MM = $ million

See Pages 9 through 22 for Explanation of Ratios and Data

Current Data Sorted by Assets / Comparative Historical Data

0-500M	500M-2MM	2-10MM	10-50MM	50-100MM	100-250MM	Type of Statement	4/1/09-3/31/10 ALL	4/1/10-3/31/11 ALL
						Unqualified	3	2
	1	1	1			Reviewed	9	8
	2	4	2			Compiled	15	17
6	4	1				Tax Returns	20	20
	5	2	1	1		Other	10	11
	2 (4/1-9/30/13)		29 (10/1/13-3/31/14)					
6	12	8	4	1		NUMBER OF STATEMENTS	57	58
%	%	%	%	%	%	ASSETS	%	%
	21.4				DATA NOT AVAILABLE	Cash & Equivalents	11.8	10.9
	2.9					Trade Receivables (net)	7.0	6.9
	10.3					Inventory	9.1	6.6
	1.3					All Other Current	3.7	6.0
	35.9					Total Current	31.5	30.5
	56.2					Fixed Assets (net)	53.5	55.2
	.0					Intangibles (net)	1.8	.2
	7.8					All Other Non-Current	13.2	14.2
	100.0					Total	100.0	100.0
						LIABILITIES		
	15.4					Notes Payable-Short Term	21.7	34.9
	11.9					Cur. Mat.-L.T.D.	6.9	10.0
	.6					Trade Payables	1.3	.7
	.0					Income Taxes Payable	.1	.0
	.8					All Other Current	20.4	6.0
	28.7					Total Current	50.4	51.7
	40.8					Long-Term Debt	26.6	35.3
	.0					Deferred Taxes	.0	.1
	.0					All Other Non-Current	4.0	3.3
	30.5					Net Worth	19.0	9.6
	100.0					Total Liabilities & Net Worth	100.0	100.0
						INCOME DATA		
	100.0					Net Sales	100.0	100.0
						Gross Profit		
	85.9					Operating Expenses	85.9	90.4
	14.1					Operating Profit	14.1	9.6
	-.8					All Other Expenses (net)	4.3	4.2
	14.9					Profit Before Taxes	9.8	5.4
						RATIOS		
	3.9						2.1	1.7
	1.2					Current	1.1	.7
	.2						.3	.2
	3.0						1.3	1.1
	.5					Quick	.6	.3
	.1						.1	.0
	0 UND						0 UND	0 UND
	0 UND					Sales/Receivables	0 UND	0 UND
	0 UND						43 8.5	30 12.2
						Cost of Sales/Inventory		
						Cost of Sales/Payables		
	5.8						5.2	4.4
	32.7					Sales/Working Capital	150.5	-21.0
	-9.5						-5.5	-3.2
	19.3						7.8	9.7
	(11) 9.4					EBIT/Interest	(46) 2.2	(52) 2.6
	3.0						.8	.5
						Net Profit + Depr., Dep., Amort./Cur. Mat. L/T/D		
	.5						.8	.8
	1.2					Fixed/Worth	1.3	1.7
	3.6						-11.8	NM
	.6						.6	.6
	1.3					Debt/Worth	1.6	2.3
	4.0						-11.8	-13.9
	101.4						38.5	43.0
	(10) 38.6					% Profit Before Taxes/Tangible Net Worth	(41) 12.0	(43) 7.7
	7.0						1.8	-2.4
	34.1						16.8	18.6
	18.5					% Profit Before Taxes/Total Assets	5.8	2.4
	4.4						-.5	-4.0
	6.0						9.2	10.3
	2.6					Sales/Net Fixed Assets	2.1	1.6
	1.3						.9	.7
	3.4						1.8	1.5
	1.1					Sales/Total Assets	1.1	.9
	.7						.5	.5
							3.1	2.5
						% Depr., Dep., Amort./Sales	(45) 7.4	(51) 7.3
							14.9	12.3
								2.7
						% Officers', Directors' Owners' Comp/Sales		(11) 4.1
								10.5
6932M	21050M	21031M	38165M	262656M		Net Sales ($)	155569M	579673M
1560M	13938M	44756M	63504M	82008M		Total Assets ($)	226656M	466863M

M = $ thousand MM = $ million

See Pages 9 through 22 for Explanation of Ratios and Data

Comparative Historical Data

Current Data Sorted by Sales

4/1/11-3/31/12 ALL	4/1/12-3/31/13 ALL	4/1/13-3/31/14 ALL	Type of Statement	0-1MM	1-3MM	3-5MM	5-10MM	10-25MM	25MM & OVER
2	3		Unqualified						
3	4	3	Reviewed		2		1		
24	11	8	Compiled	1	2	2	2	1	
15	9	11	Tax Returns	3	6	2			
10	17	9	Other	1	6	1			1
				2 (4/1-9/30/13)		29 (10/1/13-3/31/14)			
54	44	31	NUMBER OF STATEMENTS	5	16	5	3	1	1
%	%	%	**ASSETS**	%	%	%	%	%	%
11.0	16.4	18.0	Cash & Equivalents		21.7				
7.1	5.8	7.6	Trade Receivables (net)		3.6				
6.7	8.2	8.8	Inventory		8.4				
3.1	1.5	2.1	All Other Current		.3				
27.9	31.9	36.6	Total Current		33.9				
58.7	55.2	52.5	Fixed Assets (net)		55.3				
.2	1.4	1.0	Intangibles (net)		.1				
13.3	11.6	9.8	All Other Non-Current		10.7				
100.0	100.0	100.0	Total		100.0				
			LIABILITIES						
33.1	29.1	21.8	Notes Payable-Short Term		28.1				
9.0	10.7	9.2	Cur. Mat.-L.T.D.		13.4				
1.2	1.1	.8	Trade Payables		.8				
.2	.1	.0	Income Taxes Payable		.0				
6.3	5.8	1.6	All Other Current		.5				
49.7	46.8	33.3	Total Current		42.8				
38.2	34.6	36.5	Long-Term Debt		41.5				
.1	.1	.0	Deferred Taxes		.0				
1.9	1.3	.2	All Other Non-Current		.3				
10.1	17.2	29.9	Net Worth		15.4				
100.0	100.0	100.0	Total Liabilties & Net Worth		100.0				
			INCOME DATA						
100.0	100.0	100.0	Net Sales		100.0				
			Gross Profit						
86.2	87.2	89.1	Operating Expenses		89.8				
13.8	12.8	10.9	Operating Profit		10.2				
5.0	1.4	.9	All Other Expenses (net)		.9				
8.8	11.4	10.0	Profit Before Taxes		9.3				
			RATIOS						
1.9	3.5	3.0			1.4				
.7	1.2	1.3	Current		1.0				
.2	.2	.7			.4				
1.0	2.7	2.0			1.1				
.4	.5	.8	Quick		.7				
.2	.1	.2			.2				
0 UND	0 UND	0 UND			0 UND				
0 UND	0 UND	0 UND	Sales/Receivables		0 UND				
41 8.8	14 25.7	64 5.7			0 UND				
			Cost of Sales/Inventory						
			Cost of Sales/Payables						
9.2	4.9	4.6			6.9				
-28.8	26.2	33.6	Sales/Working Capital		-604.2				
-4.1	-4.3	-9.7			-6.9				
10.0	16.7	17.0			12.1				
(45) 3.6	(39) 4.4	(28) 4.9	EBIT/Interest		(15) 4.3				
1.0	2.0	2.6			2.1				
			Net Profit + Depr., Dep., Amort./Cur. Mat. L/T/D						
.9	.8	.5			.6				
1.8	1.5	1.0	Fixed/Worth		1.6				
-7.6	-9.0	4.0			-3.0				
.8	.6	.4			.6				
1.6	1.5	1.2	Debt/Worth		1.7				
-11.4	-98.3	26.3			-40.6				
80.3	61.0	56.3			61.0				
(38) 19.2	(32) 20.9	(25) 10.1	% Profit Before Taxes/Tangible Net Worth		(11) 10.1				
1.2	6.2	2.5			6.6				
25.9	30.1	21.0			20.7				
6.9	10.8	5.9	% Profit Before Taxes/Total Assets		5.5				
-.2	2.8	2.6			3.3				
6.8	8.1	8.5			8.1				
2.6	2.2	2.5	Sales/Net Fixed Assets		2.8				
1.1	1.1	.9			.9				
3.0	3.0	3.2			4.7				
1.4	1.1	1.1	Sales/Total Assets		1.1				
.6	.6	.5			.6				
2.5	1.5	1.5							
(41) 4.6	(31) 4.4	(20) 4.5	% Depr., Dep., Amort./Sales						
18.0	7.1	7.7							
3.1									
(10) 4.4			% Officers', Directors' Owners' Comp/Sales						
6.5									
380882M	632941M	349834M	Net Sales ($)	2984M	25599M	17621M	24546M	16428M	262656M
388066M	459565M	205766M	Total Assets ($)	9006M	31575M	29485M	39033M	14659M	82008M

M = $ thousand MM = $ million

See Pages 9 through 22 for Explanation of Ratios and Data

Current Data Sorted by Assets / Comparative Historical Data

0-500M	500M-2MM	2-10MM	10-50MM	50-100MM	100-250MM		4/1/09-3/31/10 ALL	4/1/10-3/31/11 ALL
						Type of Statement		
		4	6	4	2	Unqualified	21	19
1	2	3	12	4		Reviewed	41	39
3	12	21	8	3	1	Compiled	65	65
10	29	16	2		2	Tax Returns	107	82
6	10	28	21	5	3	Other	76	90
35 (4/1-9/30/13)			183 (10/1/13-3/31/14)					
20	53	72	49	16	8	**NUMBER OF STATEMENTS**	310	295
%	%	%	%	%	%	**ASSETS**	%	%
12.5	11.6	10.0	4.5	1.3		Cash & Equivalents	9.8	10.1
9.3	6.1	10.7	13.5	16.4		Trade Receivables (net)	8.8	8.8
9.8	11.4	12.4	18.9	22.8		Inventory	12.1	14.3
1.6	4.0	3.2	8.2	5.2		All Other Current	5.0	5.8
33.1	33.0	36.4	45.0	45.7		Total Current	35.7	38.9
63.6	50.0	49.4	41.2	44.3		Fixed Assets (net)	52.9	48.9
.0	3.4	4.3	1.4	3.2		Intangibles (net)	1.5	1.8
3.1	13.7	10.0	12.4	6.8		All Other Non-Current	10.0	10.3
100.0	100.0	100.0	100.0	100.0		Total	100.0	100.0
						LIABILITIES		
31.4	24.2	12.0	12.6	16.0		Notes Payable-Short Term	21.3	23.6
4.9	5.5	3.6	3.6	2.9		Cur. Mat.-L.T.D.	4.7	5.9
4.0	4.7	5.1	6.4	6.7		Trade Payables	4.0	4.6
.0	.1	.2	.6	.6		Income Taxes Payable	.5	.4
8.7	5.2	4.8	11.5	2.6		All Other Current	8.1	6.2
49.0	39.8	25.8	34.7	28.7		Total Current	38.6	40.6
34.0	38.9	29.0	19.9	28.9		Long-Term Debt	30.8	32.6
.0	.0	.0	.7	.9		Deferred Taxes	.5	.6
31.1	7.6	6.0	1.8	.7		All Other Non-Current	6.4	6.9
-14.0	13.7	39.3	42.9	40.9		Net Worth	23.7	19.3
100.0	100.0	100.0	100.0	100.0		Total Liabilties & Net Worth	100.0	100.0
						INCOME DATA		
100.0	100.0	100.0	100.0	100.0		Net Sales	100.0	100.0
						Gross Profit		
90.1	88.9	89.0	88.3	88.9		Operating Expenses	88.9	90.0
9.9	11.1	11.0	11.7	11.1		Operating Profit	11.1	10.0
3.3	1.7	3.1	1.3	2.9		All Other Expenses (net)	3.3	2.8
6.6	9.4	7.9	10.5	8.2		Profit Before Taxes	7.8	7.2
						RATIOS		
3.0	5.1	2.7	2.4	2.0			2.3	2.7
.8	1.3	1.2	1.4	1.6		Current	1.1	1.3
.1	.2	.6	1.0	1.3			.4	.6
1.7	2.9	1.5	1.5	1.0			1.3	1.3
.3	.9	(71) .5	.5	.5		Quick	(309) .4	(294) .5
.0	.1	.2	.1	.3			.1	.1
0 UND	0 UND	0 UND	10 37.7	30 12.0			0 UND	0 UND
0 UND	0 UND	11 33.1	38 9.6	39 9.3		Sales/Receivables	3 132.0	2 176.6
12 31.3	18 20.4	38 9.6	68 5.4	79 4.6			40 9.2	46 7.9
						Cost of Sales/Inventory		
						Cost of Sales/Payables		
5.0	5.7	3.5	2.6	3.1			4.7	4.0
NM	37.4	26.6	7.8	4.8		Sales/Working Capital	32.7	16.1
-6.5	-8.0	-11.5	-116.8	15.9			-8.8	-11.4
23.0	18.0	15.7	15.6	8.8			9.4	9.0
(15) 1.6	(47) 2.9	(63) 4.4	(46) 7.2	(13) 3.7		EBIT/Interest	(273) 3.1	(270) 3.3
.7	1.0	1.4	2.6	1.6			.9	1.2
							6.0	5.9
						Net Profit + Depr., Dep., Amort./Cur. Mat. L/T/D	(55) 2.3	(50) 2.7
							.9	1.2
1.2	.4	.6	.4	.9			.7	.6
8.9	1.5	1.3	.8	1.1		Fixed/Worth	1.3	1.3
-2.0	-48.7	15.4	1.8	2.1			4.3	4.4
1.1	.6	.5	.6	.9			.6	.6
10.5	3.1	1.3	1.3	1.5		Debt/Worth	1.7	1.7
-3.7	-12.0	36.4	2.9	2.9			6.8	8.1
209.5	55.3	44.3	37.6	25.0			33.8	33.0
(11) 30.8	(37) 20.9	(57) 12.1	(46) 17.3	15.8		% Profit Before Taxes/Tangible Net Worth	(257) 13.5	(238) 12.5
.0	3.8	3.0	5.8	8.6			.6	2.7
45.0	13.7	13.9	12.5	10.6			14.2	14.1
7.0	5.5	4.5	5.8	4.5		% Profit Before Taxes/Total Assets	4.9	4.9
-1.4	-.1	.8	2.4	2.0			-.4	.5
14.2	20.6	8.7	8.5	4.4			7.7	9.0
6.8	5.5	2.4	2.1	1.9		Sales/Net Fixed Assets	2.1	2.7
2.9	1.3	.7	1.1	.8			.9	.9
5.3	4.0	2.0	1.4	1.5			2.2	2.3
3.3	1.8	1.0	.8	.7		Sales/Total Assets	1.1	1.0
1.6	.9	.4	.4	.4			.5	.5
1.3	2.0	1.7	2.1	2.2			2.8	2.7
(17) 3.0	(37) 4.0	(59) 6.4	(42) 5.6	(14) 4.6		% Depr., Dep., Amort./Sales	(243) 6.6	(237) 6.3
10.2	14.4	15.2	8.2	7.3			10.7	11.7
	2.0	.9	2.6				1.5	1.8
	(22) 3.7	(15) 2.7	(10) 3.3			% Officers', Directors' Owners' Comp/Sales	(87) 3.1	(67) 4.2
	9.6	3.5	6.3				6.3	8.5
15919M	218789M	437340M	1162599M	1108446M	968152M	Net Sales ($)	4030350M	3846466M
5340M	64213M	342900M	1056165M	1185256M	1078913M	Total Assets ($)	3238317M	3612951M

M = $ thousand MM = $ million

See Pages 9 through 22 for Explanation of Ratios and Data

Comparative Historical Data				Current Data Sorted by Sales					
			Type of Statement						
15	16	16	Unqualified				1	6	9
42	35	22	Reviewed	2	1	3		6	10
57	44	48	Compiled	6	9	14	8	7	4
110	83	59	Tax Returns	18	17	8	12	2	2
79	77	73	Other	15	7	9	14	16	12
4/1/11-3/31/12	4/1/12-3/31/13	4/1/13-3/31/14		35 (4/1-9/30/13)			183 (10/1/13-3/31/14)		
ALL	ALL	ALL		0-1MM	1-3MM	3-5MM	5-10MM	10-25MM	25MM & OVER
303	255	218	**NUMBER OF STATEMENTS**	41	34	34	35	37	37
%	%	%	**ASSETS**	%	%	%	%	%	%
11.0	8.1	8.5	Cash & Equivalents	5.9	9.1	16.0	10.7	5.8	4.5
9.3	11.3	10.3	Trade Receivables (net)	6.1	5.4	8.1	12.6	12.8	17.0
11.9	14.4	14.5	Inventory	9.0	9.0	12.6	15.0	14.9	26.8
5.1	5.1	4.6	All Other Current	1.0	1.5	6.9	7.0	4.7	6.7
37.2	38.9	37.9	Total Current	22.1	24.9	43.5	45.3	38.2	55.0
48.4	49.8	48.2	Fixed Assets (net)	68.3	55.7	43.5	46.2	42.0	31.6
2.6	1.6	3.0	Intangibles (net)	.8	5.7	1.9	.7	4.8	4.4
11.9	9.7	10.8	All Other Non-Current	8.9	13.7	11.1	7.8	15.0	9.0
100.0	100.0	100.0	Total	100.0	100.0	100.0	100.0	100.0	100.0
			LIABILITIES						
21.6	17.0	17.2	Notes Payable-Short Term	13.8	13.3	34.7	15.4	12.6	14.9
7.5	5.9	4.3	Cur. Mat.-L.T.D.	4.4	7.3	3.2	2.7	3.0	5.0
5.3	6.6	5.5	Trade Payables	3.4	1.7	2.9	6.5	6.2	12.0
.5	.5	.3	Income Taxes Payable	.1	.3	.0	.3	.6	.3
6.1	6.7	6.6	All Other Current	6.2	3.5	5.7	5.2	7.5	11.0
41.0	36.6	33.8	Total Current	27.8	26.0	46.5	30.1	29.9	43.3
30.1	34.0	29.6	Long-Term Debt	44.9	42.3	21.6	27.0	22.4	17.9
.5	.5	.3	Deferred Taxes	.0	.2	.0	.0	.8	.8
8.3	5.6	7.2	All Other Non-Current	16.9	11.6	1.9	.4	9.8	1.0
20.1	23.3	29.1	Net Worth	10.4	19.9	30.0	42.5	37.0	37.1
100.0	100.0	100.0	Total Liabilties & Net Worth	100.0	100.0	100.0	100.0	100.0	100.0
			INCOME DATA						
100.0	100.0	100.0	Net Sales	100.0	100.0	100.0	100.0	100.0	100.0
			Gross Profit						
88.9	87.9	89.2	Operating Expenses	85.4	82.5	89.2	92.0	92.1	94.0
11.1	12.1	10.8	Operating Profit	14.6	17.5	10.8	8.0	7.9	6.0
1.6	2.8	2.2	All Other Expenses (net)	6.2	3.5	.8	.9	1.1	.4
9.5	9.3	8.5	Profit Before Taxes	8.4	14.0	9.9	7.1	6.8	5.6
			RATIOS						
2.8	2.5	2.7		3.4	3.8	4.6	3.5	2.6	1.9
1.4	1.3	1.3	Current	1.0	.9	1.2	1.4	1.5	1.3
.3	.5	.6		.1	.2	.7	1.0	.7	1.1
1.6	1.4	1.7		1.9	2.2	2.9	1.4	1.7	.8
.4	.5	(217) .5	Quick	(40) .5	.5	.7	.6	.7	.4
.1	.1	.2		.1	.0	.1	.2	.3	.2
0 UND	0 UND	0 UND		0 UND	0 UND	0 UND	0 UND	8 43.0	19 19.0
2 229.9	10 35.6	12 29.4	Sales/Receivables	0 UND	0 UND	4 83.8	17 21.1	25 14.6	31 11.6
38 9.5	46 8.0	43 8.4		26 14.2	6 59.2	40 9.1	63 5.8	49 7.5	55 6.6
			Cost of Sales/Inventory						
			Cost of Sales/Payables						
3.4	3.8	3.8		3.2	5.2	3.8	2.8	2.7	3.9
15.1	19.1	14.7	Sales/Working Capital	UND	NM	25.3	11.7	12.6	7.8
-9.0	-11.4	-12.3		-4.0	-4.4	-10.9	-149.3	-43.8	44.3
12.1	11.8	15.6		10.6	15.6	21.2	16.8	11.8	15.1
(270) 4.5	(228) 4.0	(191) 4.0	EBIT/Interest	(32) 1.9	(29) 3.3	(31) 3.5	(32) 5.6	(33) 4.4	(34) 6.6
1.4	1.5	1.4		.4	1.1	1.0	2.3	2.0	2.0
7.6	5.1	4.6							4.5
(42) 2.4	(39) 2.6	(29) 2.3	Net Profit + Depr., Dep., Amort./Cur. Mat. L/T/D						(14) 3.2
1.2	1.2	1.2							1.7
.7	.6	.5		1.0	1.0	.3	.4	.4	.4
1.3	1.2	1.2	Fixed/Worth	2.2	2.5	.8	1.2	1.2	1.0
9.1	6.6	5.1		NM	-7.2	1.9	2.0	4.6	1.7
.6	.6	.6		.5	.7	.4	.4	.6	.9
1.9	1.9	1.5	Debt/Worth	2.1	3.6	.9	1.2	1.4	1.5
34.2	13.7	13.1		-15.7	-3.7	151.6	3.2	7.0	3.9
48.6	46.0	37.5		32.1	75.9	69.5	25.3	38.1	32.8
(234) 21.3	(210) 20.4	(174) 16.4	% Profit Before Taxes/Tangible Net Worth	(30) 6.7	(23) 19.2	(27) 12.5	(29) 13.2	(31) 16.3	(34) 20.2
3.5	3.9	3.6		1.1	7.6	2.5	2.7	6.6	7.8
18.0	16.8	13.5		8.2	17.5	25.1	14.1	12.5	14.1
7.6	7.0	4.8	% Profit Before Taxes/Total Assets	2.2	5.4	4.6	7.5	6.0	6.0
1.1	1.6	.7		-1.6	1.3	.5	2.1	.9	2.3
10.6	8.2	10.4		1.7	5.7	15.7	13.4	12.2	10.9
2.9	2.8	2.7	Sales/Net Fixed Assets	.7	3.0	3.4	4.0	2.5	6.6
1.1	1.0	1.0		.2	1.2	1.2	1.4	1.4	1.8
2.6	2.4	2.4		1.1	2.6	2.9	2.8	2.3	2.4
1.1	1.1	1.1	Sales/Total Assets	.4	1.3	1.6	1.4	1.1	1.5
.6	.6	.5		.1	.5	.8	.6	.7	.6
2.2	2.1	2.0		2.1	3.8	3.1	1.6	1.0	1.3
(244) 5.0	(216) 5.2	(176) 5.1	% Depr., Dep., Amort./Sales	(33) 14.2	(29) 8.3	(23) 5.0	(28) 4.2	(30) 3.8	(33) 2.3
9.7	10.9	12.0		25.2	20.7	13.4	8.6	6.9	6.7
1.5	1.5	2.1		2.9	2.4			.9	
(78) 2.4	(61) 3.2	(57) 3.4	% Officers', Directors' Owners' Comp/Sales	(11) 8.3	(13) 5.2			(10) 2.8	
7.1	6.5	8.4		16.4	8.7			4.7	
3576284M	4667194M	3911245M	Net Sales ($)	19697M	55560M	135429M	249008M	597679M	2853872M
3967323M	3930933M	3732787M	Total Assets ($)	70869M	95898M	130455M	313793M	707160M	2414612M

M = $ thousand MM = $ million

See Pages 9 through 22 for Explanation of Ratios and Data

Current Data Sorted by Assets							Comparative Historical Data	
						Type of Statement		
	1		5		1	Unqualified	6	6
1		5	12			Reviewed	13	23
1	2	3	8			Compiled	28	24
15	25	20	1		2	Tax Returns	56	58
3	9	10	13	1	3	Other	31	49
18 (4/1-9/30/13)		123 (10/1/13-3/31/14)					4/1/09-3/31/10 ALL	4/1/10-3/31/11 ALL
0-500M	500M-2MM	2-10MM	10-50MM	50-100MM	100-250MM			
20	37	38	39	1	6	NUMBER OF STATEMENTS	134	160
%	%	%	%	%	%	**ASSETS**	%	%
34.3	6.3	3.4	4.8			Cash & Equivalents	8.3	6.4
5.1	1.5	4.9	7.1			Trade Receivables (net)	5.6	4.3
14.9	22.4	30.5	35.3			Inventory	26.7	25.6
5.8	3.4	2.5	3.0			All Other Current	5.6	4.3
60.0	33.7	41.3	50.3			Total Current	46.1	40.6
30.0	58.6	48.1	37.6			Fixed Assets (net)	42.3	50.1
2.6	.0	3.5	3.0			Intangibles (net)	1.7	.5
7.4	7.7	7.1	9.2			All Other Non-Current	9.9	8.7
100.0	100.0	100.0	100.0			Total	100.0	100.0
						LIABILITIES		
55.0	15.7	24.5	22.7			Notes Payable-Short Term	41.7	34.5
4.0	3.8	4.1	1.9			Cur. Mat.-L.T.D.	4.0	2.4
1.9	2.6	2.1	5.5			Trade Payables	2.2	3.4
.1	.4	.0	1.0			Income Taxes Payable	.1	.3
25.0	2.7	2.6	7.2			All Other Current	5.7	7.9
85.9	25.2	33.4	38.4			Total Current	53.6	48.4
37.3	35.3	27.3	23.4			Long-Term Debt	19.5	21.7
.0	.2	.1	.4			Deferred Taxes	.5	.2
2.8	4.4	4.5	2.0			All Other Non-Current	4.5	5.3
-26.0	34.9	34.7	35.9			Net Worth	21.7	24.3
100.0	100.0	100.0	100.0			Total Liabilties & Net Worth	100.0	100.0
						INCOME DATA		
100.0	100.0	100.0	100.0			Net Sales	100.0	100.0
						Gross Profit		
97.0	95.4	96.2	90.2			Operating Expenses	95.4	90.3
3.0	4.6	3.8	9.8			Operating Profit	4.6	9.7
.3	2.4	2.1	2.1			All Other Expenses (net)	2.2	2.0
2.7	2.2	1.7	7.7			Profit Before Taxes	2.4	7.7
						RATIOS		
1.6	6.6	1.9	2.0				1.8	2.0
1.0	1.1	1.2	1.4			Current	1.1	1.2
.2	.7	.7	1.0				.7	.6
1.2	.7	.6	.5				.7	.5
(18) .9	.1	(37) .1	.2			Quick	(132) .2	(158) .2
.1	.0	.0	.0				.0	.0
0 UND	0 UND	0 UND	0 UND				0 UND	0 UND
0 UND	0 UND	0 UND	9 40.3			Sales/Receivables	0 UND	0 UND
0 UND	0 UND	1 272.1	33 11.2				19 19.3	11 33.5
						Cost of Sales/Inventory		
						Cost of Sales/Payables		
24.0	3.5	4.3	2.6				4.3	3.5
UND	45.9	17.3	7.1			Sales/Working Capital	40.3	16.1
-2.3	-5.8	-7.2	157.2				-8.3	-7.1
5.9	4.5	5.3	11.3				4.5	5.9
(15) 1.1	(28) 1.3	(36) 1.6	(37) 3.7			EBIT/Interest	(122) 1.1	(140) 2.5
-5.0	-.7	-.9	.9				-1.2	1.1
							8.0	6.7
						Net Profit + Depr., Dep., Amort./Cur. Mat. L/T/D	(15) 2.3	(14) 2.5
							.8	.9
.0	.9	.4	.4				.4	.5
2.2	1.3	1.1	.8			Fixed/Worth	1.1	1.2
-2.0	UND	3.3	2.6				3.4	4.0
1.4	.3	1.0	.9				.7	.6
11.2	2.2	1.7	1.8			Debt/Worth	1.7	1.6
-2.8	-231.8	6.4	3.1				8.9	5.9
103.5	25.2	13.6	21.0				18.3	25.4
(13) 5.5	(27) 7.5	(31) 2.9	(36) 7.9			% Profit Before Taxes/Tangible Net Worth	(105) 2.7	(132) 7.5
-55.1	-2.7	-2.5	.7				-6.4	1.0
14.3	4.9	7.0	9.0				5.9	10.2
3.1	1.3	1.2	3.1			% Profit Before Taxes/Total Assets	.7	3.0
-10.9	-2.3	-3.2	-.2				-5.1	.1
UND	3.7	16.5	14.0				16.4	6.3
30.5	1.2	1.5	4.6			Sales/Net Fixed Assets	2.6	1.5
4.2	.3	.5	.6				.8	.6
8.0	1.4	1.3	1.4				1.9	1.5
2.5	.7	.7	.6			Sales/Total Assets	1.0	.7
1.4	.3	.3	.2				.4	.4
	1.5	2.5	.6				1.0	1.6
	(31) 6.3	(29) 7.6	(34) 2.6			% Depr., Dep., Amort./Sales	(113) 4.5	(129) 5.4
	16.2	13.0	9.5				13.0	12.7
							.8	1.6
						% Officers', Directors' Owners' Comp/Sales	(42) 2.0	(31) 3.1
							4.6	7.5
17125M	72522M	180641M	1126911M	129607M	2303444M	Net Sales ($)	1211848M	2419362M
4105M	42627M	171142M	841037M	87907M	989654M	Total Assets ($)	1243164M	1868687M

M = $ thousand MM = $ million

See Pages 9 through 22 for Explanation of Ratios and Data

Comparative Historical Data				Current Data Sorted by Sales					
			Type of Statement						
8	6	7	Unqualified	1	1		2	1	2
28	19	18	Reviewed	1		3	4	6	4
16	19	14	Compiled	2	3	3		5	1
48	50	63	Tax Returns	30	18	6	4	2	3
43	46	39	Other	7	10	6	4	3	9
4/1/11-3/31/12 ALL	4/1/12-3/31/13 ALL	4/1/13-3/31/14 ALL		18 (4/1-9/30/13)			123 (10/1/13-3/31/14)		
				0-1MM	1-3MM	3-5MM	5-10MM	10-25MM	25MM & OVER
143	140	141	**NUMBER OF STATEMENTS**	41	32	18	14	17	19
%	%	%	**ASSETS**	%	%	%	%	%	%
6.8	7.2	8.9	Cash & Equivalents	18.5	3.5	11.9	4.1	4.4	2.4
4.7	4.5	5.0	Trade Receivables (net)	.0	3.4	9.0	4.9	8.4	12.0
31.3	27.5	27.1	Inventory	10.8	24.9	22.6	45.8	45.1	40.1
5.2	5.6	3.2	All Other Current	5.3	1.4	1.6	3.5	5.2	1.6
47.9	44.8	44.3	Total Current	34.5	33.2	45.0	58.4	63.1	56.0
44.8	44.4	44.9	Fixed Assets (net)	55.8	58.7	42.0	33.0	22.5	29.3
.5	1.7	2.1	Intangibles (net)	3.4	1.4	.2	.2	5.0	1.4
6.8	9.1	8.7	All Other Non-Current	6.3	6.7	12.8	8.3	9.4	13.3
100.0	100.0	100.0	Total	100.0	100.0	100.0	100.0	100.0	100.0
			LIABILITIES						
26.4	25.9	27.9	Notes Payable-Short Term	25.6	22.3	21.3	33.6	34.9	38.4
3.9	4.1	3.3	Cur. Mat.-L.T.D.	2.4	5.6	1.7	4.0	3.7	1.9
3.1	3.5	3.1	Trade Payables	2.9	.5	1.7	3.6	2.3	10.0
.4	.3	.4	Income Taxes Payable	.0	.0	1.4	.0	1.1	.5
6.7	10.6	7.3	All Other Current	12.5	2.6	7.0	8.5	5.8	4.6
40.4	44.3	42.0	Total Current	43.3	31.1	33.2	49.8	47.8	55.4
20.2	21.4	30.3	Long-Term Debt	38.3	42.2	22.4	14.9	13.3	26.7
.1	.3	.2	Deferred Taxes	.2	.2	.3	.0	.3	.4
4.0	4.2	3.5	All Other Non-Current	5.6	2.6	4.8	1.1	1.2	2.7
35.3	29.7	24.0	Net Worth	12.5	23.9	39.3	34.2	37.4	14.8
100.0	100.0	100.0	Total Liabilties & Net Worth	100.0	100.0	100.0	100.0	100.0	100.0
			INCOME DATA						
100.0	100.0	100.0	Net Sales	100.0	100.0	100.0	100.0	100.0	100.0
			Gross Profit						
89.1	92.0	94.5	Operating Expenses	93.8	92.1	92.9	97.0	96.0	98.1
10.9	8.0	5.5	Operating Profit	6.2	7.9	7.1	3.0	4.0	1.9
3.2	2.4	1.8	All Other Expenses (net)	3.4	3.2	1.1	-.2	-.3	.3
7.7	5.6	3.7	Profit Before Taxes	2.7	4.8	6.0	3.2	4.3	1.6
			RATIOS						
2.3	2.1	2.1		4.7	1.9	3.8	1.7	1.9	2.0
1.3	1.3	1.2	Current	1.1	1.1	1.4	1.3	1.4	1.3
.8	.7	.8		.4	.7	.7	1.0	1.0	1.0
.6	.6	.9		1.2	.4	1.9	.4	.5	.7
(142) .1	(139) .1	(138) .2	Quick	(40) .4	(31) .1	.4	(13) .1	.2	.3
.0	.0	.0		.0	.0	.0	.0	.1	.0
0 UND	0 UND	0 UND		0 UND	0 UND	0 UND	0 UND	0 UND	2 155.4
0 UND	0 UND	0 UND	Sales/Receivables	0 UND	0 UND	0 UND	0 UND	17 21.7	13 29.0
8 45.1	9 41.0	6 56.2		0 UND	0 UND	5 77.1	37 9.8	31 11.8	32 11.4
			Cost of Sales/Inventory						
			Cost of Sales/Payables						
2.6	4.7	3.8		3.5	4.4	1.7	4.7	2.9	5.4
9.6	15.4	20.2	Sales/Working Capital	64.2	100.2	15.8	10.9	10.7	15.1
-14.0	-11.3	-8.4		-2.1	-4.4	-38.0	NM	358.4	157.2
10.7	7.0	6.2		6.1	3.1	7.1	7.1	11.3	9.9
(120) 3.6	(119) 2.4	(121) 2.1	EBIT/Interest	(27) 1.2	(31) 1.6	(16) 1.9	3.7	2.4	(16) 5.3
1.2	.4	-.2		-1.2	.4	-1.2	.5	-1.2	-1.0
8.2	14.4	11.6							
(12) 4.2	(13) 5.7	(12) 4.6	Net Profit + Depr., Dep., Amort./Cur. Mat. L/T/D						
1.7	.7	3.5							
.3	.4	.4		.9	.9	.3	.3	.1	.3
.9	1.2	1.2	Fixed/Worth	2.4	1.8	1.2	.6	.5	1.1
2.1	3.9	4.8		-10.3	NM	2.6	2.1	1.9	2.7
.6	.5	.8		.5	.5	.3	1.2	1.1	1.4
1.5	1.5	2.2	Debt/Worth	4.6	1.6	1.5	2.1	1.8	2.4
4.4	8.7	13.3		-7.2	-203.9	3.0	6.4	4.2	3.8
33.1	22.1	21.5		28.6	9.5	17.6	24.3	18.0	43.2
(124) 12.1	(112) 8.0	(112) 6.1	% Profit Before Taxes/Tangible Net Worth	(28) 3.3	(23) 4.0	(17) 10.6	(13) 13.6	(15) 4.4	(16) 12.4
1.1	.1	-2.5		-3.2	-2.4	-5.5	4.4	-20.0	-4.2
10.5	8.4	8.0		10.9	3.4	9.3	7.9	7.3	12.7
4.0	3.5	1.7	% Profit Before Taxes/Total Assets	1.3	1.4	2.7	3.4	2.3	5.0
-.6	-1.1	-2.3		-2.8	-1.7	-4.2	-.1	-6.8	-1.4
10.8	17.2	14.9		16.5	3.2	21.1	22.1	105.1	14.5
1.8	2.7	2.8	Sales/Net Fixed Assets	1.0	1.3	1.3	4.6	15.3	8.7
.6	.6	.7		.2	.9	.6	1.1	4.7	3.1
1.6	1.8	1.8		1.3	1.7	2.8	1.5	1.8	3.1
.8	.8	.9	Sales/Total Assets	.4	.9	.5	1.1	.9	1.4
.3	.4	.4		.2	.5	.3	.6	.6	1.1
1.6	1.2	1.5		4.9	1.9	3.7		.4	.2
(108) 5.5	(101) 5.1	(106) 5.4	% Depr., Dep., Amort./Sales	(29) 9.2	(26) 7.5	(15) 6.5		(12) 1.8	(15) .7
15.4	11.6	13.0		26.0	13.0	12.6		11.0	1.3
.6	.8	.8							
(28) 1.3	(36) 3.1	(30) 4.1	% Officers', Directors' Owners' Comp/Sales						
3.4	7.7	8.1							
1898162M	1857381M	3830250M	Net Sales ($)	15310M	54517M	68509M	103489M	283083M	3305342M
1644625M	1672057M	2136472M	Total Assets ($)	52375M	132779M	143336M	144350M	297039M	1366593M

M = $ thousand MM = $ million

See Pages 9 through 22 for Explanation of Ratios and Data

Current Data Sorted by Assets							Comparative Historical Data	
						Type of Statement		
		2	10	5	7	Unqualified	40	40
		6	16	3	3	Reviewed	51	52
	7	9	7	1	2	Compiled	32	33
3	1	2	1			Tax Returns	18	23
2	5	11	24	7	8	Other	57	70
	38 (4/1-9/30/13)		104 (10/1/13-3/31/14)				4/1/09-3/31/10 ALL	4/1/10-3/31/11 ALL
0-500M	**500M-2MM**	**2-10MM**	**10-50MM**	**50-100MM**	**100-250MM**			
5	13	30	58	16	20	**NUMBER OF STATEMENTS**	198	218
%	%	%	%	%	%	**ASSETS**	%	%
	4.0	2.1	5.1	4.9	5.2	Cash & Equivalents	4.8	4.4
	24.6	19.1	15.2	12.5	15.0	Trade Receivables (net)	15.7	14.5
	35.2	43.7	44.0	57.6	47.3	Inventory	40.5	42.5
	1.1	5.3	8.2	5.7	9.3	All Other Current	6.0	7.4
	64.9	70.2	72.5	80.7	76.8	Total Current	67.0	68.8
	25.7	25.4	20.7	15.3	16.3	Fixed Assets (net)	24.2	23.8
	2.8	.1	1.4	.0	.4	Intangibles (net)	.2	.6
	6.6	4.3	5.4	4.0	6.6	All Other Non-Current	8.6	6.8
	100.0	100.0	100.0	100.0	100.0	Total	100.0	100.0
						LIABILITIES		
	27.3	33.5	39.3	38.5	35.0	Notes Payable-Short Term	38.8	36.7
	1.3	2.4	1.0	1.0	.8	Cur. Mat.-L.T.D.	2.0	2.5
	17.6	8.2	5.5	5.5	4.9	Trade Payables	6.3	7.2
	1.1	.4	.7	.0	.2	Income Taxes Payable	.2	.2
	5.0	7.2	8.4	10.0	3.3	All Other Current	6.9	7.1
	52.2	51.7	55.0	55.0	44.2	Total Current	54.1	53.7
	15.0	14.4	10.6	8.1	8.2	Long-Term Debt	14.9	17.8
	.8	.2	.2	.0	.8	Deferred Taxes	.4	.3
	.5	3.6	1.4	1.6	2.1	All Other Non-Current	4.4	4.4
	31.5	30.2	32.9	35.2	44.8	Net Worth	26.1	23.9
	100.0	100.0	100.0	100.0	100.0	Total Liabilties & Net Worth	100.0	100.0
						INCOME DATA		
	100.0	100.0	100.0	100.0	100.0	Net Sales	100.0	100.0
						Gross Profit		
	98.3	100.1	94.8	99.8	96.8	Operating Expenses	97.1	92.5
	1.7	-.1	5.2	.2	3.2	Operating Profit	2.9	7.5
	.3	.5	.8	.3	-.3	All Other Expenses (net)	1.6	1.9
	1.4	-.7	4.4	-.1	3.5	Profit Before Taxes	1.3	5.5
						RATIOS		
	2.2	1.8	1.6	1.6	1.9		1.7	2.0
	1.2	1.2	1.2	1.4	1.6	Current	1.2	1.3
	.8	1.0	1.1	1.2	1.3		1.0	1.1
	1.6	.8	.6	.5	.9		.7	.7
	.5	(29) .3	(56) .2	.3	.4	Quick	(196) .2	(217) .3
	.4	.1	.1	.1	.1		.1	.1
	0 UND	**1** 357.7	**1** 298.0	**12** 31.2	**6** 57.0		**4** 102.4	**1** 359.2
	21 17.1	**10** 34.8	**12** 31.3	**19** 18.9	**24** 15.2	Sales/Receivables	**17** 21.0	**16** 22.8
	32 11.3	**55** 6.6	**43** 8.5	**63** 5.8	**62** 5.9		**45** 8.2	**45** 8.1
						Cost of Sales/Inventory		
						Cost of Sales/Payables		
	11.4	4.6	4.5	4.3	3.7		5.2	3.4
	51.0	17.2	10.3	6.0	6.1	Sales/Working Capital	11.3	9.1
	-313.3	NM	41.6	11.2	10.9		156.8	52.4
	17.7	4.7	7.4	4.4	10.2		5.5	7.5
	(11) 5.8	(29) 1.2	(55) 3.6	.1	(18) 5.7	EBIT/Interest	(190) 1.6	(201) 3.5
	-1.2	-1.4	.3	-7.5	3.0		-.5	1.4
			10.8				6.5	10.0
			(10) 3.1			Net Profit + Depr., Dep., Amort./Cur. Mat. L/T/D	(19) 1.8	(27) 6.8
			-.4				.2	1.7
	.2	.2	.2	.2	.1		.2	.2
	.6	.9	.5	.5	.2	Fixed/Worth	.6	.5
	NM	2.2	1.2	.8	.7		1.4	1.3
	.5	1.3	1.1	1.5	.8		1.0	.9
	5.0	2.4	2.4	1.9	1.6	Debt/Worth	2.5	2.5
	NM	7.7	5.8	3.2	2.9		5.4	6.3
	56.3	21.8	25.6	11.0	19.4		22.4	29.1
	(10) 15.0	(29) 5.2	(53) 10.9	-3.8	14.5	% Profit Before Taxes/Tangible Net Worth	(176) 5.8	(191) 15.9
	-29.7	-12.2	-4.6	-25.9	5.0		-7.0	5.2
	15.6	6.0	7.9	2.9	8.6		6.8	8.9
	8.7	.6	4.6	-1.9	4.3	% Profit Before Taxes/Total Assets	1.5	4.9
	-.8	-4.3	-1.0	-5.7	2.5		-3.2	.7
	150.1	92.5	33.8	31.4	28.6		29.0	38.9
	17.0	15.8	12.3	10.3	15.6	Sales/Net Fixed Assets	10.5	10.9
	5.8	4.1	5.8	4.6	8.6		3.8	3.9
	6.3	3.0	2.2	2.6	2.1		2.3	2.1
	3.7	2.0	1.7	1.4	1.7	Sales/Total Assets	1.6	1.4
	1.9	1.3	1.0	1.1	1.0		.9	.8
		.3	.6	.7	.4		.7	.8
		(25) 1.0	(51) 1.0	(14) 1.0	(15) .8	% Depr., Dep., Amort./Sales	(167) 1.5	(174) 1.4
		2.7	1.4	1.7	1.4		3.1	3.3
			.3				.4	.4
			(11) 1.1			% Officers', Directors' Owners' Comp/Sales	(44) 1.0	(39) 1.2
			2.6				3.7	3.6
8029M	**96581M**	**892392M**	**2768834M**	**1937908M**	**8248726M**	Net Sales ($)	**9641184M**	**8607918M**
1110M	**15953M**	**179221M**	**1471640M**	**1112835M**	**3036373M**	Total Assets ($)	**5784216M**	**6227457M**

M = $ thousand MM = $ million

See Pages 9 through 22 for Explanation of Ratios and Data

Comparative Historical Data				Current Data Sorted by Sales					
			Type of Statement						
37	31	24	Unqualified					3	21
48	34	28	Reviewed			1	1	8	18
30	32	26	Compiled	1		2	8	5	10
25	13	7	Tax Returns	3	1	1	1		1
64	67	57	Other	1	5	4	4	12	31
4/1/11-3/31/12 ALL	**4/1/12-3/31/13 ALL**	**4/1/13-3/31/14 ALL**		**38 (4/1-9/30/13)**			**104 (10/1/13-3/31/14)**		
				0-1MM	**1-3MM**	**3-5MM**	**5-10MM**	**10-25MM**	**25MM & OVER**
204	177	142	**NUMBER OF STATEMENTS**	5	6	8	14	28	81
%	%	%	**ASSETS**	%	%	%	%	%	%
4.6	5.1	5.1	Cash & Equivalents				-1.0	7.0	4.6
17.2	18.4	16.1	Trade Receivables (net)				13.3	19.1	17.1
43.4	43.9	43.9	Inventory				57.9	37.6	48.1
8.0	6.6	6.6	All Other Current				2.0	5.5	8.2
73.1	74.0	71.8	Total Current				72.1	69.2	78.1
20.3	20.0	21.1	Fixed Assets (net)				21.2	25.6	15.9
1.2	.9	.9	Intangibles (net)				.0	2.9	.1
5.2	5.1	6.2	All Other Non-Current				6.7	2.3	5.9
100.0	100.0	100.0	Total				100.0	100.0	100.0
			LIABILITIES						
37.0	35.4	35.2	Notes Payable-Short Term				41.2	38.5	36.1
2.0	1.0	1.9	Cur. Mat.-L.T.D.				.6	2.2	1.0
8.0	8.9	7.0	Trade Payables				4.9	8.2	6.7
.4	.3	.5	Income Taxes Payable				.6	1.0	.2
7.5	7.1	8.5	All Other Current				2.7	10.3	7.8
54.8	52.6	53.1	Total Current				49.9	60.1	52.0
12.1	9.9	12.2	Long-Term Debt				8.6	9.1	8.8
.3	.2	.3	Deferred Taxes				.7	.2	.3
2.9	3.0	1.8	All Other Non-Current				1.7	2.9	1.4
29.9	34.3	32.6	Net Worth				39.1	27.7	37.5
100.0	100.0	100.0	Total Liabilties & Net Worth				100.0	100.0	100.0
			INCOME DATA						
100.0	100.0	100.0	Net Sales				100.0	100.0	100.0
			Gross Profit						
93.1	95.9	97.6	Operating Expenses				91.5	96.5	98.4
6.9	4.1	2.4	Operating Profit				8.5	3.5	1.6
1.2	.9	.5	All Other Expenses (net)				-.6	.2	.1
5.6	3.1	1.8	Profit Before Taxes				9.1	3.3	1.4
			RATIOS						
1.7	1.8	1.8					2.3	1.4	1.8
1.3	1.3	1.3	Current				1.5	1.1	1.4
1.1	1.1	1.1					1.1	.8	1.2
.8	.8	.8					.9	.7	.9
(176) .3	(139) .4	.3	Quick				(11) .5	.3	.3
.1	.1	.1					.1	.1	.1
3 132.9	1 337.8	2 183.8					0 UND	2 224.2	6 66.2
18 20.3	18 20.2	15 24.7	Sales/Receivables				17 22.1	17 21.3	16 23.2
48 7.6	51 7.1	49 7.4					43 8.4	59 6.2	40 9.1
			Cost of Sales/Inventory						
			Cost of Sales/Payables						
5.1	4.9	4.7					1.6	5.8	4.7
10.6	10.7	10.4	Sales/Working Capital				8.1	44.9	9.5
39.8	39.2	50.2					51.5	-14.8	17.8
9.9	9.0	7.5					17.5	11.1	7.1
(186) 4.3	(162) 3.4	(132) 3.6	EBIT/Interest				(13) 5.6	(27) 3.8	(77) 3.3
1.7	.9	-.3					1.8	-1.5	-.5
12.1	18.9	9.2							9.3
(30) 5.7	(31) 3.8	(27) 4.1	Net Profit + Depr., Dep., Amort./Cur. Mat. L/T/D						(20) 3.8
2.6	1.5	-.2							-2.8
.1	.1	.2					.2	.3	.1
.5	.5	.5	Fixed/Worth				.5	.9	.4
1.1	1.0	1.0					.9	2.6	.7
1.0	1.0	1.0					.5	1.2	1.0
2.5	2.2	2.1	Debt/Worth				1.9	3.7	2.1
5.4	5.1	5.1					5.4	32.7	3.2
36.5	26.1	21.9					47.0	28.0	20.0
(183) 18.5	(165) 12.4	(131) 10.1	% Profit Before Taxes/Tangible Net Worth				19.9	(23) 10.4	(80) 10.3
6.0	.0	-6.7					7.5	-5.1	-8.6
10.5	9.2	8.7					12.6	10.1	7.3
5.9	3.8	3.5	% Profit Before Taxes/Total Assets				7.7	3.5	3.6
1.6	-.1	-2.4					.9	-4.0	-2.4
38.6	47.9	39.0					63.4	30.1	44.5
14.0	15.7	13.8	Sales/Net Fixed Assets				9.2	11.2	16.5
6.8	6.4	5.3					3.4	3.4	8.7
2.6	2.7	2.7					3.7	2.3	2.7
1.8	1.8	1.8	Sales/Total Assets				1.5	1.6	1.9
1.1	1.2	1.1					.9	1.1	1.3
.6	.5	.5					.4	.9	.4
(163) 1.1	(131) 1.0	(117) 1.0	% Depr., Dep., Amort./Sales				(11) .7	(23) 1.3	(70) .8
1.9	1.7	1.7					1.3	2.7	1.3
.3	.3	.2							.1
(44) .9	(39) .8	(24) .9	% Officers', Directors' Owners' Comp/Sales						(15) .4
2.0	3.0	2.6							2.3
11006120M	16489229M	13952470M	Net Sales ($)	2818M	10507M	33465M	100504M	483928M	13321248M
6396847M	6658806M	5817132M	Total Assets ($)	9621M	14794M	50376M	173652M	380317M	5188372M

M = $ thousand MM = $ million

See Pages 9 through 22 for Explanation of Ratios and Data

Current Data Sorted by Assets							Comparative Historical Data	
						Type of Statement		
			2	6	5	Unqualified	17	13
	3	57	147	16	7	Reviewed	354	448
	5	38	25	2	1	Compiled	103	102
5	18	14	2			Tax Returns	44	42
3	8	26	52	9	2	Other	68	80
	31 (4/1-9/30/13)		422 (10/1/13-3/31/14)				4/1/09-3/31/10 ALL	4/1/10-3/31/11 ALL
0-500M	500M-2MM	2-10MM	10-50MM	50-100MM	100-250MM			
8	34	135	228	33	15	**NUMBER OF STATEMENTS**	586	685
%	%	%	%	%	%	**ASSETS**	%	%
	4.8	1.7	1.3	.7	1.8	Cash & Equivalents	1.6	1.5
	4.2	6.5	8.3	7.2	17.0	Trade Receivables (net)	5.5	6.2
	14.5	14.4	14.6	14.5	12.7	Inventory	11.1	11.4
	1.3	1.8	1.7	2.3	.7	All Other Current	2.6	2.8
	24.7	24.3	25.9	24.7	32.2	Total Current	20.8	21.9
	61.8	64.0	62.7	66.0	59.1	Fixed Assets (net)	67.0	65.9
	1.6	.7	1.3	1.9	.3	Intangibles (net)	1.0	1.2
	11.8	11.0	10.1	7.4	8.4	All Other Non-Current	11.2	11.0
	100.0	100.0	100.0	100.0	100.0	Total	100.0	100.0
						LIABILITIES		
	16.5	12.1	12.8	13.9	12.7	Notes Payable-Short Term	14.8	13.8
	5.6	4.7	4.6	3.7	3.5	Cur. Mat.-L.T.D.	6.1	7.0
	2.6	5.9	4.9	5.2	4.4	Trade Payables	4.4	4.4
	.0	.0	.0	.0	.0	Income Taxes Payable	.0	.0
	9.6	3.7	3.0	2.1	6.5	All Other Current	3.1	3.6
	34.4	26.4	25.3	24.9	27.1	Total Current	28.5	28.9
	75.6	38.2	36.5	40.4	37.2	Long-Term Debt	48.7	45.2
	.0	.1	.2	.5	.4	Deferred Taxes	.2	.1
	8.0	5.5	3.2	.7	.9	All Other Non-Current	4.4	5.6
	-18.0	29.8	34.9	33.5	34.3	Net Worth	18.2	20.1
	100.0	100.0	100.0	100.0	100.0	Total Liabilties & Net Worth	100.0	100.0
						INCOME DATA		
	100.0	100.0	100.0	100.0	100.0	Net Sales	100.0	100.0
						Gross Profit		
	93.6	92.3	89.7	87.5	91.2	Operating Expenses	110.1	88.7
	6.4	7.7	10.3	12.5	8.8	Operating Profit	-10.1	11.3
	1.4	3.8	3.4	2.9	1.2	All Other Expenses (net)	7.3	5.8
	4.9	3.9	6.9	9.6	7.6	Profit Before Taxes	-17.4	5.4
						RATIOS		
	2.2	1.4	1.6	1.6	1.4		1.2	1.2
	1.0	.9	1.1	1.1	1.1	Current	.8	.8
	.2	.6	.8	.7	.9		.5	.5
	1.1	.5	.7	.6	1.0		.4	.4
	.3	.3	(227) .3	.3	.6	Quick	.2	.2
	.1	.2	.2	.2	.3		.1	.1
	0 UND	9 42.7	19 19.7	21 17.7	22 16.9		18 20.1	16 23.0
	0 UND	20 17.9	28 13.1	29 12.8	33 11.2	Sales/Receivables	24 14.9	23 16.0
	12 30.6	32 11.3	39 9.3	38 9.6	83 4.4		40 9.1	33 11.2
						Cost of Sales/Inventory		
						Cost of Sales/Payables		
	7.7	12.4	7.9	7.2	9.0		19.4	20.0
	NM	-52.0	45.5	33.0	39.8	Sales/Working Capital	-11.4	-19.5
	-7.2	-10.6	-14.0	-9.6	-49.6		-4.1	-5.6
	4.2	5.4	7.6	5.3	9.2		-.4	4.4
	(28) .8	(123) 2.9	(222) 3.8	(31) 3.7	(14) 4.1	EBIT/Interest	(555) -2.5	(648) 2.3
	-.7	.4	1.7	2.7	2.0		-5.8	1.2
							2.6	3.2
						Net Profit + Depr., Dep., Amort./Cur. Mat. L/T/D	(26) .2	(28) 1.9
							-1.0	.9
	1.0	1.3	1.2	1.6	1.1		1.5	1.5
	3.9	2.1	1.8	2.1	1.7	Fixed/Worth	2.9	2.7
	-2.6	5.2	3.2	3.3	2.9		9.8	7.6
	.4	1.1	1.0	1.3	1.4		1.5	1.3
	3.5	2.2	2.0	2.0	1.9	Debt/Worth	3.3	2.9
	-6.9	7.3	3.8	3.8	3.2		13.5	11.1
	37.8	35.5	24.1	22.5	17.2		-6.0	27.6
	(23) -.7	(120) 11.1	(207) 13.4	(32) 18.0	13.4	% Profit Before Taxes/Tangible Net Worth	(474) -29.1	(561) 13.3
	-29.5	-1.9	4.8	8.7	4.8		-71.1	3.7
	7.0	7.6	8.5	7.8	6.4		-3.1	7.8
	-1.1	3.7	4.2	5.9	5.4	% Profit Before Taxes/Total Assets	-10.0	3.5
	-5.4	-1.0	1.3	3.0	.8		-16.4	.4
	9.5	2.2	1.6	1.3	3.7		1.3	1.6
	2.8	1.6	1.2	1.0	.9	Sales/Net Fixed Assets	.8	1.0
	1.2	.9	.9	.7	.8		.6	.7
	2.6	1.2	1.0	.9	1.5		.7	.9
	1.5	.9	.8	.7	.6	Sales/Total Assets	.5	.7
	.9	.7	.6	.4	.5		.4	.5
	2.0	5.4	5.4	3.3	1.6		9.0	6.9
	(30) 6.0	(128) 7.9	(217) 7.2	(32) 5.9	(12) 8.2	% Depr., Dep., Amort./Sales	(555) 12.5	(644) 10.1
	11.8	10.4	9.3	8.4	10.2		16.4	12.9
		.8	.5				.7	.6
		(28) 1.5	(52) .8			% Officers', Directors' Owners' Comp/Sales	(137) 1.5	(146) 1.3
		4.4	1.3				2.9	2.3
17597M	72526M	819724M	4127266M	1763604M	3306681M	Net Sales ($)	8143166M	9943738M
2664M	38902M	801318M	4874945M	2259207M	2082008M	Total Assets ($)	11505553M	13611475M

M = $ thousand MM = $ million

See Pages 9 through 22 for Explanation of Ratios and Data

Comparative Historical Data				Current Data Sorted by Sales					
			Type of Statement						
14	12	13	Unqualified					1	12
413	289	230	Reviewed	1	14	14	54	101	46
108	90	71	Compiled	4	10	12	24	16	5
46	32	39	Tax Returns	10	17	6		6	
64	121	100	Other	7	13	6	21	36	17
4/1/11-3/31/12 ALL	**4/1/12-3/31/13 ALL**	**4/1/13-3/31/14 ALL**		**31 (4/1-9/30/13)**			**422 (10/1/13-3/31/14)**		
				0-1MM	**1-3MM**	**3-5MM**	**5-10MM**	**10-25MM**	**25MM & OVER**
645	544	453	**NUMBER OF STATEMENTS**	22	54	38	99	160	80
%	%	%	**ASSETS**	%	%	%	%	%	%
1.6	1.8	1.9	Cash & Equivalents	2.7	4.9	2.6	1.4	1.1	1.7
8.0	7.2	7.6	Trade Receivables (net)	.7	5.7	4.7	7.7	7.9	11.2
13.3	14.1	14.2	Inventory	3.3	12.7	10.7	16.1	15.5	15.2
3.0	2.3	1.7	All Other Current	.9	1.6	1.4	1.8	1.6	1.9
26.0	25.4	25.4	Total Current	7.6	24.9	19.3	27.1	26.1	30.0
63.0	63.8	63.1	Fixed Assets (net)	85.4	61.6	68.8	61.4	61.1	61.4
.9	.5	1.2	Intangibles (net)	2.7	1.4	.9	.9	1.4	1.1
10.1	10.3	10.2	All Other Non-Current	4.2	12.1	11.0	10.6	11.4	7.5
100.0	100.0	100.0	Total	100.0	100.0	100.0	100.0	100.0	100.0
			LIABILITIES						
12.9	14.6	13.8	Notes Payable-Short Term	4.1	10.1	17.2	16.3	14.0	13.9
6.3	5.6	4.8	Cur. Mat.-L.T.D.	9.7	3.8	6.0	4.9	4.6	4.0
5.0	6.3	4.9	Trade Payables	.6	2.8	3.7	6.7	4.3	7.4
.0	.0	.0	Income Taxes Payable	.0	.0	.0	.0	.0	.0
3.0	3.9	3.8	All Other Current	1.1	7.5	3.4	3.0	3.3	4.0
27.4	30.5	27.3	Total Current	15.6	24.2	30.3	30.9	26.1	29.3
42.4	40.7	41.7	Long-Term Debt	66.9	56.0	54.2	38.1	35.5	35.9
.2	.1	.2	Deferred Taxes	.0	.0	.3	.2	.1	.3
5.1	3.0	3.9	All Other Non-Current	2.5	6.4	1.8	6.6	3.1	1.9
24.9	25.8	26.9	Net Worth	15.0	13.4	13.4	24.1	35.1	32.6
100.0	100.0	100.0	Total Liabilties & Net Worth	100.0	100.0	100.0	100.0	100.0	100.0
			INCOME DATA						
100.0	100.0	100.0	Net Sales	100.0	100.0	100.0	100.0	100.0	100.0
			Gross Profit						
85.5	94.6	90.7	Operating Expenses	72.2	93.4	93.2	91.8	90.6	91.4
14.5	5.4	9.3	Operating Profit	27.8	6.6	6.8	8.2	9.4	8.6
4.3	3.8	3.3	All Other Expenses (net)	13.8	4.1	5.1	2.5	2.3	2.0
10.2	1.6	6.0	Profit Before Taxes	14.0	2.5	1.7	5.6	7.1	6.7
			RATIOS						
1.5	1.3	1.6		1.3	2.5	1.4	1.5	1.7	1.6
1.0	.9	1.0	Current	.4	1.1	.9	1.0	1.1	1.1
.7	.7	.7		.1	.5	.6	.7	.8	.8
.6	.5	.6		.4	1.1	.4	.5	.7	.7
(643) .3	.3	(452) .3	Quick	.1	.4	.3	(98) .3	.3	.4
.2	.2	.2		.0	.1	.2	.2	.2	.2
15 24.2	**17** 22.0	**15** 23.6		**0** UND	**0** UND	**8** 43.6	**19** 19.3	**17** 21.0	**20** 18.7
26 14.2	**23** 16.2	**22** 16.6	Sales/Receivables	**0** UND	**14** 26.5	**18** 19.8	**26** 13.8	**23** 15.6	**29** 12.8
39 9.3	**36** 10.2	**35** 10.5		**0** UND	**34** 10.7	**34** 10.6	**33** 10.9	**36** 10.1	**38** 9.6
			Cost of Sales/Inventory						
			Cost of Sales/Payables						
9.5	13.2	8.5		13.2	5.6	15.9	10.5	8.1	9.4
999.8	-41.4	417.3	Sales/Working Capital	-16.6	75.3	-29.1	-53.2	48.0	40.2
-10.1	-8.6	-11.2		-2.1	-10.7	-6.2	-12.1	-14.1	-14.5
7.7	3.2	6.4		2.9	7.3	3.9	6.4	7.7	6.8
(612) 4.2	(519) 1.4	(425) 3.2	EBIT/Interest	(13) 1.7	(45) 1.2	(35) 2.5	(97) 3.2	(158) 3.8	(77) 3.8
2.1	-.5	1.3		-.3	-.5	.1	1.3	1.8	2.2
5.9	3.2	4.2							4.7
(32) 3.0	(21) 1.7	(21) 2.7	Net Profit + Depr., Dep., Amort./Cur. Mat. L/T/D						(10) 3.0
1.1	.8	1.8							2.1
1.3	1.3	1.2		1.4	1.0	1.6	1.2	1.2	1.3
2.1	2.2	2.0	Fixed/Worth	3.2	2.3	2.0	2.2	1.7	1.9
4.7	4.5	4.1		NM	NM	5.5	4.7	3.3	3.0
1.2	1.2	1.1		.6	.6	1.2	1.1	.9	1.5
2.3	2.3	2.1	Debt/Worth	3.3	2.5	2.0	2.2	1.9	2.1
5.6	5.2	5.0		NM	NM	6.6	5.9	3.7	3.6
40.3	13.9	25.1		56.4	22.1	18.5	27.6	24.1	24.5
(562) 24.5	(484) 3.1	(399) 13.1	% Profit Before Taxes/Tangible Net Worth	(17) 4.8	(41) 2.2	(31) 10.2	(88) 12.7	(145) 14.4	(77) 18.5
10.9	-7.6	2.7		-.6	-12.6	-4.1	3.0	4.8	6.5
12.5	4.6	8.2		6.1	5.8	5.9	8.6	9.1	8.3
7.7	.8	4.0	% Profit Before Taxes/Total Assets	2.4	.7	3.7	5.1	4.7	5.7
2.9	-3.5	.5		-1.2	-3.6	-2.8	.6	1.5	2.0
2.0	1.9	2.1		1.4	3.4	1.9	2.0	2.0	2.6
1.2	1.2	1.3	Sales/Net Fixed Assets	.2	1.5	1.1	1.5	1.3	1.3
.9	.8	.9		.1	.5	.5	1.0	1.0	.9
1.1	1.0	1.1		.9	1.6	1.1	1.1	1.1	1.2
.8	.7	.8	Sales/Total Assets	.2	1.0	.8	.9	.8	.8
.6	.5	.6		.1	.4	.4	.6	.6	.6
5.6	5.7	5.0		6.2	3.8	5.7	5.3	5.1	3.2
(607) 8.1	(513) 8.3	(424) 7.1	% Depr., Dep., Amort./Sales	(20) 18.7	(47) 8.2	(36) 9.2	(92) 7.4	(152) 6.9	(77) 5.9
10.4	10.9	9.8		29.2	16.7	11.1	9.6	9.1	8.2
.5	.6	.5			3.9		.7	.6	.1
(151) .9	(120) 1.1	(97) 1.0	% Officers', Directors' Owners' Comp/Sales		(10) 4.5		(19) 1.0	(38) 1.0	(18) .3
1.8	2.4	1.9			5.5		1.6	1.3	.8
10985598M	10464691M	10107398M	Net Sales ($)	13645M	109972M	152726M	739362M	2471667M	6620026M
12596237M	11841409M	10059044M	Total Assets ($)	58498M	244729M	283180M	995794M	3250014M	5226829M

M = $ thousand MM = $ million

See Pages 9 through 22 for Explanation of Ratios and Data

Current Data Sorted by Assets / Comparative Historical Data

0-500M	500M-2MM	2-10MM	10-50MM	50-100MM	100-250MM		4/1/09-3/31/10 ALL	4/1/10-3/31/11 ALL
						Type of Statement		
		1			5	Unqualified	9	10
	1	1	2		1	Reviewed	8	9
	3	3	6			Compiled	13	9
5	9	3	1			Tax Returns	18	18
	9	6	8	2	1	Other	23	25
	10 (4/1-9/30/13)		57 (10/1/13-3/31/14)					
5	22	14	17	2	7	**NUMBER OF STATEMENTS**	71	71
%	%	%	%	%	%	**ASSETS**	%	%
	9.4	1.5	3.3			Cash & Equivalents	3.8	3.7
	4.5	3.0	8.3			Trade Receivables (net)	6.1	5.3
	9.2	26.2	38.7			Inventory	30.3	32.1
	1.9	3.4	3.5			All Other Current	2.5	3.7
	24.9	34.0	53.8			Total Current	42.8	44.9
	64.3	52.1	39.1			Fixed Assets (net)	48.8	47.2
	.2	4.4	2.5			Intangibles (net)	2.1	1.1
	10.6	9.5	4.6			All Other Non-Current	6.3	6.9
	100.0	100.0	100.0			Total	100.0	100.0
						LIABILITIES		
	17.1	16.6	38.6			Notes Payable-Short Term	28.4	25.7
	8.0	3.5	3.1			Cur. Mat.-L.T.D.	5.2	5.1
	5.3	1.3	6.8			Trade Payables	8.0	5.1
	.0	1.3	.1			Income Taxes Payable	.2	.1
	6.8	4.6	7.4			All Other Current	4.3	4.1
	37.2	27.4	55.9			Total Current	46.2	40.1
	42.1	24.2	26.8			Long-Term Debt	40.8	34.9
	.0	.3	.0			Deferred Taxes	.4	.2
	.2	2.3	3.3			All Other Non-Current	4.7	4.6
	20.5	45.8	14.0			Net Worth	8.0	20.2
	100.0	100.0	100.0			Total Liabilities & Net Worth	100.0	100.0
						INCOME DATA		
	100.0	100.0	100.0			Net Sales	100.0	100.0
						Gross Profit		
	87.6	90.9	95.3			Operating Expenses	102.9	91.4
	12.4	9.1	4.7			Operating Profit	-2.9	8.6
	1.8	.0	1.7			All Other Expenses (net)	2.4	1.6
	10.7	9.1	3.0			Profit Before Taxes	-5.3	7.0
						RATIOS		
	2.1	2.2	3.3				1.6	2.1
	.4	1.2	1.7			Current	1.2	1.3
	.1	.6	1.0				.6	.8
	1.6	.6	1.1				.5	.4
	.2	.1	(16) .2			Quick	.2	.1
	.1	.1	.1				.1	.0
	0 UND	0 UND	3 110.3				0 UND	0 UND
	0 UND	4 92.6	17 22.0			Sales/Receivables	7 53.8	4 92.8
	3 129.3	23 16.1	42 8.6				19 19.4	18 20.5
						Cost of Sales/Inventory		
						Cost of Sales/Payables		
	18.4	5.2	2.3				7.6	5.5
	-23.9	251.4	7.1			Sales/Working Capital	27.8	13.8
	-2.8	-8.4	NM				-13.6	-16.7
	18.0	15.3	11.9				1.9	8.2
	(21) 7.4	10.2	(16) 1.9			EBIT/Interest	(63) -.1	(67) 3.5
	.7	-.1	-1.9				-6.4	1.2
						Net Profit + Depr., Dep., Amort./Cur. Mat. L/T/D		
	1.0	.7	.5				.9	.7
	1.6	1.3	1.3			Fixed/Worth	1.8	1.3
	-5.2	2.1	NM				-7.1	-7.4
	.6	.4	.5				1.3	1.0
	2.2	1.2	1.5			Debt/Worth	3.6	2.3
	-8.6	2.6	-8.4				-18.3	-10.7
	66.5	27.0	20.6				16.1	39.4
	(14) 26.0	(13) 12.8	(12) 7.6			% Profit Before Taxes/Tangible Net Worth	(51) -1.0	(50) 18.7
	4.1	-8.2	-1.5				-55.9	5.6
	30.1	17.8	9.9				3.0	14.5
	11.0	9.3	1.5			% Profit Before Taxes/Total Assets	-1.5	7.1
	-1.0	-3.3	-9.8				-20.5	.1
	5.2	4.4	18.9				8.6	7.3
	2.4	1.4	2.6			Sales/Net Fixed Assets	3.1	2.9
	1.1	.6	1.1				1.2	1.0
	2.6	1.5	2.0				2.1	2.0
	1.3	.9	1.1			Sales/Total Assets	1.3	1.2
	1.0	.5	.6				.7	.7
	1.7	5.8	3.0				2.2	2.6
	(18) 14.5	(10) 10.0	(10) 6.8			% Depr., Dep., Amort./Sales	(59) 5.0	(60) 5.2
	28.2	16.7	10.6				11.9	8.7
							.6	.5
						% Officers', Directors' Owners' Comp/Sales	(15) 1.5	(15) 2.1
							5.5	4.3
2189M	86553M	82157M	441240M	201037M	1182347M	Net Sales ($)	2009538M	1780641M
1620M	26272M	74346M	341127M	142612M	834113M	Total Assets ($)	1549897M	1473391M

M = $ thousand MM = $ million

See Pages 9 through 22 for Explanation of Ratios and Data

Comparative Historical Data

Current Data Sorted by Sales

			Type of Statement						
12	11	6	Unqualified					1	5
7	6	5	Reviewed				1		4
13	17	12	Compiled	1	2	1	3	3	2
17	26	18	Tax Returns	9	4	4		1	
33	25	26	Other	3	7	3	3	3	7
				10 (4/1-9/30/13)		57 (10/1/13-3/31/14)			
4/1/11-3/31/12 ALL	4/1/12-3/31/13 ALL	4/1/13-3/31/14 ALL		0-1MM	1-3MM	3-5MM	5-10MM	10-25MM	25MM & OVER
82	85	67	NUMBER OF STATEMENTS	13	13	8	7	8	18
%	%	%	**ASSETS**	%	%	%	%	%	%
3.4	7.0	4.9	Cash & Equivalents	3.5	10.8				2.6
5.6	5.4	5.4	Trade Receivables (net)	.1	4.3				12.3
32.2	26.0	25.2	Inventory	15.0	2.7				37.8
2.3	3.2	3.1	All Other Current	.2	.1				7.3
43.4	41.6	38.6	Total Current	18.9	17.8				60.0
45.7	47.9	49.4	Fixed Assets (net)	67.8	66.7				26.2
1.9	1.5	1.7	Intangibles (net)	.3	.1				2.5
9.0	9.0	10.3	All Other Non-Current	13.0	15.3				11.3
100.0	100.0	100.0	Total	100.0	100.0				100.0
			LIABILITIES						
21.6	18.7	25.2	Notes Payable-Short Term	25.5	17.3				41.0
5.5	5.6	4.6	Cur. Mat.-L.T.D.	3.2	9.2				2.8
6.1	5.4	4.5	Trade Payables	.1	1.7				10.1
.3	.3	.3	Income Taxes Payable	.0	.0				.1
8.1	4.0	6.1	All Other Current	3.3	9.0				9.5
41.7	34.0	40.7	Total Current	32.0	37.3				63.5
30.0	38.7	30.6	Long-Term Debt	47.4	34.4				19.0
.1	.1	.1	Deferred Taxes	.0	.0				.1
3.1	5.7	1.7	All Other Non-Current	1.5	.4				3.2
25.1	21.5	26.9	Net Worth	19.1	28.0				14.2
100.0	100.0	100.0	Total Liabilties & Net Worth	100.0	100.0				100.0
			INCOME DATA						
100.0	100.0	100.0	Net Sales	100.0	100.0				100.0
			Gross Profit						
90.9	90.4	91.7	Operating Expenses	85.0	80.0				101.4
9.1	9.6	8.3	Operating Profit	15.0	20.0				-1.4
.5	2.0	1.2	All Other Expenses (net)	4.0	1.0				.5
8.6	7.5	7.2	Profit Before Taxes	11.0	19.0				-1.9
			RATIOS						
2.3	2.2	2.1		1.3	3.2				1.9
1.3	1.3	1.3	Current	.3	.8				1.4
.8	.7	.3		.1	.1				1.0
.5	.8	.7		.8	3.2				.7
.2	.2	(66) .3	Quick	.2	.4				(17) .3
.1	.1	.1		.0	.1				.1
0 UND	0 UND	0 UND		0 UND	0 UND				5 69.6
6 64.9	2 169.3	4 99.6	Sales/Receivables	0 UND	0 UND				20 18.4
18 20.1	16 22.5	22 16.5		0 UND	23 16.0				34 10.6
			Cost of Sales/Inventory						
			Cost of Sales/Payables						
5.4	4.4	5.3		254.4	11.3				6.5
11.7	16.0	17.7	Sales/Working Capital	-8.9	-134.7				13.5
-28.4	-14.3	-8.9		-2.8	-4.1				NM
11.6	10.1	14.1		9.7	19.3				8.8
(79) 5.2	(76) 3.5	(64) 4.6	EBIT/Interest	(12) 2.0	15.6				(17) 2.1
2.5	.9	.0		-.5	5.8				-3.1
6.6									
(12) 3.9			Net Profit + Depr., Dep., Amort./Cur. Mat. L/T/D						
1.2									
.5	.7	.6		1.1	1.0				.1
1.3	1.5	1.2	Fixed/Worth	2.6	1.5				.7
NM	101.6	6.8		-3.1	NM				1.5
.7	.8	.6		.4	.5				.8
1.6	2.0	1.5	Debt/Worth	5.8	1.5				1.3
-360.3	315.9	14.1		-8.4	NM				NM
43.0	36.1	28.6			141.5				15.9
(61) 22.0	(65) 17.4	(51) 12.8	% Profit Before Taxes/Tangible Net Worth		(10) 37.5				(14) 10.8
12.1	4.3	-2.3			13.2				-7.4
18.9	14.4	15.9		13.9	47.9				6.0
9.5	5.4	5.3	% Profit Before Taxes/Total Assets	9.6	15.9				.4
4.3	-1.8	-3.1		-3.3	5.2				-15.3
10.5	10.2	7.4		8.4	2.9				137.4
3.6	3.4	2.7	Sales/Net Fixed Assets	.6	2.3				7.0
1.4	1.1	1.2		.3	1.0				2.8
2.5	2.2	1.9		1.3	1.9				2.5
1.4	1.4	1.2	Sales/Total Assets	.5	1.2				1.6
.9	.6	.8		.2	.9				1.2
2.0	1.4	2.1		3.3					.9
(70) 4.4	(75) 4.7	(52) 6.3	% Depr., Dep., Amort./Sales	(11) 23.1					(13) 2.1
8.8	11.1	15.6		35.9					3.6
.7	1.5	1.3							
(14) 3.5	(17) 2.7	(13) 3.1	% Officers', Directors' Owners' Comp/Sales						
6.1	6.2	6.8							
3449927M	2956544M	1995523M	Net Sales ($)	6340M	23041M	30683M	54421M	118526M	1762512M
2204982M	1956776M	1420090M	Total Assets ($)	13267M	32776M	29969M	67601M	111811M	1164666M

M = $ thousand MM = $ million

See Pages 9 through 22 for Explanation of Ratios and Data

Current Data Sorted by Assets							Comparative Historical Data	
						Type of Statement		
				4	1	Unqualified	14	14
			3	2		Reviewed	7	6
		5	3			Compiled	5	7
1	3	3				Tax Returns	12	12
1	1	6	7	1	2	Other	15	16
	5 (4/1-9/30/13)		38 (10/1/13-3/31/14)				**4/1/09-3/31/10 ALL**	**4/1/10-3/31/11 ALL**
0-500M	**500M-2MM**	**2-10MM**	**10-50MM**	**50-100MM**	**100-250MM**			
2	4	14	13	7	3	**NUMBER OF STATEMENTS**	53	55
%	%	%	%	%	%	**ASSETS**	%	%
		15.0	16.6			Cash & Equivalents	9.8	10.6
		11.7	19.3			Trade Receivables (net)	14.1	14.5
		12.9	17.7			Inventory	16.9	15.8
		.8	2.3			All Other Current	1.9	1.2
		40.4	55.9			Total Current	42.6	42.1
		49.9	34.9			Fixed Assets (net)	48.8	51.0
		.1	.7			Intangibles (net)	1.5	1.8
		9.5	8.5			All Other Non-Current	7.1	5.1
		100.0	100.0			Total	100.0	100.0
						LIABILITIES		
		15.7	6.2			Notes Payable-Short Term	5.1	6.0
		3.0	3.3			Cur. Mat.-L.T.D.	3.9	3.6
		12.2	8.1			Trade Payables	10.3	8.1
		.0	.1			Income Taxes Payable	.6	.7
		10.8	3.7			All Other Current	5.3	7.3
		41.6	21.3			Total Current	25.1	25.8
		23.6	12.7			Long-Term Debt	25.0	25.1
		.0	.0			Deferred Taxes	1.3	.7
		3.5	1.6			All Other Non-Current	7.8	3.1
		31.3	64.3			Net Worth	40.8	45.4
		100.0	100.0			Total Liabilties & Net Worth	100.0	100.0
						INCOME DATA		
		100.0	100.0			Net Sales	100.0	100.0
						Gross Profit		
		90.6	95.4			Operating Expenses	93.0	92.4
		9.4	4.6			Operating Profit	7.0	7.6
		2.3	-.5			All Other Expenses (net)	1.5	2.0
		7.1	5.1			Profit Before Taxes	5.5	5.6
						RATIOS		
		3.6	7.0				3.0	4.2
		1.1	2.7			Current	2.0	1.9
		.4	1.6				.9	.9
		2.7	5.9				1.5	2.2
		.6	1.7			Quick	.9	.9
		.2	.8				.4	.4
		0 UND	21 17.5				0 UND	1 297.1
		12 29.5	25 14.5			Sales/Receivables	23 15.9	22 16.8
		24 15.3	33 10.9				31 11.9	36 10.1
						Cost of Sales/Inventory		
						Cost of Sales/Payables		
		10.0	3.6				5.6	6.0
		NM	6.1			Sales/Working Capital	9.1	10.4
		-8.9	17.0				-120.6	-42.8
		20.0	31.0				29.0	12.6
		(12) 3.9	(10) 18.2			EBIT/Interest	(41) 4.2	(43) 5.6
		1.2	8.0				1.8	1.1
							5.0	
						Net Profit + Depr., Dep., Amort./Cur. Mat. L/T/D	(10) 1.9	
							1.1	
		.5	.4				.5	.6
		1.4	.6			Fixed/Worth	1.0	1.0
		3.7	.8				2.5	2.9
		.5	.2				.3	.3
		1.9	.6			Debt/Worth	1.2	1.2
		4.9	1.3				2.9	3.1
		48.7	37.6				24.3	34.6
		(12) 31.6	11.3			% Profit Before Taxes/Tangible Net Worth	(48) 13.3	(49) 16.9
		2.1	7.3				5.5	4.6
		24.8	22.9				13.9	15.3
		9.6	7.8			% Profit Before Taxes/Total Assets	6.5	8.1
		.1	4.2				1.3	1.4
		19.5	22.5				10.4	7.6
		8.3	7.2			Sales/Net Fixed Assets	3.5	3.8
		1.8	3.5				1.6	1.9
		3.6	3.2				3.1	3.0
		2.8	2.3			Sales/Total Assets	1.6	1.6
		1.3	1.6				1.0	1.0
		.9	.7				1.9	2.2
		1.6	(11) 1.2			% Depr., Dep., Amort./Sales	(44) 4.5	(43) 4.5
		10.7	6.7				10.1	8.6
							.8	
						% Officers', Directors' Owners' Comp/Sales	(10) 1.5	
							2.5	
1265M	24469M	213598M	758975M	919451M	663336M	Net Sales ($)	2978291M	3258831M
249M	3436M	74957M	320314M	507628M	530414M	Total Assets ($)	1784788M	1992773M

M = $ thousand MM = $ million

See Pages 9 through 22 for Explanation of Ratios and Data

Comparative Historical Data | Current Data Sorted by Sales

			Type of Statement						
14	11	5	Unqualified						5
6	6	5	Reviewed						5
6	3	8	Compiled	1	1			4	2
9	7	7	Tax Returns	3	1	1		2	
13	15	18	Other	1			1	3	13
4/1/11-3/31/12 ALL	4/1/12-3/31/13 ALL	4/1/13-3/31/14 ALL		5 (4/1-9/30/13)			38 (10/1/13-3/31/14)		
				0-1MM	1-3MM	3-5MM	5-10MM	10-25MM	25MM & OVER
48	42	43	NUMBER OF STATEMENTS	5	2	1	1	9	25
%	%	%	ASSETS	%	%	%	%	%	%
7.8	13.6	16.6	Cash & Equivalents						15.0
15.3	9.9	13.1	Trade Receivables (net)						15.7
17.3	17.1	14.5	Inventory						17.2
2.0	2.5	1.4	All Other Current						1.9
42.3	43.1	45.7	Total Current						49.9
50.2	49.0	46.4	Fixed Assets (net)						42.6
1.4	1.0	.7	Intangibles (net)						1.0
6.0	7.0	7.2	All Other Non-Current						6.5
100.0	100.0	100.0	Total						100.0
			LIABILITIES						
8.7	9.2	13.4	Notes Payable-Short Term						6.3
2.4	3.3	3.4	Cur. Mat.-L.T.D.						3.2
10.3	9.0	8.5	Trade Payables						12.3
.3	.2	.1	Income Taxes Payable						.2
6.9	7.3	6.3	All Other Current						8.4
28.6	29.0	31.6	Total Current						30.4
25.8	30.3	25.4	Long-Term Debt						14.5
1.3	.6	.4	Deferred Taxes						.7
1.3	4.2	2.8	All Other Non-Current						2.3
42.9	35.9	39.7	Net Worth						52.0
100.0	100.0	100.0	Total Liabilties & Net Worth						100.0
			INCOME DATA						
100.0	100.0	100.0	Net Sales						100.0
			Gross Profit						
95.4	97.4	92.9	Operating Expenses						96.0
4.6	2.6	7.1	Operating Profit						4.0
2.6	2.8	1.0	All Other Expenses (net)						.1
1.9	-.2	6.2	Profit Before Taxes						4.0
			RATIOS						
3.0	3.6	3.7							3.5
2.0	1.5	1.6	Current						1.9
.8	1.0	.9							1.2
1.9	1.5	2.5							2.4
.9	.5	1.0	Quick						1.2
.3	.3	.4							.4
7 49.8	**0** UND	**0** UND							**17** 21.4
23 15.8	**17** 21.6	**21** 17.7	Sales/Receivables						**24** 15.5
34 10.8	**28** 13.2	**29** 12.8							**29** 12.7
			Cost of Sales/Inventory						
			Cost of Sales/Payables						
5.6	7.4	5.7							5.7
11.5	12.6	12.8	Sales/Working Capital						11.4
-45.1	168.2	-51.6							36.4
17.3	11.6	19.8							31.0
(38) 5.3	(30) 2.3	(36) 6.1	EBIT/Interest						(22) 8.6
.7	.3	1.6							1.9
			Net Profit + Depr., Dep., Amort./Cur. Mat. L/T/D						
.6	.5	.5							.5
.9	1.2	.8	Fixed/Worth						.8
3.0	2.7	2.8							1.2
.3	.4	.3							.3
1.2	1.4	1.2	Debt/Worth						.8
4.1	4.4	2.7							1.6
28.3	28.0	45.1							30.7
(42) 12.9	(36) 8.8	(38) 21.9	% Profit Before Taxes/Tangible Net Worth						(24) 16.1
-1.6	-.6	5.9							6.3
14.7	11.5	23.3							21.5
5.4	2.2	8.2	% Profit Before Taxes/Total Assets						8.2
-1.3	-3.1	1.4							3.0
7.7	18.3	15.0							10.9
3.7	3.5	4.5	Sales/Net Fixed Assets						4.5
2.2	1.8	2.6							2.9
3.1	3.3	3.4							3.2
1.8	1.8	2.3	Sales/Total Assets						2.3
1.3	1.1	1.5							1.5
1.0	.7	1.0							1.0
(35) 3.7	(30) 3.3	(34) 2.6	% Depr., Dep., Amort./Sales						(19) 1.7
9.9	8.9	8.8							4.5
			% Officers', Directors' Owners' Comp/Sales						
3322648M	2674084M	2581094M	Net Sales ($)	2818M	4191M	4048M	6719M	149319M	2413999M
1736542M	1683789M	1436998M	Total Assets ($)	6015M	8737M	2472M	1273M	57517M	1360984M

M = $ thousand MM = $ million

See Pages 9 through 22 for Explanation of Ratios and Data

Current Data Sorted by Assets							Comparative Historical Data	
						Type of Statement		
				2		Unqualified	1	
			1		1	Reviewed	2	3
		1				Compiled	5	2
1	5	1				Tax Returns	7	12
2	5	6	1	1		Other	12	12
	2 (4/1-9/30/13)		25 (10/1/13-3/31/14)				4/1/09-3/31/10	4/1/10-3/31/11
0-500M	500M-2MM	2-10MM	10-50MM	50-100MM	100-250MM		ALL	ALL
3	10	8	2	3	1	**NUMBER OF STATEMENTS**	27	29
%	%	%	%	%	%	**ASSETS**	%	%
	28.6					Cash & Equivalents	16.3	17.7
	18.5					Trade Receivables (net)	7.3	6.8
	17.0					Inventory	5.2	5.2
	1.2					All Other Current	5.4	7.8
	65.3					Total Current	34.2	37.4
	18.8					Fixed Assets (net)	48.7	50.1
	.1					Intangibles (net)	2.3	.4
	15.8					All Other Non-Current	14.8	12.0
	100.0					Total	100.0	100.0
						LIABILITIES		
	14.9					Notes Payable-Short Term	16.4	18.4
	4.3					Cur. Mat.-L.T.D.	7.1	3.4
	2.7					Trade Payables	8.0	9.7
	.0					Income Taxes Payable	.0	.0
	12.7					All Other Current	15.5	21.2
	34.7					Total Current	47.0	52.7
	15.2					Long-Term Debt	43.7	38.8
	.0					Deferred Taxes	.0	.0
	9.0					All Other Non-Current	4.9	11.7
	41.1					Net Worth	4.5	-3.1
	100.0					Total Liabilities & Net Worth	100.0	100.0
						INCOME DATA		
	100.0					Net Sales	100.0	100.0
						Gross Profit		
	97.0					Operating Expenses	93.0	93.0
	3.0					Operating Profit	7.0	7.0
	-.8					All Other Expenses (net)	2.2	3.5
	3.8					Profit Before Taxes	4.8	3.5
						RATIOS		
	9.6						3.0	2.1
	2.4					Current	.7	.5
	1.2						.2	.2
	9.0						1.6	1.2
	1.4					Quick	.5	.4
	.7						.2	.2
	0 UND						0 UND	0 UND
	7 49.2					Sales/Receivables	1 725.0	3 109.6
	29 12.8						43 8.4	47 7.7
						Cost of Sales/Inventory		
						Cost of Sales/Payables		
	1.9						4.4	15.9
	5.1					Sales/Working Capital	-73.8	-29.0
	89.0						-1.6	-4.5
							4.8	16.9
						EBIT/Interest	(25) 1.3	(20) 2.7
							-4.0	-1.7
						Net Profit + Depr., Dep., Amort./Cur. Mat. L/T/D		
	.0						.5	.4
	.4					Fixed/Worth	4.0	1.4
	.8						-1.7	-1.1
	.1						.8	.4
	1.1					Debt/Worth	16.3	3.3
	5.1						-4.1	-3.4
							71.8	159.0
						% Profit Before Taxes/Tangible Net Worth	(16) 3.0	(19) 12.5
							-29.7	-4.2
	28.8						17.6	22.8
	7.6					% Profit Before Taxes/Total Assets	1.6	5.3
	-3.0						-10.7	-4.0
	238.9						36.2	38.6
	19.2					Sales/Net Fixed Assets	2.1	3.1
	3.2						.7	.8
	3.2						2.5	3.8
	1.5					Sales/Total Assets	1.0	1.1
	.7						.5	.5
							3.0	2.1
						% Depr., Dep., Amort./Sales	(15) 7.1	(17) 6.6
							22.8	27.3
							1.7	.8
						% Officers', Directors' Owners' Comp/Sales	(12) 5.4	(14) 3.5
							10.6	8.3
2009M	61204M	32935M	18034M	73206M	35956M	Net Sales ($)	130833M	183138M
687M	13340M	37324M	28586M	185672M	108237M	Total Assets ($)	148793M	309322M

M = $ thousand MM = $ million

See Pages 9 through 22 for Explanation of Ratios and Data

Comparative Historical Data				Current Data Sorted by Sales					
			Type of Statement						
	1	2	Unqualified					2	
2	2	2	Reviewed					1	1
4	7	1	Compiled			1			
13	9	7	Tax Returns	1	2	1	2		1
23	14	15	Other	6	5	2		1	1
4/1/11-3/31/12 ALL	**4/1/12-3/31/13 ALL**	**4/1/13-3/31/14 ALL**			**2 (4/1-9/30/13)**			**25 (10/1/13-3/31/14)**	
				0-1MM	**1-3MM**	**3-5MM**	**5-10MM**	**10-25MM**	**25MM & OVER**
42	33	27	**NUMBER OF STATEMENTS**	7	7	4	2	4	3
%	%	%	**ASSETS**	%	%	%	%	%	%
13.5	10.0	15.6	Cash & Equivalents						
9.5	8.5	10.1	Trade Receivables (net)						
6.7	7.1	9.6	Inventory						
12.7	5.4	6.8	All Other Current						
42.3	31.0	42.1	Total Current						
41.7	49.4	37.8	Fixed Assets (net)						
5.4	4.5	5.9	Intangibles (net)						
10.6	15.1	14.2	All Other Non-Current						
100.0	100.0	100.0	Total						
			LIABILITIES						
22.9	18.5	23.3	Notes Payable-Short Term						
5.0	1.6	2.8	Cur. Mat.-L.T.D.						
6.2	4.8	3.7	Trade Payables						
.0	.0	.0	Income Taxes Payable						
15.9	37.2	8.9	All Other Current						
50.0	62.1	38.7	Total Current						
36.0	21.7	19.9	Long-Term Debt						
.0	.0	.0	Deferred Taxes						
14.8	10.1	17.9	All Other Non-Current						
-.8	6.1	23.5	Net Worth						
100.0	100.0	100.0	Total Liabilties & Net Worth						
			INCOME DATA						
100.0	100.0	100.0	Net Sales						
			Gross Profit						
91.7	91.4	91.3	Operating Expenses						
8.3	8.6	8.7	Operating Profit						
3.4	3.9	.8	All Other Expenses (net)						
4.8	4.6	7.9	Profit Before Taxes						
			RATIOS						
2.3	1.9	2.8							
1.2	1.2	1.5	Current						
.4	.2	.5							
1.4	1.1	1.6							
.3	.3	.6	Quick						
.1	.1	.1							
0 UND	**0** UND	**0** UND							
9 38.5	**2** 181.1	**8** 47.8	Sales/Receivables						
43 8.5	**35** 10.5	**52** 7.0							
			Cost of Sales/Inventory						
			Cost of Sales/Payables						
2.4	9.0	4.1							
51.0	51.4	8.8	Sales/Working Capital						
-2.8	-2.3	-6.2							
11.0	22.1	9.7							
(32) 3.9	(27) 3.0	(25) 2.9	EBIT/Interest						
-8.9	-2.8	.2							
			Net Profit + Depr., Dep., Amort./Cur. Mat. L/T/D						
.4	.3	.5							
1.3	1.1	.8	Fixed/Worth						
-1.3	-44.8	-.9							
.6	.5	.3							
1.9	1.4	1.2	Debt/Worth						
-2.7	-52.5	-3.1							
26.5	46.1	58.6							
(26) 6.5	(24) 7.6	(19) 5.9	% Profit Before Taxes/Tangible Net Worth						
-4.7	.1	-.6							
13.1	12.2	16.3							
3.4	2.5	2.6	% Profit Before Taxes/Total Assets						
-6.1	-1.8	-.9							
11.1	18.8	12.3							
2.2	2.7	3.3	Sales/Net Fixed Assets						
.8	.4	1.0							
1.3	2.9	1.8							
.8	.9	.8	Sales/Total Assets						
.3	.3	.5							
4.1	6.9	.4							
(28) 6.1	(19) 10.1	(15) 9.2	% Depr., Dep., Amort./Sales						
22.2	27.5	21.4							
2.4									
(13) 10.0			% Officers', Directors' Owners' Comp/Sales						
18.7									
174901M	**171635M**	**223344M**	Net Sales ($)	**3885M**	**12951M**	**18255M**	**12889M**	**60688M**	**114676M**
386798M	**390168M**	**373846M**	Total Assets ($)	**8330M**	**14318M**	**24286M**	**3702M**	**160687M**	**162523M**

M = $ thousand MM = $ million

See Pages 9 through 22 for Explanation of Ratios and Data

Current Data Sorted by Assets							Comparative Historical Data	
						Type of Statement		
	1	2	5	1	3	Unqualified	18	14
		2	5	1	1	Reviewed	15	18
	2	6	4	1		Compiled	19	22
6	3	4	1			Tax Returns	24	15
1	5	11	5	3	2	Other	38	43
10 (4/1-9/30/13)		65 (10/1/13-3/31/14)					4/1/09-3/31/10 ALL	4/1/10-3/31/11 ALL
0-500M	**500M-2MM**	**2-10MM**	**10-50MM**	**50-100MM**	**100-250MM**			
7	11	25	20	6	6	**NUMBER OF STATEMENTS**	114	112
%	%	%	%	%	%	**ASSETS**	%	%
	6.8	10.0	2.1			Cash & Equivalents	6.7	8.1
	3.5	8.7	7.1			Trade Receivables (net)	9.5	10.3
	28.9	19.3	22.0			Inventory	18.0	12.7
	9.4	2.7	2.2			All Other Current	3.5	4.3
	48.6	40.7	33.4			Total Current	37.7	35.4
	26.0	39.9	42.0			Fixed Assets (net)	45.0	45.3
	4.1	3.0	.9			Intangibles (net)	1.6	1.2
	21.3	16.4	23.7			All Other Non-Current	15.6	18.1
	100.0	100.0	100.0			Total	100.0	100.0
						LIABILITIES		
	16.0	12.7	13.8			Notes Payable-Short Term	15.7	14.3
	7.0	5.9	6.3			Cur. Mat.-L.T.D.	7.5	6.8
	6.4	3.5	4.7			Trade Payables	3.9	4.2
	.0	.0	.1			Income Taxes Payable	.1	.2
	13.1	18.3	8.5			All Other Current	8.5	8.5
	42.6	40.5	33.4			Total Current	35.7	34.0
	23.8	18.0	32.3			Long-Term Debt	31.6	26.2
	.0	.0	1.6			Deferred Taxes	.6	.4
	.0	4.2	1.9			All Other Non-Current	5.7	5.7
	33.7	37.3	30.8			Net Worth	26.5	33.7
	100.0	100.0	100.0			Total Liabilties & Net Worth	100.0	100.0
						INCOME DATA		
	100.0	100.0	100.0			Net Sales	100.0	100.0
						Gross Profit		
	98.2	84.5	87.3			Operating Expenses	94.1	90.5
	1.8	15.5	12.7			Operating Profit	5.9	9.5
	3.2	6.4	1.4			All Other Expenses (net)	3.0	2.8
	-1.4	9.1	11.3			Profit Before Taxes	2.9	6.7
						RATIOS		
	1.6	3.4	1.3				2.8	2.0
	1.0	1.1	.8			Current	1.1	1.2
	.7	.4	.4				.5	.6
	.9	2.9	.7				1.3	1.1
	.4	.4	.3			Quick	.4	.5
	.2	.1	.1				.2	.2
	0 UND	0 UND	1 274.0				0 UND	2 194.7
	0 UND	0 UND	10 37.0			Sales/Receivables	11 33.4	11 34.1
	11 34.3	14 26.5	30 12.2				24 15.2	26 14.3
						Cost of Sales/Inventory		
						Cost of Sales/Payables		
	22.9	4.2	15.2				5.8	9.7
	-544.0	76.0	-17.8			Sales/Working Capital	35.0	37.5
	-38.9	-5.9	-5.7				-8.3	-13.2
	9.5	24.4	11.9				4.5	7.7
	(10) 3.4	(22) 8.2	3.4			EBIT/Interest	(99) 1.3	(92) 3.1
	1.0	1.7	1.3				-.9	1.1
							4.7	6.5
						Net Profit + Depr., Dep., Amort./Cur. Mat. L/T/D	(15) 1.2	(16) 1.7
							-.7	.5
	.1	.3	.3				.5	.5
	.6	.7	1.0			Fixed/Worth	1.7	1.3
	2.0	2.2	3.0				5.3	3.7
	1.4	.3	1.0				1.0	.6
	2.1	1.4	2.2			Debt/Worth	2.3	1.8
	26.4	3.7	4.2				8.4	6.6
	115.0	64.2	50.3				26.5	34.4
	42.9	(22) 18.5	(18) 9.0			% Profit Before Taxes/Tangible Net Worth	(98) 2.6	(99) 9.6
	.0	3.6	3.9				-8.4	1.6
	17.0	19.5	9.6				7.3	9.6
	4.3	5.5	4.0			% Profit Before Taxes/Total Assets	.6	2.4
	.0	1.2	.8				-3.0	-.4
	801.5	48.6	12.0				15.6	15.7
	32.8	3.9	3.7			Sales/Net Fixed Assets	3.6	4.2
	7.0	.2	.5				.8	.9
	7.1	4.3	1.9				3.2	3.6
	4.5	1.4	.9			Sales/Total Assets	1.2	1.4
	1.9	.2	.2				.4	.5
		.2	1.7				1.0	.7
		(18) .9	(19) 3.6			% Depr., Dep., Amort./Sales	(93) 4.3	(90) 3.6
		5.4	11.3				11.4	9.4
							1.2	1.1
						% Officers', Directors' Owners' Comp/Sales	(23) 1.7	(22) 2.0
							4.3	5.0
8243M	71472M	222891M	608674M	244712M	1059648M	Net Sales ($)	1822116M	2322256M
1603M	15539M	119295M	442977M	442316M	1052250M	Total Assets ($)	2183243M	2724187M

M = $ thousand MM = $ million

See Pages 9 through 22 for Explanation of Ratios and Data

Comparative Historical Data | Current Data Sorted by Sales

4/1/11-3/31/12 ALL	4/1/12-3/31/13 ALL	4/1/13-3/31/14 ALL	Type of Statement	0-1MM	1-3MM	3-5MM	5-10MM	10-25MM	25MM & OVER
12	10	12	Unqualified	2	1		1	2	6
17	9	9	Reviewed		4	1	1	2	1
17	7	13	Compiled	1	3		2	4	3
15	22	14	Tax Returns	5	3	1	4		1
37	29	27	Other	2	5		7	7	6
				10 (4/1-9/30/13)			65 (10/1/13-3/31/14)		
98	77	75	NUMBER OF STATEMENTS	10	16	2	15	15	17
%	%	%	ASSETS	%	%	%	%	%	%
8.1	12.2	7.1	Cash & Equivalents	14.4	5.1		7.5	6.1	5.8
9.6	7.6	6.7	Trade Receivables (net)	2.5	2.2		4.9	9.3	13.7
16.4	14.8	18.3	Inventory	.0	20.4		19.2	23.7	23.9
4.4	4.4	3.3	All Other Current	.4	1.5		8.5	.9	4.3
38.6	38.9	35.5	Total Current	17.2	29.1		40.2	40.0	47.7
41.0	38.9	44.4	Fixed Assets (net)	64.7	43.6		41.8	48.7	32.8
1.8	1.8	2.1	Intangibles (net)	.4	7.1		.1	.9	1.3
18.6	20.4	18.1	All Other Non-Current	17.6	20.2		17.8	10.5	18.2
100.0	100.0	100.0	Total	100.0	100.0		100.0	100.0	100.0
			LIABILITIES						
12.8	15.4	12.3	Notes Payable-Short Term	5.3	14.3		14.9	11.5	14.2
5.9	5.3	5.1	Cur. Mat.-L.T.D.	2.0	1.2		3.6	13.2	4.9
4.1	3.6	4.8	Trade Payables	7.0	.4		4.3	7.3	6.6
.1	.0	.0	Income Taxes Payable	.0	.0		.0	.1	.0
11.8	8.1	14.6	All Other Current	2.5	5.2		34.3	2.8	9.4
34.7	32.5	36.8	Total Current	16.8	21.2		57.1	34.8	35.1
26.0	25.9	30.8	Long-Term Debt	30.2	32.0		22.9	18.9	30.7
.3	.4	.5	Deferred Taxes	.0	.0		.0	2.1	.3
7.4	4.0	2.5	All Other Non-Current	.4	5.9		.3	.1	5.1
31.5	37.2	29.3	Net Worth	52.6	40.9		19.7	44.1	28.9
100.0	100.0	100.0	Total Liabilties & Net Worth	100.0	100.0		100.0	100.0	100.0
			INCOME DATA						
100.0	100.0	100.0	Net Sales	100.0	100.0		100.0	100.0	100.0
			Gross Profit						
89.9	86.5	87.2	Operating Expenses	72.9	80.1		97.0	85.3	93.6
10.1	13.5	12.8	Operating Profit	27.1	19.9		3.0	14.7	6.4
2.7	2.4	3.3	All Other Expenses (net)	15.4	3.0		1.5	.4	.8
7.4	11.2	9.6	Profit Before Taxes	11.7	16.9		1.5	14.3	5.6
			RATIOS						
2.6	3.8	2.3	Current	3.7	7.2		6.6	1.6	3.1
1.2	1.2	1.1		.9	.7		1.0	1.1	1.5
.4	.4	.5		.2	.4		.6	.6	1.1
1.3	1.6	1.3	Quick	2.5	1.7		6.5	.9	1.2
.4	(76) .6	.4		.9	.4		.4	.3	.6
.2	.2	.2		.2	.1		.0	.1	.3
0 UND	0 UND	0 UND	Sales/Receivables	0 UND	0 UND		0 UND	0 999.8	10 38.3
10 35.1	6 66.1	0 50.7		0 UND	0 UND		7 55.6	8 43.1	17 21.9
24 15.5	19 19.2	18 19.9		7 52.8	12 29.8		12 29.4	18 19.9	41 8.9
			Cost of Sales/Inventory						
			Cost of Sales/Payables						
7.1	9.4	9.0	Sales/Working Capital	1.9	2.9		14.3	12.3	8.0
38.2	42.1	76.0		NM	-12.1		-238.1	76.0	12.2
-12.5	-11.1	-10.2		-19.6	-3.1		-10.8	-16.7	NM
9.0	10.9	15.5	EBIT/Interest		22.9		7.2	13.8	24.5
(84) 2.8	(63) 6.0	(66) 6.3			(15) 2.0		(13) 2.0	(14) 7.5	12.7
.7	1.5	1.4			1.0		1.0	3.4	1.5
2.0			Net Profit + Depr., Dep., Amort./Cur. Mat. L/T/D						
(11) 1.1									
.1									
.3	.2	.3	Fixed/Worth	.6	.3		.1	.3	.3
.8	.7	1.0		1.3	.9		1.0	1.0	1.2
3.2	2.8	2.9		2.8	NM		3.2	1.7	1.8
.6	.6	.6	Debt/Worth	.1	.3		.5	.8	1.3
1.5	1.6	1.9		.7	1.4		2.1	1.6	2.0
6.0	6.8	4.4		2.5	NM		26.4	3.6	3.9
19.7	52.6	57.6	% Profit Before Taxes/Tangible Net Worth		29.3		78.0	98.8	73.1
(85) 6.5	(68) 14.4	(66) 19.5			(12) 5.0		(14) 25.8	25.3	(15) 36.1
-2.5	4.0	2.0			.2		.5	9.0	9.1
10.4	19.1	18.2	% Profit Before Taxes/Total Assets	12.3	15.7		18.5	18.9	18.0
3.9	6.8	4.9		4.0	1.8		1.2	8.5	10.3
-1.2	.8	.5		.1	-.9		.0	4.7	1.6
33.9	67.7	22.9	Sales/Net Fixed Assets	4.8	11.7		98.5	48.9	43.3
4.4	6.0	4.2		.2	3.4		7.0	3.9	4.9
1.5	1.0	.5		.1	.3		3.2	.4	2.6
4.0	4.3	3.7	Sales/Total Assets	1.6	1.7		4.5	6.0	4.3
1.5	1.5	1.4		.1	.5		2.6	1.4	1.7
.4	.3	.2		.1	.1		.5	.3	1.2
.6	.6	.8	% Depr., Dep., Amort./Sales		.8			.4	.3
(74) 2.8	(61) 3.3	(57) 2.7			(12) 6.1			(13) 2.8	2.1
7.6	11.0	6.9			14.1			5.4	3.5
1.1	.7	1.4	% Officers', Directors' Owners' Comp/Sales						
(25) 1.9	(26) 1.6	(17) 3.2							
6.6	4.9	7.5							
2728818M	1834945M	2215640M	Net Sales ($)	4340M	30193M	8319M	116036M	246562M	1810190M
2752600M	1716518M	2073980M	Total Assets ($)	32379M	130967M	17702M	253898M	383422M	1255612M

M = $ thousand MM = $ million

See Pages 9 through 22 for Explanation of Ratios and Data

Current Data Sorted by Assets							Comparative Historical Data	
						Type of Statement		
			1		1	Unqualified	2	3
	3	5	4			Reviewed	19	14
1	4	6		1		Compiled	37	28
7	19	13	1			Tax Returns	39	34
1	6	6	5			Other	25	23
	14 (4/1-9/30/13)		70 (10/1/13-3/31/14)				4/1/09-3/31/10 ALL	4/1/10-3/31/11 ALL
0-500M	500M-2MM	2-10MM	10-50MM	50-100MM	100-250MM			
9	32	30	11	1	1	**NUMBER OF STATEMENTS**	122	102
%	%	%	%	%	%	**ASSETS**	%	%
	18.2	9.6	10.4			Cash & Equivalents	14.3	10.8
	9.0	8.5	11.1			Trade Receivables (net)	9.8	11.4
	8.2	18.4	12.6			Inventory	12.6	12.1
	3.0	2.9	3.8			All Other Current	4.7	3.4
	38.5	39.5	37.9			Total Current	41.4	37.7
	47.4	51.3	45.3			Fixed Assets (net)	48.1	50.0
	1.7	2.2	.1			Intangibles (net)	1.9	2.1
	12.4	6.9	16.7			All Other Non-Current	8.5	10.2
	100.0	100.0	100.0			Total	100.0	100.0
						LIABILITIES		
	14.9	13.0	12.5			Notes Payable-Short Term	11.4	12.2
	10.7	9.2	4.2			Cur. Mat.-L.T.D.	8.7	10.6
	5.3	6.4	3.3			Trade Payables	5.5	6.5
	.4	.4	.0			Income Taxes Payable	.1	.2
	6.4	8.0	2.8			All Other Current	7.7	5.8
	37.8	36.9	22.8			Total Current	33.4	35.3
	39.4	30.3	22.3			Long-Term Debt	34.5	30.8
	.5	1.0	.9			Deferred Taxes	.7	.9
	4.0	5.7	4.7			All Other Non-Current	4.2	8.1
	18.2	26.0	49.2			Net Worth	27.2	25.0
	100.0	100.0	100.0			Total Liabilties & Net Worth	100.0	100.0
						INCOME DATA		
	100.0	100.0	100.0			Net Sales	100.0	100.0
	49.0	37.4	34.3			Gross Profit	39.2	40.6
	45.6	35.1	19.6			Operating Expenses	36.8	38.0
	3.4	2.4	14.7			Operating Profit	2.5	2.6
	1.4	-.7	-.1			All Other Expenses (net)	.5	.1
	2.0	3.1	14.8			Profit Before Taxes	2.0	2.5
						RATIOS		
	2.9	1.4	4.0				2.5	2.0
	1.1	1.0	1.3			Current	1.3	1.1
	.2	.6	.8				.5	.6
	1.6	1.1	2.4				1.8	1.4
	.7	.5	.6			Quick	(121) .6	(101) .6
	.1	.2	.3				.2	.2
	0 UND	0 UND	0 999.8				0 UND	0 UND
	0 UND	5 72.2	15 23.9			Sales/Receivables	9 39.3	10 36.3
	15 25.1	14 25.5	27 13.6				25 14.9	28 13.2
	0 UND	0 UND	0 UND				0 UND	0 UND
	0 UND	7 50.0	0 UND			Cost of Sales/Inventory	6 57.3	2 162.5
	39 9.4	87 4.2	33 10.9				43 8.6	48 7.6
	0 UND	0 UND	2 192.5				0 UND	0 UND
	1 547.0	9 40.0	9 39.2			Cost of Sales/Payables	7 55.2	9 41.7
	18 19.9	22 16.9	27 13.5				23 15.8	33 11.0
	12.8	9.9	7.1				7.0	9.6
	60.9	NM	21.8			Sales/Working Capital	41.6	55.7
	-11.3	-19.3	-30.8				-14.4	-18.1
	5.8	9.6	19.1				4.3	6.4
	(31) 2.6	(29) 3.2	(10) 5.1			EBIT/Interest	(111) 1.7	(95) 2.7
	-.2	1.4	1.7				.1	.3
							2.9	1.1
						Net Profit + Depr., Dep., Amort./Cur. Mat. L/T/D	(17) 1.7	(15) .7
							.7	.4
	1.0	1.0	.4				.6	.8
	2.4	1.7	.9			Fixed/Worth	1.9	1.6
	350.9	NM	1.5				13.5	101.4
	1.9	.9	.1				.6	.9
	5.0	2.6	1.8			Debt/Worth	2.7	1.8
	467.2	NM	3.7				22.2	170.1
	96.7	41.5	43.9				29.8	32.9
	(26) 13.2	(23) 19.7	24.4			% Profit Before Taxes/Tangible Net Worth	(98) 9.6	(78) 11.5
	-3.8	4.2	8.6				-2.3	-.7
	13.0	11.6	18.8				11.5	12.5
	3.8	3.7	11.0			% Profit Before Taxes/Total Assets	2.7	4.7
	-1.0	.6	2.3				-1.8	-2.9
	13.0	8.1	9.5				17.6	11.3
	5.7	4.4	2.3			Sales/Net Fixed Assets	4.9	4.7
	3.1	3.1	1.9				2.7	2.3
	3.9	3.7	1.7				3.1	3.7
	2.8	2.2	1.3			Sales/Total Assets	2.2	2.1
	1.8	1.5	.9				1.6	1.3
	3.0	1.2					2.1	2.4
	(22) 11.6	(25) 6.1				% Depr., Dep., Amort./Sales	(108) 5.8	(87) 6.3
	16.4	10.7					11.3	10.4
	1.7	1.1					1.7	1.9
	(24) 3.8	(19) 1.7				% Officers', Directors' Owners' Comp/Sales	(57) 3.2	(54) 2.9
	6.4	2.5					6.4	6.6
10725M	124624M	318173M	772230M	99932M	100602M	Net Sales ($)	1110257M	1585646M
2478M	37479M	127709M	273979M	59922M	113362M	Total Assets ($)	711237M	866562M

M = $ thousand MM = $ million

See Pages 9 through 22 for Explanation of Ratios and Data

Comparative Historical Data | Current Data Sorted by Sales

4/1/11-3/31/12 ALL	4/1/12-3/31/13 ALL	4/1/13-3/31/14 ALL	Type of Statement	0-1MM	1-3MM	3-5MM	5-10MM	10-25MM	25MM & OVER
	4	2	Unqualified					1	1
10	16	12	Reviewed	1	2	1	1	5	2
25	21	12	Compiled	1	3	1	5		2
55	35	40	Tax Returns	3	14	7	9	4	3
22	25	18	Other	1	4	3	3	5	2
					14 (4/1-9/30/13)		70 (10/1/13-3/31/14)		
112	101	84	**NUMBER OF STATEMENTS**	6	23	12	18	15	10
%	%	%	**ASSETS**	%	%	%	%	%	%
11.0	9.8	15.5	Cash & Equivalents		21.1	9.4	11.4	13.2	16.9
10.1	10.8	8.4	Trade Receivables (net)		4.3	9.8	10.0	11.6	12.9
11.5	10.6	12.9	Inventory		10.6	16.2	10.0	16.9	13.4
3.1	2.4	2.9	All Other Current		3.0	2.6	6.0	.7	2.1
35.7	33.6	39.6	Total Current		39.0	38.0	37.5	42.5	45.3
50.0	52.3	48.5	Fixed Assets (net)		49.1	55.6	53.6	41.2	40.5
1.7	3.1	1.6	Intangibles (net)		1.6	1.7	3.5	.4	.7
12.6	11.0	10.3	All Other Non-Current		10.2	4.6	5.4	15.9	13.5
100.0	100.0	100.0	Total		100.0	100.0	100.0	100.0	100.0
			LIABILITIES						
15.4	14.5	19.4	Notes Payable-Short Term		10.1	22.5	8.5	17.9	10.9
9.2	8.3	8.8	Cur. Mat.-L.T.D.		11.3	8.2	10.7	8.1	2.3
7.1	6.5	5.4	Trade Payables		5.5	5.2	2.3	10.0	6.9
.1	.3	.3	Income Taxes Payable		.6	.0	.4	.2	.1
7.9	4.8	6.0	All Other Current		5.1	7.8	2.5	9.0	5.3
39.6	34.4	39.9	Total Current		32.6	43.7	24.4	45.3	25.6
41.5	34.4	33.4	Long-Term Debt		43.6	33.9	39.0	22.1	14.6
.5	.6	.7	Deferred Taxes		.6	.0	1.0	1.5	.0
4.6	5.4	5.0	All Other Non-Current		2.1	2.8	7.8	6.1	5.7
13.8	25.2	21.0	Net Worth		21.0	19.6	27.8	25.0	54.1
100.0	100.0	100.0	Total Liabilities & Net Worth		100.0	100.0	100.0	100.0	100.0
			INCOME DATA						
100.0	100.0	100.0	Net Sales		100.0	100.0	100.0	100.0	100.0
41.8	38.7	42.9	Gross Profit		55.8	43.0	39.4	31.2	27.7
39.4	34.2	38.1	Operating Expenses		50.1	43.4	36.4	28.2	13.9
2.3	4.5	4.9	Operating Profit		5.7	-.4	3.0	3.1	13.8
.1	.1	.3	All Other Expenses (net)		.9	-1.2	-1.6	.8	.0
2.3	4.4	4.5	Profit Before Taxes		4.8	.8	4.6	2.3	13.8
			RATIOS						
2.0	1.8	2.6			2.6	2.2	4.9	1.3	48.4
1.0	1.0	1.1	Current		1.3	.7	1.2	.7	1.6
.5	.4	.6			.7	.2	.7	.4	1.0
1.2	1.1	1.4			1.7	.9	2.5	.7	48.4
(110) .5	.5	(83) .6	Quick		.9	.3	.7	.4	1.0
.2	.2	.3			.2	.1	.5	.3	.4
0 UND	0 UND	0 UND			0 UND	0 UND	0 UND	4 89.9	0 999.8
7 53.9	10 37.7	4 81.6	Sales/Receivables		0 UND	1 597.0	7 53.8	14 26.8	15 24.3
19 18.8	22 16.7	15 24.0			12 29.5	15 23.8	15 24.9	19 19.5	24 15.3
0 UND	0 UND	0 UND			0 UND	0 UND	0 UND	0 UND	0 UND
1 305.9	0 842.4	0 UND	Cost of Sales/Inventory		0 UND	0 UND	0 UND	2 176.3	17 21.0
41 9.0	42 8.6	46 8.0			49 7.5	68 5.4	47 7.8	51 7.2	35 10.5
0 UND	0 UND	0 UND			0 UND	0 UND	0 UND	9 39.2	0 UND
8 46.0	8 47.4	5 67.4	Cost of Sales/Payables		4 82.5	1 567.6	0 UND	21 17.8	5 67.4
29 12.5	19 19.1	21 17.2			21 17.1	18 19.9	19 18.9	31 11.8	10 36.8
18.2	11.7	10.3			9.3	6.9	14.3	21.8	8.5
NM	431.3	60.9	Sales/Working Capital		42.5	-48.8	73.8	-45.2	34.1
-13.3	-13.5	-19.6			-18.8	-11.0	-19.9	-9.9	NM
6.3	7.3	9.2			8.7	2.9	9.7	12.7	
(108) 2.2	(96) 2.9	(79) 2.8	EBIT/Interest		3.5	-.1	(17) 3.3	2.8	
.4	.9	1.0			1.7	-2.1	1.4	1.5	
	3.3	2.3							
	(14) 1.5	(12) 1.4	Net Profit + Depr., Dep., Amort./Cur. Mat. L/T/D						
	1.1	1.0							
.9	.9	.9			1.0	1.4	1.1	.8	.2
2.5	2.0	1.7	Fixed/Worth		2.6	3.1	1.9	1.3	.7
-5.0	9.2	13.0			39.8	6.2	-5.7	9.8	1.5
1.1	1.1	1.0			.9	1.9	.8	1.1	.1
3.7	2.6	3.1	Debt/Worth		4.5	4.9	2.1	3.3	1.1
-10.4	20.8	23.9			53.0	14.6	-10.4	10.7	3.3
54.7	44.7	52.5			229.6	25.0	31.8	46.8	52.5
(80) 17.8	(80) 12.0	(68) 20.5	% Profit Before Taxes/Tangible Net Worth		(20) 30.8	(10) -3.3	(13) 19.7	(12) 10.4	22.9
1.1	.4	4.3			6.3	-72.2	7.8	.9	17.3
13.4	12.0	13.0			17.2	3.8	12.4	14.0	30.2
3.7	5.3	4.4	% Profit Before Taxes/Total Assets		6.7	-1.7	6.3	3.3	11.0
-1.5	.0	.1			2.9	-13.6	1.1	.4	4.0
16.6	12.5	10.6			9.4	8.6	9.0	23.1	55.1
5.3	4.3	4.9	Sales/Net Fixed Assets		5.4	4.5	4.5	5.4	6.0
2.7	2.3	2.7			2.7	3.0	2.6	2.6	2.2
4.7	4.3	3.9			4.0	3.8	3.7	4.4	5.5
2.7	2.4	2.3	Sales/Total Assets		2.6	2.4	2.2	3.1	2.5
1.6	1.3	1.5			1.4	1.1	1.6	1.4	1.0
2.8	2.6	1.6			5.2		3.5	.9	
(88) 6.1	(87) 6.1	(62) 7.3	% Depr., Dep., Amort./Sales		(15) 10.5		(15) 8.1	(12) 1.4	
10.7	9.9	12.8			16.2		12.0	6.5	
1.4	1.1	1.3			3.2	1.2	1.1		
(72) 2.9	(51) 2.5	(52) 3.2	% Officers', Directors' Owners' Comp/Sales		(15) 4.0	(10) 3.9	(13) 1.5		
5.4	5.4	5.8			6.0	6.6	2.3		
1068563M	1773726M	1426286M	Net Sales ($)	3622M	46186M	49981M	128895M	253712M	943890M
583930M	1031192M	614929M	Total Assets ($)	2510M	25996M	29709M	64442M	139444M	352828M

M = $ thousand MM = $ million

See Pages 9 through 22 for Explanation of Ratios and Data

Current Data Sorted by Assets / Comparative Historical Data

0-500M	500M-2MM	2-10MM	10-50MM	50-100MM	100-250MM		4/1/09-3/31/10 ALL	4/1/10-3/31/11 ALL
						Type of Statement		
1			2	6		Unqualified	9	8
	1	1				Reviewed	4	3
		1				Compiled	8	4
8	7	1				Tax Returns	14	10
4	4	6	6	2	3	Other	24	20
2 (4/1-9/30/13)			51 (10/1/13-3/31/14)					
13	12	9	8	8	3	**NUMBER OF STATEMENTS**	59	45
%	%	%	%	%	%	**ASSETS**	%	%
20.9	7.1					Cash & Equivalents	13.6	17.6
2.6	1.2					Trade Receivables (net)	4.5	6.8
7.8	3.3					Inventory	7.6	9.1
.8	.2					All Other Current	1.9	2.8
32.1	11.9					Total Current	27.6	36.2
41.5	55.2					Fixed Assets (net)	36.0	32.9
21.4	26.8					Intangibles (net)	20.2	20.3
4.9	6.1					All Other Non-Current	16.2	10.6
100.0	100.0					Total	100.0	100.0
						LIABILITIES		
56.5	6.8					Notes Payable-Short Term	27.7	43.3
15.0	7.8					Cur. Mat.-L.T.D.	6.6	5.9
5.0	6.5					Trade Payables	3.5	6.1
.0	.0					Income Taxes Payable	.1	.0
8.4	59.0					All Other Current	6.7	8.4
84.8	80.1					Total Current	44.5	63.7
53.8	40.3					Long-Term Debt	42.5	33.3
.0	.0					Deferred Taxes	.4	.5
19.9	25.1					All Other Non-Current	2.7	6.2
-58.5	-45.4					Net Worth	9.7	-3.8
100.0	100.0					Total Liabilities & Net Worth	100.0	100.0
						INCOME DATA		
100.0	100.0					Net Sales	100.0	100.0
						Gross Profit		
85.5	106.1					Operating Expenses	86.4	88.6
14.5	-6.1					Operating Profit	13.6	11.4
2.2	4.0					All Other Expenses (net)	3.9	3.0
12.2	-10.1					Profit Before Taxes	9.6	8.3
						RATIOS		
1.3	.8						2.3	1.9
.2	.1					Current	1.3	1.3
.0	.0						.3	.4
.8	.8						1.8	1.4
.2	.1					Quick	.5	.8
.0	.0						.2	.2
0 UND	0 UND						0 UND	0 UND
0 UND	0 UND					Sales/Receivables	0 UND	1 387.1
0 UND	0 UND						20 18.0	25 14.9
						Cost of Sales/Inventory		
						Cost of Sales/Payables		
NM	-372.4						5.9	8.0
-7.1	-2.4					Sales/Working Capital	20.9	45.1
-3.2	-1.0						-4.9	-10.6
							11.7	12.7
						EBIT/Interest	(54) 4.0	(40) 4.0
							.7	.6
						Net Profit + Depr., Dep., Amort./Cur. Mat. L/T/D		
NM	NM						.5	.4
-.5	-1.3					Fixed/Worth	1.7	1.8
-.3	-.4						-1.2	-1.1
-20.5	NM						.8	2.0
-2.8	-2.4					Debt/Worth	9.2	7.0
-1.5	-1.5						-2.4	-2.7
							55.6	109.5
						% Profit Before Taxes/Tangible Net Worth	(33) 26.9	(26) 37.1
							1.7	4.9
41.4	5.8						18.5	21.0
5.3	-5.6					% Profit Before Taxes/Total Assets	5.9	6.2
-9.2	-25.8						-.9	-4.1
59.1	12.0						19.6	22.7
6.2	1.4					Sales/Net Fixed Assets	3.8	6.7
3.3	.8						1.6	2.9
3.5	1.5						2.2	3.4
2.0	1.0					Sales/Total Assets	1.1	1.3
1.2	.6						.7	.7
	6.2						2.4	2.9
	(10) 16.4					% Depr., Dep., Amort./Sales	(44) 5.6	(34) 6.0
	34.5						11.7	12.8
						% Officers', Directors' Owners' Comp/Sales		
7005M	17811M	56230M	245561M	419449M	281770M	Net Sales ($)	1439716M	1383760M
3126M	13172M	37749M	210449M	573818M	332996M	Total Assets ($)	1121023M	1064440M

M = $ thousand MM = $ million

See Pages 9 through 22 for Explanation of Ratios and Data

Comparative Historical Data				Current Data Sorted by Sales					
			Type of Statement						
11	15	9	Unqualified	1				2	6
6	1	2	Reviewed		1				1
	1	1	Compiled				1		
24	15	16	Tax Returns	11	4		1		
21	19	25	Other	6	7		3		9
4/1/11-3/31/12 ALL	4/1/12-3/31/13 ALL	4/1/13-3/31/14 ALL		2 (4/1-9/30/13)		51 (10/1/13-3/31/14)			
				0-1MM	1-3MM	3-5MM	5-10MM	10-25MM	25MM & OVER
62	51	53	**NUMBER OF STATEMENTS**	18	12		5	2	16
%	%	%	**ASSETS**	%	%	%	%	%	%
11.6	10.6	10.6	Cash & Equivalents	15.4	8.4	D			4.3
5.2	3.8	5.1	Trade Receivables (net)	2.1	5.8	A			7.1
9.4	14.2	5.3	Inventory	5.6	.1	T			7.6
3.9	5.7	2.5	All Other Current	.4	1.7	A			6.0
30.0	34.3	23.5	Total Current	23.6	16.0				25.0
32.5	39.0	48.4	Fixed Assets (net)	52.9	48.6	N			49.9
15.6	18.0	20.2	Intangibles (net)	19.9	25.4	O			14.3
21.9	8.7	7.9	All Other Non-Current	3.6	9.9	T			10.7
100.0	100.0	100.0	Total	100.0	100.0				100.0
			LIABILITIES			A			
17.3	21.4	16.0	Notes Payable-Short Term	41.1	6.3	V			1.7
5.2	4.5	7.8	Cur. Mat.-L.T.D.	12.7	7.7	A			4.5
5.8	3.2	5.1	Trade Payables	7.2	1.9	I			5.4
.2	.2	.0	Income Taxes Payable	.0	.0	L			.1
12.4	4.6	21.1	All Other Current	9.2	36.3	A			6.6
41.0	33.9	50.0	Total Current	70.2	52.2	B			18.3
37.3	30.0	41.8	Long-Term Debt	52.9	33.7	L			49.0
.5	.5	.4	Deferred Taxes	.0	.0	E			1.2
5.4	12.1	11.7	All Other Non-Current	24.2	11.8				1.0
15.8	23.4	-3.9	Net Worth	-47.2	2.4				30.5
100.0	100.0	100.0	Total Liabilties & Net Worth	100.0	100.0				100.0
			INCOME DATA						
100.0	100.0	100.0	Net Sales	100.0	100.0				100.0
			Gross Profit						
86.2	90.1	91.2	Operating Expenses	91.1	85.9				93.8
13.8	9.9	8.8	Operating Profit	8.9	14.1				6.2
2.8	3.4	3.0	All Other Expenses (net)	3.8	4.6				2.3
11.0	6.5	5.7	Profit Before Taxes	5.1	9.5				3.9
			RATIOS						
2.1	2.2	1.9		.9	1.2				2.2
1.1	1.5	.9	Current	.2	.3				1.3
.2	.8	.1		.0	.1				.6
1.5	1.2	1.0		.8	1.1				1.0
.4	.5	.4	Quick	.1	.1				.6
.1	.1	.0		.0	.0				.3
0 UND	0 UND	0 UND		0 UND	0 UND				6 65.6
1 581.7	1 318.0	0 UND	Sales/Receivables	0 UND	0 UND				27 13.5
21 17.2	17 20.9	24 14.9		0 UND	0 UND				44 8.3
			Cost of Sales/Inventory						
			Cost of Sales/Payables						
7.4	5.3	11.8		-154.1	13.5				4.9
93.4	14.7	-15.1	Sales/Working Capital	-4.8	-11.6				21.5
-8.4	-23.2	-3.3		-2.0	-1.5				-10.1
14.2	14.2	8.7		3.0					8.0
(55) 5.7	(47) 4.4	(42) 2.6	EBIT/Interest	(13) -.2					3.1
1.4	1.1	-.3		-3.4					.5
			Net Profit + Depr., Dep., Amort./Cur. Mat. L/T/D						
.2	.7	1.0		NM	1.0				1.0
1.5	3.6	96.8	Fixed/Worth	-.9	NM				5.7
-1.8	-4.7	-.9		-.3	-.9				-1.8
.9	1.4	1.6		-22.2	1.4				1.1
3.0	5.3	-28.0	Debt/Worth	-2.6	NM				8.3
-5.3	-9.3	-2.3		-1.5	-2.0				-5.1
138.4	281.9	96.4							41.0
(38) 49.6	(36) 30.4	(26) 40.2	% Profit Before Taxes/Tangible Net Worth						(11) 6.1
16.3	7.9	5.0							-8.0
36.8	20.3	16.1		11.9	25.3				8.9
14.6	5.7	4.6	% Profit Before Taxes/Total Assets	2.5	4.5				3.6
1.9	.1	-4.6		-13.8	-5.0				-1.4
29.2	19.0	7.3		50.4	12.6				3.9
6.0	3.9	2.1	Sales/Net Fixed Assets	3.3	3.3				1.8
2.9	1.4	1.3		1.2	1.1				1.5
3.2	2.1	1.8		2.3	1.4				1.2
1.6	.9	.9	Sales/Total Assets	1.4	1.0				.8
.9	.7	.6		.6	.5				.6
1.9	2.3	3.5		5.6					3.4
(52) 3.9	(40) 4.4	(42) 6.6	% Depr., Dep., Amort./Sales	(12) 12.0					(14) 5.1
7.3	7.2	13.2		24.2					8.0
5.2									
(11) 8.5			% Officers', Directors' Owners' Comp/Sales						
15.0									
1357847M	2368663M	1027826M	Net Sales ($)	9651M	18384M		31306M	42810M	925675M
1432232M	1935797M	1171310M	Total Assets ($)	11695M	32231M		26043M	55892M	1045449M

M = $ thousand MM = $ million

See Pages 9 through 22 for Explanation of Ratios and Data

Current Data Sorted by Assets							Comparative Historical Data	
						Type of Statement		
			1			Unqualified	1	2
		2	1	2		Reviewed	5	5
		2	1		1	Compiled	8	10
7	14	2				Tax Returns	20	14
2	5	3	2			Other	10	19
6 (4/1-9/30/13)			39 (10/1/13-3/31/14)				4/1/09-3/31/10 ALL	4/1/10-3/31/11 ALL
0-500M	**500M-2MM**	**2-10MM**	**10-50MM**	**50-100MM**	**100-250MM**			
9	19	9	5	2	1	**NUMBER OF STATEMENTS**	44	50
%	%	%	%	%	%	**ASSETS**	%	%
	14.8					Cash & Equivalents	14.2	10.5
	1.6					Trade Receivables (net)	7.6	6.3
	.3					Inventory	4.8	5.4
	1.8					All Other Current	1.8	3.3
	18.5					Total Current	28.4	25.4
	13.0					Fixed Assets (net)	32.8	34.7
	38.9					Intangibles (net)	23.4	24.8
	29.6					All Other Non-Current	15.5	15.0
	100.0					Total	100.0	100.0
						LIABILITIES		
	3.3					Notes Payable-Short Term	9.8	9.7
	5.7					Cur. Mat.-L.T.D.	4.6	3.5
	2.5					Trade Payables	5.9	7.2
	.5					Income Taxes Payable	.0	1.4
	5.9					All Other Current	6.0	7.9
	17.9					Total Current	26.4	29.7
	50.6					Long-Term Debt	50.4	37.1
	.0					Deferred Taxes	.4	.3
	12.8					All Other Non-Current	8.6	7.0
	18.6					Net Worth	14.2	26.0
	100.0					Total Liabilties & Net Worth	100.0	100.0
						INCOME DATA		
	100.0					Net Sales	100.0	100.0
						Gross Profit		
	81.1					Operating Expenses	84.7	86.7
	18.9					Operating Profit	15.3	13.3
	4.1					All Other Expenses (net)	4.7	5.1
	14.8					Profit Before Taxes	10.7	8.2
						RATIOS		
	2.2						2.2	2.6
	.6					Current	1.2	.9
	.1						.3	.1
	2.0						1.9	1.6
	.6					Quick	.7	.5
	.1						.3	.1
	0 UND						0 UND	0 UND
	0 UND					Sales/Receivables	0 UND	0 UND
	0 UND						18 20.6	31 11.8
						Cost of Sales/Inventory		
						Cost of Sales/Payables		
	9.3						9.0	6.7
	-23.4					Sales/Working Capital	46.4	-538.7
	-4.5						-10.4	-4.1
	9.6						12.1	16.5
	(17) 4.8					EBIT/Interest	(38) 3.6	(41) 4.0
	2.8						.9	.5
						Net Profit + Depr., Dep., Amort./Cur. Mat. L/T/D		
	.3						.3	.4
	-.5					Fixed/Worth	1.0	.9
	-.1						-2.8	-6.4
	1.8						.7	.5
	-18.6					Debt/Worth	4.0	3.5
	-1.2						-2.2	-2.0
							77.0	47.1
						% Profit Before Taxes/Tangible Net Worth	(26) 29.9	(33) 20.3
							7.2	-1.5
	30.7						32.6	23.6
	13.3					% Profit Before Taxes/Total Assets	8.0	7.0
	3.5						.9	-2.3
	89.0						50.6	19.1
	14.5					Sales/Net Fixed Assets	8.7	4.9
	8.3						1.9	1.9
	1.3						2.7	1.9
	1.1					Sales/Total Assets	1.1	1.1
	.7						.6	.7
	.7						2.0	2.7
	(10) 6.0					% Depr., Dep., Amort./Sales	(32) 4.3	(37) 7.2
	10.1						10.6	12.6
							1.6	1.9
						% Officers', Directors' Owners' Comp/Sales	(17) 3.6	(15) 3.7
							8.6	10.1
10261M	22879M	65328M	103027M	87588M	68361M	Net Sales ($)	280397M	459602M
2578M	21579M	35364M	121022M	116490M	144419M	Total Assets ($)	276781M	434333M

M = $ thousand MM = $ million

See Pages 9 through 22 for Explanation of Ratios and Data

Comparative Historical Data				Current Data Sorted by Sales					
			Type of Statement						
1	1	1	Unqualified						1
9	6	5	Reviewed		1	1			3
14	11	4	Compiled				3		1
18	11	23	Tax Returns	8	14	1			
17	14	12	Other	5	3		1	1	2
4/1/11-3/31/12 ALL	**4/1/12-3/31/13 ALL**	**4/1/13-3/31/14 ALL**		**6 (4/1-9/30/13)**			**39 (10/1/13-3/31/14)**		
				0-1MM	**1-3MM**	**3-5MM**	**5-10MM**	**10-25MM**	**25MM & OVER**
59	43	45	**NUMBER OF STATEMENTS**	13	18	2	4	1	7
%	%	%	**ASSETS**	%	%	%	%	%	%
17.2	18.7	19.1	Cash & Equivalents	25.0	20.0				
4.7	5.6	3.8	Trade Receivables (net)	4.9	1.7				
7.2	5.9	5.2	Inventory	3.4	.3				
1.5	2.6	2.7	All Other Current	1.3	1.9				
30.6	32.8	30.7	Total Current	34.7	23.9				
32.7	21.8	21.6	Fixed Assets (net)	8.7	17.8				
20.7	20.0	27.6	Intangibles (net)	36.4	26.3				
16.0	25.4	20.1	All Other Non-Current	20.3	32.0				
100.0	100.0	100.0	Total	100.0	100.0				
			LIABILITIES						
6.1	6.4	5.6	Notes Payable-Short Term	.4	10.9				
5.5	5.9	6.5	Cur. Mat.-L.T.D.	4.6	9.6				
4.6	3.5	2.9	Trade Payables	2.7	1.2				
.1	.1	.3	Income Taxes Payable	.8	.0				
11.0	8.7	5.0	All Other Current	7.6	1.9				
27.3	24.6	20.3	Total Current	16.1	23.6				
37.6	24.7	50.3	Long-Term Debt	46.2	66.7				
.2	.4	.1	Deferred Taxes	.0	.0				
7.8	8.9	8.6	All Other Non-Current	8.0	13.7				
27.0	41.4	20.7	Net Worth	29.6	-4.0				
100.0	100.0	100.0	Total Liabilties & Net Worth	100.0	100.0				
			INCOME DATA						
100.0	100.0	100.0	Net Sales	100.0	100.0				
			Gross Profit						
82.2	77.3	82.1	Operating Expenses	81.5	77.2				
17.8	22.7	17.9	Operating Profit	18.5	22.8				
3.1	2.1	2.8	All Other Expenses (net)	2.7	4.1				
14.6	20.6	15.1	Profit Before Taxes	15.8	18.7				
			RATIOS						
2.2	3.8	3.3		9.2	2.0				
1.3	2.0	1.6	Current	1.9	1.4				
.3	.5	.4		.2	.3				
1.5	3.8	2.4		9.2	2.0				
.7	1.5	.9	Quick	1.6	1.4				
.2	.3	.3		.2	.3				
0 UND	0 UND	0 UND		0 UND	0 UND				
0 UND	0 UND	0 UND	Sales/Receivables	0 UND	0 UND				
11 32.0	18 20.2	4 90.0		0 UND	0 UND				
			Cost of Sales/Inventory						
			Cost of Sales/Payables						
8.5	5.5	6.0		2.6	16.3				
40.0	30.2	19.6	Sales/Working Capital	19.6	201.8				
-17.7	-19.4	-9.8		-7.2	-9.0				
16.8	27.3	21.8		7.4	22.0				
(44) 6.1	(33) 5.8	(40) 5.2	EBIT/Interest	(12) 5.2	(15) 5.9				
2.3	2.4	2.5		2.5	3.5				
			Net Profit + Depr., Dep., Amort./Cur. Mat. L/T/D						
.2	.0	.2		.0	.2				
.8	.4	1.0	Fixed/Worth	1.0	3.1				
7.4	1.4	-.3		-.2	-.2				
.7	.5	.5		.4	1.2				
3.4	1.4	12.8	Debt/Worth	18.0	NM				
-2.2	-2.9	-1.4		-1.3	-1.3				
88.4	110.1	93.5							
(42) 31.2	(29) 41.4	(25) 31.5	% Profit Before Taxes/Tangible Net Worth						
20.9	11.5	12.7							
25.2	44.6	28.0		23.5	35.1				
14.4	17.8	13.3	% Profit Before Taxes/Total Assets	10.8	15.0				
4.7	4.5	4.0		4.0	8.6				
34.9	314.3	62.6		UND	270.8				
7.9	27.5	10.7	Sales/Net Fixed Assets	19.8	10.4				
2.6	5.0	4.6		14.1	8.5				
2.3	4.6	2.2		1.9	2.7				
1.3	1.4	1.2	Sales/Total Assets	1.3	1.2				
.8	.8	.7		.6	.9				
1.6	.3	.6			.3				
(45) 4.4	(28) 3.6	(28) 3.5	% Depr., Dep., Amort./Sales		(13) 2.6				
8.3	6.7	8.1			7.6				
1.6	1.9	2.5							
(21) 3.4	(18) 3.4	(18) 5.5	% Officers', Directors' Owners' Comp/Sales						
8.4	8.9	10.7							
491269M	403974M	357444M	Net Sales ($)	9472M	28484M	6507M	33190M	10646M	269145M
483562M	389131M	441452M	Total Assets ($)	12104M	25690M	5028M	37908M	2883M	357839M

M = $ thousand MM = $ million

See Pages 9 through 22 for Explanation of Ratios and Data

Current Data Sorted by Assets							Comparative Historical Data	
						Type of Statement		
		11	2		1	Unqualified	25	23
	1	15	1			Reviewed	15	13
	1	4	1			Compiled	7	13
6	4	3			1	Tax Returns	15	21
2	3	6	4			Other	18	14
	27 (4/1-9/30/13)		39 (10/1/13-3/31/14)				4/1/09-3/31/10	4/1/10-3/31/11
0-500M	500M-2MM	2-10MM	10-50MM	50-100MM	100-250MM		ALL	ALL
8	9	39	8		2	**NUMBER OF STATEMENTS**	80	84
%	%	%	%	%	%	**ASSETS**	%	%
		16.4		DATA NOT AVAILABLE		Cash & Equivalents	12.7	12.9
		19.9				Trade Receivables (net)	14.5	15.2
		12.2				Inventory	12.6	15.0
		3.5				All Other Current	2.5	4.3
		52.0				Total Current	42.3	47.4
		35.9				Fixed Assets (net)	45.9	40.9
		.4				Intangibles (net)	.7	1.2
		11.6				All Other Non-Current	11.0	10.5
		100.0				Total	100.0	100.0
						LIABILITIES		
		5.5				Notes Payable-Short Term	9.0	12.0
		3.1				Cur. Mat.-L.T.D.	6.3	6.0
		12.7				Trade Payables	7.3	7.9
		.1				Income Taxes Payable	.1	.2
		13.9				All Other Current	15.9	10.9
		35.3				Total Current	38.5	37.1
		16.5				Long-Term Debt	21.0	23.8
		.2				Deferred Taxes	.1	.3
		1.8				All Other Non-Current	5.3	4.5
		46.2				Net Worth	35.2	34.3
		100.0				Total Liabilities & Net Worth	100.0	100.0
						INCOME DATA		
		100.0				Net Sales	100.0	100.0
						Gross Profit		
		80.5				Operating Expenses	89.0	90.3
		19.5				Operating Profit	11.0	9.7
		-.9				All Other Expenses (net)	1.5	.2
		20.4				Profit Before Taxes	9.4	9.5
						RATIOS		
		2.3					2.5	2.7
		1.4				Current	1.3	1.4
		1.2					.7	.9
		1.4					1.9	1.5
		1.2				Quick	.8	.8
		.7					.2	.3
		8 45.6					1 249.4	3 114.2
		37 9.8				Sales/Receivables	20 18.5	18 20.8
		101 3.6					44 8.3	65 5.6
						Cost of Sales/Inventory		
						Cost of Sales/Payables		
		4.3					5.2	5.2
		7.5				Sales/Working Capital	13.2	14.7
		36.7					-23.4	-39.1
		88.5					16.6	30.1
		(38) 19.0				EBIT/Interest	(61) 3.0	(69) 5.8
		5.9					.5	1.2
							4.7	3.7
						Net Profit + Depr., Dep., Amort./Cur. Mat. L/T/D	(10) 1.8	(10) 3.1
							.4	1.8
		.4					.5	.4
		.7				Fixed/Worth	.9	.8
		1.3					2.3	2.7
		.6					.4	.5
		1.1				Debt/Worth	1.1	1.8
		2.1					5.1	5.0
		65.0					38.5	40.4
		(37) 29.3				% Profit Before Taxes/Tangible Net Worth	(69) 15.8	(71) 16.3
		14.7					-.8	4.4
		28.1					16.8	15.6
		14.4				% Profit Before Taxes/Total Assets	6.7	5.4
		6.7					-1.9	.3
		10.4					8.7	15.9
		3.8				Sales/Net Fixed Assets	3.0	3.9
		2.4					1.2	1.7
		2.1					2.8	2.7
		1.3				Sales/Total Assets	1.3	1.2
		.9					.6	.7
		2.1					2.4	1.5
		(37) 4.1				% Depr., Dep., Amort./Sales	(67) 5.0	(72) 4.9
		5.6					10.0	8.7
							.8	2.3
						% Officers', Directors' Owners' Comp/Sales	(13) 2.3	(23) 5.0
							7.8	10.3
10487M	24758M	374220M	202901M		3283838M	Net Sales ($)	1589947M	1643765M
1412M	9806M	217446M	160830M		315170M	Total Assets ($)	614038M	714482M

M = $ thousand MM = $ million

See Pages 9 through 22 for Explanation of Ratios and Data

Comparative Historical Data				Current Data Sorted by Sales					
			Type of Statement						
18	20	14	Unqualified		2	5	3	3	1
10	11	17	Reviewed		1	6	3	6	1
10	6	6	Compiled			3	2	1	
19	13	14	Tax Returns	6	3	1	3		1
18	20	15	Other	1	3	2	3	1	5
4/1/11-3/31/12	**4/1/12-3/31/13**	**4/1/13-3/31/14**		**27 (4/1-9/30/13)**			**39 (10/1/13-3/31/14)**		
ALL	**ALL**	**ALL**		**0-1MM**	**1-3MM**	**3-5MM**	**5-10MM**	**10-25MM**	**25MM & OVER**
75	70	66	**NUMBER OF STATEMENTS**	7	9	17	14	11	8
%	%	%	**ASSETS**	%	%	%	%	%	%
16.4	14.8	19.6	Cash & Equivalents			16.6	23.2	15.1	
19.4	17.7	18.7	Trade Receivables (net)			16.7	20.1	20.6	
13.5	15.3	11.7	Inventory			11.2	10.1	19.2	
5.5	4.7	3.4	All Other Current			4.1	4.6	3.5	
54.7	52.6	53.5	Total Current			48.7	57.9	58.5	
35.5	36.3	34.6	Fixed Assets (net)			43.2	32.9	25.8	
1.6	1.4	1.3	Intangibles (net)			.5	.5	.0	
8.1	9.7	10.7	All Other Non-Current			7.6	8.7	15.7	
100.0	100.0	100.0	Total			100.0	100.0	100.0	
			LIABILITIES						
11.2	10.9	15.2	Notes Payable-Short Term			3.2	10.5	7.3	
4.3	4.1	3.0	Cur. Mat.-L.T.D.			2.9	3.2	1.8	
10.4	9.5	12.2	Trade Payables			6.4	18.3	14.5	
.2	.1	.2	Income Taxes Payable			.0	.5	.2	
13.9	8.4	11.9	All Other Current			13.4	8.5	17.0	
40.0	33.1	42.4	Total Current			26.0	40.9	40.8	
15.8	20.8	13.8	Long-Term Debt			15.5	10.8	15.6	
.3	.4	.2	Deferred Taxes			.0	.2	.4	
2.6	5.2	7.4	All Other Non-Current			1.3	2.1	8.1	
41.3	40.5	36.2	Net Worth			57.1	46.0	35.0	
100.0	100.0	100.0	Total Liabilties & Net Worth			100.0	100.0	100.0	
			INCOME DATA						
100.0	100.0	100.0	Net Sales			100.0	100.0	100.0	
			Gross Profit						
87.2	87.0	83.8	Operating Expenses			77.8	83.1	84.2	
12.8	13.0	16.2	Operating Profit			22.2	16.9	15.8	
.6	.5	-.7	All Other Expenses (net)			-1.1	-.8	-.4	
12.2	12.4	16.9	Profit Before Taxes			23.3	17.6	16.2	
			RATIOS						
2.3	2.6	2.6				5.3	1.9	1.6	
1.4	1.6	1.5	Current			1.8	1.5	1.3	
1.1	1.1	1.1				1.3	.9	1.1	
1.8	1.7	1.8				4.0	1.4	1.1	
.9	.8	1.2	Quick			1.4	1.3	.8	
.4	.5	.5				.8	.7	.5	
3 107.9	**3** 124.5	**3** 140.8				**6** 58.9	**3** 145.9	**4** 83.2	
18 20.8	**19** 18.9	**21** 17.7	Sales/Receivables			**34** 10.7	**29** 12.5	**31** 11.9	
57 6.4	**46** 8.0	**65** 5.6				**114** 3.2	**78** 4.7	**45** 8.2	
			Cost of Sales/Inventory						
			Cost of Sales/Payables						
6.4	4.8	4.7				4.1	4.9	6.6	
13.6	8.0	9.5	Sales/Working Capital			5.0	10.1	22.9	
66.2	252.8	35.3				10.5	-237.0	64.1	
28.3	31.9	82.3				138.0	73.7	88.8	
(59) 6.6	(63) 8.9	(58) 15.3	EBIT/Interest			(14) 42.7	(12) 22.0	12.7	
2.4	2.5	5.8				5.9	8.0	4.6	
17.3	14.3								
(11) 5.5	(12) 6.1		Net Profit + Depr., Dep., Amort./Cur. Mat. L/T/D						
1.7	2.4								
.3	.4	.4				.4	.4	.3	
.8	.7	.7	Fixed/Worth			.7	.8	.6	
2.1	1.9	1.4				1.3	1.6	1.3	
.5	.6	.6				.2	.5	1.0	
1.8	1.3	1.2	Debt/Worth			.7	1.2	1.4	
4.1	4.4	3.3				1.3	2.5	2.7	
57.6	52.8	64.3				54.9	95.7	129.1	
(68) 27.0	(63) 22.3	(58) 26.9	% Profit Before Taxes/Tangible Net Worth			(16) 25.9	(13) 35.7	(10) 21.9	
8.9	8.7	11.7				13.8	16.7	7.3	
23.5	19.3	27.0				22.7	28.7	52.8	
10.9	8.7	12.2	% Profit Before Taxes/Total Assets			13.6	21.2	11.8	
1.9	4.0	5.4				5.4	7.0	2.7	
23.5	12.5	13.3				4.0	65.8	13.5	
5.8	4.7	4.7	Sales/Net Fixed Assets			2.5	3.9	11.4	
2.4	2.5	2.6				1.3	2.5	6.6	
3.3	2.8	2.5				1.3	3.3	4.0	
1.6	1.4	1.5	Sales/Total Assets			1.0	1.3	2.5	
1.0	.9	.9				.6	1.1	1.9	
1.1	1.2	1.2				2.0	3.2	.5	
(59) 2.9	(62) 3.6	(56) 2.6	% Depr., Dep., Amort./Sales			4.6	(11) 5.1	1.9	
5.7	6.4	5.4				6.2	5.4	2.4	
1.3	1.2	1.3							
(22) 4.2	(15) 2.0	(14) 5.0	% Officers', Directors' Owners' Comp/Sales						
6.8	5.7	6.6							
907963M	**4018726M**	**3896204M**	Net Sales ($)	**2743M**	**19637M**	**63134M**	**95559M**	**192437M**	**3522694M**
536305M	**874446M**	**704664M**	Total Assets ($)	**3056M**	**120841M**	**87343M**	**68066M**	**86931M**	**338427M**

M = $ thousand MM = $ million

See Pages 9 through 22 for Explanation of Ratios and Data

Current Data Sorted by Assets							Comparative Historical Data	
						Type of Statement		
	1	2	3	1	1	Unqualified	7	8
		2	5		1	Reviewed	10	11
1	8	5	1	1		Compiled	18	14
6	3	4	2			Tax Returns	18	19
3	9	7	2		2	Other	16	25
	15 (4/1-9/30/13)		55 (10/1/13-3/31/14)				4/1/09-3/31/10	4/1/10-3/31/11
0-500M	**500M-2MM**	**2-10MM**	**10-50MM**	**50-100MM**	**100-250MM**		**ALL**	**ALL**
10	21	20	13	2	4	**NUMBER OF STATEMENTS**	69	77
%	%	%	%	%	%	**ASSETS**	%	%
17.8	11.8	12.7	14.4			Cash & Equivalents	16.1	9.5
4.6	13.3	13.2	18.4			Trade Receivables (net)	11.3	16.3
8.5	6.2	17.1	13.8			Inventory	13.7	15.6
.0	1.3	8.1	4.7			All Other Current	3.3	4.7
30.9	32.5	51.2	51.3			Total Current	44.4	46.1
63.7	57.1	34.6	43.6			Fixed Assets (net)	39.8	40.4
2.6	2.2	4.1	.1			Intangibles (net)	2.1	3.3
2.9	8.1	10.1	5.0			All Other Non-Current	13.7	10.2
100.0	100.0	100.0	100.0			Total	100.0	100.0
						LIABILITIES		
15.4	11.2	8.4	8.4			Notes Payable-Short Term	15.5	16.0
7.2	6.7	2.7	2.7			Cur. Mat.-L.T.D.	5.3	5.8
1.2	7.6	8.8	10.2			Trade Payables	4.5	9.0
.0	.1	.3	.1			Income Taxes Payable	.4	.3
4.5	4.3	7.4	5.8			All Other Current	8.5	9.7
28.3	29.9	27.6	27.2			Total Current	34.1	40.7
47.2	35.9	15.2	13.8			Long-Term Debt	28.8	26.1
.0	.2	2.1	.3			Deferred Taxes	.2	.4
1.3	24.1	11.7	2.3			All Other Non-Current	2.2	5.8
23.1	10.0	43.5	56.4			Net Worth	34.7	27.0
100.0	100.0	100.0	100.0			Total Liabilties & Net Worth	100.0	100.0
						INCOME DATA		
100.0	100.0	100.0	100.0			Net Sales	100.0	100.0
						Gross Profit		
92.2	95.8	94.6	86.9			Operating Expenses	90.2	91.8
7.8	4.2	5.4	13.1			Operating Profit	9.8	8.2
1.1	1.5	-.6	1.0			All Other Expenses (net)	2.0	1.3
6.7	2.7	6.0	12.1			Profit Before Taxes	7.7	6.8
						RATIOS		
2.7	2.6	3.1	3.4				2.6	2.7
1.0	1.0	1.8	2.2			Current	1.4	1.3
.4	.4	1.0	1.3				.6	.8
1.4	1.8	2.4	2.7				2.2	1.8
.6	.8	1.1	1.4			Quick	.7	.6
.4	.3	.5	.7				.2	.3
0 UND	**1** 320.5	**13** 27.4	**20** 17.9				**0** UND	**1** 384.7
0 UND	**12** 31.6	**21** 17.5	**30** 12.2			Sales/Receivables	**15** 23.9	**24** 15.4
2 221.7	**49** 7.4	**43** 8.5	**66** 5.5				**41** 8.9	**49** 7.5
						Cost of Sales/Inventory		
						Cost of Sales/Payables		
5.7	7.0	3.9	3.6				4.8	5.6
NM	678.8	14.2	5.0			Sales/Working Capital	15.6	19.0
-10.2	-6.8	-343.2	18.5				-38.7	-24.8
	6.1	17.0	45.9				21.4	12.7
	(19) 2.1	(17) 6.6	(12) 17.2			EBIT/Interest	(62) 4.6	(68) 4.3
	.5	1.8	1.8				1.7	1.9
							6.6	17.5
						Net Profit + Depr., Dep., Amort./Cur. Mat. L/T/D	(16) 3.3	(13) 3.5
							1.7	.6
1.0	.9	.2	.3				.3	.4
6.5	1.7	1.2	.7			Fixed/Worth	.7	1.1
-2.2	-18.4	2.8	.8				2.7	3.2
1.0	.9	.4	.2				.4	.7
8.8	2.2	1.2	.7			Debt/Worth	1.6	2.0
-3.8	-37.4	6.6	2.0				3.8	5.7
	20.8	42.4	34.4				42.5	50.2
	(15) 13.7	(18) 13.7	15.0			% Profit Before Taxes/Tangible Net Worth	(62) 21.1	(67) 20.1
	2.7	5.4	2.3				6.4	8.7
25.8	11.3	14.5	25.2				16.8	19.7
7.8	4.5	6.4	4.8			% Profit Before Taxes/Total Assets	8.1	6.7
-.4	-.2	2.1	1.2				1.7	2.0
5.5	6.1	12.6	10.5				14.4	11.8
3.3	2.8	5.9	4.7			Sales/Net Fixed Assets	8.6	5.1
1.5	1.9	2.8	1.3				2.6	2.3
3.4	2.4	1.9	2.0				2.8	2.5
2.0	1.6	1.7	1.5			Sales/Total Assets	1.7	1.5
.9	1.3	1.3	.8				1.1	1.1
	4.6	.9	1.0				1.6	2.4
	(15) 8.9	(16) 1.7	3.0			% Depr., Dep., Amort./Sales	(54) 4.8	(61) 5.2
	17.8	6.5	8.1				10.4	10.1
		1.3					1.3	1.8
		(10) 2.1				% Officers', Directors' Owners' Comp/Sales	(22) 4.6	(28) 3.4
		4.0					10.5	6.5
6062M	**55858M**	**183742M**	**343778M**	**28489M**	**440389M**	Net Sales ($)	**1600354M**	**992565M**
2664M	**24141M**	**102923M**	**265863M**	**119759M**	**603681M**	Total Assets ($)	**1071308M**	**735106M**

M = $ thousand MM = $ million

See Pages 9 through 22 for Explanation of Ratios and Data

Comparative Historical Data				Current Data Sorted by Sales					
			Type of Statement						
6	9	8	Unqualified		1		1	3	3
5	12	8	Reviewed				1	4	3
14	11	16	Compiled	1	7		3	5	
24	24	15	Tax Returns	5	4	2	2	1	1
29	28	23	Other	5	6	3	2	4	3
				15 (4/1-9/30/13)			55 (10/1/13-3/31/14)		
4/1/11-3/31/12 ALL	4/1/12-3/31/13 ALL	4/1/13-3/31/14 ALL		0-1MM	1-3MM	3-5MM	5-10MM	10-25MM	25MM & OVER
78	84	70	**NUMBER OF STATEMENTS**	11	18	5	9	17	10
%	%	%	**ASSETS**	%	%	%	%	%	%
14.8	13.4	13.7	Cash & Equivalents	9.5	16.0			14.1	16.6
12.6	19.4	12.3	Trade Receivables (net)	5.4	10.1			14.4	15.5
13.5	12.4	11.9	Inventory	6.2	3.8			19.5	18.2
5.5	4.8	3.7	All Other Current	.1	7.0			5.0	1.6
46.4	50.0	41.6	Total Current	21.2	36.8			53.0	51.9
42.8	39.0	47.0	Fixed Assets (net)	76.4	54.3			39.3	29.7
1.3	2.6	3.6	Intangibles (net)	2.3	3.2			2.7	9.3
9.5	8.4	7.9	All Other Non-Current	.1	5.7			4.9	9.1
100.0	100.0	100.0	Total	100.0	100.0			100.0	100.0
			LIABILITIES						
8.5	11.0	10.0	Notes Payable-Short Term	18.3	6.6			13.6	.7
5.6	4.6	4.5	Cur. Mat.-L.T.D.	8.3	7.2			2.3	1.3
11.6	11.3	7.2	Trade Payables	2.6	6.2			6.9	12.2
.1	.1	.3	Income Taxes Payable	.0	.2			.0	1.2
10.2	8.9	5.5	All Other Current	3.6	3.2			7.6	5.9
36.0	35.9	27.5	Total Current	32.8	23.4			30.4	21.2
29.9	26.0	25.6	Long-Term Debt	39.4	49.6			6.4	13.1
.1	.5	.7	Deferred Taxes	.0	.2			.9	.4
8.3	3.7	11.2	All Other Non-Current	3.1	21.1			9.1	1.8
25.6	33.9	35.0	Net Worth	24.6	5.7			53.3	63.5
100.0	100.0	100.0	Total Liabilties & Net Worth	100.0	100.0			100.0	100.0
			INCOME DATA						
100.0	100.0	100.0	Net Sales	100.0	100.0			100.0	100.0
			Gross Profit						
90.9	92.8	92.3	Operating Expenses	94.2	93.4			93.1	83.6
9.1	7.2	7.7	Operating Profit	5.8	6.6			6.9	16.4
1.6	.3	.5	All Other Expenses (net)	2.1	1.0			-1.2	.1
7.4	6.9	7.2	Profit Before Taxes	3.7	5.6			8.1	16.2
			RATIOS						
2.4	2.8	3.1		.8	3.6			3.4	4.2
1.3	1.5	1.6	Current	.5	1.3			1.7	2.8
.7	.9	.7		.4	.6			1.0	1.6
2.0	2.1	2.1		.8	2.5			2.7	2.7
.7	.9	.9	Quick	.4	1.0			1.3	1.8
.3	.5	.4		.3	.4			.4	.6
0 UND	**7** 53.9	**4** 92.4		**0** UND	**0** UND			**14** 27.0	**18** 20.2
16 23.2	**28** 12.9	**20** 17.9	Sales/Receivables	**1** 321.0	**7** 49.9			**28** 12.9	**24** 15.4
27 13.5	**52** 7.0	**42** 8.6		**54** 6.7	**36** 10.0			**40** 9.1	**60** 6.1
			Cost of Sales/Inventory						
			Cost of Sales/Payables						
7.2	5.1	4.1		-47.5	4.1			3.5	2.3
18.9	14.1	15.5	Sales/Working Capital	-10.3	51.6			10.3	4.5
-23.4	-69.8	-29.8		-5.0	-27.3			-142.5	17.1
8.8	15.7	19.1		3.6	6.6			14.2	
(67) 4.1	(75) 3.7	(63) 3.6	EBIT/Interest	1.8	(15) 3.7			(14) 3.5	
1.6	1.2	1.6		.0	1.1			1.9	
8.0	5.3	33.6							
(11) 2.9	(16) 2.0	(12) 3.4	Net Profit + Depr., Dep., Amort./Cur. Mat. L/T/D						
1.1	1.4	1.7							
.7	.3	.4		1.4	.8			.3	.3
1.3	.9	1.2	Fixed/Worth	2.7	2.8			.8	.7
3.3	2.5	5.4		-4.2	-6.9			1.9	.8
.9	.7	.5		.9	.9			.3	.2
2.9	1.9	1.3	Debt/Worth	2.1	3.0			.8	.5
7.4	6.5	13.4		-5.9	-8.8			3.7	1.5
58.8	55.8	33.2			65.6			29.5	
(66) 25.8	(72) 21.5	(58) 14.8	% Profit Before Taxes/Tangible Net Worth		(12) 46.0			9.8	
8.3	4.4	4.2			13.9			3.4	
17.8	20.7	13.5		12.5	18.0			12.7	23.2
6.9	8.2	6.0	% Profit Before Taxes/Total Assets	3.8	6.1			4.3	11.0
1.8	1.3	1.4		-.5	2.8			1.6	9.1
14.2	19.3	9.5		3.2	6.1			14.4	11.4
5.8	6.8	4.1	Sales/Net Fixed Assets	1.4	3.5			6.1	6.2
2.1	2.8	1.9		.8	2.2			1.3	2.1
3.0	3.1	2.0		1.3	2.4			2.0	2.2
1.9	1.8	1.6	Sales/Total Assets	1.0	1.6			1.7	1.1
1.1	1.4	1.0		.7	1.3			.9	.8
1.7	1.3	1.3			3.1			1.0	
(54) 4.5	(61) 2.4	(57) 3.5	% Depr., Dep., Amort./Sales		(13) 7.2			(15) 2.5	
12.2	9.8	10.2			16.2			7.9	
2.1	1.9	1.3							
(28) 3.8	(29) 4.1	(26) 3.3	% Officers', Directors' Owners' Comp/Sales						
8.8	5.3	9.3							
1606669M	**5374567M**	**1058318M**	Net Sales ($)	**5633M**	**33001M**	**23537M**	**71326M**	**260913M**	**663908M**
972987M	**1290959M**	**1119031M**	Total Assets ($)	**5714M**	**19896M**	**18654M**	**67751M**	**277960M**	**729056M**

Current Data Sorted by Assets							Comparative Historical Data	
						Type of Statement		
2	1	3	8	5	3	Unqualified	55	46
	5	16	21	5	1	Reviewed	51	60
	5	16	8	1		Compiled	33	35
4	7	8	2			Tax Returns	19	24
3	7	21	18	5	5	Other	72	60
	68 (4/1-9/30/13)		112 (10/1/13-3/31/14)				4/1/09-3/31/10	4/1/10-3/31/11
0-500M	**500M-2MM**	**2-10MM**	**10-50MM**	**50-100MM**	**100-250MM**		**ALL**	**ALL**
9	25	64	57	16	9	**NUMBER OF STATEMENTS**	230	225
%	%	%	%	%	%	**ASSETS**	%	%
	12.1	9.1	9.0	20.8		Cash & Equivalents	9.3	10.0
	13.6	24.7	21.5	18.8		Trade Receivables (net)	19.2	20.1
	19.9	14.8	21.5	15.8		Inventory	18.9	17.4
	8.6	4.6	5.1	5.9		All Other Current	5.5	5.2
	54.1	53.1	57.2	61.3		Total Current	52.8	52.7
	41.0	40.4	34.0	31.1		Fixed Assets (net)	38.1	37.6
	1.5	1.4	2.5	2.8		Intangibles (net)	1.6	1.7
	3.4	5.0	6.3	4.8		All Other Non-Current	7.5	8.0
	100.0	100.0	100.0	100.0		Total	100.0	100.0
						LIABILITIES		
	12.9	9.9	7.3	7.1		Notes Payable-Short Term	11.5	11.3
	4.4	4.0	3.3	2.3		Cur. Mat.-L.T.D.	4.1	3.6
	15.9	17.1	21.1	15.9		Trade Payables	14.1	13.8
	.1	.1	.1	.4		Income Taxes Payable	.2	.3
	6.9	9.1	11.8	14.5		All Other Current	10.0	11.6
	40.2	40.1	43.7	40.2		Total Current	39.8	40.6
	18.0	18.6	16.1	12.9		Long-Term Debt	20.3	18.3
	.0	.4	.9	1.1		Deferred Taxes	.6	.7
	6.0	5.2	3.2	4.4		All Other Non-Current	3.0	3.4
	35.8	35.7	36.2	41.4		Net Worth	36.3	37.0
	100.0	100.0	100.0	100.0		Total Liabilties & Net Worth	100.0	100.0
						INCOME DATA		
	100.0	100.0	100.0	100.0		Net Sales	100.0	100.0
						Gross Profit		
	88.7	93.9	87.9	85.5		Operating Expenses	91.8	89.9
	11.3	6.1	12.1	14.5		Operating Profit	8.2	10.1
	.3	.1	.1	.3		All Other Expenses (net)	1.6	1.9
	11.0	6.0	12.0	14.2		Profit Before Taxes	6.6	8.2
						RATIOS		
	3.2	2.2	1.9	2.6			1.8	1.8
	1.3	1.3	1.3	1.7		Current	1.3	1.3
	.7	.8	1.1	1.2			1.0	1.0
	1.5	1.6	1.1	1.5			1.2	1.3
	.6	.9	.8	1.1		Quick	(229) .6	(224) .7
	.3	.5	.3	.9			.3	.3
	0 UND	**13** 27.1	**16** 22.8	**27** 13.5			**11** 32.4	**9** 39.4
	13 27.6	**29** 12.7	**37** 9.8	**42** 8.6		Sales/Receivables	**32** 11.3	**34** 10.7
	29 12.8	**61** 6.0	**66** 5.5	**74** 4.9			**50** 7.2	**63** 5.8
						Cost of Sales/Inventory		
						Cost of Sales/Payables		
	9.7	8.7	5.1	3.5			5.9	6.9
	37.4	29.3	9.2	6.7		Sales/Working Capital	15.7	13.6
	-22.6	-39.8	51.3	19.0			-174.6	-114.1
	33.5	20.9	28.7	32.4			11.4	14.1
	(22) 12.0	(59) 6.0	(52) 14.1	(15) 13.8		EBIT/Interest	(219) 4.1	(210) 5.7
	1.0	1.8	2.3	9.0			1.4	2.1
			7.9				9.5	7.3
			(14) 2.8			Net Profit + Depr., Dep., Amort./Cur. Mat. L/T/D	(73) 3.4	(65) 3.7
			1.4				1.4	2.0
	.4	.3	.5	.6			.5	.4
	.8	1.0	1.0	1.0		Fixed/Worth	1.0	.9
	14.7	2.7	1.7	1.3			2.0	1.7
	.5	.8	.8	.8			.9	.8
	1.5	2.3	1.9	1.5		Debt/Worth	1.7	1.7
	29.4	4.2	6.0	3.7			3.6	3.8
	135.4	56.9	72.2	46.5			35.6	39.5
	(20) 46.4	(59) 19.3	(53) 35.6	32.7		% Profit Before Taxes/Tangible Net Worth	(208) 16.7	(207) 20.5
	18.8	5.4	10.5	23.2			4.6	7.3
	40.3	21.1	17.4	17.0			12.2	12.9
	18.4	6.3	9.9	14.2		% Profit Before Taxes/Total Assets	5.8	7.0
	.8	1.6	2.7	9.5			.9	1.8
	39.1	19.5	16.0	13.6			14.2	14.8
	9.7	9.5	4.9	4.6		Sales/Net Fixed Assets	6.1	6.0
	2.3	2.7	1.9	1.6			1.9	1.9
	4.5	3.7	2.3	2.6			2.7	2.7
	2.8	2.4	1.3	1.1		Sales/Total Assets	1.6	1.6
	1.5	1.1	.8	.7			.9	.8
	.8	.7	1.2	1.0			1.2	1.2
	(22) 2.6	(59) 1.6	(53) 3.0	2.7		% Depr., Dep., Amort./Sales	(204) 2.3	(203) 2.7
	9.9	4.6	5.8	5.5			5.8	6.8
		1.2	.4				.9	.8
		(14) 1.8	(14) .9			% Officers', Directors' Owners' Comp/Sales	(44) 1.5	(57) 1.8
		2.8	2.3				4.1	5.2
21407M	106306M	890966M	2185710M	1818028M	2575038M	Net Sales ($)	11802094M	8400474M
2109M	27594M	303428M	1304390M	1066463M	1382426M	Total Assets ($)	6712774M	5196828M

M = $ thousand MM = $ million

See Pages 9 through 22 for Explanation of Ratios and Data

Comparative Historical Data / Current Data Sorted by Sales

4/1/11-3/31/12 ALL	4/1/12-3/31/13 ALL	4/1/13-3/31/14 ALL	Type of Statement	0-1MM	1-3MM	3-5MM	5-10MM	10-25MM	25MM & OVER
39	35	22	Unqualified	1	1	2	1	7	10
56	44	48	Reviewed	1	3		4	20	20
39	30	30	Compiled	2	2	4	8	7	7
27	15	21	Tax Returns	3	7	4	3	1	3
57	69	59	Other	2	8	6	8	13	22
				68 (4/1-9/30/13)			112 (10/1/13-3/31/14)		
218	193	180	NUMBER OF STATEMENTS	9	21	16	24	48	62
%	%	%	**ASSETS**	%	%	%	%	%	%
11.9	12.5	11.3	Cash & Equivalents		14.2	9.0	11.1	9.6	12.5
21.2	20.3	20.9	Trade Receivables (net)		12.1	10.8	27.9	21.2	24.8
17.7	20.2	17.6	Inventory		8.3	10.7	20.2	18.8	21.1
4.1	3.8	5.4	All Other Current		4.6	6.5	7.4	5.0	5.6
54.9	56.7	55.2	Total Current		39.1	37.1	66.6	54.5	64.0
35.8	34.5	37.6	Fixed Assets (net)		52.8	56.3	28.4	36.9	29.6
1.7	2.7	1.8	Intangibles (net)		2.3	1.1	3.3	2.2	1.2
7.6	6.1	5.4	All Other Non-Current		5.7	5.5	1.7	6.4	5.2
100.0	100.0	100.0	Total		100.0	100.0	100.0	100.0	100.0
			LIABILITIES						
10.3	11.5	9.7	Notes Payable-Short Term		12.1	9.7	16.2	7.7	7.7
4.0	3.3	3.8	Cur. Mat.-L.T.D.		7.8	8.9	2.2	3.1	2.3
13.6	15.9	17.4	Trade Payables		10.8	8.6	22.2	17.9	22.0
.1	.1	.1	Income Taxes Payable		.1	.0	.1	.3	.1
14.9	13.6	11.8	All Other Current		16.4	4.8	10.3	12.1	12.2
42.8	44.4	42.8	Total Current		47.2	32.0	51.0	41.1	44.4
19.7	16.5	17.3	Long-Term Debt		29.5	28.8	10.0	17.4	12.3
.7	.6	.6	Deferred Taxes		.0	.7	.1	1.0	.7
4.6	6.6	5.4	All Other Non-Current		4.4	3.1	5.1	3.2	3.8
32.2	31.9	34.0	Net Worth		18.9	35.4	33.9	37.4	38.8
100.0	100.0	100.0	Total Liabilties & Net Worth		100.0	100.0	100.0	100.0	100.0
			INCOME DATA						
100.0	100.0	100.0	Net Sales		100.0	100.0	100.0	100.0	100.0
			Gross Profit						
90.6	89.4	90.5	Operating Expenses		82.3	88.4	93.4	93.0	90.2
9.4	10.6	9.5	Operating Profit		17.7	11.6	6.6	7.0	9.8
1.4	1.6	.0	All Other Expenses (net)		1.2	.5	.2	-.3	-.2
8.0	9.0	9.5	Profit Before Taxes		16.5	11.1	6.4	7.2	10.0
			RATIOS						
2.2	2.0	2.2			1.3	3.1	3.5	2.0	2.2
1.4	1.3	1.3	Current		.9	1.3	1.3	1.3	1.4
1.0	1.0	1.0			.6	.6	1.0	1.0	1.1
1.4	1.2	1.4			1.3	2.6	1.9	1.1	1.3
.8	.9	.9	Quick		.6	.9	1.0	.7	.9
.4	.4	.4			.4	.2	.3	.4	.6
15 23.7	**13** 27.9	**13** 27.7			**0** UND	**0** 807.3	**16** 23.3	**12** 29.5	**25** 14.8
33 11.2	**33** 11.1	**29** 12.4	Sales/Receivables		**19** 19.1	**20** 18.5	**47** 7.7	**22** 16.5	**38** 9.6
62 5.9	**59** 6.2	**54** 6.7			**35** 10.5	**70** 5.2	**85** 4.3	**49** 7.4	**54** 6.8
			Cost of Sales/Inventory						
			Cost of Sales/Payables						
5.8	6.3	5.8			11.5	6.0	5.1	5.8	4.4
14.7	15.5	14.3	Sales/Working Capital		-59.8	96.9	12.0	19.8	13.0
-131.7	114.6	-461.7			-14.8	-34.2	155.0	699.4	41.5
18.5	24.1	27.3			14.1	26.3	31.8	33.9	33.0
(200) 6.3	(175) 6.8	(161) 10.0	EBIT/Interest		(18) 5.6	(14) 4.4	6.5	(42) 5.0	(57) 14.4
2.2	1.7	2.0			.3	.9	1.6	2.3	3.4
7.7	8.9	5.8						2.6	9.9
(61) 3.6	(45) 3.3	(37) 2.5	Net Profit + Depr., Dep., Amort./Cur. Mat. L/T/D					(10) 2.0	(19) 4.3
1.7	1.2	1.4						1.1	1.5
.4	.5	.5			.6	.8	.2	.5	.4
.9	1.0	1.0	Fixed/Worth		2.7	1.6	.8	.9	1.0
2.2	2.2	2.5			14.7	4.0	4.1	1.7	1.4
.9	.9	.8			.9	.6	.6	.8	.8
1.6	2.0	1.8	Debt/Worth		3.6	2.4	2.1	1.5	1.7
5.6	6.1	6.0			NM	30.7	10.8	3.3	4.1
48.6	53.3	68.8			99.0	185.2	65.8	59.5	67.2
(191) 23.4	(172) 27.2	(163) 26.9	% Profit Before Taxes/Tangible Net Worth		(16) 56.4	28.5	(20) 18.6	(44) 22.6	(60) 35.0
8.3	7.1	9.1			8.5	2.3	9.5	7.0	20.6
17.7	17.4	20.0			32.2	18.4	18.6	17.2	19.1
7.9	7.0	10.0	% Profit Before Taxes/Total Assets		13.0	9.4	5.2	8.1	13.6
1.8	1.2	2.2			-.6	.6	1.6	3.2	2.8
21.0	18.9	20.1			13.5	11.6	34.9	18.5	22.2
6.7	6.3	7.1	Sales/Net Fixed Assets		2.4	2.4	13.7	7.7	7.8
2.4	2.5	2.2			1.0	.9	3.3	3.7	2.9
3.1	2.8	3.4			3.3	2.8	2.8	3.8	3.5
1.7	1.6	1.9	Sales/Total Assets		1.8	1.2	1.9	2.5	2.0
.9	.8	1.0			.6	.7	1.0	1.2	.9
1.0	.9	.9			4.5	2.0	.6	1.0	.7
(191) 2.7	(165) 2.7	(162) 2.4	% Depr., Dep., Amort./Sales		(18) 9.9	(14) 4.6	(22) 1.0	(45) 2.0	(56) 1.6
6.6	5.0	5.7			19.5	10.4	3.4	4.1	4.9
1.0	.8	.7						1.0	.4
(46) 1.4	(31) 1.6	(43) 1.7	% Officers', Directors' Owners' Comp/Sales					(12) 2.5	(15) .8
3.5	4.6	3.3						3.8	2.3
12249412M	7485533M	7597455M	Net Sales ($)	4941M	40312M	64925M	181832M	811238M	6494207M
4801384M	4696304M	4086410M	Total Assets ($)	5835M	43984M	69308M	130785M	502638M	3333860M

M = $ thousand MM = $ million

See Pages 9 through 22 for Explanation of Ratios and Data

Current Data Sorted by Assets							Comparative Historical Data	
	1	2	1		1	**Type of Statement** Unqualified	3	5
	2	2				Reviewed	5	5
	3		1			Compiled	6	8
2	2	1				Tax Returns	3	7
1	2	5	3	1		Other	2	6
	8 (4/1-9/30/13)		22 (10/1/13-3/31/14)				4/1/09-3/31/10	4/1/10-3/31/11
0-500M	500M-2MM	2-10MM	10-50MM	50-100MM	100-250MM		ALL	ALL
3	10	10	5	1	1	**NUMBER OF STATEMENTS**	19	31
%	%	%	%	%	%	**ASSETS**	%	%
	17.0	19.6				Cash & Equivalents	24.7	21.1
	11.4	6.3				Trade Receivables (net)	7.3	13.8
	10.8	14.3				Inventory	3.5	8.1
	3.7	5.5				All Other Current	6.6	6.6
	42.9	45.7				Total Current	42.1	49.6
	37.2	44.8				Fixed Assets (net)	45.1	35.4
	.1	.1				Intangibles (net)	.3	1.1
	19.8	9.5				All Other Non-Current	12.6	13.9
	100.0	100.0				Total	100.0	100.0
						LIABILITIES		
	20.0	.5				Notes Payable-Short Term	6.0	11.2
	12.5	1.9				Cur. Mat.-L.T.D.	6.1	3.3
	3.7	6.0				Trade Payables	7.8	9.2
	.0	.6				Income Taxes Payable	.0	.3
	4.2	16.0				All Other Current	9.3	10.0
	40.3	24.9				Total Current	29.2	34.0
	22.7	17.6				Long-Term Debt	20.9	17.7
	.1	.8				Deferred Taxes	1.0	.1
	1.7	11.9				All Other Non-Current	.2	2.9
	35.2	44.7				Net Worth	48.9	45.3
	100.0	100.0				Total Liabilties & Net Worth	100.0	100.0
						INCOME DATA		
	100.0	100.0				Net Sales	100.0	100.0
						Gross Profit		
	92.3	95.6				Operating Expenses	87.1	90.7
	7.7	4.4				Operating Profit	12.9	9.3
	-.3	-.8				All Other Expenses (net)	1.7	-.1
	8.0	5.2				Profit Before Taxes	11.2	9.4
						RATIOS		
	8.5	2.7					3.3	4.8
	.9	1.3				Current	1.3	1.5
	.3	.6					.4	.8
	5.9	1.5					2.9	4.4
	.6	.6				Quick	.7	1.3
	.1	.1					.0	.4
	0 UND	0 UND					0 UND	0 UND
	0 UND	1 307.8				Sales/Receivables	0 UND	15 24.6
	36 10.1	19 19.2					23 15.7	34 10.7
						Cost of Sales/Inventory		
						Cost of Sales/Payables		
	4.3	5.0					4.3	5.2
	NM	275.0				Sales/Working Capital	39.8	13.0
	-13.1	-99.8					-4.5	-16.9
							14.0	18.6
						EBIT/Interest	(15) 6.6	(22) 4.7
							4.1	2.6
						Net Profit + Depr., Dep., Amort./Cur. Mat. L/T/D		
	.2	.2					.3	.2
	1.0	.9				Fixed/Worth	1.1	.6
	-57.0	2.1					1.6	1.9
	.4	.5					.4	.5
	.9	1.1				Debt/Worth	.9	1.2
	-87.8	3.2					3.8	3.0
		38.8					52.7	50.7
		24.2				% Profit Before Taxes/Tangible Net Worth	(18) 28.4	(30) 28.4
		5.0					12.4	8.5
	24.5	13.0					21.8	19.2
	10.8	6.5				% Profit Before Taxes/Total Assets	11.6	8.0
	3.1	2.3					3.3	2.1
	20.6	36.5					17.2	28.0
	8.9	4.8				Sales/Net Fixed Assets	3.9	6.1
	3.5	2.3					1.6	2.3
	2.9	3.0					3.0	3.2
	1.9	1.5				Sales/Total Assets	1.7	1.8
	1.6	.8					.6	1.2
							2.1	1.9
						% Depr., Dep., Amort./Sales	(17) 5.5	(21) 4.7
							9.2	9.0
								.5
						% Officers', Directors' Owners' Comp/Sales		(10) 3.6
								6.3
2349M	22899M	82589M	95624M	101546M	59599M	Net Sales ($)	150428M	594759M
173M	10277M	47798M	122135M	67404M	172360M	Total Assets ($)	220297M	444401M

M = $ thousand MM = $ million

See Pages 9 through 22 for Explanation of Ratios and Data

Comparative Historical Data				Current Data Sorted by Sales					
			Type of Statement						
4	4	5	Unqualified		1		2	1	1
6	3	4	Reviewed			2	1	1	
3	1	4	Compiled		3				1
8	2	5	Tax Returns	1	3	1			
7	8	12	Other	2	2	1	1	5	1
4/1/11-3/31/12	**4/1/12-3/31/13**	**4/1/13-3/31/14**		**8 (4/1-9/30/13)**			**22 (10/1/13-3/31/14)**		
ALL	**ALL**	**ALL**		**0-1MM**	**1-3MM**	**3-5MM**	**5-10MM**	**10-25MM**	**25MM & OVER**
28	18	30	**NUMBER OF STATEMENTS**	3	9	4	4	7	3
%	%	%	**ASSETS**	%	%	%	%	%	%
26.1	28.5	21.4	Cash & Equivalents						
13.5	12.4	9.5	Trade Receivables (net)						
4.8	9.7	10.0	Inventory						
6.3	4.5	5.3	All Other Current						
50.6	55.0	46.1	Total Current						
39.6	35.1	40.3	Fixed Assets (net)						
2.6	1.1	1.0	Intangibles (net)						
7.2	8.9	12.6	All Other Non-Current						
100.0	100.0	100.0	Total						
			LIABILITIES						
12.1	10.2	7.5	Notes Payable-Short Term						
4.2	6.5	6.1	Cur. Mat.-L.T.D.						
8.4	9.1	8.7	Trade Payables						
.4	.9	.8	Income Taxes Payable						
10.9	9.3	8.9	All Other Current						
36.0	36.0	31.9	Total Current						
27.2	16.0	19.7	Long-Term Debt						
.3	.8	.4	Deferred Taxes						
5.4	1.4	18.1	All Other Non-Current						
31.0	45.8	29.9	Net Worth						
100.0	100.0	100.0	Total Liabilities & Net Worth						
			INCOME DATA						
100.0	100.0	100.0	Net Sales						
			Gross Profit						
89.3	93.7	93.0	Operating Expenses						
10.7	6.3	7.0	Operating Profit						
2.2	-.6	-.7	All Other Expenses (net)						
8.4	7.0	7.7	Profit Before Taxes						
			RATIOS						
3.6	3.8	3.1							
1.6	1.4	1.5	Current						
.7	.8	.7							
3.5	3.5	1.5							
1.2	.8	.7	Quick						
.4	.4	.2							
0 UND	**0** UND	**0** UND							
19 18.9	**15** 24.0	**5** 67.7	Sales/Receivables						
43 8.5	**53** 6.9	**39** 9.3							
			Cost of Sales/Inventory						
			Cost of Sales/Payables						
6.5	4.7	3.4							
18.1	29.9	25.6	Sales/Working Capital						
-25.9	-17.6	-27.8							
25.2	42.0	39.4							
(21) 5.3	(15) 12.0	(25) 9.5	EBIT/Interest						
2.6	2.6	3.0							
			Net Profit + Depr., Dep., Amort./Cur. Mat. L/T/D						
.2	.1	.2							
.7	.5	.9	Fixed/Worth						
5.2	1.8	2.9							
.7	.5	.5							
1.6	1.7	.9	Debt/Worth						
8.8	2.5	3.9							
95.7	54.1	33.7							
(25) 48.8	30.7	(26) 17.5	% Profit Before Taxes/Tangible Net Worth						
10.1	-.7	9.9							
25.5	25.4	16.6							
9.8	11.4	8.7	% Profit Before Taxes/Total Assets						
3.2	-.3	2.5							
27.9	46.9	22.0							
7.8	7.5	6.4	Sales/Net Fixed Assets						
3.4	3.4	2.4							
3.9	3.5	3.0							
2.4	2.0	1.7	Sales/Total Assets						
1.4	1.4	1.1							
1.1	1.1	.9							
(24) 2.4	(16) 2.1	(25) 2.3	% Depr., Dep., Amort./Sales						
4.9	5.0	7.3							
.9									
(11) 5.0			% Officers', Directors' Owners' Comp/Sales						
6.2									
354615M	**330370M**	**364606M**	Net Sales ($)	**895M**	**16891M**	**15618M**	**26279M**	**97087M**	**207836M**
299607M	**332099M**	**420147M**	Total Assets ($)	**4588M**	**7393M**	**10480M**	**21704M**	**120569M**	**255413M**

M = $ thousand MM = $ million

See Pages 9 through 22 for Explanation of Ratios and Data

Current Data Sorted by Assets							Comparative Historical Data	
						Type of Statement		
		2	2	1	1	Unqualified	12	15
1	1	2	3			Reviewed	8	10
1	5	2	1			Compiled	23	11
9	12	5				Tax Returns	31	35
1	6	8	10		2	Other	32	24
10 (4/1-9/30/13)			65 (10/1/13-3/31/14)				4/1/09-3/31/10	4/1/10-3/31/11
0-500M	500M-2MM	2-10MM	10-50MM	50-100MM	100-250MM		ALL	ALL
12	24	19	16	1	3	**NUMBER OF STATEMENTS**	106	95
%	%	%	%	%	%	**ASSETS**	%	%
24.0	16.4	14.5	17.1			Cash & Equivalents	10.6	12.0
5.5	19.0	17.3	25.0			Trade Receivables (net)	18.9	13.5
10.1	24.1	13.9	12.6			Inventory	17.0	17.7
2.7	1.1	4.5	2.9			All Other Current	2.8	3.8
42.3	60.7	50.2	57.5			Total Current	49.3	47.0
42.6	31.2	31.7	28.1			Fixed Assets (net)	34.9	40.7
11.0	1.8	4.3	1.1			Intangibles (net)	5.9	4.9
4.0	6.3	13.8	13.3			All Other Non-Current	9.9	7.4
100.0	100.0	100.0	100.0			Total	100.0	100.0
						LIABILITIES		
9.2	14.7	14.6	6.7			Notes Payable-Short Term	19.9	13.3
41.5	2.6	1.1	2.1			Cur. Mat.-L.T.D.	4.8	3.7
4.4	4.7	11.5	12.2			Trade Payables	13.5	9.6
.0	.1	.1	.0			Income Taxes Payable	.2	.2
22.8	7.1	9.5	9.3			All Other Current	9.7	9.5
77.9	29.2	36.7	30.3			Total Current	48.0	36.3
57.6	38.4	12.6	9.6			Long-Term Debt	28.1	26.0
.0	.0	.3	.1			Deferred Taxes	.4	.3
18.7	7.0	7.2	3.7			All Other Non-Current	3.4	10.3
-54.5	25.4	43.2	56.3			Net Worth	20.1	27.0
100.0	100.0	100.0	100.0			Total Liabilties & Net Worth	100.0	100.0
						INCOME DATA		
100.0	100.0	100.0	100.0			Net Sales	100.0	100.0
						Gross Profit		
89.5	92.8	94.6	95.0			Operating Expenses	94.2	93.8
10.5	7.2	5.4	5.0			Operating Profit	5.8	6.2
-1.3	1.1	4.9	.2			All Other Expenses (net)	.8	2.6
11.8	6.1	.5	4.8			Profit Before Taxes	5.0	3.6
						RATIOS		
1.9	10.5	1.8	4.9				2.0	2.3
.7	2.2	1.2	1.9			Current	1.4	1.4
.2	1.1	.5	1.3				.4	.7
.8	5.9	1.5	3.1				1.4	1.3
.5	1.4	.8	1.6			Quick	.7	(94) .6
.2	.3	.4	.7				.2	.3
0 UND	**0** UND	**6** 59.6	**22** 16.3				**3** 120.9	**0** UND
0 UND	**13** 27.3	**21** 17.6	**36** 10.0			Sales/Receivables	**19** 19.0	**17** 21.9
8 45.3	**31** 11.9	**47** 7.8	**48** 7.6				**40** 9.2	**33** 11.1
						Cost of Sales/Inventory		
						Cost of Sales/Payables		
18.8	5.8	3.6	4.1				7.2	7.7
-80.4	10.6	18.2	7.2			Sales/Working Capital	34.2	30.9
-10.4	98.4	-10.1	35.9				-17.5	-49.5
23.6	12.6	63.6	193.5				12.5	12.2
(10) 10.9	(20) 5.1	(13) 3.0	(12) 11.4			EBIT/Interest	(88) 3.3	(80) 3.6
3.6	1.7	.6	.3				.8	1.5
								15.9
						Net Profit + Depr., Dep., Amort./Cur. Mat. L/T/D		(12) 4.7
								2.3
1.0	.3	.1	.1				.3	.3
-1.7	1.3	.5	.3			Fixed/Worth	.7	1.1
-.2	NM	1.7	1.0				3.5	3.6
.9	.6	.6	.2				.7	.7
-3.1	2.7	1.4	.8			Debt/Worth	2.1	2.0
-1.7	NM	5.9	3.2				11.7	5.7
	89.6	34.0	22.9				48.5	44.9
	(18) 32.8	(17) 12.6	7.9			% Profit Before Taxes/Tangible Net Worth	(84) 10.7	(76) 15.5
	8.0	-3.1	-.9				.4	5.1
75.3	34.0	15.6	15.0				17.8	22.0
26.7	12.6	2.8	4.9			% Profit Before Taxes/Total Assets	4.4	7.7
8.2	2.8	-1.5	-.5				-.4	1.4
151.8	48.7	24.3	53.6				44.1	22.3
10.9	14.1	11.3	12.7			Sales/Net Fixed Assets	10.3	8.3
4.3	4.5	2.3	3.3				4.2	2.3
7.4	4.6	3.7	3.6				4.7	3.9
3.3	3.2	1.6	1.6			Sales/Total Assets	2.5	2.4
2.7	2.1	.5	1.2				1.4	1.1
	.7	1.5	1.2				.7	1.4
	(16) 1.7	(14) 1.8	(12) 2.3			% Depr., Dep., Amort./Sales	(78) 1.9	(71) 2.9
	5.5	16.0	4.8				4.5	6.7
	3.3						1.8	1.2
	(13) 4.1					% Officers', Directors' Owners' Comp/Sales	(47) 4.8	(35) 2.5
	12.3						9.1	7.8
9214M	76249M	255487M	1084141M	55939M	1157119M	Net Sales ($)	2585266M	2251271M
2387M	22348M	90033M	366539M	55014M	566133M	Total Assets ($)	1339829M	1101523M

M = $ thousand MM = $ million

See Pages 9 through 22 for Explanation of Ratios and Data

Comparative Historical Data				Current Data Sorted by Sales					
			Type of Statement						
12	10	6	Unqualified	1				2	3
4	6	7	Reviewed	1	1	1			4
12	11	9	Compiled	3	1	3	1		1
30	23	26	Tax Returns	9	8	4	3	1	1
25	21	27	Other	2	4	3	4	5	9
4/1/11-3/31/12 ALL	**4/1/12-3/31/13 ALL**	**4/1/13-3/31/14 ALL**		**10 (4/1-9/30/13)**			**65 (10/1/13-3/31/14)**		
				0-1MM	**1-3MM**	**3-5MM**	**5-10MM**	**10-25MM**	**25MM & OVER**
83	71	75	**NUMBER OF STATEMENTS**	16	14	11	8	8	18
%	%	%	**ASSETS**	%	%	%	%	%	%
12.3	12.5	16.6	Cash & Equivalents	18.8	23.4	8.0			12.3
18.4	15.5	17.4	Trade Receivables (net)	2.8	15.9	25.4			27.6
13.9	21.4	17.8	Inventory	6.9	23.2	15.5			23.5
3.3	3.3	2.7	All Other Current	2.8	1.4	5.9			3.1
47.9	52.7	54.5	Total Current	31.3	63.8	54.8			66.4
38.1	32.3	32.1	Fixed Assets (net)	57.5	29.4	27.7			20.7
4.9	3.0	4.1	Intangibles (net)	8.4	.1	8.6			2.5
9.1	12.1	9.3	All Other Non-Current	2.8	6.6	8.8			10.3
100.0	100.0	100.0	Total	100.0	100.0	100.0			100.0
			LIABILITIES						
16.0	14.8	12.2	Notes Payable-Short Term	8.1	8.6	19.1			14.2
3.5	2.2	8.2	Cur. Mat.-L.T.D.	31.3	2.6	4.2			.8
9.8	11.1	8.3	Trade Payables	1.7	4.8	6.9			15.4
.1	.1	.1	Income Taxes Payable	.0	.2	.0			.0
10.7	8.6	10.8	All Other Current	19.1	2.9	2.3			9.4
40.1	36.8	39.5	Total Current	60.3	19.1	32.7			39.8
25.0	18.0	27.6	Long-Term Debt	46.6	49.5	33.6			7.7
.3	.2	.1	Deferred Taxes	.0	.0	.0			.1
10.1	6.6	8.0	All Other Non-Current	19.6	7.0	8.6			4.3
24.4	38.4	24.7	Net Worth	-26.6	24.4	25.1			48.1
100.0	100.0	100.0	Total Liabilties & Net Worth	100.0	100.0	100.0			100.0
			INCOME DATA						
100.0	100.0	100.0	Net Sales	100.0	100.0	100.0			100.0
			Gross Profit						
93.0	95.7	93.4	Operating Expenses	90.5	90.1	92.0			96.7
7.0	4.3	6.6	Operating Profit	9.5	9.9	8.0			3.3
2.2	-.4	1.4	All Other Expenses (net)	6.3	.1	1.0			.0
4.8	4.7	5.2	Profit Before Taxes	3.2	9.7	7.0			3.3
			RATIOS						
3.3	3.5	3.3		1.2	17.8	2.9			2.8
1.5	1.5	1.6	Current	.6	4.3	1.3			1.7
1.0	.9	.8		.2	2.2	.8			1.1
2.1	2.6	2.1		.9	17.5	2.1			1.9
1.0	.7	.9	Quick	.4	2.2	1.0			.9
.3	.3	.4		.1	.9	.1			.5
0 UND	**0** UND	**0** UND		**0** UND	**0** UND	**14** 26.8			**12** 30.2
17 21.7	**20** 18.4	**16** 23.5	Sales/Receivables	**0** UND	**14** 25.6	**27** 13.3			**23** 16.0
43 8.5	**38** 9.5	**44** 8.3		**8** 44.1	**41** 8.8	**44** 8.3			**51** 7.1
			Cost of Sales/Inventory						
			Cost of Sales/Payables						
5.2	4.5	5.1		14.4	4.6	4.4			5.0
18.5	14.1	16.0	Sales/Working Capital	-33.7	7.4	32.5			9.6
181.3	-87.0	-108.0		-4.1	17.2	-26.7			NM
14.7	21.5	16.8		22.3	14.3	7.9			84.9
(70) 3.4	(57) 5.7	(59) 5.4	EBIT/Interest	(11) 8.0	(11) 5.4	(10) 2.7			(17) 8.0
1.4	1.7	2.0		1.6	2.0	1.0			1.2
		11.6							
		(13) 2.7	Net Profit + Depr., Dep., Amort./Cur. Mat. L/T/D						
		1.1							
.3	.2	.2		1.1	.2	.2			.0
1.0	.6	.7	Fixed/Worth	NM	.6	2.0			.5
UND	2.3	4.6		-.7	NM	-5.9			.8
.6	.4	.6		1.0	.4	1.3			.3
1.8	2.1	1.4	Debt/Worth	NM	.8	5.7			1.5
UND	4.9	7.9		-2.4	NM	-12.2			3.4
48.3	39.9	35.2			92.1				25.5
(63) 15.8	(57) 12.8	(60) 12.7	% Profit Before Taxes/Tangible Net Worth		(11) 31.5				9.1
5.3	3.6	2.8			8.5				2.1
18.1	18.3	23.7		39.5	50.4	6.8			17.0
5.6	7.2	6.8	% Profit Before Taxes/Total Assets	14.0	18.5	3.9			3.2
.9	1.1	1.5		-2.3	5.3	.1			.4
30.1	47.8	50.8		29.0	116.7	50.8			UND
9.7	12.8	11.3	Sales/Net Fixed Assets	4.1	7.8	8.0			15.2
2.6	4.4	4.2		.3	4.4	3.7			5.3
4.4	4.8	4.3		3.6	4.2	4.3			5.8
2.2	2.9	2.6	Sales/Total Assets	2.4	2.8	2.5			2.9
1.0	1.3	1.4		.3	2.2	1.0			1.5
1.4	1.4	1.1		4.3	.4				1.2
(60) 2.3	(54) 3.0	(55) 2.1	% Depr., Dep., Amort./Sales	(12) 7.8	(10) 1.7				(12) 2.3
6.1	5.2	5.8		22.0	6.6				4.8
1.9	1.5	2.3							
(31) 4.7	(29) 4.7	(27) 4.1	% Officers', Directors' Owners' Comp/Sales						
10.8	8.4	11.8							
2239355M	**1814604M**	**2638149M**	Net Sales ($)	**7754M**	**28215M**	**42279M**	**56768M**	**143448M**	**2359685M**
1110150M	**827165M**	**1102454M**	Total Assets ($)	**16841M**	**11717M**	**33354M**	**30518M**	**84406M**	**925618M**

M = $ thousand MM = $ million

See Pages 9 through 22 for Explanation of Ratios and Data

MINING

Current Data Sorted by Assets							Comparative Historical Data	
						Type of Statement		
		4	15	9	21	Unqualified	61	70
		7	3	1	1	Reviewed	9	14
	2	5	5		1	Compiled	15	18
2	4	5	1			Tax Returns	16	23
3	4	26	43	16	13	Other	107	99
23 (4/1-9/30/13)		168 (10/1/13-3/31/14)					4/1/09-3/31/10	4/1/10-3/31/11
0-500M	500M-2MM	2-10MM	10-50MM	50-100MM	100-250MM		ALL	ALL
5	10	47	67	26	36	NUMBER OF STATEMENTS	208	224
%	%	%	%	%	%	**ASSETS**	%	%
	17.2	14.6	12.9	7.6	4.8	Cash & Equivalents	10.5	9.5
	17.3	10.9	12.2	7.1	5.5	Trade Receivables (net)	11.2	14.7
	2.5	2.9	3.1	1.5	.6	Inventory	2.6	3.0
	2.6	4.9	2.4	1.4	2.5	All Other Current	6.0	4.1
	39.7	33.2	30.6	17.6	13.4	Total Current	30.2	31.4
	49.4	45.2	56.5	67.0	79.8	Fixed Assets (net)	56.3	55.5
	4.2	5.1	2.9	3.8	2.0	Intangibles (net)	2.4	3.3
	6.7	16.5	10.0	11.6	4.8	All Other Non-Current	11.1	9.9
	100.0	100.0	100.0	100.0	100.0	Total	100.0	100.0
						LIABILITIES		
	45.4	12.4	3.2	1.0	1.1	Notes Payable-Short Term	5.0	5.1
	2.4	1.9	1.7	6.4	.6	Cur. Mat.-L.T.D.	3.5	4.0
	9.6	7.0	9.1	5.1	4.2	Trade Payables	7.6	7.8
	.0	.0	.0	.0	.0	Income Taxes Payable	.1	.1
	6.1	6.8	3.1	3.5	8.1	All Other Current	7.4	7.1
	63.6	28.1	17.0	16.0	14.1	Total Current	23.6	24.1
	12.8	17.8	13.7	34.3	33.7	Long-Term Debt	29.8	20.1
	.4	.4	.7	1.1	1.1	Deferred Taxes	.8	.8
	.0	2.1	10.7	5.3	3.8	All Other Non-Current	6.6	5.6
	23.3	51.5	57.9	43.3	47.3	Net Worth	39.2	49.5
	100.0	100.0	100.0	100.0	100.0	Total Liabilties & Net Worth	100.0	100.0
						INCOME DATA		
	100.0	100.0	100.0	100.0	100.0	Net Sales	100.0	100.0
	39.2	55.2	54.5	61.8	66.2	Gross Profit	54.8	55.1
	24.7	39.8	35.7	43.5	43.4	Operating Expenses	43.5	37.8
	14.5	15.4	18.9	18.3	22.8	Operating Profit	11.3	17.3
	.2	4.9	1.8	7.9	4.8	All Other Expenses (net)	4.8	3.3
	14.3	10.5	17.0	10.4	18.0	Profit Before Taxes	6.5	14.0
						RATIOS		
	39.1	3.1	3.9	2.5	1.6		3.0	3.4
	1.0	1.4	1.8	1.4	.9	Current	1.3	1.5
	.2	.4	1.0	.9	.6		.8	.8
	38.5	2.8	3.4	2.2	1.2		2.1	2.3
	.9	.9	1.3	1.1	.8	Quick	.9	1.1
	.0	.2	.6	.6	.5		.4	.6
	0 UND	**0** UND	**12** 30.4	**28** 12.9	**32** 11.5		**11** 32.7	**18** 20.5
	0 UND	**16** 22.6	**36** 10.0	**46** 7.9	**44** 8.3	Sales/Receivables	**40** 9.2	**45** 8.2
	34 10.6	**47** 7.8	**60** 6.1	**83** 4.4	**79** 4.6		**63** 5.8	**73** 5.0
	0 UND	**0** UND	**0** UND	**0** UND	**0** UND		**0** UND	**0** UND
	0 UND	**0** UND	**0** UND	**0** UND	**0** UND	Cost of Sales/Inventory	**0** UND	**0** UND
	0 UND	**7** 49.6	**6** 63.5	**12** 30.8	**8** 45.6		**18** 20.2	**19** 19.7
	0 UND	**0** UND	**9** 42.1	**49** 7.5	**34** 10.8		**7** 53.9	**11** 34.5
	1 297.5	**31** 11.8	**32** 11.3	**94** 3.9	**111** 3.3	Cost of Sales/Payables	**36** 10.1	**47** 7.8
	30 12.2	**104** 3.5	**146** 2.5	**159** 2.3	**243** 1.5		**100** 3.7	**136** 2.7
	15.4	5.2	3.8	4.8	7.3		4.5	4.0
	NM	15.2	12.1	12.1	-74.3	Sales/Working Capital	14.7	14.3
	-2.9	-5.6	999.8	-64.6	-6.2		-15.2	-20.9
		21.1	24.0	12.2	15.4		9.7	25.6
		(35) 3.7	(53) 4.6	(25) 1.5	(33) 6.1	EBIT/Interest	(174) 2.5	(182) 5.3
		-.5	-1.4	.8	-.6		-.6	1.2
							37.0	35.7
						Net Profit + Depr., Dep., Amort./Cur. Mat. L/T/D	(20) 2.0	(18) 4.2
							.3	2.2
	.5	.4	.5	.9	1.3		.6	.7
	1.4	.8	1.0	1.7	1.8	Fixed/Worth	1.4	1.2
	-2.0	1.8	1.9	3.0	2.7		2.6	2.0
	.3	.2	.2	.7	.6		.4	.3
	3.6	.9	.6	1.3	1.1	Debt/Worth	1.2	.9
	-7.7	2.0	2.2	2.4	2.2		3.6	2.5
		27.7	39.6	23.4	29.9		22.9	39.2
		(39) 13.0	(64) 14.8	(24) 3.9	(34) 10.0	% Profit Before Taxes/Tangible Net Worth	(188) 6.2	(200) 17.0
		5.1	-1.0	-5.4	-6.8		-4.0	2.0
	22.9	13.1	20.2	10.9	12.7		12.0	18.0
	6.1	4.2	7.3	1.4	5.1	% Profit Before Taxes/Total Assets	2.8	6.8
	-.2	.7	-1.2	-1.1	-3.5		-2.4	.5
	37.6	7.2	6.0	1.9	.6		5.9	4.0
	3.5	2.2	1.2	.5	.4	Sales/Net Fixed Assets	1.1	1.3
	.8	.8	.3	.3	.2		.4	.4
	4.7	1.5	1.4	.6	.4		1.4	1.5
	1.4	.6	.5	.4	.3	Sales/Total Assets	.5	.6
	.6	.4	.3	.3	.2		.3	.3
		2.7	4.4	12.4	11.1		4.8	4.2
		(35) 6.9	(55) 11.5	(22) 16.8	(10) 19.9	% Depr., Dep., Amort./Sales	(135) 14.1	(155) 11.1
		20.1	26.3	27.6	28.7		27.5	19.8
		2.3					2.5	2.0
		(13) 3.0				% Officers', Directors' Owners' Comp/Sales	(24) 5.9	(23) 4.1
		8.1					12.2	8.5
6481M	39870M	435233M	2088041M	949514M	3252600M	Net Sales ($)	7145647M	7389944M
1206M	12188M	267878M	1763144M	1903140M	6641618M	Total Assets ($)	11651379M	11906842M

M = $ thousand MM = $ million

See Pages 9 through 22 for Explanation of Ratios and Data

Comparative Historical Data				Current Data Sorted by Sales					
			Type of Statement						
71	50	49	Unqualified		1	3	6	9	30
15	7	12	Reviewed		1	1	2	3	5
16	10	13	Compiled	1	4		3	2	3
12	10	12	Tax Returns	3	3	2	1	3	
82	115	105	Other	8	12	14	16	24	31
4/1/11-3/31/12 ALL	**4/1/12-3/31/13 ALL**	**4/1/13-3/31/14 ALL**		**23 (4/1-9/30/13)**			**168 (10/1/13-3/31/14)**		
				0-1MM	**1-3MM**	**3-5MM**	**5-10MM**	**10-25MM**	**25MM & OVER**
196	192	191	**NUMBER OF STATEMENTS**	12	21	20	28	41	69
%	%	%	**ASSETS**	%	%	%	%	%	%
12.3	11.1	11.3	Cash & Equivalents	18.1	12.2	17.0	8.2	12.2	9.0
13.6	12.0	10.4	Trade Receivables (net)	6.9	5.5	3.4	7.3	12.5	14.5
2.0	2.9	2.4	Inventory	3.4	.6	.5	1.0	3.2	3.5
4.4	3.7	3.4	All Other Current	17.1	1.6	4.1	1.4	3.2	2.2
32.3	29.7	27.5	Total Current	45.5	19.9	25.0	17.9	31.0	29.2
56.0	57.0	58.5	Fixed Assets (net)	52.8	43.3	60.5	69.4	56.7	60.1
2.7	2.1	3.4	Intangibles (net)	.0	12.8	2.2	.4	2.3	3.3
9.0	11.2	10.7	All Other Non-Current	1.7	24.0	12.3	12.3	10.0	7.4
100.0	100.0	100.0	Total	100.0	100.0	100.0	100.0	100.0	100.0
			LIABILITIES						
5.4	6.5	7.1	Notes Payable-Short Term	23.2	12.6	13.1	7.8	3.3	2.8
1.8	1.3	2.2	Cur. Mat.-L.T.D.	.0	2.2	2.9	1.2	1.2	3.3
8.7	7.8	7.1	Trade Payables	4.6	2.7	3.5	7.4	8.1	9.1
.1	.1	.0	Income Taxes Payable	.0	.0	.0	.0	.0	.1
7.5	8.4	5.6	All Other Current	11.6	5.1	3.9	4.0	3.7	6.9
23.5	24.1	21.9	Total Current	39.4	22.6	23.4	20.3	16.2	22.2
21.4	20.2	21.5	Long-Term Debt	12.8	16.7	17.0	14.8	23.3	27.5
.9	1.3	.7	Deferred Taxes	.0	.0	1.0	.1	1.1	1.0
4.8	7.0	5.7	All Other Non-Current	1.1	8.3	3.9	4.6	10.6	3.8
49.4	47.4	50.2	Net Worth	46.8	52.4	54.7	60.1	48.8	45.6
100.0	100.0	100.0	Total Liabilties & Net Worth	100.0	100.0	100.0	100.0	100.0	100.0
			INCOME DATA						
100.0	100.0	100.0	Net Sales	100.0	100.0	100.0	100.0	100.0	100.0
55.7	56.4	57.3	Gross Profit	63.9	58.2	64.2	59.2	58.3	52.6
39.3	39.1	39.2	Operating Expenses	40.7	40.2	44.9	46.5	38.1	34.6
16.4	17.3	18.1	Operating Profit	23.2	18.0	19.3	12.6	20.2	18.0
2.9	3.4	3.9	All Other Expenses (net)	1.8	4.1	6.4	.9	5.8	3.4
13.5	14.0	14.3	Profit Before Taxes	21.4	13.9	12.9	11.7	14.3	14.5
			RATIOS						
3.5	3.0	3.1	Current	18.6	1.8	2.3	3.1	5.0	2.6
1.5	1.4	1.3		5.3	.4	1.2	1.3	1.8	1.3
.7	.7	.7		.9	.1	.4	.7	1.0	.8
2.8	2.4	2.5	Quick	9.8	1.6	2.2	2.9	3.8	2.4
1.1	1.0	1.1		.8	.3	1.0	1.1	1.4	1.0
.5	.5	.5		.2	.0	.2	.5	.7	.6
9 41.8	**12** 29.7	**8** 46.7	Sales/Receivables	**0** UND	**0** UND	**0** UND	**2** 154.5	**24** 15.1	**22** 16.7
41 8.8	**39** 9.4	**35** 10.3		**0** UND	**0** UND	**13** 27.7	**29** 12.7	**41** 8.9	**42** 8.6
69 5.3	**58** 6.3	**58** 6.3		**45** 8.1	**50** 7.3	**68** 5.4	**59** 6.2	**65** 5.6	**64** 5.7
0 UND	**0** UND	**0** UND	Cost of Sales/Inventory	**0** UND	**0** UND	**0** UND	**0** UND	**0** UND	**0** UND
0 UND	**0** UND	**0** UND		**0** UND	**0** UND	**0** UND	**0** UND	**0** UND	**0** UND
4 88.2	**7** 50.3	**6** 57.1		**0** UND	**0** UND	**0** UND	**0** UND	**13** 27.1	**11** 33.4
12 29.6	**12** 30.8	**8** 48.3	Cost of Sales/Payables	**0** UND	**0** UND	**0** UND	**2** 173.5	**10** 35.8	**18** 20.0
51 7.2	**54** 6.7	**49** 7.5		**0** UND	**31** 11.8	**66** 5.5	**46** 7.9	**51** 7.1	**49** 7.4
174 2.1	**140** 2.6	**135** 2.7		**70** 5.2	**152** 2.4	**203** 1.8	**182** 2.0	**159** 2.3	**122** 3.0
4.1	5.8	4.8	Sales/Working Capital	1.0	9.7	2.8	5.4	3.8	6.0
11.9	14.7	20.7		1.7	-5.6	57.0	17.7	8.1	28.5
-12.4	-12.8	-12.7		NM	-2.6	-4.9	-8.2	-141.5	-33.2
24.8	27.6	15.1	EBIT/Interest		10.1	40.5	28.6	10.9	16.7
(154) 4.7	(161) 5.1	(157) 4.0			(17) 2.4	(17) 7.4	(21) 3.6	(32) 2.0	(65) 5.9
1.2	.0	-.4			-1.0	-1.9	-1.3	-.7	.8
41.9	18.7	8.1	Net Profit + Depr., Dep., Amort./Cur. Mat. L/T/D						
(19) 4.2	(15) 7.7	(12) 3.0							
1.4	1.2	.6							
.6	.6	.6	Fixed/Worth	.3	.1	.6	.7	.5	.8
1.2	1.2	1.2		.7	1.2	1.0	1.1	1.2	1.5
2.4	2.3	2.4		2.1	10.5	1.7	1.6	2.7	2.5
.3	.3	.3	Debt/Worth	.0	.3	.2	.1	.2	.7
.9	.8	.9		.4	1.0	.4	.5	.8	1.3
2.6	2.8	2.3		6.6	10.4	1.5	1.3	2.4	2.9
34.5	45.1	31.4	% Profit Before Taxes/Tangible Net Worth	16.8	15.5	41.1	26.0	30.6	40.7
(178) 13.5	(174) 11.5	(172) 11.3		(11) 10.1	(17) 8.0	(17) 13.0	(25) 5.9	(37) 7.8	(65) 16.1
.3	-.1	-.7		3.2	-2.3	2.2	-3.4	-4.4	.3
18.0	18.8	15.0	% Profit Before Taxes/Total Assets	17.3	8.5	32.3	18.3	15.3	15.9
6.4	5.9	4.9		6.1	4.2	7.0	3.5	3.4	8.0
.2	-1.0	-1.0		2.1	-.9	-1.5	-2.6	-1.5	-.2
6.0	6.3	5.3	Sales/Net Fixed Assets	9.3	11.1	3.2	2.2	5.5	6.1
1.2	.9	.9		.8	1.3	1.0	.4	1.2	.8
.4	.4	.4		.4	.5	.5	.2	.3	.4
1.5	1.6	1.1	Sales/Total Assets	1.1	.8	.8	.9	1.2	2.0
.5	.5	.5		.4	.5	.5	.4	.5	.5
.3	.3	.3		.2	.2	.3	.2	.3	.3
2.7	2.3	3.3	% Depr., Dep., Amort./Sales		4.6	2.8	7.1	4.4	1.9
(126) 13.0	(120) 10.7	(132) 11.2			(16) 9.9	(15) 11.5	(23) 20.4	(35) 12.2	(37) 9.3
24.1	22.6	24.1			23.7	34.9	30.5	23.7	16.0
1.2	1.4	1.5	% Officers', Directors' Owners' Comp/Sales						
(28) 3.1	(22) 3.0	(26) 2.9							
5.0	6.1	7.4							
10560257M	**7345460M**	**6771739M**	Net Sales ($)	**7340M**	**39759M**	**78398M**	**203948M**	**655449M**	**5786845M**
10567839M	**11405025M**	**10589174M**	Total Assets ($)	**21480M**	**165505M**	**228642M**	**700565M**	**1667308M**	**7805674M**

M = $ thousand MM = $ million

See Pages 9 through 22 for Explanation of Ratios and Data

Current Data Sorted by Assets | **Comparative Historical Data**

DATA NOT AVAILABLE

0-500M	500M-2MM	2-10MM	10-50MM	50-100MM	100-250MM	Type of Statement	4/1/09-3/31/10 ALL	4/1/10-3/31/11 ALL
			4	2	3	Unqualified	30	29
		1	2			Reviewed	4	7
	1	3	1			Compiled	5	8
		3				Tax Returns	7	6
	1	1	6	5	11	Other	41	37
	12 (4/1-9/30/13)		32 (10/1/13-3/31/14)					
0-500M	500M-2MM	2-10MM	10-50MM	50-100MM	100-250MM		4/1/09-3/31/10 ALL	4/1/10-3/31/11 ALL
	2	8	13	7	14	NUMBER OF STATEMENTS	87	87
%	%	%	%	%	%	ASSETS	%	%
			6.4		2.7	Cash & Equivalents	12.8	10.6
			15.7		9.3	Trade Receivables (net)	14.1	13.2
			12.5		9.5	Inventory	6.5	8.6
			1.9		.9	All Other Current	2.5	3.4
			36.4		22.4	Total Current	35.9	35.7
			41.3		62.5	Fixed Assets (net)	46.9	45.5
			9.8		8.5	Intangibles (net)	3.5	2.5
			12.5		6.6	All Other Non-Current	13.7	16.3
			100.0		100.0	Total	100.0	100.0
						LIABILITIES		
			6.2		2.7	Notes Payable-Short Term	4.3	2.9
			7.3		5.9	Cur. Mat.-L.T.D.	6.1	6.1
			12.8		5.8	Trade Payables	9.9	11.5
			.0		.0	Income Taxes Payable	.3	.2
			35.3		7.8	All Other Current	9.8	9.8
			61.7		22.2	Total Current	30.4	30.5
			13.1		23.3	Long-Term Debt	20.8	17.1
			.0		2.6	Deferred Taxes	.7	1.0
			9.0		12.9	All Other Non-Current	14.4	17.3
			16.2		39.0	Net Worth	33.8	34.1
			100.0		100.0	Total Liabilities & Net Worth	100.0	100.0
						INCOME DATA		
			100.0		100.0	Net Sales	100.0	100.0
			14.4		26.2	Gross Profit	26.4	30.4
			14.3		15.8	Operating Expenses	14.2	19.8
			.1		10.4	Operating Profit	12.2	10.5
			1.6		1.4	All Other Expenses (net)	2.1	.5
			-1.4		9.0	Profit Before Taxes	10.2	10.0
						RATIOS		
			1.8		1.3		2.0	2.0
			.9		1.1	Current	1.1	1.2
			.4		1.0		.8	.7
			1.1		.9		1.5	1.6
			.3		.7	Quick	.8	.7
			.2		.4		.4	.3
			11 32.2		**17** 21.7		**16** 22.8	**15** 23.9
			29 12.6		**28** 13.2	Sales/Receivables	**26** 13.9	**29** 12.5
			47 7.8		**38** 9.5		**40** 9.2	**38** 9.7
			1 311.5		**17** 21.9		**2** 187.6	**2** 176.6
			14 25.7		**31** 11.6	Cost of Sales/Inventory	**14** 26.1	**12** 31.0
			46 8.0		**66** 5.5		**35** 10.5	**51** 7.1
			14 25.6		**15** 24.5		**16** 22.4	**17** 21.9
			22 16.4		**23** 15.9	Cost of Sales/Payables	**23** 16.2	**26** 13.9
			30 12.2		**30** 12.3		**38** 9.5	**37** 9.8
			4.8		19.1		7.9	6.9
			-76.3		185.4	Sales/Working Capital	47.0	35.1
			-6.9		-422.7		-25.4	-20.6
			9.5		16.5		30.2	25.4
			(12) .4		13.2	EBIT/Interest	(81) 10.6	(81) 9.0
			-7.6		1.7		1.8	2.3
							8.7	
						Net Profit + Depr., Dep., Amort./Cur. Mat. L/T/D	(15) 2.3	
							.8	
			.5		1.0		.7	.6
			1.0		1.5	Fixed/Worth	1.5	1.2
			NM		-107.5		4.3	2.4
			.5		.6		.9	.7
			1.7		1.3	Debt/Worth	2.3	1.5
			NM		-207.0		10.9	4.4
			22.4				79.4	53.4
			(10) -2.4			% Profit Before Taxes/Tangible Net Worth	(73) 33.5	(78) 28.8
			-25.4				12.6	18.4
			10.4		16.5		23.5	22.0
			-.4		11.4	% Profit Before Taxes/Total Assets	13.9	10.6
			-12.4		2.4		1.5	3.2
			12.6		3.1		5.5	6.7
			6.7		1.7	Sales/Net Fixed Assets	3.0	3.6
			2.4		1.3		1.6	1.9
			2.8		1.5		2.1	2.3
			1.5		1.1	Sales/Total Assets	1.3	1.4
			.9		.8		.9	.9
			2.5				2.7	2.5
			(12) 4.7			% Depr., Dep., Amort./Sales	(62) 5.7	(65) 5.2
			8.1				8.4	8.8
						% Officers', Directors' Owners' Comp/Sales		
	20808M	168710M	576568M	579431M	2727194M	Net Sales ($)	7820633M	7318026M
	1934M	43167M	330503M	469788M	2453970M	Total Assets ($)	5922641M	5456304M

M = $ thousand MM = $ million

See Pages 9 through 22 for Explanation of Ratios and Data

Comparative Historical Data				Current Data Sorted by Sales					
			Type of Statement						
20	14	9	Unqualified						9
6	1	3	Reviewed					2	1
5	8	5	Compiled				2	2	1
7	2	3	Tax Returns					2	1
37	32	24	Other				1	3	20
				12 (4/1-9/30/13)			32 (10/1/13-3/31/14)		
4/1/11-3/31/12 ALL	4/1/12-3/31/13 ALL	4/1/13-3/31/14 ALL		0-1MM	1-3MM	3-5MM	5-10MM	10-25MM	25MM & OVER
75	57	44	**NUMBER OF STATEMENTS**				3	9	32
%	%	%	**ASSETS**	%	%	%	%	%	%
12.8	10.6	7.4	Cash & Equivalents	DATA NOT AVAILABLE	DATA NOT AVAILABLE	DATA NOT AVAILABLE			7.2
16.8	11.1	16.7	Trade Receivables (net)						13.8
4.9	5.4	9.5	Inventory						9.0
2.3	2.0	1.1	All Other Current						1.2
36.8	29.0	34.7	Total Current						31.2
43.9	47.3	45.6	Fixed Assets (net)						48.9
5.2	4.9	6.0	Intangibles (net)						7.4
14.0	18.8	13.7	All Other Non-Current						12.5
100.0	100.0	100.0	Total						100.0
			LIABILITIES						
3.7	2.5	5.5	Notes Payable-Short Term						4.0
7.6	8.8	5.8	Cur. Mat.-L.T.D.						5.7
15.7	9.2	15.5	Trade Payables						10.2
.1	.2	.1	Income Taxes Payable						.2
9.6	5.3	17.1	All Other Current						18.8
36.7	26.0	44.1	Total Current						38.9
17.8	15.4	14.4	Long-Term Debt						16.0
.8	1.3	1.2	Deferred Taxes						1.1
10.3	10.5	11.0	All Other Non-Current						12.8
34.3	46.9	29.3	Net Worth						31.1
100.0	100.0	100.0	Total Liabilties & Net Worth						100.0
			INCOME DATA						
100.0	100.0	100.0	Net Sales						100.0
25.6	25.6	20.4	Gross Profit						18.0
17.5	17.1	16.8	Operating Expenses						13.1
8.0	8.5	3.6	Operating Profit						4.9
-.3	.1	.7	All Other Expenses (net)						.9
8.4	8.3	2.9	Profit Before Taxes						4.0
			RATIOS						
1.8	2.2	1.8							1.8
1.0	1.3	1.0	Current						1.1
.4	.7	.7							.8
1.3	1.7	1.0							1.0
.7	.8	.7	Quick						.7
.3	.3	.3							.3
15 24.1	14 26.7	14 25.2							14 25.2
28 13.1	24 15.5	28 13.0	Sales/Receivables						28 13.2
42 8.7	42 8.7	39 9.3							37 9.8
0 UND	0 UND	7 55.3							8 45.5
8 45.7	11 34.0	17 21.9	Cost of Sales/Inventory						17 21.9
28 13.2	29 12.7	41 9.0							35 10.3
22 16.9	15 25.0	15 24.4							14 26.2
31 11.8	27 13.6	24 15.4	Cost of Sales/Payables						23 16.1
46 8.0	45 8.1	36 10.2							30 12.3
8.2	9.0	10.8							10.8
367.8	47.5	NM	Sales/Working Capital						185.4
-9.4	-12.3	-15.3							-43.5
27.5	21.2	15.7							15.7
(69) 7.8	(51) 6.1	(39) 2.2	EBIT/Interest						(31) 4.1
1.8	1.9	-.1							-.1
		5.7							
		(10) 2.7	Net Profit + Depr., Dep., Amort./Cur. Mat. L/T/D						
		.9							
.6	.8	.8							.9
1.2	1.1	1.3	Fixed/Worth						1.3
3.8	2.4	-354.5							NM
.6	.4	.5							.5
1.6	1.2	1.4	Debt/Worth						1.3
8.3	3.5	-452.2							NM
61.1	46.2	29.1							31.3
(63) 21.4	(54) 21.3	(32) 13.1	% Profit Before Taxes/Tangible Net Worth						(24) 15.8
8.3	5.4	-19.7							-11.6
22.0	18.0	12.6							15.6
6.3	9.7	.6	% Profit Before Taxes/Total Assets						6.8
1.9	.9	-12.3							-10.0
8.7	4.5	15.0							9.4
3.8	2.4	2.6	Sales/Net Fixed Assets						2.5
1.6	1.4	1.9							1.7
3.0	1.7	2.3							1.7
1.4	1.3	1.5	Sales/Total Assets						1.5
.9	.9	1.0							1.0
3.4	4.4	1.7							1.6
(51) 5.0	(37) 6.5	(33) 4.5	% Depr., Dep., Amort./Sales						(22) 5.5
7.3	8.4	7.4							7.5
			% Officers', Directors' Owners' Comp/Sales						
5416976M	4951510M	4072711M	Net Sales ($)				22702M	154710M	3895299M
4584676M	4343000M	3299362M	Total Assets ($)				16851M	89635M	3192876M

M = $ thousand MM = $ million

See Pages 9 through 22 for Explanation of Ratios and Data

Current Data Sorted by Assets							Comparative Historical Data	
						Type of Statement		
	1		8	1	6	Unqualified	15	15
		6	4	2		Reviewed	13	6
1		4	1			Compiled	8	7
	3	2		1		Tax Returns	9	3
		7	10	4	3	Other	32	33
	7 (4/1-9/30/13)		57 (10/1/13-3/31/14)				4/1/09-3/31/10 ALL	4/1/10-3/31/11 ALL
0-500M	500M-2MM	2-10MM	10-50MM	50-100MM	100-250MM			
1	4	19	23	8	9	NUMBER OF STATEMENTS	77	64
%	%	%	%	%	%	**ASSETS**	%	%
		10.5	6.7			Cash & Equivalents	8.2	9.1
		14.1	7.3			Trade Receivables (net)	12.1	12.5
		13.4	18.9			Inventory	15.2	13.7
		3.5	1.4			All Other Current	1.8	5.7
		41.5	34.3			Total Current	37.3	41.1
		50.5	50.2			Fixed Assets (net)	52.6	47.2
		1.0	3.1			Intangibles (net)	3.3	5.2
		7.1	12.3			All Other Non-Current	6.8	6.5
		100.0	100.0			Total	100.0	100.0
						LIABILITIES		
		2.8	3.8			Notes Payable-Short Term	12.7	4.7
		5.5	3.4			Cur. Mat.-L.T.D.	4.4	6.0
		9.0	4.2			Trade Payables	6.7	8.1
		.1	.0			Income Taxes Payable	.1	.2
		4.7	4.9			All Other Current	4.1	4.8
		22.1	16.2			Total Current	28.0	23.8
		24.2	18.5			Long-Term Debt	24.4	22.5
		1.0	.4			Deferred Taxes	1.0	1.1
		.3	2.3			All Other Non-Current	5.2	4.8
		52.3	62.5			Net Worth	41.3	47.8
		100.0	100.0			Total Liabilities & Net Worth	100.0	100.0
						INCOME DATA		
		100.0	100.0			Net Sales	100.0	100.0
		34.2	25.6			Gross Profit	33.0	30.9
		29.2	16.1			Operating Expenses	23.7	22.8
		5.0	9.5			Operating Profit	9.3	8.1
		.6	1.3			All Other Expenses (net)	2.1	1.6
		4.5	8.2			Profit Before Taxes	7.2	6.5
						RATIOS		
		4.6	3.4				4.3	3.9
		1.7	2.8			Current	2.2	2.2
		.6	1.3				1.1	1.1
		2.2	2.2				2.1	2.3
		1.1	1.1			Quick	1.1	1.0
		.6	.3				.4	.4
		25 14.6	**22** 16.5				**27** 13.7	**26** 13.8
		38 9.6	**31** 11.7			Sales/Receivables	**38** 9.5	**39** 9.5
		56 6.5	**42** 8.7				**46** 7.9	**50** 7.3
		5 76.6	**52** 7.0				**16** 22.7	**11** 32.9
		68 5.4	**122** 3.0			Cost of Sales/Inventory	**61** 6.0	**42** 8.7
		182 2.0	**203** 1.8				**118** 3.1	**123** 3.0
		15 23.9	**16** 23.0				**14** 25.3	**16** 22.5
		37 9.8	**26** 14.1			Cost of Sales/Payables	**27** 13.4	**25** 14.8
		52 7.0	**39** 9.3				**46** 7.9	**47** 7.8
		2.8	3.4				3.2	2.6
		27.8	5.1			Sales/Working Capital	6.7	6.8
		-9.5	9.5				54.5	31.9
		9.0	47.3				11.1	8.0
		(17) 4.5	(21) 2.4			EBIT/Interest	(70) 3.6	(57) 3.2
		-1.9	1.4				1.7	1.5
							11.4	3.2
						Net Profit + Depr., Dep., Amort./Cur. Mat. L/T/D	(14) 3.3	(12) 1.4
							1.4	.1
		.5	.6				.7	.7
		1.1	.9			Fixed/Worth	1.1	1.0
		2.1	1.1				2.0	1.6
		.3	.2				.4	.5
		1.1	.7			Debt/Worth	1.1	1.0
		1.8	1.2				2.7	3.4
		30.7	15.7				30.7	19.7
		(18) 12.5	(22) 4.0			% Profit Before Taxes/Tangible Net Worth	(71) 13.3	(57) 10.3
		-3.2	2.5				3.9	2.7
		13.4	11.9				10.8	9.3
		5.4	2.6			% Profit Before Taxes/Total Assets	5.2	4.9
		-3.3	1.0				1.9	1.2
		5.3	2.4				3.1	3.7
		2.9	1.4			Sales/Net Fixed Assets	1.8	2.2
		1.0	1.0				1.0	1.2
		2.1	1.0				1.4	1.3
		.9	.7			Sales/Total Assets	.9	.9
		.7	.5				.6	.7
		3.4	4.7				4.5	5.1
		(18) 5.2	8.7			% Depr., Dep., Amort./Sales	(68) 8.0	(57) 8.8
		8.5	13.7				11.8	11.4
							2.2	1.9
						% Officers', Directors' Owners' Comp/Sales	(21) 4.7	(15) 5.0
							9.4	7.1
294M	14716M	139530M	435026M	385682M	1010566M	Net Sales ($)	1953770M	2414517M
318M	5327M	95380M	564660M	568277M	1343741M	Total Assets ($)	2214606M	2364939M

M = $ thousand MM = $ million

See Pages 9 through 22 for Explanation of Ratios and Data

Comparative Historical Data				Current Data Sorted by Sales					
14	13	16	Type of Statement: Unqualified			1		5	10
11	8	12	Reviewed		2		1	7	2
8	5	6	Compiled	1		2	2	1	
10	7	6	Tax Returns		2	2	1		1
33	36	24	Other		3	3	3	8	7
4/1/11-3/31/12 ALL	4/1/12-3/31/13 ALL	4/1/13-3/31/14 ALL		7 (4/1-9/30/13)			57 (10/1/13-3/31/14)		
				0-1MM	1-3MM	3-5MM	5-10MM	10-25MM	25MM & OVER
76	69	64	NUMBER OF STATEMENTS	1	7	8	7	21	20
%	%	%	ASSETS	%	%	%	%	%	%
8.6	8.4	9.0	Cash & Equivalents					7.3	8.4
14.2	11.0	10.4	Trade Receivables (net)					7.6	12.3
12.6	13.2	13.4	Inventory					16.9	10.9
2.4	2.4	1.8	All Other Current					1.5	1.5
37.7	35.0	34.7	Total Current					33.3	33.1
49.1	52.5	48.5	Fixed Assets (net)					48.6	49.5
6.6	2.9	5.5	Intangibles (net)					8.9	7.5
6.6	9.5	11.3	All Other Non-Current					9.2	9.9
100.0	100.0	100.0	Total					100.0	100.0
			LIABILITIES						
4.0	4.5	3.5	Notes Payable-Short Term					3.6	3.2
6.5	4.8	5.0	Cur. Mat.-L.T.D.					7.7	3.2
8.6	5.4	6.3	Trade Payables					4.1	6.0
.1	.2	.1	Income Taxes Payable					.0	.3
5.4	5.4	4.0	All Other Current					4.0	2.9
24.6	20.2	18.9	Total Current					19.4	15.7
21.5	24.1	22.8	Long-Term Debt					15.5	22.8
1.2	1.0	1.2	Deferred Taxes					.5	3.2
2.8	3.4	2.9	All Other Non-Current					2.3	2.9
49.9	51.3	54.1	Net Worth					62.3	55.4
100.0	100.0	100.0	Total Liabilties & Net Worth					100.0	100.0
			INCOME DATA						
100.0	100.0	100.0	Net Sales					100.0	100.0
29.6	32.4	32.9	Gross Profit					29.3	25.8
23.8	24.2	23.4	Operating Expenses					16.8	19.7
5.8	8.3	9.5	Operating Profit					12.5	6.0
1.2	1.4	1.3	All Other Expenses (net)					1.5	.6
4.6	6.9	8.2	Profit Before Taxes					11.0	5.4
			RATIOS						
3.6	4.2	4.0	Current					5.2	3.4
2.1	2.0	2.3						2.7	2.5
1.2	1.1	1.0						1.1	1.2
2.1	2.2	2.4	Quick					3.0	1.7
1.0	1.1	1.1						1.1	1.1
.5	.4	.5						.4	.8
29 12.5	**25** 14.4	**24** 14.9	Sales/Receivables					**23** 15.8	**31** 11.7
33 10.9	**34** 10.6	**36** 10.1						**32** 11.4	**38** 9.5
46 7.9	**46** 7.9	**50** 7.3						**49** 7.5	**49** 7.5
8 43.3	**7** 53.1	**21** 17.3	Cost of Sales/Inventory					**56** 6.5	**32** 11.3
56 6.5	**61** 6.0	**74** 4.9						**114** 3.2	**55** 6.6
118 3.1	**130** 2.8	**146** 2.5						**152** 2.4	**83** 4.4
16 22.4	**13** 28.4	**16** 22.9	Cost of Sales/Payables					**15** 24.8	**21** 17.7
24 15.1	**20** 18.0	**26** 14.1						**21** 17.7	**26** 14.2
39 9.3	**34** 10.8	**45** 8.1						**33** 11.2	**38** 9.7
3.9	3.7	3.0	Sales/Working Capital					2.2	3.3
7.8	7.5	7.1						5.9	7.0
28.5	54.3	206.2						27.5	25.7
11.9	14.4	10.9	EBIT/Interest					49.9	11.1
(67) 3.7	(62) 2.7	(57) 4.5						(19) 2.9	(19) 5.7
1.2	.4	1.5						1.2	2.2
7.2	5.4	5.3	Net Profit + Depr., Dep., Amort./Cur. Mat. L/T/D						
(16) 2.5	(13) 2.7	(13) 4.3							
.7	.2	2.2							
.7	.7	.6	Fixed/Worth					.6	.7
1.1	1.0	1.0						1.0	1.0
2.2	2.1	1.9						1.6	1.5
.3	.3	.3	Debt/Worth					.2	.4
.9	.9	.9						.7	.9
2.9	2.6	1.8						1.5	1.8
23.3	19.7	21.3	% Profit Before Taxes/Tangible Net Worth					18.5	15.7
(67) 13.6	(64) 11.4	(57) 10.6						(19) 5.5	(19) 11.0
2.9	-.7	3.0						1.7	3.6
10.7	10.8	12.4	% Profit Before Taxes/Total Assets					12.5	8.7
5.6	5.1	5.0						2.9	4.5
.6	-.9	1.1						.8	1.8
4.2	2.8	3.7	Sales/Net Fixed Assets					3.1	3.7
2.1	1.8	1.7						1.3	1.8
1.2	1.1	1.1						.9	1.4
1.6	1.4	1.3	Sales/Total Assets					1.1	1.1
1.0	.9	.8						.7	.9
.7	.5	.6						.4	.8
4.4	4.4	4.4	% Depr., Dep., Amort./Sales					5.7	4.5
(69) 6.9	(60) 7.8	(57) 8.0						9.4	(16) 7.7
10.3	11.6	10.9						13.2	8.4
1.9	1.6	1.9	% Officers', Directors' Owners' Comp/Sales						
(22) 5.1	(19) 5.1	(17) 4.8							
7.0	7.3	8.3							
2257997M	2193616M	1985814M	Net Sales ($)	294M	16566M	33604M	45517M	317772M	1572061M
2635785M	2496368M	2577703M	Total Assets ($)	318M	25892M	36736M	57780M	573557M	1883420M

M = $ thousand MM = $ million

See Pages 9 through 22 for Explanation of Ratios and Data

Current Data Sorted by Assets							Comparative Historical Data	
						Type of Statement		
			8	3	3	Unqualified	11	14
		2	5	1		Reviewed	10	8
	1	3	1			Compiled	9	7
2	6		1			Tax Returns	4	5
	4	10	11	5	3	Other	23	25
	10 (4/1-9/30/13)		59 (10/1/13-3/31/14)				4/1/09-3/31/10	4/1/10-3/31/11
0-500M	**500M-2MM**	**2-10MM**	**10-50MM**	**50-100MM**	**100-250MM**		**ALL**	**ALL**
2	11	15	26	9	6	**NUMBER OF STATEMENTS**	57	59
%	%	%	%	%	%	**ASSETS**	%	%
	16.7	8.7	9.4			Cash & Equivalents	8.5	7.7
	28.7	17.6	10.3			Trade Receivables (net)	15.3	11.1
	17.1	21.6	15.8			Inventory	14.2	16.2
	1.2	1.1	1.5			All Other Current	2.4	3.9
	63.8	49.0	37.0			Total Current	40.4	38.9
	29.9	41.4	50.3			Fixed Assets (net)	48.4	47.9
	3.2	4.2	7.2			Intangibles (net)	4.8	4.6
	3.2	5.5	5.5			All Other Non-Current	6.4	8.6
	100.0	100.0	100.0			Total	100.0	100.0
						LIABILITIES		
	15.4	5.8	2.1			Notes Payable-Short Term	4.9	5.8
	5.6	4.1	3.4			Cur. Mat.-L.T.D.	5.1	5.6
	23.7	10.0	4.4			Trade Payables	9.8	6.5
	.0	.0	.1			Income Taxes Payable	.1	.0
	12.9	10.9	6.3			All Other Current	5.4	6.3
	57.6	31.0	16.3			Total Current	25.3	24.2
	30.1	17.0	17.4			Long-Term Debt	28.2	24.7
	.0	.0	2.0			Deferred Taxes	.9	1.0
	3.9	5.5	9.0			All Other Non-Current	8.1	10.1
	8.4	46.6	55.3			Net Worth	37.5	40.0
	100.0	100.0	100.0			Total Liabilties & Net Worth	100.0	100.0
						INCOME DATA		
	100.0	100.0	100.0			Net Sales	100.0	100.0
	39.8	21.0	30.2			Gross Profit	31.9	37.6
	35.5	16.2	17.7			Operating Expenses	24.6	29.1
	4.3	4.8	12.5			Operating Profit	7.3	8.4
	.9	1.1	2.0			All Other Expenses (net)	2.3	3.4
	3.4	3.7	10.5			Profit Before Taxes	5.0	5.0
						RATIOS		
	1.5	3.1	5.4				4.4	4.6
	1.3	1.9	3.3			Current	2.1	1.8
	.8	1.1	2.2				1.0	1.0
	1.5	1.9	3.8				2.0	1.8
	.7	.9	1.5			Quick	.9	.9
	.4	.3	.7				.6	.4
	19 18.8	**26** 14.2	**28** 13.0				**26** 13.9	**22** 16.7
	30 12.0	**41** 9.0	**41** 8.9			Sales/Receivables	**39** 9.4	**37** 9.8
	41 8.9	**61** 6.0	**55** 6.6				**52** 7.1	**57** 6.4
	0 UND	**14** 25.4	**42** 8.6				**20** 18.6	**23** 15.8
	7 49.5	**65** 5.6	**91** 4.0			Cost of Sales/Inventory	**71** 5.2	**87** 4.2
	65 5.6	**166** 2.2	**152** 2.4				**115** 3.2	**167** 2.2
	15 24.1	**13** 27.3	**11** 32.5				**14** 26.8	**10** 38.2
	38 9.6	**30** 12.3	**22** 16.8			Cost of Sales/Payables	**23** 15.9	**24** 15.3
	79 4.6	**50** 7.3	**29** 12.6				**47** 7.7	**65** 5.6
	12.2	3.5	2.6				2.9	2.9
	21.8	6.4	3.4			Sales/Working Capital	6.7	6.1
	-9.5	23.8	4.7				NM	-54.5
		17.1	67.7				11.5	7.2
		(14) 2.7	(24) 6.6			EBIT/Interest	(51) 2.1	(53) 3.1
		-.5	3.6				-.3	.8
			8.2				15.1	11.1
			(10) 3.6			Net Profit + Depr., Dep., Amort./Cur. Mat. L/T/D	(16) 4.7	(12) 2.0
			1.1				1.4	1.0
	.3	.4	.7				.6	.5
	2.0	.8	.9			Fixed/Worth	1.1	1.2
	25.5	2.7	1.4				4.0	15.0
	4.5	.3	.3				.3	.3
	7.8	1.3	.9			Debt/Worth	1.0	1.1
	-5.7	6.1	2.0				12.2	41.8
		17.6	30.7				23.5	20.8
		(14) 9.1	(24) 16.5			% Profit Before Taxes/Tangible Net Worth	(47) 12.3	(47) 7.2
		-2.1	3.3				1.6	.3
	13.9	9.5	13.3				14.7	12.0
	7.9	2.8	6.6			% Profit Before Taxes/Total Assets	3.2	3.3
	.0	-2.1	1.3				-2.5	-.4
	68.6	4.2	3.3				3.8	5.1
	5.4	3.4	1.7			Sales/Net Fixed Assets	2.4	2.3
	3.5	2.0	1.1				1.2	1.2
	3.5	1.9	1.1				1.4	1.4
	2.0	1.2	.9			Sales/Total Assets	1.0	.9
	1.6	.6	.5				.7	.5
		4.4	5.2				4.0	4.9
		(14) 7.0	6.9			% Depr., Dep., Amort./Sales	(48) 7.7	(53) 8.6
		8.3	10.4				12.2	12.9
								2.0
						% Officers', Directors' Owners' Comp/Sales		(11) 4.1
								5.9
415M	**36013M**	**102691M**	**487572M**	**677506M**	**898002M**	Net Sales ($)	**1582390M**	**955043M**
676M	**12980M**	**70328M**	**568928M**	**672234M**	**1143183M**	Total Assets ($)	**1581474M**	**1101097M**

M = $ thousand MM = $ million

See Pages 9 through 22 for Explanation of Ratios and Data

Comparative Historical Data / Current Data Sorted by Sales

4/1/11-3/31/12 ALL	4/1/12-3/31/13 ALL	4/1/13-3/31/14 ALL	Type of Statement	0-1MM	1-3MM	3-5MM	5-10MM	10-25MM	25MM & OVER
13	13	14	Unqualified			1		3	10
15	18	8	Reviewed		1	1	1	3	2
9	8	5	Compiled		2	1	1	1	
9	11	9	Tax Returns	2	3	3	1		
27	20	33	Other		5	2	5	13	8
					10 (4/1-9/30/13)		59 (10/1/13-3/31/14)		
73	70	69	NUMBER OF STATEMENTS	2	11	8	8	20	20
%	%	%	**ASSETS**	%	%	%	%	%	%
8.4	10.4	8.8	Cash & Equivalents		12.7			8.1	6.6
14.0	15.3	15.3	Trade Receivables (net)		10.1			13.8	13.1
14.6	14.8	16.0	Inventory		26.1			18.0	11.5
3.9	4.2	2.3	All Other Current		1.9			1.6	3.1
40.9	44.7	42.3	Total Current		50.9			41.5	34.2
48.9	43.0	47.1	Fixed Assets (net)		42.3			42.2	54.9
3.8	4.9	4.9	Intangibles (net)		5.3			9.7	3.2
6.5	7.3	5.6	All Other Non-Current		1.5			6.5	7.6
100.0	100.0	100.0	Total		100.0			100.0	100.0
			LIABILITIES						
4.2	4.4	5.5	Notes Payable-Short Term		17.5			4.9	1.6
5.8	5.4	4.1	Cur. Mat.-L.T.D.		5.3			3.2	4.1
8.0	7.5	9.1	Trade Payables		9.7			7.5	6.0
.0	.2	.1	Income Taxes Payable		.0			.1	.1
12.6	6.5	8.8	All Other Current		18.8			7.4	6.8
30.6	24.1	27.6	Total Current		51.3			23.0	18.6
27.3	17.9	24.7	Long-Term Debt		25.1			15.7	32.7
.3	.8	1.4	Deferred Taxes		.0			1.9	2.8
7.6	10.7	6.9	All Other Non-Current		5.0			7.1	5.5
34.2	46.5	39.4	Net Worth		18.6			52.3	40.4
100.0	100.0	100.0	Total Liabilties & Net Worth		100.0			100.0	100.0
			INCOME DATA						
100.0	100.0	100.0	Net Sales		100.0			100.0	100.0
35.5	35.9	28.1	Gross Profit		36.0			25.6	21.2
29.4	26.7	19.6	Operating Expenses		32.6			16.9	13.1
6.0	9.2	8.5	Operating Profit		3.4			8.6	8.1
1.5	1.6	2.0	All Other Expenses (net)		1.9			.5	.9
4.5	7.6	6.6	Profit Before Taxes		1.5			8.1	7.2
			RATIOS						
3.4	4.4	3.6	Current		2.1			4.5	4.2
1.8	2.1	2.2			1.2			2.9	2.4
.8	1.1	1.2			.6			1.6	1.3
1.9	2.8	2.1	Quick		.7			2.9	2.6
.8	1.3	.9			.4			1.3	1.3
.4	.5	.5			.3			.6	.5
29 12.8	**26** 14.0	**28** 13.1	Sales/Receivables		**17** 21.0			**30** 12.1	**22** 16.7
43 8.5	**37** 9.9	**41** 8.9			**20** 18.1			**41** 8.8	**46** 7.9
65 5.6	**51** 7.2	**60** 6.1			**34** 10.6			**54** 6.7	**76** 4.8
21 17.4	**26** 14.2	**15** 23.6	Cost of Sales/Inventory		**27** 13.7			**49** 7.4	**17** 21.3
74 4.9	**60** 6.1	**69** 5.3			**140** 2.6			**99** 3.7	**57** 6.4
135 2.7	**118** 3.1	**146** 2.5			**192** 1.9			**159** 2.3	**81** 4.5
15 24.4	**10** 36.6	**12** 29.4	Cost of Sales/Payables		**13** 27.3			**12** 31.4	**10** 36.2
32 11.5	**22** 16.4	**25** 14.6			**38** 9.6			**26** 13.9	**22** 16.9
61 6.0	**47** 7.7	**42** 8.7			**89** 4.1			**53** 6.9	**29** 12.6
3.0	3.2	3.2	Sales/Working Capital		3.5			3.0	3.3
6.2	6.4	4.9			13.9			3.6	4.6
-16.9	19.6	23.4			-6.0			6.6	19.1
12.6	14.6	13.2	EBIT/Interest		5.2			62.8	10.9
(65) 2.7	(61) 5.3	(62) 5.4			1.0			(19) 5.5	(18) 5.8
.2	1.7	1.0			-.3			2.3	.4
3.3	5.5	6.9	Net Profit + Depr., Dep., Amort./Cur. Mat. L/T/D						
(12) 1.7	(16) 1.3	(16) 2.2							
-.1	.5	.6							
.6	.6	.7	Fixed/Worth		.8			.7	.8
1.1	.9	1.0			3.9			.8	1.1
3.4	1.9	2.2			-5.6			1.5	1.6
.5	.4	.5	Debt/Worth		3.4			.3	.5
1.6	1.2	1.5			7.8			1.3	1.1
6.5	2.5	4.7			-8.3			2.0	2.4
26.0	34.8	31.3	% Profit Before Taxes/Tangible Net Worth					29.9	32.5
(61) 12.8	(63) 15.7	(61) 11.9						(19) 8.3	(19) 11.1
.5	3.2	.5						2.1	-1.7
11.0	19.1	11.2	% Profit Before Taxes/Total Assets		12.1			10.9	11.2
3.5	7.4	6.5			.0			4.1	5.4
-3.4	.6	.0			-2.1			1.0	-.6
4.3	5.1	4.1	Sales/Net Fixed Assets		4.6			4.6	2.8
2.0	2.8	2.1			3.5			1.9	1.6
1.1	1.5	1.3			1.5			1.2	1.2
1.4	1.6	1.6	Sales/Total Assets		1.8			1.2	1.3
.9	1.0	1.0			1.6			.9	1.0
.6	.8	.6			.6			.6	.7
4.0	3.2	4.4	% Depr., Dep., Amort./Sales		2.8			4.0	4.3
(67) 8.7	(64) 5.9	(59) 7.0			(10) 7.1			6.2	(15) 7.0
14.5	8.9	9.0			13.2			10.2	8.9
2.4	1.4	.8	% Officers', Directors' Owners' Comp/Sales						
(12) 5.2	(15) 3.3	(13) 1.8							
7.4	7.1	3.5							
1551972M	2024470M	2202199M	Net Sales ($)	415M	24002M	32635M	56781M	315245M	1773121M
1706602M	1806011M	2468329M	Total Assets ($)	676M	22451M	44432M	56170M	401542M	1943058M

M = $ thousand MM = $ million

See Pages 9 through 22 for Explanation of Ratios and Data

Current Data Sorted by Assets							Comparative Historical Data	
						Type of Statement		
		3	11	3	1	Unqualified	30	31
	1	12	11	1		Reviewed	30	30
1	4	9	5	1		Compiled	28	28
10	5	6	1			Tax Returns	31	22
2	6	23	13	5	3	Other	57	68
12 (4/1-9/30/13)		125 (10/1/13-3/31/14)					4/1/09-3/31/10 ALL	4/1/10-3/31/11 ALL
0-500M	**500M-2MM**	**2-10MM**	**10-50MM**	**50-100MM**	**100-250MM**			
13	16	53	41	10	4	**NUMBER OF STATEMENTS**	176	179
%	%	%	%	%	%	**ASSETS**	%	%
19.3	17.6	11.5	9.0	14.4		Cash & Equivalents	11.7	10.6
9.6	19.4	14.4	13.1	18.7		Trade Receivables (net)	13.7	15.2
4.6	11.2	11.7	11.0	7.8		Inventory	9.5	9.5
.1	1.1	2.2	1.6	1.3		All Other Current	3.4	2.8
33.7	49.2	39.8	34.7	42.2		Total Current	38.3	38.1
52.9	37.9	49.7	55.6	46.6		Fixed Assets (net)	48.1	48.8
3.3	4.9	4.1	3.4	2.2		Intangibles (net)	4.0	3.0
10.1	7.9	6.4	6.2	9.0		All Other Non-Current	9.5	10.2
100.0	100.0	100.0	100.0	100.0		Total	100.0	100.0
						LIABILITIES		
19.0	10.8	5.7	3.4	4.6		Notes Payable-Short Term	5.1	6.6
6.6	7.0	6.1	4.5	4.7		Cur. Mat.-L.T.D.	6.9	7.1
.2	11.2	7.0	6.3	8.4		Trade Payables	6.7	8.6
.0	.0	.2	.2	.0		Income Taxes Payable	.2	.2
13.6	3.7	6.9	3.9	3.3		All Other Current	6.8	6.6
39.3	32.7	25.9	18.3	21.1		Total Current	25.7	29.2
94.4	28.6	27.4	22.3	19.2		Long-Term Debt	27.4	32.2
.0	.0	.4	.7	3.2		Deferred Taxes	.5	.6
1.9	3.0	5.5	8.0	17.8		All Other Non-Current	5.7	5.1
-35.6	35.8	40.7	50.6	38.7		Net Worth	40.7	32.9
100.0	100.0	100.0	100.0	100.0		Total Liabilties & Net Worth	100.0	100.0
						INCOME DATA		
100.0	100.0	100.0	100.0	100.0		Net Sales	100.0	100.0
73.2	51.1	35.9	25.3	18.6		Gross Profit	34.2	34.3
60.5	46.1	26.8	20.1	15.2		Operating Expenses	30.8	30.3
12.6	5.0	9.0	5.2	3.4		Operating Profit	3.4	4.0
.6	3.3	1.1	.8	-.6		All Other Expenses (net)	2.1	1.7
12.0	1.7	8.0	4.3	4.0		Profit Before Taxes	1.3	2.3
						RATIOS		
3.0	3.4	3.4	4.3	7.8			3.6	2.9
.7	1.7	1.6	2.0	2.0		Current	1.7	1.5
.4	.8	1.0	1.1	.7			.9	.8
2.6	2.3	2.0	2.5	7.3			2.1	1.8
.7	1.1	.9	1.2	1.6		Quick	1.0	1.0
.3	.6	.5	.6	.4			.5	.5
0 UND	**19** 18.8	**21** 17.8	**28** 12.9	**38** 9.5			**26** 13.8	**23** 15.8
0 UND	**26** 14.3	**38** 9.7	**41** 8.8	**51** 7.1		Sales/Receivables	**41** 8.9	**40** 9.1
18 20.5	**58** 6.3	**62** 5.9	**51** 7.2	**87** 4.2			**59** 6.1	**67** 5.5
0 UND	**0** UND	**8** 47.1	**20** 18.5	**23** 16.0			**0** UND	**3** 145.2
0 UND	**2** 165.3	**42** 8.7	**38** 9.5	**29** 12.5		Cost of Sales/Inventory	**31** 11.9	**26** 13.8
8 45.3	**37** 9.8	**107** 3.4	**94** 3.9	**51** 7.2			**89** 4.1	**80** 4.6
0 UND	**7** 53.1	**9** 41.2	**14** 26.2	**17** 21.9			**11** 34.2	**11** 34.4
0 UND	**24** 15.3	**26** 13.9	**20** 18.1	**29** 12.4		Cost of Sales/Payables	**24** 15.5	**24** 15.3
0 UND	**96** 3.8	**54** 6.8	**39** 9.3	**54** 6.7			**51** 7.1	**55** 6.6
26.7	5.2	2.9	3.1	1.5			3.1	3.8
-280.0	12.4	8.0	6.2	8.2		Sales/Working Capital	8.5	11.3
-10.8	NM	-235.6	73.4	-11.3			-39.8	-20.2
34.1	6.4	6.8	11.2	15.7			9.9	5.5
(10) 12.7	(13) 2.7	(46) 3.7	(39) 5.0	5.8		EBIT/Interest	(152) 1.9	(158) 2.1
1.5	-2.9	1.5	1.2	1.7			-.3	.0
			4.0				3.9	4.8
			(11) 2.6			Net Profit + Depr., Dep., Amort./Cur. Mat. L/T/D	(33) 1.9	(36) 1.8
			1.0				1.0	1.1
2.5	.5	.7	.8	.6			.6	.7
UND	1.4	1.2	1.1	1.5		Fixed/Worth	1.2	1.3
-.9	72.0	181.0	2.3	4.1			3.0	5.3
2.1	.5	.3	.4	.8			.5	.6
UND	2.2	1.5	1.1	1.6		Debt/Worth	1.3	1.6
-2.1	96.2	341.1	2.6	6.7			4.3	11.8
	46.3	29.8	22.7	35.1			20.6	23.1
	(13) 13.7	(41) 14.7	(39) 11.3	16.6		% Profit Before Taxes/Tangible Net Worth	(149) 3.8	(144) 7.0
	-11.5	3.8	.7	1.8			-7.8	-5.6
84.4	11.0	13.0	10.5	8.1			9.7	9.6
20.7	3.8	6.9	5.4	6.3		% Profit Before Taxes/Total Assets	1.9	2.8
5.7	-4.5	1.9	.5	2.8			-3.4	-2.5
43.4	10.5	3.6	3.4	3.4			4.5	4.1
6.3	5.2	2.1	2.0	2.7		Sales/Net Fixed Assets	2.3	2.2
2.2	2.5	1.0	.9	1.4			1.0	1.2
6.9	3.6	1.5	1.5	1.6			1.6	1.6
2.5	1.6	.9	1.0	1.0		Sales/Total Assets	1.0	1.0
1.3	1.2	.6	.7	.4			.6	.6
.8	3.1	4.6	3.7				4.5	4.7
(10) 5.6	(14) 5.7	(46) 6.5	(40) 7.8			% Depr., Dep., Amort./Sales	(155) 8.4	(152) 8.7
11.4	15.5	13.5	12.8				16.4	14.5
		.9					1.5	1.5
		(21) 2.0				% Officers', Directors' Owners' Comp/Sales	(45) 3.2	(56) 2.7
		4.0					8.2	7.4
11664M	**53591M**	**283963M**	**1032739M**	**666389M**	**622989M**	Net Sales ($)	**3433877M**	**3187715M**
3717M	**23468M**	**265987M**	**943740M**	**680407M**	**566578M**	Total Assets ($)	**3224234M**	**3444222M**

M = $ thousand MM = $ million

See Pages 9 through 22 for Explanation of Ratios and Data

Comparative Historical Data / Current Data Sorted by Sales

4/1/11-3/31/12 ALL	4/1/12-3/31/13 ALL	4/1/13-3/31/14 ALL		0-1MM	1-3MM	3-5MM	5-10MM	10-25MM	25MM & OVER
			Type of Statement						
27	27	18	Unqualified			2	3	2	11
48	33	25	Reviewed		6	1	5	5	8
25	25	20	Compiled		7	1	7	4	1
23	27	22	Tax Returns	7	6	4	5		
61	54	52	Other	4	8	7	8	14	11
				12 (4/1-9/30/13)			125 (10/1/13-3/31/14)		
184	166	137	**NUMBER OF STATEMENTS**	11	27	15	28	25	31
%	%	%	**ASSETS**	%	%	%	%	%	%
8.3	11.4	12.3	Cash & Equivalents	13.0	16.0	12.3	11.3	10.0	11.4
18.2	14.7	14.5	Trade Receivables (net)	3.8	11.5	12.0	18.3	13.3	19.8
11.5	10.6	10.4	Inventory	15.2	10.9	7.8	8.8	9.9	11.3
2.6	2.5	1.6	All Other Current	.0	.6	.8	2.2	2.8	2.0
40.5	39.3	38.8	Total Current	32.0	39.1	33.0	40.6	36.0	44.4
47.0	47.7	50.3	Fixed Assets (net)	56.4	47.6	49.2	55.0	55.1	42.8
3.3	3.6	3.8	Intangibles (net)	.8	6.4	6.3	.6	4.1	3.9
9.2	9.4	7.1	All Other Non-Current	10.8	6.9	11.5	3.8	4.8	8.8
100.0	100.0	100.0	Total	100.0	100.0	100.0	100.0	100.0	100.0
			LIABILITIES						
5.9	6.4	6.7	Notes Payable-Short Term	13.9	8.8	7.4	6.9	3.5	4.3
6.6	5.5	5.6	Cur. Mat.-L.T.D.	4.9	7.4	4.1	7.3	4.8	4.2
10.0	7.7	6.7	Trade Payables	.4	4.8	7.6	7.1	7.7	9.2
.3	.1	.1	Income Taxes Payable	.0	.0	.2	.3	.2	.2
7.9	8.6	5.9	All Other Current	14.9	3.3	13.5	5.2	2.8	4.4
30.8	28.3	25.1	Total Current	34.1	24.2	32.7	26.7	19.0	22.3
24.6	25.5	31.8	Long-Term Debt	50.9	57.0	25.0	18.4	26.6	22.5
.7	.6	.6	Deferred Taxes	.0	.2	.1	.5	1.9	.5
9.1	5.6	6.5	All Other Non-Current	4.7	6.6	5.3	4.7	7.9	8.1
34.9	40.1	36.1	Net Worth	10.3	12.0	36.9	49.7	44.6	46.6
100.0	100.0	100.0	Total Liabilties & Net Worth	100.0	100.0	100.0	100.0	100.0	100.0
			INCOME DATA						
100.0	100.0	100.0	Net Sales	100.0	100.0	100.0	100.0	100.0	100.0
34.1	31.2	36.2	Gross Profit	82.5	44.7	37.6	33.5	27.2	21.5
28.8	25.0	28.9	Operating Expenses	64.6	38.4	27.3	28.6	21.3	15.3
5.3	6.2	7.3	Operating Profit	18.0	6.2	10.3	5.0	5.9	6.2
.9	.7	1.1	All Other Expenses (net)	5.9	2.2	-.4	.4	.0	.5
4.4	5.4	6.2	Profit Before Taxes	12.1	4.0	10.7	4.5	5.9	5.7
			RATIOS						
2.7	4.5	3.5		4.0	3.5	2.6	3.3	4.3	2.9
1.4	1.6	1.7	Current	.7	1.7	1.5	1.4	2.3	2.0
.9	.9	1.0		.4	1.0	.9	.9	1.1	1.3
1.7	2.2	2.2		3.1	2.2	2.1	2.6	2.8	2.1
.9	1.0	1.1	Quick	.6	1.1	1.2	.9	1.0	1.3
.5	.5	.5		.1	.4	.6	.5	.5	.8
31 11.8	**26** 13.8	**20** 17.9		**0** UND	**12** 29.7	**18** 20.5	**31** 11.7	**21** 17.3	**39** 9.4
46 7.9	**38** 9.5	**38** 9.5	Sales/Receivables	**0** UND	**25** 14.8	**22** 16.9	**40** 9.2	**38** 9.7	**48** 7.6
73 5.0	**53** 6.9	**56** 6.5		**32** 11.5	**59** 6.2	**66** 5.5	**61** 6.0	**52** 7.0	**60** 6.1
5 75.0	**4** 96.6	**5** 74.3		**0** UND	**0** UND	**6** 64.3	**7** 52.2	**5** 76.4	**20** 18.2
35 10.4	**31** 11.9	**33** 11.2	Cost of Sales/Inventory	**0** UND	**30** 12.2	**34** 10.7	**23** 15.7	**53** 6.9	**32** 11.3
96 3.8	**85** 4.3	**87** 4.2		**608** .6	**114** 3.2	**87** 4.2	**76** 4.8	**94** 3.9	**47** 7.7
12 30.0	**10** 36.9	**8** 44.8		**0** UND	**2** 168.9	**13** 27.4	**9** 40.5	**11** 34.7	**16** 22.3
28 13.1	**20** 18.2	**18** 20.8	Cost of Sales/Payables	**0** UND	**13** 27.6	**26** 13.9	**18** 20.0	**26** 14.3	**25** 14.4
66 5.5	**47** 7.8	**42** 8.6		**0** UND	**46** 8.0	**81** 4.5	**42** 8.7	**45** 8.1	**39** 9.4
4.2	3.2	3.7		3.6	3.0	4.6	3.8	3.1	4.0
11.6	10.2	8.7	Sales/Working Capital	-280.0	9.7	8.1	15.0	6.2	7.5
-50.3	-73.7	-227.6		-7.6	-131.0	-45.5	-111.9	NM	20.9
8.2	8.0	10.0			8.1	6.8	10.5	14.5	10.7
(163) 3.2	(146) 4.1	(122) 4.5	EBIT/Interest		(24) 2.1	(11) 3.7	(26) 4.5	(23) 3.1	(30) 6.3
.7	1.3	1.3			.8	2.7	.6	1.0	4.0
6.1	5.7	3.3							
(35) 2.4	(32) 2.6	(22) 2.3	Net Profit + Depr., Dep., Amort./Cur. Mat. L/T/D						
1.1	1.4	1.1							
.7	.6	.7		1.0	.7	.6	.7	.8	.7
1.2	1.2	1.4	Fixed/Worth	5.0	2.0	1.6	1.1	1.9	1.0
4.0	3.2	4.7		-7.8	-3.0	206.7	2.1	3.7	1.7
.6	.4	.5		1.5	.4	.3	.4	.4	.6
1.7	1.5	1.5	Debt/Worth	5.5	2.8	1.7	.6	1.6	1.1
6.5	4.0	7.4		-14.2	-5.5	428.9	3.0	3.3	3.0
30.6	29.0	29.6			22.7	75.3	18.7	29.6	31.6
(155) 9.5	(146) 10.4	(114) 14.2	% Profit Before Taxes/Tangible Net Worth		(18) 8.6	(12) 32.7	(25) 8.3	(22) 7.6	(30) 15.1
-.3	2.4	2.1			-1.3	7.7	-1.8	-.4	8.5
10.8	11.5	12.1		54.0	11.7	15.4	12.0	11.7	9.7
3.7	4.8	6.2	% Profit Before Taxes/Total Assets	9.5	3.1	6.9	5.4	5.4	7.3
-1.5	.9	1.2		3.3	-.2	4.5	.1	.3	5.1
5.1	4.7	4.8		6.3	5.4	5.2	4.6	3.3	5.3
2.4	2.4	2.5	Sales/Net Fixed Assets	2.2	2.3	1.8	2.3	1.6	3.2
1.1	1.2	1.2		1.4	.9	.9	1.3	.9	2.3
1.6	1.7	1.7		2.5	1.7	1.5	1.9	1.3	1.7
1.0	1.0	1.1	Sales/Total Assets	1.4	1.1	.8	1.2	.9	1.4
.6	.7	.7		1.2	.6	.7	.7	.6	1.0
3.8	4.0	3.8			4.8	5.4	3.4	5.9	3.1
(169) 7.3	(146) 7.2	(121) 6.6	% Depr., Dep., Amort./Sales		(24) 6.8	(13) 9.6	(24) 6.2	(22) 8.9	(29) 4.2
12.4	13.4	12.5			15.4	16.5	11.6	14.6	7.5
1.4	1.0	1.3					1.3		
(42) 2.5	(52) 2.4	(43) 2.2	% Officers', Directors' Owners' Comp/Sales				(14) 2.0		
6.1	7.1	5.7					3.5		
3147079M	3169104M	2671335M	Net Sales ($)	5590M	52399M	60683M	191976M	350041M	2010646M
3119564M	3260148M	2483897M	Total Assets ($)	6170M	65013M	72938M	225767M	475186M	1638823M

M = $ thousand MM = $ million

See Pages 9 through 22 for Explanation of Ratios and Data

Current Data Sorted by Assets / Comparative Historical Data

0-500M	500M-2MM	2-10MM	10-50MM	50-100MM	100-250MM	Type of Statement	4/1/09-3/31/10 ALL	4/1/10-3/31/11 ALL
	1	1	3	6	2	Unqualified	18	15
1		6	10	1	1	Reviewed	13	13
1	2	7	3			Compiled	11	14
6	6	8	4			Tax Returns	19	26
4	14	20	23	12	11	Other	64	67
15 (4/1-9/30/13)		138 (10/1/13-3/31/14)						
12	23	42	43	19	14	NUMBER OF STATEMENTS	125	135
%	%	%	%	%	%	ASSETS	%	%
34.5	15.7	10.2	14.2	4.9	8.7	Cash & Equivalents	10.5	12.0
9.3	25.4	28.2	22.1	16.1	9.7	Trade Receivables (net)	18.5	19.8
3.9	3.2	5.1	3.3	5.2	2.3	Inventory	7.6	5.2
3.3	.6	2.6	2.2	3.3	1.7	All Other Current	3.7	4.6
51.0	44.8	46.1	41.8	29.5	22.3	Total Current	40.3	41.5
43.9	44.8	41.0	47.7	55.9	57.7	Fixed Assets (net)	48.2	49.2
3.2	2.0	2.7	2.6	11.8	10.4	Intangibles (net)	5.0	3.2
1.8	8.3	10.2	7.9	2.8	9.5	All Other Non-Current	6.5	6.1
100.0	100.0	100.0	100.0	100.0	100.0	Total	100.0	100.0
						LIABILITIES		
1.5	14.7	9.1	5.9	5.0	3.3	Notes Payable-Short Term	5.2	5.8
5.4	3.3	5.1	6.1	6.8	2.0	Cur. Mat.-L.T.D.	8.2	8.3
4.8	10.2	13.7	9.1	7.5	5.0	Trade Payables	8.7	10.2
.2	1.0	.2	.6	.1	.7	Income Taxes Payable	.1	.2
20.3	8.0	7.2	5.5	5.7	2.6	All Other Current	7.6	8.0
32.1	37.3	35.3	27.2	25.0	13.6	Total Current	29.8	32.6
55.0	23.3	23.6	11.4	27.4	18.2	Long-Term Debt	26.7	29.8
.0	.0	.2	1.8	1.4	3.7	Deferred Taxes	1.1	1.0
12.3	15.5	2.0	6.3	4.9	2.3	All Other Non-Current	8.1	4.4
.5	23.9	38.8	53.4	41.4	62.3	Net Worth	34.4	32.2
100.0	100.0	100.0	100.0	100.0	100.0	Total Liabilties & Net Worth	100.0	100.0
						INCOME DATA		
100.0	100.0	100.0	100.0	100.0	100.0	Net Sales	100.0	100.0
						Gross Profit		
87.3	89.4	89.4	90.0	90.0	92.6	Operating Expenses	92.5	88.7
12.7	10.6	10.6	10.0	10.0	7.4	Operating Profit	7.5	11.3
-.4	-.2	2.9	-.4	3.1	1.0	All Other Expenses (net)	2.2	2.6
13.1	10.9	7.7	10.4	7.0	6.4	Profit Before Taxes	5.3	8.7
						RATIOS		
23.5	4.1	2.5	4.3	1.6	4.7		2.8	2.5
7.0	1.3	1.5	1.4	1.4	1.4	Current	1.3	1.4
.6	.5	.9	.9	.8	.4		.8	.7
22.4	4.1	2.0	3.7	1.1	3.9		2.1	1.9
5.2	1.1	1.2	1.2	.9	1.1	Quick	.9	1.0
.6	.5	.8	.7	.6	.4		.5	.4
0 UND	25 14.7	35 10.5	41 9.0	46 8.0	41 8.8		25 14.8	22 16.6
0 UND	36 10.1	47 7.7	53 6.9	57 6.4	45 8.1	Sales/Receivables	44 8.3	48 7.6
16 22.3	66 5.5	70 5.2	83 4.4	83 4.4	68 5.4		70 5.2	70 5.2
						Cost of Sales/Inventory		
						Cost of Sales/Payables		
6.0	5.8	6.2	3.4	6.5	3.1		5.1	5.0
26.7	33.7	14.7	9.9	10.8	13.5	Sales/Working Capital	15.5	16.1
-37.0	-8.7	-38.0	-23.1	-16.8	-5.1		-18.6	-9.5
	45.7	47.7	34.1	5.5	20.3		9.6	13.0
	(16) 16.0	(36) 11.7	(37) 11.3	2.5	(13) 6.6	EBIT/Interest	(106) 2.1	(119) 4.3
	-1.5	4.8	2.1	.5	-3.4		-.5	.6
							4.6	4.8
						Net Profit + Depr., Dep., Amort./Cur. Mat. L/T/D	(21) 2.4	(21) 1.8
							1.4	.9
.3	.3	.4	.6	1.4	.9		.6	.8
1.1	.9	.9	.9	2.2	1.1	Fixed/Worth	1.4	1.4
UND	10.0	6.8	1.4	3.5	1.4		3.4	2.9
.1	.4	.6	.3	.9	.4		.6	.7
1.4	1.8	1.4	1.0	2.6	.6	Debt/Worth	1.4	1.5
UND	15.5	8.0	1.9	6.2	1.4		5.8	6.4
242.6	199.1	74.9	42.4	48.0	33.0		47.8	58.0
(10) 68.9	(19) 66.9	(36) 24.9	(41) 19.0	(16) 15.7	(13) 14.9	% Profit Before Taxes/Tangible Net Worth	(107) 10.7	(119) 18.1
23.4	21.6	10.3	3.3	-.9	.4		-5.1	-1.2
80.6	52.6	27.7	24.0	13.6	12.1		14.6	22.0
32.7	26.7	12.5	10.0	4.0	8.7	% Profit Before Taxes/Total Assets	5.4	6.7
12.6	3.2	5.0	1.8	-.6	-2.6		-4.4	-1.1
32.9	11.2	14.3	5.1	2.7	3.0		8.1	9.5
14.6	5.5	4.6	3.1	1.3	.9	Sales/Net Fixed Assets	2.7	2.7
5.1	2.5	2.3	1.4	.9	.4		1.1	1.1
6.3	3.3	2.5	1.7	1.1	.7		2.2	2.1
4.4	2.5	1.8	1.2	.9	.6	Sales/Total Assets	1.1	1.3
2.2	1.6	1.2	.9	.7	.4		.6	.6
	3.3	4.7	4.4	7.3			3.7	4.2
	(13) 5.0	(27) 7.3	(38) 8.9	(14) 9.0		% Depr., Dep., Amort./Sales	(89) 9.1	(98) 7.9
	8.4	11.0	15.2	14.9			13.6	14.7
		1.9					1.1	1.1
		(16) 3.2				% Officers', Directors' Owners' Comp/Sales	(30) 4.6	(33) 4.1
		12.2					10.6	8.6
19654M	60433M	443396M	1293217M	1324727M	1631490M	Net Sales ($)	3106694M	3697273M
3521M	25517M	241065M	980762M	1526713M	2346422M	Total Assets ($)	3491082M	3993849M

M = $ thousand MM = $ million

See Pages 9 through 22 for Explanation of Ratios and Data

Comparative Historical Data / Current Data Sorted by Sales

	Comparative Historical Data			Current Data Sorted by Sales					
Type of Statement									
Unqualified	21	19	13		1			3	9
Reviewed	23	16	19				5	10	4
Compiled	12	15	13		2	2	2	6	1
Tax Returns	22	25	24	4	8	1	4	5	2
Other	79	70	84	5	13	4	8	21	33
	4/1/11-3/31/12 ALL	4/1/12-3/31/13 ALL	4/1/13-3/31/14 ALL	15 (4/1-9/30/13)			138 (10/1/13-3/31/14)		
				0-1MM	1-3MM	3-5MM	5-10MM	10-25MM	25MM & OVER
NUMBER OF STATEMENTS	157	145	153	9	24	7	19	45	49
ASSETS	%	%	%	%	%	%	%	%	%
Cash & Equivalents	11.0	11.3	13.2		21.7		10.8	13.2	7.5
Trade Receivables (net)	22.5	20.3	21.4		18.4		30.5	25.7	18.1
Inventory	4.6	4.7	4.0		4.3		5.0	3.2	3.8
All Other Current	3.4	3.7	2.3		2.1		1.1	3.4	2.3
Total Current	41.5	40.0	40.9		46.5		47.3	45.5	31.8
Fixed Assets (net)	47.6	49.2	47.0		41.7		43.3	41.8	54.6
Intangibles (net)	2.6	2.7	4.4		3.4		4.1	2.9	7.6
All Other Non-Current	8.3	8.1	7.6		8.4		5.3	9.7	6.0
Total	100.0	100.0	100.0		100.0		100.0	100.0	100.0
LIABILITIES									
Notes Payable-Short Term	6.7	5.1	7.4		15.3		6.6	6.5	5.4
Cur. Mat.-L.T.D.	5.1	5.5	5.1		1.9		5.6	5.1	6.5
Trade Payables	8.9	10.1	9.6		11.1		12.7	10.1	8.0
Income Taxes Payable	.4	.2	.5		.4		1.3	.5	.3
All Other Current	7.8	5.5	7.3		5.1		11.5	7.5	5.3
Total Current	28.8	26.4	29.8		33.7		37.6	29.8	25.4
Long-Term Debt	23.0	26.8	22.6		22.6		44.6	19.5	18.9
Deferred Taxes	1.2	1.7	1.1		.0		.5	1.2	1.6
All Other Non-Current	4.4	10.8	6.4		7.5		2.0	6.0	3.2
Net Worth	42.5	34.3	40.1		36.2		15.2	43.5	50.9
Total Liabilties & Net Worth	100.0	100.0	100.0		100.0		100.0	100.0	100.0
INCOME DATA									
Net Sales	100.0	100.0	100.0		100.0		100.0	100.0	100.0
Gross Profit									
Operating Expenses	86.8	89.1	89.8		90.1		92.0	90.0	90.7
Operating Profit	13.2	10.9	10.2		9.9		8.0	10.0	9.3
All Other Expenses (net)	1.6	2.1	1.1		2.0		.2	-.1	1.3
Profit Before Taxes	11.6	8.7	9.1		7.8		7.8	10.0	8.1
RATIOS									
	3.4	2.8	3.1		5.8		2.6	4.0	1.9
Current	1.5	1.4	1.4		1.8		1.8	1.6	1.2
	.8	.9	.8		.6		.9	.9	.8
	2.5	2.2	2.7		4.3		2.5	3.1	1.6
Quick	1.2	1.1	1.1		1.4		1.4	1.4	.9
	.7	.7	.7		.6		.8	.8	.6
	31 11.7	**14** 25.9	**32** 11.3		**0** UND		**39** 9.4	**38** 9.7	**42** 8.7
Sales/Receivables	**54** 6.7	**44** 8.3	**47** 7.7		**26** 14.2		**54** 6.8	**48** 7.6	**52** 7.0
	74 4.9	**62** 5.9	**70** 5.2		**64** 5.7		**96** 3.8	**72** 5.1	**72** 5.1
Cost of Sales/Inventory									
Cost of Sales/Payables									
	4.7	6.0	5.7		5.6		4.0	4.0	6.3
Sales/Working Capital	12.3	16.5	12.9		11.6		13.4	10.9	11.6
	-25.0	-65.1	-18.0		-12.9		-23.1	-191.4	-16.8
	31.6	21.5	28.9		42.6		43.3	44.9	13.8
EBIT/Interest	(138) 9.8	(130) 9.1	(129) 7.7		(16) 8.7		(18) 6.5	(41) 13.9	(46) 5.2
	2.5	3.0	2.4		-1.8		2.1	4.2	1.7
	13.3	12.0	8.2						5.5
Net Profit + Depr., Dep., Amort./Cur. Mat. L/T/D	(20) 3.2	(19) 6.5	(21) 3.9						(10) 3.9
	1.4	1.7	1.7						1.7
	.5	.7	.5		.2		.2	.5	.8
Fixed/Worth	1.1	1.2	1.0		.6		.9	.9	1.3
	2.2	2.9	2.9		9.0		9.2	3.0	2.4
	.5	.7	.5		.3		.5	.5	.6
Debt/Worth	1.2	1.5	1.2		1.6		1.2	1.1	1.0
	3.0	6.7	3.1		13.0		10.4	4.5	2.6
	76.7	73.7	65.8		161.7		123.8	46.8	48.4
% Profit Before Taxes/Tangible Net Worth	(140) 33.0	(127) 40.0	(135) 26.1		(21) 40.2		(16) 35.0	(39) 23.3	(45) 18.3
	11.4	15.8	6.9		7.3		9.9	5.8	6.7
	27.1	27.0	27.6		36.5		38.6	27.9	14.0
% Profit Before Taxes/Total Assets	13.5	14.3	11.3		19.8		10.9	13.2	7.9
	3.0	5.1	2.2		-.9		4.1	3.6	1.8
	6.6	8.5	7.2		11.6		37.6	7.8	4.3
Sales/Net Fixed Assets	2.9	3.2	3.5		5.6		3.4	4.4	1.8
	1.6	1.8	1.4		2.9		1.4	2.1	1.0
	2.2	2.6	2.4		3.0		3.3	2.3	1.6
Sales/Total Assets	1.3	1.6	1.4		2.3		1.5	1.5	1.0
	.8	.9	.9		1.4		1.0	1.0	.6
	3.5	2.9	4.6		3.7		4.7	4.2	6.4
% Depr., Dep., Amort./Sales	(94) 7.0	(96) 6.4	(101) 7.9		(13) 5.8		(12) 6.7	(36) 8.4	(31) 8.9
	12.3	11.3	13.4		7.9		10.6	12.2	15.1
	1.3	1.7	1.9					1.0	
% Officers', Directors' Owners' Comp/Sales	(43) 4.0	(42) 3.2	(40) 3.1					(12) 2.7	
	6.7	5.6	13.6					8.2	
Net Sales ($)	4860715M	7030410M	4772917M	4904M	46749M	28897M	139828M	758919M	3793620M
Total Assets ($)	5289325M	4939899M	5124000M	13183M	32252M	37855M	116186M	659291M	4265233M

M = $ thousand MM = $ million

See Pages 9 through 22 for Explanation of Ratios and Data

Current Data Sorted by Assets							Comparative Historical Data	
						Type of Statement		
1	3	10	52	31	37	Unqualified	80	85
1	2	12	25	2	1	Reviewed	36	44
4	23	46	10	6	2	Compiled	36	38
11	20	17	2			Tax Returns	32	42
14	33	113	141	75	61	Other	226	292
90 (4/1-9/30/13)			665 (10/1/13-3/31/14)				**4/1/09-3/31/10 ALL**	**4/1/10-3/31/11 ALL**
0-500M	**500M-2MM**	**2-10MM**	**10-50MM**	**50-100MM**	**100-250MM**			
31	81	198	230	114	101	**NUMBER OF STATEMENTS**	410	501
%	%	%	%	%	%	**ASSETS**	%	%
30.5	21.5	14.3	7.6	6.0	5.3	Cash & Equivalents	10.8	10.8
21.1	22.8	32.3	26.4	19.4	16.2	Trade Receivables (net)	20.7	25.9
1.8	3.8	6.6	6.1	5.3	10.1	Inventory	6.7	8.0
1.3	2.3	2.8	4.4	3.1	3.5	All Other Current	3.5	3.8
54.7	50.4	55.9	44.4	33.7	35.2	Total Current	41.7	48.4
37.0	38.0	33.2	44.0	51.8	43.9	Fixed Assets (net)	43.7	39.0
.8	2.6	3.5	5.6	10.0	15.4	Intangibles (net)	7.5	6.8
7.3	8.9	7.4	5.9	4.5	5.5	All Other Non-Current	7.1	5.8
100.0	100.0	100.0	100.0	100.0	100.0	Total	100.0	100.0
						LIABILITIES		
19.2	9.9	6.9	6.1	4.7	5.0	Notes Payable-Short Term	7.1	7.2
9.4	6.2	4.5	5.5	5.5	4.9	Cur. Mat.-L.T.D.	5.2	5.5
25.7	10.6	11.9	10.6	8.1	7.7	Trade Payables	9.6	11.1
.0	1.0	.2	.4	.6	.2	Income Taxes Payable	.3	.4
20.9	5.9	5.8	7.1	6.8	5.1	All Other Current	8.9	8.9
75.1	33.6	29.4	29.8	25.7	22.8	Total Current	31.1	33.0
37.1	23.3	17.3	18.2	28.0	19.4	Long-Term Debt	21.5	17.8
.1	.0	.3	.9	1.9	1.9	Deferred Taxes	1.2	1.1
13.4	4.2	6.2	4.0	5.6	2.6	All Other Non-Current	6.7	5.8
-25.8	38.9	46.8	47.1	38.8	53.4	Net Worth	39.5	42.4
100.0	100.0	100.0	100.0	100.0	100.0	Total Liabilities & Net Worth	100.0	100.0
						INCOME DATA		
100.0	100.0	100.0	100.0	100.0	100.0	Net Sales	100.0	100.0
						Gross Profit		
90.4	91.5	89.7	89.8	87.1	84.5	Operating Expenses	92.0	90.0
9.6	8.5	10.3	10.2	12.9	15.5	Operating Profit	8.0	10.0
1.3	.7	1.1	1.4	3.3	2.4	All Other Expenses (net)	2.8	2.6
8.4	7.8	9.3	8.8	9.6	13.0	Profit Before Taxes	5.2	7.4
						RATIOS		
2.6	5.2	3.9	2.4	2.4	2.4		2.6	3.0
1.0	1.8	2.0	1.4	1.3	1.6	Current	1.4	1.6
.4	.7	1.1	1.0	.9	1.1		.8	1.0
2.3	5.0	3.4	1.9	1.8	1.6		2.0	2.3
1.0	1.3	1.5	1.1	1.0	1.1	Quick	1.1	1.1
.3	.5	.9	.7	.7	.7		.5	.7
0 UND	**0** UND	**34** 10.7	**45** 8.1	**54** 6.7	**49** 7.5		**28** 13.2	**33** 11.0
23 16.0	**21** 17.0	**51** 7.1	**61** 6.0	**70** 5.2	**60** 6.1	Sales/Receivables	**49** 7.4	**57** 6.4
78 4.7	**45** 8.1	**72** 5.1	**78** 4.7	**87** 4.2	**73** 5.0		**69** 5.3	**78** 4.7
						Cost of Sales/Inventory		
						Cost of Sales/Payables		
10.5	6.3	4.9	5.6	3.8	4.2		5.3	4.4
213.7	17.9	8.5	12.1	10.5	8.1	Sales/Working Capital	13.8	10.7
-7.6	-29.1	53.1	-205.3	-30.7	36.7		-18.7	-166.3
10.2	27.4	39.5	20.1	12.0	19.3		12.7	20.4
(22) 4.0	(62) 8.7	(169) 12.3	(209) 6.4	(107) 4.2	(92) 6.0	EBIT/Interest	(354) 3.3	(427) 5.2
.6	.9	2.8	1.6	.9	2.7		.1	1.4
		7.7	7.1	4.9	13.2		4.9	5.1
		(25) 3.5	(41) 2.4	(28) 2.8	(20) 2.8	Net Profit + Depr., Dep., Amort./Cur. Mat. L/T/D	(84) 2.3	(92) 2.0
		1.6	1.1	1.0	1.6		1.2	1.0
.0	.2	.2	.5	1.1	.7		.5	.4
3.5	1.1	.7	1.1	2.1	1.2	Fixed/Worth	1.4	1.0
-1.3	10.7	1.9	1.8	5.0	2.2		4.0	2.6
2.2	.3	.5	.6	1.1	.5		.7	.5
9.7	1.7	1.1	1.4	2.1	1.3	Debt/Worth	1.8	1.6
-3.2	40.0	3.0	2.8	12.3	2.9		6.1	4.1
116.9	91.3	66.4	52.6	42.2	40.1		45.5	55.5
(19) 50.0	(62) 48.3	(180) 40.1	(216) 24.0	(96) 19.2	(91) 22.9	% Profit Before Taxes/Tangible Net Worth	(346) 15.8	(439) 25.5
-7.3	.8	11.4	7.4	.3	8.7		-2.3	6.7
36.9	52.3	33.9	19.8	13.9	16.0		16.4	22.9
19.6	11.7	15.7	8.2	6.8	7.9	% Profit Before Taxes/Total Assets	4.7	8.3
-1.9	-.6	3.2	1.7	.1	3.2		-1.9	1.2
486.0	35.7	31.8	8.8	3.6	6.3		12.6	18.1
18.1	10.9	8.0	3.0	1.8	2.1	Sales/Net Fixed Assets	3.0	4.4
3.7	4.1	2.8	1.6	.8	1.0		1.4	1.8
8.4	4.6	3.0	2.0	1.2	1.4		2.3	2.5
3.6	2.6	2.0	1.4	.9	.8	Sales/Total Assets	1.3	1.5
1.5	1.8	1.3	.9	.5	.5		.7	.8
.8	1.4	1.6	2.5	4.2	1.6		2.0	1.8
(10) 1.9	(52) 4.1	(135) 3.6	(205) 6.0	(87) 8.4	(53) 5.1	% Depr., Dep., Amort./Sales	(303) 5.7	(366) 5.3
22.4	11.9	7.7	10.3	11.8	9.5		12.5	10.8
3.1	2.5	1.5	.8				1.3	1.2
(10) 7.1	(36) 4.0	(49) 3.0	(25) 1.9			% Officers', Directors' Owners' Comp/Sales	(88) 3.4	(109) 2.9
17.7	7.8	5.6	6.6				8.5	5.8
55066M	333823M	2246344M	8195195M	9199367M	17691248M	Net Sales ($)	17491067M	24593546M
8493M	101341M	991611M	5531930M	8633359M	16503136M	Total Assets ($)	17354542M	17627278M

M = $ thousand MM = $ million

See Pages 9 through 22 for Explanation of Ratios and Data

Comparative Historical Data				Current Data Sorted by Sales					
			Type of Statement						
117	93	134	Unqualified	2	4		10	23	95
37	44	43	Reviewed	1	2		5	16	19
67	68	91	Compiled	5	17	12	21	23	13
53	60	50	Tax Returns	4	11	9	14	12	
344	415	437	Other	16	28	26	61	93	213
4/1/11-3/31/12	**4/1/12-3/31/13**	**4/1/13-3/31/14**		**90 (4/1-9/30/13)**			**665 (10/1/13-3/31/14)**		
ALL	**ALL**	**ALL**		**0-1MM**	**1-3MM**	**3-5MM**	**5-10MM**	**10-25MM**	**25MM & OVER**
618	680	755	**NUMBER OF STATEMENTS**	28	62	47	111	167	340
%	%	%	**ASSETS**	%	%	%	%	%	%
11.0	10.8	11.2	Cash & Equivalents	16.9	19.3	18.8	16.3	10.8	6.8
28.5	25.5	24.9	Trade Receivables (net)	18.1	15.6	20.7	29.1	25.6	26.0
7.0	6.7	6.2	Inventory	1.6	3.2	7.3	4.2	6.4	7.6
3.8	3.6	3.3	All Other Current	2.9	2.2	2.0	3.0	3.1	3.9
50.3	46.6	45.6	Total Current	39.7	40.3	48.8	52.6	45.9	44.2
37.7	41.2	41.4	Fixed Assets (net)	41.7	45.6	39.6	34.8	44.3	41.6
5.9	6.7	6.5	Intangibles (net)	1.2	1.9	1.4	6.5	4.8	9.4
6.1	5.6	6.4	All Other Non-Current	17.1	12.3	10.2	6.1	4.9	4.8
100.0	100.0	100.0	Total	100.0	100.0	100.0	100.0	100.0	100.0
			LIABILITIES						
6.1	6.9	6.9	Notes Payable-Short Term	11.3	6.9	5.9	7.1	7.8	6.2
6.0	5.2	5.4	Cur. Mat.-L.T.D.	9.2	5.1	5.4	5.7	4.7	5.4
11.8	9.6	10.8	Trade Payables	12.2	12.5	9.2	11.2	10.9	10.5
.3	.5	.4	Income Taxes Payable	2.6	.0	.1	.2	.3	.5
8.6	7.9	6.9	All Other Current	15.2	4.8	4.8	5.8	6.4	7.4
32.8	30.0	30.4	Total Current	50.5	29.3	25.4	30.0	30.0	29.9
18.7	22.1	20.9	Long-Term Debt	28.3	29.7	21.4	21.1	19.7	19.2
.9	.9	.9	Deferred Taxes	.1	.0	.1	.6	.8	1.4
5.5	5.4	5.0	All Other Non-Current	4.8	10.7	5.5	5.0	4.2	4.4
42.1	41.7	42.7	Net Worth	16.2	30.4	47.6	43.3	45.4	45.0
100.0	100.0	100.0	Total Liabilties & Net Worth	100.0	100.0	100.0	100.0	100.0	100.0
			INCOME DATA						
100.0	100.0	100.0	Net Sales	100.0	100.0	100.0	100.0	100.0	100.0
			Gross Profit						
87.3	86.3	88.9	Operating Expenses	78.6	89.9	88.2	90.4	88.6	89.3
12.7	13.7	11.1	Operating Profit	21.4	10.1	11.8	9.6	11.4	10.7
2.1	2.1	1.6	All Other Expenses (net)	3.2	2.5	1.0	1.2	1.0	1.9
10.6	11.6	9.5	Profit Before Taxes	18.2	7.6	10.9	8.4	10.4	8.8
			RATIOS						
2.8	2.9	2.9		2.7	4.7	5.4	4.0	2.9	2.4
1.7	1.6	1.5	Current	1.1	1.4	1.8	1.8	1.7	1.4
1.1	1.0	1.0		.4	.6	1.0	1.0	1.1	1.0
2.3	2.3	2.3		2.5	4.3	5.2	3.5	2.4	1.9
1.3	1.2	1.2	Quick	1.0	1.3	1.2	1.5	1.2	1.1
.7	.7	.7		.2	.4	.6	.8	.7	.7
38 9.7	**34** 10.6	**37** 9.8		**0** UND	**0** UND	**5** 78.7	**34** 10.8	**41** 9.0	**49** 7.5
61 6.0	**55** 6.6	**55** 6.6	Sales/Receivables	**25** 14.8	**20** 18.2	**45** 8.2	**51** 7.2	**54** 6.7	**61** 6.0
81 4.5	**78** 4.7	**76** 4.8		**89** 4.1	**60** 6.1	**66** 5.5	**81** 4.5	**73** 5.0	**78** 4.7
			Cost of Sales/Inventory						
			Cost of Sales/Payables						
4.8	5.0	5.1		2.8	3.9	3.4	4.7	4.9	5.7
10.3	11.2	11.0	Sales/Working Capital	16.2	20.8	8.8	9.8	10.4	12.1
90.4	131.4	-167.6		-1.9	-14.0	-87.4	138.7	61.6	-385.6
29.3	30.5	22.3		9.4	10.2	22.1	34.0	32.3	19.2
(536) 8.7	(604) 9.6	(661) 7.4	EBIT/Interest	(19) 3.3	(43) 3.1	(35) 6.6	(97) 9.2	(148) 8.5	(319) 6.6
2.3	2.5	1.5		.6	-1.2	.1	2.1	1.4	2.0
9.0	7.5	7.0					6.9	7.4	7.5
(103) 3.1	(132) 3.4	(120) 2.8	Net Profit + Depr., Dep., Amort./Cur. Mat. L/T/D				(15) 3.5	(23) 3.3	(75) 2.7
1.5	1.3	1.1					1.4	1.5	1.4
.4	.4	.4		.0	.2	.1	.2	.5	.6
.9	1.0	1.1	Fixed/Worth	1.7	1.7	.9	.9	1.1	1.2
2.3	2.6	2.6		UND	6.9	2.4	2.1	2.1	2.4
.6	.6	.6		.3	.4	.3	.5	.6	.7
1.5	1.4	1.5	Debt/Worth	3.2	1.9	1.1	1.2	1.1	1.6
4.0	3.9	3.7		UND	14.9	2.6	3.5	3.0	3.6
79.6	66.8	57.4		79.6	60.5	69.9	73.0	51.3	54.6
(550) 38.1	(591) 34.3	(664) 26.5	% Profit Before Taxes/Tangible Net Worth	(21) 28.8	(49) 15.1	(41) 25.7	(95) 31.6	(152) 27.0	(306) 26.6
13.1	11.5	6.8		.6	-7.8	.1	8.9	6.4	9.6
28.3	28.3	22.5		22.0	18.8	37.3	31.4	26.4	18.8
12.9	12.7	9.9	% Profit Before Taxes/Total Assets	10.4	5.3	9.9	12.3	10.9	9.2
3.2	3.3	1.7		-.2	-6.4	.3	3.5	2.7	2.9
18.4	14.8	14.8		317.7	19.0	20.3	30.1	11.9	11.0
4.8	4.2	3.7	Sales/Net Fixed Assets	2.7	3.7	4.8	7.9	3.5	3.0
2.0	1.7	1.6		.8	1.2	1.8	2.3	1.6	1.6
2.7	2.5	2.4		1.6	2.3	2.9	3.3	2.6	2.0
1.6	1.5	1.4	Sales/Total Assets	.7	1.4	1.9	1.9	1.5	1.3
.9	.8	.8		.2	.6	.9	1.0	.9	.8
1.7	2.0	2.0		1.5	2.2	1.8	2.3	2.6	1.7
(433) 4.9	(496) 5.5	(542) 5.5	% Depr., Dep., Amort./Sales	(12) 19.9	(40) 11.7	(34) 7.0	(73) 4.8	(138) 5.6	(245) 4.6
9.0	10.4	10.8		31.1	20.5	16.1	9.0	11.1	8.9
1.4	1.6	1.3			1.3	3.4	2.3	1.0	.8
(118) 2.8	(127) 2.9	(130) 3.2	% Officers', Directors' Owners' Comp/Sales		(19) 4.2	(13) 4.6	(39) 3.8	(35) 1.7	(21) 1.5
5.9	5.8	6.2			13.3	6.9	9.1	4.5	3.2
32913177M	**36413096M**	**37721043M**	Net Sales ($)	**12132M**	**116666M**	**186289M**	**792550M**	**2837205M**	**33776201M**
22939865M	**28111429M**	**31769870M**	Total Assets ($)	**44693M**	**199422M**	**593814M**	**842906M**	**3317345M**	**26771690M**

M = $ thousand MM = $ million

See Pages 9 through 22 for Explanation of Ratios and Data

UTILITIES

Current Data Sorted by Assets							Comparative Historical Data	
						Type of Statement		
		3	4	2	8	Unqualified	8	9
			1			Reviewed	2	1
	1					Compiled	3	1
						Tax Returns	2	
1		1	2		1	Other	9	4
	4 (4/1-9/30/13)		20 (10/1/13-3/31/14)				**4/1/09-3/31/10**	**4/1/10-3/31/11**
0-500M	**500M-2MM**	**2-10MM**	**10-50MM**	**50-100MM**	**100-250MM**		**ALL**	**ALL**
1	1	4	7	2	9	**NUMBER OF STATEMENTS**	24	15
%	%	%	%	%	%	**ASSETS**	%	%
						Cash & Equivalents	14.3	5.8
						Trade Receivables (net)	15.2	11.8
						Inventory	5.5	5.5
						All Other Current	3.3	4.8
						Total Current	38.4	27.9
						Fixed Assets (net)	45.6	57.0
						Intangibles (net)	3.2	3.9
						All Other Non-Current	12.8	11.0
						Total	100.0	100.0
						LIABILITIES		
						Notes Payable-Short Term	3.0	4.5
						Cur. Mat.-L.T.D.	3.6	4.5
						Trade Payables	6.5	4.8
						Income Taxes Payable	.8	.0
						All Other Current	14.2	5.5
						Total Current	28.1	19.3
						Long-Term Debt	16.8	29.1
						Deferred Taxes	.5	.9
						All Other Non-Current	17.0	7.7
						Net Worth	37.6	43.0
						Total Liabilties & Net Worth	100.0	100.0
						INCOME DATA		
						Net Sales	100.0	100.0
						Gross Profit		
						Operating Expenses	86.5	80.1
						Operating Profit	13.5	19.9
						All Other Expenses (net)	2.6	6.8
						Profit Before Taxes	10.9	13.1
						RATIOS		
							2.1	2.1
						Current	1.5	1.4
							.6	1.0
							1.8	1.8
						Quick	1.0	.9
							.4	.5
							28 12.8	**32** 11.4
						Sales/Receivables	**37** 9.8	**39** 9.5
							46 7.9	**43** 8.4
						Cost of Sales/Inventory		
						Cost of Sales/Payables		
							5.5	6.3
						Sales/Working Capital	13.5	14.1
							-10.4	UND
							17.4	5.4
						EBIT/Interest	(20) 5.7	2.7
							1.7	1.3
						Net Profit + Depr., Dep., Amort./Cur. Mat. L/T/D		
							.2	.7
						Fixed/Worth	1.1	1.5
							2.0	2.3
							.6	1.0
						Debt/Worth	1.3	1.4
							2.1	2.6
							49.1	15.3
						% Profit Before Taxes/Tangible Net Worth	(22) 12.6	10.3
							1.3	4.3
							16.9	8.6
						% Profit Before Taxes/Total Assets	6.5	4.2
							.3	.5
							23.7	1.5
						Sales/Net Fixed Assets	1.7	.8
							.6	.3
							2.5	1.0
						Sales/Total Assets	.6	.5
							.4	.2
							1.0	3.4
						% Depr., Dep., Amort./Sales	(22) 5.2	6.9
							9.8	13.7
						% Officers', Directors' Owners' Comp/Sales		
2307M	**119M**	**59109M**	**87909M**	**73908M**	**960354M**	Net Sales ($)	**753508M**	**471217M**
442M	**642M**	**21953M**	**230437M**	**162168M**	**1742077M**	Total Assets ($)	**862016M**	**837958M**

M = $ thousand MM = $ million

See Pages 9 through 22 for Explanation of Ratios and Data

Comparative Historical Data				Current Data Sorted by Sales					
			Type of Statement						
38	8	17	Unqualified			1	1	5	10
1	3	1	Reviewed		1				
1	1	1	Compiled	1					
2	5		Tax Returns						
8	9	5	Other		1	1		3	
4/1/11-3/31/12 ALL	**4/1/12-3/31/13 ALL**	**4/1/13-3/31/14 ALL**		**4 (4/1-9/30/13)**			**20 (10/1/13-3/31/14)**		
				0-1MM	**1-3MM**	**3-5MM**	**5-10MM**	**10-25MM**	**25MM & OVER**
50	26	24	**NUMBER OF STATEMENTS**	1	2	2	1	8	10
%	%	%	**ASSETS**	%	%	%	%	%	%
5.4	15.0	7.3	Cash & Equivalents						11.6
13.2	10.9	14.4	Trade Receivables (net)						11.0
4.1	.7	2.6	Inventory						3.6
3.3	1.7	1.8	All Other Current						1.9
26.0	28.2	26.1	Total Current						28.2
52.3	48.7	56.8	Fixed Assets (net)						55.3
5.5	4.7	2.3	Intangibles (net)						.5
16.2	18.4	14.9	All Other Non-Current						16.0
100.0	100.0	100.0	Total						100.0
			LIABILITIES						
3.5	3.6	3.4	Notes Payable-Short Term						.6
2.1	5.2	2.5	Cur. Mat.-L.T.D.						2.4
5.7	8.4	9.5	Trade Payables						12.4
.4	.3	.0	Income Taxes Payable						.0
6.0	11.8	5.3	All Other Current						6.5
17.8	29.1	20.7	Total Current						21.9
34.2	35.3	34.2	Long-Term Debt						39.9
.6	1.9	.8	Deferred Taxes						.1
13.5	1.3	3.3	All Other Non-Current						3.7
33.8	32.4	40.9	Net Worth						34.3
100.0	100.0	100.0	Total Liabilties & Net Worth						100.0
			INCOME DATA						
100.0	100.0	100.0	Net Sales						100.0
			Gross Profit						
86.8	85.8	84.5	Operating Expenses						85.4
13.2	14.2	15.5	Operating Profit						14.6
6.3	3.5	5.1	All Other Expenses (net)						4.0
6.9	10.7	10.5	Profit Before Taxes						10.7
			RATIOS						
2.1	2.4	1.9							2.8
1.4	1.0	1.1	Current						1.2
.9	.7	.8							.7
1.7	2.0	1.6							2.4
.9	.8	1.0	Quick						1.0
.7	.5	.7							.6
30 12.3	**0** UND	**29** 12.8							**29** 12.5
45 8.1	**23** 15.9	**38** 9.5	Sales/Receivables						**38** 9.5
62 5.9	**35** 10.4	**47** 7.7							**46** 7.9
			Cost of Sales/Inventory						
			Cost of Sales/Payables						
4.6	4.1	6.2							2.5
12.6	NM	65.4	Sales/Working Capital						24.8
-36.9	-7.5	-16.7							-12.3
4.7	4.8	7.2							
(44) 2.8	(20) 2.1	(20) 2.6	EBIT/Interest						
1.7	-2.5	1.6							
30.9									
(17) 5.4			Net Profit + Depr., Dep., Amort./Cur. Mat. L/T/D						
1.2									
1.0	.9	.8							.5
2.2	1.9	1.2	Fixed/Worth						1.3
3.3	NM	5.7							5.4
1.4	1.1	.5							.6
2.4	2.2	1.4	Debt/Worth						1.9
4.2	NM	11.7							60.4
18.2	43.5	19.7							
(44) 10.7	(20) 9.8	(21) 8.7	% Profit Before Taxes/Tangible Net Worth						
4.5	-.3	3.6							
5.5	11.6	7.1							7.8
3.1	1.9	3.0	% Profit Before Taxes/Total Assets						3.2
.5	-5.2	1.4							2.4
2.9	61.7	2.4							4.7
.7	.7	.7	Sales/Net Fixed Assets						.9
.5	.3	.3							.4
.9	2.1	.6							.9
.5	.5	.4	Sales/Total Assets						.5
.3	.2	.2							.3
3.7	1.3	4.3							
(46) 6.8	(22) 8.5	(21) 8.0	% Depr., Dep., Amort./Sales						
11.6	16.7	15.1							
			% Officers', Directors' Owners' Comp/Sales						
1506149M	**571268M**	**1183706M**	Net Sales ($)	**119M**	**5190M**	**6513M**	**8175M**	**147418M**	**1016291M**
2600044M	**1403875M**	**2157719M**	Total Assets ($)	**642M**	**13669M**	**24414M**	**32422M**	**488571M**	**1598001M**

M = $ thousand MM = $ million

See Pages 9 through 22 for Explanation of Ratios and Data

Current Data Sorted by Assets | Comparative Historical Data

0-500M	500M-2MM	2-10MM	10-50MM	50-100MM	100-250MM	Type of Statement	4/1/09-3/31/10 ALL	4/1/10-3/31/11 ALL
2	2	3	4	1	5	Unqualified	7	9
	3	4	1			Reviewed		
1		1	1			Compiled		
1			2			Tax Returns	1	1
2	3	6	7	2	3	Other	8	10
1 (4/1-9/30/13)		53 (10/1/13-3/31/14)					4/1/09-3/31/10	4/1/10-3/31/11
0-500M	500M-2MM	2-10MM	10-50MM	50-100MM	100-250MM		ALL	ALL
6	8	14	15	3	8	NUMBER OF STATEMENTS	16	20
%	%	%	%	%	%	ASSETS	%	%
		14.7	5.5			Cash & Equivalents	16.3	8.9
		15.2	6.8			Trade Receivables (net)	13.1	13.1
		2.3	3.3			Inventory	7.5	5.8
		3.3	6.3			All Other Current	5.6	4.0
		35.5	21.8			Total Current	42.4	31.7
		53.6	59.3			Fixed Assets (net)	47.5	48.8
		6.4	3.3			Intangibles (net)	5.6	7.5
		4.6	15.5			All Other Non-Current	4.5	12.0
		100.0	100.0			Total	100.0	100.0
						LIABILITIES		
		8.8	8.6			Notes Payable-Short Term	4.0	3.6
		25.8	3.1			Cur. Mat.-L.T.D.	1.9	9.0
		4.9	3.9			Trade Payables	13.8	10.1
		.1	.0			Income Taxes Payable	.1	.0
		11.2	6.0			All Other Current	4.7	7.8
		50.6	21.5			Total Current	24.7	30.5
		16.7	27.7			Long-Term Debt	25.2	19.3
		1.1	.0			Deferred Taxes	.8	2.3
		12.6	6.4			All Other Non-Current	7.5	12.2
		19.0	44.4			Net Worth	41.8	35.7
		100.0	100.0			Total Liabilties & Net Worth	100.0	100.0
						INCOME DATA		
		100.0	100.0			Net Sales	100.0	100.0
						Gross Profit		
		88.4	79.7			Operating Expenses	88.4	90.7
		11.6	20.3			Operating Profit	11.6	9.3
		3.8	10.2			All Other Expenses (net)	3.3	6.0
		7.8	10.1			Profit Before Taxes	8.4	3.2
						RATIOS		
		3.6	5.1				3.7	2.0
		.8	.9			Current	2.0	1.0
		.5	.2				1.3	.7
		2.6	3.9				2.3	1.9
		.7	.6			Quick	1.2	.7
		.4	.1				.7	.2
		26 14.1	13 28.7				21 17.1	17 21.9
		32 11.3	22 16.6			Sales/Receivables	29 12.7	31 11.9
		74 4.9	50 7.3				61 6.0	49 7.5
						Cost of Sales/Inventory		
						Cost of Sales/Payables		
		4.5	3.0				2.6	5.3
		-16.5	-23.3			Sales/Working Capital	6.6	NM
		-3.8	-2.3				18.9	-6.8
		8.7					11.3	9.1
		(12) 3.0				EBIT/Interest	(13) 4.5	(19) 3.4
		.1					.4	-.4
						Net Profit + Depr., Dep., Amort./Cur. Mat. L/T/D		
		.3	.7				.3	.6
		1.3	1.6			Fixed/Worth	1.1	1.5
		2.7	15.4				3.5	5.1
		.3	.2				.4	.8
		.9	1.3			Debt/Worth	1.6	1.8
		NM	15.2				3.8	9.8
		15.0	31.4				80.9	37.3
		(11) 9.2	(13) 4.0			% Profit Before Taxes/Tangible Net Worth	(14) 11.5	(17) 13.7
		3.3	-.9				.8	-4.2
		8.5	12.0				19.1	6.7
		3.0	3.4			% Profit Before Taxes/Total Assets	5.7	3.7
		-25.1	.0				-.3	-3.5
		18.9	17.8				23.5	6.8
		1.6	.7			Sales/Net Fixed Assets	.9	.9
		.2	.1				.4	.3
		2.2	.9				2.3	1.4
		.8	.4			Sales/Total Assets	.5	.5
		.2	.1				.3	.2
		1.7	6.4				.9	.3
		(12) 14.2	(13) 18.0			% Depr., Dep., Amort./Sales	(10) 6.7	(13) 7.3
		39.0	50.8				12.7	16.5
						% Officers', Directors' Owners' Comp/Sales		
1439M	8612M	71967M	216660M	145362M	479732M	Net Sales ($)	874884M	571167M
1911M	9624M	57888M	364588M	235498M	1191167M	Total Assets ($)	763855M	1018589M

M = $ thousand MM = $ million

See Pages 9 through 22 for Explanation of Ratios and Data

Comparative Historical Data | **Current Data Sorted by Sales**

4/1/11-3/31/12 ALL	4/1/12-3/31/13 ALL	4/1/13-3/31/14 ALL		0-1MM	1-3MM	3-5MM	5-10MM	10-25MM	25MM & OVER
			Type of Statement						
11	9	17	Unqualified	4	1	2		5	5
2	2	8	Reviewed	4	3			1	
	2	3	Compiled	1		2			
2	1	3	Tax Returns	3					
11	14	23	Other	4	4	1	3	6	5
					1 (4/1-9/30/13)		53 (10/1/13-3/31/14)		
26	28	54	**NUMBER OF STATEMENTS**	16	8	5	3	12	10
%	%	%	**ASSETS**	%	%	%	%	%	%
9.8	16.2	9.8	Cash & Equivalents	5.2				15.7	11.8
10.0	14.3	10.9	Trade Receivables (net)	3.7				14.9	10.8
5.1	4.0	2.9	Inventory	.0				4.2	5.1
2.8	7.1	3.9	All Other Current	1.7				1.4	8.3
27.7	41.7	27.6	Total Current	10.6				36.2	36.0
51.4	41.9	56.5	Fixed Assets (net)	77.7				53.7	31.1
5.9	5.9	4.9	Intangibles (net)	5.1				5.2	8.8
15.0	10.5	11.0	All Other Non-Current	6.5				4.9	24.1
100.0	100.0	100.0	Total	100.0				100.0	100.0
			LIABILITIES						
.5	20.2	17.4	Notes Payable-Short Term	39.6				.1	8.3
3.5	3.6	9.9	Cur. Mat.-L.T.D.	6.0				11.8	4.4
8.4	7.6	6.2	Trade Payables	6.3				5.0	6.9
.1	.1	.0	Income Taxes Payable	.0				.0	.1
7.3	12.7	6.0	All Other Current	1.1				8.3	8.3
19.9	44.2	39.5	Total Current	53.0				25.2	28.0
30.3	22.3	27.5	Long-Term Debt	38.0				27.1	18.9
2.1	1.5	.7	Deferred Taxes	.0				.0	2.5
14.7	9.2	6.3	All Other Non-Current	4.2				.8	3.1
33.0	22.8	25.9	Net Worth	4.8				47.0	47.5
100.0	100.0	100.0	Total Liabilties & Net Worth	100.0				100.0	100.0
			INCOME DATA						
100.0	100.0	100.0	Net Sales	100.0				100.0	100.0
			Gross Profit						
87.2	85.9	82.6	Operating Expenses	80.2				81.5	87.3
12.8	14.1	17.4	Operating Profit	19.8				18.5	12.7
7.4	9.8	9.7	All Other Expenses (net)	18.3				7.3	.7
5.4	4.2	7.7	Profit Before Taxes	1.5				11.3	12.0
			RATIOS						
2.1	2.6	2.9		.8				4.9	5.2
1.2	1.4	1.0	Current	.5				2.5	1.7
.9	.8	.5		.3				1.2	.8
1.6	1.8	2.4		.8				4.1	4.3
.9	.8	.8	Quick	.4				2.1	1.1
.4	.5	.4		.3				.8	.6
12 30.0	**8** 47.0	**15** 24.7		**11** 33.0				**7** 49.1	**11** 34.2
26 14.0	**32** 11.4	**31** 11.7	Sales/Receivables	**30** 12.0				**32** 11.3	**51** 7.1
45 8.1	**70** 5.2	**58** 6.3		**76** 4.8				**56** 6.5	**59** 6.2
			Cost of Sales/Inventory						
			Cost of Sales/Payables						
3.8	3.3	2.9		-10.4				2.8	2.1
13.9	12.0	NM	Sales/Working Capital	-2.6				4.8	11.3
-15.0	-22.4	-3.4		-1.7				25.8	-16.0
6.3	12.6	10.3							
(21) 2.5	(19) 3.9	(36) 3.7	EBIT/Interest						
.7	2.0	1.2							
			Net Profit + Depr., Dep., Amort./Cur. Mat. L/T/D						
1.0	.2	.3		1.5				.7	.1
1.8	1.7	1.6	Fixed/Worth	2.2				1.3	.5
UND	4.1	2.8		3.9				2.2	1.6
.9	.8	.4		.9				.3	.2
2.5	1.8	1.5	Debt/Worth	1.6				1.0	1.9
UND	5.4	3.1		3.3				17.9	4.0
54.9	19.2	22.4		9.8				44.2	
(23) 15.0	(23) 3.6	(47) 8.9	% Profit Before Taxes/Tangible Net Worth	(14) 4.6				(10) 13.9	
.7	.0	.4		-4.0				1.7	
8.6	15.5	9.0		4.1				20.3	15.2
1.7	2.6	2.9	% Profit Before Taxes/Total Assets	.4				5.0	7.9
-.6	-.2	-.8		-1.7				-4.3	1.8
5.5	45.5	9.3		.2				10.6	135.4
.6	4.5	.6	Sales/Net Fixed Assets	.1				1.3	8.3
.3	.3	.1		.1				.3	.4
.7	3.1	1.2		.2				2.3	1.3
.3	.7	.4	Sales/Total Assets	.1				.8	.8
.2	.2	.1		.1				.2	.3
6.7	.5	5.9		41.1				4.4	
(23) 11.9	(23) 8.0	(45) 20.7	% Depr., Dep., Amort./Sales	(13) 57.7				(10) 8.0	
25.8	25.0	45.1		78.4				26.4	
			% Officers', Directors' Owners' Comp/Sales						
886072M	1385076M	923772M	Net Sales ($)	5169M	13935M	20687M	21045M	198204M	664732M
1435946M	1468067M	1860676M	Total Assets ($)	48654M	47867M	92225M	57462M	632214M	982254M

M = $ thousand MM = $ million

See Pages 9 through 22 for Explanation of Ratios and Data

Current Data Sorted by Assets							Comparative Historical Data	
						Type of Statement		
5	6	13	142	139	147	Unqualified	461	151
	1	1	3			Reviewed	11	14
		2	3			Compiled	6	5
	1	1				Tax Returns	4	12
4	7	17	20	11	23	Other	73	72
	141 (4/1-9/30/13)		405 (10/1/13-3/31/14)				**4/1/09-3/31/10 ALL**	**4/1/10-3/31/11 ALL**
0-500M	**500M-2MM**	**2-10MM**	**10-50MM**	**50-100MM**	**100-250MM**			
9	15	34	168	150	170	**NUMBER OF STATEMENTS**	555	254
%	%	%	%	%	%	**ASSETS**	%	%
	22.2	15.1	6.6	4.4	4.9	Cash & Equivalents	6.5	9.6
	21.7	15.9	6.4	5.4	6.3	Trade Receivables (net)	8.7	12.0
	9.2	4.7	2.3	1.5	1.6	Inventory	2.5	4.0
	2.1	4.9	1.8	1.1	2.0	All Other Current	2.5	2.6
	55.2	40.6	17.0	12.5	14.7	Total Current	20.1	28.3
	30.5	43.7	66.3	70.8	68.4	Fixed Assets (net)	65.1	55.5
	2.2	4.0	3.5	1.2	3.0	Intangibles (net)	2.3	3.1
	12.2	11.8	13.2	15.5	13.9	All Other Non-Current	12.5	13.1
	100.0	100.0	100.0	100.0	100.0	Total	100.0	100.0
						LIABILITIES		
	.4	6.6	1.4	.9	1.7	Notes Payable-Short Term	3.2	4.3
	5.5	2.4	2.9	1.9	2.7	Cur. Mat.-L.T.D.	3.0	2.4
	8.5	9.3	4.4	4.1	4.6	Trade Payables	5.5	8.4
	1.1	.1	.3	.3	.2	Income Taxes Payable	.3	.2
	17.0	8.1	4.1	2.9	3.6	All Other Current	5.0	9.8
	32.5	26.5	13.1	10.2	12.8	Total Current	17.1	25.1
	59.6	26.5	37.4	38.7	40.5	Long-Term Debt	38.3	32.7
	.8	2.4	.8	.4	.2	Deferred Taxes	.4	1.3
	9.8	10.1	3.9	3.7	4.8	All Other Non-Current	4.5	7.8
	-2.7	34.6	44.7	47.0	41.6	Net Worth	39.7	33.1
	100.0	100.0	100.0	100.0	100.0	Total Liabilties & Net Worth	100.0	100.0
						INCOME DATA		
	100.0	100.0	100.0	100.0	100.0	Net Sales	100.0	100.0
						Gross Profit		
	76.5	88.9	87.4	91.8	90.4	Operating Expenses	90.9	88.4
	23.5	11.1	12.6	8.2	9.6	Operating Profit	9.1	11.6
	4.4	4.2	3.5	1.5	2.1	All Other Expenses (net)	2.4	3.2
	19.0	6.9	9.1	6.7	7.5	Profit Before Taxes	6.7	8.4
						RATIOS		
	4.8	4.3	1.9	1.5	1.6		1.7	2.0
	2.1	2.0	1.4	1.2	1.1	Current	1.2	1.2
	.7	.8	.9	.8	.8		.8	.8
	4.8	3.0	1.5	1.2	1.2		1.3	1.5
	1.4	1.2	1.0	.9	.8	Quick	.8	.9
	.5	.7	.6	.6	.5		.5	.5
	26 13.9	**27** 13.3	**30** 12.1	**27** 13.3	**24** 14.9		**26** 14.3	**25** 14.9
	35 10.4	**41** 9.0	**40** 9.1	**35** 10.4	**35** 10.5	Sales/Receivables	**35** 10.3	**37** 9.9
	87 4.2	**62** 5.9	**49** 7.4	**45** 8.1	**45** 8.1		**47** 7.8	**50** 7.2
						Cost of Sales/Inventory		
						Cost of Sales/Payables		
	2.3	3.4	5.9	11.2	9.6		8.7	6.1
	7.7	8.0	15.2	33.8	50.9	Sales/Working Capital	37.1	24.5
	-7.6	-22.7	-48.3	-25.7	-18.6		-20.0	-17.2
	30.6	6.5	4.3	3.9	4.1		3.5	6.0
	(13) 4.8	(26) 2.5	(146) 2.8	(141) 2.7	(162) 2.7	EBIT/Interest	(523) 2.3	(228) 3.1
	1.9	1.0	2.2	2.2	2.0		1.8	2.0
			8.1	3.9	4.6		5.8	16.3
			(19) 3.4	(16) 3.1	(16) 2.9	Net Profit + Depr., Dep., Amort./Cur. Mat. L/T/D	(62) 2.9	(48) 3.7
			1.5	2.4	1.3		1.6	1.7
	.1	.1	1.2	1.2	1.4		1.2	1.0
	.4	1.0	1.8	1.6	1.8	Fixed/Worth	1.8	1.6
	3.7	2.4	2.3	2.1	2.4		2.5	2.6
	.6	.4	.8	.7	1.1		1.0	.8
	1.9	.9	1.5	1.3	1.6	Debt/Worth	1.5	1.4
	5.8	3.3	2.2	1.9	2.2		2.4	3.0
	54.8	28.2	10.8	9.9	11.4		12.0	16.7
	(12) 27.0	(28) 8.8	(165) 7.4	7.3	(165) 8.4	% Profit Before Taxes/Tangible Net Worth	(531) 7.7	(223) 9.2
	6.9	2.4	5.2	5.5	5.8		5.0	5.8
	43.4	8.3	4.5	4.1	4.5		4.6	7.4
	12.1	3.7	3.2	3.2	3.1	% Profit Before Taxes/Total Assets	3.1	3.9
	1.5	.2	2.3	2.3	2.0		1.9	1.9
	46.9	40.8	.9	.8	.8		1.1	4.0
	10.2	1.7	.6	.6	.7	Sales/Net Fixed Assets	.7	.8
	.5	.5	.5	.5	.5		.5	.5
	2.9	2.0	.6	.6	.6		.7	1.3
	1.1	.8	.4	.4	.5	Sales/Total Assets	.5	.6
	.3	.3	.3	.4	.4		.4	.4
	1.1	1.1	5.9	5.9	5.7		5.1	3.6
	(11) 2.6	(27) 7.9	(164) 7.7	7.5	(164) 6.9	% Depr., Dep., Amort./Sales	(531) 6.7	(229) 6.1
	8.0	12.4	9.7	8.8	8.6		8.7	9.1
							1.7	1.0
						% Officers', Directors' Owners' Comp/Sales	(17) 4.4	(25) 4.0
							6.8	6.5
3129M	31363M	354715M	2908268M	6049237M	15984461M	Net Sales ($)	24178816M	11943868M
2874M	18404M	189622M	5215070M	10982387M	25954179M	Total Assets ($)	40692192M	14703407M

M = $ thousand MM = $ million

See Pages 9 through 22 for Explanation of Ratios and Data

Comparative Historical Data				Current Data Sorted by Sales					
			Type of Statement						
490	473	452	Unqualified	12	12	8	32	120	268
19	11	5	Reviewed			1	1	1	2
6	6	5	Compiled	1	1	2		1	
6	6	2	Tax Returns		2				
65	78	82	Other	7	9	5	12	20	29
4/1/11-3/31/12	**4/1/12-3/31/13**	**4/1/13-3/31/14**		**141 (4/1-9/30/13)**			**405 (10/1/13-3/31/14)**		
ALL	**ALL**	**ALL**		**0-1MM**	**1-3MM**	**3-5MM**	**5-10MM**	**10-25MM**	**25MM & OVER**
586	574	546	**NUMBER OF STATEMENTS**	20	24	16	45	142	299
%	%	%	**ASSETS**	%	%	%	%	%	%
6.5	7.7	6.6	Cash & Equivalents	10.0	19.1	5.7	8.3	4.8	6.0
8.2	7.8	7.2	Trade Receivables (net)	7.0	8.1	11.0	9.1	5.2	7.5
2.2	2.5	2.2	Inventory	3.1	4.2	5.2	3.2	1.9	1.7
1.8	2.2	1.8	All Other Current	.7	2.1	1.3	2.6	1.6	2.0
18.7	20.2	17.7	Total Current	20.8	33.4	23.2	23.2	13.5	17.2
65.8	65.3	65.5	Fixed Assets (net)	59.6	42.2	62.6	64.1	70.1	65.9
1.8	1.6	2.7	Intangibles (net)	2.1	11.3	3.5	2.7	2.6	2.1
13.7	13.0	14.1	All Other Non-Current	17.5	13.1	10.8	10.0	13.8	14.8
100.0	100.0	100.0	Total	100.0	100.0	100.0	100.0	100.0	100.0
			LIABILITIES						
2.4	2.0	1.8	Notes Payable-Short Term	3.1	.4	10.4	1.3	1.5	1.5
2.1	2.2	2.7	Cur. Mat.-L.T.D.	8.5	2.6	4.5	4.2	2.2	2.3
5.5	5.3	4.8	Trade Payables	1.8	4.9	2.1	4.1	3.5	5.8
.3	.3	.3	Income Taxes Payable	.0	.7	.1	.2	.3	.2
4.7	4.7	4.2	All Other Current	1.8	10.4	7.6	3.8	2.7	4.4
15.0	14.5	13.7	Total Current	15.1	19.0	24.7	13.6	10.2	14.3
39.5	40.1	39.8	Long-Term Debt	72.0	52.3	33.5	41.6	41.2	36.1
.4	.7	.6	Deferred Taxes	.6	3.5	3.5	.6	.5	.3
4.7	5.1	5.0	All Other Non-Current	10.9	15.4	5.0	5.0	3.0	4.7
40.4	39.6	40.9	Net Worth	1.4	9.8	33.3	39.2	45.1	44.6
100.0	100.0	100.0	Total Liabilties & Net Worth	100.0	100.0	100.0	100.0	100.0	100.0
			INCOME DATA						
100.0	100.0	100.0	Net Sales	100.0	100.0	100.0	100.0	100.0	100.0
			Gross Profit						
90.5	89.8	88.9	Operating Expenses	62.6	79.5	76.2	88.6	88.9	92.1
9.5	10.2	11.1	Operating Profit	37.4	20.5	23.8	11.4	11.1	7.9
2.7	2.3	2.6	All Other Expenses (net)	11.2	6.7	12.0	6.0	2.3	.9
6.8	7.9	8.5	Profit Before Taxes	26.1	13.8	11.8	5.4	8.8	7.0
			RATIOS						
1.8	1.9	1.7		2.6	8.5	1.6	3.1	1.9	1.6
1.2	1.2	1.2	Current	1.3	1.6	.9	1.6	1.3	1.2
.8	.9	.8		.5	1.3	.6	1.1	.9	.8
1.4	1.4	1.4		1.9	7.1	1.2	2.4	1.5	1.3
.9	.9	.9	Quick	1.0	1.5	.7	1.2	1.0	.9
.6	.6	.6		.5	.7	.3	.7	.6	.6
27 13.7	**25** 14.6	**27** 13.6		**23** 16.1	**10** 35.6	**30** 12.3	**37** 9.9	**29** 12.8	**26** 14.0
36 10.2	**35** 10.4	**36** 10.0	Sales/Receivables	**33** 11.0	**33** 11.0	**47** 7.7	**43** 8.5	**37** 9.8	**35** 10.5
46 7.9	**45** 8.1	**47** 7.8		**87** 4.2	**51** 7.2	**73** 5.0	**54** 6.7	**47** 7.7	**45** 8.1
			Cost of Sales/Inventory						
			Cost of Sales/Payables						
7.9	7.1	7.7		2.7	2.2	10.0	3.3	7.0	11.2
23.3	23.5	21.4	Sales/Working Capital	10.2	7.6	-28.8	7.7	16.4	38.0
-33.2	-31.6	-24.6		-4.6	14.5	-2.5	21.0	-39.4	-22.5
3.8	4.2	4.2		4.9	4.7	8.0	4.2	3.5	4.4
(543) 2.5	(522) 2.7	(494) 2.7	EBIT/Interest	(16) 3.8	(16) 2.9	(11) 3.7	(35) 2.6	(133) 2.6	(283) 2.8
1.8	1.9	2.1		1.7	1.5	1.9	2.1	2.1	2.1
6.5	6.1	5.2						3.3	5.2
(51) 3.3	(54) 3.6	(59) 3.2	Net Profit + Depr., Dep., Amort./Cur. Mat. L/T/D					(14) 2.6	(29) 3.4
2.0	2.2	2.0						1.5	2.4
1.2	1.2	1.2		1.1	.2	1.4	1.2	1.3	1.2
1.7	1.7	1.7	Fixed/Worth	2.2	2.3	2.6	1.5	1.8	1.7
2.3	2.3	2.3		5.4	2.7	4.4	2.5	2.2	2.2
.9	.8	.9		.9	1.0	1.5	.6	1.0	.8
1.5	1.5	1.5	Debt/Worth	2.1	2.2	2.1	1.4	1.5	1.4
2.1	2.2	2.2		7.1	-12.4	5.0	2.5	2.0	2.0
11.1	11.3	11.0		17.6	20.7	32.1	10.9	10.4	10.7
(564) 7.3	(549) 7.5	(525) 7.9	% Profit Before Taxes/Tangible Net Worth	(16) 12.2	(17) 8.7	(15) 7.7	(43) 6.5	(141) 7.9	(293) 7.8
4.9	4.8	5.5		5.3	1.6	2.9	2.2	5.9	5.7
4.6	4.9	4.6		11.0	6.9	5.0	4.6	4.2	4.5
3.0	3.1	3.2	% Profit Before Taxes/Total Assets	5.5	3.3	2.7	3.2	3.1	3.3
1.9	1.9	2.2		1.3	-.6	1.3	.9	2.4	2.3
.9	1.0	.9		7.8	31.1	2.4	1.0	.7	1.0
.7	.6	.6	Sales/Net Fixed Assets	.4	.7	.4	.6	.6	.7
.5	.5	.5		.1	.4	.1	.4	.5	.6
.7	.7	.6		1.2	1.0	1.0	.6	.5	.7
.5	.5	.4	Sales/Total Assets	.2	.4	.3	.4	.4	.5
.4	.4	.4		.1	.2	.1	.3	.3	.4
5.5	5.6	5.7		6.6	6.4	3.0	6.1	6.7	5.3
(561) 7.0	(544) 7.3	(523) 7.3	% Depr., Dep., Amort./Sales	(17) 11.1	(18) 11.0	11.6	(43) 8.9	(140) 7.9	(289) 6.5
9.1	9.3	9.2		32.3	13.8	30.6	14.0	9.6	8.2
1.2	3.3								
(18) 2.8	(12) 4.9		% Officers', Directors' Owners' Comp/Sales						
5.6	11.0								
23826736M	**24918850M**	**25331173M**	Net Sales ($)	**9130M**	**46555M**	**63331M**	**335894M**	**2461482M**	**22414781M**
43241174M	**42899803M**	**42362536M**	Total Assets ($)	**49715M**	**271394M**	**321171M**	**1058522M**	**6828676M**	**33833058M**

M = $ thousand MM = $ million

See Pages 9 through 22 for Explanation of Ratios and Data

Current Data Sorted by Assets							Comparative Historical Data	
						Type of Statement		
	2	2	21	10	21	Unqualified	47	54
	2	8	7	1		Reviewed	15	20
	2	5	1			Compiled	14	13
3	7	9	1			Tax Returns	6	9
	3	7	16	8	12	Other	57	49
	47 (4/1-9/30/13)		101 (10/1/13-3/31/14)				4/1/09-3/31/10	4/1/10-3/31/11
0-500M	500M-2MM	2-10MM	10-50MM	50-100MM	100-250MM		ALL	ALL
3	16	31	46	19	33	NUMBER OF STATEMENTS	139	145
%	%	%	%	%	%	**ASSETS**	%	%
	17.6	15.4	13.4	7.1	8.8	Cash & Equivalents	13.0	12.1
	26.5	34.3	24.4	29.9	17.0	Trade Receivables (net)	19.6	19.9
	4.0	6.2	5.0	7.0	5.5	Inventory	6.6	6.5
	15.7	1.7	3.0	6.4	4.2	All Other Current	3.1	3.2
	63.7	57.6	45.8	50.3	35.5	Total Current	42.4	41.7
	21.1	33.8	42.9	41.4	56.2	Fixed Assets (net)	46.2	46.0
	1.9	3.6	3.6	1.2	1.5	Intangibles (net)	4.3	3.8
	13.3	5.0	7.7	7.1	6.8	All Other Non-Current	7.1	8.5
	100.0	100.0	100.0	100.0	100.0	Total	100.0	100.0
						LIABILITIES		
	16.0	3.5	6.6	3.8	3.2	Notes Payable-Short Term	5.8	5.8
	2.2	2.9	1.8	1.8	1.9	Cur. Mat.-L.T.D.	2.8	2.5
	20.8	23.2	19.8	25.5	15.8	Trade Payables	16.6	16.7
	.3	.5	.1	.5	.5	Income Taxes Payable	.4	.3
	42.0	9.5	8.6	7.8	5.0	All Other Current	8.8	7.8
	81.4	39.5	37.0	39.3	26.3	Total Current	34.4	33.1
	10.5	13.1	17.1	17.5	17.4	Long-Term Debt	17.8	19.4
	.5	.9	2.3	1.5	2.9	Deferred Taxes	2.2	2.5
	6.0	2.1	3.1	6.6	2.8	All Other Non-Current	4.8	4.0
	1.7	44.4	40.5	35.1	50.6	Net Worth	40.8	41.0
	100.0	100.0	100.0	100.0	100.0	Total Liabilties & Net Worth	100.0	100.0
						INCOME DATA		
	100.0	100.0	100.0	100.0	100.0	Net Sales	100.0	100.0
						Gross Profit		
	99.0	91.6	93.4	89.3	84.9	Operating Expenses	89.4	90.2
	1.0	8.4	6.6	10.7	15.1	Operating Profit	10.6	9.8
	.4	.5	1.4	3.4	2.9	All Other Expenses (net)	2.6	2.2
	.6	8.0	5.3	7.4	12.2	Profit Before Taxes	7.9	7.6
						RATIOS		
	1.8	2.3	1.7	1.7	1.7		1.8	1.9
	1.2	1.5	1.2	1.2	1.3	Current	1.2	1.3
	.7	1.1	.9	.9	1.1		.8	.8
	1.7	1.9	1.5	1.3	1.2		1.3	1.5
	.8	1.4	1.0	1.0	.9	Quick	.9	1.0
	.3	1.0	.6	.6	.7		.5	.5
	3 111.2	**22** 16.6	**15** 23.9	**13** 28.5	**20** 18.0		**13** 28.4	**14** 25.7
	17 20.9	**43** 8.5	**36** 10.2	**43** 8.4	**32** 11.4	Sales/Receivables	**26** 13.9	**28** 12.9
	51 7.2	**55** 6.6	**55** 6.6	**70** 5.2	**47** 7.8		**45** 8.1	**45** 8.1
						Cost of Sales/Inventory		
						Cost of Sales/Payables		
	9.4	6.5	7.2	5.0	9.1		8.8	8.2
	49.2	11.9	68.4	82.1	20.0	Sales/Working Capital	44.3	32.3
	-16.5	327.9	-30.2	-366.4	51.7		-40.0	-45.3
	42.7	28.4	30.2	16.4	13.5		12.0	13.0
	(13) 5.4	(27) 11.6	(40) 11.9	(18) 3.9	(31) 4.8	EBIT/Interest	(112) 5.3	(123) 4.9
	1.1	4.0	4.2	1.6	2.7		2.0	2.4
			6.2			Net Profit + Depr., Dep.,	8.3	11.0
			(12) 3.8			Amort./Cur. Mat. L/T/D	(27) 3.4	(39) 4.3
			3.0				1.6	2.3
	.1	.1	.3	.1	.3		.5	.5
	.8	.8	1.0	1.0	1.1	Fixed/Worth	1.1	1.1
	-1.2	1.3	1.9	2.7	1.9		2.3	2.2
	.6	.7	.5	.8	.5		.7	.7
	30.9	1.2	1.6	2.5	1.5	Debt/Worth	1.7	1.8
	-6.0	3.6	3.2	5.9	2.1		3.4	2.8
		39.0	30.4	32.5	24.5	% Profit Before Taxes/Tangible	37.8	31.6
		(30) 21.6	(43) 17.1	14.7	14.0	Net Worth	(129) 17.8	(136) 15.5
		10.6	8.8	7.7	4.6		5.8	6.3
	14.8	19.2	11.9	8.9	9.0	% Profit Before Taxes/Total	12.2	10.0
	7.3	8.9	6.5	4.8	4.8	Assets	6.4	5.6
	.3	3.9	3.1	2.1	2.6		1.8	2.1
	164.7	360.1	116.3	474.8	83.0		52.7	43.5
	17.9	6.9	2.2	12.7	.6	Sales/Net Fixed Assets	2.9	2.4
	7.8	2.2	.8	.6	.3		.8	.8
	4.4	5.2	4.4	6.9	2.4		3.7	4.3
	3.2	2.6	1.3	2.7	.5	Sales/Total Assets	1.6	1.3
	1.9	1.3	.6	.4	.3		.5	.5
	1.7	.1	.2	.5	.7		.6	.5
	(11) 2.9	(27) 3.0	(40) 4.7	(14) 3.9	(29) 8.0	% Depr., Dep., Amort./Sales	(114) 4.2	(128) 4.5
	3.7	6.6	7.6	16.0	12.5		7.1	7.9
		1.5				% Officers', Directors'	.9	.8
		(12) 2.5				Owners' Comp/Sales	(24) 2.1	(23) 2.1
		3.3					2.9	3.7
2711M	**65492M**	**931177M**	**3793609M**	**5741573M**	**9833630M**	Net Sales ($)	**11249834M**	**12521125M**
787M	**18068M**	**175202M**	**1162515M**	**1434528M**	**5241494M**	Total Assets ($)	**6835692M**	**6697057M**

M = $ thousand MM = $ million

See Pages 9 through 22 for Explanation of Ratios and Data

Comparative Historical Data / Current Data Sorted by Sales

4/1/11-3/31/12 ALL	4/1/12-3/31/13 ALL	4/1/13-3/31/14 ALL	Type of Statement	0-1MM	1-3MM	3-5MM	5-10MM	10-25MM	25MM & OVER
60	56	56	Unqualified		3	2	1	10	40
13	14	18	Reviewed				7	4	7
13	7	8	Compiled	1	2	1	2		2
12	11	20	Tax Returns	4	4	3	3	4	2
56	63	46	Other	1	1	1	6	6	31
				47 (4/1-9/30/13)			101 (10/1/13-3/31/14)		
154	151	148	**NUMBER OF STATEMENTS**	6	10	7	19	24	82
%	%	%	**ASSETS**	%	%	%	%	%	%
12.1	14.0	12.7	Cash & Equivalents		28.5		8.6	9.5	11.8
21.7	20.6	25.4	Trade Receivables (net)		12.4		24.1	11.0	32.9
7.0	5.8	5.5	Inventory		3.9		4.9	4.5	6.6
3.0	4.0	5.4	All Other Current		7.6		1.7	2.4	4.3
43.8	44.4	49.1	Total Current		52.4		39.4	27.4	55.6
43.9	43.7	41.1	Fixed Assets (net)		44.8		46.7	62.8	34.2
3.6	3.4	2.6	Intangibles (net)		.1		3.4	3.8	2.4
8.7	8.4	7.3	All Other Non-Current		2.7		10.5	6.0	7.9
100.0	100.0	100.0	Total		100.0		100.0	100.0	100.0
			LIABILITIES						
6.3	7.4	5.7	Notes Payable-Short Term		2.8		14.3	2.0	5.8
3.7	3.9	2.1	Cur. Mat.-L.T.D.		1.7		2.7	2.1	1.7
16.3	14.2	20.3	Trade Payables		14.0		15.1	8.5	26.7
.3	.2	.4	Income Taxes Payable		1.3		.5	.1	.3
8.0	9.7	12.0	All Other Current		28.7		12.0	7.1	9.2
34.5	35.3	40.4	Total Current		48.3		44.6	19.9	43.7
16.6	17.1	15.5	Long-Term Debt		19.3		15.4	16.3	14.7
1.9	1.9	1.8	Deferred Taxes		1.2		2.7	2.3	1.8
7.0	5.9	3.5	All Other Non-Current		1.5		2.9	5.7	3.1
40.0	39.7	38.8	Net Worth		29.7		34.4	55.7	36.7
100.0	100.0	100.0	Total Liabilties & Net Worth		100.0		100.0	100.0	100.0
			INCOME DATA						
100.0	100.0	100.0	Net Sales		100.0		100.0	100.0	100.0
			Gross Profit						
90.5	90.7	91.3	Operating Expenses		90.1		89.2	83.4	93.7
9.5	9.3	8.7	Operating Profit		9.9		10.8	16.6	6.3
1.5	1.9	1.7	All Other Expenses (net)		2.0		2.3	4.0	.9
8.0	7.4	7.0	Profit Before Taxes		7.8		8.5	12.6	5.4
			RATIOS						
2.1	2.1	1.8			4.4		2.3	1.7	1.7
1.3	1.3	1.3	Current		2.1		1.3	1.2	1.3
.8	.8	1.0			1.1		.8	.8	1.0
1.6	1.7	1.5			3.3		2.1	1.3	1.4
.9	1.0	1.1	Quick		1.9		1.1	1.1	1.0
.5	.5	.7			.7		.6	.6	.7
17 21.0	15 24.9	15 23.9			5 78.4		22 16.9	16 22.7	19 19.4
29 12.5	31 11.8	36 10.2	Sales/Receivables		18 20.4		46 8.0	38 9.6	36 10.1
43 8.4	53 6.9	54 6.7			41 9.0		58 6.3	61 6.0	54 6.8
			Cost of Sales/Inventory						
			Cost of Sales/Payables						
7.5	6.6	8.4			5.7		10.9	4.9	10.4
36.2	21.9	24.9	Sales/Working Capital		9.8		56.8	26.2	35.0
-45.6	-36.0	-352.1			NM		-39.4	-13.8	323.1
13.7	15.0	25.2					60.3	40.1	16.1
(124) 5.7	(127) 4.8	(130) 6.7	EBIT/Interest				(17) 6.2	(22) 11.2	(73) 5.7
2.5	2.5	2.9					2.4	4.5	2.8
7.9	11.1	7.6							8.3
(30) 2.3	(35) 3.3	(28) 3.3	Net Profit + Depr., Dep., Amort./Cur. Mat. L/T/D						(17) 3.3
1.1	1.6	1.7							1.4
.5	.2	.2			.5		.6	.8	.1
1.2	1.0	1.0	Fixed/Worth		.8		1.5	1.4	.7
2.3	1.9	2.0			1.3		6.8	1.9	1.8
.6	.6	.5			.5		.2	.5	.8
1.7	1.5	1.6	Debt/Worth		.8		2.0	.8	1.9
3.9	2.9	3.6			10.8		9.2	1.5	3.5
25.1	29.2	32.4					58.6	18.3	35.6
(138) 13.0	(141) 12.3	(137) 17.1	% Profit Before Taxes/Tangible Net Worth				(17) 20.5	(23) 10.1	(79) 19.2
6.4	2.8	7.5					5.0	3.8	9.0
10.2	11.8	12.3			13.5		16.7	8.7	13.5
5.7	4.8	6.3	% Profit Before Taxes/Total Assets		9.3		6.4	5.6	6.3
2.0	1.7	2.9			6.3		3.9	3.0	2.5
89.1	85.6	108.7			43.2		67.1	2.3	329.4
3.2	2.7	5.0	Sales/Net Fixed Assets		2.4		4.2	.9	32.8
.8	.7	.8			.8		.9	.4	.9
4.7	3.7	4.6			3.8		3.3	1.5	5.3
1.5	1.4	1.7	Sales/Total Assets		1.5		1.7	.6	3.3
.6	.5	.6			.6		.8	.2	.7
.5	.4	.3					.5	5.5	.1
(125) 4.2	(131) 5.5	(123) 4.2	% Depr., Dep., Amort./Sales				(16) 3.6	(23) 8.2	(66) .6
7.0	8.7	8.4					7.0	15.9	7.3
.7	.5	1.4							
(28) 1.6	(23) 1.7	(25) 2.7	% Officers', Directors' Owners' Comp/Sales						
5.4	3.0	4.5							
15408031M	17553338M	20368192M	Net Sales ($)	4403M	21657M	28663M	155773M	414884M	19742812M
7585445M	8834069M	8032594M	Total Assets ($)	6650M	29651M	33991M	158755M	1253489M	6550058M

M = $ thousand MM = $ million

See Pages 9 through 22 for Explanation of Ratios and Data

Current Data Sorted by Assets							Comparative Historical Data	
						Type of Statement		
1	5	35	65	20	25	Unqualified	113	111
	3	5				Reviewed	14	15
	2	5	2	2		Compiled	12	22
11	4	4				Tax Returns	24	32
3	14	30	17	3	2	Other	55	58
99 (4/1-9/30/13)			159 (10/1/13-3/31/14)				4/1/09-3/31/10 ALL	4/1/10-3/31/11 ALL
0-500M	500M-2MM	2-10MM	10-50MM	50-100MM	100-250MM			
15	28	79	84	25	27	**NUMBER OF STATEMENTS**	218	238
%	%	%	%	%	%	**ASSETS**	%	%
21.4	16.7	15.4	9.0	9.2	6.5	Cash & Equivalents	9.3	11.1
16.0	14.3	9.3	2.6	3.1	2.8	Trade Receivables (net)	8.5	10.2
7.4	8.6	3.6	1.2	1.2	3.4	Inventory	3.5	4.4
2.3	2.1	1.4	.9	.8	1.0	All Other Current	1.6	2.5
47.1	41.8	29.7	13.8	14.3	13.6	Total Current	22.9	28.2
39.1	49.0	59.9	77.5	76.8	73.2	Fixed Assets (net)	66.7	59.8
1.7	4.9	4.9	2.5	3.9	6.4	Intangibles (net)	2.6	3.5
12.0	4.3	5.5	6.2	4.9	6.7	All Other Non-Current	7.8	8.5
100.0	100.0	100.0	100.0	100.0	100.0	Total	100.0	100.0
						LIABILITIES		
14.1	2.4	1.3	.8	.2	.7	Notes Payable-Short Term	3.5	5.5
10.8	1.9	3.4	2.2	4.6	4.2	Cur. Mat.-L.T.D.	3.2	3.2
9.7	11.6	5.6	1.6	1.3	1.4	Trade Payables	4.6	6.0
.0	.0	.1	.0	.0	.1	Income Taxes Payable	.1	.1
13.9	3.4	4.0	2.8	1.8	2.6	All Other Current	7.8	11.7
48.4	19.3	14.4	7.5	7.9	9.1	Total Current	19.2	26.4
25.0	25.8	31.5	33.8	36.2	36.2	Long-Term Debt	29.4	26.8
.0	.0	.0	.2	.4	2.4	Deferred Taxes	.6	.6
13.2	4.2	5.9	5.0	2.1	5.5	All Other Non-Current	7.0	9.1
13.5	50.8	48.1	53.4	53.4	46.8	Net Worth	43.8	37.0
100.0	100.0	100.0	100.0	100.0	100.0	Total Liabilities & Net Worth	100.0	100.0
						INCOME DATA		
100.0	100.0	100.0	100.0	100.0	100.0	Net Sales	100.0	100.0
						Gross Profit		
91.3	85.9	88.4	83.8	81.6	83.8	Operating Expenses	87.4	87.0
8.7	14.1	11.6	16.2	18.4	16.2	Operating Profit	12.6	13.0
1.8	4.4	6.0	6.1	4.8	4.7	All Other Expenses (net)	5.0	5.4
6.9	9.7	5.6	10.1	13.6	11.5	Profit Before Taxes	7.6	7.6
						RATIOS		
2.0	6.0	7.2	4.7	6.1	3.5		3.5	3.2
1.3	3.8	2.6	2.5	2.9	1.8	Current	1.5	1.5
.7	1.4	1.3	1.1	1.4	1.1		.7	.9
1.5	4.7	5.7	4.1	5.7	3.3		2.7	2.8
.8	2.6	2.4	2.1	2.7	1.3	Quick	1.1	1.2
.4	1.1	1.2	.9	1.3	.8		.5	.5
0 UND	9 38.9	25 14.8	23 15.6	27 13.6	27 13.5		16 22.6	17 22.1
17 20.9	29 12.4	36 10.2	33 11.2	41 8.8	37 9.9	Sales/Receivables	31 12.0	34 10.8
32 11.5	42 8.6	47 7.8	43 8.4	60 6.1	46 7.9		44 8.4	49 7.4
						Cost of Sales/Inventory		
						Cost of Sales/Payables		
5.4	2.4	1.5	1.7	1.3	1.8		3.0	3.2
45.5	6.5	3.4	3.3	3.3	4.9	Sales/Working Capital	10.5	9.3
-12.8	15.7	17.0	45.0	5.9	44.5		-19.0	-40.5
	33.3	11.0	6.1	5.9	5.2		5.7	6.3
	(18) 5.5	(67) 2.5	(66) 2.5	(20) 2.6	(20) 3.3	EBIT/Interest	(188) 2.4	(190) 2.5
	1.0	.5	1.3	1.1	1.8		1.0	1.0
							8.4	10.1
						Net Profit + Depr., Dep., Amort./Cur. Mat. L/T/D	(38) 2.8	(32) 3.6
							1.3	1.0
.4	.2	.9	1.1	1.1	1.2		1.0	.9
1.5	.9	1.3	1.5	1.5	1.7	Fixed/Worth	1.4	1.4
-11.7	1.3	2.5	2.4	3.3	2.6		3.0	4.7
1.7	.3	.3	.4	.4	.5		.5	.5
7.1	.5	.7	.8	.7	1.2	Debt/Worth	1.1	1.2
-5.8	2.6	2.6	1.8	2.9	2.6		3.1	6.4
160.3	33.9	12.6	7.5	6.5	9.6		13.4	15.5
(10) 43.1	(24) 10.6	(70) 4.2	(81) 3.3	(23) 3.9	(24) 3.2	% Profit Before Taxes/Tangible Net Worth	(197) 4.4	(201) 4.7
-1.7	.7	-1.5	.4	.6	1.5		.0	.2
21.2	14.6	6.3	3.9	4.3	3.1		6.0	6.6
11.7	6.3	2.1	1.7	1.6	1.7	% Profit Before Taxes/Total Assets	2.1	2.1
-.7	.5	-1.0	.3	.3	.6		.0	.0
18.4	46.9	3.6	.3	.3	.3		3.1	5.6
5.0	3.7	.4	.2	.2	.2	Sales/Net Fixed Assets	.3	.5
1.9	.4	.3	.2	.1	.1		.2	.2
4.5	3.4	.8	.2	.2	.2		1.0	1.7
2.6	1.0	.3	.2	.2	.1	Sales/Total Assets	.3	.3
.9	.3	.2	.1	.1	.1		.2	.2
1.6	2.1	6.8	12.6	11.8	16.4		8.2	5.3
(11) 3.0	(19) 11.2	(63) 14.8	(79) 19.0	(24) 16.6	(23) 20.8	% Depr., Dep., Amort./Sales	(197) 14.1	(204) 12.3
17.3	20.4	21.1	24.6	25.0	25.4		21.4	20.2
		2.1					2.7	1.7
		(10) 5.0				% Officers', Directors' Owners' Comp/Sales	(28) 7.5	(29) 6.7
		8.2					10.1	12.0
11415M	64482M	276037M	524060M	407270M	1199762M	Net Sales ($)	2132768M	2657332M
4145M	35175M	378238M	2085064M	1637053M	4326225M	Total Assets ($)	6318440M	6318167M

M = $ thousand MM = $ million

See Pages 9 through 22 for Explanation of Ratios and Data

	Comparative Historical Data			Current Data Sorted by Sales					
Type of Statement									
Unqualified	130	150	151	20	43	16	32	27	13
Reviewed	15	9	8	3	1	3		1	
Compiled	20	11	11	1	2	1	4	3	
Tax Returns	26	24	19	9	7	2	1		
Other	63	61	69	15	20	11	11	9	3
	4/1/11-3/31/12 ALL	4/1/12-3/31/13 ALL	4/1/13-3/31/14 ALL	99 (4/1-9/30/13)			159 (10/1/13-3/31/14)		
				0-1MM	1-3MM	3-5MM	5-10MM	10-25MM	25MM & OVER
NUMBER OF STATEMENTS	254	255	258	48	73	33	48	40	16
ASSETS	%	%	%	%	%	%	%	%	%
Cash & Equivalents	12.5	11.7	12.3	14.4	13.5	11.2	12.7	9.7	8.4
Trade Receivables (net)	7.5	7.0	6.8	4.8	4.8	6.8	7.8	10.1	10.6
Inventory	4.6	4.0	3.3	1.4	2.1	3.8	3.9	3.9	10.7
All Other Current	1.8	1.2	1.2	1.5	.8	.9	2.0	.6	2.5
Total Current	26.5	23.9	23.7	22.1	21.1	22.6	26.4	24.4	32.2
Fixed Assets (net)	62.9	66.0	66.3	69.6	69.6	65.2	63.5	66.4	51.6
Intangibles (net)	2.4	3.7	4.0	3.2	2.9	5.2	3.6	3.4	11.8
All Other Non-Current	8.2	6.4	6.0	5.1	6.4	7.0	6.5	5.8	4.4
Total	100.0	100.0	100.0	100.0	100.0	100.0	100.0	100.0	100.0
LIABILITIES									
Notes Payable-Short Term	3.5	3.7	1.8	2.7	2.8	.9	1.1	.6	1.9
Cur. Mat.-L.T.D.	3.1	3.0	3.5	2.1	4.1	2.3	3.4	4.0	6.3
Trade Payables	4.6	3.8	4.3	3.1	2.9	4.0	7.0	5.2	5.2
Income Taxes Payable	.1	.1	.1	.0	.0	.1	.1	.0	.3
All Other Current	5.9	3.9	3.8	4.2	3.7	3.7	3.3	3.3	5.4
Total Current	17.2	14.5	13.5	12.1	13.5	11.0	15.0	13.1	19.1
Long-Term Debt	31.6	32.3	32.2	30.5	38.7	27.9	29.9	31.8	25.0
Deferred Taxes	.4	.4	.4	.0	.0	.0	.4	.4	4.1
All Other Non-Current	7.3	4.7	5.4	2.4	6.1	3.7	5.0	8.2	9.1
Net Worth	43.5	48.1	48.5	55.1	41.7	57.4	49.7	46.5	42.7
Total Liabilties & Net Worth	100.0	100.0	100.0	100.0	100.0	100.0	100.0	100.0	100.0
INCOME DATA									
Net Sales	100.0	100.0	100.0	100.0	100.0	100.0	100.0	100.0	100.0
Gross Profit									
Operating Expenses	83.7	84.7	85.7	85.5	86.3	85.4	85.4	85.5	85.1
Operating Profit	16.3	15.3	14.3	14.5	13.7	14.6	14.6	14.5	14.9
All Other Expenses (net)	6.4	6.4	5.4	5.8	7.6	3.5	4.8	3.8	3.2
Profit Before Taxes	9.9	8.8	9.0	8.7	6.1	11.0	9.8	10.7	11.7
RATIOS									
Current	4.0	4.8	5.4	11.4	5.2	4.2	5.1	6.3	3.4
	2.0	2.5	2.4	3.6	2.3	2.4	2.6	2.2	1.8
	1.0	1.3	1.2	1.4	1.1	1.2	1.1	1.2	1.3
Quick	3.4	4.2	4.9	8.9	4.8	3.9	4.6	5.9	2.4
	1.6	1.9	2.1	3.5	2.1	2.2	2.1	1.9	1.1
	.7	.9	1.0	1.1	1.0	1.1	.8	1.1	.6
Sales/Receivables	**15** 24.5	**23** 15.9	**23** 15.9	**10** 37.3	**21** 17.6	**24** 15.0	**26** 14.2	**27** 13.5	**25** 14.7
	31 11.6	**35** 10.3	**33** 11.1	**30** 12.2	**32** 11.5	**33** 11.1	**33** 10.9	**38** 9.6	**45** 8.2
	44 8.3	**51** 7.2	**46** 8.0	**43** 8.5	**46** 8.0	**48** 7.6	**48** 7.6	**48** 7.6	**50** 7.3
Cost of Sales/Inventory									
Cost of Sales/Payables									
Sales/Working Capital	2.2	1.7	1.7	1.2	1.7	2.0	1.8	1.6	2.8
	5.1	3.6	3.8	2.3	3.9	4.4	3.9	4.7	7.9
	76.4	17.5	24.3	8.8	26.1	22.8	35.9	39.9	21.0
EBIT/Interest	6.7	7.0	6.3	3.3	6.0	13.7	6.7	10.0	18.8
	(203) 3.1	(203) 2.9	(200) 2.6	(34) 1.4	(60) 2.4	(26) 3.5	(34) 2.5	(32) 3.6	(14) 4.0
	1.7	1.3	1.1	.0	1.2	1.4	1.3	1.8	1.3
Net Profit + Depr., Dep., Amort./Cur. Mat. L/T/D	13.2	9.6	9.0						
	(34) 2.7	(16) 3.8	(18) 2.3						
	1.5	.9	.4						
Fixed/Worth	.9	.9	.9	.9	1.0	.9	.9	.9	.8
	1.4	1.3	1.3	1.1	1.5	1.2	1.5	1.4	1.9
	2.9	2.5	2.5	1.9	2.7	2.3	2.8	2.6	3.2
Debt/Worth	.5	.4	.4	.2	.5	.3	.3	.3	.8
	1.0	.9	.8	.7	.9	.6	.9	.8	2.0
	3.2	2.9	2.6	2.4	3.1	2.2	3.7	2.5	2.9
% Profit Before Taxes/Tangible Net Worth	16.4	10.5	10.8	7.7	9.3	10.5	10.9	11.4	43.8
	(230) 5.8	(222) 4.2	(232) 4.1	(44) 2.6	(64) 3.5	(31) 5.9	(45) 2.8	(35) 5.2	(13) 13.8
	1.7	.5	.4	-1.6	.3	.5	-.1	1.8	9.2
% Profit Before Taxes/Total Assets	7.5	5.6	5.6	5.4	4.7	8.0	4.7	5.8	17.2
	2.6	2.2	2.0	2.1	1.6	3.3	1.5	2.1	4.2
	.5	.3	.1	-.6	-.5	.7	-.2	.7	1.1
Sales/Net Fixed Assets	4.1	.9	1.3	.4	.8	1.4	7.6	3.4	10.5
	.3	.3	.3	.3	.3	.3	.2	.3	1.1
	.2	.2	.2	.2	.2	.2	.2	.2	.3
Sales/Total Assets	1.0	.5	.5	.3	.5	.7	1.0	.4	1.3
	.3	.2	.2	.2	.2	.2	.2	.2	.6
	.2	.1	.1	.2	.2	.2	.1	.1	.2
% Depr., Dep., Amort./Sales	6.4	7.3	9.7	13.3	9.0	4.4	10.0	10.8	1.5
	(222) 14.3	(233) 15.5	(219) 17.3	(40) 19.2	(64) 16.6	(29) 17.3	(41) 18.9	(34) 16.7	(11) 11.3
	21.6	22.6	22.9	22.4	23.8	22.2	23.6	23.1	16.6
% Officers', Directors' Owners' Comp/Sales	2.1	2.6	2.5						
	(37) 4.8	(29) 4.1	(20) 6.1						
	8.4	7.4	8.7						
Net Sales ($)	2749655M	1917471M	2483026M	27125M	134217M	128415M	339968M	593070M	1260231M
Total Assets ($)	6961501M	6875633M	8465900M	133738M	646848M	558257M	1783844M	3110061M	2233152M

M = $ thousand MM = $ million

See Pages 9 through 22 for Explanation of Ratios and Data

Current Data Sorted by Assets							Comparative Historical Data	
						Type of Statement		
		3	11	1	2	Unqualified	18	13
			3			Reviewed	1	
	1	2				Compiled		1
						Tax Returns	1	1
		3	5	2		Other	8	10
	14 (4/1-9/30/13)		19 (10/1/13-3/31/14)				**4/1/09-3/31/10 ALL**	**4/1/10-3/31/11 ALL**
0-500M	**500M-2MM**	**2-10MM**	**10-50MM**	**50-100MM**	**100-250MM**			
	1	8	19	3	2	**NUMBER OF STATEMENTS**	28	25
%	%	%	%	%	%	**ASSETS**	%	%
DATA NOT AVAILABLE			10.7			Cash & Equivalents	6.4	10.9
			5.1			Trade Receivables (net)	6.5	2.5
			.2			Inventory	.2	1.4
			2.9			All Other Current	1.8	2.2
			18.8			Total Current	14.9	17.0
			71.3			Fixed Assets (net)	75.0	74.0
			5.3			Intangibles (net)	1.0	1.7
			4.6			All Other Non-Current	9.1	7.3
			100.0			Total	100.0	100.0
						LIABILITIES		
			7.5			Notes Payable-Short Term	6.6	.2
			4.4			Cur. Mat.-L.T.D.	2.2	1.8
			3.3			Trade Payables	3.2	1.7
			.0			Income Taxes Payable	.2	.2
			5.8			All Other Current	2.8	3.3
			21.0			Total Current	15.0	7.2
			37.7			Long-Term Debt	36.6	34.6
			.3			Deferred Taxes	.9	.4
			4.3			All Other Non-Current	13.6	9.3
			36.8			Net Worth	33.9	48.4
			100.0			Total Liabilities & Net Worth	100.0	100.0
						INCOME DATA		
			100.0			Net Sales	100.0	100.0
						Gross Profit		
			86.6			Operating Expenses	78.4	79.3
			13.4			Operating Profit	21.6	20.7
			6.5			All Other Expenses (net)	6.0	5.0
			6.9			Profit Before Taxes	15.6	15.7
						RATIOS		
			3.9				3.1	5.2
			1.8			Current	1.4	2.1
			.4				.7	.9
			3.7				2.8	4.8
			1.8			Quick	1.0	1.9
			.4				.5	.6
			9 41.0				17 21.5	0 UND
			34 10.8			Sales/Receivables	26 13.9	25 14.3
			50 7.3				43 8.5	48 7.6
						Cost of Sales/Inventory		
						Cost of Sales/Payables		
			1.4				3.1	1.4
			24.5			Sales/Working Capital	26.0	10.8
			-3.5				-12.5	-21.8
			11.4				4.4	7.7
			(14) 3.4			EBIT/Interest	(23) 1.9	(22) 3.9
			1.8				.9	1.8
						Net Profit + Depr., Dep., Amort./Cur. Mat. L/T/D		
			1.2				1.2	1.0
			1.9			Fixed/Worth	2.3	1.3
			3.3				3.8	3.2
			.5				.5	.3
			1.3			Debt/Worth	2.2	1.2
			6.1				3.4	3.0
			9.7				29.1	14.5
			(16) 6.1			% Profit Before Taxes/Tangible Net Worth	(24) 7.2	(23) 5.5
			.4				-.3	.7
			3.9				6.7	6.1
			2.6			% Profit Before Taxes/Total Assets	2.8	3.1
			.2				-.1	1.0
			.3				.5	.5
			.3			Sales/Net Fixed Assets	.3	.2
			.1				.1	.1
			.2				.4	.3
			.2			Sales/Total Assets	.2	.2
			.1				.1	.1
			14.4				8.9	7.6
			(17) 19.5			% Depr., Dep., Amort./Sales	(26) 17.0	14.4
			32.8				23.5	23.4
						% Officers', Directors' Owners' Comp/Sales		
	3314M	6326M	129114M	41897M	29831M	Net Sales ($)	236505M	194450M
	911M	37629M	452633M	232386M	304502M	Total Assets ($)	1335788M	1076762M

M = $ thousand MM = $ million

See Pages 9 through 22 for Explanation of Ratios and Data

Comparative Historical Data				Current Data Sorted by Sales					
			Type of Statement						
13	12	17	Unqualified	5	4	1	3	4	
		3	Reviewed			1		2	
1	3	3	Compiled	1	1	1			
1	1		Tax Returns						
4	9	10	Other	2	3		2	3	
4/1/11-3/31/12 ALL	**4/1/12-3/31/13 ALL**	**4/1/13-3/31/14 ALL**		**14 (4/1-9/30/13)**			**19 (10/1/13-3/31/14)**		
				0-1MM	**1-3MM**	**3-5MM**	**5-10MM**	**10-25MM**	**25MM & OVER**
19	25	33	**NUMBER OF STATEMENTS**	8	8	3	5	9	
%	%	%	**ASSETS**	%	%	%	%	%	%
12.9	11.5	9.8	Cash & Equivalents						DATA NOT AVAILABLE
4.6	9.8	3.8	Trade Receivables (net)						
1.5	2.0	.1	Inventory						
1.0	3.4	2.2	All Other Current						
19.9	26.7	15.9	Total Current						
76.1	66.3	76.0	Fixed Assets (net)						
1.0	.8	3.2	Intangibles (net)						
3.0	6.2	4.9	All Other Non-Current						
100.0	100.0	100.0	Total						
			LIABILITIES						
1.4	2.7	5.2	Notes Payable-Short Term						
2.4	4.7	3.5	Cur. Mat.-L.T.D.						
2.4	4.7	2.1	Trade Payables						
.4	.1	.0	Income Taxes Payable						
6.0	32.1	4.6	All Other Current						
12.6	44.3	15.4	Total Current						
21.3	23.3	36.8	Long-Term Debt						
1.5	.2	.4	Deferred Taxes						
2.6	.7	3.6	All Other Non-Current						
62.0	31.6	43.8	Net Worth						
100.0	100.0	100.0	Total Liabilties & Net Worth						
			INCOME DATA						
100.0	100.0	100.0	Net Sales						
			Gross Profit						
89.4	84.2	85.3	Operating Expenses						
10.6	15.8	14.7	Operating Profit						
3.0	4.8	7.8	All Other Expenses (net)						
7.7	11.0	7.0	Profit Before Taxes						
			RATIOS						
6.9	4.6	4.5							
3.3	1.6	1.9	Current						
1.7	.4	.5							
6.5	4.3	4.4							
3.0	1.4	1.9	Quick						
1.3	.3	.4							
7 53.1	**1** 564.0	**9** 41.9							
22 16.6	**20** 17.9	**34** 10.8	Sales/Receivables						
41 8.8	**49** 7.5	**53** 6.9							
			Cost of Sales/Inventory						
			Cost of Sales/Payables						
1.1	1.6	1.5							
2.0	17.7	6.9	Sales/Working Capital						
9.2	-5.0	-5.0							
7.7	5.9	6.3							
(15) 1.6	(17) 3.4	(25) 2.5	EBIT/Interest						
.5	1.7	1.8							
			Net Profit + Depr., Dep., Amort./Cur. Mat. L/T/D						
.9	.9	1.1							
1.1	1.1	1.6	Fixed/Worth						
1.3	2.6	3.0							
.2	.2	.5							
.5	.8	1.1	Debt/Worth						
1.5	2.4	2.3							
6.6	38.4	7.7							
(17) 1.3	(23) 5.9	(30) 3.8	% Profit Before Taxes/Tangible Net Worth						
-.4	.4	.2							
4.4	7.7	3.8							
.9	3.8	2.0	% Profit Before Taxes/Total Assets						
-.2	.2	.1							
.3	7.2	.3							
.2	.3	.2	Sales/Net Fixed Assets						
.1	.1	.1							
.3	2.0	.2							
.2	.2	.2	Sales/Total Assets						
.1	.1	.1							
13.1	9.0	10.3							
17.5	(19) 17.3	(30) 19.0	% Depr., Dep., Amort./Sales						
35.0	31.0	27.5							
			% Officers', Directors' Owners' Comp/Sales						
92418M	170295M	210482M	Net Sales ($)	5016M	16597M	10978M	36090M	141801M	
580669M	526446M	1028061M	Total Assets ($)	61937M	111251M	61120M	207355M	586398M	

M = $ thousand MM = $ million

See Pages 9 through 22 for Explanation of Ratios and Data

CONSTRUCTION—GENERAL INDUSTRIES FORMAT*

Current Data Sorted by Assets							Comparative Historical Data	
						Type of Statement		
	1	14	30	13	12	Unqualified	78	67
4	21	48	37	6	2	Reviewed	192	149
6	40	66	30	2	1	Compiled	233	179
151	181	138	25	2	2	Tax Returns	904	698
64	119	216	89	17	10	Other	734	717
	99 (4/1-9/30/13)		1,248 (10/1/13-3/31/14)				4/1/09-3/31/10	4/1/10-3/31/11
0-500M	**500M-2MM**	**2-10MM**	**10-50MM**	**50-100MM**	**100-250MM**		**ALL**	**ALL**
225	362	482	211	40	27	**NUMBER OF STATEMENTS**	2141	1810
%	%	%	%	%	%	**ASSETS**	%	%
25.0	11.4	10.3	9.9	9.2	7.3	Cash & Equivalents	10.4	10.9
14.1	10.1	10.5	9.1	3.4	13.0	Trade Receivables (net)	9.5	9.4
21.7	48.2	51.4	51.9	56.4	53.0	Inventory	50.4	48.6
4.2	4.8	4.6	5.8	6.9	3.7	All Other Current	4.3	4.7
65.1	74.6	76.8	76.6	75.9	77.0	Total Current	74.6	73.6
22.6	14.7	13.7	13.0	10.3	8.6	Fixed Assets (net)	15.6	15.5
1.3	1.5	.8	.7	1.1	1.5	Intangibles (net)	.8	.8
11.1	9.3	8.8	9.6	12.7	12.8	All Other Non-Current	9.0	10.1
100.0	100.0	100.0	100.0	100.0	100.0	Total	100.0	100.0
						LIABILITIES		
35.2	28.9	30.0	28.4	26.2	43.7	Notes Payable-Short Term	34.5	32.2
3.4	2.1	1.6	2.5	5.9	.6	Cur. Mat.-L.T.D.	4.8	3.3
12.2	11.4	10.9	11.9	9.9	8.1	Trade Payables	8.1	8.7
.0	.2	.1	.1	.0	.0	Income Taxes Payable	.1	.1
13.5	18.3	16.0	13.5	8.5	11.3	All Other Current	14.1	15.4
64.4	60.9	58.6	56.4	50.6	63.8	Total Current	61.6	59.7
23.2	15.2	11.0	10.9	11.8	3.1	Long-Term Debt	15.1	14.8
.0	.0	.0	.3	.0	.5	Deferred Taxes	.1	.1
9.1	5.5	5.0	4.5	2.1	5.1	All Other Non-Current	5.3	4.8
3.3	18.4	25.4	28.0	35.6	27.5	Net Worth	18.0	20.5
100.0	100.0	100.0	100.0	100.0	100.0	Total Liabilties & Net Worth	100.0	100.0
						INCOME DATA		
100.0	100.0	100.0	100.0	100.0	100.0	Net Sales	100.0	100.0
26.6	18.7	16.3	16.8	20.0	23.0	Gross Profit	18.1	18.9
22.8	14.6	11.6	11.8	13.9	15.8	Operating Expenses	17.5	15.8
3.8	4.1	4.7	5.1	6.1	7.3	Operating Profit	.6	3.1
.8	.5	.8	.7	.6	1.5	All Other Expenses (net)	2.0	1.8
3.1	3.5	3.9	4.4	5.5	5.8	Profit Before Taxes	-1.4	1.4
						RATIOS		
3.7	2.3	2.1	1.8	1.9	2.1		2.1	2.2
1.4	1.2	1.3	1.3	1.4	1.3	Current	1.2	1.3
.6	.9	1.0	1.0	1.2	1.2		1.0	.9
2.6	.9	.9	.7	.4	1.1		.8	.8
.8	(360) .3	(481) .2	.2	.2	.2	Quick	(2138) .1	(1803) .2
.1	.1	.0	.1	.1	.1		.0	.0
0 UND	**0** UND	**0** UND	**0** UND	**0** UND	**0** UND		**0** UND	**0** UND
0 UND	**0** UND	**0** 999.8	**1** 315.4	**1** 717.9	**2** 178.7	Sales/Receivables	**0** 999.8	**0** UND
10 34.8	**15** 23.7	**20** 18.2	**21** 17.6	**5** 69.6	**36** 10.1		**17** 21.7	**15** 23.6
0 UND	**0** UND	**1** 300.2	**3** 134.0	**4** 92.9	**38** 9.5		**0** UND	**0** UND
0 UND	**101** 3.6	**152** 2.4	**174** 2.1	**174** 2.1	**228** 1.6	Cost of Sales/Inventory	**165** 2.2	**140** 2.6
32 11.4	**243** 1.5	**304** 1.2	**304** 1.2	**261** 1.4	**281** 1.3		**441** .8	**368** 1.0
0 UND	**0** UND	**1** 320.6	**10** 35.6	**13** 27.6	**10** 38.0		**0** UND	**0** UND
0 UND	**7** 52.4	**15** 23.6	**19** 19.1	**21** 17.2	**24** 15.0	Cost of Sales/Payables	**9** 40.5	**9** 39.2
11 34.6	**29** 12.8	**34** 10.6	**40** 9.2	**41** 8.9	**48** 7.6		**27** 13.3	**27** 13.7
9.3	5.1	3.6	3.7	4.2	4.2		3.2	3.5
50.8	21.1	12.1	10.3	6.7	6.3	Sales/Working Capital	11.5	11.4
-29.6	-30.9	-173.5	61.9	17.4	16.4		-45.5	-55.0
21.7	15.5	34.1	25.7	28.7	21.9		6.5	9.9
(145) 4.8	(258) 4.7	(369) 6.5	(167) 6.9	(36) 7.5	(26) 8.5	EBIT/Interest	(1602) 1.5	(1324) 2.3
.7	1.0	1.6	2.4	2.6	2.0		-1.7	-.2
		9.0	8.7				5.2	8.7
		(24) 1.7	(23) 3.2			Net Profit + Depr., Dep., Amort./Cur. Mat. L/T/D	(76) 1.1	(68) 1.8
		-.4	.8				-.1	.3
.0	.0	.0	.0	.0	.0		.0	.0
.5	.2	.2	.1	.1	.0	Fixed/Worth	.2	.2
11.4	3.8	1.2	.7	.5	.4		3.0	2.3
.9	1.7	1.4	1.4	1.0	.8		1.5	1.3
3.7	5.0	3.7	2.9	1.9	2.0	Debt/Worth	4.5	3.9
-7.8	78.9	15.2	8.4	4.8	4.9		42.3	24.4
149.1	80.6	67.3	49.0	53.1	52.0		34.1	46.6
(160) 62.2	(282) 29.6	(412) 29.2	(193) 25.7	28.4	(26) 36.0	% Profit Before Taxes/Tangible Net Worth	(1698) 7.5	(1473) 13.7
16.7	4.6	6.3	8.0	11.3	7.8		-10.0	-1.9
40.4	13.5	12.8	9.7	15.4	14.3		7.5	10.4
14.0	5.3	4.9	4.8	7.7	5.8	% Profit Before Taxes/Total Assets	1.0	2.6
-2.4	.0	.7	1.9	2.6	2.0		-4.2	-1.9
UND	999.8	478.1	315.7	201.9	313.7		316.6	407.2
74.5	75.0	69.0	78.4	54.1	151.2	Sales/Net Fixed Assets	49.0	54.8
16.4	11.9	10.6	11.9	10.7	8.5		7.6	9.0
9.8	3.2	2.6	2.1	2.2	1.8		2.7	2.9
5.3	2.0	1.5	1.4	1.6	1.3	Sales/Total Assets	1.3	1.5
2.4	1.2	.9	.8	1.2	.5		.6	.7
.3	.2	.2	.1	.2	.1		.3	.2
(98) .7	(175) .5	(260) .4	(137) .3	(31) .3	(18) .4	% Depr., Dep., Amort./Sales	(1229) .7	(956) .6
1.6	1.5	1.1	.9	.7	.8		1.7	1.7
2.9	1.8	.9	.4				1.4	1.4
(118) 4.8	(155) 3.0	(153) 1.5	(48) 1.2			% Officers', Directors' Owners' Comp/Sales	(914) 2.8	(726) 2.9
7.7	5.3	3.0	2.8				5.3	5.8
341334M	**994714M**	**4176763M**	**6637625M**	**5791675M**	**7763887M**	Net Sales ($)	**27531598M**	**25547164M**
58406M	**414455M**	**2308465M**	**4460634M**	**2937932M**	**4133285M**	Total Assets ($)	**20723665M**	**16747518M**

M = $ thousand **MM = $ million**

See Pages 9 through 22 for Explanation of Ratios and Data

Comparative Historical Data | Current Data Sorted by Sales

4/1/11-3/31/12 ALL	4/1/12-3/31/13 ALL	4/1/13-3/31/14 ALL		0-1MM	1-3MM	3-5MM	5-10MM	10-25MM	25MM & OVER
			Type of Statement						
66	83	70	Unqualified		3	1	4	13	49
172	138	118	Reviewed	2	11	14	22	37	32
153	137	145	Compiled	11	34	22	33	35	10
639	582	499	Tax Returns	145	163	71	66	41	13
574	536	515	Other	52	133	63	89	100	78
					99 (4/1-9/30/13)		1,248 (10/1/13-3/31/14)		
1604	1476	1347	**NUMBER OF STATEMENTS**	210	344	171	214	226	182
%	%	%	**ASSETS**	%	%	%	%	%	%
11.7	13.1	12.9	Cash & Equivalents	15.1	13.6	11.1	13.2	11.3	12.3
11.1	11.3	10.6	Trade Receivables (net)	6.9	8.8	11.5	9.7	14.8	13.4
44.7	44.3	45.8	Inventory	41.6	43.6	44.6	52.3	43.9	51.1
4.7	5.1	4.8	All Other Current	2.4	4.3	5.3	5.0	7.5	4.7
72.2	73.8	74.2	Total Current	66.1	70.2	72.5	80.2	77.5	81.5
16.3	15.1	15.1	Fixed Assets (net)	22.8	17.3	15.7	11.7	12.7	8.5
1.2	1.1	1.1	Intangibles (net)	1.1	1.4	1.0	.7	1.2	.8
10.3	10.0	9.6	All Other Non-Current	10.1	11.1	10.7	7.4	8.6	9.2
100.0	100.0	100.0	Total	100.0	100.0	100.0	100.0	100.0	100.0
			LIABILITIES						
28.3	30.7	30.5	Notes Payable-Short Term	36.9	28.5	31.1	30.0	26.6	31.7
3.2	3.0	2.3	Cur. Mat.-L.T.D.	1.4	2.4	3.5	1.8	2.4	2.5
10.1	11.2	11.3	Trade Payables	4.9	9.8	11.7	12.1	15.1	15.4
.1	.1	.1	Income Taxes Payable	.0	.1	.3	.2	.1	.1
14.9	15.6	15.5	All Other Current	13.5	17.2	18.2	16.7	14.2	12.1
56.6	60.5	59.7	Total Current	56.7	58.0	64.7	60.7	58.4	61.9
15.6	13.6	14.0	Long-Term Debt	24.2	17.7	12.7	10.6	8.9	6.8
.1	.0	.1	Deferred Taxes	.0	.0	.1	.0	.2	.1
5.8	5.7	5.6	All Other Non-Current	9.4	6.8	4.8	4.0	5.1	2.5
21.9	20.2	20.6	Net Worth	9.8	17.4	17.7	24.6	27.3	28.7
100.0	100.0	100.0	Total Liabilties & Net Worth	100.0	100.0	100.0	100.0	100.0	100.0
			INCOME DATA						
100.0	100.0	100.0	Net Sales	100.0	100.0	100.0	100.0	100.0	100.0
19.3	19.4	19.0	Gross Profit	28.7	20.4	17.1	15.8	14.4	16.5
16.2	15.3	14.5	Operating Expenses	23.5	16.4	13.0	11.5	9.9	11.0
3.1	4.1	4.5	Operating Profit	5.2	4.1	4.1	4.3	4.4	5.5
1.4	.9	.7	All Other Expenses (net)	2.4	.6	.2	.4	.1	.5
1.7	3.2	3.8	Profit Before Taxes	2.8	3.4	3.9	3.9	4.3	4.9
			RATIOS						
2.3	2.3	2.2		4.4	3.0	1.9	2.2	1.8	1.8
1.3	1.3	1.3	Current	1.3	1.3	1.2	1.3	1.2	1.3
.9	.9	1.0		.8	.9	.8	1.0	1.0	1.1
1.0	1.0	1.0		1.4	1.0	.9	.9	1.0	1.0
(1598) .2	(1473) .2	(1344) .2	Quick	.3	(343) .3	.2	(212) .2	.2	.2
.1	.0	.1		.0	.1	.0	.1	.1	.1
0 UND	**0** UND	**0** UND		**0** UND	**0** UND	**0** UND	**0** UND	**0** UND	**0** UND
0 999.8	**0** 999.8	**0** 999.8	Sales/Receivables	**0** UND	**0** UND	**0** UND	**0** 999.8	**2** 174.6	**2** 237.1
20 18.3	**19** 18.8	**16** 23.1		**5** 74.2	**9** 40.4	**19** 19.0	**10** 35.4	**35** 10.4	**28** 13.0
0 UND	**0** UND	**0** UND		**0** UND	**0** UND	**0** UND	**2** 197.6	**0** UND	**0** 999.8
122 3.0	**104** 3.5	**107** 3.4	Cost of Sales/Inventory	**166** 2.2	**89** 4.1	**72** 5.1	**118** 3.1	**94** 3.9	**140** 2.6
304 1.2	**261** 1.4	**261** 1.4		**608** .6	**261** 1.4	**228** 1.6	**228** 1.6	**203** 1.8	**215** 1.7
0 UND	**0** UND	**0** UND		**0** UND	**0** UND	**0** UND	**1** 345.8	**8** 46.7	**12** 29.6
11 32.4	**12** 30.3	**12** 30.0	Cost of Sales/Payables	**0** UND	**5** 67.6	**13** 27.9	**13** 27.6	**18** 19.9	**23** 16.0
30 12.0	**33** 11.2	**31** 11.6		**17** 21.6	**27** 13.6	**31** 11.8	**31** 11.9	**35** 10.4	**42** 8.6
3.4	4.2	4.5		2.2	3.5	5.6	6.5	4.8	5.1
11.4	13.2	15.1	Sales/Working Capital	12.1	16.9	25.0	15.1	15.2	10.8
-64.6	-68.3	-88.0		-11.1	-29.4	-28.2	270.3	999.8	28.3
10.0	18.0	24.4		7.7	14.6	23.9	38.1	51.1	43.3
(1199) 2.8	(1094) 4.6	(1001) 6.0	EBIT/Interest	(132) 2.6	(245) 3.5	(134) 6.5	(163) 7.5	(181) 9.0	(146) 11.3
.3	1.1	1.6		-.4	.3	1.9	1.6	3.1	2.9
6.1	5.5	10.6				5.3	4.4	4.9	17.7
(62) 2.3	(56) 2.1	(59) 2.7	Net Profit + Depr., Dep., Amort./Cur. Mat. L/T/D			(10) 1.8	(11) 1.6	(13) 2.5	(17) 5.8
-.1	.4	.4				-.2	.0	.6	1.8
.0	.0	.0		.0	.0	.0	.0	.0	.0
.2	.2	.2	Fixed/Worth	.3	.3	.4	.1	.1	.1
1.8	1.8	1.7		4.2	5.6	3.4	1.3	.9	.5
1.2	1.2	1.2		1.1	1.2	1.6	1.4	1.2	1.3
3.4	3.2	3.7	Debt/Worth	4.8	4.2	5.0	4.8	3.4	2.2
19.3	22.4	19.2		-45.0	135.3	71.6	18.8	7.8	5.5
49.6	66.4	71.8		68.4	84.1	73.0	90.1	63.2	61.7
(1313) 14.4	(1199) 23.9	(1113) 31.3	% Profit Before Taxes/Tangible Net Worth	(153) 20.0	(265) 25.4	(133) 33.7	(184) 40.2	(208) 30.8	(170) 34.9
-.2	3.3	6.8		-3.3	.9	9.4	8.8	11.2	15.0
11.6	15.7	15.1		14.8	14.3	16.8	17.7	13.1	16.7
3.2	4.9	5.8	% Profit Before Taxes/Total Assets	2.7	4.2	6.0	6.8	7.1	8.1
-1.0	.2	.7		-2.8	-1.0	1.5	1.1	2.5	3.5
574.0	734.0	548.3		UND	999.8	296.3	785.2	295.8	314.2
55.3	63.9	72.4	Sales/Net Fixed Assets	38.2	55.7	58.7	110.4	68.7	108.1
9.2	11.9	11.9		3.0	11.1	12.5	30.3	15.5	21.2
3.0	3.2	3.2		2.4	3.5	3.9	3.4	3.1	2.7
1.6	1.8	1.9	Sales/Total Assets	1.0	1.8	2.0	2.1	2.0	2.0
.7	.9	1.0		.4	.9	1.1	1.3	1.3	1.4
.2	.2	.2		.6	.2	.2	.1	.1	.1
(862) .6	(752) .5	(719) .4	% Depr., Dep., Amort./Sales	(90) 1.5	(167) .6	(91) .4	(107) .3	(132) .3	(132) .2
1.7	1.5	1.2		3.8	1.6	1.1	.7	.9	.5
1.5	1.3	1.3		3.7	2.5	1.4	1.0	.6	.3
(631) 3.1	(572) 2.6	(485) 2.7	% Officers', Directors' Owners' Comp/Sales	(71) 6.4	(137) 4.0	(79) 2.3	(88) 1.6	(79) 1.2	(31) .9
5.6	5.5	5.3		10.3	6.1	3.7	3.1	2.1	1.9
19828635M	**24567809M**	**25705998M**	Net Sales ($)	**115835M**	**651316M**	**664014M**	**1564506M**	**3503878M**	**19206449M**
13960372M	**14075862M**	**14313177M**	Total Assets ($)	**205672M**	**700136M**	**488261M**	**1074222M**	**2533386M**	**9311500M**

M = $ thousand MM = $ million

See Pages 9 through 22 for Explanation of Ratios and Data

Current Data Sorted by Assets							Comparative Historical Data	
						Type of Statement		
		4	11	8	4	Unqualified	33	27
	3	14	14			Reviewed	33	21
1	2	3	1			Compiled	13	9
8	7	5	1			Tax Returns	45	25
4	5	16	22	1	1	Other	64	44
23 (4/1-9/30/13)		112 (10/1/13-3/31/14)					4/1/09-3/31/10	4/1/10-3/31/11
0-500M	500M-2MM	2-10MM	10-50MM	50-100MM	100-250MM		ALL	ALL
13	17	42	49	9	5	**NUMBER OF STATEMENTS**	188	126
%	%	%	%	%	%	**ASSETS**	%	%
29.4	22.7	17.0	25.6			Cash & Equivalents	17.8	15.6
13.5	23.1	35.1	32.6			Trade Receivables (net)	25.5	26.9
3.6	15.5	8.3	10.6			Inventory	22.6	19.7
19.7	7.0	11.4	13.5			All Other Current	9.0	9.4
66.3	68.3	71.8	82.3			Total Current	75.0	71.5
22.6	18.5	12.8	7.6			Fixed Assets (net)	13.3	16.8
.1	2.7	1.8	1.5			Intangibles (net)	1.1	2.8
11.1	10.5	13.6	8.6			All Other Non-Current	10.6	8.9
100.0	100.0	100.0	100.0			Total	100.0	100.0
						LIABILITIES		
10.1	11.4	7.5	5.9			Notes Payable-Short Term	17.6	14.7
7.6	1.2	1.0	3.0			Cur. Mat.-L.T.D.	2.6	1.2
8.7	18.7	26.9	33.9			Trade Payables	20.1	18.9
.0	.0	.0	.3			Income Taxes Payable	.3	.1
16.4	4.8	18.9	16.1			All Other Current	14.1	15.7
42.7	36.0	54.3	59.3			Total Current	54.8	50.6
5.3	22.1	8.0	5.2			Long-Term Debt	11.0	12.4
.0	.0	.0	.0			Deferred Taxes	.2	.0
42.5	6.1	1.3	2.1			All Other Non-Current	3.8	2.5
9.6	35.7	36.4	33.3			Net Worth	30.3	34.4
100.0	100.0	100.0	100.0			Total Liabilties & Net Worth	100.0	100.0
						INCOME DATA		
100.0	100.0	100.0	100.0			Net Sales	100.0	100.0
38.5	22.5	18.0	11.4			Gross Profit	19.6	17.9
24.6	19.3	13.6	8.1			Operating Expenses	15.9	16.3
13.9	3.2	4.4	3.3			Operating Profit	3.7	1.6
1.4	2.5	1.0	.6			All Other Expenses (net)	1.1	2.0
12.5	.7	3.4	2.7			Profit Before Taxes	2.6	-.4
						RATIOS		
9.8	4.0	1.9	1.6				2.2	2.1
3.3	1.7	1.4	1.4			Current	1.4	1.3
1.0	1.0	1.0	1.1				1.1	1.1
4.8	3.8	1.5	1.2				1.4	1.5
1.3	1.6	1.2	1.1			Quick	(186) 1.0	1.0
.3	.7	.5	.6				.2	.2
0 UND	**0** UND	**9** 38.5	**3** 105.6				**0** 930.5	**0** UND
0 UND	**13** 28.6	**38** 9.6	**43** 8.4			Sales/Receivables	**33** 11.1	**33** 11.0
1 511.3	**38** 9.5	**68** 5.4	**54** 6.8				**62** 5.9	**63** 5.8
0 UND	**0** UND	**0** UND	**0** UND				**0** UND	**0** UND
0 UND	**0** UND	**0** UND	**0** UND			Cost of Sales/Inventory	**0** UND	**0** UND
0 UND	**3** 107.1	**0** UND	**0** UND				**161** 2.3	**53** 6.8
0 UND	**0** UND	**22** 16.3	**26** 14.1				**8** 45.3	**7** 50.6
1 549.0	**13** 28.5	**37** 9.8	**41** 8.9			Cost of Sales/Payables	**31** 11.8	**25** 14.4
12 31.4	**28** 12.9	**59** 6.2	**63** 5.8				**58** 6.3	**57** 6.5
7.6	4.9	5.3	8.1				5.0	5.0
58.0	13.8	13.9	16.4			Sales/Working Capital	12.1	12.1
NM	NM	-273.5	35.5				71.1	50.1
	43.6	53.6	107.6				27.6	36.1
	(13) 4.7	(26) 8.7	(29) 23.9			EBIT/Interest	(135) 3.9	(86) 4.0
	-2.3	1.3	5.5				.2	-.8
							32.6	28.5
						Net Profit + Depr., Dep., Amort./Cur. Mat. L/T/D	(21) 5.7	(14) .9
							2.4	-2.3
.0	.0	.0	.0				.0	.0
.0	.5	.1	.1			Fixed/Worth	.1	.1
.9	12.2	.5	.3				.8	1.1
.2	.6	.6	1.5				1.0	1.0
1.7	1.5	1.8	2.4			Debt/Worth	2.1	2.3
3.5	96.0	4.0	4.6				9.4	4.4
154.2	82.1	37.1	54.4				38.8	46.8
(12) 90.4	(15) 49.5	(39) 16.1	(48) 20.5			% Profit Before Taxes/Tangible Net Worth	(162) 14.8	(112) 10.0
6.4	-5.7	2.1	4.8				1.8	-6.0
135.8	25.8	13.6	14.0				10.2	11.8
48.0	7.7	4.2	6.9			% Profit Before Taxes/Total Assets	3.8	2.0
5.5	-3.3	.5	1.9				-.4	-3.6
UND	215.1	999.8	999.8				305.9	289.8
UND	51.8	91.7	185.4			Sales/Net Fixed Assets	60.2	64.8
14.3	11.0	18.7	45.7				13.4	9.0
15.6	6.1	4.3	4.1				3.4	3.7
5.6	3.0	2.4	3.1			Sales/Total Assets	2.0	2.3
2.8	1.3	1.4	2.0				.9	.4
		.2	.0				.2	.3
		(20) .6	(36) .2			% Depr., Dep., Amort./Sales	(111) .6	(77) .5
		1.3	.4				1.4	1.8
		.5	.4				1.3	1.1
		(12) 1.9	(17) .8			% Officers', Directors' Owners' Comp/Sales	(60) 2.7	(30) 2.0
		2.6	2.8				6.0	5.8
14790M	93409M	623988M	2979391M	1678851M	1411784M	Net Sales ($)	6868698M	3145290M
2701M	22146M	214466M	1028853M	569734M	794450M	Total Assets ($)	2499353M	1903792M

M = $ thousand MM = $ million

See Pages 9 through 22 for Explanation of Ratios and Data

Comparative Historical Data				Current Data Sorted by Sales					
			Type of Statement						
26	16	27	Unqualified				1	2	24
33	32	31	Reviewed		2	2	3	7	17
9	7	7	Compiled		4	2	1		
30	26	21	Tax Returns	9	7		3	2	
48	62	49	Other	2	4	3	6	12	22
				23 (4/1-9/30/13)			112 (10/1/13-3/31/14)		
4/1/11-3/31/12 ALL	**4/1/12-3/31/13 ALL**	**4/1/13-3/31/14 ALL**		**0-1MM**	**1-3MM**	**3-5MM**	**5-10MM**	**10-25MM**	**25MM & OVER**
146	143	135	**NUMBER OF STATEMENTS**	11	17	7	14	23	63
%	%	%	**ASSETS**	%	%	%	%	%	%
17.5	22.4	22.6	Cash & Equivalents	26.2	15.4		13.5	21.7	26.9
30.8	28.3	31.2	Trade Receivables (net)	1.9	20.0		28.2	38.4	39.9
18.6	17.4	8.7	Inventory	8.4	18.9		22.1	4.8	4.3
8.9	8.3	12.6	All Other Current	19.2	16.0		5.5	10.7	13.7
75.8	76.4	75.1	Total Current	55.7	70.2		69.3	75.7	84.7
9.8	12.4	11.8	Fixed Assets (net)	29.4	17.7		16.3	8.6	4.0
2.4	.9	1.6	Intangibles (net)	.2	2.0		.0	4.3	1.1
11.9	10.3	11.5	All Other Non-Current	14.8	10.0		14.4	11.3	10.1
100.0	100.0	100.0	Total	100.0	100.0		100.0	100.0	100.0
			LIABILITIES						
14.7	13.2	6.9	Notes Payable-Short Term	4.2	20.1		18.4	2.6	2.9
2.5	2.7	2.4	Cur. Mat.-L.T.D.	9.2	.7		.1	4.6	1.6
22.4	23.6	28.2	Trade Payables	1.7	14.8		17.1	31.2	40.4
.2	.1	.1	Income Taxes Payable	.0	.0		.0	.0	.2
11.7	16.5	15.8	All Other Current	16.6	4.0		18.9	14.0	17.2
51.5	56.1	53.4	Total Current	31.6	39.7		54.7	52.4	62.2
7.7	8.6	8.9	Long-Term Debt	14.6	23.6		6.4	5.5	4.2
.2	.0	.0	Deferred Taxes	.0	.0		.0	.1	.0
3.8	3.9	6.3	All Other Non-Current	5.3	32.3		7.1	.4	1.7
36.9	31.5	31.3	Net Worth	48.5	4.4		31.8	41.7	31.9
100.0	100.0	100.0	Total Liabilties & Net Worth	100.0	100.0		100.0	100.0	100.0
			INCOME DATA						
100.0	100.0	100.0	Net Sales	100.0	100.0		100.0	100.0	100.0
16.8	21.2	17.2	Gross Profit	47.9	22.3		27.1	13.8	8.1
13.9	15.4	12.6	Operating Expenses	33.8	17.4		19.3	10.7	5.4
2.9	5.9	4.6	Operating Profit	14.1	4.9		7.8	3.1	2.7
.5	.6	1.0	All Other Expenses (net)	6.8	1.3		.8	-.1	.0
2.3	5.3	3.5	Profit Before Taxes	7.3	3.6		7.0	3.2	2.6

4/1/11-3/31/12 ALL	4/1/12-3/31/13 ALL	4/1/13-3/31/14 ALL	**RATIOS**	0-1MM	1-3MM	3-5MM	5-10MM	10-25MM	25MM & OVER
2.1	2.1	2.1		11.1	9.4		1.7	2.7	1.5
1.4	1.4	1.4	Current	1.3	2.7		1.4	1.5	1.3
1.1	1.1	1.1		.3	.9		1.1	1.0	1.2
1.6	1.6	1.5		2.5	3.4		1.6	1.8	1.2
(145) 1.1	1.1	1.1	Quick	.1	1.3		1.1	1.2	1.1
.4	.4	.6		.0	.7		.2	.7	.9
0 UND	**0** 999.8	**1** 365.8		**0** UND	**0** UND		**0** UND	**13** 27.3	**24** 15.3
40 9.1	**32** 11.4	**34** 10.7	Sales/Receivables	**0** UND	**4** 88.0		**27** 13.6	**34** 10.6	**46** 7.9
68 5.4	**58** 6.3	**57** 6.4		**13** 28.6	**27** 13.4		**91** 4.0	**61** 6.0	**61** 6.0
0 UND	**0** UND	**0** UND		**0** UND	**0** UND		**0** UND	**0** UND	**0** UND
0 UND	**0** UND	**0** UND	Cost of Sales/Inventory	**0** UND	**0** UND		**0** UND	**0** UND	**0** UND
21 17.4	**35** 10.5	**0** UND		**18** 20.6	**23** 16.2		**192** 1.9	**0** UND	**0** UND
11 34.7	**9** 41.4	**15** 23.9		**0** UND	**0** UND		**16** 22.4	**17** 21.4	**29** 12.6
37 9.9	**35** 10.5	**35** 10.5	Cost of Sales/Payables	**0** UND	**8** 47.8		**31** 11.6	**36** 10.1	**49** 7.5
64 5.7	**62** 5.9	**61** 6.0		**36** 10.0	**37** 9.8		**59** 6.2	**47** 7.8	**64** 5.7
5.2	5.8	6.0		2.3	3.5		4.6	7.4	9.6
11.8	13.3	16.4	Sales/Working Capital	58.0	7.0		13.5	13.9	18.9
41.5	43.6	47.5		-1.0	-90.3		NM	-351.4	27.9
42.7	54.9	65.5			10.8		47.4	55.9	145.2
(106) 5.7	(87) 13.2	(81) 11.1	EBIT/Interest		(12) 3.8		(12) 3.1	(14) 13.3	(34) 36.0
.2	2.1	1.3			-.5		1.2	2.3	9.5
17.5	35.6	7.9							
(13) 4.2	(16) 9.2	(14) 1.4	Net Profit + Depr., Dep., Amort./Cur. Mat. L/T/D						
1.4	1.7	-.5							
.0	.0	.0		.0	.0		.1	.0	.0
.1	.1	.1	Fixed/Worth	.0	.3		.5	.1	.0
.6	.6	.5		3.9	1.1		4.2	.5	.1
.9	.9	.9		.1	.7		.9	.3	1.6
1.9	1.9	2.3	Debt/Worth	2.9	1.7		4.0	1.5	2.6
3.9	5.0	5.3		5.1	13.2		14.7	6.6	4.9
49.3	54.0	54.7		133.9	69.6		29.2	79.6	54.2
(135) 21.7	(130) 32.2	(128) 19.8	% Profit Before Taxes/Tangible Net Worth	6.8	(14) 23.9		(12) 6.2	(22) 17.6	23.8
1.6	5.7	3.7		-5.7	-10.7		2.1	1.1	8.1
17.0	18.7	15.8		121.5	31.4		15.6	19.7	13.9
5.4	8.5	6.5	% Profit Before Taxes/Total Assets	6.5	7.7		3.2	7.2	7.2
.2	1.3	.7		-1.7	-5.0		.5	.5	2.7
299.3	400.2	999.8		UND	UND		56.0	999.8	999.8
73.7	82.4	143.9	Sales/Net Fixed Assets	UND	36.1		23.5	132.5	291.8
19.5	17.7	23.9		.6	8.9		14.8	23.9	95.7
3.7	4.2	4.3		11.1	3.9		2.7	5.2	4.2
2.6	3.0	3.1	Sales/Total Assets	1.5	2.0		1.9	3.8	3.3
1.4	1.5	1.8		.2	.8		1.2	2.2	2.7
.2	.1	.1						.2	.1
(99) .4	(81) .3	(78) .2	% Depr., Dep., Amort./Sales					(12) .4	(43) .1
1.2	.8	.9						1.6	.3
1.7	1.2	.5							.5
(42) 2.6	(37) 2.5	(40) 1.9	% Officers', Directors' Owners' Comp/Sales						(17) .8
5.0	3.9	4.1							2.7

4/1/11-3/31/12 ALL	4/1/12-3/31/13 ALL	4/1/13-3/31/14 ALL		0-1MM	1-3MM	3-5MM	5-10MM	10-25MM	25MM & OVER
4880321M	**3672321M**	**6802213M**	Net Sales ($)	**4833M**	**30975M**	**25952M**	**104365M**	**402450M**	**6233638M**
2789550M	**1643748M**	**2632350M**	Total Assets ($)	**10723M**	**20994M**	**71953M**	**75447M**	**197136M**	**2256097M**

M = $ thousand MM = $ million

See Pages 9 through 22 for Explanation of Ratios and Data

Current Data Sorted by Assets / Comparative Historical Data

Type of Statement								
Unqualified		1	5	10	16	8	26	25
Reviewed	1	5	13	20	4	1	30	29
Compiled	3	12	31	23	2		29	17
Tax Returns	24	33	41	11			96	72
Other	8	32	82	73	6	7	108	94
	22 (4/1-9/30/13)		450 (10/1/13-3/31/14)				4/1/09-3/31/10 ALL	4/1/10-3/31/11 ALL
	0-500M	**500M-2MM**	**2-10MM**	**10-50MM**	**50-100MM**	**100-250MM**		
NUMBER OF STATEMENTS	36	83	172	137	28	16	289	237
ASSETS	%	%	%	%	%	%	%	%
Cash & Equivalents	35.1	8.9	8.9	8.7	6.9	9.5	8.4	11.2
Trade Receivables (net)	6.8	5.7	3.6	2.2	4.1	9.5	7.5	7.3
Inventory	17.5	60.2	67.1	70.3	66.6	64.5	52.4	48.4
All Other Current	3.6	3.4	4.1	3.3	2.4	3.2	4.3	5.0
Total Current	63.1	78.1	83.6	84.5	80.2	86.8	72.7	72.0
Fixed Assets (net)	26.6	11.1	9.0	7.6	7.7	7.6	15.8	17.9
Intangibles (net)	.9	.2	.9	.1	.2	.4	1.0	.5
All Other Non-Current	9.5	10.6	6.5	7.7	12.0	5.3	10.4	9.6
Total	100.0	100.0	100.0	100.0	100.0	100.0	100.0	100.0
LIABILITIES								
Notes Payable-Short Term	26.6	36.3	43.1	41.6	34.5	22.4	33.2	26.5
Cur. Mat.-L.T.D.	3.8	2.6	1.7	1.9	1.8	.7	3.8	1.9
Trade Payables	10.3	8.6	6.2	5.9	10.2	8.4	7.8	7.1
Income Taxes Payable	.0	.0	.1	.1	.0	.0	.1	.1
All Other Current	16.1	21.4	12.4	9.9	6.0	7.3	13.0	13.4
Total Current	56.9	68.9	63.5	59.3	52.6	38.7	57.9	49.0
Long-Term Debt	21.6	10.4	10.4	7.2	10.3	15.3	16.6	17.7
Deferred Taxes	.0	.1	.0	.0	.0	.0	.1	.1
All Other Non-Current	2.7	4.7	4.5	6.5	2.0	1.9	6.1	6.3
Net Worth	18.7	15.9	21.7	27.0	35.0	44.1	19.3	26.9
Total Liabilities & Net Worth	100.0	100.0	100.0	100.0	100.0	100.0	100.0	100.0
INCOME DATA								
Net Sales	100.0	100.0	100.0	100.0	100.0	100.0	100.0	100.0
Gross Profit	20.8	17.2	16.4	17.1	22.1	20.7	15.6	19.4
Operating Expenses	17.0	10.0	10.7	10.2	10.8	11.5	15.8	17.1
Operating Profit	3.8	7.2	5.7	6.9	11.3	9.3	-.2	2.2
All Other Expenses (net)	.6	.8	1.1	.7	.8	.1	2.3	2.5
Profit Before Taxes	3.3	6.4	4.6	6.2	10.6	9.1	-2.5	-.2
RATIOS								
Current	2.2	2.1	1.8	1.8	1.9	8.5	2.0	2.7
	1.2	1.2	1.3	1.4	1.5	1.9	1.3	1.4
	.6	.9	1.0	1.1	1.3	1.3	.9	1.0
Quick	1.7	.4	.3	.3	.3	1.2	.7	.9
	.8	.1	.1	.1	.1	.3	(286) .1	(235) .2
	.2	.0	.0	.0	.1	.1	.0	.0
Sales/Receivables	**0** UND	**0** UND	**0** UND	**0** UND	**0** UND	**0** UND	**0** UND	**0** UND
	0 UND	**0** UND	**0** UND	**0** UND	**1** 474.7	**2** 174.8	**0** 999.8	**0** 920.7
	4 82.7	**0** UND	**3** 137.1	**2** 199.7	**4** 85.8	**11** 32.2	**12** 30.5	**17** 20.9
Cost of Sales/Inventory	**0** UND	**50** 7.3	**114** 3.2	**146** 2.5	**152** 2.4	**174** 2.1	**4** 99.2	**1** 407.2
	0 UND	**146** 2.5	**174** 2.1	**215** 1.7	**203** 1.8	**281** 1.3	**209** 1.7	**200** 1.8
	5 76.9	**281** 1.3	**304** 1.2	**332** 1.1	**304** 1.2	**406** .9	**494** .7	**453** .8
Cost of Sales/Payables	**0** UND	**0** UND	**0** 983.6	**4** 95.4	**19** 19.5	**7** 54.6	**0** 999.8	**0** UND
	0 UND	**1** 295.0	**10** 36.2	**14** 26.2	**24** 15.4	**23** 16.1	**10** 37.3	**11** 32.6
	5 77.7	**16** 22.6	**20** 18.3	**26** 13.8	**37** 9.8	**38** 9.6	**29** 12.7	**33** 10.9
Sales/Working Capital	15.3	4.0	4.2	3.1	2.1	1.3	2.3	2.1
	111.2	17.4	10.8	7.8	6.2	3.4	9.4	5.9
	-26.3	-50.1	51.2	14.0	8.8	6.1	-40.9	NM
EBIT/Interest	15.6	16.6	17.7	18.8	24.8	18.2	5.1	9.3
	(27) 5.7	(56) 5.3	(132) 5.3	(97) 6.1	(24) 10.2	(11) 4.1	(221) .8	(181) 2.4
	1.2	1.9	1.6	2.7	3.6	1.9	-1.8	-.2
Net Profit + Depr., Dep., Amort./Cur. Mat. L/T/D							5.6	7.1
							(16) 1.2	(10) 1.9
							-.1	.0
Fixed/Worth	.0	.0	.0	.0	.0	.0	.0	.0
	.6	.1	.1	.1	.1	.0	.2	.1
	9.0	2.3	.6	.3	.3	.3	2.8	1.6
Debt/Worth	.8	1.9	1.7	1.5	1.0	.9	1.4	1.0
	2.5	4.6	3.9	2.8	2.3	1.6	3.9	2.4
	46.5	55.1	12.1	7.5	4.4	2.5	83.4	11.0
% Profit Before Taxes/Tangible Net Worth	153.3	98.7	75.4	67.3	55.2	36.0	28.0	31.7
	(29) 47.5	(67) 43.7	(151) 39.5	(129) 36.3	29.0	25.1	(226) 5.3	(204) 8.4
	4.2	13.7	14.2	9.7	9.6	6.2	-12.5	-5.1
% Profit Before Taxes/Total Assets	35.4	19.9	14.6	15.0	16.4	18.3	5.4	8.6
	14.5	5.1	7.2	7.6	7.5	12.2	.3	2.3
	-.2	2.2	1.4	2.4	3.4	1.8	-5.0	-2.3
Sales/Net Fixed Assets	UND	UND	999.8	486.9	224.9	528.4	220.3	625.0
	104.5	136.4	119.5	133.7	104.9	185.8	47.3	45.1
	26.6	23.2	29.4	37.0	15.8	9.9	6.2	6.7
Sales/Total Assets	13.2	2.6	2.5	2.0	1.9	1.6	2.2	2.2
	5.3	1.7	1.7	1.4	1.6	1.3	1.0	1.2
	2.5	1.0	.9	.9	.9	.8	.5	.5
% Depr., Dep., Amort./Sales	.4	.2	.1	.1	.1		.3	.2
	(17) .8	(31) .5	(65) .3	(70) .2	(13) .2		(167) .7	(124) .6
	2.0	1.0	.9	.4	.6		1.5	1.9
% Officers', Directors' Owners' Comp/Sales	2.3	1.8	1.0	.5			.9	1.3
	(20) 5.5	(27) 2.7	(48) 1.5	(30) 1.0			(92) 2.4	(75) 2.3
	9.2	5.2	3.5	2.2			5.1	5.0
Net Sales ($)	70788M	217842M	1560651M	4422298M	2859241M	3124521M	6700173M	5007047M
Total Assets ($)	9711M	107688M	861366M	3019247M	2007917M	2472433M	5848096M	4025699M

M = $ thousand MM = $ million

See Pages 9 through 22 for Explanation of Ratios and Data

Comparative Historical Data				Current Data Sorted by Sales					
			Type of Statement						
23	24	40	Unqualified	1	3	3	3	2	28
40	41	44	Reviewed	1	3	1	7	16	16
38	53	71	Compiled	2	9	11	17	12	20
58	111	109	Tax Returns	24	33	12	17	14	9
128	191	208	Other	12	33	22	37	50	54
4/1/11-3/31/12 ALL	4/1/12-3/31/13 ALL	4/1/13-3/31/14 ALL			22 (4/1-9/30/13)		450 (10/1/13-3/31/14)		
				0-1MM	1-3MM	3-5MM	5-10MM	10-25MM	25MM & OVER
287	420	472	**NUMBER OF STATEMENTS**	40	81	49	81	94	127
%	%	%	**ASSETS**	%	%	%	%	%	%
9.9	10.8	10.8	Cash & Equivalents	17.3	12.7	11.0	11.3	8.0	9.0
6.5	4.1	4.0	Trade Receivables (net)	.8	2.9	4.7	6.3	3.7	4.2
54.5	63.3	62.9	Inventory	41.8	54.8	57.8	61.4	68.9	73.2
4.4	3.2	3.6	All Other Current	2.3	1.9	3.9	3.9	5.2	3.5
75.4	81.4	81.2	Total Current	62.2	72.4	77.5	83.0	85.8	89.9
15.0	9.8	10.2	Fixed Assets (net)	27.7	15.9	11.3	7.5	7.6	4.2
.8	.5	.5	Intangibles (net)	.0	.7	.1	.4	.6	.6
8.8	8.2	8.1	All Other Non-Current	10.1	11.0	11.1	9.1	6.0	5.3
100.0	100.0	100.0	Total	100.0	100.0	100.0	100.0	100.0	100.0
			LIABILITIES						
30.6	36.7	39.0	Notes Payable-Short Term	24.7	34.4	39.5	40.1	43.8	42.0
3.3	2.1	2.0	Cur. Mat.-L.T.D.	1.5	3.2	3.4	1.1	2.5	1.2
8.1	7.6	7.1	Trade Payables	5.0	5.3	4.4	8.7	7.2	9.0
.1	.1	.1	Income Taxes Payable	.0	.1	.2	.0	.0	.1
14.2	10.6	13.0	All Other Current	31.2	14.5	15.9	9.6	10.1	9.4
56.2	57.0	61.2	Total Current	62.4	57.5	63.5	59.5	63.6	61.7
13.2	9.2	10.5	Long-Term Debt	24.0	17.1	7.5	7.3	8.2	6.9
.0	.0	.0	Deferred Taxes	.0	.0	.0	.1	.0	.0
6.4	5.0	4.7	All Other Non-Current	5.8	4.7	7.9	3.0	6.0	3.3
24.2	28.7	23.5	Net Worth	7.7	20.7	21.2	30.0	22.3	28.0
100.0	100.0	100.0	Total Liabilties & Net Worth	100.0	100.0	100.0	100.0	100.0	100.0
			INCOME DATA						
100.0	100.0	100.0	Net Sales	100.0	100.0	100.0	100.0	100.0	100.0
18.2	18.4	17.6	Gross Profit	22.1	19.5	18.8	16.9	15.7	16.2
15.5	12.1	10.9	Operating Expenses	17.3	12.8	11.2	11.2	9.2	8.7
2.7	6.3	6.6	Operating Profit	4.8	6.7	7.7	5.7	6.5	7.5
1.4	1.4	.9	All Other Expenses (net)	3.0	1.3	.5	.3	.5	.6
1.4	5.0	5.8	Profit Before Taxes	1.8	5.4	7.2	5.4	6.0	6.8
			RATIOS						
2.3	2.0	1.9		4.5	2.1	1.9	2.1	1.7	1.8
1.3	1.4	1.3	Current	1.4	1.2	1.2	1.4	1.3	1.4
1.1	1.1	1.1		.6	1.0	.8	1.1	1.1	1.2
.6	.4	.4		.8	.6	.4	.6	.3	.3
.2	(415) .2	.1	Quick	.1	.2	.1	.2	.1	.1
.0	.1	.0		.0	.0	.0	.1	.1	.1
0 UND	**0** UND	**0** UND		**0** UND	**0** UND	**0** UND	**0** UND	**0** UND	**0** UND
0 999.8	**0** UND	**0** UND	Sales/Receivables	**0** UND	**0** UND	**0** UND	**0** UND	**0** 999.8	**0** UND
14 25.3	**5** 80.5	**2** 157.2		**0** UND	**0** UND	**2** 184.1	**10** 37.1	**4** 88.3	**2** 168.6
21 17.0	**111** 3.3	**99** 3.7		**0** UND	**14** 25.3	**28** 13.0	**74** 4.9	**118** 3.1	**130** 2.8
192 1.9	**203** 1.8	**182** 2.0	Cost of Sales/Inventory	**215** 1.7	**182** 2.0	**174** 2.1	**152** 2.4	**192** 1.9	**182** 2.0
456 .8	**332** 1.1	**304** 1.2		**1217** .3	**304** 1.2	**365** 1.0	**281** 1.3	**304** 1.2	**261** 1.4
1 306.4	**1** 723.4	**0** 999.8		**0** UND	**0** UND	**0** UND	**1** 367.2	**3** 110.8	**7** 49.7
15 24.8	**14** 25.4	**10** 36.2	Cost of Sales/Payables	**0** UND	**1** 311.3	**6** 61.7	**9** 41.5	**14** 25.8	**17** 21.2
30 12.1	**27** 13.3	**23** 16.0		**5** 71.8	**17** 20.9	**18** 20.2	**22** 16.7	**25** 14.8	**27** 13.5
2.4	3.1	3.7		1.1	3.6	2.8	3.9	4.0	4.0
7.3	7.2	9.1	Sales/Working Capital	10.7	16.7	10.2	9.3	7.7	8.6
77.6	27.8	52.3		-14.4	-48.7	-6.1	45.8	23.5	14.7
12.3	18.1	17.8		5.7	9.9	31.3	24.3	22.4	28.1
(218) 3.7	(285) 5.3	(347) 5.9	EBIT/Interest	(30) 1.7	(55) 3.3	(34) 8.6	(58) 8.0	(78) 5.8	(92) 8.9
.3	1.7	2.3		-1.0	.8	2.3	2.8	2.5	3.3
		4.4							
		(10) .4	Net Profit + Depr., Dep., Amort./Cur. Mat. L/T/D						
		-2.4							
.0	.0	.0		.0	.0	.0	.0	.0	.0
.1	.1	.1	Fixed/Worth	.7	.1	.1	.1	.1	.1
1.7	.6	.6		-45.3	2.7	1.2	.4	.8	.2
1.3	1.2	1.5		1.4	1.5	1.7	1.0	1.6	1.5
3.0	2.7	3.1	Debt/Worth	3.7	4.2	3.6	2.5	3.7	2.7
12.4	7.0	11.0		-21.1	29.6	22.8	10.1	11.2	5.8
44.4	58.9	75.6		93.6	80.2	85.9	79.9	62.9	74.5
(240) 14.6	(374) 26.4	(420) 37.4	% Profit Before Taxes/Tangible Net Worth	(28) 9.7	(69) 30.5	(42) 31.3	(76) 40.9	(83) 37.1	(122) 44.0
.0	4.9	11.7		-7.8	4.1	13.3	9.0	14.2	18.9
9.8	15.0	16.6		11.2	13.2	13.9	20.2	13.7	19.0
3.7	6.7	7.6	% Profit Before Taxes/Total Assets	1.6	4.5	4.8	8.7	7.4	11.1
-1.5	1.0	2.2		-2.4	.3	2.3	2.5	2.0	5.0
403.5	999.8	999.8		UND	UND	UND	928.1	999.8	427.7
65.0	117.5	125.0	Sales/Net Fixed Assets	57.3	132.7	143.0	107.2	112.6	143.9
11.2	20.1	28.9		1.8	10.7	23.5	37.7	22.5	56.0
2.3	2.1	2.4		2.1	2.4	2.1	2.9	2.4	2.4
1.3	1.4	1.7	Sales/Total Assets	.6	1.4	1.2	1.8	1.7	1.8
.7	.8	1.0		.2	.8	.7	1.1	1.2	1.3
.2	.1	.1		1.0	.2	.1	.2	.1	.1
(154) .5	(205) .3	(203) .3	% Depr., Dep., Amort./Sales	(13) 2.1	(35) .5	(17) .6	(27) .4	(45) .3	(66) .1
1.2	.9	.8		4.8	1.3	1.1	1.4	.6	.3
.9	1.2	.9		2.7	2.2	1.4	.9	.9	.4
(76) 2.6	(126) 2.1	(127) 1.9	% Officers', Directors' Owners' Comp/Sales	(13) 5.9	(28) 4.0	(16) 2.5	(21) 1.8	(24) 1.2	(25) .9
4.6	4.4	4.7		8.9	8.8	4.8	3.4	1.7	2.0
6586246M	9845195M	12255341M	Net Sales ($)	20204M	159292M	194741M	578947M	1443053M	9859104M
4591309M	6978741M	8478362M	Total Assets ($)	43663M	179697M	310107M	437935M	1371555M	6135405M

M = $ thousand MM = $ million

See Pages 9 through 22 for Explanation of Ratios and Data

Current Data Sorted by Assets							Comparative Historical Data	
						Type of Statement		
	1		3			Unqualified	7	6
	5	8	4			Reviewed	13	8
5	9	12				Compiled	15	19
38	23	6	1			Tax Returns	34	48
20	26	13	7	1		Other	37	49
	13 (4/1-9/30/13)		169 (10/1/13-3/31/14)				4/1/09-3/31/10	4/1/10-3/31/11
0-500M	500M-2MM	2-10MM	10-50MM	50-100MM	100-250MM		ALL	ALL
63	64	39	15	1		**NUMBER OF STATEMENTS**	106	130
%	%	%	%	%	%	**ASSETS**	%	%
23.0	19.1	16.3	14.2		D	Cash & Equivalents	16.5	16.6
19.5	32.0	35.3	26.8		A	Trade Receivables (net)	28.5	28.6
6.9	6.6	10.6	13.5		T	Inventory	9.5	8.4
7.4	7.4	6.6	6.9		A	All Other Current	10.4	6.7
56.7	65.0	68.8	61.5			Total Current	65.0	60.3
29.3	23.6	17.8	19.6		N	Fixed Assets (net)	21.4	23.4
2.0	3.0	3.3	6.9		O	Intangibles (net)	6.1	8.2
11.9	8.4	10.1	12.1		T	All Other Non-Current	7.5	8.1
100.0	100.0	100.0	100.0			Total	100.0	100.0
					A	**LIABILITIES**		
34.5	9.3	9.4	12.2		V	Notes Payable-Short Term	17.3	21.5
13.0	2.2	1.2	4.6		A	Cur. Mat.-L.T.D.	4.2	7.0
18.8	16.9	16.4	18.7		I	Trade Payables	14.6	21.0
.0	.1	.0	.4		L	Income Taxes Payable	.2	.2
22.3	14.0	18.5	13.8		A	All Other Current	21.4	15.2
88.7	42.5	45.5	49.6		B	Total Current	57.7	64.8
32.6	15.9	12.3	25.0		L	Long-Term Debt	20.0	28.3
.0	.5	.0	.0		E	Deferred Taxes	.1	.2
10.1	5.9	2.8	5.6			All Other Non-Current	11.5	9.1
-31.4	35.2	39.4	19.8			Net Worth	10.7	-2.5
100.0	100.0	100.0	100.0			Total Liabilities & Net Worth	100.0	100.0
						INCOME DATA		
100.0	100.0	100.0	100.0			Net Sales	100.0	100.0
41.3	35.9	25.6	25.2			Gross Profit	32.1	34.4
36.7	29.8	21.1	18.4			Operating Expenses	29.4	29.7
4.6	6.1	4.4	6.8			Operating Profit	2.7	4.8
.2	.6	.0	1.8			All Other Expenses (net)	.6	1.2
4.4	5.5	4.5	5.0			Profit Before Taxes	2.1	3.6
						RATIOS		
2.5	4.4	2.1	1.5				2.6	2.2
.8	1.7	1.6	1.3			Current	1.4	1.1
.3	1.0	1.1	1.1				.8	.6
1.8	3.6	1.9	1.1				1.8	1.6
.6	1.2	1.2	.9			Quick	.9	.9
.2	.5	.7	.3				.4	.3
0 UND	**6** 62.1	**11** 32.4	**9** 38.9				**0** UND	**0** UND
0 999.8	**27** 13.5	**39** 9.3	**28** 12.9			Sales/Receivables	**25** 14.7	**22** 16.4
16 22.4	**58** 6.3	**66** 5.5	**79** 4.6				**51** 7.1	**45** 8.0
0 UND	**0** UND	**0** UND	**0** UND				**0** UND	**0** UND
0 UND	**0** UND	**0** UND	**0** 999.8			Cost of Sales/Inventory	**0** UND	**0** UND
4 90.9	**2** 195.7	**4** 81.2	**56** 6.5				**9** 40.8	**3** 116.1
0 UND	**4** 96.4	**9** 42.8	**21** 17.4				**1** 546.5	**1** 308.6
0 UND	**22** 16.7	**18** 19.9	**32** 11.5			Cost of Sales/Payables	**14** 25.5	**16** 22.6
27 13.6	**41** 9.0	**29** 12.6	**46** 7.9				**32** 11.2	**33** 11.1
17.8	5.7	7.4	10.3				7.8	9.7
-67.4	14.5	12.0	13.9			Sales/Working Capital	20.4	59.3
-14.4	-270.2	62.5	68.7				-41.0	-19.7
20.2	25.1	34.5	12.3				10.9	17.8
(56) 7.2	(47) 7.4	(33) 9.9	(13) 6.4			EBIT/Interest	(81) 2.9	(110) 4.2
.5	2.5	3.0	2.5				-1.2	.7
						Net Profit + Depr., Dep., Amort./Cur. Mat. L/T/D		
.5	.1	.1	.1				.2	.2
8.0	.6	.3	.4			Fixed/Worth	.8	1.0
-.7	2.5	1.0	2.8				-2.4	-1.1
3.5	.8	.7	1.3				.8	1.1
UND	1.8	1.6	3.2			Debt/Worth	3.4	3.9
-3.0	14.8	6.4	15.7				-7.7	-4.4
539.3	101.9	73.7	89.7				81.9	95.6
(34) 93.8	(53) 45.2	(36) 33.4	(12) 27.7			% Profit Before Taxes/Tangible Net Worth	(69) 34.6	(87) 35.4
-5.3	7.8	9.3	9.3				4.3	5.5
46.7	35.1	21.5	14.9				22.6	28.3
18.1	8.7	7.8	10.1			% Profit Before Taxes/Total Assets	6.7	12.4
-4.4	2.0	1.7	2.2				-2.5	-.4
90.2	76.4	225.9	87.9				81.1	117.6
32.4	33.3	22.7	60.8			Sales/Net Fixed Assets	28.3	32.6
14.7	10.4	13.0	9.1				12.0	10.7
14.0	5.1	4.2	3.3				5.6	7.2
7.6	3.4	3.0	2.0			Sales/Total Assets	3.5	3.7
3.7	2.1	1.6	1.6				2.1	2.1
.4	.3	.2	.2				.6	.3
(38) 1.1	(40) .7	(30) .7	(14) .4			% Depr., Dep., Amort./Sales	(73) 1.2	(79) 1.1
3.4	1.7	2.0	1.3				2.1	2.3
3.5	2.3	1.6					3.0	2.0
(42) 6.1	(39) 3.8	(14) 2.2				% Officers', Directors' Owners' Comp/Sales	(53) 5.5	(69) 3.8
8.8	6.2	3.1					8.5	7.3
104192M	267072M	419071M	919135M	21333M		Net Sales ($)	3148923M	3004428M
12874M	67881M	143015M	329432M	70327M		Total Assets ($)	853858M	1097109M

M = $ thousand MM = $ million

See Pages 9 through 22 for Explanation of Ratios and Data

Comparative Historical Data				Current Data Sorted by Sales					
			Type of Statement						
10	13	4	Unqualified		1				3
17	16	17	Reviewed		2	4	3	4	4
23	28	26	Compiled	1	7	6	6	5	1
60	81	68	Tax Returns	19	26	11	4	7	1
57	61	67	Other	10	25	6	10	9	7
4/1/11-3/31/12	**4/1/12-3/31/13**	**4/1/13-3/31/14**		**13 (4/1-9/30/13)**		**169 (10/1/13-3/31/14)**			
ALL	**ALL**	**ALL**		**0-1MM**	**1-3MM**	**3-5MM**	**5-10MM**	**10-25MM**	**25MM & OVER**
167	199	182	**NUMBER OF STATEMENTS**	30	61	27	23	25	16
%	%	%	**ASSETS**	%	%	%	%	%	%
16.6	19.2	19.4	Cash & Equivalents	20.8	18.3	21.9	21.9	16.6	17.3
31.4	27.7	27.9	Trade Receivables (net)	16.3	23.5	34.1	34.7	37.9	30.8
8.1	10.2	8.1	Inventory	7.3	6.9	13.3	4.7	5.3	14.7
7.9	7.2	7.5	All Other Current	9.2	6.5	5.4	7.0	10.6	7.7
64.0	64.3	62.9	Total Current	53.5	55.1	74.6	68.2	70.5	70.4
21.5	22.9	23.9	Fixed Assets (net)	32.1	30.4	15.7	21.7	16.8	11.4
5.3	3.4	3.0	Intangibles (net)	1.2	3.0	3.8	3.8	1.6	6.4
9.2	9.5	10.2	All Other Non-Current	13.1	11.6	5.8	6.3	11.0	11.7
100.0	100.0	100.0	Total	100.0	100.0	100.0	100.0	100.0	100.0
			LIABILITIES						
19.2	18.3	18.2	Notes Payable-Short Term	18.4	20.7	12.9	10.0	31.5	8.9
6.0	3.3	5.9	Cur. Mat.-L.T.D.	5.7	11.1	4.2	.6	1.9	3.3
16.9	18.1	17.5	Trade Payables	7.6	17.4	13.9	27.4	18.4	27.3
.1	.2	.1	Income Taxes Payable	.0	.0	.2	.0	.0	.3
22.4	22.0	18.3	All Other Current	16.0	15.9	14.7	22.1	29.6	14.4
64.7	61.8	60.0	Total Current	47.7	65.1	46.0	60.0	81.4	54.2
16.3	22.2	21.6	Long-Term Debt	39.3	27.3	13.9	9.9	5.8	21.0
.1	.2	.2	Deferred Taxes	.0	.0	1.1	.0	.0	.0
8.9	6.2	6.6	All Other Non-Current	12.4	8.5	3.3	3.8	1.9	6.0
10.1	9.5	11.6	Net Worth	.5	-.8	35.8	26.3	10.9	18.7
100.0	100.0	100.0	Total Liabilities & Net Worth	100.0	100.0	100.0	100.0	100.0	100.0
			INCOME DATA						
100.0	100.0	100.0	Net Sales	100.0	100.0	100.0	100.0	100.0	100.0
33.2	33.5	34.7	Gross Profit	45.1	36.2	31.9	35.0	25.4	27.9
28.7	27.9	29.4	Operating Expenses	35.3	32.6	26.2	30.8	21.4	22.3
4.5	5.6	5.2	Operating Profit	9.8	3.6	5.7	4.2	4.0	5.6
.7	1.1	.4	All Other Expenses (net)	1.4	.1	.3	.0	.0	1.4
3.8	4.5	4.8	Profit Before Taxes	8.4	3.5	5.4	4.2	4.0	4.1
			RATIOS						
1.9	2.6	2.5		4.2	2.6	4.0	4.3	1.9	1.6
1.2	1.4	1.3	Current	1.6	1.2	1.7	1.5	1.4	1.3
.7	.8	.7		.6	.5	1.1	.7	.9	1.1
1.5	2.0	1.9		3.6	1.7	3.1	3.8	1.7	1.3
(166) .9	1.0	1.0	Quick	.6	.7	1.3	1.1	1.0	1.0
.4	.4	.4		.2	.3	.5	.4	.3	.5
1 490.2	**0** UND	**0** UND		**0** UND	**0** UND	**4** 97.5	**7** 49.8	**9** 39.6	**10** 38.4
28 13.0	**23** 16.2	**16** 23.3	Sales/Receivables	**2** 149.4	**10** 37.2	**18** 20.0	**29** 12.5	**33** 11.0	**32** 11.3
54 6.8	**49** 7.5	**55** 6.6		**24** 15.4	**51** 7.2	**72** 5.1	**51** 7.1	**64** 5.7	**76** 4.8
0 UND	**0** UND	**0** UND		**0** UND	**0** UND	**0** UND	**0** UND	**0** UND	**0** UND
0 UND	**0** UND	**0** UND	Cost of Sales/Inventory	**0** UND	**0** UND	**0** UND	**0** UND	**0** UND	**0** UND
5 80.9	**9** 41.9	**3** 113.8		**1** 311.2	**3** 123.0	**19** 19.2	**4** 93.9	**0** 808.4	**38** 9.6
3 120.2	**0** UND	**0** UND		**0** UND	**0** UND	**2** 150.8	**15** 23.6	**10** 36.2	**23** 15.9
18 20.2	**16** 22.5	**17** 21.5	Cost of Sales/Payables	**0** UND	**9** 39.5	**15** 23.9	**26** 14.2	**19** 19.2	**37** 9.9
41 9.0	**35** 10.5	**33** 11.0		**35** 10.5	**30** 12.2	**31** 11.6	**41** 8.9	**29** 12.7	**48** 7.6
7.7	7.8	8.4		9.7	7.2	6.1	6.2	9.6	10.4
46.6	23.2	22.8	Sales/Working Capital	49.2	55.6	19.6	21.9	21.7	19.3
-29.9	-41.3	-33.2		-8.1	-29.9	34.3	-26.6	-22.4	59.5
27.2	25.3	24.4		17.5	18.8	35.8	27.2	36.0	13.2
(141) 6.8	(161) 6.9	(150) 7.6	EBIT/Interest	(25) 7.4	(51) 4.2	(21) 10.5	(16) 7.6	(24) 13.1	(13) 6.4
1.5	2.0	2.1		.6	.9	3.1	1.5	8.5	2.5
7.3	15.2								
(11) 2.5	(13) 4.6		Net Profit + Depr., Dep., Amort./Cur. Mat. L/T/D						
-4.0	2.4								
.1	.1	.1		.5	.2	.1	.1	.1	.1
.7	.7	.7	Fixed/Worth	3.0	1.7	.5	.3	.3	.3
UND	-45.4	UND		-1.2	-17.9	3.9	18.1	1.2	2.8
1.1	.8	.9		1.7	1.4	.7	.5	.8	1.3
3.8	3.3	3.5	Debt/Worth	35.8	4.5	2.5	.9	2.1	4.0
-164.4	-16.6	-105.4		-3.4	-15.7	55.3	48.3	21.6	16.4
94.1	113.9	103.4		569.5	137.5	80.9	103.4	91.3	102.6
(125) 35.1	(145) 43.8	(135) 45.4	% Profit Before Taxes/Tangible Net Worth	(17) 100.0	(44) 42.8	(23) 45.4	(18) 30.8	(20) 46.4	(13) 32.2
6.9	12.1	7.6		18.9	-.1	17.5	7.2	27.8	11.3
27.6	35.6	32.1		44.4	32.3	29.6	42.1	27.7	18.7
8.4	12.8	9.5	% Profit Before Taxes/Total Assets	17.8	7.1	8.7	8.0	17.2	8.4
.8	1.9	1.2		-.9	-3.0	3.4	.4	4.4	2.7
91.9	149.2	86.4		82.1	71.6	105.3	58.6	199.6	143.3
32.6	40.1	29.5	Sales/Net Fixed Assets	16.6	26.2	49.0	35.4	29.9	74.2
11.7	12.6	13.1		9.9	10.4	22.5	18.5	14.5	27.9
5.8	7.0	7.2		6.4	10.9	7.2	5.6	6.5	4.3
3.5	3.7	3.7	Sales/Total Assets	3.3	4.0	3.6	4.4	3.9	2.6
2.3	2.2	2.1		.9	1.9	2.3	3.0	2.7	1.9
.4	.4	.3		.7	.4	.2	.3	.1	.2
(124) 1.1	(131) .9	(123) .7	% Depr., Dep., Amort./Sales	(17) 2.9	(37) 1.0	(19) .6	(17) .8	(18) .5	(15) .4
2.2	2.0	2.3		3.6	2.6	1.7	2.2	1.3	.9
2.4	2.1	2.3		4.1	2.6	3.2	1.1	1.4	
(83) 4.4	(113) 4.3	(99) 3.8	% Officers', Directors' Owners' Comp/Sales	(19) 6.5	(35) 5.8	(17) 5.2	(13) 2.3	(13) 1.8	
6.9	6.6	6.6		16.2	7.6	7.1	3.8	2.6	
2933976M	**2775358M**	**1730803M**	Net Sales ($)	**16485M**	**112930M**	**110195M**	**170451M**	**366007M**	**954735M**
951552M	**818299M**	**623529M**	Total Assets ($)	**7641M**	**42047M**	**40284M**	**40575M**	**173101M**	**319881M**

M = $ thousand MM = $ million

See Pages 9 through 22 for Explanation of Ratios and Data

Current Data Sorted by Assets							Comparative Historical Data	
						Type of Statement		
	4	27	43	14	10	Unqualified	188	156
4	25	62	29	2		Reviewed	238	218
4	10	10	2	2		Compiled	51	27
20	31	13	2	2		Tax Returns	131	90
13	28	47	42	8	9	Other	196	163
84 (4/1-9/30/13)			379 (10/1/13-3/31/14)				4/1/09-3/31/10	4/1/10-3/31/11
0-500M	**500M-2MM**	**2-10MM**	**10-50MM**	**50-100MM**	**100-250MM**		**ALL**	**ALL**
41	98	159	118	28	19	**NUMBER OF STATEMENTS**	804	654
%	%	%	%	%	%	**ASSETS**	%	%
24.1	20.8	22.8	22.6	24.8	14.7	Cash & Equivalents	22.8	21.7
27.2	39.6	42.4	42.4	35.9	45.7	Trade Receivables (net)	36.1	40.1
9.4	3.5	2.0	2.2	3.1	1.5	Inventory	5.3	3.4
2.8	6.7	8.6	10.3	10.7	9.7	All Other Current	7.1	7.5
63.5	70.5	75.8	77.5	74.5	71.6	Total Current	71.3	72.7
22.9	16.9	15.0	12.7	16.8	13.4	Fixed Assets (net)	18.5	17.1
1.2	2.9	2.2	2.5	3.3	5.1	Intangibles (net)	1.2	2.1
12.3	9.7	7.0	7.2	5.4	9.9	All Other Non-Current	9.0	8.1
100.0	100.0	100.0	100.0	100.0	100.0	Total	100.0	100.0
						LIABILITIES		
28.7	6.8	4.2	2.8	3.1	2.1	Notes Payable-Short Term	8.9	8.0
5.1	2.1	1.4	1.4	2.0	2.9	Cur. Mat.-L.T.D.	2.9	2.4
11.6	23.9	30.4	31.4	22.8	24.9	Trade Payables	24.1	25.6
.2	.5	.4	.2	.3	.0	Income Taxes Payable	.4	.5
24.0	14.4	15.2	19.0	18.5	28.4	All Other Current	16.4	15.2
69.6	47.7	51.6	54.8	46.7	58.4	Total Current	52.8	51.6
29.2	7.5	7.5	4.9	6.8	6.7	Long-Term Debt	10.2	8.1
.0	.2	.3	.4	.9	.0	Deferred Taxes	.3	.3
15.1	4.6	1.8	2.5	1.9	3.3	All Other Non-Current	3.2	3.1
-13.9	39.9	38.9	37.4	43.7	31.7	Net Worth	33.5	36.9
100.0	100.0	100.0	100.0	100.0	100.0	Total Liabilties & Net Worth	100.0	100.0
						INCOME DATA		
100.0	100.0	100.0	100.0	100.0	100.0	Net Sales	100.0	100.0
37.0	26.5	16.0	13.7	17.3	11.5	Gross Profit	19.6	19.3
33.5	22.6	13.1	10.6	12.7	8.8	Operating Expenses	17.3	17.1
3.5	3.9	3.0	3.1	4.5	2.7	Operating Profit	2.2	2.2
1.2	.2	-.1	-.1	.1	.0	All Other Expenses (net)	.4	.3
2.3	3.7	3.0	3.3	4.4	2.7	Profit Before Taxes	1.8	1.8
						RATIOS		
5.5	2.9	2.0	1.7	2.4	1.4		2.1	2.1
1.5	1.5	1.5	1.3	1.6	1.2	Current	1.4	1.5
.5	1.0	1.2	1.2	1.2	1.1		1.1	1.1
5.5	2.6	1.7	1.5	1.7	1.2		1.7	1.8
.8	1.4	1.3	1.2	1.2	1.1	Quick	1.2	1.3
.3	.7	1.0	1.0	1.1	.9		.8	.9
0 UND	**26** 13.8	**33** 11.0	**44** 8.3	**38** 9.6	**60** 6.1		**25** 14.6	**33** 10.9
10 35.8	**47** 7.7	**54** 6.8	**59** 6.2	**66** 5.5	**66** 5.5	Sales/Receivables	**45** 8.1	**56** 6.6
46 8.0	**73** 5.0	**73** 5.0	**81** 4.5	**81** 4.5	**79** 4.6		**68** 5.4	**78** 4.7
0 UND	**0** UND	**0** UND	**0** UND	**0** UND	**0** UND		**0** UND	**0** UND
0 UND	**0** UND	**0** UND	**0** UND	**0** UND	**0** 999.8	Cost of Sales/Inventory	**0** UND	**0** UND
0 756.4	**0** UND	**0** UND	**0** 768.8	**3** 105.0	**4** 88.9		**1** 484.9	**1** 333.1
0 UND	**9** 40.2	**19** 18.9	**28** 13.2	**20** 18.0	**14** 26.0		**16** 23.1	**19** 19.7
0 UND	**29** 12.5	**38** 9.6	**51** 7.2	**39** 9.4	**26** 14.2	Cost of Sales/Payables	**32** 11.4	**37** 9.9
21 17.3	**59** 6.2	**63** 5.8	**69** 5.3	**62** 5.9	**55** 6.6		**56** 6.5	**62** 5.9
9.5	5.7	6.8	6.9	5.0	13.4		7.0	6.0
69.3	12.4	12.7	13.7	11.5	18.9	Sales/Working Capital	13.6	12.2
-20.5	138.9	34.5	28.2	19.7	37.6		52.2	38.9
11.9	55.4	49.6	62.8	85.6	25.7		38.3	29.0
(29) 4.0	(68) 10.0	(133) 15.5	(89) 16.0	(23) 48.0	(15) 10.9	EBIT/Interest	(612) 6.3	(500) 6.2
-.9	1.1	3.5	4.4	2.9	6.3		.6	.4
		21.3	15.5				10.8	10.6
		(34) 5.4	(33) 4.2			Net Profit + Depr., Dep., Amort./Cur. Mat. L/T/D	(152) 3.1	(111) 3.6
		2.4	1.7				.8	1.0
.0	.0	.1	.1	.1	.2		.1	.1
.6	.2	.2	.3	.2	.4	Fixed/Worth	.3	.3
-2.4	.9	.6	.6	.5	.9		.9	.8
.5	.5	.9	1.1	.8	1.8		.9	.7
5.4	1.6	1.6	2.1	2.1	2.7	Debt/Worth	1.8	1.7
-2.2	6.4	3.7	3.5	3.5	5.4		4.2	3.6
188.5	63.0	45.5	44.4	43.5	31.2		39.5	30.2
(23) 32.7	(88) 25.6	(150) 16.1	(114) 19.3	20.2	(18) 19.9	% Profit Before Taxes/Tangible Net Worth	(723) 14.3	(596) 10.7
14.3	6.0	3.4	3.6	8.3	15.6		.3	-1.7
43.1	19.3	13.2	12.2	15.6	6.4		13.3	11.0
13.1	7.4	5.5	5.8	6.7	5.5	% Profit Before Taxes/Total Assets	4.4	3.8
-29.7	1.0	1.1	1.4	3.4	3.8		-.7	-1.8
UND	191.2	137.0	85.5	89.0	52.4		92.8	80.7
56.9	34.8	36.7	32.0	20.3	17.6	Sales/Net Fixed Assets	30.6	29.2
17.1	10.8	13.9	12.5	7.7	15.6		9.6	10.5
17.4	4.2	4.0	3.3	3.3	3.0		3.9	3.6
6.7	2.8	2.9	2.6	2.2	2.5	Sales/Total Assets	2.7	2.7
2.9	1.7	1.9	1.8	1.5	1.7		1.8	1.8
.5	.2	.2	.2	.4	.2		.4	.3
(22) 1.2	(72) .9	(135) .6	(108) .6	(25) .8	(17) 1.0	% Depr., Dep., Amort./Sales	(650) .8	(541) .8
2.8	2.3	1.4	1.4	2.8	1.5		2.3	1.9
4.0	2.3	1.1	.5				1.5	1.3
(26) 7.5	(51) 4.6	(52) 2.2	(29) 1.1			% Officers', Directors' Owners' Comp/Sales	(315) 3.1	(241) 2.7
11.0	6.2	3.6	3.3				5.5	5.1
66812M	379815M	2562093M	6404761M	6494671M	7839378M	Net Sales ($)	31546146M	24363799M
9625M	120675M	819174M	2499459M	2024886M	3167357M	Total Assets ($)	12009036M	10098092M

M = $ thousand MM = $ million

See Pages 9 through 22 for Explanation of Ratios and Data

Comparative Historical Data				Current Data Sorted by Sales					
			Type of Statement						
136	99	98	Unqualified		1	1	5	20	71
203	150	122	Reviewed	3	12	17	23	32	35
35	27	28	Compiled	4	6	4	5	6	3
107	80	68	Tax Returns	11	19	13	13	6	6
159	141	147	Other	8	19	11	18	34	57
4/1/11-3/31/12 ALL	4/1/12-3/31/13 ALL	4/1/13-3/31/14 ALL		84 (4/1-9/30/13)			379 (10/1/13-3/31/14)		
				0-1MM	1-3MM	3-5MM	5-10MM	10-25MM	25MM & OVER
640	497	463	**NUMBER OF STATEMENTS**	26	57	46	64	98	172
%	%	%	**ASSETS**	%	%	%	%	%	%
21.2	21.7	22.2	Cash & Equivalents	17.4	23.3	22.6	22.0	22.7	22.3
39.9	39.8	40.2	Trade Receivables (net)	36.3	28.2	29.5	39.6	45.0	45.2
3.9	3.4	3.0	Inventory	8.1	4.2	4.7	3.8	1.4	2.1
7.8	7.9	8.3	All Other Current	2.6	5.0	6.2	6.9	8.9	10.9
72.7	72.8	73.7	Total Current	64.4	60.7	62.9	72.3	78.0	80.5
16.1	16.7	15.6	Fixed Assets (net)	24.0	22.2	21.5	18.0	12.2	11.5
2.3	1.9	2.5	Intangibles (net)	2.0	2.3	4.8	1.2	2.5	2.6
8.9	8.5	8.1	All Other Non-Current	9.4	14.8	10.8	8.5	7.3	5.4
100.0	100.0	100.0	Total	100.0	100.0	100.0	100.0	100.0	100.0
			LIABILITIES						
5.8	5.8	6.4	Notes Payable-Short Term	12.3	12.6	15.9	6.8	3.6	2.4
2.5	3.5	2.0	Cur. Mat.-L.T.D.	4.3	4.0	1.9	1.4	1.4	1.5
27.9	26.6	26.9	Trade Payables	21.4	12.7	18.0	23.9	31.3	33.4
.4	.5	.3	Income Taxes Payable	.2	.4	.1	.5	.7	.2
17.0	16.7	17.5	All Other Current	30.8	14.1	11.4	14.5	15.4	20.7
53.5	53.1	53.2	Total Current	69.0	43.7	47.4	47.1	52.4	58.1
8.3	9.3	8.7	Long-Term Debt	16.6	16.8	14.0	11.5	5.4	4.2
.3	.3	.3	Deferred Taxes	.1	.3	.4	.0	.5	.3
2.6	3.2	3.8	All Other Non-Current	19.8	8.0	2.0	3.1	1.9	1.8
35.3	34.1	34.0	Net Worth	-5.5	31.1	36.2	38.3	39.7	35.6
100.0	100.0	100.0	Total Liabilties & Net Worth	100.0	100.0	100.0	100.0	100.0	100.0
			INCOME DATA						
100.0	100.0	100.0	Net Sales	100.0	100.0	100.0	100.0	100.0	100.0
18.5	19.8	19.4	Gross Profit	36.8	32.4	28.8	22.0	13.9	12.2
15.5	15.8	16.1	Operating Expenses	33.3	27.8	25.4	17.4	11.2	9.4
3.0	3.9	3.3	Operating Profit	3.4	4.6	3.4	4.6	2.7	2.8
.4	.1	.1	All Other Expenses (net)	2.8	.5	-.4	.1	-.1	-.2
2.6	3.8	3.2	Profit Before Taxes	.6	4.1	3.8	4.4	2.8	3.0
			RATIOS						
2.2	2.0	2.1		5.6	5.5	2.9	2.2	1.9	1.6
1.4	1.4	1.4	Current	1.1	1.9	1.6	1.5	1.5	1.3
1.1	1.1	1.1		.5	.8	1.0	1.2	1.2	1.2
1.8	1.7	1.8		4.5	5.0	2.9	2.0	1.7	1.4
1.2	1.2	1.2	Quick	.8	1.9	1.4	1.4	1.3	1.2
.9	.9	.9		.4	.5	.7	1.0	1.0	1.0
32 11.5	29 12.4	32 11.5		0 UND	12 29.8	13 28.5	31 11.6	35 10.4	41 9.0
52 7.0	51 7.1	54 6.8	Sales/Receivables	50 7.3	34 10.7	47 7.7	52 7.0	55 6.6	58 6.3
76 4.8	73 5.0	74 4.9		122 3.0	64 5.7	74 4.9	70 5.2	79 4.6	74 4.9
0 UND	0 UND	0 UND		0 UND	0 UND	0 UND	0 UND	0 UND	0 UND
0 UND	0 UND	0 UND	Cost of Sales/Inventory	0 UND	0 UND	0 UND	0 UND	0 UND	0 UND
1 422.1	1 429.8	0 999.8		0 UND	3 130.0	0 UND	0 999.8	0 999.8	0 738.8
18 20.2	18 20.2	15 24.1		0 UND	2 154.1	10 38.3	12 30.1	20 17.9	24 15.0
38 9.5	36 10.2	35 10.3	Cost of Sales/Payables	12 29.9	12 29.7	24 15.1	32 11.3	37 9.8	45 8.2
64 5.7	59 6.2	61 6.0		83 4.4	57 6.4	60 6.1	64 5.7	61 6.0	63 5.8
6.3	7.3	7.0		4.3	4.2	5.0	6.9	6.7	8.3
13.2	13.9	13.5	Sales/Working Capital	23.2	9.8	12.4	10.7	13.0	15.2
38.4	47.8	35.9		-4.7	-49.0	268.7	28.0	34.0	26.3
27.6	40.1	51.7		9.7	22.8	55.0	40.2	46.6	76.8
(474) 8.6	(368) 10.7	(357) 12.8	EBIT/Interest	(16) 3.5	(44) 5.5	(36) 9.0	(48) 11.7	(78) 15.1	(135) 21.8
1.6	3.2	2.8		-10.9	-.8	2.0	3.3	2.3	5.9
10.2	9.1	15.3						16.3	27.3
(104) 3.5	(69) 3.5	(82) 4.2	Net Profit + Depr., Dep., Amort./Cur. Mat. L/T/D					(25) 4.5	(38) 5.6
1.6	1.4	1.9						2.3	2.0
.1	.1	.1		.0	.0	.1	.1	.1	.1
.3	.3	.2	Fixed/Worth	.4	.3	.3	.4	.2	.2
.8	.8	.7		-1.4	1.8	1.0	.8	.5	.5
.8	.8	.8		.4	.4	.5	.8	.8	1.2
1.8	1.8	2.0	Debt/Worth	9.6	1.1	1.2	1.5	1.7	2.3
4.0	4.2	4.3		-2.7	14.0	5.0	3.9	3.3	4.1
34.0	46.5	46.4		49.0	41.9	69.8	65.5	46.5	44.7
(581) 14.2	(455) 20.1	(421) 19.8	% Profit Before Taxes/Tangible Net Worth	(16) 29.1	(44) 14.8	(41) 23.7	(60) 21.1	(94) 17.6	(166) 20.8
1.3	6.2	5.0		14.6	-.4	-.4	6.9	2.1	8.0
12.3	15.0	15.3		19.5	22.0	20.4	18.3	12.1	12.7
4.7	6.2	6.0	% Profit Before Taxes/Total Assets	2.8	7.0	7.6	7.8	5.6	5.9
.3	1.9	1.2		-22.9	-3.6	-1.7	3.5	1.0	3.0
120.5	113.0	129.6		UND	216.7	66.2	77.0	180.9	111.2
40.4	36.7	34.0	Sales/Net Fixed Assets	44.9	21.7	20.6	29.2	44.1	37.8
11.9	11.8	12.2		4.1	6.7	7.1	11.3	15.8	15.9
3.8	3.8	3.9		3.1	4.0	4.3	4.1	4.1	3.8
2.7	2.9	2.8	Sales/Total Assets	1.7	2.3	2.4	2.9	3.0	2.9
1.8	1.9	1.8		1.1	1.4	1.4	2.0	1.9	2.2
.3	.2	.2		1.1	.3	.5	.2	.2	.2
(512) .7	(399) .7	(379) .6	% Depr., Dep., Amort./Sales	(13) 2.8	(43) 1.2	(34) 1.3	(48) .8	(85) .5	(156) .5
1.6	1.6	1.6		5.8	3.5	2.8	1.8	1.2	1.2
1.2	1.4	1.5		3.0	4.3	2.7	1.7	1.1	.5
(246) 2.5	(178) 2.8	(166) 3.0	% Officers', Directors' Owners' Comp/Sales	(12) 10.0	(33) 6.1	(23) 4.1	(27) 2.3	(33) 2.0	(38) 1.1
4.9	4.9	5.7		15.8	7.9	6.1	4.6	3.0	3.2
21860309M	20295778M	23747530M	Net Sales ($)	16075M	110216M	173665M	469407M	1685854M	21292313M
9368158M	8286980M	8641176M	Total Assets ($)	10787M	71434M	88657M	198451M	722935M	7548912M

M = $ thousand MM = $ million

See Pages 9 through 22 for Explanation of Ratios and Data

Current Data Sorted by Assets							Comparative Historical Data	
						Type of Statement		
1	11	95	181	44	48	Unqualified	437	424
10	133	354	94	3		Reviewed	617	579
10	28	20	2	2	1	Compiled	86	83
56	68	60	7		1	Tax Returns	154	146
38	99	170	134	20	24	Other	390	367
276 (4/1-9/30/13)			1,438 (10/1/13-3/31/14)				4/1/09-3/31/10 ALL	4/1/10-3/31/11 ALL
0-500M	500M-2MM	2-10MM	10-50MM	50-100MM	100-250MM			
115	339	699	418	69	74	**NUMBER OF STATEMENTS**	1684	1599
%	%	%	%	%	%	**ASSETS**	%	%
30.1	22.0	22.1	23.7	23.8	22.0	Cash & Equivalents	25.9	24.7
24.1	43.1	46.2	48.4	45.7	48.7	Trade Receivables (net)	40.2	41.3
4.7	4.7	2.1	2.1	2.0	.5	Inventory	2.7	2.4
5.4	7.5	9.9	8.6	9.1	10.3	All Other Current	8.5	9.7
64.3	77.2	80.3	82.7	80.7	81.5	Total Current	77.2	78.1
21.3	13.5	10.9	10.2	10.4	10.5	Fixed Assets (net)	14.7	13.4
2.8	1.5	1.6	1.2	2.5	1.0	Intangibles (net)	1.5	1.5
11.6	7.8	7.2	5.8	6.5	7.0	All Other Non-Current	6.6	7.1
100.0	100.0	100.0	100.0	100.0	100.0	Total	100.0	100.0
						LIABILITIES		
27.3	9.0	4.3	2.8	1.3	2.5	Notes Payable-Short Term	6.2	6.5
6.9	1.8	1.3	1.0	1.0	.9	Cur. Mat.-L.T.D.	2.0	1.9
15.4	28.0	34.6	42.0	40.5	43.0	Trade Payables	29.7	30.9
.3	.3	.4	.2	.1	.1	Income Taxes Payable	.5	.4
18.6	11.8	14.7	16.7	20.5	21.2	All Other Current	15.1	15.4
68.6	50.8	55.2	62.7	63.4	67.7	Total Current	53.5	55.1
17.9	7.4	4.2	5.4	4.4	4.2	Long-Term Debt	6.9	6.5
.0	.2	.3	.1	.2	.1	Deferred Taxes	.3	.3
7.1	4.5	2.4	2.1	2.0	2.3	All Other Non-Current	2.2	2.7
6.4	37.1	37.8	29.8	30.1	25.7	Net Worth	37.0	35.3
100.0	100.0	100.0	100.0	100.0	100.0	Total Liabilties & Net Worth	100.0	100.0
						INCOME DATA		
100.0	100.0	100.0	100.0	100.0	100.0	Net Sales	100.0	100.0
31.8	19.7	14.2	9.3	8.8	7.6	Gross Profit	16.8	16.4
28.2	16.9	11.7	7.7	7.1	6.5	Operating Expenses	14.6	14.4
3.6	2.8	2.5	1.6	1.8	1.2	Operating Profit	2.2	2.0
-.1	.1	-.2	-.1	.6	.3	All Other Expenses (net)	.3	.3
3.7	2.7	2.8	1.7	1.1	.9	Profit Before Taxes	1.9	1.7
						RATIOS		
2.5	2.6	1.9	1.6	1.4	1.4		2.1	2.0
1.1	1.6	1.4	1.3	1.2	1.2	Current	1.5	1.4
.6	1.1	1.2	1.1	1.1	1.1		1.2	1.2
2.1	2.2	1.7	1.4	1.3	1.2		1.8	1.8
1.0	1.4	1.2	1.2	1.1	1.1	Quick	1.3	(1598) 1.3
.5	.9	1.0	1.0	1.0	.9		1.0	.9
0 UND	**20** 17.9	**35** 10.3	**46** 8.0	**49** 7.5	**54** 6.8		**29** 12.5	**34** 10.8
9 40.7	**43** 8.5	**55** 6.6	**60** 6.1	**64** 5.7	**65** 5.6	Sales/Receivables	**48** 7.6	**53** 6.9
31 11.9	**65** 5.6	**76** 4.8	**78** 4.7	**76** 4.8	**74** 4.9		**68** 5.4	**75** 4.9
0 UND	**0** UND	**0** UND	**0** UND	**0** UND	**0** UND		**0** UND	**0** UND
0 UND	**0** UND	**0** UND	**0** UND	**0** UND	**0** UND	Cost of Sales/Inventory	**0** UND	**0** UND
0 UND	**0** UND	**0** UND	**0** 999.8	**0** 999.8	**0** 999.8		**0** UND	**0** UND
0 UND	**14** 25.2	**27** 13.5	**39** 9.4	**46** 8.0	**47** 7.7		**21** 17.6	**24** 15.1
6 59.5	**30** 12.1	**45** 8.2	**56** 6.5	**61** 6.0	**61** 6.0	Cost of Sales/Payables	**39** 9.3	**44** 8.3
26 13.9	**51** 7.2	**64** 5.7	**74** 4.9	**72** 5.1	**76** 4.8		**59** 6.2	**67** 5.4
12.0	7.1	6.9	9.0	10.8	10.0		6.7	6.4
144.8	13.8	12.9	16.7	18.6	21.0	Sales/Working Capital	13.2	11.9
-37.3	48.5	29.2	31.9	29.6	34.2		32.2	29.7
27.4	44.7	50.1	69.2	140.8	41.2		39.6	36.0
(77) 4.3	(261) 10.2	(514) 13.8	(313) 18.5	(45) 14.7	(50) 17.1	EBIT/Interest	(1235) 7.8	(1181) 5.8
-2.0	1.6	2.9	2.6	-2.5	4.7		.5	-1.1
	9.4	12.0	14.0	105.2	16.4		12.6	13.5
	(28) 2.7	(140) 4.4	(84) 4.6	(15) 4.0	(22) 10.2	Net Profit + Depr., Dep., Amort./Cur. Mat. L/T/D	(333) 4.4	(316) 3.7
	-.7	1.2	.9	1.0	1.0		.9	.9
.0	.1	.1	.1	.1	.1		.1	.1
.4	.2	.2	.2	.2	.2	Fixed/Worth	.2	.2
-21.0	.7	.5	.4	.4	.5		.6	.6
.7	.7	.9	1.5	1.6	1.9		.8	.8
3.1	1.4	1.8	2.7	3.1	3.6	Debt/Worth	1.8	1.8
-4.9	4.2	3.7	5.2	5.0	5.7		3.8	3.8
108.7	61.9	41.0	37.1	24.9	25.2		38.3	33.2
(76) 45.5	(307) 21.3	(671) 16.0	(403) 15.3	(67) 12.9	(71) 14.4	% Profit Before Taxes/Tangible Net Worth	(1573) 14.3	(1482) 11.7
4.0	2.9	3.6	3.5	.1	6.9		1.2	.0
39.4	19.9	12.6	8.2	6.3	6.2		12.9	11.2
14.8	8.0	5.5	4.1	2.7	3.3	% Profit Before Taxes/Total Assets	4.6	3.9
-2.9	.3	1.3	1.0	.0	.9		.1	-1.0
999.8	125.3	157.6	184.9	231.6	132.1		116.5	125.1
48.2	50.2	55.7	66.0	81.4	59.1	Sales/Net Fixed Assets	44.2	43.7
18.3	18.3	20.0	23.6	19.4	25.3		15.4	15.8
10.4	4.9	4.0	3.7	3.3	3.2		4.1	3.7
4.7	3.6	3.1	3.0	2.8	2.8	Sales/Total Assets	3.0	2.8
3.0	2.4	2.1	2.2	2.2	2.2		2.1	2.0
.4	.3	.2	.1	.1	.2		.3	.3
(52) .8	(236) .6	(588) .4	(381) .3	(65) .3	(65) .3	% Depr., Dep., Amort./Sales	(1423) .6	(1308) .6
1.5	1.4	.9	.6	.7	.6		1.4	1.5
2.4	1.6	1.1	.5	.3			1.2	1.2
(62) 6.2	(156) 3.3	(296) 1.8	(108) .7	(13) .6		% Officers', Directors' Owners' Comp/Sales	(629) 2.5	(617) 2.2
9.5	5.1	3.1	1.6	1.9			4.7	4.3
211235M	1721083M	11089246M	27110638M	12836336M	31749910M	Net Sales ($)	80513771M	62800428M
29929M	425938M	3536765M	9274053M	4745857M	11412243M	Total Assets ($)	25080585M	23347521M

M = $ thousand MM = $ million

See Pages 9 through 22 for Explanation of Ratios and Data

Comparative Historical Data / Current Data Sorted by Sales

4/1/11-3/31/12 ALL	4/1/12-3/31/13 ALL	4/1/13-3/31/14 ALL	Type of Statement	0-1MM	1-3MM	3-5MM	5-10MM	10-25MM	25MM & OVER
431	355	380	Unqualified		3	6	19	64	288
580	582	594	Reviewed	6	40	67	131	222	128
80	70	63	Compiled	5	16	14	14	8	6
185	211	192	Tax Returns	35	32	39	43	35	8
392	443	485	Other	18	55	35	82	99	196
				276 (4/1-9/30/13)			1,438 (10/1/13-3/31/14)		
1668	1661	1714	NUMBER OF STATEMENTS	64	146	161	289	428	626
%	%	%	**ASSETS**	%	%	%	%	%	%
24.3	22.9	23.1	Cash & Equivalents	25.3	24.0	22.3	21.3	23.0	23.7
42.9	43.4	44.7	Trade Receivables (net)	16.2	30.2	38.2	44.5	47.2	51.1
2.1	2.7	2.7	Inventory	9.8	6.7	4.1	2.4	1.8	1.5
8.9	8.9	8.8	All Other Current	4.6	8.1	7.0	9.8	9.1	9.1
78.3	77.8	79.3	Total Current	55.8	69.0	71.5	78.0	81.0	85.4
12.9	13.0	11.9	Fixed Assets (net)	29.2	17.7	15.8	12.7	11.1	8.0
2.2	1.8	1.6	Intangibles (net)	2.8	2.1	2.7	1.4	1.5	1.2
6.6	7.4	7.2	All Other Non-Current	12.2	11.3	10.0	7.9	6.4	5.4
100.0	100.0	100.0	Total	100.0	100.0	100.0	100.0	100.0	100.0
			LIABILITIES						
5.8	6.3	6.2	Notes Payable-Short Term	16.7	14.6	11.6	7.5	4.5	2.3
2.0	2.0	1.7	Cur. Mat.-L.T.D.	5.5	4.2	1.8	1.8	1.4	.9
33.2	32.1	34.4	Trade Payables	10.3	20.4	22.4	28.4	36.2	44.8
.4	.3	.3	Income Taxes Payable	.1	.6	.5	.4	.2	.1
15.1	15.6	15.4	All Other Current	21.3	14.0	12.2	12.6	14.6	17.8
56.5	56.3	57.9	Total Current	53.9	53.8	48.5	50.6	56.9	65.8
6.5	6.7	6.1	Long-Term Debt	25.1	9.7	9.8	5.3	4.7	3.6
.3	.2	.2	Deferred Taxes	.0	.2	.3	.3	.3	.1
2.6	2.6	3.1	All Other Non-Current	12.4	3.4	5.1	3.3	2.5	1.8
34.2	34.2	32.7	Net Worth	8.5	32.9	36.3	40.5	35.6	28.7
100.0	100.0	100.0	Total Liabilties & Net Worth	100.0	100.0	100.0	100.0	100.0	100.0
			INCOME DATA						
100.0	100.0	100.0	Net Sales	100.0	100.0	100.0	100.0	100.0	100.0
15.3	15.6	14.8	Gross Profit	33.6	25.7	22.3	17.1	13.4	8.3
13.2	13.4	12.4	Operating Expenses	29.7	22.4	19.7	14.6	10.7	6.7
2.2	2.2	2.3	Operating Profit	3.9	3.3	2.6	2.5	2.6	1.6
.1	.1	-.1	All Other Expenses (net)	.0	.3	-.1	.0	-.1	-.1
2.0	2.1	2.4	Profit Before Taxes	3.8	3.0	2.7	2.5	2.8	1.8
			RATIOS						
1.9	1.9	1.8		3.5	3.0	2.9	2.1	1.9	1.5
1.4	1.4	1.4	Current	1.1	1.4	1.7	1.6	1.4	1.3
1.2	1.1	1.1		.7	.9	1.1	1.2	1.2	1.1
1.7	1.7	1.6		2.0	2.2	2.6	1.9	1.7	1.3
1.2	1.2	1.2	Quick	.9	1.1	1.4	1.4	1.3	1.1
1.0	.9	1.0		.3	.6	1.0	1.0	1.0	1.0
34 10.8	33 11.2	33 11.0		0 UND	9 42.2	17 21.4	27 13.4	35 10.3	43 8.4
54 6.7	52 7.0	54 6.8	Sales/Receivables	6 57.9	41 8.8	49 7.5	51 7.1	54 6.8	58 6.3
74 4.9	72 5.1	74 4.9		51 7.1	78 4.7	73 5.0	74 4.9	76 4.8	73 5.0
0 UND	0 UND	0 UND		0 UND	0 UND	0 UND	0 UND	0 UND	0 UND
0 UND	0 UND	0 UND	Cost of Sales/Inventory	0 UND	0 UND	0 UND	0 UND	0 UND	0 UND
0 UND	0 UND	0 UND		18 20.4	0 UND	0 UND	0 UND	0 UND	0 UND
25 14.4	23 15.7	24 15.0		0 UND	9 42.1	11 32.8	19 19.6	28 13.1	38 9.5
45 8.1	43 8.5	46 8.0	Cost of Sales/Payables	5 67.6	33 11.1	29 12.7	35 10.4	45 8.2	55 6.6
68 5.4	63 5.8	68 5.4		51 7.1	62 5.9	57 6.4	55 6.6	66 5.5	72 5.1
7.0	7.3	7.9		4.0	4.3	5.7	6.8	7.5	11.0
13.5	14.2	15.0	Sales/Working Capital	180.5	13.6	10.7	11.7	13.7	18.9
32.6	39.0	37.4		-9.0	-63.5	38.8	30.3	37.1	33.1
39.0	48.4	52.5		6.9	30.6	37.7	41.0	56.6	83.2
(1226) 8.4	(1215) 9.0	(1260) 13.3	EBIT/Interest	(39) 1.4	(103) 6.0	(126) 7.1	(220) 10.4	(320) 16.8	(452) 19.8
1.6	1.6	2.3		-5.0	.2	1.6	1.2	3.0	3.8
15.9	13.1	13.2				3.8	10.1	16.6	16.6
(320) 4.1	(283) 3.9	(292) 4.1	Net Profit + Depr., Dep., Amort./Cur. Mat. L/T/D			(13) 1.8	(59) 4.1	(89) 3.7	(123) 5.4
.7	1.0	1.0				-3.2	.0	1.0	2.1
.1	.1	.1		.0	.1	.1	.1	.1	.1
.2	.2	.2	Fixed/Worth	.7	.3	.3	.2	.2	.2
.6	.6	.5		NM	1.0	.9	.5	.5	.4
.9	.9	1.0		.5	.5	.6	.8	1.0	1.6
2.0	2.0	2.1	Debt/Worth	3.5	1.4	1.3	1.4	1.9	2.9
4.5	4.2	4.8		-6.4	6.0	5.2	3.6	3.8	5.1
34.0	39.1	43.0		49.5	58.4	54.2	49.4	46.1	36.3
(1530) 12.6	(1524) 14.4	(1595) 16.8	% Profit Before Taxes/Tangible Net Worth	(42) 7.5	(125) 18.1	(141) 18.3	(274) 15.8	(406) 18.7	(607) 16.5
1.9	2.6	3.4		-4.9	-1.6	2.4	1.0	4.2	5.1
11.3	12.5	12.8		19.9	20.4	17.5	16.2	14.1	8.6
4.1	4.5	5.2	% Profit Before Taxes/Total Assets	2.6	6.4	6.6	6.7	6.0	4.2
.5	.4	.9		-8.8	-1.4	.8	.5	1.3	1.2
142.7	149.2	167.8		191.3	93.6	93.0	114.2	173.7	204.7
50.4	51.9	57.4	Sales/Net Fixed Assets	18.3	35.2	34.7	46.9	57.8	81.2
17.2	18.3	20.1		3.6	11.4	13.1	17.7	21.7	31.0
3.8	4.0	4.2		4.1	4.2	4.3	4.4	4.3	4.0
2.9	3.1	3.1	Sales/Total Assets	1.8	2.5	2.9	3.1	3.2	3.2
2.1	2.2	2.2		.9	1.5	1.9	2.2	2.3	2.6
.2	.2	.2		.6	.4	.3	.3	.2	.1
(1375) .5	(1348) .4	(1387) .4	% Depr., Dep., Amort./Sales	(30) 2.0	(85) 1.0	(124) .7	(222) .5	(366) .4	(560) .2
1.2	1.1	.9		4.1	1.8	1.8	1.2	.8	.5
1.1	1.1	1.0		2.7	2.4	2.1	1.5	1.0	.5
(660) 2.1	(651) 2.3	(643) 1.9	% Officers', Directors' Owners' Comp/Sales	(28) 8.7	(70) 4.1	(80) 3.4	(134) 2.4	(181) 1.7	(150) .7
4.0	4.4	3.9		12.3	6.8	5.4	4.2	2.8	1.6
75386553M	69683866M	84718448M	Net Sales ($)	35101M	289974M	627693M	2129121M	6810670M	74825889M
27258117M	24791682M	29424785M	Total Assets ($)	36339M	222415M	275425M	881397M	2685542M	25323667M

M = $ thousand MM = $ million

See Pages 9 through 22 for Explanation of Ratios and Data

Current Data Sorted by Assets / Comparative Historical Data

0-500M	500M-2MM	2-10MM	10-50MM	50-100MM	100-250MM		4/1/09-3/31/10 ALL	4/1/10-3/31/11 ALL
						Type of Statement		
1	3	26	35	7	9	Unqualified	119	112
1	18	93	22		2	Reviewed	162	141
1	11	6		2		Compiled	22	21
9	14	8				Tax Returns	42	42
4	21	45	35	11	3	Other	133	114
	74 (4/1-9/30/13)		313 (10/1/13-3/31/14)					
16	67	178	92	20	14	**NUMBER OF STATEMENTS**	478	430
%	%	%	%	%	%	**ASSETS**	%	%
27.3	17.7	17.9	17.5	14.9	15.9	Cash & Equivalents	17.1	16.2
20.5	30.2	36.3	35.6	26.3	29.8	Trade Receivables (net)	31.2	32.5
3.6	4.5	3.1	3.0	3.2	2.8	Inventory	3.9	3.5
4.8	4.7	8.9	9.0	12.7	14.5	All Other Current	7.3	8.3
56.2	57.1	66.2	65.1	57.0	62.9	Total Current	59.6	60.5
29.5	36.9	27.6	26.0	33.1	28.9	Fixed Assets (net)	31.0	30.2
.5	1.2	.8	3.3	5.8	4.6	Intangibles (net)	1.9	2.0
13.9	4.8	5.4	5.6	4.0	3.6	All Other Non-Current	7.6	7.2
100.0	100.0	100.0	100.0	100.0	100.0	Total	100.0	100.0
						LIABILITIES		
12.5	4.9	5.3	4.0	3.9	3.8	Notes Payable-Short Term	5.7	7.0
6.7	5.0	4.1	3.9	2.4	4.8	Cur. Mat.-L.T.D.	5.8	4.7
19.1	13.1	17.8	18.7	13.5	15.0	Trade Payables	15.9	18.2
.4	.3	.6	.4	.1	.0	Income Taxes Payable	.6	.5
37.3	7.3	9.1	11.8	15.5	15.7	All Other Current	9.8	8.6
76.0	30.5	36.8	38.8	35.3	39.3	Total Current	37.7	39.0
51.0	20.4	10.4	9.8	16.9	17.3	Long-Term Debt	15.9	14.3
.0	.2	1.0	.7	1.2	.6	Deferred Taxes	.9	.9
6.1	4.0	1.8	3.1	2.3	2.1	All Other Non-Current	2.8	3.9
-32.4	44.9	49.9	47.6	44.4	40.6	Net Worth	42.8	41.9
100.0	100.0	100.0	100.0	100.0	100.0	Total Liabilties & Net Worth	100.0	100.0
						INCOME DATA		
100.0	100.0	100.0	100.0	100.0	100.0	Net Sales	100.0	100.0
53.1	38.6	21.4	17.8	24.3	15.1	Gross Profit	24.3	22.3
47.9	33.1	16.1	13.5	16.1	9.5	Operating Expenses	21.6	19.7
5.2	5.5	5.4	4.4	8.2	5.6	Operating Profit	2.8	2.7
.1	.6	.1	.2	.1	-.7	All Other Expenses (net)	.2	.1
5.2	4.9	5.2	4.2	8.1	6.3	Profit Before Taxes	2.6	2.5
						RATIOS		
7.0	4.8	2.7	2.4	2.3	2.0		2.5	2.6
1.9	2.3	1.7	1.6	1.6	1.7	Current	1.6	1.7
.3	1.0	1.4	1.3	1.3	1.3		1.1	1.2
6.8	4.3	2.3	2.1	1.7	1.5		2.1	2.1
1.8	1.6	1.5	1.4	1.1	1.2	Quick	1.3	1.3
.2	.7	1.1	1.0	.9	.9		.8	.8
0 UND	26 14.0	43 8.4	52 7.0	34 10.6	41 8.9		35 10.5	36 10.1
12 31.0	39 9.4	61 6.0	70 5.2	42 8.6	62 5.9	Sales/Receivables	55 6.7	56 6.5
44 8.3	63 5.8	81 4.5	87 4.2	66 5.5	76 4.8		74 4.9	76 4.8
0 UND	0 UND	0 UND	0 UND	0 UND	0 UND		0 UND	0 UND
0 UND	0 UND	0 UND	0 UND	1 710.0	0 UND	Cost of Sales/Inventory	0 UND	0 UND
0 UND	11 33.6	7 51.8	6 58.7	23 16.1	14 25.9		6 59.6	5 66.5
0 UND	9 38.7	20 18.4	23 16.1	20 18.7	21 17.7		16 22.8	19 19.3
2 227.0	26 13.8	34 10.8	42 8.7	34 10.8	41 8.9	Cost of Sales/Payables	31 11.8	35 10.4
48 7.6	47 7.7	49 7.4	56 6.5	54 6.8	47 7.8		51 7.2	54 6.7
9.0	4.5	4.5	4.2	5.0	4.4		5.6	5.1
17.1	8.2	8.2	7.6	9.5	8.1	Sales/Working Capital	10.0	9.0
-18.9	UND	13.9	19.3	17.0	11.2		37.6	36.3
17.8	30.0	35.4	45.5	30.7	82.4		18.3	21.5
(14) 10.2	(59) 6.0	(155) 8.5	(83) 10.5	(17) 4.8	6.8	EBIT/Interest	(428) 4.4	(377) 4.3
.9	-.2	1.8	2.3	2.0	2.6		.4	-.2
		8.3	4.4	12.4			6.7	7.2
		(62) 3.1	(31) 2.5	(10) 4.7		Net Profit + Depr., Dep., Amort./Cur. Mat. L/T/D	(137) 2.2	(118) 2.5
		1.5	1.8	2.1			1.2	1.1
.3	.2	.3	.3	.4	.4		.3	.3
.8	.7	.5	.5	.8	.7	Fixed/Worth	.7	.6
NM	3.3	.9	1.1	1.4	1.7		1.4	1.4
.4	.3	.6	.6	.7	.9		.6	.6
1.4	1.0	1.0	1.1	1.7	1.6	Debt/Worth	1.2	1.2
NM	4.4	1.8	2.1	2.9	2.8		2.7	2.7
113.2	56.5	38.1	41.5	41.4	37.9		30.7	30.5
(12) 51.7	(59) 18.3	(172) 15.3	(88) 15.4	17.5	(12) 25.2	% Profit Before Taxes/Tangible Net Worth	(441) 11.8	(396) 9.5
21.1	2.3	2.4	1.8	4.0	7.5		.1	-2.0
63.7	23.3	16.6	16.8	11.9	16.1		13.8	13.3
24.7	9.1	7.6	7.1	4.2	5.7	% Profit Before Taxes/Total Assets	4.7	4.0
2.5	-.7	.9	1.3	1.8	2.7		-.6	-1.9
41.5	21.4	14.7	13.6	14.0	15.8		17.0	17.9
15.3	9.0	8.2	8.2	6.0	8.2	Sales/Net Fixed Assets	7.9	8.0
11.3	3.3	5.3	4.2	4.3	2.3		4.2	4.4
7.6	3.5	2.7	2.3	2.2	2.5		2.8	2.8
4.7	2.4	2.1	1.9	1.7	1.5	Sales/Total Assets	2.0	2.1
3.1	1.7	1.5	1.3	1.5	1.1		1.5	1.5
.4	1.9	1.4	1.3	1.8	1.4		1.8	1.6
(10) 2.9	(54) 3.6	(164) 2.8	(90) 2.8	3.4	(11) 2.7	% Depr., Dep., Amort./Sales	(414) 3.6	(385) 3.3
4.5	6.9	4.3	4.2	4.4	3.7		5.9	5.7
	3.8	1.3	.6				1.4	1.8
	(34) 5.7	(73) 2.5	(22) 1.2			% Officers', Directors' Owners' Comp/Sales	(212) 2.9	(174) 3.1
	9.3	5.0	2.3				6.1	6.1
15991M	213863M	1948506M	3711665M	2378282M	3787139M	Net Sales ($)	11964460M	11305837M
3620M	81833M	911025M	1934002M	1267674M	2200958M	Total Assets ($)	6530784M	6412005M

M = $ thousand MM = $ million

See Pages 9 through 22 for Explanation of Ratios and Data

Comparative Historical Data				Current Data Sorted by Sales					
			Type of Statement						
89	90	81	Unqualified	1	1	4	11	21	43
133	120	136	Reviewed	2	9	21	44	41	19
30	17	20	Compiled	3	7	2	5	2	1
42	32	31	Tax Returns	7	12	3	5	4	
107	128	119	Other	8	10	12	16	34	39
					74 (4/1-9/30/13)		313 (10/1/13-3/31/14)		
4/1/11-3/31/12 ALL	4/1/12-3/31/13 ALL	4/1/13-3/31/14 ALL		0-1MM	1-3MM	3-5MM	5-10MM	10-25MM	25MM & OVER
401	387	387	**NUMBER OF STATEMENTS**	21	39	42	81	102	102
%	%	%	**ASSETS**	%	%	%	%	%	%
15.1	15.7	17.9	Cash & Equivalents	17.6	22.4	17.4	18.5	18.6	15.3
34.4	36.7	33.7	Trade Receivables (net)	17.4	25.5	33.4	32.9	37.7	36.9
3.3	3.6	3.3	Inventory	2.8	4.8	5.2	2.8	3.1	2.7
8.2	7.7	8.4	All Other Current	5.6	3.9	6.5	8.5	9.3	10.5
60.8	63.8	63.3	Total Current	43.4	56.6	62.5	62.7	68.8	65.4
29.7	26.8	29.2	Fixed Assets (net)	47.3	33.9	31.2	28.9	26.0	26.5
2.6	2.6	1.9	Intangibles (net)	1.5	1.3	.2	2.3	.9	3.5
6.9	6.8	5.6	All Other Non-Current	7.9	8.2	6.2	6.0	4.4	4.6
100.0	100.0	100.0	Total	100.0	100.0	100.0	100.0	100.0	100.0
			LIABILITIES						
7.7	5.8	5.1	Notes Payable-Short Term	9.3	6.7	6.4	5.8	3.7	3.9
4.6	3.9	4.2	Cur. Mat.-L.T.D.	8.1	5.2	3.4	4.3	3.8	3.9
17.8	18.6	16.9	Trade Payables	14.4	11.0	15.6	14.9	19.4	19.5
.4	.4	.4	Income Taxes Payable	.3	.3	.6	.6	.4	.2
9.9	9.7	11.1	All Other Current	29.3	4.0	6.8	8.1	10.8	14.7
40.3	38.5	37.8	Total Current	61.4	27.3	32.7	33.8	38.1	42.1
12.4	12.2	14.3	Long-Term Debt	31.0	29.5	13.5	11.4	10.9	11.0
.8	.7	.8	Deferred Taxes	.2	.1	1.4	.9	.6	.9
4.4	4.9	2.7	All Other Non-Current	4.1	2.4	6.4	2.6	1.5	2.4
42.2	43.7	44.4	Net Worth	3.8	40.8	46.0	51.3	49.0	43.6
100.0	100.0	100.0	Total Liabilties & Net Worth	100.0	100.0	100.0	100.0	100.0	100.0
			INCOME DATA						
100.0	100.0	100.0	Net Sales	100.0	100.0	100.0	100.0	100.0	100.0
23.1	22.5	24.8	Gross Profit	54.4	40.0	29.1	24.5	19.6	16.4
20.6	17.9	19.5	Operating Expenses	43.1	36.6	22.5	19.8	14.9	11.1
2.5	4.7	5.3	Operating Profit	11.3	3.4	6.6	4.7	4.7	5.3
.2	.2	.2	All Other Expenses (net)	2.5	-.1	.0	.2	.1	.0
2.3	4.4	5.1	Profit Before Taxes	8.8	3.5	6.6	4.5	4.6	5.3
			RATIOS						
2.6	2.5	2.8		3.5	7.6	4.1	2.9	2.8	2.0
1.6	1.6	1.7	Current	1.2	2.8	2.2	1.8	1.7	1.6
1.1	1.2	1.3		.6	1.0	1.4	1.4	1.4	1.3
2.2	2.2	2.4		2.9	7.6	3.5	2.4	2.4	1.6
(400) 1.3	1.4	1.5	Quick	1.2	2.1	1.8	1.6	1.4	1.2
.9	1.0	1.0		.4	.7	1.0	.9	1.1	.9
36 10.0	42 8.7	38 9.5		0 UND	20 18.7	38 9.6	40 9.2	43 8.4	47 7.8
62 5.9	60 6.1	57 6.4	Sales/Receivables	16 23.2	38 9.6	61 6.0	56 6.5	62 5.9	62 5.9
83 4.4	81 4.5	79 4.6		42 8.6	64 5.7	96 3.8	78 4.7	83 4.4	79 4.6
0 UND	0 UND	0 UND		0 UND	0 UND	0 UND	0 UND	0 UND	0 UND
0 UND	0 UND	0 UND	Cost of Sales/Inventory	0 UND	0 UND	0 UND	0 UND	0 UND	0 UND
6 59.1	7 55.3	8 47.6		0 UND	11 33.6	11 33.2	9 40.3	6 64.7	6 64.2
19 19.2	20 18.1	18 19.8		0 UND	4 85.6	18 19.9	18 19.8	20 18.0	21 17.0
35 10.3	34 10.6	34 10.6	Cost of Sales/Payables	9 39.9	26 14.1	33 11.1	30 12.1	36 10.2	40 9.2
54 6.8	53 6.9	51 7.1		40 9.2	51 7.1	59 6.2	47 7.7	51 7.2	54 6.8
5.1	4.9	4.5		3.6	4.2	3.2	4.3	4.6	5.5
9.7	8.9	8.2	Sales/Working Capital	22.3	8.0	6.2	8.7	7.8	9.6
41.0	21.6	17.9		-12.4	UND	15.0	14.3	14.9	20.3
14.4	22.8	35.0		12.6	14.3	34.9	31.2	46.4	46.4
(354) 3.9	(344) 7.7	(342) 8.1	EBIT/Interest	(18) 2.5	(34) 4.2	(39) 9.2	(74) 10.1	(83) 10.3	(94) 8.1
.5	2.0	1.6		-2.4	-1.7	1.8	1.6	2.3	2.7
5.9	5.2	6.7				11.1	8.3	4.4	4.8
(105) 2.1	(98) 2.6	(116) 3.1	Net Profit + Depr., Dep., Amort./Cur. Mat. L/T/D			(14) 7.2	(24) 4.4	(32) 2.3	(40) 2.7
1.0	1.1	1.8				1.8	1.6	1.3	2.1
.3	.3	.3		.4	.2	.3	.3	.2	.3
.6	.6	.6	Fixed/Worth	.9	.7	.7	.6	.5	.6
1.2	1.1	1.1		4.1	5.5	1.0	1.1	.9	1.2
.5	.6	.5		.4	.2	.7	.4	.5	.8
1.3	1.2	1.0	Debt/Worth	.9	.9	1.0	.9	1.1	1.3
2.7	2.7	2.3		6.3	7.2	2.2	1.6	2.1	2.5
25.6	38.5	41.8		65.5	30.8	56.5	40.3	45.3	41.7
(360) 10.6	(359) 16.1	(363) 16.5	% Profit Before Taxes/Tangible Net Worth	(18) 19.7	(32) 13.5	(39) 15.5	(77) 15.5	(100) 18.7	(97) 17.7
.1	4.0	2.6		-7.5	-2.7	2.5	2.3	3.0	4.5
10.9	14.3	17.6		31.6	21.5	19.4	16.5	18.1	16.9
3.7	6.3	7.5	% Profit Before Taxes/Total Assets	7.6	5.0	8.8	8.2	7.5	5.7
-1.0	1.3	1.1		-13.5	-4.0	1.1	.7	1.7	2.3
17.2	19.2	15.5		15.3	22.5	10.1	13.6	25.4	16.4
8.1	9.3	8.2	Sales/Net Fixed Assets	5.0	11.1	6.7	6.9	9.3	8.8
4.3	4.9	4.6		1.7	3.7	3.4	4.2	5.7	5.4
2.6	2.8	2.7		5.6	3.3	2.4	2.6	2.8	2.6
2.0	2.2	2.1	Sales/Total Assets	1.5	2.3	1.7	1.9	2.3	2.1
1.6	1.6	1.5		.6	1.6	1.3	1.5	1.8	1.6
1.8	1.5	1.4		2.6	1.9	1.7	1.9	1.2	1.2
(357) 3.3	(340) 2.9	(349) 2.9	% Depr., Dep., Amort./Sales	(16) 6.1	(31) 4.0	(36) 3.6	(74) 3.4	(94) 2.6	(98) 2.4
5.4	4.7	4.5		12.2	6.4	6.4	5.3	3.8	3.6
1.3	1.3	1.4		3.9	4.4	2.2	1.8	.8	.5
(161) 3.1	(136) 2.6	(143) 3.2	% Officers', Directors' Owners' Comp/Sales	(11) 11.5	(23) 5.9	(20) 4.2	(33) 3.6	(36) 2.2	(20) .9
5.8	5.7	5.9		13.7	7.6	6.8	7.2	4.5	1.7
10751859M	12445847M	12055446M	Net Sales ($)	14465M	81950M	166033M	602092M	1647412M	9543494M
5709108M	5977739M	6399112M	Total Assets ($)	20585M	38057M	102847M	364298M	846483M	5026842M

M = $ thousand MM = $ million

See Pages 9 through 22 for Explanation of Ratios and Data

Current Data Sorted by Assets							Comparative Historical Data	
		1	14	7	3	**Type of Statement** Unqualified	25	18
	3	12	5			Reviewed	14	13
1	2	3				Compiled	12	10
2	4	2	1			Tax Returns	4	8
	1	22	22	8	8	Other	39	38
	24 (4/1-9/30/13)		97 (10/1/13-3/31/14)				**4/1/09-3/31/10**	**4/1/10-3/31/11**
0-500M	**500M-2MM**	**2-10MM**	**10-50MM**	**50-100MM**	**100-250MM**		**ALL**	**ALL**
3	10	40	42	15	11	**NUMBER OF STATEMENTS**	94	87
%	%	%	%	%	%	**ASSETS**	%	%
	13.7	14.7	12.7	13.5	9.6	Cash & Equivalents	15.0	14.6
	42.0	31.6	32.4	25.2	22.7	Trade Receivables (net)	24.5	28.3
	10.5	4.6	6.8	5.0	9.2	Inventory	4.5	3.4
	4.0	6.6	7.8	6.9	14.8	All Other Current	5.9	4.5
	70.2	57.5	59.7	50.6	56.4	Total Current	49.9	50.8
	15.3	33.8	33.6	33.9	24.8	Fixed Assets (net)	35.9	36.8
	8.0	4.5	3.0	11.1	17.3	Intangibles (net)	7.3	7.6
	6.6	4.3	3.7	4.4	1.5	All Other Non-Current	6.8	4.8
	100.0	100.0	100.0	100.0	100.0	Total	100.0	100.0
						LIABILITIES		
	5.8	5.3	8.0	2.8	5.2	Notes Payable-Short Term	6.0	8.2
	7.4	5.6	3.3	2.9	5.9	Cur. Mat.-L.T.D.	4.3	5.4
	17.7	14.2	12.7	11.4	12.0	Trade Payables	11.8	10.3
	.5	.2	.3	.3	.5	Income Taxes Payable	.8	.4
	5.2	13.6	9.8	8.8	12.2	All Other Current	10.1	8.9
	36.5	39.0	34.1	26.1	35.8	Total Current	33.1	33.1
	17.2	16.4	14.6	10.7	19.2	Long-Term Debt	19.4	14.7
	.0	.8	1.0	4.2	1.0	Deferred Taxes	2.0	2.4
	1.2	5.8	2.2	1.0	1.7	All Other Non-Current	3.4	3.5
	45.1	38.0	48.2	58.0	42.3	Net Worth	42.1	46.2
	100.0	100.0	100.0	100.0	100.0	Total Liabilities & Net Worth	100.0	100.0
						INCOME DATA		
	100.0	100.0	100.0	100.0	100.0	Net Sales	100.0	100.0
						Gross Profit		
	92.1	93.2	91.8	90.3	90.9	Operating Expenses	93.5	88.9
	7.9	6.8	8.2	9.7	9.1	Operating Profit	6.5	11.1
	-1.4	.8	1.4	-.4	2.1	All Other Expenses (net)	2.9	2.5
	9.4	6.1	6.7	10.0	6.9	Profit Before Taxes	3.6	8.5
						RATIOS		
	7.3	2.3	3.1	2.9	2.2		2.5	2.8
	1.6	1.6	1.7	1.7	1.7	Current	1.5	1.5
	1.0	1.0	1.3	1.1	1.3		1.0	1.0
	4.3	2.1	2.2	2.2	1.5		2.1	2.4
	1.3	1.3	1.3	1.0	.9	Quick	1.1	1.3
	.8	.7	.8	.9	.4		.7	.8
	26 14.3	**20** 18.7	**42** 8.6	**37** 9.8	**31** 11.8		**28** 13.2	**34** 10.6
	42 8.7	**41** 8.9	**57** 6.4	**51** 7.1	**63** 5.8	Sales/Receivables	**42** 8.6	**55** 6.7
	94 3.9	**64** 5.7	**81** 4.5	**73** 5.0	**81** 4.5		**57** 6.4	**76** 4.8
						Cost of Sales/Inventory		
						Cost of Sales/Payables		
	4.9	8.1	5.2	3.7	4.7		5.4	4.8
	15.8	14.6	8.9	8.5	7.2	Sales/Working Capital	13.1	12.3
	NM	83.9	18.1	108.6	10.4		NM	-160.0
		46.1	59.0	78.3	677.9		22.5	26.9
		(35) 19.3	(34) 16.0	(14) 29.7	7.0	EBIT/Interest	(86) 5.5	(76) 9.0
		2.3	5.1	5.7	3.1		.6	2.0
			13.4				9.1	7.9
			(11) 4.2			Net Profit + Depr., Dep., Amort./Cur. Mat. L/T/D	(29) 2.8	(21) 2.2
			3.3				1.1	.6
	.0	.3	.4	.3	.2		.4	.5
	.2	.8	.7	.8	1.2	Fixed/Worth	1.0	1.1
	18.3	1.8	1.1	1.2	3.1		2.7	1.9
	.3	.7	.5	.3	1.7		.6	.5
	2.7	1.4	1.1	1.1	2.6	Debt/Worth	1.9	1.3
	41.2	3.5	2.1	2.1	3.8		4.5	4.0
		74.1	56.1	66.9	56.0		44.7	65.5
		(34) 52.9	(41) 22.5	29.6	29.0	% Profit Before Taxes/Tangible Net Worth	(81) 15.7	(75) 25.6
		15.6	9.0	21.2	17.8		.2	7.5
	49.1	31.9	19.8	21.7	19.2		18.9	19.5
	11.8	17.2	12.3	16.0	7.9	% Profit Before Taxes/Total Assets	5.5	9.7
	1.1	2.6	3.5	9.3	4.2		-1.3	3.8
	548.9	27.3	16.2	19.3	18.9		13.5	13.2
	25.1	8.3	7.3	4.8	6.0	Sales/Net Fixed Assets	6.6	5.9
	9.6	4.2	3.6	2.1	1.3		3.0	3.4
	4.3	3.7	2.7	1.9	2.0		3.1	2.5
	2.9	2.5	2.0	1.6	1.3	Sales/Total Assets	1.7	1.7
	2.2	1.8	1.3	.6	.9		1.1	1.2
		.9	1.1	.5			1.1	2.2
		(28) 2.1	(37) 2.1	(13) 3.0		% Depr., Dep., Amort./Sales	(78) 3.5	(67) 4.2
		4.3	4.3	5.9			6.1	7.4
							.7	1.3
						% Officers', Directors' Owners' Comp/Sales	(23) 1.9	(17) 2.1
							10.8	5.6
2922M	**42432M**	**500046M**	**2502206M**	**1897471M**	**2390453M**	Net Sales ($)	**6162375M**	**5009040M**
776M	**12875M**	**182789M**	**1171657M**	**1126848M**	**1826038M**	Total Assets ($)	**4165268M**	**3125865M**

M = $ thousand MM = $ million

See Pages 9 through 22 for Explanation of Ratios and Data

Comparative Historical Data / Current Data Sorted by Sales

4/1/11-3/31/12 ALL	4/1/12-3/31/13 ALL	4/1/13-3/31/14 ALL		0-1MM	1-3MM	3-5MM	5-10MM	10-25MM	25MM & OVER
			Type of Statement						
25	21	25	Unqualified				1		24
16	19	20	Reviewed		1	1	3	10	5
15	13	6	Compiled		3		1	2	
8	9	9	Tax Returns	1	3	2	1	1	1
48	56	61	Other		2	2	9	19	29
				24 (4/1-9/30/13)			97 (10/1/13-3/31/14)		
112	118	121	**NUMBER OF STATEMENTS**	1	9	5	15	32	59
%	%	%	**ASSETS**	%	%	%	%	%	%
13.7	14.2	13.4	Cash & Equivalents				18.8	12.0	13.2
30.2	31.7	31.3	Trade Receivables (net)				23.3	34.7	31.6
4.9	4.5	6.2	Inventory				3.3	5.8	6.9
4.1	4.8	7.5	All Other Current				6.0	8.4	8.7
53.1	55.2	58.3	Total Current				51.3	60.8	60.4
33.4	35.7	31.2	Fixed Assets (net)				37.0	33.0	28.0
7.3	5.5	6.1	Intangibles (net)				6.2	2.7	7.9
6.3	3.5	4.4	All Other Non-Current				5.5	3.4	3.7
100.0	100.0	100.0	Total				100.0	100.0	100.0
			LIABILITIES						
5.3	5.9	6.8	Notes Payable-Short Term				5.2	4.7	6.7
5.4	4.2	4.6	Cur. Mat.-L.T.D.				6.1	5.5	3.2
12.8	10.8	13.2	Trade Payables				10.8	14.8	13.4
.2	.3	.3	Income Taxes Payable				.1	.4	.3
9.9	8.5	10.9	All Other Current				6.7	13.5	11.0
33.7	29.7	35.8	Total Current				28.8	38.9	34.7
17.0	17.8	15.3	Long-Term Debt				20.7	17.5	10.8
1.5	1.7	1.2	Deferred Taxes				.0	1.7	1.6
2.9	4.5	3.3	All Other Non-Current				9.5	2.6	1.8
44.8	46.4	44.4	Net Worth				41.0	39.3	51.1
100.0	100.0	100.0	Total Liabilties & Net Worth				100.0	100.0	100.0
			INCOME DATA						
100.0	100.0	100.0	Net Sales				100.0	100.0	100.0
			Gross Profit						
91.7	91.5	92.1	Operating Expenses				93.7	91.9	92.0
8.3	8.5	7.9	Operating Profit				6.3	8.1	8.0
1.0	.8	.8	All Other Expenses (net)				.4	1.4	.1
7.2	7.6	7.1	Profit Before Taxes				5.8	6.7	7.8
			RATIOS						
2.5	3.0	2.5					4.4	2.5	2.3
1.6	1.9	1.7	Current				1.8	1.7	1.7
1.1	1.3	1.2					1.0	1.3	1.3
2.1	2.5	2.1					4.4	1.7	1.9
1.3	1.6	1.3	Quick				1.3	1.3	1.3
.8	1.0	.8					.6	.7	.9
33 11.0	**35** 10.5	**33** 11.1					**15** 24.9	**34** 10.8	**37** 9.8
51 7.1	**52** 7.0	**49** 7.4	Sales/Receivables				**49** 7.4	**49** 7.5	**55** 6.6
74 4.9	**79** 4.6	**76** 4.8					**60** 6.1	**78** 4.7	**79** 4.6
			Cost of Sales/Inventory						
			Cost of Sales/Payables						
6.1	4.8	5.3					5.2	5.7	5.0
10.2	9.4	10.3	Sales/Working Capital				11.7	12.4	8.6
72.9	19.1	36.6					89.6	38.0	13.7
35.9	33.6	47.6					162.5	24.3	69.0
(101) 8.7	(109) 10.7	(105) 16.1	EBIT/Interest				(13) 31.7	(27) 12.2	(53) 17.6
2.0	3.1	3.3					-.3	2.4	5.7
9.3	9.1	23.0							22.3
(26) 4.0	(23) 4.7	(27) 4.9	Net Profit + Depr., Dep., Amort./Cur. Mat. L/T/D						(16) 6.2
2.1	1.9	3.3							3.3
.4	.3	.3					.3	.2	.3
.8	.9	.7	Fixed/Worth				.9	.8	.7
1.6	1.9	1.3					2.9	1.9	1.1
.5	.5	.6					.7	.7	.5
1.4	1.4	1.4	Debt/Worth				1.2	1.6	1.2
3.3	2.6	3.1					3.1	3.0	2.6
71.3	69.1	71.2					89.8	71.2	63.9
(99) 33.9	(109) 38.5	(112) 35.7	% Profit Before Taxes/Tangible Net Worth				(13) 34.1	(29) 37.6	(58) 32.3
9.1	10.6	13.7					-10.3	11.3	17.2
24.6	28.3	25.3					31.3	29.3	22.6
11.7	12.3	13.8	% Profit Before Taxes/Total Assets				16.0	12.8	15.2
2.3	3.5	3.9					-11.8	5.1	5.2
12.5	16.4	22.7					20.8	33.4	20.8
7.2	6.7	8.4	Sales/Net Fixed Assets				5.9	8.2	8.3
3.8	3.7	3.8					3.7	3.3	4.8
2.9	2.9	3.0					3.2	4.2	2.6
2.1	2.1	2.1	Sales/Total Assets				2.3	2.4	2.0
1.3	1.4	1.5					1.7	1.2	1.5
1.9	1.4	1.0					1.8	1.4	.7
(91) 3.2	(85) 3.1	(89) 2.2	% Depr., Dep., Amort./Sales				(11) 3.0	(24) 2.3	(44) 1.9
6.7	5.7	4.5					4.4	8.4	3.6
.9	.9	.9							
(25) 1.9	(29) 2.1	(20) 1.8	% Officers', Directors' Owners' Comp/Sales						
3.5	3.6	3.6							
6058293M	9098246M	7335530M	Net Sales ($)	284M	17073M	21288M	115476M	514168M	6667241M
3775078M	4506903M	4320983M	Total Assets ($)	62M	22627M	9040M	64464M	471363M	3753427M

M = $ thousand MM = $ million

See Pages 9 through 22 for Explanation of Ratios and Data

Current Data Sorted by Assets							Comparative Historical Data	
						Type of Statement		
		8	12	6	6	Unqualified	26	29
	4	31	4			Reviewed	31	37
	9	8	1	1		Compiled	17	10
9	9	5				Tax Returns	8	17
3	8	34	20	6	3	Other	37	33
24 (4/1-9/30/13)			163 (10/1/13-3/31/14)				4/1/09-3/31/10	4/1/10-3/31/11
0-500M	500M-2MM	2-10MM	10-50MM	50-100MM	100-250MM		ALL	ALL
12	30	86	37	13	9	**NUMBER OF STATEMENTS**	119	126
%	%	%	%	%	%	**ASSETS**	%	%
22.2	19.2	16.0	11.8	14.0		Cash & Equivalents	12.8	13.3
10.6	30.6	36.0	33.5	27.2		Trade Receivables (net)	37.3	35.7
7.9	4.8	5.5	5.5	6.5		Inventory	4.0	6.5
8.1	7.0	6.0	11.7	16.7		All Other Current	8.4	9.6
48.8	61.6	63.5	62.4	64.4		Total Current	62.5	65.1
34.6	29.7	25.4	30.4	22.7		Fixed Assets (net)	30.3	26.1
.2	3.0	2.2	4.6	8.0		Intangibles (net)	2.7	2.1
16.3	5.7	8.9	2.6	4.9		All Other Non-Current	4.5	6.7
100.0	100.0	100.0	100.0	100.0		Total	100.0	100.0
						LIABILITIES		
15.8	9.0	9.0	8.0	9.3		Notes Payable-Short Term	9.2	9.7
2.4	5.6	3.1	3.9	3.6		Cur. Mat.-L.T.D.	5.6	6.8
4.5	14.2	13.8	13.8	19.9		Trade Payables	15.6	17.1
.0	.3	.3	.1	.1		Income Taxes Payable	.5	.3
12.1	6.1	8.7	13.3	9.2		All Other Current	11.3	13.2
34.8	35.2	35.0	39.1	42.1		Total Current	42.1	47.1
36.7	17.1	10.6	12.6	17.7		Long-Term Debt	14.0	13.5
.0	.3	.5	.5	2.0		Deferred Taxes	.5	.4
14.8	6.6	2.6	3.1	3.4		All Other Non-Current	7.3	4.4
13.7	40.9	51.3	44.6	34.8		Net Worth	36.1	34.5
100.0	100.0	100.0	100.0	100.0		Total Liabilties & Net Worth	100.0	100.0
						INCOME DATA		
100.0	100.0	100.0	100.0	100.0		Net Sales	100.0	100.0
42.9	40.7	34.0	23.1	21.5		Gross Profit	27.5	26.8
34.7	36.5	26.9	17.0	16.5		Operating Expenses	23.1	23.1
8.3	4.2	7.0	6.1	5.0		Operating Profit	4.3	3.7
.8	-.4	1.4	.5	.6		All Other Expenses (net)	.8	.6
7.5	4.6	5.6	5.6	4.4		Profit Before Taxes	3.5	3.1
						RATIOS		
2.6	3.9	3.6	2.6	2.1			2.2	2.3
1.4	2.1	2.0	1.6	1.5		Current	1.6	1.5
.5	1.3	1.3	1.1	1.2			1.1	1.1
1.4	3.6	3.1	1.8	1.6			2.0	1.7
.9	1.6	1.6	1.2	1.0		Quick	1.2	1.1
.4	.7	1.0	.6	.7			.8	.8
0 UND	**0** UND	**37** 9.9	**38** 9.6	**40** 9.2			**38** 9.6	**34** 10.9
0 UND	**31** 11.6	**56** 6.5	**55** 6.6	**49** 7.4		Sales/Receivables	**58** 6.3	**54** 6.8
39 9.3	**66** 5.5	**83** 4.4	**74** 4.9	**64** 5.7			**72** 5.1	**74** 4.9
0 UND	**0** UND	**0** UND	**0** UND	**0** UND			**0** UND	**0** UND
0 UND	**0** UND	**0** UND	**2** 181.1	**2** 222.6		Cost of Sales/Inventory	**0** UND	**1** 481.7
0 UND	**7** 48.9	**9** 42.2	**17** 21.0	**9** 39.4			**9** 39.4	**17** 21.8
0 UND	**0** UND	**12** 29.5	**17** 22.0	**22** 16.3			**12** 31.1	**15** 25.1
0 UND	**13** 28.0	**24** 15.0	**31** 11.9	**27** 13.4		Cost of Sales/Payables	**27** 13.6	**27** 13.4
8 47.3	**36** 10.0	**51** 7.1	**53** 6.9	**63** 5.8			**47** 7.7	**54** 6.7
11.6	6.3	4.4	5.1	5.1			5.6	6.0
460.7	14.7	8.7	11.7	11.2		Sales/Working Capital	12.0	11.5
-88.2	42.5	18.5	38.0	17.6			62.2	52.5
	44.2	43.4	46.6	52.2			20.4	22.3
	(26) 15.3	(71) 10.3	(33) 10.1	(12) 15.2		EBIT/Interest	(108) 6.5	(117) 7.2
	1.4	2.7	2.9	5.3			1.1	1.9
		20.6	9.1				7.3	7.3
		(10) 3.9	(12) 4.7			Net Profit + Depr., Dep., Amort./Cur. Mat. L/T/D	(25) 2.6	(31) 2.4
		1.8	1.5				1.4	.6
.1	.2	.2	.2	.2			.3	.2
1.1	.6	.4	.6	.6		Fixed/Worth	.7	.6
-2.7	1.3	.9	1.6	NM			1.7	1.3
.6	.5	.3	.6	1.1			.8	.7
3.2	.9	.8	1.4	2.4		Debt/Worth	1.6	1.7
-5.2	2.9	2.4	2.6	NM			5.1	4.0
	139.7	48.4	55.8	80.8			59.0	50.7
	(27) 52.5	(79) 19.8	(35) 22.3	(10) 29.5		% Profit Before Taxes/Tangible Net Worth	(104) 23.9	(114) 24.4
	2.6	5.5	6.9	13.6			.8	3.5
86.5	43.1	23.7	16.8	12.2			22.5	18.0
38.1	25.7	7.7	6.0	10.0		% Profit Before Taxes/Total Assets	9.3	7.7
-6.1	.8	2.2	1.5	2.0			-.4	1.1
219.7	109.9	25.0	29.2	60.6			26.0	36.8
32.9	25.4	11.7	8.2	8.8		Sales/Net Fixed Assets	9.5	10.5
8.6	6.6	5.4	3.7	4.7			4.4	5.1
15.0	6.7	3.1	2.7	2.5			3.3	3.2
6.4	4.6	2.2	2.1	1.7		Sales/Total Assets	2.3	2.4
2.0	2.6	1.5	1.2	1.2			1.6	1.6
	.6	1.1	1.6	.4			1.4	1.4
	(23) 1.3	(69) 2.8	(33) 2.5	(12) 2.0		% Depr., Dep., Amort./Sales	(96) 2.6	(100) 2.7
	4.9	5.7	3.4	5.8			5.3	6.3
	2.1	1.3					1.1	1.4
	(14) 3.9	(34) 3.1				% Officers', Directors' Owners' Comp/Sales	(27) 2.5	(42) 3.4
	5.9	5.4					4.3	7.8
14863M	178024M	1012248M	1795759M	1668017M	2251769M	Net Sales ($)	4043366M	3517304M
2271M	36193M	430396M	860033M	916056M	1298071M	Total Assets ($)	2168586M	1911460M

M = $ thousand MM = $ million

See Pages 9 through 22 for Explanation of Ratios and Data

Comparative Historical Data | **Current Data Sorted by Sales**

4/1/11-3/31/12 ALL	4/1/12-3/31/13 ALL	4/1/13-3/31/14 ALL		0-1MM	1-3MM	3-5MM	5-10MM	10-25MM	25MM & OVER
			Type of Statement						
39	33	32	Unqualified			1	2	6	23
48	40	39	Reviewed		1	5	14	16	3
15	10	19	Compiled	2	3	3	2	7	2
17	18	23	Tax Returns	4	6	1	7	5	
55	77	74	Other	4	5	7	17	17	24
				24 (4/1-9/30/13)			163 (10/1/13-3/31/14)		
174	178	187	**NUMBER OF STATEMENTS**	10	15	17	42	51	52
%	%	%	**ASSETS**	%	%	%	%	%	%
13.2	13.0	15.6	Cash & Equivalents	20.9	13.6	17.7	17.4	16.9	11.7
37.8	39.0	32.0	Trade Receivables (net)	15.2	14.5	34.6	30.1	40.4	32.7
3.9	4.8	6.0	Inventory	14.1	.0	3.1	7.9	4.3	7.2
9.9	9.3	8.4	All Other Current	6.3	10.0	8.1	4.0	7.1	13.4
64.8	66.1	62.0	Total Current	56.6	38.1	63.5	59.3	68.6	65.1
25.2	23.7	27.6	Fixed Assets (net)	23.4	41.8	20.4	33.8	23.0	26.0
2.9	2.7	3.2	Intangibles (net)	3.5	.5	4.1	1.4	3.4	5.0
7.1	7.5	7.2	All Other Non-Current	16.5	19.5	12.0	5.5	5.0	3.9
100.0	100.0	100.0	Total	100.0	100.0	100.0	100.0	100.0	100.0
			LIABILITIES						
8.6	8.4	9.1	Notes Payable-Short Term	10.9	6.7	14.6	8.6	7.8	9.4
5.1	5.6	3.7	Cur. Mat.-L.T.D.	1.9	7.2	2.2	3.8	3.3	4.0
15.3	15.8	13.6	Trade Payables	6.0	6.6	10.3	14.4	14.7	16.3
.3	.3	.2	Income Taxes Payable	.0	.0	.8	.2	.4	.1
13.0	10.6	10.0	All Other Current	11.3	4.5	12.1	6.0	9.7	14.3
42.4	40.7	36.7	Total Current	30.1	25.1	39.9	33.0	35.9	44.1
11.6	13.3	14.4	Long-Term Debt	17.8	33.0	10.1	14.9	11.2	12.5
.4	.4	.5	Deferred Taxes	.9	.0	.1	.4	.5	1.0
4.5	3.5	4.4	All Other Non-Current	17.7	15.9	3.8	2.4	1.7	2.8
41.1	42.1	44.0	Net Worth	33.4	26.0	46.1	49.4	50.7	39.6
100.0	100.0	100.0	Total Liabilties & Net Worth	100.0	100.0	100.0	100.0	100.0	100.0
			INCOME DATA						
100.0	100.0	100.0	Net Sales	100.0	100.0	100.0	100.0	100.0	100.0
28.5	27.5	31.7	Gross Profit	35.4	49.6	37.3	40.8	26.5	21.8
24.5	21.1	25.6	Operating Expenses	30.7	37.3	34.1	36.9	19.7	15.1
4.0	6.5	6.1	Operating Profit	4.8	12.3	3.2	3.9	6.8	6.7
.4	.5	.8	All Other Expenses (net)	3.3	2.7	-.3	.4	.6	.5
3.6	6.0	5.3	Profit Before Taxes	1.4	9.6	3.4	3.5	6.1	6.2
			RATIOS						
2.5	2.6	2.9		3.2	3.8	5.4	3.2	3.3	2.1
1.7	1.7	1.8	Current	2.5	1.6	1.8	2.0	2.1	1.5
1.2	1.2	1.2		1.5	.5	1.1	1.2	1.4	1.2
2.0	2.1	2.4		2.4	3.6	4.4	3.2	2.9	1.6
1.3	1.3	1.3	Quick	1.4	1.0	1.5	1.5	1.7	1.0
.9	.9	.8		.8	.5	1.0	.8	1.1	.7
39 9.3	38 9.5	32 11.5		0 UND	0 UND	32 11.3	22 16.9	33 11.2	39 9.4
59 6.2	54 6.8	50 7.3	Sales/Receivables	54 6.8	25 14.4	65 5.6	43 8.4	54 6.7	52 7.0
76 4.8	78 4.7	72 5.1		126 2.9	70 5.2	94 3.9	70 5.2	72 5.1	65 5.6
0 UND	0 UND	0 UND		0 UND	0 UND	0 UND	0 UND	0 UND	0 UND
0 UND	0 999.8	0 999.8	Cost of Sales/Inventory	1 314.6	0 UND	0 UND	0 UND	1 539.3	8 45.6
9 39.1	10 36.0	12 30.1		215 1.7	0 UND	1 255.9	16 23.1	7 49.4	15 23.7
11 33.6	12 29.6	11 32.3		0 UND	0 UND	7 51.0	12 29.5	9 42.6	17 20.9
26 14.3	26 13.9	24 15.5	Cost of Sales/Payables	4 82.4	3 109.0	15 23.8	26 14.3	21 17.3	28 13.2
46 8.0	47 7.8	46 7.9		83 4.4	35 10.4	36 10.1	54 6.7	51 7.1	46 7.9
5.7	5.7	5.1		1.9	3.1	3.9	5.6	4.9	6.3
9.6	9.2	11.2	Sales/Working Capital	4.4	19.2	7.3	13.0	10.0	11.5
24.2	19.7	30.6		NM	-96.6	21.9	67.3	18.1	24.1
32.5	35.0	43.5			26.4	68.5	46.2	47.3	46.6
(158) 6.9	(159) 10.0	(160) 10.4	EBIT/Interest		(11) 15.7	(15) 23.0	(33) 10.3	(45) 13.3	(49) 10.4
1.4	3.3	2.8			-4.7	-7.2	-.5	3.5	3.4
13.8	7.1	8.8						32.7	7.9
(37) 3.9	(23) 2.8	(34) 3.2	Net Profit + Depr., Dep., Amort./Cur. Mat. L/T/D					(10) 3.5	(21) 3.2
1.6	1.4	1.8						1.5	2.0
.3	.2	.2		.0	.1	.2	.2	.3	.3
.6	.5	.5	Fixed/Worth	.3	1.1	.4	.7	.4	.7
1.2	1.1	1.2		NM	169.0	.9	1.6	.6	1.5
.5	.7	.5		.3	.3	.3	.5	.4	.8
1.3	1.3	1.3	Debt/Worth	2.6	1.0	.7	.9	1.0	1.8
3.3	3.0	3.2		NM	258.0	5.5	2.2	2.2	4.1
41.6	52.0	60.7			202.4	42.0	58.7	47.9	70.0
(149) 21.0	(159) 30.5	(168) 26.3	% Profit Before Taxes/Tangible Net Worth		(12) 48.1	(15) 22.1	(38) 37.5	(48) 19.5	(47) 28.9
7.6	9.9	6.9			3.7	2.6	5.3	6.7	10.9
18.2	24.1	29.8		38.6	44.7	33.9	38.2	22.2	16.0
7.9	12.5	10.3	% Profit Before Taxes/Total Assets	1.9	16.1	8.0	14.7	9.3	10.2
.8	2.6	1.7		-15.2	.1	-17.7	.9	3.0	3.1
33.2	41.6	30.9		UND	35.7	72.7	30.3	30.7	25.6
11.6	12.5	11.7	Sales/Net Fixed Assets	61.1	6.3	11.7	12.5	16.5	9.2
6.0	6.7	5.1		4.1	1.7	6.0	3.7	7.4	6.0
3.3	3.1	3.4		3.7	12.5	3.2	4.5	3.6	2.7
2.3	2.4	2.4	Sales/Total Assets	1.2	2.6	1.8	2.4	2.5	2.3
1.7	1.8	1.5		.8	.5	1.5	1.5	2.0	1.4
1.1	1.1	1.1				.6	1.0	1.1	1.4
(140) 2.4	(142) 2.4	(150) 2.5	% Depr., Dep., Amort./Sales			(14) 1.3	(36) 2.9	(43) 2.3	(44) 2.3
4.2	3.7	4.8				6.4	6.4	3.4	3.4
1.6	1.4	1.3				1.5	2.1	1.0	
(52) 3.0	(64) 3.2	(61) 3.2	% Officers', Directors' Owners' Comp/Sales			(11) 3.7	(18) 4.6	(17) 1.9	
7.5	5.3	6.2				6.0	7.4	3.7	
6968897M	7652897M	6920680M	Net Sales ($)	5140M	29200M	63614M	322761M	855899M	5644066M
3894381M	4204914M	3543020M	Total Assets ($)	6658M	29257M	32719M	190939M	357056M	2926391M

M = $ thousand MM = $ million

See Pages 9 through 22 for Explanation of Ratios and Data

Current Data Sorted by Assets / Comparative Historical Data

Type of Statement	0-500M	500M-2MM	2-10MM	10-50MM	50-100MM	100-250MM	4/1/09-3/31/10 ALL	4/1/10-3/31/11 ALL
Unqualified		2	2	8	2	5	49	31
Reviewed		4	5	8	6		51	36
Compiled	3	8	18	7	1	2	69	58
Tax Returns	16	49	74	9			263	170
Other	4	42	69	33	6	9	313	311
	23 (4/1-9/30/13)			369 (10/1/13-3/31/14)				
NUMBER OF STATEMENTS	23	105	168	65	15	16	745	606
ASSETS	%	%	%	%	%	%	%	%
Cash & Equivalents	22.5	8.2	6.0	7.8	11.5	9.1	7.5	7.2
Trade Receivables (net)	3.7	5.2	2.8	3.0	8.8	3.7	4.5	3.4
Inventory	35.3	32.7	41.0	26.6	15.0	30.7	31.5	34.0
All Other Current	6.2	3.0	3.7	2.1	10.6	2.8	4.3	4.2
Total Current	67.7	49.2	53.4	39.5	45.9	46.2	47.8	48.7
Fixed Assets (net)	21.6	36.4	33.6	36.7	18.1	39.3	36.4	38.9
Intangibles (net)	4.9	1.8	2.0	1.3	5.7	.4	1.8	1.6
All Other Non-Current	5.8	12.6	11.0	22.5	30.2	14.1	14.0	10.7
Total	100.0	100.0	100.0	100.0	100.0	100.0	100.0	100.0
LIABILITIES								
Notes Payable-Short Term	19.0	14.0	16.6	10.6	4.6	14.1	18.0	16.4
Cur. Mat.-L.T.D.	2.7	2.5	2.5	4.4	2.5	3.1	4.4	4.6
Trade Payables	4.8	4.3	3.1	3.5	10.1	3.2	3.5	2.5
Income Taxes Payable	.0	.0	.0	.1	.1	.1	.1	.0
All Other Current	22.8	15.1	11.5	8.5	13.0	8.3	12.1	11.8
Total Current	49.4	36.0	33.7	27.1	30.3	28.7	38.1	35.4
Long-Term Debt	13.7	28.7	34.1	24.6	27.5	30.1	34.3	34.3
Deferred Taxes	.0	.0	.0	.1	1.9	.0	.0	.0
All Other Non-Current	15.5	6.5	4.6	7.9	2.9	17.2	3.8	4.7
Net Worth	21.5	28.9	27.6	40.2	37.3	24.0	23.8	25.5
Total Liabilties & Net Worth	100.0	100.0	100.0	100.0	100.0	100.0	100.0	100.0
INCOME DATA								
Net Sales	100.0	100.0	100.0	100.0	100.0	100.0	100.0	100.0
Gross Profit								
Operating Expenses	68.3	77.5	81.3	84.3	87.3	78.2	82.4	81.6
Operating Profit	31.7	22.5	18.7	15.7	12.7	21.8	17.6	18.4
All Other Expenses (net)	5.4	8.7	11.5	7.5	3.7	6.9	11.8	11.3
Profit Before Taxes	26.2	13.8	7.2	8.2	9.0	14.9	5.8	7.1
RATIOS								
Current	26.2	5.9	4.9	5.6	7.1	7.0	3.0	3.9
	1.6	1.4	1.5	1.7	2.1	2.0	1.3	1.4
	.5	.4	.7	.6	1.2	.7	.5	.6
Quick	1.2	1.6	.8	2.1	2.4	1.4	1.1	1.2
	.7	.3	(167) .2	(64) .4	.9	.5	(744) .2	(605) .2
	.3	.0	.0	.1	.2	.1	.0	.0
Sales/Receivables	0 UND	0 UND	0 UND	0 UND	0 UND	0 UND	0 UND	0 UND
	0 UND	0 UND	0 UND	0 999.8	6 62.2	5 71.0	0 UND	0 UND
	0 UND	1 477.6	4 82.8	13 27.4	73 5.0	47 7.8	13 27.6	8 45.9
Cost of Sales/Inventory								
Cost of Sales/Payables								
Sales/Working Capital	1.5	1.0	.8	.9	.9	1.0	1.0	.8
	5.2	7.7	2.9	5.1	5.3	3.8	8.5	6.0
	-5.5	-4.3	-7.5	-10.2	12.1	-3.6	-3.6	-4.9
EBIT/Interest	55.6	11.1	10.0	8.6	10.2	4.2	5.2	5.4
	(13) 13.0	(67) 3.3	(89) 2.8	(47) 3.0	(13) 4.5	(10) 2.4	(401) 1.7	(321) 1.8
	2.5	1.0	.0	-.3	1.2	1.7	-.9	-.3
Net Profit + Depr., Dep., Amort./Cur. Mat. L/T/D							8.7	6.5
							(24) 1.8	(26) 2.1
							.7	1.0
Fixed/Worth	.0	.0	.0	.1	.0	.0	.0	.0
	.0	.7	.4	1.0	.1	1.4	.9	.8
	-16.3	2.8	6.1	1.9	2.6	7.7	6.3	4.9
Debt/Worth	.4	.6	.9	.6	.5	.5	1.2	.8
	5.9	2.1	3.0	1.5	3.0	2.4	3.4	2.7
	-4.2	14.4	44.7	5.4	7.6	11.6	35.2	32.0
% Profit Before Taxes/Tangible Net Worth	99.4	54.9	29.8	28.8	23.0	31.7	22.3	23.8
	(14) 50.8	(84) 12.5	(132) 5.5	(57) 8.2	(13) 6.4	(13) 6.5	(594) 3.7	(488) 5.0
	1.5	2.9	-1.9	-.1	.1	2.1	-5.4	-2.5
% Profit Before Taxes/Total Assets	53.2	13.0	7.8	10.7	9.4	11.3	4.5	5.5
	15.9	3.2	1.7	2.3	1.6	3.8	.8	1.1
	3.8	.1	-1.6	-1.7	-.2	.7	-2.1	-1.5
Sales/Net Fixed Assets	UND	UND	UND	45.3	304.5	212.2	265.7	UND
	670.0	4.7	9.8	1.7	89.1	1.7	2.9	2.8
	5.3	.5	.3	.4	2.3	.5	.2	.2
Sales/Total Assets	2.0	1.2	.6	.7	1.1	.8	.6	.7
	1.1	.4	.3	.3	.5	.3	.2	.2
	.3	.2	.1	.1	.2	.2	.1	.1
% Depr., Dep., Amort./Sales		1.2	.6	.5	.3	.2	1.2	1.7
		(40) 8.0	(75) 5.2	(43) 2.0	(10) 1.0	(10) .6	(404) 5.7	(295) 7.9
		17.5	17.4	12.1	8.6	5.3	16.4	19.8
% Officers', Directors' Owners' Comp/Sales			2.2				1.4	1.8
			(13) 5.0				(91) 3.0	(52) 3.7
			11.4				6.8	6.3
Net Sales ($)	14918M	95732M	411910M	793451M	900037M	1152063M	5060144M	4284649M
Total Assets ($)	6051M	121008M	783681M	1365695M	1023456M	2589126M	10918647M	9305336M

M = $ thousand MM = $ million

See Pages 9 through 22 for Explanation of Ratios and Data

Comparative Historical Data				Current Data Sorted by Sales					
			Type of Statement						
30	18	19	Unqualified		3	1	2	4	9
38	30	23	Reviewed	4	1	3	4	7	4
55	45	39	Compiled	16	11	2	5	1	4
188	183	148	Tax Returns	89	44	7	5	3	
235	190	163	Other	60	46	12	17	14	14
4/1/11-3/31/12 ALL	**4/1/12-3/31/13 ALL**	**4/1/13-3/31/14 ALL**			**23 (4/1-9/30/13)**		**369 (10/1/13-3/31/14)**		
				0-1MM	**1-3MM**	**3-5MM**	**5-10MM**	**10-25MM**	**25MM & OVER**
546	466	392	**NUMBER OF STATEMENTS**	169	105	25	33	29	31
%	%	%	**ASSETS**	%	%	%	%	%	%
6.8	7.3	8.2	Cash & Equivalents	6.4	8.9	5.6	10.7	13.9	9.2
3.9	3.1	3.8	Trade Receivables (net)	1.2	4.8	2.1	8.2	5.9	9.2
33.0	38.7	34.6	Inventory	32.6	40.3	40.5	32.4	33.9	25.0
3.0	3.1	3.6	All Other Current	4.2	1.3	3.1	4.7	4.8	6.4
46.7	52.3	50.2	Total Current	44.4	55.3	51.3	56.1	58.6	50.0
36.5	32.3	33.8	Fixed Assets (net)	42.9	27.3	30.7	27.5	19.6	28.2
1.6	1.5	2.1	Intangibles (net)	2.8	1.3	2.2	.3	2.0	3.0
15.3	13.9	13.9	All Other Non-Current	9.9	16.2	15.7	16.1	19.9	18.9
100.0	100.0	100.0	Total	100.0	100.0	100.0	100.0	100.0	100.0
			LIABILITIES						
18.2	16.3	14.5	Notes Payable-Short Term	10.2	21.3	7.5	21.3	12.1	15.4
3.1	2.3	2.8	Cur. Mat.-L.T.D.	3.3	.8	7.5	5.3	1.3	2.6
3.2	3.5	3.9	Trade Payables	2.8	3.4	2.1	4.7	5.3	10.3
.1	.1	.0	Income Taxes Payable	.0	.0	.0	.0	.2	.2
13.0	12.4	12.6	All Other Current	10.8	11.6	32.9	12.2	10.7	11.9
37.5	34.6	33.8	Total Current	27.0	37.0	49.9	43.5	29.6	40.5
29.0	27.2	29.5	Long-Term Debt	37.3	21.9	33.1	21.7	23.7	23.3
.1	.1	.1	Deferred Taxes	.0	.1	.0	.8	.0	.0
5.3	5.1	6.8	All Other Non-Current	6.9	6.8	5.3	4.8	5.0	10.4
28.1	33.0	29.9	Net Worth	28.8	34.2	11.6	29.2	41.7	25.8
100.0	100.0	100.0	Total Liabilties & Net Worth	100.0	100.0	100.0	100.0	100.0	100.0
			INCOME DATA						
100.0	100.0	100.0	Net Sales	100.0	100.0	100.0	100.0	100.0	100.0
			Gross Profit						
82.8	82.4	80.1	Operating Expenses	73.6	84.6	84.0	81.1	91.0	86.4
17.2	17.6	19.9	Operating Profit	26.4	15.4	16.0	18.9	9.0	13.6
11.0	8.9	9.2	All Other Expenses (net)	15.3	5.8	4.4	5.9	1.4	2.5
6.2	8.7	10.6	Profit Before Taxes	11.0	9.7	11.6	13.0	7.7	11.1
			RATIOS						
2.9	4.7	5.7		6.2	4.3	7.8	4.3	8.4	2.8
1.2	1.4	1.6	Current	1.6	1.5	2.0	1.5	2.2	1.4
.5	.6	.6		.4	.7	.7	.9	1.3	.5
1.0	1.0	1.2		1.0	.8	2.2	1.9	3.6	1.0
.2	(463) .2	(390) .3	Quick	.2	(103) .2	.2	.5	.7	.5
.0	.0	.0		.0	.0	.0	.1	.1	.2
0 UND	0 UND	0 UND		0 UND	0 UND	0 UND	0 UND	0 UND	0 UND
0 UND	0 UND	0 UND	Sales/Receivables	0 UND	0 UND	0 999.8	1 329.4	0 999.8	6 62.2
8 47.7	6 57.4	5 67.6		0 UND	5 75.2	4 94.5	13 27.3	12 29.6	76 4.8
			Cost of Sales/Inventory						
			Cost of Sales/Payables						
.9	.8	.9		.5	1.2	1.2	1.4	1.7	3.6
10.6	4.2	5.1	Sales/Working Capital	4.1	3.6	1.9	6.6	5.1	8.8
-4.1	-6.6	-6.0		-3.5	-11.4	-15.3	-514.8	13.4	-4.7
5.2	10.2	11.1		5.6	13.9	5.1	33.9	17.9	8.6
(316) 1.9	(273) 2.5	(239) 3.2	EBIT/Interest	(76) 2.5	(72) 3.6	(19) 3.0	(24) 4.1	(25) 4.5	(23) 4.5
-.8	.5	.8		.1	.5	1.3	1.1	1.2	1.7
5.3	3.9	3.0							
(20) 1.5	(20) 1.5	(11) 1.9	Net Profit + Depr., Dep., Amort./Cur. Mat. L/T/D						
.5	.5	.7							
.0	.0	.0		.0	.0	.0	.0	.0	.0
.9	.3	.6	Fixed/Worth	1.2	.1	1.0	.4	.2	.5
4.4	2.4	4.0		9.9	1.5	8.8	2.0	1.7	2.6
.8	.7	.7		.8	.6	1.0	.8	.6	.8
2.9	2.2	2.4	Debt/Worth	2.9	1.9	3.3	1.8	1.5	3.0
24.9	12.6	21.2		NM	16.9	23.9	5.2	6.6	7.6
22.1	31.1	33.2		27.4	47.2	53.4	33.3	60.5	52.3
(439) 4.6	(387) 6.7	(313) 9.3	% Profit Before Taxes/Tangible Net Worth	(127) 4.4	(86) 10.6	(21) 20.3	(28) 12.2	(25) 17.6	(26) 25.7
-3.6	-1.7	.2		-1.3	.6	7.7	1.1	2.7	5.5
5.9	8.5	10.6		5.8	12.5	10.3	17.7	17.2	13.0
1.4	2.1	2.7	% Profit Before Taxes/Total Assets	1.4	2.5	3.7	5.0	7.0	7.0
-1.8	-1.0	-.6		-1.1	-1.4	.9	.4	.7	1.4
999.8	UND	UND		UND	UND	UND	UND	236.6	95.3
4.0	12.7	8.6	Sales/Net Fixed Assets	.8	50.5	5.2	13.6	52.8	32.9
.2	.3	.4		.2	.8	.4	1.0	3.7	1.5
.7	.8	.9		.3	1.0	1.2	2.0	1.7	1.5
.3	.3	.3	Sales/Total Assets	.2	.5	.3	.7	.8	.9
.1	.1	.1		.1	.2	.2	.3	.5	.3
.9	.9	.6		3.9	.7	.3	.3	.1	.2
(271) 6.3	(200) 5.1	(184) 3.5	% Depr., Dep., Amort./Sales	(74) 13.5	(37) 2.5	(15) 1.2	(20) 1.2	(16) .5	(22) .6
18.7	16.8	14.7		23.8	13.7	10.1	8.7	3.2	2.4
1.6	1.6	2.2		5.1	2.8				
(65) 4.5	(59) 3.6	(33) 5.3	% Officers', Directors' Owners' Comp/Sales	(10) 7.0	(13) 5.3				
9.2	6.9	8.0		17.8	8.0				
3515008M	2479113M	3368111M	Net Sales ($)	69201M	180325M	94331M	226450M	429800M	2368004M
7478799M	6219655M	5889017M	Total Assets ($)	443769M	580063M	299010M	603704M	728093M	3234378M

M = $ thousand MM = $ million

See Pages 9 through 22 for Explanation of Ratios and Data

Current Data Sorted by Assets

Comparative Historical Data

0-500M	500M-2MM	2-10MM	10-50MM	50-100MM	100-250MM		4/1/09-3/31/10 ALL	4/1/10-3/31/11 ALL
						Type of Statement		
1	14	95	149	51	30	Unqualified	408	387
3	33	120	55	6		Reviewed	237	215
4	8	16	5			Compiled	45	44
11	16	18	5		1	Tax Returns	46	43
9	31	100	130	31	21	Other	272	223
137 (4/1-9/30/13)			826 (10/1/13-3/31/14)					
28	102	349	344	88	52	**NUMBER OF STATEMENTS**	1008	912
%	%	%	%	%	%	**ASSETS**	%	%
28.3	17.9	19.9	18.4	22.4	20.2	Cash & Equivalents	20.1	18.6
20.9	31.5	30.7	29.0	24.9	20.0	Trade Receivables (net)	27.3	28.7
1.1	5.0	3.5	5.3	3.7	6.3	Inventory	3.9	3.9
3.5	3.5	6.1	7.5	9.0	9.2	All Other Current	7.2	6.6
53.9	57.9	60.3	60.1	60.0	55.8	Total Current	58.4	57.8
31.4	34.2	33.0	32.1	28.8	33.5	Fixed Assets (net)	33.5	33.4
4.5	1.3	1.6	2.1	4.5	4.6	Intangibles (net)	1.3	1.9
10.3	6.5	5.1	5.7	6.7	6.1	All Other Non-Current	6.7	7.0
100.0	100.0	100.0	100.0	100.0	100.0	Total	100.0	100.0
						LIABILITIES		
24.0	8.6	4.4	3.2	2.6	1.9	Notes Payable-Short Term	4.9	5.0
6.3	3.7	4.3	4.4	3.2	3.3	Cur. Mat.-L.T.D.	5.1	5.1
15.6	14.9	16.3	16.5	15.0	12.3	Trade Payables	14.9	15.6
.0	.5	.3	.2	.3	.3	Income Taxes Payable	.5	.4
14.4	5.9	8.1	10.3	13.6	13.6	All Other Current	10.8	10.4
60.4	33.7	33.4	34.7	34.8	31.4	Total Current	36.1	36.5
30.5	15.3	13.1	13.0	14.4	11.0	Long-Term Debt	14.7	14.8
.0	.7	1.2	1.1	1.2	1.5	Deferred Taxes	1.2	1.2
9.9	3.8	2.1	2.7	3.4	3.7	All Other Non-Current	2.7	3.0
-.7	46.6	50.2	48.5	46.2	52.5	Net Worth	45.4	44.5
100.0	100.0	100.0	100.0	100.0	100.0	Total Liabilties & Net Worth	100.0	100.0
						INCOME DATA		
100.0	100.0	100.0	100.0	100.0	100.0	Net Sales	100.0	100.0
34.5	26.2	19.8	13.6	10.1	12.9	Gross Profit	18.8	18.2
34.3	22.4	15.8	10.9	8.4	9.6	Operating Expenses	15.1	15.5
.2	3.8	4.0	2.7	1.7	3.3	Operating Profit	3.8	2.7
.7	.3	.0	-.2	-.1	-.2	All Other Expenses (net)	.3	.1
-.4	3.5	4.0	2.9	1.8	3.5	Profit Before Taxes	3.5	2.6
						RATIOS		
2.6	4.2	3.2	2.5	2.5	2.4		2.5	2.5
1.0	1.7	1.9	1.7	1.6	1.7	Current	1.7	1.6
.4	1.0	1.3	1.3	1.3	1.4		1.2	1.2
2.3	2.9	2.7	1.8	2.0	1.5		2.1	2.1
.9	1.5	1.5	1.3	1.3	1.1	Quick	1.3	1.3
.3	.8	1.0	1.0	1.0	.9		.9	.9
0 UND	**17** 22.0	**28** 13.2	**34** 10.7	**29** 12.6	**29** 12.8		**28** 13.1	**30** 12.3
12 31.1	**44** 8.3	**43** 8.5	**52** 7.0	**54** 6.8	**41** 9.0	Sales/Receivables	**46** 8.0	**47** 7.7
29 12.4	**70** 5.2	**69** 5.3	**73** 5.0	**74** 4.9	**64** 5.7		**67** 5.5	**68** 5.4
0 UND	**0** UND	**0** UND	**0** UND	**0** UND	**1** 366.2		**0** UND	**0** UND
0 UND	**0** UND	**0** UND	**2** 160.6	**3** 105.3	**9** 42.0	Cost of Sales/Inventory	**0** 755.6	**1** 673.4
0 UND	**6** 57.5	**7** 56.1	**15** 23.9	**14** 26.9	**41** 9.0		**10** 38.0	**11** 34.5
0 UND	**6** 60.1	**12** 30.8	**19** 19.5	**23** 15.9	**20** 18.5		**14** 25.3	**14** 25.9
9 40.3	**19** 18.8	**25** 14.6	**32** 11.4	**34** 10.7	**28** 13.2	Cost of Sales/Payables	**28** 13.2	**28** 12.9
31 11.8	**46** 7.9	**44** 8.3	**46** 7.9	**49** 7.5	**41** 9.0		**44** 8.3	**45** 8.1
17.6	5.3	5.1	5.2	4.3	5.2		5.3	5.6
NM	12.7	9.2	8.7	8.2	7.7	Sales/Working Capital	9.5	9.6
-12.0	300.5	24.0	16.7	15.6	13.5		24.5	26.3
7.0	17.2	32.8	22.2	29.1	30.9		22.6	17.1
(19) 2.7	(86) 2.1	(308) 8.4	(316) 6.2	(80) 9.0	(46) 9.3	EBIT/Interest	(907) 5.8	(822) 5.0
-2.7	-2.5	2.1	1.5	.8	2.9		1.4	1.1
	3.8	4.5	3.6	5.7	5.9		5.9	4.8
	(17) 1.5	(92) 1.7	(113) 2.1	(46) 2.3	(21) 3.2	Net Profit + Depr., Dep., Amort./Cur. Mat. L/T/D	(339) 2.5	(285) 2.3
	.4	.7	1.2	1.5	1.9		1.2	1.1
.6	.3	.3	.4	.4	.4		.4	.4
10.1	.8	.7	.7	.7	.6	Fixed/Worth	.7	.7
-.6	1.6	1.1	1.2	1.1	1.0		1.2	1.2
.8	.5	.5	.6	.7	.6		.6	.6
20.9	1.1	.9	1.2	1.3	1.0	Debt/Worth	1.1	1.2
-2.7	2.3	2.0	2.1	2.2	1.6		2.2	2.3
130.9	30.8	36.1	22.9	21.1	20.6		30.1	27.7
(16) 15.6	(91) 12.3	(335) 14.5	(342) 10.6	(84) 9.9	(50) 12.8	% Profit Before Taxes/Tangible Net Worth	(963) 14.8	(855) 11.6
-34.0	-6.5	2.8	1.7	.5	5.5		2.4	1.2
19.9	15.4	16.8	9.6	8.3	10.1		14.3	13.3
3.3	4.5	6.7	4.9	4.7	6.3	% Profit Before Taxes/Total Assets	6.2	5.1
-26.2	-4.9	1.0	.7	-.5	2.6		.9	.2
63.0	17.7	16.3	11.6	11.3	9.9		12.9	13.3
24.4	9.5	7.3	6.3	6.1	5.2	Sales/Net Fixed Assets	6.8	6.8
8.8	4.7	4.2	4.1	4.2	3.0		3.9	3.9
8.1	3.5	3.0	2.6	2.0	2.2		2.7	2.7
6.4	2.7	2.2	2.0	1.7	1.6	Sales/Total Assets	2.0	2.0
2.9	1.8	1.7	1.5	1.3	1.3		1.5	1.5
.8	1.9	1.7	2.2	2.1	1.5		1.9	2.1
(17) 3.2	(82) 3.4	(317) 2.8	(332) 3.3	(83) 3.3	(40) 2.6	% Depr., Dep., Amort./Sales	(889) 3.4	(811) 3.4
5.3	4.9	4.7	4.6	4.7	3.9		5.2	5.3
2.2	2.6	1.4	.7	.4			1.3	1.2
(18) 4.7	(50) 4.6	(133) 2.4	(96) 1.2	(12) .8		% Officers', Directors' Owners' Comp/Sales	(332) 2.5	(296) 2.6
7.2	6.0	4.3	2.3	2.1			5.1	4.5
45623M	348294M	4381551M	16662943M	11099665M	13670495M	Net Sales ($)	46904068M	39637237M
7742M	130169M	1848189M	8146643M	6415407M	8013739M	Total Assets ($)	26038659M	21938550M

M = $ thousand MM = $ million

See Pages 9 through 22 for Explanation of Ratios and Data

Comparative Historical Data				Current Data Sorted by Sales					
			Type of Statement						
375	364	340	Unqualified		6	10	30	78	216
232	233	217	Reviewed	4	19	25	48	66	55
44	35	33	Compiled	3	6	5	11	5	3
46	51	51	Tax Returns	7	12	5	13	10	4
237	272	322	Other	9	20	17	32	79	165
4/1/11-3/31/12	**4/1/12-3/31/13**	**4/1/13-3/31/14**		**137 (4/1-9/30/13)**			**826 (10/1/13-3/31/14)**		
ALL	**ALL**	**ALL**		**0-1MM**	**1-3MM**	**3-5MM**	**5-10MM**	**10-25MM**	**25MM & OVER**
934	955	963	**NUMBER OF STATEMENTS**	23	63	62	134	238	443
%	%	%	**ASSETS**	%	%	%	%	%	%
18.2	17.9	19.7	Cash & Equivalents	19.8	25.5	18.1	20.2	20.4	18.5
30.4	30.1	28.8	Trade Receivables (net)	24.9	21.5	27.5	30.3	30.6	28.7
4.3	4.5	4.4	Inventory	5.2	2.5	5.3	3.7	3.8	5.0
7.0	6.9	6.7	All Other Current	3.3	3.3	5.6	4.5	6.1	8.5
59.9	59.4	59.5	Total Current	53.1	52.8	56.5	58.6	60.8	60.7
31.8	32.7	32.4	Fixed Assets (net)	30.2	37.9	37.4	33.6	32.1	30.8
2.0	2.3	2.3	Intangibles (net)	5.2	1.7	.9	2.2	1.4	2.9
6.2	5.6	5.8	All Other Non-Current	11.5	7.6	5.2	5.6	5.6	5.6
100.0	100.0	100.0	Total	100.0	100.0	100.0	100.0	100.0	100.0
			LIABILITIES						
5.7	4.8	4.7	Notes Payable-Short Term	11.2	11.2	8.9	5.6	4.1	2.9
4.3	4.5	4.2	Cur. Mat.-L.T.D.	1.2	4.7	4.9	4.8	4.3	3.9
17.3	17.2	15.9	Trade Payables	12.3	13.9	11.8	13.0	17.0	17.2
.3	.4	.3	Income Taxes Payable	.0	.3	1.0	.2	.2	.3
11.0	10.2	9.7	All Other Current	12.4	7.1	7.6	6.1	9.3	11.5
38.5	37.1	34.7	Total Current	37.1	37.2	34.1	29.8	34.9	35.7
12.9	13.4	13.8	Long-Term Debt	13.3	21.3	16.0	12.7	13.7	12.8
1.1	1.2	1.1	Deferred Taxes	.9	.8	.8	.8	1.1	1.2
2.9	3.3	2.9	All Other Non-Current	5.8	8.2	1.2	2.8	1.5	3.0
44.5	45.0	47.5	Net Worth	43.0	32.5	47.9	53.9	48.8	47.2
100.0	100.0	100.0	Total Liabilties & Net Worth	100.0	100.0	100.0	100.0	100.0	100.0
			INCOME DATA						
100.0	100.0	100.0	Net Sales	100.0	100.0	100.0	100.0	100.0	100.0
17.0	17.5	17.4	Gross Profit	36.0	32.2	25.5	22.6	16.9	12.0
14.3	14.5	14.3	Operating Expenses	28.7	29.4	20.2	19.2	13.0	9.7
2.7	2.9	3.2	Operating Profit	7.3	2.8	5.4	3.3	3.9	2.3
.1	-.1	.0	All Other Expenses (net)	1.7	.0	.5	-.1	-.2	-.1
2.6	3.0	3.2	Profit Before Taxes	5.6	2.8	4.8	3.4	4.0	2.4
			RATIOS						
2.4	2.5	2.8		13.5	4.5	3.1	4.0	3.0	2.3
1.6	1.6	1.7	Current	1.7	1.4	1.7	2.3	1.8	1.6
1.2	1.2	1.3		.4	.6	1.2	1.3	1.3	1.3
2.0	2.1	2.3		12.9	4.5	2.8	3.6	2.4	1.7
1.3	1.3	1.4	Quick	1.1	1.1	1.4	2.0	1.5	1.3
.9	.9	1.0		.4	.5	.8	1.1	1.0	1.0
33 11.2	**30** 12.1	**28** 13.2		**3** 113.0	**5** 74.7	**21** 17.2	**28** 13.1	**32** 11.5	**29** 12.6
48 7.6	**46** 7.9	**46** 7.9	Sales/Receivables	**31** 11.8	**37** 9.9	**41** 8.9	**47** 7.7	**46** 8.0	**49** 7.5
73 5.0	**69** 5.3	**70** 5.2		**101** 3.6	**69** 5.3	**73** 5.0	**72** 5.1	**72** 5.1	**69** 5.3
0 UND	**0** UND	**0** UND		**0** UND	**0** UND	**0** UND	**0** UND	**0** UND	**0** UND
1 395.5	**1** 526.5	**1** 487.6	Cost of Sales/Inventory	**0** UND	**0** UND	**0** UND	**0** UND	**0** UND	**3** 127.0
12 29.4	**11** 32.3	**12** 31.0		**7** 51.4	**6** 63.9	**6** 59.9	**10** 35.9	**10** 35.2	**14** 25.5
16 22.2	**16** 22.2	**15** 25.0		**4** 81.4	**6** 65.7	**6** 59.9	**8** 45.9	**15** 23.9	**20** 18.7
31 11.6	**30** 12.1	**28** 13.2	Cost of Sales/Payables	**20** 18.0	**17** 20.9	**21** 17.0	**21** 17.0	**30** 12.2	**31** 11.9
51 7.2	**46** 7.9	**45** 8.2		**87** 4.2	**45** 8.2	**49** 7.4	**36** 10.2	**46** 7.9	**45** 8.2
5.3	5.5	5.1		.8	3.7	5.2	4.4	4.9	5.5
9.9	10.0	9.1	Sales/Working Capital	10.3	19.5	10.1	7.6	8.8	9.3
27.9	28.9	21.4		-10.7	-20.8	34.5	22.8	20.2	17.5
15.2	16.8	24.6		4.6	12.6	19.2	24.3	38.4	22.6
(827) 4.2	(855) 4.8	(855) 6.6	EBIT/Interest	(10) 2.7	(50) 2.2	(57) 3.0	(116) 7.7	(218) 8.4	(404) 6.7
1.0	1.0	1.4		-2.2	-1.7	-.2	2.1	2.2	1.4
5.2	4.3	4.6			2.5	3.8	5.0	7.1	4.5
(293) 2.3	(281) 2.2	(290) 2.0	Net Profit + Depr., Dep., Amort./Cur. Mat. L/T/D		(10) 1.6	(12) 1.3	(25) 1.1	(71) 2.0	(170) 2.2
1.3	1.2	1.1			.4	.4	.4	1.1	1.3
.4	.4	.4		.0	.3	.3	.3	.3	.4
.7	.7	.7	Fixed/Worth	.6	1.1	.7	.6	.7	.7
1.2	1.3	1.2		3.0	6.2	1.2	1.1	1.2	1.1
.6	.6	.5		.1	.5	.5	.4	.5	.7
1.2	1.2	1.1	Debt/Worth	.8	1.5	.9	.7	1.0	1.2
2.3	2.2	2.1		7.2	17.0	2.2	1.6	2.1	2.2
25.5	27.3	27.3		15.5	50.8	40.5	31.4	35.9	22.9
(885) 9.4	(906) 11.3	(918) 12.2	% Profit Before Taxes/Tangible Net Worth	(18) 8.3	(49) 11.4	(56) 8.5	(129) 15.1	(231) 14.7	(435) 10.3
.4	.4	1.9		-5.8	-5.2	-7.4	2.4	3.3	1.5
11.0	12.2	12.4		13.0	15.8	17.8	16.3	14.7	9.5
3.8	5.0	5.3	% Profit Before Taxes/Total Assets	3.6	4.3	4.3	6.8	6.2	4.8
.1	.1	.5		-6.0	-8.2	-3.4	1.4	1.2	.5
14.6	14.5	13.9		463.0	23.0	15.3	13.8	15.4	12.8
7.2	7.1	6.9	Sales/Net Fixed Assets	7.0	8.4	6.2	6.2	7.0	6.9
4.3	4.2	4.2		1.5	3.5	3.6	3.8	4.0	4.4
2.7	2.8	2.8		2.6	4.6	2.8	3.0	2.7	2.6
2.0	2.1	2.0	Sales/Total Assets	.8	2.3	2.1	2.2	2.1	2.0
1.5	1.5	1.5		.4	1.3	1.5	1.6	1.6	1.6
1.9	1.8	1.8		3.7	1.9	1.9	1.8	1.6	2.0
(837) 3.0	(849) 3.0	(871) 3.1	% Depr., Dep., Amort./Sales	(13) 9.0	(52) 3.8	(52) 3.7	(118) 3.5	(221) 2.8	(415) 3.1
4.8	4.6	4.6		18.7	5.2	5.6	5.4	4.4	4.3
1.1	1.0	1.2			3.8	2.5	1.9	1.2	.6
(315) 2.2	(306) 2.2	(315) 2.2	% Officers', Directors' Owners' Comp/Sales		(30) 5.5	(32) 4.7	(54) 2.8	(86) 1.8	(106) 1.3
4.2	3.9	4.3			8.2	6.3	4.6	3.3	2.2
43846469M	**45004083M**	**46208571M**	Net Sales ($)	**13333M**	**133636M**	**236738M**	**940761M**	**3784923M**	**41099180M**
23827255M	**24347396M**	**24561889M**	Total Assets ($)	**20357M**	**79219M**	**137551M**	**537338M**	**2006116M**	**21781308M**

M = $ thousand MM = $ million

See Pages 9 through 22 for Explanation of Ratios and Data

Current Data Sorted by Assets							Comparative Historical Data	
1	4	30	34	16	14	Type of Statement Unqualified	100	107
	18	59	27	2		Reviewed	122	108
2	6	13	2	2		Compiled	24	24
15	18	18	1	1		Tax Returns	41	50
10	22	49	37	9	11	Other	100	83
76 (4/1-9/30/13)			345 (10/1/13-3/31/14)				4/1/09-3/31/10	4/1/10-3/31/11
0-500M	500M-2MM	2-10MM	10-50MM	50-100MM	100-250MM		ALL	ALL
28	68	169	101	30	25	NUMBER OF STATEMENTS	387	372
%	%	%	%	%	%	ASSETS	%	%
29.6	13.7	16.3	18.4	14.2	21.6	Cash & Equivalents	17.9	17.1
19.3	36.6	34.7	34.5	31.5	26.2	Trade Receivables (net)	30.2	30.5
4.5	4.9	3.0	.9	8.6	1.3	Inventory	3.9	4.1
6.2	3.8	6.8	8.5	8.9	12.5	All Other Current	7.2	6.7
59.7	58.9	60.8	62.4	63.2	61.6	Total Current	59.2	58.4
27.2	30.7	29.9	28.4	25.4	24.9	Fixed Assets (net)	32.3	33.0
.7	3.0	2.8	4.5	5.8	4.7	Intangibles (net)	1.9	1.9
12.1	7.5	6.4	4.8	5.6	8.8	All Other Non-Current	6.6	6.7
100.0	100.0	100.0	100.0	100.0	100.0	Total	100.0	100.0
						LIABILITIES		
23.4	6.3	6.5	3.8	4.5	1.2	Notes Payable-Short Term	6.8	6.1
6.4	5.1	4.2	3.7	4.2	2.0	Cur. Mat.-L.T.D.	5.2	5.4
9.9	17.8	18.0	17.6	18.8	14.1	Trade Payables	15.3	15.1
.0	.3	.3	.2	.3	.4	Income Taxes Payable	.5	.3
7.8	9.7	9.4	12.7	20.8	18.9	All Other Current	12.8	12.7
47.5	39.2	38.5	38.1	48.7	36.6	Total Current	40.6	39.5
29.3	19.9	13.4	10.5	13.8	11.6	Long-Term Debt	14.9	15.9
.0	.4	.8	1.4	1.2	.9	Deferred Taxes	.9	1.1
16.5	5.4	2.5	3.0	.9	1.7	All Other Non-Current	3.8	5.0
6.7	35.2	44.8	47.0	35.4	49.1	Net Worth	39.8	38.5
100.0	100.0	100.0	100.0	100.0	100.0	Total Liabilties & Net Worth	100.0	100.0
						INCOME DATA		
100.0	100.0	100.0	100.0	100.0	100.0	Net Sales	100.0	100.0
45.9	34.7	25.0	18.1	17.6	13.8	Gross Profit	23.0	24.4
37.7	31.6	20.2	14.3	11.2	8.2	Operating Expenses	20.7	20.8
8.2	3.1	4.7	3.8	6.4	5.5	Operating Profit	2.3	3.6
.5	.0	-.3	-.4	.8	-.1	All Other Expenses (net)	.5	.6
7.7	3.1	5.1	4.2	5.6	5.6	Profit Before Taxes	1.8	3.0
						RATIOS		
4.1	2.9	2.5	2.3	1.6	2.1		2.2	2.3
1.8	1.7	1.6	1.6	1.3	1.6	Current	1.5	1.6
.7	1.0	1.2	1.2	1.1	1.3		1.1	1.1
3.2	2.2	2.0	1.9	1.3	1.7		1.9	1.9
1.5	1.5	1.3	1.3	1.1	1.2	Quick	(386) 1.2	(371) 1.3
.5	.7	1.0	.9	.6	.9		.7	.8
0 UND	22 16.4	38 9.6	45 8.1	43 8.4	45 8.1		35 10.5	30 12.3
0 UND	43 8.5	60 6.1	61 6.0	61 6.0	58 6.3	Sales/Receivables	54 6.8	54 6.8
54 6.8	68 5.4	83 4.4	81 4.5	78 4.7	83 4.4		75 4.9	79 4.6
0 UND	0 UND	0 UND	0 UND	0 UND	0 UND		0 UND	0 UND
0 UND	0 UND	0 UND	0 UND	3 122.4	0 UND	Cost of Sales/Inventory	0 UND	0 UND
0 UND	3 106.2	3 106.1	2 175.1	17 21.8	3 105.5		8 45.4	8 43.7
0 UND	11 34.2	17 21.9	23 15.8	28 12.9	28 13.1		14 25.6	15 24.0
0 UND	29 12.5	34 10.6	37 9.9	39 9.3	46 7.9	Cost of Sales/Payables	27 13.3	29 12.6
36 10.0	58 6.3	57 6.4	49 7.4	55 6.6	52 7.0		47 7.8	50 7.3
6.1	6.3	5.2	4.9	6.1	3.5		5.2	5.8
20.1	13.9	9.8	9.5	13.4	8.1	Sales/Working Capital	10.5	10.6
-35.9	907.3	28.1	20.9	50.0	13.9		51.9	64.6
37.5	24.6	29.4	25.3	48.7	86.9		20.6	18.6
(19) 7.9	(58) 6.8	(153) 8.2	(88) 8.1	(24) 7.0	(20) 17.9	EBIT/Interest	(358) 4.0	(337) 3.9
.4	.4	2.0	2.6	3.0	9.6		.6	.4
		6.4	6.8		7.2		8.4	6.4
		(40) 2.2	(38) 3.4		(10) 4.6	Net Profit + Depr., Dep., Amort./Cur. Mat. L/T/D	(123) 2.4	(113) 2.6
		1.4	1.8		3.2		1.1	.9
.2	.3	.3	.3	.3	.1		.3	.3
.9	.7	.6	.7	.5	.5	Fixed/Worth	.7	.7
-.5	2.5	1.3	1.3	2.7	.7		1.6	1.6
.6	.5	.6	.6	1.2	.7		.7	.6
2.1	1.6	1.4	1.4	2.2	1.0	Debt/Worth	1.5	1.4
-3.9	8.0	2.4	2.3	5.1	1.9		2.9	3.0
148.9	75.9	46.0	32.5	39.7	30.3		34.4	34.1
(19) 91.0	(57) 39.1	(160) 21.2	(97) 16.5	(26) 24.4	(24) 15.2	% Profit Before Taxes/Tangible Net Worth	(353) 13.4	(338) 12.7
20.0	2.0	4.5	3.2	10.5	3.3		.2	.2
104.0	26.4	18.8	13.7	13.8	11.6		13.4	14.6
25.2	11.6	7.9	6.5	6.6	6.7	% Profit Before Taxes/Total Assets	4.8	4.5
-8.4	-2.5	1.5	1.4	3.2	.7		-1.5	-1.2
256.3	27.4	19.2	17.9	24.0	28.5		18.2	18.0
26.3	13.3	8.2	6.5	8.2	9.2	Sales/Net Fixed Assets	7.4	8.0
6.4	5.0	4.3	3.6	5.2	3.7		3.8	3.8
8.0	3.7	2.7	2.4	2.6	2.2		2.6	2.9
4.0	2.7	2.0	1.9	1.9	1.3	Sales/Total Assets	2.0	2.0
2.1	1.7	1.5	1.3	1.2	.9		1.4	1.4
.3	1.2	1.2	1.4	.8	.9		1.3	1.7
(11) 1.9	(50) 2.7	(146) 2.7	(92) 2.9	(27) 1.9	(19) 1.1	% Depr., Dep., Amort./Sales	(342) 3.2	(323) 3.6
5.6	5.7	5.3	4.8	4.2	2.3		6.3	6.6
2.9	2.3	1.5	.5				1.6	1.4
(14) 6.5	(33) 4.8	(65) 2.4	(30) 1.0			% Officers', Directors' Owners' Comp/Sales	(141) 3.6	(129) 3.6
11.8	5.8	4.3	3.6				6.7	6.2
28326M	250940M	1853264M	4401008M	4649691M	6737476M	Net Sales ($)	15655505M	12500507M
5294M	86054M	855448M	2215827M	2213876M	4178589M	Total Assets ($)	8215238M	6945310M

M = $ thousand MM = $ million

See Pages 9 through 22 for Explanation of Ratios and Data

Comparative Historical Data				Current Data Sorted by Sales					
			Type of Statement						
114	124	99	Unqualified	1	6	3	9	24	56
121	112	106	Reviewed		10	14	32	33	17
30	23	25	Compiled		4	4	9	5	3
61	71	53	Tax Returns	7	17	10	10	5	4
123	112	138	Other	10	13	13	22	33	47
4/1/11-3/31/12	4/1/12-3/31/13	4/1/13-3/31/14		76 (4/1-9/30/13)			345 (10/1/13-3/31/14)		
ALL	ALL	ALL		0-1MM	1-3MM	3-5MM	5-10MM	10-25MM	25MM & OVER
449	442	421	**NUMBER OF STATEMENTS**	18	50	44	82	100	127
%	%	%	**ASSETS**	%	%	%	%	%	%
17.3	16.6	17.5	Cash & Equivalents	17.8	18.8	14.0	19.8	15.4	18.2
31.5	32.2	33.2	Trade Receivables (net)	24.9	22.0	34.8	33.8	36.2	35.3
4.0	3.4	3.2	Inventory	7.1	4.8	3.1	4.0	1.5	2.9
6.6	6.3	7.2	All Other Current	6.7	2.9	3.8	6.3	8.2	9.8
59.4	58.5	61.0	Total Current	56.5	48.6	55.7	63.9	61.4	66.2
31.2	31.0	28.9	Fixed Assets (net)	23.8	39.0	31.0	27.6	31.5	23.7
2.5	2.7	3.4	Intangibles (net)	.0	3.7	4.9	3.1	1.2	5.3
6.9	7.8	6.6	All Other Non-Current	19.3	8.8	8.5	5.3	5.9	4.8
100.0	100.0	100.0	Total	100.0	100.0	100.0	100.0	100.0	100.0
			LIABILITIES						
6.8	7.2	6.5	Notes Payable-Short Term	6.4	16.5	8.1	6.1	5.4	3.2
5.3	4.9	4.3	Cur. Mat.-L.T.D.	4.8	6.2	5.5	3.9	4.3	3.2
15.4	15.5	17.2	Trade Payables	12.9	9.9	14.0	19.2	18.4	19.5
.4	.3	.3	Income Taxes Payable	.0	.1	.3	.3	.3	.3
11.4	12.5	11.5	All Other Current	9.1	11.7	6.9	6.9	10.1	17.4
39.3	40.4	39.7	Total Current	33.2	44.4	34.7	36.4	38.6	43.6
16.0	15.1	14.7	Long-Term Debt	14.9	28.5	19.8	12.7	12.3	10.8
.8	.8	.9	Deferred Taxes	.0	.5	1.0	.3	1.5	.9
4.0	3.0	3.9	All Other Non-Current	10.5	5.1	4.9	4.9	2.8	2.3
40.0	40.8	40.8	Net Worth	41.5	21.5	39.6	45.7	44.8	42.5
100.0	100.0	100.0	Total Liabilities & Net Worth	100.0	100.0	100.0	100.0	100.0	100.0
			INCOME DATA						
100.0	100.0	100.0	Net Sales	100.0	100.0	100.0	100.0	100.0	100.0
24.5	23.7	25.1	Gross Profit	51.0	40.3	28.5	25.0	21.5	17.0
20.0	18.8	20.4	Operating Expenses	40.1	38.7	25.2	19.4	17.2	12.0
4.5	4.9	4.6	Operating Profit	10.9	1.6	3.3	5.6	4.4	5.0
.2	.1	-.1	All Other Expenses (net)	.7	.4	-.6	-.6	-.2	.1
4.3	4.9	4.8	Profit Before Taxes	10.1	1.2	3.8	6.3	4.6	4.9
			RATIOS						
2.5	2.4	2.4		5.0	2.9	2.8	2.8	2.3	2.0
1.6	1.6	1.6	Current	2.5	1.3	1.8	1.7	1.6	1.5
1.1	1.1	1.2		.9	.7	1.1	1.2	1.2	1.2
2.2	2.1	2.0		3.3	1.9	2.3	2.1	2.0	1.7
1.3	1.3	1.3	Quick	2.2	1.0	1.5	1.5	1.3	1.2
.8	.8	.9		.4	.5	1.0	1.0	.9	.9
31 11.8	**31** 11.9	**34** 10.8		**0** UND	**4** 84.7	**30** 12.3	**33** 10.9	**39** 9.4	**46** 8.0
57 6.4	**55** 6.6	**57** 6.4	Sales/Receivables	**41** 8.8	**30** 12.0	**61** 6.0	**50** 7.3	**61** 6.0	**60** 6.1
81 4.5	**81** 4.5	**79** 4.6		**94** 3.9	**66** 5.5	**85** 4.3	**79** 4.6	**83** 4.4	**78** 4.7
0 UND	**0** UND	**0** UND		**0** UND	**0** UND	**0** UND	**0** UND	**0** UND	**0** UND
0 UND	**0** UND	**0** UND	Cost of Sales/Inventory	**0** UND	**0** UND	**0** UND	**0** UND	**0** UND	**0** UND
5 71.8	**5** 80.7	**3** 111.8		**0** UND	**9** 41.3	**3** 114.5	**3** 105.9	**3** 136.9	**3** 104.7
14 26.4	**14** 26.6	**19** 19.7		**0** UND	**0** UND	**9** 40.1	**16** 22.5	**21** 17.4	**27** 13.7
31 11.9	**29** 12.7	**35** 10.4	Cost of Sales/Payables	**32** 11.3	**23** 15.7	**20** 18.6	**31** 11.7	**39** 9.3	**36** 10.1
49 7.4	**48** 7.6	**54** 6.8		**87** 4.2	**54** 6.8	**42** 8.7	**62** 5.9	**60** 6.1	**51** 7.2
5.1	5.2	5.5		2.9	6.1	5.9	4.7	5.6	5.7
10.0	10.5	10.5	Sales/Working Capital	6.8	44.9	9.5	8.9	11.5	10.4
40.8	58.5	32.4		-34.3	-26.5	102.1	21.4	26.9	21.4
20.3	25.5	29.1		55.3	8.8	29.0	33.0	25.0	39.7
(383) 5.4	(388) 6.1	(362) 8.3	EBIT/Interest	(10) 18.8	(41) 4.1	(41) 5.1	(74) 9.5	(90) 8.7	(106) 10.4
1.2	1.6	2.1		3.7	-1.5	1.4	2.4	2.4	3.1
7.7	7.9	6.7					12.5	6.6	7.0
(108) 2.9	(108) 3.0	(103) 3.5	Net Profit + Depr., Dep., Amort./Cur. Mat. L/T/D				(21) 3.7	(25) 2.7	(48) 4.1
1.0	1.6	1.7					.8	1.7	2.1
.3	.3	.3		.0	.2	.5	.2	.3	.3
.7	.6	.6	Fixed/Worth	.3	1.2	.9	.5	.7	.5
1.4	1.4	1.4		4.5	9.5	2.5	1.3	1.2	1.1
.6	.6	.6		.3	.5	.7	.5	.6	.8
1.3	1.4	1.5	Debt/Worth	.8	1.4	1.7	1.3	1.4	1.7
3.2	3.4	3.0		7.6	NM	5.4	2.4	2.6	2.8
38.8	37.3	44.8		118.9	45.7	44.2	69.7	41.1	39.4
(408) 15.2	(404) 17.6	(383) 20.4	% Profit Before Taxes/Tangible Net Worth	(15) 58.6	(38) 10.0	(36) 18.0	(79) 30.1	(98) 18.8	(117) 20.4
1.6	3.1	4.5		1.1	-11.6	3.8	7.5	5.6	6.3
16.3	16.4	18.8		50.4	22.1	20.1	22.3	14.5	14.0
5.7	6.7	7.5	% Profit Before Taxes/Total Assets	7.8	4.3	6.7	10.9	7.3	6.8
.0	1.2	1.4		-2.8	-5.7	1.2	2.5	2.4	2.5
20.7	22.3	22.7		UND	32.6	21.0	19.8	18.6	29.8
8.7	8.3	8.8	Sales/Net Fixed Assets	15.4	7.2	9.7	8.7	8.2	9.5
3.8	4.1	4.3		4.2	2.5	4.2	5.0	3.7	5.5
2.7	2.9	2.9		3.2	3.0	3.0	3.1	2.7	2.7
2.0	2.0	2.0	Sales/Total Assets	2.1	1.8	2.0	2.1	2.1	2.1
1.4	1.4	1.4		1.0	1.2	1.4	1.4	1.6	1.3
1.3	1.2	1.1			2.0	1.7	.9	1.4	.8
(372) 3.0	(374) 2.9	(345) 2.6	% Depr., Dep., Amort./Sales		(33) 6.5	(33) 3.5	(72) 2.4	(89) 2.7	(112) 2.1
5.6	5.1	4.9			14.3	5.9	4.9	5.4	3.6
1.4	1.5	1.2			4.0	2.2	1.5	.9	.5
(161) 2.9	(159) 3.1	(147) 2.6	% Officers', Directors' Owners' Comp/Sales		(31) 6.0	(24) 3.0	(31) 2.4	(29) 2.0	(28) 1.0
5.2	6.0	5.4			8.4	5.4	4.3	3.4	2.3
15835944M	18619754M	17920705M	Net Sales ($)	6928M	96419M	179951M	588272M	1665445M	15383690M
8404280M	9864812M	9555088M	Total Assets ($)	8324M	74832M	96617M	336826M	928519M	8109970M

M = $ thousand MM = $ million

See Pages 9 through 22 for Explanation of Ratios and Data

Current Data Sorted by Assets							Comparative Historical Data	
						Type of Statement		
1	2	10	12	3	2	Unqualified	42	39
4	16	50	20			Reviewed	111	103
5	17	16		2	1	Compiled	53	38
45	31	14	1		1	Tax Returns	88	93
15	41	57	24	6	1	Other	152	132
45 (4/1-9/30/13)		352 (10/1/13-3/31/14)					4/1/09-3/31/10 ALL	4/1/10-3/31/11 ALL
0-500M	500M-2MM	2-10MM	10-50MM	50-100MM	100-250MM			
70	107	147	57	11	5	**NUMBER OF STATEMENTS**	446	405
%	%	%	%	%	%	**ASSETS**	%	%
24.3	12.3	12.7	16.6	14.7		Cash & Equivalents	15.6	14.9
22.9	41.5	48.2	48.5	43.0		Trade Receivables (net)	34.9	36.5
5.2	3.6	1.6	1.7	2.6		Inventory	3.8	3.8
2.2	4.4	7.2	6.7	12.1		All Other Current	6.5	6.0
54.6	61.8	69.8	73.4	72.4		Total Current	60.8	61.1
30.1	27.0	24.1	20.4	20.6		Fixed Assets (net)	29.5	29.1
4.6	2.1	1.9	1.8	.6		Intangibles (net)	2.5	2.3
10.7	9.1	4.2	4.4	6.4		All Other Non-Current	7.2	7.5
100.0	100.0	100.0	100.0	100.0		Total	100.0	100.0
						LIABILITIES		
23.1	10.6	6.8	5.9	3.9		Notes Payable-Short Term	13.0	13.2
4.3	3.9	2.7	3.0	2.1		Cur. Mat.-L.T.D.	5.2	4.4
14.7	17.4	24.9	20.3	22.6		Trade Payables	16.0	18.3
.5	.0	.2	.3	.0		Income Taxes Payable	.4	.3
17.0	11.5	9.0	13.2	17.2		All Other Current	11.3	11.7
59.5	43.4	43.6	42.7	45.9		Total Current	46.0	47.8
38.2	18.5	13.3	6.8	9.6		Long-Term Debt	18.4	19.4
.1	.1	.4	.5	.4		Deferred Taxes	.5	.6
15.8	5.2	3.1	2.5	2.0		All Other Non-Current	4.9	6.9
-13.7	32.8	39.6	47.6	42.1		Net Worth	30.2	25.4
100.0	100.0	100.0	100.0	100.0		Total Liabilties & Net Worth	100.0	100.0
						INCOME DATA		
100.0	100.0	100.0	100.0	100.0		Net Sales	100.0	100.0
43.1	33.5	23.0	18.1	12.7		Gross Profit	26.4	26.2
37.4	28.3	18.6	13.4	9.4		Operating Expenses	25.9	26.3
5.7	5.1	4.4	4.7	3.3		Operating Profit	.5	-.2
.9	.2	.0	.0	-.3		All Other Expenses (net)	.7	.4
4.7	4.9	4.4	4.7	3.6		Profit Before Taxes	-.2	-.6
						RATIOS		
3.3	2.7	2.6	2.4	1.9			2.4	2.6
1.0	1.6	1.7	1.8	1.7		Current	1.4	1.4
.4	.9	1.2	1.4	1.3			.9	.9
2.8	2.5	2.4	2.1	1.7			2.1	2.2
.9	(106) 1.5	1.4	1.6	1.1		Quick	1.2	1.2
.2	.7	1.0	1.2	1.0			.7	.7
0 UND	**28** 13.1	**45** 8.2	**60** 6.1	**59** 6.2			**30** 12.1	**28** 13.2
1 616.0	**47** 7.7	**68** 5.4	**79** 4.6	**64** 5.7		Sales/Receivables	**52** 7.0	**51** 7.1
33 10.9	**64** 5.7	**87** 4.2	**101** 3.6	**81** 4.5			**73** 5.0	**81** 4.5
0 UND	**0** UND	**0** UND	**0** UND	**0** UND			**0** UND	**0** UND
0 UND	**0** UND	**0** UND	**0** UND	**0** UND		Cost of Sales/Inventory	**0** UND	**0** UND
1 245.6	**2** 146.5	**2** 201.5	**5** 75.4	**8** 45.9			**5** 71.6	**5** 69.1
0 UND	**9** 39.9	**21** 17.6	**23** 15.8	**24** 15.5			**10** 36.4	**11** 31.7
0 769.9	**23** 15.7	**34** 10.6	**38** 9.7	**32** 11.3		Cost of Sales/Payables	**25** 14.5	**29** 12.7
26 14.1	**40** 9.2	**51** 7.1	**55** 6.6	**49** 7.4			**45** 8.1	**50** 7.2
14.1	7.7	5.8	5.1	6.2			6.3	5.5
401.3	14.1	10.1	8.2	7.9		Sales/Working Capital	13.3	14.0
-20.2	-74.9	28.6	12.3	15.2			-68.2	-83.1
19.8	21.2	39.7	28.5				9.7	9.6
(54) 5.6	(98) 8.6	(130) 11.7	(49) 10.5			EBIT/Interest	(386) 1.6	(351) 2.3
1.2	2.1	3.7	3.2				-2.9	-2.7
		14.3	8.7				6.7	5.2
		(21) 3.0	(16) 4.2			Net Profit + Depr., Dep., Amort./Cur. Mat. L/T/D	(76) 2.1	(79) 2.1
		1.6	1.2				.7	-.1
.2	.3	.1	.1	.1			.2	.3
4.4	.7	.5	.4	.4		Fixed/Worth	.7	.6
-.7	1.6	1.2	.7	1.0			2.5	3.1
1.2	.7	.8	.6	1.0			.7	.7
UND	1.6	1.4	1.2	1.5		Debt/Worth	1.6	1.7
-2.7	4.2	3.2	2.5	3.1			8.7	8.8
924.9	75.0	44.4	35.5	21.0			34.9	27.4
(37) 72.7	(93) 34.4	(136) 25.2	(56) 16.5	17.1		% Profit Before Taxes/Tangible Net Worth	(370) 10.2	(327) 8.6
26.8	8.7	12.4	5.6	8.6			-11.6	-7.5
54.6	29.1	18.9	13.5	6.2			12.2	11.3
13.9	10.8	9.3	6.1	5.3		% Profit Before Taxes/Total Assets	1.6	2.4
-.9	3.2	3.8	2.3	4.1			-9.1	-7.2
197.4	41.9	54.1	49.1	126.5			33.8	31.1
38.2	13.3	14.7	15.2	9.8		Sales/Net Fixed Assets	11.4	12.5
10.4	6.8	6.7	7.1	4.7			5.1	5.7
9.0	4.6	3.3	2.9	3.1			3.6	3.8
4.9	3.2	2.6	2.2	2.7		Sales/Total Assets	2.5	2.5
3.3	2.3	2.0	1.6	1.6			1.7	1.7
.6	.8	.4	.7	.3			1.1	1.1
(40) 1.5	(71) 2.0	(113) 1.5	(50) 1.3	(10) 1.6		% Depr., Dep., Amort./Sales	(354) 2.4	(313) 2.6
4.0	4.7	3.2	3.2	4.4			4.9	5.0
3.6	1.3	1.2	1.1				2.2	2.0
(46) 6.1	(55) 3.5	(65) 2.0	(18) 1.5			% Officers', Directors' Owners' Comp/Sales	(201) 4.1	(194) 4.1
13.6	5.3	3.8	2.4				7.2	7.6
90639M	440492M	1869309M	2556484M	1816363M	3590218M	Net Sales ($)	8409892M	8589221M
14348M	123790M	656357M	1099345M	767513M	816259M	Total Assets ($)	3447673M	3148753M

M = $ thousand MM = $ million

See Pages 9 through 22 for Explanation of Ratios and Data

Comparative Historical Data | **Current Data Sorted by Sales**

4/1/11-3/31/12 ALL	4/1/12-3/31/13 ALL	4/1/13-3/31/14 ALL		0-1MM	1-3MM	3-5MM	5-10MM	10-25MM	25MM & OVER
			Type of Statement						
43	47	30	Unqualified	1	1	2	2	7	17
117	81	90	Reviewed		9	13	17	36	15
44	33	41	Compiled	2	10	11	8	6	4
85	79	92	Tax Returns	26	29	12	17	6	2
131	109	144	Other	10	20	21	33	25	35
				45 (4/1-9/30/13)			352 (10/1/13-3/31/14)		
420	349	397	**NUMBER OF STATEMENTS**	39	69	59	77	80	73
%	%	%	**ASSETS**	%	%	%	%	%	%
15.1	13.9	15.2	Cash & Equivalents	26.8	18.5	11.9	11.7	13.9	13.7
38.7	40.7	41.5	Trade Receivables (net)	12.9	32.1	42.3	45.3	50.7	50.9
3.5	3.5	2.8	Inventory	7.9	4.1	1.4	2.6	1.7	1.6
6.3	5.5	5.5	All Other Current	2.2	2.8	5.9	5.2	7.2	8.1
63.6	63.5	65.1	Total Current	49.7	57.6	61.5	64.8	73.5	74.3
27.1	24.4	25.7	Fixed Assets (net)	31.0	30.0	30.0	25.3	21.8	20.1
2.6	4.1	2.3	Intangibles (net)	3.9	3.8	2.3	2.1	1.6	1.1
6.7	8.0	6.8	All Other Non-Current	15.3	8.6	6.1	7.8	3.0	4.4
100.0	100.0	100.0	Total	100.0	100.0	100.0	100.0	100.0	100.0
			LIABILITIES						
14.3	13.5	10.7	Notes Payable-Short Term	24.8	10.6	11.2	10.9	6.0	7.7
4.7	4.0	3.4	Cur. Mat.-L.T.D.	3.0	4.0	5.0	2.4	3.5	3.0
19.2	18.9	20.2	Trade Payables	8.0	17.4	17.1	20.7	26.5	24.2
.2	.2	.2	Income Taxes Payable	.3	.3	.1	.2	.2	.2
12.3	12.4	11.9	All Other Current	21.6	8.6	15.3	7.7	9.8	13.9
50.7	49.0	46.4	Total Current	57.8	40.8	48.6	41.9	46.0	49.0
17.0	17.9	18.2	Long-Term Debt	39.0	27.2	19.7	16.1	10.3	8.4
.5	.5	.3	Deferred Taxes	.0	.1	.3	.3	.6	.5
6.7	6.6	5.8	All Other Non-Current	19.7	9.8	4.3	2.1	3.5	2.0
25.1	26.0	29.3	Net Worth	-16.6	22.0	27.2	39.7	39.6	40.1
100.0	100.0	100.0	Total Liabilties & Net Worth	100.0	100.0	100.0	100.0	100.0	100.0
			INCOME DATA						
100.0	100.0	100.0	Net Sales	100.0	100.0	100.0	100.0	100.0	100.0
25.9	26.6	28.5	Gross Profit	50.2	38.7	31.7	26.1	19.9	16.7
23.9	22.7	23.6	Operating Expenses	42.1	33.9	27.1	21.6	15.8	11.7
2.0	3.9	4.9	Operating Profit	8.2	4.8	4.6	4.5	4.1	5.0
.2	.3	.2	All Other Expenses (net)	1.1	.3	.2	.2	-.1	.1
1.8	3.6	4.7	Profit Before Taxes	7.0	4.4	4.4	4.3	4.2	4.9
			RATIOS						
2.5	2.4	2.6		3.2	3.2	2.6	3.1	2.5	2.2
1.5	1.4	1.6	Current	.9	1.7	1.7	1.6	1.6	1.6
1.0	1.0	1.1		.2	.8	.9	1.2	1.2	1.3
2.1	2.2	2.4		2.7	3.2	2.4	2.6	2.1	1.9
1.3	1.2	(396) 1.4	Quick	.6	1.5	1.5	(76) 1.4	1.4	1.4
.7	.8	.9		.2	.6	.7	1.0	.9	1.1
27 13.7	**33** 11.1	**27** 13.3		**0** UND	**8** 45.2	**33** 10.9	**31** 11.6	**48** 7.6	**46** 8.0
54 6.7	**57** 6.4	**53** 6.9	Sales/Receivables	**0** UND	**35** 10.4	**52** 7.0	**61** 6.0	**65** 5.6	**70** 5.2
79 4.6	**83** 4.4	**79** 4.6		**24** 15.3	**57** 6.4	**74** 4.9	**85** 4.3	**87** 4.2	**87** 4.2
0 UND	**0** UND	**0** UND		**0** UND	**0** UND	**0** UND	**0** UND	**0** UND	**0** UND
0 UND	**0** UND	**0** UND	Cost of Sales/Inventory	**0** UND	**0** UND	**0** UND	**0** UND	**0** UND	**0** UND
5 75.1	**5** 69.3	**3** 142.6		**21** 17.5	**3** 131.2	**2** 177.2	**3** 126.5	**1** 390.8	**4** 94.0
10 35.7	**11** 33.6	**11** 32.1		**0** UND	**0** UND	**12** 30.7	**11** 34.5	**25** 14.8	**21** 17.3
27 13.7	**31** 11.9	**26** 13.8	Cost of Sales/Payables	**0** UND	**17** 22.1	**23** 15.7	**27** 13.4	**40** 9.2	**31** 11.6
49 7.5	**54** 6.8	**47** 7.8		**24** 15.2	**46** 8.0	**41** 9.0	**49** 7.4	**61** 6.0	**46** 7.9
6.8	6.7	6.5		11.4	8.1	7.5	6.7	5.5	6.1
14.9	14.2	12.2	Sales/Working Capital	-190.0	15.6	11.6	10.3	10.6	9.2
-482.1	564.0	135.2		-8.3	-46.7	-74.9	31.5	53.7	18.3
12.0	21.4	29.4		16.9	16.3	22.1	24.1	56.8	60.5
(356) 4.1	(310) 6.3	(345) 9.0	EBIT/Interest	(29) 3.9	(60) 7.4	(49) 7.8	(69) 9.9	(73) 14.5	(65) 13.6
-1.4	1.5	2.4		.1	.9	1.4	3.1	4.1	5.6
5.9	5.2	8.7						11.8	10.0
(71) 2.0	(61) 2.5	(49) 3.0	Net Profit + Depr., Dep., Amort./Cur. Mat. L/T/D					(16) 3.0	(20) 5.2
.7	1.2	1.3						1.5	2.0
.2	.2	.2		.2	.3	.3	.2	.1	.1
.7	.6	.6	Fixed/Worth	2.4	1.0	.8	.5	.6	.4
2.3	2.6	1.7		-.4	42.3	2.7	1.4	1.2	.8
.7	.7	.7		.6	.8	.7	.7	.7	.7
1.7	1.9	1.6	Debt/Worth	102.0	2.9	1.6	1.2	1.5	1.3
7.1	9.9	4.9		-2.5	-175.0	6.1	3.2	4.1	3.1
45.8	47.1	60.5		872.0	100.0	59.6	55.5	49.5	40.3
(340) 12.5	(280) 19.6	(337) 27.5	% Profit Before Taxes/Tangible Net Worth	(22) 75.6	(51) 42.9	(48) 22.1	(71) 27.6	(76) 27.7	(69) 18.5
-4.6	2.7	9.9		17.0	7.2	4.9	13.1	13.8	9.0
16.1	18.2	25.7		59.2	31.2	28.5	19.6	20.5	13.5
4.2	6.5	9.5	% Profit Before Taxes/Total Assets	11.5	10.9	9.2	9.7	9.5	6.7
-3.5	.5	2.8		-4.7	-.8	2.0	4.0	3.5	3.5
36.8	47.7	60.3		190.0	60.3	32.4	40.6	66.1	75.0
13.2	16.0	16.7	Sales/Net Fixed Assets	33.4	13.3	14.5	12.9	16.3	19.9
5.9	7.3	7.1		8.4	6.5	4.6	7.7	7.2	7.8
3.9	3.8	4.0		7.3	5.6	4.2	3.9	3.4	3.6
2.6	2.7	2.9	Sales/Total Assets	3.3	3.4	3.0	2.9	2.6	2.8
1.8	2.0	2.0		1.7	2.1	1.9	2.1	2.0	2.2
.9	.9	.6		.6	.8	1.3	.8	.4	.5
(323) 2.2	(267) 1.8	(287) 1.7	% Depr., Dep., Amort./Sales	(23) 1.6	(41) 3.0	(45) 2.0	(53) 1.8	(64) 1.4	(61) 1.1
4.1	3.5	3.4		4.9	4.8	5.0	3.2	2.5	3.3
1.7	1.4	1.3		5.1	2.5	1.3	1.3	1.1	.8
(198) 3.7	(165) 2.8	(187) 3.2	% Officers', Directors' Owners' Comp/Sales	(28) 10.4	(41) 4.7	(26) 3.4	(38) 2.3	(33) 1.5	(21) 1.5
6.5	5.3	5.5		15.8	6.4	5.4	4.7	2.4	2.1
9996316M	**8099289M**	**10363505M**	Net Sales ($)	**20544M**	**134232M**	**234522M**	**548089M**	**1256392M**	**8169726M**
3648127M	**3322817M**	**3477612M**	Total Assets ($)	**7614M**	**47601M**	**99137M**	**204523M**	**520063M**	**2598674M**

M = $ thousand MM = $ million

See Pages 9 through 22 for Explanation of Ratios and Data

Current Data Sorted by Assets							Comparative Historical Data	
						Type of Statement		
		8	18	4	1	Unqualified	32	28
1	8	39	17			Reviewed	63	61
3	4	10		1		Compiled	23	26
3	10	7	1		1	Tax Returns	33	29
4	12	15	15	1	1	Other	56	62
26 (4/1-9/30/13)			158 (10/1/13-3/31/14)				4/1/09-3/31/10	4/1/10-3/31/11
0-500M	500M-2MM	2-10MM	10-50MM	50-100MM	100-250MM		ALL	ALL
11	34	79	51	6	3	**NUMBER OF STATEMENTS**	207	206
%	%	%	%	%	%	**ASSETS**	%	%
9.1	12.9	16.5	15.2			Cash & Equivalents	16.0	13.1
30.1	46.2	49.3	40.7			Trade Receivables (net)	37.0	39.4
11.1	3.8	4.4	7.8			Inventory	5.9	6.1
1.1	3.6	6.4	7.7			All Other Current	8.7	8.7
51.4	66.5	76.7	71.3			Total Current	67.6	67.4
27.9	18.7	17.6	23.7			Fixed Assets (net)	24.0	24.0
6.3	6.6	2.1	.8			Intangibles (net)	2.2	1.7
14.5	8.2	3.6	4.2			All Other Non-Current	6.2	6.9
100.0	100.0	100.0	100.0			Total	100.0	100.0
						LIABILITIES		
20.0	13.2	10.2	7.0			Notes Payable-Short Term	11.4	13.3
6.8	3.2	2.7	2.3			Cur. Mat.-L.T.D.	3.5	3.4
23.5	13.0	17.6	15.1			Trade Payables	15.3	15.5
.0	.1	.4	.3			Income Taxes Payable	.5	.4
31.6	14.3	11.5	11.7			All Other Current	16.7	12.4
81.8	43.8	42.5	36.3			Total Current	47.4	45.0
30.2	10.4	10.4	9.7			Long-Term Debt	12.0	12.8
.0	.4	.5	1.2			Deferred Taxes	.6	.6
23.6	6.0	3.8	2.9			All Other Non-Current	6.1	5.3
-35.6	39.5	42.8	49.9			Net Worth	33.9	36.3
100.0	100.0	100.0	100.0			Total Liabilties & Net Worth	100.0	100.0
						INCOME DATA		
100.0	100.0	100.0	100.0			Net Sales	100.0	100.0
38.4	28.3	22.4	16.4			Gross Profit	26.5	26.0
38.4	25.0	19.0	12.7			Operating Expenses	24.7	26.4
.0	3.3	3.5	3.7			Operating Profit	1.8	-.3
.2	.3	.2	-.3			All Other Expenses (net)	.3	.4
-.3	3.0	3.3	4.0			Profit Before Taxes	1.5	-.8
						RATIOS		
1.5	2.8	2.9	3.4				2.5	2.8
.6	1.8	1.8	1.9			Current	1.7	1.6
.1	1.0	1.3	1.4				1.2	1.1
1.3	2.7	2.5	2.4				2.1	2.2
.5	1.5	1.5	1.4			Quick	1.3	1.2
.1	.9	1.0	1.0				.8	.8
2 213.4	**42** 8.7	**44** 8.3	**64** 5.7				**38** 9.6	**42** 8.6
33 11.2	**58** 6.3	**68** 5.4	**78** 4.7			Sales/Receivables	**62** 5.9	**67** 5.4
48 7.6	**74** 4.9	**96** 3.8	**104** 3.5				**84** 4.3	**101** 3.6
0 UND	**0** UND	**0** UND	**0** UND				**0** UND	**0** UND
0 UND	**0** UND	**0** UND	**5** 75.9			Cost of Sales/Inventory	**1** 365.4	**1** 268.1
7 51.7	**4** 86.1	**12** 31.0	**22** 16.6				**19** 19.6	**20** 18.1
14 25.3	**3** 112.9	**16** 23.3	**21** 17.7				**10** 36.4	**14** 26.7
25 14.5	**19** 18.9	**25** 14.4	**30** 12.3			Cost of Sales/Payables	**23** 15.6	**33** 11.1
43 8.4	**34** 10.8	**49** 7.4	**41** 8.8				**44** 8.3	**50** 7.4
10.4	6.1	4.5	3.0				4.8	4.2
-13.3	11.6	8.4	5.9			Sales/Working Capital	8.8	8.2
-5.6	-485.8	16.4	10.9				33.5	56.8
	13.5	22.4	21.6				18.4	7.0
	(25) 3.3	(70) 8.4	(48) 11.3			EBIT/Interest	(185) 4.0	(181) 2.0
	1.5	2.2	1.8				-.3	-4.1
		10.8	8.7				9.0	2.9
		(16) 3.0	(17) 4.6			Net Profit + Depr., Dep., Amort./Cur. Mat. L/T/D	(59) 4.1	(46) 1.1
		1.8	2.5				1.1	-1.1
.4	.2	.1	.2				.2	.2
-1.2	.5	.3	.4			Fixed/Worth	.5	.6
-.2	2.5	1.2	.8				1.2	1.4
7.5	.6	.7	.5				.6	.5
-4.9	1.5	1.2	1.2			Debt/Worth	1.3	1.4
-2.3	29.8	3.7	1.8				4.2	4.6
	62.7	38.1	30.1				39.2	22.7
	(27) 15.4	(71) 15.7	(50) 15.1			% Profit Before Taxes/Tangible Net Worth	(182) 13.1	(179) 3.6
	3.2	5.4	2.4				.1	-10.3
10.7	21.8	15.1	11.0				13.6	9.3
.3	4.8	6.9	6.9			% Profit Before Taxes/Total Assets	5.1	1.6
-21.1	.8	1.8	1.5				-2.7	-8.8
140.3	78.2	63.0	19.8				35.9	29.9
21.9	26.5	20.6	10.1			Sales/Net Fixed Assets	14.5	12.6
11.1	10.2	9.7	4.2				5.8	5.3
6.6	3.9	3.1	2.4				3.2	2.8
4.6	3.1	2.5	1.7			Sales/Total Assets	2.2	2.0
3.0	2.3	1.8	1.4				1.6	1.5
.4	.5	.5	1.0				.8	1.0
(10) .9	(25) 1.0	(68) 1.0	(47) 1.6			% Depr., Dep., Amort./Sales	(179) 1.8	(172) 2.0
2.0	3.8	2.1	2.4				3.7	3.7
	2.4	1.2	.8				2.3	2.3
	(21) 2.9	(28) 3.1	(16) 1.9			% Officers', Directors' Owners' Comp/Sales	(81) 4.0	(93) 4.2
	7.0	5.3	3.2				8.0	7.3
22022M	135721M	879891M	2197677M	601355M	1040569M	Net Sales ($)	6258262M	4103876M
4169M	40025M	363877M	1129592M	403546M	401344M	Total Assets ($)	2487838M	2357295M

M = $ thousand MM = $ million

See Pages 9 through 22 for Explanation of Ratios and Data

Comparative Historical Data				Current Data Sorted by Sales					
			Type of Statement						
32	30	31	Unqualified				1	12	18
52	51	65	Reviewed	1	3	4	22	27	8
20	16	18	Compiled		6	4	2	5	1
24	31	22	Tax Returns		6	5	4	4	3
58	46	48	Other	1	6	9	8	11	13
4/1/11-3/31/12 ALL	**4/1/12-3/31/13 ALL**	**4/1/13-3/31/14 ALL**		**26 (4/1-9/30/13)**			**158 (10/1/13-3/31/14)**		
				0-1MM	**1-3MM**	**3-5MM**	**5-10MM**	**10-25MM**	**25MM & OVER**
186	174	184	**NUMBER OF STATEMENTS**	2	21	22	37	59	43
%	%	%	**ASSETS**	%	%	%	%	%	%
12.6	14.4	14.8	Cash & Equivalents		8.2	15.1	15.0	20.4	10.6
43.6	44.5	44.0	Trade Receivables (net)		42.4	43.8	46.0	45.3	42.0
5.8	5.1	5.8	Inventory		9.0	4.3	4.4	4.5	8.2
7.7	7.7	6.0	All Other Current		4.2	2.8	6.3	6.1	8.5
69.7	71.7	70.7	Total Current		63.8	65.9	71.8	76.4	69.3
22.3	20.7	21.2	Fixed Assets (net)		25.3	23.4	16.7	18.4	26.2
2.2	2.9	2.9	Intangibles (net)		.4	6.3	6.3	1.8	1.0
5.7	4.6	5.2	All Other Non-Current		10.5	4.4	5.2	3.4	3.5
100.0	100.0	100.0	Total		100.0	100.0	100.0	100.0	100.0
			LIABILITIES						
11.7	13.2	10.2	Notes Payable-Short Term		12.9	13.0	15.2	6.8	7.0
4.1	2.5	2.9	Cur. Mat.-L.T.D.		5.3	2.1	3.1	2.7	2.3
18.2	17.5	16.0	Trade Payables		16.3	13.4	17.3	16.1	16.7
.3	.3	.3	Income Taxes Payable		.1	.0	.7	.1	.3
12.3	12.9	13.3	All Other Current		17.7	11.4	13.9	11.0	13.2
46.6	46.4	42.7	Total Current		52.3	39.9	50.2	36.7	39.6
12.4	10.2	11.9	Long-Term Debt		16.4	17.2	10.7	8.3	13.3
.6	1.4	.7	Deferred Taxes		.2	.4	.5	1.0	.7
6.0	6.9	5.0	All Other Non-Current		8.8	2.1	2.7	3.4	3.0
34.4	35.1	39.8	Net Worth		22.4	40.5	35.8	50.5	43.4
100.0	100.0	100.0	Total Liabilties & Net Worth		100.0	100.0	100.0	100.0	100.0
			INCOME DATA						
100.0	100.0	100.0	Net Sales		100.0	100.0	100.0	100.0	100.0
23.6	23.8	22.5	Gross Profit		36.2	25.6	23.8	21.3	15.5
22.4	20.7	19.3	Operating Expenses		34.2	22.9	21.7	16.7	11.9
1.2	3.1	3.3	Operating Profit		2.0	2.7	2.1	4.5	3.6
.0	.1	.1	All Other Expenses (net)		.6	.2	.1	-.2	.2
1.3	3.0	3.2	Profit Before Taxes		1.4	2.5	2.0	4.8	3.4
			RATIOS						
2.4	2.7	2.9			4.0	2.8	2.3	3.6	2.5
1.6	1.7	1.8	Current		1.8	1.9	1.4	2.1	1.7
1.1	1.2	1.3			.7	1.0	1.0	1.5	1.4
2.0	2.2	2.4			2.6	2.7	1.7	3.4	1.8
1.3	1.4	1.4	Quick		1.1	1.6	1.1	1.7	1.3
.9	.9	1.0			.5	.9	.9	1.3	1.0
51 7.1	**48** 7.6	**44** 8.3			**36** 10.1	**44** 8.3	**46** 8.0	**43** 8.5	**55** 6.6
74 4.9	**65** 5.6	**68** 5.4	Sales/Receivables		**49** 7.4	**63** 5.8	**68** 5.4	**66** 5.5	**69** 5.3
91 4.0	**94** 3.9	**91** 4.0			**85** 4.3	**111** 3.3	**89** 4.1	**96** 3.8	**89** 4.1
0 UND	**0** UND	**0** UND			**0** UND	**0** UND	**0** UND	**0** UND	**0** UND
0 UND	**0** UND	**0** 931.1	Cost of Sales/Inventory		**0** UND	**0** UND	**0** UND	**1** 558.5	**6** 57.4
13 27.6	**12** 31.4	**16** 22.2			**22** 16.5	**4** 86.1	**7** 55.1	**17** 21.4	**30** 12.3
15 23.6	**16** 22.7	**16** 23.4			**16** 23.2	**2** 158.5	**9** 40.3	**17** 21.1	**24** 15.4
29 12.8	**31** 11.6	**26** 14.1	Cost of Sales/Payables		**27** 13.5	**19** 19.2	**23** 16.2	**24** 14.9	**30** 12.2
48 7.6	**47** 7.8	**41** 8.9			**46** 8.0	**40** 9.2	**42** 8.7	**40** 9.1	**43** 8.4
4.9	5.2	4.4			5.7	3.7	4.4	4.1	5.4
9.0	8.6	8.5	Sales/Working Capital		10.9	10.8	12.9	6.9	7.6
30.2	20.9	18.4			-13.7	NM	-471.4	10.1	11.4
14.6	16.1	18.9			6.4	18.2	11.7	40.1	18.4
(167) 3.5	(148) 5.3	(161) 8.1	EBIT/Interest		(17) 2.6	(14) 2.0	(33) 3.8	(56) 12.5	(40) 9.6
-1.1	1.6	1.7			-2.4	-6.3	1.1	3.8	2.4
7.4	5.7	8.3						6.5	10.2
(42) 1.6	(41) 2.5	(40) 4.6	Net Profit + Depr., Dep., Amort./Cur. Mat. L/T/D					(15) 4.1	(14) 5.0
.0	1.5	2.2						2.4	2.0
.2	.2	.2			.2	.1	.2	.2	.2
.5	.5	.4	Fixed/Worth		.5	.3	.5	.3	.5
1.5	1.3	1.1			-2.3	2.5	2.3	.6	.9
.8	.9	.6			.5	.3	.9	.5	.8
1.7	1.7	1.3	Debt/Worth		1.9	1.3	3.2	1.0	1.6
5.1	3.4	3.7			-4.9	4.4	9.7	1.7	2.3
26.4	38.5	35.2			16.9	65.8	40.0	38.1	33.8
(161) 6.4	(155) 15.7	(159) 15.3	% Profit Before Taxes/Tangible Net Worth		(13) 7.8	(19) 10.0	(30) 16.1	(55) 15.7	(41) 16.1
-7.6	5.7	4.2			1.5	3.2	1.5	8.5	4.5
11.1	13.1	12.0			11.4	10.3	15.3	15.1	11.0
3.3	5.3	6.3	% Profit Before Taxes/Total Assets		3.1	3.8	4.3	7.9	6.5
-3.5	1.1	.9			-6.7	-4.9	.2	3.1	2.4
34.5	50.1	47.7			43.1	114.5	90.2	35.3	22.9
13.5	16.0	13.7	Sales/Net Fixed Assets		16.7	18.6	23.1	13.2	11.3
5.7	7.6	5.9			6.4	5.9	9.3	6.8	4.5
3.2	3.3	3.3			4.5	3.9	3.7	3.1	2.7
2.1	2.4	2.4	Sales/Total Assets		2.4	2.4	2.7	2.5	2.1
1.5	1.7	1.6			1.8	1.4	2.0	1.6	1.6
.7	.8	.6			.6	.6	.5	.7	.6
(146) 1.7	(147) 1.4	(158) 1.2	% Depr., Dep., Amort./Sales		(18) 1.0	(16) 1.7	(30) 1.0	(55) 1.2	(37) 1.6
3.4	2.7	2.4			3.4	4.4	3.3	2.3	2.3
1.6	1.6	1.4			2.6	1.0	2.6	1.1	
(72) 3.6	(69) 3.2	(72) 2.8	% Officers', Directors' Owners' Comp/Sales		(13) 4.0	(11) 2.5	(17) 3.1	(22) 2.5	
5.5	6.1	5.4			7.4	5.0	7.0	4.2	
3702424M	**4123051M**	**4877235M**	Net Sales ($)	**1436M**	**42941M**	**88496M**	**261805M**	**921086M**	**3561471M**
2143634M	**2271283M**	**2342553M**	Total Assets ($)	**575M**	**17574M**	**42798M**	**116897M**	**468950M**	**1695759M**

M = $ thousand MM = $ million

See Pages 9 through 22 for Explanation of Ratios and Data

	Current Data Sorted by Assets						Comparative Historical Data	
Type of Statement								
Unqualified		1		3				
Reviewed		2	5	1			22	15
Compiled		2	1				11	10
Tax Returns	8	8	2				21	14
Other	2	7	9	2			18	18
	6 (4/1-9/30/13)			47 (10/1/13-3/31/14)			4/1/09-3/31/10 ALL	4/1/10-3/31/11 ALL
	0-500M	500M-2MM	2-10MM	10-50MM	50-100MM	100-250MM		
NUMBER OF STATEMENTS	10	20	17	6			72	57
ASSETS	%	%	%	%	%	%	%	%
Cash & Equivalents	25.8	12.5	8.5		DATA NOT AVAILABLE	DATA NOT AVAILABLE	19.2	16.2
Trade Receivables (net)	15.9	42.7	45.2				38.7	37.4
Inventory	5.7	6.8	9.2				6.5	8.6
All Other Current	5.1	10.5	17.1				7.6	6.3
Total Current	52.4	72.4	80.1				72.0	68.5
Fixed Assets (net)	30.0	9.0	13.3				15.7	18.4
Intangibles (net)	.5	9.4	.5				4.3	2.5
All Other Non-Current	17.0	9.1	6.1				8.0	10.6
Total	100.0	100.0	100.0				100.0	100.0
LIABILITIES								
Notes Payable-Short Term	28.9	13.5	11.5				15.4	14.8
Cur. Mat.-L.T.D.	2.0	.9	1.2				4.5	2.9
Trade Payables	.8	24.2	26.3				20.4	16.2
Income Taxes Payable	.0	.3	.7				.3	.1
All Other Current	16.3	24.5	11.0				17.9	13.1
Total Current	47.9	63.5	50.8				58.5	47.1
Long-Term Debt	43.0	12.4	12.6				14.6	17.3
Deferred Taxes	.0	.2	.0				.3	.3
All Other Non-Current	5.3	5.3	13.7				5.3	6.4
Net Worth	3.8	18.6	22.9				21.3	28.9
Total Liabilties & Net Worth	100.0	100.0	100.0				100.0	100.0
INCOME DATA								
Net Sales	100.0	100.0	100.0				100.0	100.0
Gross Profit	24.0	28.0	23.4				27.8	28.1
Operating Expenses	17.8	27.1	19.9				25.8	27.1
Operating Profit	6.2	1.0	3.4				2.0	1.0
All Other Expenses (net)	.8	.3	.6				.3	.0
Profit Before Taxes	5.5	.7	2.8				1.7	1.1
RATIOS								
Current	3.7	2.3	2.3				3.0	2.4
	1.2	1.6	1.7				1.4	1.9
	.6	.6	1.3				.9	1.2
Quick		2.2	1.4				2.3	1.9
		1.4	1.2				1.1	1.2
		.4	.7				.7	.8
Sales/Receivables	0 UND	9 40.9	31 11.9				16 22.8	17 21.5
	0 UND	40 9.2	41 8.9				47 7.8	52 7.1
	14 26.2	54 6.8	57 6.4				62 5.8	74 4.9
Cost of Sales/Inventory	0 UND	0 UND	0 UND				0 UND	0 UND
	0 UND	0 UND	1 674.8				0 UND	3 145.1
	5 78.1	32 11.5	15 24.0				19 19.1	21 17.0
Cost of Sales/Payables	0 UND	2 177.4	19 19.1				5 77.8	8 44.6
	0 UND	19 19.2	32 11.5				20 18.1	18 20.6
	0 UND	38 9.5	43 8.4				34 10.8	44 8.3
Sales/Working Capital	36.6	9.5	7.0				5.1	5.7
	103.3	14.3	12.1				15.6	8.2
	-22.7	-24.6	26.0				-43.5	202.2
EBIT/Interest	28.9	28.4	92.4				7.8	6.1
	12.4	(15) 7.0	(15) 9.4				(58) 1.4	(48) 2.7
	2.0	2.2	-1.9				-3.6	-2.6
Net Profit + Depr., Dep., Amort./Cur. Mat. L/T/D								
Fixed/Worth	.1	.0	.1				.1	.1
	1.1	.2	.1				.4	.4
	-5.7	-80.3	.5				4.4	4.1
Debt/Worth	1.7	1.1	1.0				.7	.6
	5.3	3.3	1.5				2.0	1.2
	-10.2	-4.0	5.2				25.0	21.2
% Profit Before Taxes/Tangible Net Worth		45.9	43.8				45.0	29.3
		(12) 19.2	(14) 27.0				(56) 10.7	(46) 12.7
		-25.1	-.2				-10.8	-6.5
% Profit Before Taxes/Total Assets	52.0	20.5	22.1				22.6	11.6
	37.6	8.4	11.2				3.8	4.6
	13.6	-11.1	-.6				-7.6	-5.0
Sales/Net Fixed Assets	743.8	775.0	251.3				76.5	76.8
	55.4	168.6	73.6				33.6	31.6
	17.4	30.6	11.9				15.8	10.2
Sales/Total Assets	14.0	8.3	5.8				4.9	3.8
	10.7	4.4	3.2				3.2	2.7
	5.5	2.4	2.2				2.3	2.0
% Depr., Dep., Amort./Sales		.1	.2				.5	.5
		(12) .2	(10) .5				(54) 1.0	(45) 1.0
		.9	2.3				2.0	2.1
% Officers', Directors' Owners' Comp/Sales		2.7					2.0	1.8
		(11) 4.4					(42) 5.0	(30) 3.9
		5.4					8.7	7.6
Net Sales ($)	25246M	104695M	258440M	488985M			502281M	420561M
Total Assets ($)	2444M	22218M	75785M	155758M			184743M	167121M

M = $ thousand MM = $ million

See Pages 9 through 22 for Explanation of Ratios and Data

Comparative Historical Data				Current Data Sorted by Sales					
			Type of Statement						
4	5	4	Unqualified				1		3
15	18	8	Reviewed		1		1	5	1
11	8	3	Compiled			1	2		
9	12	18	Tax Returns	3	3	3	7	2	
19	21	20	Other	1	4	2	5	6	2
4/1/11-3/31/12 ALL	4/1/12-3/31/13 ALL	4/1/13-3/31/14 ALL		6 (4/1-9/30/13)			47 (10/1/13-3/31/14)		
				0-1MM	1-3MM	3-5MM	5-10MM	10-25MM	25MM & OVER
58	64	53	**NUMBER OF STATEMENTS**	4	8	6	16	13	6
%	%	%	**ASSETS**	%	%	%	%	%	%
13.7	9.4	13.8	Cash & Equivalents				13.8	12.4	
39.5	46.6	39.5	Trade Receivables (net)				44.2	44.9	
9.7	8.5	6.9	Inventory				4.4	9.0	
8.8	9.7	11.7	All Other Current				14.3	16.5	
71.7	74.4	71.8	Total Current				76.7	82.8	
16.2	15.0	14.7	Fixed Assets (net)				15.4	8.0	
4.1	3.7	4.3	Intangibles (net)				.5	1.5	
8.0	6.9	9.2	All Other Non-Current				7.5	7.7	
100.0	100.0	100.0	Total				100.0	100.0	
			LIABILITIES						
20.8	13.8	15.8	Notes Payable-Short Term				13.5	10.5	
2.6	1.7	1.3	Cur. Mat.-L.T.D.				1.9	.7	
17.5	17.7	20.4	Trade Payables				20.5	36.9	
.3	.1	.4	Income Taxes Payable				.4	.9	
10.9	13.3	17.6	All Other Current				20.4	8.7	
52.1	46.7	55.5	Total Current				56.7	57.7	
10.6	14.0	17.6	Long-Term Debt				22.0	6.1	
.1	.1	.1	Deferred Taxes				.2	.0	
6.7	8.1	7.5	All Other Non-Current				10.5	7.5	
30.5	31.2	19.3	Net Worth				10.6	28.8	
100.0	100.0	100.0	Total Liabilties & Net Worth				100.0	100.0	
			INCOME DATA						
100.0	100.0	100.0	Net Sales				100.0	100.0	
29.7	26.5	24.1	Gross Profit				23.2	19.1	
27.8	22.1	21.2	Operating Expenses				20.0	17.9	
1.8	4.4	3.0	Operating Profit				3.2	1.1	
.5	.2	.5	All Other Expenses (net)				.3	.0	
1.3	4.2	2.5	Profit Before Taxes				2.9	1.1	
			RATIOS						
2.5	2.7	2.2					2.4	2.0	
1.5	1.7	1.6	Current				1.6	1.7	
1.1	1.1	.9					.9	1.3	
1.9	2.1	1.6					1.7	1.4	
(57) 1.1	1.2	(52) 1.2	Quick				1.3	1.0	
.8	.7	.6					.8	.6	
23 15.6	**31** 11.9	**14** 26.7					**0** UND	**26** 14.2	
52 7.0	**51** 7.2	**37** 9.8	Sales/Receivables				**44** 8.3	**35** 10.4	
72 5.1	**78** 4.7	**56** 6.5					**66** 5.5	**57** 6.4	
0 UND	**0** UND	**0** UND					**0** UND	**0** UND	
0 UND	**1** 289.5	**1** 674.8	Cost of Sales/Inventory				**0** UND	**0** UND	
27 13.7	**30** 12.0	**9** 42.0					**5** 79.0	**5** 74.3	
8 43.2	**11** 32.9	**1** 318.9					**0** UND	**19** 19.1	
22 16.7	**22** 16.4	**23** 16.1	Cost of Sales/Payables				**29** 12.4	**32** 11.5	
41 8.8	**38** 9.6	**42** 8.7					**42** 8.6	**44** 8.3	
5.1	4.8	9.1					8.1	5.7	
11.3	10.3	16.5	Sales/Working Capital				15.4	12.1	
79.7	57.2	-304.0					NM	36.2	
9.6	13.7	26.8					37.3	49.0	
(51) 4.0	(54) 4.4	(46) 8.7	EBIT/Interest				(14) 12.7	(10) 5.9	
.2	1.8	1.7					-2.5	.4	
			Net Profit + Depr., Dep., Amort./Cur. Mat. L/T/D						
.1	.1	.1					.1	.1	
.3	.3	.3	Fixed/Worth				.2	.1	
1.9	1.4	1.9					NM	.5	
.8	.7	1.2					1.3	1.0	
2.2	1.9	2.0	Debt/Worth				2.0	1.4	
9.6	9.8	-283.2					-13.4	5.2	
42.3	70.8	70.9					66.6	36.4	
(47) 11.0	(55) 19.8	(39) 28.0	% Profit Before Taxes/Tangible Net Worth				(11) 25.2	(11) 5.5	
-3.1	6.0	.8					-9.8	.8	
13.8	17.3	23.8					29.0	12.8	
4.5	8.0	12.1	% Profit Before Taxes/Total Assets				13.7	.8	
-2.5	1.2	-.3					-2.3	-.6	
94.6	145.2	283.0					646.0	259.7	
34.4	57.2	79.0	Sales/Net Fixed Assets				79.5	184.1	
11.6	11.3	20.9					21.7	31.8	
4.3	4.5	7.2					9.9	6.5	
3.1	3.1	4.3	Sales/Total Assets				4.3	4.3	
2.0	2.0	2.3					3.1	2.3	
.5	.3	.2							
(36) .9	(48) .6	(31) .4	% Depr., Dep., Amort./Sales						
2.2	1.8	1.3							
2.3	1.6	2.3							
(34) 4.0	(37) 3.6	(22) 3.9	% Officers', Directors' Owners' Comp/Sales						
8.7	6.5	5.4							
750242M	**888402M**	**877366M**	Net Sales ($)	**2766M**	**14558M**	**23160M**	**113896M**	**223699M**	**499287M**
394226M	**312654M**	**256205M**	Total Assets ($)	**2011M**	**5096M**	**4240M**	**29889M**	**65671M**	**149298M**

M = $ thousand **MM = $ million**

See Pages 9 through 22 for Explanation of Ratios and Data

Current Data Sorted by Assets							Comparative Historical Data	
						Type of Statement		
	1	3	2			Unqualified	19	11
1	14	56	2			Reviewed	73	65
2	15	2				Compiled	20	22
21	14	4				Tax Returns	44	34
11	20	19	4	2	1	Other	50	43
	20 (4/1-9/30/13)		174 (10/1/13-3/31/14)				**4/1/09-3/31/10 ALL**	**4/1/10-3/31/11 ALL**
0-500M	**500M-2MM**	**2-10MM**	**10-50MM**	**50-100MM**	**100-250MM**			
35	64	84	8	2	1	**NUMBER OF STATEMENTS**	206	175
%	%	%	%	%	%	**ASSETS**	%	%
20.5	17.0	12.4				Cash & Equivalents	16.8	17.1
24.4	42.9	50.5				Trade Receivables (net)	40.2	37.4
4.3	5.3	5.6				Inventory	4.7	5.0
2.1	5.9	6.9				All Other Current	8.0	8.6
51.3	71.0	75.3				Total Current	69.7	68.2
31.6	19.9	17.6				Fixed Assets (net)	19.7	20.0
2.3	3.5	.9				Intangibles (net)	2.5	2.2
14.8	5.6	6.2				All Other Non-Current	8.0	9.6
100.0	100.0	100.0				Total	100.0	100.0
						LIABILITIES		
49.8	13.1	10.0				Notes Payable-Short Term	11.6	12.0
1.4	1.7	2.3				Cur. Mat.-L.T.D.	3.1	3.0
13.5	13.4	19.5				Trade Payables	12.3	14.8
.1	.1	.5				Income Taxes Payable	.7	.6
16.8	14.6	13.1				All Other Current	11.8	13.1
81.7	42.8	45.4				Total Current	39.6	43.6
31.3	8.9	10.3				Long-Term Debt	12.1	11.9
.0	.1	.4				Deferred Taxes	.4	.4
4.1	5.8	3.0				All Other Non-Current	4.8	4.1
-16.9	42.4	40.9				Net Worth	43.1	40.1
100.0	100.0	100.0				Total Liabilties & Net Worth	100.0	100.0
						INCOME DATA		
100.0	100.0	100.0				Net Sales	100.0	100.0
43.5	31.1	20.8				Gross Profit	26.9	26.4
38.6	25.9	17.7				Operating Expenses	25.3	26.4
4.9	5.2	3.2				Operating Profit	1.6	.0
1.0	.6	.2				All Other Expenses (net)	.3	.3
3.9	4.6	2.9				Profit Before Taxes	1.3	-.3
						RATIOS		
3.0	4.1	2.6					3.6	2.7
1.5	1.8	1.6				Current	1.8	1.6
.3	1.1	1.2					1.2	1.1
2.0	3.4	2.3					3.1	2.4
1.1	(63) 1.6	1.4				Quick	1.6	1.3
.2	.8	1.0					1.0	.8
0 UND	**24** 15.3	**59** 6.2					**33** 10.9	**33** 11.1
10 36.4	**52** 7.0	**78** 4.7				Sales/Receivables	**61** 5.9	**60** 6.1
32 11.4	**78** 4.7	**101** 3.6					**84** 4.3	**89** 4.1
0 UND	**0** UND	**0** UND					**0** UND	**0** UND
0 UND	**0** UND	**0** UND				Cost of Sales/Inventory	**0** UND	**0** UND
0 999.8	**5** 80.4	**5** 75.0					**3** 111.2	**4** 86.5
0 UND	**7** 55.8	**15** 24.7					**7** 49.2	**9** 40.5
5 70.0	**18** 19.8	**33** 11.2				Cost of Sales/Payables	**17** 22.0	**23** 16.0
19 19.6	**34** 10.8	**45** 8.1					**33** 11.1	**45** 8.0
11.7	5.0	4.9					4.9	4.9
66.7	10.0	8.7				Sales/Working Capital	8.5	10.5
-12.5	66.3	28.9					31.1	108.0
24.9	31.5	24.6					17.8	9.4
(25) 7.8	(57) 12.1	(75) 5.2				EBIT/Interest	(176) 4.5	(149) 1.9
2.1	2.6	2.3					-1.4	-2.9
		6.8					8.1	4.2
		(14) 3.5				Net Profit + Depr., Dep., Amort./Cur. Mat. L/T/D	(42) 3.8	(31) 1.4
		1.6					1.4	-1.7
.4	.1	.1					.2	.1
1.5	.4	.3				Fixed/Worth	.3	.3
-2.2	2.6	1.1					1.0	1.1
1.0	.4	.6					.4	.5
3.8	1.3	1.3				Debt/Worth	1.1	1.2
-12.4	7.2	4.0					3.0	4.9
138.1	92.5	34.1					38.9	21.8
(25) 56.9	(54) 36.6	(80) 17.1				% Profit Before Taxes/Tangible Net Worth	(180) 11.0	(148) 3.9
20.7	5.4	4.0					-2.9	-10.7
51.9	32.4	11.3					14.6	12.1
22.1	13.9	5.1				% Profit Before Taxes/Total Assets	4.3	1.6
3.4	3.0	1.7					-3.8	-5.4
71.0	51.4	45.1					37.4	42.8
33.9	24.5	17.5				Sales/Net Fixed Assets	20.3	17.4
12.4	12.4	11.5					9.9	8.1
11.3	4.1	3.2					3.5	3.3
5.7	3.2	2.5				Sales/Total Assets	2.5	2.4
4.0	2.1	1.9					1.9	1.6
.7	.5	.6					.8	1.0
(17) 2.0	(44) 1.3	(71) 1.1				% Depr., Dep., Amort./Sales	(174) 1.5	(139) 2.0
3.6	2.0	2.0					2.9	3.7
2.4	2.7	1.3					3.2	2.6
(21) 6.5	(38) 4.2	(39) 2.7				% Officers', Directors' Owners' Comp/Sales	(121) 5.8	(89) 4.5
9.8	6.3	5.7					10.3	9.4
55005M	**228983M**	**981410M**	**222334M**	**94813M**	**89046M**	Net Sales ($)	**2709288M**	**1485977M**
7879M	**66034M**	**376772M**	**101023M**	**133322M**	**101401M**	Total Assets ($)	**1113575M**	**668363M**

M = $ thousand MM = $ million

See Pages 9 through 22 for Explanation of Ratios and Data

Comparative Historical Data				Current Data Sorted by Sales					
			Type of Statement						
8	9	6	Unqualified		1	1		4	
78	70	73	Reviewed	2	6	6	34	21	4
21	24	19	Compiled	5	7	3	3	1	
38	42	39	Tax Returns	9	14	8	5	3	
62	47	57	Other	8	13	11	9	8	8
				20 (4/1-9/30/13)			174 (10/1/13-3/31/14)		
4/1/11-3/31/12 ALL	**4/1/12-3/31/13 ALL**	**4/1/13-3/31/14 ALL**		**0-1MM**	**1-3MM**	**3-5MM**	**5-10MM**	**10-25MM**	**25MM & OVER**
207	192	194	**NUMBER OF STATEMENTS**	24	41	29	51	37	12
%	%	%	**ASSETS**	%	%	%	%	%	%
15.0	14.9	16.1	Cash & Equivalents	21.8	18.3	17.3	13.9	13.4	12.3
45.3	43.2	42.5	Trade Receivables (net)	20.3	36.9	38.6	54.1	50.5	41.5
4.1	4.7	5.2	Inventory	7.6	3.5	8.0	2.7	5.1	10.0
8.2	7.7	5.6	All Other Current	3.6	3.9	4.6	7.4	6.8	5.8
72.5	70.4	69.4	Total Current	53.2	62.6	68.5	78.1	75.8	69.7
18.0	20.0	20.8	Fixed Assets (net)	30.4	25.8	19.1	15.2	18.1	21.0
1.9	2.1	2.2	Intangibles (net)	3.8	4.0	1.9	1.0	.4	4.0
7.5	7.5	7.6	All Other Non-Current	12.5	7.7	10.5	5.7	5.7	5.3
100.0	100.0	100.0	Total	100.0	100.0	100.0	100.0	100.0	100.0
			LIABILITIES						
14.7	17.4	18.1	Notes Payable-Short Term	50.4	15.3	20.6	12.3	10.0	6.8
2.8	3.5	2.1	Cur. Mat.-L.T.D.	.8	1.8	1.4	2.1	2.4	6.0
15.7	17.7	16.3	Trade Payables	12.3	12.6	14.3	17.2	20.8	23.6
.5	.6	.3	Income Taxes Payable	.2	.0	.1	.7	.3	.0
17.4	12.0	14.5	All Other Current	22.6	11.8	17.9	11.4	13.9	13.7
51.1	51.2	51.2	Total Current	86.3	41.5	54.3	43.7	47.4	50.2
10.0	13.1	13.6	Long-Term Debt	18.8	20.5	13.7	9.9	8.1	12.1
.5	.2	.2	Deferred Taxes	.0	.1	.2	.2	.5	.5
3.8	4.3	4.0	All Other Non-Current	7.6	4.6	3.3	3.9	2.6	1.9
34.5	31.2	31.0	Net Worth	-12.4	33.3	28.4	42.3	41.4	35.3
100.0	100.0	100.0	Total Liabilities & Net Worth	100.0	100.0	100.0	100.0	100.0	100.0
			INCOME DATA						
100.0	100.0	100.0	Net Sales	100.0	100.0	100.0	100.0	100.0	100.0
23.6	25.1	27.8	Gross Profit	52.2	33.4	29.5	21.0	17.9	15.7
22.8	22.8	23.7	Operating Expenses	47.1	28.4	23.7	17.9	14.8	13.3
.7	2.3	4.1	Operating Profit	5.1	5.0	5.8	3.1	3.2	2.4
.1	.2	.5	All Other Expenses (net)	2.1	.2	.6	.3	.1	-.6
.7	2.0	3.7	Profit Before Taxes	3.1	4.8	5.2	2.8	3.0	3.0
			RATIOS						
2.8	2.8	3.1		4.2	3.7	3.7	3.2	3.0	1.6
1.6	1.6	1.6	Current	1.2	1.7	1.7	1.9	1.6	1.3
1.2	1.1	1.1		.2	.9	1.2	1.3	1.1	1.1
2.3	2.2	2.4		3.2	2.6	3.0	2.6	2.8	1.4
1.3	1.3	(193) 1.4	Quick	.6	1.5	(28) 1.6	1.6	1.3	1.2
.9	.7	.8		.2	.8	.7	1.1	.8	.6
42 8.6	29 12.6	23 15.7		0 UND	7 49.0	21 17.0	54 6.7	43 8.4	35 10.5
70 5.2	60 6.1	59 6.2	Sales/Receivables	17 21.3	51 7.1	34 10.6	74 4.9	70 5.2	58 6.3
94 3.9	87 4.2	87 4.2		45 8.1	81 4.5	68 5.4	101 3.6	96 3.8	78 4.7
0 UND	0 UND	0 UND		0 UND	0 UND	0 UND	0 UND	0 UND	0 UND
0 UND	0 UND	0 UND	Cost of Sales/Inventory	0 UND	0 UND	0 UND	0 UND	0 UND	1 281.6
4 82.0	5 67.6	3 129.5		7 49.8	0 UND	17 21.4	2 190.5	3 134.6	34 10.8
10 35.8	10 35.8	8 48.5		0 UND	0 752.9	6 57.9	10 35.7	14 26.5	24 15.4
24 15.4	25 14.5	23 15.6	Cost of Sales/Payables	10 36.4	16 22.5	17 21.8	26 14.1	31 11.6	33 10.9
40 9.1	42 8.7	38 9.6		26 13.9	36 10.0	36 10.2	39 9.3	46 8.0	37 9.8
4.7	6.0	5.3		7.4	5.1	6.0	4.8	5.2	8.3
9.3	10.9	11.3	Sales/Working Capital	18.9	15.7	13.4	7.7	12.4	16.2
30.8	87.5	66.5		-6.7	-59.3	33.3	18.3	36.5	34.6
11.4	16.6	25.1		17.7	23.4	38.3	29.8	26.2	14.5
(171) 3.8	(175) 4.1	(165) 6.7	EBIT/Interest	(14) 6.3	(37) 10.4	(25) 21.6	(45) 4.9	(34) 6.5	(10) 8.2
-.9	-.9	2.4		-.8	2.5	3.2	1.4	2.7	2.3
10.4	7.4	6.9							
(41) 2.3	(33) 1.8	(23) 2.9	Net Profit + Depr., Dep., Amort./Cur. Mat. L/T/D						
.2	-.7	1.4							
.1	.1	.1		.1	.2	.1	.1	.2	.2
.3	.4	.4	Fixed/Worth	1.1	.5	.4	.3	.3	.7
1.1	1.8	1.5		NM	8.5	1.5	.7	1.0	1.2
.5	.6	.6		.6	.6	.6	.6	.5	1.6
1.4	1.7	1.5	Debt/Worth	6.0	1.4	1.3	1.0	1.7	2.4
3.3	6.0	5.3		NM	34.0	5.5	2.7	4.1	3.9
24.9	51.9	57.8		101.0	97.8	102.1	38.2	42.8	58.7
(181) 5.5	(163) 16.8	(170) 22.9	% Profit Before Taxes/Tangible Net Worth	(18) 32.7	(33) 37.5	(24) 31.4	(47) 12.8	(36) 22.1	26.0
-7.1	-.2	5.4		4.3	4.7	17.2	1.9	10.5	4.6
11.3	20.4	21.9		29.2	36.4	29.2	13.7	14.7	13.0
2.9	5.2	8.0	% Profit Before Taxes/Total Assets	8.6	11.2	15.3	4.1	6.0	5.3
-4.7	-3.1	2.0		1.6	2.0	7.7	.8	3.1	2.1
53.8	58.1	53.1		141.4	60.9	68.2	44.1	51.4	54.0
22.5	22.8	22.0	Sales/Net Fixed Assets	17.2	20.4	24.7	21.1	23.0	27.0
11.5	10.0	11.7		5.2	8.5	13.0	14.6	10.7	8.7
3.4	3.9	4.1		4.9	5.5	5.5	3.6	3.7	4.3
2.6	2.8	2.8	Sales/Total Assets	3.3	2.8	3.5	2.8	2.7	2.9
1.8	2.1	2.0		1.2	2.1	1.8	2.1	2.1	1.3
.6	.6	.6		1.8	.9	.4	.6	.5	.6
(167) 1.2	(157) 1.2	(141) 1.2	% Depr., Dep., Amort./Sales	(11) 3.5	(27) 1.8	(17) .9	(43) 1.1	(33) .9	(10) 1.1
2.2	2.3	2.1		5.9	3.0	1.8	1.9	1.4	3.9
1.9	1.9	1.7		2.4	2.6	2.3	1.8	.9	
(102) 3.7	(102) 4.0	(102) 4.0	% Officers', Directors' Owners' Comp/Sales	(12) 6.7	(25) 5.1	(17) 4.7	(28) 3.2	(16) 3.0	
7.1	7.3	7.0		11.0	7.5	6.4	5.5	5.6	
1926070M	1753656M	1671591M	Net Sales ($)	13529M	80770M	116199M	380083M	569731M	511279M
826139M	802648M	786431M	Total Assets ($)	11940M	32582M	47952M	147344M	224026M	322587M

M = $ thousand MM = $ million

See Pages 9 through 22 for Explanation of Ratios and Data

Current Data Sorted by Assets							Comparative Historical Data	
						Type of Statement		
		1	3	1	1	Unqualified	10	9
1	12	49	5			Reviewed	64	51
2	7	5				Compiled	20	18
10	15	8	1			Tax Returns	19	25
5	5	9	4			Other	27	26
26 (4/1-9/30/13)		118 (10/1/13-3/31/14)					4/1/09-3/31/10 ALL	4/1/10-3/31/11 ALL
0-500M	500M-2MM	2-10MM	10-50MM	50-100MM	100-250MM			
18	39	72	13	1	1	**NUMBER OF STATEMENTS**	140	129
%	%	%	%	%	%	**ASSETS**	%	%
24.2	13.7	14.5	15.3			Cash & Equivalents	17.5	14.9
37.2	44.5	54.5	51.7			Trade Receivables (net)	43.1	41.9
13.0	4.7	6.7	2.6			Inventory	8.6	11.0
.8	5.1	6.8	11.4			All Other Current	7.4	7.9
75.2	68.0	82.4	81.0			Total Current	76.6	75.7
20.9	22.5	12.4	14.0			Fixed Assets (net)	16.0	16.1
.4	.9	1.3	1.3			Intangibles (net)	2.2	3.3
3.6	8.7	3.8	3.7			All Other Non-Current	5.3	4.9
100.0	100.0	100.0	100.0			Total	100.0	100.0
						LIABILITIES		
23.1	14.0	9.6	7.5			Notes Payable-Short Term	13.7	11.7
2.7	3.3	1.4	.8			Cur. Mat.-L.T.D.	2.4	3.6
20.1	21.7	20.8	15.4			Trade Payables	16.6	18.6
.0	.3	.2	.0			Income Taxes Payable	.4	.4
14.8	10.5	13.2	16.1			All Other Current	16.5	13.6
60.6	49.7	45.4	39.8			Total Current	49.6	47.8
22.1	20.0	6.3	4.9			Long-Term Debt	9.2	9.6
.0	.1	.3	.0			Deferred Taxes	.3	.2
8.6	3.6	2.6	2.6			All Other Non-Current	6.3	4.3
8.7	26.5	45.4	52.7			Net Worth	34.5	38.1
100.0	100.0	100.0	100.0			Total Liabilties & Net Worth	100.0	100.0
						INCOME DATA		
100.0	100.0	100.0	100.0			Net Sales	100.0	100.0
44.1	34.0	24.5	20.3			Gross Profit	30.6	29.4
40.1	28.1	20.0	14.3			Operating Expenses	26.5	29.2
4.0	5.8	4.5	6.0			Operating Profit	4.1	.2
.3	.5	-.2	.2			All Other Expenses (net)	.5	.1
3.6	5.3	4.7	5.8			Profit Before Taxes	3.7	.1
						RATIOS		
3.0	2.6	3.0	2.4				2.6	2.5
1.6	1.6	2.0	2.0			Current	1.6	1.7
.8	.9	1.2	1.8				1.3	1.3
2.4	2.3	2.6	2.3				2.1	2.0
1.1	1.5	1.5	1.6			Quick	1.3	1.3
.6	.7	1.0	1.3				.9	.9
0 UND	**25** 14.8	**61** 6.0	**66** 5.5				**36** 10.2	**43** 8.4
26 13.8	**54** 6.7	**76** 4.8	**91** 4.0			Sales/Receivables	**54** 6.7	**68** 5.4
61 6.0	**74** 4.9	**99** 3.7	**101** 3.6				**78** 4.7	**94** 3.9
0 UND	**0** UND	**0** 999.8	**0** UND				**0** UND	**0** UND
9 39.8	**1** 290.8	**2** 153.4	**1** 343.9			Cost of Sales/Inventory	**3** 104.7	**8** 43.9
39 9.3	**13** 28.2	**16** 22.3	**3** 123.4				**18** 20.1	**29** 12.4
0 UND	**20** 17.9	**18** 20.8	**22** 16.4				**12** 29.4	**20** 18.0
26 14.2	**33** 11.0	**32** 11.4	**26** 14.2			Cost of Sales/Payables	**24** 15.0	**33** 10.9
60 6.1	**51** 7.1	**54** 6.8	**38** 9.7				**44** 8.3	**50** 7.3
8.7	6.0	4.4	4.7				5.5	4.2
25.3	13.9	7.3	5.4			Sales/Working Capital	10.0	8.3
-46.7	-40.4	16.9	7.2				21.6	18.4
20.0	41.1	36.2	55.4				32.3	10.3
(17) 8.0	(35) 6.9	(61) 15.3	(11) 18.4			EBIT/Interest	(123) 6.5	(111) 1.8
-1.0	1.8	3.7	9.6				1.4	-5.5
		47.4					13.8	8.2
		(26) 5.2				Net Profit + Depr., Dep., Amort./Cur. Mat. L/T/D	(30) 3.6	(31) 1.4
		1.6					1.6	-5.5
.1	.1	.1	.1				.1	.1
.6	.4	.2	.2			Fixed/Worth	.3	.3
-2.1	2.1	.5	.5				.7	1.0
.8	.7	.5	.6				.7	.6
6.6	1.8	1.3	.9			Debt/Worth	1.6	1.5
-5.2	5.8	2.4	1.3				3.7	4.0
88.9	83.3	44.4	30.5				44.8	17.7
(11) 53.4	(31) 34.0	(68) 22.9	18.1			% Profit Before Taxes/Tangible Net Worth	(121) 17.3	(115) 4.1
8.9	7.8	6.4	4.8				4.0	-22.2
63.2	28.0	19.4	13.8				19.2	7.5
21.9	9.0	9.4	9.8			% Profit Before Taxes/Total Assets	7.2	1.5
-4.6	2.2	3.0	2.8				1.3	-6.1
195.3	92.1	59.1	56.0				62.8	44.6
33.5	37.6	29.1	14.6			Sales/Net Fixed Assets	32.8	22.9
10.3	16.6	14.1	7.7				15.8	10.3
11.6	4.2	3.2	2.7				3.9	3.3
4.3	3.2	2.5	2.3			Sales/Total Assets	2.9	2.4
3.3	2.7	2.0	1.7				2.2	1.5
	.4	.4	.4				.5	.6
	(30) .9	(64) .7	(12) .7			% Depr., Dep., Amort./Sales	(124) 1.0	(115) 1.1
	1.3	1.2	1.1				1.6	2.1
4.1	2.3	1.9					2.5	2.7
(15) 6.9	(25) 4.5	(41) 2.8				% Officers', Directors' Owners' Comp/Sales	(80) 3.8	(73) 5.4
11.4	7.0	5.9					7.8	7.8
27159M	**171910M**	**893971M**	**413161M**	**139604M**	**179932M**	Net Sales ($)	**1752771M**	**1683187M**
4549M	**46565M**	**353356M**	**185804M**	**84005M**	**100404M**	Total Assets ($)	**708745M**	**916796M**

M = $ thousand MM = $ million

See Pages 9 through 22 for Explanation of Ratios and Data

Comparative Historical Data				Current Data Sorted by Sales					
			Type of Statement						
10	4	6	Unqualified					1	5
53	41	67	Reviewed	2	1	9	22	25	8
25	10	14	Compiled	3	3	4	4		
32	23	34	Tax Returns	5	9	5	8	5	2
34	41	23	Other	2	4	4	4	7	2
				26 (4/1-9/30/13)			118 (10/1/13-3/31/14)		
4/1/11-3/31/12 ALL	4/1/12-3/31/13 ALL	4/1/13-3/31/14 ALL		0-1MM	1-3MM	3-5MM	5-10MM	10-25MM	25MM & OVER
154	119	144	**NUMBER OF STATEMENTS**	12	17	22	38	38	17
%	%	%	**ASSETS**	%	%	%	%	%	%
13.4	10.4	15.7	Cash & Equivalents	13.5	26.5	10.9	16.4	14.8	13.6
45.3	51.2	49.3	Trade Receivables (net)	35.2	29.7	52.0	50.1	56.7	56.6
8.4	8.0	6.5	Inventory	17.6	4.1	5.2	7.7	5.8	1.6
8.4	7.4	6.1	All Other Current	.9	4.8	4.0	6.6	6.1	12.7
75.5	77.1	77.6	Total Current	67.1	65.1	72.0	80.8	83.4	84.4
15.7	14.8	16.2	Fixed Assets (net)	24.9	26.6	16.8	13.2	13.6	11.7
3.9	2.6	1.1	Intangibles (net)	.3	.2	2.3	1.9	.4	.6
4.9	5.6	5.1	All Other Non-Current	7.7	8.0	8.9	4.0	2.7	3.3
100.0	100.0	100.0	Total	100.0	100.0	100.0	100.0	100.0	100.0
			LIABILITIES						
13.3	14.3	12.2	Notes Payable-Short Term	9.4	29.9	9.5	9.7	10.3	9.5
6.2	3.8	2.0	Cur. Mat.-L.T.D.	3.7	1.5	4.1	1.7	1.3	.9
21.0	22.9	20.3	Trade Payables	22.7	18.1	22.4	18.9	21.4	18.9
.2	.2	.2	Income Taxes Payable	.0	.0	.7	.1	.1	.2
11.7	12.8	13.5	All Other Current	7.6	16.7	9.8	11.2	14.0	23.1
52.4	54.1	48.2	Total Current	43.4	66.2	46.5	41.7	47.1	52.6
11.3	10.8	11.8	Long-Term Debt	19.5	28.2	17.0	7.7	5.5	6.5
.2	.2	.2	Deferred Taxes	.0	.0	.3	.2	.3	.0
4.2	3.8	3.6	All Other Non-Current	2.7	7.6	6.5	1.7	1.0	6.6
31.9	31.0	36.3	Net Worth	34.3	-1.9	29.7	48.8	46.1	34.3
100.0	100.0	100.0	Total Liabilties & Net Worth	100.0	100.0	100.0	100.0	100.0	100.0
			INCOME DATA						
100.0	100.0	100.0	Net Sales	100.0	100.0	100.0	100.0	100.0	100.0
29.4	29.0	29.1	Gross Profit	48.0	42.5	33.3	27.4	20.5	20.2
29.2	26.2	24.2	Operating Expenses	41.8	33.8	28.5	23.6	16.8	14.2
.3	2.9	5.0	Operating Profit	6.1	8.7	4.8	3.8	3.7	6.0
.2	.6	.1	All Other Expenses (net)	.3	1.2	-.3	-.1	-.1	.0
.1	2.3	4.9	Profit Before Taxes	5.8	7.5	5.1	3.9	3.8	6.0
			RATIOS						
2.4	2.4	2.7		2.8	2.2	2.9	3.7	2.8	2.3
1.6	1.6	1.7	Current	1.8	.9	1.6	2.2	1.8	1.9
1.1	1.2	1.2		.9	.7	1.0	1.3	1.3	1.3
2.0	1.9	2.4		2.1	2.2	2.7	3.5	2.4	2.1
1.3	(118) 1.3	1.5	Quick	1.1	.7	1.4	1.6	1.5	1.5
.8	.9	1.0		.6	.4	.8	1.1	1.2	1.0
43 8.4	49 7.5	44 8.3		25 14.7	6 59.7	39 9.4	49 7.4	62 5.9	65 5.6
68 5.4	72 5.1	69 5.3	Sales/Receivables	45 8.1	17 21.8	69 5.3	65 5.6	78 4.7	76 4.8
91 4.0	94 3.9	89 4.1		59 6.2	72 5.1	78 4.7	87 4.2	101 3.6	99 3.7
0 UND	0 UND	0 UND		0 UND	0 UND	0 UND	0 UND	0 UND	0 UND
3 113.9	4 94.9	2 157.5	Cost of Sales/Inventory	26 13.9	4 96.8	2 158.8	2 167.2	1 248.5	2 184.5
18 20.0	16 22.8	15 24.6		47 7.8	9 39.8	19 18.9	19 19.4	9 40.6	4 83.0
21 17.0	23 15.8	17 21.0		0 UND	0 UND	21 17.7	14 25.6	18 19.9	24 15.5
34 10.8	41 8.9	31 11.6	Cost of Sales/Payables	47 7.7	31 11.9	30 12.1	35 10.3	28 13.0	30 12.2
54 6.7	59 6.2	51 7.2		66 5.5	57 6.4	47 7.8	48 7.6	56 6.5	37 9.8
5.1	5.5	5.3		8.5	6.7	5.0	4.6	4.7	5.4
9.0	9.0	8.4	Sales/Working Capital	20.1	-125.8	13.0	7.8	7.8	6.5
37.6	24.3	25.7		NM	-16.6	NM	18.5	13.8	13.5
11.8	19.1	36.2		29.3	42.3	38.4	24.6	54.1	108.9
(128) 2.7	(106) 5.1	(125) 11.5	EBIT/Interest	(10) .9	(16) 8.3	(20) 7.5	(33) 7.8	(32) 21.9	(14) 15.8
-3.7	1.1	2.2		-4.5	1.6	2.2	2.2	4.1	5.0
10.5	14.8	19.9						32.5	
(29) 2.7	(22) 1.7	(33) 5.5	Net Profit + Depr., Dep., Amort./Cur. Mat. L/T/D					(13) 4.3	
-3.8	.4	1.5						2.0	
.1	.1	.1		.2	.1	.1	.1	.1	.1
.4	.3	.3	Fixed/Worth	.8	1.0	.3	.3	.2	.2
1.0	.9	.7		NM	-3.3	12.9	.6	.4	.5
.7	.9	.6		.4	1.4	.7	.4	.5	.7
1.9	1.9	1.4	Debt/Worth	1.0	8.4	1.6	1.1	1.2	1.5
6.0	5.3	4.0		NM	-3.5	190.6	2.6	2.0	3.3
33.1	40.2	53.7				64.1	57.7	40.5	52.9
(131) 10.3	(102) 15.5	(125) 25.2	% Profit Before Taxes/Tangible Net Worth			(18) 29.4	(37) 25.2	(37) 17.0	(15) 29.3
-6.2	1.5	6.7				12.6	4.8	6.4	4.8
11.5	14.1	22.5		26.4	42.5	28.0	25.0	18.5	16.4
3.7	5.6	9.7	% Profit Before Taxes/Total Assets	2.8	27.2	9.1	8.2	8.5	12.2
-7.6	.1	2.5		-13.2	1.5	3.3	1.2	3.7	4.5
58.4	69.5	70.1		58.4	208.8	86.8	68.1	63.2	96.4
29.6	29.7	30.8	Sales/Net Fixed Assets	21.1	18.0	28.7	30.8	31.5	38.6
12.1	15.1	12.7		9.3	5.9	17.8	17.5	13.0	10.8
3.7	3.6	3.6		4.9	4.5	4.3	3.4	3.4	2.9
2.5	2.7	2.8	Sales/Total Assets	3.6	2.9	3.0	2.7	2.7	2.5
1.9	2.1	2.1		2.7	2.4	2.5	2.0	2.1	2.0
.6	.5	.4				.4	.4	.3	.3
(125) 1.0	(94) .8	(116) .7	% Depr., Dep., Amort./Sales			(17) .9	(32) .8	(34) .6	.6
1.6	1.1	1.2				1.4	1.2	.9	1.0
2.5	2.6	2.0			2.6	2.2	2.6	1.9	1.0
(87) 4.1	(68) 4.0	(89) 3.8	% Officers', Directors' Owners' Comp/Sales		(12) 5.1	(16) 3.8	(22) 4.7	(19) 2.2	(11) 1.4
6.8	6.6	6.9			10.2	7.0	6.6	3.7	3.9
1688143M	1135837M	1825737M	Net Sales ($)	8856M	35343M	90814M	268124M	602855M	819745M
827644M	477071M	774683M	Total Assets ($)	4191M	11801M	34352M	106892M	238827M	378620M

M = $ thousand MM = $ million

See Pages 9 through 22 for Explanation of Ratios and Data

Current Data Sorted by Assets							Comparative Historical Data	
						Type of Statement		
	2	8	4	1		Unqualified	28	31
1	37	89	12	1		Reviewed	142	142
3	13	9	1			Compiled	37	38
36	16	10			1	Tax Returns	62	67
9	32	41	17	2		Other	102	97
	43 (4/1-9/30/13)		302 (10/1/13-3/31/14)				4/1/09-3/31/10	4/1/10-3/31/11
0-500M	500M-2MM	2-10MM	10-50MM	50-100MM	100-250MM		ALL	ALL
49	100	157	34	4	1	NUMBER OF STATEMENTS	371	375
%	%	%	%	%	%	**ASSETS**	%	%
39.0	13.3	15.8	13.2			Cash & Equivalents	16.1	16.4
15.0	46.5	46.5	43.0			Trade Receivables (net)	39.8	41.4
7.7	6.2	5.8	4.9			Inventory	7.6	6.7
3.9	7.9	9.5	12.8			All Other Current	7.8	8.4
65.7	74.0	77.5	73.9			Total Current	71.3	72.8
26.0	16.9	13.7	12.7			Fixed Assets (net)	18.2	17.1
.7	2.6	1.3	5.9			Intangibles (net)	2.4	2.9
7.4	6.6	7.6	7.5			All Other Non-Current	8.0	7.2
100.0	100.0	100.0	100.0			Total	100.0	100.0
						LIABILITIES		
26.9	9.9	7.6	5.7			Notes Payable-Short Term	11.3	12.0
11.2	2.5	2.1	2.3			Cur. Mat.-L.T.D.	3.8	2.6
15.6	20.3	20.2	16.4			Trade Payables	18.8	20.4
.0	.2	.3	.2			Income Taxes Payable	.4	.4
16.4	11.1	13.2	20.2			All Other Current	14.0	12.7
70.1	44.0	43.4	44.8			Total Current	48.2	48.1
29.5	10.3	5.9	6.0			Long-Term Debt	11.2	10.3
.0	.2	.2	.2			Deferred Taxes	.4	.3
12.1	4.2	2.1	2.8			All Other Non-Current	3.5	3.9
-11.6	41.2	48.4	46.1			Net Worth	36.7	37.4
100.0	100.0	100.0	100.0			Total Liabilties & Net Worth	100.0	100.0
						INCOME DATA		
100.0	100.0	100.0	100.0			Net Sales	100.0	100.0
34.7	28.1	23.5	23.0			Gross Profit	27.9	27.0
33.3	24.0	18.9	18.5			Operating Expenses	25.8	24.4
1.5	4.1	4.6	4.5			Operating Profit	2.1	2.7
.3	.3	-.1	-.3			All Other Expenses (net)	.2	.0
1.2	3.8	4.7	4.8			Profit Before Taxes	1.9	2.6
						RATIOS		
3.3	2.6	2.9	2.2				2.7	2.6
1.6	1.7	1.9	1.6			Current	1.6	1.7
.7	1.3	1.3	1.3				1.2	1.1
2.5	2.1	2.5	2.0				1.9	2.1
1.2	1.3	1.5	1.3			Quick	1.3	1.3
.5	.9	1.0	1.0				.8	.8
0 UND	**31** 11.7	**41** 8.8	**44** 8.3				**25** 14.6	**27** 13.4
1 341.6	**48** 7.6	**56** 6.5	**78** 4.7			Sales/Receivables	**49** 7.4	**50** 7.3
15 23.8	**68** 5.4	**73** 5.0	**96** 3.8				**71** 5.1	**76** 4.8
0 UND	**0** UND	**0** UND	**1** 271.8				**0** UND	**0** UND
0 UND	**2** 188.8	**4** 98.3	**4** 81.2			Cost of Sales/Inventory	**5** 67.9	**4** 98.8
7 55.0	**12** 31.7	**13** 29.1	**19** 19.7				**17** 22.0	**13** 27.5
0 UND	**13** 28.2	**18** 20.0	**20** 18.5				**14** 26.6	**14** 26.3
3 132.0	**27** 13.6	**28** 13.1	**29** 12.8			Cost of Sales/Payables	**26** 14.1	**28** 12.9
27 13.3	**42** 8.6	**46** 7.9	**46** 7.9				**42** 8.8	**45** 8.2
14.2	6.5	5.1	4.2				6.0	6.1
52.6	13.5	8.1	8.7			Sales/Working Capital	11.9	11.2
-64.3	34.9	18.1	15.0				48.2	44.1
22.1	39.6	48.2	28.6				21.4	19.8
(36) 9.7	(84) 9.6	(137) 14.0	(27) 10.6			EBIT/Interest	(330) 3.7	(318) 5.0
-3.7	1.9	3.1	2.3				-1.3	.1
	23.5	11.1					6.3	6.7
	(10) 3.4	(34) 2.8				Net Profit + Depr., Dep., Amort./Cur. Mat. L/T/D	(85) 2.3	(90) 2.7
	1.8	.1					-.4	.6
.1	.1	.1	.1				.2	.1
.7	.3	.2	.3			Fixed/Worth	.4	.3
-8.4	.8	.5	.5				.9	1.0
.7	.6	.5	.7				.6	.6
1.6	1.3	1.0	1.1			Debt/Worth	1.4	1.3
-8.3	3.4	2.4	2.3				3.4	4.4
201.9	69.7	40.2	38.5				48.6	40.4
(34) 49.0	(91) 20.3	(148) 23.3	(31) 14.7			% Profit Before Taxes/Tangible Net Worth	(324) 13.6	(320) 14.3
.5	6.2	9.1	8.1				-.5	-.6
52.1	29.2	20.7	12.8				19.8	18.6
7.0	9.2	10.4	5.2			% Profit Before Taxes/Total Assets	4.5	5.6
-13.5	2.7	2.8	1.5				-2.3	-.7
597.8	62.8	55.5	33.7				45.5	53.0
49.0	27.2	27.3	21.9			Sales/Net Fixed Assets	23.9	26.7
16.6	17.5	15.0	10.9				12.9	14.3
16.5	4.8	3.6	2.6				4.2	4.5
7.3	3.8	2.9	2.3			Sales/Total Assets	3.0	3.1
4.2	3.0	2.3	1.7				2.3	2.3
.3	.4	.5	.7				.7	.7
(32) .7	(76) 1.0	(127) .8	(28) 1.1			% Depr., Dep., Amort./Sales	(319) 1.4	(310) 1.1
1.8	1.6	1.2	1.7				2.0	1.9
2.3	1.9	1.5					2.2	1.9
(31) 4.3	(49) 3.2	(80) 2.8				% Officers', Directors' Owners' Comp/Sales	(194) 4.0	(198) 3.5
12.4	4.8	4.9					7.0	5.7
105297M	454000M	2054431M	1608575M	681201M	765449M	Net Sales ($)	5311728M	7097060M
11368M	116207M	690342M	770475M	275698M	197943M	Total Assets ($)	2099059M	2384783M

M = $ thousand MM = $ million

See Pages 9 through 22 for Explanation of Ratios and Data

Comparative Historical Data				Current Data Sorted by Sales					
			Type of Statement						
31	17	15	Unqualified			1	2	7	5
138	134	140	Reviewed		17	14	48	46	15
36	31	26	Compiled	2	5	6	8	3	2
71	64	63	Tax Returns	13	21	6	11	9	3
111	87	101	Other	4	13	14	23	25	22
4/1/11-3/31/12	**4/1/12-3/31/13**	**4/1/13-3/31/14**		**43 (4/1-9/30/13)**			**302 (10/1/13-3/31/14)**		
ALL	**ALL**	**ALL**		**0-1MM**	**1-3MM**	**3-5MM**	**5-10MM**	**10-25MM**	**25MM & OVER**
387	333	345	**NUMBER OF STATEMENTS**	19	56	41	92	90	47
%	%	%	**ASSETS**	%	%	%	%	%	%
16.3	15.8	18.0	Cash & Equivalents	38.1	19.6	18.6	17.6	17.7	9.0
42.9	42.3	41.4	Trade Receivables (net)	11.7	31.3	45.6	43.8	46.2	48.1
5.9	5.5	6.1	Inventory	16.3	6.5	5.4	5.4	5.0	5.6
8.4	8.7	8.6	All Other Current	3.7	6.9	5.9	7.7	10.8	12.4
73.5	72.2	74.2	Total Current	69.8	64.4	75.5	74.5	79.8	75.1
17.1	17.4	16.2	Fixed Assets (net)	22.1	25.7	14.4	15.7	12.9	11.5
2.6	2.6	2.4	Intangibles (net)	3.8	.1	2.0	2.7	1.0	6.6
6.9	7.8	7.2	All Other Non-Current	3.7	9.8	8.1	7.1	6.2	6.8
100.0	100.0	100.0	Total	100.0	100.0	100.0	100.0	100.0	100.0
			LIABILITIES						
11.5	11.3	10.8	Notes Payable-Short Term	23.7	16.2	7.8	11.0	6.8	8.9
2.9	3.0	3.5	Cur. Mat.-L.T.D.	5.7	9.4	1.8	3.0	1.6	2.2
21.4	19.9	19.1	Trade Payables	9.1	16.7	20.4	19.8	20.8	20.5
.3	.4	.2	Income Taxes Payable	.0	.1	.6	.1	.3	.2
13.0	13.8	13.8	All Other Current	11.6	14.2	12.1	12.2	14.2	18.2
49.1	48.4	47.5	Total Current	50.2	56.6	42.7	46.1	43.6	50.0
9.9	10.1	10.5	Long-Term Debt	19.3	28.1	8.4	6.6	5.2	5.9
.3	.3	.2	Deferred Taxes	.0	.1	.4	.2	.2	.2
4.9	3.4	4.2	All Other Non-Current	12.6	9.4	2.8	2.2	2.9	2.6
35.9	37.7	37.5	Net Worth	18.1	5.8	45.7	44.9	48.1	41.4
100.0	100.0	100.0	Total Liabilties & Net Worth	100.0	100.0	100.0	100.0	100.0	100.0
			INCOME DATA						
100.0	100.0	100.0	Net Sales	100.0	100.0	100.0	100.0	100.0	100.0
26.4	26.8	26.4	Gross Profit	40.5	31.1	28.5	25.8	22.8	21.1
23.7	23.1	22.4	Operating Expenses	37.4	29.3	22.6	22.2	17.7	17.4
2.7	3.7	4.0	Operating Profit	3.0	1.7	5.9	3.7	5.1	3.7
.1	.3	.0	All Other Expenses (net)	.6	.2	-.2	.0	-.1	-.1
2.6	3.3	3.9	Profit Before Taxes	2.4	1.6	6.1	3.6	5.2	3.7
			RATIOS						
2.6	2.8	2.7		10.0	2.7	3.5	2.7	2.8	2.2
1.7	1.7	1.7	Current	2.7	1.7	1.7	1.6	1.9	1.5
1.2	1.2	1.3		1.0	.9	1.3	1.2	1.4	1.1
2.1	2.2	2.3		8.0	2.0	3.0	2.4	2.4	1.8
1.4	1.3	1.4	Quick	2.1	1.3	1.3	1.4	1.5	1.2
.8	.9	.9		.4	.6	.9	1.0	1.1	.9
30 12.2	**29** 12.6	**29** 12.8		**0** UND	**6** 66.2	**29** 12.4	**33** 11.2	**37** 9.8	**43** 8.4
53 6.9	**51** 7.2	**51** 7.2	Sales/Receivables	**0** UND	**36** 10.0	**51** 7.2	**52** 7.0	**56** 6.5	**57** 6.4
74 4.9	**73** 5.0	**72** 5.1		**29** 12.5	**56** 6.5	**70** 5.2	**64** 5.7	**78** 4.7	**78** 4.7
0 UND	**0** UND	**0** UND		**0** UND	**0** UND	**0** UND	**0** UND	**0** UND	**1** 440.7
2 158.5	**3** 105.7	**2** 149.0	Cost of Sales/Inventory	**6** 60.0	**1** 250.5	**2** 149.0	**2** 176.4	**3** 128.8	**4** 85.5
11 34.4	**13** 28.8	**12** 31.0		**89** 4.1	**11** 32.4	**10** 37.7	**12** 31.0	**11** 32.0	**12** 30.9
14 25.3	**13** 28.0	**13** 27.3		**0** UND	**4** 84.9	**11** 34.1	**14** 25.8	**18** 20.5	**19** 19.0
27 13.4	**26** 14.0	**25** 14.5	Cost of Sales/Payables	**2** 165.0	**20** 18.5	**29** 12.8	**24** 15.2	**28** 13.1	**25** 14.6
45 8.2	**44** 8.3	**43** 8.5		**31** 11.7	**41** 9.0	**48** 7.6	**43** 8.5	**44** 8.3	**44** 8.3
5.8	6.5	5.8		5.0	6.3	4.8	6.4	5.1	6.8
11.1	11.8	11.2	Sales/Working Capital	18.0	20.8	15.4	11.6	7.8	11.6
45.0	48.4	33.3		-30.6	-221.3	44.8	22.6	16.9	31.0
24.5	28.1	41.5		29.5	16.2	55.0	42.7	61.2	42.1
(340) 7.1	(290) 9.4	(289) 11.0	EBIT/Interest	(10) 1.0	(46) 5.1	(34) 12.3	(80) 9.8	(77) 20.6	(42) 13.8
1.0	2.3	2.1		-4.4	-2.7	3.4	1.3	4.2	4.0
8.7	9.3	12.0					4.7	36.0	16.6
(88) 3.6	(63) 3.8	(56) 2.9	Net Profit + Depr., Dep., Amort./Cur. Mat. L/T/D				(17) 2.2	(17) 10.1	(10) 5.5
.6	1.1	1.3					.0	2.6	1.9
.1	.2	.1		.0	.2	.1	.1	.1	.2
.3	.4	.3	Fixed/Worth	.1	.6	.2	.3	.2	.3
.9	.9	.6		2.1	12.1	.6	.6	.5	.6
.6	.6	.6		.2	.6	.5	.5	.5	.9
1.4	1.4	1.2	Debt/Worth	1.5	1.4	1.4	1.1	1.0	1.5
5.0	3.4	3.1		-21.7	36.9	3.1	2.7	2.4	3.6
43.9	51.7	51.4		185.7	51.0	81.7	43.9	46.0	45.5
(334) 16.2	(291) 20.6	(309) 22.9	% Profit Before Taxes/Tangible Net Worth	(14) 45.5	(44) 13.4	(39) 41.5	(83) 18.1	(86) 25.5	(43) 23.8
2.6	5.4	7.6		2.0	-5.3	12.0	3.9	12.4	13.3
18.9	21.4	23.1		55.6	20.4	38.7	19.8	24.3	15.8
5.9	8.7	8.8	% Profit Before Taxes/Total Assets	2.8	4.9	11.8	7.5	10.9	8.5
.1	1.4	1.6		-18.2	-3.6	4.6	.7	4.2	3.0
57.1	55.9	60.0		UND	55.0	77.2	54.5	63.9	54.1
29.7	29.0	27.7	Sales/Net Fixed Assets	37.8	23.1	31.7	26.1	30.6	28.3
16.5	16.2	15.9		14.5	10.2	21.9	16.0	15.6	17.3
4.5	4.2	4.5		9.2	6.1	4.9	4.5	4.1	3.8
3.1	3.2	3.2	Sales/Total Assets	4.5	3.7	3.4	3.2	3.0	2.6
2.3	2.4	2.4		1.4	2.6	2.9	2.5	2.3	2.4
.5	.6	.5		.7	.5	.3	.5	.5	.6
(322) 1.0	(270) 1.0	(268) .9	% Depr., Dep., Amort./Sales	(13) .9	(42) 1.3	(31) .8	(71) .9	(73) .8	(38) .9
1.6	1.5	1.4		2.4	2.2	1.3	1.5	1.2	1.2
1.9	2.1	1.8		3.4	2.9	1.8	2.0	1.2	.8
(208) 3.6	(167) 3.7	(168) 3.0	% Officers', Directors' Owners' Comp/Sales	(12) 12.6	(29) 4.6	(17) 2.5	(50) 3.6	(47) 2.4	(13) 1.0
6.1	6.4	5.2		15.6	7.7	4.9	4.9	4.1	5.9
7104185M	**5405410M**	**5668953M**	Net Sales ($)	**10537M**	**121113M**	**165059M**	**659415M**	**1331761M**	**3381068M**
2282175M	**2171300M**	**2062033M**	Total Assets ($)	**4252M**	**40591M**	**52378M**	**218248M**	**511902M**	**1234662M**

M = $ thousand **MM = $ million**

See Pages 9 through 22 for Explanation of Ratios and Data

Current Data Sorted by Assets | **Comparative Historical Data**

0-500M	500M-2MM	2-10MM	10-50MM	50-100MM	100-250MM		4/1/09-3/31/10 ALL	4/1/10-3/31/11 ALL
						Type of Statement		
		2	3	1		Unqualified	9	11
	3	26	6			Reviewed	21	29
	6	8				Compiled	12	9
15	6	4	2			Tax Returns	20	22
10	9	13	7	2	1	Other	23	33
14 (4/1-9/30/13)		110 (10/1/13-3/31/14)						
25	24	53	18	3	1	**NUMBER OF STATEMENTS**	85	104
%	%	%	%	%	%	**ASSETS**	%	%
19.2	12.4	12.9	12.3			Cash & Equivalents	13.6	13.4
16.4	51.7	51.3	30.6			Trade Receivables (net)	34.4	36.2
12.9	10.6	4.5	4.6			Inventory	4.3	10.1
.7	3.5	7.6	12.5			All Other Current	7.6	5.9
49.3	78.1	76.2	59.9			Total Current	59.9	65.6
34.8	17.2	17.8	30.3			Fixed Assets (net)	29.2	22.5
.2	.5	.9	6.6			Intangibles (net)	2.0	2.3
15.8	4.2	5.1	3.1			All Other Non-Current	8.9	9.6
100.0	100.0	100.0	100.0			Total	100.0	100.0
						LIABILITIES		
37.9	11.3	7.1	3.1			Notes Payable-Short Term	12.0	11.5
2.4	3.8	2.7	5.0			Cur. Mat.-L.T.D.	6.7	4.0
15.1	22.2	21.7	20.8			Trade Payables	16.0	20.5
.0	.4	.2	.0			Income Taxes Payable	.1	.2
18.3	20.3	11.4	10.2			All Other Current	15.1	9.8
73.6	58.0	43.1	39.2			Total Current	50.0	46.0
31.0	7.5	10.2	19.5			Long-Term Debt	21.4	14.2
.0	.1	.4	.0			Deferred Taxes	.5	.6
15.6	6.5	3.6	7.4			All Other Non-Current	13.0	5.1
-20.2	27.8	42.8	34.0			Net Worth	15.1	34.1
100.0	100.0	100.0	100.0			Total Liabilties & Net Worth	100.0	100.0
						INCOME DATA		
100.0	100.0	100.0	100.0			Net Sales	100.0	100.0
39.1	31.6	25.4	22.8			Gross Profit	31.8	30.9
34.4	24.7	19.3	15.9			Operating Expenses	28.6	28.1
4.7	6.9	6.1	6.9			Operating Profit	3.2	2.8
1.4	1.2	.2	1.4			All Other Expenses (net)	.6	.5
3.3	5.7	5.9	5.5			Profit Before Taxes	2.6	2.3
						RATIOS		
1.6	2.4	2.5	2.5				2.1	2.3
.7	1.4	1.7	1.4			Current	1.4	1.5
.3	1.1	1.3	1.1				.9	1.1
1.5	2.1	2.4	1.6				2.0	1.8
.4	1.3	1.5	1.2			Quick	1.1	1.1
.2	.7	1.0	.7				.6	.7
0 UND	**31** 11.9	**42** 8.7	**34** 10.7				**17** 21.8	**27** 13.6
1 587.0	**48** 7.6	**69** 5.3	**59** 6.2			Sales/Receivables	**46** 7.9	**46** 7.9
25 14.5	**62** 5.9	**99** 3.7	**79** 4.6				**67** 5.5	**65** 5.6
0 UND	**0** UND	**0** UND	**0** UND				**0** UND	**0** UND
0 UND	**0** UND	**0** UND	**5** 70.6			Cost of Sales/Inventory	**1** 435.0	**1** 434.1
8 44.5	**14** 26.3	**8** 47.6	**19** 19.7				**10** 35.6	**29** 12.8
0 UND	**14** 25.9	**16** 22.8	**21** 17.7				**5** 70.6	**15** 25.0
0 999.8	**27** 13.6	**30** 12.1	**41** 9.0			Cost of Sales/Payables	**19** 18.8	**27** 13.6
34 10.6	**42** 8.7	**54** 6.7	**61** 6.0				**41** 8.8	**51** 7.2
22.0	7.6	5.0	6.6				5.8	6.2
-121.9	17.9	8.8	11.3			Sales/Working Capital	20.8	13.5
-14.7	94.3	16.4	44.1				-90.9	49.4
33.7	18.6	44.8	36.0				11.1	16.0
(18) 4.2	(19) 7.5	(46) 11.8	(17) 6.8			EBIT/Interest	(75) 2.7	(86) 4.5
-.8	2.3	2.9	2.0				-.9	1.1
		157.9					7.2	6.1
		(11) 5.3				Net Profit + Depr., Dep., Amort./Cur. Mat. L/T/D	(18) 3.1	(22) 2.9
		.2					1.1	1.6
.1	.2	.1	.5				.3	.2
1.2	.6	.3	.9			Fixed/Worth	.8	.5
-.9	5.8	1.0	3.0				25.3	1.5
.5	.8	.6	1.1				1.1	.7
29.4	2.0	1.5	2.0			Debt/Worth	2.6	1.8
-2.6	11.0	3.0	6.2				78.0	3.5
197.9	59.3	62.0	40.4				48.1	43.2
(14) 80.0	(19) 39.8	(52) 32.6	(15) 17.2			% Profit Before Taxes/Tangible Net Worth	(65) 12.1	(92) 17.3
19.8	22.8	11.8	6.3				.3	1.8
48.7	22.1	26.8	11.3				15.9	19.9
16.3	12.4	13.9	6.9			% Profit Before Taxes/Total Assets	3.7	5.9
-10.0	1.9	3.3	1.7				-3.0	.4
600.8	48.9	69.0	24.4				27.0	46.6
36.3	29.2	22.8	7.1			Sales/Net Fixed Assets	12.8	18.6
9.3	12.0	9.4	5.5				6.6	8.5
10.2	5.1	3.7	2.4				4.0	4.3
6.6	3.4	2.7	2.1			Sales/Total Assets	2.8	2.9
3.6	2.4	2.0	1.6				1.9	1.7
.3	.6	.5	1.4				.9	.7
(14) 1.3	(19) 1.2	(42) 1.4	(16) 2.3			% Depr., Dep., Amort./Sales	(67) 2.4	(83) 1.8
2.9	2.0	2.2	4.4				4.0	3.6
3.6		1.2					2.2	1.5
(16) 5.8		(29) 2.0				% Officers', Directors' Owners' Comp/Sales	(36) 5.7	(50) 3.1
9.3		3.8					9.6	7.2
50247M	100380M	687825M	1046689M	411854M	93896M	Net Sales ($)	1518228M	2641745M
5956M	27226M	242018M	443323M	179443M	111729M	Total Assets ($)	537577M	1213838M

M = $ thousand MM = $ million

See Pages 9 through 22 for Explanation of Ratios and Data

Comparative Historical Data / Current Data Sorted by Sales

4/1/11-3/31/12 ALL	4/1/12-3/31/13 ALL	4/1/13-3/31/14 ALL	Type of Statement	0-1MM	1-3MM	3-5MM	5-10MM	10-25MM	25MM & OVER
7	13	6	Unqualified					4	2
31	25	35	Reviewed		1	2	11	14	7
9	11	14	Compiled		1	2	5	5	1
31	23	27	Tax Returns	3	10	3	6	4	1
43	46	42	Other	6	8	4	8	7	9
				14 (4/1-9/30/13)			110 (10/1/13-3/31/14)		
121	118	124	NUMBER OF STATEMENTS	9	20	11	30	34	20
%	%	%	**ASSETS**	%	%	%	%	%	%
15.4	15.8	13.6	Cash & Equivalents		11.8	8.6	15.5	13.0	12.7
35.2	38.3	40.9	Trade Receivables (net)		29.5	44.6	46.0	52.2	35.2
7.1	6.6	7.3	Inventory		13.8	12.7	6.0	2.8	3.5
5.9	7.0	6.3	All Other Current		3.8	2.0	6.1	8.3	10.6
63.6	67.7	68.2	Total Current		58.9	67.9	73.7	76.4	61.9
24.2	21.7	23.1	Fixed Assets (net)		27.2	24.6	18.5	18.7	27.4
2.2	2.6	2.1	Intangibles (net)		.1	1.0	1.1	2.3	6.6
9.9	7.9	6.7	All Other Non-Current		13.9	6.5	6.7	2.6	4.1
100.0	100.0	100.0	Total		100.0	100.0	100.0	100.0	100.0
			LIABILITIES						
16.3	13.9	13.7	Notes Payable-Short Term		22.3	30.2	10.7	4.9	5.6
4.8	4.3	3.3	Cur. Mat.-L.T.D.		2.1	3.7	2.7	3.4	4.9
19.6	20.6	20.2	Trade Payables		15.0	15.3	22.5	21.8	21.6
.1	.1	.2	Income Taxes Payable		.0	.0	.2	.1	.1
11.9	10.4	14.3	All Other Current		25.5	17.6	13.9	9.8	12.1
52.6	49.3	51.7	Total Current		64.9	66.9	50.0	40.0	44.3
14.9	12.8	15.4	Long-Term Debt		12.6	9.4	17.4	12.8	15.1
.3	.1	.2	Deferred Taxes		.0	.0	.3	.1	.6
4.9	9.7	7.1	All Other Non-Current		10.1	13.5	3.4	2.7	5.1
27.3	28.1	25.7	Net Worth		12.3	10.2	28.9	44.3	35.0
100.0	100.0	100.0	Total Liabilties & Net Worth		100.0	100.0	100.0	100.0	100.0
			INCOME DATA						
100.0	100.0	100.0	Net Sales		100.0	100.0	100.0	100.0	100.0
32.6	29.0	28.8	Gross Profit		43.0	27.2	27.2	21.8	21.4
29.4	25.3	22.6	Operating Expenses		33.7	26.4	20.9	15.5	15.5
3.1	3.8	6.2	Operating Profit		9.3	.8	6.3	6.3	5.9
.4	.0	.8	All Other Expenses (net)		1.7	.8	.4	.7	.4
2.7	3.8	5.3	Profit Before Taxes		7.6	.0	5.9	5.6	5.5
			RATIOS						
2.7	2.1	2.3	Current		3.2	2.4	2.1	3.8	1.6
1.5	1.4	1.5			1.1	1.2	1.5	1.7	1.3
1.0	1.1	1.1			.4	.9	1.3	1.4	1.1
2.2	1.8	1.9	Quick		1.6	1.6	1.9	3.3	1.3
(120) 1.1	(117) 1.2	1.3			.8	1.1	1.3	1.6	1.0
.7	.8	.7			.3	.4	.7	1.1	.8
18 20.8	**26** 14.1	**24** 15.2	Sales/Receivables		**0** UND	**30** 12.3	**30** 12.0	**38** 9.5	**36** 10.0
46 8.0	**49** 7.4	**53** 6.9			**33** 11.1	**54** 6.8	**63** 5.8	**68** 5.4	**57** 6.4
73 5.0	**74** 4.9	**76** 4.8			**54** 6.7	**64** 5.7	**111** 3.3	**89** 4.1	**68** 5.4
0 UND	**0** UND	**0** UND	Cost of Sales/Inventory		**0** UND	**0** UND	**0** UND	**0** UND	**0** UND
0 UND	**0** UND	**0** UND			**0** UND	**10** 37.1	**0** UND	**0** 999.8	**0** UND
18 20.5	**12** 29.4	**12** 30.6			**27** 13.3	**41** 8.8	**12** 31.2	**10** 36.9	**7** 53.9
6 66.2	**15** 24.9	**11** 33.9	Cost of Sales/Payables		**0** UND	**6** 65.9	**15** 24.8	**18** 20.6	**19** 19.4
28 12.9	**31** 11.8	**28** 12.9			**16** 22.6	**15** 24.6	**35** 10.4	**29** 12.6	**36** 10.0
51 7.1	**54** 6.8	**50** 7.3			**43** 8.5	**64** 5.7	**60** 6.1	**46** 8.0	**47** 7.8
6.2	7.6	6.4	Sales/Working Capital		11.3	5.7	5.0	5.2	9.2
15.8	14.9	14.2			63.1	32.0	11.2	8.9	16.5
-456.0	99.9	67.8			-19.1	-23.9	30.5	12.4	39.6
13.0	20.1	32.0	EBIT/Interest		55.3	14.9	33.7	69.1	21.4
(96) 4.5	(99) 5.5	(104) 8.1			(17) 18.6	3.9	(23) 9.0	(31) 18.9	(17) 6.8
.3	1.8	2.3			2.8	-2.3	3.5	1.9	3.0
7.6	13.3	12.1	Net Profit + Depr., Dep., Amort./Cur. Mat. L/T/D						
(21) 3.8	(18) 3.6	(19) 4.1							
.3	1.3	1.1							
.2	.2	.1	Fixed/Worth		.1	.3	.2	.1	.3
.6	.5	.6			1.1	.9	.4	.4	.9
2.8	1.5	1.9			NM	-1.7	2.2	1.0	1.7
.6	.8	.8	Debt/Worth		.9	1.8	.7	.6	1.2
1.9	1.8	2.0			4.0	2.7	1.6	1.4	2.0
8.5	7.2	8.0			NM	-8.5	8.2	3.1	4.4
55.1	66.0	63.1	% Profit Before Taxes/Tangible Net Worth		148.3		80.1	50.4	50.8
(100) 15.5	(101) 20.4	(103) 31.0			(15) 65.1		(27) 38.4	(32) 28.1	(17) 17.2
-1.5	2.0	14.4			43.9		20.8	13.1	9.9
24.5	19.2	23.9	% Profit Before Taxes/Total Assets		46.1	11.4	23.8	26.4	13.9
6.8	9.1	11.4			19.4	8.6	15.2	13.8	6.9
-2.3	1.6	2.4			8.8	-4.4	4.8	2.8	2.9
52.5	71.3	59.4	Sales/Net Fixed Assets		74.4	36.5	57.5	89.8	47.8
19.8	19.9	23.7			28.4	23.8	26.2	23.6	9.0
9.1	8.5	8.7			9.1	10.6	10.2	8.7	6.3
4.4	4.6	4.5	Sales/Total Assets		6.4	6.1	4.9	4.2	3.3
2.9	2.7	3.0			3.6	3.2	2.7	3.1	2.5
2.1	1.9	2.1			2.2	2.0	1.9	2.1	2.0
.6	.7	.6	% Depr., Dep., Amort./Sales		.7	1.1	.5	.5	1.0
(87) 1.4	(85) 1.4	(95) 1.6			(12) 1.8	(10) 1.8	(25) 1.0	(26) 1.2	(19) 2.6
3.0	2.7	2.6			2.9	2.3	1.7	2.2	3.7
2.3	1.4	1.5	% Officers', Directors' Owners' Comp/Sales		4.0		1.4	.8	
(60) 3.8	(59) 2.8	(60) 3.1			(11) 6.4		(13) 2.7	(16) 1.6	
7.0	5.9	5.3			9.7		5.0	2.2	
2223709M	2515239M	2390891M	Net Sales ($)	4930M	33040M	44690M	210583M	552893M	1544755M
880287M	1172987M	1009695M	Total Assets ($)	1652M	10451M	14495M	83633M	214909M	684555M

M = $ thousand MM = $ million

See Pages 9 through 22 for Explanation of Ratios and Data

Current Data Sorted by Assets / Comparative Historical Data

0-500M	500M-2MM	2-10MM	10-50MM	50-100MM	100-250MM		4/1/09-3/31/10 ALL	4/1/10-3/31/11 ALL
						Type of Statement		
2	5	44	66	22	12	Unqualified	194	164
6	89	290	76			Reviewed	467	447
16	42	28	6			Compiled	115	120
93	87	43	4		1	Tax Returns	210	243
46	109	130	76	10	6	Other	352	313
	211 (4/1-9/30/13)		1,098 (10/1/13-3/31/14)					
163	332	535	228	32	19	**NUMBER OF STATEMENTS**	1338	1287
%	%	%	%	%	%	**ASSETS**	%	%
29.7	16.3	14.2	14.2	10.4	8.2	Cash & Equivalents	18.2	16.7
26.6	48.2	52.5	51.5	54.7	50.3	Trade Receivables (net)	44.2	45.7
4.6	6.2	4.3	2.7	2.3	5.0	Inventory	5.8	5.7
3.3	6.4	9.3	11.4	10.5	11.1	All Other Current	7.8	8.2
64.2	77.0	80.3	79.8	78.0	74.6	Total Current	76.1	76.3
25.4	15.4	13.2	12.9	13.7	10.2	Fixed Assets (net)	16.1	15.0
1.5	1.4	1.4	2.1	3.7	11.4	Intangibles (net)	2.3	2.5
8.9	6.1	5.2	5.1	4.7	3.8	All Other Non-Current	5.5	6.2
100.0	100.0	100.0	100.0	100.0	100.0	Total	100.0	100.0
						LIABILITIES		
25.0	11.0	8.4	6.1	4.4	3.7	Notes Payable-Short Term	10.5	12.1
2.6	2.2	2.0	1.9	3.0	1.1	Cur. Mat.-L.T.D.	3.5	3.0
15.2	18.7	18.9	18.8	19.3	16.0	Trade Payables	16.9	18.9
.2	.4	.4	.2	.3	.1	Income Taxes Payable	.5	.4
21.9	13.3	16.4	20.5	23.1	25.2	All Other Current	17.0	15.2
64.9	45.6	46.1	47.5	50.1	46.2	Total Current	48.5	49.6
24.3	9.6	7.0	4.6	12.1	7.5	Long-Term Debt	9.3	10.4
.1	.4	.4	.3	.5	.9	Deferred Taxes	.5	.4
13.5	5.5	2.1	3.6	1.8	9.4	All Other Non-Current	3.9	5.1
-2.8	38.9	44.4	44.0	35.5	36.0	Net Worth	37.9	34.4
100.0	100.0	100.0	100.0	100.0	100.0	Total Liabilties & Net Worth	100.0	100.0
						INCOME DATA		
100.0	100.0	100.0	100.0	100.0	100.0	Net Sales	100.0	100.0
44.4	30.6	23.5	17.7	18.2	17.8	Gross Profit	27.6	26.6
38.7	26.2	18.5	13.6	14.3	12.6	Operating Expenses	24.5	24.3
5.7	4.4	5.0	4.1	3.9	5.2	Operating Profit	3.1	2.4
.6	.3	.2	.1	.5	1.3	All Other Expenses (net)	.4	.4
5.0	4.1	4.8	4.0	3.4	3.9	Profit Before Taxes	2.7	2.0
						RATIOS		
3.0	3.6	2.6	2.3	1.9	2.0		2.9	2.6
1.3	1.9	1.8	1.6	1.6	1.6	Current	1.7	1.7
.7	1.2	1.4	1.4	1.3	1.5		1.2	1.2
2.5	2.8	2.2	1.9	1.6	1.7		2.4	2.2
(162) 1.1	1.6	1.5	1.4	1.3	1.2	Quick	1.4	(1286) 1.4
.5	1.0	1.1	1.1	1.0	1.1		1.0	.9
0 UND	**36** 10.1	**53** 6.9	**60** 6.1	**59** 6.2	**61** 6.0		**37** 9.8	**42** 8.6
15 24.4	**53** 6.9	**69** 5.3	**76** 4.8	**78** 4.7	**72** 5.1	Sales/Receivables	**59** 6.2	**63** 5.8
43 8.5	**73** 5.0	**87** 4.2	**96** 3.8	**94** 3.9	**83** 4.4		**79** 4.6	**84** 4.3
0 UND	**0** UND	**0** UND	**0** UND	**0** UND	**0** 999.8		**0** UND	**0** UND
0 UND	**1** 406.9	**1** 418.2	**0** 973.8	**0** UND	**2** 236.8	Cost of Sales/Inventory	**1** 248.9	**1** 293.0
6 56.9	**12** 31.3	**8** 44.7	**4** 86.6	**1** 291.2	**15** 24.2		**10** 35.5	**12** 31.2
0 UND	**11** 33.5	**16** 22.4	**20** 18.3	**24** 15.4	**16** 22.5		**12** 29.5	**14** 25.3
6 64.3	**24** 15.0	**27** 13.7	**29** 12.8	**29** 12.6	**24** 15.2	Cost of Sales/Payables	**24** 15.5	**29** 12.7
32 11.3	**42** 8.7	**45** 8.2	**45** 8.2	**45** 8.1	**34** 10.6		**40** 9.2	**48** 7.7
11.7	5.4	5.1	5.3	7.2	6.8		5.4	5.2
42.3	9.8	8.1	8.1	10.8	8.9	Sales/Working Capital	9.5	9.4
-41.2	25.6	15.0	14.8	17.4	16.2		24.3	25.2
30.3	33.4	48.1	54.6	64.3	87.9		30.1	21.9
(121) 8.0	(259) 8.8	(457) 12.7	(202) 13.8	(28) 16.2	(17) 28.3	EBIT/Interest	(1107) 6.1	(1087) 3.9
.9	1.9	3.9	3.5	7.9	2.6		.3	-.8
	7.2	13.8	15.0	16.0	242.8		8.5	7.5
	(38) 2.5	(107) 4.7	(69) 8.0	(10) 3.8	(11) 21.9	Net Profit + Depr., Dep., Amort./Cur. Mat. L/T/D	(310) 2.8	(232) 2.5
	.4	1.9	2.1	.3	2.5		.9	.1
.1	.1	.1	.1	.1	.2		.1	.1
.9	.3	.2	.2	.2	.2	Fixed/Worth	.3	.3
-1.2	.8	.5	.5	1.0	1.4		.8	.9
.6	.5	.6	.8	1.1	1.2		.6	.7
3.2	1.3	1.2	1.4	1.8	1.6	Debt/Worth	1.3	1.4
-3.9	4.3	2.4	2.4	4.1	7.4		3.4	4.0
167.6	56.5	48.5	40.1	44.1	60.9		43.4	35.4
(110) 87.7	(287) 27.1	(510) 23.4	(222) 18.9	(28) 24.1	(16) 22.0	% Profit Before Taxes/Tangible Net Worth	(1197) 16.6	(1119) 12.1
25.7	6.3	7.0	5.6	11.6	13.9		2.1	-.4
66.9	25.8	20.5	16.2	12.5	12.5		18.4	14.3
26.1	10.0	9.6	8.0	6.1	8.8	% Profit Before Taxes/Total Assets	5.6	4.0
2.2	1.8	2.7	2.4	3.4	3.6		-.7	-2.6
124.6	88.6	66.6	58.6	100.3	51.3		63.4	65.4
42.4	29.1	31.1	30.9	41.1	31.7	Sales/Net Fixed Assets	29.0	32.1
17.3	14.4	16.1	12.9	17.2	17.2		14.2	14.7
10.1	4.1	3.5	3.1	3.3	3.0		3.7	3.6
5.5	3.2	2.7	2.5	2.8	2.8	Sales/Total Assets	2.9	2.7
3.5	2.5	2.2	1.9	2.0	2.6		2.2	2.1
.7	.5	.4	.4	.3	.3		.5	.5
(85) 1.4	(232) 1.0	(463) .8	(213) .7	(31) .5	(16) .5	% Depr., Dep., Amort./Sales	(1087) 1.0	(1050) 1.0
2.7	1.8	1.2	1.3	1.6	1.0		1.8	1.8
4.8	2.5	1.5	.8				2.4	2.2
(103) 7.0	(189) 4.1	(259) 2.6	(62) 1.4			% Officers', Directors' Owners' Comp/Sales	(631) 4.5	(627) 4.1
11.9	7.0	4.5	2.9				7.9	7.2
283200M	1385967M	7290650M	12347183M	5670293M	7211439M	Net Sales ($)	29257198M	26258502M
40529M	397545M	2552227M	4860169M	2100390M	2703215M	Total Assets ($)	11313277M	10603473M

M = $ thousand MM = $ million

See Pages 9 through 22 for Explanation of Ratios and Data

Comparative Historical Data / **Current Data Sorted by Sales**

	4/1/11-3/31/12 ALL	4/1/12-3/31/13 ALL	4/1/13-3/31/14 ALL	0-1MM	1-3MM	3-5MM	5-10MM	10-25MM	25MM & OVER
Type of Statement				211 (4/1-9/30/13)			1,098 (10/1/13-3/31/14)		
Unqualified	174	147	151	2	5	1	10	29	104
Reviewed	453	421	461	1	32	47	124	165	92
Compiled	119	85	92	7	28	15	17	18	7
Tax Returns	268	240	228	45	69	47	33	28	6
Other	366	344	377	26	56	42	93	73	87
NUMBER OF STATEMENTS	1380	1237	1309	81	190	152	277	313	296
ASSETS	%	%	%	%	%	%	%	%	%
Cash & Equivalents	16.6	15.5	16.5	22.3	22.1	20.6	14.9	14.7	12.5
Trade Receivables (net)	47.4	48.6	48.0	23.9	37.5	44.8	51.3	52.3	55.5
Inventory	5.1	5.0	4.5	6.6	5.0	7.6	4.4	3.8	2.8
All Other Current	7.9	8.2	8.2	4.0	5.2	6.9	7.9	9.8	10.7
Total Current	76.9	77.3	77.2	56.8	69.9	79.9	78.4	80.6	81.5
Fixed Assets (net)	14.3	14.3	15.2	28.7	19.8	14.4	13.9	13.8	11.6
Intangibles (net)	2.6	2.4	1.7	1.7	2.0	.8	1.4	1.4	2.7
All Other Non-Current	6.2	6.1	5.8	12.8	8.3	4.8	6.3	4.2	4.2
Total	100.0	100.0	100.0	100.0	100.0	100.0	100.0	100.0	100.0
LIABILITIES									
Notes Payable-Short Term	11.3	11.1	10.6	25.0	14.5	11.9	10.0	7.8	6.9
Cur. Mat.-L.T.D.	3.0	2.6	2.1	1.7	3.1	1.8	2.2	2.0	1.9
Trade Payables	20.0	19.4	18.3	11.1	16.5	16.7	19.3	19.6	19.9
Income Taxes Payable	.4	.4	.3	.3	.3	.5	.6	.2	.2
All Other Current	14.8	16.0	17.3	17.9	14.3	15.3	14.2	18.4	21.8
Total Current	49.5	49.5	48.7	56.0	48.6	46.3	46.3	48.1	50.7
Long-Term Debt	10.0	9.4	9.5	29.6	16.2	6.5	7.0	7.6	5.8
Deferred Taxes	.4	.4	.3	.1	.3	.2	.5	.2	.4
All Other Non-Current	5.4	5.0	4.7	17.3	6.8	6.1	2.9	2.6	3.3
Net Worth	34.7	35.7	36.7	-3.0	28.0	41.0	43.2	41.6	39.8
Total Liabilities & Net Worth	100.0	100.0	100.0	100.0	100.0	100.0	100.0	100.0	100.0
INCOME DATA									
Net Sales	100.0	100.0	100.0	100.0	100.0	100.0	100.0	100.0	100.0
Gross Profit	26.0	26.6	26.7	52.3	37.7	30.0	25.2	22.0	17.3
Operating Expenses	22.9	22.5	21.9	44.5	32.6	25.4	20.5	17.4	13.2
Operating Profit	3.1	4.2	4.8	7.7	5.1	4.6	4.7	4.6	4.1
All Other Expenses (net)	.3	.3	.3	1.2	.5	.1	.2	.1	.3
Profit Before Taxes	2.8	3.9	4.5	6.5	4.6	4.5	4.5	4.5	3.9
RATIOS									
Current	2.6	2.6	2.6	2.8	4.2	3.8	2.8	2.5	2.1
	1.7	1.7	1.7	1.5	1.8	1.9	1.9	1.8	1.6
	1.2	1.2	1.3	.7	1.0	1.3	1.3	1.4	1.3
Quick	2.2	2.2	2.2	2.3	3.3	2.9	2.5	2.1	1.8
	1.4	(1236) 1.4	(1308) 1.5	(80) 1.1	1.5	1.6	1.6	1.5	1.3
	1.0	1.0	1.0	.4	.7	.9	1.1	1.1	1.1
Sales/Receivables	42 8.6	42 8.6	43 8.5	0 UND	16 23.0	36 10.0	47 7.7	52 7.0	57 6.4
	63 5.8	63 5.8	63 5.8	26 14.2	43 8.4	52 7.0	65 5.6	68 5.4	73 5.0
	85 4.3	85 4.3	83 4.4	62 5.9	72 5.1	74 4.9	85 4.3	85 4.3	87 4.2
Cost of Sales/Inventory	0 UND	0 UND	0 UND	0 UND	0 UND	0 UND	0 UND	0 UND	0 UND
	1 383.2	1 435.3	0 840.4	0 UND	0 UND	2 231.0	1 688.8	1 488.9	0 890.4
	10 36.7	9 41.3	8 46.2	19 19.6	10 36.3	19 19.4	10 36.8	6 58.5	4 86.6
Cost of Sales/Payables	16 23.2	15 24.9	14 26.6	0 UND	4 104.0	9 42.3	15 24.7	17 21.5	19 18.9
	29 12.7	27 13.3	26 14.2	9 38.6	19 19.3	24 15.1	27 13.5	27 13.7	27 13.5
	46 7.9	46 7.9	43 8.4	51 7.2	41 8.9	42 8.7	42 8.6	45 8.1	40 9.1
Sales/Working Capital	5.5	5.5	5.4	6.0	5.3	4.9	5.2	5.6	6.2
	9.5	9.6	9.5	24.5	12.4	9.7	8.1	8.7	9.4
	27.3	21.7	20.7	-17.1	159.2	23.6	18.6	15.4	16.3
EBIT/Interest	24.1	31.0	41.4	16.9	30.5	37.6	53.1	57.0	43.9
	(1134) 5.5	(1039) 8.9	(1084) 11.7	(58) 5.6	(150) 8.7	(114) 8.4	(230) 12.3	(268) 14.4	(264) 13.9
	1.1	2.2	3.2	1.2	1.7	1.2	2.8	3.9	4.4
Net Profit + Depr., Dep., Amort./Cur. Mat. L/T/D	8.5	12.3	13.9		4.9	8.0	16.3	12.1	19.8
	(261) 3.0	(231) 4.6	(236) 5.5		(14) 2.1	(19) 3.3	(41) 3.5	(61) 4.9	(100) 7.8
	.5	1.7	1.7		.9	.3	.5	2.0	2.2
Fixed/Worth	.1	.1	.1	.1	.1	.1	.1	.1	.1
	.3	.3	.3	1.0	.4	.3	.2	.2	.2
	.8	.7	.7	-1.1	2.2	.7	.6	.6	.5
Debt/Worth	.7	.6	.6	.6	.5	.4	.6	.6	.9
	1.5	1.5	1.4	3.7	1.5	1.1	1.1	1.3	1.5
	4.1	3.5	3.2	-4.0	11.5	3.5	2.8	2.4	2.7
% Profit Before Taxes/Tangible Net Worth	43.5	49.1	53.8	148.8	85.5	55.1	57.0	48.6	45.0
	(1210) 16.4	(1090) 21.2	(1173) 25.2	(53) 52.9	(152) 32.2	(133) 25.9	(257) 25.0	(297) 24.1	(281) 20.9
	2.7	4.9	7.4	7.1	9.8	4.5	5.7	7.9	8.6
% Profit Before Taxes/Total Assets	17.1	19.1	22.2	47.6	31.4	27.9	24.2	20.6	16.0
	6.2	7.6	9.7	11.1	12.3	9.8	10.3	10.3	8.3
	.4	1.4	2.5	.6	2.2	1.2	2.2	3.2	2.8
Sales/Net Fixed Assets	81.9	71.5	75.9	87.3	88.0	82.0	76.3	68.5	72.8
	32.6	32.7	32.2	20.5	28.2	32.3	32.9	30.8	35.9
	15.5	15.5	15.4	6.2	11.4	18.6	15.7	16.1	18.1
Sales/Total Assets	3.7	3.8	3.8	6.1	4.8	4.1	3.8	3.7	3.4
	2.8	2.9	2.9	2.9	3.1	3.2	2.8	2.8	2.9
	2.1	2.2	2.2	1.2	2.2	2.5	2.2	2.2	2.3
% Depr., Dep., Amort./Sales	.4	.4	.4	1.1	.6	.5	.4	.4	.3
	(1086) .9	(992) .8	(1040) .8	(45) 2.1	(121) 1.4	(111) .9	(216) .8	(274) .7	(273) .6
	1.6	1.5	1.5	3.7	2.5	1.7	1.3	1.2	1.0
% Officers', Directors' Owners' Comp/Sales	1.9	1.8	1.8	7.2	3.4	2.9	1.9	1.3	.8
	(671) 3.7	(631) 3.5	(621) 3.4	(43) 11.4	(118) 6.1	(97) 4.1	(142) 2.9	(143) 2.4	(78) 1.4
	6.2	6.1	6.4	17.3	8.7	6.0	5.0	3.8	2.9
Net Sales ($)	34074837M	30846371M	34188732M	44419M	385570M	603669M	2005524M	4975814M	26173736M
Total Assets ($)	11674676M	11932476M	12654075M	31830M	137430M	202575M	783633M	1876679M	9621928M

M = $ thousand MM = $ million

See Pages 9 through 22 for Explanation of Ratios and Data

Current Data Sorted by Assets							Comparative Historical Data	
						Type of Statement		
1	4	40	57	5	8	Unqualified	121	117
4	72	275	71	1		Reviewed	407	386
13	64	37	2			Compiled	121	135
135	129	59	3		4	Tax Returns	251	251
61	133	135	80	11	6	Other	350	333
256 (4/1-9/30/13)		1,154 (10/1/13-3/31/14)					4/1/09-3/31/10 ALL	4/1/10-3/31/11 ALL
0-500M	500M-2MM	2-10MM	10-50MM	50-100MM	100-250MM			
214	402	546	213	17	18	**NUMBER OF STATEMENTS**	1250	1222
%	%	%	%	%	%	**ASSETS**	%	%
25.3	16.9	14.9	16.5	13.8	18.3	Cash & Equivalents	17.7	16.2
23.4	41.3	50.0	51.8	57.7	43.2	Trade Receivables (net)	41.4	42.4
9.9	9.7	5.3	4.1	1.1	4.9	Inventory	7.2	8.1
2.2	4.4	8.1	9.3	10.3	9.0	All Other Current	6.7	6.9
60.8	72.4	78.3	81.8	82.9	75.3	Total Current	73.1	73.5
26.6	17.2	12.9	11.0	14.1	10.3	Fixed Assets (net)	17.6	17.3
4.1	3.4	2.6	2.6	.3	8.4	Intangibles (net)	3.0	2.9
8.6	7.0	6.2	4.6	2.7	5.9	All Other Non-Current	6.3	6.3
100.0	100.0	100.0	100.0	100.0	100.0	Total	100.0	100.0
						LIABILITIES		
23.5	9.8	6.2	6.5	3.5	9.4	Notes Payable-Short Term	10.2	12.0
6.2	2.9	2.2	1.2	.7	1.0	Cur. Mat.-L.T.D.	3.3	3.1
16.6	20.9	22.4	21.6	23.5	21.3	Trade Payables	19.8	21.6
.1	.1	.4	.5	.2	.2	Income Taxes Payable	.4	.4
14.6	13.5	16.6	21.8	28.5	23.0	All Other Current	17.0	14.7
61.1	47.2	47.7	51.5	56.3	54.9	Total Current	50.7	51.8
25.5	15.3	7.0	5.7	5.5	9.9	Long-Term Debt	12.5	12.4
.1	.3	.3	.2	.0	.7	Deferred Taxes	.3	.3
11.8	4.4	4.0	3.4	1.2	3.4	All Other Non-Current	5.9	6.4
1.6	32.9	41.0	39.1	36.9	31.1	Net Worth	30.7	29.1
100.0	100.0	100.0	100.0	100.0	100.0	Total Liabilties & Net Worth	100.0	100.0
						INCOME DATA		
100.0	100.0	100.0	100.0	100.0	100.0	Net Sales	100.0	100.0
44.9	33.5	24.1	18.7	15.9	22.1	Gross Profit	28.9	29.1
40.3	30.0	20.4	15.1	11.1	18.0	Operating Expenses	25.9	27.0
4.6	3.5	3.7	3.6	4.8	4.1	Operating Profit	3.1	2.2
.6	.4	.1	.0	.3	.1	All Other Expenses (net)	.4	.3
4.0	3.1	3.5	3.7	4.5	4.0	Profit Before Taxes	2.7	1.9
						RATIOS		
2.7	2.9	2.4	2.1	1.8	2.0		2.4	2.5
1.3	1.6	1.7	1.5	1.4	1.5	Current	1.6	1.6
.6	1.1	1.3	1.3	1.3	1.1		1.2	1.1
2.2	2.4	2.1	1.7	1.6	1.6		2.0	2.0
.9	1.3	1.4	1.3	1.2	1.2	Quick	1.3	1.2
.4	.8	1.0	1.0	1.1	.8		.9	.8
0 UND	24 15.2	46 7.9	58 6.3	70 5.2	46 8.0		30 12.1	30 12.0
10 35.4	42 8.7	63 5.8	73 5.0	73 5.0	63 5.8	Sales/Receivables	50 7.3	56 6.6
33 11.1	62 5.9	85 4.3	89 4.1	101 3.6	76 4.8		72 5.1	78 4.7
0 UND	0 UND	0 UND	0 999.8	0 UND	0 UND		0 UND	0 UND
1 247.9	6 60.2	3 121.2	2 157.9	1 256.1	1 627.5	Cost of Sales/Inventory	4 88.7	5 73.0
15 24.0	24 15.4	12 29.6	9 39.2	3 115.7	8 47.7		16 22.8	18 20.2
0 UND	14 26.4	19 19.1	24 15.4	24 14.9	21 17.6		15 25.1	17 21.1
15 23.6	25 14.5	32 11.3	34 10.6	40 9.1	34 10.7	Cost of Sales/Payables	27 13.7	31 11.8
40 9.2	44 8.3	52 7.0	49 7.5	48 7.6	46 8.0		43 8.4	48 7.6
13.1	6.4	5.6	5.3	6.9	5.0		6.1	6.0
46.9	14.1	9.7	9.3	11.9	10.9	Sales/Working Capital	11.9	11.8
-26.9	56.0	19.0	18.4	17.4	48.3		34.3	41.4
16.0	24.3	44.5	38.5	47.4	133.9		24.4	18.2
(162) 6.2	(340) 6.8	(466) 11.0	(181) 13.0	(12) 18.3	(17) 8.9	EBIT/Interest	(1057) 5.3	(1034) 4.4
1.5	1.7	2.9	3.5	8.1	6.5		.8	.3
	7.6	7.8	15.2				10.6	9.9
	(37) 2.2	(124) 3.3	(62) 5.4			Net Profit + Depr., Dep., Amort./Cur. Mat. L/T/D	(258) 3.7	(230) 2.7
	.8	1.3	1.8				1.0	.8
.2	.1	.1	.1	.1	.2		.1	.1
1.3	.4	.3	.2	.4	.3	Fixed/Worth	.4	.4
-1.2	2.6	.6	.6	.6	.8		1.2	1.3
1.0	.6	.7	.9	1.3	1.0		.8	.8
6.6	1.8	1.5	1.7	2.2	3.1	Debt/Worth	1.7	1.8
-3.8	15.0	3.1	3.5	2.8	5.3		4.7	5.7
155.6	68.4	47.4	39.7	39.8	66.8		47.2	41.4
(139) 53.5	(325) 29.1	(516) 21.6	(201) 21.9	(15) 16.1	(15) 28.6	% Profit Before Taxes/Tangible Net Worth	(1048) 19.0	(1033) 13.5
15.2	6.9	6.0	5.8	12.9	15.7		2.7	1.1
47.3	21.8	18.0	14.9	11.6	22.5		18.1	15.5
17.6	8.8	8.0	7.8	8.7	7.9	% Profit Before Taxes/Total Assets	6.4	4.7
2.2	1.4	2.2	2.5	4.0	3.6		.0	-.7
105.5	66.1	61.3	77.4	106.0	75.0		57.8	56.2
32.1	28.5	32.8	38.8	28.6	24.1	Sales/Net Fixed Assets	28.7	27.2
15.6	15.4	16.3	18.7	11.2	18.5		14.2	14.2
9.8	4.7	3.6	3.2	3.5	3.5		4.1	4.0
5.8	3.5	2.9	2.6	2.8	2.5	Sales/Total Assets	3.1	3.0
3.5	2.7	2.2	2.1	1.8	1.5		2.3	2.2
.5	.5	.4	.3	.3	.4		.5	.6
(122) 1.2	(295) 1.1	(482) .8	(196) .6	(15) .6	(15) .8	% Depr., Dep., Amort./Sales	(1016) 1.1	(990) 1.0
2.2	1.8	1.3	1.1	1.4	1.2		1.8	1.8
3.5	2.4	1.3	.7				2.0	2.1
(138) 6.5	(240) 4.3	(270) 2.3	(75) 1.7			% Officers', Directors' Owners' Comp/Sales	(645) 3.9	(657) 4.2
10.6	7.5	4.3	2.5				7.4	7.4
379540M	1714476M	7747615M	10792008M	3143120M	8861350M	Net Sales ($)	29011800M	23449906M
55543M	458592M	2618232M	4196417M	1200673M	2732234M	Total Assets ($)	9908455M	8365311M

M = $ thousand MM = $ million

See Pages 9 through 22 for Explanation of Ratios and Data

Comparative Historical Data | **Current Data Sorted by Sales**

			Type of Statement						
123	110	115	Unqualified		2	1	7	33	72
408	347	423	Reviewed	1	26	37	105	166	88
109	118	116	Compiled	7	26	22	36	22	3
313	308	330	Tax Returns	53	104	76	49	40	8
413	394	426	Other	25	76	67	77	70	111
4/1/11-3/31/12 ALL	4/1/12-3/31/13 ALL	4/1/13-3/31/14 ALL		256 (4/1-9/30/13)			1,154 (10/1/13-3/31/14)		
				0-1MM	1-3MM	3-5MM	5-10MM	10-25MM	25MM & OVER
1366	1277	1410	NUMBER OF STATEMENTS	86	234	203	274	331	282
%	%	%	ASSETS	%	%	%	%	%	%
16.1	16.2	17.3	Cash & Equivalents	23.7	18.6	19.1	17.3	15.5	15.4
43.4	43.6	43.8	Trade Receivables (net)	23.2	32.0	38.4	44.6	52.0	53.2
8.2	7.3	7.0	Inventory	8.3	11.6	8.1	7.0	5.1	4.3
6.6	6.5	6.4	All Other Current	2.1	3.4	4.0	6.7	8.4	9.1
74.3	73.5	74.5	Total Current	57.3	65.6	69.6	75.6	81.0	82.0
16.4	16.7	15.9	Fixed Assets (net)	31.0	20.8	17.8	15.3	11.9	11.0
3.2	3.2	3.1	Intangibles (net)	3.9	5.3	3.0	3.3	1.9	2.4
6.1	6.5	6.5	All Other Non-Current	7.9	8.3	9.6	5.8	5.3	4.6
100.0	100.0	100.0	Total	100.0	100.0	100.0	100.0	100.0	100.0
			LIABILITIES						
11.6	11.1	9.9	Notes Payable-Short Term	17.7	16.7	12.2	7.9	6.3	6.4
2.9	3.1	2.8	Cur. Mat.-L.T.D.	5.8	5.3	2.5	2.9	1.8	1.3
21.9	21.0	21.0	Trade Payables	13.9	18.6	20.3	21.3	23.3	22.7
.4	.4	.3	Income Taxes Payable	.1	.1	.1	.3	.3	.4
14.4	14.7	16.4	All Other Current	18.3	13.3	11.8	13.1	18.5	22.4
51.3	50.2	50.4	Total Current	55.8	53.9	46.9	45.5	50.2	53.2
13.3	13.6	12.0	Long-Term Debt	31.3	20.6	15.4	9.7	6.2	5.6
.2	.3	.3	Deferred Taxes	.1	.1	.2	.5	.2	.2
6.2	6.1	5.2	All Other Non-Current	13.7	7.1	5.7	4.1	3.7	3.1
29.0	29.8	32.2	Net Worth	-.9	18.2	31.8	40.2	39.7	37.8
100.0	100.0	100.0	Total Liabilties & Net Worth	100.0	100.0	100.0	100.0	100.0	100.0
			INCOME DATA						
100.0	100.0	100.0	Net Sales	100.0	100.0	100.0	100.0	100.0	100.0
29.7	30.3	29.0	Gross Profit	49.0	40.0	32.0	29.4	22.4	18.9
26.9	26.6	25.2	Operating Expenses	42.8	36.2	29.3	25.4	18.7	15.3
2.8	3.7	3.8	Operating Profit	6.1	3.8	2.7	4.0	3.8	3.5
.5	.2	.2	All Other Expenses (net)	1.5	.4	.3	.2	.0	.0
2.4	3.5	3.5	Profit Before Taxes	4.7	3.4	2.4	3.9	3.7	3.5
			RATIOS						
2.3	2.5	2.5		4.1	2.8	3.1	2.7	2.4	2.0
1.5	1.6	1.6	Current	1.4	1.5	1.7	1.7	1.7	1.5
1.1	1.2	1.2		.6	.9	1.1	1.2	1.3	1.3
1.9	2.1	2.1		3.6	2.2	2.4	2.4	2.0	1.7
(1365) 1.2	1.3	1.3	Quick	1.1	1.1	1.4	1.4	1.4	1.3
.9	.9	.9		.4	.5	.8	.9	1.0	1.0
29 12.5	**27** 13.3	**28** 13.0		**0** UND	**10** 34.9	**19** 19.4	**28** 13.0	**45** 8.1	**52** 7.0
53 6.9	**52** 7.0	**54** 6.8	Sales/Receivables	**19** 19.2	**32** 11.3	**42** 8.6	**54** 6.8	**64** 5.7	**69** 5.3
76 4.8	**74** 4.9	**78** 4.7		**42** 8.7	**55** 6.6	**63** 5.8	**81** 4.5	**81** 4.5	**83** 4.4
0 UND	**0** UND	**0** UND		**0** UND	**0** UND	**0** UND	**0** UND	**0** UND	**0** UND
4 81.3	**4** 97.3	**3** 109.7	Cost of Sales/Inventory	**0** UND	**9** 41.5	**4** 83.9	**4** 83.2	**3** 143.8	**2** 168.7
17 20.9	**15** 23.9	**15** 24.9		**20** 17.9	**29** 12.6	**17** 20.9	**17** 21.9	**10** 35.3	**9** 42.1
16 22.4	**14** 25.3	**16** 22.9		**0** UND	**10** 36.2	**13** 27.2	**15** 24.4	**19** 19.6	**21** 17.1
30 12.0	**28** 13.1	**29** 12.4	Cost of Sales/Payables	**16** 23.0	**27** 13.5	**23** 15.8	**30** 12.2	**31** 11.9	**33** 11.2
50 7.3	**46** 8.0	**47** 7.8		**65** 5.6	**51** 7.2	**42** 8.6	**54** 6.8	**47** 7.7	**45** 8.2
6.6	6.7	6.4		5.8	7.5	6.4	5.9	5.6	6.4
12.6	12.7	11.9	Sales/Working Capital	30.8	18.7	15.4	10.2	10.2	10.3
43.0	40.3	37.1		-15.1	-62.6	138.3	28.0	20.6	19.4
19.4	28.5	34.2		12.0	15.8	22.6	38.7	49.0	44.7
(1146) 4.6	(1090) 8.3	(1178) 8.9	EBIT/Interest	(62) 3.0	(192) 5.8	(170) 5.5	(229) 9.8	(280) 13.0	(245) 16.0
.7	2.2	2.3		-1.6	1.0	.9	3.1	3.4	4.3
8.9	11.6	10.5			3.0	7.1	8.6	9.3	13.6
(237) 2.9	(222) 4.0	(234) 3.4	Net Profit + Depr., Dep., Amort./Cur. Mat. L/T/D		(13) 1.3	(23) 1.8	(47) 3.2	(69) 3.3	(81) 4.9
1.0	1.4	1.4			-.2	-2.6	1.2	1.5	2.6
.1	.1	.1		.3	.2	.1	.1	.1	.1
.4	.4	.3	Fixed/Worth	1.3	.6	.4	.3	.2	.2
1.3	1.4	1.0		-1.5	UND	5.2	.9	.6	.5
.8	.8	.7		.7	.7	.6	.6	.7	.9
1.9	1.8	1.7	Debt/Worth	5.2	3.2	1.7	1.6	1.5	1.9
6.6	6.4	5.6		-3.3	-23.7	21.1	3.8	3.1	3.3
45.7	57.7	54.3		127.0	97.9	61.8	50.1	48.9	41.3
(1141) 17.6	(1068) 24.4	(1213) 25.5	% Profit Before Taxes/Tangible Net Worth	(58) 52.1	(171) 36.9	(158) 19.0	(247) 25.4	(312) 22.0	(267) 23.0
2.7	6.9	6.9		11.6	6.2	3.4	8.5	6.0	8.4
16.6	21.5	19.9		37.0	29.1	20.7	19.7	19.1	15.7
5.7	9.0	8.8	% Profit Before Taxes/Total Assets	9.7	12.2	7.9	9.4	8.3	8.5
.0	1.8	2.2		.2	.7	.3	3.1	2.3	3.3
70.3	67.9	69.9		60.3	66.9	77.5	66.7	69.5	74.8
31.1	32.6	31.8	Sales/Net Fixed Assets	17.5	23.5	32.5	29.1	37.2	37.5
14.9	15.5	16.4		7.1	13.4	17.0	16.2	21.0	19.1
4.3	4.6	4.3		5.8	5.1	5.2	4.2	3.8	3.5
3.1	3.2	3.1	Sales/Total Assets	3.3	3.5	3.5	3.1	3.1	2.9
2.3	2.4	2.4		1.8	2.4	2.5	2.3	2.4	2.4
.5	.5	.4		.8	.7	.5	.5	.4	.3
(1048) .9	(986) .9	(1125) .8	% Depr., Dep., Amort./Sales	(41) 2.0	(156) 1.2	(156) 1.1	(221) .9	(291) .8	(260) .6
1.6	1.5	1.4		3.3	2.1	1.7	1.5	1.1	1.0
2.0	1.9	1.7		5.5	3.5	2.4	1.8	1.3	.8
(746) 4.0	(690) 3.6	(728) 3.4	% Officers', Directors' Owners' Comp/Sales	(48) 9.8	(149) 5.7	(124) 3.9	(145) 2.9	(172) 2.0	(90) 1.7
7.2	6.6	6.4		14.7	8.5	7.1	5.1	4.0	3.2
29419543M	**28572970M**	**32638109M**	Net Sales ($)	**54272M**	**457846M**	**799755M**	**1938680M**	**5319024M**	**24068532M**
9395650M	**9198207M**	**11261691M**	Total Assets ($)	**21146M**	**153326M**	**266334M**	**674521M**	**1881312M**	**8265052M**

M = $ thousand MM = $ million

See Pages 9 through 22 for Explanation of Ratios and Data

Current Data Sorted by Assets | Comparative Historical Data

0-500M	500M-2MM	2-10MM	10-50MM	50-100MM	100-250MM		4/1/09-3/31/10 ALL	4/1/10-3/31/11 ALL
						Type of Statement		
	1	4	13		1	Unqualified	31	16
1	11	41	11	1		Reviewed	69	70
	8	9	1			Compiled	27	23
21	21	12	1			Tax Returns	46	61
6	25	23	13		1	Other	57	81
	33 (4/1-9/30/13)		192 (10/1/13-3/31/14)					
28	66	89	39	1	2	**NUMBER OF STATEMENTS**	230	251
%	%	%	%	%	%	**ASSETS**	%	%
25.6	15.7	14.6	12.4			Cash & Equivalents	14.2	15.4
24.6	42.3	45.0	35.6			Trade Receivables (net)	36.6	38.4
7.1	9.6	5.9	8.0			Inventory	10.3	9.4
10.3	4.1	9.0	6.9			All Other Current	5.2	5.2
67.6	71.7	74.5	63.0			Total Current	66.4	68.5
16.9	17.2	17.6	26.4			Fixed Assets (net)	22.8	20.9
2.3	3.8	1.6	4.0			Intangibles (net)	3.7	3.1
13.2	7.3	6.2	6.7			All Other Non-Current	7.1	7.6
100.0	100.0	100.0	100.0			Total	100.0	100.0
						LIABILITIES		
30.7	13.3	9.7	6.0			Notes Payable-Short Term	13.8	11.9
.9	2.3	2.3	3.8			Cur. Mat.-L.T.D.	6.1	4.0
15.8	16.0	18.3	14.3			Trade Payables	16.8	17.1
.2	.4	.2	.2			Income Taxes Payable	.4	.4
20.0	9.2	13.5	20.8			All Other Current	14.1	12.8
67.6	41.2	44.0	45.1			Total Current	51.2	46.2
12.1	10.7	8.1	12.2			Long-Term Debt	15.1	16.1
.0	.1	.6	1.4			Deferred Taxes	.4	.3
5.9	6.8	2.1	9.2			All Other Non-Current	5.4	6.5
14.4	41.2	45.2	32.1			Net Worth	27.9	30.8
100.0	100.0	100.0	100.0			Total Liabilties & Net Worth	100.0	100.0
						INCOME DATA		
100.0	100.0	100.0	100.0			Net Sales	100.0	100.0
44.6	34.6	25.1	25.8			Gross Profit	32.0	32.2
37.8	29.9	21.5	21.7			Operating Expenses	29.8	29.7
6.8	4.6	3.6	4.1			Operating Profit	2.2	2.5
-.1	.6	.1	1.4			All Other Expenses (net)	.5	.4
6.9	4.0	3.5	2.7			Profit Before Taxes	1.7	2.1
						RATIOS		
4.2	3.2	2.5	2.3				2.7	2.9
1.9	1.9	1.7	1.3			Current	1.7	1.7
1.0	1.3	1.2	1.1				1.1	1.2
3.2	2.8	2.0	1.8				2.2	2.5
1.6	1.6	1.4	1.1			Quick	1.2	1.3
.7	1.0	.9	.7				.7	.8
0 UND	**29** 12.6	**42** 8.7	**45** 8.2				**30** 12.1	**31** 11.8
16 23.0	**44** 8.3	**60** 6.1	**64** 5.7			Sales/Receivables	**51** 7.1	**53** 6.9
43 8.5	**76** 4.8	**73** 5.0	**83** 4.4				**70** 5.2	**75** 4.8
0 UND	**0** UND	**0** UND	**0** UND				**0** UND	**0** UND
0 UND	**3** 133.3	**1** 335.3	**1** 639.3			Cost of Sales/Inventory	**6** 65.2	**2** 232.9
8 43.1	**24** 15.0	**16** 22.3	**31** 11.7				**33** 11.2	**25** 14.6
0 UND	**11** 33.4	**17** 22.0	**16** 22.4				**10** 37.2	**12** 31.7
5 72.0	**24** 15.1	**27** 13.6	**30** 12.2			Cost of Sales/Payables	**24** 15.3	**24** 15.1
19 19.5	**42** 8.7	**39** 9.4	**42** 8.7				**41** 8.8	**43** 8.5
6.7	5.4	5.8	6.2				5.4	5.3
36.1	9.9	9.8	13.8			Sales/Working Capital	10.6	10.8
-383.8	29.1	21.7	45.9				332.1	34.7
48.8	32.4	40.5	9.7				17.9	18.4
(20) 10.7	(54) 8.0	(77) 9.4	(35) 5.3			EBIT/Interest	(200) 3.7	(208) 3.8
2.0	2.1	2.2	1.9				-.4	-.1
		11.5	4.0				9.8	7.0
		(18) 3.4	(14) 2.2			Net Profit + Depr., Dep., Amort./Cur. Mat. L/T/D	(34) 3.0	(33) 2.7
		1.7	1.1				1.3	.5
.0	.1	.1	.3				.2	.1
.1	.3	.3	.8			Fixed/Worth	.4	.4
UND	1.4	.6	1.6				2.1	2.4
.3	.4	.5	.8				.6	.7
1.6	1.0	1.4	2.3			Debt/Worth	1.6	1.6
-26.2	3.6	2.7	4.7				5.9	5.5
94.2	49.6	45.5	38.0				35.7	45.6
(20) 56.0	(56) 28.0	(87) 22.6	(33) 15.4			% Profit Before Taxes/Tangible Net Worth	(188) 12.0	(211) 13.1
21.1	6.0	2.8	5.6				-3.3	-1.8
46.0	24.3	19.2	10.8				14.7	19.1
21.5	7.5	7.0	5.4			% Profit Before Taxes/Total Assets	4.8	4.6
10.3	1.5	1.1	.8				-3.2	-2.1
UND	88.5	59.2	50.7				46.6	59.9
38.9	37.6	21.7	12.8			Sales/Net Fixed Assets	19.9	22.9
17.1	12.3	9.9	3.2				8.5	8.9
10.8	4.2	3.8	2.7				3.7	3.6
5.4	3.1	2.7	2.1			Sales/Total Assets	2.8	2.6
2.7	2.3	2.2	1.2				1.9	1.8
.3	.5	.5	.4				.7	.6
(14) 2.0	(44) 1.1	(80) 1.0	(36) 1.5			% Depr., Dep., Amort./Sales	(189) 1.5	(183) 1.5
5.3	2.5	2.1	4.2				2.9	2.7
2.6	3.0	2.1					2.2	2.6
(17) 4.6	(38) 4.9	(38) 3.8				% Officers', Directors' Owners' Comp/Sales	(105) 4.7	(111) 5.3
8.8	6.7	6.0					7.7	8.2
38159M	269225M	1076800M	1914817M	72707M	217982M	Net Sales ($)	3862510M	3611445M
6824M	80028M	374614M	907205M	68913M	259997M	Total Assets ($)	2061419M	1905667M

M = $ thousand MM = $ million

See Pages 9 through 22 for Explanation of Ratios and Data

Comparative Historical Data				Current Data Sorted by Sales					
			Type of Statement						
18	16	19	Unqualified			1	2	3	13
63	57	65	Reviewed	1	3	4	28	17	12
36	25	18	Compiled		1	3	7	6	1
68	57	55	Tax Returns	11	16	12	12	4	
81	83	68	Other	6	11	10	14	15	12
					33 (4/1-9/30/13)		192 (10/1/13-3/31/14)		
4/1/11-3/31/12 ALL	4/1/12-3/31/13 ALL	4/1/13-3/31/14 ALL		0-1MM	1-3MM	3-5MM	5-10MM	10-25MM	25MM & OVER
266	238	225	**NUMBER OF STATEMENTS**	18	31	30	63	45	38
%	%	%	**ASSETS**	%	%	%	%	%	%
14.8	16.6	15.8	Cash & Equivalents	25.6	17.6	14.0	16.7	13.0	12.7
39.1	37.5	39.8	Trade Receivables (net)	27.8	30.7	46.2	40.2	47.6	38.1
10.1	7.9	7.5	Inventory	6.4	9.2	7.3	7.4	7.7	6.3
4.7	5.0	7.3	All Other Current	12.3	6.9	4.7	7.8	4.6	9.8
68.7	66.9	70.4	Total Current	72.1	64.4	72.2	72.2	72.9	66.9
19.1	22.2	18.8	Fixed Assets (net)	13.9	22.4	15.2	18.8	19.0	20.8
3.7	3.2	3.4	Intangibles (net)	4.0	3.5	4.1	1.9	1.8	6.7
8.5	7.7	7.5	All Other Non-Current	10.0	9.7	8.5	7.1	6.3	5.6
100.0	100.0	100.0	Total	100.0	100.0	100.0	100.0	100.0	100.0
			LIABILITIES						
12.8	12.7	12.6	Notes Payable-Short Term	43.1	16.9	12.6	7.9	10.3	5.1
3.3	2.9	2.4	Cur. Mat.-L.T.D.	.5	3.0	1.3	2.5	2.4	3.5
17.9	17.2	16.5	Trade Payables	17.6	13.1	15.2	16.1	20.4	15.9
.2	.2	.3	Income Taxes Payable	.0	.2	.1	.6	.1	.2
13.7	13.3	14.2	All Other Current	29.6	5.1	10.6	12.2	16.9	17.6
47.9	46.4	46.0	Total Current	90.8	38.2	39.8	39.3	50.1	42.4
14.2	13.8	10.1	Long-Term Debt	15.2	9.6	11.8	9.6	8.9	9.2
.3	.3	.6	Deferred Taxes	.0	.1	.1	.3	.7	1.7
11.2	5.8	5.2	All Other Non-Current	2.9	7.3	7.7	4.0	1.8	8.4
26.4	33.7	38.1	Net Worth	-8.9	44.7	40.6	46.8	38.5	38.4
100.0	100.0	100.0	Total Liabilties & Net Worth	100.0	100.0	100.0	100.0	100.0	100.0
			INCOME DATA						
100.0	100.0	100.0	Net Sales	100.0	100.0	100.0	100.0	100.0	100.0
32.1	34.6	30.5	Gross Profit	52.3	36.5	32.9	28.0	26.0	22.9
28.0	29.5	26.0	Operating Expenses	44.8	30.7	28.4	24.5	21.4	19.6
4.1	5.1	4.5	Operating Profit	7.5	5.8	4.5	3.5	4.6	3.4
.7	.6	.5	All Other Expenses (net)	-.3	.7	.2	.4	.5	1.2
3.4	4.5	4.0	Profit Before Taxes	7.8	5.1	4.3	3.1	4.1	2.2
			RATIOS						
3.1	2.7	2.8		31.8	3.5	3.4	2.6	2.1	2.5
1.6	1.6	1.7	Current	1.3	2.0	2.0	1.9	1.5	1.4
1.1	1.0	1.2		.5	1.1	1.3	1.4	1.2	1.2
2.5	2.4	2.2		23.6	3.2	2.7	2.2	1.7	2.2
1.2	1.3	1.3	Quick	1.0	1.7	1.7	1.5	1.2	1.1
.7	.8	.9		.4	.7	1.1	1.0	.9	.7
27 13.6	29 12.4	33 11.2		0 UND	8 43.4	29 12.7	36 10.1	37 9.8	42 8.6
50 7.3	49 7.4	50 7.3	Sales/Receivables	41 8.9	34 10.6	65 5.6	49 7.4	60 6.1	60 6.1
78 4.7	70 5.2	73 5.0		65 5.6	48 7.6	94 3.9	68 5.4	73 5.0	72 5.1
0 UND	0 UND	0 UND		0 UND	0 UND	0 UND	0 UND	0 UND	0 UND
2 206.7	2 234.5	1 302.2	Cost of Sales/Inventory	0 UND	0 UND	4 98.8	1 557.4	2 175.1	0 819.6
24 15.1	25 14.8	19 18.8		22 16.5	20 18.5	24 15.0	13 27.3	24 15.2	17 22.1
11 32.2	12 29.7	12 30.4		0 UND	4 89.5	14 25.9	13 27.6	13 27.6	19 18.9
24 15.2	26 14.0	26 14.2	Cost of Sales/Payables	15 23.6	14 25.5	28 12.9	26 14.0	30 12.3	27 13.7
53 6.9	50 7.3	40 9.2		62 5.9	42 8.7	39 9.4	38 9.6	46 8.0	39 9.4
5.4	5.8	5.7		3.1	5.8	4.7	5.5	7.0	6.2
11.6	11.9	10.9	Sales/Working Capital	380.5	12.2	8.5	9.7	17.4	12.6
131.9	121.7	35.2		-15.8	66.4	29.2	16.5	40.0	39.1
19.2	23.3	32.6		13.8	49.0	57.5	26.6	33.8	22.0
(224) 5.2	(201) 7.0	(189) 7.5	EBIT/Interest	(11) 4.8	(27) 11.5	(25) 10.5	(53) 6.7	(39) 7.5	(34) 7.9
1.3	1.9	2.0		1.4	2.5	1.7	1.3	2.8	1.7
5.2	14.1	5.9					13.6		5.7
(33) 2.4	(38) 2.5	(41) 2.5	Net Profit + Depr., Dep., Amort./Cur. Mat. L/T/D				(13) 2.7		(15) 2.6
.8	1.0	1.0					1.1		1.3
.1	.1	.1		.0	.0	.1	.2	.1	.2
.4	.5	.3	Fixed/Worth	.2	.4	.2	.3	.3	.6
1.6	1.6	1.2		-1.6	1.2	1.4	.7	1.1	1.7
.7	.7	.5		.2	.3	.5	.4	.9	.6
1.9	1.5	1.4	Debt/Worth	3.6	.6	1.0	1.2	1.7	2.0
7.9	6.2	3.6		-2.5	3.4	3.4	2.1	4.0	4.2
57.5	55.2	49.3		408.7	71.6	50.0	45.3	52.9	36.4
(223) 17.0	(199) 22.3	(197) 23.9	% Profit Before Taxes/Tangible Net Worth	(11) 52.0	(26) 28.8	(26) 23.2	(60) 13.3	(42) 25.9	(32) 17.1
2.7	5.0	5.6		20.0	10.0	5.1	1.9	6.6	5.5
20.4	20.1	21.2		42.6	30.7	27.9	18.0	19.0	11.2
6.1	8.3	7.9	% Profit Before Taxes/Total Assets	19.0	12.0	7.0	6.6	8.6	5.8
.5	1.7	1.6		1.8	3.7	1.9	.6	2.7	.1
81.5	57.1	77.5		342.3	521.3	88.6	43.7	94.6	66.3
29.4	22.0	25.2	Sales/Net Fixed Assets	32.1	33.0	32.3	24.5	27.7	15.1
10.8	7.8	9.9		9.6	14.7	9.9	9.5	9.9	7.7
4.0	3.7	4.0		5.7	5.4	3.7	3.9	4.1	3.2
2.8	2.7	2.8	Sales/Total Assets	2.9	3.3	2.8	2.9	3.1	2.4
1.9	1.9	2.0		1.3	2.1	2.3	2.0	2.4	1.6
.6	.6	.5		.4	1.1	.5	.5	.4	.4
(198) 1.2	(187) 1.3	(176) 1.2	% Depr., Dep., Amort./Sales	(10) 3.4	(16) 1.8	(21) 1.3	(57) .9	(38) 1.0	(34) 1.1
2.7	2.6	2.5		5.5	3.3	2.9	1.9	2.4	2.7
1.8	2.2	2.6			2.3	3.0	2.4	1.8	
(120) 3.8	(105) 4.1	(103) 4.3	% Officers', Directors' Owners' Comp/Sales		(21) 4.6	(20) 4.6	(32) 4.1	(14) 2.8	
6.4	6.8	6.7			6.5	7.3	6.0	5.8	
3283972M	5799017M	3589690M	Net Sales ($)	10663M	66166M	115809M	441840M	724199M	2231013M
1443856M	1554951M	1697581M	Total Assets ($)	5138M	24455M	42760M	176405M	309775M	1139048M

M = $ thousand MM = $ million

See Pages 9 through 22 for Explanation of Ratios and Data

Current Data Sorted by Assets							Comparative Historical Data	
						Type of Statement		
	3	4	17	4		Unqualified	48	43
2	16	64	22			Reviewed	131	104
3	19	9	1	1		Compiled	33	44
27	25	9	1		1	Tax Returns	62	68
12	32	35	14	4	1	Other	91	104
67 (4/1-9/30/13)		259 (10/1/13-3/31/14)					4/1/09-3/31/10 ALL	4/1/10-3/31/11 ALL
0-500M	500M-2MM	2-10MM	10-50MM	50-100MM	100-250MM			
44	95	121	55	9	2	NUMBER OF STATEMENTS	365	363
%	%	%	%	%	%	**ASSETS**	%	%
21.8	14.7	12.8	12.5			Cash & Equivalents	16.4	15.2
31.6	51.4	58.1	53.9			Trade Receivables (net)	45.6	45.7
6.8	8.2	3.5	2.8			Inventory	5.4	4.9
6.1	3.3	9.6	12.1			All Other Current	8.1	7.7
66.4	77.7	83.9	81.3			Total Current	75.4	73.4
23.6	14.4	9.8	7.2			Fixed Assets (net)	14.4	16.0
1.2	2.2	1.2	2.6			Intangibles (net)	3.1	2.7
8.7	5.7	5.2	8.9			All Other Non-Current	7.0	7.8
100.0	100.0	100.0	100.0			Total	100.0	100.0
						LIABILITIES		
24.0	10.0	11.4	7.4			Notes Payable-Short Term	17.4	17.1
2.6	2.2	1.0	1.8			Cur. Mat.-L.T.D.	2.2	2.2
16.6	19.6	17.2	15.6			Trade Payables	14.1	15.7
.5	.5	.3	.3			Income Taxes Payable	.4	.4
21.2	12.5	16.4	20.8			All Other Current	16.3	15.5
65.0	44.7	46.2	45.9			Total Current	50.4	50.8
39.2	9.0	6.2	2.4			Long-Term Debt	11.1	10.4
.0	.1	.2	.1			Deferred Taxes	.4	.3
6.8	4.0	3.5	4.5			All Other Non-Current	4.3	7.1
-11.0	42.1	43.9	47.1			Net Worth	33.8	31.4
100.0	100.0	100.0	100.0			Total Liabilities & Net Worth	100.0	100.0
						INCOME DATA		
100.0	100.0	100.0	100.0			Net Sales	100.0	100.0
35.9	26.1	18.9	14.8			Gross Profit	25.5	25.3
32.4	21.7	14.9	11.8			Operating Expenses	23.7	24.7
3.4	4.5	4.0	3.0			Operating Profit	1.8	.7
.7	-.1	.3	.2			All Other Expenses (net)	.6	.4
2.7	4.6	3.7	2.8			Profit Before Taxes	1.2	.2
						RATIOS		
3.9	3.4	2.8	2.3				3.1	3.0
1.2	1.8	1.8	1.8			Current	1.8	1.8
.5	1.2	1.3	1.4				1.2	1.1
3.6	3.0	2.4	2.0				2.5	2.7
(43) 1.1	1.6	1.6	1.4			Quick	1.5	1.4
.4	1.0	1.1	1.1				.9	.9
0 UND	36 10.1	59 6.2	63 5.8				39 9.3	40 9.0
10 35.3	56 6.5	74 4.9	81 4.5			Sales/Receivables	60 6.1	62 5.9
45 8.1	72 5.1	94 3.9	96 3.8				78 4.7	83 4.4
0 UND	0 UND	0 UND	0 UND				0 UND	0 UND
0 UND	3 132.5	0 812.8	2 166.0			Cost of Sales/Inventory	1 345.3	1 333.5
5 71.5	20 18.3	8 46.1	6 57.4				9 39.1	9 38.5
0 UND	10 35.1	15 24.7	15 23.6				9 40.9	10 38.1
11 32.0	19 18.9	24 15.5	21 17.6			Cost of Sales/Payables	17 21.3	19 19.2
30 12.0	43 8.4	37 9.8	34 10.7				32 11.5	33 10.9
12.9	5.5	4.9	5.2				5.3	5.0
69.4	9.6	7.6	7.3			Sales/Working Capital	8.7	8.8
-25.8	26.9	18.6	10.9				29.0	88.9
27.7	37.4	31.6	27.9				20.9	12.9
(36) 7.6	(77) 11.8	(107) 11.2	(48) 12.3			EBIT/Interest	(317) 5.1	(312) 3.1
-2.0	4.1	3.4	3.2				-.4	-5.0
		12.5	36.8				15.4	8.6
		(30) 6.0	(15) 9.0			Net Profit + Depr., Dep., Amort./Cur. Mat. L/T/D	(66) 3.0	(66) 3.1
		2.2	.1				.5	-.7
.0	.1	.1	.0				.1	.1
.3	.2	.2	.1			Fixed/Worth	.2	.3
-1.4	.9	.5	.2				.9	.9
.6	.4	.7	.6				.6	.6
4.3	1.4	1.4	1.1			Debt/Worth	1.3	1.3
-3.2	3.9	2.9	1.8				5.5	4.4
219.6	61.9	48.9	28.0				38.5	34.5
(27) 94.2	(82) 30.5	(116) 20.2	(54) 12.0			% Profit Before Taxes/Tangible Net Worth	(310) 13.4	(300) 7.2
14.8	10.9	5.0	3.0				.1	-5.6
73.9	24.9	20.1	15.4				17.7	12.7
31.8	12.5	6.3	4.7			% Profit Before Taxes/Total Assets	4.8	2.6
-4.4	3.9	2.0	1.6				-2.8	-7.4
641.3	113.2	127.2	106.0				77.8	75.2
68.9	35.0	46.1	49.1			Sales/Net Fixed Assets	37.2	31.0
27.9	16.9	21.8	27.6				17.2	16.8
11.6	4.2	3.5	3.0				3.8	3.8
7.0	3.2	2.7	2.5			Sales/Total Assets	2.9	2.8
4.1	2.7	2.2	2.1				2.2	2.1
.2	.4	.2	.2				.4	.4
(23) .6	(62) .8	(106) .5	(51) .4			% Depr., Dep., Amort./Sales	(300) .8	(294) .9
1.6	1.4	.8	.6				1.4	1.5
3.0	2.1	1.5	.6				2.2	2.0
(26) 5.9	(52) 3.8	(62) 2.4	(23) 1.8			% Officers', Directors' Owners' Comp/Sales	(184) 4.4	(208) 4.1
9.1	6.3	4.5	4.4				8.0	7.9
64825M	383777M	1745333M	2803021M	1563744M	940929M	Net Sales ($)	6602220M	6570339M
9192M	106175M	619430M	1111237M	682737M	306070M	Total Assets ($)	3060904M	2534927M

M = $ thousand MM = $ million

See Pages 9 through 22 for Explanation of Ratios and Data

Comparative Historical Data				Current Data Sorted by Sales					
			Type of Statement						
32	33	28	Unqualified		1	1	1	5	20
107	92	104	Reviewed	1	8	7	20	46	22
43	30	33	Compiled	1	9	9	7	4	3
68	65	63	Tax Returns	15	18	11	12	3	4
96	83	98	Other	6	17	15	20	22	18
				67 (4/1-9/30/13)		259 (10/1/13-3/31/14)			
4/1/11-3/31/12 ALL	4/1/12-3/31/13 ALL	4/1/13-3/31/14 ALL		0-1MM	1-3MM	3-5MM	5-10MM	10-25MM	25MM & OVER
346	303	326	**NUMBER OF STATEMENTS**	23	53	43	60	80	67
%	%	%	**ASSETS**	%	%	%	%	%	%
15.1	14.3	14.9	Cash & Equivalents	18.8	16.5	16.8	15.5	13.4	12.4
47.6	50.0	51.5	Trade Receivables (net)	24.1	44.0	47.3	54.8	58.6	58.1
5.1	5.1	5.1	Inventory	8.4	7.9	7.1	5.4	2.9	3.1
7.4	8.1	7.8	All Other Current	9.8	3.9	3.3	7.3	8.5	12.5
75.3	77.5	79.3	Total Current	61.1	72.3	74.4	82.9	83.4	86.1
13.5	12.3	12.5	Fixed Assets (net)	35.2	15.1	17.6	10.5	7.4	7.2
2.2	1.9	1.8	Intangibles (net)	2.0	2.0	2.3	1.0	2.2	1.5
9.0	8.2	6.4	All Other Non-Current	1.3	10.6	5.6	5.5	7.0	5.1
100.0	100.0	100.0	Total	100.0	100.0	100.0	100.0	100.0	100.0
			LIABILITIES						
14.1	14.7	11.8	Notes Payable-Short Term	20.8	17.3	10.4	12.0	8.9	8.7
2.3	2.3	1.7	Cur. Mat.-L.T.D.	2.3	2.9	2.0	1.0	1.3	1.5
16.8	17.6	17.6	Trade Payables	20.2	15.0	18.4	18.2	16.8	18.5
.3	.3	.4	Income Taxes Payable	1.0	.2	.8	.3	.2	.2
14.4	16.8	16.7	All Other Current	18.0	15.6	13.8	11.1	19.4	21.0
47.8	51.8	48.2	Total Current	62.3	51.0	45.4	42.7	46.6	49.9
9.8	10.6	11.1	Long-Term Debt	62.2	12.7	6.5	7.6	5.5	5.0
.2	.2	.1	Deferred Taxes	.0	.2	.1	.1	.2	.2
5.2	5.4	4.4	All Other Non-Current	5.9	4.4	4.3	4.2	3.8	4.7
37.0	32.0	36.2	Net Worth	-30.4	31.8	43.7	45.4	43.8	40.2
100.0	100.0	100.0	Total Liabilities & Net Worth	100.0	100.0	100.0	100.0	100.0	100.0
			INCOME DATA						
100.0	100.0	100.0	Net Sales	100.0	100.0	100.0	100.0	100.0	100.0
23.2	22.8	22.8	Gross Profit	35.6	31.8	25.3	22.6	17.5	16.1
22.3	19.8	19.0	Operating Expenses	34.8	27.1	20.4	18.6	13.3	13.3
.9	3.0	3.8	Operating Profit	.8	4.7	4.9	4.0	4.2	2.8
.3	.2	.2	All Other Expenses (net)	-.1	.6	-.1	.1	.4	.1
.6	2.8	3.6	Profit Before Taxes	.8	4.1	5.0	3.9	3.9	2.6
			RATIOS						
3.0	2.6	2.9		4.8	3.2	3.7	3.8	2.5	2.3
1.8	1.6	1.8	Current	1.1	1.9	1.7	2.0	1.9	1.7
1.1	1.2	1.2		.5	1.1	1.2	1.3	1.4	1.4
2.6	2.2	2.5		4.1	2.9	3.6	3.7	2.2	1.9
1.5	1.4	(325) 1.5	Quick	(22) .7	1.6	1.5	1.8	1.7	1.4
1.0	.9	1.0		.4	.9	1.0	1.1	1.2	1.1
41 8.8	41 8.8	43 8.5		0 UND	23 16.0	38 9.7	46 8.0	60 6.1	57 6.4
68 5.4	66 5.5	64 5.7	Sales/Receivables	15 25.0	47 7.8	57 6.4	62 5.9	73 5.0	74 4.9
89 4.1	91 4.0	87 4.2		50 7.3	76 4.8	69 5.3	91 4.0	91 4.0	91 4.0
0 UND	0 UND	0 UND		0 UND	0 UND	0 UND	0 UND	0 UND	0 UND
2 223.8	1 371.2	1 359.7	Cost of Sales/Inventory	0 UND	1 289.1	3 138.2	0 UND	1 322.2	1 258.7
12 30.7	9 41.7	10 35.1		10 35.1	18 20.1	19 19.3	13 29.1	8 47.2	6 66.3
11 32.3	13 27.7	12 29.5		0 UND	10 38.3	10 37.5	11 31.9	15 24.6	15 23.6
21 17.3	23 15.7	20 17.9	Cost of Sales/Payables	27 13.3	16 22.7	19 18.9	19 19.0	21 17.2	24 15.5
38 9.6	38 9.7	37 9.9		55 6.6	33 11.2	43 8.4	41 8.8	30 12.2	35 10.3
5.1	5.5	5.3		19.6	5.0	5.2	4.7	5.3	5.4
8.1	9.4	9.0	Sales/Working Capital	494.0	10.9	9.6	8.1	7.8	8.3
29.9	31.3	23.4		-11.4	63.0	28.3	20.9	18.6	11.9
13.1	25.2	31.6		10.8	24.9	36.1	55.8	39.4	31.0
(274) 2.6	(256) 5.7	(279) 11.1	EBIT/Interest	(17) 3.8	(42) 5.6	(37) 11.0	(51) 15.4	(70) 12.1	(62) 13.6
-3.4	1.3	3.4		-4.8	2.1	6.1	4.4	3.5	2.5
9.4	15.4	18.8						9.5	46.9
(57) 1.1	(41) 2.7	(57) 6.5	Net Profit + Depr., Dep., Amort./Cur. Mat. L/T/D					(24) 5.5	(19) 9.0
-5.4	.1	1.6						.8	5.2
.1	.1	.1		.0	.0	.2	.1	.0	.0
.2	.2	.2	Fixed/Worth	1.8	.2	.3	.2	.1	.1
.8	.8	.6		-1.4	.9	.9	.5	.3	.3
.5	.6	.6		.7	.6	.4	.4	.8	.7
1.3	1.5	1.4	Debt/Worth	8.9	1.5	1.4	.9	1.3	1.5
4.5	5.8	3.5		-2.2	4.5	7.1	3.2	2.7	2.5
27.8	46.6	55.5		299.1	75.4	74.4	57.6	43.0	37.7
(296) 7.0	(256) 16.9	(288) 20.6	% Profit Before Taxes/Tangible Net Worth	(12) 65.8	(46) 27.2	(36) 30.0	(53) 25.8	(77) 18.8	(64) 15.5
-6.6	4.1	5.3		-2.4	8.4	8.6	8.5	4.8	4.3
14.0	17.0	21.7		67.8	27.5	31.2	28.9	17.4	16.2
2.8	5.8	8.1	% Profit Before Taxes/Total Assets	10.3	11.2	14.8	12.0	6.5	5.8
-5.6	.5	2.1		-19.4	1.8	3.8	3.0	2.1	1.9
101.8	143.4	136.9		726.0	168.2	53.6	129.0	138.3	204.3
43.3	44.5	48.0	Sales/Net Fixed Assets	68.0	44.3	25.9	33.4	59.2	55.8
17.7	22.1	21.0		5.9	17.5	14.8	19.9	27.5	33.8
3.7	3.9	4.1		9.4	4.2	4.3	4.6	3.6	3.5
2.8	2.9	3.0	Sales/Total Assets	5.3	3.1	3.6	3.0	2.8	2.8
2.1	2.2	2.3		2.1	2.3	2.8	2.2	2.2	2.4
.3	.3	.2		.4	.4	.3	.3	.2	.2
(262) .7	(232) .5	(251) .5	% Depr., Dep., Amort./Sales	(12) 2.0	(27) .9	(32) .8	(50) .6	(70) .4	(60) .4
1.2	1.1	1.0		4.1	2.2	1.3	.9	.6	.6
1.9	1.7	1.6		3.2	3.4	2.3	1.7	1.4	.7
(170) 3.6	(142) 2.8	(167) 2.9	% Officers', Directors' Owners' Comp/Sales	(13) 8.0	(28) 6.2	(23) 4.5	(33) 2.7	(45) 2.1	(25) 1.4
5.7	5.6	6.1		11.0	9.9	6.3	4.3	4.2	4.2
5268244M	6441627M	7501629M	Net Sales ($)	13520M	105224M	165403M	432399M	1297309M	5487774M
2455275M	2544185M	2834841M	Total Assets ($)	4443M	40361M	60217M	161419M	537628M	2030773M

M = $ thousand MM = $ million

See Pages 9 through 22 for Explanation of Ratios and Data

Current Data Sorted by Assets | **Comparative Historical Data**

0-500M	500M-2MM	2-10MM	10-50MM	50-100MM	100-250MM	Type of Statement	4/1/09-3/31/10 ALL	4/1/10-3/31/11 ALL
	4	9	3		1	Unqualified	19	16
3	14	35	3			Reviewed	65	60
	6	6				Compiled	31	24
30	19	3				Tax Returns	33	45
10	13	27	2			Other	52	50
35 (4/1-9/30/13)			153 (10/1/13-3/31/14)					
43	56	80	8		1	NUMBER OF STATEMENTS	200	195
%	%	%	%	%	%	ASSETS	%	%
28.3	19.7	16.1		DATA NOT AVAILABLE		Cash & Equivalents	16.5	17.9
22.2	48.0	50.1				Trade Receivables (net)	44.0	41.2
1.6	1.9	2.3				Inventory	2.6	2.6
3.0	3.7	9.0				All Other Current	8.4	9.5
55.2	73.3	77.5				Total Current	71.5	71.1
32.0	17.0	15.3				Fixed Assets (net)	19.7	19.1
2.2	.3	2.1				Intangibles (net)	1.8	2.8
10.7	9.3	5.1				All Other Non-Current	7.1	7.0
100.0	100.0	100.0				Total	100.0	100.0
						LIABILITIES		
39.9	11.9	7.9				Notes Payable-Short Term	16.3	18.3
2.0	1.3	1.7				Cur. Mat.-L.T.D.	3.5	2.5
14.3	13.9	12.6				Trade Payables	12.4	12.9
.1	.1	.5				Income Taxes Payable	.6	.8
20.8	10.3	11.9				All Other Current	14.7	15.6
77.1	37.5	34.6				Total Current	47.4	50.2
20.7	6.6	5.2				Long-Term Debt	9.4	11.4
.3	1.1	.4				Deferred Taxes	.5	.3
6.6	4.5	2.3				All Other Non-Current	7.5	7.1
-4.8	50.3	57.5				Net Worth	35.2	31.1
100.0	100.0	100.0				Total Liabilities & Net Worth	100.0	100.0
						INCOME DATA		
100.0	100.0	100.0				Net Sales	100.0	100.0
41.6	33.2	25.9				Gross Profit	32.2	32.4
33.5	29.5	20.9				Operating Expenses	29.5	29.0
8.1	3.7	5.0				Operating Profit	2.7	3.4
.2	.3	.3				All Other Expenses (net)	.4	.3
7.9	3.4	4.7				Profit Before Taxes	2.2	3.1
						RATIOS		
3.2	4.8	4.5					3.6	3.9
1.0	2.2	2.5				Current	1.9	1.9
.3	1.3	1.5					1.2	1.1
2.7	4.5	3.9					3.1	3.3
.9	2.1	2.2				Quick	1.5	1.5
.3	1.2	1.1					.9	.8
0 UND	**39** 9.4	**59** 6.2					**28** 12.9	**27** 13.8
0 999.8	**64** 5.7	**73** 5.0				Sales/Receivables	**55** 6.6	**53** 6.8
32 11.5	**83** 4.4	**91** 4.0					**81** 4.5	**84** 4.4
0 UND	**0** UND	**0** UND					**0** UND	**0** UND
0 UND	**0** UND	**0** UND				Cost of Sales/Inventory	**0** UND	**0** UND
0 UND	**0** UND	**2** 211.1					**1** 248.5	**2** 199.9
0 UND	**7** 50.1	**10** 35.3					**6** 61.1	**6** 64.6
1 320.8	**20** 18.0	**18** 19.9				Cost of Sales/Payables	**14** 25.3	**16** 23.3
20 18.1	**46** 7.9	**33** 11.0					**28** 13.1	**32** 11.4
16.6	5.2	3.6					5.0	4.6
-855.8	7.7	6.5				Sales/Working Capital	9.0	9.0
-17.0	14.5	12.0					39.9	44.5
22.6	25.5	88.4					23.7	19.5
(35) 8.7	(44) 6.6	(68) 14.2				EBIT/Interest	(168) 4.4	(161) 4.1
3.4	2.7	1.6					-1.8	.0
		36.1					13.4	9.9
		(17) 8.8				Net Profit + Depr., Dep., Amort./Cur. Mat. L/T/D	(37) 2.9	(34) 3.4
		-1.5					.6	.4
.2	.1	.1					.1	.1
1.8	.3	.2				Fixed/Worth	.3	.3
-2.9	.8	.5					1.0	1.1
1.2	.3	.3					.4	.4
11.1	.9	.7				Debt/Worth	1.0	1.1
-4.6	2.3	1.6					3.1	4.0
224.1	45.5	40.1					35.7	45.8
(24) 102.8	(50) 23.6	(79) 18.6				% Profit Before Taxes/Tangible Net Worth	(172) 14.1	(165) 15.1
36.4	3.5	3.9					-2.5	1.4
122.9	27.3	18.7					19.8	21.7
30.2	8.0	9.4				% Profit Before Taxes/Total Assets	5.4	6.1
8.3	.8	.7					-4.7	-.9
178.4	89.3	59.1					58.2	66.3
36.4	33.5	22.6				Sales/Net Fixed Assets	24.0	24.8
16.3	9.5	9.7					12.2	11.8
12.8	3.6	3.2					4.4	4.4
6.7	3.0	2.5				Sales/Total Assets	3.0	2.9
4.6	2.1	1.8					2.1	2.1
.2	.5	.4					.8	.7
(22) 1.0	(35) 1.1	(68) .9				% Depr., Dep., Amort./Sales	(166) 1.3	(149) 1.3
2.4	2.5	2.0					2.3	2.3
1.8	3.1	1.2					3.1	2.9
(26) 3.4	(30) 5.8	(38) 3.2				% Officers', Directors' Owners' Comp/Sales	(113) 5.8	(108) 4.5
8.3	9.0	7.3					10.7	8.4
69662M	207317M	856655M	216691M		291136M	Net Sales ($)	3022234M	1121715M
9336M	67327M	343345M	122584M		153935M	Total Assets ($)	888566M	460905M

M = $ thousand MM = $ million

See Pages 9 through 22 for Explanation of Ratios and Data

Comparative Historical Data | Current Data Sorted by Sales

4/1/11-3/31/12 ALL	4/1/12-3/31/13 ALL	4/1/13-3/31/14 ALL	Type of Statement	0-1MM	1-3MM	3-5MM	5-10MM	10-25MM	25MM & OVER
16	16	17	Unqualified		3	2	4	4	4
71	60	55	Reviewed		10	7	18	20	
21	24	12	Compiled		1	2	5	4	
41	52	52	Tax Returns	12	23	11	3	3	
56	47	52	Other	7	8	11	11	14	1
				35 (4/1-9/30/13)			153 (10/1/13-3/31/14)		
205	199	188	NUMBER OF STATEMENTS	19	45	33	41	45	5
%	%	%	ASSETS	%	%	%	%	%	%
19.9	19.3	19.7	Cash & Equivalents	26.0	24.6	25.6	14.4	13.8	
39.8	42.3	42.8	Trade Receivables (net)	25.3	35.3	41.1	50.8	51.9	
2.2	3.1	2.0	Inventory	.1	3.7	.1	2.5	1.9	
8.7	5.9	6.3	All Other Current	3.8	3.8	2.2	7.5	9.8	
70.5	70.6	70.9	Total Current	55.3	67.4	69.0	75.2	77.4	
20.2	19.8	19.7	Fixed Assets (net)	35.6	22.7	19.5	15.9	14.4	
2.2	1.9	1.9	Intangibles (net)	2.6	.1	2.3	1.5	3.1	
7.1	7.7	7.5	All Other Non-Current	6.7	9.8	9.2	7.3	5.0	
100.0	100.0	100.0	Total	100.0	100.0	100.0	100.0	100.0	
			LIABILITIES						
16.2	18.1	16.4	Notes Payable-Short Term	36.3	15.4	23.5	13.3	7.8	
3.9	2.4	1.7	Cur. Mat.-L.T.D.	.4	2.1	1.2	1.6	2.2	
13.3	13.2	13.3	Trade Payables	20.8	11.4	9.5	13.2	14.8	
.4	.4	.4	Income Taxes Payable	.0	.0	.2	.3	1.1	
13.3	14.4	13.5	All Other Current	12.7	18.9	12.9	9.6	11.7	
47.1	48.6	45.3	Total Current	70.2	47.9	47.3	38.0	37.6	
9.5	12.6	9.3	Long-Term Debt	6.8	16.8	9.3	7.2	4.9	
.6	.3	.6	Deferred Taxes	.8	.9	.9	.5	.2	
4.9	5.0	3.9	All Other Non-Current	10.8	4.3	5.4	2.3	1.4	
37.8	33.5	40.9	Net Worth	11.5	30.1	37.1	52.0	55.9	
100.0	100.0	100.0	Total Liabilities & Net Worth	100.0	100.0	100.0	100.0	100.0	
			INCOME DATA						
100.0	100.0	100.0	Net Sales	100.0	100.0	100.0	100.0	100.0	
29.9	34.0	32.1	Gross Profit	43.7	37.4	33.0	28.3	25.6	
26.4	29.6	26.7	Operating Expenses	33.6	32.1	28.4	24.8	19.6	
3.6	4.5	5.4	Operating Profit	10.2	5.3	4.7	3.5	6.0	
.3	.2	.3	All Other Expenses (net)	.7	.1	.3	.4	.1	
3.2	4.2	5.1	Profit Before Taxes	9.4	5.1	4.4	3.1	6.0	
			RATIOS						
3.9	3.5	4.3		4.4	4.1	5.1	4.4	3.8	
1.9	1.9	2.1	Current	1.3	2.1	2.7	2.1	2.1	
1.1	1.2	1.2		.2	.9	1.1	1.4	1.5	
3.4	3.1	3.9		4.4	3.8	5.0	4.1	3.4	
1.6	1.7	1.8	Quick	1.0	2.0	2.7	1.6	1.7	
.8	.9	.9		.2	.7	1.1	1.2	1.1	
25 14.4	**28** 12.9	**27** 13.3		**0** UND	**13** 27.6	**23** 15.8	**46** 7.9	**43** 8.5	
51 7.1	**54** 6.7	**61** 6.0	Sales/Receivables	**3** 111.2	**48** 7.6	**51** 7.2	**72** 5.1	**68** 5.4	
78 4.7	**74** 4.9	**81** 4.5		**46** 7.9	**74** 4.9	**104** 3.5	**85** 4.3	**89** 4.1	
0 UND	**0** UND	**0** UND		**0** UND	**0** UND	**0** UND	**0** UND	**0** UND	
0 UND	**0** UND	**0** UND	Cost of Sales/Inventory	**0** UND	**0** UND	**0** UND	**0** UND	**0** UND	
1 413.5	**2** 177.6	**1** 480.1		**0** UND	**4** 102.1	**0** UND	**3** 111.0	**1** 428.3	
4 98.9	**8** 44.0	**6** 64.5		**0** UND	**0** UND	**1** 375.0	**12** 31.7	**9** 38.8	
16 22.2	**20** 18.7	**18** 20.7	Cost of Sales/Payables	**16** 23.5	**18** 20.4	**10** 36.8	**20** 18.4	**19** 19.2	
32 11.4	**35** 10.3	**33** 11.2		**56** 6.5	**25** 14.5	**31** 11.6	**33** 11.2	**36** 10.2	
4.6	4.6	4.4		12.6	5.6	3.7	3.8	4.7	
8.9	9.0	9.2	Sales/Working Capital	50.3	11.4	6.5	9.1	7.8	
50.9	49.9	31.0		-4.9	-103.4	NM	15.4	14.0	
28.8	36.3	34.3		14.3	19.1	44.2	24.8	106.6	
(174) 5.5	(171) 7.1	(156) 11.0	EBIT/Interest	(13) 7.2	(36) 8.1	(28) 7.9	(37) 10.9	(37) 24.8	
-.1	1.3	2.0		3.2	-2.7	2.3	1.6	5.0	
15.4	17.5	27.8						169.3	
(22) 7.2	(22) 4.8	(22) 6.1	Net Profit + Depr., Dep., Amort./Cur. Mat. L/T/D					(10) 24.1	
1.2	1.8	1.3						7.6	
.1	.1	.1		.0	.1	.1	.1	.1	
.3	.4	.3	Fixed/Worth	.7	.3	.2	.3	.2	
1.2	1.4	.9		-11.0	4.9	1.9	.8	.5	
.4	.5	.3		.7	.4	.2	.3	.3	
1.0	1.0	1.1	Debt/Worth	4.2	1.5	.7	1.2	.8	
3.9	5.0	3.9		-3.7	-36.2	5.3	2.0	2.0	
40.5	51.4	50.2		195.0	64.3	42.9	31.6	49.8	
(172) 15.8	(164) 24.2	(162) 24.9	% Profit Before Taxes/Tangible Net Worth	(12) 83.5	(33) 26.5	(28) 15.4	(39) 15.7	29.3	
.0	3.5	6.1		44.0	-1.9	4.9	1.1	10.8	
22.1	24.4	29.5		79.0	44.1	20.2	14.7	23.3	
7.1	9.0	10.3	% Profit Before Taxes/Total Assets	28.6	17.5	7.4	8.3	14.3	
-2.3	.9	2.1		7.7	-1.7	2.1	.6	5.2	
56.8	70.8	75.6		100.0	113.5	100.5	75.1	54.5	
23.3	22.8	29.3	Sales/Net Fixed Assets	29.0	27.2	42.8	30.0	29.3	
10.7	10.6	10.3		3.3	9.3	9.6	10.9	14.8	
4.3	4.5	4.3		7.1	6.6	3.7	3.2	3.8	
2.9	3.0	2.9	Sales/Total Assets	4.8	3.1	3.0	2.8	2.9	
2.0	2.2	2.0		1.3	2.4	1.7	2.0	2.1	
.7	.6	.5			.5	.5	.4	.4	
(156) 1.2	(155) 1.2	(132) .9	% Depr., Dep., Amort./Sales		(29) 1.4	(21) .9	(34) 1.1	(37) .8	
1.9	2.1	2.1			2.9	2.8	1.8	1.7	
2.8	3.4	2.2			2.0	2.5	1.5	1.1	
(111) 4.3	(107) 5.3	(97) 4.5	% Officers', Directors' Owners' Comp/Sales		(28) 6.1	(22) 5.4	(19) 4.5	(19) 2.9	
7.9	8.5	8.4			8.5	9.1	6.8	4.4	
1282241M	1159997M	1641461M	Net Sales ($)	10444M	91844M	123056M	281367M	702368M	432382M
533517M	453804M	696527M	Total Assets ($)	4368M	32184M	52336M	114515M	267780M	225344M

M = $ thousand MM = $ million

See Pages 9 through 22 for Explanation of Ratios and Data

	Current Data Sorted by Assets						Comparative Historical Data	
Type of Statement								
Unqualified			3	5			3	8
Reviewed	1	16	40	8			60	45
Compiled	6	7	7				27	24
Tax Returns	12	22	9	2			42	30
Other	10	23	23	14	1		60	73
	21 (4/1-9/30/13)		188 (10/1/13-3/31/14)				4/1/09-3/31/10 ALL	4/1/10-3/31/11 ALL
	0-500M	500M-2MM	2-10MM	10-50MM	50-100MM	100-250MM		
NUMBER OF STATEMENTS	29	68	82	29	1		192	180
ASSETS	%	%	%	%	%	%	%	%
Cash & Equivalents	21.8	11.1	10.2	2.4		DATA NOT AVAILABLE	11.5	10.4
Trade Receivables (net)	32.4	49.7	57.5	51.6			46.2	45.9
Inventory	12.3	10.4	10.0	13.4			13.1	14.4
All Other Current	3.2	5.6	8.8	9.4			7.1	5.1
Total Current	69.8	76.9	86.5	76.8			77.9	75.7
Fixed Assets (net)	21.7	12.2	7.0	7.4			14.3	13.5
Intangibles (net)	6.0	2.6	2.8	9.3			2.6	2.5
All Other Non-Current	2.5	8.3	3.7	6.4			5.2	8.2
Total	100.0	100.0	100.0	100.0			100.0	100.0
LIABILITIES								
Notes Payable-Short Term	14.8	14.6	13.6	15.1			20.7	18.8
Cur. Mat.-L.T.D.	3.2	2.7	2.2	1.3			2.4	2.3
Trade Payables	20.9	17.7	18.1	17.3			18.4	18.6
Income Taxes Payable	.4	.4	.8	.3			.3	.4
All Other Current	12.3	11.8	12.8	14.7			16.8	14.3
Total Current	51.6	47.2	47.5	48.6			58.7	54.3
Long-Term Debt	10.3	8.4	5.3	7.2			11.5	11.5
Deferred Taxes	.0	.1	.1	.9			.1	.2
All Other Non-Current	14.5	5.3	4.0	5.6			6.1	6.8
Net Worth	23.6	38.9	43.2	37.5			23.6	27.2
Total Liabilties & Net Worth	100.0	100.0	100.0	100.0			100.0	100.0
INCOME DATA								
Net Sales	100.0	100.0	100.0	100.0			100.0	100.0
Gross Profit	34.7	25.5	22.6	22.3			29.1	28.4
Operating Expenses	31.3	21.2	19.2	18.4			27.7	25.7
Operating Profit	3.4	4.4	3.4	3.9			1.4	2.7
All Other Expenses (net)	.4	.2	.1	.5			.1	.4
Profit Before Taxes	3.0	4.2	3.3	3.4			1.3	2.3
RATIOS								
	4.9	2.2	2.5	2.1			2.8	2.8
Current	1.4	1.7	1.8	1.4			1.6	1.5
	.9	1.3	1.4	1.2			1.1	1.1
	4.9	2.0	2.0	1.5			2.1	2.1
Quick	1.1	1.4	1.4	1.1			1.3	1.2
	.5	.9	1.0	.9			.8	.7
	0 UND	**25** 14.4	**55** 6.6	**51** 7.1			**31** 11.8	**28** 12.8
Sales/Receivables	**16** 22.6	**54** 6.7	**69** 5.3	**63** 5.8			**54** 6.8	**54** 6.8
	44 8.3	**73** 5.0	**83** 4.4	**89** 4.1			**78** 4.7	**76** 4.8
	0 UND	**0** UND	**0** 999.8	**1** 330.4			**0** 999.8	**1** 463.1
Cost of Sales/Inventory	**2** 196.9	**3** 106.4	**5** 74.6	**19** 19.0			**10** 37.5	**11** 32.1
	24 15.5	**16** 23.3	**20** 18.6	**39** 9.4			**28** 13.1	**34** 10.8
	0 UND	**5** 77.9	**13** 27.6	**15** 23.6			**9** 39.6	**11** 34.0
Cost of Sales/Payables	**12** 31.0	**20** 18.6	**23** 15.6	**26** 14.0			**20** 18.3	**21** 17.3
	33 11.2	**33** 10.9	**38** 9.5	**40** 9.2			**34** 10.8	**37** 9.9
	10.7	7.0	5.4	7.5			5.8	6.2
Sales/Working Capital	61.1	10.6	8.6	9.9			11.5	12.3
	-59.9	25.7	14.7	18.8			55.5	51.9
	27.5	18.6	25.5	36.9			12.0	12.2
EBIT/Interest	(20) 5.2	(59) 9.4	(72) 7.7	4.7			(166) 2.4	(157) 2.9
	1.6	3.9	3.0	2.2			-.8	.9
			10.2				11.7	3.9
Net Profit + Depr., Dep., Amort./Cur. Mat. L/T/D			(25) 3.5				(28) 2.3	(29) 1.3
			1.8				.4	.6
	.1	.1	.0	.1			.1	.1
Fixed/Worth	1.2	.2	.1	.3			.3	.3
	NM	.6	.3	.8			.8	1.0
	.3	.9	.7	1.3			.6	.7
Debt/Worth	3.3	1.5	1.7	2.2			1.7	2.2
	-4.3	4.4	3.1	5.9			5.9	7.9
	158.9	82.3	49.4	46.7			40.2	41.9
% Profit Before Taxes/Tangible Net Worth	(21) 57.0	(60) 41.9	(77) 22.4	(25) 24.0			(166) 13.3	(147) 13.4
	7.1	16.6	11.0	11.9			-.3	.3
	46.8	29.2	20.7	13.8			16.7	19.9
% Profit Before Taxes/Total Assets	11.2	13.0	8.9	7.9			3.6	4.3
	.7	3.3	2.9	2.4			-3.5	-.7
	157.9	123.8	185.0	109.9			113.6	100.3
Sales/Net Fixed Assets	60.4	55.3	72.5	60.4			44.1	46.0
	18.1	30.3	38.1	39.4			17.9	19.6
	8.6	5.1	3.8	3.4			4.3	4.2
Sales/Total Assets	5.0	3.6	3.2	2.8			3.2	3.1
	3.7	2.7	2.7	2.3			2.5	2.4
	.3	.3	.2	.3			.3	.3
% Depr., Dep., Amort./Sales	(15) .6	(42) .6	(57) .4	(23) .5			(144) .7	(140) .7
	1.3	1.3	.6	.6			1.6	1.3
	4.2	2.4	1.8				2.0	2.1
% Officers', Directors' Owners' Comp/Sales	(18) 6.2	(36) 3.3	(39) 2.6				(96) 4.6	(87) 3.5
	7.5	5.2	4.8				7.6	7.3
Net Sales ($)	54630M	351073M	1265061M	1561308M	172349M		2941922M	1729676M
Total Assets ($)	8798M	85561M	363097M	572741M	55455M		689913M	550205M

M = $ thousand MM = $ million

See Pages 9 through 22 for Explanation of Ratios and Data

Comparative Historical Data | **Current Data Sorted by Sales**

4/1/11-3/31/12 ALL	4/1/12-3/31/13 ALL	4/1/13-3/31/14 ALL	Type of Statement	0-1MM	1-3MM	3-5MM	5-10MM	10-25MM	25MM & OVER
7	7	8	Unqualified			1	1	1	5
57	51	65	Reviewed		2	8	23	20	12
19	18	20	Compiled	2	5	2	6	3	2
51	45	45	Tax Returns	1	14	12	8	8	2
67	69	71	Other	4	10	12	12	17	16
					21 (4/1-9/30/13)		188 (10/1/13-3/31/14)		
201	190	209	NUMBER OF STATEMENTS	7	31	35	50	49	37
%	%	%	**ASSETS**	%	%	%	%	%	%
8.3	11.9	11.0	Cash & Equivalents		11.4	13.3	11.5	10.6	3.0
46.7	49.2	50.6	Trade Receivables (net)		38.3	48.8	57.4	52.8	54.7
14.1	11.0	11.0	Inventory		9.8	9.4	10.9	10.9	13.7
7.4	6.9	7.0	All Other Current		6.1	4.9	6.3	7.8	9.7
76.5	79.0	79.7	Total Current		65.5	76.4	86.2	82.0	81.1
13.6	10.9	10.8	Fixed Assets (net)		17.5	16.1	7.4	9.9	5.7
2.6	3.4	4.1	Intangibles (net)		7.6	1.4	1.4	4.0	8.3
7.3	6.7	5.4	All Other Non-Current		9.4	6.0	4.9	4.1	4.9
100.0	100.0	100.0	Total		100.0	100.0	100.0	100.0	100.0
			LIABILITIES						
17.5	20.8	14.4	Notes Payable-Short Term		17.8	15.2	13.5	13.0	16.0
2.9	1.9	2.3	Cur. Mat.-L.T.D.		1.7	2.8	3.1	1.7	1.3
20.1	18.1	18.2	Trade Payables		15.5	14.4	18.6	19.6	19.2
.3	.4	.6	Income Taxes Payable		.4	1.1	.3	.9	.2
11.1	14.4	12.7	All Other Current		8.2	12.0	12.4	14.4	13.3
51.9	55.6	48.3	Total Current		43.7	45.4	48.0	49.5	50.0
10.8	10.2	7.3	Long-Term Debt		11.7	8.1	5.1	6.7	5.8
.1	.1	.2	Deferred Taxes		.0	.1	.1	.0	.8
8.2	5.2	6.1	All Other Non-Current		18.2	6.7	2.0	3.4	5.6
29.0	28.9	38.2	Net Worth		26.3	39.7	44.7	40.3	37.8
100.0	100.0	100.0	Total Liabilties & Net Worth		100.0	100.0	100.0	100.0	100.0
			INCOME DATA						
100.0	100.0	100.0	Net Sales		100.0	100.0	100.0	100.0	100.0
26.3	26.7	25.2	Gross Profit		32.7	24.9	21.4	23.5	22.2
24.1	22.8	21.4	Operating Expenses		29.0	21.0	18.1	19.2	18.6
2.2	3.9	3.8	Operating Profit		3.7	3.8	3.3	4.3	3.6
.5	.6	.2	All Other Expenses (net)		.5	.2	.2	.1	.3
1.8	3.3	3.5	Profit Before Taxes		3.2	3.6	3.2	4.2	3.3
			RATIOS						
2.4	2.6	2.4			3.2	2.2	3.0	2.2	2.3
1.6	1.6	1.7	Current		1.7	1.8	1.8	1.7	1.5
1.1	1.2	1.3			.9	1.4	1.4	1.3	1.3
1.9	2.1	1.9			2.3	1.9	2.6	1.7	1.5
1.1	1.3	1.3	Quick		1.1	1.4	1.5	1.3	1.1
.7	.9	.9			.6	1.0	1.0	.9	.9
31 11.7	**34** 10.6	**33** 11.0			**9** 38.7	**19** 19.1	**42** 8.7	**40** 9.1	**51** 7.1
54 6.7	**58** 6.3	**58** 6.3	Sales/Receivables		**32** 11.4	**59** 6.2	**62** 5.9	**59** 6.2	**63** 5.8
79 4.6	**81** 4.5	**79** 4.6			**70** 5.2	**83** 4.4	**76** 4.8	**79** 4.6	**91** 4.0
1 599.1	**0** UND	**0** UND			**0** UND	**0** UND	**0** UND	**1** 717.6	**1** 330.4
12 29.5	**6** 56.9	**4** 84.4	Cost of Sales/Inventory		**1** 339.0	**3** 129.0	**6** 64.3	**4** 93.3	**13** 29.1
31 11.8	**27** 13.7	**22** 16.5			**16** 23.0	**15** 25.0	**20** 18.3	**22** 16.5	**36** 10.2
13 27.6	**12** 30.7	**10** 38.2			**1** 518.4	**2** 194.6	**11** 32.9	**12** 29.5	**15** 23.6
25 14.4	**22** 16.6	**22** 16.3	Cost of Sales/Payables		**20** 18.5	**19** 18.9	**22** 16.3	**21** 17.1	**25** 14.7
44 8.3	**39** 9.3	**36** 10.1			**38** 9.5	**34** 10.6	**34** 10.6	**36** 10.0	**37** 9.8
7.3	6.3	6.9			9.2	6.1	5.4	8.0	7.3
11.6	11.4	10.4	Sales/Working Capital		18.1	9.0	9.3	10.6	9.9
37.0	27.1	23.5			-74.1	16.9	18.6	19.6	20.4
15.0	23.9	25.5			18.4	26.5	24.9	31.3	33.4
(175) 4.0	(164) 6.0	(181) 7.5	EBIT/Interest		(27) 5.0	(27) 10.6	(42) 6.0	(45) 12.3	(36) 6.1
1.2	1.9	2.7			1.6	3.3	2.0	5.2	2.5
11.5	10.6	10.9					8.2	26.5	41.1
(29) 4.8	(32) 3.6	(40) 6.4	Net Profit + Depr., Dep., Amort./Cur. Mat. L/T/D				(12) 2.4	(13) 8.0	(12) 9.5
1.1	1.4	1.9					1.2	1.9	4.0
.1	.1	.1			.1	.1	.1	.1	.1
.2	.2	.2	Fixed/Worth		.5	.2	.2	.1	.2
1.6	.5	.6			10.7	1.0	.3	.4	.5
.7	.7	.8			.8	.8	.6	.7	1.2
2.2	1.9	1.8	Debt/Worth		3.3	1.4	1.3	2.0	2.2
7.9	5.8	4.5			-4.6	4.5	2.6	3.5	5.9
35.1	49.8	61.7			95.2	71.3	53.5	55.9	53.3
(167) 16.8	(157) 25.6	(184) 31.8	% Profit Before Taxes/Tangible Net Worth		(23) 40.9	(31) 43.4	(47) 29.8	(46) 30.7	(32) 24.8
2.1	8.1	12.0			5.2	11.9	7.6	16.5	12.3
13.5	21.1	25.6			28.5	31.1	19.6	26.6	17.8
5.2	8.3	10.6	% Profit Before Taxes/Total Assets		10.6	10.7	10.2	13.3	8.3
.3	2.0	2.9			1.0	2.9	1.5	5.4	2.7
117.4	119.4	140.4			169.6	127.5	175.3	135.0	129.0
50.2	60.4	63.6	Sales/Net Fixed Assets		46.6	47.3	60.5	76.4	75.0
18.8	27.9	33.6			20.5	20.7	34.1	40.2	41.3
4.1	4.4	4.5			5.9	5.1	4.8	4.3	3.5
3.3	3.3	3.5	Sales/Total Assets		3.8	3.6	3.5	3.5	3.0
2.4	2.6	2.7			2.5	2.6	2.8	2.9	2.4
.3	.3	.3			.5	.3	.4	.2	.3
(146) .6	(129) .6	(138) .5	% Depr., Dep., Amort./Sales		(14) 1.0	(23) .7	(35) .5	(34) .4	(29) .4
1.2	.9	.8			2.1	1.3	.8	.5	.6
1.7	1.9	2.1			3.5	2.2	2.0	1.6	2.0
(101) 3.4	(86) 3.1	(102) 3.2	% Officers', Directors' Owners' Comp/Sales		(17) 5.6	(19) 4.4	(27) 3.0	(20) 2.5	(16) 2.8
6.7	5.7	5.5			10.1	7.1	4.8	3.6	3.8
2239028M	2447724M	3404421M	Net Sales ($)	4423M	61130M	141732M	381277M	774641M	2041218M
748990M	823829M	1085652M	Total Assets ($)	1403M	17258M	42642M	113605M	236714M	674030M

M = $ thousand MM = $ million

See Pages 9 through 22 for Explanation of Ratios and Data

Current Data Sorted by Assets							Comparative Historical Data	
						Type of Statement		
1		2				Unqualified	5	3
	5	11	5			Reviewed	16	26
1	5	2				Compiled	8	9
7	10	8				Tax Returns	25	19
6	17	14	3			Other	32	28
	19 (4/1-9/30/13)		78 (10/1/13-3/31/14)				4/1/09-3/31/10 ALL	4/1/10-3/31/11 ALL
0-500M	**500M-2MM**	**2-10MM**	**10-50MM**	**50-100MM**	**100-250MM**			
15	37	37	8			**NUMBER OF STATEMENTS**	86	85
%	%	%	%	%	%	**ASSETS**	%	%
21.3	14.1	10.8		DATA NOT AVAILABLE	DATA NOT AVAILABLE	Cash & Equivalents	13.4	12.6
13.5	32.1	40.1				Trade Receivables (net)	29.5	30.1
8.7	14.9	16.6				Inventory	15.6	14.3
3.7	4.4	6.6				All Other Current	4.8	5.5
47.3	65.5	74.1				Total Current	63.3	62.4
36.3	22.8	17.1				Fixed Assets (net)	23.7	24.3
4.4	2.2	1.8				Intangibles (net)	1.6	1.2
11.9	9.5	7.0				All Other Non-Current	11.3	12.1
100.0	100.0	100.0				Total	100.0	100.0
						LIABILITIES		
24.8	11.6	10.7				Notes Payable-Short Term	16.1	16.1
3.8	1.5	4.0				Cur. Mat.-L.T.D.	2.9	4.4
11.4	17.2	16.7				Trade Payables	17.7	19.6
.5	.1	.7				Income Taxes Payable	.3	.3
23.8	17.8	13.0				All Other Current	13.2	10.0
64.3	48.2	45.2				Total Current	50.2	50.4
22.2	17.9	10.4				Long-Term Debt	18.7	20.1
.0	.2	.2				Deferred Taxes	.1	.1
5.2	12.8	5.3				All Other Non-Current	5.4	4.2
8.4	20.9	38.9				Net Worth	25.6	25.2
100.0	100.0	100.0				Total Liabilties & Net Worth	100.0	100.0
						INCOME DATA		
100.0	100.0	100.0				Net Sales	100.0	100.0
44.8	39.5	31.1				Gross Profit	34.2	34.4
40.3	34.0	26.1				Operating Expenses	32.3	32.3
4.5	5.6	5.0				Operating Profit	1.8	2.1
.0	.8	.4				All Other Expenses (net)	.8	.8
4.5	4.8	4.6				Profit Before Taxes	1.0	1.3
						RATIOS		
2.3	2.7	2.6					2.9	3.1
1.4	1.5	1.7				Current	1.5	1.6
.4	.9	1.2					.7	.8
1.7	1.9	1.7					2.3	2.1
1.0	1.0	1.1				Quick	1.0	1.0
.2	.4	.7					.4	.4
0 UND	**13** 27.1	**49** 7.4					**10** 37.0	**18** 20.4
0 UND	**38** 9.6	**65** 5.6				Sales/Receivables	**42** 8.8	**46** 8.0
30 12.2	**76** 4.8	**85** 4.3					**69** 5.3	**79** 4.6
0 UND	**0** UND	**1** 571.0					**0** UND	**0** UND
0 UND	**14** 25.6	**20** 17.9				Cost of Sales/Inventory	**9** 39.7	**9** 38.7
0 UND	**73** 5.0	**66** 5.5					**46** 7.9	**57** 6.4
0 UND	**17** 21.2	**18** 19.9					**14** 27.0	**15** 24.9
3 120.0	**32** 11.4	**34** 10.8				Cost of Sales/Payables	**27** 13.4	**34** 10.6
33 11.2	**64** 5.7	**56** 6.5					**54** 6.7	**61** 6.0
10.9	5.3	4.4					5.4	4.7
67.9	10.2	8.0				Sales/Working Capital	12.7	9.5
-14.0	-79.6	19.6					-24.3	-34.0
9.4	16.3	16.0					8.0	5.1
(11) 6.3	(32) 5.3	(33) 6.0				EBIT/Interest	(71) 1.9	(69) 1.4
2.0	-1.9	2.3					-4.3	-3.7
							6.9	5.2
						Net Profit + Depr., Dep., Amort./Cur. Mat. L/T/D	(11) 3.2	(12) 1.6
							.5	.1
.5	.1	.1					.2	.2
.9	.6	.4				Fixed/Worth	.5	.6
-1.8	20.1	1.1					4.4	3.3
.2	.8	.7					.5	.6
3.6	2.6	1.6				Debt/Worth	1.7	1.8
-3.6	44.6	4.0					12.6	11.2
87.2	82.9	39.7					32.8	26.1
(10) 49.3	(29) 41.1	(32) 19.3				% Profit Before Taxes/Tangible Net Worth	(70) 10.6	(70) 5.6
13.4	-2.5	6.5					-9.1	-11.0
27.6	29.4	15.3					12.6	11.9
15.5	8.4	6.9				% Profit Before Taxes/Total Assets	1.8	2.0
3.5	-2.9	2.9					-7.0	-6.5
40.8	64.0	53.8					47.5	40.1
19.0	25.4	22.1				Sales/Net Fixed Assets	15.9	16.6
10.5	8.1	6.7					7.2	6.3
11.4	3.6	2.9					3.8	3.4
5.4	2.4	2.2				Sales/Total Assets	2.6	2.3
1.5	1.7	1.6					1.8	1.5
.6	.3	.4					.8	.5
(10) 1.4	(22) .9	(31) 1.1				% Depr., Dep., Amort./Sales	(68) 1.7	(69) 1.2
2.2	2.0	1.6					2.9	2.3
	4.2	2.6					2.3	2.4
	(16) 5.9	(14) 4.1				% Officers', Directors' Owners' Comp/Sales	(45) 6.0	(46) 4.6
	7.3	7.1					8.8	8.7
14914M	116454M	321770M	368596M			Net Sales ($)	1195107M	679414M
3535M	42092M	138589M	170990M			Total Assets ($)	440539M	338748M

M = $ thousand MM = $ million

See Pages 9 through 22 for Explanation of Ratios and Data

Comparative Historical Data				Current Data Sorted by Sales					
			Type of Statement						
7	4	3	Unqualified	1	1	1			
20	19	21	Reviewed		1	2	7	8	3
10	7	8	Compiled	1	3	2	1	1	
29	26	25	Tax Returns	5	9	6	4	1	
27	39	40	Other	4	13	7	8	5	3
4/1/11-3/31/12 ALL	4/1/12-3/31/13 ALL	4/1/13-3/31/14 ALL		19 (4/1-9/30/13)			78 (10/1/13-3/31/14)		
				0-1MM	1-3MM	3-5MM	5-10MM	10-25MM	25MM & OVER
93	95	97	NUMBER OF STATEMENTS	11	27	18	20	15	6
%	%	%	**ASSETS**	%	%	%	%	%	%
9.2	8.2	13.0	Cash & Equivalents	29.5	12.7	17.2	10.1	4.2	
36.9	38.3	33.1	Trade Receivables (net)	8.6	25.1	29.1	48.4	44.2	
15.6	17.7	14.3	Inventory	10.0	14.4	25.3	7.6	14.5	
6.3	5.3	5.8	All Other Current	4.2	4.1	3.7	6.5	8.3	
67.9	69.6	66.2	Total Current	52.4	56.3	75.3	72.7	71.3	
18.2	16.6	22.0	Fixed Assets (net)	33.7	30.9	17.8	14.7	16.5	
3.8	2.2	3.2	Intangibles (net)	2.6	4.5	.2	2.4	3.4	
10.0	11.6	8.5	All Other Non-Current	11.4	8.3	6.7	10.2	8.8	
100.0	100.0	100.0	Total	100.0	100.0	100.0	100.0	100.0	
			LIABILITIES						
17.4	15.5	13.6	Notes Payable-Short Term	12.4	15.7	13.2	12.4	12.3	
2.3	2.4	2.9	Cur. Mat.-L.T.D.	1.3	4.5	3.5	2.0	1.7	
22.2	21.4	15.7	Trade Payables	7.5	14.8	15.7	17.1	23.3	
.2	.2	.4	Income Taxes Payable	.0	.4	.0	1.0	.4	
15.1	18.0	16.7	All Other Current	26.7	18.4	17.8	13.3	8.7	
57.2	57.5	49.3	Total Current	48.1	53.7	50.1	45.7	46.5	
14.3	14.8	14.9	Long-Term Debt	21.0	21.4	10.7	10.8	13.3	
.1	.0	.3	Deferred Taxes	.0	.0	.5	.1	.4	
6.4	5.0	7.7	All Other Non-Current	8.5	7.7	3.1	19.3	.5	
22.1	22.7	27.8	Net Worth	22.4	17.2	35.5	24.0	39.5	
100.0	100.0	100.0	Total Liabilties & Net Worth	100.0	100.0	100.0	100.0	100.0	
			INCOME DATA						
100.0	100.0	100.0	Net Sales	100.0	100.0	100.0	100.0	100.0	
33.4	33.9	35.7	Gross Profit	50.2	44.3	33.4	28.3	28.1	
31.4	29.0	30.8	Operating Expenses	43.4	38.0	30.6	23.2	24.0	
2.0	4.8	5.0	Operating Profit	6.8	6.3	2.9	5.1	4.1	
.8	.8	.5	All Other Expenses (net)	1.3	.7	.3	.0	.4	
1.3	4.0	4.5	Profit Before Taxes	5.5	5.7	2.5	5.1	3.7	
			RATIOS						
2.4	2.3	2.4		6.0	2.3	2.6	2.4	1.9	
1.6	1.5	1.6	Current	2.6	1.2	1.5	1.9	1.5	
.9	.9	1.1		1.6	.5	1.0	1.2	1.2	
1.6	1.6	1.7		2.6	1.6	1.5	2.0	1.6	
1.1	.9	1.1	Quick	1.5	.7	1.0	1.4	1.1	
.4	.4	.5		.2	.3	.4	.7	.8	
17 21.1	**21** 17.6	**17** 20.9		**0** UND	**2** 201.0	**19** 19.1	**43** 8.5	**44** 8.3	
47 7.7	**51** 7.2	**53** 6.9	Sales/Receivables	**0** UND	**33** 11.0	**43** 8.5	**62** 5.9	**60** 6.1	
76 4.8	**76** 4.8	**78** 4.7		**18** 19.8	**81** 4.5	**68** 5.4	**83** 4.4	**85** 4.3	
0 UND	**0** UND	**0** UND		**0** UND	**0** UND	**3** 116.0	**0** UND	**3** 117.4	
14 25.3	**13** 27.7	**14** 25.6	Cost of Sales/Inventory	**0** UND	**9** 41.0	**51** 7.2	**0** UND	**15** 24.3	
43 8.5	**57** 6.4	**62** 5.9		**243** 1.5	**83** 4.4	**135** 2.7	**20** 18.2	**41** 9.0	
15 24.7	**15** 24.6	**10** 37.9		**0** UND	**9** 40.1	**14** 25.9	**15** 25.1	**22** 16.9	
30 12.1	**31** 11.8	**31** 11.9	Cost of Sales/Payables	**5** 68.0	**23** 16.2	**31** 11.6	**27** 13.5	**39** 9.3	
59 6.2	**60** 6.1	**49** 7.5		**126** 2.9	**69** 5.3	**46** 8.0	**38** 9.6	**78** 4.7	
5.6	5.5	5.2		2.6	5.7	4.2	5.0	6.5	
12.1	12.1	10.7	Sales/Working Capital	3.4	67.9	10.0	8.5	13.4	
-144.7	-114.4	130.7		40.0	-14.0	NM	23.0	20.9	
8.9	9.3	16.2			10.2	9.7	35.1	29.5	
(81) 3.3	(80) 4.0	(84) 5.7	EBIT/Interest		(23) 6.0	(15) 4.2	(18) 13.4	6.0	
-.2	1.2	1.7			.3	-2.0	3.5	1.8	
			Net Profit + Depr., Dep., Amort./Cur. Mat. L/T/D						
.1	.1	.2		.0	.3	.1	.1	.2	
.5	.4	.5	Fixed/Worth	.7	1.3	.3	.3	.4	
2.9	3.3	4.9		6.1	-3.0	7.6	7.8	.7	
.8	.8	.8		.2	.9	.6	.7	1.0	
1.9	1.7	2.1	Debt/Worth	1.5	4.2	1.6	2.3	1.6	
16.5	29.0	18.2		12.2	-7.3	19.3	30.3	3.5	
43.5	56.7	59.9			95.7	74.3	82.8	38.5	
(76) 16.4	(78) 16.7	(77) 22.3	% Profit Before Taxes/Tangible Net Worth		(19) 44.5	(15) 7.1	(16) 41.7	(13) 25.0	
2.0	4.6	5.2			-7.0	2.4	13.2	11.7	
13.8	21.4	19.3		15.5	27.6	14.6	26.6	16.5	
5.1	6.1	8.4	% Profit Before Taxes/Total Assets	3.5	11.0	4.5	11.5	6.8	
-1.5	.5	1.5		1.7	-1.3	-2.3	4.5	2.2	
72.6	76.4	56.6		280.7	57.7	42.1	53.5	83.6	
31.1	34.6	21.9	Sales/Net Fixed Assets	14.7	19.0	19.3	28.0	12.5	
9.5	12.2	8.5		3.0	3.8	11.3	19.5	7.5	
3.8	4.2	3.4		10.6	3.6	3.7	3.5	3.4	
2.7	2.7	2.4	Sales/Total Assets	1.3	2.3	2.1	2.9	2.5	
1.7	1.8	1.6		.4	1.4	1.6	2.4	2.0	
.5	.4	.4			.3	.4	.5	.3	
(73) 1.0	(59) 1.0	(70) 1.1	% Depr., Dep., Amort./Sales		(19) 1.1	(12) 1.3	(14) .9	(14) 1.1	
2.0	1.8	1.8			2.0	2.2	1.4	1.8	
2.2	2.2	3.4			4.1				
(49) 4.5	(45) 3.8	(40) 4.9	% Officers', Directors' Owners' Comp/Sales		(14) 6.3				
7.3	5.4	6.8			8.6				
1098529M	787248M	821734M	Net Sales ($)	5570M	50298M	68026M	146208M	231446M	320186M
306044M	325915M	355206M	Total Assets ($)	4768M	26361M	31501M	50841M	94660M	147075M

M = $ thousand MM = $ million

See Pages 9 through 22 for Explanation of Ratios and Data

Current Data Sorted by Assets / Comparative Historical Data

0-500M	500M-2MM	2-10MM	10-50MM	50-100MM	100-250MM	Type of Statement	4/1/09-3/31/10 ALL	4/1/10-3/31/11 ALL
		1	2		1	Unqualified	6	5
2	6	16	1			Reviewed	34	30
1	4	3				Compiled	15	9
22	12	3	2			Tax Returns	22	29
9	17	4	1		1	Other	25	40
	20 (4/1-9/30/13)		88 (10/1/13-3/31/14)					
34	39	27	6		2	NUMBER OF STATEMENTS	102	113
%	%	%	%	%	%	**ASSETS**	%	%
21.9	16.0	12.8		DATA NOT AVAILABLE		Cash & Equivalents	17.0	15.8
29.5	35.0	50.5				Trade Receivables (net)	35.7	32.7
8.4	12.4	11.8				Inventory	9.3	10.1
1.6	8.3	7.6				All Other Current	6.2	7.0
61.4	71.6	82.8				Total Current	68.3	65.7
16.5	18.5	12.6				Fixed Assets (net)	23.3	22.4
8.6	2.1	.3				Intangibles (net)	3.9	3.5
13.5	7.7	4.3				All Other Non-Current	4.6	8.4
100.0	100.0	100.0				Total	100.0	100.0
						LIABILITIES		
27.7	11.0	4.4				Notes Payable-Short Term	16.1	21.1
8.5	1.6	1.9				Cur. Mat.-L.T.D.	2.9	3.3
18.8	15.0	21.5				Trade Payables	17.2	17.1
.8	.1	.4				Income Taxes Payable	.2	.3
24.1	20.8	13.7				All Other Current	13.3	16.2
79.9	48.5	42.0				Total Current	49.6	58.0
24.4	13.5	8.0				Long-Term Debt	15.1	17.6
.0	.1	.1				Deferred Taxes	.2	.3
21.6	7.5	4.9				All Other Non-Current	10.3	5.1
-25.8	30.4	44.9				Net Worth	24.8	18.9
100.0	100.0	100.0				Total Liabilities & Net Worth	100.0	100.0
						INCOME DATA		
100.0	100.0	100.0				Net Sales	100.0	100.0
34.0	34.8	23.8				Gross Profit	32.5	32.4
31.4	30.0	20.3				Operating Expenses	30.2	31.2
2.6	4.8	3.5				Operating Profit	2.4	1.2
.3	.1	.2				All Other Expenses (net)	.5	.7
2.2	4.7	3.4				Profit Before Taxes	1.9	.5
						RATIOS		
2.5	2.7	3.1				Current	3.4	3.1
1.0	1.6	1.9					1.6	1.6
.4	1.2	1.5					.8	.9
2.3	2.6	2.4				Quick	2.6	2.3
.9	1.0	1.3					1.1	.8
.3	.6	1.0					.6	.4
0 UND	**8** 44.0	**38** 9.6				Sales/Receivables	**20** 18.5	**16** 22.4
8 44.4	**29** 12.4	**54** 6.7					**45** 8.1	**35** 10.6
28 13.1	**63** 5.8	**94** 3.9					**75** 4.9	**61** 6.0
0 UND	**0** UND	**0** UND				Cost of Sales/Inventory	**0** UND	**0** UND
0 UND	**7** 48.9	**4** 85.2					**7** 55.7	**4** 81.3
7 48.8	**37** 9.9	**40** 9.2					**28** 13.0	**29** 12.5
0 UND	**7** 55.8	**13** 28.3				Cost of Sales/Payables	**6** 56.5	**8** 48.3
7 53.8	**23** 15.9	**37** 9.9					**24** 15.0	**18** 19.8
34 10.8	**35** 10.4	**53** 6.9					**44** 8.3	**38** 9.6
20.4	6.1	3.7				Sales/Working Capital	5.3	5.5
NM	12.0	6.5					9.9	15.2
-27.8	37.7	20.7					-40.0	-50.8
16.0	39.6	26.3				EBIT/Interest	12.6	11.8
(23) 6.0	(32) 9.3	(23) 5.5					(86) 2.2	(97) 2.5
1.0	3.5	1.4					-2.3	-4.4
		9.3				Net Profit + Depr., Dep., Amort./Cur. Mat. L/T/D	5.9	30.4
		(11) 1.6					(22) 2.2	(14) 2.7
		.7					-.1	.3
.0	.1	.1				Fixed/Worth	.2	.1
.8	.5	.2					.6	.6
-.7	1.6	.6					8.4	-5.3
2.5	.9	.5				Debt/Worth	.8	.6
8.7	2.2	1.1					2.0	2.0
-1.9	9.4	3.9					165.8	-18.5
384.7	99.2	44.2				% Profit Before Taxes/Tangible Net Worth	50.7	43.4
(21) 20.0	(34) 40.1	(26) 6.3					(78) 10.1	(83) 13.9
-10.5	8.5	2.9					-5.8	-10.4
53.1	26.1	25.9				% Profit Before Taxes/Total Assets	12.4	16.4
20.4	10.0	2.1					1.2	4.5
-3.7	3.5	.6					-4.9	-7.2
UND	186.0	104.9				Sales/Net Fixed Assets	52.2	74.5
83.9	47.0	42.3					19.5	25.0
22.6	14.4	16.0					7.7	9.5
13.1	4.4	4.2				Sales/Total Assets	4.2	4.6
7.0	3.5	2.6					2.7	3.0
3.8	2.8	1.8					1.9	2.0
.5	.2	.2				% Depr., Dep., Amort./Sales	.7	.7
(14) .9	(27) .4	(22) .6					(84) 1.2	(81) 1.2
2.5	1.0	1.1					2.5	2.5
2.5	1.8	1.7				% Officers', Directors' Owners' Comp/Sales	2.4	2.3
(20) 5.5	(27) 3.5	(13) 2.4					(54) 5.0	(59) 4.8
8.8	5.7	5.7					8.5	7.7
55741M	161010M	394282M	2017443M		414483M	Net Sales ($)	1270319M	1588537M
7919M	44919M	131141M	113302M		253962M	Total Assets ($)	695967M	468320M

M = $ thousand MM = $ million

See Pages 9 through 22 for Explanation of Ratios and Data

Comparative Historical Data				Current Data Sorted by Sales					
			Type of Statement						
4	2	4	Unqualified					1	3
25	28	25	Reviewed	1	1	6	5	10	2
17	10	8	Compiled		2	2	3	1	
42	36	39	Tax Returns	9	19	4	4	1	2
27	30	32	Other	4	12	9	2	3	2
4/1/11-3/31/12 ALL	4/1/12-3/31/13 ALL	4/1/13-3/31/14 ALL			20 (4/1-9/30/13)		88 (10/1/13-3/31/14)		
				0-1MM	1-3MM	3-5MM	5-10MM	10-25MM	25MM & OVER
115	106	108	**NUMBER OF STATEMENTS**	14	34	21	14	16	9
%	%	%	**ASSETS**	%	%	%	%	%	%
14.5	16.2	16.5	Cash & Equivalents	23.0	17.6	16.7	16.2	10.5	
36.9	38.7	37.3	Trade Receivables (net)	29.7	28.3	42.5	35.9	53.6	
8.7	9.3	10.4	Inventory	16.2	10.7	8.1	11.8	9.6	
6.1	3.9	5.9	All Other Current	1.0	2.9	5.8	15.8	7.8	
66.2	68.1	70.1	Total Current	69.9	59.5	73.0	79.8	81.6	
20.6	22.0	16.8	Fixed Assets (net)	14.2	20.1	22.0	8.2	13.0	
6.2	3.6	4.5	Intangibles (net)	12.0	4.9	1.4	1.2	.2	
7.0	6.3	8.6	All Other Non-Current	3.9	15.5	3.6	10.8	5.2	
100.0	100.0	100.0	Total	100.0	100.0	100.0	100.0	100.0	
			LIABILITIES						
12.7	17.1	13.9	Notes Payable-Short Term	42.6	13.0	8.7	12.6	5.7	
2.1	4.2	3.8	Cur. Mat.-L.T.D.	10.2	5.0	1.6	2.5	1.4	
19.9	21.2	18.2	Trade Payables	31.3	10.8	19.9	16.5	17.9	
.3	.4	.4	Income Taxes Payable	1.0	.4	.2	.1	.6	
15.4	17.0	19.8	All Other Current	32.1	17.7	10.5	30.2	16.3	
50.4	60.0	56.1	Total Current	117.3	46.8	41.1	61.9	42.0	
19.0	13.9	16.5	Long-Term Debt	17.8	25.6	14.7	5.8	6.6	
.3	.1	.0	Deferred Taxes	.0	.0	.1	.2	.0	
13.1	10.5	11.5	All Other Non-Current	46.8	9.7	5.4	2.4	2.1	
17.2	15.6	15.9	Net Worth	-81.9	17.9	38.7	29.7	49.4	
100.0	100.0	100.0	Total Liabilties & Net Worth	100.0	100.0	100.0	100.0	100.0	
			INCOME DATA						
100.0	100.0	100.0	Net Sales	100.0	100.0	100.0	100.0	100.0	
34.8	34.2	31.0	Gross Profit	32.9	35.7	33.0	26.3	25.1	
32.2	30.3	27.2	Operating Expenses	32.4	31.8	27.8	22.2	21.5	
2.6	3.9	3.8	Operating Profit	.5	4.0	5.2	4.1	3.7	
1.0	.6	.3	All Other Expenses (net)	1.1	.0	.4	-.3	.1	
1.7	3.3	3.6	Profit Before Taxes	-.6	3.9	4.8	4.4	3.6	
			RATIOS						
2.7	2.7	2.7		2.3	3.5	2.6	2.2	3.3	
1.5	1.6	1.6	Current	1.0	1.3	1.8	1.7	1.9	
.9	.9	1.0		.3	.6	1.4	1.2	1.3	
2.1	2.2	2.1		2.3	3.2	2.1	1.5	2.8	
1.1	1.1	1.1	Quick	.8	.8	1.3	.9	1.4	
.6	.7	.6		.2	.4	1.0	.6	1.2	
15 25.0	17 21.6	8 44.4		0 UND	0 UND	19 18.9	0 UND	38 9.6	
39 9.4	40 9.1	36 10.0	Sales/Receivables	3 123.7	22 16.8	54 6.7	28 13.0	48 7.6	
68 5.4	62 5.9	69 5.3		24 15.1	60 6.1	73 5.0	85 4.3	85 4.3	
0 UND	0 UND	0 UND		0 UND	0 UND	0 UND	0 UND	0 UND	
1 299.7	2 167.3	1 269.9	Cost of Sales/Inventory	0 UND	1 372.4	7 48.9	2 242.5	5 67.6	
23 15.8	18 20.2	23 15.7		23 16.1	24 14.9	33 11.1	27 13.7	23 16.2	
9 40.7	10 37.5	2 151.9		0 UND	0 UND	13 27.9	7 53.0	10 38.1	
26 14.2	22 16.7	23 16.0	Cost of Sales/Payables	0 UND	9 39.7	34 10.7	23 15.9	22 16.7	
48 7.6	41 8.8	39 9.3		40 9.2	34 10.8	55 6.6	34 10.6	39 9.3	
6.4	6.0	6.5		30.4	5.8	5.9	6.6	4.9	
16.1	17.0	17.2	Sales/Working Capital	NM	36.5	10.4	10.9	8.4	
-60.1	-61.8	NM		-6.1	-30.5	19.5	28.4	23.8	
12.3	24.2	26.3			17.2	91.8	9.3	29.7	
(96) 3.6	(92) 6.6	(85) 7.9	EBIT/Interest		(26) 10.4	(17) 15.7	(11) 6.0	(14) 7.9	
-1.8	1.8	2.0			2.2	3.8	1.3	1.6	
7.3	15.0	9.3							
(11) 1.4	(11) 5.7	(15) 1.6	Net Profit + Depr., Dep., Amort./Cur. Mat. L/T/D						
-.9	.3	.7							
.1	.1	.1		.0	.1	.1	.0	.1	
.5	.7	.4	Fixed/Worth	NM	.9	.4	.2	.2	
11.0	7.6	2.3		-.1	NM	1.4	.5	.5	
.9	.7	.8		3.3	.9	.8	.7	.4	
2.7	2.0	2.7	Debt/Worth	-6.3	7.6	1.3	1.3	1.2	
-37.5	58.3	18.0		-1.5	-31.0	3.7	4.0	2.5	
62.3	66.8	85.9			257.1	82.4	100.9	51.2	
(85) 8.9	(81) 29.6	(86) 32.0	% Profit Before Taxes/Tangible Net Worth		(25) 40.9	(20) 36.5	(13) 37.4	12.2	
-6.7	5.7	5.3			5.2	6.8	3.4	3.1	
18.7	22.9	33.8		53.1	41.6	21.7	61.5	30.3	
4.1	9.1	9.3	% Profit Before Taxes/Total Assets	4.7	12.5	11.8	7.5	5.1	
-4.0	.6	1.4		-29.4	2.5	3.0	1.1	1.0	
107.8	95.9	187.7		UND	297.8	91.6	460.1	187.4	
29.3	35.8	51.9	Sales/Net Fixed Assets	105.1	60.6	33.5	119.5	41.1	
13.7	13.2	19.2		29.7	18.1	8.7	21.9	20.9	
5.2	4.8	5.5		13.1	5.0	4.9	6.4	4.3	
3.1	3.6	3.7	Sales/Total Assets	8.1	3.8	3.1	4.0	3.4	
1.9	2.3	2.5		2.9	2.9	1.8	2.5	2.4	
.5	.4	.2			.3	.2	.2	.2	
(72) .9	(78) .8	(70) .7	% Depr., Dep., Amort./Sales		(16) .7	(15) 1.0	(11) .3	(13) .5	
1.7	1.6	1.4			1.5	1.9	.7	1.3	
2.8	2.2	2.0			1.6	2.4			
(64) 4.4	(60) 4.2	(62) 3.8	% Officers', Directors' Owners' Comp/Sales		(23) 2.6	(15) 5.3			
7.6	6.6	5.8			5.6	6.2			
1073460M	1911230M	3042959M	Net Sales ($)	7084M	72512M	82991M	101710M	293[illegible]0M	2484682M
415720M	682570M	551243M	Total Assets ($)	1414M	23794M	30827M	27325M	94399M	373484M

M = $ thousand MM = $ million

See Pages 9 through 22 for Explanation of Ratios and Data

Current Data Sorted by Assets / Comparative Historical Data

0-500M	500M-2MM	2-10MM	10-50MM	50-100MM	100-250MM		4/1/09-3/31/10 ALL	4/1/10-3/31/11 ALL
						Type of Statement		
		2	7		1	Unqualified	4	11
1	8	19	2			Reviewed	31	32
4	5	8		1		Compiled	8	12
15	14	7				Tax Returns	16	28
10	23	14	3			Other	24	31
	23 (4/1-9/30/13)		121 (10/1/13-3/31/14)					
30	50	50	12	1	1	**NUMBER OF STATEMENTS**	83	114
%	%	%	%	%	%	**ASSETS**	%	%
21.8	16.1	13.4	9.4			Cash & Equivalents	14.0	15.6
26.8	34.9	41.9	48.0			Trade Receivables (net)	39.9	41.4
10.5	6.9	9.3	6.5			Inventory	7.7	10.0
1.0	8.6	7.7	9.5			All Other Current	5.7	5.7
60.1	66.6	72.2	73.3			Total Current	67.3	72.7
21.6	20.1	21.5	9.7			Fixed Assets (net)	18.9	19.2
7.0	3.8	2.4	13.1			Intangibles (net)	5.6	2.9
11.4	9.6	3.9	3.8			All Other Non-Current	8.3	5.2
100.0	100.0	100.0	100.0			Total	100.0	100.0
						LIABILITIES		
17.2	8.2	7.8	11.7			Notes Payable-Short Term	10.8	12.4
14.4	3.9	3.0	6.7			Cur. Mat.-L.T.D.	4.4	2.3
17.0	15.1	17.7	15.9			Trade Payables	16.8	20.3
.0	.1	.7	.0			Income Taxes Payable	.4	.3
25.4	13.2	18.5	17.4			All Other Current	13.0	15.1
73.9	40.5	47.7	51.7			Total Current	45.3	50.4
14.9	12.5	17.9	6.7			Long-Term Debt	15.1	13.3
.0	.3	.2	1.1			Deferred Taxes	.4	.2
15.4	6.4	4.8	1.7			All Other Non-Current	12.0	8.9
-4.2	40.4	29.4	38.7			Net Worth	27.2	27.2
100.0	100.0	100.0	100.0			Total Liabilties & Net Worth	100.0	100.0
						INCOME DATA		
100.0	100.0	100.0	100.0			Net Sales	100.0	100.0
44.6	33.1	26.8	22.4			Gross Profit	31.2	31.8
39.9	27.4	22.4	17.8			Operating Expenses	26.9	29.0
4.7	5.7	4.5	4.6			Operating Profit	4.3	2.8
.5	.9	.5	.8			All Other Expenses (net)	.5	.5
4.2	4.8	3.9	3.7			Profit Before Taxes	3.8	2.3
						RATIOS		
4.3	3.7	2.5	1.8				2.2	2.6
1.4	2.0	1.5	1.3			Current	1.6	1.6
.4	1.1	1.2	1.1				1.1	1.0
4.3	3.0	2.0	1.5				1.8	2.1
1.0	1.2	1.3	1.0			Quick	1.2	1.3
.2	.7	.8	.8				.8	.7
0 UND	13 27.4	29 12.4	39 9.3				27 13.5	21 17.5
5 71.8	45 8.2	53 6.9	70 5.2			Sales/Receivables	50 7.3	47 7.8
37 9.9	64 5.7	85 4.3	107 3.4				74 5.0	79 4.6
0 UND	0 UND	0 UND	0 UND				0 UND	0 UND
0 UND	0 UND	1 396.9	3 137.1			Cost of Sales/Inventory	4 101.9	3 134.0
21 17.7	18 20.5	23 16.1	20 18.1				16 22.6	20 17.9
0 UND	6 58.2	16 22.4	11 32.4				7 54.4	10 37.9
10 35.0	15 23.7	27 13.5	24 15.0			Cost of Sales/Payables	24 14.9	28 12.9
23 15.7	36 10.1	40 9.2	49 7.4				42 8.7	56 6.5
14.1	6.4	6.0	6.2				6.0	6.1
88.6	10.8	9.6	17.4			Sales/Working Capital	10.6	10.8
-16.6	118.4	69.8	64.6				156.8	517.7
35.9	43.4	37.9	27.5				17.4	13.8
(20) 9.1	(34) 8.6	(41) 7.8	8.0			EBIT/Interest	(73) 6.5	(98) 5.1
3.5	1.9	1.7	4.2				.6	1.6
		17.4					32.7	8.4
		(11) 3.3				Net Profit + Depr., Dep., Amort./Cur. Mat. L/T/D	(16) 2.4	(24) 3.9
		.9					.9	.1
.1	.1	.1	.1				.2	.2
.5	.4	.4	.2			Fixed/Worth	.4	.4
-1.5	2.5	1.6	.8				2.8	1.7
1.4	.3	.7	1.0				1.0	1.0
3.7	1.8	1.6	2.1			Debt/Worth	2.6	2.0
-3.3	19.3	3.4	5.3				10.8	16.8
138.0	57.4	40.4	40.5				65.2	44.3
(18) 56.4	(42) 27.8	(43) 20.0	(10) 19.8			% Profit Before Taxes/Tangible Net Worth	(66) 24.8	(92) 21.1
4.9	6.1	4.9	14.5				4.8	3.5
47.3	28.1	22.7	13.6				20.2	18.3
14.1	7.5	7.0	8.7			% Profit Before Taxes/Total Assets	8.7	6.6
2.6	1.5	1.4	3.1				-1.7	.4
467.6	92.3	63.9	83.5				53.8	73.5
50.4	22.6	23.1	50.3			Sales/Net Fixed Assets	18.8	22.4
21.4	8.5	9.3	17.8				10.3	12.3
9.8	4.0	3.4	3.3				4.2	4.4
7.3	3.4	2.8	2.3			Sales/Total Assets	2.9	3.2
3.8	2.5	2.2	2.0				1.9	2.0
.4	.4	.4	.3				.7	.4
(18) .8	(32) .9	(40) .9	(11) .6			% Depr., Dep., Amort./Sales	(62) 1.2	(87) 1.1
1.7	2.4	1.9	1.5				2.4	2.1
1.7	1.7	1.9					2.8	1.9
(19) 3.5	(26) 3.3	(26) 4.1				% Officers', Directors' Owners' Comp/Sales	(38) 4.2	(53) 3.4
7.3	5.3	5.1					7.2	6.2
67779M	197309M	685723M	657237M	144114M	403621M	Net Sales ($)	1183660M	2146532M
8448M	59475M	218230M	265016M	77825M	232295M	Total Assets ($)	514719M	824010M

M = $ thousand MM = $ million

See Pages 9 through 22 for Explanation of Ratios and Data

Comparative Historical Data / Current Data Sorted by Sales

4/1/11-3/31/12 ALL	4/1/12-3/31/13 ALL	4/1/13-3/31/14 ALL	Type of Statement	0-1MM	1-3MM	3-5MM	5-10MM	10-25MM	25MM & OVER
12	8	10	Unqualified					2	8
45	36	30	Reviewed	1	2	3	12	9	3
16	8	18	Compiled	4	3	2	4	4	1
32	27	36	Tax Returns	5	10	10	8	2	1
43	39	50	Other	2	17	8	11	8	4
				23 (4/1-9/30/13)		121 (10/1/13-3/31/14)			
148	118	144	NUMBER OF STATEMENTS	12	32	23	35	25	17
%	%	%	ASSETS	%	%	%	%	%	%
15.2	14.2	15.6	Cash & Equivalents	12.7	14.1	19.1	18.4	15.1	10.5
43.5	40.7	36.6	Trade Receivables (net)	28.4	29.7	31.8	40.5	46.0	40.3
8.5	9.2	8.9	Inventory	6.0	8.6	10.6	10.1	6.3	10.5
6.8	5.1	6.8	All Other Current	1.0	5.7	6.3	7.8	9.1	7.9
73.9	69.2	67.8	Total Current	48.0	58.0	67.9	76.8	76.5	69.2
17.3	22.0	20.1	Fixed Assets (net)	32.8	23.7	18.1	16.9	17.6	17.4
3.3	2.7	4.7	Intangibles (net)	11.7	7.0	1.5	.6	3.3	10.1
5.5	6.1	7.4	All Other Non-Current	7.5	11.3	12.5	5.7	2.6	3.4
100.0	100.0	100.0	Total	100.0	100.0	100.0	100.0	100.0	100.0
			LIABILITIES						
12.7	17.4	10.6	Notes Payable-Short Term	6.0	8.5	6.2	17.1	9.1	12.6
2.0	3.5	6.0	Cur. Mat.-L.T.D.	3.5	13.4	6.1	1.8	2.9	6.7
21.1	19.7	16.4	Trade Payables	7.3	15.5	12.7	18.9	23.1	14.5
.4	.2	.3	Income Taxes Payable	.0	.4	.0	.2	.7	.0
19.9	14.3	17.8	All Other Current	9.6	25.3	11.3	15.8	18.7	21.4
56.0	55.1	51.1	Total Current	26.4	63.0	36.4	53.7	54.6	55.2
10.9	12.1	14.4	Long-Term Debt	29.3	12.1	11.2	9.2	8.8	31.1
.3	.1	.3	Deferred Taxes	.0	.4	.0	.3	.0	.8
8.9	12.4	7.2	All Other Non-Current	4.7	16.4	4.4	4.4	7.0	1.7
24.0	20.3	27.1	Net Worth	39.6	8.1	48.1	32.4	29.5	11.2
100.0	100.0	100.0	Total Liabilities & Net Worth	100.0	100.0	100.0	100.0	100.0	100.0
			INCOME DATA						
100.0	100.0	100.0	Net Sales	100.0	100.0	100.0	100.0	100.0	100.0
31.0	30.1	32.2	Gross Profit	60.7	37.2	31.3	28.0	24.4	24.6
28.0	27.1	27.3	Operating Expenses	47.4	32.4	27.3	24.7	19.8	19.7
3.0	3.0	5.0	Operating Profit	13.2	4.8	4.0	3.3	4.6	4.9
.5	.3	.7	All Other Expenses (net)	3.9	.3	.3	.4	.1	1.0
2.5	2.7	4.3	Profit Before Taxes	9.3	4.5	3.8	2.9	4.5	3.9
			RATIOS						
2.3	2.7	2.8		4.2	3.8	4.1	3.2	2.4	1.7
1.5	1.5	1.6	Current	1.4	1.7	2.1	1.8	1.4	1.3
1.0	1.0	1.0		.8	.6	1.7	1.2	1.0	1.1
2.0	2.0	2.2		4.1	3.0	4.0	2.3	2.0	1.4
1.1	1.2	1.2	Quick	1.0	1.3	1.5	1.1	1.3	.9
.7	.7	.7		.2	.4	.6	.9	.7	.6
26 14.2	19 18.9	14 26.6		0 UND	3 145.0	1 494.3	16 23.0	29 12.5	29 12.4
50 7.3	49 7.5	41 9.0	Sales/Receivables	44 8.3	36 10.0	31 11.7	47 7.8	60 6.1	50 7.3
79 4.6	79 4.6	73 5.0		114 3.2	60 6.1	52 7.0	76 4.8	81 4.5	99 3.7
0 UND	0 UND	0 UND		0 UND	0 UND	0 UND	0 UND	0 UND	0 UND
0 905.2	2 234.4	1 612.1	Cost of Sales/Inventory	0 UND	1 380.5	0 UND	1 381.8	1 694.8	2 146.7
20 18.6	26 13.8	22 16.9		63 5.8	18 20.4	22 16.7	24 14.9	14 26.8	34 10.8
13 28.8	12 30.5	8 47.2		0 UND	2 212.9	0 UND	10 36.4	20 18.0	9 39.3
32 11.3	27 13.5	19 19.1	Cost of Sales/Payables	22 16.3	16 22.7	9 42.3	18 19.9	28 12.9	23 15.8
57 6.4	51 7.2	36 10.2		91 4.0	34 10.7	24 15.1	31 11.8	49 7.4	37 9.9
6.8	7.0	6.6		4.9	6.7	6.7	5.9	7.2	7.4
13.1	16.2	13.4	Sales/Working Capital	17.9	18.2	12.6	10.4	12.5	20.3
812.0	117.9	215.0		-25.6	-16.9	28.6	25.4	495.2	104.7
22.7	22.5	34.1			33.0	50.5	38.2	27.4	27.3
(121) 4.8	(106) 5.6	(109) 8.3	EBIT/Interest		(19) 6.8	(19) 11.5	(28) 8.0	(22) 8.1	(15) 8.1
.5	1.1	2.6			.7	2.6	1.5	3.4	5.8
8.9	8.0	5.2							
(26) 2.7	(21) 2.5	(24) 3.1	Net Profit + Depr., Dep., Amort./Cur. Mat. L/T/D						
.6	-.1	.6							
.1	.2	.1		.1	.2	.0	.1	.1	.2
.4	.5	.4	Fixed/Worth	1.4	1.7	.4	.2	.5	.4
1.3	4.1	2.1		-3.8	-.8	.8	.6	2.4	NM
.9	.9	.7		.4	1.0	.3	.6	.7	1.1
2.0	2.6	1.9	Debt/Worth	2.1	6.7	1.2	1.2	2.0	2.4
8.3	26.0	8.7		-7.7	-4.2	2.9	3.0	5.9	NM
53.6	62.2	57.6			92.3	81.0	55.0	52.0	43.0
(125) 20.8	(94) 25.5	(115) 26.2	% Profit Before Taxes/Tangible Net Worth		(20) 50.7	(22) 27.8	(31) 11.5	(21) 29.3	(13) 21.5
3.8	5.5	6.3			12.5	4.5	4.9	10.8	13.3
19.0	18.7	23.4		12.0	30.1	35.2	27.2	23.8	14.2
6.3	6.9	9.2	% Profit Before Taxes/Total Assets	4.4	13.3	17.2	6.4	9.2	8.2
-.5	-.3	1.8		1.0	-.5	1.6	1.6	2.6	3.3
87.8	68.7	86.9		42.8	123.8	416.0	202.9	61.2	72.9
28.9	25.3	29.4	Sales/Net Fixed Assets	6.5	25.1	47.0	51.4	32.5	35.7
13.5	11.0	10.9		1.4	12.0	11.5	13.9	10.9	13.0
4.2	4.3	4.5		2.6	7.4	4.8	5.0	4.3	3.6
3.0	3.0	3.2	Sales/Total Assets	1.6	3.7	3.4	3.3	2.9	2.3
2.1	2.0	2.3		.4	2.4	2.9	2.4	2.2	1.9
.4	.4	.4			.6	.2	.3	.4	.3
(107) 1.1	(91) 1.0	(103) .9	% Depr., Dep., Amort./Sales		(17) 1.0	(15) .8	(26) 1.0	(20) .5	(16) .7
1.9	1.8	1.8			2.3	1.5	1.8	1.1	1.5
2.0	2.3	1.7			1.8	1.0	1.8	1.4	
(61) 4.3	(52) 4.3	(76) 3.6	% Officers', Directors' Owners' Comp/Sales		(15) 3.4	(18) 3.2	(20) 3.5	(10) 3.3	
6.4	6.9	5.7			5.7	5.5	5.1	4.8	
2619636M	2198566M	2155783M	Net Sales ($)	6442M	62615M	95509M	249432M	400937M	1340848M
915587M	879506M	861289M	Total Assets ($)	7820M	21199M	27122M	78162M	135113M	591873M

M = $ thousand MM = $ million

See Pages 9 through 22 for Explanation of Ratios and Data

Current Data Sorted by Assets | **Comparative Historical Data**

						Type of Statement		
	6	37	49	11	4	Unqualified	158	126
7	51	157	51	1		Reviewed	333	313
10	36	32	2		2	Compiled	96	86
97	71	38	7		1	Tax Returns	229	203
24	72	86	51	8	7	Other	298	288
105 (4/1-9/30/13)			813 (10/1/13-3/31/14)				4/1/09-3/31/10	4/1/10-3/31/11
0-500M	500M-2MM	2-10MM	10-50MM	50-100MM	100-250MM		ALL	ALL
138	236	350	160	20	14	NUMBER OF STATEMENTS	1114	1016
%	%	%	%	%	%	ASSETS	%	%
21.7	14.4	11.3	14.9	14.6	7.8	Cash & Equivalents	13.0	13.0
16.5	30.3	36.0	32.4	29.0	22.2	Trade Receivables (net)	29.6	31.0
4.2	3.9	3.0	2.8	2.0	2.6	Inventory	5.0	4.4
3.0	4.2	6.0	6.6	6.8	12.3	All Other Current	6.1	6.1
45.4	52.7	56.3	56.7	52.5	44.9	Total Current	53.7	54.6
41.6	36.7	35.7	35.1	36.8	41.8	Fixed Assets (net)	36.2	35.7
2.9	2.9	2.3	3.1	6.3	5.0	Intangibles (net)	2.2	2.0
10.2	7.7	5.7	5.1	4.4	8.3	All Other Non-Current	7.9	7.7
100.0	100.0	100.0	100.0	100.0	100.0	Total	100.0	100.0
						LIABILITIES		
14.2	11.4	7.4	3.6	2.4	10.0	Notes Payable-Short Term	10.3	10.7
8.1	5.0	5.9	5.3	4.7	5.6	Cur. Mat.-L.T.D.	7.1	6.3
10.9	13.5	15.0	14.6	14.0	10.1	Trade Payables	14.7	15.7
.0	.5	.4	.4	.1	.0	Income Taxes Payable	.3	.3
14.8	8.5	8.0	10.0	11.6	12.1	All Other Current	12.7	10.9
47.9	38.8	36.6	33.8	32.8	38.0	Total Current	45.2	44.0
44.5	24.9	15.8	14.6	17.0	30.9	Long-Term Debt	19.8	21.6
.0	.5	1.0	1.2	.2	1.9	Deferred Taxes	.7	.8
13.8	4.8	3.2	2.6	3.4	2.0	All Other Non-Current	4.2	4.6
-6.3	31.0	43.4	47.8	46.6	27.3	Net Worth	30.0	29.0
100.0	100.0	100.0	100.0	100.0	100.0	Total Liabilties & Net Worth	100.0	100.0
						INCOME DATA		
100.0	100.0	100.0	100.0	100.0	100.0	Net Sales	100.0	100.0
49.7	40.8	25.9	20.8	16.2	21.9	Gross Profit	29.0	30.3
47.4	35.2	20.8	15.2	12.9	16.8	Operating Expenses	27.2	27.6
2.2	5.7	5.1	5.6	3.2	5.1	Operating Profit	1.8	2.7
.3	.2	-.1	-.2	.1	.9	All Other Expenses (net)	.8	.5
2.0	5.5	5.2	5.8	3.2	4.3	Profit Before Taxes	1.0	2.2
						RATIOS		
2.9	2.8	2.4	2.3	1.7	1.8		2.2	2.3
1.0	1.4	1.6	1.6	1.5	1.5	Current	1.4	1.4
.5	.9	1.1	1.2	1.1	1.3		.9	.9
2.4	2.3	2.1	2.0	1.4	1.6		1.8	2.0
(137) .8	1.3	1.3	1.4	1.2	1.2	Quick	(1111) 1.1	1.1
.4	.7	.9	.9	.8	.8		.6	.7
0 UND	**19** 19.7	**44** 8.3	**48** 7.6	**51** 7.1	**0** UND		**28** 12.9	**26** 14.2
0 UND	**43** 8.5	**63** 5.8	**63** 5.8	**72** 5.1	**63** 5.8	Sales/Receivables	**53** 7.0	**54** 6.8
31 11.6	**63** 5.8	**85** 4.3	**81** 4.5	**85** 4.3	**94** 3.9		**77** 4.7	**79** 4.6
0 UND	**0** UND	**0** UND	**0** UND	**0** UND	**0** UND		**0** UND	**0** UND
0 UND	**0** UND	**0** UND	**0** 999.8	**0** 999.8	**2** 162.8	Cost of Sales/Inventory	**0** UND	**0** UND
0 UND	**3** 106.7	**4** 87.9	**4** 89.3	**9** 41.7	**12** 31.6		**11** 33.9	**8** 47.4
0 UND	**6** 59.7	**15** 24.7	**22** 16.9	**21** 17.7	**0** UND		**12** 31.2	**11** 32.5
1 467.5	**22** 16.5	**30** 12.3	**33** 11.2	**42** 8.6	**27** 13.5	Cost of Sales/Payables	**25** 14.4	**28** 12.8
20 18.6	**45** 8.1	**49** 7.5	**50** 7.3	**56** 6.5	**40** 9.1		**49** 7.4	**51** 7.2
13.1	7.2	5.4	5.2	6.5	6.7		6.1	6.1
UND	16.0	10.2	9.1	9.6	10.3	Sales/Working Capital	16.2	15.2
-18.2	-110.7	37.8	22.0	40.5	49.0		-37.3	-51.8
12.5	15.9	18.6	27.6	75.2	19.2		8.5	11.0
(108) 4.5	(206) 5.0	(328) 6.8	(145) 10.3	8.1	3.6	EBIT/Interest	(981) 2.2	(912) 3.2
1.0	1.2	1.9	2.4	1.1	1.6		-1.0	-.4
	5.2	3.7	4.6				3.6	6.3
	(22) 2.4	(86) 2.0	(46) 2.7			Net Profit + Depr., Dep., Amort./Cur. Mat. L/T/D	(248) 1.7	(214) 2.2
	.6	1.2	1.4				.7	1.0
.6	.4	.4	.4	.5	.8		.4	.4
2.5	1.0	.9	.8	.9	1.3	Fixed/Worth	1.0	.9
-1.3	4.4	1.5	1.4	1.6	3.5		2.4	2.9
1.0	.8	.7	.7	.7	.8		.7	.7
6.3	1.9	1.3	1.1	1.0	2.3	Debt/Worth	1.7	1.6
-2.8	9.9	2.7	2.4	2.8	20.2		5.2	6.7
106.3	69.1	42.5	41.1	45.5	24.5		29.6	35.6
(83) 57.4	(192) 30.8	(327) 20.1	(155) 19.4	(18) 12.9	(12) 10.1	% Profit Before Taxes/Tangible Net Worth	(943) 8.9	(855) 12.5
15.0	7.2	4.3	4.3	.8	3.9		-4.2	-3.3
35.6	23.6	17.9	16.0	16.5	7.2		11.5	15.0
12.7	8.7	7.5	8.7	3.7	3.5	% Profit Before Taxes/Total Assets	3.1	4.7
-4.4	.7	1.9	1.6	.2	.5		-4.3	-3.0
51.1	22.3	12.1	10.1	7.3	6.0		18.4	17.3
12.4	7.9	5.7	5.1	4.5	4.2	Sales/Net Fixed Assets	6.0	6.6
5.0	3.7	3.4	3.0	2.1	3.1		3.1	3.4
7.5	3.4	2.6	2.3	2.0	2.3		2.9	3.0
4.3	2.5	1.9	1.7	1.4	1.4	Sales/Total Assets	2.0	2.0
2.2	1.7	1.5	1.3	1.1	1.2		1.3	1.4
1.4	1.6	1.7	2.3	3.3			1.9	2.0
(89) 3.7	(173) 3.4	(308) 3.7	(144) 3.8	4.6		% Depr., Dep., Amort./Sales	(933) 4.7	(828) 4.5
8.1	6.7	5.8	5.4	7.3			8.5	7.9
2.7	2.3	1.4	1.0				2.0	1.8
(82) 5.9	(129) 3.8	(152) 2.3	(45) 1.4			% Officers', Directors' Owners' Comp/Sales	(472) 3.5	(425) 3.7
10.7	7.1	3.7	3.8				7.1	6.9
173694M	746334M	3484013M	6748659M	2119411M	4573668M	Net Sales ($)	17516180M	13694838M
35652M	276828M	1685561M	3458332M	1403400M	2108089M	Total Assets ($)	9656220M	8565860M

M = $ thousand MM = $ million

See Pages 9 through 22 for Explanation of Ratios and Data

Comparative Historical Data				Current Data Sorted by Sales					
			Type of Statement						
151	123	107	Unqualified	1	1	4	16	31	54
319	280	267	Reviewed	11	26	39	75	81	35
122	79	82	Compiled	9	26	20	15	8	4
216	217	214	Tax Returns	57	79	28	32	9	9
335	268	248	Other	22	42	47	40	51	46
4/1/11-3/31/12	**4/1/12-3/31/13**	**4/1/13-3/31/14**		**105 (4/1-9/30/13)**		**813 (10/1/13-3/31/14)**			
ALL	**ALL**	**ALL**		**0-1MM**	**1-3MM**	**3-5MM**	**5-10MM**	**10-25MM**	**25MM & OVER**
1143	967	918	**NUMBER OF STATEMENTS**	100	174	138	178	180	148
%	%	%	**ASSETS**	%	%	%	%	%	%
13.4	13.9	14.3	Cash & Equivalents	19.1	16.6	14.8	11.4	12.9	13.3
33.6	31.8	30.6	Trade Receivables (net)	16.5	21.9	31.0	36.7	38.0	33.6
3.6	3.0	3.3	Inventory	5.3	3.7	2.7	3.1	2.8	3.1
6.0	5.8	5.3	All Other Current	2.4	2.7	6.2	5.3	6.7	7.7
56.6	54.5	53.5	Total Current	43.4	44.8	54.6	56.4	60.4	57.7
33.0	34.9	36.9	Fixed Assets (net)	44.0	42.8	35.4	34.8	32.3	34.4
2.5	2.5	2.8	Intangibles (net)	2.9	3.6	2.5	2.0	2.4	3.5
7.9	8.1	6.8	All Other Non-Current	9.7	8.8	7.4	6.7	4.9	4.4
100.0	100.0	100.0	Total	100.0	100.0	100.0	100.0	100.0	100.0
			LIABILITIES						
11.0	10.4	8.7	Notes Payable-Short Term	11.3	11.7	9.2	8.7	7.6	4.3
6.8	5.9	5.8	Cur. Mat.-L.T.D.	7.7	5.7	5.3	6.4	5.3	5.2
16.7	15.4	13.8	Trade Payables	6.7	11.8	12.5	16.1	16.9	15.8
.4	.3	.3	Income Taxes Payable	.1	.4	.8	.3	.2	.3
11.0	10.7	9.6	All Other Current	13.9	9.5	7.1	7.9	9.2	11.8
45.9	42.8	38.3	Total Current	39.7	39.0	35.0	39.4	39.3	37.3
18.6	20.0	22.5	Long-Term Debt	38.4	34.5	22.1	16.3	13.9	15.9
.8	.7	.8	Deferred Taxes	.1	.6	.8	.8	1.2	.8
4.5	5.0	5.1	All Other Non-Current	10.5	7.7	5.7	3.3	2.6	2.9
30.3	31.5	33.3	Net Worth	11.4	18.2	36.4	40.2	43.1	43.1
100.0	100.0	100.0	Total Liabilities & Net Worth	100.0	100.0	100.0	100.0	100.0	100.0
			INCOME DATA						
100.0	100.0	100.0	Net Sales	100.0	100.0	100.0	100.0	100.0	100.0
29.0	30.8	32.1	Gross Profit	54.1	44.5	35.1	28.0	20.4	19.3
25.3	26.0	27.3	Operating Expenses	50.4	38.7	30.1	23.2	16.1	14.0
3.7	4.8	4.9	Operating Profit	3.6	5.8	5.0	4.8	4.3	5.2
.5	.2	.0	All Other Expenses (net)	.5	.0	-.1	-.3	.1	.1
3.2	4.5	4.8	Profit Before Taxes	3.1	5.8	5.0	5.1	4.2	5.2
			RATIOS						
2.4	2.4	2.4		3.5	3.3	2.4	2.5	2.4	1.9
1.4	1.5	1.5	Current	1.2	1.3	1.7	1.4	1.6	1.5
1.0	1.0	1.0		.5	.6	1.1	1.0	1.2	1.2
2.0	2.0	2.1		2.9	2.3	2.2	2.0	2.0	1.7
(1142) 1.2	1.2	(917) 1.3	Quick	.9	1.2	1.4	(177) 1.2	1.3	1.2
.7	.7	.8		.4	.5	.8	.9	.9	.9
30 12.1	**26** 14.3	**27** 13.7		**0** UND	**0** UND	**22** 16.3	**42** 8.6	**44** 8.3	**47** 7.7
55 6.6	**52** 7.0	**53** 6.9	Sales/Receivables	**14** 25.7	**32** 11.4	**50** 7.3	**60** 6.1	**64** 5.7	**62** 5.9
81 4.5	**78** 4.7	**78** 4.7		**56** 6.5	**55** 6.6	**76** 4.8	**83** 4.4	**83** 4.4	**79** 4.6
0 UND	**0** UND	**0** UND		**0** UND	**0** UND	**0** UND	**0** UND	**0** UND	**0** UND
0 UND	**0** UND	**0** UND	Cost of Sales/Inventory	**0** UND	**0** UND	**0** UND	**0** UND	**0** UND	**1** 374.2
6 61.6	**3** 107.5	**4** 95.2		**0** UND	**2** 152.8	**3** 120.4	**5** 76.2	**2** 156.9	**5** 77.9
13 28.2	**10** 37.3	**10** 36.8		**0** UND	**0** UND	**8** 48.4	**17** 21.8	**19** 19.6	**20** 18.5
29 12.7	**27** 13.4	**26** 14.3	Cost of Sales/Payables	**6** 65.6	**15** 24.7	**23** 15.8	**32** 11.4	**31** 11.6	**31** 11.6
51 7.1	**47** 7.8	**46** 8.0		**21** 17.3	**42** 8.7	**42** 8.7	**55** 6.6	**48** 7.6	**46** 8.0
5.9	6.0	6.1		6.2	7.2	6.1	5.5	5.6	6.6
14.0	13.6	12.9	Sales/Working Capital	41.8	29.4	12.1	12.7	10.1	11.1
-127.0	-232.7	631.4		-15.0	-24.0	55.2	174.0	33.1	29.6
13.9	15.9	18.9		9.1	13.8	17.3	18.6	26.3	27.3
(1014) 4.0	(850) 5.5	(821) 6.5	EBIT/Interest	(78) 4.4	(148) 4.4	(124) 5.0	(167) 6.0	(167) 9.3	(137) 9.3
.6	1.5	1.5		.9	.4	1.7	1.6	2.8	2.0
3.7	3.9	3.8			7.2	3.1	3.3	4.3	4.7
(217) 2.0	(175) 2.2	(167) 2.3	Net Profit + Depr., Dep., Amort./Cur. Mat. L/T/D		(10) 2.2	(21) 1.6	(31) 1.9	(56) 2.3	(43) 2.9
1.0	1.2	1.2			.1	.7	.6	1.2	1.8
.4	.4	.4		.4	.6	.3	.4	.3	.4
.9	.9	1.0	Fixed/Worth	1.4	1.4	1.0	.9	.7	.9
2.1	2.3	2.2		NM	-5.8	2.6	1.9	1.4	1.4
.7	.7	.7		.5	.8	.7	.7	.7	.8
1.7	1.6	1.5	Debt/Worth	2.3	2.1	1.6	1.4	1.2	1.4
4.7	4.8	4.3		-11.0	-10.6	5.3	3.4	2.5	2.6
40.0	48.9	53.4		78.1	76.4	55.2	51.8	44.3	49.2
(966) 14.7	(829) 18.5	(787) 22.0	% Profit Before Taxes/Tangible Net Worth	(73) 22.9	(121) 30.7	(121) 21.4	(161) 21.5	(171) 21.8	(140) 20.5
.4	3.2	5.0		2.9	2.7	6.8	2.8	7.7	4.7
15.6	20.0	20.0		26.7	28.1	21.1	21.0	16.5	16.2
5.3	7.3	8.2	% Profit Before Taxes/Total Assets	9.3	9.1	8.6	6.8	9.2	8.0
-.6	.8	1.0		-.9	-.4	1.8	1.1	2.7	.7
21.3	19.3	17.4		22.4	22.3	24.0	14.4	14.9	11.1
7.5	7.4	6.5	Sales/Net Fixed Assets	5.6	7.0	7.6	6.1	7.5	6.1
3.8	3.9	3.6		2.4	3.3	3.6	3.5	4.0	3.7
3.2	3.2	3.0		3.3	4.3	3.3	2.7	2.8	2.5
2.2	2.2	2.1	Sales/Total Assets	1.9	2.4	2.3	2.0	2.0	2.0
1.5	1.6	1.5		1.1	1.5	1.7	1.5	1.6	1.5
1.8	1.8	1.9		3.0	2.0	1.4	2.0	1.6	1.9
(924) 4.0	(793) 3.6	(739) 3.7	% Depr., Dep., Amort./Sales	(71) 6.5	(122) 4.0	(99) 3.4	(153) 3.7	(165) 3.5	(129) 3.4
6.5	6.1	6.2		11.9	7.0	6.0	6.1	5.1	5.2
1.9	2.0	1.6		3.8	2.8	2.2	1.5	1.0	.8
(469) 3.4	(425) 3.3	(417) 3.0	% Officers', Directors' Owners' Comp/Sales	(50) 9.0	(102) 4.3	(68) 3.8	(85) 2.3	(72) 1.6	(40) 1.2
6.1	6.3	5.8		14.7	7.6	5.8	3.3	3.4	3.6
18153179M	**17386529M**	**17845779M**	Net Sales ($)	**57633M**	**345944M**	**539264M**	**1302913M**	**2790392M**	**12809633M**
10344047M	**8719510M**	**8967862M**	Total Assets ($)	**33897M**	**181642M**	**265233M**	**730202M**	**1526725M**	**6230163M**

M = $ thousand MM = $ million

See Pages 9 through 22 for Explanation of Ratios and Data

Current Data Sorted by Assets							Comparative Historical Data	
						Type of Statement		
2	5	25	34	9	7	Unqualified	112	103
4	57	167	38			Reviewed	264	303
19	54	48	4			Compiled	118	111
166	119	56	4		1	Tax Returns	283	274
54	167	156	55	11	9	Other	332	362
158 (4/1-9/30/13)			1,113 (10/1/13-3/31/14)				4/1/09-3/31/10 ALL	4/1/10-3/31/11 ALL
0-500M	500M-2MM	2-10MM	10-50MM	50-100MM	100-250MM			
245	402	452	135	20	17	NUMBER OF STATEMENTS	1109	1153
%	%	%	%	%	%	**ASSETS**	%	%
25.4	16.8	12.2	14.5	14.7	8.0	Cash & Equivalents	15.2	14.7
20.9	37.5	42.1	37.5	22.7	23.4	Trade Receivables (net)	33.0	36.0
6.3	6.9	6.9	5.1	2.8	3.2	Inventory	7.6	7.5
3.0	4.8	6.2	9.7	8.0	5.4	All Other Current	6.1	5.9
55.5	65.9	67.4	66.8	48.3	40.1	Total Current	61.9	64.1
29.4	23.4	23.1	22.1	40.8	38.7	Fixed Assets (net)	27.6	24.7
3.4	3.2	2.8	4.8	6.2	13.3	Intangibles (net)	3.1	3.0
11.7	7.5	6.6	6.3	4.7	7.9	All Other Non-Current	7.5	8.2
100.0	100.0	100.0	100.0	100.0	100.0	Total	100.0	100.0
						LIABILITIES		
23.6	9.3	6.8	5.5	4.8	2.3	Notes Payable-Short Term	11.6	13.1
5.2	4.1	3.4	3.0	4.1	4.5	Cur. Mat.-L.T.D.	5.2	4.7
11.7	17.0	17.7	18.6	10.5	12.6	Trade Payables	16.4	17.6
.1	.2	.4	.4	.9	.1	Income Taxes Payable	.3	.4
12.7	10.8	13.3	15.1	8.9	9.2	All Other Current	13.3	12.8
53.4	41.5	41.6	42.5	29.2	28.8	Total Current	46.8	48.5
27.9	18.4	12.6	10.6	22.9	29.7	Long-Term Debt	17.5	16.1
.0	.2	.8	.6	1.3	4.8	Deferred Taxes	.5	.5
14.8	3.9	3.2	3.7	6.7	2.6	All Other Non-Current	4.2	6.2
4.0	36.0	41.8	42.6	39.8	34.1	Net Worth	31.0	28.7
100.0	100.0	100.0	100.0	100.0	100.0	Total Liabilties & Net Worth	100.0	100.0
						INCOME DATA		
100.0	100.0	100.0	100.0	100.0	100.0	Net Sales	100.0	100.0
44.8	36.4	29.6	22.6	21.8	24.1	Gross Profit	32.6	32.7
39.6	30.9	23.9	16.4	13.1	17.6	Operating Expenses	29.2	29.3
5.2	5.5	5.7	6.2	8.8	6.6	Operating Profit	3.4	3.5
.4	.3	.4	.2	1.3	4.7	All Other Expenses (net)	.8	.5
4.8	5.2	5.3	6.1	7.5	1.9	Profit Before Taxes	2.7	3.0
						RATIOS		
3.1	3.2	2.5	2.3	2.3	1.8		2.6	2.6
1.5	1.8	1.6	1.5	1.8	1.4	Current	1.5	1.5
.6	1.2	1.2	1.2	1.0	1.1		1.0	1.0
2.7	2.8	2.2	1.8	2.0	1.3		2.1	2.2
1.2	1.4	1.3	1.2	1.4	1.1	Quick	1.2	1.2
.4	.9	.9	.8	.6	.8		.6	.7
0 UND	**20** 18.5	**38** 9.5	**45** 8.1	**49** 7.5	**49** 7.4		**21** 17.6	**23** 15.8
5 80.0	**39** 9.3	**58** 6.3	**64** 5.7	**60** 6.1	**62** 5.9	Sales/Receivables	**44** 8.3	**50** 7.4
30 12.0	**63** 5.8	**81** 4.5	**87** 4.2	**83** 4.4	**78** 4.7		**70** 5.2	**77** 4.7
0 UND	**0** UND	**0** UND	**0** UND	**0** UND	**0** UND		**0** UND	**0** UND
0 UND	**0** UND	**0** 999.8	**1** 608.3	**1** 367.0	**2** 151.4	Cost of Sales/Inventory	**0** 844.0	**1** 479.3
4 95.4	**12** 30.5	**13** 27.4	**12** 31.3	**24** 15.5	**15** 25.0		**17** 21.2	**19** 18.8
0 UND	**6** 60.7	**15** 24.2	**19** 19.0	**14** 26.9	**16** 22.2		**9** 39.8	**10** 35.9
2 188.7	**21** 17.2	**30** 12.3	**36** 10.2	**27** 13.3	**21** 17.5	Cost of Sales/Payables	**23** 15.7	**26** 14.2
22 16.3	**38** 9.5	**49** 7.4	**55** 6.6	**47** 7.8	**45** 8.1		**44** 8.3	**50** 7.3
14.3	6.6	5.9	5.0	3.8	8.0		6.5	6.0
45.2	12.8	11.0	9.2	5.9	20.0	Sales/Working Capital	14.1	13.4
-36.2	61.2	28.4	27.1	NM	58.4		-148.5	999.8
25.3	28.3	29.7	34.3	22.5	9.3		14.8	16.4
(184) 8.6	(339) 9.1	(397) 9.9	(124) 11.0	(17) 4.6	(14) 2.7	EBIT/Interest	(961) 3.7	(961) 4.0
2.3	2.5	3.1	3.4	1.8	1.3		.0	.6
	5.0	9.0	11.0				4.9	6.1
	(30) 2.8	(90) 4.0	(42) 4.4			Net Profit + Depr., Dep., Amort./Cur. Mat. L/T/D	(217) 1.9	(177) 2.1
	1.7	1.7	1.7				.7	.7
.2	.1	.2	.2	.1	.3		.2	.2
1.1	.5	.5	.5	1.5	1.7	Fixed/Worth	.6	.5
-8.3	1.6	1.2	1.2	2.8	7.4		2.3	2.1
.7	.6	.6	.8	.9	1.3		.7	.7
3.2	1.4	1.4	1.7	2.2	3.2	Debt/Worth	1.7	1.7
-10.8	5.0	3.0	3.2	3.4	10.4		6.7	6.5
156.0	71.9	49.6	44.0	42.4	40.1		49.0	51.1
(168) 65.9	(328) 33.0	(419) 25.7	(124) 19.9	(19) 17.6	(14) 16.7	% Profit Before Taxes/Tangible Net Worth	(936) 16.1	(960) 18.2
21.0	8.8	9.2	8.8	4.5	7.2		-.1	.7
44.3	28.8	21.1	16.8	10.3	9.2		19.3	18.2
21.0	13.1	9.1	7.7	6.9	4.0	% Profit Before Taxes/Total Assets	5.3	6.3
5.2	3.0	3.1	3.2	2.7	.5		-1.6	-.8
121.6	69.0	49.3	31.4	30.3	33.5		38.7	45.8
30.1	24.3	16.8	13.4	4.6	12.3	Sales/Net Fixed Assets	15.0	16.9
11.8	9.7	6.6	4.9	.8	1.2		5.8	6.7
10.2	4.8	3.3	2.6	1.9	2.2		3.8	3.9
5.2	3.4	2.5	1.9	1.3	1.2	Sales/Total Assets	2.6	2.6
3.4	2.3	1.9	1.4	.6	.8		1.8	1.8
.6	.5	.6	.7	.5			.8	.7
(119) 1.2	(262) 1.2	(364) 1.5	(124) 1.6	(19) 3.9		% Depr., Dep., Amort./Sales	(907) 2.0	(870) 1.7
2.7	2.8	3.0	3.7	13.5			4.2	4.0
3.4	2.3	1.5	1.0				2.2	2.1
(162) 6.5	(220) 4.1	(206) 2.7	(32) 1.6			% Officers', Directors' Owners' Comp/Sales	(567) 4.1	(575) 4.0
10.3	6.4	4.5	2.9				7.5	7.0
391542M	1677219M	5271818M	5844454M	1860258M	5048600M	Net Sales ($)	17112415M	20718826M
61357M	453630M	2023823M	2859804M	1474495M	2898674M	Total Assets ($)	8864694M	8693236M

M = $ thousand MM = $ million

See Pages 9 through 22 for Explanation of Ratios and Data

Comparative Historical Data				Current Data Sorted by Sales					
			Type of Statement						
111	86	82	Unqualified	2	1	2	9	24	44
302	274	266	Reviewed		25	34	84	90	33
174	132	125	Compiled	6	39	24	29	20	7
337	361	346	Tax Returns	66	124	63	63	24	6
385	396	452	Other	30	103	74	90	88	67
4/1/11-3/31/12 ALL	**4/1/12-3/31/13 ALL**	**4/1/13-3/31/14 ALL**		**158 (4/1-9/30/13)**			**1,113 (10/1/13-3/31/14)**		
				0-1MM	**1-3MM**	**3-5MM**	**5-10MM**	**10-25MM**	**25MM & OVER**
1309	1249	1271	**NUMBER OF STATEMENTS**	104	292	197	275	246	157
%	%	%	**ASSETS**	%	%	%	%	%	%
15.2	15.0	16.4	Cash & Equivalents	24.2	17.7	19.6	13.3	14.9	12.6
36.1	36.6	35.5	Trade Receivables (net)	15.4	29.6	35.5	39.5	45.4	37.2
7.2	7.6	6.5	Inventory	5.2	7.8	4.6	7.7	5.9	6.0
5.7	5.8	5.5	All Other Current	2.1	4.3	4.5	5.2	6.9	9.7
64.2	65.0	63.9	Total Current	46.9	59.5	64.2	65.7	73.1	65.6
23.8	23.9	24.8	Fixed Assets (net)	33.8	27.4	25.8	24.5	18.8	22.7
3.5	3.1	3.4	Intangibles (net)	5.2	4.1	2.4	2.9	1.6	6.2
8.5	8.1	7.8	All Other Non-Current	14.1	9.0	7.6	6.9	6.5	5.5
100.0	100.0	100.0	Total	100.0	100.0	100.0	100.0	100.0	100.0
			LIABILITIES						
13.0	11.1	10.6	Notes Payable-Short Term	23.5	15.0	9.5	8.8	6.5	5.0
4.4	4.1	4.0	Cur. Mat.-L.T.D.	6.8	3.9	3.8	4.7	2.8	3.0
17.9	17.5	16.2	Trade Payables	9.3	12.2	15.7	17.2	19.8	21.5
.4	.3	.3	Income Taxes Payable	.0	.2	.3	.2	.6	.4
12.7	13.6	12.5	All Other Current	11.1	12.1	11.0	12.4	13.2	15.1
48.3	46.6	43.6	Total Current	50.7	43.4	40.2	43.2	43.0	45.0
17.5	16.9	17.6	Long-Term Debt	29.9	21.2	20.1	16.4	10.4	12.7
.5	.5	.5	Deferred Taxes	.0	.3	.2	.8	.7	.8
7.3	6.5	5.8	All Other Non-Current	19.1	6.5	4.6	3.7	3.2	4.5
26.5	29.6	32.6	Net Worth	.4	28.6	34.9	35.9	42.7	36.9
100.0	100.0	100.0	Total Liabilties & Net Worth	100.0	100.0	100.0	100.0	100.0	100.0
			INCOME DATA						
100.0	100.0	100.0	Net Sales	100.0	100.0	100.0	100.0	100.0	100.0
32.1	33.1	33.7	Gross Profit	50.1	41.9	36.1	30.9	26.7	20.8
28.4	27.9	28.1	Operating Expenses	43.1	36.4	30.6	26.2	20.2	15.3
3.7	5.1	5.6	Operating Profit	7.0	5.4	5.5	4.7	6.6	5.5
.4	.5	.4	All Other Expenses (net)	.8	.4	.6	.2	.1	.7
3.3	4.7	5.2	Profit Before Taxes	6.2	5.0	4.9	4.5	6.5	4.8
			RATIOS						
2.5	2.6	2.8		3.4	3.4	3.2	2.6	2.5	2.0
1.5	1.5	1.6	Current	1.3	1.7	1.9	1.6	1.7	1.4
1.0	1.0	1.1		.5	1.0	1.2	1.1	1.2	1.1
2.0	2.1	2.3		3.0	2.8	2.7	2.1	2.2	1.5
1.2	(1247) 1.2	1.3	Quick	1.2	1.4	1.5	1.3	1.4	1.1
.7	.7	.8		.3	.7	.9	.9	1.0	.8
21 17.0	21 17.1	22 16.7		0 UND	7 53.6	18 19.8	25 14.4	39 9.4	41 8.9
48 7.6	47 7.7	46 7.9	Sales/Receivables	0 UND	34 10.6	38 9.5	48 7.6	58 6.3	58 6.3
74 4.9	74 4.9	72 5.1		29 12.6	63 5.8	69 5.3	72 5.1	81 4.5	78 4.7
0 UND	0 UND	0 UND		0 UND	0 UND	0 UND	0 UND	0 UND	0 UND
0 UND	0 999.8	0 UND	Cost of Sales/Inventory	0 UND	0 UND	0 UND	0 999.8	0 999.8	1 374.5
15 25.1	16 22.8	12 31.3		3 143.8	15 24.2	10 38.3	13 28.3	11 33.7	12 29.9
10 37.8	8 43.2	7 50.0		0 UND	0 940.3	4 101.2	11 33.3	16 22.7	17 20.9
26 14.1	25 14.4	23 16.1	Cost of Sales/Payables	3 109.1	13 27.7	20 18.1	26 14.2	30 12.1	35 10.3
46 7.9	47 7.8	45 8.1		28 13.2	38 9.6	39 9.4	41 8.8	49 7.4	54 6.8
6.6	6.4	6.3		10.5	6.6	6.0	6.6	6.0	6.0
14.2	13.6	14.0	Sales/Working Capital	90.6	15.7	14.6	13.6	10.8	12.0
753.5	139.6	79.5		-28.6	-314.4	60.0	59.3	23.7	42.1
17.0	22.7	28.3		22.5	23.8	30.0	23.6	51.4	29.7
(1108) 4.8	(1050) 6.6	(1075) 9.3	EBIT/Interest	(68) 5.1	(243) 7.7	(168) 11.5	(241) 8.3	(217) 11.8	(138) 9.9
1.0	1.8	2.8		.9	2.0	3.0	2.4	4.5	3.0
6.6	9.6	8.0			5.5	4.8	6.8	9.2	13.4
(205) 2.5	(162) 2.7	(178) 3.4	Net Profit + Depr., Dep., Amort./Cur. Mat. L/T/D		(16) 3.4	(14) 1.7	(40) 3.4	(61) 4.1	(45) 4.1
1.1	1.2	1.6			2.0	1.3	1.4	1.9	1.4
.2	.2	.2		.2	.1	.2	.1	.1	.2
.6	.6	.5	Fixed/Worth	1.4	.6	.5	.6	.4	.5
2.2	1.8	1.8		-14.0	2.1	1.7	1.9	.9	1.9
.7	.7	.7		.7	.5	.6	.7	.7	1.0
1.8	1.7	1.6	Debt/Worth	4.7	1.4	1.3	1.7	1.4	2.1
7.3	7.2	5.1		-10.0	8.1	3.5	4.6	2.8	3.8
56.3	65.9	62.8		139.1	82.8	62.2	58.3	49.3	46.1
(1074) 21.6	(1031) 26.6	(1072) 31.3	% Profit Before Taxes/Tangible Net Worth	(69) 57.8	(235) 35.1	(162) 33.9	(235) 25.0	(232) 28.8	(139) 21.0
2.6	7.0	9.5		11.5	7.9	11.3	8.3	11.8	8.9
20.8	23.9	26.1		43.3	32.4	31.7	21.2	23.8	16.4
7.7	8.9	10.9	% Profit Before Taxes/Total Assets	17.0	14.7	14.1	9.8	10.2	7.8
.1	1.5	3.1		.1	2.5	4.6	2.8	3.8	2.9
53.0	59.9	59.7		119.6	62.7	57.4	54.7	56.9	54.0
20.2	20.6	21.2	Sales/Net Fixed Assets	16.3	22.4	21.3	18.2	24.2	21.2
7.7	7.6	7.8		5.1	8.5	8.1	8.4	9.6	6.2
4.1	4.3	4.4		7.5	5.0	5.3	4.2	3.7	3.2
2.8	2.8	2.9	Sales/Total Assets	3.4	3.3	3.2	2.9	2.7	2.2
1.9	1.9	2.0		1.7	2.1	2.1	2.0	2.0	1.5
.7	.6	.6		.9	.6	.8	.6	.5	.5
(973) 1.5	(940) 1.5	(897) 1.3	% Depr., Dep., Amort./Sales	(47) 2.4	(177) 1.3	(124) 1.8	(210) 1.5	(204) 1.0	(135) 1.2
3.3	3.2	3.1		6.0	3.1	3.2	3.2	2.3	3.4
2.0	2.1	2.0		5.1	3.5	2.3	1.9	1.1	.9
(621) 3.9	(626) 3.8	(623) 3.8	% Officers', Directors' Owners' Comp/Sales	(57) 8.5	(169) 5.6	(108) 4.0	(138) 3.0	(119) 2.0	(32) 1.5
7.2	6.6	6.5		15.8	8.5	6.3	4.5	3.4	3.0
19572435M	**16937755M**	**20093891M**	Net Sales ($)	**61011M**	**577125M**	**776951M**	**1992796M**	**3805985M**	**12880023M**
9190662M	**7688215M**	**9771783M**	Total Assets ($)	**29271M**	**219435M**	**284075M**	**839010M**	**1692663M**	**6707329M**

M = $ thousand MM = $ million

See Pages 9 through 22 for Explanation of Ratios and Data

MANUFACTURING

Current Data Sorted by Assets							Comparative Historical Data	
						Type of Statement		
		3	17	6	5	Unqualified	41	45
	3	4	5	2		Reviewed	22	28
	3	6	1			Compiled	13	12
2	5	3				Tax Returns	16	14
	2	15	12	4	3	Other	47	43
	32 (4/1-9/30/13)		69 (10/1/13-3/31/14)				4/1/09-3/31/10	4/1/10-3/31/11
0-500M	500M-2MM	2-10MM	10-50MM	50-100MM	100-250MM		ALL	ALL
2	13	31	35	12	8	NUMBER OF STATEMENTS	139	142
%	%	%	%	%	%	**ASSETS**	%	%
	8.5	8.4	11.9	9.7		Cash & Equivalents	7.7	7.2
	29.2	29.6	21.2	23.4		Trade Receivables (net)	26.4	24.5
	28.9	24.5	26.0	17.5		Inventory	23.3	23.9
	.9	2.6	2.6	6.6		All Other Current	3.8	3.6
	67.5	65.2	61.6	57.2		Total Current	61.2	59.3
	18.7	24.5	26.2	21.0		Fixed Assets (net)	29.0	28.2
	3.7	5.6	5.4	9.2		Intangibles (net)	2.9	5.6
	10.0	4.8	6.8	12.6		All Other Non-Current	6.8	7.0
	100.0	100.0	100.0	100.0		Total	100.0	100.0
						LIABILITIES		
	17.3	8.2	9.3	8.8		Notes Payable-Short Term	12.0	11.4
	2.6	2.5	1.9	1.8		Cur. Mat.-L.T.D.	3.1	2.9
	18.0	25.1	15.2	12.3		Trade Payables	16.3	14.4
	.1	.1	.1	.0		Income Taxes Payable	.1	.2
	5.0	9.4	8.7	7.9		All Other Current	10.0	10.4
	43.0	45.3	35.2	30.8		Total Current	41.5	39.3
	19.5	11.7	6.8	12.9		Long-Term Debt	16.6	13.9
	.0	.0	.4	.3		Deferred Taxes	.2	.4
	.2	2.5	7.8	1.7		All Other Non-Current	3.8	3.5
	37.3	40.5	49.7	54.4		Net Worth	37.9	42.8
	100.0	100.0	100.0	100.0		Total Liabilties & Net Worth	100.0	100.0
						INCOME DATA		
	100.0	100.0	100.0	100.0		Net Sales	100.0	100.0
	22.8	23.9	20.9	20.3		Gross Profit	21.7	23.5
	21.4	17.9	13.7	14.9		Operating Expenses	16.3	17.7
	1.4	6.0	7.2	5.4		Operating Profit	5.4	5.8
	.8	.5	-.2	.1		All Other Expenses (net)	.5	.6
	.6	5.6	7.4	5.3		Profit Before Taxes	5.0	5.2
						RATIOS		
	3.1	2.6	2.6	3.3			2.5	2.5
	1.6	1.6	1.9	1.6		Current	1.4	1.4
	1.0	1.1	1.3	1.2			1.1	1.1
	2.0	1.6	1.3	2.3			1.3	1.2
	.9	.9	.8	.9		Quick	.7	.8
	.4	.5	.4	.6			.5	.5
	14 26.0	**15** 24.7	**14** 25.4	**11** 33.9			**19** 19.6	**19** 19.6
	25 14.8	**27** 13.5	**21** 17.5	**22** 16.3		Sales/Receivables	**30** 12.1	**29** 12.6
	38 9.6	**44** 8.3	**31** 11.6	**37** 9.9			**41** 8.9	**42** 8.7
	21 17.0	**18** 20.6	**15** 23.8	**12** 30.6			**14** 26.8	**19** 19.7
	43 8.4	**29** 12.6	**44** 8.3	**19** 18.9		Cost of Sales/Inventory	**32** 11.5	**39** 9.4
	56 6.5	**73** 5.0	**54** 6.7	**33** 11.2			**61** 6.0	**59** 6.1
	6 64.8	**16** 22.5	**12** 29.9	**5** 76.3			**13** 28.6	**13** 28.4
	27 13.6	**21** 17.0	**17** 21.1	**12** 29.5		Cost of Sales/Payables	**22** 16.9	**20** 18.5
	33 11.2	**32** 11.3	**26** 14.1	**19** 18.8			**34** 10.8	**30** 12.2
	9.9	7.2	5.9	7.6			7.9	8.2
	14.8	18.2	12.5	20.4		Sales/Working Capital	19.6	17.8
	NM	38.8	22.2	41.0			83.1	60.5
	3.0	22.4	128.8	164.5			18.7	22.1
	(11) 2.7	(26) 8.9	(32) 11.1	(10) 6.4		EBIT/Interest	(126) 5.5	(131) 6.8
	-7.0	3.2	3.0	2.6			1.8	2.2
							8.3	12.9
						Net Profit + Depr., Dep., Amort./Cur. Mat. L/T/D	(30) 2.9	(27) 5.2
							.6	2.5
	.1	.2	.3	.1			.4	.4
	.4	.7	.6	.6		Fixed/Worth	.8	.7
	NM	1.3	.9	1.2			1.9	1.4
	.3	.8	.6	.4			.6	.6
	2.0	1.5	1.0	.6		Debt/Worth	2.0	1.5
	NM	8.1	2.5	4.9			5.4	4.2
	36.7	78.2	36.6	38.6			59.2	47.4
	(10) 16.6	(28) 32.0	(33) 17.4	(11) 29.5		% Profit Before Taxes/Tangible Net Worth	(128) 25.9	(132) 24.3
	-3.1	13.3	9.1	13.6			9.3	9.2
	11.3	20.8	22.1	19.8			20.7	16.6
	5.9	9.7	11.4	9.1		% Profit Before Taxes/Total Assets	10.0	8.7
	-4.1	4.5	3.4	5.1			2.2	2.6
	148.6	39.6	27.2	60.9			28.4	23.8
	18.9	12.6	12.0	26.7		Sales/Net Fixed Assets	12.9	11.6
	15.0	7.5	7.3	10.2			6.2	5.6
	5.5	4.4	3.4	5.9			4.1	3.8
	3.3	3.3	2.7	3.8		Sales/Total Assets	2.9	2.8
	2.5	2.0	2.2	1.4			2.1	2.1
		1.0	.7	.2			.8	.7
		(24) 1.7	(31) 1.2	(10) .7		% Depr., Dep., Amort./Sales	(116) 1.2	(124) 1.3
		3.3	2.1	1.5			2.6	2.6
							.7	.8
						% Officers', Directors' Owners' Comp/Sales	(28) 1.7	(32) 1.7
							4.5	3.1
7913M	56269M	632752M	2104840M	2753053M	3406603M	Net Sales ($)	9605336M	11327653M
588M	14263M	167391M	710925M	776015M	1073697M	Total Assets ($)	3672779M	4187378M

M = $ thousand MM = $ million

See Pages 9 through 22 for Explanation of Ratios and Data

Comparative Historical Data				Current Data Sorted by Sales					
			Type of Statement						
45	32	31	Unqualified					2	29
16	18	14	Reviewed			3		2	9
13	8	10	Compiled			4	2	3	1
16	13	10	Tax Returns	1	2	4	1		2
51	48	36	Other			1	5	8	22
4/1/11-3/31/12 ALL	**4/1/12-3/31/13 ALL**	**4/1/13-3/31/14 ALL**		**32 (4/1-9/30/13)**			**69 (10/1/13-3/31/14)**		
				0-1MM	**1-3MM**	**3-5MM**	**5-10MM**	**10-25MM**	**25MM & OVER**
141	119	101	**NUMBER OF STATEMENTS**	1	2	12	8	15	63
%	%	%	**ASSETS**	%	%	%	%	%	%
8.8	5.7	9.6	Cash & Equivalents			8.0		7.7	10.0
24.9	26.8	25.4	Trade Receivables (net)			23.6		26.0	25.2
24.2	25.6	24.5	Inventory			28.8		19.2	24.3
3.2	2.8	2.7	All Other Current			1.0		2.9	3.2
61.0	60.9	62.2	Total Current			61.4		55.8	62.7
27.9	26.3	24.2	Fixed Assets (net)			27.7		31.7	24.1
5.6	5.4	5.4	Intangibles (net)			1.9		7.2	5.2
5.6	7.4	8.2	All Other Non-Current			8.9		5.3	7.9
100.0	100.0	100.0	Total			100.0		100.0	100.0
			LIABILITIES						
9.9	12.2	9.5	Notes Payable-Short Term			12.4		11.0	8.1
3.1	2.3	2.2	Cur. Mat.-L.T.D.			2.3		1.8	2.1
16.3	15.9	18.4	Trade Payables			11.9		19.8	18.8
.1	.2	.1	Income Taxes Payable			.0		.1	.1
9.9	8.5	8.9	All Other Current			11.8		9.3	8.9
39.4	39.0	39.1	Total Current			38.5		41.9	38.0
14.5	13.3	11.2	Long-Term Debt			16.4		15.4	8.7
.4	.5	.3	Deferred Taxes			.0		.0	.4
6.0	4.3	3.8	All Other Non-Current			.4		1.4	4.9
39.8	43.0	45.7	Net Worth			44.7		41.3	47.9
100.0	100.0	100.0	Total Liabilties & Net Worth			100.0		100.0	100.0
			INCOME DATA						
100.0	100.0	100.0	Net Sales			100.0		100.0	100.0
23.2	19.5	21.7	Gross Profit			18.5		24.0	19.6
17.6	15.5	16.3	Operating Expenses			14.9		18.3	14.1
5.6	4.0	5.5	Operating Profit			3.6		5.7	5.5
.4	.5	.2	All Other Expenses (net)			.3		.5	.0
5.2	3.5	5.2	Profit Before Taxes			3.3		5.2	5.5
			RATIOS						
2.5	2.2	2.6				3.7		1.6	2.4
1.7	1.6	1.7	Current			2.1		1.3	1.8
1.1	1.2	1.2				1.1		1.1	1.3
1.5	1.3	1.6				2.3		1.4	1.3
.8	.8	.9	Quick			1.0		.8	.9
.5	.5	.5				.4		.3	.6
18 20.7	**18** 19.8	**15** 24.9				**9** 40.5		**10** 36.8	**15** 24.1
27 13.3	**27** 13.7	**23** 16.0	Sales/Receivables			**20** 18.0		**21** 17.7	**22** 16.3
41 9.0	**38** 9.6	**36** 10.0				**32** 11.5		**44** 8.3	**35** 10.5
17 21.9	**15** 23.8	**16** 23.0				**17** 21.1		**13** 27.6	**14** 25.5
36 10.1	**32** 11.5	**32** 11.3	Cost of Sales/Inventory			**37** 9.9		**18** 20.0	**31** 11.8
63 5.8	**63** 5.8	**58** 6.3				**65** 5.6		**51** 7.1	**49** 7.4
11 32.4	**14** 26.6	**12** 31.0				**1** 478.9		**17** 21.7	**12** 29.2
22 16.6	**19** 19.0	**20** 18.1	Cost of Sales/Payables			**11** 34.1		**29** 12.6	**20** 18.7
36 10.1	**31** 11.6	**28** 13.0				**25** 14.4		**35** 10.5	**26** 14.3
8.3	9.0	7.3				6.2		11.7	7.2
15.6	17.1	15.3	Sales/Working Capital			14.9		18.2	15.4
60.3	42.2	37.1				46.1		38.8	30.0
16.3	14.8	32.6						22.4	81.5
(128) 5.2	(110) 6.3	(87) 8.2	EBIT/Interest					(14) 8.9	(56) 10.8
1.8	2.9	2.7						3.0	3.0
8.9	7.0	5.3							5.3
(25) 3.9	(20) 4.0	(12) 3.9	Net Profit + Depr., Dep., Amort./Cur. Mat. L/T/D						(12) 3.9
1.7	2.0	1.8							1.8
.4	.3	.2				.2		.7	.2
.8	.7	.6	Fixed/Worth			.7		.9	.5
1.6	1.2	1.1				1.2		1.8	.9
.7	.7	.6				.4		1.0	.6
1.5	1.6	1.2	Debt/Worth			1.1		1.7	1.0
5.0	3.4	3.4				4.2		3.4	2.5
41.0	39.0	43.6				29.3		89.8	41.7
(124) 22.9	(112) 18.4	(92) 20.0	% Profit Before Taxes/Tangible Net Worth			(10) 18.7		(14) 27.7	(59) 20.3
11.3	10.9	10.7				-16.3		8.0	10.8
17.6	13.6	19.0				12.6		20.2	20.8
8.3	7.1	9.0	% Profit Before Taxes/Total Assets			7.5		7.5	10.1
2.5	3.7	3.9				-13.0		4.5	4.0
28.4	33.4	35.2				22.2		23.9	34.7
12.6	14.7	15.3	Sales/Net Fixed Assets			15.0		10.2	15.6
6.8	6.8	8.3				9.4		5.9	8.4
4.2	4.7	4.6				5.7		4.4	4.6
3.0	3.2	3.0	Sales/Total Assets			3.9		3.3	3.0
2.1	2.1	2.2				2.0		2.3	2.3
.7	.6	.7				.7		1.0	.7
(118) 1.2	(105) 1.1	(82) 1.2	% Depr., Dep., Amort./Sales			(10) 1.0		(13) 1.4	(53) 1.2
2.2	2.0	2.1				1.8		3.2	1.9
.8	.6	.9							
(29) 1.7	(26) 1.3	(16) 2.5	% Officers', Directors' Owners' Comp/Sales						
2.9	2.5	3.8							
10475831M	**12057872M**	**8961430M**	Net Sales ($)	**735M**	**3808M**	**46389M**	**59547M**	**251889M**	**8599062M**
3484337M	**3745799M**	**2742879M**	Total Assets ($)	**544M**	**2035M**	**15722M**	**28782M**	**89858M**	**2605938M**

M = $ thousand MM = $ million

See Pages 9 through 22 for Explanation of Ratios and Data

Current Data Sorted by Assets							**Comparative Historical Data**	
						Type of Statement		
		1	4	3	8	Unqualified	18	21
			3	1		Reviewed	5	3
		3	1			Compiled	6	6
	1					Tax Returns	4	3
	1	3	7	5	8	Other	16	8
	15 (4/1-9/30/13)		34 (10/1/13-3/31/14)				**4/1/09-3/31/10**	**4/1/10-3/31/11**
0-500M	**500M-2MM**	**2-10MM**	**10-50MM**	**50-100MM**	**100-250MM**		**ALL**	**ALL**
	2	7	15	9	16	**NUMBER OF STATEMENTS**	49	41
%	%	%	%	%	%	**ASSETS**	%	%
DATA NOT AVAILABLE			3.9		5.3	Cash & Equivalents	7.5	6.1
			23.6		21.0	Trade Receivables (net)	20.1	20.9
			21.6		23.9	Inventory	26.9	26.1
			2.8		4.3	All Other Current	3.1	4.9
			51.9		54.4	Total Current	57.6	58.0
			38.9		40.2	Fixed Assets (net)	33.2	32.4
			.7		2.9	Intangibles (net)	2.6	1.9
			8.5		2.5	All Other Non-Current	6.7	7.7
			100.0		100.0	Total	100.0	100.0
						LIABILITIES		
			10.5		6.3	Notes Payable-Short Term	13.3	11.5
			2.3		2.0	Cur. Mat.-L.T.D.	3.5	2.6
			11.6		12.1	Trade Payables	11.1	11.5
			.0		.0	Income Taxes Payable	.3	.4
			5.0		8.7	All Other Current	7.0	6.9
			29.4		29.1	Total Current	35.2	32.9
			21.6		17.3	Long-Term Debt	17.5	17.2
			.7		1.4	Deferred Taxes	1.2	.8
			19.1		3.9	All Other Non-Current	3.9	6.6
			29.3		48.2	Net Worth	42.2	42.5
			100.0		100.0	Total Liabilties & Net Worth	100.0	100.0
						INCOME DATA		
			100.0		100.0	Net Sales	100.0	100.0
			22.1		11.6	Gross Profit	22.3	20.8
			16.0		7.6	Operating Expenses	15.9	14.9
			6.0		4.0	Operating Profit	6.4	5.9
			.8		.5	All Other Expenses (net)	1.6	1.2
			5.2		3.5	Profit Before Taxes	4.8	4.7
						RATIOS		
			2.8		2.5		2.5	3.3
			1.7		1.7	Current	1.6	1.9
			1.4		1.3		1.2	1.3
			1.4		1.2		1.4	1.4
			1.0		.8	Quick	.7	.9
			.7		.6		.5	.5
			26 13.9		**25** 14.4		**22** 16.5	**22** 16.6
			35 10.5		**31** 11.7	Sales/Receivables	**28** 12.9	**30** 12.1
			46 8.0		**36** 10.1		**36** 10.2	**47** 7.7
			21 17.4		**31** 11.6		**33** 11.2	**33** 11.1
			35 10.4		**41** 8.9	Cost of Sales/Inventory	**47** 7.8	**52** 7.0
			68 5.4		**54** 6.8		**65** 5.6	**78** 4.7
			11 34.6		**8** 45.1		**9** 39.1	**10** 36.2
			17 21.0		**17** 21.9	Cost of Sales/Payables	**16** 23.0	**21** 17.6
			37 9.8		**31** 11.8		**32** 11.5	**30** 12.1
			9.0		8.5		7.3	6.2
			10.9		11.3	Sales/Working Capital	12.1	8.5
			18.1		16.3		19.0	18.3
			12.2		19.9		25.6	25.9
			(14) 7.1		6.5	EBIT/Interest	5.6	(37) 6.8
			3.1		2.4		1.7	2.1
							8.4	17.0
						Net Profit + Depr., Dep., Amort./Cur. Mat. L/T/D	(19) 4.7	(12) 6.0
							1.9	1.9
			.7		.7		.3	.3
			.9		1.0	Fixed/Worth	.9	.7
			2.8		1.5		1.6	1.4
			.5		.8		.8	.7
			1.1		1.7	Debt/Worth	1.7	1.5
			9.8		1.9		3.1	3.2
			37.8		24.8		45.0	40.7
			(13) 17.7		21.1	% Profit Before Taxes/Tangible Net Worth	(48) 30.0	(39) 32.3
			8.4		6.9		13.5	15.3
			19.1		13.3		22.4	20.1
			5.9		8.4	% Profit Before Taxes/Total Assets	11.8	12.1
			4.8		2.3		2.6	3.3
			18.3		10.6		13.0	19.7
			5.3		5.7	Sales/Net Fixed Assets	8.7	8.6
			3.1		4.1		4.5	3.8
			3.0		2.5		3.1	2.7
			2.2		2.2	Sales/Total Assets	2.4	2.1
			1.9		2.1		1.9	1.6
			.9		1.1		1.1	1.3
			1.5		(11) 1.6	% Depr., Dep., Amort./Sales	(43) 1.8	(34) 1.9
			3.7		2.1		2.6	3.2
						% Officers', Directors' Owners' Comp/Sales		
	7102M	**93008M**	**904102M**	**1427783M**	**6104588M**	Net Sales ($)	**6269175M**	**3876283M**
	1896M	**30148M**	**369346M**	**682015M**	**2622116M**	Total Assets ($)	**2653058M**	**1910207M**

M = $ thousand **MM = $ million**

See Pages 9 through 22 for Explanation of Ratios and Data

Comparative Historical Data				Current Data Sorted by Sales					
			Type of Statement						
18	21	16	Unqualified			1			15
10	9	4	Reviewed						4
5	4	4	Compiled				1	1	2
2	3	1	Tax Returns				1		
14	14	24	Other		1		1	2	20
				15 (4/1-9/30/13)		34 (10/1/13-3/31/14)			
4/1/11-3/31/12 ALL	4/1/12-3/31/13 ALL	4/1/13-3/31/14 ALL		0-1MM	1-3MM	3-5MM	5-10MM	10-25MM	25MM & OVER
49	51	49	**NUMBER OF STATEMENTS**		1	1	3	3	41
%	%	%	**ASSETS**	%	%	%	%	%	%
6.5	5.8	6.1	Cash & Equivalents	DATA NOT AVAILABLE					6.6
22.2	20.2	21.8	Trade Receivables (net)						21.1
28.9	28.7	24.4	Inventory						22.9
2.7	2.9	2.7	All Other Current						3.0
60.3	57.6	55.1	Total Current						53.7
31.8	34.8	35.3	Fixed Assets (net)						37.7
3.1	2.3	4.4	Intangibles (net)						3.7
5.1	5.2	5.2	All Other Non-Current						4.9
100.0	100.0	100.0	Total						100.0
			LIABILITIES						
14.2	12.7	7.6	Notes Payable-Short Term						6.9
4.4	2.7	2.1	Cur. Mat.-L.T.D.						1.9
15.1	14.3	12.9	Trade Payables						11.2
.1	.2	.0	Income Taxes Payable						.0
6.9	5.6	6.6	All Other Current						7.4
40.7	35.5	29.2	Total Current						27.4
20.0	20.7	18.6	Long-Term Debt						19.0
.8	.7	1.0	Deferred Taxes						1.2
3.6	5.5	8.5	All Other Non-Current						9.1
35.0	37.6	42.6	Net Worth						43.3
100.0	100.0	100.0	Total Liabilties & Net Worth						100.0
			INCOME DATA						
100.0	100.0	100.0	Net Sales						100.0
20.8	17.5	18.4	Gross Profit						17.1
16.0	13.6	13.4	Operating Expenses						11.5
4.9	4.0	5.0	Operating Profit						5.6
1.0	.7	.6	All Other Expenses (net)						.6
3.9	3.3	4.4	Profit Before Taxes						5.0
			RATIOS						
2.2	2.3	2.7							2.7
1.5	1.5	2.0	Current						2.0
1.1	1.3	1.3							1.4
1.0	1.1	1.3							1.4
.7	.6	1.0	Quick						1.0
.5	.5	.6							.7
25 14.6	25 14.6	25 14.4							25 14.4
33 11.1	34 10.6	31 11.6	Sales/Receivables						31 11.6
42 8.7	41 8.8	40 9.1							38 9.5
29 12.6	39 9.3	26 13.8							27 13.6
58 6.3	49 7.4	41 8.8	Cost of Sales/Inventory						41 8.8
76 4.8	76 4.8	62 5.9							59 6.2
14 27.0	13 28.9	10 34.9							10 37.4
26 14.2	23 16.2	19 19.1	Cost of Sales/Payables						17 21.0
45 8.1	43 8.4	35 10.3							31 11.7
6.9	6.3	7.3							7.3
10.3	11.6	10.6	Sales/Working Capital						10.8
62.7	17.0	15.1							15.1
11.7	14.4	17.7							20.6
(45) 5.1	(50) 6.3	(47) 7.3	EBIT/Interest						(39) 7.8
2.1	2.6	2.4							2.8
7.4	5.7	7.6							7.8
(18) 4.2	(17) 3.9	(14) 4.2	Net Profit + Depr., Dep., Amort./Cur. Mat. L/T/D						(13) 4.2
1.8	2.1	2.1							2.7
.4	.5	.4							.5
.8	.8	.9	Fixed/Worth						.9
1.4	1.8	1.5							1.5
.8	.7	.6							.6
1.7	1.7	1.4	Debt/Worth						1.3
5.6	3.2	2.4							2.0
41.3	35.6	26.9							27.1
(45) 25.8	(47) 19.3	(46) 19.9	% Profit Before Taxes/Tangible Net Worth						(39) 22.4
15.9	11.2	6.8							7.4
14.5	12.4	14.5							16.0
8.8	8.5	7.8	% Profit Before Taxes/Total Assets						7.8
2.2	2.4	2.4							4.3
13.4	13.3	16.0							14.1
6.7	6.2	7.1	Sales/Net Fixed Assets						6.2
4.8	3.9	3.8							3.5
2.7	2.7	3.0							2.8
2.2	2.1	2.2	Sales/Total Assets						2.2
1.7	1.6	1.8							1.8
1.2	1.1	.8							.8
(40) 1.9	(45) 1.6	(43) 1.3	% Depr., Dep., Amort./Sales						(36) 1.5
2.7	3.0	2.2							2.2
.4	.5								
(10) 1.2	(11) 1.5		% Officers', Directors' Owners' Comp/Sales						
2.6	2.1								
5735476M	7524451M	8536583M	Net Sales ($)		1284M	3082M	20968M	44517M	8466732M
2688727M	3309898M	3705521M	Total Assets ($)		783M	4070M	7081M	10998M	3682589M

M = $ thousand MM = $ million

See Pages 9 through 22 for Explanation of Ratios and Data

Current Data Sorted by Assets							Comparative Historical Data	
						Type of Statement		
	1	1	3	4		Unqualified	17	12
	1	4	5			Reviewed	14	16
	1	3				Compiled	9	9
2	2		1			Tax Returns	9	7
2	4	6	5	3		Other	19	27
	16 (4/1-9/30/13)		32 (10/1/13-3/31/14)				4/1/09-3/31/10	4/1/10-3/31/11
0-500M	500M-2MM	2-10MM	10-50MM	50-100MM	100-250MM		ALL	ALL
4	9	14	14	7		NUMBER OF STATEMENTS	68	71
%	%	%	%	%	%	**ASSETS**	%	%
		19.3	12.3		DATA NOT AVAILABLE	Cash & Equivalents	9.3	10.2
		14.6	14.3			Trade Receivables (net)	15.5	16.4
		23.5	30.0			Inventory	29.2	28.4
		4.1	1.6			All Other Current	2.4	4.2
		61.5	58.2			Total Current	56.5	59.2
		31.8	33.7			Fixed Assets (net)	33.0	30.0
		1.8	4.1			Intangibles (net)	5.0	6.0
		5.0	3.9			All Other Non-Current	5.5	4.8
		100.0	100.0			Total	100.0	100.0
						LIABILITIES		
		4.4	9.6			Notes Payable-Short Term	12.1	13.5
		3.3	1.7			Cur. Mat.-L.T.D.	4.5	3.2
		7.0	9.6			Trade Payables	11.1	14.1
		.1	.0			Income Taxes Payable	.3	.2
		9.4	5.0			All Other Current	8.1	9.1
		24.2	26.0			Total Current	36.1	40.1
		13.3	15.7			Long-Term Debt	18.5	20.4
		.3	.9			Deferred Taxes	.7	.9
		17.3	4.5			All Other Non-Current	8.4	9.5
		45.0	52.8			Net Worth	36.3	29.1
		100.0	100.0			Total Liabilities & Net Worth	100.0	100.0
						INCOME DATA		
		100.0	100.0			Net Sales	100.0	100.0
		41.9	29.7			Gross Profit	35.8	35.5
		35.6	22.4			Operating Expenses	33.9	31.3
		6.3	7.3			Operating Profit	2.0	4.2
		1.6	.9			All Other Expenses (net)	1.0	1.0
		4.7	6.4			Profit Before Taxes	1.0	3.2
						RATIOS		
		5.9	4.6				2.6	3.3
		3.2	2.3			Current	1.6	1.6
		1.4	1.8				1.1	1.0
		3.1	2.7				1.4	1.4
		1.8	1.0			Quick	.7	(70) .7
		.7	.5				.3	.4
		10 35.0	**13** 27.3				**12** 30.9	**12** 29.4
		27 13.6	**23** 15.7			Sales/Receivables	**20** 18.5	**24** 15.1
		30 12.0	**40** 9.2				**32** 11.4	**36** 10.1
		51 7.1	**55** 6.6				**39** 9.3	**34** 10.6
		66 5.5	**74** 4.9			Cost of Sales/Inventory	**63** 5.8	**66** 5.5
		83 4.4	**91** 4.0				**107** 3.4	**99** 3.7
		12 31.6	**16** 22.7				**13** 27.7	**11** 31.9
		17 21.9	**21** 17.0			Cost of Sales/Payables	**24** 15.1	**26** 13.9
		27 13.4	**33** 11.0				**39** 9.3	**40** 9.2
		3.2	3.9				6.6	6.1
		5.4	6.9			Sales/Working Capital	12.2	12.9
		19.1	8.9				29.1	180.4
		45.3	27.5				12.6	10.6
		(13) 9.4	(13) 13.8			EBIT/Interest	(64) 1.8	(63) 3.8
		1.8	5.4				.0	1.1
							7.1	5.3
						Net Profit + Depr., Dep., Amort./Cur. Mat. L/T/D	(20) 2.8	(23) 3.5
							1.1	2.2
		.3	.5				.4	.4
		.5	.7			Fixed/Worth	1.1	1.0
		1.9	1.0				4.8	9.7
		.3	.5				.5	.5
		.8	.9			Debt/Worth	1.9	2.2
		2.4	1.9				UND	-107.0
		28.9	37.6				27.7	28.4
		(12) 15.6	(13) 17.1			% Profit Before Taxes/Tangible Net Worth	(52) 11.7	(53) 15.5
		6.5	13.2				-5.3	4.0
		21.5	19.6				12.1	13.6
		9.7	10.2			% Profit Before Taxes/Total Assets	2.6	7.4
		2.5	6.4				-3.6	.2
		14.4	18.5				12.4	15.2
		8.3	5.7			Sales/Net Fixed Assets	7.4	9.4
		5.0	4.0				4.1	5.1
		2.7	2.5				3.0	3.2
		2.2	2.2			Sales/Total Assets	2.1	2.6
		1.7	1.8				1.6	1.7
		1.8	1.1				1.8	1.4
		(13) 2.8	1.9			% Depr., Dep., Amort./Sales	(58) 2.7	(65) 2.2
		4.5	3.7				4.3	3.4
							2.1	1.8
						% Officers', Directors' Owners' Comp/Sales	(21) 4.4	(24) 3.8
							7.2	7.2
4868M	27471M	150619M	664625M	871582M		Net Sales ($)	1894995M	2178954M
1584M	11471M	71247M	313729M	481532M		Total Assets ($)	1025902M	1107593M

M = $ thousand MM = $ million

See Pages 9 through 22 for Explanation of Ratios and Data

Comparative Historical Data				Current Data Sorted by Sales					
			Type of Statement						
14	14	9	Unqualified				1	1	7
19	11	10	Reviewed		1		2	3	4
7	4	4	Compiled		1		2	1	
11	5	5	Tax Returns		2	2			1
19	25	20	Other	1	4	1	3	4	7
				16 (4/1-9/30/13)			32 (10/1/13-3/31/14)		
4/1/11-3/31/12 ALL	**4/1/12-3/31/13 ALL**	**4/1/13-3/31/14 ALL**		**0-1MM**	**1-3MM**	**3-5MM**	**5-10MM**	**10-25MM**	**25MM & OVER**
70	59	48	**NUMBER OF STATEMENTS**	1	8	3	8	9	19
%	%	%	**ASSETS**	%	%	%	%	%	%
12.2	13.2	13.6	Cash & Equivalents						11.0
15.1	15.7	14.9	Trade Receivables (net)						18.5
28.8	31.5	27.6	Inventory						25.3
2.9	2.4	2.8	All Other Current						.9
58.9	62.9	59.0	Total Current						55.8
28.5	27.4	32.3	Fixed Assets (net)						35.4
4.4	4.1	3.7	Intangibles (net)						5.2
8.1	5.6	5.0	All Other Non-Current						3.6
100.0	100.0	100.0	Total						100.0
			LIABILITIES						
10.0	11.6	8.9	Notes Payable-Short Term						9.5
3.0	2.2	2.9	Cur. Mat.-L.T.D.						2.4
11.8	10.2	10.0	Trade Payables						11.7
.3	.2	.1	Income Taxes Payable						.1
9.2	8.7	7.1	All Other Current						6.1
34.2	32.9	29.0	Total Current						29.9
16.7	17.7	24.1	Long-Term Debt						19.2
.8	.6	.5	Deferred Taxes						.8
9.8	8.6	11.6	All Other Non-Current						5.6
38.6	40.1	34.7	Net Worth						44.5
100.0	100.0	100.0	Total Liabilties & Net Worth						100.0
			INCOME DATA						
100.0	100.0	100.0	Net Sales						100.0
36.0	33.7	37.1	Gross Profit						26.1
30.5	27.8	30.0	Operating Expenses						17.6
5.5	5.9	7.1	Operating Profit						8.4
.9	1.2	1.4	All Other Expenses (net)						1.2
4.6	4.7	5.6	Profit Before Taxes						7.3
			RATIOS						
3.7	4.4	4.0							4.0
1.8	2.1	2.3	Current						2.0
1.3	1.4	1.5							1.5
1.9	2.5	2.4							2.0
(68) .9	(58) .9	1.0	Quick						1.0
.5	.5	.5							.5
9 42.9	**14** 26.9	**13** 28.8							**23** 16.2
24 15.2	**23** 16.2	**24** 15.1	Sales/Receivables						**28** 13.2
38 9.6	**39** 9.3	**34** 10.7							**45** 8.1
46 7.9	**47** 7.8	**49** 7.5							**41** 9.0
61 6.0	**70** 5.2	**68** 5.4	Cost of Sales/Inventory						**57** 6.4
91 4.0	**101** 3.6	**96** 3.8							**83** 4.4
11 31.8	**14** 25.9	**13** 27.8							**17** 21.7
19 19.1	**21** 17.5	**21** 17.6	Cost of Sales/Payables						**22** 16.4
37 9.9	**31** 11.7	**32** 11.5							**36** 10.0
5.2	4.6	4.1							4.7
9.9	8.4	7.5	Sales/Working Capital						7.7
28.5	14.0	14.7							10.8
20.0	23.0	40.0							60.3
(63) 4.9	(54) 6.7	(46) 6.9	EBIT/Interest						13.8
1.3	1.8	2.3							5.5
6.7	19.8								
(18) 3.5	(17) 4.9		Net Profit + Depr., Dep., Amort./Cur. Mat. L/T/D						
.8	1.7								
.4	.3	.4							.5
.6	.7	.8	Fixed/Worth						.9
2.2	2.7	3.2							2.2
.4	.4	.5							.5
.8	1.1	1.0	Debt/Worth						.9
5.0	15.5	5.0							4.3
37.1	38.4	36.3							39.6
(57) 17.4	(47) 16.7	(37) 18.5	% Profit Before Taxes/Tangible Net Worth						(17) 23.8
5.7	7.1	13.0							15.7
16.2	15.1	19.2							19.5
6.5	9.6	10.5	% Profit Before Taxes/Total Assets						13.1
1.6	2.1	4.9							7.1
15.4	15.5	14.4							7.8
9.4	8.6	6.6	Sales/Net Fixed Assets						5.0
5.4	5.0	4.5							4.1
2.9	2.9	2.8							2.4
2.4	2.4	2.2	Sales/Total Assets						1.9
1.7	1.7	1.7							1.6
1.3	1.4	1.3							1.5
(64) 2.3	(52) 2.1	(44) 2.0	% Depr., Dep., Amort./Sales						1.9
3.4	2.6	3.6							3.4
2.1	1.5	.8							
(29) 4.8	(18) 2.2	(14) 2.4	% Officers', Directors' Owners' Comp/Sales						
6.6	4.9	2.8							
2541083M	**2740762M**	**1719165M**	Net Sales ($)	**562M**	**14840M**	**11167M**	**59289M**	**138234M**	**1495073M**
1169341M	**1299022M**	**879563M**	Total Assets ($)	**263M**	**7913M**	**2944M**	**30150M**	**66217M**	**772076M**

M = $ thousand MM = $ million

See Pages 9 through 22 for Explanation of Ratios and Data

Current Data Sorted by Assets							Comparative Historical Data	
						Type of Statement		
1		1	6	3	4	Unqualified	23	19
	1	3	6	4		Reviewed	17	12
		3	2			Compiled	3	6
1	2	3	1		1	Tax Returns	8	8
	1	9	13	5	3	Other	16	27
25 (4/1-9/30/13)			48 (10/1/13-3/31/14)				4/1/09-3/31/10	4/1/10-3/31/11
0-500M	**500M-2MM**	**2-10MM**	**10-50MM**	**50-100MM**	**100-250MM**		**ALL**	**ALL**
2	4	19	28	12	8	**NUMBER OF STATEMENTS**	67	72
%	%	%	%	%	%	**ASSETS**	%	%
		6.4	3.9	3.8		Cash & Equivalents	4.8	6.0
		23.5	20.3	12.0		Trade Receivables (net)	17.5	18.3
		30.0	35.3	33.3		Inventory	35.9	34.3
		.5	4.1	2.7		All Other Current	2.7	1.8
		60.4	63.5	51.8		Total Current	61.0	60.4
		26.7	27.1	33.7		Fixed Assets (net)	30.8	29.5
		8.5	5.4	11.2		Intangibles (net)	3.1	4.6
		4.4	4.0	3.2		All Other Non-Current	5.1	5.5
		100.0	100.0	100.0		Total	100.0	100.0
						LIABILITIES		
		14.3	11.8	16.6		Notes Payable-Short Term	16.0	14.0
		4.2	2.2	2.1		Cur. Mat.-L.T.D.	4.9	3.1
		23.8	17.1	7.8		Trade Payables	14.2	15.1
		.0	.2	.1		Income Taxes Payable	.3	.1
		6.7	6.0	4.7		All Other Current	7.1	10.1
		49.0	37.3	31.3		Total Current	42.6	42.4
		23.9	13.0	14.8		Long-Term Debt	18.2	16.6
		.2	1.2	.8		Deferred Taxes	.7	.9
		29.1	5.9	7.9		All Other Non-Current	7.8	9.8
		-2.2	42.7	45.2		Net Worth	30.7	30.3
		100.0	100.0	100.0		Total Liabilties & Net Worth	100.0	100.0
						INCOME DATA		
		100.0	100.0	100.0		Net Sales	100.0	100.0
		35.8	17.5	24.5		Gross Profit	20.1	19.2
		28.5	14.0	12.7		Operating Expenses	14.9	16.9
		7.3	3.5	11.8		Operating Profit	5.2	2.4
		.5	.5	7.5		All Other Expenses (net)	1.4	1.0
		6.8	3.0	4.3		Profit Before Taxes	3.9	1.3
						RATIOS		
		2.1	2.9	2.8			2.0	2.0
		1.2	1.6	1.6		Current	1.4	1.5
		1.0	1.3	1.3			1.1	1.1
		.9	1.0	1.2			1.0	1.0
		.6	.7	.4		Quick	.5	.5
		.4	.4	.4			.3	.3
		22 16.9	**23** 15.6	**21** 17.3			**23** 16.1	**23** 15.6
		26 13.9	**31** 11.6	**26** 14.0		Sales/Receivables	**32** 11.4	**32** 11.4
		31 11.8	**41** 8.8	**34** 10.7			**42** 8.6	**43** 8.5
		17 21.5	**26** 14.1	**48** 7.6			**37** 9.8	**33** 11.0
		56 6.5	**59** 6.2	**99** 3.7		Cost of Sales/Inventory	**89** 4.1	**79** 4.6
		104 3.5	**122** 3.0	**174** 2.1			**164** 2.2	**165** 2.2
		20 18.3	**13** 27.5	**14** 25.7			**15** 25.1	**18** 20.5
		33 11.0	**29** 12.4	**24** 15.3		Cost of Sales/Payables	**31** 11.7	**29** 12.5
		40 9.1	**39** 9.4	**45** 8.2			**47** 7.8	**48** 7.7
		9.8	3.9	4.1			5.7	5.2
		32.7	10.2	6.8		Sales/Working Capital	10.6	13.2
		-56.4	18.0	21.1			47.3	88.1
		24.6	12.9	10.4			10.6	9.8
		(18) 7.4	(26) 3.9	4.1		EBIT/Interest	(66) 3.2	(69) 3.2
		1.7	1.7	2.1			1.5	.1
							3.6	7.4
						Net Profit + Depr., Dep., Amort./Cur. Mat. L/T/D	(21) 1.6	(27) 2.5
							1.2	.5
		.6	.3	.9			.5	.5
		1.3	.6	1.0		Fixed/Worth	1.0	1.0
		-.7	1.2	1.4			2.0	3.0
		2.0	.6	1.0			1.0	1.0
		3.2	1.6	1.6		Debt/Worth	2.4	2.2
		-4.3	3.2	2.4			9.7	7.9
		146.8	26.8	38.5			55.7	36.1
		(13) 62.9	(26) 12.7	(11) 9.6		% Profit Before Taxes/Tangible Net Worth	(58) 16.6	(60) 12.3
		.8	4.0	4.8			6.6	-.8
		29.6	10.4	10.5			13.8	9.8
		13.9	5.0	3.0		% Profit Before Taxes/Total Assets	5.3	3.9
		-.1	1.3	1.7			1.5	-2.3
		201.9	18.7	14.4			10.7	13.2
		14.6	8.8	4.9		Sales/Net Fixed Assets	6.3	6.8
		6.5	4.3	2.7			2.8	3.9
		4.3	3.2	1.8			2.9	3.0
		3.1	2.0	1.5		Sales/Total Assets	1.5	1.7
		1.7	1.1	1.2			1.1	1.1
		.9	1.0	2.1			1.6	1.4
		(11) 1.8	(26) 2.1	(10) 3.2		% Depr., Dep., Amort./Sales	(59) 2.5	(64) 2.5
		2.2	4.4	5.0			3.8	4.1
						% Officers', Directors' Owners' Comp/Sales		
2166M	33994M	289135M	1685821M	1192862M	2269210M	Net Sales ($)	5433830M	5175738M
816M	5852M	78988M	764957M	781375M	1503535M	Total Assets ($)	3349830M	3475145M

M = $ thousand MM = $ million

See Pages 9 through 22 for Explanation of Ratios and Data

Comparative Historical Data				Current Data Sorted by Sales					
			Type of Statement						
20	18	15	Unqualified	1				2	12
19	14	14	Reviewed		1	1	1	2	9
2	3	5	Compiled		1	1		2	1
10	5	8	Tax Returns		1	1	2	2	2
24	31	31	Other			1	1	8	21
4/1/11-3/31/12 ALL	**4/1/12-3/31/13 ALL**	**4/1/13-3/31/14 ALL**		**25 (4/1-9/30/13)**			**48 (10/1/13-3/31/14)**		
				0-1MM	**1-3MM**	**3-5MM**	**5-10MM**	**10-25MM**	**25MM & OVER**
75	71	73	**NUMBER OF STATEMENTS**	1	3	4	4	16	45
%	%	%	**ASSETS**	%	%	%	%	%	%
4.9	6.6	4.7	Cash & Equivalents					7.7	3.0
20.8	20.2	18.7	Trade Receivables (net)					24.1	17.7
34.5	31.8	32.0	Inventory					22.8	36.0
2.1	3.0	3.0	All Other Current					.3	3.8
62.3	61.6	58.5	Total Current					54.9	60.5
27.3	29.1	29.4	Fixed Assets (net)					35.2	28.0
4.8	3.8	7.4	Intangibles (net)					3.0	8.2
5.6	5.5	4.7	All Other Non-Current					6.9	3.4
100.0	100.0	100.0	Total					100.0	100.0
			LIABILITIES						
13.9	13.6	11.8	Notes Payable-Short Term					8.6	12.1
2.9	2.6	2.6	Cur. Mat.-L.T.D.					3.2	2.0
18.4	15.8	16.1	Trade Payables					23.8	13.7
.3	.1	.1	Income Taxes Payable					.0	.1
9.1	8.3	6.9	All Other Current					6.9	6.4
44.5	40.4	37.4	Total Current					42.5	34.3
16.1	14.2	18.1	Long-Term Debt					24.3	14.9
1.1	1.3	1.3	Deferred Taxes					.2	1.9
8.7	7.0	11.6	All Other Non-Current					31.9	6.2
29.7	37.1	31.6	Net Worth					1.1	42.8
100.0	100.0	100.0	Total Liabilties & Net Worth					100.0	100.0
			INCOME DATA						
100.0	100.0	100.0	Net Sales					100.0	100.0
21.0	21.5	23.3	Gross Profit					32.2	18.4
16.9	14.8	17.1	Operating Expenses					20.9	12.7
4.1	6.8	6.2	Operating Profit					11.2	5.6
.5	.8	1.6	All Other Expenses (net)					.5	2.6
3.6	6.0	4.6	Profit Before Taxes					10.8	3.0
			RATIOS						
2.0	2.1	2.4						2.6	3.0
1.4	1.5	1.6	Current					1.3	1.6
1.1	1.2	1.1						.7	1.3
.9	1.2	1.0						1.3	1.0
.5	.6	.6	Quick					.7	.6
.4	.4	.4						.5	.4
23 15.6	**24** 15.4	**21** 17.7						**21** 17.8	**21** 17.5
30 12.1	**30** 12.0	**26** 13.8	Sales/Receivables					**26** 14.0	**26** 13.8
40 9.2	**40** 9.2	**37** 9.9						**28** 12.9	**41** 8.9
26 14.3	**27** 13.7	**23** 15.6						**14** 26.3	**35** 10.5
79 4.6	**81** 4.5	**70** 5.2	Cost of Sales/Inventory					**38** 9.6	**85** 4.3
152 2.4	**114** 3.2	**122** 3.0						**61** 6.0	**135** 2.7
23 15.8	**15** 24.8	**13** 27.8						**25** 14.4	**13** 27.8
35 10.5	**28** 13.0	**28** 13.1	Cost of Sales/Payables					**33** 10.9	**23** 15.7
48 7.6	**42** 8.6	**37** 9.8						**39** 9.3	**36** 10.1
5.3	5.7	4.4						8.3	3.8
16.8	10.5	11.2	Sales/Working Capital					29.2	9.3
66.0	25.2	62.5						-30.2	20.2
11.1	17.2	15.1						76.9	12.1
(73) 4.7	(67) 8.2	(69) 4.4	EBIT/Interest					7.7	(43) 4.0
2.0	2.7	1.9						2.9	2.5
5.6	3.2	5.1							5.6
(20) 3.2	(19) 2.5	(16) 2.1	Net Profit + Depr., Dep., Amort./Cur. Mat. L/T/D						(12) 3.1
1.2	2.1	1.2							1.5
.5	.5	.4						.7	.4
1.0	.7	.9	Fixed/Worth					1.1	.7
2.5	1.5	1.7						NM	1.3
1.2	.9	.7						1.2	.7
2.6	1.8	1.9	Debt/Worth					1.9	1.7
10.8	3.4	5.8						NM	3.1
32.4	42.5	42.6						170.4	25.2
(64) 17.2	(64) 22.6	(62) 13.2	% Profit Before Taxes/Tangible Net Worth					(12) 94.3	(40) 12.4
9.1	11.5	4.0						31.9	4.9
10.8	18.4	14.0						57.8	10.0
4.6	8.6	5.7	% Profit Before Taxes/Total Assets					17.1	5.3
1.6	3.2	1.3						6.8	1.8
20.2	13.9	25.1						149.2	17.3
8.5	7.0	8.0	Sales/Net Fixed Assets					8.0	8.0
4.6	4.5	4.3						3.5	4.4
3.2	2.7	3.4						4.7	2.7
1.8	1.7	1.8	Sales/Total Assets					3.4	1.7
1.2	1.4	1.3						1.7	1.3
1.0	1.0	1.5						1.0	1.2
(67) 1.9	(57) 1.9	(54) 2.2	% Depr., Dep., Amort./Sales					(12) 2.1	(36) 2.2
3.1	3.4	4.1						3.3	3.8
1.3		.4							
(11) 2.3		(18) 1.4	% Officers', Directors' Owners' Comp/Sales						
2.6		3.1							
6582096M	7615147M	5473188M	Net Sales ($)	400M	6883M	14967M	35170M	236915M	5178853M
3626936M	3996586M	3135523M	Total Assets ($)	329M	4335M	10758M	15453M	100021M	3004627M

M = $ thousand MM = $ million

See Pages 9 through 22 for Explanation of Ratios and Data

Current Data Sorted by Assets							Comparative Historical Data	
						Type of Statement		
		3	8	4	3	Unqualified	20	19
		1	7			Reviewed	15	10
			3			Compiled	6	7
1	1	1	1			Tax Returns	5	6
	2	9	14	3	2	Other	34	26
19 (4/1-9/30/13)			44 (10/1/13-3/31/14)				4/1/09-3/31/10	4/1/10-3/31/11
0-500M	500M-2MM	2-10MM	10-50MM	50-100MM	100-250MM		ALL	ALL
1	3	14	33	7	5	**NUMBER OF STATEMENTS**	80	68
%	%	%	%	%	%	**ASSETS**	%	%
		11.5	9.1			Cash & Equivalents	7.1	5.8
		16.8	17.9			Trade Receivables (net)	19.4	21.0
		18.7	18.3			Inventory	19.8	18.4
		1.5	2.7			All Other Current	1.6	2.1
		48.5	48.0			Total Current	47.9	47.4
		44.5	38.3			Fixed Assets (net)	37.2	36.7
		2.3	8.8			Intangibles (net)	10.1	11.2
		4.6	4.9			All Other Non-Current	4.9	4.7
		100.0	100.0			Total	100.0	100.0
						LIABILITIES		
		6.2	3.7			Notes Payable-Short Term	7.6	5.5
		3.9	4.1			Cur. Mat.-L.T.D.	3.5	2.8
		16.3	11.4			Trade Payables	14.1	14.7
		.3	.0			Income Taxes Payable	.2	.3
		5.9	8.0			All Other Current	11.6	8.1
		32.7	27.3			Total Current	37.1	31.5
		21.5	17.3			Long-Term Debt	22.1	22.1
		.6	1.5			Deferred Taxes	.8	1.1
		12.2	3.0			All Other Non-Current	3.8	11.9
		33.0	51.0			Net Worth	36.2	33.4
		100.0	100.0			Total Liabilties & Net Worth	100.0	100.0
						INCOME DATA		
		100.0	100.0			Net Sales	100.0	100.0
		29.0	26.8			Gross Profit	25.4	27.1
		25.7	21.4			Operating Expenses	20.2	21.4
		3.3	5.3			Operating Profit	5.2	5.7
		2.0	-.3			All Other Expenses (net)	1.2	1.0
		1.3	5.6			Profit Before Taxes	4.0	4.8
						RATIOS		
		2.6	2.5				2.2	2.4
		1.4	1.9			Current	1.5	1.6
		.8	1.2				.9	1.2
		1.5	1.7				1.2	1.3
		.8	1.0			Quick	.7	.8
		.3	.5				.5	.6
		13 27.5	**21** 17.7				**19** 19.6	**22** 16.5
		19 18.9	**26** 13.8			Sales/Receivables	**25** 14.8	**27** 13.7
		25 14.6	**33** 11.2				**34** 10.7	**34** 10.7
		22 16.5	**28** 13.0				**24** 15.0	**23** 15.9
		38 9.7	**38** 9.7			Cost of Sales/Inventory	**35** 10.3	**32** 11.5
		55 6.6	**48** 7.6				**54** 6.7	**57** 6.4
		19 19.7	**13** 27.4				**16** 23.3	**15** 23.8
		33 11.0	**23** 16.2			Cost of Sales/Payables	**23** 16.1	**22** 16.6
		43 8.4	**31** 11.8				**33** 11.1	**35** 10.4
		10.4	8.2				8.7	8.3
		36.2	13.6			Sales/Working Capital	16.7	15.5
		-36.1	63.8				-69.6	54.8
		14.9	30.1				15.3	14.5
		(13) 7.3	(31) 8.9			EBIT/Interest	(75) 5.0	(66) 6.6
		-1.9	2.1				1.7	1.2
							5.4	6.5
						Net Profit + Depr., Dep., Amort./Cur. Mat. L/T/D	(23) 2.4	(27) 3.6
							1.7	2.0
		.6	.4				.6	.6
		1.6	1.0			Fixed/Worth	1.2	1.1
		-8.8	2.1				2.8	3.9
		.7	.5				.9	.6
		1.7	1.1			Debt/Worth	2.0	1.6
		-14.9	2.9				7.7	8.5
		45.0	51.2				57.9	55.1
		(10) 21.3	(30) 18.3			% Profit Before Taxes/Tangible Net Worth	(67) 32.9	(54) 25.1
		-31.0	9.2				12.4	8.0
		26.9	23.2				17.8	18.2
		9.4	8.1			% Profit Before Taxes/Total Assets	8.1	8.1
		-8.6	2.2				2.5	1.4
		11.5	15.9				14.2	11.7
		7.6	5.7			Sales/Net Fixed Assets	7.1	6.1
		4.5	3.6				3.8	4.0
		3.4	2.9				3.3	3.1
		3.1	2.3			Sales/Total Assets	2.5	2.3
		2.3	1.7				1.6	1.7
		1.5	1.5				1.4	1.7
		(12) 2.3	(31) 2.7			% Depr., Dep., Amort./Sales	(63) 2.3	(65) 2.5
		3.3	4.0				4.0	4.0
							1.7	1.6
						% Officers', Directors' Owners' Comp/Sales	(16) 3.2	(15) 3.2
							3.8	9.2
4311M	9742M	215726M	1844357M	1108099M	1414538M	Net Sales ($)	5440240M	4167097M
408M	3382M	72545M	772160M	563415M	789259M	Total Assets ($)	2472449M	2028724M

M = $ thousand MM = $ million

See Pages 9 through 22 for Explanation of Ratios and Data

Comparative Historical Data | **Current Data Sorted by Sales**

4/1/11-3/31/12 ALL	4/1/12-3/31/13 ALL	4/1/13-3/31/14 ALL	Type of Statement	0-1MM	1-3MM	3-5MM	5-10MM	10-25MM	25MM & OVER
16	13	18	Unqualified				1	3	14
14	15	8	Reviewed					2	6
7	6	3	Compiled						3
6	4	4	Tax Returns		1	1		1	1
32	39	30	Other		2		3	8	17
					19 (4/1-9/30/13)		44 (10/1/13-3/31/14)		
75	77	63	**NUMBER OF STATEMENTS**		3	1	4	14	41
%	%	%	**ASSETS**	%	%	%	%	%	%
6.2	6.5	9.2	Cash & Equivalents	D				6.6	8.9
22.5	19.6	18.0	Trade Receivables (net)	A				15.5	19.1
18.7	19.7	18.6	Inventory	T				16.9	20.0
2.0	3.0	2.2	All Other Current	A				.7	2.6
49.4	48.8	47.9	Total Current					39.7	50.6
36.8	36.6	39.2	Fixed Assets (net)	N				43.8	36.8
9.1	9.7	7.4	Intangibles (net)	O				12.0	6.7
4.7	4.9	5.4	All Other Non-Current	T				4.6	5.9
100.0	100.0	100.0	Total					100.0	100.0
			LIABILITIES	A					
8.5	7.6	4.7	Notes Payable-Short Term	V				7.4	3.1
4.1	3.3	4.0	Cur. Mat.-L.T.D.	A				4.0	4.3
15.8	14.4	12.7	Trade Payables	I				16.1	11.5
.1	.2	.1	Income Taxes Payable	L				.0	.1
7.9	8.3	8.5	All Other Current	A				6.1	8.4
36.4	33.8	30.1	Total Current	B				33.6	27.3
15.4	17.2	18.9	Long-Term Debt	L				25.3	16.7
.5	1.1	.9	Deferred Taxes	E				.9	1.1
5.0	6.1	5.5	All Other Non-Current					6.4	3.3
42.7	41.9	44.5	Net Worth					33.8	51.6
100.0	100.0	100.0	Total Liabilties & Net Worth					100.0	100.0
			INCOME DATA						
100.0	100.0	100.0	Net Sales					100.0	100.0
27.1	26.8	26.2	Gross Profit					29.0	24.4
23.1	21.5	22.0	Operating Expenses					26.0	18.9
4.0	5.3	4.3	Operating Profit					3.0	5.5
1.0	.7	.4	All Other Expenses (net)					-.1	.3
3.0	4.6	3.9	Profit Before Taxes					3.1	5.2
			RATIOS						
2.3	2.4	2.5						2.0	2.5
1.4	1.5	1.8	Current					1.1	2.0
1.0	1.1	1.0						.8	1.3
1.3	1.3	1.5						1.2	1.7
.7	.9	.9	Quick					.5	1.0
.5	.5	.5						.3	.6
22 16.8	**21** 17.7	**21** 17.7						**13** 27.5	**22** 16.6
28 12.9	**27** 13.6	**25** 14.5	Sales/Receivables					**19** 18.9	**27** 13.5
36 10.2	**34** 10.8	**33** 11.1						**29** 12.5	**35** 10.4
23 15.9	**24** 15.3	**28** 13.2						**22** 16.5	**29** 12.7
33 11.2	**37** 9.9	**39** 9.4	Cost of Sales/Inventory					**38** 9.5	**38** 9.7
51 7.1	**55** 6.6	**49** 7.5						**51** 7.1	**48** 7.6
18 20.6	**17** 21.6	**14** 25.3						**15** 25.0	**12** 29.9
25 14.8	**26** 13.8	**23** 15.6	Cost of Sales/Payables					**34** 10.6	**23** 16.2
36 10.0	**35** 10.3	**39** 9.4						**43** 8.4	**31** 11.6
9.1	9.3	7.9						17.0	6.6
16.7	14.7	14.6	Sales/Working Capital					90.5	10.7
-999.8	65.5	-316.5						-33.4	20.0
16.4	21.1	16.9						13.9	28.4
(72) 3.6	(72) 6.0	(59) 5.6	EBIT/Interest					4.7	(39) 8.1
.5	2.4	.8						-1.7	2.4
6.1	4.5	7.2							8.0
(24) 2.0	(22) 3.4	(19) 3.1	Net Profit + Depr., Dep., Amort./Cur. Mat. L/T/D						(17) 3.1
.7	1.8	1.2							.9
.6	.6	.5						1.4	.5
1.1	1.2	1.2	Fixed/Worth					2.6	.8
2.1	2.0	2.7						-7.0	1.6
.7	.7	.6						1.6	.5
1.6	1.6	1.6	Debt/Worth					3.3	.8
4.6	3.2	3.8						-13.9	2.3
31.9	35.6	36.1						54.7	30.6
(65) 18.0	(64) 22.0	(53) 17.4	% Profit Before Taxes/Tangible Net Worth					(10) 12.1	(37) 18.3
-.8	9.8	5.6						-31.0	8.8
13.4	16.1	19.3						26.9	18.4
4.0	8.0	7.5	% Profit Before Taxes/Total Assets					5.1	8.0
-.7	2.6	-.4						-6.8	2.3
12.9	13.3	10.1						10.5	9.6
5.5	6.8	6.7	Sales/Net Fixed Assets					5.9	6.7
4.0	4.3	3.9						3.4	4.2
3.6	3.0	3.2						3.4	2.9
2.3	2.4	2.4	Sales/Total Assets					2.8	2.1
1.6	1.8	1.7						1.6	1.8
1.4	1.5	1.6						2.1	1.6
(69) 2.5	(68) 2.4	(57) 2.7	% Depr., Dep., Amort./Sales					(11) 2.7	(38) 2.7
3.7	3.3	3.9						4.8	3.4
1.1	.7								
(16) 2.9	(15) 2.6		% Officers', Directors' Owners' Comp/Sales						
5.6	4.2								
4852933M	5911089M	4596773M	Net Sales ($)		6177M	4311M	29885M	254997M	4301403M
2117846M	2807839M	2201169M	Total Assets ($)		4648M	408M	15998M	115612M	2064503M

M = $ thousand MM = $ million

See Pages 9 through 22 for Explanation of Ratios and Data

Current Data Sorted by Assets / Comparative Historical Data

0-500M	500M-2MM	2-10MM	10-50MM	50-100MM	100-250MM	Type of Statement	4/1/09-3/31/10 ALL	4/1/10-3/31/11 ALL
	1	4	8	1	8	Unqualified	26	31
1	1	11	5	2		Reviewed	13	11
	1	4	2			Compiled	5	9
3	2					Tax Returns	6	7
1	2	8	11	6	9	Other	35	38
	27 (4/1-9/30/13)		64 (10/1/13-3/31/14)					
5	7	27	26	9	17	NUMBER OF STATEMENTS	85	96
%	%	%	%	%	%	**ASSETS**	%	%
		8.8	3.9		.7	Cash & Equivalents	5.5	5.2
		21.2	16.7		11.3	Trade Receivables (net)	17.2	15.6
		29.5	30.5		38.0	Inventory	36.4	34.3
		1.4	2.4		4.5	All Other Current	2.7	3.1
		60.9	53.5		54.5	Total Current	61.8	58.2
		30.6	35.5		30.8	Fixed Assets (net)	30.7	31.3
		5.0	7.7		10.8	Intangibles (net)	3.1	5.6
		3.4	3.3		4.0	All Other Non-Current	4.4	4.9
		100.0	100.0		100.0	Total	100.0	100.0
						LIABILITIES		
		13.3	11.1		16.9	Notes Payable-Short Term	13.3	14.2
		3.8	3.6		3.0	Cur. Mat.-L.T.D.	2.3	2.6
		14.5	10.8		10.9	Trade Payables	13.3	12.8
		.1	.1		.0	Income Taxes Payable	.3	.3
		8.2	6.7		8.5	All Other Current	8.3	6.9
		39.9	32.3		39.4	Total Current	37.6	36.7
		15.9	15.1		13.5	Long-Term Debt	16.7	16.6
		1.2	1.3		1.6	Deferred Taxes	.6	.5
		1.1	7.3		4.9	All Other Non-Current	5.4	5.6
		42.0	43.9		40.6	Net Worth	39.6	40.5
		100.0	100.0		100.0	Total Liabilties & Net Worth	100.0	100.0
						INCOME DATA		
		100.0	100.0		100.0	Net Sales	100.0	100.0
		23.1	23.8		11.9	Gross Profit	22.6	25.1
		20.5	17.8		9.5	Operating Expenses	15.2	18.3
		2.6	5.9		2.4	Operating Profit	7.4	6.7
		.8	.8		.6	All Other Expenses (net)	1.2	1.3
		1.8	5.1		1.8	Profit Before Taxes	6.2	5.5
						RATIOS		
		2.6	2.3		1.9		2.4	2.3
		1.5	1.7		1.4	Current	1.7	1.6
		1.2	1.4		1.0		1.2	1.2
		1.2	.9		.5		.9	.9
		.7	.5		.4	Quick	.5	.5
		.3	.3		.2		.4	.3
		19 19.3	**23** 15.8		**22** 16.9		**22** 16.3	**20** 17.9
		30 12.2	**29** 12.6		**28** 13.1	Sales/Receivables	**28** 12.9	**29** 12.8
		34 10.7	**41** 8.9		**36** 10.2		**37** 9.7	**35** 10.6
		29 12.5	**45** 8.2		**63** 5.8		**51** 7.2	**45** 8.2
		47 7.7	**74** 4.9		**118** 3.1	Cost of Sales/Inventory	**82** 4.4	**68** 5.3
		96 3.8	**152** 2.4		**159** 2.3		**156** 2.3	**138** 2.6
		15 24.9	**18** 19.9		**13** 28.7		**16** 22.4	**16** 23.4
		24 15.5	**26** 13.8		**23** 15.8	Cost of Sales/Payables	**24** 15.5	**24** 15.4
		38 9.6	**41** 8.9		**34** 10.7		**38** 9.6	**42** 8.7
		6.4	4.7		4.3		5.1	5.5
		13.3	7.4		7.2	Sales/Working Capital	8.2	9.5
		36.4	20.7		-772.5		27.5	25.6
		8.1	12.8		3.6		15.9	18.3
		(22) 2.5	(24) 7.4		(16) 2.5	EBIT/Interest	(80) 4.8	(88) 5.6
		.9	2.5		.8		2.5	2.4
		4.9	5.9		4.1		9.7	8.0
		(10) 3.5	(12) 3.9		(10) 2.2	Net Profit + Depr., Dep., Amort./Cur. Mat. L/T/D	(32) 4.6	(42) 4.9
		.5	1.8		1.0		2.6	2.4
		.2	.5		.6		.5	.5
		1.0	.9		.8	Fixed/Worth	.8	.9
		1.5	1.4		7.9		1.5	2.2
		1.2	.8		.9		.8	.7
		1.7	1.2		1.8	Debt/Worth	1.3	1.8
		3.2	2.9		21.5		3.0	4.3
		21.8	26.7		13.4		37.6	42.6
		(25) 7.2	(22) 15.5		(15) 5.1	% Profit Before Taxes/Tangible Net Worth	(76) 24.2	(83) 25.0
		1.4	11.9		.6		15.4	9.4
		7.2	13.6		4.5		17.3	17.7
		1.9	9.2		2.7	% Profit Before Taxes/Total Assets	9.9	7.8
		.8	3.3		.0		3.7	2.6
		15.2	8.2		5.8		13.2	11.9
		7.8	4.0		5.4	Sales/Net Fixed Assets	5.8	6.0
		4.8	3.4		4.4		3.6	3.6
		3.0	2.1		1.8		2.8	2.6
		2.2	1.7		1.3	Sales/Total Assets	1.9	1.9
		1.7	1.2		1.1		1.4	1.3
		1.0	2.2		2.1		1.1	1.5
		(25) 1.8	(24) 2.7		(14) 2.6	% Depr., Dep., Amort./Sales	(73) 2.0	(88) 2.2
		2.9	3.9		3.5		3.1	3.3
							.7	1.4
						% Officers', Directors' Owners' Comp/Sales	(20) 2.0	(16) 3.0
							3.8	5.5
7140M	28496M	328781M	1156962M	1209949M	3968142M	Net Sales ($)	7247976M	7407839M
1464M	8417M	141276M	715590M	702125M	2798289M	Total Assets ($)	3918140M	4149461M

M = $ thousand MM = $ million

See Pages 9 through 22 for Explanation of Ratios and Data

Comparative Historical Data				Current Data Sorted by Sales					
			Type of Statement						
25	23	22	Unqualified		1	1	1	4	15
12	18	20	Reviewed	1		2	2	9	6
8	12	7	Compiled	1		1	1	2	2
5	7	5	Tax Returns		4	1			
36	41	37	Other	1	1	2	2	7	24
					27 (4/1-9/30/13)			64 (10/1/13-3/31/14)	
4/1/11-3/31/12 ALL	4/1/12-3/31/13 ALL	4/1/13-3/31/14 ALL		0-1MM	1-3MM	3-5MM	5-10MM	10-25MM	25MM & OVER
86	101	91	**NUMBER OF STATEMENTS**	3	6	7	6	22	47
%	%	%	**ASSETS**	%	%	%	%	%	%
4.3	5.9	5.6	Cash & Equivalents					7.5	3.2
18.2	18.0	16.8	Trade Receivables (net)					24.3	14.1
30.9	33.7	31.7	Inventory					28.6	32.2
4.2	3.0	2.8	All Other Current					1.1	3.9
57.5	60.6	56.8	Total Current					61.5	53.3
32.8	30.8	32.5	Fixed Assets (net)					28.7	35.7
4.8	3.8	6.7	Intangibles (net)					6.0	7.5
4.9	4.9	3.9	All Other Non-Current					3.7	3.6
100.0	100.0	100.0	Total					100.0	100.0
			LIABILITIES						
12.9	12.6	14.6	Notes Payable-Short Term					13.3	13.3
2.6	4.8	3.2	Cur. Mat.-L.T.D.					2.8	3.3
16.1	15.2	12.5	Trade Payables					16.6	11.0
.3	.2	.2	Income Taxes Payable					.0	.2
8.8	7.0	7.8	All Other Current					4.6	8.3
40.6	39.8	38.2	Total Current					37.4	36.1
24.3	17.2	18.1	Long-Term Debt					15.0	16.8
1.0	1.0	1.1	Deferred Taxes					1.0	1.4
5.7	3.3	4.1	All Other Non-Current					6.1	4.4
28.4	38.6	38.4	Net Worth					40.5	41.3
100.0	100.0	100.0	Total Liabilties & Net Worth					100.0	100.0
			INCOME DATA						
100.0	100.0	100.0	Net Sales					100.0	100.0
22.2	22.9	22.7	Gross Profit					20.3	20.0
18.0	18.0	18.4	Operating Expenses					17.4	15.3
4.3	4.9	4.3	Operating Profit					3.0	4.7
1.0	.8	.8	All Other Expenses (net)					.5	.8
3.3	4.1	3.4	Profit Before Taxes					2.5	3.9
			RATIOS						
2.3	2.3	2.3						2.3	1.9
1.5	1.5	1.5	Current					1.6	1.4
1.1	1.1	1.2						1.2	1.1
.8	.9	.8						1.3	.7
.6	.5	.5	Quick					.7	.5
.4	.3	.3						.4	.3
21 17.1	**19** 19.1	**21** 17.4						**22** 16.4	**22** 16.8
26 13.9	**26** 14.0	**29** 12.7	Sales/Receivables					**26** 14.3	**29** 12.7
35 10.5	**36** 10.0	**38** 9.7						**34** 10.7	**41** 9.0
35 10.5	**46** 7.9	**38** 9.7						**27** 13.4	**59** 6.2
63 5.8	**72** 5.1	**72** 5.1	Cost of Sales/Inventory					**42** 8.6	**89** 4.1
118 3.1	**135** 2.7	**118** 3.1						**66** 5.5	**140** 2.6
17 21.8	**16** 22.8	**15** 24.9						**16** 22.2	**17** 21.7
29 12.7	**28** 13.2	**24** 15.1	Cost of Sales/Payables					**33** 11.1	**24** 15.4
47 7.8	**46** 8.0	**41** 9.0						**41** 8.9	**41** 9.0
5.8	4.9	5.5						6.2	5.4
10.3	10.1	9.3	Sales/Working Capital					12.3	9.1
49.7	71.3	40.8						37.7	40.8
9.9	10.4	9.1						9.7	9.1
(83) 4.1	(91) 3.8	(79) 2.8	EBIT/Interest					(17) 3.2	(45) 3.4
1.4	1.7	1.6						1.4	1.6
5.6	5.1	5.9							5.8
(40) 3.7	(42) 2.1	(37) 3.1	Net Profit + Depr., Dep., Amort./Cur. Mat. L/T/D						(24) 2.5
1.7	1.1	1.5							1.5
.6	.4	.5						.2	.6
1.1	.8	.9	Fixed/Worth					1.0	1.0
3.5	1.7	1.7						1.6	1.9
1.0	.8	.8						1.1	.8
2.0	1.7	1.6	Debt/Worth					2.0	1.4
8.2	4.3	3.4						3.1	2.9
33.6	31.1	26.8						41.2	25.2
(73) 18.0	(89) 15.5	(81) 13.3	% Profit Before Taxes/Tangible Net Worth					(21) 10.3	(42) 13.5
4.8	6.4	4.6						2.3	4.3
10.4	12.5	10.9						13.0	10.5
5.7	5.7	5.3	% Profit Before Taxes/Total Assets					3.5	6.0
.7	1.8	1.6						1.1	1.9
10.1	12.8	9.9						21.2	6.0
5.3	5.6	5.6	Sales/Net Fixed Assets					10.7	4.7
4.0	3.6	3.8						4.7	3.4
2.6	2.8	2.4						3.4	2.0
1.9	1.8	1.8	Sales/Total Assets					2.3	1.6
1.3	1.3	1.2						1.9	1.2
1.4	1.1	1.5						1.0	2.2
(73) 2.3	(85) 2.2	(78) 2.5	% Depr., Dep., Amort./Sales					(19) 1.4	(42) 2.7
3.0	3.2	3.5						2.8	3.8
.9	.5	1.1							
(16) 1.6	(22) 1.3	(17) 2.2	% Officers', Directors' Owners' Comp/Sales						
3.3	4.4	4.4							
7363803M	**7819477M**	**6699470M**	Net Sales ($)	**1016M**	**12295M**	**27136M**	**48604M**	**367398M**	**6243021M**
4375685M	**4791294M**	**4367161M**	Total Assets ($)	**1177M**	**4917M**	**22162M**	**24775M**	**153680M**	**4160450M**

M = $ thousand MM = $ million

See Pages 9 through 22 for Explanation of Ratios and Data

Current Data Sorted by Assets							Comparative Historical Data	
						Type of Statement		
		2	6	3	3	Unqualified	14	15
	2	2	4			Reviewed	8	6
	1					Compiled	3	3
1	2					Tax Returns	3	1
		3	2	1	2	Other	16	15
	13 (4/1-9/30/13)		21 (10/1/13-3/31/14)				4/1/09-3/31/10	4/1/10-3/31/11
0-500M	500M-2MM	2-10MM	10-50MM	50-100MM	100-250MM		ALL	ALL
1	5	7	12	4	5	**NUMBER OF STATEMENTS**	44	40
%	%	%	%	%	%	**ASSETS**	%	%
			4.1			Cash & Equivalents	5.3	6.0
			18.4			Trade Receivables (net)	19.3	17.9
			44.3			Inventory	41.7	33.2
			1.9			All Other Current	2.0	3.3
			68.6			Total Current	68.2	60.4
			24.5			Fixed Assets (net)	21.2	27.1
			2.0			Intangibles (net)	3.1	4.8
			4.8			All Other Non-Current	7.5	7.7
			100.0			Total	100.0	100.0
						LIABILITIES		
			24.4			Notes Payable-Short Term	15.3	17.5
			4.2			Cur. Mat.-L.T.D.	2.6	2.2
			14.5			Trade Payables	16.6	14.7
			.7			Income Taxes Payable	.5	.6
			6.6			All Other Current	6.0	5.9
			50.3			Total Current	41.0	40.9
			12.6			Long-Term Debt	14.2	10.6
			.2			Deferred Taxes	.4	.5
			2.5			All Other Non-Current	4.6	8.0
			34.3			Net Worth	39.8	40.0
			100.0			Total Liabilties & Net Worth	100.0	100.0
						INCOME DATA		
			100.0			Net Sales	100.0	100.0
			22.2			Gross Profit	26.4	27.4
			16.4			Operating Expenses	20.7	20.5
			5.8			Operating Profit	5.8	6.9
			1.2			All Other Expenses (net)	1.3	.7
			4.6			Profit Before Taxes	4.5	6.2
						RATIOS		
			1.8				2.3	2.3
			1.3			Current	1.5	1.4
			1.1				1.2	1.2
			.7				1.0	1.1
			.4			Quick	.5	.6
			.3				.3	.3
			29 12.6				28 12.9	19 19.1
			35 10.4			Sales/Receivables	36 10.0	38 9.6
			52 7.0				42 8.7	48 7.6
			89 4.1				58 6.3	40 9.1
			122 3.0			Cost of Sales/Inventory	129 2.8	97 3.7
			215 1.7				177 2.1	131 2.8
			25 14.4				17 21.9	16 22.3
			32 11.5			Cost of Sales/Payables	28 13.0	30 12.2
			41 8.8				83 4.4	51 7.2
			6.7				4.5	5.0
			15.6			Sales/Working Capital	8.8	9.7
			19.2				16.9	30.1
			17.6				33.1	35.6
			8.3			EBIT/Interest	(43) 5.5	5.5
			2.7				1.7	1.3
							10.6	5.3
						Net Profit + Depr., Dep., Amort./Cur. Mat. L/T/D	(15) 3.2	(13) 2.2
							1.8	-.4
			.2				.2	.4
			1.0			Fixed/Worth	.5	.8
			1.2				1.0	1.7
			1.1				.8	.8
			3.0			Debt/Worth	2.1	2.3
			5.2				2.9	4.3
			63.4				51.3	72.4
			29.8			% Profit Before Taxes/Tangible Net Worth	(42) 17.8	(37) 22.1
			10.3				5.1	5.2
			16.4				27.5	17.2
			7.0			% Profit Before Taxes/Total Assets	8.2	9.2
			4.0				1.4	1.3
			35.7				28.3	18.6
			5.7			Sales/Net Fixed Assets	10.9	6.9
			4.3				4.1	3.8
			2.1				2.3	2.4
			1.4			Sales/Total Assets	1.9	1.7
			1.1				1.2	1.2
			.6				.8	.7
			1.9			% Depr., Dep., Amort./Sales	(38) 1.6	(34) 2.2
			3.8				2.9	2.9
						% Officers', Directors' Owners' Comp/Sales		
134M	12114M	94293M	510200M	519158M	1217677M	Net Sales ($)	3003602M	2547497M
35M	6049M	46562M	335622M	286273M	862639M	Total Assets ($)	1808109M	1789015M

M = $ thousand MM = $ million

See Pages 9 through 22 for Explanation of Ratios and Data

Comparative Historical Data				Current Data Sorted by Sales					
			Type of Statement						
18	18	14	Unqualified					3	11
7	8	8	Reviewed		2			4	2
4	3	1	Compiled		1				
2	3	3	Tax Returns	1	1	1			
10	15	8	Other				1	2	5
					13 (4/1-9/30/13)			21 (10/1/13-3/31/14)	
4/1/11-3/31/12 ALL	4/1/12-3/31/13 ALL	4/1/13-3/31/14 ALL		0-1MM	1-3MM	3-5MM	5-10MM	10-25MM	25MM & OVER
41	47	34	**NUMBER OF STATEMENTS**	1	4	1	1	9	18
%	%	%	**ASSETS**	%	%	%	%	%	%
5.4	8.3	7.9	Cash & Equivalents						4.8
21.5	17.8	17.2	Trade Receivables (net)						17.3
33.8	37.9	37.4	Inventory						39.4
1.4	2.3	2.1	All Other Current						2.2
62.1	66.3	64.5	Total Current						63.6
26.0	24.1	28.7	Fixed Assets (net)						30.4
5.2	5.0	2.2	Intangibles (net)						3.8
6.7	4.7	4.6	All Other Non-Current						2.2
100.0	100.0	100.0	Total						100.0
			LIABILITIES						
10.2	13.7	13.8	Notes Payable-Short Term						13.1
2.4	3.2	2.5	Cur. Mat.-L.T.D.						3.8
16.2	19.1	13.6	Trade Payables						15.0
.3	.4	.3	Income Taxes Payable						.4
6.1	6.6	8.6	All Other Current						8.9
35.2	43.1	38.9	Total Current						41.3
17.2	14.4	16.1	Long-Term Debt						22.8
.3	.5	.3	Deferred Taxes						.3
8.5	8.1	6.0	All Other Non-Current						4.3
38.9	33.9	38.7	Net Worth						31.4
100.0	100.0	100.0	Total Liabilties & Net Worth						100.0
			INCOME DATA						
100.0	100.0	100.0	Net Sales						100.0
26.6	27.1	33.1	Gross Profit						21.4
19.2	20.3	25.8	Operating Expenses						14.5
7.4	6.8	7.3	Operating Profit						6.8
.8	.0	1.5	All Other Expenses (net)						2.7
6.6	6.8	5.8	Profit Before Taxes						4.1
			RATIOS						
2.5	2.7	2.1							1.9
1.8	1.5	1.7	Current						1.6
1.2	1.2	1.3							1.3
1.5	1.3	1.3							.8
.7	.6	.6	Quick						.4
.4	.3	.3							.3
29 12.8	**24** 15.5	**27** 13.4							**28** 13.0
38 9.6	**30** 12.3	**33** 11.2	Sales/Receivables						**31** 11.9
51 7.1	**39** 9.3	**45** 8.1							**46** 8.0
36 10.1	**47** 7.8	**69** 5.3							**73** 5.0
79 4.6	**91** 4.0	**114** 3.2	Cost of Sales/Inventory						**111** 3.3
135 2.7	**166** 2.2	**192** 1.9							**192** 1.9
17 21.3	**18** 20.0	**18** 20.6							**21** 17.2
26 13.8	**35** 10.3	**32** 11.5	Cost of Sales/Payables						**33** 11.1
55 6.6	**63** 5.8	**63** 5.8							**47** 7.8
5.1	4.4	5.1							5.5
9.3	8.4	8.7	Sales/Working Capital						8.1
22.8	19.5	17.3							16.2
29.6	25.5	32.1							16.1
(39) 6.4	(44) 4.8	(33) 10.6	EBIT/Interest						7.6
1.9	1.6	3.1							2.1
24.2	4.4								
(12) 2.5	(19) 2.6		Net Profit + Depr., Dep., Amort./Cur. Mat. L/T/D						
1.1	1.7								
.3	.4	.4							.7
.7	.9	.8	Fixed/Worth						1.0
1.5	1.8	1.1							1.2
.8	1.1	1.0							1.2
2.2	2.2	1.6	Debt/Worth						1.6
5.9	7.5	6.1							10.0
76.8	76.5	52.5							55.2
(39) 27.7	(42) 34.4	(33) 22.7	% Profit Before Taxes/Tangible Net Worth						(17) 22.7
10.3	9.7	9.2							12.4
18.7	17.5	14.3							11.1
7.7	7.8	6.6	% Profit Before Taxes/Total Assets						6.1
2.1	1.2	4.0							3.6
25.2	28.5	22.8							7.3
8.6	7.3	6.4	Sales/Net Fixed Assets						5.0
4.1	4.3	4.6							4.1
2.9	2.7	2.3							2.0
1.8	1.8	1.7	Sales/Total Assets						1.6
1.4	1.2	1.3							1.3
.9	.9	.8							1.1
(36) 2.0	(41) 2.3	(30) 2.2	% Depr., Dep., Amort./Sales						(17) 2.3
2.7	3.2	3.1							3.1
			% Officers', Directors' Owners' Comp/Sales						
3304063M	4112842M	2353576M	Net Sales ($)	134M	7907M	4207M	5271M	154182M	2181875M
1934555M	2503536M	1537180M	Total Assets ($)	35M	5062M	987M	4213M	98542M	1428341M

M = $ thousand MM = $ million

See Pages 9 through 22 for Explanation of Ratios and Data

Current Data Sorted by Assets							Comparative Historical Data	
						Type of Statement		
		1	7	7	7	Unqualified	22	21
		2				Reviewed	9	5
						Compiled	3	3
1	1					Tax Returns	6	
1	1	4	10	2	5	Other	28	23
12 (4/1-9/30/13)			36 (10/1/13-3/31/14)				4/1/09-3/31/10	4/1/10-3/31/11
0-500M	500M-2MM	2-10MM	10-50MM	50-100MM	100-250MM		ALL	ALL
1	2	7	17	9	12	**NUMBER OF STATEMENTS**	68	52
%	%	%	%	%	%	**ASSETS**	%	%
			4.2		6.1	Cash & Equivalents	8.6	7.9
			32.2		29.5	Trade Receivables (net)	24.5	30.0
			14.9		9.7	Inventory	13.5	13.1
			4.1		1.1	All Other Current	2.7	1.8
			55.4		46.3	Total Current	49.2	52.8
			39.5		45.5	Fixed Assets (net)	38.7	34.8
			1.9		1.5	Intangibles (net)	3.3	7.9
			3.1		6.7	All Other Non-Current	8.8	4.5
			100.0		100.0	Total	100.0	100.0
						LIABILITIES		
			11.8		3.6	Notes Payable-Short Term	5.5	5.4
			5.9		1.9	Cur. Mat.-L.T.D.	3.0	3.1
			23.2		20.6	Trade Payables	20.4	22.5
			.0		.0	Income Taxes Payable	.1	.1
			13.6		8.6	All Other Current	7.8	10.2
			54.4		34.7	Total Current	36.8	41.4
			8.4		28.0	Long-Term Debt	18.1	13.1
			1.5		1.0	Deferred Taxes	1.0	1.1
			6.7		1.8	All Other Non-Current	3.6	3.8
			29.1		34.4	Net Worth	40.4	40.6
			100.0		100.0	Total Liabilities & Net Worth	100.0	100.0
						INCOME DATA		
			100.0		100.0	Net Sales	100.0	100.0
			21.4		16.5	Gross Profit	26.0	20.7
			20.0		13.3	Operating Expenses	23.5	18.0
			1.3		3.2	Operating Profit	2.4	2.7
			.1		.1	All Other Expenses (net)	.2	.6
			1.2		3.2	Profit Before Taxes	2.3	2.1
						RATIOS		
			1.5		1.8		1.8	1.8
			1.0		1.5	Current	1.3	1.3
			.8		1.1		1.0	.9
			1.2		1.4		1.2	1.3
			.6		1.0	Quick	.9	.9
			.4		.8		.6	.6
			21 17.6		**20** 18.6		**21** 17.5	**20** 17.9
			29 12.6		**22** 16.8	Sales/Receivables	**26** 14.2	**24** 15.0
			34 10.6		**31** 11.8		**32** 11.3	**31** 11.8
			10 35.3		**6** 61.4		**9** 39.1	**9** 39.7
			12 29.8		**15** 25.1	Cost of Sales/Inventory	**15** 25.1	**16** 22.7
			17 21.8		**22** 16.3		**30** 12.1	**23** 15.8
			17 21.4		**17** 21.1		**18** 20.6	**18** 20.4
			25 14.4		**24** 15.4	Cost of Sales/Payables	**27** 13.7	**23** 15.6
			32 11.5		**40** 9.1		**38** 9.6	**34** 10.6
			20.8		13.6		11.8	14.0
			509.5		29.3	Sales/Working Capital	28.7	52.2
			-29.4		105.6		501.6	-90.0
			6.5		13.7		21.1	19.8
			(15) 3.9		7.0	EBIT/Interest	(63) 5.5	(47) 5.4
			-.7		4.0		2.0	1.2
							9.8	8.9
						Net Profit + Depr., Dep., Amort./Cur. Mat. L/T/D	(26) 3.8	(20) 3.2
							2.6	1.9
			.8		.9		.6	.6
			1.3		1.5	Fixed/Worth	.9	.9
			NM		1.9		1.7	2.0
			1.3		1.5		.7	.8
			2.0		2.0	Debt/Worth	1.3	1.3
			NM		2.6		3.9	4.8
			24.3		34.1		34.3	29.3
			(13) 8.5		16.8	% Profit Before Taxes/Tangible Net Worth	(64) 19.9	(48) 14.7
			-7.3		10.7		6.9	-1.4
			7.8		10.6		14.1	12.1
			4.9		5.4	% Profit Before Taxes/Total Assets	7.2	5.3
			-2.3		3.6		2.3	-.5
			17.4		25.5		16.7	29.0
			10.0		7.8	Sales/Net Fixed Assets	6.7	10.0
			6.7		3.1		5.2	5.6
			5.5		7.3		4.3	5.3
			3.8		3.7	Sales/Total Assets	3.1	3.6
			3.3		2.0		2.4	2.7
			.8				1.1	.7
			1.7			% Depr., Dep., Amort./Sales	(61) 1.9	(47) 1.5
			2.0				3.0	2.6
							.6	
						% Officers', Directors' Owners' Comp/Sales	(14) 1.6	
							2.8	
1839M	13579M	205382M	2239518M	2551098M	8890770M	Net Sales ($)	9894416M	12402166M
413M	2864M	43989M	513182M	747866M	2145598M	Total Assets ($)	2957395M	3069811M

M = $ thousand MM = $ million

See Pages 9 through 22 for Explanation of Ratios and Data

	Comparative Historical Data				Current Data Sorted by Sales					
Type of Statement										
Unqualified	27	25	22			1				21
Reviewed	7	11	2						1	1
Compiled		1								
Tax Returns	4	4	2			1		1		
Other	22	27	22				1		3	18
	4/1/11-3/31/12 ALL	4/1/12-3/31/13 ALL	4/1/13-3/31/14 ALL		12 (4/1-9/30/13)		36 (10/1/13-3/31/14)			
				0-1MM	1-3MM	3-5MM	5-10MM	10-25MM	25MM & OVER	
NUMBER OF STATEMENTS	60	68	48		2	1	1	4	40	
ASSETS	%	%	%	%	%	%	%	%	%	
Cash & Equivalents	9.4	9.5	8.0	DATA NOT AVAILABLE					6.6	
Trade Receivables (net)	28.3	25.9	28.5						30.3	
Inventory	13.3	13.8	13.4						12.4	
All Other Current	1.3	3.5	2.5						2.9	
Total Current	52.3	52.6	52.4						52.3	
Fixed Assets (net)	38.2	37.2	41.0						41.7	
Intangibles (net)	4.7	2.8	2.5						1.4	
All Other Non-Current	4.8	7.3	4.1						4.7	
Total	100.0	100.0	100.0						100.0	
LIABILITIES										
Notes Payable-Short Term	6.0	6.5	6.8						7.1	
Cur. Mat.-L.T.D.	3.0	2.0	3.7						3.7	
Trade Payables	20.7	18.8	20.5						20.7	
Income Taxes Payable	.1	.2	.0						.0	
All Other Current	10.3	9.6	11.5						12.5	
Total Current	40.0	37.1	42.6						44.0	
Long-Term Debt	14.7	15.8	17.9						16.7	
Deferred Taxes	1.3	1.2	1.2						1.1	
All Other Non-Current	4.0	4.4	7.7						4.5	
Net Worth	40.0	41.5	30.6						33.7	
Total Liabilties & Net Worth	100.0	100.0	100.0						100.0	
INCOME DATA										
Net Sales	100.0	100.0	100.0						100.0	
Gross Profit	21.1	22.9	20.0						17.9	
Operating Expenses	18.9	20.4	18.4						15.9	
Operating Profit	2.2	2.5	1.6						2.0	
All Other Expenses (net)	.5	.6	.1						.0	
Profit Before Taxes	1.7	1.9	1.5						2.0	
RATIOS										
Current	1.9	2.0	1.7						1.7	
	1.3	1.4	1.2						1.2	
	.9	1.0	.9						.8	
Quick	1.4	1.6	1.3						1.3	
	.9	.9	.9						.9	
	.6	.6	.5						.4	
Sales/Receivables	19 19.7	19 19.2	21 17.4						21 17.3	
	24 15.4	24 15.0	25 14.6						25 14.6	
	31 11.7	31 11.8	31 11.7						33 11.1	
Cost of Sales/Inventory	10 38.0	9 42.4	9 38.6						8 44.0	
	16 23.2	15 24.7	15 24.8						14 26.2	
	28 12.9	27 13.5	26 13.9						20 18.3	
Cost of Sales/Payables	14 26.4	18 20.0	17 21.2						17 21.9	
	23 15.6	23 16.2	22 16.3						25 14.5	
	29 12.5	29 12.4	33 11.1						33 11.1	
Sales/Working Capital	15.4	12.2	15.4						16.4	
	42.5	26.9	36.5						38.9	
	-114.0	NM	-62.3						-53.3	
EBIT/Interest	18.4	23.3	9.3						11.7	
	(56) 4.8	(61) 5.6	(41) 4.6						(35) 4.6	
	1.2	1.1	.0						1.9	
Net Profit + Depr., Dep., Amort./Cur. Mat. L/T/D	7.7	10.8	4.0						3.6	
	(24) 3.2	(24) 2.5	(19) 2.1						(15) 2.1	
	.3	1.9	.4						.4	
Fixed/Worth	.6	.5	.7						.7	
	1.0	.9	1.5						1.5	
	2.2	1.8	2.3						1.9	
Debt/Worth	.8	.8	1.2						1.4	
	1.8	1.4	2.0						2.0	
	3.8	2.6	3.5						3.3	
% Profit Before Taxes/Tangible Net Worth	26.8	23.0	23.6						24.1	
	(55) 13.7	(62) 15.1	(41) 11.0						(36) 12.9	
	4.6	1.9	-3.3						-1.1	
% Profit Before Taxes/Total Assets	11.3	12.7	7.9						8.5	
	4.3	5.0	4.0						5.0	
	.3	-1.1	-1.3						-.2	
Sales/Net Fixed Assets	27.1	25.1	16.6						17.7	
	9.0	9.5	8.8						8.9	
	4.7	5.4	4.0						3.9	
Sales/Total Assets	5.8	5.6	5.5						5.7	
	3.5	3.2	3.6						3.8	
	2.2	2.4	2.4						2.7	
% Depr., Dep., Amort./Sales	.5	.5	.7						.5	
	(50) 1.7	(61) 1.7	(41) 1.7						(34) 1.5	
	2.6	2.9	2.7						2.4	
% Officers', Directors' Owners' Comp/Sales		.7								
		(11) 1.1								
		1.8								
Net Sales ($)	14384324M	15820206M	13902186M		4381M	4779M	8800M	69931M	13814295M	
Total Assets ($)	3582211M	3917909M	3453912M		2696M	1399M	1465M	25415M	3422937M	

M = $ thousand MM = $ million

See Pages 9 through 22 for Explanation of Ratios and Data

Current Data Sorted by Assets							Comparative Historical Data	
						Type of Statement		
			8	2	4	Unqualified	26	21
	1	10	9	2		Reviewed	11	15
	1	4	1		1	Compiled	7	4
	1	1	1			Tax Returns	5	4
1	1	4	12	4	3	Other	32	31
16 (4/1-9/30/13)			55 (10/1/13-3/31/14)				4/1/09-3/31/10	4/1/10-3/31/11
0-500M	500M-2MM	2-10MM	10-50MM	50-100MM	100-250MM		ALL	ALL
1	4	19	31	8	8	NUMBER OF STATEMENTS	81	75
%	%	%	%	%	%	**ASSETS**	%	%
		8.2	7.6			Cash & Equivalents	7.7	6.8
		23.1	21.7			Trade Receivables (net)	20.0	22.5
		21.1	23.0			Inventory	24.7	24.7
		.8	1.9			All Other Current	2.3	3.0
		53.2	54.2			Total Current	54.8	57.0
		38.8	39.5			Fixed Assets (net)	35.1	36.8
		1.3	3.6			Intangibles (net)	3.0	2.4
		6.7	2.7			All Other Non-Current	7.1	3.8
		100.0	100.0			Total	100.0	100.0
						LIABILITIES		
		8.4	10.1			Notes Payable-Short Term	10.3	11.8
		3.5	2.5			Cur. Mat.-L.T.D.	3.2	2.3
		23.2	14.8			Trade Payables	16.5	17.6
		.1	.0			Income Taxes Payable	.2	.1
		6.1	5.6			All Other Current	7.9	5.9
		41.1	32.9			Total Current	38.0	37.7
		22.1	18.1			Long-Term Debt	18.6	17.3
		.3	1.1			Deferred Taxes	.9	1.1
		6.7	3.6			All Other Non-Current	4.8	4.1
		29.8	44.4			Net Worth	37.7	39.8
		100.0	100.0			Total Liabilties & Net Worth	100.0	100.0
						INCOME DATA		
		100.0	100.0			Net Sales	100.0	100.0
		17.7	17.7			Gross Profit	18.9	16.5
		15.0	13.1			Operating Expenses	13.3	11.9
		2.7	4.6			Operating Profit	5.6	4.5
		.4	.6			All Other Expenses (net)	1.0	.9
		2.3	4.0			Profit Before Taxes	4.7	3.6
						RATIOS		
		2.4	2.8				2.4	2.4
		1.6	1.5			Current	1.6	1.5
		.9	1.1				1.1	1.1
		1.7	1.4				1.3	1.5
		.9	.8			Quick	.7	.7
		.5	.6				.4	.5
		22 16.4	**21** 17.1				**21** 17.3	**22** 16.5
		30 12.2	**26** 14.3			Sales/Receivables	**27** 13.4	**27** 13.4
		37 9.8	**32** 11.4				**31** 11.7	**33** 10.9
		9 42.7	**19** 19.3				**16** 23.5	**16** 22.6
		28 13.2	**37** 9.8			Cost of Sales/Inventory	**36** 10.2	**28** 13.0
		54 6.7	**64** 5.7				**64** 5.7	**62** 5.9
		23 16.1	**13** 27.2				**17** 21.6	**17** 21.9
		33 11.0	**22** 16.4			Cost of Sales/Payables	**26** 14.0	**25** 14.7
		49 7.4	**35** 10.4				**37** 9.9	**34** 10.8
		11.2	7.0				7.1	8.8
		16.2	15.3			Sales/Working Capital	15.6	15.2
		-36.3	44.5				100.4	57.3
		21.3	27.3				22.9	21.1
		(18) 4.6	(29) 6.8			EBIT/Interest	(78) 6.6	(71) 7.4
		.0	2.0				2.3	2.5
			3.6				8.9	8.0
			(13) 2.4			Net Profit + Depr., Dep., Amort./Cur. Mat. L/T/D	(24) 3.6	(23) 3.9
			1.4				1.5	2.8
		.6	.5				.4	.6
		1.5	.8			Fixed/Worth	.9	1.0
		6.7	1.6				1.9	2.0
		.5	.7				.7	.6
		1.7	1.6			Debt/Worth	1.6	1.4
		16.0	2.6				3.6	3.1
		26.9	34.1				47.4	37.7
		(15) 15.2	(29) 17.4			% Profit Before Taxes/Tangible Net Worth	(74) 27.5	(68) 23.1
		-.9	10.2				11.3	11.9
		20.3	18.5				19.5	16.9
		5.5	9.1			% Profit Before Taxes/Total Assets	10.9	8.8
		-2.5	2.6				3.5	3.8
		12.9	15.6				14.8	13.7
		7.1	6.4			Sales/Net Fixed Assets	6.5	7.1
		6.4	3.0				4.3	4.7
		3.8	3.4				3.7	3.8
		3.0	2.8			Sales/Total Assets	2.6	2.8
		2.2	1.7				1.8	2.1
		1.1	1.2				1.2	1.3
		(18) 1.9	(30) 1.6			% Depr., Dep., Amort./Sales	(72) 1.8	(69) 1.8
		3.3	3.7				2.6	2.6
							.7	.7
						% Officers', Directors' Owners' Comp/Sales	(21) 1.4	(23) 1.4
							2.2	2.7
79M	18306M	317832M	1893429M	1437351M	3403360M	Net Sales ($)	7379129M	6665542M
39M	5262M	112511M	754538M	578006M	1294011M	Total Assets ($)	3040483M	2669482M

M = $ thousand MM = $ million

See Pages 9 through 22 for Explanation of Ratios and Data

Comparative Historical Data | Current Data Sorted by Sales

4/1/11-3/31/12 ALL	4/1/12-3/31/13 ALL	4/1/13-3/31/14 ALL		0-1MM	1-3MM	3-5MM	5-10MM	10-25MM	25MM & OVER
			Type of Statement						
22	16	14	Unqualified					1	13
16	16	22	Reviewed		1		3	5	13
4	1	7	Compiled		1			4	2
3	8	3	Tax Returns			1			2
22	32	25	Other	1		1	3	3	17
				16 (4/1-9/30/13)			55 (10/1/13-3/31/14)		
67	73	71	**NUMBER OF STATEMENTS**	1	2	2	6	13	47
%	%	%	**ASSETS**	%	%	%	%	%	%
7.0	7.8	8.1	Cash & Equivalents					5.1	6.5
23.1	22.8	21.0	Trade Receivables (net)					18.8	22.6
25.8	22.5	23.2	Inventory					21.9	25.9
1.7	1.7	2.0	All Other Current					1.8	2.0
57.7	54.8	54.3	Total Current					47.5	56.9
36.4	38.5	38.0	Fixed Assets (net)					45.0	36.7
.8	1.4	2.8	Intangibles (net)					6.0	2.3
5.0	5.3	4.9	All Other Non-Current					1.4	4.1
100.0	100.0	100.0	Total					100.0	100.0
			LIABILITIES						
11.5	11.4	9.1	Notes Payable-Short Term					10.9	9.6
2.8	2.4	2.5	Cur. Mat.-L.T.D.					4.2	2.0
17.3	16.8	16.8	Trade Payables					17.3	18.0
.0	.1	.0	Income Taxes Payable					.0	.0
6.3	6.0	6.3	All Other Current					4.8	5.7
38.0	36.7	34.7	Total Current					37.2	35.3
15.9	20.0	18.0	Long-Term Debt					16.9	18.2
.5	1.0	.7	Deferred Taxes					1.7	.7
4.6	5.6	3.9	All Other Non-Current					3.0	2.9
41.0	36.7	42.7	Net Worth					41.1	43.0
100.0	100.0	100.0	Total Liabilities & Net Worth					100.0	100.0
			INCOME DATA						
100.0	100.0	100.0	Net Sales					100.0	100.0
15.2	16.6	19.4	Gross Profit					17.1	15.7
11.9	12.8	15.1	Operating Expenses					13.2	11.7
3.3	3.9	4.3	Operating Profit					3.9	3.9
.3	.5	.4	All Other Expenses (net)					.8	.4
2.9	3.4	3.9	Profit Before Taxes					3.0	3.6
			RATIOS						
2.1	2.4	2.6						2.6	2.6
1.5	1.6	1.6	Current					1.1	1.7
1.1	1.1	1.0						.8	1.2
1.3	1.4	1.4						1.4	1.1
.7	.8	.8	Quick					.6	.8
.4	.6	.5						.3	.6
22 16.5	21 17.1	22 16.9						20 18.2	22 16.7
27 13.5	27 13.7	26 14.3	Sales/Receivables					33 11.1	26 13.9
33 10.9	35 10.5	33 10.9						37 9.9	32 11.5
14 26.7	15 25.1	16 23.3						16 23.3	19 19.3
28 13.0	27 13.5	37 9.8	Cost of Sales/Inventory					41 8.8	37 9.8
65 5.6	52 7.0	64 5.7						76 4.8	64 5.7
16 22.4	16 22.5	16 22.3						18 20.4	16 22.3
22 16.3	23 15.6	26 13.8	Cost of Sales/Payables					29 12.4	24 15.1
33 11.0	34 10.8	41 9.0						44 8.3	36 10.2
9.0	8.5	7.0						11.3	6.7
16.0	15.4	15.3	Sales/Working Capital					19.5	14.9
68.6	67.1	169.7						-27.0	44.5
24.8	14.7	21.6						17.9	27.3
(63) 5.5	(69) 5.4	(65) 6.6	EBIT/Interest					(12) 2.6	(45) 6.8
.9	1.9	1.4						-.2	2.3
8.8	14.1	7.0							7.8
(22) 4.4	(19) 3.1	(19) 2.4	Net Profit + Depr., Dep., Amort./Cur. Mat. L/T/D						(15) 3.1
1.7	2.0	1.3							1.7
.5	.5	.5						.7	.5
.8	1.0	.9	Fixed/Worth					2.4	.8
1.5	2.2	2.4						5.7	1.3
.9	.8	.5						.3	.7
1.4	1.5	1.4	Debt/Worth					2.9	1.4
2.6	3.8	3.2						11.9	2.3
26.2	35.2	26.9						28.7	24.9
(64) 17.5	(64) 20.2	(65) 16.9	% Profit Before Taxes/Tangible Net Worth					(12) 14.5	(44) 16.8
.5	7.2	7.5						-22.0	9.5
13.2	12.9	12.4						16.2	12.4
7.3	7.3	7.6	% Profit Before Taxes/Total Assets					5.5	8.1
.6	1.6	1.4						-2.6	2.4
13.3	14.8	11.8						6.8	11.9
7.4	7.2	6.8	Sales/Net Fixed Assets					6.4	8.2
4.8	4.8	5.0						3.1	5.1
3.7	3.5	3.3						3.2	3.7
2.8	2.8	2.7	Sales/Total Assets					2.3	2.8
1.9	2.0	1.9						1.3	2.0
1.3	1.2	1.1						1.3	1.1
(62) 1.7	(61) 1.7	(67) 1.7	% Depr., Dep., Amort./Sales					2.8	(45) 1.6
3.1	2.8	3.1						3.6	3.0
.6	.6	.7							.7
(20) 1.0	(23) 1.2	(18) 1.2	% Officers', Directors' Owners' Comp/Sales						(10) 1.1
2.2	2.2	3.2							1.7
6015370M	7540049M	7070357M	Net Sales ($)	79M	5411M	8163M	52044M	234142M	6770518M
2321805M	2929824M	2744367M	Total Assets ($)	39M	2563M	8214M	21814M	152959M	2558778M

M = $ thousand MM = $ million

See Pages 9 through 22 for Explanation of Ratios and Data

Current Data Sorted by Assets							Comparative Historical Data	
						Type of Statement		
		1	2	1	1	Unqualified	5	6
		7	1			Reviewed	3	7
						Compiled	1	2
		2	1			Tax Returns	3	5
	3	1	7			Other	12	12
	5 (4/1-9/30/13)		22 (10/1/13-3/31/14)				4/1/09-3/31/10	4/1/10-3/31/11
0-500M	**500M-2MM**	**2-10MM**	**10-50MM**	**50-100MM**	**100-250MM**		**ALL**	**ALL**
	3	11	11	1	1	**NUMBER OF STATEMENTS**	24	32
%	%	%	%	%	%	**ASSETS**	%	%
DATA NOT AVAILABLE		17.4	5.7			Cash & Equivalents	9.4	7.0
		9.9	15.2			Trade Receivables (net)	12.1	13.3
		26.1	18.2			Inventory	21.5	23.6
		1.6	1.3			All Other Current	2.6	1.4
		55.0	40.4			Total Current	45.7	45.3
		36.0	48.0			Fixed Assets (net)	32.2	38.7
		7.1	5.9			Intangibles (net)	15.6	12.2
		2.0	5.7			All Other Non-Current	6.6	3.8
		100.0	100.0			Total	100.0	100.0
						LIABILITIES		
		3.9	9.5			Notes Payable-Short Term	8.4	13.3
		3.4	5.0			Cur. Mat.-L.T.D.	2.9	4.9
		10.0	12.2			Trade Payables	12.0	12.1
		1.3	.1			Income Taxes Payable	.0	.0
		5.0	8.5			All Other Current	7.1	4.5
		23.5	35.2			Total Current	30.3	34.9
		20.7	31.9			Long-Term Debt	28.4	37.0
		.7	1.3			Deferred Taxes	.6	1.2
		7.7	7.1			All Other Non-Current	7.4	5.2
		47.3	24.5			Net Worth	33.3	21.7
		100.0	100.0			Total Liabilties & Net Worth	100.0	100.0
						INCOME DATA		
		100.0	100.0			Net Sales	100.0	100.0
		44.0	30.3			Gross Profit	42.4	39.5
		40.1	26.6			Operating Expenses	36.3	34.7
		3.9	3.7			Operating Profit	6.1	4.9
		.3	2.5			All Other Expenses (net)	3.0	1.9
		3.6	1.2			Profit Before Taxes	3.1	2.9
						RATIOS		
		4.3	1.9				2.7	2.1
		3.1	1.1			Current	1.4	1.2
		1.0	.6				.8	.8
		2.2	1.2				1.3	.9
		.9	.5			Quick	.6	.5
		.4	.3				.4	.3
		6 64.8	**12** 29.8				**13** 28.3	**12** 29.6
		13 27.5	**26** 13.9			Sales/Receivables	**19** 19.4	**19** 19.6
		17 21.2	**39** 9.4				**29** 12.7	**26** 13.9
		24 15.4	**38** 9.7				**36** 10.2	**29** 12.5
		55 6.6	**43** 8.5			Cost of Sales/Inventory	**57** 6.4	**50** 7.2
		94 3.9	**81** 4.5				**90** 4.0	**87** 4.2
		7 53.2	**21** 17.6				**16** 22.3	**15** 25.0
		22 16.7	**29** 12.7			Cost of Sales/Payables	**24** 15.2	**24** 15.2
		36 10.2	**65** 5.6				**37** 9.8	**36** 10.0
		4.9	8.6				5.0	9.5
		7.6	36.7			Sales/Working Capital	17.8	27.9
		-150.8	-8.1				-50.7	-16.7
			7.7				8.9	7.4
			3.6			EBIT/Interest	(23) 3.2	(31) 2.1
			.2				.7	1.0
								11.0
						Net Profit + Depr., Dep., Amort./Cur. Mat. L/T/D		(10) 4.5
								1.5
		.5	.9				.5	.9
		.6	1.5			Fixed/Worth	1.3	2.7
		3.3	-71.8				-5.4	-4.3
		.4	1.5				.7	1.3
		1.7	2.2			Debt/Worth	1.6	4.7
		6.4	-111.3				-15.8	-16.0
		31.3					47.0	42.5
		(10) 14.5				% Profit Before Taxes/Tangible Net Worth	(17) 27.4	(20) 22.7
		-3.0					2.6	.6
		20.4	12.9				22.1	15.9
		7.7	7.5			% Profit Before Taxes/Total Assets	4.5	3.6
		-1.7	-2.7				-1.3	.2
		13.5	6.5				19.5	18.1
		7.6	2.7			Sales/Net Fixed Assets	11.1	8.9
		4.2	2.4				4.9	2.6
		3.0	3.2				3.2	3.4
		2.5	1.6			Sales/Total Assets	2.0	2.3
		2.0	1.1				1.1	1.3
		2.0	2.3				1.2	1.4
		(10) 2.6	4.0			% Depr., Dep., Amort./Sales	(20) 2.0	(29) 2.2
		3.7	4.9				5.3	5.2
						% Officers', Directors' Owners' Comp/Sales		
	8673M	145364M	541643M	184230M	181492M	Net Sales ($)	915194M	945491M
	4644M	51645M	263257M	79491M	153831M	Total Assets ($)	495742M	564117M

M = $ thousand MM = $ million

See Pages 9 through 22 for Explanation of Ratios and Data

Comparative Historical Data				Current Data Sorted by Sales					
			Type of Statement						
6	5	5	Unqualified					2	3
8	6	8	Reviewed				3	4	1
1	1		Compiled						
2	5	3	Tax Returns				1	2	
15	15	11	Other	2	1		2	1	5
4/1/11-3/31/12 ALL	**4/1/12-3/31/13 ALL**	**4/1/13-3/31/14 ALL**		**5 (4/1-9/30/13)**			**22 (10/1/13-3/31/14)**		
				0-1MM	**1-3MM**	**3-5MM**	**5-10MM**	**10-25MM**	**25MM & OVER**
32	32	27	**NUMBER OF STATEMENTS**	2	1		6	9	9
%	%	%	**ASSETS**	%	%	%	%	%	%
3.9	5.3	12.5	Cash & Equivalents			DATA NOT AVAILABLE			
12.8	12.8	11.6	Trade Receivables (net)						
23.0	24.0	20.2	Inventory						
1.2	2.3	1.3	All Other Current						
40.9	44.4	45.6	Total Current						
44.5	42.5	40.3	Fixed Assets (net)						
8.6	10.6	8.5	Intangibles (net)						
6.0	2.5	5.6	All Other Non-Current						
100.0	100.0	100.0	Total						
			LIABILITIES						
12.8	10.4	5.8	Notes Payable-Short Term						
7.1	5.9	3.8	Cur. Mat.-L.T.D.						
11.9	12.5	10.1	Trade Payables						
.1	.0	.5	Income Taxes Payable						
7.9	6.1	5.7	All Other Current						
39.8	35.0	26.0	Total Current						
26.0	32.5	27.0	Long-Term Debt						
1.5	1.7	1.2	Deferred Taxes						
9.1	11.4	6.0	All Other Non-Current						
23.7	19.4	39.7	Net Worth						
100.0	100.0	100.0	Total Liabilties & Net Worth						
			INCOME DATA						
100.0	100.0	100.0	Net Sales						
36.0	35.2	37.5	Gross Profit						
33.1	30.5	32.7	Operating Expenses						
2.9	4.6	4.8	Operating Profit						
1.3	1.7	1.5	All Other Expenses (net)						
1.6	2.9	3.3	Profit Before Taxes						
			RATIOS						
1.5	2.1	3.7							
1.0	1.2	1.8	Current						
.7	.8	1.0							
.5	.8	1.7							
.4	.4	.9	Quick						
.2	.3	.4							
14 25.6	**7** 55.2	**12** 29.8							
19 19.5	**18** 20.8	**16** 22.8	Sales/Receivables						
28 13.1	**27** 13.6	**26** 13.9							
38 9.5	**41** 9.0	**33** 11.2							
54 6.7	**51** 7.2	**46** 7.9	Cost of Sales/Inventory						
81 4.5	**69** 5.3	**85** 4.3							
18 20.8	**18** 20.6	**13** 28.8							
30 12.0	**23** 16.0	**26** 14.2	Cost of Sales/Payables						
38 9.6	**34** 10.7	**36** 10.1							
16.0	10.0	5.1							
NM	26.8	15.5	Sales/Working Capital						
-17.3	-25.1	-150.8							
4.8	5.9	9.1							
(31) 2.1	(31) 2.6	(24) 3.4	EBIT/Interest						
.7	1.5	1.3							
7.8	4.2	3.3							
(13) 2.5	(13) 2.9	(14) 2.3	Net Profit + Depr., Dep., Amort./Cur. Mat. L/T/D						
1.4	2.0	.5							
1.2	1.5	.6							
1.8	3.2	1.4	Fixed/Worth						
-90.9	-32.9	5.2							
1.7	2.3	.7							
3.2	7.5	2.0	Debt/Worth						
-135.3	-56.7	10.1							
57.9	66.8	51.0							
(22) 26.6	(22) 29.7	(21) 24.1	% Profit Before Taxes/Tangible Net Worth						
-5.6	6.2	2.1							
13.2	10.9	14.6							
2.6	6.3	7.7	% Profit Before Taxes/Total Assets						
-1.7	1.3	.2							
8.8	10.7	11.6							
5.0	6.1	6.5	Sales/Net Fixed Assets						
2.9	3.2	2.7							
3.0	2.9	3.0							
2.2	2.3	2.0	Sales/Total Assets						
1.5	1.6	1.4							
1.6	1.8	2.1							
(29) 3.4	(30) 2.9	(25) 2.9	% Depr., Dep., Amort./Sales						
5.6	4.4	4.7							
			% Officers', Directors' Owners' Comp/Sales						
1808497M	**1500580M**	**1061402M**	Net Sales ($)	**1582M**	**1488M**		**42978M**	**156176M**	**859178M**
914839M	**833297M**	**552868M**	Total Assets ($)	**11251M**	**1674M**		**17704M**	**87820M**	**434419M**

M = $ thousand MM = $ million

See Pages 9 through 22 for Explanation of Ratios and Data

Current Data Sorted by Assets							Comparative Historical Data	
						Type of Statement		
		2	3	1		Unqualified	19	16
	2	5	3			Reviewed	18	12
3		4				Compiled	15	10
	4					Tax Returns	5	15
	3	6	9	7	3	Other	29	22
	11 (4/1-9/30/13)		44 (10/1/13-3/31/14)				4/1/09-3/31/10 ALL	4/1/10-3/31/11 ALL
0-500M	500M-2MM	2-10MM	10-50MM	50-100MM	100-250MM			
3	9	17	15	8	3	**NUMBER OF STATEMENTS**	86	75
%	%	%	%	%	%	**ASSETS**	%	%
		4.2	5.1			Cash & Equivalents	10.1	9.9
		27.6	25.2			Trade Receivables (net)	23.4	24.8
		18.8	28.2			Inventory	19.1	20.4
		1.9	2.6			All Other Current	2.7	1.7
		52.5	61.1			Total Current	55.3	56.8
		40.2	34.2			Fixed Assets (net)	36.8	34.6
		.5	2.8			Intangibles (net)	3.3	2.6
		6.9	1.9			All Other Non-Current	4.5	6.1
		100.0	100.0			Total	100.0	100.0
						LIABILITIES		
		12.1	17.5			Notes Payable-Short Term	10.7	8.2
		2.4	1.8			Cur. Mat.-L.T.D.	3.0	3.1
		13.1	13.3			Trade Payables	10.4	15.5
		.3	.0			Income Taxes Payable	.1	.3
		5.8	12.3			All Other Current	7.8	7.7
		33.7	44.9			Total Current	32.0	34.8
		22.9	14.7			Long-Term Debt	19.5	20.4
		.6	.3			Deferred Taxes	.3	.4
		3.0	6.8			All Other Non-Current	6.3	5.8
		39.8	33.3			Net Worth	41.9	38.5
		100.0	100.0			Total Liabilties & Net Worth	100.0	100.0
						INCOME DATA		
		100.0	100.0			Net Sales	100.0	100.0
		14.9	10.5			Gross Profit	22.5	18.4
		14.4	9.2			Operating Expenses	20.3	15.9
		.5	1.2			Operating Profit	2.2	2.4
		.0	.4			All Other Expenses (net)	.1	.4
		.5	.9			Profit Before Taxes	2.1	2.0
						RATIOS		
		2.3	1.6				3.3	3.0
		1.6	1.2			Current	1.7	1.7
		1.1	1.0				1.1	1.2
		1.3	1.2				2.0	1.7
		1.1	.7			Quick	1.0	1.0
		.6	.4				.5	.6
		13 27.1	14 25.4				14 25.8	15 24.5
		18 20.8	18 19.9			Sales/Receivables	21 17.8	19 18.9
		22 16.6	23 15.6				29 12.7	29 12.6
		8 44.2	12 29.2				10 36.6	11 32.2
		17 22.1	17 21.8			Cost of Sales/Inventory	19 19.1	20 18.4
		20 18.7	32 11.3				38 9.5	36 10.2
		5 69.2	5 71.5				5 76.5	6 62.4
		10 36.3	13 27.4			Cost of Sales/Payables	10 37.7	12 29.8
		13 27.5	22 16.7				20 18.1	23 15.7
		18.3	15.7				9.1	10.4
		28.3	33.7			Sales/Working Capital	23.6	20.4
		256.5	341.9				113.6	54.6
		7.9	15.9				13.0	13.3
		2.9	2.6			EBIT/Interest	(79) 3.4	(72) 3.7
		.2	-.5				.0	1.0
							4.9	6.7
						Net Profit + Depr., Dep., Amort./Cur. Mat. L/T/D	(17) 2.4	(22) 3.9
							1.7	1.1
		.5	.5				.4	.4
		.9	1.0			Fixed/Worth	.9	.9
		1.5	2.3				2.9	2.1
		.8	.8				.5	.6
		1.6	2.6			Debt/Worth	1.7	1.5
		3.2	5.7				4.9	4.2
		33.6	35.5				32.6	38.5
		7.9	(14) 22.3			% Profit Before Taxes/Tangible Net Worth	(76) 14.3	(70) 13.4
		-10.6	-15.9				1.7	.5
		12.6	6.8				13.7	13.4
		2.7	5.1			% Profit Before Taxes/Total Assets	5.4	4.7
		-3.0	-5.2				-1.1	.1
		33.2	33.1				28.2	32.8
		15.0	13.5			Sales/Net Fixed Assets	10.4	12.0
		7.5	7.5				4.4	5.3
		7.8	5.2				5.7	5.6
		5.8	4.7			Sales/Total Assets	3.4	3.9
		3.1	3.4				2.0	2.4
		.6	.4				.5	.5
		(14) 1.1	(13) 1.0			% Depr., Dep., Amort./Sales	(78) 1.5	(71) 1.1
		3.0	1.4				2.6	2.2
							1.0	.8
						% Officers', Directors' Owners' Comp/Sales	(29) 1.9	(33) 2.0
							4.8	4.0
3686M	93536M	561680M	2365960M	3645602M	1629875M	Net Sales ($)	6551663M	7072444M
433M	11190M	93385M	412271M	569263M	499857M	Total Assets ($)	1720329M	1933298M

M = $ thousand MM = $ million

See Pages 9 through 22 for Explanation of Ratios and Data

Comparative Historical Data | **Current Data Sorted by Sales**

4/1/11-3/31/12 ALL	4/1/12-3/31/13 ALL	4/1/13-3/31/14 ALL		0-1MM	1-3MM	3-5MM	5-10MM	10-25MM	25MM & OVER
			Type of Statement						
12	9	6	Unqualified					2	4
21	12	10	Reviewed				1	2	7
14	5	7	Compiled	1	2	1	1		2
9	3	4	Tax Returns	1	1		1	1	
20	28	28	Other		1		1	1	25
					11 (4/1-9/30/13)		44 (10/1/13-3/31/14)		
76	57	55	**NUMBER OF STATEMENTS**	2	4	1	4	6	38
%	%	%	**ASSETS**	%	%	%	%	%	%
5.5	6.4	6.6	Cash & Equivalents						5.9
26.4	25.5	27.4	Trade Receivables (net)						30.1
21.2	23.0	20.7	Inventory						22.4
1.4	1.9	1.6	All Other Current						1.9
54.5	56.7	56.4	Total Current						60.3
35.6	34.7	34.9	Fixed Assets (net)						32.0
4.0	3.0	4.7	Intangibles (net)						4.5
5.8	5.6	4.0	All Other Non-Current						3.2
100.0	100.0	100.0	Total						100.0
			LIABILITIES						
10.8	12.5	13.1	Notes Payable-Short Term						13.7
2.5	3.5	3.6	Cur. Mat.-L.T.D.						2.2
17.1	17.0	14.3	Trade Payables						13.1
.4	.1	.1	Income Taxes Payable						.1
8.3	10.6	11.1	All Other Current						9.9
39.1	43.7	42.3	Total Current						39.1
21.6	20.3	21.6	Long-Term Debt						15.3
.7	.4	.3	Deferred Taxes						.2
7.9	4.5	8.8	All Other Non-Current						4.7
30.6	31.1	27.0	Net Worth						40.7
100.0	100.0	100.0	Total Liabilties & Net Worth						100.0
			INCOME DATA						
100.0	100.0	100.0	Net Sales						100.0
18.7	16.0	16.1	Gross Profit						11.4
17.6	14.7	15.1	Operating Expenses						10.3
1.1	1.3	1.0	Operating Profit						1.2
.1	.2	.3	All Other Expenses (net)						.1
1.1	1.1	.7	Profit Before Taxes						1.1
			RATIOS						
2.1	2.3	2.5							2.6
1.4	1.5	1.4	Current						1.6
1.1	1.0	1.0							1.0
1.3	1.4	1.6							1.6
(74) .8	.9	.9	Quick						1.1
.5	.4	.5							.6
13 27.4	**12** 30.6	**14** 25.7							**14** 25.7
20 18.2	**17** 22.1	**18** 20.6	Sales/Receivables						**18** 20.4
27 13.5	**22** 16.5	**23** 15.9							**23** 16.1
9 42.1	**8** 46.8	**8** 44.5							**8** 44.5
19 19.2	**17** 21.0	**14** 25.9	Cost of Sales/Inventory						**14** 26.1
36 10.0	**31** 11.9	**23** 16.1							**23** 15.8
5 76.1	**5** 68.5	**5** 77.5							**5** 80.1
12 29.8	**10** 36.7	**10** 36.3	Cost of Sales/Payables						**9** 42.1
28 13.2	**19** 18.9	**16** 23.0							**15** 25.1
15.8	14.4	16.0							15.6
32.9	35.0	33.7	Sales/Working Capital						31.6
235.6	NM	437.6							231.1
10.5	10.0	10.5							15.5
(70) 3.1	(52) 2.7	(50) 4.1	EBIT/Interest						(36) 4.8
1.5	-.4	-.4							-.5
11.2	4.9	14.4	Net Profit + Depr., Dep.,						
(21) 6.0	(13) 2.6	(12) 3.0	Amort./Cur. Mat. L/T/D						
2.2	1.9	1.1							
.4	.3	.5							.5
1.0	1.0	1.0	Fixed/Worth						.9
3.3	3.7	4.7							1.9
.8	.7	.8							.7
2.5	2.6	2.5	Debt/Worth						2.1
7.3	9.0	8.8							5.3
32.9	44.2	38.3	% Profit Before Taxes/Tangible						38.1
(67) 15.4	(50) 12.8	(47) 16.9	Net Worth						(36) 19.0
1.7	-22.8	-6.2							-11.4
10.5	12.5	16.1	% Profit Before Taxes/Total						16.4
3.6	3.5	5.4	Assets						5.9
.2	-5.4	-4.2							-4.2
37.4	34.8	32.4							33.8
14.0	14.9	16.0	Sales/Net Fixed Assets						17.0
7.1	8.6	9.7							10.3
6.4	7.4	7.6							7.4
4.4	4.9	5.1	Sales/Total Assets						5.2
2.8	3.3	3.4							3.7
.5	.4	.6							.5
(66) 1.3	(50) 1.2	(45) 1.0	% Depr., Dep., Amort./Sales						(31) .9
2.2	2.1	1.6							1.3
.5	.3	.7	% Officers', Directors'						
(29) 1.2	(16) 1.6	(13) 2.2	Owners' Comp/Sales						
2.7	3.2	5.0							
7138619M	8796425M	8300339M	Net Sales ($)	1434M	8183M	3158M	25020M	108869M	8153675M
1779741M	1685424M	1586399M	Total Assets ($)	592M	2686M	2857M	9008M	19889M	1551367M

M = $ thousand MM = $ million

See Pages 9 through 22 for Explanation of Ratios and Data

Current Data Sorted by Assets							Comparative Historical Data	
						Type of Statement		
		4	11	6	3	Unqualified	33	29
1		19	10	3		Reviewed	29	43
1	4	10	3	1	1	Compiled	25	19
3	4	3	1			Tax Returns	10	19
	5	12	19	10	4	Other	53	57
19 (4/1-9/30/13)			119 (10/1/13-3/31/14)				4/1/09-3/31/10	4/1/10-3/31/11
0-500M	500M-2MM	2-10MM	10-50MM	50-100MM	100-250MM		ALL	ALL
5	13	48	44	20	8	**NUMBER OF STATEMENTS**	150	167
%	%	%	%	%	%	**ASSETS**	%	%
	14.3	9.4	8.9	4.7		Cash & Equivalents	9.7	8.8
	38.0	20.9	23.0	21.3		Trade Receivables (net)	20.5	23.3
	24.4	22.6	24.1	27.7		Inventory	23.7	22.7
	.8	1.8	.8	1.2		All Other Current	2.7	2.3
	77.5	54.7	56.8	55.0		Total Current	56.6	57.2
	17.2	37.9	36.5	39.5		Fixed Assets (net)	33.7	33.7
	.6	3.2	3.1	2.8		Intangibles (net)	4.0	4.0
	4.7	4.3	3.6	2.7		All Other Non-Current	5.7	5.2
	100.0	100.0	100.0	100.0		Total	100.0	100.0
						LIABILITIES		
	22.4	8.6	8.0	5.6		Notes Payable-Short Term	10.2	9.3
	1.0	2.7	3.0	3.3		Cur. Mat.-L.T.D.	3.4	3.1
	27.5	14.9	11.0	7.5		Trade Payables	13.2	13.2
	.0	.1	.1	.1		Income Taxes Payable	.1	.1
	8.2	5.6	6.9	7.6		All Other Current	8.3	9.0
	59.1	31.9	29.1	24.2		Total Current	35.2	34.8
	15.3	16.7	19.8	20.7		Long-Term Debt	18.1	20.2
	.1	.2	.5	.7		Deferred Taxes	.6	.5
	26.5	3.9	5.2	2.3		All Other Non-Current	6.3	7.4
	-.9	47.3	45.4	52.1		Net Worth	39.8	37.1
	100.0	100.0	100.0	100.0		Total Liabilties & Net Worth	100.0	100.0
						INCOME DATA		
	100.0	100.0	100.0	100.0		Net Sales	100.0	100.0
	17.3	22.2	21.0	16.7		Gross Profit	22.6	20.4
	15.6	20.3	16.3	11.0		Operating Expenses	18.8	17.6
	1.7	1.9	4.7	5.6		Operating Profit	3.9	2.8
	.6	-.1	.6	.4		All Other Expenses (net)	.7	.7
	1.1	2.0	4.1	5.2		Profit Before Taxes	3.2	2.1
						RATIOS		
	2.4	2.8	3.3	3.4			2.8	2.9
	1.4	1.7	2.0	2.3		Current	1.6	1.8
	.9	1.1	1.4	1.7			1.2	1.2
	1.5	1.7	1.8	1.6			1.6	1.7
	1.0	.8	1.1	1.0		Quick	.9	.9
	.5	.5	.7	.8			.5	.6
	13 27.1	**15** 24.2	**17** 21.9	**18** 19.9			**15** 23.9	**16** 23.5
	18 19.9	**20** 17.9	**21** 17.3	**25** 14.4		Sales/Receivables	**20** 18.1	**21** 17.4
	27 13.3	**26** 13.9	**30** 12.3	**35** 10.5			**26** 14.1	**26** 13.8
	5 74.8	**17** 21.2	**12** 30.4	**24** 15.1			**16** 22.7	**17** 20.9
	11 33.7	**29** 12.6	**29** 12.5	**41** 9.0		Cost of Sales/Inventory	**29** 12.5	**25** 14.8
	24 15.0	**42** 8.7	**59** 6.2	**79** 4.6			**50** 7.3	**43** 8.4
	10 34.9	**11** 33.2	**7** 52.8	**8** 48.1			**8** 44.2	**8** 45.9
	15 24.4	**16** 23.2	**12** 29.5	**10** 37.4		Cost of Sales/Payables	**14** 26.2	**13** 27.9
	22 16.4	**24** 15.2	**23** 15.9	**17** 21.1			**27** 13.6	**21** 17.3
	10.7	9.6	6.6	5.4			8.1	8.8
	39.5	21.3	12.2	9.4		Sales/Working Capital	18.6	17.6
	NM	135.1	24.6	19.5			58.0	49.9
	26.1	11.5	16.4	29.5			13.7	10.7
	(10) 2.5	(38) 2.5	(40) 8.5	(19) 19.7		EBIT/Interest	(139) 5.3	(158) 4.0
	1.4	.7	2.5	9.3			1.9	1.2
		6.8	4.2				6.0	9.8
		(12) 2.6	(12) 2.4			Net Profit + Depr., Dep., Amort./Cur. Mat. L/T/D	(41) 2.9	(43) 3.6
		2.1	.7				1.8	1.8
	.2	.4	.4	.5			.4	.4
	1.2	.8	.9	.8		Fixed/Worth	.9	.9
	-2.6	1.5	1.3	1.5			2.1	1.9
	3.9	.5	.7	.6			.6	.7
	19.1	1.2	1.1	1.0		Debt/Worth	1.7	1.6
	-5.8	2.9	2.4	1.4			4.7	3.8
		25.1	29.5	39.0			42.2	39.5
		(46) 9.2	(41) 19.4	31.6		% Profit Before Taxes/Tangible Net Worth	(136) 22.5	(148) 19.4
		2.7	6.9	15.3			9.8	4.0
	16.6	11.9	15.1	18.1			17.4	12.3
	3.7	3.9	7.2	14.5		% Profit Before Taxes/Total Assets	9.1	6.4
	-1.8	.4	3.2	8.7			2.6	.3
	195.0	27.8	24.9	16.6			22.5	20.8
	45.9	9.1	9.0	6.4		Sales/Net Fixed Assets	10.0	10.4
	13.1	5.2	4.4	4.8			5.8	5.6
	13.9	5.0	4.5	4.6			4.6	5.1
	5.5	3.5	2.9	2.6		Sales/Total Assets	3.1	3.5
	4.3	2.1	2.1	1.8			2.2	2.2
		.7	.7	.8			.8	.9
		(42) 1.4	1.7	1.8		% Depr., Dep., Amort./Sales	(135) 1.5	(149) 1.6
		2.5	2.7	2.8			2.4	2.6
		1.0	.5				.9	.9
		(17) 1.7	(13) .7			% Officers', Directors' Owners' Comp/Sales	(50) 2.3	(66) 2.0
		4.0	2.0				3.7	4.4
5038M	**163193M**	**1098498M**	**3771642M**	**4953557M**	**4170171M**	Net Sales ($)	**16301591M**	**14532540M**
1187M	**15314M**	**270369M**	**978952M**	**1468656M**	**1229924M**	Total Assets ($)	**4947888M**	**4369529M**

M = $ thousand MM = $ million

See Pages 9 through 22 for Explanation of Ratios and Data

Comparative Historical Data				Current Data Sorted by Sales					
			Type of Statement						
27	24	24	Unqualified			1	1	3	19
34	27	33	Reviewed		1		6	9	17
17	21	20	Compiled		2	1	2	4	11
19	9	11	Tax Returns	3	2		1	4	1
68	68	50	Other			2	2	9	37
4/1/11-3/31/12 ALL	**4/1/12-3/31/13 ALL**	**4/1/13-3/31/14 ALL**		**19 (4/1-9/30/13)**			**119 (10/1/13-3/31/14)**		
				0-1MM	**1-3MM**	**3-5MM**	**5-10MM**	**10-25MM**	**25MM & OVER**
165	149	138	**NUMBER OF STATEMENTS**	3	5	4	12	29	85
%	%	%	**ASSETS**	%	%	%	%	%	%
7.6	9.2	9.3	Cash & Equivalents				18.0	5.9	7.7
25.8	23.4	22.5	Trade Receivables (net)				12.9	28.0	22.9
23.0	26.4	24.3	Inventory				13.0	24.3	26.4
2.4	2.3	1.3	All Other Current				1.1	1.2	1.3
58.8	61.3	57.4	Total Current				45.0	59.4	58.3
30.8	30.8	34.9	Fixed Assets (net)				44.3	35.2	33.8
5.4	3.2	3.9	Intangibles (net)				2.8	3.0	4.7
4.9	4.7	3.9	All Other Non-Current				7.9	2.4	3.1
100.0	100.0	100.0	Total				100.0	100.0	100.0
			LIABILITIES						
11.7	12.5	9.4	Notes Payable-Short Term				4.3	11.0	9.9
2.2	2.3	2.7	Cur. Mat.-L.T.D.				1.7	3.2	2.7
16.0	14.7	13.6	Trade Payables				6.6	20.5	12.5
.1	.1	.1	Income Taxes Payable				.0	.0	.1
8.2	8.2	8.8	All Other Current				9.0	5.7	9.7
38.2	37.9	34.5	Total Current				21.6	40.3	34.8
16.8	15.8	18.3	Long-Term Debt				16.3	15.5	18.3
.5	.4	.5	Deferred Taxes				.1	.1	.7
7.2	7.0	6.0	All Other Non-Current				9.2	4.5	3.7
37.3	38.9	40.6	Net Worth				52.8	39.5	42.5
100.0	100.0	100.0	Total Liabilties & Net Worth				100.0	100.0	100.0
			INCOME DATA						
100.0	100.0	100.0	Net Sales				100.0	100.0	100.0
19.6	19.1	20.8	Gross Profit				32.3	22.5	15.9
17.0	15.9	17.5	Operating Expenses				28.9	20.1	12.9
2.6	3.2	3.2	Operating Profit				3.5	2.4	3.1
.4	.3	.4	All Other Expenses (net)				-.5	.3	.2
2.1	2.9	2.9	Profit Before Taxes				4.0	2.1	2.8
			RATIOS						
2.8	2.9	3.1					6.1	2.2	3.0
1.7	1.8	1.9	Current				1.9	1.5	2.0
1.0	1.2	1.2					1.1	1.1	1.4
1.7	1.6	1.6					4.7	1.2	1.6
.9	.9	.9	Quick				1.0	.8	.9
.5	.5	.6					.7	.6	.6
16 22.6	**15** 24.0	**16** 22.4					**17** 22.0	**18** 20.6	**16** 22.5
21 17.2	**20** 18.1	**21** 17.4	Sales/Receivables				**21** 17.2	**22** 16.3	**20** 18.4
28 13.1	**27** 13.7	**29** 12.8					**30** 12.0	**30** 12.2	**28** 12.9
15 25.1	**15** 23.7	**15** 23.9					**19** 19.5	**18** 20.0	**15** 24.1
25 14.5	**29** 12.8	**30** 12.2	Cost of Sales/Inventory				**35** 10.4	**29** 12.4	**30** 12.0
41 8.8	**51** 7.1	**46** 7.9					**55** 6.6	**50** 7.3	**45** 8.2
9 39.5	**8** 48.1	**8** 44.8					**12** 31.4	**11** 32.6	**8** 48.4
14 26.2	**13** 28.4	**13** 28.0	Cost of Sales/Payables				**16** 22.7	**18** 20.7	**12** 29.8
24 15.0	**21** 17.4	**22** 16.4					**26** 14.3	**26** 14.3	**20** 18.3
10.1	8.7	8.0					4.5	9.2	7.8
20.7	16.1	15.6	Sales/Working Capital				13.9	24.3	14.0
180.6	60.8	49.0					NM	84.7	31.0
14.0	16.4	18.8						11.9	19.3
(156) 4.0	(135) 7.5	(117) 6.9	EBIT/Interest					(26) 2.7	(74) 8.5
1.5	2.9	1.9						1.0	2.3
10.2	10.2	4.2							4.0
(40) 2.6	(36) 3.6	(31) 2.7	Net Profit + Depr., Dep., Amort./Cur. Mat. L/T/D						(22) 2.3
1.4	2.3	1.5							1.2
.4	.4	.4					.4	.5	.4
.9	.8	.9	Fixed/Worth				.6	1.0	.8
1.8	1.6	1.6					3.6	1.3	1.5
.8	.7	.6					.1	.7	.6
1.6	1.5	1.2	Debt/Worth				.8	1.4	1.2
5.8	4.6	3.9					4.9	4.9	2.9
36.7	35.0	33.6					43.6	32.7	33.6
(137) 19.1	(131) 20.5	(123) 16.7	% Profit Before Taxes/Tangible Net Worth				(11) 21.0	(26) 11.2	(79) 19.4
4.4	9.6	5.7					5.6	2.4	7.1
13.6	14.4	15.0					20.6	11.3	16.1
6.2	8.1	6.1	% Profit Before Taxes/Total Assets				4.5	2.5	8.5
1.0	2.4	1.7					3.9	-.6	2.0
27.7	21.3	25.8					8.6	39.7	22.9
13.3	11.2	9.3	Sales/Net Fixed Assets				5.3	8.8	9.4
5.8	6.4	5.5					2.5	4.1	5.6
5.6	5.4	5.1					2.3	5.2	5.4
3.7	3.5	3.5	Sales/Total Assets				2.1	3.5	3.8
2.4	2.2	2.1					1.8	2.0	2.2
.7	1.0	.7					1.4	.9	.6
(150) 1.2	(130) 1.5	(123) 1.4	% Depr., Dep., Amort./Sales				(11) 1.9	(23) 2.0	(80) 1.3
2.2	2.4	2.7					3.5	3.0	2.5
.8	.7	.8						.7	.6
(55) 1.7	(46) 1.7	(42) 1.6	% Officers', Directors' Owners' Comp/Sales					(11) 1.2	(22) 1.2
3.7	4.8	3.7						3.4	2.2
15960872M	**15017036M**	**14162099M**	Net Sales ($)	**2088M**	**9349M**	**14716M**	**92001M**	**457891M**	**13586054M**
4307513M	**4267272M**	**3964402M**	Total Assets ($)	**344M**	**3852M**	**20850M**	**52786M**	**160326M**	**3726244M**

M = $ thousand MM = $ million

See Pages 9 through 22 for Explanation of Ratios and Data

Current Data Sorted by Assets							Comparative Historical Data	
Type of Statement								
Unqualified			2	2	4	4	27	23
Reviewed			4	3			13	8
Compiled			1				1	3
Tax Returns			1				3	2
Other		3	2	10	2	7	13	24
		10 (4/1-9/30/13)		35 (10/1/13-3/31/14)			4/1/09-3/31/10 ALL	4/1/10-3/31/11 ALL
	0-500M	500M-2MM	2-10MM	10-50MM	50-100MM	100-250MM		
NUMBER OF STATEMENTS		3	10	15	6	11	57	60
ASSETS	%	%	%	%	%	%	%	%
Cash & Equivalents	DATA NOT AVAILABLE		6.2	3.5		10.8	5.2	6.9
Trade Receivables (net)			30.4	15.3		11.5	19.1	19.0
Inventory			22.7	15.9		24.4	22.5	21.3
All Other Current			2.1	5.6		2.3	2.1	2.4
Total Current			61.5	40.2		49.0	48.9	49.7
Fixed Assets (net)			27.9	52.9		37.6	42.4	41.5
Intangibles (net)			6.1	.2		5.3	2.5	2.2
All Other Non-Current			4.5	6.7		8.0	6.2	6.7
Total			100.0	100.0		100.0	100.0	100.0
LIABILITIES								
Notes Payable-Short Term			11.9	8.5		4.8	10.7	6.8
Cur. Mat.-L.T.D.			2.3	3.3		4.5	4.4	3.6
Trade Payables			23.0	11.9		7.0	13.1	13.0
Income Taxes Payable			.0	.0		2.7	.5	.6
All Other Current			11.6	5.2		5.9	8.1	6.7
Total Current			48.8	29.0		24.9	36.8	30.7
Long-Term Debt			16.9	20.2		21.6	17.8	15.3
Deferred Taxes			.7	.4		2.4	1.0	1.3
All Other Non-Current			2.8	1.2		7.0	3.5	4.4
Net Worth			30.8	49.1		44.0	40.9	48.3
Total Liabilties & Net Worth			100.0	100.0		100.0	100.0	100.0
INCOME DATA								
Net Sales			100.0	100.0		100.0	100.0	100.0
Gross Profit			15.4	17.2		15.7	16.0	18.7
Operating Expenses			12.1	13.5		12.3	11.2	14.5
Operating Profit			3.3	3.6		3.4	4.8	4.2
All Other Expenses (net)			.6	.4		-.3	.5	.4
Profit Before Taxes			2.7	3.2		3.7	4.3	3.7
RATIOS								
			1.9	2.2		3.8	2.1	2.5
Current			1.4	1.6		2.2	1.4	1.8
			.9	1.1		1.1	1.0	1.4
			1.2	1.2		2.3	1.1	1.3
Quick			.7	1.0		.7	.7	.8
			.4	.4		.4	.4	.6
			16 22.4	**7** 51.8		**12** 31.6	**15** 24.0	**14** 26.0
Sales/Receivables			**19** 19.4	**15** 24.1		**18** 20.8	**19** 18.9	**19** 18.9
			28 13.2	**21** 17.1		**22** 16.7	**28** 13.3	**28** 13.2
			11 33.1	**7** 49.6		**33** 11.1	**15** 24.0	**20** 18.6
Cost of Sales/Inventory			**24** 15.4	**21** 17.3		**43** 8.5	**30** 12.0	**33** 11.1
			39 9.4	**28** 13.2		**60** 6.1	**55** 6.7	**47** 7.8
			8 43.3	**9** 40.0		**7** 54.4	**10** 36.8	**11** 33.9
Cost of Sales/Payables			**16** 23.2	**12** 30.7		**11** 34.5	**17** 22.0	**16** 23.4
			36 10.1	**19** 19.6		**16** 22.8	**25** 14.7	**23** 16.1
			11.0	13.6		5.5	10.9	8.7
Sales/Working Capital			25.1	22.7		11.8	24.5	16.2
			-141.6	211.3		53.5	847.5	29.4
			9.7	14.2			13.2	20.2
EBIT/Interest			7.7	6.4			(53) 4.0	(58) 5.3
			3.3	.3			1.8	2.4
							19.2	8.9
Net Profit + Depr., Dep., Amort./Cur. Mat. L/T/D							(14) 2.8	(17) 4.4
							2.3	2.4
			.6	.6		.5	.7	.5
Fixed/Worth			1.4	1.2		1.2	1.3	.9
			-2.5	1.4		1.8	2.0	1.9
			1.1	.6		.4	.6	.5
Debt/Worth			2.8	1.0		1.8	1.5	1.4
			-22.7	1.3		3.0	3.4	2.5
				38.8		39.0	46.9	36.7
% Profit Before Taxes/Tangible Net Worth				16.5		(10) 17.2	(54) 18.3	18.7
				-2.6		3.4	6.2	10.3
			16.2	19.3		21.1	16.8	17.4
% Profit Before Taxes/Total Assets			7.1	4.6		6.7	8.0	7.1
			3.4	-.9		1.2	2.5	2.5
			273.7	14.7		9.0	10.7	12.6
Sales/Net Fixed Assets			8.4	6.1		6.7	6.7	7.4
			6.6	4.3		6.1	4.6	4.6
			9.9	5.3		3.1	4.6	4.1
Sales/Total Assets			3.1	3.5		2.4	2.7	2.9
			2.6	2.4		2.3	2.1	2.1
				1.1			1.2	1.3
% Depr., Dep., Amort./Sales				1.7			(48) 2.1	(51) 1.9
				3.1			2.9	3.1
% Officers', Directors' Owners' Comp/Sales								
Net Sales ($)		39538M	269966M	1531751M	1287802M	4075104M	9997169M	9045581M
Total Assets ($)		3497M	42817M	388868M	421302M	1599928M	3568712M	3488075M

M = $ thousand MM = $ million

See Pages 9 through 22 for Explanation of Ratios and Data

Comparative Historical Data				Current Data Sorted by Sales					
			Type of Statement						
18	13	12	Unqualified			1		1	10
10	9	7	Reviewed					2	5
2	2	1	Compiled				1		
3	3	1	Tax Returns					1	
10	16	24	Other				3	3	18
				10 (4/1-9/30/13)			35 (10/1/13-3/31/14)		
4/1/11-3/31/12 ALL	4/1/12-3/31/13 ALL	4/1/13-3/31/14 ALL		0-1MM	1-3MM	3-5MM	5-10MM	10-25MM	25MM & OVER
43	43	45	**NUMBER OF STATEMENTS**			1	4	7	33
%	%	%	**ASSETS**	%	%	%	%	%	%
6.4	6.5	6.2	Cash & Equivalents	DATA NOT AVAILABLE	DATA NOT AVAILABLE				6.0
16.7	16.8	18.4	Trade Receivables (net)						18.2
21.0	22.5	19.7	Inventory						21.5
2.9	2.0	3.5	All Other Current						3.3
47.1	47.8	47.9	Total Current						49.1
44.7	46.3	41.7	Fixed Assets (net)						41.6
.8	1.1	2.7	Intangibles (net)						2.0
7.4	4.8	7.8	All Other Non-Current						7.3
100.0	100.0	100.0	Total						100.0
			LIABILITIES						
8.9	8.5	7.6	Notes Payable-Short Term						7.2
4.0	4.0	3.2	Cur. Mat.-L.T.D.						3.6
11.6	13.1	14.4	Trade Payables						13.0
.3	.4	.7	Income Taxes Payable						.9
4.8	7.2	6.7	All Other Current						7.6
29.6	33.1	32.6	Total Current						32.4
18.0	18.4	20.1	Long-Term Debt						18.7
.8	.7	1.0	Deferred Taxes						1.1
3.6	2.2	3.0	All Other Non-Current						3.0
48.2	45.5	43.4	Net Worth						44.8
100.0	100.0	100.0	Total Liabilties & Net Worth						100.0
			INCOME DATA						
100.0	100.0	100.0	Net Sales						100.0
18.1	18.1	15.7	Gross Profit						13.5
15.6	14.4	12.3	Operating Expenses						10.2
2.5	3.7	3.4	Operating Profit						3.4
.4	.4	.3	All Other Expenses (net)						.2
2.1	3.3	3.1	Profit Before Taxes						3.1
			RATIOS						
2.3	2.4	2.3							2.3
1.5	1.7	1.5	Current						1.7
1.3	1.2	1.1							1.1
1.0	1.1	1.2							1.2
.7	.6	.8	Quick						.8
.4	.4	.5							.5
16 23.3	**16** 23.2	**12** 31.6							**12** 31.6
20 18.1	**19** 19.5	**18** 20.4	Sales/Receivables						**16** 23.2
26 14.1	**25** 14.5	**23** 15.9							**21** 17.7
15 23.6	**15** 25.1	**11** 32.9							**14** 25.7
30 12.0	**35** 10.5	**28** 13.2	Cost of Sales/Inventory						**28** 13.2
54 6.7	**56** 6.5	**39** 9.3							**41** 8.8
9 38.7	**10** 38.0	**9** 41.8							**8** 44.2
15 24.0	**15** 24.3	**13** 27.2	Cost of Sales/Payables						**11** 34.4
27 13.5	**27** 13.7	**18** 20.1							**17** 21.0
9.4	8.5	11.8							12.1
22.4	19.2	22.7	Sales/Working Capital						20.0
40.9	37.2	178.9							141.5
10.2	12.3	12.4							10.3
(42) 3.3	(42) 6.0	(43) 6.4	EBIT/Interest						(31) 6.4
1.2	2.2	1.6							1.2
			Net Profit + Depr., Dep., Amort./Cur. Mat. L/T/D						
.6	.6	.6							.6
1.0	1.1	1.2	Fixed/Worth						1.2
1.8	1.7	1.5							1.4
.4	.6	.9							.8
1.5	1.2	1.2	Debt/Worth						1.1
2.3	2.0	2.6							2.2
25.3	33.1	38.3							38.5
(42) 8.2	(40) 19.6	(41) 18.0	% Profit Before Taxes/Tangible Net Worth						(30) 17.2
3.6	8.5	5.2							4.7
8.1	13.7	17.5							19.6
4.3	9.0	6.7	% Profit Before Taxes/Total Assets						7.0
.3	2.4	2.1							1.4
11.2	9.4	14.1							14.1
6.7	6.3	7.1	Sales/Net Fixed Assets						6.7
3.5	3.8	5.9							5.9
4.7	3.7	4.3							4.3
2.6	2.7	3.1	Sales/Total Assets						3.2
1.8	2.0	2.4							2.4
1.3	1.2	1.2							1.2
(37) 2.1	(38) 1.8	(39) 2.1	% Depr., Dep., Amort./Sales						(28) 1.8
3.5	3.3	2.7							2.7
			% Officers', Directors' Owners' Comp/Sales						
5484435M	6746914M	7204161M	Net Sales ($)			4669M	31247M	124092M	7044153M
2220187M	2422004M	2456412M	Total Assets ($)			2900M	7375M	45217M	2400920M

M = $ thousand MM = $ million

See Pages 9 through 22 for Explanation of Ratios and Data

Current Data Sorted by Assets							Comparative Historical Data	
						Type of Statement		
		1	3		3	Unqualified	26	15
		2	5			Reviewed	19	19
	1	2				Compiled	6	3
2	1	5				Tax Returns	10	12
2	5	12	14	5	1	Other	39	35
12 (4/1-9/30/13)			52 (10/1/13-3/31/14)				4/1/09-3/31/10	4/1/10-3/31/11
0-500M	500M-2MM	2-10MM	10-50MM	50-100MM	100-250MM		ALL	ALL
4	7	22	22	5	4	**NUMBER OF STATEMENTS**	100	84
%	%	%	%	%	%	**ASSETS**	%	%
		7.8	6.3			Cash & Equivalents	7.4	9.1
		26.8	19.2			Trade Receivables (net)	21.7	21.3
		29.3	34.9			Inventory	29.1	29.8
		.6	1.7			All Other Current	3.7	3.1
		64.5	62.2			Total Current	61.9	63.3
		16.3	23.5			Fixed Assets (net)	28.9	29.3
		3.9	9.9			Intangibles (net)	4.1	3.1
		15.3	4.5			All Other Non-Current	5.1	4.3
		100.0	100.0			Total	100.0	100.0
						LIABILITIES		
		12.5	15.5			Notes Payable-Short Term	17.2	17.5
		1.6	3.5			Cur. Mat.-L.T.D.	4.1	2.5
		29.9	10.7			Trade Payables	14.4	15.5
		.0	.1			Income Taxes Payable	.2	.2
		12.1	9.0			All Other Current	7.8	10.0
		56.2	38.8			Total Current	43.7	45.7
		9.6	16.1			Long-Term Debt	12.9	12.2
		.5	.9			Deferred Taxes	.8	.9
		1.3	7.1			All Other Non-Current	5.4	8.0
		32.5	37.1			Net Worth	37.2	33.1
		100.0	100.0			Total Liabilties & Net Worth	100.0	100.0
						INCOME DATA		
		100.0	100.0			Net Sales	100.0	100.0
		14.6	16.5			Gross Profit	19.3	19.2
		14.5	15.0			Operating Expenses	16.7	14.6
		.1	1.5			Operating Profit	2.6	4.6
		-1.5	.6			All Other Expenses (net)	.2	.2
		1.5	.9			Profit Before Taxes	2.3	4.4
						RATIOS		
		2.4	2.4				2.2	1.9
		1.3	1.5			Current	1.5	1.4
		.7	1.2				1.1	1.0
		1.1	1.3				1.0	1.1
		.7	.7			Quick	.6	.6
		.4	.4				.4	.4
		25 14.6	**25** 14.4				**21** 17.4	**19** 18.8
		31 11.8	**31** 11.8			Sales/Receivables	**30** 12.2	**31** 11.7
		51 7.2	**37** 9.8				**36** 10.0	**38** 9.5
		18 20.3	**47** 7.7				**20** 18.4	**20** 18.4
		37 9.8	**64** 5.7			Cost of Sales/Inventory	**49** 7.5	**49** 7.4
		79 4.6	**81** 4.5				**94** 3.9	**85** 4.3
		22 16.8	**11** 33.6				**10** 38.0	**8** 47.9
		29 12.5	**22** 16.9			Cost of Sales/Payables	**19** 19.4	**17** 21.5
		63 5.8	**33** 10.9				**33** 10.9	**35** 10.3
		6.8	6.2				6.7	7.6
		23.2	11.1			Sales/Working Capital	14.2	17.5
		-9.8	24.9				87.3	183.8
		10.8	13.6				7.4	11.4
		(19) 5.0	2.9			EBIT/Interest	(98) 3.0	(81) 4.7
		-.6	-.7				1.2	2.2
							15.7	19.3
						Net Profit + Depr., Dep., Amort./Cur. Mat. L/T/D	(30) 3.3	(27) 3.5
							1.2	2.0
		.2	.3				.4	.3
		.6	.5			Fixed/Worth	.7	.7
		1.6	1.4				2.3	1.7
		.7	1.1				.9	1.0
		2.6	1.6			Debt/Worth	1.7	2.1
		9.7	5.1				4.5	3.8
		47.2	29.1				41.6	45.0
		(18) 28.5	(19) 6.8			% Profit Before Taxes/Tangible Net Worth	(87) 18.4	(75) 26.6
		7.3	-6.7				.8	9.6
		19.5	11.3				12.3	16.4
		6.1	4.3			% Profit Before Taxes/Total Assets	4.2	6.7
		-1.2	-2.8				.3	2.7
		49.8	27.0				38.2	28.0
		22.7	15.4			Sales/Net Fixed Assets	11.1	11.4
		9.2	5.2				4.1	4.3
		4.5	3.0				3.5	3.6
		2.7	2.3			Sales/Total Assets	2.5	2.4
		1.7	1.3				1.5	1.7
		.4	.7				.7	.6
		(17) .7	(21) 1.2			% Depr., Dep., Amort./Sales	(87) 1.5	(75) 1.4
		1.4	3.8				2.9	2.7
							1.1	.8
						% Officers', Directors' Owners' Comp/Sales	(28) 2.3	(28) 2.0
							3.4	2.9
8276M	35315M	362908M	1100422M	739061M	1197185M	Net Sales ($)	8234714M	4935088M
1159M	8180M	123891M	495670M	326552M	629597M	Total Assets ($)	3948596M	2484101M

M = $ thousand MM = $ million

See Pages 9 through 22 for Explanation of Ratios and Data

Comparative Historical Data				Current Data Sorted by Sales					
			Type of Statement						
13	21	7	Unqualified					1	6
15	14	7	Reviewed				1	2	4
5	4	3	Compiled			1		2	
14	8	8	Tax Returns	1	1	2	2	1	1
34	41	39	Other		3	1	7	6	22
				12 (4/1-9/30/13)			52 (10/1/13-3/31/14)		
4/1/11-3/31/12 ALL	4/1/12-3/31/13 ALL	4/1/13-3/31/14 ALL		0-1MM	1-3MM	3-5MM	5-10MM	10-25MM	25MM & OVER
81	88	64	**NUMBER OF STATEMENTS**	1	4	4	10	12	33
%	%	%	**ASSETS**	%	%	%	%	%	%
11.9	9.8	6.8	Cash & Equivalents				5.7	9.7	4.7
21.9	22.8	23.9	Trade Receivables (net)				26.6	31.2	22.0
28.0	36.5	30.4	Inventory				19.6	32.1	38.5
3.9	2.8	1.8	All Other Current				.2	2.5	2.2
65.6	71.9	62.8	Total Current				52.1	75.5	67.4
22.4	19.8	21.7	Fixed Assets (net)				25.5	14.7	19.5
2.7	3.1	6.2	Intangibles (net)				.8	7.1	7.1
9.3	5.2	9.3	All Other Non-Current				21.6	2.7	6.0
100.0	100.0	100.0	Total				100.0	100.0	100.0
			LIABILITIES						
21.6	22.1	19.8	Notes Payable-Short Term				8.4	14.8	20.2
2.8	2.1	2.0	Cur. Mat.-L.T.D.				2.4	.7	2.8
14.8	15.6	17.8	Trade Payables				28.6	29.9	12.0
.1	.1	.0	Income Taxes Payable				.0	.0	.1
11.1	10.9	11.2	All Other Current				19.5	7.4	8.8
50.5	50.8	50.8	Total Current				58.9	52.8	43.9
11.8	9.1	11.9	Long-Term Debt				14.7	9.2	11.7
.3	.3	.6	Deferred Taxes				.0	.8	.8
4.6	7.5	4.4	All Other Non-Current				.0	3.6	4.4
32.9	32.4	32.4	Net Worth				26.3	33.6	39.2
100.0	100.0	100.0	Total Liabilties & Net Worth				100.0	100.0	100.0
			INCOME DATA						
100.0	100.0	100.0	Net Sales				100.0	100.0	100.0
18.8	19.4	17.5	Gross Profit				19.1	16.0	12.5
15.4	15.1	15.8	Operating Expenses				23.7	15.4	9.6
3.5	4.3	1.7	Operating Profit				-4.6	.5	2.9
.2	.3	-.3	All Other Expenses (net)				-.9	-3.5	.7
3.3	4.0	2.0	Profit Before Taxes				-3.7	4.0	2.2
			RATIOS						
2.1	2.1	2.2					2.1	2.4	2.1
1.3	1.3	1.3	Current				.8	1.6	1.4
1.0	1.1	1.1					.4	1.2	1.2
1.1	1.2	1.2					1.2	1.7	1.0
.6	.6	.6	Quick				.5	.9	.6
.4	.4	.4					.2	.6	.4
12 30.7	**20** 18.5	**23** 15.9					**19** 19.3	**24** 15.2	**26** 14.1
27 13.3	**29** 12.5	**30** 12.3	Sales/Receivables				**39** 9.4	**29** 12.4	**30** 12.0
39 9.4	**38** 9.6	**39** 9.3					**58** 6.3	**45** 8.1	**38** 9.6
13 27.4	**33** 11.0	**21** 17.0					**11** 34.1	**20** 18.5	**46** 8.0
45 8.2	**62** 5.9	**47** 7.7	Cost of Sales/Inventory				**37** 9.9	**41** 9.0	**61** 6.0
83 4.4	**104** 3.5	**79** 4.6					**85** 4.3	**118** 3.1	**87** 4.2
7 51.5	**9** 38.8	**11** 34.1					**12** 30.0	**16** 23.2	**11** 33.8
16 22.5	**19** 19.1	**23** 15.6	Cost of Sales/Payables				**69** 5.3	**28** 13.2	**18** 20.5
32 11.5	**34** 10.7	**34** 10.8					**118** 3.1	**34** 10.8	**29** 12.5
8.2	5.4	6.6					12.1	6.3	6.5
18.4	13.0	16.0	Sales/Working Capital				-67.8	8.6	13.3
392.5	69.3	49.0					-3.2	36.7	29.1
8.5	14.2	10.3						19.7	9.5
(79) 4.1	(85) 5.5	(57) 4.4	EBIT/Interest					(11) 8.5	(32) 4.5
1.7	2.8	.5						3.9	1.2
8.5	32.7	15.5							
(16) 5.1	(16) 7.4	(11) 5.9	Net Profit + Depr., Dep., Amort./Cur. Mat. L/T/D						
2.0	3.3	1.3							
.2	.2	.3					.4	.3	.2
.6	.5	.6	Fixed/Worth				.7	.5	.5
1.4	1.6	1.6					NM	1.3	1.1
1.0	1.0	.7					.7	.6	1.0
2.2	2.4	2.1	Debt/Worth				5.1	2.6	1.5
7.1	5.8	8.3					NM	8.0	4.3
41.9	47.0	38.5						60.8	29.1
(73) 23.0	(78) 23.8	(52) 16.6	% Profit Before Taxes/Tangible Net Worth					(11) 35.1	(29) 12.5
9.7	11.2	4.8						21.0	5.0
12.6	17.1	14.7					17.2	17.1	12.0
7.6	6.8	5.2	% Profit Before Taxes/Total Assets				.7	9.8	4.8
1.9	3.5	.3					-14.2	4.6	.9
53.6	62.3	40.3					32.6	49.9	44.8
14.0	18.9	16.0	Sales/Net Fixed Assets				17.5	29.1	16.4
6.7	6.5	7.6					8.8	8.7	6.0
3.9	4.0	3.8					3.4	5.7	3.4
2.7	2.8	2.5	Sales/Total Assets				2.0	3.1	2.5
1.9	1.7	1.7					1.1	1.5	1.7
.5	.4	.5							.6
(69) 1.1	(77) .7	(53) 1.1	% Depr., Dep., Amort./Sales						(30) 1.1
2.6	2.0	2.3							2.3
.6	.9	1.1							
(29) 1.8	(24) 1.6	(18) 2.2	% Officers', Directors' Owners' Comp/Sales						
2.8	4.6	3.5							
7016370M	**5696701M**	**3443167M**	Net Sales ($)	**232M**	**6396M**	**16170M**	**72194M**	**213552M**	**3134623M**
2987779M	**2589849M**	**1585049M**	Total Assets ($)	**80M**	**2844M**	**7623M**	**47167M**	**87942M**	**1439393M**

M = $ thousand MM = $ million

See Pages 9 through 22 for Explanation of Ratios and Data

Current Data Sorted by Assets							Comparative Historical Data	
						Type of Statement		
			1	1	1	Unqualified	8	4
		3	4			Reviewed	9	6
6	9	4				Compiled	69	36
14	11	5			1	Tax Returns	35	33
7	4	7	8	1		Other	41	32
	5 (4/1-9/30/13)		82 (10/1/13-3/31/14)				4/1/09-3/31/10	4/1/10-3/31/11
0-500M	**500M-2MM**	**2-10MM**	**10-50MM**	**50-100MM**	**100-250MM**		**ALL**	**ALL**
27	24	19	13	2	2	**NUMBER OF STATEMENTS**	162	111
%	%	%	%	%	%	**ASSETS**	%	%
16.6	10.5	6.7	9.4			Cash & Equivalents	12.8	11.8
8.4	7.3	13.5	9.9			Trade Receivables (net)	6.6	8.6
9.7	7.8	10.5	10.5			Inventory	5.3	6.0
.1	7.7	1.2	1.5			All Other Current	2.2	1.9
34.7	33.2	31.9	31.3			Total Current	26.9	28.3
44.8	45.7	38.7	45.5			Fixed Assets (net)	43.9	46.5
13.1	11.7	26.2	12.8			Intangibles (net)	18.7	14.2
7.4	9.4	3.2	10.4			All Other Non-Current	10.5	11.0
100.0	100.0	100.0	100.0			Total	100.0	100.0
						LIABILITIES		
9.8	3.5	11.4	6.9			Notes Payable-Short Term	4.2	5.5
3.6	6.7	4.7	7.4			Cur. Mat.-L.T.D.	7.3	6.0
6.6	9.6	9.5	11.5			Trade Payables	7.3	10.0
.0	1.0	.0	.0			Income Taxes Payable	.1	.2
21.4	11.0	16.6	6.1			All Other Current	19.7	8.1
41.5	31.8	42.3	31.9			Total Current	38.6	29.8
29.7	44.8	38.9	23.4			Long-Term Debt	35.2	32.6
.0	.0	.0	.1			Deferred Taxes	.0	.2
19.0	2.6	2.4	5.7			All Other Non-Current	11.4	10.5
9.8	20.8	16.5	39.0			Net Worth	14.7	26.9
100.0	100.0	100.0	100.0			Total Liabilties & Net Worth	100.0	100.0
						INCOME DATA		
100.0	100.0	100.0	100.0			Net Sales	100.0	100.0
58.5	38.5	37.0	30.0			Gross Profit	45.3	45.7
51.1	33.4	31.9	24.4			Operating Expenses	38.7	41.1
7.4	5.1	5.2	5.7			Operating Profit	6.6	4.6
.5	.8	1.9	1.8			All Other Expenses (net)	1.5	1.0
6.9	4.3	3.3	3.8			Profit Before Taxes	5.1	3.6
						RATIOS		
2.0	1.6	1.5	1.9				1.6	1.8
1.3	1.1	.9	.7			Current	.8	1.0
.6	.5	.5	.6				.3	.4
1.7	1.1	.8	1.1				1.1	1.4
.9	.5	.5	.6			Quick	.5	(110) .7
.2	.1	.3	.3				.1	.2
0 UND	0 UND	1 670.6	3 125.9				0 UND	0 999.8
0 UND	1 393.4	20 18.0	25 14.7			Sales/Receivables	1 468.9	2 172.3
9 39.8	14 26.1	34 10.8	30 12.2				13 27.2	17 21.0
2 149.0	5 70.7	5 76.6	8 47.0				2 154.4	3 114.4
7 54.5	9 41.2	20 18.6	24 15.1			Cost of Sales/Inventory	4 81.5	8 47.1
26 14.0	14 26.0	37 9.8	46 7.9				12 31.4	20 18.3
0 UND	1 346.8	7 53.1	9 39.3				1 258.9	5 74.3
1 281.0	15 24.7	25 14.8	26 13.8			Cost of Sales/Payables	9 42.4	13 28.4
23 15.7	25 14.7	40 9.2	46 8.0				23 15.8	35 10.5
24.9	19.7	21.8	11.0				22.5	21.2
56.4	293.7	-60.8	-27.3			Sales/Working Capital	-38.1	999.8
-13.6	-22.1	-6.2	-12.7				-11.3	-14.7
12.0	15.6	9.4	8.2				11.9	13.2
(19) 3.9	(22) 3.4	3.1	(11) 4.8			EBIT/Interest	(153) 4.4	(102) 5.4
1.4	1.2	1.3	.4				1.7	1.4
							6.0	3.5
						Net Profit + Depr., Dep., Amort./Cur. Mat. L/T/D	(23) 2.5	(13) 1.5
							1.4	.1
1.1	1.6	1.1	.4				1.1	1.0
UND	6.4	-22.6	2.1			Fixed/Worth	7.6	2.3
-1.5	-2.9	-.5	NM				-1.4	-4.1
.9	1.9	2.5	.8				1.4	1.0
UND	16.5	-20.2	1.7			Debt/Worth	19.7	3.1
-4.6	-5.0	-2.1	NM				-3.4	-7.1
287.6	134.7		23.2				122.3	89.7
(14) 86.8	(13) 46.9		(10) 15.1			% Profit Before Taxes/Tangible Net Worth	(92) 54.3	(78) 43.8
1.9	15.1		9.0				20.7	8.4
43.4	22.9	10.4	12.5				25.3	23.1
17.4	9.8	4.4	7.2			% Profit Before Taxes/Total Assets	11.4	9.9
3.0	1.2	.9	.8				2.5	.5
22.3	16.3	26.4	7.4				13.5	11.7
9.8	7.9	4.9	5.7			Sales/Net Fixed Assets	6.8	6.2
5.9	3.9	3.3	2.8				3.7	3.5
7.3	5.3	2.5	2.3				4.0	3.6
4.4	2.9	1.9	1.7			Sales/Total Assets	2.6	2.6
2.8	1.6	1.6	1.3				1.7	1.8
1.0	1.2	2.0	2.4				2.2	1.8
(18) 2.0	(21) 2.3	(11) 4.4	(12) 3.4			% Depr., Dep., Amort./Sales	(142) 3.6	(95) 3.1
4.2	4.3	5.0	4.5				4.6	5.0
4.4	1.6						1.7	1.3
(15) 5.8	(14) 3.4					% Officers', Directors' Owners' Comp/Sales	(65) 3.5	(49) 3.9
7.8	5.0						5.7	6.5
28393M	88760M	161763M	541798M	432312M	1967475M	Net Sales ($)	1839260M	2681588M
6684M	24683M	78550M	304893M	154910M	370871M	Total Assets ($)	803097M	1016464M

M = $ thousand MM = $ million

See Pages 9 through 22 for Explanation of Ratios and Data

Comparative Historical Data / Current Data Sorted by Sales

Comparative Historical Data			Type of Statement	Current Data Sorted by Sales					
1	1	3	Unqualified						3
6	7	7	Reviewed			2		2	3
41	24	19	Compiled	3	8	2	3	3	
37	32	31	Tax Returns	10	11	5	3	1	1
36	27	27	Other	5	3	4	2	6	7
4/1/11-3/31/12 ALL	4/1/12-3/31/13 ALL	4/1/13-3/31/14 ALL		5 (4/1-9/30/13)			82 (10/1/13-3/31/14)		
				0-1MM	1-3MM	3-5MM	5-10MM	10-25MM	25MM & OVER
121	91	87	NUMBER OF STATEMENTS	18	22	13	8	12	14
%	%	%	**ASSETS**	%	%	%	%	%	%
10.4	14.1	11.1	Cash & Equivalents	17.7	11.5	8.1		7.7	8.6
8.6	13.6	9.9	Trade Receivables (net)	7.7	6.6	6.9		17.4	12.0
7.3	9.0	9.5	Inventory	5.7	7.8	10.2		15.3	10.6
2.6	2.2	2.6	All Other Current	4.1	2.2	5.2		.1	1.4
28.9	38.9	33.1	Total Current	35.2	28.1	30.3		40.5	32.5
45.9	43.9	44.1	Fixed Assets (net)	40.5	55.2	41.8		44.0	43.4
14.1	8.2	15.1	Intangibles (net)	16.5	11.5	19.8		12.9	10.7
11.1	9.0	7.8	All Other Non-Current	7.8	5.2	8.1		2.6	13.3
100.0	100.0	100.0	Total	100.0	100.0	100.0		100.0	100.0
			LIABILITIES						
6.0	5.0	8.3	Notes Payable-Short Term	6.3	6.1	10.4		5.6	8.1
6.0	4.9	5.4	Cur. Mat.-L.T.D.	1.1	4.8	7.9		8.3	4.9
8.9	14.2	9.7	Trade Payables	5.4	5.8	11.8		13.0	15.1
.1	.3	.3	Income Taxes Payable	.1	.8	.7		.0	.0
18.9	8.2	14.8	All Other Current	21.3	13.8	12.5		23.8	8.9
39.9	32.7	38.5	Total Current	34.2	31.3	43.3		50.7	37.0
30.2	25.6	34.2	Long-Term Debt	25.2	50.2	45.6		31.3	18.6
.0	.1	.0	Deferred Taxes	.0	.0	.0		.0	.1
14.6	10.7	9.6	All Other Non-Current	25.5	3.0	4.0		3.0	14.4
15.3	31.0	17.7	Net Worth	15.1	15.5	7.0		15.1	29.9
100.0	100.0	100.0	Total Liabilties & Net Worth	100.0	100.0	100.0		100.0	100.0
			INCOME DATA						
100.0	100.0	100.0	Net Sales	100.0	100.0	100.0		100.0	100.0
49.7	43.6	42.7	Gross Profit	63.1	45.7	43.4		28.1	28.7
44.5	36.6	36.9	Operating Expenses	54.0	40.9	38.9		23.5	23.2
5.2	7.0	5.8	Operating Profit	9.1	4.8	4.5		4.6	5.4
.6	1.7	1.1	All Other Expenses (net)	.7	.9	.9		1.8	1.6
4.6	5.3	4.7	Profit Before Taxes	8.3	3.9	3.6		2.9	3.9
			RATIOS						
2.1	2.4	1.7		3.2	1.7	1.1		1.3	1.8
.9	1.2	.9	Current	1.7	1.2	.6		.7	1.0
.3	.6	.5		.5	.3	.4		.5	.6
1.3	2.1	1.3		2.1	1.4	.8		.8	1.1
.6	.9	.6	Quick	1.1	.7	.2		.5	.7
.2	.4	.3		.3	.2	.0		.3	.3
0 UND	0 974.0	0 UND		0 UND	0 UND	0 UND		3 113.6	4 93.1
1 279.4	11 33.4	6 62.0	Sales/Receivables	0 UND	0 999.8	1 400.5		23 16.0	23 16.2
20 18.6	27 13.3	26 13.8		13 28.2	10 35.2	18 19.9		43 8.5	27 13.7
3 104.5	4 95.5	5 71.1		2 204.9	5 69.8	6 65.2		5 67.8	11 34.4
7 50.5	9 38.6	11 31.9	Cost of Sales/Inventory	8 46.2	7 52.8	12 30.3		16 23.5	17 21.7
19 19.7	26 13.9	24 15.1		27 13.3	17 21.8	21 17.8		52 7.0	29 12.4
0 877.4	8 45.5	1 288.0		0 UND	0 UND	2 221.2		7 52.0	10 37.8
12 29.5	18 20.1	16 22.8	Cost of Sales/Payables	5 81.1	3 122.3	25 14.4		18 19.8	24 15.5
30 12.0	35 10.5	29 12.6		25 14.7	21 17.5	36 10.0		43 8.5	43 8.5
18.4	10.2	23.0		11.6	24.9	NM		152.2	12.0
-179.3	66.8	-189.2	Sales/Working Capital	30.7	59.7	-33.0		-14.1	NM
-15.2	-23.2	-12.9		-12.5	-13.0	-13.1		-5.9	-12.0
14.2	10.9	12.0		16.0	8.4	9.8		13.1	17.2
(98) 4.3	(75) 5.0	(75) 3.9	EBIT/Interest	(11) 4.7	(20) 2.3	(12) 3.1		5.2	(12) 4.9
1.5	2.2	1.3		3.2	1.0	1.2		.6	3.3
	6.5	24.9							
	(21) 2.3	(13) 5.6	Net Profit + Depr., Dep., Amort./Cur. Mat. L/T/D						
	1.1	2.8							
.8	.7	1.1		.7	2.0	3.1		2.8	.4
1.7	1.8	6.0	Fixed/Worth	6.4	-11.9	-45.5		NM	1.7
-2.4	-32.0	-2.3		-1.4	-3.0	-1.0		-6.0	NM
.6	.9	1.6		.6	2.4	6.4		4.3	.8
2.3	2.6	12.6	Debt/Worth	12.1	-19.6	-61.6		NM	1.8
-4.7	-50.7	-3.9		-4.0	-6.9	-2.8		-12.7	NM
74.6	80.5	95.4		214.3	97.3				19.0
(79) 28.2	(67) 26.7	(48) 25.9	% Profit Before Taxes/Tangible Net Worth	(11) 58.4	(10) 36.4				(11) 14.8
4.8	12.0	8.4		2.6	-1.2				10.2
22.7	20.6	20.8		44.9	28.9	20.7		16.0	14.1
8.8	12.5	9.1	% Profit Before Taxes/Total Assets	17.3	8.7	9.0		4.4	7.3
1.8	3.6	1.3		7.4	.9	.6		-.9	3.6
15.2	14.3	16.4		19.8	12.3	22.1		22.5	7.7
6.3	6.8	7.2	Sales/Net Fixed Assets	7.2	6.4	14.1		3.7	5.7
3.9	3.9	3.9		5.4	3.0	4.4		2.8	3.9
4.4	3.8	4.6		5.1	5.5	6.6		4.4	2.9
2.9	2.8	2.7	Sales/Total Assets	3.1	2.8	3.0		1.9	2.1
2.0	2.0	1.6		1.8	1.6	1.5		1.5	1.5
1.5	1.2	1.4		.9	2.0	.8			2.3
(101) 2.6	(80) 2.3	(65) 2.4	% Depr., Dep., Amort./Sales	(11) 1.4	(19) 3.1	(11) 2.3			(12) 2.8
4.4	3.9	4.7		4.2	5.9	4.3			4.5
1.8	2.2	3.0			2.2				
(57) 3.9	(45) 4.9	(38) 4.4	% Officers', Directors' Owners' Comp/Sales		(13) 4.4				
5.7	8.6	7.2			5.6				
1336446M	1070941M	3220501M	Net Sales ($)	12078M	39073M	52646M	56778M	173943M	2885983M
633877M	471637M	940591M	Total Assets ($)	4676M	18247M	20251M	19501M	87058M	790858M

M = $ thousand MM = $ million

See Pages 9 through 22 for Explanation of Ratios and Data

Current Data Sorted by Assets							Comparative Historical Data	
						Type of Statement		
	1	1	9	8	6	Unqualified	41	32
	3	21	12			Reviewed	51	42
1	5	9	3			Compiled	22	23
11	8	7	1			Tax Returns	24	17
5	11	21	40	13	14	Other	62	73
27 (4/1-9/30/13)			183 (10/1/13-3/31/14)				4/1/09-3/31/10 ALL	4/1/10-3/31/11 ALL
0-500M	500M-2MM	2-10MM	10-50MM	50-100MM	100-250MM			
17	28	59	65	21	20	NUMBER OF STATEMENTS	200	187
%	%	%	%	%	%	**ASSETS**	%	%
21.8	12.0	12.3	8.9	6.5	7.0	Cash & Equivalents	10.8	8.8
10.4	20.6	21.6	15.7	15.7	15.9	Trade Receivables (net)	17.8	18.7
9.2	10.5	14.2	9.3	9.4	9.8	Inventory	10.7	11.5
.4	2.3	3.4	2.6	4.5	6.7	All Other Current	3.0	2.6
41.8	45.4	51.5	36.6	36.1	39.3	Total Current	42.4	41.6
43.1	40.0	37.8	49.9	37.6	36.9	Fixed Assets (net)	44.6	44.1
7.8	4.8	4.5	4.6	13.8	11.0	Intangibles (net)	6.1	6.3
6.9	9.8	6.3	8.9	12.4	12.8	All Other Non-Current	7.0	8.0
100.0	100.0	100.0	100.0	100.0	100.0	Total	100.0	100.0
						LIABILITIES		
19.9	10.7	5.0	2.4	5.0	2.7	Notes Payable-Short Term	6.2	5.6
1.7	3.0	3.6	4.4	2.1	4.7	Cur. Mat.-L.T.D.	5.1	4.5
8.2	9.8	18.4	11.4	9.7	12.7	Trade Payables	13.0	14.3
.0	.2	.1	.2	.3	.1	Income Taxes Payable	.2	.3
29.2	10.4	5.3	6.3	12.4	9.6	All Other Current	7.5	10.0
59.0	34.2	32.4	24.6	29.5	29.8	Total Current	31.9	34.8
38.1	24.6	16.7	26.9	20.0	28.3	Long-Term Debt	25.6	22.2
.0	.0	.6	1.0	3.1	1.0	Deferred Taxes	.6	.6
13.9	8.6	10.8	4.3	4.6	12.6	All Other Non-Current	7.4	7.3
-10.8	32.6	39.5	43.2	42.8	28.3	Net Worth	34.4	35.2
100.0	100.0	100.0	100.0	100.0	100.0	Total Liabilties & Net Worth	100.0	100.0
						INCOME DATA		
100.0	100.0	100.0	100.0	100.0	100.0	Net Sales	100.0	100.0
50.1	47.7	33.3	29.8	34.1	27.0	Gross Profit	36.8	34.5
55.8	41.3	27.8	24.5	28.3	25.3	Operating Expenses	30.7	29.5
-5.7	6.3	5.5	5.3	5.8	1.8	Operating Profit	6.1	5.1
2.2	.6	.5	1.8	.9	1.3	All Other Expenses (net)	.9	.8
-7.8	5.7	5.0	3.5	4.9	.5	Profit Before Taxes	5.3	4.2
						RATIOS		
4.1	2.6	3.1	2.0	2.1	2.1		2.3	1.9
1.2	1.8	1.5	1.4	1.3	1.3	Current	1.4	1.3
.3	.9	1.0	1.1	.9	.8		1.0	.9
3.8	2.1	2.1	1.5	1.2	1.2		1.5	1.3
.9	1.2	1.0	.9	.7	.8	Quick	.9	.8
.3	.7	.6	.6	.6	.5		.5	.5
0 UND	6 66.1	16 22.9	19 19.3	20 18.6	25 14.8		16 22.1	18 20.4
1 420.5	17 21.7	22 16.6	26 13.9	24 15.1	31 11.8	Sales/Receivables	23 15.7	25 14.5
18 20.3	34 10.7	33 11.2	33 11.0	38 9.5	37 9.8		32 11.5	34 10.6
0 UND	4 93.1	8 44.4	12 31.7	14 25.5	15 24.6		10 36.9	11 33.7
16 23.4	10 35.4	18 20.2	21 17.4	21 17.1	22 16.3	Cost of Sales/Inventory	19 19.6	20 18.2
36 10.1	28 13.0	33 11.0	32 11.5	33 11.0	33 11.0		30 12.4	30 12.0
0 UND	0 960.9	18 20.8	19 19.4	16 23.2	24 15.0		15 24.2	15 24.0
8 44.7	13 27.2	26 14.0	25 14.4	26 14.0	29 12.4	Cost of Sales/Payables	25 14.7	27 13.5
24 14.9	31 11.7	39 9.3	41 8.9	43 8.4	36 10.0		34 10.7	38 9.5
13.3	14.3	8.3	9.0	8.7	6.7		10.9	11.8
45.3	26.2	21.8	22.6	28.7	22.7	Sales/Working Capital	30.8	34.8
-9.3	NM	-420.3	99.2	-81.5	-37.4		-164.8	-65.7
3.9	16.1	39.0	13.8	22.5	8.5		13.6	13.6
(10) -.9	(25) 5.2	(51) 6.7	(60) 5.9	7.4	4.9	EBIT/Interest	(183) 4.9	(170) 4.4
-6.4	.4	2.1	2.1	3.5	-.4		2.1	1.6
		10.0	5.5	7.2			4.9	4.9
		(18) 3.0	(19) 3.1	(12) 4.3		Net Profit + Depr., Dep., Amort./Cur. Mat. L/T/D	(61) 2.9	(59) 2.8
		1.6	1.8	2.5			2.0	1.3
.3	.5	.5	.7	.7	.7		.7	.7
.9	1.0	1.1	1.4	1.5	1.2	Fixed/Worth	1.6	1.4
NM	45.6	3.1	2.9	NM	-.9		4.6	5.2
.7	.7	.6	.6	.6	.7		.9	.9
1.9	1.7	1.7	1.5	1.8	1.6	Debt/Worth	1.9	1.8
-2.3	57.8	5.4	3.8	NM	-3.1		7.6	7.7
91.7	105.1	60.6	37.7	42.1	23.0		66.5	48.8
(11) 11.8	(22) 35.6	(52) 33.7	(59) 19.6	(16) 18.6	(13) 14.9	% Profit Before Taxes/Tangible Net Worth	(170) 31.3	(158) 24.5
-11.8	-.7	12.4	7.4	6.5	3.3		10.1	7.0
16.7	27.2	23.0	15.2	13.8	9.5		20.5	17.9
-3.7	12.3	12.7	8.3	8.2	3.0	% Profit Before Taxes/Total Assets	9.1	7.4
-38.5	-1.0	2.8	3.1	1.8	-9.9		3.1	1.6
37.5	20.6	15.4	6.5	7.2	7.2		11.4	10.8
13.1	8.3	8.9	3.8	6.5	4.7	Sales/Net Fixed Assets	5.4	5.8
5.0	5.8	5.2	2.6	3.8	3.0		3.4	3.5
7.4	4.6	4.0	2.4	2.4	2.4		3.6	3.6
3.1	3.4	3.2	2.0	2.1	1.7	Sales/Total Assets	2.5	2.5
1.8	2.8	2.5	1.4	1.3	.9		1.7	1.6
.6	1.7	1.2	1.9	1.9	3.2		1.7	1.8
(11) 2.7	(21) 2.5	(50) 1.8	(62) 3.7	2.8	(13) 3.8	% Depr., Dep., Amort./Sales	(177) 2.9	(169) 2.9
8.8	3.4	3.0	4.8	4.9	4.8		4.3	4.3
		1.2	1.1				1.2	2.0
		(19) 2.5	(10) 2.8			% Officers', Directors' Owners' Comp/Sales	(74) 3.2	(67) 3.5
		3.4	3.5				5.5	6.6
16312M	113601M	1018544M	3119694M	2989117M	5894187M	Net Sales ($)	9790312M	9173462M
4185M	29866M	320164M	1577195M	1462685M	2931346M	Total Assets ($)	4669417M	4837616M

M = $ thousand MM = $ million

See Pages 9 through 22 for Explanation of Ratios and Data

Comparative Historical Data / Current Data Sorted by Sales

Comparative Historical Data				Current Data Sorted by Sales					
			Type of Statement						
32	19	25	Unqualified			1		1	23
44	33	36	Reviewed		2		6	16	12
28	13	18	Compiled	1	1	3	4	6	3
29	27	27	Tax Returns	7	8	2	6	3	1
74	76	104	Other	3	6	6	8	14	67
				27 (4/1-9/30/13)		183 (10/1/13-3/31/14)			
4/1/11-3/31/12 ALL	4/1/12-3/31/13 ALL	4/1/13-3/31/14 ALL		0-1MM	1-3MM	3-5MM	5-10MM	10-25MM	25MM & OVER
207	168	210	**NUMBER OF STATEMENTS**	11	17	12	24	40	106
%	%	%	**ASSETS**	%	%	%	%	%	%
8.6	9.6	10.9	Cash & Equivalents	16.1	19.9	8.5	15.0	11.9	7.9
18.9	17.6	17.6	Trade Receivables (net)	2.9	18.2	16.6	24.8	17.5	17.6
11.9	12.5	10.9	Inventory	8.4	6.8	9.3	15.3	11.6	10.7
2.8	3.8	3.2	All Other Current	.8	1.4	2.2	3.4	3.1	3.8
42.2	43.5	42.6	Total Current	28.2	46.3	36.6	58.5	44.2	40.0
44.2	43.1	42.2	Fixed Assets (net)	63.6	34.3	45.1	31.0	44.7	42.4
6.2	5.0	6.4	Intangibles (net)	6.6	5.6	7.4	5.0	3.2	7.8
7.3	8.4	8.9	All Other Non-Current	1.2	13.7	10.9	5.4	7.9	9.7
100.0	100.0	100.0	Total	100.0	100.0	100.0	100.0	100.0	100.0
			LIABILITIES						
6.7	7.9	6.0	Notes Payable-Short Term	10.3	20.7	10.7	3.0	4.5	3.9
4.8	4.5	3.6	Cur. Mat.-L.T.D.	2.1	3.6	2.7	2.6	3.7	4.0
15.7	14.0	12.8	Trade Payables	8.6	7.5	9.3	14.7	15.7	13.0
.1	.2	.1	Income Taxes Payable	.0	.2	.0	.0	.1	.2
10.0	7.9	9.3	All Other Current	40.8	11.8	5.2	5.8	4.9	8.6
37.3	34.5	31.8	Total Current	61.8	43.7	27.9	26.1	28.9	29.6
24.6	25.3	24.1	Long-Term Debt	60.0	27.0	20.3	19.8	18.7	23.3
.6	.8	.9	Deferred Taxes	.0	.0	.0	.2	.6	1.5
7.1	7.0	8.3	All Other Non-Current	15.2	5.6	10.8	16.1	10.4	5.2
30.4	32.3	34.9	Net Worth	-36.7	23.6	41.0	37.8	41.4	40.4
100.0	100.0	100.0	Total Liabilities & Net Worth	100.0	100.0	100.0	100.0	100.0	100.0
			INCOME DATA						
100.0	100.0	100.0	Net Sales	100.0	100.0	100.0	100.0	100.0	100.0
33.0	33.2	35.0	Gross Profit	57.6	45.3	53.4	35.0	34.3	29.2
29.4	28.7	30.7	Operating Expenses	64.7	41.3	46.4	29.1	29.2	24.6
3.6	4.5	4.3	Operating Profit	-7.1	4.0	7.0	5.9	5.1	4.6
.8	.8	1.2	All Other Expenses (net)	6.3	1.2	.7	.5	.6	1.1
2.9	3.8	3.2	Profit Before Taxes	-13.4	2.8	6.3	5.4	4.5	3.6
			RATIOS						
2.0	2.0	2.4		2.6	4.7	2.7	3.4	2.4	2.0
1.2	1.3	1.4	Current	1.2	1.1	1.8	2.5	1.5	1.4
.8	.9	.9		.2	.6	.9	1.3	.8	.9
1.3	1.4	1.7		2.3	4.2	1.6	2.4	1.8	1.3
.8	.8	.9	Quick	.9	1.0	1.0	1.5	1.0	.8
.5	.5	.6		.1	.4	.6	.9	.6	.6
16 22.6	**15** 24.0	**16** 23.2		**0** UND	**0** UND	**0** UND	**19** 19.5	**13** 27.1	**19** 18.9
24 15.1	**24** 15.2	**24** 14.9	Sales/Receivables	**0** UND	**18** 20.5	**14** 25.7	**27** 13.6	**23** 16.2	**26** 13.9
32 11.5	**30** 12.3	**33** 11.0		**4** 84.7	**31** 11.7	**40** 9.1	**36** 10.0	**32** 11.4	**33** 11.0
10 35.5	**10** 36.4	**10** 37.0		**0** UND	**0** UND	**7** 52.2	**6** 65.8	**8** 44.0	**14** 27.0
18 20.2	**19** 19.1	**19** 19.7	Cost of Sales/Inventory	**16** 22.3	**9** 41.5	**14** 26.0	**20** 17.9	**16** 22.2	**21** 17.0
30 12.1	**34** 10.7	**31** 11.7		**61** 6.0	**19** 18.8	**49** 7.5	**38** 9.6	**31** 11.7	**32** 11.5
16 22.3	**15** 25.1	**15** 24.2		**0** UND	**0** 765.4	**0** UND	**14** 26.3	**20** 18.3	**18** 20.2
27 13.7	**23** 16.2	**24** 14.9	Cost of Sales/Payables	**10** 35.2	**10** 35.9	**13** 28.8	**21** 17.8	**30** 12.2	**26** 14.0
40 9.1	**34** 10.6	**38** 9.7		**64** 5.7	**25** 14.5	**36** 10.1	**36** 10.2	**48** 7.6	**36** 10.0
12.4	11.7	8.7		11.3	11.7	16.0	5.5	9.0	8.7
46.3	31.7	26.0	Sales/Working Capital	45.3	65.5	63.5	13.3	26.0	27.3
-44.5	-66.2	-102.3		-2.7	-17.2	NM	27.7	-44.1	-102.3
11.2	14.7	16.7			16.4	16.4	28.1	36.9	13.9
(191) 4.5	(160) 4.7	(187) 5.7	EBIT/Interest		(12) 2.6	(10) 6.5	(21) 4.8	(34) 6.9	(103) 6.3
.9	1.7	1.3			.3	.9	.0	2.1	2.1
4.7	6.0	5.8						19.7	5.3
(56) 2.2	(48) 3.5	(58) 3.1	Net Profit + Depr., Dep., Amort./Cur. Mat. L/T/D					(10) 3.5	(41) 3.1
1.0	1.8	1.9						1.0	2.0
.8	.6	.6		1.7	.2	.7	.3	.5	.7
1.5	1.6	1.3	Fixed/Worth	-38.6	.6	1.3	.9	1.3	1.4
5.5	5.2	5.5		-1.4	18.9	39.5	2.3	3.7	4.7
.9	.9	.6		1.0	.4	.5	.4	.6	.7
2.1	2.0	1.5	Debt/Worth	-40.2	1.3	2.1	2.7	1.5	1.5
8.5	8.6	9.4		-2.5	-3.9	49.9	4.9	6.1	8.5
46.5	46.6	45.8			105.5	117.4	68.8	63.3	37.7
(166) 19.3	(139) 21.1	(173) 23.8	% Profit Before Taxes/Tangible Net Worth		(12) 49.5	(10) 29.2	(21) 33.8	(38) 30.0	(87) 20.3
5.2	5.7	7.4			8.7	-1.7	7.2	9.5	7.4
15.4	14.2	17.1		-2.2	35.0	27.0	19.3	21.8	14.4
6.5	6.9	8.3	% Profit Before Taxes/Total Assets	-3.7	8.5	21.5	11.0	9.8	7.5
.0	1.4	.3		-28.6	-4.5	1.1	-.7	3.9	1.6
13.0	12.4	11.1		8.2	33.1	20.0	23.6	13.5	8.1
5.7	6.3	6.5	Sales/Net Fixed Assets	3.4	11.1	8.3	9.4	7.5	5.1
3.4	4.1	3.5		1.2	6.7	3.6	5.3	3.2	3.4
3.9	3.7	3.5		4.9	5.0	4.2	3.9	3.9	2.9
2.7	2.7	2.4	Sales/Total Assets	1.6	3.5	3.2	2.9	2.7	2.1
1.8	1.9	1.6		.9	2.7	2.5	2.4	1.7	1.4
1.3	1.7	1.6				2.0	1.3	1.2	1.8
(177) 2.5	(149) 2.8	(178) 2.7	% Depr., Dep., Amort./Sales			(10) 2.6	(19) 1.8	(37) 2.5	(94) 3.4
4.1	4.3	4.4				3.2	3.0	4.5	4.5
1.4	1.5	1.4							1.3
(70) 2.7	(57) 2.9	(49) 2.8	% Officers', Directors' Owners' Comp/Sales						(13) 2.2
5.1	4.2	5.3							3.3
9333106M	7961676M	13151455M	Net Sales ($)	5864M	30769M	46630M	178215M	722180M	12167797M
5025161M	3925903M	6325441M	Total Assets ($)	18172M	8887M	16674M	74376M	326398M	5880934M

M = $ thousand MM = $ million
See Pages 9 through 22 for Explanation of Ratios and Data

Current Data Sorted by Assets							Comparative Historical Data	
						Type of Statement		
			2		1	Unqualified	3	7
		2	1			Reviewed	2	3
	1	2	1			Compiled	4	5
1	1	1				Tax Returns	3	3
		5	6	3		Other	14	14
	3 (4/1-9/30/13)		24 (10/1/13-3/31/14)				4/1/09-3/31/10	4/1/10-3/31/11
0-500M	500M-2MM	2-10MM	10-50MM	50-100MM	100-250MM		ALL	ALL
1	2	10	10	3	1	**NUMBER OF STATEMENTS**	26	32
%	%	%	%	%	%	**ASSETS**	%	%
		10.1	6.5			Cash & Equivalents	10.7	12.5
		18.6	12.2			Trade Receivables (net)	18.0	19.0
		16.8	16.2			Inventory	16.5	16.4
		4.3	1.3			All Other Current	.8	1.6
		49.7	36.1			Total Current	45.9	49.5
		37.7	48.2			Fixed Assets (net)	40.7	40.6
		8.6	5.5			Intangibles (net)	9.9	4.3
		3.9	10.2			All Other Non-Current	3.5	5.6
		100.0	100.0			Total	100.0	100.0
						LIABILITIES		
		8.2	3.8			Notes Payable-Short Term	4.2	7.3
		3.8	10.8			Cur. Mat.-L.T.D.	3.5	3.5
		13.4	11.0			Trade Payables	13.6	12.5
		.3	.2			Income Taxes Payable	.0	.1
		3.1	4.6			All Other Current	7.7	6.5
		28.8	30.3			Total Current	29.0	29.9
		20.0	25.2			Long-Term Debt	19.4	22.6
		.0	2.2			Deferred Taxes	.3	.9
		4.4	1.0			All Other Non-Current	3.5	2.6
		46.8	41.3			Net Worth	47.8	44.0
		100.0	100.0			Total Liabilities & Net Worth	100.0	100.0
						INCOME DATA		
		100.0	100.0			Net Sales	100.0	100.0
		31.4	22.0			Gross Profit	34.2	34.5
		28.8	18.2			Operating Expenses	25.8	31.1
		2.6	3.8			Operating Profit	8.4	3.4
		.4	2.4			All Other Expenses (net)	.3	.7
		2.2	1.3			Profit Before Taxes	8.1	2.7
						RATIOS		
		3.3	2.9				2.2	3.0
		1.8	1.2			Current	1.6	1.6
		1.3	.8				1.2	1.1
		2.4	1.8				1.6	2.0
		1.1	.5			Quick	1.0	1.1
		.6	.3				.6	.4
		25 14.8	**25** 14.4				**18** 20.0	**19** 19.2
		37 9.8	**31** 11.8			Sales/Receivables	**26** 14.0	**29** 12.7
		40 9.1	**41** 9.0				**31** 11.7	**45** 8.1
		9 42.5	**29** 12.7				**20** 18.6	**29** 12.7
		42 8.7	**49** 7.4			Cost of Sales/Inventory	**34** 10.8	**42** 8.6
		85 4.3	**69** 5.3				**52** 7.0	**61** 6.0
		20 18.7	**11** 32.7				**20** 17.9	**16** 22.6
		31 11.6	**51** 7.2			Cost of Sales/Payables	**26** 14.0	**28** 12.9
		46 8.0	**66** 5.5				**34** 10.7	**44** 8.4
		6.3	6.3				8.4	5.4
		8.6	24.1			Sales/Working Capital	19.3	15.0
		22.5	-26.8				36.3	62.3
		19.5					17.7	14.4
		6.8				EBIT/Interest	(24) 7.8	(28) 5.1
		1.7					1.7	-.5
						Net Profit + Depr., Dep., Amort./Cur. Mat. L/T/D		
		.6	.7				.6	.3
		.9	1.7			Fixed/Worth	1.1	1.3
		3.7	NM				2.7	2.0
		.6	.4				.8	.7
		1.5	1.9			Debt/Worth	1.4	1.4
		6.2	NM				4.0	2.7
							77.1	47.4
						% Profit Before Taxes/Tangible Net Worth	(23) 24.4	(28) 21.8
							2.6	3.0
		14.3	10.8				28.0	17.8
		9.6	6.3			% Profit Before Taxes/Total Assets	11.3	9.7
		1.2	-3.5				1.3	.1
		9.0	4.6				12.3	16.2
		5.3	2.9			Sales/Net Fixed Assets	6.7	5.5
		3.4	1.5				4.2	1.8
		2.1	1.6				3.6	2.9
		1.8	1.5			Sales/Total Assets	2.5	1.9
		1.5	.9				1.6	1.1
			2.4				1.9	1.1
			3.2			% Depr., Dep., Amort./Sales	(22) 2.4	(31) 2.9
			4.9				4.6	5.9
							2.2	
						% Officers', Directors' Owners' Comp/Sales	(12) 3.5	
							14.9	
308M	21558M	84504M	323277M	410871M	445780M	Net Sales ($)	1593332M	774759M
109M	3021M	45956M	228887M	209066M	230239M	Total Assets ($)	627932M	482995M

M = $ thousand MM = $ million

See Pages 9 through 22 for Explanation of Ratios and Data

Comparative Historical Data / Current Data Sorted by Sales

Comparative Historical Data			Type of Statement	Current Data Sorted by Sales					
6	4	3	Unqualified					1	2
4	3	3	Reviewed			2		1	
3	2	4	Compiled				2	1	1
	3	3	Tax Returns	1			1	1	
8	13	14	Other			1	2	4	7
					3 (4/1-9/30/13)		24 (10/1/13-3/31/14)		
4/1/11-3/31/12 ALL	4/1/12-3/31/13 ALL	4/1/13-3/31/14 ALL		0-1MM	1-3MM	3-5MM	5-10MM	10-25MM	25MM & OVER
21	25	27	NUMBER OF STATEMENTS	1		3	5	8	10
%	%	%	**ASSETS**	%	%	%	%	%	%
9.2	8.8	9.4	Cash & Equivalents		DATA NOT AVAILABLE				9.4
21.1	17.4	17.5	Trade Receivables (net)						11.9
20.2	18.5	16.8	Inventory						13.1
2.4	3.1	3.7	All Other Current						5.0
52.8	47.9	47.4	Total Current						39.4
38.1	39.9	39.0	Fixed Assets (net)						46.6
6.1	7.4	7.5	Intangibles (net)						5.1
3.0	4.7	6.1	All Other Non-Current						8.9
100.0	100.0	100.0	Total						100.0
			LIABILITIES						
4.5	6.3	7.1	Notes Payable-Short Term						2.5
3.4	3.2	6.1	Cur. Mat.-L.T.D.						4.9
17.1	12.4	13.7	Trade Payables						12.0
.0	.1	.3	Income Taxes Payable						.4
10.1	7.5	6.0	All Other Current						4.3
35.1	29.3	33.2	Total Current						24.2
18.7	15.4	27.1	Long-Term Debt						35.0
.7	1.7	1.4	Deferred Taxes						3.7
4.1	4.9	7.6	All Other Non-Current						16.1
41.4	48.7	30.7	Net Worth						21.0
100.0	100.0	100.0	Total Liabilities & Net Worth						100.0
			INCOME DATA						
100.0	100.0	100.0	Net Sales						100.0
29.2	32.1	29.2	Gross Profit						23.8
24.1	26.6	24.4	Operating Expenses						14.3
5.2	5.4	4.8	Operating Profit						9.5
.8	.9	1.4	All Other Expenses (net)						.7
4.4	4.5	3.5	Profit Before Taxes						8.8
			RATIOS						
1.9	2.6	2.2							2.9
1.5	1.6	1.4	Current						1.5
1.2	1.1	1.0							1.0
1.3	1.8	1.5							1.9
.8	.9	.8	Quick						.6
.6	.4	.4							.3
26 14.2	**24** 15.5	**24** 14.9							**24** 15.0
30 12.2	**31** 11.6	**34** 10.8	Sales/Receivables						**27** 13.6
46 8.0	**39** 9.4	**39** 9.3							**37** 9.9
22 16.3	**29** 12.4	**25** 14.7							**27** 13.3
51 7.2	**54** 6.7	**45** 8.1	Cost of Sales/Inventory						**38** 9.6
64 5.7	**76** 4.8	**73** 5.0							**59** 6.2
24 15.1	**23** 15.7	**17** 22.0							**11** 32.7
39 9.3	**34** 10.7	**35** 10.4	Cost of Sales/Payables						**34** 10.7
51 7.1	**51** 7.1	**57** 6.4							**65** 5.6
7.7	6.8	6.9							6.2
12.1	11.8	15.2	Sales/Working Capital						18.1
45.9	44.1	-183.8							-148.5
12.5	11.7	13.2							
(18) 9.5	(21) 4.0	(25) 7.9	EBIT/Interest						
-1.6	1.3	1.5							
			Net Profit + Depr., Dep., Amort./Cur. Mat. L/T/D						
.6	.6	.6							.5
1.0	.9	1.3	Fixed/Worth						1.3
1.9	1.7	2.4							1.8
.9	.6	.9							.4
1.4	1.2	1.8	Debt/Worth						1.3
2.7	2.4	5.5							2.6
55.2	45.8	30.6							
(19) 23.6	(23) 15.7	(22) 20.3	% Profit Before Taxes/Tangible Net Worth						
-16.0	5.0	3.4							
24.3	14.0	14.1							14.9
13.0	6.6	9.5	% Profit Before Taxes/Total Assets						10.2
-5.5	.9	1.5							6.7
29.7	9.7	8.3							5.6
5.5	4.9	4.4	Sales/Net Fixed Assets						3.6
2.1	2.1	2.5							1.5
3.3	2.8	2.2							2.1
2.0	1.6	1.8	Sales/Total Assets						1.7
1.2	1.1	1.5							1.0
.6	.6	1.7							
(20) 2.2	(24) 1.9	(25) 2.8	% Depr., Dep., Amort./Sales						
4.5	6.1	4.2							
		2.1							
		(10) 4.0	% Officers', Directors' Owners' Comp/Sales						
		5.0							
1082318M	1133914M	1286298M	Net Sales ($)	308M		13080M	37330M	119389M	1116191M
510703M	565532M	717278M	Total Assets ($)	109M		17912M	19727M	62286M	617244M

M = $ thousand MM = $ million

See Pages 9 through 22 for Explanation of Ratios and Data

Current Data Sorted by Assets							Comparative Historical Data	
						Type of Statement		
		1	3	4	2	Unqualified	7	10
	1	3	4	4	1	Reviewed	7	9
	2			1		Compiled	7	2
3	1	2				Tax Returns	1	3
	5	5	16	2	2	Other	14	13
	15 (4/1-9/30/13)		47 (10/1/13-3/31/14)				4/1/09-3/31/10 ALL	4/1/10-3/31/11 ALL
0-500M	500M-2MM	2-10MM	10-50MM	50-100MM	100-250MM			
3	9	11	23	11	5	**NUMBER OF STATEMENTS**	36	37
%	%	%	%	%	%	**ASSETS**	%	%
		3.4	8.1	2.1		Cash & Equivalents	6.4	9.6
		23.9	23.6	32.5		Trade Receivables (net)	23.4	22.4
		29.0	25.0	23.7		Inventory	27.6	29.9
		1.4	4.6	1.1		All Other Current	5.3	1.8
		57.8	61.3	59.3		Total Current	62.7	63.7
		38.4	33.6	32.8		Fixed Assets (net)	27.7	25.6
		1.8	3.5	1.5		Intangibles (net)	4.8	4.7
		2.0	1.6	6.4		All Other Non-Current	4.8	5.9
		100.0	100.0	100.0		Total	100.0	100.0
						LIABILITIES		
		11.0	11.2	18.4		Notes Payable-Short Term	17.6	15.1
		4.9	3.2	2.6		Cur. Mat.-L.T.D.	1.8	2.4
		22.4	24.5	11.7		Trade Payables	17.2	17.9
		.1	.0	.7		Income Taxes Payable	.6	.2
		16.9	9.3	2.8		All Other Current	9.5	9.4
		55.3	48.2	36.2		Total Current	46.7	45.0
		26.6	15.0	25.0		Long-Term Debt	14.1	20.2
		.8	.3	.0		Deferred Taxes	.4	.2
		2.2	1.4	5.7		All Other Non-Current	5.6	5.8
		15.1	35.2	33.1		Net Worth	33.2	28.8
		100.0	100.0	100.0		Total Liabilties & Net Worth	100.0	100.0
						INCOME DATA		
		100.0	100.0	100.0		Net Sales	100.0	100.0
		19.5	30.9	36.9		Gross Profit	28.3	25.1
		21.3	17.4	13.8		Operating Expenses	20.6	20.3
		-1.8	13.5	23.1		Operating Profit	7.7	4.8
		.6	4.7	.7		All Other Expenses (net)	.6	.8
		-2.4	8.8	22.4		Profit Before Taxes	7.1	4.0
						RATIOS		
		1.2	1.5	2.8			2.1	2.2
		1.0	1.2	1.5		Current	1.4	1.3
		.9	1.1	1.2			1.1	1.0
		.6	.9	2.2			1.1	1.1
		.5	.7	1.0		Quick	.6	.7
		.4	.5	.6			.5	.4
		29 12.6	**29** 12.5	**49** 7.5			**22** 16.8	**25** 14.4
		40 9.1	**38** 9.6	**89** 4.1		Sales/Receivables	**35** 10.4	**31** 11.7
		48 7.6	**64** 5.7	**332** 1.1			**50** 7.2	**46** 8.0
		36 10.2	**33** 11.0	**45** 8.1			**24** 15.1	**29** 12.4
		55 6.6	**52** 7.0	**65** 5.6		Cost of Sales/Inventory	**52** 7.0	**54** 6.7
		63 5.8	**66** 5.5	**332** 1.1			**83** 4.4	**87** 4.2
		17 21.5	**22** 16.6	**9** 41.0			**17** 22.0	**16** 22.7
		39 9.3	**41** 8.8	**35** 10.4		Cost of Sales/Payables	**28** 13.1	**26** 14.1
		62 5.9	**85** 4.3	**56** 6.5			**43** 8.5	**49** 7.5
		7.4	8.0	1.3			8.3	7.2
		-754.3	26.2	9.8		Sales/Working Capital	16.4	20.4
		-34.0	72.6	14.5			57.1	246.1
			16.6				10.1	7.9
			(20) 8.0			EBIT/Interest	(31) 5.3	(35) 4.5
			3.1				3.6	2.9
			14.2					5.5
			(12) 3.4			Net Profit + Depr., Dep., Amort./Cur. Mat. L/T/D		(10) 2.5
			.7					.3
		1.0	.7	.5			.4	.4
		3.0	1.0	1.1		Fixed/Worth	.7	1.1
		-1.6	1.7	2.8			3.2	4.5
		1.4	1.2	1.3			1.2	2.1
		4.5	3.0	2.4		Debt/Worth	2.5	3.7
		-5.4	3.9	5.1			8.6	10.9
			66.9	52.3			62.7	48.4
			(22) 32.7	31.7		% Profit Before Taxes/Tangible Net Worth	(31) 36.3	(31) 33.1
			2.6	22.3			16.6	17.7
		6.5	24.9	20.0			20.0	11.6
		1.3	6.6	12.6		% Profit Before Taxes/Total Assets	8.2	7.9
		-3.1	1.6	1.5			4.7	2.7
		17.3	32.5	32.3			23.6	25.7
		6.8	12.9	3.6		Sales/Net Fixed Assets	13.0	11.4
		3.2	3.0	.9			4.2	5.1
		2.9	4.3	2.6			3.4	3.4
		2.4	3.2	1.3		Sales/Total Assets	2.5	2.2
		1.7	.7	.4			1.6	1.5
		.8	.4	1.0			1.0	1.1
		(10) 1.7	1.1	2.3		% Depr., Dep., Amort./Sales	(31) 1.4	(32) 1.6
		3.0	1.5	5.9			2.3	2.5
						% Officers', Directors' Owners' Comp/Sales		
3959M	51649M	173983M	1671072M	1226852M	1299460M	Net Sales ($)	1623723M	1795125M
909M	12666M	79073M	603492M	731058M	775010M	Total Assets ($)	821941M	947430M

M = $ thousand MM = $ million

See Pages 9 through 22 for Explanation of Ratios and Data

Comparative Historical Data				Current Data Sorted by Sales					
			Type of Statement						
13	10	10	Unqualified		1	1			8
14	10	13	Reviewed				2	5	6
4	1	3	Compiled				2		1
9	10	6	Tax Returns	1	2		1	2	
26	27	30	Other	1	3	1	4	5	16
4/1/11-3/31/12 ALL	4/1/12-3/31/13 ALL	4/1/13-3/31/14 ALL		15 (4/1-9/30/13)			47 (10/1/13-3/31/14)		
				0-1MM	1-3MM	3-5MM	5-10MM	10-25MM	25MM & OVER
66	58	62	**NUMBER OF STATEMENTS**	2	6	2	9	12	31
%	%	%	**ASSETS**	%	%	%	%	%	%
8.8	6.0	8.5	Cash & Equivalents					3.5	9.3
24.1	24.5	25.6	Trade Receivables (net)					27.1	27.7
27.8	30.1	28.5	Inventory					21.1	33.4
5.4	2.8	2.4	All Other Current					1.3	3.9
66.1	63.5	64.9	Total Current					53.0	74.2
25.3	28.1	29.7	Fixed Assets (net)					42.1	21.0
3.6	3.2	2.3	Intangibles (net)					.7	2.7
4.9	5.1	3.0	All Other Non-Current					4.2	2.1
100.0	100.0	100.0	Total					100.0	100.0
			LIABILITIES						
13.5	18.9	11.1	Notes Payable-Short Term					8.1	15.9
3.1	3.1	4.4	Cur. Mat.-L.T.D.					4.4	3.2
20.2	17.9	23.7	Trade Payables					15.9	28.1
.2	.0	.1	Income Taxes Payable					.0	.3
10.3	12.3	9.7	All Other Current					14.4	8.4
47.3	52.2	49.0	Total Current					42.8	55.8
13.3	16.4	17.4	Long-Term Debt					30.7	10.5
.6	.1	.3	Deferred Taxes					.5	.5
10.4	5.3	4.1	All Other Non-Current					3.3	3.6
28.4	26.0	29.2	Net Worth					22.6	29.6
100.0	100.0	100.0	Total Liabilties & Net Worth					100.0	100.0
			INCOME DATA						
100.0	100.0	100.0	Net Sales					100.0	100.0
31.1	29.1	30.9	Gross Profit					37.9	24.0
25.1	23.4	20.3	Operating Expenses					18.8	15.8
5.9	5.7	10.6	Operating Profit					19.1	8.2
1.0	1.5	2.0	All Other Expenses (net)					1.8	.5
5.0	4.2	8.6	Profit Before Taxes					17.3	7.7
			RATIOS						
2.4	2.4	2.4						2.7	1.5
1.5	1.4	1.3	Current					1.3	1.2
1.2	1.1	1.0						1.0	1.1
1.1	1.1	1.3						2.0	.8
.7	.6	.7	Quick					.7	.6
.5	.4	.5						.5	.4
18 20.3	**20** 18.6	**23** 15.7						**38** 9.5	**24** 15.5
31 11.6	**36** 10.1	**41** 9.0	Sales/Receivables					**45** 8.2	**38** 9.6
49 7.5	**49** 7.4	**60** 6.1						**281** 1.3	**52** 7.0
29 12.8	**37** 9.8	**34** 10.6						**42** 8.7	**34** 10.7
46 7.9	**60** 6.1	**56** 6.5	Cost of Sales/Inventory					**60** 6.1	**55** 6.6
96 3.8	**91** 4.0	**87** 4.2						**281** 1.3	**83** 4.4
21 17.7	**16** 22.7	**21** 17.4						**15** 23.8	**22** 16.6
37 9.8	**32** 11.5	**38** 9.5	Cost of Sales/Payables					**43** 8.4	**41** 8.8
49 7.4	**53** 6.9	**64** 5.7						**63** 5.8	**66** 5.5
6.7	6.1	6.2						1.7	9.8
13.0	12.1	16.0	Sales/Working Capital					82.5	24.4
53.8	72.6	154.2						-395.1	62.9
14.4	18.3	15.4						8.7	31.8
(64) 4.5	(54) 5.4	(54) 8.5	EBIT/Interest					(11) 3.1	(29) 8.8
1.3	1.4	2.9						1.2	3.9
21.3	5.1	10.6							14.0
(20) 5.8	(20) 3.2	(24) 4.2	Net Profit + Depr., Dep., Amort./Cur. Mat. L/T/D						(13) 6.0
2.6	2.1	1.3							3.3
.3	.4	.5						.7	.5
.8	.9	1.2	Fixed/Worth					2.2	.9
2.1	2.2	2.9						NM	1.6
1.0	1.0	1.3						.9	2.4
2.2	2.8	3.3	Debt/Worth					2.9	3.6
8.6	7.1	6.4						NM	5.9
47.4	56.3	50.3							62.0
(60) 27.2	(51) 31.2	(55) 32.4	% Profit Before Taxes/Tangible Net Worth						(30) 33.9
8.4	11.4	5.3							20.5
16.6	18.4	20.0						18.4	25.4
6.5	5.3	9.6	% Profit Before Taxes/Total Assets					7.0	10.8
.6	.8	1.4						1.1	3.1
32.6	35.5	30.9						6.9	32.5
13.1	14.4	10.9	Sales/Net Fixed Assets					3.1	15.5
6.2	5.1	3.6						.9	8.6
3.8	3.9	3.8						2.4	3.7
2.6	2.6	2.7	Sales/Total Assets					1.6	3.2
1.6	1.6	1.2						.4	2.0
.9	.7	.6						1.6	.7
(57) 1.6	(52) 1.3	(54) 1.2	% Depr., Dep., Amort./Sales					(11) 3.8	(29) 1.1
2.8	2.3	2.6						9.3	1.5
.9	.4	1.4							
(14) 1.6	(15) 3.3	(12) 3.5	% Officers', Directors' Owners' Comp/Sales						
7.3	7.5	6.0							
4603699M	3968976M	4426975M	Net Sales ($)	1609M	9671M	8789M	59716M	198840M	4148350M
2343250M	1934652M	2202208M	Total Assets ($)	14177M	67274M	65731M	35801M	276729M	1742496M

M = $ thousand MM = $ million

See Pages 9 through 22 for Explanation of Ratios and Data

	Current Data Sorted by Assets						Comparative Historical Data	
Type of Statement								
Unqualified		1	4	9	3	5	20	18
Reviewed			9	4			15	13
Compiled	1	5	5				12	9
Tax Returns	1	4	3	1			9	17
Other		6	7	9	7	4	31	33
	20 (4/1-9/30/13)		68 (10/1/13-3/31/14)				4/1/09-3/31/10	4/1/10-3/31/11
	0-500M	500M-2MM	2-10MM	10-50MM	50-100MM	100-250MM	ALL	ALL
NUMBER OF STATEMENTS	2	16	28	23	10	9	87	90
ASSETS	%	%	%	%	%	%	%	%
Cash & Equivalents		16.7	9.2	6.4	15.3		7.6	9.6
Trade Receivables (net)		18.6	21.7	21.8	19.2		20.3	20.6
Inventory		25.6	26.5	22.0	23.9		20.2	20.4
All Other Current		.1	4.1	2.9	2.6		1.8	2.0
Total Current		61.0	61.4	53.1	61.0		49.9	52.6
Fixed Assets (net)		26.8	29.2	35.7	30.4		36.2	35.7
Intangibles (net)		3.7	6.3	7.5	5.4		7.4	6.4
All Other Non-Current		8.4	3.0	3.7	3.2		6.5	5.2
Total		100.0	100.0	100.0	100.0		100.0	100.0
LIABILITIES								
Notes Payable-Short Term		6.8	11.2	8.0	5.4		9.3	7.7
Cur. Mat.-L.T.D.		5.9	2.8	2.4	3.4		3.6	3.8
Trade Payables		20.6	20.0	16.5	14.4		14.8	16.4
Income Taxes Payable		.1	.2	.5	.2		.6	.1
All Other Current		7.3	20.1	8.1	8.2		8.8	11.8
Total Current		40.7	54.3	35.6	31.6		37.1	39.8
Long-Term Debt		31.8	12.8	17.6	51.1		25.1	23.9
Deferred Taxes		.4	.5	2.6	.7		1.1	.9
All Other Non-Current		14.1	5.1	3.6	22.7		10.6	7.4
Net Worth		12.9	27.3	40.7	-6.0		26.1	27.9
Total Liabilties & Net Worth		100.0	100.0	100.0	100.0		100.0	100.0
INCOME DATA								
Net Sales		100.0	100.0	100.0	100.0		100.0	100.0
Gross Profit		36.3	29.5	26.3	30.3		29.8	30.9
Operating Expenses		31.8	27.8	21.9	19.2		24.6	27.7
Operating Profit		4.5	1.8	4.4	11.1		5.2	3.2
All Other Expenses (net)		1.2	.9	1.2	.9		1.2	1.1
Profit Before Taxes		3.3	.9	3.2	10.2		4.0	2.1
RATIOS								
Current		3.4	2.3	1.9	2.7		2.4	2.3
		1.9	1.3	1.5	1.9		1.3	1.4
		1.2	1.1	1.1	1.5		1.0	1.0
Quick		2.3	1.0	1.1	1.5		1.4	1.4
		1.1	.7	.7	1.2		.7	.8
		.6	.5	.6	.7		.5	.5
Sales/Receivables		**13** 27.7	**17** 21.0	**28** 13.0	**25** 14.4		**22** 16.3	**18** 20.0
		20 17.9	**25** 14.8	**31** 11.8	**29** 12.5		**30** 12.3	**27** 13.3
		26 13.8	**36** 10.1	**42** 8.6	**41** 8.8		**37** 9.8	**36** 10.1
Cost of Sales/Inventory		**18** 20.1	**29** 12.4	**24** 15.5	**35** 10.5		**25** 14.3	**20** 18.4
		27 13.5	**46** 7.9	**31** 11.9	**53** 6.9		**37** 9.9	**40** 9.2
		51 7.1	**83** 4.4	**69** 5.3	**76** 4.8		**58** 6.3	**64** 5.7
Cost of Sales/Payables		**6** 60.5	**22** 16.9	**22** 16.3	**17** 22.1		**15** 24.2	**17** 22.0
		21 17.4	**25** 14.6	**27** 13.3	**28** 13.1		**25** 14.6	**24** 14.9
		41 9.0	**45** 8.1	**45** 8.1	**46** 8.0		**39** 9.3	**36** 10.2
Sales/Working Capital		7.2	8.4	6.4	5.1		8.0	8.9
		14.8	18.8	17.4	8.8		26.7	19.0
		69.2	152.4	127.6	13.5		-207.4	-825.6
EBIT/Interest		14.4	11.0	20.1	100.6		11.6	19.0
		(12) 4.9	(27) 4.0	(22) 6.6	18.7		(79) 3.8	(78) 3.0
		.3	-1.0	.9	4.4		1.5	1.1
Net Profit + Depr., Dep., Amort./Cur. Mat. L/T/D							11.0	13.2
							(35) 4.5	(27) 3.6
							1.9	1.3
Fixed/Worth		.1	.4	.5	.4		.6	.5
		1.1	.9	.9	.7		1.3	1.1
		NM	3.3	7.2	NM		-60.9	NM
Debt/Worth		.5	.7	.7	.5		1.1	.8
		3.6	1.8	1.2	3.8		2.3	1.7
		-4.8	8.4	11.4	-2.0		-56.1	NM
% Profit Before Taxes/Tangible Net Worth		127.6	33.7	38.9			50.0	37.1
		(11) 20.7	(24) 19.5	(19) 17.4			(63) 25.8	(68) 18.1
		13.3	.2	.5			11.7	3.2
% Profit Before Taxes/Total Assets		23.8	16.7	17.7	28.8		19.7	12.6
		16.3	3.5	7.0	16.0		7.9	5.6
		2.4	-4.1	-.2	10.8		1.7	.1
Sales/Net Fixed Assets		49.8	19.9	14.7	66.3		13.5	18.4
		14.9	8.8	5.7	6.8		6.3	7.4
		8.3	6.1	4.4	4.3		4.0	4.4
Sales/Total Assets		5.3	3.6	2.8	2.6		3.2	3.5
		4.1	2.6	2.2	2.1		2.3	2.5
		2.1	2.0	1.8	1.4		1.6	1.8
% Depr., Dep., Amort./Sales		.8	1.0	1.2			1.3	1.2
		(12) 2.6	(24) 2.1	(22) 2.1			(75) 2.2	(77) 1.9
		4.6	4.6	2.9			3.0	3.4
% Officers', Directors' Owners' Comp/Sales							1.9	1.5
							(21) 3.1	(27) 2.6
							5.2	5.3
Net Sales ($)	2214M	66511M	412344M	1403678M	1555537M	3028684M	5084536M	4596239M
Total Assets ($)	503M	17714M	148586M	626347M	726278M	1548682M	2580963M	2215817M

M = $ thousand MM = $ million

See Pages 9 through 22 for Explanation of Ratios and Data

Comparative Historical Data / Current Data Sorted by Sales

4/1/11-3/31/12 ALL	4/1/12-3/31/13 ALL	4/1/13-3/31/14 ALL	Type of Statement	0-1MM	1-3MM	3-5MM	5-10MM	10-25MM	25MM & OVER
18	12	22	Unqualified				1	4	17
13	10	13	Reviewed				2	6	5
8	9	11	Compiled	1	1	3	3	3	
11	10	9	Tax Returns		3	2	2	1	1
44	33	33	Other	2	2	2	4	4	19
				20 (4/1-9/30/13)			68 (10/1/13-3/31/14)		
94	74	88	NUMBER OF STATEMENTS	3	6	7	12	18	42
%	%	%	**ASSETS**	%	%	%	%	%	%
7.5	9.2	10.3	Cash & Equivalents				13.8	10.8	7.8
26.1	23.9	20.6	Trade Receivables (net)				21.3	20.3	21.1
22.8	21.4	23.9	Inventory				29.0	22.9	23.5
2.8	2.5	2.5	All Other Current				1.3	6.2	2.1
59.2	57.0	57.4	Total Current				65.3	60.3	54.6
31.3	30.7	31.7	Fixed Assets (net)				21.9	30.2	35.0
4.0	5.8	6.8	Intangibles (net)				11.7	5.2	7.2
5.4	6.4	4.1	All Other Non-Current				1.1	4.3	3.2
100.0	100.0	100.0	Total				100.0	100.0	100.0
			LIABILITIES						
7.7	7.7	7.8	Notes Payable-Short Term				13.5	8.5	6.2
3.5	2.8	3.6	Cur. Mat.-L.T.D.				3.8	2.6	2.8
18.4	16.9	17.7	Trade Payables				29.0	14.6	15.7
.1	.1	.2	Income Taxes Payable				.0	.1	.2
10.5	8.0	12.2	All Other Current				20.8	10.6	8.4
40.2	35.6	41.4	Total Current				67.1	36.5	33.5
19.5	18.6	25.0	Long-Term Debt				9.7	13.9	28.2
1.2	1.2	1.4	Deferred Taxes				.1	1.2	2.1
8.7	9.8	8.2	All Other Non-Current				20.4	4.1	8.1
30.4	34.9	24.0	Net Worth				2.6	44.3	28.1
100.0	100.0	100.0	Total Liabilties & Net Worth				100.0	100.0	100.0
			INCOME DATA						
100.0	100.0	100.0	Net Sales				100.0	100.0	100.0
28.9	28.5	29.7	Gross Profit				26.7	28.9	26.7
24.2	25.1	25.3	Operating Expenses				25.0	23.6	20.7
4.7	3.4	4.4	Operating Profit				1.8	5.3	6.0
.7	.6	1.0	All Other Expenses (net)				.3	1.0	.8
4.1	2.9	3.4	Profit Before Taxes				1.5	4.3	5.2
			RATIOS						
2.3	2.5	2.3	Current				2.7	2.8	2.2
1.4	1.5	1.6					1.4	1.6	1.7
1.1	1.1	1.1					1.1	1.1	1.2
1.2	1.7	1.3	Quick				1.3	1.3	1.3
.8	.8	.8					.8	.8	.7
.5	.5	.6					.6	.6	.6
21 17.1	**21** 17.4	**20** 18.6	Sales/Receivables				**8** 43.5	**20** 18.6	**25** 14.4
30 12.3	**27** 13.3	**28** 13.0					**15** 25.0	**30** 12.1	**32** 11.5
39 9.4	**34** 10.7	**36** 10.2					**24** 14.9	**34** 10.7	**38** 9.7
22 16.3	**22** 16.7	**26** 14.1	Cost of Sales/Inventory				**23** 15.9	**29** 12.5	**27** 13.5
39 9.4	**31** 11.6	**40** 9.1					**33** 11.2	**45** 8.1	**38** 9.5
66 5.5	**58** 6.3	**69** 5.3					**52** 7.0	**64** 5.7	**72** 5.1
17 21.8	**14** 26.1	**20** 18.1	Cost of Sales/Payables				**16** 22.2	**22** 16.4	**21** 17.2
28 13.1	**26** 14.0	**26** 14.0					**31** 11.8	**25** 14.6	**27** 13.6
44 8.3	**35** 10.3	**40** 9.1					**73** 5.0	**33** 11.1	**39** 9.3
8.1	7.2	7.0	Sales/Working Capital				8.2	7.9	6.8
18.7	16.4	13.3					20.6	12.9	12.1
140.5	129.2	55.1					69.2	41.5	40.0
15.9	16.2	17.9	EBIT/Interest				10.8	26.0	21.9
(83) 6.1	(68) 5.7	(82) 5.9					(11) 1.9	(17) 4.2	(41) 8.0
1.8	1.7	1.7					-1.0	1.3	4.2
7.2	9.5	7.7	Net Profit + Depr., Dep., Amort./Cur. Mat. L/T/D						7.4
(39) 2.5	(24) 3.7	(29) 3.9							(20) 3.3
1.3	1.3	1.9							2.1
.4	.3	.4	Fixed/Worth				.5	.4	.4
.9	1.0	1.0					1.0	.7	1.1
2.8	2.8	5.0					NM	2.1	5.4
.8	.7	.7	Debt/Worth				.6	.4	.9
2.0	1.6	2.0					7.8	1.4	1.9
10.6	9.2	15.3					-3.7	5.8	10.8
49.9	31.8	44.4	% Profit Before Taxes/Tangible Net Worth					42.7	38.9
(76) 22.4	(61) 16.2	(70) 21.8						(16) 21.8	(35) 23.1
7.6	3.5	7.3						.8	12.8
17.9	12.0	18.5	% Profit Before Taxes/Total Assets				23.8	19.9	17.7
7.6	6.4	8.0					8.5	5.5	8.2
2.7	1.1	1.2					-5.0	.2	4.0
26.6	27.0	20.5	Sales/Net Fixed Assets				94.5	15.2	20.9
8.6	10.0	8.5					18.9	8.6	6.1
4.5	5.4	4.7					7.8	4.3	4.6
3.7	4.1	3.6	Sales/Total Assets				5.3	3.3	2.9
2.5	2.8	2.5					4.0	2.6	2.2
1.9	1.9	1.8					2.1	2.0	1.7
1.0	1.2	1.2	% Depr., Dep., Amort./Sales					.9	1.1
(78) 2.0	(61) 2.0	(73) 2.2						(16) 1.8	(36) 2.2
2.8	3.0	3.5						3.6	2.6
1.2	1.4	1.1	% Officers', Directors' Owners' Comp/Sales						
(23) 2.3	(20) 2.3	(20) 4.0							
4.3	4.7	6.8							
5533510M	5235506M	6468968M	Net Sales ($)	1357M	12978M	27981M	84083M	294855M	6047714M
2332144M	2188284M	3068110M	Total Assets ($)	1781M	12091M	13404M	27700M	135947M	2877187M

M = $ thousand MM = $ million

See Pages 9 through 22 for Explanation of Ratios and Data

Current Data Sorted by Assets						Type of Statement	Comparative Historical Data	
1			5	2	6	Unqualified	10	12
		6	2			Reviewed	8	11
	2					Compiled	8	5
1	3	2	1			Tax Returns	9	12
3	5	7	13	2	1	Other	24	21
	11 (4/1-9/30/13)		51 (10/1/13-3/31/14)				4/1/09-3/31/10	4/1/10-3/31/11
0-500M	500M-2MM	2-10MM	10-50MM	50-100MM	100-250MM		ALL	ALL
5	10	15	21	4	7	NUMBER OF STATEMENTS	59	61
%	%	%	%	%	%	ASSETS	%	%
	15.0	6.0	8.0			Cash & Equivalents	7.7	6.3
	26.0	22.9	18.2			Trade Receivables (net)	21.1	21.6
	26.7	28.5	26.9			Inventory	25.2	27.5
	.1	3.8	2.9			All Other Current	2.3	2.5
	67.9	61.3	55.9			Total Current	56.3	57.8
	25.5	30.7	25.0			Fixed Assets (net)	30.6	30.2
	3.2	1.4	9.6			Intangibles (net)	8.1	5.0
	3.4	6.6	9.5			All Other Non-Current	4.9	7.0
	100.0	100.0	100.0			Total	100.0	100.0
						LIABILITIES		
	6.6	10.8	7.3			Notes Payable-Short Term	7.0	12.4
	6.3	3.6	4.4			Cur. Mat.-L.T.D.	5.1	3.8
	17.1	17.2	11.2			Trade Payables	15.0	17.9
	.0	.2	.0			Income Taxes Payable	.1	.1
	23.9	9.6	12.4			All Other Current	10.4	8.0
	53.9	41.4	35.3			Total Current	37.6	42.2
	10.4	9.0	6.2			Long-Term Debt	21.2	16.7
	.0	1.3	.4			Deferred Taxes	.4	.5
	34.4	2.4	7.8			All Other Non-Current	6.4	7.8
	1.3	45.8	50.4			Net Worth	34.4	32.9
	100.0	100.0	100.0			Total Liabilties & Net Worth	100.0	100.0
						INCOME DATA		
	100.0	100.0	100.0			Net Sales	100.0	100.0
	41.7	41.7	39.3			Gross Profit	39.0	37.5
	33.5	35.4	34.1			Operating Expenses	35.7	33.9
	8.2	6.3	5.3			Operating Profit	3.3	3.6
	.2	.7	.8			All Other Expenses (net)	.7	.7
	7.9	5.6	4.4			Profit Before Taxes	2.6	2.9
						RATIOS		
	5.5	2.0	2.6				2.9	2.1
	1.5	1.2	1.7			Current	2.1	1.4
	.7	.9	1.3				1.1	1.0
	2.3	1.2	1.2				1.5	.9
	.9	.7	.8			Quick	1.0	.7
	.3	.4	.5				.5	.4
	18 20.4	**17** 21.0	**26** 13.9				**22** 16.5	**20** 18.1
	20 18.0	**24** 15.0	**29** 12.5			Sales/Receivables	**27** 13.6	**32** 11.5
	30 12.0	**39** 9.4	**34** 10.7				**36** 10.2	**41** 8.9
	8 48.4	**35** 10.3	**45** 8.2				**37** 10.0	**40** 9.0
	23 16.0	**56** 6.5	**78** 4.7			Cost of Sales/Inventory	**53** 6.9	**56** 6.5
	54 6.7	**74** 4.9	**111** 3.3				**79** 4.6	**82** 4.4
	12 31.7	**23** 15.6	**19** 19.6				**20** 18.5	**20** 18.3
	18 20.2	**31** 11.7	**24** 15.4			Cost of Sales/Payables	**31** 11.6	**32** 11.3
	33 11.2	**50** 7.3	**46** 7.9				**48** 7.6	**58** 6.3
	8.0	7.0	5.1				5.6	7.0
	22.3	32.3	13.0			Sales/Working Capital	11.7	17.7
	-23.0	-42.8	78.9				83.9	556.0
		42.0	38.2				15.6	13.0
		(14) 14.0	(18) 7.9			EBIT/Interest	(50) 4.6	(53) 4.2
		5.0	1.3				1.8	1.4
							7.4	15.0
						Net Profit + Depr., Dep., Amort./Cur. Mat. L/T/D	(10) 4.1	(17) 5.8
							2.7	1.7
	.1	.3	.3				.3	.3
	.8	.6	.5			Fixed/Worth	1.0	.9
	NM	1.4	1.4				6.4	4.3
	.8	.8	.5				.7	.8
	1.8	1.2	1.6			Debt/Worth	1.2	2.4
	NM	2.6	2.3				17.9	8.3
		81.8	35.3				47.2	33.3
		38.2	14.0			% Profit Before Taxes/Tangible Net Worth	(46) 25.1	(50) 17.2
		19.2	2.2				13.1	10.2
	45.5	20.7	20.4				14.4	16.7
	23.1	16.9	4.3			% Profit Before Taxes/Total Assets	8.4	6.5
	11.1	6.1	.8				3.1	1.2
	62.7	20.4	20.1				24.2	25.6
	28.0	14.3	8.6			Sales/Net Fixed Assets	8.5	9.1
	6.9	6.0	4.9				5.0	4.8
	6.3	3.9	2.8				3.6	3.1
	3.5	2.9	2.2			Sales/Total Assets	2.4	2.4
	2.9	2.5	1.5				1.6	1.9
		1.3	2.2				1.3	1.4
		2.4	(19) 3.5			% Depr., Dep., Amort./Sales	(46) 2.5	(44) 1.9
		3.0	4.6				3.7	3.6
							2.4	2.6
						% Officers', Directors' Owners' Comp/Sales	(19) 3.6	(26) 4.6
							6.4	7.1
2978M	49567M	276379M	929612M	363406M	2333522M	Net Sales ($)	3179131M	2833879M
1084M	11850M	88190M	427785M	284117M	1096986M	Total Assets ($)	1675040M	1437226M

M = $ thousand MM = $ million

See Pages 9 through 22 for Explanation of Ratios and Data

Comparative Historical Data				Current Data Sorted by Sales					
			Type of Statement						
9	11	14	Unqualified	1				2	11
7	7	8	Reviewed				1	4	3
11	7	2	Compiled		1	1			
8	10	7	Tax Returns	1		1	3	1	1
30	27	31	Other	2	2	2	3	7	15
4/1/11-3/31/12 ALL	4/1/12-3/31/13 ALL	4/1/13-3/31/14 ALL		11 (4/1-9/30/13)			51 (10/1/13-3/31/14)		
				0-1MM	1-3MM	3-5MM	5-10MM	10-25MM	25MM & OVER
65	62	62	**NUMBER OF STATEMENTS**	4	3	4	7	14	30
%	%	%	**ASSETS**	%	%	%	%	%	%
8.0	8.1	8.7	Cash & Equivalents					5.5	9.9
20.1	20.1	19.3	Trade Receivables (net)					17.4	19.2
27.5	26.3	26.1	Inventory					18.6	27.2
2.5	1.5	3.6	All Other Current					5.7	2.1
58.0	56.1	57.6	Total Current					47.2	58.5
29.3	26.8	27.7	Fixed Assets (net)					36.1	23.7
5.9	7.8	7.2	Intangibles (net)					4.3	9.6
6.9	9.4	7.5	All Other Non-Current					12.4	8.3
100.0	100.0	100.0	Total					100.0	100.0
			LIABILITIES						
13.2	13.5	11.0	Notes Payable-Short Term					11.4	6.8
2.8	3.2	3.9	Cur. Mat.-L.T.D.					4.2	3.3
16.2	14.7	13.1	Trade Payables					14.0	11.3
.0	.1	.1	Income Taxes Payable					.2	.1
7.6	9.6	12.8	All Other Current					8.4	11.6
39.9	41.1	40.9	Total Current					38.3	33.0
14.8	12.7	9.2	Long-Term Debt					7.9	9.2
.9	.5	.9	Deferred Taxes					1.4	1.0
10.0	9.8	10.0	All Other Non-Current					8.1	6.4
34.5	35.9	39.0	Net Worth					44.2	50.4
100.0	100.0	100.0	Total Liabilties & Net Worth					100.0	100.0
			INCOME DATA						
100.0	100.0	100.0	Net Sales					100.0	100.0
34.2	36.0	39.5	Gross Profit					45.4	36.2
31.1	31.2	33.7	Operating Expenses					40.1	31.3
3.0	4.9	5.7	Operating Profit					5.4	4.9
.9	.7	.8	All Other Expenses (net)					.8	1.0
2.2	4.1	4.9	Profit Before Taxes					4.6	3.9
			RATIOS						
2.2	2.2	2.3						2.1	2.3
1.5	1.4	1.6	Current					1.1	1.7
1.1	1.0	1.0						.8	1.5
1.1	1.2	1.1						.8	1.2
.7	.7	.7	Quick					.4	.9
.5	.4	.4						.3	.6
20 18.4	**18** 20.0	**19** 18.9						**19** 18.9	**24** 15.3
29 12.8	**30** 12.3	**27** 13.5	Sales/Receivables					**26** 13.9	**29** 12.6
38 9.5	**38** 9.5	**32** 11.3						**29** 12.4	**34** 10.8
36 10.2	**30** 12.3	**35** 10.4						**34** 10.6	**43** 8.5
54 6.8	**57** 6.4	**58** 6.3	Cost of Sales/Inventory					**59** 6.2	**64** 5.7
94 3.9	**83** 4.4	**89** 4.1						**107** 3.4	**89** 4.1
21 17.6	**20** 18.6	**17** 21.2						**27** 13.6	**18** 20.4
31 11.7	**26** 14.0	**24** 15.3	Cost of Sales/Payables					**37** 9.8	**23** 16.0
50 7.3	**45** 8.2	**42** 8.7						**56** 6.5	**33** 11.1
6.7	8.5	6.9						9.8	6.4
10.6	15.1	12.8	Sales/Working Capital					101.1	9.9
71.7	-793.0	187.2						-20.1	16.0
9.2	24.3	32.8						34.8	71.2
(58) 3.4	(55) 6.6	(56) 10.5	EBIT/Interest					11.8	(27) 7.5
-.2	2.3	2.4						5.4	1.9
7.2	9.9	9.1							23.0
(16) 2.8	(16) 3.1	(20) 4.9	Net Profit + Depr., Dep., Amort./Cur. Mat. L/T/D						(10) 3.6
1.7	1.6	2.2							1.5
.4	.2	.3						.4	.2
.8	.9	.7	Fixed/Worth					.9	.6
1.5	3.8	1.9						1.7	1.3
.8	.7	.7						.9	.6
1.6	2.0	1.6	Debt/Worth					1.6	1.3
3.8	9.6	2.8						2.7	2.2
23.1	41.9	59.6						67.1	37.7
(56) 12.6	(50) 17.7	(57) 27.4	% Profit Before Taxes/Tangible Net Worth					35.6	(29) 14.0
4.9	9.1	8.6						15.7	2.9
9.8	14.3	20.7						20.5	20.3
4.9	7.5	9.9	% Profit Before Taxes/Total Assets					14.5	6.2
.7	2.9	2.1						8.9	.9
21.6	33.4	23.3						15.6	18.2
9.2	9.3	9.7	Sales/Net Fixed Assets					5.7	9.1
5.6	5.9	5.5						3.9	6.2
3.1	3.3	3.1						2.9	2.9
2.4	2.5	2.5	Sales/Total Assets					2.4	2.4
1.7	1.9	1.7						1.5	1.6
1.3	1.1	1.3						1.3	1.4
(51) 2.1	(47) 2.6	(50) 2.5	% Depr., Dep., Amort./Sales					2.6	(24) 2.5
3.8	4.4	3.8						3.9	3.9
1.9	2.0	1.8							
(24) 3.3	(16) 2.8	(21) 3.3	% Officers', Directors' Owners' Comp/Sales						
4.6	5.2	5.3							
3783060M	4599093M	3955464M	Net Sales ($)	1975M	4939M	16176M	53561M	242860M	3635953M
1718796M	1911572M	1910012M	Total Assets ($)	993M	1514M	5173M	19208M	161075M	1722049M

M = $ thousand MM = $ million
See Pages 9 through 22 for Explanation of Ratios and Data

Current Data Sorted by Assets							Comparative Historical Data	
						Type of Statement		
			3	1		Unqualified	9	8
			2			Reviewed	8	8
	1	5	2			Compiled	6	6
	1					Tax Returns	1	1
		4	3	3	1	Other	15	14
	4 (4/1-9/30/13)		22 (10/1/13-3/31/14)				4/1/09-3/31/10	4/1/10-3/31/11
0-500M	500M-2MM	2-10MM	10-50MM	50-100MM	100-250MM		ALL	ALL
	2	9	10	4	1	NUMBER OF STATEMENTS	39	37
%	%	%	%	%	%	**ASSETS**	%	%
D			12.9			Cash & Equivalents	12.1	9.9
A			16.6			Trade Receivables (net)	22.2	22.6
T			22.3			Inventory	26.8	28.9
A			2.4			All Other Current	3.6	2.7
			54.2			Total Current	64.8	64.1
N			30.7			Fixed Assets (net)	26.9	28.2
O			5.1			Intangibles (net)	4.5	5.3
T			10.0			All Other Non-Current	3.8	2.4
			100.0			Total	100.0	100.0
A						**LIABILITIES**		
V			2.6			Notes Payable-Short Term	7.0	7.9
A			1.7			Cur. Mat.-L.T.D.	3.2	2.7
I			8.6			Trade Payables	11.7	13.6
L			.0			Income Taxes Payable	.5	.4
A			7.2			All Other Current	7.4	5.7
B			20.1			Total Current	29.7	30.4
L			9.6			Long-Term Debt	8.4	13.6
E			1.7			Deferred Taxes	.5	.7
			2.9			All Other Non-Current	3.1	3.3
			65.6			Net Worth	58.3	52.1
			100.0			Total Liabilities & Net Worth	100.0	100.0
						INCOME DATA		
			100.0			Net Sales	100.0	100.0
			39.5			Gross Profit	35.5	36.1
			27.6			Operating Expenses	26.1	26.8
			12.0			Operating Profit	9.4	9.3
			.2			All Other Expenses (net)	.5	.5
			11.8			Profit Before Taxes	8.9	8.8
						RATIOS		
			5.1				3.1	3.9
			3.6			Current	2.4	2.5
			1.6				1.7	1.6
			3.2				1.9	2.2
			1.5			Quick	1.3	1.2
			.9				.7	.7
			33 11.1				**28** 12.8	**27** 13.5
			37 9.8			Sales/Receivables	**38** 9.6	**33** 11.2
			44 8.3				**44** 8.3	**44** 8.3
			44 8.3				**43** 8.4	**48** 7.6
			73 5.0			Cost of Sales/Inventory	**66** 5.6	**73** 5.0
			114 3.2				**116** 3.2	**104** 3.5
			9 38.5				**21** 17.3	**16** 23.2
			19 18.9			Cost of Sales/Payables	**28** 12.9	**26** 13.8
			43 8.4				**36** 10.2	**44** 8.2
			3.2				4.0	3.9
			6.1			Sales/Working Capital	6.5	6.9
			13.8				10.6	12.6
							43.5	67.6
						EBIT/Interest	(35) 13.1	(36) 12.0
							7.4	5.8
							11.9	16.3
						Net Profit + Depr., Dep., Amort./Cur. Mat. L/T/D	(16) 4.9	(14) 4.2
							2.6	2.3
			.3				.3	.3
			.6			Fixed/Worth	.5	.6
			1.0				.8	1.0
			.3				.4	.5
			.6			Debt/Worth	.7	.9
			1.4				1.3	1.9
			44.6				38.7	44.7
			24.1			% Profit Before Taxes/Tangible Net Worth	(37) 24.0	(35) 29.4
			13.1				15.6	11.1
			28.3				24.6	24.0
			13.5			% Profit Before Taxes/Total Assets	14.4	15.4
			7.7				8.5	5.7
			13.7				14.3	19.0
			5.6			Sales/Net Fixed Assets	8.7	7.9
			3.5				5.8	5.1
			2.1				3.0	2.8
			1.6			Sales/Total Assets	2.0	2.1
			1.3				1.4	1.5
							1.3	1.0
						% Depr., Dep., Amort./Sales	(36) 1.9	(35) 1.9
							3.3	3.0
							1.1	1.6
						% Officers', Directors' Owners' Comp/Sales	(10) 2.0	(10) 2.8
							3.9	13.7
	7247M	85465M	472965M	471553M	499076M	Net Sales ($)	1620797M	1785904M
	3241M	32564M	258638M	347078M	180748M	Total Assets ($)	1075065M	911587M

M = $ thousand MM = $ million

See Pages 9 through 22 for Explanation of Ratios and Data

Comparative Historical Data				Current Data Sorted by Sales					
			Type of Statement						
7	7	4	Unqualified						4
5	8	2	Reviewed					1	1
2	2	8	Compiled			2	2	3	1
1	5	1	Tax Returns			1			
19	18	11	Other			1	2	3	5
4/1/11-3/31/12 ALL	4/1/12-3/31/13 ALL	4/1/13-3/31/14 ALL		4 (4/1-9/30/13)		22 (10/1/13-3/31/14)			
				0-1MM	1-3MM	3-5MM	5-10MM	10-25MM	25MM & OVER
34	40	26	**NUMBER OF STATEMENTS**			4	4	7	11
%	%	%	**ASSETS**	%	%	%	%	%	%
8.0	8.2	10.9	Cash & Equivalents	DATA NOT AVAILABLE	DATA NOT AVAILABLE				15.1
21.8	18.1	17.3	Trade Receivables (net)						16.7
27.2	28.4	24.4	Inventory						19.7
2.6	4.3	2.9	All Other Current						2.8
59.6	59.1	55.4	Total Current						54.3
26.6	26.1	28.5	Fixed Assets (net)						25.5
8.9	7.9	8.3	Intangibles (net)						4.9
4.9	7.0	7.8	All Other Non-Current						15.3
100.0	100.0	100.0	Total						100.0
			LIABILITIES						
8.9	12.1	9.7	Notes Payable-Short Term						4.8
2.4	1.7	3.3	Cur. Mat.-L.T.D.						3.1
11.2	9.9	8.8	Trade Payables						5.6
.3	.1	.2	Income Taxes Payable						.4
7.1	11.8	5.8	All Other Current						5.5
29.9	35.6	27.8	Total Current						19.4
13.1	10.1	10.8	Long-Term Debt						8.4
2.2	.9	.9	Deferred Taxes						1.2
4.1	8.0	2.7	All Other Non-Current						2.1
50.6	45.4	57.8	Net Worth						68.9
100.0	100.0	100.0	Total Liabilties & Net Worth						100.0
			INCOME DATA						
100.0	100.0	100.0	Net Sales						100.0
36.0	37.0	36.4	Gross Profit						31.6
26.5	28.1	25.0	Operating Expenses						17.2
9.5	8.9	11.4	Operating Profit						14.4
1.0	.7	.6	All Other Expenses (net)						.3
8.4	8.2	10.8	Profit Before Taxes						14.1
			RATIOS						
3.7	3.5	4.2							5.0
1.9	2.1	2.1	Current						4.1
1.4	1.2	1.3							1.5
1.7	1.8	2.2							3.3
1.0	.8	1.0	Quick						2.0
.6	.6	.6							.7
28 13.2	**26** 14.3	**21** 17.0							**35** 10.4
36 10.0	**38** 9.6	**36** 10.1	Sales/Receivables						**38** 9.5
44 8.3	**47** 7.7	**44** 8.3							**48** 7.6
46 7.9	**51** 7.1	**40** 9.2							**41** 9.0
63 5.8	**76** 4.8	**73** 5.0	Cost of Sales/Inventory						**66** 5.5
104 3.5	**111** 3.3	**107** 3.4							**81** 4.5
16 23.2	**14** 26.4	**13** 29.1							**9** 38.7
24 15.1	**27** 13.6	**21** 17.7	Cost of Sales/Payables						**15** 23.6
38 9.5	**46** 8.0	**30** 12.0							**23** 16.0
4.7	4.3	3.9							2.9
8.4	8.2	7.6	Sales/Working Capital						4.7
16.8	20.0	18.3							9.3
42.8	61.7	24.6							
(31) 15.9	(33) 12.9	(23) 12.5	EBIT/Interest						
3.3	3.2	3.5							
7.3	15.3								
(14) 3.0	(11) 7.4		Net Profit + Depr., Dep., Amort./Cur. Mat. L/T/D						
1.7	1.9								
.3	.3	.4							.2
.6	.7	.6	Fixed/Worth						.4
1.4	1.3	1.0							.6
.5	.4	.4							.2
1.0	1.0	1.0	Debt/Worth						.4
2.1	2.6	1.7							1.3
38.3	43.0	63.4							68.9
(29) 24.6	(34) 26.5	(25) 29.1	% Profit Before Taxes/Tangible Net Worth						28.9
10.6	16.0	15.0							15.4
22.3	22.6	28.3							28.2
13.0	14.5	14.1	% Profit Before Taxes/Total Assets						11.1
4.2	5.3	7.7							9.6
21.5	36.4	21.1							34.9
8.4	8.9	7.0	Sales/Net Fixed Assets						6.9
5.5	4.3	4.3							3.7
2.8	2.7	2.4							2.3
2.1	2.0	2.0	Sales/Total Assets						1.5
1.6	1.3	1.4							1.1
1.3	1.4	1.4							1.4
(32) 1.7	(34) 2.0	(23) 2.5	% Depr., Dep., Amort./Sales						(10) 2.0
2.8	2.9	3.1							2.6
			% Officers', Directors' Owners' Comp/Sales						
1893550M	2233576M	1536306M	Net Sales ($)			14713M	28762M	142101M	1350730M
1068509M	1268542M	822269M	Total Assets ($)			8039M	12254M	73155M	728821M

M = $ thousand MM = $ million

See Pages 9 through 22 for Explanation of Ratios and Data

Current Data Sorted by Assets | Comparative Historical Data

0-500M	500M-2MM	2-10MM	10-50MM	50-100MM	100-250MM	Type of Statement	4/1/09-3/31/10 ALL	4/1/10-3/31/11 ALL
		2	1	2		Unqualified	7	6
		2	1			Reviewed	6	11
		1	2			Compiled	6	4
	3	2	2			Tax Returns	4	3
	2	2	5	1		Other	11	15
	4 (4/1-9/30/13)		24 (10/1/13-3/31/14)					
	5	9	11	3		NUMBER OF STATEMENTS	34	39
%	%	%	%	%	%	**ASSETS**	%	%
DATA NOT AVAILABLE			15.4		DATA NOT AVAILABLE	Cash & Equivalents	10.3	10.9
			18.9			Trade Receivables (net)	20.0	20.6
			19.6			Inventory	29.3	24.3
			1.2			All Other Current	1.2	1.5
			55.1			Total Current	60.7	57.3
			31.0			Fixed Assets (net)	28.8	35.5
			9.8			Intangibles (net)	6.2	4.1
			4.0			All Other Non-Current	4.3	3.0
			100.0			Total	100.0	100.0
						LIABILITIES		
			1.9			Notes Payable-Short Term	10.6	9.2
			1.7			Cur. Mat.-L.T.D.	2.6	4.2
			12.2			Trade Payables	16.2	16.5
			.0			Income Taxes Payable	.7	.3
			4.8			All Other Current	19.5	7.6
			20.7			Total Current	49.6	37.7
			9.2			Long-Term Debt	15.0	16.8
			.0			Deferred Taxes	.3	.2
			8.5			All Other Non-Current	6.1	4.9
			61.6			Net Worth	29.0	40.3
			100.0			Total Liabilties & Net Worth	100.0	100.0
						INCOME DATA		
			100.0			Net Sales	100.0	100.0
			25.2			Gross Profit	30.2	26.4
			20.1			Operating Expenses	25.9	21.2
			5.1			Operating Profit	4.3	5.3
			1.0			All Other Expenses (net)	.5	1.0
			4.2			Profit Before Taxes	3.8	4.3
						RATIOS		
			4.9				2.6	2.8
			2.8			Current	1.7	1.5
			1.6				1.0	1.1
			3.4				1.7	1.7
			1.6			Quick	.8	.7
			.7				.4	.5
			26 14.2				**21** 17.8	**23** 15.9
			30 12.2			Sales/Receivables	**28** 13.0	**32** 11.5
			42 8.7				**35** 10.4	**36** 10.0
			29 12.6				**30** 12.0	**35** 10.5
			34 10.6			Cost of Sales/Inventory	**47** 7.7	**44** 8.4
			54 6.8				**76** 4.8	**64** 5.7
			16 23.1				**16** 23.0	**17** 20.9
			22 16.8			Cost of Sales/Payables	**24** 15.2	**25** 14.7
			23 15.8				**41** 8.9	**42** 8.7
			4.2				7.5	6.7
			9.3			Sales/Working Capital	13.0	12.1
			13.0				-761.3	49.6
			38.2				24.4	13.5
			31.4			EBIT/Interest	(33) 10.2	(35) 6.1
			2.9				4.1	2.6
							9.5	9.1
						Net Profit + Depr., Dep., Amort./Cur. Mat. L/T/D	(14) 3.5	(21) 2.7
							2.2	1.5
			.4				.5	.6
			.6			Fixed/Worth	1.0	1.1
			.8				2.2	2.4
			.3				.6	.7
			.8			Debt/Worth	2.1	1.4
			1.0				3.8	3.8
			30.3				70.6	32.8
			(10) 21.2			% Profit Before Taxes/Tangible Net Worth	(30) 27.2	(37) 18.5
			6.5				13.4	8.8
			14.0				20.9	13.4
			12.5			% Profit Before Taxes/Total Assets	9.7	6.3
			1.6				4.3	3.4
			11.0				25.5	12.4
			7.0			Sales/Net Fixed Assets	8.9	7.5
			5.6				5.1	3.1
			3.4				3.7	3.2
			2.1			Sales/Total Assets	2.7	2.4
			1.3				1.6	1.5
			1.6				.8	1.2
			2.7			% Depr., Dep., Amort./Sales	(29) 1.5	(37) 2.2
			5.1				3.3	3.9
								1.5
						% Officers', Directors' Owners' Comp/Sales		(10) 2.7
								4.9
	25170M	117653M	711357M	407872M		Net Sales ($)	1828367M	1981910M
	6233M	50146M	317325M	185067M		Total Assets ($)	844840M	1031704M

M = $ thousand MM = $ million

See Pages 9 through 22 for Explanation of Ratios and Data

Comparative Historical Data				Current Data Sorted by Sales					
Type of Statement									
Unqualified	9	3	5				1	1	3
Reviewed	5	1	3					2	1
Compiled	3	3	3					2	1
Tax Returns	2	4	7		1	1	2	1	2
Other	13	14	10				2	3	5
	4/1/11-3/31/12	4/1/12-3/31/13	4/1/13-3/31/14		4 (4/1-9/30/13)		24 (10/1/13-3/31/14)		
	ALL	ALL	ALL	0-1MM	1-3MM	3-5MM	5-10MM	10-25MM	25MM & OVER
NUMBER OF STATEMENTS	32	25	28		1	1	5	9	12
ASSETS	%	%	%	%	%	%	%	%	%
Cash & Equivalents	6.8	12.7	13.1	DATA NOT AVAILABLE					12.7
Trade Receivables (net)	20.5	22.7	21.3						19.1
Inventory	27.1	24.3	22.7						19.4
All Other Current	2.7	1.9	2.3						1.5
Total Current	57.0	61.7	59.4						52.7
Fixed Assets (net)	35.5	28.9	31.3						34.4
Intangibles (net)	4.7	4.3	7.0						9.1
All Other Non-Current	2.8	5.1	2.3						3.7
Total	100.0	100.0	100.0						100.0
LIABILITIES									
Notes Payable-Short Term	13.3	8.4	3.9						3.1
Cur. Mat.-L.T.D.	4.2	2.7	3.7						2.0
Trade Payables	18.2	17.5	14.6						10.1
Income Taxes Payable	.0	.0	.1						.0
All Other Current	4.7	6.1	5.3						5.5
Total Current	40.3	34.7	27.6						20.6
Long-Term Debt	20.5	14.5	20.3						11.2
Deferred Taxes	.4	.0	.0						.0
All Other Non-Current	8.1	5.1	6.5						7.3
Net Worth	30.6	45.7	45.6						60.9
Total Liabilties & Net Worth	100.0	100.0	100.0						100.0
INCOME DATA									
Net Sales	100.0	100.0	100.0						100.0
Gross Profit	22.9	27.2	25.4						22.8
Operating Expenses	21.2	23.2	20.5						16.1
Operating Profit	1.7	4.0	4.9						6.7
All Other Expenses (net)	1.5	1.3	.9						1.2
Profit Before Taxes	.2	2.7	4.1						5.4
RATIOS									
Current	2.2	3.5	4.4						4.8
	1.4	1.7	2.1						3.0
	1.0	1.2	1.5						1.5
Quick	1.5	2.0	2.5						3.2
	.7	1.0	1.2						1.5
	.4	.6	.7						.7
Sales/Receivables	**22** 16.4	**22** 16.7	**24** 15.0						**26** 14.0
	30 12.2	**29** 12.5	**28** 13.0						**31** 11.6
	38 9.6	**35** 10.3	**38** 9.6						**41** 8.9
Cost of Sales/Inventory	**30** 12.2	**29** 12.5	**29** 12.5						**33** 10.9
	43 8.4	**37** 9.9	**38** 9.7						**38** 9.7
	66 5.5	**62** 5.9	**53** 6.9						**48** 7.6
Cost of Sales/Payables	**20** 18.0	**17** 21.1	**16** 22.5						**16** 23.1
	30 12.3	**21** 17.2	**23** 16.1						**20** 18.6
	38 9.7	**32** 11.5	**30** 12.3						**23** 15.8
Sales/Working Capital	7.0	5.8	4.7						4.2
	16.8	10.7	10.7						9.1
	609.2	32.7	15.2						15.4
EBIT/Interest	5.3	17.4	39.7						83.2
	(30) 2.5	(20) 4.9	(26) 10.1						32.1
	-1.5	3.0	2.5						5.4
Net Profit + Depr., Dep., Amort./Cur. Mat. L/T/D	4.6	7.5	9.1						
	(16) 1.8	(11) 2.4	(13) 3.9						
	.4	1.5	1.4						
Fixed/Worth	.7	.3	.4						.5
	1.7	.7	.7						.6
	3.2	1.9	2.3						.8
Debt/Worth	1.1	.6	.4						.4
	3.3	2.0	.9						.7
	5.4	3.3	4.1						.9
% Profit Before Taxes/Tangible Net Worth	32.2	49.4	38.1						30.6
	(29) 7.0	24.1	(24) 22.9						(11) 26.8
	-15.2	5.1	7.7						16.3
% Profit Before Taxes/Total Assets	8.0	15.8	13.9						18.2
	2.9	8.4	7.8						12.9
	-4.6	3.1	1.9						6.1
Sales/Net Fixed Assets	12.4	17.2	11.6						10.5
	6.9	8.7	6.8						6.7
	3.9	5.4	5.7						5.2
Sales/Total Assets	3.3	3.2	3.5						3.3
	2.5	2.5	2.5						2.1
	1.7	2.0	1.9						1.9
% Depr., Dep., Amort./Sales	1.2	.8	1.3						1.6
	(28) 2.1	(23) 1.8	(27) 2.6						2.5
	3.5	3.3	3.7						4.6
% Officers', Directors' Owners' Comp/Sales			1.6						
			(14) 3.1						
			4.5						
Net Sales ($)	1887028M	1088001M	1262052M		2840M	3030M	36476M	147310M	1072396M
Total Assets ($)	917713M	462132M	558771M		1303M	500M	13422M	68195M	475351M

M = $ thousand MM = $ million

See Pages 9 through 22 for Explanation of Ratios and Data

Current Data Sorted by Assets							Comparative Historical Data	
						Type of Statement		
			5	1	3	Unqualified	5	5
		3	3			Reviewed	4	4
1	2	4	1			Compiled	3	5
	1	1				Tax Returns	3	2
1	2	10	11	2	3	Other	13	11
14 (4/1-9/30/13)		40 (10/1/13-3/31/14)					4/1/09-3/31/10	4/1/10-3/31/11
0-500M	500M-2MM	2-10MM	10-50MM	50-100MM	100-250MM		ALL	ALL
2	5	18	20	3	6	NUMBER OF STATEMENTS	28	27
%	%	%	%	%	%	**ASSETS**	%	%
		13.3	8.9			Cash & Equivalents	8.6	7.4
		22.9	17.0			Trade Receivables (net)	19.4	21.7
		27.6	34.3			Inventory	33.8	31.8
		5.4	1.5			All Other Current	2.5	1.5
		69.2	61.6			Total Current	64.4	62.5
		23.3	22.8			Fixed Assets (net)	28.4	30.6
		1.6	9.6			Intangibles (net)	2.5	2.2
		6.0	6.0			All Other Non-Current	4.7	4.7
		100.0	100.0			Total	100.0	100.0
						LIABILITIES		
		7.1	14.5			Notes Payable-Short Term	9.7	8.2
		3.7	3.9			Cur. Mat.-L.T.D.	4.3	4.8
		16.8	10.2			Trade Payables	12.6	16.1
		.0	.8			Income Taxes Payable	1.0	.7
		33.8	6.3			All Other Current	6.3	7.0
		61.4	35.8			Total Current	33.9	36.7
		7.8	12.8			Long-Term Debt	13.7	11.7
		.0	1.7			Deferred Taxes	.4	.3
		3.4	2.2			All Other Non-Current	7.8	4.6
		27.3	47.5			Net Worth	44.3	46.7
		100.0	100.0			Total Liabilties & Net Worth	100.0	100.0
						INCOME DATA		
		100.0	100.0			Net Sales	100.0	100.0
		24.1	35.2			Gross Profit	30.3	32.2
		20.0	27.7			Operating Expenses	25.1	24.7
		4.0	7.4			Operating Profit	5.2	7.5
		.3	1.1			All Other Expenses (net)	.6	1.5
		3.8	6.4			Profit Before Taxes	4.6	6.0
						RATIOS		
		3.7	3.5				3.7	3.3
		1.9	1.6			Current	2.2	1.9
		1.2	1.1				1.5	1.1
		2.2	1.1				1.7	1.6
		.7	.6			Quick	.9	1.0
		.5	.4				.5	.5
		22 16.3	**27** 13.6				**21** 17.5	**26** 14.0
		27 13.3	**33** 11.1			Sales/Receivables	**29** 12.4	**30** 12.0
		36 10.2	**43** 8.5				**42** 8.6	**37** 9.9
		17 21.0	**73** 5.0				**55** 6.7	**54** 6.8
		62 5.9	**114** 3.2			Cost of Sales/Inventory	**85** 4.3	**70** 5.2
		73 5.0	**135** 2.7				**106** 3.5	**115** 3.2
		17 21.1	**23** 16.0				**21** 17.1	**20** 18.1
		21 17.8	**28** 13.0			Cost of Sales/Payables	**29** 12.5	**32** 11.4
		38 9.6	**41** 8.8				**37** 9.7	**49** 7.5
		5.8	4.4				4.2	3.6
		8.6	7.9			Sales/Working Capital	6.9	8.7
		NM	26.8				13.8	44.6
		68.6	16.7				20.4	88.7
		(12) 13.9	(19) 7.9			EBIT/Interest	7.0	(26) 12.6
		4.0	1.6				2.2	3.1
						Net Profit + Depr., Dep., Amort./Cur. Mat. L/T/D		
		.3	.2				.4	.3
		.5	.6			Fixed/Worth	.6	.5
		1.1	1.4				1.0	1.0
		.4	.6				.6	.4
		1.0	1.4			Debt/Worth	1.3	1.3
		2.0	3.3				3.8	4.0
		59.8	46.6				44.9	54.4
		(17) 28.2	(17) 19.2			% Profit Before Taxes/Tangible Net Worth	(26) 18.5	28.9
		22.0	12.5				10.1	9.4
		27.6	14.9				23.1	28.0
		14.2	7.7			% Profit Before Taxes/Total Assets	9.5	12.3
		6.9	2.4				2.9	3.3
		35.2	22.5				17.3	20.4
		14.4	10.0			Sales/Net Fixed Assets	10.1	9.7
		7.2	5.7				5.2	4.0
		3.7	2.4				2.8	2.8
		2.7	1.8			Sales/Total Assets	2.1	2.1
		1.9	1.2				1.3	1.6
		.4	.8				1.2	.9
		(15) 1.4	(19) 1.7			% Depr., Dep., Amort./Sales	(23) 2.0	(24) 1.5
		2.7	2.5				3.1	2.4
						% Officers', Directors' Owners' Comp/Sales		
2563M	33743M	287445M	908224M	337828M	1155559M	Net Sales ($)	1211136M	1105425M
560M	6547M	102051M	475586M	222185M	853996M	Total Assets ($)	647382M	518587M

M = $ thousand MM = $ million

See Pages 9 through 22 for Explanation of Ratios and Data

Comparative Historical Data / Current Data Sorted by Sales

Type of Statement									
Unqualified	7	7	9					1	8
Reviewed	4	4	6					1	5
Compiled	6	5	8		1	1		5	1
Tax Returns	2	2	2				2		
Other	17	28	29		2	1	4	9	13
					14 (4/1-9/30/13)		40 (10/1/13-3/31/14)		
	4/1/11-3/31/12 ALL	4/1/12-3/31/13 ALL	4/1/13-3/31/14 ALL	0-1MM	1-3MM	3-5MM	5-10MM	10-25MM	25MM & OVER
NUMBER OF STATEMENTS	36	46	54		3	2	6	16	27
ASSETS	%	%	%	%	%	%	%	%	%
Cash & Equivalents	10.4	9.4	9.0	DATA NOT AVAILABLE				10.8	9.1
Trade Receivables (net)	21.0	20.8	21.2					22.4	17.5
Inventory	34.8	32.8	32.3					25.6	39.4
All Other Current	1.9	1.3	2.8					2.6	1.7
Total Current	68.0	64.3	65.3					61.5	67.7
Fixed Assets (net)	24.9	22.3	22.8					15.9	25.2
Intangibles (net)	3.0	8.0	5.9					13.3	3.7
All Other Non-Current	4.1	5.3	6.0					9.2	3.5
Total	100.0	100.0	100.0					100.0	100.0
LIABILITIES									
Notes Payable-Short Term	7.0	10.4	10.3					7.0	13.0
Cur. Mat.-L.T.D.	2.9	2.2	3.2					2.0	3.3
Trade Payables	14.7	13.3	14.6					14.6	10.9
Income Taxes Payable	.9	.5	.4					.8	.2
All Other Current	5.8	15.2	15.2					35.4	6.0
Total Current	31.3	41.7	43.7					59.9	33.3
Long-Term Debt	10.7	10.8	11.0					8.5	13.7
Deferred Taxes	.3	.7	.9					1.0	1.3
All Other Non-Current	5.6	6.8	3.3					3.2	4.3
Net Worth	52.1	40.0	41.1					27.4	47.4
Total Liabilties & Net Worth	100.0	100.0	100.0					100.0	100.0
INCOME DATA									
Net Sales	100.0	100.0	100.0					100.0	100.0
Gross Profit	31.5	30.5	30.8					27.0	31.6
Operating Expenses	22.9	23.4	24.5					23.3	23.3
Operating Profit	8.6	7.1	6.3					3.7	8.3
All Other Expenses (net)	.7	.7	.7					1.2	.6
Profit Before Taxes	8.0	6.4	5.7					2.5	7.7
RATIOS									
Current	4.1	3.3	3.7					3.3	4.0
	2.6	2.0	1.8					1.7	2.5
	1.6	1.3	1.2					1.4	1.5
Quick	2.0	1.9	1.5					2.3	1.7
	1.1	.8	.8					.7	1.0
	.6	.5	.5					.5	.4
Sales/Receivables	**26** 13.9	**27** 13.5	**24** 15.0					**23** 16.1	**27** 13.4
	35 10.5	**32** 11.4	**31** 11.9					**30** 12.3	**31** 11.8
	41 9.0	**40** 9.2	**40** 9.1					**36** 10.0	**44** 8.3
Cost of Sales/Inventory	**63** 5.8	**49** 7.5	**45** 8.1					**21** 17.4	**69** 5.3
	78 4.7	**74** 4.9	**74** 4.9					**68** 5.4	**111** 3.3
	130 2.8	**118** 3.1	**130** 2.8					**107** 3.4	**182** 2.0
Cost of Sales/Payables	**21** 17.2	**22** 16.5	**19** 18.9					**19** 19.6	**20** 18.2
	34 10.8	**30** 12.1	**27** 13.4					**24** 14.9	**28** 13.1
	46 8.0	**37** 9.8	**39** 9.3					**33** 10.9	**42** 8.6
Sales/Working Capital	3.4	4.5	3.8					6.6	3.5
	5.6	6.8	8.1					8.1	6.4
	9.2	19.5	27.1					18.0	10.8
EBIT/Interest	58.7	29.9	32.0					52.8	35.3
	(32) 15.4	(39) 11.8	(43) 10.7					(12) 8.9	(23) 10.7
	3.7	3.8	2.0					.6	2.0
Net Profit + Depr., Dep., Amort./Cur. Mat. L/T/D	7.3	13.9	9.8						12.7
	(13) 2.6	(11) 5.8	(17) 5.3						(11) 5.8
	1.8	2.6	1.8						1.6
Fixed/Worth	.2	.2	.2					.2	.2
	.4	.6	.5					.3	.5
	1.0	1.2	1.2					1.1	1.2
Debt/Worth	.3	.5	.5					.4	.5
	1.0	1.4	1.1					1.2	1.2
	1.8	4.9	2.5					5.6	2.2
% Profit Before Taxes/Tangible Net Worth	39.0	50.2	41.8					47.1	46.6
	(34) 27.4	(41) 26.5	(49) 23.6					(13) 24.1	(25) 21.5
	16.2	13.1	14.0					9.2	14.0
% Profit Before Taxes/Total Assets	25.8	18.2	19.6					26.3	15.3
	14.5	10.4	8.0					7.6	8.5
	4.8	4.6	3.7					-.3	3.7
Sales/Net Fixed Assets	23.5	31.2	29.0					40.4	15.0
	10.2	11.8	10.0					21.0	8.3
	5.4	6.1	5.7					8.3	4.6
Sales/Total Assets	3.0	2.9	3.1					4.6	2.5
	2.1	2.1	2.0					2.1	1.9
	1.5	1.4	1.4					1.3	1.3
% Depr., Dep., Amort./Sales	.8	.8	.7					.2	.8
	(35) 1.4	(39) 1.7	(48) 1.7					(13) 1.4	1.7
	2.5	2.6	2.7					3.4	2.6
% Officers', Directors' Owners' Comp/Sales		1.4	1.8						
		(12) 3.0	(15) 2.6						
		4.6	4.0						
Net Sales ($)	1851041M	2293642M	2725362M		5097M	7267M	47709M	248847M	2416442M
Total Assets ($)	1004637M	1319206M	1660925M		1143M	4478M	31947M	128746M	1494611M

M = $ thousand MM = $ million

See Pages 9 through 22 for Explanation of Ratios and Data

Current Data Sorted by Assets | Comparative Historical Data

0-500M	500M-2MM	2-10MM	10-50MM	50-100MM	100-250MM		4/1/09-3/31/10 ALL	4/1/10-3/31/11 ALL
						Type of Statement		
		1	3	1	2	Unqualified	9	9
		1	1			Reviewed	2	6
2		3			2	Compiled	6	5
3	1	4				Tax Returns	3	4
2	1	7	8	5		Other	13	12
	11 (4/1-9/30/13)		36 (10/1/13-3/31/14)					
7	2	16	12	6	4	**NUMBER OF STATEMENTS**	33	36
%	%	%	%	%	%	**ASSETS**	%	%
		17.2	2.8			Cash & Equivalents	10.6	12.1
		19.8	17.3			Trade Receivables (net)	18.9	17.1
		13.0	16.5			Inventory	15.0	18.3
		2.0	3.1			All Other Current	1.4	1.3
		52.0	39.6			Total Current	45.8	48.8
		34.4	49.8			Fixed Assets (net)	40.0	37.8
		7.3	8.1			Intangibles (net)	8.8	9.2
		6.3	2.5			All Other Non-Current	5.4	4.2
		100.0	100.0			Total	100.0	100.0
						LIABILITIES		
		8.1	7.5			Notes Payable-Short Term	6.6	7.4
		2.1	3.9			Cur. Mat.-L.T.D.	3.1	2.6
		16.8	12.5			Trade Payables	20.0	19.7
		.6	.1			Income Taxes Payable	.2	.1
		2.7	5.2			All Other Current	9.0	9.2
		30.2	29.2			Total Current	39.0	38.8
		15.3	32.3			Long-Term Debt	23.7	24.4
		1.0	1.1			Deferred Taxes	.6	.1
		7.3	11.6			All Other Non-Current	9.4	10.1
		46.2	25.8			Net Worth	27.4	26.6
		100.0	100.0			Total Liabilties & Net Worth	100.0	100.0
						INCOME DATA		
		100.0	100.0			Net Sales	100.0	100.0
		30.7	30.2			Gross Profit	26.0	26.1
		25.1	27.7			Operating Expenses	22.9	22.2
		5.6	2.5			Operating Profit	3.1	3.9
		.5	1.1			All Other Expenses (net)	1.4	.9
		5.1	1.4			Profit Before Taxes	1.7	3.1
						RATIOS		
		3.0	2.1				2.5	2.6
		1.8	1.5			Current	1.1	1.2
		.8	.7				.8	.9
		1.8	1.0				1.6	1.7
		1.2	.6			Quick	.6	.7
		.5	.5				.4	.5
		15 24.8	**19** 19.4				**19** 19.3	**16** 22.1
		26 14.1	**23** 15.7			Sales/Receivables	**25** 14.6	**22** 16.8
		37 9.8	**37** 9.9				**31** 11.8	**29** 12.6
		12 30.6	**13** 29.0				**10** 35.9	**12** 29.7
		22 16.4	**33** 10.9			Cost of Sales/Inventory	**17** 21.0	**23** 15.7
		37 9.9	**70** 5.2				**42** 8.7	**49** 7.5
		14 25.3	**13** 27.9				**20** 18.7	**16** 22.7
		32 11.5	**24** 15.2			Cost of Sales/Payables	**30** 12.1	**30** 12.2
		47 7.8	**41** 8.9				**49** 7.5	**43** 8.5
		6.4	9.3				11.9	10.0
		17.1	18.2			Sales/Working Capital	93.5	42.1
		-39.0	-41.5				-32.4	-47.2
		23.8	5.1				13.2	24.2
		(13) 10.3	2.4			EBIT/Interest	(30) 4.7	(33) 3.0
		3.3	-2.0				1.3	1.4
							12.1	
						Net Profit + Depr., Dep., Amort./Cur. Mat. L/T/D	(10) 6.2	
							1.2	
		.3	1.2				.7	.6
		1.5	1.9			Fixed/Worth	1.7	1.4
		1.9	3.0				-9.0	-4.6
		.6	.9				1.2	.9
		1.7	2.8			Debt/Worth	3.2	2.7
		4.0	4.0				-20.7	-13.0
		68.5	47.5				74.4	49.6
		43.5	(10) 17.9			% Profit Before Taxes/Tangible Net Worth	(23) 52.8	(25) 35.0
		11.6	4.7				11.0	11.4
		22.0	9.5				14.3	17.0
		14.2	4.8			% Profit Before Taxes/Total Assets	9.5	6.7
		5.7	-3.0				2.6	2.4
		34.9	7.7				10.3	12.8
		7.3	4.2			Sales/Net Fixed Assets	6.9	7.1
		5.1	2.5				4.4	3.9
		4.0	2.7				3.6	3.8
		2.9	2.1			Sales/Total Assets	2.6	2.5
		2.0	1.6				2.1	1.8
		.8	1.7				1.2	1.2
		(13) 1.8	2.1			% Depr., Dep., Amort./Sales	(27) 2.6	(30) 2.1
		2.6	3.9				3.4	3.2
		1.5						1.8
		(10) 4.3				% Officers', Directors' Owners' Comp/Sales		(12) 4.9
		7.6						6.0
9262M	12005M	323719M	601059M	692155M	1578722M	Net Sales ($)	4059778M	4751433M
1526M	2372M	91883M	272378M	434121M	641402M	Total Assets ($)	1448473M	1851831M

M = $ thousand MM = $ million

See Pages 9 through 22 for Explanation of Ratios and Data

Comparative Historical Data							Current Data Sorted by Sales							
						Type of Statement								
	8		8		7	Unqualified				1				6
	5		1		2	Reviewed						1		1
	6		2		7	Compiled	2			2		1		2
	6		8		8	Tax Returns	1	1	1	1		2		2
	19		26		23	Other	2		1	2		6		12
	4/1/11-3/31/12		**4/1/12-3/31/13**		**4/1/13-3/31/14**		**11 (4/1-9/30/13)**			**36 (10/1/13-3/31/14)**				
	ALL		**ALL**		**ALL**		**0-1MM**	**1-3MM**	**3-5MM**	**5-10MM**		**10-25MM**		**25MM & OVER**
	44		45		47	**NUMBER OF STATEMENTS**	5	1	2	6		10		23
	%		%		%	**ASSETS**	%	%	%	%		%		%
	10.7		9.8		11.4	Cash & Equivalents						11.0		8.3
	17.6		16.9		19.4	Trade Receivables (net)						23.6		18.0
	17.3		19.8		16.0	Inventory						15.4		16.7
	3.7		2.6		3.3	All Other Current						2.8		1.7
	49.2		49.1		50.1	Total Current						52.8		44.7
	35.1		31.2		35.4	Fixed Assets (net)						32.2		36.0
	10.2		14.0		9.4	Intangibles (net)						9.2		14.0
	5.5		5.8		5.1	All Other Non-Current						5.9		5.3
	100.0		100.0		100.0	Total						100.0		100.0
						LIABILITIES								
	5.6		6.6		7.3	Notes Payable-Short Term						10.5		3.6
	2.4		3.3		2.5	Cur. Mat.-L.T.D.						2.8		2.7
	15.2		15.5		18.8	Trade Payables						12.5		17.8
	.1		.2		.3	Income Taxes Payable						1.0		.0
	7.9		4.9		4.5	All Other Current						2.6		4.9
	31.2		30.5		33.4	Total Current						29.3		29.0
	28.0		25.0		19.4	Long-Term Debt						23.7		21.8
	.2		.4		.9	Deferred Taxes						1.6		1.2
	12.5		11.3		8.2	All Other Non-Current						6.4		11.0
	28.1		32.9		38.1	Net Worth						39.0		36.9
	100.0		100.0		100.0	Total Liabilties & Net Worth						100.0		100.0
						INCOME DATA								
	100.0		100.0		100.0	Net Sales						100.0		100.0
	28.6		32.7		29.4	Gross Profit						30.0		25.8
	24.9		28.6		25.9	Operating Expenses						24.3		22.9
	3.7		4.1		3.6	Operating Profit						5.7		3.0
	1.3		.9		.8	All Other Expenses (net)						1.1		1.0
	2.4		3.2		2.7	Profit Before Taxes						4.6		1.9
						RATIOS								
	2.5		3.6		2.2							2.4		2.2
	1.7		1.8		1.6	Current						1.9		1.4
	1.0		1.0		.9							1.4		.9
	1.9		1.4		1.4							1.6		1.1
	.8		1.0		.8	Quick						1.1		.8
	.4		.6		.6							.6		.5
13	27.3	**17**	21.0	**16**	22.8						**20**	18.5	**18**	19.9
23	16.2	**25**	14.4	**26**	13.9	Sales/Receivables					**40**	9.1	**27**	13.5
33	10.9	**42**	8.6	**37**	9.9						**52**	7.0	**37**	9.9
12	29.4	**22**	16.9	**16**	22.5						**15**	23.9	**18**	20.2
26	14.1	**40**	9.2	**30**	12.0	Cost of Sales/Inventory					**27**	13.6	**30**	12.0
54	6.7	**72**	5.1	**42**	8.6						**68**	5.4	**62**	5.9
13	28.2	**17**	21.5	**19**	19.7						**7**	55.8	**21**	17.8
26	14.1	**30**	12.0	**27**	13.3	Cost of Sales/Payables					**23**	15.7	**32**	11.5
41	8.9	**45**	8.1	**45**	8.2						**42**	8.7	**41**	8.8
	9.2		5.7		8.3							5.8		8.6
	19.9		15.2		22.2	Sales/Working Capital						13.3		25.3
	NM		-599.3		-60.9							NM		-71.8
	8.9		19.9		10.7									15.7
(39)	4.3	(42)	3.8	(38)	4.5	EBIT/Interest							(21)	3.5
	1.5		.2		1.1									.4
					5.9									6.6
				(13)	2.1	Net Profit + Depr., Dep., Amort./Cur. Mat. L/T/D							(10)	2.0
					.8									.5
	.5		.4		.4							.1		.4
	1.5		1.3		1.5	Fixed/Worth						1.4		1.6
	-19.6		NM		2.6							2.4		-1.4
	.9		.8		.8							1.0		.6
	1.7		3.8		2.4	Debt/Worth						2.6		2.4
	-118.0		-17.3		5.6							4.6		-3.4
	32.9		55.0		46.8							75.8		45.4
(32)	20.4	(32)	28.2	(39)	18.9	% Profit Before Taxes/Tangible Net Worth						48.5	(17)	13.8
	5.4		4.2		7.3							16.7		6.4
	12.5		16.5		13.8							17.3		9.5
	6.0		6.0		4.6	% Profit Before Taxes/Total Assets						12.1		4.6
	2.8		-4.0		-1.9							5.2		-1.9
	16.9		16.7		20.1							56.9		17.8
	8.4		8.9		7.8	Sales/Net Fixed Assets						7.3		8.0
	4.1		4.1		4.0							4.8		3.7
	4.4		3.2		3.9							3.2		3.2
	2.4		2.1		2.4	Sales/Total Assets						2.3		2.4
	1.6		1.5		1.8							1.7		1.8
	1.3		1.0		1.2									.9
(35)	2.3	(36)	2.3	(41)	2.3	% Depr., Dep., Amort./Sales								2.0
	3.2		3.8		3.2									3.5
	1.4		1.9		.8									
(12)	2.1	(11)	2.5	(19)	3.9	% Officers', Directors' Owners' Comp/Sales								
	4.3		3.6		7.0									
	2441054M		**2504673M**		**3216922M**	Net Sales ($)	**2713M**	**1849M**	**8487M**	**46357M**		**163068M**		**2994448M**
	1194279M		**1466010M**		**1443682M**	Total Assets ($)	**954M**	**253M**	**1454M**	**19999M**		**72582M**		**1348440M**

M = $ thousand MM = $ million

See Pages 9 through 22 for Explanation of Ratios and Data

Current Data Sorted by Assets							Comparative Historical Data	
						Type of Statement		
	1	7	18	9	8	Unqualified	56	40
	2	15	17			Reviewed	37	38
1	5	10	1	1	1	Compiled	20	19
4	17	11	1			Tax Returns	34	33
10	15	26	36	12	10	Other	97	90
	47 (4/1-9/30/13)		191 (10/1/13-3/31/14)				4/1/09-3/31/10 ALL	4/1/10-3/31/11 ALL
0-500M	500M-2MM	2-10MM	10-50MM	50-100MM	100-250MM			
15	40	69	73	22	19	**NUMBER OF STATEMENTS**	244	220
%	%	%	%	%	%	**ASSETS**	%	%
20.8	15.3	6.6	7.8	3.7	6.6	Cash & Equivalents	7.2	8.4
31.2	22.1	23.2	20.9	13.9	16.4	Trade Receivables (net)	21.3	22.7
20.0	24.8	28.1	27.6	22.7	23.5	Inventory	26.6	25.2
.3	2.7	2.0	2.4	2.2	2.9	All Other Current	2.5	2.3
72.4	64.9	59.9	58.7	42.5	49.4	Total Current	57.7	58.6
22.3	22.0	30.6	31.3	42.3	28.9	Fixed Assets (net)	30.8	31.6
1.6	8.0	4.3	6.3	10.1	14.2	Intangibles (net)	5.4	5.7
3.7	5.1	5.3	3.7	5.1	7.5	All Other Non-Current	6.1	4.2
100.0	100.0	100.0	100.0	100.0	100.0	Total	100.0	100.0
						LIABILITIES		
14.4	7.8	9.0	10.6	10.5	4.8	Notes Payable-Short Term	10.2	11.4
6.5	3.5	3.2	3.4	3.3	3.8	Cur. Mat.-L.T.D.	4.3	3.6
18.9	20.9	17.0	15.0	10.9	11.1	Trade Payables	15.9	17.3
.3	.1	.2	.1	.2	.0	Income Taxes Payable	.4	.3
27.1	8.9	8.3	8.0	4.6	10.4	All Other Current	9.5	8.4
67.3	41.2	37.8	37.1	29.6	30.1	Total Current	40.4	41.1
10.3	19.2	17.5	16.8	21.7	19.9	Long-Term Debt	19.8	15.8
.0	.2	.7	.3	.6	.6	Deferred Taxes	.6	.6
33.6	14.3	8.8	7.3	8.2	5.1	All Other Non-Current	8.0	7.7
-11.4	25.0	35.3	38.4	40.0	44.3	Net Worth	31.3	34.8
100.0	100.0	100.0	100.0	100.0	100.0	Total Liabilties & Net Worth	100.0	100.0
						INCOME DATA		
100.0	100.0	100.0	100.0	100.0	100.0	Net Sales	100.0	100.0
40.7	32.7	29.7	25.9	29.5	29.2	Gross Profit	30.7	30.0
34.1	28.8	25.9	19.6	23.9	23.6	Operating Expenses	24.5	24.4
6.6	3.9	3.8	6.3	5.6	5.6	Operating Profit	6.1	5.6
.5	.7	.5	.9	.1	1.7	All Other Expenses (net)	.8	1.0
6.1	3.2	3.3	5.4	5.6	4.0	Profit Before Taxes	5.3	4.6
						RATIOS		
6.3	3.6	2.3	2.6	2.2	2.4		2.2	2.2
1.9	1.5	1.8	1.8	1.5	1.6	Current	1.5	1.4
.7	1.1	1.2	1.1	1.2	1.3		1.1	1.1
5.0	1.6	1.4	1.4	.8	1.1		1.2	1.3
1.0	.9	.8	.7	.7	.7	Quick	.7	.7
.3	.5	.5	.4	.5	.5		.4	.4
3 129.4	**10** 35.7	**20** 18.4	**23** 15.6	**21** 17.6	**24** 15.5		**20** 18.1	**22** 16.9
10 35.0	**19** 19.7	**29** 12.4	**32** 11.3	**26** 14.1	**30** 12.3	Sales/Receivables	**27** 13.4	**31** 11.9
29 12.4	**33** 11.2	**39** 9.4	**44** 8.3	**33** 11.0	**37** 9.9		**38** 9.7	**42** 8.6
7 55.3	**9** 42.1	**26** 14.3	**30** 12.2	**39** 9.3	**36** 10.0		**26** 13.9	**23** 16.2
14 25.5	**31** 11.8	**51** 7.1	**58** 6.3	**52** 7.0	**61** 6.0	Cost of Sales/Inventory	**46** 8.0	**47** 7.8
48 7.6	**70** 5.2	**85** 4.3	**101** 3.6	**83** 4.4	**89** 4.1		**78** 4.7	**80** 4.5
0 UND	**11** 31.9	**17** 21.0	**17** 21.9	**23** 15.9	**20** 18.7		**15** 24.2	**15** 23.6
6 58.3	**31** 11.6	**27** 13.4	**26** 14.2	**33** 11.1	**31** 11.9	Cost of Sales/Payables	**27** 13.5	**28** 12.9
21 17.0	**44** 8.3	**39** 9.4	**56** 6.5	**50** 7.3	**46** 7.9		**43** 8.5	**48** 7.6
5.8	7.2	7.0	5.1	9.0	6.5		7.0	6.7
11.8	12.5	12.5	11.3	16.0	11.6	Sales/Working Capital	18.0	15.8
-26.5	71.9	49.2	45.0	32.7	28.9		116.0	103.0
	17.6	18.3	24.6	29.8	21.7		14.7	15.0
	(32) 3.2	(62) 6.5	(66) 6.9	10.9	(16) 5.2	EBIT/Interest	(224) 5.1	(198) 6.0
	-.1	1.6	2.0	4.1	.5		2.2	2.2
			6.1				10.9	8.4
			(28) 2.7			Net Profit + Depr., Dep., Amort./Cur. Mat. L/T/D	(80) 4.5	(59) 3.1
			1.4				2.2	1.9
.0	.2	.3	.4	.9	.4		.4	.4
.2	1.5	.9	1.1	1.2	1.1	Fixed/Worth	.9	.9
-67.0	-3.9	3.1	2.0	1.9	12.0		3.2	2.2
.1	1.2	1.1	.7	.9	.8		.9	.8
6.0	2.9	1.8	1.8	1.7	1.6	Debt/Worth	2.1	1.8
-2.3	-13.0	6.2	4.7	3.4	22.7		7.6	6.1
	71.2	75.8	42.5	34.5	61.4		60.0	57.7
	(28) 29.0	(61) 30.5	(65) 25.9	(18) 21.1	(15) 20.1	% Profit Before Taxes/Tangible Net Worth	(207) 29.5	(190) 28.8
	-1.3	4.8	8.3	14.9	.1		11.5	10.2
45.2	19.0	22.4	17.5	12.3	17.1		18.4	20.4
24.7	7.7	9.6	9.0	9.8	5.3	% Profit Before Taxes/Total Assets	9.8	9.2
.0	-.7	1.0	3.1	4.5	-.3		3.4	2.9
UND	193.5	28.1	18.4	7.2	29.8		25.5	21.8
59.8	17.0	13.1	9.6	4.3	8.9	Sales/Net Fixed Assets	10.2	9.1
15.4	6.3	5.4	4.1	2.7	3.7		4.9	4.7
8.9	5.0	4.1	2.9	2.0	2.9		3.9	3.6
4.0	3.1	2.7	2.1	1.8	1.8	Sales/Total Assets	2.6	2.4
2.3	2.2	1.8	1.5	1.4	1.5		1.7	1.7
	.9	.6	.9	2.2	1.2		.9	1.0
	(21) 2.1	(59) 1.4	(69) 1.6	2.8	(14) 2.1	% Depr., Dep., Amort./Sales	(206) 1.5	(186) 2.0
	3.5	2.8	2.9	3.8	2.6		2.8	3.8
	1.7	1.4	1.7				1.4	1.3
	(18) 3.0	(29) 3.5	(14) 3.1			% Officers', Directors' Owners' Comp/Sales	(77) 2.7	(64) 2.8
	4.5	7.3	6.1				5.8	6.6
21598M	**179412M**	**1047287M**	**3861384M**	**2738422M**	**5817901M**	Net Sales ($)	**15563089M**	**12565106M**
3770M	**51241M**	**351915M**	**1659362M**	**1561032M**	**2787579M**	Total Assets ($)	**6499468M**	**5280339M**

M = $ thousand MM = $ million

See Pages 9 through 22 for Explanation of Ratios and Data

Comparative Historical Data / Current Data Sorted by Sales

4/1/11-3/31/12 ALL	4/1/12-3/31/13 ALL	4/1/13-3/31/14 ALL		0-1MM	1-3MM	3-5MM	5-10MM	10-25MM	25MM & OVER
			Type of Statement						
42	49	43	Unqualified	1				10	32
43	33	34	Reviewed			1	3	14	16
23	22	19	Compiled	1	1	3	7	5	2
34	31	33	Tax Returns	1	11	7	9	4	1
100	101	109	Other	6	7	10	7	25	54
					47 (4/1-9/30/13)		191 (10/1/13-3/31/14)		
242	236	238	**NUMBER OF STATEMENTS**	9	19	21	26	58	105
%	%	%	**ASSETS**	%	%	%	%	%	%
8.3	8.6	9.1	Cash & Equivalents		15.1	13.1	9.8	8.2	6.5
22.8	21.5	21.4	Trade Receivables (net)		21.3	23.6	17.1	23.1	20.5
25.8	25.3	26.0	Inventory		25.6	24.0	26.4	28.9	25.9
1.6	1.7	2.2	All Other Current		1.6	2.1	1.6	1.7	2.7
58.5	57.1	58.7	Total Current		63.7	62.9	54.9	61.8	55.6
29.5	31.3	29.8	Fixed Assets (net)		26.5	20.8	34.3	30.9	30.9
6.6	6.4	6.7	Intangibles (net)		1.9	8.0	6.0	4.3	8.6
5.4	5.2	4.8	All Other Non-Current		7.9	8.3	4.8	2.9	4.9
100.0	100.0	100.0	Total		100.0	100.0	100.0	100.0	100.0
			LIABILITIES						
12.2	10.0	9.4	Notes Payable-Short Term		11.7	10.5	5.0	10.3	9.6
2.6	3.7	3.6	Cur. Mat.-L.T.D.		7.0	2.9	3.4	3.9	3.2
17.7	17.1	16.1	Trade Payables		15.3	25.1	15.4	16.5	15.5
.2	.5	.1	Income Taxes Payable		.3	.1	.2	.2	.1
7.5	6.5	9.3	All Other Current		18.8	10.1	6.3	8.9	8.1
40.2	37.8	38.6	Total Current		53.0	48.7	30.3	39.7	36.4
17.0	17.6	17.7	Long-Term Debt		24.4	12.4	19.6	18.8	16.5
.4	.7	.5	Deferred Taxes		.0	.0	.6	.7	.4
7.1	7.6	10.5	All Other Non-Current		31.5	7.3	9.5	6.3	7.7
35.2	36.4	32.7	Net Worth		-8.9	31.6	39.9	34.4	39.0
100.0	100.0	100.0	Total Liabilties & Net Worth		100.0	100.0	100.0	100.0	100.0
			INCOME DATA						
100.0	100.0	100.0	Net Sales		100.0	100.0	100.0	100.0	100.0
30.0	29.2	29.7	Gross Profit		41.9	30.0	31.7	28.2	26.5
23.8	23.5	24.6	Operating Expenses		42.1	28.9	26.1	22.9	20.5
6.2	5.7	5.1	Operating Profit		-.2	1.1	5.5	5.3	6.0
.9	1.0	.7	All Other Expenses (net)		.5	.7	.6	.7	.7
5.3	4.7	4.4	Profit Before Taxes		-.7	.4	4.9	4.5	5.4
			RATIOS						
2.3	2.4	2.5			2.7	3.1	3.0	2.5	2.3
1.5	1.6	1.7	Current		1.6	1.3	1.8	1.7	1.7
1.0	1.1	1.1			1.0	.9	1.3	1.1	1.2
1.3	1.4	1.4			1.2	1.3	1.6	1.3	1.3
.7	.7	.8	Quick		1.0	.6	1.0	.7	.7
.5	.5	.5			.2	.3	.5	.5	.4
21 17.4	**22** 16.9	**19** 19.4			**3** 129.4	**14** 25.6	**11** 33.5	**23** 16.1	**21** 17.1
31 11.9	**28** 12.9	**29** 12.6	Sales/Receivables		**28** 13.0	**20** 18.1	**23** 15.8	**31** 11.8	**29** 12.7
41 9.0	**38** 9.7	**39** 9.3			**48** 7.6	**32** 11.3	**39** 9.3	**45** 8.1	**36** 10.1
20 18.0	**25** 14.5	**25** 14.4			**14** 25.5	**7** 52.3	**11** 34.3	**36** 10.2	**31** 11.8
49 7.5	**46** 7.9	**50** 7.3	Cost of Sales/Inventory		**48** 7.6	**34** 10.8	**39** 9.3	**57** 6.4	**51** 7.2
85 4.3	**74** 4.9	**81** 4.5			**94** 3.9	**56** 6.5	**87** 4.2	**89** 4.1	**76** 4.8
16 23.0	**16** 22.9	**15** 23.7			**4** 94.0	**16** 23.5	**15** 24.2	**15** 23.8	**18** 20.3
26 14.2	**28** 13.1	**27** 13.4	Cost of Sales/Payables		**34** 10.8	**35** 10.3	**27** 13.5	**27** 13.4	**26** 13.9
45 8.2	**41** 8.8	**43** 8.4			**68** 5.4	**51** 7.2	**37** 9.8	**42** 8.6	**44** 8.3
6.7	6.8	6.7			6.6	8.3	7.1	6.3	7.1
16.2	13.9	12.5	Sales/Working Capital		11.0	20.9	11.6	12.9	13.9
131.0	70.7	47.4			-999.8	-38.0	46.4	75.2	35.8
16.9	18.9	19.7			13.9	1.7	14.3	20.7	25.9
(216) 5.7	(206) 6.5	(203) 6.0	EBIT/Interest		(14) 2.2	(16) -.7	(22) 5.9	(52) 7.2	(96) 7.2
1.8	2.2	1.5			-.2	-3.4	3.2	2.0	2.1
7.4	7.1	6.2						5.0	7.0
(71) 3.2	(68) 2.8	(53) 2.9	Net Profit + Depr., Dep., Amort./Cur. Mat. L/T/D					(16) 1.8	(36) 3.6
1.6	1.4	1.4						.7	1.8
.4	.5	.4			.3	.1	.4	.3	.5
.9	1.0	1.1	Fixed/Worth		5.4	.5	1.1	1.2	1.0
2.6	2.4	3.1			-3.9	6.5	1.9	4.6	1.8
.9	.8	.8			1.8	.6	1.2	.8	.8
2.0	2.0	1.8	Debt/Worth		5.6	2.0	1.5	2.0	1.7
8.2	5.9	8.0			-12.4	NM	2.9	7.7	6.1
51.7	59.7	55.0			51.5	60.1	54.6	69.2	55.5
(207) 25.0	(204) 26.9	(195) 25.9	% Profit Before Taxes/Tangible Net Worth		(11) 18.9	(16) -.7	(23) 25.6	(49) 30.7	(90) 25.9
10.4	10.1	5.3			-3.0	-7.6	5.1	11.7	11.3
16.7	17.6	20.0			24.7	16.7	18.3	21.3	19.4
7.9	8.8	9.4	% Profit Before Taxes/Total Assets		5.1	-1.3	9.5	12.4	9.2
2.1	2.5	1.4			-7.4	-12.5	2.9	2.8	3.2
27.2	20.5	27.1			60.6	268.3	21.2	31.3	18.0
10.3	9.5	11.6	Sales/Net Fixed Assets		14.6	25.9	10.8	10.6	9.6
5.1	4.7	4.4			5.1	6.5	4.6	4.0	4.3
3.6	3.8	3.7			4.9	5.8	3.7	3.7	3.1
2.4	2.5	2.3	Sales/Total Assets		2.2	3.1	2.8	2.4	2.2
1.7	1.7	1.6			1.4	2.0	1.5	1.6	1.7
1.0	1.0	.9				.3	1.1	.8	.8
(195) 1.8	(199) 1.9	(188) 1.8	% Depr., Dep., Amort./Sales			(11) 1.8	(20) 1.9	(51) 1.8	(95) 1.7
3.0	3.0	3.0				3.8	2.9	2.9	2.8
1.6	1.4	1.6					2.0	1.6	.1
(74) 3.1	(68) 3.2	(70) 3.3	% Officers', Directors' Owners' Comp/Sales				(17) 4.9	(19) 3.3	(16) 1.9
6.0	5.8	5.9					8.5	5.8	3.5
13344072M	**13432230M**	**13666004M**	Net Sales ($)	**4576M**	**36925M**	**83488M**	**184514M**	**977849M**	**12378652M**
5979587M	**6426143M**	**6414899M**	Total Assets ($)	**4207M**	**18520M**	**32034M**	**92789M**	**506368M**	**5760981M**

M = $ thousand MM = $ million

See Pages 9 through 22 for Explanation of Ratios and Data

Current Data Sorted by Assets

Comparative Historical Data

0-500M	500M-2MM	2-10MM	10-50MM	50-100MM	100-250MM	Type of Statement	4/1/09-3/31/10 ALL	4/1/10-3/31/11 ALL
		1	12	4	3	Unqualified	36	37
		4	2		1	Reviewed	8	6
	1	2	1			Compiled	8	6
1		4	1			Tax Returns	5	6
	2	8	14	4	11	Other	41	34
11 (4/1-9/30/13)		65 (10/1/13-3/31/14)						
1	3	19	30	8	15	NUMBER OF STATEMENTS	98	89
%	%	%	%	%	%	**ASSETS**	%	%
		17.2	15.0		4.3	Cash & Equivalents	8.8	9.6
		17.6	15.1		12.3	Trade Receivables (net)	16.4	16.1
		15.9	13.5		11.9	Inventory	15.4	13.4
		3.2	2.9		5.0	All Other Current	2.7	3.8
		53.8	46.6		33.5	Total Current	43.2	42.8
		30.1	30.1		33.0	Fixed Assets (net)	31.8	32.7
		5.3	14.8		22.9	Intangibles (net)	14.0	15.3
		10.8	8.5		10.7	All Other Non-Current	10.9	9.2
		100.0	100.0		100.0	Total	100.0	100.0
						LIABILITIES		
		6.0	2.0		1.6	Notes Payable-Short Term	4.6	2.3
		3.0	2.1		2.1	Cur. Mat.-L.T.D.	4.4	3.7
		14.2	16.5		12.7	Trade Payables	14.2	12.7
		.3	.4		.3	Income Taxes Payable	.2	.2
		9.5	12.9		9.4	All Other Current	9.6	10.3
		33.0	34.1		26.2	Total Current	33.0	29.2
		19.2	18.6		45.6	Long-Term Debt	18.1	16.9
		.6	1.8		6.3	Deferred Taxes	1.1	1.1
		7.6	5.1		8.3	All Other Non-Current	6.0	4.0
		39.6	40.4		13.6	Net Worth	41.8	48.8
		100.0	100.0		100.0	Total Liabilties & Net Worth	100.0	100.0
						INCOME DATA		
		100.0	100.0		100.0	Net Sales	100.0	100.0
		30.6	27.6		37.7	Gross Profit	29.4	32.5
		25.0	21.5		31.2	Operating Expenses	24.3	26.4
		5.6	6.1		6.5	Operating Profit	5.1	6.1
		.2	.7		1.2	All Other Expenses (net)	.8	.8
		5.4	5.4		5.3	Profit Before Taxes	4.4	5.3
						RATIOS		
		4.2	2.9		1.5		2.7	2.8
		1.8	1.9		1.2	Current	1.5	1.6
		1.2	1.3		1.0		.9	1.1
		2.6	2.1		.8		1.8	1.7
		1.2	1.0		.6	Quick	(97) 1.0	.9
		.5	.7		.3		.4	.5
		17 21.9	21 17.1		9 41.9		19 19.5	19 19.5
		24 15.4	26 14.2		24 15.1	Sales/Receivables	25 14.3	27 13.6
		29 12.5	30 12.3		30 12.2		30 12.0	34 10.9
		12 30.6	19 19.4		19 18.8		18 20.8	19 19.6
		25 14.6	24 15.2		26 13.8	Cost of Sales/Inventory	26 14.0	27 13.3
		70 5.2	33 11.0		36 10.0		44 8.3	46 8.0
		14 25.3	17 21.1		24 15.4		13 27.8	17 21.5
		24 15.5	23 15.9		34 10.8	Cost of Sales/Payables	24 15.2	26 14.1
		34 10.6	36 10.2		48 7.6		37 9.9	41 8.9
		7.2	6.5		15.8		7.9	5.7
		11.2	10.6		63.1	Sales/Working Capital	17.6	16.0
		21.0	62.4		-544.4		-122.0	93.8
		46.6	191.8		5.4		22.9	18.6
		(13) 14.7	(28) 12.8		3.8	EBIT/Interest	(87) 5.1	(77) 5.8
		2.4	1.8		.8		1.4	2.0
							10.8	9.7
						Net Profit + Depr., Dep., Amort./Cur. Mat. L/T/D	(28) 3.8	(24) 3.3
							1.6	.8
		.2	.4		1.0		.5	.5
		.5	.8		4.4	Fixed/Worth	1.0	.9
		1.0	-1.5		-.9		16.3	2.2
		.2	.4		1.4		.5	.6
		.9	1.6		10.4	Debt/Worth	1.3	1.0
		1.6	-12.5		-2.5		91.0	4.6
		35.0	56.9				41.8	36.9
		(18) 15.6	(21) 32.3			% Profit Before Taxes/Tangible Net Worth	(75) 19.5	(72) 16.0
		6.1	6.4				4.7	3.2
		13.5	21.7		6.4		14.0	11.9
		10.9	9.5		3.9	% Profit Before Taxes/Total Assets	6.7	5.0
		2.3	1.6		-.8		1.1	2.0
		26.4	17.2		10.2		13.5	12.3
		13.5	8.7		8.4	Sales/Net Fixed Assets	7.8	6.6
		4.4	4.5		4.7		5.2	4.5
		3.4	3.3		3.1		3.0	2.9
		2.4	2.3		1.6	Sales/Total Assets	2.2	1.9
		1.7	1.4		1.5		1.6	1.3
		.4	1.5				1.8	1.9
		(18) 2.2	2.3			% Depr., Dep., Amort./Sales	(82) 2.9	(77) 2.7
		4.2	3.5				4.1	3.9
							.8	.8
						% Officers', Directors' Owners' Comp/Sales	(15) .9	(14) 2.1
							2.2	5.7
368M	16361M	284104M	1873532M	1237135M	5770085M	Net Sales ($)	9022397M	9558947M
301M	4320M	99556M	785865M	509892M	2634532M	Total Assets ($)	4448167M	4927901M

M = $ thousand MM = $ million

See Pages 9 through 22 for Explanation of Ratios and Data

Comparative Historical Data				Current Data Sorted by Sales					
			Type of Statement						
31	21	20	Unqualified						20
7	11	7	Reviewed					4	3
7	7	4	Compiled				2	1	1
6	6	6	Tax Returns	1		1	2	1	1
47	41	39	Other			2	3	7	27
4/1/11-3/31/12 ALL	4/1/12-3/31/13 ALL	4/1/13-3/31/14 ALL			11 (4/1-9/30/13)		65 (10/1/13-3/31/14)		
				0-1MM	1-3MM	3-5MM	5-10MM	10-25MM	25MM & OVER
98	86	76	**NUMBER OF STATEMENTS**	1		3	7	13	52
%	%	%	**ASSETS**	%	%	%	%	%	%
8.2	8.9	12.4	Cash & Equivalents		DATA NOT AVAILABLE			17.2	12.5
15.6	14.8	15.5	Trade Receivables (net)					16.5	15.4
14.3	15.0	15.0	Inventory					14.4	13.1
3.6	3.0	3.3	All Other Current					2.2	3.6
41.8	41.8	46.3	Total Current					50.2	44.6
30.9	34.1	30.9	Fixed Assets (net)					35.1	31.6
17.2	13.4	12.6	Intangibles (net)					8.7	14.9
10.1	10.8	10.2	All Other Non-Current					6.0	8.9
100.0	100.0	100.0	Total					100.0	100.0
			LIABILITIES						
4.1	4.9	4.0	Notes Payable-Short Term					5.3	1.8
2.8	2.4	2.3	Cur. Mat.-L.T.D.					2.7	2.1
12.9	14.8	14.8	Trade Payables					13.5	15.5
.2	.1	.3	Income Taxes Payable					.2	.4
9.2	10.7	10.4	All Other Current					12.6	10.2
29.2	33.0	31.8	Total Current					34.3	29.9
23.4	22.2	23.0	Long-Term Debt					27.0	25.8
1.7	1.7	2.3	Deferred Taxes					1.0	3.2
9.0	8.8	13.7	All Other Non-Current					10.5	5.9
36.7	34.3	29.1	Net Worth					27.2	35.2
100.0	100.0	100.0	Total Liabilities & Net Worth					100.0	100.0
			INCOME DATA						
100.0	100.0	100.0	Net Sales					100.0	100.0
32.4	32.3	31.0	Gross Profit					26.2	31.1
26.5	26.7	25.5	Operating Expenses					24.3	25.1
6.0	5.6	5.4	Operating Profit					2.0	6.0
1.1	.9	.5	All Other Expenses (net)					-.3	.7
4.8	4.6	4.9	Profit Before Taxes					2.3	5.3
			RATIOS						
2.5	2.2	2.9						3.7	2.5
1.5	1.5	1.6	Current					1.8	1.6
.9	.9	1.1						1.2	1.1
1.4	1.3	1.8						2.9	1.6
.8	.7	.9	Quick					1.2	.9
.4	.4	.5						.6	.6
20 18.5	17 22.1	17 21.6						16 22.2	16 22.3
29 12.8	25 14.6	24 15.0	Sales/Receivables					29 12.7	24 15.0
34 10.6	30 12.0	30 12.3						35 10.5	29 12.4
20 18.3	20 18.4	18 20.8						12 29.2	18 20.6
30 12.3	28 12.9	25 14.8	Cost of Sales/Inventory					25 14.6	24 15.5
51 7.1	48 7.6	42 8.6						53 6.9	32 11.4
17 21.0	17 21.7	17 21.1						17 21.4	17 21.1
30 12.2	28 13.0	24 15.0	Cost of Sales/Payables					24 15.5	25 14.5
46 7.9	46 7.9	38 9.6						41 8.8	37 9.9
6.7	9.1	7.6						5.3	8.5
18.2	20.3	13.4	Sales/Working Capital					11.2	15.3
-65.5	-65.4	65.5						43.7	72.1
15.5	11.9	53.8						40.6	88.4
(90) 3.7	(74) 4.0	(66) 5.4	EBIT/Interest					(10) 12.6	(51) 5.5
1.4	1.2	1.4						.3	2.3
3.5	4.3	5.0							2.1
(20) 2.4	(18) 3.3	(13) 2.0	Net Profit + Depr., Dep., Amort./Cur. Mat. L/T/D						(10) 1.6
1.3	1.8	1.5							1.5
.7	.7	.4						.4	.6
1.0	1.2	.9	Fixed/Worth					.7	1.2
-1.8	-1.9	-28.2						1.0	-1.3
.7	.6	.4						.3	.5
1.7	1.6	1.4	Debt/Worth					.9	1.4
-4.8	-4.7	-59.9						2.8	-7.1
45.0	29.1	43.1						32.4	50.6
(69) 16.2	(60) 11.4	(56) 14.4	% Profit Before Taxes/Tangible Net Worth					(11) 14.1	(37) 14.6
6.5	.8	5.4						5.1	6.4
12.0	11.4	13.9						13.4	17.7
4.9	5.4	6.4	% Profit Before Taxes/Total Assets					7.0	5.6
1.2	1.1	1.7						-1.3	1.9
11.2	10.6	18.5						17.2	13.2
6.3	6.6	8.8	Sales/Net Fixed Assets					6.4	8.1
4.2	4.1	4.6						3.9	4.7
2.7	3.1	3.2						3.3	3.2
1.8	2.1	2.3	Sales/Total Assets					2.3	2.4
1.3	1.5	1.5						1.5	1.6
1.6	1.7	1.3						1.5	1.6
(82) 2.8	(74) 2.8	(64) 2.1	% Depr., Dep., Amort./Sales					(12) 2.2	(42) 2.1
4.9	5.1	4.0						4.2	3.9
1.9	1.5	1.6							
(15) 3.1	(10) 3.4	(12) 2.3	% Officers', Directors' Owners' Comp/Sales						
6.6	9.7	6.8							
10841797M	10462777M	9181585M	Net Sales ($)	368M		10690M	50482M	207144M	8912901M
5682515M	5190112M	4034466M	Total Assets ($)	301M		8339M	20307M	100740M	3904779M

M = $ thousand MM = $ million

See Pages 9 through 22 for Explanation of Ratios and Data

Current Data Sorted by Assets							Comparative Historical Data	
						Type of Statement		
			2	1	2	Unqualified	14	7
		4	3			Reviewed	4	7
		1				Compiled	5	7
	1	2				Tax Returns	9	5
		3	4			Other	14	13
	4 (4/1-9/30/13)		19 (10/1/13-3/31/14)				**4/1/09-3/31/10 ALL**	**4/1/10-3/31/11 ALL**
0-500M	**500M-2MM**	**2-10MM**	**10-50MM**	**50-100MM**	**100-250MM**			
	1	10	9	1	2	**NUMBER OF STATEMENTS**	46	39
%	%	%	%	%	%	**ASSETS**	%	%
DATA NOT AVAILABLE		2.6				Cash & Equivalents	6.4	5.4
		15.4				Trade Receivables (net)	17.5	14.2
		10.8				Inventory	15.0	15.0
		.9				All Other Current	2.4	2.5
		29.8				Total Current	41.3	37.2
		45.6				Fixed Assets (net)	44.7	50.5
		19.4				Intangibles (net)	10.6	7.9
		5.2				All Other Non-Current	3.4	4.5
		100.0				Total	100.0	100.0
						LIABILITIES		
		8.6				Notes Payable-Short Term	7.5	6.0
		5.4				Cur. Mat.-L.T.D.	5.5	4.3
		14.8				Trade Payables	10.5	10.0
		.0				Income Taxes Payable	.1	.0
		6.5				All Other Current	14.3	7.1
		35.4				Total Current	37.8	27.4
		26.4				Long-Term Debt	27.5	21.9
		2.2				Deferred Taxes	.6	1.2
		13.9				All Other Non-Current	14.6	19.9
		22.1				Net Worth	19.6	29.6
		100.0				Total Liabilties & Net Worth	100.0	100.0
						INCOME DATA		
		100.0				Net Sales	100.0	100.0
		42.6				Gross Profit	40.9	42.0
		39.8				Operating Expenses	34.8	38.2
		2.8				Operating Profit	6.1	3.8
		1.9				All Other Expenses (net)	2.9	2.5
		.9				Profit Before Taxes	3.2	1.3
						RATIOS		
		1.1					2.2	2.5
		.9				Current	1.4	1.4
		.5					.6	.9
		.8					1.2	1.3
		.5				Quick	.8	.9
		.3					.4	.4
		27 13.5					23 15.6	21 17.4
		32 11.4				Sales/Receivables	29 12.6	27 13.3
		37 9.9					39 9.4	39 9.3
		23 15.9					23 15.6	26 13.8
		32 11.4				Cost of Sales/Inventory	38 9.5	36 10.1
		38 9.5					57 6.4	66 5.6
		31 11.7					12 30.3	11 34.8
		69 5.3				Cost of Sales/Payables	28 13.1	25 14.8
		74 4.9					43 8.5	48 7.6
		107.1					7.4	7.2
		-37.6				Sales/Working Capital	17.1	21.4
		-13.4					-10.7	-30.4
		3.1					7.6	4.7
		1.8				EBIT/Interest	(42) 2.7	(35) 2.0
		.6					1.4	-.9
							2.3	
						Net Profit + Depr., Dep., Amort./Cur. Mat. L/T/D	(10) 2.0	
							1.8	
		1.4					1.0	.9
		NM				Fixed/Worth	2.8	1.6
		-5.1					-4.9	4.6
		1.8					1.4	1.0
		NM				Debt/Worth	3.3	1.9
		-11.4					-9.6	4.8
							52.8	28.8
						% Profit Before Taxes/Tangible Net Worth	(31) 29.5	(32) 8.6
							5.8	-8.6
		3.2					10.2	9.0
		1.8				% Profit Before Taxes/Total Assets	5.6	3.4
		-.9					-.1	-5.7
		5.8					7.6	6.0
		4.8				Sales/Net Fixed Assets	3.6	2.9
		2.6					1.9	1.9
		2.5					2.4	2.3
		1.5				Sales/Total Assets	1.5	1.6
		1.2					1.1	1.1
							3.0	3.1
						% Depr., Dep., Amort./Sales	(37) 6.2	(32) 5.5
							8.9	8.5
						% Officers', Directors' Owners' Comp/Sales		
	3704M	95653M	356388M	75140M	539796M	Net Sales ($)	1769423M	1555569M
	1597M	58801M	198758M	52999M	245577M	Total Assets ($)	1369300M	1209866M

M = $ thousand MM = $ million

See Pages 9 through 22 for Explanation of Ratios and Data

Comparative Historical Data				Current Data Sorted by Sales					
			Type of Statement						
6	6	5	Unqualified						5
6	9	7	Reviewed				2	4	1
6	1	1	Compiled					1	
4	3	3	Tax Returns			2	1		
15	17	7	Other				3	1	3
				4 (4/1-9/30/13)		19 (10/1/13-3/31/14)			
4/1/11-3/31/12 ALL	4/1/12-3/31/13 ALL	4/1/13-3/31/14 ALL		0-1MM	1-3MM	3-5MM	5-10MM	10-25MM	25MM & OVER
37	36	23	**NUMBER OF STATEMENTS**			2	6	6	9
%	%	%	**ASSETS**	%	%	%	%	%	%
7.3	6.3	6.5	Cash & Equivalents	DATA NOT AVAILABLE	DATA NOT AVAILABLE				
14.6	13.9	13.2	Trade Receivables (net)						
8.9	15.2	13.2	Inventory						
1.6	2.5	1.5	All Other Current						
32.4	37.9	34.4	Total Current						
49.9	45.8	47.0	Fixed Assets (net)						
13.1	11.3	12.3	Intangibles (net)						
4.6	4.9	6.2	All Other Non-Current						
100.0	100.0	100.0	Total						
			LIABILITIES						
5.9	4.3	4.5	Notes Payable-Short Term						
4.8	7.0	4.9	Cur. Mat.-L.T.D.						
9.4	11.6	14.3	Trade Payables						
.3	.0	.2	Income Taxes Payable						
13.5	10.8	8.4	All Other Current						
33.9	33.7	32.3	Total Current						
22.0	23.3	27.3	Long-Term Debt						
1.7	1.5	1.7	Deferred Taxes						
7.9	10.0	23.1	All Other Non-Current						
34.5	31.4	15.6	Net Worth						
100.0	100.0	100.0	Total Liabilties & Net Worth						
			INCOME DATA						
100.0	100.0	100.0	Net Sales						
42.8	35.3	39.3	Gross Profit						
38.0	31.5	33.6	Operating Expenses						
4.8	3.8	5.7	Operating Profit						
1.4	2.4	1.9	All Other Expenses (net)						
3.3	1.4	3.7	Profit Before Taxes						
			RATIOS						
2.0	1.8	1.4							
1.3	1.2	1.0	Current						
.6	.7	.8							
1.2	1.2	.9							
.8	.6	.5	Quick						
.3	.3	.3							
26 14.2	**25** 14.4	**23** 16.1							
36 10.0	**30** 12.1	**31** 11.9	Sales/Receivables						
42 8.6	**39** 9.4	**36** 10.2							
27 13.6	**26** 14.0	**25** 14.5							
37 9.8	**36** 10.2	**31** 11.8	Cost of Sales/Inventory						
54 6.8	**48** 7.6	**51** 7.1							
17 21.5	**16** 23.2	**27** 13.6							
30 12.3	**30** 12.3	**47** 7.7	Cost of Sales/Payables						
58 6.3	**51** 7.1	**72** 5.1							
9.8	8.3	13.0							
37.3	22.2	-744.7	Sales/Working Capital						
-10.6	-15.9	-22.4							
7.5	6.3	5.0							
(35) 2.0	(34) 2.7	(22) 2.8	EBIT/Interest						
.8	1.3	1.5							
	1.9								
	(10) 1.1		Net Profit + Depr., Dep., Amort./Cur. Mat. L/T/D						
	-.8								
1.0	.8	1.5							
2.4	2.0	1.9	Fixed/Worth						
UND	NM	-15.6							
1.1	1.2	1.8							
2.7	3.2	4.5	Debt/Worth						
UND	NM	-20.0							
43.7	36.6	59.4							
(28) 18.8	(27) 9.7	(15) 27.4	% Profit Before Taxes/Tangible Net Worth						
.2	.7	7.1							
9.5	9.7	9.0							
3.8	3.4	3.3	% Profit Before Taxes/Total Assets						
-1.0	.4	1.7							
5.2	6.5	5.9							
2.7	3.7	3.0	Sales/Net Fixed Assets						
1.5	1.6	2.0							
2.0	2.3	2.3							
1.3	1.4	1.4	Sales/Total Assets						
.9	1.0	1.2							
5.2	2.7	3.3							
(31) 8.1	(30) 5.3	(20) 5.8	% Depr., Dep., Amort./Sales						
10.7	7.8	8.3							
			% Officers', Directors' Owners' Comp/Sales						
1533749M	**1510509M**	**1070681M**	Net Sales ($)			**7740M**	**46089M**	**93895M**	**922957M**
1217365M	**934959M**	**557732M**	Total Assets ($)			**4975M**	**42152M**	**54161M**	**456444M**

 M = $ thousand MM = $ million

See Pages 9 through 22 for Explanation of Ratios and Data

Current Data Sorted by Assets / Comparative Historical Data

0-500M	500M-2MM	2-10MM	10-50MM	50-100MM	100-250MM	Type of Statement	4/1/09-3/31/10 ALL	4/1/10-3/31/11 ALL
1			7	1	2	Unqualified	16	12
		6	7			Reviewed	9	7
	5	6				Compiled	6	8
4	10	6	1			Tax Returns	7	19
12	15	21	17	10	4	Other	36	35
17 (4/1-9/30/13)		118 (10/1/13-3/31/14)						
17	30	39	32	11	6	NUMBER OF STATEMENTS	74	81
%	%	%	%	%	%	**ASSETS**	%	%
24.5	14.2	6.9	6.7	1.9		Cash & Equivalents	8.7	9.2
5.5	5.8	8.2	7.7	10.7		Trade Receivables (net)	10.6	8.6
15.1	13.8	13.7	10.8	10.7		Inventory	16.0	16.8
2.3	.6	.9	1.3	1.3		All Other Current	4.0	1.6
47.5	34.5	29.7	26.5	24.7		Total Current	39.3	36.2
48.6	60.5	61.3	69.3	68.4		Fixed Assets (net)	49.1	51.6
3.4	2.6	3.4	1.7	4.2		Intangibles (net)	8.2	8.9
.8	2.4	5.7	2.5	2.7		All Other Non-Current	3.4	3.3
100.0	100.0	100.0	100.0	100.0		Total	100.0	100.0
						LIABILITIES		
6.8	6.2	3.5	1.9	8.5		Notes Payable-Short Term	3.8	5.4
1.0	3.3	4.2	3.2	5.8		Cur. Mat.-L.T.D.	5.6	2.9
7.7	6.7	8.1	6.0	8.4		Trade Payables	9.7	9.6
.0	.0	.0	.1	.5		Income Taxes Payable	.2	.0
9.2	7.5	6.8	5.3	7.2		All Other Current	10.3	6.8
24.7	23.8	22.6	16.4	30.4		Total Current	29.5	24.7
29.4	41.1	32.8	31.4	32.0		Long-Term Debt	33.3	39.1
2.5	.0	1.2	2.1	1.8		Deferred Taxes	.8	1.2
16.0	4.7	7.1	6.5	3.2		All Other Non-Current	6.3	6.8
27.5	30.4	36.3	43.6	32.7		Net Worth	30.0	28.2
100.0	100.0	100.0	100.0	100.0		Total Liabilties & Net Worth	100.0	100.0
						INCOME DATA		
100.0	100.0	100.0	100.0	100.0		Net Sales	100.0	100.0
57.8	55.2	56.7	44.2	38.1		Gross Profit	39.3	44.8
52.5	51.1	48.3	32.7	28.1		Operating Expenses	30.3	35.3
5.3	4.1	8.4	11.5	10.0		Operating Profit	9.0	9.5
.5	.7	1.3	1.5	1.5		All Other Expenses (net)	1.3	.7
4.8	3.4	7.1	10.0	8.5		Profit Before Taxes	7.8	8.7
						RATIOS		
4.6	3.3	2.2	2.1	1.2			1.9	2.3
2.1	1.5	1.3	1.6	1.0		Current	1.4	1.5
1.0	.8	.8	.9	.6			.9	.9
3.6	2.0	1.2	1.3	.6			1.1	1.3
1.2	.8	.6	.7	.5		Quick	.5	.6
.5	.3	.4	.4	.2			.3	.3
0 UND	**0** UND	**7** 50.0	**16** 23.1	**23** 15.6			**4** 82.6	**7** 55.7
0 UND	**5** 69.3	**13** 27.3	**22** 16.9	**29** 12.4		Sales/Receivables	**21** 17.3	**17** 21.7
25 14.6	**19** 19.7	**25** 14.5	**35** 10.4	**38** 9.6			**30** 12.2	**28** 13.2
17 21.5	**33** 11.1	**42** 8.7	**41** 8.8	**36** 10.1			**24** 15.3	**35** 10.5
35 10.4	**52** 7.0	**72** 5.1	**47** 7.7	**41** 8.9		Cost of Sales/Inventory	**47** 7.7	**53** 6.9
99 3.7	**99** 3.7	**94** 3.9	**79** 4.6	**65** 5.6			**67** 5.5	**79** 4.6
0 UND	**1** 475.0	**26** 14.3	**28** 13.2	**16** 23.0			**15** 23.8	**16** 23.4
0 UND	**18** 20.0	**39** 9.3	**40** 9.2	**35** 10.4		Cost of Sales/Payables	**25** 14.6	**34** 10.8
33 11.1	**46** 7.9	**50** 7.3	**54** 6.8	**54** 6.7			**44** 8.3	**49** 7.4
4.3	6.1	9.6	8.0	21.2			9.0	6.7
18.2	15.4	32.1	12.7	-351.2		Sales/Working Capital	19.7	27.7
-559.3	-41.9	-26.8	-45.7	-6.3			-51.5	-65.3
30.5	7.6	15.1	15.7	13.2			13.1	17.9
(13) 3.8	(27) 3.9	(38) 7.2	(28) 6.1	10.1		EBIT/Interest	(69) 5.5	(78) 6.6
-.5	-1.1	3.0	3.3	5.8			2.4	2.1
			4.3				5.8	6.1
			(10) 3.0			Net Profit + Depr., Dep., Amort./Cur. Mat. L/T/D	(19) 3.2	(15) 3.4
			2.7				1.8	1.7
.6	1.2	1.1	1.1	1.8			.9	1.0
1.9	2.2	2.0	1.5	2.6		Fixed/Worth	1.8	1.6
-5.2	13.1	3.5	3.0	3.7			3.2	7.4
.4	.7	.9	.7	1.2			1.0	.9
1.6	2.9	2.2	1.4	2.6		Debt/Worth	1.7	1.6
-9.0	43.3	4.5	2.7	4.6			3.6	9.7
56.7	47.5	46.4	39.6	76.0			70.3	88.1
(12) 34.6	(24) 14.6	(36) 31.9	(30) 31.2	43.7		% Profit Before Taxes/Tangible Net Worth	(59) 37.0	(64) 36.9
-2.7	-15.2	13.7	10.8	19.7			11.1	10.8
39.2	17.4	19.0	17.3	14.9			22.2	27.7
12.0	8.7	12.0	11.7	14.5		% Profit Before Taxes/Total Assets	12.8	12.8
-5.1	-4.6	4.3	3.3	7.3			4.2	2.2
20.8	5.0	4.1	2.7	2.6			9.0	8.2
6.8	2.6	2.6	1.3	1.7		Sales/Net Fixed Assets	3.8	3.4
2.5	1.6	1.7	.9	1.4			2.1	1.7
7.0	2.9	2.2	1.2	1.5			2.7	2.8
2.4	1.5	1.7	.9	1.2		Sales/Total Assets	1.8	1.5
1.2	1.2	1.0	.7	1.0			1.3	1.1
2.8	1.8	2.8	4.3	3.5			2.0	2.2
(10) 7.6	(19) 4.7	(33) 5.1	(30) 6.2	4.3		% Depr., Dep., Amort./Sales	(65) 3.7	(65) 4.3
13.9	8.9	8.9	8.0	6.3			7.0	7.0
	1.9						.8	2.2
	(14) 6.6					% Officers', Directors' Owners' Comp/Sales	(16) 2.8	(21) 3.5
	8.1						5.2	5.6
15572M	70026M	315999M	860043M	1004935M	985180M	Net Sales ($)	4000064M	3418090M
4419M	34433M	197557M	740146M	756190M	866472M	Total Assets ($)	2189696M	2388832M

M = $ thousand MM = $ million

See Pages 9 through 22 for Explanation of Ratios and Data

Comparative Historical Data				Current Data Sorted by Sales					
			Type of Statement						
18	14	11	Unqualified	1				3	7
12	14	13	Reviewed				5	6	2
5	8	11	Compiled	2	1	3	3	2	
15	22	21	Tax Returns	5	9	2	5		
42	45	79	Other	13	14	6	13	13	20
4/1/11-3/31/12	4/1/12-3/31/13	4/1/13-3/31/14		17 (4/1-9/30/13)			118 (10/1/13-3/31/14)		
ALL	ALL	ALL		0-1MM	1-3MM	3-5MM	5-10MM	10-25MM	25MM & OVER
92	103	135	**NUMBER OF STATEMENTS**	21	24	11	26	24	29
%	%	%	**ASSETS**	%	%	%	%	%	%
9.6	8.8	10.1	Cash & Equivalents	13.4	17.6	17.1	6.3	7.9	4.2
10.5	8.0	7.4	Trade Receivables (net)	5.3	3.3	8.9	8.2	9.4	9.5
13.3	13.4	12.8	Inventory	9.5	13.2	19.7	14.7	13.2	10.1
3.1	2.4	1.2	All Other Current	1.2	1.1	.3	1.1	1.8	1.0
36.6	32.5	31.5	Total Current	29.3	35.2	46.0	30.3	32.3	24.8
50.2	57.8	62.3	Fixed Assets (net)	65.7	60.6	46.2	63.6	60.1	68.0
8.1	5.1	3.1	Intangibles (net)	4.3	1.9	1.0	1.5	3.8	5.0
5.0	4.6	3.1	All Other Non-Current	.8	2.3	6.9	4.6	3.9	2.2
100.0	100.0	100.0	Total	100.0	100.0	100.0	100.0	100.0	100.0
			LIABILITIES						
3.2	3.3	4.4	Notes Payable-Short Term	7.8	8.1	1.0	2.9	2.0	3.6
3.6	3.9	3.4	Cur. Mat.-L.T.D.	2.9	2.1	2.8	3.2	4.0	4.5
10.6	9.9	7.3	Trade Payables	3.3	6.9	10.8	9.1	7.4	7.6
.2	.2	.1	Income Taxes Payable	.0	.0	.0	.0	.1	.2
7.0	11.4	7.0	All Other Current	4.1	7.6	10.7	8.2	6.1	6.9
24.6	28.5	22.2	Total Current	18.1	24.7	25.3	23.4	19.6	22.9
29.0	33.7	33.1	Long-Term Debt	36.6	35.7	43.7	31.9	31.3	27.2
1.3	1.2	1.5	Deferred Taxes	2.0	.0	.0	.6	4.1	1.7
4.9	7.2	7.8	All Other Non-Current	13.3	8.2	3.3	7.3	7.2	6.0
40.2	29.4	35.4	Net Worth	30.2	31.4	27.7	36.8	37.8	42.2
100.0	100.0	100.0	Total Liabilties & Net Worth	100.0	100.0	100.0	100.0	100.0	100.0
			INCOME DATA						
100.0	100.0	100.0	Net Sales	100.0	100.0	100.0	100.0	100.0	100.0
46.4	49.1	50.9	Gross Profit	61.0	56.4	54.9	51.6	47.0	40.1
35.5	40.7	43.0	Operating Expenses	57.3	53.4	46.4	44.7	35.5	27.3
10.9	8.4	7.9	Operating Profit	3.7	3.0	8.5	6.9	11.5	12.8
.7	1.3	1.1	All Other Expenses (net)	2.1	.9	.9	.9	.8	1.2
10.2	7.2	6.8	Profit Before Taxes	1.6	2.1	7.6	6.0	10.7	11.6
			RATIOS						
2.3	2.5	2.3		2.4	4.1	2.9	2.5	3.5	1.5
1.4	1.4	1.3	Current	1.6	1.2	1.7	1.4	1.2	1.2
.9	.9	.9		.8	.7	1.1	.8	.9	.9
1.3	1.4	1.4		1.6	2.5	1.3	1.2	1.9	.8
.7	.6	.7	Quick	.7	.6	.9	.6	.7	.5
.4	.3	.4		.2	.3	.5	.3	.4	.4
5 78.8	**5** 73.3	**5** 69.1		**0** UND	**0** UND	**3** 126.1	**6** 66.3	**11** 33.5	**19** 19.6
17 20.9	**15** 23.8	**17** 21.4	Sales/Receivables	**6** 61.9	**4** 96.9	**13** 27.2	**18** 20.5	**20** 18.5	**25** 14.7
26 14.2	**25** 14.5	**29** 12.7		**24** 15.3	**12** 31.1	**24** 15.4	**29** 12.7	**33** 11.2	**35** 10.4
23 16.1	**29** 12.4	**36** 10.1		**25** 14.5	**34** 10.6	**51** 7.1	**36** 10.1	**40** 9.2	**38** 9.6
47 7.7	**47** 7.7	**51** 7.2	Cost of Sales/Inventory	**52** 7.0	**85** 4.3	**66** 5.5	**48** 7.6	**61** 6.0	**44** 8.3
62 5.9	**79** 4.6	**85** 4.3		**107** 3.4	**126** 2.9	**79** 4.6	**79** 4.6	**83** 4.4	**64** 5.7
19 19.5	**19** 18.9	**17** 21.3		**0** UND	**0** UND	**19** 18.9	**32** 11.5	**22** 16.6	**27** 13.6
33 11.2	**31** 11.9	**36** 10.2	Cost of Sales/Payables	**4** 93.0	**18** 20.6	**26** 14.3	**43** 8.5	**36** 10.0	**39** 9.4
54 6.8	**46** 7.9	**50** 7.3		**44** 8.3	**51** 7.1	**36** 10.1	**55** 6.6	**49** 7.4	**47** 7.7
8.3	10.0	8.7		10.6	5.6	7.3	10.2	8.0	13.7
31.7	24.1	25.1	Sales/Working Capital	23.4	23.6	12.5	19.2	36.8	43.9
-101.3	-37.3	-45.6		-24.6	-28.9	81.3	-25.7	NM	-43.4
23.6	16.6	13.2		11.0	13.6		12.8	14.1	23.6
(82) 7.8	(89) 7.0	(123) 6.2	EBIT/Interest	(18) 3.1	(22) 3.7		(24) 5.0	7.9	(27) 8.0
2.6	2.8	2.8		-2.0	-.8		2.6	3.6	4.9
4.7	9.7	8.0						3.6	
(17) 3.6	(20) 4.9	(25) 3.6	Net Profit + Depr., Dep., Amort./Cur. Mat. L/T/D					(10) 2.9	
2.3	2.8	2.8						2.4	
.8	1.1	1.1		.8	1.0	.8	1.1	1.1	1.3
1.3	2.1	2.0	Fixed/Worth	2.1	2.3	2.1	2.1	1.8	1.7
2.6	5.7	3.7		-7.0	8.6	-5.3	3.1	3.3	3.1
.7	.8	.8		.7	.5	.8	.8	1.2	.8
1.4	1.7	1.7	Debt/Worth	2.2	2.9	2.4	2.0	1.5	1.4
3.1	6.6	4.6		-11.2	21.7	-10.6	5.0	3.5	3.0
71.6	66.2	45.9		36.1	38.1		45.3	41.8	75.1
(79) 40.7	(85) 28.4	(118) 31.5	% Profit Before Taxes/Tangible Net Worth	(15) 23.7	(21) 13.6		(24) 24.2	(22) 37.5	(28) 38.1
16.8	12.7	10.0		-16.8	-16.1		-3.9	31.3	14.8
29.5	20.9	17.8		16.1	15.6	29.0	17.6	17.8	21.4
13.8	10.9	10.6	% Profit Before Taxes/Total Assets	6.9	6.7	8.2	10.3	12.9	12.6
5.2	3.5	2.1		-8.7	-3.9	4.0	-.8	6.8	5.7
9.1	5.4	3.7		4.3	6.2	62.9	5.2	3.6	2.7
3.4	2.4	2.3	Sales/Net Fixed Assets	1.7	2.3	3.7	2.6	2.5	1.7
1.9	1.5	1.4		1.6	1.3	2.6	1.0	1.5	1.4
2.9	2.4	2.0		1.7	2.8	3.7	2.4	1.9	1.6
1.7	1.5	1.4	Sales/Total Assets	1.3	1.5	2.1	1.7	1.5	1.1
1.2	1.1	1.0		.9	1.0	1.4	.8	1.1	1.0
2.5	2.9	3.5		4.7	1.7		3.9	2.4	4.3
(72) 3.9	(85) 4.3	(108) 5.0	% Depr., Dep., Amort./Sales	(13) 11.1	(17) 8.0		(21) 6.5	(21) 4.2	(28) 4.5
6.2	7.2	8.2		17.2	10.7		8.5	5.4	7.2
2.1	2.1	2.4			2.1				
(25) 4.9	(26) 4.0	(30) 5.1	% Officers', Directors' Owners' Comp/Sales		(14) 5.1				
7.3	6.6	7.2			6.6				
4395337M	**3697779M**	**3251755M**	Net Sales ($)	**12562M**	**43361M**	**46985M**	**191472M**	**370211M**	**2587164M**
2834867M	**2331482M**	**2599217M**	Total Assets ($)	**12517M**	**49910M**	**26872M**	**177522M**	**291397M**	**2040999M**

M = $ thousand MM = $ million

See Pages 9 through 22 for Explanation of Ratios and Data

	Current Data Sorted by Assets						Comparative Historical Data	
Type of Statement								
Unqualified	1		3	16	7	11	24	34
Reviewed			9	24	5	2	43	46
Compiled	1	3	7	5		1	16	17
Tax Returns	3	11	10				22	21
Other	5	23	34	24	6	8	91	100
	32 (4/1-9/30/13)			187 (10/1/13-3/31/14)			4/1/09-3/31/10	4/1/10-3/31/11
	0-500M	500M-2MM	2-10MM	10-50MM	50-100MM	100-250MM	ALL	ALL
NUMBER OF STATEMENTS	10	37	63	69	18	22	196	218
ASSETS	%	%	%	%	%	%	%	%
Cash & Equivalents	24.1	6.1	4.8	3.5	3.3	3.3	3.6	3.9
Trade Receivables (net)	17.9	6.2	10.1	7.1	6.9	8.5	8.4	9.5
Inventory	34.3	48.6	51.4	41.2	38.9	37.1	46.8	43.9
All Other Current	6.5	.8	2.2	2.7	1.6	2.9	2.1	2.3
Total Current	82.9	61.7	68.5	54.5	50.8	51.9	60.9	59.6
Fixed Assets (net)	13.5	30.5	26.1	39.0	37.8	33.1	33.4	33.4
Intangibles (net)	.7	5.2	2.2	2.1	3.8	9.5	2.5	3.5
All Other Non-Current	3.1	2.5	3.2	4.3	7.6	5.5	3.1	3.4
Total	100.0	100.0	100.0	100.0	100.0	100.0	100.0	100.0
LIABILITIES								
Notes Payable-Short Term	25.6	16.3	17.9	10.8	9.9	7.7	16.1	14.2
Cur. Mat.-L.T.D.	1.5	2.4	1.6	2.9	1.5	1.5	1.8	2.4
Trade Payables	14.7	10.0	10.9	6.7	5.9	7.0	8.6	7.9
Income Taxes Payable	.0	.1	.1	.3	.5	.2	.1	.2
All Other Current	5.8	6.1	6.0	5.6	5.1	8.2	6.2	6.3
Total Current	47.7	34.8	36.4	26.5	22.9	24.5	32.8	31.1
Long-Term Debt	21.3	17.1	15.6	23.7	27.6	17.6	21.9	22.3
Deferred Taxes	.0	.0	.1	.9	.9	.3	.4	.6
All Other Non-Current	7.5	12.9	6.6	4.5	1.7	3.4	8.5	8.5
Net Worth	23.4	35.2	41.3	44.5	47.0	54.1	36.4	37.6
Total Liabilties & Net Worth	100.0	100.0	100.0	100.0	100.0	100.0	100.0	100.0
INCOME DATA								
Net Sales	100.0	100.0	100.0	100.0	100.0	100.0	100.0	100.0
Gross Profit	46.0	57.6	48.7	48.2	48.2	39.0	46.4	46.3
Operating Expenses	37.2	50.6	39.9	34.8	26.9	22.8	38.0	36.6
Operating Profit	8.8	7.0	8.8	13.4	21.4	16.1	8.4	9.7
All Other Expenses (net)	1.8	2.1	2.1	4.2	2.4	1.3	5.0	4.8
Profit Before Taxes	7.0	4.9	6.7	9.2	19.0	14.9	3.4	4.9
RATIOS								
Current	24.3	3.8	3.5	3.8	6.0	4.0	3.6	3.8
	1.7	1.5	2.0	2.1	2.3	2.9	2.0	2.1
	1.2	1.2	1.5	1.5	1.5	1.5	1.3	1.4
Quick	7.1	.9	.8	.7	1.1	1.0	.7	.8
	.7	.3	.3	.3	.5	.5	.3	.4
	.4	.1	.1	.2	.2	.3	.1	.2
Sales/Receivables	0 UND	3 116.5	15 24.1	21 17.4	19 19.0	29 12.7	15 25.0	19 19.3
	16 23.5	16 22.9	29 12.8	34 10.7	32 11.4	40 9.2	34 10.8	36 10.0
	73 5.0	31 11.9	47 7.7	58 6.3	49 7.4	68 5.4	52 7.0	55 6.7
Cost of Sales/Inventory	0 UND	174 2.1	281 1.3	406 .9	261 1.4	304 1.2	292 1.3	260 1.4
	192 1.9	332 1.1	521 .7	521 .7	521 .7	456 .8	510 .7	446 .8
	521 .7	730 .5	730 .5	730 .5	912 .4	521 .7	894 .4	741 .5
Cost of Sales/Payables	0 UND	10 35.0	25 14.4	29 12.5	27 13.5	29 12.5	18 20.6	18 20.3
	22 16.9	55 6.6	49 7.5	65 5.6	42 8.6	51 7.2	54 6.7	43 8.4
	104 3.5	118 3.1	130 2.8	99 3.7	76 4.8	70 5.2	111 3.3	86 4.2
Sales/Working Capital	2.1	2.5	1.4	1.1	1.1	1.4	1.4	1.6
	5.9	5.6	2.6	2.1	2.6	1.9	2.5	2.5
	16.2	35.5	5.7	4.2	3.7	4.3	6.0	5.6
EBIT/Interest		8.8	8.1	10.9	19.0	24.6	7.6	7.8
		(33) 3.3	(59) 2.7	(63) 4.6	(17) 4.2	7.4	(174) 2.4	(195) 2.1
		.4	.9	1.7	2.7	2.4	.5	.8
Net Profit + Depr., Dep., Amort./Cur. Mat. L/T/D				6.5		57.8	10.0	9.6
				(18) 4.3		(10) 8.0	(41) 2.5	(53) 3.1
				1.4		4.9	.6	.9
Fixed/Worth	.0	.2	.2	.5	.5	.4	.3	.3
	.1	.9	.5	1.0	1.0	.8	.9	.9
	-4.7	6.5	1.2	1.7	1.2	1.6	2.3	2.0
Debt/Worth	.1	.6	.6	.5	.7	.3	.7	.7
	3.0	2.0	1.4	1.5	1.4	1.0	1.8	1.5
	-8.4	25.9	2.9	3.1	2.4	2.6	3.9	4.4
% Profit Before Taxes/Tangible Net Worth		83.6	23.0	29.3	29.0	39.7	21.8	27.1
		(30) 27.2	(55) 11.4	(65) 11.2	(17) 23.3	(21) 16.1	(175) 8.9	(195) 9.1
		6.2	.3	1.3	6.5	3.1	-3.1	-.2
% Profit Before Taxes/Total Assets	32.3	13.6	7.0	10.9	15.2	18.4	8.5	9.8
	14.5	6.4	4.1	5.1	9.0	7.0	2.8	3.3
	-.3	-.4	-.1	.8	1.8	2.1	-1.5	-.4
Sales/Net Fixed Assets	UND	12.6	12.1	3.6	3.3	4.2	7.8	7.4
	493.8	5.8	4.0	1.3	1.3	1.9	2.5	2.4
	5.2	2.4	1.6	.8	.8	1.3	.9	1.0
Sales/Total Assets	3.1	1.8	1.1	.8	.8	.8	1.1	1.0
	1.4	1.2	.7	.5	.6	.6	.6	.7
	.7	.8	.5	.4	.4	.4	.4	.4
% Depr., Dep., Amort./Sales		2.0	1.7	3.0	3.2	3.4	2.1	2.0
		(21) 3.3	(48) 4.0	(61) 6.1	6.4	(20) 5.0	(156) 5.3	(190) 5.0
		6.7	6.8	9.4	8.8	8.4	10.4	9.3
% Officers', Directors' Owners' Comp/Sales		3.3	2.9				2.2	2.1
		(11) 5.0	(12) 4.2				(26) 5.3	(32) 4.9
		13.7	6.2				11.0	8.4
Net Sales ($)	4827M	55730M	286558M	1238049M	774892M	2532915M	3921819M	5301649M
Total Assets ($)	2755M	42591M	327835M	1877710M	1311833M	3400384M	5229794M	7057861M

M = $ thousand MM = $ million

See Pages 9 through 22 for Explanation of Ratios and Data

	Comparative Historical Data							Current Data Sorted by Sales										
						Type of Statement												
	31		36		38	Unqualified				2		1		3		10		22
	45		43		40	Reviewed				2		3		10		20		5
	24		18		17	Compiled		3		2		7		1		3		1
	26		17		24	Tax Returns		6		15		2				1		
	105		102		100	Other		11		31		15		13		12		18
										32 (4/1-9/30/13)				187 (10/1/13-3/31/14)				
	4/1/11-3/31/12 ALL		**4/1/12-3/31/13 ALL**		**4/1/13-3/31/14 ALL**			**0-1MM**		**1-3MM**		**3-5MM**		**5-10MM**		**10-25MM**		**25MM & OVER**
	231		216		219	**NUMBER OF STATEMENTS**		20		52		28		27		46		46
	%		%		%	**ASSETS**		%		%		%		%		%		%
	4.8		5.1		5.2	Cash & Equivalents		12.8		5.3		4.6		4.3		3.3		4.7
	8.0		7.5		8.4	Trade Receivables (net)		11.0		6.5		5.6		8.9		9.0		10.4
	44.0		41.5		44.4	Inventory		46.0		47.9		48.3		40.8		42.2		41.9
	3.1		2.5		2.4	All Other Current		.8		2.5		1.3		2.8		2.5		3.1
	59.9		56.6		60.5	Total Current		70.7		62.2		59.9		56.9		57.1		60.0
	32.9		34.8		32.0	Fixed Assets (net)		24.9		30.6		32.3		36.6		35.1		30.7
	3.9		4.1		3.5	Intangibles (net)		1.2		4.3		3.4		4.8		2.7		3.7
	3.3		4.5		4.0	All Other Non-Current		3.2		2.9		4.4		1.7		5.1		5.6
	100.0		100.0		100.0	Total		100.0		100.0		100.0		100.0		100.0		100.0
						LIABILITIES												
	12.4		10.3		14.1	Notes Payable-Short Term		22.6		15.8		14.0		14.9		9.7		12.4
	2.5		2.4		2.1	Cur. Mat.-L.T.D.		2.0		2.0		1.7		1.5		3.4		1.7
	8.4		7.9		8.8	Trade Payables		8.8		8.7		8.1		9.4		9.1		8.7
	.1		.2		.2	Income Taxes Payable		.0		.1		.0		.5		.3		.2
	6.3		5.8		6.0	All Other Current		9.1		4.3		2.8		6.7		5.7		8.5
	29.7		26.6		31.2	Total Current		42.4		30.9		26.6		33.0		28.2		31.5
	21.2		23.5		19.8	Long-Term Debt		23.6		19.3		17.3		18.6		25.7		15.3
	.5		.7		.4	Deferred Taxes		.0		.0		.5		1.0		.8		.3
	8.0		10.4		6.3	All Other Non-Current		9.1		10.2		9.2		3.9		3.6		3.0
	40.7		38.8		42.2	Net Worth		24.9		39.6		46.3		43.5		41.7		49.9
	100.0		100.0		100.0	Total Liabilities & Net Worth		100.0		100.0		100.0		100.0		100.0		100.0
						INCOME DATA												
	100.0		100.0		100.0	Net Sales		100.0		100.0		100.0		100.0		100.0		100.0
	47.4		48.7		48.9	Gross Profit		52.2		56.9		52.0		44.1		45.3		43.3
	37.8		36.6		37.2	Operating Expenses		44.7		48.3		43.5		30.3		31.8		27.0
	9.6		12.1		11.7	Operating Profit		7.5		8.5		8.4		13.8		13.5		16.3
	3.7		3.9		2.7	All Other Expenses (net)		2.9		3.2		1.8		3.6		2.7		2.0
	5.9		8.1		9.0	Profit Before Taxes		4.6		5.3		6.6		10.1		10.8		14.3
						RATIOS												
	4.0		4.3		4.0			9.8		4.3		5.9		3.2		5.6		3.6
	2.1		2.3		2.1	Current		1.7		2.1		2.0		2.0		2.4		2.1
	1.4		1.5		1.4			1.3		1.3		1.5		1.4		1.4		1.4
	.8		.9		.9			1.1		.7		1.3		.9		1.0		.8
	.4	(215)	.4		.3	Quick		.5		.3		.3		.4		.4		.4
	.2		.2		.2			.1		.2		.1		.2		.2		.2
14	26.6	**14**	25.3	**16**	23.0		**5**	79.5	**4**	87.5	**14**	26.8	**22**	16.4	**19**	18.8	**28**	13.1
30	12.1	**29**	12.6	**30**	12.2	Sales/Receivables	**17**	20.9	**23**	15.7	**21**	17.3	**31**	11.7	**37**	9.9	**36**	10.2
50	7.3	**46**	8.0	**51**	7.1		**42**	8.6	**40**	9.2	**40**	9.1	**58**	6.3	**55**	6.6	**58**	6.3
243	1.5	**261**	1.4	**261**	1.4		**130**	2.8	**215**	1.7	**332**	1.1	**304**	1.2	**261**	1.4	**243**	1.5
456	.8	**521**	.7	**456**	.8	Cost of Sales/Inventory	**456**	.8	**456**	.8	**521**	.7	**521**	.7	**608**	.6	**406**	.9
730	.5	**730**	.5	**730**	.5		**912**	.4	**912**	.4	**730**	.5	**730**	.5	**730**	.5	**521**	.7
18	20.2	**22**	16.5	**25**	14.4		**0**	UND	**20**	18.6	**26**	14.3	**28**	13.2	**33**	11.2	**26**	14.0
41	8.8	**56**	6.5	**55**	6.6	Cost of Sales/Payables	**54**	6.8	**60**	6.1	**56**	6.5	**51**	7.1	**60**	6.1	**48**	7.6
87	4.2	**99**	3.7	**101**	3.6		**126**	2.9	**130**	2.8	**130**	2.8	**99**	3.7	**99**	3.7	**74**	4.9
	1.5		1.3		1.4			1.5		1.4		1.6		1.2		1.1		1.4
	2.5		2.3		2.7	Sales/Working Capital		4.7		3.1		2.2		2.1		2.1		2.8
	4.8		6.0		6.6			20.3		6.6		3.9		4.6		6.1		6.7
	7.7		10.2		9.7			8.4		5.9		9.5		6.2		10.9		38.4
(209)	2.8	(194)	3.1	(200)	3.9	EBIT/Interest	(15)	2.8	(46)	2.6	(27)	3.8	(24)	3.1	(43)	5.7	(45)	7.7
	.9		1.3		1.4			.1		.6		.8		1.7		1.8		2.6
	8.6		7.8		8.0											6.6		25.6
(52)	4.2	(50)	4.1	(42)	4.8	Net Profit + Depr., Dep., Amort./Cur. Mat. L/T/D									(15)	4.7	(15)	8.7
	1.9		1.7		1.9											1.8		5.0
	.3		.3		.3			.1		.2		.2		.2		.5		.3
	.9		.9		.8	Fixed/Worth		1.1		.8		.6		.9		1.0		.7
	1.9		1.8		1.6			41.4		1.5		2.1		2.0		1.6		1.2
	.6		.6		.6			.4		.7		.6		.4		.6		.5
	1.4		1.5		1.5	Debt/Worth		6.9		1.7		1.5		1.0		1.7		1.0
	4.7		3.9		4.1			NM		4.3		2.8		5.0		3.4		2.1
	25.1		28.6		32.8			93.2		36.0		27.1		16.6		31.9		39.3
(206)	11.4	(194)	13.2	(194)	14.8	% Profit Before Taxes/Tangible Net Worth	(15)	48.6	(44)	14.7	(23)	5.5	(23)	11.2	(43)	14.6		17.7
	.8		2.5		2.7			8.1		.3		-1.3		4.5		4.2		3.8
	9.6		10.4		12.0			16.9		10.5		9.8		8.9		11.1		17.9
	3.9		4.3		5.1	% Profit Before Taxes/Total Assets		6.6		4.1		3.4		3.7		6.9		7.8
	-.3		.7		.7			-1.1		-.5		-.4		1.6		.9		2.1
	7.4		7.9		7.4			10.7		13.6		8.0		7.0		5.1		5.1
	2.5		2.0		2.5	Sales/Net Fixed Assets		5.0		4.7		3.4		1.4		1.3		2.6
	1.0		.9		1.1			2.8		1.4		1.0		.7		.9		1.4
	1.1		1.0		1.1			1.4		1.7		.9		.8		.8		1.0
	.7		.7		.7	Sales/Total Assets		.8		.8		.8		.6		.5		.7
	.4		.4		.5			.5		.5		.5		.3		.4		.5
	2.6		3.1		2.4					1.9		2.2		2.9		2.9		2.2
(187)	5.4	(170)	6.0	(171)	5.2	% Depr., Dep., Amort./Sales			(34)	4.0	(21)	5.4	(24)	6.6	(41)	6.1	(42)	4.3
	8.7		8.9		8.3					6.7		7.3		9.2		9.4		6.3
	1.5		2.6		3.1					3.2								
(31)	4.3	(29)	3.7	(27)	4.3	% Officers', Directors' Owners' Comp/Sales			(12)	4.2								
	8.5		9.1		7.7					7.5								
	4247296M		**6978910M**		**4892971M**	Net Sales ($)		**10449M**		**101685M**		**106256M**		**188282M**		**751947M**		**3734352M**
	6095148M		**7121261M**		**6963108M**	Total Assets ($)		**12500M**		**180117M**		**201967M**		**456897M**		**1596085M**		**4515542M**

M = $ thousand MM = $ million

See Pages 9 through 22 for Explanation of Ratios and Data

Current Data Sorted by Assets							Comparative Historical Data	
						Type of Statement		
			8	4		Unqualified	13	12
	2	9	2	1	1	Reviewed	12	10
	2	3	1			Compiled	5	3
		1				Tax Returns	4	1
	1	2	6	2	1	Other	16	16
	12 (4/1-9/30/13)		34 (10/1/13-3/31/14)				4/1/09-3/31/10 ALL	4/1/10-3/31/11 ALL
0-500M	500M-2MM	2-10MM	10-50MM	50-100MM	100-250MM			
	5	15	17	7	2	**NUMBER OF STATEMENTS**	50	42
%	%	%	%	%	%	**ASSETS**	%	%
DATA NOT AVAILABLE		9.1	9.8			Cash & Equivalents	7.8	6.7
		25.3	28.3			Trade Receivables (net)	24.2	26.9
		33.6	26.7			Inventory	30.5	31.6
		1.4	1.5			All Other Current	2.6	3.7
		69.3	66.2			Total Current	65.0	69.0
		24.1	26.2			Fixed Assets (net)	24.3	22.9
		1.1	1.0			Intangibles (net)	2.9	1.1
		5.5	6.5			All Other Non-Current	7.8	7.1
		100.0	100.0			Total	100.0	100.0
						LIABILITIES		
		6.3	7.5			Notes Payable-Short Term	7.0	8.2
		1.9	7.3			Cur. Mat.-L.T.D.	2.0	3.0
		15.5	14.4			Trade Payables	12.4	15.5
		.3	.4			Income Taxes Payable	.3	.3
		6.7	4.8			All Other Current	9.1	8.0
		30.7	34.4			Total Current	30.8	35.0
		11.8	18.5			Long-Term Debt	12.8	14.2
		.3	1.7			Deferred Taxes	1.0	.9
		10.1	4.8			All Other Non-Current	5.2	5.1
		47.2	40.7			Net Worth	50.1	44.9
		100.0	100.0			Total Liabilties & Net Worth	100.0	100.0
						INCOME DATA		
		100.0	100.0			Net Sales	100.0	100.0
		20.9	16.9			Gross Profit	17.4	20.0
		18.5	13.4			Operating Expenses	15.2	14.7
		2.4	3.5			Operating Profit	2.3	5.3
		.3	.5			All Other Expenses (net)	1.0	.5
		2.1	3.0			Profit Before Taxes	1.3	4.9
						RATIOS		
		3.5	3.9				3.7	3.6
		2.3	2.4			Current	2.5	2.1
		1.6	1.3				1.5	1.3
		1.9	2.4				1.9	1.8
		1.4	1.7			Quick	1.2	1.1
		.9	.7				.7	.5
		23 15.6	**33** 11.0				**32** 11.4	**31** 11.9
		34 10.6	**47** 7.8			Sales/Receivables	**44** 8.3	**39** 9.3
		53 6.9	**54** 6.7				**57** 6.4	**55** 6.6
		48 7.6	**42** 8.6				**45** 8.2	**41** 8.9
		61 6.0	**52** 7.0			Cost of Sales/Inventory	**64** 5.7	**59** 6.2
		87 4.2	**72** 5.1				**96** 3.8	**89** 4.1
		18 19.8	**18** 20.1				**14** 25.2	**15** 24.9
		29 12.7	**28** 12.9			Cost of Sales/Payables	**25** 14.4	**23** 15.9
		42 8.7	**42** 8.7				**35** 10.5	**39** 9.4
		5.0	3.7				3.7	4.0
		6.1	7.0			Sales/Working Capital	5.5	6.7
		9.6	15.6				10.1	17.1
		10.8	20.0				6.9	17.1
		(12) 4.7	(16) 6.4			EBIT/Interest	(44) 1.9	(37) 6.6
		.3	1.2				.2	2.5
							8.2	35.3
						Net Profit + Depr., Dep., Amort./Cur. Mat. L/T/D	(14) 3.4	(14) 9.1
							1.4	3.6
		.0	.2				.2	.2
		.3	.6			Fixed/Worth	.4	.4
		1.7	1.8				.9	1.0
		.5	.5				.4	.5
		1.0	1.4			Debt/Worth	.8	.9
		1.4	5.5				1.9	3.2
		30.5	41.3				12.7	51.0
		(13) 17.8	(16) 12.8			% Profit Before Taxes/Tangible Net Worth	(46) 2.8	(39) 18.2
		3.0	2.6				-3.7	6.6
		14.0	12.9				5.9	15.7
		9.1	4.0			% Profit Before Taxes/Total Assets	1.3	7.7
		1.3	.6				-1.1	3.0
		228.7	25.2				22.3	33.8
		14.2	9.4			Sales/Net Fixed Assets	8.4	13.8
		2.6	4.2				4.0	6.6
		3.2	2.6				2.4	3.0
		2.5	2.0			Sales/Total Assets	1.8	2.3
		1.1	1.7				1.3	1.8
		.2	.9				1.0	.6
		(13) .7	(16) 2.7			% Depr., Dep., Amort./Sales	(43) 2.3	(38) 1.5
		6.7	3.7				3.9	3.1
							2.2	
						% Officers', Directors' Owners' Comp/Sales	(17) 3.6	
							6.3	
	35010M	174101M	933462M	1100828M	700047M	Net Sales ($)	2544448M	3148343M
	7557M	80497M	436414M	515358M	355237M	Total Assets ($)	1394812M	1420778M

M = $ thousand MM = $ million

See Pages 9 through 22 for Explanation of Ratios and Data

Comparative Historical Data				Current Data Sorted by Sales					
			Type of Statement						
12	17	12	Unqualified					1	11
11	12	15	Reviewed		1	1	5	4	4
4	5	6	Compiled				3	2	1
3	3	1	Tax Returns					1	
24	20	12	Other				1	2	9
				12 (4/1-9/30/13)			34 (10/1/13-3/31/14)		
4/1/11-3/31/12 ALL	4/1/12-3/31/13 ALL	4/1/13-3/31/14 ALL		0-1MM	1-3MM	3-5MM	5-10MM	10-25MM	25MM & OVER
54	57	46	**NUMBER OF STATEMENTS**		1	1	9	10	25
%	%	%	**ASSETS**	%	%	%	%	%	%
10.6	8.5	8.1	Cash & Equivalents	DATA NOT AVAILABLE				14.3	7.1
22.2	24.7	26.8	Trade Receivables (net)					30.7	27.7
32.1	32.2	32.5	Inventory					35.1	29.8
1.6	2.2	1.6	All Other Current					.3	1.7
66.4	67.5	69.0	Total Current					80.3	66.3
23.4	21.6	23.5	Fixed Assets (net)					14.3	26.0
2.3	2.1	.8	Intangibles (net)					.0	.8
7.9	8.7	6.8	All Other Non-Current					5.3	6.8
100.0	100.0	100.0	Total					100.0	100.0
			LIABILITIES						
5.6	8.1	8.9	Notes Payable-Short Term					5.3	8.4
2.5	2.4	4.1	Cur. Mat.-L.T.D.					.9	5.7
13.8	14.2	16.6	Trade Payables					18.0	15.6
.2	.5	.4	Income Taxes Payable					.3	.5
9.5	9.2	7.4	All Other Current					6.1	8.3
31.7	34.3	37.4	Total Current					30.6	38.5
11.0	9.7	15.2	Long-Term Debt					7.1	17.5
.5	1.0	1.0	Deferred Taxes					.4	1.6
3.2	4.4	7.5	All Other Non-Current					10.2	4.7
53.6	50.6	38.9	Net Worth					51.7	37.8
100.0	100.0	100.0	Total Liabilties & Net Worth					100.0	100.0
			INCOME DATA						
100.0	100.0	100.0	Net Sales					100.0	100.0
17.7	16.9	16.8	Gross Profit					21.2	14.0
14.6	12.1	13.5	Operating Expenses					19.7	9.6
3.1	4.8	3.3	Operating Profit					1.5	4.4
.1	.4	.4	All Other Expenses (net)					-.6	.6
2.9	4.3	2.9	Profit Before Taxes					2.0	3.8
			RATIOS						
3.9	3.9	3.3						3.8	3.7
2.5	1.9	2.3	Current					2.5	2.3
1.3	1.5	1.2						2.2	1.1
2.0	2.2	2.0						2.3	2.3
1.2	.9	1.1	Quick					1.7	1.1
.6	.5	.5						1.0	.5
28 12.9	28 13.1	28 13.1						26 14.3	34 10.8
37 9.8	39 9.4	41 8.9	Sales/Receivables					28 13.0	45 8.2
44 8.3	47 7.8	50 7.3						41 8.9	51 7.2
44 8.3	35 10.4	43 8.4						40 9.1	40 9.1
60 6.1	56 6.5	59 6.2	Cost of Sales/Inventory					53 6.9	60 6.1
83 4.4	76 4.8	87 4.2						89 4.1	79 4.6
14 26.4	15 25.1	18 20.1						18 20.4	18 20.1
24 15.4	25 14.4	25 14.7	Cost of Sales/Payables					23 15.9	23 15.8
34 10.6	34 10.7	40 9.2						34 10.8	42 8.7
4.1	4.6	4.3						3.3	4.2
6.1	6.9	7.1	Sales/Working Capital					5.9	7.2
16.9	11.8	16.6						10.7	43.4
28.7	22.9	18.9							19.8
(47) 4.7	(47) 4.9	(42) 5.8	EBIT/Interest						(23) 6.7
2.4	1.8	1.7							2.1
7.5	7.6	4.7							
(10) 5.5	(15) 4.2	(15) 3.1	Net Profit + Depr., Dep., Amort./Cur. Mat. L/T/D						
-1.2	2.0	1.6							
.1	.2	.2						.0	.2
.4	.4	.5	Fixed/Worth					.2	.9
.7	.8	1.7						.5	1.8
.4	.4	.6						.5	.6
.6	1.2	1.2	Debt/Worth					.8	1.5
2.1	2.2	5.4						1.1	5.5
35.8	32.5	33.0							43.3
(52) 10.2	(55) 13.0	(40) 18.7	% Profit Before Taxes/Tangible Net Worth						(23) 17.5
2.5	1.0	5.2							5.8
10.7	15.2	12.5						15.9	11.9
5.7	6.6	8.8	% Profit Before Taxes/Total Assets					10.1	8.5
1.7	.8	1.8						-.3	2.6
42.8	34.0	35.4						239.1	26.3
11.6	13.8	12.0	Sales/Net Fixed Assets					17.8	7.8
5.1	5.3	4.9						9.0	4.7
3.1	3.0	3.3						4.0	2.8
2.1	2.4	2.3	Sales/Total Assets					2.6	2.1
1.6	1.7	1.7						1.6	1.8
.6	.6	.6							1.0
(46) 1.5	(48) 1.4	(40) 1.5	% Depr., Dep., Amort./Sales						(21) 1.8
2.9	3.4	3.3							3.3
1.0									
(14) 3.3			% Officers', Directors' Owners' Comp/Sales						
6.0									
5163192M	4756063M	2943448M	Net Sales ($)		2023M	4334M	64054M	158085M	2714952M
2395725M	2121132M	1395063M	Total Assets ($)		2941M	1248M	36998M	71482M	1282394M

M = $ thousand MM = $ million

See Pages 9 through 22 for Explanation of Ratios and Data

Current Data Sorted by Assets							Comparative Historical Data	
		3	9	5	1	**Type of Statement** Unqualified	15	25
	1	9	5			Reviewed	13	12
	3	3	4			Compiled	15	11
	2	2				Tax Returns	10	5
	3	6	14	4	2	Other	27	31
	16 (4/1-9/30/13)		60 (10/1/13-3/31/14)				**4/1/09-3/31/10 ALL**	**4/1/10-3/31/11 ALL**
0-500M	**500M-2MM**	**2-10MM**	**10-50MM**	**50-100MM**	**100-250MM**			
	9	23	32	9	3	**NUMBER OF STATEMENTS**	80	84
%	%	%	%	%	%	**ASSETS**	%	%
DATA NOT AVAILABLE		9.0	9.7			Cash & Equivalents	9.9	7.3
		20.5	24.9			Trade Receivables (net)	25.1	23.9
		40.8	32.2			Inventory	29.5	30.0
		1.8	1.0			All Other Current	1.9	2.5
		72.2	67.8			Total Current	66.4	63.7
		23.1	22.6			Fixed Assets (net)	22.2	23.4
		1.6	3.2			Intangibles (net)	5.6	6.2
		3.1	6.5			All Other Non-Current	5.8	6.8
		100.0	100.0			Total	100.0	100.0
						LIABILITIES		
		5.1	10.2			Notes Payable-Short Term	8.2	10.2
		3.3	2.2			Cur. Mat.-L.T.D.	5.2	3.5
		20.0	12.6			Trade Payables	15.0	14.9
		.2	.3			Income Taxes Payable	1.4	.2
		11.5	9.3			All Other Current	7.3	10.0
		40.2	34.5			Total Current	37.0	38.7
		10.8	23.0			Long-Term Debt	17.0	22.2
		.2	.6			Deferred Taxes	.6	.4
		4.0	1.7			All Other Non-Current	7.1	8.2
		44.8	40.2			Net Worth	38.3	30.5
		100.0	100.0			Total Liabilties & Net Worth	100.0	100.0
						INCOME DATA		
		100.0	100.0			Net Sales	100.0	100.0
		24.2	22.9			Gross Profit	24.5	25.3
		19.2	15.8			Operating Expenses	21.6	22.4
		5.0	7.1			Operating Profit	3.0	2.9
		.3	1.0			All Other Expenses (net)	1.2	1.3
		4.7	6.0			Profit Before Taxes	1.8	1.6
						RATIOS		
		2.7	3.6				3.7	2.9
		2.2	2.3			Current	2.0	2.0
		1.3	1.5				1.3	1.2
		1.4	1.7				2.0	1.5
		.9	.9			Quick	1.0	.9
		.4	.7				.5	.4
		14 25.8	**34** 10.8				**29** 12.8	**24** 14.9
		40 9.1	**47** 7.8			Sales/Receivables	**45** 8.2	**43** 8.5
		45 8.1	**54** 6.8				**56** 6.5	**57** 6.4
		60 6.1	**56** 6.5				**32** 11.3	**41** 9.0
		81 4.5	**78** 4.7			Cost of Sales/Inventory	**65** 5.6	**73** 5.0
		122 3.0	**104** 3.5				**114** 3.2	**106** 3.4
		19 18.8	**17** 21.2				**18** 20.0	**19** 18.8
		33 11.0	**30** 12.0			Cost of Sales/Payables	**31** 11.8	**33** 11.1
		53 6.9	**41** 8.8				**42** 8.6	**49** 7.5
		4.1	4.0				4.2	4.5
		6.1	5.7			Sales/Working Capital	7.2	6.9
		14.0	10.1				15.2	25.1
		13.6	18.8				12.3	16.4
		(20) 7.3	(27) 10.9			EBIT/Interest	(73) 3.5	(77) 5.2
		1.1	1.5				.5	1.0
							5.1	4.9
						Net Profit + Depr., Dep., Amort./Cur. Mat. L/T/D	(19) 2.6	(19) 3.3
							.4	.6
		.1	.2				.2	.2
		.3	.4			Fixed/Worth	.5	.5
		1.1	.8				1.5	1.7
		.6	.4				.6	.6
		.9	.8			Debt/Worth	1.3	1.1
		3.6	1.7				4.3	3.2
		41.3	33.3				32.3	29.3
		17.8	(29) 23.3			% Profit Before Taxes/Tangible Net Worth	(66) 10.3	(69) 15.4
		2.7	8.9				-.5	2.6
		11.9	15.2				12.7	13.0
		7.2	11.7			% Profit Before Taxes/Total Assets	4.3	6.5
		1.0	4.2				-1.5	.2
		47.8	16.5				32.5	29.4
		18.6	9.3			Sales/Net Fixed Assets	11.7	11.5
		4.0	5.8				5.4	5.4
		3.2	2.3				2.7	3.0
		2.4	1.9			Sales/Total Assets	2.0	2.0
		1.3	1.5				1.4	1.4
		.2	1.2				.8	1.1
		(20) .9	(29) 1.9			% Depr., Dep., Amort./Sales	(64) 2.3	(72) 2.5
		3.4	2.9				4.3	3.8
							1.6	.7
						% Officers', Directors' Owners' Comp/Sales	(19) 4.2	(14) 2.5
							7.0	6.9
	36305M	**309526M**	**1273201M**	**1142654M**	**1550961M**	Net Sales ($)	**3718881M**	**4242587M**
	11214M	**136348M**	**650191M**	**591244M**	**468600M**	Total Assets ($)	**1975096M**	**2088030M**

M = $ thousand MM = $ million

See Pages 9 through 22 for Explanation of Ratios and Data

Comparative Historical Data				Current Data Sorted by Sales					
			Type of Statement						
16	19	18	Unqualified					3	15
18	21	15	Reviewed		1	1	2	6	5
7	8	10	Compiled		1	1	2	2	4
6	6	4	Tax Returns		1	1	1	1	
34	37	29	Other		1	1	4	12	11
					16 (4/1-9/30/13)		60 (10/1/13-3/31/14)		
4/1/11-3/31/12 ALL	**4/1/12-3/31/13 ALL**	**4/1/13-3/31/14 ALL**		**0-1MM**	**1-3MM**	**3-5MM**	**5-10MM**	**10-25MM**	**25MM & OVER**
81	91	76	**NUMBER OF STATEMENTS**		4	4	9	24	35
%	%	%	**ASSETS**	%	%	%	%	%	%
7.9	8.2	8.7	Cash & Equivalents	**DATA NOT AVAILABLE**				8.9	7.5
24.9	24.1	24.2	Trade Receivables (net)					20.1	25.4
32.2	32.9	34.5	Inventory					37.6	33.5
1.4	1.6	1.4	All Other Current					1.7	1.6
66.4	66.7	68.8	Total Current					68.4	68.0
24.1	22.6	22.6	Fixed Assets (net)					23.1	21.3
3.6	3.5	3.5	Intangibles (net)					1.6	5.3
5.9	7.2	5.2	All Other Non-Current					6.9	5.4
100.0	100.0	100.0	Total					100.0	100.0
			LIABILITIES						
12.8	7.9	9.6	Notes Payable-Short Term					6.9	9.5
2.7	2.4	2.8	Cur. Mat.-L.T.D.					3.7	1.5
18.0	17.9	15.3	Trade Payables					17.2	14.3
.2	.2	.3	Income Taxes Payable					.5	.1
11.3	9.2	11.4	All Other Current					9.8	9.2
45.0	37.6	39.4	Total Current					38.1	34.6
19.3	15.4	17.0	Long-Term Debt					8.1	22.0
.5	.3	.5	Deferred Taxes					.3	.9
7.9	5.3	3.9	All Other Non-Current					2.3	3.6
27.3	41.4	39.2	Net Worth					51.2	38.8
100.0	100.0	100.0	Total Liabilties & Net Worth					100.0	100.0
			INCOME DATA						
100.0	100.0	100.0	Net Sales					100.0	100.0
24.6	22.4	22.3	Gross Profit					21.1	19.8
21.3	17.7	16.9	Operating Expenses					17.6	13.4
3.3	4.7	5.5	Operating Profit					3.5	6.4
.8	.8	.9	All Other Expenses (net)					.6	1.1
2.5	3.9	4.6	Profit Before Taxes					3.0	5.3
			RATIOS						
2.8	3.3	3.0						3.3	3.3
2.0	2.0	2.2	Current					2.2	2.3
1.1	1.3	1.4						1.3	1.5
1.5	1.7	1.4						1.4	1.4
1.0	1.1	.9	Quick					.8	.9
.5	.6	.6						.4	.7
29 12.6	**28** 12.9	**27** 13.3						**17** 21.9	**37** 9.9
41 8.9	**38** 9.5	**43** 8.4	Sales/Receivables					**38** 9.6	**47** 7.8
51 7.1	**54** 6.8	**51** 7.1						**49** 7.4	**51** 7.1
40 9.1	**43** 8.4	**51** 7.1						**47** 7.8	**55** 6.6
66 5.5	**73** 5.0	**73** 5.0	Cost of Sales/Inventory					**83** 4.4	**69** 5.3
104 3.5	**94** 3.9	**96** 3.8						**122** 3.0	**89** 4.1
20 18.7	**17** 21.9	**17** 21.2						**19** 19.3	**17** 21.5
34 10.8	**30** 12.0	**30** 12.1	Cost of Sales/Payables					**34** 10.6	**27** 13.4
45 8.1	**48** 7.6	**41** 8.8						**48** 7.6	**41** 8.8
4.9	4.4	4.2						3.6	4.2
7.4	6.3	6.3	Sales/Working Capital					6.3	6.3
25.1	16.7	13.5						16.1	11.9
17.8	28.0	18.8						13.2	18.8
(73) 3.3	(83) 5.6	(67) 7.5	EBIT/Interest					(20) 6.4	(32) 10.4
1.1	1.6	1.2						1.2	2.4
18.2	10.1	4.1							5.8
(22) 3.2	(24) 5.3	(21) 2.4	Net Profit + Depr., Dep., Amort./Cur. Mat. L/T/D						(10) 2.2
1.5	1.8	.7							.8
.2	.1	.1						.1	.3
.6	.4	.4	Fixed/Worth					.3	.4
1.9	1.2	1.1						.9	.8
.6	.4	.6						.5	.4
1.5	1.0	.9	Debt/Worth					.8	1.0
8.2	4.9	3.4						3.5	1.9
35.8	27.7	33.7						27.0	33.1
(67) 17.0	(81) 16.0	(68) 21.1	% Profit Before Taxes/Tangible Net Worth					15.9	(31) 22.8
2.8	5.1	6.7						7.0	6.4
15.1	14.3	13.9						11.8	15.0
6.0	5.8	7.6	% Profit Before Taxes/Total Assets					7.0	11.3
.2	1.9	1.1						2.1	2.7
26.5	35.6	37.7						30.4	20.5
10.9	9.5	10.7	Sales/Net Fixed Assets					10.1	9.3
5.8	5.8	5.6						5.2	6.6
2.9	2.8	2.9						3.2	2.5
2.1	2.0	2.0	Sales/Total Assets					1.8	2.1
1.7	1.6	1.5						1.3	1.9
1.0	.8	.6						.7	1.0
(72) 2.1	(77) 1.7	(64) 1.5	% Depr., Dep., Amort./Sales					(22) 1.3	(32) 1.9
3.0	2.6	2.5						3.6	2.4
.7	.9	.8							
(14) 1.9	(19) 2.3	(19) 1.9	% Officers', Directors' Owners' Comp/Sales						
5.4	3.8	5.9							
3221997M	5205055M	4312647M	Net Sales ($)		9381M	17359M	64651M	413221M	3808035M
1687574M	2481900M	1857597M	Total Assets ($)		4403M	7461M	39658M	228887M	1577188M

M = $ thousand MM = $ million

See Pages 9 through 22 for Explanation of Ratios and Data

Current Data Sorted by Assets | **Comparative Historical Data**

0-500M	500M-2MM	2-10MM	10-50MM	50-100MM	100-250MM	Type of Statement	4/1/09-3/31/10 ALL	4/1/10-3/31/11 ALL
		1	1	2		Unqualified	3	4
		2			1	Reviewed	3	1
						Compiled	1	1
	1	2				Tax Returns		
		1	6	4		Other	2	3
	3 (4/1-9/30/13)		18 (10/1/13-3/31/14)					
	1	6	7	6	1	NUMBER OF STATEMENTS	9	9
%	%	%	%	%	%	**ASSETS**	%	%
DATA NOT AVAILABLE						Cash & Equivalents		
						Trade Receivables (net)		
						Inventory		
						All Other Current		
						Total Current		
						Fixed Assets (net)		
						Intangibles (net)		
						All Other Non-Current		
						Total		
						LIABILITIES		
						Notes Payable-Short Term		
						Cur. Mat.-L.T.D.		
						Trade Payables		
						Income Taxes Payable		
						All Other Current		
						Total Current		
						Long-Term Debt		
						Deferred Taxes		
						All Other Non-Current		
						Net Worth		
						Total Liabilties & Net Worth		
						INCOME DATA		
						Net Sales		
						Gross Profit		
						Operating Expenses		
						Operating Profit		
						All Other Expenses (net)		
						Profit Before Taxes		
						RATIOS		
						Current		
						Quick		
						Sales/Receivables		
						Cost of Sales/Inventory		
						Cost of Sales/Payables		
						Sales/Working Capital		
						EBIT/Interest		
						Net Profit + Depr., Dep., Amort./Cur. Mat. L/T/D		
						Fixed/Worth		
						Debt/Worth		
						% Profit Before Taxes/Tangible Net Worth		
						% Profit Before Taxes/Total Assets		
						Sales/Net Fixed Assets		
						Sales/Total Assets		
						% Depr., Dep., Amort./Sales		
						% Officers', Directors' Owners' Comp/Sales		
	5774M	68897M	336314M	669046M	161666M	Net Sales ($)	684625M	364301M
	1070M	30400M	159334M	407514M	170907M	Total Assets ($)	403231M	249732M

M = $ thousand MM = $ million

See Pages 9 through 22 for Explanation of Ratios and Data

Comparative Historical Data				Current Data Sorted by Sales					
Type of Statement									
Unqualified	1	8	4						4
Reviewed	3	4	3				1	1	1
Compiled									
Tax Returns	2	3	3		1	1	1		
Other	8	15	11			1		3	7
	4/1/11-3/31/12 ALL	4/1/12-3/31/13 ALL	4/1/13-3/31/14 ALL		3 (4/1-9/30/13)		18 (10/1/13-3/31/14)		
				0-1MM	1-3MM	3-5MM	5-10MM	10-25MM	25MM & OVER
NUMBER OF STATEMENTS	14	30	21		1	2	2	4	12
ASSETS	%	%	%	%	%	%	%	%	%
Cash & Equivalents	3.6	6.1	4.8	DATA NOT AVAILABLE					2.2
Trade Receivables (net)	21.1	17.7	18.4						20.8
Inventory	23.4	22.1	24.1						24.8
All Other Current	1.6	1.1	2.7						2.2
Total Current	49.7	47.0	50.0						50.0
Fixed Assets (net)	32.2	39.6	35.7						34.5
Intangibles (net)	6.8	3.5	4.3						4.4
All Other Non-Current	11.3	9.9	10.0						11.2
Total	100.0	100.0	100.0						100.0
LIABILITIES									
Notes Payable-Short Term	11.1	8.4	12.5						12.5
Cur. Mat.-L.T.D.	6.4	5.6	5.4						6.5
Trade Payables	18.0	13.0	15.7						14.7
Income Taxes Payable	.1	.0	.1						.1
All Other Current	14.1	7.8	7.3						6.5
Total Current	49.7	34.8	41.0						40.3
Long-Term Debt	10.3	20.9	13.2						10.1
Deferred Taxes	.6	.6	.4						.7
All Other Non-Current	11.1	12.9	13.0						19.1
Net Worth	28.4	30.8	32.3						29.8
Total Liabilties & Net Worth	100.0	100.0	100.0						100.0
INCOME DATA									
Net Sales	100.0	100.0	100.0						100.0
Gross Profit	18.8	20.4	21.9						15.6
Operating Expenses	17.2	15.7	16.8						9.9
Operating Profit	1.6	4.7	5.1						5.6
All Other Expenses (net)	.1	.7	.0						-.6
Profit Before Taxes	1.5	4.0	5.1						6.2
RATIOS									
Current	1.9	2.2	1.8						1.7
	1.1	1.5	1.5						1.6
	.7	.9	.9						.8
Quick	1.0	1.1	.8						.8
	.6	.7	.6						.6
	.3	.4	.4						.4
Sales/Receivables	**31** 11.6	**29** 12.7	**20** 18.6						**33** 10.9
	36 10.1	**34** 10.7	**37** 9.8						**42** 8.7
	52 7.0	**49** 7.5	**49** 7.4						**54** 6.8
Cost of Sales/Inventory	**25** 14.4	**32** 11.4	**33** 11.0						**22** 16.6
	37 9.9	**46** 7.9	**54** 6.7						**45** 8.2
	94 3.9	**81** 4.5	**78** 4.7						**83** 4.4
Cost of Sales/Payables	**20** 18.1	**21** 17.5	**23** 16.0						**23** 16.2
	28 12.9	**33** 11.1	**29** 12.6						**25** 14.8
	50 7.3	**43** 8.5	**43** 8.4						**44** 8.3
Sales/Working Capital	8.9	6.8	7.3						7.3
	52.7	11.2	12.7						10.6
	-12.3	-87.8	-35.4						-50.6
EBIT/Interest	7.6	11.8	15.1						18.5
	(13) 1.9	(28) 7.1	6.4						6.2
	.6	1.9	2.6						2.4
Net Profit + Depr., Dep., Amort./Cur. Mat. L/T/D		7.8	4.1						
		(13) 3.6	(11) 2.4						
		1.4	1.5						
Fixed/Worth	.4	.5	.5						.5
	1.0	1.3	1.4						1.4
	NM	4.8	4.6						5.3
Debt/Worth	1.1	.9	.9						.8
	2.5	1.8	1.6						1.5
	NM	5.6	8.1						11.6
% Profit Before Taxes/Tangible Net Worth	17.1	44.3	46.8						41.6
	(11) 8.8	(27) 22.9	(18) 15.3						(10) 15.3
	-7.4	3.2	3.2						7.6
% Profit Before Taxes/Total Assets	9.1	13.4	17.8						18.6
	3.3	7.4	8.1						7.9
	-.2	3.2	2.5						3.2
Sales/Net Fixed Assets	25.6	20.8	9.3						9.2
	8.5	4.8	6.5						7.4
	5.0	1.9	3.9						4.1
Sales/Total Assets	2.7	2.6	2.3						2.7
	2.1	1.5	2.0						1.8
	1.4	1.2	1.2						1.1
% Depr., Dep., Amort./Sales	.8	1.0	1.4						1.2
	(12) 2.0	(26) 2.5	(19) 2.4						(11) 2.0
	4.7	5.1	3.1						2.5
% Officers', Directors' Owners' Comp/Sales									
Net Sales ($)	**602877M**	**1593818M**	**1241697M**		**2925M**	**9177M**	**14365M**	**90133M**	**1125097M**
Total Assets ($)	**321231M**	**1148291M**	**769225M**		**2318M**	**4616M**	**4701M**	**54019M**	**703571M**

M = $ thousand MM = $ million

See Pages 9 through 22 for Explanation of Ratios and Data

Current Data Sorted by Assets							Comparative Historical Data	
						Type of Statement		
		3	6			Unqualified	11	12
	1	12	6			Reviewed	17	19
	4	6				Compiled	6	6
1	4	2			1	Tax Returns	4	6
	5	4	5	5		Other	22	21
	13 (4/1-9/30/13)		52 (10/1/13-3/31/14)				4/1/09-3/31/10 ALL	4/1/10-3/31/11 ALL
0-500M	500M-2MM	2-10MM	10-50MM	50-100MM	100-250MM			
1	14	27	17	5	1	**NUMBER OF STATEMENTS**	60	64
%	%	%	%	%	%	**ASSETS**	%	%
	6.7	11.0	5.2			Cash & Equivalents	6.5	5.5
	24.6	27.7	26.9			Trade Receivables (net)	26.9	29.9
	30.9	32.1	33.7			Inventory	33.5	34.4
	1.7	1.7	3.0			All Other Current	1.3	2.4
	63.9	72.5	68.8			Total Current	68.1	72.2
	27.1	21.9	18.1			Fixed Assets (net)	22.1	20.7
	.2	2.2	4.8			Intangibles (net)	2.1	2.3
	8.8	3.4	8.3			All Other Non-Current	7.6	4.8
	100.0	100.0	100.0			Total	100.0	100.0
						LIABILITIES		
	15.7	14.0	13.9			Notes Payable-Short Term	13.7	14.4
	3.5	2.1	1.6			Cur. Mat.-L.T.D.	6.0	2.1
	18.6	17.4	15.1			Trade Payables	18.7	19.4
	.2	.0	.1			Income Taxes Payable	.2	.2
	10.3	5.5	8.1			All Other Current	9.0	9.0
	48.3	39.0	38.7			Total Current	47.6	45.0
	14.2	8.7	9.8			Long-Term Debt	8.5	10.8
	.0	.1	.6			Deferred Taxes	.2	.2
	29.9	3.9	7.1			All Other Non-Current	3.5	5.7
	7.5	48.2	43.8			Net Worth	40.2	38.2
	100.0	100.0	100.0			Total Liabilties & Net Worth	100.0	100.0
						INCOME DATA		
	100.0	100.0	100.0			Net Sales	100.0	100.0
	45.9	26.4	22.3			Gross Profit	26.3	25.4
	44.8	22.0	17.3			Operating Expenses	23.9	21.3
	1.2	4.4	5.0			Operating Profit	2.5	4.1
	.7	2.3	.9			All Other Expenses (net)	.9	1.3
	.5	2.1	4.1			Profit Before Taxes	1.6	2.8
						RATIOS		
	5.2	3.6	2.7				2.4	2.6
	2.9	2.3	1.9			Current	1.6	1.7
	.7	1.3	1.2				1.1	1.2
	3.3	1.9	1.4				1.4	1.5
	.8	1.2	.7			Quick	.6	.7
	.3	.6	.5				.4	.5
	16 23.4	**25** 14.6	**33** 11.1				**27** 13.4	**35** 10.5
	30 12.1	**38** 9.7	**47** 7.7			Sales/Receivables	**44** 8.3	**46** 8.0
	36 10.1	**51** 7.1	**73** 5.0				**60** 6.1	**60** 6.1
	13 27.9	**20** 18.3	**47** 7.7				**43** 8.4	**42** 8.6
	50 7.3	**83** 4.4	**73** 5.0			Cost of Sales/Inventory	**69** 5.3	**76** 4.8
	118 3.1	**118** 3.1	**135** 2.7				**126** 2.9	**107** 3.4
	15 24.4	**18** 20.8	**29** 12.4				**20** 18.1	**19** 19.6
	26 13.8	**25** 14.4	**38** 9.5			Cost of Sales/Payables	**33** 11.0	**36** 10.0
	70 5.2	**54** 6.8	**52** 7.0				**55** 6.6	**57** 6.4
	4.5	3.2	4.6				5.4	5.7
	8.5	6.3	5.5			Sales/Working Capital	12.2	9.1
	-14.7	12.7	14.3				26.3	15.3
	6.4	11.1	18.3				10.2	12.1
	(12) .7	(24) 3.6	(16) 3.9			EBIT/Interest	(54) 2.5	(56) 3.7
	-6.4	-.4	1.3				1.0	1.6
							8.8	17.2
						Net Profit + Depr., Dep., Amort./Cur. Mat. L/T/D	(13) 2.1	(11) 2.7
							-.5	1.1
	.1	.1	.2				.1	.1
	NM	.3	.3			Fixed/Worth	.5	.4
	-1.2	1.0	1.1				1.0	1.6
	.5	.5	.5				.7	.8
	NM	.9	1.2			Debt/Worth	1.5	2.0
	-3.4	2.4	3.3				3.8	4.1
		27.9	24.2				23.2	32.5
		(25) 14.7	(15) 14.9			% Profit Before Taxes/Tangible Net Worth	(57) 8.2	(60) 17.5
		.2	2.5				1.4	5.5
	13.7	10.7	13.9				8.4	10.7
	.3	4.8	5.7			% Profit Before Taxes/Total Assets	2.9	5.4
	-8.8	-2.7	.7				.8	1.2
	92.9	68.0	29.6				64.6	63.3
	12.6	26.3	13.9			Sales/Net Fixed Assets	16.1	17.6
	7.3	6.1	7.1				5.0	5.9
	3.9	3.4	2.3				2.9	2.9
	2.7	1.9	1.9			Sales/Total Assets	2.1	2.4
	1.9	1.5	1.5				1.6	1.7
		.5	.7				.4	.5
		(26) 1.2	(15) 1.3			% Depr., Dep., Amort./Sales	(51) 1.3	(49) 1.5
		2.9	2.0				3.2	2.8
		1.1					1.4	1.0
		(11) 3.3				% Officers', Directors' Owners' Comp/Sales	(21) 2.6	(16) 2.1
		6.1					5.7	5.7
411M	46698M	345451M	898123M	699329M	429400M	Net Sales ($)	2141498M	2659163M
88M	15580M	142773M	512704M	326234M	203600M	Total Assets ($)	1089623M	1305891M

M = $ thousand MM = $ million

See Pages 9 through 22 for Explanation of Ratios and Data

Comparative Historical Data				Current Data Sorted by Sales					
			Type of Statement						
5	7	9	Unqualified					2	7
16	23	19	Reviewed		2		4	6	7
5	8	10	Compiled		1	5	3	1	
5	2	8	Tax Returns	1	3	1	2		1
28	13	19	Other		3		4	2	10
4/1/11-3/31/12 ALL	**4/1/12-3/31/13 ALL**	**4/1/13-3/31/14 ALL**		**13 (4/1-9/30/13)**			**52 (10/1/13-3/31/14)**		
				0-1MM	**1-3MM**	**3-5MM**	**5-10MM**	**10-25MM**	**25MM & OVER**
59	53	65	**NUMBER OF STATEMENTS**	1	9	6	13	11	25
%	%	%	**ASSETS**	%	%	%	%	%	%
6.6	5.5	8.0	Cash & Equivalents				6.2	11.4	5.4
28.5	29.0	27.1	Trade Receivables (net)				25.6	19.3	33.4
35.6	35.7	31.3	Inventory				36.6	36.8	31.7
2.5	2.7	2.0	All Other Current				.3	4.9	1.5
73.3	72.9	68.4	Total Current				68.6	72.3	72.1
18.9	21.0	21.6	Fixed Assets (net)				22.0	20.8	14.3
1.8	1.0	3.0	Intangibles (net)				.6	2.6	5.3
6.0	5.1	7.0	All Other Non-Current				8.8	4.3	8.3
100.0	100.0	100.0	Total				100.0	100.0	100.0
			LIABILITIES						
15.0	15.6	16.2	Notes Payable-Short Term				22.5	15.5	11.5
4.8	2.1	2.4	Cur. Mat.-L.T.D.				1.9	2.1	1.9
20.6	19.1	16.6	Trade Payables				23.7	15.6	17.6
.0	.1	.1	Income Taxes Payable				.0	.0	.1
9.3	5.4	7.4	All Other Current				9.1	1.8	8.4
49.7	42.3	42.7	Total Current				57.2	35.0	39.5
10.8	8.0	12.5	Long-Term Debt				4.3	13.6	13.6
.1	.4	.2	Deferred Taxes				.0	.1	.4
5.0	6.4	12.4	All Other Non-Current				5.6	2.0	8.6
34.4	43.0	32.2	Net Worth				32.8	49.2	37.8
100.0	100.0	100.0	Total Liabilties & Net Worth				100.0	100.0	100.0
			INCOME DATA						
100.0	100.0	100.0	Net Sales				100.0	100.0	100.0
25.7	25.6	29.8	Gross Profit				31.3	24.8	21.7
21.9	22.3	26.7	Operating Expenses				26.9	21.6	16.9
3.9	3.3	3.1	Operating Profit				4.3	3.2	4.8
.5	.6	1.4	All Other Expenses (net)				2.4	2.2	1.0
3.4	2.7	1.7	Profit Before Taxes				1.9	1.0	3.8
			RATIOS						
2.8	2.7	3.3	Current				3.1	3.2	2.4
1.5	1.9	2.0					1.7	2.1	1.8
1.2	1.4	1.3					.9	1.3	1.3
1.8	1.2	1.8	Quick				1.6	1.7	1.4
.8	.8	.9					.6	.8	.9
.4	.5	.5					.3	.6	.6
28 12.9	**28** 12.9	**25** 14.6	Sales/Receivables				**21** 17.7	**27** 13.6	**37** 9.8
44 8.3	**40** 9.1	**39** 9.4					**28** 13.0	**38** 9.7	**49** 7.5
54 6.7	**52** 7.0	**54** 6.7					**45** 8.1	**51** 7.1	**61** 6.0
42 8.6	**29** 12.7	**25** 14.6	Cost of Sales/Inventory				**34** 10.6	**63** 5.8	**43** 8.4
76 4.8	**72** 5.1	**63** 5.8					**54** 6.8	**91** 4.0	**58** 6.3
118 3.1	**107** 3.4	**114** 3.2					**126** 2.9	**114** 3.2	**118** 3.1
17 21.5	**16** 23.2	**18** 20.5	Cost of Sales/Payables				**22** 16.7	**19** 19.6	**20** 18.1
28 13.0	**35** 10.4	**34** 10.6					**51** 7.1	**44** 8.3	**35** 10.5
46 8.0	**49** 7.5	**52** 7.0					**66** 5.5	**54** 6.7	**47** 7.8
5.7	5.3	4.3	Sales/Working Capital				5.7	3.5	4.8
9.9	8.5	6.7					8.9	7.7	6.8
20.8	14.1	16.1					NM	9.3	14.0
8.8	16.4	8.3	EBIT/Interest				29.5	14.1	30.6
(49) 3.9	(49) 4.4	(59) 3.1					(12) .9	(10) 3.4	(24) 3.9
1.1	1.6	.7					-5.1	1.0	1.4
5.2	2.9		Net Profit + Depr., Dep., Amort./Cur. Mat. L/T/D						
(11) 3.0	(11) 2.2								
1.9	1.4								
.1	.1	.1	Fixed/Worth				.1	.1	.1
.4	.3	.4					.5	.3	.3
1.3	.9	1.7					NM	1.1	1.1
.5	.5	.5	Debt/Worth				.4	.5	.5
1.8	1.3	1.5					1.6	.8	1.8
5.5	3.5	6.9					NM	2.5	5.8
35.6	40.9	28.8	% Profit Before Taxes/Tangible Net Worth				42.7	19.2	34.8
(51) 12.8	(51) 14.1	(52) 15.7					(10) 7.5	11.6	(22) 20.5
1.1	4.9	2.2					-1.3	-4.5	7.2
11.5	14.0	10.8	% Profit Before Taxes/Total Assets				6.4	9.0	16.3
4.5	5.4	4.4					.7	4.8	5.7
.5	1.0	-.7					-7.2	-2.7	.8
64.0	66.6	51.0	Sales/Net Fixed Assets				74.1	63.4	35.9
19.9	21.1	14.3					14.9	26.3	20.9
6.8	7.1	7.3					7.6	3.3	10.1
3.5	3.4	3.0	Sales/Total Assets				3.9	1.9	2.9
2.3	2.5	2.1					2.7	1.7	2.1
1.8	1.7	1.7					2.0	1.6	1.7
.4	.4	.6	% Depr., Dep., Amort./Sales				.6	.4	.6
(45) 1.0	(46) 1.0	(55) 1.2					(11) 1.1	1.3	(21) 1.0
2.0	2.1	2.1					2.1	3.2	1.8
1.6	1.6	1.6	% Officers', Directors' Owners' Comp/Sales						
(16) 4.9	(15) 3.8	(21) 3.3							
8.5	8.8	8.1							
2209526M	1543085M	2419412M	Net Sales ($)	411M	18777M	23045M	94354M	178510M	2104315M
1067819M	713260M	1200979M	Total Assets ($)	88M	10096M	18769M	35341M	94224M	1042461M

M = $ thousand MM = $ million

See Pages 9 through 22 for Explanation of Ratios and Data

Current Data Sorted by Assets							Comparative Historical Data	
						Type of Statement		
			3	2	1	Unqualified	9	7
	1	1	3			Reviewed	12	8
	3	1				Compiled	2	1
1	1		1			Tax Returns		3
		3	2	4		Other	15	14
	4 (4/1-9/30/13)		23 (10/1/13-3/31/14)				**4/1/09-3/31/10**	**4/1/10-3/31/11**
0-500M	**500M-2MM**	**2-10MM**	**10-50MM**	**50-100MM**	**100-250MM**		**ALL**	**ALL**
1	5	5	9	6	1	**NUMBER OF STATEMENTS**	38	33
%	%	%	%	%	%	**ASSETS**	%	%
						Cash & Equivalents	10.1	7.7
						Trade Receivables (net)	25.5	23.2
						Inventory	24.2	30.1
						All Other Current	2.4	1.5
						Total Current	62.2	62.5
						Fixed Assets (net)	28.2	26.4
						Intangibles (net)	4.4	5.9
						All Other Non-Current	5.1	5.2
						Total	100.0	100.0
						LIABILITIES		
						Notes Payable-Short Term	9.6	8.9
						Cur. Mat.-L.T.D.	5.5	3.1
						Trade Payables	13.6	14.2
						Income Taxes Payable	.2	.1
						All Other Current	9.0	7.6
						Total Current	37.9	33.8
						Long-Term Debt	16.3	17.4
						Deferred Taxes	.6	.5
						All Other Non-Current	4.7	8.4
						Net Worth	40.5	39.9
						Total Liabilities & Net Worth	100.0	100.0
						INCOME DATA		
						Net Sales	100.0	100.0
						Gross Profit	28.1	24.7
						Operating Expenses	24.1	20.2
						Operating Profit	4.0	4.5
						All Other Expenses (net)	1.0	.1
						Profit Before Taxes	3.0	4.4
						RATIOS		
							2.7	3.2
						Current	1.8	2.5
							1.1	1.3
							1.8	1.6
						Quick	.9	1.2
							.6	.6
							29 12.5	**28** 13.1
						Sales/Receivables	**47** 7.7	**45** 8.1
							55 6.6	**52** 7.0
							36 10.2	**41** 8.9
						Cost of Sales/Inventory	**53** 6.9	**63** 5.8
							85 4.3	**104** 3.5
							13 27.7	**23** 15.8
						Cost of Sales/Payables	**32** 11.5	**31** 11.6
							45 8.1	**37** 10.0
							4.6	4.7
						Sales/Working Capital	8.7	6.2
							43.7	17.2
							12.3	33.0
						EBIT/Interest	(36) 5.4	(30) 7.8
							2.3	2.5
							3.5	
						Net Profit + Depr., Dep., Amort./Cur. Mat. L/T/D	(11) 2.6	
							2.0	
							.3	.4
						Fixed/Worth	.7	.7
							2.2	1.8
							.6	.6
						Debt/Worth	1.1	1.3
							5.4	4.7
							45.4	42.1
						% Profit Before Taxes/Tangible Net Worth	(33) 23.7	(28) 25.6
							9.8	7.5
							16.9	19.3
						% Profit Before Taxes/Total Assets	8.2	9.0
							3.3	2.7
							18.6	13.0
						Sales/Net Fixed Assets	7.3	7.6
							4.2	5.1
							2.8	2.5
						Sales/Total Assets	1.9	2.0
							1.5	1.7
							.9	1.4
						% Depr., Dep., Amort./Sales	(30) 2.3	(28) 2.5
							4.0	3.7
							1.2	
						% Officers', Directors' Owners' Comp/Sales	(12) 4.6	
							13.8	
1353M	**17119M**	**35739M**	**385933M**	**843314M**	**127754M**	Net Sales ($)	**1391270M**	**1351902M**
328M	**5495M**	**21792M**	**208717M**	**467348M**	**122608M**	Total Assets ($)	**824858M**	**751467M**

M = $ thousand MM = $ million

See Pages 9 through 22 for Explanation of Ratios and Data

Comparative Historical Data | Current Data Sorted by Sales

	4/1/11-3/31/12 ALL		4/1/12-3/31/13 ALL		4/1/13-3/31/14 ALL	Type of Statement	0-1MM	1-3MM	3-5MM	5-10MM	10-25MM		25MM & OVER
	4		1		6	Unqualified					1		5
	9		7		5	Reviewed			1		1		3
	1		3		4	Compiled		1	3				
	1		5		3	Tax Returns		2					1
	16		10		9	Other			1	2			6
							4 (4/1-9/30/13)		23 (10/1/13-3/31/14)				
	31		26		27	NUMBER OF STATEMENTS		3	5	2	2		15
	%		%		%	**ASSETS**	%	%	%	%	%		%
	11.5		9.3		11.1	Cash & Equivalents	DATA NOT AVAILABLE						7.2
	25.0		23.1		28.1	Trade Receivables (net)							23.5
	27.9		29.4		27.2	Inventory							27.5
	1.4		2.4		.4	All Other Current							.7
	65.8		64.2		66.8	Total Current							58.9
	25.9		28.3		23.1	Fixed Assets (net)							26.9
	3.2		2.0		4.1	Intangibles (net)							6.5
	5.2		5.5		6.0	All Other Non-Current							7.7
	100.0		100.0		100.0	Total							100.0
						LIABILITIES							
	8.0		7.7		5.5	Notes Payable-Short Term							6.8
	2.5		3.4		2.5	Cur. Mat.-L.T.D.							3.0
	18.3		19.8		20.5	Trade Payables							18.7
	.1		.1		.1	Income Taxes Payable							.1
	6.3		5.0		7.9	All Other Current							6.2
	35.2		36.1		36.5	Total Current							34.7
	13.2		18.0		21.9	Long-Term Debt							36.9
	.1		.2		.2	Deferred Taxes							.4
	11.2		6.9		10.9	All Other Non-Current							11.8
	40.3		38.8		30.5	Net Worth							16.3
	100.0		100.0		100.0	Total Liabilties & Net Worth							100.0
						INCOME DATA							
	100.0		100.0		100.0	Net Sales							100.0
	26.9		27.2		26.9	Gross Profit							22.2
	21.6		23.4		20.8	Operating Expenses							15.1
	5.3		3.8		6.1	Operating Profit							7.1
	-.1		.4		1.4	All Other Expenses (net)							2.1
	5.4		3.4		4.7	Profit Before Taxes							5.0
						RATIOS							
	3.1		3.3		3.0								2.8
	2.4		1.9		1.9	Current							1.6
	1.5		1.4		1.2								1.2
	2.0		2.0		1.5								1.5
	1.6		1.1		1.1	Quick							.8
	.7		.6		.6								.5
34	10.8	**28**	13.2	**34**	10.6							**37**	9.9
43	8.4	**37**	9.9	**44**	8.3	Sales/Receivables						**45**	8.1
52	7.0	**47**	7.8	**53**	6.9							**56**	6.5
41	8.8	**37**	9.9	**43**	8.4							**51**	7.2
56	6.5	**53**	6.9	**60**	6.1	Cost of Sales/Inventory						**62**	5.9
83	4.4	**83**	4.4	**87**	4.2							**85**	4.3
26	14.1	**20**	17.9	**20**	18.1							**24**	15.2
34	10.7	**31**	11.6	**36**	10.0	Cost of Sales/Payables						**38**	9.5
49	7.5	**46**	7.9	**50**	7.3							**50**	7.3
	3.9		4.4		4.6								4.6
	6.1		8.0		8.2	Sales/Working Capital							10.8
	14.3		20.6		20.1								20.4
	64.4		11.8		28.3								13.8
(29)	8.3	(21)	6.7	(24)	7.5	EBIT/Interest						(14)	6.1
	4.6		1.7		3.4								3.8
	9.4												
(10)	4.9					Net Profit + Depr., Dep., Amort./Cur. Mat. L/T/D							
	3.5												
	.3		.3		.3								.6
	.7		.7		.6	Fixed/Worth							1.1
	1.0		1.1		3.0								-12.3
	.6		.4		.5								1.1
	1.2		1.2		1.7	Debt/Worth							4.8
	3.1		2.1		-49.6								-19.9
	43.6		34.9		61.2								81.2
(27)	19.4	(22)	12.1	(20)	19.5	% Profit Before Taxes/Tangible Net Worth						(10)	23.4
	11.9		1.0		4.9								7.6
	19.9		14.6		19.9								14.6
	7.6		5.5		7.3	% Profit Before Taxes/Total Assets							8.0
	3.2		.4		2.0								3.3
	13.7		22.7		17.7								13.6
	8.8		9.8		9.3	Sales/Net Fixed Assets							6.6
	4.7		4.5		4.7								4.4
	2.8		2.8		3.1								2.4
	2.1		2.4		2.2	Sales/Total Assets							1.9
	1.8		1.9		1.5								1.2
	1.1		.9		1.0								1.3
(29)	1.6	(21)	1.8	(26)	1.7	% Depr., Dep., Amort./Sales							1.9
	2.5		2.9		2.7								2.6
			2.3		2.5								
		(10)	5.2	(12)	4.8	% Officers', Directors' Owners' Comp/Sales							
			10.5		7.3								
	1518330M		946521M		1411212M	Net Sales ($)		7177M	19148M	17607M	29206M		1338074M
	806009M		432588M		826288M	Total Assets ($)		1915M	15660M	7007M	20242M		781464M

M = $ thousand MM = $ million

See Pages 9 through 22 for Explanation of Ratios and Data

Current Data Sorted by Assets							Comparative Historical Data	
			8	3		**Type of Statement** Unqualified	15	11
	1		3			Reviewed	11	9
1	4	4	1			Compiled	10	10
1	2					Tax Returns	4	5
	2	3	5	1	3	Other	22	18
9 (4/1-9/30/13)			33 (10/1/13-3/31/14)				**4/1/09-3/31/10 ALL**	**4/1/10-3/31/11 ALL**
0-500M	**500M-2MM**	**2-10MM**	**10-50MM**	**50-100MM**	**100-250MM**			
2	9	7	17	4	3	**NUMBER OF STATEMENTS**	62	53
%	%	%	%	%	%	**ASSETS**	%	%
			11.0			Cash & Equivalents	8.7	9.9
			18.4			Trade Receivables (net)	19.7	21.4
			32.0			Inventory	33.2	35.7
			5.1			All Other Current	2.8	3.9
			66.4			Total Current	64.5	70.9
			24.1			Fixed Assets (net)	24.8	22.1
			2.3			Intangibles (net)	2.5	1.5
			7.2			All Other Non-Current	8.1	5.5
			100.0			Total	100.0	100.0
						LIABILITIES		
			6.7			Notes Payable-Short Term	7.1	7.5
			2.8			Cur. Mat.-L.T.D.	2.5	3.3
			13.4			Trade Payables	19.2	21.2
			.2			Income Taxes Payable	.2	.0
			10.7			All Other Current	11.0	12.5
			33.8			Total Current	40.1	44.6
			10.8			Long-Term Debt	19.4	18.3
			.0			Deferred Taxes	.4	.4
			2.9			All Other Non-Current	4.9	1.0
			52.5			Net Worth	35.2	35.8
			100.0			Total Liabilties & Net Worth	100.0	100.0
						INCOME DATA		
			100.0			Net Sales	100.0	100.0
			25.1			Gross Profit	30.4	29.7
			20.3			Operating Expenses	26.4	26.8
			4.8			Operating Profit	4.0	2.9
			.6			All Other Expenses (net)	.7	.6
			4.2			Profit Before Taxes	3.3	2.3
						RATIOS		
			2.6				2.5	3.0
			2.0			Current	1.8	1.7
			1.6				1.3	1.2
			1.2				1.3	1.6
			.8			Quick	.7	.8
			.5				.4	.4
			18 20.1				**21** 17.4	**25** 14.8
			33 11.1			Sales/Receivables	**37** 9.9	**35** 10.4
			49 7.4				**48** 7.7	**49** 7.4
			36 10.1				**41** 8.9	**51** 7.2
			94 3.9			Cost of Sales/Inventory	**83** 4.4	**92** 4.0
			107 3.4				**137** 2.7	**122** 3.0
			18 20.3				**23** 15.8	**24** 14.9
			33 11.1			Cost of Sales/Payables	**37** 9.7	**41** 9.0
			41 8.9				**56** 6.5	**60** 6.1
			4.9				4.3	4.2
			6.7			Sales/Working Capital	6.6	6.1
			10.6				13.6	21.8
			22.0				15.6	19.5
			(14) 4.2			EBIT/Interest	(56) 4.0	(45) 4.7
			1.0				.8	-1.1
							7.3	
						Net Profit + Depr., Dep., Amort./Cur. Mat. L/T/D	(12) 2.7	
							.6	
			.3				.2	.1
			.6			Fixed/Worth	.5	.4
			.8				1.2	1.0
			.5				.6	.4
			.9			Debt/Worth	1.3	1.0
			1.8				2.7	2.6
			38.0				25.8	30.6
			11.2			% Profit Before Taxes/Tangible Net Worth	(56) 12.6	(48) 12.0
			.1				2.0	-1.5
			18.4				13.9	10.6
			5.0			% Profit Before Taxes/Total Assets	5.9	4.9
			.0				.1	-2.5
			16.6				27.5	60.1
			8.4			Sales/Net Fixed Assets	8.9	18.1
			4.9				4.1	3.9
			2.3				2.8	2.7
			1.9			Sales/Total Assets	1.9	1.8
			1.6				1.3	1.3
			1.2				1.1	1.0
			2.3			% Depr., Dep., Amort./Sales	(49) 2.4	(41) 1.8
			2.9				3.5	4.4
							2.1	2.0
						% Officers', Directors' Owners' Comp/Sales	(13) 3.0	(17) 2.7
							4.4	6.0
1917M	32325M	113810M	920453M	392945M	619921M	Net Sales ($)	3120075M	1909754M
378M	10925M	37675M	467534M	278924M	468675M	Total Assets ($)	1799781M	1253406M

M = $ thousand MM = $ million

See Pages 9 through 22 for Explanation of Ratios and Data

Comparative Historical Data				Current Data Sorted by Sales					
			Type of Statement						
7	7	11	Unqualified					1	10
9	8	4	Reviewed				1		3
6	11	10	Compiled		4	1	1	2	2
1	3	3	Tax Returns	2	1				
19	18	14	Other			2		4	8
4/1/11-3/31/12 ALL	**4/1/12-3/31/13 ALL**	**4/1/13-3/31/14 ALL**		**9 (4/1-9/30/13)**			**33 (10/1/13-3/31/14)**		
				0-1MM	**1-3MM**	**3-5MM**	**5-10MM**	**10-25MM**	**25MM & OVER**
42	47	42	**NUMBER OF STATEMENTS**	2	5	3	2	7	23
%	%	%	**ASSETS**	%	%	%	%	%	%
8.1	10.2	9.5	Cash & Equivalents						9.0
20.7	25.9	23.7	Trade Receivables (net)						18.8
35.2	32.6	31.8	Inventory						32.4
2.3	3.4	3.3	All Other Current						4.2
66.3	72.1	68.4	Total Current						64.3
24.1	18.9	21.8	Fixed Assets (net)						24.9
3.1	1.7	2.6	Intangibles (net)						4.5
6.6	7.3	7.1	All Other Non-Current						6.3
100.0	100.0	100.0	Total						100.0
			LIABILITIES						
6.3	7.5	13.6	Notes Payable-Short Term						8.6
2.4	2.3	2.0	Cur. Mat.-L.T.D.						2.2
19.7	17.8	20.5	Trade Payables						13.7
.1	.4	.1	Income Taxes Payable						.2
11.2	9.9	10.2	All Other Current						10.7
39.7	37.8	46.4	Total Current						35.3
13.9	9.2	10.6	Long-Term Debt						14.1
.4	.6	.5	Deferred Taxes						1.0
2.0	6.0	4.5	All Other Non-Current						.6
43.9	46.4	38.1	Net Worth						49.1
100.0	100.0	100.0	Total Liabilties & Net Worth						100.0
			INCOME DATA						
100.0	100.0	100.0	Net Sales						100.0
27.7	25.4	29.2	Gross Profit						23.6
22.5	21.7	25.6	Operating Expenses						18.7
5.2	3.7	3.6	Operating Profit						5.0
2.2	.7	.9	All Other Expenses (net)						1.0
3.0	3.0	2.7	Profit Before Taxes						3.9
			RATIOS						
2.6	3.2	3.0							2.8
1.9	2.0	2.0	Current						2.0
1.1	1.3	1.3							1.6
1.3	1.3	1.3							1.1
.8	.9	.8	Quick						.8
.4	.6	.5							.6
26 14.2	**24** 15.1	**22** 16.7							**24** 15.2
37 9.9	**42** 8.6	**38** 9.7	Sales/Receivables						**36** 10.2
52 7.0	**51** 7.2	**49** 7.5							**46** 8.0
41 8.9	**47** 7.8	**36** 10.1							**44** 8.3
83 4.4	**89** 4.1	**78** 4.7	Cost of Sales/Inventory						**101** 3.6
146 2.5	**122** 3.0	**111** 3.3							**111** 3.3
26 14.1	**21** 17.0	**21** 17.1							**22** 16.7
43 8.5	**31** 11.9	**34** 10.6	Cost of Sales/Payables						**34** 10.6
58 6.3	**45** 8.1	**54** 6.7							**45** 8.2
4.3	3.6	4.2							4.7
6.9	5.7	6.8	Sales/Working Capital						6.7
25.7	13.1	12.6							11.0
19.9	13.7	15.9							16.3
(34) 3.9	(34) 3.7	(36) 4.2	EBIT/Interest						(20) 4.9
.3	1.4	1.0							1.0
	4.4								
	(12) 2.2		Net Profit + Depr., Dep., Amort./Cur. Mat. L/T/D						
	2.0								
.1	.1	.2							.3
.6	.4	.4	Fixed/Worth						.6
1.1	.8	.9							.9
.6	.4	.6							.6
1.4	1.0	1.0	Debt/Worth						.9
2.5	3.4	2.9							2.1
28.1	25.1	29.9							31.8
(39) 6.5	(45) 9.6	(37) 13.4	% Profit Before Taxes/Tangible Net Worth						(21) 11.2
-2.4	2.0	2.5							.1
9.8	12.6	12.4							10.5
3.1	4.8	5.3	% Profit Before Taxes/Total Assets						6.2
-1.3	1.3	.0							.0
45.4	64.4	28.7							11.5
10.4	14.1	11.0	Sales/Net Fixed Assets						6.5
4.0	4.8	5.3							4.6
2.7	3.0	3.2							2.2
1.9	2.1	2.1	Sales/Total Assets						1.8
1.3	1.4	1.6							1.4
.7	.6	.8							1.2
(34) 1.7	(42) 1.9	(37) 1.6	% Depr., Dep., Amort./Sales						(21) 2.2
3.2	3.3	2.7							2.8
			% Officers', Directors' Owners' Comp/Sales						
2023275M	**2677542M**	**2081371M**	Net Sales ($)	**1525M**	**11040M**	**13942M**	**13318M**	**112978M**	**1928568M**
1364377M	**1625106M**	**1264111M**	Total Assets ($)	**1150M**	**4878M**	**3755M**	**4190M**	**63685M**	**1186453M**

M = $ thousand MM = $ million

See Pages 9 through 22 for Explanation of Ratios and Data

Current Data Sorted by Assets							Comparative Historical Data	
						Type of Statement		
		1	5	1	2	Unqualified	8	14
	1	8	4			Reviewed	16	17
	1	4				Compiled	5	5
3	4	2				Tax Returns	3	6
		5	10	1	2	Other	24	19
	8 (4/1-9/30/13)		46 (10/1/13-3/31/14)				**4/1/09-3/31/10**	**4/1/10-3/31/11**
0-500M	**500M-2MM**	**2-10MM**	**10-50MM**	**50-100MM**	**100-250MM**		**ALL**	**ALL**
3	6	20	19	2	4	**NUMBER OF STATEMENTS**	56	61
%	%	%	%	%	%	**ASSETS**	%	%
		9.0	12.7			Cash & Equivalents	9.8	8.2
		37.7	25.4			Trade Receivables (net)	28.7	29.3
		32.5	33.7			Inventory	30.4	34.6
		3.6	1.9			All Other Current	2.4	3.7
		82.8	73.7			Total Current	71.3	75.8
		12.7	9.9			Fixed Assets (net)	16.4	11.7
		1.4	7.8			Intangibles (net)	5.5	4.4
		3.1	8.5			All Other Non-Current	6.7	8.1
		100.0	100.0			Total	100.0	100.0
						LIABILITIES		
		8.9	14.8			Notes Payable-Short Term	13.7	13.1
		3.9	.4			Cur. Mat.-L.T.D.	4.7	3.1
		27.9	14.4			Trade Payables	15.5	17.6
		.2	.0			Income Taxes Payable	.1	.7
		9.0	11.6			All Other Current	12.9	8.7
		50.0	41.2			Total Current	46.9	43.2
		10.3	6.5			Long-Term Debt	12.6	11.3
		.0	.0			Deferred Taxes	.1	.0
		4.6	2.9			All Other Non-Current	7.4	4.5
		35.2	49.3			Net Worth	33.1	40.9
		100.0	100.0			Total Liabilties & Net Worth	100.0	100.0
						INCOME DATA		
		100.0	100.0			Net Sales	100.0	100.0
		28.1	37.1			Gross Profit	31.7	30.3
		24.1	25.0			Operating Expenses	30.5	27.0
		4.1	12.1			Operating Profit	1.2	3.2
		.1	.6			All Other Expenses (net)	.7	.6
		3.9	11.5			Profit Before Taxes	.5	2.7
						RATIOS		
		3.3	3.5				2.9	3.1
		1.5	1.8			Current	1.5	2.0
		1.2	1.3				1.2	1.2
		1.6	1.9				1.6	1.5
		.9	1.0			Quick	.8	.9
		.7	.4				.5	.5
		34 10.6	**35** 10.5				**27** 13.6	**31** 11.6
		40 9.1	**46** 8.0			Sales/Receivables	**38** 9.5	**42** 8.6
		63 5.8	**62** 5.9				**62** 5.9	**54** 6.7
		28 12.9	**60** 6.1				**43** 8.5	**47** 7.7
		51 7.1	**99** 3.7			Cost of Sales/Inventory	**65** 5.6	**68** 5.4
		96 3.8	**159** 2.3				**104** 3.5	**114** 3.2
		25 14.5	**20** 18.3				**14** 26.5	**16** 23.0
		45 8.2	**30** 12.0			Cost of Sales/Payables	**23** 15.7	**30** 12.2
		62 5.9	**45** 8.2				**44** 8.3	**48** 7.6
		4.8	2.7				5.0	4.1
		12.3	6.4			Sales/Working Capital	8.7	6.8
		21.9	17.2				24.6	19.2
		9.2	5.2				8.2	12.0
		(17) 4.9	(11) 3.6			EBIT/Interest	(45) 2.7	(52) 4.5
		2.4	1.2				.3	1.2
							3.6	5.2
						Net Profit + Depr., Dep., Amort./Cur. Mat. L/T/D	(17) 2.0	(19) 2.7
							.1	.5
		.1	.0				.1	.1
		.3	.1			Fixed/Worth	.4	.2
		.9	.4				1.7	.8
		1.0	.4				.8	.5
		1.7	1.0			Debt/Worth	1.7	1.2
		3.3	2.0				26.3	8.7
		56.4	58.2				15.5	37.4
		(18) 31.2	(16) 16.2			% Profit Before Taxes/Tangible Net Worth	(44) 7.9	(50) 11.2
		12.0	7.0				.6	3.0
		18.3	16.3				7.4	10.9
		10.4	6.5			% Profit Before Taxes/Total Assets	2.9	4.5
		2.7	3.3				-2.3	.8
		85.0	109.5				98.7	80.8
		39.6	36.3			Sales/Net Fixed Assets	26.7	34.2
		18.3	14.8				9.0	12.7
		4.1	2.6				3.0	3.0
		3.3	2.0			Sales/Total Assets	2.1	2.3
		2.3	1.0				1.6	1.8
		.2	.3				.6	.4
		(17) .5	(13) .7			% Depr., Dep., Amort./Sales	(38) 1.2	(44) 1.0
		.9	1.6				2.8	1.9
							2.2	2.1
						% Officers', Directors' Owners' Comp/Sales	(22) 3.9	(26) 4.0
							7.8	6.8
1631M	**39095M**	**272486M**	**791081M**	**225451M**	**1076249M**	Net Sales ($)	**1657826M**	**3226827M**
600M	**6911M**	**88499M**	**454261M**	**109890M**	**726238M**	Total Assets ($)	**831708M**	**1589917M**

M = $ thousand MM = $ million

See Pages 9 through 22 for Explanation of Ratios and Data

Comparative Historical Data / Current Data Sorted by Sales

4/1/11-3/31/12 ALL	4/1/12-3/31/13 ALL	4/1/13-3/31/14 ALL	Type of Statement	0-1MM	1-3MM	3-5MM	5-10MM	10-25MM	25MM & OVER
10	9	9	Unqualified					1	8
17	11	13	Reviewed			1	3	4	5
4	7	5	Compiled			1	1	2	1
6	5	9	Tax Returns	2	2	1	1	3	
13	29	18	Other			1	3	5	9
				8 (4/1-9/30/13)		46 (10/1/13-3/31/14)			
50	61	54	NUMBER OF STATEMENTS	2	2	4	8	15	23
%	%	%	ASSETS	%	%	%	%	%	%
6.5	7.3	10.3	Cash & Equivalents					10.9	8.5
28.6	30.7	27.9	Trade Receivables (net)					27.6	29.3
35.7	36.0	32.1	Inventory					35.0	35.4
1.9	2.6	2.9	All Other Current					1.8	1.9
72.7	76.5	73.2	Total Current					75.4	75.1
17.7	11.1	13.3	Fixed Assets (net)					19.3	10.7
3.5	4.8	5.3	Intangibles (net)					2.8	9.3
6.1	7.6	8.2	All Other Non-Current					2.6	5.0
100.0	100.0	100.0	Total					100.0	100.0
			LIABILITIES						
12.0	13.3	21.4	Notes Payable-Short Term					8.8	15.8
2.9	1.9	1.8	Cur. Mat.-L.T.D.					4.6	.6
19.2	17.9	19.7	Trade Payables					24.5	19.0
.3	.2	.1	Income Taxes Payable					.0	.1
9.3	10.3	9.1	All Other Current					11.6	10.3
43.7	43.6	52.1	Total Current					49.5	45.8
14.3	10.2	10.3	Long-Term Debt					10.5	5.0
.0	.0	.0	Deferred Taxes					.0	.0
6.2	6.0	3.4	All Other Non-Current					2.6	3.0
35.8	40.1	34.2	Net Worth					37.3	46.2
100.0	100.0	100.0	Total Liabilties & Net Worth					100.0	100.0
			INCOME DATA						
100.0	100.0	100.0	Net Sales					100.0	100.0
28.1	31.4	33.8	Gross Profit					35.3	26.7
24.7	26.6	26.6	Operating Expenses					29.3	19.8
3.4	4.8	7.2	Operating Profit					5.9	7.0
.7	1.0	.4	All Other Expenses (net)					1.0	.7
2.7	3.7	6.8	Profit Before Taxes					5.0	6.2
			RATIOS						
2.5	2.9	3.1						2.9	3.4
1.6	1.9	1.6	Current					1.5	1.6
1.2	1.3	1.2						1.2	1.2
1.1	1.3	1.3						1.2	1.7
.7	.8	.8	Quick					.8	.8
.4	.6	.5						.5	.5
29 12.8	**29** 12.5	**29** 12.6						**28** 13.2	**38** 9.5
46 8.0	**47** 7.7	**41** 8.9	Sales/Receivables					**35** 10.4	**56** 6.5
66 5.5	**63** 5.8	**63** 5.8						**40** 9.1	**63** 5.8
45 8.2	**43** 8.4	**38** 9.6						**39** 9.3	**63** 5.8
72 5.1	**78** 4.7	**70** 5.2	Cost of Sales/Inventory					**58** 6.3	**78** 4.7
130 2.8	**118** 3.1	**114** 3.2						**104** 3.5	**140** 2.6
21 17.7	**21** 17.4	**22** 16.8						**22** 16.4	**27** 13.7
32 11.3	**35** 10.5	**35** 10.5	Cost of Sales/Payables					**44** 8.3	**33** 11.0
54 6.7	**52** 7.0	**52** 7.0						**53** 6.9	**51** 7.1
4.6	4.0	4.4						5.9	4.8
8.5	6.8	9.7	Sales/Working Capital					19.7	8.2
24.4	21.9	24.3						35.1	23.4
7.6	8.1	9.3						45.2	23.0
(48) 3.1	(54) 4.3	(43) 4.5	EBIT/Interest					(13) 4.9	(17) 5.0
1.6	1.2	1.6						1.6	2.0
14.4	15.0								
(18) 2.4	(11) 4.9		Net Profit + Depr., Dep., Amort./Cur. Mat. L/T/D						
.8	1.2								
.1	.1	.0						.2	.1
.4	.3	.3	Fixed/Worth					.4	.3
1.5	1.1	.8						1.1	.8
.9	.7	.6						1.0	.5
2.2	1.9	1.5	Debt/Worth					1.6	1.2
4.3	5.5	4.2						3.3	4.7
25.2	40.6	66.1						80.7	62.8
(44) 16.0	(52) 21.2	(47) 24.1	% Profit Before Taxes/Tangible Net Worth					(14) 45.0	(20) 22.0
5.8	4.1	8.6						21.0	9.6
10.2	15.3	17.8						29.4	18.5
4.1	5.8	8.4	% Profit Before Taxes/Total Assets					16.1	8.0
1.6	.9	2.0						2.0	4.8
61.4	102.2	112.0						47.8	109.5
23.7	39.0	38.4	Sales/Net Fixed Assets					29.3	36.3
6.3	16.9	15.3						12.5	14.8
2.8	2.9	3.5						4.1	2.9
2.2	2.2	2.4	Sales/Total Assets					3.2	2.0
1.7	1.7	1.7						2.3	1.7
.4	.2	.2						.2	.2
(44) 1.0	(44) .6	(41) .6	% Depr., Dep., Amort./Sales					(13) .6	(19) .7
1.9	1.4	1.3						1.3	1.4
1.6	1.5	1.0							
(22) 2.6	(20) 3.0	(17) 2.7	% Officers', Directors' Owners' Comp/Sales						
4.2	4.8	9.9							
2364934M	3133478M	2405993M	Net Sales ($)	448M	2615M	15860M	61364M	200223M	2125483M
1197423M	1662992M	1386399M	Total Assets ($)	446M	926M	47599M	31615M	78496M	1227317M

M = $ thousand MM = $ million

See Pages 9 through 22 for Explanation of Ratios and Data

Current Data Sorted by Assets / Comparative Historical Data

0-500M	500M-2MM	2-10MM	10-50MM	50-100MM	100-250MM		4/1/09-3/31/10 ALL	4/1/10-3/31/11 ALL
						Type of Statement		
			3	1		Unqualified	6	6
		6	6			Reviewed	13	15
	1	1		1		Compiled	7	8
1	6	3				Tax Returns	11	10
2	5	7	8	1		Other	19	22
	15 (4/1-9/30/13)		37 (10/1/13-3/31/14)					
3	12	17	17	3		NUMBER OF STATEMENTS	56	61
%	%	%	%	%	%	**ASSETS**	%	%
	11.4	12.0	7.0		DATA NOT AVAILABLE	Cash & Equivalents	8.1	9.5
	28.6	19.9	26.3			Trade Receivables (net)	22.3	22.9
	36.8	32.2	37.4			Inventory	33.8	34.4
	1.0	2.6	3.0			All Other Current	2.7	2.4
	77.8	66.6	73.8			Total Current	67.0	69.2
	11.1	17.3	18.8			Fixed Assets (net)	21.5	21.0
	.5	4.7	2.9			Intangibles (net)	2.9	4.7
	10.6	11.5	4.6			All Other Non-Current	8.6	5.0
	100.0	100.0	100.0			Total	100.0	100.0
						LIABILITIES		
	14.8	8.6	6.7			Notes Payable-Short Term	12.4	12.7
	3.2	1.6	1.6			Cur. Mat.-L.T.D.	2.1	3.7
	15.5	10.1	13.3			Trade Payables	11.9	12.6
	.1	.4	.4			Income Taxes Payable	.2	.5
	17.2	12.2	7.1			All Other Current	9.6	10.3
	50.8	33.0	29.0			Total Current	36.2	39.7
	10.5	10.2	8.8			Long-Term Debt	9.9	11.2
	.0	.1	.4			Deferred Taxes	.1	.5
	9.2	7.7	2.6			All Other Non-Current	6.7	7.3
	29.5	49.0	59.1			Net Worth	47.2	41.4
	100.0	100.0	100.0			Total Liabilties & Net Worth	100.0	100.0
						INCOME DATA		
	100.0	100.0	100.0			Net Sales	100.0	100.0
	36.1	33.2	23.1			Gross Profit	34.4	33.7
	32.2	30.3	18.6			Operating Expenses	31.3	29.1
	3.9	2.8	4.4			Operating Profit	3.1	4.6
	.6	.6	-.2			All Other Expenses (net)	1.0	.6
	3.3	2.3	4.6			Profit Before Taxes	2.1	4.0
						RATIOS		
	3.8	3.9	4.3				2.9	3.2
	2.0	2.0	2.8			Current	1.9	2.0
	1.0	1.6	1.6				1.4	1.1
	2.5	1.8	2.0				1.5	1.5
	.7	1.1	1.4			Quick	.9	.8
	.3	.5	.7				.5	.5
	19 19.7	**14** 25.6	**33** 11.1				**26** 14.2	**26** 14.2
	30 12.3	**38** 9.5	**41** 8.9			Sales/Receivables	**34** 10.8	**39** 9.4
	49 7.4	**53** 6.9	**50** 7.3				**49** 7.4	**58** 6.3
	48 7.6	**45** 8.1	**61** 6.0				**49** 7.5	**55** 6.6
	61 6.0	**87** 4.2	**76** 4.8			Cost of Sales/Inventory	**83** 4.4	**91** 4.0
	85 4.3	**152** 2.4	**104** 3.5				**140** 2.6	**135** 2.7
	5 73.9	**15** 24.7	**11** 34.2				**10** 35.3	**16** 22.6
	17 21.9	**30** 12.2	**25** 14.6			Cost of Sales/Payables	**24** 15.5	**25** 14.6
	51 7.1	**35** 10.3	**38** 9.6				**38** 9.6	**46** 7.9
	4.8	3.9	3.6				4.7	4.0
	9.8	6.8	4.6			Sales/Working Capital	6.5	7.1
	NM	9.1	9.7				13.6	71.9
		15.2	35.1				14.5	15.6
		(15) 1.5	(15) 14.8			EBIT/Interest	(49) 3.0	(53) 4.4
		-2.1	9.1				-.1	1.5
								2.3
						Net Profit + Depr., Dep., Amort./Cur. Mat. L/T/D		(12) 1.3
								.5
	.0	.1	.1				.1	.1
	.2	.3	.4			Fixed/Worth	.3	.4
	NM	1.1	.6				.9	1.4
	.4	.6	.5				.5	.5
	1.7	.9	.7			Debt/Worth	.9	1.3
	NM	2.1	1.3				2.2	4.5
		23.5	29.2				28.9	38.6
		(15) 8.8	19.2			% Profit Before Taxes/Tangible Net Worth	(53) 12.9	(52) 11.3
		-9.3	8.5				-.5	2.6
	12.0	9.4	16.4				12.2	14.7
	3.1	.5	11.5			% Profit Before Taxes/Total Assets	5.4	5.6
	-3.9	-5.6	5.8				-1.4	.7
	202.9	46.3	23.5				35.9	31.2
	35.3	17.9	11.9			Sales/Net Fixed Assets	15.2	14.4
	15.6	7.0	6.4				6.0	7.3
	3.9	2.4	2.4				2.7	2.7
	2.9	1.9	2.0			Sales/Total Assets	2.1	2.1
	2.1	1.6	2.0				1.7	1.7
		1.0	.7				.8	.6
		(14) 1.6	(15) 1.1			% Depr., Dep., Amort./Sales	(47) 1.6	(51) 1.3
		1.9	3.1				3.3	2.5
							1.8	3.4
						% Officers', Directors' Owners' Comp/Sales	(23) 3.2	(24) 4.6
							5.7	5.8
3664M	40227M	166017M	645112M	265931M		Net Sales ($)	744325M	992763M
933M	12385M	87214M	326950M	175230M		Total Assets ($)	453440M	597058M

M = $ thousand MM = $ million

See Pages 9 through 22 for Explanation of Ratios and Data

Comparative Historical Data				Current Data Sorted by Sales					
			Type of Statement						
6	13	4	Unqualified						4
18	10	12	Reviewed				1	7	4
2	6	3	Compiled				2		1
11	15	10	Tax Returns		4	4	2		
17	11	23	Other	3	2	1	4	6	7
4/1/11-3/31/12	4/1/12-3/31/13	4/1/13-3/31/14			15 (4/1-9/30/13)			37 (10/1/13-3/31/14)	
ALL	ALL	ALL		0-1MM	1-3MM	3-5MM	5-10MM	10-25MM	25MM & OVER
54	55	52	**NUMBER OF STATEMENTS**	3	6	5	9	13	16
%	%	%	**ASSETS**	%	%	%	%	%	%
7.0	10.2	9.8	Cash & Equivalents					10.1	6.9
22.5	21.7	23.7	Trade Receivables (net)					18.0	25.4
36.0	33.9	35.2	Inventory					34.5	36.8
1.6	4.3	2.2	All Other Current					1.8	2.7
67.2	70.1	70.8	Total Current					64.4	71.9
19.4	18.2	17.2	Fixed Assets (net)					24.6	18.6
6.0	6.4	3.8	Intangibles (net)					6.9	4.6
7.3	5.4	8.3	All Other Non-Current					4.1	4.9
100.0	100.0	100.0	Total					100.0	100.0
			LIABILITIES						
12.2	8.2	11.7	Notes Payable-Short Term					5.6	7.1
1.8	1.6	2.0	Cur. Mat.-L.T.D.					1.3	2.2
11.4	13.8	12.2	Trade Payables					12.6	11.6
.2	.7	.4	Income Taxes Payable					.5	.7
9.0	10.7	17.4	All Other Current					4.2	9.0
34.6	35.0	43.7	Total Current					24.3	30.6
12.9	15.8	11.8	Long-Term Debt					12.2	15.7
.6	.2	.3	Deferred Taxes					.6	.5
7.5	2.8	7.2	All Other Non-Current					1.9	4.2
44.2	46.3	37.0	Net Worth					61.0	48.9
100.0	100.0	100.0	Total Liabilties & Net Worth					100.0	100.0
			INCOME DATA						
100.0	100.0	100.0	Net Sales					100.0	100.0
33.2	33.3	31.4	Gross Profit					29.0	25.0
27.9	28.3	28.3	Operating Expenses					24.1	21.7
5.3	5.0	3.1	Operating Profit					4.8	3.2
.8	.9	.4	All Other Expenses (net)					.5	.2
4.4	4.1	2.6	Profit Before Taxes					4.4	3.1
			RATIOS						
3.3	4.0	3.8	Current					4.4	3.6
2.0	2.6	2.1						3.3	2.4
1.3	1.3	1.5						1.7	1.5
1.7	1.7	1.8	Quick					2.5	1.7
.9	1.0	1.0						1.1	1.0
.5	.5	.5						.4	.7
25 14.4	18 20.4	22 16.4	Sales/Receivables					15 24.0	37 9.9
43 8.4	33 11.2	34 10.6						29 12.6	43 8.5
54 6.8	45 8.1	51 7.2						41 8.9	49 7.5
68 5.4	58 6.3	54 6.8	Cost of Sales/Inventory					51 7.1	62 5.9
83 4.4	78 4.7	73 5.0						91 4.0	73 5.0
140 2.6	107 3.4	118 3.1						104 3.5	135 2.7
13 28.1	13 27.3	12 30.7	Cost of Sales/Payables					21 17.7	10 36.1
24 15.1	22 16.7	21 17.0						31 11.9	24 15.5
44 8.3	38 9.6	36 10.0						35 10.3	38 9.5
4.4	3.8	3.9	Sales/Working Capital					3.8	3.5
6.3	6.0	6.6						4.6	5.1
16.8	17.3	11.9						10.0	9.7
13.4	16.3	20.2	EBIT/Interest					40.1	29.4
(47) 5.4	(50) 5.6	(44) 4.5						(11) 9.7	12.0
1.9	2.8	-.8						1.0	1.8
			Net Profit + Depr., Dep., Amort./Cur. Mat. L/T/D						
.1	.1	.1	Fixed/Worth					.1	.2
.3	.3	.3						.4	.4
1.0	.9	.9						.7	.7
.5	.5	.5	Debt/Worth					.3	.5
1.0	.9	1.0						.6	.7
4.6	4.4	3.3						1.9	1.6
29.7	38.9	27.7	% Profit Before Taxes/Tangible Net Worth					26.2	31.6
(46) 11.9	(46) 17.4	(43) 14.9						16.4	(14) 22.0
6.1	5.1	-.7						-.6	9.3
10.4	18.9	13.5	% Profit Before Taxes/Total Assets					15.6	14.5
4.9	7.3	4.9						8.3	9.2
2.0	1.8	-4.3						-.1	.9
43.2	35.0	41.8	Sales/Net Fixed Assets					44.1	21.6
13.7	17.5	17.9						11.6	11.0
6.4	7.8	8.7						4.9	6.2
2.4	2.9	2.7	Sales/Total Assets					2.2	2.5
2.1	2.2	2.0						2.0	2.0
1.5	1.9	1.8						1.8	1.6
.9	.8	.8	% Depr., Dep., Amort./Sales					1.0	.7
(45) 1.4	(46) 1.4	(38) 1.6						(12) 1.6	(14) 1.6
2.6	2.2	2.1						1.9	3.8
2.5	2.5	2.5	% Officers', Directors' Owners' Comp/Sales						
(21) 3.5	(21) 5.4	(15) 3.3							
5.3	8.8	8.1							
1070479M	1486400M	1120951M	Net Sales ($)	2051M	13469M	19010M	65272M	195087M	826062M
719593M	845618M	602712M	Total Assets ($)	975M	5156M	7915M	30903M	98125M	459638M

M = $ thousand MM = $ million

See Pages 9 through 22 for Explanation of Ratios and Data

Current Data Sorted by Assets | Comparative Historical Data

Type of Statement	0-500M	500M-2MM	2-10MM	10-50MM	50-100MM	100-250MM	4/1/09-3/31/10 ALL	4/1/10-3/31/11 ALL
Unqualified			2	5		2	21	20
Reviewed		1	21	8			19	36
Compiled		6	10	1		1	17	20
Tax Returns	1	6	9				16	18
Other	2	5	7	13	6	1	52	38
		22 (4/1-9/30/13)		85 (10/1/13-3/31/14)				
NUMBER OF STATEMENTS	3	18	49	27	6	4	125	132
ASSETS	%	%	%	%	%	%	%	%
Cash & Equivalents		18.1	8.4	8.4			7.1	11.0
Trade Receivables (net)		20.1	27.5	24.6			24.3	24.7
Inventory		30.8	38.7	33.4			33.0	32.2
All Other Current		3.1	1.1	1.9			2.3	3.8
Total Current		72.0	75.7	68.2			66.6	71.7
Fixed Assets (net)		19.3	16.6	24.3			23.1	17.9
Intangibles (net)		3.1	1.5	3.8			4.6	4.0
All Other Non-Current		5.6	6.3	3.7			5.6	6.4
Total		100.0	100.0	100.0			100.0	100.0
LIABILITIES								
Notes Payable-Short Term		13.7	8.4	10.8			13.3	10.6
Cur. Mat.-L.T.D.		1.8	1.7	2.2			4.4	3.9
Trade Payables		14.6	20.1	16.8			17.9	18.2
Income Taxes Payable		.0	.3	.3			.3	.2
All Other Current		9.4	7.7	5.1			8.2	9.5
Total Current		39.6	38.1	35.1			44.1	42.4
Long-Term Debt		11.4	7.5	9.5			16.5	15.6
Deferred Taxes		.0	.1	1.2			.6	.4
All Other Non-Current		24.8	5.1	4.8			8.3	8.2
Net Worth		24.2	49.1	49.3			30.5	33.4
Total Liabilties & Net Worth		100.0	100.0	100.0			100.0	100.0
INCOME DATA								
Net Sales		100.0	100.0	100.0			100.0	100.0
Gross Profit		35.2	25.6	23.0			28.4	30.9
Operating Expenses		30.5	22.3	15.8			25.3	25.4
Operating Profit		4.7	3.4	7.2			3.0	5.4
All Other Expenses (net)		1.1	-.1	.2			1.0	1.0
Profit Before Taxes		3.6	3.5	7.0			2.1	4.5
RATIOS								
Current		5.3	3.4	5.0			2.7	3.4
		2.0	2.3	1.9			1.6	1.9
		1.1	1.5	1.3			1.1	1.3
Quick		2.8	1.4	2.1			1.3	1.6
		.8	1.0	1.0			.7	.9
		.5	.7	.7			.5	.5
Sales/Receivables		**2** 148.3	**30** 12.0	**32** 11.3			**24** 15.2	**23** 16.0
		33 11.1	**41** 8.8	**37** 9.8			**39** 9.4	**37** 9.8
		41 9.0	**58** 6.3	**52** 7.0			**54** 6.7	**50** 7.3
Cost of Sales/Inventory		**15** 24.3	**56** 6.5	**46** 7.9			**36** 10.2	**41** 8.9
		54 6.8	**78** 4.7	**72** 5.1			**67** 5.4	**66** 5.5
		135 2.7	**140** 2.6	**111** 3.3			**120** 3.0	**114** 3.2
Cost of Sales/Payables		**8** 46.1	**22** 16.5	**15** 24.8			**17** 21.4	**18** 20.0
		17 20.9	**37** 9.9	**29** 12.6			**30** 12.3	**32** 11.5
		51 7.2	**58** 6.3	**45** 8.2			**49** 7.5	**45** 8.0
Sales/Working Capital		5.1	3.6	3.1			4.7	4.1
		10.8	4.6	7.6			7.8	7.2
		55.1	8.4	11.2			86.6	23.2
EBIT/Interest		14.4	17.8	48.1			8.3	13.4
		(17) 3.2	(43) 7.0	(26) 12.2			(116) 3.0	(123) 4.3
		1.1	2.7	5.7			-.2	1.8
Net Profit + Depr., Dep., Amort./Cur. Mat. L/T/D							5.2	8.4
							(32) 2.1	(30) 2.6
							.0	1.3
Fixed/Worth		.0	.1	.2			.2	.1
		.3	.2	.5			.6	.4
		.9	.6	1.3			1.8	1.8
Debt/Worth		1.3	.4	.4			.7	.7
		2.2	1.0	1.3			1.8	1.8
		3.7	2.7	3.4			7.2	6.6
% Profit Before Taxes/Tangible Net Worth		101.1	31.4	42.6			39.6	45.8
		(17) 31.3	17.3	(25) 23.1			(105) 14.8	(112) 22.0
		2.4	5.1	12.8			1.0	7.0
% Profit Before Taxes/Total Assets		18.2	14.0	18.7			13.0	14.9
		6.8	6.5	10.9			3.9	6.3
		.3	1.9	7.2			-1.6	2.2
Sales/Net Fixed Assets		556.0	65.2	24.8			37.5	56.1
		28.7	21.0	9.2			13.1	21.3
		7.3	9.8	4.9			7.0	9.2
Sales/Total Assets		4.1	2.7	2.6			3.1	3.2
		3.0	2.2	2.0			2.2	2.3
		1.7	1.6	1.6			1.6	1.6
% Depr., Dep., Amort./Sales		.4	.4	.6			.7	.6
		(13) .8	(42) .9	1.3			(104) 1.5	(108) 1.3
		1.2	2.4	2.4			2.8	2.7
% Officers', Directors' Owners' Comp/Sales			1.3				1.5	1.5
			(22) 2.7				(44) 3.6	(50) 2.5
			5.3				5.6	5.5
Net Sales ($)	4639M	63237M	553460M	1111886M	481030M	766961M	4049995M	3448608M
Total Assets ($)	1253M	21126M	248747M	533369M	373145M	673705M	2281048M	1775095M

M = $ thousand MM = $ million

See Pages 9 through 22 for Explanation of Ratios and Data

Comparative Historical Data				Current Data Sorted by Sales					
			Type of Statement						
17	19	9	Unqualified				1	1	7
27	33	30	Reviewed		1	2	4	14	9
16	16	18	Compiled	1		5	6	4	2
18	18	16	Tax Returns	2	4	2	2	6	
51	42	34	Other	1	2	5	6	1	19
4/1/11-3/31/12 ALL	**4/1/12-3/31/13 ALL**	**4/1/13-3/31/14 ALL**		**22 (4/1-9/30/13)**			**85 (10/1/13-3/31/14)**		
				0-1MM	**1-3MM**	**3-5MM**	**5-10MM**	**10-25MM**	**25MM & OVER**
129	128	107	**NUMBER OF STATEMENTS**	4	7	14	19	26	37
%	%	%	**ASSETS**	%	%	%	%	%	%
9.5	9.5	10.0	Cash & Equivalents			13.1	12.7	8.1	7.0
24.3	22.2	25.0	Trade Receivables (net)			22.1	19.7	32.4	23.2
33.1	32.3	33.8	Inventory			36.9	37.5	38.9	32.0
2.6	3.1	2.2	All Other Current			1.0	3.3	1.2	3.1
69.4	67.0	70.9	Total Current			73.0	73.2	80.6	65.4
19.0	21.7	19.4	Fixed Assets (net)			23.0	18.5	11.9	20.9
4.4	4.2	4.3	Intangibles (net)			1.4	.5	2.3	8.9
7.2	7.1	5.5	All Other Non-Current			2.6	7.8	5.2	4.8
100.0	100.0	100.0	Total			100.0	100.0	100.0	100.0
			LIABILITIES						
9.8	8.7	9.2	Notes Payable-Short Term			12.9	7.6	10.0	8.0
2.4	3.2	1.8	Cur. Mat.-L.T.D.			2.4	1.6	1.8	2.1
16.0	15.8	17.8	Trade Payables			12.8	16.3	21.6	17.2
.1	.2	.2	Income Taxes Payable			.2	.0	.4	.3
9.7	10.4	7.8	All Other Current			13.9	7.2	5.7	7.5
38.0	38.2	36.8	Total Current			42.1	32.7	39.5	35.1
15.5	14.5	10.5	Long-Term Debt			11.4	9.9	3.5	13.2
.6	1.3	1.2	Deferred Taxes			.0	.1	.3	3.2
8.1	7.7	8.1	All Other Non-Current			6.0	8.4	5.9	4.3
37.7	38.4	43.4	Net Worth			40.5	49.0	50.7	44.2
100.0	100.0	100.0	Total Liabilities & Net Worth			100.0	100.0	100.0	100.0
			INCOME DATA						
100.0	100.0	100.0	Net Sales			100.0	100.0	100.0	100.0
31.3	31.6	26.4	Gross Profit			37.2	26.3	23.2	23.0
26.4	26.2	21.7	Operating Expenses			30.9	22.1	19.5	16.1
4.9	5.4	4.8	Operating Profit			6.3	4.2	3.7	6.9
.6	.8	.4	All Other Expenses (net)			.7	.2	-.4	.8
4.3	4.7	4.4	Profit Before Taxes			5.6	4.0	4.1	6.1
			RATIOS						
3.5	3.7	3.9				4.4	5.6	3.3	3.5
2.0	2.2	2.2	Current			1.6	2.6	2.2	1.9
1.3	1.3	1.3				1.1	1.4	1.6	1.3
1.7	2.0	1.7				2.4	2.4	1.6	1.5
.9	.9	1.0	Quick			.7	.9	1.1	.9
.5	.6	.7				.5	.6	.7	.7
25 14.7	**23** 16.2	**30** 12.0				**2** 148.3	**21** 17.3	**30** 12.2	**33** 10.9
39 9.3	**35** 10.3	**39** 9.4	Sales/Receivables			**37** 9.9	**38** 9.5	**45** 8.2	**41** 8.9
52 7.0	**49** 7.5	**56** 6.5				**61** 6.0	**51** 7.2	**61** 6.0	**59** 6.2
41 8.8	**40** 9.1	**46** 7.9				**55** 6.6	**38** 9.7	**54** 6.7	**48** 7.6
65 5.6	**72** 5.1	**72** 5.1	Cost of Sales/Inventory			**85** 4.3	**65** 5.6	**79** 4.6	**72** 5.1
118 3.1	**118** 3.1	**126** 2.9				**135** 2.7	**192** 1.9	**126** 2.9	**101** 3.6
17 21.1	**16** 23.4	**17** 21.4				**12** 29.3	**16** 23.4	**24** 15.5	**20** 18.4
32 11.3	**30** 12.0	**31** 11.6	Cost of Sales/Payables			**27** 13.3	**32** 11.3	**34** 10.7	**30** 12.1
47 7.8	**47** 7.8	**50** 7.3				**51** 7.2	**70** 5.2	**63** 5.8	**46** 8.0
4.1	4.3	3.9				4.9	3.2	3.8	4.1
6.8	6.3	6.0	Sales/Working Capital			8.0	4.6	5.0	6.7
18.0	15.1	12.7				51.6	13.5	8.4	11.2
23.4	16.1	20.3				41.9	14.0	22.0	36.7
(117) 4.6	(117) 5.6	(96) 6.9	EBIT/Interest			(13) 4.6	(17) 7.0	(22) 7.0	(35) 10.1
1.5	1.7	2.3				2.2	2.5	4.7	2.4
11.9	6.4	3.0							3.2
(23) 1.9	(33) 2.6	(22) 1.9	Net Profit + Depr., Dep., Amort./Cur. Mat. L/T/D						(11) 2.2
.4	1.6	1.2							1.9
.2	.2	.1				.2	.1	.0	.2
.4	.5	.3	Fixed/Worth			.5	.2	.2	.5
1.4	1.5	.9				1.0	.7	.5	1.3
.5	.5	.5				.9	.5	.4	.5
1.5	1.5	1.4	Debt/Worth			2.2	1.0	.9	1.7
5.0	3.3	3.0				5.9	2.5	3.3	5.3
49.1	39.4	37.6				69.1	34.5	32.4	38.4
(114) 23.2	(112) 17.9	(101) 18.9	% Profit Before Taxes/Tangible Net Worth			31.2	17.4	16.8	(32) 20.9
6.9	5.0	5.0				7.3	3.9	7.6	11.1
17.1	17.7	14.0				14.5	17.2	13.2	15.2
8.8	8.0	7.5	% Profit Before Taxes/Total Assets			7.5	4.9	7.0	8.4
1.8	2.1	1.4				2.2	2.8	3.8	3.3
40.5	38.2	58.1				35.3	59.9	84.4	28.3
17.2	12.5	15.6	Sales/Net Fixed Assets			15.9	21.0	36.9	10.6
7.6	6.5	7.0				7.1	6.3	12.5	4.9
2.9	2.9	2.8				3.2	2.5	2.9	2.6
2.3	2.1	2.2	Sales/Total Assets			2.8	1.9	2.4	1.8
1.6	1.6	1.5				1.6	1.5	1.7	1.3
.7	.7	.5				.3	.3	.5	.5
(97) 1.2	(105) 1.4	(94) 1.1	% Depr., Dep., Amort./Sales			(13) .8	(16) .7	(22) 1.0	1.3
2.7	3.0	2.4				1.3	2.3	2.3	2.8
1.9	2.1	1.3					1.3	1.1	
(45) 3.4	(42) 3.5	(39) 3.1	% Officers', Directors' Owners' Comp/Sales				(10) 2.6	(10) 2.0	
6.4	5.6	6.6					6.8	4.3	
4095592M	**4614523M**	**2981213M**	Net Sales ($)	**3424M**	**16424M**	**55504M**	**132359M**	**395440M**	**2378062M**
2319430M	**2797484M**	**1851345M**	Total Assets ($)	**2674M**	**8135M**	**25449M**	**69014M**	**177136M**	**1568937M**

M = $ thousand MM = $ million

See Pages 9 through 22 for Explanation of Ratios and Data

Current Data Sorted by Assets							Comparative Historical Data	
						Type of Statement		
		2	4	5	2	Unqualified	32	22
	2	7	4		1	Reviewed	22	28
	3	1				Compiled	9	4
2	1	1				Tax Returns	10	11
2	1	2	5	3	4	Other	29	42
	6 (4/1-9/30/13)		46 (10/1/13-3/31/14)				4/1/09-3/31/10 ALL	4/1/10-3/31/11 ALL
0-500M	500M-2MM	2-10MM	10-50MM	50-100MM	100-250MM			
4	7	13	13	8	7	**NUMBER OF STATEMENTS**	102	107
%	%	%	%	%	%	**ASSETS**	%	%
		4.5	15.9			Cash & Equivalents	13.9	9.0
		29.3	24.9			Trade Receivables (net)	30.7	29.7
		41.8	42.1			Inventory	31.4	35.4
		4.2	2.9			All Other Current	2.5	3.4
		79.8	85.8			Total Current	78.6	77.6
		16.9	6.7			Fixed Assets (net)	10.7	9.3
		.4	.8			Intangibles (net)	3.9	5.8
		2.8	6.7			All Other Non-Current	6.8	7.4
		100.0	100.0			Total	100.0	100.0
						LIABILITIES		
		16.6	13.7			Notes Payable-Short Term	14.6	16.3
		1.4	.8			Cur. Mat.-L.T.D.	3.3	3.7
		11.1	10.6			Trade Payables	17.6	15.2
		.1	.0			Income Taxes Payable	.1	.2
		10.0	7.2			All Other Current	13.9	11.2
		39.3	32.3			Total Current	49.5	46.6
		6.6	6.4			Long-Term Debt	5.7	7.1
		.0	.0			Deferred Taxes	.2	.2
		1.7	13.3			All Other Non-Current	9.1	13.1
		52.4	48.0			Net Worth	35.5	33.0
		100.0	100.0			Total Liabilties & Net Worth	100.0	100.0
						INCOME DATA		
		100.0	100.0			Net Sales	100.0	100.0
		24.1	26.4			Gross Profit	32.8	34.9
		20.9	23.1			Operating Expenses	28.5	28.7
		3.1	3.4			Operating Profit	4.3	6.2
		.9	-.1			All Other Expenses (net)	1.1	1.0
		2.2	3.4			Profit Before Taxes	3.2	5.2
						RATIOS		
		3.1	7.1				3.7	3.0
		1.9	2.6			Current	1.8	1.7
		1.6	1.6				1.3	1.2
		1.8	3.9				2.1	1.6
		.7	1.2			Quick	1.0	.8
		.5	.6				.5	.5
		29 12.4	**21** 17.5				**25** 14.8	**24** 15.2
		45 8.1	**43** 8.5			Sales/Receivables	**42** 8.7	**43** 8.4
		74 4.9	**81** 4.5				**66** 5.5	**63** 5.8
		54 6.7	**62** 5.9				**34** 10.7	**45** 8.2
		78 4.7	**104** 3.5			Cost of Sales/Inventory	**63** 5.8	**73** 5.0
		122 3.0	**182** 2.0				**104** 3.5	**114** 3.2
		2 185.6	**13** 28.9				**13** 27.6	**11** 34.6
		22 16.9	**23** 15.7			Cost of Sales/Payables	**29** 12.8	**29** 12.7
		49 7.5	**34** 10.7				**57** 6.4	**45** 8.1
		3.8	2.0				4.0	4.0
		6.5	3.1			Sales/Working Capital	6.7	8.2
		9.9	10.9				17.9	18.9
		14.8	24.9				15.7	24.3
		3.1	(12) 12.3			EBIT/Interest	(89) 4.0	(96) 5.0
		1.1	2.5				1.1	1.4
							20.3	20.0
						Net Profit + Depr., Dep., Amort./Cur. Mat. L/T/D	(19) 2.5	(17) 8.5
							-.2	2.1
		.1	.0				.0	.0
		.2	.2			Fixed/Worth	.2	.2
		.4	.3				.6	.8
		.5	.2				.5	.7
		.8	.9			Debt/Worth	1.3	1.5
		2.5	6.0				4.6	5.8
		20.1	26.3				51.3	54.4
		5.2	(11) 14.6			% Profit Before Taxes/Tangible Net Worth	(86) 19.9	(89) 22.2
		1.5	7.5				2.5	6.0
		10.1	11.1				14.5	20.3
		2.9	6.2			% Profit Before Taxes/Total Assets	6.3	10.1
		.5	2.3				.2	1.5
		180.3	93.2				165.9	163.3
		33.7	33.6			Sales/Net Fixed Assets	48.8	54.1
		11.0	17.8				12.8	15.9
		3.4	2.5				3.3	3.3
		2.2	1.7			Sales/Total Assets	2.5	2.3
		1.5	1.3				1.7	1.8
		.3	.4				.3	.3
		(10) .6	(12) .9			% Depr., Dep., Amort./Sales	(83) .7	(80) .7
		1.5	1.1				1.4	1.4
							1.9	1.9
						% Officers', Directors' Owners' Comp/Sales	(38) 4.0	(41) 3.7
							6.7	6.1
7706M	25079M	143557M	470112M	964453M	2265490M	Net Sales ($)	5836171M	6953784M
1093M	7390M	58806M	252326M	555366M	1070013M	Total Assets ($)	2880974M	3427791M

M = $ thousand MM = $ million

See Pages 9 through 22 for Explanation of Ratios and Data

Comparative Historical Data				Current Data Sorted by Sales					
			Type of Statement						
13	21	13	Unqualified				1	4	8
25	14	14	Reviewed		1	1	4	2	6
4	3	4	Compiled		2		2		
9	7	4	Tax Returns		3	1			
29	25	17	Other	2	1		1	3	10
4/1/11-3/31/12	**4/1/12-3/31/13**	**4/1/13-3/31/14**			**6 (4/1-9/30/13)**		**46 (10/1/13-3/31/14)**		
ALL	**ALL**	**ALL**		**0-1MM**	**1-3MM**	**3-5MM**	**5-10MM**	**10-25MM**	**25MM & OVER**
80	70	52	**NUMBER OF STATEMENTS**	2	7	2	8	9	24
%	%	%	**ASSETS**	%	%	%	%	%	%
9.2	11.4	9.4	Cash & Equivalents						12.6
28.8	25.8	24.0	Trade Receivables (net)						22.1
37.6	37.7	40.7	Inventory						33.5
4.0	4.7	5.4	All Other Current						7.2
79.7	79.7	79.4	Total Current						75.3
10.0	10.2	11.1	Fixed Assets (net)						10.3
4.6	6.6	4.8	Intangibles (net)						9.8
5.6	3.6	4.7	All Other Non-Current						4.5
100.0	100.0	100.0	Total						100.0
			LIABILITIES						
12.9	15.1	16.1	Notes Payable-Short Term						13.5
2.5	2.3	1.3	Cur. Mat.-L.T.D.						1.3
17.0	16.6	14.4	Trade Payables						11.7
.1	.2	.1	Income Taxes Payable						.1
8.5	10.3	8.4	All Other Current						10.9
41.0	44.4	40.2	Total Current						37.6
9.3	6.6	9.4	Long-Term Debt						9.0
.4	.6	.1	Deferred Taxes						.3
13.0	8.4	8.2	All Other Non-Current						7.2
36.3	39.9	42.0	Net Worth						46.0
100.0	100.0	100.0	Total Liabilties & Net Worth						100.0
			INCOME DATA						
100.0	100.0	100.0	Net Sales						100.0
33.8	32.8	28.2	Gross Profit						26.6
27.4	27.5	25.3	Operating Expenses						23.3
6.4	5.3	2.9	Operating Profit						3.3
1.7	.8	.6	All Other Expenses (net)						.8
4.7	4.6	2.3	Profit Before Taxes						2.5
			RATIOS						
4.2	3.1	3.1							4.4
2.0	2.1	2.1	Current						2.2
1.4	1.4	1.5							1.4
1.6	1.6	1.6							2.3
.9	.9	.8	Quick						.8
.5	.5	.5							.5
24 14.9	**24** 15.4	**20** 18.0							**23** 15.7
51 7.2	**41** 9.0	**40** 9.1	Sales/Receivables						**37** 9.9
69 5.3	**68** 5.4	**61** 6.0							**59** 6.2
51 7.2	**56** 6.5	**58** 6.3							**58** 6.3
87 4.2	**99** 3.7	**85** 4.3	Cost of Sales/Inventory						**78** 4.7
159 2.3	**182** 2.0	**146** 2.5							**122** 3.0
13 27.1	**18** 20.7	**15** 25.0							**16** 22.4
31 11.8	**27** 13.5	**24** 15.3	Cost of Sales/Payables						**29** 12.4
54 6.7	**40** 9.1	**46** 8.0							**48** 7.6
3.2	2.7	3.1							3.0
5.5	6.2	6.4	Sales/Working Capital						6.8
11.9	12.8	10.7							10.7
19.7	19.3	18.0							21.4
(67) 3.7	(58) 4.1	(46) 5.3	EBIT/Interest						(21) 10.9
1.6	1.4	1.1							1.1
	30.3								
	(11) 4.4		Net Profit + Depr., Dep., Amort./Cur. Mat. L/T/D						
	1.4								
.0	.1	.1							.1
.2	.2	.2	Fixed/Worth						.4
.7	.9	.8							.6
.6	.6	.5							.3
1.6	1.5	1.3	Debt/Worth						1.2
5.7	9.0	6.3							8.2
41.8	65.9	40.5							39.5
(69) 16.3	(60) 16.0	(43) 14.6	% Profit Before Taxes/Tangible Net Worth						(19) 24.9
3.8	2.7	4.0							10.1
14.2	15.4	13.3							15.3
6.2	5.8	5.6	% Profit Before Taxes/Total Assets						6.9
1.1	1.1	.7							1.3
101.2	98.3	125.0							75.1
36.4	37.8	38.1	Sales/Net Fixed Assets						35.1
11.7	11.9	13.1							11.8
3.0	3.0	3.2							2.7
2.2	1.8	2.3	Sales/Total Assets						2.2
1.5	1.3	1.4							1.5
.3	.4	.4							.4
(64) .8	(56) .9	(40) .9	% Depr., Dep., Amort./Sales						(19) 1.1
1.5	1.8	1.7							1.7
1.9	1.3	1.3							
(26) 3.5	(20) 3.7	(14) 2.4	% Officers', Directors' Owners' Comp/Sales						
5.5	5.9	5.2							
5304318M	**3783631M**	**3876397M**	Net Sales ($)	**1512M**	**15724M**	**7811M**	**58835M**	**153666M**	**3638849M**
2857225M	**2008951M**	**1944994M**	Total Assets ($)	**440M**	**7905M**	**2229M**	**22083M**	**103025M**	**1809312M**

M = $ thousand MM = $ million

See Pages 9 through 22 for Explanation of Ratios and Data

Current Data Sorted by Assets							Comparative Historical Data	
						Type of Statement		
		2	1	5		Unqualified	19	16
	1	9	1	1		Reviewed	11	23
	1	4				Compiled	3	4
2	1	1				Tax Returns	5	8
	4	10	4	2	2	Other	28	27
	7 (4/1-9/30/13)		44 (10/1/13-3/31/14)				4/1/09-3/31/10	4/1/10-3/31/11
0-500M	500M-2MM	2-10MM	10-50MM	50-100MM	100-250MM		ALL	ALL
2	7	26	6	8	2	NUMBER OF STATEMENTS	66	78
%	%	%	%	%	%	**ASSETS**	%	%
		7.8				Cash & Equivalents	5.3	5.5
		21.5				Trade Receivables (net)	26.3	22.8
		46.0				Inventory	42.3	44.0
		9.2				All Other Current	3.0	6.2
		84.5				Total Current	76.9	78.5
		8.9				Fixed Assets (net)	10.2	9.1
		1.8				Intangibles (net)	5.5	4.4
		4.8				All Other Non-Current	7.5	8.1
		100.0				Total	100.0	100.0
						LIABILITIES		
		17.8				Notes Payable-Short Term	15.9	19.1
		1.7				Cur. Mat.-L.T.D.	6.5	1.9
		21.5				Trade Payables	14.8	17.9
		.0				Income Taxes Payable	.6	.2
		6.7				All Other Current	14.0	9.1
		47.8				Total Current	51.7	48.2
		2.6				Long-Term Debt	12.3	6.4
		.2				Deferred Taxes	.3	.7
		2.7				All Other Non-Current	6.0	6.9
		46.7				Net Worth	29.7	37.8
		100.0				Total Liabilties & Net Worth	100.0	100.0
						INCOME DATA		
		100.0				Net Sales	100.0	100.0
		28.1				Gross Profit	32.3	33.3
		26.2				Operating Expenses	29.4	30.3
		1.9				Operating Profit	2.8	3.0
		.6				All Other Expenses (net)	2.1	.9
		1.3				Profit Before Taxes	.7	2.1
						RATIOS		
		2.5					3.1	3.0
		1.8				Current	2.0	1.7
		1.4					1.3	1.2
		1.1					1.4	1.3
		.7				Quick	.8	.6
		.3					.3	.2
		11 32.1					**23** 15.6	**10** 37.6
		28 13.1				Sales/Receivables	**44** 8.3	**38** 9.6
		43 8.4					**73** 5.0	**58** 6.3
		40 9.2					**62** 5.9	**61** 6.0
		94 3.9				Cost of Sales/Inventory	**101** 3.6	**111** 3.3
		182 2.0					**166** 2.2	**159** 2.3
		23 16.2					**15** 24.0	**11** 31.8
		33 11.1				Cost of Sales/Payables	**26** 14.1	**27** 13.5
		52 7.0					**41** 8.9	**53** 6.9
		3.6					4.0	4.0
		5.4				Sales/Working Capital	6.0	6.6
		20.5					13.8	23.0
		8.1					6.9	7.4
		(23) 4.2				EBIT/Interest	(64) 2.1	(73) 3.5
		1.2					.5	.8
							25.6	23.8
						Net Profit + Depr., Dep., Amort./Cur. Mat. L/T/D	(14) 4.5	(14) 7.0
							1.6	3.6
		.0					.1	.1
		.1				Fixed/Worth	.2	.1
		.3					.8	1.0
		.6					.8	.7
		1.2				Debt/Worth	1.7	1.8
		1.8					10.8	6.6
		83.0					28.0	42.2
		(25) 14.8				% Profit Before Taxes/Tangible Net Worth	(56) 7.4	(69) 15.0
		.5					-4.1	2.1
		18.3					9.1	13.4
		5.9				% Profit Before Taxes/Total Assets	2.5	5.5
		.0					-2.3	.0
		332.9					91.7	121.8
		41.2				Sales/Net Fixed Assets	32.5	48.7
		15.1					11.8	21.2
		3.7					2.8	3.1
		2.2				Sales/Total Assets	2.0	2.2
		1.6					1.5	1.5
		.2					.4	.3
		(17) .3				% Depr., Dep., Amort./Sales	(53) .9	(57) .6
		1.0					1.4	1.3
							2.5	1.6
						% Officers', Directors' Owners' Comp/Sales	(17) 5.2	(21) 3.5
							7.5	6.0
2358M	28364M	351127M	313954M	973945M	177834M	Net Sales ($)	4905579M	4429643M
504M	8360M	126047M	122611M	553960M	226882M	Total Assets ($)	2357603M	2317142M

M = $ thousand MM = $ million

See Pages 9 through 22 for Explanation of Ratios and Data

Comparative Historical Data				Current Data Sorted by Sales					
			Type of Statement						
13	11	8	Unqualified					2	6
20	20	12	Reviewed		1		3	5	3
1	3	5	Compiled				4		1
9	5	4	Tax Returns	1	2		1		
36	27	22	Other		2	3	5	4	8
4/1/11-3/31/12 ALL	**4/1/12-3/31/13 ALL**	**4/1/13-3/31/14 ALL**		**7 (4/1-9/30/13)**			**44 (10/1/13-3/31/14)**		
				0-1MM	**1-3MM**	**3-5MM**	**5-10MM**	**10-25MM**	**25MM & OVER**
79	66	51	**NUMBER OF STATEMENTS**	1	5	3	13	11	18
%	%	%	**ASSETS**	%	%	%	%	%	%
9.2	8.8	8.9	Cash & Equivalents				9.7	5.3	10.2
20.3	20.4	22.3	Trade Receivables (net)				25.6	19.1	27.5
42.3	44.6	43.7	Inventory				47.1	45.9	38.7
5.9	6.2	6.0	All Other Current				7.9	6.6	6.0
77.7	80.0	80.9	Total Current				90.3	76.9	82.4
10.6	9.2	8.9	Fixed Assets (net)				6.1	14.8	6.5
4.6	4.7	2.8	Intangibles (net)				.4	3.9	5.3
7.1	6.2	7.4	All Other Non-Current				3.1	4.4	5.8
100.0	100.0	100.0	Total				100.0	100.0	100.0
			LIABILITIES						
19.9	18.8	16.7	Notes Payable-Short Term				29.6	5.4	17.5
2.7	.9	2.7	Cur. Mat.-L.T.D.				2.5	1.6	3.0
13.8	13.3	17.2	Trade Payables				16.1	26.8	12.9
.1	.1	.0	Income Taxes Payable				.1	.0	.1
7.9	14.1	8.0	All Other Current				7.9	7.8	8.3
44.4	47.2	44.7	Total Current				56.2	41.5	41.8
8.2	6.7	6.1	Long-Term Debt				3.6	4.2	2.7
.5	.4	.2	Deferred Taxes				.0	.5	.4
7.0	6.5	5.0	All Other Non-Current				1.2	.8	7.7
39.9	39.1	44.0	Net Worth				39.0	53.0	47.4
100.0	100.0	100.0	Total Liabilties & Net Worth				100.0	100.0	100.0
			INCOME DATA						
100.0	100.0	100.0	Net Sales				100.0	100.0	100.0
33.7	30.8	30.9	Gross Profit				31.3	28.2	24.7
29.8	26.1	27.5	Operating Expenses				33.0	22.6	18.6
4.0	4.8	3.4	Operating Profit				-1.7	5.7	6.1
.8	1.5	.6	All Other Expenses (net)				1.0	.2	.5
3.2	3.3	2.8	Profit Before Taxes				-2.7	5.4	5.6
			RATIOS						
3.6	3.7	2.6					2.0	2.6	4.2
2.1	2.1	1.7	Current				1.6	1.8	1.8
1.3	1.3	1.4					1.4	1.4	1.5
1.4	1.3	1.2					1.0	1.0	1.6
.7	.7	.7	Quick				.7	.4	1.0
.4	.3	.3					.3	.1	.4
8 44.7	**17** 21.3	**12** 30.7					**12** 29.3	**0** 999.8	**32** 11.3
39 9.4	**39** 9.4	**34** 10.7	Sales/Receivables				**29** 12.8	**22** 16.7	**46** 8.0
63 5.8	**57** 6.4	**56** 6.5					**56** 6.5	**41** 8.8	**69** 5.3
64 5.7	**58** 6.3	**54** 6.7					**46** 7.9	**37** 9.9	**60** 6.1
118 3.1	**118** 3.1	**104** 3.5	Cost of Sales/Inventory				**135** 2.7	**64** 5.7	**99** 3.7
192 1.9	**215** 1.7	**182** 2.0					**192** 1.9	**159** 2.3	**146** 2.5
11 32.9	**10** 35.2	**16** 22.5					**18** 20.3	**23** 15.6	**15** 25.1
28 13.1	**21** 17.7	**28** 13.1	Cost of Sales/Payables				**32** 11.5	**40** 9.1	**26** 14.2
43 8.4	**35** 10.4	**41** 8.9					**47** 7.7	**62** 5.9	**29** 12.5
2.9	3.2	3.6					3.8	3.6	2.4
5.2	5.0	5.8	Sales/Working Capital				6.0	8.4	4.2
17.6	14.3	17.7					18.8	34.4	13.6
14.3	10.0	13.4					4.2	47.8	65.6
(71) 4.5	(61) 4.2	(45) 5.2	EBIT/Interest				3.0	(10) 9.0	(14) 11.2
1.7	1.3	1.3					-1.7	5.5	3.1
11.6	5.3								
(15) 7.0	(15) 2.5		Net Profit + Depr., Dep., Amort./Cur. Mat. L/T/D						
.6	1.3								
.0	.0	.0					.0	.1	.0
.2	.2	.1	Fixed/Worth				.1	.2	.2
.9	.4	.4					.3	.7	.3
.6	.7	.6					.9	.4	.7
1.5	1.5	1.3	Debt/Worth				1.5	.6	1.4
5.0	5.1	2.2					3.2	1.3	2.3
49.8	43.8	60.5					26.8	91.0	73.2
(68) 15.8	(60) 13.3	(47) 22.6	% Profit Before Taxes/Tangible Net Worth				(12) 4.4	50.3	(17) 30.6
4.3	4.2	3.3					-30.9	2.2	14.9
14.5	13.1	16.8					8.2	23.2	15.2
6.3	4.1	7.5	% Profit Before Taxes/Total Assets				1.7	14.1	8.9
1.9	1.2	1.4					-14.3	1.6	4.7
111.3	137.0	210.6					355.1	134.1	210.9
35.8	30.4	40.1	Sales/Net Fixed Assets				53.8	39.0	31.9
11.5	14.2	14.8					21.5	15.0	12.5
2.8	2.6	3.5					3.5	4.7	3.4
1.9	2.1	2.2	Sales/Total Assets				1.9	3.1	1.9
1.3	1.4	1.6					1.6	2.2	1.2
.3	.5	.2							.4
(58) .8	(49) 1.0	(34) .6	% Depr., Dep., Amort./Sales						(15) .6
1.8	1.7	1.1							1.5
1.8	2.3	1.2							
(17) 4.9	(12) 4.6	(14) 2.3	% Officers', Directors' Owners' Comp/Sales						
10.8	8.8	6.4							
3445204M	**3180580M**	**1847582M**	Net Sales ($)	**936M**	**11212M**	**11576M**	**96747M**	**182639M**	**1544472M**
2120139M	**1855902M**	**1038364M**	Total Assets ($)	**449M**	**5287M**	**6677M**	**46665M**	**60424M**	**918862M**

M = $ thousand MM = $ million

See Pages 9 through 22 for Explanation of Ratios and Data

Current Data Sorted by Assets / Comparative Historical Data

0-500M	500M-2MM	2-10MM	10-50MM	50-100MM	100-250MM		4/1/09-3/31/10 ALL	4/1/10-3/31/11 ALL
						Type of Statement		
	1		16	5	3	Unqualified	31	47
	2	29	15			Reviewed	31	83
	2	3			1	Compiled	9	8
2	3	1				Tax Returns	8	11
1	4	15	16	2	5	Other	31	47
22 (4/1-9/30/13)			104 (10/1/13-3/31/14)					
3	12	48	47	7	9	**NUMBER OF STATEMENTS**	110	196
%	%	%	%	%	%	**ASSETS**	%	%
	15.3	9.1	11.6			Cash & Equivalents	15.2	11.0
	37.0	29.0	24.2			Trade Receivables (net)	28.3	22.9
	29.8	38.3	34.3			Inventory	32.8	38.3
	3.2	6.9	8.0			All Other Current	4.0	6.8
	85.3	83.3	78.0			Total Current	80.3	79.1
	12.6	7.3	6.5			Fixed Assets (net)	9.7	8.3
	.2	6.5	10.9			Intangibles (net)	4.9	6.9
	1.9	2.9	4.6			All Other Non-Current	5.1	5.8
	100.0	100.0	100.0			Total	100.0	100.0
						LIABILITIES		
	18.1	12.2	24.0			Notes Payable-Short Term	12.1	11.6
	.1	.6	3.0			Cur. Mat.-L.T.D.	3.6	1.9
	25.3	29.3	21.6			Trade Payables	19.8	26.1
	.0	.0	.1			Income Taxes Payable	.4	.4
	27.9	10.7	10.6			All Other Current	9.5	11.5
	71.5	52.8	59.3			Total Current	45.5	51.5
	1.3	2.0	4.1			Long-Term Debt	7.8	4.3
	.0	.0	.6			Deferred Taxes	.2	.2
	14.0	4.2	3.2			All Other Non-Current	8.2	6.8
	13.2	41.0	32.9			Net Worth	38.4	37.2
	100.0	100.0	100.0			Total Liabilties & Net Worth	100.0	100.0
						INCOME DATA		
	100.0	100.0	100.0			Net Sales	100.0	100.0
	34.5	31.3	30.7			Gross Profit	33.0	32.9
	31.1	27.3	27.6			Operating Expenses	28.6	28.9
	3.4	4.0	3.1			Operating Profit	4.4	4.0
	.6	.4	.7			All Other Expenses (net)	1.0	.8
	2.8	3.6	2.4			Profit Before Taxes	3.4	3.2
						RATIOS		
	3.1	2.5	2.0				3.2	2.5
	2.1	1.5	1.2			Current	1.9	1.6
	1.1	1.2	1.1				1.4	1.2
	2.9	1.1	.9				1.8	1.3
	1.6	.6	.6			Quick	.9	.7
	.4	.5	.3				.6	.3
	1 498.2	8 47.9	6 58.1				19 18.9	5 75.0
	25 14.4	29 12.6	35 10.5			Sales/Receivables	38 9.6	22 16.6
	49 7.4	50 7.3	61 6.0				53 6.9	46 8.0
	0 UND	38 9.6	37 9.8				31 11.6	29 12.7
	35 10.4	56 6.5	64 5.7			Cost of Sales/Inventory	61 6.0	60 6.1
	63 5.8	96 3.8	94 3.9				104 3.5	99 3.7
	4 83.5	26 14.0	19 18.9				17 21.0	20 18.3
	28 13.1	37 9.9	31 11.7			Cost of Sales/Payables	30 12.3	31 11.7
	42 8.7	60 6.1	51 7.1				48 7.6	51 7.2
	6.8	6.0	6.7				4.4	5.5
	16.6	13.3	18.0			Sales/Working Capital	7.7	11.9
	107.1	32.8	116.0				17.9	40.0
		25.2	8.8				12.5	12.9
		(40) 6.1	(42) 3.9			EBIT/Interest	(92) 3.1	(173) 3.5
		1.7	.7				1.3	1.4
			7.2				91.9	18.7
			(13) .6			Net Profit + Depr., Dep., Amort./Cur. Mat. L/T/D	(20) 3.9	(35) 3.6
			-1.7				.3	1.2
	.0	.0	.1				.0	.0
	.1	.1	.2			Fixed/Worth	.2	.2
	.5	.4	1.2				.6	.7
	.4	.7	.9				.6	.8
	3.2	1.8	2.5			Debt/Worth	1.4	1.8
	NM	5.6	13.9				4.9	6.4
		60.3	46.2				43.8	66.9
		(43) 33.4	(38) 20.7			% Profit Before Taxes/Tangible Net Worth	(94) 17.5	(167) 25.1
		3.1	2.9				2.9	5.5
	40.2	22.9	13.7				17.0	19.8
	15.6	10.8	4.4			% Profit Before Taxes/Total Assets	6.4	7.4
	5.7	1.1	.2				.9	1.2
	UND	696.3	199.1				190.9	237.5
	526.5	153.8	104.3			Sales/Net Fixed Assets	51.5	85.3
	36.6	31.1	23.1				15.9	30.2
	5.8	5.4	4.4				3.9	5.1
	5.2	3.4	2.8			Sales/Total Assets	2.6	3.3
	3.6	2.1	1.9				1.8	2.2
		.1	.1				.2	.1
		(34) .2	(37) .4			% Depr., Dep., Amort./Sales	(83) .5	(149) .4
		.4	1.5				1.1	.8
		1.2	.9				1.0	1.3
		(26) 2.2	(16) 2.1			% Officers', Directors' Owners' Comp/Sales	(50) 2.1	(77) 2.4
		3.4	3.1				4.0	4.6
1294M	64386M	880332M	3058524M	877206M	1979245M	Net Sales ($)	6311362M	9542270M
912M	13439M	225633M	983718M	462407M	1680056M	Total Assets ($)	2857768M	3942667M

M = $ thousand MM = $ million

See Pages 9 through 22 for Explanation of Ratios and Data

Comparative Historical Data | **Current Data Sorted by Sales**

4/1/11-3/31/12 ALL	4/1/12-3/31/13 ALL	4/1/13-3/31/14 ALL		0-1MM	1-3MM	3-5MM	5-10MM	10-25MM	25MM & OVER
			Type of Statement						
30	37	25	Unqualified			1	1		23
50	71	46	Reviewed			1	8	18	19
4	7	6	Compiled				2	2	2
14	10	6	Tax Returns	2		4			
42	38	43	Other	1	1	3	4	12	22
				22 (4/1-9/30/13)			104 (10/1/13-3/31/14)		
140	163	126	**NUMBER OF STATEMENTS**	3	1	9	15	32	66
%	%	%	**ASSETS**	%	%	%	%	%	%
12.5	12.2	10.0	Cash & Equivalents				5.7	11.5	9.0
27.3	26.1	26.7	Trade Receivables (net)				26.4	29.1	24.6
34.2	35.8	34.3	Inventory				45.4	34.8	33.2
5.7	5.2	6.2	All Other Current				7.9	6.2	6.8
79.7	79.3	77.1	Total Current				85.3	81.7	73.7
7.0	6.7	7.5	Fixed Assets (net)				7.1	7.4	6.6
8.0	9.0	11.7	Intangibles (net)				5.2	8.9	16.2
5.2	4.9	3.7	All Other Non-Current				2.5	2.0	3.5
100.0	100.0	100.0	Total				100.0	100.0	100.0
			LIABILITIES						
10.5	12.9	17.2	Notes Payable-Short Term				19.1	9.9	20.9
1.4	.8	1.7	Cur. Mat.-L.T.D.				.9	.6	2.5
24.7	23.5	23.4	Trade Payables				20.5	26.8	22.9
.2	.2	.1	Income Taxes Payable				.1	.0	.1
9.6	12.7	11.5	All Other Current				27.3	7.6	10.3
46.4	50.0	53.9	Total Current				68.0	44.9	56.8
5.2	5.7	5.1	Long-Term Debt				2.0	1.4	8.5
.5	.2	.3	Deferred Taxes				.0	.1	.5
9.1	6.9	4.9	All Other Non-Current				3.0	3.4	3.9
38.9	37.2	35.8	Net Worth				27.0	50.1	30.2
100.0	100.0	100.0	Total Liabilties & Net Worth				100.0	100.0	100.0
			INCOME DATA						
100.0	100.0	100.0	Net Sales				100.0	100.0	100.0
34.8	33.3	33.4	Gross Profit				35.8	31.2	31.8
29.7	29.3	28.7	Operating Expenses				33.0	26.2	27.7
5.0	4.0	4.7	Operating Profit				2.8	5.0	4.1
.7	.9	.8	All Other Expenses (net)				.4	.4	1.2
4.3	3.1	3.9	Profit Before Taxes				2.4	4.6	2.9
			RATIOS						
3.1	3.2	2.5	Current				3.2	2.9	2.0
1.9	1.7	1.5					1.8	1.6	1.4
1.3	1.2	1.1					1.1	1.3	1.1
1.5	1.5	1.1	Quick				1.6	1.1	1.0
1.0	.8	.7					.6	.7	.7
.5	.4	.4					.4	.5	.4
11 34.6	**9** 42.3	**12** 29.4	Sales/Receivables				**14** 25.9	**14** 25.5	**6** 66.1
29 12.8	**28** 13.2	**37** 9.9					**41** 8.9	**25** 14.5	**40** 9.1
52 7.0	**51** 7.1	**55** 6.6					**65** 5.6	**45** 8.1	**57** 6.4
30 12.1	**29** 12.8	**38** 9.7	Cost of Sales/Inventory				**64** 5.7	**35** 10.5	**38** 9.7
58 6.3	**55** 6.6	**64** 5.7					**89** 4.1	**59** 6.2	**63** 5.8
107 3.4	**107** 3.4	**107** 3.4					**130** 2.8	**96** 3.8	**104** 3.5
20 18.2	**19** 19.4	**22** 16.6	Cost of Sales/Payables				**13** 27.4	**23** 15.9	**22** 16.6
33 11.0	**30** 12.3	**36** 10.2					**30** 12.3	**38** 9.6	**32** 11.4
50 7.3	**44** 8.3	**57** 6.4					**61** 6.0	**61** 6.0	**46** 8.0
4.8	5.8	5.8	Sales/Working Capital				4.5	6.7	6.5
7.2	9.9	12.0					7.2	11.2	16.6
20.6	31.2	46.7					32.6	23.6	68.7
17.1	13.6	10.1	EBIT/Interest				16.9	28.8	8.1
(120) 5.3	(139) 4.4	(109) 5.3					(13) 5.2	(25) 7.4	(63) 3.7
2.1	1.9	1.2					2.1	3.0	.8
22.0	46.5	15.1	Net Profit + Depr., Dep., Amort./Cur. Mat. L/T/D						4.7
(24) 5.9	(31) 5.5	(19) .8							(14) .5
2.0	1.5	-3.4							-5.6
.0	.0	.0	Fixed/Worth				.0	.0	.1
.1	.1	.2					.1	.1	.3
.4	.5	.8					.3	.4	NM
.8	.8	.8	Debt/Worth				.6	.6	1.6
1.8	2.0	2.4					2.0	1.7	5.5
4.6	6.2	14.0					10.6	3.1	-11.6
66.6	75.2	67.5	% Profit Before Taxes/Tangible Net Worth				78.4	58.7	68.0
(123) 30.9	(135) 33.2	(100) 33.2					(12) 18.8	(29) 36.9	(48) 24.1
6.5	6.8	3.5					4.6	6.5	2.8
22.0	21.0	18.7	% Profit Before Taxes/Total Assets				15.4	28.4	13.7
8.7	9.1	8.1					5.6	12.1	4.5
2.5	1.8	.5					2.2	.9	-.1
289.0	327.5	414.2	Sales/Net Fixed Assets				999.8	539.7	207.9
78.5	125.2	100.6					91.4	153.8	95.1
34.4	41.2	29.2					35.7	28.2	30.8
4.7	4.9	4.6	Sales/Total Assets				3.8	4.7	4.6
3.0	3.2	2.8					2.5	3.2	2.8
2.0	2.1	1.9					1.9	2.1	1.8
.1	.1	.1	% Depr., Dep., Amort./Sales					.1	.2
(105) .3	(121) .3	(83) .3						(24) .3	(45) .3
.8	.8	1.0						.6	1.1
1.6	1.1	1.1	% Officers', Directors' Owners' Comp/Sales					1.3	.8
(63) 2.8	(61) 2.1	(45) 2.1						(13) 1.8	(23) 1.7
6.2	3.7	3.4						5.1	2.8
7423223M	9509216M	6860987M	Net Sales ($)	1294M	2745M	36910M	107650M	515664M	6196724M
3560306M	4157880M	3366165M	Total Assets ($)	912M	1041M	22695M	45205M	178669M	3117643M

M = $ thousand MM = $ million

See Pages 9 through 22 for Explanation of Ratios and Data

Current Data Sorted by Assets							Comparative Historical Data	
						Type of Statement		
	1	1	6	2		Unqualified	20	15
		5	3			Reviewed	12	13
	2	3				Compiled	7	3
7	7	6				Tax Returns	8	16
1	4	9	9	1	2	Other	14	20
	15 (4/1-9/30/13)		54 (10/1/13-3/31/14)				4/1/09-3/31/10	4/1/10-3/31/11
0-500M	500M-2MM	2-10MM	10-50MM	50-100MM	100-250MM		ALL	ALL
8	14	24	18	3	2	**NUMBER OF STATEMENTS**	61	67
%	%	%	%	%	%	**ASSETS**	%	%
	8.1	8.8	3.8			Cash & Equivalents	10.4	8.4
	29.4	30.6	22.0			Trade Receivables (net)	26.0	24.0
	35.1	31.6	48.0			Inventory	37.4	40.0
	3.0	5.3	6.1			All Other Current	2.8	4.1
	75.7	76.3	79.9			Total Current	76.7	76.5
	12.4	13.4	9.9			Fixed Assets (net)	11.5	12.6
	3.6	.9	5.2			Intangibles (net)	4.5	4.8
	8.3	9.4	5.1			All Other Non-Current	7.3	6.2
	100.0	100.0	100.0			Total	100.0	100.0
						LIABILITIES		
	13.5	15.2	15.6			Notes Payable-Short Term	14.8	17.5
	1.3	1.6	.5			Cur. Mat.-L.T.D.	2.0	4.1
	18.5	17.8	12.9			Trade Payables	15.9	14.5
	.0	.3	.1			Income Taxes Payable	.1	.1
	7.9	12.1	8.2			All Other Current	10.1	8.8
	41.2	47.2	37.3			Total Current	42.9	45.0
	9.5	9.1	3.5			Long-Term Debt	7.7	11.6
	.0	.4	.0			Deferred Taxes	.5	.1
	13.8	6.3	3.3			All Other Non-Current	5.7	9.1
	35.4	37.0	56.0			Net Worth	43.3	34.1
	100.0	100.0	100.0			Total Liabilties & Net Worth	100.0	100.0
						INCOME DATA		
	100.0	100.0	100.0			Net Sales	100.0	100.0
	34.2	35.5	34.3			Gross Profit	33.7	35.4
	32.2	31.3	25.6			Operating Expenses	28.2	31.2
	2.1	4.2	8.8			Operating Profit	5.5	4.2
	.6	1.0	.8			All Other Expenses (net)	.8	.5
	1.5	3.2	8.0			Profit Before Taxes	4.7	3.7
						RATIOS		
	3.2	2.7	3.2				4.4	3.5
	2.0	1.7	2.2			Current	1.8	1.8
	1.2	1.3	1.5				1.4	1.3
	1.7	1.5	1.2				2.0	1.2
	.9	.7	.7			Quick	1.0	.7
	.5	.4	.4				.4	.4
	21 17.1	**18** 20.1	**34** 10.8				**21** 17.2	**23** 16.1
	30 12.1	**46** 7.9	**51** 7.1			Sales/Receivables	**38** 9.6	**38** 9.7
	41 8.8	**69** 5.3	**63** 5.8				**49** 7.4	**52** 7.0
	18 20.8	**29** 12.6	**104** 3.5				**49** 7.5	**55** 6.6
	60 6.1	**66** 5.5	**152** 2.4			Cost of Sales/Inventory	**89** 4.1	**104** 3.5
	135 2.7	**107** 3.4	**243** 1.5				**126** 2.9	**159** 2.3
	12 31.2	**18** 20.6	**23** 16.1				**16** 22.6	**10** 35.4
	20 18.6	**40** 9.2	**39** 9.3			Cost of Sales/Payables	**28** 13.0	**29** 12.6
	39 9.4	**62** 5.9	**52** 7.0				**39** 9.3	**50** 7.3
	4.6	6.0	2.7				3.4	3.7
	11.9	8.7	4.0			Sales/Working Capital	6.2	6.3
	38.6	18.8	5.6				14.6	17.7
	11.3	9.3	64.0				21.4	16.6
	(11) 5.5	(21) 4.7	(16) 8.0			EBIT/Interest	(53) 4.9	(62) 5.7
	1.3	1.9	2.7				1.6	2.3
								30.5
						Net Profit + Depr., Dep., Amort./Cur. Mat. L/T/D		(14) 5.0
								1.4
	.1	.1	.1				.1	.1
	.1	.3	.2			Fixed/Worth	.2	.2
	3.0	.6	.3				.5	.8
	.7	.8	.4				.3	.6
	1.8	1.9	.7			Debt/Worth	1.3	1.8
	19.2	3.9	2.4				2.8	5.6
	77.0	37.8	46.4				36.7	42.0
	(12) 31.3	(23) 11.1	16.3			% Profit Before Taxes/Tangible Net Worth	(52) 24.0	(55) 18.9
	-18.4	2.4	6.3				4.3	7.4
	25.8	12.5	13.3				19.4	15.3
	7.8	4.2	7.8			% Profit Before Taxes/Total Assets	9.3	7.9
	-1.9	1.4	2.9				.9	2.3
	61.8	103.9	50.4				102.0	71.0
	31.1	34.6	33.2			Sales/Net Fixed Assets	35.6	30.2
	12.6	13.5	11.8				12.5	12.5
	4.8	3.1	2.6				3.4	2.9
	3.1	2.4	1.9			Sales/Total Assets	2.1	2.3
	1.9	1.7	1.4				1.5	1.8
	.2	.3	.4				.3	.3
	(10) .5	(18) .6	(17) .7			% Depr., Dep., Amort./Sales	(44) .9	(50) .7
	.9	1.3	1.7				1.6	1.3
		1.6					1.9	1.9
		(12) 2.7				% Officers', Directors' Owners' Comp/Sales	(30) 3.8	(37) 3.1
		3.5					5.3	6.0
8993M	49790M	317673M	607988M	515472M	439993M	Net Sales ($)	2463707M	2410511M
2163M	15726M	125867M	360939M	245419M	305081M	Total Assets ($)	1462280M	1181528M

M = $ thousand MM = $ million

See Pages 9 through 22 for Explanation of Ratios and Data

Comparative Historical Data				Current Data Sorted by Sales					
14	14	10	**Type of Statement** Unqualified		1			4	5
19	11	8	Reviewed				1	5	2
5	7	5	Compiled		1	2	1	1	
13	17	20	Tax Returns	3	7	3	4	2	1
33	26	26	Other	1	3	2	4	7	9
				15 (4/1-9/30/13)			54 (10/1/13-3/31/14)		
4/1/11-3/31/12 ALL	**4/1/12-3/31/13 ALL**	**4/1/13-3/31/14 ALL**		**0-1MM**	**1-3MM**	**3-5MM**	**5-10MM**	**10-25MM**	**25MM & OVER**
84	75	69	**NUMBER OF STATEMENTS**	4	12	7	10	19	17
%	%	%	**ASSETS**	%	%	%	%	%	%
7.9	7.2	9.6	Cash & Equivalents		17.6		12.9	7.3	4.2
25.0	24.3	25.7	Trade Receivables (net)		19.3		32.1	30.5	23.6
40.5	41.0	36.7	Inventory		35.9		29.6	38.2	47.1
3.6	3.2	4.7	All Other Current		2.0		6.0	7.9	3.2
77.0	75.6	76.6	Total Current		74.8		80.6	83.9	78.1
10.7	13.2	11.9	Fixed Assets (net)		9.6		10.7	9.1	9.6
3.9	4.6	2.8	Intangibles (net)		2.0		.5	1.2	5.4
8.4	6.5	8.7	All Other Non-Current		13.6		8.2	5.8	6.9
100.0	100.0	100.0	Total		100.0		100.0	100.0	100.0
			LIABILITIES						
13.7	14.3	13.4	Notes Payable-Short Term		14.3		8.1	18.8	16.0
2.9	2.2	1.0	Cur. Mat.-L.T.D.		.9		1.7	1.2	.6
17.1	17.1	16.8	Trade Payables		13.0		17.4	17.1	17.2
.2	.1	.1	Income Taxes Payable		.0		.0	.4	.1
10.6	11.5	11.4	All Other Current		16.6		13.2	9.3	6.7
44.5	45.2	42.8	Total Current		44.9		40.3	46.9	40.5
9.6	11.8	6.9	Long-Term Debt		3.0		9.3	4.4	2.6
.3	.3	.2	Deferred Taxes		.0		.1	.2	.3
5.3	7.6	7.9	All Other Non-Current		14.4		2.2	8.7	4.5
40.3	35.2	42.3	Net Worth		37.7		48.1	39.7	52.1
100.0	100.0	100.0	Total Liabilties & Net Worth		100.0		100.0	100.0	100.0
			INCOME DATA						
100.0	100.0	100.0	Net Sales		100.0		100.0	100.0	100.0
37.6	35.2	34.9	Gross Profit		34.4		42.3	30.1	32.5
31.3	30.9	29.8	Operating Expenses		26.8		40.1	28.1	25.6
6.3	4.3	5.1	Operating Profit		7.6		2.3	2.0	6.9
.6	.9	.8	All Other Expenses (net)		1.0		.2	1.1	.4
5.7	3.3	4.3	Profit Before Taxes		6.6		2.0	.9	6.5
			RATIOS						
3.3	3.0	2.9			3.1		3.4	3.1	2.8
1.8	2.0	2.0	Current		2.0		2.1	2.0	2.2
1.4	1.4	1.3			1.0		1.3	1.3	1.5
1.4	1.7	1.4			1.7		1.6	1.4	.9
.7	(74) .7	.7	Quick		.6		1.0	.8	.7
.4	.4	.4			.3		.5	.4	.5
20 17.9	**23** 16.2	**19** 18.8			**8** 46.6		**5** 77.9	**31** 11.6	**33** 11.2
36 10.2	**37** 9.8	**38** 9.6	Sales/Receivables		**30** 12.0		**48** 7.6	**42** 8.6	**45** 8.1
51 7.2	**49** 7.4	**59** 6.2			**51** 7.2		**72** 5.1	**66** 5.5	**59** 6.2
53 6.9	**46** 8.0	**35** 10.4			**4** 83.9		**25** 14.7	**36** 10.2	**68** 5.4
94 3.9	**104** 3.5	**89** 4.1	Cost of Sales/Inventory		**68** 5.4		**79** 4.6	**74** 4.9	**140** 2.6
203 1.8	**174** 2.1	**166** 2.2			**228** 1.6		**146** 2.5	**152** 2.4	**192** 1.9
19 19.4	**16** 22.2	**17** 21.8			**0** UND		**3** 115.7	**23** 15.7	**23** 16.2
31 11.9	**35** 10.4	**33** 11.0	Cost of Sales/Payables		**22** 16.6		**19** 19.5	**38** 9.5	**46** 8.0
57 6.4	**62** 5.9	**52** 7.0			**37** 9.9		**101** 3.6	**50** 7.3	**52** 7.0
3.9	3.7	3.7			2.5		3.0	3.6	3.4
6.2	7.7	6.6	Sales/Working Capital		12.2		6.5	6.7	4.4
14.8	15.0	16.8			NM		17.6	13.3	11.1
16.8	14.6	11.7						27.7	42.6
(76) 4.8	(68) 5.3	(58) 6.2	EBIT/Interest					(18) 3.6	(16) 9.9
2.1	1.9	2.0						.9	4.9
21.2	18.3								
(17) 4.1	(12) 4.9		Net Profit + Depr., Dep., Amort./Cur. Mat. L/T/D						
1.6	1.4								
.1	.1	.1			.0		.0	.0	.1
.2	.2	.2	Fixed/Worth		.1		.2	.2	.2
.6	.7	.6			.7		.4	.3	.3
.7	.7	.6			.6		.6	.4	.5
1.4	1.8	1.2	Debt/Worth		1.3		.9	1.3	1.0
3.9	5.0	3.8			25.1		3.3	3.6	2.1
53.8	39.3	51.0			42.0		20.1	56.5	56.8
(74) 28.1	(65) 18.6	(64) 15.8	% Profit Before Taxes/Tangible Net Worth		(10) 11.0		10.4	(18) 12.8	22.7
12.7	7.4	3.8			-34.3		2.2	-3.5	8.2
20.4	12.6	16.7			12.9		5.6	10.9	26.9
9.1	6.9	5.5	% Profit Before Taxes/Total Assets		2.5		4.1	7.0	7.2
2.5	2.3	1.3			-7.6		1.4	1.1	4.1
90.9	97.6	90.3			UND		314.3	134.1	42.3
35.7	37.7	31.3	Sales/Net Fixed Assets		31.1		56.0	48.1	28.2
13.5	11.8	13.5			13.4		11.3	18.3	13.4
3.1	2.9	3.2			5.9		2.7	3.1	2.8
2.1	2.1	2.2	Sales/Total Assets		2.8		2.4	2.0	2.0
1.6	1.6	1.6			1.2		1.6	1.7	1.5
.3	.3	.3						.3	.4
(63) .6	(59) .7	(54) .7	% Depr., Dep., Amort./Sales					(14) .6	.8
1.6	1.8	1.3						1.3	1.6
1.7	1.8	1.7							
(32) 2.5	(28) 2.8	(36) 3.1	% Officers', Directors' Owners' Comp/Sales						
3.7	4.7	5.6							
2501680M	2213614M	1939909M	Net Sales ($)	2722M	22019M	27052M	73649M	309075M	1505392M
1240245M	1082519M	1055195M	Total Assets ($)	1072M	42291M	13773M	34304M	153509M	810246M

M = $ thousand MM = $ million

See Pages 9 through 22 for Explanation of Ratios and Data

Current Data Sorted by Assets							Comparative Historical Data	
						Type of Statement		
			8	3	2	Unqualified	47	44
1	5	11	11		1	Reviewed	33	45
1	4	13	1			Compiled	23	17
14	16	11	1			Tax Returns	31	39
2	16	26	16	6	8	Other	66	81
22 (4/1-9/30/13)			155 (10/1/13-3/31/14)				4/1/09-3/31/10 ALL	4/1/10-3/31/11 ALL
0-500M	500M-2MM	2-10MM	10-50MM	50-100MM	100-250MM			
18	41	61	37	9	11	**NUMBER OF STATEMENTS**	200	226
%	%	%	%	%	%	**ASSETS**	%	%
17.9	10.3	9.6	8.8		6.8	Cash & Equivalents	11.1	10.0
12.9	23.9	20.2	28.8		25.0	Trade Receivables (net)	25.3	24.8
34.3	37.3	33.9	38.9		31.5	Inventory	36.1	39.9
.9	2.1	6.1	2.9		3.4	All Other Current	2.5	3.1
65.9	73.6	69.9	79.4		66.6	Total Current	75.0	77.8
15.6	12.9	17.3	11.2		9.1	Fixed Assets (net)	12.3	11.2
12.4	4.3	5.4	4.2		13.8	Intangibles (net)	6.0	3.7
5.9	9.2	7.5	5.3		10.5	All Other Non-Current	6.7	7.3
100.0	100.0	100.0	100.0		100.0	Total	100.0	100.0
						LIABILITIES		
9.0	14.5	12.5	15.3		8.1	Notes Payable-Short Term	18.3	16.3
.7	2.0	2.3	1.9		.9	Cur. Mat.-L.T.D.	2.4	3.5
13.6	22.3	16.3	13.6		13.7	Trade Payables	15.8	20.6
.0	.1	.0	.5		.3	Income Taxes Payable	.3	.2
11.7	10.7	9.5	8.8		8.1	All Other Current	8.6	9.3
35.0	49.6	40.7	40.1		31.2	Total Current	45.4	50.0
12.8	11.8	9.8	5.2		18.9	Long-Term Debt	12.3	8.7
.0	.1	.1	.0		1.3	Deferred Taxes	.3	.2
19.7	14.5	4.0	4.6		7.5	All Other Non-Current	7.1	7.5
32.5	23.9	45.4	50.1		41.2	Net Worth	35.0	33.6
100.0	100.0	100.0	100.0		100.0	Total Liabilties & Net Worth	100.0	100.0
						INCOME DATA		
100.0	100.0	100.0	100.0		100.0	Net Sales	100.0	100.0
52.3	41.5	37.0	31.6		32.6	Gross Profit	37.6	36.2
45.6	38.5	33.0	25.5		26.2	Operating Expenses	33.1	31.2
6.7	3.1	4.1	6.2		6.4	Operating Profit	4.4	5.0
.5	.8	.9	.8		.8	All Other Expenses (net)	1.2	.7
6.2	2.3	3.2	5.4		5.6	Profit Before Taxes	3.3	4.3
						RATIOS		
6.4	3.0	3.1	3.8		4.6		3.5	3.4
2.1	1.7	1.9	2.1		2.7	Current	1.9	1.8
.9	1.0	1.3	1.3		1.5		1.2	1.2
2.3	1.8	1.5	1.5		2.5		1.8	1.6
.8	.9	.7	.9		1.1	Quick	.8	.8
.4	.4	.4	.5		.8		.5	.4
0 UND	7 53.5	11 34.5	33 11.2		40 9.2		24 14.9	20 18.3
2 185.4	23 15.9	29 12.5	51 7.2		56 6.5	Sales/Receivables	38 9.5	35 10.5
30 12.1	58 6.3	48 7.6	65 5.6		65 5.6		57 6.4	56 6.5
0 UND	33 10.9	40 9.1	54 6.8		69 5.3		47 7.7	51 7.2
91 4.0	91 4.0	85 4.3	101 3.6		83 4.4	Cost of Sales/Inventory	96 3.8	96 3.8
130 2.8	166 2.2	146 2.5	174 2.1		140 2.6		152 2.4	146 2.5
0 UND	16 22.6	11 33.3	19 19.1		18 20.2		18 20.2	19 19.2
23 15.9	31 11.8	29 12.5	29 12.8		30 12.2	Cost of Sales/Payables	32 11.4	33 10.9
57 6.4	65 5.6	68 5.4	45 8.1		46 7.9		50 7.3	60 6.1
7.4	4.4	3.9	2.8		2.9		3.7	3.5
14.0	10.9	7.5	4.8		3.9	Sales/Working Capital	6.8	8.2
-59.8	NM	20.3	13.9		6.2		18.6	24.5
45.3	25.8	27.7	25.4				14.6	17.8
(12) 4.9	(35) 7.3	(55) 6.1	(35) 7.3			EBIT/Interest	(178) 3.4	(193) 4.3
.8	.9	2.0	2.2				1.0	1.2
							12.6	29.2
						Net Profit + Depr., Dep., Amort./Cur. Mat. L/T/D	(38) 4.8	(30) 7.0
							1.2	3.3
.0	.0	.1	.0		.1		.1	.1
.3	.2	.3	.1		.3	Fixed/Worth	.2	.2
NM	-11.1	.9	.5		2.0		1.7	1.0
.4	.8	.6	.4		.3		.6	.5
2.5	1.6	1.2	1.1		2.4	Debt/Worth	1.5	1.4
-58.5	-30.6	3.8	2.4		16.8		9.3	6.2
69.2	51.3	36.1	36.7				41.8	44.8
(12) 24.8	(30) 24.2	(56) 16.7	(35) 16.5			% Profit Before Taxes/Tangible Net Worth	(166) 17.3	(186) 20.8
.0	9.2	3.6	7.7				3.8	4.3
31.1	16.3	14.4	17.1		16.1		16.8	18.4
16.1	10.0	6.8	7.8		7.2	% Profit Before Taxes/Total Assets	5.2	7.4
3.5	.0	.8	3.0		5.0		.3	1.2
UND	313.1	77.1	137.4		52.4		85.1	113.9
42.0	40.3	21.8	34.5		16.4	Sales/Net Fixed Assets	30.1	39.5
11.6	16.1	8.6	15.3		9.1		12.7	15.8
6.0	4.4	3.3	2.8		2.2		3.0	3.2
4.0	2.7	2.3	2.0		1.7	Sales/Total Assets	2.2	2.3
2.5	1.7	1.3	1.4		1.3		1.5	1.7
	.2	.2	.2				.4	.4
	(29) .6	(45) .7	(31) .8			% Depr., Dep., Amort./Sales	(151) 1.0	(159) .7
	1.6	1.9	1.5				2.0	1.5
3.8	2.2	1.6					2.3	1.9
(13) 7.8	(24) 4.5	(27) 3.1				% Officers', Directors' Owners' Comp/Sales	(79) 3.3	(82) 3.3
10.0	8.4	3.8					5.6	5.7
18974M	152444M	716005M	1684277M	1392658M	2446344M	Net Sales ($)	7197420M	8651381M
4848M	49861M	297884M	799027M	634517M	1444336M	Total Assets ($)	3946033M	4408831M

M = $ thousand MM = $ million

See Pages 9 through 22 for Explanation of Ratios and Data

	Comparative Historical Data			Current Data Sorted by Sales					
Type of Statement									
Unqualified	32	24	13					4	9
Reviewed	41	36	29		1	1	6	9	12
Compiled	19	11	19		4	2	5	7	1
Tax Returns	50	32	42	10	15	10	5	2	
Other	78	82	74	2	9	8	11	16	28
	4/1/11-3/31/12 ALL	4/1/12-3/31/13 ALL	4/1/13-3/31/14 ALL	22 (4/1-9/30/13)		155 (10/1/13-3/31/14)			
				0-1MM	1-3MM	3-5MM	5-10MM	10-25MM	25MM & OVER
NUMBER OF STATEMENTS	220	185	177	12	29	21	27	38	50
ASSETS	%	%	%	%	%	%	%	%	%
Cash & Equivalents	10.0	9.1	10.1	16.4	10.7	12.8	12.8	8.3	7.1
Trade Receivables (net)	24.0	25.3	22.6	12.4	17.6	19.8	22.7	22.7	29.1
Inventory	38.8	35.6	36.2	28.8	36.3	31.4	37.8	36.4	39.0
All Other Current	3.8	3.1	3.6	.2	6.2	.9	2.7	5.7	2.8
Total Current	76.5	73.2	72.5	57.8	70.9	65.0	75.9	73.0	78.0
Fixed Assets (net)	12.1	13.0	14.0	18.3	14.4	15.7	14.8	15.6	10.2
Intangibles (net)	4.7	4.3	6.1	16.8	4.7	9.0	4.8	3.3	5.8
All Other Non-Current	6.6	9.5	7.4	6.9	10.0	10.2	4.5	8.0	6.1
Total	100.0	100.0	100.0	100.0	100.0	100.0	100.0	100.0	100.0
LIABILITIES									
Notes Payable-Short Term	16.6	16.3	12.7	8.0	8.5	17.6	11.7	14.5	13.4
Cur. Mat.-L.T.D.	2.7	2.0	1.9	.5	2.0	2.3	1.0	2.9	1.6
Trade Payables	18.7	18.7	16.7	12.1	15.4	21.0	23.5	13.3	15.7
Income Taxes Payable	.1	.1	.1	.0	.1	.0	.1	.1	.3
All Other Current	10.1	9.1	9.8	3.0	17.1	11.6	7.8	5.5	10.8
Total Current	48.2	46.2	41.3	23.6	43.2	52.6	44.2	36.4	41.8
Long-Term Debt	10.3	15.4	10.4	9.0	12.8	23.5	7.6	6.0	8.5
Deferred Taxes	.2	.3	.2	.0	.2	.0	.3	.0	.3
All Other Non-Current	8.7	7.7	8.5	37.9	12.9	5.1	7.3	3.2	4.9
Net Worth	32.6	30.4	39.7	29.4	31.0	18.8	40.6	54.4	44.5
Total Liabilties & Net Worth	100.0	100.0	100.0	100.0	100.0	100.0	100.0	100.0	100.0
INCOME DATA									
Net Sales	100.0	100.0	100.0	100.0	100.0	100.0	100.0	100.0	100.0
Gross Profit	38.0	36.7	38.0	47.4	46.9	45.8	39.2	31.7	31.4
Operating Expenses	33.3	32.9	33.2	43.1	44.1	41.1	34.5	26.7	25.3
Operating Profit	4.7	3.8	4.8	4.3	2.8	4.7	4.7	5.1	6.0
All Other Expenses (net)	.9	.9	.8	.7	.9	1.3	.7	.7	.6
Profit Before Taxes	3.8	2.9	4.0	3.7	1.9	3.4	4.0	4.4	5.4
RATIOS									
Current	3.0	3.7	3.4	7.2	4.8	3.0	2.7	3.6	3.6
	1.7	1.9	2.0	2.3	2.4	1.4	1.9	2.0	2.0
	1.2	1.2	1.3	.9	.9	.8	1.3	1.5	1.3
Quick	1.3	1.4	1.6	2.8	2.3	1.9	1.2	1.5	1.5
	.8	.8	.8	1.0	.9	.7	.7	.8	.9
	.4	.4	.4	.4	.4	.3	.4	.5	.5
Sales/Receivables	**16** 23.4	**18** 20.5	**16** 22.6	**0** UND	**2** 202.6	**6** 62.3	**8** 47.1	**21** 17.2	**31** 11.7
	36 10.1	**36** 10.2	**33** 11.0	**21** 17.2	**32** 11.3	**20** 18.2	**22** 16.8	**33** 11.2	**49** 7.4
	53 6.9	**51** 7.2	**55** 6.6	**30** 12.0	**65** 5.6	**50** 7.3	**42** 8.7	**51** 7.2	**62** 5.9
Cost of Sales/Inventory	**50** 7.3	**33** 11.0	**44** 8.3	**0** UND	**38** 9.5	**22** 16.5	**37** 9.9	**35** 10.3	**56** 6.5
	101 3.6	**87** 4.2	**89** 4.1	**89** 4.1	**146** 2.5	**91** 4.0	**72** 5.1	**76** 4.8	**87** 4.2
	152 2.4	**152** 2.4	**159** 2.3	**159** 2.3	**243** 1.5	**182** 2.0	**107** 3.4	**130** 2.8	**140** 2.6
Cost of Sales/Payables	**15** 24.7	**18** 20.5	**14** 26.1	**0** UND	**14** 25.2	**20** 18.1	**19** 19.4	**9** 40.0	**19** 19.5
	31 11.6	**30** 12.1	**30** 12.2	**18** 20.7	**32** 11.5	**45** 8.1	**46** 7.9	**24** 15.1	**30** 12.0
	65 5.6	**55** 6.6	**56** 6.5	**47** 7.8	**89** 4.1	**94** 3.9	**64** 5.7	**39** 9.3	**45** 8.2
Sales/Working Capital	4.0	3.8	3.7	5.3	2.2	4.9	5.8	3.2	3.3
	8.3	7.6	7.2	10.7	6.5	33.0	7.9	6.7	5.9
	23.0	30.9	32.2	NM	-58.8	-25.8	27.8	18.1	15.7
EBIT/Interest	15.3	14.2	25.9		15.9	23.9	30.3	37.8	25.1
	(187) 4.6	(163) 3.8	(154) 6.0		(25) 2.7	(18) 7.4	(24) 6.5	(35) 8.3	(45) 5.7
	1.8	1.0	2.0		.2	.4	2.5	2.7	2.2
Net Profit + Depr., Dep., Amort./Cur. Mat. L/T/D	26.4	16.9	20.1						32.1
	(28) 6.5	(25) 3.8	(25) 3.7						(12) 3.0
	.9	1.5	1.3						1.4
Fixed/Worth	.1	.1	.1	.0	.0	.1	.1	.1	.1
	.2	.2	.3	.3	.2	2.3	.3	.2	.2
	1.1	1.1	.8	55.9	NM	-.9	.8	.6	.6
Debt/Worth	.7	.6	.6	.3	.6	1.1	.6	.4	.7
	1.8	1.8	1.5	1.7	1.9	4.8	1.6	.7	1.6
	6.4	6.2	4.8	NM	-85.3	-12.0	3.6	1.6	3.6
% Profit Before Taxes/Tangible Net Worth	47.4	42.8	40.8		21.4	77.7	47.5	32.1	48.0
	(180) 21.9	(153) 21.8	(151) 19.7		(21) 7.2	(14) 34.8	(24) 23.8	(36) 15.7	(47) 18.6
	8.6	4.5	7.2		-8.3	13.4	9.1	6.2	8.3
% Profit Before Taxes/Total Assets	18.0	18.8	17.0	21.6	17.7	21.9	18.3	17.2	16.3
	8.1	5.5	7.8	12.2	6.8	10.0	9.2	8.0	7.5
	1.4	.8	2.0	-.9	-2.0	-2.2	4.5	2.4	3.6
Sales/Net Fixed Assets	111.4	121.7	117.0	UND	106.2	210.7	267.0	81.6	117.4
	40.1	32.3	31.1	29.8	29.5	22.8	35.5	24.2	39.7
	13.2	11.8	11.2	10.5	9.5	7.8	11.8	8.6	15.3
Sales/Total Assets	3.1	3.6	3.5	5.4	3.3	3.6	4.1	3.3	2.9
	2.2	2.4	2.3	2.4	2.1	2.3	3.0	2.2	2.1
	1.5	1.5	1.4	1.4	1.0	1.3	1.9	1.6	1.7
% Depr., Dep., Amort./Sales	.5	.4	.3		.5	.4	.2	.2	.2
	(163) .9	(134) .7	(128) .7		(19) 1.5	(14) 1.1	(20) .5	(31) .6	(39) .7
	1.4	1.8	1.7		2.0	2.1	.9	1.8	1.5
% Officers', Directors' Owners' Comp/Sales	1.5	1.4	1.7	6.7	1.6	2.7	2.8	1.0	1.0
	(91) 3.3	(72) 3.0	(77) 3.7	(10) 9.4	(18) 3.6	(11) 6.6	(12) 3.8	(14) 1.9	(12) 1.8
	5.6	5.6	7.6	10.9	6.3	10.5	7.5	3.2	6.4
Net Sales ($)	**6500264M**	**7193545M**	**6410702M**	**7832M**	**56721M**	**83637M**	**194963M**	**614997M**	**5452552M**
Total Assets ($)	**3500505M**	**4145311M**	**3230473M**	**3452M**	**37928M**	**44433M**	**81788M**	**309951M**	**2752921M**

M = $ thousand MM = $ million

Current Data Sorted by Assets							Comparative Historical Data	
						Type of Statement		
		1	2			Unqualified	11	10
	1	3				Reviewed	5	7
	1		2			Compiled	5	4
2		2	1			Tax Returns	5	4
	1	3	1	2		Other	11	12
	3 (4/1-9/30/13)		19 (10/1/13-3/31/14)				4/1/09-3/31/10 ALL	4/1/10-3/31/11 ALL
0-500M	500M-2MM	2-10MM	10-50MM	50-100MM	100-250MM			
2	3	9	6	2		NUMBER OF STATEMENTS	37	37
%	%	%	%	%	%	**ASSETS**	%	%
					D A T A N O T A V A I L A B L E	Cash & Equivalents	10.3	10.7
						Trade Receivables (net)	29.4	23.6
						Inventory	33.2	37.3
						All Other Current	2.3	3.7
						Total Current	75.2	75.3
						Fixed Assets (net)	12.7	11.1
						Intangibles (net)	6.3	9.2
						All Other Non-Current	5.8	4.3
						Total	100.0	100.0
						LIABILITIES		
						Notes Payable-Short Term	23.4	16.1
						Cur. Mat.-L.T.D.	5.5	6.3
						Trade Payables	14.9	18.5
						Income Taxes Payable	.3	.3
						All Other Current	7.8	5.0
						Total Current	51.9	46.2
						Long-Term Debt	12.2	5.8
						Deferred Taxes	.3	.5
						All Other Non-Current	4.5	4.0
						Net Worth	31.0	43.5
						Total Liabilties & Net Worth	100.0	100.0
						INCOME DATA		
						Net Sales	100.0	100.0
						Gross Profit	31.3	28.9
						Operating Expenses	29.4	24.1
						Operating Profit	1.8	4.8
						All Other Expenses (net)	.9	1.8
						Profit Before Taxes	.9	3.0
						RATIOS		
							2.3	2.6
						Current	1.5	1.5
							1.1	1.2
							1.3	1.5
						Quick	.9	.7
							.5	.4
							31 11.7	**22** 16.7
						Sales/Receivables	**40** 9.1	**37** 9.8
							62 5.9	**51** 7.1
							41 8.9	**44** 8.3
						Cost of Sales/Inventory	**68** 5.3	**68** 5.3
							114 3.2	**123** 3.0
							13 27.4	**16** 22.5
						Cost of Sales/Payables	**30** 12.2	**31** 11.6
							52 7.0	**59** 6.2
							4.8	4.5
						Sales/Working Capital	11.3	10.1
							33.5	26.6
							5.6	6.5
						EBIT/Interest	(34) 2.5	(34) 2.8
							.7	.8
						Net Profit + Depr., Dep., Amort./Cur. Mat. L/T/D		
							.1	.1
						Fixed/Worth	.3	.3
							2.5	.8
							.8	.8
						Debt/Worth	2.5	2.5
							13.8	5.5
							48.6	45.0
						% Profit Before Taxes/Tangible Net Worth	(33) 17.8	(34) 19.8
							3.9	2.3
							7.8	13.5
						% Profit Before Taxes/Total Assets	3.4	6.4
							-1.9	-.3
							106.3	73.7
						Sales/Net Fixed Assets	26.4	27.0
							10.9	11.3
							3.4	3.2
						Sales/Total Assets	2.3	2.4
							1.8	1.7
							.5	.4
						% Depr., Dep., Amort./Sales	(27) 1.2	(26) 1.3
							2.0	1.8
							3.0	1.2
						% Officers', Directors' Owners' Comp/Sales	(14) 4.7	(11) 3.7
							12.3	7.2
891M	20840M	130887M	342368M	485980M		Net Sales ($)	1736961M	1830039M
588M	4928M	46133M	119015M	136678M		Total Assets ($)	965221M	923960M

M = $ thousand MM = $ million

See Pages 9 through 22 for Explanation of Ratios and Data

Comparative Historical Data / Current Data Sorted by Sales

	4/1/11-3/31/12 ALL	4/1/12-3/31/13 ALL	4/1/13-3/31/14 ALL	0-1MM	1-3MM	3-5MM	5-10MM	10-25MM	25MM & OVER
Type of Statement				3 (4/1-9/30/13)			19 (10/1/13-3/31/14)		
Unqualified	7	5	3					1	2
Reviewed	9	7	4		1		2	1	
Compiled	3	5	3				1		2
Tax Returns	5	8	5	2				1	2
Other	12	11	7	1		1		1	4
NUMBER OF STATEMENTS	36	36	22	3	1	1	3	4	10
ASSETS	%	%	%	%	%	%	%	%	%
Cash & Equivalents	7.5	8.4	15.1						12.6
Trade Receivables (net)	25.0	23.3	25.4						32.1
Inventory	41.1	41.5	34.0						38.9
All Other Current	2.0	2.4	2.8						2.1
Total Current	75.6	75.5	77.4						85.7
Fixed Assets (net)	13.4	13.8	13.2						5.3
Intangibles (net)	5.7	4.7	6.9						6.6
All Other Non-Current	5.3	6.0	2.6						2.5
Total	100.0	100.0	100.0						100.0
LIABILITIES									
Notes Payable-Short Term	13.6	10.5	10.8						9.3
Cur. Mat.-L.T.D.	1.2	1.6	2.4						2.3
Trade Payables	19.3	21.0	14.5						13.4
Income Taxes Payable	.5	.3	.1						.1
All Other Current	6.6	10.4	7.9						14.1
Total Current	41.2	43.8	35.7						39.2
Long-Term Debt	8.7	13.4	22.1						12.1
Deferred Taxes	.2	.1	.2						.0
All Other Non-Current	2.6	9.1	8.4						7.7
Net Worth	47.4	33.5	33.7						40.9
Total Liabilties & Net Worth	100.0	100.0	100.0						100.0
INCOME DATA									
Net Sales	100.0	100.0	100.0						100.0
Gross Profit	29.8	30.5	25.9						20.2
Operating Expenses	25.0	25.9	22.6						14.9
Operating Profit	4.8	4.6	3.3						5.3
All Other Expenses (net)	.5	1.3	1.5						.5
Profit Before Taxes	4.3	3.3	1.8						4.8
RATIOS									
Current	3.1	3.1	5.9						6.3
	1.8	1.9	2.0						2.0
	1.3	1.3	1.6						1.6
Quick	1.4	1.3	2.3						3.7
	.8	.7	1.3						1.0
	.4	.4	.7						.5
Sales/Receivables	**22** 16.6	**20** 17.9	**22** 16.4						**25** 14.6
	38 9.7	**34** 10.8	**38** 9.5						**34** 10.6
	51 7.2	**42** 8.7	**60** 6.1						**60** 6.1
Cost of Sales/Inventory	**34** 10.7	**46** 8.0	**28** 12.9						**35** 10.3
	96 3.8	**79** 4.6	**56** 6.5						**56** 6.5
	152 2.4	**130** 2.8	**107** 3.4						**107** 3.4
Cost of Sales/Payables	**15** 23.7	**15** 24.3	**9** 41.1						**7** 49.3
	33 10.9	**37** 9.9	**23** 15.9						**21** 17.7
	61 6.0	**68** 5.4	**42** 8.7						**37** 9.9
Sales/Working Capital	3.9	4.6	2.6						2.5
	7.2	9.4	6.6						7.3
	25.4	18.7	12.4						11.5
EBIT/Interest	25.8	10.8	22.2						
	(29) 4.5	(30) 4.0	(20) 5.1						
	2.0	2.1	-.8						
Net Profit + Depr., Dep., Amort./Cur. Mat. L/T/D									
Fixed/Worth	.1	.1	.1						.1
	.2	.3	.3						.2
	.6	1.9	1.4						.7
Debt/Worth	.5	.9	.7						.6
	1.1	2.9	4.6						4.1
	4.0	7.8	10.1						10.0
% Profit Before Taxes/Tangible Net Worth	40.3	33.7	74.3						120.4
	(35) 24.9	(33) 22.2	(20) 11.8						11.2
	8.6	11.9	3.3						3.4
% Profit Before Taxes/Total Assets	18.1	11.8	14.6						18.5
	8.3	7.4	5.0						7.9
	1.8	1.9	-.4						.7
Sales/Net Fixed Assets	84.6	105.5	108.1						208.0
	21.4	29.6	34.2						48.4
	14.4	14.8	14.9						27.4
Sales/Total Assets	3.4	4.1	4.3						4.5
	2.4	2.5	2.4						2.8
	1.6	1.6	1.5						1.7
% Depr., Dep., Amort./Sales	.2	.2	.3						.2
	(32) 1.1	(33) .9	.6						.5
	1.7	1.8	1.7						1.7
% Officers', Directors' Owners' Comp/Sales	1.0	1.3	1.7						
	(14) 4.4	(16) 3.7	(12) 2.1						
	8.1	6.7	4.8						
Net Sales ($)	2074085M	885275M	980966M	1760M	2649M	3866M	22697M	53388M	896606M
Total Assets ($)	896611M	339948M	307342M	4638M	1608M	4344M	7452M	18208M	271092M

M = $ thousand MM = $ million

See Pages 9 through 22 for Explanation of Ratios and Data

Current Data Sorted by Assets							Comparative Historical Data	
						Type of Statement		
	1		4	1	1	Unqualified	6	5
	1	6	3			Reviewed	4	8
	1					Compiled		2
1	1	2				Tax Returns	3	3
	3	3	3	1	3	Other	19	23
	5 (4/1-9/30/13)		30 (10/1/13-3/31/14)				**4/1/09-3/31/10 ALL**	**4/1/10-3/31/11 ALL**
0-500M	**500M-2MM**	**2-10MM**	**10-50MM**	**50-100MM**	**100-250MM**			
1	7	11	10	2	4	**NUMBER OF STATEMENTS**	32	41
%	%	%	%	%	%	**ASSETS**	%	%
		13.7	11.2			Cash & Equivalents	12.0	11.2
		28.9	17.8			Trade Receivables (net)	27.0	23.8
		30.6	31.0			Inventory	27.1	34.3
		11.5	10.2			All Other Current	5.1	2.9
		84.7	70.2			Total Current	71.2	72.2
		7.2	20.4			Fixed Assets (net)	19.5	16.2
		3.8	2.5			Intangibles (net)	4.5	5.6
		4.3	6.9			All Other Non-Current	4.7	5.9
		100.0	100.0			Total	100.0	100.0
						LIABILITIES		
		9.9	15.6			Notes Payable-Short Term	12.2	10.8
		1.4	2.2			Cur. Mat.-L.T.D.	1.5	2.7
		7.1	8.8			Trade Payables	10.1	13.6
		.1	.0			Income Taxes Payable	.2	.1
		8.1	9.7			All Other Current	7.8	16.3
		26.6	36.4			Total Current	31.9	43.4
		4.7	9.7			Long-Term Debt	10.5	11.8
		.2	.0			Deferred Taxes	.8	.6
		21.8	.5			All Other Non-Current	8.7	9.0
		46.7	53.4			Net Worth	48.1	35.2
		100.0	100.0			Total Liabilties & Net Worth	100.0	100.0
						INCOME DATA		
		100.0	100.0			Net Sales	100.0	100.0
		30.3	26.9			Gross Profit	36.4	38.2
		28.6	22.4			Operating Expenses	30.1	30.9
		1.7	4.4			Operating Profit	6.3	7.3
		-.1	.9			All Other Expenses (net)	.7	.7
		1.8	3.5			Profit Before Taxes	5.6	6.6
						RATIOS		
		10.7	4.5				4.9	4.7
		3.0	1.9			Current	2.9	2.2
		2.0	1.3				1.6	1.5
		4.7	1.8				2.7	2.4
		1.6	.6			Quick	1.4	.9
		.6	.4				.6	.5
		29 12.6	**22** 16.3				**32** 11.5	**29** 12.4
		42 8.6	**39** 9.4			Sales/Receivables	**43** 8.5	**39** 9.4
		54 6.8	**54** 6.8				**73** 5.0	**53** 6.9
		9 41.4	**23** 15.9				**49** 7.5	**45** 8.2
		70 5.2	**111** 3.3			Cost of Sales/Inventory	**85** 4.3	**111** 3.3
		111 3.3	**130** 2.8				**126** 2.9	**174** 2.1
		6 64.0	**11** 31.8				**16** 23.3	**15** 24.4
		11 32.8	**17** 21.2			Cost of Sales/Payables	**22** 16.6	**33** 11.2
		18 20.0	**30** 12.0				**38** 9.7	**49** 7.4
		2.3	2.7				2.7	2.7
		5.2	5.5			Sales/Working Capital	4.1	4.5
		9.0	47.9				11.1	9.6
		23.9					10.7	14.5
		(10) 5.6				EBIT/Interest	(27) 3.1	(35) 5.8
		-9.3					1.2	2.7
							22.7	
						Net Profit + Depr., Dep., Amort./Cur. Mat. L/T/D	(10) 4.1	
							2.7	
		.0	.1				.1	.1
		.1	.3			Fixed/Worth	.3	.3
		.2	.9				.9	.9
		.3	.6				.4	.5
		.6	.8			Debt/Worth	1.1	1.2
		1.2	2.1				1.9	3.8
		39.3	29.5				24.5	38.4
		(10) 13.8	4.5			% Profit Before Taxes/Tangible Net Worth	(28) 15.3	(35) 20.8
		-3.5	-1.7				3.9	9.3
		19.8	8.8				14.8	16.5
		9.7	1.5			% Profit Before Taxes/Total Assets	7.9	8.2
		-4.8	-1.0				1.6	3.7
		999.8	54.7				28.7	71.3
		49.0	11.8			Sales/Net Fixed Assets	13.4	11.8
		17.7	4.3				7.3	7.2
		4.6	2.0				2.3	2.4
		2.5	1.6			Sales/Total Assets	1.8	1.9
		1.9	1.5				1.5	1.4
							.8	.5
						% Depr., Dep., Amort./Sales	(25) 1.4	(30) 1.4
							2.8	3.0
							4.4	3.5
						% Officers', Directors' Owners' Comp/Sales	(10) 6.1	(10) 5.1
							10.3	7.9
1880M	**22727M**	**168369M**	**437727M**	**225982M**	**1127887M**	Net Sales ($)	**2172566M**	**2002697M**
344M	**8335M**	**54076M**	**249965M**	**150397M**	**685461M**	Total Assets ($)	**1441252M**	**1331724M**

M = $ thousand MM = $ million

See Pages 9 through 22 for Explanation of Ratios and Data

Comparative Historical Data				Current Data Sorted by Sales					
			Type of Statement						
10	6	7	Unqualified		1				6
10	10	10	Reviewed			1	3	3	3
1	2	1	Compiled		1				
6	1	4	Tax Returns		2		2		
18	16	13	Other		1	2	1	1	8
4/1/11-3/31/12 ALL	4/1/12-3/31/13 ALL	4/1/13-3/31/14 ALL		5 (4/1-9/30/13)		30 (10/1/13-3/31/14)			
				0-1MM	**1-3MM**	**3-5MM**	**5-10MM**	**10-25MM**	**25MM & OVER**
45	35	35	**NUMBER OF STATEMENTS**		5	3	6	4	17
%	%	%	**ASSETS**	%	%	%	%	%	%
10.7	13.5	11.9	Cash & Equivalents	DATA NOT AVAILABLE					8.5
22.6	23.6	23.5	Trade Receivables (net)						22.6
36.9	35.4	30.1	Inventory						28.4
3.0	5.0	8.1	All Other Current						10.1
73.2	77.6	73.6	Total Current						69.7
14.5	11.6	14.2	Fixed Assets (net)						16.7
7.3	5.8	6.3	Intangibles (net)						7.1
5.0	5.1	5.9	All Other Non-Current						6.5
100.0	100.0	100.0	Total						100.0
			LIABILITIES						
17.2	6.8	10.0	Notes Payable-Short Term						9.3
3.0	.7	1.7	Cur. Mat.-L.T.D.						1.7
14.2	14.9	13.9	Trade Payables						8.5
.1	.1	.0	Income Taxes Payable						.0
7.4	8.2	8.8	All Other Current						8.3
42.0	30.7	34.4	Total Current						27.8
8.4	7.2	8.5	Long-Term Debt						11.1
.6	.3	.3	Deferred Taxes						.5
5.1	6.2	10.5	All Other Non-Current						3.3
43.9	55.6	46.3	Net Worth						57.3
100.0	100.0	100.0	Total Liabilties & Net Worth						100.0
			INCOME DATA						
100.0	100.0	100.0	Net Sales						100.0
37.6	35.1	34.7	Gross Profit						29.0
33.5	30.7	32.0	Operating Expenses						24.9
4.0	4.4	2.7	Operating Profit						4.1
1.1	.8	.6	All Other Expenses (net)						.4
2.9	3.6	2.1	Profit Before Taxes						3.7
			RATIOS						
4.2	5.0	5.8							5.0
2.5	2.8	2.9	Current						3.6
1.4	1.7	1.5							1.5
1.9	2.4	2.4							2.6
1.0	1.3	1.3	Quick						1.7
.5	.7	.5							.6
29 12.6	23 15.9	27 13.5							26 13.9
38 9.7	30 12.0	41 8.9	Sales/Receivables						38 9.5
59 6.2	57 6.4	56 6.5							61 6.0
66 5.5	45 8.2	30 12.0							26 14.1
114 3.2	107 3.4	99 3.7	Cost of Sales/Inventory						107 3.4
166 2.2	152 2.4	140 2.6							140 2.6
14 26.6	16 23.2	12 30.4							11 33.3
31 11.6	25 14.6	24 15.5	Cost of Sales/Payables						18 20.4
46 7.9	51 7.1	39 9.3							36 10.2
2.8	2.7	2.8							2.6
5.0	4.5	5.4	Sales/Working Capital						5.4
16.9	12.7	14.2							11.8
15.4	19.5	17.2							22.2
(39) 6.4	(30) 4.3	(32) 3.9	EBIT/Interest						(16) 9.0
1.5	.8	.8							1.4
			Net Profit + Depr., Dep., Amort./Cur. Mat. L/T/D						
.1	.0	.1							.1
.2	.2	.2	Fixed/Worth						.2
.5	.3	.9							.6
.6	.4	.5							.5
1.1	.7	.8	Debt/Worth						.7
3.0	2.1	2.7							1.2
30.8	30.8	36.8							34.1
(40) 18.0	(33) 16.6	(30) 11.2	% Profit Before Taxes/Tangible Net Worth						(16) 14.2
5.7	2.9	2.2							2.6
13.9	17.8	13.6							14.6
6.9	7.5	5.4	% Profit Before Taxes/Total Assets						7.0
1.5	.3	.0							.6
65.4	81.0	69.6							51.3
16.1	37.3	17.7	Sales/Net Fixed Assets						14.7
9.8	12.2	9.3							6.5
2.4	3.0	2.7							3.1
1.8	2.1	2.0	Sales/Total Assets						1.7
1.4	1.5	1.5							1.4
.6	.3	.6							.8
(36) 1.1	(29) .9	(28) 1.0	% Depr., Dep., Amort./Sales						(15) 1.3
2.3	1.9	2.5							3.3
			% Officers', Directors' Owners' Comp/Sales						
3428618M	3247542M	1984572M	Net Sales ($)		9679M	11862M	42947M	64878M	1855206M
2314884M	1838034M	1148578M	Total Assets ($)		4323M	6640M	19379M	36545M	1081691M

M = $ thousand MM = $ million

See Pages 9 through 22 for Explanation of Ratios and Data

Current Data Sorted by Assets							Comparative Historical Data	
						Type of Statement		
1	1	4	14	9	3	Unqualified	36	33
	1	17	18	1	2	Reviewed	34	40
	7	13	4		1	Compiled	23	26
3	14	3	3			Tax Returns	28	22
1	8	21	24	8	8	Other	65	79
	37 (4/1-9/30/13)		152 (10/1/13-3/31/14)				4/1/09-3/31/10 ALL	4/1/10-3/31/11 ALL
0-500M	500M-2MM	2-10MM	10-50MM	50-100MM	100-250MM			
5	31	58	63	18	14	**NUMBER OF STATEMENTS**	186	200
%	%	%	%	%	%	**ASSETS**	%	%
	9.9	9.0	6.5	4.1	5.7	Cash & Equivalents	6.2	5.4
	12.8	13.8	10.1	10.8	10.3	Trade Receivables (net)	11.6	10.2
	28.8	28.4	28.8	32.1	19.9	Inventory	24.5	27.9
	2.0	1.5	2.2	2.7	1.1	All Other Current	3.0	2.4
	53.4	52.6	47.6	49.7	37.0	Total Current	45.4	46.1
	36.6	34.2	40.4	35.0	50.2	Fixed Assets (net)	42.1	42.7
	2.1	2.8	1.9	3.8	1.1	Intangibles (net)	1.4	1.6
	7.9	10.4	10.1	11.5	11.6	All Other Non-Current	11.2	9.6
	100.0	100.0	100.0	100.0	100.0	Total	100.0	100.0
						LIABILITIES		
	15.4	11.8	8.7	10.4	24.3	Notes Payable-Short Term	14.3	14.6
	8.1	4.0	4.1	2.1	2.4	Cur. Mat.-L.T.D.	6.6	5.7
	5.3	6.1	5.0	5.6	4.5	Trade Payables	5.8	5.6
	.0	.1	.2	.1	.0	Income Taxes Payable	.1	.1
	11.7	5.8	7.7	5.1	2.9	All Other Current	5.4	4.7
	40.6	27.8	25.7	23.3	34.1	Total Current	32.2	30.7
	21.9	17.9	19.3	19.8	18.1	Long-Term Debt	27.4	23.7
	.0	.2	.6	1.7	2.3	Deferred Taxes	.5	.5
	6.9	3.8	4.4	6.0	6.8	All Other Non-Current	6.0	8.7
	30.6	50.3	50.0	49.2	38.7	Net Worth	33.8	36.3
	100.0	100.0	100.0	100.0	100.0	Total Liabilties & Net Worth	100.0	100.0
						INCOME DATA		
	100.0	100.0	100.0	100.0	100.0	Net Sales	100.0	100.0
	30.8	21.8	23.3	15.0	24.3	Gross Profit	17.6	24.8
	25.2	16.4	13.6	8.1	12.4	Operating Expenses	20.3	21.2
	5.6	5.4	9.7	7.0	11.9	Operating Profit	-2.8	3.6
	.8	.8	.2	.5	1.4	All Other Expenses (net)	1.3	1.7
	4.9	4.5	9.5	6.4	10.5	Profit Before Taxes	-4.1	1.9
						RATIOS		
	2.5	4.1	3.8	3.9	3.0		3.0	2.7
	1.3	1.9	2.1	2.2	2.2	Current	1.6	1.6
	.7	1.3	1.2	1.4	1.1		.9	1.0
	1.2	1.5	1.6	.9	1.4		1.3	1.0
	.3	.8	.6	.6	.9	Quick	.6	(199) .5
	.2	.4	.3	.3	.5		.2	.2
	3 130.9	12 31.0	11 32.8	15 23.8	10 35.2		12 31.5	12 31.7
	12 29.7	18 20.4	18 20.1	23 16.1	20 18.1	Sales/Receivables	20 17.9	18 20.1
	17 21.3	29 12.5	24 15.4	31 11.9	29 12.7		31 11.9	30 12.2
	22 16.9	27 13.6	40 9.1	53 6.9	30 12.3		33 11.2	32 11.3
	43 8.5	60 6.1	73 5.0	79 4.6	49 7.4	Cost of Sales/Inventory	60 6.1	66 5.5
	81 4.5	96 3.8	122 3.0	130 2.8	91 4.0		107 3.4	126 2.9
	1 327.4	4 91.1	8 47.8	6 62.8	6 58.0		5 75.2	5 72.8
	5 70.9	9 41.2	11 34.6	11 33.0	12 29.9	Cost of Sales/Payables	10 36.9	11 32.5
	12 29.7	19 19.6	20 18.3	21 17.1	21 17.4		19 19.3	21 17.6
	11.4	5.6	4.6	3.8	4.1		4.7	4.5
	28.3	9.2	8.9	7.2	7.7	Sales/Working Capital	10.8	11.2
	-18.2	40.7	17.7	13.1	73.6		-39.5	-247.8
	13.5	26.3	35.0	28.9	28.8		2.5	7.7
	(26) 4.8	(49) 6.8	(60) 10.1	7.2	(13) 16.2	EBIT/Interest	(174) .0	(187) 2.3
	1.5	3.1	3.1	3.9	4.7		-3.0	.6
		5.2	4.8				2.5	4.7
		(12) 3.8	(11) 3.0			Net Profit + Depr., Dep., Amort./Cur. Mat. L/T/D	(42) 1.4	(46) 1.7
		1.4	2.0				.5	1.0
	.6	.3	.5	.3	.4		.5	.5
	1.7	.8	.8	.8	1.2	Fixed/Worth	1.3	1.1
	115.3	1.2	1.7	1.5	2.2		3.3	3.0
	.4	.3	.4	.5	.3		.6	.6
	2.0	1.3	1.1	1.2	1.4	Debt/Worth	1.7	1.4
	237.5	2.5	2.3	3.6	2.9		5.5	4.6
	58.6	39.5	46.7	38.8	41.8		12.6	26.0
	(24) 28.8	(55) 19.2	(60) 26.2	16.2	(13) 37.0	% Profit Before Taxes/Tangible Net Worth	(160) -4.5	(170) 9.9
	11.8	7.2	12.4	9.4	14.3		-18.5	.6
	26.9	20.6	20.0	12.5	16.0		3.8	9.3
	11.5	8.6	10.4	7.7	14.6	% Profit Before Taxes/Total Assets	-3.1	2.9
	2.0	3.0	5.0	4.7	5.3		-11.4	-1.2
	17.6	14.1	7.4	12.6	6.9		6.9	8.3
	9.0	7.7	4.3	4.7	4.0	Sales/Net Fixed Assets	4.0	4.7
	6.3	4.1	2.8	3.0	1.5		1.9	2.3
	4.0	3.1	2.3	2.2	2.1		2.2	2.5
	3.3	2.5	1.7	1.3	1.3	Sales/Total Assets	1.4	1.6
	2.2	1.7	1.3	1.0	.9		.9	1.0
	1.6	1.0	2.1	1.7	1.4		2.6	2.2
	(24) 3.1	(51) 1.9	(62) 3.8	(16) 2.7	(11) 4.4	% Depr., Dep., Amort./Sales	(172) 4.6	(176) 3.8
	5.0	3.5	5.6	4.6	5.0		7.7	6.8
	.7	.9					1.7	1.1
	(14) 2.3	(19) 1.3				% Officers', Directors' Owners' Comp/Sales	(57) 2.4	(50) 1.6
	5.6	1.9					3.9	3.1
2518M	114379M	698970M	2797212M	2368305M	2512400M	Net Sales ($)	5024584M	5532922M
1093M	35082M	307753M	1464165M	1385034M	1767018M	Total Assets ($)	4710500M	4221276M

M = $ thousand MM = $ million

See Pages 9 through 22 for Explanation of Ratios and Data

Comparative Historical Data				Current Data Sorted by Sales					
			Type of Statement						
35	38	32	Unqualified	1	1	1		5	24
55	39	39	Reviewed		1	1	5	18	14
27	27	25	Compiled	2	4	2	10	3	4
23	23	23	Tax Returns	4	5	3	7	3	1
58	73	70	Other	1	3	3	12	15	36
4/1/11-3/31/12 ALL	4/1/12-3/31/13 ALL	4/1/13-3/31/14 ALL		37 (4/1-9/30/13)			152 (10/1/13-3/31/14)		
				0-1MM	1-3MM	3-5MM	5-10MM	10-25MM	25MM & OVER
198	200	189	**NUMBER OF STATEMENTS**	8	14	10	34	44	79
%	%	%	**ASSETS**	%	%	%	%	%	%
4.9	6.7	7.5	Cash & Equivalents		9.6	9.7	11.0	4.0	7.6
12.2	11.1	11.6	Trade Receivables (net)		12.3	8.5	14.5	13.0	10.7
28.0	28.5	28.4	Inventory		30.3	24.7	27.7	29.0	29.0
2.5	2.8	1.9	All Other Current		2.2	2.7	1.2	1.7	2.2
47.7	49.1	49.3	Total Current		54.5	45.6	54.4	47.8	49.6
41.0	39.4	38.5	Fixed Assets (net)		33.2	46.9	34.6	39.7	38.3
2.2	1.4	2.4	Intangibles (net)		.8	.9	3.2	2.4	2.5
9.1	10.1	9.8	All Other Non-Current		11.6	6.6	7.8	10.1	9.7
100.0	100.0	100.0	Total		100.0	100.0	100.0	100.0	100.0
			LIABILITIES						
15.9	14.6	12.0	Notes Payable-Short Term		20.0	10.6	14.4	9.9	11.6
4.3	3.7	4.4	Cur. Mat.-L.T.D.		11.2	2.8	4.5	3.5	3.2
6.5	5.6	5.3	Trade Payables		5.5	2.4	5.3	6.2	5.6
.1	.1	.1	Income Taxes Payable		.0	.0	.2	.0	.2
8.9	6.4	7.0	All Other Current		20.1	10.8	3.1	6.5	6.5
35.6	30.4	28.9	Total Current		56.8	26.7	27.5	26.1	27.2
23.0	21.6	20.1	Long-Term Debt		12.1	26.2	22.2	16.7	19.5
.4	.6	.6	Deferred Taxes		.0	.0	.1	.3	1.2
7.1	6.6	5.0	All Other Non-Current		1.8	10.4	5.6	4.3	5.2
33.8	40.7	45.5	Net Worth		29.3	36.7	44.7	52.5	47.0
100.0	100.0	100.0	Total Liabilties & Net Worth		100.0	100.0	100.0	100.0	100.0
			INCOME DATA						
100.0	100.0	100.0	Net Sales		100.0	100.0	100.0	100.0	100.0
19.9	20.2	23.9	Gross Profit		35.9	29.4	25.9	23.4	19.3
18.2	16.1	16.3	Operating Expenses		29.7	20.6	19.5	16.9	10.2
1.7	4.1	7.6	Operating Profit		6.2	8.9	6.4	6.5	9.1
.8	.7	.7	All Other Expenses (net)		.3	.1	.6	.0	.7
.9	3.4	6.9	Profit Before Taxes		5.9	8.8	5.8	6.4	8.4
			RATIOS						
2.7	3.7	3.7			1.8	8.5	6.8	3.2	3.9
1.6	1.6	2.0	Current		.8	1.9	1.9	2.0	2.1
1.0	1.1	1.2			.6	1.1	1.1	1.4	1.3
1.0	1.2	1.4			.7	3.1	3.2	1.2	1.6
.4	.5	.7	Quick		.3	.5	.8	.9	.7
.2	.3	.3			.2	.1	.3	.3	.4
12 29.2	11 34.3	11 34.5			8 43.9	2 189.5	12 29.9	12 31.1	11 32.0
19 19.4	20 18.7	17 21.3	Sales/Receivables		14 26.0	9 38.5	17 21.5	18 20.4	19 18.9
28 13.0	26 14.2	26 13.9			21 17.6	16 23.4	29 12.5	28 12.9	26 14.2
33 11.2	31 11.9	36 10.1			28 13.0	14 25.2	21 17.6	39 9.4	39 9.3
65 5.6	55 6.6	64 5.7	Cost of Sales/Inventory		63 5.8	31 11.7	65 5.6	70 5.2	69 5.3
118 3.1	107 3.4	104 3.5			111 3.3	60 6.1	96 3.8	118 3.1	104 3.5
5 72.8	6 66.0	5 72.7			0 UND	2 214.8	3 111.0	7 50.9	6 62.5
11 32.9	10 38.0	10 37.9	Cost of Sales/Payables		11 32.5	3 105.4	7 49.4	12 29.7	10 35.6
21 17.2	15 24.4	19 19.7			25 14.6	14 25.4	14 26.7	22 16.5	18 20.8
5.5	4.9	5.3			6.7	9.7	4.4	4.8	5.2
11.5	11.3	10.0	Sales/Working Capital		-21.6	15.7	8.8	9.9	8.4
301.5	120.4	40.6			-10.9	NM	89.3	26.2	17.1
5.8	10.6	26.7			8.3	26.9	21.4	29.4	31.0
(182) 1.5	(182) 3.6	(169) 6.9	EBIT/Interest		(10) 3.1	4.9	(28) 3.4	(42) 10.6	(74) 10.2
-.2	1.3	2.9			1.5	.7	2.1	2.1	3.9
4.4	5.7	5.0							4.8
(44) 1.7	(39) 2.2	(32) 3.1	Net Profit + Depr., Dep., Amort./Cur. Mat. L/T/D						(19) 3.0
1.0	1.3	1.6							1.6
.5	.4	.4			.4	.7	.4	.3	.4
1.0	1.0	.9	Fixed/Worth		2.2	.9	.8	.8	.8
2.4	2.5	1.9			NM	NM	1.9	1.3	1.8
.7	.5	.4			1.2	.6	.2	.2	.4
1.6	1.4	1.3	Debt/Worth		4.3	1.2	1.4	1.1	1.2
5.2	3.4	3.2			NM	NM	3.5	2.1	2.8
15.5	27.8	43.5			40.3		42.1	34.8	46.7
(172) 4.6	(173) 13.9	(174) 22.5	% Profit Before Taxes/Tangible Net Worth		(11) 19.2		(30) 21.0	(42) 19.4	(76) 27.5
-7.1	2.9	11.0			12.9		5.5	6.6	13.2
7.0	11.9	18.6			24.9	32.5	22.0	15.4	20.0
1.6	5.4	9.6	% Profit Before Taxes/Total Assets		10.7	10.7	8.7	8.0	10.6
-3.7	.6	3.4			2.3	-1.9	2.0	2.3	5.7
9.0	12.1	11.4			15.8	8.2	19.6	10.6	10.3
4.8	6.0	6.2	Sales/Net Fixed Assets		8.6	6.7	8.3	5.8	5.0
2.6	3.0	3.4			5.3	4.2	3.3	3.4	3.2
2.4	2.9	2.9			3.6	3.9	3.3	3.0	2.4
1.7	2.0	2.0	Sales/Total Assets		2.7	2.9	2.6	1.8	1.8
1.1	1.3	1.3			1.9	1.9	1.4	1.3	1.3
1.8	1.5	1.5				2.6	1.0	1.4	1.7
(177) 3.5	(173) 3.1	(168) 3.0	% Depr., Dep., Amort./Sales			3.4	(30) 2.6	(41) 2.1	(72) 3.3
6.0	5.3	4.8				12.4	5.4	4.5	4.6
.9	1.1	.9					1.0	.9	
(45) 2.0	(47) 1.9	(43) 1.5	% Officers', Directors' Owners' Comp/Sales				(16) 1.7	(11) 1.3	
5.1	2.9	2.6					2.4	1.5	
6301306M	8203441M	8493784M	Net Sales ($)	4696M	33247M	38072M	242531M	709420M	7465818M
4365216M	4840262M	4960145M	Total Assets ($)	5522M	14719M	43164M	128977M	554255M	4213508M

M = $ thousand MM = $ million

See Pages 9 through 22 for Explanation of Ratios and Data

Current Data Sorted by Assets							Comparative Historical Data	
			5	1		Type of Statement Unqualified	14	11
		4				Reviewed	7	10
	1	4				Compiled	6	4
	1					Tax Returns	3	3
		10	2			Other	22	18
	3 (4/1-9/30/13)		25 (10/1/13-3/31/14)				4/1/09-3/31/10 ALL	4/1/10-3/31/11 ALL
0-500M	500M-2MM	2-10MM	10-50MM	50-100MM	100-250MM			
	2	18	7	1		NUMBER OF STATEMENTS	52	46
%	%	%	%	%	%	ASSETS	%	%
DATA NOT AVAILABLE		6.2			DATA NOT AVAILABLE	Cash & Equivalents	9.2	7.4
		23.7				Trade Receivables (net)	15.7	21.8
		39.4				Inventory	32.2	31.4
		1.8				All Other Current	3.1	2.0
		71.1				Total Current	60.2	62.6
		22.8				Fixed Assets (net)	29.5	27.6
		2.7				Intangibles (net)	3.3	.7
		3.3				All Other Non-Current	7.0	9.1
		100.0				Total	100.0	100.0
						LIABILITIES		
		15.5				Notes Payable-Short Term	10.5	16.3
		.5				Cur. Mat.-L.T.D.	2.5	2.3
		9.3				Trade Payables	7.6	9.5
		.1				Income Taxes Payable	.2	.0
		4.4				All Other Current	7.5	12.8
		29.8				Total Current	28.2	41.0
		7.4				Long-Term Debt	17.1	15.5
		.0				Deferred Taxes	.1	.4
		2.3				All Other Non-Current	1.8	1.9
		60.5				Net Worth	52.7	41.2
		100.0				Total Liabilities & Net Worth	100.0	100.0
						INCOME DATA		
		100.0				Net Sales	100.0	100.0
		20.9				Gross Profit	16.1	22.4
		17.8				Operating Expenses	12.7	18.1
		3.1				Operating Profit	3.3	4.4
		.2				All Other Expenses (net)	.2	.1
		2.9				Profit Before Taxes	3.1	4.3
						RATIOS		
		3.7					4.5	3.8
		2.5				Current	2.2	2.0
		2.1					1.5	1.6
		2.0					1.6	1.6
		.9				Quick	.9	.8
		.5					.5	.4
		15 24.3					**16** 22.2	**14** 25.4
		23 15.9				Sales/Receivables	**24** 15.4	**27** 13.7
		36 10.1					**35** 10.5	**34** 10.9
		35 10.3					**39** 9.3	**32** 11.3
		54 6.8				Cost of Sales/Inventory	**57** 6.4	**60** 6.1
		81 4.5					**89** 4.1	**88** 4.2
		7 50.0					**8** 47.9	**8** 45.3
		10 38.1				Cost of Sales/Payables	**11** 32.0	**13** 28.2
		19 19.5					**20** 18.7	**19** 19.2
		5.5					4.1	4.8
		7.2				Sales/Working Capital	6.1	6.9
		8.5					15.1	14.4
		44.0					15.7	32.9
		16.8				EBIT/Interest	(46) 5.0	(44) 8.9
		3.2					1.2	2.4
							13.3	9.1
						Net Profit + Depr., Dep., Amort./Cur. Mat. L/T/D	(15) 6.1	(15) 5.5
							4.2	2.0
		.2					.3	.3
		.3				Fixed/Worth	.5	.5
		.5					1.0	1.0
		.3					.4	.3
		.6				Debt/Worth	.9	.9
		.8					1.7	1.8
		38.7					23.9	28.9
		(17) 12.6				% Profit Before Taxes/Tangible Net Worth	(50) 10.7	(43) 14.0
		4.9					4.1	5.7
		20.9					11.8	14.8
		8.4				% Profit Before Taxes/Total Assets	7.0	6.9
		3.2					.5	3.3
		43.7					17.6	19.4
		28.1				Sales/Net Fixed Assets	7.3	10.7
		7.3					5.0	5.3
		3.7					2.7	3.1
		3.0				Sales/Total Assets	2.1	2.4
		2.0					1.5	1.8
		.9					.9	.9
		(14) 1.0				% Depr., Dep., Amort./Sales	(44) 1.7	(44) 1.5
		1.6					2.4	2.7
							.4	.7
						% Officers', Directors' Owners' Comp/Sales	(13) .8	(14) 1.1
							2.7	2.9
	4502M	254005M	463536M	205027M		Net Sales ($)	3645415M	2484703M
	2284M	82831M	161065M	71517M		Total Assets ($)	2049125M	1258119M

M = $ thousand MM = $ million

See Pages 9 through 22 for Explanation of Ratios and Data

Comparative Historical Data				Current Data Sorted by Sales					
			Type of Statement						
10	10	6	Unqualified					1	5
7	5	4	Reviewed					3	1
2	5	5	Compiled		1	1	1	2	
3	1	1	Tax Returns		1				
14	19	12	Other			3	1	5	3
4/1/11-3/31/12 ALL	4/1/12-3/31/13 ALL	4/1/13-3/31/14 ALL			3 (4/1-9/30/13)		25 (10/1/13-3/31/14)		
				0-1MM	1-3MM	3-5MM	5-10MM	10-25MM	25MM & OVER
36	40	28	**NUMBER OF STATEMENTS**		2	4	2	11	9
%	%	%	**ASSETS**	%	%	%	%	%	%
7.9	5.7	7.6	Cash & Equivalents	DATA NOT AVAILABLE				4.6	
20.3	21.7	22.1	Trade Receivables (net)					24.3	
31.5	35.2	34.3	Inventory					40.0	
1.9	2.9	2.0	All Other Current					2.3	
61.6	65.6	65.9	Total Current					71.3	
29.2	23.1	27.1	Fixed Assets (net)					19.3	
1.6	1.6	2.7	Intangibles (net)					2.9	
7.6	9.7	4.2	All Other Non-Current					6.6	
100.0	100.0	100.0	Total					100.0	
			LIABILITIES						
13.5	15.9	14.0	Notes Payable-Short Term					13.8	
2.3	3.4	2.3	Cur. Mat.-L.T.D.					4.0	
10.4	9.9	9.2	Trade Payables					9.6	
.4	.0	.1	Income Taxes Payable					.2	
6.4	6.1	5.9	All Other Current					4.5	
32.8	35.4	31.5	Total Current					32.1	
21.5	12.1	9.8	Long-Term Debt					5.7	
.1	.3	.3	Deferred Taxes					.0	
.9	2.4	4.8	All Other Non-Current					.6	
44.7	49.8	53.6	Net Worth					61.6	
100.0	100.0	100.0	Total Liabilities & Net Worth					100.0	
			INCOME DATA						
100.0	100.0	100.0	Net Sales					100.0	
20.1	17.6	19.8	Gross Profit					15.9	
17.0	15.9	17.0	Operating Expenses					12.5	
3.1	1.7	2.8	Operating Profit					3.4	
.6	-.1	.4	All Other Expenses (net)					.5	
2.5	1.8	2.4	Profit Before Taxes					2.9	
			RATIOS						
3.2	2.7	3.6						4.0	
1.9	2.0	2.3	Current					2.6	
1.4	1.4	1.4						2.1	
1.5	1.1	1.9						1.9	
.7	.6	.8	Quick					1.1	
.4	.4	.4						.4	
17 21.7	**21** 17.5	**15** 24.8						**15** 25.0	
27 13.6	**34** 10.8	**23** 15.7	Sales/Receivables					**23** 15.8	
41 9.0	**41** 8.8	**37** 9.8						**35** 10.3	
28 13.0	**42** 8.7	**37** 9.8						**37** 9.9	
59 6.2	**62** 5.9	**52** 7.0	Cost of Sales/Inventory					**48** 7.6	
107 3.4	**99** 3.7	**72** 5.1						**72** 5.1	
9 41.9	**9** 39.7	**8** 47.3						**7** 49.2	
13 27.9	**15** 24.4	**10** 35.2	Cost of Sales/Payables					**9** 38.8	
26 13.8	**23** 15.7	**19** 19.0						**13** 27.7	
4.9	5.3	6.5						7.2	
6.6	7.0	8.0	Sales/Working Capital					8.2	
14.1	15.2	23.0						8.6	
15.2	28.4	34.9						54.7	
(34) 6.6	(36) 7.0	(27) 7.0	EBIT/Interest					24.2	
.1	1.9	3.3						3.7	
	5.0								
	(10) 2.6		Net Profit + Depr., Dep., Amort./Cur. Mat. L/T/D						
	-.5								
.2	.2	.2						.1	
.5	.4	.4	Fixed/Worth					.3	
2.4	.9	1.1						.4	
.4	.5	.4						.3	
.8	1.0	.8	Debt/Worth					.7	
4.2	1.6	2.1						.8	
16.4	23.4	25.3						40.6	
(33) 7.3	(38) 15.1	(27) 12.6	% Profit Before Taxes/Tangible Net Worth					18.6	
-8.7	4.7	5.6						7.4	
8.5	13.1	14.3						22.3	
4.2	6.8	6.8	% Profit Before Taxes/Total Assets					14.8	
-2.9	1.4	2.6						3.7	
22.7	35.7	40.1						51.3	
10.1	13.7	15.8	Sales/Net Fixed Assets					32.6	
5.0	5.9	4.5						7.9	
2.8	3.0	3.6						4.5	
2.1	2.6	3.0	Sales/Total Assets					3.3	
1.7	1.6	1.9						2.6	
1.1	.9	.8							
(29) 1.8	(36) 1.3	(24) 1.1	% Depr., Dep., Amort./Sales						
2.3	2.8	3.8							
			% Officers', Directors' Owners' Comp/Sales						
1741956M	**2190499M**	**927070M**	Net Sales ($)		**4502M**	**17956M**	**12695M**	**176745M**	**715172M**
882463M	**1046227M**	**317697M**	Total Assets ($)		**2284M**	**12305M**	**5500M**	**59771M**	**237837M**

M = $ thousand MM = $ million

See Pages 9 through 22 for Explanation of Ratios and Data

Current Data Sorted by Assets | **Comparative Historical Data**

0-500M	500M-2MM	2-10MM	10-50MM	50-100MM	100-250MM		4/1/09-3/31/10 ALL	4/1/10-3/31/11 ALL
						Type of Statement		
		2	5	2	2	Unqualified	12	17
	1	6	5			Reviewed	6	12
	1	5	6			Compiled	8	6
1	7	5				Tax Returns	13	3
1	4	9	8	2	3	Other	36	28
	14 (4/1-9/30/13)		61 (10/1/13-3/31/14)					
2	13	27	24	4	5	**NUMBER OF STATEMENTS**	75	66
%	%	%	%	%	%	**ASSETS**	%	%
	11.7	4.0	5.3			Cash & Equivalents	7.4	5.9
	25.2	25.1	18.4			Trade Receivables (net)	19.0	21.3
	27.5	30.4	40.5			Inventory	32.3	31.5
	.6	1.3	1.9			All Other Current	4.0	3.1
	65.0	60.7	66.1			Total Current	62.7	61.8
	24.1	21.9	25.6			Fixed Assets (net)	27.2	31.0
	7.9	10.2	1.8			Intangibles (net)	2.3	1.9
	3.0	7.2	6.4			All Other Non-Current	7.8	5.3
	100.0	100.0	100.0			Total	100.0	100.0
						LIABILITIES		
	5.4	14.3	11.8			Notes Payable-Short Term	17.3	11.3
	2.0	2.5	1.9			Cur. Mat.-L.T.D.	4.5	4.7
	15.3	11.5	6.4			Trade Payables	10.0	10.4
	1.1	.0	.0			Income Taxes Payable	.1	.1
	10.1	12.2	6.4			All Other Current	5.9	6.5
	33.8	40.6	26.5			Total Current	37.8	32.9
	6.1	12.3	13.3			Long-Term Debt	16.1	15.0
	.0	.0	.7			Deferred Taxes	.4	.5
	10.2	7.2	5.1			All Other Non-Current	6.7	5.1
	50.0	39.9	54.4			Net Worth	39.0	46.6
	100.0	100.0	100.0			Total Liabilties & Net Worth	100.0	100.0
						INCOME DATA		
	100.0	100.0	100.0			Net Sales	100.0	100.0
	23.9	18.8	23.5			Gross Profit	20.4	22.0
	20.3	17.6	18.6			Operating Expenses	23.0	18.7
	3.6	1.2	5.0			Operating Profit	-2.6	3.3
	.5	.7	1.1			All Other Expenses (net)	1.1	.6
	3.1	.5	3.8			Profit Before Taxes	-3.7	2.7
						RATIOS		
	3.2	4.4	5.1				3.4	4.3
	2.2	1.9	3.2			Current	1.8	2.2
	1.5	.9	1.8				1.2	1.3
	1.8	1.5	2.3				1.4	1.5
	1.5	.8	1.3			Quick	.6	.8
	.6	.3	.5				.4	.5
	15 24.3	**15** 24.9	**23** 16.1				**25** 14.6	**22** 16.9
	24 15.4	**41** 9.0	**38** 9.6			Sales/Receivables	**37** 9.9	**32** 11.3
	42 8.6	**66** 5.5	**59** 6.2				**52** 7.1	**45** 8.1
	12 31.7	**23** 16.0	**66** 5.5				**48** 7.7	**41** 8.8
	29 12.4	**64** 5.7	**135** 2.7			Cost of Sales/Inventory	**80** 4.6	**65** 5.6
	70 5.2	**104** 3.5	**182** 2.0				**155** 2.4	**125** 2.9
	5 78.7	**7** 53.9	**9** 41.6				**9** 40.9	**8** 44.8
	20 18.1	**10** 36.9	**14** 25.5			Cost of Sales/Payables	**14** 25.5	**15** 24.3
	42 8.7	**38** 9.6	**21** 17.3				**33** 11.1	**31** 11.7
	6.3	3.3	2.3				3.1	3.6
	9.6	7.6	4.2			Sales/Working Capital	6.7	7.3
	20.0	-61.9	8.3				13.9	15.3
	16.3	31.1	11.1				2.9	10.6
	(10) 6.0	(26) 5.0	(22) 6.0			EBIT/Interest	(69) .6	(57) 2.2
	-7.8	-4.5	1.2				-3.8	.2
							3.1	7.6
						Net Profit + Depr., Dep., Amort./Cur. Mat. L/T/D	(10) 1.7	(14) 2.6
							1.0	.5
	.0	.3	.2				.3	.3
	.6	.7	.4			Fixed/Worth	.7	.7
	NM	2.8	.9				1.5	1.1
	.3	.6	.3				.5	.5
	.7	1.9	.6			Debt/Worth	1.5	1.0
	NM	55.5	2.0				6.0	2.6
	58.7	70.4	22.1				6.3	23.2
	(10) 23.7	(21) 28.3	(23) 9.2			% Profit Before Taxes/Tangible Net Worth	(63) -2.4	(59) 9.8
	-22.8	-1.3	1.0				-14.0	-2.2
	30.4	17.1	10.5				3.5	10.7
	13.2	8.1	5.6			% Profit Before Taxes/Total Assets	-2.1	3.7
	-3.2	-5.1	.2				-9.8	-1.5
	651.0	28.0	12.7				13.7	14.4
	12.7	9.3	7.4			Sales/Net Fixed Assets	6.1	7.0
	4.9	6.3	4.5				3.8	4.0
	5.0	2.6	2.4				2.4	2.7
	2.5	2.1	1.7			Sales/Total Assets	1.8	1.9
	1.9	1.2	1.1				1.1	1.3
		1.0	1.4				1.2	1.0
		(20) 2.1	2.4			% Depr., Dep., Amort./Sales	(64) 2.2	(56) 2.2
		4.6	3.3				3.8	3.6
		.9					1.9	1.0
		(11) 2.0				% Officers', Directors' Owners' Comp/Sales	(15) 4.9	(14) 3.3
		6.7					8.3	5.5
1947M	48889M	278482M	1014388M	479179M	1543097M	Net Sales ($)	2370256M	3775436M
401M	14039M	148553M	573115M	301029M	793488M	Total Assets ($)	1578691M	1919410M

M = $ thousand MM = $ million

See Pages 9 through 22 for Explanation of Ratios and Data

Comparative Historical Data				Current Data Sorted by Sales					
			Type of Statement						
18	11	11	Unqualified				1	3	7
12	14	12	Reviewed		1	2		6	3
8	11	12	Compiled		1	1	4		6
13	6	13	Tax Returns	1	3	3	4	2	
30	19	27	Other	1	2	1	5	8	10
4/1/11-3/31/12 ALL	**4/1/12-3/31/13 ALL**	**4/1/13-3/31/14 ALL**		**14 (4/1-9/30/13)**			**61 (10/1/13-3/31/14)**		
				0-1MM	**1-3MM**	**3-5MM**	**5-10MM**	**10-25MM**	**25MM & OVER**
81	61	75	**NUMBER OF STATEMENTS**	2	7	7	14	19	26
%	%	%	**ASSETS**	%	%	%	%	%	%
6.9	6.5	6.5	Cash & Equivalents				3.3	4.7	6.1
21.6	23.8	22.0	Trade Receivables (net)				27.7	18.9	18.4
31.9	32.4	32.6	Inventory				28.8	46.8	31.8
3.2	2.4	1.5	All Other Current				.3	1.6	1.9
63.6	65.1	62.6	Total Current				60.1	71.9	58.3
29.6	26.6	25.4	Fixed Assets (net)				18.1	19.5	33.5
2.3	3.4	5.9	Intangibles (net)				14.5	5.2	1.4
4.5	4.9	6.1	All Other Non-Current				7.3	3.4	6.8
100.0	100.0	100.0	Total				100.0	100.0	100.0
			LIABILITIES						
12.8	12.7	12.0	Notes Payable-Short Term				19.7	12.9	7.9
2.5	2.1	2.3	Cur. Mat.-L.T.D.				2.4	2.4	2.5
12.3	12.1	10.3	Trade Payables				8.9	8.5	7.2
.0	.1	.2	Income Taxes Payable				.0	.0	.0
8.9	6.9	8.9	All Other Current				10.7	8.7	7.6
36.6	33.9	33.7	Total Current				41.6	32.6	25.1
17.1	18.5	13.2	Long-Term Debt				11.6	12.7	15.4
.3	.3	.3	Deferred Taxes				.0	.1	.7
7.3	5.2	7.2	All Other Non-Current				13.1	3.2	6.4
38.8	42.0	45.6	Net Worth				33.6	51.4	52.4
100.0	100.0	100.0	Total Liabilties & Net Worth				100.0	100.0	100.0
			INCOME DATA						
100.0	100.0	100.0	Net Sales				100.0	100.0	100.0
20.6	22.6	21.3	Gross Profit				18.0	20.1	21.3
18.6	17.5	17.8	Operating Expenses				18.6	17.0	14.2
2.0	5.0	3.5	Operating Profit				-.6	3.1	7.1
.8	.4	.7	All Other Expenses (net)				-1.7	.7	.8
1.2	4.6	2.7	Profit Before Taxes				1.1	2.3	6.2
			RATIOS						
3.6	4.5	4.4					3.5	5.1	3.6
2.1	2.4	2.1	Current				2.0	4.0	2.3
1.2	1.3	1.3					.9	1.7	1.6
1.7	2.1	1.8					1.7	2.1	1.9
.8	1.0	1.0	Quick				.9	1.3	.9
.5	.5	.4					.3	.3	.4
19 19.5	**20** 18.2	**18** 20.4					**14** 26.5	**15** 24.1	**19** 18.9
31 11.7	**32** 11.4	**30** 12.0	Sales/Receivables				**45** 8.1	**33** 11.0	**25** 14.4
51 7.1	**49** 7.4	**54** 6.8					**70** 5.2	**63** 5.8	**46** 8.0
33 11.2	**37** 9.8	**31** 11.8					**19** 19.3	**51** 7.2	**36** 10.1
58 6.3	**66** 5.5	**66** 5.5	Cost of Sales/Inventory				**65** 5.6	**126** 2.9	**87** 4.2
122 3.0	**130** 2.8	**130** 2.8					**83** 4.4	**215** 1.7	**140** 2.6
10 35.4	**8** 44.3	**8** 45.5					**6** 65.8	**8** 47.5	**9** 42.4
16 22.4	**17** 21.0	**15** 23.7	Cost of Sales/Payables				**9** 40.3	**12** 30.5	**16** 22.4
31 11.7	**31** 11.9	**26** 13.8					**38** 9.5	**24** 15.0	**21** 17.2
3.5	3.7	3.5					3.0	2.8	3.5
8.1	7.0	7.5	Sales/Working Capital				9.6	4.4	7.3
21.3	15.6	15.6					-52.7	12.3	14.8
7.5	29.9	21.5					36.8	9.7	38.1
(73) 2.4	(57) 6.3	(68) 5.9	EBIT/Interest				3.9	(17) 4.7	(25) 11.0
-.7	1.7	.9					-4.5	-.7	4.3
5.3		8.1							
(11) 1.6		(10) 1.8	Net Profit + Depr., Dep., Amort./Cur. Mat. L/T/D						
.5		.2							
.3	.2	.3					.2	.2	.2
.6	.6	.6	Fixed/Worth				.6	.3	.6
1.1	1.3	1.6					-8.6	2.2	1.4
.5	.4	.4					.7	.3	.4
1.0	1.0	1.0	Debt/Worth				4.0	.7	.8
4.7	3.9	5.8					-14.7	5.8	2.2
19.6	36.3	43.5						62.8	39.9
(71) 7.6	(56) 12.9	(64) 18.4	% Profit Before Taxes/Tangible Net Worth					(17) 16.8	17.2
-3.3	5.3	.3						-.2	8.3
9.6	16.5	16.0					17.8	14.7	15.1
2.2	6.6	8.1	% Profit Before Taxes/Total Assets				10.4	.9	9.2
-2.6	2.2	-.9					-8.1	-.9	4.5
16.9	18.8	15.8					476.6	28.0	10.1
7.2	7.7	9.1	Sales/Net Fixed Assets				12.2	9.3	6.9
4.5	5.0	5.1					6.9	6.0	3.8
3.1	2.9	2.7					2.7	2.4	2.6
2.1	2.0	1.9	Sales/Total Assets				2.2	1.7	2.0
1.2	1.3	1.3					1.4	1.2	1.2
1.0	1.1	1.3						1.0	1.5
(68) 2.5	(48) 2.3	(58) 2.2	% Depr., Dep., Amort./Sales					(16) 1.8	(22) 2.4
3.7	3.4	3.6						3.7	3.0
1.3	1.1	.9							
(23) 3.0	(15) 2.2	(27) 2.0	% Officers', Directors' Owners' Comp/Sales						
4.6	7.0	6.7							
2868023M	2997747M	3365982M	Net Sales ($)	1179M	16347M	27641M	102460M	307642M	2910713M
1840682M	1745407M	1830625M	Total Assets ($)	1021M	6664M	15896M	60041M	203081M	1543922M

M = $ thousand MM = $ million

See Pages 9 through 22 for Explanation of Ratios and Data

Current Data Sorted by Assets							Comparative Historical Data	
						Type of Statement		
	1					Unqualified	4	3
	2	4	2			Reviewed	16	15
1	1	5				Compiled	6	10
1	7	1				Tax Returns	7	13
3	3	6	4			Other	27	20
4 (4/1-9/30/13)			37 (10/1/13-3/31/14)				**4/1/09-3/31/10 ALL**	**4/1/10-3/31/11 ALL**
0-500M	**500M-2MM**	**2-10MM**	**10-50MM**	**50-100MM**	**100-250MM**			
5	14	16	6			**NUMBER OF STATEMENTS**	60	61
%	%	%	%	%	%	**ASSETS**	%	%
	12.0	7.4		DATA NOT AVAILABLE	DATA NOT AVAILABLE	Cash & Equivalents	9.7	9.8
	23.0	39.3				Trade Receivables (net)	19.8	21.2
	27.9	20.5				Inventory	22.4	23.7
	4.6	1.1				All Other Current	3.5	3.9
	67.5	68.2				Total Current	55.4	58.6
	25.9	25.0				Fixed Assets (net)	35.2	33.0
	1.0	4.6				Intangibles (net)	3.2	1.9
	5.7	2.2				All Other Non-Current	6.2	6.4
	100.0	100.0				Total	100.0	100.0
						LIABILITIES		
	3.4	6.4				Notes Payable-Short Term	12.7	15.0
	2.8	2.1				Cur. Mat.-L.T.D.	5.1	3.6
	7.3	25.0				Trade Payables	8.3	8.6
	.0	.0				Income Taxes Payable	.1	.0
	6.6	34.1				All Other Current	8.4	11.3
	20.1	67.5				Total Current	34.6	38.5
	19.3	5.8				Long-Term Debt	20.0	17.7
	.1	.2				Deferred Taxes	.4	.1
	17.7	5.4				All Other Non-Current	14.3	16.5
	42.8	21.1				Net Worth	30.7	27.3
	100.0	100.0				Total Liabilties & Net Worth	100.0	100.0
						INCOME DATA		
	100.0	100.0				Net Sales	100.0	100.0
	28.7	26.0				Gross Profit	30.5	28.6
	26.0	19.2				Operating Expenses	35.0	30.8
	2.8	6.8				Operating Profit	-4.5	-2.2
	.0	.0				All Other Expenses (net)	1.4	.7
	2.8	6.8				Profit Before Taxes	-5.9	-2.8
						RATIOS		
	13.1	3.9					5.1	5.4
	4.1	2.4				Current	1.7	2.0
	1.8	1.4					1.1	1.1
	6.2	2.7					2.9	2.4
	3.0	1.7				Quick	.9	1.1
	.9	1.1					.5	.5
	21 17.0	**32** 11.5					**23** 15.6	**21** 17.0
	24 15.2	**41** 8.9				Sales/Receivables	**32** 11.6	**34** 10.8
	42 8.7	**48** 7.6					**44** 8.2	**49** 7.4
	31 11.9	**15** 23.9					**34** 10.7	**35** 10.3
	41 8.9	**38** 9.6				Cost of Sales/Inventory	**53** 6.9	**55** 6.7
	55 6.6	**56** 6.5					**77** 4.8	**91** 4.0
	3 121.6	**11** 33.9					**8** 47.6	**6** 64.8
	10 36.7	**19** 19.7				Cost of Sales/Payables	**14** 26.3	**13** 29.0
	18 20.1	**31** 11.7					**24** 15.4	**24** 15.0
	4.3	5.6					4.7	4.0
	6.1	8.7				Sales/Working Capital	9.0	8.3
	12.0	23.8					93.8	56.9
	39.5	72.1					3.3	3.1
	(13) 3.5	(13) 30.1				EBIT/Interest	(55) -1.2	(51) -.3
	3.0	14.3					-9.6	-3.1
						Net Profit + Depr., Dep., Amort./Cur. Mat. L/T/D		
	.3	.2					.5	.4
	.8	.5				Fixed/Worth	1.1	.9
	2.2	.9					4.5	3.2
	.4	.4					.6	.4
	1.7	1.0				Debt/Worth	1.5	1.1
	6.5	2.2					12.2	6.9
	33.3	85.2					4.7	14.2
	(12) 17.6	(15) 42.6				% Profit Before Taxes/Tangible Net Worth	(48) -6.5	(49) -.2
	2.0	29.5					-41.2	-18.3
	19.7	31.1					2.2	4.9
	7.2	20.3				% Profit Before Taxes/Total Assets	-7.9	-2.0
	1.2	10.2					-28.4	-11.6
	19.2	50.3					12.3	13.4
	12.3	15.3				Sales/Net Fixed Assets	6.2	6.9
	6.9	7.3					3.9	4.3
	3.5	4.9					2.9	3.0
	2.9	3.1				Sales/Total Assets	2.1	2.2
	2.6	2.6					1.4	1.5
	.7	.9					1.6	2.2
	(12) 2.0	(13) 1.0				% Depr., Dep., Amort./Sales	(54) 3.7	(53) 3.1
	2.6	1.9					5.7	4.5
							2.0	1.9
						% Officers', Directors' Owners' Comp/Sales	(22) 3.3	(27) 3.6
							6.4	7.1
8924M	**44558M**	**236873M**	**273458M**			Net Sales ($)	**585655M**	**800703M**
1668M	**16121M**	**68578M**	**125797M**			Total Assets ($)	**308461M**	**462069M**

M = $ thousand MM = $ million

See Pages 9 through 22 for Explanation of Ratios and Data

Comparative Historical Data / Current Data Sorted by Sales

4/1/11-3/31/12 ALL	4/1/12-3/31/13 ALL	4/1/13-3/31/14 ALL	Type of Statement	0-1MM	1-3MM	3-5MM	5-10MM	10-25MM	25MM & OVER
5	3	1	Unqualified			1			
13	12	8	Reviewed		2			3	3
15	11	7	Compiled		1	1	2	3	
8	10	9	Tax Returns	1	2	3	2	1	
22	18	16	Other	1	4	1	3	4	3
					4 (4/1-9/30/13)		37 (10/1/13-3/31/14)		
63	54	41	NUMBER OF STATEMENTS	2	9	6	7	11	6
%	%	%	**ASSETS**	%	%	%	%	%	%
9.1	8.2	10.2	Cash & Equivalents					7.4	
22.9	28.6	30.8	Trade Receivables (net)					51.1	
22.7	24.5	22.7	Inventory					14.1	
3.9	3.4	2.6	All Other Current					1.8	
58.5	64.8	66.3	Total Current					74.4	
30.2	26.1	26.7	Fixed Assets (net)					15.8	
4.7	4.4	3.2	Intangibles (net)					7.7	
6.6	4.7	3.9	All Other Non-Current					2.0	
100.0	100.0	100.0	Total					100.0	
			LIABILITIES						
17.4	10.2	7.7	Notes Payable-Short Term					3.1	
3.5	2.4	2.1	Cur. Mat.-L.T.D.					2.3	
11.5	11.6	16.2	Trade Payables					22.5	
.1	.2	.0	Income Taxes Payable					.0	
12.0	16.8	24.5	All Other Current					10.9	
44.5	41.1	50.5	Total Current					38.8	
13.8	11.0	12.7	Long-Term Debt					6.7	
.1	.2	.1	Deferred Taxes					.2	
22.5	25.8	20.9	All Other Non-Current					7.4	
19.0	21.9	15.7	Net Worth					46.8	
100.0	100.0	100.0	Total Liabilties & Net Worth					100.0	
			INCOME DATA						
100.0	100.0	100.0	Net Sales					100.0	
29.4	27.5	27.0	Gross Profit					23.5	
30.2	26.8	22.7	Operating Expenses					17.8	
-.8	.8	4.2	Operating Profit					5.8	
1.0	.3	.2	All Other Expenses (net)					.4	
-1.8	.4	4.1	Profit Before Taxes					5.4	
			RATIOS						
4.5	4.5	6.9						2.8	
1.6	2.6	2.2	Current					2.0	
1.1	1.3	1.4						1.4	
2.1	2.1	3.4						2.1	
.8	1.1	1.5	Quick					1.5	
.5	.7	.9						1.2	
20 18.0	**29** 12.5	**22** 16.3						**41** 8.9	
32 11.4	**34** 10.6	**36** 10.0	Sales/Receivables					**48** 7.6	
43 8.4	**49** 7.5	**47** 7.7						**58** 6.3	
30 12.0	**30** 12.3	**21** 17.8						**1** 717.6	
51 7.2	**43** 8.5	**37** 9.9	Cost of Sales/Inventory					**19** 19.7	
66 5.5	**72** 5.1	**53** 6.9						**53** 6.9	
7 55.8	**7** 49.0	**7** 52.7						**11** 33.5	
14 25.4	**14** 26.0	**13** 27.9	Cost of Sales/Payables					**20** 18.0	
25 14.4	**25** 14.6	**28** 13.0						**31** 11.7	
4.9	4.6	5.5						5.7	
9.7	8.1	8.2	Sales/Working Capital					8.0	
108.7	24.2	18.5						13.1	
3.9	7.0	35.0							
(53) 1.1	(44) 2.2	(35) 7.9	EBIT/Interest						
-2.5	.1	3.1							
			Net Profit + Depr., Dep., Amort./Cur. Mat. L/T/D						
.5	.4	.3						.1	
.8	.6	.6	Fixed/Worth					.3	
10.5	1.9	1.6						.5	
.4	.4	.5						.6	
1.6	1.7	1.6	Debt/Worth					1.1	
13.3	7.1	4.7						2.3	
21.4	28.6	60.0						85.2	
(48) 5.2	(43) 11.5	(35) 30.0	% Profit Before Taxes/Tangible Net Worth					42.6	
-9.9	4.1	9.4						12.7	
5.6	10.6	23.4						32.3	
.6	3.8	9.8	% Profit Before Taxes/Total Assets					20.2	
-9.9	-1.2	3.4						3.5	
19.6	24.2	25.1						77.1	
8.2	13.1	12.9	Sales/Net Fixed Assets					24.7	
4.7	6.3	7.2						11.2	
3.3	3.5	3.9						5.4	
2.3	2.5	3.0	Sales/Total Assets					2.9	
1.5	1.8	2.4						2.0	
2.1	.9	.9							
(54) 2.7	(51) 1.7	(33) 1.2	% Depr., Dep., Amort./Sales						
4.5	3.1	2.5							
1.1	.9	.9							
(27) 3.1	(24) 2.7	(19) 3.3	% Officers', Directors' Owners' Comp/Sales						
6.3	7.3	5.3							
901636M	759800M	563813M	Net Sales ($)	653M	18133M	23613M	52693M	175624M	293097M
420735M	345936M	212164M	Total Assets ($)	743M	5640M	7570M	19618M	69580M	109013M

M = $ thousand MM = $ million

See Pages 9 through 22 for Explanation of Ratios and Data

Current Data Sorted by Assets							Comparative Historical Data	
						Type of Statement		
			5	1	1	Unqualified	12	10
	2	7	3		1	Reviewed	35	34
	8	9				Compiled	25	21
3	10	7			1	Tax Returns	46	43
1	10	9	12	2		Other	57	67
	14 (4/1-9/30/13)		78 (10/1/13-3/31/14)				4/1/09-3/31/10 ALL	4/1/10-3/31/11 ALL
0-500M	500M-2MM	2-10MM	10-50MM	50-100MM	100-250MM			
4	30	32	20	3	3	**NUMBER OF STATEMENTS**	175	175
%	%	%	%	%	%	**ASSETS**	%	%
	12.0	12.5	7.7			Cash & Equivalents	8.2	11.0
	30.3	27.2	22.9			Trade Receivables (net)	24.9	24.0
	23.6	23.6	30.4			Inventory	24.5	25.5
	.4	3.6	1.8			All Other Current	2.9	2.5
	66.3	66.8	62.7			Total Current	60.4	63.1
	22.2	23.2	31.4			Fixed Assets (net)	30.1	28.8
	3.4	2.5	2.7			Intangibles (net)	3.0	2.6
	8.1	7.5	3.2			All Other Non-Current	6.5	5.5
	100.0	100.0	100.0			Total	100.0	100.0
						LIABILITIES		
	11.0	9.7	14.2			Notes Payable-Short Term	14.9	16.2
	3.0	2.4	1.5			Cur. Mat.-L.T.D.	5.0	3.8
	17.2	12.8	10.7			Trade Payables	14.0	13.9
	.8	.1	.1			Income Taxes Payable	.2	.2
	20.4	11.5	7.2			All Other Current	11.3	11.8
	52.4	36.4	33.6			Total Current	45.3	45.8
	27.4	14.3	16.1			Long-Term Debt	21.8	18.2
	.5	.2	.4			Deferred Taxes	.4	.3
	11.4	7.4	4.0			All Other Non-Current	9.0	8.6
	8.3	41.7	45.8			Net Worth	23.5	27.1
	100.0	100.0	100.0			Total Liabilties & Net Worth	100.0	100.0
						INCOME DATA		
	100.0	100.0	100.0			Net Sales	100.0	100.0
	30.8	29.1	20.0			Gross Profit	26.0	29.5
	27.1	24.8	15.8			Operating Expenses	27.7	29.0
	3.7	4.3	4.2			Operating Profit	-1.6	.5
	1.3	.4	.5			All Other Expenses (net)	1.0	.8
	2.4	3.9	3.7			Profit Before Taxes	-2.7	-.3
						RATIOS		
	2.1	2.7	4.2				2.6	3.0
	1.5	1.7	1.9			Current	1.5	1.6
	.8	1.4	1.3				1.0	1.0
	1.7	2.1	1.7				1.5	1.6
	1.0	1.1	.9			Quick	(174) .8	.9
	.4	.7	.5				.4	.4
	18 20.0	**25** 14.6	**21** 17.1				**21** 17.4	**21** 17.1
	30 12.2	**40** 9.1	**38** 9.7			Sales/Receivables	**33** 10.9	**35** 10.4
	52 7.0	**68** 5.4	**46** 7.9				**51** 7.1	**50** 7.3
	19 19.4	**29** 12.8	**36** 10.2				**20** 18.2	**24** 15.2
	29 12.6	**51** 7.2	**62** 5.9			Cost of Sales/Inventory	**51** 7.2	**48** 7.6
	68 5.4	**76** 4.8	**96** 3.8				**84** 4.3	**93** 3.9
	12 29.2	**13** 28.8	**9** 39.3				**10** 36.0	**12** 30.3
	31 11.6	**20** 18.3	**17** 20.9			Cost of Sales/Payables	**18** 19.9	**19** 19.2
	44 8.3	**47** 7.7	**27** 13.4				**37** 9.9	**33** 10.9
	7.0	5.3	4.9				5.6	5.5
	13.4	7.9	8.7			Sales/Working Capital	11.7	10.4
	-49.9	13.9	16.8				-136.6	181.7
	18.4	22.2	12.1				3.9	6.2
	(28) 3.0	(30) 5.6	(19) 3.2			EBIT/Interest	(163) .6	(155) 1.9
	1.0	.5	2.2				-4.4	-1.8
							3.7	5.2
						Net Profit + Depr., Dep., Amort./Cur. Mat. L/T/D	(23) 2.1	(22) 2.2
							.3	.0
	.0	.3	.4				.3	.4
	.4	.5	.8			Fixed/Worth	1.0	.9
	31.2	1.6	1.3				-27.7	4.7
	1.0	.7	.7				.8	.8
	4.2	1.3	1.1			Debt/Worth	2.1	2.0
	-12.3	5.1	2.2				-59.8	12.1
	52.2	38.9	29.1				18.7	26.3
	(22) 31.5	(29) 14.7	(18) 14.9			% Profit Before Taxes/Tangible Net Worth	(131) .8	(140) 6.7
	7.0	-5.8	5.6				-21.0	-6.4
	22.6	16.7	13.5				5.0	8.2
	6.3	8.4	5.3			% Profit Before Taxes/Total Assets	-1.0	2.2
	.3	-1.3	3.4				-11.1	-5.7
	308.8	34.4	11.9				18.1	23.0
	18.9	13.6	8.5			Sales/Net Fixed Assets	9.4	10.2
	7.1	6.5	4.8				4.4	4.8
	4.4	3.2	2.9				3.2	3.4
	3.3	2.2	2.4			Sales/Total Assets	2.2	2.4
	2.1	1.7	1.9				1.6	1.6
	1.1	.9	.9				1.2	1.4
	(20) 2.2	(30) 1.7	1.3			% Depr., Dep., Amort./Sales	(143) 2.3	(144) 2.3
	3.6	2.5	2.7				3.7	3.7
	2.1	1.5					2.1	2.2
	(17) 3.3	(15) 3.3				% Officers', Directors' Owners' Comp/Sales	(63) 4.2	(74) 4.2
	6.0	6.0					8.3	7.6
4129M	112981M	376159M	993353M	426750M	1186335M	Net Sales ($)	3612346M	3460399M
818M	35185M	153197M	414251M	194219M	456956M	Total Assets ($)	2082688M	1899530M

M = $ thousand MM = $ million

See Pages 9 through 22 for Explanation of Ratios and Data

Comparative Historical Data

Type of Statement	4/1/11-3/31/12 ALL	4/1/12-3/31/13 ALL	4/1/13-3/31/14 ALL
Unqualified	6	5	7
Reviewed	29	22	13
Compiled	25	17	17
Tax Returns	43	28	21
Other	57	45	34
NUMBER OF STATEMENTS	160	117	92
ASSETS	%	%	%
Cash & Equivalents	9.8	9.7	11.3
Trade Receivables (net)	25.4	27.0	26.4
Inventory	24.2	24.1	25.4
All Other Current	1.7	2.8	1.9
Total Current	61.1	63.6	65.0
Fixed Assets (net)	28.2	25.1	25.2
Intangibles (net)	3.0	2.3	3.2
All Other Non-Current	7.7	9.0	6.6
Total	100.0	100.0	100.0
LIABILITIES			
Notes Payable-Short Term	13.9	15.7	13.6
Cur. Mat.-L.T.D.	3.8	3.2	2.6
Trade Payables	13.1	14.8	14.1
Income Taxes Payable	.2	.1	.3
All Other Current	12.2	9.8	16.3
Total Current	43.2	43.6	46.9
Long-Term Debt	19.4	17.3	19.3
Deferred Taxes	.3	.3	.4
All Other Non-Current	12.1	15.1	10.9
Net Worth	25.0	23.7	22.4
Total Liabilities & Net Worth	100.0	100.0	100.0
INCOME DATA			
Net Sales	100.0	100.0	100.0
Gross Profit	30.8	28.7	27.6
Operating Expenses	29.4	26.5	23.8
Operating Profit	1.4	2.2	3.9
All Other Expenses (net)	.8	.3	.8
Profit Before Taxes	.6	1.9	3.1
RATIOS			
Current	3.2	3.2	2.5
	1.7	1.7	1.7
	.9	1.1	1.3
Quick	1.8	1.8	1.8
	.9	.9	1.0
	.5	.5	.5
Sales/Receivables	**19** 18.8	**23** 16.1	**20** 18.0
	34 10.6	**33** 11.1	**32** 11.5
	52 7.0	**55** 6.6	**50** 7.3
Cost of Sales/Inventory	**22** 16.4	**18** 20.0	**24** 15.0
	41 8.9	**45** 8.2	**45** 8.2
	79 4.6	**81** 4.5	**74** 4.9
Cost of Sales/Payables	**9** 42.2	**12** 30.5	**12** 31.4
	19 19.3	**21** 17.6	**20** 18.3
	41 8.9	**38** 9.6	**40** 9.1
Sales/Working Capital	5.5	5.0	5.5
	10.3	9.3	8.7
	-42.3	49.3	20.5
EBIT/Interest	7.0	13.0	18.0
	(143) 1.9	(103) 3.2	(87) 3.8
	-.5	1.1	1.3
Net Profit + Depr., Dep., Amort./Cur. Mat. L/T/D	2.0	7.1	7.9
	(20) 1.2	(15) 3.3	(13) 4.9
	-.5	2.0	2.3
Fixed/Worth	.3	.3	.3
	.8	.6	.6
	NM	5.0	2.5
Debt/Worth	.8	.6	.9
	1.6	1.6	2.0
	NM	14.3	7.0
% Profit Before Taxes/Tangible Net Worth	27.2	30.0	45.7
	(120) 6.4	(94) 12.0	(73) 16.0
	-5.8	.2	1.8
% Profit Before Taxes/Total Assets	10.9	12.2	15.1
	2.8	4.6	6.3
	-4.1	.2	.6
Sales/Net Fixed Assets	29.5	28.3	34.5
	10.4	11.2	11.3
	5.2	6.1	5.7
Sales/Total Assets	3.3	3.3	3.5
	2.4	2.4	2.5
	1.7	1.8	1.8
% Depr., Dep., Amort./Sales	1.0	.8	.9
	(138) 2.0	(101) 1.7	(78) 1.9
	3.5	2.6	3.1
% Officers', Directors' Owners' Comp/Sales	2.0	2.2	1.5
	(68) 4.3	(44) 3.8	(43) 3.2
	6.8	6.3	5.1
Net Sales ($)	3077345M	3890024M	3099707M
Total Assets ($)	1494683M	1860139M	1254626M

Current Data Sorted by Sales

14 (4/1-9/30/13) — 78 (10/1/13-3/31/14)

Type of Statement	0-1MM	1-3MM	3-5MM	5-10MM	10-25MM	25MM & OVER
Unqualified						7
Reviewed		2		3	2	6
Compiled	2	5	1	6	3	
Tax Returns	1	7	4	5	3	1
Other	1	1	6	6	7	13
NUMBER OF STATEMENTS	4	15	11	20	15	27
ASSETS	%	%	%	%	%	%
Cash & Equivalents		9.1	12.5	16.1	9.1	11.2
Trade Receivables (net)		22.7	29.6	31.3	26.5	22.6
Inventory		23.1	24.8	19.6	28.3	28.8
All Other Current		.6	.3	1.5	5.4	2.0
Total Current		55.5	67.1	68.5	69.3	64.5
Fixed Assets (net)		33.1	19.1	21.7	22.6	26.8
Intangibles (net)		3.5	4.6	2.8	1.1	3.6
All Other Non-Current		7.9	9.2	7.1	7.1	5.1
Total		100.0	100.0	100.0	100.0	100.0
LIABILITIES						
Notes Payable-Short Term		17.5	13.6	6.7	11.0	12.0
Cur. Mat.-L.T.D.		2.2	2.2	2.6	.8	3.7
Trade Payables		13.4	17.5	16.8	10.7	10.6
Income Taxes Payable		.0	.0	1.3	.1	.0
All Other Current		25.6	29.7	10.4	8.8	12.3
Total Current		58.7	63.0	37.9	31.5	38.6
Long-Term Debt		29.0	39.8	14.4	11.7	13.2
Deferred Taxes		.1	.8	.4	.5	.4
All Other Non-Current		14.5	10.7	2.0	6.5	9.2
Net Worth		-2.3	-14.3	45.2	49.7	38.6
Total Liabilities & Net Worth		100.0	100.0	100.0	100.0	100.0
INCOME DATA						
Net Sales		100.0	100.0	100.0	100.0	100.0
Gross Profit		28.4	33.0	29.6	25.9	22.1
Operating Expenses		26.7	26.7	25.2	20.6	18.5
Operating Profit		1.7	6.4	4.4	5.3	3.6
All Other Expenses (net)		1.1	2.0	.4	.6	.2
Profit Before Taxes		.6	4.4	4.0	4.8	3.4
RATIOS						
Current		2.0	2.1	2.1	8.4	2.9
		1.6	1.3	1.8	2.5	1.8
		.5	.5	1.4	1.4	1.3
Quick		1.2	1.8	1.9	3.9	1.4
		.6	.8	1.3	1.2	.8
		.4	.4	.8	.6	.5
Sales/Receivables		**15** 24.1	**19** 19.7	**18** 20.5	**31** 11.8	**21** 17.7
		40 9.1	**27** 13.7	**35** 10.3	**40** 9.1	**29** 12.5
		51 7.2	**40** 9.2	**63** 5.8	**65** 5.6	**41** 9.0
Cost of Sales/Inventory		**22** 16.3	**23** 15.9	**9** 39.4	**44** 8.3	**33** 11.2
		37 9.9	**29** 12.4	**23** 15.7	**60** 6.1	**47** 7.7
		111 3.3	**69** 5.3	**68** 5.4	**76** 4.8	**73** 5.0
Cost of Sales/Payables		**11** 33.6	**18** 20.5	**8** 44.0	**11** 32.4	**11** 32.4
		21 17.5	**30** 12.2	**30** 12.2	**16** 22.9	**15** 24.1
		48 7.6	**38** 9.5	**46** 8.0	**21** 17.0	**25** 14.8
Sales/Working Capital		5.3	6.1	7.2	2.8	6.4
		7.5	24.0	9.8	5.2	9.3
		-9.4	-10.8	15.2	14.7	17.7
EBIT/Interest		18.1	24.8	31.4	14.4	18.0
		(14) 1.4	(10) 4.0	(19) 7.9	(14) 7.0	(26) 4.8
		-1.2	1.7	.6	1.4	2.4
Net Profit + Depr., Dep., Amort./Cur. Mat. L/T/D						
Fixed/Worth		.2	.0	.0	.2	.4
		1.4	1.6	.4	.4	.8
		-1.2	-1.1	.7	1.2	2.6
Debt/Worth		1.0	2.8	.7	.3	.7
		5.5	6.2	1.0	1.0	1.8
		-2.8	-3.9	2.8	1.9	7.0
% Profit Before Taxes/Tangible Net Worth				55.7	30.2	33.4
				(19) 18.9	(14) 13.3	(22) 17.1
				-5.7	1.3	5.6
% Profit Before Taxes/Total Assets		6.2	23.2	21.2	14.6	14.2
		1.4	12.3	9.9	10.3	10.1
		-4.8	2.2	-1.3	.6	2.1
Sales/Net Fixed Assets		26.2	431.3	152.4	39.4	20.0
		9.5	20.0	12.2	15.5	9.6
		4.3	8.1	6.8	6.0	5.4
Sales/Total Assets		3.9	4.6	4.1	3.0	3.4
		2.2	3.8	2.8	2.4	2.6
		1.8	1.8	1.8	1.6	2.0
% Depr., Dep., Amort./Sales		1.1		.5	1.2	.9
		(12) 2.4		(15) 1.8	(14) 1.8	(26) 1.3
		5.0		3.7	2.6	2.8
% Officers', Directors' Owners' Comp/Sales		3.0				1.5
		(10) 4.1				(10) 2.5
		8.3				4.7
Net Sales ($)	3050M	32701M	39561M	141302M	212062M	2671031M
Total Assets ($)	1957M	18269M	14135M	57038M	108588M	1054639M

M = $ thousand MM = $ million

See Pages 9 through 22 for Explanation of Ratios and Data

Current Data Sorted by Assets | **Comparative Historical Data**

						Type of Statement		
			3		1	Unqualified	9	10
		3	3			Reviewed	12	11
1	1	2	1			Compiled	13	9
2	1	4				Tax Returns	4	8
1	1	3	8	4	2	Other	23	13
11 (4/1-9/30/13)			30 (10/1/13-3/31/14)				4/1/09-3/31/10	4/1/10-3/31/11
0-500M	**500M-2MM**	**2-10MM**	**10-50MM**	**50-100MM**	**100-250MM**		**ALL**	**ALL**
4	3	12	15	4	3	**NUMBER OF STATEMENTS**	61	51
%	%	%	%	%	%	**ASSETS**	%	%
		8.3	4.1			Cash & Equivalents	6.6	5.8
		21.2	18.1			Trade Receivables (net)	12.1	15.2
		24.8	36.8			Inventory	34.6	33.9
		.9	1.3			All Other Current	2.2	1.1
		55.2	60.3			Total Current	55.6	55.9
		30.3	31.3			Fixed Assets (net)	34.7	36.7
		.0	2.0			Intangibles (net)	1.7	.7
		14.5	6.4			All Other Non-Current	8.1	6.6
		100.0	100.0			Total	100.0	100.0
						LIABILITIES		
		14.4	13.2			Notes Payable-Short Term	16.9	19.6
		3.2	1.9			Cur. Mat.-L.T.D.	6.3	4.1
		9.7	6.0			Trade Payables	8.3	12.4
		.1	.4			Income Taxes Payable	.1	.0
		10.9	7.5			All Other Current	6.8	6.0
		38.4	29.1			Total Current	38.4	42.1
		16.8	5.0			Long-Term Debt	19.2	17.7
		.0	.1			Deferred Taxes	.6	.4
		.6	2.1			All Other Non-Current	5.0	4.3
		44.1	63.7			Net Worth	36.8	35.4
		100.0	100.0			Total Liabilties & Net Worth	100.0	100.0
						INCOME DATA		
		100.0	100.0			Net Sales	100.0	100.0
		17.2	16.2			Gross Profit	17.2	20.5
		12.4	12.2			Operating Expenses	18.8	18.3
		4.8	4.0			Operating Profit	-1.6	2.2
		.4	-.1			All Other Expenses (net)	1.0	2.0
		4.4	4.1			Profit Before Taxes	-2.6	.2
						RATIOS		
		3.3	4.5				2.1	2.2
		1.5	2.1			Current	1.7	1.5
		1.1	1.3				1.1	1.1
		1.5	1.2				.8	1.0
		.8	.8			Quick	.4	.5
		.4	.5				.3	.3
		15 24.0	**15** 23.6				**12** 30.4	**13** 27.6
		25 14.7	**22** 16.3			Sales/Receivables	**23** 15.9	**21** 17.4
		35 10.4	**44** 8.3				**30** 12.2	**36** 10.0
		29 12.6	**57** 6.4				**43** 8.6	**50** 7.3
		42 8.7	**78** 4.7			Cost of Sales/Inventory	**79** 4.6	**70** 5.2
		53 6.9	**111** 3.3				**130** 2.8	**104** 3.5
		7 49.8	**4** 89.4				**7** 49.4	**6** 58.1
		14 26.7	**14** 26.3			Cost of Sales/Payables	**13** 28.6	**17** 21.7
		21 17.3	**18** 20.2				**30** 12.0	**29** 12.7
		8.1	3.4				4.7	6.2
		16.0	6.6			Sales/Working Capital	8.9	11.3
		754.4	16.2				37.9	161.1
		14.4	13.4				2.6	4.1
		5.1	(14) 8.5			EBIT/Interest	(59) .0	(46) 1.6
		2.6	4.1				-2.9	-.2
							4.5	
						Net Profit + Depr., Dep., Amort./Cur. Mat. L/T/D	(18) 1.3	
							.5	
		.4	.3				.4	.4
		.6	.5			Fixed/Worth	.8	.8
		1.3	.7				2.6	2.1
		.7	.3				.6	.6
		1.2	.6			Debt/Worth	1.5	1.6
		2.4	1.3				5.8	5.0
		37.5	35.0				12.3	21.3
		18.1	16.1			% Profit Before Taxes/Tangible Net Worth	(52) -1.8	(46) 7.6
		6.2	4.6				-17.4	-2.0
		18.2	18.9				4.0	7.8
		5.7	8.1			% Profit Before Taxes/Total Assets	-1.1	1.8
		2.2	2.5				-7.8	-1.5
		24.7	16.2				16.5	19.2
		9.2	8.6			Sales/Net Fixed Assets	5.0	7.1
		4.0	4.3				3.1	3.0
		3.2	3.0				2.7	2.9
		2.3	1.8			Sales/Total Assets	1.7	1.9
		2.0	1.7				1.0	1.4
		1.1	.9				1.9	1.1
		(11) 2.1	(13) 1.4			% Depr., Dep., Amort./Sales	(55) 3.8	(48) 2.8
		5.1	5.0				5.0	4.5
							1.5	1.8
						% Officers', Directors' Owners' Comp/Sales	(19) 4.2	(17) 3.4
							8.5	5.8
4771M	**9850M**	**154344M**	**763676M**	**525698M**	**246676M**	Net Sales ($)	**1310147M**	**1501516M**
964M	**3102M**	**60352M**	**363110M**	**292985M**	**378299M**	Total Assets ($)	**920769M**	**759962M**

M = $ thousand MM = $ million

See Pages 9 through 22 for Explanation of Ratios and Data

Comparative Historical Data | **Current Data Sorted by Sales**

4/1/11-3/31/12 ALL	4/1/12-3/31/13 ALL	4/1/13-3/31/14 ALL	**Type of Statement**	0-1MM	1-3MM	3-5MM	5-10MM	10-25MM	25MM & OVER
8	9	4	Unqualified						4
9	7	6	Reviewed				2	2	2
8	11	5	Compiled		2		1	2	
8	4	7	Tax Returns	1	2		1	3	
12	19	19	Other	1		1	1	2	14
					11 (4/1-9/30/13)		30 (10/1/13-3/31/14)		
45	50	41	**NUMBER OF STATEMENTS**	2	4	1	5	9	20
%	%	%	**ASSETS**	%	%	%	%	%	%
4.1	4.8	5.5	Cash & Equivalents						2.7
14.3	16.3	18.0	Trade Receivables (net)						16.6
36.3	33.9	26.7	Inventory						31.7
1.9	2.1	1.9	All Other Current						2.4
56.6	57.1	52.1	Total Current						53.4
31.2	34.1	34.0	Fixed Assets (net)						32.6
.9	.9	1.5	Intangibles (net)						3.0
11.2	7.9	12.4	All Other Non-Current						11.1
100.0	100.0	100.0	Total						100.0
			LIABILITIES						
18.4	18.1	12.1	Notes Payable-Short Term						13.6
4.0	4.4	5.2	Cur. Mat.-L.T.D.						3.4
9.4	11.2	8.9	Trade Payables						6.0
.1	.1	.2	Income Taxes Payable						.4
6.9	8.3	8.6	All Other Current						6.5
38.8	42.2	35.0	Total Current						29.8
20.4	21.6	25.4	Long-Term Debt						13.4
.2	.5	1.3	Deferred Taxes						2.7
7.5	5.1	4.6	All Other Non-Current						2.3
33.0	30.6	33.7	Net Worth						51.8
100.0	100.0	100.0	Total Liabilties & Net Worth						100.0
			INCOME DATA						
100.0	100.0	100.0	Net Sales						100.0
22.2	24.1	21.4	Gross Profit						17.2
19.6	20.2	17.5	Operating Expenses						13.2
2.7	3.8	3.9	Operating Profit						4.1
1.2	.9	.2	All Other Expenses (net)						.5
1.4	3.0	3.7	Profit Before Taxes						3.6
			RATIOS						
3.3	3.0	3.0							2.6
1.4	1.5	1.7	Current						1.7
1.0	1.1	1.0							1.2
1.2	1.0	1.2							1.1
.5	.6	.7	Quick						.6
.3	.3	.4							.4
14 25.6	13 27.3	16 22.8							18 20.0
25 14.8	22 16.8	24 15.4	Sales/Receivables						24 15.4
32 11.5	32 11.4	39 9.4							41 9.0
44 8.3	35 10.3	31 11.7							42 8.6
85 4.3	69 5.3	54 6.7	Cost of Sales/Inventory						73 5.0
107 3.4	122 3.0	83 4.4							99 3.7
7 53.8	6 61.9	8 48.4							9 40.7
17 21.9	14 26.1	14 26.3	Cost of Sales/Payables						14 26.0
36 10.0	27 13.7	26 14.3							20 18.5
5.0	4.5	5.1							5.1
11.3	11.5	12.2	Sales/Working Capital						7.7
NM	186.2	626.8							17.0
5.4	6.6	10.0							9.9
(41) 1.5	(46) 3.2	(38) 5.1	EBIT/Interest						(19) 5.3
.4	1.2	2.0							2.0
		6.8							
		(10) 2.7	Net Profit + Depr., Dep., Amort./Cur. Mat. L/T/D						
		1.2							
.3	.4	.3							.3
.8	.7	.6	Fixed/Worth						.6
1.9	1.7	1.3							1.0
.8	.6	.5							.5
1.7	1.5	1.2	Debt/Worth						1.2
4.8	2.9	2.6							1.9
21.0	32.1	31.1							27.1
(41) 4.7	(46) 10.9	(37) 16.1	% Profit Before Taxes/Tangible Net Worth						(19) 11.7
-2.1	3.5	5.3							.2
8.3	13.3	16.1							13.6
.9	5.0	6.0	% Profit Before Taxes/Total Assets						6.8
-1.8	.6	1.6							.7
20.4	20.3	13.8							15.2
8.2	7.5	8.3	Sales/Net Fixed Assets						7.9
3.5	4.5	3.7							2.4
3.1	3.0	3.3							3.0
2.1	2.3	2.1	Sales/Total Assets						1.8
1.4	1.4	1.4							1.0
1.1	.8	.8							.5
(38) 2.5	(42) 2.1	(33) 1.7	% Depr., Dep., Amort./Sales						(17) 1.2
4.5	4.5	5.6							3.3
1.5	1.8	1.6							
(19) 2.0	(21) 2.8	(16) 2.2	% Officers', Directors' Owners' Comp/Sales						
3.0	5.5	4.3							
921215M	1202749M	1705015M	Net Sales ($)	853M	8050M	4049M	39514M	159120M	1493429M
570433M	702700M	1098812M	Total Assets ($)	247M	2615M	2438M	18358M	80736M	994418M

M = $ thousand MM = $ million

See Pages 9 through 22 for Explanation of Ratios and Data

Current Data Sorted by Assets							Comparative Historical Data	
			4	1	2	**Type of Statement** Unqualified	7	6
	3	15	3			Reviewed	21	17
	4	3	1			Compiled	19	19
8	7	5	1			Tax Returns	24	15
3	11	8	3	1	2	Other	32	36
15 (4/1-9/30/13)		70 (10/1/13-3/31/14)					4/1/09-3/31/10 ALL	4/1/10-3/31/11 ALL
0-500M	500M-2MM	2-10MM	10-50MM	50-100MM	100-250MM			
11	25	31	12	2	4	**NUMBER OF STATEMENTS**	103	93
%	%	%	%	%	%	**ASSETS**	%	%
16.5	8.3	6.6	4.6			Cash & Equivalents	7.5	7.8
27.7	29.3	30.1	14.2			Trade Receivables (net)	23.2	25.7
22.2	26.3	30.1	37.3			Inventory	26.2	25.1
2.6	1.7	2.7	4.2			All Other Current	3.3	2.7
68.9	65.7	69.4	60.3			Total Current	60.3	61.2
23.3	22.2	23.2	29.3			Fixed Assets (net)	27.9	26.9
2.8	1.2	1.3	6.2			Intangibles (net)	4.2	3.1
5.0	10.9	6.1	4.1			All Other Non-Current	7.7	8.8
100.0	100.0	100.0	100.0			Total	100.0	100.0
						LIABILITIES		
31.2	12.1	12.6	11.8			Notes Payable-Short Term	15.5	22.2
2.8	1.9	3.4	6.2			Cur. Mat.-L.T.D.	5.9	7.5
16.0	19.9	16.4	8.1			Trade Payables	14.1	15.2
.0	.0	.1	.9			Income Taxes Payable	.1	.2
18.0	9.1	10.0	10.8			All Other Current	8.2	8.0
68.0	43.0	42.5	37.7			Total Current	43.8	53.0
29.6	21.9	14.9	14.2			Long-Term Debt	24.1	22.6
.0	.0	.6	1.6			Deferred Taxes	.2	.1
8.6	10.4	3.5	3.1			All Other Non-Current	10.7	15.7
-6.2	24.7	38.5	43.4			Net Worth	21.2	8.6
100.0	100.0	100.0	100.0			Total Liabilties & Net Worth	100.0	100.0
						INCOME DATA		
100.0	100.0	100.0	100.0			Net Sales	100.0	100.0
33.0	31.9	22.7	20.6			Gross Profit	27.8	28.0
32.2	30.0	18.4	17.3			Operating Expenses	28.5	28.5
.8	1.9	4.3	3.3			Operating Profit	-.7	-.4
.4	.4	.5	1.1			All Other Expenses (net)	1.6	1.3
.4	1.6	3.8	2.1			Profit Before Taxes	-2.3	-1.7
						RATIOS		
2.7	4.0	3.1	2.5				3.0	2.3
1.3	1.5	1.6	1.7			Current	1.6	1.3
.4	1.0	1.1	1.2				1.0	.8
2.5	2.6	1.9	.9				1.6	1.3
1.0	.9	.9	.5			Quick	.8	.7
.3	.4	.5	.2				.4	.4
1 342.0	**27** 13.3	**24** 15.3	**13** 28.2				**21** 17.2	**21** 17.5
11 34.1	**39** 9.4	**41** 8.8	**23** 16.2			Sales/Receivables	**36** 10.2	**36** 10.2
41 8.9	**49** 7.4	**79** 4.6	**31** 11.9				**53** 6.9	**49** 7.4
0 UND	**15** 24.0	**4** 89.1	**36** 10.0				**15** 24.3	**12** 29.2
9 41.1	**40** 9.2	**56** 6.5	**111** 3.3			Cost of Sales/Inventory	**50** 7.2	**49** 7.5
26 14.0	**72** 5.1	**118** 3.1	**140** 2.6				**115** 3.2	**93** 3.9
0 UND	**13** 27.1	**13** 28.0	**9** 40.7				**10** 36.5	**10** 37.1
10 35.7	**30** 12.1	**23** 16.0	**15** 25.0			Cost of Sales/Payables	**20** 18.0	**20** 18.3
25 14.6	**50** 7.3	**49** 7.4	**27** 13.6				**42** 8.8	**47** 7.7
8.6	6.1	5.0	5.5				4.5	6.3
102.6	8.0	7.8	7.5			Sales/Working Capital	11.2	17.7
-23.8	NM	29.4	18.1				119.2	-30.3
	9.1	11.8	10.4				3.9	3.9
	(24) 3.7	(28) 4.8	3.4			EBIT/Interest	(92) 1.1	(80) 1.0
	.4	1.5	1.2				-3.9	-2.8
							3.3	6.0
						Net Profit + Depr., Dep., Amort./Cur. Mat. L/T/D	(19) 1.0	(15) 3.0
							-.3	.1
.0	.1	.3	.4				.4	.4
.7	.5	.6	.8			Fixed/Worth	.9	1.0
-.5	-3.0	1.4	2.4				-15.0	-3.0
2.2	.5	.7	.7				.7	1.0
6.9	2.1	1.6	1.7			Debt/Worth	2.5	3.2
-4.3	-7.8	4.4	4.7				-30.0	-7.9
	25.9	39.9	46.4				24.4	32.9
	(17) 4.5	(27) 18.1	(11) 13.7			% Profit Before Taxes/Tangible Net Worth	(74) 1.3	(65) 4.2
	-17.5	1.5	3.5				-30.6	-19.3
9.6	17.4	15.8	9.5				7.6	9.0
3.4	7.1	4.2	4.5			% Profit Before Taxes/Total Assets	.3	.7
-6.7	-1.5	.7	.1				-10.8	-11.4
UND	57.5	25.8	13.2				19.0	22.3
47.1	19.6	11.5	6.5			Sales/Net Fixed Assets	8.4	10.7
17.5	8.1	4.8	3.6				5.3	5.6
10.1	3.6	2.8	2.2				3.4	3.4
5.2	2.6	1.8	1.8			Sales/Total Assets	2.2	2.2
2.7	2.4	1.5	1.4				1.4	1.6
	.5	.6	1.0				1.6	1.4
	(18) 1.8	(28) 1.6	(11) 1.6			% Depr., Dep., Amort./Sales	(90) 2.5	(76) 2.3
	3.4	3.1	3.6				4.0	3.7
	2.1	.9					2.0	1.1
	(11) 4.7	(10) 1.4				% Officers', Directors' Owners' Comp/Sales	(51) 3.7	(39) 3.8
	10.3	1.9					6.1	7.6
17164M	76826M	307274M	438169M	229066M	1035210M	Net Sales ($)	1358415M	1095088M
2884M	27066M	159435M	233885M	138380M	621352M	Total Assets ($)	836125M	595136M

M = $ thousand MM = $ million

See Pages 9 through 22 for Explanation of Ratios and Data

Comparative Historical Data / Current Data Sorted by Sales

4/1/11-3/31/12 ALL	4/1/12-3/31/13 ALL	4/1/13-3/31/14 ALL	Type of Statement	0-1MM	1-3MM	3-5MM	5-10MM	10-25MM	25MM & OVER
4	6	7	Unqualified					2	5
21	20	21	Reviewed		1	2	6	9	3
19	17	8	Compiled		3		4		1
20	16	21	Tax Returns	2	10	4	3	1	1
32	24	28	Other	2	7	4	7	2	6
				15 (4/1-9/30/13)			70 (10/1/13-3/31/14)		
96	83	85	NUMBER OF STATEMENTS	4	21	10	20	14	16
%	%	%	**ASSETS**	%	%	%	%	%	%
6.5	7.4	7.7	Cash & Equivalents		11.7	5.4	7.2	6.3	3.2
30.1	28.7	26.6	Trade Receivables (net)		28.5	30.9	28.4	31.2	18.0
22.4	26.6	28.8	Inventory		27.1	22.2	29.8	31.1	34.3
3.4	2.0	2.5	All Other Current		2.2	.4	1.6	4.1	2.9
62.4	64.7	65.5	Total Current		69.4	58.9	66.9	72.8	58.4
26.8	23.2	24.7	Fixed Assets (net)		19.6	31.2	25.8	15.3	31.9
3.5	3.5	2.7	Intangibles (net)		.9	.0	1.6	5.2	4.7
7.2	8.6	7.0	All Other Non-Current		10.1	9.9	5.6	6.6	5.0
100.0	100.0	100.0	Total		100.0	100.0	100.0	100.0	100.0
			LIABILITIES						
18.8	15.6	14.3	Notes Payable-Short Term		20.4	8.9	12.9	15.1	9.4
6.4	3.1	3.4	Cur. Mat.-L.T.D.		1.9	1.8	2.1	4.8	6.4
16.3	16.0	15.6	Trade Payables		20.7	17.8	13.9	18.9	8.5
.3	.1	.2	Income Taxes Payable		.0	.1	.1	.1	.7
8.6	11.5	10.7	All Other Current		5.5	13.1	9.0	14.3	8.0
50.3	46.3	44.2	Total Current		48.5	41.6	38.0	53.3	33.0
16.9	18.0	19.8	Long-Term Debt		27.4	17.7	17.5	9.4	19.5
.3	.4	.6	Deferred Taxes		.0	.4	.7	1.3	1.1
15.9	10.5	6.2	All Other Non-Current		6.1	4.2	11.5	.8	3.7
16.6	24.8	29.2	Net Worth		18.0	36.1	32.3	35.1	42.7
100.0	100.0	100.0	Total Liabilties & Net Worth		100.0	100.0	100.0	100.0	100.0
			INCOME DATA						
100.0	100.0	100.0	Net Sales		100.0	100.0	100.0	100.0	100.0
28.4	29.5	27.0	Gross Profit		34.6	25.0	27.6	20.4	22.5
27.5	25.6	23.9	Operating Expenses		33.4	23.4	22.6	17.0	17.9
1.0	3.9	3.1	Operating Profit		1.2	1.6	5.0	3.4	4.5
1.0	1.4	.6	All Other Expenses (net)		.1	.5	.5	.9	1.1
.0	2.5	2.4	Profit Before Taxes		1.1	1.1	4.5	2.5	3.4
			RATIOS						
2.1	2.7	3.0			2.9	4.3	5.1	2.3	2.6
1.3	1.3	1.6	Current		1.5	1.4	1.7	1.5	1.7
.9	1.0	1.1			.9	.8	1.1	.8	1.2
1.2	1.4	1.9			2.5	2.7	3.3	1.0	.9
.7	.8	.8	Quick		.8	1.1	1.6	.7	.7
.5	.4	.4			.4	.4	.4	.3	.4
21 17.1	**23** 15.8	**21** 17.6			**22** 16.5	**25** 14.8	**24** 15.3	**16** 22.7	**22** 16.7
39 9.4	**34** 10.8	**36** 10.0	Sales/Receivables		**37** 9.8	**39** 9.3	**41** 9.0	**35** 10.5	**26** 14.2
54 6.7	**55** 6.6	**50** 7.3			**43** 8.4	**61** 6.0	**54** 6.7	**89** 4.1	**50** 7.3
10 38.4	**8** 45.5	**12** 31.2			**6** 63.2	**16** 23.5	**5** 76.6	**3** 126.4	**30** 12.0
33 10.9	**38** 9.6	**40** 9.2	Cost of Sales/Inventory		**29** 12.6	**33** 10.9	**63** 5.8	**44** 8.3	**101** 3.6
83 4.4	**104** 3.5	**114** 3.2			**94** 3.9	**42** 8.7	**126** 2.9	**101** 3.6	**140** 2.6
12 30.8	**13** 28.8	**10** 35.5			**9** 40.9	**2** 234.8	**12** 30.2	**12** 31.2	**10** 36.1
22 16.8	**24** 15.2	**22** 16.4	Cost of Sales/Payables		**25** 14.6	**18** 20.7	**21** 17.5	**22** 16.6	**20** 18.1
43 8.4	**45** 8.1	**42** 8.7			**51** 7.1	**45** 8.1	**30** 12.2	**64** 5.7	**35** 10.5
6.5	6.4	5.3			5.3	6.5	5.2	5.0	4.4
17.0	21.3	10.1	Sales/Working Capital		14.6	22.3	7.6	9.1	8.7
-91.1	99.7	83.6			-68.5	-20.0	29.0	-28.4	18.1
6.2	13.4	10.3			6.8	7.0	9.3	21.6	19.6
(86) 1.7	(74) 3.8	(76) 3.7	EBIT/Interest		(16) 2.2	1.8	(18) 4.6	(13) 6.5	3.4
-1.6	1.0	1.0			.1	-1.0	2.3	.1	1.7
14.8	7.3	4.6							
(11) 3.5	(12) 2.9	(16) 2.7	Net Profit + Depr., Dep., Amort./Cur. Mat. L/T/D						
1.4	1.5	1.2							
.4	.2	.2			.1	.2	.3	.2	.3
1.0	.7	.6	Fixed/Worth		.5	.6	.7	.5	.6
11.4	2.8	3.6			-3.0	NM	3.3	NM	3.2
1.1	.8	.8			.9	.6	.5	1.1	.7
2.8	2.1	2.2	Debt/Worth		4.7	1.0	2.0	1.9	1.7
56.3	9.6	14.7			-6.4	-17.6	12.3	NM	4.7
27.3	33.3	37.1			37.1		36.8	40.9	46.1
(75) 6.0	(67) 14.1	(67) 10.7	% Profit Before Taxes/Tangible Net Worth		(14) 10.1		(17) 19.5	(11) 24.9	10.9
-17.1	1.4	.3			-20.2		2.0	-3.1	3.7
10.7	13.8	13.3			12.1	11.5	16.8	19.1	10.1
2.5	5.2	3.9	% Profit Before Taxes/Total Assets		3.9	1.8	9.7	7.7	4.5
-5.9	.0	.1			-1.6	-1.4	1.1	-1.7	1.7
29.6	34.3	41.6			163.3	36.0	19.0	137.1	12.4
10.8	12.1	12.4	Sales/Net Fixed Assets		41.4	10.5	9.1	20.0	7.1
5.8	5.8	5.8			9.7	4.7	5.4	4.7	3.6
3.7	3.3	3.2			6.0	4.1	3.3	2.8	2.2
2.4	2.4	2.4	Sales/Total Assets		2.9	2.7	2.2	2.1	1.8
1.7	1.6	1.7			2.4	2.1	1.3	1.6	1.4
1.0	.9	1.0			.7		1.3	.3	1.1
(81) 2.1	(68) 1.6	(66) 1.6	% Depr., Dep., Amort./Sales		(13) 2.2		(18) 2.0	(13) .8	(14) 1.5
3.1	3.2	3.2			3.5		3.4	2.5	2.8
1.4	1.0	1.5			2.3				
(47) 3.3	(29) 2.8	(32) 2.9	% Officers', Directors' Owners' Comp/Sales		(12) 8.3				
5.8	5.9	8.8			10.4				
1429672M	1493810M	2103709M	Net Sales ($)	2551M	43029M	39607M	143407M	219841M	1655274M
924239M	747593M	1183002M	Total Assets ($)	1040M	14586M	14500M	80792M	107478M	964606M

M = $ thousand MM = $ million

See Pages 9 through 22 for Explanation of Ratios and Data

Current Data Sorted by Assets							Comparative Historical Data	
						Type of Statement		
		2	5		3	Unqualified	7	5
1	5	10	10	1		Reviewed	30	25
1	8	6	2	1	1	Compiled	28	25
4	11	7				Tax Returns	35	39
5	14	19	5	4		Other	44	52
28 (4/1-9/30/13)			97 (10/1/13-3/31/14)				4/1/09-3/31/10	4/1/10-3/31/11
0-500M	500M-2MM	2-10MM	10-50MM	50-100MM	100-250MM		ALL	ALL
11	38	44	22	6	4	**NUMBER OF STATEMENTS**	144	146
%	%	%	%	%	%	**ASSETS**	%	%
16.9	7.7	9.0	1.6			Cash & Equivalents	8.5	8.1
24.4	37.6	30.8	32.2			Trade Receivables (net)	26.1	27.1
32.1	22.7	22.2	16.5			Inventory	22.7	22.9
.5	1.7	1.4	1.9			All Other Current	2.1	1.9
73.9	69.6	63.4	52.2			Total Current	59.4	60.1
18.4	22.0	28.8	21.5			Fixed Assets (net)	29.3	28.5
3.3	3.9	4.4	12.8			Intangibles (net)	4.6	4.7
4.4	4.4	3.4	13.5			All Other Non-Current	6.7	6.7
100.0	100.0	100.0	100.0			Total	100.0	100.0
						LIABILITIES		
34.7	11.7	14.8	16.0			Notes Payable-Short Term	15.7	14.2
6.5	3.2	3.7	2.7			Cur. Mat.-L.T.D.	4.5	4.2
17.3	16.5	13.0	17.5			Trade Payables	12.4	13.1
.0	1.4	.1	.0			Income Taxes Payable	.2	.1
25.7	15.8	4.3	4.8			All Other Current	6.2	7.4
84.1	48.6	35.9	41.1			Total Current	39.0	38.9
7.8	19.0	13.2	12.1			Long-Term Debt	19.2	16.2
.0	.0	.3	.3			Deferred Taxes	.1	.2
1.8	8.3	2.4	3.7			All Other Non-Current	5.6	5.3
6.3	24.0	48.2	42.9			Net Worth	36.0	39.5
100.0	100.0	100.0	100.0			Total Liabilties & Net Worth	100.0	100.0
						INCOME DATA		
100.0	100.0	100.0	100.0			Net Sales	100.0	100.0
41.5	30.0	23.9	19.8			Gross Profit	28.3	26.0
39.4	25.2	19.4	16.9			Operating Expenses	25.1	23.3
2.1	4.8	4.5	2.9			Operating Profit	3.2	2.7
.2	.1	.6	.3			All Other Expenses (net)	.8	.7
1.8	4.7	3.9	2.6			Profit Before Taxes	2.4	2.1
						RATIOS		
5.6	3.1	3.4	1.7				3.0	2.9
1.0	2.0	1.7	1.3			Current	1.6	1.8
.4	1.3	1.1	.9				1.1	1.2
2.1	2.0	2.6	1.0				2.0	2.0
.5	1.2	1.1	.9			Quick	.8	1.0
.1	.8	.7	.6				.5	.6
0 UND	24 15.2	27 13.3	36 10.1				25 14.5	24 15.2
18 20.4	31 11.8	35 10.4	41 9.0			Sales/Receivables	34 10.8	33 10.9
27 13.7	41 9.0	42 8.6	51 7.1				44 8.3	43 8.5
14 27.0	12 30.7	15 23.7	15 23.6				24 15.4	20 18.3
35 10.5	26 13.8	27 13.3	32 11.3			Cost of Sales/Inventory	43 8.5	37 10.0
81 4.5	46 8.0	50 7.3	45 8.1				74 4.9	58 6.3
2 222.7	10 37.5	9 39.9	14 25.8				9 39.3	10 38.3
7 51.5	21 17.6	17 21.1	24 14.9			Cost of Sales/Payables	19 19.5	17 21.7
33 11.0	34 10.8	24 15.1	47 7.7				37 9.9	31 11.7
9.2	7.3	6.4	8.9				6.3	6.9
-999.8	12.4	12.8	19.0			Sales/Working Capital	12.3	12.0
-9.1	30.3	52.7	-43.6				130.8	39.4
	22.6	16.5	9.5				6.4	14.5
	(32) 6.3	(40) 5.9	4.0			EBIT/Interest	(137) 2.3	(140) 4.2
	1.0	2.6	1.8				.9	.5
							5.6	6.1
						Net Profit + Depr., Dep., Amort./Cur. Mat. L/T/D	(19) 2.6	(21) 2.5
							1.5	1.0
.1	.2	.3	.1				.3	.3
.5	.5	.8	.8			Fixed/Worth	.8	.7
-.7	1.9	1.2	1.7				3.0	1.8
.4	.6	.5	.9				.7	.6
32.5	2.3	1.4	2.1			Debt/Worth	1.9	1.5
-3.0	7.1	3.1	3.9				7.4	3.8
	77.5	32.1	29.0				35.8	37.8
	(33) 38.2	(43) 17.7	(20) 14.5			% Profit Before Taxes/Tangible Net Worth	(120) 13.2	(128) 16.4
	1.8	5.9	4.6				.4	2.4
32.9	30.3	16.7	8.4				10.6	16.0
6.0	11.8	8.5	4.7			% Profit Before Taxes/Total Assets	3.8	6.2
-9.6	.1	3.3	1.1				-.1	-1.0
100.0	79.6	27.7	93.2				26.5	27.1
57.9	27.9	11.2	13.8			Sales/Net Fixed Assets	11.5	11.6
13.1	8.1	5.6	5.0				4.9	5.6
10.5	5.1	4.1	2.8				3.6	4.0
5.5	4.0	2.7	2.1			Sales/Total Assets	2.6	2.8
3.7	3.0	2.0	1.7				1.7	1.8
	.6	1.3	.6				1.4	1.2
	(30) 1.1	(39) 2.0	(19) 1.4			% Depr., Dep., Amort./Sales	(129) 2.4	(127) 2.1
	2.6	3.3	3.9				4.3	3.7
	1.9	1.1					1.7	1.6
	(19) 2.9	(19) 2.6				% Officers', Directors' Owners' Comp/Sales	(62) 3.0	(65) 3.5
	3.7	5.1					5.9	5.2
15972M	189539M	586662M	1096142M	909186M	900720M	Net Sales ($)	2288525M	2505454M
2784M	47502M	190940M	493016M	414502M	725374M	Total Assets ($)	1274339M	1432085M

M = $ thousand MM = $ million

See Pages 9 through 22 for Explanation of Ratios and Data

Comparative Historical Data				Current Data Sorted by Sales					
			Type of Statement						
10	6	10	Unqualified				1	2	7
26	22	27	Reviewed		2	2	5	7	11
31	27	19	Compiled		5	3	5	2	4
33	34	22	Tax Returns	2	5	7	5	3	
52	49	47	Other	1	6	4	12	15	9
				28 (4/1-9/30/13)			97 (10/1/13-3/31/14)		
4/1/11-3/31/12 ALL	**4/1/12-3/31/13 ALL**	**4/1/13-3/31/14 ALL**		**0-1MM**	**1-3MM**	**3-5MM**	**5-10MM**	**10-25MM**	**25MM & OVER**
152	138	125	**NUMBER OF STATEMENTS**	3	18	16	28	29	31
%	%	%	**ASSETS**	%	%	%	%	%	%
6.5	5.9	7.5	Cash & Equivalents		7.8	10.1	11.1	6.5	1.9
31.6	30.2	32.3	Trade Receivables (net)		29.0	23.4	37.2	34.1	34.0
23.1	21.8	22.2	Inventory		26.5	28.0	24.8	19.8	17.5
1.8	2.0	1.6	All Other Current		.2	3.9	1.0	1.1	2.1
63.0	59.9	63.5	Total Current		63.5	65.3	74.1	61.5	55.5
26.6	28.5	25.2	Fixed Assets (net)		27.8	22.8	19.1	29.5	25.4
4.4	4.8	5.7	Intangibles (net)		5.2	6.3	3.6	4.1	8.7
6.1	6.9	5.6	All Other Non-Current		3.5	5.6	3.1	4.9	10.3
100.0	100.0	100.0	Total		100.0	100.0	100.0	100.0	100.0
			LIABILITIES						
11.7	15.7	15.9	Notes Payable-Short Term		11.5	9.5	13.5	15.9	16.3
3.4	4.2	3.5	Cur. Mat.-L.T.D.		6.3	3.2	2.3	4.7	2.2
15.1	16.8	15.4	Trade Payables		11.5	11.9	14.6	16.4	18.0
.0	.1	.5	Income Taxes Payable		.0	.0	1.9	.2	.0
9.2	11.5	9.8	All Other Current		16.8	29.0	5.6	4.8	5.2
39.4	48.3	45.1	Total Current		46.2	53.6	37.9	42.0	41.7
14.5	18.6	14.0	Long-Term Debt		17.4	14.9	14.6	16.1	10.4
.3	.3	.3	Deferred Taxes		.1	.0	.1	.4	.8
5.0	5.8	4.6	All Other Non-Current		13.0	4.7	1.3	3.6	4.2
40.8	26.9	36.0	Net Worth		23.3	26.9	46.1	37.9	42.9
100.0	100.0	100.0	Total Liabilities & Net Worth		100.0	100.0	100.0	100.0	100.0
			INCOME DATA						
100.0	100.0	100.0	Net Sales		100.0	100.0	100.0	100.0	100.0
24.7	26.3	26.2	Gross Profit		33.0	35.3	25.6	21.1	20.1
21.5	22.9	21.8	Operating Expenses		28.9	31.4	19.6	18.4	15.4
3.1	3.4	4.3	Operating Profit		4.1	3.9	6.1	2.8	4.7
.2	.3	.3	All Other Expenses (net)		.0	.2	.8	.3	.1
2.9	3.1	4.0	Profit Before Taxes		4.1	3.7	5.2	2.5	4.6
			RATIOS						
2.7	2.3	3.0			4.1	5.4	2.8	2.9	1.9
1.8	1.5	1.7	Current		1.4	3.0	1.9	1.5	1.4
1.2	1.1	1.1			.8	1.4	1.5	1.0	1.1
1.7	1.5	1.7			2.7	2.7	2.2	1.7	1.2
1.0	.9	1.0	Quick		1.0	1.0	1.3	.9	.9
.6	.6	.6			.3	.8	.7	.7	.7
27 13.7	**26** 14.3	**26** 14.0			**10** 36.1	**20** 18.7	**26** 14.1	**28** 13.2	**37** 9.8
35 10.3	**33** 10.9	**35** 10.3	Sales/Receivables		**28** 13.1	**28** 13.1	**35** 10.3	**33** 11.1	**41** 9.0
44 8.3	**41** 8.9	**44** 8.3			**40** 9.1	**41** 9.0	**42** 8.7	**42** 8.6	**53** 6.9
17 21.4	**13** 28.0	**14** 25.9			**14** 26.9	**29** 12.4	**11** 32.8	**15** 24.6	**9** 42.7
34 10.8	**31** 11.7	**29** 12.4	Cost of Sales/Inventory		**26** 13.8	**40** 9.1	**26** 13.9	**25** 14.7	**33** 11.2
51 7.2	**51** 7.2	**49** 7.5			**83** 4.4	**72** 5.1	**46** 7.9	**35** 10.3	**49** 7.5
10 36.0	**11** 32.4	**10** 35.2			**2** 197.4	**4** 87.6	**9** 38.6	**11** 34.0	**16** 22.4
19 19.4	**21** 17.0	**20** 18.5	Cost of Sales/Payables		**13** 28.3	**19** 19.2	**21** 17.6	**21** 17.7	**24** 15.5
29 12.6	**33** 10.9	**31** 11.6			**31** 11.9	**33** 11.1	**28** 12.9	**24** 14.9	**47** 7.8
7.9	9.7	7.3			7.0	5.8	5.9	8.8	8.8
12.2	17.8	13.2	Sales/Working Capital		21.4	11.6	11.6	14.1	16.7
31.6	111.4	60.5			-43.5	17.8	15.9	240.9	77.2
11.0	11.4	15.1			26.2	9.9	30.4	9.5	23.2
(135) 4.0	(130) 4.7	(110) 5.7	EBIT/Interest		(14) 1.2	(10) 1.9	(26) 7.5	(28) 3.8	7.7
1.2	1.6	1.8			-1.3	.2	4.3	.7	2.9
4.7	5.1	6.8							
(30) 2.8	(24) 1.7	(13) 4.1	Net Profit + Depr., Dep., Amort./Cur. Mat. L/T/D						
1.6	.9	2.9							
.2	.4	.2			.5	.2	.1	.5	.2
.6	.9	.8	Fixed/Worth		1.6	.3	.3	.9	.8
1.8	2.4	1.7			-1.3	1.5	.9	2.2	1.3
.6	.8	.7			.6	.4	.5	1.0	.8
1.3	1.9	1.7	Debt/Worth		3.0	1.6	1.3	1.9	2.0
4.1	6.1	4.5			-8.5	2.8	2.6	5.1	4.1
37.0	48.8	42.6			70.5	73.5	57.8	26.7	40.5
(136) 17.9	(119) 18.2	(111) 21.7	% Profit Before Taxes/Tangible Net Worth		(12) 23.8	(15) 5.9	(27) 28.2	(28) 16.6	(28) 26.2
3.9	4.0	4.5			1.0	-13.2	14.5	-1.1	10.5
13.6	16.6	18.8			26.2	27.0	19.9	15.5	16.0
6.0	8.1	7.6	% Profit Before Taxes/Total Assets		4.4	3.3	11.9	4.5	6.9
.9	.9	1.1			-4.1	-2.6	7.1	-.1	3.0
34.7	37.5	56.2			54.5	59.5	89.1	28.8	92.7
13.7	15.7	15.8	Sales/Net Fixed Assets		12.5	35.8	21.4	15.6	13.3
6.6	6.1	6.4			6.5	6.1	7.4	6.0	4.1
4.5	4.7	4.6			4.9	4.2	5.4	4.7	3.5
3.1	3.2	3.1	Sales/Total Assets		3.3	3.2	3.8	3.8	2.1
2.1	2.1	2.0			2.3	2.0	2.4	2.5	1.5
1.0	.9	.9			.8	.6	1.1	1.0	.5
(127) 2.0	(117) 1.7	(101) 1.7	% Depr., Dep., Amort./Sales		(14) 2.1	(13) 1.0	(20) 1.7	(27) 1.8	(25) 1.4
3.3	3.4	3.2			5.1	2.1	2.7	3.8	3.4
1.5	1.3	1.1					1.5		
(66) 3.0	(61) 2.7	(43) 2.7	% Officers', Directors' Owners' Comp/Sales				(17) 2.6		
4.8	4.5	4.7					3.7		
4044864M	**3440931M**	**3698221M**	Net Sales ($)	**1461M**	**34329M**	**63169M**	**200770M**	**489385M**	**2909107M**
1517231M	**1688854M**	**1874118M**	Total Assets ($)	**370M**	**12798M**	**23591M**	**67613M**	**163640M**	**1606106M**

M = $ thousand MM = $ million

See Pages 9 through 22 for Explanation of Ratios and Data

Current Data Sorted by Assets / Comparative Historical Data

0-500M	500M-2MM	2-10MM	10-50MM	50-100MM	100-250MM	Type of Statement	4/1/09-3/31/10 ALL	4/1/10-3/31/11 ALL
			2			Unqualified	10	8
	1	3	1			Reviewed	11	6
	1	2				Compiled	8	3
						Tax Returns		2
	1	6	2	1	1	Other	11	8
	2 (4/1-9/30/13)		19 (10/1/13-3/31/14)					
0-500M	500M-2MM	2-10MM	10-50MM	50-100MM	100-250MM		4/1/09-3/31/10 ALL	4/1/10-3/31/11 ALL
	3	11	5	1	1	**NUMBER OF STATEMENTS**	40	27
%	%	%	%	%	%	**ASSETS**	%	%
DATA NOT AVAILABLE		17.3				Cash & Equivalents	16.8	14.5
		21.9				Trade Receivables (net)	13.3	18.5
		24.4				Inventory	25.1	24.4
		8.2				All Other Current	3.7	2.4
		71.9				Total Current	58.9	59.7
		21.9				Fixed Assets (net)	29.2	29.6
		.7				Intangibles (net)	3.3	3.0
		5.5				All Other Non-Current	8.6	7.7
		100.0				Total	100.0	100.0
						LIABILITIES		
		6.1				Notes Payable-Short Term	9.4	7.1
		.8				Cur. Mat.-L.T.D.	3.0	4.6
		10.5				Trade Payables	9.2	15.6
		.4				Income Taxes Payable	.1	.0
		14.3				All Other Current	13.3	15.2
		32.0				Total Current	35.0	42.5
		10.9				Long-Term Debt	26.6	29.1
		.3				Deferred Taxes	.4	.2
		4.4				All Other Non-Current	6.3	7.6
		52.4				Net Worth	31.7	20.5
		100.0				Total Liabilties & Net Worth	100.0	100.0
						INCOME DATA		
		100.0				Net Sales	100.0	100.0
		18.2				Gross Profit	17.5	21.8
		16.7				Operating Expenses	22.1	20.5
		1.5				Operating Profit	-4.6	1.4
		.6				All Other Expenses (net)	1.0	2.6
		.9				Profit Before Taxes	-5.6	-1.2
						RATIOS		
		4.6					3.5	2.4
		1.9				Current	1.8	1.6
		1.3					1.1	1.2
		3.3					2.4	1.5
		1.0				Quick	.8	.8
		.7					.4	.5
		21 17.8					11 32.1	14 26.1
		28 13.0				Sales/Receivables	25 14.3	38 9.5
		44 8.3					33 11.0	50 7.3
		22 16.6					24 15.3	19 19.1
		29 12.5				Cost of Sales/Inventory	53 6.8	56 6.5
		74 4.9					104 3.5	85 4.3
		8 43.8					5 74.7	9 41.9
		15 24.9				Cost of Sales/Payables	10 35.9	15 25.0
		38 9.7					24 15.2	41 8.9
		5.3					3.4	5.0
		12.2				Sales/Working Capital	6.7	8.1
		31.2					33.4	37.6
							4.8	15.9
						EBIT/Interest	(36) 1.1	(22) 1.7
							-9.9	-.4
						Net Profit + Depr., Dep., Amort./Cur. Mat. L/T/D		
		.1					.3	.2
		.4				Fixed/Worth	.6	.8
		1.3					4.6	1.9
		.3					.7	.9
		1.2				Debt/Worth	1.0	1.5
		1.8					7.2	5.1
		13.4					11.7	29.7
		6.6				% Profit Before Taxes/Tangible Net Worth	(32) 1.3	(23) 3.3
		-11.2					-16.6	-17.6
		5.7					5.9	13.9
		3.9				% Profit Before Taxes/Total Assets	-.3	1.8
		-6.3					-15.4	-5.3
		42.2					15.2	28.0
		23.8				Sales/Net Fixed Assets	6.6	8.4
		4.5					3.2	4.4
		3.8					2.5	2.3
		3.0				Sales/Total Assets	1.6	1.7
		1.5					1.1	1.3
							.9	.6
						% Depr., Dep., Amort./Sales	(32) 1.8	(18) 1.7
							2.7	4.2
						% Officers', Directors' Owners' Comp/Sales		
	10835M	173098M	252600M	181075M	101300M	Net Sales ($)	1144337M	1659367M
	3337M	60122M	104354M	65982M	116500M	Total Assets ($)	1043870M	1229046M

M = $ thousand MM = $ million

See Pages 9 through 22 for Explanation of Ratios and Data

Comparative Historical Data

4/1/11-3/31/12 ALL	4/1/12-3/31/13 ALL	4/1/13-3/31/14 ALL	
			Type of Statement
9	10	2	Unqualified
4	5	5	Reviewed
7	2	3	Compiled
	1		Tax Returns
11	13	11	Other
31	31	21	**NUMBER OF STATEMENTS**
%	%	%	**ASSETS**
18.4	16.7	18.7	Cash & Equivalents
17.8	18.8	17.1	Trade Receivables (net)
25.6	22.9	28.5	Inventory
3.8	7.4	6.0	All Other Current
65.5	65.8	70.3	Total Current
25.9	25.2	18.1	Fixed Assets (net)
2.0	2.6	1.2	Intangibles (net)
6.6	6.4	10.4	All Other Non-Current
100.0	100.0	100.0	Total
			LIABILITIES
4.8	6.6	22.4	Notes Payable-Short Term
4.1	2.5	.6	Cur. Mat.-L.T.D.
10.3	10.4	9.4	Trade Payables
.1	.3	.2	Income Taxes Payable
17.9	18.2	14.5	All Other Current
37.3	38.0	47.1	Total Current
14.1	14.2	9.2	Long-Term Debt
.3	.2	.1	Deferred Taxes
5.2	9.9	6.9	All Other Non-Current
43.1	37.7	36.6	Net Worth
100.0	100.0	100.0	Total Liabilties & Net Worth
			INCOME DATA
100.0	100.0	100.0	Net Sales
18.3	22.3	17.0	Gross Profit
17.4	17.1	14.9	Operating Expenses
.9	5.2	2.2	Operating Profit
.1	.0	.3	All Other Expenses (net)
.8	5.2	1.8	Profit Before Taxes
			RATIOS
3.4	3.5	4.1	
1.7	1.7	1.9	Current
1.2	1.2	1.2	
2.6	2.8	3.2	
.9	.9	1.0	Quick
.4	.5	.4	
17 21.2	**21** 17.8	**12** 30.3	
26 14.3	**29** 12.5	**24** 14.9	Sales/Receivables
50 7.3	**36** 10.1	**29** 12.4	
20 18.4	**22** 16.9	**22** 16.7	
38 9.6	**34** 10.8	**38** 9.7	Cost of Sales/Inventory
101 3.6	**79** 4.6	**78** 4.7	
7 54.6	**7** 50.1	**8** 45.7	
12 29.9	**14** 26.5	**12** 31.5	Cost of Sales/Payables
23 15.6	**31** 11.7	**25** 14.7	
4.7	4.7	5.1	
8.6	7.3	9.7	Sales/Working Capital
20.4	18.4	33.8	
29.4	32.9	39.1	
(29) 3.9	(27) 9.4	(16) 3.6	EBIT/Interest
-.2	1.3	-3.7	
			Net Profit + Depr., Dep., Amort./Cur. Mat. L/T/D
.2	.3	.1	
.4	.7	.3	Fixed/Worth
1.6	2.2	.7	
.4	.6	.4	
1.1	1.1	.7	Debt/Worth
4.7	5.8	1.6	
34.7	45.0	23.6	
(27) 9.6	(27) 12.7	(19) 7.6	% Profit Before Taxes/Tangible Net Worth
-1.7	1.0	-2.2	
10.3	13.2	12.0	
4.2	5.1	4.0	% Profit Before Taxes/Total Assets
-2.7	.0	-4.0	
20.1	18.3	47.7	
9.0	12.3	16.9	Sales/Net Fixed Assets
5.7	7.1	11.9	
2.7	2.6	3.7	
2.0	2.0	2.5	Sales/Total Assets
1.5	1.6	1.9	
.7	.5	.5	
(27) 1.4	(25) 1.1	(16) .7	% Depr., Dep., Amort./Sales
2.2	1.8	1.1	
			% Officers', Directors' Owners' Comp/Sales
2199357M	**2154281M**	**718908M**	Net Sales ($)
1029282M	**955738M**	**350295M**	Total Assets ($)

Current Data Sorted by Sales

	0-1MM	1-3MM	3-5MM	5-10MM	10-25MM	25MM & OVER
	2 (4/1-9/30/13)		19 (10/1/13-3/31/14)			
Type of Statement						
Unqualified						2
Reviewed			1		2	2
Compiled			1	1		1
Tax Returns						
Other			1	1	5	4
NUMBER OF STATEMENTS			3	2	7	9
ASSETS	%	%	%	%	%	%
(all rows)	DATA NOT AVAILABLE	DATA NOT AVAILABLE				
Net Sales ($)			**10835M**	**12590M**	**98135M**	**597348M**
Total Assets ($)			**3337M**	**8741M**	**38935M**	**299282M**

M = $ thousand MM = $ million

See Pages 9 through 22 for Explanation of Ratios and Data

Current Data Sorted by Assets | **Comparative Historical Data**

Type of Statement								
Unqualified				2			7	8
Reviewed			6	2			15	14
Compiled			4		1		3	3
Tax Returns	2	3	3				6	5
Other		1	4	5	2		14	20
	6 (4/1-9/30/13)			29 (10/1/13-3/31/14)				
	0-500M	500M-2MM	2-10MM	10-50MM	50-100MM	100-250MM	4/1/09-3/31/10 ALL	4/1/10-3/31/11 ALL
NUMBER OF STATEMENTS	2	4	17	9	3		45	50
ASSETS	%	%	%	%	%	%	%	%
Cash & Equivalents			9.0			DATA NOT AVAILABLE	8.4	9.1
Trade Receivables (net)			24.2				17.2	21.2
Inventory			29.1				24.5	26.0
All Other Current			4.0				2.5	4.0
Total Current			66.3				52.6	60.3
Fixed Assets (net)			23.6				32.9	28.1
Intangibles (net)			2.2				6.1	5.1
All Other Non-Current			7.9				8.4	6.5
Total			100.0				100.0	100.0
LIABILITIES								
Notes Payable-Short Term			12.0				16.2	17.3
Cur. Mat.-L.T.D.			1.1				3.1	3.7
Trade Payables			16.6				10.0	10.8
Income Taxes Payable			.1				.1	.0
All Other Current			16.3				19.5	14.3
Total Current			46.2				48.9	46.0
Long-Term Debt			9.9				18.1	13.1
Deferred Taxes			1.7				.6	.3
All Other Non-Current			2.8				5.0	7.3
Net Worth			39.4				27.4	33.3
Total Liabilities & Net Worth			100.0				100.0	100.0
INCOME DATA								
Net Sales			100.0				100.0	100.0
Gross Profit			21.5				28.1	26.5
Operating Expenses			19.9				31.9	26.6
Operating Profit			1.6				-3.9	-.1
All Other Expenses (net)			.1				1.8	1.3
Profit Before Taxes			1.5				-5.6	-1.4
RATIOS								
Current			3.2				1.9	2.2
			1.8				1.2	1.3
			1.3				.8	.9
Quick			1.5				1.0	1.0
			.9				.5	.6
			.5				.2	.3
Sales/Receivables			**17** 22.1				**9** 38.5	**10** 38.2
			26 14.1				**29** 12.6	**28** 12.8
			54 6.7				**55** 6.6	**53** 6.9
Cost of Sales/Inventory			**16** 23.5				**27** 13.5	**22** 16.8
			42 8.7				**74** 4.9	**52** 7.0
			107 3.4				**114** 3.2	**97** 3.8
Cost of Sales/Payables			**14** 26.0				**9** 40.1	**6** 57.8
			20 18.3				**25** 14.5	**18** 19.9
			41 8.9				**38** 9.6	**40** 9.2
Sales/Working Capital			4.8				6.8	6.8
			9.9				18.9	16.8
			17.3				-15.6	-24.4
EBIT/Interest			28.2				6.7	6.5
			(15) 13.7				(41) .7	(48) 1.2
			2.2				-3.8	-1.8
Net Profit + Depr., Dep., Amort./Cur. Mat. L/T/D							4.5	
							(12) 2.2	
							-3.2	
Fixed/Worth			.2				.4	.4
			.6				.9	.8
			1.6				3.7	2.1
Debt/Worth			.3				1.0	1.1
			1.7				2.1	2.4
			3.0				14.4	6.0
% Profit Before Taxes/Tangible Net Worth			90.7				22.4	40.2
			(15) 20.6				(37) 1.4	(43) 5.4
			6.7				-28.2	-11.8
% Profit Before Taxes/Total Assets			21.4				5.2	8.5
			7.6				-.6	.7
			-.8				-13.7	-6.0
Sales/Net Fixed Assets			38.2				13.2	27.2
			11.8				5.8	10.1
			5.8				2.7	3.1
Sales/Total Assets			3.3				2.6	3.0
			2.4				1.6	2.0
			1.9				.9	1.2
% Depr., Dep., Amort./Sales			.6				1.7	1.5
			(15) 1.0				(37) 2.8	(41) 1.9
			1.8				4.3	3.9
% Officers', Directors' Owners' Comp/Sales								1.5
								(10) 2.6
								8.4
Net Sales ($)	2599M	10735M	221408M	441836M	404219M		793099M	1156259M
Total Assets ($)	481M	4400M	84042M	225030M	210576M		424912M	653899M

M = $ thousand MM = $ million

See Pages 9 through 22 for Explanation of Ratios and Data

Comparative Historical Data				Current Data Sorted by Sales					
			Type of Statement						
7	5	2	Unqualified						2
12	9	8	Reviewed				2	3	3
7	6	5	Compiled				3	1	1
4	6	8	Tax Returns		4		4		
20	13	12	Other		1		1	3	7
4/1/11-3/31/12 ALL	**4/1/12-3/31/13 ALL**	**4/1/13-3/31/14 ALL**		**6 (4/1-9/30/13)**			**29 (10/1/13-3/31/14)**		
				0-1MM	**1-3MM**	**3-5MM**	**5-10MM**	**10-25MM**	**25MM & OVER**
50	39	35	**NUMBER OF STATEMENTS**		5		10	7	13
%	%	%	**ASSETS**	%	%	%	%	%	%
8.9	9.3	12.3	Cash & Equivalents	DATA NOT AVAILABLE		DATA NOT AVAILABLE	13.5		12.6
20.6	22.9	20.0	Trade Receivables (net)				22.2		19.6
27.1	26.4	31.0	Inventory				33.1		32.7
2.6	2.5	3.7	All Other Current				2.5		6.5
59.3	61.2	67.1	Total Current				71.4		71.4
28.6	26.4	22.6	Fixed Assets (net)				18.8		21.3
4.4	3.7	2.5	Intangibles (net)				1.9		3.3
7.7	8.7	7.8	All Other Non-Current				7.9		4.0
100.0	100.0	100.0	Total				100.0		100.0
			LIABILITIES						
14.6	17.7	9.8	Notes Payable-Short Term				8.8		15.5
1.8	1.3	1.4	Cur. Mat.-L.T.D.				.8		1.5
11.9	11.2	13.1	Trade Payables				10.5		13.7
.2	.1	.2	Income Taxes Payable				.2		.5
17.1	14.2	17.8	All Other Current				8.3		25.8
45.7	44.4	42.3	Total Current				28.6		56.9
12.7	13.8	14.9	Long-Term Debt				4.8		8.7
.3	.1	1.0	Deferred Taxes				1.3		1.7
7.7	3.7	2.0	All Other Non-Current				1.2		1.7
33.6	38.0	39.8	Net Worth				64.2		31.0
100.0	100.0	100.0	Total Liabilties & Net Worth				100.0		100.0
			INCOME DATA						
100.0	100.0	100.0	Net Sales				100.0		100.0
25.0	24.2	23.4	Gross Profit				25.9		19.0
23.6	20.3	21.6	Operating Expenses				24.0		17.5
1.4	3.9	1.8	Operating Profit				1.9		1.6
1.0	1.2	.3	All Other Expenses (net)				.2		.3
.4	2.6	1.5	Profit Before Taxes				1.7		1.3
			RATIOS						
2.1	2.3	3.2					9.6		2.4
1.3	1.4	1.8	Current				2.7		1.6
.9	.9	1.1					1.7		1.0
1.2	1.4	1.7					6.6		1.4
.7	.7	.9	Quick				1.5		.7
.3	.3	.5					.7		.2
11 34.4	**13** 28.5	**16** 22.9					**17** 21.7		**8** 46.8
29 12.7	**26** 14.2	**25** 14.8	Sales/Receivables				**21** 17.0		**28** 13.2
51 7.2	**51** 7.2	**47** 7.7					**44** 8.3		**51** 7.1
21 17.7	**18** 20.4	**17** 21.8					**0** UND		**18** 20.4
56 6.5	**40** 9.2	**46** 8.0	Cost of Sales/Inventory				**60** 6.1		**42** 8.7
101 3.6	**91** 4.0	**122** 3.0					**114** 3.2		**135** 2.7
9 39.0	**11** 34.7	**13** 28.1					**9** 42.4		**13** 28.1
21 17.4	**20** 18.0	**19** 19.7	Cost of Sales/Payables				**20** 18.6		**17** 22.1
37 9.9	**34** 10.7	**41** 8.9					**31** 11.9		**40** 9.2
7.1	4.6	4.7					4.5		4.1
17.9	15.7	9.3	Sales/Working Capital				5.3		9.3
-94.0	-40.4	124.7					12.5		-181.3
9.4	9.7	28.2							19.2
(47) 4.4	(32) 5.4	(31) 6.7	EBIT/Interest						(12) 6.1
-.9	1.4	.3							-7.4
			Net Profit + Depr., Dep., Amort./Cur. Mat. L/T/D						
.4	.2	.2					.0		.4
.9	.5	.6	Fixed/Worth				.3		.7
2.4	2.1	1.7					.8		1.4
.6	.5	.3					.1		.6
2.2	1.5	1.7	Debt/Worth				.4		2.0
6.3	5.1	3.2					1.8		3.6
43.1	37.9	49.8					24.5		41.8
(43) 10.6	(36) 17.0	(32) 18.5	% Profit Before Taxes/Tangible Net Worth				17.4		(12) 15.4
-10.6	3.9	3.1					5.5		-27.3
13.8	10.6	20.4					20.9		10.4
2.8	5.4	7.6	% Profit Before Taxes/Total Assets				11.0		4.5
-5.0	1.1	-3.2					2.1		-10.6
26.4	32.7	47.4					600.1		45.8
9.7	11.8	11.6	Sales/Net Fixed Assets				15.7		9.7
4.1	4.4	5.6					8.7		4.9
3.4	3.6	3.0					3.0		3.5
2.1	2.1	2.1	Sales/Total Assets				2.4		2.1
1.5	1.3	1.7					2.0		1.5
.7	.7	.6							.5
(44) 1.5	(35) 1.3	(28) 1.1	% Depr., Dep., Amort./Sales						(11) 1.1
2.3	2.6	1.7							1.4
	1.5	2.1							
	(10) 3.2	(11) 5.0	% Officers', Directors' Owners' Comp/Sales						
	9.3	10.6							
1089581M	**760220M**	**1080797M**	Net Sales ($)		**7749M**		**77507M**	**97112M**	**898429M**
533357M	**416017M**	**524529M**	Total Assets ($)		**3705M**		**33693M**	**51200M**	**435931M**

M = $ thousand MM = $ million

See Pages 9 through 22 for Explanation of Ratios and Data

Current Data Sorted by Assets							Comparative Historical Data	
						Type of Statement		
	1	5	8	2	4	Unqualified	20	25
	2	18	9		1	Reviewed	44	35
1	10	7	1		1	Compiled	24	24
12	21	9			1	Tax Returns	48	37
8	10	19	22	7	1	Other	72	58
30 (4/1-9/30/13)		150 (10/1/13-3/31/14)					4/1/09-3/31/10 ALL	4/1/10-3/31/11 ALL
0-500M	500M-2MM	2-10MM	10-50MM	50-100MM	100-250MM			
21	44	58	40	9	8	**NUMBER OF STATEMENTS**	208	179
%	%	%	%	%	%	**ASSETS**	%	%
18.1	8.1	7.0	5.6			Cash & Equivalents	9.2	6.8
22.4	22.6	22.1	17.8			Trade Receivables (net)	18.7	18.2
13.2	33.2	27.5	32.5			Inventory	29.7	31.6
.3	2.5	3.2	1.9			All Other Current	2.3	2.8
53.9	66.5	59.8	57.8			Total Current	59.8	59.5
31.0	24.9	31.8	29.5			Fixed Assets (net)	29.9	30.9
3.8	1.5	2.5	6.3			Intangibles (net)	3.5	4.4
11.2	7.1	6.0	6.4			All Other Non-Current	6.8	5.2
100.0	100.0	100.0	100.0			Total	100.0	100.0
						LIABILITIES		
23.0	16.5	10.2	10.1			Notes Payable-Short Term	16.5	15.0
2.9	5.1	2.1	2.3			Cur. Mat.-L.T.D.	5.1	4.4
19.9	18.0	12.3	9.9			Trade Payables	11.4	11.5
.0	.0	.3	.2			Income Taxes Payable	.2	.2
25.7	9.5	8.6	6.3			All Other Current	7.6	8.4
71.5	49.0	33.5	28.7			Total Current	40.8	39.5
27.3	11.8	19.6	14.6			Long-Term Debt	19.1	19.0
.0	.1	.3	.8			Deferred Taxes	.2	.5
16.0	10.4	7.8	8.5			All Other Non-Current	8.1	8.3
-14.9	28.7	38.8	47.4			Net Worth	31.7	32.8
100.0	100.0	100.0	100.0			Total Liabilties & Net Worth	100.0	100.0
						INCOME DATA		
100.0	100.0	100.0	100.0			Net Sales	100.0	100.0
47.6	30.9	25.0	22.4			Gross Profit	28.5	29.4
44.2	26.3	21.2	15.5			Operating Expenses	26.0	26.4
3.5	4.6	3.8	6.9			Operating Profit	2.5	3.0
1.8	.7	.1	.6			All Other Expenses (net)	1.2	.9
1.7	3.9	3.7	6.3			Profit Before Taxes	1.3	2.1
						RATIOS		
3.2	2.6	3.2	2.8				3.1	3.2
1.5	1.6	1.7	2.0			Current	1.6	1.7
.5	.9	1.2	1.4				1.0	1.1
2.7	1.2	1.5	1.5				1.4	1.4
1.3	.7	.8	.9			Quick	.6	.7
.3	.3	.5	.5				.3	.3
0 UND	**13** 28.8	**18** 20.4	**22** 16.5				**15** 24.0	**17** 22.1
12 29.8	**29** 12.8	**29** 12.5	**30** 12.3			Sales/Receivables	**27** 13.4	**30** 12.2
26 14.0	**38** 9.6	**47** 7.7	**45** 8.1				**45** 8.1	**45** 8.1
0 UND	**16** 22.4	**21** 17.1	**36** 10.0				**28** 13.0	**35** 10.5
5 76.5	**51** 7.1	**54** 6.8	**69** 5.3			Cost of Sales/Inventory	**63** 5.8	**76** 4.8
24 15.2	**99** 3.7	**101** 3.6	**122** 3.0				**130** 2.8	**130** 2.8
2 205.7	**12** 30.4	**9** 40.7	**13** 28.7				**10** 35.1	**9** 41.3
11 34.7	**25** 14.4	**20** 18.5	**20** 18.5			Cost of Sales/Payables	**21** 17.3	**21** 17.6
26 14.0	**45** 8.2	**39** 9.4	**30** 12.0				**37** 9.9	**34** 10.6
11.1	5.9	4.5	4.4				4.9	4.5
32.7	15.4	10.7	7.6			Sales/Working Capital	9.9	8.5
-13.8	-42.5	28.6	17.2				160.4	40.5
34.8	17.3	18.7	24.3				6.4	8.1
(16) 6.2	(39) 4.6	(57) 6.2	(39) 9.5			EBIT/Interest	(187) 2.3	(165) 2.9
-.1	1.4	1.8	4.2				-.3	.3
		30.9	27.1				3.3	4.8
		(10) 13.3	(12) 6.8			Net Profit + Depr., Dep., Amort./Cur. Mat. L/T/D	(45) 1.3	(34) 2.6
		1.9	3.9				.5	1.1
.4	.2	.3	.3				.3	.4
.9	.6	.8	.5			Fixed/Worth	.7	.8
-1.0	107.0	1.6	1.4				2.5	2.3
.3	.7	.7	.6				.7	.7
4.5	2.2	1.2	1.0			Debt/Worth	1.9	1.7
-3.1	340.8	4.0	2.2				8.0	5.8
96.3	41.8	48.8	35.8				32.7	32.4
(14) 53.4	(34) 15.7	(53) 24.6	(37) 22.9			% Profit Before Taxes/Tangible Net Worth	(177) 9.2	(152) 11.8
22.1	7.3	6.0	14.7				-5.3	-2.5
53.4	17.0	17.5	13.1				10.5	12.9
27.8	8.9	9.2	8.6			% Profit Before Taxes/Total Assets	2.9	4.3
-7.9	2.5	1.3	5.2				-4.4	-2.3
68.2	55.4	20.1	15.5				23.8	20.4
40.3	16.8	8.3	8.5			Sales/Net Fixed Assets	7.8	8.2
8.0	6.2	4.3	4.2				3.9	3.7
9.8	3.9	3.4	2.7				3.0	2.8
5.5	2.6	2.2	1.9			Sales/Total Assets	1.9	1.9
3.2	1.9	1.7	1.3				1.3	1.3
.5	.8	1.1	1.0				1.1	1.2
(13) .9	(36) 1.7	(49) 1.5	(39) 1.5			% Depr., Dep., Amort./Sales	(176) 2.5	(153) 2.1
2.2	3.2	3.5	2.8				4.9	5.3
5.3	2.3	.9					2.6	2.2
(12) 9.0	(26) 5.2	(16) 1.7				% Officers', Directors' Owners' Comp/Sales	(78) 4.2	(76) 3.7
14.7	7.9	4.8					6.8	7.1
29722M	163673M	671316M	1871230M	1004005M	2255171M	Net Sales ($)	3303002M	2825732M
5077M	50480M	280350M	910994M	586248M	1254988M	Total Assets ($)	2234232M	1895535M

M = $ thousand MM = $ million

See Pages 9 through 22 for Explanation of Ratios and Data

Comparative Historical Data				Current Data Sorted by Sales					
			Type of Statement						
20	16	20	Unqualified		1	1	5	1	12
46	32	30	Reviewed		1		5	16	8
30	22	20	Compiled	2	5	4	4	4	1
44	46	43	Tax Returns	6	15	9	7	4	2
58	56	67	Other	4	7	5	10	13	28
					30 (4/1-9/30/13)		150 (10/1/13-3/31/14)		
4/1/11-3/31/12 ALL	4/1/12-3/31/13 ALL	4/1/13-3/31/14 ALL		0-1MM	1-3MM	3-5MM	5-10MM	10-25MM	25MM & OVER
198	172	180	**NUMBER OF STATEMENTS**	12	29	19	31	38	51
%	%	%	**ASSETS**	%	%	%	%	%	%
8.1	8.2	8.0	Cash & Equivalents	9.3	14.6	8.9	9.8	5.4	4.4
20.4	19.9	20.8	Trade Receivables (net)	18.6	17.2	24.6	20.6	23.4	20.3
28.7	29.3	27.7	Inventory	20.8	24.7	28.1	29.0	26.9	30.8
3.1	1.9	2.2	All Other Current	3.3	.5	1.4	4.3	1.4	2.6
60.2	59.3	58.8	Total Current	51.9	57.0	63.0	63.6	57.0	58.1
28.8	29.3	30.6	Fixed Assets (net)	30.6	28.9	29.6	27.5	34.5	30.8
4.8	4.7	4.0	Intangibles (net)	.4	4.0	2.5	3.7	2.8	6.5
6.2	6.6	6.7	All Other Non-Current	17.1	10.1	4.9	5.2	5.6	4.6
100.0	100.0	100.0	Total	100.0	100.0	100.0	100.0	100.0	100.0
			LIABILITIES						
12.4	12.9	13.0	Notes Payable-Short Term	23.2	20.0	6.7	12.0	12.1	10.1
5.5	2.9	2.9	Cur. Mat.-L.T.D.	.9	3.9	5.1	3.3	2.9	1.7
11.4	14.3	13.7	Trade Payables	24.9	9.0	19.9	13.8	13.9	11.1
.1	.1	.2	Income Taxes Payable	.0	.0	.0	.2	.3	.2
9.7	8.3	10.1	All Other Current	35.2	9.5	7.9	11.5	7.0	6.6
39.2	38.6	39.8	Total Current	84.2	42.4	39.7	40.8	36.2	29.9
15.5	16.6	17.3	Long-Term Debt	24.1	15.9	19.3	14.9	20.2	14.9
.5	.4	.4	Deferred Taxes	.0	.3	.0	.2	.1	1.1
8.6	10.0	9.5	All Other Non-Current	16.7	12.7	10.9	9.7	5.7	8.1
36.2	34.4	33.1	Net Worth	-25.1	28.6	30.1	34.5	37.8	46.1
100.0	100.0	100.0	Total Liabilties & Net Worth	100.0	100.0	100.0	100.0	100.0	100.0
			INCOME DATA						
100.0	100.0	100.0	Net Sales	100.0	100.0	100.0	100.0	100.0	100.0
29.2	27.1	28.5	Gross Profit	46.5	40.0	25.2	28.6	24.3	22.0
26.3	22.9	23.4	Operating Expenses	43.4	34.9	21.1	22.5	20.7	15.4
2.9	4.2	5.1	Operating Profit	3.1	5.1	4.1	6.1	3.6	6.6
.7	.9	.6	All Other Expenses (net)	3.6	.4	.0	.5	.3	.7
2.2	3.3	4.5	Profit Before Taxes	-.5	4.7	4.1	5.6	3.3	5.9
			RATIOS						
3.4	3.8	3.0		4.1	2.9	3.1	3.6	2.8	2.8
1.7	1.7	1.8	Current	.9	1.8	1.6	2.1	1.4	2.1
1.1	1.2	1.1		.5	.7	1.1	1.2	1.1	1.4
1.4	1.7	1.5		1.3	1.9	2.0	1.6	1.2	1.5
.8	.8	.8	Quick	.5	.8	.9	.9	.8	.9
.3	.4	.4		.1	.3	.4	.5	.5	.6
16 22.8	**15** 24.6	**16** 22.4		**1** 306.4	**12** 29.5	**13** 28.8	**10** 37.8	**18** 20.7	**24** 15.5
27 13.4	**28** 12.9	**29** 12.8	Sales/Receivables	**26** 13.8	**26** 14.1	**25** 14.4	**29** 12.8	**25** 14.7	**31** 11.9
44 8.3	**43** 8.4	**41** 8.9		**38** 9.7	**35** 10.3	**40** 9.2	**42** 8.6	**43** 8.4	**50** 7.3
22 16.6	**25** 14.7	**16** 22.4		**0** UND	**5** 75.3	**15** 24.5	**15** 24.8	**22** 16.9	**35** 10.4
61 6.0	**57** 6.4	**54** 6.7	Cost of Sales/Inventory	**5** 77.2	**45** 8.1	**46** 7.9	**49** 7.5	**45** 8.1	**62** 5.9
111 3.3	**104** 3.5	**89** 4.1		**107** 3.4	**83** 4.4	**83** 4.4	**107** 3.4	**76** 4.8	**94** 3.9
10 35.6	**9** 42.4	**10** 35.5		**9** 42.9	**2** 153.2	**11** 32.5	**8** 46.5	**12** 31.0	**12** 29.3
19 19.7	**20** 18.7	**19** 19.0	Cost of Sales/Payables	**24** 14.9	**19** 19.1	**22** 16.9	**14** 26.0	**21** 17.8	**17** 20.9
35 10.5	**34** 10.6	**34** 10.6		**66** 5.5	**43** 8.4	**50** 7.3	**29** 12.7	**36** 10.1	**30** 12.2
4.7	5.0	5.0		3.4	4.4	5.8	4.6	6.3	4.8
9.5	9.9	11.6	Sales/Working Capital	NM	14.2	16.6	7.7	18.6	7.6
46.7	48.6	49.1		-10.1	-18.7	25.0	75.5	165.7	17.4
7.2	9.9	20.7			28.8	25.3	19.9	12.5	24.6
(174) 2.2	(152) 3.4	(167) 6.6	EBIT/Interest		(27) 5.6	(17) 9.4	(28) 10.2	5.0	(49) 8.9
.9	1.4	2.7			2.2	2.2	2.6	1.3	3.9
4.0	8.2	18.6							15.0
(43) 2.1	(25) 3.2	(33) 6.5	Net Profit + Depr., Dep., Amort./Cur. Mat. L/T/D						(15) 4.1
1.1	1.4	2.6							3.2
.3	.3	.3		.2	.2	.3	.1	.3	.4
.8	.8	.7	Fixed/Worth	NM	.9	.6	.5	.9	.7
1.9	1.8	1.9		-1.0	2.6	-2.6	1.9	1.9	1.4
.6	.7	.6		.2	.7	.7	.6	.9	.6
1.6	1.5	1.3	Debt/Worth	NM	1.7	1.3	1.2	1.2	1.1
5.4	5.0	4.3		-2.7	5.5	-15.2	4.1	3.8	2.4
26.0	35.7	43.7			51.1	50.2	41.3	42.5	40.6
(169) 10.0	(146) 20.8	(154) 25.4	% Profit Before Taxes/Tangible Net Worth		(24) 29.8	(14) 11.9	(28) 26.1	(35) 22.9	(47) 26.4
1.1	4.3	10.3			8.8	-3.5	15.0	3.7	15.0
12.8	16.6	19.3		74.3	28.2	21.6	19.6	14.9	16.2
3.1	5.8	9.4	% Profit Before Taxes/Total Assets	12.1	10.6	9.1	10.2	6.6	9.3
-.2	1.2	3.2		-29.3	4.0	.1	3.1	.6	5.1
26.5	26.1	24.9		49.2	41.3	55.4	55.4	21.6	15.3
8.6	10.6	10.2	Sales/Net Fixed Assets	12.8	16.2	15.9	15.3	7.9	8.3
4.5	4.2	4.4		3.2	3.2	4.5	5.0	4.5	3.7
3.2	3.2	3.6		5.2	4.7	3.9	3.7	3.7	3.0
2.2	2.4	2.3	Sales/Total Assets	2.9	2.6	2.4	2.7	2.2	1.9
1.5	1.6	1.6		1.1	1.7	2.0	1.7	1.7	1.4
1.0	.9	.9			.8	.6	.8	1.3	1.0
(166) 2.5	(148) 2.0	(150) 1.6	% Depr., Dep., Amort./Sales		(24) 1.5	(15) 2.1	(25) 1.4	(31) 1.8	(47) 1.5
4.2	4.2	3.3			3.2	4.3	3.7	3.2	2.6
2.0	1.4	1.5			4.6	2.3	1.2	.7	
(75) 4.2	(63) 3.0	(61) 3.6	% Officers', Directors' Owners' Comp/Sales		(16) 6.7	(10) 3.2	(10) 1.5	(14) 1.9	
7.8	5.6	8.0			9.0	6.7	3.3	3.3	
3012408M	4213645M	5995117M	Net Sales ($)	7245M	49783M	71931M	215718M	573774M	5076666M
1716678M	2101857M	3088137M	Total Assets ($)	3804M	26069M	28989M	114714M	275419M	2639142M

M = $ thousand MM = $ million

See Pages 9 through 22 for Explanation of Ratios and Data

Current Data Sorted by Assets							Comparative Historical Data	
		1	9	3	4	**Type of Statement** Unqualified	23	27
		3	2			Reviewed	13	11
		1				Compiled	3	5
1	1	3				Tax Returns	3	1
	2	4	9	3	6	Other	43	39
	15 (4/1-9/30/13)		37 (10/1/13-3/31/14)				4/1/09-3/31/10 ALL	4/1/10-3/31/11 ALL
0-500M	500M-2MM	2-10MM	10-50MM	50-100MM	100-250MM			
1	3	12	20	6	10	**NUMBER OF STATEMENTS**	85	83
%	%	%	%	%	%	**ASSETS**	%	%
		4.4	9.1		7.6	Cash & Equivalents	4.7	5.8
		24.6	19.7		14.8	Trade Receivables (net)	24.8	24.7
		22.4	24.6		25.5	Inventory	23.5	20.9
		3.0	1.8		3.8	All Other Current	2.5	3.2
		54.4	55.1		51.7	Total Current	55.5	54.5
		32.9	33.3		34.1	Fixed Assets (net)	35.2	34.7
		.3	4.2		8.0	Intangibles (net)	2.4	3.9
		12.4	7.3		6.2	All Other Non-Current	6.9	7.0
		100.0	100.0		100.0	Total	100.0	100.0
						LIABILITIES		
		7.0	6.3		2.1	Notes Payable-Short Term	10.3	7.2
		3.9	6.0		3.8	Cur. Mat.-L.T.D.	4.0	5.3
		16.4	12.2		10.4	Trade Payables	17.6	16.9
		.0	.1		.3	Income Taxes Payable	.4	.4
		5.0	8.7		4.1	All Other Current	12.5	6.1
		32.3	33.2		20.7	Total Current	44.9	35.9
		26.8	18.3		26.9	Long-Term Debt	20.8	17.4
		2.1	.4		1.7	Deferred Taxes	1.1	1.4
		2.8	8.2		9.1	All Other Non-Current	5.3	7.7
		36.0	40.1		41.6	Net Worth	27.8	37.6
		100.0	100.0		100.0	Total Liabilties & Net Worth	100.0	100.0
						INCOME DATA		
		100.0	100.0		100.0	Net Sales	100.0	100.0
		25.5	15.2		21.8	Gross Profit	21.7	21.3
		20.3	12.2		13.4	Operating Expenses	15.8	15.5
		5.2	3.0		8.4	Operating Profit	6.0	5.8
		1.4	.7		2.5	All Other Expenses (net)	.9	1.5
		3.8	2.4		5.8	Profit Before Taxes	5.1	4.3
						RATIOS		
		2.7	2.5		4.9		2.2	2.3
		1.5	2.1		2.1	Current	1.4	1.5
		1.0	1.0		1.7		1.0	1.1
		1.4	1.7		2.0		1.2	1.4
		.8	1.0		.8	Quick	.7	.8
		.5	.4		.7		.5	.5
		8 43.7	**24** 15.2		**30** 12.2		**27** 13.8	**26** 13.9
		27 13.3	**31** 11.6		**35** 10.3	Sales/Receivables	**35** 10.3	**38** 9.7
		38 9.7	**40** 9.1		**43** 8.4		**45** 8.2	**46** 7.9
		22 16.9	**34** 10.7		**57** 6.4		**27** 13.6	**22** 16.8
		33 11.1	**39** 9.4		**72** 5.1	Cost of Sales/Inventory	**43** 8.5	**36** 10.2
		54 6.7	**57** 6.4		**96** 3.8		**65** 5.6	**65** 5.7
		9 38.8	**13** 27.1		**14** 25.8		**21** 17.2	**20** 18.2
		26 14.1	**23** 16.0		**29** 12.8	Cost of Sales/Payables	**29** 12.4	**28** 13.2
		36 10.0	**32** 11.5		**41** 9.0		**40** 9.1	**37** 9.9
		7.1	5.0		3.6		6.9	6.5
		16.0	7.6		6.1	Sales/Working Capital	17.7	13.9
		NM	-164.0		8.1		NM	75.0
		6.3	18.6		7.7		8.0	10.7
		(11) 2.4	(19) 4.4		2.7	EBIT/Interest	(80) 3.9	(78) 4.5
		.1	-2.6		-6.1		.7	1.7
							4.8	12.1
						Net Profit + Depr., Dep., Amort./Cur. Mat. L/T/D	(23) 2.5	(32) 3.2
							1.3	1.9
		.3	.5		.7		.5	.5
		.7	.9		1.5	Fixed/Worth	1.2	1.0
		119.8	3.4		3.6		3.3	2.2
		1.2	.9		.3		.8	1.1
		1.5	1.7		3.3	Debt/Worth	2.4	2.0
		262.0	5.1		10.4		9.3	3.7
		20.1	38.2				48.4	48.1
		(10) 9.2	(18) 8.9			% Profit Before Taxes/Tangible Net Worth	(70) 24.2	(73) 21.0
		-.2	-24.1				4.6	7.0
		8.7	19.7		10.4		14.1	14.8
		2.9	4.5		4.5	% Profit Before Taxes/Total Assets	7.2	8.9
		-1.5	-6.2		-2.1		.5	1.2
		27.7	9.9		9.7		19.4	13.3
		7.5	7.8		5.3	Sales/Net Fixed Assets	6.4	7.4
		3.8	5.4		2.7		3.0	3.8
		4.2	2.7		1.8		3.2	3.5
		2.5	2.2		1.4	Sales/Total Assets	2.2	2.2
		1.7	1.7		1.2		1.5	1.6
		.6	1.0				1.1	1.2
		(11) 1.9	(18) 2.0			% Depr., Dep., Amort./Sales	(75) 2.2	(76) 2.1
		3.3	3.1				4.4	4.1
								1.4
						% Officers', Directors', Owners' Comp/Sales		(13) 2.3
								2.9
1058M	**13585M**	**167824M**	**1309288M**	**761260M**	**2085604M**	Net Sales ($)	**7062022M**	**8309090M**
338M	**3395M**	**65029M**	**573108M**	**489486M**	**1349449M**	Total Assets ($)	**3517311M**	**3719323M**

M = $ thousand   MM = $ million

See Pages 9 through 22 for Explanation of Ratios and Data

Comparative Historical Data				Current Data Sorted by Sales					
			Type of Statement						
21	14	17	Unqualified					1	16
8	6	5	Reviewed					2	3
2		1	Compiled					1	
3	2	5	Tax Returns		1		2	2	
30	23	24	Other	2		1	1	2	18
					15 (4/1-9/30/13)			37 (10/1/13-3/31/14)	
4/1/11-3/31/12 ALL	4/1/12-3/31/13 ALL	4/1/13-3/31/14 ALL		0-1MM	1-3MM	3-5MM	5-10MM	10-25MM	25MM & OVER
64	45	52	**NUMBER OF STATEMENTS**	2	1	1	3	8	37
%	%	%	**ASSETS**	%	%	%	%	%	%
4.3	6.4	8.1	Cash & Equivalents						8.2
21.7	18.4	19.1	Trade Receivables (net)						18.0
23.4	23.9	24.1	Inventory						23.6
2.5	2.8	2.4	All Other Current						2.4
52.0	51.5	53.8	Total Current						52.3
37.4	38.3	33.0	Fixed Assets (net)						35.1
4.5	3.5	4.0	Intangibles (net)						4.9
6.1	6.7	9.2	All Other Non-Current						7.7
100.0	100.0	100.0	Total						100.0
			LIABILITIES						
10.3	6.3	6.9	Notes Payable-Short Term						5.6
5.3	4.0	4.0	Cur. Mat.-L.T.D.						4.6
17.1	13.7	12.4	Trade Payables						11.3
.4	.5	.1	Income Taxes Payable						.2
8.8	6.5	5.8	All Other Current						6.3
41.8	31.1	29.2	Total Current						28.0
21.1	17.1	22.5	Long-Term Debt						23.6
1.9	2.4	1.6	Deferred Taxes						1.5
7.1	8.4	9.5	All Other Non-Current						10.3
28.1	41.0	37.1	Net Worth						36.6
100.0	100.0	100.0	Total Liabilties & Net Worth						100.0
			INCOME DATA						
100.0	100.0	100.0	Net Sales						100.0
17.3	20.1	20.1	Gross Profit						17.2
13.1	13.7	15.0	Operating Expenses						12.0
4.3	6.3	5.1	Operating Profit						5.3
1.4	.8	1.3	All Other Expenses (net)						1.5
2.9	5.5	3.7	Profit Before Taxes						3.8
			RATIOS						
2.1	2.6	3.1							4.0
1.3	1.7	2.1	Current						2.1
.9	1.2	1.2							1.1
1.2	1.5	1.7							2.0
.6	.7	.8	Quick						1.0
.4	.5	.5							.5
26 13.9	**25** 14.4	**24** 15.5							**26** 14.1
32 11.3	**30** 12.0	**31** 11.6	Sales/Receivables						**34** 10.7
45 8.2	**36** 10.0	**39** 9.3							**39** 9.3
28 12.9	**30** 12.3	**30** 12.0							**34** 10.7
44 8.3	**45** 8.2	**46** 7.9	Cost of Sales/Inventory						**47** 7.8
72 5.1	**72** 5.1	**68** 5.4							**70** 5.2
17 21.9	**19** 19.4	**13** 27.2							**14** 26.5
24 15.3	**26** 14.0	**26** 14.3	Cost of Sales/Payables						**25** 14.4
41 9.0	**33** 11.1	**33** 10.9							**33** 11.2
8.5	5.8	5.0							4.9
23.5	10.9	8.0	Sales/Working Capital						7.7
-40.1	23.2	73.0							145.6
8.4	12.5	11.3							16.4
(60) 3.6	(42) 6.9	(49) 3.3	EBIT/Interest						(36) 2.9
1.7	2.4	-1.0							-2.2
3.8	5.9	2.8							2.9
(23) 2.3	(20) 2.9	(16) 1.8	Net Profit + Depr., Dep., Amort./Cur. Mat. L/T/D						(11) 2.4
1.3	1.1	-.3							-.5
.6	.6	.5							.6
1.3	1.1	.9	Fixed/Worth						1.2
2.3	2.6	3.4							4.3
1.0	.7	1.1							1.0
2.2	1.6	1.9	Debt/Worth						2.8
4.8	4.0	7.2							8.2
41.2	35.5	36.1							45.8
(54) 19.0	(42) 21.1	(45) 9.4	% Profit Before Taxes/Tangible Net Worth						(32) 15.2
5.1	11.0	-16.9							-18.5
12.4	13.5	10.8							15.2
6.2	8.1	4.3	% Profit Before Taxes/Total Assets						4.4
.1	3.9	-3.4							-3.6
11.1	9.9	11.7							9.7
6.6	6.2	6.3	Sales/Net Fixed Assets						6.5
3.3	2.8	3.8							4.0
3.0	2.7	2.7							2.6
2.0	1.9	2.0	Sales/Total Assets						2.0
1.5	1.4	1.4							1.4
1.2	1.3	1.4							1.5
(62) 2.3	(44) 2.8	(45) 2.5	% Depr., Dep., Amort./Sales						(33) 2.3
3.5	4.3	3.5							3.1
1.2	1.0	1.3							
(11) 2.4	(10) 2.9	(12) 3.4	% Officers', Directors' Owners' Comp/Sales						
2.7	6.4	7.6							
5746716M	**4148197M**	**4338619M**	Net Sales ($)	**1294M**	**1058M**	**4653M**	**19990M**	**125311M**	**4186313M**
3112820M	**2553505M**	**2480805M**	Total Assets ($)	**4310M**	**338M**	**1042M**	**6740M**	**57045M**	**2411330M**

M = $ thousand MM = $ million

See Pages 9 through 22 for Explanation of Ratios and Data

Current Data Sorted by Assets / Comparative Historical Data

0-500M	500M-2MM	2-10MM	10-50MM	50-100MM	100-250MM		4/1/09-3/31/10 ALL	4/1/10-3/31/11 ALL
						Type of Statement		
1		5	13	2	5	Unqualified	32	34
	3	36	22	2		Reviewed	73	69
	7	19	2	1		Compiled	25	31
1	5	11			1	Tax Returns	14	21
1	5	32	41	6	7	Other	72	91
41 (4/1-9/30/13)			187 (10/1/13-3/31/14)					
3	20	103	78	11	13	**NUMBER OF STATEMENTS**	216	246
%	%	%	%	%	%	**ASSETS**	%	%
	15.3	8.8	6.4	6.9	1.3	Cash & Equivalents	6.9	7.0
	39.4	32.2	26.0	18.3	23.8	Trade Receivables (net)	28.0	29.6
	21.2	19.2	17.7	12.2	15.7	Inventory	15.9	17.7
	1.0	1.2	2.0	2.8	1.3	All Other Current	1.8	1.9
	76.8	61.4	52.1	40.2	42.1	Total Current	52.5	56.2
	15.9	29.8	38.3	50.0	36.0	Fixed Assets (net)	36.0	32.5
	.8	3.0	2.0	7.4	18.5	Intangibles (net)	4.3	4.5
	6.5	5.8	7.5	2.4	3.3	All Other Non-Current	7.3	6.7
	100.0	100.0	100.0	100.0	100.0	Total	100.0	100.0
						LIABILITIES		
	6.0	8.5	9.7	4.1	9.7	Notes Payable-Short Term	9.0	9.4
	4.7	4.1	4.2	3.7	2.2	Cur. Mat.-L.T.D.	5.2	4.2
	25.4	19.0	15.9	12.3	14.3	Trade Payables	18.0	20.2
	.0	.1	.2	.2	.0	Income Taxes Payable	.2	.1
	8.7	7.0	5.5	4.3	8.0	All Other Current	5.8	8.1
	44.8	38.8	35.5	24.5	34.3	Total Current	38.3	42.1
	11.4	15.7	17.7	26.7	18.2	Long-Term Debt	19.9	18.7
	.6	.6	1.6	2.5	1.0	Deferred Taxes	.9	.8
	5.5	4.2	5.5	2.1	5.8	All Other Non-Current	7.3	5.7
	37.7	40.8	39.7	44.2	40.8	Net Worth	33.6	32.8
	100.0	100.0	100.0	100.0	100.0	Total Liabilties & Net Worth	100.0	100.0
						INCOME DATA		
	100.0	100.0	100.0	100.0	100.0	Net Sales	100.0	100.0
	26.7	24.7	20.4	23.9	25.7	Gross Profit	24.0	26.9
	23.4	19.8	15.3	19.0	19.0	Operating Expenses	21.8	22.3
	3.4	4.9	5.1	4.9	6.7	Operating Profit	2.2	4.5
	.3	.3	.3	-1.0	1.0	All Other Expenses (net)	.6	.4
	3.1	4.7	4.8	5.9	5.7	Profit Before Taxes	1.6	4.1
						RATIOS		
	3.9	3.0	2.6	2.3	1.6		2.3	2.2
	2.0	1.5	1.4	1.6	1.4	Current	1.3	1.4
	1.1	1.1	1.0	1.2	1.1		1.0	1.0
	3.0	2.1	1.8	2.0	1.1		1.5	1.5
	1.1	1.0	.9	.9	.9	Quick	.9	.9
	.8	.7	.6	.8	.6		.6	.6
	27 13.3	**31** 11.9	**30** 12.0	**25** 14.6	**37** 9.8		**32** 11.3	**32** 11.5
	33 10.9	**38** 9.5	**39** 9.3	**39** 9.4	**41** 8.9	Sales/Receivables	**39** 9.3	**41** 9.0
	38 9.5	**45** 8.2	**49** 7.5	**59** 6.2	**55** 6.6		**47** 7.8	**48** 7.6
	15 24.1	**15** 23.6	**21** 17.7	**26** 13.9	**16** 23.3		**18** 20.1	**18** 20.0
	20 18.7	**28** 13.2	**33** 10.9	**41** 9.0	**36** 10.2	Cost of Sales/Inventory	**28** 12.9	**30** 12.1
	36 10.0	**45** 8.2	**45** 8.2	**55** 6.6	**58** 6.3		**42** 8.6	**47** 7.8
	11 34.0	**14** 26.0	**15** 25.0	**24** 15.5	**20** 18.7		**16** 22.6	**19** 19.1
	27 13.4	**24** 15.3	**27** 13.5	**32** 11.4	**26** 14.2	Cost of Sales/Payables	**30** 12.3	**31** 11.7
	50 7.3	**43** 8.5	**38** 9.6	**56** 6.5	**61** 6.0		**46** 8.0	**49** 7.5
	6.3	6.5	6.2	6.4	10.8		7.4	8.2
	12.1	12.5	16.1	9.8	22.3	Sales/Working Capital	20.7	19.5
	81.9	120.7	328.2	27.1	NM		-302.6	-986.1
	52.8	20.0	25.3	12.4	39.5		7.6	16.4
	(16) 4.7	(94) 6.4	(73) 9.9	(10) 6.1	20.4	EBIT/Interest	(206) 2.8	(228) 5.0
	.8	2.2	3.1	2.1	3.7		1.0	2.8
		4.6	4.6				4.5	6.1
		(33) 2.1	(37) 3.0			Net Profit + Depr., Dep., Amort./Cur. Mat. L/T/D	(71) 2.3	(83) 2.9
		.8	1.5				1.3	1.4
	.0	.3	.6	1.0	1.3		.6	.5
	.2	.7	1.1	1.8	1.5	Fixed/Worth	1.1	1.1
	1.4	2.3	2.7	2.9	NM		2.8	2.7
	.4	.6	.6	.8	1.1		.9	.9
	1.0	1.5	1.6	2.8	1.4	Debt/Worth	1.9	2.0
	6.4	6.2	5.7	4.1	NM		5.9	5.7
	41.1	52.8	47.5	42.0	43.2		31.1	47.7
	(17) 28.6	(92) 21.4	(72) 30.7	24.6	(10) 40.7	% Profit Before Taxes/Tangible Net Worth	(185) 12.2	(212) 23.9
	2.7	7.5	12.1	2.6	37.0		2.6	11.3
	19.7	16.4	16.9	12.4	13.6		9.3	16.8
	5.6	8.5	8.7	5.1	9.9	% Profit Before Taxes/Total Assets	3.8	8.2
	.9	2.6	4.2	2.4	5.1		-.5	3.4
	443.2	22.2	12.7	5.1	12.9		15.0	20.9
	83.4	10.4	6.8	2.5	4.9	Sales/Net Fixed Assets	7.3	8.4
	12.5	5.8	3.8	1.8	3.6		4.0	4.6
	4.8	3.7	3.1	2.1	2.2		3.1	3.5
	4.3	2.8	2.3	1.2	1.7	Sales/Total Assets	2.4	2.5
	3.7	2.2	1.8	1.1	1.6		1.8	1.9
	.1	1.0	1.3	2.0	1.9		1.6	1.3
	(11) 1.5	(91) 1.7	(77) 1.9	2.9	(12) 2.2	% Depr., Dep., Amort./Sales	(199) 2.5	(223) 2.2
	2.4	2.5	3.3	6.5	2.3		3.7	3.2
	1.9	.9	1.2				1.6	1.3
	(13) 5.0	(38) 2.1	(17) 2.2			% Officers', Directors' Owners' Comp/Sales	(69) 3.2	(78) 3.3
	6.3	4.4	4.5				6.3	5.6
2417M	114953M	1579375M	4603764M	992680M	3377632M	Net Sales ($)	7401077M	9779006M
965M	26321M	550632M	1875279M	654620M	1831002M	Total Assets ($)	3754560M	4541492M

M = $ thousand MM = $ million

See Pages 9 through 22 for Explanation of Ratios and Data

Comparative Historical Data				Current Data Sorted by Sales					
			Type of Statement						
34	29	26	Unqualified	1			1	6	18
77	58	63	Reviewed			2	11	31	19
27	18	29	Compiled			4	11	12	2
30	25	18	Tax Returns		3	1	7	4	3
73	94	92	Other	1	3	2	5	22	59
4/1/11-3/31/12 ALL	**4/1/12-3/31/13 ALL**	**4/1/13-3/31/14 ALL**		**41 (4/1-9/30/13)**			**187 (10/1/13-3/31/14)**		
				0-1MM	**1-3MM**	**3-5MM**	**5-10MM**	**10-25MM**	**25MM & OVER**
241	224	228	**NUMBER OF STATEMENTS**	2	6	9	35	75	101
%	%	%	**ASSETS**	%	%	%	%	%	%
7.2	7.0	8.2	Cash & Equivalents				11.4	8.6	5.6
28.0	29.1	29.5	Trade Receivables (net)				31.4	31.2	28.0
17.4	17.9	18.3	Inventory				19.3	18.2	18.0
1.6	1.9	1.6	All Other Current				1.5	1.0	1.9
54.1	55.9	57.5	Total Current				63.6	59.1	53.6
33.4	33.8	32.7	Fixed Assets (net)				24.2	33.1	36.4
4.2	2.8	3.6	Intangibles (net)				4.4	2.2	4.6
8.3	7.5	6.1	All Other Non-Current				7.8	5.7	5.4
100.0	100.0	100.0	Total				100.0	100.0	100.0
			LIABILITIES						
8.4	8.9	8.5	Notes Payable-Short Term				7.3	9.4	8.8
4.2	3.9	4.0	Cur. Mat.-L.T.D.				3.4	4.1	3.8
16.9	19.2	17.8	Trade Payables				17.0	19.7	17.3
.1	.1	.2	Income Taxes Payable				.1	.2	.1
7.4	6.6	6.5	All Other Current				8.2	5.7	6.2
37.0	38.7	37.0	Total Current				36.1	39.1	36.3
18.8	17.0	17.2	Long-Term Debt				12.5	17.0	17.3
1.0	.9	1.0	Deferred Taxes				.6	.7	1.6
6.5	4.8	4.7	All Other Non-Current				6.0	3.5	4.9
36.7	38.5	40.0	Net Worth				44.8	39.7	39.9
100.0	100.0	100.0	Total Liabilties & Net Worth				100.0	100.0	100.0
			INCOME DATA						
100.0	100.0	100.0	Net Sales				100.0	100.0	100.0
26.5	25.0	23.7	Gross Profit				23.4	24.1	21.3
21.9	20.7	18.6	Operating Expenses				20.1	19.2	16.2
4.6	4.3	5.1	Operating Profit				3.3	4.9	5.0
.4	.2	.3	All Other Expenses (net)				-.5	.4	.3
4.2	4.1	4.8	Profit Before Taxes				3.8	4.5	4.7
			RATIOS						
2.4	2.6	2.6					4.0	2.6	2.3
1.5	1.5	1.5	Current				2.2	1.5	1.5
1.1	1.0	1.1					1.1	1.0	1.1
1.7	1.7	1.9					3.1	2.0	1.5
1.0	.9	1.0	Quick				1.2	.9	.9
.6	.6	.6					.8	.6	.6
31 11.7	**30** 12.0	**31** 11.8					**32** 11.5	**30** 12.1	**31** 11.7
38 9.7	**38** 9.6	**39** 9.4	Sales/Receivables				**38** 9.7	**38** 9.6	**39** 9.3
45 8.1	**46** 7.9	**47** 7.8					**44** 8.3	**47** 7.8	**49** 7.5
17 21.2	**18** 20.0	**17** 21.1					**17** 21.3	**15** 24.2	**21** 17.7
30 12.1	**31** 11.9	**30** 12.0	Cost of Sales/Inventory				**30** 12.2	**27** 13.4	**33** 11.0
46 8.0	**46** 8.0	**45** 8.1					**50** 7.3	**47** 7.8	**43** 8.5
16 23.2	**14** 25.6	**15** 24.8					**14** 26.9	**14** 26.4	**16** 22.9
29 12.5	**29** 12.8	**26** 14.3	Cost of Sales/Payables				**23** 16.0	**24** 15.2	**27** 13.4
46 7.9	**48** 7.6	**42** 8.6					**41** 8.9	**46** 7.9	**42** 8.7
7.4	7.4	6.5					6.0	7.1	7.7
14.9	13.8	12.9	Sales/Working Capital				9.5	12.9	16.4
125.1	150.3	98.0					81.3	224.5	64.0
16.0	17.5	24.8					21.2	19.8	36.6
(221) 6.1	(202) 5.5	(209) 7.5	EBIT/Interest				(30) 3.0	(70) 5.6	(94) 9.8
2.4	2.1	2.4					.7	2.7	3.4
5.6	4.7	4.6					6.6	4.1	5.8
(84) 3.0	(87) 2.7	(82) 2.6	Net Profit + Depr., Dep., Amort./Cur. Mat. L/T/D				(12) 2.7	(25) 2.0	(43) 3.0
1.5	1.4	1.2					.8	.7	1.8
.5	.4	.4					.2	.3	.6
1.0	.9	1.0	Fixed/Worth				.7	.8	1.1
2.1	1.9	2.5					3.5	1.7	2.8
.6	.7	.6					.3	.6	.7
1.9	1.6	1.5	Debt/Worth				1.5	1.5	1.8
5.1	4.2	5.8					8.7	4.0	5.7
41.6	43.6	49.1					39.6	53.5	48.6
(208) 23.1	(203) 19.8	(204) 27.6	% Profit Before Taxes/Tangible Net Worth				(29) 10.7	(69) 27.0	(93) 33.7
11.3	7.8	9.7					1.5	9.2	15.4
16.6	16.3	16.4					19.9	16.3	16.4
7.6	7.0	8.6	% Profit Before Taxes/Total Assets				4.5	8.3	11.4
3.1	2.3	3.2					-.1	3.4	4.7
18.6	16.2	17.2					42.4	19.4	13.2
8.2	7.2	8.0	Sales/Net Fixed Assets				13.3	9.0	7.0
4.6	4.8	4.5					6.3	4.5	4.1
3.5	3.5	3.7					4.1	3.7	3.3
2.5	2.6	2.6	Sales/Total Assets				2.8	2.7	2.4
1.9	1.9	1.8					2.1	2.1	1.8
1.2	1.3	1.2					.7	1.1	1.2
(214) 2.1	(203) 2.1	(203) 1.9	% Depr., Dep., Amort./Sales				(30) 1.5	(66) 2.0	(99) 1.9
3.3	3.3	2.9					2.2	2.9	2.9
2.0	1.5	1.0					1.8	1.0	.8
(73) 3.7	(65) 2.7	(71) 2.2	% Officers', Directors' Owners' Comp/Sales				(18) 4.7	(27) 2.0	(18) 1.4
5.5	5.2	4.8					5.8	3.0	4.1
9040774M	**9752617M**	**10670821M**	Net Sales ($)	**1257M**	**11911M**	**37628M**	**263307M**	**1231083M**	**9125635M**
4337652M	**4429879M**	**4938819M**	Total Assets ($)	**660M**	**11121M**	**14767M**	**104098M**	**567405M**	**4240768M**

M = $ thousand MM = $ million

See Pages 9 through 22 for Explanation of Ratios and Data

Current Data Sorted by Assets							Comparative Historical Data	
						Type of Statement		
		3	7	2		Unqualified	12	15
	2	4	8	1		Reviewed	18	20
		4				Compiled	4	6
	2	1				Tax Returns	4	4
	1	3	10	5	1	Other	28	23
	13 (4/1-9/30/13)		41 (10/1/13-3/31/14)				4/1/09-3/31/10 ALL	4/1/10-3/31/11 ALL
0-500M	500M-2MM	2-10MM	10-50MM	50-100MM	100-250MM			
	5	15	25	8	1	**NUMBER OF STATEMENTS**	66	68
%	%	%	%	%	%	**ASSETS**	%	%
DATA NOT AVAILABLE		6.1	2.9			Cash & Equivalents	4.9	6.8
		23.0	20.0			Trade Receivables (net)	21.4	22.7
		24.8	21.9			Inventory	21.9	20.4
		1.7	1.0			All Other Current	2.9	2.6
		55.7	45.9			Total Current	51.1	52.5
		31.4	47.6			Fixed Assets (net)	41.1	38.7
		5.9	1.5			Intangibles (net)	2.9	2.9
		7.0	5.1			All Other Non-Current	4.9	5.9
		100.0	100.0			Total	100.0	100.0
						LIABILITIES		
		2.8	13.0			Notes Payable-Short Term	10.5	8.5
		7.6	5.0			Cur. Mat.-L.T.D.	5.5	4.9
		9.3	11.2			Trade Payables	13.1	11.1
		.2	.3			Income Taxes Payable	.1	.1
		5.8	4.2			All Other Current	5.8	8.8
		25.8	33.9			Total Current	35.1	33.5
		27.2	24.9			Long-Term Debt	25.6	20.2
		.5	3.0			Deferred Taxes	.8	1.3
		2.9	3.2			All Other Non-Current	5.4	3.2
		43.6	35.0			Net Worth	33.0	41.9
		100.0	100.0			Total Liabilties & Net Worth	100.0	100.0
						INCOME DATA		
		100.0	100.0			Net Sales	100.0	100.0
		34.0	21.0			Gross Profit	24.1	25.8
		28.2	15.8			Operating Expenses	20.0	19.1
		5.8	5.3			Operating Profit	4.1	6.7
		.8	.8			All Other Expenses (net)	1.2	.9
		5.0	4.4			Profit Before Taxes	2.9	5.8
						RATIOS		
		4.0	2.2				2.4	3.2
		2.0	1.4			Current	1.4	1.5
		1.2	1.1				1.1	1.1
		3.3	1.1				1.2	1.6
		.9	.6			Quick	.7	.8
		.4	.5				.5	.6
		24 15.5	**36** 10.0				**29** 12.5	**32** 11.5
		38 9.7	**47** 7.8			Sales/Receivables	**38** 9.7	**39** 9.3
		57 6.4	**50** 7.3				**47** 7.8	**48** 7.6
		27 13.6	**45** 8.2				**38** 9.7	**36** 10.1
		50 7.3	**54** 6.7			Cost of Sales/Inventory	**52** 7.0	**50** 7.3
		111 3.3	**70** 5.2				**68** 5.3	**68** 5.3
		10 36.0	**15** 24.9				**16** 23.3	**14** 25.5
		23 15.9	**30** 12.1			Cost of Sales/Payables	**29** 12.6	**25** 14.7
		32 11.3	**45** 8.2				**44** 8.3	**38** 9.6
		4.6	7.8				6.2	5.7
		12.6	14.1			Sales/Working Capital	16.4	12.1
		34.8	NM				39.7	66.4
		12.5	16.0				6.7	21.7
		(14) 6.5	4.4			EBIT/Interest	(64) 3.2	(63) 7.1
		1.7	2.1				1.3	2.8
			3.9				3.8	5.8
			(15) 2.7			Net Profit + Depr., Dep., Amort./Cur. Mat. L/T/D	(27) 2.4	(29) 2.7
			1.6				1.2	1.6
		.4	.8				.7	.5
		1.0	1.2			Fixed/Worth	1.3	1.0
		1.3	2.4				2.8	2.3
		1.0	.9				.8	.6
		1.6	2.2			Debt/Worth	2.0	1.8
		3.2	3.3				5.0	3.9
		50.4	29.8				34.4	46.3
		24.3	(23) 21.3			% Profit Before Taxes/Tangible Net Worth	(57) 18.3	(61) 28.8
		5.7	10.6				1.1	13.1
		20.4	13.2				11.4	17.0
		9.8	6.0			% Profit Before Taxes/Total Assets	6.1	11.4
		2.4	3.1				2.0	4.5
		12.6	5.1				7.3	8.7
		7.2	3.7			Sales/Net Fixed Assets	4.5	4.9
		4.0	2.5				3.2	3.3
		2.5	2.1				2.5	2.4
		1.9	1.8			Sales/Total Assets	1.9	1.9
		1.7	1.3				1.6	1.6
		1.6	2.7				2.2	2.1
		(14) 4.4	3.8			% Depr., Dep., Amort./Sales	(60) 3.3	(62) 2.9
		5.9	4.9				4.5	4.2
							.8	1.3
						% Officers', Directors' Owners' Comp/Sales	(11) 3.5	(14) 2.2
							6.3	4.6
	13097M	217803M	1028280M	926051M	257035M	Net Sales ($)	2476104M	2593453M
	5641M	100539M	563364M	523821M	156190M	Total Assets ($)	1485675M	1537303M

M = $ thousand MM = $ million

See Pages 9 through 22 for Explanation of Ratios and Data

Comparative Historical Data | Current Data Sorted by Sales

			Type of Statement						
12	19	12	Unqualified					4	8
17	20	15	Reviewed		1	1	1	5	7
7	4	4	Compiled				1	3	
3	4	3	Tax Returns		1	1	1		
28	21	20	Other		1		1	3	15
					13 (4/1-9/30/13)		41 (10/1/13-3/31/14)		
4/1/11-3/31/12 ALL	4/1/12-3/31/13 ALL	4/1/13-3/31/14 ALL		0-1MM	1-3MM	3-5MM	5-10MM	10-25MM	25MM & OVER
67	68	54	NUMBER OF STATEMENTS		3	2	4	15	30
%	%	%	**ASSETS**	%	%	%	%	%	%
6.3	5.4	5.1	Cash & Equivalents	DATA NOT AVAILABLE				4.8	4.0
23.7	22.5	20.9	Trade Receivables (net)					23.1	19.6
22.6	22.1	23.4	Inventory					18.9	22.9
1.8	2.0	1.6	All Other Current					1.2	1.9
54.5	52.2	50.9	Total Current					48.1	48.3
36.1	40.1	39.3	Fixed Assets (net)					39.0	42.8
4.9	2.9	3.8	Intangibles (net)					5.4	3.0
4.5	4.9	6.0	All Other Non-Current					7.5	5.9
100.0	100.0	100.0	Total					100.0	100.0
			LIABILITIES						
9.9	9.2	8.2	Notes Payable-Short Term					5.9	11.0
4.8	5.3	5.3	Cur. Mat.-L.T.D.					5.9	5.2
14.4	13.6	10.4	Trade Payables					11.0	10.8
.1	.5	.2	Income Taxes Payable					.2	.3
7.1	6.4	5.1	All Other Current					5.7	4.8
36.3	35.0	29.2	Total Current					28.6	32.1
21.9	20.6	23.7	Long-Term Debt					29.0	19.3
1.2	1.6	1.7	Deferred Taxes					.6	2.7
4.4	4.2	4.0	All Other Non-Current					3.1	4.0
36.2	38.7	41.4	Net Worth					38.7	42.0
100.0	100.0	100.0	Total Liabilties & Net Worth					100.0	100.0
			INCOME DATA						
100.0	100.0	100.0	Net Sales					100.0	100.0
25.8	23.7	25.2	Gross Profit					29.4	20.0
19.9	18.7	19.7	Operating Expenses					23.2	14.8
5.8	5.0	5.5	Operating Profit					6.2	5.3
.7	.8	.7	All Other Expenses (net)					1.2	.5
5.1	4.2	4.8	Profit Before Taxes					5.0	4.8
			RATIOS						
2.8	2.7	2.7						2.7	2.3
1.4	1.5	1.5	Current					1.4	1.4
1.1	1.0	1.2						1.0	1.2
1.7	1.7	1.4						2.3	1.1
.8	.8	.7	Quick					.7	.7
.5	.4	.5						.5	.5
33 11.0	**30** 12.0	**29** 12.7						**28** 12.9	**30** 12.0
41 8.8	**42** 8.7	**41** 9.0	Sales/Receivables					**41** 8.8	**41** 9.0
51 7.1	**47** 7.8	**50** 7.3						**58** 6.3	**48** 7.6
38 9.5	**36** 10.1	**40** 9.2						**27** 13.6	**43** 8.5
59 6.2	**50** 7.3	**53** 6.9	Cost of Sales/Inventory					**50** 7.3	**51** 7.1
81 4.5	**66** 5.5	**83** 4.4						**66** 5.5	**76** 4.8
14 26.3	**16** 22.4	**14** 26.4						**17** 21.3	**15** 24.9
29 12.6	**27** 13.7	**25** 14.5	Cost of Sales/Payables					**27** 13.6	**29** 12.6
44 8.3	**41** 9.0	**41** 9.0						**51** 7.2	**41** 9.0
4.6	5.8	5.5						6.1	6.9
12.9	12.4	12.1	Sales/Working Capital					15.1	12.6
99.9	UND	41.8						-891.2	34.0
13.6	11.5	16.0						11.8	21.8
(63) 4.9	(66) 4.9	(53) 5.3	EBIT/Interest					2.8	7.7
2.3	2.2	2.1						1.8	2.2
3.9	3.6	3.5							3.8
(32) 2.0	(38) 2.4	(26) 2.7	Net Profit + Depr., Dep., Amort./Cur. Mat. L/T/D						(16) 2.6
1.5	1.8	1.9							1.6
.5	.6	.7						.5	.7
1.2	1.2	1.2	Fixed/Worth					1.2	1.1
3.2	2.1	2.2						2.5	2.1
.9	.9	.7						1.4	.6
2.1	1.8	1.7	Debt/Worth					1.7	1.8
5.1	3.5	3.2						3.3	3.1
32.6	35.7	36.7						40.6	29.8
(56) 19.5	(64) 19.8	(51) 22.3	% Profit Before Taxes/Tangible Net Worth					25.3	(27) 21.1
11.0	12.6	10.6						17.2	10.6
16.1	14.8	14.8						16.5	14.6
8.6	7.8	8.2	% Profit Before Taxes/Total Assets					5.2	8.1
3.2	3.5	3.8						4.1	3.1
10.6	8.2	8.5						8.6	6.4
4.5	4.6	4.4	Sales/Net Fixed Assets					6.2	3.8
3.4	3.3	3.3						3.6	3.3
2.3	2.5	2.2						2.5	2.1
1.8	1.9	1.8	Sales/Total Assets					1.8	1.8
1.5	1.5	1.5						1.3	1.6
1.8	2.3	2.4						3.1	2.7
(65) 3.0	(65) 3.3	(51) 3.7	% Depr., Dep., Amort./Sales					4.5	(29) 3.7
4.7	5.1	5.0						5.6	5.1
1.1	1.3	1.4							
(15) 1.3	(16) 2.2	(12) 2.8	% Officers', Directors' Owners' Comp/Sales						
6.9	5.0	4.8							
3002075M	2946497M	2442266M	Net Sales ($)		6139M	6958M	30939M	247299M	2150931M
1761451M	1653017M	1349555M	Total Assets ($)		2364M	3277M	17041M	142807M	1184066M

M = $ thousand MM = $ million

See Pages 9 through 22 for Explanation of Ratios and Data

Current Data Sorted by Assets | **Comparative Historical Data**

0-500M	500M-2MM	2-10MM	10-50MM	50-100MM	100-250MM	Type of Statement	4/1/09-3/31/10 ALL	4/1/10-3/31/11 ALL
			1	1	2	Unqualified	7	5
	1	4	4	1		Reviewed	11	16
		2				Compiled	6	5
		2				Tax Returns	2	2
	2	2	5			Other	22	19
	4 (4/1-9/30/13)		23 (10/1/13-3/31/14)					
	3	10	10	2	2	NUMBER OF STATEMENTS	48	47
%	%	%	%	%	%	**ASSETS**	%	%
DATA NOT AVAILABLE		9.5	4.2			Cash & Equivalents	7.9	7.0
		26.0	25.1			Trade Receivables (net)	26.2	22.6
		18.1	26.4			Inventory	19.7	20.9
		.5	.3			All Other Current	3.4	2.2
		54.2	56.0			Total Current	57.2	52.7
		38.4	40.1			Fixed Assets (net)	38.1	41.6
		2.7	.9			Intangibles (net)	1.4	1.1
		4.7	3.0			All Other Non-Current	3.3	4.6
		100.0	100.0			Total	100.0	100.0
						LIABILITIES		
		6.1	7.5			Notes Payable-Short Term	8.9	6.6
		4.5	2.6			Cur. Mat.-L.T.D.	4.8	3.1
		14.9	14.5			Trade Payables	14.6	12.1
		.0	.0			Income Taxes Payable	.1	.0
		3.4	3.7			All Other Current	7.2	7.4
		28.9	28.4			Total Current	35.5	29.3
		14.2	23.8			Long-Term Debt	20.7	19.5
		.6	.1			Deferred Taxes	1.0	1.0
		4.3	2.5			All Other Non-Current	2.5	10.6
		52.1	45.1			Net Worth	40.1	39.6
		100.0	100.0			Total Liabilities & Net Worth	100.0	100.0
						INCOME DATA		
		100.0	100.0			Net Sales	100.0	100.0
		28.5	22.7			Gross Profit	23.7	23.5
		24.2	19.5			Operating Expenses	19.9	19.7
		4.2	3.2			Operating Profit	3.7	3.8
		.5	.1			All Other Expenses (net)	1.0	.4
		3.7	3.1			Profit Before Taxes	2.7	3.4
						RATIOS		
		3.6	2.5				2.4	3.5
		1.5	1.8			Current	1.7	1.8
		1.3	1.5				1.3	1.2
		2.4	1.9				1.6	2.0
		1.0	1.2			Quick	1.1	1.2
		.7	.7				.6	.7
		25 14.6	**33** 11.0				**31** 11.7	**29** 12.4
		39 9.4	**38** 9.5			Sales/Receivables	**38** 9.7	**38** 9.5
		56 6.5	**48** 7.6				**52** 7.0	**50** 7.3
		27 13.7	**25** 14.5				**23** 16.2	**23** 16.0
		33 11.1	**41** 8.9			Cost of Sales/Inventory	**35** 10.4	**31** 11.7
		57 6.4	**111** 3.3				**51** 7.2	**55** 6.6
		10 35.1	**14** 26.3				**16** 22.8	**16** 23.3
		19 18.9	**25** 14.8			Cost of Sales/Payables	**27** 13.3	**22** 16.6
		64 5.7	**36** 10.0				**36** 10.2	**33** 11.1
		7.2	7.8				5.4	5.3
		11.6	8.4			Sales/Working Capital	11.9	9.2
		22.3	14.0				28.9	34.4
		35.4	29.3				8.1	26.6
		14.4	6.2			EBIT/Interest	(45) 4.2	(45) 5.4
		2.6	.9				.6	1.5
							3.9	7.8
						Net Profit + Depr., Dep., Amort./Cur. Mat. L/T/D	(17) 3.1	(13) 5.8
							1.5	2.3
		.3	.5				.5	.5
		.7	1.0			Fixed/Worth	1.1	1.0
		1.5	1.3				1.5	1.6
		.7	.7				.8	.7
		1.0	1.2			Debt/Worth	1.5	1.3
		1.5	2.4				2.3	3.2
		25.1	37.3				32.7	32.1
		19.1	15.0			% Profit Before Taxes/Tangible Net Worth	(44) 13.7	(43) 21.2
		7.4	-.4				3.0	7.6
		19.3	18.6				11.3	15.9
		9.6	7.5			% Profit Before Taxes/Total Assets	6.0	7.5
		2.4	-.1				-.8	1.8
		24.1	16.5				10.2	9.2
		5.0	5.3			Sales/Net Fixed Assets	5.5	4.8
		4.1	3.5				3.5	3.9
		2.9	2.8				2.7	2.6
		2.3	2.5			Sales/Total Assets	2.1	2.2
		1.9	1.8				1.7	1.9
		1.7	1.0				1.4	1.9
		2.6	3.0			% Depr., Dep., Amort./Sales	(44) 3.3	(43) 2.7
		4.1	4.2				4.2	4.8
							.8	1.0
						% Officers', Directors' Owners' Comp/Sales	(19) 1.9	(21) 1.9
							5.1	3.1
	17535M	145653M	563073M	276517M	551475M	Net Sales ($)	1744433M	2043947M
	4490M	57172M	242747M	179888M	267243M	Total Assets ($)	1044630M	1035511M

M = $ thousand MM = $ million

See Pages 9 through 22 for Explanation of Ratios and Data

Comparative Historical Data				Current Data Sorted by Sales					
			Type of Statement						
3	5	4	Unqualified						4
16	11	10	Reviewed			1		4	5
6	5	2	Compiled			1		1	
6	1	2	Tax Returns			1		1	
15	11	9	Other		1	1		2	5
					4 (4/1-9/30/13)		23 (10/1/13-3/31/14)		
4/1/11-3/31/12 ALL	4/1/12-3/31/13 ALL	4/1/13-3/31/14 ALL		0-1MM	1-3MM	3-5MM	5-10MM	10-25MM	25MM & OVER
46	33	27	**NUMBER OF STATEMENTS**		1	4		8	14
%	%	%	**ASSETS**	%	%	%	%	%	%
6.0	7.4	6.1	Cash & Equivalents	D			D		4.7
27.6	27.8	26.5	Trade Receivables (net)	A			A		24.8
21.4	22.7	21.5	Inventory	T			T		24.2
1.4	.7	.8	All Other Current	A			A		1.0
56.3	58.6	54.9	Total Current						54.7
37.2	34.7	38.0	Fixed Assets (net)	N			N		40.1
1.8	1.4	2.5	Intangibles (net)	O			O		1.7
4.7	5.2	4.6	All Other Non-Current	T			T		3.4
100.0	100.0	100.0	Total						100.0
			LIABILITIES	A			A		
9.3	10.4	9.0	Notes Payable-Short Term	V			V		8.5
4.3	4.3	3.8	Cur. Mat.-L.T.D.	A			A		3.3
15.8	16.1	15.9	Trade Payables	I			I		14.0
.1	.3	.0	Income Taxes Payable	L			L		.1
6.7	6.2	4.2	All Other Current	A			A		4.9
36.3	37.3	32.8	Total Current	B			B		30.8
17.6	16.3	21.1	Long-Term Debt	L			L		22.1
.8	.2	.7	Deferred Taxes	E			E		.9
4.8	4.4	3.1	All Other Non-Current						2.4
40.6	41.8	42.3	Net Worth						43.9
100.0	100.0	100.0	Total Liabilties & Net Worth						100.0
			INCOME DATA						
100.0	100.0	100.0	Net Sales						100.0
22.5	21.6	24.9	Gross Profit						20.8
19.1	16.1	20.9	Operating Expenses						16.7
3.5	5.5	4.1	Operating Profit						4.1
.0	.6	.5	All Other Expenses (net)						.3
3.4	4.9	3.6	Profit Before Taxes						3.8
			RATIOS						
2.5	2.3	2.4	Current						2.7
1.7	1.7	1.6							1.8
1.0	1.2	1.3							1.4
1.8	1.5	1.6	Quick						1.7
1.1	1.0	1.0							1.2
.6	.7	.7							.6
29 12.7	27 13.4	31 11.9	Sales/Receivables						33 11.0
38 9.5	34 10.8	38 9.5							39 9.3
47 7.7	46 7.9	55 6.6							52 7.0
26 14.1	24 15.1	27 13.7	Cost of Sales/Inventory						27 13.4
36 10.1	32 11.5	37 9.9							43 8.4
51 7.2	59 6.2	55 6.6							66 5.5
13 28.2	16 23.2	15 24.8	Cost of Sales/Payables						15 25.0
26 14.2	22 16.4	28 13.2							27 13.6
41 9.0	34 10.6	45 8.1							36 10.0
6.6	6.5	7.3	Sales/Working Capital						6.7
12.2	10.8	12.4							8.4
-236.2	39.1	28.0							17.3
18.5	17.3	28.6	EBIT/Interest						28.9
(45) 4.3	(31) 9.9	5.4							6.2
2.0	4.3	2.2							2.0
7.5			Net Profit + Depr., Dep., Amort./Cur. Mat. L/T/D						
(14) 3.0									
1.4									
.5	.3	.6	Fixed/Worth						.6
1.0	.8	1.1							1.0
1.6	1.3	2.3							1.6
.8	.8	.8	Debt/Worth						.7
1.6	1.5	1.2							1.2
3.1	2.3	3.7							3.8
41.8	36.5	37.6	% Profit Before Taxes/Tangible Net Worth						39.2
(43) 17.4	(31) 22.9	(25) 20.6							19.5
5.9	15.3	7.0							3.8
15.4	16.2	13.7	% Profit Before Taxes/Total Assets						14.8
6.6	8.3	7.4							7.1
2.2	5.6	2.3							1.8
13.1	14.8	13.2	Sales/Net Fixed Assets						10.7
5.3	6.6	5.4							5.2
4.0	4.6	3.8							3.5
3.1	2.9	2.7	Sales/Total Assets						2.7
2.5	2.3	2.4							2.4
2.1	2.1	1.8							1.4
1.6	1.6	1.6	% Depr., Dep., Amort./Sales						1.6
(44) 2.6	(31) 2.3	2.7							3.2
4.4	3.5	4.1							4.9
.9	.9		% Officers', Directors' Owners' Comp/Sales						
(22) 2.0	(11) 1.8								
3.8	3.2								
1976617M	1436585M	1554253M	Net Sales ($)		2797M	14690M		145701M	1391065M
858722M	574794M	751540M	Total Assets ($)		1282M	9354M		51026M	689878M

M = $ thousand MM = $ million

See Pages 9 through 22 for Explanation of Ratios and Data

Current Data Sorted by Assets							Comparative Historical Data	
						Type of Statement		
1		5	17	10	11	Unqualified	63	52
	3	15	16			Reviewed	51	65
2	4	14	2	1		Compiled	27	23
	5	5				Tax Returns	24	21
	9	22	23	8	7	Other	91	85
	32 (4/1-9/30/13)		148 (10/1/13-3/31/14)				4/1/09-3/31/10	4/1/10-3/31/11
0-500M	**500M-2MM**	**2-10MM**	**10-50MM**	**50-100MM**	**100-250MM**		**ALL**	**ALL**
3	21	61	58	19	18	**NUMBER OF STATEMENTS**	256	246
%	%	%	%	%	%	**ASSETS**	%	%
	10.6	8.5	7.6	9.9	5.3	Cash & Equivalents	6.1	6.9
	31.0	31.2	24.1	19.3	18.5	Trade Receivables (net)	24.3	25.5
	24.6	28.0	25.9	18.8	20.5	Inventory	23.5	25.1
	2.1	1.1	3.5	1.9	2.1	All Other Current	2.3	1.9
	68.2	68.8	61.1	49.9	46.3	Total Current	56.2	59.4
	22.2	23.7	27.6	28.3	27.6	Fixed Assets (net)	31.0	29.6
	.4	4.5	4.5	12.9	22.3	Intangibles (net)	7.3	6.6
	9.3	3.0	6.7	8.9	3.8	All Other Non-Current	5.4	4.4
	100.0	100.0	100.0	100.0	100.0	Total	100.0	100.0
						LIABILITIES		
	6.5	11.7	8.0	1.9	11.0	Notes Payable-Short Term	11.2	11.7
	2.0	5.4	5.0	3.4	2.7	Cur. Mat.-L.T.D.	4.6	3.9
	23.3	21.3	15.0	8.8	11.1	Trade Payables	15.3	16.9
	.0	.1	.1	.2	.7	Income Taxes Payable	.3	.1
	12.1	6.9	6.5	5.2	8.0	All Other Current	7.8	6.6
	43.9	45.5	34.6	19.5	33.6	Total Current	39.2	39.3
	12.4	15.1	12.3	17.2	18.6	Long-Term Debt	18.4	16.9
	.0	.2	1.0	1.3	2.3	Deferred Taxes	.8	1.0
	13.8	5.9	4.7	6.5	10.8	All Other Non-Current	8.1	6.4
	30.0	33.3	47.3	55.5	34.6	Net Worth	33.5	36.4
	100.0	100.0	100.0	100.0	100.0	Total Liabilties & Net Worth	100.0	100.0
						INCOME DATA		
	100.0	100.0	100.0	100.0	100.0	Net Sales	100.0	100.0
	32.5	28.6	22.8	22.0	20.6	Gross Profit	25.1	25.3
	28.6	23.3	16.4	16.8	14.4	Operating Expenses	21.4	19.7
	3.9	5.4	6.4	5.2	6.2	Operating Profit	3.7	5.6
	.2	.3	.6	.9	3.0	All Other Expenses (net)	1.4	.9
	3.7	5.0	5.8	4.3	3.3	Profit Before Taxes	2.3	4.7
						RATIOS		
	3.2	2.1	3.5	3.8	2.0		2.4	2.6
	1.8	1.5	1.9	2.5	1.2	Current	1.5	1.6
	1.2	1.2	1.4	1.7	1.0		1.0	1.1
	1.6	1.4	1.7	2.3	1.0		1.5	1.5
	1.0	.8	1.0	1.4	.6	Quick	.8	.8
	.7	.6	.6	.8	.5		.5	.5
	25 14.4	**30** 12.0	**30** 12.2	**33** 10.9	**26** 13.8		**31** 11.8	**30** 12.1
	36 10.1	**38** 9.6	**38** 9.5	**39** 9.4	**38** 9.5	Sales/Receivables	**40** 9.1	**38** 9.5
	45 8.1	**53** 6.9	**49** 7.5	**46** 8.0	**54** 6.8		**49** 7.5	**49** 7.5
	15 24.5	**33** 11.1	**41** 8.9	**41** 9.0	**42** 8.7		**33** 11.0	**34** 10.7
	28 13.1	**46** 7.9	**56** 6.5	**56** 6.5	**61** 6.0	Cost of Sales/Inventory	**49** 7.4	**52** 7.0
	66 5.5	**76** 4.8	**83** 4.4	**63** 5.8	**76** 4.8		**73** 5.0	**73** 5.0
	21 17.3	**18** 20.1	**18** 20.7	**14** 26.0	**21** 17.8		**18** 20.0	**20** 18.0
	34 10.8	**35** 10.5	**29** 12.4	**20** 18.0	**31** 11.6	Cost of Sales/Payables	**28** 12.9	**30** 12.3
	54 6.7	**54** 6.7	**42** 8.7	**27** 13.3	**45** 8.2		**46** 7.9	**42** 8.6
	7.4	7.5	5.1	4.0	9.2		6.0	5.9
	13.0	10.5	8.1	6.6	16.3	Sales/Working Capital	12.8	11.9
	43.0	52.1	17.2	8.9	120.0		115.7	54.7
	11.0	25.1	31.0	13.5	3.9		9.3	14.6
	(15) 5.8	(56) 7.5	(53) 12.4	(15) 4.4	(15) 1.6	EBIT/Interest	(235) 3.3	(230) 5.2
	4.8	2.8	3.2	1.7	.5		1.0	2.0
		6.3	4.7				4.7	5.2
		(13) 2.8	(16) 3.7			Net Profit + Depr., Dep., Amort./Cur. Mat. L/T/D	(74) 2.3	(77) 2.8
		1.4	2.1				.8	1.5
	.4	.3	.3	.4	.8		.4	.4
	.6	.9	.5	.6	2.5	Fixed/Worth	1.1	1.0
	1.4	2.0	1.3	2.5	-.6		4.9	2.9
	1.0	1.0	.5	.4	1.7		.9	.7
	2.0	2.1	1.2	.8	3.8	Debt/Worth	2.3	2.2
	8.1	5.8	2.5	3.0	-3.5		10.8	6.9
	49.6	66.2	46.9	21.1	46.2		42.0	48.7
	(19) 19.7	(53) 32.4	(52) 26.2	(16) 16.0	(11) 12.8	% Profit Before Taxes/Tangible Net Worth	(203) 15.6	(207) 25.9
	8.5	7.8	13.6	4.3	.1		1.8	8.1
	16.5	22.5	19.3	9.9	9.4		13.5	17.8
	7.9	11.6	11.7	4.4	5.6	% Profit Before Taxes/Total Assets	5.7	7.5
	4.7	2.5	5.9	.9	-1.1		.0	2.1
	55.7	78.3	14.7	8.5	9.3		14.3	17.3
	17.4	14.4	8.7	5.0	6.6	Sales/Net Fixed Assets	7.5	7.7
	6.4	6.9	4.8	4.4	4.0		4.0	4.7
	4.1	3.2	2.5	2.3	2.2		2.9	2.9
	3.3	2.7	2.1	1.7	1.3	Sales/Total Assets	2.1	2.2
	1.9	2.0	1.7	1.1	1.1		1.5	1.7
	.3	.5	1.1	2.1	1.8		1.4	1.2
	(16) 1.7	(51) 1.4	(53) 2.0	(18) 3.7	(14) 2.2	% Depr., Dep., Amort./Sales	(220) 2.7	(217) 2.4
	3.1	2.8	3.4	6.4	3.8		4.2	3.7
	2.4	1.9	1.1				1.4	1.6
	(10) 3.6	(21) 3.6	(12) 2.1			% Officers', Directors' Owners' Comp/Sales	(64) 2.4	(81) 2.7
	7.4	6.8	3.0				5.7	4.7
2013M	**77429M**	**930876M**	**2951963M**	**2099439M**	**4279503M**	Net Sales ($)	**13335068M**	**11617797M**
626M	**24774M**	**344148M**	**1442916M**	**1308739M**	**2694174M**	Total Assets ($)	**7598804M**	**6636511M**

M = $ thousand MM = $ million

See Pages 9 through 22 for Explanation of Ratios and Data

Comparative Historical Data				Current Data Sorted by Sales					
			Type of Statement						
51	27	44	Unqualified	1			1	6	36
49	35	34	Reviewed		1	1	3	14	15
26	16	23	Compiled	1	2	3	6	7	4
24	16	10	Tax Returns	1		3	3	3	
103	96	69	Other	1	3	6	6	17	36
				32 (4/1-9/30/13)			148 (10/1/13-3/31/14)		
4/1/11-3/31/12 ALL	4/1/12-3/31/13 ALL	4/1/13-3/31/14 ALL		0-1MM	1-3MM	3-5MM	5-10MM	10-25MM	25MM & OVER
253	190	180	**NUMBER OF STATEMENTS**	4	6	13	19	47	91
%	%	%	**ASSETS**	%	%	%	%	%	%
6.1	7.2	8.5	Cash & Equivalents			11.2	11.4	8.7	6.9
27.2	25.9	26.1	Trade Receivables (net)			26.8	31.2	30.3	23.0
27.7	25.4	24.9	Inventory			20.5	23.1	27.6	25.0
2.2	2.5	2.2	All Other Current			2.4	.8	1.7	2.8
63.2	60.9	61.6	Total Current			60.9	66.5	68.3	57.6
26.4	28.1	26.0	Fixed Assets (net)			21.6	24.3	23.5	27.3
5.6	6.4	6.7	Intangibles (net)			5.0	4.9	4.6	9.0
4.8	4.6	5.7	All Other Non-Current			12.5	4.3	3.6	6.1
100.0	100.0	100.0	Total			100.0	100.0	100.0	100.0
			LIABILITIES						
11.5	9.8	8.8	Notes Payable-Short Term			7.2	10.8	8.5	9.0
3.8	3.5	4.3	Cur. Mat.-L.T.D.			4.5	2.1	7.3	3.6
18.4	17.8	16.9	Trade Payables			19.7	20.3	20.8	13.6
.2	.2	.2	Income Taxes Payable			.0	.2	.2	.2
8.1	6.7	7.3	All Other Current			9.2	6.1	5.3	7.4
42.1	38.0	37.5	Total Current			40.5	39.5	42.1	33.8
16.0	15.6	14.3	Long-Term Debt			19.8	12.3	15.2	14.5
.9	.9	.8	Deferred Taxes			.1	.0	.4	1.3
6.9	6.2	6.9	All Other Non-Current			16.0	8.5	7.6	5.1
34.1	39.3	40.6	Net Worth			23.5	39.7	34.7	45.3
100.0	100.0	100.0	Total Liabilties & Net Worth			100.0	100.0	100.0	100.0
			INCOME DATA						
100.0	100.0	100.0	Net Sales			100.0	100.0	100.0	100.0
24.7	24.6	25.6	Gross Profit			34.7	34.1	25.7	22.1
20.3	20.0	20.2	Operating Expenses			32.7	28.7	19.9	16.0
4.4	4.5	5.5	Operating Profit			2.0	5.4	5.9	6.1
1.0	1.0	.7	All Other Expenses (net)			-.5	.1	.7	1.0
3.3	3.6	4.8	Profit Before Taxes			2.6	5.3	5.1	5.1
			RATIOS						
2.5	2.5	2.8				1.9	3.5	2.6	2.8
1.5	1.7	1.7	Current			1.6	1.5	1.7	1.7
1.1	1.3	1.2				1.1	1.0	1.4	1.2
1.3	1.4	1.6				1.5	2.0	1.7	1.4
.8	.9	.9	Quick			1.0	.9	1.0	.8
.5	.6	.6				.5	.6	.6	.6
30 12.3	30 12.0	30 12.0				18 20.3	31 11.6	30 12.1	31 11.9
39 9.3	38 9.6	38 9.7	Sales/Receivables			31 11.9	43 8.5	39 9.3	38 9.7
51 7.1	46 7.9	49 7.5				47 7.7	63 5.8	49 7.4	46 7.9
39 9.3	32 11.3	34 10.7				14 26.0	31 11.9	33 10.9	41 9.0
55 6.6	54 6.8	53 6.9	Cost of Sales/Inventory			26 14.2	51 7.1	46 7.9	57 6.4
73 5.0	73 5.0	76 4.8				66 5.5	91 4.0	72 5.1	79 4.6
20 18.4	17 21.0	17 21.2				21 17.3	19 19.0	21 17.0	17 21.6
31 11.7	27 13.3	29 12.6	Cost of Sales/Payables			33 11.1	49 7.4	35 10.4	25 14.4
46 7.9	45 8.1	47 7.7				54 6.8	60 6.1	54 6.8	40 9.1
5.7	5.8	5.8				7.8	7.3	5.9	5.4
12.2	10.4	9.9	Sales/Working Capital			13.3	10.3	8.8	9.5
43.9	23.9	25.8				453.4	162.9	16.9	23.9
12.0	14.5	20.9				10.7	16.0	24.5	22.9
(237) 4.0	(176) 5.0	(156) 7.7	EBIT/Interest			(12) 5.4	(15) 7.1	(45) 9.8	(79) 7.7
1.6	1.8	2.5				2.4	4.6	3.0	2.1
4.7	5.0	5.0						9.5	4.3
(80) 2.6	(56) 2.7	(41) 2.8	Net Profit + Depr., Dep., Amort./Cur. Mat. L/T/D					(12) 4.8	(25) 2.8
.8	1.2	1.7						1.9	1.7
.3	.3	.3				.5	.1	.3	.4
.9	.8	.7	Fixed/Worth			1.0	1.0	.7	.7
2.5	2.0	1.9				2.6	2.1	1.9	2.1
.7	.7	.7				1.4	1.2	.8	.5
2.2	1.6	1.6	Debt/Worth			4.0	2.4	1.4	1.5
7.5	5.9	5.2				14.6	7.1	4.2	4.9
41.3	44.3	48.2				57.3	68.4	49.9	47.0
(210) 22.2	(164) 23.3	(154) 24.1	% Profit Before Taxes/Tangible Net Worth			(11) 19.4	(17) 31.4	(39) 29.2	(78) 23.6
5.4	5.6	9.4				4.6	18.5	7.8	10.6
14.8	16.3	17.5				12.6	20.1	20.7	16.2
6.0	7.7	9.3	% Profit Before Taxes/Total Assets			7.6	10.2	11.6	9.1
1.4	1.3	2.7				2.1	3.4	2.5	3.1
24.2	16.4	21.6				92.3	61.5	28.1	13.5
9.8	8.9	9.1	Sales/Net Fixed Assets			19.7	19.8	13.1	7.4
4.9	4.9	5.0				7.6	6.7	7.2	4.7
3.2	3.0	3.0				4.2	3.3	3.2	2.6
2.2	2.3	2.2	Sales/Total Assets			3.2	2.4	2.6	2.0
1.7	1.7	1.7				1.9	1.8	1.9	1.3
1.0	1.1	1.0				.2	.3	1.0	1.1
(214) 2.0	(163) 1.9	(155) 2.0	% Depr., Dep., Amort./Sales			(10) 1.2	(14) 1.3	(39) 1.9	(83) 2.2
3.7	4.0	3.5				2.6	3.5	3.4	3.7
1.9	1.9	1.4						1.3	1.1
(79) 3.5	(51) 3.4	(46) 3.1	% Officers', Directors' Owners' Comp/Sales					(17) 2.9	(13) 2.3
7.4	7.2	4.8						4.8	3.9
12432027M	10864966M	10341223M	Net Sales ($)	2366M	10547M	53896M	141309M	841068M	9292037M
6681693M	6088097M	5815377M	Total Assets ($)	2406M	4920M	23585M	66636M	371001M	5346829M

M = $ thousand MM = $ million

See Pages 9 through 22 for Explanation of Ratios and Data

Current Data Sorted by Assets							Comparative Historical Data	
						Type of Statement		
		1	5	2		Unqualified	12	12
		7	2			Reviewed	18	17
		1				Compiled	5	6
	4					Tax Returns	8	3
2	1	9	7			Other	20	15
	7 (4/1-9/30/13)		34 (10/1/13-3/31/14)				4/1/09-3/31/10	4/1/10-3/31/11
0-500M	500M-2MM	2-10MM	10-50MM	50-100MM	100-250MM		ALL	ALL
2	5	18	14	2		**NUMBER OF STATEMENTS**	63	53
%	%	%	%	%	%	**ASSETS**	%	%
		4.2	3.2		DATA NOT AVAILABLE	Cash & Equivalents	6.1	8.0
		27.1	31.7			Trade Receivables (net)	31.5	31.8
		26.2	23.6			Inventory	22.6	22.9
		3.7	1.7			All Other Current	2.1	2.2
		61.2	60.2			Total Current	62.3	64.9
		29.1	16.3			Fixed Assets (net)	28.9	25.2
		5.2	20.3			Intangibles (net)	5.0	3.9
		4.4	3.2			All Other Non-Current	3.7	6.1
		100.0	100.0			Total	100.0	100.0
						LIABILITIES		
		12.1	13.8			Notes Payable-Short Term	15.1	11.6
		2.6	3.4			Cur. Mat.-L.T.D.	4.1	4.9
		13.4	16.7			Trade Payables	21.9	16.6
		.4	.0			Income Taxes Payable	.1	.3
		13.6	8.9			All Other Current	10.4	9.2
		42.1	42.8			Total Current	51.6	42.7
		9.2	20.6			Long-Term Debt	21.2	18.5
		2.3	.6			Deferred Taxes	.8	1.0
		2.9	9.4			All Other Non-Current	8.8	5.6
		43.4	26.6			Net Worth	17.8	32.2
		100.0	100.0			Total Liabilties & Net Worth	100.0	100.0
						INCOME DATA		
		100.0	100.0			Net Sales	100.0	100.0
		32.6	27.1			Gross Profit	24.4	27.4
		31.6	23.8			Operating Expenses	22.5	24.1
		1.0	3.3			Operating Profit	1.9	3.2
		-.4	1.8			All Other Expenses (net)	.8	.8
		1.4	1.5			Profit Before Taxes	1.1	2.5
						RATIOS		
		2.2	1.9				2.0	2.5
		1.5	1.4			Current	1.4	1.5
		1.1	1.1				1.0	1.1
		1.3	1.2				1.5	1.7
		.7	.8			Quick	.8	.9
		.5	.5				.6	.6
		35 10.5	33 11.1				37 9.9	37 9.9
		39 9.4	47 7.8			Sales/Receivables	46 8.0	48 7.6
		53 6.9	57 6.4				58 6.3	61 6.0
		31 11.7	27 13.3				21 17.4	28 13.2
		46 8.0	51 7.2			Cost of Sales/Inventory	41 9.0	41 8.8
		111 3.3	99 3.7				68 5.4	76 4.8
		15 24.4	22 16.8				20 18.0	18 20.2
		23 16.0	24 14.9			Cost of Sales/Payables	35 10.4	26 13.8
		41 9.0	38 9.6				48 7.6	48 7.6
		6.9	6.8				7.7	5.2
		10.7	12.8			Sales/Working Capital	14.0	10.4
		NM	42.2				233.2	37.2
		18.9	11.9				4.0	10.7
		(17) 3.8	3.9			EBIT/Interest	(57) 1.9	(48) 3.4
		1.0	-1.6				-.9	1.3
		3.9					3.0	3.9
		(10) 2.3				Net Profit + Depr., Dep., Amort./Cur. Mat. L/T/D	(14) 1.7	(24) 2.4
		1.7					.7	1.6
		.5	.6				.5	.3
		1.0	1.4			Fixed/Worth	1.2	.8
		1.5	-1.9				4.9	2.2
		.9	1.5				1.3	1.1
		1.4	13.2			Debt/Worth	2.3	2.0
		2.9	-5.7				8.8	7.0
		23.1	64.8				28.4	31.8
		(17) 11.1	(10) 43.5			% Profit Before Taxes/Tangible Net Worth	(49) 12.0	(46) 15.2
		3.8	-127.5				-9.7	2.0
		6.5	13.1				7.6	9.4
		3.8	6.1			% Profit Before Taxes/Total Assets	1.9	5.3
		1.3	-6.1				-4.0	.0
		18.9	25.4				18.5	17.7
		8.3	13.3			Sales/Net Fixed Assets	9.3	10.4
		5.1	9.6				4.9	6.4
		2.9	2.8				2.9	3.0
		2.3	2.3			Sales/Total Assets	2.2	2.2
		1.8	1.6				1.9	1.7
		.6	1.1				1.1	1.3
		1.8	(12) 2.1			% Depr., Dep., Amort./Sales	(53) 2.2	(45) 2.1
		4.4	3.6				3.3	3.1
							1.6	1.7
						% Officers', Directors' Owners' Comp/Sales	(18) 4.2	(14) 3.4
							6.9	9.6
4529M	15355M	253053M	782126M	349568M		Net Sales ($)	3260828M	4208476M
628M	6053M	111725M	378836M	180553M		Total Assets ($)	1457677M	1977922M

M = $ thousand MM = $ million

See Pages 9 through 22 for Explanation of Ratios and Data

Comparative Historical Data				Current Data Sorted by Sales					
			Type of Statement						
13	7	8	Unqualified					1	7
15	10	9	Reviewed				4	3	2
3	1	1	Compiled				1		
8	2	4	Tax Returns		3	1			
16	27	19	Other	1	1	1		10	6
					7 (4/1-9/30/13)			34 (10/1/13-3/31/14)	
4/1/11-3/31/12 ALL	**4/1/12-3/31/13 ALL**	**4/1/13-3/31/14 ALL**		**0-1MM**	**1-3MM**	**3-5MM**	**5-10MM**	**10-25MM**	**25MM & OVER**
55	47	41	**NUMBER OF STATEMENTS**	1	4	2	5	14	15
%	%	%	**ASSETS**	%	%	%	%	%	%
6.9	5.4	3.9	Cash & Equivalents					4.6	2.9
29.0	29.9	30.1	Trade Receivables (net)					23.7	31.7
22.3	24.6	24.5	Inventory					25.8	27.8
3.5	3.0	2.4	All Other Current					1.9	1.8
61.7	62.9	61.0	Total Current					56.0	64.1
28.0	22.6	24.4	Fixed Assets (net)					27.0	17.7
4.2	8.1	9.9	Intangibles (net)					12.7	15.1
6.1	6.4	4.8	All Other Non-Current					4.3	3.1
100.0	100.0	100.0	Total					100.0	100.0
			LIABILITIES						
12.6	12.6	12.5	Notes Payable-Short Term					10.0	15.8
4.0	4.3	3.3	Cur. Mat.-L.T.D.					3.1	3.0
16.3	15.7	20.0	Trade Payables					9.6	18.5
.2	.1	.2	Income Taxes Payable					.5	.0
6.2	8.5	10.0	All Other Current					10.0	7.1
39.3	41.3	46.0	Total Current					33.3	44.5
16.9	14.6	18.0	Long-Term Debt					11.7	18.8
.8	1.4	1.2	Deferred Taxes					2.7	.6
9.3	6.7	9.1	All Other Non-Current					2.7	10.1
33.8	36.0	25.6	Net Worth					49.6	26.0
100.0	100.0	100.0	Total Liabilties & Net Worth					100.0	100.0
			INCOME DATA						
100.0	100.0	100.0	Net Sales					100.0	100.0
27.1	27.8	29.2	Gross Profit					35.4	23.4
24.3	24.6	27.3	Operating Expenses					31.3	22.0
2.7	3.3	1.9	Operating Profit					4.2	1.4
1.1	.4	.6	All Other Expenses (net)					.6	1.3
1.6	2.9	1.3	Profit Before Taxes					3.5	.1
			RATIOS						
2.3	2.5	2.0						2.5	1.9
1.6	1.6	1.4	Current					1.8	1.4
1.1	1.2	.9						1.2	1.2
1.6	1.8	1.2						1.7	1.2
.9	.8	.7	Quick					.7	.7
.6	.6	.5						.5	.6
34 10.8	**33** 11.0	**34** 10.7						**31** 11.8	**35** 10.3
43 8.5	**43** 8.5	**44** 8.3	Sales/Receivables					**38** 9.7	**46** 7.9
52 7.0	**61** 6.0	**54** 6.7						**42** 8.6	**55** 6.6
24 15.1	**29** 12.5	**28** 12.9						**32** 11.3	**30** 12.3
33 10.9	**46** 8.0	**44** 8.3	Cost of Sales/Inventory					**53** 6.9	**44** 8.3
59 6.2	**126** 2.9	**101** 3.6						**111** 3.3	**96** 3.8
16 23.2	**17** 22.0	**21** 17.1						**14** 26.6	**23** 15.9
22 16.7	**25** 14.6	**28** 13.1	Cost of Sales/Payables					**18** 20.8	**27** 13.3
48 7.6	**49** 7.4	**47** 7.7						**23** 15.6	**47** 7.7
6.0	5.1	6.7						6.9	6.5
12.4	9.0	15.0	Sales/Working Capital					10.0	10.7
36.7	42.5	-90.2						20.8	31.4
8.6	13.3	9.8						29.4	9.8
(52) 2.4	(41) 4.3	(39) 3.8	EBIT/Interest					(13) 4.8	3.8
.3	.6	.2						2.3	-1.1
2.8	10.8	3.9							
(19) 1.7	(15) 2.1	(18) 2.0	Net Profit + Depr., Dep., Amort./Cur. Mat. L/T/D						
.9	.8	.9							
.3	.2	.5						.5	.6
.8	.7	1.1	Fixed/Worth					.8	1.1
3.3	2.7	NM						1.4	-6.4
.9	1.0	1.3						.9	1.6
2.1	2.0	2.7	Debt/Worth					1.3	11.5
9.3	14.1	NM						2.7	-25.8
25.6	39.5	40.8						33.1	55.9
(49) 8.7	(38) 13.3	(31) 11.1	% Profit Before Taxes/Tangible Net Worth					(13) 11.7	(11) 42.8
-6.1	4.3	-3.2						5.0	-104.1
8.7	12.8	8.2						12.8	12.6
3.4	5.3	3.2	% Profit Before Taxes/Total Assets					5.5	2.8
-2.3	-.5	-.1						2.3	-5.6
15.2	29.6	21.3						19.2	17.6
9.6	10.7	10.7	Sales/Net Fixed Assets					10.5	11.8
5.5	6.8	6.6						5.1	8.5
2.9	3.2	2.8						2.5	2.8
2.3	2.2	2.3	Sales/Total Assets					2.3	2.4
1.7	1.4	1.8						1.8	1.7
1.4	1.1	.8						.6	.9
(47) 2.1	(36) 1.7	(36) 1.8	% Depr., Dep., Amort./Sales					1.3	(13) 1.8
3.0	3.1	3.9						4.4	3.4
2.3	1.5	.7							
(18) 3.7	(13) 2.5	(10) 2.3	% Officers', Directors' Owners' Comp/Sales						
10.4	5.6	6.0							
3096036M	**3552186M**	**1404631M**	Net Sales ($)	**156M**	**10504M**	**9224M**	**36512M**	**231192M**	**1117043M**
1507137M	**1786924M**	**677795M**	Total Assets ($)	**202M**	**4632M**	**1847M**	**17276M**	**126345M**	**527493M**

M = $ thousand MM = $ million

See Pages 9 through 22 for Explanation of Ratios and Data

Current Data Sorted by Assets							Comparative Historical Data	
						Type of Statement		
		1		1	5	Unqualified	14	8
		1	2			Reviewed	4	6
		1	2			Compiled	6	8
						Tax Returns		1
		1	9	5	4	Other	10	22
	3 (4/1-9/30/13)		29 (10/1/13-3/31/14)				4/1/09-3/31/10	4/1/10-3/31/11
0-500M	500M-2MM	2-10MM	10-50MM	50-100MM	100-250MM		ALL	ALL
		4	13	6	9	**NUMBER OF STATEMENTS**	34	45
%	%	%	%	%	%	**ASSETS**	%	%
DATA NOT AVAILABLE	DATA NOT AVAILABLE		4.5			Cash & Equivalents	5.2	6.1
			22.8			Trade Receivables (net)	20.9	20.9
			27.8			Inventory	19.9	22.0
			1.2			All Other Current	4.3	2.1
			56.3			Total Current	50.4	51.1
			33.5			Fixed Assets (net)	39.5	40.9
			4.5			Intangibles (net)	6.1	3.9
			5.7			All Other Non-Current	4.1	4.1
			100.0			Total	100.0	100.0
						LIABILITIES		
			10.6			Notes Payable-Short Term	6.4	7.3
			5.0			Cur. Mat.-L.T.D.	4.0	4.4
			17.2			Trade Payables	14.4	16.3
			.1			Income Taxes Payable	.1	.0
			5.0			All Other Current	7.1	7.4
			37.9			Total Current	32.0	35.4
			22.8			Long-Term Debt	22.5	23.0
			.3			Deferred Taxes	1.2	1.9
			7.8			All Other Non-Current	2.3	3.6
			31.3			Net Worth	42.0	36.0
			100.0			Total Liabilties & Net Worth	100.0	100.0
						INCOME DATA		
			100.0			Net Sales	100.0	100.0
			21.8			Gross Profit	25.0	21.8
			14.7			Operating Expenses	14.0	15.3
			7.2			Operating Profit	11.0	6.5
			1.2			All Other Expenses (net)	1.4	1.6
			5.9			Profit Before Taxes	9.6	4.8
						RATIOS		
			2.2				2.2	2.1
			1.5			Current	1.7	1.4
			1.1				1.1	.9
			1.3				1.3	1.1
			.7			Quick	.8	.8
			.3				.5	.5
			28 13.2				26 14.0	23 16.2
			33 11.1			Sales/Receivables	32 11.3	30 12.0
			42 8.6				45 8.2	41 8.9
			42 8.7				29 12.5	37 9.7
			52 7.0			Cost of Sales/Inventory	48 7.6	50 7.4
			74 4.9				75 4.8	72 5.1
			27 13.5				19 19.1	20 18.7
			28 13.2			Cost of Sales/Payables	35 10.4	34 10.9
			34 10.8				46 8.0	47 7.8
			8.2				6.7	7.5
			14.3			Sales/Working Capital	12.5	15.0
			43.6				36.1	-43.6
			33.3				18.0	11.5
			3.6			EBIT/Interest	(31) 10.5	(43) 4.7
			2.4				4.0	1.8
								11.1
						Net Profit + Depr., Dep., Amort./Cur. Mat. L/T/D		(13) 3.1
								1.3
			.6				.6	.5
			1.2			Fixed/Worth	1.0	1.5
			2.6				2.4	3.0
			.9				.8	1.0
			2.3			Debt/Worth	1.7	2.3
			5.5				3.2	4.4
			58.4				60.8	35.4
			(11) 19.9			% Profit Before Taxes/Tangible Net Worth	(32) 46.6	(42) 16.2
			15.1				26.2	6.1
			22.9				21.1	13.2
			6.8			% Profit Before Taxes/Total Assets	12.5	5.6
			4.5				7.7	2.3
			14.2				15.4	14.7
			6.5			Sales/Net Fixed Assets	5.7	5.0
			4.3				2.7	3.0
			2.7				3.0	2.6
			2.1			Sales/Total Assets	2.1	2.1
			1.7				1.0	1.3
			1.9				1.3	1.9
			2.4			% Depr., Dep., Amort./Sales	(29) 2.5	(39) 2.7
			3.8				4.2	5.6
						% Officers', Directors' Owners' Comp/Sales		
		38163M	831268M	770296M	1763760M	Net Sales ($)	3400060M	3747873M
		16110M	332274M	403977M	1378150M	Total Assets ($)	2108431M	2308542M

M = $ thousand MM = $ million

See Pages 9 through 22 for Explanation of Ratios and Data

Comparative Historical Data / Current Data Sorted by Sales

4/1/11-3/31/12 ALL	4/1/12-3/31/13 ALL	4/1/13-3/31/14 ALL		0-1MM	1-3MM	3-5MM	5-10MM	10-25MM	25MM & OVER
			Type of Statement						
6	7	7	Unqualified				1		6
2	3	3	Reviewed				1		2
3	5	3	Compiled					3	
4	2		Tax Returns						
16	22	19	Other				1		18
					3 (4/1-9/30/13)		29 (10/1/13-3/31/14)		
31	39	32	**NUMBER OF STATEMENTS**				3	3	26
%	%	%	**ASSETS**	%	%	%	%	%	%
7.5	5.4	3.8	Cash & Equivalents	DATA NOT AVAILABLE	DATA NOT AVAILABLE	DATA NOT AVAILABLE			3.7
18.6	23.9	17.8	Trade Receivables (net)						18.8
20.5	18.1	23.0	Inventory						22.2
2.1	1.3	1.1	All Other Current						1.4
48.8	48.6	45.8	Total Current						46.1
41.4	35.7	40.4	Fixed Assets (net)						38.0
5.8	11.1	9.7	Intangibles (net)						11.8
4.1	4.6	4.2	All Other Non-Current						4.1
100.0	100.0	100.0	Total						100.0
			LIABILITIES						
9.2	15.7	8.1	Notes Payable-Short Term						7.2
4.5	5.3	4.8	Cur. Mat.-L.T.D.						4.9
15.1	14.6	14.1	Trade Payables						13.6
.0	.2	.1	Income Taxes Payable						.1
6.9	7.0	5.2	All Other Current						5.5
35.6	42.8	32.3	Total Current						31.4
28.8	22.8	28.1	Long-Term Debt						28.1
1.4	1.1	2.0	Deferred Taxes						2.4
6.0	7.6	6.2	All Other Non-Current						6.0
28.2	25.8	31.4	Net Worth						32.1
100.0	100.0	100.0	Total Liabilities & Net Worth						100.0
			INCOME DATA						
100.0	100.0	100.0	Net Sales						100.0
25.7	21.1	21.6	Gross Profit						21.4
16.2	13.8	14.7	Operating Expenses						14.4
9.5	7.3	6.9	Operating Profit						7.0
2.5	1.9	1.8	All Other Expenses (net)						1.8
6.9	5.4	5.1	Profit Before Taxes						5.2
			RATIOS						
2.7	2.4	2.0							2.3
1.7	1.3	1.5	Current						1.6
1.1	1.0	1.1							1.2
1.4	1.3	1.0							1.1
.9	.7	.7	Quick						.8
.4	.4	.4							.4
16 22.8	**25** 14.5	**26** 14.2							**27** 13.3
30 12.3	**33** 11.0	**33** 11.1	Sales/Receivables						**33** 11.0
43 8.5	**46** 8.0	**41** 9.0							**41** 9.0
33 11.2	**36** 10.1	**40** 9.1							**41** 9.0
53 6.9	**48** 7.6	**51** 7.2	Cost of Sales/Inventory						**53** 6.9
74 4.9	**72** 5.1	**70** 5.2							**73** 5.0
16 23.3	**24** 15.2	**25** 14.4							**25** 14.7
31 11.7	**31** 11.7	**28** 13.0	Cost of Sales/Payables						**28** 13.2
49 7.5	**48** 7.6	**37** 9.8							**38** 9.7
5.5	6.2	8.6							7.8
10.0	15.8	14.4	Sales/Working Capital						13.7
51.3	-648.9	48.6							32.0
13.2	9.9	8.0							8.5
(28) 4.3	(38) 3.6	3.4	EBIT/Interest						4.0
1.7	1.9	2.0							1.9
		5.2							5.2
		(10) 2.8	Net Profit + Depr., Dep., Amort./Cur. Mat. L/T/D						(10) 2.8
		1.2							1.2
.7	.7	1.1							.8
2.0	1.8	1.9	Fixed/Worth						2.0
3.6	-8.6	4.3							NM
1.3	1.4	1.4							1.2
2.7	2.7	2.4	Debt/Worth						2.6
10.2	-16.7	7.4							NM
27.1	31.0	38.1							38.5
(25) 16.0	(28) 19.6	(25) 19.9	% Profit Before Taxes/Tangible Net Worth						(20) 20.7
10.1	8.8	10.2							15.0
18.4	11.2	10.0							10.3
6.2	7.5	5.3	% Profit Before Taxes/Total Assets						5.5
2.7	3.1	3.3							3.2
15.6	11.7	11.8							12.7
4.7	5.1	4.4	Sales/Net Fixed Assets						4.6
1.8	2.9	2.6							2.5
2.4	2.2	2.4							2.3
1.8	1.6	1.8	Sales/Total Assets						1.8
1.0	1.0	1.3							1.3
1.2	2.0	2.3							2.2
(28) 2.8	(34) 3.5	(31) 2.6	% Depr., Dep., Amort./Sales						(25) 2.4
5.5	4.8	4.8							4.5
			% Officers', Directors' Owners' Comp/Sales						
1679917M	**2968406M**	**3403487M**	Net Sales ($)				**25357M**	**42178M**	**3335952M**
1207037M	**2449990M**	**2130511M**	Total Assets ($)				**11525M**	**36309M**	**2082677M**

M = $ thousand MM = $ million

See Pages 9 through 22 for Explanation of Ratios and Data

Current Data Sorted by Assets							Comparative Historical Data	
						Type of Statement		
		2	9	6	3	Unqualified	30	30
		15	5			Reviewed	17	25
	4	10	1			Compiled	9	13
3	4	4	1			Tax Returns	9	10
1	3	8	14	6	5	Other	48	31
	26 (4/1-9/30/13)		78 (10/1/13-3/31/14)				4/1/09-3/31/10 ALL	4/1/10-3/31/11 ALL
0-500M	500M-2MM	2-10MM	10-50MM	50-100MM	100-250MM			
4	11	39	30	12	8	**NUMBER OF STATEMENTS**	113	109
%	%	%	%	%	%	**ASSETS**	%	%
	13.1	10.0	5.0	4.1		Cash & Equivalents	7.5	8.9
	28.5	27.9	24.5	24.4		Trade Receivables (net)	27.0	23.3
	27.1	25.0	24.4	20.7		Inventory	24.6	24.7
	.2	1.1	1.5	1.6		All Other Current	1.8	2.0
	68.9	63.8	55.4	50.8		Total Current	60.8	58.8
	24.4	25.0	38.5	30.9		Fixed Assets (net)	29.0	29.6
	3.5	5.6	1.4	11.1		Intangibles (net)	5.8	6.2
	3.2	5.6	4.7	7.2		All Other Non-Current	4.4	5.4
	100.0	100.0	100.0	100.0		Total	100.0	100.0
						LIABILITIES		
	8.4	7.1	7.9	8.1		Notes Payable-Short Term	10.5	10.6
	1.4	3.3	4.5	2.7		Cur. Mat.-L.T.D.	4.3	3.6
	23.7	14.0	17.9	10.8		Trade Payables	17.1	16.2
	.5	.0	.1	.1		Income Taxes Payable	.1	.1
	7.6	6.8	4.7	10.9		All Other Current	7.8	6.9
	41.6	31.2	35.2	32.7		Total Current	39.8	37.5
	11.7	11.3	33.0	19.5		Long-Term Debt	17.3	17.9
	.8	.2	.9	2.8		Deferred Taxes	.5	.7
	25.6	4.1	3.4	6.0		All Other Non-Current	5.9	5.9
	20.2	53.2	27.5	39.1		Net Worth	36.5	37.9
	100.0	100.0	100.0	100.0		Total Liabilties & Net Worth	100.0	100.0
						INCOME DATA		
	100.0	100.0	100.0	100.0		Net Sales	100.0	100.0
	21.9	26.4	18.9	22.1		Gross Profit	23.7	24.4
	21.0	20.5	13.5	16.4		Operating Expenses	19.2	18.7
	.9	5.9	5.4	5.7		Operating Profit	4.5	5.7
	.1	.8	1.4	1.0		All Other Expenses (net)	1.4	.8
	.8	5.1	4.0	4.8		Profit Before Taxes	3.1	4.9
						RATIOS		
	2.9	5.8	2.6	3.6			2.5	2.4
	1.5	2.4	1.4	1.4		Current	1.7	1.6
	1.2	1.3	1.1	1.2			1.1	1.1
	1.4	3.8	1.3	1.4			1.4	1.4
	1.1	1.9	.8	.9		Quick	.8	.9
	.7	.6	.5	.6			.5	.5
	11 33.5	**26** 14.0	**27** 13.5	**33** 11.0			**30** 12.0	**27** 13.5
	30 12.1	**36** 10.0	**37** 9.8	**41** 9.0		Sales/Receivables	**40** 9.1	**37** 9.9
	40 9.1	**53** 6.9	**46** 7.9	**68** 5.4			**48** 7.5	**48** 7.7
	4 83.6	**29** 12.6	**25** 14.7	**44** 8.3			**27** 13.7	**28** 13.0
	17 20.9	**54** 6.8	**41** 9.0	**56** 6.5		Cost of Sales/Inventory	**44** 8.2	**46** 7.9
	54 6.8	**70** 5.2	**58** 6.3	**73** 5.0			**76** 4.8	**78** 4.7
	10 37.8	**9** 41.7	**19** 19.6	**21** 17.2			**19** 18.9	**17** 21.0
	17 22.0	**25** 14.4	**31** 11.8	**28** 13.2		Cost of Sales/Payables	**29** 12.7	**29** 12.8
	31 11.9	**36** 10.0	**43** 8.5	**34** 10.6			**44** 8.3	**44** 8.2
	7.4	4.2	7.1	4.4			6.2	6.1
	14.9	6.6	15.0	11.2		Sales/Working Capital	10.1	10.8
	68.1	20.0	107.6	39.3			54.4	73.1
	21.7	57.6	17.6	17.1			9.3	21.0
	(10) 6.3	(33) 8.1	(29) 4.6	(11) 3.6		EBIT/Interest	(102) 3.9	(100) 6.1
	3.3	1.5	2.6	2.2			1.8	2.7
							6.3	7.9
						Net Profit + Depr., Dep., Amort./Cur. Mat. L/T/D	(24) 3.3	(16) 3.4
							1.7	1.3
	.1	.2	.6	.5			.3	.3
	.9	.4	1.6	1.2		Fixed/Worth	.8	.8
	-1.0	1.4	2.9	NM			2.5	2.7
	1.1	.2	.7	.8			.7	.7
	1.8	.9	2.2	1.9		Debt/Worth	2.1	1.7
	-29.9	4.4	4.7	NM			5.5	6.1
		47.8	46.3				47.6	51.6
		(36) 30.3	(27) 20.6			% Profit Before Taxes/Tangible Net Worth	(100) 24.9	(94) 26.1
		11.5	12.5				8.7	10.8
	17.8	28.1	16.6	13.2			15.5	16.8
	8.3	12.3	7.6	7.3		% Profit Before Taxes/Total Assets	7.2	8.6
	4.0	1.4	3.1	2.0			2.7	3.7
	254.7	33.0	13.8	13.1			30.6	18.2
	21.5	15.0	6.9	5.7		Sales/Net Fixed Assets	10.5	10.0
	9.0	4.5	3.8	2.6			4.1	4.0
	8.6	3.3	3.3	2.2			3.0	3.0
	3.2	2.4	2.5	1.6		Sales/Total Assets	2.2	2.2
	2.6	1.5	1.8	1.2			1.5	1.5
		1.0	1.1	1.7			1.1	1.0
		(34) 2.1	(28) 1.9	2.0		% Depr., Dep., Amort./Sales	(94) 2.2	(97) 2.0
		4.3	3.6	3.6			4.8	3.9
		2.0					1.9	2.3
		(13) 4.8				% Officers', Directors' Owners' Comp/Sales	(26) 2.9	(22) 3.3
		7.5					6.0	6.2
4988M	76949M	448437M	1697024M	1466872M	1797346M	Net Sales ($)	5583491M	6160664M
877M	13133M	190745M	639431M	881505M	1273204M	Total Assets ($)	2820257M	3047839M

M = $ thousand MM = $ million

See Pages 9 through 22 for Explanation of Ratios and Data

Comparative Historical Data				Current Data Sorted by Sales					
			Type of Statement						
26	22	20	Unqualified					2	18
22	18	20	Reviewed			1	6	8	5
18	7	15	Compiled		2	4	5	3	1
16	13	12	Tax Returns	1	3	3	3	2	
33	39	37	Other		1	2	4	6	24
4/1/11-3/31/12 ALL	4/1/12-3/31/13 ALL	4/1/13-3/31/14 ALL		26 (4/1-9/30/13)			78 (10/1/13-3/31/14)		
				0-1MM	1-3MM	3-5MM	5-10MM	10-25MM	25MM & OVER
115	99	104	**NUMBER OF STATEMENTS**	1	6	10	18	21	48
%	%	%	**ASSETS**	%	%	%	%	%	%
7.4	8.1	8.2	Cash & Equivalents			8.7	12.3	7.8	6.4
25.1	24.4	26.9	Trade Receivables (net)			27.8	25.0	28.3	25.0
24.7	24.1	23.7	Inventory			29.6	23.7	26.5	23.4
1.8	1.6	1.2	All Other Current			.3	1.7	.9	1.5
59.1	58.2	60.0	Total Current			66.3	62.7	63.6	56.2
31.1	30.5	29.1	Fixed Assets (net)			21.4	24.5	29.6	31.5
6.0	6.1	5.8	Intangibles (net)			4.0	9.0	2.5	6.9
3.9	5.1	5.2	All Other Non-Current			8.2	3.8	4.3	5.4
100.0	100.0	100.0	Total			100.0	100.0	100.0	100.0
			LIABILITIES						
10.0	9.2	8.2	Notes Payable-Short Term			9.4	4.0	9.2	8.1
4.2	2.8	3.6	Cur. Mat.-L.T.D.			5.3	2.5	2.3	4.2
15.3	17.5	16.8	Trade Payables			18.4	12.8	15.1	17.4
.2	.2	.1	Income Taxes Payable			.1	.0	.0	.1
6.6	7.7	6.9	All Other Current			5.7	7.9	7.3	6.4
36.3	37.5	35.6	Total Current			38.9	27.3	33.9	36.2
17.2	15.5	19.5	Long-Term Debt			17.3	8.5	12.3	26.4
.6	.6	.8	Deferred Taxes			.0	.1	1.2	.9
6.1	7.0	7.2	All Other Non-Current			20.4	9.1	3.0	5.6
39.9	39.4	36.9	Net Worth			23.4	55.1	49.5	30.9
100.0	100.0	100.0	Total Liabilities & Net Worth			100.0	100.0	100.0	100.0
			INCOME DATA						
100.0	100.0	100.0	Net Sales			100.0	100.0	100.0	100.0
25.8	26.0	23.1	Gross Profit			26.6	25.4	23.8	18.9
20.8	20.9	17.9	Operating Expenses			27.7	19.1	17.7	13.2
5.1	5.1	5.2	Operating Profit			-1.2	6.3	6.1	5.7
.7	.8	1.0	All Other Expenses (net)			.6	.3	.9	1.4
4.4	4.4	4.1	Profit Before Taxes			-1.7	6.0	5.3	4.3
			RATIOS						
2.9	2.8	3.5				3.8	7.4	5.6	3.3
1.5	1.5	1.5	Current			2.3	3.2	1.5	1.4
1.1	1.1	1.1				1.3	1.5	1.0	1.1
1.6	1.5	1.9				2.0	4.2	3.3	1.4
.9	.8	.9	Quick			1.2	2.0	1.2	.8
.5	.5	.5				.6	.6	.5	.5
29 12.5	28 13.2	28 12.9				38 9.7	17 21.8	30 12.1	30 12.3
38 9.6	35 10.3	38 9.7	Sales/Receivables			39 9.3	26 13.8	39 9.3	37 9.9
46 7.9	45 8.1	49 7.4				62 5.9	53 6.9	49 7.5	48 7.6
28 13.0	27 13.6	26 14.2				23 15.7	20 18.6	28 13.2	30 12.2
45 8.1	48 7.6	44 8.3	Cost of Sales/Inventory			76 4.8	46 8.0	49 7.4	43 8.5
74 4.9	73 5.0	69 5.3				101 3.6	68 5.4	65 5.6	65 5.6
14 26.1	17 21.3	17 22.0				16 23.1	2 201.8	14 26.2	20 18.3
25 14.7	24 15.1	26 14.3	Cost of Sales/Payables			26 13.8	14 26.0	26 14.3	31 11.8
35 10.3	41 9.0	42 8.7				66 5.5	32 11.5	38 9.7	42 8.6
5.8	5.9	5.5				5.0	3.8	5.1	6.4
12.7	13.7	11.6	Sales/Working Capital			7.9	5.5	12.6	12.2
55.5	51.1	64.0				10.5	23.6	NM	64.0
14.2	16.0	20.3				10.6	70.0	71.9	17.6
(106) 6.6	(90) 7.0	(93) 5.2	EBIT/Interest			4.2	(14) 17.6	(19) 8.1	(45) 4.6
2.0	2.7	2.5				-184.5	4.4	2.6	2.3
6.3	7.3	6.4							5.9
(26) 2.8	(24) 2.7	(25) 2.5	Net Profit + Depr., Dep., Amort./Cur. Mat. L/T/D						(14) 2.6
.9	1.7	1.5							1.6
.3	.3	.3				.1	.2	.2	.5
.9	1.0	1.1	Fixed/Worth			.6	.6	.5	1.4
2.2	2.2	2.8				NM	NM	1.7	4.9
.6	.6	.6				1.0	.2	.3	.7
1.7	1.8	1.8	Debt/Worth			1.9	.6	1.3	2.5
4.8	3.6	7.6				NM	NM	3.1	9.4
43.8	42.7	45.8					41.1	51.3	42.0
(102) 24.3	(84) 26.8	(87) 24.5	% Profit Before Taxes/Tangible Net Worth				(14) 32.9	24.9	(38) 22.0
9.7	10.1	12.5					12.9	12.4	12.6
17.5	17.3	17.7				12.8	30.3	18.3	16.1
8.5	7.8	8.5	% Profit Before Taxes/Total Assets			6.0	17.7	7.8	7.9
3.1	4.0	3.2				-14.6	1.1	3.5	3.0
17.2	17.0	28.0				40.3	60.2	33.3	15.4
8.6	9.5	9.5	Sales/Net Fixed Assets			11.6	17.7	15.0	6.9
4.3	4.0	4.2				6.6	4.1	3.7	4.2
3.1	3.2	3.3				3.2	3.3	3.5	3.2
2.2	2.3	2.3	Sales/Total Assets			2.2	2.5	2.4	2.2
1.7	1.6	1.6				1.6	1.4	1.6	1.6
1.2	1.2	1.1					1.1	.9	1.4
(102) 2.2	(84) 2.2	(91) 1.9	% Depr., Dep., Amort./Sales				(13) 2.8	(19) 1.3	(44) 1.9
3.7	3.8	3.4					4.6	4.5	3.2
2.1	2.1	1.9							
(25) 2.9	(22) 3.4	(27) 3.5	% Officers', Directors' Owners' Comp/Sales						
7.2	8.0	8.0							
4572546M	4875094M	5491616M	Net Sales ($)	577M	10165M	38419M	136339M	340617M	4965499M
2452531M	2756866M	2998895M	Total Assets ($)	150M	5762M	20554M	66652M	160871M	2744906M

M = $ thousand MM = $ million

See Pages 9 through 22 for Explanation of Ratios and Data

Current Data Sorted by Assets							Comparative Historical Data	
						Type of Statement		
		12	45	11	4	Unqualified	143	142
1	17	94	52	2		Reviewed	240	244
10	44	64	7	1		Compiled	143	176
60	83	41	2		2	Tax Returns	186	202
22	81	140	94	15	12	Other	430	421
158 (4/1-9/30/13)			758 (10/1/13-3/31/14)				4/1/09-3/31/10	4/1/10-3/31/11
0-500M	500M-2MM	2-10MM	10-50MM	50-100MM	100-250MM		ALL	ALL
93	225	351	200	29	18	**NUMBER OF STATEMENTS**	1142	1185
%	%	%	%	%	%	**ASSETS**	%	%
18.4	12.5	10.3	9.6	6.1	6.5	Cash & Equivalents	9.6	10.2
27.7	32.4	29.6	25.7	21.2	23.7	Trade Receivables (net)	26.5	27.3
9.8	11.5	11.9	12.3	14.6	11.0	Inventory	10.6	11.1
1.8	1.6	1.4	2.3	1.4	1.7	All Other Current	2.5	2.2
57.6	57.9	53.2	49.9	43.4	43.0	Total Current	49.2	50.7
25.5	29.3	37.0	38.6	34.6	23.2	Fixed Assets (net)	38.8	37.2
7.7	6.5	4.7	6.0	16.5	30.1	Intangibles (net)	6.1	5.8
9.2	6.3	5.1	5.5	5.5	3.7	All Other Non-Current	5.9	6.2
100.0	100.0	100.0	100.0	100.0	100.0	Total	100.0	100.0
						LIABILITIES		
18.2	9.5	6.8	6.4	4.3	6.3	Notes Payable-Short Term	10.0	9.2
6.6	6.0	4.9	5.7	5.5	6.3	Cur. Mat.-L.T.D.	7.3	6.9
21.3	19.2	15.5	12.9	11.7	9.7	Trade Payables	14.9	15.1
.0	.1	.2	.2	.0	.1	Income Taxes Payable	.2	.2
15.1	8.3	8.7	8.9	6.1	7.6	All Other Current	9.7	10.0
61.2	43.2	36.1	34.1	27.5	30.0	Total Current	42.1	41.5
40.5	28.5	23.0	22.8	23.9	27.2	Long-Term Debt	28.2	27.4
.0	.2	.8	1.2	2.4	1.4	Deferred Taxes	.7	.8
18.8	10.4	5.2	5.5	4.0	22.7	All Other Non-Current	6.4	8.6
-20.6	17.7	34.8	36.5	42.2	18.7	Net Worth	22.6	21.7
100.0	100.0	100.0	100.0	100.0	100.0	Total Liabilties & Net Worth	100.0	100.0
						INCOME DATA		
100.0	100.0	100.0	100.0	100.0	100.0	Net Sales	100.0	100.0
49.5	45.1	35.0	27.3	24.3	28.1	Gross Profit	35.7	36.8
45.7	41.1	30.9	22.2	18.4	24.0	Operating Expenses	34.1	33.3
3.8	4.0	4.0	5.1	5.9	4.1	Operating Profit	1.5	3.5
.5	.6	.8	1.1	1.6	5.0	All Other Expenses (net)	1.6	1.3
3.3	3.4	3.2	4.0	4.3	-.9	Profit Before Taxes	.0	2.2
						RATIOS		
2.6	2.4	2.4	2.3	2.2	1.8		2.1	2.2
1.2	1.5	1.5	1.5	1.5	1.4	Current	1.2	1.3
.7	.9	1.1	1.0	1.0	1.1		.8	.9
2.2	1.8	1.8	1.6	1.4	1.4		1.6	1.7
1.0	1.1	1.1	1.0	.9	.9	Quick	.9	1.0
.5	.6	.8	.6	.6	.7		.6	.6
3 115.2	**26** 13.8	**33** 10.9	**36** 10.1	**36** 10.0	**41** 8.9		**31** 11.8	**31** 11.7
22 16.6	**38** 9.7	**43** 8.4	**47** 7.8	**46** 8.0	**52** 7.0	Sales/Receivables	**42** 8.6	**42** 8.6
36 10.2	**49** 7.4	**56** 6.5	**62** 5.9	**60** 6.1	**73** 5.0		**55** 6.6	**57** 6.4
1 447.6	**5** 71.2	**13** 28.1	**16** 22.9	**29** 12.8	**18** 20.4		**9** 40.7	**10** 36.0
8 43.3	**15** 23.7	**23** 16.1	**25** 14.8	**37** 9.8	**35** 10.5	Cost of Sales/Inventory	**20** 18.3	**22** 16.3
22 16.3	**35** 10.5	**42** 8.7	**47** 7.8	**73** 5.0	**68** 5.4		**39** 9.3	**39** 9.3
0 UND	**18** 19.8	**20** 18.6	**19** 19.0	**19** 19.3	**16** 22.3		**18** 20.8	**18** 20.4
22 16.8	**35** 10.4	**30** 12.0	**28** 12.9	**31** 11.6	**33** 11.1	Cost of Sales/Payables	**31** 11.9	**31** 11.9
39 9.4	**60** 6.1	**46** 7.9	**43** 8.5	**47** 7.8	**45** 8.1		**51** 7.1	**50** 7.3
12.9	7.4	6.9	6.8	6.3	7.6		8.0	8.1
65.9	21.1	14.1	13.8	14.5	11.4	Sales/Working Capital	27.3	19.2
-24.1	-96.6	68.0	362.1	-540.5	NM		-25.9	-50.1
8.8	12.5	10.1	12.8	20.5	6.0		4.1	6.0
(77) 3.0	(195) 2.8	(332) 4.1	(188) 4.1	(27) 3.0	(16) 2.2	EBIT/Interest	(1062) 1.3	(1110) 2.3
.0	1.1	1.5	1.3	1.1	-.5		-1.1	.4
	3.8	3.1	3.1	3.8			2.2	3.4
	(24) 1.6	(77) 2.1	(70) 2.0	(17) 2.1		Net Profit + Depr., Dep., Amort./Cur. Mat. L/T/D	(287) 1.3	(286) 1.7
	.9	1.4	1.3	1.2			.3	.9
.4	.4	.6	.6	.6	1.1		.7	.7
30.4	1.3	1.2	1.2	1.7	-1.4	Fixed/Worth	1.8	1.6
-.4	-3.3	2.9	3.2	NM	-.3		-133.2	40.2
1.0	1.0	.9	.8	.9	1.4		1.0	1.0
-103.7	3.1	2.1	1.8	2.0	-4.7	Debt/Worth	2.9	2.7
-2.3	-8.9	6.5	5.1	NM	-2.0		-75.2	-999.8
83.2	78.9	39.6	43.6	22.9			29.5	39.2
(46) 37.2	(155) 24.7	(303) 17.8	(174) 18.6	(22) 16.4		% Profit Before Taxes/Tangible Net Worth	(847) 6.5	(888) 15.7
4.2	1.1	4.1	4.2	3.7			-12.6	-.2
28.9	20.7	13.8	12.4	10.8	7.5		8.2	11.8
7.4	6.9	5.5	5.0	4.2	2.0	% Profit Before Taxes/Total Assets	1.1	3.9
-2.8	.3	1.0	.7	.5	-7.7		-7.0	-1.9
62.6	30.6	11.9	9.0	8.0	18.0		13.5	13.7
21.9	13.9	6.1	5.2	4.7	7.2	Sales/Net Fixed Assets	5.3	6.2
11.1	5.5	3.8	3.2	3.0	3.7		3.1	3.5
6.5	3.9	2.8	2.4	1.9	1.8		2.9	2.9
4.3	2.8	2.3	1.9	1.4	1.3	Sales/Total Assets	2.1	2.2
3.0	2.1	1.7	1.5	1.0	1.0		1.4	1.6
.5	1.2	2.3	2.9	2.8			2.6	2.5
(64) 1.5	(167) 2.4	(315) 3.7	(189) 4.5	4.8		% Depr., Dep., Amort./Sales	(986) 4.4	(1033) 4.1
4.3	4.6	5.5	6.2	6.6			7.0	6.3
4.8	3.1	2.1	1.5				2.6	2.4
(59) 8.2	(136) 4.7	(150) 3.5	(48) 2.2			% Officers', Directors' Owners' Comp/Sales	(478) 4.7	(492) 4.3
13.1	6.7	5.8	3.5				8.3	7.9
124657M	**827041M**	**3936014M**	**8142371M**	**3195714M**	**4295930M**	Net Sales ($)	**19181611M**	**21346805M**
24704M	**275045M**	**1713945M**	**4243433M**	**2162145M**	**2939251M**	Total Assets ($)	**11260810M**	**12775107M**

M = $ thousand MM = $ million

See Pages 9 through 22 for Explanation of Ratios and Data

Comparative Historical Data				Current Data Sorted by Sales					
			Type of Statement						
126	78	72	Unqualified				6	14	52
224	192	166	Reviewed		9	11	26	70	50
175	132	126	Compiled	7	20	27	41	23	8
240	208	188	Tax Returns	31	66	39	34	15	3
406	377	364	Other	16	38	50	77	81	102
4/1/11-3/31/12	**4/1/12-3/31/13**	**4/1/13-3/31/14**		**158 (4/1-9/30/13)**			**758 (10/1/13-3/31/14)**		
ALL	**ALL**	**ALL**		**0-1MM**	**1-3MM**	**3-5MM**	**5-10MM**	**10-25MM**	**25MM & OVER**
1171	987	916	**NUMBER OF STATEMENTS**	54	133	127	184	203	215
%	%	%	**ASSETS**	%	%	%	%	%	%
10.2	10.3	11.3	Cash & Equivalents	19.9	12.1	13.2	10.7	10.6	8.7
28.0	27.8	28.9	Trade Receivables (net)	18.8	30.4	28.6	30.6	30.8	27.3
11.2	11.2	11.7	Inventory	6.8	10.9	11.7	11.4	12.2	13.4
2.5	2.3	1.7	All Other Current	2.8	1.3	1.9	.9	1.8	2.3
51.8	51.7	53.6	Total Current	48.3	54.6	55.5	53.5	55.3	51.6
35.9	35.5	33.9	Fixed Assets (net)	30.7	30.4	32.3	36.5	34.9	34.8
6.3	6.6	6.6	Intangibles (net)	10.0	8.6	6.6	3.9	4.8	8.7
6.0	6.3	5.9	All Other Non-Current	11.0	6.4	5.6	6.2	5.0	4.9
100.0	100.0	100.0	Total	100.0	100.0	100.0	100.0	100.0	100.0
			LIABILITIES						
9.2	9.1	8.4	Notes Payable-Short Term	11.8	11.7	9.5	7.9	7.8	5.9
6.8	6.0	5.6	Cur. Mat.-L.T.D.	5.9	6.5	5.9	5.2	5.2	5.4
16.0	15.2	16.2	Trade Payables	12.9	19.8	18.8	15.4	16.2	13.9
.2	.2	.2	Income Taxes Payable	.0	.2	.1	.2	.2	.2
10.0	9.6	9.2	All Other Current	13.3	9.3	10.3	7.8	8.8	9.0
42.1	40.1	39.6	Total Current	43.9	47.6	44.7	36.5	38.2	34.4
26.4	28.1	26.2	Long-Term Debt	41.3	38.6	26.9	24.0	20.5	21.6
.8	.7	.7	Deferred Taxes	.0	.3	.2	.8	1.0	1.3
9.2	9.0	8.2	All Other Non-Current	23.6	9.8	10.8	6.2	5.2	6.5
21.6	22.2	25.3	Net Worth	-8.8	3.7	17.4	32.6	35.1	36.2
100.0	100.0	100.0	Total Liabilties & Net Worth	100.0	100.0	100.0	100.0	100.0	100.0
			INCOME DATA						
100.0	100.0	100.0	Net Sales	100.0	100.0	100.0	100.0	100.0	100.0
37.5	36.5	36.8	Gross Profit	54.1	47.2	43.6	38.5	29.9	27.0
33.7	32.6	32.5	Operating Expenses	50.8	43.7	39.1	34.0	26.2	21.7
3.8	3.9	4.3	Operating Profit	3.3	3.5	4.5	4.5	3.7	5.3
1.2	1.0	.9	All Other Expenses (net)	1.0	.6	.9	.7	.8	1.3
2.7	2.9	3.4	Profit Before Taxes	2.2	2.9	3.6	3.8	2.9	4.0
			RATIOS						
2.3	2.3	2.3		4.1	2.1	2.4	2.4	2.3	2.2
1.4	1.4	1.5	Current	1.2	1.4	1.4	1.5	1.4	1.5
.9	.9	1.0		.7	.8	.9	1.1	1.0	1.1
1.7	1.7	1.8		2.6	1.8	1.8	1.9	1.7	1.5
1.0	1.0	1.1	Quick	.9	1.0	1.1	1.1	1.1	1.0
.6	.6	.7		.4	.5	.6	.8	.7	.7
31 11.8	**30** 12.3	**30** 12.1		**4** 99.2	**22** 16.6	**28** 13.2	**32** 11.5	**36** 10.1	**36** 10.1
42 8.6	**41** 8.8	**41** 8.8	Sales/Receivables	**22** 16.7	**35** 10.5	**39** 9.3	**41** 9.0	**46** 7.9	**46** 8.0
54 6.7	**54** 6.7	**55** 6.6		**36** 10.0	**49** 7.5	**51** 7.1	**52** 7.0	**58** 6.3	**62** 5.9
9 41.8	**8** 43.4	**10** 37.1		**0** UND	**2** 197.3	**7** 52.0	**9** 40.3	**14** 26.1	**17** 21.4
21 17.0	**21** 17.6	**21** 17.3	Cost of Sales/Inventory	**11** 33.4	**13** 28.5	**19** 19.3	**20** 17.9	**23** 16.2	**28** 13.1
39 9.3	**38** 9.5	**40** 9.2		**23** 15.6	**33** 11.1	**40** 9.2	**43** 8.5	**37** 9.8	**48** 7.6
18 20.2	**17** 21.0	**18** 19.8		**0** UND	**12** 31.2	**21** 17.1	**18** 20.7	**19** 19.4	**20** 18.4
31 11.9	**30** 12.1	**30** 12.2	Cost of Sales/Payables	**28** 13.0	**29** 12.8	**33** 10.9	**29** 12.8	**30** 12.2	**31** 11.8
51 7.1	**49** 7.4	**47** 7.7		**63** 5.8	**60** 6.1	**59** 6.2	**46** 7.9	**44** 8.3	**44** 8.3
8.2	7.9	7.3		8.0	8.2	6.3	7.5	7.0	7.2
18.7	19.5	15.8	Sales/Working Capital	106.8	22.7	21.2	14.7	14.9	13.6
-62.8	-64.4	UND		-18.5	-35.1	-87.6	70.5	136.9	36.4
7.6	7.9	11.0		7.1	6.1	9.5	14.0	9.5	16.3
(1090) 2.7	(916) 3.4	(835) 3.4	EBIT/Interest	(42) 1.7	(114) 2.2	(113) 3.0	(176) 4.0	(192) 4.1	(198) 4.5
.9	.9	1.2		-1.0	.5	1.0	1.8	1.5	1.2
3.1	3.5	3.1			1.8	3.5	3.1	3.6	3.1
(277) 1.9	(237) 1.8	(191) 2.0	Net Profit + Depr., Dep., Amort./Cur. Mat. L/T/D		(13) .9	(15) 1.8	(30) 2.1	(51) 2.2	(82) 2.1
1.1	1.1	1.2			.2	1.5	1.4	1.2	1.3
.6	.6	.5		.4	.5	.4	.6	.6	.6
1.6	1.6	1.2	Fixed/Worth	18.4	1.9	1.6	1.1	1.1	1.2
11.9	34.1	8.4		-.5	-1.2	-3.4	3.6	2.6	3.8
1.0	1.1	.9		.7	1.1	1.0	.8	.8	.9
2.7	2.8	2.3	Debt/Worth	21.2	3.8	3.9	2.0	2.1	1.8
43.7	-999.8	22.5		-2.7	-4.4	-7.9	7.8	6.1	6.2
45.5	47.4	46.8		80.4	57.3	65.5	50.1	38.5	42.8
(896) 15.6	(739) 18.0	(706) 18.7	% Profit Before Taxes/Tangible Net Worth	(28) 22.3	(82) 16.6	(85) 17.9	(154) 20.5	(180) 15.5	(177) 20.8
1.5	2.8	3.6		1.2	-1.1	3.7	3.9	3.7	4.9
13.1	13.4	14.8		19.9	17.9	15.0	17.3	12.2	13.3
4.7	5.6	5.7	% Profit Before Taxes/Total Assets	4.1	6.1	6.0	6.5	4.5	5.6
-.2	-.2	.5		-3.5	-.4	-.4	1.7	.9	.6
15.0	15.9	17.6		35.8	30.9	25.6	15.9	13.4	10.2
6.7	7.1	7.4	Sales/Net Fixed Assets	17.9	13.9	9.1	6.4	6.7	5.9
3.6	3.8	4.0		7.0	5.0	4.6	3.8	3.9	3.7
3.1	3.3	3.2		4.2	4.2	3.5	3.4	2.9	2.5
2.3	2.2	2.3	Sales/Total Assets	3.1	2.8	2.4	2.5	2.2	2.0
1.6	1.7	1.7		2.0	1.8	1.9	1.8	1.7	1.4
2.2	2.0	2.0		1.1	.9	1.5	1.9	2.3	2.5
(1015) 3.8	(849) 3.7	(771) 3.6	% Depr., Dep., Amort./Sales	(36) 2.9	(100) 2.4	(98) 3.3	(158) 3.9	(183) 3.7	(196) 3.9
5.8	5.6	5.5		6.5	4.8	5.7	5.6	5.3	5.6
2.7	2.4	2.3		6.7	3.6	2.2	2.6	2.0	1.1
(496) 4.6	(427) 4.0	(399) 4.3	% Officers', Directors' Owners' Comp/Sales	(32) 11.8	(85) 5.5	(65) 4.3	(92) 4.3	(82) 3.3	(43) 1.9
7.3	7.2	7.1		17.0	8.4	6.0	6.7	5.0	3.2
22080606M	18503730M	20521727M	Net Sales ($)	35015M	266497M	507583M	1344088M	3186856M	15181688M
12457500M	9987682M	11358523M	Total Assets ($)	15843M	118926M	220720M	608618M	1568005M	8826411M

M = $ thousand MM = $ million

See Pages 9 through 22 for Explanation of Ratios and Data

Current Data Sorted by Assets							Comparative Historical Data	
						Type of Statement		
		2	3		3	Unqualified	10	6
	2	12	4	1	1	Reviewed	29	25
2	10	8	2			Compiled	17	19
16	9	4				Tax Returns	13	24
7	12	12	12		4	Other	40	34
	11 (4/1-9/30/13)		115 (10/1/13-3/31/14)				4/1/09-3/31/10	4/1/10-3/31/11
0-500M	500M-2MM	2-10MM	10-50MM	50-100MM	100-250MM		ALL	ALL
25	33	38	21	1	8	NUMBER OF STATEMENTS	109	108
%	%	%	%	%	%	**ASSETS**	%	%
20.2	10.4	8.7	10.1			Cash & Equivalents	9.8	9.4
24.5	32.7	25.1	28.8			Trade Receivables (net)	28.3	29.1
10.1	11.6	21.1	17.2			Inventory	18.4	19.8
3.1	2.5	2.0	3.6			All Other Current	3.0	1.7
57.9	57.2	56.9	59.8			Total Current	59.5	59.9
32.1	28.3	32.4	26.0			Fixed Assets (net)	28.9	28.4
5.1	5.5	5.7	9.0			Intangibles (net)	6.2	7.2
5.0	9.0	5.0	5.2			All Other Non-Current	5.5	4.4
100.0	100.0	100.0	100.0			Total	100.0	100.0
						LIABILITIES		
22.6	9.7	11.0	12.3			Notes Payable-Short Term	9.4	10.0
4.9	3.1	4.3	2.1			Cur. Mat.-L.T.D.	5.3	5.1
15.9	20.8	15.2	17.0			Trade Payables	14.7	16.4
.0	.0	.0	.3			Income Taxes Payable	.1	.1
6.5	6.4	7.2	10.9			All Other Current	10.0	8.1
49.9	40.1	37.7	42.6			Total Current	39.6	39.6
28.2	31.5	23.2	11.8			Long-Term Debt	21.7	24.6
.0	.0	.2	.3			Deferred Taxes	.3	.1
7.7	8.1	2.4	6.3			All Other Non-Current	6.5	5.0
14.2	20.3	36.5	39.0			Net Worth	31.9	30.6
100.0	100.0	100.0	100.0			Total Liabilties & Net Worth	100.0	100.0
						INCOME DATA		
100.0	100.0	100.0	100.0			Net Sales	100.0	100.0
55.0	43.4	35.1	26.1			Gross Profit	38.7	38.7
52.6	40.7	30.2	20.9			Operating Expenses	37.0	34.6
2.4	2.6	4.9	5.2			Operating Profit	1.7	4.1
1.0	.9	.9	.4			All Other Expenses (net)	1.2	1.1
1.4	1.7	4.0	4.9			Profit Before Taxes	.5	3.0
						RATIOS		
4.1	2.7	2.6	2.1				2.6	2.4
1.0	1.7	1.8	1.3			Current	1.5	1.7
.7	.8	1.0	1.0				1.1	1.1
3.1	2.4	1.7	1.5				1.9	1.7
.9	.9	.9	.9			Quick	1.0	1.0
.5	.6	.5	.6				.5	.6
6 63.0	**20** 18.0	**23** 16.1	**38** 9.6				**28** 13.0	**25** 14.6
17 21.4	**31** 11.7	**38** 9.5	**56** 6.5			Sales/Receivables	**41** 8.9	**36** 10.0
29 12.5	**54** 6.8	**49** 7.4	**65** 5.6				**57** 6.4	**53** 6.8
0 UND	**3** 132.5	**20** 18.7	**17** 21.4				**10** 38.2	**14** 26.0
10 37.1	**15** 23.6	**41** 8.8	**31** 11.6			Cost of Sales/Inventory	**41** 8.9	**42** 8.7
30 12.2	**31** 11.7	**63** 5.8	**56** 6.5				**77** 4.7	**69** 5.3
0 UND	**20** 17.9	**19** 19.0	**23** 15.7				**17** 21.1	**14** 25.3
14 25.2	**37** 9.8	**27** 13.4	**40** 9.2			Cost of Sales/Payables	**32** 11.5	**27** 13.6
49 7.5	**61** 6.0	**41** 8.9	**52** 7.0				**43** 8.5	**51** 7.2
9.5	7.9	7.1	6.5				5.9	7.1
-361.3	22.6	10.8	18.5			Sales/Working Capital	12.1	11.8
-21.0	-24.3	NM	NM				99.3	77.2
10.4	16.5	12.7	30.7				5.5	9.4
(22) 5.0	(32) 3.3	(35) 3.7	(17) 8.9			EBIT/Interest	(97) 1.5	(98) 2.9
1.0	.5	1.3	1.5				-2.2	.9
							5.4	5.2
						Net Profit + Depr., Dep., Amort./Cur. Mat. L/T/D	(21) 1.6	(20) 1.9
							.5	.8
.4	.3	.6	.3				.3	.3
3.7	2.5	1.0	.9			Fixed/Worth	1.0	1.0
-1.4	21.4	3.7	NM				4.0	2.3
1.1	.7	.8	.8				.8	.7
4.2	7.4	1.7	2.1			Debt/Worth	2.0	1.9
-4.7	NM	7.9	NM				18.6	10.5
94.3	56.6	50.8	71.1				36.8	41.9
(16) 49.4	(25) 14.0	(33) 28.9	(16) 30.6			% Profit Before Taxes/Tangible Net Worth	(86) 6.5	(86) 14.8
9.7	-6.2	3.4	8.5				-8.5	2.1
22.8	15.6	21.2	21.5				11.0	14.2
12.3	4.7	6.3	5.4			% Profit Before Taxes/Total Assets	1.7	5.2
-.2	-2.8	.9	1.0				-6.5	-.2
75.3	38.8	23.5	32.6				27.1	28.9
20.4	11.5	8.2	16.3			Sales/Net Fixed Assets	11.5	12.3
6.3	6.9	4.2	4.2				4.4	5.3
7.4	4.2	3.3	2.7				3.4	3.7
5.0	3.0	2.4	2.2			Sales/Total Assets	2.1	2.6
3.0	2.1	2.0	1.5				1.6	1.9
.5	.7	1.1	.8				1.3	.9
(16) 2.0	(24) 2.5	(32) 2.1	(19) 2.1			% Depr., Dep., Amort./Sales	(92) 2.6	(96) 2.1
4.4	4.6	4.1	3.3				4.5	4.1
4.1	3.2	1.5					3.3	2.7
(16) 7.9	(23) 7.0	(20) 2.8				% Officers', Directors' Owners' Comp/Sales	(46) 5.7	(55) 4.5
11.7	9.4	6.6					9.5	10.0
34130M	124115M	389540M	881454M	80869M	1721233M	Net Sales ($)	1683417M	2248477M
6783M	37723M	157196M	377562M	66810M	1114063M	Total Assets ($)	872355M	1300395M

M = $ thousand MM = $ million

See Pages 9 through 22 for Explanation of Ratios and Data

Comparative Historical Data | Current Data Sorted by Sales

4/1/11-3/31/12 ALL	4/1/12-3/31/13 ALL	4/1/13-3/31/14 ALL		0-1MM	1-3MM	3-5MM	5-10MM	10-25MM	25MM & OVER
			Type of Statement						
10	10	8	Unqualified				1	2	5
25	15	20	Reviewed		1	1	7	6	5
20	16	22	Compiled	1	5	4	9	1	2
26	21	29	Tax Returns	3	14	8	4		
43	43	47	Other	7	7	5	4	11	13
				11 (4/1-9/30/13)			115 (10/1/13-3/31/14)		
124	105	126	**NUMBER OF STATEMENTS**	11	27	18	25	20	25
%	%	%	**ASSETS**	%	%	%	%	%	%
9.1	10.8	11.5	Cash & Equivalents	7.9	17.3	14.6	7.6	10.8	8.8
26.7	28.1	27.2	Trade Receivables (net)	19.8	28.9	29.8	26.7	24.6	29.5
21.0	16.2	16.2	Inventory	8.3	9.7	12.6	21.3	18.7	22.0
3.5	2.8	3.0	All Other Current	6.4	.6	3.1	1.5	3.6	4.9
60.3	58.0	57.8	Total Current	42.4	56.5	60.1	57.1	57.7	65.2
28.0	27.4	29.3	Fixed Assets (net)	37.9	31.1	25.6	36.9	25.6	21.4
6.1	6.7	6.9	Intangibles (net)	14.3	4.7	5.6	2.9	10.0	8.4
5.7	7.9	6.0	All Other Non-Current	5.4	7.7	8.7	3.1	6.8	5.0
100.0	100.0	100.0	Total	100.0	100.0	100.0	100.0	100.0	100.0
			LIABILITIES						
14.4	10.7	12.8	Notes Payable-Short Term	20.9	18.5	11.0	9.0	12.1	9.0
5.8	5.6	3.7	Cur. Mat.-L.T.D.	7.8	2.8	2.8	4.1	4.2	2.7
17.4	15.5	16.7	Trade Payables	15.1	13.9	18.3	14.3	23.5	16.4
.2	.1	.1	Income Taxes Payable	.0	.0	.0	.0	.3	.3
8.6	8.4	8.3	All Other Current	5.1	6.1	6.1	7.7	7.3	14.9
46.4	40.3	41.7	Total Current	48.8	41.3	38.3	35.1	47.4	43.3
24.1	24.8	23.6	Long-Term Debt	43.9	30.2	26.4	23.9	17.1	10.6
.1	.2	.1	Deferred Taxes	.0	.0	.1	.2	.2	.2
8.0	6.6	6.3	All Other Non-Current	18.2	7.2	5.0	1.0	4.8	7.7
21.4	28.1	28.2	Net Worth	-10.8	21.3	30.2	39.8	30.4	38.2
100.0	100.0	100.0	Total Liabilties & Net Worth	100.0	100.0	100.0	100.0	100.0	100.0
			INCOME DATA						
100.0	100.0	100.0	Net Sales	100.0	100.0	100.0	100.0	100.0	100.0
37.0	40.5	39.4	Gross Profit	57.1	50.6	43.6	37.7	29.6	26.3
33.0	34.0	35.6	Operating Expenses	54.3	47.9	41.3	32.8	23.5	22.2
4.0	6.6	3.9	Operating Profit	2.8	2.7	2.3	4.8	6.1	4.1
1.0	1.0	.9	All Other Expenses (net)	2.0	1.2	.4	.7	1.0	.4
3.0	5.5	3.0	Profit Before Taxes	.8	1.6	1.9	4.2	5.0	3.8
			RATIOS						
2.3	2.7	2.5		1.7	3.6	3.2	2.5	2.0	2.2
1.5	1.6	1.5	Current	.9	1.3	2.2	1.8	1.2	1.7
1.1	.9	.9		.4	.7	.9	1.1	.8	1.1
1.5	2.0	1.9		.9	2.5	2.8	1.7	1.2	1.7
.9	1.0	.9	Quick	.6	1.2	1.4	.9	.7	.9
.5	.5	.6		.4	.6	.6	.5	.5	.6
25 14.7	**24** 15.4	**20** 18.1		**9** 38.5	**13** 28.8	**19** 19.1	**22** 16.4	**25** 14.5	**38** 9.6
37 9.9	**40** 9.1	**36** 10.1	Sales/Receivables	**18** 19.8	**22** 16.4	**31** 11.6	**33** 11.1	**43** 8.5	**48** 7.6
51 7.2	**53** 6.9	**52** 7.0		**26** 14.2	**51** 7.1	**50** 7.3	**46** 7.9	**55** 6.6	**62** 5.9
14 25.8	**7** 55.7	**9** 38.7		**0** UND	**0** UND	**2** 153.2	**23** 16.0	**13** 27.9	**21** 17.4
43 8.5	**31** 11.6	**27** 13.4	Cost of Sales/Inventory	**13** 29.0	**12** 30.3	**16** 22.2	**48** 7.6	**32** 11.3	**50** 7.3
78 4.7	**58** 6.3	**51** 7.1		**28** 13.2	**33** 11.0	**39** 9.3	**66** 5.5	**42** 8.6	**79** 4.6
16 22.7	**19** 19.7	**16** 23.0		**11** 32.8	**4** 91.0	**19** 18.8	**18** 20.0	**19** 19.1	**23** 16.1
32 11.5	**30** 12.3	**29** 12.7	Cost of Sales/Payables	**20** 18.1	**26** 14.1	**34** 10.7	**24** 15.0	**35** 10.3	**36** 10.1
51 7.2	**44** 8.3	**49** 7.4		**146** 2.5	**52** 7.0	**62** 5.9	**41** 8.9	**54** 6.8	**45** 8.2
7.3	6.5	7.3		24.5	7.0	7.3	7.0	9.3	6.2
13.4	10.6	13.1	Sales/Working Capital	-50.0	55.5	12.0	9.9	24.5	8.9
94.5	-176.0	-73.5		-4.0	-19.7	-39.7	210.1	-29.3	38.0
9.9	17.5	13.7		5.5	9.8	25.4	13.9	15.0	27.5
(107) 2.7	(95) 6.3	(114) 4.5	EBIT/Interest	2.7	(24) 3.9	(17) 2.2	(24) 7.4	(19) 5.8	(19) 10.4
.8	1.9	1.1		-1.2	.7	.4	1.6	1.6	.1
4.8	10.1	7.0							16.0
(19) 2.6	(22) 4.3	(19) 3.5	Net Profit + Depr., Dep., Amort./Cur. Mat. L/T/D						(10) 3.5
1.6	2.1	1.9							2.2
.4	.4	.4		3.8	.4	.2	.5	.5	.2
1.0	.8	1.1	Fixed/Worth	-7.0	1.3	1.6	.9	1.3	.7
4.3	6.7	19.5		-.7	17.8	NM	4.2	5.0	-9.8
.9	.8	.8		4.2	1.1	.5	.7	1.8	.7
2.7	2.1	2.3	Debt/Worth	-45.5	2.3	3.1	1.2	3.6	1.5
15.5	14.0	73.9		-2.0	67.5	NM	5.1	16.6	-35.6
45.7	66.6	58.7			62.6	63.0	49.4	65.4	62.3
(98) 16.6	(83) 28.2	(96) 26.7	% Profit Before Taxes/Tangible Net Worth		(22) 28.3	(14) 13.2	(22) 29.0	(16) 35.2	(18) 32.8
1.2	11.0	4.6			-2.2	2.3	1.9	9.0	8.1
15.4	25.1	20.6		19.9	19.1	14.4	22.6	22.9	21.1
4.3	10.7	6.4	% Profit Before Taxes/Total Assets	4.4	6.4	3.4	8.7	7.8	7.4
-.2	2.8	.2		-13.5	-1.6	-.8	2.4	2.8	-3.3
28.8	30.1	30.2		29.3	60.8	44.5	24.3	27.7	38.9
11.1	12.8	12.1	Sales/Net Fixed Assets	12.7	13.0	13.8	7.7	14.4	17.4
5.7	6.2	5.2		2.6	6.5	7.1	2.7	5.3	5.2
3.4	3.6	3.9		7.3	5.5	4.4	3.3	3.6	3.1
2.6	2.8	2.5	Sales/Total Assets	2.5	3.4	3.2	2.3	2.5	2.2
1.8	1.9	1.9		1.1	2.0	2.3	2.1	1.5	1.5
1.0	1.0	.8			1.3	.7	.6	1.2	.7
(96) 2.2	(83) 2.3	(97) 2.0	% Depr., Dep., Amort./Sales		(18) 2.7	(14) 1.3	(22) 2.1	(16) 2.0	(21) 1.7
3.9	3.5	3.8			4.8	3.4	4.4	4.2	3.1
2.2	2.8	2.6			3.3	3.5	1.6		
(54) 4.2	(48) 4.4	(63) 4.6	% Officers', Directors' Owners' Comp/Sales		(19) 7.5	(14) 6.5	(14) 2.9		
10.1	9.1	9.1			10.0	9.4	6.0		
3581740M	2343198M	3231341M	Net Sales ($)	7240M	51650M	72714M	178814M	312441M	2608482M
2026913M	1119893M	1760137M	Total Assets ($)	5548M	16945M	23976M	77479M	158516M	1477673M

M = $ thousand MM = $ million

See Pages 9 through 22 for Explanation of Ratios and Data

Current Data Sorted by Assets							Comparative Historical Data	
						Type of Statement		
			1	1	1	Unqualified	6	11
		3	1			Reviewed	7	7
1	2	2	1			Compiled	1	2
1	1					Tax Returns	1	5
			6	2	1	Other	12	8
8 (4/1-9/30/13)			16 (10/1/13-3/31/14)				4/1/09-3/31/10 ALL	4/1/10-3/31/11 ALL
0-500M	500M-2MM	2-10MM	10-50MM	50-100MM	100-250MM			
2	3	5	9	3	2	**NUMBER OF STATEMENTS**	27	33
%	%	%	%	%	%	**ASSETS**	%	%
						Cash & Equivalents	8.7	10.3
						Trade Receivables (net)	24.3	29.1
						Inventory	11.7	15.2
						All Other Current	2.3	3.3
						Total Current	47.0	57.9
						Fixed Assets (net)	41.0	30.1
						Intangibles (net)	4.5	4.2
						All Other Non-Current	7.5	7.8
						Total	100.0	100.0
						LIABILITIES		
						Notes Payable-Short Term	4.3	5.1
						Cur. Mat.-L.T.D.	6.6	5.9
						Trade Payables	9.1	13.0
						Income Taxes Payable	.1	.1
						All Other Current	7.7	11.3
						Total Current	27.8	35.4
						Long-Term Debt	20.9	11.9
						Deferred Taxes	1.4	.9
						All Other Non-Current	11.5	9.0
						Net Worth	38.5	42.8
						Total Liabilties & Net Worth	100.0	100.0
						INCOME DATA		
						Net Sales	100.0	100.0
						Gross Profit	30.8	28.0
						Operating Expenses	26.6	25.4
						Operating Profit	4.2	2.6
						All Other Expenses (net)	1.1	-.1
						Profit Before Taxes	3.2	2.7
						RATIOS		
							2.8	3.7
						Current	2.2	1.7
							1.0	1.0
							2.3	2.5
						Quick	1.3	1.1
							.7	.6
							36 10.2	**36** 10.0
						Sales/Receivables	**44** 8.3	**53** 6.9
							58 6.2	**59** 6.2
							10 37.5	**9** 41.2
						Cost of Sales/Inventory	**19** 19.4	**28** 13.1
							44 8.3	**55** 6.6
							19 19.5	**17** 21.5
						Cost of Sales/Payables	**22** 16.6	**25** 14.7
							31 11.6	**43** 8.5
							5.0	4.0
						Sales/Working Capital	6.5	6.8
							232.0	NM
							6.1	11.0
						EBIT/Interest	(22) 1.5	(29) 2.9
							-3.0	.8
						Net Profit + Depr., Dep., Amort./Cur. Mat. L/T/D		
							.6	.3
						Fixed/Worth	.7	.7
							2.5	1.9
							.3	.4
						Debt/Worth	1.0	1.1
							5.1	10.4
							37.7	35.5
						% Profit Before Taxes/Tangible Net Worth	(24) 10.9	(31) 9.1
							-3.7	-.2
							7.9	12.5
						% Profit Before Taxes/Total Assets	4.7	2.7
							-1.6	.0
							7.6	15.7
						Sales/Net Fixed Assets	4.0	7.5
							3.1	3.8
							2.3	2.4
						Sales/Total Assets	1.8	1.9
							1.4	1.5
							3.6	2.5
						% Depr., Dep., Amort./Sales	(22) 4.8	(27) 4.1
							6.1	5.7
						% Officers', Directors' Owners' Comp/Sales		
1655M	**7697M**	**85429M**	**245654M**	**291877M**	**557543M**	Net Sales ($)	**1248912M**	**1377868M**
416M	**3664M**	**30622M**	**165637M**	**191357M**	**427088M**	Total Assets ($)	**856195M**	**897359M**

M = $ thousand MM = $ million

See Pages 9 through 22 for Explanation of Ratios and Data

Comparative Historical Data / Current Data Sorted by Sales

			Type of Statement						
8	1	3	Unqualified						3
6	5	4	Reviewed					3	1
2	4	6	Compiled	1	2		1	2	
5	3	2	Tax Returns	1		1			
15	8	9	Other					2	7
4/1/11-3/31/12 ALL	4/1/12-3/31/13 ALL	4/1/13-3/31/14 ALL		8 (4/1-9/30/13)			16 (10/1/13-3/31/14)		
				0-1MM	1-3MM	3-5MM	5-10MM	10-25MM	25MM & OVER
36	21	24	NUMBER OF STATEMENTS	2	2	1	1	7	11
%	%	%	ASSETS	%	%	%	%	%	%
9.7	11.1	14.0	Cash & Equivalents						8.2
28.2	31.0	27.9	Trade Receivables (net)						26.4
12.7	11.7	17.1	Inventory						18.2
1.9	.9	.8	All Other Current						1.3
52.6	54.8	59.7	Total Current						54.1
33.8	39.7	29.8	Fixed Assets (net)						30.6
2.7	2.4	6.4	Intangibles (net)						12.4
10.9	3.1	4.1	All Other Non-Current						2.9
100.0	100.0	100.0	Total						100.0
			LIABILITIES						
8.2	7.4	7.7	Notes Payable-Short Term						6.2
7.1	3.7	2.0	Cur. Mat.-L.T.D.						1.4
14.6	11.0	12.1	Trade Payables						9.6
.1	.0	.0	Income Taxes Payable						.0
6.4	10.5	8.2	All Other Current						9.1
36.4	32.5	30.0	Total Current						26.4
13.4	29.6	21.9	Long-Term Debt						13.4
.9	.5	.7	Deferred Taxes						.1
7.9	7.2	15.4	All Other Non-Current						13.1
41.3	30.1	32.1	Net Worth						47.1
100.0	100.0	100.0	Total Liabilties & Net Worth						100.0
			INCOME DATA						
100.0	100.0	100.0	Net Sales						100.0
28.2	31.3	28.4	Gross Profit						28.0
25.4	25.2	27.4	Operating Expenses						26.1
2.8	6.2	.9	Operating Profit						1.9
.2	1.4	.3	All Other Expenses (net)						.6
2.7	4.7	.7	Profit Before Taxes						1.3
			RATIOS						
3.4	3.3	4.3							2.6
1.6	1.5	2.4	Current						2.0
1.0	1.0	1.6							1.4
2.3	2.6	3.0							1.5
1.1	1.2	1.4	Quick						1.2
.7	.8	.9							.9
36 10.0	**33** 11.0	**38** 9.7							**41** 8.8
49 7.4	**46** 7.9	**51** 7.2	Sales/Receivables						**61** 6.0
58 6.3	**63** 5.8	**66** 5.5							**72** 5.1
8 43.3	**4** 95.3	**10** 36.7							**33** 11.0
28 13.1	**31** 11.7	**38** 9.7	Cost of Sales/Inventory						**52** 7.0
46 8.0	**49** 7.5	**70** 5.2							**111** 3.3
19 19.2	**16** 22.3	**18** 20.0							**18** 19.8
25 14.4	**22** 16.9	**20** 18.7	Cost of Sales/Payables						**24** 15.1
39 9.3	**35** 10.5	**41** 9.0							**43** 8.4
5.2	5.1	3.6							3.0
12.0	13.6	6.0	Sales/Working Capital						7.4
NM	412.4	14.4							17.2
6.5	17.5	30.9							
(32) 1.7	(19) 1.4	(17) 3.5	EBIT/Interest						
.0	.5	1.1							
			Net Profit + Depr., Dep., Amort./Cur. Mat. L/T/D						
.5	.3	.3							.7
.7	.9	.8	Fixed/Worth						.8
1.5	NM	NM							17.2
.4	.5	.4							.4
1.0	2.2	1.0	Debt/Worth						1.2
7.6	NM	NM							71.4
20.5	27.2	33.7							
(31) 5.3	(16) 4.6	(18) 5.4	% Profit Before Taxes/Tangible Net Worth						
-.7	-3.0	-7.6							
6.7	7.3	7.1							7.2
1.8	1.9	1.5	% Profit Before Taxes/Total Assets						1.4
-.6	-.4	-7.1							-.7
12.3	14.2	16.0							9.5
6.6	6.5	8.6	Sales/Net Fixed Assets						4.9
3.0	3.1	3.5							3.4
2.6	2.7	2.5							1.8
2.0	2.1	1.8	Sales/Total Assets						1.5
1.4	1.6	1.4							1.2
2.6	2.4	2.0							
(29) 3.6	(18) 3.7	(17) 3.6	% Depr., Dep., Amort./Sales						
6.2	4.6	5.9							
2.2									
(10) 3.7			% Officers', Directors' Owners' Comp/Sales						
7.3									
1547205M	765265M	1189855M	Net Sales ($)	1655M	3200M	4497M	5439M	129633M	1045431M
1072425M	497637M	818784M	Total Assets ($)	416M	1745M	1919M	2255M	68293M	744156M

M = $ thousand MM = $ million

See Pages 9 through 22 for Explanation of Ratios and Data

Current Data Sorted by Assets							Comparative Historical Data	
						Type of Statement		
			3			Unqualified	5	10
	1	11	2			Reviewed	22	22
3	6	1	3			Compiled	8	11
3	2	3				Tax Returns	8	5
1	3	5	2			Other	20	22
	12 (4/1-9/30/13)		37 (10/1/13-3/31/14)				4/1/09-3/31/10 ALL	4/1/10-3/31/11 ALL
0-500M	500M-2MM	2-10MM	10-50MM	50-100MM	100-250MM			
7	12	20	10			**NUMBER OF STATEMENTS**	63	70
%	%	%	%	%	%	**ASSETS**	%	%
	19.7	8.0	21.1	DATA NOT AVAILABLE	DATA NOT AVAILABLE	Cash & Equivalents	9.7	8.9
	28.3	28.4	20.8			Trade Receivables (net)	30.3	28.9
	4.7	11.7	14.8			Inventory	10.6	10.4
	4.0	2.2	1.3			All Other Current	2.7	1.8
	56.7	50.3	58.0			Total Current	53.2	50.0
	29.7	36.6	33.6			Fixed Assets (net)	35.8	36.5
	8.1	4.2	2.0			Intangibles (net)	4.4	4.7
	5.4	8.9	6.4			All Other Non-Current	6.6	8.8
	100.0	100.0	100.0			Total	100.0	100.0
						LIABILITIES		
	6.3	8.3	.8			Notes Payable-Short Term	12.5	10.1
	4.4	4.7	1.9			Cur. Mat.-L.T.D.	7.8	5.9
	9.7	11.7	4.4			Trade Payables	12.0	11.3
	.0	.0	.4			Income Taxes Payable	.2	.1
	13.7	8.1	10.8			All Other Current	8.7	8.4
	34.1	32.8	18.3			Total Current	41.3	35.8
	13.6	18.5	12.4			Long-Term Debt	26.3	27.9
	.0	.9	.8			Deferred Taxes	.3	.5
	16.5	22.9	5.5			All Other Non-Current	12.5	13.7
	35.8	24.9	63.0			Net Worth	19.6	22.2
	100.0	100.0	100.0			Total Liabilties & Net Worth	100.0	100.0
						INCOME DATA		
	100.0	100.0	100.0			Net Sales	100.0	100.0
	43.2	34.6	27.8			Gross Profit	35.9	33.4
	39.5	29.8	23.7			Operating Expenses	32.8	30.0
	3.8	4.8	4.1			Operating Profit	3.1	3.4
	-.1	1.0	-1.3			All Other Expenses (net)	1.5	.8
	3.8	3.8	5.4			Profit Before Taxes	1.6	2.6
						RATIOS		
	2.6	2.8	6.3				2.7	3.3
	2.2	1.6	2.6			Current	1.4	1.4
	1.2	1.1	2.1				.8	1.0
	2.4	2.1	6.2				2.1	2.2
	2.0	1.3	1.9			Quick	1.0	1.2
	1.1	.8	1.2				.6	.7
	32 11.5	**36** 10.1	**41** 8.8				**36** 10.2	**39** 9.4
	42 8.7	**46** 8.0	**48** 7.6			Sales/Receivables	**48** 7.6	**51** 7.2
	50 7.3	**58** 6.3	**65** 5.6				**63** 5.8	**64** 5.7
	0 UND	**7** 54.4	**15** 24.7				**2** 153.6	**0** UND
	4 85.4	**14** 26.0	**28** 13.0			Cost of Sales/Inventory	**17** 21.0	**19** 19.3
	11 31.8	**31** 11.6	**89** 4.1				**34** 10.8	**42** 8.7
	14 25.8	**15** 24.2	**5** 77.4				**10** 35.6	**11** 33.8
	23 16.0	**21** 17.8	**8** 43.3			Cost of Sales/Payables	**24** 15.3	**22** 16.4
	47 7.8	**43** 8.4	**27** 13.3				**41** 9.0	**38** 9.5
	7.2	5.9	2.2				5.5	4.7
	10.6	14.1	5.0			Sales/Working Capital	16.0	15.4
	53.3	105.1	7.0				-25.6	-106.8
	85.6	14.8					5.9	7.8
	6.4	(18) 3.9				EBIT/Interest	(60) 1.8	(68) 2.7
	-.8	1.0					-.9	.7
							4.9	6.5
						Net Profit + Depr., Dep., Amort./Cur. Mat. L/T/D	(15) 1.0	(15) 3.0
							.2	1.6
	.3	.4	.2				.5	.5
	1.1	.9	.6			Fixed/Worth	1.6	1.5
	2.8	4.3	1.1				-29.7	3.3
	.6	.5	.4				.9	.8
	1.5	1.5	.8			Debt/Worth	2.4	1.9
	5.9	10.3	.9				-195.0	7.3
	57.3	48.3	26.4				27.1	54.4
	(10) 23.4	(17) 8.0	12.6			% Profit Before Taxes/Tangible Net Worth	(47) 11.5	(59) 14.2
	-33.8	2.2	1.1				-12.0	.7
	20.8	15.1	13.4				12.0	13.9
	12.5	4.9	6.7			% Profit Before Taxes/Total Assets	3.0	4.6
	-9.4	.6	.8				-5.1	-.1
	28.9	14.6	10.5				17.6	12.4
	8.3	6.3	6.4			Sales/Net Fixed Assets	6.6	6.1
	4.3	4.2	2.8				3.2	3.3
	3.8	2.8	1.9				2.9	2.6
	2.3	2.4	1.5			Sales/Total Assets	2.0	2.0
	1.9	1.7	.9				1.4	1.4
	1.0	2.9					2.2	2.1
	3.0	(17) 4.7				% Depr., Dep., Amort./Sales	(53) 4.5	(59) 4.2
	6.3	5.9					7.1	6.2
							2.7	2.6
						% Officers', Directors' Owners' Comp/Sales	(24) 4.0	(30) 4.4
							8.8	8.1
5812M	42208M	201635M	296503M			Net Sales ($)	709566M	829413M
1716M	15426M	88326M	223543M			Total Assets ($)	387189M	499254M

M = $ thousand MM = $ million

See Pages 9 through 22 for Explanation of Ratios and Data

Comparative Historical Data				Current Data Sorted by Sales					
			Type of Statement						
6	5	3	Unqualified					1	2
17	12	14	Reviewed		1		6	5	2
14	11	13	Compiled	1	5	3	1	3	
10	7	8	Tax Returns	3	2	1	2		
19	16	11	Other	1	1	1	5	1	2
4/1/11-3/31/12	**4/1/12-3/31/13**	**4/1/13-3/31/14**		**12 (4/1-9/30/13)**			**37 (10/1/13-3/31/14)**		
ALL	**ALL**	**ALL**		**0-1MM**	**1-3MM**	**3-5MM**	**5-10MM**	**10-25MM**	**25MM & OVER**
66	51	49	**NUMBER OF STATEMENTS**	5	9	5	14	10	6
%	%	%	**ASSETS**	%	%	%	%	%	%
10.5	12.9	13.3	Cash & Equivalents				12.9	17.6	
28.8	26.9	28.5	Trade Receivables (net)				29.5	27.3	
9.2	12.5	11.0	Inventory				13.8	9.3	
1.8	1.8	2.2	All Other Current				1.9	1.6	
50.2	54.1	55.1	Total Current				58.1	55.9	
35.6	31.7	33.3	Fixed Assets (net)				28.7	32.7	
4.6	4.7	4.2	Intangibles (net)				6.2	.2	
9.6	9.5	7.4	All Other Non-Current				6.9	11.1	
100.0	100.0	100.0	Total				100.0	100.0	
			LIABILITIES						
12.5	11.7	11.5	Notes Payable-Short Term				5.8	8.7	
5.7	4.6	3.7	Cur. Mat.-L.T.D.				6.4	3.8	
13.6	10.7	9.6	Trade Payables				13.5	8.3	
.1	.0	.1	Income Taxes Payable				.0	.2	
7.8	8.8	13.0	All Other Current				10.0	8.0	
39.8	35.9	37.8	Total Current				35.7	29.0	
24.3	20.1	17.1	Long-Term Debt				17.3	14.3	
.3	.4	.7	Deferred Taxes				.7	.4	
13.4	14.7	14.5	All Other Non-Current				8.6	36.1	
22.3	28.9	29.8	Net Worth				37.8	20.3	
100.0	100.0	100.0	Total Liabilties & Net Worth				100.0	100.0	
			INCOME DATA						
100.0	100.0	100.0	Net Sales				100.0	100.0	
34.5	34.1	37.2	Gross Profit				35.6	26.8	
32.0	28.8	33.3	Operating Expenses				28.9	24.3	
2.4	5.3	3.9	Operating Profit				6.7	2.5	
.7	.8	.2	All Other Expenses (net)				1.6	-1.0	
1.7	4.5	3.7	Profit Before Taxes				5.1	3.6	
			RATIOS						
2.7	2.9	2.7					3.0	6.3	
1.3	1.4	1.7	Current				1.9	1.7	
.9	1.0	1.1					1.2	1.0	
2.3	2.2	2.2					2.1	6.2	
1.2	1.0	1.4	Quick				1.4	1.3	
.7	.6	.9					1.0	.9	
36 10.1	**38** 9.6	**37** 9.9					**25** 14.6	**38** 9.6	
46 8.0	**46** 7.9	**47** 7.8	Sales/Receivables				**41** 9.0	**51** 7.1	
61 6.0	**60** 6.1	**59** 6.2					**65** 5.6	**63** 5.8	
2 162.3	**4** 96.8	**2** 178.5					**3** 114.8	**0** UND	
15 24.9	**17** 21.9	**14** 26.1	Cost of Sales/Inventory				**16** 22.7	**13** 27.1	
37 9.9	**37** 9.8	**31** 11.9					**36** 10.1	**61** 6.0	
13 27.8	**13** 27.5	**10** 37.4					**12** 30.5	**7** 51.1	
24 15.2	**24** 15.0	**21** 17.8	Cost of Sales/Payables				**21** 17.8	**21** 17.5	
46 8.0	**31** 11.6	**33** 11.2					**53** 6.9	**27** 13.6	
5.8	6.6	6.0					6.2	2.2	
28.1	13.7	10.6	Sales/Working Capital				11.3	12.0	
-48.5	-892.1	65.5					31.7	NM	
5.9	32.1	36.1					39.4		
(60) 1.8	(48) 3.4	(44) 5.7	EBIT/Interest				4.9		
.0	.7	.8					2.3		
4.5	5.1								
(12) 2.2	(11) 1.9		Net Profit + Depr., Dep., Amort./Cur. Mat. L/T/D						
.6	.4								
.3	.3	.3					.2	.2	
1.2	1.2	.9	Fixed/Worth				.9	.6	
5.8	4.2	3.2					5.1	3.3	
.7	.5	.6					.6	.3	
2.0	1.8	1.2	Debt/Worth				1.7	.8	
8.3	9.6	5.9					11.0	7.0	
31.1	63.1	48.3					51.7		
(54) 12.4	(42) 25.5	(41) 12.3	% Profit Before Taxes/Tangible Net Worth				(12) 32.4		
-4.6	-1.9	.8					9.1		
12.2	25.3	17.5					23.7	10.3	
3.8	6.1	5.9	% Profit Before Taxes/Total Assets				7.0	4.7	
-1.9	-.7	-.1					3.3	.4	
12.8	16.2	16.5					29.8	11.1	
7.3	8.2	7.3	Sales/Net Fixed Assets				9.4	8.9	
3.2	4.5	5.0					5.1	5.2	
2.9	2.9	3.0					2.7	3.3	
2.1	2.2	2.3	Sales/Total Assets				2.6	1.7	
1.5	1.5	1.7					2.0	.9	
2.5	2.0	2.4					2.4		
(58) 3.7	(43) 3.6	(43) 3.7	% Depr., Dep., Amort./Sales				(11) 4.7		
6.4	6.6	6.0					6.0		
3.9	1.6	2.2							
(23) 6.9	(12) 3.8	(19) 4.0	% Officers', Directors' Owners' Comp/Sales						
11.2	6.3	10.0							
643858M	**642855M**	**546158M**	Net Sales ($)	**2984M**	**15662M**	**19047M**	**102907M**	**168912M**	**236646M**
360098M	**469598M**	**329011M**	Total Assets ($)	**959M**	**12624M**	**8421M**	**46114M**	**136231M**	**124662M**

M = $ thousand MM = $ million

See Pages 9 through 22 for Explanation of Ratios and Data

	Current Data Sorted by Assets						Comparative Historical Data	
Type of Statement								
Unqualified		1		5	3		12	8
Reviewed			1				7	4
Compiled			1				3	4
Tax Returns								2
Other	2	2	5	9	3	1	21	15
	7 (4/1-9/30/13)			26 (10/1/13-3/31/14)			4/1/09-3/31/10	4/1/10-3/31/11
	0-500M	500M-2MM	2-10MM	10-50MM	50-100MM	100-250MM	ALL	ALL
NUMBER OF STATEMENTS	2	3	7	14	6	1	43	33
ASSETS	%	%	%	%	%	%	%	%
Cash & Equivalents				9.1			13.0	13.9
Trade Receivables (net)				22.0			23.4	22.6
Inventory				14.4			17.8	18.1
All Other Current				2.1			3.0	4.5
Total Current				47.6			57.1	59.1
Fixed Assets (net)				43.8			32.2	31.1
Intangibles (net)				3.1			2.0	2.0
All Other Non-Current				5.6			8.7	7.8
Total				100.0			100.0	100.0
LIABILITIES								
Notes Payable-Short Term				8.2			5.4	4.6
Cur. Mat.-L.T.D.				3.2			2.7	2.0
Trade Payables				15.8			20.9	20.6
Income Taxes Payable				.7			.5	.2
All Other Current				5.5			14.7	8.1
Total Current				33.5			44.1	35.5
Long-Term Debt				17.0			8.5	13.3
Deferred Taxes				2.1			1.2	.5
All Other Non-Current				5.9			4.5	3.7
Net Worth				41.5			41.6	46.9
Total Liabilities & Net Worth				100.0			100.0	100.0
INCOME DATA								
Net Sales				100.0			100.0	100.0
Gross Profit				25.8			17.2	18.1
Operating Expenses				23.6			13.5	13.2
Operating Profit				2.3			3.7	4.9
All Other Expenses (net)				1.9			-.3	.0
Profit Before Taxes				.4			4.1	4.9
RATIOS								
Current				2.1			2.4	2.6
				1.6			1.3	1.7
				.8			1.0	1.2
Quick				1.5			1.8	1.8
				.8			1.0	1.0
				.5			.5	.6
Sales/Receivables				16 22.4			14 26.2	16 23.5
				29 12.4			23 16.2	26 14.1
				47 7.7			40 9.1	50 7.4
Cost of Sales/Inventory				8 46.5			5 71.4	7 56.1
				22 16.5			15 24.8	17 21.1
				34 10.7			36 10.2	51 7.1
Cost of Sales/Payables				16 22.4			13 28.4	14 25.4
				24 15.4			21 17.3	28 13.1
				38 9.5			32 11.3	39 9.3
Sales/Working Capital				10.1			6.2	5.8
				23.8			31.5	15.7
				-220.7			999.8	60.5
EBIT/Interest				29.7			39.2	45.2
				(12) 8.3			(35) 7.5	(29) 12.9
				2.5			1.5	3.4
Net Profit + Depr., Dep., Amort./Cur. Mat. L/T/D								
Fixed/Worth				.3			.3	.2
				1.2			.8	.5
				1.7			1.8	1.2
Debt/Worth				1.0			.4	.5
				1.5			1.0	.9
				2.7			6.4	2.5
% Profit Before Taxes/Tangible Net Worth				65.7			38.1	36.1
				(13) 21.4			(39) 17.9	(31) 22.3
				3.1			2.5	3.9
% Profit Before Taxes/Total Assets				18.3			14.7	17.2
				9.0			8.1	8.3
				1.4			.8	2.5
Sales/Net Fixed Assets				15.1			24.7	38.1
				8.2			10.9	14.8
				2.8			5.5	3.1
Sales/Total Assets				4.8			5.4	4.9
				2.7			3.3	2.5
				1.0			1.5	1.2
% Depr., Dep., Amort./Sales				1.2			.6	.4
				(12) 1.8			(36) 1.1	(27) 1.1
				3.9			2.4	2.3
% Officers', Directors' Owners' Comp/Sales								
Net Sales ($)	9106M	11749M	217578M	1256026M	1739642M	528543M	8695400M	8090066M
Total Assets ($)	335M	3885M	43959M	425632M	388641M	168140M	2205486M	2322361M

M = $ thousand MM = $ million

See Pages 9 through 22 for Explanation of Ratios and Data

Comparative Historical Data				Current Data Sorted by Sales					
15	6	9	Unqualified		1	1			7
1	2	1	Reviewed						1
9	3	1	Compiled				1		
3	1		Tax Returns						
23	24	22	Other		2	3	2	1	14
4/1/11-3/31/12 ALL	4/1/12-3/31/13 ALL	4/1/13-3/31/14 ALL			7 (4/1-9/30/13)		26 (10/1/13-3/31/14)		
				0-1MM	1-3MM	3-5MM	5-10MM	10-25MM	25MM & OVER
51	36	33	NUMBER OF STATEMENTS		3	4	3	1	22
%	%	%	ASSETS	%	%	%	%	%	%
10.0	12.2	8.3	Cash & Equivalents	DATA NOT AVAILABLE					7.3
21.6	21.9	23.2	Trade Receivables (net)						23.0
18.1	19.2	16.7	Inventory						19.6
2.9	2.1	1.7	All Other Current						1.4
52.6	55.5	49.9	Total Current						51.4
30.6	35.4	41.2	Fixed Assets (net)						39.0
3.5	3.9	2.6	Intangibles (net)						3.5
13.3	5.3	6.4	All Other Non-Current						6.0
100.0	100.0	100.0	Total						100.0
			LIABILITIES						
5.2	4.1	4.3	Notes Payable-Short Term						4.2
3.3	3.2	3.9	Cur. Mat.-L.T.D.						4.9
19.1	20.7	23.3	Trade Payables						25.0
.5	.4	.4	Income Taxes Payable						.6
11.5	6.9	7.5	All Other Current						7.0
39.7	35.3	39.3	Total Current						41.7
13.2	13.7	17.7	Long-Term Debt						16.5
1.0	2.0	1.1	Deferred Taxes						1.6
4.0	6.5	6.1	All Other Non-Current						5.4
42.1	42.5	35.7	Net Worth						34.8
100.0	100.0	100.0	Total Liabilties & Net Worth						100.0
			INCOME DATA						
100.0	100.0	100.0	Net Sales						100.0
22.6	20.0	24.0	Gross Profit						15.3
16.9	12.2	19.8	Operating Expenses						12.1
5.7	7.8	4.1	Operating Profit						3.1
.4	.6	1.1	All Other Expenses (net)						.8
5.3	7.2	3.0	Profit Before Taxes						2.3
			RATIOS						
2.4	2.9	2.0							1.8
1.3	1.5	1.5	Current						1.3
.9	1.0	.9							.9
1.5	1.6	1.5							1.1
.7	.9	.8	Quick						.8
.4	.5	.5							.5
11 34.4	10 37.7	12 30.6							11 32.9
27 13.5	22 16.3	22 16.6	Sales/Receivables						21 17.6
37 9.9	38 9.7	48 7.6							29 12.8
7 51.8	1 395.3	3 108.2							8 46.5
16 23.4	15 24.8	12 30.3	Cost of Sales/Inventory						15 24.1
39 9.3	41 8.9	29 12.5							34 10.7
11 32.0	10 35.8	11 34.4							11 33.6
26 13.9	22 16.3	22 16.6	Cost of Sales/Payables						21 17.1
37 9.9	32 11.3	35 10.5							35 10.5
9.0	8.5	10.9							16.1
30.0	19.9	26.6	Sales/Working Capital						28.5
-98.4	323.8	-297.4							-275.1
26.0	30.9	19.3							19.3
(43) 8.0	(31) 11.4	(29) 7.0	EBIT/Interest						(21) 7.0
2.1	1.1	3.4							3.1
5.6									
(11) 3.1			Net Profit + Depr., Dep., Amort./Cur. Mat. L/T/D						
.7									
.3	.3	.6							.6
.8	.9	1.2	Fixed/Worth						1.3
1.7	1.8	1.8							1.7
.5	.6	1.0							1.0
1.5	1.5	1.8	Debt/Worth						1.6
3.2	2.9	3.1							2.4
46.0	50.6	49.2							43.7
(48) 28.7	(33) 25.5	(30) 20.4	% Profit Before Taxes/Tangible Net Worth						(20) 24.0
7.5	2.7	8.5							10.2
21.8	23.4	17.7							15.1
9.7	8.9	7.3	% Profit Before Taxes/Total Assets						8.4
3.1	.3	2.4							3.1
31.9	23.4	20.7							17.3
11.4	8.5	10.0	Sales/Net Fixed Assets						10.2
6.9	4.1	3.9							5.7
4.5	4.2	6.7							7.0
3.2	3.0	2.9	Sales/Total Assets						3.2
1.8	1.1	2.1							2.3
.7	.6	.8							.5
(42) 1.0	(29) .9	(27) 1.2	% Depr., Dep., Amort./Sales						(20) 1.2
2.2	2.6	3.1							2.1
			% Officers', Directors' Owners' Comp/Sales						
10624347M	8329103M	3762644M	Net Sales ($)		6112M	18542M	18329M	10748M	3708913M
2469095M	2548178M	1030592M	Total Assets ($)		48044M	3428M	47387M	28632M	903101M

M = $ thousand MM = $ million

See Pages 9 through 22 for Explanation of Ratios and Data

Current Data Sorted by Assets							Comparative Historical Data	
						Type of Statement		
	1	9	12	1	8	Unqualified	32	34
	3	18	4			Reviewed	27	24
	1	3				Compiled	9	8
4	3	6				Tax Returns	13	10
	2	18	13	4	4	Other	42	38
	17 (4/1-9/30/13)		97 (10/1/13-3/31/14)				4/1/09-3/31/10	4/1/10-3/31/11
0-500M	**500M-2MM**	**2-10MM**	**10-50MM**	**50-100MM**	**100-250MM**		**ALL**	**ALL**
4	10	54	29	5	12	**NUMBER OF STATEMENTS**	123	114
%	%	%	%	%	%	**ASSETS**	%	%
	18.4	11.8	11.1		9.7	Cash & Equivalents	14.9	13.7
	20.6	26.8	20.6		13.1	Trade Receivables (net)	25.5	24.1
	13.9	12.6	19.6		17.5	Inventory	11.5	12.3
	1.3	2.3	6.2		4.5	All Other Current	4.4	3.1
	54.3	53.6	57.6		44.8	Total Current	56.3	53.3
	35.7	35.7	33.9		37.3	Fixed Assets (net)	33.7	35.2
	.2	3.3	3.5		6.8	Intangibles (net)	2.0	4.8
	9.8	7.4	5.0		11.2	All Other Non-Current	8.0	6.8
	100.0	100.0	100.0		100.0	Total	100.0	100.0
						LIABILITIES		
	13.5	4.8	5.3		3.9	Notes Payable-Short Term	5.9	6.2
	2.9	4.5	4.0		2.6	Cur. Mat.-L.T.D.	3.5	3.4
	7.8	13.8	11.8		10.8	Trade Payables	14.0	13.3
	.5	.5	.3		.5	Income Taxes Payable	.3	.4
	17.2	7.9	6.1		7.5	All Other Current	8.2	4.9
	42.0	31.6	27.5		25.4	Total Current	32.0	28.1
	8.9	16.8	17.5		10.0	Long-Term Debt	14.0	17.2
	1.2	1.1	1.6		1.9	Deferred Taxes	.7	.7
	.4	7.3	1.7		1.0	All Other Non-Current	4.3	4.6
	47.5	43.2	51.7		61.9	Net Worth	48.9	49.3
	100.0	100.0	100.0		100.0	Total Liabilties & Net Worth	100.0	100.0
						INCOME DATA		
	100.0	100.0	100.0		100.0	Net Sales	100.0	100.0
	18.0	22.6	18.0		9.1	Gross Profit	23.9	24.3
	17.7	17.3	11.9		7.3	Operating Expenses	17.9	17.6
	.3	5.3	6.1		1.8	Operating Profit	6.0	6.7
	2.6	.6	.4		-1.0	All Other Expenses (net)	.5	.0
	-2.3	4.7	5.7		2.8	Profit Before Taxes	5.5	6.7
						RATIOS		
	4.9	3.0	4.1		3.5		4.0	3.4
	2.4	1.6	2.2		2.0	Current	2.0	1.7
	.4	1.2	1.3		1.3		1.2	1.3
	4.2	2.2	2.1		1.9		2.9	2.5
	1.5	1.4	1.0		1.4	Quick	1.4	1.3
	.1	.7	.6		.2		.8	.7
	6 58.3	**14** 26.6	**20** 17.9		**20** 18.1		**26** 14.0	**20** 18.4
	25 14.8	**34** 10.7	**29** 12.4		**40** 9.2	Sales/Receivables	**38** 9.5	**38** 9.5
	50 7.3	**70** 5.2	**57** 6.4		**54** 6.7		**60** 6.0	**59** 6.2
	0 UND	**7** 53.5	**8** 47.5		**13** 28.0		**4** 81.3	**5** 70.2
	1 487.1	**21** 17.3	**38** 9.7		**50** 7.3	Cost of Sales/Inventory	**22** 16.9	**19** 19.3
	31 11.8	**39** 9.4	**78** 4.7		**73** 5.0		**44** 8.3	**46** 7.9
	1 393.5	**9** 39.1	**14** 26.1		**18** 19.8		**12** 30.3	**14** 26.2
	10 38.3	**21** 17.3	**21** 17.6		**28** 13.0	Cost of Sales/Payables	**24** 15.4	**25** 14.7
	32 11.3	**44** 8.3	**39** 9.3		**36** 10.1		**44** 8.3	**42** 8.6
	3.5	5.2	3.5		3.8		4.1	4.0
	10.4	10.3	8.9		5.7	Sales/Working Capital	8.8	9.6
	-32.5	45.4	21.2		24.9		31.7	30.5
		25.2	28.0		40.5		26.2	21.4
		(49) 7.0	(26) 5.6		10.3	EBIT/Interest	(107) 7.4	(99) 6.0
		2.2	2.4		1.6		2.8	2.6
		4.4					8.8	8.4
		(17) 2.1				Net Profit + Depr., Dep., Amort./Cur. Mat. L/T/D	(32) 4.2	(32) 3.0
		1.1					2.6	1.9
	.1	.4	.4		.4		.3	.4
	.5	.9	.8		.8	Fixed/Worth	.7	.9
	2.6	1.7	1.3		1.0		1.4	1.8
	.2	.5	.4		.4		.3	.4
	.5	1.3	1.2		.7	Debt/Worth	.9	1.1
	2.1	3.3	2.7		1.2		2.6	2.5
		53.7	29.2		11.2		44.0	40.7
		(50) 13.4	20.2		5.8	% Profit Before Taxes/Tangible Net Worth	(115) 20.2	(106) 19.6
		6.3	7.9		1.9		6.1	8.5
	5.5	15.3	15.7		5.3		20.0	20.5
	-.6	8.2	6.8		4.5	% Profit Before Taxes/Total Assets	9.8	9.7
	-17.5	1.5	2.8		1.0		2.0	3.5
	19.8	13.5	10.8		7.7		13.4	13.7
	10.5	6.3	6.1		4.0	Sales/Net Fixed Assets	7.1	6.3
	4.4	4.1	4.0		2.6		3.6	3.4
	3.4	3.0	2.6		1.6		2.9	3.2
	2.2	2.1	2.0		1.4	Sales/Total Assets	2.2	2.1
	2.0	1.7	1.3		.9		1.4	1.3
		1.2	1.7				1.7	1.6
		(51) 2.5	(26) 2.8			% Depr., Dep., Amort./Sales	(109) 2.8	(98) 2.5
		5.1	3.7				4.5	4.8
		1.2					2.2	1.1
		(22) 2.0				% Officers', Directors' Owners' Comp/Sales	(33) 3.4	(30) 2.7
		3.0					5.3	4.8
3292M	32305M	709808M	1433026M	594576M	2664888M	Net Sales ($)	5781325M	5713780M
814M	13123M	309533M	694122M	344095M	1957590M	Total Assets ($)	2813036M	3239420M

M = $ thousand MM = $ million

See Pages 9 through 22 for Explanation of Ratios and Data

Comparative Historical Data							Current Data Sorted by Sales								
						Type of Statement									
	39		28		31	Unqualified		2			3		7		19
	27		30		25	Reviewed		2	1		6		9		7
	10		9		4	Compiled			1		3				
	7		9		13	Tax Returns	2	3	2		1		5		
	39		38		41	Other		2	1		6		13		19
	4/1/11-3/31/12		4/1/12-3/31/13		4/1/13-3/31/14		17 (4/1-9/30/13)				97 (10/1/13-3/31/14)				
	ALL		ALL		ALL		0-1MM	1-3MM	3-5MM		5-10MM		10-25MM		25MM & OVER
	122		114		114	**NUMBER OF STATEMENTS**	2	9	5		19		34		45
	%		%		%	**ASSETS**	%	%	%		%		%		%
	14.3		10.8		12.7	Cash & Equivalents					12.8		12.7		9.6
	23.1		23.6		22.0	Trade Receivables (net)					23.6		25.9		20.4
	12.2		14.8		14.8	Inventory					10.1		12.1		20.7
	3.2		3.6		3.3	All Other Current					.9		2.0		5.4
	52.9		52.7		52.9	Total Current					47.5		52.7		56.1
	34.9		35.9		36.0	Fixed Assets (net)					42.5		36.2		32.5
	3.2		3.5		3.7	Intangibles (net)					2.4		4.3		4.5
	8.9		7.8		7.5	All Other Non-Current					7.6		6.8		6.8
	100.0		100.0		100.0	Total					100.0		100.0		100.0
						LIABILITIES									
	6.9		8.2		5.6	Notes Payable-Short Term					2.8		5.2		5.9
	4.1		4.5		4.0	Cur. Mat.-L.T.D.					5.1		4.3		3.5
	13.1		12.9		11.8	Trade Payables					11.8		12.7		13.0
	.2		.3		.4	Income Taxes Payable					.3		.7		.3
	6.7		7.1		8.0	All Other Current					8.8		6.7		6.7
	31.0		32.9		29.8	Total Current					28.8		29.5		29.3
	15.2		15.3		18.8	Long-Term Debt					22.7		15.1		14.1
	.7		.8		1.3	Deferred Taxes					2.6		.7		1.4
	3.7		3.6		4.7	All Other Non-Current					8.0		7.4		1.8
	49.4		47.4		45.4	Net Worth					37.9		47.3		53.4
	100.0		100.0		100.0	Total Liabilties & Net Worth					100.0		100.0		100.0
						INCOME DATA									
	100.0		100.0		100.0	Net Sales					100.0		100.0		100.0
	19.9		19.4		20.8	Gross Profit					21.7		21.7		15.0
	14.8		15.5		15.9	Operating Expenses					15.8		17.4		10.2
	5.1		4.0		4.9	Operating Profit					5.8		4.4		4.8
	.5		.0		.6	All Other Expenses (net)					2.0		.6		-.1
	4.6		3.9		4.2	Profit Before Taxes					3.8		3.8		4.9
						RATIOS									
	3.5		3.4		3.5						3.7		3.0		3.6
	1.7		1.5		1.7	Current					1.4		2.1		1.9
	1.1		1.1		1.2						.9		1.3		1.3
	2.2		2.1		2.2						2.6		2.4		1.9
	1.3		1.1		1.4	Quick					1.3		1.5		1.0
	.7		.5		.7						.6		.9		.6
20	18.7	**16**	22.9	**17**	21.6					**9**	40.2	**21**	17.5	**19**	19.4
35	10.5	**33**	11.1	**30**	12.1	Sales/Receivables				**35**	10.3	**34**	10.7	**29**	12.4
59	6.2	**59**	6.2	**62**	5.9					**76**	4.8	**64**	5.7	**54**	6.7
6	59.6	**9**	40.2	**6**	58.3					**8**	47.4	**6**	58.8	**11**	32.5
20	18.3	**25**	14.7	**23**	15.6	Cost of Sales/Inventory				**27**	13.4	**15**	24.4	**42**	8.7
41	9.0	**57**	6.4	**53**	6.9					**41**	8.8	**38**	9.7	**76**	4.8
11	32.0	**11**	32.0	**10**	36.6					**9**	38.5	**8**	46.8	**16**	23.3
23	15.6	**19**	19.0	**21**	17.8	Cost of Sales/Payables				**20**	18.1	**18**	20.6	**24**	15.2
36	10.2	**35**	10.5	**38**	9.7					**49**	7.4	**38**	9.6	**37**	9.9
	5.0		4.8		4.3						4.3		4.8		3.9
	11.9		12.1		9.8	Sales/Working Capital					9.8		10.4		8.9
	55.1		73.7		37.6						-30.8		-29.7		24.6
	21.6		18.6		22.6						24.3		22.4		28.0
(113)	5.9	(102)	4.7	(103)	5.6	EBIT/Interest				(17)	5.6	(31)	6.9	(42)	6.9
	2.8		2.8		1.9						2.0		2.1		2.4
	7.9		5.0		4.5								6.7		5.9
(35)	2.7	(41)	2.7	(35)	2.6	Net Profit + Depr., Dep., Amort./Cur. Mat. L/T/D						(14)	2.8	(12)	2.8
	1.3		1.7		1.2								1.4		1.3
	.4		.4		.4						.4		.5		.4
	.8		.8		.8	Fixed/Worth					.8		1.0		.7
	1.5		1.5		1.4						2.5		1.2		1.2
	.4		.4		.4						.4		.5		.4
	1.1		1.3		1.2	Debt/Worth					.8		1.2		1.2
	2.4		2.6		2.7						4.3		2.9		2.6
	32.4		31.5		28.9						30.5		29.0		29.2
(116)	15.1	(107)	13.6	(108)	12.6	% Profit Before Taxes/Tangible Net Worth				(17)	9.9	(32)	13.7		12.8
	7.8		5.2		6.0						5.8		6.4		6.8
	16.1		14.6		12.3						10.9		15.1		12.4
	7.2		6.0		5.8	% Profit Before Taxes/Total Assets					5.6		6.6		6.0
	2.6		2.0		1.5						1.0		1.6		2.6
	12.0		12.4		11.7						6.4		15.2		11.6
	5.8		6.5		6.3	Sales/Net Fixed Assets					4.1		6.5		7.1
	3.8		3.6		3.9						3.1		4.3		4.0
	3.1		3.1		2.8						2.1		3.2		2.8
	2.1		2.3		2.1	Sales/Total Assets					1.7		2.3		2.0
	1.4		1.4		1.5						1.3		2.0		1.3
	1.6		1.8		1.7						2.1		1.3		1.7
(100)	2.5	(104)	2.7	(101)	2.7	% Depr., Dep., Amort./Sales				(18)	3.1	(32)	2.8	(38)	2.6
	4.1		4.1		4.5						4.9		6.0		3.4
	1.0		1.9		1.0								1.4		
(31)	2.3	(32)	3.5	(40)	2.2	% Officers', Directors' Owners' Comp/Sales						(17)	2.4		
	4.3		5.5		4.0								3.3		
	6469944M		6011893M		5437895M	Net Sales ($)	501M	18007M	19660M		141660M		535994M		4722073M
	3786752M		3387834M		3319277M	Total Assets ($)	449M	16949M	9906M		92074M		287809M		2912090M

M = $ thousand MM = $ million

See Pages 9 through 22 for Explanation of Ratios and Data

Current Data Sorted by Assets							Comparative Historical Data	
						Type of Statement		
		1	4	2	3	Unqualified	11	13
	1	9	5			Reviewed	7	11
	2	4	1			Compiled	7	5
1	2	2				Tax Returns		3
	1	10	9	2	3	Other	28	15
	13 (4/1-9/30/13)		49 (10/1/13-3/31/14)				4/1/09-3/31/10	4/1/10-3/31/11
0-500M	500M-2MM	2-10MM	10-50MM	50-100MM	100-250MM		ALL	ALL
1	6	26	19	4	6	**NUMBER OF STATEMENTS**	53	47
%	%	%	%	%	%	**ASSETS**	%	%
		13.3	13.2			Cash & Equivalents	11.0	10.2
		29.4	26.0			Trade Receivables (net)	27.6	29.0
		24.6	30.1			Inventory	28.8	28.3
		1.5	1.7			All Other Current	4.2	1.8
		68.7	70.9			Total Current	71.7	69.2
		19.4	18.9			Fixed Assets (net)	22.3	23.1
		5.5	5.5			Intangibles (net)	2.5	3.9
		6.4	4.7			All Other Non-Current	3.5	3.8
		100.0	100.0			Total	100.0	100.0
						LIABILITIES		
		8.8	3.6			Notes Payable-Short Term	14.9	10.7
		2.1	1.5			Cur. Mat.-L.T.D.	2.5	3.5
		14.5	12.5			Trade Payables	15.6	16.9
		.1	.4			Income Taxes Payable	.2	.5
		7.0	9.1			All Other Current	7.5	6.1
		32.4	27.1			Total Current	40.6	37.6
		9.6	7.4			Long-Term Debt	8.3	8.7
		.3	1.1			Deferred Taxes	.6	.7
		8.0	8.4			All Other Non-Current	5.8	4.1
		49.6	56.0			Net Worth	44.6	48.8
		100.0	100.0			Total Liabilties & Net Worth	100.0	100.0
						INCOME DATA		
		100.0	100.0			Net Sales	100.0	100.0
		31.7	32.0			Gross Profit	31.8	30.8
		25.1	24.7			Operating Expenses	27.0	24.7
		6.6	7.3			Operating Profit	4.8	6.1
		.2	.2			All Other Expenses (net)	.6	.4
		6.4	7.1			Profit Before Taxes	4.2	5.7
						RATIOS		
		3.8	5.4				3.5	4.5
		2.6	2.6			Current	2.0	1.9
		1.4	1.9				1.3	1.4
		2.7	3.7				2.5	2.7
		1.6	1.5			Quick	1.0	1.1
		.8	1.0				.6	.6
		26 14.1	**33** 11.2				**29** 12.7	**31** 11.9
		43 8.5	**46** 8.0			Sales/Receivables	**42** 8.7	**43** 8.4
		51 7.2	**53** 6.9				**52** 7.0	**50** 7.3
		29 12.7	**46** 8.0				**34** 10.7	**41** 8.9
		44 8.3	**72** 5.1			Cost of Sales/Inventory	**57** 6.4	**65** 5.6
		63 5.8	**91** 4.0				**89** 4.1	**88** 4.1
		19 19.5	**17** 21.6				**17** 21.4	**21** 17.3
		27 13.6	**26** 14.3			Cost of Sales/Payables	**27** 13.5	**32** 11.5
		40 9.2	**41** 8.9				**39** 9.3	**44** 8.2
		4.3	2.9				3.6	3.9
		6.2	6.7			Sales/Working Capital	7.0	7.6
		16.4	7.9				19.8	17.3
		29.3	113.5				21.4	38.8
		(24) 8.2	(17) 20.4			EBIT/Interest	(50) 8.6	(44) 7.3
		4.4	1.7				3.1	2.1
							13.0	24.8
						Net Profit + Depr., Dep., Amort./Cur. Mat. L/T/D	(17) 5.5	(16) 8.2
							2.4	2.9
		.1	.2				.2	.2
		.4	.4			Fixed/Worth	.4	.4
		.7	.7				1.2	1.0
		.6	.3				.4	.4
		1.0	.6			Debt/Worth	1.1	1.0
		2.7	1.7				2.4	2.0
		42.9	46.8				47.4	51.3
		(25) 28.0	(18) 24.8			% Profit Before Taxes/Tangible Net Worth	(50) 25.1	(43) 23.7
		17.3	7.9				6.0	7.5
		21.7	25.9				22.1	18.6
		13.6	14.1			% Profit Before Taxes/Total Assets	9.5	9.3
		6.9	.6				2.6	1.6
		65.4	19.2				25.5	26.6
		15.8	12.9			Sales/Net Fixed Assets	14.3	11.9
		6.4	9.9				7.8	8.2
		3.7	2.7				3.1	3.1
		2.3	2.1			Sales/Total Assets	2.5	2.5
		1.9	1.8				1.8	1.7
		.4	.9				.6	.8
		(22) .9	(17) 1.3			% Depr., Dep., Amort./Sales	(49) 1.3	(42) 1.1
		2.4	2.0				1.9	1.8
		.9					1.4	
		(12) 2.4				% Officers', Directors' Owners' Comp/Sales	(12) 2.6	
		4.6					14.2	
2262M	50656M	359567M	1168871M	692367M	1508858M	Net Sales ($)	3144010M	3820227M
335M	8842M	130668M	501219M	282160M	924754M	Total Assets ($)	1427310M	1408409M

M = $ thousand MM = $ million

See Pages 9 through 22 for Explanation of Ratios and Data

Comparative Historical Data				Current Data Sorted by Sales					
			Type of Statement						
16	16	10	Unqualified					1	9
11	15	15	Reviewed				3	9	3
6	7	7	Compiled		1	1	1	3	1
3	3	5	Tax Returns		1		3		1
31	34	25	Other			1	5	4	15
				13 (4/1-9/30/13)			49 (10/1/13-3/31/14)		
4/1/11-3/31/12 ALL	4/1/12-3/31/13 ALL	4/1/13-3/31/14 ALL		0-1MM	1-3MM	3-5MM	5-10MM	10-25MM	25MM & OVER
67	75	62	**NUMBER OF STATEMENTS**		2	2	12	17	29
%	%	%	**ASSETS**	%	%	%	%	%	%
8.7	10.6	12.7	Cash & Equivalents	DATA NOT AVAILABLE			10.6	15.1	11.1
30.5	29.0	27.5	Trade Receivables (net)				31.4	27.2	25.4
26.3	24.6	25.1	Inventory				29.0	24.1	24.4
2.1	1.5	1.6	All Other Current				.2	2.2	2.1
67.7	65.7	67.0	Total Current				71.2	68.6	63.0
20.2	23.2	20.9	Fixed Assets (net)				19.0	20.0	22.0
6.6	4.4	6.1	Intangibles (net)				6.7	3.4	8.3
5.5	6.7	6.0	All Other Non-Current				3.1	8.0	6.8
100.0	100.0	100.0	Total				100.0	100.0	100.0
			LIABILITIES						
8.0	9.7	7.7	Notes Payable-Short Term				14.2	6.5	5.4
2.2	2.1	1.8	Cur. Mat.-L.T.D.				2.7	1.6	1.6
18.1	18.2	13.7	Trade Payables				15.6	13.2	13.0
.2	.2	.2	Income Taxes Payable				.2	.1	.3
7.4	11.1	7.5	All Other Current				9.8	5.3	7.3
35.9	41.3	30.8	Total Current				42.5	26.6	27.5
11.7	10.4	10.7	Long-Term Debt				10.8	9.3	8.9
.8	.9	.9	Deferred Taxes				.0	.5	1.6
7.0	7.7	7.4	All Other Non-Current				7.0	6.9	8.0
44.6	39.7	50.2	Net Worth				39.7	56.6	54.0
100.0	100.0	100.0	Total Liabilties & Net Worth				100.0	100.0	100.0
			INCOME DATA						
100.0	100.0	100.0	Net Sales				100.0	100.0	100.0
30.2	27.5	33.0	Gross Profit				37.0	31.7	29.2
23.9	21.8	26.0	Operating Expenses				28.8	25.6	22.1
6.2	5.7	6.9	Operating Profit				8.3	6.2	7.1
.5	.1	.3	All Other Expenses (net)				.7	-.1	.3
5.8	5.7	6.6	Profit Before Taxes				7.6	6.3	6.7
			RATIOS						
3.2	3.4	3.9					3.3	4.3	3.9
1.8	1.7	2.5	Current				1.8	2.8	2.4
1.4	1.2	1.5					1.2	1.8	1.5
2.0	2.2	2.6					1.8	3.2	2.6
1.1	1.0	1.3	Quick				1.0	1.9	1.2
.7	.7	.8					.6	1.1	.7
33 10.9	**27** 13.4	**26** 13.9					**36** 10.0	**24** 14.9	**24** 14.9
43 8.5	**34** 10.6	**42** 8.6	Sales/Receivables				**43** 8.5	**38** 9.6	**42** 8.6
50 7.3	**46** 8.0	**51** 7.2					**50** 7.3	**51** 7.1	**52** 7.0
32 11.3	**30** 12.1	**34** 10.6					**36** 10.1	**29** 12.8	**38** 9.6
53 6.9	**47** 7.7	**54** 6.8	Cost of Sales/Inventory				**55** 6.6	**42** 8.7	**64** 5.7
79 4.6	**73** 5.0	**83** 4.4					**83** 4.4	**55** 6.6	**89** 4.1
16 22.7	**17** 21.3	**18** 20.6					**21** 17.0	**17** 21.1	**15** 24.7
27 13.4	**26** 14.2	**26** 14.1	Cost of Sales/Payables				**31** 11.6	**21** 17.7	**25** 14.4
50 7.3	**45** 8.2	**40** 9.2					**45** 8.1	**29** 12.5	**35** 10.3
5.0	4.8	3.9					4.7	4.0	3.8
8.4	10.4	6.7	Sales/Working Capital				9.2	6.1	6.8
18.0	43.0	11.8					28.6	12.5	11.8
42.7	51.9	42.9					40.5	31.1	95.8
(62) 10.4	(69) 8.9	(57) 10.9	EBIT/Interest				8.2	(15) 10.9	(26) 18.1
3.1	3.2	3.3					3.7	4.9	2.0
19.1	14.3	7.0							8.6
(22) 3.5	(26) 3.5	(18) 3.4	Net Profit + Depr., Dep., Amort./Cur. Mat. L/T/D						(13) 5.0
1.7	2.0	2.2							1.7
.1	.2	.2					.1	.2	.2
.4	.6	.5	Fixed/Worth				.6	.3	.4
1.5	1.2	.9					1.1	.6	.8
.8	.7	.5					.8	.5	.4
1.3	1.3	1.0	Debt/Worth				2.0	.8	.9
3.8	4.0	2.5					5.0	2.2	1.8
61.6	65.3	48.5					57.1	36.5	55.6
(61) 33.4	(67) 25.8	(58) 25.8	% Profit Before Taxes/Tangible Net Worth				(11) 38.9	22.3	(27) 24.5
11.7	14.4	16.2					20.4	17.3	9.8
21.0	18.3	22.9					28.8	19.9	24.1
10.3	10.7	12.6	% Profit Before Taxes/Total Assets				17.0	10.3	11.8
4.9	5.1	5.1					3.9	7.9	1.3
70.3	28.2	34.7					219.2	55.2	16.6
12.9	12.0	12.3	Sales/Net Fixed Assets				19.8	14.0	11.1
6.3	6.2	8.0					5.5	6.3	8.5
3.6	3.6	3.6					3.6	3.7	2.8
2.5	2.5	2.3	Sales/Total Assets				2.2	2.3	2.3
1.7	1.7	1.8					1.9	1.7	1.7
.6	.7	.6					.3	.5	1.1
(56) 1.3	(66) 1.2	(54) 1.2	% Depr., Dep., Amort./Sales				(11) .9	(14) .8	(26) 1.4
2.1	2.1	2.2					3.0	1.4	2.2
1.5	1.6	1.1							
(16) 3.7	(17) 3.8	(22) 3.6	% Officers', Directors' Owners' Comp/Sales						
6.7	5.8	6.3							
4895190M	6385517M	3782581M	Net Sales ($)		4531M	8644M	92021M	266314M	3411071M
2190701M	2576665M	1847978M	Total Assets ($)		2072M	2536M	38060M	118965M	1686345M

M = $ thousand MM = $ million

See Pages 9 through 22 for Explanation of Ratios and Data

Current Data Sorted by Assets							Comparative Historical Data	
						Type of Statement		
			2	2		Unqualified	14	10
1			4			Reviewed	1	1
	1		1			Compiled	5	4
	1					Tax Returns	3	4
1	1		5		1	Other	12	12
3 (4/1-9/30/13)			17 (10/1/13-3/31/14)				4/1/09-3/31/10	4/1/10-3/31/11
0-500M	500M-2MM	2-10MM	10-50MM	50-100MM	100-250MM		ALL	ALL
2	3		12	2	1	**NUMBER OF STATEMENTS**	35	31
%	%	%	%	%	%	**ASSETS**	%	%
		DATA NOT AVAILABLE	20.0			Cash & Equivalents	12.6	10.1
			21.7			Trade Receivables (net)	20.8	24.1
			19.0			Inventory	17.2	20.6
			1.9			All Other Current	1.6	1.7
			62.7			Total Current	52.1	56.4
			31.9			Fixed Assets (net)	35.5	34.2
			2.9			Intangibles (net)	6.4	3.3
			2.5			All Other Non-Current	5.9	6.1
			100.0			Total	100.0	100.0
						LIABILITIES		
			7.5			Notes Payable-Short Term	11.4	5.1
			2.6			Cur. Mat.-L.T.D.	2.8	4.1
			10.6			Trade Payables	11.6	15.1
			.0			Income Taxes Payable	.2	.1
			5.0			All Other Current	7.4	9.3
			25.7			Total Current	33.4	33.6
			17.6			Long-Term Debt	22.9	18.5
			.6			Deferred Taxes	.4	.1
			3.7			All Other Non-Current	2.7	3.3
			52.4			Net Worth	40.6	44.5
			100.0			Total Liabilties & Net Worth	100.0	100.0
						INCOME DATA		
			100.0			Net Sales	100.0	100.0
			29.8			Gross Profit	29.3	24.6
			16.9			Operating Expenses	24.3	18.2
			12.9			Operating Profit	5.0	6.4
			.0			All Other Expenses (net)	1.5	1.7
			12.9			Profit Before Taxes	3.5	4.7
						RATIOS		
			5.6				3.5	4.1
			2.9			Current	1.6	1.7
			1.0				1.0	1.1
			3.9				2.4	2.5
			1.9			Quick	1.1	(30) .9
			.8				.6	.7
			12 30.3				16 22.2	15 23.7
			42 8.7			Sales/Receivables	38 9.5	36 10.1
			54 6.7				60 6.1	53 6.8
			9 38.8				19 18.9	8 44.4
			38 9.6			Cost of Sales/Inventory	37 10.0	30 12.2
			61 6.0				65 5.6	79 4.6
			13 28.8				10 36.8	12 30.3
			24 15.1			Cost of Sales/Payables	27 13.7	20 18.0
			36 10.1				34 10.8	38 9.6
			3.1				4.8	5.1
			5.2			Sales/Working Capital	7.4	9.6
			NM				168.5	59.7
			56.9				9.2	14.5
			(11) 23.0			EBIT/Interest	(32) 3.0	(27) 3.8
			3.1				.1	1.4
						Net Profit + Depr., Dep., Amort./Cur. Mat. L/T/D		
			.0				.5	.2
			.5			Fixed/Worth	1.0	.7
			1.7				4.2	1.6
			.3				.5	.6
			1.0			Debt/Worth	2.1	1.4
			2.4				8.5	4.1
			82.7				57.3	57.6
			32.6			% Profit Before Taxes/Tangible Net Worth	(28) 19.4	(30) 21.6
			16.6				-1.9	2.2
			30.1				14.8	11.8
			14.8			% Profit Before Taxes/Total Assets	4.6	5.6
			3.7				-1.3	1.2
			UND				18.2	35.2
			7.8			Sales/Net Fixed Assets	7.2	10.3
			3.2				2.2	3.2
			3.6				2.5	4.0
			2.3			Sales/Total Assets	1.9	1.8
			1.2				1.1	1.4
							1.3	.7
						% Depr., Dep., Amort./Sales	(29) 2.5	(25) 1.9
							4.9	4.5
							.5	
						% Officers', Directors' Owners' Comp/Sales	(10) 2.6	
							10.0	
871M	8181M		621556M	266932M	168682M	Net Sales ($)	1352138M	2060186M
206M	3192M		284800M	147179M	100266M	Total Assets ($)	1020180M	965550M

M = $ thousand MM = $ million

See Pages 9 through 22 for Explanation of Ratios and Data

Comparative Historical Data				Current Data Sorted by Sales					
			Type of Statement						
4	5	4	Unqualified						4
4	3	5	Reviewed	1					4
6	4	2	Compiled				1		1
2		1	Tax Returns	1					
10	3	8	Other	1	1			3	3
				3 (4/1-9/30/13)			17 (10/1/13-3/31/14)		
4/1/11-3/31/12 ALL	**4/1/12-3/31/13 ALL**	**4/1/13-3/31/14 ALL**		**0-1MM**	**1-3MM**	**3-5MM**	**5-10MM**	**10-25MM**	**25MM & OVER**
26	15	20	**NUMBER OF STATEMENTS**	3	1		1	3	12
%	%	%	**ASSETS**	%	%	%	%	%	%
11.8	7.9	14.2	Cash & Equivalents			DATA NOT AVAILABLE			13.6
28.2	25.4	20.6	Trade Receivables (net)						21.5
23.2	17.3	16.1	Inventory						19.6
4.3	2.6	3.0	All Other Current						4.6
67.5	53.1	53.9	Total Current						59.3
28.4	39.4	41.9	Fixed Assets (net)						36.6
.9	1.5	2.2	Intangibles (net)						1.7
3.3	6.0	2.0	All Other Non-Current						2.4
100.0	100.0	100.0	Total						100.0
			LIABILITIES						
9.9	8.9	7.0	Notes Payable-Short Term						8.6
4.2	4.7	2.9	Cur. Mat.-L.T.D.						3.5
16.8	16.6	11.0	Trade Payables						11.3
.1	.2	.0	Income Taxes Payable						.0
10.2	4.0	14.3	All Other Current						5.6
41.2	34.3	35.3	Total Current						29.1
21.3	28.7	18.9	Long-Term Debt						13.3
.3	.2	.4	Deferred Taxes						.6
6.5	1.0	12.5	All Other Non-Current						3.7
30.7	35.8	33.0	Net Worth						53.3
100.0	100.0	100.0	Total Liabilties & Net Worth						100.0
			INCOME DATA						
100.0	100.0	100.0	Net Sales						100.0
20.0	13.8	26.0	Gross Profit						19.5
14.9	11.4	15.8	Operating Expenses						13.5
5.1	2.4	10.2	Operating Profit						6.0
.4	-.4	.3	All Other Expenses (net)						.4
4.6	2.8	9.9	Profit Before Taxes						5.6
			RATIOS						
3.1	2.7	3.0							3.0
1.4	1.5	1.8	Current						2.3
1.1	1.0	.9							1.1
2.0	1.5	2.3							2.3
.9	.7	1.1	Quick						1.3
.5	.6	.6							.6
16 23.2	**5** 78.2	**11** 32.7							**4** 83.6
30 12.3	**37** 9.9	**33** 10.9	Sales/Receivables						**39** 9.4
57 6.4	**43** 8.4	**51** 7.2							**51** 7.2
3 105.9	**1** 264.6	**2** 146.2							**3** 137.9
30 12.0	**20** 18.1	**29** 12.8	Cost of Sales/Inventory						**27** 13.7
85 4.3	**49** 7.4	**57** 6.4							**57** 6.4
10 37.9	**6** 65.1	**9** 41.8							**7** 52.2
27 13.6	**22** 16.5	**20** 18.1	Cost of Sales/Payables						**20** 17.9
48 7.6	**27** 13.4	**36** 10.1							**36** 10.1
6.5	6.3	5.0							5.0
17.4	23.8	16.0	Sales/Working Capital						8.4
163.6	-539.0	NM							31.5
19.2	13.9	24.6							24.8
(24) 5.2	(13) 1.9	(17) 7.8	EBIT/Interest						13.4
2.3	-1.1	2.3							2.2
			Net Profit + Depr., Dep., Amort./Cur. Mat. L/T/D						
.2	.6	.3							.0
.6	1.3	1.2	Fixed/Worth						.6
1.6	2.7	2.7							1.8
.5	.6	.5							.3
1.9	1.1	1.7	Debt/Worth						.8
3.2	6.1	5.4							2.4
52.9	29.7	42.6							32.9
(25) 25.5	(12) 19.7	(17) 23.8	% Profit Before Taxes/Tangible Net Worth						19.6
4.7	5.4	7.4							6.4
23.3	14.4	29.7							25.9
9.5	3.4	11.7	% Profit Before Taxes/Total Assets						8.5
2.0	-6.2	3.7							2.5
38.1	45.7	17.3							UND
15.1	8.4	5.4	Sales/Net Fixed Assets						7.8
4.8	3.7	2.7							3.2
5.8	4.3	3.4							3.6
2.6	3.3	2.2	Sales/Total Assets						2.3
1.4	1.8	1.4							1.7
.6	.8	1.9							
(20) 1.7	(13) 1.7	(13) 3.9	% Depr., Dep., Amort./Sales						
2.8	7.4	6.9							
			% Officers', Directors' Owners' Comp/Sales						
1598467M	**1044729M**	**1066222M**	Net Sales ($)	**1860M**	**1846M**		**5346M**	**49437M**	**1007733M**
524711M	**290559M**	**535643M**	Total Assets ($)	**955M**	**887M**		**1556M**	**78142M**	**454103M**

M = $ thousand MM = $ million

See Pages 9 through 22 for Explanation of Ratios and Data

	Current Data Sorted by Assets						Comparative Historical Data	
Type of Statement								
Unqualified			2	5	6	8	37	24
Reviewed			8	8			21	27
Compiled				2			8	5
Tax Returns		2					8	7
Other	1	2	5	20	8	3	53	60
	19 (4/1-9/30/13)			61 (10/1/13-3/31/14)			4/1/09-3/31/10	4/1/10-3/31/11
	0-500M	500M-2MM	2-10MM	10-50MM	50-100MM	100-250MM	ALL	ALL
NUMBER OF STATEMENTS	1	4	15	35	14	11	127	123
ASSETS	%	%	%	%	%	%	%	%
Cash & Equivalents			10.6	12.3	6.3	7.5	10.3	9.2
Trade Receivables (net)			32.8	21.6	21.3	16.1	23.6	23.5
Inventory			25.2	21.1	16.3	15.0	21.9	20.9
All Other Current			3.0	2.4	1.8	.3	2.1	2.6
Total Current			71.7	57.5	45.6	38.9	57.9	56.2
Fixed Assets (net)			18.6	30.8	38.4	24.8	29.1	32.5
Intangibles (net)			1.3	4.3	8.8	31.9	5.4	5.7
All Other Non-Current			8.4	7.4	7.1	4.4	7.5	5.6
Total			100.0	100.0	100.0	100.0	100.0	100.0
LIABILITIES								
Notes Payable-Short Term			16.3	5.2	10.5	3.9	8.7	8.0
Cur. Mat.-L.T.D.			2.7	2.9	2.7	2.2	3.5	3.1
Trade Payables			15.0	14.1	9.5	7.7	15.2	13.9
Income Taxes Payable			.0	.1	.0	.1	.3	.4
All Other Current			6.8	8.2	5.3	5.6	9.9	7.1
Total Current			40.9	30.5	28.1	19.5	37.6	32.4
Long-Term Debt			10.1	14.9	15.0	20.4	14.3	16.4
Deferred Taxes			.2	.6	2.4	2.4	.8	1.2
All Other Non-Current			5.6	4.2	4.4	7.3	7.5	4.5
Net Worth			43.3	49.9	50.1	50.4	39.7	45.4
Total Liabilties & Net Worth			100.0	100.0	100.0	100.0	100.0	100.0
INCOME DATA								
Net Sales			100.0	100.0	100.0	100.0	100.0	100.0
Gross Profit			29.4	30.1	26.5	23.2	32.2	33.0
Operating Expenses			19.7	21.4	17.8	16.8	23.9	24.0
Operating Profit			9.7	8.7	8.7	6.3	8.2	9.0
All Other Expenses (net)			.4	.6	.5	3.4	1.0	1.0
Profit Before Taxes			9.3	8.1	8.1	2.9	7.2	8.0
RATIOS								
Current			2.1	2.9	2.8	5.4	2.6	2.9
			1.7	2.2	1.6	1.9	1.8	1.9
			1.3	1.4	1.0	.9	1.2	1.3
Quick			1.5	2.2	1.5	2.3	1.8	1.6
			1.0	1.2	.9	.9	1.0	1.1
			.6	.8	.7	.4	.6	.7
Sales/Receivables			**38** 9.6	**29** 12.4	**45** 8.1	**34** 10.8	**35** 10.4	**32** 11.3
			49 7.4	**43** 8.4	**51** 7.1	**47** 7.8	**45** 8.2	**43** 8.4
			61 6.0	**54** 6.8	**57** 6.4	**69** 5.3	**54** 6.8	**54** 6.7
Cost of Sales/Inventory			**36** 10.1	**39** 9.3	**22** 16.7	**38** 9.5	**36** 10.0	**31** 11.7
			55 6.6	**59** 6.2	**43** 8.4	**46** 8.0	**59** 6.2	**54** 6.8
			69 5.3	**74** 4.9	**61** 6.0	**59** 6.2	**107** 3.4	**85** 4.3
Cost of Sales/Payables			**13** 28.2	**25** 14.5	**23** 15.9	**19** 19.1	**22** 16.4	**23** 15.8
			33 11.2	**32** 11.5	**33** 11.2	**23** 15.7	**33** 10.9	**30** 12.3
			52 7.0	**43** 8.5	**49** 7.4	**35** 10.3	**51** 7.1	**48** 7.6
Sales/Working Capital			5.0	4.5	4.7	5.1	4.5	4.6
			9.0	6.9	11.2	7.2	10.1	8.5
			18.2	19.4	NM	-66.6	27.0	20.6
EBIT/Interest			32.1	62.8	16.8	66.2	16.5	33.7
			(13) 10.6	(31) 10.5	(13) 8.6	(10) 4.2	(117) 7.4	(111) 8.4
			4.3	4.4	7.0	1.3	2.3	3.3
Net Profit + Depr., Dep., Amort./Cur. Mat. L/T/D							12.9	11.9
							(44) 3.2	(42) 4.4
							1.8	2.4
Fixed/Worth			.1	.2	.5	.6	.4	.4
			.2	.6	.8	3.4	.8	.8
			1.0	1.0	2.3	-.5	1.7	1.7
Debt/Worth			.5	.4	.7	.3	.6	.6
			1.4	1.1	1.0	6.5	1.5	1.3
			4.0	2.6	2.2	-2.8	4.1	3.7
% Profit Before Taxes/Tangible Net Worth			55.9	40.5	21.9		52.3	56.7
			(13) 35.0	(32) 28.3	(12) 14.4		(114) 29.4	(116) 29.6
			14.1	16.5	10.4		8.1	11.2
% Profit Before Taxes/Total Assets			20.8	17.8	14.5	11.9	20.6	20.4
			15.8	12.1	6.5	5.5	10.5	11.9
			11.3	9.1	4.4	.0	2.2	4.7
Sales/Net Fixed Assets			36.9	14.6	8.3	10.8	16.9	12.3
			13.3	4.9	3.3	5.1	6.2	6.1
			5.2	3.5	2.0	3.6	3.3	3.5
Sales/Total Assets			2.7	2.4	2.0	1.9	2.5	2.8
			2.4	1.9	1.5	1.6	1.8	1.9
			2.0	1.3	.9	1.0	1.1	1.3
% Depr., Dep., Amort./Sales			.5	.7	2.7		1.0	1.2
			(14) 1.5	2.1	4.4		(111) 2.5	(112) 2.3
			2.4	4.0	6.0		5.0	4.4
% Officers', Directors' Owners' Comp/Sales							1.0	1.1
							(25) 1.9	(28) 1.7
							7.3	6.8
Net Sales ($)	1574M	17234M	186140M	1531816M	1626096M	3163709M	5609599M	6256278M
Total Assets ($)	483M	5074M	80455M	785152M	1036203M	1971441M	3827538M	4017161M

M = $ thousand MM = $ million

See Pages 9 through 22 for Explanation of Ratios and Data

Comparative Historical Data				Current Data Sorted by Sales					
			Type of Statement						
22	20	21	Unqualified			1		2	18
20	15	16	Reviewed				3	5	8
4	7	2	Compiled						2
6	7	2	Tax Returns		1	1			
59	47	39	Other		2		2	9	26
					19 (4/1-9/30/13)		61 (10/1/13-3/31/14)		
4/1/11-3/31/12 ALL	**4/1/12-3/31/13 ALL**	**4/1/13-3/31/14 ALL**		**0-1MM**	**1-3MM**	**3-5MM**	**5-10MM**	**10-25MM**	**25MM & OVER**
111	96	80	**NUMBER OF STATEMENTS**		3	2	5	16	54
%	%	%	**ASSETS**	%	%	%	%	%	%
7.9	8.0	10.5	Cash & Equivalents	DATA NOT AVAILABLE				8.4	9.7
25.0	25.3	23.5	Trade Receivables (net)					30.2	20.7
22.5	21.3	19.5	Inventory					21.3	19.5
2.3	2.1	2.1	All Other Current					1.3	2.2
57.7	56.7	55.7	Total Current					61.2	52.1
30.3	31.6	28.9	Fixed Assets (net)					27.9	30.2
6.2	6.7	8.1	Intangibles (net)					1.1	11.4
5.8	5.0	7.2	All Other Non-Current					9.8	6.4
100.0	100.0	100.0	Total					100.0	100.0
			LIABILITIES						
10.7	9.7	7.9	Notes Payable-Short Term					15.4	6.4
3.7	3.2	2.8	Cur. Mat.-L.T.D.					4.3	2.2
13.7	14.6	13.1	Trade Payables					15.0	12.1
.5	.1	.1	Income Taxes Payable					.0	.1
7.9	7.3	6.9	All Other Current					3.6	8.3
36.5	34.9	30.8	Total Current					38.1	29.0
14.9	16.6	15.3	Long-Term Debt					21.5	13.1
1.1	.5	1.0	Deferred Taxes					.2	1.5
9.4	7.1	4.9	All Other Non-Current					6.6	4.9
38.2	40.9	48.0	Net Worth					33.6	51.6
100.0	100.0	100.0	Total Liabilties & Net Worth					100.0	100.0
			INCOME DATA						
100.0	100.0	100.0	Net Sales					100.0	100.0
32.3	31.3	29.4	Gross Profit					28.9	27.2
24.6	22.1	21.1	Operating Expenses					20.4	19.1
7.7	9.2	8.3	Operating Profit					8.5	8.1
.5	1.2	.9	All Other Expenses (net)					.2	1.2
7.1	8.0	7.4	Profit Before Taxes					8.2	6.9
			RATIOS						
2.5	2.4	3.0						2.5	3.0
1.6	1.6	2.0	Current					1.7	2.0
1.1	1.2	1.2						1.0	1.2
1.4	1.6	1.8						1.7	1.6
.9	.9	1.1	Quick					1.1	1.1
.6	.6	.7						.6	.7
34 10.7	**33** 11.0	**36** 10.1						**42** 8.6	**34** 10.8
43 8.4	**43** 8.5	**47** 7.8	Sales/Receivables					**51** 7.1	**46** 8.0
55 6.6	**55** 6.6	**56** 6.5						**68** 5.4	**54** 6.8
33 11.2	**29** 12.4	**33** 11.0						**30** 12.3	**39** 9.4
56 6.5	**47** 7.8	**53** 6.9	Cost of Sales/Inventory					**51** 7.1	**52** 7.0
87 4.2	**74** 4.9	**70** 5.2						**87** 4.2	**66** 5.5
20 18.7	**20** 17.9	**22** 16.7						**23** 16.1	**22** 16.5
33 11.0	**34** 10.8	**31** 11.6	Cost of Sales/Payables					**32** 11.3	**31** 11.8
49 7.4	**46** 8.0	**45** 8.1						**51** 7.1	**45** 8.1
4.5	5.0	5.0						4.0	5.2
10.7	10.6	7.6	Sales/Working Capital					10.9	7.6
66.8	25.3	22.5						313.9	24.8
20.7	20.4	42.5						40.4	44.4
(98) 6.3	(88) 8.6	(72) 10.1	EBIT/Interest					(15) 4.7	(48) 9.5
2.7	3.0	4.2						4.2	4.4
19.2	8.6	7.6							7.3
(37) 5.4	(20) 4.2	(26) 3.8	Net Profit + Depr., Dep., Amort./Cur. Mat. L/T/D						(22) 3.8
2.2	1.9	1.8							1.9
.4	.3	.2						.1	.3
.9	.9	.7	Fixed/Worth					.7	.7
1.9	1.8	1.5						2.5	1.9
.7	.7	.5						.8	.4
1.7	1.7	1.2	Debt/Worth					1.6	1.1
5.2	4.6	3.1						5.8	2.9
58.7	55.7	42.5						47.7	35.0
(96) 29.1	(84) 30.4	(68) 25.1	% Profit Before Taxes/Tangible Net Worth					(13) 30.2	(45) 22.2
12.6	15.7	13.6						11.2	12.2
19.8	21.0	18.1						20.3	14.8
10.8	10.4	11.7	% Profit Before Taxes/Total Assets					15.4	11.4
3.6	4.9	4.9						3.5	4.6
17.0	20.0	16.0						31.0	14.3
6.4	6.2	6.0	Sales/Net Fixed Assets					8.0	4.9
3.4	2.8	3.6						4.4	3.4
2.8	2.7	2.5						2.5	2.4
1.9	1.9	1.9	Sales/Total Assets					2.0	1.7
1.3	1.2	1.3						1.4	1.2
1.2	1.1	.9						.7	.9
(95) 2.3	(80) 2.5	(74) 2.8	% Depr., Dep., Amort./Sales					(15) 1.6	(50) 3.1
3.9	4.6	4.7						3.1	4.8
1.3	.6	.4							
(22) 2.0	(22) 2.3	(14) 1.3	% Officers', Directors' Owners' Comp/Sales						
5.5	3.8	3.0							
6835639M	**6166336M**	**6526569M**	Net Sales ($)		**6099M**	**8629M**	**37591M**	**276074M**	**6198176M**
4154576M	**4019241M**	**3878808M**	Total Assets ($)		**2626M**	**6311M**	**18907M**	**185907M**	**3665057M**

M = $ thousand MM = $ million

See Pages 9 through 22 for Explanation of Ratios and Data

Current Data Sorted by Assets							Comparative Historical Data	
						Type of Statement		
			3	7	9	Unqualified	32	40
						Reviewed		1
						Compiled	1	1
						Tax Returns		
			1	5	6	Other	10	13
	6 (4/1-9/30/13)		25 (10/1/13-3/31/14)				**4/1/09-3/31/10**	**4/1/10-3/31/11**
0-500M	**500M-2MM**	**2-10MM**	**10-50MM**	**50-100MM**	**100-250MM**		**ALL**	**ALL**
			4	12	15	**NUMBER OF STATEMENTS**	43	55
%	%	%	%	%	%	**ASSETS**	%	%
DATA NOT AVAILABLE	DATA NOT AVAILABLE	DATA NOT AVAILABLE		15.3	10.8	Cash & Equivalents	7.7	7.8
				10.2	13.7	Trade Receivables (net)	6.2	8.7
				10.7	12.0	Inventory	8.1	10.6
				.8	3.4	All Other Current	1.2	3.2
				37.0	39.9	Total Current	23.1	30.3
				56.0	57.4	Fixed Assets (net)	71.1	64.9
				5.2	.1	Intangibles (net)	.6	.7
				1.7	2.6	All Other Non-Current	5.3	4.2
				100.0	100.0	Total	100.0	100.0
						LIABILITIES		
				.0	1.3	Notes Payable-Short Term	2.6	4.3
				4.1	7.4	Cur. Mat.-L.T.D.	5.9	5.4
				6.1	8.0	Trade Payables	5.0	5.7
				.1	.0	Income Taxes Payable	.0	.0
				2.6	7.4	All Other Current	4.1	5.3
				12.9	24.1	Total Current	17.5	20.7
				15.0	17.4	Long-Term Debt	33.5	27.6
				1.5	.1	Deferred Taxes	.0	.0
				.3	3.0	All Other Non-Current	1.6	2.3
				70.3	55.4	Net Worth	47.4	49.4
				100.0	100.0	Total Liabilities & Net Worth	100.0	100.0
						INCOME DATA		
				100.0	100.0	Net Sales	100.0	100.0
				18.8	11.3	Gross Profit	14.4	18.8
				10.0	5.9	Operating Expenses	13.2	11.2
				8.8	5.4	Operating Profit	1.2	7.6
				1.1	.9	All Other Expenses (net)	1.8	1.2
				7.7	4.5	Profit Before Taxes	-.6	6.4
						RATIOS		
				5.0	2.6		2.0	2.7
				2.0	1.7	Current	1.5	1.7
				1.5	1.3		1.1	1.1
				4.4	1.8		1.3	1.6
				1.4	1.0	Quick	.9	.8
				.5	.8		.5	.5
				6 59.3	**7** 51.9		**11** 33.7	**10** 35.3
				11 32.6	**14** 26.9	Sales/Receivables	**15** 24.8	**15** 24.6
				36 10.2	**17** 21.0		**19** 19.0	**22** 16.4
				10 36.4	**10** 34.8		**13** 27.2	**15** 23.7
				13 28.9	**15** 24.3	Cost of Sales/Inventory	**22** 16.6	**23** 15.7
				32 11.3	**22** 16.7		**41** 9.0	**39** 9.4
				7 51.4	**5** 69.8		**5** 73.2	**6** 57.3
				10 37.2	**7** 50.9	Cost of Sales/Payables	**11** 33.6	**10** 37.5
				27 13.7	**18** 20.3		**26** 14.0	**21** 17.7
				5.2	12.1		10.4	9.2
				8.1	17.0	Sales/Working Capital	20.9	13.1
				34.5	65.0		149.2	92.2
				42.1	15.5		4.5	7.9
				(11) 9.8	11.7	EBIT/Interest	(42) 1.8	(53) 4.4
				2.7	2.1		-.5	2.9
						Net Profit + Depr., Dep., Amort./Cur. Mat. L/T/D		
				.6	.8		1.1	1.0
				.9	1.0	Fixed/Worth	1.8	1.4
				1.3	1.3		2.1	1.8
				.2	.5		.7	.5
				.4	.6	Debt/Worth	1.4	1.0
				.7	1.0		2.0	1.6
				29.3	28.2		17.6	26.8
				19.0	18.0	% Profit Before Taxes/Tangible Net Worth	2.1	(54) 17.6
				9.0	14.0		-13.5	9.4
				21.5	17.0		7.4	13.8
				10.0	10.5	% Profit Before Taxes/Total Assets	1.1	9.4
				3.8	3.1		-4.2	3.4
				5.5	5.5		2.0	2.7
				3.3	3.2	Sales/Net Fixed Assets	1.6	2.0
				2.7	2.7		1.3	1.5
				2.6	2.8		1.5	1.6
				2.1	2.1	Sales/Total Assets	1.2	1.3
				1.8	2.0		1.0	1.2
				2.4	1.4		3.6	3.2
				(10) 2.5	(11) 2.1	% Depr., Dep., Amort./Sales	(36) 4.8	(49) 4.5
				3.2	2.5		6.1	5.1
						% Officers', Directors' Owners' Comp/Sales		
			662876M	**1591576M**	**11087613M**	Net Sales ($)	**5965772M**	**10783174M**
			152302M	**857207M**	**2345007M**	Total Assets ($)	**4515816M**	**5659212M**

M = $ thousand MM = $ million

See Pages 9 through 22 for Explanation of Ratios and Data

Comparative Historical Data				Current Data Sorted by Sales					
			Type of Statement						
41	29	19	Unqualified					1	18
			Reviewed						
	1		Compiled						
			Tax Returns						
21	22	12	Other				1		11
4/1/11-3/31/12 ALL	4/1/12-3/31/13 ALL	4/1/13-3/31/14 ALL		6 (4/1-9/30/13)			25 (10/1/13-3/31/14)		
				0-1MM	1-3MM	3-5MM	5-10MM	10-25MM	25MM & OVER
62	52	31	**NUMBER OF STATEMENTS**				1	1	29
%	%	%	**ASSETS**	%	%	%	%	%	%
9.3	5.9	12.6	Cash & Equivalents	DATA NOT AVAILABLE	DATA NOT AVAILABLE	DATA NOT AVAILABLE			12.6
8.7	9.6	11.8	Trade Receivables (net)						12.6
12.4	13.5	11.6	Inventory						12.4
2.4	2.5	2.4	All Other Current						2.6
32.8	31.4	38.4	Total Current						40.1
63.6	64.2	57.1	Fixed Assets (net)						56.7
.7	.5	2.1	Intangibles (net)						.7
2.9	3.8	2.4	All Other Non-Current						2.5
100.0	100.0	100.0	Total						100.0
			LIABILITIES						
2.5	5.2	.7	Notes Payable-Short Term						.7
6.0	3.5	5.1	Cur. Mat.-L.T.D.						5.4
5.6	6.4	7.3	Trade Payables						7.6
.0	.0	.0	Income Taxes Payable						.0
5.4	4.6	7.0	All Other Current						7.4
19.5	19.7	20.1	Total Current						21.1
24.3	23.1	16.1	Long-Term Debt						15.3
.1	.3	1.0	Deferred Taxes						.7
2.9	3.5	1.7	All Other Non-Current						1.8
53.1	53.4	61.0	Net Worth						61.1
100.0	100.0	100.0	Total Liabilties & Net Worth						100.0
			INCOME DATA						
100.0	100.0	100.0	Net Sales						100.0
14.3	7.5	16.5	Gross Profit						15.1
7.8	8.0	8.7	Operating Expenses						8.6
6.5	-.5	7.8	Operating Profit						6.6
1.1	.7	.7	All Other Expenses (net)						.9
5.4	-1.2	7.1	Profit Before Taxes						5.7
			RATIOS						
2.4	2.2	3.3							3.4
1.9	1.7	1.8	Current						1.8
1.5	1.2	1.4							1.4
1.3	1.0	2.6							2.6
1.1	.7	1.1	Quick						1.0
.7	.5	.7							.7
8 46.3	**6** 66.0	**7** 54.8							**7** 53.3
11 33.2	**12** 31.3	**11** 32.0	Sales/Receivables						**12** 31.4
17 21.4	**17** 21.7	**17** 21.0							**18** 20.3
14 26.8	**12** 30.4	**10** 34.8							**11** 34.2
19 19.2	**17** 22.0	**14** 26.9	Cost of Sales/Inventory						**15** 24.3
29 12.5	**32** 11.4	**22** 16.5							**23** 16.2
5 79.1	**5** 77.3	**6** 63.2							**5** 66.5
8 47.7	**7** 54.6	**9** 38.7	Cost of Sales/Payables						**9** 39.8
11 32.9	**12** 30.3	**21** 17.2							**18** 20.8
10.3	14.3	7.5							7.8
15.7	23.0	17.0	Sales/Working Capital						20.0
25.3	53.9	38.4							38.4
9.6	2.1	16.0							16.4
(60) 6.7	(49) .0	(29) 10.7	EBIT/Interest						(27) 10.9
3.0	-2.8	3.3							2.7
3.5									
(10) 2.8			Net Profit + Depr., Dep., Amort./Cur. Mat. L/T/D						
.9									
.9	1.0	.8							.7
1.3	1.3	1.0	Fixed/Worth						.9
1.7	1.8	1.3							1.3
.4	.4	.3							.2
.9	1.0	.6	Debt/Worth						.6
1.7	1.2	1.0							.9
27.6	4.3	29.0							29.7
19.9	-3.3	20.4	% Profit Before Taxes/Tangible Net Worth						20.4
13.9	-10.9	14.0							14.2
15.6	2.4	20.8							21.9
11.5	-2.3	11.8	% Profit Before Taxes/Total Assets						12.4
6.5	-6.3	4.5							4.0
4.1	4.5	5.8							5.8
2.9	3.0	3.3	Sales/Net Fixed Assets						3.5
2.3	2.4	2.7							2.8
2.5	2.7	2.8							2.9
2.1	2.0	2.2	Sales/Total Assets						2.2
1.7	1.8	1.9							2.0
2.2	1.9	1.8							1.8
(52) 2.5	(40) 2.5	(25) 2.5	% Depr., Dep., Amort./Sales						(23) 2.4
3.3	3.2	2.8							2.6
			% Officers', Directors' Owners' Comp/Sales						
19494983M	**18060918M**	**13342065M**	Net Sales ($)				**7734M**	**19056M**	**13315275M**
7084768M	**5659505M**	**3354516M**	Total Assets ($)				**25113M**	**98776M**	**3230627M**

M = $ thousand MM = $ million

See Pages 9 through 22 for Explanation of Ratios and Data

Current Data Sorted by Assets							Comparative Historical Data	
						Type of Statement		
		2	18	30	16	Unqualified	72	69
		6	9			Reviewed	23	17
		6	1			Compiled	12	8
		3				Tax Returns	6	8
2	4	10	13	8	12	Other	50	49
	22 (4/1-9/30/13)		118 (10/1/13-3/31/14)				**4/1/09-3/31/10**	**4/1/10-3/31/11**
0-500M	**500M-2MM**	**2-10MM**	**10-50MM**	**50-100MM**	**100-250MM**		**ALL**	**ALL**
2	4	27	41	38	28	**NUMBER OF STATEMENTS**	163	151
%	%	%	%	%	%	**ASSETS**	%	%
		6.4	8.2	9.1	10.1	Cash & Equivalents	8.8	9.2
		29.8	19.6	12.4	11.9	Trade Receivables (net)	18.0	19.0
		29.7	22.8	14.3	12.5	Inventory	17.2	17.1
		.9	3.2	2.9	3.0	All Other Current	2.6	3.7
		66.8	53.8	38.6	37.4	Total Current	46.6	48.9
		27.7	33.5	50.4	47.3	Fixed Assets (net)	42.8	39.7
		1.3	10.7	2.1	10.0	Intangibles (net)	4.9	5.7
		4.1	1.9	8.8	5.3	All Other Non-Current	5.7	5.7
		100.0	100.0	100.0	100.0	Total	100.0	100.0
						LIABILITIES		
		11.9	5.3	1.7	2.2	Notes Payable-Short Term	5.9	6.8
		2.4	3.7	3.8	5.5	Cur. Mat.-L.T.D.	4.1	3.8
		20.0	9.9	10.4	7.0	Trade Payables	12.2	12.3
		.0	.2	.0	1.1	Income Taxes Payable	.2	.2
		7.7	7.2	4.4	6.4	All Other Current	6.6	8.0
		42.1	26.3	20.3	22.2	Total Current	28.8	31.0
		6.6	14.7	10.9	19.8	Long-Term Debt	19.4	17.2
		.5	1.7	.3	1.6	Deferred Taxes	.6	.8
		6.5	5.8	4.9	4.7	All Other Non-Current	5.3	6.4
		44.2	51.5	63.6	51.8	Net Worth	45.9	44.4
		100.0	100.0	100.0	100.0	Total Liabilties & Net Worth	100.0	100.0
						INCOME DATA		
		100.0	100.0	100.0	100.0	Net Sales	100.0	100.0
		31.3	27.8	13.3	19.2	Gross Profit	22.3	25.1
		24.9	20.0	8.9	10.2	Operating Expenses	18.3	18.3
		6.5	7.8	4.4	9.0	Operating Profit	4.0	6.8
		.5	1.6	.1	1.5	All Other Expenses (net)	1.3	.9
		6.0	6.2	4.3	7.5	Profit Before Taxes	2.8	5.8
						RATIOS		
		2.7	3.0	2.8	2.6		2.5	2.8
		1.5	2.1	1.9	1.9	Current	1.7	1.9
		1.0	1.6	1.4	1.3		1.2	1.2
		1.5	1.8	1.5	1.5		1.4	1.6
		.9	1.1	1.1	1.1	Quick	.9	1.0
		.5	.6	.6	.8		.6	.6
		31 11.8	**25** 14.8	**12** 29.5	**10** 37.4		**19** 19.3	**17** 21.1
		40 9.2	**39** 9.4	**18** 20.7	**21** 17.1	Sales/Receivables	**37** 9.8	**40** 9.2
		49 7.5	**48** 7.6	**40** 9.1	**51** 7.2		**51** 7.1	**53** 6.9
		40 9.2	**38** 9.5	**14** 26.2	**15** 25.0		**24** 15.1	**24** 15.1
		57 6.4	**64** 5.7	**25** 14.5	**23** 15.7	Cost of Sales/Inventory	**43** 8.5	**40** 9.1
		85 4.3	**104** 3.5	**45** 8.1	**51** 7.1		**70** 5.2	**69** 5.3
		17 21.8	**12** 29.7	**6** 56.8	**7** 55.2		**15** 25.1	**12** 30.0
		37 9.9	**30** 12.2	**21** 17.2	**23** 16.2	Cost of Sales/Payables	**28** 13.0	**27** 13.7
		66 5.5	**38** 9.6	**35** 10.4	**29** 12.6		**47** 7.8	**41** 8.8
		5.6	5.2	7.2	6.2		4.9	5.2
		17.0	7.8	14.0	13.1	Sales/Working Capital	9.9	9.1
		127.2	18.3	22.1	23.4		30.4	22.3
		52.1	22.3	33.4	26.6		10.8	18.8
		(22) 13.8	(36) 6.7	(35) 17.5	11.6	EBIT/Interest	(153) 4.7	(139) 7.8
		3.7	2.4	2.3	3.2		.7	2.7
			14.8		30.1		9.7	14.8
			(17) 3.4		(10) 6.5	Net Profit + Depr., Dep., Amort./Cur. Mat. L/T/D	(42) 3.7	(38) 4.1
			2.2		2.7		1.6	2.0
		.3	.4	.6	.8		.4	.4
		.6	.8	.8	1.1	Fixed/Worth	1.0	.9
		1.3	1.9	1.1	2.4		2.2	1.6
		.4	.4	.2	.5		.5	.5
		1.1	1.0	.5	1.2	Debt/Worth	1.1	1.0
		3.8	3.9	.8	3.4		3.4	2.7
		72.3	60.1	29.1	38.3		29.1	38.0
		(24) 45.4	(36) 29.8	(37) 20.0	(25) 25.2	% Profit Before Taxes/Tangible Net Worth	(149) 13.1	(137) 19.3
		18.7	3.7	6.0	13.6		-1.0	8.4
		33.3	19.2	17.3	18.4		11.3	18.9
		16.8	9.9	12.0	11.3	% Profit Before Taxes/Total Assets	6.2	8.8
		4.8	1.8	3.0	6.3		-.8	3.4
		29.1	12.5	5.7	6.0		13.9	14.2
		12.3	5.9	4.0	4.0	Sales/Net Fixed Assets	3.5	4.4
		6.0	3.4	3.0	2.6		1.8	2.1
		3.8	2.7	2.3	2.2		2.1	2.1
		2.6	1.8	2.1	1.8	Sales/Total Assets	1.4	1.5
		2.1	1.2	1.7	1.3		1.1	1.2
		.5	1.3	2.0	2.3		1.4	1.3
		(24) 1.0	(36) 3.1	2.6	(20) 2.6	% Depr., Dep., Amort./Sales	(139) 3.6	(129) 3.5
		2.0	4.7	3.6	2.8		5.7	5.0
		1.4					1.0	.9
		(10) 3.1				% Officers', Directors' Owners' Comp/Sales	(34) 2.4	(24) 3.4
		4.7					5.2	5.3
313M	18272M	395513M	2145322M	5894435M	7207759M	Net Sales ($)	10966745M	11509455M
315M	5540M	139402M	1021666M	2848193M	4105512M	Total Assets ($)	8233160M	7839544M

M = $ thousand MM = $ million

See Pages 9 through 22 for Explanation of Ratios and Data

Comparative Historical Data				Current Data Sorted by Sales					
			Type of Statement						
70	57	66	Unqualified				1	4	61
18	19	15	Reviewed				2	9	4
8	6	7	Compiled				1	5	1
6	5	3	Tax Returns			1	1	1	
58	51	49	Other	2	3		5	10	29
4/1/11-3/31/12 ALL	**4/1/12-3/31/13 ALL**	**4/1/13-3/31/14 ALL**		**22 (4/1-9/30/13)**			**118 (10/1/13-3/31/14)**		
				0-1MM	**1-3MM**	**3-5MM**	**5-10MM**	**10-25MM**	**25MM & OVER**
160	138	140	**NUMBER OF STATEMENTS**	2	3	1	10	29	95
%	%	%	**ASSETS**	%	%	%	%	%	%
8.7	7.0	8.6	Cash & Equivalents				11.4	6.9	8.8
17.7	18.1	18.0	Trade Receivables (net)				22.7	26.0	15.3
20.0	23.0	19.5	Inventory				25.3	26.5	17.1
2.4	2.7	2.6	All Other Current				3.9	1.7	2.8
48.9	50.9	48.8	Total Current				63.3	61.1	44.1
39.5	40.1	39.3	Fixed Assets (net)				23.9	28.0	44.5
6.2	4.4	6.6	Intangibles (net)				7.2	5.2	6.5
5.4	4.7	5.4	All Other Non-Current				5.5	5.7	5.0
100.0	100.0	100.0	Total				100.0	100.0	100.0
			LIABILITIES						
5.1	4.6	4.9	Notes Payable-Short Term				1.1	10.9	3.4
3.5	3.9	3.8	Cur. Mat.-L.T.D.				2.5	2.8	4.3
12.9	11.4	11.7	Trade Payables				18.9	14.7	10.1
.2	.3	.3	Income Taxes Payable				.0	.2	.3
7.2	7.1	6.3	All Other Current				17.2	5.7	5.4
28.9	27.3	27.0	Total Current				39.6	34.3	23.5
17.5	18.2	13.1	Long-Term Debt				4.4	8.9	14.9
.9	.9	1.0	Deferred Taxes				.0	1.7	1.0
6.8	3.9	6.1	All Other Non-Current				13.1	5.7	4.0
45.9	49.7	52.8	Net Worth				42.9	49.3	56.7
100.0	100.0	100.0	Total Liabilities & Net Worth				100.0	100.0	100.0
			INCOME DATA						
100.0	100.0	100.0	Net Sales				100.0	100.0	100.0
22.4	19.7	23.3	Gross Profit				34.6	37.8	16.8
16.1	14.8	15.8	Operating Expenses				32.3	28.1	10.3
6.3	5.0	7.4	Operating Profit				2.4	9.7	6.5
.7	.9	1.4	All Other Expenses (net)				2.8	.6	.8
5.6	4.0	6.0	Profit Before Taxes				-.4	9.1	5.7
			RATIOS						
2.8	3.0	2.8					3.6	2.3	2.8
1.8	1.9	1.9	Current				2.0	1.9	2.0
1.3	1.4	1.3					1.0	1.2	1.4
1.6	1.5	1.6					2.0	1.5	1.6
.9	.9	1.0	Quick				1.0	1.0	1.1
.6	.6	.6					.4	.6	.7
15 24.4	**15** 23.8	**17** 22.0					**29** 12.6	**31** 11.8	**13** 29.0
36 10.0	**29** 12.4	**31** 11.6	Sales/Receivables				**45** 8.2	**40** 9.2	**22** 16.7
52 7.0	**45** 8.1	**48** 7.6					**50** 7.3	**52** 7.0	**46** 8.0
21 17.3	**22** 16.6	**20** 18.6					**20** 18.1	**41** 8.8	**15** 24.7
41 9.0	**46** 8.0	**43** 8.5	Cost of Sales/Inventory				**78** 4.7	**83** 4.4	**34** 10.7
81 4.5	**79** 4.6	**81** 4.5					**104** 3.5	**118** 3.1	**54** 6.7
10 35.4	**12** 31.4	**11** 34.2					**19** 19.6	**14** 25.9	**7** 49.1
25 14.6	**20** 17.9	**26** 13.8	Cost of Sales/Payables				**45** 8.1	**40** 9.2	**23** 15.9
44 8.3	**35** 10.4	**39** 9.3					**114** 3.2	**60** 6.1	**32** 11.4
5.3	5.7	5.9					3.6	4.3	6.5
10.2	12.1	12.1	Sales/Working Capital				8.8	7.8	12.4
22.7	25.7	22.8					NM	44.9	22.3
29.9	21.8	29.6						43.3	27.7
(150) 8.6	(129) 5.1	(125) 10.9	EBIT/Interest					(23) 19.0	(92) 11.6
2.6	-.3	3.2						3.9	2.8
13.1	6.6	12.2						11.8	17.7
(39) 3.5	(38) 2.2	(42) 4.1	Net Profit + Depr., Dep., Amort./Cur. Mat. L/T/D					(12) 4.1	(29) 4.6
1.9	.8	2.1						2.8	2.0
.4	.4	.5					.1	.4	.6
.9	.9	.8	Fixed/Worth				.5	.7	.9
1.7	1.4	1.5					NM	1.3	1.5
.4	.4	.4					.3	.5	.3
1.1	.9	.8	Debt/Worth				1.0	1.0	.6
3.2	1.9	2.6					NM	2.8	2.3
38.3	36.1	48.2						72.5	37.3
(137) 20.6	(130) 10.8	(127) 25.2	% Profit Before Taxes/Tangible Net Worth					(27) 46.4	(88) 22.7
12.7	-3.0	7.6						23.4	6.4
17.3	13.8	19.3					17.7	33.1	18.0
10.7	5.9	12.1	% Profit Before Taxes/Total Assets				1.2	17.1	11.6
4.2	-1.3	3.6					-9.1	6.6	3.7
14.5	12.0	11.1					64.2	15.2	7.8
4.6	4.9	5.5	Sales/Net Fixed Assets				15.9	7.6	4.5
2.8	3.3	3.2					3.9	5.0	3.0
2.4	2.7	2.7					3.4	2.8	2.6
1.9	2.0	2.0	Sales/Total Assets				2.2	2.0	2.1
1.4	1.6	1.4					.9	1.2	1.6
1.5	1.7	1.7						.7	1.9
(136) 2.5	(115) 2.6	(121) 2.5	% Depr., Dep., Amort./Sales					(27) 1.8	(85) 2.6
3.9	3.7	3.5						2.7	3.7
1.2	1.6	1.3							
(25) 2.4	(22) 3.2	(14) 1.8	% Officers', Directors' Owners' Comp/Sales						
3.6	5.0	4.4							
16300553M	**15330664M**	**15661614M**	Net Sales ($)	**313M**	**5614M**	**4853M**	**69592M**	**485498M**	**15095744M**
9142768M	**7715121M**	**8120628M**	Total Assets ($)	**315M**	**5334M**	**2097M**	**52387M**	**328024M**	**7732471M**

 M = $ thousand MM = $ million

See Pages 9 through 22 for Explanation of Ratios and Data

Current Data Sorted by Assets							Comparative Historical Data	
						Type of Statement		
		6	19	1	7	Unqualified	52	52
		18	13			Reviewed	42	45
	5	5				Compiled	17	15
4	4	5	1			Tax Returns	16	14
1	6	21	33	9	12	Other	87	86
	22 (4/1-9/30/13)		148 (10/1/13-3/31/14)				4/1/09-3/31/10	4/1/10-3/31/11
0-500M	**500M-2MM**	**2-10MM**	**10-50MM**	**50-100MM**	**100-250MM**		**ALL**	**ALL**
5	15	55	66	10	19	**NUMBER OF STATEMENTS**	214	212
%	%	%	%	%	%	**ASSETS**	%	%
	16.1	10.4	6.2	5.7	9.0	Cash & Equivalents	7.4	7.2
	28.0	26.9	25.0	20.2	22.9	Trade Receivables (net)	25.8	27.6
	23.8	25.4	26.6	22.3	18.6	Inventory	24.6	25.9
	3.9	1.6	2.6	2.6	2.5	All Other Current	2.9	2.5
	71.8	64.3	60.5	50.9	53.0	Total Current	60.7	63.2
	23.5	29.0	31.3	25.7	31.1	Fixed Assets (net)	29.3	27.1
	2.8	2.3	4.8	15.7	10.8	Intangibles (net)	5.0	5.7
	2.0	4.5	3.3	7.7	5.1	All Other Non-Current	5.0	4.1
	100.0	100.0	100.0	100.0	100.0	Total	100.0	100.0
						LIABILITIES		
	8.0	7.8	12.1	4.0	4.8	Notes Payable-Short Term	13.4	10.3
	2.7	3.7	2.1	1.3	2.4	Cur. Mat.-L.T.D.	3.8	2.8
	11.5	16.2	16.7	12.5	14.2	Trade Payables	16.8	17.3
	.1	.1	.1	.8	.1	Income Taxes Payable	.3	.1
	10.5	8.1	6.1	6.6	16.4	All Other Current	6.7	9.2
	32.8	35.9	37.2	25.2	38.0	Total Current	41.0	39.7
	18.2	15.5	14.0	19.3	23.0	Long-Term Debt	14.8	13.8
	.0	.3	.9	2.7	3.7	Deferred Taxes	.7	.7
	.2	7.7	3.9	12.2	5.3	All Other Non-Current	7.5	7.0
	48.8	40.5	44.0	40.5	30.1	Net Worth	36.0	38.8
	100.0	100.0	100.0	100.0	100.0	Total Liabilties & Net Worth	100.0	100.0
						INCOME DATA		
	100.0	100.0	100.0	100.0	100.0	Net Sales	100.0	100.0
	32.1	29.9	20.4	18.9	18.4	Gross Profit	25.3	25.9
	29.8	23.1	15.3	11.2	11.0	Operating Expenses	21.1	19.9
	2.3	6.8	5.1	7.7	7.4	Operating Profit	4.2	6.0
	-.9	.7	.8	1.2	2.1	All Other Expenses (net)	1.0	1.0
	3.2	6.1	4.3	6.5	5.3	Profit Before Taxes	3.1	4.9
						RATIOS		
	4.4	3.4	2.6	2.7	2.9		2.5	2.5
	2.2	2.0	1.6	1.9	1.6	Current	1.6	1.7
	1.3	1.3	1.2	1.5	1.4		1.1	1.1
	2.7	2.2	1.4	1.8	1.7		1.5	1.6
	1.1	1.0	.8	.8	.9	Quick	.8	.9
	.6	.6	.5	.6	.6		.5	.5
	24 15.1	**30** 12.0	**30** 12.1	**34** 10.8	**35** 10.3		**36** 10.1	**38** 9.6
	37 9.9	**42** 8.7	**41** 9.0	**39** 9.4	**45** 8.1	Sales/Receivables	**47** 7.8	**47** 7.8
	41 8.8	**51** 7.1	**53** 6.9	**63** 5.8	**59** 6.2		**57** 6.5	**56** 6.5
	6 58.8	**30** 12.3	**42** 8.6	**38** 9.7	**29** 12.4		**36** 10.0	**38** 9.6
	25 14.5	**55** 6.6	**57** 6.4	**57** 6.4	**47** 7.7	Cost of Sales/Inventory	**55** 6.6	**58** 6.2
	85 4.3	**85** 4.3	**83** 4.4	**73** 5.0	**70** 5.2		**83** 4.4	**84** 4.4
	8 44.5	**18** 20.2	**19** 19.2	**19** 18.8	**21** 17.1		**22** 16.3	**24** 15.5
	15 24.0	**33** 11.0	**32** 11.3	**29** 12.8	**39** 9.3	Cost of Sales/Payables	**36** 10.0	**36** 10.2
	34 10.6	**44** 8.3	**48** 7.6	**39** 9.3	**45** 8.1		**49** 7.4	**51** 7.1
	4.1	5.2	6.0	5.1	4.7		5.4	5.5
	8.2	7.3	10.2	8.0	8.6	Sales/Working Capital	11.8	9.4
	14.3	17.5	23.5	9.9	14.9		77.2	29.8
	10.9	32.0	22.5	26.3	24.4		11.1	17.1
	(13) 4.1	(46) 7.1	(65) 7.2	9.5	(16) 6.0	EBIT/Interest	(196) 4.0	(189) 6.0
	2.8	1.6	2.7	3.6	3.4		1.0	2.0
			21.0				5.3	11.6
			(17) 3.8			Net Profit + Depr., Dep., Amort./Cur. Mat. L/T/D	(48) 2.4	(60) 5.3
			1.6				.8	2.1
	.1	.3	.4	.6	.4		.3	.3
	.3	.6	.8	.9	1.4	Fixed/Worth	.7	.7
	1.9	1.8	1.5	-1.3	-4.6		2.1	2.3
	.3	.5	.6	.9	.9		.6	.7
	.9	1.1	1.5	2.0	3.1	Debt/Worth	1.9	1.7
	2.8	3.6	3.6	-7.5	-13.6		5.8	7.1
	48.8	61.2	35.4		42.3		40.0	54.8
	(14) 11.8	(46) 29.6	(61) 17.4		(12) 22.0	% Profit Before Taxes/Tangible Net Worth	(187) 18.4	(182) 24.7
	5.2	10.8	6.8		14.7		5.3	8.7
	18.5	27.6	14.7	17.2	12.8		12.6	16.9
	5.0	10.7	6.9	8.6	9.8	% Profit Before Taxes/Total Assets	5.5	7.9
	3.7	1.7	2.2	5,4	5.0		.0	2.4
	94.6	35.5	11.2	12.3	9.6		18.7	19.4
	19.8	7.7	7.0	7.2	5.2	Sales/Net Fixed Assets	6.5	7.0
	5.0	3.9	4.3	3.6	3.9		4.2	4.5
	4.6	3.1	2.5	2.0	2.0		2.7	2.7
	2.6	2.2	2.0	1.5	1.7	Sales/Total Assets	1.9	2.1
	1.7	1.7	1.7	1.1	1.2		1.4	1.5
	1.4	1.2	1.1		1.3		1.1	1.3
	(11) 1.7	(45) 2.3	(64) 1.9		(11) 2.4	% Depr., Dep., Amort./Sales	(181) 2.5	(178) 2.3
	3.4	3.1	3.0		3.2		4.5	3.9
	4.1	1.5	1.1				1.7	1.3
	(10) 6.6	(15) 3.0	(11) 1.5			% Officers', Directors' Owners' Comp/Sales	(57) 3.7	(59) 3.4
	8.9	8.4	3.1				8.0	7.0
6160M	**51828M**	**684558M**	**3291411M**	**1258347M**	**6131005M**	Net Sales ($)	**11283485M**	**11989088M**
1227M	**17877M**	**292804M**	**1465913M**	**707996M**	**3202316M**	Total Assets ($)	**6707986M**	**6706966M**

M = $ thousand MM = $ million

See Pages 9 through 22 for Explanation of Ratios and Data

Comparative Historical Data				Current Data Sorted by Sales					
			Type of Statement						
59	38	33	Unqualified				5	2	26
47	37	31	Reviewed				13	9	9
16	11	10	Compiled		5	2	2		1
15	9	14	Tax Returns	2	3	2	4	1	2
90	81	82	Other	1	2	4	9	20	46
4/1/11-3/31/12 ALL	**4/1/12-3/31/13 ALL**	**4/1/13-3/31/14 ALL**		22 (4/1-9/30/13)			148 (10/1/13-3/31/14)		
				0-1MM	**1-3MM**	**3-5MM**	**5-10MM**	**10-25MM**	**25MM & OVER**
227	176	170	**NUMBER OF STATEMENTS**	3	10	8	33	32	84
%	%	%	**ASSETS**	%	%	%	%	%	%
9.4	8.7	9.6	Cash & Equivalents		20.0		10.3	9.5	7.3
26.3	25.3	25.4	Trade Receivables (net)		14.4		23.6	25.0	26.6
25.0	25.9	24.4	Inventory		18.7		27.3	24.6	24.4
2.4	2.2	2.3	All Other Current		1.4		1.8	1.5	2.8
63.2	62.0	61.7	Total Current		54.6		63.0	60.6	61.1
26.7	29.8	29.1	Fixed Assets (net)		35.7		30.3	31.3	28.1
4.7	3.9	5.0	Intangibles (net)		4.2		2.8	4.7	6.7
5.3	4.3	4.2	All Other Non-Current		5.5		3.9	3.4	4.1
100.0	100.0	100.0	Total		100.0		100.0	100.0	100.0
			LIABILITIES						
9.3	9.5	9.3	Notes Payable-Short Term		10.7		7.2	10.6	9.1
3.8	3.1	2.8	Cur. Mat.-L.T.D.		4.5		3.9	2.8	2.0
16.7	15.4	15.5	Trade Payables		3.6		12.4	15.6	17.5
.1	.2	.1	Income Taxes Payable		.0		.1	.1	.2
10.1	11.4	8.4	All Other Current		4.5		11.6	6.3	8.6
40.1	39.7	36.2	Total Current		23.3		35.2	35.4	37.3
14.4	13.7	16.0	Long-Term Debt		22.4		13.5	18.7	15.3
.9	1.1	1.0	Deferred Taxes		.0		.1	.6	1.8
6.1	6.5	5.4	All Other Non-Current		.1		3.4	3.5	6.0
38.4	39.0	41.4	Net Worth		54.1		47.8	41.8	39.7
100.0	100.0	100.0	Total Liabilties & Net Worth		100.0		100.0	100.0	100.0
			INCOME DATA						
100.0	100.0	100.0	Net Sales		100.0		100.0	100.0	100.0
26.4	24.8	25.1	Gross Profit		38.8		28.9	27.3	19.5
20.3	18.5	19.2	Operating Expenses		34.9		22.0	22.4	13.0
6.1	6.3	5.9	Operating Profit		4.0		6.9	4.9	6.5
1.0	.8	.8	All Other Expenses (net)		-1.5		.5	.7	1.1
5.1	5.5	5.1	Profit Before Taxes		5.5		6.4	4.2	5.4
			RATIOS						
3.0	3.0	2.9			7.2		3.1	2.9	2.8
1.7	1.7	1.8	Current		2.4		2.1	1.4	1.8
1.3	1.3	1.3			1.0		1.3	1.1	1.4
1.8	1.6	1.9			3.2		1.9	2.1	1.5
.9	.9	.9	Quick		1.5		1.0	.7	.9
.6	.5	.6			.7		.5	.5	.6
33 11.1	**33** 10.9	**30** 12.1			**0** UND		**26** 14.1	**31** 11.9	**33** 10.9
42 8.6	**41** 8.8	**41** 9.0	Sales/Receivables		**27** 13.7		**40** 9.1	**45** 8.2	**42** 8.7
56 6.5	**52** 7.0	**51** 7.1			**38** 9.5		**47** 7.7	**60** 6.1	**54** 6.8
36 10.1	**37** 9.9	**32** 11.5			**0** UND		**31** 11.9	**41** 9.0	**35** 10.5
56 6.5	**54** 6.8	**54** 6.8	Cost of Sales/Inventory		**13** 27.1		**70** 5.2	**69** 5.3	**52** 7.0
78 4.7	**83** 4.4	**81** 4.5			**94** 3.9		**94** 3.9	**91** 4.0	**69** 5.3
22 16.7	**17** 21.4	**18** 20.8			**0** UND		**14** 26.1	**19** 19.1	**21** 17.0
33 10.9	**31** 11.9	**32** 11.3	Cost of Sales/Payables		**7** 54.4		**31** 11.7	**35** 10.5	**33** 11.2
49 7.4	**47** 7.8	**45** 8.1			**23** 15.6		**43** 8.4	**47** 7.7	**45** 8.2
4.6	4.8	5.4			2.4		5.6	5.9	5.4
8.5	9.1	8.5	Sales/Working Capital		7.9		7.0	9.9	9.0
21.6	20.5	19.1			NM		19.5	35.7	17.7
22.7	23.8	25.8					32.5	19.4	32.3
(205) 6.7	(154) 7.1	(154) 6.8	EBIT/Interest				(28) 5.5	(29) 4.5	(79) 8.0
2.6	2.6	2.7					1.4	2.2	3.2
8.5	11.7	12.9							18.1
(71) 3.8	(53) 3.8	(32) 3.8	Net Profit + Depr., Dep., Amort./Cur. Mat. L/T/D						(25) 3.8
1.1	2.2	1.9							2.0
.3	.4	.3			.1		.2	.4	.4
.7	.7	.7	Fixed/Worth		.8		.5	1.0	.7
1.8	1.4	1.8			2.8		1.3	1.8	2.1
.7	.7	.5			.2		.4	.6	.6
1.6	1.3	1.5	Debt/Worth		.6		.9	2.0	1.9
4.4	3.5	4.0			5.0		2.9	4.1	4.7
45.0	47.3	45.0					43.1	40.4	45.5
(203) 22.3	(156) 23.1	(144) 21.0	% Profit Before Taxes/Tangible Net Worth				(29) 19.9	(29) 17.6	(69) 23.5
10.1	10.2	9.4					7.3	6.5	10.8
15.3	17.8	18.4			31.2		24.6	16.3	16.5
8.3	9.4	8.2	% Profit Before Taxes/Total Assets		4.6		10.6	5.0	8.4
2.8	2.5	2.3			-4.6		.8	2.0	3.5
19.2	13.7	18.4			60.1		37.0	8.8	14.3
8.7	7.8	7.6	Sales/Net Fixed Assets		12.4		12.2	6.3	7.7
5.1	4.3	4.3			3.1		3.4	3.9	4.6
2.8	2.9	2.9			5.3		3.1	2.3	2.9
2.1	2.1	2.0	Sales/Total Assets		2.1		2.2	1.7	2.0
1.5	1.5	1.6			1.5		1.7	1.5	1.6
1.0	1.1	1.1					1.2	1.9	.9
(192) 1.7	(156) 1.8	(145) 2.0	% Depr., Dep., Amort./Sales				(27) 2.3	(28) 2.3	(72) 1.5
3.4	3.3	3.0					3.4	2.8	2.7
1.7	1.5	1.5					2.1		
(57) 3.2	(43) 3.7	(39) 4.1	% Officers', Directors' Owners' Comp/Sales				(11) 4.3		
5.2	6.6	7.7					10.2		
14360501M	**12560570M**	**11423309M**	Net Sales ($)	**2327M**	**21679M**	**31435M**	**243995M**	**573416M**	**10550457M**
7384258M	**6482924M**	**5688133M**	Total Assets ($)	**988M**	**10943M**	**14082M**	**133912M**	**310483M**	**5217725M**

M = $ thousand MM = $ million

See Pages 9 through 22 for Explanation of Ratios and Data

Current Data Sorted by Assets							Comparative Historical Data	
						Type of Statement		
	1	1	4	3	2	Unqualified	17	15
		3	2			Reviewed	13	15
	2	1				Compiled	4	7
	1	2				Tax Returns	3	4
1	1	4	3	1	2	Other	10	16
	8 (4/1-9/30/13)		26 (10/1/13-3/31/14)				4/1/09-3/31/10 ALL	4/1/10-3/31/11 ALL
0-500M	500M-2MM	2-10MM	10-50MM	50-100MM	100-250MM			
1	5	11	9	4	4	**NUMBER OF STATEMENTS**	47	57
%	%	%	%	%	%	**ASSETS**	%	%
		7.4				Cash & Equivalents	8.5	8.6
		22.7				Trade Receivables (net)	25.4	21.5
		35.0				Inventory	31.4	27.0
		3.3				All Other Current	1.6	3.4
		68.4				Total Current	66.9	60.4
		23.5				Fixed Assets (net)	25.4	31.6
		1.5				Intangibles (net)	2.8	2.7
		6.6				All Other Non-Current	5.0	5.3
		100.0				Total	100.0	100.0
						LIABILITIES		
		5.5				Notes Payable-Short Term	16.0	11.2
		4.4				Cur. Mat.-L.T.D.	3.5	4.2
		17.9				Trade Payables	18.5	12.7
		.4				Income Taxes Payable	.5	.6
		6.8				All Other Current	7.9	7.6
		35.0				Total Current	46.4	36.2
		18.4				Long-Term Debt	13.5	19.9
		1.1				Deferred Taxes	.9	.6
		11.5				All Other Non-Current	2.5	3.8
		34.1				Net Worth	36.7	39.4
		100.0				Total Liabilties & Net Worth	100.0	100.0
						INCOME DATA		
		100.0				Net Sales	100.0	100.0
		27.1				Gross Profit	30.8	33.8
		23.0				Operating Expenses	23.9	25.9
		4.1				Operating Profit	6.9	7.9
		.9				All Other Expenses (net)	1.6	1.1
		3.2				Profit Before Taxes	5.3	6.8
						RATIOS		
		3.4					2.4	2.5
		2.3				Current	1.7	1.7
		1.5					1.2	1.2
		1.4					1.3	1.5
		1.1				Quick	.7	.8
		.4					.5	.5
		18 20.5					18 20.0	19 19.0
		32 11.5				Sales/Receivables	30 12.3	31 11.7
		42 8.6					62 5.9	58 6.3
		38 9.5					44 8.3	42 8.8
		46 7.9				Cost of Sales/Inventory	84 4.3	61 6.0
		107 3.4					123 3.0	102 3.6
		16 22.7					21 17.3	20 18.2
		23 16.0				Cost of Sales/Payables	36 10.1	29 12.6
		50 7.3					71 5.2	46 7.9
		5.3					6.0	5.4
		8.4				Sales/Working Capital	8.8	9.5
		14.3					22.4	17.5
		20.0					10.7	15.4
		5.9				EBIT/Interest	(44) 4.3	(51) 4.1
		2.0					1.7	1.9
							5.6	49.1
						Net Profit + Depr., Dep., Amort./Cur. Mat. L/T/D	(14) 2.1	(14) 3.0
							1.2	1.6
		.3					.4	.4
		.9				Fixed/Worth	.6	.8
		1.2					1.2	1.6
		.5					.6	.6
		1.7				Debt/Worth	1.4	1.4
		5.2					3.8	3.2
		35.7					37.2	40.7
		(10) 21.6				% Profit Before Taxes/Tangible Net Worth	(40) 20.3	(51) 22.3
		13.5					8.5	13.0
		9.9					15.6	15.6
		8.5				% Profit Before Taxes/Total Assets	6.7	8.0
		1.8					2.5	2.7
		20.0					17.3	12.5
		12.4				Sales/Net Fixed Assets	9.5	8.2
		5.8					5.9	4.3
		4.0					2.8	2.7
		2.6				Sales/Total Assets	2.1	2.0
		1.8					1.6	1.4
		.9					.9	1.2
		1.3				% Depr., Dep., Amort./Sales	(39) 1.4	(50) 2.2
		2.2					2.7	3.4
							3.2	1.9
						% Officers', Directors' Owners' Comp/Sales	(15) 4.5	(17) 4.6
							6.8	9.6
206M	22349M	168285M	312888M	392851M	815698M	Net Sales ($)	2604101M	1892888M
105M	7877M	58434M	146348M	263763M	589043M	Total Assets ($)	1109116M	994920M

M = $ thousand MM = $ million

See Pages 9 through 22 for Explanation of Ratios and Data

Comparative Historical Data / Current Data Sorted by Sales

	4/1/11-3/31/12 ALL		4/1/12-3/31/13 ALL		4/1/13-3/31/14 ALL		0-1MM	1-3MM	3-5MM	5-10MM	10-25MM		25MM & OVER
						Type of Statement							
		10		10		11	Unqualified		1			2		8
		7		4		5	Reviewed				1	2		2
		5		2		3	Compiled			1	1	1		
		9		3		3	Tax Returns		1		2			
		16		12		12	Other	1		2		3		6
								8 (4/1-9/30/13)			26 (10/1/13-3/31/14)			
		47		31		34	**NUMBER OF STATEMENTS**	1	2	3	4	8		16
	%		%		%	**ASSETS**	%	%	%	%	%		%
	8.5		5.5		7.5	Cash & Equivalents							6.8
	19.4		20.1		20.9	Trade Receivables (net)							23.3
	30.9		37.5		30.1	Inventory							34.2
	2.6		2.0		2.3	All Other Current							1.5
	61.5		65.0		60.8	Total Current							65.9
	31.0		27.2		30.0	Fixed Assets (net)							23.5
	2.6		2.7		4.6	Intangibles (net)							6.2
	4.9		4.9		4.6	All Other Non-Current							4.3
	100.0		100.0		100.0	Total							100.0
						LIABILITIES							
	30.4		13.2		11.0	Notes Payable-Short Term							14.4
	4.3		3.1		3.5	Cur. Mat.-L.T.D.							3.5
	16.1		16.6		16.5	Trade Payables							13.9
	.3		.3		.6	Income Taxes Payable							.5
	9.3		10.0		6.6	All Other Current							8.6
	60.4		43.3		38.2	Total Current							40.9
	18.4		13.9		18.2	Long-Term Debt							9.5
	.9		.5		.7	Deferred Taxes							.4
	4.1		1.2		7.9	All Other Non-Current							3.0
	16.1		40.9		34.9	Net Worth							46.1
	100.0		100.0		100.0	Total Liabilties & Net Worth							100.0
						INCOME DATA							
	100.0		100.0		100.0	Net Sales							100.0
	31.4		32.2		30.1	Gross Profit							24.0
	24.5		24.7		24.3	Operating Expenses							19.0
	6.9		7.5		5.8	Operating Profit							5.0
	1.1		.8		.9	All Other Expenses (net)							.4
	5.8		6.7		4.9	Profit Before Taxes							4.7
						RATIOS							
	2.0		2.3		2.6								2.6
	1.4		1.6		1.8	Current							1.7
	1.2		1.1		1.1								1.2
	1.0		1.1		1.3								1.3
	.6		.5		.8	Quick							.7
	.4		.3		.4								.4
18	20.7	**19**	19.1	**21**	17.6							**25**	14.4
29	12.6	**34**	10.6	**30**	12.1	Sales/Receivables						**31**	11.7
46	8.0	**43**	8.4	**40**	9.1							**40**	9.2
42	8.6	**57**	6.4	**40**	9.2							**47**	7.7
78	4.7	**81**	4.5	**74**	4.9	Cost of Sales/Inventory						**78**	4.7
126	2.9	**126**	2.9	**107**	3.4							**104**	3.5
19	19.1	**23**	15.9	**19**	19.0							**18**	20.0
28	12.9	**41**	9.0	**28**	12.9	Cost of Sales/Payables						**28**	13.2
53	6.9	**50**	7.3	**48**	7.6							**42**	8.7
	6.4		6.2		5.3								5.7
	11.0		10.0		8.6	Sales/Working Capital							8.9
	25.3		22.8		48.4								25.5
	21.4		27.0		18.1								18.9
	6.4	(30)	7.7	(32)	5.6	EBIT/Interest						(14)	5.9
	2.7		2.6		1.9								1.7
	4.7				2.8								
(15)	1.9			(12)	2.4	Net Profit + Depr., Dep., Amort./Cur. Mat. L/T/D							
	.1				1.8								
	.5		.4		.5								.4
	.7		.6		.9	Fixed/Worth							.6
	1.3		1.1		2.3								1.3
	.9		.7		.8								.5
	1.7		1.4		1.8	Debt/Worth							1.6
	4.6		3.8		5.7								4.6
	53.8		45.3		41.8								48.1
(41)	23.6	(29)	20.6	(29)	25.2	% Profit Before Taxes/Tangible Net Worth						(15)	25.2
	12.4		11.6		12.8								10.0
	21.2		23.8		15.5								24.9
	8.1		6.1		8.4	% Profit Before Taxes/Total Assets							8.2
	4.6		3.7		1.6								1.9
	16.6		18.2		13.5								15.8
	9.8		9.7		9.2	Sales/Net Fixed Assets							10.2
	4.4		5.7		4.9								6.2
	2.9		2.9		3.4								3.4
	1.9		1.9		2.1	Sales/Total Assets							2.2
	1.4		1.3		1.4								1.4
	.9		.8		1.0								.9
(44)	1.8	(30)	1.1		1.6	% Depr., Dep., Amort./Sales							1.3
	3.3		2.6		2.4								2.0
	1.4		2.3										
(14)	4.2	(10)	4.5			% Officers', Directors' Owners' Comp/Sales							
	9.3		9.4										
	2277748M		**1799477M**		**1712277M**	Net Sales ($)	**206M**	**5604M**	**10265M**	**29903M**	**134780M**		**1531519M**
	1226782M		**987905M**		**1065570M**	Total Assets ($)	**105M**	**4299M**	**4915M**	**10311M**	**77304M**		**968636M**

M = $ thousand MM = $ million

See Pages 9 through 22 for Explanation of Ratios and Data

Current Data Sorted by Assets							Comparative Historical Data	
		1	5	3	2	**Type of Statement** Unqualified	13	12
		9	4	1		Reviewed	2	7
		2	1	1		Compiled	6	4
	5		1			Tax Returns	8	4
	2	4	5		2	Other	7	10
	13 (4/1-9/30/13)		35 (10/1/13-3/31/14)				4/1/09- 3/31/10	4/1/10- 3/31/11
0-500M	**500M-2MM**	**2-10MM**	**10-50MM**	**50-100MM**	**100-250MM**		**ALL**	**ALL**
	7	16	16	5	4	**NUMBER OF STATEMENTS**	36	37
%	%	%	%	%	%	**ASSETS**	%	%
D		8.5	4.1			Cash & Equivalents	8.4	9.5
A		18.2	23.0			Trade Receivables (net)	21.7	24.9
T		30.8	34.0			Inventory	24.1	26.0
A		.6	2.1			All Other Current	3.2	2.4
		58.2	63.3			Total Current	57.3	62.7
N		36.7	29.8			Fixed Assets (net)	34.5	31.1
O		1.2	2.5			Intangibles (net)	3.8	1.4
T		4.0	4.4			All Other Non-Current	4.4	4.8
		100.0	100.0			Total	100.0	100.0
A						**LIABILITIES**		
V		14.6	15.9			Notes Payable-Short Term	13.0	12.0
A		4.1	2.5			Cur. Mat.-L.T.D.	5.2	3.0
I		11.1	13.4			Trade Payables	12.9	16.0
L		.4	.2			Income Taxes Payable	.2	.1
A		12.8	9.5			All Other Current	11.6	11.1
B		42.9	41.5			Total Current	42.9	42.2
L		11.7	10.9			Long-Term Debt	19.4	20.9
E		2.7	1.2			Deferred Taxes	.8	.9
		10.5	7.1			All Other Non-Current	5.6	5.5
		32.2	39.3			Net Worth	31.3	30.5
		100.0	100.0			Total Liabilties & Net Worth	100.0	100.0
						INCOME DATA		
		100.0	100.0			Net Sales	100.0	100.0
		30.1	21.8			Gross Profit	30.8	29.0
		26.3	19.3			Operating Expenses	27.3	22.0
		3.8	2.6			Operating Profit	3.6	7.0
		-.1	-.2			All Other Expenses (net)	.1	.0
		3.9	2.7			Profit Before Taxes	3.5	7.0
						RATIOS		
		2.2	1.8				2.1	2.0
		1.3	1.5			Current	1.3	1.5
		1.1	1.3				1.0	1.1
		.9	.8				1.1	1.3
		.7	.8			Quick	.7	.8
		.3	.4				.4	.5
		13 27.4	**28** 13.0				**17** 21.4	**27** 13.8
		25 14.5	**37** 9.9			Sales/Receivables	**30** 12.0	**37** 9.8
		34 10.7	**49** 7.5				**49** 7.5	**47** 7.7
		25 14.4	**45** 8.2				**21** 17.6	**31** 11.7
		78 4.7	**72** 5.1			Cost of Sales/Inventory	**55** 6.6	**61** 6.0
		114 3.2	**122** 3.0				**92** 4.0	**109** 3.3
		10 37.2	**16** 23.0				**14** 25.7	**18** 20.1
		25 14.7	**26** 14.0			Cost of Sales/Payables	**22** 16.3	**27** 13.3
		38 9.5	**51** 7.2				**49** 7.5	**42** 8.7
		8.1	7.6				7.6	6.8
		17.6	10.0			Sales/Working Capital	18.2	12.2
		45.3	13.0				-241.8	76.6
		11.7	18.6				9.5	16.4
		6.4	7.1			EBIT/Interest	(35) 3.7	(35) 6.0
		1.9	1.9				1.0	2.4
								15.5
						Net Profit + Depr., Dep., Amort./Cur. Mat. L/T/D		(10) 4.5
								1.4
		.8	.5				.6	.5
		.9	.8			Fixed/Worth	1.3	.9
		1.5	1.2				3.7	2.0
		1.2	.9				1.2	.9
		1.6	1.5			Debt/Worth	3.9	2.7
		3.8	2.9				12.8	5.4
		40.6	31.4				61.1	55.3
		(15) 26.4	(15) 19.9			% Profit Before Taxes/Tangible Net Worth	(33) 29.9	(34) 33.5
		14.6	7.6				3.1	8.7
		14.7	15.0				14.8	18.0
		9.3	7.4			% Profit Before Taxes/Total Assets	8.4	7.7
		2.6	2.0				.5	3.5
		12.4	8.9				18.1	15.3
		6.2	6.8			Sales/Net Fixed Assets	6.7	11.0
		3.7	4.5				3.3	4.8
		3.5	2.4				3.3	2.9
		2.2	2.0			Sales/Total Assets	2.0	2.1
		1.5	1.6				1.5	1.5
		1.4	1.3				.8	.9
		2.2	2.2			% Depr., Dep., Amort./Sales	(34) 2.1	(34) 1.9
		4.1	4.6				3.9	3.3
								1.6
						% Officers', Directors' Owners' Comp/Sales		(13) 3.9
								5.1
	25921M	204312M	686671M	901331M	887967M	Net Sales ($)	2192171M	1672121M
	5887M	84272M	343228M	378818M	663997M	Total Assets ($)	1052433M	715306M

M = $ thousand MM = $ million

See Pages 9 through 22 for Explanation of Ratios and Data

Comparative Historical Data				Current Data Sorted by Sales					
			Type of Statement						
11	8	11	Unqualified					1	10
8	13	14	Reviewed				3	6	5
6	4	4	Compiled				1	1	2
4	7	6	Tax Returns		2	2	1		1
11	7	13	Other		1	1	3	2	6
				13 (4/1-9/30/13)			35 (10/1/13-3/31/14)		
4/1/11-3/31/12 ALL	**4/1/12-3/31/13 ALL**	**4/1/13-3/31/14 ALL**		**0-1MM**	**1-3MM**	**3-5MM**	**5-10MM**	**10-25MM**	**25MM & OVER**
40	39	48	**NUMBER OF STATEMENTS**		3	3	8	10	24
%	%	%	**ASSETS**	%	%	%	%	%	%
6.8	5.9	8.5	Cash & Equivalents	**DATA NOT AVAILABLE**				6.6	6.5
25.6	19.4	20.7	Trade Receivables (net)					22.4	22.6
28.0	28.8	31.2	Inventory					29.6	31.5
2.7	2.7	2.3	All Other Current					.8	3.9
63.1	56.9	62.6	Total Current					59.5	64.6
30.5	34.2	29.7	Fixed Assets (net)					36.8	26.1
3.1	3.5	3.6	Intangibles (net)					1.9	4.6
3.3	5.3	4.1	All Other Non-Current					1.8	4.7
100.0	100.0	100.0	Total					100.0	100.0
			LIABILITIES						
12.5	13.1	13.2	Notes Payable-Short Term					12.8	12.7
5.6	3.5	2.5	Cur. Mat.-L.T.D.					3.5	2.5
16.4	11.4	13.9	Trade Payables					10.8	13.2
.3	.1	.4	Income Taxes Payable					.5	.6
9.4	15.6	18.7	All Other Current					9.4	10.1
44.2	43.6	48.7	Total Current					37.0	39.0
15.9	15.9	13.4	Long-Term Debt					12.2	14.2
1.6	1.6	1.8	Deferred Taxes					3.7	1.6
5.7	8.7	11.6	All Other Non-Current					15.8	7.4
32.7	30.1	24.5	Net Worth					31.3	37.7
100.0	100.0	100.0	Total Liabilties & Net Worth					100.0	100.0
			INCOME DATA						
100.0	100.0	100.0	Net Sales					100.0	100.0
31.3	30.6	25.6	Gross Profit					30.8	21.4
25.0	25.6	21.4	Operating Expenses					26.3	16.7
6.4	5.0	4.2	Operating Profit					4.5	4.7
.1	-.1	.1	All Other Expenses (net)					.8	-.1
6.2	5.1	4.1	Profit Before Taxes					3.8	4.8
			RATIOS						
2.0	2.2	2.1						2.9	2.0
1.4	1.3	1.5	Current					1.5	1.6
1.1	1.0	1.1						1.2	1.4
1.5	1.1	.9						1.5	.9
.7	.6	.7	Quick					.9	.8
.5	.4	.5						.3	.5
27 13.3	**18** 19.9	**18** 20.1						**19** 19.2	**29** 12.7
38 9.6	**30** 12.0	**30** 12.3	Sales/Receivables					**26** 13.9	**37** 9.9
62 5.9	**42** 8.6	**45** 8.2						**62** 5.9	**49** 7.5
32 11.4	**29** 12.7	**38** 9.5						**31** 11.6	**43** 8.4
69 5.3	**74** 4.9	**69** 5.3	Cost of Sales/Inventory					**76** 4.8	**68** 5.4
122 3.0	**99** 3.7	**111** 3.3						**104** 3.5	**107** 3.4
21 17.1	**15** 24.9	**14** 26.4						**7** 49.1	**16** 22.6
33 11.1	**25** 14.8	**27** 13.6	Cost of Sales/Payables					**20** 18.0	**25** 14.8
58 6.3	**45** 8.1	**43** 8.4						**46** 7.9	**35** 10.5
7.1	7.4	6.7						4.9	5.8
13.2	22.1	10.7	Sales/Working Capital					10.6	9.5
34.5	312.8	24.9						27.5	14.0
15.0	14.6	15.1						14.4	20.7
(38) 5.8	(38) 6.5	(47) 9.0	EBIT/Interest					5.0	(23) 9.9
1.8	2.3	2.6						1.6	2.8
8.9	18.6	7.9							
(11) 2.7	(11) 4.6	(15) 4.4	Net Profit + Depr., Dep., Amort./Cur. Mat. L/T/D						
1.7	1.5	1.7							
.5	.7	.6						.8	.5
1.0	1.0	.9	Fixed/Worth					1.0	.7
2.1	1.5	1.4						2.1	1.3
.9	1.1	1.0						1.1	.8
2.3	2.0	1.8	Debt/Worth					1.3	1.9
6.7	4.4	4.1						5.9	4.6
53.9	54.0	40.1							48.3
(36) 29.4	(35) 35.0	(42) 24.2	% Profit Before Taxes/Tangible Net Worth						(21) 22.7
12.7	21.7	12.8							12.6
18.2	15.7	15.8						15.8	15.7
8.6	10.5	10.5	% Profit Before Taxes/Total Assets					8.7	11.6
2.7	3.9	2.5						1.9	4.1
17.9	11.9	13.8						11.7	16.2
7.8	6.8	7.3	Sales/Net Fixed Assets					6.2	7.4
4.2	3.7	4.2						3.7	5.1
3.2	3.0	3.1						3.3	2.8
1.9	2.0	2.2	Sales/Total Assets					1.9	2.2
1.2	1.5	1.5						1.4	1.6
1.3	1.3	1.2						1.4	1.1
(34) 2.1	2.8	(46) 2.0	% Depr., Dep., Amort./Sales					2.2	1.7
4.2	4.6	4.2						4.7	3.0
	2.1	2.3							
	(11) 3.5	(10) 3.0	% Officers', Directors' Owners' Comp/Sales						
	4.6	4.0							
2021303M	**1835256M**	**2706202M**	Net Sales ($)		**5120M**	**13499M**	**56737M**	**167251M**	**2463595M**
1125759M	**974453M**	**1476202M**	Total Assets ($)		**1916M**	**5015M**	**28690M**	**86490M**	**1354091M**

M = $ thousand MM = $ million

See Pages 9 through 22 for Explanation of Ratios and Data

Current Data Sorted by Assets							Comparative Historical Data	
						Type of Statement		
		1	4	1	3	Unqualified	21	15
		1	5			Reviewed	8	8
	2	1				Compiled	5	4
	1	1	2			Tax Returns	1	5
	2	5	5	2	4	Other	13	17
	12 (4/1-9/30/13)		28 (10/1/13-3/31/14)				4/1/09-3/31/10 ALL	4/1/10-3/31/11 ALL
0-500M	500M-2MM	2-10MM	10-50MM	50-100MM	100-250MM			
	5	9	16	3	7	**NUMBER OF STATEMENTS**	48	49
%	%	%	%	%	%	**ASSETS**	%	%
DATA NOT AVAILABLE			18.5			Cash & Equivalents	15.4	14.1
			18.7			Trade Receivables (net)	21.2	24.8
			24.2			Inventory	29.4	26.4
			1.5			All Other Current	4.5	2.8
			62.9			Total Current	70.5	68.1
			20.5			Fixed Assets (net)	19.9	17.0
			7.8			Intangibles (net)	6.6	8.9
			8.7			All Other Non-Current	3.0	6.0
			100.0			Total	100.0	100.0
						LIABILITIES		
			3.5			Notes Payable-Short Term	8.4	6.6
			1.9			Cur. Mat.-L.T.D.	2.4	2.8
			11.0			Trade Payables	15.7	15.3
			.3			Income Taxes Payable	.7	.4
			13.5			All Other Current	12.5	11.6
			30.2			Total Current	39.7	36.6
			9.7			Long-Term Debt	14.4	14.2
			.7			Deferred Taxes	.4	.8
			3.1			All Other Non-Current	9.1	6.4
			56.3			Net Worth	36.4	41.9
			100.0			Total Liabilties & Net Worth	100.0	100.0
						INCOME DATA		
			100.0			Net Sales	100.0	100.0
			39.7			Gross Profit	35.0	34.8
			31.2			Operating Expenses	27.6	26.2
			8.5			Operating Profit	7.4	8.6
			1.0			All Other Expenses (net)	.8	.6
			7.5			Profit Before Taxes	6.5	8.0
						RATIOS		
			4.1				3.2	3.2
			1.9			Current	1.8	2.2
			1.5				1.2	1.3
			2.0				2.1	1.9
			1.2			Quick	1.0	1.2
			.7				.4	.6
			22 16.3				**21** 17.6	**26** 14.2
			34 10.8			Sales/Receivables	**36** 10.3	**44** 8.3
			45 8.2				**46** 7.9	**61** 6.0
			42 8.6				**54** 6.8	**48** 7.5
			76 4.8			Cost of Sales/Inventory	**80** 4.6	**91** 4.0
			114 3.2				**129** 2.8	**133** 2.7
			13 27.6				**14** 25.6	**22** 16.4
			27 13.5			Cost of Sales/Payables	**42** 8.7	**34** 10.7
			55 6.6				**65** 5.7	**56** 6.5
			4.0				4.1	3.3
			6.6			Sales/Working Capital	7.5	5.2
			12.4				21.8	10.5
			88.9				19.8	60.8
			(14) 19.6			EBIT/Interest	(42) 7.5	(45) 7.3
			4.5				3.3	2.8
							14.0	31.6
						Net Profit + Depr., Dep., Amort./Cur. Mat. L/T/D	(13) 8.4	(14) 5.2
							3.0	3.0
			.2				.2	.1
			.5			Fixed/Worth	.5	.3
			.9				2.3	2.0
			.3				.5	.5
			.9			Debt/Worth	2.0	1.8
			2.4				10.9	9.9
			43.5				58.0	47.9
			(15) 25.2			% Profit Before Taxes/Tangible Net Worth	(40) 35.3	(41) 26.1
			14.4				19.9	15.9
			25.1				27.5	18.0
			9.8			% Profit Before Taxes/Total Assets	12.1	10.9
			5.8				5.2	5.4
			21.9				34.0	29.8
			13.3			Sales/Net Fixed Assets	12.5	13.2
			6.9				5.6	6.7
			2.3				2.8	2.3
			1.8			Sales/Total Assets	1.8	1.7
			1.5				1.5	1.3
			1.2				.9	1.2
			(15) 1.7			% Depr., Dep., Amort./Sales	(41) 1.7	(41) 2.2
			2.7				3.1	3.0
							1.0	1.0
						% Officers', Directors' Owners' Comp/Sales	(11) 1.9	(11) 1.9
							7.2	5.9
	10269M	109491M	591957M	222408M	1451283M	Net Sales ($)	2677307M	3205041M
	5464M	45773M	336185M	227809M	1095717M	Total Assets ($)	1476161M	1689373M

M = $ thousand MM = $ million

See Pages 9 through 22 for Explanation of Ratios and Data

Comparative Historical Data							Current Data Sorted by Sales						
						Type of Statement							
	19		12		9	Unqualified				1	1		7
	7		6		6	Reviewed			1		1		4
	4		4		3	Compiled	1		1		1		
	4		7		4	Tax Returns		1		1	1		1
	19		25		18	Other	1	1		3	2		11
							12 (4/1-9/30/13)			28 (10/1/13-3/31/14)			
	4/1/11-3/31/12 ALL		**4/1/12-3/31/13 ALL**		**4/1/13-3/31/14 ALL**		**0-1MM**	**1-3MM**	**3-5MM**	**5-10MM**	**10-25MM**		**25MM & OVER**
	53		54		40	**NUMBER OF STATEMENTS**	2	2	2	5	6		23
	%		%		%	**ASSETS**	%	%	%	%	%		%
	14.2		12.8		18.8	Cash & Equivalents							15.9
	25.6		21.3		24.7	Trade Receivables (net)							21.2
	31.6		30.4		26.6	Inventory							27.5
	3.7		4.7		3.2	All Other Current							4.4
	75.2		69.2		73.3	Total Current							69.0
	15.6		16.2		14.2	Fixed Assets (net)							16.4
	4.9		7.1		5.4	Intangibles (net)							6.1
	4.4		7.5		7.1	All Other Non-Current							8.4
	100.0		100.0		100.0	Total							100.0
						LIABILITIES							
	9.6		10.4		7.3	Notes Payable-Short Term							6.7
	2.1		3.5		2.4	Cur. Mat.-L.T.D.							2.1
	15.5		14.0		12.4	Trade Payables							13.5
	.8		.6		.8	Income Taxes Payable							1.2
	12.5		10.2		12.3	All Other Current							13.3
	40.4		38.7		35.1	Total Current							36.8
	11.1		9.8		7.9	Long-Term Debt							7.8
	.4		.4		.3	Deferred Taxes							.4
	10.2		9.7		3.3	All Other Non-Current							3.8
	37.8		41.5		53.4	Net Worth							51.2
	100.0		100.0		100.0	Total Liabilties & Net Worth							100.0
						INCOME DATA							
	100.0		100.0		100.0	Net Sales							100.0
	35.5		34.8		40.3	Gross Profit							38.5
	28.0		26.8		30.3	Operating Expenses							29.3
	7.4		8.0		10.0	Operating Profit							9.2
	1.8		1.4		.3	All Other Expenses (net)							1.2
	5.7		6.6		9.6	Profit Before Taxes							8.1
						RATIOS							
	3.5		3.6		4.3								3.2
	2.0		2.0		2.1	Current							1.8
	1.3		1.4		1.5								1.4
	1.7		1.8		2.7								2.1
	1.1		1.0		1.3	Quick							1.1
	.6		.6		.8								.5
27	13.5	**27**	13.5	**29**	12.5							**29**	12.7
41	8.8	**36**	10.0	**43**	8.5	Sales/Receivables						**43**	8.4
62	5.9	**56**	6.5	**63**	5.8							**59**	6.2
70	5.2	**58**	6.3	**60**	6.1							**65**	5.6
91	4.0	**89**	4.1	**87**	4.2	Cost of Sales/Inventory						**89**	4.1
126	2.9	**126**	2.9	**146**	2.5							**159**	2.3
19	19.2	**17**	21.0	**20**	18.3							**22**	16.4
40	9.2	**32**	11.4	**29**	12.5	Cost of Sales/Payables						**30**	12.3
55	6.6	**46**	8.0	**55**	6.6							**54**	6.7
	3.2		3.5		2.8								3.0
	5.8		6.1		4.7	Sales/Working Capital							6.0
	11.2		12.4		8.9								17.2
	29.8		25.3		47.2								93.0
(48)	7.2	(49)	4.8	(33)	10.9	EBIT/Interest						(21)	9.4
	2.1		2.0		5.6								3.8
	13.6		49.5		7.9								
(12)	4.7	(15)	3.7	(13)	4.5	Net Profit + Depr., Dep., Amort./Cur. Mat. L/T/D							
	2.2		1.1		1.9								
	.1		.1		.1								.1
	.3		.3		.2	Fixed/Worth							.2
	1.7		.9		.7								1.0
	.6		.6		.3								.3
	1.6		1.6		1.0	Debt/Worth							1.0
	4.9		3.7		2.5								4.1
	53.3		48.4		51.5								45.3
(46)	27.6	(47)	26.8	(37)	29.2	% Profit Before Taxes/Tangible Net Worth						(22)	26.0
	8.3		6.4		15.6								12.2
	17.6		18.6		26.7								19.9
	9.2		10.0		11.5	% Profit Before Taxes/Total Assets							9.8
	2.1		3.2		6.2								5.0
	40.4		50.0		25.5								15.9
	15.4		14.5		14.6	Sales/Net Fixed Assets							12.3
	7.9		7.7		8.1								7.5
	2.5		2.6		2.2								2.1
	1.8		1.9		1.7	Sales/Total Assets							1.6
	1.5		1.3		1.3								1.1
	.6		.8		1.2								1.2
(43)	2.0	(45)	1.8	(31)	1.8	% Depr., Dep., Amort./Sales						(19)	2.0
	2.7		3.0		2.7								2.7
	1.3		2.7										
(11)	4.0	(14)	4.6			% Officers', Directors' Owners' Comp/Sales							
	5.2		5.3										
	3931313M		**3025644M**		**2385408M**	Net Sales ($)	**1660M**	**3769M**	**9124M**	**42377M**	**111689M**		**2216789M**
	1854651M		**1728234M**		**1710948M**	Total Assets ($)	**1632M**	**1980M**	**4190M**	**24439M**	**61812M**		**1616895M**

M = $ thousand MM = $ million

See Pages 9 through 22 for Explanation of Ratios and Data

Current Data Sorted by Assets							Comparative Historical Data	
						Type of Statement		
		2	9	3	7	Unqualified	27	24
		2	6	1	1	Reviewed	11	15
	2	3	2			Compiled	5	7
2	3	4				Tax Returns	10	
1	4	14	15	6	8	Other	33	53
18 (4/1-9/30/13)			77 (10/1/13-3/31/14)				4/1/09-3/31/10	4/1/10-3/31/11
0-500M	**500M-2MM**	**2-10MM**	**10-50MM**	**50-100MM**	**100-250MM**		**ALL**	**ALL**
3	9	25	32	10	16	**NUMBER OF STATEMENTS**	86	99
%	%	%	%	%	%	**ASSETS**	%	%
		18.5	6.9	11.7	12.5	Cash & Equivalents	12.5	12.5
		20.1	16.7	11.4	13.3	Trade Receivables (net)	17.8	18.1
		29.8	27.3	24.2	19.5	Inventory	25.7	24.8
		.8	3.4	4.5	3.7	All Other Current	2.8	2.9
		69.2	54.3	51.8	48.9	Total Current	58.8	58.3
		21.6	25.8	14.8	19.8	Fixed Assets (net)	23.7	23.1
		4.2	15.4	28.0	27.2	Intangibles (net)	11.3	12.9
		5.0	4.5	5.4	4.0	All Other Non-Current	6.2	5.6
		100.0	100.0	100.0	100.0	Total	100.0	100.0
						LIABILITIES		
		5.6	5.0	5.2	3.9	Notes Payable-Short Term	6.4	8.8
		5.1	3.4	3.5	2.6	Cur. Mat.-L.T.D.	2.6	3.2
		17.7	10.8	10.7	6.9	Trade Payables	14.6	14.6
		.4	.1	1.1	.4	Income Taxes Payable	.5	.5
		14.7	8.0	17.4	7.1	All Other Current	10.9	9.6
		43.6	27.3	37.9	20.8	Total Current	35.0	36.8
		17.2	20.4	17.7	23.0	Long-Term Debt	16.1	13.9
		.5	1.0	3.1	2.0	Deferred Taxes	.8	1.1
		8.7	2.9	6.2	3.6	All Other Non-Current	10.3	7.4
		30.1	48.3	35.2	50.5	Net Worth	37.9	40.9
		100.0	100.0	100.0	100.0	Total Liabilties & Net Worth	100.0	100.0
						INCOME DATA		
		100.0	100.0	100.0	100.0	Net Sales	100.0	100.0
		45.2	39.3	48.8	48.8	Gross Profit	48.5	45.3
		36.8	28.3	39.3	31.2	Operating Expenses	39.4	37.0
		8.4	11.0	9.5	17.7	Operating Profit	9.0	8.3
		1.3	4.5	.8	2.8	All Other Expenses (net)	1.5	1.7
		7.1	6.5	8.7	14.9	Profit Before Taxes	7.5	6.6
						RATIOS		
		2.6	2.8	1.9	3.4		2.6	2.9
		1.9	1.9	1.4	2.2	Current	1.7	1.8
		1.1	1.6	1.1	1.5		1.3	1.2
		2.1	1.2	.9	1.7		1.4	1.4
		.7	.8	.7	1.1	Quick	.7	.9
		.5	.5	.4	.6		.4	.5
		22 16.5	**27** 13.3	**3** 143.5	**14** 26.8		**19** 18.7	**26** 13.9
		33 11.1	**43** 8.5	**36** 10.0	**52** 7.0	Sales/Receivables	**34** 10.7	**38** 9.5
		49 7.4	**57** 6.4	**52** 7.0	**63** 5.8		**48** 7.5	**50** 7.3
		34 10.6	**66** 5.5	**78** 4.7	**74** 4.9		**59** 6.2	**63** 5.8
		83 4.4	**107** 3.4	**104** 3.5	**111** 3.3	Cost of Sales/Inventory	**102** 3.6	**104** 3.5
		192 1.9	**146** 2.5	**166** 2.2	**166** 2.2		**149** 2.4	**143** 2.6
		22 16.4	**25** 14.6	**34** 10.7	**23** 15.9		**28** 13.1	**26** 14.2
		51 7.2	**36** 10.0	**50** 7.3	**33** 10.9	Cost of Sales/Payables	**43** 8.4	**40** 9.0
		81 4.5	**58** 6.3	**57** 6.4	**54** 6.8		**65** 5.6	**63** 5.8
		4.4	3.7	6.2	3.6		4.5	4.3
		8.2	6.6	11.1	5.6	Sales/Working Capital	8.2	7.3
		44.3	9.1	NM	8.6		22.0	27.0
		19.1	22.4		67.7		38.7	28.8
		(20) 4.9	(29) 2.8		(14) 9.7	EBIT/Interest	(76) 8.9	(83) 6.9
		-.5	1.6		4.1		2.6	2.0
			9.6				18.2	7.4
			(12) 2.7			Net Profit + Depr., Dep., Amort./Cur. Mat. L/T/D	(26) 4.8	(32) 2.4
			.9				1.5	1.2
		.2	.5	.2	.5		.3	.4
		.6	.9	2.4	.8	Fixed/Worth	.8	.8
		NM	5.8	-.3	-.6		2.5	6.3
		.9	.8	1.3	.6		.7	.7
		2.9	1.6	5.0	1.9	Debt/Worth	1.9	1.6
		-29.6	21.5	-4.3	-4.3		5.7	36.5
		80.3	35.5		47.6		90.8	56.2
		(18) 35.8	(25) 15.7		(11) 26.0	% Profit Before Taxes/Tangible Net Worth	(72) 42.9	(78) 29.8
		1.6	7.5		22.8		16.0	13.4
		33.7	17.0	15.6	19.0		24.1	22.0
		13.5	8.3	6.1	12.4	% Profit Before Taxes/Total Assets	10.0	9.6
		.4	1.9	3.8	8.1		2.9	2.9
		63.5	10.0	49.3	12.8		26.4	22.1
		11.6	6.6	24.5	6.8	Sales/Net Fixed Assets	9.6	9.8
		6.7	3.3	4.1	4.8		4.0	4.2
		3.1	2.0	3.2	1.5		2.7	2.5
		2.2	1.4	1.3	1.1	Sales/Total Assets	1.8	1.7
		1.7	1.1	1.2	.8		1.2	1.1
		1.0	1.6		1.4		1.3	1.3
		(22) 1.7	(30) 2.9		(12) 2.6	% Depr., Dep., Amort./Sales	(71) 2.2	(81) 2.3
		2.6	4.2		4.2		3.7	3.7
			1.3				1.4	1.1
			(11) 2.6			% Officers', Directors' Owners' Comp/Sales	(19) 2.9	(15) 2.1
			3.4				4.6	3.5
4525M	52593M	356395M	1026226M	1434676M	3089747M	Net Sales ($)	5303972M	7674174M
740M	13472M	141989M	727075M	743454M	2711417M	Total Assets ($)	3205736M	5014963M

M = $ thousand MM = $ million

See Pages 9 through 22 for Explanation of Ratios and Data

Comparative Historical Data / Current Data Sorted by Sales

4/1/11-3/31/12 ALL	4/1/12-3/31/13 ALL	4/1/13-3/31/14 ALL		0-1MM	1-3MM	3-5MM	5-10MM	10-25MM	25MM & OVER
			Type of Statement						
21	18	21	Unqualified					4	17
11	9	10	Reviewed					3	7
8	8	7	Compiled			2	2	2	1
10	8	9	Tax Returns	1		3	4	1	
44	48	48	Other	1	1	2	5	17	22
				18 (4/1-9/30/13)			77 (10/1/13-3/31/14)		
94	91	95	**NUMBER OF STATEMENTS**	2	1	7	11	27	47
%	%	%	**ASSETS**	%	%	%	%	%	%
13.9	14.8	13.0	Cash & Equivalents				9.4	11.0	11.8
19.3	17.5	18.3	Trade Receivables (net)				28.5	18.4	15.7
27.2	24.9	26.1	Inventory				25.1	29.1	25.7
2.4	2.7	2.7	All Other Current				1.7	1.5	4.1
62.8	59.9	60.1	Total Current				64.7	60.1	57.3
19.6	22.7	21.7	Fixed Assets (net)				19.3	17.6	23.0
11.7	12.7	13.8	Intangibles (net)				12.2	15.3	16.1
5.8	4.7	4.4	All Other Non-Current				3.8	7.1	3.6
100.0	100.0	100.0	Total				100.0	100.0	100.0
			LIABILITIES						
6.8	7.2	5.6	Notes Payable-Short Term				7.4	5.4	5.5
3.9	2.6	3.6	Cur. Mat.-L.T.D.				4.6	4.3	2.9
15.0	13.8	14.5	Trade Payables				22.2	14.7	10.7
.3	.4	.3	Income Taxes Payable				.4	.3	.5
11.3	10.6	10.4	All Other Current				6.1	12.3	11.3
37.3	34.7	34.4	Total Current				40.7	37.0	30.8
14.1	15.9	18.1	Long-Term Debt				14.5	16.0	19.8
.7	.9	1.1	Deferred Taxes				.0	1.7	1.3
6.8	6.8	5.4	All Other Non-Current				9.1	5.7	4.2
41.2	41.6	41.0	Net Worth				35.7	39.6	43.8
100.0	100.0	100.0	Total Liabilties & Net Worth				100.0	100.0	100.0
			INCOME DATA						
100.0	100.0	100.0	Net Sales				100.0	100.0	100.0
45.4	44.2	44.0	Gross Profit				44.6	42.6	42.0
36.8	35.2	33.0	Operating Expenses				37.0	32.7	30.8
8.6	9.0	10.9	Operating Profit				7.6	9.9	11.3
2.1	2.0	2.5	All Other Expenses (net)				3.2	3.8	1.9
6.5	7.0	8.4	Profit Before Taxes				4.4	6.1	9.3
			RATIOS						
2.9	3.4	2.6					1.9	2.9	2.4
1.9	1.8	1.8	Current				1.6	1.9	1.7
1.2	1.3	1.3					1.3	1.1	1.5
1.6	2.1	1.4					1.2	1.5	1.3
.9	.8	.9	Quick				1.1	.8	.7
.6	.5	.5					.5	.5	.5
23 16.2	**17** 21.5	**22** 16.5					**12** 30.5	**29** 12.8	**20** 17.9
38 9.5	**31** 11.9	**37** 9.9	Sales/Receivables				**35** 10.5	**36** 10.2	**42** 8.6
49 7.4	**48** 7.6	**53** 6.9					**49** 7.4	**54** 6.7	**54** 6.8
56 6.5	**54** 6.7	**54** 6.7					**29** 12.7	**54** 6.7	**69** 5.3
99 3.7	**94** 3.9	**99** 3.7	Cost of Sales/Inventory				**66** 5.5	**94** 3.9	**101** 3.6
159 2.3	**135** 2.7	**146** 2.5					**114** 3.2	**159** 2.3	**152** 2.4
26 14.0	**23** 15.8	**24** 14.9					**21** 17.0	**23** 15.9	**24** 14.9
43 8.5	**36** 10.1	**42** 8.6	Cost of Sales/Payables				**39** 9.3	**41** 8.9	**37** 9.8
66 5.5	**59** 6.2	**63** 5.8					**60** 6.1	**78** 4.7	**54** 6.7
4.4	4.7	4.6					6.9	3.7	5.3
6.9	7.3	7.1	Sales/Working Capital				15.5	5.8	7.1
20.8	16.2	13.3					24.3	44.9	10.2
37.4	40.8	22.9						14.6	27.9
(79) 8.6	(77) 7.3	(79) 5.9	EBIT/Interest					(24) 3.8	(41) 8.6
2.2	2.0	1.9						-.5	2.3
6.8	5.4	7.8							8.9
(23) 3.8	(29) 2.9	(30) 2.7	Net Profit + Depr., Dep., Amort./Cur. Mat. L/T/D						(22) 3.6
2.2	1.8	1.1							1.5
.3	.3	.3					.2	.3	.5
.7	.8	.7	Fixed/Worth				.8	.5	.8
4.8	106.5	7.1					-3.4	-4.5	7.1
.6	.7	.9					.9	.7	.9
1.7	1.4	1.9	Debt/Worth				3.5	1.8	1.8
17.8	999.8	-999.8					-16.1	-18.4	27.1
50.6	77.1	55.8						55.8	42.3
(74) 27.4	(69) 30.5	(71) 24.6	% Profit Before Taxes/Tangible Net Worth					(19) 18.3	(36) 22.3
11.3	9.4	10.2						-16.5	12.3
19.7	23.1	20.7					27.7	17.1	20.4
8.6	9.0	11.2	% Profit Before Taxes/Total Assets				22.7	8.0	9.9
2.8	2.9	2.4					-2.6	-.5	3.6
33.1	24.3	23.3					61.1	20.6	17.9
12.6	10.3	9.5	Sales/Net Fixed Assets				25.9	10.4	7.7
5.3	4.6	4.9					6.3	5.6	4.1
2.5	2.8	2.7					5.3	2.6	2.0
1.8	1.7	1.6	Sales/Total Assets				3.0	1.8	1.4
1.2	1.2	1.2					1.4	1.2	1.1
1.0	.8	1.2						1.2	1.4
(74) 1.7	(70) 2.3	(76) 2.2	% Depr., Dep., Amort./Sales					(23) 2.0	(41) 2.5
3.1	4.1	3.5						3.3	3.8
1.4	2.0	1.6							1.0
(29) 2.5	(21) 3.4	(30) 3.1	% Officers', Directors' Owners' Comp/Sales						(10) 1.6
5.3	8.2	6.9							2.6
5950368M	6122275M	5964162M	Net Sales ($)	1104M	2698M	27203M	78971M	464787M	5389399M
4336893M	3950287M	4338147M	Total Assets ($)	315M	738M	18033M	46618M	477404M	3795039M

M = $ thousand MM = $ million

See Pages 9 through 22 for Explanation of Ratios and Data

	Current Data Sorted by Assets						Comparative Historical Data	
Type of Statement								
Unqualified	1	1	8	13	10	8	46	50
Reviewed		1	4	11	1	1	27	24
Compiled		3	7	1	1		13	20
Tax Returns	2	2	5				17	12
Other		7	18	40	16	13	100	90
	27 (4/1-9/30/13)			147 (10/1/13-3/31/14)			4/1/09-3/31/10	4/1/10-3/31/11
	0-500M	500M-2MM	2-10MM	10-50MM	50-100MM	100-250MM	ALL	ALL
NUMBER OF STATEMENTS	3	14	42	65	28	22	203	196
ASSETS	%	%	%	%	%	%	%	%
Cash & Equivalents		7.8	15.9	11.7	18.4	16.9	14.0	15.4
Trade Receivables (net)		26.9	24.0	20.4	16.6	13.1	22.0	21.6
Inventory		31.2	19.4	24.1	18.0	12.6	19.8	20.1
All Other Current		2.3	1.7	3.4	3.3	4.8	3.2	3.6
Total Current		68.3	61.0	59.7	56.4	47.5	59.0	60.8
Fixed Assets (net)		23.5	25.3	25.7	22.2	17.1	24.9	24.5
Intangibles (net)		1.8	2.6	10.7	13.7	29.2	11.0	8.9
All Other Non-Current		6.4	11.0	4.0	7.8	6.2	5.1	5.8
Total		100.0	100.0	100.0	100.0	100.0	100.0	100.0
LIABILITIES								
Notes Payable-Short Term		15.5	6.2	6.0	1.6	1.8	6.2	5.5
Cur. Mat.-L.T.D.		1.1	3.1	8.2	4.1	3.0	3.6	2.9
Trade Payables		15.1	14.8	14.4	13.4	10.7	12.1	12.6
Income Taxes Payable		.1	.1	.3	.3	.6	.3	.3
All Other Current		6.9	10.0	11.0	13.6	9.6	12.4	10.4
Total Current		38.6	34.3	39.9	33.0	25.6	34.7	31.7
Long-Term Debt		11.2	12.4	17.4	19.0	16.1	15.5	11.8
Deferred Taxes		.3	.1	.4	1.6	3.6	.7	.6
All Other Non-Current		4.7	4.4	6.8	3.8	8.4	5.7	6.5
Net Worth		45.2	48.8	35.5	42.6	46.3	43.4	49.5
Total Liabilties & Net Worth		100.0	100.0	100.0	100.0	100.0	100.0	100.0
INCOME DATA								
Net Sales		100.0	100.0	100.0	100.0	100.0	100.0	100.0
Gross Profit		41.1	46.5	42.9	52.7	58.5	42.1	44.7
Operating Expenses		35.1	37.1	33.6	38.8	39.9	35.2	35.8
Operating Profit		6.0	9.4	9.3	14.0	18.5	6.9	8.9
All Other Expenses (net)		.5	.2	.9	3.9	5.1	1.7	.9
Profit Before Taxes		5.5	9.2	8.4	10.1	13.5	5.2	8.0
RATIOS								
Current		2.8	3.8	3.4	4.1	3.2	3.1	3.5
		1.6	2.0	1.9	1.8	1.9	1.8	2.0
		1.3	1.2	1.0	1.1	1.4	1.2	1.3
Quick		1.2	2.0	2.2	2.5	1.8	1.9	2.1
		.8	1.0	.8	1.0	1.1	1.0	1.2
		.7	.6	.5	.6	.9	.6	.7
Sales/Receivables		**17** 21.9	**29** 12.7	**34** 10.7	**36** 10.0	**32** 11.4	**30** 12.2	**30** 12.1
		30 12.3	**36** 10.1	**44** 8.3	**49** 7.4	**52** 7.0	**43** 8.5	**41** 8.9
		47 7.7	**48** 7.6	**62** 5.9	**61** 6.0	**61** 6.0	**59** 6.2	**58** 6.3
Cost of Sales/Inventory		**37** 9.8	**12** 30.9	**60** 6.1	**65** 5.6	**51** 7.2	**40** 9.0	**39** 9.3
		65 5.6	**54** 6.7	**91** 4.0	**104** 3.5	**111** 3.3	**74** 4.9	**87** 4.2
		73 5.0	**104** 3.5	**130** 2.8	**140** 2.6	**182** 2.0	**119** 3.1	**131** 2.8
Cost of Sales/Payables		**22** 16.9	**20** 18.6	**24** 15.2	**36** 10.2	**31** 11.6	**20** 18.6	**20** 17.9
		31 11.6	**35** 10.3	**38** 9.7	**51** 7.2	**52** 7.0	**36** 10.1	**36** 10.3
		38 9.5	**62** 5.9	**66** 5.5	**76** 4.8	**114** 3.2	**57** 6.4	**56** 6.6
Sales/Working Capital		6.6	4.8	3.4	2.6	2.3	3.5	3.4
		11.3	7.5	7.8	5.4	5.3	7.2	6.0
		23.8	34.5	75.0	55.6	10.6	22.7	18.8
EBIT/Interest		12.8	49.6	32.2	60.6	58.5	17.1	32.1
		(11) 3.9	(35) 7.0	(54) 7.2	(25) 6.4	(18) 7.8	(168) 4.2	(166) 10.2
		1.3	2.1	2.3	1.8	.7	1.6	2.6
Net Profit + Depr., Dep., Amort./Cur. Mat. L/T/D			8.4	7.3	35.0	20.5	6.1	13.4
			(10) 4.3	(26) 3.5	(13) 2.0	(11) 8.6	(57) 1.9	(66) 3.3
			1.5	.6	1.2	3.6	.7	1.6
Fixed/Worth		.2	.2	.3	.3	.3	.2	.2
		.5	.5	.7	.5	.9	.7	.6
		.7	1.9	2.3	578.1	-.2	2.4	1.5
Debt/Worth		.6	.5	.5	.3	.5	.6	.4
		1.1	1.1	1.5	1.3	1.4	1.6	1.1
		3.7	3.4	7.5	817.1	-2.8	6.8	3.2
% Profit Before Taxes/Tangible Net Worth		80.6	83.1	49.9	228.4	50.1	52.7	52.5
		16.4	(40) 30.0	(53) 22.6	(22) 29.7	(14) 24.6	(173) 23.1	(176) 28.2
		4.5	11.0	8.1	11.3	15.8	6.2	9.1
% Profit Before Taxes/Total Assets		31.6	29.4	18.7	31.4	25.0	16.3	22.9
		6.3	12.0	9.5	12.3	10.5	7.6	10.1
		1.5	3.5	3.0	5.2	1.2	2.1	3.8
Sales/Net Fixed Assets		41.8	28.6	25.3	29.7	62.0	30.0	28.4
		22.0	10.5	8.6	8.2	11.1	8.3	9.5
		6.9	4.6	3.7	3.2	3.9	3.2	3.0
Sales/Total Assets		3.9	4.0	2.2	2.2	1.5	2.6	2.5
		2.9	2.0	1.5	1.1	.9	1.5	1.5
		2.4	1.4	1.0	.9	.5	.9	1.0
% Depr., Dep., Amort./Sales		.7	.7	1.2	1.7	1.4	1.1	1.2
		(11) 1.1	(34) 1.5	(56) 2.1	(24) 3.1	(15) 2.9	(161) 2.6	(170) 2.3
		1.4	3.8	3.5	3.8	4.8	4.7	4.3
% Officers', Directors' Owners' Comp/Sales			2.0	1.4			1.6	1.9
			(12) 2.6	(15) 2.4			(36) 3.0	(43) 2.9
			3.5	4.6			5.6	5.8
Net Sales ($)	4434M	69058M	615049M	2227305M	3159280M	3523365M	11077764M	10372922M
Total Assets ($)	745M	20261M	235525M	1530103M	2053282M	3474310M	9093741M	8045271M

M = $ thousand MM = $ million

See Pages 9 through 22 for Explanation of Ratios and Data

Comparative Historical Data | **Current Data Sorted by Sales**

4/1/11-3/31/12 ALL	4/1/12-3/31/13 ALL	4/1/13-3/31/14 ALL		0-1MM	1-3MM	3-5MM	5-10MM	10-25MM	25MM & OVER
			Type of Statement						
46	36	41	Unqualified	1		3	3	5	29
28	23	18	Reviewed			1	1	7	9
20	13	12	Compiled		1	3	4	1	3
15	10	9	Tax Returns		1	2	4	2	
78	88	94	Other		2	3	9	16	64
				27 (4/1-9/30/13)		147 (10/1/13-3/31/14)			
187	170	174	**NUMBER OF STATEMENTS**	1	4	12	21	31	105
%	%	%	**ASSETS**	%	%	%	%	%	%
13.5	12.7	14.2	Cash & Equivalents			14.5	8.7	17.7	14.5
20.7	19.7	20.3	Trade Receivables (net)			23.7	20.5	17.7	20.7
22.0	20.4	20.8	Inventory			18.1	22.6	19.5	20.9
2.8	3.0	3.1	All Other Current			3.1	1.3	2.8	3.6
59.1	55.8	58.4	Total Current			59.3	53.0	57.8	59.7
24.9	25.2	23.9	Fixed Assets (net)			19.3	29.2	31.4	20.8
10.4	11.8	10.9	Intangibles (net)			9.3	9.2	4.6	13.3
5.6	7.1	6.8	All Other Non-Current			12.0	8.6	6.3	6.1
100.0	100.0	100.0	Total			100.0	100.0	100.0	100.0
			LIABILITIES						
8.6	7.7	5.5	Notes Payable-Short Term			6.5	9.3	4.8	4.5
2.8	3.7	5.0	Cur. Mat.-L.T.D.			1.7	3.5	3.0	6.4
14.0	14.8	13.9	Trade Payables			14.1	13.3	10.3	15.4
.3	.4	.3	Income Taxes Payable			.2	.0	.1	.4
12.1	11.3	10.6	All Other Current			5.9	8.4	11.0	11.5
37.9	38.0	35.2	Total Current			28.4	34.6	29.2	38.3
14.4	20.1	17.4	Long-Term Debt			16.5	14.6	16.0	16.4
.6	.8	.9	Deferred Taxes			.4	.2	.1	1.4
5.9	6.6	5.7	All Other Non-Current			7.8	5.9	3.1	6.2
41.2	34.5	40.8	Net Worth			47.0	44.7	51.6	37.8
100.0	100.0	100.0	Total Liabilties & Net Worth			100.0	100.0	100.0	100.0
			INCOME DATA						
100.0	100.0	100.0	Net Sales			100.0	100.0	100.0	100.0
43.7	43.3	47.4	Gross Profit			49.6	44.5	52.8	46.0
35.7	34.9	36.4	Operating Expenses			38.7	41.0	41.1	33.7
8.0	8.3	11.0	Operating Profit			10.9	3.4	11.7	12.3
1.2	2.2	1.8	All Other Expenses (net)			1.8	.4	-.6	2.7
6.8	6.1	9.2	Profit Before Taxes			9.1	3.0	12.3	9.6
			RATIOS						
3.3	3.0	3.4				3.8	2.5	4.0	3.4
2.0	1.8	1.9	Current			2.0	1.6	1.9	1.9
1.1	1.2	1.2				1.5	1.2	1.0	1.2
2.1	1.8	2.0				2.4	1.5	2.4	2.1
1.0	.9	1.0	Quick			1.3	1.0	1.1	1.0
.6	.5	.6				.7	.6	.6	.6
31 11.8	**29** 12.8	**31** 11.7				**27** 13.6	**27** 13.6	**24** 15.5	**33** 10.9
45 8.1	**41** 8.9	**42** 8.7	Sales/Receivables			**35** 10.5	**39** 9.4	**37** 9.9	**45** 8.2
60 6.1	**61** 6.0	**57** 6.4				**55** 6.6	**54** 6.7	**49** 7.5	**60** 6.1
51 7.2	**46** 7.9	**47** 7.7				**37** 9.9	**4** 85.3	**33** 11.1	**54** 6.7
91 4.0	**85** 4.3	**89** 4.1	Cost of Sales/Inventory			**66** 5.5	**55** 6.6	**91** 4.0	**91** 4.0
135 2.7	**130** 2.8	**126** 2.9				**104** 3.5	**99** 3.7	**146** 2.5	**130** 2.8
27 13.7	**25** 14.8	**25** 14.5				**30** 12.3	**20** 18.7	**15** 24.7	**28** 12.9
40 9.1	**40** 9.1	**39** 9.3	Cost of Sales/Payables			**36** 10.0	**36** 10.1	**26** 13.8	**44** 8.3
73 5.0	**78** 4.7	**65** 5.6				**61** 6.0	**70** 5.2	**46** 7.9	**68** 5.4
3.3	3.6	3.7				4.9	5.8	3.7	3.2
6.7	7.7	7.5	Sales/Working Capital			9.3	13.3	7.1	7.3
30.1	33.5	26.9				21.1	66.2	999.8	31.9
28.4	23.7	39.7				97.1	6.7	50.8	44.1
(165) 7.3	(149) 6.3	(145) 6.4	EBIT/Interest			(10) 11.4	(17) 3.9	(27) 6.3	(88) 8.1
1.8	1.8	1.8				3.1	-5.4	2.1	2.1
15.0	10.0	10.5							11.2
(50) 6.0	(52) 4.4	(62) 4.3	Net Profit + Depr., Dep., Amort./Cur. Mat. L/T/D						(48) 4.0
1.9	1.9	1.4							1.2
.2	.3	.2				.1	.2	.3	.2
.6	.7	.6	Fixed/Worth			.3	.7	.7	.7
2.3	3.0	2.7				.6	2.1	1.6	16.2
.5	.6	.5				.4	.9	.4	.5
1.3	1.7	1.3	Debt/Worth			1.5	1.3	.9	1.6
5.9	10.3	8.5				7.2	3.3	3.4	63.5
43.4	51.5	63.2				84.8	59.5	71.4	62.9
(152) 21.6	(137) 23.8	(145) 23.5	% Profit Before Taxes/Tangible Net Worth			(11) 23.3	(18) 11.6	(29) 32.4	(83) 23.5
7.3	6.7	9.1				7.0	-11.8	11.2	12.2
18.7	16.8	23.6				23.7	16.0	33.2	21.7
8.2	8.2	9.8	% Profit Before Taxes/Total Assets			8.9	8.5	14.1	9.8
1.3	2.1	2.9				3.5	-6.3	4.3	3.4
25.5	24.7	29.1				82.9	32.3	19.3	28.8
7.5	7.1	9.8	Sales/Net Fixed Assets			15.3	16.0	6.6	10.3
3.4	3.7	4.2				6.9	3.5	3.5	4.2
2.1	2.4	2.5				3.0	3.2	2.2	2.3
1.5	1.6	1.7	Sales/Total Assets			2.3	2.0	1.5	1.5
.9	1.0	1.0				1.4	1.3	1.1	.9
1.3	1.3	1.0					1.0	1.2	1.0
(151) 2.7	(128) 2.7	(143) 2.0	% Depr., Dep., Amort./Sales				(18) 1.4	(26) 2.3	(87) 2.1
4.8	4.7	3.7					6.0	4.2	3.5
1.2	1.7	1.4						1.9	.9
(35) 2.0	(39) 3.3	(36) 2.4	% Officers', Directors' Owners' Comp/Sales					(10) 2.7	(12) 1.6
5.4	6.3	3.6						3.7	4.0
9878289M	8486699M	9598491M	Net Sales ($)	22M	7389M	51781M	142960M	505328M	8891011M
8181178M	7144190M	7314226M	Total Assets ($)	43M	4820M	48662M	84858M	394722M	6781121M

M = $ thousand MM = $ million

See Pages 9 through 22 for Explanation of Ratios and Data

Current Data Sorted by Assets							Comparative Historical Data	
						Type of Statement		
		2	6	1	3	Unqualified	15	14
		21	11		1	Reviewed	33	28
	5	13				Compiled	16	19
3	7	3	1			Tax Returns	18	9
2	8	12	7	4	5	Other	58	55
19 (4/1-9/30/13)			96 (10/1/13-3/31/14)				4/1/09-3/31/10 ALL	4/1/10-3/31/11 ALL
0-500M	500M-2MM	2-10MM	10-50MM	50-100MM	100-250MM			
5	20	51	25	5	9	**NUMBER OF STATEMENTS**	140	125
%	%	%	%	%	%	**ASSETS**	%	%
	11.0	12.4	10.5			Cash & Equivalents	9.4	7.8
	29.1	25.1	25.7			Trade Receivables (net)	24.4	23.4
	31.8	25.6	30.0			Inventory	25.0	28.2
	.4	1.2	1.4			All Other Current	3.0	2.6
	72.3	64.3	67.7			Total Current	61.8	62.1
	19.8	20.3	18.3			Fixed Assets (net)	24.2	21.8
	1.9	9.2	9.8			Intangibles (net)	7.1	8.3
	5.9	6.2	4.2			All Other Non-Current	6.9	7.9
	100.0	100.0	100.0			Total	100.0	100.0
						LIABILITIES		
	9.6	6.9	7.6			Notes Payable-Short Term	9.5	10.2
	3.8	2.2	2.2			Cur. Mat.-L.T.D.	4.5	3.5
	20.9	13.4	12.6			Trade Payables	13.9	14.1
	1.1	.1	.2			Income Taxes Payable	.2	.1
	4.2	6.5	8.5			All Other Current	7.9	8.3
	39.6	29.1	31.1			Total Current	35.9	36.3
	12.7	13.0	7.7			Long-Term Debt	13.0	15.3
	.2	.5	1.0			Deferred Taxes	.5	.6
	14.9	4.8	6.8			All Other Non-Current	9.5	7.3
	32.6	52.6	53.3			Net Worth	41.0	40.5
	100.0	100.0	100.0			Total Liabilties & Net Worth	100.0	100.0
						INCOME DATA		
	100.0	100.0	100.0			Net Sales	100.0	100.0
	40.9	33.0	32.7			Gross Profit	35.6	35.1
	35.1	25.2	25.0			Operating Expenses	31.7	28.8
	5.8	7.8	7.7			Operating Profit	3.9	6.3
	.2	.1	.3			All Other Expenses (net)	1.0	1.2
	5.5	7.6	7.4			Profit Before Taxes	3.0	5.1
						RATIOS		
	3.1	4.5	3.3				3.3	3.5
	1.9	2.4	2.6			Current	1.8	2.1
	1.3	1.3	1.6				1.2	1.2
	1.5	2.8	2.2				1.9	2.0
	1.0	1.2	1.3			Quick	.9	.9
	.5	.8	.7				.6	.6
	20 18.7	**29** 12.4	**33** 11.1				**31** 12.0	**31** 11.8
	33 11.1	**38** 9.5	**51** 7.2			Sales/Receivables	**41** 8.9	**42** 8.7
	46 7.9	**47** 7.7	**61** 6.0				**51** 7.1	**51** 7.2
	34 10.7	**29** 12.7	**59** 6.2				**43** 8.4	**50** 7.3
	51 7.2	**65** 5.6	**76** 4.8			Cost of Sales/Inventory	**68** 5.4	**72** 5.1
	99 3.7	**101** 3.6	**104** 3.5				**99** 3.7	**104** 3.5
	18 20.6	**14** 26.2	**22** 16.9				**18** 20.2	**21** 17.7
	45 8.1	**23** 15.6	**31** 11.9			Cost of Sales/Payables	**30** 12.2	**32** 11.5
	51 7.2	**41** 9.0	**42** 8.7				**47** 7.8	**48** 7.7
	4.6	4.2	3.7				4.3	4.5
	9.5	6.1	5.6			Sales/Working Capital	7.3	6.9
	27.6	18.7	8.6				19.2	18.5
	31.3	23.0	97.6				11.3	15.7
	(17) 5.4	(42) 11.0	(23) 11.5			EBIT/Interest	(127) 3.6	(111) 5.6
	2.6	3.5	4.5				-.1	1.9
		6.1	21.0				8.7	6.6
		(15) 3.4	(15) 9.9			Net Profit + Depr., Dep., Amort./Cur. Mat. L/T/D	(42) 3.2	(36) 2.9
		2.2	5.9				1.2	1.1
	.1	.1	.2				.2	.2
	.4	.4	.3			Fixed/Worth	.5	.5
	2.0	1.2	1.0				2.3	2.0
	.7	.4	.4				.5	.5
	1.4	.7	.9			Debt/Worth	1.2	1.3
	8.0	2.5	3.0				5.1	4.2
	106.2	52.8	58.4				28.8	45.8
	(18) 30.2	(43) 32.0	(24) 23.4			% Profit Before Taxes/Tangible Net Worth	(118) 11.3	(105) 21.1
	5.7	10.4	9.7				1.6	8.7
	38.0	27.0	20.3				12.4	13.7
	9.5	12.3	10.1			% Profit Before Taxes/Total Assets	4.4	7.3
	2.4	5.0	4.3				-.2	3.2
	82.7	44.3	25.9				24.8	27.7
	17.7	14.3	11.3			Sales/Net Fixed Assets	10.9	12.9
	11.7	5.5	6.8				4.9	5.6
	3.8	3.1	2.6				2.9	2.7
	2.9	2.2	2.0			Sales/Total Assets	2.0	2.1
	2.3	1.6	1.4				1.4	1.5
	.1	.5	.7				.9	.8
	(14) 1.0	(44) 1.0	1.2			% Depr., Dep., Amort./Sales	(126) 1.6	(110) 1.4
	1.9	1.7	1.8				2.7	2.3
	4.3	1.8					2.0	2.0
	(11) 5.2	(14) 3.1				% Officers', Directors' Owners' Comp/Sales	(52) 4.9	(39) 3.4
	7.3	6.7					7.9	7.2
8313M	70199M	672215M	1194084M	629688M	1392963M	Net Sales ($)	4122661M	3768406M
1170M	24980M	288645M	580409M	354797M	1377453M	Total Assets ($)	2569791M	2529773M

M = $ thousand MM = $ million

See Pages 9 through 22 for Explanation of Ratios and Data

Comparative Historical Data | Current Data Sorted by Sales

			Type of Statement						
21	12	12	Unqualified				1	1	10
28	24	33	Reviewed		1		5	18	9
18	9	18	Compiled		1	3	7	5	2
17	16	14	Tax Returns	1	4	2	5	2	
60	52	38	Other	2	7	3	4	5	17
4/1/11-3/31/12 ALL	4/1/12-3/31/13 ALL	4/1/13-3/31/14 ALL		19 (4/1-9/30/13)			96 (10/1/13-3/31/14)		
				0-1MM	1-3MM	3-5MM	5-10MM	10-25MM	25MM & OVER
144	113	115	NUMBER OF STATEMENTS	3	13	8	22	31	38
%	%	%	ASSETS	%	%	%	%	%	%
10.5	9.5	11.6	Cash & Equivalents		10.5		15.2	9.7	11.3
25.1	24.8	24.0	Trade Receivables (net)		29.0		21.4	25.5	23.8
26.7	25.6	25.9	Inventory		26.6		29.5	24.6	24.7
1.7	2.3	1.8	All Other Current		.4		.6	1.6	1.9
64.0	62.2	63.2	Total Current		66.6		66.7	61.3	61.7
22.0	22.2	20.8	Fixed Assets (net)		22.9		15.5	25.7	17.4
7.2	8.2	9.9	Intangibles (net)		4.5		9.0	9.1	15.1
6.8	7.4	6.1	All Other Non-Current		6.0		8.8	3.8	5.7
100.0	100.0	100.0	Total		100.0		100.0	100.0	100.0
			LIABILITIES						
9.6	7.6	6.8	Notes Payable-Short Term		10.3		2.5	10.7	5.1
2.5	3.0	2.3	Cur. Mat.-L.T.D.		3.4		1.9	3.2	1.5
14.4	15.4	13.2	Trade Payables		16.9		12.4	15.6	10.7
.3	.2	.3	Income Taxes Payable		.0		.0	.1	.2
8.0	8.2	6.3	All Other Current		3.2		4.2	7.8	7.5
35.0	34.4	28.9	Total Current		33.8		21.0	37.4	25.1
16.3	16.4	12.7	Long-Term Debt		13.3		9.1	14.8	11.3
.8	.8	.8	Deferred Taxes		.0		.4	.7	1.3
9.7	8.5	8.5	All Other Non-Current		17.1		2.5	6.2	7.1
38.3	39.9	49.1	Net Worth		35.8		67.0	40.8	55.3
100.0	100.0	100.0	Total Liabilties & Net Worth		100.0		100.0	100.0	100.0
			INCOME DATA						
100.0	100.0	100.0	Net Sales		100.0		100.0	100.0	100.0
35.3	35.5	36.1	Gross Profit		45.1		34.6	31.8	33.8
29.4	29.0	28.6	Operating Expenses		38.4		26.9	25.5	24.6
5.8	6.6	7.5	Operating Profit		6.6		7.6	6.4	9.2
.8	.9	.5	All Other Expenses (net)		.6		-.9	.9	1.1
5.0	5.7	6.9	Profit Before Taxes		6.0		8.5	5.5	8.2
			RATIOS						
3.5	3.4	4.3			4.8		7.9	2.6	4.2
1.9	2.1	2.5	Current		2.1		3.9	1.9	2.9
1.3	1.3	1.5			1.5		1.8	1.2	1.8
2.1	1.9	2.5			2.8		3.2	1.5	2.4
1.0	(112) 1.2	(114) 1.2	Quick		1.2		1.6	.9	1.6
.6	.6	.8			.5		1.0	.6	.8
31 11.8	32 11.5	29 12.8			20 18.1		27 13.7	31 11.8	34 10.7
40 9.2	40 9.2	40 9.2	Sales/Receivables		38 9.6		31 11.9	41 9.0	45 8.1
52 7.0	52 7.0	51 7.1			58 6.3		47 7.8	52 7.0	53 6.9
41 9.0	40 9.1	41 8.8			22 16.6		35 10.5	22 16.3	54 6.8
69 5.3	68 5.4	68 5.4	Cost of Sales/Inventory		43 8.5		62 5.9	65 5.6	76 4.8
94 3.9	101 3.6	101 3.6			135 2.7		104 3.5	96 3.8	99 3.7
20 18.6	18 20.1	17 21.1			10 37.0		11 33.9	20 18.7	22 16.7
30 12.3	31 11.7	30 12.0	Cost of Sales/Payables		41 8.8		23 16.1	31 11.9	31 11.9
51 7.2	48 7.6	43 8.4			65 5.6		42 8.7	49 7.5	39 9.4
4.3	4.5	3.9			3.6		3.3	5.3	3.4
6.8	7.2	5.9	Sales/Working Capital		5.7		5.6	8.6	5.3
18.3	20.0	12.3			19.5		11.6	29.3	7.3
17.0	27.3	29.9			22.0		37.8	15.3	93.3
(130) 5.8	(101) 8.4	(96) 10.8	EBIT/Interest		(10) 2.7		(17) 16.9	(28) 6.3	(33) 12.8
1.9	1.8	3.0			1.2		6.5	2.4	4.4
6.1	12.6	12.7						9.9	36.7
(46) 2.3	(39) 4.8	(38) 4.7	Net Profit + Depr., Dep., Amort./Cur. Mat. L/T/D					(12) 3.3	(17) 9.9
1.1	1.4	2.0						1.7	4.5
.2	.2	.2			.1		.1	.3	.2
.5	.6	.5	Fixed/Worth		.6		.2	.8	.4
2.0	1.5	1.3			1.6		.6	1.8	1.1
.6	.6	.4			.5		.2	.6	.3
1.7	1.2	1.0	Debt/Worth		1.3		.4	2.0	1.0
4.2	4.1	3.4			3.8		1.0	4.7	3.2
44.8	58.3	60.1			95.3		57.8	47.1	69.6
(123) 25.0	(97) 25.4	(98) 27.4	% Profit Before Taxes/Tangible Net Worth		(12) 12.4		(21) 11.4	(24) 27.6	(32) 30.5
8.8	9.2	9.9			1.6		6.4	12.1	10.7
16.0	20.7	21.9			36.6		33.6	17.3	21.6
9.0	7.1	10.1	% Profit Before Taxes/Total Assets		3.0		8.5	9.1	11.1
2.8	2.6	4.2			.2		4.3	4.8	4.2
29.9	32.7	31.4			115.3		87.0	26.8	24.5
11.8	11.4	12.0	Sales/Net Fixed Assets		15.0		21.4	11.2	10.5
5.9	5.4	5.8			6.1		8.7	4.7	5.8
2.9	3.0	3.0			3.7		3.2	3.1	2.7
2.2	2.1	2.2	Sales/Total Assets		2.8		2.2	2.2	1.8
1.6	1.5	1.4			1.2		1.4	1.6	1.2
.7	.8	.7					.8	.6	.7
(126) 1.4	(90) 1.4	(98) 1.2	% Depr., Dep., Amort./Sales				(16) 1.0	(30) 1.3	(35) 1.3
2.2	2.8	2.3					1.5	2.3	2.9
3.0	2.2	2.3							
(46) 4.9	(32) 3.7	(30) 4.2	% Officers', Directors' Owners' Comp/Sales						
7.6	6.3	6.9							
4190266M	4203801M	3967462M	Net Sales ($)	977M	28263M	35186M	156434M	492956M	3253646M
2703332M	2826578M	2627454M	Total Assets ($)	649M	19025M	16016M	77293M	234742M	2279729M

M = $ thousand MM = $ million

See Pages 9 through 22 for Explanation of Ratios and Data

Current Data Sorted by Assets | **Comparative Historical Data**

Type of Statement	0-500M	500M-2MM	2-10MM	10-50MM	50-100MM	100-250MM	4/1/09-3/31/10 ALL	4/1/10-3/31/11 ALL
Unqualified		1	1	8	1	3	16	13
Reviewed			16	9			18	19
Compiled			2		1		4	5
Tax Returns	1	2	9				5	9
Other		3	12	18	2	5	32	21
	12 (4/1-9/30/13)			82 (10/1/13-3/31/14)				
NUMBER OF STATEMENTS	1	6	40	35	4	8	75	67
	%	%	%	%	%	%	%	%
ASSETS								
Cash & Equivalents			10.2	5.5			6.2	9.0
Trade Receivables (net)			26.6	23.0			25.9	26.8
Inventory			30.4	26.6			26.3	29.1
All Other Current			1.0	1.9			3.0	1.9
Total Current			68.2	56.9			61.3	66.8
Fixed Assets (net)			20.2	22.3			21.4	18.4
Intangibles (net)			3.4	14.0			8.9	6.7
All Other Non-Current			8.3	6.9			8.3	8.1
Total			100.0	100.0			100.0	100.0
LIABILITIES								
Notes Payable-Short Term			9.3	7.5			9.3	9.5
Cur. Mat.-L.T.D.			2.1	3.4			4.1	4.9
Trade Payables			16.8	12.4			14.3	15.5
Income Taxes Payable			.2	.1			.4	.2
All Other Current			9.8	7.9			7.6	8.5
Total Current			38.1	31.3			35.7	38.5
Long-Term Debt			12.7	14.4			14.5	11.4
Deferred Taxes			.2	2.7			1.1	.7
All Other Non-Current			3.3	3.8			8.8	8.1
Net Worth			45.6	47.8			39.8	41.3
Total Liabilties & Net Worth			100.0	100.0			100.0	100.0
INCOME DATA								
Net Sales			100.0	100.0			100.0	100.0
Gross Profit			32.2	28.3			32.8	33.6
Operating Expenses			27.5	20.1			27.3	27.4
Operating Profit			4.7	8.3			5.5	6.2
All Other Expenses (net)			-.1	1.7			1.1	.6
Profit Before Taxes			4.8	6.6			4.4	5.6
RATIOS								
Current			2.8	2.7			2.7	2.7
			1.9	1.8			1.9	1.8
			1.2	1.4			1.3	1.3
Quick			1.6	1.6			1.5	1.4
			1.1	.9			.9	.9
			.7	.6			.6	.6
Sales/Receivables			**29** 12.4	**38** 9.6			**39** 9.4	**33** 10.9
			37 9.9	**43** 8.4			**47** 7.8	**44** 8.3
			43 8.4	**53** 6.9			**52** 7.0	**55** 6.7
Cost of Sales/Inventory			**45** 8.2	**49** 7.5			**50** 7.3	**55** 6.7
			63 5.8	**65** 5.6			**67** 5.4	**70** 5.2
			101 3.6	**94** 3.9			**97** 3.8	**103** 3.5
Cost of Sales/Payables			**22** 16.4	**23** 16.0			**25** 14.5	**22** 16.9
			32 11.4	**30** 12.2			**32** 11.4	**32** 11.3
			51 7.2	**36** 10.1			**45** 8.1	**56** 6.5
Sales/Working Capital			4.7	4.9			5.4	4.9
			8.1	6.9			7.2	7.4
			22.9	14.5			22.4	20.2
EBIT/Interest			28.1	28.7			12.3	18.4
			(36) 9.7	(34) 8.9			(70) 3.8	(59) 5.9
			3.2	5.2			1.5	2.9
Net Profit + Depr., Dep., Amort./Cur. Mat. L/T/D				8.3			7.6	5.2
				(16) 2.8			(24) 2.8	(19) 2.8
				1.4			1.3	2.1
Fixed/Worth			.2	.3			.2	.2
			.5	.7			.7	.5
			1.2	2.0			1.6	1.3
Debt/Worth			.6	.7			.8	.6
			1.3	1.1			1.9	1.7
			2.9	7.9			4.9	3.3
% Profit Before Taxes/Tangible Net Worth			45.8	40.0			41.6	54.8
			(37) 20.3	(28) 22.8			(68) 20.6	(62) 31.4
			9.5	14.0			5.5	11.1
% Profit Before Taxes/Total Assets			16.3	19.0			14.9	18.6
			9.8	9.3			6.1	8.3
			3.4	6.4			1.9	3.9
Sales/Net Fixed Assets			32.8	17.5			23.6	41.0
			12.6	10.5			10.9	14.6
			7.7	5.7			6.0	7.1
Sales/Total Assets			3.0	2.5			2.5	2.6
			2.4	1.9			2.0	2.1
			2.0	1.6			1.6	1.6
% Depr., Dep., Amort./Sales			.7	.8			.8	.9
			(36) 1.3	1.6			(61) 1.7	(54) 1.4
			1.9	2.7			2.5	2.1
% Officers', Directors' Owners' Comp/Sales			2.1				3.0	2.8
			(21) 2.8				(20) 6.1	(26) 4.3
			8.3				8.6	7.8
Net Sales ($)	1002M	23081M	503695M	1635612M	411637M	1628134M	2598491M	2289217M
Total Assets ($)	374M	7956M	203885M	902116M	229865M	1333277M	1634189M	1275718M

M = $ thousand MM = $ million

See Pages 9 through 22 for Explanation of Ratios and Data

Comparative Historical Data				Current Data Sorted by Sales					
			Type of Statement						
15	19	14	Unqualified		1			3	10
22	14	25	Reviewed				4	9	12
7	4	3	Compiled					2	1
8	3	12	Tax Returns		1	1	6	4	
33	34	40	Other		2		8	7	23
4/1/11-3/31/12 ALL	4/1/12-3/31/13 ALL	4/1/13-3/31/14 ALL		12 (4/1-9/30/13)			82 (10/1/13-3/31/14)		
				0-1MM	1-3MM	3-5MM	5-10MM	10-25MM	25MM & OVER
85	74	94	**NUMBER OF STATEMENTS**		4	1	18	25	46
%	%	%	**ASSETS**	%	%	%	%	%	%
9.3	9.3	8.9	Cash & Equivalents	DATA NOT AVAILABLE			12.9	9.2	7.2
28.2	25.6	25.8	Trade Receivables (net)				26.2	26.1	24.9
28.0	25.5	27.1	Inventory				29.3	29.9	24.5
2.2	1.8	1.3	All Other Current				1.6	.4	1.8
67.6	62.2	63.1	Total Current				69.9	65.6	58.4
19.6	19.6	21.0	Fixed Assets (net)				17.9	16.4	24.5
7.6	9.9	9.2	Intangibles (net)				6.4	8.9	10.8
5.3	8.3	6.7	All Other Non-Current				5.8	9.1	6.3
100.0	100.0	100.0	Total				100.0	100.0	100.0
			LIABILITIES						
9.1	9.5	8.3	Notes Payable-Short Term				7.2	10.1	7.8
3.0	2.4	2.4	Cur. Mat.-L.T.D.				2.7	1.6	2.9
16.6	13.3	14.0	Trade Payables				17.3	13.3	13.5
.2	.7	.3	Income Taxes Payable				.2	.2	.4
13.9	8.2	10.4	All Other Current				11.2	10.3	10.8
42.8	34.2	35.4	Total Current				38.5	35.6	35.4
13.9	14.5	13.9	Long-Term Debt				16.6	9.0	15.3
.9	1.2	1.4	Deferred Taxes				.1	1.8	1.7
8.6	6.6	4.9	All Other Non-Current				5.5	2.6	5.9
33.8	43.4	44.4	Net Worth				39.2	50.9	41.7
100.0	100.0	100.0	Total Liabilities & Net Worth				100.0	100.0	100.0
			INCOME DATA						
100.0	100.0	100.0	Net Sales				100.0	100.0	100.0
30.6	29.2	31.2	Gross Profit				39.9	29.4	28.2
24.7	22.5	24.2	Operating Expenses				35.7	23.1	20.7
5.9	6.8	7.0	Operating Profit				4.2	6.3	7.4
.9	1.2	.8	All Other Expenses (net)				.3	.2	1.2
5.0	5.6	6.3	Profit Before Taxes				3.9	6.1	6.2
			RATIOS						
3.0	3.0	2.8					2.8	3.0	2.5
1.9	1.8	1.8	Current				1.7	2.2	1.6
1.3	1.4	1.3					1.3	1.2	1.3
1.6	2.0	1.6					1.5	1.7	1.5
.9	1.0	1.0	Quick				1.0	1.3	.9
.7	.7	.6					.7	.6	.6
32 11.3	**33** 11.2	**32** 11.3					**29** 12.6	**32** 11.3	**34** 10.6
42 8.7	**40** 9.1	**41** 8.8	Sales/Receivables				**35** 10.4	**40** 9.1	**43** 8.4
51 7.1	**54** 6.8	**52** 7.0					**45** 8.2	**51** 7.2	**58** 6.3
46 7.9	**43** 8.5	**47** 7.8					**44** 8.3	**46** 8.0	**45** 8.1
64 5.7	**55** 6.6	**65** 5.6	Cost of Sales/Inventory				**65** 5.6	**68** 5.4	**61** 6.0
85 4.3	**79** 4.6	**94** 3.9					**111** 3.3	**118** 3.1	**81** 4.5
21 17.2	**20** 18.2	**23** 15.9					**24** 15.5	**14** 26.9	**26** 14.0
32 11.4	**30** 12.3	**30** 12.0	Cost of Sales/Payables				**35** 10.4	**24** 15.1	**31** 11.9
46 8.0	**41** 8.9	**41** 8.9					**60** 6.1	**36** 10.0	**38** 9.7
4.8	4.4	4.4					4.0	3.9	5.1
7.5	8.3	7.9	Sales/Working Capital				11.4	7.5	9.3
15.2	16.2	16.5					19.1	20.2	16.6
24.0	28.3	29.7					13.4	35.1	41.3
(72) 6.4	(72) 9.1	(85) 9.4	EBIT/Interest				(14) 3.7	(23) 11.1	(45) 10.8
2.5	2.9	4.5					2.4	4.4	5.7
7.2	11.5	11.5							8.6
(26) 3.3	(28) 3.7	(28) 3.7	Net Profit + Depr., Dep., Amort./Cur. Mat. L/T/D						(21) 3.7
2.0	1.7	2.3							2.0
.2	.2	.2					.1	.1	.3
.6	.5	.6	Fixed/Worth				.6	.4	.7
1.8	1.0	1.4					NM	.9	1.4
.7	.7	.6					.7	.6	.7
1.7	1.3	1.2	Debt/Worth				1.6	.9	1.1
4.5	3.6	3.4					NM	3.9	3.1
49.8	47.1	43.8					50.9	26.5	44.0
(70) 23.3	(66) 24.3	(80) 23.2	% Profit Before Taxes/Tangible Net Worth				(14) 17.2	(22) 17.9	(39) 26.9
10.7	13.8	12.5					5.6	8.9	16.7
16.6	15.0	17.2					16.4	16.8	16.5
9.8	9.5	9.8	% Profit Before Taxes/Total Assets				7.3	10.1	9.6
3.4	4.3	5.1					2.7	4.6	7.1
31.9	24.7	23.7					64.3	30.9	16.4
13.4	11.0	11.2	Sales/Net Fixed Assets				13.6	12.4	9.2
6.0	6.6	6.0					7.5	7.9	5.3
3.2	2.8	2.7					3.0	2.8	2.5
2.4	2.0	2.1	Sales/Total Assets				2.5	2.3	1.9
1.7	1.5	1.6					1.9	1.6	1.5
.9	.9	.7					.3	.8	.8
(69) 1.5	(65) 1.5	(85) 1.6	% Depr., Dep., Amort./Sales				(15) 1.5	(23) 1.3	1.8
2.6	2.2	2.6					3.7	1.6	2.9
1.9	1.7	2.1					2.6	2.1	
(21) 3.0	(18) 3.0	(29) 3.2	% Officers', Directors' Owners' Comp/Sales				(10) 6.8	(11) 2.8	
4.2	7.1	7.6					19.6	4.1	
3357288M	3748834M	4203161M	Net Sales ($)		7104M	3967M	126876M	360113M	3705101M
2071015M	2407291M	2677473M	Total Assets ($)		4073M	2715M	53792M	228192M	2388701M

M = $ thousand MM = $ million

See Pages 9 through 22 for Explanation of Ratios and Data

Current Data Sorted by Assets | **Comparative Historical Data**

0-500M	500M-2MM	2-10MM	10-50MM	50-100MM	100-250MM		4/1/09-3/31/10 ALL	4/1/10-3/31/11 ALL
						Type of Statement		
		2	6	2	1	Unqualified	6	3
	2	3	5			Reviewed	9	13
		2	1			Compiled	5	6
4	3	2				Tax Returns	13	17
2	2	7	8	3	2	Other	26	29
	9 (4/1-9/30/13)		48 (10/1/13-3/31/14)					
6	7	16	20	5	3	**NUMBER OF STATEMENTS**	59	68
%	%	%	%	%	%	**ASSETS**	%	%
		4.3	3.3			Cash & Equivalents	8.0	7.4
		30.8	24.2			Trade Receivables (net)	25.7	23.5
		31.3	28.3			Inventory	26.4	28.5
		3.5	2.1			All Other Current	2.4	1.8
		69.9	57.8			Total Current	62.5	61.2
		19.3	26.0			Fixed Assets (net)	22.8	25.4
		4.4	10.7			Intangibles (net)	7.3	7.7
		6.4	5.5			All Other Non-Current	7.4	5.8
		100.0	100.0			Total	100.0	100.0
						LIABILITIES		
		12.8	12.9			Notes Payable-Short Term	11.8	11.0
		1.9	3.5			Cur. Mat.-L.T.D.	7.1	5.2
		17.2	12.1			Trade Payables	15.0	15.8
		.2	.0			Income Taxes Payable	.1	.1
		8.2	7.4			All Other Current	10.1	7.4
		40.3	36.0			Total Current	44.2	39.4
		8.2	11.0			Long-Term Debt	15.6	17.7
		.2	.2			Deferred Taxes	.6	.3
		3.8	11.4			All Other Non-Current	3.9	6.4
		47.6	41.5			Net Worth	35.7	36.2
		100.0	100.0			Total Liabilties & Net Worth	100.0	100.0
						INCOME DATA		
		100.0	100.0			Net Sales	100.0	100.0
		39.0	25.7			Gross Profit	42.2	38.7
		31.6	20.7			Operating Expenses	34.4	32.8
		7.4	5.0			Operating Profit	7.7	5.9
		1.1	1.0			All Other Expenses (net)	1.0	1.0
		6.2	4.1			Profit Before Taxes	6.8	4.9
						RATIOS		
		2.9	2.2				2.8	2.7
		1.8	1.6			Current	1.8	1.6
		1.3	1.3				1.0	1.2
		1.7	1.1				1.9	1.4
		.9	.7			Quick	.9	.9
		.5	.5				.5	.5
		21 17.6	**33** 10.9				**31** 11.9	**27** 13.7
		36 10.0	**42** 8.7			Sales/Receivables	**40** 9.2	**37** 9.9
		68 5.4	**59** 6.2				**50** 7.3	**49** 7.5
		42 8.6	**54** 6.8				**39** 9.4	**38** 9.5
		85 4.3	**65** 5.6			Cost of Sales/Inventory	**68** 5.3	**66** 5.5
		122 3.0	**94** 3.9				**113** 3.2	**109** 3.3
		25 14.8	**22** 16.9				**21** 17.5	**20** 18.7
		41 9.0	**26** 13.9			Cost of Sales/Payables	**36** 10.0	**36** 10.0
		64 5.7	**34** 10.8				**59** 6.2	**52** 7.0
		4.4	6.7				4.4	5.4
		8.4	10.4			Sales/Working Capital	10.0	9.9
		29.7	22.5				-999.8	24.6
		45.9	14.7				17.4	19.8
		(15) 10.0	7.5			EBIT/Interest	(52) 4.9	(66) 5.0
		1.9	1.9				2.5	2.5
			12.4				4.4	3.7
			(11) 4.0			Net Profit + Depr., Dep., Amort./Cur. Mat. L/T/D	(15) 1.8	(16) 1.8
			.2				1.1	1.0
		.1	.5				.2	.3
		.5	.7			Fixed/Worth	.6	.8
		.8	1.3				2.4	2.4
		.5	1.0				.9	1.0
		1.1	1.5			Debt/Worth	2.0	1.6
		2.1	4.3				4.3	6.5
		69.2	76.6				79.0	67.9
		(15) 23.4	(18) 27.0			% Profit Before Taxes/Tangible Net Worth	(50) 30.0	(58) 29.6
		3.3	5.6				8.8	10.3
		26.0	19.8				22.1	19.0
		12.9	8.1			% Profit Before Taxes/Total Assets	8.6	7.4
		1.1	2.1				3.3	2.6
		106.8	13.9				33.7	31.4
		16.4	8.7			Sales/Net Fixed Assets	14.6	12.4
		7.4	5.0				6.3	6.1
		3.4	2.4				2.9	2.9
		2.5	2.0			Sales/Total Assets	2.2	2.3
		1.8	1.7				1.7	1.8
		.4	1.6				1.1	1.0
		(14) .8	2.1			% Depr., Dep., Amort./Sales	(46) 1.9	(61) 1.8
		1.8	3.3				3.1	3.1
							1.7	1.4
						% Officers', Directors' Owners' Comp/Sales	(24) 3.5	(30) 4.4
							6.0	6.9
7229M	35153M	167333M	887943M	807696M	630259M	Net Sales ($)	1479425M	2049846M
1717M	10682M	71911M	440050M	379948M	511204M	Total Assets ($)	737978M	1115874M

M = $ thousand MM = $ million

See Pages 9 through 22 for Explanation of Ratios and Data

Comparative Historical Data / Current Data Sorted by Sales

4/1/11-3/31/12 ALL	4/1/12-3/31/13 ALL	4/1/13-3/31/14 ALL		0-1MM	1-3MM	3-5MM	5-10MM	10-25MM	25MM & OVER
			Type of Statement						
8	5	11	Unqualified				1	2	8
14	8	10	Reviewed				4	2	4
3	2	3	Compiled			2			1
14	8	9	Tax Returns	1	4	2		2	
24	26	24	Other	1	1	2	2	6	12
				9 (4/1-9/30/13)			48 (10/1/13-3/31/14)		
63	49	57	**NUMBER OF STATEMENTS**	2	5	6	7	12	25
%	%	%	**ASSETS**	%	%	%	%	%	%
8.9	7.4	8.1	Cash & Equivalents					5.0	5.0
25.8	28.5	25.8	Trade Receivables (net)					36.9	22.4
28.3	27.7	28.4	Inventory					27.7	25.2
1.9	1.6	2.3	All Other Current					.3	2.7
65.0	65.1	64.5	Total Current					69.9	55.2
22.6	16.3	19.9	Fixed Assets (net)					18.7	23.0
6.7	12.8	9.1	Intangibles (net)					4.2	14.9
5.7	5.7	6.6	All Other Non-Current					7.2	6.9
100.0	100.0	100.0	Total					100.0	100.0
			LIABILITIES						
10.5	11.2	13.6	Notes Payable-Short Term					10.5	9.7
4.3	2.4	4.2	Cur. Mat.-L.T.D.					3.8	2.4
19.5	23.3	14.7	Trade Payables					13.8	12.3
.3	.0	.1	Income Taxes Payable					.3	.0
5.8	7.3	8.0	All Other Current					8.6	7.4
40.4	44.3	40.6	Total Current					37.0	31.9
15.9	14.2	16.5	Long-Term Debt					6.0	13.0
.4	.5	.3	Deferred Taxes					.2	.5
5.7	6.5	14.7	All Other Non-Current					8.3	8.7
37.6	34.5	28.0	Net Worth					48.5	45.9
100.0	100.0	100.0	Total Liabilities & Net Worth					100.0	100.0
			INCOME DATA						
100.0	100.0	100.0	Net Sales					100.0	100.0
36.9	36.9	34.4	Gross Profit					31.8	26.7
31.9	32.0	28.6	Operating Expenses					25.9	21.4
5.1	4.8	5.8	Operating Profit					5.9	5.3
.4	1.0	.8	All Other Expenses (net)					.3	1.2
4.7	3.8	5.0	Profit Before Taxes					5.6	4.1
			RATIOS						
2.9	2.9	2.6						2.5	2.4
1.7	1.9	1.8	Current					1.8	1.8
1.3	1.2	1.2						1.5	1.3
1.7	1.6	1.5						1.8	1.4
.9	.9	.9	Quick					1.0	.9
.6	.6	.5						.5	.6
28 13.2	**29** 12.6	**25** 14.7						**31** 11.9	**33** 11.1
38 9.7	**41** 9.0	**38** 9.7	Sales/Receivables					**40** 9.1	**38** 9.5
47 7.8	**48** 7.6	**50** 7.3						**78** 4.7	**50** 7.3
35 10.4	**38** 9.7	**42** 8.7						**35** 10.4	**45** 8.1
58 6.3	**59** 6.2	**69** 5.3	Cost of Sales/Inventory					**85** 4.3	**59** 6.2
94 3.9	**96** 3.8	**91** 4.0						**94** 3.9	**85** 4.3
22 16.3	**20** 18.2	**23** 15.6						**24** 15.1	**22** 16.8
34 10.7	**35** 10.3	**30** 12.3	Cost of Sales/Payables					**26** 13.8	**26** 13.9
62 5.9	**54** 6.7	**44** 8.3						**36** 10.1	**35** 10.3
5.4	5.8	5.9						5.3	5.6
9.2	8.4	9.5	Sales/Working Capital					8.9	9.0
25.4	21.4	23.5						14.6	19.6
17.2	44.7	31.5						48.3	18.6
(54) 4.3	(47) 8.1	(54) 8.6	EBIT/Interest					17.4	10.8
1.3	3.2	1.9						2.1	1.6
	12.2	8.5							8.3
	(11) 8.0	(19) 3.7	Net Profit + Depr., Dep., Amort./Cur. Mat. L/T/D						(13) 3.7
	1.9	.3							1.1
.1	.1	.2						.0	.5
.5	.5	.7	Fixed/Worth					.4	.7
1.4	2.2	1.3						.8	1.3
.6	.5	.7						.5	1.1
1.5	1.3	1.5	Debt/Worth					.9	1.5
3.0	35.6	30.5						1.7	4.0
64.1	68.7	61.4						69.7	57.5
(54) 22.5	(39) 30.6	(45) 23.7	% Profit Before Taxes/Tangible Net Worth					(11) 33.1	(21) 23.7
2.3	11.1	7.8						4.0	8.9
24.7	19.7	22.2						26.0	14.0
7.7	9.6	8.8	% Profit Before Taxes/Total Assets					14.9	8.2
.2	1.7	1.7						1.9	1.3
52.9	54.1	39.4						154.9	14.1
13.4	20.3	13.8	Sales/Net Fixed Assets					13.0	9.1
6.3	8.4	8.0						7.4	6.9
3.3	3.5	3.2						3.4	2.4
2.4	2.4	2.2	Sales/Total Assets					2.5	2.1
2.0	1.9	1.7						1.8	1.6
.8	.8	.8						.7	1.5
(51) 1.6	(38) 1.2	(49) 1.5	% Depr., Dep., Amort./Sales					(10) 1.3	(23) 2.1
2.7	2.0	2.8						2.3	3.4
2.2	1.2	1.4							
(26) 3.5	(19) 1.6	(16) 4.2	% Officers', Directors' Owners' Comp/Sales						
6.0	5.9	10.6							
1712845M	1744423M	2535613M	Net Sales ($)	600M	9382M	23755M	50464M	190929M	2260483M
954888M	1127852M	1415512M	Total Assets ($)	289M	2325M	15569M	19398M	91614M	1286317M

M = $ thousand MM = $ million

See Pages 9 through 22 for Explanation of Ratios and Data

Current Data Sorted by Assets							Comparative Historical Data	
						Type of Statement		
1		2	7	2	1	Unqualified	14	16
		6	6			Reviewed	21	16
1	2	2				Compiled	7	11
1		2				Tax Returns	7	10
	2	7	10		1	Other	18	14
5 (4/1-9/30/13)		48 (10/1/13-3/31/14)					4/1/09-3/31/10 ALL	4/1/10-3/31/11 ALL
0-500M	**500M-2MM**	**2-10MM**	**10-50MM**	**50-100MM**	**100-250MM**			
3	4	19	23	2	2	**NUMBER OF STATEMENTS**	67	67
%	%	%	%	%	%	**ASSETS**	%	%
		11.1	7.6			Cash & Equivalents	9.8	11.4
		33.0	25.8			Trade Receivables (net)	28.5	27.4
		31.8	25.9			Inventory	25.2	26.9
		1.0	3.1			All Other Current	2.0	2.0
		76.9	62.4			Total Current	65.5	67.7
		9.6	26.5			Fixed Assets (net)	18.6	20.2
		7.2	6.0			Intangibles (net)	7.4	6.8
		6.3	5.1			All Other Non-Current	8.5	5.3
		100.0	100.0			Total	100.0	100.0
						LIABILITIES		
		13.0	11.0			Notes Payable-Short Term	10.9	9.2
		1.1	4.0			Cur. Mat.-L.T.D.	2.3	2.4
		20.2	12.9			Trade Payables	16.3	15.4
		.0	.0			Income Taxes Payable	.1	.2
		10.9	8.8			All Other Current	8.0	8.6
		45.2	36.7			Total Current	37.7	35.9
		3.0	10.4			Long-Term Debt	12.5	10.6
		.3	.3			Deferred Taxes	.3	.3
		.2	2.8			All Other Non-Current	13.8	4.3
		51.4	49.7			Net Worth	35.6	49.0
		100.0	100.0			Total Liabilties & Net Worth	100.0	100.0
						INCOME DATA		
		100.0	100.0			Net Sales	100.0	100.0
		38.0	33.2			Gross Profit	37.9	40.7
		34.6	26.7			Operating Expenses	32.1	34.9
		3.3	6.5			Operating Profit	5.8	5.7
		.2	.6			All Other Expenses (net)	.9	.6
		3.1	5.9			Profit Before Taxes	4.9	5.1
						RATIOS		
		2.5	2.2				2.7	3.7
		1.6	1.7			Current	1.8	1.8
		1.3	1.2				1.3	1.2
		1.3	1.1				1.8	2.5
		.9	.9			Quick	1.0	1.0
		.8	.6				.6	.6
		33 11.2	**34** 10.6				**34** 10.8	**31** 11.9
		34 10.7	**41** 9.0			Sales/Receivables	**41** 8.9	**39** 9.4
		54 6.8	**50** 7.3				**47** 7.7	**50** 7.3
		33 10.9	**43** 8.4				**41** 8.8	**48** 7.5
		47 7.8	**61** 6.0			Cost of Sales/Inventory	**63** 5.8	**62** 5.9
		63 5.8	**91** 4.0				**84** 4.3	**102** 3.6
		26 13.8	**17** 21.2				**19** 19.1	**16** 22.4
		40 9.1	**25** 14.4			Cost of Sales/Payables	**35** 10.3	**32** 11.3
		56 6.5	**46** 8.0				**50** 7.2	**49** 7.5
		6.8	6.9				5.6	4.2
		14.0	11.9			Sales/Working Capital	8.0	8.5
		18.4	17.0				22.2	18.7
		11.6	23.4				12.3	24.0
		(16) 7.7	(20) 6.4			EBIT/Interest	(59) 7.7	(57) 6.9
		5.1	2.4				2.6	3.0
			10.9				8.5	4.8
			(11) 3.3			Net Profit + Depr., Dep., Amort./Cur. Mat. L/T/D	(20) 3.7	(15) 2.5
			1.5				1.1	1.0
		.1	.3				.2	.2
		.2	.6			Fixed/Worth	.5	.4
		.4	.8				1.0	1.0
		.7	.7				.7	.5
		1.3	1.4			Debt/Worth	1.6	1.1
		1.9	1.9				4.4	2.3
		47.7	32.7				46.3	49.3
		(18) 20.1	22.6			% Profit Before Taxes/Tangible Net Worth	(58) 24.3	(60) 24.7
		3.2	10.0				9.5	7.4
		14.2	15.1				24.5	19.3
		8.8	10.2			% Profit Before Taxes/Total Assets	9.8	10.5
		1.1	2.4				2.8	4.2
		69.3	16.3				30.4	36.8
		34.8	11.2			Sales/Net Fixed Assets	16.6	14.6
		19.3	5.1				9.1	7.2
		4.4	2.5				3.1	3.2
		3.1	2.3			Sales/Total Assets	2.4	2.4
		2.6	1.7				1.7	1.5
		.4	1.2				1.1	1.1
		(14) 1.1	(22) 1.9			% Depr., Dep., Amort./Sales	(57) 1.4	(59) 1.5
		1.4	2.7				2.2	2.4
							1.7	2.9
						% Officers', Directors' Owners' Comp/Sales	(22) 3.2	(23) 5.0
							8.2	8.8
3510M	**14074M**	**284555M**	**1333073M**	**167078M**	**352763M**	Net Sales ($)	**2881152M**	**2461353M**
748M	**4858M**	**89109M**	**594035M**	**161517M**	**253927M**	Total Assets ($)	**1388903M**	**1217113M**

M = $ thousand MM = $ million

See Pages 9 through 22 for Explanation of Ratios and Data

Comparative Historical Data / Current Data Sorted by Sales

4/1/11-3/31/12 ALL	4/1/12-3/31/13 ALL	4/1/13-3/31/14 ALL		0-1MM	1-3MM	3-5MM	5-10MM	10-25MM	25MM & OVER
			Type of Statement						
6	11	13	Unqualified		1			2	10
19	19	12	Reviewed				2	2	8
7	6	5	Compiled	1	1	1		2	
8	2	3	Tax Returns	1			1	1	
22	15	20	Other		1	2	3	4	10
				5 (4/1-9/30/13)			48 (10/1/13-3/31/14)		
62	53	53	**NUMBER OF STATEMENTS**	2	3	3	6	11	28
%	%	%	**ASSETS**	%	%	%	%	%	%
10.3	9.7	10.2	Cash & Equivalents					8.7	8.2
28.7	28.6	29.3	Trade Receivables (net)					35.5	27.0
28.1	27.6	28.4	Inventory					27.6	27.3
1.7	1.7	1.9	All Other Current					.9	2.9
68.9	67.6	69.8	Total Current					72.7	65.3
17.3	19.5	18.6	Fixed Assets (net)					17.2	23.4
6.7	4.1	5.8	Intangibles (net)					3.3	6.2
7.1	8.8	5.8	All Other Non-Current					6.8	5.1
100.0	100.0	100.0	Total					100.0	100.0
			LIABILITIES						
10.9	9.3	11.8	Notes Payable-Short Term					14.5	11.1
2.4	3.2	2.7	Cur. Mat.-L.T.D.					1.8	3.7
15.5	14.8	16.2	Trade Payables					16.4	13.4
.5	.1	.1	Income Taxes Payable					.1	.1
9.0	8.9	9.1	All Other Current					12.7	8.3
38.3	36.2	39.8	Total Current					45.4	36.6
8.6	10.9	9.2	Long-Term Debt					5.4	11.4
.1	.2	.3	Deferred Taxes					.4	.3
3.7	5.3	1.8	All Other Non-Current					.2	2.8
49.3	47.3	48.9	Net Worth					48.5	48.9
100.0	100.0	100.0	Total Liabilties & Net Worth					100.0	100.0
			INCOME DATA						
100.0	100.0	100.0	Net Sales					100.0	100.0
36.6	35.6	36.5	Gross Profit					47.1	31.4
31.2	29.3	30.0	Operating Expenses					41.4	25.4
5.4	6.2	6.5	Operating Profit					5.7	6.0
.4	.2	.4	All Other Expenses (net)					.6	.3
5.0	6.0	6.0	Profit Before Taxes					5.0	5.6
			RATIOS						
3.0	4.2	2.6						1.8	2.5
1.8	1.8	1.7	Current					1.5	1.7
1.3	1.4	1.3						1.4	1.3
2.1	1.7	1.4						1.1	1.4
1.1	1.1	.9	Quick					1.0	.8
.6	.6	.6						.7	.7
32 11.3	**31** 11.9	**33** 11.0						**33** 11.2	**34** 10.6
40 9.2	**37** 9.8	**39** 9.4	Sales/Receivables					**33** 10.9	**41** 8.9
48 7.6	**46** 7.9	**53** 6.9						**55** 6.6	**50** 7.3
42 8.6	**42** 8.7	**42** 8.7						**33** 10.9	**45** 8.1
58 6.3	**62** 5.9	**56** 6.5	Cost of Sales/Inventory					**56** 6.5	**64** 5.7
79 4.6	**101** 3.6	**94** 3.9						**114** 3.2	**89** 4.1
17 21.0	**16** 23.1	**19** 18.8						**17** 20.9	**18** 20.7
32 11.4	**27** 13.3	**32** 11.4	Cost of Sales/Payables					**30** 12.3	**26** 13.9
46 8.0	**45** 8.1	**47** 7.7						**45** 8.2	**43** 8.4
5.9	4.9	5.8						8.4	5.0
8.2	8.1	9.9	Sales/Working Capital					14.0	9.9
15.6	20.8	17.0						18.4	16.2
23.1	25.0	23.4						11.8	32.3
(51) 6.1	(47) 7.1	(44) 7.4	EBIT/Interest					(10) 6.3	(24) 7.0
2.0	2.8	3.1						4.5	2.8
16.9	6.9	10.3							9.7
(15) 6.8	(14) 2.1	(16) 3.4	Net Profit + Depr., Dep., Amort./Cur. Mat. L/T/D						(13) 3.3
1.6	.9	1.4							1.2
.2	.2	.2						.2	.3
.4	.5	.4	Fixed/Worth					.2	.6
.8	1.1	.8						.4	.8
.5	.6	.7						.8	.8
1.3	1.2	1.4	Debt/Worth					1.3	1.5
3.0	3.5	2.1						1.6	2.1
45.6	52.5	46.3						59.6	32.7
(59) 20.3	(50) 25.7	(52) 23.1	% Profit Before Taxes/Tangible Net Worth					26.6	16.2
6.7	6.8	7.0						3.3	8.3
21.7	20.3	16.8						29.4	12.9
7.6	10.6	10.0	% Profit Before Taxes/Total Assets					11.8	9.0
2.0	2.4	3.0						1.1	3.1
33.8	43.0	63.7						69.3	17.8
16.0	14.7	18.3	Sales/Net Fixed Assets					34.8	11.7
10.2	6.6	6.7						18.3	6.2
3.3	3.2	3.5						4.7	2.8
2.5	2.3	2.5	Sales/Total Assets					3.1	2.3
2.0	1.7	1.8						2.5	1.7
.8	.7	.8						.4	1.3
(53) 1.4	(47) 1.3	(44) 1.6	% Depr., Dep., Amort./Sales					(10) 1.1	(27) 1.8
2.2	2.0	2.2						2.2	2.5
2.4		2.8							
(19) 3.8		(10) 7.0	% Officers', Directors' Owners' Comp/Sales						
10.6		9.6							
2555041M	**2367928M**	**2155053M**	Net Sales ($)	**690M**	**6787M**	**11281M**	**47941M**	**171215M**	**1917139M**
1351638M	**1227404M**	**1104194M**	Total Assets ($)	**372M**	**4678M**	**3432M**	**21293M**	**63344M**	**1011075M**

M = $ thousand MM = $ million

See Pages 9 through 22 for Explanation of Ratios and Data

Current Data Sorted by Assets							Comparative Historical Data	
						Type of Statement		
			8	4	6	Unqualified	26	16
		5	14			Reviewed	22	15
		7	1			Compiled	5	9
1	3	5				Tax Returns	3	6
	3	19	23	10	4	Other	38	49
11 (4/1-9/30/13)			102 (10/1/13-3/31/14)				4/1/09-3/31/10	4/1/10-3/31/11
0-500M	**500M-2MM**	**2-10MM**	**10-50MM**	**50-100MM**	**100-250MM**		**ALL**	**ALL**
1	6	36	46	14	10	**NUMBER OF STATEMENTS**	94	95
%	%	%	%	%	%	**ASSETS**	%	%
		10.9	9.5	2.1	7.0	Cash & Equivalents	7.0	10.1
		25.7	24.0	19.0	13.2	Trade Receivables (net)	25.9	25.2
		35.0	27.6	23.2	17.4	Inventory	30.2	29.2
		2.1	2.3	1.4	2.9	All Other Current	4.3	2.4
		73.5	63.4	45.7	40.5	Total Current	67.4	66.9
		13.1	18.8	6.4	12.9	Fixed Assets (net)	16.3	16.7
		8.9	13.7	43.8	40.4	Intangibles (net)	10.4	12.5
		4.4	4.1	4.1	6.2	All Other Non-Current	5.9	3.9
		100.0	100.0	100.0	100.0	Total	100.0	100.0
						LIABILITIES		
		15.2	8.7	7.6	.0	Notes Payable-Short Term	13.2	9.3
		1.6	1.3	3.0	1.9	Cur. Mat.-L.T.D.	2.8	2.3
		18.7	12.1	11.1	9.2	Trade Payables	21.1	16.5
		.2	.3	.1	.0	Income Taxes Payable	.4	.2
		6.9	7.9	5.0	9.0	All Other Current	9.4	10.0
		42.6	30.3	26.8	20.2	Total Current	46.9	38.2
		9.2	14.5	22.3	26.8	Long-Term Debt	10.4	11.8
		.7	1.4	3.3	3.9	Deferred Taxes	.4	.5
		11.9	13.0	5.3	4.9	All Other Non-Current	3.6	9.7
		35.7	40.8	42.3	44.1	Net Worth	38.8	39.7
		100.0	100.0	100.0	100.0	Total Liabilties & Net Worth	100.0	100.0
						INCOME DATA		
		100.0	100.0	100.0	100.0	Net Sales	100.0	100.0
		41.3	38.6	35.9	38.4	Gross Profit	37.4	40.0
		34.6	29.7	30.3	32.2	Operating Expenses	31.5	33.8
		6.7	8.9	5.6	6.2	Operating Profit	5.9	6.2
		.3	1.9	2.7	1.2	All Other Expenses (net)	1.3	1.5
		6.5	6.9	2.9	5.0	Profit Before Taxes	4.6	4.7
						RATIOS		
		2.8	4.4	2.4	3.3		2.1	2.9
		1.6	1.9	1.8	2.2	Current	1.5	1.9
		1.4	1.5	1.4	1.9		1.1	1.3
		1.9	2.1	1.1	1.4		1.2	1.6
		.7	1.1	.8	1.2	Quick	.8	.8
		.5	.7	.5	.9		.5	.6
		27 13.4	**36** 10.2	**32** 11.4	**29** 12.6		**31** 11.9	**31** 11.8
		35 10.4	**45** 8.2	**37** 9.9	**43** 8.5	Sales/Receivables	**43** 8.4	**44** 8.2
		51 7.1	**62** 5.9	**68** 5.4	**58** 6.3		**60** 6.0	**61** 6.0
		59 6.2	**57** 6.4	**76** 4.8	**50** 7.3		**55** 6.6	**60** 6.1
		79 4.6	**91** 4.0	**94** 3.9	**94** 3.9	Cost of Sales/Inventory	**92** 4.0	**93** 3.9
		130 2.8	**118** 3.1	**146** 2.5	**126** 2.9		**141** 2.6	**144** 2.5
		21 17.1	**24** 15.2	**29** 12.5	**27** 13.6		**32** 11.4	**24** 15.0
		42 8.7	**36** 10.0	**41** 8.8	**39** 9.4	Cost of Sales/Payables	**50** 7.3	**43** 8.5
		57 6.4	**54** 6.7	**49** 7.4	**54** 6.7		**77** 4.7	**73** 5.0
		5.4	3.5	3.6	3.2		5.2	3.9
		9.2	6.2	6.1	5.5	Sales/Working Capital	10.1	6.3
		13.0	13.4	24.5	9.1		29.9	12.9
		16.9	40.6	5.7			17.5	22.7
		(31) 7.4	(43) 7.8	3.6		EBIT/Interest	(87) 5.2	(85) 6.6
		4.3	.7	.8			1.5	1.8
			6.7				13.3	18.0
			(11) 3.7			Net Profit + Depr., Dep., Amort./Cur. Mat. L/T/D	(21) 5.9	(18) 8.1
			-2.9				2.2	1.7
		.1	.2	.2	.2		.2	.2
		.4	.4	NM	NM	Fixed/Worth	.7	.5
		2.6	5.2	-.1	-.2		1.5	2.0
		.7	.5	1.7	.6		1.1	.6
		1.6	1.2	NM	NM	Debt/Worth	2.3	1.8
		7.1	9.1	-1.8	-2.2		4.8	5.1
		76.6	78.2				53.8	54.6
		(29) 40.8	(36) 38.1			% Profit Before Taxes/Tangible Net Worth	(79) 28.2	(77) 29.4
		14.6	16.4				8.0	11.3
		23.8	29.0	7.6	13.3		14.6	18.9
		11.1	11.4	4.4	8.7	% Profit Before Taxes/Total Assets	8.1	7.4
		5.4	-.4	-.5	-3.4		1.1	1.3
		176.9	39.9	76.1	20.2		36.3	35.1
		17.4	11.1	30.9	15.1	Sales/Net Fixed Assets	15.4	14.2
		11.0	8.0	23.7	5.1		7.6	7.7
		3.2	2.4	1.8	2.4		2.6	2.8
		2.6	1.9	1.3	1.1	Sales/Total Assets	2.0	2.0
		1.7	1.4	.7	.6		1.4	1.2
		.6	1.0				.8	.7
		(29) 1.1	(37) 1.5			% Depr., Dep., Amort./Sales	(77) 1.8	(79) 1.5
		2.2	2.3				3.0	2.4
		1.0					1.3	2.1
		(15) 2.4				% Officers', Directors' Owners' Comp/Sales	(25) 3.2	(26) 4.2
		7.7					5.3	7.6
2081M	31905M	436214M	2079793M	1414857M	2056193M	Net Sales ($)	4223748M	4036205M
415M	7039M	191552M	1147559M	1028678M	1626476M	Total Assets ($)	2642988M	2628769M

M = $ thousand MM = $ million

See Pages 9 through 22 for Explanation of Ratios and Data

Comparative Historical Data				Current Data Sorted by Sales					
			Type of Statement						
19	18	18	Unqualified					1	17
22	10	19	Reviewed				3	4	12
9	7	8	Compiled				4	3	1
3	8	9	Tax Returns		2	1	2	4	
39	55	59	Other			4	8	9	38
					11 (4/1-9/30/13)		102 (10/1/13-3/31/14)		
4/1/11-3/31/12 ALL	**4/1/12-3/31/13 ALL**	**4/1/13-3/31/14 ALL**		**0-1MM**	**1-3MM**	**3-5MM**	**5-10MM**	**10-25MM**	**25MM & OVER**
92	98	113	**NUMBER OF STATEMENTS**		2	5	17	21	68
%	%	%	**ASSETS**	%	%	%	%	%	%
6.9	7.7	9.2	Cash & Equivalents	DATA NOT AVAILABLE			11.6	10.3	7.9
24.0	23.7	22.6	Trade Receivables (net)				16.4	31.8	21.8
31.5	32.8	28.9	Inventory				33.5	37.1	25.1
2.4	1.9	2.0	All Other Current				2.6	1.3	2.2
64.8	66.0	62.7	Total Current				64.1	80.5	57.0
17.3	16.5	15.1	Fixed Assets (net)				19.2	13.4	14.1
13.4	12.6	17.6	Intangibles (net)				13.7	3.8	24.0
4.4	4.8	4.6	All Other Non-Current				2.9	2.2	5.0
100.0	100.0	100.0	Total				100.0	100.0	100.0
			LIABILITIES						
11.7	11.1	10.2	Notes Payable-Short Term				10.6	12.9	9.0
2.5	2.4	1.6	Cur. Mat.-L.T.D.				2.5	1.1	1.7
17.1	17.8	14.1	Trade Payables				13.4	22.3	12.2
.1	.2	.2	Income Taxes Payable				.0	.4	.2
13.5	11.6	7.1	All Other Current				10.5	5.6	7.1
44.9	43.0	33.1	Total Current				36.9	42.3	30.2
11.0	15.3	14.2	Long-Term Debt				12.0	10.1	16.9
.8	1.2	1.5	Deferred Taxes				.8	.6	2.2
9.1	9.1	10.3	All Other Non-Current				20.7	3.4	10.7
34.2	31.3	40.8	Net Worth				29.6	43.6	40.0
100.0	100.0	100.0	Total Liabilties & Net Worth				100.0	100.0	100.0
			INCOME DATA						
100.0	100.0	100.0	Net Sales				100.0	100.0	100.0
38.0	36.9	40.3	Gross Profit				44.8	39.8	38.0
31.0	29.1	32.9	Operating Expenses				38.3	33.7	29.8
6.9	7.8	7.4	Operating Profit				6.5	6.0	8.1
1.1	1.1	1.3	All Other Expenses (net)				1.6	.0	1.9
5.9	6.7	6.1	Profit Before Taxes				4.9	6.0	6.2
			RATIOS						
2.6	2.8	3.2					3.3	3.1	3.2
1.6	1.7	1.8	Current				1.5	1.8	1.9
1.2	1.2	1.4					1.2	1.4	1.5
1.3	1.4	1.8					1.7	2.2	1.6
.7	.7	.9	Quick				.6	.8	1.0
.5	.5	.6					.3	.6	.7
31 11.7	**33** 10.9	**29** 12.7					**17** 21.2	**31** 11.6	**32** 11.5
44 8.3	**45** 8.2	**41** 8.9	Sales/Receivables				**29** 12.7	**49** 7.4	**42** 8.6
57 6.4	**58** 6.3	**59** 6.2					**41** 9.0	**60** 6.1	**62** 5.9
64 5.7	**63** 5.8	**59** 6.2					**60** 6.1	**44** 8.3	**59** 6.2
89 4.1	**85** 4.3	**89** 4.1	Cost of Sales/Inventory				**104** 3.5	**76** 4.8	**89** 4.1
126 2.9	**135** 2.7	**122** 3.0					**152** 2.4	**135** 2.7	**114** 3.2
24 15.0	**27** 13.7	**26** 14.2					**20** 18.4	**23** 16.2	**28** 13.2
38 9.6	**38** 9.5	**38** 9.5	Cost of Sales/Payables				**30** 12.0	**44** 8.3	**38** 9.6
73 5.0	**68** 5.4	**54** 6.8					**59** 6.2	**59** 6.2	**53** 6.9
4.6	4.6	4.1					5.0	4.5	3.7
9.5	8.3	7.2	Sales/Working Capital				12.9	8.9	6.3
25.8	21.5	13.8					24.5	11.6	12.7
15.8	24.6	23.3					6.1	30.7	26.7
(82) 7.2	(88) 6.0	(103) 6.5	EBIT/Interest				(14) 4.4	(20) 16.5	(63) 5.2
2.1	2.0	1.7					-.3	6.8	.8
6.7	24.9	7.8							6.1
(20) 2.3	(26) 4.7	(22) 3.9	Net Profit + Depr., Dep., Amort./Cur. Mat. L/T/D						(17) 3.3
1.3	2.0	1.3							.6
.2	.1	.2					.1	.1	.2
.5	.5	.5	Fixed/Worth				.8	.4	.8
3.7	27.1	-51.6					NM	.6	-.3
.8	.8	.7					1.2	.6	.7
1.9	2.2	1.6	Debt/Worth				1.7	1.5	2.0
14.7	-44.7	-182.9					NM	1.9	-3.6
57.9	62.8	71.5					142.3	60.3	80.3
(71) 25.6	(73) 35.6	(84) 34.2	% Profit Before Taxes/Tangible Net Worth				(13) 25.0	(19) 35.7	(45) 35.7
10.6	16.9	16.7					1.2	22.4	16.6
17.6	22.0	23.2					17.7	20.0	23.2
7.0	9.0	10.0	% Profit Before Taxes/Total Assets				5.6	14.6	8.1
2.7	2.4	2.2					-.9	8.5	-.2
45.3	72.7	56.7					76.0	143.9	48.5
18.5	19.6	17.9	Sales/Net Fixed Assets				16.0	20.9	19.6
8.2	8.9	9.1					6.9	11.3	9.0
3.0	2.5	2.8					3.0	3.8	2.4
1.9	2.0	2.0	Sales/Total Assets				2.1	2.7	1.8
1.3	1.3	1.3					1.0	1.9	1.2
.8	.7	.8					.8	.4	1.0
(70) 1.6	(71) 1.4	(81) 1.4	% Depr., Dep., Amort./Sales				(15) 2.4	(17) 1.0	(45) 1.7
2.6	2.6	2.5					3.9	1.3	3.3
1.4	.9	1.2							
(24) 2.5	(24) 1.7	(25) 2.4	% Officers', Directors' Owners' Comp/Sales						
4.9	5.5	6.0							
3528057M	**5155827M**	**6021043M**	Net Sales ($)		**5003M**	**20085M**	**125006M**	**330975M**	**5539974M**
2654752M	**3482680M**	**4001719M**	Total Assets ($)		**1091M**	**8900M**	**85581M**	**137611M**	**3768536M**

M = $ thousand MM = $ million

See Pages 9 through 22 for Explanation of Ratios and Data

Current Data Sorted by Assets							Comparative Historical Data	
						Type of Statement		
			2		1	Unqualified	8	8
		3	1			Reviewed	10	9
	2	1				Compiled	3	5
	3					Tax Returns	12	2
	4	8	6		1	Other	17	12
	4 (4/1-9/30/13)		28 (10/1/13-3/31/14)				4/1/09-3/31/10 ALL	4/1/10-3/31/11 ALL
0-500M	500M-2MM	2-10MM	10-50MM	50-100MM	100-250MM			
	9	12	9		2	NUMBER OF STATEMENTS	50	36
%	%	%	%	%	%	**ASSETS**	%	%
DATA NOT AVAILABLE		7.5		DATA NOT AVAILABLE		Cash & Equivalents	10.8	6.3
		26.2				Trade Receivables (net)	27.5	31.2
		35.2				Inventory	27.5	27.2
		1.8				All Other Current	1.9	2.3
		70.6				Total Current	67.7	67.1
		19.6				Fixed Assets (net)	19.8	17.6
		3.7				Intangibles (net)	4.6	9.7
		6.1				All Other Non-Current	7.9	5.5
		100.0				Total	100.0	100.0
						LIABILITIES		
		9.8				Notes Payable-Short Term	9.1	11.1
		4.9				Cur. Mat.-L.T.D.	1.9	2.0
		22.0				Trade Payables	18.2	18.6
		.1				Income Taxes Payable	.2	.2
		8.4				All Other Current	8.8	8.0
		45.3				Total Current	38.1	39.9
		6.8				Long-Term Debt	12.2	18.7
		1.0				Deferred Taxes	1.4	.8
		2.0				All Other Non-Current	3.7	3.6
		44.9				Net Worth	44.7	36.9
		100.0				Total Liabilities & Net Worth	100.0	100.0
						INCOME DATA		
		100.0				Net Sales	100.0	100.0
		32.1				Gross Profit	36.7	32.9
		28.8				Operating Expenses	29.7	26.8
		3.3				Operating Profit	7.0	6.0
		.6				All Other Expenses (net)	.4	1.1
		2.6				Profit Before Taxes	6.6	4.9
						RATIOS		
		3.2					2.9	2.5
		1.4				Current	1.7	1.8
		1.3					1.2	1.2
		1.9					1.5	1.6
		.7				Quick	.9	.8
		.5					.7	.5
		31 11.7					**32** 11.4	**39** 9.3
		34 10.6				Sales/Receivables	**42** 8.8	**46** 8.0
		54 6.8					**52** 7.0	**58** 6.3
		41 8.9					**34** 10.8	**29** 12.7
		85 4.3				Cost of Sales/Inventory	**59** 6.1	**74** 4.9
		114 3.2					**107** 3.4	**109** 3.3
		13 28.8					**20** 18.5	**23** 15.9
		36 10.0				Cost of Sales/Payables	**33** 11.0	**32** 11.5
		58 6.3					**55** 6.6	**57** 6.4
		5.2					4.9	4.7
		9.3				Sales/Working Capital	7.4	9.2
		22.3					22.3	18.8
		11.9					21.5	27.4
		4.9				EBIT/Interest	(47) 7.7	(35) 6.1
		1.6					3.0	2.3
							15.4	26.4
						Net Profit + Depr., Dep., Amort./Cur. Mat. L/T/D	(15) 3.7	(12) 4.7
							1.6	2.8
		.2					.2	.3
		.5				Fixed/Worth	.5	.6
		.6					1.0	1.5
		.4					.5	.8
		1.5				Debt/Worth	1.2	3.2
		3.6					3.5	5.8
		27.2					69.4	45.1
		13.4				% Profit Before Taxes/Tangible Net Worth	(46) 25.0	(31) 30.2
		3.1					5.9	7.5
		13.3					19.8	17.1
		3.4				% Profit Before Taxes/Total Assets	10.5	9.1
		1.2					3.7	1.4
		26.8					33.1	39.3
		14.8				Sales/Net Fixed Assets	16.9	12.5
		8.6					7.2	7.0
		2.9					3.4	2.6
		2.4				Sales/Total Assets	2.2	2.2
		2.0					1.8	1.6
		.4					.9	.9
		(11) 1.0				% Depr., Dep., Amort./Sales	(38) 1.4	(30) 1.6
		2.3					3.5	2.6
							1.6	1.5
						% Officers', Directors' Owners' Comp/Sales	(16) 4.9	(10) 4.2
							12.2	8.0
	30140M	141304M	517392M		845389M	Net Sales ($)	1677961M	1391165M
	10203M	59977M	210234M		415033M	Total Assets ($)	866795M	709838M

M = $ thousand MM = $ million

See Pages 9 through 22 for Explanation of Ratios and Data

Comparative Historical Data				Current Data Sorted by Sales					
			Type of Statement						
7	3	3	Unqualified						3
9	4	4	Reviewed				1	2	1
3	2	3	Compiled		2		1		
5	4	3	Tax Returns		2		1		
10	16	19	Other	1	2	1	2	6	7
4/1/11-3/31/12	**4/1/12-3/31/13**	**4/1/13-3/31/14**		**4 (4/1-9/30/13)**			**28 (10/1/13-3/31/14)**		
ALL	**ALL**	**ALL**		**0-1MM**	**1-3MM**	**3-5MM**	**5-10MM**	**10-25MM**	**25MM & OVER**
34	29	32	**NUMBER OF STATEMENTS**	1	6	1	5	8	11
%	%	%	**ASSETS**	%	%	%	%	%	%
5.8	8.4	7.9	Cash & Equivalents						6.2
30.3	27.2	24.9	Trade Receivables (net)						25.2
31.1	31.8	32.4	Inventory						31.5
3.0	1.6	2.1	All Other Current						3.8
70.2	69.1	67.4	Total Current						66.8
18.0	17.1	19.7	Fixed Assets (net)						21.6
5.1	7.1	8.8	Intangibles (net)						8.0
6.7	6.7	4.1	All Other Non-Current						3.6
100.0	100.0	100.0	Total						100.0
			LIABILITIES						
11.2	11.9	14.1	Notes Payable-Short Term						12.0
1.9	3.2	2.6	Cur. Mat.-L.T.D.						1.9
20.5	17.2	19.1	Trade Payables						19.4
.1	.1	.1	Income Taxes Payable						.1
11.1	7.3	8.3	All Other Current						5.9
44.8	39.8	44.2	Total Current						39.3
15.8	15.9	8.4	Long-Term Debt						8.4
.6	.7	.5	Deferred Taxes						.4
5.6	4.9	5.2	All Other Non-Current						5.0
33.2	38.7	41.7	Net Worth						46.9
100.0	100.0	100.0	Total Liabilties & Net Worth						100.0
			INCOME DATA						
100.0	100.0	100.0	Net Sales						100.0
29.3	34.6	35.4	Gross Profit						32.6
24.4	27.8	31.5	Operating Expenses						26.9
4.9	6.8	3.9	Operating Profit						5.7
.7	.7	.9	All Other Expenses (net)						.6
4.2	6.1	3.0	Profit Before Taxes						5.1
			RATIOS						
2.3	3.0	2.8							3.1
1.7	1.7	1.6	Current						1.7
1.2	1.3	1.1							1.4
1.2	1.4	1.5							1.3
.8	.8	.8	Quick						.9
.5	.6	.5							.5
35 10.3	**32** 11.3	**30** 12.0							**36** 10.2
40 9.2	**43** 8.5	**35** 10.3	Sales/Receivables						**43** 8.4
50 7.3	**48** 7.6	**48** 7.6							**52** 7.0
38 9.5	**57** 6.4	**42** 8.6							**62** 5.9
65 5.6	**74** 4.9	**72** 5.1	Cost of Sales/Inventory						**69** 5.3
101 3.6	**94** 3.9	**111** 3.3							**99** 3.7
25 14.4	**24** 15.5	**29** 12.8							**30** 12.1
45 8.2	**31** 11.6	**38** 9.6	Cost of Sales/Payables						**37** 9.8
54 6.7	**59** 6.2	**51** 7.1							**52** 7.0
6.2	5.0	5.2							5.0
10.7	8.4	9.7	Sales/Working Capital						6.8
22.0	17.4	31.1							11.6
20.4	21.9	22.8							
6.5	(25) 8.5	(29) 6.8	EBIT/Interest						
1.7	1.4	1.6							
16.6									
(14) 3.2			Net Profit + Depr., Dep., Amort./Cur. Mat. L/T/D						
1.8									
.2	.3	.2							.3
.6	.6	.5	Fixed/Worth						.5
1.1	1.2	2.4							3.9
.9	.8	.7							.7
2.3	2.0	1.6	Debt/Worth						.8
5.1	6.3	7.4							7.5
87.3	69.1	37.0							
(31) 24.7	(26) 16.9	(26) 15.6	% Profit Before Taxes/Tangible Net Worth						
6.5	5.0	6.4							
17.4	18.0	15.1							21.0
9.2	6.0	7.6	% Profit Before Taxes/Total Assets						9.3
1.1	1.0	1.2							4.9
47.3	29.3	36.2							22.1
17.2	17.0	16.7	Sales/Net Fixed Assets						9.3
7.1	10.4	8.1							7.3
3.6	3.1	3.1							2.5
2.3	2.3	2.4	Sales/Total Assets						2.2
1.8	1.9	1.9							1.9
.6	.4	.8							
(23) 1.1	(26) 1.2	(25) 1.7	% Depr., Dep., Amort./Sales						
1.8	2.2	2.2							
			% Officers', Directors' Owners' Comp/Sales						
1134270M	**1532838M**	**1534225M**	Net Sales ($)	**372M**	**13436M**	**4884M**	**41097M**	**111655M**	**1362781M**
593031M	**696367M**	**695447M**	Total Assets ($)	**1173M**	**5659M**	**2187M**	**15512M**	**45649M**	**625267M**

M = $ thousand MM = $ million

See Pages 9 through 22 for Explanation of Ratios and Data

Current Data Sorted by Assets							Comparative Historical Data	
						Type of Statement		
			2	1	3	Unqualified	7	7
			2			Reviewed	4	1
			2			Compiled	2	3
	2	2	1			Tax Returns	4	2
	6	7	9	3	2	Other	13	15
	6 (4/1-9/30/13)		36 (10/1/13-3/31/14)				4/1/09-3/31/10	4/1/10-3/31/11
0-500M	500M-2MM	2-10MM	10-50MM	50-100MM	100-250MM		ALL	ALL
	8	9	16	4	5	**NUMBER OF STATEMENTS**	30	28
%	%	%	%	%	%	**ASSETS**	%	%
D			7.1			Cash & Equivalents	6.6	9.2
A			28.6			Trade Receivables (net)	24.2	28.2
T			24.9			Inventory	18.1	23.3
A			2.5			All Other Current	2.0	2.3
			63.2			Total Current	50.9	63.0
N			27.6			Fixed Assets (net)	39.7	26.1
O			7.2			Intangibles (net)	5.5	5.5
T			2.1			All Other Non-Current	3.9	5.3
			100.0			Total	100.0	100.0
A						**LIABILITIES**		
V			10.2			Notes Payable-Short Term	9.1	9.4
A			2.0			Cur. Mat.-L.T.D.	6.3	2.6
I			13.9			Trade Payables	15.3	19.5
L			.0			Income Taxes Payable	.6	.2
A			5.9			All Other Current	4.8	6.1
B			32.0			Total Current	36.1	37.8
L			15.5			Long-Term Debt	19.7	14.6
E			1.0			Deferred Taxes	.3	.5
			4.6			All Other Non-Current	3.5	8.2
			46.9			Net Worth	40.4	38.9
			100.0			Total Liabilties & Net Worth	100.0	100.0
						INCOME DATA		
			100.0			Net Sales	100.0	100.0
			21.4			Gross Profit	25.5	28.3
			13.7			Operating Expenses	21.4	20.8
			7.7			Operating Profit	4.2	7.5
			1.2			All Other Expenses (net)	1.3	.8
			6.4			Profit Before Taxes	2.9	6.7
						RATIOS		
			3.4				2.3	2.4
			2.1			Current	1.4	1.9
			1.3				.8	1.1
			2.7				1.4	1.5
			1.0			Quick	.7	1.1
			.6				.4	.5
			30 12.1				**37** 9.9	**33** 11.1
			48 7.6			Sales/Receivables	**54** 6.8	**42** 8.6
			53 6.9				**64** 5.7	**60** 6.1
			27 13.4				**33** 11.2	**37** 9.9
			61 6.0			Cost of Sales/Inventory	**46** 8.0	**58** 6.3
			81 4.5				**76** 4.8	**77** 4.8
			19 19.7				**26** 14.2	**23** 15.9
			23 15.7			Cost of Sales/Payables	**42** 8.7	**40** 9.2
			33 11.2				**61** 5.9	**68** 5.4
			5.5				5.7	6.3
			7.4			Sales/Working Capital	15.6	7.7
			13.8				-13.4	59.5
			36.5				8.0	38.8
			(14) 4.6			EBIT/Interest	(28) 1.7	(24) 7.3
			2.5				-.2	1.5
						Net Profit + Depr., Dep., Amort./Cur. Mat. L/T/D		
			.3				.6	.4
			.6			Fixed/Worth	1.0	.6
			2.7				2.8	3.0
			.6				.7	.8
			1.2			Debt/Worth	1.7	1.3
			4.9				3.8	8.9
			49.6				20.9	76.9
			(14) 25.9			% Profit Before Taxes/Tangible Net Worth	(27) 5.2	(24) 35.3
			7.2				-10.7	12.4
			17.3				9.1	29.7
			5.2			% Profit Before Taxes/Total Assets	3.1	16.6
			3.1				-3.1	3.1
			13.6				9.1	17.8
			10.6			Sales/Net Fixed Assets	4.7	9.7
			3.8				1.9	5.1
			3.3				2.3	3.0
			2.3			Sales/Total Assets	1.5	2.4
			1.3				1.1	1.6
			.8				1.9	1.9
			1.8			% Depr., Dep., Amort./Sales	(25) 4.5	(20) 2.7
			2.6				8.1	3.6
							1.4	2.3
						% Officers', Directors' Owners' Comp/Sales	(12) 3.8	(11) 5.2
							6.6	6.7
	45275M	165904M	1105034M	591255M	1681900M	Net Sales ($)	1335316M	1555397M
	10431M	56945M	460760M	270015M	1070755M	Total Assets ($)	809849M	884354M

M = $ thousand MM = $ million

See Pages 9 through 22 for Explanation of Ratios and Data

Comparative Historical Data				Current Data Sorted by Sales					
			Type of Statement						
8	5	6	Unqualified						6
4	5	2	Reviewed						2
3	4	2	Compiled						2
3	2	5	Tax Returns			1	2	1	1
25	17	27	Other		3	1	2	8	13
4/1/11-3/31/12 ALL	4/1/12-3/31/13 ALL	4/1/13-3/31/14 ALL			6 (4/1-9/30/13)		36 (10/1/13-3/31/14)		
				0-1MM	1-3MM	3-5MM	5-10MM	10-25MM	25MM & OVER
43	33	42	**NUMBER OF STATEMENTS**		3	2	4	9	24
%	%	%	**ASSETS**	%	%	%	%	%	%
8.4	8.0	10.6	Cash & Equivalents	DATA NOT AVAILABLE					8.1
28.7	25.4	27.4	Trade Receivables (net)						28.3
21.4	27.2	21.3	Inventory						22.1
2.1	1.3	1.8	All Other Current						2.8
60.6	61.9	61.2	Total Current						61.4
27.8	27.7	27.1	Fixed Assets (net)						28.2
5.0	3.0	7.5	Intangibles (net)						7.1
6.5	7.3	4.2	All Other Non-Current						3.3
100.0	100.0	100.0	Total						100.0
			LIABILITIES						
9.3	10.0	9.1	Notes Payable-Short Term						9.0
3.2	3.3	2.6	Cur. Mat.-L.T.D.						2.2
18.4	17.4	15.1	Trade Payables						13.8
.1	.4	.2	Income Taxes Payable						.0
6.5	6.0	5.9	All Other Current						6.4
37.4	37.1	32.8	Total Current						31.4
16.0	20.0	18.5	Long-Term Debt						15.4
.5	.2	.9	Deferred Taxes						1.2
4.2	3.5	6.0	All Other Non-Current						4.6
41.9	39.3	41.8	Net Worth						47.4
100.0	100.0	100.0	Total Liabilities & Net Worth						100.0
			INCOME DATA						
100.0	100.0	100.0	Net Sales						100.0
27.2	28.3	27.2	Gross Profit						19.6
19.8	20.1	18.6	Operating Expenses						12.2
7.4	8.2	8.6	Operating Profit						7.4
.3	1.0	.9	All Other Expenses (net)						.8
7.1	7.2	7.7	Profit Before Taxes						6.6
			RATIOS						
2.8	2.8	3.3							3.3
1.8	1.8	2.0	Current						1.9
1.2	1.1	1.2							1.3
1.7	1.6	2.4							2.7
1.1	.8	1.1	Quick						1.1
.6	.5	.6							.5
25 14.5	**33** 10.9	**28** 13.0							**29** 12.4
41 9.0	**38** 9.5	**42** 8.6	Sales/Receivables						**47** 7.7
49 7.4	**45** 8.2	**51** 7.2							**51** 7.2
20 18.6	**42** 8.7	**25** 14.6							**26** 13.9
45 8.1	**64** 5.7	**45** 8.1	Cost of Sales/Inventory						**45** 8.1
57 6.4	**81** 4.5	**74** 4.9							**68** 5.4
19 19.0	**25** 14.8	**19** 19.5							**19** 19.7
27 13.3	**38** 9.7	**28** 13.0	Cost of Sales/Payables						**24** 15.2
42 8.6	**55** 6.6	**43** 8.4							**38** 9.7
5.5	6.2	5.6							5.5
10.5	9.6	8.6	Sales/Working Capital						8.6
48.0	23.7	30.1							14.6
42.7	21.9	51.5							94.4
(37) 11.4	(31) 6.4	(36) 8.9	EBIT/Interest						(23) 10.2
1.8	1.8	3.4							2.8
			Net Profit + Depr., Dep., Amort./Cur. Mat. L/T/D						
.3	.4	.4							.3
.5	.6	.8	Fixed/Worth						.6
1.4	2.2	2.7							2.8
.8	.7	.5							.5
1.4	1.6	1.5	Debt/Worth						1.2
3.8	3.3	6.5							4.9
60.9	61.1	101.2							51.0
(40) 36.2	(30) 22.4	(34) 37.6	% Profit Before Taxes/Tangible Net Worth						(20) 33.3
8.9	7.2	11.9							9.8
38.3	22.2	25.2							24.5
13.0	8.1	11.7	% Profit Before Taxes/Total Assets						9.5
2.4	2.3	4.9							3.2
18.6	20.2	16.1							14.8
10.5	10.9	10.0	Sales/Net Fixed Assets						10.5
5.8	3.9	4.5							4.3
3.2	3.3	3.4							3.3
2.8	2.5	2.3	Sales/Total Assets						2.3
1.7	1.6	1.7							1.4
1.3	1.1	1.2							.8
(32) 2.0	(29) 2.1	(31) 2.1	% Depr., Dep., Amort./Sales						(20) 1.8
3.6	3.3	2.7							2.5
1.0									
(12) 2.1			% Officers', Directors' Owners' Comp/Sales						
4.1									
3395605M	2288016M	3589368M	Net Sales ($)		6804M	8742M	28406M	144475M	3400941M
1377597M	1056403M	1868906M	Total Assets ($)		2661M	4648M	10380M	93118M	1758099M

M = $ thousand MM = $ million

See Pages 9 through 22 for Explanation of Ratios and Data

Current Data Sorted by Assets							Comparative Historical Data	
						Type of Statement		
		5	14	9	10	Unqualified	48	35
	5	17	13			Reviewed	43	48
1	7	8	1		1	Compiled	19	16
6	13	10				Tax Returns	21	22
2	20	26	32	20	10	Other	95	108
41 (4/1-9/30/13)			**189 (10/1/13-3/31/14)**				**4/1/09-3/31/10**	**4/1/10-3/31/11**
0-500M	**500M-2MM**	**2-10MM**	**10-50MM**	**50-100MM**	**100-250MM**		**ALL**	**ALL**
9	45	66	60	29	21	**NUMBER OF STATEMENTS**	226	229
%	%	%	%	%	%	**ASSETS**	%	%
	11.6	9.8	7.0	6.1	6.6	Cash & Equivalents	9.4	8.9
	31.4	27.4	26.2	20.0	17.8	Trade Receivables (net)	26.5	28.3
	26.0	23.8	26.7	25.8	16.3	Inventory	23.3	25.5
	3.0	3.2	2.3	3.0	2.0	All Other Current	3.5	2.8
	72.1	64.2	62.1	54.9	42.8	Total Current	62.8	65.5
	17.9	22.8	23.8	26.6	34.8	Fixed Assets (net)	25.8	22.3
	3.6	5.2	9.0	13.6	15.2	Intangibles (net)	5.6	6.1
	6.5	7.9	5.1	4.9	7.2	All Other Non-Current	5.8	6.2
	100.0	100.0	100.0	100.0	100.0	Total	100.0	100.0
						LIABILITIES		
	6.6	11.3	10.5	12.9	5.6	Notes Payable-Short Term	10.9	9.2
	5.5	2.8	3.0	3.6	2.9	Cur. Mat.-L.T.D.	3.8	3.5
	19.9	15.8	17.5	12.8	10.4	Trade Payables	15.8	15.4
	.0	.3	.4	.4	.2	Income Taxes Payable	.2	.3
	9.1	7.4	7.3	4.8	5.2	All Other Current	10.5	8.7
	41.1	37.7	38.7	34.6	24.3	Total Current	41.1	37.2
	19.2	15.8	12.9	13.6	23.6	Long-Term Debt	15.1	14.3
	.2	.3	.4	1.9	3.5	Deferred Taxes	.7	.7
	13.1	4.2	4.7	4.2	6.3	All Other Non-Current	6.2	7.0
	26.4	42.0	43.3	45.7	42.3	Net Worth	36.9	40.8
	100.0	100.0	100.0	100.0	100.0	Total Liabilities & Net Worth	100.0	100.0
						INCOME DATA		
	100.0	100.0	100.0	100.0	100.0	Net Sales	100.0	100.0
	41.2	36.5	30.3	23.9	22.7	Gross Profit	33.3	34.7
	37.5	30.4	23.3	15.8	14.8	Operating Expenses	27.7	27.3
	3.6	6.1	7.0	8.1	7.8	Operating Profit	5.5	7.3
	.6	1.1	.8	1.1	1.9	All Other Expenses (net)	1.1	.8
	3.1	4.9	6.2	7.0	5.9	Profit Before Taxes	4.4	6.5
						RATIOS		
	3.6	2.8	2.5	2.4	2.5		2.7	3.0
	2.2	1.7	1.6	1.8	2.0	Current	1.7	1.8
	1.3	1.1	1.2	1.3	1.4		1.2	1.3
	2.5	1.7	1.5	1.6	1.6		1.6	1.8
	1.0	1.0	.9	.9	1.2	Quick	.9	1.0
	.7	.6	.5	.5	1.0		.6	.6
	24 15.2	**33** 10.9	**34** 10.8	**35** 10.5	**43** 8.5		**29** 12.7	**31** 11.6
	41 8.8	**41** 8.8	**46** 8.0	**47** 7.8	**50** 7.3	Sales/Receivables	**42** 8.7	**44** 8.3
	53 6.9	**54** 6.8	**54** 6.8	**58** 6.3	**60** 6.1		**54** 6.7	**55** 6.6
	22 16.6	**36** 10.2	**39** 9.3	**38** 9.6	**31** 11.7		**28** 13.1	**35** 10.5
	48 7.6	**57** 6.4	**65** 5.6	**59** 6.2	**48** 7.6	Cost of Sales/Inventory	**57** 6.4	**56** 6.5
	87 4.2	**89** 4.1	**111** 3.3	**94** 3.9	**79** 4.6		**93** 3.9	**96** 3.8
	11 34.3	**22** 16.6	**19** 19.5	**24** 15.0	**24** 15.2		**20** 18.6	**21** 17.7
	27 13.3	**32** 11.4	**34** 10.7	**34** 10.6	**31** 11.7	Cost of Sales/Payables	**31** 11.6	**32** 11.5
	62 5.9	**55** 6.6	**49** 7.4	**44** 8.3	**45** 8.1		**50** 7.3	**52** 7.1
	4.6	4.6	5.6	4.2	3.9		4.9	4.6
	8.7	10.1	10.1	8.2	6.0	Sales/Working Capital	10.0	8.7
	18.4	56.8	22.4	18.3	15.7		26.8	18.9
	17.5	32.3	17.5	29.5	12.7		18.0	22.0
	(35) 3.9	(58) 6.6	(52) 8.4	(26) 6.9	(20) 7.0	EBIT/Interest	(197) 5.3	(197) 6.3
	1.0	1.7	3.4	3.3	1.8		1.5	2.9
		5.2	7.0	4.0			13.9	9.6
		(17) 4.1	(19) 3.3	(12) 2.8		Net Profit + Depr., Dep., Amort./Cur. Mat. L/T/D	(55) 3.0	(63) 3.4
		1.1	2.6	1.2			1.1	1.8
	.1	.1	.3	.4	.5		.3	.2
	.3	.5	.7	.8	1.5	Fixed/Worth	.7	.5
	NM	1.4	1.8	2.3	4.8		1.6	1.5
	.3	.6	.6	.6	.8		.7	.7
	1.2	1.5	1.9	1.8	2.0	Debt/Worth	1.6	1.5
	NM	3.9	5.7	9.6	12.7		4.6	5.4
	43.9	48.6	52.3	51.6	40.1		50.0	61.4
	(34) 20.4	(60) 20.4	(50) 25.1	(26) 30.3	(17) 20.0	% Profit Before Taxes/Tangible Net Worth	(190) 25.6	(206) 32.6
	5.5	7.3	12.5	19.2	12.4		5.8	13.6
	21.5	17.0	15.7	15.4	12.2		20.8	22.1
	8.8	9.0	10.3	7.7	8.6	% Profit Before Taxes/Total Assets	8.5	10.8
	1.6	1.2	4.6	3.6	1.7		1.2	4.2
	103.5	27.4	28.5	12.9	5.8		30.8	42.9
	22.7	19.0	9.4	7.1	4.1	Sales/Net Fixed Assets	10.4	12.1
	11.2	5.5	4.9	4.1	2.7		4.3	5.2
	3.7	3.0	2.6	2.1	1.8		3.0	3.0
	3.2	2.2	1.8	1.7	1.2	Sales/Total Assets	2.1	2.2
	2.0	1.5	1.4	1.2	.9		1.4	1.5
	.2	.7	.8	1.2	1.9		.8	.7
	(32) 1.0	(53) 1.2	(54) 1.6	(25) 1.7	(15) 3.6	% Depr., Dep., Amort./Sales	(185) 1.8	(193) 1.8
	2.5	2.6	2.8	3.6	6.9		3.9	3.3
	3.4	1.4					2.0	1.9
	(19) 4.5	(26) 2.7				% Officers', Directors' Owners' Comp/Sales	(56) 4.7	(60) 3.7
	17.5	6.0					8.2	6.8
15843M	**154252M**	**819037M**	**2623360M**	**3409105M**	**5050096M**	Net Sales ($)	**10746757M**	**9914218M**
2700M	**52902M**	**339050M**	**1320754M**	**2043072M**	**3661160M**	Total Assets ($)	**6177397M**	**5483814M**

M = $ thousand MM = $ million

See Pages 9 through 22 for Explanation of Ratios and Data

Comparative Historical Data | Current Data Sorted by Sales

	4/1/11-3/31/12 ALL	4/1/12-3/31/13 ALL	4/1/13-3/31/14 ALL	0-1MM	1-3MM	3-5MM	5-10MM	10-25MM	25MM & OVER
Type of Statement									
Unqualified	45	34	38				1	5	32
Reviewed	34	30	35		4	2	6	7	16
Compiled	24	19	18		4	3	5	4	2
Tax Returns	28	34	29		11	9	5	3	1
Other	107	114	110	3	13	8	11	20	55
				41 (4/1-9/30/13)		189 (10/1/13-3/31/14)			
NUMBER OF STATEMENTS	238	231	230	3	32	22	28	39	106
ASSETS	%	%	%	%	%	%	%	%	%
Cash & Equivalents	10.0	11.5	8.9		10.8	12.7	11.2	10.6	6.6
Trade Receivables (net)	26.9	26.2	26.3		27.4	28.4	25.6	29.1	24.8
Inventory	24.2	24.2	24.3		23.0	28.6	17.4	26.5	25.0
All Other Current	2.5	2.9	2.7		4.6	.8	4.1	2.3	2.3
Total Current	63.6	64.8	62.1		65.7	70.6	58.3	68.5	58.7
Fixed Assets (net)	24.0	22.5	23.6		16.7	18.2	31.7	19.3	25.1
Intangibles (net)	6.9	6.1	7.8		8.1	2.5	3.1	6.3	10.7
All Other Non-Current	5.5	6.6	6.5		9.5	8.7	6.8	5.8	5.5
Total	100.0	100.0	100.0		100.0	100.0	100.0	100.0	100.0
LIABILITIES									
Notes Payable-Short Term	7.8	8.9	11.1		17.5	4.5	11.8	9.1	10.9
Cur. Mat.-L.T.D.	3.5	2.8	3.6		5.7	2.3	4.6	3.2	2.7
Trade Payables	15.2	14.8	15.8		16.1	17.2	13.4	15.8	16.4
Income Taxes Payable	.3	.2	.3		.0	.0	.5	.4	.3
All Other Current	8.9	8.0	8.0		9.7	7.9	14.7	6.3	6.4
Total Current	35.8	34.8	38.8		49.1	31.9	44.8	34.8	36.8
Long-Term Debt	16.8	14.3	16.5		20.0	21.2	19.2	11.4	14.1
Deferred Taxes	.8	.8	.8		.2	.1	.1	.9	1.3
All Other Non-Current	6.1	7.3	6.9		18.0	2.0	3.9	2.6	5.1
Net Worth	40.5	42.8	37.0		12.8	44.9	31.9	50.3	42.7
Total Liabilties & Net Worth	100.0	100.0	100.0		100.0	100.0	100.0	100.0	100.0
INCOME DATA									
Net Sales	100.0	100.0	100.0		100.0	100.0	100.0	100.0	100.0
Gross Profit	32.3	31.9	33.2		38.5	47.5	37.9	32.8	26.8
Operating Expenses	25.8	24.5	27.0		35.1	43.3	31.9	25.5	19.5
Operating Profit	6.5	7.4	6.2		3.4	4.1	6.0	7.3	7.3
All Other Expenses (net)	.5	.7	1.0		1.3	1.2	.9	.6	1.0
Profit Before Taxes	5.9	6.7	5.2		2.1	3.0	5.1	6.7	6.3
RATIOS									
Current	2.8	3.4	2.8		3.7	7.5	2.7	2.8	2.4
	1.8	1.8	1.8		1.5	2.8	1.3	1.9	1.7
	1.3	1.2	1.2		.9	1.5	.8	1.3	1.3
Quick	1.8	2.0	1.7		2.3	3.9	1.5	2.2	1.5
	1.0	1.1	1.0		.8	1.6	.8	1.1	.9
	.6	.6	.6		.5	.8	.5	.7	.5
Sales/Receivables	29 12.7	30 12.0	33 11.2		25 14.7	29 12.6	29 12.8	34 10.8	34 10.8
	42 8.6	41 9.0	44 8.3		47 7.8	42 8.7	39 9.4	43 8.4	46 8.0
	55 6.6	52 7.0	55 6.6		63 5.8	51 7.2	43 8.4	55 6.6	55 6.6
Cost of Sales/Inventory	31 11.8	31 11.9	36 10.1		9 40.4	40 9.1	21 17.8	45 8.2	36 10.1
	54 6.7	51 7.1	54 6.8		50 7.3	69 5.3	46 8.0	62 5.9	54 6.8
	87 4.2	81 4.5	91 4.0		111 3.3	118 3.1	65 5.6	89 4.1	94 3.9
Cost of Sales/Payables	18 20.1	17 21.5	20 18.4		6 58.0	16 22.3	12 31.6	24 15.0	22 16.3
	29 12.6	29 12.4	31 11.6		33 10.9	29 12.6	26 14.1	33 11.1	32 11.3
	50 7.3	46 8.0	49 7.4		72 5.1	64 5.7	45 8.1	43 8.5	46 7.9
Sales/Working Capital	4.7	4.6	5.1		4.0	3.9	7.2	3.9	5.5
	8.7	8.4	9.6		12.3	6.7	19.1	7.0	9.9
	22.3	21.7	25.4		-46.4	12.0	-20.7	14.0	21.8
EBIT/Interest	22.2	34.7	18.5		9.4	16.4	53.8	39.5	18.8
	(206) 6.4	(193) 8.4	(197) 7.0		(25) 2.8	(16) 2.3	(26) 6.6	(33) 8.8	(94) 7.8
	2.0	2.1	1.9		-1.2	1.2	.9	4.4	3.1
Net Profit + Depr., Dep., Amort./Cur. Mat. L/T/D	4.8	10.8	5.1						4.5
	(61) 2.3	(65) 4.0	(62) 3.1						(41) 3.3
	1.4	1.8	1.8						2.5
Fixed/Worth	.2	.1	.2		.1	.1	.3	.1	.3
	.6	.6	.7		.5	.3	1.3	.4	.7
	2.1	1.7	2.5		NM	2.3	10.4	.9	1.9
Debt/Worth	.6	.5	.6		.4	.3	.9	.5	.7
	1.6	1.3	1.7		2.9	1.1	2.2	1.4	2.0
	6.1	4.6	6.8		-124.5	4.5	11.9	2.2	7.2
% Profit Before Taxes/Tangible Net Worth	55.3	55.9	47.6		38.6	25.2	63.8	46.4	52.3
	(201) 25.4	(198) 27.3	(191) 23.3		(23) 18.8	(18) 11.5	(23) 33.4	(37) 20.6	(90) 25.1
	8.7	8.7	9.4		-27.9	5.5	8.1	9.4	15.9
% Profit Before Taxes/Total Assets	20.3	22.9	15.9		17.3	14.3	22.7	22.2	15.3
	8.4	9.5	8.7		7.4	6.1	8.1	9.2	8.7
	2.3	2.4	2.5		-1.9	2.1	-1.2	3.9	4.2
Sales/Net Fixed Assets	40.2	42.8	32.8		201.4	68.2	36.1	32.7	23.9
	11.7	13.2	12.6		20.4	18.8	10.6	19.1	8.7
	5.2	5.3	4.9		5.6	14.1	3.7	6.2	4.5
Sales/Total Assets	3.1	3.1	3.0		3.4	3.5	3.7	3.0	2.6
	2.2	2.2	2.1		2.1	3.0	2.3	2.3	1.8
	1.4	1.4	1.4		1.1	1.9	1.6	1.7	1.3
% Depr., Dep., Amort./Sales	.8	.7	.7		.6	.2	.6	.7	.8
	(181) 1.7	(191) 1.6	(183) 1.4		(22) 1.6	(19) 1.1	(20) 1.1	(33) 1.2	(88) 1.7
	3.3	2.9	2.9		3.4	2.6	5.4	2.8	3.1
% Officers', Directors' Owners' Comp/Sales	1.3	2.4	1.4			2.5	3.2	1.4	.5
	(74) 3.9	(55) 3.8	(59) 3.6			(13) 4.0	(13) 5.5	(15) 1.7	(11) .9
	7.4	5.8	7.8			15.5	9.2	3.6	2.4
Net Sales ($)	10845296M	11489948M	12071693M	1915M	61802M	84298M	185922M	647225M	11090531M
Total Assets ($)	5756635M	6191949M	7419638M	3309M	39989M	36522M	100610M	512340M	6726868M

M = $ thousand MM = $ million

See Pages 9 through 22 for Explanation of Ratios and Data

Current Data Sorted by Assets / Comparative Historical Data

0-500M	500M-2MM	2-10MM	10-50MM	50-100MM	100-250MM		4/1/09-3/31/10 ALL	4/1/10-3/31/11 ALL
11 (4/1-9/30/13)		74 (10/1/13-3/31/14)				**Type of Statement**		
		1	7	4	3	Unqualified	9	9
	2	9	4			Reviewed	3	9
	2	3	1		1	Compiled	5	4
1	8	7	2			Tax Returns	6	13
1	2	10	9	5	3	Other	21	23
2	14	30	23	9	7	**NUMBER OF STATEMENTS**	44	58
%	%	%	%	%	%	**ASSETS**	%	%
	14.3	9.2	6.1			Cash & Equivalents	3.5	6.9
	24.9	29.8	24.9			Trade Receivables (net)	29.5	28.0
	23.7	29.6	25.4			Inventory	24.0	23.8
	4.1	1.5	2.6			All Other Current	2.7	3.5
	67.0	70.0	59.1			Total Current	59.7	62.1
	21.8	22.4	24.6			Fixed Assets (net)	30.9	27.0
	2.9	4.5	5.7			Intangibles (net)	4.3	4.7
	8.2	3.1	10.6			All Other Non-Current	5.1	6.3
	100.0	100.0	100.0			Total	100.0	100.0
						LIABILITIES		
	10.9	14.3	8.1			Notes Payable-Short Term	18.4	10.1
	.3	3.4	3.7			Cur. Mat.-L.T.D.	3.7	6.9
	13.1	22.1	17.6			Trade Payables	19.6	19.0
	.0	.0	.1			Income Taxes Payable	.1	.3
	5.2	5.0	12.0			All Other Current	7.7	4.1
	29.4	44.8	41.5			Total Current	49.6	40.5
	12.8	17.2	11.2			Long-Term Debt	16.2	17.2
	.0	.5	1.0			Deferred Taxes	.6	.8
	10.9	7.2	3.7			All Other Non-Current	3.3	6.0
	46.8	30.3	42.6			Net Worth	30.2	35.5
	100.0	100.0	100.0			Total Liabilities & Net Worth	100.0	100.0
						INCOME DATA		
	100.0	100.0	100.0			Net Sales	100.0	100.0
	43.7	25.3	21.5			Gross Profit	26.5	27.7
	36.2	22.6	16.4			Operating Expenses	22.0	22.4
	7.4	2.8	5.1			Operating Profit	4.5	5.3
	2.4	.4	.5			All Other Expenses (net)	1.5	1.4
	5.1	2.4	4.6			Profit Before Taxes	3.0	3.9
						RATIOS		
	8.0	2.1	1.9				1.9	2.5
	2.8	1.7	1.5			Current	1.3	1.7
	1.5	1.3	1.0				1.0	1.1
	5.0	1.5	1.2				1.1	1.6
	1.5	.8	.7			Quick	.6	.8
	.8	.6	.6				.4	.5
	21 17.2	**28** 13.0	**30** 12.2				**34** 10.8	**28** 13.3
	46 8.0	**37** 9.8	**34** 10.7			Sales/Receivables	**42** 8.7	**41** 9.0
	54 6.8	**50** 7.3	**47** 7.8				**52** 7.0	**48** 7.6
	18 20.0	**33** 10.9	**32** 11.5				**32** 11.5	**30** 12.1
	53 6.9	**48** 7.6	**56** 6.5			Cost of Sales/Inventory	**52** 7.0	**49** 7.4
	140 2.6	**70** 5.2	**72** 5.1				**69** 5.3	**73** 5.0
	10 37.1	**27** 13.7	**23** 16.1				**25** 14.4	**19** 19.7
	22 16.9	**42** 8.7	**33** 10.9			Cost of Sales/Payables	**35** 10.4	**33** 11.2
	41 8.9	**58** 6.3	**42** 8.7				**50** 7.2	**51** 7.1
	4.2	6.2	7.2				10.7	5.9
	6.0	8.8	15.6			Sales/Working Capital	21.8	12.0
	26.2	18.7	94.5				269.2	50.0
	31.4	10.0	46.7				10.0	11.1
	(10) 11.7	(27) 6.2	(21) 10.6			EBIT/Interest	(43) 2.4	(54) 4.3
	2.5	1.8	5.6				1.4	2.0
							4.0	3.5
						Net Profit + Depr., Dep., Amort./Cur. Mat. L/T/D	(15) 2.5	(16) 2.5
							1.2	1.2
	.1	.2	.2				.5	.3
	.3	.7	.7			Fixed/Worth	1.1	.9
	.9	1.5	1.8				3.3	2.6
	.4	1.0	.6				.9	.9
	1.1	2.1	1.5			Debt/Worth	2.9	1.7
	3.0	17.7	5.0				9.0	5.3
	66.6	40.6	44.6				35.6	42.1
	(13) 17.1	(26) 25.1	(21) 20.6			% Profit Before Taxes/Tangible Net Worth	(38) 18.2	(49) 23.9
	2.5	5.2	12.4				6.4	7.7
	26.7	15.7	17.2				13.5	17.6
	10.5	8.1	10.1			% Profit Before Taxes/Total Assets	4.6	8.6
	.9	2.5	4.0				1.1	2.1
	48.6	35.8	22.6				17.4	33.8
	27.3	10.8	12.8			Sales/Net Fixed Assets	7.4	11.9
	6.4	5.5	6.0				4.7	5.7
	4.2	3.2	2.8				2.9	3.7
	2.2	2.5	2.7			Sales/Total Assets	2.3	2.3
	1.5	2.1	1.6				1.8	1.7
	.6	.5	.7				1.4	.8
	(12) 1.9	(24) 1.7	(22) 2.4			% Depr., Dep., Amort./Sales	(40) 2.8	(51) 2.0
	4.4	3.7	3.2				3.6	3.2
		1.4					1.7	1.4
		(12) 1.9				% Officers', Directors' Owners' Comp/Sales	(16) 4.5	(23) 3.0
		4.1					7.8	4.6
1775M	51918M	345896M	1243939M	824826M	1747717M	Net Sales ($)	1491034M	1702900M
530M	17651M	136802M	554710M	584149M	1197400M	Total Assets ($)	735641M	923715M

M = $ thousand MM = $ million

See Pages 9 through 22 for Explanation of Ratios and Data

Comparative Historical Data / Current Data Sorted by Sales

4/1/11-3/31/12 ALL	4/1/12-3/31/13 ALL	4/1/13-3/31/14 ALL	Type of Statement	0-1MM	1-3MM	3-5MM	5-10MM	10-25MM	25MM & OVER
11	8	15	Unqualified					2	13
7	4	15	Reviewed				4	7	4
5	8	7	Compiled		1		2	2	2
18	9	18	Tax Returns	2	4	3	4	3	2
42	45	30	Other	2	3		5	3	17
				11 (4/1-9/30/13)			74 (10/1/13-3/31/14)		
83	74	85	NUMBER OF STATEMENTS	4	8	3	15	17	38
%	%	%	**ASSETS**	%	%	%	%	%	%
4.8	6.4	9.0	Cash & Equivalents				11.8	6.9	4.3
26.7	25.3	25.2	Trade Receivables (net)				25.7	30.6	23.3
23.5	23.9	25.5	Inventory				27.6	28.1	25.0
1.4	3.2	2.2	All Other Current				4.1	1.3	2.1
56.4	58.8	61.9	Total Current				69.2	67.0	54.7
31.9	29.9	26.0	Fixed Assets (net)				26.3	19.0	30.5
4.7	6.4	5.9	Intangibles (net)				2.1	5.4	8.3
7.0	4.9	6.3	All Other Non-Current				2.4	8.6	6.4
100.0	100.0	100.0	Total				100.0	100.0	100.0
			LIABILITIES						
8.2	9.0	11.8	Notes Payable-Short Term				10.0	14.7	10.4
4.0	4.7	3.3	Cur. Mat.-L.T.D.				4.1	2.5	4.6
19.5	18.6	17.0	Trade Payables				15.3	27.6	15.8
.1	.1	.0	Income Taxes Payable				.0	.0	.0
9.1	8.1	7.3	All Other Current				4.5	7.1	8.6
40.8	40.4	39.4	Total Current				33.9	52.0	39.4
20.9	20.3	18.7	Long-Term Debt				22.9	9.5	23.1
.8	1.3	.7	Deferred Taxes				.2	.6	1.1
7.5	4.0	6.1	All Other Non-Current				12.1	.8	4.5
29.9	34.0	35.1	Net Worth				30.8	37.1	31.9
100.0	100.0	100.0	Total Liabilties & Net Worth				100.0	100.0	100.0
			INCOME DATA						
100.0	100.0	100.0	Net Sales				100.0	100.0	100.0
23.7	26.7	26.3	Gross Profit				32.9	20.0	19.0
18.2	20.6	21.7	Operating Expenses				27.4	17.7	14.6
5.5	6.2	4.6	Operating Profit				5.5	2.4	4.4
1.7	1.5	1.2	All Other Expenses (net)				.6	.0	1.6
3.8	4.7	3.4	Profit Before Taxes				4.9	2.4	2.7
			RATIOS						
2.7	2.5	2.3	Current				3.3	2.0	2.0
1.6	1.7	1.6					1.7	1.3	1.5
1.1	1.0	1.1					1.4	.8	1.0
1.3	1.3	1.4	Quick				1.9	1.2	1.1
.9	.8	.8					1.1	.7	.6
.5	.5	.5					.8	.4	.5
29 12.8	**32** 11.3	**29** 12.4	Sales/Receivables				**28** 13.0	**24** 15.2	**33** 11.2
39 9.4	**41** 8.9	**38** 9.6					**34** 10.7	**32** 11.4	**40** 9.1
49 7.5	**51** 7.1	**50** 7.3					**45** 8.1	**48** 7.6	**50** 7.3
27 13.5	**35** 10.5	**34** 10.8	Cost of Sales/Inventory				**31** 11.8	**26** 14.2	**44** 8.3
43 8.5	**53** 6.9	**55** 6.6					**68** 5.4	**45** 8.2	**59** 6.2
69 5.3	**79** 4.6	**72** 5.1					**89** 4.1	**62** 5.9	**72** 5.1
22 16.5	**24** 15.5	**23** 15.6	Cost of Sales/Payables				**26** 14.0	**25** 14.7	**27** 13.4
33 11.2	**39** 9.3	**33** 11.0					**29** 12.8	**41** 8.9	**33** 10.9
49 7.5	**54** 6.8	**47** 7.7					**47** 7.8	**57** 6.4	**42** 8.6
6.7	6.2	5.6	Sales/Working Capital				4.6	7.4	7.2
13.1	8.5	10.0					8.1	24.8	12.5
59.5	-136.0	56.2					13.7	-50.0	NM
14.2	22.3	18.0	EBIT/Interest				12.5	18.0	18.7
(75) 6.8	(66) 7.3	(75) 6.2					(13) 6.2	(15) 8.2	(36) 5.2
2.9	2.9	2.1					2.0	3.1	2.1
4.8	4.8	5.5	Net Profit + Depr., Dep., Amort./Cur. Mat. L/T/D						5.5
(20) 2.7	(21) 3.4	(19) 2.5							(15) 2.5
1.6	1.6	1.9							2.0
.4	.3	.2	Fixed/Worth				.3	.1	.5
1.0	1.0	.7					.8	.5	1.5
2.7	2.7	2.1					1.5	1.2	4.9
1.1	.9	.8	Debt/Worth				.6	1.0	1.1
1.9	1.7	2.1					2.1	1.3	2.3
7.3	9.3	7.3					6.8	94.2	27.1
42.9	51.9	45.6	% Profit Before Taxes/Tangible Net Worth				93.4	36.8	47.1
(68) 23.4	(61) 24.7	(73) 18.4					(13) 39.2	(15) 15.7	(31) 18.4
13.8	12.1	6.5					12.4	2.6	11.9
17.3	16.3	15.8	% Profit Before Taxes/Total Assets				20.0	14.7	13.1
8.1	9.7	7.3					14.5	7.7	5.2
3.4	2.7	2.3					3.7	1.1	2.8
16.4	20.2	25.6	Sales/Net Fixed Assets				28.3	82.2	14.8
8.0	8.3	10.5					9.9	21.8	8.1
4.1	3.9	4.5					5.6	9.8	3.9
3.1	2.9	3.0	Sales/Total Assets				3.1	4.2	2.8
2.3	2.1	2.3					2.4	3.0	2.0
1.7	1.4	1.5					2.1	2.0	1.4
1.3	1.1	.9	% Depr., Dep., Amort./Sales				.4	.3	1.1
(70) 2.8	(66) 2.6	(70) 2.6					(13) 1.6	(14) 1.3	(33) 2.8
5.2	4.0	3.8					3.6	3.8	3.8
1.3	1.2	1.8	% Officers', Directors' Owners' Comp/Sales						
(27) 2.7	(22) 3.1	(27) 3.0							
4.7	4.6	7.9							
2794794M	3812180M	4216071M	Net Sales ($)	2946M	15521M	11044M	122666M	259071M	3804823M
1621457M	2313318M	2491242M	Total Assets ($)	3030M	13166M	3644M	52294M	102025M	2317083M

M = $ thousand MM = $ million

See Pages 9 through 22 for Explanation of Ratios and Data

Current Data Sorted by Assets							Comparative Historical Data	
						Type of Statement		
		3	6		3	Unqualified	8	12
		4	3			Reviewed	8	8
		2	1			Compiled	1	3
1	2	2			1	Tax Returns	2	4
	2	8	11	5	4	Other	11	17
	8 (4/1-9/30/13)		50 (10/1/13-3/31/14)				4/1/09-3/31/10	4/1/10-3/31/11
0-500M	**500M-2MM**	**2-10MM**	**10-50MM**	**50-100MM**	**100-250MM**		**ALL**	**ALL**
1	4	19	21	5	8	**NUMBER OF STATEMENTS**	30	44
%	%	%	%	%	%	**ASSETS**	%	%
		7.2	5.7			Cash & Equivalents	7.5	6.8
		31.4	21.5			Trade Receivables (net)	28.9	27.7
		25.1	23.2			Inventory	21.7	25.9
		1.0	2.3			All Other Current	2.6	2.7
		64.7	52.7			Total Current	60.7	63.0
		25.1	35.0			Fixed Assets (net)	27.2	26.4
		7.0	4.1			Intangibles (net)	4.4	5.9
		3.1	8.2			All Other Non-Current	7.7	4.6
		100.0	100.0			Total	100.0	100.0
						LIABILITIES		
		11.2	9.5			Notes Payable-Short Term	11.5	9.5
		4.5	4.3			Cur. Mat.-L.T.D.	4.7	2.1
		22.1	16.2			Trade Payables	16.0	19.1
		.0	.1			Income Taxes Payable	.4	.3
		6.9	6.9			All Other Current	6.8	10.9
		44.7	37.0			Total Current	39.4	41.9
		13.2	19.7			Long-Term Debt	16.4	20.4
		.3	.4			Deferred Taxes	.7	1.0
		5.1	5.4			All Other Non-Current	8.8	8.7
		36.7	37.4			Net Worth	34.9	28.0
		100.0	100.0			Total Liabilities & Net Worth	100.0	100.0
						INCOME DATA		
		100.0	100.0			Net Sales	100.0	100.0
		25.8	23.7			Gross Profit	25.9	24.8
		21.5	19.3			Operating Expenses	21.5	19.4
		4.3	4.3			Operating Profit	4.4	5.4
		.2	1.0			All Other Expenses (net)	1.7	1.1
		4.1	3.4			Profit Before Taxes	2.8	4.3
						RATIOS		
		2.3	2.2				2.6	2.5
		1.6	1.4			Current	1.8	1.6
		1.0	1.1				1.1	1.1
		1.4	1.2				1.5	1.5
		.9	.8			Quick	.8	.8
		.5	.4				.6	.6
		24 15.5	29 12.8				33 11.2	37 10.0
		38 9.6	36 10.2			Sales/Receivables	45 8.1	43 8.5
		50 7.3	44 8.3				53 6.9	49 7.4
		28 13.2	35 10.5				33 10.9	43 8.4
		39 9.3	54 6.8			Cost of Sales/Inventory	49 7.5	56 6.5
		62 5.9	76 4.8				68 5.4	77 4.8
		21 17.7	22 16.5				22 16.8	24 15.1
		39 9.3	35 10.5			Cost of Sales/Payables	36 10.2	33 11.2
		51 7.1	53 6.9				52 7.0	50 7.3
		6.6	6.4				7.2	4.8
		19.6	15.0			Sales/Working Capital	9.3	9.1
		-264.2	89.0				55.5	33.6
		19.8	11.5				24.5	18.4
		(18) 5.2	(20) 4.4			EBIT/Interest	(28) 4.4	(39) 5.5
		1.9	2.0				1.8	2.0
							16.9	15.7
						Net Profit + Depr., Dep., Amort./Cur. Mat. L/T/D	(12) 5.5	(16) 4.6
							1.0	1.4
		.3	.4				.3	.4
		1.1	1.0			Fixed/Worth	.8	.7
		9.8	2.7				3.3	7.0
		1.0	.7				.7	.8
		1.6	1.6			Debt/Worth	1.9	2.3
		23.7	9.0				8.6	13.2
		67.7	21.4				68.3	63.6
		(16) 26.8	(19) 13.4			% Profit Before Taxes/Tangible Net Worth	(26) 25.3	(35) 33.5
		12.9	7.6				8.0	15.9
		27.5	11.8				17.6	18.2
		6.9	5.6			% Profit Before Taxes/Total Assets	6.7	8.1
		2.3	1.8				.7	3.7
		29.3	8.3				18.4	11.6
		13.9	5.5			Sales/Net Fixed Assets	7.3	7.4
		7.0	4.3				4.3	5.7
		3.7	2.5				2.7	2.6
		2.8	1.9			Sales/Total Assets	2.0	2.0
		1.9	1.5				1.4	1.5
		1.0	1.9				1.1	1.8
		(18) 1.4	(20) 2.6			% Depr., Dep., Amort./Sales	(24) 1.8	(40) 2.5
		2.6	4.2				4.4	3.5
								1.6
						% Officers', Directors' Owners' Comp/Sales		(12) 3.9
								6.2
9785M	16987M	260965M	808089M	458532M	3904959M	Net Sales ($)	2409572M	5191951M
436M	3691M	90322M	398076M	336996M	1447597M	Total Assets ($)	1359816M	2176469M

M = $ thousand MM = $ million

See Pages 9 through 22 for Explanation of Ratios and Data

Comparative Historical Data | **Current Data Sorted by Sales**

4/1/11-3/31/12 ALL	4/1/12-3/31/13 ALL	4/1/13-3/31/14 ALL	Type of Statement	0-1MM	1-3MM	3-5MM	5-10MM	10-25MM	25MM & OVER
12	9	12	Unqualified				1	2	9
7	10	7	Reviewed					4	3
2	3	3	Compiled				1	1	1
9	7	6	Tax Returns			1	2	2	1
23	28	30	Other		2		3	9	16
				8 (4/1-9/30/13)			50 (10/1/13-3/31/14)		
53	57	58	**NUMBER OF STATEMENTS**		2	1	7	18	30
%	%	%	**ASSETS**	%	%	%	%	%	%
5.7	10.3	6.9	Cash & Equivalents	DATA NOT AVAILABLE				8.2	4.6
26.7	24.6	25.5	Trade Receivables (net)					28.2	20.0
22.2	22.5	22.8	Inventory					25.8	21.5
3.4	1.5	1.9	All Other Current					1.4	2.7
58.0	59.0	57.1	Total Current					63.5	48.9
29.8	30.8	29.1	Fixed Assets (net)					26.3	32.8
6.1	6.3	8.9	Intangibles (net)					7.3	12.0
6.0	3.8	4.8	All Other Non-Current					2.8	6.4
100.0	100.0	100.0	Total					100.0	100.0
			LIABILITIES						
10.8	8.7	8.0	Notes Payable-Short Term					8.8	8.5
4.2	3.7	4.0	Cur. Mat.-L.T.D.					4.8	3.2
17.8	16.8	17.5	Trade Payables					23.3	12.2
.7	.2	.0	Income Taxes Payable					.0	.0
5.9	5.5	6.4	All Other Current					7.3	6.2
39.5	34.8	36.0	Total Current					44.2	30.2
18.4	15.7	17.3	Long-Term Debt					14.7	18.6
1.1	.5	.5	Deferred Taxes					.3	.8
8.1	6.4	12.2	All Other Non-Current					8.1	4.6
32.9	42.6	33.9	Net Worth					32.6	45.9
100.0	100.0	100.0	Total Liabilties & Net Worth					100.0	100.0
			INCOME DATA						
100.0	100.0	100.0	Net Sales					100.0	100.0
22.5	23.3	23.9	Gross Profit					25.2	22.2
17.8	17.9	19.2	Operating Expenses					22.2	17.0
4.7	5.4	4.7	Operating Profit					2.9	5.2
1.3	.9	.9	All Other Expenses (net)					.7	1.0
3.4	4.5	3.9	Profit Before Taxes					2.2	4.2
			RATIOS						
2.2	2.6	2.3	Current					2.4	2.3
1.5	1.7	1.7						1.5	1.7
1.1	1.1	1.1						1.0	1.2
1.3	1.6	1.4	Quick					1.4	1.3
.8	.9	.9						.8	.9
.5	.5	.5						.4	.6
33 11.2	**29** 12.4	**29** 12.7	Sales/Receivables					**27** 13.3	**30** 12.1
40 9.2	**39** 9.4	**38** 9.7						**42** 8.7	**37** 9.8
49 7.4	**46** 8.0	**47** 7.7						**51** 7.1	**45** 8.2
35 10.4	**27** 13.6	**33** 10.9	Cost of Sales/Inventory					**34** 10.6	**34** 10.6
49 7.4	**47** 7.7	**43** 8.4						**47** 7.7	**45** 8.2
65 5.6	**69** 5.3	**63** 5.8						**76** 4.8	**61** 6.0
19 19.2	**17** 21.5	**20** 18.4	Cost of Sales/Payables					**36** 10.0	**16** 22.9
35 10.3	**28** 13.1	**34** 10.8						**46** 7.9	**25** 14.6
47 7.8	**47** 7.7	**46** 8.0						**60** 6.1	**37** 9.9
6.6	6.7	6.7	Sales/Working Capital					5.9	6.6
12.3	13.1	10.6						10.6	12.3
65.4	47.3	48.7						-205.5	37.1
26.1	20.8	13.2	EBIT/Interest					10.4	15.1
(49) 6.9	(52) 7.9	(54) 4.1						(17) 3.0	(29) 6.7
1.8	2.3	1.5						-.1	2.3
	5.3	5.6	Net Profit + Depr., Dep., Amort./Cur. Mat. L/T/D						11.4
	(19) 3.0	(16) 3.1							(10) 4.4
	1.8	1.3							1.5
.4	.3	.4	Fixed/Worth					.3	.5
1.1	.9	1.1						1.4	1.1
4.3	2.0	2.7						NM	2.2
.9	.6	.9	Debt/Worth					1.0	.7
2.9	1.9	1.8						3.9	1.6
17.1	5.1	9.5						NM	5.1
49.2	60.8	43.7	% Profit Before Taxes/Tangible Net Worth					33.8	31.1
(43) 28.5	(50) 28.3	(49) 18.7						(14) 17.9	(26) 19.7
12.9	13.4	9.5						-4.7	11.2
18.6	16.8	14.2	% Profit Before Taxes/Total Assets					13.6	12.4
9.9	9.0	6.5						5.2	6.7
2.5	4.0	2.2						-3.3	3.3
40.1	33.1	16.4	Sales/Net Fixed Assets					29.6	11.9
8.1	6.6	7.8						11.1	5.7
4.1	3.6	4.2						5.1	3.9
3.8	3.5	3.3	Sales/Total Assets					3.2	2.8
2.2	2.1	2.1						2.2	1.9
1.4	1.3	1.5						1.6	1.4
1.2	.8	1.2	% Depr., Dep., Amort./Sales					1.0	1.8
(43) 2.6	(50) 2.2	(51) 2.3						(17) 1.9	(26) 2.7
3.6	3.5	3.6						4.7	3.7
1.2	1.6	1.3	% Officers', Directors' Owners' Comp/Sales						
(13) 2.4	(16) 3.0	(14) 2.6							
4.6	5.7	4.2							
3835516M	3143426M	5459317M	Net Sales ($)		4420M	3458M	50759M	292333M	5108347M
2519646M	1902552M	2277118M	Total Assets ($)		1412M	596M	17102M	155890M	2102118M

M = $ thousand MM = $ million

See Pages 9 through 22 for Explanation of Ratios and Data

Current Data Sorted by Assets							Comparative Historical Data	
						Type of Statement		
		1	6	3	1	Unqualified	21	19
	1	9	5			Reviewed	23	24
		5				Compiled	10	7
	1					Tax Returns	21	16
	1	3	11	3	1	Other	41	36
	11 (4/1-9/30/13)		40 (10/1/13-3/31/14)				**4/1/09-3/31/10 ALL**	**4/1/10-3/31/11 ALL**
0-500M	**500M-2MM**	**2-10MM**	**10-50MM**	**50-100MM**	**100-250MM**			
	3	18	22	6	2	**NUMBER OF STATEMENTS**	116	102
%	%	%	%	%	%	**ASSETS**	%	%
DATA NOT AVAILABLE		9.6	6.6			Cash & Equivalents	8.3	7.4
		29.0	24.7			Trade Receivables (net)	27.3	27.1
		36.2	27.7			Inventory	23.9	27.5
		1.8	1.4			All Other Current	2.4	2.5
		76.7	60.5			Total Current	61.8	64.6
		16.5	31.2			Fixed Assets (net)	30.0	28.6
		1.5	5.3			Intangibles (net)	3.1	2.6
		5.2	3.1			All Other Non-Current	5.1	4.3
		100.0	100.0			Total	100.0	100.0
						LIABILITIES		
		13.0	8.8			Notes Payable-Short Term	9.0	8.4
		2.0	2.3			Cur. Mat.-L.T.D.	4.4	3.4
		18.1	17.8			Trade Payables	17.4	15.9
		.1	.0			Income Taxes Payable	.3	.3
		14.3	6.2			All Other Current	9.3	16.0
		47.4	35.2			Total Current	40.4	43.9
		8.1	12.3			Long-Term Debt	14.1	17.1
		.4	1.6			Deferred Taxes	.5	.5
		2.0	2.9			All Other Non-Current	3.8	3.8
		42.2	48.1			Net Worth	41.1	34.6
		100.0	100.0			Total Liabilties & Net Worth	100.0	100.0
						INCOME DATA		
		100.0	100.0			Net Sales	100.0	100.0
		22.2	18.6			Gross Profit	27.0	25.3
		16.7	13.5			Operating Expenses	21.6	19.4
		5.5	5.1			Operating Profit	5.4	5.8
		.0	.4			All Other Expenses (net)	.7	1.0
		5.5	4.7			Profit Before Taxes	4.7	4.9
						RATIOS		
		3.1	2.2				2.3	2.7
		2.1	1.8			Current	1.6	1.9
		1.1	1.2				1.1	1.2
		1.7	1.2				1.6	1.7
		1.1	.7			Quick	.9	.9
		.4	.6				.6	.5
		28 12.9	**28** 13.1				**34** 10.8	**32** 11.3
		32 11.3	**36** 10.2			Sales/Receivables	**45** 8.2	**41** 8.8
		36 10.1	**50** 7.3				**54** 6.8	**52** 7.0
		36 10.2	**41** 8.8				**36** 10.2	**37** 9.9
		48 7.6	**53** 6.9			Cost of Sales/Inventory	**54** 6.8	**54** 6.8
		63 5.8	**76** 4.8				**73** 5.0	**72** 5.1
		16 23.2	**15** 23.7				**23** 16.2	**18** 20.8
		27 13.4	**31** 11.7			Cost of Sales/Payables	**37** 9.8	**29** 12.6
		35 10.3	**44** 8.3				**51** 7.2	**44** 8.4
		5.6	5.9				5.6	5.7
		8.4	8.6			Sales/Working Capital	11.0	8.6
		NM	23.1				41.7	23.5
		88.4	34.3				21.7	14.8
		(17) 17.0	(19) 10.3			EBIT/Interest	(105) 4.9	(89) 5.5
		6.5	4.1				2.1	2.0
							5.4	5.4
						Net Profit + Depr., Dep., Amort./Cur. Mat. L/T/D	(34) 2.4	(28) 3.9
							.4	2.0
		.1	.5				.3	.3
		.5	.8			Fixed/Worth	.7	.8
		1.1	1.3				1.3	1.7
		.4	.5				.7	.7
		1.1	1.4			Debt/Worth	1.6	1.6
		5.9	2.5				3.7	3.6
		53.8	37.3				38.7	40.8
		(16) 33.8	(21) 21.0			% Profit Before Taxes/Tangible Net Worth	(110) 20.8	(90) 25.0
		19.6	17.5				5.4	9.0
		25.5	14.1				16.0	17.6
		12.9	8.5			% Profit Before Taxes/Total Assets	7.0	8.2
		8.1	4.3				2.2	3.0
		44.0	12.6				25.1	20.7
		23.6	7.5			Sales/Net Fixed Assets	8.3	9.4
		11.3	4.7				4.0	5.1
		4.1	2.7				2.8	3.0
		3.4	2.3			Sales/Total Assets	2.2	2.3
		2.7	1.8				1.6	1.7
		.5	1.2				1.3	1.1
		(17) 1.1	2.2			% Depr., Dep., Amort./Sales	(98) 2.4	(86) 2.2
		2.2	4.7				4.1	3.8
							1.2	1.1
						% Officers', Directors' Owners' Comp/Sales	(46) 2.6	(28) 2.3
							4.6	5.3
	8791M	295648M	1162365M	804179M	285582M	Net Sales ($)	5303131M	3912484M
	2869M	92175M	544251M	479152M	314985M	Total Assets ($)	3044119M	2121116M

M = $ thousand MM = $ million

See Pages 9 through 22 for Explanation of Ratios and Data

Comparative Historical Data				Current Data Sorted by Sales					
			Type of Statement						
18	12	11	Unqualified				1		10
17	20	15	Reviewed		1		2	6	6
8	4	5	Compiled				1	3	1
9	4	1	Tax Returns			1			
37	28	19	Other		1			4	14
				11 (4/1-9/30/13)			40 (10/1/13-3/31/14)		
4/1/11-3/31/12 ALL	**4/1/12-3/31/13 ALL**	**4/1/13-3/31/14 ALL**		**0-1MM**	**1-3MM**	**3-5MM**	**5-10MM**	**10-25MM**	**25MM & OVER**
89	68	51	**NUMBER OF STATEMENTS**		2	1	4	13	31
%	%	%	**ASSETS**	%	%	%	%	%	%
5.9	8.5	8.2	Cash & Equivalents	DATA NOT AVAILABLE				13.6	5.1
25.2	23.5	25.6	Trade Receivables (net)					29.8	23.4
25.5	28.9	29.8	Inventory					34.1	27.5
2.1	2.1	1.8	All Other Current					1.9	1.7
58.7	63.0	65.4	Total Current					79.3	57.6
32.5	28.3	24.1	Fixed Assets (net)					11.9	29.7
4.1	2.7	4.3	Intangibles (net)					1.9	6.3
4.8	6.0	6.2	All Other Non-Current					7.0	6.4
100.0	100.0	100.0	Total					100.0	100.0
			LIABILITIES						
11.2	8.1	9.1	Notes Payable-Short Term					10.1	8.4
3.6	2.7	2.3	Cur. Mat.-L.T.D.					1.5	2.5
18.4	16.0	16.4	Trade Payables					15.2	16.7
.3	.4	.1	Income Taxes Payable					.1	.1
7.1	8.1	9.8	All Other Current					11.6	5.9
40.6	35.3	37.7	Total Current					38.6	33.7
17.9	10.8	10.5	Long-Term Debt					8.8	12.1
.8	.8	1.0	Deferred Taxes					.3	1.4
3.6	6.3	3.6	All Other Non-Current					.7	4.8
37.1	46.7	47.2	Net Worth					51.6	48.0
100.0	100.0	100.0	Total Liabilties & Net Worth					100.0	100.0
			INCOME DATA						
100.0	100.0	100.0	Net Sales					100.0	100.0
24.5	23.6	22.3	Gross Profit					22.7	20.8
19.5	18.2	16.6	Operating Expenses					17.8	15.1
5.0	5.4	5.7	Operating Profit					4.9	5.7
.4	.3	.9	All Other Expenses (net)					-.1	1.5
4.7	5.1	4.8	Profit Before Taxes					5.1	4.2
			RATIOS						
2.3	2.9	2.9						3.5	2.4
1.5	1.8	1.9	Current					3.0	1.9
1.0	1.3	1.3						1.5	1.3
1.2	1.6	1.7						2.1	1.2
.7	.8	.9	Quick					1.6	.8
.5	.5	.5						.6	.6
30 12.1	**27** 13.3	**29** 12.4						**27** 13.4	**29** 12.8
42 8.6	**35** 10.3	**35** 10.3	Sales/Receivables					**31** 11.8	**40** 9.2
50 7.3	**46** 8.0	**46** 8.0						**34** 10.6	**50** 7.3
39 9.3	**43** 8.5	**43** 8.5						**30** 12.2	**46** 8.0
53 6.9	**55** 6.6	**53** 6.9	Cost of Sales/Inventory					**46** 7.9	**58** 6.3
72 5.1	**81** 4.5	**74** 4.9						**64** 5.7	**78** 4.7
23 15.9	**16** 22.2	**17** 21.0						**12** 30.6	**26** 14.0
34 10.6	**27** 13.3	**30** 12.1	Cost of Sales/Payables					**24** 14.9	**32** 11.4
51 7.1	**40** 9.2	**35** 10.4						**29** 12.5	**36** 10.2
7.5	5.3	5.6						5.0	5.9
11.4	8.2	7.8	Sales/Working Capital					7.7	7.8
160.2	18.0	22.7						18.7	21.7
23.1	46.7	54.6						116.2	36.8
(81) 5.7	(61) 14.2	(47) 15.0	EBIT/Interest					(12) 35.8	(28) 13.2
1.7	3.5	4.8						9.6	4.2
6.4	6.5	8.7							
(30) 3.9	(18) 3.8	(12) 3.3	Net Profit + Depr., Dep., Amort./Cur. Mat. L/T/D						
2.1	1.5	1.9							
.4	.3	.3						.1	.3
1.0	.5	.6	Fixed/Worth					.2	.7
2.2	1.3	1.3						.5	1.3
.7	.5	.4						.3	.5
2.1	1.1	1.2	Debt/Worth					.5	1.3
5.6	2.5	3.2						4.0	2.3
42.6	40.0	43.3						49.7	34.3
(81) 30.0	(62) 25.0	(47) 21.9	% Profit Before Taxes/Tangible Net Worth					(12) 33.8	(29) 21.0
10.7	14.3	14.9						15.1	16.2
16.4	19.4	22.2						25.8	16.1
9.2	11.4	10.2	% Profit Before Taxes/Total Assets					11.8	8.6
2.2	5.0	5.5						9.2	5.4
15.0	18.8	23.8						124.4	14.4
6.5	8.8	9.7	Sales/Net Fixed Assets					41.1	6.7
3.7	4.6	5.4						20.0	4.0
3.0	2.8	3.4						4.2	2.6
2.1	2.2	2.3	Sales/Total Assets					3.8	2.1
1.5	1.7	1.8						2.8	1.5
1.5	1.2	1.1						.2	1.4
(79) 2.8	(62) 2.3	(48) 1.9	% Depr., Dep., Amort./Sales					(12) .5	(30) 2.5
4.2	3.5	3.2						1.5	4.6
.9	.4	.3							
(22) 1.8	(13) 2.1	(12) 1.2	% Officers', Directors' Owners' Comp/Sales						
4.0	3.9	4.5							
4404129M	**4402405M**	**2556565M**	Net Sales ($)		**3959M**	**4832M**	**34043M**	**228910M**	**2284821M**
2628888M	**2343120M**	**1433432M**	Total Assets ($)		**1406M**	**1463M**	**17573M**	**71161M**	**1341829M**

M = $ thousand MM = $ million

See Pages 9 through 22 for Explanation of Ratios and Data

Current Data Sorted by Assets											Comparative Historical Data	
								Type of Statement				
1			2		1	1	2	Unqualified		16		16
	2		5		7			Reviewed		16		19
1	2		1		1			Compiled		10		7
	3		3					Tax Returns		5		9
1			5		4	4	3	Other		28		19
	7 (4/1-9/30/13)				42 (10/1/13-3/31/14)					4/1/09-3/31/10		4/1/10-3/31/11
0-500M	500M-2MM		2-10MM		10-50MM	50-100MM	100-250MM			ALL		ALL
3	7		16		13	5	5	**NUMBER OF STATEMENTS**		75		70
%	%		%		%	%	%	**ASSETS**		%		%
			5.5		9.5			Cash & Equivalents		7.4		7.5
			25.7		17.8			Trade Receivables (net)		22.0		22.4
			23.6		22.9			Inventory		22.8		23.7
			3.1		3.4			All Other Current		1.4		1.8
			58.0		53.8			Total Current		53.6		55.4
			33.1		33.3			Fixed Assets (net)		32.0		30.3
			1.5		9.0			Intangibles (net)		6.2		5.9
			7.4		4.0			All Other Non-Current		8.2		8.3
			100.0		100.0			Total		100.0		100.0
								LIABILITIES				
			8.6		5.0			Notes Payable-Short Term		11.4		11.0
			1.8		4.7			Cur. Mat.-L.T.D.		5.0		4.2
			17.6		11.4			Trade Payables		13.0		13.9
			.0		.1			Income Taxes Payable		.3		.1
			6.8		4.9			All Other Current		6.9		5.4
			34.9		26.2			Total Current		36.6		34.6
			16.7		14.4			Long-Term Debt		17.1		16.9
			.8		.0			Deferred Taxes		.8		.7
			4.2		9.4			All Other Non-Current		5.2		8.2
			43.4		49.9			Net Worth		40.3		39.5
			100.0		100.0			Total Liabilties & Net Worth		100.0		100.0
								INCOME DATA				
			100.0		100.0			Net Sales		100.0		100.0
			29.0		28.0			Gross Profit		30.3		32.3
			22.9		18.9			Operating Expenses		26.8		26.5
			6.1		9.1			Operating Profit		3.5		5.8
			.9		.6			All Other Expenses (net)		1.3		1.4
			5.1		8.5			Profit Before Taxes		2.2		4.3
								RATIOS				
			2.3		3.8					2.7		2.4
			1.9		2.2			Current		1.6		1.5
			1.1		.9					1.1		1.1
			1.3		2.1					1.6		1.3
			.9		.8			Quick		.9		.8
			.5		.5					.5		.5
		17	21.0	**29**	12.7				**35**	10.6	**34**	10.6
		40	9.2	**38**	9.5			Sales/Receivables	**42**	8.7	**45**	8.1
		50	7.3	**49**	7.5				**52**	7.0	**53**	6.9
		26	14.3	**38**	9.5				**48**	7.6	**43**	8.4
		47	7.7	**55**	6.6			Cost of Sales/Inventory	**68**	5.4	**68**	5.4
		81	4.5	**101**	3.6				**110**	3.3	**97**	3.8
		21	17.0	**20**	18.7				**20**	18.1	**20**	18.5
		31	11.9	**25**	14.4			Cost of Sales/Payables	**37**	9.9	**34**	10.7
		46	8.0	**47**	7.7				**51**	7.1	**55**	6.7
			6.7		3.2					4.8		4.5
			11.1		5.9			Sales/Working Capital		9.5		9.7
			71.1		-511.4					54.9		79.0
			22.5		27.4					7.0		10.6
			7.6	(12)	11.5			EBIT/Interest	(69)	2.5	(62)	3.7
			1.9		.3					.6		1.3
										4.1		4.1
								Net Profit + Depr., Dep., Amort./Cur. Mat. L/T/D	(22)	2.1	(22)	3.0
										.9		1.8
			.3		.4					.4		.3
			.7		.7			Fixed/Worth		.9		.9
			1.4		2.1					2.1		2.2
			.7		.3					.6		.7
			1.2		1.2			Debt/Worth		1.4		1.5
			2.7		3.4					4.8		4.5
			59.4		55.0					34.9		49.7
		(15)	30.5	(12)	39.4			% Profit Before Taxes/Tangible Net Worth	(66)	14.5	(63)	19.7
			6.5		14.1					-3.2		3.2
			19.6		23.1					10.8		13.7
			9.9		15.0			% Profit Before Taxes/Total Assets		4.2		6.4
			2.3		-1.6					-1.5		1.5
			20.9		8.9					13.2		16.8
			6.4		6.2			Sales/Net Fixed Assets		5.6		7.0
			4.5		3.7					3.7		3.4
			3.5		2.5					2.2		2.4
			2.0		1.8			Sales/Total Assets		1.8		1.7
			1.6		1.1					1.1		1.2
			1.3		1.8					1.8		1.4
		(14)	3.0		3.1			% Depr., Dep., Amort./Sales	(63)	3.3	(63)	3.2
			4.8		5.4					5.1		4.6
										1.9		3.2
								% Officers', Directors' Owners' Comp/Sales	(29)	3.7	(28)	5.8
										7.4		7.5
3051M	**31058M**		**198867M**		**361646M**	**541355M**	**1172822M**	Net Sales ($)		**2066496M**		**1429814M**
997M	**10222M**		**87086M**		**204273M**	**372612M**	**861042M**	Total Assets ($)		**1574492M**		**1008948M**

M = $ thousand MM = $ million

See Pages 9 through 22 for Explanation of Ratios and Data

Comparative Historical Data / Current Data Sorted by Sales

	4/1/11-3/31/12 ALL	4/1/12-3/31/13 ALL	4/1/13-3/31/14 ALL	0-1MM	1-3MM	3-5MM	5-10MM	10-25MM	25MM & OVER
Type of Statement				7 (4/1-9/30/13)			42 (10/1/13-3/31/14)		
Unqualified	12	7	7	1				3	3
Reviewed	14	10	14			1	2	8	3
Compiled	10	4	5	1		2		1	1
Tax Returns	11	4	6		2		4		
Other	25	27	17		1		3	4	9
NUMBER OF STATEMENTS	72	52	49	2	3	3	9	16	16
ASSETS	%	%	%	%	%	%	%	%	%
Cash & Equivalents	7.7	9.6	5.9					9.8	3.2
Trade Receivables (net)	24.1	22.7	22.5					19.2	20.5
Inventory	25.0	23.4	24.5					26.1	23.9
All Other Current	2.2	3.0	2.2					.7	3.5
Total Current	59.0	58.6	55.2					55.8	51.2
Fixed Assets (net)	29.2	30.6	32.3					28.5	35.2
Intangibles (net)	7.8	5.1	6.5					8.1	9.6
All Other Non-Current	4.0	5.8	6.0					7.6	4.0
Total	100.0	100.0	100.0					100.0	100.0
LIABILITIES									
Notes Payable-Short Term	9.1	7.3	7.4					8.7	5.6
Cur. Mat.-L.T.D.	4.2	3.3	2.7					2.7	3.7
Trade Payables	15.0	13.4	17.4					11.2	14.8
Income Taxes Payable	.1	.1	.0					.0	.1
All Other Current	6.5	5.9	6.5					5.7	6.4
Total Current	34.9	30.0	34.0					28.4	30.6
Long-Term Debt	15.0	14.6	19.5					9.2	26.4
Deferred Taxes	.6	1.0	.8					.8	1.6
All Other Non-Current	8.7	8.2	8.0					8.9	3.2
Net Worth	40.8	46.1	37.7					52.7	38.2
Total Liabilties & Net Worth	100.0	100.0	100.0					100.0	100.0
INCOME DATA									
Net Sales	100.0	100.0	100.0					100.0	100.0
Gross Profit	28.4	28.4	28.0					28.0	24.1
Operating Expenses	24.8	22.7	23.6					21.6	17.8
Operating Profit	3.6	5.7	4.4					6.4	6.3
All Other Expenses (net)	.8	.8	.8					1.1	2.0
Profit Before Taxes	2.8	4.9	3.6					5.3	4.3
RATIOS									
Current	3.0	3.3	2.4					3.9	2.7
	1.7	1.9	1.8					2.2	1.8
	1.1	1.3	1.1					.9	1.3
Quick	1.6	1.8	1.4					2.0	1.2
	.9	1.0	.9					1.1	.7
	.6	.6	.5					.5	.5
Sales/Receivables	28 12.9	29 12.4	28 13.1					25 14.5	31 11.6
	40 9.2	44 8.3	38 9.5					38 9.7	41 8.8
	51 7.1	52 7.0	49 7.5					49 7.4	49 7.5
Cost of Sales/Inventory	43 8.4	39 9.4	35 10.3					38 9.5	42 8.6
	64 5.7	63 5.8	54 6.7					68 5.4	69 5.3
	83 4.4	104 3.5	94 3.9					94 3.9	111 3.3
Cost of Sales/Payables	21 17.5	19 19.1	24 15.4					19 18.9	25 14.6
	30 12.2	34 10.8	34 10.7					29 12.7	37 9.8
	47 7.8	47 7.7	53 6.9					38 9.5	51 7.2
Sales/Working Capital	4.8	4.0	5.7					3.0	5.7
	9.8	8.5	10.3					8.8	8.0
	29.9	16.2	49.2					-78.3	19.2
EBIT/Interest	19.0	20.7	20.8					20.4	27.4
	(65) 5.3	(43) 6.6	(48) 6.3					(15) 4.3	10.7
	1.8	2.0	.2					-.2	1.5
Net Profit + Depr., Dep., Amort./Cur. Mat. L/T/D	8.5	5.1	5.2						
	(23) 4.5	(10) 3.5	(10) 2.7						
	2.0	1.2	2.1						
Fixed/Worth	.4	.3	.5					.3	.7
	.9	.7	.8					.6	1.0
	1.9	1.4	3.8					1.4	4.3
Debt/Worth	.7	.6	.7					.3	.9
	1.9	1.1	1.4					.7	1.5
	4.7	3.4	8.2					2.6	9.6
% Profit Before Taxes/Tangible Net Worth	46.3	40.2	45.7					45.3	82.8
	(65) 26.6	(46) 17.7	(41) 25.3					(15) 37.7	(13) 30.5
	8.0	7.0	6.7					-.2	9.5
% Profit Before Taxes/Total Assets	16.1	14.3	16.5					19.9	15.7
	6.8	7.2	7.6					5.7	7.7
	1.7	2.6	-2.3					-3.6	-2.1
Sales/Net Fixed Assets	17.1	14.5	9.0					10.8	8.0
	7.6	7.1	6.2					6.4	4.8
	4.0	3.4	4.1					4.3	3.5
Sales/Total Assets	2.7	2.3	2.7					2.9	2.6
	1.9	1.7	1.9					1.7	1.7
	1.4	1.3	1.4					1.1	1.2
% Depr., Dep., Amort./Sales	1.5	1.2	1.8					1.5	1.8
	(62) 3.0	(43) 2.6	(41) 3.1					3.0	(12) 3.1
	4.8	3.8	4.3					4.1	4.5
% Officers', Directors' Owners' Comp/Sales	3.0	2.9	1.6						
	(26) 4.8	(18) 5.0	(15) 3.4						
	8.2	8.7	10.5						
Net Sales ($)	2835464M	2334092M	2308799M	1329M	6550M	12053M	65596M	265132M	1958139M
Total Assets ($)	1750159M	1617066M	1536232M	527M	3034M	4728M	29111M	161827M	1337005M

M = $ thousand MM = $ million

See Pages 9 through 22 for Explanation of Ratios and Data

Current Data Sorted by Assets | **Comparative Historical Data**

0-500M	500M-2MM	2-10MM	10-50MM	50-100MM	100-250MM	Type of Statement	4/1/09-3/31/10 ALL	4/1/10-3/31/11 ALL
		2	8	3	4	Unqualified	30	27
	3	5	10			Reviewed	19	23
	7	8	2			Compiled	22	24
1	5	3				Tax Returns	6	2
	4	8	8	3	2	Other	38	31
	12 (4/1-9/30/13)		74 (10/1/13-3/31/14)					
1	19	26	28	6	6	**NUMBER OF STATEMENTS**	115	107
%	%	%	%	%	%	**ASSETS**	%	%
	13.6	11.7	7.5			Cash & Equivalents	7.6	7.9
	28.5	23.4	23.2			Trade Receivables (net)	23.0	24.4
	26.7	27.7	29.0			Inventory	26.5	27.3
	.7	.7	1.1			All Other Current	2.8	1.1
	69.5	63.6	60.8			Total Current	59.9	60.7
	27.3	27.1	31.0			Fixed Assets (net)	29.2	29.0
	.5	2.5	2.3			Intangibles (net)	4.5	5.0
	2.8	6.9	6.0			All Other Non-Current	6.4	5.3
	100.0	100.0	100.0			Total	100.0	100.0
						LIABILITIES		
	4.8	12.4	7.1			Notes Payable-Short Term	12.3	11.2
	4.8	2.3	3.4			Cur. Mat.-L.T.D.	3.7	4.6
	15.9	14.4	13.0			Trade Payables	12.6	12.4
	.0	.1	.6			Income Taxes Payable	.1	.1
	5.0	6.6	5.7			All Other Current	8.5	8.6
	30.6	35.9	29.7			Total Current	37.2	36.9
	19.3	11.5	14.8			Long-Term Debt	14.5	15.9
	.2	.3	1.0			Deferred Taxes	.7	.8
	30.9	6.9	5.6			All Other Non-Current	8.5	8.4
	19.0	45.4	48.9			Net Worth	39.2	37.9
	100.0	100.0	100.0			Total Liabilities & Net Worth	100.0	100.0
						INCOME DATA		
	100.0	100.0	100.0			Net Sales	100.0	100.0
	28.2	26.3	28.4			Gross Profit	24.2	26.9
	23.9	19.9	20.6			Operating Expenses	22.9	22.0
	4.3	6.4	7.8			Operating Profit	1.3	4.9
	-.2	1.3	.4			All Other Expenses (net)	1.5	1.0
	4.5	5.0	7.4			Profit Before Taxes	-.3	3.9
						RATIOS		
	4.7	3.9	3.6				3.3	3.4
	2.5	1.6	2.3			Current	1.7	1.6
	1.3	1.1	1.5				1.1	1.2
	2.9	2.8	1.7				1.8	1.8
	1.1	.9	1.0			Quick	.8	.9
	.8	.5	.6				.5	.5
	25 14.8	**24** 15.3	**41** 9.0				**36** 10.2	**36** 10.2
	38 9.6	**41** 8.9	**45** 8.1			Sales/Receivables	**48** 7.7	**43** 8.4
	51 7.2	**56** 6.5	**55** 6.6				**63** 5.8	**59** 6.2
	27 13.3	**36** 10.1	**46** 7.9				**41** 8.8	**43** 8.6
	42 8.7	**51** 7.1	**79** 4.6			Cost of Sales/Inventory	**64** 5.7	**59** 6.2
	74 4.9	**85** 4.3	**146** 2.5				**98** 3.7	**106** 3.4
	16 22.9	**8** 45.8	**20** 18.3				**17** 21.4	**15** 24.4
	25 14.4	**26** 13.8	**31** 11.9			Cost of Sales/Payables	**30** 12.1	**27** 13.7
	40 9.2	**47** 7.7	**47** 7.7				**43** 8.4	**41** 8.8
	4.0	3.8	3.5				4.2	4.1
	4.8	11.1	5.4			Sales/Working Capital	7.6	9.5
	30.7	NM	11.0				25.5	22.3
	9.4	14.4	15.6				6.4	9.4
	(14) 3.1	(20) 4.8	(25) 8.2			EBIT/Interest	(107) 1.2	(97) 3.9
	1.2	2.1	4.0				-5.3	1.3
			6.8				3.1	7.4
			(14) 3.5			Net Profit + Depr., Dep., Amort./Cur. Mat. L/T/D	(34) 1.3	(31) 3.5
			1.3				.0	1.6
	.4	.4	.3				.3	.4
	.8	.6	.6			Fixed/Worth	.7	.8
	2.3	1.0	1.2				1.8	1.7
	.6	.7	.5				.4	.6
	1.6	1.5	.9			Debt/Worth	1.5	1.5
	10.3	4.0	1.5				4.6	3.4
	89.0	36.1	33.3				24.4	33.7
	(16) 31.4	(24) 20.9	(25) 17.3			% Profit Before Taxes/Tangible Net Worth	(100) 1.8	(95) 16.4
	2.4	7.8	8.6				-19.6	3.8
	26.4	17.4	15.6				9.6	13.8
	7.9	6.8	12.1			% Profit Before Taxes/Total Assets	.9	6.6
	.6	1.3	4.9				-9.4	1.2
	61.6	23.6	13.3				13.1	13.1
	9.5	7.4	5.6			Sales/Net Fixed Assets	6.4	6.6
	6.4	4.8	3.2				3.6	4.2
	3.1	2.5	2.1				2.2	2.4
	2.6	1.9	1.7			Sales/Total Assets	1.7	1.9
	2.2	1.6	1.3				1.3	1.4
	.8	1.6	1.3				1.8	1.6
	(16) 2.7	(21) 3.4	2.2			% Depr., Dep., Amort./Sales	(103) 3.4	(94) 2.9
	4.0	4.3	3.1				5.4	4.5
	3.7	1.0					1.9	1.7
	(11) 5.8	(11) 2.5				% Officers', Directors' Owners' Comp/Sales	(34) 4.2	(40) 4.3
	7.1	5.4					5.8	6.3
67M	57642M	272885M	1100405M	674812M	1537381M	Net Sales ($)	4101749M	4428017M
111M	22163M	135911M	666568M	420997M	1029209M	Total Assets ($)	2980570M	2898334M

M = $ thousand MM = $ million

See Pages 9 through 22 for Explanation of Ratios and Data

Comparative Historical Data				Current Data Sorted by Sales					
			Type of Statement						
22	10	17	Unqualified					3	14
29	22	18	Reviewed		1	2	3	4	8
22	20	17	Compiled	1	5		7	2	2
3	6	9	Tax Returns	1	3	2	2	1	
37	37	25	Other		3	1	4	7	10
4/1/11-3/31/12	**4/1/12-3/31/13**	**4/1/13-3/31/14**		**12 (4/1-9/30/13)**			**74 (10/1/13-3/31/14)**		
ALL	**ALL**	**ALL**		**0-1MM**	**1-3MM**	**3-5MM**	**5-10MM**	**10-25MM**	**25MM & OVER**
113	95	86	**NUMBER OF STATEMENTS**	2	12	5	16	17	34
%	%	%	**ASSETS**	%	%	%	%	%	%
6.9	7.9	9.7	Cash & Equivalents		17.5		9.8	10.1	6.5
25.4	24.5	24.0	Trade Receivables (net)		27.7		21.5	26.9	22.8
27.9	29.6	28.0	Inventory		24.0		27.4	32.1	26.8
2.2	1.8	1.0	All Other Current		.7		.1	1.4	1.4
62.4	63.8	62.7	Total Current		70.0		58.9	70.6	57.5
28.6	25.3	28.4	Fixed Assets (net)		28.5		29.8	24.6	29.4
2.7	3.8	4.0	Intangibles (net)		.7		3.5	.4	7.9
6.3	7.1	4.9	All Other Non-Current		.9		7.8	4.4	5.2
100.0	100.0	100.0	Total		100.0		100.0	100.0	100.0
			LIABILITIES						
11.9	10.9	8.9	Notes Payable-Short Term		5.0		14.2	10.2	8.5
2.9	3.4	3.3	Cur. Mat.-L.T.D.		2.0		3.8	2.1	3.3
14.5	13.0	13.8	Trade Payables		11.0		17.1	14.7	11.8
.2	.2	.4	Income Taxes Payable		.0		.2	.4	.7
7.0	8.2	7.0	All Other Current		5.3		7.9	5.6	8.5
36.4	35.7	33.3	Total Current		23.4		43.2	33.1	32.8
14.7	15.6	15.6	Long-Term Debt		6.6		13.6	5.8	18.1
.7	.5	.6	Deferred Taxes		.3		.0	.9	1.0
10.2	9.1	11.3	All Other Non-Current		41.9		10.1	1.8	5.2
38.0	39.1	39.3	Net Worth		27.8		33.1	58.3	42.9
100.0	100.0	100.0	Total Liabilties & Net Worth		100.0		100.0	100.0	100.0
			INCOME DATA						
100.0	100.0	100.0	Net Sales		100.0		100.0	100.0	100.0
25.8	27.7	27.0	Gross Profit		25.7		24.6	25.4	26.2
21.2	21.5	20.2	Operating Expenses		20.9		19.4	19.7	17.9
4.6	6.2	6.8	Operating Profit		4.7		5.2	5.6	8.3
.6	.8	.7	All Other Expenses (net)		-.9		-.1	.6	.7
3.9	5.4	6.0	Profit Before Taxes		5.6		5.3	5.0	7.6
			RATIOS						
3.0	2.8	3.7			4.9		2.0	7.2	3.3
1.6	1.8	1.8	Current		4.0		1.2	1.7	2.1
1.2	1.3	1.3			1.6		1.0	1.5	1.3
1.6	1.6	2.0			3.9		1.2	4.2	1.5
.8	.9	.9	Quick		2.7		.7	.9	.8
.6	.6	.6			1.2		.4	.6	.6
35 10.4	**33** 10.9	**30** 12.1			**29** 12.7		**23** 15.6	**34** 10.8	**37** 9.8
46 7.9	**46** 8.0	**43** 8.5	Sales/Receivables		**37** 9.9		**36** 10.2	**45** 8.1	**46** 8.0
57 6.4	**54** 6.8	**55** 6.6			**54** 6.8		**54** 6.7	**64** 5.7	**56** 6.5
35 10.4	**40** 9.1	**39** 9.3			**29** 12.6		**27** 13.3	**43** 8.4	**45** 8.2
62 5.9	**72** 5.1	**69** 5.3	Cost of Sales/Inventory		**41** 8.8		**47** 7.8	**69** 5.3	**79** 4.6
107 3.4	**122** 3.0	**114** 3.2			**69** 5.3		**111** 3.3	**111** 3.3	**126** 2.9
17 21.3	**18** 20.4	**17** 21.0			**13** 27.1		**20** 18.6	**10** 35.0	**18** 20.3
30 12.0	**26** 14.2	**28** 13.0	Cost of Sales/Payables		**20** 18.7		**29** 12.5	**30** 12.3	**27** 13.3
48 7.6	**46** 8.0	**41** 8.9			**33** 11.2		**46** 8.0	**64** 5.7	**35** 10.4
4.4	3.9	3.9			3.8		5.7	3.1	3.9
9.7	8.2	6.8	Sales/Working Capital		4.3		19.6	6.9	6.1
23.1	14.6	20.8			26.3		NM	12.1	15.1
12.7	20.7	12.6					16.3	8.2	19.0
(105) 5.1	(85) 7.2	(70) 6.2	EBIT/Interest				(15) 4.9	(13) 3.3	(30) 8.3
1.9	1.9	2.6					3.2	1.7	4.2
7.6	7.7	6.5							7.3
(33) 4.2	(24) 3.2	(26) 3.5	Net Profit + Depr., Dep., Amort./Cur. Mat. L/T/D						(17) 3.8
1.9	1.3	1.5							1.5
.4	.3	.4			.1		.6	.2	.3
.7	.7	.7	Fixed/Worth		.4		1.0	.4	.8
1.5	1.6	1.6			2.1		1.9	.8	NM
.6	.7	.6			.4		1.2	.2	.6
1.4	1.5	1.3	Debt/Worth		.8		1.6	.7	1.2
3.3	4.1	4.0			2.5		6.2	1.5	NM
39.5	42.2	36.7			50.9		44.1	21.8	34.1
(102) 20.5	(83) 23.3	(73) 20.2	% Profit Before Taxes/Tangible Net Worth		(10) 8.7		(15) 35.0	11.4	(26) 21.2
6.1	4.1	7.8			2.0		11.4	2.5	14.2
14.5	18.0	16.0			28.9		16.6	17.0	15.4
6.9	8.4	9.8	% Profit Before Taxes/Total Assets		5.1		13.9	5.3	11.3
2.1	2.8	2.7			.8		3.7	1.3	5.5
13.0	17.4	14.3			68.7		8.6	28.9	9.3
6.9	7.7	6.8	Sales/Net Fixed Assets		8.9		7.4	6.5	6.3
4.2	4.6	4.4			4.9		4.8	4.3	3.9
2.6	2.6	2.5			2.9		2.5	2.5	2.2
2.1	1.9	1.9	Sales/Total Assets		2.3		1.9	1.9	1.7
1.4	1.3	1.3			2.0		1.5	1.4	1.3
1.4	1.3	1.6			.7		1.6	1.7	1.5
(102) 2.8	(84) 2.0	(77) 2.3	% Depr., Dep., Amort./Sales		(11) 1.8		(14) 3.0	(14) 2.5	(33) 2.1
3.8	3.5	3.7			4.1		4.2	3.6	3.3
1.6	2.8	1.8							
(43) 3.0	(29) 3.8	(27) 3.7	% Officers', Directors' Owners' Comp/Sales						
6.2	7.1	6.3							
5570072M	5122907M	3643192M	Net Sales ($)	761M	26397M	18959M	114538M	284221M	3198316M
3365815M	3439917M	2274959M	Total Assets ($)	4021M	11985M	6792M	62022M	154571M	2035568M

M = $ thousand MM = $ million

See Pages 9 through 22 for Explanation of Ratios and Data

Current Data Sorted by Assets							Comparative Historical Data	
						Type of Statement		
		2	7	1	1	Unqualified	10	13
		5	4			Reviewed	13	14
		1				Compiled	8	2
2	1					Tax Returns	2	4
1	1	8	6	1	3	Other	23	16
	5 (4/1-9/30/13)		39 (10/1/13-3/31/14)				**4/1/09-3/31/10**	**4/1/10-3/31/11**
0-500M	**500M-2MM**	**2-10MM**	**10-50MM**	**50-100MM**	**100-250MM**		**ALL**	**ALL**
3	2	16	17	2	4	**NUMBER OF STATEMENTS**	56	49
%	%	%	%	%	%	**ASSETS**	%	%
		11.2	7.5			Cash & Equivalents	4.4	7.5
		24.9	19.7			Trade Receivables (net)	23.5	23.3
		31.2	34.3			Inventory	26.6	29.3
		.8	1.7			All Other Current	1.4	2.5
		68.2	63.1			Total Current	55.9	62.6
		23.9	27.1			Fixed Assets (net)	26.5	26.4
		1.7	2.5			Intangibles (net)	12.3	5.1
		6.3	7.3			All Other Non-Current	5.3	5.9
		100.0	100.0			Total	100.0	100.0
						LIABILITIES		
		9.7	14.9			Notes Payable-Short Term	9.4	9.1
		2.8	3.8			Cur. Mat.-L.T.D.	8.3	3.7
		15.0	17.0			Trade Payables	15.3	14.2
		.1	.1			Income Taxes Payable	.2	.4
		4.2	3.6			All Other Current	7.1	6.5
		31.8	39.5			Total Current	40.4	33.9
		12.2	10.6			Long-Term Debt	22.2	18.7
		.5	.7			Deferred Taxes	.9	1.1
		2.9	6.9			All Other Non-Current	7.3	6.8
		52.6	42.3			Net Worth	29.3	39.5
		100.0	100.0			Total Liabilties & Net Worth	100.0	100.0
						INCOME DATA		
		100.0	100.0			Net Sales	100.0	100.0
		26.7	25.2			Gross Profit	27.8	27.4
		20.2	19.2			Operating Expenses	23.2	22.0
		6.5	6.0			Operating Profit	4.6	5.4
		.8	.4			All Other Expenses (net)	1.7	1.7
		5.7	5.6			Profit Before Taxes	2.9	3.7
						RATIOS		
		4.0	4.3				2.4	2.5
		2.9	1.5			Current	1.3	1.9
		1.3	1.0				1.0	1.3
		2.0	2.0				1.4	1.6
		1.5	.6			Quick	.7	1.0
		.7	.4				.5	.5
		28 13.0	**27** 13.7				**32** 11.5	**29** 12.4
		34 10.8	**37** 9.8			Sales/Receivables	**40** 9.2	**42** 8.8
		41 9.0	**51** 7.2				**51** 7.1	**54** 6.7
		39 9.3	**72** 5.1				**39** 9.3	**43** 8.5
		51 7.1	**87** 4.2			Cost of Sales/Inventory	**57** 6.5	**65** 5.6
		83 4.4	**111** 3.3				**100** 3.6	**116** 3.2
		20 18.5	**36** 10.2				**20** 18.1	**20** 18.0
		26 13.8	**42** 8.6			Cost of Sales/Payables	**35** 10.4	**30** 12.3
		33 11.1	**55** 6.6				**48** 7.6	**51** 7.2
		4.4	3.4				5.2	5.3
		7.1	8.2			Sales/Working Capital	14.6	7.7
		18.7	NM				536.7	12.7
		79.2	11.9				4.2	15.8
		(13) 12.7	(15) 5.4			EBIT/Interest	(50) 1.7	(46) 3.0
		4.8	1.9				.9	.7
							2.8	6.4
						Net Profit + Depr., Dep., Amort./Cur. Mat. L/T/D	(18) 1.6	(19) 2.0
							.2	1.4
		.2	.2				.6	.4
		.6	.7			Fixed/Worth	1.3	.6
		.9	2.0				-5.2	2.1
		.3	.4				1.2	.7
		.8	2.2			Debt/Worth	3.3	1.6
		3.4	4.3				-15.4	10.4
		40.5	34.2				41.4	48.8
		31.6	(16) 21.2			% Profit Before Taxes/Tangible Net Worth	(40) 15.0	(42) 14.6
		18.9	7.6				2.7	2.9
		21.9	13.0				8.7	16.5
		11.2	4.0			% Profit Before Taxes/Total Assets	3.1	6.3
		7.8	1.8				.1	.4
		19.1	18.2				17.1	18.4
		9.7	8.1			Sales/Net Fixed Assets	7.8	8.9
		6.4	3.9				4.8	3.6
		2.8	2.3				2.5	2.4
		2.3	1.7			Sales/Total Assets	2.0	1.9
		1.9	1.5				1.5	1.5
		.5	1.0				1.4	1.2
		(15) 1.1	(16) 1.8			% Depr., Dep., Amort./Sales	(48) 2.3	(43) 2.3
		2.1	3.2				4.2	4.3
							1.8	.4
						% Officers', Directors' Owners' Comp/Sales	(18) 4.3	(18) 2.7
							6.0	4.9
3938M	**5422M**	**256808M**	**729082M**	**139126M**	**895753M**	Net Sales ($)	**2017690M**	**1909197M**
1147M	**1603M**	**103492M**	**388205M**	**169484M**	**496334M**	Total Assets ($)	**1342283M**	**1177700M**

M = $ thousand MM = $ million

See Pages 9 through 22 for Explanation of Ratios and Data

Comparative Historical Data				Current Data Sorted by Sales					
			Type of Statement						
10	5	11	Unqualified				1	1	9
12	9	9	Reviewed				2	6	1
1	1	1	Compiled				1		
3	6	3	Tax Returns	1	2				
15	17	20	Other		2		2	4	12
4/1/11-3/31/12 ALL	**4/1/12-3/31/13 ALL**	**4/1/13-3/31/14 ALL**		**5 (4/1-9/30/13)**			**39 (10/1/13-3/31/14)**		
				0-1MM	**1-3MM**	**3-5MM**	**5-10MM**	**10-25MM**	**25MM & OVER**
41	38	44	**NUMBER OF STATEMENTS**	1	4		6	11	22
%	%	%	**ASSETS**	%	%	%	%	%	%
7.9	9.2	9.0	Cash & Equivalents			D		11.7	4.4
23.5	23.2	23.5	Trade Receivables (net)			A		19.7	21.2
33.8	27.2	29.0	Inventory			T		33.7	31.6
1.3	1.4	2.0	All Other Current			A		1.0	2.1
66.5	60.9	63.5	Total Current					66.1	59.3
24.5	28.1	25.5	Fixed Assets (net)			N		26.6	26.4
4.1	4.8	4.0	Intangibles (net)			O		.4	6.6
4.8	6.3	7.1	All Other Non-Current			T		6.8	7.7
100.0	100.0	100.0	Total					100.0	100.0
			LIABILITIES			A			
10.2	8.1	11.6	Notes Payable-Short Term			V		10.0	16.8
2.5	2.9	3.1	Cur. Mat.-L.T.D.			A		1.6	4.5
17.0	14.4	15.4	Trade Payables			I		12.0	17.2
.1	.5	.1	Income Taxes Payable			L		.2	.1
5.7	9.4	8.5	All Other Current			A		2.6	6.9
35.5	35.2	38.8	Total Current			B		26.3	45.6
17.9	14.3	10.7	Long-Term Debt			L		11.5	11.7
1.2	.7	.7	Deferred Taxes			E		.8	.2
6.5	7.3	4.2	All Other Non-Current					5.6	4.3
38.9	42.4	45.7	Net Worth					55.8	38.2
100.0	100.0	100.0	Total Liabilities & Net Worth					100.0	100.0
			INCOME DATA						
100.0	100.0	100.0	Net Sales					100.0	100.0
26.2	27.6	25.0	Gross Profit					26.3	21.6
20.3	22.1	19.2	Operating Expenses					19.1	16.6
5.8	5.6	5.8	Operating Profit					7.2	5.1
.8	1.1	.7	All Other Expenses (net)					.8	.8
5.0	4.4	5.2	Profit Before Taxes					6.4	4.3
			RATIOS						
3.0	2.9	4.0						4.3	2.6
2.0	2.1	2.1	Current					3.8	1.3
1.3	1.3	1.2						1.4	.8
1.6	2.0	2.0						2.4	1.1
.8	1.0	.9	Quick					2.0	.5
.5	.6	.4						.5	.3
31 11.9	**29** 12.5	**28** 13.0						**28** 13.1	**27** 13.7
38 9.6	**38** 9.7	**38** 9.7	Sales/Receivables					**33** 11.0	**36** 10.2
47 7.7	**46** 7.9	**47** 7.8						**41** 9.0	**48** 7.6
57 6.4	**33** 11.0	**43** 8.5						**53** 6.9	**51** 7.1
89 4.1	**64** 5.7	**66** 5.5	Cost of Sales/Inventory					**85** 4.3	**73** 5.0
118 3.1	**94** 3.9	**96** 3.8						**101** 3.6	**101** 3.6
27 13.4	**22** 16.6	**21** 17.4						**19** 18.8	**22** 16.8
35 10.4	**32** 11.4	**31** 11.7	Cost of Sales/Payables					**26** 13.8	**40** 9.1
47 7.7	**41** 9.0	**43** 8.4						**47** 7.8	**55** 6.6
4.1	5.0	4.5						4.0	6.7
6.5	7.7	8.9	Sales/Working Capital					4.7	15.9
15.1	28.1	22.5						13.2	-12.4
13.1	25.5	15.6							12.6
(38) 4.1	(33) 4.7	(38) 5.9	EBIT/Interest						(21) 5.0
1.8	1.7	2.4							1.7
11.7	3.2	4.4							
(12) 2.5	(14) 2.2	(12) 2.8	Net Profit + Depr., Dep., Amort./Cur. Mat. L/T/D						
1.0	1.8	1.3							
.3	.3	.3						.3	.4
.8	.6	.7	Fixed/Worth					.4	.8
1.5	1.5	1.6						1.5	2.2
.8	.5	.4						.2	.9
1.6	1.3	1.4	Debt/Worth					.5	2.4
4.6	3.9	3.4						3.6	5.7
43.7	48.6	40.5						43.4	34.0
(36) 19.1	(33) 20.7	(40) 28.2	% Profit Before Taxes/Tangible Net Worth					32.4	(19) 26.9
7.3	4.3	13.8						3.4	12.8
15.7	15.8	16.6						22.8	11.3
4.8	6.0	8.7	% Profit Before Taxes/Total Assets					8.7	4.1
1.3	.8	2.6						2.5	1.5
16.8	17.7	19.1						18.4	17.6
8.6	9.5	8.5	Sales/Net Fixed Assets					9.0	6.5
5.5	5.3	4.7						4.6	3.9
2.5	2.9	2.7						2.7	2.4
1.9	2.3	2.0	Sales/Total Assets					2.0	1.9
1.5	1.7	1.7						1.6	1.5
1.0	1.3	.9						.9	1.0
(36) 1.7	(36) 2.2	(41) 1.6	% Depr., Dep., Amort./Sales					(10) 1.7	(21) 2.1
3.9	4.0	2.6						2.5	3.4
1.8	2.1	1.8							
(13) 3.0	(11) 3.8	(11) 2.3	% Officers', Directors' Owners' Comp/Sales						
5.1	4.7	4.8							
1799102M	**1412842M**	**2030129M**	Net Sales ($)	**891M**	**8469M**		**49690M**	**199066M**	**1772013M**
1050866M	**866459M**	**1160265M**	Total Assets ($)	**389M**	**2361M**		**24813M**	**100029M**	**1032673M**

M = $ thousand MM = $ million

See Pages 9 through 22 for Explanation of Ratios and Data

Current Data Sorted by Assets							Comparative Historical Data	
						Type of Statement		
		2	6	2	1	Unqualified	18	15
	3	8	1			Reviewed	14	13
	2	5	1			Compiled	8	5
1	4	3				Tax Returns	3	4
	2	8	4	3	1	Other	23	33
	10 (4/1-9/30/13)		47 (10/1/13-3/31/14)				4/1/09-3/31/10 ALL	4/1/10-3/31/11 ALL
0-500M	500M-2MM	2-10MM	10-50MM	50-100MM	100-250MM			
1	11	26	12	5	2	**NUMBER OF STATEMENTS**	66	70
%	%	%	%	%	%	**ASSETS**	%	%
	17.8	13.9	5.9			Cash & Equivalents	7.5	6.0
	30.7	28.5	26.0			Trade Receivables (net)	25.1	26.4
	25.7	22.8	23.0			Inventory	19.8	22.0
	.4	.5	2.1			All Other Current	2.6	1.9
	74.6	65.7	56.9			Total Current	55.0	56.3
	19.4	30.2	32.1			Fixed Assets (net)	34.0	30.8
	2.1	1.8	9.4			Intangibles (net)	5.5	5.9
	3.9	2.3	1.5			All Other Non-Current	5.5	7.1
	100.0	100.0	100.0			Total	100.0	100.0
						LIABILITIES		
	14.0	9.2	8.5			Notes Payable-Short Term	9.0	12.1
	.9	1.2	3.0			Cur. Mat.-L.T.D.	6.0	4.5
	21.9	14.4	13.4			Trade Payables	14.5	16.9
	.1	.2	.0			Income Taxes Payable	.0	.0
	4.9	7.3	6.6			All Other Current	7.0	8.5
	41.8	32.2	31.5			Total Current	36.6	42.1
	15.8	11.4	16.9			Long-Term Debt	17.0	19.3
	.2	.0	.6			Deferred Taxes	.5	.7
	45.4	.8	1.7			All Other Non-Current	8.6	8.8
	-3.2	55.6	49.4			Net Worth	37.2	29.1
	100.0	100.0	100.0			Total Liabilties & Net Worth	100.0	100.0
						INCOME DATA		
	100.0	100.0	100.0			Net Sales	100.0	100.0
	37.3	30.1	19.5			Gross Profit	25.8	26.0
	35.5	23.2	13.2			Operating Expenses	23.4	21.0
	1.8	6.9	6.3			Operating Profit	2.4	5.0
	.3	.7	.7			All Other Expenses (net)	1.6	1.2
	1.5	6.2	5.6			Profit Before Taxes	.8	3.8
						RATIOS		
	2.9	4.3	3.3				2.8	2.4
	2.2	2.5	2.0			Current	1.6	1.5
	.9	1.3	.9				1.0	1.1
	1.7	3.1	1.8				1.7	1.3
	1.2	1.4	1.0			Quick	.9	.8
	.6	.8	.5				.5	.5
	23 15.8	33 11.2	36 10.0				32 11.3	32 11.3
	29 12.4	41 9.0	47 7.7			Sales/Receivables	47 7.8	45 8.2
	43 8.4	50 7.3	61 6.0				57 6.4	53 6.9
	28 13.0	33 10.9	29 12.5				30 12.0	32 11.6
	38 9.7	49 7.4	38 9.7			Cost of Sales/Inventory	43 8.5	44 8.3
	57 6.4	74 4.9	69 5.3				67 5.5	72 5.1
	27 13.4	7 49.9	13 27.5				15 24.7	20 18.1
	30 12.0	24 15.1	27 13.4			Cost of Sales/Payables	28 13.0	31 11.7
	57 6.4	37 9.8	47 7.8				44 8.3	45 8.1
	5.7	4.0	3.9				5.3	6.1
	7.4	6.7	12.9			Sales/Working Capital	12.0	12.5
	-100.3	19.7	NM				NM	45.2
		64.7	33.0				8.6	14.3
		(24) 9.7	(11) 11.1			EBIT/Interest	(57) 2.7	(68) 4.9
		3.8	3.8				-1.2	1.2
							7.8	6.4
						Net Profit + Depr., Dep., Amort./Cur. Mat. L/T/D	(22) 3.7	(23) 3.5
							1.1	1.4
	.2	.4	.4				.5	.5
	.8	.5	.9			Fixed/Worth	1.1	1.1
	-23.8	.7	1.6				3.8	3.5
	.6	.3	.6				.8	.7
	3.2	1.0	1.4			Debt/Worth	1.8	1.8
	-56.6	2.1	2.7				8.4	7.2
		37.5	38.9				42.8	47.9
		26.4	(11) 19.6			% Profit Before Taxes/Tangible Net Worth	(57) 15.7	(57) 17.7
		8.8	11.6				-8.8	2.5
	18.8	25.4	14.5				15.0	12.4
	8.3	11.7	7.1			% Profit Before Taxes/Total Assets	3.9	6.5
	-2.4	4.3	4.7				-10.1	.4
	37.8	14.5	10.7				13.2	14.5
	21.7	9.3	6.4			Sales/Net Fixed Assets	7.1	6.4
	9.2	4.3	4.2				3.4	4.0
	3.8	2.9	2.4				2.6	2.6
	3.1	2.1	1.9			Sales/Total Assets	2.0	1.9
	2.5	1.5	1.7				1.5	1.5
	.6	1.2	2.1				2.2	1.6
	(10) 1.3	(22) 1.8	2.6			% Depr., Dep., Amort./Sales	(62) 3.1	(63) 2.8
	2.7	2.9	4.4				5.3	4.7
							.7	.9
						% Officers', Directors' Owners' Comp/Sales	(16) 4.4	(17) 2.3
							9.0	4.2
2987M	40628M	310724M	612821M	586286M	611973M	Net Sales ($)	2526183M	2696067M
496M	12841M	130856M	299707M	340457M	314361M	Total Assets ($)	1500331M	1478391M

M = $ thousand MM = $ million

See Pages 9 through 22 for Explanation of Ratios and Data

Comparative Historical Data				Current Data Sorted by Sales					
			Type of Statement						
17	12	11	Unqualified			1		2	8
8	12	12	Reviewed		1	3	3	5	
6	5	8	Compiled			2	3	2	1
2	6	8	Tax Returns		3	1	3	1	
27	28	18	Other		1	1	4	4	8
4/1/11-3/31/12	**4/1/12-3/31/13**	**4/1/13-3/31/14**			**10 (4/1-9/30/13)**		**47 (10/1/13-3/31/14)**		
ALL	**ALL**	**ALL**		**0-1MM**	**1-3MM**	**3-5MM**	**5-10MM**	**10-25MM**	**25MM & OVER**
60	63	57	**NUMBER OF STATEMENTS**		5	8	13	14	17
%	%	%	**ASSETS**	%	%	%	%	%	%
8.4	10.3	12.5	Cash & Equivalents	D			20.5	5.8	7.1
27.0	24.4	28.0	Trade Receivables (net)	A			27.5	32.7	24.9
23.6	23.7	23.2	Inventory	T			19.6	25.7	24.0
2.2	1.5	1.0	All Other Current	A			.3	1.0	2.0
61.1	59.9	64.7	Total Current				68.0	65.2	57.9
30.5	31.6	29.0	Fixed Assets (net)	N			29.4	28.0	33.0
2.8	2.5	3.5	Intangibles (net)	O			.8	4.1	5.8
5.6	6.0	2.8	All Other Non-Current	T			1.8	2.7	3.2
100.0	100.0	100.0	Total				100.0	100.0	100.0
			LIABILITIES	A					
6.8	8.1	10.2	Notes Payable-Short Term	V			1.5	15.2	7.9
3.3	2.6	1.9	Cur. Mat.-L.T.D.	A			.9	2.6	2.8
12.0	13.6	16.4	Trade Payables	I			15.8	19.5	13.5
.0	.2	.1	Income Taxes Payable	L			.1	.4	.0
7.2	6.3	6.6	All Other Current	A			5.2	7.1	8.5
29.4	30.9	35.2	Total Current	B			23.6	44.8	32.8
17.8	16.9	14.0	Long-Term Debt	L			11.6	12.8	14.8
.6	.5	.3	Deferred Taxes	E			.1	.1	.7
7.6	6.3	9.7	All Other Non-Current				3.5	.1	1.9
44.6	45.4	40.8	Net Worth				61.2	42.2	49.8
100.0	100.0	100.0	Total Liabilities & Net Worth				100.0	100.0	100.0
			INCOME DATA						
100.0	100.0	100.0	Net Sales				100.0	100.0	100.0
24.4	23.5	27.5	Gross Profit				32.7	26.3	19.9
19.3	17.4	22.4	Operating Expenses				24.8	20.0	15.1
5.1	6.1	5.2	Operating Profit				7.9	6.2	4.8
1.1	.9	.7	All Other Expenses (net)				.7	.7	.8
4.0	5.2	4.5	Profit Before Taxes				7.3	5.5	4.0
			RATIOS						
3.9	3.5	3.4					6.9	2.3	3.0
1.9	2.0	2.2	Current				4.0	1.4	1.4
1.5	1.3	1.2					2.5	1.0	1.2
2.0	2.3	2.3					4.7	1.3	1.5
1.2	1.2	1.1	Quick				2.3	1.0	.9
.7	.6	.7					1.4	.5	.6
29 12.4	**29** 12.8	**29** 12.6					**27** 13.5	**30** 12.0	**31** 11.7
41 8.8	**38** 9.6	**41** 8.9	Sales/Receivables				**41** 8.8	**45** 8.2	**42** 8.7
56 6.5	**50** 7.3	**51** 7.2					**47** 7.7	**55** 6.6	**58** 6.3
33 10.9	**31** 11.6	**30** 12.3					**30** 12.1	**24** 15.0	**36** 10.2
47 7.8	**47** 7.8	**42** 8.6	Cost of Sales/Inventory				**57** 6.4	**36** 10.0	**41** 8.8
59 6.2	**76** 4.8	**72** 5.1					**74** 4.9	**89** 4.1	**72** 5.1
13 28.2	**14** 27.0	**16** 22.5					**5** 69.3	**24** 15.4	**17** 20.9
23 16.2	**26** 14.0	**28** 13.0	Cost of Sales/Payables				**24** 15.4	**40** 9.2	**28** 13.1
38 9.5	**46** 8.0	**43** 8.5					**31** 11.8	**51** 7.1	**39** 9.4
4.4	4.8	4.5					3.9	5.1	4.4
7.5	7.6	7.4	Sales/Working Capital				4.8	16.2	18.7
16.9	20.5	25.3					7.1	-266.0	21.5
21.9	38.7	35.8					113.5	45.8	40.3
(55) 4.6	(58) 6.1	(51) 7.1	EBIT/Interest				(11) 17.6	5.8	(16) 13.8
1.5	1.9	2.0					5.0	3.0	1.6
12.4	8.8	9.3							
(22) 3.0	(21) 3.5	(17) 2.9	Net Profit + Depr., Dep., Amort./Cur. Mat. L/T/D						
1.9	1.4	1.8							
.4	.4	.4					.2	.4	.5
.6	.6	.6	Fixed/Worth				.5	.6	.7
1.9	1.5	1.4					.7	1.1	1.5
.5	.5	.5					.2	.8	.5
1.2	1.1	1.2	Debt/Worth				.5	1.8	1.2
3.4	2.8	2.8					2.3	2.5	2.6
33.7	41.4	36.9					36.9	46.2	39.0
(54) 17.5	(57) 20.1	(52) 21.5	% Profit Before Taxes/Tangible Net Worth				22.7	(13) 29.1	14.1
4.8	10.2	8.7					10.1	18.8	9.2
15.7	19.6	17.0					26.9	25.6	10.9
6.8	8.1	7.3	% Profit Before Taxes/Total Assets				16.0	10.7	6.7
1.9	2.5	2.4					4.3	4.1	2.2
13.6	14.6	17.3					34.3	15.2	11.6
6.6	6.9	8.7	Sales/Net Fixed Assets				8.7	9.5	6.9
4.2	4.2	4.9					3.9	5.2	4.5
2.6	2.7	2.9					2.9	3.6	2.5
2.0	2.1	2.1	Sales/Total Assets				2.0	2.2	2.0
1.8	1.7	1.7					1.6	1.7	1.6
1.5	1.5	1.2					1.1	1.2	1.6
(54) 2.5	(56) 2.2	(52) 2.1	% Depr., Dep., Amort./Sales				(10) 1.5	(13) 2.1	2.2
4.8	4.1	3.6					4.6	3.5	4.5
.9	1.7	2.3							
(14) 3.7	(17) 3.8	(15) 3.8	% Officers', Directors' Owners' Comp/Sales						
5.6	6.5	6.7							
2968466M	**3017984M**	**2165419M**	Net Sales ($)		**10308M**	**29517M**	**86039M**	**261669M**	**1777886M**
1673956M	**1646492M**	**1098718M**	Total Assets ($)		**4773M**	**14635M**	**46106M**	**113853M**	**919351M**

M = $ thousand MM = $ million

See Pages 9 through 22 for Explanation of Ratios and Data

Current Data Sorted by Assets							Comparative Historical Data	
						Type of Statement		
		3	2	1	2	Unqualified	5	7
	1	1	3			Reviewed	5	4
	2	1	2	1		Compiled	1	3
	2	1				Tax Returns	1	
	2	4	8	2	2	Other	7	11
	6 (4/1-9/30/13)		34 (10/1/13-3/31/14)				**4/1/09-3/31/10 ALL**	**4/1/10-3/31/11 ALL**
0-500M	**500M-2MM**	**2-10MM**	**10-50MM**	**50-100MM**	**100-250MM**			
	7	10	15	4	4	**NUMBER OF STATEMENTS**	19	25
%	%	%	%	%	%	**ASSETS**	%	%
DATA NOT AVAILABLE		4.9	7.9			Cash & Equivalents	8.5	6.8
		32.8	28.2			Trade Receivables (net)	20.4	25.0
		24.9	19.5			Inventory	16.0	16.4
		6.8	3.5			All Other Current	2.5	5.9
		69.3	59.1			Total Current	47.4	54.1
		25.6	27.7			Fixed Assets (net)	37.6	32.0
		1.6	6.7			Intangibles (net)	7.0	9.7
		3.5	6.4			All Other Non-Current	8.0	4.2
		100.0	100.0			Total	100.0	100.0
						LIABILITIES		
		13.4	7.2			Notes Payable-Short Term	23.6	9.9
		2.1	2.9			Cur. Mat.-L.T.D.	3.9	5.4
		20.0	16.9			Trade Payables	24.4	13.5
		.0	.2			Income Taxes Payable	.0	.1
		6.3	5.5			All Other Current	6.1	6.1
		41.8	32.7			Total Current	58.0	34.9
		9.9	15.1			Long-Term Debt	22.9	21.8
		.0	.6			Deferred Taxes	.3	.3
		3.0	1.7			All Other Non-Current	7.0	6.9
		45.3	49.9			Net Worth	11.8	36.2
		100.0	100.0			Total Liabilities & Net Worth	100.0	100.0
						INCOME DATA		
		100.0	100.0			Net Sales	100.0	100.0
		24.9	23.1			Gross Profit	27.1	28.0
		17.3	17.3			Operating Expenses	21.1	19.5
		7.7	5.8			Operating Profit	6.0	8.5
		.9	1.4			All Other Expenses (net)	1.5	1.6
		6.7	4.5			Profit Before Taxes	4.5	6.9
						RATIOS		
		5.8	3.0				1.8	2.1
		1.5	2.2			Current	1.5	1.6
		1.3	1.2				.8	1.2
		2.1	2.0				1.3	1.3
		.8	1.1			Quick	.9	.9
		.7	.7				.5	.7
		33 11.1	**34** 10.6				**18** 20.6	**26** 14.2
		43 8.5	**43** 8.4			Sales/Receivables	**34** 10.6	**40** 9.2
		54 6.8	**54** 6.8				**42** 8.8	**51** 7.1
		24 14.9	**26** 13.9				**12** 29.9	**24** 15.4
		39 9.3	**34** 10.6			Cost of Sales/Inventory	**36** 10.1	**31** 11.6
		51 7.1	**55** 6.6				**49** 7.4	**52** 7.0
		6 65.0	**16** 22.2				**22** 16.8	**17** 21.9
		31 11.6	**28** 12.9			Cost of Sales/Payables	**28** 12.9	**28** 13.1
		49 7.5	**32** 11.3				**39** 9.3	**35** 10.4
		6.6	5.6				8.2	7.8
		10.3	9.1			Sales/Working Capital	15.3	13.0
		NM	27.5				-70.0	30.0
			25.1				16.7	14.1
			(12) 10.8			EBIT/Interest	(17) 5.0	(22) 6.5
			1.7				1.9	2.7
						Net Profit + Depr., Dep., Amort./Cur. Mat. L/T/D		
		.4	.3				.5	.5
		.5	.4			Fixed/Worth	1.1	1.2
		1.4	.9				2.7	-2.4
		.6	.3				.9	.5
		1.2	1.1			Debt/Worth	1.6	2.0
		5.1	2.0				4.1	-14.0
		78.1	36.9				60.0	52.1
		43.8	(14) 18.4			% Profit Before Taxes/Tangible Net Worth	(16) 43.6	(18) 40.5
		26.4	12.0				4.2	21.1
		23.7	15.5				26.4	21.8
		18.0	8.8			% Profit Before Taxes/Total Assets	12.2	15.5
		8.6	1.6				4.8	7.2
		13.3	18.6				16.7	21.7
		12.4	8.1			Sales/Net Fixed Assets	9.9	8.5
		10.6	5.6				2.9	4.5
		3.7	3.0				2.9	2.9
		3.0	2.4			Sales/Total Assets	2.6	2.3
		2.2	1.9				1.7	1.7
			1.0				1.1	1.3
			(14) 1.6			% Depr., Dep., Amort./Sales	(17) 2.3	(21) 2.3
			2.7				4.1	3.4
						% Officers', Directors' Owners' Comp/Sales		
	28067M	132438M	529027M	582156M	907096M	Net Sales ($)	476368M	556337M
	8254M	46175M	223685M	266157M	680339M	Total Assets ($)	221001M	265124M

M = $ thousand MM = $ million

See Pages 9 through 22 for Explanation of Ratios and Data

Comparative Historical Data				Current Data Sorted by Sales					
			Type of Statement						
6	8	8	Unqualified					3	5
4	4	5	Reviewed			1			4
4	7	6	Compiled		2		1	1	2
2	1	3	Tax Returns				2	1	
9	11	18	Other			1	3	4	10
					6 (4/1-9/30/13)		34 (10/1/13-3/31/14)		
4/1/11-3/31/12 ALL	4/1/12-3/31/13 ALL	4/1/13-3/31/14 ALL		0-1MM	1-3MM	3-5MM	5-10MM	10-25MM	25MM & OVER
25	31	40	**NUMBER OF STATEMENTS**		2	2	6	9	21
%	%	%	**ASSETS**	%	%	%	%	%	%
6.2	5.4	8.2	Cash & Equivalents	DATA NOT AVAILABLE					10.3
26.9	29.5	28.4	Trade Receivables (net)						28.0
19.2	22.7	23.0	Inventory						20.7
6.1	5.5	4.3	All Other Current						2.4
58.4	63.0	63.9	Total Current						61.3
30.4	25.9	26.1	Fixed Assets (net)						24.7
5.8	4.5	4.7	Intangibles (net)						7.3
5.4	6.6	5.3	All Other Non-Current						6.7
100.0	100.0	100.0	Total						100.0
			LIABILITIES						
8.0	9.8	8.3	Notes Payable-Short Term						5.4
3.4	2.0	4.1	Cur. Mat.-L.T.D.						4.6
15.7	17.0	16.8	Trade Payables						14.5
.2	.1	.2	Income Taxes Payable						.2
5.7	9.3	9.2	All Other Current						5.6
33.0	38.1	38.6	Total Current						30.3
15.7	14.8	12.6	Long-Term Debt						15.4
.5	.2	.7	Deferred Taxes						1.3
4.2	9.6	2.7	All Other Non-Current						2.9
46.6	37.2	45.3	Net Worth						50.1
100.0	100.0	100.0	Total Liabilties & Net Worth						100.0
			INCOME DATA						
100.0	100.0	100.0	Net Sales						100.0
28.7	26.8	25.5	Gross Profit						21.5
21.9	19.7	19.2	Operating Expenses						16.1
6.8	7.1	6.3	Operating Profit						5.4
.5	.3	.8	All Other Expenses (net)						.9
6.3	6.8	5.5	Profit Before Taxes						4.6
			RATIOS						
2.8	2.5	3.3							3.4
1.9	1.8	1.9	Current						2.9
1.5	1.2	1.2							1.4
1.4	1.4	2.0							2.4
1.1	1.0	1.0	Quick						1.4
.7	.6	.7							.8
30 12.3	35 10.5	34 10.8							34 10.7
40 9.2	41 8.8	43 8.5	Sales/Receivables						43 8.4
52 7.0	50 7.3	52 7.0							51 7.2
24 15.3	28 12.9	27 13.3							28 13.0
33 11.2	42 8.7	41 8.9	Cost of Sales/Inventory						36 10.1
56 6.5	61 6.0	62 5.9							58 6.3
13 28.2	21 17.1	17 22.1							17 21.3
24 15.1	26 14.0	28 13.1	Cost of Sales/Payables						28 12.9
42 8.6	40 9.1	38 9.5							35 10.3
6.0	5.9	5.5							3.7
9.8	9.7	9.2	Sales/Working Capital						5.9
20.5	26.7	25.8							20.0
29.0	28.0	27.1							42.9
(21) 5.7	(26) 7.7	(34) 11.6	EBIT/Interest						(18) 10.8
3.4	4.5	3.8							2.9
			Net Profit + Depr., Dep., Amort./Cur. Mat. L/T/D						
.3	.3	.3							.3
.6	.6	.5	Fixed/Worth						.5
1.6	2.2	1.0							.9
.6	.6	.5							.4
1.0	1.2	1.2	Debt/Worth						1.1
2.2	3.5	3.3							2.8
40.2	65.5	50.9							43.6
(22) 25.6	(28) 32.2	(38) 25.7	% Profit Before Taxes/Tangible Net Worth						(20) 21.7
14.4	18.4	12.5							11.8
20.1	20.9	18.5							14.7
8.9	11.7	10.2	% Profit Before Taxes/Total Assets						8.4
5.5	6.7	5.7							3.9
14.8	21.3	16.2							17.7
8.6	10.8	11.1	Sales/Net Fixed Assets						8.0
4.7	7.3	6.6							6.0
3.0	3.1	3.5							2.9
2.2	2.6	2.4	Sales/Total Assets						2.4
1.7	2.1	1.9							1.7
1.2	1.0	1.0							1.0
(23) 2.2	(28) 1.5	(36) 1.6	% Depr., Dep., Amort./Sales						(20) 1.4
3.4	2.0	2.6							2.6
	.9	1.1							
	(10) 3.7	(13) 3.7	% Officers', Directors' Owners' Comp/Sales						
	7.2	5.6							
1829458M	1195514M	2178784M	Net Sales ($)		4239M	6683M	41585M	147872M	1978405M
536417M	487014M	1224610M	Total Assets ($)		1130M	3381M	13697M	65444M	1140958M

M = $ thousand MM = $ million

See Pages 9 through 22 for Explanation of Ratios and Data

Current Data Sorted by Assets							Comparative Historical Data	
						Type of Statement		
		2	2		3	Unqualified	12	12
		4				Reviewed	7	5
						Compiled		1
	4	1				Tax Returns	2	1
		4	10	2	4	Other	13	15
	8 (4/1-9/30/13)		28 (10/1/13-3/31/14)				4/1/09-3/31/10	4/1/10-3/31/11
0-500M	500M-2MM	2-10MM	10-50MM	50-100MM	100-250MM		ALL	ALL
	4	11	12	2	7	**NUMBER OF STATEMENTS**	34	34
%	%	%	%	%	%	**ASSETS**	%	%
DATA NOT AVAILABLE		6.3	2.3			Cash & Equivalents	7.0	7.3
		20.9	20.3			Trade Receivables (net)	18.3	21.9
		22.8	19.5			Inventory	17.2	20.3
		2.5	1.5			All Other Current	4.4	4.1
		52.5	43.6			Total Current	46.9	53.6
		43.7	36.6			Fixed Assets (net)	43.6	37.3
		.0	17.4			Intangibles (net)	5.5	3.2
		3.8	2.4			All Other Non-Current	4.0	5.9
		100.0	100.0			Total	100.0	100.0
						LIABILITIES		
		6.6	6.5			Notes Payable-Short Term	5.0	8.3
		3.3	5.9			Cur. Mat.-L.T.D.	4.3	5.6
		14.3	10.6			Trade Payables	11.2	13.6
		.8	.0			Income Taxes Payable	.2	.0
		5.7	10.1			All Other Current	14.2	10.7
		30.6	33.0			Total Current	34.9	38.1
		19.0	18.3			Long-Term Debt	22.1	16.5
		.0	.3			Deferred Taxes	.7	.5
		.6	4.4			All Other Non-Current	1.8	8.9
		49.8	44.0			Net Worth	40.6	36.0
		100.0	100.0			Total Liabilties & Net Worth	100.0	100.0
						INCOME DATA		
		100.0	100.0			Net Sales	100.0	100.0
		26.1	21.4			Gross Profit	23.0	24.8
		21.5	15.0			Operating Expenses	17.2	18.8
		4.6	6.3			Operating Profit	5.8	6.0
		1.1	2.2			All Other Expenses (net)	1.7	1.2
		3.5	4.2			Profit Before Taxes	4.1	4.9
						RATIOS		
		2.3	2.3				2.6	2.4
		1.8	1.5			Current	1.3	1.4
		1.3	.9				.9	.9
		1.3	1.4				1.3	1.4
		.9	.9			Quick	.8	.7
		.4	.4				.4	.4
		30 12.0	**36** 10.2				**28** 12.9	**27** 13.5
		36 10.2	**42** 8.7			Sales/Receivables	**37** 10.0	**36** 10.2
		46 7.9	**51** 7.1				**47** 7.8	**46** 7.9
		43 8.5	**34** 10.6				**27** 13.6	**24** 15.1
		52 7.0	**43** 8.4			Cost of Sales/Inventory	**39** 9.3	**39** 9.3
		94 3.9	**76** 4.8				**77** 4.7	**85** 4.3
		22 16.3	**21** 17.8				**16** 23.3	**15** 23.6
		33 11.1	**29** 12.6			Cost of Sales/Payables	**31** 11.9	**24** 15.2
		49 7.4	**37** 9.9				**44** 8.3	**55** 6.6
		5.7	7.4				5.9	6.9
		10.2	11.4			Sales/Working Capital	14.0	17.2
		14.7	-94.7				-74.1	-19.2
		13.9	24.6				15.9	16.2
		3.3	(10) 4.1			EBIT/Interest	(30) 4.4	(30) 3.7
		1.7	-.2				1.8	1.9
								8.1
						Net Profit + Depr., Dep., Amort./Cur. Mat. L/T/D		(11) 2.3
								1.2
		.3	.6				.7	.2
		.8	1.7			Fixed/Worth	1.4	1.5
		1.8	4.8				3.2	3.8
		.6	.7				.6	.7
		1.0	3.0			Debt/Worth	2.1	2.1
		2.4	8.1				6.2	9.1
		19.2	49.5				33.8	58.1
		15.7	(10) 30.0			% Profit Before Taxes/Tangible Net Worth	(30) 18.0	(29) 23.5
		8.4	-16.5				11.5	11.3
		11.0	19.4				16.9	22.4
		4.8	7.9			% Profit Before Taxes/Total Assets	7.0	6.9
		2.5	-6.5				2.7	3.4
		14.6	7.6				8.2	32.7
		4.1	4.8			Sales/Net Fixed Assets	3.4	5.7
		2.4	2.8				2.1	2.5
		2.7	2.2				2.8	3.4
		1.7	1.6			Sales/Total Assets	1.6	2.0
		1.4	1.3				1.2	1.2
		1.1					.8	1.1
		(10) 3.8				% Depr., Dep., Amort./Sales	(22) 2.9	(27) 2.8
		5.9					5.7	5.9
						% Officers', Directors' Owners' Comp/Sales		
	14682M	123301M	491182M	210023M	1481641M	Net Sales ($)	2406121M	1924576M
	5068M	56726M	297829M	131306M	1194248M	Total Assets ($)	1748470M	1084282M

M = $ thousand MM = $ million

See Pages 9 through 22 for Explanation of Ratios and Data

Comparative Historical Data				Current Data Sorted by Sales					
			Type of Statement						
14	4	7	Unqualified			1	1		5
7	6	4	Reviewed		1		1	1	1
2	2		Compiled						
1	3	5	Tax Returns		1	3		1	
12	16	20	Other			1	1	5	13
					8 (4/1-9/30/13)		28 (10/1/13-3/31/14)		
4/1/11-3/31/12 ALL	4/1/12-3/31/13 ALL	4/1/13-3/31/14 ALL		0-1MM	1-3MM	3-5MM	5-10MM	10-25MM	25MM & OVER
36	31	36	**NUMBER OF STATEMENTS**		2	5	3	7	19
%	%	%	**ASSETS**	%	%	%	%	%	%
7.0	5.8	4.7	Cash & Equivalents	DATA NOT AVAILABLE					5.0
21.6	18.4	20.1	Trade Receivables (net)						21.2
17.5	18.3	19.0	Inventory						17.1
4.8	4.5	1.9	All Other Current						2.2
51.0	47.0	45.7	Total Current						45.5
36.4	41.3	38.3	Fixed Assets (net)						32.9
7.1	5.4	11.7	Intangibles (net)						16.3
5.5	6.3	4.4	All Other Non-Current						5.4
100.0	100.0	100.0	Total						100.0
			LIABILITIES						
6.6	6.1	7.7	Notes Payable-Short Term						6.9
4.2	4.4	4.5	Cur. Mat.-L.T.D.						3.2
15.4	12.2	14.5	Trade Payables						14.1
.3	.3	.4	Income Taxes Payable						.3
10.0	10.1	7.2	All Other Current						8.7
36.5	33.1	34.3	Total Current						33.2
20.9	23.5	24.8	Long-Term Debt						22.5
1.3	1.3	.9	Deferred Taxes						1.5
6.1	10.1	5.0	All Other Non-Current						6.7
35.3	32.1	35.0	Net Worth						36.0
100.0	100.0	100.0	Total Liabilties & Net Worth						100.0
			INCOME DATA						
100.0	100.0	100.0	Net Sales						100.0
24.6	23.1	24.5	Gross Profit						20.9
18.7	18.1	19.4	Operating Expenses						14.6
5.9	5.0	5.1	Operating Profit						6.3
1.4	1.2	1.7	All Other Expenses (net)						2.9
4.5	3.8	3.4	Profit Before Taxes						3.4
			RATIOS						
2.3	2.6	2.2							2.3
1.5	1.3	1.5	Current						1.5
1.0	1.0	.9							.9
1.6	1.3	1.2							1.3
.8	.7	.8	Quick						.8
.5	.5	.4							.5
24 15.1	25 14.4	31 11.8							34 10.6
38 9.5	35 10.5	38 9.7	Sales/Receivables						43 8.5
52 7.0	54 6.8	50 7.3							52 7.0
21 17.7	29 12.4	34 10.7							31 11.7
34 10.8	43 8.5	46 8.0	Cost of Sales/Inventory						40 9.1
56 6.5	69 5.3	79 4.6							69 5.3
24 14.9	14 26.7	27 13.5							29 12.8
32 11.5	28 12.9	35 10.4	Cost of Sales/Payables						38 9.7
49 7.4	42 8.6	47 7.8							48 7.6
6.4	5.7	6.9							6.8
14.7	19.0	12.0	Sales/Working Capital						10.7
289.8	-379.4	-37.0							-61.5
16.0	7.9	12.4							13.3
4.2	(30) 2.9	(34) 2.9	EBIT/Interest						(18) 1.3
1.2	1.0	.1							-.3
4.0									
(15) 2.5			Net Profit + Depr., Dep., Amort./Cur. Mat. L/T/D						
1.7									
.3	.5	.6							.4
1.5	1.5	1.6	Fixed/Worth						1.4
4.5	3.8	NM							-1.6
1.1	1.0	.8							.8
2.4	2.5	2.9	Debt/Worth						3.1
10.5	32.4	NM							-7.6
57.4	35.5	32.9							41.8
(30) 24.9	(25) 10.1	(27) 15.7	% Profit Before Taxes/Tangible Net Worth						(14) 16.4
6.9	1.2	.5							-2.4
13.1	10.2	12.7							19.2
5.4	4.0	5.0	% Profit Before Taxes/Total Assets						2.4
.4	.0	-2.2							-8.0
12.3	9.0	7.6							7.6
5.3	4.2	4.6	Sales/Net Fixed Assets						4.7
2.3	2.2	2.7							3.6
2.9	2.7	2.4							2.4
1.9	1.6	1.6	Sales/Total Assets						1.4
1.2	1.3	1.2							1.1
2.3	2.8	3.6							3.7
(29) 3.7	(24) 4.0	(28) 4.8	% Depr., Dep., Amort./Sales						(14) 4.5
5.3	5.4	6.3							6.4
		1.8							
		(10) 4.1	% Officers', Directors' Owners' Comp/Sales						
		5.9							
2501878M	2709813M	2320829M	Net Sales ($)		5880M	18958M	26954M	107203M	2161834M
1299766M	1399631M	1685177M	Total Assets ($)		3594M	10266M	17592M	64678M	1589047M

M = $ thousand MM = $ million

See Pages 9 through 22 for Explanation of Ratios and Data

Current Data Sorted by Assets / Comparative Historical Data

DATA NOT AVAILABLE

0-500M	500M-2MM	2-10MM	10-50MM	50-100MM	100-250MM			4/1/09-3/31/10 ALL		4/1/10-3/31/11 ALL
						Type of Statement				
			3	2	2	Unqualified		8		7
		1				Reviewed		6		3
		1				Compiled		1		4
	2	1				Tax Returns		2		1
	3	3	2	1	3	Other		14		12
	5 (4/1-9/30/13)		19 (10/1/13-3/31/14)					4/1/09-3/31/10 ALL		4/1/10-3/31/11 ALL
0-500M	500M-2MM	2-10MM	10-50MM	50-100MM	100-250MM					
	5	6	5	3	5	**NUMBER OF STATEMENTS**		31		27
%	%	%	%	%	%	**ASSETS**		%		%
						Cash & Equivalents		6.5		6.5
						Trade Receivables (net)		23.7		18.4
						Inventory		25.9		25.7
						All Other Current		5.5		3.0
						Total Current		61.6		53.6
						Fixed Assets (net)		24.8		28.0
						Intangibles (net)		8.8		12.4
						All Other Non-Current		4.8		6.0
						Total		100.0		100.0
						LIABILITIES				
						Notes Payable-Short Term		9.8		9.1
						Cur. Mat.-L.T.D.		3.3		3.8
						Trade Payables		15.4		11.2
						Income Taxes Payable		.2		.6
						All Other Current		9.7		10.3
						Total Current		38.4		34.9
						Long-Term Debt		15.8		18.1
						Deferred Taxes		.3		1.2
						All Other Non-Current		7.8		11.3
						Net Worth		37.8		34.5
						Total Liabilities & Net Worth		100.0		100.0
						INCOME DATA				
						Net Sales		100.0		100.0
						Gross Profit		29.9		30.6
						Operating Expenses		25.2		25.9
						Operating Profit		4.6		4.7
						All Other Expenses (net)		1.0		2.8
						Profit Before Taxes		3.6		1.9
						RATIOS				
								2.9		2.4
						Current		1.7		1.7
								1.1		1.2
								1.7		1.2
						Quick		1.1		.8
								.5		.4
							30	12.2	**25**	14.7
						Sales/Receivables	**40**	9.1	**41**	9.0
							59	6.2	**52**	7.0
							44	8.4	**43**	8.6
						Cost of Sales/Inventory	**63**	5.8	**61**	6.0
							79	4.6	**92**	4.0
							27	13.3	**23**	15.8
						Cost of Sales/Payables	**32**	11.3	**33**	11.0
							42	8.7	**48**	7.6
								4.2		4.1
						Sales/Working Capital		12.1		7.6
								48.0		27.3
								22.3		9.1
						EBIT/Interest	(27)	4.9	(23)	2.2
								.3		1.2
								6.7		
						Net Profit + Depr., Dep., Amort./Cur. Mat. L/T/D	(10)	2.6		
								.5		
								.3		.4
						Fixed/Worth		.9		1.1
								7.3		-1.9
								.7		.8
						Debt/Worth		1.6		2.0
								33.7		-5.7
								50.1		35.6
						% Profit Before Taxes/Tangible Net Worth	(24)	22.4	(19)	16.8
								3.5		6.1
								19.8		12.5
						% Profit Before Taxes/Total Assets		5.3		3.4
								-3.4		.5
								16.5		12.5
						Sales/Net Fixed Assets		8.3		6.4
								6.1		3.7
								2.9		2.5
						Sales/Total Assets		2.1		1.7
								1.5		1.2
								1.6		1.4
						% Depr., Dep., Amort./Sales	(26)	2.3	(19)	2.6
								4.6		4.5
						% Officers', Directors' Owners' Comp/Sales				
	14213M	114416M	206122M	316679M	1323780M	Net Sales ($)		1402315M		1238139M
	5304M	38032M	116614M	207061M	859704M	Total Assets ($)		909841M		1126126M

M = $ thousand MM = $ million

See Pages 9 through 22 for Explanation of Ratios and Data

Comparative Historical Data				Current Data Sorted by Sales					
			Type of Statement						
7	4	7	Unqualified					1	6
3	6	1	Reviewed					1	
1	2	1	Compiled					1	
3	4	3	Tax Returns		1	1		1	
10	14	12	Other	1	1		1	4	5
4/1/11-3/31/12 ALL	**4/1/12-3/31/13 ALL**	**4/1/13-3/31/14 ALL**		**5 (4/1-9/30/13)**			**19 (10/1/13-3/31/14)**		
				0-1MM	**1-3MM**	**3-5MM**	**5-10MM**	**10-25MM**	**25MM & OVER**
24	30	24	**NUMBER OF STATEMENTS**	1	2	1	1	8	11
%	%	%	**ASSETS**	%	%	%	%	%	%
9.9	5.5	5.9	Cash & Equivalents						5.6
20.4	27.1	26.3	Trade Receivables (net)						25.2
25.4	25.5	24.5	Inventory						21.8
2.9	3.7	1.7	All Other Current						1.9
58.6	61.8	58.4	Total Current						54.6
22.2	19.4	24.2	Fixed Assets (net)						24.0
14.8	11.8	13.7	Intangibles (net)						18.1
4.4	7.0	3.7	All Other Non-Current						3.3
100.0	100.0	100.0	Total						100.0
			LIABILITIES						
8.6	9.3	13.3	Notes Payable-Short Term						7.9
2.9	3.0	1.4	Cur. Mat.-L.T.D.						1.3
13.6	15.1	14.0	Trade Payables						11.1
.1	.7	.0	Income Taxes Payable						.0
11.4	7.4	11.1	All Other Current						9.0
36.5	35.5	39.8	Total Current						29.4
29.3	15.4	19.5	Long-Term Debt						17.4
.6	.5	.3	Deferred Taxes						.6
12.8	7.1	8.6	All Other Non-Current						3.6
20.8	41.5	31.7	Net Worth						49.0
100.0	100.0	100.0	Total Liabilities & Net Worth						100.0
			INCOME DATA						
100.0	100.0	100.0	Net Sales						100.0
28.3	28.8	26.4	Gross Profit						26.3
24.9	22.6	23.3	Operating Expenses						20.3
3.5	6.2	3.1	Operating Profit						5.9
1.1	.4	.7	All Other Expenses (net)						1.4
2.4	5.8	2.4	Profit Before Taxes						4.5
			RATIOS						
2.8	2.9	2.4							2.9
1.9	1.7	1.4	Current						2.1
1.1	1.2	1.1							1.2
1.5	1.5	1.4							2.0
1.0	1.0	.8	Quick						.8
.6	.6	.4							.6
18 20.2	**32** 11.5	**30** 12.1							**52** 7.0
37 9.9	**39** 9.3	**47** 7.8	Sales/Receivables						**54** 6.7
52 7.0	**57** 6.4	**58** 6.3							**69** 5.3
31 11.9	**32** 11.4	**32** 11.3							**41** 8.8
58 6.3	**53** 6.9	**54** 6.7	Cost of Sales/Inventory						**58** 6.3
76 4.8	**72** 5.1	**78** 4.7							**122** 3.0
16 22.8	**21** 17.2	**21** 17.6							**24** 15.4
30 12.2	**30** 12.1	**33** 11.2	Cost of Sales/Payables						**34** 10.7
42 8.7	**42** 8.6	**37** 9.8							**38** 9.7
5.0	5.7	6.3							4.1
8.6	9.4	14.8	Sales/Working Capital						7.4
64.3	25.1	30.5							15.3
5.6	26.2	21.0							39.8
(22) 3.3	(25) 10.6	(22) 6.9	EBIT/Interest						9.6
1.9	2.4	1.3							1.5
			Net Profit + Depr., Dep., Amort./Cur. Mat. L/T/D						
.5	.3	.4							.4
1.2	.5	1.0	Fixed/Worth						.9
-.7	1.6	-.8							1.9
1.5	.7	.7							.4
8.2	1.6	1.8	Debt/Worth						1.5
-4.0	6.7	-6.4							3.7
57.7	41.7	51.3							
(15) 16.8	(25) 27.0	(17) 21.7	% Profit Before Taxes/Tangible Net Worth						
11.0	1.4	10.3							
11.5	20.7	20.0							9.1
6.2	12.6	6.1	% Profit Before Taxes/Total Assets						6.3
2.1	3.2	.1							1.6
25.5	20.7	20.1							13.0
12.1	12.2	11.2	Sales/Net Fixed Assets						8.5
7.7	6.8	6.0							4.5
3.0	3.0	3.2							1.9
2.1	2.1	1.9	Sales/Total Assets						1.6
1.5	1.6	1.4							1.2
1.1	.8	1.4							
(21) 1.9	(28) 1.6	(18) 2.3	% Depr., Dep., Amort./Sales						
3.6	2.6	3.2							
			% Officers', Directors' Owners' Comp/Sales						
1428444M	2133160M	1975210M	Net Sales ($)	418M	4700M	3894M	5201M	147161M	1813836M
778102M	1214708M	1226715M	Total Assets ($)	655M	2279M	826M	1544M	58326M	1163085M

M = $ thousand MM = $ million

See Pages 9 through 22 for Explanation of Ratios and Data

	Current Data Sorted by Assets						Comparative Historical Data	
Type of Statement								
Unqualified		2	13	44	22	15	153	139
Reviewed	1	7	88	58	7	3	187	180
Compiled	5	23	47	14	1		76	91
Tax Returns	20	33	26				61	95
Other	6	33	98	112	38	34	313	322
	108 (4/1-9/30/13)			642 (10/1/13-3/31/14)			4/1/09-3/31/10	4/1/10-3/31/11
	0-500M	**500M-2MM**	**2-10MM**	**10-50MM**	**50-100MM**	**100-250MM**	**ALL**	**ALL**
NUMBER OF STATEMENTS	32	98	272	228	68	52	790	827
ASSETS	%	%	%	%	%	%	%	%
Cash & Equivalents	19.5	11.5	8.6	6.4	7.3	4.4	8.3	8.1
Trade Receivables (net)	24.4	27.4	26.0	24.0	20.2	19.9	24.4	26.0
Inventory	25.2	28.1	26.5	23.9	17.7	18.1	22.8	22.7
All Other Current	2.6	1.2	1.8	2.1	2.1	3.8	2.3	2.3
Total Current	71.7	68.2	62.9	56.4	47.3	46.2	57.8	59.1
Fixed Assets (net)	16.3	25.4	29.7	33.0	34.1	31.8	32.1	30.4
Intangibles (net)	2.0	3.1	3.5	5.6	13.4	14.6	5.2	5.7
All Other Non-Current	9.9	3.3	4.0	4.9	5.2	7.4	4.8	4.9
Total	100.0	100.0	100.0	100.0	100.0	100.0	100.0	100.0
LIABILITIES								
Notes Payable-Short Term	20.1	9.6	9.8	9.6	5.5	3.7	11.3	9.6
Cur. Mat.-L.T.D.	3.5	4.2	3.4	4.2	3.8	1.3	4.7	4.2
Trade Payables	13.0	19.2	14.7	12.6	13.1	13.2	14.5	15.1
Income Taxes Payable	.0	.1	.1	.4	.4	.3	.2	.2
All Other Current	6.8	9.0	8.5	7.6	7.9	8.6	8.1	7.8
Total Current	43.3	42.2	36.4	34.4	30.7	27.1	38.8	37.0
Long-Term Debt	19.0	20.1	17.4	15.4	17.7	24.0	18.2	17.7
Deferred Taxes	.0	.1	.4	1.0	1.4	1.6	.7	.7
All Other Non-Current	25.3	11.7	4.9	5.9	4.1	8.6	6.7	7.7
Net Worth	12.4	25.9	40.9	43.3	46.1	38.7	35.6	37.0
Total Liabilties & Net Worth	100.0	100.0	100.0	100.0	100.0	100.0	100.0	100.0
INCOME DATA								
Net Sales	100.0	100.0	100.0	100.0	100.0	100.0	100.0	100.0
Gross Profit	42.7	34.0	28.2	24.4	24.9	22.4	27.6	28.7
Operating Expenses	36.7	30.2	22.9	16.6	16.5	15.4	23.6	22.7
Operating Profit	6.0	3.8	5.3	7.8	8.4	7.0	4.1	6.0
All Other Expenses (net)	.8	1.1	.6	1.1	1.1	2.0	1.5	1.2
Profit Before Taxes	5.1	2.7	4.7	6.7	7.3	4.9	2.5	4.8
RATIOS								
Current	9.2	3.3	3.0	2.6	2.0	2.5	2.5	2.8
	2.2	1.7	1.7	1.7	1.6	1.8	1.6	1.7
	1.0	1.1	1.2	1.3	1.1	1.3	1.1	1.2
Quick	5.6	2.1	2.0	1.5	1.5	1.3	1.5	1.6
	1.3	.9	.9	.9	.8	.9	.8	.9
	.4	.5	.6	.6	.5	.7	.5	.6
Sales/Receivables	**5** 67.1	**22** 16.4	**31** 11.8	**35** 10.3	**36** 10.0	**39** 9.4	**34** 10.8	**34** 10.8
	30 12.3	**32** 11.3	**43** 8.5	**45** 8.1	**45** 8.1	**47** 7.7	**46** 8.0	**45** 8.2
	37 9.8	**48** 7.6	**54** 6.8	**56** 6.5	**59** 6.2	**59** 6.2	**59** 6.2	**57** 6.4
Cost of Sales/Inventory	**3** 115.6	**29** 12.4	**36** 10.2	**39** 9.3	**34** 10.8	**36** 10.0	**36** 10.0	**33** 10.9
	32 11.5	**50** 7.3	**60** 6.1	**55** 6.6	**54** 6.8	**49** 7.4	**56** 6.5	**52** 7.0
	76 4.8	**81** 4.5	**89** 4.1	**81** 4.5	**76** 4.8	**76** 4.8	**85** 4.3	**79** 4.6
Cost of Sales/Payables	**0** UND	**18** 20.8	**18** 20.1	**19** 18.9	**25** 14.6	**22** 16.3	**20** 18.1	**19** 19.2
	18 19.8	**32** 11.5	**29** 12.8	**30** 12.0	**36** 10.2	**37** 9.9	**33** 11.2	**31** 11.9
	35 10.4	**51** 7.1	**44** 8.3	**42** 8.6	**48** 7.6	**51** 7.2	**49** 7.4	**47** 7.7
Sales/Working Capital	5.1	5.2	4.9	5.2	6.0	4.9	5.0	5.1
	8.6	10.1	8.8	8.7	10.1	8.7	9.8	8.8
	-196.9	53.9	18.7	17.2	33.4	17.7	44.6	27.6
EBIT/Interest	15.0	15.0	18.2	32.1	29.4	15.6	8.7	14.6
	(19) 4.0	(86) 3.7	(247) 4.8	(217) 10.3	(60) 7.0	(46) 6.7	(721) 3.2	(739) 4.9
	1.1	1.3	1.7	3.2	2.4	1.5	.7	1.7
Net Profit + Depr., Dep., Amort./Cur. Mat. L/T/D		3.2	7.3	6.9	5.4	39.3	5.6	6.8
		(10) 1.5	(62) 3.1	(79) 3.1	(27) 3.1	(14) 6.3	(245) 2.3	(261) 3.1
		.8	1.5	1.8	1.8	4.1	.9	1.7
Fixed/Worth	.0	.2	.4	.4	.6	.7	.4	.4
	.4	.9	.7	.8	1.1	1.2	1.0	.9
	-1.6	4.1	1.7	1.6	2.2	4.4	2.8	2.3
Debt/Worth	.2	.8	.6	.6	.9	1.0	.7	.7
	2.2	2.4	1.5	1.2	1.6	2.6	1.9	1.7
	-4.3	15.0	4.5	2.8	4.7	8.0	6.0	5.2
% Profit Before Taxes/Tangible Net Worth	56.9	69.9	45.3	45.5	53.8	41.8	35.5	45.4
	(21) 14.3	(79) 18.8	(245) 23.5	(211) 24.8	(59) 25.5	(42) 22.9	(667) 14.2	(715) 22.5
	2.3	5.5	8.5	11.3	10.2	10.4	.7	8.2
% Profit Before Taxes/Total Assets	40.8	17.8	18.4	18.4	14.4	13.3	12.7	15.8
	10.5	5.0	7.8	9.5	8.6	6.8	4.3	7.8
	.7	.9	2.3	4.0	4.0	2.6	-1.0	2.0
Sales/Net Fixed Assets	UND	35.1	17.2	9.8	8.4	7.1	13.0	15.0
	25.6	14.9	8.0	6.2	4.8	4.9	5.9	7.1
	13.5	6.1	4.3	3.7	3.1	3.6	3.4	4.0
Sales/Total Assets	4.7	3.7	2.8	2.3	2.0	1.8	2.5	2.6
	3.3	2.7	2.1	1.8	1.5	1.6	1.8	2.0
	2.4	2.0	1.6	1.4	1.2	1.2	1.3	1.5
% Depr., Dep., Amort./Sales	.5	.7	1.3	1.7	2.6	2.3	1.8	1.6
	(15) 2.4	(76) 1.6	(235) 2.4	(220) 2.7	(59) 4.3	(32) 2.9	(675) 3.3	(730) 3.0
	3.4	2.9	3.8	4.2	5.7	3.7	5.2	4.7
% Officers', Directors' Owners' Comp/Sales	4.8	2.8	1.7	1.0			2.0	2.0
	(18) 7.5	(51) 4.9	(96) 3.0	(39) 2.0			(223) 3.9	(257) 3.8
	11.6	8.1	4.9	2.8			7.0	6.4
Net Sales ($)	35971M	354255M	3126831M	9167104M	7595824M	12755501M	25747316M	27942850M
Total Assets ($)	9166M	121335M	1394832M	4916566M	4889831M	8417344M	16248296M	17313322M

M = $ thousand MM = $ million

See Pages 9 through 22 for Explanation of Ratios and Data

Comparative Historical Data | **Current Data Sorted by Sales**

4/1/11-3/31/12 ALL	4/1/12-3/31/13 ALL	4/1/13-3/31/14 ALL	Type of Statement	0-1MM	1-3MM	3-5MM	5-10MM	10-25MM	25MM & OVER
150	107	96	Unqualified		1	2	2	19	72
183	159	164	Reviewed		5	7	35	65	52
106	86	90	Compiled	3	13	13	20	31	10
98	102	79	Tax Returns	10	33	15	12	9	
303	315	321	Other	6	20	20	46	67	162
				108 (4/1-9/30/13)			642 (10/1/13-3/31/14)		
840	769	750	**NUMBER OF STATEMENTS**	19	72	57	115	191	296
%	%	%	**ASSETS**	%	%	%	%	%	%
8.3	8.1	8.4	Cash & Equivalents	23.1	8.6	11.4	8.7	9.1	6.2
25.6	25.1	24.5	Trade Receivables (net)	16.6	26.6	22.3	25.9	25.9	23.6
23.7	24.6	24.5	Inventory	27.2	25.8	25.7	28.2	24.0	22.6
2.3	2.2	2.0	All Other Current	.0	1.2	2.2	1.6	2.1	2.5
59.9	60.1	59.4	Total Current	66.9	62.2	61.5	64.4	61.0	54.9
29.9	29.1	30.1	Fixed Assets (net)	22.7	29.7	29.5	28.3	30.4	31.3
5.3	6.2	5.7	Intangibles (net)	1.0	3.3	2.7	4.0	4.9	8.3
4.9	4.7	4.8	All Other Non-Current	9.2	4.8	6.3	3.3	3.7	5.5
100.0	100.0	100.0	Total	100.0	100.0	100.0	100.0	100.0	100.0
			LIABILITIES						
10.2	10.0	9.3	Notes Payable-Short Term	17.3	9.7	10.6	11.6	9.6	7.4
3.7	3.8	3.6	Cur. Mat.-L.T.D.	3.2	4.5	3.9	3.4	3.6	3.5
15.6	15.4	14.3	Trade Payables	10.1	16.1	13.5	15.0	14.8	13.7
.2	.2	.2	Income Taxes Payable	.0	.1	.1	.1	.1	.5
8.8	9.4	8.2	All Other Current	1.8	8.0	13.9	8.6	6.3	8.6
38.5	38.9	35.7	Total Current	32.4	38.4	42.0	38.6	34.4	33.7
16.5	17.0	17.7	Long-Term Debt	18.2	29.0	20.8	15.8	16.4	15.9
.7	.7	.7	Deferred Taxes	.0	.2	.4	.2	.7	1.2
7.9	7.1	7.1	All Other Non-Current	9.5	22.1	3.4	6.0	4.6	6.2
36.4	36.3	38.8	Net Worth	40.0	10.3	33.4	39.4	43.9	43.1
100.0	100.0	100.0	Total Liabilties & Net Worth	100.0	100.0	100.0	100.0	100.0	100.0
			INCOME DATA						
100.0	100.0	100.0	Net Sales	100.0	100.0	100.0	100.0	100.0	100.0
27.9	27.5	27.7	Gross Profit	41.9	38.3	34.4	29.7	25.7	23.4
22.2	21.4	21.4	Operating Expenses	33.8	35.2	29.5	24.5	19.1	16.0
5.8	6.1	6.3	Operating Profit	8.1	3.1	4.9	5.2	6.6	7.4
1.1	.9	1.0	All Other Expenses (net)	3.0	1.4	.4	.7	.8	1.1
4.7	5.2	5.3	Profit Before Taxes	5.1	1.7	4.5	4.5	5.9	6.3
			RATIOS						
2.8	2.7	2.8		9.9	3.4	3.2	2.9	3.0	2.5
1.7	1.7	1.7	Current	3.3	1.7	1.7	1.6	1.8	1.7
1.1	1.2	1.2		1.2	1.1	1.1	1.2	1.3	1.3
1.6	1.5	1.6		5.6	2.1	2.2	1.7	1.9	1.5
.9	.9	.9	Quick	1.1	.9	.9	.8	1.0	.9
.6	.6	.6		.4	.5	.5	.5	.6	.6
33 11.2	31 11.6	31 11.8		24 15.3	26 14.0	24 15.3	28 13.0	32 11.3	35 10.3
42 8.6	42 8.7	42 8.6	Sales/Receivables	31 11.6	36 10.2	35 10.5	42 8.7	43 8.4	45 8.2
55 6.6	54 6.8	54 6.7		54 6.7	54 6.8	51 7.1	51 7.1	54 6.8	56 6.5
34 10.7	34 10.6	36 10.2		0 UND	28 13.1	30 12.0	38 9.7	36 10.0	36 10.0
53 6.9	55 6.6	55 6.6	Cost of Sales/Inventory	68 5.4	62 5.9	53 6.9	63 5.8	56 6.5	52 7.0
79 4.6	83 4.4	83 4.4		130 2.8	104 3.5	81 4.5	99 3.7	79 4.6	76 4.8
19 19.1	18 19.9	19 19.0		0 UND	17 21.3	14 26.7	20 18.7	19 19.0	21 17.4
31 11.8	31 11.8	30 12.1	Cost of Sales/Payables	20 18.0	37 9.9	26 14.2	27 13.6	29 12.5	31 11.8
47 7.7	45 8.1	46 8.0		36 10.1	58 6.3	50 7.3	44 8.3	44 8.3	45 8.1
5.2	5.1	5.1		3.5	5.3	4.5	5.3	4.9	5.4
9.0	9.4	8.9	Sales/Working Capital	6.3	10.0	9.6	9.1	8.2	9.2
33.4	28.1	20.6		21.8	49.1	46.2	18.9	18.4	17.7
16.2	21.2	21.3		12.9	10.1	21.3	15.0	21.5	34.4
(759) 5.6	(687) 6.4	(675) 6.6	EBIT/Interest	(10) 2.5	(63) 1.8	(51) 3.9	(104) 5.0	(173) 6.5	(274) 10.8
1.8	2.1	2.0		-1.6	-.7	1.3	1.8	2.7	3.0
6.9	6.2	6.8				5.5	7.8	6.6	6.9
(233) 3.3	(220) 2.9	(194) 3.2	Net Profit + Depr., Dep., Amort./Cur. Mat. L/T/D			(10) 1.1	(19) 2.9	(59) 2.8	(98) 3.9
1.7	1.8	1.7				.7	1.7	1.4	2.2
.4	.4	.4		.0	.4	.3	.3	.4	.5
.9	.8	.8	Fixed/Worth	.4	1.2	.9	.7	.8	.9
2.3	2.1	2.0		1.9	-6.3	2.4	1.6	1.8	1.7
.7	.7	.7		.1	1.2	.8	.7	.5	.7
1.7	1.7	1.6	Debt/Worth	2.3	3.7	1.8	1.8	1.4	1.4
5.5	5.2	4.8		4.3	-14.1	7.7	4.8	3.9	3.6
44.4	47.4	46.5		42.2	46.1	49.0	55.7	46.9	46.3
(704) 22.3	(654) 23.5	(657) 24.0	% Profit Before Taxes/Tangible Net Worth	(15) 12.1	(51) 15.5	(48) 18.1	(106) 23.8	(173) 24.9	(264) 24.8
7.5	8.7	8.9		-.9	.0	4.9	6.4	12.1	11.7
16.3	17.7	17.9		29.8	14.4	18.1	19.0	18.7	17.7
7.5	8.9	8.2	% Profit Before Taxes/Total Assets	3.5	3.1	6.6	7.3	8.7	9.4
1.9	2.5	2.6		-7.7	-1.7	1.4	2.7	3.4	3.7
14.9	16.3	14.9		UND	30.8	21.7	19.4	12.8	10.4
7.2	7.5	7.1	Sales/Net Fixed Assets	24.2	10.3	9.0	8.9	7.0	6.3
4.3	4.4	4.1		4.3	4.5	3.8	4.4	4.2	3.8
2.8	2.7	2.7		3.1	3.1	3.3	3.0	2.7	2.4
2.0	2.1	2.0	Sales/Total Assets	2.1	2.3	2.0	2.2	2.0	1.8
1.5	1.5	1.5		1.2	1.6	1.6	1.6	1.6	1.4
1.5	1.4	1.6			.6	1.1	1.5	1.6	1.7
(722) 2.7	(654) 2.6	(637) 2.6	% Depr., Dep., Amort./Sales		(52) 2.1	(48) 2.5	(97) 2.5	(170) 2.6	(261) 2.7
4.4	4.1	4.1			3.4	4.4	4.2	4.0	4.2
2.0	1.9	1.8			4.2	3.0	1.6	1.4	1.1
(250) 3.9	(247) 3.4	(209) 3.3	% Officers', Directors' Owners' Comp/Sales		(39) 6.8	(35) 5.4	(38) 3.0	(59) 2.2	(32) 2.2
6.2	5.7	5.9			8.1	8.0	3.9	3.5	4.1
31461245M	28670447M	33035486M	Net Sales ($)	10715M	151754M	230925M	860572M	3080694M	28700826M
18820427M	17446842M	19749074M	Total Assets ($)	7052M	96526M	124443M	429744M	1648715M	17442594M

M = $ thousand MM = $ million

See Pages 9 through 22 for Explanation of Ratios and Data

Current Data Sorted by Assets							Comparative Historical Data	
						Type of Statement		
		3	1			Unqualified	4	4
	1	4	1	1		Reviewed	4	10
		1	1			Compiled	8	4
2						Tax Returns	14	12
		2	3			Other	13	10
	3 (4/1-9/30/13)		17 (10/1/13-3/31/14)				4/1/09-3/31/10 ALL	4/1/10-3/31/11 ALL
0-500M	500M-2MM	2-10MM	10-50MM	50-100MM	100-250MM			
2	1	10	6	1		**NUMBER OF STATEMENTS**	43	40
%	%	%	%	%	%	**ASSETS**	%	%
		4.6			D A T A N O T A V A I L A B L E	Cash & Equivalents	9.5	11.5
		17.1				Trade Receivables (net)	22.4	20.4
		35.6				Inventory	34.5	32.0
		8.4				All Other Current	1.4	2.7
		65.7				Total Current	67.9	66.7
		18.6				Fixed Assets (net)	20.5	24.0
		8.7				Intangibles (net)	4.1	4.0
		7.0				All Other Non-Current	7.5	5.3
		100.0				Total	100.0	100.0
						LIABILITIES		
		11.7				Notes Payable-Short Term	8.2	7.8
		3.2				Cur. Mat.-L.T.D.	4.4	3.1
		18.6				Trade Payables	26.6	29.4
		.0				Income Taxes Payable	.1	.1
		9.0				All Other Current	9.1	5.9
		42.5				Total Current	48.4	46.3
		15.3				Long-Term Debt	20.2	18.5
		.3				Deferred Taxes	.1	.2
		8.8				All Other Non-Current	4.6	4.7
		33.0				Net Worth	26.7	30.3
		100.0				Total Liabilities & Net Worth	100.0	100.0
						INCOME DATA		
		100.0				Net Sales	100.0	100.0
		27.3				Gross Profit	31.2	31.7
		26.9				Operating Expenses	29.0	28.9
		.4				Operating Profit	2.2	2.8
		.3				All Other Expenses (net)	.5	.1
		.1				Profit Before Taxes	1.7	2.7
						RATIOS		
		2.4					2.2	1.8
		1.7				Current	1.4	1.4
		.8					1.0	1.1
		1.0					1.3	1.0
		.4				Quick	.6	.6
		.3					.3	.4
		21 17.3					**12** 29.6	**19** 18.8
		27 13.4				Sales/Receivables	**32** 11.6	**30** 12.1
		38 9.6					**46** 7.9	**39** 9.4
		54 6.8					**33** 11.2	**41** 9.0
		63 5.8				Cost of Sales/Inventory	**64** 5.7	**60** 6.1
		87 4.2					**97** 3.7	**91** 4.0
		20 18.1					**31** 11.8	**33** 11.1
		48 7.6				Cost of Sales/Payables	**54** 6.7	**63** 5.8
		62 5.9					**76** 4.8	**78** 4.7
		5.5					6.8	8.4
		13.9				Sales/Working Capital	16.4	15.6
		-16.2					106.0	42.4
		29.5					8.6	11.8
		7.9				EBIT/Interest	(38) 2.7	(34) 5.2
		-2.8					.8	3.0
							4.1	16.2
						Net Profit + Depr., Dep., Amort./Cur. Mat. L/T/D	(10) 1.0	(10) 7.3
							.4	3.2
		.2					.2	.3
		.3				Fixed/Worth	.5	.8
		NM					6.8	4.0
		.7					.8	1.0
		1.6				Debt/Worth	2.7	2.3
		NM					12.3	9.3
							42.7	41.9
						% Profit Before Taxes/Tangible Net Worth	(37) 10.2	(34) 17.1
							1.2	8.5
		15.1					9.0	9.2
		9.9				% Profit Before Taxes/Total Assets	3.1	5.3
		-2.5					.3	2.4
		26.8					37.1	27.7
		20.8				Sales/Net Fixed Assets	14.4	14.9
		10.5					7.2	7.0
		3.3					3.9	3.2
		2.4				Sales/Total Assets	2.8	2.7
		1.6					1.9	1.9
		1.0					.8	.7
		1.4				% Depr., Dep., Amort./Sales	(37) 1.6	(35) 1.5
		2.6					2.8	2.6
							.7	.8
						% Officers', Directors' Owners' Comp/Sales	(16) 1.3	(16) 1.5
							3.0	2.3
1350M	3167M	175524M	393839M	156898M		Net Sales ($)	1411025M	1425960M
377M	1407M	65486M	148470M	55573M		Total Assets ($)	552404M	705932M

M = $ thousand MM = $ million

See Pages 9 through 22 for Explanation of Ratios and Data

Comparative Historical Data / Current Data Sorted by Sales

4/1/11-3/31/12 ALL	4/1/12-3/31/13 ALL	4/1/13-3/31/14 ALL	Type of Statement	0-1MM	1-3MM	3-5MM	5-10MM	10-25MM	25MM & OVER
				3 (4/1-9/30/13)		17 (10/1/13-3/31/14)			
3		4	Unqualified					2	2
10	12	7	Reviewed			1	1	1	4
5	3	2	Compiled				1		1
5	5	2	Tax Returns	2					
6	8	5	Other	1				1	3
29	28	20	NUMBER OF STATEMENTS	3		1	2	4	10
%	%	%	**ASSETS**	%	%	%	%	%	%
10.7	10.2	7.1	Cash & Equivalents		DATA NOT AVAILABLE				4.6
20.9	26.1	16.5	Trade Receivables (net)						22.3
33.6	32.4	28.5	Inventory						29.3
2.9	8.2	8.0	All Other Current						6.2
68.0	76.9	60.1	Total Current						62.4
23.9	15.1	26.7	Fixed Assets (net)						30.3
3.7	1.9	5.2	Intangibles (net)						2.6
4.3	6.1	8.0	All Other Non-Current						4.8
100.0	100.0	100.0	Total						100.0
			LIABILITIES						
8.7	6.8	7.2	Notes Payable-Short Term						5.8
2.4	2.4	2.5	Cur. Mat.-L.T.D.						2.3
26.3	26.2	19.8	Trade Payables						21.8
.1	.1	.0	Income Taxes Payable						.0
8.2	7.7	9.4	All Other Current						10.3
45.6	43.2	38.8	Total Current						40.2
14.5	9.6	32.1	Long-Term Debt						17.7
.3	.3	.3	Deferred Taxes						.2
1.4	.9	8.2	All Other Non-Current						8.5
38.1	46.0	20.6	Net Worth						33.4
100.0	100.0	100.0	Total Liabilties & Net Worth						100.0
			INCOME DATA						
100.0	100.0	100.0	Net Sales						100.0
32.4	29.0	30.2	Gross Profit						29.4
27.3	23.4	26.4	Operating Expenses						24.1
5.0	5.6	3.9	Operating Profit						5.3
1.4	.1	.2	All Other Expenses (net)						.1
3.6	5.5	3.6	Profit Before Taxes						5.2
			RATIOS						
1.9	3.2	2.1	Current						1.9
1.5	1.9	1.5							1.5
1.1	1.3	1.2							1.3
1.0	1.6	1.2	Quick						1.1
.6	.8	.5							.5
.4	.6	.2							.3
10 36.1	17 21.0	5 78.8	Sales/Receivables						7 51.6
26 14.2	31 11.9	24 15.3							24 15.3
40 9.2	49 7.4	38 9.7							41 8.9
31 11.7	28 12.9	38 9.5	Cost of Sales/Inventory						3 110.3
53 6.9	55 6.6	56 6.5							49 7.5
94 3.9	85 4.3	78 4.7							76 4.8
23 15.7	14 26.5	20 18.1	Cost of Sales/Payables						11 34.5
49 7.4	30 12.2	46 8.0							36 10.2
87 4.2	73 5.0	65 5.6							52 7.0
6.5	4.9	6.7	Sales/Working Capital						11.8
15.5	9.8	14.3							14.3
47.7	29.5	54.1							21.3
35.6	28.7	39.5	EBIT/Interest						
(27) 8.6	(22) 13.4	(18) 14.4							
2.9	4.5	6.0							
			Net Profit + Depr., Dep., Amort./Cur. Mat. L/T/D						
.2	.1	.2	Fixed/Worth						.3
.7	.2	.4							1.0
1.4	.5	3.6							2.2
.9	.6	.7	Debt/Worth						1.4
1.7	.9	1.7							2.1
4.7	2.5	4.4							4.3
66.1	50.1	44.8	% Profit Before Taxes/Tangible Net Worth						
(28) 25.1	(27) 23.5	(16) 25.2							
7.9	8.7	10.3							
12.5	16.9	21.5	% Profit Before Taxes/Total Assets						27.1
8.0	11.2	9.9							10.2
3.6	2.4	4.9							6.2
30.5	96.9	24.2	Sales/Net Fixed Assets						22.0
16.2	22.0	15.7							14.7
7.1	10.7	5.4							5.4
3.4	3.7	3.2	Sales/Total Assets						4.2
2.8	3.2	2.7							2.9
2.1	2.1	1.9							1.9
.9	.7	1.0	% Depr., Dep., Amort./Sales						
(27) 1.6	(23) 1.0	(19) 1.4							
2.5	2.1	2.5							
	.8		% Officers', Directors' Owners' Comp/Sales						
	(10) 1.2								
	2.6								
1205806M	1105938M	730778M	Net Sales ($)	2282M		3167M	17280M	67429M	640620M
428900M	383990M	271313M	Total Assets ($)	2635M		1407M	11781M	28237M	227253M

M = $ thousand MM = $ million

See Pages 9 through 22 for Explanation of Ratios and Data

Current Data Sorted by Assets							Comparative Historical Data	
						Type of Statement		
		2	1	1	1	Unqualified	11	12
	1	2	1			Reviewed	6	12
						Compiled	5	6
	4					Tax Returns	2	4
	4	6	7	2		Other	16	18
	3 (4/1-9/30/13)		29 (10/1/13-3/31/14)				**4/1/09-3/31/10**	**4/1/10-3/31/11**
0-500M	**500M-2MM**	**2-10MM**	**10-50MM**	**50-100MM**	**100-250MM**		**ALL**	**ALL**
	9	10	9	3	1	**NUMBER OF STATEMENTS**	40	52
%	%	%	%	%	%	**ASSETS**	%	%
	DATA NOT AVAILABLE	7.1				Cash & Equivalents	8.1	9.3
		28.4				Trade Receivables (net)	22.8	22.5
		31.3				Inventory	29.7	28.7
		1.4				All Other Current	4.1	1.7
		68.2				Total Current	64.6	62.2
		20.5				Fixed Assets (net)	20.7	22.3
		.6				Intangibles (net)	6.4	9.6
		10.7				All Other Non-Current	8.3	5.9
		100.0				Total	100.0	100.0
						LIABILITIES		
		8.4				Notes Payable-Short Term	9.0	7.9
		2.8				Cur. Mat.-L.T.D.	3.4	4.5
		11.9				Trade Payables	11.2	13.9
		1.0				Income Taxes Payable	.1	.4
		5.3				All Other Current	8.7	8.2
		29.3				Total Current	32.4	35.0
		10.4				Long-Term Debt	11.4	11.3
		.6				Deferred Taxes	.5	.7
		10.9				All Other Non-Current	8.7	5.6
		48.8				Net Worth	47.0	47.4
		100.0				Total Liabilties & Net Worth	100.0	100.0
						INCOME DATA		
		100.0				Net Sales	100.0	100.0
		29.4				Gross Profit	31.7	30.8
		24.1				Operating Expenses	24.7	22.0
		5.3				Operating Profit	7.1	8.8
		.3				All Other Expenses (net)	.8	.5
		5.0				Profit Before Taxes	6.3	8.3
						RATIOS		
		3.7					3.9	3.1
		2.1				Current	2.1	2.1
		1.7					1.4	1.2
		2.1					1.9	1.8
		1.1				Quick	(39) 1.1	.9
		.6					.7	.5
		29 12.7					**40** 9.1	**36** 10.2
		56 6.5				Sales/Receivables	**48** 7.6	**46** 8.0
		61 6.0					**56** 6.5	**53** 6.9
		46 8.0					**63** 5.8	**59** 6.2
		57 6.4				Cost of Sales/Inventory	**99** 3.7	**81** 4.5
		140 2.6					**140** 2.6	**118** 3.1
		19 18.8					**18** 19.8	**18** 19.9
		26 13.9				Cost of Sales/Payables	**30** 12.3	**35** 10.5
		41 8.9					**41** 9.0	**58** 6.3
		3.0					2.8	3.4
		5.2				Sales/Working Capital	6.1	6.9
		8.5					10.5	19.9
		20.9					16.8	34.2
		10.4				EBIT/Interest	(37) 8.6	(48) 11.6
		3.6					2.2	3.7
							6.6	7.5
						Net Profit + Depr., Dep., Amort./Cur. Mat. L/T/D	(15) 4.0	(20) 5.2
							2.0	1.2
		.1					.2	.2
		.4				Fixed/Worth	.5	.6
		.5					.9	1.5
		.5					.7	.5
		.8				Debt/Worth	1.2	1.4
		1.2					2.4	3.7
							39.5	50.2
						% Profit Before Taxes/Tangible Net Worth	(35) 21.4	(47) 23.1
							5.0	16.2
		14.5					18.4	18.6
		7.9				% Profit Before Taxes/Total Assets	7.2	11.7
		4.5					2.1	5.7
		27.4					17.6	16.1
		10.0				Sales/Net Fixed Assets	7.8	8.8
		5.8					4.7	5.3
		2.5					2.1	2.3
		2.1				Sales/Total Assets	1.6	1.8
		1.3					1.1	1.2
							.7	.9
						% Depr., Dep., Amort./Sales	(33) 1.5	(48) 1.7
							2.6	2.6
							1.9	1.8
						% Officers', Directors' Owners' Comp/Sales	(12) 3.1	(18) 2.5
							5.6	4.1
	26050M	112017M	423515M	352890M	176706M	Net Sales ($)	1495493M	2816813M
	9747M	57237M	213017M	201586M	124855M	Total Assets ($)	1050821M	1792060M

M = $ thousand MM = $ million

See Pages 9 through 22 for Explanation of Ratios and Data

Comparative Historical Data				Current Data Sorted by Sales					
			Type of Statement						
5	7	5	Unqualified					2	3
8	8	4	Reviewed			1	1	1	1
6	1		Compiled						
2	6	4	Tax Returns		3		1		
19	17	19	Other	1	2	1	3	5	7
4/1/11-3/31/12 ALL	**4/1/12-3/31/13 ALL**	**4/1/13-3/31/14 ALL**			**3 (4/1-9/30/13)**		**29 (10/1/13-3/31/14)**		
				0-1MM	**1-3MM**	**3-5MM**	**5-10MM**	**10-25MM**	**25MM & OVER**
40	39	32	**NUMBER OF STATEMENTS**	1	5	2	5	8	11
%	%	%	**ASSETS**	%	%	%	%	%	%
9.1	11.4	9.6	Cash & Equivalents						9.7
24.4	24.3	24.9	Trade Receivables (net)						21.0
31.3	33.9	28.0	Inventory						29.2
1.7	2.5	2.0	All Other Current						2.6
66.5	72.0	64.5	Total Current						62.5
21.4	19.3	22.5	Fixed Assets (net)						20.0
8.2	2.2	6.5	Intangibles (net)						14.0
3.9	6.5	6.5	All Other Non-Current						3.5
100.0	100.0	100.0	Total						100.0
			LIABILITIES						
7.7	7.7	6.8	Notes Payable-Short Term						6.4
2.6	2.2	3.4	Cur. Mat.-L.T.D.						3.8
15.2	15.5	12.5	Trade Payables						10.9
.3	.3	.4	Income Taxes Payable						.0
8.0	11.0	9.6	All Other Current						8.5
33.8	36.6	32.6	Total Current						29.7
8.8	12.0	12.4	Long-Term Debt						6.2
1.4	.6	.8	Deferred Taxes						1.7
4.0	11.7	14.2	All Other Non-Current						11.8
52.0	39.1	39.9	Net Worth						50.5
100.0	100.0	100.0	Total Liabilties & Net Worth						100.0
			INCOME DATA						
100.0	100.0	100.0	Net Sales						100.0
27.6	31.2	33.3	Gross Profit						27.3
20.8	24.4	27.2	Operating Expenses						16.4
6.8	6.8	6.1	Operating Profit						10.9
.1	.5	.6	All Other Expenses (net)						.7
6.7	6.3	5.5	Profit Before Taxes						10.2
			RATIOS						
3.8	3.9	3.2							3.1
2.1	2.2	2.1	Current						2.1
1.3	1.7	1.6							1.5
2.0	1.7	1.7							1.3
.9	1.1	1.0	Quick						.8
.5	.7	.7							.7
33 11.0	**33** 11.2	**32** 11.3							**33** 11.2
44 8.3	**36** 10.0	**41** 9.0	Sales/Receivables						**40** 9.1
54 6.8	**47** 7.8	**56** 6.5							**51** 7.1
51 7.2	**51** 7.2	**47** 7.7							**58** 6.3
79 4.6	**94** 3.9	**68** 5.4	Cost of Sales/Inventory						**81** 4.5
135 2.7	**135** 2.7	**126** 2.9							**114** 3.2
19 18.9	**27** 13.6	**22** 16.5							**14** 26.3
32 11.4	**39** 9.3	**33** 11.1	Cost of Sales/Payables						**32** 11.3
53 6.9	**55** 6.6	**48** 7.6							**45** 8.2
3.3	3.3	3.3							3.6
6.0	6.6	6.0	Sales/Working Capital						7.7
13.5	9.3	10.8							10.9
41.4	37.2	20.5							
(34) 12.2	(35) 9.4	(26) 10.4	EBIT/Interest						
6.5	2.3	3.0							
6.6	39.0								
(16) 4.2	(12) 6.1		Net Profit + Depr., Dep., Amort./Cur. Mat. L/T/D						
1.5	2.8								
.2	.2	.2							.3
.5	.4	.4	Fixed/Worth						.7
1.0	2.9	.9							.9
.5	.4	.7							.8
1.0	1.1	1.1	Debt/Worth						1.2
2.8	7.7	2.6							3.0
40.4	47.3	48.5							61.4
(39) 24.0	(31) 28.4	(28) 20.3	% Profit Before Taxes/Tangible Net Worth						(10) 43.1
14.0	15.4	9.9							21.2
16.4	19.6	19.4							25.6
10.7	12.1	11.0	% Profit Before Taxes/Total Assets						14.0
5.9	3.9	4.7							10.6
22.0	27.4	23.0							18.8
9.6	15.1	10.6	Sales/Net Fixed Assets						10.0
5.5	6.7	6.1							7.3
2.4	2.8	2.8							2.7
1.8	2.1	2.1	Sales/Total Assets						2.1
1.3	1.5	1.2							1.1
.6	.6	.8							.8
(38) 1.5	(36) 1.4	(26) 1.6	% Depr., Dep., Amort./Sales						1.6
2.3	2.6	3.0							3.0
1.4	1.7	1.2							
(10) 1.9	(12) 4.3	(10) 3.4	% Officers', Directors' Owners' Comp/Sales						
5.0	7.1	8.5							
2033279M	**1348460M**	**1091178M**	Net Sales ($)	**892M**	**10010M**	**8213M**	**34874M**	**111879M**	**925310M**
1274548M	**702269M**	**606442M**	Total Assets ($)	**903M**	**4377M**	**4403M**	**18733M**	**65032M**	**512994M**

M = $ thousand MM = $ million

See Pages 9 through 22 for Explanation of Ratios and Data

Current Data Sorted by Assets							Comparative Historical Data	
						Type of Statement		
		1	2	1	1	Unqualified	14	6
		6	3			Reviewed	4	9
	1	6				Compiled	5	5
	3					Tax Returns	5	3
1	2	6	3	1	1	Other	18	14
	5 (4/1-9/30/13)		33 (10/1/13-3/31/14)				**4/1/09-3/31/10 ALL**	**4/1/10-3/31/11 ALL**
0-500M	**500M-2MM**	**2-10MM**	**10-50MM**	**50-100MM**	**100-250MM**			
1	6	19	8	2	2	**NUMBER OF STATEMENTS**	46	37
%	%	%	%	%	%	**ASSETS**	%	%
		5.4				Cash & Equivalents	8.0	10.0
		32.0				Trade Receivables (net)	25.0	29.2
		30.8				Inventory	24.6	21.5
		1.0				All Other Current	3.8	2.7
		69.3				Total Current	61.5	63.5
		23.0				Fixed Assets (net)	27.9	25.1
		3.3				Intangibles (net)	3.4	5.7
		4.5				All Other Non-Current	7.2	5.8
		100.0				Total	100.0	100.0
						LIABILITIES		
		13.2				Notes Payable-Short Term	12.8	11.6
		2.5				Cur. Mat.-L.T.D.	4.0	4.3
		14.4				Trade Payables	13.2	13.2
		.1				Income Taxes Payable	.4	.5
		5.9				All Other Current	14.1	10.9
		36.0				Total Current	44.6	40.5
		7.9				Long-Term Debt	9.3	10.6
		.4				Deferred Taxes	.8	1.3
		2.3				All Other Non-Current	13.9	7.5
		53.4				Net Worth	31.4	40.1
		100.0				Total Liabilties & Net Worth	100.0	100.0
						INCOME DATA		
		100.0				Net Sales	100.0	100.0
		26.9				Gross Profit	33.7	30.3
		22.8				Operating Expenses	28.2	20.7
		4.0				Operating Profit	5.5	9.7
		.5				All Other Expenses (net)	.8	1.1
		3.5				Profit Before Taxes	4.7	8.5
						RATIOS		
		3.0					3.3	3.5
		1.9				Current	1.4	1.8
		1.5					1.0	1.2
		1.6					1.3	2.3
		1.1				Quick	.7	1.0
		.8					.5	.6
		34 10.6					**30** 12.3	**37** 9.9
		45 8.1				Sales/Receivables	**47** 7.8	**48** 7.6
		52 7.0					**58** 6.3	**59** 6.2
		44 8.3					**35** 10.3	**41** 8.9
		52 7.0				Cost of Sales/Inventory	**59** 6.2	**47** 7.8
		69 5.3					**82** 4.4	**65** 5.6
		17 21.3					**17** 21.9	**17** 21.7
		20 17.9				Cost of Sales/Payables	**29** 12.8	**24** 15.1
		41 8.9					**46** 7.9	**38** 9.6
		5.5					5.0	4.5
		8.7				Sales/Working Capital	13.2	7.6
		13.0					-296.1	23.7
		18.0					10.1	18.9
		6.8				EBIT/Interest	(41) 3.6	(34) 7.6
		1.8					1.6	5.3
							8.7	4.5
						Net Profit + Depr., Dep., Amort./Cur. Mat. L/T/D	(15) 3.6	(13) 3.2
							.9	1.3
		.3					.2	.3
		.5				Fixed/Worth	1.0	.7
		.7					2.5	1.7
		.4					.6	.5
		1.0				Debt/Worth	2.0	1.5
		1.3					6.1	3.9
		36.9					44.9	62.7
		12.2				% Profit Before Taxes/Tangible Net Worth	(37) 17.7	(33) 35.5
		5.6					4.0	19.8
		21.0					13.7	22.1
		5.3				% Profit Before Taxes/Total Assets	6.7	12.6
		1.3					1.1	8.6
		28.4					21.4	17.5
		10.5				Sales/Net Fixed Assets	8.2	8.2
		7.2					3.5	4.8
		3.2					2.6	2.9
		2.5				Sales/Total Assets	1.8	2.1
		2.2					1.3	1.4
		.9					1.7	1.1
		(18) 1.5				% Depr., Dep., Amort./Sales	(37) 3.4	(35) 2.2
		2.4					5.3	4.4
								2.6
						% Officers', Directors' Owners' Comp/Sales		(13) 4.1
								4.9
2134M	22563M	297961M	307222M	147830M	469699M	Net Sales ($)	728776M	964564M
497M	7447M	114603M	169779M	130063M	253689M	Total Assets ($)	547832M	569730M

M = $ thousand MM = $ million

See Pages 9 through 22 for Explanation of Ratios and Data

Comparative Historical Data				Current Data Sorted by Sales					
			Type of Statement						
8	5	5	Unqualified					3	2
8	8	9	Reviewed				3	4	2
7	6	7	Compiled				2	4	1
5	7	3	Tax Returns		2	1			
14	14	14	Other		2	1	2	3	6
					5 (4/1-9/30/13)		33 (10/1/13-3/31/14)		
4/1/11-3/31/12 ALL	**4/1/12-3/31/13 ALL**	**4/1/13-3/31/14 ALL**		**0-1MM**	**1-3MM**	**3-5MM**	**5-10MM**	**10-25MM**	**25MM & OVER**
42	40	38	**NUMBER OF STATEMENTS**		4	2	7	14	11
%	%	%	**ASSETS**	%	%	%	%	%	%
10.4	8.4	12.1	Cash & Equivalents	DATA NOT AVAILABLE				6.3	12.7
30.6	32.9	30.3	Trade Receivables (net)					31.7	32.8
22.0	26.8	24.7	Inventory					27.9	18.3
1.6	2.3	1.5	All Other Current					1.0	2.4
64.6	70.3	68.6	Total Current					67.0	66.4
25.6	23.3	22.7	Fixed Assets (net)					25.3	23.0
6.7	1.2	2.8	Intangibles (net)					3.4	5.4
3.1	5.2	5.9	All Other Non-Current					4.3	5.3
100.0	100.0	100.0	Total					100.0	100.0
			LIABILITIES						
8.9	9.7	11.9	Notes Payable-Short Term					9.5	8.6
2.8	4.0	2.9	Cur. Mat.-L.T.D.					2.6	.8
12.0	13.5	12.9	Trade Payables					12.2	13.7
.3	.0	.1	Income Taxes Payable					.1	.4
11.3	10.8	9.3	All Other Current					9.5	11.2
35.3	38.1	37.1	Total Current					33.9	34.8
13.8	12.5	8.3	Long-Term Debt					8.2	8.7
1.3	.5	.6	Deferred Taxes					.6	.7
11.5	10.1	4.3	All Other Non-Current					2.1	8.4
38.0	38.9	49.7	Net Worth					55.2	47.5
100.0	100.0	100.0	Total Liabilties & Net Worth					100.0	100.0
			INCOME DATA						
100.0	100.0	100.0	Net Sales					100.0	100.0
28.5	26.9	29.5	Gross Profit					29.3	22.3
19.4	21.6	23.0	Operating Expenses					23.5	16.0
9.1	5.3	6.5	Operating Profit					5.8	6.3
.9	.6	.2	All Other Expenses (net)					.5	-.4
8.3	4.7	6.3	Profit Before Taxes					5.3	6.7
			RATIOS						
3.5	2.8	2.8	Current					3.2	2.4
2.2	2.1	1.8						1.9	1.9
1.5	1.6	1.5						1.4	1.5
2.2	1.8	1.8	Quick					1.8	1.7
1.3	1.2	1.1						1.0	1.2
.9	.8	.8						.8	.9
42 8.7	32 11.5	34 10.6	Sales/Receivables					40 9.2	34 10.6
49 7.4	44 8.3	46 7.9						46 7.9	47 7.8
61 6.0	57 6.4	57 6.4						66 5.5	70 5.2
35 10.4	29 12.7	35 10.3	Cost of Sales/Inventory					43 8.4	26 13.9
57 6.4	47 7.7	57 6.4						59 6.2	44 8.3
73 5.0	74 4.9	70 5.2						101 3.6	56 6.5
14 26.4	13 27.2	15 24.1	Cost of Sales/Payables					14 27.0	19 19.1
22 16.8	25 14.8	24 15.5						23 16.0	32 11.4
35 10.3	37 9.8	41 8.8						41 8.8	47 7.8
3.9	5.6	5.3	Sales/Working Capital					5.5	3.7
6.9	7.4	7.6						6.4	9.2
17.7	12.4	11.4						12.1	11.3
17.0	27.6	41.0	EBIT/Interest					31.1	62.5
(39) 7.2	(37) 6.2	(33) 9.8						(13) 4.1	(10) 20.8
4.1	3.0	3.3						3.4	8.8
9.8	11.9	248.6	Net Profit + Depr., Dep., Amort./Cur. Mat. L/T/D						
(11) 4.7	(13) 3.3	(12) 17.5							
1.4	1.7	2.0							
.2	.2	.2	Fixed/Worth					.2	.2
.8	.4	.5						.5	.7
1.8	1.3	.9						.9	.9
.6	.6	.5	Debt/Worth					.4	.7
1.3	1.3	1.0						.8	1.1
4.3	2.4	2.2						2.1	2.8
59.9	39.2	38.6	% Profit Before Taxes/Tangible Net Worth					34.7	41.8
(36) 30.3	(38) 19.9	(37) 23.1						19.8	32.8
13.1	8.6	9.7						8.9	13.1
24.0	20.2	21.3	% Profit Before Taxes/Total Assets					20.6	21.0
14.2	8.6	9.5						8.5	15.6
6.7	5.0	3.8						3.8	4.7
16.1	29.7	28.7	Sales/Net Fixed Assets					17.4	30.4
8.2	13.8	10.5						10.5	7.5
4.9	5.6	5.7						5.5	5.1
2.9	3.2	3.1	Sales/Total Assets					2.6	3.3
2.1	2.4	2.3						2.2	2.2
1.4	1.9	1.7						1.7	1.4
1.4	.7	.9	% Depr., Dep., Amort./Sales					1.2	
(36) 2.5	(33) 1.6	(34) 1.5						(13) 1.9	
3.7	3.1	2.7						2.9	
1.6	1.5	1.8	% Officers', Directors' Owners' Comp/Sales						
(14) 3.1	(15) 3.8	(13) 2.9							
5.0	7.0	6.9							
1306719M	933785M	1247409M	Net Sales ($)		10541M	8789M	51790M	237573M	938716M
831938M	393624M	676078M	Total Assets ($)		3674M	3060M	27716M	116044M	525584M

M = $ thousand MM = $ million

See Pages 9 through 22 for Explanation of Ratios and Data

Current Data Sorted by Assets							Comparative Historical Data	
						Type of Statement		
		2	7	3	1	Unqualified	25	24
	1	17	8			Reviewed	24	35
	1	10	1			Compiled	14	18
1	8	7				Tax Returns	14	10
6	4	8	16	5	2	Other	45	44
	19 (4/1-9/30/13)		89 (10/1/13-3/31/14)				4/1/09-3/31/10 ALL	4/1/10-3/31/11 ALL
0-500M	500M-2MM	2-10MM	10-50MM	50-100MM	100-250MM			
7	14	44	32	8	3	**NUMBER OF STATEMENTS**	122	131
%	%	%	%	%	%	**ASSETS**	%	%
	13.3	7.7	4.8			Cash & Equivalents	9.2	9.4
	30.2	25.6	25.1			Trade Receivables (net)	26.7	25.0
	23.0	25.1	24.3			Inventory	24.2	26.9
	1.2	2.0	2.0			All Other Current	2.7	2.6
	67.6	60.4	56.2			Total Current	62.9	63.8
	21.7	27.8	31.7			Fixed Assets (net)	27.2	25.7
	6.6	4.7	4.6			Intangibles (net)	4.1	4.4
	4.1	7.1	7.5			All Other Non-Current	5.9	6.0
	100.0	100.0	100.0			Total	100.0	100.0
						LIABILITIES		
	7.8	9.0	10.9			Notes Payable-Short Term	12.5	11.6
	.9	2.3	3.4			Cur. Mat.-L.T.D.	3.2	2.8
	17.5	13.6	10.1			Trade Payables	14.8	13.6
	.4	.4	.1			Income Taxes Payable	.1	.2
	4.3	7.1	7.4			All Other Current	7.9	8.1
	30.9	32.4	31.9			Total Current	38.6	36.3
	9.6	11.3	9.4			Long-Term Debt	16.2	14.0
	.4	1.4	.8			Deferred Taxes	.7	.9
	1.8	1.8	7.5			All Other Non-Current	10.2	9.5
	57.4	53.1	50.4			Net Worth	34.3	39.3
	100.0	100.0	100.0			Total Liabilties & Net Worth	100.0	100.0
						INCOME DATA		
	100.0	100.0	100.0			Net Sales	100.0	100.0
	37.8	29.9	26.4			Gross Profit	29.6	30.8
	31.3	25.1	19.2			Operating Expenses	25.1	24.6
	6.4	4.8	7.2			Operating Profit	4.5	6.1
	.1	.5	.5			All Other Expenses (net)	1.6	1.0
	6.4	4.3	6.7			Profit Before Taxes	2.9	5.2
						RATIOS		
	4.9	3.1	2.6				3.3	3.6
	2.6	1.9	1.8			Current	1.9	2.1
	1.5	1.3	1.2				1.2	1.3
	3.0	2.0	1.6				2.0	2.1
	1.4	.9	1.1			Quick	1.0	1.0
	.7	.6	.6				.6	.6
	21 17.0	32 11.4	34 10.7				35 10.3	33 10.9
	34 10.6	43 8.4	47 7.8			Sales/Receivables	45 8.0	43 8.5
	48 7.6	53 6.9	58 6.3				56 6.5	53 6.8
	18 20.5	34 10.6	42 8.6				34 10.6	35 10.3
	46 7.9	55 6.6	65 5.6			Cost of Sales/Inventory	54 6.8	66 5.5
	81 4.5	91 4.0	96 3.8				92 4.0	110 3.3
	18 19.8	19 19.1	17 21.6				20 18.3	19 19.5
	22 16.8	29 12.4	22 16.7			Cost of Sales/Payables	29 12.7	29 12.7
	45 8.1	42 8.7	33 11.1				43 8.6	42 8.8
	3.6	4.9	5.0				4.4	4.3
	10.4	8.4	8.3			Sales/Working Capital	7.9	7.4
	24.5	15.3	18.0				26.9	16.7
	84.1	28.1	98.8				11.4	13.1
	(10) 16.0	(36) 7.1	(30) 12.9			EBIT/Interest	(105) 3.3	(109) 5.4
	6.2	3.4	3.9				1.1	2.3
		13.1					7.0	4.5
		(17) 3.8				Net Profit + Depr., Dep., Amort./Cur. Mat. L/T/D	(32) 3.1	(32) 3.2
		1.8					.6	1.7
	.1	.3	.3				.3	.2
	.3	.6	.7			Fixed/Worth	.8	.5
	1.0	1.1	1.0				2.6	1.5
	.1	.4	.3				.5	.4
	.6	.9	.9			Debt/Worth	1.7	1.3
	2.5	2.1	1.5				10.1	3.6
	75.4	33.1	31.7				32.8	36.4
	(13) 33.1	(43) 18.9	(29) 19.5			% Profit Before Taxes/Tangible Net Worth	(98) 15.6	(117) 18.5
	6.2	8.5	8.9				.4	7.0
	23.3	17.2	19.1				13.9	14.7
	19.8	6.9	10.4			% Profit Before Taxes/Total Assets	5.2	8.6
	5.2	3.5	5.5				.0	3.2
	47.6	14.1	13.8				25.3	30.2
	27.5	8.0	5.9			Sales/Net Fixed Assets	9.0	9.9
	10.1	5.4	3.6				4.7	5.2
	4.8	2.9	2.2				2.9	2.8
	3.2	2.0	1.9			Sales/Total Assets	2.0	1.9
	2.3	1.7	1.3				1.4	1.5
	.3	.9	1.1				1.3	1.0
	(10) .6	(41) 1.9	(31) 2.2			% Depr., Dep., Amort./Sales	(101) 2.0	(113) 2.1
	2.4	3.3	3.2				4.1	3.4
		2.6					1.9	1.8
		(16) 3.5				% Officers', Directors' Owners' Comp/Sales	(33) 4.0	(37) 4.4
		4.6					6.3	8.7
7211M	50195M	480624M	1245306M	877677M	655921M	Net Sales ($)	4246318M	4313680M
1525M	16655M	231676M	684252M	546388M	543878M	Total Assets ($)	2517611M	2392069M

M = $ thousand MM = $ million

See Pages 9 through 22 for Explanation of Ratios and Data

Comparative Historical Data / Current Data Sorted by Sales

						Type of Statement												
	16		14		13	Unqualified							1		1		11
	27		23		26	Reviewed			2		1		7		13		3
	19		13		12	Compiled					1		4		7		
	15		12		16	Tax Returns			5		4		3		4		
	41		46		41	Other	3		3		5		3		8		19
	4/1/11-3/31/12 ALL		4/1/12-3/31/13 ALL		4/1/13-3/31/14 ALL		19 (4/1-9/30/13)						89 (10/1/13-3/31/14)				
							0-1MM		1-3MM		3-5MM		5-10MM		10-25MM		25MM & OVER
	118		108		108	NUMBER OF STATEMENTS	3		10		11		18		33		33
	%		%		%	ASSETS	%		%		%		%		%		%
	9.5		8.1		9.2	Cash & Equivalents			13.2		7.5		7.8		7.4		10.0
	27.5		25.9		25.3	Trade Receivables (net)			19.8		29.6		24.4		27.3		24.8
	27.2		26.0		24.3	Inventory			24.7		23.5		27.0		21.6		25.2
	1.6		3.7		2.6	All Other Current			11.1		.9		1.6		2.7		1.3
	65.8		63.7		61.4	Total Current			68.8		61.4		60.7		59.0		61.3
	23.9		25.4		26.7	Fixed Assets (net)			15.9		26.4		28.4		29.8		28.6
	3.6		4.0		4.5	Intangibles (net)			9.4		7.7		4.3		2.4		4.6
	6.7		6.9		7.3	All Other Non-Current			5.9		4.5		6.5		8.7		5.5
	100.0		100.0		100.0	Total			100.0		100.0		100.0		100.0		100.0
						LIABILITIES											
	10.2		12.8		9.2	Notes Payable-Short Term			7.7		7.2		4.3		11.4		10.4
	2.7		4.8		2.3	Cur. Mat.-L.T.D.			2.3		1.4		2.6		2.0		2.9
	14.9		14.5		13.1	Trade Payables			19.0		16.8		14.2		12.6		10.5
	.3		.2		.2	Income Taxes Payable			.6		.0		.7		.1		.1
	9.1		8.8		7.1	All Other Current			7.9		3.1		7.9		5.9		9.3
	37.2		41.1		32.0	Total Current			37.6		28.5		29.6		32.1		33.2
	10.1		11.8		9.4	Long-Term Debt			10.4		8.8		14.9		8.8		7.7
	1.1		.8		.9	Deferred Taxes			.5		.6		1.8		.7		.9
	8.4		6.1		6.4	All Other Non-Current			20.1		1.7		1.2		2.0		10.5
	43.3		40.2		51.4	Net Worth			31.4		60.5		52.5		56.5		47.6
	100.0		100.0		100.0	Total Liabilties & Net Worth			100.0		100.0		100.0		100.0		100.0
						INCOME DATA											
	100.0		100.0		100.0	Net Sales			100.0		100.0		100.0		100.0		100.0
	30.1		31.6		32.1	Gross Profit			48.7		33.0		33.6		25.6		28.7
	24.8		25.8		25.4	Operating Expenses			44.2		27.4		26.5		20.5		20.6
	5.3		5.8		6.7	Operating Profit			4.5		5.6		7.1		5.1		8.0
	.6		.3		.6	All Other Expenses (net)			.8		.2		.6		.4		.5
	4.7		5.4		6.1	Profit Before Taxes			3.7		5.3		6.4		4.7		7.6
						RATIOS											
	3.2		3.0		3.3	Current			4.4		6.7		3.1		3.1		3.1
	2.0		1.8		2.0				2.8		1.7		2.4		2.0		1.8
	1.3		1.2		1.3				1.6		1.5		1.4		1.2		1.3
	2.1		1.8		2.0	Quick			2.0		3.2		1.9		2.0		2.0
	1.0		.8		1.1				1.0		1.1		1.1		1.1		1.1
	.6		.5		.6				.4		.7		.7		.6		.6
33	11.2	**32**	11.5	**30**	12.1	Sales/Receivables		**0**	UND	**26**	14.2	**30**	12.3	**35**	10.3	**31**	11.8
42	8.7	**43**	8.5	**42**	8.6			**24**	15.3	**43**	8.4	**36**	10.2	**49**	7.5	**43**	8.5
54	6.8	**54**	6.8	**56**	6.5			**38**	9.5	**61**	6.0	**46**	8.0	**61**	6.0	**58**	6.3
37	9.9	**37**	9.8	**35**	10.3	Cost of Sales/Inventory		**31**	11.6	**25**	14.4	**39**	9.3	**29**	12.4	**44**	8.3
60	6.1	**61**	6.0	**55**	6.6			**55**	6.6	**72**	5.1	**60**	6.1	**46**	8.0	**61**	6.0
96	3.8	**96**	3.8	**91**	4.0			**118**	3.1	**85**	4.3	**107**	3.4	**79**	4.6	**94**	3.9
20	18.2	**20**	18.3	**18**	20.2	Cost of Sales/Payables		**10**	37.1	**17**	21.0	**20**	18.5	**19**	19.0	**17**	21.8
30	12.2	**28**	12.9	**23**	15.8			**20**	18.5	**26**	14.0	**25**	14.4	**29**	12.8	**22**	16.9
44	8.3	**45**	8.1	**41**	9.0			**51**	7.2	**47**	7.7	**46**	8.0	**37**	9.9	**34**	10.8
	4.6		4.7		4.9	Sales/Working Capital			4.8		3.6		4.9		4.5		4.5
	7.3		9.1		8.4				8.4		9.3		8.5		8.2		8.3
	18.3		29.2		15.3				NM		16.0		14.5		17.7		12.5
	23.8		25.2		43.7	EBIT/Interest							29.9		55.0		46.7
(94)	7.6	(95)	7.4	(90)	10.2							(15)	12.5	(30)	7.6	(29)	11.7
	2.0		1.7		3.9								3.9		3.6		4.7
	8.4		8.3		13.1	Net Profit + Depr., Dep., Amort./Cur. Mat. L/T/D									21.9		
(30)	4.4	(32)	3.3	(29)	4.4									(10)	6.8		
	.7		2.2		2.0										1.8		
	.2		.2		.2	Fixed/Worth			.1		.0		.3		.3		.3
	.5		.6		.5				.2		.4		.5		.6		.6
	1.3		1.8		1.0				NM		1.1		1.1		.9		1.1
	.4		.4		.3	Debt/Worth			.2		.1		.4		.3		.3
	1.1		1.5		.9				.8		.9		1.0		.8		1.1
	2.9		3.5		1.9				NM		2.2		2.3		1.5		1.8
	36.3		38.3		39.1	% Profit Before Taxes/Tangible Net Worth					62.6		73.7		22.2		36.1
(105)	18.3	(93)	20.2	(102)	20.7						18.8		28.5	(32)	15.6	(30)	23.7
	5.4		4.0		9.7						3.8		11.4		7.3		15.0
	16.6		18.3		21.0	% Profit Before Taxes/Total Assets			32.5		21.7		21.5		12.2		20.5
	8.8		9.7		11.3				20.2		17.0		12.4		5.9		12.4
	1.9		1.5		4.2				-14.2		1.7		3.6		3.4		6.2
	27.1		28.4		23.8	Sales/Net Fixed Assets			90.0		95.1		20.0		13.0		21.2
	9.9		9.1		8.0				27.5		20.4		11.9		7.1		6.9
	5.1		4.7		4.8				9.3		5.4		4.6		4.5		4.3
	3.2		2.8		2.9	Sales/Total Assets			5.8		3.5		3.1		2.9		2.2
	2.2		2.1		2.0				3.2		2.7		2.0		1.9		2.0
	1.6		1.5		1.6				1.4		1.8		1.8		1.5		1.5
	.9		1.0		.8	% Depr., Dep., Amort./Sales							1.3		1.1		1.1
(105)	1.6	(95)	2.0	(92)	2.0								2.9	(31)	1.7	(31)	2.2
	3.7		3.2		3.1								3.7		3.4		2.6
	1.2		1.9		1.6	% Officers', Directors' Owners' Comp/Sales									1.9		
(39)	3.6	(31)	4.1	(30)	3.8									(10)	3.5		
	7.2		7.9		7.5										5.8		
	3488431M		**3159310M**		**3316934M**	Net Sales ($)	**1332M**		**18309M**		**44340M**		**133245M**		**511027M**		**2608681M**
	1965660M		**1880778M**		**2024374M**	Total Assets ($)	**398M**		**8971M**		**20910M**		**66450M**		**293526M**		**1634119M**

M = $ thousand MM = $ million

See Pages 9 through 22 for Explanation of Ratios and Data

Current Data Sorted by Assets | Comparative Historical Data

Type of Statement	0-500M	500M-2MM	2-10MM	10-50MM	50-100MM	100-250MM	4/1/09-3/31/10 ALL	4/1/10-3/31/11 ALL
Unqualified			2	2	4	1	22	14
Reviewed		1	5	7	1		19	15
Compiled			1				5	4
Tax Returns	1	5					12	9
Other	2	1	6	12	3	4	40	36
	8 (4/1-9/30/13)			50 (10/1/13-3/31/14)				
NUMBER OF STATEMENTS	3	7	14	21	8	5	98	78
ASSETS	%	%	%	%	%	%	%	%
Cash & Equivalents			3.9	9.6			7.7	8.6
Trade Receivables (net)			31.0	18.8			19.0	17.7
Inventory			34.1	29.2			27.1	24.0
All Other Current			.9	2.4			2.8	3.1
Total Current			69.9	59.9			56.5	53.3
Fixed Assets (net)			21.8	29.3			30.1	32.6
Intangibles (net)			3.1	4.3			6.1	4.8
All Other Non-Current			5.2	6.5			7.3	9.4
Total			100.0	100.0			100.0	100.0
LIABILITIES								
Notes Payable-Short Term			12.5	5.4			7.1	7.2
Cur. Mat.-L.T.D.			10.1	3.7			4.6	3.3
Trade Payables			16.8	6.8			10.4	9.7
Income Taxes Payable			2.3	.0			.4	.1
All Other Current			6.6	7.6			10.9	7.2
Total Current			48.2	23.5			33.4	27.5
Long-Term Debt			15.5	14.3			19.6	18.4
Deferred Taxes			.0	1.3			1.0	1.0
All Other Non-Current			12.9	3.3			5.2	7.2
Net Worth			23.4	57.6			40.8	45.8
Total Liabilties & Net Worth			100.0	100.0			100.0	100.0
INCOME DATA								
Net Sales			100.0	100.0			100.0	100.0
Gross Profit			29.0	29.6			32.0	31.6
Operating Expenses			23.0	23.3			30.3	29.3
Operating Profit			5.9	6.3			1.7	2.4
All Other Expenses (net)			.9	.8			1.6	1.2
Profit Before Taxes			5.0	5.6			.1	1.1
RATIOS								
Current			1.9	7.5			3.0	3.8
			1.7	2.7			2.0	2.4
			1.0	1.8			1.2	1.4
Quick			1.5	3.9			1.3	2.2
			.6	1.4			.8	.8
			.3	.6			.5	.5
Sales/Receivables			**28** 12.9	**34** 10.6			**31** 11.8	**32** 11.3
			37 9.9	**41** 8.8			**39** 9.4	**41** 8.9
			63 5.8	**54** 6.8			**49** 7.4	**47** 7.7
Cost of Sales/Inventory			**34** 10.7	**69** 5.3			**65** 5.6	**54** 6.7
			70 5.2	**101** 3.6			**91** 4.0	**94** 3.9
			174 2.1	**174** 2.1			**182** 2.0	**182** 2.0
Cost of Sales/Payables			**21** 17.5	**15** 24.3			**17** 22.1	**16** 23.2
			27 13.5	**22** 16.9			**26** 14.0	**29** 12.8
			62 5.9	**29** 12.7			**41** 8.9	**38** 9.6
Sales/Working Capital			5.8	2.3			3.5	2.4
			11.2	2.9			6.4	4.6
			56.7	7.1			17.3	15.5
EBIT/Interest			15.9	53.1			7.1	13.3
			(13) 5.3	(19) 12.8			(89) 2.4	(69) 2.1
			1.8	1.0			-.6	-1.6
Net Profit + Depr., Dep., Amort./Cur. Mat. L/T/D							3.2	6.1
							(20) 2.0	(14) 1.7
							.7	.7
Fixed/Worth			.2	.2			.3	.3
			.9	.4			.8	.7
			13.1	1.0			2.2	1.6
Debt/Worth			1.2	.3			.5	.5
			1.8	.8			1.5	1.2
			27.8	1.3			4.7	2.5
% Profit Before Taxes/Tangible Net Worth			109.8	31.0			23.2	29.1
			(12) 24.4	16.0			(83) 5.2	(69) 9.9
			10.0	.7			-11.9	-8.0
% Profit Before Taxes/Total Assets			11.2	18.2			9.2	10.7
			5.9	7.9			2.4	4.4
			3.0	.2			-5.0	-4.2
Sales/Net Fixed Assets			31.1	10.5			20.5	22.8
			21.8	4.5			5.8	3.9
			3.1	2.4			2.1	1.4
Sales/Total Assets			3.2	1.8			2.3	2.3
			2.2	1.1			1.3	1.3
			1.1	.8			.8	.7
% Depr., Dep., Amort./Sales			.9	1.7			1.5	1.4
			(13) 1.3	3.2			(76) 3.5	(63) 4.2
			2.9	5.4			7.0	6.8
% Officers', Directors' Owners' Comp/Sales							2.3	2.8
							(18) 6.0	(19) 4.7
							8.9	5.8
Net Sales ($)	2907M	28005M	165051M	585361M	774601M	486450M	3661316M	2802125M
Total Assets ($)	877M	9590M	73446M	460138M	591013M	721132M	3733265M	2875973M

M = $ thousand MM = $ million

See Pages 9 through 22 for Explanation of Ratios and Data

Comparative Historical Data / Current Data Sorted by Sales

4/1/11-3/31/12 ALL	4/1/12-3/31/13 ALL	4/1/13-3/31/14 ALL	Type of Statement	0-1MM	1-3MM	3-5MM	5-10MM	10-25MM	25MM & OVER
13	14	9	Unqualified			1		2	6
14	14	14	Reviewed		1		2	7	4
2	3	1	Compiled					1	
7	7	6	Tax Returns		3	2	1		
34	29	28	Other	1	1	1	5	6	14
				8 (4/1-9/30/13)			50 (10/1/13-3/31/14)		
70	67	58	NUMBER OF STATEMENTS	1	5	4	8	16	24
%	%	%	**ASSETS**	%	%	%	%	%	%
5.4	8.7	8.3	Cash & Equivalents					9.4	7.8
22.3	22.5	23.4	Trade Receivables (net)					23.9	20.4
27.5	26.9	29.0	Inventory					28.3	27.4
2.6	2.1	1.9	All Other Current					.4	3.2
57.9	60.2	62.6	Total Current					62.0	58.8
31.7	27.2	27.4	Fixed Assets (net)					25.1	31.2
3.6	2.8	2.8	Intangibles (net)					7.5	1.0
6.7	9.8	7.1	All Other Non-Current					5.4	8.9
100.0	100.0	100.0	Total					100.0	100.0
			LIABILITIES						
8.0	8.8	10.1	Notes Payable-Short Term					10.3	5.4
5.7	2.8	6.3	Cur. Mat.-L.T.D.					2.6	6.0
10.1	10.0	14.0	Trade Payables					8.8	8.1
.2	.2	.6	Income Taxes Payable					.0	.0
8.9	15.3	10.9	All Other Current					4.6	17.2
32.8	37.2	41.9	Total Current					26.4	36.6
14.1	10.2	13.7	Long-Term Debt					13.8	8.3
1.1	1.2	.9	Deferred Taxes					1.4	1.0
7.5	6.7	8.0	All Other Non-Current					3.1	9.8
44.5	44.7	35.6	Net Worth					55.2	44.3
100.0	100.0	100.0	Total Liabilties & Net Worth					100.0	100.0
			INCOME DATA						
100.0	100.0	100.0	Net Sales					100.0	100.0
27.9	29.3	28.5	Gross Profit					29.8	24.9
26.7	26.9	23.8	Operating Expenses					23.5	21.3
1.2	2.4	4.7	Operating Profit					6.3	3.6
.9	.7	1.1	All Other Expenses (net)					.6	1.4
.4	1.8	3.6	Profit Before Taxes					5.8	2.2
			RATIOS						
3.4	3.0	2.7						5.8	4.0
1.9	1.8	1.8	Current					2.3	1.9
1.3	1.3	1.0						1.6	1.0
1.7	2.0	1.6						4.0	1.7
.8	.8	.8	Quick					1.3	.9
.4	.5	.3						.6	.3
33 11.0	**34** 10.6	**31** 11.7						**35** 10.4	**33** 10.9
45 8.1	**45** 8.2	**41** 8.8	Sales/Receivables					**43** 8.5	**42** 8.6
57 6.4	**60** 6.1	**54** 6.8						**58** 6.3	**53** 6.9
65 5.6	**63** 5.8	**54** 6.7						**64** 5.7	**68** 5.4
114 3.2	**96** 3.8	**89** 4.1	Cost of Sales/Inventory					**118** 3.1	**89** 4.1
182 2.0	**152** 2.4	**135** 2.7						**182** 2.0	**130** 2.8
18 20.3	**17** 21.7	**19** 19.7						**17** 21.7	**18** 20.8
27 13.3	**25** 14.6	**26** 13.8	Cost of Sales/Payables					**22** 16.3	**23** 15.9
43 8.5	**41** 8.9	**43** 8.4						**29** 12.8	**34** 10.6
3.0	3.1	2.8						2.3	2.6
4.8	7.2	7.5	Sales/Working Capital					3.9	7.1
12.6	13.9	56.7						10.7	NM
14.0	24.6	18.1						53.1	28.0
(65) 2.2	(61) 4.2	(51) 4.3	EBIT/Interest					(15) 8.8	(21) 4.3
-1.7	.3	.6						1.1	-.6
3.2	18.2	2.1							
(14) .9	(16) 3.0	(10) .7	Net Profit + Depr., Dep., Amort./Cur. Mat. L/T/D						
.0	.3	-.4							
.3	.2	.2						.2	.1
.7	.5	.7	Fixed/Worth					.3	.6
1.7	1.2	7.9						.8	1.6
.5	.6	.6						.3	.5
1.3	1.1	1.5	Debt/Worth					.9	1.0
2.9	3.6	23.1						1.6	3.6
29.1	26.1	31.9						30.1	28.2
(63) 10.8	(61) 11.3	(47) 16.0	% Profit Before Taxes/Tangible Net Worth					(15) 14.3	(21) 16.0
-13.9	-.4	.4						1.1	.3
13.4	12.2	14.8						16.4	15.7
3.8	4.3	6.5	% Profit Before Taxes/Total Assets					5.9	4.9
-5.8	-1.2	-.4						.4	-2.4
16.7	26.4	27.2						25.9	15.1
4.1	5.6	6.5	Sales/Net Fixed Assets					6.6	3.6
1.5	2.4	2.6						2.6	1.8
2.1	2.5	2.8						2.5	2.4
1.3	1.4	1.4	Sales/Total Assets					1.2	1.2
.7	.9	.9						.8	.9
1.2	1.1	1.1						.9	.9
(57) 4.3	(55) 2.6	(49) 2.7	% Depr., Dep., Amort./Sales					(15) 2.7	(22) 3.9
8.5	5.1	5.3						5.5	5.9
2.6	2.0	1.8							
(17) 3.6	(12) 2.8	(11) 3.2	% Officers', Directors' Owners' Comp/Sales						
6.2	4.3	5.3							
2447501M	2503347M	2042375M	Net Sales ($)	171M	10703M	15953M	51265M	255243M	1709040M
2581217M	2472215M	1856196M	Total Assets ($)	41M	4762M	9852M	34595M	232122M	1574824M

M = $ thousand MM = $ million

See Pages 9 through 22 for Explanation of Ratios and Data

Current Data Sorted by Assets							Comparative Historical Data	
						Type of Statement		
						Unqualified	6	4
		5	2			Reviewed	3	7
	1					Compiled	1	4
2	3	2	1			Tax Returns	6	2
	2	5	1	1		Other	6	16
	3 (4/1-9/30/13)		22 (10/1/13-3/31/14)				**4/1/09-3/31/10**	**4/1/10-3/31/11**
0-500M	**500M-2MM**	**2-10MM**	**10-50MM**	**50-100MM**	**100-250MM**		**ALL**	**ALL**
2	6	12	4	1		**NUMBER OF STATEMENTS**	22	33
%	%	%	%	%	%	**ASSETS**	%	%
		9.4			DATA NOT AVAILABLE	Cash & Equivalents	8.9	7.6
		35.3				Trade Receivables (net)	25.8	26.9
		14.6				Inventory	18.3	24.1
		2.0				All Other Current	2.0	2.7
		61.3				Total Current	55.1	61.4
		35.0				Fixed Assets (net)	36.9	30.5
		1.5				Intangibles (net)	5.2	5.3
		2.2				All Other Non-Current	2.9	2.8
		100.0				Total	100.0	100.0
						LIABILITIES		
		10.1				Notes Payable-Short Term	6.7	9.8
		4.8				Cur. Mat.-L.T.D.	5.6	3.5
		17.3				Trade Payables	15.6	17.0
		.6				Income Taxes Payable	.2	.7
		8.2				All Other Current	9.5	7.1
		41.0				Total Current	37.6	38.0
		10.4				Long-Term Debt	22.7	15.0
		.4				Deferred Taxes	.7	.4
		15.2				All Other Non-Current	5.2	7.1
		33.0				Net Worth	33.9	39.5
		100.0				Total Liabilties & Net Worth	100.0	100.0
						INCOME DATA		
		100.0				Net Sales	100.0	100.0
		35.1				Gross Profit	34.4	31.4
		29.8				Operating Expenses	33.6	28.0
		5.3				Operating Profit	.8	3.3
		-.5				All Other Expenses (net)	1.3	.9
		5.7				Profit Before Taxes	-.5	2.4
						RATIOS		
		2.3					2.6	3.3
		1.7				Current	1.6	1.7
		1.1					1.0	1.2
		2.0					1.5	2.1
		1.3				Quick	.9	1.2
		.8					.6	.7
		24 15.3					**26** 14.1	**22** 16.2
		39 9.4				Sales/Receivables	**34** 10.7	**39** 9.3
		51 7.2					**58** 6.3	**56** 6.5
		1 331.9					**18** 20.3	**18** 20.5
		22 16.9				Cost of Sales/Inventory	**32** 11.2	**34** 10.7
		35 10.3					**78** 4.7	**62** 5.9
		17 21.7					**18** 20.3	**18** 20.1
		20 18.5				Cost of Sales/Payables	**36** 10.0	**30** 12.1
		57 6.4					**53** 6.8	**51** 7.1
		7.5					5.9	5.2
		13.0				Sales/Working Capital	13.3	9.6
		77.5					NM	62.5
		36.4					3.9	10.6
		(10) 17.0				EBIT/Interest	(20) 2.6	(28) 2.2
		8.4					-1.7	-1.0
						Net Profit + Depr., Dep., Amort./Cur. Mat. L/T/D		
		.5					.8	.5
		.9				Fixed/Worth	1.3	.7
		2.3					2.0	1.9
		.4					1.1	.4
		1.3				Debt/Worth	2.2	1.4
		5.7					5.2	3.5
		79.5					24.0	54.6
		(11) 30.2				% Profit Before Taxes/Tangible Net Worth	(19) 10.6	(29) 11.7
		17.0					-25.1	-1.2
		25.6					8.5	15.0
		15.3				% Profit Before Taxes/Total Assets	3.9	6.1
		6.9					-7.3	-3.1
		28.3					22.4	27.7
		10.7				Sales/Net Fixed Assets	6.5	9.7
		5.5					3.7	4.0
		3.5					3.3	4.0
		3.3				Sales/Total Assets	2.4	2.2
		2.5					1.4	1.6
		1.1					1.7	1.2
		1.9				% Depr., Dep., Amort./Sales	(20) 3.5	(29) 2.5
		3.7					5.5	5.5
								2.0
						% Officers', Directors' Owners' Comp/Sales		(10) 6.2
								10.7
1238M	**25542M**	**179932M**	**137938M**	**123971M**		Net Sales ($)	**1065927M**	**812452M**
371M	**8196M**	**61744M**	**56314M**	**75831M**		Total Assets ($)	**496376M**	**400512M**

M = $ thousand   MM = $ million

See Pages 9 through 22 for Explanation of Ratios and Data

Comparative Historical Data

		4/1/11-3/31/12 ALL		4/1/12-3/31/13 ALL		4/1/13-3/31/14 ALL
Type of Statement						
Unqualified		4		3		
Reviewed		6		8		7
Compiled		5		1		1
Tax Returns		7		4		8
Other		18		9		9
NUMBER OF STATEMENTS		40		24		25
ASSETS		%		%		%
Cash & Equivalents		11.5		10.5		9.2
Trade Receivables (net)		27.2		26.5		34.9
Inventory		22.2		17.7		18.0
All Other Current		3.4		3.6		2.2
Total Current		64.3		58.4		64.3
Fixed Assets (net)		29.6		28.4		31.4
Intangibles (net)		2.3		7.7		1.9
All Other Non-Current		3.7		5.5		2.4
Total		100.0		100.0		100.0
LIABILITIES						
Notes Payable-Short Term		6.2		6.9		11.4
Cur. Mat.-L.T.D.		3.7		3.0		4.6
Trade Payables		17.6		14.0		15.9
Income Taxes Payable		.0		.1		.3
All Other Current		10.8		11.1		13.1
Total Current		38.3		35.1		45.3
Long-Term Debt		14.8		13.6		13.5
Deferred Taxes		.4		.8		.4
All Other Non-Current		7.6		10.9		11.7
Net Worth		38.8		39.5		29.1
Total Liabilties & Net Worth		100.0		100.0		100.0
INCOME DATA						
Net Sales		100.0		100.0		100.0
Gross Profit		35.2		36.9		31.8
Operating Expenses		32.3		33.1		27.9
Operating Profit		2.9		3.8		4.0
All Other Expenses (net)		.5		.2		.0
Profit Before Taxes		2.4		3.7		4.0
RATIOS						
Current		3.5		5.2		2.5
		1.9		1.7		1.8
		1.3		1.2		1.2
Quick		2.4		2.6		2.0
		1.1		1.1		1.3
		.6		.6		.7
Sales/Receivables	**23**	15.8	**27**	13.7	**29**	12.6
	39	9.3	**41**	8.9	**40**	9.1
	57	6.4	**51**	7.1	**51**	7.1
Cost of Sales/Inventory	**12**	31.1	**9**	41.5	**10**	35.7
	43	8.5	**30**	12.0	**30**	12.0
	89	4.1	**68**	5.4	**51**	7.2
Cost of Sales/Payables	**16**	22.5	**11**	34.3	**17**	22.1
	33	11.2	**33**	11.0	**20**	18.0
	59	6.2	**40**	9.1	**41**	8.9
Sales/Working Capital		4.7		4.6		7.2
		8.6		8.8		9.1
		23.8		35.5		64.2
EBIT/Interest		8.4		12.6		26.8
	(34)	3.6	(20)	8.2	(20)	10.5
		-2.5		1.2		1.3
Net Profit + Depr., Dep., Amort./Cur. Mat. L/T/D						
Fixed/Worth		.5		.3		.5
		.8		.8		.9
		1.7		2.7		3.2
Debt/Worth		.5		.4		.5
		1.7		1.6		1.8
		6.2		5.9		7.5
% Profit Before Taxes/Tangible Net Worth		27.5		25.1		60.2
	(37)	13.7	(21)	13.2	(21)	24.8
		-5.0		3.7		11.7
% Profit Before Taxes/Total Assets		10.3		15.3		22.5
		4.0		5.0		8.2
		-8.2		.9		2.6
Sales/Net Fixed Assets		20.3		35.5		32.0
		7.5		7.1		10.5
		4.1		4.2		5.2
Sales/Total Assets		3.0		3.4		3.5
		2.0		2.2		3.1
		1.4		1.5		2.3
% Depr., Dep., Amort./Sales		1.7		1.1		1.0
	(34)	2.8	(21)	2.6	(24)	1.9
		4.8		3.9		3.3
% Officers', Directors' Owners' Comp/Sales		2.1				2.2
	(19)	3.1			(11)	2.7
		6.9				7.3
Net Sales ($)		**898625M**		**451759M**		**468621M**
Total Assets ($)		**492156M**		**269876M**		**202456M**

Current Data Sorted by Sales

	0-1MM	1-3MM	3-5MM	5-10MM	10-25MM	25MM & OVER
	3 (4/1-9/30/13)			22 (10/1/13-3/31/14)		
Type of Statement						
Unqualified						
Reviewed				1	4	2
Compiled			1			
Tax Returns	1	2	1	3		1
Other			2	1	3	3
NUMBER OF STATEMENTS	1	2	4	5	7	6
ASSETS	%	%	%	%	%	%
Net Sales ($)	**238M**	**3323M**	**16845M**	**37278M**	**116823M**	**294114M**
Total Assets ($)	**51M**	**969M**	**5602M**	**20042M**	**40632M**	**135160M**

M = $ thousand MM = $ million

See Pages 9 through 22 for Explanation of Ratios and Data

Current Data Sorted by Assets							Comparative Historical Data	
						Type of Statement		
		1	4			Unqualified	21	9
	3	18	5			Reviewed	32	26
	2	8	1			Compiled	10	14
6	6	5	1			Tax Returns	18	21
4	6	7	12	1		Other	46	53
	18 (4/1-9/30/13)		72 (10/1/13-3/31/14)				**4/1/09-3/31/10 ALL**	**4/1/10-3/31/11 ALL**
0-500M	**500M-2MM**	**2-10MM**	**10-50MM**	**50-100MM**	**100-250MM**			
10	17	39	23	1		**NUMBER OF STATEMENTS**	127	123
%	%	%	%	%	%	**ASSETS**	%	%
18.2	8.9	9.2	8.6		D A T A N O T A V A I L A B L E	Cash & Equivalents	8.2	10.2
28.7	37.6	29.5	27.0			Trade Receivables (net)	24.7	26.1
24.9	22.6	24.3	18.2			Inventory	21.8	22.9
.0	1.3	2.9	2.6			All Other Current	2.4	2.8
71.8	70.4	65.9	56.3			Total Current	57.1	62.0
16.2	25.3	27.6	33.2			Fixed Assets (net)	31.4	29.5
4.5	2.3	1.9	7.4			Intangibles (net)	4.1	3.7
7.6	2.0	4.6	3.1			All Other Non-Current	7.4	4.8
100.0	100.0	100.0	100.0			Total	100.0	100.0
						LIABILITIES		
17.3	26.5	8.8	6.9			Notes Payable-Short Term	11.1	8.5
3.4	6.1	3.1	3.3			Cur. Mat.-L.T.D.	5.1	4.2
24.7	14.0	15.0	11.6			Trade Payables	14.2	12.9
.0	.6	.3	.0			Income Taxes Payable	.1	.3
43.2	17.9	12.1	9.4			All Other Current	13.7	10.8
88.6	65.1	39.3	31.3			Total Current	44.3	36.7
20.9	14.4	18.7	15.8			Long-Term Debt	23.4	17.0
.0	.1	.1	.5			Deferred Taxes	.5	.4
.4	3.7	5.4	6.9			All Other Non-Current	5.6	7.7
-9.8	16.6	36.4	45.5			Net Worth	26.2	38.2
100.0	100.0	100.0	100.0			Total Liabilties & Net Worth	100.0	100.0
						INCOME DATA		
100.0	100.0	100.0	100.0			Net Sales	100.0	100.0
44.4	42.6	30.2	29.8			Gross Profit	31.6	33.3
46.1	37.8	26.0	22.2			Operating Expenses	30.2	29.7
-1.7	4.8	4.2	7.6			Operating Profit	1.4	3.5
.8	1.6	.3	.7			All Other Expenses (net)	1.0	.8
-2.5	3.3	3.9	6.9			Profit Before Taxes	.5	2.8
						RATIOS		
1.4	3.0	3.2	2.7				2.6	3.7
1.1	1.5	1.8	1.7			Current	1.5	1.8
.5	.8	1.2	1.3				.9	1.2
1.0	1.8	2.2	1.9				1.4	2.2
.5	.8	1.1	1.0			Quick	.8	1.0
.3	.4	.5	.8				.4	.6
0 UND	**26** 13.9	**29** 12.5	**33** 11.2				**31** 11.9	**35** 10.5
17 21.6	**51** 7.1	**41** 9.0	**40** 9.1			Sales/Receivables	**42** 8.8	**44** 8.3
62 5.9	**89** 4.1	**60** 6.1	**60** 6.1				**55** 6.7	**55** 6.6
0 UND	**9** 38.8	**17** 21.2	**22** 16.4				**23** 16.1	**24** 15.5
34 10.8	**40** 9.2	**40** 9.1	**40** 9.1			Cost of Sales/Inventory	**47** 7.7	**47** 7.7
61 6.0	**130** 2.8	**94** 3.9	**66** 5.5				**91** 4.0	**95** 3.8
0 UND	**11** 32.4	**16** 22.6	**16** 23.2				**14** 26.1	**17** 22.0
41 8.9	**29** 12.6	**32** 11.4	**24** 15.5			Cost of Sales/Payables	**29** 12.7	**29** 12.6
89 4.1	**66** 5.5	**45** 8.1	**49** 7.4				**49** 7.4	**45** 8.1
13.4	4.9	4.6	5.3				5.0	4.1
NM	11.1	8.3	9.8			Sales/Working Capital	14.4	8.0
-19.5	-12.4	22.1	18.6				-36.6	32.2
	13.4	29.0	22.5				7.3	9.5
	(13) 4.9	(37) 9.8	(19) 9.3			EBIT/Interest	(116) 1.9	(104) 2.9
	-.2	2.9	2.6				-1.8	-.2
		13.0					3.3	3.8
		(10) 3.6				Net Profit + Depr., Dep., Amort./Cur. Mat. L/T/D	(32) 1.5	(29) 1.7
		1.8					.4	.4
.0	.2	.1	.3				.5	.3
.7	1.0	.7	1.0			Fixed/Worth	1.1	.7
-.7	-3.3	2.3	1.9				19.5	2.0
2.0	1.5	.5	.6				.8	.6
6.7	2.1	1.2	1.2			Debt/Worth	2.2	1.5
-2.7	-9.7	4.0	2.9				73.6	4.7
	61.6	52.7	47.5				36.2	30.5
	(11) 36.8	(33) 26.4	(21) 23.8			% Profit Before Taxes/Tangible Net Worth	(97) 11.9	(104) 13.6
	16.4	6.2	17.0				-6.1	-3.3
8.2	19.6	19.1	17.8				10.8	15.4
1.0	8.7	10.3	13.1			% Profit Before Taxes/Total Assets	3.1	4.1
-19.5	-5.1	2.7	4.2				-8.0	-2.0
UND	32.0	29.2	19.0				17.1	21.4
46.2	9.9	11.1	8.0			Sales/Net Fixed Assets	7.2	8.3
24.2	3.6	5.3	3.2				3.5	3.9
5.5	3.6	3.1	2.5				2.8	2.5
3.8	1.9	2.1	2.0			Sales/Total Assets	1.9	1.9
2.2	1.2	1.6	1.7				1.3	1.4
	2.0	.9	1.3				1.3	1.5
	(11) 3.2	(38) 2.2	2.8			% Depr., Dep., Amort./Sales	(112) 2.7	(101) 2.9
	6.4	3.3	4.0				5.6	4.9
		1.6					2.1	2.0
		(20) 3.3				% Officers', Directors' Owners' Comp/Sales	(36) 3.6	(44) 4.1
		5.4					7.7	6.9
10920M	42533M	461892M	904988M	112712M		Net Sales ($)	3541699M	2706676M
3046M	18970M	190130M	463206M	51757M		Total Assets ($)	2366352M	1771591M

M = $ thousand MM = $ million

See Pages 9 through 22 for Explanation of Ratios and Data

Comparative Historical Data / Current Data Sorted by Sales

			Type of Statement						
6	8	5	Unqualified					2	3
26	30	26	Reviewed	1	2	2	6	9	6
19	19	11	Compiled		2	2	3	3	1
21	16	18	Tax Returns	3	7	2	3	2	1
50	33	30	Other	4	4	1	3	7	11
4/1/11-3/31/12	**4/1/12-3/31/13**	**4/1/13-3/31/14**			**18 (4/1-9/30/13)**			**72 (10/1/13-3/31/14)**	
ALL	**ALL**	**ALL**		**0-1MM**	**1-3MM**	**3-5MM**	**5-10MM**	**10-25MM**	**25MM & OVER**
122	106	90	**NUMBER OF STATEMENTS**	8	15	7	15	23	22
%	%	%	**ASSETS**	%	%	%	%	%	%
10.1	8.7	10.1	Cash & Equivalents		6.2		10.9	10.3	8.6
27.6	30.7	30.2	Trade Receivables (net)		34.1		35.0	31.8	26.6
22.3	22.6	22.4	Inventory		21.3		16.3	28.2	19.3
2.3	2.4	2.2	All Other Current		1.3		4.9	1.2	3.2
62.2	64.4	64.9	Total Current		62.9		67.2	71.6	57.6
26.1	28.2	27.3	Fixed Assets (net)		30.6		23.7	24.7	32.3
4.6	3.0	3.8	Intangibles (net)		5.4		3.0	2.1	7.3
7.1	4.4	4.0	All Other Non-Current		1.2		6.1	1.7	2.8
100.0	100.0	100.0	Total		100.0		100.0	100.0	100.0
			LIABILITIES						
10.1	8.9	12.5	Notes Payable-Short Term		24.6		4.1	11.9	6.5
3.0	3.6	3.7	Cur. Mat.-L.T.D.		2.8		2.7	3.0	2.9
15.7	15.1	15.0	Trade Payables		18.4		13.5	14.6	13.5
.3	.2	.2	Income Taxes Payable		.6		.5	.0	.2
11.6	10.5	15.9	All Other Current		18.0		12.6	9.8	12.2
40.6	38.4	47.3	Total Current		64.4		33.3	39.4	35.3
18.8	17.9	17.3	Long-Term Debt		18.5		12.9	21.0	14.2
.6	.4	.2	Deferred Taxes		.2		.0	.1	.7
7.8	7.5	5.0	All Other Non-Current		.9		3.0	8.5	7.2
32.1	35.8	30.1	Net Worth		16.1		50.7	31.1	42.6
100.0	100.0	100.0	Total Liabilties & Net Worth		100.0		100.0	100.0	100.0
			INCOME DATA						
100.0	100.0	100.0	Net Sales		100.0		100.0	100.0	100.0
33.8	33.0	33.8	Gross Profit		43.0		33.3	29.8	27.5
30.0	29.0	29.3	Operating Expenses		44.7		27.4	23.5	20.7
3.9	4.0	4.5	Operating Profit		-1.8		5.9	6.2	6.8
.8	.5	.7	All Other Expenses (net)		.7		.2	.3	.7
3.0	3.5	3.8	Profit Before Taxes		-2.5		5.7	5.9	6.0
			RATIOS						
2.8	3.2	2.6			1.6		3.7	3.6	2.5
1.6	1.7	1.6	Current		1.3		2.3	1.9	1.8
1.1	1.2	1.1			.9		1.2	1.2	1.4
1.5	1.7	1.8			1.5		2.5	2.4	1.8
.9	1.0	.9	Quick		.8		1.5	1.1	1.0
.6	.6	.5			.4		.6	.5	.6
30 12.1	**30** 12.1	**29** 12.6			**19** 18.9		**33** 11.0	**30** 12.2	**31** 11.6
42 8.6	**41** 9.0	**40** 9.1	Sales/Receivables		**51** 7.1		**50** 7.3	**38** 9.7	**39** 9.4
57 6.4	**55** 6.6	**61** 6.0			**78** 4.7		**65** 5.6	**58** 6.3	**60** 6.1
22 16.4	**21** 17.5	**17** 21.5			**11** 32.1		**2** 195.4	**26** 14.1	**26** 14.3
46 8.0	**46** 8.0	**39** 9.3	Cost of Sales/Inventory		**33** 11.0		**40** 9.1	**50** 7.3	**38** 9.7
83 4.4	**81** 4.5	**81** 4.5			**104** 3.5		**94** 3.9	**99** 3.7	**49** 7.5
20 18.0	**16** 23.0	**14** 25.5			**11** 32.1		**14** 26.5	**14** 25.8	**16** 23.4
33 11.1	**27** 13.4	**29** 12.5	Cost of Sales/Payables		**48** 7.6		**26** 14.0	**28** 13.2	**25** 14.4
51 7.1	**45** 8.1	**51** 7.2			**81** 4.5		**38** 9.6	**53** 6.9	**46** 8.0
4.9	4.4	5.2			8.4		4.8	4.2	5.9
10.3	9.5	9.1	Sales/Working Capital		21.5		5.9	5.8	9.2
43.1	35.0	53.5			-25.5		18.3	22.6	18.5
9.2	16.6	17.0			8.9		41.0	37.0	22.5
(101) 2.6	(94) 4.5	(77) 7.1	EBIT/Interest		(12) 4.0		(14) 9.9	(21) 10.9	(19) 9.8
.3	1.3	2.2			-5.9		3.3	2.7	3.1
5.8	5.8	13.2							
(24) 3.0	(25) 2.6	(20) 3.6	Net Profit + Depr., Dep., Amort./Cur. Mat. L/T/D						
1.3	1.5	1.7							
.3	.2	.2			.5		.1	.2	.4
.7	.7	.8	Fixed/Worth		1.1		.5	.7	1.0
2.5	2.6	2.3			4.0		2.3	3.4	1.9
.8	.7	.7			1.7		.4	.5	.7
2.0	1.8	1.8	Debt/Worth		3.2		.9	1.3	1.1
7.0	5.5	5.5			-14.1		2.7	4.4	3.2
32.1	36.3	50.9			94.0		52.4	59.5	43.5
(100) 13.4	(90) 18.5	(72) 26.3	% Profit Before Taxes/Tangible Net Worth		(11) 16.4		(14) 30.3	(19) 26.8	(19) 26.4
-.1	3.9	10.2			-18.2		9.1	19.2	15.5
13.6	15.9	16.0			8.7		25.4	21.9	18.2
3.2	6.4	9.1	% Profit Before Taxes/Total Assets		-.9		13.9	12.9	13.7
-1.7	1.0	2.5			-17.0		3.5	4.5	4.5
26.5	28.3	30.9			58.5		42.0	30.8	20.7
10.0	9.9	9.8	Sales/Net Fixed Assets		8.0		21.9	10.9	8.4
4.6	4.1	4.2			3.0		6.9	5.4	3.6
2.8	3.1	3.0			4.6		3.2	3.1	2.6
2.0	2.3	2.1	Sales/Total Assets		2.6		2.6	2.3	2.1
1.5	1.5	1.6			1.3		1.8	1.8	1.7
1.2	1.0	1.1			.7		.9	1.0	1.2
(98) 2.6	(88) 2.3	(79) 2.3	% Depr., Dep., Amort./Sales		(12) 2.5		(11) 2.4	1.9	2.4
4.0	3.8	3.9			6.0		3.6	3.1	4.1
1.9	1.8	1.7						1.4	
(49) 3.9	(47) 3.0	(38) 3.5	% Officers', Directors' Owners' Comp/Sales					(10) 2.2	
6.1	6.4	6.2						3.9	
3573822M	**1773659M**	**1533045M**	Net Sales ($)	**5077M**	**24609M**	**28379M**	**108696M**	**368905M**	**997379M**
2216686M	**993498M**	**727109M**	Total Assets ($)	**5216M**	**12749M**	**15584M**	**45468M**	**161455M**	**486637M**

M = $ thousand MM = $ million

See Pages 9 through 22 for Explanation of Ratios and Data

Current Data Sorted by Assets							Comparative Historical Data	
						Type of Statement		
		5	12	5	6	Unqualified	46	38
1	2	18	18	2		Reviewed	53	40
1	5	10	2		2	Compiled	43	27
1	9	15				Tax Returns	24	30
1	7	19	22	5	4	Other	69	95
	20 (4/1-9/30/13)		152 (10/1/13-3/31/14)				4/1/09-3/31/10	4/1/10-3/31/11
0-500M	500M-2MM	2-10MM	10-50MM	50-100MM	100-250MM		ALL	ALL
4	23	67	54	12	12	**NUMBER OF STATEMENTS**	235	230
%	%	%	%	%	%	**ASSETS**	%	%
	15.8	9.9	10.0	9.6	3.5	Cash & Equivalents	10.7	9.8
	26.8	28.0	19.7	19.5	17.4	Trade Receivables (net)	20.2	21.6
	8.4	9.2	10.2	6.0	7.1	Inventory	8.3	8.3
	4.2	2.1	1.9	2.6	3.9	All Other Current	2.6	3.1
	55.1	49.3	41.9	37.5	32.0	Total Current	41.8	42.7
	36.0	41.1	42.7	44.0	56.2	Fixed Assets (net)	46.6	45.6
	4.5	2.8	6.4	6.6	5.4	Intangibles (net)	4.1	3.6
	4.3	6.8	9.1	11.9	6.4	All Other Non-Current	7.6	8.1
	100.0	100.0	100.0	100.0	100.0	Total	100.0	100.0
						LIABILITIES		
	6.3	5.5	6.0	7.3	3.0	Notes Payable-Short Term	5.7	7.3
	5.5	4.1	5.4	4.2	5.1	Cur. Mat.-L.T.D.	5.8	5.9
	21.0	17.4	9.7	8.6	7.8	Trade Payables	10.2	12.6
	.3	.0	.1	.3	.4	Income Taxes Payable	.2	.2
	15.1	7.3	6.1	4.3	6.8	All Other Current	7.3	8.0
	48.2	34.3	27.3	24.8	23.2	Total Current	29.2	33.9
	16.0	20.9	19.0	12.2	18.6	Long-Term Debt	26.0	23.9
	.2	.4	1.3	3.1	1.5	Deferred Taxes	.7	.8
	14.3	5.3	4.2	2.3	6.2	All Other Non-Current	4.3	5.4
	21.3	39.1	48.2	57.6	50.5	Net Worth	39.7	35.9
	100.0	100.0	100.0	100.0	100.0	Total Liabilities & Net Worth	100.0	100.0
						INCOME DATA		
	100.0	100.0	100.0	100.0	100.0	Net Sales	100.0	100.0
	29.6	30.8	20.6	18.7	13.9	Gross Profit	27.5	26.2
	29.0	28.6	19.4	16.4	10.1	Operating Expenses	28.3	26.0
	.6	2.2	1.2	2.3	3.7	Operating Profit	-.8	.2
	-.3	-.3	-.2	-.4	-.3	All Other Expenses (net)	.8	1.0
	.9	2.6	1.5	2.7	4.0	Profit Before Taxes	-1.5	-.7
						RATIOS		
	2.8	2.3	2.3	1.9	2.0		3.0	2.8
	1.4	1.5	1.6	1.5	1.2	Current	1.5	1.4
	.8	1.1	1.0	1.2	1.2		.9	.9
	2.5	1.8	1.9	1.4	1.1		2.1	2.0
	.9	1.2	1.1	1.0	1.0	Quick	1.0	1.0
	.7	.7	.6	.7	.7		.6	.6
	27 13.7	**34** 10.6	**34** 10.7	**38** 9.5	**35** 10.3		**30** 12.3	**30** 12.2
	33 10.9	**45** 8.1	**45** 8.2	**52** 7.0	**52** 7.0	Sales/Receivables	**42** 8.6	**42** 8.6
	48 7.6	**54** 6.7	**57** 6.4	**63** 5.8	**63** 5.8		**57** 6.4	**58** 6.3
	1 316.8	**6** 57.6	**14** 25.3	**11** 32.8	**3** 121.8		**7** 49.4	**7** 49.1
	15 24.5	**16** 22.4	**26** 13.9	**19** 19.7	**18** 20.1	Cost of Sales/Inventory	**20** 18.7	**17** 21.9
	24 15.1	**29** 12.8	**52** 7.0	**51** 7.2	**46** 8.0		**39** 9.3	**35** 10.3
	22 16.9	**23** 16.0	**19** 19.2	**16** 22.4	**18** 20.1		**14** 26.6	**15** 24.4
	30 12.2	**33** 10.9	**28** 13.0	**26** 14.0	**28** 13.0	Cost of Sales/Payables	**26** 14.1	**29** 12.7
	60 6.1	**60** 6.1	**43** 8.4	**38** 9.5	**35** 10.5		**43** 8.5	**53** 6.9
	7.6	7.3	6.5	6.5	7.0		5.3	5.7
	27.5	10.9	10.2	13.6	20.6	Sales/Working Capital	13.1	16.5
	-26.1	121.3	291.2	36.1	30.3		-43.9	-33.7
	20.1	10.0	7.7	16.3	10.9		3.9	5.1
	(16) 5.0	(61) 3.4	(52) 2.8	(10) 7.3	(11) 2.2	EBIT/Interest	(213) 1.1	(212) 1.4
	1.4	1.0	.1	.7	1.4		-1.9	-2.1
		4.6	2.9			Net Profit + Depr., Dep.,	3.1	2.4
		(11) 2.0	(18) 1.7			Amort./Cur. Mat. L/T/D	(60) 1.3	(51) 1.2
		.9	.9				.4	.4
	.5	.6	.6	.4	.9		.6	.6
	1.3	1.0	1.0	1.0	1.2	Fixed/Worth	1.2	1.2
	-2.0	3.3	1.7	1.3	1.9		3.3	3.6
	.6	.7	.6	.5	.5		.5	.6
	2.1	1.5	1.2	.7	1.3	Debt/Worth	1.4	1.4
	-6.3	12.5	2.3	1.6	2.1		5.5	5.4
	76.0	37.6	11.9	16.2	20.8	% Profit Before Taxes/Tangible	16.1	23.9
	(16) 7.6	(57) 9.1	(50) 5.0	11.6	6.2	Net Worth	(199) 2.2	(191) 3.8
	-16.9	2.8	-5.5	3.7	2.0		-14.9	-8.2
	24.6	11.1	5.2	9.6	8.3	% Profit Before Taxes/Total	5.3	8.0
	5.7	3.8	2.3	7.0	2.5	Assets	.4	1.3
	-3.5	.2	-1.8	1.0	.9		-7.0	-5.9
	13.8	7.5	6.0	6.7	2.6		6.1	7.2
	7.5	5.5	3.6	2.4	2.4	Sales/Net Fixed Assets	3.2	3.7
	5.3	3.6	2.2	1.4	1.8		1.9	2.0
	3.6	2.9	1.8	1.6	1.4		2.0	2.2
	2.8	2.1	1.4	1.2	1.3	Sales/Total Assets	1.5	1.5
	2.2	1.6	1.1	.8	1.0		1.1	1.1
	1.3	2.3	2.8	3.1	2.8		3.5	3.6
	(21) 3.3	(63) 3.4	(53) 4.0	(11) 6.4	(11) 4.7	% Depr., Dep., Amort./Sales	(210) 5.8	(212) 5.9
	4.4	5.0	5.9	8.7	6.8		8.9	8.3
	1.9	1.7	.5			% Officers', Directors'	1.3	1.4
	(13) 4.6	(30) 2.5	(15) 1.3			Owners' Comp/Sales	(72) 2.8	(70) 2.6
	6.8	5.5	2.9				6.6	5.6
4765M	76621M	797041M	1926985M	980626M	1744537M	Net Sales ($)	7509555M	6252213M
1024M	25550M	355632M	1391750M	827496M	1429465M	Total Assets ($)	6044683M	4996099M

M = $ thousand MM = $ million

See Pages 9 through 22 for Explanation of Ratios and Data

Comparative Historical Data				Current Data Sorted by Sales					
			Type of Statement						
37	31	28	Unqualified				1	9	18
47	35	41	Reviewed		3	2	7	12	17
33	29	20	Compiled		1	7	4	3	5
38	34	25	Tax Returns		6	5	8	5	1
58	69	58	Other	2	4	4	7	17	24
				20 (4/1-9/30/13)			152 (10/1/13-3/31/14)		
4/1/11-3/31/12 ALL	**4/1/12-3/31/13 ALL**	**4/1/13-3/31/14 ALL**		**0-1MM**	**1-3MM**	**3-5MM**	**5-10MM**	**10-25MM**	**25MM & OVER**
213	198	172	**NUMBER OF STATEMENTS**	2	14	18	27	46	65
%	%	%	**ASSETS**	%	%	%	%	%	%
8.6	9.6	10.1	Cash & Equivalents		13.2	11.6	12.1	9.5	8.7
24.1	25.3	23.7	Trade Receivables (net)		20.0	23.9	25.9	27.2	21.3
9.0	8.2	9.1	Inventory		9.3	10.9	7.7	7.9	9.6
3.2	2.5	2.5	All Other Current		4.9	2.7	1.7	2.1	2.5
44.9	45.6	45.3	Total Current		47.4	49.1	47.3	46.8	42.1
43.5	43.0	42.6	Fixed Assets (net)		38.5	42.4	42.5	42.7	43.0
4.3	4.3	4.7	Intangibles (net)		8.2	2.6	2.8	3.8	6.2
7.3	7.1	7.3	All Other Non-Current		6.0	5.8	7.4	6.8	8.7
100.0	100.0	100.0	Total		100.0	100.0	100.0	100.0	100.0
			LIABILITIES						
5.8	7.0	6.1	Notes Payable-Short Term		5.2	10.8	3.7	5.2	5.7
6.1	5.4	4.9	Cur. Mat.-L.T.D.		6.9	3.8	4.1	4.1	5.7
14.0	14.7	14.0	Trade Payables		15.3	16.4	14.9	18.0	9.9
.1	.2	.1	Income Taxes Payable		.0	.3	.0	.0	.2
8.5	12.1	8.4	All Other Current		12.9	9.3	7.2	7.6	6.3
34.5	39.5	33.5	Total Current		40.3	40.6	29.9	34.8	27.8
23.8	23.1	20.5	Long-Term Debt		25.5	18.7	20.6	22.7	16.1
.4	.8	.9	Deferred Taxes		.0	.2	.3	.8	1.6
6.5	7.9	6.2	All Other Non-Current		12.5	5.2	12.2	4.5	4.1
34.8	28.8	38.8	Net Worth		21.7	35.3	36.9	37.2	50.5
100.0	100.0	100.0	Total Liabilties & Net Worth		100.0	100.0	100.0	100.0	100.0
			INCOME DATA						
100.0	100.0	100.0	Net Sales		100.0	100.0	100.0	100.0	100.0
25.2	26.4	25.9	Gross Profit		34.8	39.0	27.1	26.4	18.8
25.6	24.6	24.0	Operating Expenses		35.0	32.4	26.7	25.2	16.8
-.4	1.7	1.8	Operating Profit		-.3	6.5	.4	1.3	2.1
.2	.2	-.3	All Other Expenses (net)		.6	-.4	-.2	-.4	-.3
-.5	1.6	2.1	Profit Before Taxes		-.8	7.0	.6	1.7	2.4
			RATIOS						
2.5	2.2	2.2			2.3	3.4	3.0	2.1	2.1
1.4	1.5	1.5	Current		1.3	1.3	2.0	1.3	1.6
1.0	.9	1.0			1.0	1.0	.8	.9	1.2
1.8	1.7	1.8			1.2	3.0	2.6	1.8	1.4
1.0	1.0	1.0	Quick		1.0	1.0	1.4	1.0	1.0
.6	.6	.7			.6	.5	.8	.7	.7
34 10.8	**33** 11.1	**34** 10.8			**23** 15.9	**25** 14.8	**35** 10.4	**34** 10.7	**36** 10.2
45 8.1	**44** 8.3	**43** 8.5	Sales/Receivables		**29** 12.6	**35** 10.5	**45** 8.1	**46** 8.0	**48** 7.6
60 6.1	**59** 6.2	**56** 6.5			**42** 8.6	**54** 6.8	**54** 6.8	**58** 6.3	**59** 6.2
9 42.4	**8** 44.9	**9** 39.2			**5** 76.1	**2** 207.9	**8** 45.5	**7** 51.9	**11** 32.5
18 20.1	**16** 22.2	**18** 20.2	Cost of Sales/Inventory		**19** 19.6	**13** 28.0	**15** 23.7	**17** 21.9	**24** 15.0
43 8.5	**34** 10.6	**38** 9.7			**26** 14.0	**36** 10.1	**28** 13.0	**30** 12.1	**47** 7.8
18 20.2	**20** 18.5	**21** 17.3			**23** 16.2	**24** 15.1	**16** 22.7	**24** 15.5	**18** 20.7
31 11.9	**30** 12.2	**30** 12.2	Cost of Sales/Payables		**29** 12.4	**33** 10.9	**29** 12.5	**35** 10.3	**27** 13.3
56 6.5	**54** 6.8	**47** 7.7			**41** 8.9	**60** 6.1	**54** 6.8	**63** 5.8	**34** 10.6
6.8	7.0	7.0			6.9	3.9	5.6	8.4	6.8
12.5	13.2	13.3	Sales/Working Capital		34.6	13.4	9.4	23.8	11.6
-207.6	-39.5	181.6			NM	NM	-25.8	-88.4	26.4
5.5	9.0	10.4			17.5	16.7	5.8	11.4	10.2
(195) 1.9	(185) 3.1	(154) 3.4	EBIT/Interest		(10) 1.6	(16) 7.0	(24) 1.8	(42) 2.0	(61) 4.0
-1.3	.1	.7			-3.3	4.4	-1.2	.5	1.4
1.9	3.4	2.6							2.6
(38) 1.4	(41) 1.8	(46) 1.7	Net Profit + Depr., Dep., Amort./Cur. Mat. L/T/D						(27) 2.2
.4	1.1	.9							.9
.6	.7	.6			.4	.7	.5	.6	.6
1.1	1.2	1.1	Fixed/Worth		2.0	1.2	.8	1.3	1.0
4.1	5.6	2.6			-8.8	4.3	6.3	5.5	1.5
.6	.6	.6			.7	.8	.3	.7	.6
1.4	1.5	1.3	Debt/Worth		1.9	1.5	1.3	1.7	1.1
7.3	11.1	3.9			-18.9	8.9	16.7	12.9	1.8
18.0	27.0	21.9			25.7	85.9	17.2	31.0	16.0
(179) 4.7	(160) 9.4	(149) 7.3	% Profit Before Taxes/Tangible Net Worth		(10) -.2	(15) 40.5	(22) 4.4	(38) 4.6	(63) 8.6
-8.1	.8	.0			-33.5	7.3	-8.5	.1	1.5
7.2	9.6	8.5			4.7	25.5	6.6	9.3	7.6
1.5	3.9	3.1	% Profit Before Taxes/Total Assets		-2.5	13.4	1.8	1.9	3.9
-5.2	-1.3	-1.1			-18.5	4.9	-2.3	-.8	.6
7.6	8.0	7.5			12.5	12.0	7.5	7.4	6.3
4.0	4.7	4.8	Sales/Net Fixed Assets		7.1	5.2	5.9	5.4	3.4
2.3	2.8	2.6			5.5	2.8	3.7	3.6	2.4
2.4	2.6	2.4			3.4	3.6	2.6	2.9	1.8
1.7	1.8	1.8	Sales/Total Assets		2.4	1.9	2.2	2.0	1.4
1.2	1.3	1.3			1.8	1.0	1.4	1.5	1.1
3.0	2.7	2.7			2.7	1.1	2.5	2.0	2.9
(193) 5.1	(178) 4.3	(161) 3.6	% Depr., Dep., Amort./Sales		(11) 3.5	(17) 3.5	3.4	(44) 3.5	(61) 4.0
7.5	6.1	5.7			5.4	5.5	4.6	6.4	6.0
1.3	1.4	1.4			4.2	2.1	1.7	1.7	.5
(70) 2.5	(68) 2.9	(62) 2.7	% Officers', Directors' Owners' Comp/Sales		(10) 5.4	(11) 4.6	(14) 2.2	(14) 2.7	(13) 1.0
5.0	5.6	4.7			7.0	7.4	3.3	5.1	1.5
6467927M	**6557853M**	**5530575M**	Net Sales ($)	**1419M**	**27043M**	**71160M**	**192136M**	**781327M**	**4457490M**
4906741M	**4523725M**	**4030917M**	Total Assets ($)	**967M**	**12051M**	**45340M**	**105672M**	**510306M**	**3356581M**

M = $ thousand MM = $ million

See Pages 9 through 22 for Explanation of Ratios and Data

Current Data Sorted by Assets							Comparative Historical Data	
						Type of Statement		
		1	11	4	1	Unqualified	16	14
	4	4	7	1		Reviewed	23	27
	2	1	1			Compiled	15	12
1	4	4				Tax Returns	11	9
	5	11	8	3	2	Other	55	45
	7 (4/1-9/30/13)		68 (10/1/13-3/31/14)				**4/1/09-3/31/10 ALL**	**4/1/10-3/31/11 ALL**
0-500M	**500M-2MM**	**2-10MM**	**10-50MM**	**50-100MM**	**100-250MM**			
1	15	21	27	8	3	**NUMBER OF STATEMENTS**	120	107
%	%	%	%	%	%	**ASSETS**	%	%
	8.9	7.4	5.8			Cash & Equivalents	8.5	8.1
	23.3	21.2	19.1			Trade Receivables (net)	16.3	16.4
	27.3	25.4	23.7			Inventory	21.6	18.1
	3.6	3.1	1.1			All Other Current	4.1	2.9
	63.1	57.1	49.6			Total Current	50.6	45.4
	31.0	31.5	44.0			Fixed Assets (net)	40.1	45.0
	1.7	5.5	2.5			Intangibles (net)	3.2	3.9
	4.2	6.0	3.8			All Other Non-Current	6.2	5.7
	100.0	100.0	100.0			Total	100.0	100.0
						LIABILITIES		
	16.9	9.6	8.3			Notes Payable-Short Term	8.3	7.9
	3.7	2.0	3.3			Cur. Mat.-L.T.D.	7.1	4.8
	14.7	11.8	9.2			Trade Payables	9.5	9.4
	.0	.0	.1			Income Taxes Payable	.0	.1
	5.5	5.8	6.6			All Other Current	8.1	8.3
	40.7	29.2	27.5			Total Current	33.0	30.4
	20.4	16.9	22.0			Long-Term Debt	24.2	23.5
	.1	.3	.2			Deferred Taxes	.6	.4
	8.9	11.2	9.0			All Other Non-Current	9.2	8.1
	30.0	42.5	41.2			Net Worth	32.9	37.6
	100.0	100.0	100.0			Total Liabilities & Net Worth	100.0	100.0
						INCOME DATA		
	100.0	100.0	100.0			Net Sales	100.0	100.0
	31.3	30.5	30.5			Gross Profit	33.4	29.9
	30.5	29.1	26.5			Operating Expenses	32.0	28.5
	.7	1.4	4.0			Operating Profit	1.4	1.5
	.7	1.2	1.0			All Other Expenses (net)	2.2	2.5
	.0	.2	3.0			Profit Before Taxes	-.8	-1.0
						RATIOS		
	2.8	3.8	4.3				3.9	3.2
	1.6	2.3	2.2			Current	1.9	1.9
	1.0	1.1	1.2				1.1	1.1
	1.7	1.7	2.1				1.9	2.0
	.7	1.1	1.0			Quick	.8	.9
	.4	.5	.6				.3	.4
	20 18.4	**28** 12.9	**31** 11.7				**26** 14.0	**27** 13.8
	34 10.8	**39** 9.3	**47** 7.8			Sales/Receivables	**36** 10.1	**40** 9.1
	49 7.5	**63** 5.8	**61** 6.0				**53** 6.9	**57** 6.4
	34 10.7	**35** 10.3	**55** 6.6				**40** 9.2	**44** 8.4
	53 6.9	**73** 5.0	**96** 3.8			Cost of Sales/Inventory	**78** 4.7	**78** 4.7
	101 3.6	**152** 2.4	**135** 2.7				**127** 2.9	**115** 3.2
	15 24.4	**15** 24.0	**19** 19.1				**14** 26.3	**17** 22.1
	34 10.6	**38** 9.6	**26** 14.1			Cost of Sales/Payables	**26** 14.0	**26** 14.0
	49 7.5	**69** 5.3	**50** 7.3				**43** 8.4	**43** 8.4
	3.7	4.3	3.6				3.2	4.0
	8.0	5.4	5.9			Sales/Working Capital	6.1	7.3
	-81.4	40.0	19.2				62.8	45.4
	10.8	5.6	7.9				4.4	4.8
	(12) 5.5	(18) 3.5	(26) 3.9			EBIT/Interest	(105) 1.5	(93) 1.1
	-.8	.0	1.3				-1.6	-1.7
							2.7	8.3
						Net Profit + Depr., Dep., Amort./Cur. Mat. L/T/D	(28) 1.4	(21) 2.2
							.2	1.1
	.4	.4	.7				.5	.7
	1.3	.7	1.1			Fixed/Worth	1.2	1.4
	5.4	1.6	1.7				3.6	3.3
	.4	.5	.4				.5	.6
	2.6	2.0	1.7			Debt/Worth	1.6	1.6
	18.5	4.2	7.8				6.1	7.1
	62.6	22.2	20.9				16.2	14.2
	(12) 27.6	(18) 7.7	(24) 11.4			% Profit Before Taxes/Tangible Net Worth	(101) 5.5	(88) 3.3
	-4.1	-4.5	4.9				-10.0	-11.1
	14.9	8.4	7.3				6.1	6.4
	10.9	3.8	4.6			% Profit Before Taxes/Total Assets	1.6	.2
	-7.4	-2.7	.9				-6.5	-6.1
	16.2	9.4	5.6				8.1	5.1
	9.7	5.9	2.9			Sales/Net Fixed Assets	3.6	2.6
	5.8	3.2	1.8				1.8	1.5
	2.7	2.2	1.7				1.9	1.8
	2.4	1.7	1.4			Sales/Total Assets	1.2	1.1
	1.9	1.1	1.0				.9	.8
	1.5	1.7	2.8				2.7	3.1
	(14) 2.1	(20) 3.0	(24) 5.1			% Depr., Dep., Amort./Sales	(105) 4.9	(87) 5.7
	4.9	5.8	6.7				7.6	7.7
							2.1	1.5
						% Officers', Directors' Owners' Comp/Sales	(36) 3.4	(30) 2.8
							5.5	4.9
566M	45217M	169642M	790012M	517957M	266533M	Net Sales ($)	3167171M	2805353M
154M	20370M	114307M	610139M	520969M	456556M	Total Assets ($)	3304976M	2816022M

M = $ thousand MM = $ million

See Pages 9 through 22 for Explanation of Ratios and Data

Comparative Historical Data				Current Data Sorted by Sales					
			Type of Statement						
14	21	17	Unqualified					4	13
19	17	16	Reviewed		2	3	2	5	4
9	10	4	Compiled		2		1	1	
8	7	9	Tax Returns	1	2	2	2	2	
41	30	29	Other	2	2	5	5	4	11
4/1/11-3/31/12 ALL	**4/1/12-3/31/13 ALL**	**4/1/13-3/31/14 ALL**		**7 (4/1-9/30/13)**		**68 (10/1/13-3/31/14)**			
				0-1MM	**1-3MM**	**3-5MM**	**5-10MM**	**10-25MM**	**25MM & OVER**
91	85	75	**NUMBER OF STATEMENTS**	3	8	10	10	16	28
%	%	%	**ASSETS**	%	%	%	%	%	%
7.8	8.5	7.2	Cash & Equivalents			13.7	4.0	6.5	6.6
17.3	18.5	20.4	Trade Receivables (net)			23.7	27.4	14.3	19.2
18.9	20.2	23.2	Inventory			28.3	19.5	30.1	19.9
2.7	2.8	2.4	All Other Current			.8	.7	.3	2.2
46.8	50.0	53.2	Total Current			66.4	51.6	51.3	47.9
40.9	39.6	37.1	Fixed Assets (net)			22.2	42.0	42.8	39.8
4.7	4.8	3.5	Intangibles (net)			7.0	2.7	.5	4.1
7.6	5.6	6.2	All Other Non-Current			4.3	3.7	5.4	8.2
100.0	100.0	100.0	Total			100.0	100.0	100.0	100.0
			LIABILITIES						
8.2	7.8	9.9	Notes Payable-Short Term			12.8	9.8	9.6	7.5
5.1	3.6	3.5	Cur. Mat.-L.T.D.			2.3	2.6	2.8	3.2
10.6	10.5	10.9	Trade Payables			15.0	17.4	7.2	9.5
.1	.2	.1	Income Taxes Payable			.0	.1	.0	.1
9.1	8.3	5.6	All Other Current			7.2	6.4	6.5	4.8
33.2	30.4	30.0	Total Current			37.3	36.4	26.1	25.1
21.2	18.5	21.1	Long-Term Debt			19.3	17.4	16.6	19.5
.7	.3	.5	Deferred Taxes			.3	.4	.3	1.0
10.2	7.7	8.4	All Other Non-Current			4.7	11.4	17.2	3.7
34.7	43.0	40.1	Net Worth			38.4	34.5	39.8	50.7
100.0	100.0	100.0	Total Liabilities & Net Worth			100.0	100.0	100.0	100.0
			INCOME DATA						
100.0	100.0	100.0	Net Sales			100.0	100.0	100.0	100.0
30.1	35.4	30.2	Gross Profit			34.6	30.2	24.2	29.9
29.3	30.6	27.7	Operating Expenses			31.6	28.6	22.2	25.2
.9	4.8	2.5	Operating Profit			3.0	1.6	2.0	4.7
2.4	1.2	.9	All Other Expenses (net)			.0	.9	.5	.6
-1.5	3.6	1.6	Profit Before Taxes			3.0	.7	1.5	4.1
			RATIOS						
2.8	4.0	3.8				3.9	2.2	4.8	4.2
1.7	2.3	2.1	Current			2.5	1.4	2.7	2.2
1.0	1.1	1.1				1.1	1.1	1.2	1.3
1.8	2.1	1.7				2.3	1.2	1.6	2.3
.8	1.0	1.1	Quick			1.7	1.0	1.0	1.1
.3	.5	.6				.4	.5	.5	.6
31 11.7	**26** 14.2	**30** 12.2				**22** 16.6	**26** 14.2	**30** 12.1	**33** 10.9
38 9.5	**40** 9.1	**42** 8.7	Sales/Receivables			**36** 10.2	**43** 8.4	**35** 10.5	**47** 7.8
51 7.1	**57** 6.4	**61** 6.0				**54** 6.8	**87** 4.2	**53** 6.9	**61** 6.0
46 8.0	**36** 10.0	**49** 7.5				**18** 20.1	**13** 27.8	**73** 5.0	**55** 6.6
73 5.0	**79** 4.6	**81** 4.5	Cost of Sales/Inventory			**78** 4.7	**54** 6.8	**126** 2.9	**81** 4.5
122 3.0	**126** 2.9	**118** 3.1				**99** 3.7	**83** 4.4	**203** 1.8	**104** 3.5
18 19.8	**17** 21.2	**19** 19.1				**10** 35.2	**24** 15.2	**13** 28.7	**21** 17.0
29 12.8	**27** 13.5	**28** 13.1	Cost of Sales/Payables			**32** 11.3	**46** 8.0	**23** 16.0	**28** 13.0
51 7.1	**47** 7.7	**50** 7.3				**69** 5.3	**66** 5.5	**40** 9.2	**47** 7.7
3.9	3.8	3.7				3.6	9.3	2.1	3.7
8.3	5.8	6.9	Sales/Working Capital			6.2	21.4	4.4	7.2
-68.3	42.0	25.8				NM	57.5	23.6	13.5
5.5	6.9	7.8						11.4	8.0
(85) 1.2	(75) 2.6	(68) 3.6	EBIT/Interest					(15) 2.3	5.3
-1.3	.4	.8						-.6	1.6
3.0	3.3	3.6							
(24) 1.1	(16) 2.1	(13) 2.0	Net Profit + Depr., Dep., Amort./Cur. Mat. L/T/D						
-.2	.8	1.1							
.6	.6	.5				.3	.6	.6	.5
1.2	.9	1.1	Fixed/Worth			.5	1.1	1.0	.9
4.9	1.9	1.7				-51.5	1.8	3.2	1.3
.7	.4	.4				.3	.7	.4	.4
2.0	1.3	1.4	Debt/Worth			1.6	1.8	2.0	1.1
17.5	4.0	5.7				-159.5	4.1	6.6	1.9
15.6	19.8	22.9						14.7	17.4
(73) 3.5	(72) 9.9	(65) 10.1	% Profit Before Taxes/Tangible Net Worth					(14) 6.2	(27) 11.0
-7.4	-1.1	.1						-2.1	3.3
6.1	7.7	9.4				11.7	10.7	5.7	8.0
.4	4.0	4.4	% Profit Before Taxes/Total Assets			9.0	4.6	2.4	5.0
-5.1	-1.0	-.2				-2.0	-.6	-2.4	1.4
7.0	6.8	9.7				13.2	8.2	6.6	5.6
2.8	3.7	3.8	Sales/Net Fixed Assets			10.4	4.9	2.9	3.0
1.7	2.1	2.1				8.6	3.4	1.5	1.9
1.8	2.0	2.2				2.8	2.5	1.7	1.6
1.3	1.4	1.5	Sales/Total Assets			2.3	2.2	1.2	1.3
.8	.9	1.0				1.8	1.5	.8	.9
2.8	2.5	1.9						2.5	2.0
(80) 5.2	(74) 4.3	(68) 3.4	% Depr., Dep., Amort./Sales					(15) 4.8	(24) 4.9
7.6	7.3	6.7						6.8	6.9
1.9	2.7	2.2							
(24) 3.8	(28) 4.5	(24) 3.9	% Officers', Directors' Owners' Comp/Sales						
5.2	7.0	5.7							
2307420M	1732239M	1789927M	Net Sales ($)	2070M	17103M	38750M	70054M	241222M	1420728M
2270615M	1769843M	1722495M	Total Assets ($)	4973M	20499M	24745M	38406M	248590M	1385282M

M = $ thousand MM = $ million

See Pages 9 through 22 for Explanation of Ratios and Data

Current Data Sorted by Assets							Comparative Historical Data	
						Type of Statement		
			1	2		Unqualified	6	6
		1	1			Reviewed	3	3
		4	1			Compiled	5	5
	2	2				Tax Returns	1	1
	2	3	5	1	1	Other	8	14
	5 (4/1-9/30/13)		21 (10/1/13-3/31/14)				**4/1/09-3/31/10**	**4/1/10-3/31/11**
0-500M	**500M-2MM**	**2-10MM**	**10-50MM**	**50-100MM**	**100-250MM**		**ALL**	**ALL**
	4	10	8	3	1	**NUMBER OF STATEMENTS**	23	29
%	%	%	%	%	%	**ASSETS**	%	%
DATA NOT AVAILABLE		15.2				Cash & Equivalents	9.7	9.7
		27.4				Trade Receivables (net)	21.1	20.1
		17.1				Inventory	17.4	20.5
		1.2				All Other Current	1.4	2.2
		60.9				Total Current	49.6	52.5
		32.8				Fixed Assets (net)	41.3	34.8
		2.9				Intangibles (net)	3.7	6.1
		3.4				All Other Non-Current	5.4	6.6
		100.0				Total	100.0	100.0
						LIABILITIES		
		4.7				Notes Payable-Short Term	4.8	9.4
		1.2				Cur. Mat.-L.T.D.	3.3	3.2
		13.0				Trade Payables	9.1	9.3
		.0				Income Taxes Payable	.2	.0
		2.4				All Other Current	3.7	5.2
		21.3				Total Current	21.1	27.1
		13.4				Long-Term Debt	25.3	16.0
		.3				Deferred Taxes	.6	1.2
		13.2				All Other Non-Current	4.6	9.5
		51.7				Net Worth	48.3	46.2
		100.0				Total Liabilties & Net Worth	100.0	100.0
						INCOME DATA		
		100.0				Net Sales	100.0	100.0
		26.6				Gross Profit	25.4	24.5
		21.2				Operating Expenses	23.9	23.5
		5.4				Operating Profit	1.5	1.0
		-.1				All Other Expenses (net)	1.2	2.0
		5.5				Profit Before Taxes	.3	-1.0
						RATIOS		
		5.6					4.6	4.0
		3.4				Current	2.6	2.3
		2.7					1.5	1.4
		4.1					3.4	2.1
		2.5				Quick	1.1	1.0
		1.5					.7	.6
		36 10.0					**39** 9.5	**37** 9.8
		47 7.8				Sales/Receivables	**51** 7.1	**50** 7.3
		65 5.6					**61** 6.0	**67** 5.5
		18 19.9					**41** 8.9	**44** 8.3
		51 7.2				Cost of Sales/Inventory	**74** 4.9	**73** 5.0
		83 4.4					**92** 4.0	**91** 4.0
		18 20.8					**13** 28.7	**14** 26.7
		24 15.0				Cost of Sales/Payables	**23** 15.9	**26** 14.2
		35 10.3					**42** 8.8	**37** 9.8
		3.0					3.2	3.5
		4.9				Sales/Working Capital	4.5	5.7
		8.4					10.4	14.7
							5.2	4.6
						EBIT/Interest	1.0	(28) .2
							-.1	-2.0
								19.3
						Net Profit + Depr., Dep., Amort./Cur. Mat. L/T/D		(10) 2.1
								.5
		.3					.5	.6
		.6				Fixed/Worth	1.1	1.0
		1.6					1.6	1.6
		.3					.4	.6
		.9				Debt/Worth	1.0	.8
		4.6					3.5	3.4
		53.6					21.2	20.2
		13.5				% Profit Before Taxes/Tangible Net Worth	(22) 1.0	(25) -.7
		7.9					-9.7	-8.5
		16.9					5.7	9.8
		6.8				% Profit Before Taxes/Total Assets	.1	-.7
		2.6					-2.9	-4.9
		18.3					4.7	8.1
		4.0				Sales/Net Fixed Assets	3.3	4.0
		2.3					2.0	2.2
		2.8					1.8	2.1
		1.4				Sales/Total Assets	1.4	1.6
		1.2					1.0	.9
		.9					3.4	2.9
		4.0				% Depr., Dep., Amort./Sales	(22) 5.0	(26) 4.8
		6.5					7.2	5.8
							1.2	1.5
						% Officers', Directors' Owners' Comp/Sales	(12) 2.2	(10) 2.6
							4.8	5.7
	8467M	72048M	251192M	289209M	113269M	Net Sales ($)	700018M	1094833M
	3464M	41747M	230102M	243774M	114044M	Total Assets ($)	568819M	855052M

M = $ thousand MM = $ million

See Pages 9 through 22 for Explanation of Ratios and Data

Comparative Historical Data							Current Data Sorted by Sales					
						Type of Statement						
	3		4		3	Unqualified						3
	4		2		2	Reviewed				1	1	
	5		3		5	Compiled			2	2		1
	1		3		4	Tax Returns		2	1		1	
	14		18		12	Other		2		2	4	4
	4/1/11-3/31/12		**4/1/12-3/31/13**		**4/1/13-3/31/14**			**5 (4/1-9/30/13)**		**21 (10/1/13-3/31/14)**		
	ALL		**ALL**		**ALL**		**0-1MM**	**1-3MM**	**3-5MM**	**5-10MM**	**10-25MM**	**25MM & OVER**
	27		30		26	**NUMBER OF STATEMENTS**		4	3	5	6	8
	%		%		%	**ASSETS**	%	%	%	%	%	%
	14.0		6.0		9.8	Cash & Equivalents	**DATA NOT AVAILABLE**					
	17.6		20.7		22.5	Trade Receivables (net)						
	19.5		21.2		17.4	Inventory						
	4.2		2.4		1.6	All Other Current						
	55.3		50.3		51.3	Total Current						
	36.8		40.5		39.5	Fixed Assets (net)						
	2.9		3.2		4.3	Intangibles (net)						
	5.0		6.0		5.0	All Other Non-Current						
	100.0		100.0		100.0	Total						
						LIABILITIES						
	4.9		8.1		8.6	Notes Payable-Short Term						
	2.8		3.5		2.0	Cur. Mat.-L.T.D.						
	8.2		12.6		11.5	Trade Payables						
	.6		.2		.1	Income Taxes Payable						
	6.0		4.2		4.0	All Other Current						
	22.4		28.7		26.2	Total Current						
	14.5		17.1		21.0	Long-Term Debt						
	1.0		.9		.3	Deferred Taxes						
	7.0		11.0		16.2	All Other Non-Current						
	55.1		42.3		36.3	Net Worth						
	100.0		100.0		100.0	Total Liabilities & Net Worth						
						INCOME DATA						
	100.0		100.0		100.0	Net Sales						
	27.2		25.5		25.0	Gross Profit						
	24.7		21.5		19.6	Operating Expenses						
	2.5		4.0		5.4	Operating Profit						
	-.2		.9		.8	All Other Expenses (net)						
	2.7		3.1		4.6	Profit Before Taxes						
						RATIOS						
	4.8		2.4		3.4							
	2.9		1.7		2.6	Current						
	1.8		1.3		1.3							
	3.5		1.3		2.4							
	1.4		.8		1.2	Quick						
	.8		.6		.8							
31	11.9	**35**	10.5	**38**	9.7							
49	7.4	**49**	7.4	**46**	7.9	Sales/Receivables						
68	5.4	**73**	5.0	**64**	5.7							
38	9.5	**40**	9.1	**33**	10.9							
83	4.4	**78**	4.7	**59**	6.2	Cost of Sales/Inventory						
104	3.5	**99**	3.7	**94**	3.9							
19	18.8	**24**	15.3	**15**	24.6							
31	11.6	**33**	10.9	**26**	14.2	Cost of Sales/Payables						
42	8.6	**56**	6.5	**39**	9.3							
	2.5		4.9		3.9							
	4.1		6.8		5.8	Sales/Working Capital						
	8.9		13.1		21.1							
	8.9		6.9		19.7							
(24)	2.1	(28)	3.0	(24)	7.5	EBIT/Interest						
	-1.5		.4		1.2							
						Net Profit + Depr., Dep., Amort./Cur. Mat. L/T/D						
	.4		.7		.5							
	.8		1.0		1.0	Fixed/Worth						
	1.1		1.3		2.3							
	.4		.7		.7							
	.8		1.4		1.5	Debt/Worth						
	1.6		2.9		4.7							
	25.4		27.9		43.7							
	5.5	(29)	7.6	(23)	17.3	% Profit Before Taxes/Tangible Net Worth						
	-6.7		-2.1		3.3							
	10.1		9.5		15.8							
	3.5		3.3		8.6	% Profit Before Taxes/Total Assets						
	-3.7		-.6		1.2							
	6.0		6.6		9.2							
	3.7		2.7		3.3	Sales/Net Fixed Assets						
	2.3		2.0		2.2							
	1.9		1.9		2.0							
	1.2		1.2		1.4	Sales/Total Assets						
	.9		1.0		1.0							
	2.8		2.5		1.5							
	4.4	(29)	4.3	(24)	3.8	% Depr., Dep., Amort./Sales						
	6.0		5.4		6.1							
	1.7		.7									
(11)	3.1	(11)	2.5			% Officers', Directors' Owners' Comp/Sales						
	6.3		4.9									
	748091M		**1265747M**		**734185M**	Net Sales ($)		**8467M**	**10521M**	**36587M**	**108399M**	**570211M**
	723373M		**1076983M**		**633131M**	Total Assets ($)		**3464M**	**9244M**	**24570M**	**146402M**	**449451M**

M = $ thousand MM = $ million

See Pages 9 through 22 for Explanation of Ratios and Data

Current Data Sorted by Assets							Comparative Historical Data	
						Type of Statement		
		4	7	4	2	Unqualified	29	25
1	3	13	11	2		Reviewed	35	30
1	2	14			1	Compiled	23	25
6	4	6				Tax Returns	16	19
1	6	16	18	2	1	Other	65	52
	16 (4/1-9/30/13)		109 (10/1/13-3/31/14)				**4/1/09-3/31/10 ALL**	**4/1/10-3/31/11 ALL**
0-500M	**500M-2MM**	**2-10MM**	**10-50MM**	**50-100MM**	**100-250MM**			
9	15	53	36	8	4	**NUMBER OF STATEMENTS**	168	151
%	%	%	%	%	%	**ASSETS**	%	%
	8.0	9.0	9.5			Cash & Equivalents	10.2	12.1
	29.0	26.0	31.1			Trade Receivables (net)	24.5	24.8
	24.4	18.0	13.7			Inventory	17.0	14.8
	4.5	3.5	2.8			All Other Current	3.0	3.6
	66.0	56.6	57.1			Total Current	54.6	55.3
	24.8	35.0	35.1			Fixed Assets (net)	36.4	35.4
	7.2	3.2	2.6			Intangibles (net)	2.6	3.1
	2.0	5.2	5.3			All Other Non-Current	6.4	6.2
	100.0	100.0	100.0			Total	100.0	100.0
						LIABILITIES		
	4.1	6.7	8.7			Notes Payable-Short Term	9.1	8.9
	3.2	4.2	3.8			Cur. Mat.-L.T.D.	5.4	4.4
	12.4	12.8	13.2			Trade Payables	12.4	12.0
	.0	.0	.4			Income Taxes Payable	.4	.4
	15.6	7.5	8.7			All Other Current	11.0	7.9
	35.3	31.1	34.8			Total Current	38.3	33.7
	19.9	18.3	11.9			Long-Term Debt	18.3	20.4
	.0	.4	1.3			Deferred Taxes	.5	.4
	8.1	7.1	4.1			All Other Non-Current	5.2	4.8
	36.7	43.0	47.8			Net Worth	37.7	40.7
	100.0	100.0	100.0			Total Liabilties & Net Worth	100.0	100.0
						INCOME DATA		
	100.0	100.0	100.0			Net Sales	100.0	100.0
	39.3	32.8	24.2			Gross Profit	31.1	31.9
	30.1	26.5	18.0			Operating Expenses	28.1	28.0
	9.2	6.3	6.2			Operating Profit	3.1	3.8
	3.2	1.1	.5			All Other Expenses (net)	1.2	.8
	5.9	5.2	5.7			Profit Before Taxes	1.9	3.0
						RATIOS		
	3.5	3.6	2.9				2.7	3.2
	2.9	1.7	1.5			Current	1.7	1.7
	.9	1.1	1.2				1.1	1.1
	2.6	2.0	2.1				2.1	2.2
	.9	1.1	1.1			Quick	1.0	1.1
	.5	.6	.7				.5	.6
	24 14.9	**24** 14.9	**54** 6.8				**33** 11.0	**36** 10.2
	45 8.2	**46** 8.0	**63** 5.8			Sales/Receivables	**46** 8.0	**54** 6.8
	60 6.1	**74** 4.9	**83** 4.4				**68** 5.4	**71** 5.2
	13 28.7	**14** 26.8	**16** 22.5				**19** 19.7	**14** 25.2
	40 9.1	**51** 7.1	**39** 9.4			Cost of Sales/Inventory	**44** 8.3	**44** 8.2
	126 2.9	**99** 3.7	**69** 5.3				**89** 4.1	**85** 4.3
	3 145.7	**16** 23.0	**18** 20.0				**16** 22.6	**16** 23.2
	21 17.5	**30** 12.1	**40** 9.1			Cost of Sales/Payables	**29** 12.6	**31** 11.8
	55 6.6	**56** 6.5	**58** 6.3				**46** 8.0	**51** 7.2
	3.6	3.9	3.8				4.3	3.9
	6.5	8.2	7.7			Sales/Working Capital	8.1	7.3
	-51.1	29.6	16.3				47.9	48.1
	23.3	25.3	24.4				9.0	8.8
	(10) 4.3	(48) 4.2	(33) 6.8			EBIT/Interest	(150) 2.1	(134) 2.1
	1.8	1.3	2.3				-.2	-.6
		4.4	7.2				7.7	5.1
		(11) 3.0	(16) 3.2			Net Profit + Depr., Dep., Amort./Cur. Mat. L/T/D	(42) 1.8	(32) 2.0
		.8	2.2				.8	.4
	.0	.4	.4				.5	.4
	.4	.8	.8			Fixed/Worth	.8	.8
	5.5	1.9	1.5				3.0	2.6
	.3	.5	.4				.6	.6
	1.7	1.3	1.5			Debt/Worth	1.2	1.2
	-12.1	4.3	2.7				5.5	4.6
	51.1	38.6	27.6				28.3	33.8
	(11) 32.9	(50) 11.6	(35) 14.2			% Profit Before Taxes/Tangible Net Worth	(143) 8.9	(132) 9.6
	8.8	1.2	7.9				-3.6	-4.8
	27.4	19.8	11.2				12.3	12.4
	11.4	4.8	6.6			% Profit Before Taxes/Total Assets	2.4	3.5
	2.7	.3	3.1				-2.5	-1.8
	110.4	10.7	7.1				9.2	10.9
	9.7	6.3	4.4			Sales/Net Fixed Assets	4.5	4.8
	4.8	3.3	2.8				2.8	2.7
	4.3	2.7	2.0				2.1	2.1
	2.4	2.0	1.6			Sales/Total Assets	1.6	1.6
	1.2	1.2	1.1				1.2	1.1
		1.8	2.1				2.1	2.3
		(46) 3.3	(35) 2.8			% Depr., Dep., Amort./Sales	(142) 3.5	(130) 3.8
		4.4	4.0				5.5	5.8
		1.1					2.1	1.5
		(21) 2.0				% Officers', Directors' Owners' Comp/Sales	(45) 4.5	(54) 3.3
		4.3					5.9	5.7
12453M	56681M	493885M	1338095M	814998M	966640M	Net Sales ($)	5775116M	4874716M
3199M	20381M	269797M	872681M	562562M	688042M	Total Assets ($)	3950254M	3661902M

M = $ thousand MM = $ million

See Pages 9 through 22 for Explanation of Ratios and Data

Comparative Historical Data				Current Data Sorted by Sales					
			Type of Statement						
20	18	17	Unqualified				1	4	12
39	23	30	Reviewed	1	3		6	12	8
22	18	18	Compiled	1	1	5	8	2	1
25	12	16	Tax Returns	3	7		6		
56	37	44	Other	1	3	4	6	15	15
4/1/11-3/31/12	**4/1/12-3/31/13**	**4/1/13-3/31/14**			**16 (4/1-9/30/13)**		**109 (10/1/13-3/31/14)**		
ALL	**ALL**	**ALL**		**0-1MM**	**1-3MM**	**3-5MM**	**5-10MM**	**10-25MM**	**25MM & OVER**
162	108	125	**NUMBER OF STATEMENTS**	6	14	9	27	33	36
%	%	%	**ASSETS**	%	%	%	%	%	%
9.4	8.3	10.2	Cash & Equivalents		17.4		8.9	8.9	9.0
26.9	28.8	27.3	Trade Receivables (net)		19.9		26.5	29.9	31.3
15.0	19.2	17.4	Inventory		25.5		21.3	13.2	15.2
3.3	2.9	3.8	All Other Current		.4		2.8	2.0	4.3
54.6	59.1	58.8	Total Current		63.2		59.5	53.9	59.9
34.5	30.5	33.3	Fixed Assets (net)		32.2		29.0	35.9	33.8
4.7	4.2	3.2	Intangibles (net)		1.1		6.8	3.8	1.4
6.2	6.2	4.8	All Other Non-Current		3.5		4.7	6.4	4.9
100.0	100.0	100.0	Total		100.0		100.0	100.0	100.0
			LIABILITIES						
11.3	8.1	6.8	Notes Payable-Short Term		6.9		5.4	10.3	6.6
3.4	3.4	3.6	Cur. Mat.-L.T.D.		4.4		3.4	4.3	3.5
13.5	11.7	12.7	Trade Payables		12.8		14.4	12.4	13.3
.2	.0	.1	Income Taxes Payable		.0		.0	.1	.4
8.4	7.9	10.1	All Other Current		3.4		10.3	8.0	10.6
36.8	31.1	33.3	Total Current		27.5		33.5	35.1	34.4
18.2	19.0	16.7	Long-Term Debt		35.2		15.4	14.7	11.5
.5	.4	.7	Deferred Taxes		.1		.0	1.2	1.3
6.9	5.7	6.2	All Other Non-Current		15.4		2.9	6.9	4.9
37.6	43.8	43.1	Net Worth		21.9		48.2	42.2	47.9
100.0	100.0	100.0	Total Liabilties & Net Worth		100.0		100.0	100.0	100.0
			INCOME DATA						
100.0	100.0	100.0	Net Sales		100.0		100.0	100.0	100.0
30.9	30.1	30.2	Gross Profit		37.5		31.8	28.1	23.4
27.6	25.9	24.0	Operating Expenses		31.8		26.2	21.9	17.6
3.3	4.3	6.2	Operating Profit		5.7		5.6	6.2	5.8
1.0	.4	1.0	All Other Expenses (net)		2.0		.9	1.3	.1
2.3	3.8	5.2	Profit Before Taxes		3.7		4.6	4.9	5.7
			RATIOS						
2.8	3.7	3.3			3.5		4.3	2.6	2.8
1.5	1.9	1.7	Current		2.7		1.8	1.4	1.7
1.0	1.3	1.2			1.4		1.1	1.0	1.3
1.8	2.1	2.1			2.5		2.1	2.2	1.6
(161) 1.0	1.2	1.0	Quick		1.2		1.1	.9	1.1
.6	.7	.6			.6		.6	.6	.7
33 11.0	**33** 11.2	**29** 12.4			**17** 21.3		**21** 17.5	**39** 9.4	**56** 6.5
54 6.7	**56** 6.5	**55** 6.6	Sales/Receivables		**51** 7.2		**44** 8.3	**54** 6.8	**69** 5.3
78 4.7	**72** 5.1	**76** 4.8			**70** 5.2		**65** 5.6	**76** 4.8	**83** 4.4
12 31.2	**15** 24.2	**13** 27.8			**16** 22.8		**14** 26.9	**9** 40.4	**15** 23.9
39 9.3	**46** 7.9	**40** 9.1	Cost of Sales/Inventory		**50** 7.3		**61** 6.0	**31** 11.7	**38** 9.7
79 4.6	**99** 3.7	**83** 4.4			**81** 4.5		**96** 3.8	**64** 5.7	**72** 5.1
17 21.7	**15** 24.3	**16** 23.1			**22** 16.9		**12** 29.9	**16** 23.0	**20** 18.6
33 11.1	**27** 13.4	**31** 11.6	Cost of Sales/Payables		**41** 8.9		**30** 12.1	**24** 15.2	**35** 10.3
55 6.6	**46** 7.9	**52** 7.0			**73** 5.0		**47** 7.7	**60** 6.1	**51** 7.1
4.9	4.2	4.0			3.1		4.3	5.2	3.8
9.9	6.9	7.6	Sales/Working Capital		6.3		8.9	10.8	6.6
127.8	14.3	22.9			14.5		23.6	NM	13.6
6.2	8.8	20.7			13.0		22.2	31.6	25.4
(147) 2.3	(94) 3.0	(109) 4.5	EBIT/Interest		3.8		(22) 4.3	(31) 2.6	(33) 7.2
.2	1.3	1.9			1.8		1.0	1.7	2.8
8.7	4.4	5.6						6.3	7.0
(30) 1.5	(26) 2.5	(34) 3.1	Net Profit + Depr., Dep., Amort./Cur. Mat. L/T/D					(10) 2.7	(18) 3.5
.5	1.3	1.8						1.7	2.8
.5	.3	.4			.2		.4	.4	.5
.8	.7	.7	Fixed/Worth		1.8		.6	1.1	.7
2.3	1.5	1.9			NM		1.4	2.2	1.2
.6	.5	.5			.9		.4	.7	.5
1.7	1.3	1.5	Debt/Worth		4.3		1.1	1.8	1.4
6.9	3.0	3.5			NM		2.9	3.4	2.0
28.4	26.7	36.5			84.6		45.2	26.4	30.8
(137) 8.0	(99) 12.0	(115) 15.4	% Profit Before Taxes/Tangible Net Worth		(11) 30.3		(25) 13.9	(31) 15.2	13.9
-1.6	3.0	4.8			5.1		1.4	2.4	7.7
10.0	15.1	17.7			22.0		19.2	19.3	13.0
2.6	4.3	5.9	% Profit Before Taxes/Total Assets		6.6		4.8	3.3	7.5
-1.1	.7	1.5			2.4		-.3	1.3	3.5
11.2	13.7	10.7			52.8		15.2	9.9	8.2
5.4	6.6	5.6	Sales/Net Fixed Assets		7.7		8.7	5.6	4.6
3.0	3.6	3.1			1.6		4.4	3.4	3.0
2.4	2.4	2.5			4.3		3.0	2.7	2.0
1.7	1.9	1.8	Sales/Total Assets		2.1		2.1	2.0	1.5
1.2	1.4	1.2			.8		1.3	1.3	1.3
1.7	1.9	1.9			1.7		1.9	2.0	1.9
(142) 3.4	(92) 3.3	(106) 3.0	% Depr., Dep., Amort./Sales		(10) 2.7		(21) 3.6	(30) 3.0	(35) 2.7
5.1	4.6	4.0			5.5		4.8	3.8	3.6
1.3	1.3	1.4					1.6	.7	
(64) 3.1	(38) 2.5	(42) 2.3	% Officers', Directors' Owners' Comp/Sales				(15) 2.0	(10) 2.1	
5.6	5.7	4.9					4.5	5.3	
3586337M	**3214111M**	**3682752M**	Net Sales ($)	**3834M**	**27727M**	**39005M**	**195013M**	**490066M**	**2927107M**
2448342M	**2009033M**	**2416662M**	Total Assets ($)	**5521M**	**27779M**	**26400M**	**104105M**	**313642M**	**1939215M**

M = $ thousand MM = $ million

See Pages 9 through 22 for Explanation of Ratios and Data

Current Data Sorted by Assets							Comparative Historical Data	
						Type of Statement		
		2	2		3	Unqualified	8	9
		10	4			Reviewed	12	21
	2	1				Compiled	6	12
	2	5				Tax Returns	5	5
1	3	8	5	6		Other	27	28
	8 (4/1-9/30/13)		46 (10/1/13-3/31/14)				4/1/09-3/31/10	4/1/10-3/31/11
0-500M	500M-2MM	2-10MM	10-50MM	50-100MM	100-250MM		ALL	ALL
1	7	26	11	6	3	**NUMBER OF STATEMENTS**	58	75
%	%	%	%	%	%	**ASSETS**	%	%
		8.0	13.6			Cash & Equivalents	7.8	11.5
		26.9	18.9			Trade Receivables (net)	23.5	28.0
		35.9	24.1			Inventory	30.4	27.8
		1.9	1.0			All Other Current	4.3	2.0
		72.8	57.7			Total Current	65.9	69.4
		16.7	32.9			Fixed Assets (net)	22.1	22.7
		3.9	1.1			Intangibles (net)	3.6	2.6
		6.6	8.3			All Other Non-Current	8.3	5.4
		100.0	100.0			Total	100.0	100.0
						LIABILITIES		
		12.2	8.1			Notes Payable-Short Term	13.1	10.6
		3.9	.8			Cur. Mat.-L.T.D.	4.5	4.4
		19.7	9.5			Trade Payables	13.1	14.8
		.0	.1			Income Taxes Payable	.7	.2
		8.3	10.0			All Other Current	7.5	7.8
		44.1	28.4			Total Current	38.8	37.8
		8.5	10.8			Long-Term Debt	12.0	12.2
		.1	.7			Deferred Taxes	.5	.3
		5.6	6.5			All Other Non-Current	7.5	8.6
		41.7	53.6			Net Worth	41.2	41.2
		100.0	100.0			Total Liabilties & Net Worth	100.0	100.0
						INCOME DATA		
		100.0	100.0			Net Sales	100.0	100.0
		30.1	33.3			Gross Profit	28.5	31.0
		25.2	26.6			Operating Expenses	26.7	23.6
		4.9	6.7			Operating Profit	1.8	7.5
		.7	1.0			All Other Expenses (net)	1.3	.8
		4.2	5.7			Profit Before Taxes	.5	6.7
						RATIOS		
		3.7	3.6				2.9	3.5
		1.6	1.7			Current	1.9	1.9
		1.2	1.3				1.2	1.4
		1.4	2.3				1.6	2.2
		.9	1.1			Quick	.9	1.0
		.4	.6				.5	.7
		29 12.6	**17** 21.3				**32** 11.4	**35** 10.4
		45 8.1	**45** 8.1			Sales/Receivables	**51** 7.2	**46** 8.0
		62 5.9	**60** 6.1				**64** 5.7	**57** 6.5
		36 10.0	**43** 8.5				**47** 7.7	**36** 10.1
		81 4.5	**85** 4.3			Cost of Sales/Inventory	**91** 4.0	**69** 5.3
		135 2.7	**91** 4.0				**143** 2.6	**115** 3.2
		19 19.5	**12** 31.3				**16** 22.8	**17** 22.1
		38 9.6	**20** 17.9			Cost of Sales/Payables	**27** 13.6	**30** 12.0
		56 6.5	**30** 12.3				**46** 8.0	**44** 8.3
		3.9	3.3				3.0	3.6
		8.1	9.4			Sales/Working Capital	6.9	7.1
		17.2	15.1				16.2	16.5
		19.0					15.2	22.5
		(25) 6.4				EBIT/Interest	(53) 2.9	(66) 7.6
		1.1					-2.0	1.7
							3.6	10.8
						Net Profit + Depr., Dep., Amort./Cur. Mat. L/T/D	(13) .1	(20) 2.8
							-1.1	2.1
		.2	.4				.2	.2
		.4	.6			Fixed/Worth	.4	.4
		1.0	.9				2.1	1.2
		.7	.4				.4	.5
		2.0	.9			Debt/Worth	1.2	1.1
		4.8	1.6				5.0	3.3
		32.7	15.2				22.5	47.6
		(23) 11.8	9.2			% Profit Before Taxes/Tangible Net Worth	(50) 5.5	(68) 22.3
		.0	1.0				-5.9	4.6
		10.8	9.3				9.2	19.9
		3.9	3.6			% Profit Before Taxes/Total Assets	1.8	9.8
		-.3	.8				-4.2	1.6
		26.2	11.8				18.9	34.7
		17.1	5.1			Sales/Net Fixed Assets	9.1	11.4
		7.9	3.4				4.5	6.0
		2.9	2.7				2.2	2.7
		2.1	1.9			Sales/Total Assets	1.5	2.1
		1.4	1.1				1.1	1.5
		.6	1.3				1.2	.7
		(21) 1.1	2.8			% Depr., Dep., Amort./Sales	(49) 2.2	(67) 1.6
		2.1	4.7				4.4	3.0
							2.3	2.0
						% Officers', Directors' Owners' Comp/Sales	(21) 5.0	(27) 5.3
							9.3	7.4
1595M	25597M	272458M	524080M	557440M	506916M	Net Sales ($)	1013674M	2115838M
159M	7889M	135535M	288936M	439849M	466917M	Total Assets ($)	824788M	1093877M

M = $ thousand MM = $ million

See Pages 9 through 22 for Explanation of Ratios and Data

Comparative Historical Data				Current Data Sorted by Sales					
			Type of Statement						
13	8	7	Unqualified			1		1	5
9	17	14	Reviewed				4	7	3
11	9	3	Compiled			2		1	
8	9	7	Tax Returns		1	2	4		
32	25	23	Other		2	3	2	7	9
4/1/11-3/31/12 ALL	**4/1/12-3/31/13 ALL**	**4/1/13-3/31/14 ALL**		**8 (4/1-9/30/13)**			**46 (10/1/13-3/31/14)**		
				0-1MM	**1-3MM**	**3-5MM**	**5-10MM**	**10-25MM**	**25MM & OVER**
73	68	54	**NUMBER OF STATEMENTS**		3	8	10	16	17
%	%	%	**ASSETS**	%	%	%	%	%	%
12.0	10.6	11.8	Cash & Equivalents	DATA NOT AVAILABLE			4.8	7.8	21.8
25.0	22.8	22.4	Trade Receivables (net)				34.3	20.8	17.9
25.1	28.6	29.5	Inventory				35.5	29.2	22.4
3.8	2.9	2.2	All Other Current				3.1	2.3	2.9
65.8	64.9	65.9	Total Current				77.7	60.1	65.1
24.1	21.8	22.8	Fixed Assets (net)				14.0	30.9	21.9
4.7	5.6	4.1	Intangibles (net)				.1	3.8	6.2
5.4	7.6	7.2	All Other Non-Current				8.2	5.2	6.8
100.0	100.0	100.0	Total				100.0	100.0	100.0
			LIABILITIES						
10.0	13.1	11.6	Notes Payable-Short Term				15.7	7.0	5.5
3.6	2.9	2.6	Cur. Mat.-L.T.D.				5.0	1.7	.7
15.2	12.2	15.6	Trade Payables				27.3	13.9	9.8
.0	.2	.0	Income Taxes Payable				.0	.0	.1
9.8	10.6	8.4	All Other Current				5.7	8.1	9.3
38.6	39.1	38.2	Total Current				53.7	30.6	25.5
13.9	15.6	14.4	Long-Term Debt				7.0	12.4	4.8
.4	.2	.6	Deferred Taxes				.0	.1	1.6
4.1	5.8	6.8	All Other Non-Current				4.0	9.0	4.7
42.9	39.4	40.0	Net Worth				35.3	47.8	63.4
100.0	100.0	100.0	Total Liabilties & Net Worth				100.0	100.0	100.0
			INCOME DATA						
100.0	100.0	100.0	Net Sales				100.0	100.0	100.0
32.2	29.4	32.2	Gross Profit				31.7	31.4	30.1
24.8	23.8	25.3	Operating Expenses				22.0	26.1	18.7
7.5	5.6	6.9	Operating Profit				9.7	5.3	11.4
.7	.6	.8	All Other Expenses (net)				-.3	1.7	.6
6.8	5.0	6.1	Profit Before Taxes				10.1	3.7	10.8
			RATIOS						
3.5	2.9	3.7					6.0	3.0	4.4
1.7	1.8	1.8	Current				1.4	2.1	2.6
1.2	1.2	1.3					1.0	1.4	1.5
1.7	1.8	1.7					3.1	1.5	2.6
1.0	.9	.9	Quick				.7	1.0	1.5
.5	.6	.6					.5	.5	.9
32 11.5	**27** 13.5	**27** 13.5					**43** 8.4	**25** 14.5	**26** 13.9
41 8.9	**39** 9.3	**40** 9.1	Sales/Receivables				**51** 7.2	**36** 10.1	**41** 8.9
51 7.1	**47** 7.7	**53** 6.9					**78** 4.7	**55** 6.6	**48** 7.6
15 24.0	**23** 15.8	**38** 9.5					**28** 13.2	**27** 13.4	**39** 9.4
56 6.5	**63** 5.8	**72** 5.1	Cost of Sales/Inventory				**81** 4.5	**83** 4.4	**66** 5.5
99 3.7	**96** 3.8	**101** 3.6					**135** 2.7	**101** 3.6	**94** 3.9
15 24.2	**13** 28.8	**19** 19.3					**15** 25.0	**17** 22.1	**16** 23.5
26 13.8	**24** 14.9	**30** 12.3	Cost of Sales/Payables				**46** 8.0	**30** 12.3	**24** 15.5
46 7.9	**40** 9.2	**48** 7.6					**104** 3.5	**45** 8.2	**35** 10.3
3.9	4.4	3.4					3.4	3.5	2.5
7.4	9.5	7.9	Sales/Working Capital				11.5	7.3	5.1
32.4	25.6	18.2					NM	15.3	10.0
27.7	21.2	22.2					36.3	11.2	653.5
(67) 8.1	(65) 6.1	(50) 5.9	EBIT/Interest				11.4	(15) 3.0	(14) 18.4
2.6	1.9	1.4					1.1	1.0	5.9
44.3	5.7								
(10) 5.0	(13) 4.5		Net Profit + Depr., Dep., Amort./Cur. Mat. L/T/D						
2.1	1.0								
.2	.2	.2					.1	.2	.2
.5	.5	.5	Fixed/Worth				.5	.7	.4
1.1	1.2	1.1					1.0	1.3	.7
.6	.6	.5					.8	.5	.3
1.4	1.4	1.2	Debt/Worth				2.3	1.3	.6
3.0	3.5	4.4					9.4	2.4	1.2
52.6	48.7	27.2						11.8	28.3
(67) 23.8	(59) 23.3	(45) 11.8	% Profit Before Taxes/Tangible Net Worth					(15) 9.1	(16) 15.2
12.6	6.4	4.2						-.3	8.2
19.7	16.5	13.1					40.8	7.0	17.6
8.6	7.4	5.1	% Profit Before Taxes/Total Assets				10.7	2.7	9.3
3.4	1.2	1.0					.6	-.1	4.3
24.7	42.4	20.5					39.1	18.4	16.9
13.9	14.9	12.4	Sales/Net Fixed Assets				19.0	8.6	9.4
6.1	5.9	5.1					7.7	3.6	4.7
2.9	3.4	2.9					2.8	3.4	2.6
2.1	2.3	2.0	Sales/Total Assets				2.3	1.9	1.5
1.4	1.5	1.2					1.4	1.2	1.1
1.2	.8	.9						1.2	1.1
(57) 1.8	(54) 1.5	(47) 1.6	% Depr., Dep., Amort./Sales					(14) 1.9	(16) 1.9
3.2	2.7	2.9						3.7	3.7
.8	2.1	2.1							
(25) 3.8	(29) 4.2	(14) 3.1	% Officers', Directors' Owners' Comp/Sales						
5.7	7.6	5.3							
3054921M	1646249M	1888086M	Net Sales ($)		6029M	31602M	73541M	231367M	1545547M
1788812M	992301M	1339285M	Total Assets ($)		1934M	17736M	40921M	201918M	1076776M

M = $ thousand MM = $ million

See Pages 9 through 22 for Explanation of Ratios and Data

Current Data Sorted by Assets							Comparative Historical Data	
						Type of Statement		
		3	4		2	Unqualified	8	9
	1	7	7	1		Reviewed	17	18
3	8	7				Compiled	17	13
8	11	9			1	Tax Returns	20	20
4	9	13	4	2	2	Other	52	42
	11 (4/1-9/30/13)		95 (10/1/13-3/31/14)				4/1/09-3/31/10	4/1/10-3/31/11
0-500M	**500M-2MM**	**2-10MM**	**10-50MM**	**50-100MM**	**100-250MM**		**ALL**	**ALL**
15	29	39	15	3	5	**NUMBER OF STATEMENTS**	114	102
%	%	%	%	%	%	**ASSETS**	%	%
17.8	11.6	9.2	6.7			Cash & Equivalents	7.0	6.5
14.1	16.9	24.1	18.9			Trade Receivables (net)	19.8	17.6
27.5	28.6	27.9	28.2			Inventory	24.0	27.9
.6	1.3	1.8	2.8			All Other Current	2.8	3.3
60.0	58.4	63.1	56.7			Total Current	53.7	55.2
28.5	29.7	27.9	30.1			Fixed Assets (net)	34.1	30.7
1.4	3.7	2.2	5.1			Intangibles (net)	4.5	4.3
10.1	8.1	6.8	8.1			All Other Non-Current	7.7	9.8
100.0	100.0	100.0	100.0			Total	100.0	100.0
						LIABILITIES		
18.2	10.4	7.2	7.6			Notes Payable-Short Term	14.4	12.1
5.6	4.8	3.8	3.1			Cur. Mat.-L.T.D.	4.6	5.2
8.0	15.1	14.8	13.5			Trade Payables	12.5	13.1
.1	.0	.0	.3			Income Taxes Payable	.2	.5
6.4	16.1	11.7	17.7			All Other Current	10.9	12.0
38.3	46.5	37.5	42.2			Total Current	42.7	42.9
47.3	26.3	18.3	13.7			Long-Term Debt	28.3	24.4
.0	.0	.2	.3			Deferred Taxes	.2	.3
23.8	8.4	8.2	5.2			All Other Non-Current	6.1	7.2
-9.3	18.8	35.8	38.7			Net Worth	22.7	25.2
100.0	100.0	100.0	100.0			Total Liabilities & Net Worth	100.0	100.0
						INCOME DATA		
100.0	100.0	100.0	100.0			Net Sales	100.0	100.0
48.0	39.7	33.5	28.3			Gross Profit	37.0	34.9
44.1	36.8	28.9	19.2			Operating Expenses	35.7	32.2
3.9	2.9	4.7	9.0			Operating Profit	1.3	2.7
.0	.2	.3	.8			All Other Expenses (net)	1.7	1.2
3.9	2.7	4.3	8.2			Profit Before Taxes	-.4	1.5
						RATIOS		
7.4	2.6	2.8	3.6				2.5	2.3
1.8	1.3	1.7	1.5			Current	1.5	1.3
.5	.9	1.2	1.1				.9	.9
2.8	1.1	1.6	1.1				1.5	1.1
.9	.7	1.0	.7			Quick	.7	.6
.3	.3	.4	.4				.3	.3
0 UND	**6** 59.9	**24** 15.1	**33** 11.2				**22** 16.3	**21** 17.5
7 54.5	**18** 20.3	**35** 10.3	**43** 8.5			Sales/Receivables	**34** 10.6	**36** 10.3
29 12.6	**41** 8.9	**48** 7.6	**46** 7.9				**51** 7.2	**49** 7.5
0 UND	**31** 11.6	**26** 14.2	**43** 8.4				**22** 16.7	**41** 8.9
43 8.4	**62** 5.9	**52** 7.0	**70** 5.2			Cost of Sales/Inventory	**60** 6.1	**73** 5.0
104 3.5	**122** 3.0	**99** 3.7	**140** 2.6				**144** 2.5	**142** 2.6
0 UND	**8** 44.4	**11** 34.1	**20** 18.1				**12** 30.4	**16** 23.1
6 58.1	**23** 15.9	**27** 13.4	**33** 11.1			Cost of Sales/Payables	**25** 14.5	**28** 13.2
27 13.4	**41** 9.0	**43** 8.5	**53** 6.9				**47** 7.8	**51** 7.1
5.4	6.8	5.8	2.8				4.6	4.9
18.1	22.5	7.9	15.8			Sales/Working Capital	12.9	12.6
-29.9	-52.0	24.4	27.9				-38.2	-42.7
48.4	6.1	26.0	26.1				6.6	9.0
(12) 4.9	(28) 2.3	(36) 9.0	(14) 6.8			EBIT/Interest	(107) 1.6	(93) 1.9
-.8	.4	1.6	2.8				-1.2	-.9
							2.0	15.9
						Net Profit + Depr., Dep., Amort./Cur. Mat. L/T/D	(20) 1.1	(26) 3.7
							-.1	1.0
.1	.6	.4	.5				.6	.4
1.3	1.4	.7	1.0			Fixed/Worth	1.6	1.1
56.0	-4.0	2.1	1.9				-27.2	7.2
.9	.9	.8	.7				1.0	.8
2.3	3.2	1.9	1.6			Debt/Worth	2.7	2.1
-2.3	-16.8	5.3	4.7				-26.6	15.5
84.7	56.7	52.9	45.0				26.6	27.8
(11) 37.8	(21) 7.4	(33) 30.5	(13) 29.9			% Profit Before Taxes/Tangible Net Worth	(84) 6.7	(82) 7.4
-34.2	-5.7	11.2	14.6				-21.8	-14.5
45.4	16.1	20.2	18.4				10.1	8.8
20.8	3.6	8.5	7.4			% Profit Before Taxes/Total Assets	2.0	2.2
-1.7	-2.4	.7	5.0				-9.5	-6.4
68.3	21.7	28.6	12.3				14.9	15.7
27.5	12.8	9.7	4.8			Sales/Net Fixed Assets	6.9	6.2
14.1	3.4	4.2	3.3				2.9	3.0
6.5	4.1	3.4	2.3				3.2	2.7
4.2	2.3	2.2	1.5			Sales/Total Assets	1.8	1.6
1.8	1.5	1.6	1.2				1.1	1.1
.5	.6	1.0	1.3				1.8	1.9
(10) 1.5	(23) 2.0	(32) 1.8	(14) 2.1			% Depr., Dep., Amort./Sales	(104) 3.2	(88) 3.6
3.4	4.4	3.3	4.1				6.1	6.5
	3.2	2.0					2.6	2.0
	(16) 4.9	(18) 3.4				% Officers', Directors' Owners' Comp/Sales	(45) 4.7	(46) 3.4
	10.0	5.6					7.1	5.8
16523M	**103680M**	**364580M**	**578061M**	**184022M**	**850212M**	Net Sales ($)	**1231173M**	**1739160M**
4347M	**36010M**	**158589M**	**342421M**	**198831M**	**831888M**	Total Assets ($)	**1010825M**	**1299224M**

M = $ thousand MM = $ million

See Pages 9 through 22 for Explanation of Ratios and Data

Comparative Historical Data

Current Data Sorted by Sales

4/1/11-3/31/12 ALL	4/1/12-3/31/13 ALL	4/1/13-3/31/14 ALL	Type of Statement	0-1MM	1-3MM	3-5MM	5-10MM	10-25MM	25MM & OVER
9	5	9	Unqualified				2	3	4
11	15	16	Reviewed		1	1	5	3	6
14	15	18	Compiled	1	7	4	2	4	
21	27	29	Tax Returns	5	9	6	3	5	1
43	33	34	Other	2	7	3	10	5	7
				11 (4/1-9/30/13)			95 (10/1/13-3/31/14)		
98	95	106	**NUMBER OF STATEMENTS**	8	24	14	22	20	18
%	%	%	**ASSETS**	%	%	%	%	%	%
7.8	6.6	10.2	Cash & Equivalents		11.9	7.2	13.2	8.6	6.4
22.2	24.9	19.3	Trade Receivables (net)		17.5	16.7	22.4	27.7	18.7
25.9	24.9	27.7	Inventory		26.8	28.5	26.4	29.8	24.7
4.3	3.5	1.7	All Other Current		1.6	.5	3.0	1.7	1.7
60.2	59.9	58.9	Total Current		57.7	52.9	65.0	67.8	51.6
28.3	31.0	30.0	Fixed Assets (net)		29.1	30.4	28.2	24.5	36.2
4.3	2.2	3.0	Intangibles (net)		4.0	4.5	1.8	3.1	2.6
7.2	6.8	8.1	All Other Non-Current		9.2	12.1	5.0	4.5	9.5
100.0	100.0	100.0	Total		100.0	100.0	100.0	100.0	100.0
			LIABILITIES						
12.8	13.4	9.6	Notes Payable-Short Term		10.1	13.6	8.1	8.7	6.2
5.3	6.4	4.2	Cur. Mat.-L.T.D.		3.0	5.3	4.6	3.2	3.4
15.9	15.7	13.4	Trade Payables		14.4	17.2	14.2	14.0	12.9
.2	.2	.1	Income Taxes Payable		.1	.0	.0	.0	.3
12.4	16.7	12.9	All Other Current		10.1	16.7	10.3	11.5	17.1
46.5	52.4	40.1	Total Current		37.7	52.8	37.3	37.4	39.9
20.6	23.4	24.2	Long-Term Debt		35.0	21.1	19.8	14.4	17.2
.1	.1	.1	Deferred Taxes		.0	.0	.4	.0	.4
9.7	11.6	9.6	All Other Non-Current		17.3	4.9	3.8	12.4	1.7
23.1	12.4	25.9	Net Worth		10.0	21.2	38.8	35.8	40.8
100.0	100.0	100.0	Total Liabilties & Net Worth		100.0	100.0	100.0	100.0	100.0
			INCOME DATA						
100.0	100.0	100.0	Net Sales		100.0	100.0	100.0	100.0	100.0
37.7	34.4	36.4	Gross Profit		43.0	34.8	35.7	29.9	30.0
33.5	30.6	31.2	Operating Expenses		40.8	31.1	28.0	25.8	20.2
4.2	3.8	5.2	Operating Profit		2.2	3.7	7.7	4.0	9.8
1.2	.6	.4	All Other Expenses (net)		.5	.2	.7	.3	.6
3.0	3.2	4.9	Profit Before Taxes		1.7	3.5	7.0	3.7	9.2
			RATIOS						
2.5	2.4	2.7			3.7	1.8	3.0	3.4	2.3
1.6	1.5	1.6	Current		1.7	.9	1.9	1.8	1.4
.9	1.0	1.1			1.0	.7	1.2	1.1	1.1
1.3	1.2	1.4			1.8	1.2	1.6	1.7	1.0
.7	.7	.8	Quick		1.0	.4	1.0	1.0	.7
.3	.4	.4			.3	.2	.5	.6	.4
16 23.0	**20** 18.7	**14** 25.4			**9** 40.4	**9** 42.0	**17** 22.1	**29** 12.5	**38** 9.5
33 11.1	**35** 10.5	**34** 10.6	Sales/Receivables		**21** 17.1	**38** 9.5	**33** 11.2	**37** 9.9	**43** 8.5
51 7.2	**51** 7.2	**44** 8.3			**42** 8.7	**45** 8.1	**48** 7.6	**43** 8.5	**49** 7.5
20 18.3	**30** 12.0	**31** 11.6			**42** 8.6	**21** 17.0	**24** 15.5	**20** 18.5	**45** 8.2
53 6.9	**52** 7.0	**61** 6.0	Cost of Sales/Inventory		**65** 5.6	**51** 7.1	**54** 6.8	**49** 7.4	**85** 4.3
104 3.5	**99** 3.7	**118** 3.1			**118** 3.1	**182** 2.0	**96** 3.8	**94** 3.9	**135** 2.7
17 21.4	**17** 21.8	**11** 34.6			**3** 121.9	**12** 31.3	**12** 30.8	**17** 21.0	**19** 19.0
29 12.7	**31** 11.7	**26** 14.0	Cost of Sales/Payables		**22** 16.3	**27** 13.7	**33** 11.1	**26** 13.8	**35** 10.3
51 7.2	**48** 7.6	**42** 8.7			**33** 10.9	**64** 5.7	**47** 7.7	**32** 11.5	**68** 5.4
4.9	5.9	5.7			5.6	5.1	5.8	6.2	5.0
15.4	14.0	12.6	Sales/Working Capital		9.2	-99.5	7.1	11.0	14.7
-90.4	-176.4	106.4			NM	-15.0	26.7	28.4	29.8
11.3	12.3	14.4			7.3	14.7	49.1	22.8	25.2
(91) 3.2	(93) 3.8	(97) 5.7	EBIT/Interest		(19) 1.3	5.2	(21) 9.3	5.4	(16) 6.8
1.0	1.1	1.2			-3.3	1.2	2.5	.7	3.2
7.7	8.4	6.0							
(18) 1.4	(23) 3.2	(15) 3.1	Net Profit + Depr., Dep., Amort./Cur. Mat. L/T/D						
.9	.9	.9							
.4	.5	.4			.3	.8	.4	.4	.6
1.2	1.2	1.0	Fixed/Worth		1.4	1.8	.8	.6	1.0
4.1	4.2	3.2			-1.4	-2.5	1.6	1.4	1.9
.9	1.1	.8			.9	1.1	.8	.5	.7
2.3	2.3	2.0	Debt/Worth		4.0	7.3	1.6	1.8	1.3
16.5	26.8	20.4			-4.8	-10.0	3.4	3.4	4.2
39.8	49.4	50.5			60.1		67.5	50.0	37.7
(78) 17.8	(74) 17.7	(86) 28.2	% Profit Before Taxes/Tangible Net Worth		(17) 4.6		(20) 37.7	(17) 29.4	(17) 27.8
2.0	3.6	6.4			-30.4		15.7	14.8	17.3
14.4	14.0	19.1			27.3	12.6	32.8	19.5	15.5
4.8	6.1	8.5	% Profit Before Taxes/Total Assets		2.5	4.9	14.5	8.3	10.8
.0	.1	.6			-3.9	.6	3.7	-1.9	4.6
26.2	20.0	23.8			26.5	17.2	21.3	29.3	9.0
10.0	8.4	9.8	Sales/Net Fixed Assets		14.3	8.0	10.5	17.9	3.6
4.4	3.6	3.4			4.6	3.6	4.1	5.8	2.1
3.6	3.4	3.5			4.2	3.1	3.5	3.9	2.1
2.1	2.2	2.1	Sales/Total Assets		2.2	2.2	2.6	3.0	1.4
1.4	1.5	1.4			1.3	1.4	1.7	1.9	1.0
1.7	1.5	1.0			.4	1.2	.7	.8	1.3
(75) 3.1	(82) 2.6	(87) 2.0	% Depr., Dep., Amort./Sales		(16) 1.6	(11) 2.3	(19) 2.4	(17) 1.7	3.2
4.7	4.6	4.0			4.0	3.0	3.6	3.1	4.7
1.9	1.6	2.4			3.6				
(42) 4.3	(42) 2.8	(46) 3.8	% Officers', Directors' Owners' Comp/Sales		(13) 6.6				
7.7	5.0	6.7			10.5				
1652149M	**1807510M**	**2097078M**	Net Sales ($)	**4456M**	**41947M**	**55515M**	**164172M**	**291570M**	**1539418M**
1115168M	**1126873M**	**1572086M**	Total Assets ($)	**3065M**	**22541M**	**42536M**	**79267M**	**122326M**	**1302351M**

M = $ thousand MM = $ million

See Pages 9 through 22 for Explanation of Ratios and Data

Current Data Sorted by Assets | **Comparative Historical Data**

0-500M	500M-2MM	2-10MM	10-50MM	50-100MM	100-250MM	Type of Statement	4/1/09-3/31/10 ALL	4/1/10-3/31/11 ALL
			2	1		Unqualified	6	4
	1	4	2			Reviewed	13	8
						Compiled	3	2
2	1	1	1			Tax Returns	3	3
	2	10	3		2	Other	9	12
	3 (4/1-9/30/13)		29 (10/1/13-3/31/14)					
2	4	15	8	1	2	**NUMBER OF STATEMENTS**	34	29
%	%	%	%	%	%	**ASSETS**	%	%
		10.9				Cash & Equivalents	10.9	12.9
		22.4				Trade Receivables (net)	20.6	17.9
		23.1				Inventory	22.5	22.4
		2.1				All Other Current	3.5	3.0
		58.5				Total Current	57.4	56.1
		28.0				Fixed Assets (net)	31.1	33.0
		6.5				Intangibles (net)	4.2	5.9
		7.0				All Other Non-Current	7.3	4.9
		100.0				Total	100.0	100.0
						LIABILITIES		
		4.1				Notes Payable-Short Term	8.6	4.6
		3.5				Cur. Mat.-L.T.D.	3.5	2.8
		15.4				Trade Payables	12.0	11.8
		.3				Income Taxes Payable	.1	.0
		8.5				All Other Current	9.9	4.3
		31.9				Total Current	34.1	23.6
		17.1				Long-Term Debt	15.6	15.3
		.4				Deferred Taxes	.3	1.5
		11.0				All Other Non-Current	6.6	9.9
		39.8				Net Worth	43.4	49.8
		100.0				Total Liabilties & Net Worth	100.0	100.0
						INCOME DATA		
		100.0				Net Sales	100.0	100.0
		35.4				Gross Profit	30.0	32.8
		29.4				Operating Expenses	26.3	25.5
		6.0				Operating Profit	3.7	7.3
		1.3				All Other Expenses (net)	.5	-.1
		4.7				Profit Before Taxes	3.2	7.4
						RATIOS		
		4.1					3.2	4.3
		2.7				Current	2.1	2.5
		1.6					1.2	1.5
		2.5					2.2	2.3
		1.6				Quick	1.0	1.2
		.5					.6	.7
		33 11.1					**30** 12.3	**25** 14.9
		49 7.5				Sales/Receivables	**44** 8.3	**46** 7.9
		60 6.1					**60** 6.0	**63** 5.8
		5 80.4					**27** 13.5	**35** 10.5
		66 5.5				Cost of Sales/Inventory	**65** 5.6	**76** 4.8
		140 2.6					**105** 3.5	**109** 3.3
		21 17.3					**14** 25.7	**16** 22.2
		36 10.2				Cost of Sales/Payables	**18** 20.3	**29** 12.5
		89 4.1					**43** 8.5	**53** 6.9
		3.8					3.4	2.7
		4.7				Sales/Working Capital	7.4	4.7
		7.4					29.2	13.6
		22.6					20.8	25.2
		(12) 2.9				EBIT/Interest	(30) 4.7	(24) 6.7
		-2.3					.8	.0
							7.3	
						Net Profit + Depr., Dep., Amort./Cur. Mat. L/T/D	(10) 3.8	
							.5	
		.2					.4	.3
		.5				Fixed/Worth	.7	.8
		1.6					1.4	1.4
		.7					.6	.4
		2.2				Debt/Worth	1.3	1.3
		5.1					3.9	3.3
		57.5					32.7	39.1
		(13) 20.1				% Profit Before Taxes/Tangible Net Worth	(29) 14.5	(26) 19.4
		-8.2					-2.0	-1.9
		22.6					13.4	17.3
		3.6				% Profit Before Taxes/Total Assets	5.9	6.4
		-3.0					-.3	-1.2
		34.3					15.7	15.2
		9.6				Sales/Net Fixed Assets	6.6	4.6
		3.1					2.9	3.0
		2.0					2.5	2.2
		1.5				Sales/Total Assets	1.6	1.4
		1.3					.9	.8
		1.9					1.5	1.7
		(10) 4.3				% Depr., Dep., Amort./Sales	(33) 3.3	(26) 2.7
		9.5					4.2	5.3
						% Officers', Directors' Owners' Comp/Sales		
6266M	15681M	170900M	212465M	102422M	565702M	Net Sales ($)	679323M	526216M
884M	4983M	100657M	131921M	60876M	461491M	Total Assets ($)	578745M	458990M

M = $ thousand MM = $ million

See Pages 9 through 22 for Explanation of Ratios and Data

Comparative Historical Data				Current Data Sorted by Sales					
Type of Statement									
Unqualified	5	5	3				1		2
Reviewed	9	7	7				2	5	
Compiled	2	3							
Tax Returns	3	5	5		2	2		1	
Other	12	5	17		2	1	3	8	3
	4/1/11-3/31/12 ALL	**4/1/12-3/31/13 ALL**	**4/1/13-3/31/14 ALL**		**3 (4/1-9/30/13)**		**29 (10/1/13-3/31/14)**		
				0-1MM	**1-3MM**	**3-5MM**	**5-10MM**	**10-25MM**	**25MM & OVER**
NUMBER OF STATEMENTS	31	25	32		4	3	6	14	5
ASSETS	%	%	%	%	%	%	%	%	%
Cash & Equivalents	12.1	16.8	14.5	**DATA NOT AVAILABLE**				12.7	
Trade Receivables (net)	23.2	20.1	24.6					23.4	
Inventory	25.3	25.5	20.6					22.4	
All Other Current	3.1	2.7	2.2					1.8	
Total Current	63.7	65.1	61.8					60.3	
Fixed Assets (net)	21.7	26.4	26.2					26.2	
Intangibles (net)	8.4	1.9	3.7					2.6	
All Other Non-Current	6.1	6.6	8.3					10.9	
Total	100.0	100.0	100.0					100.0	
LIABILITIES									
Notes Payable-Short Term	7.4	3.1	3.6					1.9	
Cur. Mat.-L.T.D.	2.0	2.0	2.8					1.6	
Trade Payables	10.2	12.0	15.9					12.9	
Income Taxes Payable	.2	.2	.2					.3	
All Other Current	9.8	5.3	8.2					6.3	
Total Current	29.7	22.6	30.8					23.1	
Long-Term Debt	4.7	9.5	18.0					14.1	
Deferred Taxes	1.7	.7	.5					.8	
All Other Non-Current	5.9	8.8	7.5					8.5	
Net Worth	58.0	58.3	43.3					53.6	
Total Liabilties & Net Worth	100.0	100.0	100.0					100.0	
INCOME DATA									
Net Sales	100.0	100.0	100.0					100.0	
Gross Profit	31.1	35.7	32.9					27.7	
Operating Expenses	22.0	25.4	25.8					21.0	
Operating Profit	9.1	10.3	7.1					6.8	
All Other Expenses (net)	.7	.1	1.3					.7	
Profit Before Taxes	8.3	10.2	5.8					6.1	
RATIOS									
Current	5.5	5.6	4.4					3.9	
	3.0	3.3	2.3					2.5	
	1.7	1.9	1.6					1.8	
Quick	4.3	3.7	2.4					2.5	
	1.2	1.5	1.5					1.4	
	.7	.9	.9					.9	
Sales/Receivables	**34** 10.7	**31** 11.6	**31** 11.8					**30** 12.0	
	47 7.7	**43** 8.5	**50** 7.3					**46** 7.9	
	56 6.5	**57** 6.4	**60** 6.1					**62** 5.9	
Cost of Sales/Inventory	**35** 10.5	**47** 7.7	**26** 14.3					**0** UND	
	72 5.1	**78** 4.7	**57** 6.4					**65** 5.6	
	104 3.5	**140** 2.6	**126** 2.9					**135** 2.7	
Cost of Sales/Payables	**11** 33.2	**12** 31.2	**18** 20.7					**18** 20.1	
	22 16.5	**22** 16.6	**23** 15.6					**23** 16.1	
	41 8.9	**63** 5.8	**79** 4.6					**54** 6.7	
Sales/Working Capital	2.8	2.9	4.2					4.1	
	5.7	4.0	5.2					4.8	
	11.0	7.0	11.0					7.6	
EBIT/Interest	46.5	116.5	55.4					28.0	
	(24) 23.7	(18) 13.1	(27) 5.5					(11) 5.5	
	4.9	1.7	.1					-.5	
Net Profit + Depr., Dep., Amort./Cur. Mat. L/T/D									
Fixed/Worth	.2	.1	.2					.2	
	.3	.3	.3					.4	
	1.1	.9	1.2					1.1	
Debt/Worth	.3	.3	.4					.3	
	.9	.5	1.0					.9	
	1.8	2.2	4.5					2.5	
% Profit Before Taxes/Tangible Net Worth	46.4	43.2	45.1					44.6	
	(29) 24.7	(24) 20.3	(28) 20.2					17.6	
	10.1	1.5	1.4					-5.4	
% Profit Before Taxes/Total Assets	22.7	29.3	22.0					22.9	
	12.4	11.9	10.9					10.1	
	3.7	1.0	-.7					-1.1	
Sales/Net Fixed Assets	32.2	33.0	32.4					28.5	
	10.5	12.9	10.6					5.8	
	4.3	3.0	3.3					3.2	
Sales/Total Assets	2.2	2.2	2.6					2.1	
	1.6	1.6	1.7					1.6	
	1.1	.9	1.3					1.3	
% Depr., Dep., Amort./Sales	.8	1.0	1.4					1.2	
	(27) 1.6	(21) 2.9	(21) 2.4					(10) 2.2	
	5.5	4.2	6.0					4.2	
% Officers', Directors' Owners' Comp/Sales									
Net Sales ($)	708664M	470289M	1073436M		9485M	12446M	46625M	227993M	776887M
Total Assets ($)	444498M	351295M	760812M		6503M	3388M	41628M	136730M	572563M

M = $ thousand MM = $ million

See Pages 9 through 22 for Explanation of Ratios and Data

Current Data Sorted by Assets							Comparative Historical Data	
						Type of Statement		
	1		3	7	8	Unqualified	38	37
	1	8	6			Reviewed	25	23
1	1	3				Compiled	13	9
2	3	3				Tax Returns	5	11
	3	13	13	8	4	Other	65	58
19 (4/1-9/30/13)			69 (10/1/13-3/31/14)				4/1/09-3/31/10 ALL	4/1/10-3/31/11 ALL
0-500M	**500M-2MM**	**2-10MM**	**10-50MM**	**50-100MM**	**100-250MM**			
3	9	27	22	15	12	**NUMBER OF STATEMENTS**	146	138
%	%	%	%	%	%	**ASSETS**	%	%
		10.6	11.7	7.3	3.9	Cash & Equivalents	8.5	8.8
		34.0	23.8	18.3	22.3	Trade Receivables (net)	24.5	24.8
		23.1	25.5	32.0	29.2	Inventory	23.3	23.8
		1.4	.7	3.4	3.3	All Other Current	3.4	3.3
		69.2	61.7	61.0	58.8	Total Current	59.7	60.8
		26.0	27.7	26.2	30.2	Fixed Assets (net)	30.6	27.2
		.9	3.9	9.5	3.2	Intangibles (net)	3.2	3.6
		3.9	6.7	3.3	7.7	All Other Non-Current	6.5	8.4
		100.0	100.0	100.0	100.0	Total	100.0	100.0
						LIABILITIES		
		12.4	12.8	5.0	8.7	Notes Payable-Short Term	10.6	12.1
		3.0	2.6	1.1	.6	Cur. Mat.-L.T.D.	4.5	3.3
		18.6	13.5	11.1	13.4	Trade Payables	14.2	15.8
		.4	.1	.4	.5	Income Taxes Payable	.3	.4
		8.2	7.0	6.0	13.6	All Other Current	10.9	10.7
		42.6	36.0	23.5	36.7	Total Current	40.4	42.4
		10.7	13.0	10.6	8.9	Long-Term Debt	17.8	13.8
		1.3	1.0	2.7	.2	Deferred Taxes	.9	1.0
		5.3	6.0	5.1	6.2	All Other Non-Current	7.6	10.0
		40.1	44.0	58.1	48.0	Net Worth	33.4	32.8
		100.0	100.0	100.0	100.0	Total Liabilties & Net Worth	100.0	100.0
						INCOME DATA		
		100.0	100.0	100.0	100.0	Net Sales	100.0	100.0
		21.9	18.8	13.9	16.2	Gross Profit	21.6	20.6
		18.0	13.3	8.1	7.9	Operating Expenses	20.0	17.3
		3.9	5.5	5.7	8.3	Operating Profit	1.6	3.4
		.1	.7	.1	.6	All Other Expenses (net)	1.8	.8
		3.8	4.8	5.6	7.7	Profit Before Taxes	-.2	2.6
						RATIOS		
		2.6	2.5	4.7	2.8		3.2	3.1
		1.7	1.9	3.0	1.7	Current	1.4	1.5
		1.3	1.3	1.6	1.2		1.0	1.1
		1.7	1.8	1.6	1.2		1.6	1.8
		1.2	1.1	1.5	.9	Quick	.8	.9
		.6	.5	.7	.3		.4	.5
		32 11.3	33 11.1	26 14.0	36 10.1		31 11.8	30 12.0
		39 9.3	43 8.4	36 10.1	41 8.8	Sales/Receivables	43 8.4	42 8.6
		78 4.7	61 6.0	63 5.8	60 6.1		60 6.1	60 6.1
		23 15.7	29 12.8	41 9.0	34 10.8		21 17.8	18 19.8
		38 9.7	58 6.3	91 4.0	73 5.0	Cost of Sales/Inventory	51 7.2	49 7.4
		69 5.3	94 3.9	122 3.0	89 4.1		85 4.3	89 4.1
		21 17.7	20 18.1	18 20.2	13 28.8		16 23.1	17 21.5
		32 11.5	28 12.9	31 11.7	30 12.0	Cost of Sales/Payables	31 11.9	33 11.1
		39 9.3	36 10.0	41 8.8	45 8.2		46 8.0	47 7.8
		5.8	4.1	2.5	3.3		4.4	4.4
		8.8	7.5	3.6	6.9	Sales/Working Capital	10.0	9.2
		16.3	13.7	6.8	28.9		NM	38.5
		32.0	52.9	41.7	67.3		7.3	15.1
		(21) 8.6	(20) 13.4	(14) 12.3	(10) 4.6	EBIT/Interest	(127) 1.6	(124) 4.0
		1.5	1.3	5.6	-2.2		-1.3	.3
							6.5	6.0
						Net Profit + Depr., Dep., Amort./Cur. Mat. L/T/D	(36) 2.3	(36) 2.2
							.2	1.2
		.3	.4	.2	.4		.3	.3
		.6	.7	.6	.6	Fixed/Worth	.8	.7
		1.2	.9	1.0	1.1		2.1	2.3
		.6	.5	.4	.4		.7	.6
		1.3	1.0	.8	1.0	Debt/Worth	1.7	1.8
		4.4	2.2	2.0	6.4		4.9	10.7
		53.0	26.4	30.1	33.1		25.8	37.3
		(24) 27.4	(20) 14.2	26.0	(11) 6.3	% Profit Before Taxes/Tangible Net Worth	(122) 7.3	(112) 15.2
		2.4	7.6	10.1	-4.0		-8.1	1.5
		17.1	12.8	15.3	18.7		9.8	13.5
		8.4	7.4	10.6	3.4	% Profit Before Taxes/Total Assets	2.0	4.4
		2.0	2.4	5.7	-1.9		-6.8	-1.8
		31.7	24.8	15.3	10.2		17.6	21.4
		12.2	5.7	5.8	5.4	Sales/Net Fixed Assets	7.0	8.6
		5.6	3.0	3.3	4.3		3.1	4.3
		3.1	2.7	2.3	2.2		2.5	2.7
		2.3	1.8	1.8	1.7	Sales/Total Assets	1.8	1.9
		1.9	1.1	.9	1.2		1.2	1.3
		.6	1.2	.8			1.0	1.0
		(25) 1.4	(21) 1.9	(13) 1.6		% Depr., Dep., Amort./Sales	(122) 2.2	(113) 1.9
		4.6	3.0	4.5			4.3	3.6
		1.2					1.9	1.8
		(10) 2.3				% Officers', Directors' Owners' Comp/Sales	(25) 3.3	(31) 3.2
		6.3					6.8	6.8
5218M	25274M	341697M	915808M	1733196M	3669135M	Net Sales ($)	6356190M	8290763M
1107M	12402M	142394M	515498M	1036245M	2012299M	Total Assets ($)	3900991M	5008287M

M = $ thousand MM = $ million

See Pages 9 through 22 for Explanation of Ratios and Data

Comparative Historical Data				Current Data Sorted by Sales					
			Type of Statement						
33	21	19	Unqualified		1				18
19	13	15	Reviewed		1		4	4	6
15	9	5	Compiled		1	1	1	2	
8	6	8	Tax Returns	1	2	2	3		
54	37	41	Other		1	2	6	8	24
4/1/11-3/31/12 ALL	**4/1/12-3/31/13 ALL**	**4/1/13-3/31/14 ALL**		**19 (4/1-9/30/13)**			**69 (10/1/13-3/31/14)**		
				0-1MM	**1-3MM**	**3-5MM**	**5-10MM**	**10-25MM**	**25MM & OVER**
129	86	88	**NUMBER OF STATEMENTS**	1	6	5	14	14	48
%	%	%	**ASSETS**	%	%	%	%	%	%
7.1	7.6	8.8	Cash & Equivalents				13.8	13.3	6.7
26.5	24.5	25.6	Trade Receivables (net)				33.7	29.7	22.9
27.5	22.9	25.3	Inventory				15.7	26.8	29.6
3.3	5.5	2.7	All Other Current				.3	2.4	2.2
64.4	60.5	62.5	Total Current				63.4	72.2	61.4
26.9	30.2	27.7	Fixed Assets (net)				31.6	21.0	27.8
2.2	2.3	3.7	Intangibles (net)				.5	3.4	5.0
6.5	7.0	6.1	All Other Non-Current				4.6	3.4	5.9
100.0	100.0	100.0	Total				100.0	100.0	100.0
			LIABILITIES						
11.1	12.5	12.5	Notes Payable-Short Term				6.6	11.0	11.4
2.5	3.1	2.1	Cur. Mat.-L.T.D.				2.2	3.6	1.7
16.9	13.3	15.5	Trade Payables				15.9	17.8	13.6
.3	.2	.3	Income Taxes Payable				.8	.0	.3
16.3	11.8	9.5	All Other Current				7.9	7.4	8.6
47.2	40.9	39.9	Total Current				33.3	39.8	35.7
13.6	16.3	12.9	Long-Term Debt				12.4	7.6	11.6
.9	1.1	1.2	Deferred Taxes				1.5	1.1	1.3
5.8	5.6	5.2	All Other Non-Current				5.4	4.0	6.1
32.6	36.1	40.8	Net Worth				47.4	47.5	45.2
100.0	100.0	100.0	Total Liabilties & Net Worth				100.0	100.0	100.0
			INCOME DATA						
100.0	100.0	100.0	Net Sales				100.0	100.0	100.0
20.8	22.4	21.3	Gross Profit				25.7	20.8	15.8
15.4	18.4	15.0	Operating Expenses				19.5	16.5	10.3
5.4	4.0	6.2	Operating Profit				6.2	4.3	5.5
.6	.8	1.0	All Other Expenses (net)				-.2	.2	.6
4.8	3.3	5.3	Profit Before Taxes				6.4	4.1	4.9
			RATIOS						
2.7	2.7	2.9					2.7	3.4	3.0
1.5	1.6	1.7	Current				1.9	1.8	1.9
1.1	1.1	1.3					1.5	1.2	1.4
1.5	1.5	1.6					1.8	2.5	1.6
.7	.8	1.1	Quick				1.3	1.1	1.0
.4	.4	.5					1.2	.6	.5
28 13.2	**28** 12.9	**30** 12.3					**36** 10.2	**30** 12.2	**29** 12.5
39 9.3	**41** 8.9	**39** 9.4	Sales/Receivables				**59** 6.2	**36** 10.1	**41** 8.9
52 7.0	**56** 6.5	**61** 6.0					**81** 4.5	**61** 6.0	**61** 6.0
18 20.8	**15** 24.6	**26** 14.3					**15** 24.2	**25** 14.8	**37** 9.9
52 7.0	**52** 7.0	**54** 6.7	Cost of Sales/Inventory				**29** 12.4	**49** 7.4	**73** 5.0
85 4.3	**83** 4.4	**91** 4.0					**62** 5.9	**79** 4.6	**96** 3.8
17 20.9	**18** 20.0	**21** 17.6					**17** 22.1	**20** 18.3	**21** 17.3
30 12.3	**28** 12.9	**31** 11.8	Cost of Sales/Payables				**32** 11.5	**27** 13.6	**30** 12.3
43 8.5	**42** 8.7	**41** 9.0					**41** 8.8	**37** 9.9	**39** 9.3
5.1	4.7	4.1					4.7	3.4	3.3
10.4	9.6	7.6	Sales/Working Capital				7.0	8.9	6.8
53.0	52.0	16.3					12.0	20.4	13.4
31.8	17.0	35.4					45.3		46.9
(113) 7.8	(73) 4.1	(75) 8.6	EBIT/Interest				(12) 15.8		(44) 11.7
2.4	1.0	1.5					2.0		1.6
7.6	15.5	6.1							6.6
(32) 3.9	(21) 3.3	(15) 3.6	Net Profit + Depr., Dep., Amort./Cur. Mat. L/T/D						(12) 4.5
1.3	.2	1.6							2.2
.3	.3	.3					.4	.2	.4
.7	.7	.7	Fixed/Worth				.7	.4	.7
1.7	2.1	1.1					.8	1.8	1.1
.7	.7	.5					.5	.3	.5
1.9	1.7	1.3	Debt/Worth				1.0	1.6	1.1
7.1	4.9	3.3					2.3	5.6	2.1
55.8	39.1	32.9					49.4	35.3	31.7
(106) 24.8	(76) 15.4	(76) 17.1	% Profit Before Taxes/Tangible Net Worth				(13) 27.1	(13) 18.3	(44) 16.6
10.7	3.8	5.7					2.6	-4.3	6.4
19.4	15.2	15.3					18.6	17.3	13.8
8.3	5.9	7.6	% Profit Before Taxes/Total Assets				10.8	8.5	7.4
2.5	.4	2.1					1.9	.1	2.4
23.7	20.3	25.3					12.9	48.7	15.2
9.4	7.8	7.3	Sales/Net Fixed Assets				7.2	22.2	6.3
4.9	3.4	3.3					2.9	5.1	3.8
3.1	2.9	2.7					2.7	3.0	2.6
2.2	2.0	2.0	Sales/Total Assets				2.0	2.3	1.8
1.6	1.4	1.4					1.5	1.9	1.1
.8	.9	1.0					.9	.3	1.0
(111) 1.5	(77) 1.6	(76) 1.6	% Depr., Dep., Amort./Sales				(13) 2.0	(13) 2.0	(40) 1.6
2.8	3.0	3.7					5.1	4.3	3.0
1.1	1.6	1.3							
(22) 2.1	(19) 3.1	(23) 2.8	% Officers', Directors' Owners' Comp/Sales						
5.5	5.5	5.8							
8698795M	**5998928M**	**6690328M**	Net Sales ($)	**41M**	**12365M**	**18086M**	**106061M**	**217320M**	**6336455M**
4156177M	**3225573M**	**3719945M**	Total Assets ($)	**405M**	**6807M**	**6297M**	**65225M**	**116511M**	**3524700M**

M = $ thousand MM = $ million

See Pages 9 through 22 for Explanation of Ratios and Data

Current Data Sorted by Assets							Comparative Historical Data	
						Type of Statement		
			10	2	5	Unqualified	33	36
2		15	9	1		Reviewed	42	38
1	2	10	1		1	Compiled	14	20
5	5	12	1			Tax Returns	19	23
1	8	19	23	2	7	Other	73	67
	18 (4/1-9/30/13)		124 (10/1/13-3/31/14)				4/1/09-3/31/10 ALL	4/1/10-3/31/11 ALL
0-500M	500M-2MM	2-10MM	10-50MM	50-100MM	100-250MM			
9	15	56	44	5	13	**NUMBER OF STATEMENTS**	181	184
%	%	%	%	%	%	**ASSETS**	%	%
	9.6	10.2	5.1		4.5	Cash & Equivalents	8.7	8.0
	38.2	26.1	27.0		14.3	Trade Receivables (net)	25.7	25.8
	23.8	29.9	31.3		24.0	Inventory	26.3	25.3
	.2	1.3	2.9		3.6	All Other Current	4.3	3.6
	71.8	67.6	66.3		46.4	Total Current	65.0	62.8
	24.1	22.1	25.4		39.5	Fixed Assets (net)	25.9	25.7
	.7	2.0	4.5		5.8	Intangibles (net)	3.9	4.9
	3.4	8.4	3.8		8.3	All Other Non-Current	5.2	6.7
	100.0	100.0	100.0		100.0	Total	100.0	100.0
						LIABILITIES		
	15.3	13.1	10.6		8.5	Notes Payable-Short Term	10.4	10.1
	3.5	1.9	2.9		2.5	Cur. Mat.-L.T.D.	3.9	3.5
	21.9	19.6	16.2		11.6	Trade Payables	14.1	14.4
	.1	.2	.1		.4	Income Taxes Payable	.1	.1
	4.4	6.9	7.9		10.5	All Other Current	13.8	12.6
	45.2	41.7	37.8		33.6	Total Current	42.2	40.7
	20.7	10.4	17.7		30.9	Long-Term Debt	14.8	17.2
	.0	.3	.4		2.6	Deferred Taxes	.4	.5
	7.9	6.0	5.8		6.8	All Other Non-Current	4.6	5.9
	26.1	41.5	38.4		26.1	Net Worth	37.9	35.7
	100.0	100.0	100.0		100.0	Total Liabilities & Net Worth	100.0	100.0
						INCOME DATA		
	100.0	100.0	100.0		100.0	Net Sales	100.0	100.0
	35.5	26.0	19.5		14.2	Gross Profit	25.8	25.4
	31.8	20.5	14.1		12.9	Operating Expenses	23.3	20.9
	3.8	5.5	5.4		1.3	Operating Profit	2.5	4.5
	1.0	.4	.8		2.8	All Other Expenses (net)	1.3	.6
	2.7	5.1	4.6		-1.5	Profit Before Taxes	1.2	3.9
						RATIOS		
	3.0	3.2	3.3		2.7		3.1	3.2
	2.2	2.1	1.8		1.4	Current	1.7	1.7
	1.0	1.2	1.3		1.0		1.1	1.0
	2.8	1.8	1.6		1.2		1.6	1.9
	1.1	.9	.8		.8	Quick	.8	.8
	.5	.4	.6		.4		.5	.4
	22 16.4	**22** 16.9	**38** 9.6		**25** 14.6		**29** 12.6	**32** 11.3
	41 9.0	**35** 10.3	**45** 8.2		**43** 8.5	Sales/Receivables	**43** 8.5	**45** 8.2
	87 4.2	**48** 7.6	**54** 6.7		**58** 6.3		**58** 6.3	**57** 6.4
	9 40.5	**29** 12.6	**41** 9.0		**28** 13.1		**25** 14.4	**29** 12.4
	38 9.6	**54** 6.8	**64** 5.7		**76** 4.8	Cost of Sales/Inventory	**60** 6.1	**53** 6.8
	63 5.8	**94** 3.9	**81** 4.5		**114** 3.2		**108** 3.4	**97** 3.8
	24 15.5	**18** 19.9	**16** 22.5		**15** 24.7		**15** 24.0	**17** 21.7
	32 11.5	**29** 12.8	**29** 12.6		**32** 11.5	Cost of Sales/Payables	**27** 13.4	**29** 12.7
	49 7.4	**52** 7.0	**47** 7.8		**50** 7.3		**47** 7.8	**45** 8.0
	5.5	3.5	5.4		3.4		4.3	4.7
	7.6	7.1	8.5		9.8	Sales/Working Capital	8.7	8.1
	183.8	41.4	17.2		NM		60.0	154.0
	9.4	21.9	16.4		10.9		10.5	14.0
	(14) 2.8	(46) 4.9	(42) 7.9		3.1	EBIT/Interest	(162) 2.4	(164) 4.0
	-.5	1.9	2.5		.7		-1.4	1.5
			24.0				6.0	4.8
			(14) 3.8			Net Profit + Depr., Dep., Amort./Cur. Mat. L/T/D	(35) 1.5	(32) 3.1
			2.2				-.1	1.6
	.2	.1	.3		.6		.2	.3
	.9	.5	.6		1.5	Fixed/Worth	.7	.8
	-29.0	1.3	1.2		-8.1		2.9	2.1
	.6	.5	.8		1.5		.5	.6
	1.9	1.3	1.8		3.4	Debt/Worth	1.7	1.7
	-74.6	4.3	5.2		-12.8		7.7	6.1
	59.6	46.6	35.0				34.7	39.6
	(11) 26.3	(53) 23.2	(41) 18.7			% Profit Before Taxes/Tangible Net Worth	(152) 8.9	(152) 17.8
	-2.1	6.5	15.2				-4.6	6.0
	17.2	19.7	13.8		9.9		11.8	14.3
	5.6	7.6	8.1		2.5	% Profit Before Taxes/Total Assets	3.5	6.6
	-2.6	2.2	3.1		-1.3		-3.7	1.6
	34.4	37.7	26.0		8.6		26.1	25.2
	20.3	13.0	10.3		3.3	Sales/Net Fixed Assets	8.4	9.0
	6.5	6.6	4.9		1.7		4.1	4.6
	3.4	3.0	2.6		1.8		2.7	2.8
	3.0	2.3	2.2		1.4	Sales/Total Assets	1.8	2.0
	2.4	1.6	1.7		.7		1.3	1.4
	.5	.5	.8		.1		.9	1.0
	(12) 1.7	(50) 1.6	(42) 1.5		(10) 2.1	% Depr., Dep., Amort./Sales	(148) 2.1	(158) 2.2
	2.4	2.6	2.6		3.3		4.4	3.4
		1.5					1.7	1.5
		(23) 3.8				% Officers', Directors' Owners' Comp/Sales	(54) 3.4	(54) 3.7
		7.1					7.3	8.0
8860M	50912M	653132M	2222449M	430126M	2959179M	Net Sales ($)	7609908M	8068340M
2713M	17525M	285303M	1015085M	310822M	2368901M	Total Assets ($)	4298495M	4643634M

M = $ thousand MM = $ million

See Pages 9 through 22 for Explanation of Ratios and Data

Comparative Historical Data				Current Data Sorted by Sales					
			Type of Statement						
31	19	17	Unqualified					1	16
35	20	27	Reviewed	1	1		4	12	9
21	16	15	Compiled	1	1	2	3	6	2
30	24	23	Tax Returns	3	6	5	7	1	1
60	72	60	Other		6	3	8	15	28
				18 (4/1-9/30/13)			124 (10/1/13-3/31/14)		
4/1/11-3/31/12 ALL	**4/1/12-3/31/13 ALL**	**4/1/13-3/31/14 ALL**		**0-1MM**	**1-3MM**	**3-5MM**	**5-10MM**	**10-25MM**	**25MM & OVER**
177	151	142	**NUMBER OF STATEMENTS**	5	14	10	22	35	56
%	%	%	**ASSETS**	%	%	%	%	%	%
7.7	7.9	8.6	Cash & Equivalents		24.5	9.7	10.8	7.3	4.6
26.9	26.2	26.9	Trade Receivables (net)		33.1	18.7	30.5	26.0	25.6
27.2	28.2	28.8	Inventory		14.9	27.4	27.4	32.3	30.6
1.3	3.2	1.8	All Other Current		.0	.3	.6	2.9	2.4
63.0	65.4	66.1	Total Current		72.5	56.1	69.3	68.6	63.3
25.2	23.8	25.0	Fixed Assets (net)		18.7	32.6	23.6	23.8	26.7
5.8	4.3	2.9	Intangibles (net)		.2	.4	2.2	2.0	5.1
6.0	6.5	6.0	All Other Non-Current		8.6	10.9	4.9	5.6	4.9
100.0	100.0	100.0	Total		100.0	100.0	100.0	100.0	100.0
			LIABILITIES						
10.6	11.5	12.8	Notes Payable-Short Term		16.5	11.8	10.8	16.7	10.2
3.2	2.4	2.3	Cur. Mat.-L.T.D.		2.3	3.9	1.1	2.7	2.4
14.0	15.9	16.9	Trade Payables		19.9	13.7	15.4	22.6	14.8
.2	.2	.1	Income Taxes Payable		.1	.0	.2	.1	.2
13.4	10.0	7.3	All Other Current		1.5	8.8	5.7	7.5	9.3
41.4	39.9	39.4	Total Current		40.4	38.2	33.3	49.5	36.9
16.2	17.7	15.7	Long-Term Debt		10.0	28.4	11.6	10.5	18.7
.5	.4	.6	Deferred Taxes		.0	.0	.4	.4	1.0
5.8	5.4	6.5	All Other Non-Current		6.9	16.0	1.7	3.1	7.5
36.1	36.6	37.9	Net Worth		42.7	17.4	53.0	36.4	35.9
100.0	100.0	100.0	Total Liabilties & Net Worth		100.0	100.0	100.0	100.0	100.0
			INCOME DATA						
100.0	100.0	100.0	Net Sales		100.0	100.0	100.0	100.0	100.0
23.9	24.7	24.1	Gross Profit		36.7	34.9	29.3	22.5	15.8
18.4	18.5	19.1	Operating Expenses		29.4	33.9	21.6	17.8	11.7
5.5	6.2	5.0	Operating Profit		7.3	1.1	7.8	4.7	4.0
.8	1.0	.8	All Other Expenses (net)		.8	1.0	.5	.3	1.2
4.8	5.2	4.3	Profit Before Taxes		6.5	.1	7.3	4.4	2.8
			RATIOS						
2.9	3.3	3.4			7.3	5.5	4.2	2.5	3.1
1.7	1.7	2.0	Current		2.5	2.0	2.4	1.4	1.8
1.2	1.2	1.2			1.4	.8	1.6	1.0	1.3
1.7	1.7	1.9			5.5	3.4	2.3	1.6	1.5
.9	.9	.9	Quick		2.2	.5	1.6	.7	.8
.6	.5	.5			.8	.3	.8	.4	.6
31 11.8	27 13.7	28 13.1			18 20.2	15 25.1	32 11.3	22 16.3	39 9.4
43 8.5	40 9.2	43 8.5	Sales/Receivables		53 6.9	21 17.3	46 8.0	34 10.7	46 8.0
59 6.2	53 6.9	57 6.4			85 4.3	35 10.4	59 6.2	48 7.6	56 6.5
27 13.3	31 11.9	33 11.0			0 UND	16 23.5	25 14.8	21 17.6	41 8.9
55 6.6	54 6.8	57 6.4	Cost of Sales/Inventory		23 15.8	42 8.6	66 5.5	46 8.0	66 5.5
99 3.7	99 3.7	96 3.8			68 5.4	146 2.5	89 4.1	104 3.5	94 3.9
14 26.0	14 25.8	16 22.6			17 21.2	9 41.8	13 27.9	18 20.1	17 21.6
27 13.5	29 12.7	29 12.8	Cost of Sales/Payables		41 9.0	22 16.3	27 13.5	29 12.8	29 12.6
40 9.1	46 7.9	47 7.7			55 6.6	40 9.2	51 7.2	54 6.8	42 8.6
4.9	5.0	4.3			3.8	3.9	3.4	6.4	4.0
8.4	8.6	7.4	Sales/Working Capital		6.3	16.1	6.1	14.7	7.4
32.9	27.5	20.8			NM	-16.7	11.4	-159.1	16.6
18.7	30.8	16.6					36.4	20.0	14.1
(158) 6.2	(138) 8.9	(125) 6.2	EBIT/Interest				(17) 5.1	(33) 6.9	(54) 7.7
1.5	2.3	2.1					1.4	2.5	2.2
12.6	7.8	6.0							5.8
(43) 2.9	(32) 4.6	(24) 2.9	Net Profit + Depr., Dep., Amort./Cur. Mat. L/T/D						(17) 2.9
.8	2.3	1.4							1.8
.3	.3	.2			.1	.7	.0	.3	.3
.7	.6	.6	Fixed/Worth		.5	1.3	.2	.5	.6
1.7	1.6	1.5			-1.4	-22.3	1.5	1.2	1.4
.7	.7	.6			.2	1.2	.5	.7	1.0
1.7	1.7	1.6	Debt/Worth		.5	4.1	.8	1.6	2.0
6.1	5.7	5.1			-14.0	-56.8	2.4	4.8	5.8
41.6	61.7	47.5			54.0		42.5	48.5	47.5
(149) 21.2	(130) 30.1	(127) 21.8	% Profit Before Taxes/Tangible Net Worth		(10) 18.6		25.3	(34) 30.9	(49) 18.7
6.4	13.3	8.7			4.2		5.8	8.9	13.0
16.9	21.2	17.2			34.4	13.2	23.4	20.1	11.9
8.3	11.2	7.9	% Profit Before Taxes/Total Assets		10.5	4.0	13.8	7.5	7.9
1.1	2.8	2.1			-1.6	-8.0	3.0	2.6	2.1
23.7	25.3	32.0			44.3	14.9	84.0	20.6	21.0
10.1	10.3	10.6	Sales/Net Fixed Assets		25.6	6.9	20.1	12.5	10.0
5.2	5.6	5.8			6.4	4.4	5.6	7.2	4.4
2.8	2.9	2.9			3.1	3.2	2.8	3.3	2.6
2.1	2.2	2.2	Sales/Total Assets		2.5	2.7	2.2	2.5	2.0
1.6	1.6	1.6			1.2	1.0	1.6	1.7	1.4
1.1	.6	.6				1.5	.5	.6	.6
(150) 1.9	(132) 1.5	(122) 1.7	% Depr., Dep., Amort./Sales			2.0	(20) 1.9	(31) 1.5	(50) 1.4
3.5	2.6	2.6				3.7	3.0	2.6	2.5
1.3	1.7	1.5					1.7		
(60) 3.0	(44) 4.0	(38) 3.1	% Officers', Directors' Owners' Comp/Sales				(14) 3.6		
5.3	7.4	5.5					7.7		
9043726M	7678995M	6324658M	Net Sales ($)	2719M	29985M	37158M	168552M	571103M	5515141M
4656611M	4327468M	4000349M	Total Assets ($)	1582M	16772M	22939M	98156M	248744M	3612156M

M = $ thousand MM = $ million

See Pages 9 through 22 for Explanation of Ratios and Data

Current Data Sorted by Assets							Comparative Historical Data	
						Type of Statement		
			14	1	3	Unqualified	13	7
		6	1			Reviewed	21	15
2	4	3	4			Compiled	11	10
	3	3	2			Tax Returns	12	7
1	5	5	19	8	2	Other	35	40
	20 (4/1-9/30/13)		66 (10/1/13-3/31/14)				4/1/09-3/31/10 ALL	4/1/10-3/31/11 ALL
0-500M	500M-2MM	2-10MM	10-50MM	50-100MM	100-250MM			
3	12	17	40	9	5	**NUMBER OF STATEMENTS**	92	79
%	%	%	%	%	%	**ASSETS**	%	%
	9.3	9.5	5.1			Cash & Equivalents	9.4	6.6
	38.8	26.2	20.7			Trade Receivables (net)	23.4	26.9
	19.3	31.4	33.6			Inventory	28.8	29.9
	1.1	1.0	1.3			All Other Current	2.9	.8
	68.5	68.1	60.8			Total Current	64.5	64.2
	25.4	26.8	28.5			Fixed Assets (net)	27.1	27.5
	4.0	1.3	5.7			Intangibles (net)	3.1	2.5
	2.2	3.9	5.0			All Other Non-Current	5.3	5.8
	100.0	100.0	100.0			Total	100.0	100.0
						LIABILITIES		
	13.8	10.3	14.8			Notes Payable-Short Term	11.5	16.0
	7.4	1.3	3.8			Cur. Mat.-L.T.D.	3.0	3.0
	19.6	16.8	13.5			Trade Payables	14.4	17.1
	.0	.1	.0			Income Taxes Payable	.2	.1
	8.8	23.4	5.6			All Other Current	7.0	7.9
	49.6	51.9	37.8			Total Current	36.2	44.0
	21.2	13.5	18.7			Long-Term Debt	12.8	16.0
	.0	.1	.9			Deferred Taxes	.7	.4
	4.1	6.8	5.2			All Other Non-Current	7.0	9.0
	25.1	27.7	37.4			Net Worth	43.3	30.6
	100.0	100.0	100.0			Total Liabilties & Net Worth	100.0	100.0
						INCOME DATA		
	100.0	100.0	100.0			Net Sales	100.0	100.0
	34.1	25.7	20.1			Gross Profit	20.8	22.1
	26.8	21.2	13.0			Operating Expenses	18.3	16.9
	7.3	4.5	7.1			Operating Profit	2.4	5.2
	.2	.9	1.2			All Other Expenses (net)	1.0	1.2
	7.1	3.6	5.9			Profit Before Taxes	1.4	4.0
						RATIOS		
	2.9	4.1	3.4				3.9	2.3
	1.4	1.9	1.4			Current	1.8	1.3
	.9	1.1	1.1				1.1	1.1
	1.9	2.2	1.6				1.8	1.3
	.9	.7	.6			Quick	.8	.7
	.5	.5	.4				.5	.4
	34 10.8	**33** 11.2	**27** 13.7				**29** 12.7	**38** 9.7
	56 6.5	**43** 8.5	**38** 9.5			Sales/Receivables	**43** 8.6	**46** 7.9
	101 3.6	**55** 6.6	**45** 8.1				**55** 6.7	**55** 6.7
	10 36.7	**38** 9.6	**46** 7.9				**33** 11.0	**36** 10.2
	44 8.3	**51** 7.2	**63** 5.8			Cost of Sales/Inventory	**61** 6.0	**58** 6.3
	65 5.6	**111** 3.3	**99** 3.7				**86** 4.2	**87** 4.2
	30 12.3	**15** 24.4	**20** 18.6				**14** 25.6	**21** 17.0
	36 10.1	**22** 16.9	**26** 13.8			Cost of Sales/Payables	**24** 15.1	**32** 11.5
	72 5.1	**43** 8.5	**35** 10.3				**44** 8.4	**47** 7.8
	6.4	4.1	4.1				3.8	4.9
	18.3	9.1	11.8			Sales/Working Capital	7.9	13.7
	NM	NM	51.0				52.4	41.4
	14.9	15.2	13.4				7.0	9.2
	(11) 6.2	(15) 5.2	(35) 4.9			EBIT/Interest	(82) 2.2	(73) 3.3
	1.6	4.2	1.7				-1.1	1.5
			7.1				13.3	4.9
			(17) 2.4			Net Profit + Depr., Dep., Amort./Cur. Mat. L/T/D	(22) 2.8	(16) 3.2
			1.4				.3	1.9
	.6	.0	.4				.3	.4
	1.4	1.1	.7			Fixed/Worth	.6	.9
	4.3	2.5	3.8				1.8	1.9
	1.4	.6	.7				.5	.9
	5.5	2.0	1.8			Debt/Worth	1.6	2.0
	11.8	12.8	5.5				3.4	7.3
	75.7	59.2	33.2				24.0	38.6
	(10) 37.5	(15) 31.0	(32) 15.7			% Profit Before Taxes/Tangible Net Worth	(82) 8.6	(69) 19.0
	13.7	11.0	4.2				-7.8	3.8
	14.4	16.8	14.7				8.2	13.4
	6.9	5.3	7.4			% Profit Before Taxes/Total Assets	3.0	5.1
	1.8	3.1	1.6				-5.0	.8
	36.2	204.4	18.0				20.4	22.1
	13.8	15.3	8.8			Sales/Net Fixed Assets	8.2	9.8
	5.4	3.4	4.6				4.0	4.1
	3.3	2.8	2.6				2.7	2.6
	2.4	2.2	2.1			Sales/Total Assets	1.9	2.1
	1.6	1.3	1.4				1.4	1.4
		.6	.9				1.0	.8
		(13) 1.0	(38) 1.4			% Depr., Dep., Amort./Sales	(76) 1.8	(72) 1.7
		4.1	2.5				4.0	3.6
							1.5	1.4
						% Officers', Directors' Owners' Comp/Sales	(25) 2.3	(16) 2.7
							4.2	4.7
1282M	33690M	219746M	2008794M	1092877M	1954917M	Net Sales ($)	4122993M	2931624M
775M	14235M	98518M	963861M	640437M	761802M	Total Assets ($)	2133776M	1526783M

M = $ thousand MM = $ million

See Pages 9 through 22 for Explanation of Ratios and Data

Comparative Historical Data				Current Data Sorted by Sales					
			Type of Statement						
20	14	18	Unqualified				1	2	15
17	14	7	Reviewed			1		5	1
11	10	13	Compiled	2	3	1	3	3	1
3	6	8	Tax Returns		1	2	2	1	2
21	30	40	Other	2	1	3	3	5	26
4/1/11-3/31/12 ALL	**4/1/12-3/31/13 ALL**	**4/1/13-3/31/14 ALL**		**20 (4/1-9/30/13)**			**66 (10/1/13-3/31/14)**		
				0-1MM	**1-3MM**	**3-5MM**	**5-10MM**	**10-25MM**	**25MM & OVER**
72	74	86	**NUMBER OF STATEMENTS**	4	5	7	9	16	45
%	%	%	**ASSETS**	%	%	%	%	%	%
8.1	7.7	6.7	Cash & Equivalents					11.5	3.5
28.4	26.7	24.4	Trade Receivables (net)					21.0	23.9
26.7	28.2	30.1	Inventory					30.5	35.7
1.8	1.4	1.2	All Other Current					1.7	1.3
65.1	63.9	62.5	Total Current					64.7	64.4
26.8	27.0	27.7	Fixed Assets (net)					28.1	24.1
1.6	4.9	5.2	Intangibles (net)					3.5	5.7
6.4	4.2	4.6	All Other Non-Current					3.8	5.8
100.0	100.0	100.0	Total					100.0	100.0
			LIABILITIES						
11.3	14.0	12.2	Notes Payable-Short Term					10.4	15.4
2.0	3.1	3.5	Cur. Mat.-L.T.D.					1.7	3.5
15.8	16.1	15.2	Trade Payables					13.1	16.5
.3	.1	.0	Income Taxes Payable					.0	.0
8.1	9.2	10.8	All Other Current					7.9	7.8
37.5	42.5	41.7	Total Current					33.1	43.2
15.6	13.9	18.2	Long-Term Debt					15.8	15.0
.7	.6	.7	Deferred Taxes					.9	.8
7.1	6.2	6.1	All Other Non-Current					1.2	7.2
39.0	36.7	33.4	Net Worth					48.9	33.8
100.0	100.0	100.0	Total Liabilities & Net Worth					100.0	100.0
			INCOME DATA						
100.0	100.0	100.0	Net Sales					100.0	100.0
21.6	21.5	23.2	Gross Profit					29.1	14.7
15.9	16.6	16.7	Operating Expenses					19.4	9.5
5.7	4.9	6.5	Operating Profit					9.7	5.2
.6	.4	1.0	All Other Expenses (net)					.5	1.1
5.1	4.5	5.5	Profit Before Taxes					9.2	4.0
			RATIOS						
3.2	2.4	2.9						5.3	2.5
1.8	1.6	1.5	Current					2.1	1.5
1.2	1.0	1.1						1.2	1.1
1.7	1.2	1.7						2.8	1.3
1.0	.8	.7	Quick					.8	.6
.7	.5	.5						.5	.4
38 9.7	34 10.8	31 11.9						25 14.5	32 11.4
47 7.7	41 8.8	41 8.8	Sales/Receivables					38 9.6	41 8.9
61 6.0	47 7.7	49 7.5						51 7.1	46 7.9
30 12.0	27 13.5	40 9.2						45 8.1	45 8.2
56 6.5	51 7.2	62 5.9	Cost of Sales/Inventory					65 5.6	63 5.8
81 4.5	79 4.6	99 3.7						111 3.3	94 3.9
18 20.8	15 24.1	20 18.0						17 22.1	21 17.7
30 12.3	26 14.3	30 12.1	Cost of Sales/Payables					26 13.8	30 12.0
44 8.3	41 9.0	41 8.8						41 8.9	40 9.2
4.3	6.3	4.9						2.7	5.3
8.6	12.0	9.1	Sales/Working Capital					5.0	10.2
34.7	285.2	50.9						29.1	44.8
16.8	21.7	13.1						20.7	12.8
(63) 7.7	(70) 9.0	(75) 5.2	EBIT/Interest					(12) 7.3	(40) 5.0
2.9	2.3	1.7						4.4	1.7
8.3	7.0	7.9							7.9
(21) 5.4	(19) 3.7	(29) 3.0	Net Profit + Depr., Dep., Amort./Cur. Mat. L/T/D						(21) 4.0
3.3	1.6	1.6							1.4
.4	.3	.4						.2	.4
.7	.9	.8	Fixed/Worth					.7	.7
1.7	5.1	2.9						3.0	2.5
.6	.7	.9						.2	.9
1.4	1.7	2.0	Debt/Worth					1.0	1.8
8.3	10.2	7.2						6.7	5.4
43.2	40.8	40.3						53.9	32.9
(59) 23.2	(58) 22.8	(70) 21.5	% Profit Before Taxes/Tangible Net Worth					(14) 32.9	(36) 14.8
6.3	8.9	8.5						15.3	3.8
15.6	15.7	14.2						22.5	11.0
10.2	7.1	6.6	% Profit Before Taxes/Total Assets					11.3	5.6
3.5	2.0	2.9						5.5	1.5
18.2	19.4	24.4						31.5	24.8
10.2	10.1	9.0	Sales/Net Fixed Assets					7.9	9.1
5.3	5.1	4.3						3.1	6.0
2.8	2.9	2.7						2.6	2.8
2.2	2.3	2.1	Sales/Total Assets					1.8	2.3
1.5	1.7	1.4						1.0	1.6
.6	.8	.9						.8	.8
(65) 1.3	(67) 1.3	(75) 1.6	% Depr., Dep., Amort./Sales					(13) 1.2	(44) 1.4
2.8	2.3	2.7						3.1	2.1
1.3	.9	1.6							
(15) 5.0	(16) 1.9	(19) 3.7	% Officers', Directors' Owners' Comp/Sales						
6.7	5.5	6.3							
4492833M	**4382557M**	**5311306M**	Net Sales ($)	**1359M**	**10116M**	**26437M**	**65022M**	**290645M**	**4917727M**
2081815M	**1949076M**	**2479628M**	Total Assets ($)	**2228M**	**5350M**	**11288M**	**58408M**	**189064M**	**2213290M**

M = $ thousand MM = $ million

See Pages 9 through 22 for Explanation of Ratios and Data

Current Data Sorted by Assets							Comparative Historical Data	
						Type of Statement		
			3			Unqualified	5	6
		3	4			Reviewed	8	12
	1	2				Compiled	4	5
	1					Tax Returns	6	1
1		4	9	3	2	Other	18	13
	4 (4/1-9/30/13)		29 (10/1/13-3/31/14)				**4/1/09-3/31/10 ALL**	**4/1/10-3/31/11 ALL**
0-500M	**500M-2MM**	**2-10MM**	**10-50MM**	**50-100MM**	**100-250MM**			
1	2	9	16	3	2	**NUMBER OF STATEMENTS**	41	37
%	%	%	%	%	%	**ASSETS**	%	%
			8.3			Cash & Equivalents	9.3	7.4
			27.5			Trade Receivables (net)	27.2	26.7
			31.0			Inventory	27.3	35.8
			2.2			All Other Current	4.4	1.8
			69.1			Total Current	68.2	71.7
			20.5			Fixed Assets (net)	21.7	22.5
			7.9			Intangibles (net)	1.8	1.5
			2.5			All Other Non-Current	8.4	4.4
			100.0			Total	100.0	100.0
						LIABILITIES		
			14.1			Notes Payable-Short Term	14.8	14.7
			2.1			Cur. Mat.-L.T.D.	3.1	1.9
			17.6			Trade Payables	17.8	19.4
			.2			Income Taxes Payable	.1	.1
			11.3			All Other Current	5.4	7.8
			45.4			Total Current	41.1	43.9
			12.9			Long-Term Debt	9.2	12.2
			3.0			Deferred Taxes	.4	.5
			.8			All Other Non-Current	13.7	3.5
			37.9			Net Worth	35.5	39.9
			100.0			Total Liabilties & Net Worth	100.0	100.0
						INCOME DATA		
			100.0			Net Sales	100.0	100.0
			18.4			Gross Profit	21.8	23.4
			12.7			Operating Expenses	21.4	18.7
			5.6			Operating Profit	.3	4.8
			2.0			All Other Expenses (net)	.2	.6
			3.6			Profit Before Taxes	.1	4.2
						RATIOS		
			2.0				3.8	3.5
			1.5			Current	1.9	1.5
			1.2				1.1	1.1
			.9				2.3	1.5
			.8			Quick	.9	.7
			.5				.6	.5
			29 12.6				**34** 10.8	**37** 10.0
			42 8.6			Sales/Receivables	**41** 8.8	**46** 7.9
			57 6.4				**54** 6.8	**53** 6.9
			39 9.3				**34** 10.8	**49** 7.4
			65 5.6			Cost of Sales/Inventory	**55** 6.6	**68** 5.3
			118 3.1				**96** 3.8	**135** 2.7
			10 34.9				**13** 28.4	**23** 15.7
			27 13.7			Cost of Sales/Payables	**26** 14.2	**37** 9.7
			40 9.2				**60** 6.1	**58** 6.3
			5.5				3.6	4.2
			10.7			Sales/Working Capital	8.2	7.9
			17.7				62.3	78.7
			29.8				11.4	17.6
			(15) 4.7			EBIT/Interest	(33) 2.6	(34) 4.3
			.2				-4.2	1.2
						Net Profit + Depr., Dep., Amort./Cur. Mat. L/T/D		
			.3				.1	.2
			.7			Fixed/Worth	.5	.5
			1.6				1.1	1.6
			1.0				.5	.6
			2.2			Debt/Worth	1.4	1.7
			5.7				4.7	5.8
			58.7				29.4	51.2
			(14) 15.2			% Profit Before Taxes/Tangible Net Worth	(36) 9.7	(36) 17.8
			-5.5				-17.2	1.7
			11.5				7.5	15.5
			5.0			% Profit Before Taxes/Total Assets	2.8	5.0
			-2.7				-10.2	1.0
			28.7				66.4	34.6
			12.0			Sales/Net Fixed Assets	11.6	13.5
			6.4				6.4	5.3
			3.2				3.0	3.0
			2.3			Sales/Total Assets	2.0	2.0
			1.1				1.5	1.5
			.6				.8	1.0
			1.3			% Depr., Dep., Amort./Sales	(31) 1.5	(32) 1.5
			4.2				2.5	2.9
						% Officers', Directors' Owners' Comp/Sales		
9M	**8866M**	**78075M**	**964142M**	**375603M**	**718368M**	Net Sales ($)	**2115329M**	**1522054M**
7M	**3872M**	**40879M**	**448511M**	**216993M**	**347899M**	Total Assets ($)	**1295253M**	**705620M**

M = $ thousand MM = $ million

See Pages 9 through 22 for Explanation of Ratios and Data

Comparative Historical Data			Type of Statement	Current Data Sorted by Sales					
4	7	3	Unqualified						3
8	9	7	Reviewed		1	1	1	2	2
4	1	3	Compiled				2	1	
2	1	1	Tax Returns		1				
20	18	19	Other	1		1		3	14
4/1/11-3/31/12 ALL	4/1/12-3/31/13 ALL	4/1/13-3/31/14 ALL			4 (4/1-9/30/13)		29 (10/1/13-3/31/14)		
				0-1MM	1-3MM	3-5MM	5-10MM	10-25MM	25MM & OVER
38	36	33	NUMBER OF STATEMENTS	1	2	2	3	6	19
%	%	%	**ASSETS**	%	%	%	%	%	%
6.6	5.3	6.0	Cash & Equivalents						7.6
28.5	26.2	27.5	Trade Receivables (net)						27.0
32.3	32.7	32.5	Inventory						31.5
1.2	1.3	1.7	All Other Current						2.5
68.7	65.4	67.8	Total Current						68.6
25.1	25.9	24.3	Fixed Assets (net)						23.6
3.6	3.0	5.3	Intangibles (net)						6.7
2.6	5.7	2.5	All Other Non-Current						1.2
100.0	100.0	100.0	Total						100.0
			LIABILITIES						
9.2	14.2	11.9	Notes Payable-Short Term						11.9
1.5	1.6	1.8	Cur. Mat.-L.T.D.						1.9
18.5	18.8	18.9	Trade Payables						17.7
.1	.3	.1	Income Taxes Payable						.2
6.6	6.6	9.8	All Other Current						8.3
36.0	41.4	42.5	Total Current						40.1
11.7	12.9	10.4	Long-Term Debt						13.4
.6	.8	1.7	Deferred Taxes						2.7
3.6	2.2	4.3	All Other Non-Current						1.5
48.2	42.7	41.1	Net Worth						42.3
100.0	100.0	100.0	Total Liabilties & Net Worth						100.0
			INCOME DATA						
100.0	100.0	100.0	Net Sales						100.0
19.9	21.1	19.4	Gross Profit						17.7
14.0	15.0	15.2	Operating Expenses						11.7
5.8	6.1	4.3	Operating Profit						5.9
.9	.9	1.1	All Other Expenses (net)						1.7
5.0	5.2	3.2	Profit Before Taxes						4.3
			RATIOS						
3.7	2.9	2.5							2.8
2.2	1.6	1.6	Current						1.7
1.2	1.1	1.2							1.2
1.6	1.3	1.2							1.4
1.2	.8	.8	Quick						.8
.6	.4	.5							.5
34 10.6	32 11.3	33 11.2							29 12.6
46 8.0	42 8.7	43 8.4	Sales/Receivables						40 9.1
56 6.5	56 6.5	61 6.0							52 7.0
42 8.7	44 8.3	52 7.0							50 7.3
66 5.5	62 5.9	66 5.5	Cost of Sales/Inventory						62 5.9
107 3.4	111 3.3	111 3.3							111 3.3
17 21.3	18 20.4	18 20.5							17 20.9
31 11.8	32 11.5	38 9.7	Cost of Sales/Payables						33 11.0
53 6.9	59 6.2	49 7.5							40 9.2
3.9	4.6	5.1							4.1
6.0	13.6	9.0	Sales/Working Capital						8.3
24.9	48.2	18.0							17.8
30.1	28.4	32.8							37.1
(34) 9.5	(34) 9.8	(29) 7.5	EBIT/Interest						(18) 11.6
2.3	4.2	.8							2.4
			Net Profit + Depr., Dep., Amort./Cur. Mat. L/T/D						
.2	.3	.3							.3
.6	.7	.6	Fixed/Worth						.6
1.1	1.2	1.3							1.5
.5	.7	.7							.5
1.0	1.3	1.3	Debt/Worth						1.4
3.0	4.3	5.0							3.8
30.2	41.4	37.8							46.2
(34) 21.9	(34) 19.0	(29) 12.1	% Profit Before Taxes/Tangible Net Worth						(17) 19.1
8.9	5.9	-2.9							-4.8
17.5	16.3	12.5							12.8
7.0	8.3	5.0	% Profit Before Taxes/Total Assets						8.0
2.3	2.7	-1.3							-1.7
31.2	27.9	25.0							26.6
8.0	10.0	10.4	Sales/Net Fixed Assets						10.4
5.1	4.7	4.2							5.5
2.8	2.9	2.9							3.0
1.9	2.0	1.7	Sales/Total Assets						2.4
1.6	1.5	1.2							1.4
.4	.6	.7							.7
(35) 1.3	(34) 1.4	(30) 1.3	% Depr., Dep., Amort./Sales						1.3
2.8	2.7	4.2							4.2
			% Officers', Directors' Owners' Comp/Sales						
2737836M	2588787M	2145063M	Net Sales ($)	9M	4688M	7399M	23421M	96447M	2013099M
1361216M	1252008M	1058161M	Total Assets ($)	7M	4242M	6360M	9050M	68872M	969630M

M = $ thousand MM = $ million

See Pages 9 through 22 for Explanation of Ratios and Data

Current Data Sorted by Assets							Comparative Historical Data	
		1	11	3	3	**Type of Statement** Unqualified	24	21
		9	6			Reviewed	11	17
	1		1			Compiled	3	5
1		3	1			Tax Returns	3	6
	2	7	14	4	3	Other	35	40
	12 (4/1-9/30/13)		58 (10/1/13-3/31/14)				**4/1/09-3/31/10**	**4/1/10-3/31/11**
0-500M	**500M-2MM**	**2-10MM**	**10-50MM**	**50-100MM**	**100-250MM**		**ALL**	**ALL**
1	3	20	33	7	6	**NUMBER OF STATEMENTS**	76	89
%	%	%	%	%	%	**ASSETS**	%	%
		10.2	5.0			Cash & Equivalents	6.8	6.2
		29.3	26.2			Trade Receivables (net)	24.6	27.9
		26.8	23.9			Inventory	23.3	26.3
		2.6	1.2			All Other Current	3.9	2.2
		68.9	56.4			Total Current	58.6	62.6
		28.0	36.7			Fixed Assets (net)	32.4	30.4
		1.9	4.1			Intangibles (net)	3.1	2.3
		1.1	2.8			All Other Non-Current	5.9	4.7
		100.0	100.0			Total	100.0	100.0
						LIABILITIES		
		11.7	9.3			Notes Payable-Short Term	13.8	14.4
		10.1	3.3			Cur. Mat.-L.T.D.	4.3	4.2
		19.5	15.4			Trade Payables	14.9	16.3
		.1	.1			Income Taxes Payable	.2	.2
		9.0	8.1			All Other Current	10.4	8.1
		50.3	36.1			Total Current	43.6	43.2
		9.1	19.1			Long-Term Debt	19.9	16.9
		.6	.5			Deferred Taxes	.7	.8
		11.0	2.1			All Other Non-Current	5.5	6.5
		28.9	42.1			Net Worth	30.3	32.5
		100.0	100.0			Total Liabilities & Net Worth	100.0	100.0
						INCOME DATA		
		100.0	100.0			Net Sales	100.0	100.0
		20.7	17.3			Gross Profit	20.7	20.2
		16.3	11.1			Operating Expenses	18.1	16.5
		4.5	6.1			Operating Profit	2.6	3.7
		.6	.7			All Other Expenses (net)	.8	.6
		3.8	5.5			Profit Before Taxes	1.9	3.1
						RATIOS		
		5.0	2.0				2.6	2.4
		1.9	1.5			Current	1.6	1.6
		1.1	1.2				.9	1.2
		3.7	1.2				1.4	1.5
		1.0	.9			Quick	.9	.8
		.5	.6				.4	.5
		28 13.0	**26** 14.2				**30** 12.0	**34** 10.6
		36 10.2	**34** 10.8			Sales/Receivables	**41** 8.9	**43** 8.5
		53 6.9	**46** 8.0				**53** 6.9	**54** 6.8
		26 13.9	**28** 13.1				**25** 14.6	**25** 14.4
		37 9.8	**36** 10.0			Cost of Sales/Inventory	**40** 9.1	**42** 8.7
		55 6.6	**54** 6.7				**79** 4.6	**79** 4.6
		18 20.2	**17** 21.1				**16** 23.4	**20** 18.4
		24 14.9	**25** 14.6			Cost of Sales/Payables	**25** 14.6	**30** 12.3
		40 9.2	**34** 10.8				**43** 8.5	**43** 8.5
		4.0	8.5				5.8	5.5
		6.4	13.3			Sales/Working Capital	9.8	9.9
		132.0	32.7				-94.0	35.3
		19.6	48.9				8.8	18.7
		(19) 8.4	(32) 9.5			EBIT/Interest	(71) 2.3	(84) 4.9
		1.6	2.7				-.6	1.3
							4.2	6.3
						Net Profit + Depr., Dep., Amort./Cur. Mat. L/T/D	(19) 1.8	(24) 2.9
							.1	.9
		.2	.5				.3	.2
		.6	1.0			Fixed/Worth	1.1	.8
		1.5	2.1				3.5	2.2
		.4	.9				.6	.7
		1.1	1.6			Debt/Worth	1.9	1.7
		5.5	3.7				5.8	4.8
		30.8	48.7				33.8	34.3
		(17) 23.6	(31) 27.0			% Profit Before Taxes/Tangible Net Worth	(63) 9.1	(73) 17.2
		13.6	12.0				-8.2	5.0
		15.1	25.5				11.6	14.2
		10.4	8.4			% Profit Before Taxes/Total Assets	2.3	7.2
		2.5	3.8				-3.8	.5
		29.3	13.4				16.7	24.5
		13.2	7.3			Sales/Net Fixed Assets	6.7	7.8
		5.3	4.7				4.2	4.1
		3.3	3.7				2.6	2.9
		2.8	2.5			Sales/Total Assets	2.1	2.1
		2.0	1.9				1.5	1.6
		.7	1.4				1.3	1.1
		1.2	2.0			% Depr., Dep., Amort./Sales	(62) 2.4	(76) 1.9
		2.0	3.1				4.1	3.3
			.8				1.0	.8
			(10) 1.0			% Officers', Directors' Owners' Comp/Sales	(16) 1.6	(23) 2.1
			3.1				3.7	11.4
649M	**6348M**	**287252M**	**1840598M**	**1524631M**	**1176697M**	Net Sales ($)	**3307076M**	**4801031M**
383M	**3879M**	**101749M**	**683336M**	**542293M**	**855678M**	Total Assets ($)	**1839329M**	**2542730M**

M = $ thousand MM = $ million

See Pages 9 through 22 for Explanation of Ratios and Data

Comparative Historical Data				Current Data Sorted by Sales					
			Type of Statement						
27	21	18	Unqualified				1	3	14
19	18	15	Reviewed				2	5	8
2	2	2	Compiled			1			1
2	7	5	Tax Returns	1		2	1	1	
25	29	30	Other	1	1	1	1	4	22
				12 (4/1-9/30/13)			58 (10/1/13-3/31/14)		
4/1/11-3/31/12 ALL	**4/1/12-3/31/13 ALL**	**4/1/13-3/31/14 ALL**		**0-1MM**	**1-3MM**	**3-5MM**	**5-10MM**	**10-25MM**	**25MM & OVER**
75	77	70	**NUMBER OF STATEMENTS**	2	1	4	5	13	45
%	%	%	**ASSETS**	%	%	%	%	%	%
5.2	6.5	6.6	Cash & Equivalents					6.5	5.5
27.3	25.6	27.5	Trade Receivables (net)					29.9	27.0
24.9	26.7	24.1	Inventory					24.8	25.5
2.0	2.2	2.1	All Other Current					2.6	2.1
59.4	61.1	60.4	Total Current					63.9	60.1
31.8	31.1	33.1	Fixed Assets (net)					29.3	35.5
4.3	2.8	3.6	Intangibles (net)					5.0	1.2
4.5	5.0	2.9	All Other Non-Current					1.8	3.2
100.0	100.0	100.0	Total					100.0	100.0
			LIABILITIES						
13.2	12.8	10.2	Notes Payable-Short Term					9.7	10.0
3.7	5.8	5.0	Cur. Mat.-L.T.D.					5.0	2.6
16.8	14.6	15.8	Trade Payables					19.1	16.7
.2	.1	.1	Income Taxes Payable					.1	.1
6.7	7.3	8.1	All Other Current					11.3	7.1
40.6	40.6	39.3	Total Current					45.2	36.5
17.2	13.1	14.8	Long-Term Debt					16.0	16.6
1.4	1.2	.7	Deferred Taxes					.9	.9
4.8	4.7	8.2	All Other Non-Current					12.3	7.1
36.1	40.3	37.0	Net Worth					25.6	38.9
100.0	100.0	100.0	Total Liabilities & Net Worth					100.0	100.0
			INCOME DATA						
100.0	100.0	100.0	Net Sales					100.0	100.0
18.5	22.5	19.5	Gross Profit					16.3	16.7
13.0	15.5	13.7	Operating Expenses					13.9	10.3
5.5	7.0	5.8	Operating Profit					2.4	6.4
.7	.8	.7	All Other Expenses (net)					.1	.8
4.8	6.2	5.1	Profit Before Taxes					2.2	5.6
			RATIOS						
2.2	2.6	3.5						1.9	2.3
1.6	1.8	1.7	Current					1.4	1.7
1.2	1.1	1.2						1.1	1.2
1.5	1.6	1.9						1.2	1.4
.9	.9	.9	Quick					.9	.9
.5	.5	.6						.4	.6
33 11.2	**28** 13.1	**28** 13.1						**28** 12.9	**26** 14.3
42 8.6	**38** 9.7	**36** 10.0	Sales/Receivables					**35** 10.4	**35** 10.5
53 6.9	**45** 8.1	**48** 7.6						**58** 6.3	**47** 7.7
27 13.3	**29** 12.4	**27** 13.6						**20** 18.7	**27** 13.3
41 8.9	**49** 7.5	**38** 9.6	Cost of Sales/Inventory					**33** 11.2	**36** 10.0
68 5.4	**72** 5.1	**69** 5.3						**61** 6.0	**69** 5.3
16 22.5	**17** 21.1	**18** 20.6						**21** 17.1	**17** 21.1
26 14.2	**25** 14.4	**25** 14.4	Cost of Sales/Payables					**27** 13.5	**26** 14.2
42 8.7	**32** 11.4	**36** 10.1						**41** 8.9	**36** 10.1
5.9	4.8	5.2						6.4	6.2
11.1	10.8	12.0	Sales/Working Capital					12.2	13.0
58.5	56.7	32.6						93.9	40.9
23.1	20.6	23.7						16.5	30.7
(71) 5.5	(66) 6.6	(67) 7.8	EBIT/Interest					7.8	(44) 7.9
2.6	3.4	2.5						-1.8	3.7
5.9	7.9	16.6							22.0
(24) 3.5	(23) 2.3	(22) 4.8	Net Profit + Depr., Dep., Amort./Cur. Mat. L/T/D						(16) 4.8
2.0	.9	1.7							1.8
.5	.3	.4						.2	.5
1.0	1.0	1.0	Fixed/Worth					1.3	1.0
1.9	1.8	2.5						22.1	2.1
.9	.6	.8						1.1	.9
1.5	1.4	1.7	Debt/Worth					2.0	1.9
3.8	4.6	5.3						71.2	4.1
38.3	49.6	44.0						33.9	49.0
(64) 24.6	(68) 24.8	(62) 26.9	% Profit Before Taxes/Tangible Net Worth					(11) 23.6	(42) 31.1
10.0	10.1	13.2						3.5	13.5
15.8	16.3	15.7						11.6	17.1
9.6	10.9	9.9	% Profit Before Taxes/Total Assets					8.1	10.1
2.4	2.6	2.6						-2.7	4.6
17.0	19.7	17.8						25.0	15.0
7.5	8.0	7.3	Sales/Net Fixed Assets					10.9	7.3
4.1	4.1	4.5						5.4	4.7
3.1	3.2	3.2						3.3	3.7
2.1	2.2	2.4	Sales/Total Assets					2.7	2.5
1.7	1.7	1.8						2.1	1.8
1.2	1.1	1.0						.8	1.4
(68) 2.0	(70) 2.0	(67) 1.9	% Depr., Dep., Amort./Sales					1.0	(43) 2.0
3.0	2.9	3.1						1.9	3.1
.7	.9	.8							.7
(14) 1.0	(20) 3.5	(21) 1.1	% Officers', Directors' Owners' Comp/Sales						(12) .9
2.1	7.9	5.1							2.3
5608463M	5881177M	4836175M	Net Sales ($)	1370M	1036M	16555M	41200M	225078M	4550936M
2717426M	2818099M	2187318M	Total Assets ($)	1094M	1401M	8206M	28809M	94881M	2052927M

M = $ thousand MM = $ million

See Pages 9 through 22 for Explanation of Ratios and Data

Current Data Sorted by Assets | **Comparative Historical Data**

0-500M	500M-2MM	2-10MM	10-50MM	50-100MM	100-250MM		4/1/09-3/31/10 ALL	4/1/10-3/31/11 ALL
						Type of Statement		
			5	2	1	Unqualified	12	10
		1	2	1		Reviewed	14	15
						Compiled	4	4
						Tax Returns	5	3
			8	6	4	Other	28	33
	3 (4/1-9/30/13)		27 (10/1/13-3/31/14)					
		1	15	9	5	**NUMBER OF STATEMENTS**	63	65
%	%	%	%	%	%	**ASSETS**	%	%
DATA NOT AVAILABLE	DATA NOT AVAILABLE		2.8			Cash & Equivalents	8.7	6.3
			26.8			Trade Receivables (net)	27.0	31.0
			26.5			Inventory	27.8	29.9
			3.4			All Other Current	4.2	2.1
			59.6			Total Current	67.7	69.2
			25.7			Fixed Assets (net)	22.2	20.3
			3.2			Intangibles (net)	3.0	3.9
			11.6			All Other Non-Current	7.1	6.6
			100.0			Total	100.0	100.0
						LIABILITIES		
			14.8			Notes Payable-Short Term	11.7	16.3
			2.4			Cur. Mat.-L.T.D.	2.2	2.0
			16.0			Trade Payables	16.8	18.4
			.1			Income Taxes Payable	.7	.2
			8.2			All Other Current	8.9	7.4
			41.5			Total Current	40.3	44.3
			7.6			Long-Term Debt	15.4	12.1
			1.1			Deferred Taxes	.7	.7
			6.3			All Other Non-Current	7.1	8.0
			43.4			Net Worth	36.4	34.8
			100.0			Total Liabilties & Net Worth	100.0	100.0
						INCOME DATA		
			100.0			Net Sales	100.0	100.0
			15.9			Gross Profit	20.5	17.6
			11.4			Operating Expenses	17.3	14.4
			4.4			Operating Profit	3.2	3.2
			1.4			All Other Expenses (net)	1.7	1.2
			3.1			Profit Before Taxes	1.5	1.9
						RATIOS		
			1.9				3.1	2.7
			1.4			Current	1.7	1.6
			1.2				1.2	1.1
			.9				1.7	1.3
			.8			Quick	.9	.8
			.5				.5	.5
			33 11.0				34 10.8	39 9.4
			38 9.5			Sales/Receivables	48 7.6	48 7.6
			49 7.5				61 6.0	61 6.0
			35 10.3				34 10.6	38 9.6
			49 7.5			Cost of Sales/Inventory	73 5.0	54 6.7
			83 4.4				101 3.6	85 4.3
			21 17.8				21 17.5	15 23.8
			34 10.7			Cost of Sales/Payables	35 10.5	31 11.7
			41 8.9				49 7.5	47 7.7
			6.3				3.8	4.8
			13.0			Sales/Working Capital	7.9	10.1
			45.7				17.7	42.8
			11.9				8.8	9.8
			(14) 4.2			EBIT/Interest	(58) 2.7	(57) 4.6
			.3				.1	.9
							7.5	5.4
						Net Profit + Depr., Dep., Amort./Cur. Mat. L/T/D	(18) 2.6	(15) 4.6
							.4	.9
			.3				.2	.2
			.6			Fixed/Worth	.6	.7
			.9				1.5	1.5
			1.1				.7	.6
			1.4			Debt/Worth	2.1	2.3
			2.0				5.2	8.3
			22.2				30.5	46.8
			15.8			% Profit Before Taxes/Tangible Net Worth	(57) 11.7	(61) 16.3
			-1.6				-.8	3.7
			8.0				8.1	10.2
			6.1			% Profit Before Taxes/Total Assets	3.2	4.7
			-.7				-1.8	.3
			23.4				30.3	37.9
			7.0			Sales/Net Fixed Assets	11.0	12.9
			4.8				4.7	7.1
			2.7				2.7	3.2
			2.4			Sales/Total Assets	1.9	2.3
			1.4				1.3	1.6
			1.0				1.0	.6
			(14) 2.3			% Depr., Dep., Amort./Sales	(52) 1.7	(56) 1.2
			3.3				3.8	2.7
							2.5	3.4
						% Officers', Directors' Owners' Comp/Sales	(16) 3.8	(15) 4.2
							7.0	9.5
		17311M	821320M	1346473M	1359116M	Net Sales ($)	4762125M	7332203M
		5804M	352046M	623013M	829268M	Total Assets ($)	2341610M	2837832M

Comparative Historical Data				Current Data Sorted by Sales					
			Type of Statement						
6	8	8	Unqualified					1	7
8	4	4	Reviewed					1	3
4	1		Compiled						
4	2		Tax Returns						
20	22	18	Other					1	17
				3 (4/1-9/30/13)		27 (10/1/13-3/31/14)			
4/1/11-3/31/12 ALL	**4/1/12-3/31/13 ALL**	**4/1/13-3/31/14 ALL**		**0-1MM**	**1-3MM**	**3-5MM**	**5-10MM**	**10-25MM**	**25MM & OVER**
42	37	30	**NUMBER OF STATEMENTS**					3	27
%	%	%	**ASSETS**	%	%	%	%	%	%
8.8	6.7	4.0	Cash & Equivalents	DATA NOT AVAILABLE	DATA NOT AVAILABLE	DATA NOT AVAILABLE	DATA NOT AVAILABLE		4.3
28.0	28.7	26.8	Trade Receivables (net)						27.5
28.8	28.3	27.1	Inventory						27.0
2.1	3.7	3.6	All Other Current						4.0
67.7	67.4	61.5	Total Current						62.8
19.4	21.9	20.6	Fixed Assets (net)						20.8
4.1	3.8	9.2	Intangibles (net)						7.0
8.7	6.9	8.7	All Other Non-Current						9.4
100.0	100.0	100.0	Total						100.0
			LIABILITIES						
15.2	15.7	13.8	Notes Payable-Short Term						13.4
1.8	.9	3.1	Cur. Mat.-L.T.D.						3.2
17.4	15.3	12.2	Trade Payables						12.3
1.4	.1	.3	Income Taxes Payable						.3
6.9	6.8	6.3	All Other Current						6.5
42.6	38.8	35.7	Total Current						35.6
8.2	6.0	9.8	Long-Term Debt						10.5
.9	1.3	1.6	Deferred Taxes						1.7
5.2	6.4	5.2	All Other Non-Current						5.2
43.1	47.4	47.6	Net Worth						46.9
100.0	100.0	100.0	Total Liabilties & Net Worth						100.0
			INCOME DATA						
100.0	100.0	100.0	Net Sales						100.0
19.4	16.1	16.9	Gross Profit						14.7
13.9	10.7	11.7	Operating Expenses						10.6
5.5	5.4	5.2	Operating Profit						4.1
.4	.6	1.2	All Other Expenses (net)						1.2
5.1	4.7	4.0	Profit Before Taxes						2.8
			RATIOS						
2.8	2.7	3.1							3.0
1.6	1.7	1.7	Current						1.7
1.1	1.2	1.3							1.2
1.2	1.2	1.5							1.4
.8	.8	.8	Quick						.8
.5	.7	.6							.7
27 13.6	34 10.7	36 10.2							34 10.6
39 9.3	41 9.0	46 8.0	Sales/Receivables						45 8.1
50 7.3	49 7.5	51 7.1							52 7.0
33 10.9	33 11.1	39 9.3							35 10.3
51 7.2	48 7.6	49 7.4	Cost of Sales/Inventory						49 7.4
76 4.8	69 5.3	73 5.0							62 5.9
10 35.6	17 21.9	12 30.1							9 38.7
25 14.4	26 14.0	23 15.6	Cost of Sales/Payables						23 16.0
45 8.2	34 10.7	37 9.9							36 10.0
4.4	5.6	5.3							5.7
13.3	9.6	8.8	Sales/Working Capital						8.7
37.5	23.6	18.9							19.5
22.7	27.0	15.6							12.1
(35) 5.0	(32) 6.8	(28) 4.5	EBIT/Interest						(26) 4.5
2.2	2.0	2.8							2.6
50.7	15.8	7.2							8.5
(11) 8.1	(13) 6.3	(12) 2.8	Net Profit + Depr., Dep., Amort./Cur. Mat. L/T/D						(11) 3.0
4.0	3.3	1.4							1.4
.2	.3	.2							.2
.5	.5	.7	Fixed/Worth						.6
1.0	.8	.9							1.0
.6	.4	.9							.9
1.7	1.5	1.4	Debt/Worth						1.4
3.6	3.4	3.6							3.4
46.4	32.4	36.6							22.7
(39) 20.0	(36) 17.3	(29) 15.8	% Profit Before Taxes/Tangible Net Worth						(26) 14.9
9.6	8.5	4.2							3.7
15.4	15.5	9.0							8.0
7.4	5.6	5.7	% Profit Before Taxes/Total Assets						5.6
2.3	2.7	2.2							2.0
34.7	26.7	25.2							22.0
18.2	14.3	12.3	Sales/Net Fixed Assets						12.2
8.8	6.9	6.5							6.5
3.4	3.1	2.7							2.6
2.6	2.6	2.3	Sales/Total Assets						2.4
1.8	1.6	1.4							1.4
.4	.6	.7							.7
(40) .8	(34) 1.1	(27) 1.2	% Depr., Dep., Amort./Sales						(24) 1.3
1.3	2.1	2.6							2.4
1.4									
(10) 2.2			% Officers', Directors' Owners' Comp/Sales						
7.9									
6603462M	4823359M	3544220M	Net Sales ($)					61032M	3483188M
2375713M	1901949M	1810131M	Total Assets ($)					78938M	1731193M

M = $ thousand MM = $ million

See Pages 9 through 22 for Explanation of Ratios and Data

Current Data Sorted by Assets							Comparative Historical Data	
						Type of Statement		
		2	3	3	1	Unqualified	4	8
		4	3			Reviewed	14	10
	1	2	1			Compiled	4	4
		2	1			Tax Returns	6	2
	1	3	6	2	4	Other	21	20
	5 (4/1-9/30/13)		34 (10/1/13-3/31/14)				4/1/09-3/31/10	4/1/10-3/31/11
0-500M	500M-2MM	2-10MM	10-50MM	50-100MM	100-250MM		ALL	ALL
	2	13	14	5	5	**NUMBER OF STATEMENTS**	49	44
%	%	%	%	%	%	**ASSETS**	%	%
DATA NOT AVAILABLE		9.0	8.9			Cash & Equivalents	10.9	8.2
		27.8	19.2			Trade Receivables (net)	23.8	23.7
		21.3	20.7			Inventory	26.9	27.7
		1.7	1.4			All Other Current	2.8	2.6
		59.9	50.3			Total Current	64.4	62.2
		26.1	31.5			Fixed Assets (net)	26.7	24.5
		12.4	7.3			Intangibles (net)	3.7	7.9
		1.6	11.0			All Other Non-Current	5.1	5.4
		100.0	100.0			Total	100.0	100.0
						LIABILITIES		
		10.4	9.1			Notes Payable-Short Term	14.2	13.1
		4.2	5.3			Cur. Mat.-L.T.D.	2.9	4.6
		9.4	10.9			Trade Payables	15.4	15.3
		.2	.0			Income Taxes Payable	.2	.6
		9.3	10.2			All Other Current	7.6	7.4
		33.4	35.6			Total Current	40.4	40.9
		25.5	17.0			Long-Term Debt	14.6	15.5
		1.4	1.1			Deferred Taxes	1.0	2.0
		2.0	3.5			All Other Non-Current	19.8	8.8
		37.7	42.9			Net Worth	24.2	32.8
		100.0	100.0			Total Liabilities & Net Worth	100.0	100.0
						INCOME DATA		
		100.0	100.0			Net Sales	100.0	100.0
		26.5	19.6			Gross Profit	23.4	26.3
		19.7	16.2			Operating Expenses	20.0	20.3
		6.8	3.4			Operating Profit	3.4	6.0
		1.3	.4			All Other Expenses (net)	.6	1.6
		5.5	3.0			Profit Before Taxes	2.8	4.4
						RATIOS		
		2.9	2.9				2.7	3.0
		2.0	1.3			Current	1.6	1.4
		1.8	.9				1.2	1.0
		2.0	1.5				1.5	1.3
		1.2	.8			Quick	.9	.7
		1.0	.4				.5	.4
		43 8.4	**33** 11.1				**29** 12.5	**35** 10.5
		51 7.1	**38** 9.5			Sales/Receivables	**45** 8.1	**44** 8.2
		59 6.2	**49** 7.5				**53** 6.8	**52** 7.0
		31 11.6	**32** 11.3				**33** 11.1	**39** 9.3
		57 6.4	**53** 6.9			Cost of Sales/Inventory	**55** 6.6	**69** 5.3
		64 5.7	**99** 3.7				**109** 3.4	**101** 3.6
		15 24.5	**17** 21.6				**14** 26.9	**22** 16.3
		25 14.6	**20** 18.5			Cost of Sales/Payables	**27** 13.7	**33** 10.9
		36 10.2	**27** 13.4				**44** 8.3	**51** 7.2
		3.5	4.9				3.5	4.8
		5.3	19.1			Sales/Working Capital	9.6	10.2
		15.2	-65.2				21.8	67.5
		14.5	11.0				14.1	9.3
		4.2	(13) 2.1			EBIT/Interest	(46) 2.0	(40) 3.2
		2.5	-2.2				.1	1.8
						Net Profit + Depr., Dep.,	3.9	5.0
						Amort./Cur. Mat. L/T/D	(12) .6	(13) 2.2
							.1	.6
		.3	.5				.3	.3
		1.0	.7			Fixed/Worth	.7	.7
		6.9	2.0				2.7	2.0
		1.0	.8				.7	.8
		2.8	1.6			Debt/Worth	1.8	2.2
		15.3	4.6				6.0	5.9
		42.3	9.9			% Profit Before Taxes/Tangible	34.7	44.8
		(11) 28.4	(13) 2.4			Net Worth	(40) 10.2	(37) 20.4
		21.4	-12.5				-4.4	9.8
		11.5	3.2			% Profit Before Taxes/Total	12.8	12.0
		8.3	1.1			Assets	3.0	6.7
		4.3	-5.6				-2.7	2.1
		13.4	28.0				32.0	20.2
		6.8	4.7			Sales/Net Fixed Assets	9.3	12.3
		4.2	2.6				4.4	4.1
		2.5	2.6				2.9	2.8
		1.9	1.4			Sales/Total Assets	1.9	1.9
		1.3	.8				1.2	1.3
		1.0	.9				.5	.9
		2.9	(12) 4.2			% Depr., Dep., Amort./Sales	(39) 1.7	(34) 1.3
		5.3	5.8				3.6	2.1
						% Officers', Directors'	2.4	
						Owners' Comp/Sales	(11) 4.0	
							6.5	
	20455M	176263M	741416M	739129M	1251814M	Net Sales ($)	2154322M	2389894M
	1528M	82139M	398679M	369849M	760801M	Total Assets ($)	1331559M	1527805M

M = $ thousand MM = $ million

See Pages 9 through 22 for Explanation of Ratios and Data

Comparative Historical Data / Current Data Sorted by Sales

4/1/11-3/31/12 ALL	4/1/12-3/31/13 ALL	4/1/13-3/31/14 ALL	Type of Statement	0-1MM	1-3MM	3-5MM	5-10MM	10-25MM	25MM & OVER
8	10	9	Unqualified				2		7
9	5	7	Reviewed				1	4	2
4	6	4	Compiled			1	2	1	
6	8	3	Tax Returns			1	1		1
16	11	16	Other		1	1	2		12
				5 (4/1-9/30/13)			34 (10/1/13-3/31/14)		
43	40	39	NUMBER OF STATEMENTS		1	3	8	5	22
%	%	%	**ASSETS**	%	%	%	%	%	%
6.7	5.7	7.3	Cash & Equivalents	DATA NOT AVAILABLE					6.0
26.9	24.5	23.4	Trade Receivables (net)						23.9
29.3	27.2	22.2	Inventory						24.8
2.4	3.4	1.7	All Other Current						2.1
65.2	60.8	54.6	Total Current						56.9
21.9	28.6	28.6	Fixed Assets (net)						30.4
7.9	5.7	11.0	Intangibles (net)						8.3
5.0	4.8	5.8	All Other Non-Current						4.3
100.0	100.0	100.0	Total						100.0
			LIABILITIES						
18.7	11.8	10.6	Notes Payable-Short Term						9.6
2.3	4.1	4.8	Cur. Mat.-L.T.D.						6.3
14.7	12.3	11.4	Trade Payables						13.4
.4	.2	.5	Income Taxes Payable						.7
7.8	7.7	10.0	All Other Current						6.5
43.9	36.1	37.3	Total Current						36.5
15.5	17.6	18.4	Long-Term Debt						15.4
.6	1.5	1.2	Deferred Taxes						.9
8.0	8.1	8.8	All Other Non-Current						4.1
31.9	36.7	34.3	Net Worth						43.1
100.0	100.0	100.0	Total Liabilties & Net Worth						100.0
			INCOME DATA						
100.0	100.0	100.0	Net Sales						100.0
26.4	24.1	19.9	Gross Profit						14.1
19.9	19.1	16.3	Operating Expenses						12.2
6.5	5.0	3.6	Operating Profit						2.0
1.2	.9	1.2	All Other Expenses (net)						1.2
5.3	4.1	2.4	Profit Before Taxes						.7
			RATIOS						
2.7	3.7	2.5	Current						3.2
1.5	1.7	1.7							1.7
1.2	1.3	1.1							1.1
1.5	2.1	1.5	Quick						1.5
.7	1.0	1.0							.9
.6	.5	.6							.6
33 10.9	32 11.3	36 10.2	Sales/Receivables						34 10.6
40 9.1	42 8.7	43 8.4							43 8.5
54 6.8	51 7.1	51 7.1							51 7.2
34 10.6	35 10.4	29 12.6	Cost of Sales/Inventory						28 12.9
59 6.2	66 5.5	57 6.4							54 6.7
94 3.9	96 3.8	81 4.5							85 4.3
21 17.7	9 40.8	17 20.9	Cost of Sales/Payables						19 19.1
29 12.5	23 16.0	24 15.4							25 14.4
44 8.3	33 11.0	35 10.5							36 10.0
4.8	4.4	4.7	Sales/Working Capital						4.6
10.3	8.7	9.3							12.1
28.5	24.7	52.3							51.2
12.7	10.1	13.9	EBIT/Interest						13.6
(41) 4.1	(34) 6.7	(38) 3.8							3.8
2.4	2.0	1.5							-.1
5.6	3.6	4.4	Net Profit + Depr., Dep., Amort./Cur. Mat. L/T/D						
(13) 3.2	(10) 2.0	(16) 2.4							
.9	.8	1.6							
.3	.5	.5	Fixed/Worth						.5
.8	.7	.8							.7
1.2	2.4	2.6							2.0
1.1	.6	1.0	Debt/Worth						.8
2.6	2.2	2.1							2.1
9.9	4.8	6.4							4.6
50.4	44.4	40.6	% Profit Before Taxes/Tangible Net Worth						27.2
(35) 26.3	(35) 18.6	(32) 21.4							(19) 8.1
11.4	5.9	2.8							1.3
15.6	14.4	11.7	% Profit Before Taxes/Total Assets						11.0
8.2	8.9	4.0							2.8
2.5	2.0	.5							-3.3
23.1	21.6	15.6	Sales/Net Fixed Assets						19.2
13.9	9.6	6.8							6.1
4.2	4.2	3.6							3.3
3.1	2.9	2.5	Sales/Total Assets						3.1
2.5	2.2	1.5							1.8
1.3	1.5	1.2							1.3
.6	.5	.8	% Depr., Dep., Amort./Sales						.8
(40) 1.2	(36) 1.4	(35) 2.8							(19) 1.9
2.5	3.1	4.9							4.9
.9	.8	1.0	% Officers', Directors' Owners' Comp/Sales						
(12) 3.2	(16) 2.0	(12) 2.2							
5.6	5.5	3.4							
2432258M	2644620M	2929077M	Net Sales ($)		2928M	11573M	70625M	94225M	2749726M
1034417M	1301888M	1612996M	Total Assets ($)		822M	11712M	67556M	62416M	1470490M

M = $ thousand MM = $ million

See Pages 9 through 22 for Explanation of Ratios and Data

Current Data Sorted by Assets							Comparative Historical Data	
						Type of Statement		
			4	3	1	Unqualified	17	14
		3	6			Reviewed	7	5
	1					Compiled	2	4
2	3	2				Tax Returns	2	4
	2	6	5	4	4	Other	21	22
	11 (4/1-9/30/13)		35 (10/1/13-3/31/14)				4/1/09-3/31/10 ALL	4/1/10-3/31/11 ALL
0-500M	500M-2MM	2-10MM	10-50MM	50-100MM	100-250MM			
2	6	11	15	7	5	**NUMBER OF STATEMENTS**	49	49
%	%	%	%	%	%	**ASSETS**	%	%
		7.2	6.7			Cash & Equivalents	9.2	8.5
		25.4	24.2			Trade Receivables (net)	24.3	25.4
		27.6	38.1			Inventory	31.5	34.5
		7.0	1.9			All Other Current	4.0	4.8
		67.2	70.9			Total Current	68.9	73.1
		29.1	20.8			Fixed Assets (net)	21.3	20.4
		.2	4.5			Intangibles (net)	2.7	2.3
		3.5	3.7			All Other Non-Current	7.1	4.2
		100.0	100.0			Total	100.0	100.0
						LIABILITIES		
		9.3	20.3			Notes Payable-Short Term	17.8	20.0
		3.6	2.1			Cur. Mat.-L.T.D.	2.9	2.1
		17.4	13.8			Trade Payables	17.3	14.9
		.0	.0			Income Taxes Payable	.2	.2
		10.0	5.0			All Other Current	11.2	10.9
		40.3	41.2			Total Current	49.6	48.2
		8.4	4.8			Long-Term Debt	9.8	13.5
		.7	2.0			Deferred Taxes	.5	.3
		3.7	1.9			All Other Non-Current	4.6	6.9
		46.9	50.1			Net Worth	35.5	31.2
		100.0	100.0			Total Liabilties & Net Worth	100.0	100.0
						INCOME DATA		
		100.0	100.0			Net Sales	100.0	100.0
		29.5	13.5			Gross Profit	16.7	18.2
		28.1	10.7			Operating Expenses	13.3	12.9
		1.4	2.7			Operating Profit	3.4	5.3
		.2	.4			All Other Expenses (net)	.0	.6
		1.2	2.3			Profit Before Taxes	3.4	4.6
						RATIOS		
		3.7	2.3				2.6	2.4
		1.5	1.8			Current	1.5	1.6
		1.2	1.2				1.1	1.2
		1.4	1.3				1.3	1.1
		.7	.7			Quick	.7	.7
		.4	.4				.5	.4
		5 79.5	**31** 11.7				**20** 18.6	**14** 26.8
		33 10.9	**48** 7.6			Sales/Receivables	**36** 10.2	**43** 8.5
		38 9.7	**54** 6.7				**53** 6.9	**56** 6.6
		13 27.2	**27** 13.6				**26** 14.0	**23** 15.8
		30 12.0	**59** 6.2			Cost of Sales/Inventory	**43** 8.4	**52** 7.0
		43 8.5	**114** 3.2				**69** 5.3	**78** 4.7
		3 132.0	**17** 21.1				**10** 35.1	**9** 42.8
		26 14.2	**25** 14.5			Cost of Sales/Payables	**24** 15.4	**24** 15.2
		52 7.0	**42** 8.7				**43** 8.5	**39** 9.4
		8.0	4.8				5.0	5.6
		17.2	9.9			Sales/Working Capital	13.1	12.0
		70.7	20.3				86.1	38.9
		7.9	18.3				18.4	33.2
		(10) 2.1	(14) 3.3			EBIT/Interest	(47) 4.0	(46) 9.7
		-10.2	1.4				-.4	3.7
							10.9	27.5
						Net Profit + Depr., Dep., Amort./Cur. Mat. L/T/D	(16) 1.6	(12) 13.5
							.2	2.3
		.2	.1				.2	.1
		.7	.5			Fixed/Worth	.5	.5
		1.1	.8				1.3	1.7
		.4	.7				.7	1.0
		1.7	1.1			Debt/Worth	2.0	2.3
		3.0	2.6				5.7	8.2
		33.7	18.0				46.7	93.9
		4.3	5.5			% Profit Before Taxes/Tangible Net Worth	(43) 20.5	(46) 37.4
		-5.3	1.1				-.2	18.1
		11.9	7.0				16.8	20.2
		1.6	2.8			% Profit Before Taxes/Total Assets	6.5	13.4
		-3.4	.5				-2.6	6.4
		81.7	32.9				55.0	53.6
		15.0	12.5			Sales/Net Fixed Assets	14.7	15.4
		7.3	8.6				6.8	7.7
		6.4	2.8				3.9	4.1
		4.3	2.3			Sales/Total Assets	2.7	2.6
		2.8	1.8				1.5	1.7
			.6				.4	.2
			1.1			% Depr., Dep., Amort./Sales	(44) 1.2	(44) .7
			1.4				3.0	2.2
								1.5
						% Officers', Directors' Owners' Comp/Sales		(11) 3.7
								5.5
839M	**61738M**	**281896M**	**914062M**	**1381533M**	**1585423M**	Net Sales ($)	**6001347M**	**6482624M**
502M	**7068M**	**65306M**	**414989M**	**539199M**	**775167M**	Total Assets ($)	**1944277M**	**2314652M**

M = $ thousand MM = $ million

See Pages 9 through 22 for Explanation of Ratios and Data

Comparative Historical Data				Current Data Sorted by Sales					
			Type of Statement						
16	9	8	Unqualified						8
6	6	9	Reviewed				1		8
6	5	1	Compiled					1	
1	3	7	Tax Returns	2		1	1	3	
22	20	21	Other			1		7	13
4/1/11-3/31/12 ALL	4/1/12-3/31/13 ALL	4/1/13-3/31/14 ALL		11 (4/1-9/30/13)			35 (10/1/13-3/31/14)		
				0-1MM	1-3MM	3-5MM	5-10MM	10-25MM	25MM & OVER
51	43	46	**NUMBER OF STATEMENTS**	2		2	2	11	29
%	%	%	**ASSETS**	%	%	%	%	%	%
9.7	11.2	8.8	Cash & Equivalents		DATA NOT AVAILABLE			12.2	5.4
22.8	22.6	21.6	Trade Receivables (net)					21.4	24.0
36.9	35.4	29.3	Inventory					25.9	33.3
4.3	4.8	5.8	All Other Current					6.7	5.9
73.8	74.0	65.5	Total Current					66.3	68.6
17.3	18.7	23.7	Fixed Assets (net)					28.1	19.8
4.4	2.0	5.0	Intangibles (net)					.2	7.8
4.5	5.3	5.8	All Other Non-Current					5.5	3.8
100.0	100.0	100.0	Total					100.0	100.0
			LIABILITIES						
16.9	16.2	15.5	Notes Payable-Short Term					14.5	15.2
1.7	1.9	2.6	Cur. Mat.-L.T.D.					3.7	1.6
17.7	16.8	13.0	Trade Payables					13.4	14.6
.3	.1	.1	Income Taxes Payable					.0	.2
10.6	7.8	8.3	All Other Current					10.9	7.1
47.3	42.9	39.5	Total Current					42.5	38.6
9.7	8.3	9.9	Long-Term Debt					8.9	8.1
.8	.4	1.4	Deferred Taxes					.1	2.2
7.6	6.0	4.6	All Other Non-Current					3.5	3.7
34.6	42.4	44.5	Net Worth					45.1	47.4
100.0	100.0	100.0	Total Liabilties & Net Worth					100.0	100.0
			INCOME DATA						
100.0	100.0	100.0	Net Sales					100.0	100.0
19.1	19.7	23.1	Gross Profit					24.7	15.1
14.2	14.6	17.5	Operating Expenses					23.2	11.2
4.9	5.1	5.5	Operating Profit					1.5	3.9
.2	.5	1.2	All Other Expenses (net)					.4	.2
4.7	4.5	4.4	Profit Before Taxes					1.1	3.8
			RATIOS						
3.5	3.3	2.8						2.9	2.8
1.7	1.7	1.8	Current					1.8	1.8
1.3	1.2	1.2						1.1	1.2
1.6	1.1	1.4						1.4	1.3
.8	.8	.7	Quick					.7	.7
.4	.4	.5						.5	.5
8 43.5	5 70.2	7 49.1						0 UND	23 15.8
29 12.7	31 11.6	33 11.0	Sales/Receivables					32 11.4	37 9.9
44 8.3	48 7.6	46 8.0						38 9.7	48 7.6
28 13.0	21 17.5	22 16.9						7 49.6	31 11.8
49 7.5	39 9.3	40 9.2	Cost of Sales/Inventory					24 15.1	48 7.6
101 3.6	76 4.8	94 3.9						35 10.4	99 3.7
8 45.7	7 55.0	7 51.0						1 243.7	15 24.2
21 17.8	19 18.9	23 16.2	Cost of Sales/Payables					7 49.3	25 14.5
39 9.4	34 10.8	41 8.8						52 7.0	41 9.0
5.1	5.0	5.8						8.0	4.7
10.5	11.5	13.2	Sales/Working Capital					20.3	10.9
24.7	32.5	32.7						73.6	17.4
36.0	86.5	15.7						8.2	26.9
(43) 11.2	(41) 9.4	(42) 3.9	EBIT/Interest					2.3	(28) 4.3
3.0	1.9	1.6						-4.0	2.0
25.6	8.3	14.0							13.4
(17) 5.0	(11) 3.2	(14) 4.1	Net Profit + Depr., Dep., Amort./Cur. Mat. L/T/D						(12) 4.1
2.0	2.3	1.6							2.1
.2	.1	.2						.1	.2
.4	.4	.6	Fixed/Worth					.6	.5
1.1	.8	1.0						1.1	.9
.7	.5	.6						.5	.7
1.9	1.4	1.4	Debt/Worth					.8	1.5
6.2	4.2	3.2						3.0	3.2
68.0	33.8	33.7						35.3	29.5
(43) 29.9	(37) 18.2	(42) 15.9	% Profit Before Taxes/Tangible Net Worth					10.8	(28) 14.6
13.1	5.2	1.7						-18.7	2.8
21.8	18.8	10.5						11.9	9.5
14.5	6.4	4.4	% Profit Before Taxes/Total Assets					3.6	4.0
3.7	1.3	1.0						-7.0	1.3
72.4	94.6	46.7						172.9	42.4
24.8	40.9	13.1	Sales/Net Fixed Assets					13.2	12.5
10.4	12.8	6.3						7.3	7.0
5.1	4.7	4.3						13.8	3.1
3.0	3.1	2.7	Sales/Total Assets					4.3	2.6
1.8	1.9	1.8						2.8	1.8
.3	.3	.6							.6
(41) .8	(37) .8	(40) .9	% Depr., Dep., Amort./Sales						1.1
2.0	1.4	1.9							2.2
1.2	.8	.9							
(14) 1.7	(17) 1.3	(14) 1.6	% Officers', Directors' Owners' Comp/Sales						
4.8	2.4	3.5							
7040742M	4187058M	4225491M	Net Sales ($)	839M		6417M	12280M	208515M	3997440M
2851719M	1658608M	1802231M	Total Assets ($)	502M		3375M	4532M	55355M	1738467M

M = $ thousand MM = $ million

See Pages 9 through 22 for Explanation of Ratios and Data

Current Data Sorted by Assets							Comparative Historical Data	
		3	6	2	1	**Type of Statement** Unqualified	13	18
		6	3			Reviewed	11	9
		3				Compiled	6	9
	2	1				Tax Returns	1	1
	1	8	9	4	3	Other	27	27
	13 (4/1-9/30/13)		39 (10/1/13-3/31/14)				4/1/09-3/31/10	4/1/10-3/31/11
0-500M	500M-2MM	2-10MM	10-50MM	50-100MM	100-250MM		ALL	ALL
	3	21	18	6	4	**NUMBER OF STATEMENTS**	58	64
%	%	%	%	%	%	**ASSETS**	%	%
DATA NOT AVAILABLE		12.3	9.6			Cash & Equivalents	7.6	8.5
		22.0	25.8			Trade Receivables (net)	21.2	27.6
		16.8	18.3			Inventory	18.2	17.7
		2.0	.9			All Other Current	3.5	2.8
		53.0	54.6			Total Current	50.5	56.6
		37.4	37.0			Fixed Assets (net)	36.9	32.2
		.5	2.2			Intangibles (net)	4.3	4.3
		9.0	6.2			All Other Non-Current	8.2	6.9
		100.0	100.0			Total	100.0	100.0
						LIABILITIES		
		3.3	9.6			Notes Payable-Short Term	10.6	8.4
		4.2	3.3			Cur. Mat.-L.T.D.	4.4	4.6
		10.8	12.4			Trade Payables	11.0	14.2
		.0	.2			Income Taxes Payable	.1	.3
		5.4	7.6			All Other Current	7.9	9.0
		23.8	33.1			Total Current	34.1	36.4
		24.9	12.4			Long-Term Debt	13.9	15.1
		1.5	1.5			Deferred Taxes	1.0	.7
		16.2	2.9			All Other Non-Current	6.2	3.5
		33.6	50.0			Net Worth	44.8	44.2
		100.0	100.0			Total Liabilties & Net Worth	100.0	100.0
						INCOME DATA		
		100.0	100.0			Net Sales	100.0	100.0
		20.9	16.9			Gross Profit	20.6	21.4
		15.7	12.7			Operating Expenses	19.6	15.5
		5.2	4.1			Operating Profit	1.0	5.8
		1.0	.3			All Other Expenses (net)	1.5	1.0
		4.2	3.9			Profit Before Taxes	-.5	4.9
						RATIOS		
		4.3	2.8				3.5	2.9
		2.4	1.4			Current	1.8	1.9
		1.4	1.2				1.0	1.0
		2.7	2.2				1.8	2.0
		1.5	.9			Quick	.8	1.0
		.9	.7				.5	.6
		33 10.9	**43** 8.4				**38** 9.5	**44** 8.3
		42 8.7	**50** 7.3			Sales/Receivables	**44** 8.3	**55** 6.7
		55 6.6	**55** 6.6				**53** 6.9	**67** 5.5
		26 14.2	**24** 15.5				**25** 14.4	**23** 15.7
		42 8.7	**35** 10.3			Cost of Sales/Inventory	**45** 8.2	**42** 8.7
		59 6.2	**57** 6.4				**70** 5.2	**63** 5.8
		15 24.9	**19** 18.9				**15** 24.9	**24** 15.4
		28 13.1	**24** 15.3			Cost of Sales/Payables	**21** 17.2	**31** 11.6
		37 9.9	**43** 8.4				**36** 10.1	**45** 8.1
		3.5	4.7				3.3	3.8
		7.8	11.6			Sales/Working Capital	10.5	9.0
		15.3	27.7				-193.3	-851.2
		12.0	10.2				4.9	23.4
		(18) 6.5	(15) 5.0			EBIT/Interest	(50) 1.4	(58) 4.6
		2.2	-.1				-1.3	1.5
							4.7	7.7
						Net Profit + Depr., Dep., Amort./Cur. Mat. L/T/D	(16) 2.9	(20) 3.7
							.9	2.5
		.4	.4				.4	.3
		.8	.7			Fixed/Worth	.9	.9
		1.1	1.5				3.3	1.7
		.3	.5				.4	.6
		.7	1.1			Debt/Worth	1.1	1.2
		1.9	2.0				8.4	4.3
		18.6	43.6				19.5	37.4
		(19) 7.9	13.3			% Profit Before Taxes/Tangible Net Worth	(52) 3.0	(60) 18.9
		-2.1	-1.7				-10.5	4.7
		10.6	18.9				8.9	16.0
		5.2	5.4			% Profit Before Taxes/Total Assets	.7	8.1
		.4	-.7				-6.3	1.2
		7.9	10.4				7.7	9.4
		5.3	5.3			Sales/Net Fixed Assets	4.8	6.2
		3.6	3.0				2.6	3.3
		2.3	2.4				2.0	2.0
		1.7	1.8			Sales/Total Assets	1.6	1.7
		1.4	1.5				1.0	1.3
		2.2	2.1				1.7	2.1
		(20) 3.4	3.8			% Depr., Dep., Amort./Sales	(52) 3.7	(59) 3.0
		4.2	5.8				5.2	4.8
							1.4	.8
						% Officers', Directors' Owners' Comp/Sales	(15) 3.3	(15) 2.6
							5.3	4.6
	8826M	236663M	801382M	842463M	998591M	Net Sales ($)	2036623M	2083810M
	4188M	131672M	441250M	481690M	775728M	Total Assets ($)	1820589M	1486105M

M = $ thousand MM = $ million

See Pages 9 through 22 for Explanation of Ratios and Data

Comparative Historical Data				Current Data Sorted by Sales					
			Type of Statement						
17	12	12	Unqualified				1	2	9
10	7	9	Reviewed				4	2	3
6	3	3	Compiled			1	1	1	
4	2	3	Tax Returns			2		1	
26	19	25	Other		1	1	1	8	14
4/1/11-3/31/12 ALL	4/1/12-3/31/13 ALL	4/1/13-3/31/14 ALL			13 (4/1-9/30/13)		39 (10/1/13-3/31/14)		
				0-1MM	1-3MM	3-5MM	5-10MM	10-25MM	25MM & OVER
63	43	52	**NUMBER OF STATEMENTS**		1	4	7	14	26
%	%	%	**ASSETS**	%	%	%	%	%	%
8.6	8.8	9.3	Cash & Equivalents	DATA NOT AVAILABLE				12.1	6.4
28.7	26.0	22.8	Trade Receivables (net)					23.6	24.6
18.8	17.8	17.6	Inventory					18.6	15.5
2.5	3.7	2.2	All Other Current					1.6	2.5
58.6	56.3	52.0	Total Current					55.9	49.1
32.4	32.7	35.6	Fixed Assets (net)					35.1	35.4
3.8	2.6	5.1	Intangibles (net)					.3	9.4
5.2	8.4	7.3	All Other Non-Current					8.7	6.0
100.0	100.0	100.0	Total					100.0	100.0
			LIABILITIES						
6.5	9.6	5.8	Notes Payable-Short Term					4.0	6.6
2.4	2.7	3.7	Cur. Mat.-L.T.D.					5.3	3.7
16.5	14.1	11.7	Trade Payables					9.7	13.0
.4	.1	.1	Income Taxes Payable					.1	.1
8.5	8.0	6.3	All Other Current					7.7	6.5
34.3	34.5	27.6	Total Current					26.8	29.9
13.8	16.7	20.0	Long-Term Debt					25.1	17.7
1.6	1.6	2.0	Deferred Taxes					1.1	2.7
4.4	7.3	9.5	All Other Non-Current					19.7	5.0
45.9	39.8	41.0	Net Worth					27.2	44.7
100.0	100.0	100.0	Total Liabilities & Net Worth					100.0	100.0
			INCOME DATA						
100.0	100.0	100.0	Net Sales					100.0	100.0
20.4	18.2	20.0	Gross Profit					23.2	18.1
14.2	13.9	14.7	Operating Expenses					16.5	12.4
6.2	4.3	5.2	Operating Profit					6.7	5.7
.6	.4	1.0	All Other Expenses (net)					.6	1.0
5.6	3.9	4.2	Profit Before Taxes					6.1	4.7
			RATIOS						
2.8	3.3	3.2						3.8	2.6
1.8	1.8	1.9	Current					2.0	1.4
1.1	1.0	1.2						1.3	1.2
2.0	2.0	2.3						2.7	2.0
1.2	.9	1.1	Quick					1.5	.8
.7	.6	.7						.9	.7
41 8.8	**41** 9.0	**35** 10.5						**34** 10.7	**42** 8.7
49 7.5	**45** 8.2	**48** 7.6	Sales/Receivables					**49** 7.4	**49** 7.5
58 6.3	**54** 6.8	**55** 6.6						**54** 6.7	**62** 5.9
20 18.6	**19** 19.6	**23** 15.6						**26** 14.0	**20** 18.1
33 11.2	**30** 12.3	**38** 9.5	Cost of Sales/Inventory					**41** 8.9	**37** 9.9
58 6.3	**57** 6.4	**57** 6.4						**56** 6.5	**56** 6.5
18 20.4	**18** 20.3	**20** 18.6						**15** 25.1	**20** 18.0
30 12.0	**28** 12.9	**27** 13.7	Cost of Sales/Payables					**27** 13.7	**29** 12.4
41 8.8	**38** 9.7	**41** 9.0						**33** 11.0	**42** 8.6
4.3	4.4	3.9						3.8	4.8
8.6	9.7	8.8	Sales/Working Capital					6.6	14.2
33.6	170.5	21.1						15.0	27.7
18.8	16.8	11.8						12.4	18.8
(54) 7.2	(39) 6.2	(45) 5.2	EBIT/Interest					(11) 9.4	(24) 7.7
2.3	2.2	1.0						4.5	.1
9.3	7.1	14.0							
(22) 5.5	(16) 3.4	(19) 2.6	Net Profit + Depr., Dep., Amort./Cur. Mat. L/T/D						
1.9	2.2	1.6							
.4	.5	.4						.4	.5
.8	.9	.8	Fixed/Worth					.7	.8
1.3	2.0	1.5						1.0	2.1
.5	.6	.5						.3	.7
1.2	1.5	1.1	Debt/Worth					.8	1.3
2.7	3.1	2.4						2.3	3.0
42.5	42.6	37.3						30.6	45.3
(59) 21.6	(39) 17.4	(45) 10.4	% Profit Before Taxes/Tangible Net Worth					(13) 10.4	(22) 20.0
10.4	3.6	2.1						1.7	.6
18.7	20.0	14.2						15.4	18.9
9.2	9.0	5.9	% Profit Before Taxes/Total Assets					7.9	7.1
3.6	2.4	-.2						1.9	-.7
12.6	11.1	9.1						11.5	9.5
6.3	7.2	5.4	Sales/Net Fixed Assets					5.2	5.1
4.0	3.3	3.1						3.5	2.6
2.5	2.6	2.3						2.3	2.4
1.9	2.0	1.7	Sales/Total Assets					1.8	1.6
1.5	1.4	1.3						1.4	1.2
1.8	1.8	2.1						2.2	1.5
(58) 2.7	(41) 2.7	(47) 3.2	% Depr., Dep., Amort./Sales					(13) 3.4	(22) 2.8
4.2	3.9	4.2						4.5	5.3
.8	.9	1.2							
(13) 1.7	(11) 2.0	(10) 2.0	% Officers', Directors' Owners' Comp/Sales						
3.4	3.0	2.9							
3280526M	2104663M	2887925M	Net Sales ($)		1548M	15537M	50092M	219564M	2601184M
1892415M	1042338M	1834528M	Total Assets ($)		629M	10636M	32553M	125263M	1665447M

M = $ thousand MM = $ million

See Pages 9 through 22 for Explanation of Ratios and Data

Current Data Sorted by Assets							Comparative Historical Data	
						Type of Statement		
		3	2		1	Unqualified	9	9
		2	1			Reviewed	14	16
						Compiled	8	7
	1					Tax Returns	1	2
1	1	3	8	4	4	Other	14	10
	4 (4/1-9/30/13)		27 (10/1/13-3/31/14)				4/1/09-3/31/10	4/1/10-3/31/11
0-500M	500M-2MM	2-10MM	10-50MM	50-100MM	100-250MM		ALL	ALL
1	2	8	11	4	5	**NUMBER OF STATEMENTS**	46	44
%	%	%	%	%	%	**ASSETS**	%	%
			10.4			Cash & Equivalents	9.2	8.4
			20.8			Trade Receivables (net)	27.8	31.9
			23.5			Inventory	25.5	25.9
			2.9			All Other Current	2.4	2.4
			57.6			Total Current	64.9	68.6
			31.8			Fixed Assets (net)	28.7	25.0
			1.2			Intangibles (net)	2.9	2.1
			9.4			All Other Non-Current	3.5	4.4
			100.0			Total	100.0	100.0
						LIABILITIES		
			11.8			Notes Payable-Short Term	9.4	9.3
			1.7			Cur. Mat.-L.T.D.	3.8	2.7
			13.2			Trade Payables	16.5	18.0
			.0			Income Taxes Payable	.1	.1
			9.3			All Other Current	8.7	11.2
			36.0			Total Current	38.4	41.2
			13.2			Long-Term Debt	12.7	13.9
			.5			Deferred Taxes	.1	.4
			5.1			All Other Non-Current	13.6	7.4
			45.1			Net Worth	35.2	37.1
			100.0			Total Liabilties & Net Worth	100.0	100.0
						INCOME DATA		
			100.0			Net Sales	100.0	100.0
			21.1			Gross Profit	20.8	25.1
			16.7			Operating Expenses	20.6	19.6
			4.4			Operating Profit	.1	5.5
			.2			All Other Expenses (net)	1.2	.8
			4.2			Profit Before Taxes	-1.1	4.7
						RATIOS		
			3.0				2.9	2.8
			1.8			Current	1.8	1.7
			1.1				1.1	1.1
			1.3				1.9	1.5
			1.2			Quick	1.0	1.1
			.7				.6	.7
			27 13.7				**35** 10.3	**41** 8.8
			49 7.5			Sales/Receivables	**51** 7.2	**57** 6.4
			54 6.7				**58** 6.3	**70** 5.2
			36 10.2				**27** 13.7	**30** 12.2
			61 6.0			Cost of Sales/Inventory	**48** 7.6	**48** 7.6
			122 3.0				**96** 3.8	**86** 4.2
			15 24.9				**17** 21.8	**19** 19.7
			40 9.1			Cost of Sales/Payables	**27** 13.3	**33** 11.0
			46 8.0				**48** 7.6	**56** 6.5
			3.5				4.2	4.2
			5.6			Sales/Working Capital	7.9	6.7
			70.2				27.9	38.2
							7.0	22.3
						EBIT/Interest	(43) 2.6	(38) 7.1
							-2.8	2.2
							5.0	8.3
						Net Profit + Depr., Dep., Amort./Cur. Mat. L/T/D	(13) 1.0	(13) 2.6
							-.3	1.5
			.6				.3	.3
			.8			Fixed/Worth	.6	.6
			1.9				2.1	1.4
			.4				.6	.7
			2.0			Debt/Worth	1.5	1.4
			5.6				4.9	5.0
			42.6				19.3	39.5
			18.3			% Profit Before Taxes/Tangible Net Worth	(40) 5.9	(40) 18.7
			2.3				-11.6	6.5
			11.2				6.6	14.0
			7.0			% Profit Before Taxes/Total Assets	2.0	9.3
			1.1				-5.5	2.4
			12.5				16.1	21.5
			3.6			Sales/Net Fixed Assets	7.2	9.7
			2.2				4.7	5.7
			2.7				2.8	2.6
			1.4			Sales/Total Assets	1.8	2.0
			1.0				1.5	1.5
			.8				.9	.8
			2.3			% Depr., Dep., Amort./Sales	(43) 2.4	(41) 1.8
			5.0				3.6	2.6
							2.2	1.8
						% Officers', Directors' Owners' Comp/Sales	(10) 3.8	(12) 3.1
							4.9	5.5
401M	2127M	123971M	623890M	333888M	900006M	Net Sales ($)	2120873M	1934673M
342M	3140M	53756M	333178M	246231M	733704M	Total Assets ($)	1130338M	1037131M

M = $ thousand MM = $ million

See Pages 9 through 22 for Explanation of Ratios and Data

	Comparative Historical Data			Current Data Sorted by Sales					
Type of Statement									
Unqualified	11	6	6					2	4
Reviewed	10	8	3				1	1	1
Compiled	4	1							
Tax Returns		1	1		1				
Other	15	15	21	2			1	6	12
	4/1/11-3/31/12	4/1/12-3/31/13	4/1/13-3/31/14	4 (4/1-9/30/13)		27 (10/1/13-3/31/14)			
	ALL	ALL	ALL	0-1MM	1-3MM	3-5MM	5-10MM	10-25MM	25MM & OVER
NUMBER OF STATEMENTS	40	31	31	2	1		2	9	17
ASSETS	%	%	%	%	%	%	%	%	%
Cash & Equivalents	7.1	8.1	8.6			DATA NOT AVAILABLE			7.4
Trade Receivables (net)	29.1	27.3	24.3						24.3
Inventory	27.7	27.7	19.7						21.0
All Other Current	1.9	3.6	2.8						3.2
Total Current	65.9	66.8	55.4						55.9
Fixed Assets (net)	25.7	26.6	33.2						30.5
Intangibles (net)	2.9	2.4	2.8						3.7
All Other Non-Current	5.6	4.2	8.7						9.8
Total	100.0	100.0	100.0						100.0
LIABILITIES									
Notes Payable-Short Term	10.9	11.1	8.5						9.3
Cur. Mat.-L.T.D.	2.4	2.6	2.1						2.4
Trade Payables	17.8	19.1	14.0						15.4
Income Taxes Payable	.3	.2	.1						.1
All Other Current	8.2	12.7	7.3						7.9
Total Current	39.5	45.7	32.0						35.2
Long-Term Debt	9.9	12.4	12.5						12.7
Deferred Taxes	.5	.6	.7						.8
All Other Non-Current	8.1	6.7	5.0						4.6
Net Worth	42.1	34.6	49.7						46.6
Total Liabilties & Net Worth	100.0	100.0	100.0						100.0
INCOME DATA									
Net Sales	100.0	100.0	100.0						100.0
Gross Profit	23.2	25.4	20.7						18.2
Operating Expenses	16.3	17.2	15.2						11.3
Operating Profit	7.0	8.2	5.5						7.0
All Other Expenses (net)	.3	.1	1.7						1.4
Profit Before Taxes	6.7	8.1	3.8						5.6
RATIOS									
Current	2.7	2.7	3.3						3.0
	1.9	2.1	2.2						1.8
	1.2	1.4	1.1						1.2
Quick	1.7	1.4	2.1						1.4
	1.0	.9	1.2						1.0
	.6	.7	.7						.6
Sales/Receivables	**38** 9.5	**40** 9.2	**36** 10.1						**41** 8.9
	49 7.5	**49** 7.5	**52** 7.0						**51** 7.1
	61 6.0	**60** 6.1	**76** 4.8						**56** 6.5
Cost of Sales/Inventory	**30** 12.1	**25** 14.7	**33** 11.2						**36** 10.1
	56 6.5	**55** 6.6	**54** 6.7						**54** 6.8
	91 4.0	**114** 3.2	**76** 4.8						**83** 4.4
Cost of Sales/Payables	**20** 18.7	**17** 21.9	**14** 26.4						**10** 37.8
	33 11.1	**28** 13.1	**33** 11.2						**33** 11.2
	48 7.6	**47** 7.7	**45** 8.2						**44** 8.3
Sales/Working Capital	5.2	4.0	3.5						3.4
	7.0	7.4	5.2						5.6
	23.8	16.1	70.2						42.0
EBIT/Interest	17.1	85.9	34.4						36.4
	(33) 8.9	(29) 5.5	(25) 6.7						(15) 7.6
	2.9	.1	1.8						1.6
Net Profit + Depr., Dep., Amort./Cur. Mat. L/T/D	12.6	12.5							
	(12) 5.3	(10) 6.3							
	2.8	.3							
Fixed/Worth	.4	.3	.4						.5
	.6	.5	.7						.7
	1.4	1.6	1.7						1.8
Debt/Worth	.7	.4	.4						.4
	1.6	1.1	.7						1.4
	3.9	4.5	4.7						6.0
% Profit Before Taxes/Tangible Net Worth	58.3	40.8	43.0						45.2
	(36) 28.5	(28) 27.7	(30) 17.8						19.7
	8.8	1.9	1.9						9.5
% Profit Before Taxes/Total Assets	24.1	27.6	14.3						14.5
	10.0	9.7	8.1						8.3
	4.1	-.1	.8						1.5
Sales/Net Fixed Assets	14.9	15.5	12.5						13.1
	9.4	10.7	4.6						4.6
	5.7	4.4	2.1						2.6
Sales/Total Assets	2.7	2.8	2.5						2.6
	2.1	2.2	1.4						1.5
	1.6	1.5	1.0						1.0
% Depr., Dep., Amort./Sales	1.0	.8	1.5						1.0
	(38) 1.6	(26) 1.8	(28) 2.5						(16) 2.1
	2.2	3.0	4.9						4.8
% Officers', Directors' Owners' Comp/Sales									
Net Sales ($)	**1904446M**	**1925480M**	**1984283M**	**890M**	**1638M**		**16285M**	**147054M**	**1818416M**
Total Assets ($)	**1071997M**	**1058533M**	**1370351M**	**1976M**	**1506M**		**18895M**	**134072M**	**1213902M**

M = $ thousand   MM = $ million

See Pages 9 through 22 for Explanation of Ratios and Data

Current Data Sorted by Assets / Comparative Historical Data

0-500M	500M-2MM	2-10MM	10-50MM	50-100MM	100-250MM		4/1/09-3/31/10 ALL	4/1/10-3/31/11 ALL
						Type of Statement		
		1	8	5	2	Unqualified	14	16
		9	7			Reviewed	19	16
	2	8	1			Compiled	17	19
	2	3				Tax Returns	4	8
1	1	5	11	4	3	Other	31	26
13 (4/1-9/30/13)			60 (10/1/13-3/31/14)					
1	5	26	27	9	5	**NUMBER OF STATEMENTS**	85	85
%	%	%	%	%	%	**ASSETS**	%	%
		9.6	8.8			Cash & Equivalents	9.3	7.7
		23.6	27.6			Trade Receivables (net)	23.4	28.5
		23.0	16.1			Inventory	19.2	21.0
		2.1	2.3			All Other Current	3.1	1.7
		58.2	54.7			Total Current	55.0	58.9
		32.2	32.5			Fixed Assets (net)	34.3	30.4
		2.3	7.0			Intangibles (net)	2.9	4.0
		7.2	5.7			All Other Non-Current	7.9	6.7
		100.0	100.0			Total	100.0	100.0
						LIABILITIES		
		9.1	9.1			Notes Payable-Short Term	9.9	12.5
		3.4	2.7			Cur. Mat.-L.T.D.	4.3	4.6
		13.3	16.4			Trade Payables	12.5	16.1
		.1	.1			Income Taxes Payable	.1	.1
		8.9	13.1			All Other Current	10.0	8.7
		34.9	41.4			Total Current	36.9	42.0
		23.4	16.7			Long-Term Debt	22.0	18.6
		.8	1.0			Deferred Taxes	.9	.4
		11.7	4.1			All Other Non-Current	7.5	5.6
		29.2	36.8			Net Worth	32.8	33.5
		100.0	100.0			Total Liabilties & Net Worth	100.0	100.0
						INCOME DATA		
		100.0	100.0			Net Sales	100.0	100.0
		24.9	15.3			Gross Profit	21.0	22.9
		19.4	10.9			Operating Expenses	20.4	18.9
		5.5	4.5			Operating Profit	.5	4.0
		.8	1.5			All Other Expenses (net)	1.5	1.2
		4.7	2.9			Profit Before Taxes	-1.0	2.8
						RATIOS		
		3.2	2.0				2.5	2.7
		2.0	1.4			Current	1.5	1.7
		1.2	.8				1.0	1.1
		1.7	1.6				1.6	1.9
		1.0	.9			Quick	.9	.9
		.6	.6				.5	.6
		23 15.7	**34** 10.7				**41** 8.8	**36** 10.0
		39 9.4	**47** 7.8			Sales/Receivables	**51** 7.2	**52** 7.0
		57 6.4	**65** 5.6				**66** 5.5	**63** 5.8
		22 16.7	**23** 15.7				**27** 13.4	**24** 15.2
		49 7.4	**31** 11.8			Cost of Sales/Inventory	**42** 8.6	**44** 8.3
		94 3.9	**51** 7.2				**78** 4.7	**78** 4.7
		13 28.6	**22** 16.5				**19** 19.7	**22** 16.6
		29 12.6	**33** 11.0			Cost of Sales/Payables	**31** 11.9	**34** 10.8
		38 9.7	**46** 7.9				**49** 7.5	**50** 7.3
		4.7	6.2				4.6	4.9
		7.3	11.3			Sales/Working Capital	8.7	9.9
		16.3	-25.2				59.1	56.2
		11.6	28.3				6.7	17.2
		(23) 4.7	(25) 4.7			EBIT/Interest	(81) 1.3	(80) 4.7
		1.7	.4				-1.8	1.6
							9.3	15.6
						Net Profit + Depr., Dep., Amort./Cur. Mat. L/T/D	(27) 2.1	(23) 2.5
							.3	1.7
		.5	.5				.5	.5
		.8	.9			Fixed/Worth	1.2	.8
		3.0	1.9				2.3	2.1
		.6	.5				.6	.7
		.9	1.2			Debt/Worth	2.1	1.7
		10.5	5.7				6.8	5.7
		42.8	32.6				16.4	29.9
		(21) 23.0	(23) 15.6			% Profit Before Taxes/Tangible Net Worth	(71) 3.2	(71) 18.4
		13.4	-7.9				-5.6	8.8
		17.3	15.5				4.6	14.0
		8.9	10.3			% Profit Before Taxes/Total Assets	.8	6.5
		3.0	-1.2				-5.3	2.5
		15.8	12.4				11.2	12.9
		5.8	6.3			Sales/Net Fixed Assets	4.1	6.3
		4.3	3.8				2.7	3.6
		2.5	2.8				2.0	2.5
		2.1	2.0			Sales/Total Assets	1.6	1.7
		1.7	1.6				1.2	1.4
		1.5	1.5				1.8	1.4
		(23) 2.4	2.8			% Depr., Dep., Amort./Sales	(73) 3.4	(76) 2.6
		3.8	4.0				5.9	3.7
							1.8	1.5
						% Officers', Directors' Owners' Comp/Sales	(33) 3.4	(32) 3.2
							5.1	4.3
1042M	**11222M**	**270670M**	**1498078M**	**1103041M**	**1060726M**	Net Sales ($)	**2669229M**	**4234257M**
190M	**4970M**	**129436M**	**693553M**	**654596M**	**889903M**	Total Assets ($)	**1894443M**	**2047895M**

M = $ thousand MM = $ million

See Pages 9 through 22 for Explanation of Ratios and Data

Comparative Historical Data | **Current Data Sorted by Sales**

4/1/11-3/31/12 ALL	4/1/12-3/31/13 ALL	4/1/13-3/31/14 ALL	Type of Statement	0-1MM	1-3MM	3-5MM	5-10MM	10-25MM	25MM & OVER
				13 (4/1-9/30/13)			60 (10/1/13-3/31/14)		
11	12	16	Unqualified						16
18	11	16	Reviewed			1	5	3	7
10	13	11	Compiled		1	3	4	2	1
5	4	5	Tax Returns	1	1		3		
26	33	25	Other		1	1	3	4	16
70	73	73	**NUMBER OF STATEMENTS**	1	3	5	15	9	40
%	%	%	**ASSETS**	%	%	%	%	%	%
8.7	8.8	9.4	Cash & Equivalents				9.8		8.7
29.3	26.9	24.6	Trade Receivables (net)				16.9		25.9
19.4	17.7	19.5	Inventory				23.7		17.6
2.9	2.9	2.2	All Other Current				3.5		2.3
60.3	56.3	55.7	Total Current				53.9		54.5
31.1	33.8	32.4	Fixed Assets (net)				37.7		31.4
2.5	3.4	5.7	Intangibles (net)				3.9		7.9
6.0	6.4	6.2	All Other Non-Current				4.5		6.2
100.0	100.0	100.0	Total				100.0		100.0
			LIABILITIES						
8.2	8.7	8.2	Notes Payable-Short Term				7.3		9.0
4.4	3.0	2.9	Cur. Mat.-L.T.D.				2.9		3.2
17.1	15.6	14.3	Trade Payables				14.2		15.1
.1	.1	.1	Income Taxes Payable				.0		.1
8.9	8.4	10.1	All Other Current				6.1		12.3
38.8	36.0	35.6	Total Current				30.4		39.8
16.5	18.5	19.1	Long-Term Debt				22.1		15.7
.6	.9	1.1	Deferred Taxes				1.3		1.0
6.1	7.2	7.6	All Other Non-Current				7.2		9.2
38.0	37.5	36.7	Net Worth				38.9		34.3
100.0	100.0	100.0	Total Liabilties & Net Worth				100.0		100.0
			INCOME DATA						
100.0	100.0	100.0	Net Sales				100.0		100.0
20.4	20.7	20.8	Gross Profit				25.9		17.7
15.2	14.9	15.3	Operating Expenses				20.3		10.6
5.3	5.8	5.5	Operating Profit				5.6		7.1
.6	1.0	1.1	All Other Expenses (net)				.6		1.0
4.6	4.8	4.4	Profit Before Taxes				5.0		6.0
			RATIOS						
2.6	2.7	2.7					2.7		2.1
1.7	1.7	1.8	Current				1.7		1.5
1.3	1.2	1.1					1.2		.9
1.6	1.8	1.6					1.3		1.6
1.0	1.1	.9	Quick				.8		.9
.7	.7	.6					.6		.6
38 9.6	**35** 10.4	**33** 11.2					**8** 46.2		**36** 10.1
49 7.4	**47** 7.7	**45** 8.1	Sales/Receivables				**33** 10.9		**47** 7.8
62 5.9	**62** 5.9	**58** 6.3					**42** 8.7		**64** 5.7
22 16.5	**18** 19.8	**24** 15.2					**19** 19.3		**24** 15.2
34 10.7	**33** 11.2	**36** 10.2	Cost of Sales/Inventory				**69** 5.3		**34** 10.7
55 6.6	**56** 6.5	**68** 5.4					**107** 3.4		**58** 6.3
23 15.7	**19** 18.8	**16** 23.5					**15** 23.7		**19** 18.9
35 10.4	**33** 11.1	**28** 13.2	Cost of Sales/Payables				**31** 11.8		**30** 12.1
42 8.6	**46** 8.0	**42** 8.7					**38** 9.5		**46** 8.0
4.7	4.5	5.1					4.4		5.6
9.2	9.0	9.4	Sales/Working Capital				9.4		11.4
16.1	24.1	31.4					13.4		NM
22.2	15.7	20.7					14.0		32.1
(65) 7.6	(62) 6.7	(67) 5.4	EBIT/Interest				(14) 5.0		(38) 9.5
1.8	1.6	1.4					2.6		3.4
6.2	9.3	13.1							13.7
(24) 3.0	(22) 6.6	(23) 4.9	Net Profit + Depr., Dep., Amort./Cur. Mat. L/T/D						(16) 7.4
1.7	2.5	2.0							1.8
.5	.5	.5					.6		.5
.7	.9	.7	Fixed/Worth				1.0		.9
1.2	2.7	1.9					2.8		1.9
.6	.6	.6					.6		.6
1.1	1.7	1.2	Debt/Worth				.9		1.4
4.0	5.0	6.0					9.7		5.5
40.5	34.9	40.2					57.6		41.2
(64) 18.6	(63) 25.1	(62) 20.8	% Profit Before Taxes/Tangible Net Worth				(13) 23.0		(35) 20.3
7.2	7.0	5.6					17.5		5.9
14.1	18.8	16.5					17.0		17.3
8.7	9.5	9.6	% Profit Before Taxes/Total Assets				8.9		11.1
2.1	2.5	2.3					3.2		5.0
11.2	10.7	13.3					8.9		13.3
6.8	6.0	5.6	Sales/Net Fixed Assets				5.4		6.2
4.3	3.7	3.6					2.7		3.5
2.6	2.5	2.6					2.5		2.6
2.0	1.8	1.9	Sales/Total Assets				2.1		1.9
1.6	1.5	1.5					1.6		1.4
1.6	1.9	1.7					1.4		1.4
(65) 2.8	(68) 2.8	(67) 2.8	% Depr., Dep., Amort./Sales				(14) 2.4		(38) 2.9
3.9	4.1	4.1					4.3		4.0
1.9	1.6	2.1							
(30) 2.8	(20) 3.5	(16) 4.4	% Officers', Directors' Owners' Comp/Sales						
5.2	7.5	7.3							
3430988M	4077304M	3944779M	Net Sales ($)	669M	4993M	18959M	113276M	158652M	3648230M
1769427M	2376512M	2372648M	Total Assets ($)	534M	1821M	9854M	63443M	99116M	2197880M

M = $ thousand MM = $ million

See Pages 9 through 22 for Explanation of Ratios and Data

Current Data Sorted by Assets							Comparative Historical Data	
		2	1	1		Type of Statement Unqualified	4	3
		6				Reviewed	11	8
		1	1			Compiled	6	5
						Tax Returns	3	2
		4	5		1	Other	9	10
4 (4/1-9/30/13)		18 (10/1/13-3/31/14)					4/1/09-3/31/10 ALL	4/1/10-3/31/11 ALL
0-500M	500M-2MM	2-10MM	10-50MM	50-100MM	100-250MM			
		13	7	1	1	NUMBER OF STATEMENTS	33	28
%	%	%	%	%	%	ASSETS	%	%
D	D	8.4				Cash & Equivalents	12.1	9.8
A	A	32.1				Trade Receivables (net)	25.5	29.4
T	T	19.8				Inventory	17.0	16.3
A	A	2.6				All Other Current	1.3	1.1
		62.9				Total Current	55.9	56.6
N	N	30.5				Fixed Assets (net)	38.2	35.2
O	O	5.5				Intangibles (net)	2.8	3.0
T	T	1.2				All Other Non-Current	3.1	5.1
		100.0				Total	100.0	100.0
A	A					LIABILITIES		
V	V	5.4				Notes Payable-Short Term	8.7	15.0
A	A	2.9				Cur. Mat.-L.T.D.	5.1	3.9
I	I	15.0				Trade Payables	13.3	14.5
L	L	.3				Income Taxes Payable	.0	.2
A	A	8.1				All Other Current	6.9	7.0
B	B	31.8				Total Current	34.0	40.6
L	L	15.4				Long-Term Debt	20.9	16.6
E	E	2.2				Deferred Taxes	.7	.9
		5.7				All Other Non-Current	1.8	4.0
		44.9				Net Worth	42.7	37.9
		100.0				Total Liabilties & Net Worth	100.0	100.0
						INCOME DATA		
		100.0				Net Sales	100.0	100.0
		25.1				Gross Profit	24.6	27.6
		17.1				Operating Expenses	21.9	21.5
		8.0				Operating Profit	2.7	6.1
		1.1				All Other Expenses (net)	1.2	1.4
		6.8				Profit Before Taxes	1.5	4.7
						RATIOS		
		3.1					3.4	3.0
		2.0				Current	2.1	1.9
		1.4					1.2	1.0
		1.8					2.5	2.4
		1.0				Quick	1.4	1.2
		.9					.6	.6
		37 9.8					**38** 9.6	**40** 9.2
		48 7.6				Sales/Receivables	**45** 8.2	**53** 6.8
		73 5.0					**65** 5.6	**70** 5.2
		19 19.0					**29** 12.5	**28** 13.2
		42 8.7				Cost of Sales/Inventory	**40** 9.2	**42** 8.7
		69 5.3					**57** 6.4	**66** 5.5
		20 17.9					**13** 28.1	**19** 19.2
		28 12.9				Cost of Sales/Payables	**24** 15.1	**29** 12.5
		48 7.6					**39** 9.4	**54** 6.8
		5.1					4.3	5.3
		6.7				Sales/Working Capital	8.2	9.0
		14.5					386.1	NM
		21.2					13.1	21.1
		(11) 5.8				EBIT/Interest	(31) 2.6	(25) 4.2
		3.1					1.1	1.2
						Net Profit + Depr., Dep., Amort./Cur. Mat. L/T/D		
		.3					.4	.4
		1.0				Fixed/Worth	.8	.7
		1.4					2.3	2.1
		.8					.4	.4
		1.4				Debt/Worth	1.6	1.5
		2.8					3.8	4.2
		61.4					23.7	32.9
		28.0				% Profit Before Taxes/Tangible Net Worth	(28) 7.4	(24) 20.9
		17.3					.2	2.6
		17.6					10.7	16.1
		10.4				% Profit Before Taxes/Total Assets	1.9	6.9
		3.2					-1.0	.6
		15.7					12.1	12.6
		6.7				Sales/Net Fixed Assets	5.1	6.8
		3.9					2.7	3.7
		2.5					2.5	2.6
		2.2				Sales/Total Assets	1.8	2.1
		1.7					1.2	1.4
		1.5					2.4	1.8
		(12) 2.2				% Depr., Dep., Amort./Sales	(32) 3.5	(26) 3.1
		2.7					5.9	5.0
							2.3	
						% Officers', Directors' Owners' Comp/Sales	(11) 5.8	
							10.5	
		142234M	244135M	110847M	149992M	Net Sales ($)	406035M	264766M
		68264M	133754M	80671M	118888M	Total Assets ($)	236574M	159329M

M = $ thousand MM = $ million

See Pages 9 through 22 for Explanation of Ratios and Data

Comparative Historical Data				Current Data Sorted by Sales					
			Type of Statement						
7	5	4	Unqualified					1	3
8	7	6	Reviewed			1	4	1	
3	2	2	Compiled					1	1
1	1		Tax Returns						
11	12	10	Other				3	3	4
				4 (4/1-9/30/13)		18 (10/1/13-3/31/14)			
4/1/11-3/31/12 ALL	4/1/12-3/31/13 ALL	4/1/13-3/31/14 ALL		0-1MM	1-3MM	3-5MM	5-10MM	10-25MM	25MM & OVER
30	27	22	**NUMBER OF STATEMENTS**			1	7	6	8
%	%	%	**ASSETS**	%	%	%	%	%	%
9.5	7.9	6.3	Cash & Equivalents	D	D				
28.0	25.3	28.9	Trade Receivables (net)	A	A				
20.5	21.6	22.8	Inventory	T	T				
1.6	2.6	2.1	All Other Current	A	A				
59.5	57.4	60.1	Total Current						
32.6	33.8	33.1	Fixed Assets (net)	N	N				
4.1	5.0	4.5	Intangibles (net)	O	O				
3.8	3.8	2.3	All Other Non-Current	T	T				
100.0	100.0	100.0	Total						
			LIABILITIES	A	A				
4.5	9.5	10.0	Notes Payable-Short Term	V	V				
3.1	3.2	2.9	Cur. Mat.-L.T.D.	A	A				
13.2	12.0	13.4	Trade Payables	I	I				
.2	.1	.2	Income Taxes Payable	L	L				
8.1	8.3	9.6	All Other Current	A	A				
29.2	33.2	36.1	Total Current	B	B				
14.3	13.5	13.5	Long-Term Debt	L	L				
.8	1.2	1.7	Deferred Taxes	E	E				
6.3	7.9	4.0	All Other Non-Current						
49.4	44.2	44.7	Net Worth						
100.0	100.0	100.0	Total Liabilties & Net Worth						
			INCOME DATA						
100.0	100.0	100.0	Net Sales						
28.3	26.1	24.2	Gross Profit						
19.4	17.8	17.4	Operating Expenses						
8.9	8.3	6.8	Operating Profit						
2.1	1.2	.4	All Other Expenses (net)						
6.8	7.0	6.3	Profit Before Taxes						
			RATIOS						
4.0	3.5	3.0							
2.4	1.8	1.7	Current						
1.3	1.1	1.1							
2.5	2.2	1.7							
1.5	1.1	1.0	Quick						
.8	.6	.6							
37 9.8	36 10.2	38 9.6							
49 7.4	45 8.1	50 7.3	Sales/Receivables						
62 5.9	55 6.6	65 5.6							
27 13.7	25 14.4	28 13.1							
50 7.3	49 7.5	54 6.8	Cost of Sales/Inventory						
70 5.2	72 5.1	87 4.2							
18 20.4	17 21.1	22 16.9							
29 12.5	27 13.4	31 11.9	Cost of Sales/Payables						
47 7.7	41 8.8	42 8.7							
3.6	4.5	5.1							
6.4	7.6	7.8	Sales/Working Capital						
18.2	63.0	37.2							
30.5	14.5	19.5							
(27) 8.0	(24) 6.7	(20) 5.8	EBIT/Interest						
4.0	3.7	3.3							
			Net Profit + Depr., Dep., Amort./Cur. Mat. L/T/D						
.3	.4	.4							
.7	1.2	1.0	Fixed/Worth						
1.6	1.9	1.5							
.4	.6	.9							
1.2	1.4	1.7	Debt/Worth						
2.8	4.1	2.5							
50.8	49.8	36.8							
(28) 23.6	(25) 20.0	23.5	% Profit Before Taxes/Tangible Net Worth						
11.2	9.4	11.9							
20.5	14.4	16.0							
10.0	9.5	9.1	% Profit Before Taxes/Total Assets						
3.9	5.1	3.8							
11.8	10.9	8.9							
5.6	4.8	5.4	Sales/Net Fixed Assets						
4.7	3.9	4.1							
2.7	2.5	2.3							
2.0	1.9	2.1	Sales/Total Assets						
1.4	1.4	1.5							
1.5	1.5	1.8							
(25) 1.9	(25) 2.5	(21) 2.4	% Depr., Dep., Amort./Sales						
3.8	4.4	2.9							
			% Officers', Directors' Owners' Comp/Sales						
714987M	1012409M	647208M	Net Sales ($)			4638M	58795M	95155M	488620M
426241M	630414M	401577M	Total Assets ($)			2321M	29729M	56466M	313061M

M = $ thousand MM = $ million

See Pages 9 through 22 for Explanation of Ratios and Data

Current Data Sorted by Assets / Comparative Historical Data

0-500M	500M-2MM	2-10MM	10-50MM	50-100MM	100-250MM	Type of Statement	4/1/09-3/31/10 ALL	4/1/10-3/31/11 ALL
		3	2	3	2	Unqualified	20	22
	2	7	6	1		Reviewed	19	21
	3	7	3			Compiled	12	11
2	4	1	3			Tax Returns	11	12
1	4	17	20	6	2	Other	60	54
16 (4/1-9/30/13)		83 (10/1/13-3/31/14)						
3	13	35	34	10	4	NUMBER OF STATEMENTS	122	120
%	%	%	%	%	%	**ASSETS**	%	%
	7.7	10.1	9.8	11.3		Cash & Equivalents	9.8	8.0
	32.0	24.2	21.7	17.5		Trade Receivables (net)	21.7	23.8
	23.4	21.7	24.9	20.5		Inventory	24.2	28.0
	.6	3.8	2.5	1.6		All Other Current	3.0	1.4
	63.7	59.8	58.9	50.8		Total Current	58.7	61.2
	27.4	31.9	33.9	35.9		Fixed Assets (net)	32.0	29.9
	2.3	2.7	2.5	10.1		Intangibles (net)	4.5	4.2
	6.5	5.5	4.7	3.2		All Other Non-Current	4.8	4.7
	100.0	100.0	100.0	100.0		Total	100.0	100.0
						LIABILITIES		
	6.8	10.3	7.1	2.8		Notes Payable-Short Term	10.3	9.4
	4.5	3.3	4.9	1.1		Cur. Mat.-L.T.D.	3.5	3.8
	14.0	12.6	13.5	7.1		Trade Payables	10.8	14.0
	.1	.1	.1	.0		Income Taxes Payable	.1	.1
	5.8	8.2	5.5	6.0		All Other Current	10.0	10.9
	31.2	34.5	31.1	17.0		Total Current	34.8	38.2
	26.5	13.7	13.6	15.4		Long-Term Debt	18.8	14.0
	.2	.8	1.6	2.2		Deferred Taxes	.8	1.0
	12.0	5.6	9.0	3.5		All Other Non-Current	10.7	11.7
	30.1	45.4	44.7	61.9		Net Worth	35.0	35.2
	100.0	100.0	100.0	100.0		Total Liabilties & Net Worth	100.0	100.0
						INCOME DATA		
	100.0	100.0	100.0	100.0		Net Sales	100.0	100.0
	29.5	22.0	23.4	18.1		Gross Profit	26.1	24.3
	25.3	17.7	15.7	15.5		Operating Expenses	21.4	18.4
	4.1	4.3	7.7	2.5		Operating Profit	4.7	5.9
	.6	1.1	.2	1.8		All Other Expenses (net)	1.3	1.6
	3.5	3.1	7.5	.7		Profit Before Taxes	3.3	4.2
						RATIOS		
	3.3	3.1	3.9	5.4			3.4	2.9
	2.8	2.1	2.0	3.2		Current	1.9	1.8
	1.4	.9	1.3	1.9			1.2	1.2
	1.9	2.1	2.5	3.7			2.1	1.8
	1.7	.8	1.0	1.7		Quick	.9	.8
	.8	.4	.5	.7			.6	.5
	24 15.1	30 12.1	35 10.4	44 8.3			33 11.1	37 9.8
	34 10.8	41 8.8	48 7.6	49 7.5		Sales/Receivables	44 8.4	48 7.6
	55 6.6	54 6.7	59 6.2	54 6.8			60 6.1	58 6.3
	22 16.8	18 20.8	40 9.2	49 7.5			35 10.4	44 8.4
	38 9.7	43 8.5	59 6.2	60 6.1		Cost of Sales/Inventory	59 6.2	75 4.9
	70 5.2	78 4.7	94 3.9	122 3.0			111 3.3	123 3.0
	11 33.0	14 25.4	13 28.7	16 23.4			15 24.6	22 16.9
	21 17.3	23 15.7	26 14.3	22 16.4		Cost of Sales/Payables	26 13.8	33 10.9
	34 10.7	44 8.3	40 9.1	42 8.7			42 8.6	47 7.8
	5.7	4.4	3.4	2.4			3.7	3.8
	6.9	7.7	6.2	4.0		Sales/Working Capital	7.2	7.3
	21.6	-56.7	11.9	6.6			27.9	18.8
	23.4	12.8	26.0				14.6	17.2
	4.1	(30) 5.2	(32) 8.0			EBIT/Interest	(113) 2.6	(111) 5.0
	-2.0	1.2	2.6				-.5	1.1
							4.1	5.4
						Net Profit + Depr., Dep., Amort./Cur. Mat. L/T/D	(28) 1.6	(29) 2.1
							.5	1.3
	.3	.3	.3	.4			.4	.4
	.8	.5	.8	.7		Fixed/Worth	.7	.8
	34.3	2.7	1.5	3.2			3.2	2.7
	.4	.4	.5	.2			.7	.6
	3.7	1.0	1.4	.8		Debt/Worth	1.5	1.8
	NM	2.7	3.5	5.5			7.1	7.1
	117.3	35.9	42.3				39.9	41.3
	(10) 19.1	(30) 16.4	(32) 22.6			% Profit Before Taxes/Tangible Net Worth	(102) 14.5	(101) 19.5
	-2.6	3.9	8.1				-6.0	4.5
	17.1	15.9	15.8	10.4			14.5	17.0
	10.1	4.7	13.4	7.4		% Profit Before Taxes/Total Assets	3.3	5.5
	-2.9	1.6	1.3	-.2			-4.6	.2
	46.1	15.8	9.9	4.7			11.1	13.1
	15.3	7.2	5.4	3.2		Sales/Net Fixed Assets	5.3	6.8
	5.3	4.3	2.9	2.7			3.4	3.5
	3.4	2.8	2.3	2.0			2.2	2.2
	2.6	1.9	1.6	1.3		Sales/Total Assets	1.6	1.8
	2.0	1.4	1.2	.7			1.2	1.2
	.8	1.8	1.9	2.9			1.7	1.5
	(10) 1.5	(31) 2.5	(32) 2.6	3.8		% Depr., Dep., Amort./Sales	(103) 3.0	(110) 2.8
	3.5	3.7	5.0	5.1			5.2	4.7
							1.8	1.4
						% Officers', Directors' Owners' Comp/Sales	(34) 3.8	(33) 2.7
							8.2	4.6
4159M	54446M	379931M	1108631M	893181M	1327748M	Net Sales ($)	5149694M	4663866M
970M	17773M	190924M	663787M	673176M	618338M	Total Assets ($)	3388856M	2999544M

M = $ thousand MM = $ million

See Pages 9 through 22 for Explanation of Ratios and Data

Comparative Historical Data / Current Data Sorted by Sales

Comparative Historical Data			Type of Statement	Current Data Sorted by Sales					
28	18	10	Unqualified				1	2	7
23	21	16	Reviewed				7	2	7
12	14	13	Compiled	1	1	2	4	3	2
14	23	10	Tax Returns		4	2	1	3	
64	42	50	Other	1	2	3	8	15	21
4/1/11-3/31/12	4/1/12-3/31/13	4/1/13-3/31/14		16 (4/1-9/30/13)			83 (10/1/13-3/31/14)		
ALL	ALL	ALL		0-1MM	1-3MM	3-5MM	5-10MM	10-25MM	25MM & OVER
141	118	99	**NUMBER OF STATEMENTS**	2	7	7	21	25	37
%	%	%	**ASSETS**	%	%	%	%	%	%
8.6	8.9	10.3	Cash & Equivalents				10.4	13.4	7.9
25.9	24.4	23.9	Trade Receivables (net)				24.5	24.1	23.2
25.7	25.4	22.5	Inventory				21.8	24.2	23.9
1.2	1.9	2.5	All Other Current				4.8	2.0	2.5
61.3	60.6	59.3	Total Current				61.6	63.8	57.6
29.0	31.6	32.1	Fixed Assets (net)				30.4	26.1	34.3
5.3	3.7	3.4	Intangibles (net)				4.4	3.0	4.1
4.4	4.2	5.2	All Other Non-Current				3.7	7.1	4.1
100.0	100.0	100.0	Total				100.0	100.0	100.0
			LIABILITIES						
9.2	7.0	7.3	Notes Payable-Short Term				11.1	7.0	6.5
3.1	3.8	3.8	Cur. Mat.-L.T.D.				2.6	3.0	4.7
16.4	14.3	13.0	Trade Payables				11.1	14.3	12.5
.1	.1	.1	Income Taxes Payable				.1	.2	.0
8.2	6.9	7.2	All Other Current				6.8	5.6	6.6
36.9	32.1	31.4	Total Current				31.7	30.0	30.4
17.9	16.8	15.3	Long-Term Debt				12.3	12.3	13.9
.9	.9	1.1	Deferred Taxes				1.0	1.8	1.2
9.7	7.2	7.1	All Other Non-Current				7.7	6.0	8.4
34.5	43.1	45.1	Net Worth				47.3	50.0	46.1
100.0	100.0	100.0	Total Liabilties & Net Worth				100.0	100.0	100.0
			INCOME DATA						
100.0	100.0	100.0	Net Sales				100.0	100.0	100.0
26.4	27.0	23.5	Gross Profit				19.4	22.5	21.1
19.4	21.1	18.1	Operating Expenses				14.8	15.3	15.9
7.0	5.9	5.4	Operating Profit				4.6	7.1	5.2
.5	.5	.8	All Other Expenses (net)				.5	-.1	.8
6.5	5.4	4.7	Profit Before Taxes				4.1	7.2	4.4
			RATIOS						
2.9	3.3	3.4					3.2	4.0	3.6
1.9	2.0	2.1	Current				2.4	3.0	1.9
1.2	1.4	1.2					1.2	1.3	1.6
1.8	1.7	2.2					2.1	2.4	2.1
.9	1.1	1.3	Quick				.8	1.9	1.0
.6	.5	.6					.4	.6	.6
36 10.1	**31** 11.7	**33** 11.2					**31** 11.7	**33** 11.1	**36** 10.2
45 8.1	**41** 8.9	**44** 8.3	Sales/Receivables				**38** 9.5	**45** 8.1	**48** 7.6
58 6.3	**53** 6.9	**56** 6.5					**53** 6.9	**60** 6.1	**58** 6.3
38 9.7	**36** 10.1	**32** 11.3					**14** 26.2	**38** 9.5	**41** 8.8
62 5.9	**56** 6.5	**51** 7.1	Cost of Sales/Inventory				**38** 9.7	**58** 6.3	**54** 6.7
96 3.8	**101** 3.6	**85** 4.3					**81** 4.5	**99** 3.7	**81** 4.5
19 19.3	**17** 21.1	**14** 25.4					**6** 64.9	**13** 27.3	**16** 22.7
37 9.9	**29** 12.8	**24** 15.2	Cost of Sales/Payables				**21** 17.7	**27** 13.4	**28** 13.1
56 6.5	**47** 7.8	**41** 8.8					**34** 10.8	**45** 8.1	**41** 8.9
4.1	4.5	4.0					4.9	3.4	3.4
8.4	7.3	6.5	Sales/Working Capital				7.7	4.4	6.2
26.9	19.0	17.6					30.9	9.6	13.5
20.1	20.2	23.3					16.1	42.2	26.9
(126) 7.1	(109) 7.6	(87) 6.8	EBIT/Interest				(19) 4.9	(22) 8.2	(35) 7.9
1.9	1.9	1.6					-1.6	3.1	4.9
10.3	9.1	11.7							11.7
(44) 5.9	(39) 3.5	(22) 4.6	Net Profit + Depr., Dep., Amort./Cur. Mat. L/T/D						(12) 6.6
3.0	1.5	1.4							2.4
.3	.4	.4					.3	.2	.4
.8	.7	.6	Fixed/Worth				.5	.5	.8
2.7	1.7	1.6					2.0	1.5	1.4
.7	.6	.4					.4	.4	.5
2.1	1.2	1.2	Debt/Worth				1.2	.7	1.3
6.9	4.3	4.0					3.9	2.5	3.1
51.2	50.0	36.7					60.6	37.8	33.2
(122) 28.2	(108) 22.0	(88) 17.9	% Profit Before Taxes/Tangible Net Worth				(20) 12.1	(22) 19.4	(34) 19.6
12.6	5.2	4.8					-2.0	5.4	9.8
19.2	16.9	15.6					15.8	19.6	14.5
10.5	9.7	9.6	% Profit Before Taxes/Total Assets				2.8	14.3	9.3
3.1	2.1	1.6					-2.7	1.9	3.4
13.8	13.8	15.0					17.7	37.1	9.5
7.8	6.2	5.7	Sales/Net Fixed Assets				7.2	8.9	5.2
4.0	3.7	3.2					3.6	3.6	3.1
2.5	2.7	2.8					3.1	2.4	2.7
1.9	1.9	1.9	Sales/Total Assets				2.0	1.8	1.8
1.3	1.4	1.2					1.3	1.2	1.2
1.5	1.4	1.8					1.8	.5	1.9
(121) 2.5	(104) 2.4	(88) 2.6	% Depr., Dep., Amort./Sales				(18) 2.3	(22) 2.7	(34) 2.7
4.0	4.1	4.5					3.9	3.5	4.5
1.9	2.1	3.1							
(45) 2.9	(37) 5.1	(24) 4.3	% Officers', Directors' Owners' Comp/Sales						
5.5	10.0	6.9							
6364880M	**4844803M**	**3768096M**	Net Sales ($)	**1368M**	**12495M**	**29976M**	**157876M**	**420655M**	**3145726M**
3665503M	**2951083M**	**2164968M**	Total Assets ($)	**2792M**	**5079M**	**16635M**	**95537M**	**273135M**	**1771790M**

M = $ thousand MM = $ million

See Pages 9 through 22 for Explanation of Ratios and Data

Current Data Sorted by Assets | Comparative Historical Data

0-500M	500M-2MM	2-10MM	10-50MM	50-100MM	100-250MM	Type of Statement		
		2	3	2		Unqualified	4	6
		6	2		1	Reviewed	2	9
	2	3	1			Compiled	13	14
2						Tax Returns	6	3
		4	6	2	1	Other	12	14
12 (4/1-9/30/13)			25 (10/1/13-3/31/14)				4/1/09-3/31/10	4/1/10-3/31/11
0-500M	500M-2MM	2-10MM	10-50MM	50-100MM	100-250MM		ALL	ALL
2	2	15	12	4	2	**NUMBER OF STATEMENTS**	37	46
%	%	%	%	%	%	**ASSETS**	%	%
		6.7	9.4			Cash & Equivalents	12.8	7.8
		29.3	27.6			Trade Receivables (net)	23.2	24.3
		19.3	28.3			Inventory	17.8	23.4
		.2	.8			All Other Current	.5	.8
		55.6	66.1			Total Current	54.4	56.3
		38.4	26.2			Fixed Assets (net)	31.7	31.6
		3.8	2.2			Intangibles (net)	9.1	6.5
		2.2	5.4			All Other Non-Current	4.8	5.7
		100.0	100.0			Total	100.0	100.0
						LIABILITIES		
		6.2	6.0			Notes Payable-Short Term	4.8	7.2
		6.7	1.8			Cur. Mat.-L.T.D.	4.9	4.6
		13.5	11.6			Trade Payables	14.7	16.1
		.3	.8			Income Taxes Payable	.0	.4
		7.6	6.9			All Other Current	4.9	5.9
		34.3	27.1			Total Current	29.2	34.3
		25.9	10.4			Long-Term Debt	30.3	26.5
		.0	.4			Deferred Taxes	.8	.5
		9.8	12.1			All Other Non-Current	15.3	7.8
		30.0	50.0			Net Worth	24.5	31.0
		100.0	100.0			Total Liabilties & Net Worth	100.0	100.0
						INCOME DATA		
		100.0	100.0			Net Sales	100.0	100.0
		29.7	29.5			Gross Profit	28.8	28.4
		20.0	21.2			Operating Expenses	27.2	24.4
		9.7	8.3			Operating Profit	1.6	4.0
		1.7	.2			All Other Expenses (net)	2.2	1.9
		8.0	8.1			Profit Before Taxes	-.6	2.2
						RATIOS		
		3.2	6.1				4.2	3.1
		2.0	2.8			Current	2.5	1.8
		1.0	1.8				1.4	1.1
		2.2	3.0				3.4	1.8
		1.4	1.6			Quick	1.5	1.1
		.5	1.1				.9	.5
		36 10.0	40 9.2				31 11.9	33 11.2
		47 7.7	47 7.8			Sales/Receivables	45 8.0	52 7.0
		58 6.3	64 5.7				56 6.5	62 5.9
		28 12.9	49 7.5				17 21.0	35 10.5
		47 7.7	76 4.8			Cost of Sales/Inventory	52 7.0	64 5.7
		60 6.1	94 3.9				89 4.1	117 3.1
		18 19.9	19 18.8				10 35.3	20 18.2
		33 11.1	24 15.0			Cost of Sales/Payables	26 14.1	41 8.9
		53 6.9	43 8.4				42 8.7	70 5.2
		5.2	3.8				3.5	4.1
		7.6	4.3			Sales/Working Capital	6.1	7.7
		97.2	9.9				17.2	30.5
		21.6					5.3	12.0
		13.8				EBIT/Interest	(33) .5	(44) 2.5
		1.6					-1.7	.3
						Net Profit + Depr., Dep., Amort./Cur. Mat. L/T/D		
		.6	.3				.3	.4
		1.0	.6			Fixed/Worth	1.0	1.0
		3.6	2.0				-10.2	NM
		.9	.2				.4	.5
		1.8	1.0			Debt/Worth	2.2	2.0
		7.6	3.1				-15.7	NM
		87.5	40.1				33.3	32.3
		(13) 49.6	(10) 28.9			% Profit Before Taxes/Tangible Net Worth	(26) 12.7	(35) 13.0
		33.9	7.4				-7.8	-6.1
		27.1	23.6				10.8	13.5
		20.3	13.5			% Profit Before Taxes/Total Assets	-.6	3.9
		3.3	4.7				-7.3	-3.0
		9.2	17.0				13.7	13.3
		5.7	9.2			Sales/Net Fixed Assets	6.2	6.3
		2.5	5.0				3.2	3.3
		2.7	2.5				2.6	2.5
		2.2	2.0			Sales/Total Assets	1.9	1.6
		1.2	1.5				1.0	1.2
		1.7	.7				2.1	2.0
		(14) 3.1	(11) 1.8			% Depr., Dep., Amort./Sales	(29) 4.1	(42) 3.6
		6.1	3.3				7.0	6.2
							3.0	2.3
						% Officers', Directors' Owners' Comp/Sales	(12) 3.9	(14) 3.4
							9.1	11.9
1676M	4820M	159916M	471094M	343567M	1026342M	Net Sales ($)	579752M	695012M
464M	2447M	86168M	246841M	295946M	480875M	Total Assets ($)	533166M	489730M

M = $ thousand MM = $ million

See Pages 9 through 22 for Explanation of Ratios and Data

Comparative Historical Data				Current Data Sorted by Sales					
			Type of Statement						
4	4	7	Unqualified				1	1	5
7	12	9	Reviewed				3	3	3
12	9	6	Compiled		2	1	1	1	1
4	3	2	Tax Returns	1	1				
16	19	13	Other			1	3	2	7
4/1/11-3/31/12	**4/1/12-3/31/13**	**4/1/13-3/31/14**		**12 (4/1-9/30/13)**			**25 (10/1/13-3/31/14)**		
ALL	**ALL**	**ALL**		**0-1MM**	**1-3MM**	**3-5MM**	**5-10MM**	**10-25MM**	**25MM & OVER**
43	47	37	**NUMBER OF STATEMENTS**	1	3	2	8	7	16
%	%	%	**ASSETS**	%	%	%	%	%	%
9.2	7.7	10.4	Cash & Equivalents						6.6
25.6	25.5	26.8	Trade Receivables (net)						26.5
20.8	22.4	21.4	Inventory						23.9
.8	2.5	1.3	All Other Current						2.5
56.4	58.1	59.9	Total Current						59.5
29.7	30.2	31.2	Fixed Assets (net)						27.8
6.2	4.3	5.5	Intangibles (net)						8.9
7.7	7.4	3.5	All Other Non-Current						3.8
100.0	100.0	100.0	Total						100.0
			LIABILITIES						
12.8	8.4	7.4	Notes Payable-Short Term						9.4
3.8	3.7	4.4	Cur. Mat.-L.T.D.						3.0
17.2	15.9	11.8	Trade Payables						12.8
.1	.3	.4	Income Taxes Payable						.2
5.3	7.5	6.8	All Other Current						7.1
39.2	35.9	30.9	Total Current						32.4
24.8	16.8	18.3	Long-Term Debt						12.1
.1	.3	.2	Deferred Taxes						.5
14.6	10.2	11.0	All Other Non-Current						8.6
21.2	36.8	39.6	Net Worth						46.4
100.0	100.0	100.0	Total Liabilties & Net Worth						100.0
			INCOME DATA						
100.0	100.0	100.0	Net Sales						100.0
31.5	25.0	31.1	Gross Profit						26.6
23.5	20.5	21.8	Operating Expenses						19.5
8.0	4.4	9.3	Operating Profit						7.1
2.3	.9	1.0	All Other Expenses (net)						.8
5.7	3.5	8.3	Profit Before Taxes						6.3
			RATIOS						
3.6	3.2	3.5							2.8
1.7	1.6	2.1	Current						1.8
1.2	1.3	1.4							1.4
1.7	2.0	2.4							1.6
1.1	.8	1.4	Quick						1.0
.5	.6	.8							.8
30 12.2	**35** 10.3	**39** 9.3							**41** 8.9
43 8.5	**47** 7.8	**47** 7.7	Sales/Receivables						**51** 7.1
58 6.3	**60** 6.1	**61** 6.0							**63** 5.8
26 14.3	**38** 9.6	**37** 9.8							**43** 8.5
52 7.0	**54** 6.7	**56** 6.5	Cost of Sales/Inventory						**69** 5.3
85 4.3	**72** 5.1	**81** 4.5							**94** 3.9
20 18.3	**17** 21.0	**18** 19.8							**24** 15.5
34 10.7	**34** 10.6	**33** 11.1	Cost of Sales/Payables						**34** 10.7
57 6.4	**48** 7.6	**41** 8.8							**42** 8.7
5.0	5.5	4.3							4.3
8.1	9.4	7.1	Sales/Working Capital						6.7
31.8	23.3	11.1							11.2
15.3	12.2	19.7							16.9
(38) 6.5	(44) 6.7	(33) 7.2	EBIT/Interest						(14) 7.1
2.1	1.1	3.2							3.8
			Net Profit + Depr., Dep., Amort./Cur. Mat. L/T/D						
.4	.3	.5							.4
1.1	.8	.9	Fixed/Worth						.8
-31.4	3.1	3.5							2.6
.7	.6	.6							.6
2.2	1.7	1.7	Debt/Worth						1.8
-143.3	10.8	6.2							4.3
54.7	45.9	68.6							46.9
(32) 21.7	(41) 14.2	(30) 40.7	% Profit Before Taxes/Tangible Net Worth						(13) 34.7
4.3	.0	28.0							10.9
20.6	15.4	23.3							16.1
10.0	6.0	12.6	% Profit Before Taxes/Total Assets						9.4
1.3	-.2	5.4							4.5
31.9	19.7	10.6							17.0
7.8	7.0	7.5	Sales/Net Fixed Assets						5.9
2.7	3.5	3.1							3.2
3.1	2.8	2.7							2.5
1.9	2.0	2.1	Sales/Total Assets						1.9
1.3	1.4	1.3							1.2
1.0	1.4	1.6							.7
(37) 2.7	(43) 2.9	(33) 3.0	% Depr., Dep., Amort./Sales						(15) 2.7
5.5	4.4	5.0							4.7
2.4	1.3	3.2							
(14) 3.4	(13) 2.6	(12) 4.9	% Officers', Directors' Owners' Comp/Sales						
6.3	5.3	7.2							
693288M	**1447107M**	**2007415M**	Net Sales ($)	**308M**	**6188M**	**9395M**	**69975M**	**128324M**	**1793225M**
467878M	**1088176M**	**1112741M**	Total Assets ($)	**111M**	**2800M**	**7420M**	**43441M**	**64920M**	**994049M**

M = $ thousand MM = $ million

See Pages 9 through 22 for Explanation of Ratios and Data

Current Data Sorted by Assets							Comparative Historical Data	
						Type of Statement		
		3	16	7	3	Unqualified	34	30
	2	24	18	2		Reviewed	72	79
1	5	24	3			Compiled	31	37
1	11	8	1			Tax Returns	19	30
2	10	30	41	7	2	Other	117	99
	38 (4/1-9/30/13)		**183 (10/1/13-3/31/14)**				**4/1/09-3/31/10**	**4/1/10-3/31/11**
0-500M	**500M-2MM**	**2-10MM**	**10-50MM**	**50-100MM**	**100-250MM**		**ALL**	**ALL**
4	28	89	79	16	5	**NUMBER OF STATEMENTS**	273	275
%	%	%	%	%	%	**ASSETS**	%	%
	9.6	7.5	7.8	8.5		Cash & Equivalents	7.2	7.8
	35.7	28.1	23.1	22.8		Trade Receivables (net)	23.4	25.8
	21.2	23.9	23.3	17.6		Inventory	22.7	23.5
	1.0	1.7	3.2	5.8		All Other Current	2.9	1.6
	67.5	61.2	57.3	54.7		Total Current	56.1	58.7
	26.9	32.4	31.7	32.7		Fixed Assets (net)	33.6	31.6
	1.7	2.3	5.3	4.6		Intangibles (net)	5.0	3.4
	3.9	4.1	5.7	8.1		All Other Non-Current	5.3	6.3
	100.0	100.0	100.0	100.0		Total	100.0	100.0
						LIABILITIES		
	14.9	9.8	7.1	6.7		Notes Payable-Short Term	11.2	9.9
	4.1	4.0	3.0	1.5		Cur. Mat.-L.T.D.	4.7	4.4
	16.9	14.9	12.5	13.1		Trade Payables	13.8	14.7
	.0	.3	.2	.1		Income Taxes Payable	.1	.1
	9.0	7.4	7.1	7.2		All Other Current	7.8	7.6
	44.9	36.4	29.9	28.6		Total Current	37.6	36.8
	22.9	13.4	14.3	13.8		Long-Term Debt	18.5	16.2
	.0	.8	.7	.4		Deferred Taxes	.4	.5
	9.5	2.7	4.5	2.8		All Other Non-Current	7.9	5.9
	22.7	46.7	50.7	54.3		Net Worth	35.5	40.6
	100.0	100.0	100.0	100.0		Total Liabilties & Net Worth	100.0	100.0
						INCOME DATA		
	100.0	100.0	100.0	100.0		Net Sales	100.0	100.0
	29.0	24.8	21.6	19.2		Gross Profit	23.4	25.6
	27.7	20.5	14.1	14.8		Operating Expenses	21.5	20.0
	1.2	4.3	7.5	4.5		Operating Profit	1.9	5.6
	.2	.3	.5	-.6		All Other Expenses (net)	1.0	.9
	1.0	4.0	7.0	5.1		Profit Before Taxes	.9	4.7
						RATIOS		
	3.0	2.9	3.6	3.4			2.7	3.0
	1.7	1.7	2.0	2.2		Current	1.5	1.7
	1.2	1.1	1.3	1.1			1.0	1.1
	1.9	1.8	1.9	1.5			1.5	1.8
	1.2	.9	1.0	1.1		Quick	.8	1.0
	.8	.6	.6	.8			.5	.6
	29 12.8	**33** 10.9	**40** 9.2	**38** 9.5			**35** 10.3	**38** 9.6
	43 8.5	**47** 7.8	**48** 7.6	**51** 7.2		Sales/Receivables	**50** 7.3	**47** 7.7
	57 6.4	**57** 6.4	**58** 6.3	**65** 5.6			**64** 5.7	**60** 6.1
	16 22.8	**33** 10.9	**36** 10.2	**32** 11.4			**36** 10.1	**38** 9.7
	36 10.0	**51** 7.2	**59** 6.2	**45** 8.1		Cost of Sales/Inventory	**58** 6.3	**54** 6.7
	59 6.2	**73** 5.0	**89** 4.1	**65** 5.6			**85** 4.3	**81** 4.5
	15 24.9	**20** 17.9	**19** 19.5	**24** 15.2			**19** 19.1	**20** 18.2
	25 14.5	**31** 11.8	**27** 13.4	**27** 13.3		Cost of Sales/Payables	**30** 12.1	**32** 11.4
	42 8.6	**41** 9.0	**39** 9.4	**41** 8.9			**50** 7.3	**47** 7.7
	5.8	5.3	3.8	4.1			4.6	4.7
	11.7	10.0	7.0	6.2		Sales/Working Capital	9.8	8.9
	34.4	35.9	18.4	26.8			250.0	36.1
	8.0	25.5	26.0	298.1			6.5	13.0
	(26) 2.1	(82) 6.8	(74) 8.4	(14) 11.3		EBIT/Interest	(255) 1.6	(241) 5.2
	-.2	2.6	2.8	2.1			-1.0	1.8
		5.9	6.9				3.5	7.9
		(13) 2.8	(29) 3.2			Net Profit + Depr., Dep., Amort./Cur. Mat. L/T/D	(59) 1.6	(64) 3.8
		1.0	1.5				.6	1.9
	.2	.4	.4	.3			.5	.4
	.8	.8	.7	.7		Fixed/Worth	1.0	.8
	68.2	1.6	1.2	1.8			2.6	1.8
	1.0	.6	.5	.3			.6	.5
	2.1	1.2	1.0	.8		Debt/Worth	1.8	1.5
	111.0	2.7	2.9	3.3			5.6	3.6
	58.5	38.0	40.4	28.4			24.8	37.5
	(22) 8.6	(86) 19.8	(77) 25.4	14.3		% Profit Before Taxes/Tangible Net Worth	(237) 6.2	(246) 19.2
	4.0	3.4	12.5	2.8			-10.7	4.7
	10.2	17.8	16.2	11.6			8.2	14.5
	3.2	9.4	9.4	9.0		% Profit Before Taxes/Total Assets	1.4	8.4
	-.9	1.3	4.4	1.9			-5.0	2.0
	38.6	13.8	9.8	7.6			10.7	11.8
	11.0	7.3	5.9	4.9		Sales/Net Fixed Assets	5.3	6.1
	5.5	4.5	3.8	2.9			3.3	4.2
	3.6	2.6	2.2	1.9			2.2	2.4
	2.9	2.2	1.7	1.5		Sales/Total Assets	1.6	1.9
	2.2	1.8	1.3	1.2			1.2	1.4
	1.1	1.4	1.8	2.1			2.2	1.9
	(21) 1.5	(85) 2.6	(75) 2.5	(12) 2.9		% Depr., Dep., Amort./Sales	(238) 3.8	(247) 3.1
	5.3	4.1	3.5	4.2			5.9	4.6
	3.1	2.0	.9				2.1	2.0
	(17) 5.4	(36) 4.2	(13) 2.0			% Officers', Directors' Owners' Comp/Sales	(87) 3.7	(99) 3.3
	8.4	5.8	3.5				7.1	6.3
5363M	**106456M**	**997432M**	**2991082M**	**1837517M**	**1172515M**	Net Sales ($)	**5759291M**	**7123651M**
1129M	**37913M**	**453574M**	**1718881M**	**1105876M**	**694677M**	Total Assets ($)	**4021800M**	**4408137M**

M = $ thousand MM = $ million

See Pages 9 through 22 for Explanation of Ratios and Data

Comparative Historical Data | Current Data Sorted by Sales

4/1/11-3/31/12 ALL	4/1/12-3/31/13 ALL	4/1/13-3/31/14 ALL		0-1MM	1-3MM	3-5MM	5-10MM	10-25MM	25MM & OVER
			Type of Statement						
29	27	29	Unqualified				2	6	21
91	60	46	Reviewed		3	2	5	20	16
37	32	33	Compiled		3	6	13	10	1
25	24	21	Tax Returns		5	7	5	4	
93	104	92	Other	1	4	7	16	27	37
				38 (4/1-9/30/13)			183 (10/1/13-3/31/14)		
275	247	221	**NUMBER OF STATEMENTS**	1	15	22	41	67	75
%	%	%	**ASSETS**	%	%	%	%	%	%
7.1	8.3	8.0	Cash & Equivalents		8.2	10.3	8.5	8.1	6.8
27.1	25.4	26.8	Trade Receivables (net)		26.2	30.3	29.1	27.0	24.2
24.4	24.2	22.6	Inventory		18.0	20.8	25.7	23.5	21.9
1.6	2.2	2.4	All Other Current		.1	.3	2.8	3.1	2.7
60.2	60.1	59.8	Total Current		52.5	61.6	66.1	61.7	55.6
30.9	30.6	31.5	Fixed Assets (net)		41.6	33.0	26.1	31.5	31.8
3.2	4.0	3.8	Intangibles (net)		3.6	1.1	1.8	2.2	7.4
5.7	5.3	4.9	All Other Non-Current		2.2	4.3	6.0	4.6	5.2
100.0	100.0	100.0	Total		100.0	100.0	100.0	100.0	100.0
			LIABILITIES						
10.2	8.7	9.3	Notes Payable-Short Term		15.2	10.0	10.8	9.8	6.6
4.0	3.7	3.5	Cur. Mat.-L.T.D.		5.2	4.9	3.3	3.5	2.6
15.3	14.2	14.6	Trade Payables		14.7	12.0	14.9	15.5	13.5
.2	.2	.2	Income Taxes Payable		.0	.0	.5	.1	.3
8.8	9.0	7.8	All Other Current		17.4	5.6	9.4	5.8	7.3
38.4	35.9	35.4	Total Current		52.4	32.5	38.9	34.8	30.4
15.5	17.8	17.5	Long-Term Debt		39.4	22.4	13.2	13.6	12.5
.5	.5	.6	Deferred Taxes		.0	.7	.5	.6	.9
5.8	5.4	4.3	All Other Non-Current		10.7	4.6	2.6	4.2	3.9
39.8	40.3	42.3	Net Worth		-2.5	39.8	44.8	46.8	52.4
100.0	100.0	100.0	Total Liabilties & Net Worth		100.0	100.0	100.0	100.0	100.0
			INCOME DATA						
100.0	100.0	100.0	Net Sales		100.0	100.0	100.0	100.0	100.0
24.4	23.7	24.3	Gross Profit		36.6	31.3	25.8	22.9	19.4
18.6	18.4	19.2	Operating Expenses		39.1	27.6	22.5	16.0	12.9
5.7	5.4	5.1	Operating Profit		-2.5	3.6	3.3	6.9	6.5
.5	.5	.3	All Other Expenses (net)		1.2	1.0	-.3	.3	.3
5.2	4.9	4.8	Profit Before Taxes		-3.6	2.6	3.6	6.6	6.2
			RATIOS						
2.7	3.1	3.1			1.9	4.1	3.4	2.9	3.4
1.7	1.8	1.8	Current		1.2	2.0	1.7	1.9	1.9
1.2	1.2	1.2			.7	1.2	1.2	1.1	1.2
1.6	1.7	1.7			1.4	2.5	1.4	2.0	1.5
.9	1.0	1.0	Quick		1.0	1.4	1.0	.9	1.0
.6	.6	.6			.2	.8	.7	.6	.7
36 10.0	**36** 10.2	**35** 10.3			**26** 13.8	**37** 9.8	**33** 11.1	**38** 9.7	**39** 9.4
46 7.9	**44** 8.3	**47** 7.8	Sales/Receivables		**43** 8.5	**46** 8.0	**44** 8.3	**47** 7.8	**49** 7.5
59 6.2	**56** 6.5	**58** 6.3			**54** 6.7	**53** 6.9	**62** 5.9	**56** 6.5	**60** 6.1
35 10.5	**32** 11.3	**32** 11.3			**6** 57.7	**20** 17.9	**31** 11.9	**35** 10.5	**33** 10.9
54 6.7	**52** 7.0	**49** 7.5	Cost of Sales/Inventory		**46** 8.0	**56** 6.5	**53** 6.9	**54** 6.8	**48** 7.6
85 4.3	**81** 4.5	**74** 4.9			**62** 5.9	**85** 4.3	**74** 4.9	**83** 4.4	**72** 5.1
20 18.0	**17** 20.9	**19** 19.1			**21** 17.5	**12** 29.4	**19** 19.3	**22** 16.4	**19** 18.9
31 11.9	**28** 13.0	**28** 13.0	Cost of Sales/Payables		**41** 9.0	**17** 21.2	**29** 12.7	**31** 11.8	**27** 13.6
46 7.9	**43** 8.5	**42** 8.7			**51** 7.2	**33** 11.2	**42** 8.6	**46** 7.9	**38** 9.6
5.2	4.6	4.7			7.6	4.8	4.7	4.5	4.2
9.1	7.9	8.3	Sales/Working Capital		55.9	7.8	10.3	7.1	7.4
27.4	22.5	30.4			-16.3	23.0	24.6	28.7	25.1
16.6	16.2	23.6			2.4	12.3	14.4	31.7	33.8
(253) 6.7	(222) 5.4	(205) 6.1	EBIT/Interest		(14) .6	(21) 5.6	(36) 4.7	(63) 11.7	(70) 9.3
2.2	2.2	2.0			-6.6	1.5	2.0	3.1	3.0
8.6	7.1	4.7						15.4	4.7
(67) 3.3	(66) 3.3	(51) 2.9	Net Profit + Depr., Dep., Amort./Cur. Mat. L/T/D					(14) 3.3	(24) 3.2
1.6	1.9	1.5						1.2	1.8
.4	.4	.4			1.2	.2	.3	.4	.4
.8	.8	.8	Fixed/Worth		-53.3	.8	.7	.8	.7
1.8	1.8	1.7			-1.0	2.2	1.1	1.5	1.2
.6	.6	.6			1.8	.6	.6	.5	.4
1.6	1.3	1.2	Debt/Worth		-60.2	1.8	1.1	1.2	.9
3.5	3.8	3.3			-2.7	3.9	2.4	2.8	3.0
44.1	44.6	40.4				40.4	40.4	43.2	40.6
(253) 21.1	(224) 21.5	(205) 22.4	% Profit Before Taxes/Tangible Net Worth			(21) 12.6	(40) 17.9	(65) 26.8	(72) 24.0
8.1	9.1	5.0				3.9	2.1	10.9	11.5
16.6	14.3	16.1			10.8	10.1	15.4	19.8	16.0
9.7	7.8	8.5	% Profit Before Taxes/Total Assets		.3	5.9	5.6	9.7	10.4
2.7	2.6	1.7			-10.3	1.1	1.2	4.6	3.4
12.8	12.6	11.7			10.7	24.2	24.7	11.4	9.8
7.0	6.4	6.7	Sales/Net Fixed Assets		6.2	5.7	8.0	6.5	6.4
4.5	4.3	4.4			2.5	3.7	5.2	4.2	4.1
2.6	2.6	2.6			3.0	3.0	2.9	2.4	2.3
2.0	2.0	2.0	Sales/Total Assets		2.2	2.2	2.3	2.0	1.8
1.5	1.6	1.5			1.2	1.4	1.7	1.7	1.4
1.7	1.7	1.5			1.1	1.2	1.2	1.4	1.8
(247) 2.6	(225) 2.7	(198) 2.6	% Depr., Dep., Amort./Sales		(14) 2.2	(16) 3.4	(38) 2.0	(62) 2.5	(68) 2.6
3.9	3.9	3.9			10.4	5.6	3.8	4.1	3.4
1.9	1.9	1.9				2.5	1.0	2.0	.4
(106) 3.7	(79) 3.4	(72) 3.6	% Officers', Directors' Owners' Comp/Sales			(10) 3.9	(24) 4.7	(18) 3.6	(12) 1.3
6.2	6.2	6.2				6.3	8.1	5.2	2.3
7874277M	7307804M	7110365M	Net Sales ($)	343M	30540M	91717M	293961M	1189804M	5504000M
4452976M	4276015M	4012050M	Total Assets ($)	67M	18194M	46890M	145935M	632911M	3168053M

M = $ thousand MM = $ million

See Pages 9 through 22 for Explanation of Ratios and Data

Current Data Sorted by Assets							Comparative Historical Data	
						Type of Statement		
			4	1	1	Unqualified	19	15
	3	12	9	3		Reviewed	24	29
	2	4			1	Compiled	10	10
2	3	5	1			Tax Returns	8	9
1	4	11	5	3	1	Other	30	29
	21 (4/1-9/30/13)		**55 (10/1/13-3/31/14)**				**4/1/09-3/31/10**	**4/1/10-3/31/11**
0-500M	**500M-2MM**	**2-10MM**	**10-50MM**	**50-100MM**	**100-250MM**		**ALL**	**ALL**
3	12	32	19	7	3	**NUMBER OF STATEMENTS**	91	92
%	%	%	%	%	%	**ASSETS**	%	%
	10.3	10.6	10.2			Cash & Equivalents	7.2	9.0
	34.0	20.3	19.8			Trade Receivables (net)	20.1	19.9
	31.8	36.6	33.7			Inventory	35.7	31.4
	1.0	1.7	2.4			All Other Current	2.1	1.8
	77.1	69.2	66.0			Total Current	65.1	62.2
	18.0	22.8	20.9			Fixed Assets (net)	23.0	26.2
	1.5	4.9	7.4			Intangibles (net)	6.8	4.2
	3.4	3.1	5.7			All Other Non-Current	5.1	7.4
	100.0	100.0	100.0			Total	100.0	100.0
						LIABILITIES		
	8.8	8.8	6.1			Notes Payable-Short Term	8.4	7.5
	3.8	4.5	2.3			Cur. Mat.-L.T.D.	3.3	3.3
	18.8	10.8	10.9			Trade Payables	9.4	11.2
	.3	.1	.7			Income Taxes Payable	.3	.2
	25.5	10.3	7.9			All Other Current	8.6	8.9
	57.2	34.5	27.9			Total Current	30.0	31.1
	13.0	16.1	7.9			Long-Term Debt	17.2	14.2
	.8	.9	.7			Deferred Taxes	.7	.6
	6.7	4.3	5.1			All Other Non-Current	8.4	6.6
	22.3	44.2	58.5			Net Worth	43.7	47.5
	100.0	100.0	100.0			Total Liabilties & Net Worth	100.0	100.0
						INCOME DATA		
	100.0	100.0	100.0			Net Sales	100.0	100.0
	33.7	32.3	31.3			Gross Profit	34.3	34.7
	30.4	26.4	24.3			Operating Expenses	31.8	29.6
	3.2	5.9	7.0			Operating Profit	2.4	5.1
	.5	1.3	.3			All Other Expenses (net)	1.3	1.1
	2.7	4.6	6.6			Profit Before Taxes	1.1	4.0
						RATIOS		
	4.3	2.9	4.3				4.0	4.2
	2.7	2.1	2.8			Current	2.3	2.5
	1.1	1.6	1.6				1.5	1.5
	2.3	1.7	2.2				1.6	2.1
	1.1	.7	1.2			Quick	.9	1.0
	.6	.5	.8				.5	.5
	30 12.1	**28** 12.9	**34** 10.8				**33** 11.2	**31** 11.6
	38 9.6	**39** 9.3	**43** 8.4			Sales/Receivables	**42** 8.7	**43** 8.4
	45 8.1	**50** 7.3	**49** 7.5				**53** 6.9	**57** 6.4
	31 11.8	**57** 6.4	**62** 5.9				**79** 4.6	**64** 5.7
	54 6.7	**104** 3.5	**114** 3.2			Cost of Sales/Inventory	**130** 2.8	**99** 3.7
	122 3.0	**174** 2.1	**159** 2.3				**182** 2.0	**166** 2.2
	21 17.6	**14** 25.4	**18** 20.8				**15** 24.6	**14** 26.5
	31 11.7	**27** 13.5	**28** 12.9			Cost of Sales/Payables	**24** 15.3	**28** 13.1
	39 9.3	**43** 8.5	**49** 7.4				**43** 8.4	**50** 7.3
	3.9	3.4	2.9				2.8	2.8
	6.9	5.1	3.7			Sales/Working Capital	5.0	4.8
	196.0	8.9	7.4				9.1	11.1
	17.6	15.8	74.4				8.6	16.6
	(11) 6.8	(29) 6.1	(18) 17.9			EBIT/Interest	(84) 2.4	(87) 4.3
	-.1	1.4	8.8				-.6	1.7
							5.1	10.8
						Net Profit + Depr., Dep., Amort./Cur. Mat. L/T/D	(30) 1.3	(27) 4.4
							.4	1.8
	.1	.1	.1				.2	.2
	.3	.6	.5			Fixed/Worth	.6	.5
	2.9	1.5	1.2				1.7	1.0
	.7	.7	.3				.6	.5
	.9	1.5	.5			Debt/Worth	1.3	1.0
	88.8	2.9	2.7				4.8	2.7
	61.7	42.4	37.7				21.6	25.4
	(10) 16.3	(27) 20.3	(17) 23.6			% Profit Before Taxes/Tangible Net Worth	(75) 6.7	(82) 9.5
	1.3	4.2	9.4				-5.7	3.2
	13.8	16.1	18.2				8.9	11.8
	4.3	10.9	10.7			% Profit Before Taxes/Total Assets	2.5	5.1
	-1.8	.6	5.6				-4.9	1.4
	67.7	50.9	48.2				30.5	18.0
	13.1	8.7	8.8			Sales/Net Fixed Assets	8.7	7.6
	8.2	4.9	4.7				4.4	4.1
	4.2	2.2	2.0				2.1	2.0
	2.5	1.7	1.7			Sales/Total Assets	1.5	1.6
	2.2	1.4	1.4				1.1	1.2
		.7	.7				1.5	1.7
		(28) 2.0	(18) 1.7			% Depr., Dep., Amort./Sales	(76) 2.9	(80) 3.1
		3.7	2.4				5.1	4.7
		1.8					2.9	2.3
		(10) 3.6				% Officers', Directors' Owners' Comp/Sales	(27) 4.8	(39) 3.5
		8.3					7.4	5.8
2209M	42202M	293216M	620667M	914517M	868375M	Net Sales ($)	2391102M	2102477M
973M	14350M	153549M	376417M	526470M	468595M	Total Assets ($)	1887311M	1533248M

M = $ thousand MM = $ million

See Pages 9 through 22 for Explanation of Ratios and Data

Comparative Historical Data				Current Data Sorted by Sales					
			Type of Statement						
20	7	6	Unqualified					1	5
29	18	27	Reviewed		2	2	7	5	11
9	8	7	Compiled				6		1
13	17	11	Tax Returns	2	3	2	3	1	
24	28	25	Other	1	4	2	6	5	7
				21 (4/1-9/30/13)			55 (10/1/13-3/31/14)		
4/1/11-3/31/12 ALL	4/1/12-3/31/13 ALL	4/1/13-3/31/14 ALL		0-1MM	1-3MM	3-5MM	5-10MM	10-25MM	25MM & OVER
95	78	76	**NUMBER OF STATEMENTS**	3	9	6	22	12	24
%	%	%	**ASSETS**	%	%	%	%	%	%
9.7	8.6	11.4	Cash & Equivalents				9.6	7.7	9.4
23.1	23.8	22.5	Trade Receivables (net)				22.6	22.1	22.0
32.3	33.9	33.8	Inventory				37.7	34.8	31.2
1.4	2.6	1.7	All Other Current				1.3	2.6	2.0
66.5	68.9	69.4	Total Current				71.1	67.1	64.7
22.4	21.2	21.1	Fixed Assets (net)				22.1	23.6	21.9
5.6	5.0	5.0	Intangibles (net)				4.8	4.9	7.0
5.5	4.9	4.4	All Other Non-Current				2.0	4.4	6.4
100.0	100.0	100.0	Total				100.0	100.0	100.0
			LIABILITIES						
8.0	8.8	7.8	Notes Payable-Short Term				8.1	8.6	6.9
4.1	4.1	3.3	Cur. Mat.-L.T.D.				4.8	2.9	2.6
11.0	11.3	12.0	Trade Payables				13.5	10.7	11.5
.3	.1	.3	Income Taxes Payable				.1	.7	.3
8.0	8.2	11.4	All Other Current				6.7	7.6	10.3
31.5	32.5	34.7	Total Current				33.1	30.4	31.6
14.3	15.9	12.6	Long-Term Debt				14.3	14.9	11.2
.3	.7	.8	Deferred Taxes				.7	1.6	.4
7.4	6.5	4.8	All Other Non-Current				4.0	5.9	5.1
46.5	44.3	47.1	Net Worth				47.9	47.3	51.6
100.0	100.0	100.0	Total Liabilties & Net Worth				100.0	100.0	100.0
			INCOME DATA						
100.0	100.0	100.0	Net Sales				100.0	100.0	100.0
33.6	38.5	32.5	Gross Profit				28.0	34.3	29.4
26.5	31.0	26.5	Operating Expenses				22.3	27.3	22.3
7.1	7.5	5.9	Operating Profit				5.7	7.0	7.0
.9	.6	.7	All Other Expenses (net)				1.2	.5	.2
6.2	6.9	5.2	Profit Before Taxes				4.5	6.5	6.8
			RATIOS						
4.3	4.2	4.0					3.0	4.1	4.2
2.7	2.3	2.5	Current				2.3	2.4	2.5
1.4	1.5	1.6					1.6	1.4	1.4
2.3	2.2	2.1					1.9	2.1	2.0
1.1	1.0	1.0	Quick				.8	1.0	1.0
.6	.6	.6					.5	.5	.7
34 10.8	**32** 11.4	**33** 11.1					**28** 13.1	**33** 11.2	**35** 10.4
43 8.4	**43** 8.5	**41** 8.9	Sales/Receivables				**38** 9.6	**48** 7.6	**41** 8.9
53 6.9	**55** 6.6	**49** 7.4					**49** 7.4	**50** 7.3	**50** 7.3
60 6.1	**57** 6.4	**54** 6.7					**55** 6.6	**68** 5.4	**62** 5.9
89 4.1	**107** 3.4	**96** 3.8	Cost of Sales/Inventory				**94** 3.9	**111** 3.3	**96** 3.8
152 2.4	**166** 2.2	**146** 2.5					**130** 2.8	**146** 2.5	**122** 3.0
16 22.6	**16** 23.2	**16** 22.3					**14** 26.3	**25** 14.7	**16** 22.3
26 13.9	**25** 14.5	**28** 13.0	Cost of Sales/Payables				**27** 13.5	**28** 12.9	**31** 11.6
42 8.6	**38** 9.6	**43** 8.5					**39** 9.3	**44** 8.3	**42** 8.6
2.8	2.8	3.2					4.1	2.7	3.2
5.1	5.0	4.8	Sales/Working Capital				5.1	6.4	4.5
12.2	11.4	9.0					8.9	13.1	10.9
17.3	17.9	23.3					18.3	83.6	57.5
(88) 8.2	(71) 6.9	(68) 10.2	EBIT/Interest				(20) 10.0	16.0	(21) 19.4
3.0	3.2	2.5					4.1	5.5	4.5
10.2	6.9	7.9							10.7
(32) 3.6	(25) 3.4	(25) 3.3	Net Profit + Depr., Dep., Amort./Cur. Mat. L/T/D						(11) 4.3
1.8	2.2	1.9							2.3
.1	.2	.1					.1	.1	.3
.4	.4	.5	Fixed/Worth				.6	.6	.5
1.2	1.0	1.4					1.4	1.9	1.2
.4	.5	.4					.7	.4	.3
1.1	1.0	.9	Debt/Worth				1.2	.9	.9
3.5	3.0	2.9					3.0	3.0	3.0
35.5	33.8	39.8					42.2	43.8	36.9
(87) 21.7	(69) 19.1	(67) 20.3	% Profit Before Taxes/Tangible Net Worth				(20) 22.6	(11) 23.6	(21) 22.4
8.9	8.5	6.4					6.5	9.3	8.8
17.9	17.3	16.3					15.8	17.3	17.6
8.2	10.0	10.4	% Profit Before Taxes/Total Assets				11.2	11.9	11.9
3.7	4.2	2.3					4.2	6.5	4.1
32.2	38.4	46.0					61.5	42.8	21.0
9.9	11.8	10.1	Sales/Net Fixed Assets				12.7	7.9	8.8
4.8	5.9	5.1					4.9	4.8	4.9
2.2	2.5	2.4					2.6	2.2	2.2
1.7	1.9	1.8	Sales/Total Assets				1.8	1.7	1.7
1.3	1.3	1.4					1.5	1.5	1.4
.9	.9	.8					.8	.7	1.0
(80) 2.3	(59) 1.8	(64) 2.0	% Depr., Dep., Amort./Sales				(17) 1.8	(11) 2.1	(22) 2.0
4.3	3.0	3.4					3.0	5.8	2.9
2.2	2.6	1.7							
(38) 3.4	(29) 4.9	(21) 4.1	% Officers', Directors' Owners' Comp/Sales						
6.8	10.1	10.3							
2643448M	1784873M	2741186M	Net Sales ($)	2209M	22782M	24910M	158535M	194893M	2337857M
1693875M	1050558M	1540354M	Total Assets ($)	973M	19461M	15247M	88465M	116196M	1300012M

M = $ thousand MM = $ million

See Pages 9 through 22 for Explanation of Ratios and Data

Current Data Sorted by Assets							Comparative Historical Data	
						Type of Statement		
		1	12	3	3	Unqualified	16	15
		15	2			Reviewed	11	19
	3	6	2			Compiled	12	9
4	8	8	1			Tax Returns	11	14
2	4	18	8	2	6	Other	39	38
	19 (4/1-9/30/13)		89 (10/1/13-3/31/14)				4/1/09-3/31/10 ALL	4/1/10-3/31/11 ALL
0-500M	500M-2MM	2-10MM	10-50MM	50-100MM	100-250MM			
6	15	48	25	5	9	**NUMBER OF STATEMENTS**	89	95
%	%	%	%	%	%	**ASSETS**	%	%
	11.8	12.6	9.3			Cash & Equivalents	14.9	13.4
	27.6	26.0	27.1			Trade Receivables (net)	22.8	25.6
	24.3	29.2	23.3			Inventory	25.2	23.5
	6.7	1.9	5.2			All Other Current	3.2	2.8
	70.5	69.7	64.9			Total Current	66.1	65.3
	22.3	21.4	25.5			Fixed Assets (net)	25.1	26.3
	.8	5.2	5.4			Intangibles (net)	2.3	3.6
	6.4	3.6	4.2			All Other Non-Current	6.5	4.8
	100.0	100.0	100.0			Total	100.0	100.0
						LIABILITIES		
	8.5	12.0	6.7			Notes Payable-Short Term	10.2	9.7
	2.7	2.1	1.7			Cur. Mat.-L.T.D.	4.0	6.5
	14.1	18.6	11.2			Trade Payables	15.0	16.6
	1.3	.2	.2			Income Taxes Payable	.2	.3
	6.3	14.4	11.4			All Other Current	13.2	13.6
	32.9	47.3	31.1			Total Current	42.7	46.7
	17.1	11.6	13.6			Long-Term Debt	17.3	16.1
	.0	.2	.2			Deferred Taxes	.7	.3
	7.2	8.5	6.4			All Other Non-Current	11.2	4.6
	42.7	32.4	48.7			Net Worth	28.0	32.2
	100.0	100.0	100.0			Total Liabilties & Net Worth	100.0	100.0
						INCOME DATA		
	100.0	100.0	100.0			Net Sales	100.0	100.0
	33.7	26.9	23.5			Gross Profit	32.2	27.7
	30.4	21.8	19.2			Operating Expenses	30.1	25.8
	3.3	5.1	4.3			Operating Profit	2.1	1.8
	.3	.5	.5			All Other Expenses (net)	1.7	.6
	2.9	4.5	3.9			Profit Before Taxes	.5	1.2
						RATIOS		
	5.5	2.2	3.6				3.5	3.3
	2.4	1.6	2.2			Current	1.7	1.8
	1.2	1.1	1.6				1.2	1.1
	1.7	1.1	2.3				2.3	2.0
	1.3	.8	1.0			Quick	1.0	.9
	.7	.5	.5				.4	.5
	19 19.2	**26** 14.3	**33** 11.0				**19** 19.7	**24** 15.5
	42 8.7	**34** 10.6	**51** 7.2			Sales/Receivables	**36** 10.3	**42** 8.7
	60 6.1	**58** 6.3	**81** 4.5				**58** 6.3	**67** 5.4
	3 135.9	**35** 10.5	**28** 13.2				**21** 17.4	**18** 20.1
	24 15.2	**52** 7.0	**54** 6.8			Cost of Sales/Inventory	**48** 7.6	**43** 8.6
	94 3.9	**72** 5.1	**99** 3.7				**107** 3.4	**104** 3.5
	12 31.3	**15** 23.7	**19** 18.8				**14** 26.1	**19** 19.7
	20 18.1	**34** 10.7	**26** 14.1			Cost of Sales/Payables	**29** 12.7	**31** 11.8
	47 7.8	**53** 6.9	**38** 9.5				**50** 7.3	**49** 7.4
	4.7	5.8	2.7				3.8	3.6
	8.9	11.3	5.8			Sales/Working Capital	7.5	7.8
	25.5	39.9	11.9				31.1	136.6
	11.8	20.4	24.5				9.1	23.0
	(12) 5.5	(45) 7.3	(21) 7.9			EBIT/Interest	(81) 1.4	(84) 3.5
	.9	2.9	.6				-2.5	-.4
							16.7	4.9
						Net Profit + Depr., Dep., Amort./Cur. Mat. L/T/D	(26) 2.8	(22) 1.5
							.8	.6
	.2	.2	.2				.3	.3
	.3	.7	.6			Fixed/Worth	.7	.7
	14.4	1.9	1.6				1.5	1.9
	.4	.9	.4				.7	.5
	.9	2.0	1.4			Debt/Worth	1.8	2.0
	48.9	6.3	3.0				5.3	5.1
	38.1	61.8	34.5				27.5	38.3
	(12) 11.2	(40) 36.2	(24) 15.1			% Profit Before Taxes/Tangible Net Worth	(75) 6.1	(82) 9.1
	3.1	9.5	.3				-13.3	-3.2
	19.5	20.6	10.2				11.5	15.7
	4.3	10.4	8.2			% Profit Before Taxes/Total Assets	1.6	4.4
	-.5	3.0	-.9				-7.4	-3.9
	44.0	36.4	15.7				25.2	21.0
	15.4	13.1	9.6			Sales/Net Fixed Assets	11.3	9.9
	9.0	7.6	4.4				6.0	5.4
	4.0	3.5	2.5				3.0	3.0
	2.8	2.5	1.9			Sales/Total Assets	2.1	2.1
	2.2	1.7	1.0				1.6	1.4
	.9	.7	.9				.7	.9
	(12) 1.7	(36) 1.5	1.3			% Depr., Dep., Amort./Sales	(76) 1.8	(78) 2.1
	4.2	2.1	3.6				2.9	3.5
	3.2	1.0					2.4	2.1
	(12) 5.7	(20) 1.5				% Officers', Directors' Owners' Comp/Sales	(32) 6.0	(37) 3.7
	12.2	3.1					9.5	7.0
12879M	**54126M**	**609191M**	**825405M**	**980925M**	**3312253M**	Net Sales ($)	**3756233M**	**3157082M**
1784M	**18442M**	**240228M**	**455188M**	**390509M**	**1431704M**	Total Assets ($)	**1957229M**	**1779015M**

M = $ thousand MM = $ million

See Pages 9 through 22 for Explanation of Ratios and Data

Comparative Historical Data				Current Data Sorted by Sales					
Type of Statement									
Unqualified	13	14	19				2	3	14
Reviewed	19	14	17			1	4	10	2
Compiled	11	8	11		2	1	4	4	
Tax Returns	20	16	21	2	3	6	6	3	1
Other	38	56	40	1	2	4	4	13	16
	4/1/11-3/31/12	4/1/12-3/31/13	4/1/13-3/31/14	19 (4/1-9/30/13)		89 (10/1/13-3/31/14)			
	ALL	ALL	ALL	0-1MM	1-3MM	3-5MM	5-10MM	10-25MM	25MM & OVER
NUMBER OF STATEMENTS	101	108	108	3	7	12	20	33	33
ASSETS	%	%	%	%	%	%	%	%	%
Cash & Equivalents	12.0	11.0	12.8			17.8	15.3	11.5	6.8
Trade Receivables (net)	26.4	26.2	26.0			24.4	20.0	26.4	28.7
Inventory	25.5	28.1	25.9			17.9	24.6	34.1	22.5
All Other Current	3.1	2.4	3.6			1.4	6.0	2.0	5.3
Total Current	67.1	67.8	68.3			61.5	65.9	73.9	63.4
Fixed Assets (net)	24.2	25.2	22.5			25.7	21.1	19.5	27.1
Intangibles (net)	2.6	3.7	4.5			3.9	8.2	2.1	5.4
All Other Non-Current	6.1	3.4	4.7			8.8	4.9	4.5	4.0
Total	100.0	100.0	100.0			100.0	100.0	100.0	100.0
LIABILITIES									
Notes Payable-Short Term	16.3	7.1	10.7			9.4	8.5	15.1	3.6
Cur. Mat.-L.T.D.	5.4	2.0	2.0			1.9	3.3	2.1	1.4
Trade Payables	15.3	14.3	15.0			14.3	11.9	17.9	15.5
Income Taxes Payable	.2	.1	.4			.0	.8	.0	.2
All Other Current	16.4	12.1	12.9			12.8	9.1	13.5	15.4
Total Current	53.5	35.7	41.0			38.4	33.6	48.6	36.1
Long-Term Debt	17.0	14.2	16.0			24.9	14.4	10.6	15.7
Deferred Taxes	.3	.3	.3			.0	.5	.0	.7
All Other Non-Current	8.0	5.9	6.7			3.2	9.5	6.6	5.2
Net Worth	21.1	43.9	36.1			33.5	41.9	34.2	42.3
Total Liabilties & Net Worth	100.0	100.0	100.0			100.0	100.0	100.0	100.0
INCOME DATA									
Net Sales	100.0	100.0	100.0			100.0	100.0	100.0	100.0
Gross Profit	28.3	27.5	26.9			31.0	29.7	21.8	25.1
Operating Expenses	23.6	22.2	22.5			27.1	23.4	18.0	20.1
Operating Profit	4.6	5.3	4.4			3.9	6.3	3.7	5.1
All Other Expenses (net)	.8	.4	.6			.3	.5	.3	.4
Profit Before Taxes	3.8	4.9	3.8			3.6	5.9	3.4	4.7
RATIOS									
Current	3.3	3.5	2.5			4.3	6.2	2.8	2.2
	1.8	1.9	1.8			1.5	2.0	1.7	1.7
	1.2	1.3	1.2			1.0	1.3	1.1	1.3
Quick	1.7	1.8	1.6			1.6	1.9	1.7	1.5
	.8	1.0	.9			1.0	.8	.9	.9
	.5	.6	.6			.8	.5	.4	.7
Sales/Receivables	**27** 13.6	**23** 16.2	**24** 14.9			**18** 20.8	**16** 22.2	**26** 14.3	**25** 14.8
	38 9.7	**38** 9.7	**38** 9.7			**51** 7.1	**29** 12.7	**45** 8.2	**35** 10.5
	60 6.1	**63** 5.8	**60** 6.1			**65** 5.6	**55** 6.6	**65** 5.6	**54** 6.7
Cost of Sales/Inventory	**17** 22.1	**32** 11.4	**26** 14.2			**0** UND	**25** 14.8	**38** 9.5	**21** 17.3
	49 7.4	**53** 6.9	**47** 7.7			**29** 12.5	**50** 7.3	**63** 5.8	**41** 8.8
	91 4.0	**96** 3.8	**76** 4.8			**89** 4.1	**68** 5.4	**94** 3.9	**64** 5.7
Cost of Sales/Payables	**14** 26.2	**13** 28.7	**15** 23.7			**10** 38.0	**6** 64.3	**21** 17.8	**16** 23.2
	28 13.0	**26** 14.1	**27** 13.4			**25** 14.4	**27** 13.3	**33** 10.9	**25** 14.6
	46 8.0	**42** 8.7	**42** 8.6			**51** 7.2	**41** 8.9	**46** 8.0	**36** 10.1
Sales/Working Capital	4.4	4.4	5.0			5.0	3.8	4.2	6.3
	7.9	7.3	10.6			17.0	9.0	8.4	11.8
	49.4	15.2	25.0			NM	15.2	32.7	14.9
EBIT/Interest	19.5	22.8	20.2			78.4	16.4	18.3	85.6
	(87) 4.5	(90) 7.5	(95) 8.6			(10) 8.6	(19) 5.2	(30) 8.6	(30) 12.6
	1.4	2.1	2.1			1.4	2.1	2.9	2.0
Net Profit + Depr., Dep., Amort./Cur. Mat. L/T/D	6.2	15.6	9.0						41.6
	(20) 3.9	(22) 3.8	(20) 3.4						(11) 6.8
	.7	1.6	2.0						2.7
Fixed/Worth	.2	.2	.2			.2	.2	.2	.5
	.6	.5	.6			2.3	.5	.5	.6
	1.9	1.4	1.6			-11.5	1.6	2.1	1.5
Debt/Worth	.5	.5	.7			.5	.4	.6	.7
	1.3	1.3	1.6			3.6	1.7	1.3	1.5
	5.5	3.1	6.2			-30.0	4.9	6.8	2.6
% Profit Before Taxes/Tangible Net Worth	27.8	49.5	53.4				59.1	57.9	50.6
	(83) 11.8	(99) 21.8	(93) 27.6				(17) 33.5	(29) 16.8	(31) 27.9
	2.0	3.7	7.7				11.2	6.9	17.2
% Profit Before Taxes/Total Assets	13.1	15.2	17.3			23.8	17.7	12.6	19.4
	5.7	8.1	8.4			11.0	6.4	8.3	10.2
	1.4	1.0	2.1			-.3	3.4	2.6	2.5
Sales/Net Fixed Assets	30.9	23.4	30.1			55.6	38.8	27.2	12.9
	12.2	11.8	12.2			10.4	14.1	13.8	9.9
	7.4	4.8	7.1			3.2	7.2	5.4	7.6
Sales/Total Assets	3.1	3.2	3.4			3.2	3.6	3.3	3.4
	2.2	2.1	2.3			2.3	2.1	2.2	2.4
	1.6	1.5	1.7			1.3	1.5	1.5	2.1
% Depr., Dep., Amort./Sales	.7	.7	.8				1.0	.7	1.0
	(90) 1.4	(90) 1.5	(89) 1.5				(14) 1.9	(26) 1.3	1.5
	2.3	2.5	2.3				3.6	2.6	2.0
% Officers', Directors' Owners' Comp/Sales	2.1	1.5	1.4				1.5	1.0	
	(47) 4.3	(38) 3.6	(41) 3.1				(11) 2.5	(12) 1.8	
	7.9	7.0	5.7				4.7	4.0	
Net Sales ($)	3530453M	4884481M	5794779M	1444M	15481M	46799M	147274M	511373M	5072408M
Total Assets ($)	1818878M	2222892M	2537855M	1488M	7118M	22109M	75369M	299900M	2131871M

M = $ thousand MM = $ million

See Pages 9 through 22 for Explanation of Ratios and Data

Current Data Sorted by Assets							Comparative Historical Data	
	1	12	29	8	2	Type of Statement Unqualified	61	64
	14	71	37	4		Reviewed	126	150
2	18	21	6			Compiled	50	64
11	18	23	1			Tax Returns	50	68
6	27	64	55	10	8	Other	146	155
	80 (4/1-9/30/13)		368 (10/1/13-3/31/14)				4/1/09-3/31/10	4/1/10-3/31/11
0-500M	500M-2MM	2-10MM	10-50MM	50-100MM	100-250MM		ALL	ALL
19	78	191	128	22	10	NUMBER OF STATEMENTS	433	501
%	%	%	%	%	%	ASSETS	%	%
12.1	12.6	12.3	10.7	18.2	3.4	Cash & Equivalents	14.2	12.5
31.6	34.7	34.0	30.7	22.0	34.8	Trade Receivables (net)	29.7	30.2
13.0	16.7	17.4	17.2	23.6	10.7	Inventory	18.1	18.3
3.2	4.1	5.8	6.6	5.8	11.5	All Other Current	5.0	5.2
59.9	68.2	69.5	65.2	69.6	60.5	Total Current	66.9	66.2
26.1	25.2	23.9	27.3	22.0	27.0	Fixed Assets (net)	25.6	25.7
2.0	2.0	1.5	3.0	5.5	4.3	Intangibles (net)	2.7	2.4
12.0	4.7	5.1	4.5	2.8	8.2	All Other Non-Current	4.7	5.7
100.0	100.0	100.0	100.0	100.0	100.0	Total	100.0	100.0
						LIABILITIES		
13.9	9.8	8.1	7.4	8.2	1.5	Notes Payable-Short Term	9.9	11.6
7.7	2.5	2.5	2.5	2.1	.9	Cur. Mat.-L.T.D.	3.4	3.6
19.1	18.2	14.8	13.5	9.2	12.6	Trade Payables	13.5	14.4
.1	.1	.2	.4	.0	.1	Income Taxes Payable	.3	.3
16.9	9.9	9.0	11.3	13.6	20.9	All Other Current	10.9	9.0
57.7	40.5	34.6	35.1	33.1	36.0	Total Current	38.0	38.9
40.4	18.7	10.4	13.2	12.3	9.5	Long-Term Debt	12.9	13.9
.0	.1	.7	.6	.5	.9	Deferred Taxes	.5	.4
20.8	6.1	6.1	4.2	3.5	1.6	All Other Non-Current	4.2	4.8
-18.9	34.6	48.2	47.0	50.6	52.0	Net Worth	44.4	42.1
100.0	100.0	100.0	100.0	100.0	100.0	Total Liabilities & Net Worth	100.0	100.0
						INCOME DATA		
100.0	100.0	100.0	100.0	100.0	100.0	Net Sales	100.0	100.0
50.1	33.0	26.1	20.9	23.4	15.1	Gross Profit	25.1	25.9
41.4	27.6	20.3	14.9	15.3	10.1	Operating Expenses	22.8	23.9
8.7	5.4	5.8	6.0	8.1	4.9	Operating Profit	2.4	2.0
.2	.5	.3	.6	.5	.4	All Other Expenses (net)	.7	.8
8.6	4.9	5.5	5.4	7.6	4.5	Profit Before Taxes	1.7	1.3
						RATIOS		
2.4	3.3	3.5	2.7	4.0	1.8		3.3	3.4
1.1	2.0	1.9	1.8	1.9	1.8	Current	1.8	1.9
.7	1.2	1.4	1.3	1.4	1.5		1.3	1.2
1.5	2.3	2.4	1.9	2.7	1.2		2.1	2.3
.8	1.4	1.2	1.2	1.0	1.0	Quick	1.1	1.1
.3	.8	.8	.7	.7	.9		.7	.7
12 29.2	**26** 14.2	**35** 10.4	**40** 9.2	**39** 9.4	**52** 7.0		**34** 10.8	**38** 9.7
30 12.2	**42** 8.6	**52** 7.0	**53** 6.9	**45** 8.2	**73** 5.0	Sales/Receivables	**49** 7.4	**54** 6.8
40 9.1	**69** 5.3	**72** 5.1	**73** 5.0	**59** 6.2	**94** 3.9		**70** 5.2	**75** 4.8
0 UND	**1** 272.2	**8** 45.5	**10** 36.5	**44** 8.3	**10** 35.6		**11** 32.8	**13** 28.1
4 82.6	**24** 15.1	**30** 12.2	**33** 10.9	**61** 6.0	**18** 20.5	Cost of Sales/Inventory	**35** 10.3	**37** 9.8
32 11.3	**52** 7.0	**64** 5.7	**68** 5.4	**101** 3.6	**41** 9.0		**70** 5.2	**72** 5.1
11 32.3	**13** 27.2	**17** 21.5	**18** 20.8	**19** 19.7	**15** 23.8		**15** 24.4	**17** 20.9
29 12.8	**30** 12.0	**26** 14.0	**27** 13.3	**22** 16.5	**30** 12.1	Cost of Sales/Payables	**26** 14.0	**32** 11.6
47 7.8	**51** 7.2	**42** 8.6	**40** 9.2	**34** 10.6	**41** 8.8		**41** 8.8	**48** 7.6
5.6	5.5	4.6	4.0	2.1	5.1		4.0	3.7
40.4	10.5	7.2	7.3	6.0	8.4	Sales/Working Capital	7.4	6.9
-33.8	22.2	13.8	14.6	10.6	10.3		19.6	18.3
33.9	13.9	25.3	21.0	123.4	84.1		13.0	13.4
(17) 5.5	(66) 6.4	(167) 7.9	(116) 7.9	(20) 14.6	12.4	EBIT/Interest	(389) 3.3	(444) 3.8
.9	1.6	2.5	3.0	3.5	6.6		-.1	-1.0
		5.8	7.8				8.6	4.1
		(39) 3.0	(38) 3.5			Net Profit + Depr., Dep., Amort./Cur. Mat. L/T/D	(114) 2.0	(114) 1.7
		2.1	1.8				.7	.2
.0	.3	.2	.2	.3	.5		.2	.2
.7	.7	.5	.5	.5	.6	Fixed/Worth	.5	.5
-106.0	2.0	.9	1.1	1.1	.7		1.4	1.4
1.2	.7	.4	.5	.5	.7		.5	.5
3.4	1.9	1.1	1.2	1.2	1.0	Debt/Worth	1.2	1.2
-142.3	6.5	2.1	2.3	2.3	1.3		3.1	3.2
154.0	96.5	46.6	38.3	59.0	33.1		30.1	29.6
(14) 75.2	(66) 28.8	(184) 22.8	(120) 17.8	(20) 17.9	13.8	% Profit Before Taxes/Tangible Net Worth	(392) 10.7	(450) 9.7
24.5	6.2	5.4	7.0	5.8	5.5		-.9	-4.6
41.4	28.4	20.0	15.9	15.7	14.4		12.5	12.0
14.7	10.1	10.3	8.4	8.0	6.4	% Profit Before Taxes/Total Assets	4.4	3.9
-2.9	1.4	2.4	3.5	4.9	2.7		-2.6	-3.8
111.3	34.6	26.3	19.0	10.7	9.7		21.3	18.1
27.6	13.5	12.7	7.9	7.9	5.8	Sales/Net Fixed Assets	9.7	8.8
10.5	5.7	6.1	4.5	6.3	4.7		4.7	5.0
5.3	3.5	3.0	2.4	2.1	2.5		2.6	2.5
4.6	2.8	2.3	1.9	1.5	1.8	Sales/Total Assets	2.0	2.0
2.6	2.1	1.7	1.5	1.2	1.3		1.5	1.4
.3	.8	1.0	.9	1.2			.9	1.1
(12) 2.0	(64) 1.3	(167) 1.8	(126) 1.7	1.9		% Depr., Dep., Amort./Sales	(386) 1.8	(456) 2.0
3.1	2.7	3.0	2.7	3.1			3.6	3.7
4.5	3.3	1.3	1.1				1.8	2.1
(14) 7.6	(47) 4.3	(89) 2.4	(33) 2.4			% Officers', Directors' Owners' Comp/Sales	(175) 3.9	(200) 4.2
14.9	6.3	4.5	4.9				7.3	7.4
25247M	288801M	2204467M	5526308M	2541026M	3035573M	Net Sales ($)	12949647M	10742603M
5892M	97058M	942279M	2749725M	1544591M	1680785M	Total Assets ($)	7552121M	6692463M

M = $ thousand MM = $ million

See Pages 9 through 22 for Explanation of Ratios and Data

Comparative Historical Data				Current Data Sorted by Sales					
			Type of Statement						
68	56	52	Unqualified		1		1	20	30
130	117	126	Reviewed		6	14	30	44	32
74	50	47	Compiled	1	10	7	13	13	3
71	64	53	Tax Returns	5	14	11	17	5	1
162	170	170	Other	2	13	17	29	46	63
				80 (4/1-9/30/13)			368 (10/1/13-3/31/14)		
4/1/11-3/31/12 ALL	4/1/12-3/31/13 ALL	4/1/13-3/31/14 ALL		0-1MM	1-3MM	3-5MM	5-10MM	10-25MM	25MM & OVER
505	457	448	**NUMBER OF STATEMENTS**	8	44	49	90	128	129
%	%	%	**ASSETS**	%	%	%	%	%	%
10.8	11.0	12.0	Cash & Equivalents		10.8	10.3	12.1	13.4	11.2
35.0	33.2	32.5	Trade Receivables (net)		35.9	31.6	31.4	33.3	32.2
17.7	17.4	17.2	Inventory		12.1	15.1	18.3	17.3	18.7
5.4	5.6	5.7	All Other Current		5.0	5.4	5.5	6.0	6.2
68.9	67.1	67.4	Total Current		63.7	62.5	67.3	70.1	68.2
23.1	24.4	25.2	Fixed Assets (net)		25.9	30.8	24.2	24.2	24.3
2.5	3.0	2.3	Intangibles (net)		2.5	.6	2.1	1.8	3.4
5.4	5.6	5.1	All Other Non-Current		7.8	6.1	6.4	3.9	4.1
100.0	100.0	100.0	Total		100.0	100.0	100.0	100.0	100.0
			LIABILITIES						
12.5	9.9	8.3	Notes Payable-Short Term		11.2	10.4	8.9	6.7	7.2
3.4	2.5	2.7	Cur. Mat.-L.T.D.		3.5	3.0	2.7	2.0	2.5
17.2	15.6	14.9	Trade Payables		16.8	16.3	15.6	14.1	14.1
.2	.3	.2	Income Taxes Payable		.1	.1	.2	.4	.2
12.1	11.4	10.7	All Other Current		14.7	7.3	9.2	9.6	12.9
45.4	39.6	36.7	Total Current		46.3	37.1	36.6	32.8	36.8
11.1	13.7	14.0	Long-Term Debt		15.3	18.8	12.8	11.3	11.1
.4	.5	.5	Deferred Taxes		.0	.5	.5	.6	.6
6.7	5.0	6.0	All Other Non-Current		9.6	5.7	3.9	5.1	5.5
36.5	41.2	42.8	Net Worth		28.8	37.9	46.1	50.2	46.0
100.0	100.0	100.0	Total Liabilties & Net Worth		100.0	100.0	100.0	100.0	100.0
			INCOME DATA						
100.0	100.0	100.0	Net Sales		100.0	100.0	100.0	100.0	100.0
25.6	27.3	26.5	Gross Profit		40.3	28.7	25.7	25.2	20.6
22.0	21.4	20.4	Operating Expenses		33.9	24.5	21.0	18.2	14.6
3.6	5.9	6.0	Operating Profit		6.4	4.1	4.6	7.0	6.0
.3	.5	.4	All Other Expenses (net)		.9	.5	.0	.5	.6
3.3	5.4	5.6	Profit Before Taxes		5.5	3.6	4.6	6.5	5.4
			RATIOS						
2.8	3.1	3.2			4.1	3.0	3.1	3.8	2.6
1.6	1.8	1.8	Current		1.9	1.8	1.8	2.0	1.8
1.1	1.2	1.4			1.0	1.2	1.3	1.4	1.4
2.0	2.0	2.1			2.5	2.0	2.1	2.5	1.8
1.1	1.1	1.2	Quick		1.1	1.2	1.2	1.2	1.2
.7	.7	.8			.8	.7	.8	1.0	.8
40 9.1	34 10.6	34 10.8			31 11.8	30 12.1	28 13.1	36 10.2	39 9.4
57 6.4	51 7.2	50 7.3	Sales/Receivables		46 7.9	47 7.8	46 8.0	51 7.1	53 6.9
74 4.9	73 5.0	70 5.2			74 4.9	83 4.4	63 5.8	72 5.1	73 5.0
8 45.5	7 48.7	8 48.0			1 514.2	0 796.0	7 50.9	10 36.1	12 31.3
33 11.0	33 11.2	30 12.1	Cost of Sales/Inventory		13 27.8	22 16.5	31 11.6	31 11.6	35 10.3
64 5.7	61 6.0	63 5.8			48 7.6	60 6.1	66 5.5	63 5.8	68 5.4
19 19.7	17 21.9	16 22.2			14 25.2	17 21.0	15 24.5	15 23.6	18 20.3
33 11.1	29 12.6	27 13.7	Cost of Sales/Payables		33 11.1	29 12.4	25 14.6	25 14.6	26 13.8
53 6.9	48 7.6	43 8.4			63 5.8	58 6.3	41 8.8	42 8.7	40 9.2
4.4	4.6	4.6			5.3	5.3	5.5	4.2	4.2
8.5	8.0	7.9	Sales/Working Capital		9.6	9.5	9.6	6.4	8.1
31.6	18.5	15.6			NM	20.8	17.0	13.3	13.3
15.6	22.5	22.0			12.9	13.9	16.7	26.1	25.5
(429) 4.2	(389) 6.5	(396) 8.0	EBIT/Interest		(37) 5.3	(46) 5.1	(78) 7.1	(108) 9.0	(120) 9.9
.8	2.3	2.6			1.1	1.4	1.9	3.6	3.8
5.4	8.9	7.1					5.3	7.6	13.3
(100) 2.3	(93) 3.9	(97) 3.3	Net Profit + Depr., Dep., Amort./Cur. Mat. L/T/D				(16) 2.3	(25) 3.2	(43) 3.9
.5	1.5	2.0					1.4	2.1	1.9
.2	.2	.2			.3	.3	.2	.2	.3
.5	.5	.5	Fixed/Worth		.8	.8	.5	.5	.5
1.2	1.2	1.1			29.8	2.0	.9	.9	1.0
.6	.6	.6			.6	.7	.6	.4	.6
1.4	1.3	1.2	Debt/Worth		2.7	1.8	1.1	1.2	1.2
4.1	3.1	2.6			78.7	3.7	2.0	2.2	2.1
39.0	45.3	47.4			80.9	60.2	44.1	48.7	41.3
(449) 15.8	(403) 20.5	(414) 22.6	% Profit Before Taxes/Tangible Net Worth		(34) 25.7	(45) 17.4	(85) 19.4	(123) 25.9	(121) 21.3
1.6	7.2	6.3			3.1	4.5	3.6	7.5	9.8
15.3	17.5	18.9			26.0	16.1	19.0	21.3	16.3
6.1	8.3	9.4	% Profit Before Taxes/Total Assets		6.9	7.6	9.6	11.2	8.9
.1	2.3	2.4			.5	1.4	1.7	3.9	4.1
24.6	27.0	24.0			49.8	14.9	24.5	28.5	20.6
11.5	11.0	10.4	Sales/Net Fixed Assets		13.3	9.6	12.6	11.7	9.1
5.9	5.7	5.5			4.7	4.5	6.0	5.7	5.2
2.9	2.8	3.0			3.5	3.0	3.1	2.8	2.7
2.2	2.2	2.2	Sales/Total Assets		2.4	2.4	2.4	2.1	2.1
1.6	1.6	1.7			1.9	1.6	1.7	1.7	1.6
.9	.9	.9			1.1	.8	1.1	.8	.9
(435) 1.8	(393) 1.9	(400) 1.7	% Depr., Dep., Amort./Sales		(32) 2.4	(44) 1.3	(78) 1.7	(115) 1.8	(126) 1.6
3.1	3.2	2.8			3.8	2.5	3.0	3.0	2.6
1.7	1.7	1.6			4.8	2.8	1.4	1.0	1.1
(219) 3.0	(190) 3.3	(185) 3.3	% Officers', Directors' Owners' Comp/Sales		(26) 6.6	(27) 4.1	(51) 2.7	(45) 2.2	(30) 2.3
6.1	5.7	5.9			11.1	6.1	4.7	4.8	4.1
12591259M	14959540M	13621422M	Net Sales ($)	5249M	91096M	190871M	661318M	2060957M	10611931M
7317535M	8017338M	7020330M	Total Assets ($)	1934M	45216M	92113M	307497M	1049524M	5524046M

M = $ thousand MM = $ million

See Pages 9 through 22 for Explanation of Ratios and Data

Current Data Sorted by Assets							Comparative Historical Data	
						Type of Statement		
		1	6	1	2	Unqualified	19	24
	1	16	6	1		Reviewed	27	30
	5	3				Compiled	24	16
1	9	3	1			Tax Returns	15	12
	4	16	12	5		Other	49	49
	15 (4/1-9/30/13)		78 (10/1/13-3/31/14)				4/1/09-3/31/10 ALL	4/1/10-3/31/11 ALL
0-500M	500M-2MM	2-10MM	10-50MM	50-100MM	100-250MM			
1	19	39	25	7	2	**NUMBER OF STATEMENTS**	134	131
%	%	%	%	%	%	**ASSETS**	%	%
	11.1	8.6	11.9			Cash & Equivalents	14.1	13.3
	31.5	29.8	21.0			Trade Receivables (net)	21.1	23.4
	22.9	19.3	21.9			Inventory	18.9	23.7
	1.0	4.5	2.7			All Other Current	4.1	4.1
	66.6	62.2	57.5			Total Current	58.2	64.5
	28.2	26.1	32.0			Fixed Assets (net)	30.7	25.5
	1.0	1.0	3.7			Intangibles (net)	3.4	3.5
	4.2	10.7	6.8			All Other Non-Current	7.7	6.5
	100.0	100.0	100.0			Total	100.0	100.0
						LIABILITIES		
	15.8	10.5	7.0			Notes Payable-Short Term	7.3	10.2
	3.8	2.5	2.8			Cur. Mat.-L.T.D.	4.2	4.0
	15.8	12.5	7.4			Trade Payables	10.8	12.6
	.5	.6	.1			Income Taxes Payable	.2	.2
	7.5	11.9	10.1			All Other Current	11.2	11.5
	43.4	37.9	27.3			Total Current	33.7	38.5
	28.5	10.7	16.2			Long-Term Debt	17.1	13.2
	.0	.4	1.1			Deferred Taxes	.3	.3
	3.3	4.2	3.9			All Other Non-Current	8.9	6.0
	24.8	46.8	51.6			Net Worth	39.9	41.9
	100.0	100.0	100.0			Total Liabilties & Net Worth	100.0	100.0
						INCOME DATA		
	100.0	100.0	100.0			Net Sales	100.0	100.0
	36.0	29.1	25.1			Gross Profit	29.5	29.2
	34.5	23.4	19.6			Operating Expenses	26.9	24.4
	1.6	5.7	5.5			Operating Profit	2.6	4.8
	.7	1.0	.3			All Other Expenses (net)	1.2	1.0
	.9	4.8	5.2			Profit Before Taxes	1.4	3.8
						RATIOS		
	2.2	2.7	4.0				3.4	3.2
	1.5	1.6	2.4			Current	2.0	1.8
	1.1	1.2	1.3				1.1	1.2
	1.8	1.7	2.2				2.0	2.0
	.8	1.0	1.2			Quick	1.1	.9
	.6	.6	.7				.5	.5
	28 13.0	**39** 9.3	**31** 11.6				**26** 13.8	**34** 10.6
	40 9.2	**51** 7.2	**49** 7.4			Sales/Receivables	**44** 8.4	**45** 8.2
	50 7.3	**64** 5.7	**59** 6.2				**58** 6.2	**58** 6.3
	10 37.7	**28** 13.1	**39** 9.3				**22** 16.7	**26** 13.8
	33 11.2	**47** 7.7	**91** 4.0			Cost of Sales/Inventory	**49** 7.5	**60** 6.1
	63 5.8	**74** 4.9	**140** 2.6				**92** 3.9	**115** 3.2
	15 24.1	**21** 17.3	**14** 25.6				**15** 25.0	**18** 20.4
	27 13.3	**30** 12.2	**21** 17.0			Cost of Sales/Payables	**25** 14.5	**30** 12.2
	46 7.9	**40** 9.1	**28** 13.1				**43** 8.4	**43** 8.6
	5.9	4.5	2.6				3.4	3.4
	15.8	8.4	4.2			Sales/Working Capital	6.0	6.3
	52.3	18.6	17.6				146.6	17.2
	11.1	21.2	34.9				10.9	13.6
	(17) 1.6	(35) 4.0	10.0			EBIT/Interest	(116) 2.2	(114) 4.4
	-10.3	1.3	4.5				-1.5	1.3
							9.1	5.0
						Net Profit + Depr., Dep., Amort./Cur. Mat. L/T/D	(30) 2.0	(33) 2.2
							.6	.8
	.3	.2	.3				.2	.2
	1.1	.5	.7			Fixed/Worth	.7	.6
	6.8	1.0	1.2				1.8	1.4
	1.0	.6	.6				.5	.6
	1.7	.9	1.0			Debt/Worth	1.3	1.4
	15.8	1.9	2.3				3.9	3.3
	69.8	37.9	30.2				36.3	30.9
	(15) 31.4	(36) 14.5	13.2			% Profit Before Taxes/Tangible Net Worth	(113) 11.3	(115) 16.0
	-15.9	1.5	7.1				-2.5	4.9
	26.0	19.7	12.6				12.1	13.7
	4.3	8.0	8.1			% Profit Before Taxes/Total Assets	3.3	6.6
	-11.4	.3	3.5				-4.3	1.3
	49.7	24.7	9.0				16.1	18.2
	10.7	7.9	4.7			Sales/Net Fixed Assets	6.4	8.5
	6.6	4.9	2.3				3.1	4.3
	3.3	2.4	1.6				2.3	2.4
	2.9	1.9	1.4			Sales/Total Assets	1.6	1.8
	2.2	1.5	1.1				1.1	1.2
		1.0	2.1				1.3	1.6
		(36) 2.5	(23) 3.8			% Depr., Dep., Amort./Sales	(115) 2.9	(117) 2.4
		3.4	5.7				4.5	4.0
	2.8	2.9					2.8	2.1
	(12) 4.4	(12) 3.9				% Officers', Directors' Owners' Comp/Sales	(43) 5.6	(41) 3.9
	17.9	5.1					8.3	7.0
707M	74669M	372852M	699036M	684852M	233153M	Net Sales ($)	2909449M	2883687M
43M	24485M	193506M	495320M	524453M	248280M	Total Assets ($)	1970590M	1988726M

M = $ thousand MM = $ million

See Pages 9 through 22 for Explanation of Ratios and Data

Comparative Historical Data				Current Data Sorted by Sales					
			Type of Statement						
13	13	10	Unqualified				1	4	5
27	27	24	Reviewed			3	5	12	4
16	10	8	Compiled		1	1	5	1	
11	10	14	Tax Returns	1	4	3	5		
41	48	37	Other		1	8	6	13	9
4/1/11-3/31/12 ALL	4/1/12-3/31/13 ALL	4/1/13-3/31/14 ALL		15 (4/1-9/30/13)		78 (10/1/13-3/31/14)			
				0-1MM	1-3MM	3-5MM	5-10MM	10-25MM	25MM & OVER
108	108	93	**NUMBER OF STATEMENTS**	1	6	15	22	30	19
%	%	%	**ASSETS**	%	%	%	%	%	%
12.1	13.4	11.0	Cash & Equivalents			7.1	10.4	11.0	11.8
28.7	27.8	26.5	Trade Receivables (net)			22.5	36.0	23.0	23.9
20.4	19.4	21.1	Inventory			26.4	18.7	21.4	23.5
3.6	3.3	3.1	All Other Current			1.3	4.9	3.7	2.7
64.8	63.9	61.7	Total Current			57.4	70.0	59.1	61.9
25.2	28.3	28.0	Fixed Assets (net)			30.2	20.7	29.6	28.3
3.6	2.4	2.2	Intangibles (net)			1.8	.2	2.6	3.9
6.3	5.4	8.1	All Other Non-Current			10.6	9.1	8.6	5.8
100.0	100.0	100.0	Total			100.0	100.0	100.0	100.0
			LIABILITIES						
8.5	8.4	11.6	Notes Payable-Short Term			10.5	13.6	7.5	8.0
3.0	3.1	2.8	Cur. Mat.-L.T.D.			1.3	2.5	3.3	2.8
12.4	13.0	11.7	Trade Payables			14.8	14.7	8.9	9.5
.3	.4	.4	Income Taxes Payable			.5	.3	.6	.1
11.2	12.3	12.3	All Other Current			7.0	8.6	12.6	13.5
35.3	37.2	38.7	Total Current			34.2	39.6	33.0	33.9
13.2	15.2	15.2	Long-Term Debt			12.5	10.7	18.3	9.8
.4	.5	.6	Deferred Taxes			.0	.2	.9	1.0
6.3	4.3	4.5	All Other Non-Current			3.4	5.8	2.1	7.0
44.7	42.7	41.1	Net Worth			49.9	43.7	45.8	48.2
100.0	100.0	100.0	Total Liabilties & Net Worth			100.0	100.0	100.0	100.0
			INCOME DATA						
100.0	100.0	100.0	Net Sales			100.0	100.0	100.0	100.0
28.4	29.3	30.3	Gross Profit			30.9	28.3	27.9	29.1
22.6	22.7	25.2	Operating Expenses			28.4	24.9	20.0	21.5
5.7	6.6	5.0	Operating Profit			2.5	3.4	7.8	7.6
1.1	1.0	.7	All Other Expenses (net)			-.3	1.0	.9	.4
4.7	5.6	4.4	Profit Before Taxes			2.8	2.4	6.9	7.2
			RATIOS						
2.9	2.9	2.6				2.2	3.0	3.5	2.4
2.0	1.8	1.8	Current			1.6	1.7	2.1	2.1
1.2	1.2	1.2				1.3	1.2	1.3	1.2
2.0	1.9	1.7				1.3	1.7	2.0	1.6
1.2	(107) 1.1	.9	Quick			.7	1.1	1.0	1.1
.6	.6	.6				.4	.7	.6	.8
36 10.2	28 13.2	37 9.9				28 13.0	36 10.0	37 9.8	39 9.4
51 7.2	45 8.2	47 7.8	Sales/Receivables			47 7.7	50 7.3	46 8.0	47 7.7
63 5.8	58 6.3	61 6.0				59 6.2	69 5.3	56 6.5	63 5.8
16 23.2	14 26.5	28 12.9				39 9.4	21 17.0	35 10.5	19 19.1
44 8.3	38 9.5	49 7.5	Cost of Sales/Inventory			63 5.8	32 11.5	56 6.5	91 4.0
79 4.6	81 4.5	101 3.6				101 3.6	52 7.0	118 3.1	130 2.8
15 23.6	17 21.8	17 21.9				21 17.1	15 24.9	18 20.5	16 22.6
27 13.7	25 14.5	27 13.6	Cost of Sales/Payables			30 12.0	28 13.0	25 14.4	21 17.0
39 9.4	32 11.3	38 9.7				59 6.2	42 8.6	32 11.5	43 8.5
3.8	4.5	3.9				5.1	4.7	3.6	3.1
7.0	8.6	8.2	Sales/Working Capital			9.4	8.4	6.1	3.8
25.3	36.0	29.7				26.8	33.7	15.0	20.3
33.7	24.5	18.0				12.5	39.3	21.2	17.2
(91) 7.4	(97) 8.0	(85) 6.7	EBIT/Interest			(14) 3.0	(21) 3.6	(27) 8.1	(18) 10.0
1.8	2.2	1.6				-7.6	-9.2	4.0	6.1
4.8	7.3	4.1							
(22) 3.3	(27) 3.2	(20) 2.8	Net Profit + Depr., Dep., Amort./Cur. Mat. L/T/D						
1.6	1.2	1.3							
.2	.3	.3				.3	.2	.3	.4
.6	.7	.6	Fixed/Worth			.6	.5	.6	.7
1.2	1.5	1.2				1.1	.8	1.2	1.2
.5	.5	.6				.5	.8	.6	.7
1.1	1.5	1.1	Debt/Worth			.6	1.2	.9	1.3
3.7	3.1	2.4				1.7	2.5	2.1	2.1
59.1	53.5	32.7				41.8	53.7	32.5	30.1
(97) 19.4	(98) 24.2	(85) 13.5	% Profit Before Taxes/Tangible Net Worth			(14) 9.6	(21) 16.8	(27) 18.3	17.2
3.9	7.7	5.9				-6.9	-2.4	8.7	8.1
19.0	21.5	15.0				15.7	19.2	16.1	12.0
7.9	10.8	6.6	% Profit Before Taxes/Total Assets			4.8	6.1	8.8	7.4
1.5	2.8	2.0				-3.9	-3.7	3.5	3.2
19.6	20.2	16.8				17.7	46.3	12.3	9.7
10.2	9.0	7.8	Sales/Net Fixed Assets			9.2	20.1	6.5	6.2
4.6	4.0	4.0				3.6	5.6	3.2	3.9
3.0	3.0	2.7				2.8	3.3	2.1	1.6
1.9	2.1	1.8	Sales/Total Assets			1.9	2.7	1.7	1.5
1.4	1.5	1.3				1.2	1.7	1.2	1.1
1.3	1.1	1.3				1.5	.8	1.3	2.0
(90) 2.3	(88) 2.0	(78) 2.7	% Depr., Dep., Amort./Sales			(10) 3.6	(18) 1.9	(29) 3.0	(17) 2.6
3.5	3.6	4.9				6.8	2.9	5.3	4.9
1.8	1.8	2.7							
(37) 3.2	(37) 2.8	(31) 3.7	% Officers', Directors' Owners' Comp/Sales						
5.8	7.2	6.1							
2568571M	2684500M	2065269M	Net Sales ($)	707M	10615M	59366M	168120M	476149M	1350312M
1717276M	1794989M	1486087M	Total Assets ($)	43M	5713M	33775M	87154M	334889M	1024513M

M = $ thousand MM = $ million

See Pages 9 through 22 for Explanation of Ratios and Data

Current Data Sorted by Assets							Comparative Historical Data	
						Type of Statement		
		3	9	1	1	Unqualified	23	20
	1	12	7	1		Reviewed	34	34
1	6	8	1			Compiled	16	10
1	7	1				Tax Returns	11	10
1	2	15	11	4	2	Other	53	57
	6 (4/1-9/30/13)		89 (10/1/13-3/31/14)				**4/1/09-3/31/10 ALL**	**4/1/10-3/31/11 ALL**
0-500M	**500M-2MM**	**2-10MM**	**10-50MM**	**50-100MM**	**100-250MM**			
3	16	39	28	6	3	**NUMBER OF STATEMENTS**	137	131
%	%	%	%	%	%	**ASSETS**	%	%
	6.4	11.0	11.6			Cash & Equivalents	11.7	10.1
	36.7	27.8	22.7			Trade Receivables (net)	25.9	29.0
	25.9	26.8	22.1			Inventory	22.0	24.7
	2.2	4.2	2.4			All Other Current	3.9	2.7
	71.2	69.8	58.7			Total Current	63.5	66.5
	23.5	18.9	27.2			Fixed Assets (net)	26.4	22.9
	.9	5.5	6.5			Intangibles (net)	4.6	4.9
	4.4	5.7	7.5			All Other Non-Current	5.5	5.7
	100.0	100.0	100.0			Total	100.0	100.0
						LIABILITIES		
	5.0	8.8	5.1			Notes Payable-Short Term	11.6	9.0
	4.8	2.1	2.3			Cur. Mat.-L.T.D.	3.3	3.3
	20.7	11.4	11.2			Trade Payables	12.5	13.4
	.0	.1	.2			Income Taxes Payable	.1	.2
	11.1	8.0	10.2			All Other Current	9.5	11.8
	41.5	30.4	29.0			Total Current	37.1	37.8
	17.3	10.8	10.8			Long-Term Debt	20.0	13.2
	.0	.2	1.4			Deferred Taxes	.6	.5
	7.5	9.2	7.9			All Other Non-Current	9.6	6.7
	33.7	49.3	50.9			Net Worth	32.7	41.7
	100.0	100.0	100.0			Total Liabilties & Net Worth	100.0	100.0
						INCOME DATA		
	100.0	100.0	100.0			Net Sales	100.0	100.0
	36.7	30.2	28.9			Gross Profit	31.2	30.3
	33.2	26.6	24.1			Operating Expenses	28.3	27.3
	3.5	3.7	4.8			Operating Profit	3.0	3.0
	.3	.2	.3			All Other Expenses (net)	1.5	.9
	3.3	3.5	4.5			Profit Before Taxes	1.4	2.1
						RATIOS		
	3.2	4.8	3.2				3.8	3.4
	1.9	2.6	2.5			Current	1.9	1.9
	1.2	1.7	1.4				1.2	1.3
	1.7	2.3	1.9				2.2	2.2
	1.2	1.3	1.2			Quick	1.1	1.1
	.7	.7	.7				.6	.6
	24 15.4	**26** 13.9	**30** 12.1				**31** 11.7	**31** 11.7
	31 11.6	**45** 8.1	**38** 9.6			Sales/Receivables	**40** 9.2	**44** 8.4
	60 6.1	**55** 6.6	**62** 5.9				**57** 6.4	**62** 5.8
	12 30.1	**31** 11.7	**33** 10.9				**26** 14.1	**33** 11.1
	46 8.0	**55** 6.6	**53** 6.9			Cost of Sales/Inventory	**50** 7.3	**51** 7.1
	68 5.4	**96** 3.8	**87** 4.2				**78** 4.7	**81** 4.5
	15 24.1	**14** 26.2	**14** 26.5				**11** 33.1	**14** 25.2
	32 11.4	**21** 17.4	**24** 14.9			Cost of Sales/Payables	**23** 15.8	**25** 14.8
	63 5.8	**41** 9.0	**42** 8.6				**37** 9.8	**40** 9.0
	6.4	3.4	4.1				4.1	4.7
	11.6	6.5	5.9			Sales/Working Capital	8.3	7.2
	24.1	12.5	14.1				24.1	18.3
	45.7	29.1	27.3				12.3	16.4
	11.9	(35) 5.2	(23) 10.2			EBIT/Interest	(123) 2.6	(120) 3.6
	1.0	1.9	2.4				.5	.1
		8.5	13.0				4.8	6.0
		(10) 2.8	(14) 4.2			Net Profit + Depr., Dep., Amort./Cur. Mat. L/T/D	(37) 1.7	(40) 2.3
		.7	1.8				-.1	.4
	.3	.1	.3				.3	.3
	.5	.4	.5			Fixed/Worth	.7	.6
	7.5	.8	1.2				5.7	1.7
	.7	.5	.5				.6	.6
	1.7	1.2	1.1			Debt/Worth	1.7	1.6
	36.5	2.3	1.8				13.4	4.1
	49.6	39.7	23.9				36.0	35.2
	(13) 13.0	(36) 20.6	(27) 16.1			% Profit Before Taxes/Tangible Net Worth	(109) 13.9	(118) 13.1
	-11.9	2.2	6.7				-2.5	.8
	25.8	16.6	13.1				13.0	11.9
	9.3	8.3	8.3			% Profit Before Taxes/Total Assets	5.6	4.2
	-.1	1.0	3.4				-1.7	-1.5
	38.4	38.0	13.8				24.5	27.1
	24.0	15.6	7.0			Sales/Net Fixed Assets	12.3	12.1
	9.6	5.2	4.7				4.8	5.7
	4.2	2.8	2.7				3.1	2.9
	3.4	2.3	1.8			Sales/Total Assets	2.2	2.3
	2.8	1.4	1.5				1.5	1.7
	.4	.7	1.0				.8	.9
	(11) .7	(36) 1.1	2.1			% Depr., Dep., Amort./Sales	(120) 1.7	(114) 1.6
	1.3	1.8	2.6				3.0	2.8
	2.7						1.7	2.1
	(12) 3.4					% Officers', Directors' Owners' Comp/Sales	(38) 3.7	(32) 2.7
	6.4						6.0	5.7
2591M	59227M	462137M	1008405M	663599M	544565M	Net Sales ($)	3845685M	4147856M
973M	17938M	204055M	526135M	417002M	410819M	Total Assets ($)	2388586M	2310785M

M = $ thousand MM = $ million

See Pages 9 through 22 for Explanation of Ratios and Data

Comparative Historical Data				Current Data Sorted by Sales					
			Type of Statement						
14	10	14	Unqualified				2	4	8
27	22	21	Reviewed			4	2	8	7
8	9	16	Compiled	1	2	3	8	1	1
15	14	9	Tax Returns	1	4	2	2		
56	66	35	Other		2	2	6	10	15
4/1/11-3/31/12 ALL	**4/1/12-3/31/13 ALL**	**4/1/13-3/31/14 ALL**		**6 (4/1-9/30/13)**			**89 (10/1/13-3/31/14)**		
				0-1MM	**1-3MM**	**3-5MM**	**5-10MM**	**10-25MM**	**25MM & OVER**
120	121	95	**NUMBER OF STATEMENTS**	2	8	11	20	23	31
%	%	%	**ASSETS**	%	%	%	%	%	%
8.7	8.9	10.4	Cash & Equivalents			10.4	8.2	11.5	11.8
28.4	26.2	26.2	Trade Receivables (net)			32.4	25.0	31.8	21.4
25.1	24.0	24.2	Inventory			17.6	28.4	25.4	18.9
3.5	3.3	3.2	All Other Current			3.5	5.9	2.1	3.1
65.6	62.4	64.0	Total Current			63.8	67.5	70.7	55.1
24.6	22.9	22.4	Fixed Assets (net)			24.6	18.3	24.3	23.1
4.6	7.2	6.5	Intangibles (net)			1.9	9.0	.9	12.1
5.2	7.5	7.1	All Other Non-Current			9.7	5.2	4.1	9.7
100.0	100.0	100.0	Total			100.0	100.0	100.0	100.0
			LIABILITIES						
9.1	9.9	6.6	Notes Payable-Short Term			7.7	10.9	7.5	2.1
2.8	2.8	2.5	Cur. Mat.-L.T.D.			2.2	3.7	2.7	1.7
17.1	14.9	12.3	Trade Payables			18.9	10.7	13.4	9.5
.2	.1	.1	Income Taxes Payable			.0	.2	.1	.2
10.4	10.0	10.0	All Other Current			8.1	10.7	6.6	10.2
39.6	37.6	31.4	Total Current			36.9	36.2	30.4	23.6
12.1	15.4	12.8	Long-Term Debt			15.3	9.4	12.1	12.1
.5	.6	.6	Deferred Taxes			.4	.1	.3	1.4
9.8	8.7	7.6	All Other Non-Current			12.4	8.7	9.2	6.3
38.0	37.6	47.6	Net Worth			35.1	45.6	48.1	56.6
100.0	100.0	100.0	Total Liabilties & Net Worth			100.0	100.0	100.0	100.0
			INCOME DATA						
100.0	100.0	100.0	Net Sales			100.0	100.0	100.0	100.0
29.4	31.1	30.7	Gross Profit			35.2	32.3	29.2	28.4
28.1	27.3	26.3	Operating Expenses			30.5	29.9	23.8	23.0
1.3	3.8	4.3	Operating Profit			4.6	2.4	5.4	5.4
.5	.8	.2	All Other Expenses (net)			-.4	.1	.4	.3
.8	3.0	4.1	Profit Before Taxes			5.0	2.3	5.0	5.1
			RATIOS						
2.8	3.1	3.4				3.5	3.4	3.7	3.4
1.9	2.1	2.6	Current			1.5	2.5	2.7	2.7
1.3	1.1	1.3				1.2	1.2	1.7	1.7
1.9	2.0	2.0				1.9	1.8	2.5	2.5
(119) .9	1.0	1.2	Quick			1.1	1.2	1.6	1.5
.6	.6	.7				.7	.5	.8	.8
28 12.9	**26** 14.1	**26** 13.9				**23** 15.8	**21** 17.7	**28** 13.0	**26** 13.8
40 9.1	**38** 9.7	**40** 9.2	Sales/Receivables			**46** 8.0	**41** 8.8	**46** 8.0	**33** 11.1
58 6.3	**54** 6.7	**55** 6.6				**76** 4.8	**51** 7.2	**65** 5.6	**52** 7.0
33 11.2	**32** 11.5	**29** 12.4				**12** 31.6	**38** 9.7	**34** 10.8	**30** 12.3
54 6.7	**48** 7.6	**51** 7.1	Cost of Sales/Inventory			**45** 8.1	**64** 5.7	**46** 8.0	**40** 9.1
83 4.4	**72** 5.1	**76** 4.8				**65** 5.6	**118** 3.1	**85** 4.3	**63** 5.8
14 25.9	**14** 25.2	**14** 26.6				**15** 25.0	**10** 34.8	**14** 25.6	**13** 28.4
27 13.4	**26** 13.8	**21** 17.1	Cost of Sales/Payables			**51** 7.2	**17** 21.8	**23** 15.8	**20** 18.1
47 7.7	**41** 8.9	**41** 8.8				**64** 5.7	**41** 8.9	**47** 7.8	**28** 13.0
5.1	4.8	4.5				6.0	3.3	4.3	4.5
8.1	7.5	6.8	Sales/Working Capital			13.3	6.0	6.8	5.5
24.2	33.2	14.7				17.4	27.3	9.4	14.1
8.8	19.6	28.9				48.0	39.9	23.6	30.2
(109) 2.7	(108) 5.8	(84) 7.9	EBIT/Interest			15.4	(18) 4.1	(21) 6.4	(26) 11.6
-.6	.9	2.0				1.0	.4	4.0	3.3
5.9	4.9	11.1							25.1
(29) 2.5	(25) 2.7	(26) 4.2	Net Profit + Depr., Dep., Amort./Cur. Mat. L/T/D						(13) 6.9
.6	1.0	1.5							2.8
.3	.2	.2				.4	.2	.1	.2
.6	.6	.5	Fixed/Worth			.5	.5	.4	.5
1.7	2.3	1.2				2.2	2.4	1.3	1.1
.6	.5	.5				1.0	.6	.5	.4
1.5	1.7	1.2	Debt/Worth			1.8	1.4	1.2	.9
4.4	5.7	2.9				10.8	6.8	2.1	1.9
28.0	30.5	33.5					51.1	34.9	26.5
(106) 9.2	(100) 16.0	(87) 17.0	% Profit Before Taxes/Tangible Net Worth				(16) 13.5	22.7	(29) 16.5
-4.1	3.1	3.4					1.1	9.4	8.6
10.1	14.0	15.6				25.4	22.1	21.6	13.2
2.4	7.0	8.1	% Profit Before Taxes/Total Assets			7.6	4.8	9.6	9.0
-3.8	.2	1.5				.1	.5	4.8	4.6
31.5	27.0	27.3				24.8	38.0	34.3	14.6
12.3	12.7	10.1	Sales/Net Fixed Assets			15.2	17.4	9.6	7.6
5.2	6.0	5.5				4.7	5.1	4.3	5.7
3.1	3.2	3.0				3.6	3.0	3.0	2.7
2.3	2.3	2.2	Sales/Total Assets			2.2	1.8	2.5	2.0
1.6	1.6	1.5				1.4	1.3	1.6	1.6
.9	.8	.8					.6	.6	1.3
(105) 1.7	(100) 1.5	(84) 1.3	% Depr., Dep., Amort./Sales				(17) 1.2	(21) 1.0	(30) 2.2
2.8	2.4	2.4					1.8	2.0	2.6
1.7	2.1	2.5					2.0		
(40) 3.0	(30) 3.6	(24) 2.9	% Officers', Directors' Owners' Comp/Sales				(10) 2.8		
5.2	7.2	5.4					3.9		
3596830M	**5471529M**	**2740524M**	Net Sales ($)	**1114M**	**17530M**	**43605M**	**152001M**	**380686M**	**2145588M**
1870944M	**3285030M**	**1576922M**	Total Assets ($)	**645M**	**9593M**	**22232M**	**86042M**	**174197M**	**1284213M**

M = $ thousand MM = $ million

See Pages 9 through 22 for Explanation of Ratios and Data

	Current Data Sorted by Assets						Comparative Historical Data	
Type of Statement								
Unqualified		1	6	10	2	2	28	24
Reviewed	1	11	50	13	1	1	79	95
Compiled	2	12	34	3	1		54	56
Tax Returns	9	29	14	1			52	54
Other	7	18	43	24	4	1	87	91
	47 (4/1-9/30/13)			253 (10/1/13-3/31/14)			4/1/09-3/31/10 ALL	4/1/10-3/31/11 ALL
	0-500M	500M-2MM	2-10MM	10-50MM	50-100MM	100-250MM		
NUMBER OF STATEMENTS	19	71	147	51	8	4	300	320
ASSETS	%	%	%	%	%	%	%	%
Cash & Equivalents	16.6	10.7	12.5	14.1			10.8	10.6
Trade Receivables (net)	24.5	37.2	27.7	23.6			27.7	29.9
Inventory	22.5	18.9	19.4	22.2			20.3	18.6
All Other Current	1.5	2.0	2.5	2.8			3.3	2.6
Total Current	65.1	68.7	62.1	62.7			62.0	61.7
Fixed Assets (net)	29.8	22.6	30.3	26.5			28.5	28.3
Intangibles (net)	.9	3.9	3.0	4.1			3.4	3.5
All Other Non-Current	4.1	4.8	4.5	6.7			6.2	6.5
Total	100.0	100.0	100.0	100.0			100.0	100.0
LIABILITIES								
Notes Payable-Short Term	15.6	11.2	7.0	7.7			11.3	12.2
Cur. Mat.-L.T.D.	2.1	4.1	4.1	3.0			4.8	3.8
Trade Payables	15.6	15.8	12.6	11.5			12.9	14.7
Income Taxes Payable	.0	.2	.2	.1			.1	.2
All Other Current	30.9	9.0	9.8	9.5			8.1	8.2
Total Current	64.2	40.4	33.7	31.8			37.2	39.2
Long-Term Debt	41.0	19.9	14.3	16.5			18.8	17.0
Deferred Taxes	.0	.6	.6	.7			.4	.4
All Other Non-Current	13.2	6.2	5.6	1.4			8.5	6.1
Net Worth	-18.6	33.0	45.7	49.7			35.0	37.3
Total Liabilties & Net Worth	100.0	100.0	100.0	100.0			100.0	100.0
INCOME DATA								
Net Sales	100.0	100.0	100.0	100.0			100.0	100.0
Gross Profit	38.4	35.7	27.9	24.0			29.7	29.9
Operating Expenses	32.4	31.9	23.2	17.9			27.0	25.7
Operating Profit	6.0	3.8	4.7	6.1			2.7	4.2
All Other Expenses (net)	.7	.5	.4	.6			1.0	.8
Profit Before Taxes	5.3	3.2	4.4	5.5			1.7	3.4
RATIOS								
Current	3.8	4.1	3.1	3.4			3.7	3.2
	1.1	1.6	1.9	2.0			1.8	1.7
	.4	1.2	1.2	1.5			1.2	1.2
Quick	3.8	3.0	2.2	2.3			2.2	2.1
	.8	1.2	1.1	1.2			1.1	1.1
	.1	.7	.7	.6			.6	.7
Sales/Receivables	0 965.3	31 11.8	31 11.8	31 11.9			29 12.6	33 11.0
	13 28.0	46 8.0	44 8.3	38 9.5			42 8.6	48 7.5
	53 6.9	66 5.5	56 6.5	53 6.9			57 6.4	64 5.7
Cost of Sales/Inventory	0 UND	10 38.1	18 20.5	22 16.3			17 21.4	14 26.5
	12 30.5	26 13.8	40 9.1	50 7.3			42 8.6	43 8.5
	43 8.4	69 5.3	66 5.5	96 3.8			73 5.0	75 4.9
Cost of Sales/Payables	0 UND	11 33.0	17 21.9	18 20.5			13 27.9	17 21.9
	11 33.5	27 13.7	25 14.8	23 16.2			22 16.4	27 13.3
	41 8.8	57 6.4	34 10.6	34 10.8			40 9.2	43 8.5
Sales/Working Capital	5.5	5.7	4.5	3.7			5.0	4.6
	21.7	11.2	9.3	6.0			9.0	8.8
	-17.6	29.3	25.0	13.2			26.2	26.9
EBIT/Interest	36.7	13.1	20.6	25.7			9.1	12.3
	(11) 9.0	(61) 2.6	(135) 7.3	(46) 6.3			(274) 2.7	(285) 4.2
	.8	-.8	2.5	2.2			-.4	.9
Net Profit + Depr., Dep., Amort./Cur. Mat. L/T/D		6.0	6.5				7.5	4.6
		(11) 4.2	(25) 4.1				(72) 2.4	(67) 2.8
		.7	2.5				.9	1.2
Fixed/Worth	.0	.2	.3	.3			.3	.3
	3.3	.6	.7	.7			.7	.7
	-.7	3.7	1.4	1.2			2.6	1.8
Debt/Worth	1.2	.5	.4	.4			.7	.6
	-18.6	1.9	1.1	1.1			1.7	1.6
	-2.8	12.3	3.0	2.7			6.7	4.6
% Profit Before Taxes/Tangible Net Worth		53.1	34.3	33.8			38.1	40.6
		(59) 22.8	(139) 17.5	(48) 16.3			(250) 13.6	(275) 14.8
		1.4	6.6	5.3			-.3	3.2
% Profit Before Taxes/Total Assets	56.3	18.2	13.9	18.3			13.7	15.2
	19.6	6.0	6.9	6.7			4.0	6.1
	-1.4	-1.2	2.0	1.9			-2.0	.1
Sales/Net Fixed Assets	341.0	49.5	18.2	15.1			23.8	23.8
	32.4	17.0	7.7	8.8			9.6	8.7
	9.2	7.4	4.2	4.4			4.4	4.3
Sales/Total Assets	10.7	3.4	2.7	2.5			3.0	2.8
	3.3	2.8	2.1	2.0			2.2	2.1
	2.5	1.8	1.6	1.3			1.6	1.5
% Depr., Dep., Amort./Sales		.7	1.1	1.2			1.1	1.1
		(55) 2.1	(135) 2.1	(50) 2.0			(266) 2.5	(285) 2.6
		3.2	4.0	3.4			4.4	4.4
% Officers', Directors' Owners' Comp/Sales		2.8	1.6	1.1			2.6	2.0
		(53) 5.1	(66) 2.7	(13) 2.9			(147) 4.4	(147) 3.3
		9.2	5.8	4.3			8.5	6.0
Net Sales ($)	21353M	258628M	1534204M	2077863M	1007622M	787772M	5258063M	5335244M
Total Assets ($)	4623M	89694M	706331M	1059736M	626694M	593167M	2775498M	3021722M

M = $ thousand MM = $ million

See Pages 9 through 22 for Explanation of Ratios and Data

Comparative Historical Data / Current Data Sorted by Sales

4/1/11-3/31/12 ALL	4/1/12-3/31/13 ALL	4/1/13-3/31/14 ALL	Type of Statement	0-1MM	1-3MM	3-5MM	5-10MM	10-25MM	25MM & OVER
28	30	21	Unqualified				4	4	13
89	85	77	Reviewed	1	8	6	22	32	8
39	52	52	Compiled	1	11	2	16	20	2
52	43	53	Tax Returns	5	18	10	12	7	1
93	94	97	Other	3	13	14	17	24	26
				47 (4/1-9/30/13)			253 (10/1/13-3/31/14)		
301	304	300	NUMBER OF STATEMENTS	10	50	32	71	87	50
%	%	%	**ASSETS**	%	%	%	%	%	%
10.8	10.9	12.6	Cash & Equivalents	23.0	7.8	11.7	13.9	13.6	12.5
30.3	30.6	28.7	Trade Receivables (net)	28.7	27.3	37.5	28.6	28.0	25.8
19.3	20.5	20.2	Inventory	24.5	18.9	15.6	18.8	20.9	24.2
3.4	3.1	2.4	All Other Current	2.5	2.0	1.4	2.2	2.6	3.3
63.9	65.0	63.9	Total Current	78.7	56.0	66.2	63.4	65.1	65.7
26.4	27.0	27.6	Fixed Assets (net)	18.6	29.7	27.4	29.1	27.4	25.6
4.4	2.6	3.3	Intangibles (net)	1.0	6.5	2.3	3.1	2.8	2.6
5.4	5.3	5.2	All Other Non-Current	1.6	7.8	4.0	4.5	4.7	6.1
100.0	100.0	100.0	Total	100.0	100.0	100.0	100.0	100.0	100.0
			LIABILITIES						
9.8	9.5	8.7	Notes Payable-Short Term	14.9	12.3	11.4	6.0	7.1	8.7
3.9	3.5	3.7	Cur. Mat.-L.T.D.	1.1	4.1	3.2	4.4	3.9	2.5
15.4	14.4	13.3	Trade Payables	17.1	12.3	14.6	13.5	13.0	13.0
.1	.1	.2	Income Taxes Payable	.0	.2	.5	.2	.1	.1
8.1	10.2	10.9	All Other Current	26.9	12.4	10.5	7.3	11.9	10.1
37.4	37.8	36.8	Total Current	60.1	41.3	40.2	31.3	36.1	34.4
15.0	16.6	17.4	Long-Term Debt	14.5	30.9	15.9	17.1	12.8	13.7
.5	.7	.6	Deferred Taxes	.0	.4	.0	.8	.9	.6
8.1	4.9	5.4	All Other Non-Current	11.9	8.3	6.2	5.1	4.8	2.1
39.0	40.0	39.8	Net Worth	13.4	19.1	37.6	45.6	45.4	49.2
100.0	100.0	100.0	Total Liabilities & Net Worth	100.0	100.0	100.0	100.0	100.0	100.0
			INCOME DATA						
100.0	100.0	100.0	Net Sales	100.0	100.0	100.0	100.0	100.0	100.0
28.4	28.9	29.9	Gross Profit	30.4	38.8	36.0	29.8	25.5	24.5
23.5	23.2	24.9	Operating Expenses	27.3	34.4	30.3	25.3	20.5	18.3
4.9	5.7	5.0	Operating Profit	3.1	4.4	5.7	4.5	5.0	6.1
.6	.5	.5	All Other Expenses (net)	.9	.8	.1	.4	.4	.6
4.2	5.2	4.5	Profit Before Taxes	2.3	3.6	5.7	4.2	4.6	5.6
			RATIOS						
3.0	3.3	3.4		4.1	3.8	3.9	3.8	3.1	3.3
1.7	1.9	1.8	Current	1.3	1.4	1.7	2.2	1.8	1.9
1.2	1.2	1.2		.7	.9	1.2	1.5	1.3	1.4
1.7	2.2	2.3		2.3	2.8	3.2	3.0	2.0	2.3
1.1	1.1	1.1	Quick	.9	1.0	1.2	1.5	1.1	1.0
.7	.7	.6		.5	.4	.7	.8	.7	.6
33 11.1	29 12.4	30 12.3		0 UND	28 12.9	35 10.4	29 12.5	30 12.2	31 11.7
45 8.1	42 8.6	42 8.6	Sales/Receivables	19 19.2	48 7.6	56 6.5	41 8.9	41 8.8	40 9.2
62 5.9	60 6.1	58 6.3		64 5.7	64 5.7	74 4.9	56 6.5	54 6.7	49 7.4
15 23.6	17 22.0	14 26.1		0 UND	9 39.2	7 51.7	16 22.3	14 25.9	23 16.1
41 8.8	40 9.1	40 9.2	Cost of Sales/Inventory	22 16.9	32 11.4	33 10.9	37 9.9	40 9.1	54 6.7
70 5.2	72 5.1	73 5.0		118 3.1	89 4.1	65 5.6	64 5.7	65 5.6	99 3.7
18 20.6	15 23.7	15 24.9		0 UND	10 36.6	15 24.5	15 24.5	15 25.0	18 19.8
28 13.0	25 14.4	24 15.2	Cost of Sales/Payables	17 21.1	24 14.9	25 14.8	24 15.0	24 15.3	23 16.0
44 8.3	36 10.0	40 9.1		64 5.7	56 6.5	56 6.5	38 9.5	31 11.6	38 9.5
5.0	4.7	4.6		4.4	4.0	3.9	4.8	4.3	5.0
8.6	8.8	8.5	Sales/Working Capital	17.6	12.0	8.7	7.5	9.6	7.2
24.2	23.9	23.9		-85.8	-50.0	29.3	14.6	20.5	14.4
18.0	23.3	20.6			9.0	33.7	22.3	14.7	48.5
(267) 5.6	(271) 7.3	(263) 5.9	EBIT/Interest		(43) 2.2	(30) 9.6	(64) 7.0	(76) 5.9	(46) 6.4
1.8	2.8	1.8			.3	2.0	1.4	2.7	2.4
5.7	6.6	8.2						9.6	20.8
(65) 2.8	(56) 3.8	(48) 4.3	Net Profit + Depr., Dep., Amort./Cur. Mat. L/T/D					(18) 4.9	(10) 4.1
1.3	1.7	2.3						3.1	2.9
.3	.3	.3		.0	.3	.3	.2	.4	.3
.7	.6	.6	Fixed/Worth	.2	1.0	.5	.6	.7	.5
1.6	1.5	1.5		-1.0	-2.0	1.2	1.8	1.3	1.1
.6	.6	.4		.6	.7	.7	.3	.5	.4
1.5	1.3	1.3	Debt/Worth	4.6	3.0	1.7	.9	1.2	1.3
4.6	3.5	4.4		-4.8	-9.4	7.2	4.7	2.8	2.7
44.2	44.1	41.7			51.2	49.2	39.3	34.5	35.1
(266) 20.8	(272) 21.7	(267) 18.2	% Profit Before Taxes/Tangible Net Worth		(35) 18.2	(28) 27.8	(66) 16.2	(83) 17.5	(49) 14.2
7.0	9.4	5.7			.6	8.7	5.8	6.5	6.7
16.5	18.8	17.2		29.7	18.5	21.0	15.7	13.5	18.5
7.6	8.9	7.0	% Profit Before Taxes/Total Assets	9.2	4.5	13.9	7.7	6.9	7.3
1.9	3.5	1.6		-25.0	-1.0	3.8	1.2	2.7	1.9
24.4	27.4	26.0		UND	36.2	28.8	17.0	21.9	15.3
9.7	10.3	9.8	Sales/Net Fixed Assets	226.2	10.1	13.3	9.6	8.0	9.5
5.3	5.0	4.7		5.9	4.2	4.7	4.4	4.4	5.4
3.0	3.2	3.0		7.9	3.0	3.2	3.2	2.8	2.7
2.2	2.3	2.2	Sales/Total Assets	2.5	1.8	2.5	2.3	2.2	2.1
1.6	1.7	1.7		1.6	1.4	1.7	1.8	1.6	1.5
1.1	1.0	1.1			.7	1.1	1.1	1.1	1.2
(256) 2.1	(259) 2.0	(258) 2.1	% Depr., Dep., Amort./Sales		(35) 2.5	(27) 2.0	(61) 2.1	(83) 2.1	(48) 1.8
3.3	3.5	3.6			6.5	3.3	3.8	3.8	2.3
2.1	1.9	1.8			2.9	2.7	1.7	1.5	1.2
(132) 3.7	(126) 3.4	(141) 3.7	% Officers', Directors' Owners' Comp/Sales		(35) 5.6	(19) 5.1	(40) 3.3	(34) 2.7	(10) 2.2
6.0	6.2	7.1			9.0	8.9	6.1	4.5	3.5
5691862M	6795143M	5687442M	Net Sales ($)	5566M	98227M	126314M	495351M	1306377M	3655607M
3201136M	3100735M	3080245M	Total Assets ($)	2080M	65911M	57171M	230144M	671529M	2053410M

M = $ thousand MM = $ million

See Pages 9 through 22 for Explanation of Ratios and Data

	Current Data Sorted by Assets						Comparative Historical Data	
Type of Statement								
Unqualified			4	1			5	8
Reviewed			12	4			29	23
Compiled		3	1				7	8
Tax Returns	3	9	4				5	12
Other	4	7	7	7		2	42	33
	10 (4/1-9/30/13)		58 (10/1/13-3/31/14)				4/1/09-3/31/10	4/1/10-3/31/11
	0-500M	500M-2MM	2-10MM	10-50MM	50-100MM	100-250MM	ALL	ALL
NUMBER OF STATEMENTS	7	19	28	12		2	88	84
ASSETS	%	%	%	%	%	%	%	%
Cash & Equivalents		11.7	8.3	7.0	DATA NOT AVAILABLE		8.0	8.9
Trade Receivables (net)		42.9	39.9	28.5			32.1	29.2
Inventory		14.5	15.5	18.9			18.7	17.6
All Other Current		1.7	8.4	3.8			5.8	6.2
Total Current		70.7	72.0	58.1			64.6	61.9
Fixed Assets (net)		16.2	20.2	21.3			23.6	22.7
Intangibles (net)		1.1	5.3	12.6			3.9	7.0
All Other Non-Current		12.1	2.4	7.9			8.0	8.4
Total		100.0	100.0	100.0			100.0	100.0
LIABILITIES								
Notes Payable-Short Term		14.7	12.3	8.0			10.0	13.6
Cur. Mat.-L.T.D.		3.8	2.7	4.5			3.1	2.3
Trade Payables		12.7	16.0	14.5			14.1	14.0
Income Taxes Payable		.1	.0	.0			.5	.3
All Other Current		13.5	10.5	15.2			13.9	11.3
Total Current		44.7	41.5	42.2			41.6	41.5
Long-Term Debt		17.7	9.3	12.1			16.2	17.6
Deferred Taxes		.1	.0	.5			.9	.2
All Other Non-Current		20.8	3.9	10.1			7.5	7.4
Net Worth		16.7	45.3	35.0			33.9	33.3
Total Liabilties & Net Worth		100.0	100.0	100.0			100.0	100.0
INCOME DATA								
Net Sales		100.0	100.0	100.0			100.0	100.0
Gross Profit		36.5	30.2	30.3			33.7	33.2
Operating Expenses		34.1	25.4	21.4			31.1	30.3
Operating Profit		2.4	4.8	8.8			2.6	2.9
All Other Expenses (net)		.6	.6	2.7			1.2	1.2
Profit Before Taxes		1.8	4.2	6.1			1.4	1.7
RATIOS								
Current		5.0	2.2	1.9			2.5	2.7
		2.1	1.7	1.3			1.6	1.6
		.9	1.3	1.1			1.2	1.2
Quick		4.6	1.5	1.3			1.7	1.7
		1.7	1.2	.8			.9	1.0
		.5	.8	.5			.6	.6
Sales/Receivables		**51** 7.1	**36** 10.2	**43** 8.4			**34** 10.8	**31** 11.7
		54 6.7	**56** 6.5	**53** 6.9			**50** 7.2	**47** 7.8
		72 5.1	**85** 4.3	**60** 6.1			**69** 5.3	**68** 5.4
Cost of Sales/Inventory		**10** 34.9	**6** 62.0	**18** 19.9			**13** 28.7	**9** 38.6
		23 15.9	**31** 11.7	**32** 11.4			**46** 7.9	**45** 8.1
		76 4.8	**70** 5.2	**104** 3.5			**86** 4.2	**75** 4.9
Cost of Sales/Payables		**8** 46.5	**22** 16.5	**22** 16.5			**17** 21.7	**17** 21.1
		22 16.5	**34** 10.7	**31** 11.7			**28** 13.1	**28** 13.3
		45 8.1	**45** 8.2	**56** 6.5			**48** 7.5	**49** 7.5
Sales/Working Capital		5.5	6.1	8.3			4.7	4.9
		5.9	7.3	13.8			8.4	10.1
		-62.4	16.2	26.8			47.8	21.2
EBIT/Interest		21.5	27.2	26.3			8.4	11.2
		(16) 5.2	(24) 6.6	(10) 4.8			(80) 3.1	(76) 3.4
		.8	3.2	2.8			.4	.0
Net Profit + Depr., Dep., Amort./Cur. Mat. L/T/D							7.2	4.7
							(18) 1.5	(16) 1.1
							.4	.1
Fixed/Worth		.0	.2	.6			.3	.2
		.4	.5	1.0			.7	.7
		-7.4	.9	NM			3.3	14.2
Debt/Worth		.8	.7	1.2			.7	.7
		3.3	1.4	2.8			1.8	2.3
		-4.8	2.3	NM			11.9	34.8
% Profit Before Taxes/Tangible Net Worth		49.9	35.4				34.6	59.3
		(12) 18.0	(26) 10.6				(73) 11.6	(67) 18.6
		5.6	4.0				.3	1.6
% Profit Before Taxes/Total Assets		16.0	17.0	22.9			11.1	14.8
		5.9	6.3	13.5			4.4	5.3
		.5	1.6	3.7			-3.0	-2.1
Sales/Net Fixed Assets		126.3	25.8	14.3			25.3	31.7
		23.0	12.8	11.4			10.1	12.3
		7.9	8.3	7.6			5.7	5.5
Sales/Total Assets		3.4	2.8	3.0			2.7	2.8
		2.7	2.4	2.3			2.0	2.1
		2.0	1.9	1.2			1.4	1.6
% Depr., Dep., Amort./Sales		1.1	.5	1.1			1.1	.8
		(12) 1.9	(27) .8	(10) 1.4			(71) 1.7	(74) 2.0
		2.9	1.8	2.0			3.4	3.1
% Officers', Directors' Owners' Comp/Sales			1.1				2.5	2.1
			(13) 1.9				(32) 4.0	(32) 5.5
			5.6				7.3	8.4
Net Sales ($)	7901M	66161M	316598M	540149M		523143M	2212404M	1930195M
Total Assets ($)	1924M	23966M	140586M	280870M		379126M	1262990M	1092006M

M = $ thousand MM = $ million

See Pages 9 through 22 for Explanation of Ratios and Data

Comparative Historical Data / **Current Data Sorted by Sales**

	4/1/11-3/31/12 ALL	4/1/12-3/31/13 ALL	4/1/13-3/31/14 ALL	0-1MM	1-3MM	3-5MM	5-10MM	10-25MM	25MM & OVER
Type of Statement									
Unqualified	7	8	5					4	1
Reviewed	26	25	16				5	7	4
Compiled	6	5	4		2	1	1		
Tax Returns	18	18	16	2	4	4	4	2	
Other	34	37	27	3	2	8	2	6	6
				10 (4/1-9/30/13)		58 (10/1/13-3/31/14)			
NUMBER OF STATEMENTS	91	93	68	5	8	13	12	19	11
	%	%	%	%	%	%	%	%	%
ASSETS									
Cash & Equivalents	7.7	8.2	10.3			13.2	9.1	7.1	10.7
Trade Receivables (net)	33.0	35.4	37.7			40.3	51.5	33.6	30.2
Inventory	17.4	21.0	16.5			11.7	10.2	20.4	16.6
All Other Current	6.6	4.7	4.8			3.3	5.9	7.3	5.0
Total Current	64.6	69.3	69.3			68.4	76.8	68.3	62.5
Fixed Assets (net)	20.8	18.1	19.9			19.1	15.7	18.3	25.6
Intangibles (net)	4.4	5.9	4.7			.7	6.4	7.5	7.3
All Other Non-Current	10.2	6.7	6.0			11.8	1.1	5.8	4.6
Total	100.0	100.0	100.0			100.0	100.0	100.0	100.0
LIABILITIES									
Notes Payable-Short Term	11.2	12.7	11.9			9.9	11.6	13.3	7.5
Cur. Mat.-L.T.D.	3.8	3.5	3.0			2.9	2.7	3.3	4.0
Trade Payables	16.2	15.1	14.1			9.3	16.4	15.9	13.9
Income Taxes Payable	.4	.4	.0			.2	.0	.0	.1
All Other Current	13.3	12.9	14.6			15.4	14.7	7.6	17.6
Total Current	44.8	44.6	43.7			37.6	45.3	40.0	43.0
Long-Term Debt	20.5	15.4	12.0			10.2	11.1	9.3	10.3
Deferred Taxes	.3	.4	.2			.0	.0	.1	.9
All Other Non-Current	8.6	9.2	10.4			18.4	5.1	8.0	5.4
Net Worth	25.7	30.3	33.8			33.8	38.4	42.6	40.4
Total Liabilties & Net Worth	100.0	100.0	100.0			100.0	100.0	100.0	100.0
INCOME DATA									
Net Sales	100.0	100.0	100.0			100.0	100.0	100.0	100.0
Gross Profit	34.9	33.9	33.7			36.8	27.6	32.6	28.6
Operating Expenses	33.5	28.4	29.2			35.2	24.1	25.9	20.6
Operating Profit	1.4	5.5	4.4			1.5	3.6	6.7	8.1
All Other Expenses (net)	.6	.8	1.0			-.7	.7	1.6	1.2
Profit Before Taxes	.8	4.6	3.5			2.3	2.9	5.0	6.9
RATIOS									
Current	2.8	2.5	3.4			9.2	2.2	2.2	3.7
	1.5	1.6	1.7			4.2	1.6	1.7	1.3
	1.1	1.2	1.2			1.0	1.3	1.2	1.1
Quick	1.7	1.8	1.9			4.9	1.9	1.5	2.7
	.9	(92) 1.0	1.2			2.1	1.4	1.0	.8
	.5	.6	.7			.7	.8	.6	.8
Sales/Receivables	**29** 12.4	**29** 12.5	**37** 9.9			**17** 22.1	**41** 8.8	**35** 10.3	**42** 8.6
	49 7.4	**54** 6.8	**53** 6.9			**52** 7.0	**66** 5.5	**51** 7.1	**55** 6.6
	72 5.1	**69** 5.3	**70** 5.2			**59** 6.2	**111** 3.3	**72** 5.1	**62** 5.9
Cost of Sales/Inventory	**5** 76.4	**9** 41.1	**11** 33.4			**5** 79.8	**1** 308.1	**18** 20.1	**17** 21.1
	30 12.3	**49** 7.5	**26** 14.1			**37** 9.8	**6** 58.5	**63** 5.8	**25** 14.8
	79 4.6	**89** 4.1	**76** 4.8			**47** 7.8	**34** 10.8	**83** 4.4	**99** 3.7
Cost of Sales/Payables	**15** 24.1	**16** 22.9	**18** 20.4			**8** 47.4	**20** 18.1	**21** 17.1	**24** 15.0
	34 10.8	**29** 12.4	**29** 12.6			**20** 18.2	**30** 12.3	**36** 10.1	**30** 12.3
	50 7.3	**47** 7.7	**45** 8.2			**33** 11.1	**38** 9.6	**58** 6.3	**43** 8.5
Sales/Working Capital	5.4	5.8	5.8			5.6	6.1	6.0	7.7
	11.9	10.3	7.7			6.9	8.3	7.1	13.4
	57.3	27.1	23.6			NM	16.2	22.0	27.1
EBIT/Interest	18.0	17.8	25.9				27.5	27.3	
	(83) 4.1	(75) 4.2	(57) 5.5				(11) 5.9	(17) 6.5	
	-2.0	1.0	1.5				3.6	1.7	
Net Profit + Depr., Dep., Amort./Cur. Mat. L/T/D	4.2	4.2	11.8						
	(19) 1.4	(12) 1.6	(11) 2.1						
	.3	.6	1.2						
Fixed/Worth	.3	.2	.2			.1	.2	.3	.3
	.6	.6	.6			.3	.5	.6	.9
	-26.3	4.0	1.3			1.5	.9	1.2	1.1
Debt/Worth	1.0	.9	1.0			.3	.8	1.0	1.0
	3.1	2.5	1.8			1.1	1.5	1.7	2.5
	-94.7	48.2	4.3			NM	3.9	3.4	2.8
% Profit Before Taxes/Tangible Net Worth	72.6	64.6	40.7			32.0	25.8	36.4	78.6
	(68) 22.9	(71) 30.8	(54) 18.2			(10) 18.0	(10) 10.6	(16) 13.0	(10) 48.7
	.3	7.4	7.6			4.1	7.7	-10.6	20.3
% Profit Before Taxes/Total Assets	16.3	18.7	17.7			20.9	10.2	16.0	23.2
	6.2	4.9	7.0			6.5	4.7	7.5	19.5
	-3.9	.5	1.6			1.8	3.3	1.3	4.5
Sales/Net Fixed Assets	47.6	48.9	27.4			77.1	56.8	25.9	11.8
	14.7	21.1	13.8			14.2	25.3	13.1	9.1
	7.7	9.2	8.2			7.1	9.7	9.0	5.9
Sales/Total Assets	2.9	3.3	3.2			3.4	3.3	2.7	3.1
	2.3	2.4	2.5			2.7	2.7	2.4	2.3
	1.5	1.8	1.9			2.3	1.9	1.7	1.7
% Depr., Dep., Amort./Sales	.7	.6	.7					.5	
	(76) 1.4	(69) 1.2	(53) 1.3					(18) 1.5	
	2.4	2.0	2.2					2.8	
% Officers', Directors' Owners' Comp/Sales	1.8	1.7	1.6					1.1	
	(40) 5.0	(42) 4.4	(28) 3.8					(10) 1.4	
	8.5	8.1	7.6					4.7	
Net Sales ($)	1411394M	1729658M	1453952M	2399M	14666M	52766M	93339M	289611M	1001171M
Total Assets ($)	767959M	922748M	826472M	2053M	5708M	19803M	38067M	159173M	601668M

M = $ thousand MM = $ million

See Pages 9 through 22 for Explanation of Ratios and Data

Current Data Sorted by Assets							Comparative Historical Data	
			3	3		Type of Statement Unqualified	11	12
	1	7	3			Reviewed	7	11
1	2	3	3			Compiled	6	10
		6	1			Tax Returns	7	9
1	2	5	6	3	2	Other	27	26
	7 (4/1-9/30/13)		45 (10/1/13-3/31/14)				4/1/09-3/31/10 ALL	4/1/10-3/31/11 ALL
0-500M	500M-2MM	2-10MM	10-50MM	50-100MM	100-250MM			
2	5	21	16	6	2	NUMBER OF STATEMENTS	58	68
%	%	%	%	%	%	ASSETS	%	%
		14.9	5.9			Cash & Equivalents	7.5	9.7
		24.8	29.8			Trade Receivables (net)	25.6	26.0
		19.0	20.4			Inventory	22.3	24.6
		3.2	4.4			All Other Current	4.0	2.3
		62.0	60.6			Total Current	59.4	62.6
		31.8	23.0			Fixed Assets (net)	28.1	27.3
		1.8	7.1			Intangibles (net)	8.7	6.2
		4.5	9.3			All Other Non-Current	3.7	3.9
		100.0	100.0			Total	100.0	100.0
						LIABILITIES		
		8.3	9.1			Notes Payable-Short Term	8.1	9.9
		2.8	1.4			Cur. Mat.-L.T.D.	3.6	3.8
		10.0	10.4			Trade Payables	13.5	14.9
		1.3	2.0			Income Taxes Payable	.2	.2
		17.4	16.7			All Other Current	8.9	13.5
		39.8	39.6			Total Current	34.2	42.4
		15.9	14.9			Long-Term Debt	18.2	20.1
		1.0	.5			Deferred Taxes	1.0	.8
		4.1	10.3			All Other Non-Current	6.3	4.1
		39.3	34.7			Net Worth	40.3	32.6
		100.0	100.0			Total Liabilties & Net Worth	100.0	100.0
						INCOME DATA		
		100.0	100.0			Net Sales	100.0	100.0
		28.8	27.4			Gross Profit	29.0	28.7
		22.9	19.3			Operating Expenses	25.2	24.3
		5.9	8.1			Operating Profit	3.8	4.4
		.4	.6			All Other Expenses (net)	1.8	1.0
		5.5	7.5			Profit Before Taxes	2.1	3.4
						RATIOS		
		2.3	3.5				3.2	2.3
		1.5	1.7			Current	1.6	1.6
		1.2	1.1				1.2	1.2
		1.5	1.7				1.8	1.5
		1.1	1.1			Quick	.9	.9
		.6	.5				.6	.5
		25 14.5	**37** 9.8				**37** 9.7	**34** 10.8
		37 9.8	**55** 6.6			Sales/Receivables	**50** 7.4	**44** 8.3
		57 6.4	**70** 5.2				**60** 6.1	**57** 6.4
		14 25.7	**40** 9.2				**29** 12.6	**32** 11.6
		40 9.1	**56** 6.5			Cost of Sales/Inventory	**51** 7.1	**52** 7.1
		58 6.3	**96** 3.8				**100** 3.7	**102** 3.6
		14 26.0	**12** 31.6				**19** 18.8	**17** 21.5
		22 16.7	**26** 14.2			Cost of Sales/Payables	**32** 11.6	**31** 11.9
		36 10.2	**49** 7.4				**49** 7.5	**52** 7.0
		7.8	4.8				4.1	5.6
		11.2	6.7			Sales/Working Capital	9.3	10.1
		25.6	61.6				20.0	21.2
		34.2	27.3				5.5	16.8
		(15) 10.8	(15) 14.8			EBIT/Interest	(55) 2.4	(62) 4.9
		3.9	6.6				-1.3	1.5
							6.1	7.4
						Net Profit + Depr., Dep., Amort./Cur. Mat. L/T/D	(14) 2.1	(13) 4.5
							-.1	.9
		.2	.4				.4	.3
		.4	.9			Fixed/Worth	.9	.7
		2.3	5.3				1.8	2.4
		.7	.6				.9	.7
		1.8	2.3			Debt/Worth	1.7	1.7
		4.0	12.4				6.7	6.4
		77.0	52.1				36.8	39.7
		(19) 36.1	(13) 29.4			% Profit Before Taxes/Tangible Net Worth	(49) 14.2	(57) 12.7
		6.1	15.8				-2.0	3.1
		24.8	16.1				11.6	10.0
		10.3	10.6			% Profit Before Taxes/Total Assets	2.7	6.4
		2.1	4.7				-2.2	1.3
		26.6	22.2				16.8	17.5
		13.5	8.3			Sales/Net Fixed Assets	7.4	10.7
		3.4	4.2				3.7	5.7
		3.2	2.6				2.5	2.7
		2.1	1.6			Sales/Total Assets	1.8	2.0
		1.5	1.1				1.2	1.4
		1.0	.9				1.4	1.0
		(17) 1.5	(13) 1.1			% Depr., Dep., Amort./Sales	(48) 2.6	(60) 2.1
		3.4	2.6				4.2	3.3
							1.3	1.3
						% Officers', Directors' Owners' Comp/Sales	(15) 7.4	(21) 3.6
							11.6	11.1
2807M	17639M	235904M	680205M	796043M	159301M	Net Sales ($)	2050580M	2057114M
553M	5840M	110868M	375060M	389002M	255944M	Total Assets ($)	1537366M	1355753M

M = $ thousand MM = $ million

See Pages 9 through 22 for Explanation of Ratios and Data

Comparative Historical Data | Current Data Sorted by Sales

			Type of Statement						
10	11	6	Unqualified						6
10	13	11	Reviewed		1	1	2	5	2
11	6	9	Compiled		4			3	2
8	12	7	Tax Returns				2	4	1
31	22	19	Other	1	1	2	2	4	9
4/1/11-3/31/12 ALL	4/1/12-3/31/13 ALL	4/1/13-3/31/14 ALL			7 (4/1-9/30/13)			45 (10/1/13-3/31/14)	
				0-1MM	1-3MM	3-5MM	5-10MM	10-25MM	25MM & OVER
70	64	52	NUMBER OF STATEMENTS	1	6	3	6	16	20
%	%	%	ASSETS	%	%	%	%	%	%
7.7	10.5	10.7	Cash & Equivalents					15.0	2.9
28.3	21.3	24.2	Trade Receivables (net)					27.9	28.4
26.5	24.5	19.3	Inventory					18.0	23.7
1.8	4.8	3.4	All Other Current					3.2	3.2
64.3	61.1	57.6	Total Current					64.1	58.2
24.8	24.1	28.4	Fixed Assets (net)					27.8	22.0
6.1	7.7	7.1	Intangibles (net)					4.6	12.4
4.7	7.1	6.9	All Other Non-Current					3.5	7.4
100.0	100.0	100.0	Total					100.0	100.0
			LIABILITIES						
8.2	10.9	9.2	Notes Payable-Short Term					8.1	9.3
2.6	3.7	2.4	Cur. Mat.-L.T.D.					1.2	1.8
17.9	10.5	10.3	Trade Payables					9.3	10.9
.3	.5	1.2	Income Taxes Payable					1.7	1.6
9.4	9.3	13.5	All Other Current					19.1	15.4
38.3	34.9	36.5	Total Current					39.6	39.0
14.6	16.3	15.7	Long-Term Debt					14.6	12.2
.6	1.0	1.1	Deferred Taxes					1.7	1.4
5.3	5.6	7.4	All Other Non-Current					4.7	10.3
41.2	42.3	39.4	Net Worth					39.5	37.0
100.0	100.0	100.0	Total Liabilties & Net Worth					100.0	100.0
			INCOME DATA						
100.0	100.0	100.0	Net Sales					100.0	100.0
27.9	33.0	30.7	Gross Profit					26.8	23.5
22.0	26.4	23.6	Operating Expenses					17.0	17.7
5.8	6.6	7.1	Operating Profit					9.8	5.9
.8	.6	.8	All Other Expenses (net)					.7	.8
5.1	6.0	6.4	Profit Before Taxes					9.1	5.0
			RATIOS						
2.6	3.1	2.4						2.4	2.4
1.6	1.8	1.6	Current					1.6	1.6
1.3	1.2	1.1						1.3	1.0
1.5	1.7	1.5						1.7	1.2
.9	.9	1.1	Quick					1.4	.9
.6	.6	.6						.9	.6
33 11.2	28 13.0	27 13.3						30 12.3	33 11.0
41 8.9	39 9.4	40 9.1	Sales/Receivables					47 7.8	40 9.1
57 6.4	51 7.1	57 6.4						58 6.3	57 6.4
25 14.7	31 11.6	17 21.7						16 23.4	40 9.2
47 7.7	51 7.1	45 8.1	Cost of Sales/Inventory					35 10.5	53 6.9
94 3.9	87 4.2	68 5.4						59 6.2	68 5.4
23 15.9	16 22.5	14 26.9						7 50.6	14 26.9
32 11.3	24 15.0	26 14.1	Cost of Sales/Payables					23 15.8	25 14.4
53 6.9	37 9.8	37 9.9						32 11.5	36 10.2
4.9	4.4	5.7						5.9	6.1
9.9	7.5	10.2	Sales/Working Capital					10.1	11.2
29.9	38.5	29.7						16.5	NM
21.3	25.1	35.4						21.2	48.6
(62) 4.9	(55) 10.2	(45) 12.3	EBIT/Interest					(12) 11.6	13.6
2.0	1.9	3.9						7.3	3.4
12.5	10.1								
(10) 5.1	(13) 4.8		Net Profit + Depr., Dep., Amort./Cur. Mat. L/T/D						
2.0	2.5								
.3	.2	.3						.2	.3
.7	.6	.7	Fixed/Worth					.6	1.0
2.0	2.3	2.9						2.4	4.3
.7	.6	.6						.8	.7
1.7	1.3	2.0	Debt/Worth					1.9	2.7
6.0	5.4	6.5						4.3	7.2
54.3	36.5	61.6						91.9	46.7
(62) 29.5	(53) 24.0	(45) 29.4	% Profit Before Taxes/Tangible Net Worth					(15) 43.3	(16) 29.2
6.0	6.3	13.9						15.9	15.4
20.9	18.8	17.4						24.9	16.1
8.5	10.1	10.0	% Profit Before Taxes/Total Assets					10.8	10.4
2.2	2.5	4.4						6.3	4.4
27.8	24.2	21.7						49.6	22.2
12.4	10.3	9.6	Sales/Net Fixed Assets					14.4	10.9
6.2	5.2	3.9						3.3	4.9
3.3	2.6	2.9						3.2	2.6
2.3	2.0	2.0	Sales/Total Assets					2.1	2.0
1.7	1.2	1.5						1.4	1.5
.8	1.0	1.0						.6	1.0
(60) 1.6	(54) 1.7	(40) 1.8	% Depr., Dep., Amort./Sales					(12) 1.9	(17) 1.5
2.7	3.0	3.3						3.3	2.8
1.2	1.2	1.0							
(29) 2.4	(20) 3.3	(20) 2.3	% Officers', Directors' Owners' Comp/Sales						
4.3	6.0	4.9							
2582633M	1756368M	1891899M	Net Sales ($)	607M	14251M	12945M	39374M	233860M	1590862M
1331960M	1300159M	1137267M	Total Assets ($)	253M	20050M	8615M	29951M	128232M	950166M

M = $ thousand MM = $ million

See Pages 9 through 22 for Explanation of Ratios and Data

Current Data Sorted by Assets							Comparative Historical Data	
						Type of Statement		
		2	11		3	Unqualified	18	24
		12	2	1		Reviewed	14	15
	7	4	2			Compiled	20	16
3	6	7			1	Tax Returns	16	17
5	3	10	10	3	4	Other	37	38
	18 (4/1-9/30/13)		78 (10/1/13-3/31/14)				**4/1/09-3/31/10 ALL**	**4/1/10-3/31/11 ALL**
0-500M	**500M-2MM**	**2-10MM**	**10-50MM**	**50-100MM**	**100-250MM**			
8	16	35	25	4	8	**NUMBER OF STATEMENTS**	105	110
%	%	%	%	%	%	**ASSETS**	%	%
	11.4	11.8	5.3			Cash & Equivalents	9.3	8.0
	18.0	27.0	21.4			Trade Receivables (net)	22.4	21.5
	36.9	32.6	29.9			Inventory	34.5	32.8
	3.3	1.3	1.5			All Other Current	2.3	2.8
	69.5	72.6	58.0			Total Current	68.6	65.2
	17.2	20.1	22.6			Fixed Assets (net)	20.3	19.5
	4.7	2.4	13.1			Intangibles (net)	4.0	6.4
	8.6	4.8	6.3			All Other Non-Current	7.2	8.9
	100.0	100.0	100.0			Total	100.0	100.0
						LIABILITIES		
	9.7	10.9	9.9			Notes Payable-Short Term	13.0	11.6
	4.2	4.1	2.9			Cur. Mat.-L.T.D.	3.2	2.7
	25.7	13.6	12.3			Trade Payables	11.8	11.4
	.1	.0	.2			Income Taxes Payable	.3	.2
	2.5	7.0	6.6			All Other Current	10.9	7.8
	42.2	35.6	31.9			Total Current	39.2	33.7
	22.7	11.6	17.6			Long-Term Debt	12.6	14.4
	.0	.2	1.1			Deferred Taxes	.5	.5
	9.0	13.0	10.3			All Other Non-Current	8.9	7.2
	26.1	39.6	39.0			Net Worth	38.9	44.1
	100.0	100.0	100.0			Total Liabilties & Net Worth	100.0	100.0
						INCOME DATA		
	100.0	100.0	100.0			Net Sales	100.0	100.0
	36.0	34.0	29.8			Gross Profit	32.4	32.5
	32.1	27.3	23.0			Operating Expenses	29.4	26.6
	3.9	6.8	6.8			Operating Profit	3.0	5.8
	-.4	.5	.9			All Other Expenses (net)	1.5	1.1
	4.3	6.3	5.9			Profit Before Taxes	1.5	4.7
						RATIOS		
	4.3	4.3	3.3				3.8	3.9
	1.8	2.2	1.7			Current	2.4	2.2
	1.0	1.1	1.3				1.3	1.3
	2.7	2.9	1.6				1.8	2.0
	.8	1.0	.9			Quick	.9	.9
	.3	.6	.5				.5	.5
	12 31.3	**31** 11.6	**33** 11.0				**27** 13.7	**27** 13.4
	30 12.0	**41** 9.0	**42** 8.6			Sales/Receivables	**39** 9.5	**39** 9.3
	46 7.9	**57** 6.4	**54** 6.8				**50** 7.2	**52** 7.0
	53 6.9	**51** 7.2	**60** 6.1				**50** 7.3	**58** 6.3
	126 2.9	**78** 4.7	**96** 3.8			Cost of Sales/Inventory	**87** 4.2	**94** 3.9
	152 2.4	**159** 2.3	**122** 3.0				**167** 2.2	**148** 2.5
	5 71.1	**19** 19.2	**16** 22.3				**12** 30.4	**14** 25.5
	41 9.0	**27** 13.6	**30** 12.1			Cost of Sales/Payables	**24** 15.4	**29** 12.6
	111 3.3	**36** 10.1	**48** 7.6				**50** 7.3	**43** 8.6
	3.9	3.4	4.2				3.3	3.6
	9.3	5.4	7.4			Sales/Working Capital	5.3	6.0
	755.0	29.8	14.1				12.9	11.6
	13.2	49.6	17.6				9.6	12.0
	(13) 5.0	(32) 9.4	(21) 5.8			EBIT/Interest	(91) 2.6	(89) 5.7
	1.9	3.0	2.7				.1	1.8
							45.8	11.4
						Net Profit + Depr., Dep., Amort./Cur. Mat. L/T/D	(20) 3.6	(23) 2.6
							.6	1.1
	.1	.1	.4				.2	.2
	.5	.3	.7			Fixed/Worth	.4	.4
	-4.9	1.5	NM				1.0	.9
	.9	.6	.7				.5	.5
	4.1	1.2	1.7			Debt/Worth	1.3	1.1
	-21.2	3.2	NM				4.1	3.6
	76.6	72.6	36.3				31.0	49.3
	(11) 31.2	(30) 28.8	(19) 25.2			% Profit Before Taxes/Tangible Net Worth	(96) 9.1	(99) 18.1
	5.0	11.3	5.5				.8	7.0
	26.8	30.2	13.9				11.1	15.8
	10.5	9.1	9.4			% Profit Before Taxes/Total Assets	3.9	7.8
	1.4	2.2	4.4				-.6	1.7
	153.1	46.5	14.0				26.8	28.8
	40.5	13.4	11.1			Sales/Net Fixed Assets	10.7	11.6
	4.6	6.9	6.0				5.5	5.3
	4.1	2.9	2.3				2.7	2.4
	2.0	2.2	1.8			Sales/Total Assets	1.8	1.7
	1.2	1.5	1.3				1.3	1.3
	.2	.6	1.3				1.0	1.0
	(10) 1.0	(29) 1.9	(22) 2.0			% Depr., Dep., Amort./Sales	(88) 2.3	(90) 1.9
	3.7	4.3	3.5				4.0	3.3
	3.8	3.1					1.9	2.7
	(10) 5.5	(12) 3.5				% Officers', Directors' Owners' Comp/Sales	(48) 3.8	(36) 3.5
	8.0	6.2					7.4	5.2
7059M	43499M	328126M	1059830M	301099M	1353466M	Net Sales ($)	2621460M	2707056M
2106M	18749M	153822M	599585M	271634M	1395512M	Total Assets ($)	1767648M	1918460M

Comparative Historical Data | **Current Data Sorted by Sales**

Type of Statement	4/1/11-3/31/12 ALL	4/1/12-3/31/13 ALL	4/1/13-3/31/14 ALL	0-1MM	1-3MM	3-5MM	5-10MM	10-25MM	25MM & OVER
				18 (4/1-9/30/13)			78 (10/1/13-3/31/14)		
Unqualified	19	14	16				1	4	11
Reviewed	21	16	15			1	4	8	2
Compiled	13	8	13	2	3	2	3	1	2
Tax Returns	17	19	17	1	5	5	5		1
Other	39	42	35	5	4	1	5	6	14
NUMBER OF STATEMENTS	109	99	96	8	12	9	18	19	30
ASSETS	%	%	%	%	%	%	%	%	%
Cash & Equivalents	9.7	8.5	9.8		13.6		13.5	10.9	5.1
Trade Receivables (net)	23.3	21.7	21.2		15.3		27.1	25.8	18.4
Inventory	33.5	32.3	30.0		36.4		38.1	30.0	26.7
All Other Current	1.8	2.5	1.8		.1		2.4	1.2	2.1
Total Current	68.4	65.0	62.8		65.4		81.2	67.9	52.3
Fixed Assets (net)	17.9	19.2	20.5		21.4		14.7	18.9	21.5
Intangibles (net)	7.4	7.6	8.9		7.0		.8	8.5	18.6
All Other Non-Current	6.4	8.2	7.8		6.2		3.3	4.8	7.6
Total	100.0	100.0	100.0		100.0		100.0	100.0	100.0
LIABILITIES									
Notes Payable-Short Term	10.2	9.5	8.9		10.0		7.4	12.9	7.6
Cur. Mat.-L.T.D.	2.5	2.6	3.3		1.1		2.5	2.7	2.5
Trade Payables	13.1	13.7	13.8		20.1		16.4	15.7	9.4
Income Taxes Payable	.2	.2	.1		.2		.1	.1	.1
All Other Current	7.2	5.9	6.3		5.9		5.5	9.3	6.8
Total Current	33.1	32.0	32.5		37.3		31.8	40.7	26.4
Long-Term Debt	13.8	16.2	19.1		34.7		8.6	15.0	24.1
Deferred Taxes	.6	.8	.8		.0		.2	1.1	1.7
All Other Non-Current	10.2	7.6	11.1		5.4		7.6	5.3	13.9
Net Worth	42.2	43.4	36.6		22.6		51.8	38.0	33.9
Total Liabilties & Net Worth	100.0	100.0	100.0		100.0		100.0	100.0	100.0
INCOME DATA									
Net Sales	100.0	100.0	100.0		100.0		100.0	100.0	100.0
Gross Profit	33.1	36.1	34.9		41.3		37.3	33.9	30.6
Operating Expenses	27.6	30.1	27.8		35.5		28.1	23.9	23.7
Operating Profit	5.5	6.0	7.1		5.8		9.2	10.0	6.9
All Other Expenses (net)	1.4	.9	1.2		-.4		.5	1.0	2.9
Profit Before Taxes	4.1	5.1	5.9		6.2		8.7	9.0	4.0
RATIOS									
Current	4.0	3.5	3.9		5.0		5.3	2.8	3.7
	2.4	2.1	2.0		1.9		3.1	1.7	2.1
	1.5	1.4	1.3		1.3		1.7	1.2	1.4
Quick	2.3	1.9	2.1		1.9		3.6	1.7	1.8
	1.0	.9	1.0		1.0		1.0	.8	1.0
	.6	.5	.5		.3		.7	.5	.5
Sales/Receivables	**30** 12.3	**26** 14.0	**28** 12.9		**9** 40.4		**29** 12.6	**31** 11.6	**31** 11.8
	39 9.3	**38** 9.7	**40** 9.1		**21** 17.4		**37** 9.9	**41** 8.9	**41** 8.8
	51 7.1	**49** 7.5	**53** 6.9		**42** 8.6		**57** 6.4	**48** 7.6	**54** 6.7
Cost of Sales/Inventory	**54** 6.8	**57** 6.4	**52** 7.0		**40** 9.2		**50** 7.3	**52** 7.0	**65** 5.6
	87 4.2	**94** 3.9	**91** 4.0		**87** 4.2		**96** 3.8	**68** 5.4	**94** 3.9
	146 2.5	**146** 2.5	**135** 2.7		**146** 2.5		**203** 1.8	**114** 3.2	**114** 3.2
Cost of Sales/Payables	**16** 22.2	**15** 23.9	**15** 24.0		**2** 153.8		**14** 25.5	**19** 19.2	**18** 20.8
	29 12.8	**27** 13.6	**27** 13.5		**20** 18.4		**25** 14.7	**30** 12.1	**29** 12.6
	45 8.1	**48** 7.6	**44** 8.3		**111** 3.3		**38** 9.6	**50** 7.3	**44** 8.3
Sales/Working Capital	3.4	4.3	4.0		6.0		2.6	4.1	4.3
	5.6	5.9	6.3		9.0		4.4	8.8	5.9
	9.6	10.6	17.1		19.1		6.2	22.1	10.1
EBIT/Interest	20.8	20.8	24.8				62.1	54.8	19.9
	(91) 5.1	(86) 9.7	(79) 5.0				(16) 21.9	(18) 9.3	(25) 3.7
	1.2	2.2	2.7				3.7	3.5	2.3
Net Profit + Depr., Dep., Amort./Cur. Mat. L/T/D	8.6	7.8	5.7						
	(24) 3.3	(23) 2.4	(17) 2.9						
	1.3	1.6	1.5						
Fixed/Worth	.1	.2	.3		.2		.0	.3	.4
	.4	.4	.5		1.2		.1	.5	.8
	1.5	1.4	10.5		-14.8		.6	2.9	-.8
Debt/Worth	.4	.5	.7		1.0		.6	.6	.7
	1.2	1.5	1.6		2.0		1.1	2.3	1.6
	4.3	4.2	28.9		-88.9		1.7	26.8	-3.5
% Profit Before Taxes/Tangible Net Worth	43.2	60.3	55.4				68.7	84.9	41.2
	(90) 18.8	(84) 28.4	(73) 25.9				35.1	(15) 34.3	(20) 20.2
	4.8	9.9	9.1				7.8	16.8	5.4
% Profit Before Taxes/Total Assets	14.3	20.6	21.3		21.0		33.4	21.4	14.1
	6.5	9.6	9.2		10.6		16.5	10.4	6.5
	.5	3.5	2.9		4.7		3.1	4.9	2.2
Sales/Net Fixed Assets	48.8	45.8	45.6		94.8		217.5	36.3	11.9
	11.7	12.2	11.4		37.4		23.0	14.0	10.4
	6.5	6.1	5.8		4.1		7.2	6.9	5.4
Sales/Total Assets	2.6	2.7	2.7		5.1		3.2	3.1	2.1
	1.8	2.1	1.7		2.7		2.3	2.2	1.4
	1.3	1.4	1.2		1.3		1.3	1.6	1.1
% Depr., Dep., Amort./Sales	1.0	1.0	.8				.5	.7	1.4
	(84) 1.8	(75) 1.9	(71) 2.2				(13) 1.9	(17) 1.7	(23) 2.6
	3.4	3.5	3.8				4.5	3.2	4.1
% Officers', Directors' Owners' Comp/Sales	1.6	2.6	3.1						
	(35) 3.6	(35) 4.3	(27) 4.2						
	9.6	6.3	6.3						
Net Sales ($)	3085425M	3199054M	3093079M	4828M	23201M	35737M	136265M	321702M	2571346M
Total Assets ($)	2313724M	2450948M	2441408M	7090M	11527M	21656M	71637M	169413M	2160085M

M = $ thousand MM = $ million

See Pages 9 through 22 for Explanation of Ratios and Data

Current Data Sorted by Assets							Comparative Historical Data	
						Type of Statement		
			2	1		Unqualified	7	7
	1	7	5			Reviewed	14	13
	2	7				Compiled	9	9
1	2	1	1			Tax Returns	6	9
	1	7	2		1	Other	21	17
	4 (4/1-9/30/13)		37 (10/1/13-3/31/14)				4/1/09-3/31/10 ALL	4/1/10-3/31/11 ALL
0-500M	500M-2MM	2-10MM	10-50MM	50-100MM	100-250MM			
1	6	22	10	1	1	**NUMBER OF STATEMENTS**	57	55
%	%	%	%	%	%	**ASSETS**	%	%
		11.4	12.1			Cash & Equivalents	9.0	9.9
		23.5	17.5			Trade Receivables (net)	22.2	23.6
		24.2	32.3			Inventory	27.4	27.9
		.6	1.6			All Other Current	3.8	2.0
		59.6	63.6			Total Current	62.3	63.3
		29.6	25.9			Fixed Assets (net)	27.6	26.9
		5.3	6.7			Intangibles (net)	5.7	3.9
		5.5	3.8			All Other Non-Current	4.5	5.9
		100.0	100.0			Total	100.0	100.0
						LIABILITIES		
		9.7	6.7			Notes Payable-Short Term	12.4	13.0
		2.8	1.6			Cur. Mat.-L.T.D.	4.2	2.8
		10.4	11.2			Trade Payables	9.1	10.1
		.2	.0			Income Taxes Payable	.3	.4
		7.3	4.0			All Other Current	5.6	7.8
		30.5	23.5			Total Current	31.7	34.0
		12.5	2.3			Long-Term Debt	15.9	20.9
		.2	.8			Deferred Taxes	.3	.7
		4.3	8.8			All Other Non-Current	7.5	8.9
		52.6	64.6			Net Worth	44.7	35.5
		100.0	100.0			Total Liabilties & Net Worth	100.0	100.0
						INCOME DATA		
		100.0	100.0			Net Sales	100.0	100.0
		34.7	23.9			Gross Profit	27.3	33.6
		24.3	18.1			Operating Expenses	23.5	25.1
		10.3	5.8			Operating Profit	3.9	8.5
		.7	-.1			All Other Expenses (net)	2.1	1.2
		9.7	5.9			Profit Before Taxes	1.8	7.3
						RATIOS		
		4.0	10.2				4.1	3.5
		2.5	3.2			Current	2.1	2.0
		1.2	1.4				1.3	1.4
		2.6	6.0				2.5	1.8
		1.3	1.6			Quick	1.0	1.0
		.6	.5				.5	.6
		30 12.3	**25** 14.7				**38** 9.6	**36** 10.2
		42 8.6	**39** 9.3			Sales/Receivables	**52** 7.0	**46** 7.9
		57 6.4	**47** 7.8				**66** 5.5	**53** 6.9
		45 8.2	**31** 11.6				**51** 7.1	**55** 6.6
		54 6.8	**63** 5.8			Cost of Sales/Inventory	**79** 4.6	**70** 5.2
		107 3.4	**146** 2.5				**118** 3.1	**104** 3.5
		15 23.7	**11** 32.0				**14** 26.8	**16** 23.4
		24 15.2	**24** 15.0			Cost of Sales/Payables	**27** 13.7	**23** 16.2
		43 8.5	**42** 8.7				**37** 9.8	**40** 9.1
		5.0	2.2				3.2	3.5
		5.5	4.9			Sales/Working Capital	5.9	6.3
		39.5	21.3				13.2	12.2
		194.2					7.7	14.8
		(21) 18.4				EBIT/Interest	(49) 1.6	(49) 5.1
		7.0					-.5	2.6
							7.5	10.4
						Net Profit + Depr., Dep., Amort./Cur. Mat. L/T/D	(16) 2.5	(12) 3.8
							.3	1.9
		.3	.2				.4	.3
		.6	.5			Fixed/Worth	.9	.7
		1.7	.9				1.7	4.2
		.4	.1				.4	.5
		.7	.3			Debt/Worth	2.1	1.6
		4.6	2.0				4.9	7.8
		98.3					19.8	45.0
		32.3				% Profit Before Taxes/Tangible Net Worth	(51) 4.6	(46) 25.2
		21.6					-14.2	13.0
		23.1	16.8				6.4	16.7
		14.2	11.2			% Profit Before Taxes/Total Assets	1.6	9.9
		8.5	1.3				-3.2	5.6
		13.4	72.3				11.5	18.7
		8.7	6.6			Sales/Net Fixed Assets	6.2	7.4
		4.7	3.6				3.4	4.0
		2.6	2.2				2.0	2.2
		1.9	1.7			Sales/Total Assets	1.5	1.7
		1.6	1.4				1.1	1.5
		1.6	1.3				2.1	1.1
		2.3	2.3			% Depr., Dep., Amort./Sales	(52) 3.1	(53) 3.0
		2.8	4.9				5.1	4.2
							3.6	2.0
						% Officers', Directors' Owners' Comp/Sales	(17) 6.9	(26) 3.6
							10.0	8.3
1372M	25328M	270784M	333858M	81886M	134303M	Net Sales ($)	902238M	1063334M
390M	8877M	132363M	202522M	51273M	241654M	Total Assets ($)	650162M	629124M

M = $ thousand MM = $ million

See Pages 9 through 22 for Explanation of Ratios and Data

Comparative Historical Data				Current Data Sorted by Sales					
			Type of Statement						
3	3	3	Unqualified					1	2
15	13	13	Reviewed		1		2	5	5
5	9	9	Compiled		1	2	3	3	
10	3	5	Tax Returns		1	1	1	1	1
18	19	11	Other			1	2	7	1
4/1/11-3/31/12 ALL	**4/1/12-3/31/13 ALL**	**4/1/13-3/31/14 ALL**			**4 (4/1-9/30/13)**		**37 (10/1/13-3/31/14)**		
				0-1MM	**1-3MM**	**3-5MM**	**5-10MM**	**10-25MM**	**25MM & OVER**
51	47	41	**NUMBER OF STATEMENTS**		3	4	8	17	9
%	%	%	**ASSETS**	%	%	%	%	%	%
9.4	7.9	11.3	Cash & Equivalents	**DATA NOT AVAILABLE**				10.9	
24.9	21.0	21.8	Trade Receivables (net)					22.3	
26.0	29.1	28.3	Inventory					31.5	
.9	.9	.8	All Other Current					1.2	
61.2	58.9	62.2	Total Current					65.9	
25.6	29.9	26.0	Fixed Assets (net)					28.2	
5.5	4.8	5.7	Intangibles (net)					.3	
7.7	6.3	6.1	All Other Non-Current					5.6	
100.0	100.0	100.0	Total					100.0	
			LIABILITIES						
8.1	10.6	8.7	Notes Payable-Short Term					12.5	
3.9	3.1	2.2	Cur. Mat.-L.T.D.					1.1	
11.2	10.2	11.4	Trade Payables					10.8	
.6	.8	.1	Income Taxes Payable					.2	
8.2	9.7	5.9	All Other Current					7.2	
32.0	34.4	28.2	Total Current					31.8	
19.8	13.4	9.5	Long-Term Debt					9.1	
.6	.6	.3	Deferred Taxes					.5	
6.9	8.7	7.5	All Other Non-Current					4.3	
40.8	42.9	54.5	Net Worth					54.3	
100.0	100.0	100.0	Total Liabilties & Net Worth					100.0	
			INCOME DATA						
100.0	100.0	100.0	Net Sales					100.0	
29.6	30.2	32.6	Gross Profit					31.3	
23.4	22.5	23.4	Operating Expenses					23.6	
6.2	7.7	9.1	Operating Profit					7.7	
.7	.8	.5	All Other Expenses (net)					.6	
5.5	7.0	8.6	Profit Before Taxes					7.1	
			RATIOS						
3.4	4.0	4.6						3.9	
1.9	2.0	2.5	Current					2.5	
1.3	1.3	1.4						1.2	
2.0	2.0	2.5						2.1	
1.2	1.1	1.5	Quick					1.2	
.8	.6	.6						.5	
33 10.9	**27** 13.5	**26** 14.0						**33** 10.9	
46 7.9	**36** 10.1	**40** 9.1	Sales/Receivables					**46** 8.0	
55 6.6	**51** 7.1	**51** 7.1						**61** 6.0	
38 9.5	**45** 8.1	**46** 7.9						**53** 6.9	
65 5.6	**68** 5.4	**61** 6.0	Cost of Sales/Inventory					**81** 4.5	
94 3.9	**114** 3.2	**107** 3.4						**122** 3.0	
13 27.7	**13** 28.5	**13** 27.4						**20** 18.1	
24 14.9	**21** 17.4	**24** 15.0	Cost of Sales/Payables					**30** 12.0	
35 10.5	**33** 11.2	**42** 8.6						**46** 8.0	
3.6	3.7	3.5						3.2	
6.9	6.8	5.5	Sales/Working Capital					5.4	
16.9	15.2	16.8						33.1	
21.4	27.2	108.8						108.8	
(47) 10.5	(43) 8.4	(36) 16.6	EBIT/Interest					(16) 21.8	
3.6	2.5	5.7						3.9	
17.1	10.6								
(16) 4.4	(12) 6.0		Net Profit + Depr., Dep., Amort./Cur. Mat. L/T/D						
2.9	2.9								
.3	.4	.3						.2	
.6	.6	.5	Fixed/Worth					.5	
1.5	2.1	1.1						1.5	
.4	.4	.2						.3	
1.2	1.2	.7	Debt/Worth					.5	
4.0	4.0	4.4						3.0	
48.6	43.6	72.1						41.5	
(47) 20.6	(41) 25.0	(40) 27.1	% Profit Before Taxes/Tangible Net Worth					19.6	
13.4	8.9	17.1						12.8	
15.9	18.3	21.9						18.9	
10.3	8.8	14.4	% Profit Before Taxes/Total Assets					13.8	
4.4	4.5	7.7						4.1	
14.8	11.0	16.5						15.2	
7.7	6.4	9.7	Sales/Net Fixed Assets					5.7	
4.5	4.4	4.7						3.7	
2.2	2.5	2.6						2.1	
1.8	1.9	2.0	Sales/Total Assets					1.7	
1.5	1.5	1.5						1.5	
1.7	1.5	1.0						1.1	
(44) 2.6	(45) 2.4	2.2	% Depr., Dep., Amort./Sales					1.8	
3.5	4.3	3.3						2.9	
2.1	3.9	1.7							
(18) 6.3	(11) 5.3	(14) 4.2	% Officers', Directors' Owners' Comp/Sales						
9.0	11.5	6.7							
1031784M	**1099157M**	**847531M**	Net Sales ($)		**5839M**	**17332M**	**55193M**	**267790M**	**501377M**
536802M	**680890M**	**637079M**	Total Assets ($)		**2676M**	**9451M**	**22393M**	**161371M**	**441188M**

M = $ thousand MM = $ million

See Pages 9 through 22 for Explanation of Ratios and Data

Current Data Sorted by Assets							Comparative Historical Data	
						Type of Statement		
		3	7	8	2	Unqualified	24	17
	3	16	10			Reviewed	33	35
	1	9	2			Compiled	14	8
1	6	6				Tax Returns	9	12
2	5	13	17	4	6	Other	52	54
	26 (4/1-9/30/13)		95 (10/1/13-3/31/14)				4/1/09-3/31/10	4/1/10-3/31/11
0-500M	500M-2MM	2-10MM	10-50MM	50-100MM	100-250MM		ALL	ALL
3	15	47	36	12	8	**NUMBER OF STATEMENTS**	132	126
%	%	%	%	%	%	**ASSETS**	%	%
	10.4	11.5	7.7	3.4		Cash & Equivalents	8.0	8.7
	24.1	29.7	26.0	21.6		Trade Receivables (net)	24.5	26.4
	30.3	30.5	28.8	27.1		Inventory	31.3	30.3
	.9	2.3	2.3	1.7		All Other Current	3.3	2.6
	65.6	74.0	64.9	53.9		Total Current	67.0	68.1
	28.4	17.7	27.5	34.8		Fixed Assets (net)	25.4	22.9
	1.1	4.0	3.5	7.2		Intangibles (net)	3.4	2.8
	4.9	4.3	4.1	4.0		All Other Non-Current	4.2	6.1
	100.0	100.0	100.0	100.0		Total	100.0	100.0
						LIABILITIES		
	10.6	11.8	12.5	8.0		Notes Payable-Short Term	13.8	13.0
	1.3	2.2	2.4	3.3		Cur. Mat.-L.T.D.	4.1	3.0
	12.9	18.5	14.3	10.5		Trade Payables	15.4	16.6
	.1	.1	.4	.0		Income Taxes Payable	.3	.2
	10.0	6.8	7.0	6.5		All Other Current	6.7	8.7
	35.0	39.5	36.5	28.2		Total Current	40.3	41.5
	10.2	7.9	16.3	26.2		Long-Term Debt	13.6	12.8
	.2	.2	.5	2.2		Deferred Taxes	.4	.4
	.3	10.5	4.9	3.5		All Other Non-Current	8.0	4.1
	54.4	42.0	41.8	40.0		Net Worth	37.7	41.3
	100.0	100.0	100.0	100.0		Total Liabilties & Net Worth	100.0	100.0
						INCOME DATA		
	100.0	100.0	100.0	100.0		Net Sales	100.0	100.0
	30.7	28.1	21.2	22.6		Gross Profit	23.8	26.0
	27.1	23.7	15.5	15.8		Operating Expenses	22.5	22.1
	3.6	4.4	5.7	6.8		Operating Profit	1.3	3.9
	-.2	.1	.7	.6		All Other Expenses (net)	1.1	.6
	3.8	4.3	4.9	6.3		Profit Before Taxes	.2	3.3
						RATIOS		
	4.1	4.0	2.5	3.6			2.6	2.9
	2.0	1.8	1.8	1.7		Current	1.8	1.6
	1.3	1.4	1.3	1.3			1.2	1.3
	1.7	2.5	1.5	1.1			1.3	1.3
	1.4	1.1	.9	.9		Quick	.8	.8
	.6	.7	.6	.8			.5	.5
	18 20.1	**33** 10.9	**36** 10.0	**39** 9.3			**32** 11.3	**34** 10.8
	26 14.0	**41** 9.0	**42** 8.7	**45** 8.2		Sales/Receivables	**43** 8.6	**43** 8.5
	43 8.4	**51** 7.1	**46** 7.9	**54** 6.8			**57** 6.4	**54** 6.8
	12 30.2	**41** 8.8	**41** 8.8	**51** 7.1			**43** 8.4	**35** 10.3
	38 9.6	**59** 6.2	**60** 6.1	**69** 5.3		Cost of Sales/Inventory	**75** 4.9	**65** 5.6
	135 2.7	**94** 3.9	**99** 3.7	**126** 2.9			**113** 3.2	**111** 3.3
	7 53.7	**19** 19.5	**15** 23.8	**23** 15.9			**17** 21.1	**18** 19.9
	21 17.8	**26** 14.1	**25** 14.6	**30** 12.3		Cost of Sales/Payables	**30** 12.3	**31** 11.7
	49 7.4	**49** 7.4	**38** 9.6	**38** 9.5			**47** 7.8	**49** 7.4
	6.1	4.7	4.9	3.0			4.0	4.4
	13.4	7.3	9.0	8.0		Sales/Working Capital	6.7	8.6
	28.1	13.4	21.8	16.4			27.5	19.6
	60.4	35.9	27.1	17.0			8.6	12.3
	10.5	(39) 4.4	(32) 6.0	(11) 8.7		EBIT/Interest	(123) 1.6	(112) 4.0
	2.1	2.1	2.1	3.6			-1.3	1.7
			9.9				3.6	11.4
			(13) 4.0			Net Profit + Depr., Dep., Amort./Cur. Mat. L/T/D	(38) 1.5	(37) 3.2
			2.2				.2	1.6
	.3	.2	.4	.6			.3	.2
	.6	.4	.8	1.5		Fixed/Worth	.6	.5
	1.0	.8	1.1	2.2			1.4	1.1
	.3	.4	.8	1.2			.6	.6
	.8	1.3	1.3	1.6		Debt/Worth	1.7	1.5
	1.4	6.2	2.7	7.3			3.9	4.1
	30.0	42.6	42.1	45.1			21.9	35.5
	(14) 12.6	(41) 23.4	(34) 26.1	(11) 18.2		% Profit Before Taxes/Tangible Net Worth	(115) 6.1	(112) 19.4
	1.9	7.9	9.5	11.4			-10.9	5.4
	13.9	18.8	18.7	12.4			8.5	12.7
	7.7	7.3	10.0	7.6		% Profit Before Taxes/Total Assets	1.5	6.5
	1.5	3.4	1.9	5.1			-7.2	1.2
	44.2	45.0	19.4	9.0			17.9	23.7
	9.5	20.3	7.2	6.1		Sales/Net Fixed Assets	8.4	10.4
	4.8	9.4	4.9	3.3			4.4	5.2
	4.1	3.0	2.7	2.5			2.4	2.8
	2.5	2.3	2.1	1.5		Sales/Total Assets	1.8	2.0
	1.8	1.9	1.6	1.2			1.4	1.5
	.5	.6	1.1	2.3			1.5	1.1
	(12) 1.1	(42) 1.5	1.5	2.7		% Depr., Dep., Amort./Sales	(113) 2.4	(112) 2.0
	2.2	2.3	2.2	4.5			4.0	2.9
	2.3	1.6	2.6				2.0	2.8
	(10) 5.8	(16) 3.3	(10) 4.3			% Officers', Directors' Owners' Comp/Sales	(42) 3.0	(43) 5.3
	10.2	5.7	5.9				7.9	8.3
2289M	**65130M**	**609347M**	**1747140M**	**1516609M**	**1412572M**	Net Sales ($)	**4196284M**	**8333343M**
762M	**18248M**	**252820M**	**776589M**	**886756M**	**1270956M**	Total Assets ($)	**2581220M**	**2088308M**

M = $ thousand MM = $ million

See Pages 9 through 22 for Explanation of Ratios and Data

Comparative Historical Data							Current Data Sorted by Sales								
						Type of Statement									
	27		22		20	Unqualified							5		15
	28		21		29	Reviewed		2	1		6		14		6
	15		13		12	Compiled		1	1		5		4		1
	16		12		13	Tax Returns	2	4	2				5		
	46		47		47	Other	2	1	3		6		9		26
	4/1/11-3/31/12 ALL		**4/1/12-3/31/13 ALL**		**4/1/13-3/31/14 ALL**		**26 (4/1-9/30/13)**			**95 (10/1/13-3/31/14)**					
							0-1MM	**1-3MM**	**3-5MM**		**5-10MM**		**10-25MM**		**25MM & OVER**
	132		115		121	**NUMBER OF STATEMENTS**	4	8	7		17		37		48
	%		%		%	**ASSETS**	%	%	%		%		%		%
	9.7		8.4		9.0	Cash & Equivalents					5.9		13.1		6.0
	28.6		26.8		26.2	Trade Receivables (net)					30.4		28.8		24.3
	31.0		32.1		28.1	Inventory					29.3		28.8		27.4
	2.0		1.6		2.0	All Other Current					1.6		2.8		2.1
	71.2		68.9		65.3	Total Current					67.2		73.5		59.7
	21.4		21.9		25.1	Fixed Assets (net)					21.6		20.3		29.1
	2.5		4.3		4.5	Intangibles (net)					7.0		3.8		5.6
	4.9		4.9		5.1	All Other Non-Current					4.2		2.4		5.5
	100.0		100.0		100.0	Total					100.0		100.0		100.0
						LIABILITIES									
	14.8		12.6		11.2	Notes Payable-Short Term					12.4		11.1		10.6
	2.5		2.4		2.4	Cur. Mat.-L.T.D.					2.4		2.4		2.3
	16.0		14.4		15.0	Trade Payables					13.7		16.7		13.4
	.1		.2		.2	Income Taxes Payable					.9		.1		.0
	9.5		6.7		7.6	All Other Current					5.1		7.7		7.1
	43.0		36.3		36.5	Total Current					34.4		38.2		33.4
	13.5		14.5		15.9	Long-Term Debt					4.1		13.3		19.4
	.4		.4		.6	Deferred Taxes					.3		.1		1.2
	6.4		8.3		8.5	All Other Non-Current					12.8		9.8		4.5
	36.7		40.5		38.6	Net Worth					48.4		38.6		41.6
	100.0		100.0		100.0	Total Liabilties & Net Worth					100.0		100.0		100.0
						INCOME DATA									
	100.0		100.0		100.0	Net Sales					100.0		100.0		100.0
	27.9		25.7		26.8	Gross Profit					25.7		25.7		22.6
	22.4		20.9		21.9	Operating Expenses					23.5		21.1		16.0
	5.4		4.8		4.9	Operating Profit					2.2		4.6		6.6
	.6		.9		.5	All Other Expenses (net)					.3		.7		.8
	4.9		3.9		4.3	Profit Before Taxes					1.9		3.9		5.8
						RATIOS									
	2.8		3.5		3.3						4.4		4.5		2.5
	1.7		1.9		1.8	Current					2.0		1.8		1.8
	1.3		1.4		1.3						1.4		1.3		1.3
	1.5		1.6		1.6						2.0		2.3		1.2
	.9		.9		.9	Quick					1.5		1.1		.9
	.6		.6		.6						.6		.7		.6
31	11.6	**33**	11.2	**33**	11.0					**33**	11.1	**33**	10.9	**38**	9.5
42	8.6	**40**	9.1	**41**	9.0	Sales/Receivables				**41**	9.0	**40**	9.1	**43**	8.4
58	6.3	**49**	7.4	**49**	7.5					**52**	7.0	**51**	7.1	**49**	7.5
39	9.4	**40**	9.1	**38**	9.5					**32**	11.3	**36**	10.0	**43**	8.4
74	4.9	**72**	5.1	**60**	6.1	Cost of Sales/Inventory				**60**	6.1	**54**	6.8	**61**	6.0
107	3.4	**107**	3.4	**99**	3.7					**104**	3.5	**91**	4.0	**91**	4.0
16	23.5	**16**	22.5	**17**	21.6					**14**	27.0	**16**	23.2	**18**	20.5
31	11.6	**29**	12.8	**27**	13.3	Cost of Sales/Payables				**24**	15.4	**26**	14.1	**29**	12.8
45	8.1	**41**	8.9	**41**	8.8					**50**	7.3	**40**	9.1	**39**	9.3
	4.7		4.0		4.9						5.1		4.2		4.9
	8.1		6.8		8.4	Sales/Working Capital					7.3		7.8		8.7
	20.2		14.6		18.0						13.4		20.9		16.5
	18.5		17.5		26.2						13.4		38.0		25.8
(118)	6.3	(101)	4.9	(106)	5.2	EBIT/Interest				(16)	3.6	(31)	5.4	(43)	7.3
	1.8		1.8		2.3						.6		2.1		2.7
	10.6		12.4		6.9										5.9
(36)	4.2	(35)	3.1	(35)	4.0	Net Profit + Depr., Dep., Amort./Cur. Mat. L/T/D								(22)	4.0
	1.7		1.4		2.2										2.1
	.2		.2		.3						.3		.2		.4
	.5		.6		.6	Fixed/Worth					.5		.5		.8
	1.1		1.2		1.5						1.0		1.8		1.6
	.5		.6		.6						.3		.4		.9
	1.6		1.5		1.4	Debt/Worth					1.0		1.6		1.4
	3.5		3.1		4.2						4.2		9.1		3.1
	36.6		32.8		39.4						35.5		62.8		44.0
(118)	21.7	(99)	17.4	(106)	19.8	% Profit Before Taxes/Tangible Net Worth				(15)	6.6	(32)	24.2	(44)	25.4
	7.1		3.6		8.4						-.2		8.5		10.9
	16.1		14.6		16.0						8.3		18.7		15.6
	7.8		6.5		7.3	% Profit Before Taxes/Total Assets					3.9		7.0		9.2
	1.7		1.6		3.0						-1.5		2.6		4.0
	40.1		33.7		29.6						35.5		45.9		11.6
	11.2		11.1		9.5	Sales/Net Fixed Assets					11.6		20.2		6.9
	6.3		5.6		5.0						5.3		6.5		4.8
	2.7		2.8		2.9						3.1		3.5		2.6
	2.1		2.2		2.2	Sales/Total Assets					2.4		2.3		2.0
	1.6		1.5		1.5						1.9		1.8		1.4
	.9		.7		.8						.8		.5		1.2
(113)	1.6	(103)	1.5	(110)	1.7	% Depr., Dep., Amort./Sales				(16)	1.6	(33)	1.3	(46)	2.1
	2.9		2.7		2.8						2.7		2.1		3.5
	2.2		1.8		2.0								2.1		1.5
(48)	3.6	(37)	4.0	(40)	4.7	% Officers', Directors' Owners' Comp/Sales						(12)	3.7	(10)	3.2
	7.3		6.8		6.3								5.7		5.9
	4431253M		5357107M		5353087M	Net Sales ($)	3243M	18950M	29667M		124568M		641298M		4535361M
	2314689M		2973903M		3206131M	Total Assets ($)	1399M	12405M	16127M		64858M		286915M		2824427M

M = $ thousand MM = $ million

See Pages 9 through 22 for Explanation of Ratios and Data

Current Data Sorted by Assets | **Comparative Historical Data**

	0-500M	500M-2MM	2-10MM	10-50MM	50-100MM	100-250MM	4/1/09-3/31/10 ALL	4/1/10-3/31/11 ALL
Type of Statement								
Unqualified		1	11	17	4		38	32
Reviewed		14	65	35		1	141	156
Compiled	5	54	84	5	1		155	175
Tax Returns	54	95	55	3		1	170	220
Other	15	74	114	49	7	4	245	301
	145 (4/1-9/30/13)			623 (10/1/13-3/31/14)				
NUMBER OF STATEMENTS	74	238	329	109	12	6	749	884
ASSETS	%	%	%	%	%	%	%	%
Cash & Equivalents	15.3	14.6	10.3	7.4	4.4		10.3	10.5
Trade Receivables (net)	29.0	28.0	22.6	21.2	22.1		21.9	25.6
Inventory	10.6	14.8	19.7	20.8	21.9		18.3	17.8
All Other Current	1.7	1.2	1.6	3.7	6.0		2.1	1.8
Total Current	56.6	58.7	54.2	53.1	54.5		52.6	55.7
Fixed Assets (net)	35.5	32.2	38.4	37.1	40.0		38.0	35.2
Intangibles (net)	3.0	3.3	2.8	5.3	1.6		3.5	3.6
All Other Non-Current	4.9	5.8	4.6	4.5	4.0		5.9	5.5
Total	100.0	100.0	100.0	100.0	100.0		100.0	100.0
LIABILITIES								
Notes Payable-Short Term	22.0	7.6	6.7	7.3	9.0		10.0	9.1
Cur. Mat.-L.T.D.	11.2	5.9	5.0	4.6	4.6		6.3	6.8
Trade Payables	12.5	10.8	9.9	10.1	13.2		10.1	10.8
Income Taxes Payable	.1	.1	.3	.1	1.1		.2	.1
All Other Current	9.5	8.2	5.9	6.9	8.7		7.7	6.5
Total Current	55.4	32.6	27.8	29.0	36.5		34.2	33.3
Long-Term Debt	45.5	29.4	22.6	20.3	24.1		26.0	24.4
Deferred Taxes	.0	.3	.6	1.1	.6		.6	.6
All Other Non-Current	7.9	5.9	5.7	5.0	12.6		7.0	5.8
Net Worth	-8.8	31.9	43.2	44.6	26.2		32.3	35.9
Total Liabilties & Net Worth	100.0	100.0	100.0	100.0	100.0		100.0	100.0
INCOME DATA								
Net Sales	100.0	100.0	100.0	100.0	100.0		100.0	100.0
Gross Profit	54.4	41.6	33.0	24.9	13.8		34.7	36.7
Operating Expenses	50.8	35.5	26.6	16.4	9.0		31.6	29.9
Operating Profit	3.7	6.1	6.4	8.5	4.8		3.0	6.8
All Other Expenses (net)	.8	.7	.8	.6	1.5		1.5	1.3
Profit Before Taxes	2.8	5.4	5.6	7.9	3.3		1.5	5.6
RATIOS								
	3.4	3.7	3.5	2.9	2.0		3.2	3.3
Current	1.6	1.9	2.1	1.9	1.5		1.6	1.7
	.6	1.1	1.3	1.2	1.1		1.0	1.1
	2.8	2.8	2.4	1.5	1.1		2.1	2.2
Quick	1.3	1.3	1.2	1.0	.7		1.0	1.1
	.5	.7	.7	.6	.4		.5	.6
	5 72.8	**25** 14.6	**33** 11.0	**35** 10.3	**23** 15.6		**29** 12.6	**33** 11.2
Sales/Receivables	**30** 12.2	**40** 9.2	**46** 8.0	**47** 7.8	**44** 8.3		**43** 8.5	**47** 7.8
	44 8.3	**55** 6.6	**57** 6.4	**63** 5.8	**65** 5.6		**58** 6.2	**61** 6.0
	0 UND	**2** 171.8	**21** 17.0	**35** 10.4	**29** 12.4		**14** 25.5	**13** 28.1
Cost of Sales/Inventory	**2** 202.8	**21** 17.3	**46** 7.9	**54** 6.7	**43** 8.4		**45** 8.0	**43** 8.4
	30 12.1	**63** 5.8	**91** 4.0	**96** 3.8	**61** 6.0		**91** 4.0	**84** 4.3
	0 UND	**11** 31.8	**15** 24.5	**17** 22.1	**21** 17.7		**13** 28.7	**13** 27.5
Cost of Sales/Payables	**18** 20.5	**21** 17.2	**25** 14.5	**26** 14.3	**27** 13.4		**23** 15.9	**27** 13.6
	36 10.1	**34** 10.7	**40** 9.2	**39** 9.3	**33** 11.0		**42** 8.8	**41** 9.0
	8.5	5.3	4.2	3.8	5.1		4.5	4.7
Sales/Working Capital	25.2	8.4	6.9	6.5	9.3		9.6	9.1
	-22.1	63.2	17.3	18.4	NM		160.3	42.3
	13.8	15.1	17.4	21.3	14.3		6.6	12.5
EBIT/Interest	(61) 2.5	(221) 4.8	(312) 6.4	(105) 10.3	6.5		(686) 2.0	(802) 4.2
	-2.2	1.3	1.8	2.8	2.3		-.7	1.5
		4.0	4.4	5.4			3.3	4.5
Net Profit + Depr., Dep., Amort./Cur. Mat. L/T/D		(25) 1.7	(66) 2.4	(37) 2.9			(151) 1.6	(151) 2.0
		1.2	1.5	1.6			.4	1.2
	.7	.4	.5	.6	.8		.5	.4
Fixed/Worth	2.9	.9	.9	.9	1.2		1.1	1.0
	-.7	5.1	2.1	1.7	2.5		3.5	2.6
	1.1	.6	.6	.6	1.5		.7	.6
Debt/Worth	6.1	1.7	1.3	1.2	2.5		1.9	1.6
	-3.2	10.5	3.7	2.7	4.1		7.4	5.4
	74.2	56.7	46.5	40.4	34.6		35.5	47.4
% Profit Before Taxes/Tangible Net Worth	(44) 27.9	(188) 25.4	(300) 20.9	(99) 20.9	(11) 19.0		(618) 8.9	(750) 20.6
	8.3	6.0	5.5	12.2	13.3		-7.0	5.8
	20.8	22.4	17.8	15.1	11.2		12.4	18.3
% Profit Before Taxes/Total Assets	8.7	8.9	7.9	10.4	6.5		3.0	7.5
	-7.6	1.6	1.4	3.9	2.7		-4.6	1.3
	43.8	20.1	9.0	6.0	8.3		10.4	12.7
Sales/Net Fixed Assets	16.8	9.5	4.6	4.4	6.7		4.9	6.1
	6.9	4.5	2.8	2.7	3.2		2.8	3.3
	6.3	3.3	2.2	2.0	2.5		2.4	2.6
Sales/Total Assets	4.0	2.4	1.7	1.5	2.0		1.7	1.9
	2.7	1.7	1.3	1.1	1.5		1.2	1.4
	1.3	1.6	2.5	2.5	2.0		2.3	2.2
% Depr., Dep., Amort./Sales	(46) 2.6	(175) 3.6	(293) 4.4	(106) 4.2	3.0		(682) 4.5	(756) 4.0
	4.5	6.1	7.8	6.3	5.0		7.6	6.4
	4.4	3.8	2.2	1.0			2.7	2.8
% Officers', Directors' Owners' Comp/Sales	(55) 8.0	(157) 5.6	(163) 3.5	(34) 1.9			(405) 5.4	(463) 5.1
	12.4	7.9	5.8	3.2			9.2	9.4
Net Sales ($)	92448M	742929M	2616368M	3754612M	1670721M	981040M	8498431M	10198177M
Total Assets ($)	20605M	287221M	1472200M	2346509M	775866M	744075M	5087063M	6166129M

M = $ thousand MM = $ million

See Pages 9 through 22 for Explanation of Ratios and Data

Comparative Historical Data | Current Data Sorted by Sales

			Type of Statement						
33	34	33	Unqualified			3	6	10	14
146	121	115	Reviewed		7	19	38	33	18
164	141	149	Compiled	6	37	41	41	18	6
242	206	208	Tax Returns	35	66	51	43	9	4
320	285	263	Other	12	54	44	66	48	39
4/1/11-3/31/12	4/1/12-3/31/13	4/1/13-3/31/14		145 (4/1-9/30/13)			623 (10/1/13-3/31/14)		
ALL	ALL	ALL		0-1MM	1-3MM	3-5MM	5-10MM	10-25MM	25MM & OVER
905	787	768	NUMBER OF STATEMENTS	53	164	158	194	118	81
%	%	%	ASSETS	%	%	%	%	%	%
11.4	12.6	11.6	Cash & Equivalents	10.9	15.7	12.1	11.1	9.2	7.6
26.0	24.6	24.7	Trade Receivables (net)	21.5	24.5	27.3	24.3	24.0	23.8
17.9	17.5	17.5	Inventory	13.0	13.3	16.4	19.0	20.7	23.1
2.0	1.9	1.9	All Other Current	2.1	.6	1.3	2.3	2.6	3.1
57.3	56.6	55.7	Total Current	47.4	54.1	57.1	56.7	56.6	57.7
33.6	34.9	36.0	Fixed Assets (net)	40.6	37.0	34.8	35.3	36.2	34.4
3.8	3.4	3.4	Intangibles (net)	6.3	2.9	2.8	3.1	3.0	4.9
5.3	5.1	5.0	All Other Non-Current	5.7	6.0	5.3	4.9	4.3	3.0
100.0	100.0	100.0	Total	100.0	100.0	100.0	100.0	100.0	100.0
			LIABILITIES						
10.7	8.3	8.6	Notes Payable-Short Term	24.5	8.2	7.9	6.7	7.4	6.5
5.3	5.2	5.8	Cur. Mat.-L.T.D.	12.4	5.3	5.7	5.7	4.7	4.6
11.6	10.2	10.5	Trade Payables	7.1	9.2	10.5	11.8	11.0	11.5
.2	.1	.2	Income Taxes Payable	.0	.1	.1	.1	.5	.2
7.5	8.1	7.2	All Other Current	9.4	6.9	7.7	6.2	7.4	7.2
35.3	32.0	32.2	Total Current	53.4	29.6	32.0	30.4	31.0	30.1
24.5	25.1	26.6	Long-Term Debt	46.6	34.2	26.4	23.5	18.2	18.2
.5	.5	.5	Deferred Taxes	.1	.2	.4	.7	.8	.7
6.6	5.5	6.0	All Other Non-Current	7.3	4.1	8.3	6.5	4.6	5.3
33.1	37.0	34.7	Net Worth	-7.4	31.9	32.9	38.9	45.4	45.7
100.0	100.0	100.0	Total Liabilties & Net Worth	100.0	100.0	100.0	100.0	100.0	100.0
			INCOME DATA						
100.0	100.0	100.0	Net Sales	100.0	100.0	100.0	100.0	100.0	100.0
36.8	36.7	36.3	Gross Profit	56.3	45.0	36.4	33.7	29.2	21.6
29.0	28.3	29.9	Operating Expenses	53.3	39.1	31.1	26.6	21.8	13.7
7.7	8.3	6.3	Operating Profit	2.9	5.9	5.3	7.1	7.4	7.9
.9	.8	.7	All Other Expenses (net)	1.6	.7	.7	.7	.4	.6
6.8	7.5	5.6	Profit Before Taxes	1.3	5.2	4.6	6.4	7.0	7.3
			RATIOS						
3.3	3.6	3.4		3.1	5.0	3.4	3.3	3.5	2.9
1.7	2.0	1.9	Current	1.7	2.2	1.9	1.9	2.1	1.8
1.1	1.2	1.2		.6	1.1	1.2	1.3	1.2	1.3
2.2	2.6	2.3		2.1	3.5	2.4	2.3	2.1	1.4
1.1	1.2	1.2	Quick	.8	1.5	1.3	1.2	1.1	1.0
.6	.7	.7		.4	.7	.7	.7	.6	.7
31 11.9	28 13.0	30 12.2		14 25.4	25 14.5	28 13.0	32 11.3	37 9.9	34 10.6
43 8.4	41 8.8	43 8.5	Sales/Receivables	34 10.7	39 9.4	42 8.6	43 8.4	46 7.9	47 7.8
57 6.4	56 6.5	56 6.5		50 7.3	55 6.6	56 6.5	55 6.6	57 6.4	60 6.1
8 44.7	9 42.0	10 37.7		0 UND	0 UND	5 78.7	21 17.7	25 14.5	36 10.0
38 9.6	37 9.9	37 9.8	Cost of Sales/Inventory	14 26.4	26 14.2	25 14.6	42 8.6	49 7.5	50 7.3
79 4.6	73 5.0	83 4.4		83 4.4	72 5.1	70 5.2	87 4.2	89 4.1	78 4.7
13 27.1	11 31.9	13 27.5		0 UND	10 36.2	12 31.5	16 22.5	14 26.5	17 20.9
25 14.5	22 16.9	24 15.3	Cost of Sales/Payables	19 19.4	21 17.3	22 16.7	26 14.1	26 14.3	26 14.2
43 8.5	36 10.1	38 9.6		43 8.4	36 10.2	38 9.5	41 9.0	39 9.3	33 11.0
4.9	4.8	4.6		5.9	4.5	5.0	4.6	4.0	4.3
9.9	8.8	8.2	Sales/Working Capital	18.0	8.2	8.2	7.8	6.5	7.2
46.2	25.5	27.5		-13.3	58.2	48.2	19.0	22.5	17.4
17.7	17.3	17.1		9.6	11.8	14.1	20.1	22.0	21.7
(817) 6.0	(717) 6.4	(716) 6.1	EBIT/Interest	(45) 1.3	(147) 4.2	(151) 4.9	(187) 6.2	(108) 8.8	(78) 12.5
1.9	2.4	1.7		-3.9	1.0	1.3	2.1	2.7	4.8
4.3	4.8	4.5			4.6	2.4	4.4	5.4	7.0
(146) 2.3	(134) 2.5	(134) 2.4	Net Profit + Depr., Dep., Amort./Cur. Mat. L/T/D		(11) 1.9	(27) 1.9	(35) 2.4	(35) 3.4	(25) 3.7
1.3	1.2	1.5			1.4	1.1	1.4	1.7	1.8
.4	.4	.4		.9	.4	.4	.4	.4	.4
.9	.9	.9	Fixed/Worth	4.8	1.0	1.0	.9	.8	.8
2.9	2.4	2.7		-.6	44.9	2.6	2.3	1.8	1.3
.6	.6	.6		1.1	.6	.7	.7	.5	.6
1.6	1.6	1.5	Debt/Worth	9.3	1.5	1.6	1.5	1.2	1.3
6.5	5.2	5.1		-3.0	289.8	4.8	4.0	3.0	2.5
54.2	61.4	50.1		68.1	50.0	51.7	56.4	49.7	38.4
(744) 27.2	(681) 30.3	(647) 21.7	% Profit Before Taxes/Tangible Net Worth	(30) 12.7	(124) 20.8	(133) 19.0	(174) 22.3	(111) 20.4	(75) 24.5
11.7	9.9	7.2		-5.9	3.8	5.3	7.3	9.0	15.5
21.5	24.5	18.7		17.2	18.8	21.7	21.2	18.2	15.3
10.4	10.6	9.0	% Profit Before Taxes/Total Assets	5.0	8.0	7.5	9.9	10.1	10.7
3.0	3.4	1.8		-12.8	.2	1.3	2.2	2.9	5.6
16.2	15.4	13.6		17.9	17.4	18.4	13.3	8.8	7.7
6.8	6.7	5.9	Sales/Net Fixed Assets	8.2	6.3	7.2	5.9	4.7	5.3
3.8	3.5	3.2		2.5	3.1	3.2	3.3	2.9	3.7
2.9	2.9	2.7		4.3	3.0	3.2	2.6	2.3	2.4
2.1	2.0	2.0	Sales/Total Assets	2.4	2.0	2.1	1.9	1.8	1.9
1.5	1.5	1.4		1.3	1.4	1.4	1.4	1.3	1.5
1.9	1.8	2.2		1.4	2.5	1.9	2.2	2.5	2.1
(705) 3.5	(635) 3.4	(635) 4.0	% Depr., Dep., Amort./Sales	(40) 3.5	(117) 4.3	(128) 3.9	(170) 4.0	(103) 3.8	(77) 3.6
5.8	5.9	6.7		7.1	7.8	7.2	7.1	6.5	5.1
2.5	2.5	2.6		4.9	3.9	3.5	2.1	1.7	.5
(480) 4.6	(424) 4.7	(410) 4.5	% Officers', Directors' Owners' Comp/Sales	(35) 8.4	(111) 5.9	(88) 5.3	(108) 3.2	(48) 2.9	(20) 1.2
7.9	8.2	7.4		16.4	9.2	6.7	5.6	4.6	2.9
11231150M	9286639M	9858118M	Net Sales ($)	35242M	332337M	631724M	1365011M	1841127M	5652677M
6222225M	5287442M	5646476M	Total Assets ($)	17639M	190347M	341528M	781619M	1154851M	3160492M

M = $ thousand MM = $ million

See Pages 9 through 22 for Explanation of Ratios and Data

Current Data Sorted by Assets | **Comparative Historical Data**

	0-500M	500M-2MM	2-10MM	10-50MM	50-100MM	100-250MM	4/1/09-3/31/10 ALL	4/1/10-3/31/11 ALL
Type of Statement								
Unqualified			1	5	2	2	14	13
Reviewed		1	34	18	1		56	59
Compiled		8	23	4			35	45
Tax Returns	3	10	9	2		1	21	20
Other		12	31	27	2	6	48	64
		42 (4/1-9/30/13)		160 (10/1/13-3/31/14)				
NUMBER OF STATEMENTS	3	31	98	56	5	9	174	201
ASSETS	%	%	%	%	%	%	%	%
Cash & Equivalents		13.5	11.7	4.9			7.7	7.6
Trade Receivables (net)		21.3	22.6	21.1			20.5	25.2
Inventory		19.0	25.4	21.6			24.1	25.0
All Other Current		.7	1.1	2.1			1.8	1.0
Total Current		54.6	60.7	49.7			54.2	58.7
Fixed Assets (net)		41.0	33.0	39.6			37.1	32.5
Intangibles (net)		1.9	1.5	5.1			3.2	3.5
All Other Non-Current		2.5	4.8	5.6			5.5	5.3
Total		100.0	100.0	100.0			100.0	100.0
LIABILITIES								
Notes Payable-Short Term		7.1	7.1	9.1			10.2	9.2
Cur. Mat.-L.T.D.		6.4	4.8	5.6			7.4	5.8
Trade Payables		9.5	10.6	12.1			10.8	13.3
Income Taxes Payable		.4	.4	.1			.2	.2
All Other Current		3.5	5.2	5.4			6.1	7.3
Total Current		26.9	28.1	32.3			34.8	35.9
Long-Term Debt		31.2	17.4	19.4			22.3	19.6
Deferred Taxes		.4	1.1	1.6			.8	.7
All Other Non-Current		6.0	5.9	5.7			8.4	5.7
Net Worth		35.5	47.5	40.9			33.7	38.1
Total Liabilties & Net Worth		100.0	100.0	100.0			100.0	100.0
INCOME DATA								
Net Sales		100.0	100.0	100.0			100.0	100.0
Gross Profit		41.0	26.4	22.2			28.0	28.0
Operating Expenses		34.2	20.1	15.2			26.3	22.8
Operating Profit		6.7	6.3	7.0			1.8	5.2
All Other Expenses (net)		.7	.5	1.2			1.6	1.2
Profit Before Taxes		6.1	5.8	5.8			.2	4.0
RATIOS								
Current		4.1	3.6	2.9			2.6	2.6
		1.8	2.3	1.6			1.6	1.6
		1.0	1.5	1.1			1.1	1.2
Quick		2.4	2.2	1.6			1.5	1.5
		1.0	1.2	.7			(173) .8	.9
		.6	.7	.5			.4	.5
Sales/Receivables		22 16.7	33 10.9	42 8.6			30 12.1	36 10.3
		39 9.3	42 8.7	53 6.9			44 8.3	49 7.5
		51 7.2	54 6.8	58 6.3			59 6.2	61 6.0
Cost of Sales/Inventory		12 30.3	41 9.0	41 8.8			42 8.7	35 10.5
		34 10.7	69 5.3	68 5.4			66 5.5	59 6.2
		83 4.4	96 3.8	94 3.9			106 3.4	98 3.7
Cost of Sales/Payables		15 25.0	13 27.7	25 14.7			13 27.6	20 18.2
		26 14.2	24 15.1	37 9.9			27 13.6	32 11.2
		43 8.5	35 10.5	47 7.7			48 7.6	45 8.1
Sales/Working Capital		4.5	3.9	4.4			4.6	4.9
		10.2	6.2	8.1			8.4	10.0
		-999.8	12.0	53.2			46.4	21.0
EBIT/Interest		9.8	17.8	16.7			3.6	11.5
		(27) 3.9	(95) 6.1	4.8			(162) .7	(192) 3.8
		1.6	2.0	2.2			-2.1	1.4
Net Profit + Depr., Dep., Amort./Cur. Mat. L/T/D			3.7	5.6			3.1	3.9
			(29) 2.4	(21) 2.3			(51) 1.3	(65) 1.8
			1.6	2.1			.5	1.2
Fixed/Worth		.6	.4	.7			.6	.5
		1.0	.8	1.3			1.2	.9
		3.8	1.3	1.7			2.6	1.7
Debt/Worth		.9	.5	.9			.8	.8
		2.0	1.1	1.9			1.8	1.5
		8.0	2.1	3.0			6.2	3.7
% Profit Before Taxes/Tangible Net Worth		42.9	38.5	42.5			21.2	41.3
		(25) 23.9	(94) 17.2	(53) 20.8			(145) 1.3	(183) 17.4
		3.6	5.8	8.7			-17.0	3.2
% Profit Before Taxes/Total Assets		17.8	15.0	14.2			7.7	14.5
		7.7	7.7	7.4			.3	6.1
		2.8	2.0	2.7			-7.0	.5
Sales/Net Fixed Assets		14.7	10.7	6.3			9.3	11.8
		5.4	5.7	3.5			4.6	6.1
		2.9	3.4	2.5			2.8	3.6
Sales/Total Assets		3.6	2.4	2.0			2.1	2.4
		2.1	1.7	1.5			1.6	1.8
		1.4	1.5	1.1			1.2	1.4
% Depr., Dep., Amort./Sales		1.8	2.1	2.6			3.2	2.2
		(26) 4.5	(91) 3.8	4.0			(155) 5.1	(181) 4.0
		7.2	5.2	6.3			7.2	6.3
% Officers', Directors' Owners' Comp/Sales		4.8	1.8	1.1			1.9	1.8
		(21) 6.0	(48) 3.1	(16) 1.9			(90) 4.2	(90) 3.6
		9.4	5.2	3.3			8.1	6.1
Net Sales ($)	3907M	85218M	947766M	1870470M	468362M	2329132M	2094630M	3163788M
Total Assets ($)	822M	35818M	502886M	1269066M	338812M	1385054M	1572376M	1856429M

M = $ thousand MM = $ million

See Pages 9 through 22 for Explanation of Ratios and Data

Comparative Historical Data				Current Data Sorted by Sales					
			Type of Statement						
10	12	10	Unqualified					1	9
58	44	54	Reviewed			3	20	22	9
37	39	35	Compiled	3	4	6	12	9	1
25	29	25	Tax Returns	2	6	4	5	5	3
69	74	78	Other	1	7	9	11	25	25
4/1/11-3/31/12 ALL	**4/1/12-3/31/13 ALL**	**4/1/13-3/31/14 ALL**		**42 (4/1-9/30/13)**			**160 (10/1/13-3/31/14)**		
				0-1MM	**1-3MM**	**3-5MM**	**5-10MM**	**10-25MM**	**25MM & OVER**
199	198	202	**NUMBER OF STATEMENTS**	6	17	22	48	62	47
%	%	%	**ASSETS**	%	%	%	%	%	%
8.2	8.4	10.2	Cash & Equivalents		15.7	14.4	11.3	9.0	6.6
24.4	22.4	21.6	Trade Receivables (net)		17.8	19.4	22.4	23.0	21.7
24.2	24.1	22.6	Inventory		21.8	19.2	26.0	23.3	21.6
1.9	1.8	1.3	All Other Current		.1	1.0	1.2	1.8	1.6
58.7	56.7	55.7	Total Current		55.4	54.0	60.8	57.0	51.4
31.4	33.9	35.6	Fixed Assets (net)		35.2	38.9	33.1	37.0	32.1
4.5	4.2	4.1	Intangibles (net)		6.2	1.5	.8	2.0	11.2
5.3	5.2	4.6	All Other Non-Current		3.2	5.7	5.4	3.9	5.3
100.0	100.0	100.0	Total		100.0	100.0	100.0	100.0	100.0
			LIABILITIES						
8.9	8.1	7.5	Notes Payable-Short Term		8.7	6.1	6.1	9.2	7.6
5.1	5.0	5.5	Cur. Mat.-L.T.D.		6.0	6.2	4.8	5.1	6.4
12.7	11.7	10.6	Trade Payables		7.9	7.6	11.0	11.1	12.4
.2	.2	.3	Income Taxes Payable		.0	.5	.2	.5	.1
6.5	7.0	4.9	All Other Current		2.5	3.4	6.4	4.5	5.8
33.4	31.9	28.8	Total Current		25.1	23.8	28.5	30.3	32.2
22.5	22.1	21.2	Long-Term Debt		28.9	28.6	16.7	18.8	20.7
.9	1.0	1.2	Deferred Taxes		.5	.4	1.3	1.6	1.2
5.8	7.1	6.0	All Other Non-Current		6.9	2.3	8.1	3.2	8.0
37.4	37.9	42.9	Net Worth		38.7	44.9	45.4	46.1	37.9
100.0	100.0	100.0	Total Liabilties & Net Worth		100.0	100.0	100.0	100.0	100.0
			INCOME DATA						
100.0	100.0	100.0	Net Sales		100.0	100.0	100.0	100.0	100.0
30.0	29.1	27.3	Gross Profit		43.8	30.2	27.9	23.6	21.7
23.5	23.0	20.8	Operating Expenses		33.4	24.6	22.0	17.1	15.0
6.5	6.1	6.5	Operating Profit		10.4	5.6	6.0	6.4	6.7
.6	1.0	.8	All Other Expenses (net)		1.3	.4	.5	.8	1.4
5.9	5.1	5.7	Profit Before Taxes		9.0	5.1	5.5	5.6	5.3
			RATIOS						
2.9	3.0	3.2			4.2	4.7	3.8	3.0	2.6
1.7	1.9	1.9	Current		2.6	2.6	2.3	1.9	1.8
1.3	1.2	1.3			1.0	1.3	1.5	1.3	1.1
1.5	1.8	1.9			2.7	2.5	2.1	1.9	1.4
.9	1.0	1.0	Quick		1.1	1.4	1.2	1.0	.8
.6	.6	.6			.6	.8	.7	.5	.6
34 10.6	**32** 11.4	**35** 10.4			**22** 16.9	**23** 15.9	**35** 10.5	**35** 10.3	**43** 8.4
49 7.5	**42** 8.6	**45** 8.1	Sales/Receivables		**36** 10.0	**38** 9.5	**42** 8.6	**46** 7.9	**53** 6.9
58 6.3	**56** 6.5	**56** 6.5			**49** 7.4	**54** 6.7	**54** 6.7	**56** 6.5	**60** 6.1
35 10.4	**34** 10.6	**37** 9.9			**11** 33.9	**23** 16.1	**40** 9.1	**39** 9.3	**47** 7.8
60 6.1	**61** 6.0	**66** 5.5	Cost of Sales/Inventory		**83** 4.4	**52** 7.0	**74** 4.9	**66** 5.5	**69** 5.3
104 3.5	**96** 3.8	**96** 3.8			**140** 2.6	**81** 4.5	**111** 3.3	**85** 4.3	**99** 3.7
19 18.9	**16** 23.5	**17** 22.1			**7** 54.9	**6** 60.7	**16** 23.0	**17** 22.0	**26** 13.9
30 12.3	**26** 14.3	**28** 13.2	Cost of Sales/Payables		**24** 15.0	**16** 22.6	**26** 14.1	**26** 13.8	**35** 10.3
44 8.3	**41** 9.0	**41** 8.9			**50** 7.3	**29** 12.8	**35** 10.5	**41** 9.0	**45** 8.1
4.6	4.6	4.1			3.7	3.8	3.7	4.5	4.3
8.1	8.0	6.9	Sales/Working Capital		10.0	7.5	5.0	7.0	7.8
19.9	19.8	18.1			NM	19.7	12.1	17.0	37.4
15.2	13.8	12.7			11.0	9.2	17.7	15.2	20.3
(187) 5.5	(186) 4.3	(195) 4.9	EBIT/Interest		(15) 3.5	(20) 5.8	6.3	(60) 5.4	5.0
1.9	1.7	2.0			1.4	2.7	1.4	2.1	2.1
5.0	4.4	3.9					5.4	3.3	4.9
(51) 2.2	(58) 2.4	(61) 2.1	Net Profit + Depr., Dep., Amort./Cur. Mat. L/T/D				(15) 2.6	(20) 2.1	(15) 3.2
1.3	1.4	1.7					1.6	1.7	2.0
.4	.5	.5			.4	.4	.4	.5	.5
.9	1.0	.9	Fixed/Worth		1.5	.9	.9	.8	1.3
2.0	2.1	1.7			NM	2.2	1.1	1.7	3.5
.7	.7	.7			.5	.7	.6	.6	1.2
1.7	1.7	1.5	Debt/Worth		2.6	1.2	1.0	1.3	2.2
3.9	4.5	3.3			NM	2.2	1.7	2.4	6.0
47.7	43.6	41.9			126.6	42.2	35.9	37.2	53.7
(175) 21.4	(176) 22.9	(184) 18.7	% Profit Before Taxes/Tangible Net Worth		(13) 34.2	(20) 17.3	(46) 15.2	(60) 17.4	(39) 22.6
7.4	7.2	6.8			14.5	4.7	1.0	7.3	10.4
15.9	15.8	15.0			46.3	15.9	17.8	13.3	14.3
9.0	6.7	7.4	% Profit Before Taxes/Total Assets		7.7	8.2	5.7	7.6	7.4
2.3	2.1	2.2			2.4	5.1	.5	2.8	2.4
14.2	10.2	9.6			24.0	7.5	11.5	10.1	8.1
6.4	5.8	4.9	Sales/Net Fixed Assets		5.4	5.1	5.1	4.9	4.4
3.6	3.2	2.9			3.3	3.2	3.3	2.8	3.2
2.5	2.5	2.3			3.1	2.5	2.3	2.4	2.0
1.8	1.9	1.7	Sales/Total Assets		1.7	2.0	1.6	1.9	1.5
1.4	1.3	1.2			1.3	1.3	1.4	1.3	1.0
2.1	2.1	2.3			1.1	2.3	3.1	2.1	2.4
(176) 3.5	(181) 3.9	(183) 3.9	% Depr., Dep., Amort./Sales		(13) 5.3	(20) 4.1	(43) 4.0	(60) 3.7	(41) 3.4
5.8	5.5	5.5			6.9	5.4	5.2	6.2	5.8
1.8	1.7	1.7			3.9	3.1	2.1	1.1	1.1
(85) 3.9	(82) 3.9	(88) 3.5	% Officers', Directors' Owners' Comp/Sales		(12) 4.9	(12) 5.0	(23) 3.5	(28) 2.0	(10) 2.5
6.7	7.0	6.7			7.5	7.6	6.6	4.4	4.4
2869298M	**3135835M**	**5704855M**	Net Sales ($)	**4730M**	**33835M**	**84648M**	**349576M**	**995642M**	**4236424M**
1873052M	**2164868M**	**3532458M**	Total Assets ($)	**4567M**	**19894M**	**49293M**	**213656M**	**634242M**	**2610806M**

M = $ thousand MM = $ million

See Pages 9 through 22 for Explanation of Ratios and Data

Current Data Sorted by Assets							Comparative Historical Data	
						Type of Statement		
		3	9	6	3	Unqualified	15	19
	2	16	8	1		Reviewed	25	30
2	2	4	4			Compiled	8	11
2	6	7				Tax Returns	11	11
1	1	23	15	2	4	Other	49	47
26 (4/1-9/30/13)			95 (10/1/13-3/31/14)				4/1/09-3/31/10 ALL	4/1/10-3/31/11 ALL
0-500M	500M-2MM	2-10MM	10-50MM	50-100MM	100-250MM			
5	11	53	36	9	7	**NUMBER OF STATEMENTS**	108	118
%	%	%	%	%	%	**ASSETS**	%	%
	5.7	7.9	5.4			Cash & Equivalents	9.1	6.7
	36.5	26.2	21.7			Trade Receivables (net)	21.6	24.0
	24.7	34.8	32.5			Inventory	31.9	29.7
	.5	1.0	2.1			All Other Current	2.4	1.8
	67.3	69.9	61.7			Total Current	64.9	62.2
	27.8	24.1	29.5			Fixed Assets (net)	24.7	27.2
	2.5	1.3	3.1			Intangibles (net)	4.4	3.5
	2.3	4.6	5.6			All Other Non-Current	6.0	7.1
	100.0	100.0	100.0			Total	100.0	100.0
						LIABILITIES		
	7.5	11.5	9.1			Notes Payable-Short Term	13.3	9.2
	4.0	2.6	3.2			Cur. Mat.-L.T.D.	3.2	4.5
	16.1	14.9	13.2			Trade Payables	12.5	14.1
	.7	.2	.1			Income Taxes Payable	.3	.3
	7.7	5.7	8.4			All Other Current	7.4	6.0
	36.0	34.9	34.0			Total Current	36.6	34.0
	41.6	19.8	10.8			Long-Term Debt	13.3	17.9
	.0	.9	.7			Deferred Taxes	.8	.7
	6.1	3.7	5.0			All Other Non-Current	4.4	9.2
	16.2	40.7	49.5			Net Worth	44.9	38.2
	100.0	100.0	100.0			Total Liabilties & Net Worth	100.0	100.0
						INCOME DATA		
	100.0	100.0	100.0			Net Sales	100.0	100.0
	30.7	28.1	25.6			Gross Profit	29.4	29.8
	26.7	21.8	17.6			Operating Expenses	27.3	24.2
	4.0	6.3	8.0			Operating Profit	2.1	5.6
	1.1	.7	.2			All Other Expenses (net)	1.3	1.4
	2.8	5.6	7.8			Profit Before Taxes	.9	4.2
						RATIOS		
	5.3	2.8	3.1				4.1	2.9
	2.1	2.1	2.0			Current	1.9	1.9
	1.0	1.5	1.3				1.2	1.3
	3.2	1.4	1.4				1.9	1.6
	1.2	1.0	.9			Quick	.8	1.0
	.5	.6	.5				.4	.5
	34 10.8	**35** 10.4	**35** 10.4				**36** 10.2	**39** 9.3
	45 8.2	**43** 8.5	**42** 8.7			Sales/Receivables	**48** 7.7	**46** 7.9
	57 6.4	**52** 7.0	**56** 6.5				**60** 6.0	**58** 6.3
	21 17.6	**46** 8.0	**48** 7.6				**58** 6.2	**53** 6.9
	38 9.5	**85** 4.3	**87** 4.2			Cost of Sales/Inventory	**102** 3.6	**82** 4.4
	76 4.8	**111** 3.3	**135** 2.7				**138** 2.6	**125** 2.9
	12 29.7	**21** 17.6	**22** 16.4				**15** 23.9	**19** 19.1
	34 10.7	**32** 11.4	**38** 9.5			Cost of Sales/Payables	**31** 11.7	**32** 11.4
	46 7.9	**48** 7.6	**54** 6.7				**46** 7.9	**50** 7.2
	3.3	4.0	3.8				3.5	4.0
	9.0	6.9	5.9			Sales/Working Capital	6.0	6.1
	167.6	9.2	16.4				18.0	14.2
	53.0	20.1	30.0				8.1	16.2
	3.9	(47) 7.5	(32) 9.3			EBIT/Interest	(92) 1.4	(109) 4.1
	.1	2.5	3.4				-2.1	1.1
		8.8	10.1				6.0	8.2
		(17) 1.5	(10) 5.4			Net Profit + Depr., Dep., Amort./Cur. Mat. L/T/D	(32) 2.6	(40) 2.5
		1.0	2.2				1.0	.9
	.2	.2	.4				.2	.3
	4.0	.4	.5			Fixed/Worth	.6	.8
	-.8	1.0	1.1				1.3	2.1
	.5	.7	.4				.3	.5
	6.9	1.2	1.0			Debt/Worth	1.3	1.4
	-7.2	2.7	2.5				4.8	5.9
		34.6	41.7				23.2	42.4
		(50) 17.8	24.7			% Profit Before Taxes/Tangible Net Worth	(96) 1.5	(106) 14.5
		8.3	13.4				-8.1	3.8
	14.1	17.3	23.2				9.3	13.0
	11.0	8.9	10.6			% Profit Before Taxes/Total Assets	.4	6.1
	-3.1	3.0	3.6				-4.9	.5
	48.5	22.1	9.0				14.9	13.7
	10.3	10.1	6.0			Sales/Net Fixed Assets	7.8	7.4
	6.6	4.5	4.0				4.1	3.8
	3.0	2.5	2.3				2.2	2.3
	2.4	2.1	1.6			Sales/Total Assets	1.6	1.8
	2.0	1.6	1.2				1.3	1.3
		.7	1.5				1.2	1.4
		(46) 1.9	(34) 2.4			% Depr., Dep., Amort./Sales	(94) 2.5	(110) 2.5
		3.0	3.7				4.9	4.7
		1.3					2.5	2.4
		(19) 2.4				% Officers', Directors' Owners' Comp/Sales	(34) 6.4	(36) 5.4
		5.9					11.1	11.3
4141M	40003M	569457M	1536267M	1027442M	1884997M	Net Sales ($)	2876032M	2741341M
1602M	15856M	278524M	881591M	642058M	1222473M	Total Assets ($)	1778024M	1721027M

M = $ thousand MM = $ million

See Pages 9 through 22 for Explanation of Ratios and Data

Comparative Historical Data				Current Data Sorted by Sales					
			Type of Statement						
19	19	21	Unqualified				2	1	18
29	26	27	Reviewed		1	1	8	11	6
9	11	12	Compiled	2	1	1	4	2	2
8	5	15	Tax Returns	3	1	2	8	1	
55	60	46	Other	1	1	4	6	13	21
4/1/11-3/31/12	**4/1/12-3/31/13**	**4/1/13-3/31/14**		**26 (4/1-9/30/13)**			**95 (10/1/13-3/31/14)**		
ALL	**ALL**	**ALL**		**0-1MM**	**1-3MM**	**3-5MM**	**5-10MM**	**10-25MM**	**25MM & OVER**
120	121	121	**NUMBER OF STATEMENTS**	6	4	8	28	28	47
%	%	%	**ASSETS**	%	%	%	%	%	%
6.7	6.9	6.7	Cash & Equivalents				7.3	6.1	5.9
25.9	23.8	24.8	Trade Receivables (net)				27.6	25.5	23.6
33.2	31.8	31.5	Inventory				29.7	37.2	30.1
1.8	2.4	2.5	All Other Current				.2	1.6	2.8
67.6	64.9	65.4	Total Current				64.7	70.4	62.4
23.2	26.0	26.3	Fixed Assets (net)				27.8	23.9	26.5
2.5	4.2	3.5	Intangibles (net)				2.5	1.5	5.9
6.7	4.9	4.8	All Other Non-Current				5.0	4.2	5.1
100.0	100.0	100.0	Total				100.0	100.0	100.0
			LIABILITIES						
10.6	10.6	9.4	Notes Payable-Short Term				8.5	11.8	7.4
2.7	2.8	2.8	Cur. Mat.-L.T.D.				2.4	3.4	2.6
15.4	11.9	14.1	Trade Payables				14.4	16.0	12.7
.3	.3	.2	Income Taxes Payable				.1	.3	.1
7.6	8.3	7.1	All Other Current				4.9	6.9	7.8
36.7	33.8	33.6	Total Current				30.2	38.3	30.5
15.1	17.4	18.9	Long-Term Debt				29.1	15.9	12.2
.8	1.1	1.1	Deferred Taxes				.5	.9	1.8
7.1	5.6	4.5	All Other Non-Current				2.2	5.8	5.1
40.4	42.1	41.9	Net Worth				37.9	39.0	50.3
100.0	100.0	100.0	Total Liabilties & Net Worth				100.0	100.0	100.0
			INCOME DATA						
100.0	100.0	100.0	Net Sales				100.0	100.0	100.0
27.7	29.8	27.5	Gross Profit				28.2	25.5	25.4
21.8	22.0	20.3	Operating Expenses				22.5	19.6	16.0
6.0	7.8	7.2	Operating Profit				5.7	5.9	9.4
.9	.6	.6	All Other Expenses (net)				.7	.7	.5
5.1	7.2	6.5	Profit Before Taxes				5.0	5.2	8.9
			RATIOS						
3.4	3.3	3.2					3.6	2.6	3.7
1.9	2.0	2.1	Current				2.1	1.8	2.4
1.3	1.4	1.4					1.4	1.4	1.5
1.6	1.6	1.5					2.1	1.3	1.6
.9	.9	1.0	Quick				1.0	.9	1.1
.6	.5	.6					.8	.6	.6
37 9.8	**34** 10.8	**35** 10.4					**35** 10.5	**35** 10.3	**37** 9.9
46 8.0	**43** 8.4	**43** 8.5	Sales/Receivables				**47** 7.8	**41** 9.0	**44** 8.3
57 6.4	**52** 7.0	**54** 6.8					**55** 6.6	**50** 7.3	**58** 6.3
54 6.7	**49** 7.4	**44** 8.3					**42** 8.7	**55** 6.6	**47** 7.8
78 4.7	**79** 4.6	**76** 4.8	Cost of Sales/Inventory				**73** 5.0	**87** 4.2	**74** 4.9
118 3.1	**130** 2.8	**122** 3.0					**107** 3.4	**111** 3.3	**122** 3.0
18 20.1	**18** 20.6	**21** 17.4					**21** 17.1	**21** 17.7	**21** 17.2
34 10.8	**32** 11.4	**34** 10.6	Cost of Sales/Payables				**35** 10.4	**28** 13.2	**37** 9.8
53 6.9	**43** 8.5	**47** 7.7					**51** 7.1	**54** 6.8	**46** 8.0
3.9	3.5	3.8					4.0	4.5	3.8
6.3	6.1	6.1	Sales/Working Capital				6.5	7.4	5.4
13.5	15.0	11.9					10.1	11.7	11.1
32.5	24.2	27.3					20.1	26.3	49.5
(110) 6.7	(110) 7.9	(108) 8.2	EBIT/Interest				(26) 7.3	(24) 8.2	(43) 14.9
2.2	2.8	2.7					1.2	1.7	3.8
11.6	7.5	7.5						58.7	7.9
(38) 3.5	(38) 3.3	(34) 2.7	Net Profit + Depr., Dep., Amort./Cur. Mat. L/T/D					(10) 2.7	(14) 4.6
1.8	1.8	1.2						1.1	2.2
.2	.3	.3					.2	.2	.4
.5	.6	.5	Fixed/Worth				.6	.5	.5
1.4	1.4	1.4					1.4	1.8	1.0
.5	.6	.5					.5	.7	.4
1.4	1.3	1.2	Debt/Worth				1.2	1.6	1.0
3.3	3.4	3.1					2.7	4.0	2.5
41.5	44.3	38.6					27.7	40.4	49.1
(110) 21.8	(109) 23.8	(110) 21.2	% Profit Before Taxes/Tangible Net Worth				(26) 16.3	(26) 18.6	(43) 26.4
8.2	8.7	10.1					6.2	9.9	14.3
15.1	16.6	17.4					14.7	17.2	23.0
8.4	10.4	9.4	% Profit Before Taxes/Total Assets				10.9	8.1	11.1
2.7	3.4	3.2					1.0	3.1	5.5
19.9	16.7	17.6					31.0	23.0	10.3
9.6	8.5	8.1	Sales/Net Fixed Assets				8.2	11.4	6.4
5.5	4.9	4.4					3.3	5.4	4.6
2.5	2.4	2.4					2.6	2.6	2.3
2.1	1.8	2.0	Sales/Total Assets				2.0	2.2	1.8
1.5	1.5	1.4					1.3	1.8	1.3
1.0	.9	1.3					1.1	1.0	1.3
(111) 1.9	(107) 2.1	(104) 2.0	% Depr., Dep., Amort./Sales				(23) 2.1	(25) 1.9	(43) 2.0
2.9	3.4	3.5					3.9	3.3	3.3
1.9	2.2	1.7					3.6	1.0	
(33) 4.3	(33) 4.7	(35) 4.2	% Officers', Directors' Owners' Comp/Sales				(10) 7.3	(11) 2.0	
7.3	7.0	7.4					10.3	5.0	
3592184M	4384449M	5062307M	Net Sales ($)	4203M	9580M	32955M	196438M	423728M	4395403M
2082829M	2700395M	3042104M	Total Assets ($)	2402M	4973M	23000M	118872M	215480M	2677377M

M = $ thousand MM = $ million

See Pages 9 through 22 for Explanation of Ratios and Data

Current Data Sorted by Assets / Comparative Historical Data

0-500M	500M-2MM	2-10MM	10-50MM	50-100MM	100-250MM	Type of Statement	4/1/09-3/31/10 ALL	4/1/10-3/31/11 ALL
	1	1	2	1		Unqualified	4	8
	1	10	6			Reviewed	20	15
	6	4				Compiled	17	16
2	4	2				Tax Returns	7	12
2	4	13	13	1	1	Other	40	32
	6 (4/1-9/30/13)		68 (10/1/13-3/31/14)					
4	16	30	21	2	1	NUMBER OF STATEMENTS	88	83
%	%	%	%	%	%	**ASSETS**	%	%
	10.1	9.1	8.3			Cash & Equivalents	9.4	11.1
	32.1	23.4	20.3			Trade Receivables (net)	22.4	25.6
	7.8	9.4	6.9			Inventory	9.4	7.6
	1.5	2.1	1.6			All Other Current	3.3	2.2
	51.4	44.0	37.1			Total Current	44.6	46.5
	30.8	48.5	48.6			Fixed Assets (net)	43.5	40.4
	8.3	1.9	8.2			Intangibles (net)	6.4	6.4
	9.5	5.7	6.1			All Other Non-Current	5.5	6.7
	100.0	100.0	100.0			Total	100.0	100.0
						LIABILITIES		
	9.1	5.1	10.0			Notes Payable-Short Term	9.4	9.3
	6.2	3.7	2.7			Cur. Mat.-L.T.D.	6.4	6.2
	8.8	10.3	7.9			Trade Payables	9.5	9.4
	.2	.0	.1			Income Taxes Payable	.1	.3
	5.8	8.7	5.4			All Other Current	8.1	6.9
	30.0	27.9	26.1			Total Current	33.5	32.1
	45.8	23.1	15.4			Long-Term Debt	24.9	29.0
	.0	1.5	.3			Deferred Taxes	1.0	.9
	7.2	5.5	12.2			All Other Non-Current	11.6	8.1
	17.0	42.0	46.1			Net Worth	29.0	29.9
	100.0	100.0	100.0			Total Liabilities & Net Worth	100.0	100.0
						INCOME DATA		
	100.0	100.0	100.0			Net Sales	100.0	100.0
	40.0	40.8	36.9			Gross Profit	35.2	39.7
	32.7	31.2	25.4			Operating Expenses	35.5	31.4
	7.4	9.6	11.5			Operating Profit	-.3	8.4
	.1	1.2	-.2			All Other Expenses (net)	1.9	1.9
	7.3	8.4	11.8			Profit Before Taxes	-2.1	6.5
						RATIOS		
	4.4	2.9	2.5				2.6	2.6
	1.7	2.2	1.7			Current	1.4	1.7
	1.3	1.1	.9				.8	1.1
	2.4	2.8	2.1				2.0	2.1
	1.4	1.4	1.3			Quick	.9	1.2
	.8	.7	.6				.6	.7
	37 9.9	34 10.6	48 7.6				34 10.6	40 9.2
	42 8.6	41 8.9	57 6.4			Sales/Receivables	46 7.9	51 7.2
	50 7.3	59 6.2	69 5.3				57 6.4	62 5.9
	0 UND	0 UND	0 UND				0 UND	0 UND
	2 158.6	0 UND	0 UND			Cost of Sales/Inventory	6 59.7	3 121.3
	33 11.1	19 19.1	25 14.6				35 10.5	41 8.9
	7 49.8	8 46.7	22 16.8				14 26.8	16 23.3
	16 22.6	21 17.8	26 14.2			Cost of Sales/Payables	24 15.5	24 14.9
	33 11.2	43 8.5	54 6.8				41 8.9	48 7.6
	7.6	5.9	5.5				5.5	5.4
	14.3	8.9	10.8			Sales/Working Capital	30.1	11.9
	29.8	73.6	-32.1				-18.5	33.7
	19.7	49.1	15.0				4.8	24.2
	(13) 4.2	(29) 8.1	(19) 7.3			EBIT/Interest	(79) .6	(74) 4.5
	1.7	2.9	2.7				-4.7	2.1
							3.3	4.8
						Net Profit + Depr., Dep., Amort./Cur. Mat. L/T/D	(22) 1.9	(18) 2.1
							.7	1.4
	.6	.7	.8				.6	.5
	1.5	1.4	1.1			Fixed/Worth	1.3	1.1
	-5.9	2.2	2.6				21.3	4.5
	.6	.7	.5				.5	.5
	2.5	1.4	1.6			Debt/Worth	1.3	1.7
	-13.1	3.0	4.8				NM	7.1
	36.4	46.4	48.5				17.1	64.0
	(11) 29.4	(29) 19.9	(18) 23.5			% Profit Before Taxes/Tangible Net Worth	(66) 3.2	(69) 24.7
	12.3	7.4	9.3				-13.6	10.2
	22.4	23.1	17.3				7.7	21.5
	8.8	7.9	12.7			% Profit Before Taxes/Total Assets	.7	10.0
	2.9	2.2	3.4				-10.6	2.8
	30.2	8.0	3.8				7.9	8.4
	7.2	3.0	2.8			Sales/Net Fixed Assets	4.1	4.5
	3.9	2.0	1.5				1.8	2.5
	3.5	2.3	1.6				2.7	2.7
	2.3	1.5	1.1			Sales/Total Assets	1.5	1.7
	1.5	1.1	.9				1.0	1.0
	1.3	2.2	5.7				2.8	2.9
	(14) 3.3	(28) 5.8	(20) 7.5			% Depr., Dep., Amort./Sales	(73) 4.7	(66) 4.7
	4.9	8.3	9.7				9.9	7.6
		5.2					4.6	2.8
		(12) 8.5				% Officers', Directors' Owners' Comp/Sales	(27) 6.1	(32) 5.3
		11.5					11.6	9.4
3135M	53058M	220867M	601617M	245937M	211342M	Net Sales ($)	1297227M	1415400M
1054M	21232M	136375M	482293M	148695M	236875M	Total Assets ($)	1122232M	1183089M

M = $ thousand MM = $ million

See Pages 9 through 22 for Explanation of Ratios and Data

Comparative Historical Data				Current Data Sorted by Sales					
			Type of Statement						
3	5	5	Unqualified	1				1	3
21	15	17	Reviewed		1	1	7	6	2
18	8	10	Compiled		3	3	3	1	
10	9	8	Tax Returns	2	2	3	1		
37	24	34	Other	2	5	5	5	10	7
				6 (4/1-9/30/13)		68 (10/1/13-3/31/14)			
4/1/11-3/31/12 ALL	4/1/12-3/31/13 ALL	4/1/13-3/31/14 ALL		0-1MM	1-3MM	3-5MM	5-10MM	10-25MM	25MM & OVER
89	61	74	**NUMBER OF STATEMENTS**	5	11	12	16	18	12
%	%	%	**ASSETS**	%	%	%	%	%	%
8.6	9.3	8.6	Cash & Equivalents		4.3	14.3	9.6	9.8	5.7
25.7	24.7	24.9	Trade Receivables (net)		18.0	40.1	21.4	22.8	23.0
8.3	7.8	8.6	Inventory		9.1	2.5	8.5	7.9	15.5
1.0	1.3	1.7	All Other Current		.8	1.5	3.1	1.2	1.8
43.6	43.1	43.7	Total Current		32.2	58.4	42.6	41.7	46.0
39.7	44.0	43.1	Fixed Assets (net)		48.5	27.6	53.5	45.7	43.2
5.8	4.6	6.5	Intangibles (net)		5.6	2.6	.7	7.0	7.1
10.9	8.3	6.6	All Other Non-Current		13.7	11.4	3.2	5.6	3.7
100.0	100.0	100.0	Total		100.0	100.0	100.0	100.0	100.0
			LIABILITIES						
10.1	8.4	8.0	Notes Payable-Short Term		7.2	6.7	6.0	6.0	12.0
5.7	3.9	3.8	Cur. Mat.-L.T.D.		4.3	6.6	4.7	3.4	1.7
8.9	8.3	9.0	Trade Payables		4.1	11.7	10.5	7.9	10.3
.1	.0	.1	Income Taxes Payable		.0	.2	.0	.0	.2
9.3	6.9	9.6	All Other Current		9.0	6.1	10.3	5.7	7.0
34.2	27.5	30.4	Total Current		24.6	31.3	31.6	22.9	31.2
24.5	24.5	24.8	Long-Term Debt		53.9	23.4	26.7	19.0	9.9
.7	.7	.7	Deferred Taxes		.0	.1	2.1	.7	.5
9.7	11.3	8.6	All Other Non-Current		4.0	7.1	9.4	5.2	13.7
31.0	35.9	35.4	Net Worth		17.5	38.0	30.2	52.1	44.6
100.0	100.0	100.0	Total Liabilties & Net Worth		100.0	100.0	100.0	100.0	100.0
			INCOME DATA						
100.0	100.0	100.0	Net Sales		100.0	100.0	100.0	100.0	100.0
41.1	42.5	39.1	Gross Profit		43.3	39.5	43.1	37.9	30.0
31.3	32.8	29.4	Operating Expenses		33.9	33.1	33.0	26.3	20.8
9.8	9.8	9.8	Operating Profit		9.4	6.5	10.1	11.7	9.2
1.0	.9	.5	All Other Expenses (net)		1.4	.3	.8	-.3	.6
8.8	8.9	9.3	Profit Before Taxes		8.0	6.2	9.3	12.0	8.5
			RATIOS						
2.5	3.0	2.8			3.2	4.7	2.6	2.9	2.5
1.5	1.7	1.8	Current		1.3	2.3	1.3	2.1	1.8
1.0	.9	1.0			.7	1.4	.7	1.2	1.1
2.4	2.6	2.4			2.6	4.1	1.8	2.7	1.8
1.1	1.5	1.3	Quick		1.0	2.1	1.2	1.7	1.1
.6	.6	.7			.6	1.2	.7	.7	.7
37 9.8	**36** 10.2	**38** 9.7			**30** 12.1	**41** 8.8	**34** 10.6	**44** 8.3	**42** 8.6
47 7.7	**43** 8.4	**45** 8.2	Sales/Receivables		**40** 9.1	**45** 8.1	**38** 9.7	**53** 6.9	**55** 6.6
56 6.5	**60** 6.1	**63** 5.8			**51** 7.1	**62** 5.9	**42** 8.6	**70** 5.2	**65** 5.6
0 UND	**0** UND	**0** UND			**0** UND	**0** UND	**0** UND	**0** UND	**0** UND
6 62.8	**4** 90.3	**2** 216.5	Cost of Sales/Inventory		**0** UND	**0** UND	**0** UND	**0** UND	**51** 7.1
37 9.9	**43** 8.4	**36** 10.2			**34** 10.6	**8** 48.6	**14** 26.0	**20** 18.0	**87** 4.2
12 30.3	**14** 25.7	**11** 33.1			**6** 64.8	**11** 31.8	**11** 33.8	**11** 32.2	**23** 16.1
23 16.0	**24** 15.3	**23** 15.9	Cost of Sales/Payables		**7** 51.8	**17** 21.0	**27** 13.3	**24** 15.0	**29** 12.8
36 10.1	**40** 9.2	**40** 9.1			**38** 9.5	**24** 15.4	**39** 9.4	**54** 6.7	**53** 6.9
6.5	5.2	5.9			8.7	4.6	6.6	4.3	5.5
12.9	12.1	9.4	Sales/Working Capital		13.9	7.2	36.4	8.4	8.7
126.1	-70.5	NM			-26.4	13.0	-17.2	19.0	49.0
19.4	20.3	24.1				81.9	17.5	39.5	24.4
(76) 5.8	(53) 4.6	(68) 7.8	EBIT/Interest			(10) 15.6	5.8	(17) 8.3	(11) 8.7
1.9	1.3	2.6				2.4	2.5	4.6	2.7
5.5	10.1	7.8	Net Profit + Depr., Dep.,						
(19) 2.5	(15) 3.7	(19) 2.0	Amort./Cur. Mat. L/T/D						
1.6	2.3	1.8							
.6	.6	.7			.7	.1	1.0	.7	.6
1.2	1.1	1.4	Fixed/Worth		1.5	.6	1.9	1.0	1.0
4.2	4.0	2.9			-4.3	1.6	4.3	2.2	2.7
.7	.5	.7			.5	.4	1.2	.6	.4
2.1	1.5	1.6	Debt/Worth		2.2	1.1	2.6	.8	1.3
7.7	5.4	4.6			-10.6	1.4	4.8	2.5	5.0
64.9	48.5	45.2	% Profit Before Taxes/Tangible			32.6	118.7	50.2	54.1
(73) 37.3	(49) 29.6	(62) 26.1	Net Worth			(11) 28.4	(15) 28.7	(16) 21.2	(11) 33.2
14.0	8.4	11.8				12.3	15.3	9.2	22.2
23.1	24.3	21.1	% Profit Before Taxes/Total		24.2	20.3	27.5	23.8	17.5
14.4	11.1	10.5	Assets		6.9	11.1	8.1	13.1	13.4
3.5	1.5	3.6			.1	3.4	2.9	4.5	4.2
10.5	7.4	8.3			5.9	52.4	8.4	4.5	4.6
5.0	3.8	3.4	Sales/Net Fixed Assets		3.1	13.5	3.4	2.9	3.3
2.6	1.9	2.2			1.3	3.3	1.9	1.9	2.0
2.8	2.5	2.4			1.6	4.2	2.9	1.6	1.9
1.8	1.5	1.5	Sales/Total Assets		1.4	2.2	2.0	1.2	1.4
1.1	1.0	1.1			1.0	1.2	1.3	1.0	1.1
1.8	2.3	2.6			.9	1.3	2.4	4.6	4.9
(76) 3.9	(54) 4.7	(67) 5.6	% Depr., Dep., Amort./Sales		3.6	(10) 2.7	(14) 6.1	6.5	(10) 6.8
6.3	6.6	7.9			7.0	5.0	9.2	7.7	9.9
2.0	4.9	3.5	% Officers', Directors'						
(31) 4.5	(26) 7.3	(31) 6.1	Owners' Comp/Sales						
7.3	13.2	11.3							
1351561M	1047251M	1335956M	Net Sales ($)	3678M	22091M	51723M	114776M	282860M	860828M
964785M	811401M	1026524M	Total Assets ($)	2972M	23280M	29564M	85417M	236497M	648794M

M = $ thousand MM = $ million

See Pages 9 through 22 for Explanation of Ratios and Data

Current Data Sorted by Assets							Comparative Historical Data	
						Type of Statement		
		2	2	4		Unqualified	17	12
1	3	9	9			Reviewed	23	31
	9	8	1			Compiled	22	23
10	7	6				Tax Returns	17	17
2	9	17	16	4	5	Other	53	51
	18 (4/1-9/30/13)		106 (10/1/13-3/31/14)				4/1/09-3/31/10	4/1/10-3/31/11
0-500M	500M-2MM	2-10MM	10-50MM	50-100MM	100-250MM		ALL	ALL
13	28	42	28	8	5	NUMBER OF STATEMENTS	132	134
%	%	%	%	%	%	**ASSETS**	%	%
27.1	9.0	15.1	7.8			Cash & Equivalents	10.7	12.0
24.8	35.8	27.2	27.0			Trade Receivables (net)	26.6	28.4
11.9	10.8	10.9	19.1			Inventory	11.6	12.3
.0	2.5	1.7	1.2			All Other Current	2.9	2.4
63.8	58.0	54.8	55.2			Total Current	51.7	55.2
29.4	33.0	31.5	32.2			Fixed Assets (net)	35.4	34.1
3.0	3.2	6.8	9.8			Intangibles (net)	5.2	4.7
3.9	5.7	6.9	2.8			All Other Non-Current	7.7	6.0
100.0	100.0	100.0	100.0			Total	100.0	100.0
						LIABILITIES		
21.0	10.2	9.0	10.6			Notes Payable-Short Term	12.4	10.5
8.1	6.7	4.5	3.8			Cur. Mat.-L.T.D.	4.3	3.6
8.6	15.3	13.2	11.7			Trade Payables	10.2	11.7
.0	.1	.1	.1			Income Taxes Payable	.2	.2
40.9	4.9	6.8	10.1			All Other Current	9.0	9.0
78.7	37.2	33.5	36.4			Total Current	36.1	35.1
35.4	27.2	19.4	16.6			Long-Term Debt	24.1	22.2
.0	.3	.6	1.5			Deferred Taxes	.5	.5
8.7	2.8	8.7	3.6			All Other Non-Current	5.1	9.4
-22.8	32.5	37.7	41.9			Net Worth	34.2	32.9
100.0	100.0	100.0	100.0			Total Liabilities & Net Worth	100.0	100.0
						INCOME DATA		
100.0	100.0	100.0	100.0			Net Sales	100.0	100.0
39.4	38.8	31.2	30.4			Gross Profit	34.6	35.3
32.7	31.4	23.2	22.1			Operating Expenses	31.5	29.5
6.7	7.4	8.0	8.3			Operating Profit	3.0	5.8
.4	.9	1.1	2.1			All Other Expenses (net)	1.6	.9
6.3	6.5	6.9	6.2			Profit Before Taxes	1.5	4.9
						RATIOS		
10.9	2.7	3.7	2.3				3.4	3.2
1.2	1.6	1.7	1.5			Current	1.7	1.8
.4	1.1	.8	1.1				.9	1.2
8.0	2.3	3.0	1.7				2.4	2.7
1.2	1.4	1.2	1.0			Quick	1.2	1.3
.3	.8	.6	.5				.6	.7
0 UND	**28** 12.9	**34** 10.6	**36** 10.1				**35** 10.4	**37** 9.9
5 66.8	**43** 8.5	**45** 8.1	**50** 7.3			Sales/Receivables	**43** 8.4	**45** 8.1
43 8.5	**51** 7.1	**51** 7.1	**60** 6.1				**56** 6.5	**57** 6.4
0 UND	**2** 191.8	**6** 59.9	**25** 14.5				**3** 109.8	**9** 38.4
4 100.5	**16** 22.8	**14** 25.6	**54** 6.8			Cost of Sales/Inventory	**22** 16.5	**26** 14.2
34 10.8	**29** 12.7	**43** 8.4	**76** 4.8				**46** 7.9	**50** 7.3
0 UND	**7** 53.2	**14** 25.8	**23** 16.2				**12** 31.0	**12** 31.5
4 81.6	**24** 15.3	**24** 15.5	**29** 12.8			Cost of Sales/Payables	**24** 15.5	**26** 14.2
21 17.7	**35** 10.3	**35** 10.4	**45** 8.2				**42** 8.8	**38** 9.6
5.2	9.1	4.7	6.4				5.0	4.9
38.3	18.2	9.7	10.0			Sales/Working Capital	10.8	9.1
-11.1	52.5	-21.0	45.3				-53.6	27.1
	12.7	28.9	14.4				9.2	21.0
	(22) 3.5	(33) 5.4	(25) 5.5			EBIT/Interest	(121) 2.4	(122) 5.7
	.7	1.6	2.3				-.7	1.5
		4.6	8.0				2.9	5.9
		(10) 3.4	(10) 3.4			Net Profit + Depr., Dep., Amort./Cur. Mat. L/T/D	(26) 1.6	(31) 3.4
		1.9	2.4				.2	2.2
.2	.3	.3	.5				.4	.3
1.0	1.2	.7	1.0			Fixed/Worth	.9	.8
-.2	2.3	5.7	4.0				7.1	2.9
.3	.4	.5	.8				.5	.5
2.6	2.1	1.4	1.7			Debt/Worth	1.4	1.3
-2.2	4.7	22.4	5.3				9.9	5.2
	81.2	57.0	34.9				32.6	45.5
	(24) 16.9	(35) 33.4	(22) 18.3			% Profit Before Taxes/Tangible Net Worth	(104) 13.6	(110) 24.8
	-3.2	4.5	11.4				-3.7	6.7
47.2	33.3	30.7	21.6				15.6	19.2
16.6	10.6	9.1	7.7			% Profit Before Taxes/Total Assets	4.4	8.1
-10.4	-.8	1.3	3.1				-6.1	1.3
88.2	24.8	21.6	12.9				14.3	15.2
32.0	11.8	7.2	9.1			Sales/Net Fixed Assets	6.9	7.1
12.1	5.8	3.1	2.9				2.8	3.2
9.8	4.8	2.8	2.6				2.9	2.9
3.9	3.1	2.0	2.0			Sales/Total Assets	2.0	2.1
3.2	2.3	1.3	1.0				1.2	1.4
.6	.9	1.4	1.7				1.8	1.4
(10) 1.0	(25) 2.4	(35) 2.5	(25) 2.4			% Depr., Dep., Amort./Sales	(110) 3.3	(117) 2.7
3.3	3.8	4.1	5.4				6.1	4.6
	2.7	3.1					3.6	3.3
	(16) 5.4	(20) 5.7				% Officers', Directors' Owners' Comp/Sales	(48) 5.7	(47) 6.7
	6.5	10.3					10.1	9.5
20034M	102113M	433769M	934351M	788171M	679173M	Net Sales ($)	2170995M	2635396M
2830M	30443M	205895M	490124M	512418M	753839M	Total Assets ($)	1546595M	1577231M

M = $ thousand MM = $ million

See Pages 9 through 22 for Explanation of Ratios and Data

Comparative Historical Data				Current Data Sorted by Sales					
			Type of Statement						
14	14	8	Unqualified					2	6
28	22	22	Reviewed		2	4	4	6	6
23	15	18	Compiled		4	5	6	3	
27	23	23	Tax Returns	4	8	4	7		
56	53	53	Other	2	5	5	6	14	21
				18 (4/1-9/30/13)			106 (10/1/13-3/31/14)		
4/1/11-3/31/12 ALL	4/1/12-3/31/13 ALL	4/1/13-3/31/14 ALL		0-1MM	1-3MM	3-5MM	5-10MM	10-25MM	25MM & OVER
148	127	124	**NUMBER OF STATEMENTS**	6	19	18	23	25	33
%	%	%	**ASSETS**	%	%	%	%	%	%
11.4	11.4	12.6	Cash & Equivalents		8.3	11.8	18.8	12.7	7.4
28.6	28.5	27.6	Trade Receivables (net)		29.5	28.8	28.6	26.1	26.7
13.6	10.7	13.2	Inventory		9.0	8.4	14.1	13.2	17.8
2.0	1.6	1.6	All Other Current		1.6	.5	2.4	2.5	1.1
55.7	52.3	55.0	Total Current		48.3	49.5	64.0	54.6	53.0
31.5	35.7	32.5	Fixed Assets (net)		36.9	39.5	27.0	30.6	32.1
7.6	4.7	7.0	Intangibles (net)		5.8	4.4	4.4	9.6	10.1
5.2	7.3	5.5	All Other Non-Current		9.0	6.6	4.5	5.2	4.9
100.0	100.0	100.0	Total		100.0	100.0	100.0	100.0	100.0
			LIABILITIES						
9.6	10.4	10.3	Notes Payable-Short Term		12.1	9.6	8.3	7.4	9.9
3.7	5.6	4.9	Cur. Mat.-L.T.D.		5.2	6.9	4.9	5.3	2.6
13.4	14.3	12.4	Trade Payables		12.5	12.6	12.1	13.6	11.7
.2	.1	.3	Income Taxes Payable		.1	.0	.1	.0	.8
10.1	13.6	10.9	All Other Current		6.2	16.1	7.8	5.9	9.9
37.1	44.0	38.7	Total Current		36.1	45.1	33.2	32.2	34.9
19.5	25.7	21.9	Long-Term Debt		24.6	47.3	16.4	15.0	14.3
.3	.7	1.0	Deferred Taxes		.5	.3	1.1	.7	2.0
9.1	6.1	5.8	All Other Non-Current		7.6	2.7	13.5	2.1	4.6
34.0	23.6	32.6	Net Worth		31.2	4.5	35.8	49.9	44.1
100.0	100.0	100.0	Total Liabilties & Net Worth		100.0	100.0	100.0	100.0	100.0
			INCOME DATA						
100.0	100.0	100.0	Net Sales		100.0	100.0	100.0	100.0	100.0
35.0	34.6	32.9	Gross Profit		38.8	36.5	34.6	30.6	25.8
27.5	27.2	24.8	Operating Expenses		34.5	31.6	26.8	19.4	16.5
7.5	7.4	8.2	Operating Profit		4.3	4.9	7.7	11.2	9.3
.9	.8	1.3	All Other Expenses (net)		.7	1.6	1.5	.6	1.9
6.6	6.6	6.9	Profit Before Taxes		3.7	3.3	6.2	10.6	7.4
			RATIOS						
3.2	2.8	3.2			3.3	2.3	8.0	3.7	1.9
1.8	1.6	1.6	Current		1.5	1.7	2.0	1.9	1.5
1.1	1.0	1.0			.5	1.1	1.3	.8	1.2
2.3	2.1	2.4			3.0	2.2	7.9	2.8	1.3
1.2	1.2	1.1	Quick		1.1	1.3	1.5	1.1	.9
.7	.7	.6			.4	.9	.7	.6	.7
37 9.9	**32** 11.5	**34** 10.7			**34** 10.7	**27** 13.6	**31** 11.9	**42** 8.6	**35** 10.4
47 7.7	**45** 8.1	**45** 8.1	Sales/Receivables		**39** 9.4	**43** 8.5	**44** 8.3	**50** 7.3	**49** 7.5
57 6.4	**55** 6.6	**54** 6.8			**49** 7.4	**49** 7.5	**51** 7.1	**60** 6.1	**58** 6.3
8 46.1	**7** 51.6	**6** 57.3			**4** 100.5	**0** UND	**5** 72.4	**10** 34.9	**17** 21.2
24 15.5	**18** 20.6	**21** 17.6	Cost of Sales/Inventory		**13** 28.4	**10** 35.5	**29** 12.4	**15** 23.9	**51** 7.2
57 6.4	**43** 8.4	**57** 6.4			**28** 13.0	**28** 13.0	**48** 7.6	**65** 5.6	**62** 5.9
17 22.0	**16** 22.3	**13** 28.6			**13** 28.8	**8** 45.4	**10** 38.0	**20** 18.6	**22** 16.9
27 13.6	**27** 13.6	**25** 14.8	Cost of Sales/Payables		**21** 17.1	**23** 16.2	**21** 17.6	**27** 13.6	**29** 12.7
41 8.8	**40** 9.1	**36** 10.0			**30** 12.2	**40** 9.1	**37** 9.9	**53** 6.9	**38** 9.5
5.2	5.8	6.4			5.7	8.3	4.7	4.5	8.3
9.4	11.6	10.4	Sales/Working Capital		15.1	23.3	9.1	9.6	12.3
47.3	-411.6	NM			-12.5	99.3	29.6	-18.7	25.7
19.0	26.5	17.2			4.6	11.1	9.6	20.8	78.7
(132) 6.2	(115) 6.6	(100) 5.5	EBIT/Interest		(11) 1.7	(17) 2.3	(19) 5.4	(19) 9.8	(31) 11.0
1.9	2.7	1.8			-.1	.2	1.5	3.3	3.8
5.5	6.2	6.2							6.9
(25) 2.5	(24) 3.7	(30) 3.5	Net Profit + Depr., Dep., Amort./Cur. Mat. L/T/D						(13) 3.6
1.6	1.8	2.0							2.8
.4	.4	.4			.3	.7	.2	.3	.5
.9	1.0	1.0	Fixed/Worth		1.5	1.4	.5	.6	.9
4.6	5.4	4.1			28.8	NM	2.0	3.4	1.9
.6	.6	.5			.5	.5	.4	.4	.8
1.5	1.9	1.4	Debt/Worth		3.2	3.1	1.1	1.4	1.3
7.9	7.6	5.8			31.4	NM	3.8	4.5	4.6
50.0	52.9	53.2			73.4	46.9	42.9	63.6	74.4
(120) 28.1	(102) 28.2	(100) 22.6	% Profit Before Taxes/Tangible Net Worth		(15) 9.6	(14) 12.3	(20) 17.2	(20) 35.4	(27) 23.4
12.0	8.6	7.0			-21.5	-1.3	-2.5	13.0	14.7
24.1	22.9	25.9			21.4	19.8	17.3	30.6	22.4
10.7	11.2	9.1	% Profit Before Taxes/Total Assets		-.6	2.4	9.2	9.4	11.1
3.4	3.4	1.4			-4.8	-3.0	1.1	5.4	5.3
18.0	15.3	17.3			22.0	13.4	41.0	12.4	12.9
7.6	6.8	8.1	Sales/Net Fixed Assets		14.0	8.4	14.3	7.3	7.1
4.1	3.1	4.5			2.1	4.6	4.8	3.8	4.1
3.0	3.2	3.4			3.8	4.0	3.9	2.5	2.7
2.1	2.2	2.3	Sales/Total Assets		2.4	2.7	2.7	1.6	2.2
1.5	1.5	1.3			1.2	2.1	1.3	1.3	1.2
1.2	1.3	1.4			.9	1.6	.9	1.5	1.6
(127) 2.7	(107) 2.2	(108) 2.5	% Depr., Dep., Amort./Sales		(14) 2.5	2.4	(19) 2.2	(22) 2.4	(31) 3.0
4.5	4.2	4.2			4.3	4.5	3.0	4.7	4.3
3.8	2.7	3.0			2.4	4.0	3.9		
(67) 6.1	(55) 6.0	(49) 5.8	% Officers', Directors' Owners' Comp/Sales		(11) 5.9	(10) 5.4	(16) 8.9		
9.5	8.7	7.8			7.6	6.3	10.7		
3932044M	**2992552M**	**2957611M**	Net Sales ($)	**2357M**	**38186M**	**72533M**	**156391M**	**357302M**	**2330842M**
1973444M	**1623263M**	**1995549M**	Total Assets ($)	**688M**	**20252M**	**30697M**	**92833M**	**211345M**	**1639734M**

M = $ thousand MM = $ million

See Pages 9 through 22 for Explanation of Ratios and Data

Current Data Sorted by Assets | **Comparative Historical Data**

Type of Statement	0-500M	500M-2MM	2-10MM	10-50MM	50-100MM	100-250MM	4/1/09-3/31/10 ALL	4/1/10-3/31/11 ALL
Unqualified			2	5		1	11	8
Reviewed		3	21	2	1		28	24
Compiled	1	11	10	1			23	37
Tax Returns	4	7	5				15	21
Other	1	13	28	9			53	46
	24 (4/1-9/30/13)		101 (10/1/13-3/31/14)					
NUMBER OF STATEMENTS	6	34	66	17	1	1	130	136
ASSETS	%	%	%	%	%	%	%	%
Cash & Equivalents		14.1	11.3	8.3			7.0	9.2
Trade Receivables (net)		30.8	25.7	22.6			27.3	29.7
Inventory		11.4	8.0	20.7			12.5	11.3
All Other Current		2.7	1.9	2.5			3.3	2.5
Total Current		59.0	46.9	54.0			50.2	52.7
Fixed Assets (net)		32.4	44.1	29.3			38.1	34.6
Intangibles (net)		3.0	4.1	8.7			3.9	4.8
All Other Non-Current		5.7	5.0	8.0			7.8	7.9
Total		100.0	100.0	100.0			100.0	100.0
LIABILITIES								
Notes Payable-Short Term		12.9	6.3	11.1			12.1	8.4
Cur. Mat.-L.T.D.		3.4	4.2	4.9			5.0	3.8
Trade Payables		12.8	9.5	12.5			14.4	13.0
Income Taxes Payable		.0	.1	.8			.0	.1
All Other Current		11.3	8.4	7.0			8.6	10.2
Total Current		40.3	28.5	36.3			40.2	35.5
Long-Term Debt		23.6	23.6	17.7			21.0	23.5
Deferred Taxes		.0	.5	1.6			.7	.7
All Other Non-Current		4.4	4.6	11.8			10.0	5.6
Net Worth		31.7	42.8	32.5			28.1	34.7
Total Liabilties & Net Worth		100.0	100.0	100.0			100.0	100.0
INCOME DATA								
Net Sales		100.0	100.0	100.0			100.0	100.0
Gross Profit		39.5	33.3	27.8			33.5	35.5
Operating Expenses		33.3	24.0	17.3			30.8	28.8
Operating Profit		6.2	9.4	10.4			2.7	6.7
All Other Expenses (net)		.5	1.3	2.4			1.4	1.6
Profit Before Taxes		5.6	8.1	8.0			1.3	5.1
RATIOS								
Current		4.3	3.8	2.4			2.7	3.4
		2.8	1.8	1.5			1.2	1.5
		.7	1.0	1.1			.9	1.1
Quick		3.3	2.9	1.7			1.8	2.5
		1.6	1.3	.8			.9	1.1
		.6	.7	.6			.6	.7
Sales/Receivables		**31** 11.7	**39** 9.3	**36** 10.0			**38** 9.7	**40** 9.2
		38 9.5	**47** 7.8	**41** 8.9			**47** 7.8	**50** 7.3
		49 7.4	**55** 6.6	**54** 6.7			**58** 6.3	**60** 6.0
Cost of Sales/Inventory		**3** 107.5	**6** 62.5	**15** 23.8			**8** 45.5	**7** 55.0
		12 31.0	**12** 29.6	**37** 9.8			**18** 20.7	**16** 23.3
		28 13.2	**24** 14.9	**72** 5.1			**45** 8.1	**47** 7.7
Cost of Sales/Payables		**9** 42.9	**12** 30.3	**17** 22.1			**17** 20.9	**12** 29.8
		20 18.4	**23** 16.1	**28** 13.1			**32** 11.4	**25** 14.7
		33 11.2	**37** 9.9	**38** 9.5			**46** 8.0	**41** 8.9
Sales/Working Capital		4.1	5.2	5.6			6.4	5.0
		13.3	10.9	10.8			22.1	11.7
		-18.0	131.0	NM			-33.5	95.1
EBIT/Interest		19.2	21.8	44.7			6.9	19.0
		(26) 8.9	(61) 6.4	(16) 4.3			(120) 2.4	(125) 4.2
		1.6	1.7	2.0			-.4	1.4
Net Profit + Depr., Dep., Amort./Cur. Mat. L/T/D			7.7				3.7	6.4
			(16) 3.3				(29) 1.6	(36) 2.4
			1.6				.6	1.6
Fixed/Worth		.4	.6	.5			.6	.5
		1.4	1.1	.8			1.2	1.0
		-7.1	3.1	-2.6			7.4	2.9
Debt/Worth		.5	.5	.6			.8	.5
		2.3	1.3	1.2			2.0	1.6
		-23.0	3.9	-8.2			15.9	5.0
% Profit Before Taxes/Tangible Net Worth		54.8	54.3	44.5			31.5	47.9
		(24) 27.2	(57) 24.6	(12) 24.3			(103) 8.5	(109) 20.4
		12.3	6.7	7.3			-.5	5.9
% Profit Before Taxes/Total Assets		28.8	27.0	16.2			8.8	21.9
		11.8	10.6	12.2			3.2	8.1
		1.6	1.9	2.8			-2.9	1.8
Sales/Net Fixed Assets		27.9	9.3	16.6			10.8	17.0
		11.5	4.7	7.3			5.3	6.0
		3.7	2.3	4.0			2.9	3.2
Sales/Total Assets		3.8	2.4	2.3			2.8	3.0
		2.4	2.0	2.0			1.9	2.0
		1.8	1.3	1.2			1.4	1.4
% Depr., Dep., Amort./Sales		1.2	1.7	1.3			1.3	1.3
		(27) 2.3	(63) 2.7	3.6			(113) 3.3	(120) 2.5
		4.2	5.6	4.4			5.2	4.6
% Officers', Directors' Owners' Comp/Sales		4.9	1.9				2.6	2.6
		(23) 7.1	(26) 3.8				(62) 5.5	(61) 6.0
		11.2	8.2				7.8	9.9
Net Sales ($)	6687M	116518M	664015M	659948M	120803M	104047M	1175684M	2260223M
Total Assets ($)	1963M	40080M	344090M	336395M	65478M	112965M	728761M	1130875M

M = $ thousand MM = $ million

See Pages 9 through 22 for Explanation of Ratios and Data

Comparative Historical Data				Current Data Sorted by Sales					
			Type of Statement						
8	6	8	Unqualified					2	6
29	22	27	Reviewed		2	2	11	9	3
40	21	23	Compiled		6	3	10	4	
30	22	16	Tax Returns	3	9		2	1	1
46	53	51	Other	2	11	3	13	18	4
4/1/11-3/31/12 ALL	4/1/12-3/31/13 ALL	4/1/13-3/31/14 ALL		24 (4/1-9/30/13)			101 (10/1/13-3/31/14)		
				0-1MM	1-3MM	3-5MM	5-10MM	10-25MM	25MM & OVER
153	124	125	**NUMBER OF STATEMENTS**	5	28	8	36	34	14
%	%	%	**ASSETS**	%	%	%	%	%	%
10.0	9.2	11.9	Cash & Equivalents		14.4		10.2	12.0	6.5
30.3	28.0	27.6	Trade Receivables (net)		23.3		30.3	28.4	25.3
11.1	13.5	10.5	Inventory		8.7		8.8	10.3	21.2
3.0	2.8	2.1	All Other Current		3.1		2.0	2.2	1.9
54.4	53.5	52.1	Total Current		49.4		51.3	52.9	54.8
34.9	35.3	37.9	Fixed Assets (net)		40.5		42.8	34.5	30.8
4.7	6.1	4.6	Intangibles (net)		5.0		2.1	6.8	6.7
6.0	5.0	5.3	All Other Non-Current		5.1		3.8	5.9	7.7
100.0	100.0	100.0	Total		100.0		100.0	100.0	100.0
			LIABILITIES						
10.4	12.1	9.1	Notes Payable-Short Term		9.2		10.0	5.8	13.2
3.2	3.6	3.9	Cur. Mat.-L.T.D.		3.8		3.8	5.0	2.7
16.1	14.2	10.9	Trade Payables		8.0		12.5	10.0	15.3
.1	.1	.2	Income Taxes Payable		.0		.1	.5	.1
16.6	10.7	9.1	All Other Current		8.1		4.9	12.2	7.8
46.3	40.7	33.2	Total Current		29.2		31.2	33.4	39.2
21.7	18.6	22.1	Long-Term Debt		32.1		19.7	22.4	18.1
.5	.5	.5	Deferred Taxes		.0		.5	1.0	.7
10.9	8.9	5.8	All Other Non-Current		1.7		7.5	2.4	16.0
20.6	31.3	38.5	Net Worth		37.0		41.1	40.8	26.0
100.0	100.0	100.0	Total Liabilties & Net Worth		100.0		100.0	100.0	100.0
			INCOME DATA						
100.0	100.0	100.0	Net Sales		100.0		100.0	100.0	100.0
35.2	35.2	35.0	Gross Profit		46.8		34.0	31.7	23.6
28.3	27.7	26.6	Operating Expenses		40.3		25.4	21.5	14.9
6.9	7.5	8.4	Operating Profit		6.5		8.6	10.2	8.6
.8	.9	1.1	All Other Expenses (net)		.1		1.7	1.2	1.9
6.0	6.7	7.2	Profit Before Taxes		6.3		6.9	9.0	6.7
			RATIOS						
3.4	3.2	3.2			4.2		3.2	3.3	2.2
1.6	1.7	1.8	Current		2.5		1.8	2.0	1.4
.9	1.0	1.0			.8		.9	1.2	.9
2.5	2.4	2.9			3.0		2.9	2.6	1.4
1.2	1.3	1.3	Quick		1.7		1.3	1.4	.8
.7	.6	.7			.7		.7	.9	.6
36 10.2	**36** 10.1	**36** 10.0			**34** 10.8		**35** 10.3	**42** 8.7	**32** 11.5
45 8.2	**45** 8.1	**45** 8.1	Sales/Receivables		**41** 8.8		**43** 8.4	**51** 7.1	**41** 9.0
54 6.8	**52** 7.0	**53** 6.9			**52** 7.0		**51** 7.1	**62** 5.9	**47** 7.8
2 174.3	**5** 75.0	**6** 60.8			**2** 146.1		**6** 60.8	**7** 49.0	**15** 23.7
11 33.1	**17** 21.8	**14** 26.4	Cost of Sales/Inventory		**11** 32.1		**14** 25.8	**13** 28.9	**41** 9.0
38 9.5	**54** 6.7	**31** 11.7			**24** 15.1		**25** 14.7	**26** 14.0	**64** 5.7
14 27.0	**13** 27.2	**12** 30.8			**8** 45.5		**11** 32.9	**12** 29.2	**21** 17.8
28 13.2	**24** 14.9	**24** 15.3	Cost of Sales/Payables		**27** 13.6		**22** 16.4	**19** 19.3	**28** 13.1
45 8.2	**39** 9.3	**35** 10.4			**37** 9.8		**36** 10.0	**32** 11.3	**37** 9.9
5.9	6.1	5.2			4.0		5.9	4.9	8.0
12.2	11.8	10.8	Sales/Working Capital		8.3		13.3	9.4	16.2
-85.5	-109.6	-111.4			-24.1		-38.4	29.0	-115.6
13.2	20.5	19.2			19.6		13.9	42.2	72.3
(132) 4.4	(109) 5.1	(109) 6.2	EBIT/Interest		(23) 4.4		(32) 5.1	(31) 8.3	4.4
1.7	2.0	1.7			1.0		1.7	2.0	1.3
11.0	12.6	5.1						7.4	
(28) 4.1	(18) 4.8	(24) 2.9	Net Profit + Depr., Dep., Amort./Cur. Mat. L/T/D					(12) 3.1	
3.6	2.8	1.6						1.3	
.4	.4	.5			.5		.5	.5	.4
1.0	1.0	1.2	Fixed/Worth		1.5		1.5	.8	.9
NM	31.0	3.8			-7.4		3.7	2.4	-3.1
.6	.5	.5			.5		.6	.5	.7
1.7	1.4	1.3	Debt/Worth		1.0		1.7	1.1	1.7
-35.1	82.4	8.5			-21.5		5.9	4.3	-9.7
48.1	54.0	53.6			52.1		61.3	58.4	56.4
(114) 25.0	(94) 25.9	(100) 24.7	% Profit Before Taxes/Tangible Net Worth		(20) 20.8		(32) 24.7	(28) 29.6	(10) 25.6
11.2	10.9	8.0			12.3		6.2	12.0	10.1
19.5	23.4	23.6			19.5		32.7	22.4	23.1
9.2	10.5	11.6	% Profit Before Taxes/Total Assets		6.7		10.4	14.3	11.7
2.5	3.1	1.9			.4		1.8	3.6	1.1
18.2	16.2	14.1			18.1		13.1	10.9	16.5
7.0	6.5	6.5	Sales/Net Fixed Assets		7.0		6.2	7.5	7.0
3.5	3.3	3.2			2.4		2.3	4.1	3.9
3.3	3.2	2.9			2.6		3.4	2.4	3.0
2.2	2.0	2.1	Sales/Total Assets		1.9		2.3	2.0	2.3
1.5	1.5	1.5			1.3		1.5	1.5	1.8
1.2	1.2	1.3			1.4		1.5	1.1	1.2
(132) 2.6	(104) 2.7	(114) 2.7	% Depr., Dep., Amort./Sales		(25) 2.8		(31) 2.6	2.1	3.4
4.7	4.8	4.5			5.5		5.7	3.4	4.3
2.1	2.1	3.1			6.5		2.0	1.6	
(75) 5.6	(54) 4.9	(53) 6.6	% Officers', Directors' Owners' Comp/Sales		(19) 8.1		(15) 4.7	(13) 3.1	
10.3	7.1	9.3			11.2		7.1	7.8	
1767315M	1612117M	1672018M	Net Sales ($)	3829M	58753M	29734M	254091M	490678M	834933M
845271M	975514M	900971M	Total Assets ($)	2132M	39977M	20585M	132282M	267199M	438796M

M = $ thousand MM = $ million

See Pages 9 through 22 for Explanation of Ratios and Data

Current Data Sorted by Assets							Comparative Historical Data	
						Type of Statement		
	1	8	8	4		Unqualified	13	11
	3	11	8			Reviewed	23	20
2	2	11	2			Compiled	32	28
7	20	9				Tax Returns	42	38
4	18	22	17	4	4	Other	63	77
	17 (4/1-9/30/13)		148 (10/1/13-3/31/14)				4/1/09-3/31/10 ALL	4/1/10-3/31/11 ALL
0-500M	500M-2MM	2-10MM	10-50MM	50-100MM	100-250MM			
13	44	61	35	8	4	NUMBER OF STATEMENTS	173	174
%	%	%	%	%	%	**ASSETS**	%	%
13.3	13.6	11.8	10.9			Cash & Equivalents	10.2	10.3
33.4	35.4	23.3	20.2			Trade Receivables (net)	23.0	26.4
11.5	21.9	30.5	32.5			Inventory	25.9	26.1
4.2	1.6	2.4	2.2			All Other Current	2.2	2.0
62.4	72.5	68.0	65.8			Total Current	61.2	64.8
21.6	20.8	23.1	23.0			Fixed Assets (net)	28.7	25.7
10.0	2.2	5.3	6.7			Intangibles (net)	3.8	4.5
6.0	4.5	3.6	4.5			All Other Non-Current	6.3	4.9
100.0	100.0	100.0	100.0			Total	100.0	100.0
						LIABILITIES		
15.8	6.2	8.8	5.9			Notes Payable-Short Term	11.1	11.9
1.9	5.5	3.5	1.7			Cur. Mat.-L.T.D.	5.3	5.2
52.2	15.9	14.4	7.6			Trade Payables	13.1	12.7
.0	.0	.3	.2			Income Taxes Payable	.3	.2
9.3	7.9	7.3	12.5			All Other Current	11.1	9.5
79.2	35.7	34.3	27.9			Total Current	40.9	39.6
23.1	31.3	14.1	7.3			Long-Term Debt	24.0	19.3
.0	.1	.1	.9			Deferred Taxes	.2	.3
10.3	2.3	5.1	5.2			All Other Non-Current	9.8	10.3
-12.6	30.6	46.4	58.6			Net Worth	25.1	30.5
100.0	100.0	100.0	100.0			Total Liabilties & Net Worth	100.0	100.0
						INCOME DATA		
100.0	100.0	100.0	100.0			Net Sales	100.0	100.0
46.2	40.0	32.0	32.7			Gross Profit	37.7	38.6
41.0	34.6	23.7	23.2			Operating Expenses	33.0	31.3
5.2	5.4	8.3	9.5			Operating Profit	4.6	7.3
-.3	.5	.8	1.0			All Other Expenses (net)	1.4	1.2
5.5	4.8	7.5	8.5			Profit Before Taxes	3.3	6.1
						RATIOS		
4.3	4.0	3.5	4.4				2.9	3.6
1.4	2.2	1.9	3.3			Current	1.7	1.9
.6	1.5	1.3	2.0				1.1	1.1
2.5	3.0	2.0	2.1				1.7	1.9
1.2	1.4	1.0	1.5			Quick	.8	1.1
.4	.8	.6	.8				.5	.5
0 UND	31 11.6	30 12.3	33 11.0				28 13.0	33 11.0
32 11.3	43 8.5	42 8.7	49 7.5			Sales/Receivables	44 8.2	48 7.6
44 8.3	57 6.4	56 6.5	57 6.4				58 6.3	61 6.0
0 UND	8 45.5	33 10.9	66 5.5				24 15.2	23 15.9
9 41.0	43 8.4	72 5.1	126 2.9			Cost of Sales/Inventory	72 5.1	68 5.4
27 13.5	78 4.7	152 2.4	152 2.4				129 2.8	138 2.6
0 UND	16 23.3	17 21.1	15 24.9				15 24.2	18 20.1
46 7.9	27 13.5	28 13.2	26 14.0			Cost of Sales/Payables	29 12.6	31 11.8
78 4.7	49 7.4	57 6.4	33 11.2				50 7.3	53 7.0
5.4	4.5	3.1	2.6				4.1	3.5
20.2	7.3	7.4	3.7			Sales/Working Capital	8.3	7.0
-37.1	18.0	15.4	6.6				80.1	68.3
	21.9	40.8	104.3				8.7	15.7
	(35) 6.2	(55) 13.1	(28) 31.1			EBIT/Interest	(162) 2.8	(154) 4.7
	1.4	2.3	1.9				.1	1.6
		8.4	8.4				5.7	7.9
		(10) 2.1	(12) 4.1			Net Profit + Depr., Dep., Amort./Cur. Mat. L/T/D	(35) 1.8	(25) 3.4
		1.1	1.8				.9	2.0
.4	.1	.2	.2				.3	.2
1.3	.5	.5	.4			Fixed/Worth	.8	.8
-.3	2.2	1.5	.8				5.6	4.8
2.6	.4	.5	.3				.8	.6
5.1	1.8	1.4	.6			Debt/Worth	2.3	2.0
-2.3	9.4	4.4	1.3				9.5	18.5
	60.5	62.1	34.2				51.7	72.9
	(35) 32.2	(53) 32.5	(32) 22.2			% Profit Before Taxes/Tangible Net Worth	(136) 21.3	(143) 31.4
	11.6	9.6	11.8				-.1	11.2
69.3	27.9	24.9	18.3				19.4	22.4
18.5	13.8	14.6	13.6			% Profit Before Taxes/Total Assets	5.1	10.7
1.7	2.7	3.2	5.1				-2.7	1.9
94.0	107.8	24.4	16.8				18.2	18.5
21.7	18.7	9.5	9.0			Sales/Net Fixed Assets	9.4	9.3
11.7	9.2	5.1	4.6				4.4	4.9
6.6	3.7	2.6	2.0				2.5	2.7
4.0	2.8	2.0	1.5			Sales/Total Assets	1.9	2.0
3.1	2.2	1.4	1.3				1.3	1.4
	.9	.9	.8				1.3	1.1
	(25) 2.1	(45) 2.1	(29) 2.0			% Depr., Dep., Amort./Sales	(142) 2.6	(151) 2.3
	4.9	4.0	2.9				4.8	4.5
	3.2	1.9					2.7	2.4
	(30) 5.2	(27) 4.7				% Officers', Directors' Owners' Comp/Sales	(89) 4.5	(75) 4.5
	9.2	8.5					7.9	7.8
17494M	141308M	623180M	1121950M	632477M	783670M	Net Sales ($)	4124465M	2910968M
3871M	49353M	317806M	739009M	570194M	587964M	Total Assets ($)	2340692M	2022480M

M = $ thousand MM = $ million

See Pages 9 through 22 for Explanation of Ratios and Data

Comparative Historical Data / **Current Data Sorted by Sales**

4/1/11-3/31/12 ALL	4/1/12-3/31/13 ALL	4/1/13-3/31/14 ALL	Type of Statement	0-1MM	1-3MM	3-5MM	5-10MM	10-25MM	25MM & OVER
17	9	21	Unqualified		2	1	3	7	8
19	16	22	Reviewed		2	2	4	10	4
33	27	17	Compiled		3	2	4	6	2
53	32	36	Tax Returns	4	9	14	8	1	
71	86	69	Other	3	14	8	9	16	19
				17 (4/1-9/30/13)		148 (10/1/13-3/31/14)			
193	170	165	**NUMBER OF STATEMENTS**	7	30	27	28	40	33
%	%	%	**ASSETS**	%	%	%	%	%	%
11.5	12.3	11.9	Cash & Equivalents		10.5	14.4	10.1	13.9	10.2
27.8	26.8	26.3	Trade Receivables (net)		28.8	36.5	27.1	21.6	21.2
23.1	25.6	27.1	Inventory		22.8	18.6	29.6	32.7	32.0
2.1	1.9	2.3	All Other Current		2.9	.8	1.3	2.4	2.4
64.5	66.6	67.6	Total Current		65.1	70.3	68.1	70.5	65.8
24.4	22.2	21.7	Fixed Assets (net)		26.0	17.9	21.5	22.8	16.7
4.8	6.5	6.2	Intangibles (net)		4.3	5.8	6.6	3.4	11.6
6.3	4.8	4.4	All Other Non-Current		4.6	5.9	3.8	3.3	5.8
100.0	100.0	100.0	Total		100.0	100.0	100.0	100.0	100.0
			LIABILITIES						
9.3	9.2	8.0	Notes Payable-Short Term		7.4	7.9	10.9	5.2	9.5
3.6	2.6	3.4	Cur. Mat.-L.T.D.		8.2	2.6	4.2	1.9	1.3
13.5	14.1	15.9	Trade Payables		14.9	17.1	15.5	12.0	9.2
.2	.3	.2	Income Taxes Payable		.0	.0	.2	.4	.2
13.3	8.8	8.6	All Other Current		9.5	8.8	7.6	8.8	9.4
40.0	35.0	36.1	Total Current		39.9	36.4	38.4	28.4	29.6
17.9	18.9	18.0	Long-Term Debt		42.6	16.5	13.8	8.2	9.5
.4	.4	.3	Deferred Taxes		.0	.2	.1	.5	.7
8.1	7.5	5.2	All Other Non-Current		1.7	5.1	4.1	6.6	6.9
33.7	38.2	40.4	Net Worth		15.7	41.8	43.6	56.4	53.3
100.0	100.0	100.0	Total Liabilties & Net Worth		100.0	100.0	100.0	100.0	100.0
			INCOME DATA						
100.0	100.0	100.0	Net Sales		100.0	100.0	100.0	100.0	100.0
39.2	38.1	35.6	Gross Profit		45.2	36.6	32.7	34.2	30.6
30.9	29.2	28.1	Operating Expenses		41.0	28.5	25.3	23.2	23.3
8.3	9.0	7.5	Operating Profit		4.2	8.1	7.4	11.0	7.3
.9	1.0	.9	All Other Expenses (net)		1.3	.1	.9	.3	2.0
7.4	8.0	6.6	Profit Before Taxes		2.9	8.0	6.5	10.8	5.3
			RATIOS						
3.9	4.7	4.0			3.9	6.0	3.0	4.6	4.3
2.0	2.1	2.3	Current		1.8	2.1	1.7	3.0	2.7
1.2	1.2	1.4			.9	1.4	1.3	1.6	1.8
2.2	3.1	2.2			2.3	3.1	1.8	2.5	2.0
1.1	1.0	1.2	Quick		1.1	1.5	.9	1.3	1.2
.6	.6	.7			.5	.8	.6	.7	.8
33 10.9	30 12.3	31 11.8			33 11.0	29 12.5	31 11.8	29 12.5	38 9.5
45 8.1	41 8.8	44 8.3	Sales/Receivables		40 9.2	50 7.3	42 8.6	37 9.9	50 7.3
59 6.2	54 6.7	57 6.4			51 7.1	72 5.1	58 6.3	56 6.5	57 6.4
13 28.5	27 13.5	29 12.5			19 18.8	4 95.3	24 15.0	48 7.6	69 5.3
52 7.0	59 6.2	70 5.2	Cost of Sales/Inventory		59 6.2	33 11.0	65 5.6	79 4.6	130 2.8
101 3.6	122 3.0	135 2.7			118 3.1	60 6.1	140 2.6	146 2.5	166 2.2
16 23.2	14 25.6	16 23.0			16 23.2	13 27.2	19 19.0	14 25.5	24 15.5
29 12.5	28 13.1	27 13.4	Cost of Sales/Payables		31 11.6	27 13.4	28 13.0	22 16.5	28 13.2
49 7.5	55 6.6	49 7.5			63 5.8	43 8.5	55 6.6	41 9.0	40 9.1
4.0	3.4	3.3			5.6	3.2	3.6	3.0	2.4
7.4	7.4	6.1	Sales/Working Capital		10.5	7.0	9.6	5.1	3.7
21.6	25.0	15.3			-104.0	21.0	17.5	7.9	7.4
19.4	31.6	38.2			7.1	41.8	19.8	76.6	34.2
(157) 6.0	(146) 9.0	(135) 10.0	EBIT/Interest		(23) 4.5	(21) 16.5	(25) 6.1	(35) 38.0	(27) 5.2
2.0	2.8	1.8			1.2	2.5	1.5	17.9	1.2
6.7	8.2	15.1						5.8	49.7
(29) 3.1	(27) 3.2	(26) 3.2	Net Profit + Depr., Dep., Amort./Cur. Mat. L/T/D					(12) 2.7	(10) 6.3
1.6	1.3	1.6						2.0	1.6
.2	.2	.2			.3	.0	.2	.2	.2
.6	.5	.5	Fixed/Worth		.9	.5	.5	.4	.3
2.4	2.2	1.6			-5.5	2.3	2.1	.7	1.0
.6	.5	.4			1.1	.2	.6	.4	.4
1.7	1.5	1.3	Debt/Worth		2.6	1.6	1.7	.7	.8
6.5	5.6	5.2			-11.9	10.5	5.7	1.5	2.7
67.7	60.7	50.1			80.2	61.8	49.7	69.8	31.2
(163) 30.2	(139) 33.0	(137) 29.5	% Profit Before Taxes/Tangible Net Worth		(21) 18.5	(21) 32.2	(24) 28.5	34.1	(27) 20.4
12.7	11.7	11.7			11.2	14.2	4.0	20.5	7.1
25.2	24.9	24.7			19.1	33.8	22.7	31.7	14.4
13.2	12.8	13.6	% Profit Before Taxes/Total Assets		7.9	22.0	11.5	18.0	9.3
3.7	3.4	2.9			.2	3.2	1.2	11.4	1.0
29.4	31.9	27.3			30.4	111.9	49.2	21.9	15.7
10.5	13.3	12.5	Sales/Net Fixed Assets		14.6	21.4	10.0	13.2	10.1
5.4	6.2	6.2			6.9	7.3	4.8	5.1	6.1
3.3	3.1	3.0			3.9	3.7	2.7	2.4	2.0
2.2	2.1	2.0	Sales/Total Assets		2.6	2.7	2.0	1.9	1.5
1.4	1.4	1.4			1.8	1.9	1.3	1.5	1.2
1.1	.8	.9			1.6	.9	.5	.8	.8
(143) 2.1	(120) 1.9	(114) 2.1	% Depr., Dep., Amort./Sales		(17) 3.9	(14) 2.2	(19) 1.8	(33) 1.6	(26) 1.8
4.0	3.0	3.6			5.6	4.1	4.7	2.8	3.0
2.5	2.6	2.5			3.7	2.7	3.9	1.5	
(92) 4.3	(69) 4.9	(67) 4.7	% Officers', Directors' Owners' Comp/Sales		(20) 6.2	(14) 4.0	(16) 4.7	(11) 4.1	
7.5	8.3	8.5			10.6	9.4	8.4	6.8	
2961021M	3279442M	3320079M	Net Sales ($)	4322M	63344M	107306M	207799M	638608M	2298700M
1842863M	2274868M	2268197M	Total Assets ($)	2519M	31019M	48949M	128047M	364640M	1693023M

M = $ thousand MM = $ million

See Pages 9 through 22 for Explanation of Ratios and Data

Current Data Sorted by Assets							Comparative Historical Data	
						Type of Statement		
		1	4	2	3	Unqualified	8	12
		5	6		2	Reviewed	14	18
	2	1			1	Compiled	7	9
	1	1				Tax Returns	10	4
	1	8	9	1	2	Other	15	23
	12 (4/1-9/30/13)		38 (10/1/13-3/31/14)				4/1/09-3/31/10 ALL	4/1/10-3/31/11 ALL
0-500M	500M-2MM	2-10MM	10-50MM	50-100MM	100-250MM			
	4	16	19	3	8	NUMBER OF STATEMENTS	54	66
%	%	%	%	%	%	**ASSETS**	%	%
DATA NOT AVAILABLE		8.9	12.5			Cash & Equivalents	13.1	11.1
		23.8	23.9			Trade Receivables (net)	25.5	25.7
		33.3	31.3			Inventory	31.3	29.5
		5.7	1.1			All Other Current	3.9	3.4
		71.8	68.7			Total Current	73.8	69.7
		19.8	22.5			Fixed Assets (net)	17.0	21.7
		1.8	2.7			Intangibles (net)	3.0	3.5
		6.6	6.1			All Other Non-Current	6.2	5.0
		100.0	100.0			Total	100.0	100.0
						LIABILITIES		
		10.9	10.1			Notes Payable-Short Term	6.9	9.3
		3.1	3.1			Cur. Mat.-L.T.D.	3.2	2.9
		7.8	9.9			Trade Payables	10.7	10.9
		.0	.1			Income Taxes Payable	.5	.5
		7.4	6.2			All Other Current	10.7	8.8
		29.2	29.4			Total Current	31.9	32.3
		10.5	10.3			Long-Term Debt	7.9	8.7
		.3	1.0			Deferred Taxes	.4	.7
		1.3	5.0			All Other Non-Current	5.8	3.9
		58.7	54.3			Net Worth	54.0	54.4
		100.0	100.0			Total Liabilties & Net Worth	100.0	100.0
						INCOME DATA		
		100.0	100.0			Net Sales	100.0	100.0
		35.9	29.0			Gross Profit	34.8	35.0
		27.9	20.1			Operating Expenses	27.9	25.3
		7.9	8.9			Operating Profit	6.9	9.7
		.5	.5			All Other Expenses (net)	.9	.9
		7.4	8.4			Profit Before Taxes	6.1	8.8
						RATIOS		
		6.1	4.6				6.3	4.5
		2.8	2.4			Current	2.8	2.5
		1.6	1.5				1.6	1.4
		2.0	2.7				3.6	2.4
		.9	1.7			Quick	1.1	1.2
		.6	.7				.7	.6
		33 11.2	**40** 9.2				**36** 10.1	**36** 10.1
		41 9.0	**50** 7.3			Sales/Receivables	**46** 7.9	**50** 7.3
		52 7.0	**60** 6.1				**60** 6.1	**60** 6.1
		34 10.6	**62** 5.9				**53** 6.9	**44** 8.2
		118 3.1	**91** 4.0			Cost of Sales/Inventory	**95** 3.8	**93** 3.9
		159 2.3	**122** 3.0				**150** 2.4	**140** 2.6
		10 35.5	**18** 19.8				**13** 28.0	**17** 21.0
		13 27.5	**26** 14.3			Cost of Sales/Payables	**22** 16.3	**28** 13.0
		30 12.3	**36** 10.2				**37** 10.0	**42** 8.6
		3.4	2.9				2.5	2.5
		5.3	5.1			Sales/Working Capital	4.0	4.8
		9.3	9.0				9.2	11.3
		83.2	33.1				17.4	21.4
		(14) 8.0	(17) 17.2			EBIT/Interest	(46) 3.8	(52) 11.1
		1.1	5.1				-.4	4.6
							3.5	12.7
						Net Profit + Depr., Dep., Amort./Cur. Mat. L/T/D	(15) 2.1	(17) 5.8
							.4	1.9
		.1	.2				.1	.2
		.4	.5			Fixed/Worth	.3	.4
		.8	1.2				.6	.9
		.2	.4				.3	.3
		.9	1.0			Debt/Worth	1.1	.8
		2.0	4.1				2.0	1.9
		55.4	43.8				37.1	43.3
		24.0	27.3			% Profit Before Taxes/Tangible Net Worth	(53) 17.6	(62) 26.5
		2.4	12.1				-1.7	17.2
		28.1	18.4				21.1	23.6
		13.5	8.9			% Profit Before Taxes/Total Assets	8.0	12.6
		1.4	5.9				-1.4	8.8
		48.1	16.9				40.3	28.2
		9.3	10.3			Sales/Net Fixed Assets	13.7	10.1
		5.3	3.8				6.5	4.3
		3.1	2.3				2.4	2.4
		2.0	1.8			Sales/Total Assets	1.6	1.6
		1.4	1.5				1.3	1.2
		1.1	1.2				.6	1.4
		(12) 1.8	(18) 1.9			% Depr., Dep., Amort./Sales	(44) 1.5	(53) 2.7
		3.6	3.4				3.0	4.3
							1.7	1.7
						% Officers', Directors' Owners' Comp/Sales	(12) 3.5	(17) 2.1
							9.9	3.8
	9528M	179193M	785858M	385927M	1623466M	Net Sales ($)	1570930M	2478124M
	3658M	82878M	438550M	217797M	1174875M	Total Assets ($)	1160848M	1860694M

M = $ thousand MM = $ million

See Pages 9 through 22 for Explanation of Ratios and Data

Comparative Historical Data				Current Data Sorted by Sales					
			Type of Statement						
12	11	10	Unqualified				1	2	7
16	17	13	Reviewed				2	5	6
7	6	4	Compiled		2				2
6	4	2	Tax Returns		1			1	
22	22	21	Other		1	2	2	4	12
4/1/11-3/31/12 ALL	**4/1/12-3/31/13 ALL**	**4/1/13-3/31/14 ALL**			**12 (4/1-9/30/13)**		**38 (10/1/13-3/31/14)**		
				0-1MM	**1-3MM**	**3-5MM**	**5-10MM**	**10-25MM**	**25MM & OVER**
63	60	50	**NUMBER OF STATEMENTS**		4	2	5	12	27
%	%	%	**ASSETS**	%	%	%	%	%	%
10.2	14.0	10.7	Cash & Equivalents	**D**				15.4	10.7
24.0	25.0	23.0	Trade Receivables (net)	**A**				26.8	21.5
32.2	29.8	32.5	Inventory	**T**				28.9	31.8
2.8	3.0	2.8	All Other Current	**A**				.6	4.0
69.2	71.8	69.1	Total Current					71.8	68.0
20.4	19.6	21.0	Fixed Assets (net)	**N**				21.2	22.6
6.0	3.8	4.8	Intangibles (net)	**O**				2.5	4.8
4.4	4.7	5.2	All Other Non-Current	**T**				4.5	4.6
100.0	100.0	100.0	Total					100.0	100.0
			LIABILITIES	**A**					
6.5	8.6	9.1	Notes Payable-Short Term	**V**				10.5	8.1
2.0	2.8	2.7	Cur. Mat.-L.T.D.	**A**				3.5	2.2
11.1	10.3	9.5	Trade Payables	**I**				9.6	9.9
.3	.5	.1	Income Taxes Payable	**L**				.0	.3
10.4	9.3	6.7	All Other Current	**A**				3.5	7.6
30.3	31.5	28.1	Total Current	**B**				27.0	28.1
10.6	13.6	11.6	Long-Term Debt	**L**				10.6	12.5
.6	.4	.8	Deferred Taxes	**E**				.8	1.0
5.4	5.1	5.0	All Other Non-Current					.9	5.3
53.0	49.3	54.5	Net Worth					60.7	53.0
100.0	100.0	100.0	Total Liabilties & Net Worth					100.0	100.0
			INCOME DATA						
100.0	100.0	100.0	Net Sales					100.0	100.0
33.3	34.9	31.5	Gross Profit					31.4	29.8
23.7	24.8	22.4	Operating Expenses					23.5	20.1
9.6	10.1	9.1	Operating Profit					7.9	9.8
.6	.5	.7	All Other Expenses (net)					.3	.6
9.0	9.6	8.4	Profit Before Taxes					7.6	9.2
			RATIOS						
4.3	5.1	4.5						7.3	4.3
2.4	2.5	2.6	Current					2.9	2.4
1.6	1.6	1.7						1.6	1.7
2.1	2.5	2.2						4.2	1.9
1.1	1.2	1.1	Quick					1.4	1.0
.7	.7	.7						.8	.7
39 9.4	**32** 11.5	**38** 9.7						**37** 9.8	**38** 9.6
44 8.3	**40** 9.2	**44** 8.3	Sales/Receivables					**43** 8.5	**50** 7.3
56 6.5	**51** 7.1	**56** 6.5						**61** 6.0	**58** 6.3
52 7.0	**39** 9.3	**59** 6.2						**29** 12.5	**62** 5.9
87 4.2	**87** 4.2	**91** 4.0	Cost of Sales/Inventory					**81** 4.5	**79** 4.6
130 2.8	**118** 3.1	**140** 2.6						**130** 2.8	**135** 2.7
21 17.3	**16** 23.4	**15** 24.1						**11** 33.1	**19** 19.3
27 13.7	**22** 16.6	**25** 14.7	Cost of Sales/Payables					**18** 20.8	**26** 14.0
43 8.4	**36** 10.2	**36** 10.2						**40** 9.2	**36** 10.0
3.0	3.4	3.2						3.3	3.2
4.6	5.3	4.9	Sales/Working Capital					4.4	5.1
9.8	9.0	8.6						14.8	8.5
58.3	46.8	33.1						122.5	30.1
(55) 12.9	(49) 14.2	(41) 9.9	EBIT/Interest					(11) 9.3	(22) 12.8
4.7	5.6	3.6						3.3	4.9
14.9	18.4	20.9							44.0
(14) 8.9	(14) 5.8	(13) 2.7	Net Profit + Depr., Dep., Amort./Cur. Mat. L/T/D						(10) 3.0
1.9	2.4	1.7							2.1
.3	.1	.2						.1	.3
.4	.5	.4	Fixed/Worth					.5	.4
.9	.7	1.1						.7	1.2
.3	.3	.4						.2	.4
.9	1.1	1.0	Debt/Worth					.7	1.0
2.4	2.1	2.7						2.0	2.7
49.3	55.6	51.2						55.4	46.4
(60) 31.4	(56) 36.5	(47) 28.0	% Profit Before Taxes/Tangible Net Worth					33.0	(25) 29.0
15.3	14.1	12.3						4.8	13.3
22.3	34.4	21.8						37.6	18.4
12.9	15.0	12.5	% Profit Before Taxes/Total Assets					18.1	8.6
6.4	7.2	5.8						2.4	5.9
23.6	36.8	24.3						57.5	16.9
10.9	12.2	9.9	Sales/Net Fixed Assets					11.3	9.0
5.2	5.4	5.2						4.6	5.0
2.4	2.8	2.5						3.0	2.3
1.7	2.1	1.8	Sales/Total Assets					2.0	1.6
1.3	1.5	1.4						1.5	1.3
1.0	.8	1.0						1.1	1.2
(52) 2.0	(52) 1.6	(43) 1.8	% Depr., Dep., Amort./Sales					(10) 1.9	(25) 1.8
3.2	2.8	3.3						4.5	2.9
1.1	1.2	1.3							
(14) 1.8	(21) 2.4	(13) 1.8	% Officers', Directors' Owners' Comp/Sales						
3.1	10.3	3.4							
2862461M	**2538034M**	**2983972M**	Net Sales ($)		**8621M**	**7801M**	**36074M**	**182970M**	**2748506M**
1931373M	**1564737M**	**1917758M**	Total Assets ($)		**6738M**	**4559M**	**21543M**	**99264M**	**1785654M**

 M = $ thousand MM = $ million

See Pages 9 through 22 for Explanation of Ratios and Data

Current Data Sorted by Assets / Comparative Historical Data

DATA NOT AVAILABLE

						Type of Statement				
		1	1		3	Unqualified		11		8
		2				Reviewed		8		8
		1				Compiled				2
		1	1			Tax Returns		2		3
	1	3	5	1	3	Other		11		10
	4 (4/1-9/30/13)		19 (10/1/13-3/31/14)					4/1/09-3/31/10		4/1/10-3/31/11
0-500M	500M-2MM	2-10MM	10-50MM	50-100MM	100-250MM			ALL		ALL
	1	8	7	1	6	NUMBER OF STATEMENTS		32		31
%	%	%	%	%	%	ASSETS		%		%
						Cash & Equivalents		11.1		8.9
						Trade Receivables (net)		21.8		22.7
						Inventory		31.2		28.6
						All Other Current		4.3		4.3
						Total Current		68.3		64.6
						Fixed Assets (net)		19.5		17.5
						Intangibles (net)		7.2		10.2
						All Other Non-Current		4.9		7.7
						Total		100.0		100.0
						LIABILITIES				
						Notes Payable-Short Term		9.8		12.0
						Cur. Mat.-L.T.D.		2.4		3.4
						Trade Payables		10.6		8.6
						Income Taxes Payable		.5		.5
						All Other Current		9.8		8.7
						Total Current		33.2		33.2
						Long-Term Debt		16.2		18.2
						Deferred Taxes		.2		.7
						All Other Non-Current		6.7		12.4
						Net Worth		43.7		35.5
						Total Liabilties & Net Worth		100.0		100.0
						INCOME DATA				
						Net Sales		100.0		100.0
						Gross Profit		34.7		35.2
						Operating Expenses		30.7		31.6
						Operating Profit		4.0		3.6
						All Other Expenses (net)		1.3		.7
						Profit Before Taxes		2.7		2.9
						RATIOS				
								4.4		4.8
						Current		2.2		2.3
								1.4		1.3
								2.2		2.3
						Quick		.7		1.1
								.6		.5
							36	10.0	**35**	10.4
						Sales/Receivables	**44**	8.3	**43**	8.5
							54	6.8	**57**	6.4
							68	5.4	**52**	7.0
						Cost of Sales/Inventory	**102**	3.6	**87**	4.2
							134	2.7	**159**	2.3
							21	17.4	**11**	34.4
						Cost of Sales/Payables	**25**	14.3	**23**	15.7
							37	9.8	**34**	10.8
								3.1		2.9
						Sales/Working Capital		4.9		4.5
								10.8		17.7
								16.5		12.3
						EBIT/Interest	(29)	2.6	(27)	3.0
								1.1		-.1
								9.0		
						Net Profit + Depr., Dep., Amort./Cur. Mat. L/T/D	(16)	4.0		
								.8		
								.2		.2
						Fixed/Worth		.6		.5
								2.0		11.9
								.5		.6
						Debt/Worth		1.7		1.8
								7.8		26.5
								33.3		34.0
						% Profit Before Taxes/Tangible Net Worth	(27)	13.6	(24)	20.8
								3.0		9.0
								14.1		13.6
						% Profit Before Taxes/Total Assets		4.4		6.7
								.7		-3.3
								16.8		27.4
						Sales/Net Fixed Assets		9.9		12.6
								6.2		7.0
								2.2		2.3
						Sales/Total Assets		1.9		1.8
								1.3		1.2
								1.2		.9
						% Depr., Dep., Amort./Sales	(28)	2.0	(22)	1.7
								3.3		2.7
						% Officers', Directors' Owners' Comp/Sales				
	4569M	132649M	321844M	113748M	1340391M	Net Sales ($)		2084224M		1685821M
	1477M	46166M	198337M	56482M	931111M	Total Assets ($)		1377117M		1170908M

M = $ thousand MM = $ million

See Pages 9 through 22 for Explanation of Ratios and Data

Comparative Historical Data				Current Data Sorted by Sales					
			Type of Statement						
5	4	5	Unqualified					1	4
6	6	2	Reviewed					2	
3	4	1	Compiled						1
5	4	2	Tax Returns				2		
17	14	13	Other			1	1	2	9
				4 (4/1-9/30/13)		19 (10/1/13-3/31/14)			
4/1/11-3/31/12 ALL	**4/1/12-3/31/13 ALL**	**4/1/13-3/31/14 ALL**		**0-1MM**	**1-3MM**	**3-5MM**	**5-10MM**	**10-25MM**	**25MM & OVER**
36	32	23	**NUMBER OF STATEMENTS**			1	3	5	14
%	%	%	**ASSETS**	%	%	%	%	%	%
10.5	9.5	11.2	Cash & Equivalents	DATA NOT AVAILABLE	DATA NOT AVAILABLE				14.0
25.6	27.0	26.4	Trade Receivables (net)						23.8
31.7	34.4	31.4	Inventory						24.6
2.2	4.3	3.7	All Other Current						4.0
69.9	75.1	72.7	Total Current						66.4
18.3	15.0	11.8	Fixed Assets (net)						13.5
7.9	6.8	11.2	Intangibles (net)						16.1
3.8	3.1	4.4	All Other Non-Current						4.0
100.0	100.0	100.0	Total						100.0
			LIABILITIES						
12.0	10.7	7.0	Notes Payable-Short Term						6.3
1.6	1.7	2.3	Cur. Mat.-L.T.D.						1.5
15.2	17.2	18.2	Trade Payables						14.0
.1	.4	.3	Income Taxes Payable						.4
8.5	8.3	11.4	All Other Current						10.8
37.4	38.4	39.1	Total Current						33.0
16.4	11.0	14.4	Long-Term Debt						11.4
.8	1.1	.5	Deferred Taxes						.6
4.9	2.6	7.1	All Other Non-Current						8.8
40.4	46.9	38.9	Net Worth						46.2
100.0	100.0	100.0	Total Liabilties & Net Worth						100.0
			INCOME DATA						
100.0	100.0	100.0	Net Sales						100.0
34.9	37.5	32.0	Gross Profit						30.7
30.9	29.1	27.8	Operating Expenses						23.4
4.0	8.4	4.2	Operating Profit						7.3
1.0	.5	.5	All Other Expenses (net)						.7
3.0	7.9	3.7	Profit Before Taxes						6.6
			RATIOS						
3.9	4.8	4.5	Current						3.7
1.8	1.9	1.9							2.2
1.2	1.3	1.4							1.4
1.7	1.8	1.9	Quick						1.9
.8	1.1	1.4							1.4
.5	.5	.5							.6
35 10.4	**32** 11.4	**33** 10.9	Sales/Receivables						**37** 9.8
42 8.7	**47** 7.7	**42** 8.6							**42** 8.6
61 6.0	**60** 6.1	**56** 6.5							**58** 6.3
72 5.1	**62** 5.9	**46** 8.0	Cost of Sales/Inventory						**42** 8.7
101 3.6	**96** 3.8	**79** 4.6							**78** 4.7
130 2.8	**166** 2.2	**135** 2.7							**99** 3.7
19 18.8	**17** 21.5	**20** 18.3	Cost of Sales/Payables						**15** 24.3
33 11.2	**35** 10.5	**34** 10.8							**32** 11.5
41 8.9	**51** 7.2	**49** 7.4							**48** 7.6
3.2	2.7	2.9	Sales/Working Capital						2.9
5.0	4.2	6.6							5.2
22.7	10.8	14.5							16.5
21.0	39.3	38.1	EBIT/Interest						38.1
(30) 4.7	(28) 9.1	(19) 4.5							(11) 7.3
.2	3.9	1.6							1.6
			Net Profit + Depr., Dep., Amort./Cur. Mat. L/T/D						
.2	.2	.2	Fixed/Worth						.2
.5	.3	.4							.4
1.6	.9	1.9							NM
.5	.4	.4	Debt/Worth						.4
1.3	1.4	1.3							1.2
8.4	3.2	-7.9							-6.9
33.2	56.8	27.3	% Profit Before Taxes/Tangible Net Worth						25.7
(29) 13.8	(28) 25.1	(17) 23.0							(10) 23.0
2.7	12.4	10.3							14.2
10.8	22.7	16.6	% Profit Before Taxes/Total Assets						19.1
6.5	10.3	8.3							11.1
-3.4	3.8	2.3							2.3
32.6	36.0	46.3	Sales/Net Fixed Assets						33.2
11.4	16.4	19.0							13.7
6.5	7.0	9.1							7.9
2.4	2.4	2.9	Sales/Total Assets						2.3
1.8	2.0	2.0							1.7
1.2	1.3	1.3							1.3
1.2	1.0	.8	% Depr., Dep., Amort./Sales						1.2
(25) 2.0	(24) 1.6	(19) 1.7							(11) 1.9
3.8	2.8	2.5							3.9
			% Officers', Directors' Owners' Comp/Sales						
1937965M	1776610M	1913201M	Net Sales ($)			4569M	22979M	77976M	1807677M
1303868M	1176242M	1233573M	Total Assets ($)			1477M	20022M	30601M	1181473M

M = $ thousand MM = $ million

See Pages 9 through 22 for Explanation of Ratios and Data

Current Data Sorted by Assets / Comparative Historical Data

0-500M	500M-2MM	2-10MM	10-50MM	50-100MM	100-250MM		4/1/09-3/31/10 ALL	4/1/10-3/31/11 ALL
						Type of Statement		
		1	6	2	4	Unqualified	20	23
	2	10	5			Reviewed	16	12
	3	6	3			Compiled	11	9
5	6	6				Tax Returns	13	15
	3	10	6	2	3	Other	38	40
	13 (4/1-9/30/13)		70 (10/1/13-3/31/14)					
5	14	33	20	4	7	**NUMBER OF STATEMENTS**	98	99
%	%	%	%	%	%	**ASSETS**	%	%
	13.6	10.0	10.7			Cash & Equivalents	9.7	11.1
	32.4	21.6	23.2			Trade Receivables (net)	23.1	25.8
	14.4	39.4	35.2			Inventory	28.1	30.2
	2.9	.7	1.7			All Other Current	2.7	2.2
	63.3	71.7	70.8			Total Current	63.5	69.3
	20.0	24.4	22.0			Fixed Assets (net)	23.8	20.7
	4.0	1.8	2.5			Intangibles (net)	6.3	4.4
	12.6	2.1	4.8			All Other Non-Current	6.3	5.6
	100.0	100.0	100.0			Total	100.0	100.0
						LIABILITIES		
	7.0	7.7	2.9			Notes Payable-Short Term	7.5	8.7
	5.7	3.4	2.7			Cur. Mat.-L.T.D.	5.4	3.2
	14.1	11.0	9.1			Trade Payables	11.3	12.5
	.1	.9	.0			Income Taxes Payable	.1	.3
	6.1	5.1	12.6			All Other Current	7.1	7.8
	33.0	28.1	27.3			Total Current	31.4	32.5
	16.5	16.1	11.4			Long-Term Debt	22.8	13.8
	.8	.4	.4			Deferred Taxes	.4	.4
	.4	4.4	4.3			All Other Non-Current	7.5	4.8
	49.3	51.0	56.6			Net Worth	37.8	48.5
	100.0	100.0	100.0			Total Liabilties & Net Worth	100.0	100.0
						INCOME DATA		
	100.0	100.0	100.0			Net Sales	100.0	100.0
	43.2	32.7	29.0			Gross Profit	31.4	31.3
	34.6	23.1	19.3			Operating Expenses	27.1	25.1
	8.6	9.6	9.7			Operating Profit	4.4	6.3
	1.0	1.2	.0			All Other Expenses (net)	1.4	.7
	7.6	8.4	9.7			Profit Before Taxes	3.0	5.6
						RATIOS		
	4.9	4.8	4.8				3.6	3.8
	1.7	2.8	2.8			Current	2.1	2.1
	1.1	1.8	1.7				1.4	1.4
	3.6	2.1	2.3				2.0	2.1
	1.2	1.0	1.3			Quick	1.1	1.2
	.5	.7	.8				.6	.7
	31 11.8	32 11.3	38 9.7				35 10.5	37 9.8
	47 7.7	41 8.9	42 8.6			Sales/Receivables	45 8.1	51 7.1
	61 6.0	49 7.4	52 7.0				60 6.1	66 5.5
	0 UND	57 6.4	81 4.5				47 7.7	54 6.7
	16 23.3	107 3.4	99 3.7			Cost of Sales/Inventory	85 4.3	96 3.8
	111 3.3	182 2.0	146 2.5				142 2.6	131 2.8
	15 24.0	20 18.5	18 20.5				17 21.2	19 18.8
	21 17.4	26 14.0	24 15.1			Cost of Sales/Payables	28 13.2	34 10.8
	55 6.6	50 7.3	29 12.6				43 8.4	52 7.0
	4.5	2.9	3.0				3.7	2.7
	12.5	4.2	4.3			Sales/Working Capital	5.3	4.8
	49.3	7.4	6.8				14.2	10.5
	34.0	21.1	56.6				10.5	21.1
	(11) 17.8	(30) 6.3	(16) 22.9			EBIT/Interest	(87) 3.7	(85) 5.4
	2.2	3.9	10.0				.7	1.2
		10.6					6.7	9.2
		(12) 6.3				Net Profit + Depr., Dep., Amort./Cur. Mat. L/T/D	(42) 2.0	(32) 2.8
		2.4					.7	1.3
	.1	.2	.3				.2	.2
	.4	.4	.4			Fixed/Worth	.6	.4
	1.1	1.5	.6				2.2	1.0
	.3	.5	.3				.7	.5
	.9	.8	.6			Debt/Worth	1.6	1.1
	4.3	2.8	1.5				6.8	3.0
	50.4	53.8	30.3				40.2	27.8
	(12) 29.0	27.7	(19) 25.1			% Profit Before Taxes/Tangible Net Worth	(82) 17.8	(92) 16.4
	6.6	11.1	20.7				-1.6	3.3
	30.4	21.1	20.0				12.8	14.0
	18.7	12.1	16.9			% Profit Before Taxes/Total Assets	6.0	6.7
	4.7	3.8	10.0				-1.4	1.9
	48.4	19.4	15.4				17.4	23.7
	15.9	9.6	8.5			Sales/Net Fixed Assets	8.4	9.6
	11.0	4.4	4.8				4.7	5.1
	3.2	2.3	2.2				2.3	2.0
	2.8	1.8	1.8			Sales/Total Assets	1.8	1.6
	2.1	1.4	1.5				1.2	1.3
	.8	1.0	1.2				1.1	1.0
	(10) 1.9	(31) 1.6	(17) 1.9			% Depr., Dep., Amort./Sales	(88) 2.0	(79) 2.3
	2.7	2.9	3.2				5.3	3.5
		1.3					2.7	1.6
		(13) 5.5				% Officers', Directors' Owners' Comp/Sales	(30) 4.7	(21) 4.7
		11.8					8.2	9.6
14792M	44397M	346538M	862109M	470746M	1444887M	Net Sales ($)	2674664M	3614183M
1473M	15548M	187580M	472242M	293237M	1216388M	Total Assets ($)	1749954M	2351384M

M = $ thousand MM = $ million

See Pages 9 through 22 for Explanation of Ratios and Data

Comparative Historical Data | **Current Data Sorted by Sales**

4/1/11-3/31/12 ALL	4/1/12-3/31/13 ALL	4/1/13-3/31/14 ALL	Type of Statement	0-1MM	1-3MM	3-5MM	5-10MM	10-25MM	25MM & OVER
9	10	13	Unqualified					4	9
19	22	17	Reviewed		1	1	3	8	4
10	11	12	Compiled		1	2	4	2	3
14	12	17	Tax Returns	1	6	5	4	1	
28	34	24	Other		2	3	5	3	11
					13 (4/1-9/30/13)		70 (10/1/13-3/31/14)		
80	89	83	**NUMBER OF STATEMENTS**	1	10	11	16	18	27
%	%	%	**ASSETS**	%	%	%	%	%	%
12.1	10.1	12.3	Cash & Equivalents		15.2	14.5	11.6	10.4	12.1
27.1	22.2	23.5	Trade Receivables (net)		34.0	12.4	26.8	22.6	23.4
30.2	33.7	31.4	Inventory		17.0	27.3	30.7	41.8	29.8
1.3	1.9	2.0	All Other Current		.4	4.0	1.1	.7	3.2
70.7	68.0	69.1	Total Current		66.7	58.1	70.1	75.5	68.6
18.8	20.0	23.6	Fixed Assets (net)		16.8	32.1	25.3	22.0	23.7
4.4	4.7	2.2	Intangibles (net)		4.8	2.6	2.0	.4	2.6
6.1	7.3	5.1	All Other Non-Current		11.8	7.2	2.6	2.1	5.1
100.0	100.0	100.0	Total		100.0	100.0	100.0	100.0	100.0
			LIABILITIES						
10.2	7.6	8.4	Notes Payable-Short Term		5.1	10.8	16.6	6.1	5.7
3.6	3.5	3.2	Cur. Mat.-L.T.D.		4.6	4.0	3.5	2.7	2.6
14.2	11.5	12.3	Trade Payables		17.3	16.1	12.3	11.4	9.7
.1	.1	.4	Income Taxes Payable		.1	2.4	.0	.1	.1
8.3	6.2	7.3	All Other Current		5.7	4.9	4.4	13.1	7.1
36.5	29.0	31.7	Total Current		32.8	38.2	36.8	33.4	25.2
14.1	15.0	14.4	Long-Term Debt		11.3	23.6	17.2	9.0	11.4
.7	.5	.6	Deferred Taxes		.3	.7	.4	1.1	.5
4.1	3.6	3.4	All Other Non-Current		.2	1.3	6.1	2.0	4.9
44.6	51.9	50.0	Net Worth		55.4	36.2	39.4	54.5	58.0
100.0	100.0	100.0	Total Liabilties & Net Worth		100.0	100.0	100.0	100.0	100.0
			INCOME DATA						
100.0	100.0	100.0	Net Sales		100.0	100.0	100.0	100.0	100.0
34.6	31.6	32.7	Gross Profit		43.3	33.2	32.5	32.1	28.9
26.9	23.1	23.4	Operating Expenses		38.5	25.5	24.5	21.2	17.8
7.7	8.5	9.3	Operating Profit		4.9	7.7	8.0	10.9	11.0
.5	1.2	.8	All Other Expenses (net)		1.1	1.4	1.1	.0	.4
7.1	7.3	8.5	Profit Before Taxes		3.7	6.3	6.8	10.8	10.7
			RATIOS						
4.2	4.5	4.9			8.4	3.7	5.9	5.1	6.1
2.3	2.5	2.4	Current		2.0	1.9	2.3	2.7	2.6
1.6	1.5	1.5			1.1	1.1	1.5	1.5	1.8
2.3	2.2	2.3			5.5	1.7	2.0	2.3	3.1
1.2	1.0	1.1	Quick		1.7	.5	1.3	.9	1.3
.8	.7	.8			.6	.4	.8	.6	.9
36 10.0	**29** 12.5	**35** 10.3			**33** 11.2	**5** 70.9	**33** 11.1	**34** 10.6	**39** 9.3
50 7.3	**40** 9.1	**43** 8.4	Sales/Receivables		**47** 7.7	**33** 11.1	**41** 9.0	**42** 8.6	**45** 8.2
63 5.8	**57** 6.4	**53** 6.9			**61** 6.0	**55** 6.6	**62** 5.9	**49** 7.4	**61** 6.0
38 9.7	**49** 7.5	**43** 8.4			**0** UND	**12** 31.5	**44** 8.3	**65** 5.6	**70** 5.2
91 4.0	**94** 3.9	**94** 3.9	Cost of Sales/Inventory		**35** 10.3	**99** 3.7	**69** 5.3	**114** 3.2	**89** 4.1
166 2.2	**159** 2.3	**146** 2.5			**111** 3.3	**228** 1.6	**174** 2.1	**182** 2.0	**130** 2.8
17 21.3	**14** 25.3	**18** 20.6			**16** 22.5	**15** 23.7	**17** 21.5	**20** 18.5	**17** 21.1
31 11.9	**23** 16.2	**26** 14.1	Cost of Sales/Payables		**40** 9.1	**23** 15.6	**25** 14.8	**26** 14.2	**26** 14.1
50 7.3	**41** 9.0	**46** 7.9			**57** 6.4	**55** 6.6	**49** 7.5	**46** 7.9	**35** 10.3
3.2	3.3	2.9			3.2	3.8	2.5	3.0	2.5
4.8	5.3	4.9	Sales/Working Capital		9.1	10.1	5.8	3.8	3.8
8.4	9.7	9.4			42.8	82.0	13.6	11.8	6.2
23.0	21.8	31.4					11.7	34.2	59.0
(65) 9.0	(74) 7.4	(70) 10.9	EBIT/Interest				(15) 6.4	(15) 14.8	(23) 18.9
1.6	2.5	3.9					4.6	3.9	6.7
4.8	14.1	9.8							
(26) 2.8	(26) 3.3	(21) 5.1	Net Profit + Depr., Dep., Amort./Cur. Mat. L/T/D						
1.6	1.8	2.6							
.1	.2	.2			.0	.3	.2	.2	.2
.3	.3	.4	Fixed/Worth		.2	.8	.6	.4	.4
.8	.8	.8			.9	4.9	1.7	.6	.7
.6	.5	.4			.1	.4	.6	.4	.3
1.2	1.1	.8	Debt/Worth		.6	1.3	1.6	.8	.6
2.6	2.1	2.8			6.1	38.7	3.2	2.0	1.6
43.3	41.8	46.3					81.4	49.7	39.4
(74) 19.9	(84) 22.5	(78) 25.7	% Profit Before Taxes/Tangible Net Worth				(15) 27.0	25.2	(26) 25.2
4.8	12.5	13.2					11.1	16.4	17.1
20.0	21.2	22.6			26.0	18.6	22.8	38.4	20.6
11.6	11.5	13.5	% Profit Before Taxes/Total Assets		16.8	8.6	13.2	13.6	13.9
2.1	4.3	4.5			-.9	1.0	3.4	5.7	9.7
40.7	35.3	21.3			UND	15.0	21.8	20.0	15.5
11.9	11.2	10.9	Sales/Net Fixed Assets		29.2	9.9	10.2	12.2	6.9
5.1	5.7	4.8			11.2	3.5	4.9	5.4	4.4
2.7	2.7	2.5			3.2	2.9	2.8	2.3	2.2
1.8	1.9	1.8	Sales/Total Assets		2.6	1.8	1.8	1.9	1.7
1.2	1.3	1.4			2.1	.9	1.6	1.6	1.3
.8	.8	1.1				1.2	.7	1.0	1.6
(67) 2.1	(71) 2.1	(70) 2.1	% Depr., Dep., Amort./Sales			(10) 1.5	(15) 1.6	(17) 1.5	(22) 2.3
3.3	3.4	3.0				2.5	3.0	3.3	4.1
1.7	1.5	1.7							
(24) 6.0	(26) 3.9	(24) 5.6	% Officers', Directors' Owners' Comp/Sales						
10.9	6.5	11.9							
1988704M	**3215138M**	**3183469M**	Net Sales ($)	**144M**	**17444M**	**45104M**	**115385M**	**297758M**	**2707634M**
1494544M	**2230161M**	**2186468M**	Total Assets ($)	**296M**	**7528M**	**32364M**	**58337M**	**161685M**	**1926258M**

M = $ thousand MM = $ million

See Pages 9 through 22 for Explanation of Ratios and Data

Current Data Sorted by Assets							Comparative Historical Data	
						Type of Statement		
			4			Unqualified	12	6
		1	2			Reviewed	6	6
		2				Compiled	1	2
	2	3				Tax Returns	3	3
	2	2	5		1	Other	14	12
	4 (4/1-9/30/13)		20 (10/1/13-3/31/14)				4/1/09-3/31/10	4/1/10-3/31/11
0-500M	**500M-2MM**	**2-10MM**	**10-50MM**	**50-100MM**	**100-250MM**		**ALL**	**ALL**
	4	8	11		1	**NUMBER OF STATEMENTS**	36	29
%	%	%	%	%	%	**ASSETS**	%	%
DATA NOT AVAILABLE			7.2	DATA NOT AVAILABLE		Cash & Equivalents	10.9	9.3
			21.5			Trade Receivables (net)	21.5	24.0
			31.0			Inventory	28.2	31.4
			3.4			All Other Current	2.8	2.1
			63.0			Total Current	63.3	66.8
			23.0			Fixed Assets (net)	24.2	22.1
			4.6			Intangibles (net)	4.2	8.4
			9.4			All Other Non-Current	8.3	2.8
			100.0			Total	100.0	100.0
DATA NOT AVAILABLE				DATA NOT AVAILABLE		**LIABILITIES**		
			4.8			Notes Payable-Short Term	9.3	11.8
			2.6			Cur. Mat.-L.T.D.	3.0	2.9
			15.4			Trade Payables	9.3	14.3
			.0			Income Taxes Payable	.0	.1
			6.8			All Other Current	9.4	6.1
			29.6			Total Current	31.0	35.2
			12.9			Long-Term Debt	14.6	9.3
			1.8			Deferred Taxes	.6	.2
			16.9			All Other Non-Current	4.4	5.4
			38.9			Net Worth	49.4	49.8
			100.0			Total Liabilities & Net Worth	100.0	100.0
						INCOME DATA		
			100.0			Net Sales	100.0	100.0
			26.3			Gross Profit	26.4	28.0
			20.2			Operating Expenses	22.0	20.1
			6.1			Operating Profit	4.4	7.9
			1.0			All Other Expenses (net)	1.7	1.6
			5.1			Profit Before Taxes	2.7	6.4
						RATIOS		
			4.3				4.2	3.6
			2.1			Current	2.1	1.8
			1.2				1.2	1.1
			1.5				2.5	2.0
			.9			Quick	.9	.8
			.6				.4	.5
			32 11.3				**30** 12.0	**40** 9.1
			40 9.2			Sales/Receivables	**47** 7.8	**47** 7.8
			66 5.5				**66** 5.5	**58** 6.2
			41 8.9				**46** 7.9	**51** 7.2
			89 4.1			Cost of Sales/Inventory	**81** 4.5	**85** 4.3
			182 2.0				**147** 2.5	**143** 2.6
			13 28.6				**12** 29.6	**20** 18.0
			27 13.5			Cost of Sales/Payables	**26** 14.1	**33** 11.1
			63 5.8				**46** 8.0	**50** 7.2
			2.7				2.8	3.5
			5.3			Sales/Working Capital	5.2	8.3
			24.3				13.8	27.8
			39.4				12.5	27.3
			(10) 10.9			EBIT/Interest	(33) 2.9	4.6
			2.7				.4	1.6
							2.9	
						Net Profit + Depr., Dep., Amort./Cur. Mat. L/T/D	(10) 1.1	
							.4	
			.1				.2	.2
			.8			Fixed/Worth	.6	.4
			1.2				1.5	1.6
			.7				.3	.5
			1.5			Debt/Worth	1.9	1.4
			2.4				2.6	3.0
			17.5				16.7	33.7
			(10) 9.8			% Profit Before Taxes/Tangible Net Worth	(34) 4.5	(27) 16.5
			4.8				-5.6	7.3
			12.4				9.0	15.2
			4.0			% Profit Before Taxes/Total Assets	1.8	7.6
			1.2				-1.2	1.6
			15.5				14.1	22.2
			11.4			Sales/Net Fixed Assets	5.5	12.3
			3.6				4.2	5.2
			2.0				1.9	2.4
			1.7			Sales/Total Assets	1.4	1.7
			1.2				1.1	1.3
			.6				1.8	1.1
			1.6			% Depr., Dep., Amort./Sales	(31) 2.6	(27) 1.9
			4.5				3.3	3.5
						% Officers', Directors' Owners' Comp/Sales		
	18175M	85131M	440882M		253233M	Net Sales ($)	1843572M	1683530M
	5643M	48560M	284900M		185421M	Total Assets ($)	1483999M	1026379M

M = $ thousand MM = $ million

See Pages 9 through 22 for Explanation of Ratios and Data

Comparative Historical Data				Current Data Sorted by Sales					
			Type of Statement						
11	5	4	Unqualified					1	3
8	7	3	Reviewed					2	1
3	1	2	Compiled				1	1	
3	1	5	Tax Returns		1	1		3	
11	11	10	Other			1	2	3	4
					4 (4/1-9/30/13)		20 (10/1/13-3/31/14)		
4/1/11-3/31/12 ALL	**4/1/12-3/31/13 ALL**	**4/1/13-3/31/14 ALL**		**0-1MM**	**1-3MM**	**3-5MM**	**5-10MM**	**10-25MM**	**25MM & OVER**
36	25	24	**NUMBER OF STATEMENTS**		1	2	3	10	8
%	%	%	**ASSETS**	%	%	%	%	%	%
10.7	10.0	12.7	Cash & Equivalents	D				17.2	
23.7	20.8	23.1	Trade Receivables (net)	A				28.7	
33.1	27.6	30.0	Inventory	T				20.0	
2.2	3.3	4.3	All Other Current	A				5.1	
69.6	61.6	70.2	Total Current					71.0	
22.6	29.4	17.6	Fixed Assets (net)	N				19.9	
4.4	4.8	3.4	Intangibles (net)	O				5.0	
3.5	4.2	8.9	All Other Non-Current	T				4.0	
100.0	100.0	100.0	Total					100.0	
			LIABILITIES	A					
7.0	10.5	7.7	Notes Payable-Short Term	V				8.2	
2.4	2.3	1.5	Cur. Mat.-L.T.D.	A				2.1	
13.4	12.7	12.6	Trade Payables	I				14.9	
.0	.5	.0	Income Taxes Payable	L				.0	
6.0	7.9	5.9	All Other Current	A				5.6	
28.7	33.8	27.7	Total Current	B				30.8	
11.1	16.8	8.2	Long-Term Debt	L				8.5	
.2	1.1	.9	Deferred Taxes	E				.9	
6.5	5.5	21.1	All Other Non-Current					2.6	
53.4	42.9	42.1	Net Worth					57.2	
100.0	100.0	100.0	Total Liabilties & Net Worth					100.0	
			INCOME DATA						
100.0	100.0	100.0	Net Sales					100.0	
30.3	26.5	32.7	Gross Profit					31.3	
23.3	19.3	24.5	Operating Expenses					24.0	
7.0	7.2	8.2	Operating Profit					7.3	
.6	1.1	.9	All Other Expenses (net)					.7	
6.4	6.1	7.3	Profit Before Taxes					6.6	
			RATIOS						
5.0	3.8	5.3						8.9	
2.8	2.2	2.7	Current					2.3	
1.6	1.3	1.5						1.0	
3.0	1.9	3.1						5.3	
1.3	.7	.9	Quick					1.6	
.6	.5	.6						.6	
40 9.1	**34** 10.6	**32** 11.3						**36** 10.2	
45 8.1	**41** 8.9	**39** 9.3	Sales/Receivables					**52** 7.0	
51 7.2	**47** 7.7	**54** 6.8						**72** 5.1	
51 7.1	**42** 8.6	**35** 10.5						**32** 11.4	
101 3.6	**70** 5.2	**72** 5.1	Cost of Sales/Inventory					**47** 7.7	
159 2.3	**122** 3.0	**140** 2.6						**76** 4.8	
15 23.9	**13** 27.2	**11** 32.2						**11** 34.1	
29 12.6	**21** 17.7	**21** 17.0	Cost of Sales/Payables					**18** 20.5	
55 6.6	**47** 7.7	**47** 7.8						**47** 7.8	
2.5	3.6	2.1						1.9	
4.5	5.7	4.9	Sales/Working Capital					5.3	
11.2	18.5	9.4						100.7	
85.7	20.5	61.8							
(29) 6.0	(20) 5.1	(19) 8.3	EBIT/Interest						
1.4	2.2	3.5							
			Net Profit + Depr., Dep., Amort./Cur. Mat. L/T/D						
.2	.3	.1						.0	
.3	.8	.3	Fixed/Worth					.3	
1.6	1.9	.8						1.3	
.2	.2	.2						.1	
.8	1.3	.7	Debt/Worth					1.3	
4.5	4.5	2.4						3.2	
36.8	30.1	28.1						28.1	
(34) 17.1	(23) 17.1	(22) 12.8	% Profit Before Taxes/Tangible Net Worth					16.4	
3.4	10.1	8.0						8.3	
19.1	15.7	20.9						18.7	
6.6	6.1	8.1	% Profit Before Taxes/Total Assets					7.8	
.7	4.2	3.6						1.2	
25.4	16.0	31.6						64.7	
11.4	7.2	12.4	Sales/Net Fixed Assets					10.6	
4.6	2.9	7.7						6.5	
2.4	2.5	2.4						2.4	
1.7	1.8	1.8	Sales/Total Assets					1.8	
1.2	1.2	1.2						1.4	
1.2	1.3	.7							
(30) 1.9	(22) 2.3	(20) 1.5	% Depr., Dep., Amort./Sales						
4.1	4.8	3.3							
		2.6							
		(10) 4.2	% Officers', Directors' Owners' Comp/Sales						
		7.4							
1176893M	1010543M	797421M	Net Sales ($)		1354M	6594M	19586M	158858M	611029M
802811M	673802M	524524M	Total Assets ($)		1211M	9225M	7588M	111247M	395253M

M = $ thousand MM = $ million

See Pages 9 through 22 for Explanation of Ratios and Data

Current Data Sorted by Assets							Comparative Historical Data	
			2	2	2	**Type of Statement** Unqualified	15	10
		5				Reviewed	4	3
		2	1			Compiled	4	
2						Tax Returns		
1	1	3	3	3	2	Other	8	12
5 (4/1-9/30/13)		24 (10/1/13-3/31/14)					4/1/09-3/31/10	4/1/10-3/31/11
0-500M	500M-2MM	2-10MM	10-50MM	50-100MM	100-250MM		ALL	ALL
3	1	10	6	5	4	**NUMBER OF STATEMENTS**	31	25
%	%	%	%	%	%	**ASSETS**	%	%
		18.9				Cash & Equivalents	12.0	12.1
		15.8				Trade Receivables (net)	19.9	18.7
		37.4				Inventory	34.3	30.7
		.7				All Other Current	2.8	2.1
		72.8				Total Current	69.0	63.4
		22.6				Fixed Assets (net)	15.9	19.2
		2.0				Intangibles (net)	7.3	11.7
		2.7				All Other Non-Current	7.9	5.7
		100.0				Total	100.0	100.0
						LIABILITIES		
		6.0				Notes Payable-Short Term	8.0	7.3
		1.3				Cur. Mat.-L.T.D.	2.3	1.5
		18.3				Trade Payables	11.2	8.6
		.8				Income Taxes Payable	.5	.2
		6.6				All Other Current	10.0	12.0
		33.0				Total Current	31.9	29.7
		5.4				Long-Term Debt	19.1	18.8
		.2				Deferred Taxes	1.3	1.7
		5.0				All Other Non-Current	5.0	9.9
		56.5				Net Worth	42.7	39.9
		100.0				Total Liabilities & Net Worth	100.0	100.0
						INCOME DATA		
		100.0				Net Sales	100.0	100.0
		39.4				Gross Profit	35.0	35.6
		26.2				Operating Expenses	23.9	25.2
		13.2				Operating Profit	11.1	10.4
		.0				All Other Expenses (net)	1.6	2.2
		13.1				Profit Before Taxes	9.5	8.1
						RATIOS		
		9.5					4.3	3.4
		2.0				Current	2.5	2.3
		1.6					1.5	1.6
		4.9					2.4	1.6
		1.2				Quick	.9	1.1
		.2					.6	.6
		6 63.6					27 13.5	27 13.3
		22 16.5				Sales/Receivables	39 9.3	52 7.0
		41 8.8					61 6.0	76 4.8
		12 30.7					72 5.1	76 4.8
		68 5.4				Cost of Sales/Inventory	99 3.7	99 3.7
		130 2.8					126 2.9	174 2.1
		14 26.5					16 23.5	19 19.6
		23 16.2				Cost of Sales/Payables	24 15.3	36 10.1
		33 11.0					42 8.6	52 7.0
		2.9					3.5	2.7
		6.0				Sales/Working Capital	5.2	5.0
		19.7					8.6	8.8
		186.9					27.9	37.8
		65.0				EBIT/Interest	(27) 6.0	(24) 4.0
		32.4					2.1	1.5
							24.3	4.5
						Net Profit + Depr., Dep., Amort./Cur. Mat. L/T/D	(12) 4.0	(12) 2.6
							1.6	1.3
		.1					.2	.3
		.5				Fixed/Worth	.3	.7
		NM					1.1	-.7
		.1					.4	.4
		.6				Debt/Worth	1.2	2.7
		NM					4.3	-9.1
							55.5	51.2
						% Profit Before Taxes/Tangible Net Worth	(25) 43.9	(18) 17.7
							10.4	5.1
		34.2					28.5	15.9
		26.6				% Profit Before Taxes/Total Assets	14.9	6.0
		5.0					3.6	1.1
		499.4					23.6	14.9
		10.3				Sales/Net Fixed Assets	11.1	8.1
		6.9					7.5	6.0
		2.6					2.4	1.6
		2.4				Sales/Total Assets	1.7	1.3
		1.8					1.4	.9
							1.3	1.5
						% Depr., Dep., Amort./Sales	(27) 1.7	(23) 2.6
							2.5	3.7
						% Officers', Directors' Owners' Comp/Sales		
7160M	1550M	103944M	328325M	1016214M	817162M	Net Sales ($)	2675728M	1519471M
879M	548M	40583M	201366M	371251M	569293M	Total Assets ($)	1778991M	1424556M

M = $ thousand MM = $ million

See Pages 9 through 22 for Explanation of Ratios and Data

Comparative Historical Data				Current Data Sorted by Sales					
			Type of Statement						
12	12	6	Unqualified						6
5	2	5	Reviewed				4	1	
2	3	3	Compiled				1	1	1
6	4	2	Tax Returns		2				
16	12	13	Other		1	2	1	1	8
					5 (4/1-9/30/13)		24 (10/1/13-3/31/14)		
4/1/11-3/31/12 ALL	4/1/12-3/31/13 ALL	4/1/13-3/31/14 ALL		0-1MM	1-3MM	3-5MM	5-10MM	10-25MM	25MM & OVER
41	33	29	**NUMBER OF STATEMENTS**		3	2	6	3	15
%	%	%	**ASSETS**	%	%	%	%	%	%
8.1	16.8	19.8	Cash & Equivalents	DATA NOT AVAILABLE					9.0
16.7	20.4	16.2	Trade Receivables (net)						18.3
36.9	36.2	35.8	Inventory						38.9
3.6	2.8	1.9	All Other Current						3.2
65.2	76.3	73.7	Total Current						69.4
21.8	17.1	18.1	Fixed Assets (net)						18.1
6.0	2.1	5.0	Intangibles (net)						8.3
7.0	4.6	3.2	All Other Non-Current						4.3
100.0	100.0	100.0	Total						100.0
			LIABILITIES						
6.8	7.0	6.9	Notes Payable-Short Term						4.4
2.7	1.5	1.9	Cur. Mat.-L.T.D.						2.9
15.1	14.3	11.8	Trade Payables						10.4
.2	.2	.4	Income Taxes Payable						.1
9.4	17.8	12.1	All Other Current						17.9
34.1	40.8	33.1	Total Current						35.6
12.3	13.0	12.2	Long-Term Debt						20.1
.8	.4	.9	Deferred Taxes						1.6
9.2	6.7	3.8	All Other Non-Current						1.2
43.5	39.1	50.0	Net Worth						41.5
100.0	100.0	100.0	Total Liabilties & Net Worth						100.0
			INCOME DATA						
100.0	100.0	100.0	Net Sales						100.0
36.1	32.1	39.7	Gross Profit						37.3
27.8	22.3	24.4	Operating Expenses						20.6
8.3	9.8	15.3	Operating Profit						16.7
1.1	1.0	.3	All Other Expenses (net)						.9
7.2	8.8	15.0	Profit Before Taxes						15.8
			RATIOS						
3.2	3.3	5.3							3.7
2.0	2.1	2.0	Current						1.9
1.4	1.4	1.6							1.5
1.6	1.6	3.5							1.3
.8	1.1	1.1	Quick						.9
.4	.5	.5							.4
25 14.4	17 22.0	17 21.4							26 14.0
34 10.7	29 12.7	26 13.8	Sales/Receivables						31 11.9
55 6.6	54 6.7	40 9.2							42 8.7
89 4.1	37 9.8	68 5.4							89 4.1
101 3.6	101 3.6	99 3.7	Cost of Sales/Inventory						104 3.5
174 2.1	140 2.6	130 2.8							140 2.6
29 12.4	14 25.2	11 33.0							17 21.6
38 9.5	34 10.8	22 16.4	Cost of Sales/Payables						32 11.3
57 6.4	50 7.3	34 10.6							40 9.2
3.3	3.5	3.9							5.1
5.4	6.1	6.0	Sales/Working Capital						6.0
11.6	8.0	10.0							9.2
44.0	58.4	159.2							139.1
(38) 7.6	(31) 12.4	(25) 51.0	EBIT/Interest						(12) 22.1
2.9	3.4	19.1							11.3
14.6	53.3								
(14) 5.4	(10) 13.5		Net Profit + Depr., Dep., Amort./Cur. Mat. L/T/D						
2.9	4.9								
.2	.1	.1							.2
.5	.3	.4	Fixed/Worth						.4
2.0	.8	2.1							2.1
.6	.5	.2							.3
1.4	1.3	.8	Debt/Worth						1.6
5.0	4.5	2.9							3.0
40.1	96.7	97.8							76.8
(33) 16.0	(30) 33.3	(24) 57.9	% Profit Before Taxes/Tangible Net Worth						(12) 56.9
6.5	15.1	38.1							28.2
18.5	34.2	54.2							48.6
8.3	13.3	26.8	% Profit Before Taxes/Total Assets						20.2
2.8	2.3	15.5							14.8
26.5	70.5	95.0							58.7
10.4	13.6	15.5	Sales/Net Fixed Assets						9.7
5.0	5.7	7.8							7.2
1.9	2.6	3.1							2.4
1.6	1.8	2.4	Sales/Total Assets						2.0
1.3	1.4	1.6							1.2
.9	.7	.6							.5
(35) 1.9	(25) 1.6	(21) 1.4	% Depr., Dep., Amort./Sales						(14) 1.3
4.3	3.5	3.5							3.5
			% Officers', Directors' Owners' Comp/Sales						
2418742M	1794718M	2274355M	Net Sales ($)		5125M	7649M	46348M	53532M	2161701M
1903288M	1195623M	1183920M	Total Assets ($)		1268M	3797M	19640M	17305M	1141910M

M = $ thousand MM = $ million

See Pages 9 through 22 for Explanation of Ratios and Data

Current Data Sorted by Assets							Comparative Historical Data	
		6	6	1	4	Type of Statement Unqualified	22	21
	1	10	8	1		Reviewed	18	17
	1	4		1		Compiled	7	13
	6	5				Tax Returns	4	8
	5	10	13	1	4	Other	42	38
	14 (4/1-9/30/13)		73 (10/1/13-3/31/14)				4/1/09-3/31/10	4/1/10-3/31/11
0-500M	500M-2MM	2-10MM	10-50MM	50-100MM	100-250MM		ALL	ALL
	13	35	27	4	8	NUMBER OF STATEMENTS	93	97
%	%	%	%	%	%	ASSETS	%	%
DATA NOT AVAILABLE	11.2	20.3	7.3			Cash & Equivalents	11.1	12.7
	20.6	27.0	25.8			Trade Receivables (net)	26.6	26.6
	45.2	22.7	27.3			Inventory	24.0	24.6
	.3	4.2	3.8			All Other Current	4.6	3.4
	77.3	74.2	64.2			Total Current	66.4	67.4
	18.1	21.6	26.9			Fixed Assets (net)	24.6	22.0
	1.5	.8	3.6			Intangibles (net)	4.5	5.1
	3.2	3.3	5.3			All Other Non-Current	4.5	5.5
	100.0	100.0	100.0			Total	100.0	100.0
						LIABILITIES		
	6.2	8.5	9.8			Notes Payable-Short Term	11.3	9.8
	2.5	1.9	3.4			Cur. Mat.-L.T.D.	3.1	2.6
	17.5	15.2	13.0			Trade Payables	12.6	12.6
	.1	.4	.1			Income Taxes Payable	.6	.4
	7.6	12.9	10.4			All Other Current	9.7	10.5
	33.9	38.9	36.8			Total Current	37.3	35.9
	13.8	4.6	10.9			Long-Term Debt	12.0	10.9
	.0	.6	1.0			Deferred Taxes	.6	.7
	11.9	1.4	5.7			All Other Non-Current	4.3	4.5
	40.5	54.5	45.6			Net Worth	45.7	48.0
	100.0	100.0	100.0			Total Liabilties & Net Worth	100.0	100.0
						INCOME DATA		
	100.0	100.0	100.0			Net Sales	100.0	100.0
	32.4	29.3	23.6			Gross Profit	27.2	30.9
	25.5	22.3	18.6			Operating Expenses	21.0	24.6
	7.0	7.0	5.0			Operating Profit	6.2	6.4
	-.2	-.4	.4			All Other Expenses (net)	.9	.9
	7.2	7.4	4.6			Profit Before Taxes	5.3	5.4
						RATIOS		
	4.0	4.6	2.8				3.0	3.3
	2.5	1.9	1.9			Current	1.9	2.3
	1.5	1.1	1.2				1.2	1.3
	2.1	3.3	1.3				1.9	2.0
	1.1	1.2	.8			Quick	1.0	1.2
	.5	.6	.5				.6	.7
	20 18.6	29 12.7	45 8.2				34 10.9	37 9.7
	28 13.1	43 8.5	52 7.0			Sales/Receivables	49 7.5	51 7.1
	35 10.5	54 6.7	68 5.4				62 5.9	67 5.4
	39 9.3	15 24.7	54 6.7				31 11.8	35 10.4
	107 3.4	48 7.6	76 4.8			Cost of Sales/Inventory	56 6.5	63 5.8
	140 2.6	83 4.4	99 3.7				96 3.8	114 3.2
	14 26.8	13 28.3	18 20.2				14 25.2	18 20.6
	27 13.5	28 13.1	26 14.2			Cost of Sales/Payables	24 15.1	31 11.8
	41 8.8	45 8.2	38 9.6				40 9.1	45 8.1
	3.7	3.4	4.5				4.3	3.5
	7.5	5.2	6.2			Sales/Working Capital	7.2	5.9
	14.1	41.7	15.0				25.7	13.2
	55.2	29.1	40.8				14.1	20.5
	(12) 11.1	(24) 14.9	(24) 4.4			EBIT/Interest	(85) 4.5	(78) 6.1
	1.6	3.1	1.6				1.5	1.7
							8.0	6.2
						Net Profit + Depr., Dep., Amort./Cur. Mat. L/T/D	(28) 2.5	(23) 3.1
							1.6	1.1
	.1	.1	.4				.2	.2
	.4	.4	.7			Fixed/Worth	.5	.4
	1.5	1.0	1.0				1.6	1.0
	.6	.2	.6				.6	.4
	1.6	.7	1.3			Debt/Worth	1.4	1.1
	2.1	2.9	2.5				3.3	4.1
	84.1	41.8	25.5				54.3	38.9
	(11) 48.3	(34) 26.7	(25) 12.0			% Profit Before Taxes/Tangible Net Worth	(86) 20.5	(88) 18.7
	.3	10.0	2.6				4.1	4.6
	35.9	26.5	10.8				21.2	17.6
	17.4	10.6	5.7			% Profit Before Taxes/Total Assets	7.6	8.9
	5.7	4.1	2.1				.9	1.8
	89.3	45.1	24.5				23.8	29.4
	20.0	14.7	5.3			Sales/Net Fixed Assets	9.1	11.5
	7.9	6.3	3.3				4.5	4.8
	3.5	2.9	2.1				2.9	2.6
	2.8	2.3	1.7			Sales/Total Assets	2.0	1.9
	2.3	1.7	1.4				1.4	1.3
	.2	.5	.9				1.0	1.2
	(10) .6	(29) 1.6	(24) 2.3			% Depr., Dep., Amort./Sales	(84) 2.2	(85) 2.1
	2.2	2.4	3.8				3.2	3.5
		2.7					2.1	1.8
		(14) 4.4				% Officers', Directors' Owners' Comp/Sales	(28) 3.1	(24) 3.1
		5.9					5.7	4.8
	50401M	477034M	1013251M	330538M	1700305M	Net Sales ($)	5533458M	2661239M
	17555M	182027M	614343M	254020M	1108810M	Total Assets ($)	2251811M	1884726M

M = $ thousand MM = $ million

See Pages 9 through 22 for Explanation of Ratios and Data

Comparative Historical Data / Current Data Sorted by Sales

4/1/11-3/31/12 ALL	4/1/12-3/31/13 ALL	4/1/13-3/31/14 ALL	Type of Statement	0-1MM	1-3MM	3-5MM	5-10MM	10-25MM	25MM & OVER
				14 (4/1-9/30/13)			73 (10/1/13-3/31/14)		
20	14	17	Unqualified			1	2	3	11
20	13	20	Reviewed			1	6	7	6
13	11	6	Compiled			1	1	3	1
9	6	11	Tax Returns		3	3	2	2	1
36	39	33	Other		3	1	6	7	16
98	83	87	NUMBER OF STATEMENTS		6	7	17	22	35
%	%	%	ASSETS	%	%	%	%	%	%
11.5	11.9	14.3	Cash & Equivalents	DATA NOT AVAILABLE			18.6	16.8	13.1
28.7	30.3	24.4	Trade Receivables (net)				28.9	22.2	26.0
21.1	24.3	27.7	Inventory				20.9	28.5	24.1
3.7	4.9	3.5	All Other Current				1.2	5.0	4.4
65.1	71.5	69.8	Total Current				69.7	72.5	67.6
23.9	21.1	23.1	Fixed Assets (net)				24.0	22.7	22.2
5.5	3.0	3.1	Intangibles (net)				.9	1.5	5.3
5.5	4.4	4.0	All Other Non-Current				5.3	3.3	4.9
100.0	100.0	100.0	Total				100.0	100.0	100.0
			LIABILITIES						
9.4	9.5	8.5	Notes Payable-Short Term				7.3	7.9	10.4
4.5	4.4	2.6	Cur. Mat.-L.T.D.				1.8	2.1	3.2
15.4	16.8	14.5	Trade Payables				14.9	19.4	12.1
.5	.2	.2	Income Taxes Payable				.3	.1	.3
10.2	12.1	10.5	All Other Current				8.3	6.4	13.0
39.9	42.9	36.4	Total Current				32.6	35.9	39.0
12.9	11.4	9.5	Long-Term Debt				4.6	7.4	11.2
.8	.7	.9	Deferred Taxes				.8	.5	1.4
5.9	3.9	6.6	All Other Non-Current				2.8	.8	10.1
40.5	41.1	46.7	Net Worth				59.2	55.4	38.4
100.0	100.0	100.0	Total Liabilties & Net Worth				100.0	100.0	100.0
			INCOME DATA						
100.0	100.0	100.0	Net Sales				100.0	100.0	100.0
28.1	26.3	27.3	Gross Profit				35.3	25.7	21.3
22.0	21.0	20.9	Operating Expenses				26.7	18.3	16.7
6.1	5.3	6.4	Operating Profit				8.6	7.4	4.6
.6	.5	.0	All Other Expenses (net)				-.4	-.2	.6
5.5	4.8	6.4	Profit Before Taxes				9.0	7.7	4.0
			RATIOS						
2.8	3.1	3.6					6.4	4.5	2.7
1.6	1.7	2.1	Current				2.5	1.9	2.1
1.2	1.2	1.3					1.2	1.2	1.4
1.8	2.2	2.1					4.4	2.8	1.6
1.0	.9	1.1	Quick				1.6	.8	1.0
.6	.6	.6					.7	.5	.7
36 10.0	36 10.2	31 11.7					33 10.9	30 12.2	37 9.9
49 7.4	47 7.8	44 8.3	Sales/Receivables				43 8.4	43 8.5	49 7.4
62 5.9	62 5.9	54 6.7					78 4.7	51 7.1	58 6.3
23 15.7	24 15.2	25 14.8					21 17.7	21 17.4	21 17.0
49 7.5	66 5.5	73 5.0	Cost of Sales/Inventory				46 7.9	66 5.5	73 5.0
83 4.4	96 3.8	107 3.4					101 3.6	111 3.3	94 3.9
20 17.9	18 20.1	17 22.1					13 27.1	23 15.8	17 22.1
36 10.2	29 12.4	26 13.8	Cost of Sales/Payables				31 11.6	29 12.8	25 14.5
50 7.3	42 8.6	44 8.3					51 7.2	50 7.3	38 9.7
4.6	4.0	3.6					2.8	3.4	3.9
8.7	6.9	5.5	Sales/Working Capital				5.2	4.5	6.2
19.6	20.0	19.2					223.4	14.7	25.3
18.6	33.1	25.9					137.0	33.4	19.1
(84) 6.4	(70) 9.5	(71) 8.8	EBIT/Interest				(15) 25.9	(13) 5.6	(31) 7.4
2.5	1.9	2.6					2.7	3.3	2.2
11.1	22.0	7.3							7.3
(31) 3.4	(28) 6.8	(20) 2.6	Net Profit + Depr., Dep., Amort./Cur. Mat. L/T/D						(12) 2.8
1.6	2.0	1.1							.9
.2	.2	.2					.1	.1	.2
.6	.6	.5	Fixed/Worth				.4	.4	.7
1.8	1.2	1.1					.7	1.0	1.6
.7	.5	.5					.3	.3	.8
1.6	1.2	1.3	Debt/Worth				.6	.8	1.6
3.7	3.7	2.9					1.5	2.3	6.3
53.6	42.6	39.8					59.0	41.8	30.1
(85) 29.0	(74) 18.0	(79) 19.7	% Profit Before Taxes/Tangible Net Worth				23.9	22.2	(29) 12.0
15.2	7.9	5.0					10.6	7.7	.9
20.5	17.9	19.4					31.3	26.5	14.3
11.5	7.6	9.3	% Profit Before Taxes/Total Assets				16.1	8.5	7.5
3.8	1.5	3.1					4.4	2.8	1.2
34.2	41.9	32.8					52.5	36.1	27.0
12.3	14.3	12.3	Sales/Net Fixed Assets				10.4	14.8	12.1
4.9	5.4	4.4					5.8	3.3	4.4
2.6	2.9	2.7					3.3	2.7	2.6
2.0	2.2	1.9	Sales/Total Assets				2.2	1.8	1.7
1.6	1.6	1.4					1.4	1.6	1.4
.8	.8	.7					.4	.7	.9
(86) 1.7	(69) 1.8	(72) 1.8	% Depr., Dep., Amort./Sales				(16) 1.1	(17) 1.7	(29) 1.9
3.7	3.2	2.9					3.0	3.3	2.5
1.9	2.2	2.4							
(31) 3.7	(14) 3.4	(30) 4.1	% Officers', Directors' Owners' Comp/Sales						
6.1	5.6	6.1							
3640794M	3467176M	3571529M	Net Sales ($)		13996M	26553M	122453M	343707M	3064820M
1988568M	2002356M	2176755M	Total Assets ($)		6497M	14590M	77992M	212727M	1864949M

M = $ thousand MM = $ million

See Pages 9 through 22 for Explanation of Ratios and Data

	Current Data Sorted by Assets						Comparative Historical Data	
Type of Statement								
Unqualified	1	2	10	24	8	8	58	57
Reviewed	1	6	69	34			114	123
Compiled	7	16	39	6			96	89
Tax Returns	24	60	30	6			109	108
Other	17	45	73	56	9	10	183	199
	92 (4/1-9/30/13)		469 (10/1/13-3/31/14)				4/1/09-3/31/10	4/1/10-3/31/11
	0-500M	500M-2MM	2-10MM	10-50MM	50-100MM	100-250MM	ALL	ALL
NUMBER OF STATEMENTS	50	129	221	126	17	18	560	576
ASSETS	%	%	%	%	%	%	%	%
Cash & Equivalents	19.0	15.0	10.8	12.7	8.6	8.9	10.5	10.2
Trade Receivables (net)	27.6	30.6	26.3	21.0	20.1	18.2	22.4	26.1
Inventory	19.3	21.6	23.6	24.3	23.5	20.1	23.4	22.8
All Other Current	2.5	1.3	2.2	2.7	2.2	3.5	2.8	2.6
Total Current	68.4	68.5	63.0	60.8	54.4	50.8	59.1	61.7
Fixed Assets (net)	19.7	21.2	28.4	26.8	25.7	26.1	28.8	27.7
Intangibles (net)	4.1	4.5	4.2	6.3	13.3	16.7	5.8	5.3
All Other Non-Current	7.8	5.8	4.4	6.1	6.7	6.4	6.3	5.3
Total	100.0	100.0	100.0	100.0	100.0	100.0	100.0	100.0
LIABILITIES								
Notes Payable-Short Term	12.9	11.7	9.4	8.1	6.4	6.3	11.9	10.9
Cur. Mat.-L.T.D.	5.6	4.1	3.4	2.9	2.7	1.7	4.5	4.7
Trade Payables	14.7	16.3	13.4	10.6	9.0	10.2	12.1	14.5
Income Taxes Payable	.0	.1	.3	.3	.5	.1	.1	.2
All Other Current	12.0	8.8	10.6	11.2	10.8	8.1	8.9	8.2
Total Current	45.2	41.1	37.1	33.1	29.4	26.4	37.6	38.4
Long-Term Debt	26.0	22.7	15.9	13.5	16.6	22.9	19.3	17.6
Deferred Taxes	.1	.2	.6	.5	.4	2.6	.5	.5
All Other Non-Current	21.7	7.4	5.6	3.4	11.8	6.0	8.1	7.5
Net Worth	7.1	28.7	40.9	49.5	41.7	42.0	34.5	36.0
Total Liabilties & Net Worth	100.0	100.0	100.0	100.0	100.0	100.0	100.0	100.0
INCOME DATA								
Net Sales	100.0	100.0	100.0	100.0	100.0	100.0	100.0	100.0
Gross Profit	47.9	34.8	30.5	27.4	25.7	30.2	31.0	32.1
Operating Expenses	42.3	30.1	23.9	19.6	19.4	20.5	27.6	27.1
Operating Profit	5.6	4.7	6.5	7.8	6.3	9.7	3.4	5.0
All Other Expenses (net)	.8	.7	.8	1.0	1.7	1.4	1.7	.9
Profit Before Taxes	4.8	4.0	5.7	6.9	4.5	8.4	1.7	4.1
RATIOS								
Current	4.2	3.4	3.2	4.0	3.0	3.6	3.3	2.9
	2.0	2.1	1.9	1.7	1.8	2.4	1.8	1.8
	1.0	1.2	1.2	1.2	1.2	1.4	1.1	1.2
Quick	2.8	2.6	2.2	1.9	1.3	1.9	2.0	1.8
	1.4	1.3	1.0	1.0	1.1	.9	.9	1.0
	.6	.7	.6	.6	.6	.7	.5	.6
Sales/Receivables	**3** 111.7	**22** 16.5	**29** 12.6	**31** 11.7	**33** 11.2	**36** 10.2	**27** 13.3	**31** 11.6
	23 16.2	**35** 10.3	**41** 8.8	**42** 8.6	**41** 8.8	**49** 7.4	**39** 9.3	**43** 8.4
	40 9.1	**54** 6.8	**54** 6.7	**58** 6.3	**65** 5.6	**63** 5.8	**52** 7.0	**57** 6.4
Cost of Sales/Inventory	**0** UND	**4** 92.8	**24** 15.3	**38** 9.6	**45** 8.1	**62** 5.9	**24** 14.9	**24** 15.5
	17 21.5	**24** 15.4	**52** 7.0	**68** 5.4	**78** 4.7	**81** 4.5	**57** 6.4	**53** 6.9
	43 8.5	**81** 4.5	**87** 4.2	**101** 3.6	**111** 3.3	**104** 3.5	**101** 3.6	**96** 3.8
Cost of Sales/Payables	**6** 57.3	**12** 30.1	**15** 24.0	**18** 20.5	**14** 25.4	**24** 15.3	**14** 26.9	**17** 21.0
	14 26.0	**27** 13.6	**26** 14.3	**26** 14.1	**27** 13.6	**32** 11.5	**24** 15.5	**30** 12.3
	29 12.6	**45** 8.1	**42** 8.6	**36** 10.1	**43** 8.5	**49** 7.5	**40** 9.1	**45** 8.1
Sales/Working Capital	7.1	4.9	4.5	3.2	3.5	3.0	4.1	4.6
	15.4	9.8	8.5	7.3	5.4	4.5	8.1	8.4
	UND	36.6	20.8	20.7	22.7	12.6	42.5	29.3
EBIT/Interest	17.6	18.4	21.1	28.9	13.2	33.1	8.0	11.7
	(38) 5.9	(109) 5.8	(191) 6.6	(117) 10.2	(14) 6.8	(16) 12.6	(499) 2.1	(520) 4.0
	.2	1.6	1.3	2.7	.3	3.0	-1.2	1.0
Net Profit + Depr., Dep., Amort./Cur. Mat. L/T/D		18.7	6.2	6.9			5.0	5.4
		(10) 5.1	(38) 2.6	(34) 4.0			(140) 2.0	(133) 2.1
		.7	1.5	2.1			.4	1.0
Fixed/Worth	.2	.2	.3	.2	.4	.4	.3	.3
	.8	.5	.8	.6	.8	.7	.8	.7
	-.5	3.5	2.0	1.3	4.9	NM	3.5	2.7
Debt/Worth	.7	.7	.5	.5	.7	.6	.6	.6
	4.2	2.3	1.4	1.3	1.4	2.1	1.8	1.5
	-4.1	15.0	4.9	3.1	22.8	NM	14.4	7.6
% Profit Before Taxes/Tangible Net Worth	128.5	51.7	51.0	36.5	77.8	30.9	33.8	46.4
	(33) 51.8	(101) 29.3	(194) 25.1	(118) 22.6	(14) 23.4	(14) 21.3	(441) 10.4	(477) 19.9
	5.6	6.0	8.9	10.8	9.2	10.6	-6.2	2.4
% Profit Before Taxes/Total Assets	43.4	22.6	20.8	16.8	16.7	14.6	12.5	15.9
	20.6	9.4	9.3	9.3	11.0	7.8	2.9	7.1
	-1.0	1.5	1.5	3.5	-2.2	3.5	-5.2	.3
Sales/Net Fixed Assets	106.1	58.1	19.9	16.3	11.9	8.9	18.3	19.3
	33.9	18.7	8.3	6.8	7.6	4.8	8.2	8.4
	14.0	7.7	4.6	3.7	3.6	3.2	4.1	4.4
Sales/Total Assets	6.6	3.7	2.8	2.1	2.0	1.6	2.7	2.7
	4.3	2.7	2.1	1.7	1.4	1.3	1.9	2.0
	2.7	2.0	1.5	1.3	1.0	.9	1.3	1.5
% Depr., Dep., Amort./Sales	.5	.9	1.0	1.2	1.5	2.2	1.4	1.3
	(18) 1.5	(86) 2.3	(189) 2.3	(121) 2.1	(12) 1.9	(14) 3.3	(481) 2.8	(500) 2.5
	3.1	4.0	4.0	3.8	3.4	4.2	5.5	4.6
% Officers', Directors' Owners' Comp/Sales	3.7	3.1	1.9	1.1			2.5	2.5
	(26) 8.6	(80) 5.0	(90) 3.1	(36) 1.8			(236) 5.0	(227) 4.2
	15.0	7.6	5.1	3.2			8.4	7.3
Net Sales ($)	56515M	542926M	2198021M	4228898M	1906755M	3760501M	12290038M	17117542M
Total Assets ($)	12623M	157261M	1001895M	2471709M	1188737M	3001788M	8151597M	6863810M

M = $ thousand MM = $ million

See Pages 9 through 22 for Explanation of Ratios and Data

Comparative Historical Data / Current Data Sorted by Sales

4/1/11-3/31/12 ALL	4/1/12-3/31/13 ALL	4/1/13-3/31/14 ALL	Type of Statement	0-1MM	1-3MM	3-5MM	5-10MM	10-25MM	25MM & OVER
60	47	53	Unqualified	1	1	1	2	13	35
136	116	110	Reviewed	1	1	13	33	43	19
91	57	68	Compiled	4	11	10	27	12	4
137	130	120	Tax Returns	13	45	19	24	15	4
246	230	210	Other	13	33	24	39	49	52
				92 (4/1-9/30/13)			469 (10/1/13-3/31/14)		
670	580	561	NUMBER OF STATEMENTS	32	91	67	125	132	114
%	%	%	**ASSETS**	%	%	%	%	%	%
10.6	11.8	12.8	Cash & Equivalents	16.9	14.6	13.4	11.2	14.5	9.8
26.7	26.3	25.7	Trade Receivables (net)	21.8	29.0	27.3	27.3	25.1	22.3
23.8	22.8	22.8	Inventory	22.0	18.9	23.5	22.0	23.5	25.8
3.3	3.0	2.2	All Other Current	3.3	.9	1.3	2.7	2.5	2.5
64.4	63.9	63.6	Total Current	64.1	63.5	65.5	63.2	65.7	60.4
25.2	25.5	25.5	Fixed Assets (net)	23.7	24.4	22.7	29.0	24.8	25.3
5.0	5.1	5.4	Intangibles (net)	3.1	5.9	5.6	3.0	4.8	9.1
5.4	5.6	5.5	All Other Non-Current	9.2	6.3	6.3	4.9	4.6	5.3
100.0	100.0	100.0	Total	100.0	100.0	100.0	100.0	100.0	100.0
			LIABILITIES						
9.9	10.8	9.7	Notes Payable-Short Term	11.2	14.3	8.2	10.8	6.3	9.5
4.0	3.3	3.6	Cur. Mat.-L.T.D.	2.1	4.7	3.7	5.0	2.7	2.4
14.5	13.7	13.3	Trade Payables	12.3	13.0	14.2	14.0	13.4	12.4
.2	.2	.3	Income Taxes Payable	.1	.0	.3	.4	.3	.3
9.6	10.4	10.4	All Other Current	13.6	8.5	7.6	9.9	11.5	11.9
38.2	38.5	37.2	Total Current	39.3	40.5	34.0	40.1	34.1	36.5
15.8	18.6	18.1	Long-Term Debt	24.5	24.3	26.7	17.4	12.1	13.9
.5	.6	.5	Deferred Taxes	.1	.3	.3	.4	.5	.9
8.6	7.3	7.1	All Other Non-Current	30.0	8.7	4.6	6.8	3.5	5.4
36.8	35.0	37.1	Net Worth	6.1	26.2	34.4	35.3	49.7	43.2
100.0	100.0	100.0	Total Liabilties & Net Worth	100.0	100.0	100.0	100.0	100.0	100.0
			INCOME DATA						
100.0	100.0	100.0	Net Sales	100.0	100.0	100.0	100.0	100.0	100.0
32.3	32.8	32.2	Gross Profit	46.4	39.3	36.4	31.5	27.4	26.4
26.3	26.4	25.8	Operating Expenses	40.6	34.5	30.3	25.9	19.2	19.4
6.0	6.4	6.4	Operating Profit	5.8	4.8	6.0	5.6	8.1	7.0
.8	.7	.9	All Other Expenses (net)	1.5	1.1	.8	.8	.3	1.2
5.2	5.6	5.5	Profit Before Taxes	4.2	3.7	5.2	4.8	7.8	5.8
			RATIOS						
3.1	3.1	3.5		9.6	3.3	4.4	2.8	4.2	3.3
1.9	1.9	1.9	Current	2.4	2.1	2.1	1.7	2.0	1.7
1.2	1.2	1.2		1.0	1.1	1.4	1.1	1.3	1.1
1.9	2.0	2.2		6.7	2.6	2.7	2.0	2.3	1.5
1.0	1.0	1.1	Quick	1.4	1.4	1.2	1.0	1.2	.9
.6	.6	.6		.5	.7	.6	.5	.7	.6
30 12.2	**29** 12.5	**27** 13.7		**7** 54.6	**25** 14.4	**28** 13.0	**26** 14.3	**30** 12.1	**31** 11.9
43 8.4	**41** 9.0	**40** 9.1	Sales/Receivables	**24** 14.9	**40** 9.2	**40** 9.2	**38** 9.5	**43** 8.5	**41** 8.8
57 6.4	**56** 6.5	**54** 6.8		**42** 8.6	**58** 6.3	**54** 6.7	**54** 6.7	**52** 7.0	**58** 6.3
22 16.6	**19** 19.5	**18** 20.2		**0** UND	**5** 74.0	**13** 27.3	**14** 26.1	**29** 12.4	**38** 9.5
54 6.8	**48** 7.6	**48** 7.6	Cost of Sales/Inventory	**21** 17.8	**34** 10.6	**52** 7.0	**41** 9.0	**54** 6.7	**70** 5.2
96 3.8	**89** 4.1	**91** 4.0		**130** 2.8	**83** 4.4	**99** 3.7	**85** 4.3	**81** 4.5	**99** 3.7
17 22.0	**15** 24.8	**14** 25.2		**7** 53.3	**13** 27.4	**13** 28.3	**15** 24.8	**16** 23.4	**18** 19.9
29 12.8	**25** 14.4	**25** 14.5	Cost of Sales/Payables	**13** 28.1	**24** 15.4	**28** 12.9	**26** 14.2	**25** 14.7	**27** 13.6
47 7.8	**44** 8.3	**41** 8.8		**40** 9.1	**46** 7.9	**45** 8.2	**46** 8.0	**36** 10.1	**39** 9.4
4.5	4.4	4.3		4.3	4.5	4.1	5.3	3.8	3.9
8.4	9.0	8.4	Sales/Working Capital	9.0	7.9	7.9	10.8	7.3	8.0
23.3	29.5	25.7		155.7	81.4	17.3	49.5	17.0	30.4
18.0	18.9	20.4		10.4	11.9	19.1	15.4	39.5	24.4
(594) 6.2	(513) 6.8	(485) 7.1	EBIT/Interest	(21) 3.0	(77) 3.7	(57) 9.4	(113) 6.3	(114) 14.1	(103) 10.1
1.6	2.1	1.6		-4.1	.5	1.3	1.2	4.7	2.4
7.4	7.0	7.3					3.9	6.5	10.1
(141) 2.9	(108) 3.4	(93) 3.2	Net Profit + Depr., Dep., Amort./Cur. Mat. L/T/D				(25) 2.4	(28) 3.7	(30) 4.2
1.4	1.7	1.6					1.0	2.1	2.0
.3	.3	.3		.2	.3	.2	.3	.2	.3
.6	.7	.7	Fixed/Worth	.7	.8	.6	.9	.5	.7
1.8	2.1	2.1		-2.2	415.5	2.1	2.4	1.1	2.1
.6	.6	.6		.5	.6	.6	.7	.4	.6
1.7	1.6	1.5	Debt/Worth	2.6	2.7	1.7	1.6	1.2	1.4
5.5	7.5	6.1		-4.8	-14.2	5.9	6.1	2.9	4.9
54.0	51.8	49.3		57.1	63.5	44.0	46.8	64.8	36.2
(570) 22.8	(481) 26.0	(474) 25.0	% Profit Before Taxes/Tangible Net Worth	(22) 21.9	(67) 15.7	(56) 25.9	(106) 26.2	(126) 29.0	(97) 22.8
6.0	9.9	8.6		-1.1	1.0	4.7	9.6	11.7	12.0
18.8	20.6	20.7		33.0	21.5	24.2	21.1	21.0	16.8
8.6	9.7	9.5	% Profit Before Taxes/Total Assets	3.6	5.4	11.8	9.0	12.2	8.0
1.5	2.5	2.0		-9.9	-.7	1.5	1.2	5.4	3.3
27.2	27.1	29.4		84.0	56.1	40.3	19.8	34.1	16.8
10.0	10.1	10.3	Sales/Net Fixed Assets	16.1	16.5	13.7	8.5	10.2	7.9
5.2	5.1	5.0		8.3	5.9	4.9	4.9	4.8	4.5
2.9	3.2	3.0		4.4	3.4	3.5	3.2	2.7	2.4
2.1	2.2	2.1	Sales/Total Assets	2.8	2.4	2.4	2.3	2.0	1.9
1.6	1.5	1.5		1.6	1.5	1.4	1.6	1.4	1.4
1.1	.9	1.1		.6	1.4	1.2	1.0	1.0	1.1
(539) 2.3	(471) 1.9	(440) 2.2	% Depr., Dep., Amort./Sales	(14) 1.9	(57) 3.3	(44) 2.2	(103) 2.0	(118) 2.4	(104) 1.9
4.1	3.9	3.8		4.3	4.9	4.4	3.9	3.7	3.5
2.1	1.9	2.0		3.7	3.6	2.2	2.1	1.1	1.1
(285) 4.2	(240) 3.7	(236) 3.7	% Officers', Directors' Owners' Comp/Sales	(13) 13.8	(54) 5.6	(35) 4.2	(54) 3.8	(56) 2.6	(24) 1.9
7.4	7.0	7.1		23.3	8.3	7.7	5.3	4.2	3.3
15336733M	13365738M	12693616M	Net Sales ($)	16463M	193940M	261360M	906209M	2136390M	9179254M
7990842M	7421931M	7834013M	Total Assets ($)	8796M	98212M	130572M	448860M	1229481M	5918092M

M = $ thousand MM = $ million

See Pages 9 through 22 for Explanation of Ratios and Data

Current Data Sorted by Assets							Comparative Historical Data	
Type of Statement								
Unqualified		1	8	12	2	2	31	29
Reviewed			15	11	2	1	30	22
Compiled		9	10	4			29	21
Tax Returns	4	4	7	1			9	22
Other		3	12	21	5	4	42	54
	29 (4/1-9/30/13)			109 (10/1/13-3/31/14)			4/1/09-3/31/10 ALL	4/1/10-3/31/11 ALL
	0-500M	500M-2MM	2-10MM	10-50MM	50-100MM	100-250MM		
NUMBER OF STATEMENTS	4	17	52	49	9	7	141	148
	%	%	%	%	%	%	%	%
ASSETS								
Cash & Equivalents		14.5	9.4	10.4			7.5	9.9
Trade Receivables (net)		11.8	19.9	15.7			19.4	20.6
Inventory		45.7	41.8	44.5			42.3	40.4
All Other Current		2.0	2.1	2.3			2.1	1.6
Total Current		74.1	73.1	72.8			71.3	72.5
Fixed Assets (net)		15.6	19.5	19.0			19.6	18.6
Intangibles (net)		1.9	3.5	3.7			3.8	3.0
All Other Non-Current		8.4	3.8	4.5			5.3	5.9
Total		100.0	100.0	100.0			100.0	100.0
LIABILITIES								
Notes Payable-Short Term		16.5	9.5	12.0			14.7	12.6
Cur. Mat.-L.T.D.		3.1	3.5	2.6			3.1	2.3
Trade Payables		10.9	11.8	10.5			9.5	10.0
Income Taxes Payable		.0	.0	.2			.3	.3
All Other Current		6.6	11.1	14.6			11.6	11.3
Total Current		37.0	35.9	39.9			39.2	36.5
Long-Term Debt		8.1	18.6	8.5			13.9	12.5
Deferred Taxes		.0	.3	.2			.6	.2
All Other Non-Current		4.4	5.5	4.7			6.0	6.2
Net Worth		50.6	39.7	46.7			40.4	44.6
Total Liabilities & Net Worth		100.0	100.0	100.0			100.0	100.0
INCOME DATA								
Net Sales		100.0	100.0	100.0			100.0	100.0
Gross Profit		29.9	29.4	24.1			29.4	29.2
Operating Expenses		22.1	22.0	18.1			25.8	23.8
Operating Profit		7.7	7.4	6.0			3.7	5.4
All Other Expenses (net)		-.1	.6	.0			1.0	.8
Profit Before Taxes		7.8	6.8	6.0			2.6	4.6
RATIOS								
Current		5.0	3.8	3.1			3.1	3.5
		1.9	2.0	1.7			2.0	2.1
		1.2	1.4	1.3			1.3	1.4
Quick		3.0	1.7	1.3			1.3	1.6
		.7	.7	.6			.7	.8
		.1	.4	.3			.4	.4
Sales/Receivables		**2** 146.2	**14** 25.4	**20** 18.5			**19** 19.2	**25** 14.5
		8 44.1	**25** 14.5	**33** 11.2			**34** 10.6	**38** 9.6
		27 13.6	**39** 9.4	**43** 8.4			**56** 6.5	**56** 6.5
Cost of Sales/Inventory		**9** 39.0	**59** 6.2	**78** 4.7			**70** 5.2	**67** 5.5
		126 2.9	**85** 4.3	**118** 3.1			**126** 2.9	**113** 3.2
		159 2.3	**140** 2.6	**182** 2.0			**209** 1.7	**177** 2.1
Cost of Sales/Payables		**7** 54.6	**12** 29.2	**11** 31.9			**11** 31.8	**13** 28.7
		14 26.7	**23** 15.6	**23** 16.0			**20** 18.0	**23** 15.9
		35 10.3	**34** 10.7	**38** 9.5			**35** 10.3	**35** 10.5
Sales/Working Capital		4.4	3.8	3.4			3.2	3.1
		7.7	6.9	6.9			5.5	4.6
		30.6	11.9	9.7			11.1	11.2
EBIT/Interest		51.0	24.6	36.3			10.8	20.3
		(15) 19.4	(49) 8.5	(47) 10.3			(129) 3.7	(134) 5.7
		3.2	2.9	3.6			.9	1.8
Net Profit + Depr., Dep., Amort./Cur. Mat. L/T/D				6.2			16.7	19.1
				(15) 1.8			(34) 4.2	(28) 5.5
				.8			1.6	2.7
Fixed/Worth		.0	.1	.2			.2	.1
		.2	.3	.5			.4	.4
		.9	1.2	.7			1.0	.8
Debt/Worth		.3	.5	.7			.6	.4
		1.1	1.1	1.4			1.1	1.1
		3.8	2.6	2.0			3.5	2.6
% Profit Before Taxes/Tangible Net Worth		66.8	50.1	40.3			29.8	41.0
		(16) 34.7	(45) 24.9	(47) 19.3			(127) 12.1	(140) 19.2
		16.0	12.5	10.8			1.2	5.6
% Profit Before Taxes/Total Assets		24.0	22.0	20.1			11.4	16.8
		13.3	11.5	8.0			5.2	7.5
		4.5	4.1	3.1			-.3	1.6
Sales/Net Fixed Assets		455.9	33.3	24.6			33.8	29.7
		33.5	16.6	10.3			11.1	12.0
		9.4	7.8	5.3			5.1	5.3
Sales/Total Assets		3.0	3.0	2.2			2.2	2.4
		2.4	2.4	1.7			1.6	1.8
		1.7	1.7	1.3			1.2	1.2
% Depr., Dep., Amort./Sales		1.1	.9	.7			1.1	1.0
		(11) 1.4	(46) 1.4	1.4			(126) 1.9	(125) 1.8
		2.7	1.8	2.5			3.2	3.0
% Officers', Directors' Owners' Comp/Sales			1.0	.4			1.5	1.2
			(18) 1.8	(10) 1.2			(39) 2.8	(43) 2.7
			5.2	2.6			5.9	4.3
Net Sales ($)	2297M	53387M	653388M	2101915M	1250382M	1854130M	4407935M	4989419M
Total Assets ($)	1202M	21264M	283093M	1203907M	673481M	1157686M	2889923M	3050177M

M = $ thousand MM = $ million

See Pages 9 through 22 for Explanation of Ratios and Data

Comparative Historical Data				Current Data Sorted by Sales					
			Type of Statement						
30	27	25	Unqualified		1	1	3	5	15
28	23	29	Reviewed				4	12	13
23	24	23	Compiled		4	2	9	7	1
18	20	16	Tax Returns	5	3		2	5	1
53	54	45	Other		2	2	4	11	26
4/1/11-3/31/12 ALL	4/1/12-3/31/13 ALL	4/1/13-3/31/14 ALL		29 (4/1-9/30/13)			109 (10/1/13-3/31/14)		
				0-1MM	1-3MM	3-5MM	5-10MM	10-25MM	25MM & OVER
152	148	138	**NUMBER OF STATEMENTS**	5	10	5	22	40	56
%	%	%	**ASSETS**	%	%	%	%	%	%
9.4	9.6	9.8	Cash & Equivalents		15.5		11.7	8.5	9.1
19.9	18.5	17.3	Trade Receivables (net)		9.2		14.8	21.7	16.6
40.6	42.8	43.3	Inventory		42.2		39.7	41.0	43.4
1.9	1.9	2.1	All Other Current		3.3		1.3	2.1	2.6
71.8	72.7	72.6	Total Current		70.2		67.4	73.4	71.7
19.0	18.9	18.2	Fixed Assets (net)		17.1		22.5	20.0	17.5
2.8	3.8	4.3	Intangibles (net)		.8		6.5	2.2	5.9
6.4	4.6	4.9	All Other Non-Current		11.8		3.6	4.5	4.9
100.0	100.0	100.0	Total		100.0		100.0	100.0	100.0
			LIABILITIES						
9.4	14.3	11.8	Notes Payable-Short Term		16.2		9.2	11.5	10.3
2.1	2.0	2.8	Cur. Mat.-L.T.D.		1.8		5.1	3.5	1.7
14.2	12.8	12.5	Trade Payables		8.8		12.2	11.4	12.0
.2	.1	.1	Income Taxes Payable		.0		.0	.1	.1
12.4	11.9	11.9	All Other Current		6.3		9.5	10.1	15.9
38.3	41.1	39.1	Total Current		33.0		36.1	36.5	40.1
14.0	13.1	12.5	Long-Term Debt		6.0		13.9	20.6	8.3
.3	.5	.4	Deferred Taxes		.0		.0	.3	.7
3.0	3.7	5.3	All Other Non-Current		4.8		11.0	2.8	5.5
44.3	41.6	42.7	Net Worth		56.1		39.1	39.9	45.4
100.0	100.0	100.0	Total Liabilties & Net Worth		100.0		100.0	100.0	100.0
			INCOME DATA						
100.0	100.0	100.0	Net Sales		100.0		100.0	100.0	100.0
28.5	28.0	26.7	Gross Profit		33.4		28.6	27.4	23.7
22.7	20.3	20.0	Operating Expenses		24.0		22.2	20.1	17.2
5.8	7.7	6.7	Operating Profit		9.4		6.4	7.3	6.5
.5	.8	.3	All Other Expenses (net)		-.3		.7	.5	.3
5.3	7.0	6.4	Profit Before Taxes		9.6		5.7	6.9	6.2
			RATIOS						
3.2	3.0	3.4			5.1		3.8	4.3	2.6
1.8	1.8	1.8	Current		2.8		1.8	2.0	1.7
1.3	1.3	1.3			1.1		1.2	1.3	1.4
1.4	1.4	1.3			3.0		1.0	2.0	1.2
.8	.6	.7	Quick		.8		.7	.8	.6
.4	.3	.4			.1		.4	.4	.3
18 20.8	**18** 20.6	**16** 23.1			**0** UND		**13** 27.7	**17** 21.1	**22** 16.3
33 10.9	**31** 11.6	**28** 12.9	Sales/Receivables		**6** 65.6		**21** 17.5	**28** 13.2	**32** 11.3
54 6.8	**43** 8.4	**41** 9.0			**15** 24.7		**37** 9.9	**51** 7.2	**41** 9.0
52 7.0	**62** 5.9	**60** 6.1			**0** UND		**60** 6.1	**55** 6.6	**62** 5.9
104 3.5	**101** 3.6	**99** 3.7	Cost of Sales/Inventory		**159** 2.3		**76** 4.8	**91** 4.0	**111** 3.3
166 2.2	**152** 2.4	**159** 2.3			**166** 2.2		**159** 2.3	**135** 2.7	**159** 2.3
15 24.2	**13** 27.1	**12** 31.0			**7** 50.2		**13** 28.4	**12** 29.4	**14** 25.5
26 13.8	**22** 16.4	**23** 15.6	Cost of Sales/Payables		**11** 32.0		**26** 14.2	**22** 16.3	**24** 14.9
41 9.0	**39** 9.3	**38** 9.5			**39** 9.4		**39** 9.3	**31** 11.8	**43** 8.5
3.5	4.0	3.9			3.0		3.5	3.9	4.1
6.7	6.5	7.0	Sales/Working Capital		5.9		8.1	6.9	6.7
17.5	13.5	11.4			48.0		19.8	11.9	9.7
31.5	34.0	28.1					18.8	24.9	32.4
(139) 8.0	(133) 10.6	(128) 10.3	EBIT/Interest				(20) 7.5	(39) 8.5	(53) 14.1
3.1	3.6	3.2					2.9	2.2	5.5
9.1	10.5	10.7							8.6
(28) 3.2	(32) 4.8	(28) 2.4	Net Profit + Depr., Dep., Amort./Cur. Mat. L/T/D						(17) 1.8
1.3	2.2	1.2							1.2
.2	.1	.1			.0		.1	.2	.2
.3	.4	.4	Fixed/Worth		.2		.7	.4	.4
.8	.8	.8			.5		3.4	.9	.7
.6	.6	.6			.3		.6	.6	.7
1.1	1.2	1.3	Debt/Worth		.5		1.8	1.1	1.3
2.9	2.9	2.5			2.3		5.8	2.1	2.1
46.0	49.6	47.3					49.4	53.3	45.8
(141) 23.1	(141) 27.5	(123) 22.7	% Profit Before Taxes/Tangible Net Worth				(18) 22.4	(37) 21.4	(51) 22.5
8.9	13.8	11.9					13.3	9.8	12.8
17.6	21.9	19.9			48.5		16.2	22.0	20.4
8.0	12.0	10.1	% Profit Before Taxes/Total Assets		17.1		10.5	12.6	9.8
3.1	3.8	3.5			2.4		4.2	2.8	4.0
37.4	40.3	34.2			397.0		36.9	30.2	25.1
13.4	12.8	12.4	Sales/Net Fixed Assets		23.7		11.4	15.5	10.7
5.9	5.9	7.0			5.4		4.9	5.0	7.3
2.7	2.8	2.7			2.7		3.3	3.0	2.4
2.0	2.0	2.0	Sales/Total Assets		2.1		1.8	2.3	1.9
1.3	1.5	1.5			1.4		1.5	1.5	1.4
.7	.8	.8					1.1	.6	.7
(125) 1.4	(123) 1.5	(120) 1.4	% Depr., Dep., Amort./Sales				(20) 1.5	(36) 1.6	(53) 1.2
2.5	2.5	2.2					2.5	2.5	2.1
1.2	1.1	1.1					1.7	.7	.9
(47) 2.8	(37) 1.9	(34) 2.0	% Officers', Directors' Owners' Comp/Sales				(11) 2.1	(11) 1.4	(10) 1.2
4.7	3.8	4.4					6.2	4.3	2.6
6474979M	**6426469M**	**5915499M**	Net Sales ($)	**3203M**	**19679M**	**18867M**	**164214M**	**657232M**	**5052304M**
3704357M	**3806926M**	**3340633M**	Total Assets ($)	**2075M**	**10595M**	**11317M**	**88791M**	**350146M**	**2877709M**

M = $ thousand MM = $ million

See Pages 9 through 22 for Explanation of Ratios and Data

Current Data Sorted by Assets | **Comparative Historical Data**

0-500M	500M-2MM	2-10MM	2-10MM	10-50MM	50-100MM	100-250MM		4/1/09-3/31/10 ALL	4/1/09-3/31/10 ALL	4/1/10-3/31/11 ALL	4/1/10-3/31/11 ALL
							Type of Statement				
			1	2	1		Unqualified		8		5
	1		4	1			Reviewed		6		6
	3		3	1			Compiled		5		6
1				1			Tax Returns		4		2
			2	2	1		Other		16		15
8 (4/1-9/30/13)				16 (10/1/13-3/31/14)							
1	4		10	7	2		**NUMBER OF STATEMENTS**		39		34
%	%		%	%	%	%	**ASSETS**		%		%
			9.3			DATA NOT AVAILABLE	Cash & Equivalents		10.4		11.1
			17.5				Trade Receivables (net)		14.8		17.3
			38.7				Inventory		42.7		40.8
			1.0				All Other Current		1.9		2.7
			66.5				Total Current		69.8		71.9
			18.4				Fixed Assets (net)		17.6		18.2
			13.1				Intangibles (net)		5.0		6.0
			2.0				All Other Non-Current		7.7		4.0
			100.0				Total		100.0		100.0
							LIABILITIES				
			9.5				Notes Payable-Short Term		17.5		15.0
			3.3				Cur. Mat.-L.T.D.		3.3		2.6
			16.3				Trade Payables		17.4		17.3
			.4				Income Taxes Payable		.4		.5
			7.5				All Other Current		10.6		7.6
			37.1				Total Current		49.2		42.9
			11.0				Long-Term Debt		8.1		12.2
			.3				Deferred Taxes		.3		.3
			8.7				All Other Non-Current		10.7		4.2
			42.9				Net Worth		31.7		40.4
			100.0				Total Liabilties & Net Worth		100.0		100.0
							INCOME DATA				
			100.0				Net Sales		100.0		100.0
			32.1				Gross Profit		30.9		29.1
			26.0				Operating Expenses		28.9		24.1
			6.1				Operating Profit		2.0		5.0
			.7				All Other Expenses (net)		1.4		.8
			5.4				Profit Before Taxes		.6		4.2
							RATIOS				
			2.8				Current		5.5		2.9
			1.7						1.5		1.5
			1.1						1.2		1.2
			1.4				Quick		1.6		1.3
			.6						.6		.6
			.3						.2		.3
		1	270.8				Sales/Receivables	**8**	48.4	**13**	29.0
		17	21.0					**27**	13.6	**36**	10.2
		52	7.0					**47**	7.8	**49**	7.5
		69	5.3				Cost of Sales/Inventory	**69**	5.3	**81**	4.5
		91	4.0					**120**	3.0	**107**	3.4
		152	2.4					**178**	2.0	**166**	2.2
		17	21.8				Cost of Sales/Payables	**11**	33.5	**22**	16.8
		26	13.9					**20**	18.6	**38**	9.7
		62	5.9					**48**	7.6	**55**	6.6
			4.0				Sales/Working Capital		3.5		4.3
			8.0						7.2		8.2
			20.8						20.2		17.1
							EBIT/Interest		10.3		18.2
								(37)	1.6	(33)	6.0
									-1.9		1.1
							Net Profit + Depr., Dep., Amort./Cur. Mat. L/T/D				
			.2				Fixed/Worth		.1		.1
			.6						.4		.4
			1.2						1.1		1.3
			.8				Debt/Worth		.7		.7
			1.9						1.2		1.8
			5.5						2.7		4.4
							% Profit Before Taxes/Tangible Net Worth		19.2		81.5
								(34)	3.9	(31)	18.7
									-19.1		.3
			23.5				% Profit Before Taxes/Total Assets		9.6		15.7
			5.4						1.1		7.1
			.1						-6.8		.2
			29.2				Sales/Net Fixed Assets		51.8		52.8
			18.2						15.6		21.6
			4.2						6.1		5.5
			2.5				Sales/Total Assets		2.6		2.3
			1.8						1.7		1.7
			1.6						1.3		1.2
			1.1				% Depr., Dep., Amort./Sales		.6		.6
			1.5					(38)	1.5	(27)	1.4
			2.1						2.4		1.9
							% Officers', Directors' Owners' Comp/Sales		1.7		1.1
								(16)	3.0	(14)	2.4
									6.8		3.6
1108M	**17150M**		**132480M**	**355832M**	**251021M**		Net Sales ($)		**1634538M**		**1566709M**
272M	**4262M**		**63003M**	**156617M**	**123234M**		Total Assets ($)		**808964M**		**729859M**

M = $ thousand MM = $ million

See Pages 9 through 22 for Explanation of Ratios and Data

Comparative Historical Data				Current Data Sorted by Sales					
			Type of Statement						
5	3	4	Unqualified					1	3
3	3	6	Reviewed			1	1	3	1
5	4	7	Compiled		1	5			1
2	2	2	Tax Returns		1			1	
7	11	5	Other						5
4/1/11-3/31/12 ALL	**4/1/12-3/31/13 ALL**	**4/1/13-3/31/14 ALL**			**8 (4/1-9/30/13)**			**16 (10/1/13-3/31/14)**	
				0-1MM	**1-3MM**	**3-5MM**	**5-10MM**	**10-25MM**	**25MM & OVER**
22	23	24	**NUMBER OF STATEMENTS**		2	6	1	5	10
%	%	%	**ASSETS**	%	%	%	%	%	%
8.0	5.6	7.9	Cash & Equivalents	**DATA NOT AVAILABLE**					5.2
18.0	13.6	14.8	Trade Receivables (net)						18.3
43.2	49.7	43.3	Inventory						46.0
2.2	1.6	1.5	All Other Current						2.5
71.3	70.4	67.5	Total Current						72.0
19.9	21.0	17.2	Fixed Assets (net)						15.1
5.5	4.2	8.1	Intangibles (net)						6.4
3.4	4.4	7.3	All Other Non-Current						6.5
100.0	100.0	100.0	Total						100.0
			LIABILITIES						
15.5	9.7	11.5	Notes Payable-Short Term						13.3
2.5	6.0	2.6	Cur. Mat.-L.T.D.						2.8
20.2	23.5	19.5	Trade Payables						24.2
.1	.0	.3	Income Taxes Payable						.2
10.9	9.4	7.6	All Other Current						12.0
49.1	48.5	41.4	Total Current						52.5
11.7	12.7	8.8	Long-Term Debt						7.3
.7	.3	.3	Deferred Taxes						.4
9.9	2.5	12.8	All Other Non-Current						19.7
28.6	36.0	36.8	Net Worth						20.2
100.0	100.0	100.0	Total Liabilties & Net Worth						100.0
			INCOME DATA						
100.0	100.0	100.0	Net Sales						100.0
29.8	24.3	26.5	Gross Profit						22.2
22.9	20.3	22.1	Operating Expenses						17.9
6.9	4.1	4.4	Operating Profit						4.3
1.5	.3	.7	All Other Expenses (net)						1.0
5.4	3.8	3.7	Profit Before Taxes						3.3
			RATIOS						
3.0	2.3	3.0							2.1
1.6	1.5	1.8	Current						1.6
1.1	1.2	1.3							1.2
1.1	.7	1.0							1.0
.4	.4	.6	Quick						.6
.3	.2	.3							.2
11 32.4	**11** 34.2	**6** 64.9							**8** 48.2
33 11.0	**27** 13.5	**15** 24.3	Sales/Receivables						**26** 14.1
58 6.3	**36** 10.0	**38** 9.5							**41** 9.0
83 4.4	**78** 4.7	**65** 5.6							**68** 5.4
107 3.4	**107** 3.4	**94** 3.9	Cost of Sales/Inventory						**85** 4.3
174 2.1	**159** 2.3	**135** 2.7							**114** 3.2
28 12.9	**21** 17.3	**16** 22.6							**28** 12.9
49 7.4	**42** 8.6	**40** 9.1	Cost of Sales/Payables						**44** 8.3
79 4.6	**73** 5.0	**70** 5.2							**65** 5.6
3.9	5.8	5.7							6.6
7.2	8.2	8.7	Sales/Working Capital						8.9
30.2	24.6	16.0							NM
11.1	21.8	37.5							137.2
(21) 3.8	(20) 6.4	(22) 4.5	EBIT/Interest						8.0
1.5	2.2	.2							-.1
			Net Profit + Depr., Dep., Amort./Cur. Mat. L/T/D						
.1	.3	.2							.2
.5	.6	.5	Fixed/Worth						.5
2.1	1.8	1.4							-1.4
.7	.7	.8							.7
3.4	1.7	1.4	Debt/Worth						1.2
7.0	6.7	4.7							-16.4
50.6	52.6	63.6							
(18) 17.4	(22) 26.3	(20) 24.7	% Profit Before Taxes/Tangible Net Worth						
7.3	12.7	5.0							
10.6	14.9	18.5							23.1
4.6	6.2	5.5	% Profit Before Taxes/Total Assets						6.2
1.8	4.7	.0							-1.4
75.2	47.6	27.9							28.1
15.7	13.4	19.8	Sales/Net Fixed Assets						23.1
4.7	5.4	8.3							11.7
2.6	2.8	3.0							3.0
1.7	2.1	2.5	Sales/Total Assets						2.6
1.1	1.5	1.6							2.2
.9	.7	1.0							.8
(15) 1.7	(16) 1.1	(22) 1.4	% Depr., Dep., Amort./Sales						1.3
3.0	2.2	2.0							1.9
			% Officers', Directors' Owners' Comp/Sales						
717780M	**1488638M**	**757591M**	Net Sales ($)		**3880M**	**22818M**	**6237M**	**88027M**	**636629M**
413851M	**748900M**	**347388M**	Total Assets ($)		**1326M**	**15601M**	**920M**	**54344M**	**275197M**

M = $ thousand MM = $ million

See Pages 9 through 22 for Explanation of Ratios and Data

Current Data Sorted by Assets							Comparative Historical Data	
						Type of Statement		
		1	9	1	4	Unqualified	36	26
1	1	10	8	1		Reviewed	20	23
		4	1			Compiled	9	11
1	6	4				Tax Returns	9	6
	4	5	14	8	3	Other	59	53
12 (4/1-9/30/13)			74 (10/1/13-3/31/14)				4/1/09-3/31/10	4/1/10-3/31/11
0-500M	500M-2MM	2-10MM	10-50MM	50-100MM	100-250MM		ALL	ALL
2	11	24	32	10	7	NUMBER OF STATEMENTS	133	119
%	%	%	%	%	%	**ASSETS**	%	%
	-.9	6.7	8.0	16.9		Cash & Equivalents	10.9	10.2
	41.1	24.1	17.2	14.2		Trade Receivables (net)	18.5	20.2
	32.5	31.7	31.8	37.6		Inventory	34.1	32.2
	.9	5.3	3.3	2.7		All Other Current	4.8	3.7
	73.5	67.9	60.4	71.5		Total Current	68.3	66.3
	20.4	20.0	32.1	13.9		Fixed Assets (net)	23.5	23.6
	3.2	2.3	4.2	9.9		Intangibles (net)	3.0	5.1
	2.8	9.8	3.3	4.7		All Other Non-Current	5.3	5.0
	100.0	100.0	100.0	100.0		Total	100.0	100.0
						LIABILITIES		
	9.9	9.6	6.5	9.8		Notes Payable-Short Term	12.5	12.5
	2.1	3.0	2.6	3.6		Cur. Mat.-L.T.D.	2.8	3.6
	20.0	18.0	9.0	7.1		Trade Payables	10.6	11.2
	.0	.1	.5	.2		Income Taxes Payable	.2	.3
	9.6	13.1	11.6	8.2		All Other Current	14.2	13.0
	41.6	44.0	30.2	29.0		Total Current	40.3	40.5
	29.5	8.3	18.0	7.5		Long-Term Debt	13.1	11.5
	.0	.2	.9	.9		Deferred Taxes	.4	.5
	7.3	7.8	4.2	5.8		All Other Non-Current	6.3	5.8
	21.6	39.7	46.7	56.8		Net Worth	39.8	41.7
	100.0	100.0	100.0	100.0		Total Liabilities & Net Worth	100.0	100.0
						INCOME DATA		
	100.0	100.0	100.0	100.0		Net Sales	100.0	100.0
	33.7	27.5	29.6	23.6		Gross Profit	26.5	28.7
	27.6	22.6	22.4	17.6		Operating Expenses	26.6	24.8
	6.1	4.9	7.2	6.1		Operating Profit	-.1	4.0
	.5	1.3	2.0	.2		All Other Expenses (net)	.6	.7
	5.6	3.7	5.2	5.8		Profit Before Taxes	-.7	3.3
						RATIOS		
	2.5	2.1	3.2	6.8			3.5	3.4
	2.1	1.5	2.0	2.5		Current	1.8	1.8
	1.4	1.1	1.4	1.9			1.2	1.3
	1.9	1.2	1.4	3.5			1.5	1.5
	1.0	.7	.9	1.6		Quick	.7	.7
	.3	.4	.5	.6			.3	.5
	17 21.6	**27** 13.7	**32** 11.3	**35** 10.5			**29** 12.6	**34** 10.7
	48 7.6	**38** 9.7	**49** 7.5	**42** 8.6		Sales/Receivables	**45** 8.2	**48** 7.6
	63 5.8	**46** 7.9	**59** 6.2	**49** 7.5			**62** 5.9	**59** 6.2
	13 27.8	**28** 12.9	**60** 6.1	**76** 4.8			**68** 5.3	**58** 6.2
	45 8.2	**73** 5.0	**114** 3.2	**152** 2.4		Cost of Sales/Inventory	**118** 3.1	**122** 3.0
	83 4.4	**118** 3.1	**159** 2.3	**182** 2.0			**199** 1.8	**178** 2.0
	16 23.4	**14** 25.6	**13** 28.7	**20** 18.1			**16** 23.5	**18** 19.9
	28 13.0	**31** 11.7	**24** 15.5	**22** 16.5		Cost of Sales/Payables	**23** 15.6	**33** 10.9
	60 6.1	**63** 5.8	**53** 6.9	**38** 9.5			**46** 8.0	**50** 7.3
	7.7	6.3	2.9	1.6			2.6	3.0
	10.3	11.0	5.0	3.5		Sales/Working Capital	5.3	5.1
	23.0	81.6	13.0	4.3			13.2	14.8
	16.5	21.1	24.4				6.7	12.2
	(10) 6.7	(22) 8.0	(29) 8.7			EBIT/Interest	(120) 2.3	(106) 3.6
	1.1	3.0	2.7				-2.9	1.8
			8.7				6.2	9.5
			(13) 7.3			Net Profit + Depr., Dep., Amort./Cur. Mat. L/T/D	(37) 1.4	(34) 3.5
			2.9				.0	.9
	.0	.1	.3	.1			.2	.2
	.7	.5	.5	.3		Fixed/Worth	.6	.5
	2.5	.9	1.5	NM			1.8	1.3
	1.1	.7	.4	.1			.6	.5
	2.8	1.7	1.1	.6		Debt/Worth	1.4	1.3
	6.1	2.7	1.9	NM			4.1	2.8
		47.3	24.0				21.1	25.5
		(22) 27.1	(29) 15.3			% Profit Before Taxes/Tangible Net Worth	(119) 5.2	(105) 11.1
		11.9	8.2				-8.4	3.1
	46.6	18.7	11.8	12.3			7.3	9.6
	12.6	8.0	7.1	6.4		% Profit Before Taxes/Total Assets	2.1	4.9
	.3	3.5	4.3	2.9			-5.0	1.2
	UND	62.4	11.8	19.9			18.2	13.9
	26.5	23.2	8.0	11.2		Sales/Net Fixed Assets	7.5	8.8
	10.1	6.9	2.3	7.3			3.7	4.6
	5.2	3.1	1.8	1.4			2.1	2.2
	3.0	2.2	1.4	1.1		Sales/Total Assets	1.3	1.4
	2.1	1.5	1.0	1.0			.9	1.0
		.5	1.1				1.3	1.5
		(21) 1.1	(30) 2.1			% Depr., Dep., Amort./Sales	(112) 2.3	(104) 2.2
		3.5	5.2				4.0	4.1
							1.2	1.9
						% Officers', Directors' Owners' Comp/Sales	(26) 2.9	(33) 3.5
							7.1	5.8
1786M	48694M	270836M	949899M	864804M	1101449M	Net Sales ($)	4111564M	4033972M
408M	13929M	126558M	694766M	729440M	1031609M	Total Assets ($)	3820166M	3668005M

M = $ thousand MM = $ million

See Pages 9 through 22 for Explanation of Ratios and Data

Comparative Historical Data / Current Data Sorted by Sales

4/1/11-3/31/12 ALL	4/1/12-3/31/13 ALL	4/1/13-3/31/14 ALL	Type of Statement	0-1MM	1-3MM	3-5MM	5-10MM	10-25MM	25MM & OVER
13	14	15	Unqualified					5	10
30	20	21	Reviewed		1	1	5	10	4
13	7	5	Compiled			1	2	2	
13	6	11	Tax Returns	1	2	1	5	2	
41	44	34	Other		3	1	2	6	22
				12 (4/1-9/30/13)			74 (10/1/13-3/31/14)		
110	91	86	NUMBER OF STATEMENTS	1	6	4	14	25	36
%	%	%	**ASSETS**	%	%	%	%	%	%
9.5	10.2	9.0	Cash & Equivalents				-2.7	11.1	10.0
19.7	18.1	21.6	Trade Receivables (net)				32.6	23.5	17.3
33.1	35.9	33.1	Inventory				28.1	29.8	38.2
3.2	3.2	3.4	All Other Current				4.1	3.6	3.6
65.6	67.4	67.1	Total Current				62.0	68.1	69.1
23.8	22.2	23.2	Fixed Assets (net)				22.5	24.3	19.4
4.0	4.9	4.3	Intangibles (net)				4.0	1.8	7.3
6.5	5.5	5.4	All Other Non-Current				11.4	5.9	4.2
100.0	100.0	100.0	Total				100.0	100.0	100.0
			LIABILITIES						
13.3	9.8	8.3	Notes Payable-Short Term				13.3	4.4	9.6
4.1	4.1	2.6	Cur. Mat.-L.T.D.				3.2	1.7	2.7
14.4	12.6	14.0	Trade Payables				16.4	14.4	11.6
.1	.4	.3	Income Taxes Payable				.0	.6	.3
11.4	10.7	11.8	All Other Current				11.0	11.5	12.9
43.2	37.5	37.1	Total Current				44.0	32.6	37.0
14.1	13.7	13.9	Long-Term Debt				19.0	9.0	11.6
.5	.8	.5	Deferred Taxes				.0	1.2	.4
3.9	5.6	8.4	All Other Non-Current				16.0	4.1	3.8
38.2	42.4	40.0	Net Worth				21.0	53.1	47.1
100.0	100.0	100.0	Total Liabilties & Net Worth				100.0	100.0	100.0
			INCOME DATA						
100.0	100.0	100.0	Net Sales				100.0	100.0	100.0
27.2	27.3	28.0	Gross Profit				30.6	30.1	23.6
23.9	21.8	22.2	Operating Expenses				26.7	23.6	18.1
3.3	5.5	5.9	Operating Profit				3.8	6.5	5.5
.9	.4	1.2	All Other Expenses (net)				2.5	.0	1.0
2.5	5.1	4.7	Profit Before Taxes				1.3	6.4	4.4
			RATIOS						
2.9	3.5	2.9					2.3	4.0	2.9
1.6	2.1	1.9	Current				1.4	2.4	1.8
1.1	1.2	1.3					.9	1.4	1.4
1.3	1.5	1.4					1.1	1.8	1.2
.6	.8	.8	Quick				.4	1.2	.7
.4	.5	.5					.3	.7	.5
24 15.1	**22** 16.4	**31** 11.7					**29** 12.7	**32** 11.3	**30** 12.2
45 8.2	**41** 8.9	**43** 8.4	Sales/Receivables				**41** 8.9	**46** 7.9	**44** 8.3
60 6.1	**55** 6.6	**56** 6.5					**53** 6.9	**63** 5.8	**56** 6.5
46 7.9	**55** 6.6	**49** 7.4					**13** 28.1	**33** 11.1	**64** 5.7
111 3.3	**114** 3.2	**96** 3.8	Cost of Sales/Inventory				**72** 5.1	**94** 3.9	**130** 2.8
174 2.1	**159** 2.3	**146** 2.5					**130** 2.8	**135** 2.7	**174** 2.1
20 18.0	**16** 23.1	**15** 24.7					**19** 19.2	**13** 28.0	**20** 18.6
36 10.1	**24** 15.5	**29** 12.8	Cost of Sales/Payables				**32** 11.5	**23** 16.2	**27** 13.4
52 7.0	**51** 7.1	**52** 7.0					**68** 5.4	**51** 7.2	**50** 7.3
3.2	3.2	3.7					8.7	3.5	3.4
6.3	5.4	6.6	Sales/Working Capital				19.8	5.5	4.5
31.9	16.5	15.3					-98.2	11.0	10.4
13.8	25.8	21.7					11.9	27.4	34.5
(100) 4.2	(83) 7.1	(76) 8.5	EBIT/Interest				(13) 5.1	(21) 12.9	(34) 11.6
1.0	2.7	3.8					1.7	4.0	5.6
5.5	6.5	9.2							8.2
(25) 1.6	(21) 4.0	(24) 6.2	Net Profit + Depr., Dep., Amort./Cur. Mat. L/T/D						(14) 6.2
1.1	.7	2.2							3.1
.2	.1	.1					.2	.1	.2
.6	.4	.5	Fixed/Worth				.7	.4	.4
1.5	1.1	1.3					-2.4	.8	.9
.7	.6	.5					1.0	.4	.4
1.6	1.3	1.3	Debt/Worth				2.4	.9	1.3
5.3	2.9	2.8					-14.9	2.1	2.4
31.4	32.7	37.4					145.9	43.5	25.6
(99) 10.7	(84) 14.7	(76) 16.8	% Profit Before Taxes/Tangible Net Worth				(10) 22.7	16.6	(32) 17.2
1.2	4.5	6.4					3.0	5.9	8.9
9.8	12.3	13.9					14.2	19.9	11.8
4.5	6.2	7.6	% Profit Before Taxes/Total Assets				8.0	9.3	7.6
-.8	2.6	3.2					1.7	3.5	5.0
18.1	26.7	29.6					45.6	28.1	17.7
8.5	10.7	11.2	Sales/Net Fixed Assets				24.6	8.8	10.6
4.2	4.3	4.3					7.8	3.7	5.6
2.0	1.9	2.5					5.1	2.7	1.8
1.6	1.5	1.7	Sales/Total Assets				2.3	1.7	1.4
1.1	1.0	1.1					1.4	1.1	1.0
1.0	.5	.8						.7	.7
(99) 2.0	(78) 1.6	(72) 1.7	% Depr., Dep., Amort./Sales					(24) 1.3	(32) 1.9
4.6	4.4	3.8						3.8	3.6
1.5	1.1	.8							
(35) 2.4	(20) 3.6	(18) 2.5	% Officers', Directors' Owners' Comp/Sales						
4.7	5.6	4.2							
2830359M	**3223691M**	**3237468M**	Net Sales ($)	**454M**	**12858M**	**16490M**	**93558M**	**397997M**	**2716111M**
2363314M	**2667653M**	**2596710M**	Total Assets ($)	**35M**	**26918M**	**15307M**	**51973M**	**271037M**	**2231440M**

M = $ thousand MM = $ million

See Pages 9 through 22 for Explanation of Ratios and Data

	Current Data Sorted by Assets						Comparative Historical Data	
Type of Statement								
Unqualified		1	1		1	1	12	11
Reviewed			2	4			13	10
Compiled		3	3	1			2	9
Tax Returns	1	1	3		1		3	3
Other		1	8	14	3	3	24	26
	12 (4/1-9/30/13)			40 (10/1/13-3/31/14)			4/1/09-3/31/10 ALL	4/1/10-3/31/11 ALL
	0-500M	500M-2MM	2-10MM	10-50MM	50-100MM	100-250MM		
NUMBER OF STATEMENTS	1	6	17	19	5	4	54	59
ASSETS	%	%	%	%	%	%	%	%
Cash & Equivalents			5.3	7.7			7.4	9.3
Trade Receivables (net)			24.4	22.2			20.2	22.5
Inventory			32.9	42.2			36.2	29.7
All Other Current			3.7	1.8			4.3	4.7
Total Current			66.3	73.9			68.2	66.2
Fixed Assets (net)			26.8	19.4			24.1	24.6
Intangibles (net)			3.4	4.4			4.0	3.1
All Other Non-Current			3.6	2.4			3.7	6.1
Total			100.0	100.0			100.0	100.0
LIABILITIES								
Notes Payable-Short Term			11.3	10.9			12.0	9.7
Cur. Mat.-L.T.D.			3.6	3.0			4.5	4.5
Trade Payables			18.0	12.8			11.6	13.9
Income Taxes Payable			.3	.3			.9	.5
All Other Current			6.4	9.7			10.3	10.6
Total Current			39.7	36.7			39.3	39.3
Long-Term Debt			22.4	11.9			14.6	17.6
Deferred Taxes			.7	.9			.6	.6
All Other Non-Current			3.6	8.3			7.0	3.3
Net Worth			33.6	42.2			38.6	39.2
Total Liabilties & Net Worth			100.0	100.0			100.0	100.0
INCOME DATA								
Net Sales			100.0	100.0			100.0	100.0
Gross Profit			28.0	27.7			28.9	32.5
Operating Expenses			23.0	20.2			25.1	26.2
Operating Profit			5.0	7.5			3.8	6.2
All Other Expenses (net)			.8	1.0			.7	1.6
Profit Before Taxes			4.1	6.4			3.0	4.7
RATIOS								
Current			2.7	2.9			2.6	2.7
			2.0	2.1			1.7	1.5
			1.2	1.3			1.3	1.2
Quick			1.3	1.3			1.5	1.6
			.9	.8			.7	.8
			.6	.5			.3	.4
Sales/Receivables			**32** 11.4	**33** 11.2			**29** 12.5	**37** 9.9
			38 9.6	**49** 7.4			**41** 8.9	**52** 7.0
			55 6.6	**73** 5.0			**62** 5.9	**66** 5.5
Cost of Sales/Inventory			**33** 11.1	**83** 4.4			**56** 6.5	**62** 5.9
			62 5.9	**130** 2.8			**110** 3.3	**98** 3.7
			126 2.9	**182** 2.0			**202** 1.8	**158** 2.3
Cost of Sales/Payables			**22** 16.5	**19** 19.6			**19** 19.2	**23** 15.8
			36 10.1	**37** 9.8			**30** 12.0	**42** 8.7
			59 6.2	**47** 7.7			**51** 7.2	**63** 5.8
Sales/Working Capital			4.1	2.5			3.0	3.2
			6.2	4.8			5.8	7.0
			50.1	9.5			15.6	16.9
EBIT/Interest			8.4	16.9			16.0	16.7
			(16) 4.0	(18) 8.6			(50) 3.6	(53) 5.8
			.3	4.7			-.7	2.0
Net Profit + Depr., Dep., Amort./Cur. Mat. L/T/D							13.9	18.4
							(18) 3.6	(19) 2.4
							1.3	1.1
Fixed/Worth			.2	.4			.3	.3
			.8	.5			.7	.6
			1.6	.8			1.5	1.2
Debt/Worth			.9	.7			.7	.6
			2.2	1.1			1.9	1.6
			6.5	2.3			3.2	4.1
% Profit Before Taxes/Tangible Net Worth			41.2	46.5			37.9	37.1
			(16) 20.9	(16) 23.3			(48) 18.4	(52) 21.6
			6.3	15.3			2.8	13.3
% Profit Before Taxes/Total Assets			12.9	16.2			16.1	14.3
			4.9	8.1			5.3	7.9
			-.3	4.7			-3.7	2.1
Sales/Net Fixed Assets			30.5	15.1			13.4	19.5
			14.3	9.7			7.0	7.1
			4.1	6.2			4.2	4.4
Sales/Total Assets			2.7	1.9			2.1	2.1
			2.2	1.6			1.6	1.5
			1.6	1.0			1.0	1.1
% Depr., Dep., Amort./Sales			.9	1.1			1.5	1.4
			2.0	2.4			(50) 2.8	(53) 2.2
			3.6	5.7			4.4	3.8
% Officers', Directors' Owners' Comp/Sales								.9
								(14) 1.5
								2.6
Net Sales ($)	744M	12250M	180444M	522974M	452093M	802100M	2032245M	2017088M
Total Assets ($)	189M	6060M	91367M	341158M	371047M	481440M	1260229M	1690271M

M = $ thousand MM = $ million

See Pages 9 through 22 for Explanation of Ratios and Data

Comparative Historical Data				Current Data Sorted by Sales					
			Type of Statement						
10	8	4	Unqualified		1			1	2
10	10	6	Reviewed					2	4
3	4	7	Compiled	1	1	1	3	1	
5	5	6	Tax Returns	1	1		3		1
28	25	29	Other		1		4	11	13
4/1/11-3/31/12 ALL	**4/1/12-3/31/13 ALL**	**4/1/13-3/31/14 ALL**		**12 (4/1-9/30/13)**			**40 (10/1/13-3/31/14)**		
				0-1MM	**1-3MM**	**3-5MM**	**5-10MM**	**10-25MM**	**25MM & OVER**
56	52	52	**NUMBER OF STATEMENTS**	2	4	1	10	15	20
%	%	%	**ASSETS**	%	%	%	%	%	%
6.5	7.5	7.2	Cash & Equivalents				5.1	8.4	4.7
24.7	21.2	23.7	Trade Receivables (net)				22.7	25.3	20.1
32.7	34.1	34.6	Inventory				33.1	39.3	35.0
3.2	2.9	2.3	All Other Current				5.6	1.5	1.6
67.0	65.7	67.8	Total Current				66.5	74.5	61.5
24.8	25.3	22.1	Fixed Assets (net)				27.0	18.9	21.5
3.2	5.2	6.2	Intangibles (net)				5.2	3.0	11.2
5.0	3.7	3.9	All Other Non-Current				1.3	3.6	5.8
100.0	100.0	100.0	Total				100.0	100.0	100.0
			LIABILITIES						
9.8	6.1	10.6	Notes Payable-Short Term				12.4	10.2	11.6
2.8	4.0	3.9	Cur. Mat.-L.T.D.				4.5	1.5	5.6
14.7	13.5	15.2	Trade Payables				17.2	16.7	11.8
.2	.3	.2	Income Taxes Payable				.6	.0	.3
12.3	11.2	9.5	All Other Current				3.6	10.2	12.0
39.8	35.1	39.4	Total Current				38.3	38.7	41.3
11.3	15.6	15.8	Long-Term Debt				27.9	10.0	14.5
.8	1.7	1.0	Deferred Taxes				.7	1.0	1.5
5.0	5.0	5.3	All Other Non-Current				.5	11.4	4.9
42.9	42.5	38.6	Net Worth				32.6	38.9	37.8
100.0	100.0	100.0	Total Liabilties & Net Worth				100.0	100.0	100.0
			INCOME DATA						
100.0	100.0	100.0	Net Sales				100.0	100.0	100.0
32.8	29.4	28.0	Gross Profit				28.6	25.5	28.1
24.7	23.5	22.7	Operating Expenses				24.5	19.9	20.7
8.1	5.8	5.3	Operating Profit				4.1	5.7	7.5
1.2	.8	1.1	All Other Expenses (net)				.9	.5	2.0
6.9	5.0	4.2	Profit Before Taxes				3.2	5.1	5.5
			RATIOS						
2.7	3.6	2.7					2.8	4.0	2.0
1.7	1.8	1.8	Current				2.0	2.2	1.3
1.2	1.2	1.2					1.5	1.2	1.2
1.4	1.3	1.3					1.3	1.5	.8
.7	.8	.8	Quick				.9	.9	.6
.5	.5	.5					.7	.5	.4
39 9.4	**29** 12.4	**34** 10.6					**31** 11.6	**37** 9.8	**27** 13.3
46 8.0	**38** 9.7	**46** 8.0	Sales/Receivables				**38** 9.6	**49** 7.4	**46** 8.0
61 6.0	**51** 7.1	**66** 5.5					**51** 7.1	**107** 3.4	**65** 5.6
56 6.5	**56** 6.5	**54** 6.7					**0** UND	**47** 7.7	**70** 5.2
99 3.7	**83** 4.4	**104** 3.5	Cost of Sales/Inventory				**73** 5.0	**126** 2.9	**114** 3.2
146 2.5	**130** 2.8	**152** 2.4					**135** 2.7	**174** 2.1	**130** 2.8
26 14.2	**17** 22.1	**22** 16.5					**22** 16.5	**19** 19.2	**23** 16.2
38 9.5	**31** 11.9	**39** 9.3	Cost of Sales/Payables				**39** 9.3	**41** 8.8	**36** 10.1
55 6.6	**45** 8.2	**51** 7.1					**57** 6.4	**53** 6.9	**51** 7.1
4.0	3.9	4.1					3.9	2.2	4.8
7.0	7.3	5.8	Sales/Working Capital				5.2	4.2	9.5
15.3	25.3	24.8					23.5	36.7	24.8
38.5	24.5	11.2						11.9	16.3
(52) 8.1	(49) 7.7	(50) 5.9	EBIT/Interest					(14) 6.5	7.7
2.9	1.9	.5						2.0	3.2
11.6	19.2	4.2							4.5
(17) 3.5	(19) 2.3	(20) 2.0	Net Profit + Depr., Dep., Amort./Cur. Mat. L/T/D						(13) 1.7
1.2	.9	.7							.3
.3	.2	.4					.3	.1	.4
.6	.7	.6	Fixed/Worth				.7	.6	.7
1.0	1.6	2.7					2.4	2.0	10.4
.8	.7	.8					1.1	.5	1.1
1.7	1.7	1.8	Debt/Worth				1.9	1.0	2.1
2.9	4.6	6.9					6.8	7.4	27.7
47.9	57.2	40.2						40.9	46.5
(54) 27.2	(47) 32.1	(45) 21.4	% Profit Before Taxes/Tangible Net Worth					(13) 15.4	(16) 26.0
10.9	15.5	6.7						10.6	16.5
18.1	19.2	14.7					11.6	10.4	15.8
9.3	12.4	7.4	% Profit Before Taxes/Total Assets				3.3	6.7	9.0
3.5	2.6	-1.0					-2.4	2.5	5.3
23.4	28.2	28.3					29.6	34.9	18.4
7.6	9.3	10.3	Sales/Net Fixed Assets				10.2	15.1	8.3
4.7	4.4	4.3					3.6	4.2	4.2
2.3	2.4	2.2					2.6	2.2	1.9
1.8	1.8	1.7	Sales/Total Assets				2.0	1.6	1.7
1.3	1.4	1.3					1.1	1.0	1.3
1.2	.9	1.1					1.1	.8	1.4
(52) 2.0	(46) 1.6	(51) 2.4	% Depr., Dep., Amort./Sales				2.8	1.4	2.4
3.6	3.5	3.7					5.2	4.5	4.1
1.4	1.1	1.7							
(13) 2.1	(12) 2.1	(14) 3.0	% Officers', Directors' Owners' Comp/Sales						
9.8	3.4	4.3							
2326805M	**2197103M**	**1970605M**	Net Sales ($)	**1659M**	**8331M**	**3004M**	**77515M**	**243094M**	**1637002M**
1612407M	**1509850M**	**1291261M**	Total Assets ($)	**1318M**	**3633M**	**1298M**	**46604M**	**168380M**	**1070028M**

M = $ thousand MM = $ million

See Pages 9 through 22 for Explanation of Ratios and Data

	Current Data Sorted by Assets						Comparative Historical Data	
Type of Statement								
Unqualified			2	15	8	3	18	25
Reviewed	1	1	5	3	1		8	14
Compiled		2	9				10	8
Tax Returns		1	3	4			7	12
Other	3	9	26	23	10	10	51	60
	18 (4/1-9/30/13)		121 (10/1/13-3/31/14)				**4/1/09-3/31/10 ALL**	**4/1/10-3/31/11 ALL**
	0-500M	**500M-2MM**	**2-10MM**	**10-50MM**	**50-100MM**	**100-250MM**		
NUMBER OF STATEMENTS	4	13	45	45	19	13	94	119
ASSETS	%	%	%	%	%	%	%	%
Cash & Equivalents		7.7	17.0	10.9	9.0	12.2	12.1	12.1
Trade Receivables (net)		34.7	31.0	23.2	22.1	16.5	18.2	23.4
Inventory		15.2	24.5	22.9	18.8	17.3	21.8	22.3
All Other Current		.5	3.6	3.9	5.3	7.0	5.8	6.2
Total Current		58.0	76.1	60.8	55.2	53.0	58.0	64.0
Fixed Assets (net)		27.9	18.5	28.8	28.4	24.8	24.8	22.8
Intangibles (net)		6.9	.9	5.5	12.4	18.1	9.2	6.6
All Other Non-Current		7.2	4.4	4.9	3.9	4.0	8.0	6.6
Total		100.0	100.0	100.0	100.0	100.0	100.0	100.0
LIABILITIES								
Notes Payable-Short Term		16.3	6.6	5.9	2.0	1.1	6.3	6.7
Cur. Mat.-L.T.D.		2.3	1.1	4.7	3.7	3.9	2.6	3.5
Trade Payables		19.7	17.0	15.8	10.0	8.5	9.0	12.5
Income Taxes Payable		.0	.6	.3	.2	.5	.4	.4
All Other Current		11.9	10.3	12.0	11.4	10.0	9.6	9.3
Total Current		50.1	35.7	38.7	27.3	24.0	28.0	32.5
Long-Term Debt		15.0	9.7	14.0	22.8	12.8	16.8	13.4
Deferred Taxes		.0	.3	.5	1.0	1.1	1.3	1.2
All Other Non-Current		3.1	10.4	3.3	3.6	2.2	6.2	5.4
Net Worth		31.7	43.9	43.4	45.3	59.9	47.7	47.5
Total Liabilties & Net Worth		100.0	100.0	100.0	100.0	100.0	100.0	100.0
INCOME DATA								
Net Sales		100.0	100.0	100.0	100.0	100.0	100.0	100.0
Gross Profit		48.8	36.2	35.6	34.6	40.5	35.1	37.5
Operating Expenses		39.9	26.2	24.0	22.8	26.6	29.3	28.5
Operating Profit		8.9	10.0	11.6	11.8	13.9	5.8	8.9
All Other Expenses (net)		1.2	.8	.8	1.4	1.9	1.9	1.7
Profit Before Taxes		7.7	9.2	10.8	10.4	12.0	4.0	7.2
RATIOS								
Current		2.6	3.7	3.3	4.2	4.1	3.6	3.3
		1.2	2.1	2.0	1.7	2.3	2.2	2.1
		.4	1.5	1.1	1.4	1.8	1.3	1.4
Quick		1.5	2.1	1.8	2.0	2.7	2.0	2.0
		1.0	1.4	1.1	1.2	1.2	1.0	1.0
		.4	.9	.6	.7	.9	.5	.7
Sales/Receivables		**22** 16.4	**28** 13.0	**35** 10.5	**43** 8.5	**38** 9.5	**28** 13.3	**38** 9.7
		42 8.7	**54** 6.7	**56** 6.5	**63** 5.8	**73** 5.0	**50** 7.3	**57** 6.4
		60 6.1	**68** 5.4	**78** 4.7	**70** 5.2	**89** 4.1	**66** 5.5	**74** 4.9
Cost of Sales/Inventory		**0** UND	**10** 37.0	**30** 12.3	**3** 119.5	**36** 10.0	**16** 22.8	**13** 27.8
		3 109.5	**47** 7.8	**81** 4.5	**69** 5.3	**140** 2.6	**88** 4.1	**78** 4.7
		61 6.0	**130** 2.8	**140** 2.6	**107** 3.4	**243** 1.5	**165** 2.2	**166** 2.2
Cost of Sales/Payables		**8** 45.8	**19** 18.9	**27** 13.4	**20** 17.9	**24** 15.2	**14** 26.7	**20** 18.2
		25 14.5	**33** 11.2	**36** 10.0	**37** 9.8	**46** 8.0	**26** 14.0	**42** 8.7
		53 6.9	**72** 5.1	**68** 5.4	**73** 5.0	**96** 3.8	**50** 7.3	**66** 5.5
Sales/Working Capital		7.1	4.0	3.4	3.4	1.8	2.8	2.9
		26.0	6.1	5.6	5.3	2.7	4.7	4.8
		-6.6	8.6	24.6	10.8	7.3	11.7	10.1
EBIT/Interest		34.4	57.5	29.2	44.9	39.1	23.1	23.1
		(11) 12.7	(39) 23.6	(43) 11.3	(17) 9.4	(10) 15.8	(81) 4.7	(101) 7.9
		2.4	6.5	5.2	5.8	3.1	1.2	1.3
Net Profit + Depr., Dep., Amort./Cur. Mat. L/T/D							6.4	11.4
							(20) 1.8	(26) 3.2
							.2	1.7
Fixed/Worth		.2	.1	.3	.3	.3	.2	.2
		.6	.3	.7	.9	.4	.5	.4
		-20.9	.7	1.2	2.0	2.4	1.3	1.4
Debt/Worth		.9	.4	.5	.9	.4	.4	.5
		2.0	.9	1.4	2.4	1.0	1.1	1.2
		-32.6	2.4	3.2	4.2	4.9	3.7	3.9
% Profit Before Taxes/Tangible Net Worth			76.2	50.1	54.1	59.5	30.1	55.4
			(42) 37.6	(44) 30.5	(17) 30.0	(11) 24.5	(82) 14.9	(106) 17.3
			18.9	13.0	17.9	8.2	2.4	4.4
% Profit Before Taxes/Total Assets		33.6	27.7	24.1	20.3	20.4	14.3	18.2
		20.7	17.9	13.8	8.7	13.2	6.2	8.9
		2.4	8.3	3.4	6.0	2.3	.4	.7
Sales/Net Fixed Assets		349.2	51.3	9.9	28.3	6.1	15.6	23.3
		9.6	17.0	5.9	6.5	4.2	7.0	7.7
		3.5	5.5	2.7	2.9	2.4	3.0	4.2
Sales/Total Assets		5.2	3.2	1.9	1.9	1.1	1.8	2.1
		2.5	2.2	1.4	1.3	.8	1.3	1.4
		1.5	1.8	1.0	.9	.5	.7	1.0
% Depr., Dep., Amort./Sales		.2	.6	1.3	1.4	3.4	1.2	1.2
		(10) 2.1	(31) 1.3	(42) 2.6	(16) 3.7	(11) 4.8	(77) 3.0	(88) 2.6
		11.3	3.8	4.6	5.0	5.5	6.3	4.9
% Officers', Directors' Owners' Comp/Sales			.9				2.6	1.8
			(17) 1.7				(25) 4.3	(21) 4.1
			5.1				7.6	7.3
Net Sales ($)	6424M	64615M	572889M	1536549M	1930826M	1565789M	2948531M	3456107M
Total Assets ($)	953M	17647M	247631M	1005377M	1417522M	2035371M	3056738M	3396330M

M = $ thousand MM = $ million

See Pages 9 through 22 for Explanation of Ratios and Data

Comparative Historical Data				Current Data Sorted by Sales					
			Type of Statement						
24	20	28	Unqualified			1	1	7	19
12	9	11	Reviewed		1		3	6	1
10	12	11	Compiled			2	3	6	
6	13	8	Tax Returns				1	5	2
64	68	81	Other	2	7	8	4	26	34
				18 (4/1-9/30/13)			121 (10/1/13-3/31/14)		
4/1/11-3/31/12 ALL	**4/1/12-3/31/13 ALL**	**4/1/13-3/31/14 ALL**		**0-1MM**	**1-3MM**	**3-5MM**	**5-10MM**	**10-25MM**	**25MM & OVER**
116	122	139	**NUMBER OF STATEMENTS**	2	8	11	12	50	56
%	%	%	**ASSETS**	%	%	%	%	%	%
9.8	11.4	12.4	Cash & Equivalents			10.7	11.2	14.6	10.7
28.7	26.2	26.2	Trade Receivables (net)			24.6	29.2	29.3	24.2
21.2	20.8	22.4	Inventory			27.6	25.5	21.4	20.9
6.6	4.3	3.9	All Other Current			4.3	3.4	2.6	5.6
66.2	62.8	64.9	Total Current			67.3	69.3	67.8	61.4
23.0	23.9	24.3	Fixed Assets (net)			27.4	20.3	24.0	24.1
6.3	6.6	6.1	Intangibles (net)			1.2	1.1	2.9	10.8
4.5	6.7	4.7	All Other Non-Current			4.1	9.3	5.3	3.6
100.0	100.0	100.0	Total			100.0	100.0	100.0	100.0
			LIABILITIES						
8.3	7.8	6.1	Notes Payable-Short Term			14.1	15.9	4.5	3.9
3.4	2.4	3.1	Cur. Mat.-L.T.D.			2.6	2.4	2.4	4.0
13.7	14.7	15.1	Trade Payables			17.7	20.5	14.7	14.6
.7	.5	.4	Income Taxes Payable			.5	.1	.6	.3
11.6	10.2	11.4	All Other Current			6.2	5.9	12.9	11.8
37.7	35.7	36.1	Total Current			41.1	44.8	35.1	34.6
12.8	10.9	16.8	Long-Term Debt			11.7	9.4	11.0	16.3
.7	.8	.5	Deferred Taxes			.0	.0	.6	.6
5.4	3.9	6.4	All Other Non-Current			22.6	5.2	4.8	3.5
43.3	48.8	40.3	Net Worth			24.5	40.6	48.6	44.9
100.0	100.0	100.0	Total Liabilties & Net Worth			100.0	100.0	100.0	100.0
			INCOME DATA						
100.0	100.0	100.0	Net Sales			100.0	100.0	100.0	100.0
36.9	39.2	37.6	Gross Profit			34.1	30.6	37.9	34.7
24.9	29.3	26.6	Operating Expenses			24.7	25.1	25.8	23.2
12.0	9.9	11.0	Operating Profit			9.4	5.5	12.1	11.5
1.5	1.0	1.0	All Other Expenses (net)			.1	.7	.8	1.4
10.5	8.9	10.0	Profit Before Taxes			9.2	4.8	11.4	10.1
			RATIOS						
3.3	3.3	3.6				5.2	2.0	3.8	3.5
1.8	1.9	2.1	Current			2.8	1.7	2.1	1.9
1.3	1.2	1.3				1.2	1.3	1.3	1.3
2.0	1.8	2.0				2.1	1.6	2.4	2.0
.9	1.0	1.1	Quick			1.1	1.0	1.4	1.1
.5	.7	.7				.7	.3	.8	.7
42 8.6	**33** 11.0	**33** 10.9				**26** 13.8	**19** 19.7	**35** 10.3	**39** 9.4
61 6.0	**54** 6.7	**56** 6.5	Sales/Receivables			**44** 8.3	**41** 9.0	**56** 6.5	**61** 6.0
74 4.9	**73** 5.0	**73** 5.0				**64** 5.7	**63** 5.8	**73** 5.0	**78** 4.7
16 23.5	**16** 23.1	**13** 27.8				**20** 18.4	**4** 95.9	**13** 28.2	**23** 16.1
62 5.9	**62** 5.9	**64** 5.7	Cost of Sales/Inventory			**60** 6.1	**65** 5.6	**48** 7.6	**72** 5.1
140 2.6	**135** 2.7	**140** 2.6				**94** 3.9	**140** 2.6	**140** 2.6	**140** 2.6
21 17.1	**21** 17.3	**22** 16.8				**10** 37.6	**16** 23.4	**23** 16.2	**22** 16.6
38 9.5	**37** 9.8	**36** 10.0	Cost of Sales/Payables			**39** 9.4	**32** 11.3	**32** 11.4	**37** 9.8
70 5.2	**61** 6.0	**70** 5.2				**58** 6.3	**74** 4.9	**66** 5.5	**73** 5.0
3.6	4.0	3.4				2.4	4.5	4.0	3.1
5.9	6.2	5.9	Sales/Working Capital			5.6	10.6	6.0	5.4
16.1	14.5	14.9				26.0	17.3	11.2	13.8
31.7	28.5	39.1					23.8	58.4	30.4
(99) 9.6	(100) 12.6	(121) 13.7	EBIT/Interest				(11) 4.0	(46) 23.2	(50) 12.3
2.2	3.0	5.1					1.3	7.5	3.7
8.6	8.0	11.5							9.1
(25) 3.9	(26) 4.3	(24) 5.2	Net Profit + Depr., Dep., Amort./Cur. Mat. L/T/D						(11) 5.1
2.3	1.7	1.5							1.5
.2	.2	.2				.3	.1	.1	.3
.6	.5	.5	Fixed/Worth			.9	.5	.4	.7
1.3	1.1	1.3				-.2	1.2	1.0	1.8
.5	.5	.5				.5	.7	.5	.7
1.4	1.1	1.5	Debt/Worth			.8	1.8	.9	1.7
5.9	3.3	3.6				-20.4	2.5	2.4	4.2
69.7	62.8	62.1					61.8	74.4	56.7
(99) 33.4	(115) 36.7	(125) 32.3	% Profit Before Taxes/Tangible Net Worth				21.1	(48) 37.4	(51) 31.3
11.9	13.6	16.1					3.1	20.0	13.8
25.3	25.1	25.8				23.9	21.6	28.6	23.7
10.1	13.4	14.9	% Profit Before Taxes/Total Assets			14.9	8.1	18.2	9.7
4.1	4.1	5.8				3.1	.7	8.3	5.5
23.1	30.9	30.0				46.9	21.4	46.1	17.4
10.3	11.4	6.7	Sales/Net Fixed Assets			7.2	11.8	10.6	6.4
4.3	4.1	3.3				3.3	5.0	3.2	3.2
2.2	2.7	2.5				2.6	2.5	2.8	2.0
1.6	1.7	1.7	Sales/Total Assets			2.0	2.2	1.8	1.4
1.1	1.0	1.1				1.3	1.4	1.2	.9
1.1	1.1	1.1					.2	.8	1.5
(85) 2.4	(90) 2.4	(111) 2.8	% Depr., Dep., Amort./Sales				(10) 2.0	(42) 1.6	(47) 2.9
4.1	5.5	4.6					4.3	4.4	5.1
.8	1.9	1.1						.9	
(23) 2.2	(28) 3.1	(29) 2.7	% Officers', Directors' Owners' Comp/Sales					(16) 2.2	
6.8	5.9	6.1						4.6	
4715495M	**5514925M**	**5677092M**	Net Sales ($)	**1696M**	**15476M**	**43926M**	**86527M**	**884898M**	**4644569M**
4163690M	**4424901M**	**4724501M**	Total Assets ($)	**1651M**	**12240M**	**28312M**	**50957M**	**564869M**	**4066472M**

M = $ thousand MM = $ million

See Pages 9 through 22 for Explanation of Ratios and Data

Current Data Sorted by Assets							Comparative Historical Data	
		2	7		2	**Type of Statement** Unqualified	11	12
		3	12	1		Reviewed	20	21
		5				Compiled	8	4
	1	2				Tax Returns	9	6
1	4	9	15	1	3	Other	28	47
12 (4/1-9/30/13)		56 (10/1/13-3/31/14)					4/1/09-3/31/10 ALL	4/1/10-3/31/11 ALL
0-500M	500M-2MM	2-10MM	10-50MM	50-100MM	100-250MM			
1	5	21	34	2	5	**NUMBER OF STATEMENTS**	76	90
%	%	%	%	%	%	**ASSETS**	%	%
		8.3	15.7			Cash & Equivalents	14.0	12.5
		23.8	18.4			Trade Receivables (net)	18.1	23.4
		35.8	30.0			Inventory	29.4	28.9
		1.1	2.7			All Other Current	3.3	4.0
		69.0	66.8			Total Current	64.8	68.9
		15.3	20.0			Fixed Assets (net)	20.1	17.8
		4.5	6.1			Intangibles (net)	8.9	7.4
		11.2	7.1			All Other Non-Current	6.2	6.0
		100.0	100.0			Total	100.0	100.0
						LIABILITIES		
		6.6	4.8			Notes Payable-Short Term	6.3	4.6
		1.6	1.0			Cur. Mat.-L.T.D.	2.6	2.2
		12.4	10.1			Trade Payables	11.3	12.1
		.3	.3			Income Taxes Payable	.3	.4
		27.7	19.6			All Other Current	16.1	24.3
		48.5	35.9			Total Current	36.7	43.6
		7.1	8.3			Long-Term Debt	13.6	10.2
		.4	.6			Deferred Taxes	.4	.4
		9.8	6.1			All Other Non-Current	10.6	4.9
		34.1	49.2			Net Worth	38.8	41.0
		100.0	100.0			Total Liabilties & Net Worth	100.0	100.0
						INCOME DATA		
		100.0	100.0			Net Sales	100.0	100.0
		37.9	33.8			Gross Profit	35.5	32.8
		33.7	27.8			Operating Expenses	32.2	27.5
		4.2	6.1			Operating Profit	3.3	5.3
		1.1	1.3			All Other Expenses (net)	1.2	1.0
		3.1	4.7			Profit Before Taxes	2.1	4.3
						RATIOS		
		2.8	3.1				2.9	2.6
		2.0	1.8			Current	1.9	1.5
		1.2	1.5				1.4	1.2
		1.2	1.4				1.8	1.3
		.7	1.0			Quick	.9	.8
		.3	.6				.5	.5
		33 11.2	**28** 13.1				**27** 13.3	**34** 10.7
		40 9.1	**43** 8.5			Sales/Receivables	**38** 9.7	**43** 8.5
		57 6.4	**51** 7.1				**47** 7.7	**61** 6.0
		48 7.6	**81** 4.5				**50** 7.3	**43** 8.4
		130 2.8	**111** 3.3			Cost of Sales/Inventory	**91** 4.0	**94** 3.9
		192 1.9	**152** 2.4				**146** 2.5	**146** 2.5
		14 26.3	**21** 17.3				**16** 23.0	**20** 18.0
		39 9.3	**30** 12.3			Cost of Sales/Payables	**29** 12.8	**31** 11.8
		48 7.6	**38** 9.6				**48** 7.6	**56** 6.5
		3.7	3.3				4.1	4.2
		5.7	5.0			Sales/Working Capital	6.2	7.1
		10.5	9.0				10.7	17.7
		46.8	45.8				23.5	31.7
		(19) 4.2	(28) 8.8			EBIT/Interest	(67) 6.7	(77) 12.3
		1.1	2.0				1.3	1.3
			17.4				13.4	12.0
			(12) 5.9			Net Profit + Depr., Dep., Amort./Cur. Mat. L/T/D	(20) 4.1	(29) 5.2
			4.3				2.5	1.9
		.2	.1				.2	.2
		.5	.3			Fixed/Worth	.5	.4
		1.1	.9				1.3	1.8
		.5	.6				.6	.7
		1.5	1.1			Debt/Worth	1.3	1.7
		14.1	2.2				4.7	5.9
		38.5	26.4				29.4	39.2
		(18) 24.3	(33) 13.8			% Profit Before Taxes/Tangible Net Worth	(65) 15.5	(78) 23.4
		3.0	4.3				4.9	4.1
		17.1	13.0				13.2	15.6
		4.9	6.2			% Profit Before Taxes/Total Assets	6.2	7.2
		.4	2.4				.1	.3
		41.3	17.6				22.8	32.4
		13.8	12.7			Sales/Net Fixed Assets	9.4	13.3
		6.7	4.4				4.8	5.6
		2.6	1.9				2.2	2.4
		1.6	1.5			Sales/Total Assets	1.6	1.6
		1.2	1.0				1.2	1.3
		1.2	1.0				1.0	.6
		(18) 1.8	(32) 1.5			% Depr., Dep., Amort./Sales	(64) 2.0	(71) 1.4
		2.9	3.0				3.1	2.9
							3.3	1.8
						% Officers', Directors' Owners' Comp/Sales	(22) 4.5	(21) 4.2
							9.6	5.1
368M	9676M	194549M	1142743M	220315M	1937312M	Net Sales ($)	2510089M	3709413M
155M	5948M	117799M	759226M	174746M	970662M	Total Assets ($)	1706534M	2505778M

M = $ thousand MM = $ million

See Pages 9 through 22 for Explanation of Ratios and Data

Comparative Historical Data				Current Data Sorted by Sales					
			Type of Statement						
11	11	11	Unqualified					4	7
21	15	16	Reviewed				1	7	8
6	1	5	Compiled			1	3	1	
8	11	3	Tax Returns		1		1	1	
43	30	33	Other	3	3		6	8	13
4/1/11-3/31/12 ALL	**4/1/12-3/31/13 ALL**	**4/1/13-3/31/14 ALL**		**12 (4/1-9/30/13)**			**56 (10/1/13-3/31/14)**		
				0-1MM	**1-3MM**	**3-5MM**	**5-10MM**	**10-25MM**	**25MM & OVER**
89	68	68	**NUMBER OF STATEMENTS**	3	4	1	11	21	28
%	%	%	**ASSETS**	%	%	%	%	%	%
11.6	13.1	12.5	Cash & Equivalents				6.5	12.9	15.6
24.1	20.3	20.4	Trade Receivables (net)				24.2	20.2	20.9
27.1	28.5	30.6	Inventory				37.7	30.9	28.3
4.9	3.1	2.4	All Other Current				.6	2.8	3.1
67.8	65.0	66.0	Total Current				69.0	66.7	67.9
17.5	17.8	20.7	Fixed Assets (net)				16.9	19.2	18.8
8.8	10.0	6.1	Intangibles (net)				8.1	4.5	8.2
5.9	7.2	7.2	All Other Non-Current				6.1	9.7	5.1
100.0	100.0	100.0	Total				100.0	100.0	100.0
			LIABILITIES						
4.9	5.4	4.7	Notes Payable-Short Term				7.9	3.3	4.8
1.6	1.8	1.2	Cur. Mat.-L.T.D.				1.7	1.5	.9
13.0	11.5	10.3	Trade Payables				9.0	12.6	10.9
.4	.5	.4	Income Taxes Payable				.5	.1	.6
22.3	21.3	22.5	All Other Current				13.5	31.5	20.3
42.2	40.5	39.1	Total Current				32.6	49.1	37.5
12.2	13.7	8.0	Long-Term Debt				4.8	9.2	8.4
.4	.8	.4	Deferred Taxes				.0	.9	.3
4.0	4.5	6.6	All Other Non-Current				18.6	7.2	3.3
41.2	40.6	45.8	Net Worth				44.1	33.6	50.5
100.0	100.0	100.0	Total Liabilties & Net Worth				100.0	100.0	100.0
			INCOME DATA						
100.0	100.0	100.0	Net Sales				100.0	100.0	100.0
32.5	34.5	36.5	Gross Profit				36.4	34.2	33.2
26.1	26.6	30.8	Operating Expenses				31.9	29.7	25.9
6.4	7.9	5.7	Operating Profit				4.5	4.5	7.3
.6	.7	1.2	All Other Expenses (net)				1.7	1.7	.7
5.8	7.3	4.5	Profit Before Taxes				2.8	2.8	6.6
			RATIOS						
3.1	2.6	2.8					4.0	2.3	2.7
1.6	1.8	1.7	Current				2.4	1.5	1.7
1.1	1.3	1.4					2.0	1.2	1.4
1.5	1.3	1.4					2.5	1.3	1.4
.9	.9	.8	Quick				1.1	.8	.9
.5	.5	.5					.7	.4	.6
31 11.6	**30** 12.2	**28** 13.0					**33** 11.0	**28** 13.1	**32** 11.4
43 8.5	**39** 9.3	**41** 8.8	Sales/Receivables				**37** 9.9	**42** 8.7	**43** 8.5
57 6.4	**54** 6.7	**51** 7.1					**53** 6.9	**53** 6.9	**50** 7.3
53 6.9	**48** 7.6	**70** 5.2					**68** 5.4	**63** 5.8	**70** 5.2
87 4.2	**89** 4.1	**111** 3.3	Cost of Sales/Inventory				**130** 2.8	**111** 3.3	**94** 3.9
122 3.0	**130** 2.8	**182** 2.0					**182** 2.0	**182** 2.0	**135** 2.7
19 19.4	**21** 17.5	**17** 21.2					**13** 28.4	**20** 18.2	**21** 17.1
33 11.0	**30** 12.2	**29** 12.4	Cost of Sales/Payables				**39** 9.3	**30** 12.1	**29** 12.7
46 7.9	**45** 8.2	**46** 7.9					**48** 7.6	**46** 7.9	**38** 9.7
3.9	3.9	3.5					3.8	3.7	3.9
7.4	5.8	5.4	Sales/Working Capital				4.4	6.0	5.5
21.4	19.2	12.3					6.2	16.0	13.4
41.8	25.1	46.8						47.5	68.8
(80) 13.1	(55) 11.1	(55) 8.4	EBIT/Interest					(18) 4.0	(23) 13.6
2.9	3.3	1.9						1.0	7.0
12.4	10.4	15.8							26.3
(29) 5.2	(22) 4.8	(22) 5.9	Net Profit + Depr., Dep., Amort./Cur. Mat. L/T/D						(11) 6.6
3.2	2.3	2.6							5.2
.2	.2	.2					.2	.2	.2
.5	.5	.5	Fixed/Worth				.4	.5	.4
1.2	1.1	1.0					1.4	1.7	.8
.6	.8	.5					.3	.9	.6
1.8	1.9	1.2	Debt/Worth				.5	1.9	1.0
6.8	5.7	4.2					28.7	4.4	3.7
55.2	52.8	33.7						31.8	38.6
(75) 29.9	(61) 29.9	(63) 17.8	% Profit Before Taxes/Tangible Net Worth					(20) 12.7	(26) 23.4
7.6	16.8	3.5						1.7	8.9
20.0	16.6	14.2					14.9	9.5	14.2
9.2	10.0	6.8	% Profit Before Taxes/Total Assets				8.4	4.2	11.5
2.4	4.5	1.3					-.1	.8	4.4
30.1	27.1	19.3					60.4	23.6	16.3
11.9	12.3	12.7	Sales/Net Fixed Assets				13.3	14.8	12.1
6.4	4.8	4.7					6.6	4.3	6.7
2.3	2.2	2.1					2.7	1.8	2.2
1.8	1.5	1.5	Sales/Total Assets				1.7	1.5	1.7
1.3	1.1	1.2					1.3	1.2	1.2
.7	.8	1.1						1.1	1.0
(77) 1.6	(54) 1.5	(58) 1.9	% Depr., Dep., Amort./Sales					(19) 1.6	(25) 1.4
2.6	2.7	3.1						3.9	2.3
1.6	1.5	1.6							
(18) 2.8	(18) 2.1	(11) 4.8	% Officers', Directors' Owners' Comp/Sales						
5.9	6.1	7.9							
3292665M	**3447736M**	**3504963M**	Net Sales ($)	**1170M**	**7803M**	**3078M**	**76642M**	**386855M**	**3029415M**
2078857M	**2246005M**	**2028536M**	Total Assets ($)	**1980M**	**14232M**	**5498M**	**46928M**	**275996M**	**1683902M**

M = $ thousand **MM = $ million**

See Pages 9 through 22 for Explanation of Ratios and Data

Current Data Sorted by Assets								Comparative Historical Data			
							Type of Statement				
					1		Unqualified		6		3
1	1		7	1			Reviewed		11		8
			2	2			Compiled		9		8
1	2		1				Tax Returns		3		3
	1		6	4	3	1	Other		22		25
9 (4/1-9/30/13)				25 (10/1/13-3/31/14)					4/1/09-3/31/10 ALL		4/1/10-3/31/11 ALL
0-500M	**500M-2MM**		**2-10MM**	**10-50MM**	**50-100MM**	**100-250MM**					
2	4		16	7	4	1	**NUMBER OF STATEMENTS**		51		47
%	%		%	%	%	%	**ASSETS**		%		%
			9.2				Cash & Equivalents		15.5		10.6
			21.4				Trade Receivables (net)		20.7		22.4
			40.3				Inventory		30.4		31.8
			.9				All Other Current		4.4		4.6
			71.8				Total Current		70.9		69.4
			19.2				Fixed Assets (net)		22.0		18.5
			4.3				Intangibles (net)		2.5		5.7
			4.7				All Other Non-Current		4.6		6.4
			100.0				Total		100.0		100.0
							LIABILITIES				
			16.3				Notes Payable-Short Term		12.6		11.0
			3.5				Cur. Mat.-L.T.D.		2.7		2.8
			14.1				Trade Payables		13.3		10.9
			.9				Income Taxes Payable		.1		.1
			13.0				All Other Current		14.6		15.9
			47.8				Total Current		43.3		40.7
			11.0				Long-Term Debt		11.8		17.1
			.1				Deferred Taxes		.6		.6
			15.4				All Other Non-Current		8.4		10.2
			25.7				Net Worth		35.8		31.4
			100.0				Total Liabilities & Net Worth		100.0		100.0
							INCOME DATA				
			100.0				Net Sales		100.0		100.0
			28.1				Gross Profit		32.6		33.3
			22.2				Operating Expenses		29.8		27.9
			5.8				Operating Profit		2.8		5.4
			.9				All Other Expenses (net)		.6		.8
			4.9				Profit Before Taxes		2.2		4.6
							RATIOS				
			2.2						3.4		3.1
			1.8				Current		1.7		1.9
			1.0						1.1		1.2
			1.3						1.8		1.7
			.5				Quick		.7		.8
			.4						.4		.5
		24	15.0					**28**	13.1	**30**	12.2
		39	9.3				Sales/Receivables	**40**	9.1	**48**	7.6
		52	7.0					**53**	6.9	**57**	6.4
		64	5.7					**42**	8.7	**54**	6.7
		101	3.6				Cost of Sales/Inventory	**85**	4.3	**87**	4.2
		182	2.0					**135**	2.7	**159**	2.3
		22	16.6					**17**	21.7	**13**	27.1
		29	12.5				Cost of Sales/Payables	**31**	11.6	**32**	11.5
		60	6.1					**52**	7.0	**52**	7.0
			3.8						3.0		3.6
			5.6				Sales/Working Capital		7.0		5.4
			108.7						45.3		13.9
			12.4						8.5		13.1
		(15)	4.2				EBIT/Interest	(45)	1.8	(41)	3.4
			3.0						-1.0		1.4
									2.6		
							Net Profit + Depr., Dep., Amort./Cur. Mat. L/T/D	(10)	.6		
									-3.4		
			.1						.2		.2
			.4				Fixed/Worth		.5		.6
			1.2						3.3		4.2
			.9						.5		.6
			2.0				Debt/Worth		1.1		2.2
			5.3						22.1		21.5
			41.4						20.9		37.0
		(15)	27.3				% Profit Before Taxes/Tangible Net Worth	(41)	7.4	(36)	20.5
			10.7						-4.2		7.0
			13.3						6.1		12.8
			6.3				% Profit Before Taxes/Total Assets		2.9		6.6
			4.3						-3.8		.9
			38.5						19.5		27.3
			14.3				Sales/Net Fixed Assets		9.1		10.5
			12.8						5.3		5.8
			2.5						2.3		2.2
			1.8				Sales/Total Assets		1.7		1.7
			1.5						1.2		1.3
			.9						.9		1.1
		(15)	1.9				% Depr., Dep., Amort./Sales	(46)	1.6	(40)	1.5
			2.4						2.8		3.3
									2.5		1.6
							% Officers', Directors' Owners' Comp/Sales	(10)	4.8	(18)	3.9
									6.5		5.8
890M	**17290M**		**161578M**	**235025M**	**360618M**	**191521M**	Net Sales ($)		**2898545M**		**1545400M**
81M	**4912M**		**77400M**	**147787M**	**254907M**	**217240M**	Total Assets ($)		**1348982M**		**1306122M**

M = $ thousand MM = $ million

See Pages 9 through 22 for Explanation of Ratios and Data

Comparative Historical Data / Current Data Sorted by Sales

4/1/11-3/31/12 ALL	4/1/12-3/31/13 ALL	4/1/13-3/31/14 ALL		0-1MM	1-3MM	3-5MM	5-10MM	10-25MM	25MM & OVER
			Type of Statement						
10	3	1	Unqualified						1
10	6	10	Reviewed	1		1	4	3	1
6	5	4	Compiled			1	1		2
9	5	4	Tax Returns	1		2			1
31	22	15	Other		1	1	3	2	8
				9 (4/1-9/30/13)			25 (10/1/13-3/31/14)		
66	41	34	**NUMBER OF STATEMENTS**	2	1	5	8	5	13
%	%	%	**ASSETS**	%	%	%	%	%	%
11.5	11.7	10.3	Cash & Equivalents						10.7
23.3	22.0	21.8	Trade Receivables (net)						20.5
32.5	33.9	37.1	Inventory						34.4
3.0	2.8	1.9	All Other Current						4.2
70.3	70.5	71.1	Total Current						69.9
21.0	20.1	16.1	Fixed Assets (net)						16.9
3.2	5.0	4.6	Intangibles (net)						6.7
5.5	4.4	7.9	All Other Non-Current						6.5
100.0	100.0	100.0	Total						100.0
			LIABILITIES						
7.5	9.4	10.8	Notes Payable-Short Term						13.8
3.1	2.5	2.4	Cur. Mat.-L.T.D.						1.7
12.6	11.3	11.7	Trade Payables						9.1
.1	.3	.5	Income Taxes Payable						.0
17.6	16.4	15.7	All Other Current						18.1
40.9	39.9	41.1	Total Current						42.8
10.5	10.4	9.7	Long-Term Debt						7.9
.3	.3	.1	Deferred Taxes						.1
6.0	7.8	11.0	All Other Non-Current						23.0
42.4	41.5	37.8	Net Worth						26.2
100.0	100.0	100.0	Total Liabilities & Net Worth						100.0
			INCOME DATA						
100.0	100.0	100.0	Net Sales						100.0
33.8	33.4	29.9	Gross Profit						27.2
26.4	24.8	24.4	Operating Expenses						22.9
7.4	8.6	5.4	Operating Profit						4.4
1.1	1.1	.4	All Other Expenses (net)						.0
6.2	7.6	5.0	Profit Before Taxes						4.3
			RATIOS						
3.2	3.0	3.0							4.1
1.9	1.8	1.9	Current						1.6
1.2	1.2	1.1							1.0
1.6	1.7	1.8							1.9
.9	.9	.7	Quick						.7
.5	.4	.4							.4
32 11.5	**31** 11.8	**28** 12.9							**35** 10.5
43 8.4	**46** 8.0	**39** 9.3	Sales/Receivables						**44** 8.3
54 6.7	**57** 6.4	**54** 6.7							**61** 6.0
56 6.5	**74** 4.9	**78** 4.7							**79** 4.6
96 3.8	**118** 3.1	**107** 3.4	Cost of Sales/Inventory						**114** 3.2
135 2.7	**152** 2.4	**146** 2.5							**126** 2.9
18 20.4	**19** 19.5	**16** 22.6							**15** 23.7
31 11.7	**29** 12.7	**28** 12.9	Cost of Sales/Payables						**29** 12.8
46 8.0	**41** 8.8	**38** 9.7							**32** 11.3
3.8	2.9	3.4							2.7
5.6	6.2	5.6	Sales/Working Capital						7.2
14.2	16.7	61.9							NM
62.6	38.8	24.8							128.6
(54) 6.9	(36) 5.2	(31) 4.2	EBIT/Interest						(12) 3.9
2.4	2.6	3.0							2.2
11.4		16.9							
(14) 1.1		(13) 4.9	Net Profit + Depr., Dep., Amort./Cur. Mat. L/T/D						
.2		2.4							
.2	.2	.1							.2
.4	.5	.4	Fixed/Worth						.7
1.5	1.4	.9							1.2
.6	.8	.7							.7
1.2	1.4	1.8	Debt/Worth						2.1
5.7	4.5	4.7							7.5
57.4	56.7	40.1							33.5
(59) 22.0	(39) 27.4	(32) 22.3	% Profit Before Taxes/Tangible Net Worth						(11) 16.5
9.0	8.7	4.5							.7
17.4	18.9	14.2							13.8
7.9	8.4	6.5	% Profit Before Taxes/Total Assets						7.6
3.8	2.7	2.6							.4
29.5	26.8	38.6							19.1
11.9	13.4	16.3	Sales/Net Fixed Assets						14.8
6.2	5.6	9.7							8.0
2.5	2.3	2.7							2.3
1.7	1.7	1.7	Sales/Total Assets						1.6
1.4	1.3	1.4							1.3
.7	.6	.9							.9
(56) 1.4	(36) 1.5	(28) 1.5	% Depr., Dep., Amort./Sales						(11) 1.5
3.2	3.1	2.4							2.1
1.8	3.5								
(20) 3.5	(13) 5.4		% Officers', Directors' Owners' Comp/Sales						
7.1	9.2								
2223001M	1227715M	966922M	Net Sales ($)	890M	2629M	20189M	54227M	59201M	829786M
1315950M	832139M	702327M	Total Assets ($)	81M	2151M	11469M	29241M	36026M	623359M

M = $ thousand MM = $ million

See Pages 9 through 22 for Explanation of Ratios and Data

Current Data Sorted by Assets | Comparative Historical Data

0-500M	500M-2MM	2-10MM	10-50MM	50-100MM	100-250MM	Type of Statement	4/1/09-3/31/10 ALL	4/1/10-3/31/11 ALL
			2	1	1	Unqualified	8	2
		3	2			Reviewed	11	8
	1	2				Compiled	2	5
1		2				Tax Returns	8	5
	1	4	3	4	2	Other	23	17
	6 (4/1-9/30/13)		23 (10/1/13-3/31/14)					
1	2	11	7	5	3	NUMBER OF STATEMENTS	52	37
%	%	%	%	%	%	**ASSETS**	%	%
		12.1				Cash & Equivalents	9.9	9.3
		16.4				Trade Receivables (net)	21.9	25.0
		34.4				Inventory	30.2	25.1
		2.0				All Other Current	2.9	4.2
		65.0				Total Current	64.9	63.7
		22.8				Fixed Assets (net)	20.6	18.0
		9.3				Intangibles (net)	7.9	11.0
		2.8				All Other Non-Current	6.6	7.4
		100.0				Total	100.0	100.0
						LIABILITIES		
		16.6				Notes Payable-Short Term	8.4	9.2
		2.4				Cur. Mat.-L.T.D.	7.0	6.5
		16.5				Trade Payables	18.6	13.1
		.0				Income Taxes Payable	.2	.2
		18.9				All Other Current	13.3	17.9
		54.4				Total Current	47.5	46.9
		18.2				Long-Term Debt	23.3	10.0
		.3				Deferred Taxes	.3	.5
		5.3				All Other Non-Current	6.4	10.5
		21.8				Net Worth	22.5	32.2
		100.0				Total Liabilties & Net Worth	100.0	100.0
						INCOME DATA		
		100.0				Net Sales	100.0	100.0
		36.0				Gross Profit	34.2	35.1
		32.2				Operating Expenses	34.1	29.0
		3.8				Operating Profit	.1	6.1
		1.0				All Other Expenses (net)	1.9	1.4
		2.8				Profit Before Taxes	-1.8	4.7
						RATIOS		
		2.6					2.2	2.3
		1.2				Current	1.5	1.5
		1.0					1.1	.9
		1.1					1.4	1.0
		.7				Quick	.7	.7
		.4					.4	.5
		19 19.6					**32** 11.5	**38** 9.5
		36 10.2				Sales/Receivables	**49** 7.5	**46** 8.0
		51 7.1					**61** 6.0	**59** 6.2
		43 8.5					**43** 8.5	**35** 10.3
		140 2.6				Cost of Sales/Inventory	**78** 4.7	**68** 5.4
		166 2.2					**159** 2.3	**104** 3.5
		18 20.4					**21** 17.5	**24** 15.3
		30 12.3				Cost of Sales/Payables	**39** 9.3	**34** 10.7
		72 5.1					**54** 6.8	**53** 6.9
		4.8					4.6	5.3
		20.5				Sales/Working Capital	8.6	11.4
		-169.6					43.2	-28.0
							11.1	13.3
						EBIT/Interest	(50) 2.1	(36) 3.4
							-.7	1.4
							5.7	
						Net Profit + Depr., Dep., Amort./Cur. Mat. L/T/D	(16) 1.2	
							-1.9	
		.4					.3	.2
		1.8				Fixed/Worth	.6	.5
		-1.1					5.1	21.5
		3.0					1.0	.8
		4.9				Debt/Worth	2.5	3.2
		-3.5					54.5	NM
							38.9	69.7
						% Profit Before Taxes/Tangible Net Worth	(40) 14.6	(28) 29.2
							-26.0	1.8
		6.6					11.8	15.0
		3.4				% Profit Before Taxes/Total Assets	1.8	4.3
		1.0					-9.4	.5
		54.1					33.8	44.1
		18.2				Sales/Net Fixed Assets	10.4	13.3
		3.8					5.6	6.3
		2.0					2.1	2.3
		1.5				Sales/Total Assets	1.7	1.8
		1.2					1.2	1.3
		.5					1.2	.6
		(10) 1.3				% Depr., Dep., Amort./Sales	(43) 3.0	(32) 2.2
		2.6					4.7	3.7
							1.9	1.6
						% Officers', Directors' Owners' Comp/Sales	(16) 5.7	(11) 2.9
							7.1	10.0
3127M	4314M	85485M	183542M	418860M	431430M	Net Sales ($)	1647637M	1358419M
441M	1693M	53858M	119779M	343546M	365964M	Total Assets ($)	1241141M	912354M

M = $ thousand MM = $ million

See Pages 9 through 22 for Explanation of Ratios and Data

Comparative Historical Data / Current Data Sorted by Sales

4/1/11-3/31/12 ALL	4/1/12-3/31/13 ALL	4/1/13-3/31/14 ALL		0-1MM	1-3MM	3-5MM	5-10MM	10-25MM	25MM & OVER
			Type of Statement						
3	6	4	Unqualified						4
5	6	5	Reviewed				2	3	
6	3	3	Compiled		1		1	1	
1	2	3	Tax Returns		1	1		1	
14	15	14	Other		2		4	1	7
					6 (4/1-9/30/13)		23 (10/1/13-3/31/14)		
29	32	29	**NUMBER OF STATEMENTS**		4	1	7	6	11
%	%	%	**ASSETS**	%	%	%	%	%	%
9.4	12.5	15.1	Cash & Equivalents	DATA NOT AVAILABLE					19.9
26.1	24.5	19.6	Trade Receivables (net)						19.3
27.4	28.0	27.5	Inventory						21.6
3.6	4.3	5.5	All Other Current						5.7
66.4	69.3	67.6	Total Current						66.5
15.8	14.7	16.0	Fixed Assets (net)						11.0
11.9	9.4	12.1	Intangibles (net)						19.3
5.9	6.6	4.2	All Other Non-Current						3.2
100.0	100.0	100.0	Total						100.0
			LIABILITIES						
7.7	9.5	9.9	Notes Payable-Short Term						3.2
4.6	2.9	2.2	Cur. Mat.-L.T.D.						2.8
16.0	15.2	12.1	Trade Payables						8.4
.1	.3	.1	Income Taxes Payable						.1
17.0	16.3	19.6	All Other Current						24.5
45.4	44.2	43.9	Total Current						39.0
10.3	8.6	14.0	Long-Term Debt						16.0
.5	.5	.4	Deferred Taxes						.8
2.9	4.4	5.4	All Other Non-Current						3.8
40.9	42.3	36.3	Net Worth						40.5
100.0	100.0	100.0	Total Liabilities & Net Worth						100.0
			INCOME DATA						
100.0	100.0	100.0	Net Sales						100.0
34.6	34.6	36.2	Gross Profit						37.1
29.9	29.7	32.0	Operating Expenses						33.0
4.7	4.9	4.2	Operating Profit						4.1
1.0	1.3	1.1	All Other Expenses (net)						1.6
3.8	3.7	3.1	Profit Before Taxes						2.5
			RATIOS						
2.1	2.7	3.3							2.8
1.5	1.4	1.6	Current						2.0
1.1	1.2	1.1							1.2
1.2	1.4	1.8							2.2
.9	.9	.8	Quick						.9
.5	.6	.5							.6
38 9.7	36 10.0	33 11.2							42 8.7
47 7.7	51 7.1	45 8.1	Sales/Receivables						54 6.7
59 6.2	62 5.9	56 6.5							59 6.2
52 7.0	54 6.8	41 8.9							50 7.3
94 3.9	89 4.1	91 4.0	Cost of Sales/Inventory						89 4.1
122 3.0	135 2.7	152 2.4							135 2.7
25 14.7	20 18.7	15 25.0							17 20.9
33 11.1	36 10.0	31 11.6	Cost of Sales/Payables						31 11.6
58 6.3	61 6.0	55 6.6							58 6.3
5.0	3.4	3.5							2.9
9.5	9.9	7.4	Sales/Working Capital						5.5
22.3	22.7	27.6							18.0
28.0	22.8	8.9							
(24) 6.4	(25) 3.3	(22) 3.5	EBIT/Interest						
.9	.1	.1							
			Net Profit + Depr., Dep., Amort./Cur. Mat. L/T/D						
.2	.1	.1							.1
.4	.4	.5	Fixed/Worth						.4
1.1	3.5	UND							-1.8
.7	.5	.6							.5
2.2	3.1	3.8	Debt/Worth						3.3
8.5	15.6	UND							-5.6
91.9	66.0	47.1							
(26) 12.7	(27) 11.7	(22) 17.6	% Profit Before Taxes/Tangible Net Worth						
-.1	1.8	1.3							
10.0	11.9	12.3							11.2
6.3	5.1	5.9	% Profit Before Taxes/Total Assets						5.7
-.2	1.4	.4							-.1
38.8	45.6	36.9							42.5
19.2	14.2	15.7	Sales/Net Fixed Assets						15.7
6.5	8.2	7.1							9.0
2.0	2.6	2.0							1.6
1.5	1.6	1.5	Sales/Total Assets						1.3
1.3	1.1	1.1							1.0
.7	.7	.7							1.6
(26) 1.7	(29) 1.2	(25) 1.6	% Depr., Dep., Amort./Sales						(10) 2.0
2.4	2.3	3.2							3.1
			% Officers', Directors' Owners' Comp/Sales						
1064304M	1066236M	1126758M	Net Sales ($)		7696M	3127M	57250M	88651M	970034M
734966M	784316M	885281M	Total Assets ($)		7032M	441M	43218M	58847M	775743M

M = $ thousand MM = $ million

See Pages 9 through 22 for Explanation of Ratios and Data

Current Data Sorted by Assets							Comparative Historical Data	
						Type of Statement		
	2	8	24	4	3	Unqualified	60	46
	5	26	24	3	1	Reviewed	72	64
2	12	14	4	1		Compiled	36	38
14	15	9				Tax Returns	33	33
4	23	57	43	10	9	Other	124	122
57 (4/1-9/30/13)		260 (10/1/13-3/31/14)					4/1/09-3/31/10	4/1/10-3/31/11
0-500M	500M-2MM	2-10MM	10-50MM	50-100MM	100-250MM		ALL	ALL
20	57	114	95	18	13	**NUMBER OF STATEMENTS**	325	303
%	%	%	%	%	%	**ASSETS**	%	%
17.5	15.6	12.5	14.0	9.6	12.9	Cash & Equivalents	12.7	13.3
25.7	31.7	27.2	21.0	20.5	16.4	Trade Receivables (net)	22.8	24.0
27.5	23.7	30.2	24.7	24.4	21.9	Inventory	26.1	25.6
.7	3.0	3.5	7.0	9.9	8.5	All Other Current	5.1	3.9
71.4	73.9	73.3	66.6	64.4	59.7	Total Current	66.8	66.8
18.5	16.6	18.8	18.7	15.8	19.7	Fixed Assets (net)	20.8	21.1
2.0	2.1	4.1	6.4	11.7	15.2	Intangibles (net)	4.9	5.0
8.1	7.4	3.9	8.2	8.1	5.4	All Other Non-Current	7.5	7.1
100.0	100.0	100.0	100.0	100.0	100.0	Total	100.0	100.0
						LIABILITIES		
36.7	8.7	7.2	8.3	12.9	8.5	Notes Payable-Short Term	10.4	7.7
1.8	3.4	2.0	1.7	2.4	.8	Cur. Mat.-L.T.D.	3.2	3.6
18.8	18.1	15.3	9.2	14.5	8.5	Trade Payables	12.7	13.3
.0	.1	.3	.2	.4	.4	Income Taxes Payable	.3	.3
24.8	17.3	19.3	19.1	19.5	16.9	All Other Current	16.2	16.7
82.1	47.6	44.0	38.5	49.7	35.1	Total Current	42.8	41.7
21.4	18.1	12.9	8.9	8.4	11.1	Long-Term Debt	13.2	12.0
.0	.0	.3	.4	.2	1.5	Deferred Taxes	.5	.5
9.5	4.9	7.2	3.4	6.9	5.6	All Other Non-Current	7.3	8.2
-13.0	29.4	35.6	48.7	34.8	46.7	Net Worth	36.3	37.6
100.0	100.0	100.0	100.0	100.0	100.0	Total Liabilties & Net Worth	100.0	100.0
						INCOME DATA		
100.0	100.0	100.0	100.0	100.0	100.0	Net Sales	100.0	100.0
46.4	36.6	31.0	28.9	24.9	22.1	Gross Profit	31.0	33.2
39.8	33.0	23.8	21.7	18.8	20.1	Operating Expenses	27.6	27.5
6.6	3.6	7.2	7.2	6.1	2.1	Operating Profit	3.3	5.7
1.1	.6	1.0	.6	.6	1.2	All Other Expenses (net)	1.4	1.2
5.5	3.1	6.2	6.6	5.5	.8	Profit Before Taxes	2.0	4.6
						RATIOS		
2.4	3.9	3.2	2.5	1.8	2.3		2.6	3.0
1.4	1.9	1.5	1.7	1.4	1.8	Current	1.6	1.7
.7	1.1	1.2	1.3	1.0	1.2		1.1	1.2
2.0	3.8	1.9	1.4	.8	1.2		1.5	1.6
.7	1.2	.9	.9	.6	.9	Quick	.8	1.0
.2	.7	.6	.6	.5	.5		.5	.5
0 UND	**24** 15.5	**31** 11.9	**29** 12.6	**37** 9.9	**41** 8.8		**29** 12.5	**33** 10.9
14 26.2	**41** 9.0	**44** 8.3	**44** 8.3	**47** 7.7	**50** 7.3	Sales/Receivables	**46** 7.9	**46** 7.9
37 9.9	**66** 5.5	**65** 5.6	**63** 5.8	**61** 6.0	**65** 5.6		**62** 5.9	**68** 5.4
0 UND	**0** UND	**37** 9.8	**53** 6.9	**22** 16.3	**27** 13.5		**34** 10.6	**37** 9.9
15 25.1	**32** 11.3	**70** 5.2	**79** 4.6	**74** 4.9	**94** 3.9	Cost of Sales/Inventory	**74** 4.9	**81** 4.5
87 4.2	**114** 3.2	**135** 2.7	**122** 3.0	**135** 2.7	**152** 2.4		**146** 2.5	**135** 2.7
0 UND	**13** 28.7	**16** 22.3	**17** 21.3	**26** 14.0	**25** 14.6		**16** 22.5	**21** 17.8
15 25.0	**29** 12.7	**32** 11.4	**27** 13.6	**41** 8.8	**27** 13.6	Cost of Sales/Payables	**29** 12.8	**32** 11.5
68 5.4	**45** 8.1	**51** 7.1	**38** 9.5	**48** 7.6	**36** 10.1		**54** 6.8	**54** 6.7
8.2	3.9	3.4	3.4	5.8	2.9		3.6	3.6
19.0	7.4	7.5	5.5	9.7	7.7	Sales/Working Capital	7.4	6.0
-24.4	83.1	23.2	13.6	NM	14.8		27.9	30.2
9.4	13.7	21.2	26.1	34.5	20.5		10.5	22.0
(14) 4.7	(38) 3.3	(95) 6.0	(74) 10.7	(17) 5.2	(11) 1.0	EBIT/Interest	(279) 2.1	(263) 5.3
1.2	.7	1.6	3.5	2.7	.2		-.4	1.7
		9.6	12.2	11.9			5.3	11.2
		(24) 3.5	(21) 3.6	(10) 3.4		Net Profit + Depr., Dep., Amort./Cur. Mat. L/T/D	(102) 1.6	(86) 2.5
		1.1	1.8	1.5			-.3	1.2
.0	.1	.2	.1	.4	.3		.2	.2
.9	.3	.4	.4	.8	.7	Fixed/Worth	.5	.5
-.9	7.0	1.9	1.1	-.8	NM		2.5	1.7
.8	.7	.6	.5	.8	.8		.6	.6
3.9	1.7	1.9	1.3	3.4	2.6	Debt/Worth	1.5	1.7
-3.5	25.7	6.7	2.5	-12.0	NM		10.8	5.7
184.0	49.5	54.6	43.7	92.8	33.4		31.4	47.2
(13) 128.7	(44) 16.5	(96) 23.1	(87) 24.6	(12) 20.9	(10) 5.1	% Profit Before Taxes/Tangible Net Worth	(266) 8.9	(262) 19.4
33.1	3.3	4.5	9.5	13.4	-6.2		-3.0	5.5
66.1	18.6	19.7	15.9	12.3	8.6		11.2	16.7
10.2	6.7	9.8	10.1	7.4	-.1	% Profit Before Taxes/Total Assets	2.6	6.7
3.2	-.2	1.6	3.9	4.5	-4.6		-3.2	1.3
UND	94.4	36.5	24.0	34.6	11.3		23.6	25.6
157.6	23.9	13.4	10.7	13.1	7.0	Sales/Net Fixed Assets	10.3	10.8
16.9	9.4	6.6	5.7	5.8	4.3		5.0	5.3
5.5	3.6	2.6	1.9	1.9	1.5		2.3	2.3
4.5	2.6	1.9	1.5	1.6	1.2	Sales/Total Assets	1.6	1.6
3.1	1.4	1.4	1.2	1.1	1.0		1.1	1.2
	.4	.6	.9	.6			1.0	.9
	(36) 1.4	(100) 1.3	(81) 2.0	(15) 1.4		% Depr., Dep., Amort./Sales	(271) 2.0	(261) 1.9
	3.5	2.5	3.6	2.5			4.5	3.9
5.9	3.6	2.4	1.4				2.3	2.6
(14) 8.4	(22) 5.6	(20) 3.1	(10) 2.2			% Officers', Directors' Owners' Comp/Sales	(98) 4.8	(90) 4.5
13.4	10.9	4.6	6.0				9.8	8.5
27098M	215344M	1259331M	3437856M	2216953M	2495158M	Net Sales ($)	7997456M	7516848M
5126M	73254M	627499M	2165596M	1398121M	2109300M	Total Assets ($)	5760093M	5924546M

M = $ thousand MM = $ million

See Pages 9 through 22 for Explanation of Ratios and Data

Comparative Historical Data				Current Data Sorted by Sales					
			Type of Statement						
50	33	41	Unqualified			1	4	11	25
87	48	59	Reviewed		3	5	9	25	17
31	44	33	Compiled	4	4	6	6	9	4
40	43	38	Tax Returns	7	11	9	8	3	
139	137	146	Other	10	5	14	29	42	46
4/1/11-3/31/12	**4/1/12-3/31/13**	**4/1/13-3/31/14**		**57 (4/1-9/30/13)**		**260 (10/1/13-3/31/14)**			
ALL	**ALL**	**ALL**		**0-1MM**	**1-3MM**	**3-5MM**	**5-10MM**	**10-25MM**	**25MM & OVER**
347	305	317	**NUMBER OF STATEMENTS**	21	23	35	56	90	92
%	%	%	**ASSETS**	%	%	%	%	%	%
12.6	14.8	13.7	Cash & Equivalents	14.9	13.7	15.2	15.6	12.5	12.7
26.5	26.9	25.2	Trade Receivables (net)	26.4	23.0	24.3	29.0	27.3	21.5
25.8	26.5	26.5	Inventory	23.2	34.3	29.0	26.6	25.6	25.3
5.4	5.0	4.8	All Other Current	2.3	.4	3.6	2.9	4.4	8.6
70.4	73.2	70.2	Total Current	66.8	71.4	72.1	74.1	69.8	68.1
18.7	16.8	18.2	Fixed Assets (net)	19.1	22.2	18.1	19.2	18.3	16.4
4.3	4.3	5.2	Intangibles (net)	1.5	1.0	3.7	3.2	5.5	8.5
6.6	5.7	6.4	All Other Non-Current	12.6	5.4	6.1	3.5	6.5	7.0
100.0	100.0	100.0	Total	100.0	100.0	100.0	100.0	100.0	100.0
			LIABILITIES						
7.8	8.0	10.0	Notes Payable-Short Term	32.6	12.0	7.9	5.9	8.1	9.7
2.6	2.6	2.1	Cur. Mat.-L.T.D.	5.9	2.2	1.0	1.9	2.2	1.7
13.3	14.6	13.9	Trade Payables	25.6	15.0	14.8	11.2	14.1	11.9
.2	.3	.2	Income Taxes Payable	.2	.0	.1	.5	.1	.3
18.5	17.4	19.1	All Other Current	22.9	14.5	15.9	19.5	19.2	20.3
42.5	42.9	45.4	Total Current	87.0	43.7	39.7	38.9	43.8	43.9
11.6	11.0	12.9	Long-Term Debt	17.1	23.1	20.6	12.5	10.7	8.8
.5	.4	.3	Deferred Taxes	.0	.0	.4	.3	.3	.4
8.5	8.6	5.7	All Other Non-Current	11.7	5.2	5.7	7.0	4.7	4.6
36.9	37.1	35.8	Net Worth	-15.8	27.9	33.6	41.3	40.6	42.3
100.0	100.0	100.0	Total Liabilities & Net Worth	100.0	100.0	100.0	100.0	100.0	100.0
			INCOME DATA						
100.0	100.0	100.0	Net Sales	100.0	100.0	100.0	100.0	100.0	100.0
32.0	32.7	31.6	Gross Profit	48.1	35.7	38.9	31.5	28.5	27.2
25.1	25.6	25.4	Operating Expenses	42.5	32.6	32.3	24.8	22.5	20.3
6.9	7.0	6.2	Operating Profit	5.6	3.1	6.6	6.8	6.0	7.0
.8	.7	.8	All Other Expenses (net)	1.4	.6	1.0	.9	.4	1.0
6.1	6.4	5.5	Profit Before Taxes	4.2	2.5	5.6	5.9	5.6	6.0
			RATIOS						
2.6	3.1	2.8		5.6	2.6	3.6	4.0	2.7	2.3
1.8	1.8	1.7	Current	1.5	1.9	1.9	2.1	1.5	1.6
1.2	1.2	1.2		.6	1.0	1.4	1.3	1.2	1.2
1.5	1.7	1.6		5.2	2.1	2.5	2.3	1.4	1.2
.9	1.0	.9	Quick	.8	.9	1.1	1.3	.9	.8
.6	.6	.6		.3	.3	.6	.7	.6	.5
31 11.7	**28** 13.1	**29** 12.8		**22** 16.7	**8** 45.1	**23** 15.8	**33** 11.0	**29** 12.5	**31** 11.8
47 7.7	**43** 8.4	**43** 8.5	Sales/Receivables	**46** 8.0	**38** 9.7	**38** 9.6	**45** 8.2	**47** 7.8	**43** 8.4
62 5.9	**64** 5.7	**63** 5.8		**174** 2.1	**53** 6.9	**51** 7.2	**55** 6.6	**68** 5.4	**61** 6.0
35 10.5	**31** 11.9	**30** 12.1		**0** UND	**7** 53.7	**22** 16.7	**12** 29.6	**39** 9.3	**38** 9.5
69 5.3	**68** 5.4	**66** 5.5	Cost of Sales/Inventory	**29** 12.4	**49** 7.5	**72** 5.1	**61** 6.0	**68** 5.4	**69** 5.3
118 3.1	**118** 3.1	**122** 3.0		**152** 2.4	**159** 2.3	**174** 2.1	**146** 2.5	**118** 3.1	**118** 3.1
19 19.3	**17** 21.8	**15** 23.8		**6** 59.4	**14** 26.1	**16** 22.8	**12** 30.8	**17** 21.4	**22** 16.3
30 12.0	**29** 12.4	**29** 12.7	Cost of Sales/Payables	**40** 9.1	**31** 11.9	**38** 9.5	**23** 15.6	**27** 13.3	**29** 12.7
51 7.2	**47** 7.7	**45** 8.1		**166** 2.2	**53** 6.9	**61** 6.0	**41** 8.8	**41** 8.9	**42** 8.6
3.9	3.7	3.7		1.4	3.6	4.4	3.2	4.0	4.0
6.9	6.8	7.3	Sales/Working Capital	7.8	14.6	7.4	5.4	7.5	7.5
17.0	18.6	23.0		-5.4	-170.5	19.5	14.5	22.7	22.4
31.3	43.8	20.8		4.6	12.3	31.0	16.2	29.6	24.2
(287) 9.1	(244) 10.6	(249) 6.0	EBIT/Interest	(15) 1.9	(18) 4.9	(27) 5.1	(40) 5.3	(72) 8.4	(77) 9.4
2.9	2.4	1.6		-7.2	.7	2.2	.8	3.3	1.8
12.4	9.9	10.2						19.2	6.9
(73) 4.3	(59) 3.0	(63) 3.4	Net Profit + Depr., Dep., Amort./Cur. Mat. L/T/D					(22) 4.7	(28) 3.5
2.1	1.3	1.0						.9	1.2
.2	.1	.2		.0	.1	.2	.1	.2	.2
.5	.3	.5	Fixed/Worth	.4	.6	.5	.3	.4	.6
1.3	1.4	1.6		-1.4	1.6	6.6	1.1	1.2	1.7
.7	.6	.6		.6	1.1	.6	.6	.6	.7
1.6	1.5	1.7	Debt/Worth	13.2	2.5	2.5	1.3	1.6	1.7
5.2	6.3	7.7		-3.5	15.5	16.9	3.8	4.9	8.4
50.5	56.2	51.4		32.1	123.7	82.9	51.2	43.4	53.0
(300) 27.5	(265) 27.6	(262) 24.1	% Profit Before Taxes/Tangible Net Worth	(12) 6.6	(20) 17.9	(28) 19.2	(50) 28.3	(77) 19.9	(75) 29.4
11.4	12.7	7.0		-14.3	3.3	11.0	4.0	5.6	11.6
16.9	19.5	16.5		12.7	9.1	18.7	22.5	16.0	15.9
9.9	9.8	9.0	% Profit Before Taxes/Total Assets	2.7	4.5	9.1	11.5	8.7	11.0
3.8	3.4	1.6		-10.8	.0	2.1	.3	2.9	3.9
35.0	48.5	41.9		321.8	223.9	35.8	52.3	34.6	35.0
14.8	17.5	14.2	Sales/Net Fixed Assets	12.0	10.9	19.3	13.0	14.8	13.4
6.5	7.0	6.2		3.1	5.1	6.5	6.7	6.1	6.3
2.7	2.7	2.6		3.3	4.7	3.1	3.2	2.4	2.1
1.8	1.9	1.8	Sales/Total Assets	1.0	2.3	2.3	2.0	1.7	1.6
1.4	1.4	1.3		.6	1.4	1.4	1.4	1.4	1.3
.8	.5	.7		.3	1.3	.6	.6	.7	.9
(292) 1.7	(247) 1.3	(246) 1.4	% Depr., Dep., Amort./Sales	(11) 1.9	(11) 3.4	(27) 1.4	(41) 1.4	(81) 1.3	(75) 1.6
3.0	2.8	2.8		20.0	4.8	2.7	2.7	2.7	2.6
2.4	2.2	2.7			3.0	4.0	2.2	1.4	
(84) 3.9	(88) 4.0	(66) 4.8	% Officers', Directors' Owners' Comp/Sales		(11) 5.6	(15) 5.2	(17) 3.0	(11) 2.0	
6.7	9.2	8.4			6.9	6.4	5.0	3.0	
10214873M	**7705983M**	**9651740M**	Net Sales ($)	**14913M**	**44439M**	**141745M**	**403289M**	**1500634M**	**7546720M**
6584595M	**5244376M**	**6378896M**	Total Assets ($)	**17314M**	**23563M**	**81375M**	**225144M**	**944187M**	**5087313M**

M = $ thousand MM = $ million

See Pages 9 through 22 for Explanation of Ratios and Data

Current Data Sorted by Assets							Comparative Historical Data	
		1	2	1	1	**Type of Statement** Unqualified	13	14
		5	4			Reviewed	16	19
	1	2				Compiled	5	5
	3	1	3			Tax Returns	5	6
	2	11	14	2	3	Other	23	26
	9 (4/1-9/30/13)		47 (10/1/13-3/31/14)				**4/1/09-3/31/10**	**4/1/10-3/31/11**
0-500M	**500M-2MM**	**2-10MM**	**10-50MM**	**50-100MM**	**100-250MM**		**ALL**	**ALL**
	6	20	23	3	4	**NUMBER OF STATEMENTS**	62	70
%	%	%	%	%	%	**ASSETS**	%	%
DATA NOT AVAILABLE		14.8	7.5			Cash & Equivalents	11.2	11.8
		20.5	15.7			Trade Receivables (net)	21.6	21.7
		29.4	21.7			Inventory	28.6	25.6
		1.6	4.1			All Other Current	2.7	2.7
		66.3	49.0			Total Current	64.1	61.7
		21.8	33.0			Fixed Assets (net)	22.9	22.2
		8.4	13.1			Intangibles (net)	8.5	8.5
		3.6	4.9			All Other Non-Current	4.4	7.6
		100.0	100.0			Total	100.0	100.0
						LIABILITIES		
		5.1	4.9			Notes Payable-Short Term	7.8	6.9
		2.9	6.7			Cur. Mat.-L.T.D.	2.9	2.1
		9.1	7.6			Trade Payables	12.4	11.6
		.1	.7			Income Taxes Payable	.2	.3
		10.5	8.0			All Other Current	10.9	12.2
		27.7	27.8			Total Current	34.2	33.1
		12.1	17.6			Long-Term Debt	11.3	14.8
		.0	.9			Deferred Taxes	.9	.5
		3.5	2.9			All Other Non-Current	6.0	9.9
		56.7	50.8			Net Worth	47.6	41.7
		100.0	100.0			Total Liabilties & Net Worth	100.0	100.0
						INCOME DATA		
		100.0	100.0			Net Sales	100.0	100.0
		35.3	36.9			Gross Profit	36.8	40.3
		33.1	33.4			Operating Expenses	31.8	33.0
		2.2	3.5			Operating Profit	5.0	7.2
		1.2	3.3			All Other Expenses (net)	1.5	.9
		1.0	.2			Profit Before Taxes	3.4	6.3
						RATIOS		
		4.2	3.9				3.4	3.4
		2.9	2.0			Current	2.0	1.9
		2.0	1.1				1.4	1.4
		2.8	1.7				1.6	1.8
		1.1	1.0			Quick	1.0	1.0
		.8	.6				.6	.6
		34 10.8	**30** 12.0				**34** 10.7	**36** 10.1
		42 8.7	**39** 9.4			Sales/Receivables	**42** 8.6	**49** 7.5
		58 6.3	**55** 6.6				**53** 6.9	**59** 6.2
		44 8.3	**52** 7.0				**53** 6.9	**51** 7.2
		94 3.9	**91** 4.0			Cost of Sales/Inventory	**92** 4.0	**92** 4.0
		166 2.2	**192** 1.9				**140** 2.6	**135** 2.7
		18 20.5	**18** 20.3				**14** 26.5	**20** 18.1
		28 13.0	**24** 15.1			Cost of Sales/Payables	**29** 12.7	**39** 9.5
		40 9.1	**46** 7.9				**49** 7.4	**56** 6.5
		2.3	2.5				3.6	3.4
		4.4	5.7			Sales/Working Capital	6.2	5.8
		8.4	34.3				10.9	16.3
		6.4	15.2				8.9	14.2
		(16) 1.9	(22) 5.4			EBIT/Interest	(49) 3.8	(57) 6.2
		.1	-1.9				2.5	1.7
			3.8				3.4	11.1
			(11) 3.1			Net Profit + Depr., Dep., Amort./Cur. Mat. L/T/D	(16) 2.7	(22) 5.9
			.1				1.6	2.6
		.1	.5				.2	.2
		.5	.9			Fixed/Worth	.5	.5
		1.4	1.5				1.2	1.6
		.3	.5				.5	.7
		.9	1.1			Debt/Worth	1.2	1.2
		3.8	2.5				3.0	3.8
		17.4	24.7				38.3	48.9
		7.9	(21) 9.0			% Profit Before Taxes/Tangible Net Worth	(59) 15.5	(61) 21.6
		-.8	-17.3				3.3	5.2
		6.8	11.0				9.5	17.3
		2.4	4.4			% Profit Before Taxes/Total Assets	6.0	9.7
		-.6	-6.8				.9	1.8
		33.7	10.3				29.5	28.5
		7.9	4.4			Sales/Net Fixed Assets	10.1	8.7
		4.3	2.6				4.2	4.9
		2.2	1.7				2.3	2.1
		1.6	1.3			Sales/Total Assets	1.8	1.7
		1.0	.8				1.2	1.3
		1.5	3.1				1.5	1.4
		(18) 4.9	(21) 3.8			% Depr., Dep., Amort./Sales	(50) 3.3	(57) 2.6
		6.3	5.1				4.8	5.8
		2.3					1.5	2.9
		(12) 4.1				% Officers', Directors' Owners' Comp/Sales	(20) 5.0	(25) 4.3
		6.6					8.8	7.2
	28477M	171711M	638454M	213540M	722471M	Net Sales ($)	2381115M	2371571M
	8657M	100683M	514847M	229395M	556171M	Total Assets ($)	1425778M	1615438M

M = $ thousand MM = $ million

See Pages 9 through 22 for Explanation of Ratios and Data

Comparative Historical Data | **Current Data Sorted by Sales**

4/1/11-3/31/12 ALL	4/1/12-3/31/13 ALL	4/1/13-3/31/14 ALL	Type of Statement	0-1MM	1-3MM	3-5MM	5-10MM	10-25MM	25MM & OVER
13	9	5	Unqualified			1		1	3
9	15	9	Reviewed		1	1	2	4	1
3	6	3	Compiled			1	2		
6	7	7	Tax Returns		1	1	2	2	1
23	20	32	Other			4	7	7	14
					9 (4/1-9/30/13)		47 (10/1/13-3/31/14)		
54	57	56	NUMBER OF STATEMENTS		2	8	13	14	19
%	%	%	**ASSETS**	%	%	%	%	%	%
10.7	12.5	13.4	Cash & Equivalents	DATA NOT AVAILABLE			12.1	7.9	13.2
22.0	20.6	18.3	Trade Receivables (net)				17.9	15.6	18.1
26.8	28.7	24.5	Inventory				29.2	26.4	21.6
3.2	3.8	3.0	All Other Current				2.6	3.5	2.8
62.7	65.5	59.1	Total Current				61.7	53.4	55.7
24.2	24.1	26.6	Fixed Assets (net)				26.9	36.5	24.1
7.2	5.0	9.8	Intangibles (net)				4.9	7.7	13.4
5.9	5.4	4.5	All Other Non-Current				6.4	2.4	6.8
100.0	100.0	100.0	Total				100.0	100.0	100.0
			LIABILITIES						
6.1	7.4	5.0	Notes Payable-Short Term				5.4	4.8	4.6
3.6	2.6	4.0	Cur. Mat.-L.T.D.				3.3	3.0	6.5
11.6	11.0	8.7	Trade Payables				7.4	7.5	10.5
.3	.4	.3	Income Taxes Payable				.2	.2	.7
9.4	13.8	9.9	All Other Current				5.0	11.1	6.8
31.0	35.1	28.1	Total Current				21.3	26.7	29.1
15.4	10.4	14.1	Long-Term Debt				18.1	14.8	13.0
.5	.5	.5	Deferred Taxes				.0	1.3	.4
2.9	6.5	3.2	All Other Non-Current				6.4	4.3	2.0
50.1	47.4	54.1	Net Worth				54.2	52.9	55.6
100.0	100.0	100.0	Total Liabilties & Net Worth				100.0	100.0	100.0
			INCOME DATA						
100.0	100.0	100.0	Net Sales				100.0	100.0	100.0
37.5	38.4	39.6	Gross Profit				41.7	34.7	42.7
31.1	33.8	35.1	Operating Expenses				39.0	33.6	35.5
6.4	4.6	4.5	Operating Profit				2.7	1.1	7.2
.4	.6	1.7	All Other Expenses (net)				.5	1.2	2.5
6.1	3.9	2.9	Profit Before Taxes				2.2	-.1	4.7
			RATIOS						
3.1	3.3	3.9					4.5	4.1	3.7
1.9	2.3	2.4	Current				3.2	1.8	2.4
1.5	1.8	1.5					2.0	1.3	1.1
1.7	1.9	2.3					2.9	1.9	2.4
1.0	1.1	1.1	Quick				1.1	.9	1.2
.5	.6	.7					.9	.4	.7
30 12.3	**29** 12.4	**31** 11.8					**26** 14.0	**31** 11.8	**29** 12.7
42 8.6	**45** 8.1	**41** 9.0	Sales/Receivables				**39** 9.3	**43** 8.5	**38** 9.6
53 6.9	**58** 6.3	**58** 6.3					**60** 6.1	**61** 6.0	**70** 5.2
48 7.6	**46** 8.0	**52** 7.0					**36** 10.0	**78** 4.7	**52** 7.0
87 4.2	**94** 3.9	**99** 3.7	Cost of Sales/Inventory				**87** 4.2	**101** 3.6	**107** 3.4
126 2.9	**174** 2.1	**166** 2.2					**215** 1.7	**174** 2.1	**130** 2.8
19 18.9	**20** 18.6	**19** 19.7					**15** 24.4	**13** 27.7	**19** 18.9
31 11.9	**28** 13.0	**30** 12.3	Cost of Sales/Payables				**25** 14.5	**34** 10.6	**32** 11.3
44 8.3	**47** 7.8	**43** 8.4					**46** 7.9	**41** 8.9	**61** 6.0
3.7	2.7	2.6					2.4	2.2	3.5
6.1	5.1	5.6	Sales/Working Capital				3.1	5.4	5.6
12.5	9.0	10.3					9.3	20.8	30.8
45.0	31.6	21.7					36.0	12.8	58.6
(44) 10.5	(51) 4.6	(48) 4.8	EBIT/Interest				1.9	(12) 5.0	(16) 15.3
2.4	-.3	.7					.4	-9.2	-.7
14.7	9.9	3.6							
(14) 4.7	(19) 3.1	(20) 2.6	Net Profit + Depr., Dep., Amort./Cur. Mat. L/T/D						
2.1	2.0	.8							
.2	.2	.3					.3	.5	.3
.5	.5	.6	Fixed/Worth				.7	.8	.6
1.2	1.0	1.3					1.4	1.6	1.7
.4	.5	.4					.4	.3	.3
1.0	.9	1.1	Debt/Worth				1.3	1.0	1.0
2.3	2.6	2.6					2.4	2.3	2.9
50.5	46.9	37.6					20.1	27.0	43.1
(50) 26.1	(51) 11.7	(54) 11.4	% Profit Before Taxes/Tangible Net Worth				8.2	(13) 13.1	(18) 17.3
6.5	-.5	-1.6					-.5	-8.3	-10.9
23.1	19.8	14.6					10.1	12.2	17.7
10.5	5.5	4.7	% Profit Before Taxes/Total Assets				2.9	6.6	7.2
2.7	-2.1	-.5					-.4	-4.2	-4.2
24.0	24.7	15.6					23.6	5.3	14.6
8.5	9.5	6.2	Sales/Net Fixed Assets				6.5	3.8	7.9
5.5	5.3	3.8					1.9	2.5	4.4
2.5	2.6	2.1					2.8	1.5	2.0
1.8	1.6	1.5	Sales/Total Assets				1.8	1.3	1.6
1.4	1.3	1.0					.9	.9	1.1
1.3	1.2	2.0					1.7	2.5	2.8
(44) 2.5	(45) 2.8	(50) 3.7	% Depr., Dep., Amort./Sales				(11) 4.9	3.8	(17) 3.5
4.2	6.9	5.3					8.2	7.1	4.0
1.8	2.8	2.3							
(19) 4.1	(16) 5.6	(21) 4.2	% Officers', Directors' Owners' Comp/Sales						
7.5	7.5	6.3							
1710692M	1604828M	1774653M	Net Sales ($)		3843M	34107M	91189M	254388M	1391126M
1142868M	934277M	1409753M	Total Assets ($)		2668M	25630M	72111M	243595M	1065749M

M = $ thousand MM = $ million

See Pages 9 through 22 for Explanation of Ratios and Data

Current Data Sorted by Assets							Comparative Historical Data	
						Type of Statement		
		5	15	4	3	Unqualified	40	37
2		21	22			Reviewed	64	46
2	9	16	7			Compiled	55	28
4	14	15				Tax Returns	71	33
4	15	35	30	4	9	Other	122	100
42 (4/1-9/30/13)		194 (10/1/13-3/31/14)					4/1/09-3/31/10 ALL	4/1/10-3/31/11 ALL
0-500M	500M-2MM	2-10MM	10-50MM	50-100MM	100-250MM			
12	38	92	74	8	12	**NUMBER OF STATEMENTS**	352	244
%	%	%	%	%	%	**ASSETS**	%	%
26.4	11.6	13.7	10.0		11.2	Cash & Equivalents	10.4	11.0
15.1	28.8	28.0	23.3		13.6	Trade Receivables (net)	26.8	26.9
24.8	28.4	27.4	28.2		19.0	Inventory	25.9	25.3
2.7	1.1	4.0	4.6		3.7	All Other Current	3.4	4.8
69.1	69.8	73.1	66.1		47.4	Total Current	66.4	68.0
20.7	18.4	16.9	21.1		17.5	Fixed Assets (net)	20.9	20.2
7.9	4.4	3.2	5.7		27.9	Intangibles (net)	4.9	5.2
2.2	7.4	6.8	7.1		7.2	All Other Non-Current	7.8	6.7
100.0	100.0	100.0	100.0		100.0	Total	100.0	100.0
						LIABILITIES		
13.3	7.7	10.0	7.8		4.3	Notes Payable-Short Term	10.4	9.6
1.0	5.2	9.2	3.0		2.2	Cur. Mat.-L.T.D.	3.6	2.8
21.6	18.3	16.5	12.4		7.7	Trade Payables	14.7	13.8
.0	.0	.5	.2		.1	Income Taxes Payable	.2	.2
21.1	19.2	15.6	15.1		16.5	All Other Current	11.8	14.7
57.0	50.4	51.7	38.4		30.9	Total Current	40.7	41.2
29.8	16.4	8.3	12.0		13.5	Long-Term Debt	15.7	14.4
.0	.0	.3	.9		2.4	Deferred Taxes	.3	.3
13.7	19.2	5.5	8.1		9.0	All Other Non-Current	6.1	7.9
-.5	13.9	34.2	40.6		44.3	Net Worth	37.2	36.2
100.0	100.0	100.0	100.0		100.0	Total Liabilities & Net Worth	100.0	100.0
						INCOME DATA		
100.0	100.0	100.0	100.0		100.0	Net Sales	100.0	100.0
48.7	40.2	34.1	30.7		38.4	Gross Profit	34.4	35.6
42.8	35.2	28.9	24.3		34.2	Operating Expenses	31.6	29.9
5.9	5.0	5.2	6.4		4.2	Operating Profit	2.9	5.7
.6	.9	.4	.7		3.5	All Other Expenses (net)	.9	.8
5.3	4.2	4.7	5.7		.7	Profit Before Taxes	2.0	4.9
						RATIOS		
7.9	3.3	3.1	2.8		2.4		2.8	3.2
1.6	2.0	1.7	1.8		2.0	Current	1.7	1.7
.6	1.1	1.1	1.3		1.1		1.2	1.2
7.9	1.9	2.1	1.6		1.3		1.6	1.9
.8	.9	1.0	.9		.9	Quick	.9	.9
.3	.5	.5	.5		.5		.5	.6
0 UND	**21** 17.2	**30** 12.2	**28** 13.0		**30** 12.3		**31** 11.8	**29** 12.8
12 29.5	**36** 10.1	**40** 9.1	**44** 8.3		**40** 9.2	Sales/Receivables	**42** 8.6	**45** 8.2
31 11.7	**50** 7.3	**60** 6.1	**62** 5.9		**51** 7.2		**57** 6.4	**64** 5.7
0 UND	**26** 14.2	**17** 21.9	**36** 10.0		**76** 4.8		**28** 12.9	**24** 15.3
29 12.8	**59** 6.2	**61** 6.0	**91** 4.0		**89** 4.1	Cost of Sales/Inventory	**63** 5.8	**60** 6.1
52 7.0	**166** 2.2	**122** 3.0	**135** 2.7		**174** 2.1		**114** 3.2	**111** 3.3
0 UND	**12** 29.2	**15** 24.2	**17** 21.2		**22** 16.6		**17** 21.4	**16** 22.8
21 17.5	**23** 15.6	**33** 11.1	**29** 12.5		**35** 10.5	Cost of Sales/Payables	**30** 12.1	**30** 12.2
65 5.6	**54** 6.8	**48** 7.6	**45** 8.2		**79** 4.6		**51** 7.2	**50** 7.3
8.9	4.9	4.7	3.9		3.1		4.7	4.3
25.2	9.0	7.3	7.1		5.5	Sales/Working Capital	8.2	8.6
-25.6	48.3	33.6	15.9		NM		27.8	21.7
	28.1	39.7	27.8		13.7		9.0	27.7
	(32) 6.7	(74) 8.9	(71) 8.3		(10) 8.0	EBIT/Interest	(302) 2.8	(206) 6.0
	1.4	2.1	3.2		.0		.3	1.4
		6.6	12.4				4.6	11.0
		(16) 2.7	(29) 4.5			Net Profit + Depr., Dep., Amort./Cur. Mat. L/T/D	(67) 2.1	(52) 3.0
		1.4	2.2				.5	1.4
.0	.1	.1	.2		.5		.2	.2
.8	.6	.3	.6		.7	Fixed/Worth	.5	.5
-.4	-10.3	1.3	1.8		-7.6		1.6	1.5
.3	1.0	.6	.8		.9		.7	.7
NM	2.6	1.7	1.7		2.3	Debt/Worth	1.9	1.7
-1.9	-20.8	4.9	4.6		-25.2		5.1	4.8
	80.4	52.4	43.1				37.2	51.3
	(28) 44.6	(85) 27.8	(60) 17.8			% Profit Before Taxes/Tangible Net Worth	(305) 14.5	(214) 21.6
	12.1	6.4	8.7				.5	7.0
57.5	22.6	22.7	17.7		8.6		11.8	19.8
26.4	10.2	7.5	7.1		4.7	% Profit Before Taxes/Total Assets	4.1	7.8
.9	1.3	1.4	2.8		-1.5		-1.3	1.4
806.2	85.9	66.2	32.8		7.9		37.0	38.9
86.2	27.1	25.0	14.0		6.4	Sales/Net Fixed Assets	15.8	15.4
12.1	6.9	9.3	3.8		4.3		5.9	6.2
12.8	3.3	3.0	2.5		1.5		2.8	2.8
3.3	2.8	2.2	1.6		1.0	Sales/Total Assets	2.0	2.1
2.3	1.7	1.4	1.3		.7		1.3	1.5
	.4	.5	.7				.8	.9
	(26) 1.6	(73) 1.0	(68) 1.3			% Depr., Dep., Amort./Sales	(275) 1.9	(196) 1.6
	2.3	2.4	3.0				3.7	2.6
	2.6	1.6					2.4	2.3
	(23) 5.6	(33) 2.6				% Officers', Directors' Owners' Comp/Sales	(138) 4.5	(81) 4.2
	12.6	4.9					7.6	7.7
20675M	114131M	1044136M	2694664M	782637M	1888708M	Net Sales ($)	7507435M	6596399M
3498M	41774M	443354M	1475602M	542315M	1740379M	Total Assets ($)	4705504M	3819888M

M = $ thousand MM = $ million

See Pages 9 through 22 for Explanation of Ratios and Data

Comparative Historical Data				Current Data Sorted by Sales					
			Type of Statement						
42	24	27	Unqualified				3	4	20
58	53	45	Reviewed	2			12	14	17
42	23	34	Compiled		6	5	9	7	7
29	39	33	Tax Returns	5	9	8	4	6	1
90	111	97	Other	3	11	10	15	25	33
				42 (4/1-9/30/13)			194 (10/1/13-3/31/14)		
4/1/11-3/31/12 ALL	4/1/12-3/31/13 ALL	4/1/13-3/31/14 ALL		0-1MM	1-3MM	3-5MM	5-10MM	10-25MM	25MM & OVER
261	250	236	**NUMBER OF STATEMENTS**	10	26	23	43	56	78
%	%	%	**ASSETS**	%	%	%	%	%	%
11.0	11.4	12.6	Cash & Equivalents	9.7	14.7	22.7	13.4	11.0	10.1
27.4	27.5	24.8	Trade Receivables (net)	13.2	23.6	27.0	25.3	26.7	24.6
26.0	25.5	27.1	Inventory	35.5	26.2	25.0	25.2	29.6	26.2
4.2	4.1	3.7	All Other Current	3.3	1.3	1.0	5.2	3.5	4.6
68.6	68.6	68.3	Total Current	61.7	65.8	75.7	69.1	70.7	65.5
17.6	18.0	18.7	Fixed Assets (net)	32.5	17.1	15.6	18.6	19.2	18.2
7.3	5.3	6.2	Intangibles (net)	3.1	8.9	4.3	3.5	3.4	9.8
6.5	8.1	6.8	All Other Non-Current	2.7	8.2	4.4	8.9	6.6	6.5
100.0	100.0	100.0	Total	100.0	100.0	100.0	100.0	100.0	100.0
			LIABILITIES						
9.2	9.6	8.7	Notes Payable-Short Term	2.1	9.0	8.1	7.2	13.5	6.9
3.4	2.4	5.6	Cur. Mat.-L.T.D.	1.8	1.8	17.5	11.5	2.7	2.7
14.6	13.6	15.1	Trade Payables	15.7	17.4	14.0	14.9	18.4	12.3
.2	.2	.2	Income Taxes Payable	.1	.0	.0	.8	.2	.2
14.4	14.4	16.3	All Other Current	21.2	14.8	21.8	16.3	14.9	15.7
41.8	40.2	45.9	Total Current	40.9	43.0	61.4	50.8	49.6	37.7
12.9	12.0	12.1	Long-Term Debt	32.7	22.4	10.1	8.9	9.2	10.4
.4	.3	.5	Deferred Taxes	.0	.0	.0	.3	.2	1.3
7.5	6.7	9.5	All Other Non-Current	12.8	25.4	7.3	6.0	4.4	9.9
37.5	40.7	32.0	Net Worth	13.6	9.2	21.2	34.0	36.5	40.7
100.0	100.0	100.0	Total Liabilties & Net Worth	100.0	100.0	100.0	100.0	100.0	100.0
			INCOME DATA						
100.0	100.0	100.0	Net Sales	100.0	100.0	100.0	100.0	100.0	100.0
33.6	33.1	35.1	Gross Profit	43.2	46.9	38.0	35.0	32.0	31.5
27.8	26.9	29.5	Operating Expenses	43.7	40.8	32.2	28.0	27.5	25.3
5.8	6.2	5.6	Operating Profit	-.5	6.0	5.8	7.0	4.5	6.1
.9	.6	.8	All Other Expenses (net)	2.7	1.0	.2	.5	.0	1.5
4.9	5.6	4.7	Profit Before Taxes	-3.3	5.0	5.6	6.5	4.4	4.7
			RATIOS						
2.8	3.3	3.0		5.3	3.3	3.9	3.7	2.3	2.8
1.6	1.8	1.8	Current	2.0	2.1	1.8	2.0	1.5	1.8
1.2	1.2	1.2		.6	1.0	1.0	1.2	1.2	1.3
1.6	1.9	1.7		1.2	2.4	2.8	2.6	1.4	1.4
.9	.9	.9	Quick	.5	1.0	1.4	1.0	.8	1.0
.6	.5	.5		.2	.6	.7	.4	.4	.6
30 12.2	**30** 12.2	**27** 13.3		**16** 22.6	**11** 31.8	**30** 12.0	**30** 12.2	**28** 12.9	**28** 13.0
46 8.0	**46** 8.0	**38** 9.5	Sales/Receivables	**28** 12.9	**30** 12.1	**41** 8.9	**43** 8.5	**41** 9.0	**38** 9.5
63 5.8	**64** 5.7	**58** 6.3		**42** 8.6	**47** 7.8	**76** 4.8	**62** 5.9	**59** 6.2	**57** 6.4
29 12.6	**26** 14.3	**28** 13.1		**39** 9.3	**0** UND	**18** 20.2	**12** 30.4	**38** 9.6	**35** 10.3
68 5.4	**65** 5.6	**72** 5.1	Cost of Sales/Inventory	**203** 1.8	**50** 7.3	**48** 7.6	**50** 7.3	**72** 5.1	**83** 4.4
118 3.1	**114** 3.2	**126** 2.9		**456** .8	**99** 3.7	**135** 2.7	**126** 2.9	**122** 3.0	**122** 3.0
18 20.3	**17** 21.7	**16** 23.4		**11** 32.0	**10** 35.3	**6** 61.2	**14** 26.4	**21** 17.4	**17** 21.2
33 11.0	**30** 12.1	**30** 12.3	Cost of Sales/Payables	**60** 6.1	**23** 15.7	**20** 18.7	**30** 12.2	**38** 9.6	**28** 13.1
51 7.1	**46** 7.9	**49** 7.4		**152** 2.4	**64** 5.7	**52** 7.0	**45** 8.1	**46** 7.9	**47** 7.8
4.4	3.9	4.4		1.5	5.7	3.5	3.6	4.9	4.5
8.2	7.4	7.6	Sales/Working Capital	7.7	11.1	7.8	6.1	7.8	7.7
23.5	25.3	25.2		-8.7	-121.4	-543.8	26.8	35.6	18.2
18.3	26.2	34.9			32.6	75.8	34.0	41.2	33.5
(223) 5.7	(203) 7.1	(202) 8.1	EBIT/Interest		(21) 6.6	(18) 11.1	(36) 8.9	(49) 7.0	(72) 9.2
1.5	2.0	2.1			.8	2.4	2.4	1.8	4.3
16.8	8.1	8.7						9.6	12.2
(62) 3.3	(56) 2.9	(59) 3.8	Net Profit + Depr., Dep., Amort./Cur. Mat. L/T/D					(13) 5.9	(34) 3.7
.9	1.4	2.0						1.6	2.2
.1	.1	.1		.5	.0	.1	.1	.2	.2
.4	.4	.5	Fixed/Worth	NM	.6	.3	.4	.4	.6
1.2	1.2	1.8		-1.3	-2.0	5.0	1.5	1.6	1.7
.8	.6	.7		.9	1.0	.6	.4	.8	.8
1.8	1.7	1.8	Debt/Worth	NM	2.6	2.1	1.3	1.8	1.7
5.0	4.3	7.1		-5.2	-3.7	24.1	3.6	4.9	4.8
50.5	51.7	51.6			82.0	48.8	45.3	45.3	47.2
(229) 25.3	(217) 24.0	(193) 27.4	% Profit Before Taxes/Tangible Net Worth		(18) 59.3	(18) 20.6	(40) 24.9	(49) 27.4	(63) 28.3
6.4	5.9	8.9			18.6	3.4	5.4	2.5	10.0
16.7	18.4	20.4		18.6	33.4	20.1	29.0	19.4	16.9
7.9	8.1	8.0	% Profit Before Taxes/Total Assets	1.2	11.3	6.7	12.3	5.7	8.3
1.7	1.7	1.5		-11.9	.4	1.7	1.7	.8	4.1
59.1	53.0	53.3		64.4	321.0	85.1	91.7	38.4	38.8
16.8	16.8	17.9	Sales/Net Fixed Assets	3.6	36.5	30.3	17.6	16.5	15.7
6.8	6.1	5.9		2.3	6.9	12.6	5.1	6.5	6.2
2.7	2.8	2.8		2.3	3.6	2.9	2.7	3.0	2.7
1.9	1.9	2.0	Sales/Total Assets	1.3	2.8	2.2	1.9	2.1	1.8
1.3	1.3	1.3		.7	1.7	1.3	1.3	1.4	1.3
.6	.7	.6		.4	1.1	.4	.5	.6	.7
(199) 1.5	(197) 1.5	(190) 1.4	% Depr., Dep., Amort./Sales	1.7	(13) 2.3	(17) .9	(31) 1.5	(50) 1.2	(69) 1.4
2.9	2.9	2.8		5.7	4.5	2.3	3.0	3.0	2.9
2.1	1.9	2.0			2.5	4.0	2.0	1.6	
(76) 3.7	(81) 3.7	(72) 3.5	% Officers', Directors' Owners' Comp/Sales		(15) 4.3	(14) 6.1	(13) 3.5	(15) 2.6	
6.2	6.6	7.8			9.0	9.1	4.8	2.9	
7474184M	7603552M	6544951M	Net Sales ($)	6024M	56438M	90108M	309954M	883856M	5198571M
5097036M	4980288M	4246922M	Total Assets ($)	6095M	25699M	51775M	187900M	494687M	3480766M

M = $ thousand MM = $ million

See Pages 9 through 22 for Explanation of Ratios and Data

Current Data Sorted by Assets							Comparative Historical Data	
						Type of Statement		
		3	2	2		Unqualified	13	17
	4	6	3		1	Reviewed	12	12
	2	3	2			Compiled	5	8
2	5	3				Tax Returns	10	12
1	2	10	11	3	5	Other	26	29
7 (4/1-9/30/13)			63 (10/1/13-3/31/14)				4/1/09-3/31/10 ALL	4/1/10-3/31/11 ALL
0-500M	**500M-2MM**	**2-10MM**	**10-50MM**	**50-100MM**	**100-250MM**			
3	13	25	18	5	6	**NUMBER OF STATEMENTS**	66	78
%	%	%	%	%	%	**ASSETS**	%	%
	19.0	13.6	5.9			Cash & Equivalents	12.7	13.9
	27.5	25.4	31.4			Trade Receivables (net)	24.1	30.7
	33.1	24.7	19.0			Inventory	23.6	22.0
	1.0	5.3	6.6			All Other Current	3.9	4.9
	80.7	69.1	62.9			Total Current	64.3	71.5
	12.7	18.5	22.2			Fixed Assets (net)	21.7	17.7
	3.3	7.5	12.0			Intangibles (net)	6.4	5.3
	3.3	4.9	2.9			All Other Non-Current	7.7	5.5
	100.0	100.0	100.0			Total	100.0	100.0
						LIABILITIES		
	5.6	3.7	7.2			Notes Payable-Short Term	5.9	6.1
	3.7	1.5	3.4			Cur. Mat.-L.T.D.	1.7	2.1
	23.7	11.6	9.9			Trade Payables	10.2	13.2
	.0	.1	.2			Income Taxes Payable	.3	.4
	6.4	11.1	19.7			All Other Current	11.7	15.6
	39.4	28.1	40.3			Total Current	29.9	37.4
	30.9	6.9	14.5			Long-Term Debt	12.3	11.3
	.0	.1	.3			Deferred Taxes	.7	.7
	27.5	6.9	8.6			All Other Non-Current	5.6	4.6
	2.3	58.0	36.2			Net Worth	51.6	46.1
	100.0	100.0	100.0			Total Liabilties & Net Worth	100.0	100.0
						INCOME DATA		
	100.0	100.0	100.0			Net Sales	100.0	100.0
	30.2	36.6	34.2			Gross Profit	35.8	33.0
	28.7	28.2	27.6			Operating Expenses	29.4	26.1
	1.4	8.4	6.6			Operating Profit	6.4	6.8
	.5	.4	.6			All Other Expenses (net)	.5	.6
	.9	8.0	6.0			Profit Before Taxes	5.9	6.2
						RATIOS		
	3.0	5.1	2.1				4.4	3.0
	2.1	3.2	1.7			Current	2.1	1.9
	1.6	1.6	1.2				1.4	1.4
	1.6	3.0	1.5				2.0	1.7
	1.1	1.3	1.0			Quick	1.2	1.2
	.8	1.0	.6				.8	.9
	19 19.2	**26** 14.3	**41** 9.0				**33** 11.1	**37** 9.9
	30 12.1	**41** 8.8	**51** 7.1			Sales/Receivables	**46** 7.9	**54** 6.8
	36 10.0	**47** 7.7	**69** 5.3				**61** 6.0	**68** 5.4
	20 18.0	**27** 13.7	**32** 11.4				**36** 10.2	**24** 15.2
	52 7.0	**59** 6.2	**51** 7.1			Cost of Sales/Inventory	**68** 5.4	**64** 5.7
	99 3.7	**94** 3.9	**87** 4.2				**94** 3.9	**91** 4.0
	21 17.4	**11** 33.2	**16** 23.3				**13** 27.5	**18** 19.9
	36 10.2	**22** 16.8	**27** 13.4			Cost of Sales/Payables	**28** 12.9	**31** 11.9
	49 7.4	**47** 7.7	**33** 11.0				**41** 9.0	**47** 7.7
	5.1	3.0	6.0				3.8	3.7
	7.5	4.7	8.3			Sales/Working Capital	5.8	6.2
	11.1	11.5	23.0				11.3	12.5
		56.0	35.1				23.3	33.3
		(19) 14.3	(16) 3.8			EBIT/Interest	(60) 6.8	(64) 8.9
		9.4	2.5				1.9	2.1
			5.5				12.2	10.5
			(11) 3.0			Net Profit + Depr., Dep., Amort./Cur. Mat. L/T/D	(18) 7.4	(19) 4.3
			1.1				2.0	1.3
	.0	.1	.4				.2	.1
	.3	.3	.8			Fixed/Worth	.5	.4
	NM	.7	NM				.8	1.0
	.6	.4	.9				.4	.5
	1.5	.8	2.0			Debt/Worth	1.1	1.2
	NM	1.2	NM				2.4	4.0
	35.5	60.7	67.3				33.1	49.0
	(10) 24.0	(24) 28.2	(14) 25.6			% Profit Before Taxes/Tangible Net Worth	(60) 19.6	(72) 22.0
	2.4	14.0	3.9				7.7	7.5
	19.9	30.4	16.3				14.6	18.4
	3.0	10.6	11.7			% Profit Before Taxes/Total Assets	7.6	9.7
	-4.3	5.2	6.6				3.1	2.0
	223.0	23.8	16.1				22.7	42.0
	37.8	17.1	13.5			Sales/Net Fixed Assets	9.3	12.7
	12.4	6.5	5.3				4.9	6.3
	3.9	2.8	2.6				2.5	2.7
	2.9	2.1	2.2			Sales/Total Assets	1.8	2.0
	2.4	1.8	1.8				1.3	1.4
	.3	.7	1.1				1.3	.6
	(11) .7	(23) 1.6	(17) 1.7			% Depr., Dep., Amort./Sales	(54) 1.8	(65) 1.7
	1.1	2.2	2.9				2.8	2.5
							3.8	2.9
						% Officers', Directors' Owners' Comp/Sales	(19) 5.1	(26) 4.9
							6.8	8.1
4972M	**44561M**	**264370M**	**1104645M**	**358901M**	**1350702M**	Net Sales ($)	**2586741M**	**3818535M**
939M	**14652M**	**127457M**	**482449M**	**395660M**	**956371M**	Total Assets ($)	**1800918M**	**2306369M**

M = $ thousand MM = $ million

See Pages 9 through 22 for Explanation of Ratios and Data

Comparative Historical Data				Current Data Sorted by Sales					
			Type of Statement						
13	5	7	Unqualified					4	3
18	10	14	Reviewed		1	3	2	3	5
14	9	7	Compiled		1	1	2	1	2
7	8	10	Tax Returns	1	4	4	1		
31	31	32	Other	1	1	2	5	7	16
4/1/11-3/31/12	**4/1/12-3/31/13**	**4/1/13-3/31/14**		**7 (4/1-9/30/13)**		**63 (10/1/13-3/31/14)**			
ALL	**ALL**	**ALL**		**0-1MM**	**1-3MM**	**3-5MM**	**5-10MM**	**10-25MM**	**25MM & OVER**
83	63	70	**NUMBER OF STATEMENTS**	2	7	10	10	15	26
%	%	%	**ASSETS**	%	%	%	%	%	%
16.2	11.6	13.1	Cash & Equivalents			18.6	9.3	11.7	9.2
28.2	26.8	26.0	Trade Receivables (net)			27.1	34.4	23.7	28.4
21.6	20.2	23.8	Inventory			37.8	17.8	22.8	17.3
4.5	6.5	4.5	All Other Current			1.6	6.8	4.2	6.6
70.5	65.2	67.4	Total Current			85.0	68.3	62.4	61.4
16.7	17.4	17.3	Fixed Assets (net)			13.6	12.8	22.0	19.1
4.7	10.7	10.3	Intangibles (net)			.3	12.6	6.9	15.1
8.1	6.7	5.0	All Other Non-Current			1.0	6.3	8.8	4.4
100.0	100.0	100.0	Total			100.0	100.0	100.0	100.0
			LIABILITIES						
6.6	9.1	4.6	Notes Payable-Short Term			2.9	5.0	4.6	5.3
1.8	1.7	2.5	Cur. Mat.-L.T.D.			2.2	3.9	1.6	3.3
13.4	12.1	14.4	Trade Payables			24.5	14.0	9.6	11.2
.3	.3	.1	Income Taxes Payable			.0	.0	.1	.2
15.5	14.0	13.2	All Other Current			3.3	10.5	12.7	18.3
37.7	37.2	34.9	Total Current			32.9	33.4	28.5	38.3
10.8	11.2	14.1	Long-Term Debt			18.4	18.8	7.1	15.6
.5	.6	.3	Deferred Taxes			.3	.0	.2	.6
6.5	8.5	10.3	All Other Non-Current			6.7	24.4	9.9	6.6
44.6	42.5	40.4	Net Worth			41.7	23.4	54.3	38.8
100.0	100.0	100.0	Total Liabilties & Net Worth			100.0	100.0	100.0	100.0
			INCOME DATA						
100.0	100.0	100.0	Net Sales			100.0	100.0	100.0	100.0
31.9	35.1	35.0	Gross Profit			32.7	35.3	36.2	34.3
25.2	26.4	28.1	Operating Expenses			26.7	29.1	27.6	26.1
6.7	8.7	6.9	Operating Profit			6.1	6.2	8.6	8.2
.8	.6	.7	All Other Expenses (net)			.6	-.7	.6	1.3
5.9	8.2	6.2	Profit Before Taxes			5.5	6.9	8.0	6.9
			RATIOS						
3.6	2.8	3.6				6.4	4.5	4.1	2.1
1.9	2.1	1.9	Current			3.1	1.8	1.9	1.6
1.3	1.4	1.4				1.8	1.6	1.7	1.2
1.7	1.6	1.7				3.4	3.0	1.4	1.4
1.2	1.2	1.1	Quick			1.3	1.2	1.1	.9
.8	.8	.8				.9	.9	1.0	.6
35 10.4	**32** 11.5	**30** 12.2				**30** 12.1	**36** 10.0	**25** 14.4	**41** 9.0
51 7.2	**51** 7.2	**43** 8.4	Sales/Receivables			**35** 10.3	**46** 7.9	**41** 8.8	**53** 6.9
62 5.9	**64** 5.7	**63** 5.8				**40** 9.1	**73** 5.0	**70** 5.2	**69** 5.3
25 14.7	**22** 16.5	**27** 13.3				**37** 9.9	**0** UND	**41** 8.9	**28** 12.9
43 8.4	**60** 6.1	**59** 6.2	Cost of Sales/Inventory			**83** 4.4	**34** 10.6	**59** 6.2	**51** 7.2
81 4.5	**87** 4.2	**87** 4.2				**118** 3.1	**69** 5.3	**111** 3.3	**76** 4.8
20 18.7	**18** 19.8	**16** 22.9				**16** 22.9	**8** 44.3	**7** 55.8	**22** 16.4
30 12.1	**31** 11.8	**29** 12.6	Cost of Sales/Payables			**33** 11.1	**32** 11.3	**31** 11.6	**28** 13.0
43 8.5	**44** 8.3	**44** 8.3				**51** 7.2	**56** 6.5	**43** 8.5	**44** 8.3
4.4	4.0	4.1				2.7	3.8	4.1	6.0
7.6	6.9	7.1	Sales/Working Capital			5.3	6.0	5.8	9.0
12.6	10.9	12.7				10.2	21.7	10.0	18.1
41.1	32.9	42.3						32.5	35.1
(71) 10.3	(53) 8.0	(55) 11.3	EBIT/Interest					(12) 10.6	(24) 10.3
2.3	3.9	3.0						3.7	2.9
9.0	10.9	5.7							6.9
(23) 2.6	(19) 4.7	(21) 2.8	Net Profit + Depr., Dep., Amort./Cur. Mat. L/T/D						(13) 3.0
1.6	2.6	1.1							1.2
.1	.1	.2				.0	.1	.1	.5
.4	.5	.5	Fixed/Worth			.2	.2	.4	.8
1.0	1.1	1.1				.4	NM	.9	NM
.6	.7	.5				.4	.2	.5	.9
1.2	1.2	1.1	Debt/Worth			.8	.7	1.0	2.5
3.5	3.5	5.5				5.7	NM	1.3	NM
60.1	52.8	58.5						70.9	66.4
(76) 21.0	(55) 30.8	(59) 25.8	% Profit Before Taxes/Tangible Net Worth					20.3	(20) 29.0
6.9	14.7	11.8						7.7	13.3
20.3	21.3	18.7				22.9	38.2	20.7	16.2
9.6	12.9	9.7	% Profit Before Taxes/Total Assets			12.4	5.7	8.3	11.7
2.2	6.2	3.2				5.9	-5.9	3.8	7.4
48.7	44.1	30.8				182.1	38.4	19.1	16.1
15.5	17.5	15.2	Sales/Net Fixed Assets			38.4	19.4	9.8	12.3
6.9	5.9	6.9				12.6	13.6	5.5	6.8
2.7	2.7	2.9				3.7	3.2	2.6	2.5
2.2	1.8	2.1	Sales/Total Assets			2.7	2.5	2.1	1.9
1.5	1.3	1.5				2.0	1.6	1.4	1.5
.6	.6	.6						.8	1.3
(68) 1.4	(53) 1.4	(62) 1.5	% Depr., Dep., Amort./Sales					(13) 1.8	(24) 1.7
1.9	2.3	2.6						3.5	2.7
2.2	2.4	1.8							
(28) 3.4	(21) 3.2	(19) 3.2	% Officers', Directors' Owners' Comp/Sales						
8.4	11.2	11.2							
3997828M	**3002495M**	**3128151M**	Net Sales ($)	**917M**	**14916M**	**41039M**	**74463M**	**214888M**	**2781928M**
2207363M	**1976626M**	**1977528M**	Total Assets ($)	**912M**	**7233M**	**16247M**	**43939M**	**158306M**	**1750891M**

M = $ thousand MM = $ million

See Pages 9 through 22 for Explanation of Ratios and Data

Current Data Sorted by Assets							Comparative Historical Data	
						Type of Statement		
		4	9	2	2	Unqualified	19	23
	2	10	3	1		Reviewed	23	22
			2			Compiled	6	8
2	1	2	1			Tax Returns	4	6
1	3	2	11	2	5	Other	30	23
18 (4/1-9/30/13)			47 (10/1/13-3/31/14)				4/1/09-3/31/10 ALL	4/1/10-3/31/11 ALL
0-500M	500M-2MM	2-10MM	10-50MM	50-100MM	100-250MM			
3	6	18	26	5	7	**NUMBER OF STATEMENTS**	82	82
%	%	%	%	%	%	**ASSETS**	%	%
		7.6	10.5			Cash & Equivalents	10.5	10.8
		25.4	24.3			Trade Receivables (net)	26.6	30.6
		37.2	30.2			Inventory	31.8	27.9
		2.3	4.1			All Other Current	3.7	3.7
		72.4	69.1			Total Current	72.6	73.1
		19.5	15.0			Fixed Assets (net)	17.4	14.6
		2.4	9.6			Intangibles (net)	3.6	5.1
		5.7	6.3			All Other Non-Current	6.4	7.1
		100.0	100.0			Total	100.0	100.0
						LIABILITIES		
		13.4	3.2			Notes Payable-Short Term	12.1	10.5
		3.4	1.7			Cur. Mat.-L.T.D.	2.5	2.9
		14.0	10.3			Trade Payables	13.2	15.8
		.2	.4			Income Taxes Payable	.2	.4
		13.9	16.6			All Other Current	12.8	13.9
		44.9	32.1			Total Current	40.8	43.4
		18.2	7.4			Long-Term Debt	10.8	7.8
		.4	1.2			Deferred Taxes	.5	.4
		1.4	8.5			All Other Non-Current	8.1	9.1
		35.2	50.8			Net Worth	39.7	39.4
		100.0	100.0			Total Liabilties & Net Worth	100.0	100.0
						INCOME DATA		
		100.0	100.0			Net Sales	100.0	100.0
		33.1	33.5			Gross Profit	32.2	32.8
		27.0	25.7			Operating Expenses	26.9	26.8
		6.1	7.9			Operating Profit	5.3	6.0
		.5	.9			All Other Expenses (net)	1.1	1.0
		5.6	7.0			Profit Before Taxes	4.2	5.0
						RATIOS		
		3.6	3.2				3.0	2.5
		1.7	2.2			Current	2.0	1.8
		1.2	1.4				1.3	1.2
		1.3	1.7				1.7	1.7
		.7	1.1			Quick	.9	.9
		.5	.8				.5	.5
		33 11.1	**34** 10.6				**34** 10.8	**37** 9.8
		43 8.5	**45** 8.1			Sales/Receivables	**44** 8.4	**50** 7.4
		50 7.3	**60** 6.1				**57** 6.4	**67** 5.5
		64 5.7	**57** 6.4				**46** 8.0	**34** 10.8
		94 3.9	**81** 4.5			Cost of Sales/Inventory	**94** 3.9	**69** 5.3
		146 2.5	**126** 2.9				**129** 2.8	**107** 3.4
		13 27.3	**17** 20.9				**18** 20.1	**19** 19.6
		25 14.8	**23** 16.0			Cost of Sales/Payables	**28** 13.1	**33** 11.2
		54 6.8	**39** 9.4				**44** 8.3	**53** 6.9
		4.3	3.1				3.7	3.9
		7.1	5.7			Sales/Working Capital	6.3	7.0
		22.7	11.4				12.4	23.4
		17.2	97.2				20.8	19.5
		5.0	(24) 23.3			EBIT/Interest	(75) 5.4	(72) 7.3
		3.0	5.3				1.6	2.0
							9.6	8.8
						Net Profit + Depr., Dep., Amort./Cur. Mat. L/T/D	(20) 2.4	(22) 4.0
							.5	.7
		.2	.2				.2	.1
		.4	.4			Fixed/Worth	.5	.4
		1.5	.8				1.1	1.1
		.8	.5				.6	.7
		1.8	1.0			Debt/Worth	1.6	1.6
		4.7	2.3				5.6	5.4
		60.9	52.8				44.0	51.0
		(16) 37.1	(23) 20.8			% Profit Before Taxes/Tangible Net Worth	(72) 10.6	(73) 19.1
		8.3	9.9				3.1	7.8
		19.7	21.0				17.0	15.2
		9.5	7.8			% Profit Before Taxes/Total Assets	4.4	7.6
		2.7	4.6				.9	1.1
		33.9	19.9				31.8	63.9
		14.7	12.6			Sales/Net Fixed Assets	16.3	23.6
		5.5	8.0				5.0	7.9
		2.7	2.3				2.7	2.7
		2.0	1.8			Sales/Total Assets	1.8	2.1
		1.6	1.4				1.3	1.4
		.5	.8				.8	.7
		(17) 1.0	(23) 1.2			% Depr., Dep., Amort./Sales	(68) 1.4	(69) 1.1
		1.7	2.3				2.6	2.5
							1.1	1.6
						% Officers', Directors' Owners' Comp/Sales	(17) 3.2	(20) 3.7
							5.0	9.2
4558M	**19532M**	**199794M**	**1197726M**	**519733M**	**1382443M**	Net Sales ($)	**3527014M**	**2758642M**
854M	**7166M**	**97939M**	**689170M**	**302212M**	**1082135M**	Total Assets ($)	**1998068M**	**1553290M**

M = $ thousand MM = $ million

See Pages 9 through 22 for Explanation of Ratios and Data

Comparative Historical Data / Current Data Sorted by Sales

4/1/11-3/31/12 ALL	4/1/12-3/31/13 ALL	4/1/13-3/31/14 ALL	Type of Statement	0-1MM	1-3MM	3-5MM	5-10MM	10-25MM	25MM & OVER
21	17	17	Unqualified			1	1	3	12
15	16	16	Reviewed	1			7	6	2
7	2	2	Compiled						2
8	7	6	Tax Returns	1	2		2	1	
30	24	24	Other		3		1	2	18
				18 (4/1-9/30/13)			47 (10/1/13-3/31/14)		
81	66	65	NUMBER OF STATEMENTS	2	5	1	11	12	34
%	%	%	**ASSETS**	%	%	%	%	%	%
13.2	11.8	8.9	Cash & Equivalents				9.8	9.5	8.1
28.9	27.4	26.6	Trade Receivables (net)				32.4	19.2	26.1
27.6	27.5	30.7	Inventory				36.8	36.6	25.7
3.5	5.0	4.0	All Other Current				1.7	3.0	5.9
73.2	71.7	70.1	Total Current				80.6	68.3	65.8
15.2	17.1	15.8	Fixed Assets (net)				15.5	19.1	16.7
6.9	6.3	9.3	Intangibles (net)				2.9	3.7	12.4
4.7	4.9	4.7	All Other Non-Current				1.0	8.8	5.1
100.0	100.0	100.0	Total				100.0	100.0	100.0
			LIABILITIES						
7.2	6.9	6.4	Notes Payable-Short Term				14.6	8.0	3.3
2.4	2.0	2.2	Cur. Mat.-L.T.D.				2.2	3.8	1.3
14.3	12.5	13.7	Trade Payables				17.6	7.6	11.1
.1	.2	.3	Income Taxes Payable				.0	.3	.4
16.8	19.1	15.4	All Other Current				11.4	14.8	18.2
40.9	40.7	38.0	Total Current				46.0	34.4	34.4
12.9	11.6	11.2	Long-Term Debt				15.6	14.7	8.6
.6	.7	1.0	Deferred Taxes				.1	.7	1.6
8.8	9.4	6.4	All Other Non-Current				5.7	4.0	8.8
36.7	37.6	43.3	Net Worth				32.6	46.3	46.6
100.0	100.0	100.0	Total Liabilties & Net Worth				100.0	100.0	100.0
			INCOME DATA						
100.0	100.0	100.0	Net Sales				100.0	100.0	100.0
33.4	32.5	33.5	Gross Profit				31.6	37.4	31.5
27.8	28.2	27.2	Operating Expenses				27.3	28.0	24.5
5.6	4.2	6.3	Operating Profit				4.3	9.4	6.9
.9	.4	.8	All Other Expenses (net)				.8	.9	1.0
4.7	3.9	5.6	Profit Before Taxes				3.5	8.5	5.9
			RATIOS						
2.9	2.9	3.2					3.6	3.8	2.8
1.8	1.7	2.1	Current				2.1	2.8	2.0
1.3	1.3	1.3					1.2	1.2	1.4
1.6	1.5	1.5					1.6	2.0	1.4
1.0	.9	.9	Quick				1.2	.8	1.0
.7	.6	.6					.6	.5	.7
36 10.1	33 10.9	34 10.7					37 9.9	26 14.0	40 9.2
47 7.8	49 7.4	45 8.1	Sales/Receivables				47 7.8	34 10.6	49 7.5
70 5.2	66 5.5	58 6.3					56 6.5	56 6.5	65 5.6
32 11.5	33 11.0	51 7.1					55 6.6	58 6.3	43 8.4
78 4.7	73 5.0	78 4.7	Cost of Sales/Inventory				78 4.7	152 2.4	65 5.6
104 3.5	126 2.9	140 2.6					126 2.9	192 1.9	101 3.6
18 20.8	16 23.3	16 22.2					24 15.2	13 28.2	20 18.4
32 11.3	27 13.6	24 15.0	Cost of Sales/Payables				26 14.1	16 23.1	24 14.9
51 7.1	47 7.8	50 7.3					49 7.4	47 7.8	39 9.4
3.6	3.9	3.4					4.7	2.4	3.9
7.0	6.9	6.0	Sales/Working Capital				6.1	4.3	6.0
13.8	17.0	15.4					8.8	18.1	12.4
20.0	15.4	26.9					22.5	62.8	73.7
(70) 6.0	(53) 7.7	(59) 9.0	EBIT/Interest				5.2	(11) 8.7	(31) 16.3
1.2	2.4	3.1					2.8	3.8	4.9
5.7	8.9	10.6							21.5
(20) 1.7	(19) 4.5	(17) 4.4	Net Profit + Depr., Dep., Amort./Cur. Mat. L/T/D						(11) 4.4
.4	1.0	2.1							2.2
.1	.2	.2					.2	.1	.2
.4	.6	.4	Fixed/Worth				.3	.4	.5
1.2	1.5	1.1					1.1	1.6	1.0
.7	.7	.7					.8	.4	.7
1.7	1.6	1.3	Debt/Worth				1.8	1.3	1.2
9.5	9.4	4.1					5.0	4.4	4.0
44.2	44.3	56.0						64.4	68.8
(69) 22.1	(55) 18.9	(56) 20.3	% Profit Before Taxes/Tangible Net Worth					(11) 34.5	(30) 20.6
4.5	7.2	9.7						9.9	11.9
14.9	16.0	17.3					18.9	20.4	14.5
7.3	7.2	8.5	% Profit Before Taxes/Total Assets				8.4	10.0	8.5
.9	2.3	4.4					1.7	6.0	4.5
45.4	33.1	32.1					42.8	16.0	20.2
20.1	13.5	13.0	Sales/Net Fixed Assets				18.1	10.5	11.3
8.7	8.3	8.0					11.2	5.5	7.8
2.8	2.7	2.5					3.0	2.0	2.3
2.1	2.0	1.8	Sales/Total Assets				2.5	1.7	1.8
1.4	1.4	1.4					1.6	1.3	1.4
.8	.8	.7					.4	.6	.8
(64) 1.2	(55) 1.2	(55) 1.2	% Depr., Dep., Amort./Sales				(10) .6	1.2	(29) 1.8
2.4	2.3	2.4					1.6	1.8	2.8
1.9	2.8								
(21) 3.3	(13) 3.8		% Officers', Directors' Owners' Comp/Sales						
6.5	9.4								
2696459M	2528393M	3323786M	Net Sales ($)	1029M	11621M	4597M	78438M	203042M	3025059M
1939973M	1804507M	2179476M	Total Assets ($)	1171M	3697M	2256M	37814M	142133M	1992405M

M = $ thousand MM = $ million

See Pages 9 through 22 for Explanation of Ratios and Data

Current Data Sorted by Assets							Comparative Historical Data	
						Type of Statement		
		2	13	5	2	Unqualified	26	29
	2	19	8			Reviewed	22	29
	4	4				Compiled	19	12
3		3	1			Tax Returns	9	6
1	2	24	15	5	3	Other	44	48
25 (4/1-9/30/13)			91 (10/1/13-3/31/14)				4/1/09-3/31/10	4/1/10-3/31/11
0-500M	500M-2MM	2-10MM	10-50MM	50-100MM	100-250MM		ALL	ALL
4	8	52	37	10	5	**NUMBER OF STATEMENTS**	120	124
%	%	%	%	%	%	**ASSETS**	%	%
		9.6	10.5	9.9		Cash & Equivalents	13.7	9.5
		29.3	25.5	29.6		Trade Receivables (net)	29.5	30.5
		31.6	22.1	18.9		Inventory	25.7	26.3
		2.3	3.4	4.2		All Other Current	3.3	3.8
		72.8	61.5	62.6		Total Current	72.2	70.1
		17.3	22.0	16.7		Fixed Assets (net)	17.7	18.4
		3.1	8.5	15.1		Intangibles (net)	5.6	6.0
		6.8	8.0	5.6		All Other Non-Current	4.4	5.5
		100.0	100.0	100.0		Total	100.0	100.0
						LIABILITIES		
		9.0	7.0	2.2		Notes Payable-Short Term	7.1	8.5
		1.4	1.6	4.0		Cur. Mat.-L.T.D.	3.2	2.4
		18.6	10.2	17.9		Trade Payables	13.3	16.1
		.2	.5	.0		Income Taxes Payable	.7	.6
		15.7	14.6	16.7		All Other Current	12.1	12.5
		44.8	33.9	40.9		Total Current	36.5	40.0
		7.9	11.2	14.7		Long-Term Debt	11.4	11.3
		.7	.7	.2		Deferred Taxes	.9	.5
		2.4	3.4	6.3		All Other Non-Current	7.5	6.6
		44.2	50.8	38.0		Net Worth	43.7	41.6
		100.0	100.0	100.0		Total Liabilties & Net Worth	100.0	100.0
						INCOME DATA		
		100.0	100.0	100.0		Net Sales	100.0	100.0
		27.4	25.9	19.5		Gross Profit	30.1	28.7
		23.2	20.4	13.9		Operating Expenses	24.7	23.2
		4.2	5.5	5.6		Operating Profit	5.4	5.6
		.3	1.1	.3		All Other Expenses (net)	.7	1.0
		3.8	4.4	5.2		Profit Before Taxes	4.7	4.6
						RATIOS		
		2.4	3.1	2.7			3.6	2.7
		1.8	1.7	1.6		Current	2.0	1.8
		1.2	1.2	1.2			1.4	1.3
		1.4	2.1	1.8			2.3	1.5
		.9	1.0	1.1		Quick	1.2	1.0
		.5	.6	.5			.8	.5
		30 12.0	**34** 10.6	**37** 9.8			**31** 11.7	**33** 11.0
		41 8.9	**48** 7.6	**55** 6.6		Sales/Receivables	**42** 8.6	**46** 7.9
		54 6.7	**59** 6.2	**68** 5.4			**54** 6.7	**69** 5.3
		35 10.3	**35** 10.4	**7** 55.7			**26** 14.1	**32** 11.3
		61 6.0	**63** 5.8	**56** 6.5		Cost of Sales/Inventory	**57** 6.3	**65** 5.6
		99 3.7	**76** 4.8	**83** 4.4			**100** 3.6	**99** 3.7
		16 23.0	**14** 26.0	**19** 19.7			**14** 26.5	**19** 19.3
		29 12.7	**22** 16.4	**36** 10.1		Cost of Sales/Payables	**28** 13.1	**30** 12.2
		44 8.3	**32** 11.4	**53** 6.9			**37** 10.0	**48** 7.7
		5.3	4.3	3.6			3.7	4.0
		8.6	7.0	8.9		Sales/Working Capital	7.2	7.7
		25.7	22.0	NM			15.9	17.3
		21.5	19.2	804.2			22.6	25.1
		(41) 6.9	(29) 7.8	8.9		EBIT/Interest	(104) 7.2	(110) 7.0
		1.8	2.0	1.3			1.3	1.7
			10.9				12.8	10.8
			(14) 3.8			Net Profit + Depr., Dep., Amort./Cur. Mat. L/T/D	(32) 3.5	(38) 4.2
			1.9				1.0	1.8
		.2	.2	.3			.2	.2
		.3	.5	.8		Fixed/Worth	.4	.5
		.7	1.3	-.6			1.1	1.2
		.7	.5	.8			.5	.7
		1.3	1.1	1.9		Debt/Worth	1.4	1.5
		2.8	3.2	-4.5			3.7	3.8
		49.6	30.0				46.5	40.6
		(49) 17.4	(33) 18.5			% Profit Before Taxes/Tangible Net Worth	(107) 19.2	(110) 21.8
		3.8	8.8				5.1	7.2
		17.5	12.5	19.8			18.4	15.6
		5.9	8.1	5.9		% Profit Before Taxes/Total Assets	7.9	6.7
		1.5	4.6	1.7			.9	2.2
		59.5	22.0	28.4			40.2	36.0
		21.5	11.9	14.6		Sales/Net Fixed Assets	17.1	14.7
		7.8	4.7	7.1			8.1	7.7
		3.3	2.5	2.7			3.1	2.9
		2.5	1.9	1.9		Sales/Total Assets	2.2	2.1
		1.8	1.3	1.6			1.6	1.4
		.4	1.0				.6	.7
		(44) .8	(35) 1.4			% Depr., Dep., Amort./Sales	(99) 1.3	(108) 1.3
		2.1	2.2				2.5	2.2
		1.1					1.7	1.3
		(17) 3.5				% Officers', Directors' Owners' Comp/Sales	(30) 2.9	(31) 2.8
		9.9					5.1	6.0
15850M	43119M	729178M	1837090M	1275217M	1560553M	Net Sales ($)	4427381M	5656547M
1136M	12191M	266853M	926981M	674446M	870398M	Total Assets ($)	2383913M	3146715M

M = $ thousand MM = $ million

See Pages 9 through 22 for Explanation of Ratios and Data

Comparative Historical Data				Current Data Sorted by Sales					
			Type of Statement						
33	19	22	Unqualified				1	1	20
32	29	29	Reviewed		1		3	18	7
12	9	8	Compiled		1	2	2	3	
6	14	7	Tax Returns		2	1	2	2	
49	56	50	Other		3	3	10	12	22
4/1/11-3/31/12 ALL	4/1/12-3/31/13 ALL	4/1/13-3/31/14 ALL			25 (4/1-9/30/13)		91 (10/1/13-3/31/14)		
				0-1MM	1-3MM	3-5MM	5-10MM	10-25MM	25MM & OVER
132	127	116	**NUMBER OF STATEMENTS**		7	6	18	36	49
%	%	%	**ASSETS**	%	%	%	%	%	%
8.4	11.0	11.4	Cash & Equivalents	DATA NOT AVAILABLE			11.1	8.5	10.7
31.1	28.7	27.6	Trade Receivables (net)				31.7	27.3	29.0
27.7	26.7	26.1	Inventory				28.5	26.8	23.9
3.7	2.6	2.8	All Other Current				2.4	1.9	3.8
70.9	69.0	67.8	Total Current				73.7	64.6	67.5
20.7	18.7	18.2	Fixed Assets (net)				14.7	22.4	16.4
4.8	6.2	6.7	Intangibles (net)				4.5	4.3	10.2
3.6	6.0	7.2	All Other Non-Current				7.1	8.7	5.9
100.0	100.0	100.0	Total				100.0	100.0	100.0
			LIABILITIES						
8.6	8.8	8.4	Notes Payable-Short Term				8.9	10.9	5.9
2.5	2.1	1.5	Cur. Mat.-L.T.D.				.4	1.7	2.0
17.6	16.4	16.1	Trade Payables				14.1	15.4	15.2
.4	.4	.4	Income Taxes Payable				.3	.4	.2
12.5	13.5	14.9	All Other Current				15.7	14.1	17.3
41.6	41.3	41.3	Total Current				39.4	42.6	40.6
9.6	12.0	10.5	Long-Term Debt				10.5	10.8	11.0
.7	.7	.7	Deferred Taxes				1.3	.7	.5
7.5	6.6	4.9	All Other Non-Current				2.0	1.8	5.7
40.6	39.5	42.6	Net Worth				46.9	44.1	42.2
100.0	100.0	100.0	Total Liabilties & Net Worth				100.0	100.0	100.0
			INCOME DATA						
100.0	100.0	100.0	Net Sales				100.0	100.0	100.0
28.6	29.7	26.8	Gross Profit				26.7	27.0	24.1
23.0	23.4	22.1	Operating Expenses				22.9	22.4	18.7
5.6	6.3	4.8	Operating Profit				3.8	4.6	5.4
.7	.7	.8	All Other Expenses (net)				1.3	.5	1.0
4.9	5.7	4.0	Profit Before Taxes				2.5	4.1	4.5
			RATIOS						
2.6	2.7	2.5					3.2	2.2	2.5
1.7	1.7	1.7	Current				2.3	1.5	1.7
1.2	1.2	1.2					1.3	1.1	1.2
1.7	1.5	1.5					1.7	1.4	1.6
.9	.9	1.0	Quick				1.2	.8	1.0
.6	.6	.5					.6	.5	.6
28 12.9	**25** 14.4	**31** 11.9					**30** 12.2	**27** 13.3	**33** 10.9
41 8.8	**43** 8.4	**45** 8.1	Sales/Receivables				**38** 9.6	**43** 8.4	**50** 7.3
61 6.0	**58** 6.3	**58** 6.3					**54** 6.7	**54** 6.7	**59** 6.2
26 14.1	**26** 14.3	**32** 11.4					**26** 13.9	**28** 13.2	**32** 11.3
56 6.5	**55** 6.6	**59** 6.2	Cost of Sales/Inventory				**64** 5.7	**57** 6.4	**52** 7.0
91 4.0	**91** 4.0	**83** 4.4					**99** 3.7	**76** 4.8	**74** 4.9
15 24.7	**16** 22.6	**16** 23.3					**12** 29.7	**12** 30.9	**19** 19.6
27 13.6	**26** 14.3	**25** 14.4	Cost of Sales/Payables				**25** 14.6	**26** 14.2	**26** 14.3
47 7.8	**41** 8.9	**41** 9.0					**31** 11.6	**45** 8.1	**37** 9.8
4.5	5.1	4.8					4.7	6.7	4.6
10.1	10.6	8.2	Sales/Working Capital				6.9	13.3	7.8
22.7	23.3	25.7					26.3	66.2	22.8
28.1	27.2	24.5					14.8	20.7	45.0
(111) 7.9	(111) 8.9	(91) 7.4	EBIT/Interest				(14) 3.7	(30) 6.0	(41) 9.5
2.5	2.7	1.7					-7.2	1.9	2.1
22.4	13.9	10.2							16.4
(36) 4.2	(38) 5.5	(29) 3.4	Net Profit + Depr., Dep., Amort./Cur. Mat. L/T/D						(19) 4.0
1.5	2.6	2.1							2.8
.3	.2	.2					.1	.2	.2
.6	.5	.4	Fixed/Worth				.3	.6	.4
1.1	1.2	1.2					.7	1.0	1.3
.8	.6	.7					.5	.7	.7
1.5	1.4	1.4	Debt/Worth				1.0	1.6	1.5
4.0	4.6	3.6					2.6	2.8	5.7
49.0	49.5	45.0					47.0	45.9	48.9
(118) 22.4	(106) 24.3	(100) 17.6	% Profit Before Taxes/Tangible Net Worth				(17) 9.3	(34) 21.5	(38) 23.9
9.0	11.1	6.1					-9.7	5.9	13.3
18.6	18.6	16.6					17.8	17.7	16.9
8.2	9.4	6.4	% Profit Before Taxes/Total Assets				4.3	6.5	8.3
2.4	3.2	2.2					-5.2	1.7	4.5
36.9	46.6	40.6					47.7	50.3	39.8
16.2	18.1	17.5	Sales/Net Fixed Assets				22.7	14.2	17.3
7.2	8.6	7.4					12.7	6.4	8.3
3.5	3.6	3.0					3.6	3.3	2.7
2.4	2.5	2.3	Sales/Total Assets				2.6	2.5	2.1
1.7	1.7	1.6					2.0	1.8	1.8
.6	.6	.6					.4	.4	.8
(111) 1.2	(105) 1.2	(102) 1.3	% Depr., Dep., Amort./Sales				(16) .8	(32) 1.1	(46) 1.4
2.0	2.0	2.2					1.7	2.4	2.1
1.3	2.3	1.3						.9	
(31) 2.6	(28) 3.1	(28) 3.5	% Officers', Directors' Owners' Comp/Sales					(11) 1.6	
7.2	4.3	8.6						3.9	
5163211M	6180463M	5461007M	Net Sales ($)		13490M	21603M	142248M	589043M	4694623M
2476829M	3120630M	2752005M	Total Assets ($)		11530M	17142M	65235M	279303M	2378795M

M = $ thousand MM = $ million

See Pages 9 through 22 for Explanation of Ratios and Data

Current Data Sorted by Assets							Comparative Historical Data	
						Type of Statement		
1		2	4	3	1	Unqualified	7	5
	1	14	8			Reviewed	38	42
1	9	9	1			Compiled	21	37
6	12	8	1			Tax Returns	12	16
2	9	20	9	7		Other	33	48
29 (4/1-9/30/13)			99 (10/1/13-3/31/14)				4/1/09-3/31/10 ALL	4/1/10-3/31/11 ALL
0-500M	**500M-2MM**	**2-10MM**	**10-50MM**	**50-100MM**	**100-250MM**			
10	31	53	23	10	1	**NUMBER OF STATEMENTS**	111	148
%	%	%	%	%	%	**ASSETS**	%	%
35.7	11.4	15.0	7.9	5.7		Cash & Equivalents	8.5	9.5
20.0	26.0	26.6	29.0	31.7		Trade Receivables (net)	24.9	27.2
7.9	20.4	16.4	21.0	23.7		Inventory	19.1	19.5
.8	1.6	1.6	5.3	1.4		All Other Current	1.7	3.1
64.5	59.3	59.6	63.2	62.6		Total Current	54.2	59.4
23.3	29.6	30.7	28.4	31.2		Fixed Assets (net)	36.5	33.1
.0	6.4	1.9	4.6	2.3		Intangibles (net)	3.9	2.9
12.2	4.6	7.8	3.8	3.9		All Other Non-Current	5.4	4.6
100.0	100.0	100.0	100.0	100.0		Total	100.0	100.0
						LIABILITIES		
8.1	10.0	6.1	9.2	18.1		Notes Payable-Short Term	11.9	11.4
5.8	6.1	3.6	3.9	4.0		Cur. Mat.-L.T.D.	6.9	4.7
18.4	11.4	9.7	11.8	12.8		Trade Payables	12.0	12.0
.1	.7	.4	.4	.0		Income Taxes Payable	.1	.3
13.9	8.4	8.9	10.6	8.1		All Other Current	9.6	9.9
46.3	36.6	28.7	36.0	43.1		Total Current	40.5	38.3
47.9	24.9	11.4	17.7	12.8		Long-Term Debt	23.5	19.0
.0	.4	1.7	1.0	.2		Deferred Taxes	.7	.4
.1	7.1	4.6	2.5	7.0		All Other Non-Current	6.4	8.9
5.7	31.0	53.7	42.9	36.8		Net Worth	28.9	33.4
100.0	100.0	100.0	100.0	100.0		Total Liabilties & Net Worth	100.0	100.0
						INCOME DATA		
100.0	100.0	100.0	100.0	100.0		Net Sales	100.0	100.0
48.0	37.3	31.9	17.6	16.8		Gross Profit	27.2	28.8
37.1	29.8	23.0	12.2	9.2		Operating Expenses	26.2	24.7
10.9	7.5	8.9	5.4	7.6		Operating Profit	1.0	4.1
1.3	1.0	.5	1.8	.7		All Other Expenses (net)	1.5	1.0
9.6	6.5	8.4	3.6	6.9		Profit Before Taxes	-.5	3.1
						RATIOS		
18.1	3.4	3.6	2.5	1.7			2.3	2.7
2.8	1.9	2.3	2.1	1.5		Current	1.4	1.7
.6	1.0	1.5	1.2	1.2			1.0	1.1
18.1	2.2	2.5	1.7	1.2			1.3	1.7
2.8	1.2	1.6	1.0	.9		Quick	.8	(147) 1.1
.3	.7	1.0	.7	.7			.6	.6
0 UND	**22** 16.5	**37** 9.9	**52** 7.0	**58** 6.3			**33** 11.1	**37** 9.9
5 72.1	**35** 10.4	**51** 7.2	**65** 5.6	**99** 3.7		Sales/Receivables	**44** 8.3	**53** 6.9
72 5.1	**54** 6.8	**73** 5.0	**79** 4.6	**146** 2.5			**69** 5.3	**69** 5.3
0 UND	**17** 21.5	**19** 19.5	**36** 10.2	**41** 9.0			**22** 16.8	**20** 18.0
0 UND	**38** 9.5	**34** 10.8	**55** 6.6	**76** 4.8		Cost of Sales/Inventory	**40** 9.2	**37** 9.9
14 25.3	**64** 5.7	**68** 5.4	**81** 4.5	**118** 3.1			**79** 4.6	**76** 4.8
0 UND	**10** 36.6	**14** 26.1	**21** 17.6	**35** 10.5			**13** 28.4	**15** 25.1
0 UND	**20** 18.4	**22** 16.7	**33** 10.9	**41** 8.8		Cost of Sales/Payables	**27** 13.4	**27** 13.4
69 5.3	**36** 10.1	**32** 11.5	**38** 9.5	**57** 6.4			**46** 7.9	**43** 8.4
4.1	6.4	3.9	4.1	3.5			5.2	4.7
16.7	10.6	6.1	5.6	7.5		Sales/Working Capital	13.8	9.5
-32.3	598.7	11.7	19.4	18.7			-135.8	36.2
	10.8	38.8	32.7	16.6			5.4	9.8
	(28) 4.4	(49) 13.9	4.9	7.3		EBIT/Interest	(103) 1.9	(135) 3.8
	2.2	5.3	.6	5.4			-2.2	1.2
		13.2					2.1	3.8
		(15) 6.3				Net Profit + Depr., Dep., Amort./Cur. Mat. L/T/D	(34) 1.4	(41) 2.3
		1.7					.6	1.0
.4	.5	.2	.4	.6			.6	.4
1.9	1.0	.5	.7	1.1		Fixed/Worth	1.4	1.0
-.2	-44.2	1.0	1.6	1.8			3.2	2.5
.4	1.0	.4	.6	1.1			.9	.8
3.0	3.1	.9	1.2	2.4		Debt/Worth	2.1	1.9
-3.0	-102.0	1.8	2.8	3.9			8.3	6.2
	81.8	40.0	26.4	54.5			31.8	41.7
	(22) 43.5	(52) 21.9	(22) 12.8	29.4		% Profit Before Taxes/Tangible Net Worth	(92) 5.8	(129) 17.3
	13.6	14.1	3.0	13.5			-13.2	3.8
61.5	17.6	19.0	10.4	10.8			7.4	13.2
23.8	11.0	11.5	4.3	9.0		% Profit Before Taxes/Total Assets	1.7	4.7
9.4	2.4	7.3	-1.3	6.2			-6.4	.4
101.9	27.8	18.1	10.6	7.3			10.3	11.4
17.7	8.6	6.0	6.9	3.9		Sales/Net Fixed Assets	4.8	5.3
5.9	4.6	3.0	3.1	2.8			2.8	3.3
7.8	3.2	2.4	2.1	1.6			2.4	2.5
2.7	2.5	1.6	1.7	1.1		Sales/Total Assets	1.7	1.8
2.0	1.4	1.2	1.2	.9			1.3	1.2
	2.2	1.8	1.8	2.2			2.3	2.2
	(21) 3.3	(43) 3.2	2.7	3.0		% Depr., Dep., Amort./Sales	(105) 4.3	(134) 3.6
	5.1	5.8	4.5	4.0			7.3	6.1
	1.9	2.5					2.0	2.3
	(19) 3.4	(23) 4.0				% Officers', Directors' Owners' Comp/Sales	(57) 4.2	(69) 4.2
	6.7	6.0					6.3	6.5
8717M	**93648M**	**445670M**	**694730M**	**862837M**	**114940M**	Net Sales ($)	**1508111M**	**1903505M**
2571M	**40326M**	**245383M**	**429627M**	**663898M**	**129394M**	Total Assets ($)	**1074581M**	**1355116M**

M = $ thousand MM = $ million

See Pages 9 through 22 for Explanation of Ratios and Data

Comparative Historical Data				Current Data Sorted by Sales					
			Type of Statement						
6	3	11	Unqualified	1			1	3	6
41	25	23	Reviewed		1	1	9	9	3
37	22	20	Compiled	1	5	6	5	3	
25	21	27	Tax Returns	4	9	4	7	3	
34	54	47	Other	3	7	8	4	10	15
4/1/11-3/31/12	**4/1/12-3/31/13**	**4/1/13-3/31/14**			**29 (4/1-9/30/13)**			**99 (10/1/13-3/31/14)**	
ALL	**ALL**	**ALL**		**0-1MM**	**1-3MM**	**3-5MM**	**5-10MM**	**10-25MM**	**25MM & OVER**
143	125	128	**NUMBER OF STATEMENTS**	9	22	19	26	28	24
%	%	%	**ASSETS**	%	%	%	%	%	%
11.4	10.2	13.7	Cash & Equivalents		13.8	13.9	14.2	14.0	5.9
29.6	26.5	26.7	Trade Receivables (net)		23.4	25.2	24.1	32.1	31.7
20.2	20.1	18.2	Inventory		11.5	18.2	20.8	20.8	22.2
2.9	2.0	2.2	All Other Current		.4	2.7	2.4	1.8	4.0
64.0	58.8	60.6	Total Current		49.1	60.0	61.6	68.8	63.8
27.7	32.5	29.5	Fixed Assets (net)		39.1	31.0	29.7	25.6	27.5
3.6	3.6	3.5	Intangibles (net)		4.8	6.1	1.0	1.9	4.5
4.7	5.1	6.3	All Other Non-Current		7.1	2.9	7.7	3.7	4.2
100.0	100.0	100.0	Total		100.0	100.0	100.0	100.0	100.0
			LIABILITIES						
10.4	10.1	8.6	Notes Payable-Short Term		9.3	9.1	5.6	6.2	15.2
5.4	3.9	4.5	Cur. Mat.-L.T.D.		6.9	3.3	3.9	4.3	3.2
13.3	12.5	11.4	Trade Payables		14.0	9.3	8.0	13.0	15.2
.2	.3	.5	Income Taxes Payable		1.1	.0	.4	.3	.7
11.8	11.0	9.4	All Other Current		5.9	6.4	11.9	10.7	8.3
41.2	37.8	34.4	Total Current		37.2	28.1	29.8	34.6	42.5
15.3	19.6	19.0	Long-Term Debt		26.8	16.3	13.3	12.6	16.1
.6	.5	1.0	Deferred Taxes		.4	.6	2.3	1.1	.7
5.4	8.6	4.6	All Other Non-Current		7.3	3.7	2.3	5.4	4.3
37.4	33.5	41.0	Net Worth		28.2	51.3	52.3	46.4	36.4
100.0	100.0	100.0	Total Liabilties & Net Worth		100.0	100.0	100.0	100.0	100.0
			INCOME DATA						
100.0	100.0	100.0	Net Sales		100.0	100.0	100.0	100.0	100.0
30.5	31.5	30.6	Gross Profit		42.1	34.1	29.6	27.5	15.5
24.0	22.8	22.7	Operating Expenses		34.0	24.9	22.7	19.1	10.0
6.6	8.7	8.0	Operating Profit		8.1	9.2	6.9	8.4	5.5
.4	1.1	1.0	All Other Expenses (net)		1.6	.6	.1	.4	1.9
6.1	7.6	7.0	Profit Before Taxes		6.4	8.6	6.8	8.0	3.6
			RATIOS						
2.8	2.8	3.0			3.1	3.5	3.8	3.4	2.1
1.7	1.6	2.0	Current		2.0	2.2	2.2	2.1	1.5
1.1	1.1	1.2			.9	1.6	1.4	1.4	1.2
2.0	1.8	2.3			2.3	1.9	2.6	2.4	1.2
1.1	1.1	1.2	Quick		1.3	1.6	1.5	1.2	.8
.6	.6	.7			.7	1.0	.7	.9	.6
36 10.1	**30** 12.3	**30** 12.0			**23** 16.1	**25** 14.4	**27** 13.5	**39** 9.4	**59** 6.2
51 7.1	**45** 8.1	**51** 7.1	Sales/Receivables		**41** 8.8	**44** 8.3	**51** 7.2	**51** 7.2	**66** 5.5
68 5.4	**63** 5.8	**72** 5.1			**62** 5.9	**72** 5.1	**74** 4.9	**69** 5.3	**91** 4.0
21 17.3	**25** 14.8	**19** 19.1			**0** UND	**8** 48.6	**28** 13.1	**27** 13.5	**31** 11.9
43 8.4	**42** 8.6	**41** 8.8	Cost of Sales/Inventory		**20** 18.2	**38** 9.6	**37** 9.8	**51** 7.1	**58** 6.3
79 4.6	**69** 5.3	**74** 4.9			**45** 8.2	**62** 5.9	**107** 3.4	**76** 4.8	**87** 4.2
17 21.4	**13** 28.0	**13** 27.4			**7** 49.5	**10** 36.6	**13** 28.8	**21** 17.5	**30** 12.1
27 13.3	**25** 14.5	**24** 15.3	Cost of Sales/Payables		**16** 22.3	**23** 16.0	**17** 21.1	**26** 14.3	**36** 10.0
45 8.1	**41** 8.9	**38** 9.5			**44** 8.3	**33** 11.1	**26** 13.9	**38** 9.5	**51** 7.2
4.2	4.6	4.3			6.3	5.1	3.7	4.0	4.2
8.3	10.8	6.8	Sales/Working Capital		14.2	6.9	5.6	5.7	7.5
31.4	63.9	19.1			-47.5	9.9	12.5	14.4	19.1
18.9	21.8	26.0			14.3	33.0	30.0	105.8	9.5
(132) 8.1	(115) 7.7	(119) 6.7	EBIT/Interest		(20) 3.8	(17) 7.6	(25) 10.2	(27) 17.2	(23) 5.6
2.5	2.6	3.3			1.8	4.3	4.9	4.7	1.1
6.1	5.5	9.0							6.5
(33) 3.3	(29) 3.2	(32) 3.0	Net Profit + Depr., Dep., Amort./Cur. Mat. L/T/D						(12) 2.6
1.6	1.5	1.4							1.9
.3	.3	.4			.7	.2	.4	.3	.5
.7	1.0	.8	Fixed/Worth		1.7	.9	.5	.6	1.0
1.8	2.2	1.7			-70.5	1.4	.9	1.0	1.8
.7	.8	.6			.9	.4	.5	.6	.8
1.3	1.6	1.3	Debt/Worth		2.2	1.0	.9	1.3	2.3
5.1	5.1	3.3			-169.8	3.1	1.3	2.4	4.7
58.7	51.3	52.5			94.7	63.8	33.1	53.7	48.8
(124) 26.7	(107) 29.2	(114) 22.4	% Profit Before Taxes/Tangible Net Worth		(16) 41.3	(17) 30.4	(25) 19.5	(27) 21.2	(23) 15.7
10.6	11.1	11.3			7.3	19.0	15.6	11.2	5.5
19.2	19.2	18.9			22.2	19.4	14.7	27.3	10.4
9.2	9.5	10.4	% Profit Before Taxes/Total Assets		9.8	15.6	11.2	11.7	7.4
4.2	3.6	3.2			2.3	5.6	7.7	3.4	.8
21.6	14.7	17.6			17.1	27.8	13.3	17.8	10.6
7.9	6.6	7.0	Sales/Net Fixed Assets		6.0	7.2	6.3	8.7	5.2
3.9	3.8	3.3			2.4	2.8	3.2	4.9	2.8
2.7	2.6	2.6			3.2	3.2	2.6	2.4	2.4
2.1	1.9	1.8	Sales/Total Assets		2.1	2.1	1.7	2.0	1.3
1.4	1.3	1.2			1.0	1.4	1.2	1.6	1.0
1.4	1.9	1.8			1.0	.8	2.7	1.5	1.5
(122) 3.2	(101) 3.1	(107) 3.0	% Depr., Dep., Amort./Sales		(16) 3.3	(15) 4.7	(22) 4.0	(24) 2.6	2.9
4.6	4.9	4.9			5.7	6.9	5.6	3.4	4.2
2.0	2.2	1.9			2.1	1.5	3.1	.8	
(74) 4.0	(60) 3.8	(56) 3.7	% Officers', Directors' Owners' Comp/Sales		(10) 6.0	(11) 3.3	(14) 4.6	(15) 1.9	
7.0	6.6	6.3			11.2	4.8	6.4	2.7	
2004744M	**2273843M**	**2220542M**	Net Sales ($)	**5702M**	**45204M**	**76074M**	**174008M**	**428027M**	**1491527M**
1308529M	**1392681M**	**1511199M**	Total Assets ($)	**4370M**	**28228M**	**45868M**	**109550M**	**236490M**	**1086693M**

M = $ thousand MM = $ million

See Pages 9 through 22 for Explanation of Ratios and Data

Current Data Sorted by Assets							Comparative Historical Data	
						Type of Statement		
		8	13	1	2	Unqualified	26	26
1	9	35	14	1		Reviewed	85	89
5	20	15	2		1	Compiled	57	66
7	25	14				Tax Returns	30	45
5	18	29	37	7	2	Other	89	85
51 (4/1-9/30/13)		220 (10/1/13-3/31/14)					4/1/09-3/31/10	4/1/10-3/31/11
0-500M	500M-2MM	2-10MM	10-50MM	50-100MM	100-250MM		ALL	ALL
18	72	101	66	9	5	**NUMBER OF STATEMENTS**	287	311
%	%	%	%	%	%	**ASSETS**	%	%
21.3	13.0	11.9	7.4			Cash & Equivalents	10.1	9.7
22.9	35.9	25.7	23.5			Trade Receivables (net)	27.3	30.1
17.8	15.4	20.6	18.8			Inventory	17.3	16.3
2.3	2.6	2.4	8.8			All Other Current	4.4	3.7
64.4	66.9	60.6	58.6			Total Current	59.1	59.9
30.4	28.3	30.6	29.5			Fixed Assets (net)	33.2	31.7
.8	1.1	2.7	5.8			Intangibles (net)	2.7	2.6
4.4	3.7	6.1	6.1			All Other Non-Current	5.0	5.8
100.0	100.0	100.0	100.0			Total	100.0	100.0
						LIABILITIES		
16.5	9.1	5.1	9.1			Notes Payable-Short Term	10.7	9.6
7.9	5.7	4.7	3.8			Cur. Mat.-L.T.D.	6.0	5.4
10.3	13.0	11.8	8.2			Trade Payables	10.9	12.8
.0	.0	.2	.2			Income Taxes Payable	.1	.1
14.6	9.7	10.1	12.9			All Other Current	9.6	10.6
49.3	37.6	31.9	34.2			Total Current	37.4	38.6
27.0	18.1	17.3	16.5			Long-Term Debt	19.7	16.3
.1	.3	1.0	1.0			Deferred Taxes	.7	.7
1.5	9.1	6.0	6.9			All Other Non-Current	6.3	6.0
22.1	35.0	43.8	41.3			Net Worth	36.0	38.5
100.0	100.0	100.0	100.0			Total Liabilties & Net Worth	100.0	100.0
						INCOME DATA		
100.0	100.0	100.0	100.0			Net Sales	100.0	100.0
45.0	34.2	29.2	24.7			Gross Profit	25.6	28.3
39.5	27.0	21.1	16.0			Operating Expenses	25.7	23.2
5.4	7.2	8.1	8.7			Operating Profit	-.1	5.2
1.3	.4	.9	1.1			All Other Expenses (net)	1.1	.8
4.1	6.8	7.2	7.5			Profit Before Taxes	-1.2	4.4
						RATIOS		
3.0	2.9	3.2	2.6				3.3	3.2
1.7	1.9	2.0	1.7			Current	1.7	1.7
.8	1.3	1.4	1.4				1.1	1.1
2.8	2.2	2.5	1.5				2.2	2.2
1.0	1.4	1.1	1.0			Quick	1.0	1.0
.4	.9	.7	.7				.6	.7
13 28.4	**37** 9.9	**36** 10.1	**43** 8.5				**41** 9.0	**41** 8.9
30 12.1	**49** 7.5	**51** 7.2	**61** 6.0			Sales/Receivables	**54** 6.7	**54** 6.8
42 8.6	**61** 6.0	**64** 5.7	**81** 4.5				**75** 4.8	**72** 5.1
0 UND	**5** 69.6	**22** 16.7	**26** 14.2				**21** 17.5	**15** 25.1
17 21.8	**23** 16.1	**46** 8.0	**47** 7.7			Cost of Sales/Inventory	**45** 8.2	**36** 10.2
89 4.1	**47** 7.7	**99** 3.7	**111** 3.3				**72** 5.1	**63** 5.8
4 103.0	**11** 33.2	**17** 21.1	**19** 19.5				**15** 23.6	**16** 22.2
14 25.6	**24** 15.0	**28** 13.2	**25** 14.5			Cost of Sales/Payables	**26** 14.2	**28** 13.0
34 10.7	**40** 9.2	**41** 8.9	**35** 10.5				**42** 8.7	**43** 8.5
5.4	5.4	4.2	3.8				3.4	4.0
14.0	9.2	6.3	6.8			Sales/Working Capital	7.4	8.0
-27.8	16.7	14.1	10.5				75.2	77.9
7.7	18.1	24.7	22.9				5.5	12.2
(13) 3.6	(63) 7.8	(89) 6.1	(63) 7.3			EBIT/Interest	(266) 1.8	(285) 4.1
2.3	2.5	2.5	3.0				-1.2	1.3
		2.5	4.8				2.6	4.1
		(19) 1.6	(26) 2.6			Net Profit + Depr., Dep., Amort./Cur. Mat. L/T/D	(81) 1.6	(72) 2.4
		.6	1.7				.5	1.1
.2	.3	.3	.4				.3	.3
.8	.7	.7	.8			Fixed/Worth	.9	.8
-2.7	2.3	1.8	1.8				2.6	1.8
.8	.5	.5	.7				.6	.5
2.4	1.4	1.1	1.9			Debt/Worth	1.7	1.4
-6.1	5.7	3.7	3.0				5.9	4.6
56.1	73.2	46.5	41.8				17.7	40.2
(12) 29.3	(61) 40.8	(90) 19.9	(60) 21.5			% Profit Before Taxes/Tangible Net Worth	(249) 4.7	(271) 17.0
-10.1	5.0	7.3	11.6				-12.3	3.6
30.9	28.0	18.8	16.0				6.6	14.3
10.4	12.3	9.3	9.1			% Profit Before Taxes/Total Assets	1.4	6.4
-9.5	2.9	3.1	4.7				-6.7	.9
50.2	19.3	11.3	7.9				10.8	12.4
13.0	8.0	5.8	5.1			Sales/Net Fixed Assets	5.4	6.4
5.9	5.3	3.3	3.2				2.9	3.5
3.8	3.4	2.2	1.8				2.1	2.5
2.8	2.4	1.8	1.5			Sales/Total Assets	1.5	1.8
2.0	1.8	1.3	1.0				1.1	1.3
.5	2.0	2.1	2.2				2.5	2.0
(15) 2.3	(61) 2.9	(88) 3.5	(63) 3.2			% Depr., Dep., Amort./Sales	(259) 4.5	(279) 3.8
3.4	5.2	5.1	5.0				6.7	5.9
9.3	3.6	1.4	1.3				2.5	2.4
(12) 13.9	(51) 5.8	(51) 3.1	(13) 2.0			% Officers', Directors' Owners' Comp/Sales	(138) 4.5	(173) 4.7
19.5	9.4	5.4	3.6				8.1	9.0
20192M	218720M	885241M	2191910M	824028M	860018M	Net Sales ($)	3883346M	4212257M
5805M	86692M	494307M	1543515M	680891M	688464M	Total Assets ($)	3093038M	2977928M

M = $ thousand MM = $ million

See Pages 9 through 22 for Explanation of Ratios and Data

Comparative Historical Data				Current Data Sorted by Sales					
			Type of Statement						
20	18	24	Unqualified				1	9	14
92	61	60	Reviewed	1	8	5	19	19	8
64	45	43	Compiled	2	14	14	6	5	2
39	39	46	Tax Returns	4	16	12	11	3	
100	101	98	Other	5	12	10	23	22	26
				51 (4/1-9/30/13)			220 (10/1/13-3/31/14)		
4/1/11-3/31/12 ALL	4/1/12-3/31/13 ALL	4/1/13-3/31/14 ALL		0-1MM	1-3MM	3-5MM	5-10MM	10-25MM	25MM & OVER
315	264	271	**NUMBER OF STATEMENTS**	12	50	41	60	58	50
%	%	%	**ASSETS**	%	%	%	%	%	%
9.2	10.4	11.4	Cash & Equivalents	12.9	15.3	14.6	12.1	9.9	5.3
30.4	28.9	27.6	Trade Receivables (net)	14.7	30.7	32.5	27.6	26.5	25.0
18.0	18.0	18.8	Inventory	18.6	15.1	17.3	20.7	20.8	19.0
4.6	4.1	4.2	All Other Current	2.3	2.0	2.7	2.8	7.9	5.1
62.2	61.4	61.9	Total Current	48.5	63.0	67.1	63.3	65.1	54.4
29.3	29.2	29.7	Fixed Assets (net)	38.4	31.0	26.1	28.8	27.8	32.2
3.2	3.6	3.3	Intangibles (net)	.4	1.6	1.6	2.5	2.6	8.7
5.3	5.8	5.2	All Other Non-Current	12.6	4.3	5.2	5.4	4.5	4.6
100.0	100.0	100.0	Total	100.0	100.0	100.0	100.0	100.0	100.0
			LIABILITIES						
11.3	9.5	8.2	Notes Payable-Short Term	18.4	10.7	6.4	5.0	8.5	8.1
4.0	4.1	4.9	Cur. Mat.-L.T.D.	9.4	4.7	7.2	4.0	4.1	4.1
12.9	11.7	10.9	Trade Payables	6.8	11.2	11.9	12.1	11.1	9.4
.1	.2	.1	Income Taxes Payable	.0	.0	.0	.1	.4	.1
10.0	9.4	11.1	All Other Current	8.7	12.9	9.6	11.1	10.4	11.8
38.4	34.9	35.2	Total Current	43.2	39.6	35.2	32.3	34.5	33.4
15.9	17.9	18.0	Long-Term Debt	34.6	15.5	19.8	19.0	13.2	19.4
.6	.6	.8	Deferred Taxes	.0	.3	.3	1.5	.5	1.3
8.0	6.5	6.6	All Other Non-Current	1.3	11.4	5.2	6.2	5.6	5.8
37.1	40.2	39.4	Net Worth	20.9	33.3	39.5	41.0	46.2	40.1
100.0	100.0	100.0	Total Liabilties & Net Worth	100.0	100.0	100.0	100.0	100.0	100.0
			INCOME DATA						
100.0	100.0	100.0	Net Sales	100.0	100.0	100.0	100.0	100.0	100.0
28.5	30.2	30.2	Gross Profit	51.1	35.8	31.6	29.5	27.5	22.4
22.0	22.9	22.4	Operating Expenses	41.7	28.7	25.0	22.0	18.6	13.9
6.5	7.3	7.8	Operating Profit	9.3	7.1	6.6	7.5	8.9	8.5
.5	.6	.9	All Other Expenses (net)	5.6	.8	.3	.4	.4	1.3
6.1	6.7	7.0	Profit Before Taxes	3.7	6.2	6.3	7.1	8.4	7.1
			RATIOS						
3.0	3.1	2.9		2.8	2.8	3.0	3.4	3.3	2.2
1.8	1.8	1.8	Current	1.6	1.8	1.9	1.8	2.0	1.7
1.2	1.2	1.3		.3	1.3	1.4	1.4	1.4	1.3
1.9	2.2	2.1		2.6	2.2	2.4	2.6	2.2	1.3
1.1	1.1	1.1	Quick	.4	1.3	1.2	1.3	1.1	1.0
.6	.7	.7		.1	.7	.9	.7	.7	.6
41 9.0	37 9.9	37 9.9		12 29.8	36 10.0	36 10.1	36 10.0	38 9.5	41 8.8
54 6.8	51 7.1	51 7.2	Sales/Receivables	24 14.9	47 7.7	51 7.2	51 7.2	54 6.7	59 6.2
70 5.2	69 5.3	66 5.5		41 9.0	60 6.1	63 5.8	68 5.4	65 5.6	79 4.6
17 21.7	18 20.5	14 25.2		0 UND	2 194.0	7 48.8	21 17.1	16 23.5	35 10.3
42 8.7	43 8.5	40 9.1	Cost of Sales/Inventory	8 46.7	24 15.1	30 12.2	44 8.3	47 7.8	46 7.9
83 4.4	81 4.5	83 4.4		166 2.2	78 4.7	57 6.4	114 3.2	89 4.1	81 4.5
17 21.0	14 25.3	16 23.3		4 91.4	10 37.7	16 22.8	15 24.6	16 22.3	23 16.2
31 11.7	26 14.2	26 14.1	Cost of Sales/Payables	32 11.4	25 14.5	24 15.0	27 13.7	23 16.0	27 13.5
47 7.7	40 9.2	37 9.8		60 6.1	45 8.2	33 10.9	42 8.7	33 11.1	36 10.2
4.2	4.4	4.2		3.7	3.8	5.1	4.2	3.7	4.0
7.4	7.9	7.4	Sales/Working Capital	14.0	9.3	8.1	6.3	6.3	7.8
28.2	17.0	14.3		-5.6	23.9	16.6	14.1	9.9	13.8
16.8	22.1	17.8			13.5	21.6	25.0	26.0	22.6
(285) 6.3	(238) 8.2	(241) 6.7	EBIT/Interest		(42) 5.5	(37) 7.1	(53) 6.1	(52) 12.7	(49) 5.7
2.2	2.8	2.7			1.4	2.6	2.2	4.7	2.7
7.7	6.3	4.8					2.2	4.9	6.2
(70) 2.7	(68) 3.0	(55) 2.2	Net Profit + Depr., Dep., Amort./Cur. Mat. L/T/D				(13) 1.6	(11) 3.7	(22) 2.8
1.7	1.7	1.4					.4	2.0	2.0
.4	.4	.3		.1	.3	.2	.3	.3	.5
.8	.7	.7	Fixed/Worth	3.1	.7	.8	.6	.6	1.2
1.9	1.7	2.1		NM	4.3	1.8	1.7	1.1	2.3
.6	.6	.6		.8	.5	.7	.5	.6	.8
1.7	1.5	1.4	Debt/Worth	3.3	1.1	1.7	1.1	1.1	2.0
4.4	3.8	4.5		NM	23.0	5.5	4.5	2.4	4.7
49.5	48.1	51.3			63.1	79.7	41.4	50.6	45.1
(278) 25.4	(232) 24.6	(235) 22.6	% Profit Before Taxes/Tangible Net Worth		(39) 13.4	(38) 38.4	(51) 19.2	(55) 27.3	(43) 22.1
8.6	9.4	7.8			.5	7.2	6.1	12.8	12.7
17.1	19.2	18.7		22.2	20.8	23.0	20.6	21.6	16.5
8.7	10.4	9.8	% Profit Before Taxes/Total Assets	2.9	9.4	11.8	9.5	10.2	8.2
3.1	3.4	3.2		-11.6	.0	2.9	2.8	5.5	4.7
15.2	13.8	12.6		41.8	12.8	22.8	15.5	13.7	7.3
7.0	6.6	6.1	Sales/Net Fixed Assets	5.7	6.0	10.8	5.6	6.1	5.1
4.0	3.9	3.7		1.1	3.9	6.1	3.3	3.8	3.4
2.5	2.5	2.4		2.2	2.7	3.1	2.9	2.0	1.8
1.8	1.8	1.8	Sales/Total Assets	1.8	2.1	2.4	1.7	1.7	1.5
1.3	1.3	1.3		.4	1.4	1.8	1.2	1.4	1.0
1.6	1.7	2.1		.6	2.1	1.5	1.7	2.0	2.3
(276) 3.0	(236) 3.2	(238) 3.2	% Depr., Dep., Amort./Sales	(11) 2.4	(43) 3.2	(35) 2.8	(53) 3.2	(51) 3.2	(45) 3.3
4.7	5.1	5.0		7.2	5.3	4.7	5.2	4.5	5.7
2.6	2.6	2.2			4.4	3.1	1.8	1.3	
(154) 4.8	(129) 4.3	(128) 4.3	% Officers', Directors' Owners' Comp/Sales		(38) 7.3	(26) 5.5	(31) 3.2	(22) 2.2	
8.3	7.8	7.7			10.3	6.8	5.4	3.4	
5353138M	4650699M	5000109M	Net Sales ($)	7089M	97060M	154469M	422600M	959648M	3359243M
3788953M	3183895M	3499674M	Total Assets ($)	11021M	52104M	74722M	282969M	630819M	2448039M

M = $ thousand MM = $ million

See Pages 9 through 22 for Explanation of Ratios and Data

Current Data Sorted by Assets							Comparative Historical Data	
						Type of Statement		
		1	4	4	1	Unqualified	13	7
	1	10	3	2		Reviewed	31	25
2	6	13	3			Compiled	29	23
1	10	9				Tax Returns	15	11
1	9	15	14	9	2	Other	47	46
	18 (4/1-9/30/13)		102 (10/1/13-3/31/14)				4/1/09-3/31/10	4/1/10-3/31/11
0-500M	500M-2MM	2-10MM	10-50MM	50-100MM	100-250MM		ALL	ALL
4	26	48	24	15	3	**NUMBER OF STATEMENTS**	135	112
%	%	%	%	%	%	**ASSETS**	%	%
	13.0	11.9	7.3	7.9		Cash & Equivalents	8.7	8.4
	29.8	25.0	21.0	16.9		Trade Receivables (net)	21.2	23.9
	22.4	26.3	25.1	32.9		Inventory	27.1	24.9
	1.8	2.1	3.7	2.1		All Other Current	3.0	2.5
	67.0	65.2	57.1	59.7		Total Current	60.0	59.7
	30.1	28.1	31.3	28.0		Fixed Assets (net)	26.3	28.3
	.9	2.7	5.4	6.4		Intangibles (net)	6.0	5.4
	2.0	4.1	6.3	5.8		All Other Non-Current	7.7	6.6
	100.0	100.0	100.0	100.0		Total	100.0	100.0
						LIABILITIES		
	7.4	6.6	6.4	1.9		Notes Payable-Short Term	11.0	9.7
	4.5	3.3	3.1	1.0		Cur. Mat.-L.T.D.	5.4	5.9
	15.8	9.3	8.5	8.7		Trade Payables	9.7	11.7
	.0	.0	.3	.1		Income Taxes Payable	.1	.1
	6.3	7.3	8.5	14.7		All Other Current	8.5	8.4
	34.0	26.5	26.8	26.5		Total Current	34.7	35.8
	22.2	16.0	13.5	18.5		Long-Term Debt	16.3	16.2
	.2	.8	1.3	1.3		Deferred Taxes	.8	.7
	10.0	9.0	5.5	3.2		All Other Non-Current	12.6	9.5
	33.7	47.8	52.9	50.5		Net Worth	35.5	37.8
	100.0	100.0	100.0	100.0		Total Liabilties & Net Worth	100.0	100.0
						INCOME DATA		
	100.0	100.0	100.0	100.0		Net Sales	100.0	100.0
	45.6	33.6	31.8	28.7		Gross Profit	33.5	34.3
	41.0	26.5	22.3	21.5		Operating Expenses	33.6	28.0
	4.6	7.2	9.6	7.1		Operating Profit	-.1	6.2
	.5	.5	2.0	1.5		All Other Expenses (net)	1.7	1.3
	4.1	6.7	7.5	5.6		Profit Before Taxes	-1.8	5.0
						RATIOS		
	3.4	4.2	3.2	4.0			3.4	3.1
	2.1	2.2	2.1	2.6		Current	1.8	1.7
	1.2	1.7	1.5	1.6			1.2	1.2
	2.4	2.1	1.8	1.6			1.8	1.5
	1.3	1.5	1.2	1.0		Quick	.8	.9
	.7	.9	.6	.5			.5	.6
	31 11.6	**40** 9.2	**43** 8.4	**42** 8.7			**36** 10.0	**42** 8.7
	42 8.7	**49** 7.5	**50** 7.3	**50** 7.3		Sales/Receivables	**48** 7.6	**50** 7.3
	53 6.9	**64** 5.7	**62** 5.9	**54** 6.8			**62** 5.9	**62** 5.9
	19 19.3	**36** 10.2	**60** 6.1	**85** 4.3			**39** 9.3	**38** 9.6
	39 9.3	**79** 4.6	**85** 4.3	**130** 2.8		Cost of Sales/Inventory	**99** 3.7	**76** 4.8
	79 4.6	**122** 3.0	**135** 2.7	**182** 2.0			**162** 2.2	**135** 2.7
	18 20.6	**15** 25.0	**16** 22.6	**23** 16.2			**15** 25.1	**22** 16.9
	32 11.4	**23** 15.6	**30** 12.0	**35** 10.4		Cost of Sales/Payables	**27** 13.6	**35** 10.5
	58 6.3	**39** 9.3	**40** 9.1	**42** 8.7			**43** 8.5	**47** 7.8
	5.4	2.9	3.5	2.8			2.9	2.9
	7.6	5.5	5.6	3.8		Sales/Working Capital	5.8	7.2
	23.7	7.9	9.0	5.8			30.2	18.3
	16.8	19.1	43.9	97.8			5.7	11.1
	(23) 4.9	(38) 8.5	(22) 19.4	(14) 10.3		EBIT/Interest	(121) 1.4	(103) 3.6
	1.4	3.4	2.4	2.9			-2.8	1.4
							1.9	3.4
						Net Profit + Depr., Dep., Amort./Cur. Mat. L/T/D	(41) 1.1	(34) 1.6
							-.4	.9
	.3	.2	.3	.4			.3	.4
	1.0	.6	.6	.7		Fixed/Worth	.7	.9
	2.1	1.2	1.1	1.0			2.2	1.8
	.8	.6	.4	.5			.6	.6
	1.4	1.1	.9	1.2		Debt/Worth	1.6	1.8
	4.0	2.0	2.5	2.2			9.0	4.2
	64.7	40.4	28.3	19.4			16.0	39.9
	(22) 16.2	(45) 21.4	(23) 19.5	(13) 14.4		% Profit Before Taxes/Tangible Net Worth	(113) 3.6	(96) 15.9
	.3	5.1	13.1	6.7			-13.0	3.3
	25.0	21.0	14.8	10.9			6.1	14.5
	6.0	10.6	11.7	4.6		% Profit Before Taxes/Total Assets	.8	5.3
	.4	3.3	3.7	1.9			-5.9	.7
	21.3	17.1	7.1	7.3			14.7	14.5
	9.6	6.1	4.4	5.1		Sales/Net Fixed Assets	6.9	5.8
	5.6	4.2	3.0	2.4			3.3	3.6
	3.1	2.0	1.8	1.5			1.9	2.0
	2.6	1.6	1.5	1.2		Sales/Total Assets	1.4	1.6
	2.0	1.4	1.0	1.0			1.0	1.1
	1.1	1.4	.9	1.7			1.7	1.7
	(20) 2.4	(41) 3.2	(23) 2.8	2.4		% Depr., Dep., Amort./Sales	(121) 3.6	(102) 3.1
	3.7	6.5	4.2	7.3			5.8	5.3
	5.4	2.5					2.8	2.5
	(17) 8.0	(28) 4.2				% Officers', Directors' Owners' Comp/Sales	(57) 5.9	(42) 6.7
	15.1	5.8					9.6	9.9
2240M	83461M	393504M	781570M	1267113M	649960M	Net Sales ($)	2146988M	2477793M
1116M	32448M	224511M	545353M	983261M	557636M	Total Assets ($)	1777538M	2017759M

M = $ thousand MM = $ million

See Pages 9 through 22 for Explanation of Ratios and Data

Comparative Historical Data / Current Data Sorted by Sales

4/1/11-3/31/12 ALL	4/1/12-3/31/13 ALL	4/1/13-3/31/14 ALL	Type of Statement	0-1MM	1-3MM	3-5MM	5-10MM	10-25MM	25MM & OVER
8	9	10	Unqualified				1	2	7
32	21	16	Reviewed				4	8	4
28	27	24	Compiled	1	6	5	7	3	2
22	17	20	Tax Returns	2	5	8	5		
47	41	50	Other	1	6	8	6	8	21
				18 (4/1-9/30/13)			102 (10/1/13-3/31/14)		
137	115	120	**NUMBER OF STATEMENTS**	4	17	21	23	21	34
%	%	%	**ASSETS**	%	%	%	%	%	%
9.7	10.4	10.3	Cash & Equivalents		8.2	15.5	10.8	12.7	7.2
26.0	27.0	23.8	Trade Receivables (net)		24.0	27.8	28.0	21.3	21.0
23.6	23.3	25.5	Inventory		24.4	24.6	24.7	26.1	29.4
2.3	2.6	2.4	All Other Current		1.2	2.1	1.9	2.9	3.6
61.5	63.2	62.0	Total Current		57.7	70.0	65.4	62.9	61.1
25.5	27.3	30.1	Fixed Assets (net)		32.1	25.9	30.2	28.1	28.5
7.6	3.2	3.2	Intangibles (net)		7.5	.2	.4	4.7	4.3
5.3	6.3	4.7	All Other Non-Current		2.7	3.9	4.0	4.3	6.1
100.0	100.0	100.0	Total		100.0	100.0	100.0	100.0	100.0
			LIABILITIES						
6.9	5.6	6.1	Notes Payable-Short Term		7.7	7.6	7.2	3.6	5.7
4.9	4.0	3.2	Cur. Mat.-L.T.D.		4.1	3.6	3.2	3.8	1.6
12.2	10.9	10.5	Trade Payables		13.3	11.6	7.9	11.7	10.1
.1	.1	.1	Income Taxes Payable		.1	.0	.0	.2	.2
7.8	13.4	9.0	All Other Current		4.1	7.1	6.6	9.3	11.9
31.9	34.1	28.8	Total Current		29.3	30.0	24.8	28.6	29.4
16.1	21.1	16.4	Long-Term Debt		19.8	19.9	19.1	10.4	14.8
.7	.7	.9	Deferred Taxes		.4	.2	.5	1.6	1.4
8.4	8.9	10.6	All Other Non-Current		18.2	6.4	10.0	5.2	3.3
42.9	35.3	43.3	Net Worth		32.3	43.5	45.6	54.1	51.1
100.0	100.0	100.0	Total Liabilties & Net Worth		100.0	100.0	100.0	100.0	100.0
			INCOME DATA						
100.0	100.0	100.0	Net Sales		100.0	100.0	100.0	100.0	100.0
36.9	36.1	35.2	Gross Profit		39.7	40.6	36.6	32.8	29.0
27.8	28.3	28.6	Operating Expenses		37.3	35.5	27.1	22.0	22.4
9.1	7.8	6.5	Operating Profit		2.4	5.1	9.6	10.8	6.6
1.2	.8	.9	All Other Expenses (net)		.5	.0	.8	1.4	1.4
7.9	7.1	5.7	Profit Before Taxes		1.9	5.1	8.7	9.4	5.3
			RATIOS						
3.5	3.6	3.8			3.3	5.5	4.9	3.8	3.4
2.1	2.3	2.2	Current		2.0	2.5	2.4	2.1	2.2
1.4	1.6	1.6			1.3	1.6	1.7	1.6	1.6
2.0	2.5	2.0			2.0	3.7	2.2	2.3	1.7
1.2	1.5	1.3	Quick		1.0	1.7	1.5	1.3	1.0
.7	.8	.7			.7	.8	1.3	.6	.6
41 9.0	**36** 10.2	**39** 9.4			**35** 10.5	**33** 11.2	**37** 9.9	**34** 10.7	**44** 8.3
50 7.3	**51** 7.2	**47** 7.7	Sales/Receivables		**45** 8.1	**42** 8.6	**55** 6.6	**45** 8.1	**51** 7.2
63 5.8	**60** 6.1	**59** 6.2			**55** 6.6	**53** 6.9	**65** 5.6	**51** 7.2	**59** 6.2
33 10.9	**25** 14.5	**35** 10.4			**31** 11.7	**26** 13.8	**29** 12.7	**51** 7.1	**69** 5.3
74 4.9	**56** 6.5	**78** 4.7	Cost of Sales/Inventory		**57** 6.4	**53** 6.9	**72** 5.1	**83** 4.4	**96** 3.8
122 3.0	**126** 2.9	**126** 2.9			**126** 2.9	**122** 3.0	**96** 3.8	**130** 2.8	**146** 2.5
21 17.8	**14** 26.4	**16** 23.5			**15** 24.5	**19** 19.3	**13** 29.0	**15** 23.9	**26** 14.0
32 11.3	**29** 12.5	**28** 13.0	Cost of Sales/Payables		**28** 13.1	**25** 14.5	**23** 16.2	**26** 13.9	**34** 10.6
52 7.0	**42** 8.6	**42** 8.7			**51** 7.1	**39** 9.4	**38** 9.7	**42** 8.6	**42** 8.7
3.5	3.7	3.6			5.1	2.8	3.7	3.8	3.0
6.3	6.4	5.8	Sales/Working Capital		7.1	6.7	5.0	6.2	4.3
11.2	10.3	9.6			18.1	13.4	8.6	7.7	7.8
21.5	21.9	23.4			13.5	20.7	38.2	32.5	36.4
(123) 9.1	(97) 7.2	(102) 7.7	EBIT/Interest		(16) 4.3	(18) 5.2	(18) 10.0	(17) 11.5	(31) 8.2
2.4	3.1	2.6			.0	1.4	3.2	6.4	2.7
5.5	9.0	7.6							10.9
(30) 2.4	(29) 3.1	(25) 3.5	Net Profit + Depr., Dep., Amort./Cur. Mat. L/T/D						(11) 4.4
1.5	1.9	1.2							3.5
.3	.3	.3			.5	.2	.2	.3	.3
.6	.7	.6	Fixed/Worth		1.3	.5	.6	.6	.6
1.4	1.6	1.3			NM	1.4	1.3	.8	1.1
.7	.6	.5			1.1	.5	.6	.4	.4
1.5	1.2	1.2	Debt/Worth		1.9	1.3	.9	.8	1.1
3.4	3.3	2.4			NM	2.5	2.0	1.3	2.3
54.3	45.3	39.0			56.6	19.4	76.8	39.6	20.8
(122) 28.9	(98) 27.0	(109) 18.9	% Profit Before Taxes/Tangible Net Worth		(13) 34.7	(19) 8.9	(22) 26.7	(20) 32.8	(32) 14.5
14.3	13.1	5.6			-3.7	.6	6.3	20.0	7.1
20.1	19.4	15.9			16.3	9.9	26.0	21.9	12.7
11.2	12.0	7.6	% Profit Before Taxes/Total Assets		6.4	4.4	12.1	15.0	7.5
4.1	4.6	2.3			-2.0	.4	3.7	9.0	2.3
17.8	18.3	12.8			17.7	24.5	15.0	12.7	8.0
6.8	6.8	5.9	Sales/Net Fixed Assets		6.0	9.5	6.0	5.4	4.8
3.7	4.6	3.8			3.8	5.5	4.1	3.1	3.5
2.2	2.6	2.2			2.7	2.8	2.0	2.5	1.8
1.6	1.9	1.7	Sales/Total Assets		2.0	2.3	1.8	1.7	1.4
1.2	1.4	1.2			1.3	1.5	1.5	1.1	1.1
1.0	1.4	1.4			1.7	1.3	2.4	.8	1.6
(118) 2.6	(96) 2.3	(105) 2.8	% Depr., Dep., Amort./Sales		(14) 3.2	(17) 2.6	(19) 3.2	(19) 3.4	(33) 2.5
4.2	4.3	5.3			7.1	3.5	7.3	5.1	5.0
2.7	3.2	3.0				4.3	3.6		
(56) 5.1	(50) 4.8	(50) 5.0	% Officers', Directors' Owners' Comp/Sales			(13) 5.9	(16) 4.8		
7.8	8.6	9.5				15.1	7.2		
2785044M	2673329M	3177848M	Net Sales ($)	1733M	37227M	88082M	160554M	327148M	2563104M
2027763M	1851398M	2344325M	Total Assets ($)	1654M	26053M	49208M	89479M	225322M	1952609M

M = $ thousand MM = $ million

See Pages 9 through 22 for Explanation of Ratios and Data

Current Data Sorted by Assets | Comparative Historical Data

						Type of Statement		
		7	15	6	2	Unqualified	34	38
	2	32	17	1		Reviewed	81	77
1	17	19	2			Compiled	51	55
6	23	8				Tax Returns	33	38
2	13	29	23	7	3	Other	90	97
46 (4/1-9/30/13)		189 (10/1/13-3/31/14)					4/1/09-3/31/10	4/1/10-3/31/11
0-500M	500M-2MM	2-10MM	10-50MM	50-100MM	100-250MM		ALL	ALL
9	55	95	57	14	5	NUMBER OF STATEMENTS	289	305
%	%	%	%	%	%	ASSETS	%	%
	16.1	10.3	9.6	12.4		Cash & Equivalents	8.9	9.8
	29.9	27.0	23.8	15.9		Trade Receivables (net)	23.4	25.6
	16.0	25.3	24.8	15.2		Inventory	24.9	24.2
	1.2	1.9	7.1	6.1		All Other Current	5.0	2.8
	63.2	64.6	65.2	49.6		Total Current	62.2	62.4
	28.2	25.9	25.9	26.6		Fixed Assets (net)	29.2	28.3
	1.3	3.6	3.3	17.8		Intangibles (net)	3.6	3.6
	7.4	5.9	5.5	6.0		All Other Non-Current	5.1	5.7
	100.0	100.0	100.0	100.0		Total	100.0	100.0
						LIABILITIES		
	10.9	8.2	6.4	2.7		Notes Payable-Short Term	11.7	11.6
	4.5	3.7	2.4	2.2		Cur. Mat.-L.T.D.	4.2	4.6
	14.7	13.8	12.6	8.5		Trade Payables	11.4	12.4
	.1	.3	.2	.2		Income Taxes Payable	.2	.1
	7.6	11.0	14.5	15.4		All Other Current	11.4	12.8
	37.7	37.0	36.2	29.0		Total Current	39.0	41.6
	22.5	17.0	11.4	9.5		Long-Term Debt	15.5	16.9
	.3	.8	1.0	1.5		Deferred Taxes	.5	.5
	7.8	4.9	6.8	7.5		All Other Non-Current	6.1	7.4
	31.6	40.3	44.6	52.6		Net Worth	38.9	33.6
	100.0	100.0	100.0	100.0		Total Liabilties & Net Worth	100.0	100.0
						INCOME DATA		
	100.0	100.0	100.0	100.0		Net Sales	100.0	100.0
	37.9	31.9	26.9	27.1		Gross Profit	30.5	32.7
	34.0	25.3	18.8	18.8		Operating Expenses	29.3	27.3
	3.9	6.7	8.1	8.4		Operating Profit	1.3	5.4
	.8	.7	.8	-.6		All Other Expenses (net)	1.2	1.0
	3.2	6.0	7.3	9.0		Profit Before Taxes	.0	4.4
						RATIOS		
	3.3	2.7	2.6	3.6			2.7	2.6
	2.0	1.7	1.7	1.6		Current	1.8	1.7
	1.1	1.2	1.4	1.2			1.1	1.1
	2.6	1.6	1.4	2.3			1.5	1.6
	1.3	1.0	.9	.9		Quick	.8	.9
	.8	.6	.5	.6			.5	.6
	27 13.3	33 11.0	40 9.1	39 9.4			34 10.8	35 10.3
	41 9.0	45 8.1	51 7.1	45 8.1		Sales/Receivables	47 7.8	51 7.2
	60 6.1	63 5.8	65 5.6	52 7.0			61 6.0	66 5.5
	1 288.2	28 13.0	37 9.8	30 12.0			31 11.7	31 11.9
	20 18.3	69 5.3	83 4.4	60 6.1		Cost of Sales/Inventory	66 5.5	66 5.5
	61 6.0	107 3.4	130 2.8	81 4.5			114 3.2	118 3.1
	10 37.9	17 21.5	22 16.3	18 19.9			15 23.8	19 19.0
	21 17.7	30 12.3	32 11.3	31 11.6		Cost of Sales/Payables	26 13.8	31 11.8
	49 7.4	42 8.7	45 8.1	59 6.2			45 8.2	51 7.2
	4.8	4.7	3.3	2.7			4.0	4.0
	9.9	7.5	5.6	7.4		Sales/Working Capital	7.7	7.9
	45.0	20.4	9.9	158.4			44.1	34.3
	20.1	19.5	33.1	106.4			7.9	13.2
	(51) 5.7	(84) 7.6	(52) 11.1	(12) 10.1		EBIT/Interest	(267) 1.8	(286) 4.1
	1.9	1.8	2.5	5.2			-2.9	1.2
		5.0	12.8				3.5	4.6
		(25) 2.9	(21) 4.3			Net Profit + Depr., Dep., Amort./Cur. Mat. L/T/D	(74) 1.3	(66) 1.8
		1.2	2.2				.4	1.1
	.3	.3	.2	.4			.3	.3
	.8	.6	.5	.6		Fixed/Worth	.7	.7
	1.9	1.6	1.2	1.9			2.0	2.3
	.5	.7	.6	.6			.7	.7
	1.7	1.7	1.4	1.3		Debt/Worth	1.6	1.8
	6.6	3.6	2.3	2.9			4.2	5.2
	60.6	54.0	41.1	47.6			24.9	42.6
	(45) 23.1	(85) 27.6	(55) 21.3	(13) 28.2		% Profit Before Taxes/Tangible Net Worth	(264) 5.3	(266) 16.6
	9.1	8.2	7.1	13.5			-15.9	4.3
	18.7	22.5	15.5	15.7			10.4	14.1
	8.2	9.3	9.1	9.1		% Profit Before Taxes/Total Assets	1.8	6.0
	1.1	1.7	3.1	5.6			-6.7	.8
	33.1	19.0	21.5	9.6			16.0	17.1
	11.1	9.6	7.9	5.1		Sales/Net Fixed Assets	6.8	6.9
	5.4	4.5	3.5	2.8			3.8	4.0
	3.5	2.6	1.8	1.5			2.3	2.4
	2.5	1.8	1.5	1.2		Sales/Total Assets	1.7	1.7
	1.6	1.4	1.1	.9			1.2	1.2
	1.0	1.1	1.0	1.8			1.3	1.5
	(42) 2.0	(84) 2.6	(53) 2.1	(12) 4.5		% Depr., Dep., Amort./Sales	(257) 3.0	(261) 3.0
	4.3	4.2	3.6	6.2			5.6	5.5
	2.7	2.2	1.1				2.8	2.2
	(33) 6.7	(41) 3.6	(13) 2.0			% Officers', Directors' Owners' Comp/Sales	(120) 5.0	(113) 3.7
	11.0	5.7	5.5				9.3	7.2
5752M	197419M	906338M	1836523M	1107021M	908123M	Net Sales ($)	5097126M	4694087M
1702M	69815M	463240M	1236203M	902876M	851814M	Total Assets ($)	3895289M	3594147M

M = $ thousand MM = $ million

See Pages 9 through 22 for Explanation of Ratios and Data

Comparative Historical Data | **Current Data Sorted by Sales**

Type of Statement	4/1/11-3/31/12 ALL	4/1/12-3/31/13 ALL	4/1/13-3/31/14 ALL	0-1MM	1-3MM	3-5MM	5-10MM	10-25MM	25MM & OVER
Unqualified	42	33	30				1	13	16
Reviewed	69	48	52			7	13	24	8
Compiled	55	42	39	2	9	6	11	10	1
Tax Returns	53	38	37	3	18	8	5	3	
Other	96	96	77	3	8	5	22	13	26
				46 (4/1-9/30/13)			189 (10/1/13-3/31/14)		
NUMBER OF STATEMENTS	315	257	235	8	35	26	52	63	51
ASSETS	%	%	%	%	%	%	%	%	%
Cash & Equivalents	10.2	11.2	11.7		16.0	15.9	10.5	10.4	9.8
Trade Receivables (net)	26.3	26.8	26.6		25.9	24.9	28.1	27.5	23.0
Inventory	22.8	21.1	21.8		14.5	16.1	21.9	27.7	24.2
All Other Current	3.2	3.2	3.3		1.5	1.3	2.0	4.6	5.6
Total Current	62.5	62.2	63.3		57.9	58.2	62.5	70.2	62.7
Fixed Assets (net)	28.6	28.7	26.3		33.6	27.6	27.6	21.7	24.4
Intangibles (net)	3.4	3.7	3.8		1.4	6.3	5.4	1.1	6.5
All Other Non-Current	5.5	5.3	6.6		7.1	7.9	4.5	7.0	6.4
Total	100.0	100.0	100.0		100.0	100.0	100.0	100.0	100.0
LIABILITIES									
Notes Payable-Short Term	9.0	8.7	8.5		11.7	7.1	6.6	8.7	5.3
Cur. Mat.-L.T.D.	5.0	4.2	3.8		5.8	4.7	4.4	2.5	2.3
Trade Payables	12.9	12.5	13.5		11.6	9.6	15.3	15.2	12.8
Income Taxes Payable	.2	.2	.2		.2	.1	.2	.3	.3
All Other Current	12.7	12.8	11.6		10.0	8.0	8.9	12.8	17.2
Total Current	39.9	38.3	37.6		39.3	29.5	35.4	39.4	37.9
Long-Term Debt	17.1	16.6	17.3		31.3	18.6	19.4	11.5	8.6
Deferred Taxes	.7	.8	.8		.1	1.6	.3	.6	1.5
All Other Non-Current	5.1	4.7	6.1		7.3	3.7	3.6	5.3	6.8
Net Worth	37.2	39.6	38.3		22.1	46.7	41.3	43.1	45.2
Total Liabilties & Net Worth	100.0	100.0	100.0		100.0	100.0	100.0	100.0	100.0
INCOME DATA									
Net Sales	100.0	100.0	100.0		100.0	100.0	100.0	100.0	100.0
Gross Profit	32.0	32.3	32.9		41.3	33.8	33.9	28.4	26.4
Operating Expenses	24.1	25.2	26.7		37.2	28.6	27.3	20.4	19.0
Operating Profit	7.9	7.0	6.2		4.1	5.2	6.6	8.0	7.3
All Other Expenses (net)	.8	.7	.6		.5	1.0	.8	.7	.1
Profit Before Taxes	7.1	6.4	5.5		3.5	4.2	5.8	7.3	7.2
RATIOS									
Current	2.7	2.8	2.8		2.5	3.4	3.2	2.8	2.4
	1.7	1.7	1.7		1.8	2.2	1.7	2.0	1.5
	1.2	1.2	1.2		1.0	1.4	1.2	1.2	1.3
Quick	1.6	1.7	1.7		2.3	2.1	1.8	1.5	1.2
	.9	1.0	1.0		1.2	1.6	1.0	1.0	.8
	.6	.6	.6		.6	.8	.5	.6	.6
Sales/Receivables	34 10.6	35 10.4	34 10.7		30 12.2	31 11.9	28 12.9	34 10.7	40 9.1
	48 7.6	47 7.8	46 8.0		41 9.0	43 8.4	47 7.7	41 8.9	50 7.3
	65 5.6	63 5.8	62 5.9		58 6.3	62 5.9	63 5.8	66 5.5	63 5.8
Cost of Sales/Inventory	21 17.4	19 19.7	17 21.4		0 UND	10 35.6	24 15.0	29 12.5	34 10.6
	59 6.2	51 7.2	52 7.0		24 15.3	29 12.6	53 6.9	72 5.1	74 4.9
	107 3.4	101 3.6	107 3.4		61 6.0	83 4.4	104 3.5	122 3.0	126 2.9
Cost of Sales/Payables	16 23.1	16 22.5	16 22.4		10 37.9	13 28.8	16 22.3	22 16.9	21 17.0
	29 12.5	27 13.3	30 12.3		22 16.9	17 21.9	30 12.3	30 12.2	33 11.0
	46 8.0	45 8.2	45 8.1		69 5.3	36 10.2	49 7.5	42 8.6	55 6.6
Sales/Working Capital	4.6	4.5	4.5		4.8	4.6	4.9	3.5	3.7
	7.7	8.1	7.3		9.9	7.1	7.8	6.2	7.2
	23.9	22.2	18.2		999.8	18.2	29.0	15.5	13.3
EBIT/Interest	17.2	20.8	22.1		19.5	13.9	15.7	24.2	43.5
	(275) 5.9	(234) 7.5	(210) 7.9		(33) 5.2	(24) 4.2	(47) 6.9	(56) 12.0	(46) 13.3
	2.9	2.9	2.3		1.0	.6	2.5	3.0	4.6
Net Profit + Depr., Dep., Amort./Cur. Mat. L/T/D	5.9	6.4	8.8					8.6	14.8
	(75) 2.7	(71) 3.2	(62) 3.2					(23) 3.4	(20) 5.3
	1.6	1.8	1.5					1.9	2.2
Fixed/Worth	.3	.3	.3		.5	.2	.3	.1	.3
	.7	.7	.6		1.3	.7	.7	.4	.5
	1.9	1.6	1.6		-12.6	2.2	1.6	.9	1.3
Debt/Worth	.7	.7	.6		.5	.5	.8	.6	.6
	1.5	1.5	1.6		3.0	.9	2.2	1.2	1.5
	4.0	4.0	3.8		-26.6	3.9	5.1	2.4	2.9
% Profit Before Taxes/Tangible Net Worth	48.1	53.2	49.8		33.4	67.4	50.3	57.0	46.9
	(280) 25.4	(233) 25.3	(207) 23.8		(24) 17.2	(23) 27.0	(47) 23.2	(60) 26.1	(49) 26.3
	12.6	10.2	8.1		9.5	5.7	8.0	9.3	8.1
% Profit Before Taxes/Total Assets	19.0	18.5	18.0		11.4	20.9	20.1	22.9	16.1
	10.2	10.4	8.3		7.9	6.2	9.2	12.4	7.4
	3.9	2.8	2.0		.0	-.7	2.1	4.5	4.2
Sales/Net Fixed Assets	18.7	19.6	22.1		15.8	22.2	18.1	45.1	16.5
	7.6	7.7	9.1		7.4	8.8	10.1	11.0	6.6
	4.1	4.1	4.3		4.0	5.0	4.4	5.7	3.5
Sales/Total Assets	2.5	2.6	2.6		2.9	2.7	3.0	2.8	2.0
	1.9	1.9	1.8		1.9	2.2	1.9	1.8	1.4
	1.3	1.4	1.3		1.5	1.3	1.4	1.4	1.1
% Depr., Dep., Amort./Sales	1.5	1.3	1.1		1.4	1.4	1.2	.7	1.1
	(261) 2.7	(221) 2.6	(203) 2.4		(30) 2.7	(21) 3.3	(44) 2.6	(56) 1.8	(47) 2.5
	4.6	4.6	4.3		5.0	5.6	3.6	3.1	4.2
% Officers', Directors' Owners' Comp/Sales	2.0	2.5	2.2		4.2	3.8	2.1	1.7	
	(114) 3.9	(104) 4.5	(94) 4.2		(22) 7.3	(16) 7.1	(24) 2.8	(21) 2.9	
	6.9	7.7	7.8		12.4	8.3	5.4	4.8	
Net Sales ($)	5927554M	5737778M	4961176M	3492M	72909M	105299M	372945M	1000837M	3405694M
Total Assets ($)	4469040M	3771261M	3525650M	2103M	40747M	60726M	235051M	595856M	2591167M

M = $ thousand MM = $ million

See Pages 9 through 22 for Explanation of Ratios and Data

Current Data Sorted by Assets							Comparative Historical Data	
						Type of Statement		
		2	3	3	1	Unqualified	7	9
1		19	5	1		Reviewed	14	28
1	2	8	2			Compiled	13	10
2	6	5	1			Tax Returns	13	15
2	7	10	12	3	1	Other	27	24
	20 (4/1-9/30/13)		77 (10/1/13-3/31/14)				4/1/09-3/31/10	4/1/10-3/31/11
0-500M	500M-2MM	2-10MM	10-50MM	50-100MM	100-250MM		ALL	ALL
6	15	44	23	7	2	**NUMBER OF STATEMENTS**	74	86
%	%	%	%	%	%	**ASSETS**	%	%
	13.4	17.8	8.3			Cash & Equivalents	13.4	15.1
	22.2	25.7	18.4			Trade Receivables (net)	21.8	24.1
	28.8	24.1	27.5			Inventory	21.0	21.2
	2.0	4.2	7.7			All Other Current	5.0	6.3
	66.5	71.7	61.8			Total Current	61.1	66.7
	24.4	19.4	25.4			Fixed Assets (net)	28.7	22.9
	4.3	2.6	7.6			Intangibles (net)	5.7	4.9
	4.8	6.3	5.2			All Other Non-Current	4.5	5.5
	100.0	100.0	100.0			Total	100.0	100.0
						LIABILITIES		
	17.4	5.6	7.0			Notes Payable-Short Term	7.8	7.4
	4.0	2.5	4.4			Cur. Mat.-L.T.D.	3.9	3.8
	9.5	10.3	7.3			Trade Payables	12.1	14.6
	.0	.3	.1			Income Taxes Payable	.1	.1
	11.8	16.8	13.2			All Other Current	14.0	12.2
	42.6	35.5	32.0			Total Current	37.9	38.1
	19.8	13.2	11.8			Long-Term Debt	24.0	21.0
	.0	.2	.6			Deferred Taxes	.2	.3
	3.8	4.1	7.2			All Other Non-Current	9.1	6.4
	33.9	47.1	48.4			Net Worth	28.9	34.2
	100.0	100.0	100.0			Total Liabilties & Net Worth	100.0	100.0
						INCOME DATA		
	100.0	100.0	100.0			Net Sales	100.0	100.0
	39.0	34.1	30.3			Gross Profit	32.3	29.8
	34.3	27.1	20.7			Operating Expenses	30.3	25.7
	4.7	7.0	9.6			Operating Profit	2.0	4.2
	-.2	-.2	1.9			All Other Expenses (net)	1.4	.8
	4.9	7.2	7.7			Profit Before Taxes	.6	3.3
						RATIOS		
	4.4	3.7	2.7				4.3	3.2
	2.1	2.4	1.8			Current	1.9	1.6
	1.1	1.3	1.5				1.1	1.2
	1.9	2.7	1.5				2.0	1.8
	.8	1.2	.7			Quick	1.0	1.0
	.4	.7	.4				.6	.6
	11 33.0	**34** 10.7	**35** 10.3				**24** 15.3	**27** 13.5
	28 12.9	**43** 8.5	**41** 8.9			Sales/Receivables	**39** 9.3	**44** 8.3
	57 6.4	**58** 6.3	**61** 6.0				**57** 6.4	**61** 6.0
	10 37.6	**33** 10.9	**49** 7.5				**15** 24.4	**10** 37.9
	51 7.2	**69** 5.3	**111** 3.3			Cost of Sales/Inventory	**54** 6.8	**49** 7.4
	118 3.1	**104** 3.5	**228** 1.6				**111** 3.3	**114** 3.2
	16 23.4	**13** 27.7	**13** 27.6				**10** 38.3	**16** 23.5
	20 18.1	**28** 13.2	**21** 17.4			Cost of Sales/Payables	**21** 17.5	**29** 12.5
	22 16.4	**39** 9.4	**32** 11.4				**38** 9.5	**49** 7.4
	3.9	3.5	2.5				3.1	3.1
	6.4	5.8	5.1			Sales/Working Capital	6.4	7.1
	33.1	11.3	7.6				54.2	22.5
	12.7	92.9	28.5				7.3	14.0
	9.9	(38) 17.9	(20) 12.0			EBIT/Interest	(65) 2.2	(72) 3.4
	4.2	2.0	1.9				-.8	.7
		6.1					5.1	2.8
		(10) 1.6				Net Profit + Depr., Dep., Amort./Cur. Mat. L/T/D	(15) 1.8	(13) 1.5
		1.0					.2	.5
	.1	.1	.2				.3	.2
	.5	.3	.4			Fixed/Worth	.9	.6
	1.7	1.0	1.6				10.9	1.5
	.9	.4	.4				.6	.6
	1.6	1.1	1.2			Debt/Worth	1.5	1.4
	3.5	2.9	2.4				104.1	5.4
	40.8	38.9	51.5				25.0	40.0
	(13) 33.3	(41) 20.6	(21) 25.1			% Profit Before Taxes/Tangible Net Worth	(57) 9.8	(73) 14.9
	5.5	8.1	2.2				-2.0	1.3
	19.5	20.5	17.0				9.3	15.0
	11.5	11.9	7.9			% Profit Before Taxes/Total Assets	2.1	4.8
	4.6	2.3	1.4				-3.3	-.2
	75.1	48.9	15.8				19.4	44.4
	14.1	16.3	8.5			Sales/Net Fixed Assets	7.1	9.3
	12.5	6.3	3.1				3.3	3.9
	3.3	2.4	1.9				2.6	2.5
	2.8	2.2	1.5			Sales/Total Assets	1.5	1.6
	2.0	1.6	.9				.9	1.0
		.6	1.1				1.0	.9
		(36) 1.3	(21) 2.3			% Depr., Dep., Amort./Sales	(63) 3.0	(65) 2.8
		4.8	3.8				5.5	5.7
	3.0	2.5					1.8	2.1
	(10) 3.7	(15) 3.5				% Officers', Directors' Owners' Comp/Sales	(31) 4.6	(30) 5.2
	8.1	5.5					7.7	8.6
7034M	**50002M**	**416654M**	**640306M**	**517155M**	**187263M**	Net Sales ($)	**1077046M**	**1566500M**
1955M	**19567M**	**204668M**	**527389M**	**490682M**	**370583M**	Total Assets ($)	**1024900M**	**1261691M**

M = $ thousand MM = $ million

See Pages 9 through 22 for Explanation of Ratios and Data

Comparative Historical Data / Current Data Sorted by Sales

4/1/11-3/31/12 ALL	4/1/12-3/31/13 ALL	4/1/13-3/31/14 ALL	Type of Statement	0-1MM	1-3MM	3-5MM	5-10MM	10-25MM	25MM & OVER
				20 (4/1-9/30/13)			77 (10/1/13-3/31/14)		
12	6	9	Unqualified					5	4
15	13	26	Reviewed		2	2	7	12	3
23	12	13	Compiled		3	2	5	2	1
26	19	14	Tax Returns	1	4	3	4	2	
33	42	35	Other	1	8	4	6	4	12
109	92	97	NUMBER OF STATEMENTS	2	17	11	22	25	20
%	%	%	**ASSETS**	%	%	%	%	%	%
11.0	11.7	13.6	Cash & Equivalents		7.9	18.3	18.7	14.4	10.6
26.9	24.3	23.7	Trade Receivables (net)		20.6	26.4	26.5	22.5	23.3
22.4	25.3	24.2	Inventory		21.1	29.2	23.1	24.5	23.8
4.8	4.3	4.6	All Other Current		2.0	1.8	1.1	11.2	4.5
65.0	65.7	66.1	Total Current		51.6	75.7	69.3	72.6	62.2
23.6	20.8	21.9	Fixed Assets (net)		39.0	13.2	20.3	16.5	20.0
6.7	5.6	5.2	Intangibles (net)		2.7	6.0	2.7	4.2	10.6
4.7	7.9	6.8	All Other Non-Current		6.7	5.1	7.7	6.8	7.1
100.0	100.0	100.0	Total		100.0	100.0	100.0	100.0	100.0
			LIABILITIES						
11.0	9.5	8.1	Notes Payable-Short Term		9.0	13.1	6.2	7.4	5.8
3.2	2.5	3.0	Cur. Mat.-L.T.D.		3.8	3.8	2.3	2.6	3.6
13.2	14.2	10.8	Trade Payables		16.0	11.2	8.5	11.2	8.4
.2	.2	.2	Income Taxes Payable		.0	.4	.1	.2	.2
10.0	15.6	15.3	All Other Current		11.1	7.0	16.1	20.2	17.4
37.7	41.9	37.4	Total Current		40.0	35.5	33.2	41.6	35.5
13.5	13.4	13.1	Long-Term Debt		21.8	15.4	14.4	9.0	3.7
.5	.4	.3	Deferred Taxes		.0	.0	.3	.2	.6
11.0	6.8	6.6	All Other Non-Current		11.9	4.4	7.4	6.0	4.0
37.4	37.5	42.6	Net Worth		26.3	44.8	44.7	43.1	56.2
100.0	100.0	100.0	Total Liabilties & Net Worth		100.0	100.0	100.0	100.0	100.0
			INCOME DATA						
100.0	100.0	100.0	Net Sales		100.0	100.0	100.0	100.0	100.0
34.3	35.8	34.0	Gross Profit		46.0	33.1	31.9	28.8	30.1
26.6	29.2	26.5	Operating Expenses		39.2	26.3	27.2	20.1	20.4
7.7	6.6	7.5	Operating Profit		6.8	6.8	4.7	8.7	9.7
.7	.1	.5	All Other Expenses (net)		1.6	-.2	-.5	1.0	.3
7.0	6.4	7.1	Profit Before Taxes		5.2	7.0	5.2	7.7	9.3
			RATIOS						
3.1	2.9	3.4			4.0	5.3	5.1	3.7	2.3
1.8	1.8	2.0	Current		1.7	2.2	2.2	1.6	1.8
1.2	1.1	1.3			1.2	1.3	1.5	1.1	1.4
1.8	1.8	2.2			2.1	3.8	3.4	2.2	1.6
.9	.9	1.0	Quick		.9	1.2	1.2	.7	.9
.6	.5	.5			.4	.4	.9	.4	.6
34 10.8	**24** 15.2	**30** 12.0			**12** 30.8	**28** 12.9	**30** 12.0	**30** 12.3	**41** 8.9
49 7.4	**44** 8.3	**44** 8.3	Sales/Receivables		**34** 10.7	**45** 8.2	**41** 9.0	**41** 9.0	**57** 6.4
66 5.5	**64** 5.7	**61** 6.0			**48** 7.6	**57** 6.4	**65** 5.6	**58** 6.3	**83** 4.4
16 22.5	**21** 17.8	**33** 11.1			**9** 41.2	**46** 7.9	**31** 11.7	**20** 18.1	**37** 9.9
54 6.7	**62** 5.9	**69** 5.3	Cost of Sales/Inventory		**38** 9.5	**69** 5.3	**54** 6.8	**79** 4.6	**79** 4.6
111 3.3	**152** 2.4	**114** 3.2			**243** 1.5	**99** 3.7	**107** 3.4	**107** 3.4	**126** 2.9
17 21.9	**16** 22.5	**15** 23.9			**13** 27.6	**16** 23.4	**9** 41.5	**13** 28.3	**15** 23.6
29 12.7	**30** 12.3	**22** 16.4	Cost of Sales/Payables		**21** 17.8	**22** 16.5	**20** 18.1	**21** 17.4	**28** 13.0
51 7.2	**59** 6.2	**40** 9.2			**43** 8.4	**40** 9.1	**35** 10.4	**40** 9.1	**51** 7.1
4.2	3.6	3.5			5.1	2.1	3.5	3.5	3.6
7.4	7.5	6.2	Sales/Working Capital		8.5	6.3	5.4	6.0	5.6
18.5	24.9	12.9			32.7	12.5	9.7	46.0	8.7
19.7	35.4	43.1			23.7	30.4	277.8	57.4	27.2
(93) 5.9	(75) 7.6	(83) 11.2	EBIT/Interest		(14) 9.7	(10) 13.4	(20) 5.2	(20) 16.7	(17) 14.8
2.2	2.0	2.2			4.1	9.0	1.2	2.0	2.2
9.5		2.8							
(14) 3.6		(19) 1.8	Net Profit + Depr., Dep., Amort./Cur. Mat. L/T/D						
1.6		1.0							
.2	.2	.1			.3	.0	.2	.1	.3
.5	.5	.5	Fixed/Worth		1.0	.1	.5	.2	.4
1.3	1.5	1.4			NM	.6	1.1	1.4	.9
.7	.5	.4			.6	.4	.5	.3	.4
1.4	1.4	1.2	Debt/Worth		.9	1.4	1.2	1.2	.7
3.5	5.5	3.4			NM	2.8	3.2	3.8	2.4
50.1	53.3	43.5			40.7	46.9	32.7	45.0	61.5
(96) 20.8	(79) 24.7	(86) 22.6	% Profit Before Taxes/Tangible Net Worth		(13) 22.7	(10) 35.3	(20) 12.6	(23) 24.1	(19) 25.1
8.9	9.7	6.9			6.6	6.4	1.4	12.4	7.0
18.7	23.0	19.6			19.9	27.9	20.3	21.5	16.3
7.2	9.7	11.0	% Profit Before Taxes/Total Assets		16.2	14.7	6.3	11.0	10.4
3.1	2.1	2.3			2.0	4.6	.0	2.7	2.6
35.8	42.7	34.4			44.9	112.9	32.2	51.1	14.6
12.5	12.3	12.7	Sales/Net Fixed Assets		5.4	29.0	13.3	18.9	8.8
5.3	6.7	4.6			2.1	13.1	7.2	5.3	5.1
2.9	2.8	2.5			3.6	3.3	2.7	2.4	2.0
1.9	1.8	1.9	Sales/Total Assets		2.0	2.1	2.4	1.9	1.3
1.2	1.3	1.3			1.2	1.6	1.7	1.5	.9
.7	.8	.6			.7		.8	.5	.9
(88) 1.9	(73) 2.0	(77) 1.7	% Depr., Dep., Amort./Sales		(12) 6.4		(16) 2.0	(23) 1.0	2.2
3.7	3.3	4.8			9.7		5.7	2.9	3.2
2.2	1.7	2.1					3.1		
(41) 3.8	(33) 3.5	(32) 3.5	% Officers', Directors' Owners' Comp/Sales				(11) 3.8		
6.5	6.8	6.4					5.5		
2553095M	1687793M	1818414M	Net Sales ($)	1325M	33767M	44305M	165475M	391030M	1182512M
2024356M	1260172M	1614844M	Total Assets ($)	2747M	37592M	21093M	102650M	342489M	1108273M

M = $ thousand MM = $ million

See Pages 9 through 22 for Explanation of Ratios and Data

Current Data Sorted by Assets							Comparative Historical Data	
						Type of Statement		
		2		1	1	Unqualified	7	10
	1	6	3			Reviewed	6	10
		1	1			Compiled	5	3
	1					Tax Returns	2	3
	1	5	6	1	4	Other	13	9
	6 (4/1-9/30/13)		28 (10/1/13-3/31/14)				4/1/09-3/31/10	4/1/10-3/31/11
0-500M	500M-2MM	2-10MM	10-50MM	50-100MM	100-250MM		ALL	ALL
	3	14	10	2	5	**NUMBER OF STATEMENTS**	33	35
%	%	%	%	%	%	**ASSETS**	%	%
DATA NOT AVAILABLE		7.3	7.5			Cash & Equivalents	8.9	8.1
		23.3	15.0			Trade Receivables (net)	20.5	21.6
		27.7	25.3			Inventory	29.9	29.9
		1.3	3.5			All Other Current	2.2	2.2
		59.6	51.2			Total Current	61.4	61.7
		31.3	36.3			Fixed Assets (net)	29.1	30.8
		4.2	8.8			Intangibles (net)	3.9	1.9
		4.9	3.7			All Other Non-Current	5.6	5.6
		100.0	100.0			Total	100.0	100.0
						LIABILITIES		
		7.4	10.2			Notes Payable-Short Term	11.6	3.6
		9.4	3.5			Cur. Mat.-L.T.D.	3.4	5.0
		9.0	8.0			Trade Payables	12.0	12.1
		.0	.0			Income Taxes Payable	.1	.2
		9.4	3.1			All Other Current	10.7	7.0
		35.3	24.7			Total Current	37.9	27.9
		12.2	18.1			Long-Term Debt	18.3	22.3
		.3	1.4			Deferred Taxes	.7	.7
		7.5	.6			All Other Non-Current	9.6	8.3
		44.7	55.1			Net Worth	33.4	40.8
		100.0	100.0			Total Liabilties & Net Worth	100.0	100.0
						INCOME DATA		
		100.0	100.0			Net Sales	100.0	100.0
		28.5	21.3			Gross Profit	26.9	26.9
		22.4	16.0			Operating Expenses	27.6	20.6
		6.1	5.2			Operating Profit	-.7	6.3
		.7	.9			All Other Expenses (net)	1.2	1.7
		5.4	4.3			Profit Before Taxes	-2.0	4.6
						RATIOS		
		2.5	4.1				4.1	3.6
		1.8	2.2			Current	2.0	2.5
		1.3	1.1				1.2	1.6
		1.3	2.4				1.8	1.7
		.8	.9			Quick	1.0	1.3
		.6	.4				.5	.7
		27 13.3	**35** 10.5				**35** 10.3	**40** 9.1
		38 9.5	**42** 8.7			Sales/Receivables	**47** 7.8	**52** 7.0
		52 7.0	**50** 7.3				**53** 6.9	**62** 5.9
		56 6.5	**56** 6.5				**57** 6.4	**82** 4.4
		65 5.6	**73** 5.0			Cost of Sales/Inventory	**98** 3.7	**96** 3.8
		126 2.9	**104** 3.5				**124** 2.9	**119** 3.1
		5 73.1	**14** 26.6				**11** 31.8	**17** 21.0
		18 20.5	**30** 12.1			Cost of Sales/Payables	**25** 14.7	**31** 11.6
		28 12.9	**38** 9.5				**54** 6.8	**47** 7.7
		5.1	3.8				2.9	3.0
		8.9	5.6			Sales/Working Capital	4.9	4.4
		16.2	NM				32.0	7.2
		16.8					5.4	9.0
		9.1				EBIT/Interest	(29) 1.2	(34) 3.3
		3.2					-1.7	1.1
							3.5	19.9
						Net Profit + Depr., Dep., Amort./Cur. Mat. L/T/D	(11) 1.0	(11) 2.9
							-1.4	1.6
		.4	.4				.4	.3
		.7	.9			Fixed/Worth	.9	.8
		1.5	1.9				2.6	1.8
		.8	.4				.9	.9
		1.3	1.3			Debt/Worth	2.3	1.7
		2.7	2.8				4.1	3.3
		48.9					15.9	37.3
		(13) 25.2				% Profit Before Taxes/Tangible Net Worth	(27) .0	12.5
		13.7					-35.7	1.3
		18.0	16.1				9.5	12.2
		8.5	5.7			% Profit Before Taxes/Total Assets	.1	5.5
		5.9	-.3				-9.1	.5
		16.6	24.7				22.6	15.4
		7.4	3.6			Sales/Net Fixed Assets	6.8	5.2
		3.6	1.1				2.1	2.3
		2.3	1.5				2.1	2.1
		2.1	.9			Sales/Total Assets	1.5	1.5
		1.5	.7				1.0	1.1
		1.6	1.0				1.6	1.9
		(13) 2.5	3.6			% Depr., Dep., Amort./Sales	(29) 3.2	(33) 3.1
		4.0	8.9				5.3	6.6
						% Officers', Directors' Owners' Comp/Sales		
	8676M	130281M	304849M	251995M	637645M	Net Sales ($)	1021026M	1120241M
	4581M	68314M	257916M	120451M	795091M	Total Assets ($)	752441M	860232M

M = $ thousand MM = $ million

See Pages 9 through 22 for Explanation of Ratios and Data

Comparative Historical Data / Current Data Sorted by Sales

4/1/11-3/31/12 ALL	4/1/12-3/31/13 ALL	4/1/13-3/31/14 ALL		0-1MM	1-3MM	3-5MM	5-10MM	10-25MM	25MM & OVER
			Type of Statement						
9	6	4	Unqualified					2	2
13	7	10	Reviewed			1	4	4	1
5	2	2	Compiled		1			1	
4	2	1	Tax Returns		1				
17	15	17	Other		1	1	2	4	9
					6 (4/1-9/30/13)		28 (10/1/13-3/31/14)		
48	32	34	**NUMBER OF STATEMENTS**		3	2	6	11	12
%	%	%	**ASSETS**	%	%	%	%	%	%
9.1	9.5	8.5	Cash & Equivalents	DATA NOT AVAILABLE				12.7	3.6
22.1	24.0	19.6	Trade Receivables (net)					19.6	17.8
27.4	27.5	24.2	Inventory					27.5	26.7
1.8	2.1	2.2	All Other Current					4.0	1.9
60.5	63.2	54.4	Total Current					63.8	50.1
32.1	27.6	29.7	Fixed Assets (net)					32.1	20.8
3.6	5.9	9.4	Intangibles (net)					.3	21.3
3.9	3.4	6.5	All Other Non-Current					3.8	7.9
100.0	100.0	100.0	Total					100.0	100.0
			LIABILITIES						
6.1	6.5	6.7	Notes Payable-Short Term					6.4	5.4
4.1	3.8	5.4	Cur. Mat.-L.T.D.					7.0	1.5
9.6	9.9	8.8	Trade Payables					6.9	11.6
.0	.4	.0	Income Taxes Payable					.0	.1
9.3	11.4	7.9	All Other Current					5.9	9.0
29.1	32.0	28.9	Total Current					26.1	27.5
19.0	20.3	15.8	Long-Term Debt					9.1	20.2
1.0	1.0	.7	Deferred Taxes					.4	1.7
5.0	3.5	8.5	All Other Non-Current					4.2	7.5
45.9	43.3	46.1	Net Worth					60.2	43.1
100.0	100.0	100.0	Total Liabilties & Net Worth					100.0	100.0
			INCOME DATA						
100.0	100.0	100.0	Net Sales					100.0	100.0
30.5	27.4	28.2	Gross Profit					20.9	26.9
24.3	21.3	21.8	Operating Expenses					15.5	18.7
6.1	6.1	6.4	Operating Profit					5.5	8.3
1.1	.4	3.0	All Other Expenses (net)					-.1	7.8
5.1	5.7	3.3	Profit Before Taxes					5.6	.4
			RATIOS						
4.0	2.9	3.7						5.2	3.5
2.0	1.8	2.1	Current					2.4	2.4
1.4	1.4	1.4						1.7	1.5
1.9	1.6	2.0						3.1	2.0
.9	1.0	1.0	Quick					1.2	1.1
.6	.7	.6						.6	.7
37 9.8	**35** 10.3	**35** 10.5						**31** 11.8	**42** 8.7
47 7.7	**44** 8.3	**43** 8.5	Sales/Receivables					**36** 10.0	**52** 7.0
66 5.5	**63** 5.8	**53** 6.9						**52** 7.0	**72** 5.1
55 6.6	**49** 7.5	**52** 7.0						**56** 6.5	**65** 5.6
91 4.0	**72** 5.1	**69** 5.3	Cost of Sales/Inventory					**76** 4.8	**79** 4.6
130 2.8	**111** 3.3	**107** 3.4						**122** 3.0	**104** 3.5
15 24.5	**9** 41.6	**8** 45.3						**5** 71.2	**27** 13.5
30 12.2	**23** 15.6	**26** 14.2	Cost of Sales/Payables					**13** 27.9	**35** 10.5
43 8.5	**39** 9.3	**37** 9.9						**23** 15.9	**49** 7.5
3.2	4.5	4.0						2.5	4.2
5.6	6.9	6.0	Sales/Working Capital					5.2	5.6
9.6	9.3	11.3						6.9	7.7
12.4	20.0	16.8						11.4	28.0
(46) 6.2	(30) 8.3	(33) 6.4	EBIT/Interest					(10) 10.2	5.0
1.4	2.2	1.6						3.1	2.0
10.9	4.2								
(16) 3.2	(12) 2.1		Net Profit + Depr., Dep., Amort./Cur. Mat. L/T/D						
1.2	1.0								
.4	.2	.4						.3	.4
.8	.8	.8	Fixed/Worth					.5	.9
1.3	1.8	1.6						.9	-25.1
.9	.9	.7						.4	1.0
1.6	1.6	1.6	Debt/Worth					.8	2.1
2.5	2.8	3.8						1.0	-49.3
44.2	47.3	38.5						30.9	
(46) 25.4	(29) 24.5	(28) 19.6	% Profit Before Taxes/Tangible Net Worth					22.2	
4.2	12.4	5.0						16.2	
17.1	16.7	15.5						16.4	11.2
9.4	10.6	8.2	% Profit Before Taxes/Total Assets					11.6	4.4
2.3	4.2	1.3						8.2	1.1
10.8	29.0	16.4						20.6	18.2
4.5	7.4	7.4	Sales/Net Fixed Assets					7.4	9.1
2.5	3.0	2.5						2.6	2.9
1.8	2.6	2.2						2.2	1.9
1.5	1.8	1.6	Sales/Total Assets					1.6	1.1
1.3	1.2	.8						.9	.6
1.7	1.2	1.3						1.2	1.1
(45) 3.9	(27) 2.6	(31) 2.5	% Depr., Dep., Amort./Sales					3.0	(11) 1.4
5.6	4.7	5.5						5.7	2.7
1.8	1.7								
(15) 4.9	(10) 3.5		% Officers', Directors' Owners' Comp/Sales						
7.8	7.8								
1607148M	**1146580M**	**1333446M**	Net Sales ($)		**5633M**	**8240M**	**38786M**	**163056M**	**1117731M**
1183052M	**700598M**	**1246353M**	Total Assets ($)		**5290M**	**5553M**	**26201M**	**136007M**	**1073302M**

M = $ thousand MM = $ million

See Pages 9 through 22 for Explanation of Ratios and Data

Current Data Sorted by Assets							Comparative Historical Data	
						Type of Statement		
		2	6	2	1	Unqualified	12	10
	1	10	3			Reviewed	7	15
	2	1				Compiled	2	6
						Tax Returns	2	1
	2	6	12			Other	19	19
10 (4/1-9/30/13)		38 (10/1/13-3/31/14)					4/1/09-3/31/10 ALL	4/1/10-3/31/11 ALL
0-500M	500M-2MM	2-10MM	10-50MM	50-100MM	100-250MM			
	5	19	21	2	1	**NUMBER OF STATEMENTS**	42	51
%	%	%	%	%	%	**ASSETS**	%	%
DATA NOT AVAILABLE		4.9	9.6			Cash & Equivalents	7.5	8.8
		24.2	18.4			Trade Receivables (net)	21.3	26.2
		37.9	36.4			Inventory	33.9	33.6
		1.3	3.9			All Other Current	4.2	1.3
		68.3	68.3			Total Current	66.9	69.9
		27.0	22.6			Fixed Assets (net)	21.1	21.2
		2.4	3.7			Intangibles (net)	5.7	1.9
		2.4	5.4			All Other Non-Current	6.3	6.9
		100.0	100.0			Total	100.0	100.0
						LIABILITIES		
		9.6	8.3			Notes Payable-Short Term	13.0	6.6
		3.8	2.6			Cur. Mat.-L.T.D.	4.1	5.0
		13.4	9.0			Trade Payables	9.6	11.7
		.3	.1			Income Taxes Payable	.2	.4
		5.2	17.5			All Other Current	13.0	12.4
		32.2	37.5			Total Current	39.8	36.0
		11.4	13.2			Long-Term Debt	12.1	12.5
		1.1	.9			Deferred Taxes	1.1	.9
		4.5	.7			All Other Non-Current	10.3	4.9
		50.7	47.6			Net Worth	36.6	45.6
		100.0	100.0			Total Liabilties & Net Worth	100.0	100.0
						INCOME DATA		
		100.0	100.0			Net Sales	100.0	100.0
		34.4	26.4			Gross Profit	33.7	33.9
		24.3	19.7			Operating Expenses	29.1	25.3
		10.1	6.7			Operating Profit	4.6	8.6
		1.0	-.3			All Other Expenses (net)	1.5	.7
		9.1	7.0			Profit Before Taxes	3.1	7.8
						RATIOS		
		2.7	2.5				3.2	3.3
		2.5	1.8			Current	1.9	2.0
		1.4	1.3				1.3	1.5
		1.7	1.4				1.5	2.1
		.9	.8			Quick	.8	1.0
		.5	.4				.4	.6
		31 11.8	**24** 15.1				**34** 10.8	**37** 9.9
		42 8.6	**41** 8.8			Sales/Receivables	**47** 7.8	**53** 6.9
		62 5.9	**49** 7.5				**69** 5.3	**66** 5.5
		62 5.9	**68** 5.4				**52** 7.0	**62** 5.9
		91 4.0	**111** 3.3			Cost of Sales/Inventory	**119** 3.1	**92** 4.0
		243 1.5	**146** 2.5				**247** 1.5	**163** 2.2
		15 24.0	**12** 31.2				**21** 17.4	**23** 15.7
		25 14.4	**28** 13.1			Cost of Sales/Payables	**29** 12.7	**29** 12.5
		74 4.9	**38** 9.5				**41** 8.9	**49** 7.5
		3.3	2.9				2.6	3.0
		4.3	6.3			Sales/Working Capital	5.0	4.5
		12.5	14.2				13.5	12.6
		41.2	21.0				14.3	23.0
		(18) 7.8	(16) 10.9			EBIT/Interest	(35) 3.0	(44) 8.4
		3.9	3.0				-.6	3.3
							6.3	4.6
						Net Profit + Depr., Dep., Amort./Cur. Mat. L/T/D	(12) 3.1	(17) 3.2
							.8	2.2
		.3	.2				.2	.2
		.5	.5			Fixed/Worth	.5	.5
		.8	1.0				1.0	.7
		.5	.8				.6	.6
		.9	1.3			Debt/Worth	1.3	1.1
		2.1	2.1				3.3	2.1
		66.6	37.5				38.3	37.2
		(18) 22.6	(20) 24.5			% Profit Before Taxes/Tangible Net Worth	(37) 14.0	(49) 23.4
		13.0	9.4				-.4	12.0
		22.6	15.2				16.9	19.1
		8.3	11.5			% Profit Before Taxes/Total Assets	5.6	10.0
		3.6	3.5				-4.5	5.3
		19.2	14.5				24.0	21.7
		8.5	8.8			Sales/Net Fixed Assets	6.9	9.8
		3.3	4.4				3.6	3.9
		2.5	2.3				2.0	2.1
		1.9	1.8			Sales/Total Assets	1.3	1.7
		1.2	1.1				.9	1.3
		1.3	1.0				1.6	1.0
		(18) 3.4	(19) 1.5			% Depr., Dep., Amort./Sales	(34) 2.9	(47) 2.0
		5.7	2.9				5.7	4.5
								1.3
						% Officers', Directors' Owners' Comp/Sales		(11) 3.0
								6.4
	15550M	215746M	744332M	299074M	143007M	Net Sales ($)	1153264M	1240847M
	4540M	118928M	423077M	162677M	189932M	Total Assets ($)	1106907M	924059M

M = $ thousand MM = $ million

See Pages 9 through 22 for Explanation of Ratios and Data

Comparative Historical Data / Current Data Sorted by Sales

4/1/11-3/31/12 ALL	4/1/12-3/31/13 ALL	4/1/13-3/31/14 ALL	Type of Statement	0-1MM	1-3MM	3-5MM	5-10MM	10-25MM	25MM & OVER
13	4	11	Unqualified					5	6
20	12	14	Reviewed			1	6	4	3
5		3	Compiled		1	1		1	
5	4		Tax Returns						
20	19	20	Other	1	1	1	5	5	7
				10 (4/1-9/30/13)			38 (10/1/13-3/31/14)		
63	39	48	NUMBER OF STATEMENTS	1	2	3	11	15	16
%	%	%	**ASSETS**	%	%	%	%	%	%
5.8	6.6	7.1	Cash & Equivalents				11.2	7.4	5.2
24.7	22.6	21.1	Trade Receivables (net)				18.6	22.8	22.4
37.1	36.1	38.2	Inventory				31.4	36.4	37.6
2.0	1.8	2.3	All Other Current				.8	4.9	1.8
69.5	67.1	68.7	Total Current				62.0	71.4	67.1
21.1	26.5	24.2	Fixed Assets (net)				29.7	22.1	24.1
4.8	1.7	3.1	Intangibles (net)				3.6	3.2	3.7
4.6	4.8	4.0	All Other Non-Current				4.8	3.3	5.1
100.0	100.0	100.0	Total				100.0	100.0	100.0
			LIABILITIES						
10.9	9.1	8.4	Notes Payable-Short Term				4.9	8.2	12.1
2.9	2.9	4.1	Cur. Mat.-L.T.D.				7.5	2.1	3.3
16.5	14.2	12.4	Trade Payables				13.0	12.0	11.7
.4	.3	.2	Income Taxes Payable				.4	.2	.1
12.8	9.5	17.3	All Other Current				34.9	10.7	15.7
43.4	36.1	42.4	Total Current				60.7	33.2	43.0
16.2	19.5	17.1	Long-Term Debt				29.1	9.0	13.5
.9	.7	.9	Deferred Taxes				.8	1.3	.3
3.6	6.0	3.6	All Other Non-Current				.9	1.6	1.9
35.9	37.7	36.0	Net Worth				8.5	54.8	41.3
100.0	100.0	100.0	Total Liabilties & Net Worth				100.0	100.0	100.0
			INCOME DATA						
100.0	100.0	100.0	Net Sales				100.0	100.0	100.0
33.4	34.3	30.8	Gross Profit				36.3	27.8	26.8
26.9	27.1	23.9	Operating Expenses				30.6	16.6	21.0
6.5	7.1	6.9	Operating Profit				5.7	11.2	5.8
.9	.8	.3	All Other Expenses (net)				-.9	.4	.4
5.6	6.3	6.6	Profit Before Taxes				6.6	10.8	5.3
			RATIOS						
2.4	3.1	2.6					5.7	2.7	2.5
1.9	2.0	2.1	Current				2.2	2.4	1.6
1.3	1.3	1.4					1.4	1.4	1.2
1.2	1.4	1.7					2.0	1.7	.9
.7	.9	.8	Quick				.9	.8	.7
.4	.5	.5					.5	.5	.5
34 10.8	**27** 13.3	**28** 13.1					**26** 14.2	**31** 11.8	**26** 13.9
44 8.3	**41** 9.0	**42** 8.7	Sales/Receivables				**37** 9.9	**39** 9.4	**45** 8.2
56 6.5	**47** 7.8	**51** 7.2					**48** 7.6	**51** 7.2	**51** 7.2
54 6.8	**65** 5.6	**68** 5.4					**62** 5.9	**78** 4.7	**64** 5.7
101 3.6	**87** 4.2	**101** 3.6	Cost of Sales/Inventory				**122** 3.0	**99** 3.7	**83** 4.4
166 2.2	**140** 2.6	**182** 2.0					**281** 1.3	**146** 2.5	**126** 2.9
22 16.3	**19** 19.4	**17** 21.4					**15** 24.0	**10** 38.4	**22** 16.7
38 9.6	**28** 13.2	**28** 13.1	Cost of Sales/Payables				**31** 11.9	**23** 15.9	**28** 12.9
51 7.1	**51** 7.2	**41** 9.0					**61** 6.0	**40** 9.1	**36** 10.0
4.0	4.2	3.0					1.6	3.0	5.3
5.9	5.5	5.4	Sales/Working Capital				4.3	4.0	11.2
14.0	10.8	13.6					14.4	9.4	16.4
27.1	20.3	21.4						65.3	20.1
(56) 9.8	(38) 8.6	(41) 9.8	EBIT/Interest					(12) 15.8	(14) 10.9
3.7	3.0	3.2						4.6	3.5
23.1		5.2							
(15) 4.6		(14) 2.6	Net Profit + Depr., Dep., Amort./Cur. Mat. L/T/D						
2.4		1.5							
.2	.2	.3					.3	.2	.3
.5	.5	.5	Fixed/Worth				.5	.3	.6
1.0	1.8	.9					.8	.7	1.0
.6	.6	.7					.1	.4	.9
1.4	1.2	1.2	Debt/Worth				1.0	.9	1.6
3.7	3.8	2.6					2.2	1.8	2.5
55.3	60.5	42.4					66.6	42.1	38.0
(56) 28.9	(35) 25.0	(45) 24.8	% Profit Before Taxes/Tangible Net Worth				(10) 16.5	28.6	(15) 24.8
19.0	8.8	9.8					4.6	15.2	9.1
18.7	20.7	17.0					17.4	22.6	14.4
10.9	10.2	8.1	% Profit Before Taxes/Total Assets				7.5	12.5	10.0
4.1	4.1	3.7					1.3	5.7	4.4
32.8	33.5	16.6					15.3	20.2	15.1
9.0	6.5	9.4	Sales/Net Fixed Assets				8.8	12.1	8.4
5.3	4.0	4.3					3.1	4.2	4.5
2.5	2.7	2.5					3.0	2.2	2.5
1.9	1.9	1.8	Sales/Total Assets				1.2	1.7	1.9
1.4	1.5	1.1					.9	1.5	1.5
.8	.9	1.2					1.2	1.1	1.0
(53) 2.1	(33) 2.1	(43) 1.7	% Depr., Dep., Amort./Sales				(10) 1.8	(14) 1.9	(14) 1.7
4.2	4.5	4.3					6.4	4.2	3.8
1.5	.8	.5							
(12) 3.7	(14) 2.0	(11) 1.6	% Officers', Directors' Owners' Comp/Sales						
6.4	7.0	5.2							
1569027M	**792180M**	**1417709M**	Net Sales ($)	**270M**	**4261M**	**13485M**	**82601M**	**264651M**	**1052441M**
1090915M	**485552M**	**899154M**	Total Assets ($)	**580M**	**1607M**	**7947M**	**73178M**	**175371M**	**640471M**

M = $ thousand MM = $ million

See Pages 9 through 22 for Explanation of Ratios and Data

Current Data Sorted by Assets							Comparative Historical Data	
						Type of Statement		
	1	2	11	6	2	Unqualified	26	24
	1	7	7	2		Reviewed	25	34
	4	8	2			Compiled	14	12
1	4	3	1			Tax Returns	14	20
3	5	12	17	1	4	Other	38	40
	17 (4/1-9/30/13)		87 (10/1/13-3/31/14)				4/1/09-3/31/10	4/1/10-3/31/11
0-500M	500M-2MM	2-10MM	10-50MM	50-100MM	100-250MM		ALL	ALL
4	15	32	38	9	6	NUMBER OF STATEMENTS	117	130
%	%	%	%	%	%	**ASSETS**	%	%
	11.3	11.2	10.2			Cash & Equivalents	10.2	10.6
	32.6	30.5	23.9			Trade Receivables (net)	25.5	25.6
	31.9	31.7	27.7			Inventory	31.8	31.6
	1.1	2.9	2.7			All Other Current	3.4	3.8
	76.9	76.3	64.5			Total Current	70.9	71.5
	17.4	13.8	24.8			Fixed Assets (net)	20.1	20.3
	4.8	2.0	5.7			Intangibles (net)	3.5	2.9
	.9	7.9	4.9			All Other Non-Current	5.5	5.3
	100.0	100.0	100.0			Total	100.0	100.0
						LIABILITIES		
	14.3	8.9	5.2			Notes Payable-Short Term	8.1	5.6
	2.0	1.8	2.2			Cur. Mat.-L.T.D.	3.9	2.6
	17.9	17.2	8.0			Trade Payables	13.3	13.9
	1.9	.4	.4			Income Taxes Payable	.4	.3
	7.1	10.9	12.0			All Other Current	14.7	13.3
	43.3	39.1	27.7			Total Current	40.4	35.7
	7.7	9.8	12.8			Long-Term Debt	11.6	11.5
	.1	1.0	1.4			Deferred Taxes	.9	.6
	11.2	2.9	5.0			All Other Non-Current	3.0	5.3
	37.6	47.2	53.1			Net Worth	44.2	46.8
	100.0	100.0	100.0			Total Liabilties & Net Worth	100.0	100.0
						INCOME DATA		
	100.0	100.0	100.0			Net Sales	100.0	100.0
	38.8	35.2	36.7			Gross Profit	34.2	34.7
	34.0	27.3	26.4			Operating Expenses	29.2	27.3
	4.8	7.9	10.3			Operating Profit	5.1	7.3
	.5	1.1	.7			All Other Expenses (net)	1.0	.3
	4.3	6.9	9.6			Profit Before Taxes	4.1	7.1
						RATIOS		
	4.3	3.0	5.0				4.0	3.8
	1.6	1.9	3.0			Current	2.0	2.1
	1.4	1.4	1.5				1.3	1.4
	2.4	1.8	3.6				2.0	2.0
	1.0	1.0	1.2			Quick	1.0	1.0
	.7	.7	.7				.6	.6
	32 11.3	**29** 12.6	**41** 9.0				**33** 11.2	**35** 10.5
	41 9.0	**51** 7.1	**54** 6.7			Sales/Receivables	**47** 7.7	**47** 7.7
	55 6.6	**70** 5.2	**66** 5.5				**65** 5.6	**66** 5.6
	32 11.3	**41** 8.8	**63** 5.8				**47** 7.7	**55** 6.6
	59 6.2	**78** 4.7	**111** 3.3			Cost of Sales/Inventory	**87** 4.2	**91** 4.0
	89 4.1	**152** 2.4	**152** 2.4				**146** 2.5	**145** 2.5
	7 49.7	**21** 17.4	**14** 26.3				**17** 21.7	**17** 21.4
	33 11.1	**34** 10.6	**26** 13.9			Cost of Sales/Payables	**28** 12.9	**33** 11.1
	46 7.9	**68** 5.4	**35** 10.3				**47** 7.8	**51** 7.2
	5.7	3.2	2.9				3.0	3.2
	8.0	5.7	3.8			Sales/Working Capital	5.9	5.4
	14.0	10.1	8.6				13.5	11.8
	21.8	38.4	32.7				26.6	31.8
	(13) 8.0	(27) 10.0	(29) 9.4			EBIT/Interest	(108) 5.8	(116) 8.0
	3.9	2.4	4.4				1.0	2.8
		7.3	8.7				9.4	16.9
		(11) 3.0	(15) 3.7			Net Profit + Depr., Dep., Amort./Cur. Mat. L/T/D	(44) 2.8	(38) 5.1
		.8	2.5				.9	1.4
	.2	.1	.3				.2	.2
	.3	.3	.5			Fixed/Worth	.4	.3
	1.1	.6	1.4				1.0	.9
	.5	.6	.4				.4	.4
	1.7	1.4	.8			Debt/Worth	1.4	1.1
	4.3	2.1	3.4				2.5	2.1
	66.3	45.7	40.3				34.3	34.5
	(14) 42.4	25.5	(36) 27.6			% Profit Before Taxes/Tangible Net Worth	(106) 15.7	(120) 18.2
	22.8	10.4	13.5				3.6	6.2
	21.6	21.6	19.1				15.3	19.6
	16.6	9.8	13.7			% Profit Before Taxes/Total Assets	7.0	10.0
	3.9	4.1	5.5				.0	2.3
	43.2	51.5	9.8				25.2	25.9
	22.5	21.9	6.6			Sales/Net Fixed Assets	13.0	11.7
	7.6	7.5	3.8				5.6	6.2
	3.8	2.7	1.8				2.5	2.4
	2.8	1.8	1.6			Sales/Total Assets	1.8	1.9
	2.3	1.6	1.2				1.3	1.4
		.7	.9				.8	.9
		(27) 1.0	(32) 1.8			% Depr., Dep., Amort./Sales	(98) 1.6	(115) 1.7
		1.5	3.3				2.9	2.7
	2.7	1.7					1.9	.8
	(10) 4.5	(12) 3.4				% Officers', Directors' Owners' Comp/Sales	(36) 4.1	(35) 2.6
	6.1	6.8					8.4	6.0
4612M	47396M	339611M	1226147M	1037718M	834197M	Net Sales ($)	3632628M	3897707M
1228M	15965M	169950M	806237M	640867M	882621M	Total Assets ($)	2475141M	2298859M

M = $ thousand MM = $ million

See Pages 9 through 22 for Explanation of Ratios and Data

Comparative Historical Data				Current Data Sorted by Sales					
			Type of Statement						
29	16	22	Unqualified			1	1	5	15
21	17	17	Reviewed				2	9	6
10	18	14	Compiled		2	3	6	1	2
20	17	9	Tax Returns		3	3	1	2	
45	43	42	Other	2	4	4	4	12	16
4/1/11-3/31/12 ALL	**4/1/12-3/31/13 ALL**	**4/1/13-3/31/14 ALL**		**17 (4/1-9/30/13)**			**87 (10/1/13-3/31/14)**		
				0-1MM	**1-3MM**	**3-5MM**	**5-10MM**	**10-25MM**	**25MM & OVER**
125	111	104	**NUMBER OF STATEMENTS**	2	9	11	14	29	39
%	%	%	**ASSETS**	%	%	%	%	%	%
9.9	10.3	11.0	Cash & Equivalents			14.7	10.2	10.6	10.4
28.0	25.2	26.6	Trade Receivables (net)			27.2	33.0	27.2	24.2
32.5	34.3	29.3	Inventory			33.6	24.3	31.0	27.1
2.8	2.4	2.4	All Other Current			2.4	3.5	2.6	2.6
73.3	72.1	69.3	Total Current			77.9	71.1	71.3	64.3
16.5	18.7	19.5	Fixed Assets (net)			14.8	18.6	17.8	23.7
4.7	3.8	5.2	Intangibles (net)			5.7	1.8	4.8	5.2
5.5	5.3	6.0	All Other Non-Current			1.6	8.5	6.1	6.9
100.0	100.0	100.0	Total			100.0	100.0	100.0	100.0
			LIABILITIES						
8.2	7.6	7.7	Notes Payable-Short Term			6.6	9.7	7.4	4.7
2.5	1.7	2.3	Cur. Mat.-L.T.D.			1.1	1.7	2.5	2.1
17.1	12.7	12.5	Trade Payables			16.2	16.7	13.9	8.9
.4	.3	.6	Income Taxes Payable			.1	.8	.4	.3
13.1	12.0	10.2	All Other Current			12.2	6.6	11.0	12.0
41.3	34.3	33.3	Total Current			36.2	35.4	35.2	28.1
8.5	10.4	10.8	Long-Term Debt			11.5	10.4	9.9	11.6
.6	.7	1.1	Deferred Taxes			.0	1.4	1.2	1.6
4.4	6.0	5.8	All Other Non-Current			5.1	3.4	2.9	5.8
45.2	48.5	49.0	Net Worth			47.2	49.5	50.8	52.9
100.0	100.0	100.0	Total Liabilties & Net Worth			100.0	100.0	100.0	100.0
			INCOME DATA						
100.0	100.0	100.0	Net Sales			100.0	100.0	100.0	100.0
33.8	35.8	35.7	Gross Profit			38.9	34.4	37.5	34.0
27.0	26.9	26.7	Operating Expenses			32.2	29.2	27.4	23.3
6.8	9.0	9.0	Operating Profit			6.7	5.1	10.1	10.7
.6	.3	.6	All Other Expenses (net)			.3	.9	1.2	.3
6.2	8.7	8.4	Profit Before Taxes			6.5	4.2	8.9	10.5
			RATIOS						
3.2	4.3	4.4				4.5	4.2	3.4	4.6
1.9	2.4	2.4	Current			2.5	2.4	2.0	2.7
1.3	1.4	1.4				1.6	1.4	1.5	1.4
1.7	2.2	2.4				2.4	2.1	2.5	3.2
.9	1.1	1.0	Quick			1.3	1.3	.9	1.2
.6	.6	.7				.7	.8	.7	.8
37 9.8	**33** 11.1	**36** 10.1				**31** 11.6	**29** 12.4	**39** 9.4	**39** 9.3
47 7.8	**46** 8.0	**51** 7.2	Sales/Receivables			**36** 10.2	**54** 6.8	**54** 6.7	**54** 6.8
62 5.9	**62** 5.9	**66** 5.5				**56** 6.5	**72** 5.1	**69** 5.3	**68** 5.4
54 6.8	**57** 6.4	**52** 7.0				**49** 7.5	**22** 16.7	**52** 7.0	**56** 6.5
85 4.3	**114** 3.2	**87** 4.2	Cost of Sales/Inventory			**79** 4.6	**64** 5.7	**111** 3.3	**85** 4.3
130 2.8	**159** 2.3	**140** 2.6				**114** 3.2	**146** 2.5	**159** 2.3	**140** 2.6
21 17.5	**15** 23.9	**16** 23.4				**7** 49.7	**29** 12.8	**15** 24.6	**15** 25.1
36 10.0	**26** 13.9	**29** 12.7	Cost of Sales/Payables			**37** 9.9	**34** 10.6	**28** 13.1	**28** 13.1
54 6.8	**48** 7.6	**47** 7.7				**76** 4.8	**49** 7.4	**70** 5.2	**37** 9.9
3.8	2.7	3.0				3.1	4.0	2.7	2.8
6.0	4.6	5.3	Sales/Working Capital			5.7	5.7	5.1	4.3
13.2	9.9	11.3				10.2	12.3	9.6	9.8
29.5	44.7	30.6					38.4	49.3	33.2
(103) 10.9	(94) 14.8	(82) 9.4	EBIT/Interest				(11) 4.1	(26) 10.1	(28) 10.1
2.4	4.2	4.1					2.1	6.8	4.5
8.1	13.9	6.3						6.3	6.1
(39) 4.4	(32) 5.5	(35) 3.3	Net Profit + Depr., Dep., Amort./Cur. Mat. L/T/D					(12) 3.4	(16) 3.8
1.8	2.7	1.8						1.7	1.9
.1	.1	.2				.1	.1	.2	.2
.3	.4	.4	Fixed/Worth			.2	.3	.4	.4
.6	.8	.9				.5	.8	.7	1.5
.5	.4	.5				.4	.4	.5	.4
1.2	1.2	1.3	Debt/Worth			1.4	1.3	1.0	1.2
3.2	3.1	2.6				4.9	2.4	2.0	3.3
47.3	42.9	46.8				72.0	38.1	45.7	40.4
(113) 25.0	(102) 24.9	(99) 29.2	% Profit Before Taxes/Tangible Net Worth			44.4	15.4	(28) 27.2	(37) 30.0
11.5	12.6	12.7				10.0	5.3	12.5	14.4
19.2	20.0	21.3				35.2	18.0	21.4	21.3
10.4	11.5	12.3	% Profit Before Taxes/Total Assets			18.3	5.8	14.3	13.7
5.2	3.9	4.2				4.1	2.4	5.3	5.3
50.6	47.3	26.4				61.0	57.3	25.5	11.3
15.5	11.9	9.5	Sales/Net Fixed Assets			22.1	29.1	13.9	7.2
6.5	5.8	5.8				7.4	4.8	4.9	4.9
2.6	2.5	2.4				3.8	2.9	2.5	1.8
2.0	1.7	1.8	Sales/Total Assets			2.6	1.8	1.7	1.7
1.5	1.2	1.3				1.3	1.6	1.2	1.2
.7	.7	.8					.5	.9	.8
(98) 1.5	(88) 1.6	(81) 1.4	% Depr., Dep., Amort./Sales				(11) 1.1	(24) 1.2	(33) 1.8
3.1	2.8	2.8					1.3	3.2	2.6
1.8	1.1	1.9							
(38) 3.3	(31) 4.5	(32) 3.9	% Officers', Directors' Owners' Comp/Sales						
6.9	8.3	6.5							
3482747M	**3238555M**	**3489681M**	Net Sales ($)	**1007M**	**18163M**	**42364M**	**106579M**	**493702M**	**2827866M**
2071563M	**2356374M**	**2516868M**	Total Assets ($)	**536M**	**9484M**	**25640M**	**59787M**	**345429M**	**2075992M**

M = $ thousand MM = $ million

See Pages 9 through 22 for Explanation of Ratios and Data

Current Data Sorted by Assets | **Comparative Historical Data**

0-500M	500M-2MM	2-10MM	10-50MM	50-100MM	100-250MM	**Type of Statement**	4/1/09-3/31/10 ALL	4/1/10-3/31/11 ALL
			6	3	1	Unqualified	4	6
	2	4	1	1		Reviewed	5	12
		3				Compiled	2	
	1	2				Tax Returns	2	4
1	1	5	6		1	Other	18	13
	9 (4/1-9/30/13)		29 (10/1/13-3/31/14)					
1	4	14	13	4	2	**NUMBER OF STATEMENTS**	31	35
%	%	%	%	%	%	**ASSETS**	%	%
		8.8	6.0			Cash & Equivalents	9.7	10.8
		25.4	26.0			Trade Receivables (net)	22.9	24.4
		32.3	29.4			Inventory	29.7	27.4
		3.3	10.1			All Other Current	4.8	2.4
		69.8	71.5			Total Current	67.2	65.0
		25.1	17.2			Fixed Assets (net)	22.3	18.4
		2.5	6.0			Intangibles (net)	4.3	8.9
		2.6	5.3			All Other Non-Current	6.2	7.6
		100.0	100.0			Total	100.0	100.0
						LIABILITIES		
		10.0	13.8			Notes Payable-Short Term	11.4	10.3
		3.8	2.8			Cur. Mat.-L.T.D.	3.8	3.7
		16.1	11.5			Trade Payables	11.1	14.3
		.2	.5			Income Taxes Payable	.1	.1
		9.6	10.0			All Other Current	12.0	12.7
		39.9	38.6			Total Current	38.4	41.2
		19.3	13.0			Long-Term Debt	12.7	8.1
		1.3	1.1			Deferred Taxes	1.5	1.2
		1.0	8.5			All Other Non-Current	7.6	3.6
		38.6	38.9			Net Worth	39.8	46.0
		100.0	100.0			Total Liabilities & Net Worth	100.0	100.0
						INCOME DATA		
		100.0	100.0			Net Sales	100.0	100.0
		30.7	26.5			Gross Profit	35.0	36.4
		27.1	19.7			Operating Expenses	28.6	28.4
		3.6	6.9			Operating Profit	6.4	8.0
		.4	.5			All Other Expenses (net)	.6	3.0
		3.2	6.3			Profit Before Taxes	5.8	5.0
						RATIOS		
		3.9	2.7				3.4	2.7
		1.5	1.9			Current	2.2	1.6
		1.2	1.5				1.2	1.2
		1.8	1.5				1.7	1.5
		.7	.7			Quick	1.0	1.0
		.6	.7				.5	.6
		39 9.3	**36** 10.2				**35** 10.6	**30** 12.4
		43 8.4	**64** 5.7			Sales/Receivables	**46** 8.0	**46** 8.0
		47 7.7	**73** 5.0				**59** 6.2	**69** 5.3
		49 7.5	**40** 9.1				**62** 5.9	**50** 7.3
		66 5.5	**111** 3.3			Cost of Sales/Inventory	**92** 4.0	**100** 3.6
		118 3.1	**135** 2.7				**141** 2.6	**124** 2.9
		13 27.8	**19** 19.7				**20** 18.5	**18** 20.2
		27 13.3	**33** 11.1			Cost of Sales/Payables	**25** 14.4	**33** 11.0
		48 7.6	**48** 7.6				**49** 7.5	**60** 6.1
		3.8	3.5				3.1	3.3
		7.3	4.9			Sales/Working Capital	5.3	6.7
		26.8	7.4				26.0	16.6
		27.0	19.0				19.1	87.8
		(13) 5.1	(12) 7.8			EBIT/Interest	(27) 5.4	(32) 12.5
		2.1	5.5				3.1	2.1
						Net Profit + Depr., Dep., Amort./Cur. Mat. L/T/D		
		.1	.4				.2	.2
		.4	.5			Fixed/Worth	.4	.3
		1.0	.8				2.5	.8
		.4	1.0				.5	.6
		1.7	1.7			Debt/Worth	1.7	1.4
		3.4	3.3				3.2	3.2
		21.4	47.7				34.3	40.1
		(12) 9.0	(12) 22.8			% Profit Before Taxes/Tangible Net Worth	(27) 14.1	(31) 25.6
		1.4	11.5				4.9	12.2
		8.1	12.4				16.0	15.0
		5.7	10.1			% Profit Before Taxes/Total Assets	6.3	8.0
		.6	4.5				2.9	2.2
		34.0	21.3				31.3	43.0
		11.8	8.5			Sales/Net Fixed Assets	8.9	11.4
		4.8	6.0				4.0	7.3
		2.8	2.1				2.2	2.0
		1.9	1.5			Sales/Total Assets	1.7	1.7
		1.7	1.3				1.1	1.0
		.7	.8				1.1	.8
		1.0	(11) 1.6			% Depr., Dep., Amort./Sales	(24) 1.9	(29) 1.8
		2.2	2.5				3.4	3.1
							.8	1.4
						% Officers', Directors' Owners' Comp/Sales	(14) 2.1	(10) 2.7
							9.7	9.7
793M	15831M	134097M	690117M	390891M	96270M	Net Sales ($)	848497M	1285990M
288M	5362M	64881M	420902M	285957M	295955M	Total Assets ($)	707836M	1170167M

M = $ thousand MM = $ million

See Pages 9 through 22 for Explanation of Ratios and Data

Comparative Historical Data				Current Data Sorted by Sales					
			Type of Statement						
5	9	10	Unqualified						10
9	6	8	Reviewed			1	3	3	1
6	1	3	Compiled				2	1	
4	7	3	Tax Returns		1		1	1	
10	9	14	Other	1		2	3	1	7
				9 (4/1-9/30/13)		29 (10/1/13-3/31/14)			
4/1/11-3/31/12 ALL	4/1/12-3/31/13 ALL	4/1/13-3/31/14 ALL		0-1MM	1-3MM	3-5MM	5-10MM	10-25MM	25MM & OVER
34	32	38	**NUMBER OF STATEMENTS**	1	1	3	9	6	18
%	%	%	**ASSETS**	%	%	%	%	%	%
12.3	9.0	8.2	Cash & Equivalents						7.2
25.1	24.3	23.9	Trade Receivables (net)						25.2
31.9	28.4	29.4	Inventory						21.8
2.5	1.9	5.9	All Other Current						9.5
71.8	63.6	67.3	Total Current						63.6
16.8	21.4	20.8	Fixed Assets (net)						18.9
6.0	9.1	7.3	Intangibles (net)						12.7
5.3	5.9	4.6	All Other Non-Current						4.7
100.0	100.0	100.0	Total						100.0
			LIABILITIES						
10.9	6.5	11.0	Notes Payable-Short Term						12.1
2.6	3.7	3.0	Cur. Mat.-L.T.D.						2.6
16.8	12.0	14.2	Trade Payables						10.2
.1	.2	.4	Income Taxes Payable						.6
14.0	10.3	9.9	All Other Current						11.9
44.3	32.7	38.4	Total Current						37.4
11.0	18.7	14.4	Long-Term Debt						14.2
.3	1.1	1.4	Deferred Taxes						1.5
2.9	2.5	4.1	All Other Non-Current						7.2
41.5	45.0	41.7	Net Worth						39.7
100.0	100.0	100.0	Total Liabilties & Net Worth						100.0
			INCOME DATA						
100.0	100.0	100.0	Net Sales						100.0
33.0	36.7	32.1	Gross Profit						32.5
25.2	25.5	26.7	Operating Expenses						25.7
7.8	11.2	5.4	Operating Profit						6.9
1.1	1.2	.9	All Other Expenses (net)						1.6
6.6	10.0	4.5	Profit Before Taxes						5.3
			RATIOS						
2.3	3.4	3.0							2.3
1.8	2.0	1.6	Current						1.6
1.3	1.4	1.2							1.4
1.3	1.6	1.5							1.5
.8	1.0	.7	Quick						.8
.6	.5	.6							.6
27 13.5	36 10.2	35 10.5							46 8.0
46 8.0	49 7.5	47 7.8	Sales/Receivables						64 5.7
52 7.0	60 6.1	65 5.6							78 4.7
47 7.8	33 11.1	49 7.5							29 12.6
74 4.9	72 5.1	83 4.4	Cost of Sales/Inventory						76 4.8
126 2.9	122 3.0	118 3.1							118 3.1
20 18.7	17 21.6	19 18.9							22 16.5
36 10.2	29 12.8	34 10.7	Cost of Sales/Payables						37 9.8
53 6.9	59 6.2	50 7.3							49 7.5
3.4	3.3	3.8							4.0
7.9	6.6	5.5	Sales/Working Capital						5.4
12.5	10.7	24.0							8.6
35.3	30.2	22.7							15.8
(29) 11.8	(28) 13.4	(35) 6.2	EBIT/Interest						(17) 7.8
4.8	2.8	2.3							3.8
	74.5	9.8							
	(11) 11.8	(16) 3.5	Net Profit + Depr., Dep., Amort./Cur. Mat. L/T/D						
	5.2	1.7							
.1	.1	.3							.4
.3	.3	.5	Fixed/Worth						.5
.8	1.0	1.1							2.4
.7	.6	.8							1.2
1.2	1.3	1.6	Debt/Worth						1.8
5.4	3.0	4.0							69.5
53.4	46.2	36.9							49.9
(30) 27.8	(28) 35.6	(33) 11.4	% Profit Before Taxes/Tangible Net Worth						(15) 17.6
18.8	17.4	4.7							11.1
19.0	24.1	10.7							11.1
11.2	16.9	5.6	% Profit Before Taxes/Total Assets						6.6
7.0	6.5	.6							3.8
47.8	39.7	33.3							22.3
21.4	15.0	11.8	Sales/Net Fixed Assets						8.5
9.7	7.2	5.3							5.2
3.3	2.7	2.4							2.1
2.0	1.9	1.8	Sales/Total Assets						1.3
1.5	1.1	1.3							1.1
.6	.5	.7							.8
(27) 1.0	(26) .9	(34) 1.3	% Depr., Dep., Amort./Sales						(14) 1.9
2.0	2.6	2.3							2.9
1.0		1.5							
(13) 3.1		(12) 3.4	% Officers', Directors' Owners' Comp/Sales						
5.0		6.7							
926226M	1149364M	1327999M	Net Sales ($)	793M	1521M	12712M	61218M	96517M	1155238M
663021M	949456M	1073345M	Total Assets ($)	288M	617M	5464M	31688M	46881M	988407M

M = $ thousand MM = $ million

See Pages 9 through 22 for Explanation of Ratios and Data

Current Data Sorted by Assets							Comparative Historical Data	
						Type of Statement		
	1	1	9	3	1	Unqualified	21	15
	3	15	12			Reviewed	43	38
	4	8	2			Compiled	13	17
	2	2	1			Tax Returns	3	4
	2	13	13	2	3	Other	35	39
	20 (4/1-9/30/13)		77 (10/1/13-3/31/14)				4/1/09-3/31/10 ALL	4/1/10-3/31/11 ALL
0-500M	500M-2MM	2-10MM	10-50MM	50-100MM	100-250MM			
	12	39	37	5	4	**NUMBER OF STATEMENTS**	115	113
%	%	%	%	%	%	**ASSETS**	%	%
DATA NOT AVAILABLE	14.4	10.6	15.4			Cash & Equivalents	11.3	13.2
	25.8	36.0	28.1			Trade Receivables (net)	26.9	31.3
	22.4	23.4	21.0			Inventory	24.9	25.1
	6.0	3.7	6.9			All Other Current	5.0	3.5
	68.6	73.7	71.5			Total Current	68.1	73.1
	19.5	19.3	12.6			Fixed Assets (net)	20.0	17.2
	5.5	2.2	8.3			Intangibles (net)	5.3	4.3
	6.3	4.8	7.7			All Other Non-Current	6.6	5.3
	100.0	100.0	100.0			Total	100.0	100.0
						LIABILITIES		
	6.6	8.1	4.1			Notes Payable-Short Term	11.1	8.1
	1.4	2.5	2.4			Cur. Mat.-L.T.D.	2.6	2.9
	20.0	15.5	14.8			Trade Payables	13.2	15.9
	.9	.4	.3			Income Taxes Payable	.3	.2
	12.8	17.5	20.0			All Other Current	15.6	18.9
	41.7	44.1	41.6			Total Current	42.8	46.0
	14.3	7.7	4.8			Long-Term Debt	10.0	9.6
	.3	.3	.5			Deferred Taxes	.3	.3
	1.5	3.7	2.9			All Other Non-Current	6.0	5.2
	42.2	44.3	50.2			Net Worth	41.0	38.8
	100.0	100.0	100.0			Total Liabilties & Net Worth	100.0	100.0
						INCOME DATA		
	100.0	100.0	100.0			Net Sales	100.0	100.0
	35.5	33.3	29.9			Gross Profit	30.1	31.6
	32.1	26.7	21.0			Operating Expenses	27.8	27.3
	3.4	6.6	8.9			Operating Profit	2.3	4.2
	.4	.1	.5			All Other Expenses (net)	1.3	.7
	3.0	6.5	8.4			Profit Before Taxes	1.0	3.5
						RATIOS		
	2.4	2.7	3.1				2.7	2.5
	2.1	1.7	1.7			Current	1.7	1.6
	.9	1.2	1.3				1.2	1.2
	1.5	1.9	1.9				1.6	1.7
	.7	1.0	1.2			Quick	.9	1.0
	.4	.6	.7				.6	.6
	23 15.6	**38** 9.6	**41** 8.8				**35** 10.4	**43** 8.4
	31 11.9	**57** 6.4	**52** 7.0			Sales/Receivables	**49** 7.4	**56** 6.5
	45 8.2	**70** 5.2	**64** 5.7				**71** 5.1	**75** 4.9
	11 33.2	**20** 18.4	**32** 11.4				**35** 10.4	**34** 10.6
	35 10.3	**49** 7.5	**55** 6.6			Cost of Sales/Inventory	**60** 6.1	**61** 6.0
	78 4.7	**91** 4.0	**96** 3.8				**105** 3.5	**108** 3.4
	26 13.8	**21** 17.4	**21** 17.6				**17** 22.0	**26** 14.1
	38 9.7	**32** 11.5	**33** 11.0			Cost of Sales/Payables	**30** 12.2	**36** 10.2
	61 6.0	**45** 8.1	**51** 7.1				**52** 7.1	**53** 6.9
	7.3	4.5	3.2				4.1	3.9
	8.5	8.0	7.3			Sales/Working Capital	6.9	6.8
	UND	18.2	12.2				20.9	18.8
	23.7	37.7	158.7				8.0	17.3
	(11) 4.3	(34) 10.2	(26) 21.5			EBIT/Interest	(103) 2.6	(98) 3.9
	-.3	3.3	6.7				-.7	1.0
							3.8	10.2
						Net Profit + Depr., Dep., Amort./Cur. Mat. L/T/D	(34) 1.4	(29) 2.5
							.2	1.0
	.2	.2	.1				.2	.2
	.4	.4	.3			Fixed/Worth	.5	.4
	2.4	.9	.6				1.3	1.0
	.7	.6	.4				.6	.7
	2.0	1.2	1.3			Debt/Worth	1.9	1.6
	5.1	3.9	3.6				4.1	4.3
	48.4	61.5	50.3				29.9	40.1
	(11) 24.7	(36) 25.6	(33) 35.1			% Profit Before Taxes/Tangible Net Worth	(104) 8.9	(99) 13.9
	-5.0	14.3	17.6				-3.4	2.5
	14.0	21.0	21.8				10.6	15.0
	6.5	10.9	14.7			% Profit Before Taxes/Total Assets	2.2	5.0
	-1.8	3.8	6.6				-1.7	.1
	43.4	45.3	35.6				26.3	32.9
	22.5	16.3	19.5			Sales/Net Fixed Assets	12.0	12.6
	11.8	6.4	8.8				5.7	6.9
	4.1	2.8	2.6				2.5	2.4
	3.0	2.6	1.8			Sales/Total Assets	1.9	1.8
	1.7	1.7	1.3				1.3	1.4
	.3	.6	.5				.9	.8
	(11) .7	(35) 1.4	(35) 1.2			% Depr., Dep., Amort./Sales	(98) 1.6	(98) 1.6
	2.6	2.4	2.2				2.8	2.7
		1.6					2.0	1.8
		(15) 3.2				% Officers', Directors' Owners' Comp/Sales	(23) 4.1	(28) 2.9
		9.8					6.1	8.6
	43836M	465628M	1530836M	440731M	520970M	Net Sales ($)	3651681M	3268132M
	15029M	197884M	827079M	332279M	654993M	Total Assets ($)	2283906M	1833982M

M = $ thousand MM = $ million

See Pages 9 through 22 for Explanation of Ratios and Data

Comparative Historical Data | **Current Data Sorted by Sales**

4/1/11-3/31/12 ALL	4/1/12-3/31/13 ALL	4/1/13-3/31/14 ALL		0-1MM	1-3MM	3-5MM	5-10MM	10-25MM	25MM & OVER
			Type of Statement						
21	11	15	Unqualified				1	2	12
35	25	30	Reviewed		3	2	2	16	7
17	14	14	Compiled		2	3	4	2	3
9	5	5	Tax Returns		2	1	1	1	
36	41	33	Other			1	6	11	15
				20 (4/1-9/30/13)			77 (10/1/13-3/31/14)		
118	96	97	**NUMBER OF STATEMENTS**		7	7	14	32	37
%	%	%	**ASSETS**	%	%	%	%	%	%
14.6	13.6	13.2	Cash & Equivalents	DATA NOT AVAILABLE			14.5	12.6	14.4
32.0	32.6	29.6	Trade Receivables (net)				27.3	33.0	27.7
23.4	23.4	21.4	Inventory				21.3	22.2	20.0
4.0	5.2	5.3	All Other Current				3.5	5.3	6.7
74.1	74.9	69.6	Total Current				66.6	73.2	68.8
16.7	13.1	16.5	Fixed Assets (net)				18.2	18.8	11.8
4.8	5.3	8.1	Intangibles (net)				1.7	3.9	15.0
4.4	6.7	5.9	All Other Non-Current				13.5	4.1	4.4
100.0	100.0	100.0	Total				100.0	100.0	100.0
			LIABILITIES						
6.9	6.3	6.1	Notes Payable-Short Term				6.4	4.4	4.6
1.9	1.7	2.3	Cur. Mat.-L.T.D.				1.2	2.4	2.7
16.7	15.6	15.0	Trade Payables				15.2	15.5	15.1
.2	.3	.5	Income Taxes Payable				.4	.3	.5
21.1	17.8	17.5	All Other Current				14.0	17.6	20.1
46.8	41.7	41.4	Total Current				37.1	40.2	43.0
7.7	7.0	8.3	Long-Term Debt				5.7	7.1	7.2
.4	.3	.8	Deferred Taxes				.6	.1	1.7
6.0	5.5	3.2	All Other Non-Current				1.2	4.8	2.3
39.0	45.5	46.3	Net Worth				55.3	47.8	45.8
100.0	100.0	100.0	Total Liabilities & Net Worth				100.0	100.0	100.0
			INCOME DATA						
100.0	100.0	100.0	Net Sales				100.0	100.0	100.0
30.0	31.7	32.5	Gross Profit				34.5	33.2	29.4
23.9	24.5	25.2	Operating Expenses				25.5	25.6	21.1
6.1	7.2	7.3	Operating Profit				9.1	7.5	8.2
.6	.6	.6	All Other Expenses (net)				.0	.3	1.0
5.4	6.6	6.7	Profit Before Taxes				9.1	7.2	7.3
			RATIOS						
2.6	3.0	2.7					5.4	3.0	2.6
1.6	1.7	1.7	Current				2.0	2.1	1.5
1.2	1.3	1.2					1.2	1.5	1.2
1.6	1.7	1.8					4.6	1.9	1.5
1.1	1.0	1.0	Quick				1.0	1.3	1.0
.7	.7	.6					.6	.7	.6
38 9.6	**38** 9.6	**38** 9.6					**28** 13.2	**38** 9.7	**39** 9.4
49 7.4	**47** 7.8	**47** 7.7	Sales/Receivables				**47** 7.7	**47** 7.7	**49** 7.4
70 5.2	**65** 5.6	**61** 6.0					**64** 5.7	**65** 5.6	**61** 6.0
26 14.0	**22** 16.4	**30** 12.3					**10** 35.6	**27** 13.6	**30** 12.0
50 7.3	**58** 6.3	**49** 7.5	Cost of Sales/Inventory				**54** 6.8	**50** 7.3	**48** 7.6
101 3.6	**104** 3.5	**94** 3.9					**91** 4.0	**99** 3.7	**81** 4.5
20 18.0	**18** 20.6	**22** 16.9					**13** 28.5	**19** 18.8	**23** 16.0
33 11.1	**30** 12.0	**33** 11.0	Cost of Sales/Payables				**30** 12.3	**35** 10.5	**31** 11.7
46 8.0	**51** 7.1	**47** 7.8					**49** 7.5	**45** 8.2	**51** 7.1
4.1	3.8	4.6					4.0	3.6	5.2
6.5	6.9	8.0	Sales/Working Capital				8.1	7.3	8.4
18.6	13.4	17.0					17.9	11.8	18.5
39.6	67.1	52.6					65.7	30.7	115.1
(100) 10.7	(73) 9.8	(79) 12.4	EBIT/Interest				(10) 12.5	(27) 10.3	(29) 19.7
2.5	3.6	3.9					2.9	4.3	6.5
35.1	29.3	30.7							7.6
(22) 5.6	(24) 5.5	(26) 7.6	Net Profit + Depr., Dep., Amort./Cur. Mat. L/T/D						(12) 2.7
2.3	1.9	1.6							1.5
.2	.1	.2					.1	.2	.2
.4	.2	.4	Fixed/Worth				.4	.4	.4
1.1	.8	1.3					.9	.9	2.4
.7	.6	.6					.2	.6	.6
1.7	1.3	1.6	Debt/Worth				.6	1.0	1.9
4.7	3.5	4.3					3.3	2.6	12.4
47.3	55.7	56.9					52.4	60.0	61.4
(105) 24.7	(85) 25.9	(86) 31.2	% Profit Before Taxes/Tangible Net Worth				(13) 21.0	(30) 27.0	(31) 44.9
9.2	8.6	15.1					11.1	12.8	27.3
16.4	25.4	19.4					18.1	20.4	21.7
8.5	11.6	10.3	% Profit Before Taxes/Total Assets				10.3	9.7	12.7
2.2	3.4	4.8					4.0	3.9	7.5
36.9	44.5	32.2					55.7	28.8	40.5
14.5	23.3	16.3	Sales/Net Fixed Assets				15.9	13.7	21.4
7.7	9.6	7.8					6.6	6.8	10.4
2.6	2.7	2.7					3.1	2.8	2.6
2.0	2.0	2.1	Sales/Total Assets				2.4	2.5	2.0
1.6	1.6	1.4					1.5	1.5	1.3
.7	.5	.5					.4	.7	.4
(96) 1.4	(82) 1.0	(89) 1.3	% Depr., Dep., Amort./Sales				(12) 1.4	(30) 1.4	(34) 1.2
2.4	1.8	2.4					2.8	2.4	2.2
1.6	1.5	2.2						1.6	
(33) 2.5	(25) 3.3	(30) 3.8	% Officers', Directors' Owners' Comp/Sales					(11) 2.6	
4.5	7.5	8.7						9.8	
3448510M	2555981M	3002001M	Net Sales ($)		15522M	30334M	104614M	517783M	2333748M
1862033M	1404278M	2027264M	Total Assets ($)		7942M	18591M	61733M	297581M	1641417M

M = $ thousand MM = $ million

See Pages 9 through 22 for Explanation of Ratios and Data

Current Data Sorted by Assets							Comparative Historical Data	
						Type of Statement		
			2	1	1	Unqualified	5	6
		5	3			Reviewed	8	10
	1	4				Compiled	8	9
	4	3				Tax Returns	3	1
	2	7	7	1		Other	17	16
	7 (4/1-9/30/13)		34 (10/1/13-3/31/14)				4/1/09-3/31/10	4/1/10-3/31/11
0-500M	500M-2MM	2-10MM	10-50MM	50-100MM	100-250MM		ALL	ALL
	7	19	12	2	1	**NUMBER OF STATEMENTS**	41	42
%	%	%	%	%	%	**ASSETS**	%	%
DATA NOT AVAILABLE		10.7	15.5			Cash & Equivalents	16.0	9.2
		35.4	24.2			Trade Receivables (net)	23.4	35.5
		23.6	28.2			Inventory	27.9	27.3
		3.9	6.2			All Other Current	4.9	4.0
		73.6	74.1			Total Current	72.2	76.0
		14.7	21.4			Fixed Assets (net)	17.5	15.4
		3.1	1.2			Intangibles (net)	3.8	4.3
		8.6	3.3			All Other Non-Current	6.6	4.3
		100.0	100.0			Total	100.0	100.0
						LIABILITIES		
		9.5	8.2			Notes Payable-Short Term	14.3	8.9
		2.3	1.1			Cur. Mat.-L.T.D.	2.1	2.1
		15.7	11.8			Trade Payables	10.0	17.1
		.1	.0			Income Taxes Payable	.0	.0
		14.4	13.1			All Other Current	14.5	16.8
		42.0	34.3			Total Current	40.9	44.9
		12.4	8.4			Long-Term Debt	9.1	8.7
		.6	.4			Deferred Taxes	.7	.8
		2.5	1.9			All Other Non-Current	2.3	3.8
		42.5	55.0			Net Worth	47.0	41.8
		100.0	100.0			Total Liabilities & Net Worth	100.0	100.0
						INCOME DATA		
		100.0	100.0			Net Sales	100.0	100.0
		35.7	26.0			Gross Profit	29.1	30.1
		28.1	17.5			Operating Expenses	24.9	27.7
		7.5	8.5			Operating Profit	4.2	2.4
		.1	.3			All Other Expenses (net)	2.1	1.2
		7.4	8.3			Profit Before Taxes	2.1	1.2
						RATIOS		
		2.8	3.2				4.7	3.4
		1.9	2.2			Current	2.1	1.8
		1.4	1.4				1.3	1.3
		1.6	1.8				2.5	1.8
		1.0	.9			Quick	1.1	1.0
		.8	.7				.6	.7
		30 12.0	**31** 11.8				**28** 12.8	**49** 7.5
		41 8.9	**54** 6.8			Sales/Receivables	**41** 8.9	**59** 6.1
		68 5.4	**74** 4.9				**56** 6.6	**74** 4.9
		22 16.4	**55** 6.6				**26** 14.3	**32** 11.3
		47 7.8	**85** 4.3			Cost of Sales/Inventory	**60** 6.1	**60** 6.1
		78 4.7	**104** 3.5				**129** 2.8	**113** 3.2
		19 19.0	**17** 21.1				**11** 32.1	**25** 14.4
		31 11.6	**33** 11.0			Cost of Sales/Payables	**22** 16.8	**41** 9.0
		44 8.3	**46** 7.9				**38** 9.6	**57** 6.4
		4.7	3.0				3.0	3.7
		8.7	4.2			Sales/Working Capital	6.1	7.3
		14.9	9.8				18.8	15.4
		36.0	359.7				13.9	13.3
		19.1	(10) 11.1			EBIT/Interest	(34) 4.2	(37) 1.9
		6.2	2.1				1.0	-.1
							44.8	
						Net Profit + Depr., Dep., Amort./Cur. Mat. L/T/D	(12) 10.4	
							1.6	
		.2	.1				.1	.2
		.3	.3			Fixed/Worth	.4	.4
		.8	1.2				1.0	.8
		.8	.3				.3	.4
		1.9	.7			Debt/Worth	1.2	1.5
		3.5	2.6				3.2	4.9
		73.8	53.9				34.1	28.1
		39.8	24.5			% Profit Before Taxes/Tangible Net Worth	(38) 10.8	(38) 9.7
		12.6	11.9				.9	-4.4
		23.7	22.7				12.7	8.5
		11.4	11.7			% Profit Before Taxes/Total Assets	5.8	3.0
		3.9	5.7				.0	-1.7
		35.8	26.2				38.2	34.3
		19.5	9.5			Sales/Net Fixed Assets	16.7	17.8
		12.1	4.6				7.2	8.6
		3.4	2.0				3.2	2.9
		2.6	1.8			Sales/Total Assets	2.1	2.0
		1.8	1.2				1.4	1.5
		.6	.5				.9	.6
		(18) 1.1	(10) 1.5			% Depr., Dep., Amort./Sales	(34) 1.5	(37) 1.3
		2.1	4.5				2.5	2.3
							1.9	2.3
						% Officers', Directors' Owners' Comp/Sales	(14) 3.1	(14) 4.8
							8.0	7.8
	38066M	229205M	555298M	156616M	404170M	Net Sales ($)	1402363M	1366955M
	9453M	91708M	334740M	144270M	226669M	Total Assets ($)	1016205M	1097221M

M = $ thousand MM = $ million

See Pages 9 through 22 for Explanation of Ratios and Data

Comparative Historical Data | **Current Data Sorted by Sales**

						Type of Statement								
	5		3		4	Unqualified								4
	10		9		8	Reviewed				3		4		1
	10		9		5	Compiled			1	2		2		
	2		4		7	Tax Returns		1	2	2		2		
	21		20		17	Other			1	2		5		9
								7 (4/1-9/30/13)		34 (10/1/13-3/31/14)				
	4/1/11-3/31/12 ALL		4/1/12-3/31/13 ALL		4/1/13-3/31/14 ALL		0-1MM	1-3MM	3-5MM	5-10MM		10-25MM		25MM & OVER
	48		45		41	NUMBER OF STATEMENTS		1	4	9		13		14
	%		%		%	ASSETS	%	%	%	%		%		%
	10.5		10.6		15.3	Cash & Equivalents	DATA NOT AVAILABLE					11.8		20.3
	29.6		30.9		30.5	Trade Receivables (net)						37.2		26.0
	25.9		28.1		22.6	Inventory						22.1		26.0
	4.8		3.5		4.1	All Other Current						2.9		7.3
	70.8		73.2		72.5	Total Current						73.9		79.7
	19.1		17.7		19.0	Fixed Assets (net)						17.9		16.7
	5.2		4.3		2.2	Intangibles (net)						1.0		1.5
	4.9		4.8		6.3	All Other Non-Current						7.1		2.1
	100.0		100.0		100.0	Total						100.0		100.0
						LIABILITIES								
	8.2		8.6		7.8	Notes Payable-Short Term						7.9		8.4
	1.6		1.5		1.7	Cur. Mat.-L.T.D.						2.3		.8
	15.0		18.5		15.2	Trade Payables						17.4		11.5
	.3		.2		.2	Income Taxes Payable						.1		.5
	15.8		12.9		13.1	All Other Current						14.3		13.0
	40.9		41.8		38.1	Total Current						42.2		34.1
	13.6		15.0		13.8	Long-Term Debt						8.5		3.7
	.4		.4		.6	Deferred Taxes						.0		.8
	2.6		2.6		3.3	All Other Non-Current						3.3		1.9
	42.4		40.2		44.2	Net Worth						46.1		59.5
	100.0		100.0		100.0	Total Liabilties & Net Worth						100.0		100.0
						INCOME DATA								
	100.0		100.0		100.0	Net Sales						100.0		100.0
	28.9		31.1		33.5	Gross Profit						34.7		27.2
	22.6		23.4		26.0	Operating Expenses						29.9		16.4
	6.3		7.6		7.6	Operating Profit						4.9		10.9
	.6		1.0		.2	All Other Expenses (net)						.2		-.3
	5.7		6.6		7.4	Profit Before Taxes						4.7		11.1
						RATIOS								
	2.3		2.7		3.2							3.2		3.4
	1.7		1.9		2.0	Current						1.9		2.6
	1.2		1.3		1.3							1.3		1.8
	1.3		1.5		2.0							2.5		2.1
	.9		.9		1.0	Quick						1.0		1.7
	.6		.6		.8							.8		.8
39	9.3	30	12.0	28	12.9						27	13.6	34	10.6
57	6.4	42	8.6	47	7.8	Sales/Receivables					46	7.9	58	6.3
70	5.2	54	6.7	66	5.5						68	5.4	73	5.0
22	16.6	27	13.6	21	17.4						2	167.2	51	7.2
63	5.8	58	6.3	51	7.1	Cost of Sales/Inventory					41	9.0	73	5.0
126	2.9	94	3.9	91	4.0						72	5.1	104	3.5
27	13.5	24	15.5	18	20.0						17	21.6	16	22.8
36	10.2	32	11.3	33	11.0	Cost of Sales/Payables					26	14.0	32	11.3
47	7.7	48	7.6	44	8.3						43	8.4	48	7.6
	3.7		4.2		3.6							5.5		2.4
	7.8		8.4		6.2	Sales/Working Capital						8.7		3.6
	16.5		20.2		14.3							18.5		5.8
	65.9		53.3		91.1							27.0		206.9
(43)	12.3	(41)	24.2	(39)	14.9	EBIT/Interest						11.6	(12)	64.8
	3.4		6.5		5.1							4.1		10.2
	14.8													
(11)	8.8					Net Profit + Depr., Dep., Amort./Cur. Mat. L/T/D								
	2.2													
	.1		.1		.2							.3		.1
	.4		.4		.4	Fixed/Worth						.4		.2
	1.1		1.5		.8							.6		.4
	.6		.5		.5							.5		.3
	1.7		1.8		1.2	Debt/Worth						1.7		.7
	5.2		3.8		3.6							3.0		1.2
	41.1		71.9		58.8							55.8		48.3
(44)	27.2	(39)	39.3	(38)	30.7	% Profit Before Taxes/Tangible Net Worth						19.3		27.7
	8.3		16.7		12.3							6.9		16.4
	16.4		21.6		23.6							20.4		24.3
	7.7		15.9		13.6	% Profit Before Taxes/Total Assets						8.2		18.0
	1.7		6.7		5.2							1.9		9.2
	39.6		49.9		27.4							30.9		43.1
	15.0		20.9		18.1	Sales/Net Fixed Assets						18.4		11.4
	6.9		10.6		7.3							12.1		5.0
	2.5		3.5		3.0							3.8		1.9
	1.7		2.3		2.1	Sales/Total Assets						3.0		1.8
	1.2		1.6		1.5							2.2		1.2
	.8		.5		.7							1.0		.5
(43)	1.3	(41)	1.1	(37)	1.3	% Depr., Dep., Amort./Sales					(12)	1.3	(12)	.8
	2.6		1.6		2.4							2.2		2.6
	1.8		1.8		2.6									
(16)	3.2	(15)	5.4	(15)	4.8	% Officers', Directors' Owners' Comp/Sales								
	5.4		6.4		6.9									
	1345467M		1032531M		1383355M	Net Sales ($)		1740M	15998M	66651M		191131M		1107835M
	966331M		539437M		806840M	Total Assets ($)		1169M	6806M	35013M		71467M		692385M

M = $ thousand MM = $ million

See Pages 9 through 22 for Explanation of Ratios and Data

Current Data Sorted by Assets | **Comparative Historical Data**

0-500M	500M-2MM	2-10MM	10-50MM	50-100MM	100-250MM	Type of Statement	4/1/09-3/31/10 ALL	4/1/10-3/31/11 ALL
			6	3	3	Unqualified	9	13
	2	4	4		1	Reviewed	10	7
	2	2	2			Compiled	6	6
	2	4			1	Tax Returns	6	7
1	4	7	10	1	3	Other	28	18
	11 (4/1-9/30/13)		51 (10/1/13-3/31/14)					
1	10	17	22	4	8	NUMBER OF STATEMENTS	59	51
%	%	%	%	%	%	**ASSETS**	%	%
	23.6	6.5	6.5			Cash & Equivalents	7.8	6.5
	35.5	24.9	25.2			Trade Receivables (net)	18.5	22.9
	28.4	37.0	34.5			Inventory	33.9	38.0
	.4	2.3	1.6			All Other Current	3.8	2.7
	87.8	70.7	67.9			Total Current	64.0	70.1
	10.5	21.9	19.8			Fixed Assets (net)	25.1	20.0
	.9	4.7	3.8			Intangibles (net)	6.2	5.0
	.8	2.7	8.4			All Other Non-Current	4.7	4.8
	100.0	100.0	100.0			Total	100.0	100.0
						LIABILITIES		
	11.6	15.8	10.6			Notes Payable-Short Term	9.7	13.7
	.6	2.3	2.7			Cur. Mat.-L.T.D.	4.4	2.9
	8.9	16.2	14.4			Trade Payables	9.7	18.1
	.2	.9	.1			Income Taxes Payable	.3	.1
	10.0	11.8	11.4			All Other Current	12.2	10.4
	31.3	46.9	39.2			Total Current	36.3	45.3
	9.5	19.6	13.6			Long-Term Debt	16.7	15.8
	.0	.2	.3			Deferred Taxes	.4	.6
	4.6	2.7	1.7			All Other Non-Current	5.8	10.8
	54.6	30.7	45.3			Net Worth	40.7	27.5
	100.0	100.0	100.0			Total Liabilties & Net Worth	100.0	100.0
						INCOME DATA		
	100.0	100.0	100.0			Net Sales	100.0	100.0
	30.2	24.6	25.8			Gross Profit	23.8	24.2
	26.9	18.5	18.5			Operating Expenses	23.7	21.3
	3.3	6.1	7.3			Operating Profit	.2	2.9
	.2	-.2	.8			All Other Expenses (net)	1.5	.7
	3.1	6.4	6.5			Profit Before Taxes	-1.3	2.2
						RATIOS		
	14.0	2.1	2.3				3.1	2.5
	2.7	1.6	1.8			Current	1.8	1.8
	1.4	1.2	1.3				1.2	1.2
	9.1	1.0	1.2				1.5	1.0
	1.7	.7	.8			Quick	.7	.7
	1.1	.5	.5				.4	.4
	8 46.4	22 16.7	24 15.0				21 17.0	23 15.8
	33 11.2	38 9.7	42 8.6			Sales/Receivables	36 10.2	41 9.0
	70 5.2	61 6.0	63 5.8				57 6.4	55 6.6
	0 UND	42 8.6	63 5.8				51 7.1	63 5.8
	36 10.0	64 5.7	85 4.3			Cost of Sales/Inventory	90 4.1	88 4.2
	74 4.9	111 3.3	140 2.6				144 2.5	113 3.2
	1 284.4	17 21.3	20 18.5				13 28.5	19 19.1
	10 36.3	28 12.9	34 10.6			Cost of Sales/Payables	23 16.2	35 10.3
	24 14.9	42 8.6	46 8.0				36 10.1	58 6.3
	3.8	5.8	4.5				3.1	4.4
	6.0	8.7	6.8			Sales/Working Capital	7.4	7.5
	17.5	26.5	12.4				23.0	19.9
		25.2	28.2				6.2	8.7
		(15) 5.1	(21) 10.0			EBIT/Interest	(54) 1.7	(49) 3.4
		-.3	4.9				-3.2	-.9
							10.6	3.5
						Net Profit + Depr., Dep., Amort./Cur. Mat. L/T/D	(20) 3.4	(17) 2.4
							.3	1.1
	.0	.3	.1				.2	.2
	.1	.6	.6			Fixed/Worth	.7	.6
	.5	NM	.9				1.8	-69.6
	.1	.9	.8				.6	.7
	.9	1.4	1.5			Debt/Worth	1.6	2.3
	4.6	NM	2.4				9.3	-325.7
	56.6	59.5	50.8				17.2	42.6
	14.6	(13) 37.9	(21) 26.1			% Profit Before Taxes/Tangible Net Worth	(51) 6.2	(38) 19.3
	3.8	4.0	14.0				-11.0	5.4
	17.3	23.4	19.2				5.8	13.9
	3.7	12.0	10.4			% Profit Before Taxes/Total Assets	1.3	4.6
	1.9	-2.5	6.0				-8.0	-5.1
	296.1	23.0	56.3				19.9	29.1
	104.5	12.0	12.1			Sales/Net Fixed Assets	8.4	10.5
	20.0	7.9	5.6				4.4	5.8
	4.5	3.0	2.8				2.6	2.8
	3.2	2.5	2.0			Sales/Total Assets	1.8	2.1
	2.6	1.7	1.3				1.2	1.4
		.6	.6				1.2	.8
		.8	(19) 1.2			% Depr., Dep., Amort./Sales	(52) 2.7	(46) 1.5
		1.3	2.4				4.3	2.8
							1.8	1.2
						% Officers', Directors' Owners' Comp/Sales	(14) 2.9	(15) 2.2
							4.0	4.3
2220M	31011M	236593M	1134193M	650177M	2335380M	Net Sales ($)	1940310M	1201507M
222M	8619M	91665M	500671M	300340M	1350888M	Total Assets ($)	1280121M	713684M

M = $ thousand MM = $ million

See Pages 9 through 22 for Explanation of Ratios and Data

Comparative Historical Data				Current Data Sorted by Sales					
			Type of Statement						
11	8	12	Unqualified					2	10
12	9	11	Reviewed				3	2	6
4	5	6	Compiled		1	1	2	1	1
3	6	7	Tax Returns		1	1	2	2	1
21	27	26	Other		5		2	8	11
					11 (4/1-9/30/13)		51 (10/1/13-3/31/14)		
4/1/11-3/31/12 ALL	4/1/12-3/31/13 ALL	4/1/13-3/31/14 ALL		0-1MM	1-3MM	3-5MM	5-10MM	10-25MM	25MM & OVER
51	55	62	**NUMBER OF STATEMENTS**		7	2	9	15	29
%	%	%	**ASSETS**	%	%	%	%	%	%
9.1	9.5	10.5	Cash & Equivalents	DATA NOT AVAILABLE				2.8	8.7
23.3	21.8	25.7	Trade Receivables (net)					28.1	24.6
35.4	38.5	34.7	Inventory					38.5	36.8
2.2	2.7	1.9	All Other Current					2.6	2.2
70.0	72.6	72.8	Total Current					72.0	72.2
19.0	17.5	19.0	Fixed Assets (net)					17.5	19.5
6.3	4.5	4.1	Intangibles (net)					2.1	4.9
4.6	5.5	4.1	All Other Non-Current					8.4	3.4
100.0	100.0	100.0	Total					100.0	100.0
			LIABILITIES						
11.7	14.9	12.3	Notes Payable-Short Term					18.1	10.2
2.2	1.9	2.1	Cur. Mat.-L.T.D.					2.9	2.4
14.4	15.7	13.5	Trade Payables					15.5	15.4
.2	.2	.4	Income Taxes Payable					1.0	.3
13.5	13.8	12.7	All Other Current					8.4	15.4
42.0	46.5	40.9	Total Current					45.9	43.7
13.3	9.3	13.5	Long-Term Debt					16.9	9.9
.9	.4	.5	Deferred Taxes					.4	.8
5.3	7.2	5.0	All Other Non-Current					3.4	6.5
38.6	36.6	40.0	Net Worth					33.4	39.1
100.0	100.0	100.0	Total Liabilties & Net Worth					100.0	100.0
			INCOME DATA						
100.0	100.0	100.0	Net Sales					100.0	100.0
27.8	25.0	26.5	Gross Profit					27.1	22.6
22.5	19.5	20.5	Operating Expenses					21.1	16.2
5.3	5.5	5.9	Operating Profit					6.1	6.3
.3	.2	.4	All Other Expenses (net)					.2	.6
5.0	5.3	5.6	Profit Before Taxes					5.8	5.7
			RATIOS						
2.8	2.5	2.6						2.3	2.5
1.5	1.6	1.8	Current					1.7	1.8
1.2	1.2	1.3						1.5	1.2
1.4	1.4	1.5						1.0	1.2
.9	.7	.8	Quick					.7	.8
.5	.4	.5						.5	.4
29 12.8	**16** 22.3	**21** 17.7						**38** 9.7	**21** 17.4
41 8.9	**35** 10.3	**39** 9.4	Sales/Receivables					**53** 6.9	**39** 9.4
51 7.2	**51** 7.2	**62** 5.9						**68** 5.4	**55** 6.6
47 7.7	**52** 7.0	**42** 8.6						**52** 7.0	**48** 7.6
74 4.9	**79** 4.6	**70** 5.2	Cost of Sales/Inventory					**111** 3.3	**68** 5.4
126 2.9	**122** 3.0	**122** 3.0						**152** 2.4	**107** 3.4
18 20.6	**16** 22.3	**14** 25.3						**25** 14.4	**20** 18.7
29 12.6	**29** 12.7	**29** 12.8	Cost of Sales/Payables					**39** 9.4	**32** 11.5
43 8.4	**42** 8.7	**44** 8.3						**47** 7.8	**45** 8.1
4.9	4.5	4.5						4.5	4.5
10.1	7.9	7.5	Sales/Working Capital					7.8	7.9
30.2	13.7	15.4						10.1	25.1
25.7	13.4	29.3						36.6	28.7
(50) 7.4	(52) 7.5	(55) 8.5	EBIT/Interest					5.1	(28) 9.6
2.6	2.5	3.2						.8	3.9
18.3	22.7	9.5							
(11) 5.5	(16) 5.2	(14) 5.7	Net Profit + Depr., Dep., Amort./Cur. Mat. L/T/D						
1.9	2.2	1.5							
.2	.2	.1						.1	.3
.6	.4	.4	Fixed/Worth					.4	.5
1.4	1.2	1.3						1.1	1.2
.7	.7	.8						.7	.8
2.0	1.9	1.4	Debt/Worth					1.4	1.6
7.0	4.7	3.5						2.9	4.8
63.0	48.2	50.6						36.5	51.5
(46) 34.8	(50) 31.1	(55) 29.1	% Profit Before Taxes/Tangible Net Worth					(12) 13.2	(26) 35.9
12.7	6.4	10.1						-.2	21.9
14.1	16.2	18.9						20.4	19.0
7.1	8.1	9.6	% Profit Before Taxes/Total Assets					7.3	9.9
2.2	3.2	3.4						-.4	5.5
49.1	45.1	37.4						28.6	22.3
15.1	13.8	14.2	Sales/Net Fixed Assets					17.2	13.5
6.6	6.8	7.5						6.8	7.5
3.0	2.9	3.0						3.0	2.8
2.3	2.2	2.3	Sales/Total Assets					2.3	2.0
1.6	1.5	1.7						1.2	1.7
.5	.4	.6						.6	.6
(42) 1.2	(46) .9	(48) 1.0	% Depr., Dep., Amort./Sales					(14) 1.2	(22) 1.0
1.9	1.7	1.6						2.2	1.4
1.1	1.0	2.0							
(12) 2.1	(14) 3.6	(11) 3.0	% Officers', Directors' Owners' Comp/Sales						
8.2	5.0	8.2							
2549001M	2816760M	4389574M	Net Sales ($)		13789M	7748M	60286M	247427M	4060324M
1312349M	1500974M	2252405M	Total Assets ($)		4296M	1780M	31289M	142507M	2072533M

M = $ thousand MM = $ million

See Pages 9 through 22 for Explanation of Ratios and Data

Current Data Sorted by Assets							Comparative Historical Data	
						Type of Statement		
			2			Unqualified	7	14
	3	12	1			Reviewed	9	19
	1	1	2			Compiled	5	3
4	1	3	2			Tax Returns	4	11
	2	8	10	2		Other	23	26
	11 (4/1-9/30/13)		43 (10/1/13-3/31/14)				4/1/09-3/31/10	4/1/10-3/31/11
0-500M	500M-2MM	2-10MM	10-50MM	50-100MM	100-250MM		ALL	ALL
4	7	24	17	2		**NUMBER OF STATEMENTS**	48	73
%	%	%	%	%	%	**ASSETS**	%	%
		7.9	14.7		DATA NOT AVAILABLE	Cash & Equivalents	11.6	11.2
		26.9	21.9			Trade Receivables (net)	26.0	27.1
		35.1	31.2			Inventory	24.2	26.1
		2.0	5.3			All Other Current	4.9	4.8
		71.9	73.0			Total Current	66.7	69.3
		14.9	16.6			Fixed Assets (net)	21.5	19.0
		5.4	5.4			Intangibles (net)	4.6	4.1
		7.8	5.0			All Other Non-Current	7.3	7.5
		100.0	100.0			Total	100.0	100.0
						LIABILITIES		
		10.3	14.2			Notes Payable-Short Term	13.0	8.8
		2.0	1.7			Cur. Mat.-L.T.D.	4.7	2.6
		8.5	6.8			Trade Payables	14.1	12.3
		.5	.5			Income Taxes Payable	.4	.1
		7.2	8.0			All Other Current	9.4	13.4
		28.4	31.1			Total Current	41.6	37.1
		9.4	7.6			Long-Term Debt	11.4	9.2
		.6	1.4			Deferred Taxes	.7	.8
		6.9	10.4			All Other Non-Current	9.1	7.1
		54.7	49.5			Net Worth	37.3	45.7
		100.0	100.0			Total Liabilties & Net Worth	100.0	100.0
						INCOME DATA		
		100.0	100.0			Net Sales	100.0	100.0
		33.1	33.2			Gross Profit	28.8	32.6
		27.6	24.5			Operating Expenses	27.2	26.0
		5.5	8.7			Operating Profit	1.5	6.5
		.3	.9			All Other Expenses (net)	1.5	1.9
		5.3	7.8			Profit Before Taxes	.0	4.6
						RATIOS		
		4.6	5.3				2.9	3.2
		2.9	2.9			Current	1.7	1.9
		1.7	1.8				1.1	1.3
		2.1	3.3				2.0	2.0
		1.4	1.2			Quick	.8	1.0
		.8	.7				.4	.6
		40 9.2	**38** 9.5				**41** 8.8	**41** 9.0
		49 7.5	**51** 7.2			Sales/Receivables	**62** 5.9	**58** 6.3
		60 6.1	**61** 6.0				**67** 5.4	**73** 5.0
		62 5.9	**50** 7.3				**28** 12.9	**43** 8.5
		99 3.7	**81** 4.5			Cost of Sales/Inventory	**80** 4.6	**83** 4.4
		174 2.1	**146** 2.5				**146** 2.5	**142** 2.6
		11 33.2	**12** 31.5				**15** 25.0	**20** 18.2
		16 23.1	**19** 19.3			Cost of Sales/Payables	**27** 13.6	**27** 13.6
		39 9.3	**36** 10.2				**45** 8.1	**54** 6.8
		2.9	2.2				2.8	2.9
		4.1	3.4			Sales/Working Capital	6.3	5.7
		7.6	7.4				34.7	16.0
		20.3	202.0				5.5	20.9
		(20) 11.7	(16) 10.1			EBIT/Interest	(44) .5	(67) 6.8
		2.9	1.8				-6.9	2.1
							2.1	11.8
						Net Profit + Depr., Dep., Amort./Cur. Mat. L/T/D	(10) .2	(19) 2.2
							-2.3	.5
		.1	.1				.2	.2
		.2	.4			Fixed/Worth	.6	.4
		.9	2.5				5.0	1.1
		.3	.4				.6	.6
		.6	.7			Debt/Worth	1.5	1.2
		4.4	4.3				19.0	3.8
		41.4	41.7				23.0	45.2
		20.6	(14) 21.1			% Profit Before Taxes/Tangible Net Worth	(39) .5	(68) 15.3
		9.6	5.6				-23.7	3.5
		14.9	30.3				9.5	15.7
		9.9	11.5			% Profit Before Taxes/Total Assets	-.9	6.5
		5.7	1.3				-11.0	1.9
		33.2	47.3				20.5	21.7
		15.3	11.6			Sales/Net Fixed Assets	8.9	10.3
		8.0	7.2				5.6	6.2
		2.4	2.1				2.2	2.1
		1.9	1.9			Sales/Total Assets	1.5	1.6
		1.4	1.1				1.2	1.2
		.9	1.1				1.2	1.1
		(23) 1.4	(14) 1.7			% Depr., Dep., Amort./Sales	(40) 2.4	(58) 1.8
		1.9	2.2				3.9	3.2
							1.8	1.8
						% Officers', Directors' Owners' Comp/Sales	(16) 2.9	(18) 4.8
							5.4	6.1
3830M	32119M	240891M	1265047M	135538M		Net Sales ($)	1487270M	1458017M
987M	8813M	128833M	432078M	153701M		Total Assets ($)	833306M	937268M

M = $ thousand MM = $ million

See Pages 9 through 22 for Explanation of Ratios and Data

Comparative Historical Data				Current Data Sorted by Sales					
			Type of Statement						
7	3	2	Unqualified					1	1
14	10	16	Reviewed		2	3	5	5	1
3	5	4	Compiled				2	1	1
5	5	10	Tax Returns	3	1	1	3		2
22	17	22	Other		1	1	4	8	8
4/1/11-3/31/12 ALL	4/1/12-3/31/13 ALL	4/1/13-3/31/14 ALL		11 (4/1-9/30/13)			43 (10/1/13-3/31/14)		
				0-1MM	1-3MM	3-5MM	5-10MM	10-25MM	25MM & OVER
51	40	54	**NUMBER OF STATEMENTS**	3	4	5	14	15	13
%	%	%	**ASSETS**	%	%	%	%	%	%
9.5	11.6	10.3	Cash & Equivalents				10.4	13.1	9.3
26.2	28.6	26.1	Trade Receivables (net)				25.7	23.8	23.3
26.4	29.7	33.5	Inventory				36.2	34.4	27.8
4.8	2.8	2.7	All Other Current				2.4	1.5	6.6
66.9	72.7	72.7	Total Current				74.7	72.8	67.0
20.5	17.3	14.2	Fixed Assets (net)				10.6	15.9	15.2
4.1	3.4	6.7	Intangibles (net)				6.9	6.1	11.9
8.5	6.6	6.4	All Other Non-Current				7.9	5.1	5.9
100.0	100.0	100.0	Total				100.0	100.0	100.0
			LIABILITIES						
7.7	11.8	10.0	Notes Payable-Short Term				6.8	7.9	17.9
1.7	.9	1.6	Cur. Mat.-L.T.D.				1.6	2.1	1.4
11.5	10.2	9.8	Trade Payables				8.4	10.4	5.6
.1	.1	.6	Income Taxes Payable				.7	.5	.9
10.3	10.5	7.7	All Other Current				9.9	10.1	6.7
31.3	33.6	29.8	Total Current				27.5	31.0	32.5
11.8	7.4	9.6	Long-Term Debt				10.4	7.5	7.7
.5	1.3	.7	Deferred Taxes				.2	1.2	.4
6.7	3.9	7.7	All Other Non-Current				.8	4.7	11.1
49.8	53.9	52.3	Net Worth				61.1	55.5	48.3
100.0	100.0	100.0	Total Liabilties & Net Worth				100.0	100.0	100.0
			INCOME DATA						
100.0	100.0	100.0	Net Sales				100.0	100.0	100.0
31.4	30.9	32.7	Gross Profit				30.2	35.0	29.1
24.6	24.0	27.4	Operating Expenses				26.1	27.7	19.9
6.8	6.9	5.3	Operating Profit				4.0	7.3	9.2
1.8	1.3	.5	All Other Expenses (net)				-.3	.7	.7
4.9	5.6	4.8	Profit Before Taxes				4.3	6.6	8.4
			RATIOS						
4.0	3.5	4.7					5.8	4.6	4.9
2.0	2.3	2.7	Current				3.3	2.7	2.2
1.5	1.4	1.7					1.8	1.5	1.6
1.9	2.3	2.4					2.3	2.5	2.7
1.1	1.1	1.2	Quick				1.9	1.2	1.2
.7	.7	.7					.8	.6	.8
35 10.4	**27** 13.5	**35** 10.4					**30** 12.0	**41** 8.9	**39** 9.4
49 7.4	**44** 8.3	**48** 7.6	Sales/Receivables				**50** 7.3	**45** 8.1	**59** 6.2
65 5.6	**56** 6.5	**61** 6.0					**59** 6.2	**55** 6.6	**65** 5.6
28 12.9	**27** 13.4	**42** 8.6					**32** 11.5	**85** 4.3	**39** 9.3
85 4.3	**74** 4.9	**91** 4.0	Cost of Sales/Inventory				**85** 4.3	**122** 3.0	**56** 6.5
140 2.6	**118** 3.1	**140** 2.6					**126** 2.9	**159** 2.3	**81** 4.5
15 24.8	**12** 30.7	**11** 32.1					**2** 177.4	**17** 21.4	**8** 44.1
28 12.9	**20** 18.1	**19** 19.6	Cost of Sales/Payables				**14** 25.3	**30** 12.0	**17** 21.6
45 8.1	**34** 10.7	**38** 9.5					**24** 14.9	**41** 8.8	**24** 15.3
3.6	3.4	2.7					2.8	2.0	3.0
5.0	5.7	4.7	Sales/Working Capital				5.3	4.3	5.0
9.4	11.1	8.6					8.4	9.4	9.4
21.9	28.9	29.1					22.7	13.2	608.0
(42) 8.0	(33) 10.7	(44) 11.4	EBIT/Interest				(11) 14.8	(13) 8.5	(12) 25.4
1.7	1.8	2.0					4.2	2.2	9.0
12.5		8.9							
(10) 7.2		(12) 3.2	Net Profit + Depr., Dep., Amort./Cur. Mat. L/T/D						
2.7		.7							
.1	.1	.1					.1	.1	.1
.3	.3	.2	Fixed/Worth				.1	.2	.4
1.3	.6	1.0					.3	2.0	4.0
.4	.3	.3					.3	.3	.5
.9	.7	.7	Debt/Worth				.5	.8	.7
4.4	2.7	3.6					2.4	3.4	9.7
44.2	37.7	41.8					25.8	42.4	54.9
(48) 24.4	(38) 19.3	(50) 20.6	% Profit Before Taxes/Tangible Net Worth				12.8	(14) 24.1	(11) 39.8
10.4	3.2	7.2					8.9	5.2	12.9
19.0	18.8	15.5					14.3	15.4	30.3
8.9	9.2	9.9	% Profit Before Taxes/Total Assets				7.7	11.3	15.7
2.4	1.4	4.1					5.7	4.9	4.7
29.2	41.7	43.8					138.6	42.2	53.7
10.0	16.4	18.3	Sales/Net Fixed Assets				23.5	19.4	11.6
8.1	8.3	8.3					12.7	7.6	8.3
2.2	2.9	2.4					2.7	2.2	2.2
1.9	2.1	1.9	Sales/Total Assets				2.3	1.8	1.9
1.4	1.6	1.3					1.4	1.2	1.3
.9	.6	.9					.3	1.1	1.0
(46) 1.5	(31) 1.0	(46) 1.4	% Depr., Dep., Amort./Sales				(12) 1.0	(14) 1.4	(11) 1.6
2.5	1.6	1.9					1.7	1.9	1.9
2.6	3.3	2.3							
(17) 4.5	(10) 5.1	(12) 4.9	% Officers', Directors' Owners' Comp/Sales						
6.2	8.2	10.0							
863298M	979032M	1677425M	Net Sales ($)	1161M	10674M	20230M	100083M	255969M	1289308M
530660M	531103M	724412M	Total Assets ($)	566M	4234M	12700M	52931M	162240M	491741M

M = $ thousand MM = $ million

See Pages 9 through 22 for Explanation of Ratios and Data

Current Data Sorted by Assets | **Comparative Historical Data**

	0-500M	500M-2MM	2-10MM	10-50MM	50-100MM	100-250MM	4/1/09-3/31/10 ALL	4/1/10-3/31/11 ALL
Type of Statement								
Unqualified			2	6	4	2	15	16
Reviewed		1	10	7			20	26
Compiled		4	3	1			6	7
Tax Returns		3	5				5	14
Other	1	2	10	12	2	2	22	33
		21 (4/1-9/30/13)		56 (10/1/13-3/31/14)				
NUMBER OF STATEMENTS	1	10	30	26	6	4	68	96
	%	%	%	%	%	%	%	%
ASSETS								
Cash & Equivalents		8.6	15.6	13.6			11.6	13.4
Trade Receivables (net)		19.0	21.8	22.2			19.7	23.2
Inventory		32.6	30.9	32.7			35.6	31.4
All Other Current		5.6	1.6	4.1			4.4	5.0
Total Current		65.8	69.9	72.6			71.3	72.9
Fixed Assets (net)		25.7	17.2	13.2			15.4	15.8
Intangibles (net)		1.2	5.8	5.6			5.0	4.6
All Other Non-Current		7.3	7.1	8.6			8.3	6.6
Total		100.0	100.0	100.0			100.0	100.0
LIABILITIES								
Notes Payable-Short Term		16.9	8.1	5.1			8.1	5.9
Cur. Mat.-L.T.D.		5.6	2.4	2.2			2.2	3.9
Trade Payables		19.9	11.5	9.1			11.0	14.3
Income Taxes Payable		.1	.2	.1			.3	.5
All Other Current		24.3	25.5	23.8			24.2	30.3
Total Current		66.8	47.7	40.4			45.8	54.9
Long-Term Debt		23.0	9.1	5.2			6.2	6.6
Deferred Taxes		.0	.1	.8			.4	.4
All Other Non-Current		13.6	6.0	1.8			8.6	12.9
Net Worth		-3.4	37.0	51.8			39.0	25.2
Total Liabilties & Net Worth		100.0	100.0	100.0			100.0	100.0
INCOME DATA								
Net Sales		100.0	100.0	100.0			100.0	100.0
Gross Profit		33.3	36.8	27.9			34.7	34.3
Operating Expenses		31.9	31.7	21.6			32.7	29.3
Operating Profit		1.4	5.1	6.4			2.0	4.9
All Other Expenses (net)		1.3	.6	-.3			.9	.7
Profit Before Taxes		.1	4.5	6.7			1.1	4.2
RATIOS								
Current		1.8	2.0	3.0			2.7	2.5
		1.1	1.2	1.7			1.6	1.6
		.6	1.1	1.2			1.1	1.1
Quick		.9	1.5	1.4			1.3	1.3
		.3	.6	.8			.7	.7
		.2	.4	.5			.4	.5
Sales/Receivables		**16** 22.6	**26** 13.8	**31** 11.9			**28** 12.8	**28** 13.1
		25 14.6	**38** 9.7	**47** 7.7			**39** 9.5	**42** 8.8
		40 9.1	**60** 6.1	**65** 5.6			**58** 6.3	**54** 6.8
Cost of Sales/Inventory		**0** UND	**42** 8.6	**51** 7.2			**55** 6.6	**46** 7.9
		61 6.0	**94** 3.9	**99** 3.7			**126** 2.9	**78** 4.7
		159 2.3	**135** 2.7	**152** 2.4			**189** 1.9	**141** 2.6
Cost of Sales/Payables		**10** 37.8	**20** 18.6	**11** 32.1			**11** 32.6	**15** 23.9
		31 11.9	**32** 11.4	**24** 15.3			**24** 15.1	**30** 12.0
		74 4.9	**47** 7.8	**33** 11.1			**50** 7.4	**52** 7.0
Sales/Working Capital		6.9	5.2	3.4			3.7	4.1
		NM	15.1	5.9			6.5	8.2
		-4.9	67.9	20.4			44.2	45.1
EBIT/Interest			49.3	62.6			22.8	51.6
			(26) 7.3	(18) 12.7			(58) 5.1	(82) 8.2
			1.8	5.2			.1	2.6
Net Profit + Depr., Dep., Amort./Cur. Mat. L/T/D							14.3	8.4
							(13) 1.3	(24) 2.6
							-.8	.6
Fixed/Worth		.2	.1	.1			.1	.1
		4.2	.3	.2			.4	.4
		-1.6	1.7	.6			1.4	.9
Debt/Worth		1.8	.9	.5			.6	.7
		34.2	3.2	1.1			1.8	1.8
		-3.2	6.1	2.5			5.2	4.2
% Profit Before Taxes/Tangible Net Worth			40.0	47.3			27.9	49.4
			(29) 15.0	23.4			(59) 15.6	(86) 23.4
			4.8	9.5			.9	8.8
% Profit Before Taxes/Total Assets		19.7	15.6	16.6			11.2	17.6
		.9	4.2	10.1			4.6	8.7
		-4.9	1.0	4.8			-.4	2.1
Sales/Net Fixed Assets		32.8	88.8	33.4			39.1	53.8
		18.5	21.8	19.7			15.3	19.9
		4.9	5.6	6.7			7.7	9.1
Sales/Total Assets		3.3	2.6	2.2			2.1	2.6
		2.7	1.9	1.7			1.7	1.9
		1.4	1.3	1.1			1.2	1.3
% Depr., Dep., Amort./Sales			.4	.7			.8	.8
			(25) 1.2	1.2			(60) 1.3	(78) 1.4
			2.8	2.2			1.8	2.4
% Officers', Directors' Owners' Comp/Sales			1.5				2.2	2.5
			(13) 2.4				(20) 4.2	(30) 4.0
			8.5				6.8	6.9
Net Sales ($)	337M	29713M	331928M	1038756M	625134M	1045229M	1534465M	2189584M
Total Assets ($)	201M	11891M	176899M	650863M	395530M	642480M	1031965M	1460732M

M = $ thousand MM = $ million

See Pages 9 through 22 for Explanation of Ratios and Data

Comparative Historical Data			Type of Statement	Current Data Sorted by Sales					
11	9	14	Unqualified				1	3	10
18	20	18	Reviewed	1		2	2	6	7
12	7	8	Compiled		2	3	1	1	1
9	7	8	Tax Returns		1	2	4	1	
25	31	29	Other	1		2	5	6	15
4/1/11-3/31/12 ALL	4/1/12-3/31/13 ALL	4/1/13-3/31/14 ALL		21 (4/1-9/30/13)			56 (10/1/13-3/31/14)		
				0-1MM	1-3MM	3-5MM	5-10MM	10-25MM	25MM & OVER
75	74	77	NUMBER OF STATEMENTS	2	3	9	13	17	33
%	%	%	ASSETS	%	%	%	%	%	%
9.9	9.7	12.2	Cash & Equivalents				16.6	16.1	10.6
23.3	22.7	21.5	Trade Receivables (net)				18.6	24.3	23.2
32.3	32.0	31.5	Inventory				29.7	30.7	30.6
3.5	4.5	3.7	All Other Current				1.0	2.1	5.2
68.9	68.9	68.8	Total Current				65.9	73.3	69.5
16.8	16.6	18.0	Fixed Assets (net)				18.4	11.9	18.7
7.4	7.5	5.9	Intangibles (net)				8.7	5.3	5.6
7.0	7.1	7.3	All Other Non-Current				7.0	9.5	6.2
100.0	100.0	100.0	Total				100.0	100.0	100.0
			LIABILITIES						
9.4	9.1	7.8	Notes Payable-Short Term				7.1	7.6	5.0
2.3	3.0	2.7	Cur. Mat.-L.T.D.				2.3	.8	2.8
15.5	13.7	12.6	Trade Payables				8.3	11.5	10.1
.3	.2	.1	Income Taxes Payable				.2	.3	.1
20.1	18.5	24.6	All Other Current				22.2	28.4	24.6
47.6	44.4	47.8	Total Current				40.1	48.6	42.6
8.4	8.4	10.5	Long-Term Debt				8.0	4.5	9.8
.5	.3	.4	Deferred Taxes				.0	.0	.9
5.7	6.5	6.0	All Other Non-Current				9.5	3.2	4.5
37.9	40.5	35.1	Net Worth				42.4	43.7	42.3
100.0	100.0	100.0	Total Liabilties & Net Worth				100.0	100.0	100.0
			INCOME DATA						
100.0	100.0	100.0	Net Sales				100.0	100.0	100.0
32.3	33.4	31.3	Gross Profit				40.8	33.8	26.0
25.8	27.4	26.5	Operating Expenses				33.1	29.9	20.6
6.5	5.9	4.7	Operating Profit				7.7	3.9	5.4
.6	.5	.4	All Other Expenses (net)				.2	.4	.1
5.9	5.4	4.3	Profit Before Taxes				7.5	3.5	5.3
			RATIOS						
2.1	2.3	2.1					4.0	2.7	2.3
1.5	1.6	1.4	Current				1.7	1.2	1.6
1.1	1.1	1.0					1.1	1.1	1.1
1.2	1.4	1.2					2.9	1.6	1.2
.7	.7	.7	Quick				.8	.8	.7
.4	.4	.4					.4	.4	.5
32 11.5	**29** 12.4	**27** 13.3					**26** 14.1	**25** 14.6	**31** 11.7
42 8.7	**40** 9.1	**42** 8.6	Sales/Receivables				**39** 9.3	**45** 8.2	**49** 7.5
52 7.0	**51** 7.2	**63** 5.8					**69** 5.3	**60** 6.1	**66** 5.5
46 8.0	**45** 8.1	**43** 8.5					**54** 6.7	**57** 6.4	**41** 9.0
89 4.1	**96** 3.8	**87** 4.2	Cost of Sales/Inventory				**99** 3.7	**94** 3.9	**83** 4.4
130 2.8	**152** 2.4	**135** 2.7					**159** 2.3	**140** 2.6	**114** 3.2
18 20.0	**15** 23.9	**15** 24.0					**17** 21.0	**11** 32.5	**14** 25.2
31 11.7	**27** 13.3	**29** 12.7	Cost of Sales/Payables				**41** 8.9	**26** 14.1	**24** 15.0
61 6.0	**51** 7.1	**43** 8.5					**55** 6.6	**39** 9.3	**35** 10.5
4.6	4.8	4.6					3.6	5.4	3.8
10.2	8.5	8.5	Sales/Working Capital				8.5	15.1	7.6
33.5	34.5	122.6					36.6	95.4	33.3
25.4	24.0	41.6					45.4	77.8	49.9
(54) 5.6	(58) 7.2	(63) 6.3	EBIT/Interest				(10) 6.9	(14) 8.8	(27) 11.7
1.6	2.7	1.8					1.4	4.9	2.6
9.5	14.1	15.4							23.3
(18) 2.5	(24) 2.4	(21) 3.5	Net Profit + Depr., Dep., Amort./Cur. Mat. L/T/D						(12) 4.6
1.1	.9	2.2							2.7
.2	.1	.1					.1	.0	.1
.5	.4	.4	Fixed/Worth				.5	.2	.4
1.6	1.1	1.5					1.4	1.4	1.3
.7	.6	.9					.8	.5	.8
2.2	1.8	2.5	Debt/Worth				2.8	2.0	1.6
4.7	4.8	6.0					5.3	5.8	3.5
50.2	56.8	46.2					117.1	58.4	39.6
(66) 23.4	(67) 22.6	(70) 20.9	% Profit Before Taxes/Tangible Net Worth				10.3	15.0	(32) 21.8
10.9	10.1	7.8					3.7	7.8	9.7
16.2	15.6	15.5					29.8	14.4	15.3
9.5	8.1	6.4	% Profit Before Taxes/Total Assets				4.0	7.8	9.8
2.2	2.9	1.2					1.0	2.1	2.9
31.1	44.2	34.5					96.1	90.2	31.6
15.1	15.4	17.2	Sales/Net Fixed Assets				12.6	28.4	12.0
8.5	8.2	6.0					4.6	8.4	6.3
2.9	2.5	2.5					2.4	2.7	2.3
1.7	1.8	1.8	Sales/Total Assets				1.3	1.9	1.7
1.3	1.3	1.2					1.2	1.2	1.2
.7	.7	.7					.3	.8	.8
(64) 1.4	(64) 1.3	(69) 1.5	% Depr., Dep., Amort./Sales				(11) 1.2	(14) 1.5	(32) 1.7
2.0	2.3	2.8					2.8	2.1	3.0
2.0	2.2	1.8							
(26) 3.4	(18) 4.2	(20) 4.5	% Officers', Directors' Owners' Comp/Sales						
4.8	9.7	7.1							
1806985M	1916550M	3071097M	Net Sales ($)	1006M	4409M	36308M	101847M	263280M	2664247M
1088296M	1121289M	1877864M	Total Assets ($)	1373M	2689M	21183M	70696M	159531M	1622392M

M = $ thousand MM = $ million

See Pages 9 through 22 for Explanation of Ratios and Data

Current Data Sorted by Assets							Comparative Historical Data	
						Type of Statement		
		3	2	1	2	Unqualified	8	14
	3	9	1			Reviewed	13	13
	2	1				Compiled	5	3
	1	3				Tax Returns	2	7
	1	5	10		1	Other	12	9
10 (4/1-9/30/13)		35 (10/1/13-3/31/14)					4/1/09-3/31/10	4/1/10-3/31/11
0-500M	500M-2MM	2-10MM	10-50MM	50-100MM	100-250MM		ALL	ALL
	7	21	13	1	3	NUMBER OF STATEMENTS	40	46
%	%	%	%	%	%	**ASSETS**	%	%
DATA NOT AVAILABLE		14.4	20.3			Cash & Equivalents	15.1	18.3
		31.7	23.9			Trade Receivables (net)	29.3	32.5
		28.1	15.3			Inventory	20.3	17.7
		1.9	8.3			All Other Current	4.9	5.0
		76.2	67.9			Total Current	69.5	73.5
		13.1	15.2			Fixed Assets (net)	17.9	15.3
		2.9	9.1			Intangibles (net)	4.9	6.5
		7.9	7.9			All Other Non-Current	7.7	4.7
		100.0	100.0			Total	100.0	100.0
						LIABILITIES		
		10.9	3.3			Notes Payable-Short Term	12.2	9.9
		2.4	.4			Cur. Mat.-L.T.D.	4.0	3.2
		18.9	10.7			Trade Payables	12.3	14.4
		.2	.7			Income Taxes Payable	.9	.4
		18.0	34.8			All Other Current	20.3	27.6
		50.5	49.9			Total Current	49.7	55.5
		10.1	4.3			Long-Term Debt	11.3	13.3
		.1	.4			Deferred Taxes	.2	.3
		1.2	7.5			All Other Non-Current	7.0	6.4
		38.2	37.9			Net Worth	31.8	24.5
		100.0	100.0			Total Liabilties & Net Worth	100.0	100.0
						INCOME DATA		
		100.0	100.0			Net Sales	100.0	100.0
		30.7	28.0			Gross Profit	30.1	34.0
		24.0	22.3			Operating Expenses	26.1	27.4
		6.7	5.7			Operating Profit	4.0	6.7
		.3	.5			All Other Expenses (net)	1.4	.4
		6.4	5.2			Profit Before Taxes	2.7	6.3
						RATIOS		
		2.4	2.5				2.0	2.4
		1.6	1.5			Current	1.5	1.7
		1.1	1.3				1.1	1.1
		1.8	1.3				1.4	1.9
		.9	1.1			Quick	.9	1.1
		.6	.8				.6	.7
		31 11.7	**40** 9.2				**38** 9.6	**42** 8.7
		47 7.8	**49** 7.4			Sales/Receivables	**50** 7.2	**57** 6.5
		72 5.1	**70** 5.2				**71** 5.1	**75** 4.9
		37 9.8	**21** 17.7				**10** 35.9	**18** 20.3
		68 5.4	**50** 7.3			Cost of Sales/Inventory	**37** 9.8	**47** 7.8
		94 3.9	**73** 5.0				**101** 3.6	**81** 4.5
		17 21.6	**20** 18.4				**18** 19.9	**17** 21.3
		29 12.6	**32** 11.4			Cost of Sales/Payables	**30** 12.0	**39** 9.4
		46 7.9	**40** 9.1				**43** 8.5	**59** 6.2
		3.5	3.4				4.4	3.9
		9.9	6.2			Sales/Working Capital	10.9	7.5
		25.1	9.9				56.1	48.5
		58.6	558.2				15.7	25.1
		(19) 8.5	(11) 36.5			EBIT/Interest	(37) 3.2	(39) 6.8
		2.6	3.0				.8	2.1
							5.3	
						Net Profit + Depr., Dep., Amort./Cur. Mat. L/T/D	(11) 2.3	
							-10.5	
		.1	.2				.2	.1
		.3	.5			Fixed/Worth	.7	.4
		.7	.8				1.4	1.8
		.7	.9				.9	1.0
		1.7	1.9			Debt/Worth	2.7	2.9
		4.2	2.9				8.7	8.7
		53.3	53.8				62.5	59.7
		(20) 32.0	(12) 34.7			% Profit Before Taxes/Tangible Net Worth	(37) 10.0	(39) 24.4
		5.6	16.3				.2	10.4
		23.9	24.9				10.7	19.6
		7.4	10.0			% Profit Before Taxes/Total Assets	2.3	9.3
		1.3	3.3				.0	2.1
		49.1	45.7				43.3	67.2
		16.4	13.6			Sales/Net Fixed Assets	13.7	15.7
		11.7	5.3				5.7	9.8
		3.1	2.1				2.8	3.1
		2.3	1.5			Sales/Total Assets	1.9	1.8
		1.6	.7				1.1	1.3
		.4	.5				.7	.7
		(17) .9	(12) 1.0			% Depr., Dep., Amort./Sales	(36) 1.0	(36) 1.3
		1.6	2.2				2.7	2.8
							1.6	2.0
						% Officers', Directors' Owners' Comp/Sales	(13) 4.9	(12) 2.7
							6.1	5.4
	31697M	215698M	389624M	131696M	742657M	Net Sales ($)	866085M	1158252M
	8845M	99808M	270172M	80864M	494588M	Total Assets ($)	545403M	694442M

M = $ thousand MM = $ million

See Pages 9 through 22 for Explanation of Ratios and Data

Comparative Historical Data / Current Data Sorted by Sales

4/1/11-3/31/12 ALL	4/1/12-3/31/13 ALL	4/1/13-3/31/14 ALL	Type of Statement	0-1MM	1-3MM	3-5MM	5-10MM	10-25MM	25MM & OVER
14	11	8	Unqualified				1	3	4
14	8	13	Reviewed		1	2	6	3	1
5	6	3	Compiled				3		
6	3	4	Tax Returns		1		2	1	
10	20	17	Other		1	2	2	6	6
					10 (4/1-9/30/13)		35 (10/1/13-3/31/14)		
49	48	45	NUMBER OF STATEMENTS		3	4	14	13	11
%	%	%	ASSETS	%	%	%	%	%	%
14.8	16.1	15.6	Cash & Equivalents	DATA NOT AVAILABLE			9.8	18.7	20.2
34.2	30.2	30.2	Trade Receivables (net)				34.8	25.1	30.8
18.0	19.8	23.7	Inventory				27.7	21.6	16.0
5.9	5.3	4.8	All Other Current				3.4	2.3	10.2
72.8	71.4	74.2	Total Current				75.7	67.6	77.3
15.6	16.1	13.6	Fixed Assets (net)				15.7	12.4	9.9
4.6	6.7	5.4	Intangibles (net)				2.7	9.4	7.2
6.9	5.8	6.8	All Other Non-Current				5.9	10.5	5.6
100.0	100.0	100.0	Total				100.0	100.0	100.0
			LIABILITIES						
5.6	6.8	8.5	Notes Payable-Short Term				13.6	3.9	3.5
1.8	2.8	4.5	Cur. Mat.-L.T.D.				3.1	1.1	4.1
14.9	14.2	16.2	Trade Payables				22.4	12.6	13.5
.7	.3	.7	Income Taxes Payable				.3	.6	1.1
27.0	21.9	22.4	All Other Current				17.1	29.5	28.6
50.1	46.0	52.2	Total Current				56.5	47.7	50.8
9.6	12.2	8.2	Long-Term Debt				11.5	3.4	3.6
.4	.7	.3	Deferred Taxes				.0	.5	.6
9.4	9.5	5.3	All Other Non-Current				3.3	.8	14.4
30.5	31.6	34.0	Net Worth				28.7	47.6	30.6
100.0	100.0	100.0	Total Liabilties & Net Worth				100.0	100.0	100.0
			INCOME DATA						
100.0	100.0	100.0	Net Sales				100.0	100.0	100.0
30.9	33.5	29.4	Gross Profit				26.4	34.3	27.4
24.0	25.0	23.2	Operating Expenses				20.7	27.3	19.5
6.9	8.5	6.2	Operating Profit				5.7	7.0	7.9
.4	1.0	.5	All Other Expenses (net)				.3	.3	1.0
6.4	7.5	5.7	Profit Before Taxes				5.4	6.7	6.9
			RATIOS						
2.1	2.7	2.5					1.8	2.4	2.4
1.4	1.8	1.6	Current				1.5	1.9	1.5
1.1	1.2	1.1					1.0	1.3	1.0
1.3	1.7	1.5					1.3	1.6	1.6
.9	1.1	1.0	Quick				.8	1.1	1.0
.7	.7	.7					.5	.9	.7
43 8.4	**35** 10.4	**34** 10.7					**29** 12.4	**34** 10.6	**45** 8.2
57 6.4	**51** 7.1	**48** 7.6	Sales/Receivables				**45** 8.2	**48** 7.6	**56** 6.5
73 5.0	**68** 5.4	**72** 5.1					**57** 6.4	**73** 5.0	**74** 4.9
20 18.4	**24** 15.0	**27** 13.5					**22** 16.6	**37** 9.8	**27** 13.7
38 9.7	**47** 7.8	**60** 6.1	Cost of Sales/Inventory				**51** 7.1	**68** 5.4	**48** 7.6
73 5.0	**76** 4.8	**81** 4.5					**81** 4.5	**114** 3.2	**66** 5.5
19 19.1	**19** 19.2	**16** 23.1					**15** 24.6	**18** 19.9	**21** 17.8
34 10.6	**26** 13.9	**29** 12.6	Cost of Sales/Payables				**35** 10.4	**20** 18.3	**33** 11.0
46 8.0	**49** 7.4	**45** 8.1					**51** 7.1	**34** 10.7	**40** 9.1
5.5	4.7	4.1					8.6	3.5	5.6
9.3	6.6	8.3	Sales/Working Capital				11.0	6.3	6.9
28.6	18.9	25.1					110.7	16.6	-109.1
91.5	159.3	125.4					10.6	499.5	424.0
(44) 12.4	(43) 13.8	(40) 12.1	EBIT/Interest				(12) 5.7	(12) 52.0	(10) 31.4
2.5	2.8	3.0					2.1	4.1	7.5
4.2		10.4							
(11) 1.6		(14) 1.8	Net Profit + Depr., Dep., Amort./Cur. Mat. L/T/D						
.7		-1.0							
.2	.2	.1					.2	.1	.2
.5	.4	.4	Fixed/Worth				.5	.3	.4
1.4	1.6	.8					1.1	.6	.9
.9	.9	.7					1.6	.7	1.2
2.7	2.6	1.9	Debt/Worth				2.6	.8	2.1
8.3	10.3	5.2					5.5	2.1	14.3
66.9	68.1	53.3					54.2	46.2	89.1
(43) 26.0	(40) 36.1	(41) 33.9	% Profit Before Taxes/Tangible Net Worth				(13) 21.7	(12) 35.9	(10) 32.9
9.4	17.6	8.6					6.3	10.8	21.6
21.3	21.9	21.3					20.8	21.1	27.0
5.5	11.3	7.4	% Profit Before Taxes/Total Assets				4.0	10.0	13.5
1.5	3.7	1.7					1.3	4.1	4.9
55.1	44.5	45.7					49.3	61.2	43.5
22.4	15.8	17.3	Sales/Net Fixed Assets				15.8	21.4	19.8
8.1	7.5	11.3					11.6	6.6	11.1
2.6	3.1	3.1					3.5	2.4	2.3
1.9	1.8	2.0	Sales/Total Assets				2.8	1.6	1.8
1.5	1.6	1.5					2.0	.9	1.5
.5	.5	.5					.5	.4	.5
(45) .9	(41) 1.1	(38) .9	% Depr., Dep., Amort./Sales				(11) 1.2	(12) .7	.8
2.0	2.1	1.6					2.9	1.3	2.3
2.1	2.0	2.1							
(12) 3.1	(12) 2.5	(12) 2.9	% Officers', Directors' Owners' Comp/Sales						
6.5	5.3	4.3							
1460917M	1911256M	1511372M	Net Sales ($)		7434M	17544M	107055M	227121M	1152218M
951611M	1248245M	954277M	Total Assets ($)		4455M	6625M	50754M	177560M	714883M

M = $ thousand MM = $ million

See Pages 9 through 22 for Explanation of Ratios and Data

Current Data Sorted by Assets | **Comparative Historical Data**

0-500M	500M-2MM	2-10MM	10-50MM	50-100MM	100-250MM		4/1/09-3/31/10 ALL	4/1/10-3/31/11 ALL
						Type of Statement		
1		6	13	6	2	Unqualified	37	37
	3	26	19	1		Reviewed	58	60
3	6	14	3	1		Compiled	39	39
6	20	11	1			Tax Returns	34	44
8	22	33	22	3	5	Other	86	88
36 (4/1-9/30/13)			199 (10/1/13-3/31/14)					
18	51	90	58	11	7	**NUMBER OF STATEMENTS**	254	268
%	%	%	%	%	%	**ASSETS**	%	%
14.8	15.3	15.3	14.2	10.4		Cash & Equivalents	10.5	11.4
26.8	32.5	26.7	23.2	22.0		Trade Receivables (net)	23.8	26.7
25.7	21.3	26.1	24.8	15.1		Inventory	24.2	24.0
11.1	3.4	1.8	3.4	11.3		All Other Current	4.8	5.0
78.5	72.4	69.9	65.6	58.8		Total Current	63.4	67.1
19.1	18.6	20.0	20.9	11.8		Fixed Assets (net)	24.5	21.4
.3	3.0	4.8	7.1	20.7		Intangibles (net)	5.8	5.3
2.5	6.0	5.3	6.5	8.6		All Other Non-Current	6.4	6.1
100.0	100.0	100.0	100.0	100.0		Total	100.0	100.0
						LIABILITIES		
19.8	8.1	8.0	7.9	5.6		Notes Payable-Short Term	11.7	9.3
3.8	3.1	2.6	2.1	1.6		Cur. Mat.-L.T.D.	3.4	3.9
20.1	12.8	13.7	10.0	9.3		Trade Payables	12.9	13.4
.2	.3	.2	.2	.1		Income Taxes Payable	.3	.3
8.8	12.0	13.5	15.9	14.0		All Other Current	14.2	13.5
52.8	36.3	38.0	36.2	30.6		Total Current	42.4	40.4
13.6	13.6	11.9	9.3	9.0		Long-Term Debt	15.2	13.0
.0	.1	.5	.8	1.5		Deferred Taxes	.5	.5
18.4	10.2	7.5	8.0	7.6		All Other Non-Current	8.8	10.0
15.3	39.8	42.2	45.7	51.2		Net Worth	33.0	36.1
100.0	100.0	100.0	100.0	100.0		Total Liabilties & Net Worth	100.0	100.0
						INCOME DATA		
100.0	100.0	100.0	100.0	100.0		Net Sales	100.0	100.0
44.8	42.1	33.1	31.6	32.4		Gross Profit	31.4	35.0
38.3	34.9	28.4	24.7	22.6		Operating Expenses	28.6	27.9
6.5	7.2	4.7	6.8	9.9		Operating Profit	2.8	7.1
-.9	.1	.4	.3	1.6		All Other Expenses (net)	1.4	1.1
7.3	7.1	4.3	6.6	8.2		Profit Before Taxes	1.5	6.0
						RATIOS		
4.0	5.0	2.9	3.2	3.7			3.2	3.2
1.5	2.2	1.8	1.8	2.1		Current	1.6	1.8
1.2	1.2	1.3	1.2	1.3			1.0	1.2
2.7	3.3	1.9	1.6	2.3			1.9	1.8
1.0	(50) 1.3	1.2	1.0	1.0		Quick	.8	1.0
.4	.8	.6	.6	.5			.5	.6
7 51.0	**28** 13.1	**28** 12.9	**38** 9.5	**41** 8.9			**29** 12.4	**34** 10.8
17 21.7	**43** 8.5	**45** 8.2	**55** 6.6	**59** 6.2		Sales/Receivables	**43** 8.4	**48** 7.5
35 10.5	**57** 6.4	**62** 5.9	**76** 4.8	**65** 5.6			**58** 6.3	**66** 5.6
0 UND	**8** 43.2	**30** 12.1	**60** 6.1	**5** 76.6			**26** 13.9	**25** 14.7
19 19.4	**47** 7.7	**55** 6.6	**89** 4.1	**70** 5.2		Cost of Sales/Inventory	**62** 5.9	**64** 5.7
96 3.8	**114** 3.2	**122** 3.0	**122** 3.0	**182** 2.0			**121** 3.0	**116** 3.1
6 63.3	**10** 36.1	**15** 24.9	**17** 21.0	**25** 14.7			**16** 23.5	**18** 19.9
16 23.3	**26** 14.1	**26** 13.8	**27** 13.7	**36** 10.1		Cost of Sales/Payables	**27** 13.7	**32** 11.2
55 6.6	**53** 6.9	**50** 7.3	**49** 7.4	**45** 8.2			**44** 8.3	**50** 7.3
7.0	4.4	4.0	3.2	3.2			4.0	3.6
13.6	8.2	7.0	5.2	4.9		Sales/Working Capital	9.0	6.8
51.0	24.2	16.0	18.1	10.2			264.5	21.5
30.9	17.3	28.4	40.6	29.3			8.2	15.7
(12) 4.2	(39) 6.6	(77) 5.7	(52) 10.6	(10) 17.0		EBIT/Interest	(227) 2.5	(230) 5.5
-2.5	2.0	1.7	2.3	3.5			-.4	1.5
		16.0	14.3				5.3	8.8
		(18) 2.5	(20) 6.0			Net Profit + Depr., Dep., Amort./Cur. Mat. L/T/D	(53) 1.8	(56) 3.8
		.5	3.6				.9	1.8
.1	.1	.2	.2	.1			.2	.2
.6	.5	.4	.4	.4		Fixed/Worth	.7	.5
NM	1.9	1.3	1.4	-.6			4.0	2.1
1.0	.4	.6	.5	.5			.6	.6
2.3	1.8	1.4	1.5	.8		Debt/Worth	2.1	1.6
NM	15.5	4.5	7.5	-5.3			18.4	9.0
152.5	86.9	43.3	38.5				37.1	48.5
(14) 69.0	(42) 32.1	(82) 23.6	(51) 21.2			% Profit Before Taxes/Tangible Net Worth	(203) 14.5	(218) 22.6
8.4	8.4	5.4	6.9				-.5	6.6
41.2	25.3	18.8	16.3	13.9			11.7	19.0
16.8	9.9	6.5	8.2	10.5		% Profit Before Taxes/Total Assets	3.9	7.5
5.5	2.1	1.2	1.5	5.7			-2.6	1.9
316.2	45.7	36.7	20.1	20.9			25.0	28.6
21.1	20.9	14.1	8.7	14.6		Sales/Net Fixed Assets	9.9	11.4
10.4	9.9	6.4	4.7	10.0			4.4	5.4
6.4	3.7	2.8	1.9	1.8			2.5	2.4
3.8	2.6	2.1	1.4	1.4		Sales/Total Assets	1.8	1.7
2.1	1.8	1.5	1.1	.9			1.2	1.3
	.4	.8	1.1				1.0	1.1
	(33) 1.5	(76) 1.6	(55) 1.6			% Depr., Dep., Amort./Sales	(216) 2.3	(221) 2.0
	3.3	2.9	2.8				4.3	3.6
	3.2	2.1					2.5	2.2
	(26) 4.5	(43) 4.0				% Officers', Directors' Owners' Comp/Sales	(86) 4.9	(100) 4.9
	8.8	8.4					7.6	8.2
24244M	171128M	882045M	1976024M	1111804M	1200689M	Net Sales ($)	5313990M	5472542M
5626M	63347M	428509M	1288577M	806319M	973440M	Total Assets ($)	3509307M	3759169M

M = $ thousand MM = $ million

See Pages 9 through 22 for Explanation of Ratios and Data

Comparative Historical Data | **Current Data Sorted by Sales**

						Type of Statement												
	35		30		28	Unqualified		1		1				2		5		19
	55		50		49	Reviewed				3		4		14		18		10
	34		37		27	Compiled		1		6		2		10		7		1
	35		45		38	Tax Returns		4		11		10		9		4		
	87		89		93	Other		4		12		16		15		26		20
								36 (4/1-9/30/13)						199 (10/1/13-3/31/14)				
	4/1/11-3/31/12 ALL		4/1/12-3/31/13 ALL		4/1/13-3/31/14 ALL			0-1MM		1-3MM		3-5MM		5-10MM		10-25MM		25MM & OVER
	246		251		235	NUMBER OF STATEMENTS		10		33		32		50		60		50
	%		%		%	**ASSETS**		%		%		%		%		%		%
	11.4		13.9		14.5	Cash & Equivalents		6.9		16.4		16.8		14.7		15.7		11.9
	26.7		25.5		26.8	Trade Receivables (net)		30.4		22.0		27.4		28.5		27.5		26.2
	25.3		24.6		24.0	Inventory		22.6		24.0		22.1		24.7		25.0		23.4
	4.3		4.6		4.0	All Other Current		15.6		4.0		2.8		2.5		1.7		6.7
	67.7		68.7		69.3	Total Current		75.7		66.4		69.2		70.4		69.9		68.1
	18.7		19.3		19.4	Fixed Assets (net)		13.4		23.4		16.9		21.2		21.4		15.1
	7.2		5.6		5.7	Intangibles (net)		.3		6.4		2.9		4.3		4.4		11.1
	6.5		6.4		5.7	All Other Non-Current		11.4		3.8		10.9		4.0		4.3		5.6
	100.0		100.0		100.0	Total		100.0		100.0		100.0		100.0		100.0		100.0
						LIABILITIES												
	10.6		11.1		8.7	Notes Payable-Short Term		19.5		9.0		9.1		8.0		8.6		6.7
	3.0		2.7		2.6	Cur. Mat.-L.T.D.		2.8		5.1		2.4		2.9		1.8		1.5
	13.6		14.8		12.8	Trade Payables		10.9		12.3		14.9		12.8		12.8		12.0
	.3		.2		.2	Income Taxes Payable		.4		.3		.3		.2		.1		.1
	14.9		14.5		13.5	All Other Current		4.5		11.9		6.6		16.2		14.1		17.4
	42.4		43.2		37.7	Total Current		38.1		38.6		33.2		40.2		37.4		37.8
	10.4		9.1		11.6	Long-Term Debt		13.8		16.7		10.7		13.8		9.6		8.7
	.5		.7		.6	Deferred Taxes		.0		.0		.3		.4		.7		1.2
	8.5		10.0		8.9	All Other Non-Current		24.9		11.9		9.1		10.0		5.4		6.8
	38.2		37.0		41.2	Net Worth		23.1		32.8		46.7		35.7		46.9		45.6
	100.0		100.0		100.0	Total Liabilties & Net Worth		100.0		100.0		100.0		100.0		100.0		100.0
						INCOME DATA												
	100.0		100.0		100.0	Net Sales		100.0		100.0		100.0		100.0		100.0		100.0
	33.3		33.4		35.4	Gross Profit		54.4		41.6		41.6		32.6		30.3		32.4
	27.0		26.9		29.2	Operating Expenses		41.7		38.1		31.8		28.3		25.3		24.9
	6.3		6.5		6.1	Operating Profit		12.8		3.4		9.8		4.4		5.0		7.5
	.8		.9		.4	All Other Expenses (net)		1.1		-.3		-.1		.3		.0		1.9
	5.6		5.6		5.7	Profit Before Taxes		11.6		3.7		9.9		4.0		5.0		5.6
						RATIOS												
	3.0		3.2		3.4			7.8		5.3		4.0		3.2		2.8		3.1
	1.7		1.9		1.9	Current		1.4		2.4		2.1		1.8		1.8		1.8
	1.1		1.2		1.3			1.2		1.1		1.3		1.2		1.3		1.3
	1.6		2.0		2.0			3.7		3.7		2.4		1.8		1.7		1.7
	.9		1.0	(234)	1.2	Quick		.8	(32)	1.2		1.4		1.2		1.2		1.0
	.5		.6		.6			.3		.6		.7		.6		.7		.6
33	11.1	**31**	11.6	**31**	11.8		**15**	24.8	**14**	25.5	**26**	13.9	**32**	11.3	**33**	11.2	**41**	8.9
49	7.5	**43**	8.5	**45**	8.1	Sales/Receivables	**31**	11.8	**38**	9.7	**43**	8.4	**42**	8.6	**49**	7.5	**57**	6.4
63	5.8	**60**	6.1	**64**	5.7		**101**	3.6	**61**	6.0	**61**	6.0	**54**	6.8	**65**	5.6	**76**	4.8
28	13.0	**25**	14.5	**25**	14.7		**0**	UND	**3**	106.5	**11**	33.1	**25**	14.8	**33**	11.2	**38**	9.7
72	5.1	**65**	5.6	**66**	5.5	Cost of Sales/Inventory	**87**	4.2	**70**	5.2	**45**	8.2	**58**	6.3	**64**	5.7	**83**	4.4
118	3.1	**118**	3.1	**118**	3.1		**140**	2.6	**122**	3.0	**114**	3.2	**130**	2.8	**99**	3.7	**126**	2.9
19	19.6	**14**	25.5	**14**	26.8		**8**	45.9	**7**	50.7	**12**	29.5	**13**	28.1	**14**	25.9	**20**	17.9
30	12.1	**26**	13.8	**27**	13.7	Cost of Sales/Payables	**53**	6.9	**20**	18.4	**30**	12.1	**22**	16.8	**26**	14.1	**35**	10.3
50	7.3	**46**	7.9	**49**	7.4		**146**	2.5	**51**	7.2	**51**	7.1	**49**	7.5	**42**	8.7	**49**	7.5
	3.8		3.9		3.7			2.4		3.8		4.3		4.1		4.1		3.4
	7.8		6.7		6.5	Sales/Working Capital		7.7		10.1		7.3		7.9		5.9		5.0
	32.7		19.5		18.0			UND		43.3		27.4		19.4		16.3		9.0
	24.8		29.4		26.5					9.9		36.9		35.5		34.2		25.6
(210)	7.3	(205)	7.1	(195)	7.4	EBIT/Interest			(27)	5.4	(25)	9.7	(43)	6.6	(53)	8.6	(41)	12.6
	2.4		1.7		1.9					2.4		1.9		1.6		.4		2.9
	9.2		10.7		14.3											15.7		30.2
(70)	4.8	(47)	4.2	(44)	4.7	Net Profit + Depr., Dep., Amort./Cur. Mat. L/T/D									(17)	5.9	(16)	5.9
	1.9		2.0		1.5											1.8		3.8
	.2		.2		.2			.0		.2		.1		.2		.2		.2
	.5		.4		.4	Fixed/Worth		.2		1.0		.3		.5		.4		.4
	1.7		1.6		1.6			NM		UND		1.0		2.2		.9		.9
	.7		.5		.6			.6		.5		.4		.5		.6		.6
	1.6		1.3		1.5	Debt/Worth		1.9		1.9		.9		2.4		1.3		1.4
	8.1		5.6		6.0			NM		UND		3.6		12.9		2.8		4.5
	49.2		47.4		53.2					84.7		89.0		54.8		36.7		49.9
(207)	25.6	(211)	23.9	(203)	23.5	% Profit Before Taxes/Tangible Net Worth			(25)	21.8	(28)	31.8	(43)	27.2	(58)	19.2	(41)	21.9
	10.4		5.4		6.9					4.0		9.2		9.1		2.5		12.2
	18.2		20.5		19.8			25.7		19.7		42.6		20.0		17.3		15.8
	9.0		8.5		9.1	% Profit Before Taxes/Total Assets		18.0		5.1		12.1		7.9		7.5		9.8
	2.4		1.7		1.8			-5.3		.2		2.7		1.7		-.5		2.2
	30.3		37.4		32.4			UND		33.6		85.1		29.5		24.5		28.5
	12.8		14.2		13.6	Sales/Net Fixed Assets		17.7		19.5		16.8		12.3		10.7		13.9
	6.6		6.4		6.2			7.6		5.6		9.3		5.6		6.0		5.9
	2.6		2.8		2.8			2.3		3.9		3.6		2.8		2.8		2.1
	1.9		2.1		1.9	Sales/Total Assets		2.0		2.0		2.7		2.1		1.9		1.6
	1.4		1.5		1.4			1.2		1.4		1.8		1.5		1.4		1.2
	.8		.6		.9					1.1		.4		.8		.9		1.0
(204)	1.6	(203)	1.5	(189)	1.5	% Depr., Dep., Amort./Sales			(24)	1.9	(22)	1.4	(38)	1.7	(56)	1.5	(44)	1.3
	2.8		3.0		2.9					6.5		3.0		3.5		2.8		2.7
	2.5		1.8		2.5					3.6		3.4		2.4		2.0		
(81)	4.1	(79)	3.3	(88)	4.1	% Officers', Directors' Owners' Comp/Sales			(13)	5.2	(17)	4.3	(25)	4.2	(26)	3.3		
	6.5		7.3		8.0					9.9		8.0		9.5		5.7		
	6243810M		**6115634M**		**5365934M**	Net Sales ($)		**7149M**		**69053M**		**118888M**		**348690M**		**964547M**		**3857607M**
	4140643M		**3963105M**		**3565818M**	Total Assets ($)		**4531M**		**39591M**		**67104M**		**202853M**		**600712M**		**2651027M**

 M = $ thousand MM = $ million

See Pages 9 through 22 for Explanation of Ratios and Data

Current Data Sorted by Assets | **Comparative Historical Data**

0-500M	500M-2MM	2-10MM	10-50MM	50-100MM	100-250MM		4/1/09-3/31/10 ALL	4/1/10-3/31/11 ALL
						Type of Statement		
	1	1		1	3	Unqualified	14	11
	1	5	1			Reviewed	15	10
	1	4				Compiled	3	9
3	1	6			1	Tax Returns	17	14
3	7	14	6			Other	35	28
8 (4/1-9/30/13)			51 (10/1/13-3/31/14)					
6	11	30	7	1	4	**NUMBER OF STATEMENTS**	84	72
%	%	%	%	%	%	**ASSETS**	%	%
	25.7	13.5				Cash & Equivalents	13.3	12.4
	26.2	31.2				Trade Receivables (net)	29.3	30.1
	17.1	32.6				Inventory	23.9	29.4
	.9	5.5				All Other Current	3.3	1.7
	70.0	82.8				Total Current	69.7	73.6
	13.5	9.7				Fixed Assets (net)	15.3	12.5
	6.9	1.4				Intangibles (net)	7.2	5.6
	9.6	6.2				All Other Non-Current	7.8	8.3
	100.0	100.0				Total	100.0	100.0
						LIABILITIES		
	9.9	19.9				Notes Payable-Short Term	14.2	14.5
	3.3	1.1				Cur. Mat.-L.T.D.	2.9	2.1
	25.2	15.8				Trade Payables	14.1	15.5
	.0	.1				Income Taxes Payable	.6	.4
	23.3	9.6				All Other Current	12.4	12.1
	61.7	46.5				Total Current	44.3	44.7
	14.8	5.0				Long-Term Debt	10.9	13.4
	.0	.0				Deferred Taxes	.3	.1
	5.4	8.6				All Other Non-Current	6.7	8.1
	18.0	39.9				Net Worth	37.8	33.7
	100.0	100.0				Total Liabilties & Net Worth	100.0	100.0
						INCOME DATA		
	100.0	100.0				Net Sales	100.0	100.0
	56.4	33.1				Gross Profit	40.2	37.3
	50.9	29.6				Operating Expenses	38.0	32.3
	5.5	3.5				Operating Profit	2.1	5.0
	.5	.9				All Other Expenses (net)	.9	1.4
	5.0	2.6				Profit Before Taxes	1.3	3.6
						RATIOS		
	2.0	2.8					2.4	2.6
	1.3	1.9				Current	1.5	1.6
	.9	1.3					1.1	1.3
	1.3	1.4					1.8	1.4
	1.1	.9				Quick	.9	.9
	.5	.5					.6	.6
	11 34.4	**23** 16.2					**33** 11.1	**29** 12.8
	30 12.1	**40** 9.2				Sales/Receivables	**47** 7.8	**42** 8.7
	45 8.1	**68** 5.4					**62** 5.9	**57** 6.4
	5 66.6	**19** 19.6					**26** 14.2	**31** 11.9
	58 6.3	**78** 4.7				Cost of Sales/Inventory	**59** 6.2	**61** 6.0
	174 2.1	**174** 2.1					**106** 3.5	**103** 3.6
	19 19.4	**16** 23.5					**17** 20.9	**13** 27.2
	48 7.6	**28** 13.2				Cost of Sales/Payables	**34** 10.7	**32** 11.5
	159 2.3	**49** 7.4					**54** 6.8	**58** 6.2
	6.4	4.2					4.1	5.1
	20.1	5.9				Sales/Working Capital	9.0	9.2
	-26.8	17.2					33.7	20.4
		10.7					15.1	15.1
		(23) 5.5				EBIT/Interest	(66) 3.7	(60) 4.7
		.6					.4	1.6
							12.3	19.8
						Net Profit + Depr., Dep., Amort./Cur. Mat. L/T/D	(16) 1.7	(10) 2.0
							-.9	.4
	.0	.1					.1	.1
	.2	.2				Fixed/Worth	.3	.2
	-7.6	.5					1.6	1.0
	1.2	.6					.8	.6
	2.8	1.8				Debt/Worth	2.0	1.7
	-34.0	4.5					4.6	3.9
		44.2					43.2	48.2
		(28) 9.6				% Profit Before Taxes/Tangible Net Worth	(74) 13.2	(61) 20.1
		.2					-.6	4.8
	29.8	15.6					15.1	16.9
	11.2	4.1				% Profit Before Taxes/Total Assets	3.6	7.3
	2.9	-1.3					-2.0	2.0
	173.1	206.4					68.2	130.0
	83.8	61.1				Sales/Net Fixed Assets	28.6	42.7
	10.6	16.3					10.1	15.4
	4.2	3.6					3.5	3.5
	2.8	2.4				Sales/Total Assets	2.2	2.5
	2.1	1.6					1.2	1.6
		.3					.8	.4
		(20) .7				% Depr., Dep., Amort./Sales	(52) 1.6	(47) 1.2
		1.5					3.2	2.1
		2.1					1.9	1.2
		(15) 3.5				% Officers', Directors' Owners' Comp/Sales	(27) 3.5	(22) 2.0
		4.3					8.0	4.3
4169M	52456M	398892M	491214M	340162M	1979161M	Net Sales ($)	2576889M	2016636M
1053M	14432M	124194M	183847M	57027M	610182M	Total Assets ($)	1760336M	1005988M

M = $ thousand MM = $ million

See Pages 9 through 22 for Explanation of Ratios and Data

Comparative Historical Data				Current Data Sorted by Sales					
			Type of Statement						
9	7	6	Unqualified		1			1	4
10	8	7	Reviewed		1	1	2		3
9	5	5	Compiled				3	1	1
16	12	11	Tax Returns	2	2	3	3		1
41	26	30	Other	2	5	2	7	8	6
4/1/11-3/31/12 ALL	**4/1/12-3/31/13 ALL**	**4/1/13-3/31/14 ALL**		**8 (4/1-9/30/13)**			**51 (10/1/13-3/31/14)**		
				0-1MM	**1-3MM**	**3-5MM**	**5-10MM**	**10-25MM**	**25MM & OVER**
85	58	59	**NUMBER OF STATEMENTS**	4	9	6	15	10	15
%	%	%	**ASSETS**	%	%	%	%	%	%
15.0	16.3	15.2	Cash & Equivalents				14.5	15.4	4.4
32.1	32.3	32.4	Trade Receivables (net)				31.7	28.3	47.5
26.0	26.5	26.7	Inventory				30.6	39.9	24.5
2.4	2.0	3.8	All Other Current				1.5	5.2	5.2
75.5	77.0	78.0	Total Current				78.3	88.8	81.6
12.7	10.9	11.1	Fixed Assets (net)				14.5	8.1	4.1
3.8	6.6	4.3	Intangibles (net)				2.1	1.2	8.8
7.9	5.6	6.6	All Other Non-Current				5.1	1.9	5.5
100.0	100.0	100.0	Total				100.0	100.0	100.0
			LIABILITIES						
10.4	11.9	17.3	Notes Payable-Short Term				16.0	27.3	12.9
2.1	1.8	1.7	Cur. Mat.-L.T.D.				2.2	.4	1.2
18.1	20.4	21.3	Trade Payables				15.1	18.1	33.2
.3	.4	.3	Income Taxes Payable				.2	.0	.0
13.4	11.9	12.7	All Other Current				5.4	6.3	12.5
44.4	46.5	53.3	Total Current				39.0	52.1	59.8
14.1	19.7	10.0	Long-Term Debt				6.4	2.7	14.6
.3	.4	.1	Deferred Taxes				.0	.0	.3
20.0	12.9	7.7	All Other Non-Current				14.8	5.8	5.9
21.3	20.6	28.9	Net Worth				39.8	39.4	19.4
100.0	100.0	100.0	Total Liabilties & Net Worth				100.0	100.0	100.0
			INCOME DATA						
100.0	100.0	100.0	Net Sales				100.0	100.0	100.0
39.2	37.1	36.5	Gross Profit				40.9	26.1	19.7
34.0	30.6	32.4	Operating Expenses				37.1	20.8	17.3
5.2	6.5	4.0	Operating Profit				3.8	5.4	2.4
1.1	1.3	.8	All Other Expenses (net)				.7	.6	.8
4.1	5.2	3.2	Profit Before Taxes				3.2	4.8	1.6
			RATIOS						
2.9	3.3	2.3					3.5	2.8	2.1
1.8	1.7	1.6	Current				2.0	1.5	1.4
1.3	1.2	1.2					1.3	1.3	1.1
1.7	1.6	1.4					1.7	1.6	1.1
1.0	1.0	.9	Quick				1.2	.6	.9
.7	.7	.6					.8	.5	.7
29 12.4	**29** 12.4	**23** 16.1					**30** 12.1	**16** 23.0	**27** 13.6
41 8.9	**43** 8.4	**40** 9.2	Sales/Receivables				**36** 10.1	**36** 10.0	**52** 7.0
61 6.0	**62** 5.9	**62** 5.9					**66** 5.5	**61** 6.0	**68** 5.4
24 15.4	**18** 20.2	**12** 30.1					**14** 26.2	**27** 13.4	**7** 48.7
51 7.2	**49** 7.5	**58** 6.3	Cost of Sales/Inventory				**76** 4.8	**63** 5.8	**26** 14.1
107 3.4	**104** 3.5	**122** 3.0					**215** 1.7	**114** 3.2	**60** 6.1
15 24.7	**19** 19.4	**18** 20.1					**23** 16.1	**11** 32.6	**20** 18.1
30 12.3	**36** 10.0	**33** 11.0	Cost of Sales/Payables				**36** 10.0	**22** 16.3	**36** 10.2
51 7.1	**52** 7.0	**53** 6.9					**55** 6.6	**47** 7.7	**49** 7.4
4.7	4.2	4.8					4.7	4.8	9.3
8.1	9.4	10.0	Sales/Working Capital				6.3	13.6	22.0
21.3	23.5	30.9					11.6	16.6	46.8
18.5	19.5	12.9					20.7		15.7
(68) 4.7	(44) 3.7	(45) 3.9	EBIT/Interest				(12) 5.5		3.4
1.8	1.1	.4					.7		-3.7
			Net Profit + Depr., Dep., Amort./Cur. Mat. L/T/D						
.1	.0	.0					.1	.1	.0
.2	.2	.2	Fixed/Worth				.2	.1	.1
1.2	1.1	.8					1.1	.4	.6
.7	.8	.9					.8	.6	1.0
1.2	2.0	2.1	Debt/Worth				1.4	2.3	2.2
8.3	6.4	6.8					5.7	3.7	11.1
50.2	64.2	52.6					50.7	61.1	50.0
(69) 25.8	(48) 27.4	(48) 12.0	% Profit Before Taxes/Tangible Net Worth				(13) 9.3	35.0	(12) 6.8
4.6	.5	.9					-6.0	6.3	-.1
19.6	28.3	19.5					18.1	30.2	17.1
8.0	7.0	4.1	% Profit Before Taxes/Total Assets				4.6	10.0	1.8
.6	.0	-.8					-1.2	.9	-.8
178.8	245.8	198.1					106.9	256.0	286.0
49.2	48.6	59.3	Sales/Net Fixed Assets				59.1	94.2	131.8
13.5	12.4	18.4					9.8	35.6	43.1
3.7	3.7	4.2					3.6	4.0	6.0
2.7	2.5	2.6	Sales/Total Assets				2.4	3.2	3.5
1.7	1.8	1.9					1.9	2.3	2.4
.4	.2	.4					.3		.1
(52) 1.0	(33) .7	(37) .8	% Depr., Dep., Amort./Sales				(10) .7		(12) .5
2.5	1.7	1.7					1.9		1.1
1.5	1.6	1.9							
(31) 3.1	(16) 2.1	(27) 3.7	% Officers', Directors' Owners' Comp/Sales						
6.7	4.4	10.6							
2291861M	2141262M	3266054M	Net Sales ($)	1315M	18838M	24479M	106473M	146524M	2968425M
1102078M	1008698M	990735M	Total Assets ($)	244M	17321M	13846M	47844M	51433M	860047M

M = $ thousand MM = $ million

See Pages 9 through 22 for Explanation of Ratios and Data

Current Data Sorted by Assets							Comparative Historical Data	
						Type of Statement		
		3	2	4	4	Unqualified	27	25
		8	2			Reviewed	11	13
	1		1		1	Compiled	6	3
1	2	5				Tax Returns	3	13
	5	8	17	5	7	Other	54	45
	14 (4/1-9/30/13)		62 (10/1/13-3/31/14)				4/1/09-3/31/10	4/1/10-3/31/11
0-500M	**500M-2MM**	**2-10MM**	**10-50MM**	**50-100MM**	**100-250MM**		**ALL**	**ALL**
1	8	24	22	9	12	**NUMBER OF STATEMENTS**	101	99
%	%	%	%	%	%	**ASSETS**	%	%
		14.4	10.2		14.4	Cash & Equivalents	14.3	15.2
		27.0	28.0		27.8	Trade Receivables (net)	26.5	24.7
		33.9	23.1		22.2	Inventory	23.6	26.8
		5.2	3.5		6.5	All Other Current	4.7	5.3
		80.4	64.8		70.9	Total Current	69.1	71.9
		10.5	14.2		8.1	Fixed Assets (net)	13.4	11.8
		4.3	13.4		12.6	Intangibles (net)	9.9	9.4
		4.8	7.6		8.4	All Other Non-Current	7.6	6.9
		100.0	100.0		100.0	Total	100.0	100.0
						LIABILITIES		
		10.4	5.7		3.8	Notes Payable-Short Term	9.6	7.4
		2.9	3.3		1.6	Cur. Mat.-L.T.D.	2.3	2.4
		14.6	19.9		20.2	Trade Payables	14.3	15.0
		.2	.3		.2	Income Taxes Payable	.3	.3
		10.5	14.0		12.7	All Other Current	14.1	14.0
		38.6	43.2		38.5	Total Current	40.6	39.1
		13.2	12.5		26.4	Long-Term Debt	10.1	9.1
		.4	.3		.1	Deferred Taxes	.5	.5
		7.6	11.4		10.1	All Other Non-Current	9.2	8.1
		40.3	32.5		24.9	Net Worth	39.6	43.2
		100.0	100.0		100.0	Total Liabilties & Net Worth	100.0	100.0
						INCOME DATA		
		100.0	100.0		100.0	Net Sales	100.0	100.0
		35.0	30.9		38.7	Gross Profit	36.1	36.3
		29.5	26.7		29.7	Operating Expenses	34.6	34.0
		5.5	4.2		9.0	Operating Profit	1.5	2.3
		.1	1.2		4.2	All Other Expenses (net)	.8	.8
		5.3	2.9		4.8	Profit Before Taxes	.7	1.5
						RATIOS		
		3.4	2.4		2.9		3.3	3.2
		2.2	1.5		1.9	Current	1.8	1.7
		1.5	.9		1.4		1.3	1.4
		1.7	1.3		1.5		2.1	1.9
		1.2	.8		1.2	Quick	1.0	1.0
		.6	.6		.7		.6	.6
		27 13.5	**29** 12.6		**42** 8.6		**35** 10.4	**34** 10.6
		41 9.0	**43** 8.4		**52** 7.0	Sales/Receivables	**49** 7.5	**51** 7.2
		50 7.3	**60** 6.1		**63** 5.8		**61** 6.0	**63** 5.8
		51 7.1	**30** 12.3		**46** 8.0		**33** 11.2	**45** 8.2
		78 4.7	**62** 5.9		**53** 6.9	Cost of Sales/Inventory	**65** 5.6	**79** 4.6
		114 3.2	**87** 4.2		**72** 5.1		**114** 3.2	**130** 2.8
		13 28.1	**29** 12.8		**37** 9.8		**22** 16.6	**21** 17.8
		28 12.9	**39** 9.4		**58** 6.3	Cost of Sales/Payables	**34** 10.8	**44** 8.3
		48 7.6	**73** 5.0		**79** 4.6		**54** 6.7	**62** 5.9
		4.1	4.1		4.2		3.2	3.3
		6.6	10.8		5.6	Sales/Working Capital	6.9	5.6
		11.8	-59.4		8.5		16.5	13.6
		20.7	23.4		38.6		11.8	15.8
		(22) 6.5	(18) 9.1		(10) 6.7	EBIT/Interest	(84) 2.5	(84) 3.0
		3.8	1.7		-3.8		-.1	.6
							4.4	7.9
						Net Profit + Depr., Dep., Amort./Cur. Mat. L/T/D	(26) 2.1	(28) 3.2
							1.0	1.6
		.1	.1		.1		.1	.1
		.4	.4		.2	Fixed/Worth	.4	.2
		.8	-1.2		UND		1.2	.8
		.9	1.0		.7		.5	.7
		2.0	2.4		2.6	Debt/Worth	1.8	1.4
		4.2	-8.5		UND		5.0	5.3
		59.8	35.9		52.8		31.6	37.4
		(23) 24.2	(16) 23.6		(10) 15.1	% Profit Before Taxes/Tangible Net Worth	(86) 11.2	(85) 15.2
		4.6	18.0		-2.4		-.1	1.4
		17.8	12.2		12.9		9.1	12.5
		8.1	8.5		10.3	% Profit Before Taxes/Total Assets	2.7	5.3
		2.5	3.8		.9		-2.6	-.3
		97.3	88.4		53.9		45.7	62.9
		33.9	30.9		26.4	Sales/Net Fixed Assets	21.2	24.2
		16.9	10.2		15.3		9.4	11.4
		3.3	2.8		2.6		2.5	2.5
		2.3	1.9		1.6	Sales/Total Assets	1.9	1.8
		1.6	1.3		1.2		1.2	1.1
		.6	.7		.8		.9	.7
		(18) 1.1	(19) 1.4		(10) 1.2	% Depr., Dep., Amort./Sales	(71) 1.8	(78) 1.3
		2.0	3.1		2.0		3.1	2.8
							3.7	.9
						% Officers', Directors' Owners' Comp/Sales	(15) 5.6	(21) 4.2
							8.4	6.3
2586M	**29509M**	**276902M**	**1100627M**	**944029M**	**3146147M**	Net Sales ($)	**4341067M**	**4788790M**
230M	**9803M**	**105027M**	**489749M**	**647773M**	**1623178M**	Total Assets ($)	**2597399M**	**3359505M**

M = $ thousand MM = $ million

See Pages 9 through 22 for Explanation of Ratios and Data

Comparative Historical Data | **Current Data Sorted by Sales**

4/1/11-3/31/12 ALL	4/1/12-3/31/13 ALL	4/1/13-3/31/14 ALL	Type of Statement	0-1MM	1-3MM	3-5MM	5-10MM	10-25MM	25MM & OVER
18	19	13	Unqualified		1			3	9
12	15	10	Reviewed				6	2	2
6	7	3	Compiled				1		2
12	9	8	Tax Returns		1		6	1	
47	49	42	Other	1	1	5	2	6	27
				14 (4/1-9/30/13)			62 (10/1/13-3/31/14)		
95	99	76	**NUMBER OF STATEMENTS**	1	3	5	15	12	40
%	%	%	**ASSETS**	%	%	%	%	%	%
12.1	16.1	13.5	Cash & Equivalents				14.1	11.8	12.6
28.8	26.4	27.4	Trade Receivables (net)				30.7	21.0	28.9
25.4	25.8	27.1	Inventory				32.9	27.7	23.2
4.3	4.0	4.6	All Other Current				2.8	5.5	5.4
70.5	72.3	72.6	Total Current				80.6	65.9	70.1
12.7	9.6	10.8	Fixed Assets (net)				10.5	16.0	10.1
10.0	11.1	10.4	Intangibles (net)				5.5	13.8	12.9
6.8	7.1	6.2	All Other Non-Current				3.4	4.3	6.8
100.0	100.0	100.0	Total				100.0	100.0	100.0
			LIABILITIES						
7.5	8.9	7.9	Notes Payable-Short Term				10.1	10.7	5.2
1.9	2.5	2.4	Cur. Mat.-L.T.D.				2.9	3.3	2.5
18.2	18.1	18.7	Trade Payables				18.5	12.6	20.4
.3	.5	.2	Income Taxes Payable				.2	.1	.3
12.0	12.6	11.6	All Other Current				11.4	6.1	13.7
40.0	42.7	40.8	Total Current				43.0	32.8	42.1
9.4	11.0	14.0	Long-Term Debt				18.4	15.2	14.6
.5	.6	.2	Deferred Taxes				.0	.4	.2
8.0	9.5	9.1	All Other Non-Current				7.1	7.9	11.0
42.1	36.3	35.8	Net Worth				31.5	43.7	32.1
100.0	100.0	100.0	Total Liabilties & Net Worth				100.0	100.0	100.0
			INCOME DATA						
100.0	100.0	100.0	Net Sales				100.0	100.0	100.0
37.4	35.4	34.5	Gross Profit				33.2	34.1	33.8
30.7	30.3	28.6	Operating Expenses				29.1	27.8	27.7
6.7	5.1	5.9	Operating Profit				4.1	6.3	6.0
1.1	1.0	1.3	All Other Expenses (net)				.4	1.3	1.8
5.6	4.1	4.6	Profit Before Taxes				3.7	5.0	4.2
			RATIOS						
3.0	2.6	2.8					2.8	3.7	2.6
1.9	1.8	1.7	Current				2.0	1.6	1.7
1.4	1.2	1.3					1.5	1.3	1.3
1.9	1.7	1.6					1.6	2.4	1.5
1.0	1.0	1.1	Quick				1.2	.8	1.0
.8	.6	.6					.7	.3	.6
36 10.1	32 11.5	32 11.3					35 10.4	21 17.8	38 9.7
51 7.2	46 7.9	49 7.5	Sales/Receivables				43 8.4	33 11.2	54 6.8
63 5.8	62 5.9	62 5.9					64 5.7	50 7.3	64 5.7
50 7.3	41 9.0	45 8.1					51 7.1	51 7.2	42 8.7
74 4.9	61 6.0	65 5.6	Cost of Sales/Inventory				69 5.3	72 5.1	58 6.3
118 3.1	114 3.2	104 3.5					107 3.4	114 3.2	89 4.1
23 15.7	25 14.8	24 14.9					19 19.0	19 19.7	30 12.0
41 9.0	35 10.4	36 10.1	Cost of Sales/Payables				28 13.2	41 8.8	41 8.9
59 6.2	59 6.2	63 5.8					55 6.6	55 6.6	74 4.9
3.9	4.2	4.3					4.8	3.6	4.3
6.0	6.0	7.3	Sales/Working Capital				7.3	10.2	7.0
12.7	17.3	14.9					8.8	23.3	15.5
22.7	26.4	23.4					16.7	33.3	28.4
(80) 5.8	(77) 5.1	(64) 7.5	EBIT/Interest				(14) 5.0	(11) 9.7	(32) 9.1
1.6	1.7	2.7					3.4	.7	3.3
10.4	6.4	10.9							18.6
(27) 1.9	(27) 2.1	(20) 4.1	Net Profit + Depr., Dep., Amort./Cur. Mat. L/T/D						(13) 4.3
1.4	.7	1.4							1.5
.1	.1	.1					.1	.3	.1
.2	.2	.4	Fixed/Worth				.4	.5	.2
1.0	1.1	1.6					1.2	2.4	UND
.6	.6	.9					1.7	.5	.9
1.6	1.6	2.2	Debt/Worth				2.4	2.0	2.3
5.0	12.0	7.5					6.2	19.8	UND
42.7	47.0	53.7					61.5	93.6	43.5
(79) 14.0	(77) 17.7	(62) 24.3	% Profit Before Taxes/Tangible Net Worth				(14) 31.8	(10) 38.0	(30) 23.4
2.9	1.8	5.9					5.2	-1.0	9.6
14.8	18.6	16.1					18.5	24.3	12.0
6.3	6.5	8.1	% Profit Before Taxes/Total Assets				8.3	10.5	8.5
.5	.2	3.7					3.6	-1.1	5.3
89.4	89.8	84.9					104.9	59.0	57.2
30.4	34.5	30.9	Sales/Net Fixed Assets				44.7	19.3	26.8
10.0	13.9	15.1					17.8	7.6	12.6
2.7	2.7	3.1					3.5	2.9	2.7
2.0	2.1	1.9	Sales/Total Assets				2.8	2.0	1.7
1.2	1.3	1.4					1.8	1.3	1.3
.6	.6	.7					.3		.7
(65) 1.2	(73) 1.1	(58) 1.4	% Depr., Dep., Amort./Sales				(11) .8		(35) 1.4
2.2	2.2	1.9					1.5		1.8
1.3	1.3	.7							
(25) 3.4	(17) 2.9	(14) 3.0	% Officers', Directors' Owners' Comp/Sales						
5.5	7.6	6.3							
5432142M	7142859M	5499800M	Net Sales ($)	907M	7785M	17765M	111678M	187327M	5174338M
3386596M	3871306M	2875760M	Total Assets ($)	1582M	3441M	7770M	49404M	118728M	2694835M

M = $ thousand MM = $ million

See Pages 9 through 22 for Explanation of Ratios and Data

Current Data Sorted by Assets | **Comparative Historical Data**

0-500M	500M-2MM	2-10MM	10-50MM	50-100MM	100-250MM	Type of Statement	4/1/09-3/31/10 ALL	4/1/10-3/31/11 ALL
		3	2	1		Unqualified	9	9
	1	5	2			Reviewed	4	3
		1				Compiled	2	
	1	2				Tax Returns	4	3
	2	6	7	3	3	Other	22	21
	9 (4/1-9/30/13)		30 (10/1/13-3/31/14)					
	4	17	11	4	3	**NUMBER OF STATEMENTS**	41	36
%	%	%	%	%	%	**ASSETS**	%	%
DATA NOT AVAILABLE		21.1	13.3			Cash & Equivalents	19.3	20.0
		23.6	24.5			Trade Receivables (net)	29.0	27.7
		30.5	27.3			Inventory	21.4	21.5
		3.0	5.0			All Other Current	6.0	2.9
		78.2	70.1			Total Current	75.6	72.0
		9.1	17.8			Fixed Assets (net)	12.0	11.4
		7.4	9.4			Intangibles (net)	6.1	6.6
		5.3	2.7			All Other Non-Current	6.3	10.0
		100.0	100.0			Total	100.0	100.0
						LIABILITIES		
		8.2	5.2			Notes Payable-Short Term	7.5	4.8
		1.4	1.2			Cur. Mat.-L.T.D.	5.8	1.8
		13.9	15.6			Trade Payables	17.3	17.3
		.0	.1			Income Taxes Payable	.1	.2
		10.4	7.3			All Other Current	16.6	16.5
		34.0	29.4			Total Current	47.4	40.6
		9.7	8.5			Long-Term Debt	6.2	6.4
		.2	1.6			Deferred Taxes	.3	.3
		3.8	4.4			All Other Non-Current	13.1	8.6
		52.3	56.1			Net Worth	33.1	44.1
		100.0	100.0			Total Liabilties & Net Worth	100.0	100.0
						INCOME DATA		
		100.0	100.0			Net Sales	100.0	100.0
		42.9	40.0			Gross Profit	42.2	41.3
		38.3	32.5			Operating Expenses	41.3	36.4
		4.6	7.5			Operating Profit	.9	4.9
		.9	.7			All Other Expenses (net)	1.7	1.5
		3.7	6.8			Profit Before Taxes	-.8	3.4
						RATIOS		
		5.0	4.3				3.2	3.8
		2.1	3.3			Current	1.6	2.1
		1.5	1.9				1.2	1.2
		1.9	2.6				2.0	2.3
		1.2	1.5			Quick	1.0	1.3
		.9	.7				.7	.9
		21 17.3	**29** 12.5				**38** 9.7	**39** 9.4
		44 8.3	**47** 7.8			Sales/Receivables	**54** 6.7	**47** 7.7
		54 6.7	**78** 4.7				**63** 5.8	**65** 5.6
		46 7.9	**49** 7.5				**34** 10.7	**33** 11.0
		111 3.3	**99** 3.7			Cost of Sales/Inventory	**79** 4.6	**84** 4.4
		152 2.4	**126** 2.9				**131** 2.8	**138** 2.6
		15 24.1	**16** 22.7				**24** 15.0	**24** 15.1
		41 8.8	**24** 15.1			Cost of Sales/Payables	**43** 8.4	**42** 8.7
		73 5.0	**73** 5.0				**71** 5.2	**75** 4.9
		3.2	3.1				3.2	3.1
		5.2	5.1			Sales/Working Capital	7.0	4.3
		12.9	7.7				31.8	31.9
		36.1					17.4	36.3
		(12) 15.3				EBIT/Interest	(33) 1.8	(29) 5.2
		1.2					-4.6	1.9
							7.5	
						Net Profit + Depr., Dep., Amort./Cur. Mat. L/T/D	(13) 3.4	
							-4.4	
		.0	.2				.1	.1
		.2	.5			Fixed/Worth	.2	.2
		.4	.6				3.5	1.3
		.3	.3				.5	.4
		.8	.7			Debt/Worth	1.5	.9
		2.1	6.4				18.8	7.8
		35.6	28.6				25.4	58.5
		(15) 11.0	(10) 14.7			% Profit Before Taxes/Tangible Net Worth	(33) 10.3	(30) 21.7
		1.3	-.7				-22.0	5.0
		22.0	13.1				13.4	19.8
		6.4	5.5			% Profit Before Taxes/Total Assets	.9	7.2
		.3	.6				-16.2	1.4
		85.0	40.7				52.2	56.3
		35.5	9.7			Sales/Net Fixed Assets	26.6	29.2
		13.7	6.3				12.0	9.2
		3.0	2.4				3.0	3.1
		2.1	1.9			Sales/Total Assets	1.8	1.9
		1.6	1.4				1.0	1.2
		.4					.8	.6
		(11) .9				% Depr., Dep., Amort./Sales	(31) 1.4	(27) 1.4
		1.2					2.0	1.8
						% Officers', Directors' Owners' Comp/Sales		
	17062M	208434M	450007M	337096M	692569M	Net Sales ($)	2231526M	2209204M
	4162M	94369M	259267M	277226M	386539M	Total Assets ($)	1724293M	1662396M

M = $ thousand MM = $ million

See Pages 9 through 22 for Explanation of Ratios and Data

Comparative Historical Data				Current Data Sorted by Sales					
			Type of Statement						
7	8	6	Unqualified			1		1	4
4	1	8	Reviewed			1	1	5	1
1	2	1	Compiled				1		
6	5	3	Tax Returns			1	1	1	
22	23	21	Other		2		3	4	12
					9 (4/1-9/30/13)		30 (10/1/13-3/31/14)		
4/1/11-3/31/12 ALL	4/1/12-3/31/13 ALL	4/1/13-3/31/14 ALL		0-1MM	1-3MM	3-5MM	5-10MM	10-25MM	25MM & OVER
40	39	39	**NUMBER OF STATEMENTS**		2	3	6	11	17
%	%	%	**ASSETS**	%	%	%	%	%	%
15.6	13.3	15.1	Cash & Equivalents	DATA NOT AVAILABLE				18.6	11.6
30.1	26.8	23.9	Trade Receivables (net)					28.5	23.4
26.6	27.8	29.8	Inventory					29.3	25.0
2.6	4.6	7.1	All Other Current					3.3	8.2
74.9	72.5	75.9	Total Current					79.7	68.2
12.9	14.6	11.1	Fixed Assets (net)					10.0	16.5
6.4	6.4	8.2	Intangibles (net)					3.6	9.7
5.8	6.5	4.7	All Other Non-Current					6.7	5.5
100.0	100.0	100.0	Total					100.0	100.0
			LIABILITIES						
7.7	6.2	7.5	Notes Payable-Short Term					15.6	2.8
1.7	3.5	1.8	Cur. Mat.-L.T.D.					1.6	.7
21.6	17.7	16.1	Trade Payables					18.1	13.4
.2	.2	.1	Income Taxes Payable					.0	.1
15.8	12.5	13.4	All Other Current					12.5	15.2
47.0	40.1	38.8	Total Current					47.8	32.3
7.4	14.2	9.4	Long-Term Debt					3.2	9.0
.3	.3	.6	Deferred Taxes					.0	1.2
3.3	7.9	7.0	All Other Non-Current					5.1	10.7
41.9	37.6	44.2	Net Worth					43.9	46.7
100.0	100.0	100.0	Total Liabilties & Net Worth					100.0	100.0
			INCOME DATA						
100.0	100.0	100.0	Net Sales					100.0	100.0
42.3	42.3	40.5	Gross Profit					41.3	39.0
36.0	39.3	36.8	Operating Expenses					36.1	34.7
6.3	2.9	3.7	Operating Profit					5.1	4.3
.9	.6	.8	All Other Expenses (net)					.4	1.1
5.4	2.4	2.9	Profit Before Taxes					4.7	3.2
			RATIOS						
3.3	3.4	4.0						2.3	4.9
2.2	1.9	1.9	Current					1.7	2.2
1.1	1.2	1.3						1.2	1.4
2.2	1.6	1.8						1.3	2.3
1.1	1.0	1.1	Quick					.9	1.3
.7	.7	.6						.7	.6
35 10.4	30 12.1	26 13.8						21 17.5	37 9.8
47 7.7	49 7.4	46 7.9	Sales/Receivables					26 13.8	47 7.8
63 5.8	64 5.7	59 6.2						54 6.7	65 5.6
30 12.0	29 12.5	43 8.4						52 7.0	43 8.4
85 4.3	76 4.8	99 3.7	Cost of Sales/Inventory					74 4.9	99 3.7
126 2.9	130 2.8	146 2.5						126 2.9	130 2.8
22 16.9	23 15.6	18 20.4						17 21.7	18 19.9
50 7.3	36 10.2	36 10.1	Cost of Sales/Payables					47 7.8	29 12.4
78 4.7	62 5.9	74 4.9						76 4.8	54 6.8
3.2	3.9	3.3						5.2	2.8
6.3	8.5	5.6	Sales/Working Capital					9.2	5.1
57.6	23.7	14.0						25.5	8.8
42.6	26.2	30.1						39.3	176.2
(34) 12.0	(33) 8.4	(29) 4.8	EBIT/Interest					(10) 3.1	(13) 9.2
3.1	-1.2	1.3						-.3	1.9
			Net Profit + Depr., Dep., Amort./Cur. Mat. L/T/D						
.1	.1	.1						.1	.2
.2	.2	.2	Fixed/Worth					.3	.4
.9	1.5	.5						.5	1.5
.4	.6	.4						.6	.3
.9	1.2	1.1	Debt/Worth					1.7	.7
8.1	9.2	7.1						6.4	7.2
77.5	49.8	32.6						72.4	28.6
(36) 32.3	(32) 21.4	(34) 14.7	% Profit Before Taxes/Tangible Net Worth					15.9	(14) 15.5
4.8	2.3	1.2						.6	1.2
23.1	17.7	13.3						35.9	12.7
12.7	8.1	4.5	% Profit Before Taxes/Total Assets					6.4	4.0
2.0	-6.3	.5						.2	.7
169.2	92.0	78.6						68.0	43.6
24.4	24.3	35.5	Sales/Net Fixed Assets					36.1	9.7
9.4	10.9	9.3						16.1	6.1
3.3	3.0	2.7						4.0	2.2
2.4	2.1	2.0	Sales/Total Assets					2.4	1.9
1.6	1.3	1.6						2.0	1.2
1.3	.4	.7							.8
(26) 1.8	(28) 1.6	(24) 1.3	% Depr., Dep., Amort./Sales						(12) 2.2
2.9	2.5	2.6							3.5
2.2									
(10) 4.6			% Officers', Directors' Owners' Comp/Sales						
6.9									
1714527M	2456041M	1705168M	Net Sales ($)		4922M	12457M	40919M	185557M	1461313M
1111321M	1554063M	1021563M	Total Assets ($)		5763M	12561M	18071M	75685M	909483M

M = $ thousand MM = $ million

See Pages 9 through 22 for Explanation of Ratios and Data

Current Data Sorted by Assets							Comparative Historical Data	
						Type of Statement		
	2	2	7	3	1	Unqualified	30	28
		7	7			Reviewed	15	7
		1			1	Compiled	5	6
2	1	5				Tax Returns	5	6
2	3	14	15	2	7	Other	45	40
10 (4/1-9/30/13)		72 (10/1/13-3/31/14)					**4/1/09-3/31/10**	**4/1/10-3/31/11**
0-500M	**500M-2MM**	**2-10MM**	**10-50MM**	**50-100MM**	**100-250MM**		**ALL**	**ALL**
4	6	29	29	5	9	**NUMBER OF STATEMENTS**	100	87
%	%	%	%	%	%	**ASSETS**	%	%
		17.1	9.0			Cash & Equivalents	13.8	17.8
		28.3	24.5			Trade Receivables (net)	22.8	21.5
		30.9	30.0			Inventory	26.7	26.4
		2.8	5.2			All Other Current	6.0	3.5
		79.1	68.6			Total Current	69.3	69.2
		14.7	13.0			Fixed Assets (net)	16.9	14.5
		.8	12.0			Intangibles (net)	7.5	8.3
		5.4	6.4			All Other Non-Current	6.4	8.0
		100.0	100.0			Total	100.0	100.0
						LIABILITIES		
		8.4	10.4			Notes Payable-Short Term	11.1	6.3
		2.1	3.2			Cur. Mat.-L.T.D.	3.0	1.7
		16.1	15.2			Trade Payables	13.5	11.9
		1.1	.3			Income Taxes Payable	.2	.3
		12.9	12.6			All Other Current	10.7	12.7
		40.6	41.8			Total Current	38.5	32.9
		6.2	20.8			Long-Term Debt	13.0	11.6
		.5	1.5			Deferred Taxes	.4	.3
		12.9	14.6			All Other Non-Current	3.8	4.7
		39.9	21.5			Net Worth	44.3	50.5
		100.0	100.0			Total Liabilities & Net Worth	100.0	100.0
						INCOME DATA		
		100.0	100.0			Net Sales	100.0	100.0
		43.9	35.1			Gross Profit	39.4	41.6
		36.6	32.3			Operating Expenses	34.1	34.6
		7.3	2.7			Operating Profit	5.4	7.0
		1.2	2.0			All Other Expenses (net)	2.0	1.4
		6.0	.7			Profit Before Taxes	3.4	5.6
						RATIOS		
		3.7	2.7				3.5	4.3
		2.2	1.8			Current	2.0	2.5
		1.5	1.2				1.3	1.5
		2.0	1.3				2.0	2.4
		1.1	1.0			Quick	1.1	1.4
		.7	.5				.5	.6
		27 13.3	**33** 11.0				**29** 12.6	**30** 12.0
		36 10.0	**42** 8.6			Sales/Receivables	**44** 8.4	**47** 7.8
		50 7.3	**65** 5.6				**62** 5.9	**64** 5.7
		42 8.7	**61** 6.0				**38** 9.5	**61** 6.0
		87 4.2	**99** 3.7			Cost of Sales/Inventory	**87** 4.2	**90** 4.0
		166 2.2	**159** 2.3				**148** 2.5	**176** 2.1
		16 22.2	**18** 20.1				**20** 18.4	**23** 15.8
		32 11.3	**33** 11.2			Cost of Sales/Payables	**34** 10.7	**37** 9.8
		72 5.1	**60** 6.1				**49** 7.5	**59** 6.2
		3.9	4.2				2.7	2.9
		7.6	5.5			Sales/Working Capital	5.1	4.8
		9.9	37.5				13.8	8.0
		79.2	21.3				17.8	15.4
		(26) 18.2	5.2			EBIT/Interest	(80) 2.6	(73) 5.3
		4.4	-3.3				-1.3	.0
			9.2			Net Profit + Depr., Dep.,	5.2	8.9
			(10) 1.2			Amort./Cur. Mat. L/T/D	(26) 2.6	(20) 2.0
			-4.4				.4	.4
		.1	.2				.1	.1
		.3	.3			Fixed/Worth	.3	.3
		.7	NM				1.0	.8
		.6	.6				.4	.4
		1.2	2.4			Debt/Worth	1.3	1.0
		2.5	NM				4.5	3.1
		80.5	41.9			% Profit Before Taxes/Tangible	35.6	53.1
		(28) 35.9	(22) 8.0			Net Worth	(87) 11.6	(82) 13.2
		10.8	-9.0				-6.3	-1.2
		25.1	7.9			% Profit Before Taxes/Total	13.1	17.8
		10.1	3.9			Assets	4.0	6.1
		3.7	-13.0				-3.7	-1.7
		129.9	41.2				38.9	33.2
		20.3	16.7			Sales/Net Fixed Assets	14.6	15.7
		11.0	7.6				6.4	7.3
		3.0	2.4				2.3	2.3
		2.3	1.5			Sales/Total Assets	1.7	1.4
		1.6	1.2				1.2	1.0
		.9	1.1				.8	.8
		(19) 1.3	(24) 1.9			% Depr., Dep., Amort./Sales	(76) 1.8	(64) 2.0
		3.6	3.6				3.1	3.3
		.9				% Officers', Directors'	2.2	1.7
		(10) 4.0				Owners' Comp/Sales	(21) 6.0	(16) 7.2
		5.2					13.7	9.6
3875M	**22649M**	**337515M**	**1210724M**	**541245M**	**1393014M**	Net Sales ($)	**4589267M**	**5211697M**
762M	**5731M**	**137515M**	**686264M**	**359836M**	**1521098M**	Total Assets ($)	**3013765M**	**3816153M**

M = $ thousand MM = $ million

See Pages 9 through 22 for Explanation of Ratios and Data

Comparative Historical Data / Current Data Sorted by Sales

			Type of Statement						
30	21	15	Unqualified		1	1	1	3	9
20	16	14	Reviewed		1		5	5	3
6	4	2	Compiled				1		1
11	4	8	Tax Returns	1	2			5	
45	38	43	Other	1	2	2	8	6	24
				10 (4/1-9/30/13)			72 (10/1/13-3/31/14)		
4/1/11-3/31/12 ALL	4/1/12-3/31/13 ALL	4/1/13-3/31/14 ALL		0-1MM	1-3MM	3-5MM	5-10MM	10-25MM	25MM & OVER
112	83	82	NUMBER OF STATEMENTS	2	6	3	15	19	37
%	%	%	ASSETS	%	%	%	%	%	%
16.0	13.4	15.0	Cash & Equivalents				14.6	17.8	13.2
24.9	25.0	25.8	Trade Receivables (net)				23.8	28.2	24.3
27.7	29.3	27.9	Inventory				32.6	25.7	27.5
4.0	4.9	3.9	All Other Current				2.9	2.3	5.4
72.6	72.6	72.6	Total Current				73.9	74.0	70.4
12.9	13.2	13.0	Fixed Assets (net)				17.7	12.3	11.8
7.8	8.1	7.4	Intangibles (net)				.7	8.3	11.1
6.8	6.0	7.0	All Other Non-Current				7.7	5.3	6.7
100.0	100.0	100.0	Total				100.0	100.0	100.0
			LIABILITIES						
7.3	8.6	7.6	Notes Payable-Short Term				10.8	5.5	7.7
1.9	1.7	2.4	Cur. Mat.-L.T.D.				3.0	1.5	2.6
13.1	15.7	15.3	Trade Payables				23.4	9.4	14.9
.8	.4	.5	Income Taxes Payable				1.0	.6	.4
12.2	8.3	13.5	All Other Current				9.0	12.5	11.3
35.3	34.7	39.4	Total Current				47.2	29.5	37.0
10.5	8.4	12.0	Long-Term Debt				6.9	6.0	18.8
.4	.3	.8	Deferred Taxes				.4	.5	1.3
9.3	7.2	12.2	All Other Non-Current				7.4	5.1	14.5
44.4	49.4	35.6	Net Worth				38.1	58.9	28.4
100.0	100.0	100.0	Total Liabilities & Net Worth				100.0	100.0	100.0
			INCOME DATA						
100.0	100.0	100.0	Net Sales				100.0	100.0	100.0
40.6	39.2	39.9	Gross Profit				40.1	42.1	38.0
33.7	32.3	35.2	Operating Expenses				34.4	35.0	33.4
6.9	6.9	4.7	Operating Profit				5.7	7.0	4.6
1.5	.8	1.5	All Other Expenses (net)				.6	.9	2.1
5.4	6.1	3.3	Profit Before Taxes				5.1	6.1	2.6
			RATIOS						
3.9	4.2	3.6					3.6	3.9	3.7
2.1	2.5	2.2	Current				1.5	2.3	2.5
1.4	1.6	1.5					1.1	1.9	1.5
2.3	2.2	1.9					1.2	2.4	2.0
1.2	1.2	1.1	Quick				.9	1.3	1.2
.7	.7	.7					.6	1.1	.6
32 11.5	31 11.6	31 11.6					25 14.8	29 12.5	39 9.4
48 7.6	46 7.9	43 8.4	Sales/Receivables				32 11.5	41 8.9	50 7.3
70 5.2	66 5.5	62 5.9					38 9.6	52 7.0	69 5.3
46 7.9	53 6.9	49 7.4					22 16.7	49 7.4	61 6.0
104 3.5	104 3.5	94 3.9	Cost of Sales/Inventory				96 3.8	83 4.4	107 3.4
140 2.6	135 2.7	159 2.3					228 1.6	130 2.8	159 2.3
22 16.9	25 14.5	19 19.4					26 14.0	15 24.4	27 13.3
40 9.2	39 9.4	34 10.6	Cost of Sales/Payables				52 7.0	26 14.3	36 10.2
57 6.4	54 6.7	61 6.0					111 3.3	54 6.7	59 6.2
2.5	2.9	3.9					3.5	3.8	2.6
5.0	4.6	5.5	Sales/Working Capital				8.8	5.6	4.9
11.0	8.7	10.3					28.7	8.0	9.7
36.7	42.8	38.0					65.0	168.6	27.1
(93) 9.5	(62) 9.1	(70) 8.3	EBIT/Interest				(14) 6.1	(17) 16.3	(30) 8.6
1.8	2.3	1.7					3.7	3.8	-.2
19.0	11.4	6.6							7.5
(22) 4.6	(19) 2.9	(21) 1.7	Net Profit + Depr., Dep., Amort./Cur. Mat. L/T/D						(11) 1.7
2.3	.2	-.9							-2.3
.1	.1	.1					.2	.0	.1
.2	.2	.3	Fixed/Worth				.4	.2	.3
.6	.6	.9					1.2	.4	22.4
.4	.4	.6					.6	.5	.5
.9	1.0	1.3	Debt/Worth				1.3	.7	1.3
2.3	2.3	4.2					5.5	1.7	550.0
40.3	39.5	45.7					65.7	63.9	38.9
(98) 21.1	(74) 19.1	(70) 15.0	% Profit Before Taxes/Tangible Net Worth				(14) 15.0	(18) 37.1	(29) 8.7
2.8	5.9	1.9					2.6	11.3	-3.9
18.0	17.1	14.3					10.1	24.4	9.4
7.8	7.3	6.3	% Profit Before Taxes/Total Assets				7.1	13.7	4.2
.5	1.7	.1					1.8	4.2	-2.9
46.5	59.0	47.8					28.6	206.0	31.0
22.4	22.6	20.4	Sales/Net Fixed Assets				17.9	23.5	19.0
11.4	7.9	7.9					4.8	10.1	7.8
2.5	2.5	2.6					2.4	3.1	2.4
1.6	1.8	1.9	Sales/Total Assets				1.9	2.4	1.5
1.2	1.2	1.2					1.1	1.4	.9
.6	.6	1.1					.6	1.1	1.0
(85) 1.6	(58) 1.3	(58) 1.8	% Depr., Dep., Amort./Sales				(12) 1.3	(10) 1.8	(30) 2.6
3.0	2.6	3.7					1.9	3.6	3.7
2.7	1.4	1.6							
(22) 4.0	(13) 4.9	(14) 4.1	% Officers', Directors' Owners' Comp/Sales						
6.1	6.2	5.3							
5641973M	4061336M	3509022M	Net Sales ($)	588M	11964M	11805M	107997M	320917M	3055751M
3960280M	2935872M	2711206M	Total Assets ($)	237M	5836M	4284M	63785M	165505M	2471559M

M = $ thousand MM = $ million

See Pages 9 through 22 for Explanation of Ratios and Data

Current Data Sorted by Assets							Comparative Historical Data	
						Type of Statement		
		4	7	4	3	Unqualified	21	14
	1	8		1		Reviewed	16	11
		2	2			Compiled	5	3
1	3	5				Tax Returns	6	7
	4	9	13	4	3	Other	38	48
	15 (4/1-9/30/13)		59 (10/1/13-3/31/14)				4/1/09-3/31/10 ALL	4/1/10-3/31/11 ALL
0-500M	500M-2MM	2-10MM	10-50MM	50-100MM	100-250MM			
1	8	28	22	9	6	**NUMBER OF STATEMENTS**	86	83
%	%	%	%	%	%	**ASSETS**	%	%
		12.5	11.4			Cash & Equivalents	13.5	12.3
		26.3	27.2			Trade Receivables (net)	30.4	30.5
		30.2	25.7			Inventory	24.0	23.9
		2.5	4.9			All Other Current	4.5	4.9
		71.5	69.2			Total Current	72.4	71.6
		20.3	16.1			Fixed Assets (net)	14.6	14.1
		3.5	11.8			Intangibles (net)	7.6	8.3
		4.7	2.9			All Other Non-Current	5.4	6.0
		100.0	100.0			Total	100.0	100.0
						LIABILITIES		
		9.9	3.1			Notes Payable-Short Term	12.0	12.4
		2.5	3.3			Cur. Mat.-L.T.D.	2.6	2.2
		16.4	14.2			Trade Payables	15.9	17.0
		.0	.2			Income Taxes Payable	.2	.1
		12.1	8.6			All Other Current	11.0	10.9
		40.9	29.3			Total Current	41.8	42.6
		15.5	17.3			Long-Term Debt	9.5	9.0
		1.6	.4			Deferred Taxes	.4	.4
		13.8	10.9			All Other Non-Current	7.5	8.2
		28.2	42.1			Net Worth	40.8	39.8
		100.0	100.0			Total Liabilties & Net Worth	100.0	100.0
						INCOME DATA		
		100.0	100.0			Net Sales	100.0	100.0
		37.2	40.0			Gross Profit	39.5	42.0
		35.1	32.3			Operating Expenses	34.8	34.9
		2.2	7.6			Operating Profit	4.7	7.1
		1.5	1.3			All Other Expenses (net)	1.8	1.5
		.6	6.4			Profit Before Taxes	2.9	5.6
						RATIOS		
		3.1	3.7				3.1	2.9
		1.9	2.2			Current	1.9	2.0
		1.3	1.7				1.2	1.2
		1.7	2.1				1.9	1.8
		.9	1.2			Quick	1.1	1.1
		.5	.9				.6	.6
		30 12.0	**41** 8.9				**46** 8.0	**39** 9.4
		42 8.6	**51** 7.2			Sales/Receivables	**56** 6.6	**52** 7.0
		53 6.9	**62** 5.9				**71** 5.1	**67** 5.4
		55 6.6	**38** 9.6				**50** 7.3	**37** 9.8
		101 3.6	**96** 3.8			Cost of Sales/Inventory	**78** 4.7	**78** 4.7
		135 2.7	**146** 2.5				**109** 3.3	**122** 3.0
		25 14.4	**26** 13.8				**24** 15.0	**23** 16.0
		39 9.4	**46** 8.0			Cost of Sales/Payables	**39** 9.4	**43** 8.5
		74 4.9	**68** 5.4				**62** 5.9	**73** 5.0
		3.7	2.9				3.0	3.5
		5.9	5.2			Sales/Working Capital	6.2	5.9
		13.9	7.6				17.0	16.2
		8.0	100.2				12.7	35.8
		(24) 2.4	(20) 19.5			EBIT/Interest	(71) 3.6	(71) 5.4
		.7	4.9				1.0	1.1
							9.0	11.6
						Net Profit + Depr., Dep., Amort./Cur. Mat. L/T/D	(22) 4.3	(20) 2.8
							1.8	.2
		.1	.2				.1	.1
		.4	.4			Fixed/Worth	.4	.3
		1.8	1.3				1.2	2.0
		.9	.7				.5	.6
		2.2	1.0			Debt/Worth	1.5	1.5
		6.5	5.5				8.1	18.5
		48.7	79.8				51.4	60.2
		(24) 25.0	(18) 36.4			% Profit Before Taxes/Tangible Net Worth	(71) 15.0	(67) 32.7
		2.8	12.7				2.7	6.4
		13.3	20.8				20.3	24.8
		3.4	12.5			% Profit Before Taxes/Total Assets	6.3	7.3
		-1.0	6.5				-3.0	.3
		85.3	33.0				53.7	51.2
		21.9	15.3			Sales/Net Fixed Assets	17.5	20.6
		5.5	9.3				7.2	10.0
		2.8	2.1				2.7	2.7
		2.0	1.6			Sales/Total Assets	1.8	1.9
		1.5	1.4				1.2	1.3
		.5	.7				.7	.8
		(24) 1.3	(19) 1.6			% Depr., Dep., Amort./Sales	(67) 1.5	(60) 1.4
		3.8	2.2				3.6	3.1
		2.4					2.9	2.0
		(11) 4.1				% Officers', Directors' Owners' Comp/Sales	(18) 5.1	(21) 4.6
		7.8					8.5	8.1
418M	31880M	306168M	796943M	996824M	619668M	Net Sales ($)	3855652M	4444921M
144M	9634M	142501M	438193M	652725M	804118M	Total Assets ($)	2760872M	2877188M

M = $ thousand MM = $ million

See Pages 9 through 22 for Explanation of Ratios and Data

Comparative Historical Data / Current Data Sorted by Sales

4/1/11-3/31/12 ALL	4/1/12-3/31/13 ALL	4/1/13-3/31/14 ALL	Type of Statement	0-1MM	1-3MM	3-5MM	5-10MM	10-25MM	25MM & OVER
18	14	18	Unqualified			1		4	13
13	13	10	Reviewed		1		2	6	1
8	6	4	Compiled			1		2	1
6	10	9	Tax Returns	2	1	3	3		
33	34	33	Other		2	3	5	9	14
				15 (4/1-9/30/13)			59 (10/1/13-3/31/14)		
78	77	74	NUMBER OF STATEMENTS	2	4	8	10	21	29
%	%	%	**ASSETS**	%	%	%	%	%	%
11.3	11.1	14.2	Cash & Equivalents				14.7	11.5	18.0
28.2	30.7	27.3	Trade Receivables (net)				24.4	31.3	26.7
23.7	25.9	24.2	Inventory				25.8	31.5	19.3
4.7	3.7	3.5	All Other Current				1.5	3.7	5.5
67.8	71.5	69.2	Total Current				66.5	78.0	69.5
16.8	15.2	16.8	Fixed Assets (net)				17.2	16.3	12.3
7.2	9.0	8.7	Intangibles (net)				8.9	3.4	13.8
8.2	4.4	5.3	All Other Non-Current				7.4	2.3	4.4
100.0	100.0	100.0	Total				100.0	100.0	100.0
			LIABILITIES						
9.1	10.0	8.1	Notes Payable-Short Term				14.3	11.5	1.5
3.3	2.6	2.9	Cur. Mat.-L.T.D.				1.0	3.5	2.9
16.0	17.1	14.3	Trade Payables				17.4	18.1	10.5
.2	.2	.1	Income Taxes Payable				.0	.1	.2
11.1	18.0	11.8	All Other Current				6.3	10.6	10.9
39.8	47.9	37.2	Total Current				39.0	43.8	26.0
11.0	11.0	15.1	Long-Term Debt				14.6	11.8	11.4
.4	.6	.8	Deferred Taxes				.0	.4	.6
16.5	9.4	10.6	All Other Non-Current				6.3	11.7	6.1
32.4	31.1	36.2	Net Worth				40.1	32.4	55.9
100.0	100.0	100.0	Total Liabilties & Net Worth				100.0	100.0	100.0
			INCOME DATA						
100.0	100.0	100.0	Net Sales				100.0	100.0	100.0
38.6	36.8	38.8	Gross Profit				37.4	34.2	41.2
33.8	30.9	35.4	Operating Expenses				37.1	29.1	37.1
4.8	5.9	3.4	Operating Profit				.3	5.1	4.2
1.5	1.6	1.3	All Other Expenses (net)				1.0	.6	1.2
3.3	4.2	2.1	Profit Before Taxes				-.8	4.5	2.9
			RATIOS						
3.0	2.7	3.3					3.7	2.5	3.8
1.9	1.9	2.0	Current				1.8	1.7	2.7
1.3	1.3	1.5					1.0	1.3	1.9
1.9	1.8	1.9					1.9	1.5	2.6
1.2	1.1	1.2	Quick				.9	.8	1.7
.6	.7	.6					.6	.5	1.2
39 9.4	42 8.6	36 10.1					29 12.7	31 11.6	46 8.0
52 7.0	53 6.9	49 7.4	Sales/Receivables				35 10.5	49 7.5	57 6.4
62 5.9	68 5.4	64 5.7					55 6.6	63 5.8	73 5.0
33 10.9	29 12.4	37 9.9					47 7.7	32 11.4	48 7.6
69 5.3	78 4.7	79 4.6	Cost of Sales/Inventory				101 3.6	64 5.7	74 4.9
118 3.1	122 3.0	130 2.8					159 2.3	126 2.9	118 3.1
25 14.5	21 17.1	24 15.0					14 25.5	26 14.1	23 15.8
37 9.8	33 10.9	38 9.5	Cost of Sales/Payables				47 7.7	35 10.4	34 10.8
62 5.9	73 5.0	64 5.7					76 4.8	64 5.7	55 6.6
3.9	3.8	2.7					3.1	3.9	2.2
6.8	7.1	5.7	Sales/Working Capital				6.1	7.8	3.4
16.7	12.3	10.9					NM	13.3	5.9
19.6	16.0	18.5						21.4	73.3
(73) 4.9	(66) 3.8	(64) 3.3	EBIT/Interest					(19) 5.0	(25) 6.9
1.2	1.1	-.2						1.9	1.6
6.4	8.3	19.4							26.8
(19) 2.7	(22) 1.9	(17) 2.9	Net Profit + Depr., Dep., Amort./Cur. Mat. L/T/D						(11) 3.3
1.5	.8	.8							1.7
.1	.1	.1					.1	.1	.1
.3	.4	.3	Fixed/Worth				.2	.4	.2
3.1	1.4	1.5					1.8	1.4	.5
.5	.7	.7					.7	1.0	.4
1.6	1.7	1.6	Debt/Worth				1.4	2.3	.8
31.3	10.0	7.1					7.9	4.4	2.3
47.6	43.8	49.0						62.9	29.1
(61) 17.5	(62) 16.0	(61) 19.3	% Profit Before Taxes/Tangible Net Worth					(20) 49.0	(25) 10.7
2.8	1.9	.8						24.3	-2.7
16.1	16.7	16.7					5.8	21.9	16.2
5.2	6.1	6.1	% Profit Before Taxes/Total Assets				-2.6	9.0	6.5
-.2	.7	-1.6					-8.3	2.2	.0
35.5	77.9	50.0					114.8	88.1	31.5
22.9	28.3	20.5	Sales/Net Fixed Assets				21.9	22.8	20.0
8.6	10.1	9.7					8.6	9.5	10.8
2.6	2.7	2.5					3.2	2.9	2.1
1.9	2.0	1.8	Sales/Total Assets				1.7	2.0	1.5
1.3	1.4	1.2					1.3	1.6	.9
.6	.5	.6						.5	1.1
(66) 1.4	(58) 1.4	(59) 1.6	% Depr., Dep., Amort./Sales					(18) 1.2	(23) 1.6
2.6	3.3	2.9						2.2	2.8
1.4	2.8	2.7							
(19) 4.2	(24) 4.6	(19) 4.1	% Officers', Directors' Owners' Comp/Sales						
5.5	10.2	6.8							
3986842M	2877746M	2751901M	Net Sales ($)	1411M	10091M	30865M	73010M	359076M	2277448M
2302124M	1924221M	2047315M	Total Assets ($)	1327M	9604M	16900M	49198M	178680M	1791606M

M = $ thousand MM = $ million

See Pages 9 through 22 for Explanation of Ratios and Data

Current Data Sorted by Assets							Comparative Historical Data	
						Type of Statement		
	1	1	11	3	2	Unqualified	16	21
	2	6	4			Reviewed	9	15
		4				Compiled	7	5
2	5	3				Tax Returns	10	9
	7	14	14	4	7	Other	41	55
	23 (4/1-9/30/13)		67 (10/1/13-3/31/14)				**4/1/09-3/31/10**	**4/1/10-3/31/11**
0-500M	**500M-2MM**	**2-10MM**	**10-50MM**	**50-100MM**	**100-250MM**		**ALL**	**ALL**
2	15	28	29	7	9	**NUMBER OF STATEMENTS**	83	105
%	%	%	%	%	%	**ASSETS**	%	%
	11.5	16.1	10.5			Cash & Equivalents	13.3	11.6
	35.8	22.8	21.5			Trade Receivables (net)	29.1	29.3
	28.9	38.2	35.2			Inventory	31.1	32.7
	1.1	3.9	7.0			All Other Current	3.4	3.1
	77.3	81.0	74.1			Total Current	76.9	76.7
	16.5	8.1	10.8			Fixed Assets (net)	13.0	12.3
	.3	5.1	6.6			Intangibles (net)	5.5	6.5
	6.0	5.7	8.4			All Other Non-Current	4.6	4.6
	100.0	100.0	100.0			Total	100.0	100.0
						LIABILITIES		
	16.7	11.5	7.9			Notes Payable-Short Term	10.4	8.7
	1.8	1.9	1.4			Cur. Mat.-L.T.D.	2.6	4.6
	22.4	21.3	12.1			Trade Payables	15.8	17.2
	.3	.5	.4			Income Taxes Payable	.2	.5
	30.0	8.9	14.8			All Other Current	14.2	11.6
	71.2	44.1	36.6			Total Current	43.2	42.6
	16.5	6.4	25.3			Long-Term Debt	7.9	13.9
	.0	.0	1.0			Deferred Taxes	.1	.3
	3.5	5.7	9.3			All Other Non-Current	6.4	8.3
	8.7	43.8	27.8			Net Worth	42.3	34.9
	100.0	100.0	100.0			Total Liabilities & Net Worth	100.0	100.0
						INCOME DATA		
	100.0	100.0	100.0			Net Sales	100.0	100.0
	45.2	43.1	36.1			Gross Profit	41.1	40.0
	41.1	36.5	30.2			Operating Expenses	37.8	33.5
	4.1	6.7	6.0			Operating Profit	3.3	6.4
	.5	.5	1.7			All Other Expenses (net)	1.0	1.3
	3.6	6.2	4.3			Profit Before Taxes	2.3	5.1
						RATIOS		
	3.2	5.0	3.6				3.9	3.3
	1.6	1.7	2.2			Current	1.8	2.0
	.8	1.3	1.4				1.3	1.2
	1.7	2.8	2.0				2.0	1.7
	1.1	.9	.8			Quick	1.0	.9
	.3	.4	.5				.6	.7
	17 21.7	**21** 17.7	**37** 9.8				**34** 10.7	**34** 10.8
	33 11.2	**32** 11.3	**43** 8.5			Sales/Receivables	**45** 8.1	**45** 8.1
	44 8.3	**59** 6.2	**50** 7.3				**69** 5.3	**64** 5.7
	6 64.7	**49** 7.5	**83** 4.4				**53** 6.9	**58** 6.3
	70 5.2	**89** 4.1	**118** 3.1			Cost of Sales/Inventory	**85** 4.3	**106** 3.4
	135 2.7	**182** 2.0	**166** 2.2				**148** 2.5	**141** 2.6
	13 28.5	**26** 14.0	**18** 20.5				**18** 20.0	**23** 15.6
	26 13.9	**51** 7.2	**35** 10.3			Cost of Sales/Payables	**35** 10.5	**40** 9.2
	55 6.6	**78** 4.7	**56** 6.5				**57** 6.5	**69** 5.3
	4.9	3.6	2.6				3.2	3.6
	19.0	6.1	4.9			Sales/Working Capital	7.2	5.6
	-57.4	13.4	13.4				15.9	15.4
	29.9	63.3	19.4				16.0	24.4
	(14) 6.5	(22) 6.3	(24) 5.1			EBIT/Interest	(69) 3.7	(87) 3.7
	1.7	1.1	1.1				.3	.9
							13.8	7.2
						Net Profit + Depr., Dep., Amort./Cur. Mat. L/T/D	(19) 3.5	(24) 2.0
							1.0	.5
	.2	.1	.1				.1	.1
	.4	.3	.2			Fixed/Worth	.2	.2
	5.5	.9	NM				.9	1.0
	.9	.2	.5				.4	.6
	2.1	1.4	.9			Debt/Worth	1.2	1.6
	57.5	7.6	NM				5.2	6.9
	63.5	91.1	22.3				29.8	46.7
	(12) 22.8	(25) 37.8	(22) 11.7			% Profit Before Taxes/Tangible Net Worth	(71) 9.7	(85) 23.2
	9.8	2.2	.0				.7	2.0
	25.3	23.1	14.9				11.1	19.2
	12.2	11.3	4.2			% Profit Before Taxes/Total Assets	4.6	8.7
	2.6	.8	-.1				-.2	.0
	85.8	96.3	64.8				66.4	78.0
	43.3	33.4	41.8			Sales/Net Fixed Assets	27.6	35.6
	17.8	18.9	13.4				10.3	12.5
	6.7	2.8	2.4				2.8	2.7
	3.9	2.3	1.9			Sales/Total Assets	2.2	2.1
	2.7	1.7	1.1				1.3	1.5
	.5	.6	.8				.6	.6
	(10) .9	(19) .8	(21) 1.3			% Depr., Dep., Amort./Sales	(57) 1.4	(69) 1.4
	2.2	1.1	2.6				2.5	2.3
	1.5	1.4					2.7	2.2
	(10) 4.4	(15) 3.2				% Officers', Directors' Owners' Comp/Sales	(23) 4.7	(26) 4.4
	6.0	7.7					6.1	7.6
6401M	**69952M**	**330397M**	**1254352M**	**625807M**	**1740800M**	Net Sales ($)	**4158422M**	**5122526M**
819M	**17335M**	**139724M**	**678589M**	**543960M**	**1441264M**	Total Assets ($)	**2403481M**	**2921870M**

M = $ thousand MM = $ million

See Pages 9 through 22 for Explanation of Ratios and Data

	Comparative Historical Data			Current Data Sorted by Sales					
Type of Statement									
Unqualified	20	9	18			1		1	16
Reviewed	19	14	12			3	4	4	1
Compiled	8	1	4					3	1
Tax Returns	19	14	10		2	2	5	1	
Other	44	56	46		3	2	7	14	20
	4/1/11-3/31/12 ALL	4/1/12-3/31/13 ALL	4/1/13-3/31/14 ALL		23 (4/1-9/30/13)		67 (10/1/13-3/31/14)		
				0-1MM	1-3MM	3-5MM	5-10MM	10-25MM	25MM & OVER
NUMBER OF STATEMENTS	110	94	90		5	8	16	23	38
	%	%	%	%	%	%	%	%	%
ASSETS				DATA NOT AVAILABLE					
Cash & Equivalents	11.4	10.0	13.3				8.4	20.7	9.6
Trade Receivables (net)	26.8	25.9	24.5				31.6	19.0	22.2
Inventory	33.4	35.7	32.6				40.7	30.9	32.3
All Other Current	3.1	4.1	5.1				1.8	4.1	8.0
Total Current	74.6	75.8	75.4				82.6	74.7	72.1
Fixed Assets (net)	13.1	12.1	10.8				7.1	13.7	9.2
Intangibles (net)	7.9	6.3	7.3				2.8	6.0	11.1
All Other Non-Current	4.3	5.8	6.4				7.6	5.6	7.6
Total	100.0	100.0	100.0				100.0	100.0	100.0
LIABILITIES									
Notes Payable-Short Term	11.0	16.1	9.8				18.2	4.7	7.2
Cur. Mat.-L.T.D.	3.1	2.7	3.8				3.6	.8	6.8
Trade Payables	15.2	18.4	17.2				17.6	18.6	13.0
Income Taxes Payable	.3	.3	.4				.3	.6	.4
All Other Current	13.2	12.1	15.0				7.9	9.5	15.9
Total Current	42.7	49.5	46.3				47.6	34.2	43.2
Long-Term Debt	11.7	9.4	15.4				9.8	6.9	23.9
Deferred Taxes	.2	.3	.5				.0	.5	.8
All Other Non-Current	13.0	12.6	7.0				7.8	5.3	7.5
Net Worth	32.3	28.2	30.8				34.8	53.0	24.6
Total Liabilities & Net Worth	100.0	100.0	100.0				100.0	100.0	100.0
INCOME DATA									
Net Sales	100.0	100.0	100.0				100.0	100.0	100.0
Gross Profit	40.8	39.9	41.1				40.3	43.2	38.4
Operating Expenses	35.0	35.8	36.1				34.9	38.3	33.1
Operating Profit	5.8	4.1	5.0				5.4	4.9	5.3
All Other Expenses (net)	1.4	1.0	1.5				.7	.5	2.8
Profit Before Taxes	4.4	3.0	3.5				4.8	4.4	2.5
RATIOS									
Current	3.5	2.7	3.3				3.1	8.5	2.8
	1.9	1.8	1.9				1.6	3.3	2.0
	1.3	1.3	1.3				1.2	1.2	1.6
Quick	1.7	1.3	1.7				1.8	5.1	1.3
	.9	.8	.9				.9	1.4	.8
	.5	.5	.5				.4	.7	.6
Sales/Receivables	**27** 13.5	**32** 11.3	**25** 14.6				**27** 13.4	**22** 16.4	**35** 10.4
	47 7.8	**44** 8.3	**41** 9.0				**37** 9.8	**39** 9.4	**45** 8.1
	66 5.5	**62** 5.9	**51** 7.2				**57** 6.4	**49** 7.5	**54** 6.8
Cost of Sales/Inventory	**62** 5.9	**65** 5.6	**54** 6.8				**41** 8.8	**59** 6.2	**72** 5.1
	111 3.3	**107** 3.4	**101** 3.6				**122** 3.0	**99** 3.7	**111** 3.3
	166 2.2	**166** 2.2	**166** 2.2				**192** 1.9	**166** 2.2	**152** 2.4
Cost of Sales/Payables	**20** 18.5	**23** 16.1	**21** 17.2				**18** 20.3	**16** 23.5	**27** 13.6
	38 9.6	**45** 8.2	**42** 8.7				**38** 9.5	**38** 9.5	**45** 8.1
	68 5.4	**70** 5.2	**63** 5.8				**66** 5.5	**64** 5.7	**60** 6.1
Sales/Working Capital	3.7	3.5	3.5				5.0	2.0	3.8
	6.0	6.3	5.9				8.5	4.4	4.8
	14.8	15.0	20.5				23.0	24.9	9.7
EBIT/Interest	17.3	24.9	22.2				26.8	48.7	24.0
	(98) 5.5	(81) 4.9	(76) 5.2				(15) 7.3	(16) 2.8	(33) 5.2
	1.3	.6	1.1				1.9	-8.5	.8
Net Profit + Depr., Dep., Amort./Cur. Mat. L/T/D	7.7	15.2	15.8						16.8
	(27) 3.8	(19) 2.7	(21) 3.8						(13) 3.8
	1.2	.2	.6						.5
Fixed/Worth	.1	.1	.1				.1	.1	.1
	.3	.3	.3				.3	.3	.2
	2.0	.9	1.2				.9	.7	-.4
Debt/Worth	.7	.8	.7				1.0	.2	.7
	1.8	1.8	1.6				2.3	.8	1.8
	17.9	4.7	8.1				6.7	5.2	-8.8
% Profit Before Taxes/Tangible Net Worth	49.4	53.1	49.8				73.5	55.4	34.1
	(85) 21.0	(79) 23.8	(72) 16.4				(14) 41.3	(21) 7.8	(27) 16.9
	3.5	.8	.0				11.1	-1.1	-2.9
% Profit Before Taxes/Total Assets	17.1	20.1	17.6				20.3	20.5	15.2
	7.4	6.2	4.9				13.2	3.9	4.2
	.3	-1.9	.1				3.7	-.5	-2.0
Sales/Net Fixed Assets	55.5	52.6	76.0				219.8	43.9	60.8
	28.1	26.0	32.0				55.6	21.9	31.7
	11.9	12.9	14.6				22.4	11.0	12.3
Sales/Total Assets	2.7	2.5	2.8				3.7	2.9	2.5
	2.0	2.0	2.1				2.4	2.2	1.8
	1.4	1.4	1.3				1.9	1.1	1.1
% Depr., Dep., Amort./Sales	.8	.4	.6					.6	.8
	(83) 1.3	(69) 1.2	(61) 1.1					(19) .9	(25) 1.4
	2.1	2.2	2.2					1.3	2.9
% Officers', Directors' Owners' Comp/Sales	3.0	2.1	1.6					2.8	
	(30) 5.3	(25) 4.3	(30) 4.6					(12) 5.3	
	8.8	7.5	7.2					10.4	
Net Sales ($)	4579914M	5157111M	4027709M		8422M	33946M	115921M	362194M	3507226M
Total Assets ($)	2606371M	2778027M	2821691M		3733M	11866M	48441M	232137M	2525514M

M = $ thousand MM = $ million

See Pages 9 through 22 for Explanation of Ratios and Data

Current Data Sorted by Assets							Comparative Historical Data	
						Type of Statement		
		1	5		1	Unqualified	14	13
	3	13	3			Reviewed	22	20
1	4	7	1			Compiled	11	18
	3	5	2			Tax Returns	6	15
	4	16	12			Other	49	46
	10 (4/1-9/30/13)		71 (10/1/13-3/31/14)				4/1/09-3/31/10 ALL	4/1/10-3/31/11 ALL
0-500M	**500M-2MM**	**2-10MM**	**10-50MM**	**50-100MM**	**100-250MM**			
1	14	42	23		1	**NUMBER OF STATEMENTS**	102	112
%	%	%	%	%	%	**ASSETS**	%	%
	10.6	12.0	9.0	DATA NOT AVAILABLE		Cash & Equivalents	8.0	10.7
	40.6	29.7	24.9			Trade Receivables (net)	28.9	27.3
	26.7	28.9	32.7			Inventory	26.7	27.7
	.6	1.1	1.5			All Other Current	1.6	1.0
	78.4	71.7	68.2			Total Current	65.1	66.8
	18.2	20.4	19.7			Fixed Assets (net)	23.8	21.4
	.9	2.5	5.8			Intangibles (net)	5.9	7.0
	2.5	5.4	6.3			All Other Non-Current	5.2	4.9
	100.0	100.0	100.0			Total	100.0	100.0
						LIABILITIES		
	12.1	9.0	10.7			Notes Payable-Short Term	11.8	9.9
	1.9	3.1	2.0			Cur. Mat.-L.T.D.	4.3	3.8
	29.4	19.7	12.8			Trade Payables	18.2	18.3
	.3	.2	.3			Income Taxes Payable	.2	.3
	6.6	5.6	9.3			All Other Current	8.3	6.3
	50.3	37.6	35.0			Total Current	42.9	38.6
	7.6	10.5	11.6			Long-Term Debt	12.4	12.7
	.0	1.3	.4			Deferred Taxes	.5	.5
	16.7	4.2	5.1			All Other Non-Current	7.9	8.3
	25.4	46.4	47.9			Net Worth	36.3	39.9
	100.0	100.0	100.0			Total Liabilities & Net Worth	100.0	100.0
						INCOME DATA		
	100.0	100.0	100.0			Net Sales	100.0	100.0
	35.0	25.8	23.7			Gross Profit	26.8	29.0
	31.6	22.4	15.9			Operating Expenses	24.4	22.4
	3.4	3.4	7.9			Operating Profit	2.4	6.7
	.5	.3	.9			All Other Expenses (net)	1.5	.4
	3.0	3.1	7.0			Profit Before Taxes	.9	6.2
						RATIOS		
	3.7	3.4	3.6				2.4	2.8
	1.8	2.2	2.2			Current	1.6	1.8
	1.0	1.4	1.3				1.2	1.4
	2.2	2.1	1.8				1.4	1.8
	1.1	1.2	1.0			Quick	.9	.9
	.4	.8	.7				.6	.6
	29 12.5	**37** 9.9	**38** 9.5				**39** 9.4	**38** 9.7
	44 8.3	**47** 7.7	**49** 7.4			Sales/Receivables	**48** 7.6	**48** 7.6
	53 6.9	**56** 6.5	**57** 6.4				**62** 5.9	**58** 6.3
	19 19.4	**39** 9.4	**58** 6.3				**28** 12.9	**31** 11.6
	40 9.1	**66** 5.5	**79** 4.6			Cost of Sales/Inventory	**59** 6.2	**64** 5.7
	64 5.7	**107** 3.4	**126** 2.9				**93** 3.9	**100** 3.6
	27 13.4	**25** 14.7	**20** 18.0				**21** 17.6	**22** 16.3
	47 7.8	**34** 10.8	**26** 14.2			Cost of Sales/Payables	**33** 11.2	**42** 8.6
	66 5.5	**46** 8.0	**37** 9.8				**54** 6.7	**60** 6.0
	4.7	3.8	4.2				5.3	4.6
	11.5	6.9	5.1			Sales/Working Capital	8.9	7.8
	NM	11.3	10.5				20.1	14.7
	26.8	15.1	18.2				6.8	27.1
	(11) 9.2	(39) 5.3	(20) 11.3			EBIT/Interest	(95) 1.9	(103) 8.1
	-.5	1.8	3.2				-.4	2.8
		4.1					4.8	9.5
		(11) 1.6				Net Profit + Depr., Dep., Amort./Cur. Mat. L/T/D	(31) 2.3	(26) 2.2
		.7					1.3	1.5
	.0	.1	.2				.2	.2
	.3	.4	.5			Fixed/Worth	.6	.6
	NM	1.1	.8				1.9	1.8
	.7	.5	.3				.8	.6
	1.9	.9	1.1			Debt/Worth	1.8	1.4
	NM	2.3	2.3				4.8	5.1
	51.1	29.4	46.3				22.4	49.3
	(11) 37.9	(37) 17.1	(21) 28.1			% Profit Before Taxes/Tangible Net Worth	(88) 7.6	(93) 23.6
	10.1	4.4	11.7				-3.3	8.0
	22.1	16.4	20.0				8.7	23.5
	11.6	9.0	11.7			% Profit Before Taxes/Total Assets	2.8	9.3
	.0	2.0	4.7				-2.1	3.5
	187.8	27.1	25.2				24.0	31.6
	49.3	16.0	9.3			Sales/Net Fixed Assets	13.1	14.8
	10.7	6.7	6.0				4.2	5.7
	4.6	2.6	2.3				2.5	2.7
	3.2	2.1	1.7			Sales/Total Assets	2.0	2.0
	2.1	1.8	1.4				1.5	1.6
		1.0	1.0				1.4	1.1
		(36) 2.1	(21) 2.2			% Depr., Dep., Amort./Sales	(89) 2.3	(92) 1.9
		3.8	2.7				3.8	3.2
	1.3	1.8					2.9	2.2
	(10) 3.3	(15) 2.8				% Officers', Directors' Owners' Comp/Sales	(30) 4.8	(40) 3.8
	6.9	6.1					12.6	6.0
983M	**57178M**	**504127M**	**788199M**		**198440M**	Net Sales ($)	**3507220M**	**4282370M**
188M	**16383M**	**218828M**	**410257M**		**117589M**	Total Assets ($)	**2235898M**	**2599465M**

M = $ thousand MM = $ million

See Pages 9 through 22 for Explanation of Ratios and Data

Comparative Historical Data / Current Data Sorted by Sales

4/1/11-3/31/12 ALL	4/1/12-3/31/13 ALL	4/1/13-3/31/14 ALL	Type of Statement	0-1MM	1-3MM	3-5MM	5-10MM	10-25MM	25MM & OVER
12	7	7	Unqualified				1	2	4
24	21	19	Reviewed			1	9	5	4
11	9	13	Compiled	1	3	1	5	2	1
19	13	10	Tax Returns		2	1	3	4	
38	39	32	Other	1		3	6	14	8
					10 (4/1-9/30/13)		71 (10/1/13-3/31/14)		
104	89	81	NUMBER OF STATEMENTS	2	5	6	24	27	17
%	%	%	ASSETS	%	%	%	%	%	%
9.5	12.9	11.1	Cash & Equivalents				14.3	10.4	7.6
29.1	26.1	29.7	Trade Receivables (net)				31.8	25.5	33.0
28.9	24.4	29.4	Inventory				25.9	32.7	32.6
1.5	2.6	1.2	All Other Current				.6	1.4	1.8
68.9	66.0	71.4	Total Current				72.6	70.0	74.9
20.4	23.4	20.1	Fixed Assets (net)				19.1	22.1	15.2
5.4	5.0	3.5	Intangibles (net)				2.9	2.8	5.7
5.2	5.6	5.1	All Other Non-Current				5.3	5.0	4.2
100.0	100.0	100.0	Total				100.0	100.0	100.0
			LIABILITIES						
10.7	9.0	10.0	Notes Payable-Short Term				6.1	10.3	14.0
2.7	2.6	2.5	Cur. Mat.-L.T.D.				2.4	3.4	1.6
18.2	13.4	19.2	Trade Payables				23.9	13.9	22.5
.3	.1	.2	Income Taxes Payable				.2	.3	.2
8.4	7.1	6.8	All Other Current				4.6	8.3	6.8
40.2	32.3	38.7	Total Current				37.1	36.1	45.1
10.3	16.9	10.1	Long-Term Debt				8.5	12.3	8.6
.6	.5	.8	Deferred Taxes				1.1	1.0	.7
5.8	6.8	6.5	All Other Non-Current				3.9	2.9	6.9
43.2	43.6	43.8	Net Worth				49.4	47.6	38.7
100.0	100.0	100.0	Total Liabilties & Net Worth				100.0	100.0	100.0
			INCOME DATA						
100.0	100.0	100.0	Net Sales				100.0	100.0	100.0
28.4	31.7	26.9	Gross Profit				23.6	25.6	22.3
22.9	26.8	22.2	Operating Expenses				21.4	19.3	15.3
5.4	4.9	4.7	Operating Profit				2.2	6.3	7.0
1.3	.7	.5	All Other Expenses (net)				.4	.5	.8
4.2	4.2	4.1	Profit Before Taxes				1.9	5.9	6.2
			RATIOS						
2.8	4.3	3.5	Current				3.7	3.3	3.5
1.7	2.5	2.2					2.4	2.0	1.6
1.3	1.4	1.3					1.3	1.5	1.3
1.6	2.5	2.2	Quick				2.6	1.8	1.7
1.0	1.5	1.1					1.5	1.0	.7
.6	.7	.7					.9	.7	.6
36 10.2	33 11.1	34 10.7	Sales/Receivables				32 11.4	38 9.7	37 9.9
46 7.9	42 8.6	47 7.7					49 7.5	47 7.7	45 8.1
59 6.2	50 7.3	55 6.6					60 6.1	57 6.4	53 6.9
32 11.4	24 15.3	40 9.1	Cost of Sales/Inventory				23 15.8	54 6.8	46 7.9
62 5.9	51 7.2	68 5.4					55 6.6	83 4.4	70 5.2
101 3.6	94 3.9	107 3.4					104 3.5	122 3.0	96 3.8
21 17.0	18 20.2	23 15.6	Cost of Sales/Payables				24 15.4	24 15.5	21 17.5
33 11.0	26 14.3	33 10.9					34 10.8	34 10.6	26 14.2
51 7.2	40 9.1	47 7.8					47 7.8	43 8.5	50 7.3
5.4	4.2	4.1	Sales/Working Capital				3.5	3.9	4.5
8.2	6.7	7.0					6.9	6.1	7.5
17.8	17.0	14.0					16.6	10.8	15.8
19.8	23.9	17.6	EBIT/Interest				16.9	17.6	49.7
(91) 5.6	(72) 6.6	(71) 8.7					(19) 4.7	11.4	(14) 8.2
2.7	1.6	2.0					1.6	3.5	2.3
6.5	5.9	7.3	Net Profit + Depr., Dep., Amort./Cur. Mat. L/T/D						
(26) 2.9	(18) 3.1	(19) 3.0							
2.1	1.8	1.3							
.2	.2	.1	Fixed/Worth				.1	.2	.2
.6	.5	.4					.3	.5	.6
1.1	1.4	1.0					1.0	.8	.8
.5	.3	.5	Debt/Worth				.5	.6	.5
1.5	1.1	1.0					.8	1.0	1.9
3.0	3.7	2.7					3.3	1.9	7.1
48.8	40.1	36.0	% Profit Before Taxes/Tangible Net Worth				31.6	30.5	67.5
(94) 24.7	(78) 17.4	(71) 21.6					(22) 15.9	(25) 21.0	(14) 32.1
7.4	2.6	5.5					4.5	9.3	4.3
19.5	19.6	19.7	% Profit Before Taxes/Total Assets				19.7	20.3	21.2
7.5	5.8	9.4					7.9	10.4	11.7
3.1	.9	2.0					1.9	4.1	4.4
27.7	28.7	31.9	Sales/Net Fixed Assets				51.5	25.2	33.4
14.3	11.3	14.7					16.8	9.3	17.0
7.1	6.8	6.5					7.4	5.4	9.1
2.8	2.9	2.8	Sales/Total Assets				3.1	2.5	2.9
2.2	2.1	2.1					2.1	2.1	2.3
1.7	1.6	1.7					1.8	1.4	1.7
1.1	1.1	1.0	% Depr., Dep., Amort./Sales				.9	1.1	.8
(91) 1.7	(74) 1.8	(66) 2.1					(20) 1.9	(23) 2.2	(16) 2.1
2.5	3.3	3.5					3.8	3.7	2.5
1.9	1.9	1.7	% Officers', Directors' Owners' Comp/Sales				1.5		
(35) 3.4	(37) 3.0	(31) 3.0					(12) 3.1		
4.4	6.2	5.9					5.6		
3151289M	2021078M	1548927M	Net Sales ($)	1888M	11287M	24390M	184111M	417052M	910199M
1620834M	1173949M	763245M	Total Assets ($)	773M	5440M	10870M	86349M	231240M	428573M

M = $ thousand MM = $ million

See Pages 9 through 22 for Explanation of Ratios and Data

Current Data Sorted by Assets							Comparative Historical Data	
Type of Statement								
Unqualified		1	2	6	1	10	30	26
Reviewed			8	3			7	9
Compiled	1		3				4	2
Tax Returns	2	4	4				9	18
Other	1	1	13	20	3	13	42	41
	17 (4/1-9/30/13)		79 (10/1/13-3/31/14)				**4/1/09-3/31/10 ALL**	**4/1/10-3/31/11 ALL**
	0-500M	**500M-2MM**	**2-10MM**	**10-50MM**	**50-100MM**	**100-250MM**		
NUMBER OF STATEMENTS	4	6	30	29	4	23	92	96
	%	%	%	%	%	%	%	%
ASSETS								
Cash & Equivalents			14.3	15.8		24.8	19.1	17.5
Trade Receivables (net)			25.0	23.2		18.9	21.4	24.7
Inventory			28.0	24.0		16.7	20.3	24.0
All Other Current			4.6	2.9		3.4	3.3	3.4
Total Current			71.9	65.9		63.8	64.1	69.6
Fixed Assets (net)			20.5	22.4		17.7	22.1	19.8
Intangibles (net)			2.2	3.8		13.9	6.4	5.4
All Other Non-Current			5.3	8.0		4.6	7.5	5.1
Total			100.0	100.0		100.0	100.0	100.0
LIABILITIES								
Notes Payable-Short Term			7.2	8.3		1.2	6.1	5.8
Cur. Mat.-L.T.D.			3.2	2.1		1.4	2.4	3.4
Trade Payables			10.7	10.6		12.2	13.5	14.2
Income Taxes Payable			.0	.3		.4	.3	.2
All Other Current			15.9	13.8		12.2	13.9	16.9
Total Current			37.0	35.1		27.5	36.2	40.6
Long-Term Debt			15.4	13.1		11.9	9.6	12.8
Deferred Taxes			.5	.8		.9	.4	.3
All Other Non-Current			11.5	4.8		5.7	6.7	6.9
Net Worth			35.5	46.2		54.0	47.2	39.4
Total Liabilities & Net Worth			100.0	100.0		100.0	100.0	100.0
INCOME DATA								
Net Sales			100.0	100.0		100.0	100.0	100.0
Gross Profit			38.7	31.0		28.2	38.0	38.6
Operating Expenses			32.5	25.5		27.1	36.6	31.6
Operating Profit			6.2	5.4		1.2	1.5	7.0
All Other Expenses (net)			1.2	.6		2.6	.8	.4
Profit Before Taxes			5.0	4.8		-1.4	.7	6.6
RATIOS								
Current			4.7	4.2		6.4	3.8	3.4
			2.3	2.4		2.9	2.1	2.2
			1.3	1.2		1.7	1.3	1.3
Quick			3.3	2.4		4.3	2.2	2.1
			1.2	1.4		1.9	1.3	1.2
			.7	.6		.8	.8	.7
Sales/Receivables			**38** 9.6	**48** 7.6		**42** 8.6	**30** 12.1	**34** 10.9
			47 7.8	**58** 6.3		**54** 6.7	**46** 7.9	**48** 7.7
			59 6.2	**73** 5.0		**73** 5.0	**65** 5.6	**65** 5.6
Cost of Sales/Inventory			**47** 7.7	**32** 11.3		**61** 6.0	**42** 8.7	**46** 7.9
			94 3.9	**99** 3.7		**70** 5.2	**74** 4.9	**78** 4.7
			166 2.2	**166** 2.2		**122** 3.0	**129** 2.8	**112** 3.3
Cost of Sales/Payables			**11** 32.9	**15** 24.3		**30** 12.1	**22** 16.8	**20** 18.7
			23 15.9	**35** 10.4		**39** 9.3	**43** 8.4	**36** 10.0
			56 6.5	**59** 6.2		**53** 6.9	**73** 5.0	**63** 5.8
Sales/Working Capital			3.3	2.3		1.1	2.6	3.0
			4.2	4.2		3.3	5.2	4.9
			16.0	17.7		5.9	14.9	15.3
EBIT/Interest			17.7	29.8		18.9	14.0	36.9
			(26) 4.8	(23) 3.7		(16) 1.1	(76) 3.3	(73) 9.0
			.6	.6		-7.0	-3.1	2.5
Net Profit + Depr., Dep., Amort./Cur. Mat. L/T/D							20.9	67.9
							(18) 5.5	(20) 3.5
							.9	1.3
Fixed/Worth			.1	.1		.1	.2	.1
			.5	.5		.5	.5	.4
			1.4	1.2		1.5	1.0	1.2
Debt/Worth			.3	.4		.2	.4	.5
			1.2	.8		.9	1.1	1.1
			3.5	3.4		3.1	3.3	3.8
% Profit Before Taxes/Tangible Net Worth			43.1	32.4		14.3	28.6	64.0
			(26) 11.8	(26) 21.5		(19) .8	(81) 13.3	(84) 27.0
			-.7	-.6		-14.0	-5.4	8.5
% Profit Before Taxes/Total Assets			17.0	17.1		8.2	10.3	25.9
			6.3	7.0		.4	3.0	9.8
			-1.1	-.5		-7.0	-4.9	2.0
Sales/Net Fixed Assets			37.9	19.0		14.7	20.2	30.0
			15.0	11.9		7.7	10.9	13.3
			5.4	3.8		3.4	3.8	5.2
Sales/Total Assets			2.0	1.8		1.5	1.9	2.4
			1.7	1.3		.9	1.4	1.6
			1.3	1.0		.6	.9	1.2
% Depr., Dep., Amort./Sales			.8	1.1		.7	1.3	1.3
			(27) 2.1	(24) 3.1		(15) 3.4	(64) 3.1	(70) 2.4
			3.4	4.9		6.8	7.8	4.8
% Officers', Directors' Owners' Comp/Sales							1.8	3.6
							(22) 4.4	(22) 7.2
							10.7	16.3
Net Sales ($)	**2371M**	**39734M**	**334189M**	**983002M**	**502722M**	**4428418M**	**5369432M**	**5313774M**
Total Assets ($)	**1011M**	**6446M**	**168510M**	**638369M**	**367891M**	**3879615M**	**3782796M**	**2993971M**

M = $ thousand MM = $ million

See Pages 9 through 22 for Explanation of Ratios and Data

Comparative Historical Data				Current Data Sorted by Sales					
			Type of Statement						
21	11	20	Unqualified		1	1	1	3	14
13	12	11	Reviewed			1	3	6	1
6	4	4	Compiled	1			1	2	
8	10	10	Tax Returns	1	3	2	4		
43	48	51	Other	1	1	2	5	15	27
4/1/11-3/31/12 ALL	**4/1/12-3/31/13 ALL**	**4/1/13-3/31/14 ALL**		**17 (4/1-9/30/13)**			**79 (10/1/13-3/31/14)**		
				0-1MM	**1-3MM**	**3-5MM**	**5-10MM**	**10-25MM**	**25MM & OVER**
91	85	96	**NUMBER OF STATEMENTS**	3	5	6	14	26	42
%	%	%	**ASSETS**	%	%	%	%	%	%
15.9	17.7	19.1	Cash & Equivalents				20.8	13.9	23.8
23.5	25.3	23.1	Trade Receivables (net)				17.8	23.3	22.5
26.4	24.0	22.1	Inventory				24.3	28.7	18.9
3.7	3.4	3.8	All Other Current				2.9	2.5	4.5
69.4	70.4	68.2	Total Current				65.8	68.4	69.7
19.7	19.1	19.7	Fixed Assets (net)				20.4	22.7	17.2
6.4	4.2	5.4	Intangibles (net)				.3	5.6	8.3
4.6	6.3	6.8	All Other Non-Current				13.4	3.2	4.8
100.0	100.0	100.0	Total				100.0	100.0	100.0
			LIABILITIES						
5.7	6.3	5.4	Notes Payable-Short Term				9.0	9.3	2.5
3.2	2.8	2.7	Cur. Mat.-L.T.D.				2.0	2.6	2.4
14.6	14.4	12.3	Trade Payables				8.8	10.4	13.3
.3	.1	.2	Income Taxes Payable				.0	.2	.4
10.7	11.4	16.7	All Other Current				13.2	16.3	13.7
34.4	35.1	37.3	Total Current				32.9	38.8	32.3
7.5	9.5	18.9	Long-Term Debt				11.5	12.7	10.7
.6	.5	.6	Deferred Taxes				.5	.8	.8
11.8	12.2	7.2	All Other Non-Current				20.3	3.8	5.4
45.7	42.7	36.0	Net Worth				34.7	43.9	50.8
100.0	100.0	100.0	Total Liabilties & Net Worth				100.0	100.0	100.0
			INCOME DATA						
100.0	100.0	100.0	Net Sales				100.0	100.0	100.0
36.1	34.1	34.1	Gross Profit				34.5	32.3	29.7
29.9	31.0	29.9	Operating Expenses				30.9	28.1	27.3
6.2	3.1	4.2	Operating Profit				3.5	4.2	2.4
1.0	.2	1.3	All Other Expenses (net)				.7	.1	1.8
5.2	2.9	2.8	Profit Before Taxes				2.8	4.1	.5
			RATIOS						
4.2	4.6	4.5					6.9	4.1	4.5
2.2	2.2	2.3	Current				2.4	2.3	2.7
1.4	1.4	1.3					1.4	1.2	1.5
2.5	2.7	2.8					4.6	2.8	2.9
1.2	1.2	1.3	Quick				2.3	1.1	1.3
.6	.7	.7					.5	.6	.8
35 10.3	**33** 11.1	**38** 9.5					**36** 10.0	**38** 9.6	**41** 9.0
45 8.2	**45** 8.1	**51** 7.2	Sales/Receivables				**42** 8.6	**53** 6.9	**51** 7.1
60 6.1	**65** 5.6	**68** 5.4					**83** 4.4	**60** 6.1	**69** 5.3
51 7.1	**33** 11.0	**35** 10.5					**3** 126.7	**54** 6.7	**41** 8.9
85 4.3	**76** 4.8	**79** 4.6	Cost of Sales/Inventory				**94** 3.9	**101** 3.6	**70** 5.2
135 2.7	**140** 2.6	**135** 2.7					**182** 2.0	**166** 2.2	**122** 3.0
21 17.6	**20** 18.0	**15** 23.7					**7** 54.0	**11** 33.4	**20** 18.1
35 10.3	**32** 11.5	**34** 10.7	Cost of Sales/Payables				**16** 22.9	**22** 16.7	**38** 9.5
70 5.2	**54** 6.8	**59** 6.2					**61** 6.0	**50** 7.3	**59** 6.2
3.0	2.8	2.7					2.2	3.2	1.9
4.9	5.9	4.3	Sales/Working Capital				3.8	6.0	3.5
9.5	12.6	14.1					21.6	27.0	12.8
29.7	23.8	19.5					11.2	22.6	16.4
(71) 6.2	(69) 5.3	(76) 3.6	EBIT/Interest				(12) 4.0	(23) 3.2	(29) 1.9
.7	.4	-.5					1.2	.1	-3.7
15.7	3.9	6.7							4.8
(19) 2.3	(19) 1.6	(23) 1.6	Net Profit + Depr., Dep., Amort./Cur. Mat. L/T/D						(11) 1.3
.6	.7	-.7							-.7
.1	.1	.1					.1	.2	.1
.3	.5	.5	Fixed/Worth				.4	.5	.4
2.2	1.0	1.4					NM	1.5	1.1
.3	.5	.3					.2	.4	.3
1.2	1.3	1.4	Debt/Worth				1.2	1.2	.9
5.2	3.5	4.7					NM	4.1	2.8
37.4	40.8	30.5					44.0	30.6	26.1
(76) 18.9	(76) 13.1	(80) 12.9	% Profit Before Taxes/Tangible Net Worth				(11) 11.0	(23) 15.2	(37) 8.7
.5	-.6	-5.8					-5.3	-1.2	-8.3
19.0	14.1	13.4					17.1	16.4	11.9
7.8	5.6	5.3	% Profit Before Taxes/Total Assets				5.1	4.0	3.1
-1.1	-3.4	-3.6					-1.4	-1.0	-4.4
33.2	30.8	34.2					36.7	17.5	34.8
13.0	11.7	12.7	Sales/Net Fixed Assets				20.3	8.9	10.9
4.5	5.4	4.1					4.0	4.1	4.0
2.3	2.5	2.0					2.0	1.9	2.0
1.6	1.7	1.4	Sales/Total Assets				1.6	1.4	1.3
1.1	1.2	1.1					1.1	1.2	.8
.7	.8	.9					.9	1.3	.6
(68) 1.9	(68) 1.9	(74) 2.4	% Depr., Dep., Amort./Sales				(12) 2.1	(21) 2.3	(31) 3.0
4.1	3.8	4.9					4.4	4.3	5.4
3.4	2.8	1.7							
(19) 4.7	(22) 5.1	(14) 3.5	% Officers', Directors' Owners' Comp/Sales						
15.3	8.3	5.1							
6177014M	**5344739M**	**6290436M**	Net Sales ($)	**1163M**	**11358M**	**23821M**	**106833M**	**403989M**	**5743272M**
4149907M	**3514528M**	**5061842M**	Total Assets ($)	**526M**	**7225M**	**13651M**	**116441M**	**274900M**	**4649099M**

M = $ thousand MM = $ million

See Pages 9 through 22 for Explanation of Ratios and Data

Current Data Sorted by Assets							Comparative Historical Data	
Type of Statement								
Unqualified			3	4	2	1	10	5
Reviewed		1	4				10	12
Compiled		1	1				3	2
Tax Returns							1	2
Other		4	4	7	1	4	20	11
	8 (4/1-9/30/13)		29 (10/1/13-3/31/14)				4/1/09-3/31/10 ALL	4/1/10-3/31/11 ALL
	0-500M	500M-2MM	2-10MM	10-50MM	50-100MM	100-250MM		
NUMBER OF STATEMENTS		6	12	11	3	5	44	32
ASSETS	%	%	%	%	%	%	%	%
Cash & Equivalents	DATA NOT AVAILABLE		8.7	10.6			8.4	11.8
Trade Receivables (net)			20.3	24.1			28.9	26.2
Inventory			27.2	31.4			26.0	27.9
All Other Current			1.6	4.1			3.8	2.8
Total Current			57.7	70.2			67.2	68.7
Fixed Assets (net)			25.0	19.2			23.8	23.4
Intangibles (net)			7.5	6.3			3.5	3.7
All Other Non-Current			9.7	4.3			5.6	4.3
Total			100.0	100.0			100.0	100.0
LIABILITIES								
Notes Payable-Short Term			7.8	9.6			9.7	7.5
Cur. Mat.-L.T.D.			4.7	6.6			3.1	3.4
Trade Payables			7.5	12.9			16.4	13.1
Income Taxes Payable			.7	.0			.5	.4
All Other Current			6.9	9.3			12.8	10.4
Total Current			27.7	38.4			42.4	34.8
Long-Term Debt			21.9	14.7			13.6	17.6
Deferred Taxes			.5	1.2			.4	.6
All Other Non-Current			3.0	4.8			6.7	6.6
Net Worth			46.9	40.8			36.9	40.4
Total Liabilties & Net Worth			100.0	100.0			100.0	100.0
INCOME DATA								
Net Sales			100.0	100.0			100.0	100.0
Gross Profit			26.7	29.2			31.1	30.6
Operating Expenses			22.9	27.2			26.1	23.2
Operating Profit			3.8	2.0			5.1	7.3
All Other Expenses (net)			.5	.5			1.0	.9
Profit Before Taxes			3.4	1.6			4.1	6.5
RATIOS								
Current			4.0	3.1			3.4	4.2
			2.1	1.6			1.8	2.7
			1.1	1.4			1.2	1.5
Quick			1.8	2.0			1.6	2.1
			1.0	.8			.9	1.4
			.5	.6			.7	.6
Sales/Receivables			**32** 11.3	**43** 8.5			**45** 8.2	**35** 10.5
			38 9.7	**54** 6.8			**58** 6.3	**51** 7.1
			53 6.9	**68** 5.4			**70** 5.2	**63** 5.8
Cost of Sales/Inventory			**51** 7.2	**78** 4.7			**46** 8.0	**40** 9.2
			69 5.3	**96** 3.8			**85** 4.3	**74** 4.9
			107 3.4	**146** 2.5			**135** 2.7	**122** 3.0
Cost of Sales/Payables			**7** 50.8	**28** 12.9			**23** 15.6	**19** 19.2
			16 23.4	**41** 9.0			**37** 9.9	**29** 12.7
			29 12.6	**50** 7.3			**63** 5.8	**38** 9.7
Sales/Working Capital			4.0	2.8			3.0	3.1
			6.4	4.9			7.9	4.7
			19.3	13.1			14.5	11.7
EBIT/Interest			14.1	25.3			21.4	17.7
			(11) 6.7	5.8			(38) 5.1	(27) 5.9
			.0	-5.3			1.3	2.8
Net Profit + Depr., Dep., Amort./Cur. Mat. L/T/D							23.9	18.5
							(13) 3.2	(10) 6.3
							1.3	2.2
Fixed/Worth			.3	.2			.3	.3
			.4	.5			.6	.5
			NM	4.0			1.3	1.1
Debt/Worth			.5	.6			.7	.7
			.9	1.3			1.9	1.0
			NM	17.9			3.8	2.8
% Profit Before Taxes/Tangible Net Worth							37.4	55.7
							(41) 16.9	(29) 21.4
							3.6	10.3
% Profit Before Taxes/Total Assets			14.6	13.1			16.4	18.3
			9.4	7.5			6.9	9.6
			-1.9	-3.0			.5	4.9
Sales/Net Fixed Assets			15.7	15.7			18.7	14.5
			9.4	7.5			8.2	9.5
			4.9	3.8			4.1	5.5
Sales/Total Assets			2.4	2.1			2.3	2.3
			1.8	1.6			1.8	1.8
			1.2	1.1			1.1	1.3
% Depr., Dep., Amort./Sales							.9	1.3
							(34) 2.0	1.8
							3.0	2.9
% Officers', Directors' Owners' Comp/Sales								
Net Sales ($)		21959M	110450M	447192M	178196M	1171927M	1801007M	821209M
Total Assets ($)		7116M	64186M	300238M	187315M	860274M	1278264M	556089M

M = $ thousand MM = $ million

See Pages 9 through 22 for Explanation of Ratios and Data

Comparative Historical Data				Current Data Sorted by Sales					
			Type of Statement						
9	7	10	Unqualified		1			2	7
9	5	5	Reviewed			2	2	1	
1		2	Compiled				2		
2	2		Tax Returns						
11	9	20	Other		3	1	2	3	11
4/1/11-3/31/12	**4/1/12-3/31/13**	**4/1/13-3/31/14**			**8 (4/1-9/30/13)**		**29 (10/1/13-3/31/14)**		
ALL	**ALL**	**ALL**		**0-1MM**	**1-3MM**	**3-5MM**	**5-10MM**	**10-25MM**	**25MM & OVER**
32	23	37	**NUMBER OF STATEMENTS**		4	3	6	6	18
%	%	%	**ASSETS**	%	%	%	%	%	%
14.3	15.7	9.9	Cash & Equivalents	DATA NOT AVAILABLE					9.0
23.9	24.6	23.4	Trade Receivables (net)						19.9
26.7	27.6	28.4	Inventory						30.9
4.6	2.6	4.3	All Other Current						7.6
69.4	70.5	66.0	Total Current						67.4
21.4	20.6	18.9	Fixed Assets (net)						19.4
4.7	2.1	9.2	Intangibles (net)						8.7
4.4	6.8	5.8	All Other Non-Current						4.4
100.0	100.0	100.0	Total						100.0
			LIABILITIES						
6.4	6.1	9.2	Notes Payable-Short Term						8.6
3.3	3.1	4.2	Cur. Mat.-L.T.D.						5.0
10.3	12.9	13.1	Trade Payables						16.9
.8	.6	.4	Income Taxes Payable						.3
8.7	7.4	9.3	All Other Current						10.8
29.5	30.1	36.0	Total Current						41.5
14.5	11.9	14.4	Long-Term Debt						12.7
.8	.8	.6	Deferred Taxes						.9
5.5	1.2	5.8	All Other Non-Current						4.1
49.8	56.0	43.2	Net Worth						40.7
100.0	100.0	100.0	Total Liabilities & Net Worth						100.0
			INCOME DATA						
100.0	100.0	100.0	Net Sales						100.0
29.8	28.9	27.9	Gross Profit						24.1
22.2	23.7	26.1	Operating Expenses						23.2
7.7	5.2	1.8	Operating Profit						.9
.3	.2	.4	All Other Expenses (net)						.5
7.4	5.0	1.4	Profit Before Taxes						.4
			RATIOS						
4.4	4.6	4.0							3.3
2.4	2.7	1.7	Current						1.6
1.6	1.6	1.1							1.1
2.6	2.9	1.8							1.3
1.2	1.4	.8	Quick						.6
.6	.9	.5							.3
32 11.3	**38** 9.5	**33** 11.2							**30** 12.1
42 8.7	**47** 7.7	**43** 8.5	Sales/Receivables						**53** 6.9
62 5.9	**66** 5.5	**62** 5.9							**70** 5.2
34 10.8	**45** 8.1	**48** 7.6							**63** 5.8
76 4.8	**81** 4.5	**78** 4.7	Cost of Sales/Inventory						**94** 3.9
114 3.2	**130** 2.8	**126** 2.9							**152** 2.4
13 27.5	**14** 26.3	**16** 23.5							**29** 12.4
26 14.0	**26** 13.9	**30** 12.0	Cost of Sales/Payables						**36** 10.1
42 8.6	**36** 10.0	**50** 7.3							**73** 5.0
3.1	2.5	3.4							2.7
4.2	4.7	6.5	Sales/Working Capital						5.0
8.0	7.6	18.6							57.8
27.2	12.6	17.8							15.7
(27) 9.6	(19) 7.3	(36) 7.1	EBIT/Interest						4.4
4.4	3.2	-2.9							-4.2
38.5		6.3							
(12) 5.8		(13) 4.6	Net Profit + Depr., Dep., Amort./Cur. Mat. L/T/D						
1.8		1.4							
.3	.3	.3							.4
.4	.4	.5	Fixed/Worth						.6
.6	.5	NM							2.6
.5	.3	.5							.7
.9	.7	1.3	Debt/Worth						1.5
1.9	1.5	NM							15.3
45.1	42.3	27.8							29.1
(28) 23.9	16.5	(28) 16.9	% Profit Before Taxes/Tangible Net Worth						(15) 15.4
14.4	1.7	-4.8							-8.3
21.8	16.4	12.5							9.6
11.3	9.5	5.8	% Profit Before Taxes/Total Assets						3.0
8.2	1.4	-2.5							-3.3
23.6	15.9	31.8							19.6
10.0	7.0	10.3	Sales/Net Fixed Assets						6.6
5.7	4.6	5.3							3.8
2.6	2.5	2.3							2.1
1.8	1.8	1.8	Sales/Total Assets						1.5
1.3	1.3	1.2							1.0
1.2	1.1	1.3							1.7
(29) 1.8	(22) 1.9	(27) 2.2	% Depr., Dep., Amort./Sales						(15) 2.3
2.2	3.2	3.0							3.0
			% Officers', Directors' Owners' Comp/Sales						
977058M	**531982M**	**1929724M**	Net Sales ($)		**10480M**	**13371M**	**40394M**	**81784M**	**1783695M**
691366M	**365417M**	**1419129M**	Total Assets ($)		**4938M**	**5837M**	**20152M**	**50704M**	**1337498M**

M = $ thousand MM = $ million

See Pages 9 through 22 for Explanation of Ratios and Data

Current Data Sorted by Assets							Comparative Historical Data	
			1	1	2	**Type of Statement** Unqualified	6	6
	1	5	1			Reviewed	4	6
	2	4				Compiled	11	5
1	1					Tax Returns	3	1
	3	6	3		1	Other	23	22
7 (4/1-9/30/13)		25 (10/1/13-3/31/14)					4/1/09-3/31/10	4/1/10-3/31/11
0-500M	500M-2MM	2-10MM	10-50MM	50-100MM	100-250MM		ALL	ALL
1	7	15	5	1	3	**NUMBER OF STATEMENTS**	47	40
%	%	%	%	%	%	**ASSETS**	%	%
		11.6				Cash & Equivalents	12.9	15.4
		28.5				Trade Receivables (net)	26.8	23.2
		31.4				Inventory	29.1	25.8
		.9				All Other Current	2.5	3.6
		72.3				Total Current	71.3	68.0
		17.7				Fixed Assets (net)	18.3	17.2
		5.2				Intangibles (net)	6.4	13.1
		4.7				All Other Non-Current	4.0	1.7
		100.0				Total	100.0	100.0
						LIABILITIES		
		10.1				Notes Payable-Short Term	9.9	4.6
		2.8				Cur. Mat.-L.T.D.	3.1	4.9
		21.8				Trade Payables	14.3	12.3
		.0				Income Taxes Payable	.1	.4
		7.8				All Other Current	7.5	6.6
		42.5				Total Current	34.9	28.7
		15.3				Long-Term Debt	10.6	16.9
		.3				Deferred Taxes	.8	1.1
		.4				All Other Non-Current	5.7	5.1
		41.5				Net Worth	48.0	48.1
		100.0				Total Liabilties & Net Worth	100.0	100.0
						INCOME DATA		
		100.0				Net Sales	100.0	100.0
		36.2				Gross Profit	35.3	35.9
		27.8				Operating Expenses	29.5	26.6
		8.4				Operating Profit	5.8	9.2
		1.1				All Other Expenses (net)	.2	1.0
		7.3				Profit Before Taxes	5.6	8.2
						RATIOS		
		3.1					3.6	5.7
		2.2				Current	2.5	3.1
		1.2					1.6	1.6
		2.3					2.1	2.9
		1.1				Quick	1.2	1.5
		.5					.6	.7
		28 13.0					**34** 10.8	**36** 10.0
		51 7.1				Sales/Receivables	**43** 8.4	**45** 8.1
		68 5.4					**55** 6.6	**56** 6.5
		39 9.3					**46** 7.9	**57** 6.4
		81 4.5				Cost of Sales/Inventory	**89** 4.1	**87** 4.2
		159 2.3					**112** 3.3	**125** 2.9
		24 15.5					**22** 16.3	**21** 17.2
		35 10.4				Cost of Sales/Payables	**33** 11.1	**33** 11.1
		81 4.5					**52** 7.0	**47** 7.7
		3.1					3.5	2.8
		10.1				Sales/Working Capital	5.4	4.5
		19.2					11.5	8.7
		17.3					18.9	59.3
		(12) 5.2				EBIT/Interest	(39) 3.8	(34) 13.8
		3.5					1.6	3.5
							11.3	14.3
						Net Profit + Depr., Dep., Amort./Cur. Mat. L/T/D	(14) 5.2	(12) 4.4
							1.9	2.5
		.0					.1	.1
		.2				Fixed/Worth	.2	.3
		1.8					1.1	1.6
		.5					.4	.4
		2.1				Debt/Worth	.8	.9
		4.1					3.7	7.1
		84.4					38.7	46.1
		(14) 29.9				% Profit Before Taxes/Tangible Net Worth	(41) 26.1	(31) 25.0
		11.2					7.2	14.3
		25.0					20.3	21.8
		10.3				% Profit Before Taxes/Total Assets	11.9	13.0
		4.4					2.1	4.5
		137.9					61.2	31.4
		28.9				Sales/Net Fixed Assets	18.3	17.8
		7.3					6.2	6.5
		2.5					2.7	2.2
		2.1				Sales/Total Assets	2.0	1.6
		1.4					1.6	1.3
		.4					.6	.8
		(11) .6				% Depr., Dep., Amort./Sales	(36) 2.1	(30) 2.1
		2.5					3.7	4.0
							2.7	
						% Officers', Directors' Owners' Comp/Sales	(13) 4.6	
							7.7	
432M	28230M	172934M	215010M	70350M	503935M	Net Sales ($)	1353985M	1614227M
253M	10876M	81640M	149185M	66147M	371902M	Total Assets ($)	908006M	1202708M

M = $ thousand MM = $ million

See Pages 9 through 22 for Explanation of Ratios and Data

Comparative Historical Data / Current Data Sorted by Sales

4/1/11-3/31/12 ALL	4/1/12-3/31/13 ALL	4/1/13-3/31/14 ALL	Type of Statement	0-1MM	1-3MM	3-5MM	5-10MM	10-25MM	25MM & OVER
13	9	4	Unqualified						4
5	10	7	Reviewed				2	4	1
7	6	6	Compiled		1	1	3	1	
6	5	2	Tax Returns	1		1			
17	13	13	Other		1	2	4	3	3
					7 (4/1-9/30/13)		25 (10/1/13-3/31/14)		
48	43	32	NUMBER OF STATEMENTS	1	2	4	9	8	8
%	%	%	**ASSETS**	%	%	%	%	%	%
11.6	13.8	10.8	Cash & Equivalents						
26.8	27.9	29.0	Trade Receivables (net)						
30.6	28.3	31.2	Inventory						
6.2	2.2	1.0	All Other Current						
75.2	72.1	72.0	Total Current						
16.9	16.8	17.5	Fixed Assets (net)						
5.5	8.6	7.1	Intangibles (net)						
2.4	2.4	3.5	All Other Non-Current						
100.0	100.0	100.0	Total						
			LIABILITIES						
15.0	9.6	9.8	Notes Payable-Short Term						
3.8	2.4	2.5	Cur. Mat.-L.T.D.						
18.0	12.8	17.5	Trade Payables						
.3	.5	.2	Income Taxes Payable						
6.6	9.9	6.4	All Other Current						
43.8	35.1	36.5	Total Current						
13.3	12.7	16.3	Long-Term Debt						
.5	.9	.5	Deferred Taxes						
4.9	2.9	3.5	All Other Non-Current						
37.7	48.4	43.3	Net Worth						
100.0	100.0	100.0	Total Liabilties & Net Worth						
			INCOME DATA						
100.0	100.0	100.0	Net Sales						
36.9	34.7	33.6	Gross Profit						
29.4	27.9	28.7	Operating Expenses						
7.5	6.7	5.0	Operating Profit						
1.0	1.0	1.1	All Other Expenses (net)						
6.5	5.7	3.8	Profit Before Taxes						
			RATIOS						
5.2	4.2	3.5							
2.1	2.3	2.4	Current						
1.3	1.4	1.4							
2.2	2.5	2.1							
1.1	1.1	1.1	Quick						
.5	.6	.6							
38 9.7	38 9.5	31 11.6							
46 7.9	51 7.2	52 7.0	Sales/Receivables						
55 6.6	62 5.9	68 5.4							
47 7.8	49 7.4	61 6.0							
94 3.9	91 4.0	96 3.8	Cost of Sales/Inventory						
135 2.7	122 3.0	140 2.6							
18 20.4	18 19.9	21 17.7							
31 11.7	25 14.8	34 10.6	Cost of Sales/Payables						
46 8.0	47 7.7	62 5.9							
3.3	3.0	2.9							
5.9	5.3	4.6	Sales/Working Capital						
17.4	9.9	16.1							
20.3	20.3	10.3							
(38) 4.7	(33) 4.1	(26) 4.3	EBIT/Interest						
2.2	1.4	1.3							
15.9	7.7								
(14) 3.5	(15) 2.6		Net Profit + Depr., Dep., Amort./Cur. Mat. L/T/D						
2.1	1.2								
.1	.1	.0							
.3	.4	.4	Fixed/Worth						
2.0	1.2	1.3							
.4	.4	.5							
1.2	1.8	2.0	Debt/Worth						
29.5	3.5	4.0							
37.3	57.7	60.8							
(38) 20.2	(37) 25.1	(30) 15.8	% Profit Before Taxes/Tangible Net Worth						
4.3	2.2	.0							
16.5	21.0	14.4							
8.9	7.5	5.8	% Profit Before Taxes/Total Assets						
2.4	.5	.0							
76.9	38.8	123.7							
23.3	14.1	18.3	Sales/Net Fixed Assets						
5.7	6.0	5.6							
3.1	2.6	2.5							
1.8	1.9	2.0	Sales/Total Assets						
1.3	1.2	1.1							
.7	.7	.4							
(33) 1.8	(31) 1.8	(24) 1.2	% Depr., Dep., Amort./Sales						
3.3	4.8	4.0							
2.4	2.6	3.4							
(16) 5.0	(15) 3.4	(12) 4.7	% Officers', Directors' Owners' Comp/Sales						
5.8	6.3	9.7							
1243468M	1386473M	990891M	Net Sales ($)	432M	4693M	14514M	58975M	125889M	786388M
817675M	1020245M	680003M	Total Assets ($)	253M	4390M	5878M	37491M	72714M	559277M

M = $ thousand MM = $ million

See Pages 9 through 22 for Explanation of Ratios and Data

Current Data Sorted by Assets							Comparative Historical Data	
						Type of Statement		
			5	1		Unqualified	4	3
	1	8	4			Reviewed	10	12
	1	4				Compiled		2
	4	2				Tax Returns	1	3
1	4	14	6		2	Other	8	8
	10 (4/1-9/30/13)		47 (10/1/13-3/31/14)				4/1/09-3/31/10 ALL	4/1/10-3/31/11 ALL
0-500M	500M-2MM	2-10MM	10-50MM	50-100MM	100-250MM			
1	10	28	15	1	2	**NUMBER OF STATEMENTS**	23	28
%	%	%	%	%	%	**ASSETS**	%	%
	19.6	6.6	10.3			Cash & Equivalents	5.0	7.0
	39.5	29.6	27.8			Trade Receivables (net)	29.7	31.2
	20.1	28.2	23.8			Inventory	34.2	36.9
	2.9	.9	6.9			All Other Current	1.6	1.5
	82.2	65.3	68.8			Total Current	70.5	76.5
	12.9	24.7	13.7			Fixed Assets (net)	18.3	15.6
	.9	5.0	15.5			Intangibles (net)	7.8	3.8
	4.0	5.0	2.0			All Other Non-Current	3.4	4.0
	100.0	100.0	100.0			Total	100.0	100.0
						LIABILITIES		
	.6	10.6	7.9			Notes Payable-Short Term	10.5	11.0
	4.9	2.0	2.1			Cur. Mat.-L.T.D.	2.6	6.2
	21.2	19.4	13.5			Trade Payables	17.7	22.1
	.0	.5	.8			Income Taxes Payable	.1	.8
	16.7	9.3	6.4			All Other Current	6.5	7.2
	43.4	41.8	30.7			Total Current	37.5	47.2
	7.5	13.3	13.8			Long-Term Debt	10.4	15.3
	.0	.4	2.5			Deferred Taxes	.8	.3
	43.1	6.5	4.6			All Other Non-Current	2.7	2.9
	6.0	38.0	48.4			Net Worth	48.6	34.3
	100.0	100.0	100.0			Total Liabilties & Net Worth	100.0	100.0
						INCOME DATA		
	100.0	100.0	100.0			Net Sales	100.0	100.0
	33.5	30.0	21.1			Gross Profit	23.9	27.6
	28.5	24.7	13.5			Operating Expenses	19.6	22.3
	5.0	5.3	7.5			Operating Profit	4.3	5.3
	-.5	.5	2.0			All Other Expenses (net)	.8	.8
	5.5	4.7	5.6			Profit Before Taxes	3.4	4.5
						RATIOS		
	3.3	2.7	3.2				3.3	2.7
	2.2	1.6	2.3			Current	1.9	1.9
	1.5	1.2	1.5				1.4	1.3
	2.4	1.2	1.8				1.7	1.4
	1.5	1.0	1.3			Quick	.9	.9
	1.0	.6	.9				.7	.6
	32 11.5	**33** 11.2	**55** 6.6				**43** 8.6	**37** 9.9
	53 6.9	**44** 8.3	**62** 5.9			Sales/Receivables	**54** 6.8	**44** 8.2
	61 6.0	**53** 6.9	**73** 5.0				**62** 5.9	**54** 6.7
	1 258.6	**34** 10.6	**47** 7.7				**47** 7.8	**53** 6.9
	36 10.2	**59** 6.2	**65** 5.6			Cost of Sales/Inventory	**90** 4.1	**78** 4.7
	54 6.7	**91** 4.0	**91** 4.0				**112** 3.3	**96** 3.8
	28 13.0	**26** 14.2	**20** 18.3				**25** 14.6	**28** 13.0
	34 10.7	**37** 9.9	**33** 11.1			Cost of Sales/Payables	**36** 10.2	**41** 8.9
	49 7.5	**52** 7.0	**48** 7.6				**53** 6.8	**59** 6.2
	4.4	6.0	3.2				4.5	5.7
	8.5	10.6	5.1			Sales/Working Capital	6.0	7.1
	NM	18.2	10.6				10.7	14.4
		32.5	32.1				15.1	27.9
		(25) 5.7	(13) 13.8			EBIT/Interest	(21) 4.4	(24) 6.9
		2.4	.8				1.3	.7
							4.8	15.4
						Net Profit + Depr., Dep., Amort./Cur. Mat. L/T/D	(12) 3.8	(11) 5.6
							1.5	1.3
	.1	.4	.2				.2	.1
	.3	.8	.4			Fixed/Worth	.5	.4
	NM	1.1	-2.0				.8	1.8
	.6	.8	.6				.7	.7
	2.4	2.0	1.2			Debt/Worth	1.5	1.8
	NM	4.3	-13.5				2.1	4.0
		59.6	43.6				31.5	77.7
		(26) 33.6	(11) 28.5			% Profit Before Taxes/Tangible Net Worth	(22) 15.9	(25) 31.9
		14.2	5.1				4.6	5.7
	36.5	19.3	19.6				13.0	33.6
	10.0	9.1	11.8			% Profit Before Taxes/Total Assets	5.1	13.3
	2.6	2.0	-.4				1.0	.9
	326.0	22.8	25.2				28.4	62.0
	51.4	11.4	12.2			Sales/Net Fixed Assets	12.9	18.1
	11.7	5.9	10.3				8.4	11.4
	4.4	3.0	2.2				2.2	2.9
	3.7	2.2	1.7			Sales/Total Assets	2.0	2.3
	2.1	1.8	1.2				1.7	1.9
		1.5	1.9				1.3	1.2
		(23) 2.5	(14) 2.0			% Depr., Dep., Amort./Sales	(22) 2.2	(22) 2.1
		3.2	3.0				3.1	2.7
								2.8
						% Officers', Directors' Owners' Comp/Sales		(12) 3.9
								9.9
1014M	51561M	350535M	539726M	140946M	388037M	Net Sales ($)	1005854M	995478M
315M	12899M	145788M	340294M	88935M	227875M	Total Assets ($)	546574M	505497M

M = $ thousand MM = $ million

See Pages 9 through 22 for Explanation of Ratios and Data

Comparative Historical Data | **Current Data Sorted by Sales**

Type of Statement	4/1/11-3/31/12 ALL	4/1/12-3/31/13 ALL	4/1/13-3/31/14 ALL	0-1MM	1-3MM	3-5MM	5-10MM	10-25MM	25MM & OVER
Unqualified	5	3	6					3	3
Reviewed	5	10	13			1	4	5	3
Compiled	6	5	5			2	2	1	
Tax Returns	9	7	6		3	1	1	1	
Other	22	16	27		2	4	4	8	9
					10 (4/1-9/30/13)		47 (10/1/13-3/31/14)		
NUMBER OF STATEMENTS	47	41	57		5	8	11	18	15
ASSETS	%	%	%	%	%	%	%	%	%
Cash & Equivalents	7.4	7.2	9.5	DATA NOT AVAILABLE			6.6	11.7	8.3
Trade Receivables (net)	27.5	28.8	31.2				35.3	29.9	28.1
Inventory	30.2	32.4	25.7				27.0	29.4	23.3
All Other Current	7.9	2.1	2.9				1.6	1.0	7.3
Total Current	73.1	70.5	69.3				70.4	72.0	67.0
Fixed Assets (net)	19.2	20.9	19.0				22.4	20.1	15.2
Intangibles (net)	4.8	5.6	7.6				3.8	3.7	15.8
All Other Non-Current	2.9	2.9	4.1				3.3	4.2	2.0
Total	100.0	100.0	100.0				100.0	100.0	100.0
LIABILITIES									
Notes Payable-Short Term	8.7	7.6	8.7				5.6	12.9	5.8
Cur. Mat.-L.T.D.	1.6	2.7	2.6				2.1	2.2	2.3
Trade Payables	15.8	18.4	18.1				18.5	20.0	16.5
Income Taxes Payable	.2	.3	.4				.2	.9	.5
All Other Current	13.1	8.8	10.0				13.8	9.2	8.2
Total Current	39.4	37.9	39.8				40.2	45.1	33.4
Long-Term Debt	8.9	15.9	14.8				14.4	4.9	18.2
Deferred Taxes	.2	.6	.9				.4	1.0	2.0
All Other Non-Current	10.9	3.8	12.5				2.6	9.6	4.7
Net Worth	40.6	41.8	32.0				42.4	39.4	41.7
Total Liabilties & Net Worth	100.0	100.0	100.0				100.0	100.0	100.0
INCOME DATA									
Net Sales	100.0	100.0	100.0				100.0	100.0	100.0
Gross Profit	29.7	29.2	27.6				29.0	22.8	20.9
Operating Expenses	22.0	22.4	21.9				24.6	17.4	14.6
Operating Profit	7.7	6.7	5.8				4.5	5.4	6.4
All Other Expenses (net)	.6	1.0	1.0				.1	.7	2.7
Profit Before Taxes	7.1	5.7	4.7				4.4	4.7	3.6
RATIOS									
Current	3.0	2.9	2.9				3.8	2.9	2.4
	2.3	1.7	2.0				1.7	1.7	2.1
	1.4	1.4	1.2				1.3	1.1	1.5
Quick	1.4	1.4	1.7				2.0	1.5	1.5
	1.0	1.0	1.0				1.2	1.0	1.2
	.6	.7	.6				.6	.6	.6
Sales/Receivables	**29** 12.5	**35** 10.3	**40** 9.1				**33** 11.0	**38** 9.6	**41** 9.0
	43 8.5	**45** 8.2	**48** 7.6				**48** 7.6	**47** 7.8	**56** 6.5
	53 6.9	**54** 6.7	**64** 5.7				**57** 6.4	**65** 5.6	**73** 5.0
Cost of Sales/Inventory	**31** 11.6	**36** 10.2	**32** 11.5				**24** 15.0	**33** 11.2	**47** 7.7
	69 5.3	**63** 5.8	**56** 6.5				**50** 7.3	**59** 6.2	**63** 5.8
	96 3.8	**99** 3.7	**89** 4.1				**107** 3.4	**91** 4.0	**78** 4.7
Cost of Sales/Payables	**21** 17.5	**23** 15.7	**24** 15.0				**22** 16.6	**19** 19.3	**25** 14.7
	32 11.4	**39** 9.3	**36** 10.0				**30** 12.3	**39** 9.3	**36** 10.0
	46 8.0	**52** 7.0	**50** 7.3				**47** 7.8	**51** 7.1	**49** 7.5
Sales/Working Capital	4.6	5.5	4.8				5.9	5.3	3.8
	6.9	8.9	7.5				11.1	8.6	5.7
	12.6	13.2	16.4				16.6	NM	11.2
EBIT/Interest	25.4	18.3	29.7				35.3	31.8	24.8
	(40) 7.9	(38) 8.0	(49) 7.1				14.0	(17) 7.1	(13) 6.9
	3.1	2.7	1.8				3.3	1.0	-.4
Net Profit + Depr., Dep., Amort./Cur. Mat. L/T/D	13.3	8.4	6.1						
	(11) 8.7	(13) 2.7	(20) 2.4						
	4.1	1.7	.6						
Fixed/Worth	.2	.3	.3				.5	.2	.3
	.4	.5	.7				.8	.5	.7
	1.1	1.7	1.4				1.0	1.1	-1.6
Debt/Worth	.6	.7	.7				.7	.4	.8
	1.4	1.5	2.1				2.2	2.0	1.5
	2.9	5.0	8.3				3.6	5.4	-9.6
% Profit Before Taxes/Tangible Net Worth	50.1	48.0	57.3				59.6	56.2	43.6
	(42) 31.7	(36) 27.6	(47) 28.5				28.8	(16) 37.9	(11) 28.5
	18.1	6.4	6.5				5.9	17.5	1.9
% Profit Before Taxes/Total Assets	23.4	18.4	19.7				18.5	21.7	15.2
	13.0	11.3	9.8				14.8	11.6	9.3
	4.1	2.9	2.0				2.0	.2	-8.1
Sales/Net Fixed Assets	33.0	30.1	31.4				41.3	31.2	20.6
	13.7	15.5	12.6				13.7	11.4	12.2
	9.5	7.9	7.9				5.9	9.8	8.0
Sales/Total Assets	3.0	3.3	3.0				3.9	3.0	2.2
	2.3	2.4	2.2				2.2	2.4	1.7
	1.9	1.7	1.7				1.8	1.8	1.6
% Depr., Dep., Amort./Sales	1.0	1.4	1.6					1.5	1.9
	(38) 1.7	(31) 1.8	(45) 2.2					(16) 2.1	(14) 2.3
	2.2	2.9	3.2					3.1	3.4
% Officers', Directors' Owners' Comp/Sales	2.6	2.4	2.3						
	(19) 4.1	(16) 5.0	(18) 5.3						
	10.4	7.3	6.9						
Net Sales ($)	1355451M	1623411M	1471819M		10264M	31073M	87096M	323616M	1019770M
Total Assets ($)	694438M	759888M	816106M		9927M	14833M	35651M	148886M	606809M

M = $ thousand MM = $ million

See Pages 9 through 22 for Explanation of Ratios and Data

Current Data Sorted by Assets							Comparative Historical Data	
						Type of Statement		
	1	5	11	5	2	Unqualified	34	34
	6	15	10			Reviewed	57	45
	10	13	4	1		Compiled	23	22
3	12	8	1			Tax Returns	22	28
2	11	26	26	8	3	Other	102	106
	38 (4/1-9/30/13)		145 (10/1/13-3/31/14)				4/1/09-3/31/10 ALL	4/1/10-3/31/11 ALL
0-500M	500M-2MM	2-10MM	10-50MM	50-100MM	100-250MM			
5	40	67	52	14	5	**NUMBER OF STATEMENTS**	238	235
%	%	%	%	%	%	**ASSETS**	%	%
	11.0	12.5	16.2	10.2		Cash & Equivalents	11.5	10.2
	31.8	27.3	20.4	25.6		Trade Receivables (net)	26.0	28.0
	33.1	28.8	25.7	18.5		Inventory	28.3	29.9
	2.3	4.2	3.3	1.8		All Other Current	3.0	2.6
	78.2	72.8	65.6	56.0		Total Current	68.8	70.7
	12.7	19.2	20.4	15.8		Fixed Assets (net)	19.6	16.5
	4.5	4.6	7.5	22.7		Intangibles (net)	6.1	6.9
	4.6	3.4	6.4	5.4		All Other Non-Current	5.5	6.0
	100.0	100.0	100.0	100.0		Total	100.0	100.0
						LIABILITIES		
	12.1	8.7	5.4	10.3		Notes Payable-Short Term	9.9	10.6
	4.1	4.0	1.9	1.7		Cur. Mat.-L.T.D.	2.7	3.4
	20.6	14.4	9.7	13.0		Trade Payables	15.5	14.5
	.1	.2	.2	.2		Income Taxes Payable	.1	.2
	8.0	9.0	8.6	9.8		All Other Current	10.5	10.0
	44.8	36.3	25.8	35.0		Total Current	38.7	38.8
	12.9	10.1	13.5	16.5		Long-Term Debt	13.4	13.2
	.1	.6	.8	.7		Deferred Taxes	.4	.6
	12.6	4.5	6.9	5.5		All Other Non-Current	8.3	6.7
	29.7	48.5	53.0	42.3		Net Worth	39.3	40.6
	100.0	100.0	100.0	100.0		Total Liabilties & Net Worth	100.0	100.0
						INCOME DATA		
	100.0	100.0	100.0	100.0		Net Sales	100.0	100.0
	36.2	37.4	31.4	24.0		Gross Profit	33.2	34.2
	35.7	29.7	25.1	21.0		Operating Expenses	28.1	26.6
	.5	7.7	6.4	3.1		Operating Profit	5.1	7.6
	.6	.1	.9	2.5		All Other Expenses (net)	1.1	1.1
	-.1	7.6	5.5	.5		Profit Before Taxes	4.0	6.4
						RATIOS		
	3.1	3.2	4.6	2.3			3.3	3.1
	2.1	2.1	2.8	1.6		Current	1.9	2.0
	1.3	1.4	1.7	1.3			1.3	1.3
	2.1	2.5	2.3	1.6			1.8	1.8
	.9	1.0	1.4	.9		Quick	1.0	1.0
	.5	.6	.8	.7			.6	.6
	31 11.9	**29** 12.5	**38** 9.7	**49** 7.5			**36** 10.1	**35** 10.3
	41 8.9	**41** 8.9	**47** 7.7	**58** 6.3		Sales/Receivables	**48** 7.6	**51** 7.2
	54 6.8	**54** 6.7	**59** 6.2	**69** 5.3			**60** 6.1	**62** 5.9
	45 8.1	**41** 9.0	**69** 5.3	**50** 7.3			**38** 9.6	**46** 7.9
	78 4.7	**73** 5.0	**99** 3.7	**62** 5.9		Cost of Sales/Inventory	**78** 4.7	**79** 4.6
	126 2.9	**114** 3.2	**140** 2.6	**91** 4.0			**122** 3.0	**126** 2.9
	15 23.9	**18** 19.9	**16** 22.3	**20** 18.3			**21** 17.3	**21** 17.4
	37 9.9	**29** 12.6	**27** 13.4	**32** 11.4		Cost of Sales/Payables	**33** 11.1	**33** 11.0
	65 5.6	**45** 8.1	**39** 9.3	**50** 7.3			**53** 6.9	**52** 7.0
	4.0	4.2	2.6	4.0			3.9	4.0
	6.9	6.3	4.0	8.4		Sales/Working Capital	6.1	6.3
	18.1	12.7	7.9	14.7			14.9	13.9
	14.7	33.9	41.6	20.0			14.1	20.8
	(31) 1.8	(60) 12.7	(45) 6.1	(10) 2.6		EBIT/Interest	(205) 3.7	(201) 7.3
	-2.1	2.4	1.0	-2.0			.9	2.1
		8.9	5.3				5.4	8.3
		(14) 1.4	(14) 2.4			Net Profit + Depr., Dep., Amort./Cur. Mat. L/T/D	(68) 2.7	(70) 2.8
		.3	1.3				.7	1.3
	.1	.1	.1	.3			.1	.1
	.3	.4	.4	.7		Fixed/Worth	.5	.4
	.8	.8	1.1	-1.6			1.4	1.2
	.6	.5	.4	1.2			.6	.6
	2.7	1.2	.8	2.0		Debt/Worth	1.4	1.4
	7.3	3.3	3.0	-8.6			4.1	5.2
	37.3	47.7	37.7				45.8	52.0
	(32) 5.3	(61) 26.5	(47) 18.6			% Profit Before Taxes/Tangible Net Worth	(208) 15.5	(200) 29.7
	-5.7	9.0	.9				1.8	9.1
	14.6	23.7	18.9	11.7			19.0	20.1
	1.7	12.4	6.7	4.2		% Profit Before Taxes/Total Assets	4.6	9.5
	-2.4	1.9	.1	-7.6			.2	2.6
	111.6	32.9	19.9	18.5			39.4	39.2
	31.0	17.8	8.6	7.9		Sales/Net Fixed Assets	13.3	18.3
	12.6	7.3	5.5	5.8			5.8	8.4
	3.4	2.9	2.1	2.5			2.6	2.6
	2.4	2.2	1.5	1.2		Sales/Total Assets	1.9	1.9
	1.9	1.7	1.1	.7			1.4	1.5
	.3	.9	1.2	1.1			.8	.7
	(28) .9	(54) 2.2	(47) 2.1	(12) 1.7		% Depr., Dep., Amort./Sales	(195) 2.2	(193) 1.7
	1.7	3.2	4.7	3.6			3.6	2.9
	3.2	2.0					2.6	3.2
	(24) 5.6	(29) 3.3				% Officers', Directors' Owners' Comp/Sales	(78) 4.5	(65) 5.5
	9.8	6.1					8.2	9.9
7877M	154582M	790577M	1594487M	1760512M	854904M	Net Sales ($)	5244465M	9206643M
1492M	57108M	365254M	1114290M	1098414M	775089M	Total Assets ($)	3428392M	5297105M

M = $ thousand MM = $ million

See Pages 9 through 22 for Explanation of Ratios and Data

Comparative Historical Data				Current Data Sorted by Sales					
			Type of Statement						
43	31	24	Unqualified		1	1		7	15
37	29	31	Reviewed		3	2	10	8	8
26	17	28	Compiled		3	4	11	7	3
23	27	24	Tax Returns	1	5	8	3	7	
103	91	76	Other	2	7	7	7	29	24
4/1/11-3/31/12 ALL	4/1/12-3/31/13 ALL	4/1/13-3/31/14 ALL		38 (4/1-9/30/13)		145 (10/1/13-3/31/14)			
				0-1MM	1-3MM	3-5MM	5-10MM	10-25MM	25MM & OVER
232	195	183	**NUMBER OF STATEMENTS**	3	19	22	31	58	50
%	%	%	**ASSETS**	%	%	%	%	%	%
13.4	12.0	13.7	Cash & Equivalents		11.8	16.1	15.9	14.8	10.6
27.9	26.2	26.1	Trade Receivables (net)		19.7	30.8	27.1	25.0	25.8
27.6	29.5	27.6	Inventory		30.9	29.3	27.9	29.0	24.3
3.1	2.7	3.2	All Other Current		4.2	.5	3.9	3.0	4.0
71.9	70.4	70.6	Total Current		66.5	76.6	74.7	71.8	64.7
17.0	17.1	17.4	Fixed Assets (net)		18.1	17.3	18.4	16.9	17.9
6.2	6.8	7.0	Intangibles (net)		8.0	2.3	4.5	5.8	12.1
4.9	5.7	5.0	All Other Non-Current		7.4	3.8	2.4	5.6	5.3
100.0	100.0	100.0	Total		100.0	100.0	100.0	100.0	100.0
			LIABILITIES						
7.4	9.5	9.0	Notes Payable-Short Term		11.4	14.3	7.8	6.9	8.4
2.8	3.4	3.1	Cur. Mat.-L.T.D.		2.6	3.0	4.2	4.1	1.7
15.5	14.4	14.2	Trade Payables		13.1	19.0	14.4	12.1	14.6
.3	.2	.2	Income Taxes Payable		.1	.0	.2	.2	.3
10.7	8.3	8.4	All Other Current		9.1	5.3	9.1	9.3	8.3
36.6	35.9	34.8	Total Current		36.2	41.7	35.7	32.5	33.2
12.1	14.9	13.7	Long-Term Debt		24.0	6.7	11.6	10.0	19.0
.5	.5	.5	Deferred Taxes		.3	.1	.3	.8	.8
7.4	5.3	6.9	All Other Non-Current		17.3	3.7	4.9	6.3	6.8
43.3	43.4	44.1	Net Worth		22.2	47.9	47.5	50.4	40.2
100.0	100.0	100.0	Total Liabilties & Net Worth		100.0	100.0	100.0	100.0	100.0
			INCOME DATA						
100.0	100.0	100.0	Net Sales		100.0	100.0	100.0	100.0	100.0
35.2	35.0	34.1	Gross Profit		41.3	36.2	34.9	37.2	26.8
27.8	27.3	28.6	Operating Expenses		40.7	36.5	28.6	28.5	20.8
7.5	7.6	5.5	Operating Profit		.6	-.3	6.3	8.8	6.0
.8	.9	.9	All Other Expenses (net)		.3	-.4	.2	.7	2.0
6.7	6.8	4.6	Profit Before Taxes		.4	.2	6.1	8.1	4.0
			RATIOS						
3.1	3.6	3.8			3.8	3.4	4.9	4.0	3.3
2.1	2.0	2.3	Current		2.3	2.3	2.0	2.3	2.2
1.4	1.4	1.4			1.6	1.3	1.4	1.7	1.4
1.9	2.0	2.2			2.4	3.3	2.9	2.2	1.8
1.2	1.0	1.1	Quick		.9	1.2	1.3	1.2	1.0
.7	.6	.7			.4	.5	.6	.7	.7
35 10.4	33 11.1	34 10.7			23 16.1	32 11.5	28 13.1	34 10.7	45 8.2
47 7.8	45 8.1	45 8.1	Sales/Receivables		35 10.5	45 8.1	39 9.3	44 8.3	53 6.9
60 6.1	58 6.3	59 6.2			47 7.7	60 6.1	51 7.1	54 6.7	66 5.5
38 9.5	52 7.0	46 7.9			46 8.0	27 13.7	35 10.4	54 6.8	51 7.1
73 5.0	85 4.3	83 4.4	Cost of Sales/Inventory		104 3.5	78 4.7	74 4.9	91 4.0	74 4.9
118 3.1	135 2.7	122 3.0			152 2.4	104 3.5	122 3.0	140 2.6	104 3.5
20 18.7	18 19.9	17 21.4			14 26.7	16 22.5	19 19.6	17 21.6	21 17.6
33 11.2	30 12.1	31 11.9	Cost of Sales/Payables		28 12.9	37 9.8	32 11.5	26 14.2	38 9.7
51 7.1	47 7.7	49 7.4			78 4.7	51 7.2	42 8.7	38 9.6	54 6.7
3.6	3.5	3.2			3.3	4.7	3.1	2.8	3.6
6.4	5.8	5.8	Sales/Working Capital		4.6	6.2	6.8	5.1	5.8
12.4	13.0	11.6			13.0	20.0	11.6	10.3	12.0
23.1	20.8	26.9			8.1	20.5	40.4	35.5	26.0
(190) 8.5	(164) 7.3	(152) 6.5	EBIT/Interest		(16) 1.7	(17) 4.6	(26) 5.4	(50) 15.3	(42) 5.9
2.2	2.4	1.1			-3.4	-.7	1.7	2.1	1.0
10.6	6.8	6.7						6.5	6.8
(60) 4.5	(50) 2.5	(38) 2.3	Net Profit + Depr., Dep., Amort./Cur. Mat. L/T/D					(18) 2.1	(11) 4.0
1.8	1.1	.7						.3	2.3
.1	.1	.1			.0	.1	.1	.1	.3
.4	.4	.4	Fixed/Worth		.3	.3	.5	.4	.5
1.0	1.0	.9			1.3	.6	.9	.9	1.3
.6	.5	.5			.7	.4	.2	.5	.6
1.4	1.2	1.3	Debt/Worth		2.6	.7	1.5	1.0	1.4
3.5	4.0	4.2			-13.6	3.3	5.4	3.4	6.7
58.6	44.3	43.5			44.3	34.3	34.1	61.5	40.7
(202) 26.7	(170) 20.6	(158) 19.9	% Profit Before Taxes/Tangible Net Worth		(14) 4.1	(21) 10.8	(26) 23.3	(54) 22.9	(40) 20.3
8.1	8.4	2.3			-19.9	-1.5	2.9	4.7	6.8
21.9	18.4	20.2			11.7	19.5	21.4	24.1	17.9
10.0	9.2	7.7	% Profit Before Taxes/Total Assets		4.6	2.5	9.0	10.7	7.6
2.4	2.8	.5			-12.9	-3.3	1.3	2.2	.3
44.0	48.3	42.4			167.0	51.5	32.9	43.8	23.2
18.7	13.8	15.1	Sales/Net Fixed Assets		13.2	23.9	16.4	17.7	11.3
7.9	7.4	7.1			6.8	9.9	6.8	7.2	6.5
2.9	2.8	2.7			2.4	3.4	2.9	2.8	2.4
2.0	1.9	2.0	Sales/Total Assets		1.7	2.5	2.2	2.0	1.7
1.4	1.3	1.2			1.2	2.0	1.7	1.4	1.1
.7	.9	.9			.5	.6	.4	.9	1.1
(169) 1.7	(142) 1.6	(144) 1.7	% Depr., Dep., Amort./Sales		(12) 1.5	(18) 1.1	(25) 1.6	(48) 2.1	(41) 1.9
3.1	2.9	3.3			3.6	3.5	3.1	3.7	3.4
2.5	2.2	2.2			4.4	2.9	1.8	2.3	
(68) 4.6	(67) 4.0	(61) 3.7	% Officers', Directors' Owners' Comp/Sales		(10) 7.6	(13) 4.4	(16) 3.7	(20) 3.6	
9.7	8.5	7.2			13.9	7.1	11.0	4.2	
9868791M	6321435M	5162939M	Net Sales ($)	951M	43026M	89304M	221989M	916323M	3891346M
5793533M	3980150M	3411647M	Total Assets ($)	747M	25494M	48201M	155849M	578588M	2602768M

M = $ thousand MM = $ million

See Pages 9 through 22 for Explanation of Ratios and Data

Current Data Sorted by Assets							Comparative Historical Data	
						Type of Statement		
		3	7	2		Unqualified	19	13
		3	2			Reviewed	11	7
		3			1	Compiled	1	1
	3	5				Tax Returns	5	7
1	1	7	5	1	6	Other	27	35
	7 (4/1-9/30/13)		43 (10/1/13-3/31/14)				4/1/09-3/31/10 ALL	4/1/10-3/31/11 ALL
0-500M	500M-2MM	2-10MM	10-50MM	50-100MM	100-250MM			
1	4	21	14	3	7	NUMBER OF STATEMENTS	63	63
%	%	%	%	%	%	**ASSETS**	%	%
		15.9	13.3			Cash & Equivalents	15.6	16.8
		25.0	25.9			Trade Receivables (net)	23.9	26.3
		28.5	23.2			Inventory	20.2	21.2
		5.0	4.4			All Other Current	3.4	2.9
		74.4	66.7			Total Current	63.1	67.2
		16.0	14.4			Fixed Assets (net)	20.0	15.1
		5.4	14.9			Intangibles (net)	10.4	10.8
		4.2	4.0			All Other Non-Current	6.4	6.9
		100.0	100.0			Total	100.0	100.0
						LIABILITIES		
		7.1	6.4			Notes Payable-Short Term	7.7	5.4
		2.3	1.8			Cur. Mat.-L.T.D.	2.9	1.7
		10.8	10.0			Trade Payables	10.5	10.8
		.0	.2			Income Taxes Payable	.2	.3
		14.2	17.0			All Other Current	16.1	13.1
		34.6	35.3			Total Current	37.4	31.4
		10.6	7.0			Long-Term Debt	8.6	9.0
		.6	.6			Deferred Taxes	.8	.6
		7.2	22.8			All Other Non-Current	8.0	11.5
		47.0	34.2			Net Worth	45.3	47.5
		100.0	100.0			Total Liabilities & Net Worth	100.0	100.0
						INCOME DATA		
		100.0	100.0			Net Sales	100.0	100.0
		51.7	53.2			Gross Profit	44.0	46.8
		45.2	47.8			Operating Expenses	40.5	41.0
		6.5	5.5			Operating Profit	3.5	5.8
		.2	1.3			All Other Expenses (net)	1.3	1.9
		6.2	4.2			Profit Before Taxes	2.2	3.9
						RATIOS		
		3.7	4.2				3.3	4.9
		2.3	1.5			Current	1.8	2.6
		1.4	1.3				1.2	1.5
		2.9	2.7				2.5	3.1
		1.1	1.0			Quick	1.0	1.4
		.7	.7				.5	.8
		26 13.8	**47** 7.8				**35** 10.4	**33** 11.0
		37 9.8	**54** 6.7			Sales/Receivables	**46** 7.9	**47** 7.7
		53 6.9	**73** 5.0				**57** 6.5	**67** 5.5
		51 7.1	**64** 5.7				**49** 7.4	**49** 7.5
		81 4.5	**111** 3.3			Cost of Sales/Inventory	**77** 4.7	**83** 4.4
		203 1.8	**159** 2.3				**123** 3.0	**141** 2.6
		15 25.1	**21** 17.6				**16** 23.2	**21** 17.7
		35 10.5	**50** 7.3			Cost of Sales/Payables	**32** 11.4	**35** 10.5
		46 7.9	**107** 3.4				**54** 6.8	**63** 5.8
		4.3	3.4				4.0	2.3
		5.9	5.4			Sales/Working Capital	6.9	4.8
		10.7	11.5				18.1	10.8
		18.6	87.2				14.0	44.9
		(19) 6.6	(12) 11.9			EBIT/Interest	(50) 3.6	(52) 4.9
		2.2	.7				.9	-.2
							3.2	
						Net Profit + Depr., Dep., Amort./Cur. Mat. L/T/D	(15) 2.1	
							1.3	
		.1	.1				.1	.1
		.5	.5			Fixed/Worth	.5	.3
		1.0	-.8				1.3	1.3
		.5	.3				.4	.3
		1.3	1.5			Debt/Worth	1.0	.9
		4.3	-3.5				4.8	7.9
		52.9	33.3				41.3	55.9
		(19) 20.5	(10) 20.4			% Profit Before Taxes/Tangible Net Worth	(52) 14.9	(53) 20.5
		4.9	6.0				1.5	-2.9
		21.5	13.5				16.0	21.9
		8.1	6.7			% Profit Before Taxes/Total Assets	3.8	8.8
		2.9	-1.5				-3.7	-2.2
		41.8	58.9				39.6	37.3
		25.2	11.3			Sales/Net Fixed Assets	13.4	17.1
		6.8	7.2				4.2	8.9
		2.9	2.1				2.4	2.4
		2.2	1.5			Sales/Total Assets	1.5	1.6
		1.7	1.0				1.1	1.1
		.7					1.3	.9
		(19) 1.2				% Depr., Dep., Amort./Sales	(50) 2.4	(43) 2.3
		2.3					5.4	4.9
							1.3	4.6
						% Officers', Directors' Owners' Comp/Sales	(16) 3.1	(10) 7.7
							10.6	10.4
1468M	7368M	266537M	460053M	349378M	1138091M	Net Sales ($)	2249239M	2263576M
487M	2572M	114119M	312005M	235303M	1161710M	Total Assets ($)	1882904M	1954256M

M = $ thousand MM = $ million

See Pages 9 through 22 for Explanation of Ratios and Data

Comparative Historical Data / Current Data Sorted by Sales

	4/1/11-3/31/12 ALL	4/1/12-3/31/13 ALL	4/1/13-3/31/14 ALL	0-1MM	1-3MM	3-5MM	5-10MM	10-25MM	25MM & OVER
Type of Statement									
Unqualified	14	6	12					3	9
Reviewed	4	4	5				1	4	
Compiled	3	1	4				3		1
Tax Returns	8	3	8		2	1	3	2	
Other	35	32	21	1	1		3	5	11
				7 (4/1-9/30/13)			43 (10/1/13-3/31/14)		
NUMBER OF STATEMENTS	64	46	50	1	3	1	10	14	21
ASSETS	%	%	%	%	%	%	%	%	%
Cash & Equivalents	14.7	16.7	15.9				16.7	11.2	18.7
Trade Receivables (net)	24.0	25.4	22.6				19.3	25.3	23.2
Inventory	20.7	21.9	25.4				33.6	24.8	17.7
All Other Current	3.4	3.5	4.4				7.1	2.8	5.2
Total Current	62.9	67.5	68.4				76.8	64.1	64.9
Fixed Assets (net)	19.0	15.8	14.7				11.6	20.1	14.8
Intangibles (net)	10.9	12.5	11.4				5.3	12.2	16.4
All Other Non-Current	7.3	4.2	5.5				6.4	3.7	3.9
Total	100.0	100.0	100.0				100.0	100.0	100.0
LIABILITIES									
Notes Payable-Short Term	5.1	7.0	5.6				2.4	9.2	4.4
Cur. Mat.-L.T.D.	2.2	2.6	2.0				2.6	2.4	1.7
Trade Payables	12.6	12.1	10.9				6.8	12.6	9.1
Income Taxes Payable	.3	.3	.1				.0	.0	.2
All Other Current	11.0	14.0	14.8				16.0	12.5	15.1
Total Current	31.3	36.0	33.5				27.8	36.8	30.6
Long-Term Debt	14.3	12.6	10.1				4.4	12.1	10.6
Deferred Taxes	.4	.4	.5				.0	1.2	.4
All Other Non-Current	4.9	6.4	10.7				12.4	14.1	9.9
Net Worth	49.1	44.7	45.3				55.3	35.9	48.6
Total Liabilties & Net Worth	100.0	100.0	100.0				100.0	100.0	100.0
INCOME DATA									
Net Sales	100.0	100.0	100.0				100.0	100.0	100.0
Gross Profit	44.8	44.5	51.1				56.0	52.8	48.3
Operating Expenses	38.1	38.4	43.7				48.2	46.9	41.5
Operating Profit	6.7	6.1	7.4				7.8	5.9	6.9
All Other Expenses (net)	1.1	.9	.6				1.1	.3	.6
Profit Before Taxes	5.6	5.2	6.8				6.7	5.6	6.3
RATIOS									
Current	3.8	3.8	4.2				11.2	2.8	5.1
	2.3	1.9	2.2				3.3	1.9	1.9
	1.5	1.3	1.4				1.5	1.3	1.4
Quick	2.9	2.4	2.7				4.5	1.5	3.3
	1.2	1.1	1.1				2.2	.9	1.1
	.7	.6	.8				.4	.6	.9
Sales/Receivables	36 10.1	38 9.7	32 11.3				21 17.1	27 13.4	40 9.1
	47 7.7	47 7.8	44 8.3				36 10.1	45 8.2	51 7.2
	63 5.8	68 5.4	59 6.2				51 7.1	60 6.1	65 5.6
Cost of Sales/Inventory	29 12.5	42 8.6	54 6.7				51 7.2	59 6.2	47 7.8
	89 4.1	89 4.1	87 4.2				152 2.4	89 4.1	78 4.7
	135 2.7	159 2.3	182 2.0				261 1.4	192 1.9	140 2.6
Cost of Sales/Payables	22 16.9	24 15.0	17 21.5				4 88.2	28 13.0	15 24.1
	33 11.1	45 8.2	42 8.7				18 19.8	42 8.7	45 8.1
	56 6.5	58 6.3	65 5.6				47 7.8	89 4.1	68 5.4
Sales/Working Capital	3.5	3.3	3.2				2.4	4.7	2.3
	5.4	6.2	5.8				4.3	6.6	5.1
	12.9	12.3	9.8				8.7	16.6	8.5
EBIT/Interest	16.9	40.3	25.5					14.5	101.9
	(50) 3.8	(39) 6.3	(42) 8.0					(13) 6.6	(16) 15.9
	1.2	.7	1.0					.8	2.5
Net Profit + Depr., Dep., Amort./Cur. Mat. L/T/D	11.1	5.8	4.5						
	(16) 2.5	(11) 1.7	(12) 2.5						
	.7	.9	1.5						
Fixed/Worth	.1	.1	.1				.1	.4	.1
	.5	.5	.5				.3	.5	.5
	1.6	2.2	1.1				.6	3.6	NM
Debt/Worth	.4	.4	.4				.4	.6	.4
	1.0	1.5	1.1				.8	1.5	1.5
	5.7	10.0	5.4				3.5	13.0	NM
% Profit Before Taxes/Tangible Net Worth	56.5	56.2	49.2					48.5	43.4
	(51) 20.1	(38) 25.0	(41) 19.5					(12) 17.6	(16) 19.1
	1.9	1.9	1.4					5.7	.5
% Profit Before Taxes/Total Assets	22.0	19.0	18.1				26.6	15.4	16.0
	6.6	6.9	8.0				9.9	6.5	9.8
	.9	-.1	1.5				1.8	1.3	.9
Sales/Net Fixed Assets	36.6	37.5	49.3				58.6	30.5	23.7
	12.8	16.2	18.0				26.4	15.1	11.8
	4.8	5.9	7.0				9.7	6.0	7.0
Sales/Total Assets	2.4	2.2	2.3				2.3	2.8	2.2
	1.6	1.6	1.8				2.1	1.9	1.3
	1.1	1.1	1.1				1.5	1.3	.9
% Depr., Dep., Amort./Sales	1.3	1.3	.7					1.2	.5
	(47) 2.5	(30) 2.0	(36) 1.5					(11) 2.1	(14) 2.1
	4.3	4.0	3.2					3.3	3.8
% Officers', Directors' Owners' Comp/Sales	3.7		2.5						
	(13) 7.9		(12) 4.3						
	11.8		5.4						
Net Sales ($)	2297684M	2245347M	2222895M	198M	4534M	4104M	72615M	229255M	1912189M
Total Assets ($)	2257053M	2011154M	1826196M	574M	1870M	615M	42131M	130396M	1650610M

M = $ thousand MM = $ million

See Pages 9 through 22 for Explanation of Ratios and Data

Current Data Sorted by Assets							Comparative Historical Data	
						Type of Statement		
		4	5	1	3	Unqualified	29	18
	1	8	2		1	Reviewed	16	12
	1	4		1		Compiled	2	2
	1	3				Tax Returns	1	5
1	2	11	16	3	3	Other	21	36
13 (4/1-9/30/13)			58 (10/1/13-3/31/14)				4/1/09-3/31/10	4/1/10-3/31/11
0-500M	500M-2MM	2-10MM	10-50MM	50-100MM	100-250MM		ALL	ALL
1	5	30	23	5	7	**NUMBER OF STATEMENTS**	69	73
%	%	%	%	%	%	**ASSETS**	%	%
		19.4	13.6			Cash & Equivalents	14.0	13.1
		23.1	18.5			Trade Receivables (net)	22.1	23.9
		21.7	25.0			Inventory	27.8	26.6
		6.0	4.8			All Other Current	6.1	4.9
		70.2	61.9			Total Current	70.1	68.5
		19.2	14.6			Fixed Assets (net)	16.2	16.2
		4.1	15.7			Intangibles (net)	9.6	9.7
		6.5	7.8			All Other Non-Current	4.1	5.6
		100.0	100.0			Total	100.0	100.0
						LIABILITIES		
		5.9	8.1			Notes Payable-Short Term	4.9	15.2
		1.9	5.2			Cur. Mat.-L.T.D.	2.7	2.6
		17.8	9.6			Trade Payables	9.8	11.2
		.5	.6			Income Taxes Payable	.9	.7
		17.6	11.2			All Other Current	12.8	15.2
		43.7	34.8			Total Current	31.2	44.9
		9.5	5.8			Long-Term Debt	10.0	15.8
		.3	2.3			Deferred Taxes	.8	1.0
		6.7	5.9			All Other Non-Current	4.8	5.4
		39.8	51.3			Net Worth	53.2	33.0
		100.0	100.0			Total Liabilties & Net Worth	100.0	100.0
						INCOME DATA		
		100.0	100.0			Net Sales	100.0	100.0
		40.5	39.3			Gross Profit	37.7	40.8
		33.3	31.8			Operating Expenses	30.9	33.7
		7.2	7.6			Operating Profit	6.8	7.1
		.2	2.1			All Other Expenses (net)	2.0	1.5
		7.0	5.4			Profit Before Taxes	4.8	5.5
						RATIOS		
		3.0	2.6				4.4	3.0
		1.9	2.0			Current	2.6	2.0
		1.2	1.4				1.5	1.4
		2.2	1.5				2.5	2.0
		1.1	.7			Quick	1.1	.9
		.5	.5				.6	.7
		21 17.6	**35** 10.5				**34** 10.6	**35** 10.4
		33 11.1	**46** 7.9			Sales/Receivables	**48** 7.6	**48** 7.5
		49 7.4	**61** 6.0				**65** 5.6	**63** 5.8
		13 27.1	**70** 5.2				**65** 5.7	**45** 8.2
		73 5.0	**107** 3.4			Cost of Sales/Inventory	**123** 3.0	**107** 3.4
		126 2.9	**135** 2.7				**163** 2.2	**169** 2.2
		15 25.0	**22** 16.7				**18** 20.3	**18** 20.5
		40 9.1	**45** 8.1			Cost of Sales/Payables	**28** 12.9	**30** 12.3
		66 5.5	**70** 5.2				**51** 7.2	**55** 6.6
		3.8	3.2				2.4	3.0
		7.3	4.7			Sales/Working Capital	4.0	4.8
		19.6	8.9				9.4	11.2
		52.7	25.3				66.8	28.8
		(23) 8.7	(20) 7.2			EBIT/Interest	(61) 6.5	(65) 5.4
		1.5	-1.9				.8	1.5
							10.1	67.5
						Net Profit + Depr., Dep., Amort./Cur. Mat. L/T/D	(19) 2.4	(23) 4.6
							1.3	1.5
		.2	.1				.1	.1
		.4	.3			Fixed/Worth	.3	.4
		2.8	1.1				.7	2.3
		.4	.5				.4	.5
		1.1	1.7			Debt/Worth	1.0	1.4
		7.8	3.8				2.5	12.6
		91.6	78.0				36.6	50.9
		(26) 33.5	(19) 27.6			% Profit Before Taxes/Tangible Net Worth	(61) 13.6	(59) 25.5
		9.4	-8.0				2.1	8.5
		40.9	20.2				18.2	15.8
		9.9	9.3			% Profit Before Taxes/Total Assets	7.0	8.3
		2.7	-4.9				-.6	1.2
		54.7	24.0				23.2	30.7
		13.1	14.8			Sales/Net Fixed Assets	11.9	16.2
		6.6	7.8				6.3	7.0
		2.7	1.7				2.0	2.2
		2.1	1.3			Sales/Total Assets	1.4	1.5
		1.5	1.0				1.1	1.1
		.7	1.5				1.2	1.1
		(24) 1.5	(19) 1.9			% Depr., Dep., Amort./Sales	(58) 2.1	(54) 2.3
		2.4	4.8				3.0	3.3
							2.4	2.5
						% Officers', Directors' Owners' Comp/Sales	(12) 5.1	(12) 6.9
							7.8	10.0
1045M	18119M	355673M	686432M	438561M	1233013M	Net Sales ($)	3383935M	3222760M
263M	6991M	155825M	482994M	367509M	1171213M	Total Assets ($)	2805987M	2862142M

M = $ thousand MM = $ million

See Pages 9 through 22 for Explanation of Ratios and Data

Comparative Historical Data | **Current Data Sorted by Sales**

4/1/11-3/31/12 ALL	4/1/12-3/31/13 ALL	4/1/13-3/31/14 ALL	Type of Statement	0-1MM	1-3MM	3-5MM	5-10MM	10-25MM	25MM & OVER
15	18	13	Unqualified		1			4	8
7	9	12	Reviewed		1	1	2	6	2
6	9	6	Compiled		1	1	2	1	1
5	5	4	Tax Returns				3	1	
27	31	36	Other		2		8	12	14
					13 (4/1-9/30/13)		58 (10/1/13-3/31/14)		
60	72	71	NUMBER OF STATEMENTS		5	2	15	24	25
%	%	%	ASSETS	%	%	%	%	%	%
12.4	14.1	15.3	Cash & Equivalents	DATA NOT AVAILABLE			23.2	13.6	13.1
25.0	23.5	21.8	Trade Receivables (net)				23.2	22.1	19.7
29.1	29.1	22.9	Inventory				23.5	23.4	19.8
4.7	2.8	5.3	All Other Current				2.2	6.5	6.9
71.3	69.5	65.3	Total Current				72.0	65.6	59.5
15.7	14.5	16.4	Fixed Assets (net)				19.0	16.5	12.9
8.2	9.6	12.0	Intangibles (net)				3.1	9.3	22.0
4.9	6.5	6.3	All Other Non-Current				5.9	8.6	5.6
100.0	100.0	100.0	Total				100.0	100.0	100.0
			LIABILITIES						
8.2	5.8	7.1	Notes Payable-Short Term				3.8	8.5	4.3
1.9	1.9	2.9	Cur. Mat.-L.T.D.				1.7	2.8	3.7
13.7	11.4	13.1	Trade Payables				11.3	17.7	8.6
.2	.2	.6	Income Taxes Payable				.9	.3	.5
10.2	12.5	18.0	All Other Current				9.4	18.3	18.5
34.2	31.9	41.7	Total Current				27.2	47.5	35.7
12.8	11.5	8.2	Long-Term Debt				5.7	9.9	7.7
.6	.8	1.5	Deferred Taxes				.0	.6	3.4
3.6	6.5	8.7	All Other Non-Current				6.8	8.4	6.8
48.8	49.3	40.0	Net Worth				60.3	33.5	46.4
100.0	100.0	100.0	Total Liabilties & Net Worth				100.0	100.0	100.0
			INCOME DATA						
100.0	100.0	100.0	Net Sales				100.0	100.0	100.0
36.2	41.0	40.2	Gross Profit				46.2	35.1	38.3
27.9	33.4	33.4	Operating Expenses				35.3	32.2	29.1
8.3	7.6	6.8	Operating Profit				11.0	2.9	9.2
1.0	.9	1.3	All Other Expenses (net)				.2	1.7	1.9
7.3	6.8	5.5	Profit Before Taxes				10.7	1.2	7.2
			RATIOS						
3.9	4.1	2.7					7.6	2.2	2.6
2.2	2.4	1.7	Current				2.9	1.7	1.6
1.6	1.5	1.2					2.0	1.2	1.2
2.2	2.5	1.6					4.1	1.3	1.5
1.1	1.2	.8	Quick				1.7	.7	.9
.7	.7	.6					.6	.5	.6
38 9.6	37 9.8	29 12.7					13 28.3	32 11.5	34 10.6
49 7.4	48 7.6	46 7.9	Sales/Receivables				22 16.6	42 8.6	49 7.4
68 5.4	64 5.7	62 5.9					65 5.6	50 7.3	69 5.3
61 6.0	46 7.9	38 9.7					5 75.8	43 8.5	39 9.3
122 3.0	118 3.1	89 4.1	Cost of Sales/Inventory				47 7.7	104 3.5	76 4.8
166 2.2	182 2.0	135 2.7					203 1.8	126 2.9	104 3.5
22 16.7	18 20.7	20 18.3					11 34.0	26 14.0	21 17.4
36 10.2	30 12.1	37 9.9	Cost of Sales/Payables				20 18.3	49 7.5	30 12.2
51 7.2	47 7.7	65 5.6					64 5.7	69 5.3	61 6.0
2.8	2.9	3.8					3.5	4.3	4.1
4.7	4.4	6.2	Sales/Working Capital				3.8	7.3	5.9
9.3	7.8	18.7					6.2	23.6	21.3
32.6	58.7	34.8					197.0	23.2	35.7
(53) 7.5	(64) 11.2	(59) 8.2	EBIT/Interest				(10) 24.6	(20) 3.9	(22) 10.5
1.7	1.9	-.6					-1.6	-2.6	.7
56.0	29.1	32.3							
(13) 3.8	(16) 5.8	(14) 3.8	Net Profit + Depr., Dep., Amort./Cur. Mat. L/T/D						
2.3	1.3	2.0							
.1	.1	.1					.1	.1	.2
.3	.3	.4	Fixed/Worth				.3	.4	.5
1.2	.9	3.6					.5	NM	-5.8
.4	.4	.5					.3	.7	.5
1.0	.9	1.7	Debt/Worth				.5	1.9	1.9
3.8	3.4	8.2					1.1	NM	-15.5
56.4	41.8	64.7					60.7	80.9	85.9
(52) 20.7	(62) 20.4	(56) 28.1	% Profit Before Taxes/Tangible Net Worth				22.5	(18) 30.6	(17) 43.5
3.9	9.1	6.5					1.3	4.4	21.6
19.6	18.3	19.2					48.1	13.5	26.0
10.5	9.2	8.2	% Profit Before Taxes/Total Assets				14.2	7.9	9.3
.8	1.7	-.3					.7	-3.8	.4
34.4	47.2	27.4					92.3	26.7	24.5
15.6	15.2	12.7	Sales/Net Fixed Assets				12.1	14.0	11.4
7.7	7.9	7.3					5.8	7.5	8.4
2.3	2.3	2.4					2.9	2.6	1.8
1.6	1.6	1.6	Sales/Total Assets				1.8	1.7	1.4
1.2	1.1	1.2					1.5	1.1	.9
.9	.8	.8					.8	1.0	1.1
(50) 1.7	(57) 1.6	(55) 1.8	% Depr., Dep., Amort./Sales				(11) 1.3	(20) 1.7	(19) 2.6
2.9	2.5	3.1					3.2	2.7	4.4
3.3	1.4	2.4							
(15) 5.7	(19) 6.1	(17) 4.9	% Officers', Directors' Owners' Comp/Sales						
10.2	12.7	11.9							
3008039M	2394062M	2732843M	Net Sales ($)		10907M	8588M	104407M	404237M	2204704M
2372186M	2007454M	2184795M	Total Assets ($)		6998M	6041M	55228M	255878M	1860650M

M = $ thousand MM = $ million

See Pages 9 through 22 for Explanation of Ratios and Data

Current Data Sorted by Assets | **Comparative Historical Data**

5 (4/1-9/30/13) | 24 (10/1/13-3/31/14)

0-500M	500M-2MM	2-10MM	10-50MM	50-100MM	100-250MM	Type of Statement	4/1/09-3/31/10 ALL	4/1/10-3/31/11 ALL
	1	1	4		2	Unqualified	6	7
		3	1			Reviewed	9	13
	1	4	1			Compiled	5	7
		2				Tax Returns	3	6
	2	2	4	1		Other	11	25
	4	12	10	1	2	**NUMBER OF STATEMENTS**	34	58
%	%	%	%	%	%	**ASSETS**	%	%
		13.2	11.1			Cash & Equivalents	13.7	10.2
D		37.0	29.0			Trade Receivables (net)	38.3	36.0
A		25.9	26.5			Inventory	22.0	24.0
T		4.1	7.2			All Other Current	4.6	6.9
A		80.2	73.7			Total Current	78.6	77.1
		12.7	18.0			Fixed Assets (net)	12.4	13.9
N		.3	1.3			Intangibles (net)	4.1	4.1
O		6.8	7.0			All Other Non-Current	5.0	5.0
T		100.0	100.0			Total	100.0	100.0
A						**LIABILITIES**		
V		8.5	8.2			Notes Payable-Short Term	9.6	8.4
A		1.5	1.4			Cur. Mat.-L.T.D.	3.1	3.9
I		12.0	8.3			Trade Payables	13.2	14.3
L		.0	1.2			Income Taxes Payable	.0	.3
A		17.6	15.2			All Other Current	16.6	13.6
B		39.6	34.3			Total Current	42.6	40.5
L		8.7	9.1			Long-Term Debt	6.5	8.4
E		.2	1.8			Deferred Taxes	.7	.3
		3.9	3.5			All Other Non-Current	9.0	2.8
		47.6	51.3			Net Worth	41.1	48.1
		100.0	100.0			Total Liabilties & Net Worth	100.0	100.0
						INCOME DATA		
		100.0	100.0			Net Sales	100.0	100.0
		35.4	39.3			Gross Profit	37.5	37.7
		28.9	32.6			Operating Expenses	29.5	31.7
		6.5	6.7			Operating Profit	7.9	6.0
		-.3	-.3			All Other Expenses (net)	.4	.3
		6.7	7.0			Profit Before Taxes	7.5	5.7
						RATIOS		
		4.4	3.5				3.6	3.3
		2.3	2.0			Current	2.0	2.1
		1.7	1.7				1.2	1.3
		3.7	2.7				2.2	2.0
		1.1	1.1			Quick	1.3	1.1
		.9	.5				.8	.7
		33 10.9	**46** 8.0				**36** 10.2	**41** 8.9
		45 8.1	**56** 6.5			Sales/Receivables	**48** 7.6	**54** 6.8
		51 7.2	**78** 4.7				**62** 5.9	**65** 5.6
		2 191.0	**60** 6.1				**7** 51.0	**21** 17.7
		39 9.4	**122** 3.0			Cost of Sales/Inventory	**50** 7.3	**56** 6.5
		135 2.7	**166** 2.2				**96** 3.8	**88** 4.2
		12 29.2	**15** 23.6				**11** 32.7	**18** 20.6
		18 19.8	**35** 10.5			Cost of Sales/Payables	**24** 15.0	**31** 11.9
		37 9.9	**56** 6.5				**39** 9.3	**49** 7.4
		4.7	2.5				4.4	3.9
		6.9	3.7			Sales/Working Capital	6.7	6.4
		10.2	7.4				21.2	14.7
		104.8					210.9	34.1
		(10) 8.7				EBIT/Interest	(29) 12.0	(48) 10.9
		2.4					1.9	1.6
								6.1
						Net Profit + Depr., Dep., Amort./Cur. Mat. L/T/D		(13) 1.9
								.3
		.1	.1				.1	.1
		.2	.3			Fixed/Worth	.3	.2
		1.0	.6				.5	.8
		.3	.6				.6	.4
		1.1	1.0			Debt/Worth	1.0	1.0
		3.3	1.6				3.1	3.3
		139.4	51.8				57.3	52.1
		(11) 26.2	14.3			% Profit Before Taxes/Tangible Net Worth	(32) 30.4	(52) 18.4
		11.6	2.4				9.1	6.0
		29.4	22.7				32.7	25.8
		9.3	7.3			% Profit Before Taxes/Total Assets	15.0	9.5
		6.8	1.1				1.1	2.5
		88.9	26.7				63.6	50.7
		39.6	9.6			Sales/Net Fixed Assets	25.0	19.9
		21.8	5.1				12.0	13.0
		3.9	2.1				3.5	3.2
		2.8	1.4			Sales/Total Assets	2.6	2.1
		1.8	1.2				1.7	1.7
		.3	1.7				.4	.9
		(11) .6	2.5			% Depr., Dep., Amort./Sales	(27) 1.1	(49) 1.4
		.7	3.4				1.8	2.3
							2.8	2.7
						% Officers', Directors' Owners' Comp/Sales	(11) 4.8	(17) 5.6
							9.9	7.1
	13610M	121985M	313995M	264433M	436748M	Net Sales ($)	1322198M	1868725M
	4136M	42059M	191525M	82917M	331070M	Total Assets ($)	592043M	1060483M

M = $ thousand MM = $ million

See Pages 9 through 22 for Explanation of Ratios and Data

Comparative Historical Data				Current Data Sorted by Sales					
			Type of Statement						
9	3	8	Unqualified			1		3	4
6	7	4	Reviewed					4	
9	7	6	Compiled			1	4		1
3	3	2	Tax Returns				1	1	
21	18	9	Other		1	2	1	2	3
4/1/11-3/31/12 ALL	4/1/12-3/31/13 ALL	4/1/13-3/31/14 ALL			5 (4/1-9/30/13)		24 (10/1/13-3/31/14)		
				0-1MM	1-3MM	3-5MM	5-10MM	10-25MM	25MM & OVER
48	38	29	**NUMBER OF STATEMENTS**		1	4	6	10	8
%	%	%	**ASSETS**	%	%	%	%	%	%
12.8	10.9	13.0	Cash & Equivalents	DATA NOT AVAILABLE				12.7	
37.1	32.7	32.5	Trade Receivables (net)					29.5	
18.4	27.0	23.5	Inventory					27.7	
6.1	5.3	4.8	All Other Current					6.0	
74.4	75.8	73.7	Total Current					75.8	
16.0	13.7	16.7	Fixed Assets (net)					16.8	
3.6	4.5	3.7	Intangibles (net)					.4	
6.1	6.0	6.0	All Other Non-Current					7.0	
100.0	100.0	100.0	Total					100.0	
			LIABILITIES						
7.7	10.0	8.0	Notes Payable-Short Term					10.8	
3.7	2.4	1.5	Cur. Mat.-L.T.D.					1.7	
16.0	15.2	9.6	Trade Payables					11.9	
.4	.1	.5	Income Taxes Payable					.1	
14.2	15.0	17.1	All Other Current					14.1	
42.0	42.7	36.6	Total Current					38.7	
9.9	7.7	10.8	Long-Term Debt					8.2	
.7	.5	1.0	Deferred Taxes					1.5	
4.7	2.3	3.2	All Other Non-Current					.2	
42.7	46.8	48.4	Net Worth					51.4	
100.0	100.0	100.0	Total Liabilties & Net Worth					100.0	
			INCOME DATA						
100.0	100.0	100.0	Net Sales					100.0	
38.2	38.6	37.7	Gross Profit					33.9	
30.7	34.6	30.8	Operating Expenses					27.9	
7.5	4.0	7.0	Operating Profit					6.0	
.4	.4	.0	All Other Expenses (net)					-1.4	
7.2	3.6	6.9	Profit Before Taxes					7.4	
			RATIOS						
2.7	2.7	3.3						4.1	
1.8	1.7	2.1	Current					2.5	
1.2	1.5	1.6						1.4	
1.9	1.6	2.4						3.4	
1.2	1.1	1.2	Quick					1.1	
.7	.6	.9						.3	
41 8.8	33 11.1	34 10.6						28 13.2	
55 6.6	51 7.2	46 8.0	Sales/Receivables					47 7.7	
72 5.1	65 5.6	62 5.9						64 5.7	
11 33.9	33 11.2	22 16.5						5 72.7	
34 10.7	58 6.3	48 7.6	Cost of Sales/Inventory					114 3.2	
76 4.8	111 3.3	135 2.7						166 2.2	
22 16.6	18 20.2	13 27.9						14 25.5	
38 9.5	36 10.1	24 14.9	Cost of Sales/Payables					33 11.2	
57 6.4	55 6.6	37 9.8						56 6.5	
4.4	4.5	3.7						2.9	
7.9	7.9	6.4	Sales/Working Capital					6.9	
17.7	13.0	10.0						258.0	
45.3	29.0	44.2							
(42) 9.0	(34) 8.1	(25) 6.7	EBIT/Interest						
3.0	.9	2.9							
10.0									
(17) 3.6			Net Profit + Depr., Dep., Amort./Cur. Mat. L/T/D						
2.0									
.1	.1	.1						.2	
.4	.2	.4	Fixed/Worth					.3	
1.3	.6	.9						.8	
.6	.5	.6						.4	
1.4	1.3	1.1	Debt/Worth					.7	
3.8	2.8	2.3						1.6	
45.7	51.6	48.4							
(42) 26.3	(34) 17.8	(27) 22.4	% Profit Before Taxes/Tangible Net Worth						
14.2	5.5	11.6							
19.6	16.8	28.3						30.2	
11.7	8.1	8.7	% Profit Before Taxes/Total Assets					6.6	
3.6	1.2	6.0						-.5	
41.8	74.7	63.7						60.7	
19.4	36.5	22.1	Sales/Net Fixed Assets					18.1	
9.7	9.9	7.6						5.1	
3.4	3.5	3.2						4.2	
2.2	2.4	2.2	Sales/Total Assets					1.8	
1.6	1.6	1.5						1.2	
.7	.5	.5							
(42) 1.2	(31) .8	(26) .9	% Depr., Dep., Amort./Sales						
2.8	1.6	2.3							
1.7									
(10) 3.0			% Officers', Directors' Owners' Comp/Sales						
5.4									
1440844M	1036409M	1150771M	Net Sales ($)		2568M	14371M	40440M	175938M	917454M
767301M	644886M	651707M	Total Assets ($)		1065M	5170M	18396M	102323M	524753M

M = $ thousand MM = $ million

See Pages 9 through 22 for Explanation of Ratios and Data

Current Data Sorted by Assets							Comparative Historical Data	
						Type of Statement		
		5	11	6	6	Unqualified	29	29
	1	27	10	1		Reviewed	32	34
		7				Compiled	9	11
2	2	3				Tax Returns	3	7
	10	21	17	2	2	Other	50	50
31 (4/1-9/30/13)		102 (10/1/13-3/31/14)					**4/1/09-3/31/10 ALL**	**4/1/10-3/31/11 ALL**
0-500M	**500M-2MM**	**2-10MM**	**10-50MM**	**50-100MM**	**100-250MM**	**NUMBER OF STATEMENTS**	123	131
2	13	63	38	9	8			
%	%	%	%	%	%	**ASSETS**	%	%
	5.8	9.3	16.8			Cash & Equivalents	14.0	14.0
	35.5	30.7	23.4			Trade Receivables (net)	24.2	26.2
	30.2	30.0	24.7			Inventory	25.2	25.7
	.2	4.6	3.8			All Other Current	5.8	5.4
	71.6	74.7	68.7			Total Current	69.2	71.3
	18.9	14.6	19.1			Fixed Assets (net)	15.4	15.9
	2.2	4.4	7.1			Intangibles (net)	9.0	6.8
	7.3	6.3	5.1			All Other Non-Current	6.4	5.9
	100.0	100.0	100.0			Total	100.0	100.0
						LIABILITIES		
	15.1	8.6	4.8			Notes Payable-Short Term	8.9	8.8
	1.4	2.0	2.9			Cur. Mat.-L.T.D.	2.6	2.6
	23.0	13.7	9.3			Trade Payables	9.9	11.2
	.0	.2	.2			Income Taxes Payable	.9	.3
	11.0	11.0	12.1			All Other Current	11.6	15.8
	50.6	35.5	29.1			Total Current	33.9	38.8
	11.1	8.1	7.7			Long-Term Debt	10.8	8.0
	.4	.3	.3			Deferred Taxes	.5	.6
	17.1	4.8	2.4			All Other Non-Current	9.6	8.3
	20.8	51.3	60.6			Net Worth	45.2	44.3
	100.0	100.0	100.0			Total Liabilties & Net Worth	100.0	100.0
						INCOME DATA		
	100.0	100.0	100.0			Net Sales	100.0	100.0
	43.3	35.9	39.7			Gross Profit	41.2	39.4
	43.0	30.8	32.3			Operating Expenses	35.1	31.8
	.3	5.1	7.4			Operating Profit	6.2	7.6
	1.5	.5	1.0			All Other Expenses (net)	1.4	1.2
	-1.1	4.6	6.3			Profit Before Taxes	4.8	6.4
						RATIOS		
	2.1	3.6	3.6				3.5	3.8
	1.5	2.2	2.7			Current	2.3	2.3
	1.0	1.4	1.5				1.4	1.4
	1.2	1.8	2.3				2.1	2.1
	1.1	1.2	1.3			Quick	1.3	1.2
	.4	.7	.9				.7	.7
	37 9.8	**38** 9.5	**41** 8.9				**40** 9.1	**41** 8.8
	43 8.5	**51** 7.2	**49** 7.5			Sales/Receivables	**51** 7.2	**54** 6.8
	51 7.2	**64** 5.7	**65** 5.6				**64** 5.7	**63** 5.8
	26 14.2	**51** 7.2	**47** 7.8				**56** 6.5	**50** 7.3
	64 5.7	**83** 4.4	**85** 4.3			Cost of Sales/Inventory	**88** 4.1	**87** 4.2
	135 2.7	**130** 2.8	**166** 2.2				**126** 2.9	**118** 3.1
	22 16.3	**18** 20.6	**21** 17.1				**19** 19.0	**19** 19.3
	29 12.4	**34** 10.6	**30** 12.0			Cost of Sales/Payables	**30** 12.0	**32** 11.4
	49 7.4	**52** 7.0	**46** 7.9				**46** 8.0	**50** 7.3
	7.6	3.6	2.8				2.9	2.9
	14.7	5.6	4.1			Sales/Working Capital	4.4	4.5
	NM	13.1	7.6				9.9	9.9
	9.4	34.7	72.9				26.4	25.4
	(12) 1.7	(55) 12.1	(32) 19.1			EBIT/Interest	(108) 3.1	(115) 8.8
	-1.0	2.2	5.0				.9	2.1
		17.6	30.4				11.1	10.6
		(19) 3.7	(13) 15.9			Net Profit + Depr., Dep., Amort./Cur. Mat. L/T/D	(41) 3.9	(41) 2.6
		1.6	2.5				1.0	.9
	.1	.1	.1				.1	.1
	.3	.2	.3			Fixed/Worth	.3	.4
	2.3	.7	.6				1.6	1.3
	.7	.5	.3				.4	.4
	3.0	.9	.7			Debt/Worth	1.2	1.2
	21.2	2.7	1.4				5.9	4.2
	28.7	52.5	30.8				35.2	49.1
	(11) 7.8	(60) 15.6	(37) 20.6			% Profit Before Taxes/Tangible Net Worth	(101) 17.8	(112) 19.7
	-1.5	5.2	8.7				5.2	10.9
	6.1	18.9	15.8				14.5	16.9
	2.9	7.5	8.3			% Profit Before Taxes/Total Assets	5.4	8.5
	-8.3	1.6	4.0				.7	2.6
	134.6	50.3	34.1				30.6	29.2
	29.2	17.0	13.0			Sales/Net Fixed Assets	13.0	15.6
	9.6	10.4	5.8				6.8	7.8
	4.6	2.6	2.0				2.1	2.3
	3.1	2.1	1.5			Sales/Total Assets	1.6	1.8
	1.8	1.5	1.2				1.1	1.1
	.7	.6	1.2				1.1	.9
	(10) 1.2	(51) 1.1	(28) 1.9			% Depr., Dep., Amort./Sales	(103) 1.6	(105) 1.5
	1.6	2.2	2.9				2.8	2.6
		1.6					2.5	2.5
		(21) 3.1				% Officers', Directors' Owners' Comp/Sales	(22) 6.7	(29) 3.4
		5.9					9.6	7.8
2327M	48715M	623147M	1222712M	729104M	1529537M	Net Sales ($)	4138665M	4677691M
845M	16012M	307928M	778882M	675258M	1280438M	Total Assets ($)	3684322M	3490302M

M = $ thousand MM = $ million

See Pages 9 through 22 for Explanation of Ratios and Data

Comparative Historical Data | **Current Data Sorted by Sales**

	4/1/11-3/31/12 ALL		4/1/12-3/31/13 ALL		4/1/13-3/31/14 ALL		0-1MM	1-3MM		3-5MM		5-10MM		10-25MM		25MM & OVER
						Type of Statement										
	24		24		28	Unqualified						3		5		20
	50		28		39	Reviewed				5		11		17		6
	9		9		7	Compiled				2		4		1		
	10		5		7	Tax Returns	1	1		1		2		2		
	50		55		52	Other		4		6		13		15		14
							31 (4/1-9/30/13)					102 (10/1/13-3/31/14)				
	143		121		133	**NUMBER OF STATEMENTS**	1	5		14		33		40		40
	%		%		%	**ASSETS**	%	%		%		%		%		%
	12.8		12.0		12.1	Cash & Equivalents				6.2		7.7		14.1		17.1
	28.8		28.3		27.4	Trade Receivables (net)				30.7		30.5		26.2		24.5
	26.1		26.5		27.1	Inventory				27.3		28.2		31.3		19.2
	3.7		4.4		3.7	All Other Current				3.9		5.5		2.8		3.4
	71.4		71.2		70.3	Total Current				68.2		71.9		74.5		64.2
	14.3		15.3		15.8	Fixed Assets (net)				22.3		13.0		15.5		16.6
	8.5		7.9		8.2	Intangibles (net)				1.9		6.6		6.8		13.5
	5.7		5.6		5.6	All Other Non-Current				7.6		8.6		3.2		5.6
	100.0		100.0		100.0	Total				100.0		100.0		100.0		100.0
						LIABILITIES										
	7.8		7.3		8.1	Notes Payable-Short Term				12.9		10.1		4.3		4.1
	2.2		2.4		2.2	Cur. Mat.-L.T.D.				.7		1.8		2.9		2.4
	12.6		12.1		12.4	Trade Payables				12.1		14.1		12.7		9.4
	.4		.2		.2	Income Taxes Payable				.0		.0		.4		.2
	14.4		12.2		11.3	All Other Current				6.4		13.7		10.4		13.2
	37.5		34.2		34.3	Total Current				32.2		39.7		30.6		29.3
	7.3		10.7		9.3	Long-Term Debt				12.6		7.4		8.0		8.6
	.8		.7		.4	Deferred Taxes				.4		.3		.2		.7
	8.3		5.3		6.3	All Other Non-Current				4.4		2.9		3.7		3.8
	46.1		49.1		49.8	Net Worth				50.5		49.7		57.4		57.6
	100.0		100.0		100.0	Total Liabilties & Net Worth				100.0		100.0		100.0		100.0
						INCOME DATA										
	100.0		100.0		100.0	Net Sales				100.0		100.0		100.0		100.0
	39.5		40.0		38.4	Gross Profit				44.2		37.3		37.6		37.8
	31.2		32.4		32.7	Operating Expenses				39.1		33.9		30.0		30.6
	8.3		7.6		5.7	Operating Profit				5.0		3.4		7.6		7.2
	.9		1.1		.9	All Other Expenses (net)				.8		.4		.6		1.2
	7.3		6.5		4.8	Profit Before Taxes				4.3		3.0		7.0		6.0
						RATIOS										
	3.5		3.4		3.5					3.9		3.6		3.9		3.6
	2.1		2.3		2.2	Current				2.2		1.6		2.5		2.7
	1.4		1.5		1.4					1.3		1.2		1.6		1.4
	2.1		2.0		2.0					2.0		1.7		2.0		2.4
	1.2		1.3		1.2	Quick				1.2		1.1		1.2		1.4
	.8		.8		.7					.9		.6		.8		.9
36	10.2	**38**	9.7	**40**	9.2				**39**	9.3	**40**	9.2	**34**	10.7	**47**	7.7
54	6.7	**50**	7.3	**49**	7.4	Sales/Receivables			**46**	7.9	**51**	7.2	**46**	8.0	**56**	6.5
72	5.1	**63**	5.8	**64**	5.7				**76**	4.8	**61**	6.0	**63**	5.8	**65**	5.6
43	8.5	**47**	7.8	**50**	7.3				**28**	13.1	**46**	7.9	**54**	6.7	**41**	8.8
89	4.1	**91**	4.0	**83**	4.4	Cost of Sales/Inventory			**76**	4.8	**74**	4.9	**99**	3.7	**79**	4.6
135	2.7	**130**	2.8	**135**	2.7				**130**	2.8	**130**	2.8	**152**	2.4	**122**	3.0
19	18.8	**18**	20.1	**21**	17.4				**22**	16.5	**17**	21.5	**23**	15.8	**22**	16.8
32	11.3	**32**	11.5	**33**	11.0	Cost of Sales/Payables			**31**	11.7	**32**	11.3	**35**	10.3	**31**	11.6
47	7.7	**49**	7.5	**47**	7.7				**45**	8.1	**51**	7.2	**47**	7.8	**43**	8.5
	3.0		3.7		3.1					2.7		3.9		2.8		3.2
	5.3		5.0		5.3	Sales/Working Capital				4.9		7.2		5.1		4.7
	11.1		9.6		14.6					20.8		31.8		8.6		9.5
	79.0		38.2		44.0					30.9		8.6		49.5		73.6
(124)	13.0	(100)	8.2	(116)	10.3	EBIT/Interest			(13)	10.6	(27)	3.7	(35)	23.7	(35)	27.5
	3.7		2.2		2.3					1.9		1.1		8.4		3.5
	27.0		13.0		23.7									9.4		180.3
(34)	4.7	(33)	3.8	(38)	7.6	Net Profit + Depr., Dep., Amort./Cur. Mat. L/T/D							(14)	3.7	(16)	18.4
	2.2		1.2		1.5									2.1		1.8
	.1		.1		.1					.1		.2		.1		.2
	.3		.3		.3	Fixed/Worth				.3		.3		.2		.4
	.7		.8		.8					1.4		.8		.6		.9
	.4		.5		.4					.3		.5		.4		.4
	1.2		1.1		1.0	Debt/Worth				1.0		1.1		.8		.9
	3.2		3.5		3.4					3.4		3.5		1.8		2.8
	45.5		46.6		43.1					39.1		42.2		61.9		32.5
(127)	22.3	(110)	24.5	(121)	16.3	% Profit Before Taxes/Tangible Net Worth			(13)	11.5	(31)	8.1	(39)	27.1	(36)	17.7
	10.6		7.3		6.0					5.8		.4		8.5		8.4
	19.6		19.1		14.9					10.0		13.0		24.0		14.2
	8.9		10.5		6.6	% Profit Before Taxes/Total Assets				5.4		4.0		12.3		8.6
	4.1		2.9		2.4					2.2		.1		4.1		4.0
	37.1		36.3		38.2					43.7		70.2		47.9		24.1
	15.9		16.6		16.3	Sales/Net Fixed Assets				27.4		21.6		16.9		11.8
	8.2		7.8		8.6					5.4		10.4		9.8		6.9
	2.5		2.5		2.5					3.3		2.8		2.5		2.2
	1.8		1.8		1.8	Sales/Total Assets				1.6		2.3		1.9		1.6
	1.2		1.4		1.3					1.5		1.6		1.4		1.1
	.6		.6		.7					.5		.6		.9		1.4
(116)	1.6	(103)	1.2	(103)	1.6	% Depr., Dep., Amort./Sales			(10)	.9	(26)	1.0	(33)	1.6	(30)	2.1
	2.5		2.1		2.5					1.6		2.5		2.3		2.7
	1.8		1.6		1.8							2.9		1.5		
(36)	3.6	(28)	2.8	(33)	4.3	% Officers', Directors' Owners' Comp/Sales					(10)	4.8	(13)	2.1		
	8.2		8.1		7.6							7.5		4.5		
	4708718M		3502041M		4155542M	Net Sales ($)	658M	9811M		57045M		237871M		654126M		3196031M
	3534440M		2329567M		3059363M	Total Assets ($)	346M	7385M		31454M		128823M		449458M		2441897M

M = $ thousand MM = $ million

See Pages 9 through 22 for Explanation of Ratios and Data

Current Data Sorted by Assets							Comparative Historical Data	
						Type of Statement		
		1		1		Unqualified	6	8
		1	1	1	1	Reviewed	10	11
			1	1		Compiled	2	3
		1	1			Tax Returns	4	4
			3	5		2	Other	13	14
	6 (4/1-9/30/13)		14 (10/1/13-3/31/14)				4/1/09-3/31/10 ALL	4/1/10-3/31/11 ALL
0-500M	500M-2MM	2-10MM	10-50MM	50-100MM	100-250MM	**NUMBER OF STATEMENTS**	35	40
	3	6	8	1	2			
%	%	%	%	%	%	**ASSETS**	%	%
DATA NOT AVAILABLE						Cash & Equivalents	9.0	10.1
						Trade Receivables (net)	20.7	24.4
						Inventory	34.6	30.2
						All Other Current	6.7	6.3
						Total Current	70.9	71.0
						Fixed Assets (net)	16.9	18.3
						Intangibles (net)	4.1	4.9
						All Other Non-Current	8.1	5.8
						Total	100.0	100.0
						LIABILITIES		
						Notes Payable-Short Term	10.3	6.3
						Cur. Mat.-L.T.D.	2.4	2.8
						Trade Payables	11.1	13.2
						Income Taxes Payable	.1	.4
						All Other Current	12.6	17.2
						Total Current	36.5	39.9
						Long-Term Debt	6.2	11.3
						Deferred Taxes	.4	.8
						All Other Non-Current	9.5	12.3
						Net Worth	47.4	35.6
						Total Liabilties & Net Worth	100.0	100.0
						INCOME DATA		
						Net Sales	100.0	100.0
						Gross Profit	38.8	38.5
						Operating Expenses	36.5	32.1
						Operating Profit	2.3	6.5
						All Other Expenses (net)	.4	1.6
						Profit Before Taxes	1.9	4.9
						RATIOS		
						Current	3.5 1.9 1.5	3.3 2.1 1.4
						Quick	1.4 1.0 .5	1.7 1.0 .6
						Sales/Receivables	**37** 10.0 **49** 7.5 **63** 5.8	**36** 10.1 **43** 8.6 **65** 5.6
						Cost of Sales/Inventory	**75** 4.9 **111** 3.3 **173** 2.1	**78** 4.7 **102** 3.6 **143** 2.6
						Cost of Sales/Payables	**21** 17.5 **35** 10.4 **51** 7.1	**20** 18.4 **38** 9.7 **52** 7.1
						Sales/Working Capital	2.5 4.5 8.2	2.8 5.5 9.8
						EBIT/Interest	8.9 (26) 3.3 .3	32.0 (32) 5.8 2.4
						Net Profit + Depr., Dep., Amort./Cur. Mat. L/T/D		
						Fixed/Worth	.1 .3 .6	.2 .4 .9
						Debt/Worth	.5 .8 1.4	.6 1.0 4.8
						% Profit Before Taxes/Tangible Net Worth	25.0 (32) 12.4 1.0	32.6 (33) 16.7 5.9
						% Profit Before Taxes/Total Assets	11.9 5.0 -1.3	17.3 7.7 2.0
						Sales/Net Fixed Assets	22.3 14.0 6.9	25.6 12.4 5.6
						Sales/Total Assets	2.3 1.5 1.2	2.4 1.8 1.2
						% Depr., Dep., Amort./Sales	1.1 (30) 1.8 2.9	.9 (35) 2.1 3.6
						% Officers', Directors' Owners' Comp/Sales		
	19136M	57647M	306631M	146283M	393638M	Net Sales ($)	724305M	1302535M
	4424M	28222M	213185M	82316M	336391M	Total Assets ($)	503755M	910184M

M = $ thousand MM = $ million

See Pages 9 through 22 for Explanation of Ratios and Data

Comparative Historical Data

Current Data Sorted by Sales

	4/1/11-3/31/12 ALL		4/1/12-3/31/13 ALL		4/1/13-3/31/14 ALL	Type of Statement	0-1MM	1-3MM	3-5MM	5-10MM	10-25MM		25MM & OVER
	7		4		2	Unqualified			1				1
	8		10		4	Reviewed				1	1		2
	6		3		2	Compiled			1				1
	1		1		2	Tax Returns			2				
	12		7		10	Other				1	3		6
							6 (4/1-9/30/13)		14 (10/1/13-3/31/14)				
	34		25		20	NUMBER OF STATEMENTS			4	2	4		10
	%		%		%	**ASSETS**	%	%	%	%	%		%
	14.0		12.9		12.1	Cash & Equivalents	DATA NOT AVAILABLE	DATA NOT AVAILABLE					8.2
	22.3		27.1		27.4	Trade Receivables (net)							25.5
	33.7		27.4		28.9	Inventory							26.6
	3.5		4.8		4.4	All Other Current							4.9
	73.5		72.2		72.8	Total Current							65.3
	17.4		18.2		14.3	Fixed Assets (net)							14.4
	6.2		7.0		8.1	Intangibles (net)							15.1
	3.0		2.6		4.8	All Other Non-Current							5.3
	100.0		100.0		100.0	Total							100.0
						LIABILITIES							
	6.3		5.2		6.8	Notes Payable-Short Term							5.0
	2.7		2.3		.9	Cur. Mat.-L.T.D.							.6
	10.6		14.3		11.8	Trade Payables							11.1
	.1		.1		.1	Income Taxes Payable							.3
	13.5		16.1		16.1	All Other Current							15.1
	33.2		38.1		35.7	Total Current							32.1
	7.3		6.1		9.4	Long-Term Debt							10.7
	.7		.9		.3	Deferred Taxes							.5
	10.8		13.5		7.0	All Other Non-Current							11.2
	48.0		41.4		47.7	Net Worth							45.5
	100.0		100.0		100.0	Total Liabilities & Net Worth							100.0
						INCOME DATA							
	100.0		100.0		100.0	Net Sales							100.0
	38.4		35.9		35.6	Gross Profit							35.8
	32.3		29.8		28.5	Operating Expenses							27.7
	6.1		6.0		7.1	Operating Profit							8.2
	1.1		.5		1.1	All Other Expenses (net)							1.6
	5.0		5.5		5.9	Profit Before Taxes							6.6
						RATIOS							
	4.1		3.4		3.3	Current							3.0
	2.2		2.4		1.9								1.9
	1.5		1.2		1.5								1.4
	2.0		2.0		2.0	Quick							1.6
	.9		1.0		.9								1.0
	.8		.7		.7								.8
31	11.8	**37**	9.8	**38**	9.7	Sales/Receivables						**44**	8.3
45	8.1	**45**	8.1	**45**	8.1							**56**	6.5
56	6.5	**69**	5.3	**66**	5.5							**76**	4.8
81	4.5	**36**	10.1	**59**	6.2	Cost of Sales/Inventory						**73**	5.0
111	3.3	**99**	3.7	**91**	4.0							**99**	3.7
135	2.7	**146**	2.5	**122**	3.0							**114**	3.2
19	19.3	**15**	24.9	**9**	41.6	Cost of Sales/Payables						**17**	21.2
26	13.8	**33**	11.2	**34**	10.6							**41**	8.9
41	9.0	**56**	6.5	**46**	7.9							**55**	6.6
	3.0		2.8		3.2	Sales/Working Capital							3.3
	4.3		5.4		6.0								5.9
	8.2		14.7		8.6								7.2
	22.7		64.5		313.7	EBIT/Interest							
(27)	9.0	(19)	21.4	(17)	11.5								
	3.2		4.4		1.7								
						Net Profit + Depr., Dep., Amort./Cur. Mat. L/T/D							
	.2		.1		.1	Fixed/Worth							.2
	.3		.4		.2								.3
	.8		.9		.7								.8
	.4		.5		.5	Debt/Worth							.5
	.9		1.0		1.0								1.2
	2.4		4.8		3.2								3.6
	24.1		37.4		40.7	% Profit Before Taxes/Tangible Net Worth							
(30)	13.2	(22)	23.1	(19)	25.6								
	6.8		10.3		10.6								
	12.8		17.3		19.5	% Profit Before Taxes/Total Assets							31.6
	7.4		8.3		8.3								8.3
	2.7		5.9		1.8								-4.3
	30.6		40.6		45.2	Sales/Net Fixed Assets							17.6
	13.4		14.1		16.4								12.9
	7.8		5.6		6.0								5.9
	2.2		2.3		2.5	Sales/Total Assets							2.3
	1.8		1.6		2.0								1.3
	1.3		1.2		1.2								1.0
	1.1		1.2		1.0	% Depr., Dep., Amort./Sales							
(31)	1.6	(22)	2.0	(17)	1.5								
	3.0		3.7		3.8								
						% Officers', Directors' Owners' Comp/Sales							
	1206870M		**943899M**		**923335M**	Net Sales ($)			**15461M**	**16556M**	**68310M**		**823008M**
	786789M		**620135M**		**664538M**	Total Assets ($)			**7686M**	**8225M**	**36286M**		**612341M**

M = $ thousand MM = $ million

See Pages 9 through 22 for Explanation of Ratios and Data

Current Data Sorted by Assets							Comparative Historical Data	
						Type of Statement		
		3	2		1	Unqualified	15	7
	1	3	2			Reviewed	10	9
1	1	2				Compiled	6	7
1	3	1				Tax Returns	6	3
3	5	8	8	2	1	Other	17	23
	10 (4/1-9/30/13)		38 (10/1/13-3/31/14)				4/1/09-3/31/10 ALL	4/1/10-3/31/11 ALL
0-500M	500M-2MM	2-10MM	10-50MM	50-100MM	100-250MM			
5	10	17	12	2	2	NUMBER OF STATEMENTS	54	49
%	%	%	%	%	%	**ASSETS**	%	%
	10.8	11.9	16.7			Cash & Equivalents	14.4	10.5
	32.4	32.5	18.6			Trade Receivables (net)	24.6	25.8
	34.9	29.7	19.2			Inventory	27.6	28.2
	1.1	2.7	7.1			All Other Current	2.5	6.3
	79.1	76.8	61.5			Total Current	69.2	70.9
	10.8	11.4	19.4			Fixed Assets (net)	15.5	19.0
	1.8	6.8	8.3			Intangibles (net)	6.2	5.2
	8.3	5.0	10.8			All Other Non-Current	9.1	4.9
	100.0	100.0	100.0			Total	100.0	100.0
						LIABILITIES		
	12.9	4.9	5.7			Notes Payable-Short Term	7.7	9.1
	1.7	2.9	1.3			Cur. Mat.-L.T.D.	3.6	2.6
	10.4	13.0	6.3			Trade Payables	10.7	13.4
	.2	.3	.3			Income Taxes Payable	.2	.3
	5.7	13.3	21.0			All Other Current	11.9	16.2
	30.9	34.4	34.6			Total Current	34.3	41.7
	5.2	11.0	8.0			Long-Term Debt	11.4	11.8
	.0	.3	.1			Deferred Taxes	.4	.3
	.2	5.9	13.6			All Other Non-Current	6.4	8.7
	63.7	48.3	43.7			Net Worth	47.5	37.4
	100.0	100.0	100.0			Total Liabilities & Net Worth	100.0	100.0
						INCOME DATA		
	100.0	100.0	100.0			Net Sales	100.0	100.0
	52.6	49.0	45.2			Gross Profit	42.6	45.7
	43.7	40.5	39.8			Operating Expenses	37.8	35.6
	8.9	8.5	5.4			Operating Profit	4.8	10.1
	.9	1.3	.0			All Other Expenses (net)	1.1	1.3
	8.1	7.2	5.3			Profit Before Taxes	3.7	8.8
						RATIOS		
	4.3	4.7	6.4				3.3	2.8
	2.9	2.5	2.4			Current	2.1	1.9
	1.7	1.5	1.2				1.4	1.4
	2.9	2.5	5.6				2.1	1.6
	1.3	1.5	1.1			Quick	1.2	.9
	.7	.8	.5				.7	.5
	11 33.8	**37** 9.8	**43** 8.5				**34** 10.8	**39** 9.3
	40 9.1	**46** 7.9	**53** 6.9			Sales/Receivables	**49** 7.4	**49** 7.5
	61 6.0	**60** 6.1	**69** 5.3				**67** 5.4	**63** 5.8
	49 7.4	**47** 7.8	**36** 10.1				**72** 5.1	**49** 7.4
	89 4.1	**94** 3.9	**78** 4.7			Cost of Sales/Inventory	**107** 3.4	**104** 3.5
	140 2.6	**159** 2.3	**140** 2.6				**146** 2.5	**142** 2.6
	12 31.3	**21** 17.8	**12** 30.6				**16** 22.3	**17** 21.2
	19 19.2	**27** 13.7	**23** 16.2			Cost of Sales/Payables	**32** 11.3	**37** 10.0
	29 12.8	**49** 7.4	**51** 7.1				**44** 8.3	**64** 5.7
	4.1	3.1	2.0				2.9	3.6
	6.3	6.1	3.7			Sales/Working Capital	4.6	6.1
	11.0	10.8	9.5				10.4	8.7
		46.4					29.3	25.6
		(15) 15.5				EBIT/Interest	(45) 4.4	(40) 7.1
		5.9					1.1	3.2
							7.5	18.6
						Net Profit + Depr., Dep., Amort./Cur. Mat. L/T/D	(17) 3.0	(13) 5.2
							.8	3.0
	.0	.1	.2				.1	.2
	.2	.2	.4			Fixed/Worth	.4	.5
	.3	.8	.6				.8	1.0
	.3	.4	.3				.5	.7
	.5	1.2	.8			Debt/Worth	1.1	1.8
	1.3	3.7	3.5				2.9	4.6
	92.2	48.7	37.6				44.0	70.4
	33.4	(15) 21.8	(10) 19.8			% Profit Before Taxes/Tangible Net Worth	(47) 14.1	(41) 38.3
	-8.6	16.2	4.7				1.4	10.1
	74.9	25.0	15.6				16.1	28.5
	14.1	8.2	5.3			% Profit Before Taxes/Total Assets	6.3	11.1
	-4.3	4.0	1.6				.0	3.0
	343.4	67.6	17.4				26.5	29.1
	55.6	24.7	10.5			Sales/Net Fixed Assets	12.9	13.6
	17.0	13.3	4.9				6.5	7.5
	4.7	3.0	1.5				2.3	2.5
	2.7	2.4	1.3			Sales/Total Assets	1.6	1.9
	2.1	1.5	.7				1.2	1.5
		.8	1.6				1.1	1.2
		(15) 1.4	(11) 2.1			% Depr., Dep., Amort./Sales	(44) 2.1	(42) 1.7
		2.2	3.7				3.4	4.0
							3.1	
						% Officers', Directors' Owners' Comp/Sales	(14) 5.9	
							9.6	
5437M	43517M	208202M	349805M	82322M	221575M	Net Sales ($)	1390867M	1128126M
2092M	13831M	88523M	288132M	105495M	363976M	Total Assets ($)	1165929M	772925M

M = $ thousand MM = $ million

See Pages 9 through 22 for Explanation of Ratios and Data

Comparative Historical Data / Current Data Sorted by Sales

		4/1/11-3/31/12 ALL		4/1/12-3/31/13 ALL		4/1/13-3/31/14 ALL	0-1MM	1-3MM	3-5MM	5-10MM		10-25MM		25MM & OVER
Type of Statement														
Unqualified		12		1		6						4		2
Reviewed		12		9		6			2	2		1		1
Compiled		3		5		4		2		1		1		
Tax Returns		7		8		5	1	1	1			2		
Other		22		29		27	4	1	2	5		7		8
							10 (4/1-9/30/13)			38 (10/1/13-3/31/14)				
NUMBER OF STATEMENTS		56		52		48	5	4	5	8		15		11
ASSETS		%		%		%	%	%	%	%		%		%
Cash & Equivalents		11.2		11.3		15.3						14.8		14.1
Trade Receivables (net)		25.9		27.7		26.2						29.4		18.0
Inventory		30.9		32.3		26.6						23.7		24.1
All Other Current		6.1		3.4		3.3						4.5		6.3
Total Current		74.2		74.7		71.4						72.4		62.4
Fixed Assets (net)		13.8		13.3		13.5						13.9		16.3
Intangibles (net)		4.7		4.7		7.2						4.6		10.2
All Other Non-Current		7.3		7.3		7.9						9.1		11.1
Total		100.0		100.0		100.0						100.0		100.0
LIABILITIES														
Notes Payable-Short Term		6.3		8.8		6.4						8.1		1.8
Cur. Mat.-L.T.D.		2.7		2.3		1.9						.3		1.6
Trade Payables		18.2		13.2		11.2						8.0		12.3
Income Taxes Payable		.3		.4		.2						.4		.0
All Other Current		15.1		13.4		13.7						18.4		16.8
Total Current		42.6		38.2		33.3						35.2		32.6
Long-Term Debt		9.1		8.7		8.2						4.8		12.8
Deferred Taxes		.4		.2		.2						.4		.1
All Other Non-Current		7.0		5.2		6.9						3.6		16.5
Net Worth		40.8		47.7		51.4						55.9		38.0
Total Liabilities & Net Worth		100.0		100.0		100.0						100.0		100.0
INCOME DATA														
Net Sales		100.0		100.0		100.0						100.0		100.0
Gross Profit		41.5		40.8		49.1						51.7		40.0
Operating Expenses		33.3		34.2		42.5						40.2		36.3
Operating Profit		8.2		6.6		6.6						11.5		3.7
All Other Expenses (net)		.9		.7		.6						-.2		.5
Profit Before Taxes		7.3		5.9		5.9						11.7		3.2
RATIOS														
		4.1		3.6		4.6						6.9		3.6
Current		1.9		2.2		2.5						2.5		1.7
		1.4		1.4		1.5						1.4		1.3
		2.2		1.8		2.8						4.0		2.3
Quick		.9		.9		1.5						1.4		.9
		.6		.6		.7						.8		.4
	33	11.0	32	11.3	36	10.2					38	9.6	42	8.6
Sales/Receivables	47	7.8	43	8.5	49	7.4					51	7.1	61	6.0
	70	5.2	68	5.4	65	5.6					74	4.9	65	5.6
	59	6.2	44	8.3	45	8.1					34	10.8	36	10.0
Cost of Sales/Inventory	101	3.6	104	3.5	99	3.7					81	4.5	118	3.1
	159	2.3	182	2.0	146	2.5					135	2.7	152	2.4
	15	23.7	12	29.2	13	28.9					13	27.3	20	18.5
Cost of Sales/Payables	39	9.4	29	12.6	25	14.6					23	15.7	36	10.0
	60	6.1	49	7.5	59	6.2					30	12.0	68	5.4
		3.0		3.7		3.0						2.0		3.4
Sales/Working Capital		5.8		6.1		5.6						6.1		5.9
		7.7		10.8		10.5						11.8		20.0
		71.8		45.2		31.3						133.9		51.1
EBIT/Interest	(44)	11.3	(42)	13.0	(39)	12.0					(10)	20.1		20.9
		2.7		1.6		2.9						4.7		2.9
		10.2		10.1		7.8								
Net Profit + Depr., Dep., Amort./Cur. Mat. L/T/D	(13)	4.1	(11)	2.8	(14)	2.7								
		.5		.2		.5								
		.1		.1		.1						.1		.1
Fixed/Worth		.3		.3		.3						.2		.4
		.7		.6		.6						.6		.6
		.4		.4		.4						.2		.7
Debt/Worth		1.5		1.1		.7						.5		1.7
		2.3		2.9		2.7						2.9		3.0
		46.6		53.9		45.2						72.5		30.7
% Profit Before Taxes/Tangible Net Worth	(50)	24.3	(47)	22.1	(43)	19.9					(13)	26.2	(10)	20.8
		6.5		6.9		4.3						12.3		5.3
		24.2		26.3		18.4						39.2		8.9
% Profit Before Taxes/Total Assets		10.8		7.8		6.4						14.8		4.4
		2.3		2.8		1.5						4.6		1.6
		50.6		86.0		60.7						68.4		19.4
Sales/Net Fixed Assets		19.2		19.7		21.1						24.7		9.1
		7.7		8.6		7.7						7.7		5.0
		2.3		2.6		2.7						2.7		1.5
Sales/Total Assets		1.8		2.0		1.8						1.7		1.2
		1.3		1.5		1.2						.8		.6
		.7		.7		.8						.2		
% Depr., Dep., Amort./Sales	(42)	1.7	(38)	1.5	(38)	1.8					(14)	1.3		
		2.2		2.8		3.5						3.5		
		2.1		3.1		2.5								
% Officers', Directors' Owners' Comp/Sales	(11)	2.8	(16)	4.3	(13)	3.0								
		4.3		6.0		9.0								
Net Sales ($)		1299879M		1088964M		910858M	3379M	9920M	22149M	59592M		244101M		571717M
Total Assets ($)		962984M		681493M		862049M	3618M	3440M	10896M	27578M		183167M		633350M

M = $ thousand MM = $ million

See Pages 9 through 22 for Explanation of Ratios and Data

Current Data Sorted by Assets							Comparative Historical Data	
		2	3	3		Type of Statement Unqualified	21	18
		5	2	2		Reviewed	6	11
	1	3	1			Compiled	1	4
	2	2	1			Tax Returns	3	7
	4	11	6	2	3	Other	25	30
	12 (4/1-9/30/13)		41 (10/1/13-3/31/14)				4/1/09-3/31/10 ALL	4/1/10-3/31/11 ALL
0-500M	500M-2MM	2-10MM	10-50MM	50-100MM	100-250MM			
	7	23	13	7	3	NUMBER OF STATEMENTS	56	70
%	%	%	%	%	%	ASSETS	%	%
DATA NOT AVAILABLE		12.7	18.6			Cash & Equivalents	17.5	15.9
		31.2	24.3			Trade Receivables (net)	23.6	24.2
		33.3	22.0			Inventory	24.7	24.5
		2.9	1.7			All Other Current	1.6	3.5
		80.2	66.6			Total Current	67.5	68.1
		12.6	17.9			Fixed Assets (net)	15.3	15.5
		3.5	8.4			Intangibles (net)	11.6	11.2
		3.6	7.1			All Other Non-Current	5.6	5.2
		100.0	100.0			Total	100.0	100.0
						LIABILITIES		
		9.4	4.6			Notes Payable-Short Term	5.6	6.4
		2.2	1.1			Cur. Mat.-L.T.D.	1.6	1.8
		17.8	5.5			Trade Payables	10.3	11.9
		.2	.3			Income Taxes Payable	.1	.3
		13.0	17.7			All Other Current	10.7	11.7
		42.6	29.2			Total Current	28.3	32.1
		6.1	5.3			Long-Term Debt	12.7	7.5
		.3	.0			Deferred Taxes	.6	.5
		6.9	.3			All Other Non-Current	6.5	6.0
		44.1	65.3			Net Worth	52.0	54.0
		100.0	100.0			Total Liabilities & Net Worth	100.0	100.0
						INCOME DATA		
		100.0	100.0			Net Sales	100.0	100.0
		44.8	44.2			Gross Profit	47.0	46.5
		40.1	33.4			Operating Expenses	41.5	38.5
		4.7	10.9			Operating Profit	5.5	8.0
		.7	1.3			All Other Expenses (net)	1.2	.7
		4.0	9.5			Profit Before Taxes	4.3	7.3
						RATIOS		
		3.8	5.5				4.5	3.7
		2.2	2.3			Current	2.7	2.6
		1.4	1.5				1.8	1.3
		2.2	3.8				2.7	2.4
		1.1	1.5			Quick	1.6	1.7
		.5	.8				1.0	.7
		41 9.0	36 10.0				47 7.8	39 9.3
		55 6.6	52 7.0			Sales/Receivables	54 6.8	51 7.2
		70 5.2	73 5.0				64 5.7	71 5.1
		45 8.2	58 6.3				66 5.6	63 5.8
		146 2.5	94 3.9			Cost of Sales/Inventory	104 3.5	100 3.6
		192 1.9	174 2.1				149 2.4	147 2.5
		29 12.7	13 28.6				25 14.8	24 15.0
		45 8.2	24 15.1			Cost of Sales/Payables	35 10.4	38 9.6
		64 5.7	36 10.0				60 6.1	64 5.7
		2.8	2.5				2.4	2.5
		3.9	4.7			Sales/Working Capital	3.8	3.7
		10.0	15.1				6.3	14.7
		13.0					12.6	21.1
		(21) 4.4				EBIT/Interest	(49) 3.2	(53) 8.8
		3.4					-2.2	2.1
							5.5	8.0
						Net Profit + Depr., Dep., Amort./Cur. Mat. L/T/D	(15) 2.4	(15) 4.6
							-1.5	2.8
		.0	.1				.2	.1
		.2	.2			Fixed/Worth	.3	.3
		1.0	1.2				.8	.7
		.4	.3				.3	.4
		1.4	.5			Debt/Worth	.9	.9
		2.1	1.1				2.7	3.1
		20.3	53.0				36.8	42.8
		(20) 12.3	(12) 25.7			% Profit Before Taxes/Tangible Net Worth	(48) 8.8	(63) 20.3
		6.2	4.1				-8.0	6.4
		8.5	37.3				13.6	17.3
		5.5	7.7			% Profit Before Taxes/Total Assets	5.8	10.4
		2.8	.3				-3.0	3.5
		93.1	28.7				27.1	34.1
		34.0	10.9			Sales/Net Fixed Assets	13.0	13.2
		9.9	4.0				5.1	5.4
		2.5	1.9				1.9	2.3
		1.8	1.3			Sales/Total Assets	1.5	1.5
		1.6	1.0				1.0	1.1
		.5	1.2				1.4	.9
		(22) .9	(12) 2.0			% Depr., Dep., Amort./Sales	(44) 2.3	(55) 2.0
		1.9	4.6				3.6	3.0
		2.4					3.2	2.9
		(11) 3.0				% Officers', Directors' Owners' Comp/Sales	(12) 6.9	(15) 5.8
		6.0					20.7	13.8
	27421M	257665M	375487M	628168M	421431M	Net Sales ($)	2128205M	2563347M
	8607M	129894M	273855M	504811M	448192M	Total Assets ($)	1901666M	2137070M

M = $ thousand MM = $ million

See Pages 9 through 22 for Explanation of Ratios and Data

Comparative Historical Data | **Current Data Sorted by Sales**

4/1/11-3/31/12 ALL	4/1/12-3/31/13 ALL	4/1/13-3/31/14 ALL	**Type of Statement**	0-1MM	1-3MM	3-5MM	5-10MM	10-25MM	25MM & OVER
12	15	8	Unqualified				1	1	6
11	10	9	Reviewed					5	4
7	3	5	Compiled			2	2	1	
5	5	5	Tax Returns		1	1	1	2	
25	29	26	Other		1	2	7	7	9
					12 (4/1-9/30/13)		41 (10/1/13-3/31/14)		
60	62	53	**NUMBER OF STATEMENTS**		2	5	11	16	19
%	%	%	**ASSETS**	%	%	%	%	%	%
16.0	18.5	15.6	Cash & Equivalents	DATA NOT AVAILABLE			10.1	14.7	18.0
25.8	24.7	27.2	Trade Receivables (net)				27.6	29.5	24.2
25.1	23.9	28.6	Inventory				31.0	31.8	22.6
2.4	1.6	2.4	All Other Current				1.9	3.2	2.2
69.3	68.8	73.8	Total Current				70.6	79.2	67.1
14.8	16.1	13.2	Fixed Assets (net)				13.1	15.7	13.7
10.0	9.3	7.1	Intangibles (net)				12.9	1.2	9.4
5.9	5.8	5.8	All Other Non-Current				3.4	3.9	9.8
100.0	100.0	100.0	Total				100.0	100.0	100.0
			LIABILITIES						
5.3	6.4	5.9	Notes Payable-Short Term				11.7	6.4	4.0
1.4	1.9	1.5	Cur. Mat.-L.T.D.				2.3	1.8	1.4
10.4	9.1	12.8	Trade Payables				8.6	18.2	9.3
.2	.4	.2	Income Taxes Payable				.3	.0	.3
12.9	15.1	13.4	All Other Current				12.8	12.3	16.8
30.1	32.9	33.8	Total Current				35.8	38.7	31.8
6.9	9.4	6.5	Long-Term Debt				7.8	7.8	7.1
.6	.6	.2	Deferred Taxes				.2	.2	.1
5.6	8.1	4.6	All Other Non-Current				10.6	2.7	2.8
56.7	49.1	55.0	Net Worth				45.7	50.5	58.1
100.0	100.0	100.0	Total Liabilties & Net Worth				100.0	100.0	100.0
			INCOME DATA						
100.0	100.0	100.0	Net Sales				100.0	100.0	100.0
49.2	49.2	46.2	Gross Profit				49.7	42.6	45.4
39.0	42.8	38.4	Operating Expenses				48.1	36.4	35.2
10.2	6.4	7.8	Operating Profit				1.6	6.2	10.2
.9	1.0	.8	All Other Expenses (net)				.6	.5	1.5
9.3	5.4	7.0	Profit Before Taxes				1.0	5.8	8.7
			RATIOS						
4.8	4.2	4.1	Current				2.5	4.4	3.8
2.8	2.3	2.3					2.2	2.4	2.3
1.4	1.5	1.6					1.4	1.6	1.6
3.3	2.7	2.5	Quick				1.9	2.4	2.5
1.3	1.5	1.4					.8	1.2	1.5
.8	.9	.8					.2	.9	.8
44 8.3	40 9.2	39 9.4	Sales/Receivables				16 22.7	43 8.5	48 7.6
52 7.0	52 7.0	52 7.0					42 8.7	53 6.9	55 6.6
70 5.2	64 5.7	66 5.5					87 4.2	69 5.3	66 5.5
64 5.7	69 5.3	63 5.8	Cost of Sales/Inventory				72 5.1	49 7.4	62 5.9
114 3.2	111 3.3	114 3.2					146 2.5	159 2.3	94 3.9
146 2.5	159 2.3	182 2.0					182 2.0	215 1.7	159 2.3
21 17.3	21 17.1	21 17.6	Cost of Sales/Payables				20 18.3	35 10.3	23 16.0
33 11.1	31 11.8	36 10.2					33 11.2	46 7.9	35 10.5
55 6.6	46 7.9	55 6.6					50 7.3	64 5.7	52 7.0
2.5	2.7	2.5	Sales/Working Capital				2.8	2.6	2.2
3.4	4.4	3.9					5.5	3.7	3.5
11.7	8.7	9.0					11.2	7.9	10.6
49.7	33.2	34.7	EBIT/Interest				6.7	24.3	268.1
(50) 11.1	(51) 6.9	(43) 7.6					(10) 3.9	(15) 6.5	(15) 16.0
4.7	1.8	3.0					-1.6	3.9	2.4
18.0	41.7	23.7	Net Profit + Depr., Dep., Amort./Cur. Mat. L/T/D						
(13) 3.8	(18) 4.1	(15) 3.5							
2.1	2.4	2.0							
.1	.1	.1	Fixed/Worth				.1	.1	.1
.3	.3	.2					.2	.3	.2
.8	1.1	1.0					1.0	.6	1.2
.2	.4	.3	Debt/Worth				.8	.4	.3
.9	1.3	.8					1.5	.9	.8
3.1	3.6	2.0					3.1	2.0	4.1
48.1	39.9	32.0	% Profit Before Taxes/Tangible Net Worth					22.0	49.6
(54) 20.0	(54) 16.4	(47) 18.6						(14) 15.2	(18) 20.8
8.1	3.4	6.2						6.0	3.1
21.5	18.5	15.9	% Profit Before Taxes/Total Assets				8.2	15.1	23.0
9.7	5.8	6.6					3.9	6.0	7.7
3.1	.7	2.6					.4	2.8	2.1
35.2	35.1	80.9	Sales/Net Fixed Assets				77.7	78.8	24.0
15.4	11.9	17.9					22.7	31.1	11.2
6.6	6.2	7.9					6.5	5.8	7.0
2.2	2.1	2.4	Sales/Total Assets				1.9	2.5	1.8
1.6	1.4	1.7					1.7	1.9	1.3
1.2	1.2	1.2					1.3	1.2	1.0
.8	1.0	.7	% Depr., Dep., Amort./Sales					.5	1.3
(47) 1.9	(49) 2.3	(47) 1.7						1.0	(18) 2.0
3.7	3.7	3.0						2.7	3.4
2.0	3.5	2.4	% Officers', Directors' Owners' Comp/Sales						
(15) 3.4	(18) 5.3	(16) 2.9							
6.5	13.4	5.7							
2195193M	2292075M	1710172M	Net Sales ($)		3370M	20209M	84063M	222226M	1380304M
1705321M	1568527M	1365359M	Total Assets ($)		1208M	7828M	61584M	131737M	1163002M

M = $ thousand MM = $ million

See Pages 9 through 22 for Explanation of Ratios and Data

Current Data Sorted by Assets							Comparative Historical Data	
						Type of Statement		
		8	11	4	3	Unqualified	26	24
	1	15	12			Reviewed	28	33
	3	5	2			Compiled	12	15
2	6	6	1			Tax Returns	8	5
1	4	18	20	4	5	Other	34	43
	19 (4/1-9/30/13)		112 (10/1/13-3/31/14)				4/1/09-3/31/10 ALL	4/1/10-3/31/11 ALL
0-500M	500M-2MM	2-10MM	10-50MM	50-100MM	100-250MM			
3	14	52	46	8	8	**NUMBER OF STATEMENTS**	108	120
%	%	%	%	%	%	**ASSETS**	%	%
	26.1	14.0	13.1			Cash & Equivalents	11.2	12.5
	20.3	27.9	23.6			Trade Receivables (net)	25.2	27.2
	22.0	28.3	22.5			Inventory	26.3	23.0
	1.1	5.5	6.5			All Other Current	4.6	6.2
	69.5	75.7	65.8			Total Current	67.3	68.9
	14.5	11.3	13.6			Fixed Assets (net)	18.8	16.7
	5.9	6.4	15.4			Intangibles (net)	9.0	8.6
	10.1	6.6	5.2			All Other Non-Current	5.0	5.8
	100.0	100.0	100.0			Total	100.0	100.0
						LIABILITIES		
	8.4	7.0	7.0			Notes Payable-Short Term	9.1	8.1
	1.0	2.1	2.0			Cur. Mat.-L.T.D.	2.7	2.1
	8.5	10.9	8.0			Trade Payables	10.4	10.0
	.1	1.1	.3			Income Taxes Payable	1.2	.5
	6.8	18.2	16.2			All Other Current	13.1	16.2
	24.9	39.3	33.3			Total Current	36.4	36.8
	10.5	5.4	5.6			Long-Term Debt	11.0	7.8
	.0	.1	.4			Deferred Taxes	.5	.6
	5.5	4.9	3.0			All Other Non-Current	9.1	5.0
	59.1	50.3	57.7			Net Worth	43.0	49.7
	100.0	100.0	100.0			Total Liabilties & Net Worth	100.0	100.0
						INCOME DATA		
	100.0	100.0	100.0			Net Sales	100.0	100.0
	52.3	45.8	41.5			Gross Profit	43.1	41.4
	49.3	35.7	34.6			Operating Expenses	37.9	32.7
	3.0	10.1	6.9			Operating Profit	5.2	8.6
	.9	.3	.8			All Other Expenses (net)	.8	1.0
	2.2	9.7	6.1			Profit Before Taxes	4.4	7.6
						RATIOS		
	7.1	4.1	3.9				4.1	3.1
	4.7	2.0	2.4			Current	1.9	2.1
	1.1	1.4	1.5				1.4	1.3
	5.2	2.0	2.2				2.1	2.2
	2.4	1.1	1.3			Quick	(107) 1.0	1.1
	.7	.7	.6				.6	.6
	16 22.6	**33** 11.1	**38** 9.6				**35** 10.3	**39** 9.4
	34 10.6	**44** 8.3	**54** 6.7			Sales/Receivables	**50** 7.3	**48** 7.6
	51 7.1	**65** 5.6	**70** 5.2				**68** 5.4	**68** 5.4
	30 12.3	**68** 5.4	**43** 8.4				**43** 8.5	**35** 10.4
	76 4.8	**99** 3.7	**85** 4.3			Cost of Sales/Inventory	**99** 3.7	**81** 4.5
	114 3.2	**152** 2.4	**152** 2.4				**152** 2.4	**130** 2.8
	1 277.3	**18** 19.9	**15** 23.8				**14** 25.3	**16** 22.2
	17 21.7	**29** 12.4	**28** 13.0			Cost of Sales/Payables	**32** 11.4	**32** 11.5
	54 6.7	**43** 8.4	**43** 8.5				**53** 6.9	**45** 8.1
	2.8	3.4	2.8				3.5	3.5
	3.9	6.0	4.5			Sales/Working Capital	5.0	5.5
	NM	10.9	8.7				11.0	14.7
	13.3	119.7	72.2				15.8	60.6
	(10) 6.6	(39) 14.9	(34) 11.8			EBIT/Interest	(88) 4.3	(98) 7.8
	-6.4	3.7	2.6				.9	1.9
			11.2				6.0	10.8
			(14) 5.0			Net Profit + Depr., Dep., Amort./Cur. Mat. L/T/D	(25) 2.1	(37) 4.2
			2.2				1.5	1.6
	.0	.1	.1				.1	.1
	.2	.2	.3			Fixed/Worth	.5	.4
	.9	.5	.7				1.4	1.1
	.2	.5	.3				.5	.4
	.6	1.0	.8			Debt/Worth	1.1	1.0
	2.6	2.7	2.1				3.8	3.5
	55.8	54.5	37.1				33.8	53.5
	(13) 23.5	(48) 31.8	(43) 24.4			% Profit Before Taxes/Tangible Net Worth	(91) 14.4	(109) 23.4
	1.5	12.4	6.0				1.9	5.6
	22.1	31.7	16.8				15.2	22.3
	10.6	12.0	8.0			% Profit Before Taxes/Total Assets	5.5	10.6
	-1.4	5.6	3.5				.4	1.6
	107.1	54.0	31.7				27.0	38.6
	24.9	24.1	14.4			Sales/Net Fixed Assets	12.5	13.8
	10.7	14.5	6.9				6.6	6.9
	2.4	2.4	2.0				2.4	2.4
	2.2	1.9	1.4			Sales/Total Assets	1.6	1.6
	1.7	1.6	1.0				1.2	1.2
	.2	.7	1.0				1.0	.8
	(12) .5	(41) 1.0	(42) 1.7			% Depr., Dep., Amort./Sales	(87) 1.8	(106) 1.3
	2.0	1.6	3.0				2.9	2.3
		3.1					2.7	2.6
		(15) 6.7				% Officers', Directors' Owners' Comp/Sales	(28) 4.8	(33) 4.3
		8.5					7.7	6.6
3944M	35544M	515480M	1332023M	699692M	1663311M	Net Sales ($)	2951792M	3533566M
962M	16674M	258261M	907950M	610961M	1272699M	Total Assets ($)	2484095M	2675582M

M = $ thousand MM = $ million

See Pages 9 through 22 for Explanation of Ratios and Data

Comparative Historical Data | **Current Data Sorted by Sales**

4/1/11-3/31/12 ALL	4/1/12-3/31/13 ALL	4/1/13-3/31/14 ALL	Type of Statement	0-1MM	1-3MM	3-5MM	5-10MM	10-25MM	25MM & OVER
29	19	26	Unqualified		1		3	8	14
39	23	28	Reviewed		1		8	11	8
9	5	10	Compiled		2	2	3	2	1
13	8	15	Tax Returns	2	4	3	3	3	
43	50	52	Other		5	4	8	12	23
					19 (4/1-9/30/13)		112 (10/1/13-3/31/14)		
133	105	131	**NUMBER OF STATEMENTS**	2	13	9	25	36	46
%	%	%	**ASSETS**	%	%	%	%	%	%
13.2	13.8	15.8	Cash & Equivalents		25.7		11.3	11.4	15.9
26.4	23.8	24.2	Trade Receivables (net)		22.6		25.1	26.8	24.0
25.9	27.3	24.4	Inventory		24.8		27.6	26.7	21.9
4.3	5.7	5.4	All Other Current		3.7		8.0	4.0	6.7
69.7	70.5	69.7	Total Current		76.7		71.9	68.9	68.5
16.5	15.2	13.0	Fixed Assets (net)		8.5		9.9	12.0	14.7
7.8	7.7	10.5	Intangibles (net)		4.6		13.3	11.7	10.5
6.0	6.6	6.8	All Other Non-Current		10.1		5.0	7.5	6.2
100.0	100.0	100.0	Total		100.0		100.0	100.0	100.0
			LIABILITIES						
8.6	6.4	6.5	Notes Payable-Short Term		9.8		7.4	7.8	4.4
2.8	2.2	1.8	Cur. Mat.-L.T.D.		.4		1.8	2.3	1.8
11.0	10.8	9.5	Trade Payables		8.6		9.0	10.4	9.1
.9	1.2	.6	Income Taxes Payable		.1		.2	1.5	.3
14.9	13.1	15.9	All Other Current		11.5		15.9	18.7	15.7
38.3	33.7	34.2	Total Current		30.5		34.3	40.8	31.3
10.4	8.8	6.9	Long-Term Debt		1.3		8.1	6.3	6.4
.6	.5	.2	Deferred Taxes		.0		.3	.2	.3
4.1	7.0	4.6	All Other Non-Current		7.5		3.3	6.2	3.2
46.6	49.9	54.1	Net Worth		60.7		54.0	46.5	58.9
100.0	100.0	100.0	Total Liabilties & Net Worth		100.0		100.0	100.0	100.0
			INCOME DATA						
100.0	100.0	100.0	Net Sales		100.0		100.0	100.0	100.0
40.7	44.2	44.1	Gross Profit		53.4		43.9	44.8	38.7
32.7	35.2	36.9	Operating Expenses		51.3		36.5	35.3	32.3
8.0	9.1	7.2	Operating Profit		2.0		7.4	9.5	6.4
.8	.4	.6	All Other Expenses (net)		.0		.8	.9	.3
7.2	8.7	6.7	Profit Before Taxes		2.0		6.6	8.6	6.1
			RATIOS						
3.4	3.4	4.0			7.5		5.4	2.6	3.7
2.0	2.3	2.4	Current		3.1		2.1	1.9	2.6
1.3	1.5	1.5			1.4		1.5	1.1	1.6
1.9	1.9	2.3			5.5		2.4	1.7	2.3
1.1	1.2	1.2	Quick		2.1		1.1	1.0	1.5
.6	.7	.7			.9		.7	.6	.8
38 9.7	35 10.5	33 10.9			15 23.8		26 13.8	36 10.2	41 9.0
49 7.4	45 8.1	45 8.1	Sales/Receivables		42 8.6		42 8.6	44 8.3	52 7.0
64 5.7	58 6.3	65 5.6			61 6.0		64 5.7	65 5.6	68 5.4
47 7.8	64 5.7	55 6.6			16 22.4		59 6.2	70 5.2	41 8.9
91 4.0	104 3.5	91 4.0	Cost of Sales/Inventory		87 4.2		99 3.7	94 3.9	85 4.3
146 2.5	152 2.4	146 2.5			152 2.4		159 2.3	146 2.5	146 2.5
18 20.0	19 19.6	16 23.5			12 30.9		16 23.3	16 22.4	17 22.1
30 12.1	31 11.7	29 12.4	Cost of Sales/Payables		32 11.3		31 11.6	25 14.7	31 11.9
49 7.4	49 7.5	49 7.5			60 6.1		38 9.7	49 7.4	49 7.4
3.3	2.9	3.0			2.6		3.1	3.6	2.4
5.5	4.4	4.5	Sales/Working Capital		3.8		4.1	6.1	4.2
16.5	10.3	10.0			10.4		8.9	NM	8.6
46.7	35.8	71.4					26.8	145.0	81.8
(103) 9.1	(86) 8.3	(97) 11.4	EBIT/Interest				(17) 10.2	(31) 11.2	(35) 25.0
2.1	2.4	2.4					4.4	2.3	3.4
7.1	8.7	11.5							15.3
(33) 4.1	(34) 4.2	(25) 7.4	Net Profit + Depr., Dep., Amort./Cur. Mat. L/T/D						(12) 8.9
1.6	1.6	2.0							1.8
.1	.1	.1			.0		.0	.1	.1
.3	.3	.3	Fixed/Worth		.2		.2	.3	.2
.8	.7	.6			.6		.6	.8	.5
.5	.5	.4			.2		.5	.6	.4
1.1	.9	.9	Debt/Worth		.3		.9	1.6	.7
3.3	2.7	2.6			3.3		3.3	3.9	1.7
49.6	58.2	49.0			46.6		38.9	98.7	33.3
(118) 24.6	(94) 26.5	(120) 25.3	% Profit Before Taxes/Tangible Net Worth		(12) 10.6		(22) 27.6	(31) 34.8	(45) 22.3
11.7	8.4	6.7			-62.4		11.7	17.6	5.5
21.4	21.4	20.2			27.2		16.9	34.7	17.8
11.5	9.5	10.8	% Profit Before Taxes/Total Assets		10.1		9.0	10.3	11.2
2.8	3.1	2.7			-3.4		5.0	3.4	3.4
39.3	39.0	41.2			88.0		73.8	34.8	28.4
14.1	16.2	16.6	Sales/Net Fixed Assets		28.9		38.3	16.2	14.0
7.0	7.6	10.3			14.0		13.8	12.2	5.9
2.4	2.3	2.3			2.3		2.1	2.6	1.9
1.7	1.7	1.7	Sales/Total Assets		2.2		1.7	1.8	1.5
1.4	1.3	1.3			1.5		1.6	1.4	1.1
.9	.6	.7			.2		.7	.8	1.0
(109) 1.4	(91) 1.4	(111) 1.3	% Depr., Dep., Amort./Sales		(11) .6		(19) .8	(31) 1.3	(43) 1.7
2.6	2.7	2.2			2.9		1.0	2.1	2.4
3.3	3.2	3.2							
(36) 5.2	(23) 5.1	(29) 6.9	% Officers', Directors' Owners' Comp/Sales						
7.4	8.6	11.4							
4013576M	3390683M	4249994M	Net Sales ($)	1369M	27536M	35428M	181628M	564341M	3439692M
2922461M	2466017M	3067507M	Total Assets ($)	1094M	23770M	20522M	126793M	406488M	2488840M

M = $ thousand MM = $ million

See Pages 9 through 22 for Explanation of Ratios and Data

Current Data Sorted by Assets							Comparative Historical Data	
						Type of Statement		
		1	3	1	2	Unqualified	6	10
		3	1			Reviewed	6	11
1		2	2			Compiled	1	4
	3	1				Tax Returns	8	
1	1	6	5	2		Other	19	19
8 (4/1-9/30/13)		27 (10/1/13-3/31/14)					4/1/09-3/31/10	4/1/10-3/31/11
0-500M	500M-2MM	2-10MM	10-50MM	50-100MM	100-250MM		ALL	ALL
2	4	13	11	3	2	**NUMBER OF STATEMENTS**	40	44
%	%	%	%	%	%	**ASSETS**	%	%
		15.3	5.0			Cash & Equivalents	9.7	8.3
		22.9	22.6			Trade Receivables (net)	21.8	22.9
		37.1	39.8			Inventory	36.2	33.9
		2.3	4.2			All Other Current	4.4	3.1
		77.6	71.5			Total Current	72.1	68.1
		14.0	18.8			Fixed Assets (net)	17.6	17.1
		1.7	2.6			Intangibles (net)	6.1	6.8
		6.6	7.1			All Other Non-Current	4.2	7.9
		100.0	100.0			Total	100.0	100.0
						LIABILITIES		
		9.3	15.9			Notes Payable-Short Term	11.9	13.6
		1.2	1.3			Cur. Mat.-L.T.D.	4.8	1.6
		21.5	12.8			Trade Payables	10.6	12.7
		2.3	.1			Income Taxes Payable	.0	1.0
		7.6	13.1			All Other Current	8.4	11.6
		41.9	43.2			Total Current	35.7	40.5
		13.9	13.1			Long-Term Debt	15.0	17.0
		.0	.2			Deferred Taxes	.3	.2
		9.0	5.7			All Other Non-Current	5.4	3.8
		35.2	37.8			Net Worth	43.6	38.4
		100.0	100.0			Total Liabilities & Net Worth	100.0	100.0
						INCOME DATA		
		100.0	100.0			Net Sales	100.0	100.0
		35.8	42.6			Gross Profit	41.6	42.4
		29.2	38.2			Operating Expenses	38.4	37.3
		6.6	4.5			Operating Profit	3.2	5.0
		.2	1.3			All Other Expenses (net)	1.6	1.1
		6.4	3.2			Profit Before Taxes	1.6	4.0
						RATIOS		
		3.2	2.1				4.4	3.3
		2.1	1.6			Current	1.9	1.7
		1.4	1.4				1.2	1.3
		1.5	1.0				2.3	1.5
		1.0	.7			Quick	.8	.8
		.6	.4				.4	.4
		14 25.2	**24** 15.5				**27** 13.5	**28** 13.2
		43 8.4	**44** 8.3			Sales/Receivables	**44** 8.4	**49** 7.5
		60 6.1	**51** 7.2				**59** 6.2	**59** 6.2
		54 6.8	**83** 4.4				**63** 5.8	**66** 5.5
		85 4.3	**152** 2.4			Cost of Sales/Inventory	**112** 3.3	**111** 3.3
		126 2.9	**192** 1.9				**187** 1.9	**168** 2.2
		1 251.6	**25** 14.6				**21** 17.1	**27** 13.7
		45 8.1	**32** 11.4			Cost of Sales/Payables	**29** 12.6	**35** 10.5
		72 5.1	**69** 5.3				**45** 8.2	**63** 5.8
		4.4	4.0				2.9	3.1
		6.5	6.2			Sales/Working Capital	5.8	7.9
		19.2	15.8				15.9	17.5
			19.8				12.6	14.6
			12.1			EBIT/Interest	(38) 2.4	(41) 3.8
			1.5				-1.7	.4
								25.2
						Net Profit + Depr., Dep., Amort./Cur. Mat. L/T/D		(14) .9
								-.4
		.1	.1				.2	.1
		.2	.3			Fixed/Worth	.4	.5
		2.7	.8				.9	1.0
		.6	.9				.5	.9
		1.6	1.4			Debt/Worth	1.7	1.9
		5.7	2.7				4.5	3.9
		89.4	34.1				15.4	68.4
		(11) 23.0	(10) 18.6			% Profit Before Taxes/Tangible Net Worth	(35) 4.9	(39) 8.8
		9.6	-.3				-14.7	-2.7
		31.0	10.5				6.2	10.6
		6.2	6.6			% Profit Before Taxes/Total Assets	3.2	4.6
		1.8	2.6				-4.0	-1.1
		59.1	46.9				47.1	62.1
		24.9	31.3			Sales/Net Fixed Assets	12.2	14.4
		12.5	6.8				6.2	6.0
		3.0	2.4				2.4	2.2
		2.7	1.7			Sales/Total Assets	1.7	1.7
		2.0	1.2				1.4	1.4
		.1					.7	.7
		(11) .8				% Depr., Dep., Amort./Sales	(34) 1.5	(34) 1.6
		1.6					2.7	3.5
							2.0	1.2
						% Officers', Directors' Owners' Comp/Sales	(11) 3.6	(14) 2.6
							8.9	3.7
1238M	17094M	191300M	458965M	485231M	493427M	Net Sales ($)	1229861M	1671436M
598M	4694M	74646M	242955M	237241M	398596M	Total Assets ($)	752605M	1085201M

M = $ thousand MM = $ million

See Pages 9 through 22 for Explanation of Ratios and Data

Comparative Historical Data | Current Data Sorted by Sales

4/1/11-3/31/12 ALL	4/1/12-3/31/13 ALL	4/1/13-3/31/14 ALL	Type of Statement	0-1MM	1-3MM	3-5MM	5-10MM	10-25MM	25MM & OVER
6	4	7	Unqualified				1		6
11	5	4	Reviewed				2	1	1
4	7	5	Compiled	1			1	3	
4	3	4	Tax Returns	1	2			1	
12	12	15	Other	1		1		6	7
				8 (4/1-9/30/13)			27 (10/1/13-3/31/14)		
37	31	35	**NUMBER OF STATEMENTS**	3	2	1	4	11	14
%	%	%	**ASSETS**	%	%	%	%	%	%
6.6	6.9	12.0	Cash & Equivalents					14.9	6.8
24.2	22.4	22.3	Trade Receivables (net)					18.2	28.4
39.8	38.6	37.1	Inventory					33.4	35.6
3.2	3.8	2.8	All Other Current					3.4	3.1
73.8	71.7	74.3	Total Current					69.9	73.8
15.4	18.9	15.7	Fixed Assets (net)					20.5	13.7
5.1	6.0	4.1	Intangibles (net)					.5	8.5
5.7	3.4	6.0	All Other Non-Current					9.1	4.0
100.0	100.0	100.0	Total					100.0	100.0
			LIABILITIES						
13.6	8.6	15.1	Notes Payable-Short Term					10.4	13.0
1.2	3.3	1.2	Cur. Mat.-L.T.D.					1.3	1.3
12.8	15.1	19.1	Trade Payables					22.0	12.9
1.0	1.3	.9	Income Taxes Payable					.0	.1
11.1	11.9	8.8	All Other Current					7.4	12.3
39.7	40.2	45.0	Total Current					41.2	39.5
10.6	14.3	14.6	Long-Term Debt					22.1	13.8
.3	.1	.3	Deferred Taxes					.0	.8
5.2	6.5	5.4	All Other Non-Current					9.0	5.1
44.1	38.8	34.7	Net Worth					27.6	40.8
100.0	100.0	100.0	Total Liabilties & Net Worth					100.0	100.0
			INCOME DATA						
100.0	100.0	100.0	Net Sales					100.0	100.0
43.4	41.9	41.1	Gross Profit					37.2	41.2
38.0	36.0	35.8	Operating Expenses					31.2	34.0
5.4	5.9	5.3	Operating Profit					6.0	7.2
1.5	.4	1.0	All Other Expenses (net)					.3	2.0
3.9	5.5	4.3	Profit Before Taxes					5.7	5.2
			RATIOS						
3.8	2.8	3.0						3.4	2.5
2.0	1.9	2.0	Current					1.6	2.0
1.3	1.4	1.4						1.1	1.4
1.4	1.0	1.2						1.5	1.1
.8	.7	.9	Quick					.9	1.0
.4	.3	.5						.4	.7
26 14.2	21 17.7	17 21.2						1 571.4	35 10.3
43 8.5	40 9.1	43 8.4	Sales/Receivables					33 11.1	49 7.5
58 6.3	54 6.8	58 6.3						44 8.3	69 5.3
55 6.6	73 5.0	63 5.8						41 8.8	64 5.7
135 2.7	96 3.8	104 3.5	Cost of Sales/Inventory					68 5.4	114 3.2
192 1.9	182 2.0	174 2.1						107 3.4	174 2.1
22 16.7	21 17.8	18 20.3						18 20.3	23 15.8
35 10.5	34 10.7	35 10.3	Cost of Sales/Payables					45 8.1	32 11.5
54 6.8	57 6.4	55 6.6						85 4.3	48 7.6
3.3	3.9	3.9						5.6	3.7
6.5	6.0	6.5	Sales/Working Capital					7.4	6.7
14.2	14.2	17.6						37.0	12.3
17.0	23.7	72.4							47.4
(32) 3.9	(28) 5.3	(29) 9.3	EBIT/Interest						(13) 12.1
1.3	2.1	3.6							3.6
			Net Profit + Depr., Dep., Amort./Cur. Mat. L/T/D						
.1	.2	.1						.1	.2
.3	.6	.5	Fixed/Worth					.5	.5
.7	3.8	3.4						129.5	.8
.5	.7	.5						.4	.5
1.4	1.5	1.6	Debt/Worth					2.1	1.3
3.5	4.1	20.7						176.9	7.2
27.3	40.7	76.2							50.9
(33) 9.3	(25) 17.1	(29) 27.0	% Profit Before Taxes/Tangible Net Worth						(12) 25.0
4.2	6.8	13.8							13.7
10.3	17.3	19.4						41.3	18.2
5.1	6.9	8.2	% Profit Before Taxes/Total Assets					6.2	9.3
.8	2.7	2.6						-1.2	3.3
99.3	48.3	46.9						69.0	48.0
19.4	17.2	28.7	Sales/Net Fixed Assets					29.0	24.2
7.4	6.7	8.8						6.9	8.5
2.3	2.4	2.9						3.1	2.6
2.1	2.1	2.1	Sales/Total Assets					2.7	2.0
1.5	1.5	1.6						1.6	1.7
.6	.6	.6							.7
(23) 1.4	(26) 1.3	(27) .9	% Depr., Dep., Amort./Sales						(10) 1.0
2.5	2.3	1.9							2.3
1.0	1.2	.4							
(12) 2.6	(15) 2.9	(13) 2.1	% Officers', Directors' Owners' Comp/Sales						
4.7	4.1	8.5							
1122795M	1145087M	1647255M	Net Sales ($)	2208M	5529M	4484M	32300M	178073M	1424661M
647707M	627879M	958730M	Total Assets ($)	1197M	2156M	2252M	18269M	84330M	850526M

M = $ thousand MM = $ million

See Pages 9 through 22 for Explanation of Ratios and Data

Current Data Sorted by Assets | **Comparative Historical Data**

						Type of Statement		
		4	2	4		Unqualified	14	10
1	2	10	4			Reviewed	21	11
2	2	3	1			Compiled	5	8
2	2	5				Tax Returns	14	14
	3	10	10	5	4	Other	31	30
12 (4/1-9/30/13)			64 (10/1/13-3/31/14)				4/1/09-3/31/10 ALL	4/1/10-3/31/11 ALL
0-500M	500M-2MM	2-10MM	10-50MM	50-100MM	100-250MM			
5	9	32	17	9	4	NUMBER OF STATEMENTS	85	73
%	%	%	%	%	%	ASSETS	%	%
		10.2	10.1			Cash & Equivalents	11.0	11.2
		30.5	27.8			Trade Receivables (net)	24.1	26.1
		35.9	25.8			Inventory	29.4	33.3
		2.9	2.5			All Other Current	2.9	3.7
		79.5	66.2			Total Current	67.5	74.3
		13.8	18.4			Fixed Assets (net)	19.6	17.8
		3.7	7.3			Intangibles (net)	8.0	4.3
		2.9	8.2			All Other Non-Current	4.9	3.6
		100.0	100.0			Total	100.0	100.0
						LIABILITIES		
		10.2	3.7			Notes Payable-Short Term	14.0	11.3
		1.5	1.7			Cur. Mat.-L.T.D.	2.8	4.0
		17.7	14.6			Trade Payables	16.3	15.0
		.3	.1			Income Taxes Payable	.1	.1
		8.7	13.2			All Other Current	11.6	15.6
		38.4	33.3			Total Current	44.9	46.1
		9.3	10.0			Long-Term Debt	14.3	10.6
		.2	.4			Deferred Taxes	.4	.4
		5.1	4.1			All Other Non-Current	6.7	5.1
		47.0	52.3			Net Worth	33.7	37.9
		100.0	100.0			Total Liabilties & Net Worth	100.0	100.0
						INCOME DATA		
		100.0	100.0			Net Sales	100.0	100.0
		40.7	35.7			Gross Profit	37.5	37.9
		33.9	29.0			Operating Expenses	32.9	32.3
		6.8	6.7			Operating Profit	4.6	5.6
		.4	.9			All Other Expenses (net)	1.4	1.3
		6.4	5.8			Profit Before Taxes	3.2	4.3
						RATIOS		
		3.1	3.0				2.6	2.7
		2.1	2.2			Current	1.6	1.9
		1.6	1.4				1.1	1.3
		1.6	1.8				1.3	1.4
		1.1	1.2			Quick	.8	.8
		.7	.9				.5	.6
		29 12.4	**41** 8.8				**32** 11.3	**31** 11.9
		47 7.7	**45** 8.2			Sales/Receivables	**44** 8.3	**46** 8.0
		59 6.2	**54** 6.8				**59** 6.2	**59** 6.2
		53 6.9	**53** 6.9				**55** 6.7	**54** 6.7
		104 3.5	**61** 6.0			Cost of Sales/Inventory	**90** 4.1	**89** 4.1
		130 2.8	**96** 3.8				**140** 2.6	**140** 2.6
		23 15.9	**28** 13.2				**15** 23.8	**18** 20.6
		35 10.5	**39** 9.3			Cost of Sales/Payables	**36** 10.0	**33** 11.1
		61 6.0	**46** 8.0				**61** 6.0	**51** 7.2
		3.5	5.0				3.9	3.9
		5.6	6.3			Sales/Working Capital	7.9	7.2
		10.9	11.9				35.5	16.6
		22.1	67.4				6.7	16.8
		(29) 12.0	(15) 22.7			EBIT/Interest	(75) 3.0	(63) 4.7
		3.6	5.6				.7	1.7
							4.5	3.1
						Net Profit + Depr., Dep., Amort./Cur. Mat. L/T/D	(25) 2.1	(18) 1.5
							.9	.2
		.1	.1				.2	.1
		.2	.2			Fixed/Worth	.8	.5
		.4	.9				2.3	1.3
		.6	.5				.9	.9
		1.1	.8			Debt/Worth	1.9	1.7
		1.8	1.6				9.9	6.5
		47.8	38.5				55.6	60.0
		(30) 23.7	(16) 32.2			% Profit Before Taxes/Tangible Net Worth	(67) 11.3	(62) 17.6
		8.8	10.9				-.4	2.1
		20.3	17.9				15.0	16.9
		9.9	11.2			% Profit Before Taxes/Total Assets	3.0	5.7
		3.5	3.5				-.5	1.0
		55.2	33.2				36.3	53.0
		28.6	19.1			Sales/Net Fixed Assets	13.6	15.5
		11.8	7.1				5.6	6.9
		2.9	2.4				2.4	2.7
		2.3	2.1			Sales/Total Assets	2.0	2.1
		1.8	1.6				1.4	1.6
		.4	.9				.9	.9
		(24) .9	(16) 1.5			% Depr., Dep., Amort./Sales	(67) 1.8	(54) 1.7
		1.6	2.5				2.7	2.7
		3.5					3.0	1.9
		(10) 4.5				% Officers', Directors' Owners' Comp/Sales	(29) 3.8	(31) 4.2
		10.2					5.6	6.5
4629M	47844M	364080M	752589M	1005388M	892049M	Net Sales ($)	2733627M	2438164M
1568M	12744M	148325M	370623M	693589M	582124M	Total Assets ($)	1915509M	1340634M

M = $ thousand MM = $ million

See Pages 9 through 22 for Explanation of Ratios and Data

Comparative Historical Data / Current Data Sorted by Sales

4/1/11-3/31/12 ALL	4/1/12-3/31/13 ALL	4/1/13-3/31/14 ALL	Type of Statement	0-1MM	1-3MM	3-5MM	5-10MM	10-25MM	25MM & OVER
14	9	10	Unqualified				1	4	5
11	9	17	Reviewed		2	2	5	5	3
9	9	8	Compiled	2		2	3		1
13	11	9	Tax Returns	1	1		4	3	
32	26	32	Other		1	2	5	6	18
					12 (4/1-9/30/13)		64 (10/1/13-3/31/14)		
79	64	76	**NUMBER OF STATEMENTS**	3	4	6	18	18	27
%	%	%	**ASSETS**	%	%	%	%	%	%
11.7	7.9	9.5	Cash & Equivalents				10.7	9.0	7.6
29.0	29.9	28.2	Trade Receivables (net)				27.4	32.5	30.2
33.2	32.3	32.8	Inventory				37.6	30.1	27.9
3.3	3.6	3.5	All Other Current				1.5	4.0	2.9
77.1	73.8	74.0	Total Current				77.1	75.6	68.5
16.1	16.7	16.0	Fixed Assets (net)				12.5	16.4	17.3
3.6	4.7	5.2	Intangibles (net)				6.3	5.3	6.3
3.1	4.7	4.8	All Other Non-Current				4.1	2.7	7.8
100.0	100.0	100.0	Total				100.0	100.0	100.0
			LIABILITIES						
14.0	9.8	10.3	Notes Payable-Short Term				6.2	8.6	8.9
2.0	2.2	2.0	Cur. Mat.-L.T.D.				2.0	1.2	2.4
16.1	17.8	16.8	Trade Payables				16.4	20.7	13.9
.2	.3	.2	Income Taxes Payable				.3	.1	.4
13.3	9.9	11.7	All Other Current				7.7	12.1	13.0
45.7	39.9	41.0	Total Current				32.5	42.8	38.6
10.1	11.5	8.8	Long-Term Debt				11.4	7.3	9.4
.4	.4	.2	Deferred Taxes				.1	.1	.5
6.5	6.7	6.5	All Other Non-Current				5.3	4.3	5.5
37.3	41.6	43.5	Net Worth				50.6	45.5	46.0
100.0	100.0	100.0	Total Liabilties & Net Worth				100.0	100.0	100.0
			INCOME DATA						
100.0	100.0	100.0	Net Sales				100.0	100.0	100.0
37.2	36.9	38.1	Gross Profit				42.2	37.4	34.0
32.9	29.0	32.3	Operating Expenses				34.1	31.5	27.5
4.3	7.9	5.8	Operating Profit				8.0	5.9	6.5
.6	.7	.7	All Other Expenses (net)				.7	.1	1.4
3.6	7.2	5.1	Profit Before Taxes				7.3	5.8	5.1
			RATIOS						
2.7	3.0	3.0	Current				3.2	2.4	2.9
1.7	2.1	2.0					2.4	1.6	2.1
1.3	1.3	1.4					1.9	1.4	1.3
1.4	1.6	1.6	Quick				1.6	1.3	1.7
.8	1.0	1.0					1.2	1.0	1.2
.6	.6	.6					.8	.7	.7
34 10.7	**33** 11.2	**33** 11.0	Sales/Receivables				**31** 11.7	**34** 10.7	**42** 8.7
47 7.8	**44** 8.3	**45** 8.2					**48** 7.6	**45** 8.2	**60** 6.1
58 6.3	**59** 6.2	**62** 5.9					**61** 6.0	**52** 7.0	**73** 5.0
51 7.2	**43** 8.5	**54** 6.7	Cost of Sales/Inventory				**74** 4.9	**35** 10.5	**54** 6.7
81 4.5	**73** 5.0	**87** 4.2					**104** 3.5	**63** 5.8	**83** 4.4
118 3.1	**122** 3.0	**130** 2.8					**140** 2.6	**130** 2.8	**111** 3.3
18 20.2	**19** 19.6	**23** 15.6	Cost of Sales/Payables				**24** 15.3	**27** 13.6	**21** 17.7
33 11.1	**37** 9.9	**36** 10.2					**33** 11.1	**34** 10.8	**39** 9.3
52 7.0	**55** 6.6	**57** 6.4					**62** 5.9	**62** 5.9	**48** 7.6
3.7	4.0	3.7	Sales/Working Capital				3.3	5.1	4.4
7.5	6.5	6.1					5.3	11.2	5.9
14.8	18.3	13.4					9.4	19.0	11.5
15.3	32.2	24.7	EBIT/Interest				33.1	38.3	29.0
(67) 5.3	(57) 12.1	(66) 10.3					(16) 10.5	(17) 16.7	(23) 10.9
1.8	3.1	3.4					3.3	5.2	4.1
10.8	9.6	9.5	Net Profit + Depr., Dep., Amort./Cur. Mat. L/T/D						
(13) 5.2	(17) 4.8	(18) 4.3							
1.9	.4	2.5							
.1	.2	.1	Fixed/Worth				.1	.1	.2
.4	.4	.3					.2	.2	.4
.9	1.1	.6					.3	.5	.9
.7	.7	.7	Debt/Worth				.6	.9	.5
1.6	1.2	1.3					.8	1.5	1.5
4.5	3.9	2.4					1.5	2.6	3.1
59.1	65.6	42.7	% Profit Before Taxes/Tangible Net Worth				65.3	50.2	41.8
(71) 13.4	(54) 38.1	(69) 24.4					(16) 23.7	22.3	(24) 34.6
2.3	11.2	8.7					9.4	8.4	10.9
15.9	26.7	13.9	% Profit Before Taxes/Total Assets				27.8	14.6	19.5
5.6	10.3	8.3					10.7	11.1	10.2
.9	3.4	1.7					3.6	2.2	1.0
49.4	52.4	41.8	Sales/Net Fixed Assets				46.3	246.6	29.2
17.3	20.9	20.0					18.5	30.9	14.3
8.3	9.1	9.7					12.4	10.4	6.2
3.2	3.0	2.7	Sales/Total Assets				3.0	3.7	2.5
2.1	2.2	2.2					2.2	2.3	1.9
1.7	1.6	1.6					1.6	1.8	1.4
.8	.3	.8	% Depr., Dep., Amort./Sales				.5	.3	.9
(58) 1.7	(56) .9	(58) 1.4					(15) .8	(11) 1.5	(24) 1.4
2.5	1.8	2.6					2.7	2.4	2.6
3.3	1.4	2.3	% Officers', Directors' Owners' Comp/Sales						
(26) 4.9	(22) 4.0	(23) 4.1							
7.2	7.4	8.8							
2280470M	**2600561M**	**3066579M**	Net Sales ($)	**1307M**	**7497M**	**23530M**	**126286M**	**309323M**	**2598636M**
1241899M	**1209555M**	**1808973M**	Total Assets ($)	**700M**	**3073M**	**10641M**	**59362M**	**152233M**	**1582964M**

M = $ thousand MM = $ million

See Pages 9 through 22 for Explanation of Ratios and Data

Current Data Sorted by Assets							Comparative Historical Data	
						Type of Statement		
		1	1		1	Unqualified	10	12
		1	2			Reviewed	12	11
1	3	3	1			Compiled	3	7
	3	3				Tax Returns	8	9
	2	6	7	3	1	Other	18	29
	5 (4/1-9/30/13)		34 (10/1/13-3/31/14)				**4/1/09-3/31/10 ALL**	**4/1/10-3/31/11 ALL**
0-500M	**500M-2MM**	**2-10MM**	**10-50MM**	**50-100MM**	**100-250MM**			
1	8	14	11	3	2	**NUMBER OF STATEMENTS**	51	68
%	%	%	%	%	%	**ASSETS**	%	%
		16.3	9.0			Cash & Equivalents	12.9	12.4
		28.1	25.1			Trade Receivables (net)	24.4	22.9
		31.9	24.5			Inventory	30.3	33.8
		.7	1.6			All Other Current	2.0	3.4
		77.1	60.2			Total Current	69.5	72.6
		12.3	32.6			Fixed Assets (net)	21.2	16.5
		3.4	3.3			Intangibles (net)	2.6	4.7
		7.3	3.8			All Other Non-Current	6.6	6.2
		100.0	100.0			Total	100.0	100.0
						LIABILITIES		
		8.2	7.1			Notes Payable-Short Term	14.7	12.3
		1.6	2.7			Cur. Mat.-L.T.D.	2.8	2.4
		11.5	13.4			Trade Payables	12.7	14.5
		.0	.0			Income Taxes Payable	.4	.2
		7.4	5.6			All Other Current	6.9	10.4
		28.6	28.9			Total Current	37.5	39.9
		5.1	14.0			Long-Term Debt	10.0	10.7
		.0	.6			Deferred Taxes	.2	.3
		4.2	6.5			All Other Non-Current	4.3	5.8
		62.1	50.0			Net Worth	48.0	43.4
		100.0	100.0			Total Liabilties & Net Worth	100.0	100.0
						INCOME DATA		
		100.0	100.0			Net Sales	100.0	100.0
		40.9	31.4			Gross Profit	36.9	39.2
		29.4	21.9			Operating Expenses	32.9	32.9
		11.5	9.5			Operating Profit	4.0	6.4
		.2	1.3			All Other Expenses (net)	.8	1.0
		11.3	8.2			Profit Before Taxes	3.2	5.4
						RATIOS		
		4.3	6.7				3.2	3.7
		2.9	1.5			Current	2.2	1.9
		1.4	1.1				1.3	1.2
		4.0	4.2				1.9	1.7
		1.4	.9			Quick	1.0	.9
		.8	.6				.5	.5
		30 12.0	**34** 10.8				**29** 12.5	**28** 12.8
		41 8.8	**46** 7.9			Sales/Receivables	**44** 8.3	**40** 9.2
		51 7.1	**59** 6.2				**57** 6.4	**57** 6.4
		20 18.7	**42** 8.7				**54** 6.8	**65** 5.6
		66 5.5	**81** 4.5			Cost of Sales/Inventory	**84** 4.4	**96** 3.8
		111 3.3	**99** 3.7				**128** 2.8	**159** 2.3
		9 39.0	**19** 19.2				**15** 24.3	**18** 20.6
		28 13.2	**29** 12.7			Cost of Sales/Payables	**30** 12.2	**37** 9.9
		43 8.5	**50** 7.3				**43** 8.5	**57** 6.4
		3.2	3.2				3.0	3.0
		7.0	10.8			Sales/Working Capital	6.9	5.9
		11.8	56.9				13.7	17.9
			244.8				17.3	36.0
			(10) 18.8			EBIT/Interest	(42) 3.9	(55) 7.2
			2.6				1.2	2.6
								11.0
						Net Profit + Depr., Dep., Amort./Cur. Mat. L/T/D		(10) 3.7
								2.5
		.0	.2				.2	.1
		.1	.8			Fixed/Worth	.5	.3
		.4	2.1				1.0	.9
		.2	.4				.4	.5
		.5	1.2			Debt/Worth	1.1	1.1
		1.5	3.2				2.3	3.8
		96.9	60.3				34.0	38.6
		(13) 44.5	40.3			% Profit Before Taxes/Tangible Net Worth	(47) 11.9	(58) 13.6
		19.4	10.4				1.1	3.1
		47.9	29.5				13.7	18.8
		25.8	15.5			% Profit Before Taxes/Total Assets	5.2	5.4
		10.5	3.0				.7	2.0
		332.2	25.3				38.0	51.2
		52.7	7.5			Sales/Net Fixed Assets	15.3	19.7
		9.5	3.3				4.6	6.2
		3.5	2.4				2.6	2.8
		2.4	1.8			Sales/Total Assets	2.0	2.0
		1.9	1.4				1.2	1.3
			.5				.8	.6
			(10) 2.1			% Depr., Dep., Amort./Sales	(45) 1.5	(57) 1.4
			4.1				3.1	2.9
							2.1	2.0
						% Officers', Directors' Owners' Comp/Sales	(13) 5.1	(25) 5.0
							9.3	8.7
3257M	27449M	139586M	423751M	400197M	510983M	Net Sales ($)	1583344M	2068620M
491M	9436M	54990M	231736M	224878M	408042M	Total Assets ($)	988559M	1274726M

M = $ thousand MM = $ million

See Pages 9 through 22 for Explanation of Ratios and Data

Comparative Historical Data				Current Data Sorted by Sales					
			Type of Statement						
9	12	3	Unqualified					1	2
10	4	3	Reviewed				1		2
4	9	8	Compiled	1		1	4	1	1
11	6	6	Tax Returns		2	2	1	1	
21	23	19	Other	1	1		1	8	8
4/1/11-3/31/12 ALL	4/1/12-3/31/13 ALL	4/1/13-3/31/14 ALL		5 (4/1-9/30/13)		34 (10/1/13-3/31/14)			
				0-1MM	1-3MM	3-5MM	5-10MM	10-25MM	25MM & OVER
55	54	39	**NUMBER OF STATEMENTS**	2	3	3	7	11	13
%	%	%	**ASSETS**	%	%	%	%	%	%
12.3	12.5	13.4	Cash & Equivalents					19.6	7.8
22.4	24.0	26.1	Trade Receivables (net)					21.6	24.9
30.9	28.5	27.0	Inventory					30.0	28.8
3.8	1.8	1.7	All Other Current					.8	1.8
69.4	66.8	68.2	Total Current					72.0	63.2
19.5	18.4	16.7	Fixed Assets (net)					18.9	23.5
2.9	6.1	7.6	Intangibles (net)					2.9	9.4
8.2	8.7	7.5	All Other Non-Current					6.2	3.8
100.0	100.0	100.0	Total					100.0	100.0
			LIABILITIES						
8.1	9.5	5.8	Notes Payable-Short Term					8.9	4.7
1.5	2.3	1.5	Cur. Mat.-L.T.D.					.6	2.8
14.1	16.1	13.3	Trade Payables					11.0	11.6
.1	.1	.0	Income Taxes Payable					.0	.0
7.5	13.9	10.8	All Other Current					4.6	6.7
31.3	41.9	31.4	Total Current					25.1	25.8
9.7	14.2	9.3	Long-Term Debt					7.4	17.2
.3	.3	.3	Deferred Taxes					.0	.9
3.5	9.1	4.5	All Other Non-Current					3.7	6.9
55.2	34.5	54.5	Net Worth					63.8	49.2
100.0	100.0	100.0	Total Liabilities & Net Worth					100.0	100.0
			INCOME DATA						
100.0	100.0	100.0	Net Sales					100.0	100.0
38.3	37.3	37.5	Gross Profit					39.4	33.0
33.4	32.4	30.3	Operating Expenses					30.3	23.0
4.8	4.9	7.2	Operating Profit					9.2	10.0
.9	.9	.9	All Other Expenses (net)					.7	2.2
3.9	4.0	6.2	Profit Before Taxes					8.5	7.8
			RATIOS						
4.7	3.6	4.6						8.4	5.6
2.7	1.6	2.5	Current					3.1	3.0
1.4	1.2	1.3						1.3	1.3
2.3	1.9	2.7						5.9	2.1
1.3	.8	1.5	Quick					1.3	1.5
.6	.5	.7						.6	.8
24 15.2	**26** 14.0	**24** 15.2						**24** 15.3	**37** 9.8
40 9.1	**46** 8.0	**43** 8.5	Sales/Receivables					**34** 10.8	**49** 7.5
55 6.6	**61** 6.0	**59** 6.2						**46** 8.0	**61** 6.0
33 11.0	**24** 15.1	**23** 15.9						**40** 9.2	**45** 8.1
85 4.3	**78** 4.7	**68** 5.4	Cost of Sales/Inventory					**68** 5.4	**96** 3.8
152 2.4	**130** 2.8	**107** 3.4						**87** 4.2	**126** 2.9
18 20.3	**20** 18.0	**18** 20.6						**19** 19.2	**18** 19.9
32 11.3	**33** 11.2	**29** 12.4	Cost of Sales/Payables					**23** 15.8	**29** 12.7
49 7.4	**51** 7.1	**50** 7.3						**38** 9.7	**45** 8.2
2.7	3.4	3.0						2.2	3.1
5.2	7.8	7.2	Sales/Working Capital					8.1	4.7
13.2	48.5	15.9						20.0	16.3
44.5	36.7	91.1							45.9
(43) 6.8	(42) 5.8	(27) 16.7	EBIT/Interest						(12) 12.3
1.5	-2.0	6.0							7.3
			Net Profit + Depr., Dep., Amort./Cur. Mat. L/T/D						
.1	.1	.1						.0	.1
.3	.5	.3	Fixed/Worth					.2	.5
.5	2.0	.8						1.9	1.7
.2	.5	.2						.1	.3
.7	1.5	.9	Debt/Worth					.4	1.1
2.0	NM	3.2						3.2	3.0
36.0	56.5	69.3						97.8	67.1
(52) 18.0	(41) 28.6	(36) 42.4	% Profit Before Taxes/Tangible Net Worth					18.5	(12) 46.3
5.8	5.3	9.4						3.9	12.9
19.8	24.5	29.5						73.7	29.4
6.6	11.6	15.5	% Profit Before Taxes/Total Assets					14.6	15.5
1.7	-5.1	.4						.2	3.6
43.8	66.1	141.6						160.1	26.2
16.2	21.4	22.5	Sales/Net Fixed Assets					33.5	8.8
6.2	5.9	7.5						4.7	5.3
2.8	2.7	2.9						4.0	2.4
2.0	2.1	2.0	Sales/Total Assets					2.3	1.7
1.2	1.3	1.4						1.4	1.5
.7	1.0	.4							.4
(43) 1.2	(44) 1.7	(26) 1.8	% Depr., Dep., Amort./Sales						(12) 2.8
2.7	2.9	3.4							4.7
2.9	3.2								
(19) 7.2	(12) 5.8		% Officers', Directors' Owners' Comp/Sales						
11.8	10.2								
2067049M	2351692M	1505223M	Net Sales ($)	583M	5963M	12166M	51177M	155031M	1280303M
1254759M	1524688M	929573M	Total Assets ($)	2419M	3496M	3698M	18046M	76537M	825377M

M = $ thousand MM = $ million

See Pages 9 through 22 for Explanation of Ratios and Data

	Current Data Sorted by Assets						Comparative Historical Data	
Type of Statement								
Unqualified			2	6	3	4	18	25
Reviewed			4	4			15	15
Compiled			1		1		2	3
Tax Returns		2	1				8	7
Other		3	11	13	8	4	38	32
		13 (4/1-9/30/13)		54 (10/1/13-3/31/14)			4/1/09-3/31/10	4/1/10-3/31/11
	0-500M	500M-2MM	2-10MM	10-50MM	50-100MM	100-250MM	ALL	ALL
NUMBER OF STATEMENTS		5	19	23	12	8	81	82
ASSETS	%	%	%	%	%	%	%	%
Cash & Equivalents	D		9.8	8.9	9.7		12.3	10.4
Trade Receivables (net)	A		31.7	22.5	18.2		24.1	27.0
Inventory	T		32.2	22.4	15.9		30.5	27.6
All Other Current	A		1.7	5.7	5.7		3.0	3.1
Total Current			75.4	59.4	49.5		69.8	68.1
Fixed Assets (net)	N		13.8	20.4	19.9		19.4	19.9
Intangibles (net)	O		3.1	12.0	24.3		5.6	6.4
All Other Non-Current	T		7.7	8.1	6.4		5.2	5.7
Total			100.0	100.0	100.0		100.0	100.0
LIABILITIES	A							
Notes Payable-Short Term	V		17.5	8.1	4.9		10.9	9.4
Cur. Mat.-L.T.D.	A		1.5	2.4	2.1		2.0	2.6
Trade Payables	I		20.1	9.9	6.2		15.4	14.1
Income Taxes Payable	L		.0	.2	.2		.3	.3
All Other Current	A		10.0	9.5	6.1		12.6	10.9
Total Current	B		49.2	30.1	19.6		41.3	37.2
Long-Term Debt	L		10.8	10.7	14.1		9.4	10.3
Deferred Taxes	E		.1	1.1	2.2		.5	.5
All Other Non-Current			3.3	9.5	2.2		4.7	3.0
Net Worth			36.7	48.6	62.0		44.1	49.1
Total Liabilties & Net Worth			100.0	100.0	100.0		100.0	100.0
INCOME DATA								
Net Sales			100.0	100.0	100.0		100.0	100.0
Gross Profit			33.8	24.3	28.5		28.0	28.6
Operating Expenses			25.8	20.0	21.1		24.0	22.8
Operating Profit			8.0	4.3	7.4		4.0	5.9
All Other Expenses (net)			.6	2.2	2.1		1.0	.6
Profit Before Taxes			7.5	2.1	5.3		2.9	5.2
RATIOS								
Current			2.1	3.3	4.9		3.3	3.4
			1.5	2.4	2.5		1.8	2.1
			1.1	1.3	1.6		1.2	1.4
Quick			1.6	2.1	2.7		1.9	1.8
			.7	1.0	1.5		.9	1.0
			.4	.6	.8		.6	.7
Sales/Receivables			**41** 8.9	**39** 9.3	**39** 9.4		**30** 12.0	**38** 9.7
			47 7.8	**49** 7.5	**53** 6.9		**42** 8.7	**51** 7.1
			55 6.6	**55** 6.6	**72** 5.1		**53** 6.9	**66** 5.5
Cost of Sales/Inventory			**48** 7.6	**35** 10.3	**43** 8.5		**44** 8.2	**47** 7.8
			78 4.7	**64** 5.7	**72** 5.1		**66** 5.6	**76** 4.8
			96 3.8	**96** 3.8	**130** 2.8		**105** 3.5	**110** 3.3
Cost of Sales/Payables			**30** 12.3	**16** 23.0	**22** 16.7		**15** 24.3	**18** 20.5
			37 9.8	**25** 14.6	**27** 13.4		**28** 13.0	**29** 12.7
			47 7.8	**33** 11.0	**31** 11.7		**47** 7.8	**47** 7.7
Sales/Working Capital			6.2	3.8	2.0		4.3	3.9
			11.3	5.0	4.9		7.4	5.5
			40.3	13.0	7.2		17.3	14.4
EBIT/Interest			49.3	20.7			20.6	26.9
			(14) 5.5	(22) 2.1			(71) 6.8	(70) 7.3
			1.6	-.2			1.0	2.3
Net Profit + Depr., Dep., Amort./Cur. Mat. L/T/D							10.1	8.8
							(25) 5.2	(26) 2.5
							1.3	1.2
Fixed/Worth			.1	.3	.2		.2	.2
			.4	.6	.8		.4	.4
			1.3	1.3	1.6		.8	1.0
Debt/Worth			.9	.4	.2		.5	.3
			2.0	1.4	1.5		1.2	1.1
			4.9	2.7	3.5		3.1	1.9
% Profit Before Taxes/Tangible Net Worth			91.9	17.3	29.8		50.4	43.1
			(18) 43.5	(20) 8.3	(10) 20.2		(75) 16.6	(73) 16.1
			10.4	-3.8	9.7		.8	6.3
% Profit Before Taxes/Total Assets			37.1	11.4	10.7		16.0	15.0
			7.2	2.8	6.1		5.6	7.7
			2.3	-2.9	2.0		-.5	2.4
Sales/Net Fixed Assets			45.7	22.1	12.4		38.2	24.5
			23.9	8.6	7.0		13.4	11.4
			11.0	4.9	4.8		7.5	6.1
Sales/Total Assets			3.1	2.1	1.6		3.2	2.8
			2.6	1.6	1.1		2.1	1.8
			1.8	1.2	.6		1.4	1.4
% Depr., Dep., Amort./Sales			.5	1.3			.6	.8
			(15) .8	(19) 1.7			(70) 1.4	(76) 1.7
			1.0	2.5			2.6	2.5
% Officers', Directors' Owners' Comp/Sales							2.1	1.9
							(15) 3.6	(18) 3.5
							5.6	7.3
Net Sales ($)		13078M	235086M	1048227M	857358M	1675122M	3121359M	3683169M
Total Assets ($)		3975M	100970M	595630M	800712M	1146553M	1870953M	2517753M

M = $ thousand MM = $ million

See Pages 9 through 22 for Explanation of Ratios and Data

Comparative Historical Data				Current Data Sorted by Sales					
21	12	15	**Type of Statement** Unqualified				1	2	12
14	12	8	Reviewed					5	3
4	7	2	Compiled					1	1
5	7	3	Tax Returns			2	1		
32	39	39	Other	1	2	1	7	8	20
4/1/11-3/31/12 ALL	**4/1/12-3/31/13 ALL**	**4/1/13-3/31/14 ALL**		**13 (4/1-9/30/13)**		**54 (10/1/13-3/31/14)**			
				0-1MM	**1-3MM**	**3-5MM**	**5-10MM**	**10-25MM**	**25MM & OVER**
76	77	67	**NUMBER OF STATEMENTS**	1	2	3	9	16	36
%	%	%	**ASSETS**	%	%	%	%	%	%
10.7	11.2	10.8	Cash & Equivalents					10.2	10.8
28.7	25.7	24.4	Trade Receivables (net)					25.6	23.4
28.1	27.5	24.0	Inventory					27.5	20.1
3.6	4.7	4.0	All Other Current					2.1	6.2
71.0	69.1	63.1	Total Current					65.4	60.5
18.7	19.2	20.3	Fixed Assets (net)					18.2	23.0
4.8	7.2	10.2	Intangibles (net)					9.8	11.2
5.6	4.6	6.4	All Other Non-Current					6.7	5.3
100.0	100.0	100.0	Total					100.0	100.0
			LIABILITIES						
10.7	7.3	9.3	Notes Payable-Short Term					13.4	6.4
1.8	1.4	1.9	Cur. Mat.-L.T.D.					2.3	2.3
15.9	11.8	11.7	Trade Payables					14.6	8.9
.2	.1	.1	Income Taxes Payable					.0	.2
19.8	15.1	10.2	All Other Current					8.9	12.1
48.5	35.6	33.1	Total Current					39.3	29.9
6.8	13.8	11.4	Long-Term Debt					13.9	10.0
.3	.6	.8	Deferred Taxes					.4	1.3
5.8	6.2	5.3	All Other Non-Current					6.7	3.0
38.6	43.8	49.3	Net Worth					39.7	55.8
100.0	100.0	100.0	Total Liabilties & Net Worth					100.0	100.0
			INCOME DATA						
100.0	100.0	100.0	Net Sales					100.0	100.0
26.5	31.2	28.8	Gross Profit					27.6	24.4
20.4	24.6	22.4	Operating Expenses					20.3	18.9
6.1	6.6	6.4	Operating Profit					7.3	5.5
.4	.9	1.4	All Other Expenses (net)					1.8	1.2
5.6	5.7	4.9	Profit Before Taxes					5.5	4.3
			RATIOS						
3.4	4.6	4.0						2.7	4.1
1.9	2.4	2.1	Current					1.4	2.2
1.3	1.4	1.3						1.2	1.3
1.8	2.2	2.1						1.9	2.0
1.1	1.2	1.1	Quick					.7	1.4
.6	.7	.6						.4	.7
41 9.0	**34** 10.7	**38** 9.5						**41** 8.9	**40** 9.2
48 7.6	**46** 8.0	**47** 7.7	Sales/Receivables					**45** 8.2	**50** 7.3
60 6.1	**54** 6.8	**63** 5.8						**49** 7.5	**64** 5.7
39 9.3	**40** 9.1	**40** 9.1						**43** 8.5	**27** 13.5
62 5.9	**73** 5.0	**69** 5.3	Cost of Sales/Inventory					**73** 5.0	**61** 6.0
107 3.4	**122** 3.0	**96** 3.8						**96** 3.8	**83** 4.4
19 19.4	**15** 23.9	**18** 20.8						**22** 16.8	**16** 23.1
29 12.5	**25** 14.4	**27** 13.6	Cost of Sales/Payables					**26** 14.1	**26** 14.1
47 7.8	**45** 8.1	**40** 9.1						**43** 8.4	**31** 11.7
4.0	4.1	3.8						4.8	3.0
7.0	6.6	6.7	Sales/Working Capital					12.5	5.2
15.9	11.5	13.9						39.3	12.5
38.9	62.8	42.7						40.8	36.3
(67) 6.6	(67) 8.4	(55) 4.8	EBIT/Interest					(14) 3.3	(31) 4.8
1.7	1.9	1.2						1.5	.7
23.9	15.7	4.3							4.3
(19) 8.0	(24) 4.3	(17) 1.7	Net Profit + Depr., Dep., Amort./Cur. Mat. L/T/D						(13) 1.8
1.9	1.9	.4							.3
.1	.2	.2						.3	.2
.4	.5	.5	Fixed/Worth					.7	.5
1.0	1.2	1.3						2.3	1.1
.4	.3	.4						.9	.3
1.2	1.1	1.4	Debt/Worth					2.0	1.1
2.9	3.8	3.1						8.5	2.7
40.2	60.8	41.9						75.0	28.1
(64) 16.7	(64) 27.1	(61) 21.8	% Profit Before Taxes/Tangible Net Worth					(14) 37.2	(34) 16.0
4.7	7.0	4.5						9.2	.1
24.2	25.6	21.1						22.9	12.7
7.9	12.1	4.8	% Profit Before Taxes/Total Assets					4.7	6.1
2.3	1.9	.5						2.0	.0
29.4	31.7	23.9						29.4	18.1
13.7	14.2	10.7	Sales/Net Fixed Assets					15.3	7.4
7.1	7.0	6.0						7.1	4.7
3.0	2.9	2.5						2.8	1.9
2.2	2.2	1.6	Sales/Total Assets					2.0	1.6
1.4	1.4	1.3						1.4	1.2
.8	.8	1.0						.8	1.3
(65) 1.3	(67) 1.4	(54) 1.6	% Depr., Dep., Amort./Sales					(14) 1.0	(32) 1.8
2.0	2.0	2.6						1.4	2.9
1.8	1.8	1.8							
(17) 2.9	(17) 2.6	(12) 2.5	% Officers', Directors' Owners' Comp/Sales						
3.5	6.3	5.2							
3743559M	3589990M	3828871M	Net Sales ($)	803M	4156M	11291M	69069M	251164M	3492388M
2225223M	2139549M	2647840M	Total Assets ($)	608M	1959M	8643M	44444M	139558M	2452628M

M = $ thousand MM = $ million

See Pages 9 through 22 for Explanation of Ratios and Data

Current Data Sorted by Assets							Comparative Historical Data	
						Type of Statement		
		1	5	4		Unqualified	15	18
	1	3	5			Reviewed	11	7
	4	5				Compiled	7	8
	2			1		Tax Returns	2	3
	3	10	9	3	4	Other	20	27
	12 (4/1-9/30/13)		48 (10/1/13-3/31/14)				4/1/09-3/31/10	4/1/10-3/31/11
0-500M	500M-2MM	2-10MM	10-50MM	50-100MM	100-250MM		ALL	ALL
	10	19	19	8	4	**NUMBER OF STATEMENTS**	55	63
%	%	%	%	%	%	**ASSETS**	%	%
DATA NOT AVAILABLE	8.0	10.4	13.0			Cash & Equivalents	6.4	9.3
	32.2	28.4	27.6			Trade Receivables (net)	28.5	26.6
	27.4	20.1	26.7			Inventory	26.8	28.0
	.1	3.9	2.1			All Other Current	2.1	3.7
	67.8	62.9	69.4			Total Current	63.8	67.7
	29.5	21.3	16.1			Fixed Assets (net)	23.5	21.9
	1.5	3.7	9.7			Intangibles (net)	7.2	5.4
	1.3	12.2	4.8			All Other Non-Current	5.5	5.0
	100.0	100.0	100.0			Total	100.0	100.0
						LIABILITIES		
	2.8	3.5	4.8			Notes Payable-Short Term	11.4	9.1
	3.7	2.0	2.0			Cur. Mat.-L.T.D.	2.6	2.0
	18.6	13.2	13.7			Trade Payables	14.5	16.3
	.0	.5	.1			Income Taxes Payable	.5	.1
	12.2	14.8	10.6			All Other Current	9.2	11.3
	37.3	33.9	31.2			Total Current	38.3	38.8
	20.9	13.5	7.6			Long-Term Debt	14.0	11.9
	.1	.5	.3			Deferred Taxes	.6	.6
	4.6	5.4	11.3			All Other Non-Current	4.5	8.2
	37.1	46.6	49.7			Net Worth	42.6	40.4
	100.0	100.0	100.0			Total Liabilities & Net Worth	100.0	100.0
						INCOME DATA		
	100.0	100.0	100.0			Net Sales	100.0	100.0
	38.0	31.8	29.5			Gross Profit	29.3	28.1
	36.7	26.0	20.9			Operating Expenses	24.0	24.2
	1.3	5.9	8.6			Operating Profit	5.3	3.9
	-.4	.6	1.1			All Other Expenses (net)	2.3	.7
	1.7	5.3	7.5			Profit Before Taxes	3.0	3.2
						RATIOS		
	2.8	3.3	3.5				2.4	2.7
	2.4	2.6	2.4			Current	1.8	2.1
	1.3	1.4	1.7				1.3	1.2
	1.7	1.9	2.2				1.4	1.6
	1.3	1.3	1.7			Quick	.9	1.0
	.8	.8	.8				.6	.6
	31 11.8	35 10.4	39 9.4				40 9.1	39 9.5
	34 10.8	46 7.9	52 7.0			Sales/Receivables	49 7.4	47 7.8
	49 7.4	61 6.0	79 4.6				57 6.4	58 6.3
	34 10.6	24 15.1	54 6.7				51 7.2	50 7.3
	45 8.2	52 7.0	81 4.5			Cost of Sales/Inventory	66 5.5	66 5.6
	96 3.8	74 4.9	122 3.0				87 4.2	111 3.3
	16 22.7	7 53.0	19 19.5				22 17.0	20 18.0
	33 10.9	29 12.5	26 14.2			Cost of Sales/Payables	31 11.8	35 10.4
	57 6.4	51 7.1	46 7.9				44 8.4	54 6.8
	5.2	3.6	2.6				4.6	3.9
	8.5	6.9	4.1			Sales/Working Capital	7.4	6.6
	NM	17.8	6.8				15.9	18.2
		42.5	54.9				11.9	17.8
		(15) 9.9	(17) 12.7			EBIT/Interest	(49) 3.9	(56) 6.2
		4.0	2.2				-1.3	1.6
							6.2	8.6
						Net Profit + Depr., Dep., Amort./Cur. Mat. L/T/D	(20) 3.0	(21) 2.6
							.5	1.1
	.3	.2	.2				.3	.3
	.9	.5	.3			Fixed/Worth	.6	.6
	1.8	.9	2.4				1.4	1.6
	1.0	.6	.3				.7	.5
	2.2	1.2	.6			Debt/Worth	1.3	1.4
	5.8	2.3	5.1				3.9	4.8
	31.9	40.7	39.8				27.3	39.6
	13.6	(17) 26.0	(15) 25.8			% Profit Before Taxes/Tangible Net Worth	(48) 10.0	(55) 18.7
	3.1	6.3	10.3				-8.0	5.0
	9.5	21.4	21.0				11.8	15.8
	4.2	7.5	9.2			% Profit Before Taxes/Total Assets	4.7	6.6
	-.5	2.5	5.0				-1.2	1.1
	40.9	30.0	33.9				16.0	30.7
	9.1	9.1	12.7			Sales/Net Fixed Assets	8.6	9.6
	4.9	6.6	6.3				6.0	5.4
	3.5	2.7	2.1				2.5	2.5
	2.7	2.0	1.7			Sales/Total Assets	1.9	1.8
	2.3	1.5	1.3				1.5	1.3
	.7	.8	.7				.9	.9
	1.1	(15) 1.4	(14) 2.0			% Depr., Dep., Amort./Sales	(50) 1.9	(59) 1.8
	2.8	1.8	2.9				2.8	2.9
							1.2	1.7
						% Officers', Directors' Owners' Comp/Sales	(13) 2.1	(18) 5.1
							6.1	6.5
	45473M	183219M	704375M	742953M	729033M	Net Sales ($)	2074779M	2716906M
	14813M	86587M	433113M	535995M	516522M	Total Assets ($)	1288442M	1642577M

M = $ thousand MM = $ million

See Pages 9 through 22 for Explanation of Ratios and Data

Comparative Historical Data				Current Data Sorted by Sales					
			Type of Statement						
14	11	10	Unqualified				1		9
8	5	9	Reviewed				1	5	3
7	4	9	Compiled		1	2	3	3	
6	6	3	Tax Returns		1		1		1
31	29	29	Other		2	3	4	6	14
4/1/11-3/31/12 ALL	4/1/12-3/31/13 ALL	4/1/13-3/31/14 ALL		12 (4/1-9/30/13)			48 (10/1/13-3/31/14)		
				0-1MM	1-3MM	3-5MM	5-10MM	10-25MM	25MM & OVER
66	55	60	**NUMBER OF STATEMENTS**		4	5	10	14	27
%	%	%	**ASSETS**	%	%	%	%	%	%
8.5	8.1	11.7	Cash & Equivalents	DATA NOT AVAILABLE			5.4	10.2	13.1
32.0	29.5	28.2	Trade Receivables (net)				28.1	33.7	28.0
29.2	30.7	23.7	Inventory				25.9	22.8	24.0
2.6	3.3	2.5	All Other Current				3.1	1.3	2.8
72.3	71.6	66.1	Total Current				62.5	68.0	67.8
18.0	18.0	21.1	Fixed Assets (net)				25.2	15.9	19.8
4.7	4.1	6.5	Intangibles (net)				.3	10.4	8.5
4.9	6.2	6.2	All Other Non-Current				12.0	5.7	3.9
100.0	100.0	100.0	Total				100.0	100.0	100.0
			LIABILITIES						
7.4	8.1	3.7	Notes Payable-Short Term				3.0	4.0	4.6
2.3	2.0	2.2	Cur. Mat.-L.T.D.				2.4	2.0	1.7
15.3	16.9	14.1	Trade Payables				13.5	14.9	14.4
.2	.1	.2	Income Taxes Payable				.0	.7	.2
12.3	12.1	13.9	All Other Current				10.5	18.1	14.5
37.4	39.2	34.2	Total Current				29.4	39.7	35.4
10.3	11.0	12.4	Long-Term Debt				19.5	9.7	8.4
.6	.3	.3	Deferred Taxes				.5	.4	.4
5.6	6.0	7.8	All Other Non-Current				3.8	10.1	9.5
46.1	43.4	45.3	Net Worth				46.8	40.1	46.3
100.0	100.0	100.0	Total Liabilties & Net Worth				100.0	100.0	100.0
			INCOME DATA						
100.0	100.0	100.0	Net Sales				100.0	100.0	100.0
29.6	30.4	30.6	Gross Profit				37.5	30.4	24.8
23.2	25.4	25.0	Operating Expenses				31.3	27.0	17.8
6.4	5.0	5.5	Operating Profit				6.2	3.4	7.0
.5	-.2	.6	All Other Expenses (net)				1.1	1.5	.4
5.9	5.2	5.0	Profit Before Taxes				5.1	1.9	6.6
			RATIOS						
3.0	2.8	3.3					3.4	2.8	3.0
2.2	2.0	2.2	Current				2.5	1.8	2.1
1.3	1.3	1.4					1.4	1.4	1.4
1.6	1.3	1.9					1.7	2.0	2.0
1.0	1.0	1.2	Quick				1.3	1.2	1.1
.8	.7	.8					.9	.9	.7
42 8.6	**38** 9.6	**35** 10.5					**27** 13.6	**45** 8.2	**43** 8.4
51 7.1	**47** 7.8	**50** 7.3	Sales/Receivables				**34** 10.7	**52** 7.0	**54** 6.8
64 5.7	**60** 6.1	**61** 6.0					**45** 8.1	**68** 5.4	**79** 4.6
41 8.9	**46** 8.0	**35** 10.4					**0** UND	**31** 11.8	**36** 10.0
74 4.9	**70** 5.2	**64** 5.7	Cost of Sales/Inventory				**63** 5.8	**54** 6.8	**76** 4.8
111 3.3	**118** 3.1	**99** 3.7					**94** 3.9	**91** 4.0	**104** 3.5
19 19.1	**20** 17.9	**16** 23.5					**8** 47.8	**9** 42.4	**19** 19.1
31 11.9	**30** 12.2	**29** 12.7	Cost of Sales/Payables				**23** 15.8	**25** 14.7	**29** 12.5
43 8.4	**47** 7.8	**49** 7.5					**44** 8.3	**64** 5.7	**46** 7.9
3.7	4.0	3.7					4.6	4.6	3.6
5.5	7.3	6.4	Sales/Working Capital				6.6	7.6	5.0
16.4	13.3	12.5					27.8	19.7	11.9
30.5	76.5	39.9					44.2	27.6	110.8
(50) 9.6	(48) 11.9	(53) 9.4	EBIT/Interest				9.5	(13) 9.4	(25) 12.7
3.6	4.8	2.3					1.9	.4	3.7
18.6		39.3							
(18) 7.3		(16) 5.3	Net Profit + Depr., Dep., Amort./Cur. Mat. L/T/D						
2.6		1.9							
.2	.2	.2					.3	.1	.2
.4	.4	.5	Fixed/Worth				.4	.6	.3
.9	.9	1.5					.9	NM	1.5
.6	.5	.5					.6	.8	.4
1.3	1.6	1.4	Debt/Worth				1.2	1.4	1.3
2.8	3.0	3.3					2.4	NM	2.9
45.3	42.6	32.6					76.0	44.0	32.2
(60) 24.8	(51) 22.3	(53) 18.7	% Profit Before Taxes/Tangible Net Worth				13.7	(11) 26.7	(23) 20.3
9.3	6.1	7.2					3.6	8.6	10.3
17.6	15.2	16.2					28.6	19.8	16.3
10.7	7.2	7.4	% Profit Before Taxes/Total Assets				4.3	9.3	8.9
4.7	3.0	2.3					2.2	-.5	3.4
50.5	31.2	31.4					30.1	60.6	19.0
12.2	12.4	9.1	Sales/Net Fixed Assets				9.3	26.4	8.3
6.4	7.6	5.6					8.1	8.8	5.3
3.0	3.0	2.6					3.5	2.8	2.0
2.0	2.1	2.0	Sales/Total Assets				2.7	2.3	1.6
1.4	1.5	1.3					2.0	2.0	1.2
.6	.7	.8						.6	1.1
(57) 1.4	(47) 1.3	(51) 1.5	% Depr., Dep., Amort./Sales					(11) 1.3	(24) 2.3
2.4	2.3	2.6						1.7	3.0
1.0	1.7								
(17) 4.0	(12) 1.8		% Officers', Directors' Owners' Comp/Sales						
7.4	5.1								
3030146M	2973102M	2405053M	Net Sales ($)		9211M	20888M	65903M	215539M	2093512M
1735699M	1637730M	1587030M	Total Assets ($)		5901M	13381M	27442M	125024M	1415282M

M = $ thousand MM = $ million

See Pages 9 through 22 for Explanation of Ratios and Data

Current Data Sorted by Assets							Comparative Historical Data	
						Type of Statement		
			1	2		Unqualified	10	7
		9	2			Reviewed	16	14
		3				Compiled	9	10
2	1	2				Tax Returns	6	7
1	2	1	3		2	Other	7	9
4 (4/1-9/30/13)		27 (10/1/13-3/31/14)					4/1/09-3/31/10	4/1/10-3/31/11
0-500M	**500M-2MM**	**2-10MM**	**10-50MM**	**50-100MM**	**100-250MM**		**ALL**	**ALL**
3	3	15	6	2	2	**NUMBER OF STATEMENTS**	48	47
%	%	%	%	%	%	**ASSETS**	%	%
		17.9				Cash & Equivalents	16.2	13.6
		42.0				Trade Receivables (net)	30.2	33.4
		23.1				Inventory	23.6	23.7
		.9				All Other Current	3.7	3.9
		84.0				Total Current	73.7	74.6
		12.8				Fixed Assets (net)	17.5	17.0
		.8				Intangibles (net)	4.9	2.2
		2.4				All Other Non-Current	4.0	6.1
		100.0				Total	100.0	100.0
						LIABILITIES		
		6.7				Notes Payable-Short Term	14.6	14.4
		.6				Cur. Mat.-L.T.D.	2.7	1.8
		17.7				Trade Payables	15.7	16.5
		.4				Income Taxes Payable	.3	.2
		9.0				All Other Current	9.3	10.4
		34.4				Total Current	42.6	43.3
		2.9				Long-Term Debt	8.2	7.8
		.2				Deferred Taxes	.5	.3
		3.4				All Other Non-Current	8.4	5.2
		59.2				Net Worth	40.3	43.4
		100.0				Total Liabilties & Net Worth	100.0	100.0
						INCOME DATA		
		100.0				Net Sales	100.0	100.0
		31.8				Gross Profit	30.0	31.5
		24.7				Operating Expenses	26.9	25.1
		7.1				Operating Profit	3.1	6.3
		.1				All Other Expenses (net)	1.1	1.0
		7.0				Profit Before Taxes	2.1	5.3
						RATIOS		
		4.5					3.6	3.4
		2.7				Current	2.2	1.8
		1.7					1.4	1.3
		3.0					2.5	2.3
		1.8				Quick	1.3	1.0
		1.4					.8	.7
		35 10.4					**38** 9.6	**41** 8.9
		54 6.7				Sales/Receivables	**46** 7.9	**51** 7.2
		68 5.4					**57** 6.5	**65** 5.6
		21 17.6					**32** 11.3	**29** 12.5
		42 8.7				Cost of Sales/Inventory	**53** 6.9	**56** 6.5
		76 4.8					**87** 4.2	**77** 4.7
		15 24.3					**20** 18.1	**21** 17.6
		24 15.3				Cost of Sales/Payables	**32** 11.2	**32** 11.5
		52 7.0					**47** 7.7	**49** 7.4
		3.3					4.1	4.3
		6.3				Sales/Working Capital	6.4	7.8
		9.6					12.0	14.7
		130.4					22.1	24.3
		(14) 40.4				EBIT/Interest	(41) 2.9	(42) 6.0
		10.7					-2.5	2.1
							10.5	8.7
						Net Profit + Depr., Dep., Amort./Cur. Mat. L/T/D	(15) 3.7	(14) 2.9
							1.8	.8
		.1					.1	.1
		.2				Fixed/Worth	.3	.3
		.4					.8	.5
		.3					.5	.4
		.6				Debt/Worth	1.1	1.4
		1.4					2.6	3.1
		42.9					32.3	35.0
		(14) 28.1				% Profit Before Taxes/Tangible Net Worth	(40) 11.5	(42) 18.9
		15.1					-2.9	4.1
		31.3					14.2	23.4
		14.2				% Profit Before Taxes/Total Assets	3.8	7.9
		5.7					-5.7	1.0
		88.9					44.6	44.5
		26.1				Sales/Net Fixed Assets	16.9	18.4
		14.6					7.1	8.9
		3.7					2.9	2.8
		2.5				Sales/Total Assets	2.1	2.3
		2.1					1.4	1.8
		.4					.6	.7
		(11) .7				% Depr., Dep., Amort./Sales	(41) 1.2	(42) 1.2
		1.0					2.7	2.3
		2.5					1.6	2.1
		(10) 7.2				% Officers', Directors' Owners' Comp/Sales	(18) 4.1	(20) 3.8
		10.2					12.9	11.3
1631M	6402M	212035M	293747M	277451M	382123M	Net Sales ($)	1178867M	1303929M
636M	2887M	77477M	131447M	156370M	352449M	Total Assets ($)	884635M	763031M

M = $ thousand MM = $ million

See Pages 9 through 22 for Explanation of Ratios and Data

Comparative Historical Data				Current Data Sorted by Sales					
			Type of Statement						
5	1	3	Unqualified						3
8	11	11	Reviewed				2	6	3
7	7	3	Compiled				2	1	
5	1	5	Tax Returns	2	1		2		
17	16	9	Other	1	1	1	1		5
4/1/11-3/31/12 ALL	4/1/12-3/31/13 ALL	4/1/13-3/31/14 ALL		4 (4/1-9/30/13)		27 (10/1/13-3/31/14)			
				0-1MM	1-3MM	3-5MM	5-10MM	10-25MM	25MM & OVER
42	36	31	**NUMBER OF STATEMENTS**	3	2	1	7	7	11
%	%	%	**ASSETS**	%	%	%	%	%	%
13.1	17.2	16.2	Cash & Equivalents						17.4
34.5	29.3	37.1	Trade Receivables (net)						28.8
25.0	30.6	21.9	Inventory						22.7
5.3	3.3	1.9	All Other Current						3.3
77.9	80.4	77.1	Total Current						72.3
14.3	13.6	12.6	Fixed Assets (net)						12.8
4.8	3.4	4.0	Intangibles (net)						10.0
3.1	2.5	6.3	All Other Non-Current						4.9
100.0	100.0	100.0	Total						100.0
			LIABILITIES						
11.6	8.1	9.1	Notes Payable-Short Term						5.6
2.3	.9	1.2	Cur. Mat.-L.T.D.						.6
15.5	15.1	18.5	Trade Payables						15.0
.3	.0	.4	Income Taxes Payable						.2
8.3	17.1	23.6	All Other Current						12.0
38.0	41.4	52.7	Total Current						33.3
5.9	4.7	4.3	Long-Term Debt						5.6
.4	.2	.1	Deferred Taxes						.1
8.8	8.7	14.1	All Other Non-Current						34.9
46.9	45.0	28.8	Net Worth						26.1
100.0	100.0	100.0	Total Liabilties & Net Worth						100.0
			INCOME DATA						
100.0	100.0	100.0	Net Sales						100.0
33.1	35.1	34.2	Gross Profit						32.7
25.8	30.2	27.8	Operating Expenses						24.8
7.3	5.0	6.4	Operating Profit						8.0
.2	.4	.2	All Other Expenses (net)						.5
7.1	4.6	6.3	Profit Before Taxes						7.5
			RATIOS						
3.7	4.2	3.6							3.4
2.4	2.4	2.6	Current						2.6
1.4	1.5	1.6							1.6
2.2	2.1	2.7							1.9
1.4	1.4	1.5	Quick						1.3
.9	.8	.8							.8
44 8.3	**34** 10.7	**38** 9.7							**38** 9.5
51 7.1	**45** 8.2	**50** 7.3	Sales/Receivables						**45** 8.1
69 5.3	**61** 6.0	**66** 5.5							**54** 6.7
27 13.5	**41** 9.0	**29** 12.6							**38** 9.6
57 6.4	**66** 5.5	**51** 7.2	Cost of Sales/Inventory						**57** 6.4
79 4.6	**111** 3.3	**78** 4.7							**126** 2.9
19 19.2	**16** 22.8	**19** 19.3							**19** 19.3
30 12.3	**29** 12.6	**37** 9.9	Cost of Sales/Payables						**36** 10.0
44 8.3	**48** 7.6	**54** 6.8							**46** 7.9
3.3	3.2	3.3							3.1
5.5	5.3	6.2	Sales/Working Capital						5.0
11.7	9.1	9.9							8.9
24.1	81.9	128.8							
(36) 10.3	(29) 10.5	(27) 25.4	EBIT/Interest						
4.9	5.3	5.3							
7.1									
(16) 3.6			Net Profit + Depr., Dep., Amort./Cur. Mat. L/T/D						
1.5									
.1	.1	.1							.1
.3	.3	.2	Fixed/Worth						.2
.5	.5	.6							.8
.5	.6	.4							.6
1.0	.9	.9	Debt/Worth						1.0
3.1	1.9	2.5							4.1
44.2	47.1	54.6							62.2
(39) 27.7	(33) 21.9	(27) 31.7	% Profit Before Taxes/Tangible Net Worth						(10) 45.0
10.5	11.9	15.7							22.6
18.8	24.6	21.3							17.5
10.7	10.4	13.1	% Profit Before Taxes/Total Assets						13.8
4.0	3.5	5.4							7.9
50.8	58.7	70.9							53.1
18.4	21.0	26.1	Sales/Net Fixed Assets						24.9
8.5	9.4	10.9							7.4
2.9	2.9	3.2							2.8
2.1	2.2	2.4	Sales/Total Assets						2.0
1.7	1.7	1.9							1.2
.5	.4	.6							
(38) 1.0	(31) 1.0	(23) .8	% Depr., Dep., Amort./Sales						
1.7	1.8	1.5							
3.1	2.6	2.3							
(14) 6.6	(13) 6.9	(13) 8.0	% Officers', Directors' Owners' Comp/Sales						
10.6	16.3	10.5							
1365480M	1319200M	1173389M	Net Sales ($)	1631M	3256M	3146M	57184M	129833M	978339M
824004M	827192M	721266M	Total Assets ($)	636M	2036M	851M	26879M	43817M	647047M

M = $ thousand MM = $ million

See Pages 9 through 22 for Explanation of Ratios and Data

Current Data Sorted by Assets | **Comparative Historical Data**

0-500M	500M-2MM	2-10MM	10-50MM	50-100MM	100-250MM	Type of Statement	4/1/09-3/31/10 ALL	4/1/10-3/31/11 ALL
		1	4	3		Unqualified	13	15
	1	11	4	1		Reviewed	16	20
	4	4	3			Compiled	13	10
2	2	1	1			Tax Returns	7	13
	2	8	11	4	4	Other	23	32
10 (4/1-9/30/13)			61 (10/1/13-3/31/14)					
2	9	25	23	8	4	**NUMBER OF STATEMENTS**	72	90
%	%	%	%	%	%	**ASSETS**	%	%
		13.1	15.0			Cash & Equivalents	13.4	13.4
		30.7	26.1			Trade Receivables (net)	26.6	29.7
		31.6	30.5			Inventory	28.6	27.0
		4.9	4.3			All Other Current	3.5	4.9
		80.3	75.9			Total Current	72.1	75.0
		13.8	13.9			Fixed Assets (net)	16.1	12.9
		3.3	5.6			Intangibles (net)	6.4	4.5
		2.6	4.5			All Other Non-Current	5.4	7.7
		100.0	100.0			Total	100.0	100.0
						LIABILITIES		
		10.6	4.4			Notes Payable-Short Term	9.5	7.2
		3.0	1.1			Cur. Mat.-L.T.D.	2.6	3.1
		14.4	8.7			Trade Payables	10.5	14.2
		.0	.1			Income Taxes Payable	.1	.1
		12.4	10.8			All Other Current	11.8	12.4
		40.3	25.0			Total Current	34.4	37.0
		9.3	6.9			Long-Term Debt	9.9	9.7
		.0	.3			Deferred Taxes	.3	.4
		7.4	10.9			All Other Non-Current	7.2	7.2
		42.9	57.0			Net Worth	48.2	45.7
		100.0	100.0			Total Liabilties & Net Worth	100.0	100.0
						INCOME DATA		
		100.0	100.0			Net Sales	100.0	100.0
		37.7	35.2			Gross Profit	35.9	37.7
		29.7	23.0			Operating Expenses	30.9	30.1
		8.0	12.2			Operating Profit	5.0	7.6
		.7	1.0			All Other Expenses (net)	1.0	.6
		7.2	11.2			Profit Before Taxes	4.0	7.0
						RATIOS		
		4.1	5.7				4.2	3.5
		2.5	3.1			Current	2.1	2.1
		1.6	2.0				1.4	1.4
		2.4	4.2				2.4	2.4
		1.4	1.5			Quick	1.3	1.2
		.6	.9				.7	.7
		33 11.2	47 7.8				37 10.0	35 10.6
		41 9.0	54 6.7			Sales/Receivables	47 7.7	52 7.1
		68 5.4	65 5.6				59 6.1	64 5.7
		38 9.6	53 6.9				50 7.3	34 10.7
		79 4.6	104 3.5			Cost of Sales/Inventory	95 3.8	80 4.6
		159 2.3	192 1.9				132 2.8	140 2.6
		16 23.2	16 22.8				13 29.1	22 16.8
		24 15.1	29 12.6			Cost of Sales/Payables	23 15.9	30 12.2
		59 6.2	41 8.8				40 9.0	49 7.5
		3.6	1.9				3.7	3.2
		4.9	3.9			Sales/Working Capital	5.1	5.6
		7.5	5.4				10.8	11.0
		18.3	149.9				18.4	40.5
		(19) 8.0	(19) 27.6			EBIT/Interest	(61) 2.7	(76) 10.3
		2.7	10.0				.5	1.9
							11.8	6.7
						Net Profit + Depr., Dep., Amort./Cur. Mat. L/T/D	(17) 4.5	(19) 4.5
							.2	1.6
		.2	.1				.1	.1
		.3	.2			Fixed/Worth	.4	.3
		.9	.4				.9	.6
		.5	.2				.4	.4
		1.2	.6			Debt/Worth	1.0	1.2
		5.0	1.4				3.5	2.8
		111.8	44.3				38.6	49.4
		(24) 40.5	(21) 29.9			% Profit Before Taxes/Tangible Net Worth	(64) 13.7	(83) 22.8
		23.2	14.1				-.3	8.9
		27.2	28.2				16.1	22.7
		14.6	16.7			% Profit Before Taxes/Total Assets	4.6	8.5
		5.9	7.5				-.2	2.3
		42.1	26.9				40.7	60.8
		17.1	13.1			Sales/Net Fixed Assets	16.2	17.5
		11.3	8.9				7.2	9.1
		2.5	2.1				2.8	2.7
		2.1	1.7			Sales/Total Assets	1.9	1.9
		1.6	1.2				1.4	1.3
		.6	.6				.6	.8
		(21) 1.3	(21) 1.4			% Depr., Dep., Amort./Sales	(64) 1.4	(77) 1.3
		1.8	2.4				2.4	2.6
							2.5	2.1
						% Officers', Directors' Owners' Comp/Sales	(24) 5.1	(29) 3.4
							11.2	10.0
2457M	34947M	256736M	806361M	1090986M	742103M	Net Sales ($)	1609917M	1993208M
548M	11463M	111329M	521372M	572803M	534525M	Total Assets ($)	1056357M	1279070M

M = $ thousand MM = $ million

See Pages 9 through 22 for Explanation of Ratios and Data

Comparative Historical Data / Current Data Sorted by Sales

Type of Statement	4/1/11-3/31/12 ALL	4/1/12-3/31/13 ALL	4/1/13-3/31/14 ALL	0-1MM	1-3MM	3-5MM	5-10MM	10-25MM	25MM & OVER
Unqualified	15	9	8					2	6
Reviewed	18	15	17			1	9	2	5
Compiled	11	9	11			5	3	2	1
Tax Returns	13	8	6	1	2	1		1	1
Other	21	21	29		2	2	2	6	17
				10 (4/1-9/30/13)			61 (10/1/13-3/31/14)		
NUMBER OF STATEMENTS	78	62	71	1	4	9	14	13	30
ASSETS	%	%	%	%	%	%	%	%	%
Cash & Equivalents	12.7	12.9	15.3				11.0	15.0	18.6
Trade Receivables (net)	32.7	27.5	28.3				32.2	24.7	27.6
Inventory	25.7	29.7	28.0				34.8	27.4	24.0
All Other Current	3.0	4.0	4.7				3.0	9.8	4.4
Total Current	74.1	74.1	76.2				81.1	76.9	74.6
Fixed Assets (net)	14.3	15.0	13.4				12.2	12.2	15.0
Intangibles (net)	5.4	4.7	5.0				3.0	4.0	6.9
All Other Non-Current	6.2	6.2	5.3				3.8	6.8	3.5
Total	100.0	100.0	100.0				100.0	100.0	100.0
LIABILITIES									
Notes Payable-Short Term	7.1	8.4	6.4				6.7	2.4	5.8
Cur. Mat.-L.T.D.	2.0	1.6	1.8				3.5	.4	1.0
Trade Payables	13.8	12.5	13.1				17.1	8.4	10.9
Income Taxes Payable	.4	.1	.2				.0	.0	.5
All Other Current	15.2	11.9	11.7				14.8	11.6	12.2
Total Current	38.4	34.4	33.1				42.1	22.9	30.3
Long-Term Debt	6.0	9.8	8.9				10.2	4.9	6.6
Deferred Taxes	.4	.3	.4				.0	.0	.9
All Other Non-Current	14.4	10.8	9.0				5.2	9.9	12.0
Net Worth	40.8	44.6	48.5				42.6	62.4	50.3
Total Liabilities & Net Worth	100.0	100.0	100.0				100.0	100.0	100.0
INCOME DATA									
Net Sales	100.0	100.0	100.0				100.0	100.0	100.0
Gross Profit	35.0	34.9	34.8				38.0	41.7	30.7
Operating Expenses	26.7	29.0	26.0				30.4	29.8	20.6
Operating Profit	8.3	5.9	8.8				7.6	12.0	10.0
All Other Expenses (net)	.5	.9	.8				.9	.3	.9
Profit Before Taxes	7.8	5.0	8.0				6.7	11.7	9.1
RATIOS									
Current	3.5	4.2	5.0				2.8	7.1	5.4
	2.0	2.1	2.6				2.1	4.3	2.7
	1.3	1.5	1.6				1.4	3.0	2.0
Quick	2.1	2.3	3.2				1.8	4.2	3.3
	1.3	1.2	1.5				1.2	2.5	1.7
	.8	.8	.9				.5	.9	1.1
Sales/Receivables	38 9.5	32 11.5	38 9.7				33 11.0	33 11.2	46 8.0
	46 7.9	43 8.5	49 7.5				45 8.1	45 8.2	54 6.7
	61 6.0	52 7.0	64 5.7				76 4.8	56 6.5	64 5.7
Cost of Sales/Inventory	29 12.8	33 11.0	41 9.0				62 5.9	33 11.1	38 9.5
	66 5.5	81 4.5	73 5.0				81 4.5	126 2.9	65 5.6
	107 3.4	152 2.4	152 2.4				166 2.2	182 2.0	126 2.9
Cost of Sales/Payables	13 27.2	14 26.5	16 22.8				18 20.0	11 33.3	18 20.4
	26 13.9	27 13.3	26 13.9				36 10.2	24 15.0	25 14.5
	40 9.2	45 8.1	43 8.4				85 4.3	36 10.1	43 8.4
Sales/Working Capital	3.7	3.1	2.9				4.1	2.1	2.0
	6.3	5.4	4.6				5.3	3.4	4.0
	17.5	11.9	7.8				7.5	4.6	6.7
EBIT/Interest	50.6	36.7	75.3				18.2		81.0
	(65) 14.3	(51) 11.0	(54) 12.5				(12) 9.2		(22) 30.1
	4.8	2.2	2.6				3.1		8.8
Net Profit + Depr., Dep., Amort./Cur. Mat. L/T/D	33.9	5.9	41.9						
	(19) 6.5	(13) 3.8	(14) 9.2						
	1.1	1.3	1.4						
Fixed/Worth	.1	.1	.1				.2	.1	.1
	.3	.3	.3				.3	.2	.3
	.8	.8	.7				1.3	.2	1.1
Debt/Worth	.4	.4	.3				.6	.2	.2
	1.2	1.0	1.0				1.5	.5	.7
	2.8	3.3	3.6				5.7	1.9	3.2
% Profit Before Taxes/Tangible Net Worth	53.8	43.2	50.7				101.3	59.4	36.4
	(68) 29.4	(57) 22.4	(65) 29.9				38.8	35.5	(25) 26.4
	16.6	5.3	14.8				26.1	14.6	15.3
% Profit Before Taxes/Total Assets	25.3	17.2	26.2				19.5	34.2	26.7
	13.1	11.7	13.9				12.4	25.1	13.7
	4.6	3.0	4.9				6.1	7.0	5.8
Sales/Net Fixed Assets	45.0	79.9	55.1				48.5	81.5	23.4
	18.6	17.9	16.1				16.8	17.1	14.0
	8.2	8.1	9.4				11.0	10.1	8.9
Sales/Total Assets	3.0	2.6	2.7				2.4	2.3	2.6
	2.3	2.0	2.1				2.1	2.1	1.7
	1.7	1.6	1.4				1.4	1.3	1.3
% Depr., Dep., Amort./Sales	.6	.6	.6				.6	.4	.6
	(67) 1.1	(53) 1.2	(58) 1.4				(11) 1.3	(11) 1.4	(28) 1.4
	2.4	2.0	2.2				1.8	2.5	2.3
% Officers', Directors' Owners' Comp/Sales	1.9	1.9	1.7						
	(26) 3.3	(23) 4.5	(17) 2.5						
	8.3	9.3	8.3						
Net Sales ($)	2322900M	1820121M	2933590M	528M	9882M	34798M	97405M	208224M	2582753M
Total Assets ($)	1365412M	1034315M	1752040M	262M	6125M	14971M	54761M	134054M	1541867M

M = $ thousand MM = $ million

See Pages 9 through 22 for Explanation of Ratios and Data

	Current Data Sorted by Assets						Comparative Historical Data	
Type of Statement								
Unqualified				2			5	6
Reviewed			4	1			3	5
Compiled			1	1			1	2
Tax Returns		2					4	6
Other	2	1	3	6	2	3	7	8
		9 (4/1-9/30/13)		19 (10/1/13-3/31/14)			4/1/09-3/31/10 ALL	4/1/10-3/31/11 ALL
	0-500M	500M-2MM	2-10MM	10-50MM	50-100MM	100-250MM		
NUMBER OF STATEMENTS	2	3	8	10	2	3	20	27
	%	%	%	%	%	%	%	%
ASSETS								
Cash & Equivalents				13.6			12.0	7.8
Trade Receivables (net)				25.8			26.1	27.5
Inventory				28.4			27.2	27.4
All Other Current				4.1			4.1	1.3
Total Current				71.9			69.5	64.0
Fixed Assets (net)				16.2			17.0	21.3
Intangibles (net)				4.3			4.2	6.1
All Other Non-Current				7.6			9.3	8.6
Total				100.0			100.0	100.0
LIABILITIES								
Notes Payable-Short Term				2.4			10.3	6.9
Cur. Mat.-L.T.D.				1.7			2.8	2.2
Trade Payables				11.3			17.2	15.3
Income Taxes Payable				.0			.2	.1
All Other Current				9.7			11.3	10.8
Total Current				25.2			41.8	35.3
Long-Term Debt				7.3			16.5	16.2
Deferred Taxes				1.6			.4	.5
All Other Non-Current				.1			15.2	7.0
Net Worth				65.8			26.1	41.1
Total Liabilties & Net Worth				100.0			100.0	100.0
INCOME DATA								
Net Sales				100.0			100.0	100.0
Gross Profit				22.9			35.9	35.1
Operating Expenses				14.0			30.0	27.4
Operating Profit				8.9			5.9	7.7
All Other Expenses (net)				.2			1.3	1.3
Profit Before Taxes				8.6			4.6	6.3
RATIOS								
Current				5.7			2.5	3.6
				2.1			1.8	2.0
				1.8			1.4	1.2
Quick				3.3			1.3	1.9
				1.4			.8	1.1
				.5			.5	.6
Sales/Receivables				23 15.9			26 14.1	28 13.0
				30 12.1			50 7.4	50 7.3
				66 5.5			56 6.5	62 5.9
Cost of Sales/Inventory				51 7.2			36 10.1	44 8.3
				59 6.2			62 5.9	91 4.0
				74 4.9			117 3.1	114 3.2
Cost of Sales/Payables				0 UND			26 13.9	24 15.3
				17 21.7			47 7.8	39 9.5
				34 10.7			61 5.9	61 6.0
Sales/Working Capital				3.1			4.4	3.5
				5.5			7.5	6.3
				9.2			15.8	28.1
EBIT/Interest							14.9	15.8
							(18) 3.4	(24) 5.5
							1.3	2.1
Net Profit + Depr., Dep., Amort./Cur. Mat. L/T/D								
Fixed/Worth				.1			.2	.2
				.2			1.1	.5
				.5			3.8	1.7
Debt/Worth				.2			.9	.7
				.6			3.2	1.3
				1.0			18.1	9.0
% Profit Before Taxes/Tangible Net Worth				31.6			61.1	52.0
				22.3			(16) 24.2	(23) 29.1
				16.6			6.1	10.3
% Profit Before Taxes/Total Assets				22.1			13.0	21.1
				16.2			7.0	8.5
				6.4			1.8	3.4
Sales/Net Fixed Assets				91.7			76.4	45.4
				18.4			12.3	14.9
				5.7			5.5	6.2
Sales/Total Assets				2.8			2.7	2.6
				2.3			2.1	2.2
				1.7			1.4	1.4
% Depr., Dep., Amort./Sales							.9	.8
							(15) 2.2	(21) 1.8
							3.1	3.4
% Officers', Directors' Owners' Comp/Sales								2.7
								(10) 3.8
								5.9
Net Sales ($)	2709M	8481M	99289M	749453M	275030M	868889M	829271M	1080586M
Total Assets ($)	774M	4739M	32203M	259850M	169903M	535748M	446119M	495412M

M = $ thousand MM = $ million

See Pages 9 through 22 for Explanation of Ratios and Data

Comparative Historical Data				Current Data Sorted by Sales					
			Type of Statement						
7	7	2	Unqualified					1	1
3	2	5	Reviewed				1	3	1
1	2	2	Compiled			1			1
6	5	2	Tax Returns		2				
15	15	17	Other	1	1	1	3		11
4/1/11-3/31/12	**4/1/12-3/31/13**	**4/1/13-3/31/14**		**9 (4/1-9/30/13)**			**19 (10/1/13-3/31/14)**		
ALL	**ALL**	**ALL**		**0-1MM**	**1-3MM**	**3-5MM**	**5-10MM**	**10-25MM**	**25MM & OVER**
32	31	28	**NUMBER OF STATEMENTS**	1	3	2	4	4	14
%	%	%	**ASSETS**	%	%	%	%	%	%
6.4	5.1	8.4	Cash & Equivalents						11.2
28.6	37.8	27.9	Trade Receivables (net)						30.6
30.3	29.2	30.3	Inventory						29.4
1.4	.4	3.9	All Other Current						3.5
66.7	72.6	70.4	Total Current						74.7
23.1	16.1	15.2	Fixed Assets (net)						17.1
4.2	5.3	6.8	Intangibles (net)						6.0
6.0	6.1	7.5	All Other Non-Current						2.2
100.0	100.0	100.0	Total						100.0
			LIABILITIES						
11.5	11.7	17.0	Notes Payable-Short Term						3.5
4.0	4.5	3.6	Cur. Mat.-L.T.D.						1.9
18.7	26.3	19.2	Trade Payables						17.8
.3	.0	.1	Income Taxes Payable						.1
9.6	8.6	10.6	All Other Current						8.2
44.0	51.0	50.6	Total Current						31.3
20.7	15.1	13.3	Long-Term Debt						14.8
.5	.8	1.0	Deferred Taxes						1.2
3.9	3.6	3.1	All Other Non-Current						3.3
31.0	29.4	31.9	Net Worth						49.3
100.0	100.0	100.0	Total Liabilties & Net Worth						100.0
			INCOME DATA						
100.0	100.0	100.0	Net Sales						100.0
34.8	27.7	24.2	Gross Profit						18.1
30.5	22.9	17.7	Operating Expenses						13.1
4.3	4.8	6.5	Operating Profit						5.1
.6	.8	1.3	All Other Expenses (net)						1.5
3.7	4.0	5.3	Profit Before Taxes						3.5
			RATIOS						
3.1	2.2	3.2							4.6
1.9	1.6	1.9	Current						2.0
1.1	1.2	1.3							1.6
1.6	1.3	2.2							2.7
.8	1.0	1.0	Quick						1.2
.5	.7	.5							.8
34 10.8	**41** 8.8	**25** 14.6							**26** 14.2
46 7.9	**54** 6.8	**43** 8.4	Sales/Receivables						**58** 6.3
59 6.2	**61** 6.0	**64** 5.7							**69** 5.3
53 6.9	**33** 11.1	**49** 7.4							**48** 7.6
78 4.7	**56** 6.5	**69** 5.3	Cost of Sales/Inventory						**55** 6.6
111 3.3	**111** 3.3	**94** 3.9							**73** 5.0
30 12.2	**27** 13.5	**14** 25.2							**10** 36.8
38 9.6	**35** 10.3	**37** 9.8	Cost of Sales/Payables						**34** 10.6
55 6.6	**59** 6.2	**60** 6.1							**54** 6.8
4.0	6.6	4.1							3.1
7.4	8.9	7.9	Sales/Working Capital						6.2
48.5	33.2	14.0							9.6
11.6	43.5	34.6							
(28) 4.4	(29) 5.6	(22) 4.8	EBIT/Interest						
.7	1.5	1.1							
	5.9								
	(11) 2.3		Net Profit + Depr., Dep., Amort./Cur. Mat. L/T/D						
	1.0								
.2	.1	.0							.1
1.3	.4	.4	Fixed/Worth						.3
6.3	2.4	6.0							3.2
.8	.9	.3							.3
1.8	2.8	1.6	Debt/Worth						.9
23.1	13.9	69.0							6.8
60.8	68.6	102.2							35.6
(25) 36.7	(28) 32.3	(22) 27.0	% Profit Before Taxes/Tangible Net Worth						(12) 18.6
6.5	10.4	3.3							5.9
21.5	18.0	21.0							20.3
10.5	7.5	8.9	% Profit Before Taxes/Total Assets						12.1
1.4	.4	1.0							1.1
36.7	78.0	127.2							91.7
16.0	21.4	19.0	Sales/Net Fixed Assets						18.4
4.5	8.1	7.4							7.0
2.7	3.5	3.1							2.8
2.2	2.0	2.5	Sales/Total Assets						2.3
1.5	1.8	1.5							1.6
.7	.7	.5							
(25) 1.8	(24) 1.9	(20) 1.2	% Depr., Dep., Amort./Sales						
3.1	2.6	2.2							
2.8	1.4								
(13) 3.3	(11) 2.4		% Officers', Directors' Owners' Comp/Sales						
7.0	6.2								
1386377M	2152474M	2003851M	Net Sales ($)	865M	6304M	7392M	31032M	72150M	1886108M
667372M	986009M	1003217M	Total Assets ($)	335M	4112M	3497M	13900M	38870M	942503M

M = $ thousand MM = $ million

See Pages 9 through 22 for Explanation of Ratios and Data

Current Data Sorted by Assets							Comparative Historical Data	
						Type of Statement		
		2	5	3	2	Unqualified	15	13
		6	4			Reviewed	11	16
	1	5	2			Compiled	11	14
	4	1				Tax Returns	4	8
	1	7	8	1	3	Other	22	21
	5 (4/1-9/30/13)		50 (10/1/13-3/31/14)				4/1/09-3/31/10	4/1/10-3/31/11
0-500M	**500M-2MM**	**2-10MM**	**10-50MM**	**50-100MM**	**100-250MM**		**ALL**	**ALL**
	6	21	19	4	5	**NUMBER OF STATEMENTS**	63	72
%	%	%	%	%	%	**ASSETS**	%	%
DATA NOT AVAILABLE		9.1	14.7			Cash & Equivalents	10.6	12.3
		29.3	22.9			Trade Receivables (net)	23.9	27.2
		40.3	29.0			Inventory	29.3	30.5
		.8	1.8			All Other Current	2.1	2.4
		79.5	68.4			Total Current	65.9	72.5
		15.9	19.2			Fixed Assets (net)	20.2	17.2
		.8	9.7			Intangibles (net)	6.5	5.3
		3.8	2.7			All Other Non-Current	7.4	5.0
		100.0	100.0			Total	100.0	100.0
						LIABILITIES		
		9.3	8.4			Notes Payable-Short Term	7.4	10.0
		2.1	.9			Cur. Mat.-L.T.D.	3.6	2.5
		15.5	10.1			Trade Payables	12.1	16.5
		.2	.3			Income Taxes Payable	.1	.2
		9.0	8.5			All Other Current	8.9	11.2
		36.1	28.2			Total Current	32.2	40.5
		11.2	5.9			Long-Term Debt	10.3	10.8
		.2	1.4			Deferred Taxes	1.0	.5
		4.8	.4			All Other Non-Current	6.2	4.6
		47.6	64.2			Net Worth	50.2	43.6
		100.0	100.0			Total Liabilities & Net Worth	100.0	100.0
						INCOME DATA		
		100.0	100.0			Net Sales	100.0	100.0
		29.1	32.6			Gross Profit	30.4	32.9
		24.4	24.1			Operating Expenses	25.1	25.9
		4.7	8.5			Operating Profit	5.4	7.0
		.6	.6			All Other Expenses (net)	1.0	1.0
		4.1	7.9			Profit Before Taxes	4.4	5.9
						RATIOS		
		3.3	7.0				3.7	3.4
		2.6	3.4			Current	2.2	2.0
		1.6	1.3				1.3	1.3
		1.8	3.6				2.2	2.0
		1.1	1.5			Quick	1.2	1.0
		.6	.7				.6	.5
		30 12.0	**38** 9.6				**33** 11.1	**37** 9.9
		40 9.1	**45** 8.2			Sales/Receivables	**46** 7.9	**45** 8.1
		46 8.0	**59** 6.2				**52** 7.0	**52** 7.0
		54 6.8	**72** 5.1				**53** 6.9	**49** 7.4
		81 4.5	**89** 4.1			Cost of Sales/Inventory	**84** 4.3	**85** 4.3
		126 2.9	**130** 2.8				**118** 3.1	**114** 3.2
		16 22.4	**13** 27.9				**17** 21.0	**23** 16.1
		26 14.0	**21** 17.3			Cost of Sales/Payables	**28** 13.2	**33** 11.0
		40 9.1	**30** 12.0				**43** 8.4	**47** 7.7
		4.0	2.9				3.6	3.8
		5.6	4.8			Sales/Working Capital	6.2	7.1
		8.9	10.6				13.0	13.2
		16.1	144.9				16.9	17.1
		(18) 7.7	(14) 33.2			EBIT/Interest	(54) 4.4	(59) 6.8
		2.9	4.7				.4	2.7
							8.0	4.9
						Net Profit + Depr., Dep., Amort./Cur. Mat. L/T/D	(19) 2.9	(19) 3.3
							.2	2.1
		.2	.1				.2	.1
		.3	.2			Fixed/Worth	.5	.4
		.5	.4				.9	1.4
		.5	.2				.5	.5
		1.1	.4			Debt/Worth	1.1	1.4
		2.6	2.4				3.3	6.1
		37.5	28.9				39.9	45.0
		17.2	(18) 22.4			% Profit Before Taxes/Tangible Net Worth	(57) 14.8	(65) 28.2
		7.7	9.2				-1.4	12.2
		18.1	20.6				18.7	20.6
		6.8	13.8			% Profit Before Taxes/Total Assets	5.9	11.6
		3.9	5.4				-.2	4.3
		44.9	29.2				34.6	46.5
		13.5	11.8			Sales/Net Fixed Assets	12.0	16.1
		8.9	5.9				5.1	7.4
		3.0	2.5				2.4	2.7
		2.4	1.9			Sales/Total Assets	2.0	2.2
		1.9	1.2				1.4	1.6
		.5	.7				.9	.7
		1.4	1.3			% Depr., Dep., Amort./Sales	(52) 2.1	(56) 1.4
		2.4	2.6				3.4	2.6
		2.0					2.7	2.9
		(10) 3.0				% Officers', Directors' Owners' Comp/Sales	(19) 4.4	(22) 6.4
		7.2					7.0	9.8
	21240M	363995M	904020M	434929M	1994561M	Net Sales ($)	4269545M	3614802M
	8511M	119644M	493180M	261588M	1042954M	Total Assets ($)	2479891M	1883250M

M = $ thousand MM = $ million

See Pages 9 through 22 for Explanation of Ratios and Data

Comparative Historical Data				Current Data Sorted by Sales					
			Type of Statement						
14	12	12	Unqualified					3	9
10	9	10	Reviewed			1	1	5	3
8	11	8	Compiled		1	1	2	1	3
8	4	5	Tax Returns		1	3		1	
22	29	20	Other			1	2	5	12
					5 (4/1-9/30/13)		50 (10/1/13-3/31/14)		
4/1/11-3/31/12 ALL	**4/1/12-3/31/13 ALL**	**4/1/13-3/31/14 ALL**		**0-1MM**	**1-3MM**	**3-5MM**	**5-10MM**	**10-25MM**	**25MM & OVER**
62	65	55	**NUMBER OF STATEMENTS**		2	6	5	15	27
%	%	%	**ASSETS**	%	%	%	%	%	%
8.6	8.2	10.7	Cash & Equivalents	DATA NOT AVAILABLE				9.1	11.5
29.2	26.8	25.5	Trade Receivables (net)					24.2	26.0
32.1	32.4	33.4	Inventory					39.0	31.2
1.2	2.3	1.7	All Other Current					.6	2.4
71.1	69.7	71.3	Total Current					72.9	71.0
19.8	16.3	18.3	Fixed Assets (net)					19.7	15.0
4.8	9.0	6.2	Intangibles (net)					1.6	9.6
4.3	4.9	4.2	All Other Non-Current					5.8	4.4
100.0	100.0	100.0	Total					100.0	100.0
			LIABILITIES						
10.2	8.4	7.9	Notes Payable-Short Term					8.9	5.0
2.9	1.9	1.7	Cur. Mat.-L.T.D.					1.3	1.7
13.5	12.9	12.6	Trade Payables					12.7	14.6
.2	.2	.4	Income Taxes Payable					.2	.7
11.2	6.3	8.1	All Other Current					8.9	8.5
38.0	29.7	30.7	Total Current					32.0	30.6
9.7	15.2	10.5	Long-Term Debt					5.8	9.7
.8	.8	.9	Deferred Taxes					.1	1.6
4.0	5.6	3.2	All Other Non-Current					6.3	2.4
47.6	48.8	54.8	Net Worth					55.8	55.7
100.0	100.0	100.0	Total Liabilties & Net Worth					100.0	100.0
			INCOME DATA						
100.0	100.0	100.0	Net Sales					100.0	100.0
30.3	27.0	31.4	Gross Profit					33.8	28.0
24.4	21.6	24.9	Operating Expenses					28.1	20.9
5.9	5.5	6.5	Operating Profit					5.7	7.0
1.2	1.2	.8	All Other Expenses (net)					.4	.8
4.7	4.2	5.7	Profit Before Taxes					5.3	6.2
			RATIOS						
3.0	3.9	3.6						3.9	3.7
1.9	2.4	2.6	Current					2.6	2.6
1.3	1.7	1.6						1.6	1.7
1.7	2.3	2.0						1.7	2.1
1.0	1.1	1.2	Quick					1.1	1.3
.6	.7	.7						.5	.7
40 9.1	**34** 10.8	**33** 11.1						**33** 11.1	**33** 10.9
46 7.9	**42** 8.7	**43** 8.4	Sales/Receivables					**40** 9.1	**44** 8.3
53 6.9	**56** 6.5	**49** 7.4						**47** 7.7	**49** 7.4
54 6.8	**52** 7.0	**61** 6.0						**51** 7.1	**61** 6.0
73 5.0	**72** 5.1	**81** 4.5	Cost of Sales/Inventory					**89** 4.1	**76** 4.8
101 3.6	**118** 3.1	**122** 3.0						**152** 2.4	**118** 3.1
18 20.1	**19** 19.3	**14** 25.4						**19** 19.2	**14** 26.5
30 12.1	**28** 13.0	**24** 15.0	Cost of Sales/Payables					**30** 12.0	**24** 15.0
45 8.1	**38** 9.5	**36** 10.2						**43** 8.5	**33** 10.9
4.1	3.8	3.6						2.6	4.0
6.9	5.3	5.0	Sales/Working Capital					6.5	4.8
16.8	8.4	10.3						10.3	10.6
36.3	26.8	30.1						96.0	53.1
(56) 8.2	(56) 6.5	(45) 8.2	EBIT/Interest					(13) 8.1	(20) 8.7
2.6	1.9	2.9						3.0	2.3
9.0	9.1	19.4							
(18) 2.5	(19) 5.3	(18) 3.5	Net Profit + Depr., Dep., Amort./Cur. Mat. L/T/D						
1.6	1.0	2.0							
.1	.1	.2						.2	.1
.4	.4	.3	Fixed/Worth					.2	.3
1.1	.7	.6						.6	.6
.6	.5	.4						.3	.3
1.2	1.2	.9	Debt/Worth					.8	.8
3.5	3.0	2.1						2.1	2.6
46.0	36.1	36.4						25.4	38.3
(58) 27.7	(56) 26.2	(53) 21.2	% Profit Before Taxes/Tangible Net Worth					18.0	(25) 23.4
6.7	9.9	8.7						4.8	9.7
18.5	20.2	20.4						17.0	20.6
11.1	8.7	10.4	% Profit Before Taxes/Total Assets					6.4	11.0
2.7	2.7	2.8						2.5	3.1
34.0	35.3	30.7						30.7	39.2
14.0	14.2	12.7	Sales/Net Fixed Assets					12.7	13.1
6.7	9.3	7.4						5.4	8.1
2.8	2.7	2.6						3.0	2.6
2.2	2.1	2.0	Sales/Total Assets					2.0	2.0
1.8	1.6	1.7						1.5	1.6
.6	.5	.8						.7	.6
(56) 1.5	(55) 1.2	(50) 1.4	% Depr., Dep., Amort./Sales					2.3	(23) 1.1
2.7	2.3	2.7						2.9	1.7
1.8	1.1	1.5							
(20) 3.2	(19) 2.6	(20) 2.7	% Officers', Directors' Owners' Comp/Sales						
5.7	6.0	6.5							
4022982M	5372810M	3718745M	Net Sales ($)		4852M	24877M	41852M	239084M	3408080M
2000236M	2869282M	1925877M	Total Assets ($)		2705M	11206M	28337M	128205M	1755424M

M = $ thousand MM = $ million

See Pages 9 through 22 for Explanation of Ratios and Data

Current Data Sorted by Assets | **Comparative Historical Data**

0-500M	500M-2MM	2-10MM	10-50MM	50-100MM	100-250MM		4/1/09-3/31/10 ALL	4/1/10-3/31/11 ALL
						Type of Statement		
		9	10	5	4	Unqualified	46	29
	2	17	8			Reviewed	38	47
2	7	12	6			Compiled	28	32
3	9	16	1			Tax Returns	33	33
7	13	40	25	5	11	Other	101	122
21 (4/1-9/30/13)		191 (10/1/13-3/31/14)						
12	31	94	50	10	15	**NUMBER OF STATEMENTS**	246	263
%	%	%	%	%	%	**ASSETS**	%	%
19.4	14.6	13.1	12.7	6.8	13.7	Cash & Equivalents	10.5	11.5
25.6	29.1	27.9	24.2	18.5	17.7	Trade Receivables (net)	26.5	29.5
33.2	32.3	26.8	30.0	22.5	16.8	Inventory	29.4	28.3
.4	2.4	2.6	2.1	1.7	9.8	All Other Current	3.6	3.3
78.7	78.4	70.4	69.0	49.4	58.0	Total Current	70.0	72.6
13.3	13.1	18.8	15.5	9.8	9.7	Fixed Assets (net)	17.3	14.1
.3	5.5	4.6	11.0	31.8	27.2	Intangibles (net)	7.6	6.9
7.7	3.0	6.2	4.5	9.0	5.1	All Other Non-Current	5.2	6.4
100.0	100.0	100.0	100.0	100.0	100.0	Total	100.0	100.0
						LIABILITIES		
18.1	13.3	7.7	9.2	10.2	2.9	Notes Payable-Short Term	10.9	9.6
2.3	1.2	2.0	2.3	1.5	1.3	Cur. Mat.-L.T.D.	3.2	2.4
18.7	13.1	19.3	12.2	7.6	9.7	Trade Payables	14.1	15.2
.0	.3	.1	.3	.1	.6	Income Taxes Payable	.3	.2
43.4	5.4	11.5	8.4	8.3	14.2	All Other Current	12.1	10.9
82.5	33.3	40.7	32.4	27.6	28.7	Total Current	40.6	38.3
4.2	12.3	14.1	11.7	10.3	20.0	Long-Term Debt	12.3	10.3
.0	.1	.2	.8	2.5	2.0	Deferred Taxes	.3	.4
11.8	5.2	4.2	6.2	14.1	3.4	All Other Non-Current	5.3	4.9
1.5	49.2	40.9	48.9	45.5	45.9	Net Worth	41.4	46.1
100.0	100.0	100.0	100.0	100.0	100.0	Total Liabilities & Net Worth	100.0	100.0
						INCOME DATA		
100.0	100.0	100.0	100.0	100.0	100.0	Net Sales	100.0	100.0
43.9	45.8	36.5	34.5	35.9	35.8	Gross Profit	34.6	35.8
41.0	39.4	29.9	27.8	26.1	27.1	Operating Expenses	30.1	29.1
3.0	6.4	6.6	6.7	9.8	8.7	Operating Profit	4.4	6.7
-.1	.1	.7	.4	3.7	2.8	All Other Expenses (net)	1.3	.8
3.1	6.3	5.9	6.3	6.1	5.9	Profit Before Taxes	3.2	5.9
						RATIOS		
2.9	6.6	3.1	4.1	3.6	3.3		3.1	3.6
1.5	2.9	1.7	2.3	2.0	2.0	Current	1.8	2.0
.6	1.5	1.2	1.5	1.5	1.3		1.2	1.3
1.5	5.4	2.0	2.4	1.6	2.0		1.7	1.9
.8	1.2	1.1	1.3	1.0	1.1	Quick	.9	1.1
.1	.6	.6	.7	.6	.4		.5	.6
13 28.6	**22** 16.9	**29** 12.6	**43** 8.5	**43** 8.4	**46** 8.0		**32** 11.6	**34** 10.6
32 11.4	**37** 9.8	**45** 8.2	**50** 7.3	**50** 7.3	**54** 6.7	Sales/Receivables	**44** 8.3	**48** 7.6
45 8.1	**51** 7.2	**62** 5.9	**62** 5.9	**58** 6.3	**65** 5.6		**59** 6.2	**60** 6.0
19 18.9	**11** 34.0	**34** 10.8	**68** 5.4	**73** 5.0	**43** 8.4		**44** 8.4	**39** 9.4
36 10.1	**72** 5.1	**69** 5.3	**94** 3.9	**122** 3.0	**70** 5.2	Cost of Sales/Inventory	**75** 4.9	**72** 5.1
152 2.4	**182** 2.0	**114** 3.2	**182** 2.0	**166** 2.2	**130** 2.8		**115** 3.2	**120** 3.0
17 21.2	**10** 35.4	**23** 16.0	**19** 18.9	**17** 21.1	**31** 11.6		**19** 19.3	**18** 19.9
33 11.1	**21** 17.7	**41** 8.9	**35** 10.4	**33** 11.2	**46** 7.9	Cost of Sales/Payables	**31** 11.8	**34** 10.7
56 6.5	**52** 7.0	**69** 5.3	**54** 6.8	**49** 7.5	**64** 5.7		**50** 7.4	**52** 7.0
5.5	2.8	4.0	2.7	2.8	2.8		3.8	3.8
22.5	5.5	7.0	4.3	5.0	3.4	Sales/Working Capital	7.6	6.7
NM	15.9	24.1	8.1	10.5	12.7		18.4	18.0
	23.0	30.4	60.5		57.2		15.8	28.8
	(26) 5.8	(78) 6.3	(40) 11.1		(11) 3.3	EBIT/Interest	(221) 4.0	(219) 10.5
	1.7	2.6	1.9		.2		1.0	2.3
		10.7	8.8			Net Profit + Depr., Dep.,	4.6	5.7
		(13) 4.4	(14) 4.4			Amort./Cur. Mat. L/T/D	(56) 2.2	(54) 2.3
		.8	3.2				.4	1.0
.2	.1	.1	.1	.2	.1		.2	.1
.3	.2	.3	.4	.6	.3	Fixed/Worth	.4	.3
NM	.7	1.3	.9	-.9	-.3		1.4	.8
1.0	.3	.6	.5	1.5	.5		.7	.5
4.0	1.1	1.8	1.0	3.8	2.2	Debt/Worth	1.6	1.3
NM	5.4	4.6	3.0	-4.2	-2.7		5.3	3.1
	69.9	54.3	42.6			% Profit Before Taxes/Tangible	45.0	55.0
	(27) 20.4	(84) 26.6	(42) 23.8			Net Worth	(212) 18.5	(230) 28.4
	4.6	8.9	7.8				1.9	9.0
33.6	26.0	19.7	18.4	18.1	14.9	% Profit Before Taxes/Total	14.9	21.9
16.9	11.6	9.8	9.3	7.9	7.7	Assets	6.2	10.6
-4.1	2.3	2.7	3.0	3.0	-1.8		.1	2.5
87.0	53.6	59.5	35.4	25.5	44.0		51.4	54.9
28.5	27.6	17.0	14.2	11.2	21.4	Sales/Net Fixed Assets	16.0	20.1
14.6	12.9	7.8	6.2	7.4	7.4		6.7	10.3
3.8	4.3	2.8	2.2	2.4	1.5		3.0	3.1
3.0	2.7	2.1	1.6	.9	1.2	Sales/Total Assets	2.0	2.1
1.5	1.7	1.7	1.1	.6	.7		1.5	1.5
	.5	.5	.6				.7	.6
	(20) .8	(72) 1.3	(43) 1.1			% Depr., Dep., Amort./Sales	(195) 1.6	(200) 1.4
	2.1	2.2	2.7				3.4	2.6
	4.5	2.0				% Officers', Directors'	2.5	2.3
	(18) 5.8	(28) 2.9				Owners' Comp/Sales	(73) 4.6	(90) 3.9
	9.3	5.2					9.0	6.9
12095M	109547M	1065951M	2010288M	944591M	2543219M	Net Sales ($)	8400981M	8144131M
3843M	37736M	474299M	1172798M	760107M	2356021M	Total Assets ($)	4978297M	4959778M

M = $ thousand MM = $ million

See Pages 9 through 22 for Explanation of Ratios and Data

Comparative Historical Data | **Current Data Sorted by Sales**

4/1/11-3/31/12 ALL	4/1/12-3/31/13 ALL	4/1/13-3/31/14 ALL	Type of Statement	0-1MM	1-3MM	3-5MM	5-10MM	10-25MM	25MM & OVER
47	32	28	Unqualified				4	6	18
56	28	27	Reviewed			2	9	9	7
37	24	27	Compiled		7	2	7	9	2
40	48	29	Tax Returns	4	5	1	10	9	
103	119	101	Other	7	8	8	19	29	30
					21 (4/1-9/30/13)		191 (10/1/13-3/31/14)		
283	251	212	NUMBER OF STATEMENTS	11	20	13	49	62	57
%	%	%	**ASSETS**	%	%	%	%	%	%
10.3	11.4	13.3	Cash & Equivalents	18.1	16.0	8.6	12.7	15.8	10.5
29.0	26.7	25.9	Trade Receivables (net)	18.7	29.1	31.2	25.0	28.1	23.5
29.4	30.7	27.8	Inventory	32.0	27.3	31.9	28.6	27.6	25.8
2.5	2.9	2.8	All Other Current	2.4	1.9	2.0	1.9	2.2	4.7
71.3	71.7	69.8	Total Current	71.3	74.2	73.7	68.1	73.7	64.4
16.5	16.1	15.8	Fixed Assets (net)	18.6	15.2	20.6	18.2	14.8	13.5
7.1	6.1	8.9	Intangibles (net)	2.7	2.9	1.2	8.4	7.3	16.1
5.2	6.1	5.4	All Other Non-Current	7.4	7.7	4.4	5.2	4.3	6.0
100.0	100.0	100.0	Total	100.0	100.0	100.0	100.0	100.0	100.0
			LIABILITIES						
9.9	11.0	9.2	Notes Payable-Short Term	9.5	16.4	10.4	8.6	8.5	7.8
2.6	1.8	1.9	Cur. Mat.-L.T.D.	1.6	2.1	.6	2.1	1.8	2.2
15.8	14.1	15.5	Trade Payables	15.8	12.5	12.1	14.7	20.1	12.7
.2	.2	.2	Income Taxes Payable	.0	.0	.7	.2	.0	.4
12.3	10.2	11.7	All Other Current	34.1	13.8	6.4	7.2	13.0	10.5
40.9	37.2	38.6	Total Current	61.1	44.8	30.3	32.8	43.4	33.6
10.5	10.8	12.9	Long-Term Debt	19.8	8.4	13.5	17.7	7.8	14.5
.5	.4	.5	Deferred Taxes	.0	.1	.0	.1	.5	1.2
9.1	10.3	5.7	All Other Non-Current	18.1	4.6	.8	4.6	4.5	6.8
39.0	41.4	42.3	Net Worth	1.0	42.1	55.4	44.7	43.7	43.9
100.0	100.0	100.0	Total Liabilties & Net Worth	100.0	100.0	100.0	100.0	100.0	100.0
			INCOME DATA						
100.0	100.0	100.0	Net Sales	100.0	100.0	100.0	100.0	100.0	100.0
36.7	35.6	37.7	Gross Profit	44.6	51.4	38.8	37.6	37.5	31.6
29.2	29.9	31.0	Operating Expenses	39.2	42.9	35.1	33.7	29.5	23.8
7.5	5.7	6.7	Operating Profit	5.5	8.5	3.7	3.9	8.0	7.9
.9	.7	.8	All Other Expenses (net)	-.1	.0	.3	.8	.5	1.7
6.6	5.1	5.9	Profit Before Taxes	5.6	8.5	3.5	3.1	7.5	6.2
			RATIOS						
3.1	3.9	4.0		3.2	7.9	5.2	5.1	3.0	3.2
1.8	2.1	1.9	Current	1.7	2.6	2.5	2.1	1.6	1.9
1.3	1.4	1.3		.9	1.1	1.5	1.3	1.2	1.5
1.6	2.1	2.1		1.3	7.1	2.8	2.8	1.9	1.8
1.0	1.1	1.1	Quick	.6	1.4	1.3	1.2	.9	1.1
.6	.6	.6		.2	.5	.8	.7	.6	.6
35 10.5	**30** 12.0	**34** 10.7		**15** 24.5	**21** 17.3	**35** 10.3	**29** 12.6	**29** 12.5	**45** 8.2
49 7.5	**46** 8.0	**46** 8.0	Sales/Receivables	**37** 9.8	**42** 8.7	**51** 7.2	**40** 9.1	**46** 8.0	**49** 7.4
61 6.0	**58** 6.3	**61** 6.0		**46** 8.0	**64** 5.7	**59** 6.2	**65** 5.6	**63** 5.8	**58** 6.3
43 8.4	**43** 8.4	**41** 8.8		**6** 58.5	**0** UND	**41** 8.8	**42** 8.7	**35** 10.3	**55** 6.6
78 4.7	**79** 4.6	**79** 4.6	Cost of Sales/Inventory	**32** 11.3	**54** 6.8	**73** 5.0	**74** 4.9	**83** 4.4	**83** 4.4
126 2.9	**140** 2.6	**140** 2.6		**304** 1.2	**166** 2.2	**146** 2.5	**135** 2.7	**152** 2.4	**130** 2.8
21 17.2	**18** 20.8	**20** 18.4		**30** 12.0	**11** 32.0	**6** 63.4	**19** 18.8	**21** 17.5	**23** 15.9
33 11.0	**29** 12.5	**37** 9.9	Cost of Sales/Payables	**68** 5.4	**25** 14.7	**15** 25.1	**40** 9.2	**45** 8.2	**35** 10.5
54 6.7	**50** 7.3	**58** 6.3		**114** 3.2	**45** 8.2	**57** 6.4	**55** 6.6	**76** 4.8	**54** 6.8
3.9	3.2	3.3		3.0	2.7	3.0	3.6	3.2	3.3
6.6	6.1	6.0	Sales/Working Capital	9.4	5.3	5.4	6.1	7.2	5.5
15.8	15.3	15.2		-157.2	90.7	10.9	19.7	17.0	10.1
30.5	34.6	30.1			20.8	71.0	18.9	40.1	40.4
(246) 8.3	(205) 8.7	(169) 6.4	EBIT/Interest		(15) 6.4	5.7	(41) 5.7	(51) 16.0	(43) 4.0
3.1	2.1	2.0			2.1	-.3	1.9	4.4	.3
8.6	12.2	7.9						15.0	8.7
(62) 2.5	(35) 3.3	(37) 4.4	Net Profit + Depr., Dep., Amort./Cur. Mat. L/T/D					(10) 6.2	(18) 7.0
1.2	1.0	2.9						3.7	2.8
.1	.1	.1		.1	.1	.1	.1	.1	.2
.4	.3	.3	Fixed/Worth	.3	.3	.2	.3	.3	.4
1.1	.9	1.2		-.6	1.1	.8	1.6	.9	5.8
.6	.4	.5		1.3	.4	.3	.4	.6	.6
1.7	1.2	1.6	Debt/Worth	5.4	.9	.6	2.2	1.5	1.8
5.4	4.2	5.2		-2.8	6.3	1.8	6.2	4.1	12.9
55.7	54.1	51.2			145.7	48.2	46.1	55.8	50.5
(245) 32.8	(224) 26.4	(178) 25.7	% Profit Before Taxes/Tangible Net Worth		(18) 37.8	(12) 13.3	(42) 20.3	(55) 26.6	(44) 31.0
11.9	6.8	9.3			11.2	-2.0	3.5	16.4	18.7
20.0	21.1	18.4		18.4	35.7	14.1	18.5	19.3	18.2
11.2	8.5	9.8	% Profit Before Taxes/Total Assets	3.4	14.6	4.0	6.3	12.1	10.9
4.4	1.8	2.6		-5.1	3.5	.1	1.3	6.5	.9
44.7	67.9	46.9		150.2	53.3	45.5	43.4	79.3	35.2
16.8	20.8	18.9	Sales/Net Fixed Assets	19.6	22.7	20.4	16.8	24.0	15.1
7.8	8.1	8.0		5.3	11.0	5.0	6.0	9.1	7.7
2.9	3.0	2.7		3.0	3.6	3.7	2.7	2.8	2.3
2.0	2.0	2.0	Sales/Total Assets	1.4	2.3	1.9	2.0	2.1	1.7
1.4	1.3	1.4		1.1	1.7	1.5	1.5	1.5	1.0
.6	.6	.6			.8		.8	.4	.6
(216) 1.4	(176) 1.4	(157) 1.3	% Depr., Dep., Amort./Sales		(11) 1.0		(37) 1.7	(49) 1.1	(46) 1.2
2.9	2.5	2.7			3.6		3.7	2.0	3.4
2.4	2.8	2.4					2.4	2.3	
(93) 4.2	(84) 5.5	(56) 4.5	% Officers', Directors' Owners' Comp/Sales				(20) 4.4	(15) 3.3	
7.0	8.2	6.7					5.5	4.7	
9587254M	7319423M	6685691M	Net Sales ($)	6649M	43511M	50356M	360732M	966550M	5257893M
5880610M	4705374M	4804804M	Total Assets ($)	6476M	25835M	24842M	202610M	551092M	3993949M

M = $ thousand MM = $ million

See Pages 9 through 22 for Explanation of Ratios and Data

Current Data Sorted by Assets							Comparative Historical Data	
						Type of Statement		
1			3		4	Unqualified	6	4
		1	2			Reviewed	9	3
	1	2				Compiled	3	3
	2					Tax Returns	5	9
		2	1	3		Other	20	16
	2 (4/1-9/30/13)		20 (10/1/13-3/31/14)				4/1/09-3/31/10	4/1/10-3/31/11
0-500M	500M-2MM	2-10MM	10-50MM	50-100MM	100-250MM		ALL	ALL
1	3	5	6	3	4	**NUMBER OF STATEMENTS**	43	35
%	%	%	%	%	%	**ASSETS**	%	%
						Cash & Equivalents	9.9	8.9
						Trade Receivables (net)	20.1	21.4
						Inventory	30.7	32.8
						All Other Current	5.2	6.1
						Total Current	65.7	69.1
						Fixed Assets (net)	23.2	18.2
						Intangibles (net)	3.3	6.3
						All Other Non-Current	7.8	6.4
						Total	100.0	100.0
						LIABILITIES		
						Notes Payable-Short Term	18.0	15.6
						Cur. Mat.-L.T.D.	4.6	4.4
						Trade Payables	13.7	13.4
						Income Taxes Payable	.2	.3
						All Other Current	14.2	14.2
						Total Current	50.7	48.0
						Long-Term Debt	9.3	12.1
						Deferred Taxes	.4	.3
						All Other Non-Current	7.9	16.4
						Net Worth	31.6	23.2
						Total Liabilties & Net Worth	100.0	100.0
						INCOME DATA		
						Net Sales	100.0	100.0
						Gross Profit	21.9	28.6
						Operating Expenses	21.5	26.2
						Operating Profit	.4	2.4
						All Other Expenses (net)	.9	1.7
						Profit Before Taxes	-.5	.7
						RATIOS		
							1.9	2.1
						Current	1.4	1.8
							1.1	1.1
							1.0	1.2
						Quick	.5	.5
							.2	.3
							15 24.7	16 22.8
						Sales/Receivables	37 9.8	38 9.5
							61 6.0	63 5.8
							27 13.6	17 21.7
						Cost of Sales/Inventory	57 6.4	66 5.5
							118 3.1	169 2.2
							15 24.9	14 25.9
						Cost of Sales/Payables	31 11.7	23 15.9
							53 6.8	46 8.0
							5.6	4.5
						Sales/Working Capital	11.3	7.0
							63.2	18.1
							6.6	9.4
						EBIT/Interest	(40) 2.6	(32) 3.7
							-1.6	-.5
							4.3	
						Net Profit + Depr., Dep., Amort./Cur. Mat. L/T/D	(13) 1.9	
							-.1	
							.2	.2
						Fixed/Worth	.9	.7
							2.2	-3.7
							1.0	1.0
						Debt/Worth	2.3	2.6
							5.8	-71.0
							27.2	25.7
						% Profit Before Taxes/Tangible Net Worth	(35) 7.0	(26) 13.2
							-14.2	-4.1
							8.3	10.6
						% Profit Before Taxes/Total Assets	3.1	5.9
							-4.6	-3.3
							34.6	41.8
						Sales/Net Fixed Assets	13.1	12.4
							4.0	8.5
							2.6	2.4
						Sales/Total Assets	1.6	1.7
							1.1	1.2
							.9	.9
						% Depr., Dep., Amort./Sales	(33) 2.0	(27) 2.0
							4.7	3.5
							1.9	1.6
						% Officers', Directors' Owners' Comp/Sales	(10) 3.4	(12) 3.2
							7.1	6.1
155M	11325M	39422M	456501M	858651M	1062078M	Net Sales ($)	1582955M	1753192M
166M	2726M	22061M	221338M	200948M	765874M	Total Assets ($)	1084126M	874965M

M = $ thousand MM = $ million

See Pages 9 through 22 for Explanation of Ratios and Data

Comparative Historical Data / Current Data Sorted by Sales

4/1/11-3/31/12 ALL	4/1/12-3/31/13 ALL	4/1/13-3/31/14 ALL	Type of Statement	0-1MM	1-3MM	3-5MM	5-10MM	10-25MM	25MM & OVER
5	5	8	Unqualified	1					7
5	2	3	Reviewed				1		2
3	4	3	Compiled			1	1	1	
4	1	2	Tax Returns	1			1		
17	10	6	Other			1		1	4
					2 (4/1-9/30/13)		20 (10/1/13-3/31/14)		
34	22	22	NUMBER OF STATEMENTS	2		2	3	2	13
%	%	%	**ASSETS**	%	%	%	%	%	%
13.5	12.2	13.1	Cash & Equivalents		DATA NOT AVAILABLE				13.6
15.8	23.5	26.4	Trade Receivables (net)						21.8
32.2	26.4	21.8	Inventory						19.8
4.5	7.0	3.5	All Other Current						4.4
66.0	69.1	64.9	Total Current						59.6
20.0	21.1	28.7	Fixed Assets (net)						33.5
3.0	3.5	2.0	Intangibles (net)						2.7
11.2	6.2	4.5	All Other Non-Current						4.2
100.0	100.0	100.0	Total						100.0
			LIABILITIES						
10.9	9.6	10.6	Notes Payable-Short Term						9.2
3.6	10.1	4.1	Cur. Mat.-L.T.D.						4.6
13.2	15.9	14.9	Trade Payables						16.0
.3	.3	.2	Income Taxes Payable						.2
16.8	14.2	20.5	All Other Current						19.1
44.9	50.1	50.2	Total Current						49.1
9.5	10.1	10.2	Long-Term Debt						9.6
.2	.2	.6	Deferred Taxes						.4
11.4	3.6	5.4	All Other Non-Current						7.8
34.0	36.1	33.6	Net Worth						33.1
100.0	100.0	100.0	Total Liabilities & Net Worth						100.0
			INCOME DATA						
100.0	100.0	100.0	Net Sales						100.0
26.0	21.9	24.0	Gross Profit						15.9
25.0	19.3	19.9	Operating Expenses						11.9
1.0	2.5	4.1	Operating Profit						4.0
-.5	.1	.6	All Other Expenses (net)						.3
1.5	2.4	3.5	Profit Before Taxes						3.7
			RATIOS						
2.6	2.1	2.5							1.7
1.5	1.4	1.5	Current						1.3
1.0	1.1	1.0							1.0
1.3	1.2	1.9							1.1
.6	.8	.8	Quick						.7
.3	.5	.6							.4
15 24.7	**14** 25.4	**21** 17.7							**18** 20.6
35 10.4	**31** 11.8	**32** 11.3	Sales/Receivables						**28** 12.9
57 6.4	**57** 6.4	**66** 5.5							**68** 5.4
31 11.7	**16** 23.5	**17** 22.0							**16** 22.2
76 4.8	**47** 7.7	**40** 9.2	Cost of Sales/Inventory						**39** 9.4
215 1.7	**122** 3.0	**73** 5.0							**47** 7.7
12 30.9	**9** 40.4	**18** 20.2							**15** 23.7
27 13.6	**23** 16.2	**23** 15.9	Cost of Sales/Payables						**23** 15.6
52 7.0	**54** 6.7	**54** 6.8							**45** 8.1
3.8	7.0	6.2							7.0
7.7	11.4	9.5	Sales/Working Capital						12.5
-310.3	NM	-202.8							-159.6
12.9	62.6	59.4							
(27) 5.0	(20) 4.0	(17) 4.5	EBIT/Interest						
1.3	1.7	-.1							
			Net Profit + Depr., Dep., Amort./Cur. Mat. L/T/D						
.2	.1	.3							.4
.5	.6	.7	Fixed/Worth						.7
5.0	-4.1	3.7							3.9
.6	.5	.5							.8
2.9	2.3	1.8	Debt/Worth						3.4
26.7	-21.3	7.0							8.8
24.8	29.0	47.4							49.7
(28) 9.8	(16) 14.2	(18) 19.6	% Profit Before Taxes/Tangible Net Worth						(11) 19.7
.4	1.5	-4.3							-5.4
9.0	10.1	19.0							14.3
1.7	3.9	7.9	% Profit Before Taxes/Total Assets						8.3
-.1	1.6	-1.8							1.5
32.5	62.8	32.4							30.0
12.6	10.3	6.8	Sales/Net Fixed Assets						4.9
4.8	4.4	3.5							3.1
2.1	3.1	2.9							2.6
1.7	2.3	1.8	Sales/Total Assets						1.6
1.1	1.5	1.3							1.3
.7	.7	.5							.3
(23) 1.6	(14) 1.9	(17) 3.1	% Depr., Dep., Amort./Sales						(11) 3.1
3.4	3.2	4.6							4.2
1.7									
(11) 3.7			% Officers', Directors' Owners' Comp/Sales						
5.8									
1884463M	1799204M	2428132M	Net Sales ($)	1028M		6757M	20016M	23101M	2377230M
1380162M	1064558M	1213113M	Total Assets ($)	726M		2687M	12120M	9420M	1188160M

M = $ thousand MM = $ million

See Pages 9 through 22 for Explanation of Ratios and Data

Current Data Sorted by Assets							Comparative Historical Data	
						Type of Statement		
		4	9	3	7	Unqualified	25	35
		10	6	2		Reviewed	32	21
2	5	5				Compiled	9	17
3	8	3	1			Tax Returns	13	13
1	3	11	7	3	5	Other	54	49
	21 (4/1-9/30/13)		77 (10/1/13-3/31/14)				**4/1/09-3/31/10**	**4/1/10-3/31/11**
0-500M	**500M-2MM**	**2-10MM**	**10-50MM**	**50-100MM**	**100-250MM**		**ALL**	**ALL**
6	16	33	23	8	12	**NUMBER OF STATEMENTS**	133	135
%	%	%	%	%	%	**ASSETS**	%	%
	12.6	11.3	7.9		10.7	Cash & Equivalents	8.4	9.7
	28.1	20.6	17.3		20.7	Trade Receivables (net)	20.5	21.6
	34.2	43.7	34.7		22.3	Inventory	36.0	34.6
	.1	1.5	3.6		5.1	All Other Current	3.2	3.3
	75.0	77.1	63.5		58.8	Total Current	68.1	69.2
	12.9	16.5	23.7		29.5	Fixed Assets (net)	20.6	19.4
	5.4	2.5	2.6		7.0	Intangibles (net)	5.3	4.0
	6.7	4.0	10.2		4.7	All Other Non-Current	6.0	7.4
	100.0	100.0	100.0		100.0	Total	100.0	100.0
						LIABILITIES		
	10.7	12.0	11.8		12.5	Notes Payable-Short Term	15.7	14.1
	.8	2.0	2.5		5.3	Cur. Mat.-L.T.D.	4.3	3.3
	23.2	18.8	8.1		11.6	Trade Payables	15.7	17.2
	.0	.2	.3		.1	Income Taxes Payable	.4	.3
	11.8	16.0	12.9		10.4	All Other Current	16.6	13.6
	46.6	49.0	35.5		39.9	Total Current	52.7	48.6
	16.8	15.2	11.4		12.3	Long-Term Debt	13.8	10.9
	.0	.3	.3		.6	Deferred Taxes	.5	.5
	16.8	5.2	4.1		3.6	All Other Non-Current	7.8	7.7
	19.9	30.4	48.7		43.5	Net Worth	25.3	32.3
	100.0	100.0	100.0		100.0	Total Liabilties & Net Worth	100.0	100.0
						INCOME DATA		
	100.0	100.0	100.0		100.0	Net Sales	100.0	100.0
	24.8	20.9	18.5		17.2	Gross Profit	20.7	23.8
	22.1	17.6	13.5		10.8	Operating Expenses	20.1	20.4
	2.7	3.3	5.1		6.4	Operating Profit	.6	3.4
	.5	.5	.6		1.0	All Other Expenses (net)	1.6	.7
	2.1	2.8	4.5		5.4	Profit Before Taxes	-1.0	2.7
						RATIOS		
	4.3	2.4	3.1		2.3		2.1	2.7
	1.4	1.5	1.9		1.9	Current	1.4	1.6
	1.0	1.2	1.3		1.1		1.0	1.1
	2.0	1.0	1.4		1.2		1.1	1.4
	.8	.5	.8		1.0	Quick	.5	.7
	.5	.4	.5		.4		.3	.3
	16 22.7	**17** 21.4	**16** 22.8		**30** 12.1		**15** 24.6	**18** 20.0
	27 13.6	**32** 11.5	**29** 12.7		**41** 8.9	Sales/Receivables	**37** 9.9	**32** 11.3
	36 10.2	**43** 8.5	**41** 8.8		**57** 6.4		**49** 7.5	**51** 7.2
	12 31.7	**51** 7.2	**33** 11.1		**38** 9.5		**43** 8.4	**42** 8.7
	49 7.4	**79** 4.6	**57** 6.4		**56** 6.5	Cost of Sales/Inventory	**67** 5.4	**69** 5.3
	64 5.7	**111** 3.3	**107** 3.4		**79** 4.6		**112** 3.3	**113** 3.2
	15 25.1	**13** 27.7	**10** 35.5		**16** 23.2		**12** 29.4	**15** 25.0
	18 19.8	**24** 15.4	**14** 26.0		**23** 15.8	Cost of Sales/Payables	**21** 17.1	**28** 13.1
	43 8.5	**54** 6.7	**21** 17.5		**50** 7.3		**47** 7.8	**43** 8.6
	7.0	5.2	6.4		4.2		5.6	4.8
	13.3	11.0	8.2		6.9	Sales/Working Capital	10.7	9.3
	NM	21.3	15.4		126.0		-186.1	38.5
	18.7	24.1	35.1		27.2		6.3	12.4
	(14) 3.5	(29) 5.3	(21) 9.4		(11) 6.4	EBIT/Interest	(117) 1.4	(122) 4.0
	-.7	1.4	2.1		2.9		-1.3	1.2
							4.2	7.9
						Net Profit + Depr., Dep., Amort./Cur. Mat. L/T/D	(33) 1.4	(33) 2.0
							-.2	.7
	.0	.3	.1		.4		.2	.2
	.4	.5	.5		.6	Fixed/Worth	.6	.5
	12.1	1.3	2.1		2.0		4.1	1.5
	.6	.8	.3		.6		.8	.7
	2.1	2.0	1.0		.9	Debt/Worth	2.4	1.5
	NM	7.2	7.1		4.1		22.0	7.9
	73.8	39.2	53.4		30.4		30.6	36.8
	(12) 26.0	(28) 15.6	21.1		(11) 24.6	% Profit Before Taxes/Tangible Net Worth	(102) 5.2	(111) 13.9
	-3.3	5.0	8.6		17.3		-9.7	4.0
	27.1	11.6	15.5		13.6		8.3	12.7
	3.8	5.9	9.7		7.3	% Profit Before Taxes/Total Assets	1.1	5.0
	-3.3	1.5	3.5		4.4		-6.8	.6
	356.7	72.7	49.3		8.7		34.7	47.3
	88.8	15.1	8.5		6.0	Sales/Net Fixed Assets	15.1	14.3
	14.5	9.9	5.8		3.7		5.5	6.7
	5.0	3.6	2.7		2.2		3.1	3.2
	3.8	2.8	2.0		1.6	Sales/Total Assets	2.1	2.3
	2.8	1.8	1.5		1.3		1.3	1.5
		.5	.8				.7	.6
		(30) 1.0	(20) 2.0			% Depr., Dep., Amort./Sales	(109) 1.5	(108) 1.4
		2.0	3.2				3.3	2.6
		1.3					1.4	1.5
		(10) 1.5				% Officers', Directors' Owners' Comp/Sales	(44) 2.6	(45) 2.4
		3.1					4.4	5.5
5907M	70611M	443101M	1335981M	999227M	3740608M	Net Sales ($)	6331370M	6953406M
1355M	18988M	166497M	569252M	587350M	2080589M	Total Assets ($)	3622413M	3785140M

M = $ thousand MM = $ million

See Pages 9 through 22 for Explanation of Ratios and Data

Comparative Historical Data / Current Data Sorted by Sales

4/1/11-3/31/12 ALL	4/1/12-3/31/13 ALL	4/1/13-3/31/14 ALL		0-1MM	1-3MM	3-5MM	5-10MM	10-25MM	25MM & OVER
			Type of Statement						
26	23	23	Unqualified				2	2	19
23	29	18	Reviewed			1	4	4	9
17	12	12	Compiled	1	2	3	1	5	
16	11	15	Tax Returns	3	2	5	3	1	1
48	47	30	Other	1	2	2	5	8	12
				21 (4/1-9/30/13)			77 (10/1/13-3/31/14)		
130	122	98	**NUMBER OF STATEMENTS**	5	6	11	15	20	41
%	%	%	**ASSETS**	%	%	%	%	%	%
9.5	8.8	10.3	Cash & Equivalents			14.7	13.9	8.0	9.6
22.6	21.3	21.2	Trade Receivables (net)			26.5	23.4	18.9	20.4
35.7	39.5	35.8	Inventory			25.6	32.2	48.4	32.4
2.3	3.7	2.3	All Other Current			.1	.7	1.4	4.0
70.2	73.4	69.7	Total Current			67.0	70.2	76.7	66.3
19.3	17.3	20.0	Fixed Assets (net)			16.1	12.8	20.5	23.7
3.8	3.1	3.4	Intangibles (net)			4.9	1.9	1.3	4.2
6.7	6.3	7.0	All Other Non-Current			12.0	15.1	1.6	5.8
100.0	100.0	100.0	Total			100.0	100.0	100.0	100.0
			LIABILITIES						
14.7	14.2	12.5	Notes Payable-Short Term			5.6	7.7	16.9	12.6
3.5	1.7	2.4	Cur. Mat.-L.T.D.			1.3	1.1	2.4	3.4
17.2	16.7	16.5	Trade Payables			16.9	17.9	16.1	15.2
.1	.1	.2	Income Taxes Payable			.0	.3	.0	.2
14.0	16.1	13.2	All Other Current			11.8	12.3	18.6	10.3
49.6	48.9	44.7	Total Current			35.7	39.2	54.0	41.7
11.1	9.2	17.2	Long-Term Debt			13.5	9.9	14.9	14.8
.3	.5	.3	Deferred Taxes			.0	.2	.0	.5
8.1	8.8	6.5	All Other Non-Current			23.3	10.2	1.4	4.2
30.8	32.7	31.4	Net Worth			27.5	40.5	29.6	38.8
100.0	100.0	100.0	Total Liabilties & Net Worth			100.0	100.0	100.0	100.0
			INCOME DATA						
100.0	100.0	100.0	Net Sales			100.0	100.0	100.0	100.0
22.4	22.3	22.1	Gross Profit			27.6	21.7	17.8	17.9
18.2	17.6	17.7	Operating Expenses			22.0	19.6	15.6	11.9
4.2	4.7	4.4	Operating Profit			5.6	2.2	2.1	6.0
.7	.6	.7	All Other Expenses (net)			.6	.2	.5	.9
3.5	4.1	3.7	Profit Before Taxes			4.9	2.0	1.6	5.1
			RATIOS						
2.9	2.6	2.6				4.5	5.2	1.9	2.5
1.5	1.7	1.6	Current			1.8	1.8	1.4	1.8
1.1	1.1	1.1				1.0	1.1	1.2	1.1
1.4	1.3	1.2				3.0	4.0	.8	1.2
.7	.6	.7	Quick			.8	1.0	.4	.8
.3	.4	.4				.6	.5	.3	.4
19 18.9	**13** 27.3	**17** 21.4				**19** 18.9	**27** 13.4	**12** 30.7	**24** 15.0
33 11.2	**29** 12.4	**31** 11.9	Sales/Receivables			**28** 13.0	**41** 8.8	**18** 20.0	**34** 10.7
50 7.3	**51** 7.1	**42** 8.7				**35** 10.5	**52** 7.0	**35** 10.4	**45** 8.1
35 10.4	**43** 8.5	**38** 9.6				**13** 27.9	**51** 7.1	**46** 8.0	**35** 10.4
66 5.5	**78** 4.7	**65** 5.6	Cost of Sales/Inventory			**42** 8.6	**81** 4.5	**74** 4.9	**59** 6.2
114 3.2	**122** 3.0	**104** 3.5				**64** 5.7	**104** 3.5	**152** 2.4	**101** 3.6
16 22.9	**12** 31.0	**13** 27.5				**14** 25.3	**13** 27.3	**8** 46.4	**13** 27.9
31 11.9	**25** 14.4	**20** 18.0	Cost of Sales/Payables			**17** 21.7	**26** 13.9	**16** 22.9	**20** 17.9
43 8.5	**42** 8.7	**42** 8.7				**34** 10.7	**58** 6.3	**25** 14.6	**42** 8.7
5.4	5.2	5.2				6.1	4.1	8.7	4.8
10.4	9.0	9.6	Sales/Working Capital			10.0	6.7	11.0	8.7
99.3	44.9	44.2				-388.7	43.3	19.8	44.7
20.1	24.3	27.8					35.4	22.4	29.2
(117) 3.7	(106) 4.0	(87) 6.2	EBIT/Interest				(13) 1.5	(19) 4.6	(38) 7.8
1.4	1.3	1.5					-1.4	1.3	2.8
9.9	29.6	31.2							32.7
(24) 3.0	(21) 3.7	(17) 3.8	Net Profit + Depr., Dep., Amort./Cur. Mat. L/T/D						(15) 15.4
1.8	1.9	1.5							1.7
.2	.2	.1				.0	.0	.3	.3
.5	.4	.5	Fixed/Worth			.1	.3	.5	.5
1.7	1.9	2.0				2.8	-2.7	1.5	1.8
.6	.5	.6				.5	.2	1.1	.6
2.0	1.8	1.7	Debt/Worth			.9	1.2	2.7	1.2
8.9	9.3	7.2				168.3	-19.9	6.5	4.2
41.5	44.7	43.9					11.2	43.9	39.2
(109) 14.8	(100) 19.1	(85) 23.5	% Profit Before Taxes/Tangible Net Worth				(11) 5.9	(19) 27.3	(37) 24.6
4.4	5.2	5.4					-12.4	5.7	12.7
13.6	14.7	15.5				30.3	7.1	12.2	15.7
5.1	6.2	7.8	% Profit Before Taxes/Total Assets			15.3	2.3	6.0	9.7
1.1	1.3	1.2				-2.5	-2.3	1.0	5.9
57.0	56.2	67.0				999.8	91.6	49.6	23.5
16.7	19.1	14.9	Sales/Net Fixed Assets			50.8	38.5	13.1	8.8
6.5	9.0	7.4				8.3	6.8	8.3	5.7
3.6	3.3	3.6				4.6	2.9	3.8	2.9
2.3	2.4	2.2	Sales/Total Assets			3.7	2.1	2.9	2.0
1.5	1.5	1.6				2.8	1.0	1.8	1.5
.5	.6	.6					.5	.6	.8
(96) 1.3	(99) 1.0	(77) 1.1	% Depr., Dep., Amort./Sales				(11) 1.6	(18) 1.5	(34) 1.3
2.3	2.0	2.4					2.2	2.3	3.1
1.4	.8	.8							
(37) 2.4	(38) 1.7	(26) 1.9	% Officers', Directors' Owners' Comp/Sales						
4.7	4.2	3.6							
6771879M	**6748678M**	**6595435M**	Net Sales ($)	**2759M**	**13520M**	**44827M**	**106242M**	**293530M**	**6134557M**
3362036M	**3669840M**	**3424031M**	Total Assets ($)	**1945M**	**8200M**	**14455M**	**81457M**	**125120M**	**3192854M**

M = $ thousand MM = $ million

See Pages 9 through 22 for Explanation of Ratios and Data

Current Data Sorted by Assets							Comparative Historical Data	
						Type of Statement		
		1	3	1	2	Unqualified	8	18
		4	8			Reviewed	8	14
	2	5		1		Compiled	16	11
4	2	2				Tax Returns	6	8
1	4	8	10	3	4	Other	33	30
10 (4/1-9/30/13)		55 (10/1/13-3/31/14)					4/1/09-3/31/10	4/1/10-3/31/11
0-500M	500M-2MM	2-10MM	10-50MM	50-100MM	100-250MM		ALL	ALL
5	8	20	21	5	6	**NUMBER OF STATEMENTS**	71	81
%	%	%	%	%	%	**ASSETS**	%	%
		8.4	6.4			Cash & Equivalents	7.9	8.3
		16.7	15.6			Trade Receivables (net)	14.4	16.4
		39.1	45.2			Inventory	38.6	38.7
		.9	3.6			All Other Current	3.6	3.6
		65.1	70.8			Total Current	64.5	67.1
		24.9	21.4			Fixed Assets (net)	23.0	21.5
		5.7	4.2			Intangibles (net)	6.0	5.5
		4.3	3.6			All Other Non-Current	6.6	5.9
		100.0	100.0			Total	100.0	100.0
						LIABILITIES		
		11.6	12.7			Notes Payable-Short Term	15.8	14.7
		3.5	5.7			Cur. Mat.-L.T.D.	3.8	5.7
		11.7	13.9			Trade Payables	15.6	17.7
		.1	.2			Income Taxes Payable	.1	.2
		5.2	12.8			All Other Current	13.7	16.5
		31.9	45.2			Total Current	48.9	54.9
		11.2	13.7			Long-Term Debt	15.5	19.6
		.1	.5			Deferred Taxes	.8	.6
		6.9	3.1			All Other Non-Current	9.5	15.5
		49.8	37.4			Net Worth	25.2	9.5
		100.0	100.0			Total Liabilties & Net Worth	100.0	100.0
						INCOME DATA		
		100.0	100.0			Net Sales	100.0	100.0
		22.9	17.7			Gross Profit	18.7	19.5
		16.8	10.7			Operating Expenses	18.2	15.2
		6.1	7.0			Operating Profit	.4	4.3
		.0	.8			All Other Expenses (net)	1.2	.7
		6.1	6.2			Profit Before Taxes	-.8	3.6
						RATIOS		
		4.5	2.3				2.8	3.8
		2.4	1.6			Current	1.8	1.7
		1.2	1.3				1.1	1.0
		2.4	.7				1.0	1.2
		.8	.4			Quick	.6	.5
		.3	.2				.2	.2
		8 44.5	**5** 75.6				**7** 51.4	**8** 46.1
		16 23.0	**17** 21.4			Sales/Receivables	**20** 18.3	**23** 15.8
		28 13.2	**38** 9.6				**31** 11.7	**40** 9.1
		35 10.4	**45** 8.2				**46** 8.0	**43** 8.4
		52 7.0	**65** 5.6			Cost of Sales/Inventory	**68** 5.4	**62** 5.9
		87 4.2	**99** 3.7				**108** 3.4	**104** 3.5
		9 40.7	**10** 36.5				**9** 41.2	**9** 42.3
		14 25.6	**18** 20.4			Cost of Sales/Payables	**17** 21.3	**18** 20.0
		30 12.0	**31** 11.6				**34** 10.8	**40** 9.1
		7.0	5.6				4.6	4.9
		9.3	10.3			Sales/Working Capital	9.4	10.9
		31.0	27.4				40.8	NM
		35.3	20.5				10.6	11.3
		(18) 13.9	(19) 10.0			EBIT/Interest	(66) 1.9	(74) 4.8
		5.9	1.5				-2.8	1.4
							7.1	12.2
						Net Profit + Depr., Dep., Amort./Cur. Mat. L/T/D	(12) 2.8	(19) 2.0
							-.2	.4
		.2	.2				.3	.3
		.4	.5			Fixed/Worth	.7	.9
		.9	1.1				5.2	NM
		.4	1.0				.7	.8
		.7	1.9			Debt/Worth	2.6	2.3
		3.4	4.6				16.8	NM
		74.9	46.4				27.0	43.9
		(19) 46.5	30.3			% Profit Before Taxes/Tangible Net Worth	(55) 5.1	(61) 17.8
		18.6	10.7				-18.9	2.1
		36.3	16.8				9.9	16.2
		18.9	10.3			% Profit Before Taxes/Total Assets	2.2	7.2
		6.4	1.5				-9.0	1.4
		40.7	41.7				39.5	46.4
		13.5	14.9			Sales/Net Fixed Assets	12.3	13.8
		6.7	7.9				5.5	6.2
		4.3	3.5				3.6	3.8
		3.5	2.9			Sales/Total Assets	2.3	2.6
		1.8	2.0				1.4	1.5
		.4	.5				.8	.8
		(17) 1.0	(20) .9			% Depr., Dep., Amort./Sales	(57) 1.3	(65) 1.4
		2.8	1.9				2.5	2.7
							1.2	1.1
						% Officers', Directors' Owners' Comp/Sales	(19) 3.0	(22) 2.3
							4.5	4.0
11678M	36150M	311165M	1251416M	878400M	2064987M	Net Sales ($)	3672471M	4048113M
1161M	13893M	95381M	455073M	363722M	1243382M	Total Assets ($)	1970602M	2053933M

M = $ thousand MM = $ million

See Pages 9 through 22 for Explanation of Ratios and Data

Comparative Historical Data / Current Data Sorted by Sales

4/1/11-3/31/12 ALL	4/1/12-3/31/13 ALL	4/1/13-3/31/14 ALL		0-1MM	1-3MM	3-5MM	5-10MM	10-25MM	25MM & OVER
			Type of Statement						
12	6	7	Unqualified						7
14	11	12	Reviewed				1	1	10
15	6	8	Compiled			1	4	2	1
7	18	8	Tax Returns	2	2	2	1	1	
31	40	30	Other	1	1	3	3	7	15
				10 (4/1-9/30/13)			55 (10/1/13-3/31/14)		
79	81	65	**NUMBER OF STATEMENTS**	3	3	6	9	11	33
%	%	%	**ASSETS**	%	%	%	%	%	%
9.7	11.8	9.6	Cash & Equivalents					8.5	7.0
15.9	14.3	15.3	Trade Receivables (net)					21.6	15.4
41.4	39.2	40.3	Inventory					37.6	41.9
2.0	2.8	2.4	All Other Current					.3	2.8
69.0	68.1	67.6	Total Current					68.0	67.1
20.7	20.1	21.8	Fixed Assets (net)					18.9	22.7
6.5	3.8	6.1	Intangibles (net)					9.6	6.2
3.8	8.0	4.5	All Other Non-Current					3.5	4.1
100.0	100.0	100.0	Total					100.0	100.0
			LIABILITIES						
11.2	9.1	13.2	Notes Payable-Short Term					11.2	13.1
2.4	2.3	3.2	Cur. Mat.-L.T.D.					1.3	4.0
16.1	14.2	13.6	Trade Payables					13.2	15.1
.2	.3	.1	Income Taxes Payable					.0	.2
12.7	20.3	9.7	All Other Current					4.9	12.8
42.6	46.3	39.9	Total Current					30.7	45.1
14.1	13.7	15.8	Long-Term Debt					14.6	12.6
.5	.5	.5	Deferred Taxes					.0	1.0
5.5	9.5	5.7	All Other Non-Current					3.9	4.8
37.2	30.1	38.0	Net Worth					50.8	36.5
100.0	100.0	100.0	Total Liabilties & Net Worth					100.0	100.0
			INCOME DATA						
100.0	100.0	100.0	Net Sales					100.0	100.0
20.1	24.2	23.6	Gross Profit					20.6	15.6
16.5	16.8	17.7	Operating Expenses					16.4	11.2
3.5	7.5	5.9	Operating Profit					4.1	4.4
.7	.6	.7	All Other Expenses (net)					1.5	.7
2.8	6.9	5.2	Profit Before Taxes					2.6	3.7
			RATIOS						
3.5	4.0	3.2						4.8	2.1
1.8	1.6	1.7	Current					3.2	1.5
1.1	1.1	1.2						1.1	1.2
1.2	1.2	1.3						2.5	.7
.6	.6	.6	Quick					1.4	.5
.3	.3	.3						.4	.3
7 51.1	**4** 86.9	**7** 49.1						**11** 33.1	**8** 44.4
19 18.9	**12** 29.9	**20** 18.4	Sales/Receivables					**26** 13.8	**22** 16.4
30 12.3	**31** 11.7	**34** 10.6						**49** 7.4	**34** 10.6
40 9.2	**29** 12.6	**41** 9.0						**40** 9.2	**45** 8.2
64 5.7	**64** 5.7	**62** 5.9	Cost of Sales/Inventory					**66** 5.5	**61** 6.0
111 3.3	**99** 3.7	**89** 4.1						**135** 2.7	**74** 4.9
8 44.9	**7** 50.7	**10** 37.1						**17** 22.1	**11** 33.7
21 17.1	**23** 16.2	**19** 19.3	Cost of Sales/Payables					**26** 14.3	**19** 19.3
37 9.9	**37** 9.8	**38** 9.6						**32** 11.4	**39** 9.3
5.7	5.8	6.3						3.2	8.0
12.0	13.9	9.9	Sales/Working Capital					7.3	10.7
55.6	54.5	39.7						33.2	44.2
14.0	25.2	23.0							19.4
(72) 5.5	(70) 6.3	(57) 8.6	EBIT/Interest						(32) 8.4
1.6	3.3	2.5							3.6
4.3	5.2								
(22) 1.2	(17) 2.6		Net Profit + Depr., Dep., Amort./Cur. Mat. L/T/D						
.4	1.5								
.3	.2	.2						.1	.2
.7	.6	.5	Fixed/Worth					.4	.9
1.4	1.3	2.0						2.4	1.9
.6	.7	.6						.4	1.0
2.4	1.7	1.9	Debt/Worth					.9	2.4
7.5	4.8	4.6						4.1	6.1
50.8	66.0	58.4						74.9	61.6
(68) 25.5	(69) 36.7	(58) 33.5	% Profit Before Taxes/Tangible Net Worth					25.5	(31) 34.8
4.6	19.2	16.5						-14.7	20.8
16.0	21.8	22.6						28.5	16.8
6.9	12.0	11.3	% Profit Before Taxes/Total Assets					10.6	10.3
2.3	5.1	2.1						-2.7	4.1
44.8	67.9	44.1						61.1	35.4
15.1	15.2	14.1	Sales/Net Fixed Assets					31.2	14.4
7.3	8.0	7.9						7.4	8.4
3.8	4.2	3.7						3.5	3.6
2.6	3.1	2.8	Sales/Total Assets					2.7	2.9
1.9	1.8	1.9						1.6	2.1
.7	.7	.5						.4	.5
(68) 1.1	(64) 1.2	(50) 1.1	% Depr., Dep., Amort./Sales					(10) .4	(27) .9
2.0	1.9	2.3						2.5	1.5
1.0	.8	.6							
(18) 1.8	(21) 2.0	(17) 1.4	% Officers', Directors' Owners' Comp/Sales						
2.8	3.6	3.1							
4898135M	5241821M	4553796M	Net Sales ($)	1312M	7077M	23464M	65510M	163327M	4293106M
2418604M	2228282M	2172612M	Total Assets ($)	14867M	4323M	10381M	21906M	75037M	2046098M

M = $ thousand MM = $ million

See Pages 9 through 22 for Explanation of Ratios and Data

Current Data Sorted by Assets							Comparative Historical Data	
						Type of Statement		
		2	2	1	2	Unqualified	10	8
		1	2			Reviewed	9	8
1	2	2				Compiled	10	6
		1			1	Tax Returns	2	2
	5	5	1		1	Other	11	18
4 (4/1-9/30/13)			25 (10/1/13-3/31/14)				**4/1/09-3/31/10**	**4/1/10-3/31/11**
0-500M	**500M-2MM**	**2-10MM**	**10-50MM**	**50-100MM**	**100-250MM**		**ALL**	**ALL**
1	7	11	5	1	4	**NUMBER OF STATEMENTS**	42	42
%	%	%	%	%	%	**ASSETS**	%	%
		9.8				Cash & Equivalents	11.2	10.4
		9.7				Trade Receivables (net)	13.8	19.4
		44.1				Inventory	48.1	40.5
		4.1				All Other Current	3.2	3.3
		67.8				Total Current	76.3	73.7
		28.5				Fixed Assets (net)	13.0	12.6
		1.0				Intangibles (net)	6.0	4.8
		2.7				All Other Non-Current	4.7	8.9
		100.0				Total	100.0	100.0
						LIABILITIES		
		5.6				Notes Payable-Short Term	17.7	11.0
		3.7				Cur. Mat.-L.T.D.	3.6	1.8
		8.4				Trade Payables	11.4	12.9
		1.3				Income Taxes Payable	.2	.2
		14.3				All Other Current	16.5	16.6
		33.3				Total Current	49.4	42.4
		16.9				Long-Term Debt	15.8	10.1
		.4				Deferred Taxes	.0	.1
		5.5				All Other Non-Current	11.1	19.0
		43.9				Net Worth	23.6	28.3
		100.0				Total Liabilties & Net Worth	100.0	100.0
						INCOME DATA		
		100.0				Net Sales	100.0	100.0
		30.9				Gross Profit	15.4	17.5
		21.1				Operating Expenses	18.5	15.9
		9.8				Operating Profit	-3.1	1.6
		.9				All Other Expenses (net)	1.5	.5
		9.0				Profit Before Taxes	-4.6	1.0
						RATIOS		
		3.2					2.8	2.8
		1.8				Current	1.4	1.9
		1.3					1.0	1.2
		1.0					1.1	1.2
		.4				Quick	.5	.8
		.1					.3	.5
		3 108.5					**6** 64.0	**5** 67.2
		10 36.6				Sales/Receivables	**14** 25.6	**18** 20.0
		16 23.2					**31** 11.9	**33** 11.2
		39 9.4					**48** 7.7	**36** 10.0
		73 5.0				Cost of Sales/Inventory	**70** 5.2	**54** 6.7
		203 1.8					**139** 2.6	**79** 4.6
		4 94.4					**7** 54.8	**7** 49.6
		12 30.9				Cost of Sales/Payables	**14** 26.1	**15** 24.5
		24 15.2					**28** 13.2	**24** 14.9
		5.7					4.7	5.7
		6.9				Sales/Working Capital	21.6	10.6
		13.6					-687.4	40.0
							11.6	25.8
						EBIT/Interest	(39) -.5	(35) 5.3
							-7.7	.7
						Net Profit + Depr., Dep., Amort./Cur. Mat. L/T/D		
		.1					.2	.1
		1.0				Fixed/Worth	.8	.3
		1.3					3.9	1.8
		.4					1.4	.9
		1.1				Debt/Worth	6.3	2.8
		2.2					86.9	NM
		94.7					80.9	80.5
		(10) 10.4				% Profit Before Taxes/Tangible Net Worth	(34) .7	(32) 34.3
		4.5					-66.2	-.4
		18.7					9.9	17.4
		9.2				% Profit Before Taxes/Total Assets	-4.3	5.3
		2.3					-16.5	-3.7
		78.0					62.1	101.4
		20.1				Sales/Net Fixed Assets	35.5	47.6
		2.2					12.1	17.0
		4.6					3.9	4.5
		2.8				Sales/Total Assets	2.8	3.4
		1.1					1.6	2.0
		.4					.4	.4
		(10) 1.0				% Depr., Dep., Amort./Sales	(33) 1.0	(35) .6
		7.8					1.4	1.1
							2.2	.8
						% Officers', Directors' Owners' Comp/Sales	(11) 2.8	(10) 2.2
							3.7	3.6
1342M	**25605M**	**147468M**	**570743M**	**174029M**	**2746950M**	Net Sales ($)	**2309508M**	**3099385M**
417M	**8205M**	**50382M**	**123772M**	**92903M**	**792120M**	Total Assets ($)	**964214M**	**1188081M**

M = $ thousand MM = $ million

See Pages 9 through 22 for Explanation of Ratios and Data

Comparative Historical Data | **Current Data Sorted by Sales**

			Type of Statement						
8	9	7	Unqualified				1		6
1	5	3	Reviewed				1		2
2	2	5	Compiled		1	2		1	1
1	3	2	Tax Returns					1	1
17	9	12	Other	1	3	3	2	1	2
4/1/11-3/31/12 ALL	4/1/12-3/31/13 ALL	4/1/13-3/31/14 ALL			4 (4/1-9/30/13)		25 (10/1/13-3/31/14)		
				0-1MM	1-3MM	3-5MM	5-10MM	10-25MM	25MM & OVER
29	28	29	NUMBER OF STATEMENTS	1	4	5	4	3	12
%	%	%	ASSETS	%	%	%	%	%	%
7.9	6.5	6.1	Cash & Equivalents						5.7
21.4	20.2	18.8	Trade Receivables (net)						24.0
40.6	41.6	45.3	Inventory						43.3
3.5	2.2	2.5	All Other Current						2.7
73.4	70.6	72.8	Total Current						75.7
12.9	18.0	21.3	Fixed Assets (net)						13.6
8.5	7.8	4.1	Intangibles (net)						9.1
5.2	3.5	1.8	All Other Non-Current						1.6
100.0	100.0	100.0	Total						100.0
			LIABILITIES						
7.7	12.1	13.1	Notes Payable-Short Term						9.1
.8	1.9	2.1	Cur. Mat.-L.T.D.						3.3
14.4	13.7	11.4	Trade Payables						13.5
.2	.1	.5	Income Taxes Payable						.8
21.1	18.1	20.2	All Other Current						23.4
44.1	45.9	47.2	Total Current						50.1
10.7	17.1	16.7	Long-Term Debt						17.6
.6	1.0	.4	Deferred Taxes						.9
9.1	7.9	8.5	All Other Non-Current						14.6
35.8	28.1	27.2	Net Worth						16.8
100.0	100.0	100.0	Total Liabilties & Net Worth						100.0
			INCOME DATA						
100.0	100.0	100.0	Net Sales						100.0
19.2	18.3	24.1	Gross Profit						18.8
17.0	14.2	18.4	Operating Expenses						13.6
2.2	4.1	5.7	Operating Profit						5.1
.7	.7	.9	All Other Expenses (net)						1.0
1.5	3.4	4.7	Profit Before Taxes						4.1
			RATIOS						
2.6	1.9	2.0							1.9
1.9	1.4	1.5	Current						1.5
1.1	1.1	1.3							1.3
1.0	.8	.8							.9
.6	.5	.6	Quick						.6
.3	.3	.3							.3
15 24.9	**15** 24.1	**10** 35.8							**13** 27.5
23 16.0	**18** 20.2	**20** 18.0	Sales/Receivables						**21** 17.6
39 9.3	**31** 11.6	**31** 11.6							**30** 12.1
39 9.4	**35** 10.3	**41** 8.8							**29** 12.8
55 6.6	**45** 8.1	**65** 5.6	Cost of Sales/Inventory						**47** 7.8
126 2.9	**73** 5.0	**101** 3.6							**76** 4.8
8 44.4	**11** 34.2	**7** 55.3							**6** 57.8
17 22.1	**18** 20.3	**13** 28.6	Cost of Sales/Payables						**18** 20.7
42 8.6	**32** 11.3	**27** 13.7							**28** 13.0
5.7	9.4	6.5							10.1
8.0	14.5	12.6	Sales/Working Capital						15.4
37.8	52.7	20.3							21.8
9.4	25.9	16.7							115.7
(22) 2.0	5.6	(26) 3.9	EBIT/Interest						(11) 2.9
.1	1.0	1.7							1.3
			Net Profit + Depr., Dep., Amort./Cur. Mat. L/T/D						
.1	.1	.2							.2
.3	.6	.9	Fixed/Worth						.7
9.1	NM	-9.4							-.8
.8	1.1	.9							1.1
1.9	1.7	2.0	Debt/Worth						2.4
26.5	-16.7	-26.4							-3.7
31.0	61.6	73.1							
(23) 9.1	(20) 37.1	(21) 25.5	% Profit Before Taxes/Tangible Net Worth						
-1.0	19.6	4.1							
10.7	20.6	17.8							27.5
1.8	9.5	9.1	% Profit Before Taxes/Total Assets						13.9
-1.0	.1	1.2							1.7
69.0	83.9	46.5							76.4
22.0	24.8	26.3	Sales/Net Fixed Assets						34.7
9.0	10.2	8.6							14.2
4.3	5.1	4.3							5.0
2.8	4.0	3.2	Sales/Total Assets						4.3
1.7	2.0	2.3							3.3
.4	.3	.3							.2
(20) 1.1	(27) .7	(25) .6	% Depr., Dep., Amort./Sales						.4
1.7	1.4	1.5							1.3
		1.3							
		(11) 4.9	% Officers', Directors' Owners' Comp/Sales						
		11.2							
3239735M	3031039M	3666137M	Net Sales ($)	353M	8674M	18052M	26005M	54586M	3558467M
1180832M	859673M	1067799M	Total Assets ($)	5290M	4990M	7495M	13459M	15572M	1020993M

M = $ thousand MM = $ million

See Pages 9 through 22 for Explanation of Ratios and Data

Current Data Sorted by Assets							Comparative Historical Data	
						Type of Statement		
		3	3	3	2	Unqualified	6	8
		2	3			Reviewed	5	5
		2	1			Compiled	5	7
	1					Tax Returns	2	4
		3	4	3		Other	13	16
	4 (4/1-9/30/13)		26 (10/1/13-3/31/14)				**4/1/09-3/31/10 ALL**	**4/1/10-3/31/11 ALL**
0-500M	**500M-2MM**	**2-10MM**	**10-50MM**	**50-100MM**	**100-250MM**			
	1	10	11	6	2	**NUMBER OF STATEMENTS**	31	40
%	%	%	%	%	%	**ASSETS**	%	%
DATA NOT AVAILABLE		7.0	5.9			Cash & Equivalents	6.7	6.0
		20.0	20.6			Trade Receivables (net)	21.5	23.6
		47.3	27.7			Inventory	34.4	32.8
		.7	2.8			All Other Current	2.1	1.4
		74.9	57.0			Total Current	64.7	63.8
		13.0	33.3			Fixed Assets (net)	22.7	28.2
		5.2	4.0			Intangibles (net)	5.5	4.2
		6.9	5.8			All Other Non-Current	7.1	3.7
		100.0	100.0			Total	100.0	100.0
						LIABILITIES		
		17.9	11.3			Notes Payable-Short Term	19.0	12.9
		1.4	6.3			Cur. Mat.-L.T.D.	4.2	4.2
		10.8	11.2			Trade Payables	10.9	15.8
		.0	.0			Income Taxes Payable	.0	.1
		7.4	4.6			All Other Current	6.1	10.9
		37.5	33.5			Total Current	40.3	43.8
		3.0	14.4			Long-Term Debt	13.0	19.3
		.0	.9			Deferred Taxes	.7	.9
		15.6	3.2			All Other Non-Current	2.7	6.8
		43.9	48.0			Net Worth	43.3	29.2
		100.0	100.0			Total Liabilties & Net Worth	100.0	100.0
						INCOME DATA		
		100.0	100.0			Net Sales	100.0	100.0
		32.4	32.5			Gross Profit	30.7	29.3
		23.5	22.0			Operating Expenses	27.3	26.1
		8.9	10.5			Operating Profit	3.3	3.2
		.6	1.2			All Other Expenses (net)	1.8	1.5
		8.3	9.3			Profit Before Taxes	1.5	1.7
						RATIOS		
		3.9	2.6				4.1	2.5
		2.8	2.0			Current	1.6	1.5
		1.5	1.2				1.0	1.0
		1.5	1.1				1.4	1.2
		.8	.8			Quick	.7	.7
		.4	.5				.4	.4
		28 13.2	**30** 12.0				**26** 13.8	**28** 12.9
		41 8.9	**41** 8.8			Sales/Receivables	**39** 9.4	**45** 8.2
		46 7.9	**56** 6.5				**65** 5.6	**68** 5.4
		99 3.7	**32** 11.3				**59** 6.2	**57** 6.4
		152 2.4	**146** 2.5			Cost of Sales/Inventory	**99** 3.7	**101** 3.6
		228 1.6	**174** 2.1				**152** 2.4	**152** 2.4
		18 19.9	**13** 29.0				**13** 27.3	**22** 16.3
		25 14.5	**27** 13.6			Cost of Sales/Payables	**28** 13.2	**32** 11.5
		43 8.4	**51** 7.1				**46** 8.0	**76** 4.8
		3.2	3.8				3.3	4.1
		5.4	5.1			Sales/Working Capital	10.9	10.8
		8.2	24.4				70.3	-67.5
			14.8				7.2	11.1
			9.2			EBIT/Interest	(24) 1.1	(36) 2.5
			3.2				-1.8	.7
						Net Profit + Depr., Dep., Amort./Cur. Mat. L/T/D		
		.1	.4				.2	.4
		.3	.7			Fixed/Worth	.4	1.1
		NM	1.4				2.0	4.7
		.4	.6				.5	.6
		1.0	1.0			Debt/Worth	.7	3.2
		NM	2.0				7.7	36.8
			27.1				25.0	52.0
			6.4			% Profit Before Taxes/Tangible Net Worth	(27) 3.3	(32) 14.6
			3.5				-14.1	.8
		26.4	15.0				13.8	8.1
		12.3	2.2			% Profit Before Taxes/Total Assets	1.6	4.6
		-.2	1.6				-7.7	-.7
		42.8	21.4				18.6	16.8
		20.1	3.4			Sales/Net Fixed Assets	8.2	7.2
		9.8	2.4				4.7	3.2
		2.5	2.3				2.9	2.3
		1.9	1.5			Sales/Total Assets	1.7	1.7
		1.3	1.0				1.1	1.0
			1.6				1.5	1.3
			4.6			% Depr., Dep., Amort./Sales	(28) 3.4	(35) 3.3
			6.6				7.9	5.6
						% Officers', Directors' Owners' Comp/Sales		
	2402M	**116500M**	**474312M**	**517293M**	**467169M**	Net Sales ($)	**793335M**	**1249701M**
	1069M	**60072M**	**289194M**	**419678M**	**352739M**	Total Assets ($)	**588352M**	**910413M**

M = $ thousand MM = $ million

See Pages 9 through 22 for Explanation of Ratios and Data

Comparative Historical Data / Current Data Sorted by Sales

4/1/11-3/31/12 ALL	4/1/12-3/31/13 ALL	4/1/13-3/31/14 ALL		0-1MM	1-3MM	3-5MM	5-10MM	10-25MM	25MM & OVER
			Type of Statement						
12	4	11	Unqualified				2	1	8
3	3	5	Reviewed				1	2	2
5	2	3	Compiled			1		2	
4	2	1	Tax Returns		1				
25	19	10	Other				2	2	6
					4 (4/1-9/30/13)		26 (10/1/13-3/31/14)		
49	30	30	**NUMBER OF STATEMENTS**		1	1	5	7	16
%	%	%	**ASSETS**	%	%	%	%	%	%
4.1	6.7	5.0	Cash & Equivalents						5.0
23.2	16.4	19.0	Trade Receivables (net)						21.0
31.8	30.5	32.4	Inventory						23.8
3.5	3.0	1.7	All Other Current						2.6
62.7	56.5	58.1	Total Current						52.3
24.9	26.1	28.2	Fixed Assets (net)						34.0
7.0	9.8	7.4	Intangibles (net)						9.2
5.4	7.6	6.4	All Other Non-Current						4.4
100.0	100.0	100.0	Total						100.0
			LIABILITIES						
10.4	5.8	11.4	Notes Payable-Short Term						7.7
3.8	2.6	4.1	Cur. Mat.-L.T.D.						5.0
15.0	16.2	11.0	Trade Payables						12.3
.7	.1	.1	Income Taxes Payable						.2
15.4	12.5	5.7	All Other Current						6.8
45.3	37.2	32.4	Total Current						32.0
11.2	12.9	11.9	Long-Term Debt						13.9
1.2	1.6	1.1	Deferred Taxes						2.0
5.5	8.8	9.4	All Other Non-Current						6.1
36.9	39.5	45.2	Net Worth						46.0
100.0	100.0	100.0	Total Liabilities & Net Worth						100.0
			INCOME DATA						
100.0	100.0	100.0	Net Sales						100.0
30.8	27.4	28.5	Gross Profit						23.5
25.3	20.0	20.2	Operating Expenses						17.4
5.4	7.4	8.3	Operating Profit						6.1
1.4	.9	1.0	All Other Expenses (net)						.7
4.0	6.5	7.3	Profit Before Taxes						5.4
			RATIOS						
2.5	2.9	2.8							2.3
1.6	1.7	1.9	Current						1.6
1.1	1.0	1.4							1.2
1.1	1.2	1.1							1.1
.7	.6	.7	Quick						.7
.4	.4	.5							.5
22 16.4	22 16.5	33 11.2							33 11.0
37 9.9	34 10.8	42 8.7	Sales/Receivables						45 8.1
59 6.2	54 6.8	53 6.9							54 6.7
42 8.6	42 8.7	43 8.4							33 11.0
79 4.6	81 4.5	104 3.5	Cost of Sales/Inventory						52 7.0
135 2.7	192 1.9	166 2.2							135 2.7
20 18.5	20 18.5	20 18.4							21 17.0
32 11.3	34 10.7	31 11.9	Cost of Sales/Payables						31 11.9
53 6.9	58 6.3	48 7.6							46 8.0
4.8	3.5	4.5							5.3
8.9	6.5	5.6	Sales/Working Capital						7.7
105.4	NM	14.0							23.3
9.4	22.3	14.1							12.0
(42) 3.6	(25) 8.9	(28) 6.1	EBIT/Interest						(15) 5.0
1.4	2.9	2.6							2.5
3.7									
(11) 1.8			Net Profit + Depr., Dep., Amort./Cur. Mat. L/T/D						
.9									
.3	.3	.2							.4
.9	1.0	.8	Fixed/Worth						1.2
2.8	2.4	1.5							1.8
.6	.6	.7							.7
2.1	1.3	1.5	Debt/Worth						1.9
16.4	7.3	3.6							3.8
48.1	58.5	45.6							49.2
(41) 17.7	(25) 31.3	(28) 21.0	% Profit Before Taxes/Tangible Net Worth						14.2
2.8	7.3	3.8							3.3
14.4	21.9	15.7							9.0
3.7	6.9	5.7	% Profit Before Taxes/Total Assets						5.5
.7	2.7	1.5							1.6
25.4	45.0	23.7							18.8
10.0	5.4	5.6	Sales/Net Fixed Assets						4.0
4.5	3.1	3.1							2.6
2.5	1.9	2.2							2.3
1.8	1.6	1.5	Sales/Total Assets						1.5
1.1	1.0	1.0							1.1
1.3	1.0	1.1							1.6
(32) 2.0	(24) 2.8	(25) 2.7	% Depr., Dep., Amort./Sales						(14) 4.6
4.2	4.5	6.1							6.1
			% Officers', Directors' Owners' Comp/Sales						
2278661M	1795100M	1577676M	Net Sales ($)		2402M	4911M	34977M	123043M	1412343M
1587143M	1473973M	1122752M	Total Assets ($)		1069M	2512M	27307M	102002M	989862M

DATA NOT AVAILABLE

M = $ thousand MM = $ million

See Pages 9 through 22 for Explanation of Ratios and Data

Current Data Sorted by Assets							Comparative Historical Data	
						Type of Statement		
			1		3	Unqualified	4	8
		3	3	1		Reviewed	6	7
1	1	2				Compiled	4	2
		2				Tax Returns		5
	3	4	3	3	5	Other	16	20
	5 (4/1-9/30/13)		30 (10/1/13-3/31/14)				**4/1/09-3/31/10**	**4/1/10-3/31/11**
0-500M	**500M-2MM**	**2-10MM**	**10-50MM**	**50-100MM**	**100-250MM**		**ALL**	**ALL**
1	4	11	7	4	8	**NUMBER OF STATEMENTS**	30	42
%	%	%	%	%	%	**ASSETS**	%	%
		15.2				Cash & Equivalents	8.4	10.1
		31.8				Trade Receivables (net)	25.9	26.9
		33.7				Inventory	34.8	28.8
		3.6				All Other Current	2.7	3.6
		84.2				Total Current	71.7	69.5
		10.5				Fixed Assets (net)	17.9	18.9
		2.2				Intangibles (net)	5.0	7.5
		3.1				All Other Non-Current	5.5	4.1
		100.0				Total	100.0	100.0
						LIABILITIES		
		9.9				Notes Payable-Short Term	13.5	7.0
		1.7				Cur. Mat.-L.T.D.	2.8	3.4
		24.7				Trade Payables	15.2	18.3
		.0				Income Taxes Payable	.1	.2
		10.3				All Other Current	5.6	9.1
		46.7				Total Current	37.1	38.0
		11.4				Long-Term Debt	14.6	8.6
		.3				Deferred Taxes	.2	.5
		18.2				All Other Non-Current	8.3	7.7
		23.5				Net Worth	39.8	45.1
		100.0				Total Liabilties & Net Worth	100.0	100.0
						INCOME DATA		
		100.0				Net Sales	100.0	100.0
		26.3				Gross Profit	28.5	26.4
		21.0				Operating Expenses	25.5	19.1
		5.3				Operating Profit	3.0	7.3
		.4				All Other Expenses (net)	1.2	1.5
		4.8				Profit Before Taxes	1.9	5.8
						RATIOS		
		2.6					3.0	3.1
		2.0				Current	1.7	2.3
		1.5					1.4	1.3
		1.6					1.6	1.9
		1.4				Quick	1.0	.9
		.6					.5	.6
		39 9.4					**35** 10.4	**35** 10.3
		52 7.0				Sales/Receivables	**57** 6.4	**46** 8.0
		69 5.3					**63** 5.8	**61** 6.0
		25 14.7					**66** 5.5	**30** 12.0
		55 6.6				Cost of Sales/Inventory	**99** 3.7	**64** 5.7
		159 2.3					**146** 2.5	**114** 3.2
		38 9.7					**30** 12.2	**26** 13.8
		54 6.8				Cost of Sales/Payables	**39** 9.4	**39** 9.3
		66 5.5					**54** 6.7	**59** 6.2
		3.4					3.8	3.7
		6.1				Sales/Working Capital	7.6	6.8
		10.0					9.3	13.3
		34.3					11.4	36.5
		12.6				EBIT/Interest	(27) 2.9	(34) 7.8
		2.5					.4	2.3
						Net Profit + Depr., Dep., Amort./Cur. Mat. L/T/D		
		.1					.1	.2
		.5				Fixed/Worth	.4	.5
		3.1					1.0	2.1
		.6					.8	.5
		4.0				Debt/Worth	1.7	1.3
		13.9					4.5	5.2
							18.2	62.7
						% Profit Before Taxes/Tangible Net Worth	(27) 6.1	(37) 32.7
							-5.9	11.9
		30.2					8.0	19.6
		10.4				% Profit Before Taxes/Total Assets	1.9	10.3
		4.4					-1.6	3.2
		64.5					33.0	36.0
		29.1				Sales/Net Fixed Assets	14.2	14.9
		17.7					6.7	5.2
		2.7					2.1	2.6
		2.1				Sales/Total Assets	1.7	1.9
		1.8					1.2	1.4
							1.3	.8
						% Depr., Dep., Amort./Sales	(21) 1.9	(34) 1.7
							3.4	3.3
								1.9
						% Officers', Directors' Owners' Comp/Sales		(11) 3.6
								4.5
870M	**8887M**	**132282M**	**326343M**	**367322M**	**1074220M**	Net Sales ($)	**910373M**	**2935301M**
125M	**5607M**	**57531M**	**156291M**	**244809M**	**1112514M**	Total Assets ($)	**656237M**	**1661596M**

M = $ thousand MM = $ million

See Pages 9 through 22 for Explanation of Ratios and Data

Comparative Historical Data | **Current Data Sorted by Sales**

	4/1/11-3/31/12 ALL		4/1/12-3/31/13 ALL		4/1/13-3/31/14 ALL		0-1MM	1-3MM	3-5MM	5-10MM	10-25MM		25MM & OVER
						Type of Statement							
	6		6		4	Unqualified					1		3
	7		5		7	Reviewed					3		4
	4		6		4	Compiled	1	1		2			
	2		4		2	Tax Returns				1	1		
	17		19		18	Other		3		3	1		11
							5 (4/1-9/30/13)		30 (10/1/13-3/31/14)				
	36		40		35	**NUMBER OF STATEMENTS**	1	4		6	6		18
	%		%		%	**ASSETS**	%	%	%	%	%		%
	8.2		6.7		8.7	Cash & Equivalents			DATA NOT AVAILABLE				5.5
	28.6		25.3		24.6	Trade Receivables (net)							21.3
	27.3		30.0		28.8	Inventory							22.2
	5.0		3.3		2.7	All Other Current							1.4
	69.2		65.4		64.9	Total Current							50.3
	17.0		19.2		16.6	Fixed Assets (net)							20.3
	10.7		12.4		15.2	Intangibles (net)							26.1
	3.2		3.1		3.2	All Other Non-Current							3.3
	100.0		100.0		100.0	Total							100.0
						LIABILITIES							
	8.0		8.6		10.6	Notes Payable-Short Term							8.0
	1.7		5.8		2.2	Cur. Mat.-L.T.D.							2.4
	21.8		19.8		17.3	Trade Payables							14.8
	.2		.1		.0	Income Taxes Payable							.0
	9.4		9.2		7.6	All Other Current							7.2
	41.0		43.5		37.7	Total Current							32.4
	13.7		13.7		14.7	Long-Term Debt							18.6
	.7		.7		.5	Deferred Taxes							.8
	7.8		12.7		14.8	All Other Non-Current							6.3
	36.8		29.4		32.4	Net Worth							41.9
	100.0		100.0		100.0	Total Liabilities & Net Worth							100.0
						INCOME DATA							
	100.0		100.0		100.0	Net Sales							100.0
	27.8		33.1		34.4	Gross Profit							35.2
	20.5		25.8		27.0	Operating Expenses							24.1
	7.3		7.4		7.5	Operating Profit							11.1
	2.5		2.2		2.1	All Other Expenses (net)							3.9
	4.8		5.2		5.4	Profit Before Taxes							7.2
						RATIOS							
	2.9		2.6		2.4								2.0
	2.1		1.5		1.8	Current							1.4
	1.3		1.1		1.2								.7
	1.8		1.1		1.5								1.2
	.9		.8		.8	Quick							.6
	.6		.5		.4								.3
36	10.2	**33**	11.2	**24**	15.0							**18**	20.5
50	7.3	**46**	8.0	**47**	7.8	Sales/Receivables						**49**	7.5
61	6.0	**55**	6.6	**63**	5.8							**63**	5.8
33	11.2	**49**	7.5	**40**	9.1							**40**	9.1
64	5.7	**74**	4.9	**62**	5.9	Cost of Sales/Inventory						**51**	7.1
104	3.5	**118**	3.1	**114**	3.2							**114**	3.2
22	16.6	**24**	15.4	**35**	10.4							**36**	10.0
34	10.6	**37**	9.8	**43**	8.5	Cost of Sales/Payables						**41**	8.8
50	7.3	**65**	5.6	**59**	6.2							**59**	6.2
	4.1		4.3		5.0								5.9
	6.2		9.4		8.3	Sales/Working Capital							8.9
	18.3		31.4		21.8								-18.6
	43.1		22.0		24.2								34.0
(30)	11.0	(35)	10.8	(30)	7.4	EBIT/Interest						(15)	11.1
	3.2		1.9		2.2								2.2
			7.1										
		(11)	3.6			Net Profit + Depr., Dep., Amort./Cur. Mat. L/T/D							
			1.6										
	.2		.4		.2								.3
	.5		.8		.6	Fixed/Worth							.6
	18.7		NM		-1.6								-.6
	.4		1.0		.8								.8
	1.6		2.6		2.7	Debt/Worth							2.2
	41.1		NM		-4.6								-1.8
	64.4		58.4		80.7								71.1
(28)	36.7	(30)	23.8	(26)	40.8	% Profit Before Taxes/Tangible Net Worth						(13)	38.1
	12.1		9.3		12.5								13.3
	25.9		17.4		23.5								24.2
	9.8		8.9		6.7	% Profit Before Taxes/Total Assets							6.9
	2.3		2.1		2.1								2.7
	68.7		24.4		30.5								25.7
	16.1		13.0		14.7	Sales/Net Fixed Assets							9.0
	8.6		6.9		7.8								3.0
	3.0		2.3		2.4								2.4
	2.1		1.9		1.9	Sales/Total Assets							1.5
	1.3		1.5		1.3								.6
	.4		.4		.8								1.3
(27)	1.3	(35)	1.9	(28)	1.9	% Depr., Dep., Amort./Sales						(16)	2.3
	2.3		3.2		3.4								8.9
			1.7										
		(12)	3.7			% Officers', Directors' Owners' Comp/Sales							
			8.0										
	1647529M		2697305M		1909924M	Net Sales ($)	870M	8887M		44790M	107883M		1747494M
	1032889M		1798770M		1576877M	Total Assets ($)	125M	5607M		24675M	43300M		1503170M

M = $ thousand MM = $ million

See Pages 9 through 22 for Explanation of Ratios and Data

Current Data Sorted by Assets							Comparative Historical Data	
						Type of Statement		
		1	1	1		Unqualified	3	5
	1	3		1		Reviewed	1	4
			1			Compiled	3	1
						Tax Returns		4
		4	6	1	2	Other	9	9
	3 (4/1-9/30/13)		19 (10/1/13-3/31/14)				4/1/09-3/31/10 ALL	4/1/10-3/31/11 ALL
0-500M	500M-2MM	2-10MM	10-50MM	50-100MM	100-250MM			
	1	8	8	3	2	NUMBER OF STATEMENTS	16	23
%	%	%	%	%	%	**ASSETS**	%	%
DATA NOT AVAILABLE						Cash & Equivalents	5.4	4.4
						Trade Receivables (net)	16.9	23.6
						Inventory	28.9	34.1
						All Other Current	3.2	4.4
						Total Current	54.4	66.5
						Fixed Assets (net)	29.4	21.4
						Intangibles (net)	12.6	8.7
						All Other Non-Current	3.7	3.4
						Total	100.0	100.0
						LIABILITIES		
						Notes Payable-Short Term	5.9	10.2
						Cur. Mat.-L.T.D.	4.4	3.4
						Trade Payables	10.6	18.7
						Income Taxes Payable	.1	.4
						All Other Current	7.2	8.0
						Total Current	28.2	40.7
						Long-Term Debt	20.5	18.4
						Deferred Taxes	.9	1.1
						All Other Non-Current	10.2	5.8
						Net Worth	40.2	34.1
						Total Liabilties & Net Worth	100.0	100.0
						INCOME DATA		
						Net Sales	100.0	100.0
						Gross Profit	25.8	27.2
						Operating Expenses	20.9	20.9
						Operating Profit	5.0	6.3
						All Other Expenses (net)	2.8	1.2
						Profit Before Taxes	2.2	5.1
						RATIOS		
						Current	2.8	3.2
							1.9	1.5
							1.3	1.2
						Quick	1.3	1.0
							.7	.8
							.5	.5
						Sales/Receivables	**24** 15.0	**27** 13.7
							41 8.9	**35** 10.4
							59 6.1	**53** 6.9
						Cost of Sales/Inventory	**49** 7.4	**42** 8.7
							113 3.2	**79** 4.6
							149 2.4	**117** 3.1
						Cost of Sales/Payables	**20** 18.0	**26** 14.0
							38 9.7	**31** 11.7
							49 7.5	**47** 7.8
						Sales/Working Capital	3.4	4.3
							6.2	8.4
							13.0	22.8
						EBIT/Interest	7.4	15.3
							(15) 1.3	(21) 4.9
							-1.0	2.0
						Net Profit + Depr., Dep., Amort./Cur. Mat. L/T/D		
						Fixed/Worth	.5	.2
							.8	.8
							NM	4.9
						Debt/Worth	.8	1.1
							1.8	2.3
							NM	16.8
						% Profit Before Taxes/Tangible Net Worth	39.0	121.0
							(12) 6.3	(20) 30.7
							-12.4	9.7
						% Profit Before Taxes/Total Assets	12.8	17.3
							1.5	8.4
							-3.1	4.0
						Sales/Net Fixed Assets	14.5	45.6
							5.0	18.4
							2.0	4.3
						Sales/Total Assets	1.9	2.9
							1.3	2.2
							.9	1.3
						% Depr., Dep., Amort./Sales	2.0	.6
							(13) 2.7	(20) 1.5
							5.0	5.4
						% Officers', Directors' Owners' Comp/Sales		
	1676M	106179M	309346M	384470M	704196M	Net Sales ($)	606227M	1545197M
	919M	47167M	172548M	200598M	370954M	Total Assets ($)	392550M	746971M

M = $ thousand MM = $ million

Comparative Historical Data | Current Data Sorted by Sales

						Type of Statement							
	3				3	Unqualified					1		2
	8		7		5	Reviewed		1	1	2			1
	1				1	Compiled							
	2		1			Tax Returns					1		
	16		12		13	Other			1		3		9
	4/1/11-3/31/12 ALL		4/1/12-3/31/13 ALL		4/1/13-3/31/14 ALL		3 (4/1-9/30/13)			19 (10/1/13-3/31/14)			
							0-1MM	1-3MM	3-5MM	5-10MM	10-25MM		25MM & OVER
	30		20		22	NUMBER OF STATEMENTS		1	2	2	5		12
	%		%		%	ASSETS	%	%	%	%	%		%
	9.0		7.7		10.3	Cash & Equivalents	DATA NOT AVAILABLE						5.7
	22.6		23.9		23.2	Trade Receivables (net)							24.7
	29.2		32.2		27.5	Inventory							25.2
	2.1		2.6		4.8	All Other Current							2.5
	62.9		66.4		65.8	Total Current							58.2
	27.7		18.1		23.1	Fixed Assets (net)							28.5
	5.7		6.9		4.3	Intangibles (net)							7.0
	3.7		8.6		6.8	All Other Non-Current							6.3
	100.0		100.0		100.0	Total							100.0
						LIABILITIES							
	11.9		8.3		8.8	Notes Payable-Short Term							7.2
	3.9		5.4		2.9	Cur. Mat.-L.T.D.							4.1
	13.9		16.4		16.6	Trade Payables							16.3
	.1		.4		.0	Income Taxes Payable							.1
	11.0		7.6		8.3	All Other Current							7.2
	40.8		38.0		36.7	Total Current							34.9
	19.9		12.7		15.9	Long-Term Debt							18.3
	.8		1.1		.7	Deferred Taxes							1.3
	5.4		16.5		13.5	All Other Non-Current							19.6
	33.2		31.7		33.2	Net Worth							26.0
	100.0		100.0		100.0	Total Liabilities & Net Worth							100.0
						INCOME DATA							
	100.0		100.0		100.0	Net Sales							100.0
	25.3		25.9		30.5	Gross Profit							27.7
	20.3		17.9		23.6	Operating Expenses							19.3
	5.1		8.0		6.9	Operating Profit							8.4
	1.0		1.9		1.6	All Other Expenses (net)							2.4
	4.1		6.0		5.3	Profit Before Taxes							6.0
						RATIOS							
	2.2		3.2		3.5								2.5
	1.4		1.6		1.6	Current							1.5
	1.2		1.1		1.2								1.1
	1.3		1.0		1.7								1.5
	.8		.7		.9	Quick							.8
	.5		.6		.6								.6
26	14.1	29	12.5	35	10.4							38	9.5
38	9.6	40	9.1	43	8.5	Sales/Receivables						41	8.9
46	7.9	51	7.2	56	6.5							52	7.0
33	11.1	38	9.7	34	10.6							36	10.2
53	6.9	74	4.9	55	6.6	Cost of Sales/Inventory						54	6.8
107	3.4	91	4.0	118	3.1							104	3.5
20	18.3	19	19.2	24	15.4							30	12.3
27	13.4	34	10.8	41	9.0	Cost of Sales/Payables						37	9.9
34	10.8	46	7.9	57	6.4							55	6.6
	5.7		4.0		4.5								4.7
	10.5		8.8		7.6	Sales/Working Capital							10.2
	30.1		33.0		23.1								42.0
	13.5		8.6		22.4								30.3
(26)	4.2	(18)	3.3	(20)	6.8	EBIT/Interest							8.5
	1.9		2.0		1.0								1.0
			9.2										
		(10)	3.2			Net Profit + Depr., Dep., Amort./Cur. Mat. L/T/D							
			1.6										
	.4		.1		.2								.6
	.9		.8		.7	Fixed/Worth							1.6
	2.7		1.3		2.0								3.2
	.7		.8		1.0								1.3
	2.2		2.4		2.7	Debt/Worth							3.5
	6.2		5.0		6.0								5.5
	63.6		60.5		56.6								59.4
(27)	26.8	(16)	22.7	(20)	33.9	% Profit Before Taxes/Tangible Net Worth						(10)	48.0
	5.1		9.1		-.2								7.7
	16.1		18.6		23.5								21.3
	10.0		12.3		11.6	% Profit Before Taxes/Total Assets							14.0
	3.3		2.9		-.8								1.5
	20.6		30.4		15.0								14.3
	8.7		15.2		9.0	Sales/Net Fixed Assets							8.1
	4.4		6.7		6.5								5.9
	3.0		2.8		2.6								2.7
	2.1		2.2		1.8	Sales/Total Assets							2.1
	1.5		1.5		1.4								1.5
	1.1		.4		1.1								1.3
(26)	2.3	(19)	1.2	(21)	1.7	% Depr., Dep., Amort./Sales						(11)	1.7
	5.2		4.3		3.7								3.2
						% Officers', Directors' Owners' Comp/Sales							
	1164960M		861875M		1505867M	Net Sales ($)		1676M	9004M	17135M	83424M		1394628M
	615344M		454867M		792186M	Total Assets ($)		919M	6485M	9435M	47675M		727672M

M = $ thousand MM = $ million

See Pages 9 through 22 for Explanation of Ratios and Data

Current Data Sorted by Assets							Comparative Historical Data	
						Type of Statement		
		1	5	4	4	Unqualified	14	13
		3	4		1	Reviewed	6	7
1		2				Compiled	4	4
1						Tax Returns	3	4
1	1	5	11	3	1	Other	19	27
7 (4/1-9/30/13)			41 (10/1/13-3/31/14)				**4/1/09-3/31/10**	**4/1/10-3/31/11**
0-500M	**500M-2MM**	**2-10MM**	**10-50MM**	**50-100MM**	**100-250MM**		**ALL**	**ALL**
3	1	11	20	7	6	**NUMBER OF STATEMENTS**	46	55
%	%	%	%	%	%	**ASSETS**	%	%
		12.6	15.3			Cash & Equivalents	9.0	10.2
		32.3	24.5			Trade Receivables (net)	27.2	30.3
		30.2	25.9			Inventory	24.5	27.4
		6.4	3.6			All Other Current	2.8	3.3
		81.6	69.2			Total Current	63.5	71.2
		12.0	21.1			Fixed Assets (net)	23.8	19.3
		4.0	4.5			Intangibles (net)	6.1	3.9
		2.4	5.3			All Other Non-Current	6.7	5.6
		100.0	100.0			Total	100.0	100.0
						LIABILITIES		
		5.1	8.9			Notes Payable-Short Term	9.3	12.5
		1.9	1.2			Cur. Mat.-L.T.D.	3.8	1.7
		16.2	20.4			Trade Payables	14.1	21.0
		.0	.3			Income Taxes Payable	.1	.0
		15.2	17.1			All Other Current	13.8	10.5
		38.4	47.8			Total Current	41.1	45.8
		5.0	7.6			Long-Term Debt	25.1	5.1
		.1	.5			Deferred Taxes	.7	.4
		3.7	6.6			All Other Non-Current	14.3	10.5
		52.8	37.5			Net Worth	18.7	38.2
		100.0	100.0			Total Liabilties & Net Worth	100.0	100.0
						INCOME DATA		
		100.0	100.0			Net Sales	100.0	100.0
		28.9	21.5			Gross Profit	22.2	24.7
		19.6	15.7			Operating Expenses	21.8	19.2
		9.4	5.8			Operating Profit	.3	5.5
		1.9	.2			All Other Expenses (net)	1.5	.7
		7.5	5.5			Profit Before Taxes	-1.2	4.8
						RATIOS		
		5.6	2.4				2.9	2.8
		3.2	1.6			Current	1.5	1.4
		1.2	.9				1.1	1.2
		2.3	1.3				1.3	1.6
		1.0	.8			Quick	.9	(54) .9
		.8	.5				.5	.6
		26 14.3	**25** 14.4				**32** 11.2	**28** 13.3
		31 11.7	**43** 8.4			Sales/Receivables	**55** 6.6	**45** 8.1
		54 6.7	**51** 7.2				**73** 5.0	**58** 6.3
		26 13.8	**34** 10.6				**20** 18.3	**29** 12.6
		41 8.9	**44** 8.3			Cost of Sales/Inventory	**41** 8.9	**44** 8.4
		118 3.1	**62** 5.9				**98** 3.7	**64** 5.7
		10 34.9	**23** 15.8				**15** 24.9	**18** 20.7
		17 21.8	**34** 10.7			Cost of Sales/Payables	**32** 11.5	**34** 10.7
		54 6.8	**42** 8.6				**58** 6.3	**51** 7.2
		3.3	5.9				4.9	5.9
		5.9	8.4			Sales/Working Capital	11.9	13.9
		35.2	-57.1				54.1	25.6
			35.1				4.0	32.6
			(18) 8.5			EBIT/Interest	(42) 1.4	(45) 7.6
			1.6				-3.3	3.4
							2.5	32.4
						Net Profit + Depr., Dep., Amort./Cur. Mat. L/T/D	(11) .9	(13) 3.1
							-1.6	1.5
		.0	.1				.2	.2
		.1	.8			Fixed/Worth	.6	.5
		.8	1.6				2.5	1.0
		.2	.7				.8	.4
		.7	1.4			Debt/Worth	2.0	1.7
		4.2	5.2				7.7	3.6
		86.5	55.5				28.1	57.5
		(10) 28.5	(18) 31.7			% Profit Before Taxes/Tangible Net Worth	(37) 5.8	(46) 22.4
		4.5	9.1				-10.2	9.3
		25.0	17.7				5.3	18.9
		11.8	9.9			% Profit Before Taxes/Total Assets	1.7	9.7
		1.7	2.9				-8.9	3.9
		728.8	46.9				22.5	59.7
		49.1	16.3			Sales/Net Fixed Assets	11.1	16.3
		12.7	6.1				4.8	8.0
		3.2	3.0				2.5	3.0
		3.0	2.3			Sales/Total Assets	1.9	2.7
		2.6	1.9				1.2	2.0
			.7				1.0	.9
			(18) 1.5			% Depr., Dep., Amort./Sales	(36) 2.4	(46) 1.4
			2.4				4.6	2.6
						% Officers', Directors' Owners' Comp/Sales		
8860M	6102M	174701M	1095689M	1699816M	1858524M	Net Sales ($)	2166401M	3228228M
888M	848M	63535M	481638M	525932M	1030295M	Total Assets ($)	1304020M	1470636M

M = $ thousand MM = $ million

See Pages 9 through 22 for Explanation of Ratios and Data

Comparative Historical Data				Current Data Sorted by Sales					
			Type of Statement						
10	8	14	Unqualified				1	1	12
7	6	8	Reviewed				2	1	5
5	2	3	Compiled				2	1	
3	1	1	Tax Returns	1					
13	22	22	Other		1		2	1	18
					7 (4/1-9/30/13)		41 (10/1/13-3/31/14)		
4/1/11-3/31/12 ALL	**4/1/12-3/31/13 ALL**	**4/1/13-3/31/14 ALL**		**0-1MM**	**1-3MM**	**3-5MM**	**5-10MM**	**10-25MM**	**25MM & OVER**
38	39	48	**NUMBER OF STATEMENTS**	1	1		7	4	35
%	%	%	**ASSETS**	%	%	%	%	%	%
10.5	11.5	13.8	Cash & Equivalents			DATA NOT AVAILABLE			12.5
30.6	25.8	27.1	Trade Receivables (net)						27.0
23.2	25.6	23.8	Inventory						22.1
3.3	3.6	4.7	All Other Current						4.5
67.6	66.6	69.5	Total Current						66.1
21.8	21.1	22.0	Fixed Assets (net)						25.3
5.6	3.2	3.8	Intangibles (net)						3.7
5.0	9.1	4.7	All Other Non-Current						4.9
100.0	100.0	100.0	Total						100.0
			LIABILITIES						
10.7	8.0	7.1	Notes Payable-Short Term						8.9
2.0	1.0	1.4	Cur. Mat.-L.T.D.						1.4
18.1	14.1	19.0	Trade Payables						22.6
.1	.2	.1	Income Taxes Payable						.1
13.2	12.2	16.6	All Other Current						17.3
44.0	35.5	44.4	Total Current						50.3
9.9	9.7	9.2	Long-Term Debt						8.2
.7	.6	.6	Deferred Taxes						.9
5.8	6.4	6.6	All Other Non-Current						5.3
39.4	47.8	39.2	Net Worth						35.3
100.0	100.0	100.0	Total Liabilties & Net Worth						100.0
			INCOME DATA						
100.0	100.0	100.0	Net Sales						100.0
19.4	24.7	21.0	Gross Profit						15.8
14.8	18.6	15.3	Operating Expenses						10.9
4.6	6.0	5.7	Operating Profit						4.9
.4	.1	.8	All Other Expenses (net)						.9
4.2	6.0	4.9	Profit Before Taxes						4.0
			RATIOS						
3.2	3.6	3.2	Current						2.1
1.6	1.8	1.6							1.4
1.1	1.4	1.0							.9
1.8	1.9	1.4	Quick						1.2
.9	1.0	.9							.7
.5	.7	.6							.5
29 12.6	**25** 14.4	**25** 14.4	Sales/Receivables						**26** 14.3
37 9.8	**38** 9.6	**39** 9.3							**42** 8.7
59 6.2	**49** 7.4	**51** 7.2							**53** 6.9
23 15.9	**22** 16.5	**24** 15.3	Cost of Sales/Inventory						**23** 15.8
41 9.0	**43** 8.5	**40** 9.1							**39** 9.3
57 6.4	**73** 5.0	**65** 5.6							**57** 6.4
15 24.2	**12** 29.9	**13** 28.4	Cost of Sales/Payables						**15** 23.6
30 12.2	**26** 13.8	**30** 12.1							**33** 10.9
46 8.0	**42** 8.7	**47** 7.8							**47** 7.8
5.2	5.0	5.4	Sales/Working Capital						6.0
11.6	8.7	9.3							11.1
30.6	16.8	200.9							-47.6
31.2	18.0	33.2	EBIT/Interest						35.2
(34) 9.5	(31) 7.8	(40) 7.8							(31) 7.6
3.0	2.1	-.1							-.6
9.8	51.4	12.7	Net Profit + Depr., Dep., Amort./Cur. Mat. L/T/D						12.9
(13) 3.4	(11) 5.3	(12) 5.9							(11) 2.4
.8	2.6	1.6							1.4
.3	.1	.1	Fixed/Worth						.3
.5	.4	.8							.9
1.1	1.0	1.7							2.0
.6	.4	.4	Debt/Worth						.9
1.4	1.1	1.4							1.7
4.7	2.6	6.0							7.4
46.7	46.1	47.8	% Profit Before Taxes/Tangible Net Worth						39.9
(35) 15.9	(36) 22.8	(41) 24.5							(30) 23.1
9.2	8.5	8.7							8.9
16.6	14.6	19.5	% Profit Before Taxes/Total Assets						17.5
6.9	8.7	8.1							7.1
3.0	4.2	.5							.5
34.5	56.6	51.9	Sales/Net Fixed Assets						30.4
10.7	13.8	12.1							9.6
7.2	6.8	5.9							4.7
3.2	3.3	3.1	Sales/Total Assets						3.0
2.5	2.5	2.6							2.3
2.1	1.9	1.8							1.8
.9	.5	.7	% Depr., Dep., Amort./Sales						.6
(31) 1.5	(33) 1.4	(38) 1.7							(31) 1.7
2.6	2.3	2.8							2.8
			% Officers', Directors' Owners' Comp/Sales						
2851193M	3357323M	4843692M	Net Sales ($)	593M	1023M		55440M	62510M	4724126M
1427610M	1457238M	2103136M	Total Assets ($)	214M	269M		24044M	33905M	2044704M

M = $ thousand MM = $ million

See Pages 9 through 22 for Explanation of Ratios and Data

Current Data Sorted by Assets | **Comparative Historical Data**

0-500M	500M-2MM	2-10MM	10-50MM	50-100MM	100-250MM	**Type of Statement**	4/1/09-3/31/10 ALL	4/1/10-3/31/11 ALL
		1	8	2	1	Unqualified	12	15
	1	8	11	1		Reviewed	15	12
	2	8	1			Compiled	3	4
						Tax Returns	2	1
1	1	8	15	8	12	Other	35	33
	16 (4/1-9/30/13)		73 (10/1/13-3/31/14)					
0-500M	**500M-2MM**	**2-10MM**	**10-50MM**	**50-100MM**	**100-250MM**		**4/1/09-3/31/10 ALL**	**4/1/10-3/31/11 ALL**
1	4	25	35	11	13	**NUMBER OF STATEMENTS**	67	65
%	%	%	%	%	%	**ASSETS**	%	%
		13.6	6.7	2.6	3.7	Cash & Equivalents	6.2	5.7
		32.8	26.8	25.6	30.0	Trade Receivables (net)	25.1	26.6
		21.9	22.2	19.4	14.6	Inventory	16.3	17.6
		1.1	3.7	3.5	4.1	All Other Current	2.2	3.0
		69.4	59.4	51.0	52.4	Total Current	49.7	52.9
		20.8	33.2	34.9	33.9	Fixed Assets (net)	40.3	38.1
		3.8	.8	5.4	5.8	Intangibles (net)	3.7	3.2
		6.0	6.6	8.7	7.9	All Other Non-Current	6.3	5.8
		100.0	100.0	100.0	100.0	Total	100.0	100.0
						LIABILITIES		
		12.1	9.6	7.5	4.8	Notes Payable-Short Term	10.8	12.0
		1.5	3.4	4.3	2.0	Cur. Mat.-L.T.D.	4.6	4.5
		21.0	15.3	16.3	20.5	Trade Payables	15.3	18.5
		.2	.1	.1	.1	Income Taxes Payable	.0	.2
		8.2	8.5	6.5	6.1	All Other Current	8.7	8.5
		43.1	37.0	34.8	33.4	Total Current	39.4	43.8
		11.6	13.7	16.7	26.6	Long-Term Debt	19.1	16.8
		.4	.9	.9	.6	Deferred Taxes	.7	.9
		3.1	2.5	6.5	14.5	All Other Non-Current	7.0	7.6
		41.9	45.9	41.1	24.9	Net Worth	33.8	30.9
		100.0	100.0	100.0	100.0	Total Liabilties & Net Worth	100.0	100.0
						INCOME DATA		
		100.0	100.0	100.0	100.0	Net Sales	100.0	100.0
		22.7	17.5	15.0	17.3	Gross Profit	16.2	19.1
		15.9	12.9	8.5	12.6	Operating Expenses	16.9	14.8
		6.8	4.6	6.5	4.7	Operating Profit	-.6	4.3
		.8	.4	.6	1.3	All Other Expenses (net)	1.0	.4
		6.0	4.2	6.0	3.4	Profit Before Taxes	-1.6	4.0
						RATIOS		
		2.4	3.0	2.3	2.2		2.2	1.7
		1.5	1.8	1.5	1.6	Current	1.2	1.3
		1.2	1.0	1.2	1.3		.9	.9
		1.5	1.6	1.1	1.3		1.2	1.0
		1.0	1.0	.8	1.0	Quick	.8	.8
		.7	.6	.6	.8		.6	.5
		42 8.6	**40** 9.2	**54** 6.7	**47** 7.7		**46** 7.9	**40** 9.2
		54 6.7	**52** 7.0	**62** 5.9	**60** 6.1	Sales/Receivables	**60** 6.1	**52** 7.1
		68 5.4	**61** 6.0	**72** 5.1	**64** 5.7		**69** 5.3	**63** 5.8
		35 10.5	**32** 11.3	**37** 9.8	**17** 21.5		**29** 12.7	**29** 12.8
		48 7.6	**47** 7.7	**59** 6.2	**24** 15.5	Cost of Sales/Inventory	**38** 9.6	**35** 10.3
		56 6.5	**73** 5.0	**73** 5.0	**61** 6.0		**64** 5.7	**53** 6.9
		27 13.7	**21** 17.8	**37** 9.8	**33** 11.2		**24** 15.3	**27** 13.5
		43 8.4	**33** 11.0	**42** 8.7	**43** 8.4	Cost of Sales/Payables	**41** 9.0	**41** 8.9
		58 6.3	**54** 6.8	**59** 6.2	**53** 6.9		**59** 6.2	**52** 7.0
		5.3	4.1	6.1	6.7		5.6	8.6
		8.0	7.7	8.4	11.4	Sales/Working Capital	20.3	24.3
		30.0	-85.2	17.9	17.1		-42.3	-43.4
		54.9	26.6	19.5	12.3		4.1	9.7
		(23) 7.8	(34) 5.1	(10) 8.9	(12) 4.4	EBIT/Interest	(66) .5	(60) 4.8
		2.4	1.3	2.9	1.5		-2.9	1.6
							1.9	4.8
						Net Profit + Depr., Dep., Amort./Cur. Mat. L/T/D	(15) .9	(23) 3.2
							.1	1.6
		.2	.5	.6	.9		.7	.8
		.4	.8	1.1	1.3	Fixed/Worth	1.3	1.3
		1.1	1.7	4.5	8.1		2.3	5.5
		.6	.5	.5	1.3		.8	.9
		1.4	1.2	1.4	3.4	Debt/Worth	1.9	2.6
		2.8	2.8	6.0	21.2		4.7	9.3
		59.7	35.3	56.2	65.3		14.7	37.7
		(22) 29.2	(33) 13.5	(10) 18.9	(11) 20.0	% Profit Before Taxes/Tangible Net Worth	(60) -.3	(54) 18.3
		12.6	6.5	16.6	1.3		-19.2	5.1
		18.9	12.6	13.2	11.4		6.4	12.8
		11.4	6.1	8.9	6.1	% Profit Before Taxes/Total Assets	-.6	5.4
		1.9	.9	3.8	.8		-7.6	1.2
		19.0	8.3	6.1	9.6		7.1	8.2
		13.1	6.1	5.0	5.0	Sales/Net Fixed Assets	4.3	5.9
		8.3	4.0	2.8	3.8		2.6	3.3
		2.6	2.5	1.8	2.3		2.0	2.4
		2.2	2.0	1.5	1.8	Sales/Total Assets	1.5	1.8
		1.8	1.2	1.3	1.5		1.0	1.4
		1.0	1.6	2.6			2.6	2.4
		(23) 1.5	(33) 2.4	3.5		% Depr., Dep., Amort./Sales	(57) 4.3	(59) 3.3
		2.1	3.2	4.3			5.9	5.3
		1.4					2.2	.9
		(11) 2.8				% Officers', Directors' Owners' Comp/Sales	(16) 4.8	(11) 1.8
		3.9					6.4	4.9
26M	8968M	336879M	1474362M	1351250M	3859418M	Net Sales ($)	3059438M	5241893M
13M	4998M	151900M	780253M	863569M	1916727M	Total Assets ($)	2036772M	2805535M

M = $ thousand MM = $ million

See Pages 9 through 22 for Explanation of Ratios and Data

Comparative Historical Data / Current Data Sorted by Sales

4/1/11-3/31/12 ALL	4/1/12-3/31/13 ALL	4/1/13-3/31/14 ALL	Type of Statement	0-1MM	1-3MM	3-5MM	5-10MM	10-25MM	25MM & OVER
15	13	12	Unqualified			1		1	10
13	16	21	Reviewed			1	3	9	8
8	5	11	Compiled	1		2	3	5	
	2		Tax Returns						
36	32	45	Other	2			2	10	31
				16 (4/1-9/30/13)			73 (10/1/13-3/31/14)		
72	68	89	NUMBER OF STATEMENTS	3		4	8	25	49
%	%	%	**ASSETS**	%	%	%	%	%	%
5.5	7.1	7.6	Cash & Equivalents		DATA NOT AVAILABLE			12.5	4.2
28.6	26.8	28.2	Trade Receivables (net)					27.7	28.6
19.2	18.8	20.4	Inventory					21.2	19.9
2.6	2.5	2.8	All Other Current					.8	4.3
55.9	55.2	59.0	Total Current					62.2	57.1
33.4	36.1	30.9	Fixed Assets (net)					28.0	32.9
4.4	1.8	3.4	Intangibles (net)					2.6	3.3
6.3	6.9	6.7	All Other Non-Current					7.2	6.8
100.0	100.0	100.0	Total					100.0	100.0
			LIABILITIES						
10.7	8.6	9.7	Notes Payable-Short Term					8.9	7.9
3.1	2.9	2.7	Cur. Mat.-L.T.D.					1.7	3.5
16.7	17.2	17.5	Trade Payables					18.5	18.0
.1	.3	.2	Income Taxes Payable					.3	.1
10.8	12.8	9.7	All Other Current					7.0	8.0
41.4	41.7	39.8	Total Current					36.4	37.5
12.7	19.6	19.5	Long-Term Debt					10.6	17.9
1.1	1.2	.8	Deferred Taxes					.3	.9
4.4	4.4	5.0	All Other Non-Current					1.5	6.6
40.3	33.1	34.9	Net Worth					51.2	37.1
100.0	100.0	100.0	Total Liabilties & Net Worth					100.0	100.0
			INCOME DATA						
100.0	100.0	100.0	Net Sales					100.0	100.0
18.2	17.5	19.5	Gross Profit					21.3	16.7
13.1	13.7	14.2	Operating Expenses					15.6	11.5
5.1	3.8	5.3	Operating Profit					5.7	5.2
.4	.5	.8	All Other Expenses (net)					.1	.7
4.8	3.3	4.5	Profit Before Taxes					5.6	4.5
			RATIOS						
2.0	2.2	2.4	Current					3.0	2.4
1.4	1.5	1.5						1.4	1.6
1.0	1.0	1.2						1.1	1.2
1.2	1.4	1.4	Quick					1.8	1.4
.8	.9	1.0						.9	1.0
.6	.6	.6						.7	.6
43 8.4	**41** 8.9	**41** 8.8	Sales/Receivables					**38** 9.6	**42** 8.7
55 6.6	**52** 7.0	**54** 6.7						**51** 7.2	**54** 6.7
68 5.4	**63** 5.8	**66** 5.5						**65** 5.6	**64** 5.7
27 13.3	**24** 15.4	**29** 12.6	Cost of Sales/Inventory					**41** 9.0	**27** 13.5
41 9.0	**38** 9.5	**46** 8.0						**54** 6.8	**44** 8.3
56 6.5	**63** 5.8	**65** 5.6						**62** 5.9	**66** 5.5
24 15.0	**22** 16.6	**27** 13.6	Cost of Sales/Payables					**27** 13.7	**27** 13.6
39 9.3	**35** 10.4	**39** 9.4						**39** 9.3	**38** 9.6
51 7.1	**47** 7.8	**55** 6.6						**55** 6.6	**54** 6.7
6.1	6.2	5.0	Sales/Working Capital					5.0	6.0
15.3	12.7	8.6						8.0	8.6
580.9	152.9	33.9						40.8	18.6
24.7	17.0	19.2	EBIT/Interest					53.5	19.2
(70) 6.7	(65) 5.6	(83) 6.7						(22) 6.7	(47) 6.8
2.4	1.4	2.3						1.9	2.6
8.8	8.1	6.7	Net Profit + Depr., Dep., Amort./Cur. Mat. L/T/D						5.5
(23) 4.8	(31) 4.7	(23) 3.5							(18) 3.4
2.1	2.5	2.8							2.6
.6	.6	.5	Fixed/Worth					.2	.6
.9	.9	.8						.5	.9
1.8	2.0	2.1						1.3	2.4
.8	.7	.6	Debt/Worth					.4	.7
1.6	1.4	1.6						1.4	1.9
4.0	3.6	5.3						2.2	5.8
42.9	34.1	43.8	% Profit Before Taxes/Tangible Net Worth					48.4	40.4
(66) 24.0	(60) 21.1	(80) 22.3						17.1	(44) 22.7
7.9	4.5	7.4						6.9	9.2
17.9	14.0	15.3	% Profit Before Taxes/Total Assets					16.4	12.9
8.6	6.2	8.2						8.2	8.4
2.3	.7	2.0						2.3	2.9
12.5	10.7	12.9	Sales/Net Fixed Assets					18.9	8.8
6.1	5.1	6.5						9.1	5.7
3.7	3.2	4.2						3.9	4.3
2.5	2.5	2.5	Sales/Total Assets					2.6	2.4
2.0	2.0	2.0						2.0	2.0
1.3	1.5	1.5						1.2	1.5
1.6	1.6	1.4	% Depr., Dep., Amort./Sales					1.0	1.9
(68) 2.8	(64) 2.9	(79) 2.3						(23) 1.8	(43) 2.6
4.5	4.4	3.4						3.3	3.6
1.4	1.6	.9	% Officers', Directors' Owners' Comp/Sales						
(16) 3.8	(12) 3.6	(17) 2.1							
5.1	4.1	3.7							
5245787M	6161272M	7030903M	Net Sales ($)	1282M		16140M	70278M	434125M	6509078M
2782210M	3373530M	3717460M	Total Assets ($)	2064M		8170M	45915M	266143M	3395168M

M = $ thousand MM = $ million

See Pages 9 through 22 for Explanation of Ratios and Data

Current Data Sorted by Assets							Comparative Historical Data	
						Type of Statement		
		10	25	19	20	Unqualified	75	55
	2	22	22	2		Reviewed	61	64
1	5	17	5	2		Compiled	35	37
3	6	10	1			Tax Returns	20	27
	17	28	39	24	37	Other	165	157
37 (4/1-9/30/13)			280 (10/1/13-3/31/14)				**4/1/09-3/31/10 ALL**	**4/1/10-3/31/11 ALL**
0-500M	**500M-2MM**	**2-10MM**	**10-50MM**	**50-100MM**	**100-250MM**			
4	30	87	92	47	57	**NUMBER OF STATEMENTS**	356	340
%	%	%	%	%	%	**ASSETS**	%	%
	18.6	10.2	9.9	5.2	5.9	Cash & Equivalents	8.4	9.2
	26.1	23.5	24.3	19.8	22.5	Trade Receivables (net)	23.8	24.2
	28.3	30.8	26.3	21.6	15.3	Inventory	28.0	28.1
	1.2	2.3	3.0	5.3	4.2	All Other Current	3.0	2.8
	74.2	66.9	63.4	51.9	47.9	Total Current	63.3	64.3
	16.2	24.7	28.9	33.0	29.5	Fixed Assets (net)	26.8	25.5
	4.6	5.5	2.9	9.9	16.7	Intangibles (net)	4.9	5.0
	5.0	2.9	4.8	5.3	5.9	All Other Non-Current	4.9	5.2
	100.0	100.0	100.0	100.0	100.0	Total	100.0	100.0
						LIABILITIES		
	10.3	10.4	10.0	7.6	5.5	Notes Payable-Short Term	12.5	11.2
	1.9	3.1	2.9	2.7	3.2	Cur. Mat.-L.T.D.	4.0	3.5
	19.2	16.7	15.9	13.4	16.7	Trade Payables	16.6	15.5
	.2	.1	.3	.3	.4	Income Taxes Payable	.1	.3
	29.5	10.2	10.3	9.9	10.5	All Other Current	10.0	9.3
	61.1	40.4	39.4	34.0	36.3	Total Current	43.3	39.7
	11.5	13.3	11.9	12.7	23.0	Long-Term Debt	15.6	13.2
	.1	.2	.9	1.4	2.2	Deferred Taxes	.6	.8
	11.4	5.4	3.2	5.9	7.1	All Other Non-Current	7.4	5.9
	16.0	40.7	44.6	46.0	31.4	Net Worth	33.1	40.3
	100.0	100.0	100.0	100.0	100.0	Total Liabilties & Net Worth	100.0	100.0
						INCOME DATA		
	100.0	100.0	100.0	100.0	100.0	Net Sales	100.0	100.0
	33.3	31.1	20.8	17.3	19.2	Gross Profit	24.8	27.6
	28.3	24.6	14.5	12.6	13.0	Operating Expenses	22.9	21.9
	5.1	6.5	6.2	4.7	6.2	Operating Profit	1.9	5.7
	.4	2.0	.4	1.0	1.8	All Other Expenses (net)	1.5	.9
	4.7	4.5	5.9	3.7	4.4	Profit Before Taxes	.4	4.9
						RATIOS		
	3.3	3.8	2.8	2.2	1.9		2.6	2.8
	2.1	1.8	1.6	1.6	1.5	Current	1.5	1.6
	1.1	1.1	1.2	1.1	1.1		1.1	1.1
	1.7	1.7	1.5	1.2	1.1		1.3	1.4
	1.3	.9	.9	.7	.9	Quick	.8	.8
	.6	.5	.6	.5	.6		.5	.5
	20 18.1	**25** 14.8	**30** 12.1	**30** 12.1	**35** 10.3		**30** 12.2	**29** 12.4
	30 12.2	**37** 9.9	**41** 9.0	**36** 10.1	**47** 7.8	Sales/Receivables	**45** 8.1	**43** 8.4
	43 8.4	**53** 6.9	**58** 6.3	**47** 7.7	**62** 5.9		**63** 5.8	**56** 6.5
	21 17.7	**39** 9.3	**26** 13.9	**30** 12.1	**26** 14.1		**36** 10.0	**35** 10.4
	33 11.1	**70** 5.2	**52** 7.0	**47** 7.7	**45** 8.2	Cost of Sales/Inventory	**66** 5.5	**66** 5.5
	114 3.2	**118** 3.1	**79** 4.6	**94** 3.9	**79** 4.6		**111** 3.3	**114** 3.2
	7 55.5	**17** 22.0	**17** 21.2	**19** 19.5	**29** 12.7		**19** 19.6	**19** 19.5
	20 18.5	**31** 11.6	**27** 13.6	**28** 12.9	**43** 8.4	Cost of Sales/Payables	**35** 10.4	**33** 11.1
	40 9.2	**49** 7.5	**38** 9.5	**47** 7.8	**53** 6.9		**54** 6.8	**51** 7.1
	4.2	4.1	4.3	5.4	5.8		4.4	4.5
	8.5	7.5	10.1	8.9	10.0	Sales/Working Capital	9.3	9.4
	84.3	35.9	30.4	45.7	54.2		48.9	39.8
	29.5	28.1	27.4	52.5	20.3		6.4	20.1
	(25) 5.7	(78) 6.4	(81) 12.0	(43) 4.7	(55) 6.3	EBIT/Interest	(328) 2.2	(314) 5.8
	1.9	2.1	4.0	2.1	1.7		-1.0	1.7
		20.0	8.8	52.1	15.0		4.4	8.8
		(17) 4.6	(28) 4.5	(19) 5.7	(18) 7.1	Net Profit + Depr., Dep., Amort./Cur. Mat. L/T/D	(102) 2.0	(99) 3.3
		1.5	1.7	1.5	1.5		.6	1.3
	.1	.1	.3	.5	.8		.3	.3
	.4	.6	.6	.8	1.9	Fixed/Worth	.8	.7
	2.3	1.8	1.5	3.0	-2.9		2.0	1.5
	.5	.6	.6	.6	1.1		.7	.6
	1.1	1.9	1.4	1.4	4.4	Debt/Worth	2.0	1.5
	7.8	4.6	2.8	4.6	-8.8		5.7	4.5
	62.6	55.3	56.8	33.4	46.4		33.6	46.8
	(24) 17.0	(74) 21.3	(88) 29.1	(41) 24.9	(39) 22.5	% Profit Before Taxes/Tangible Net Worth	(298) 7.6	(301) 20.8
	7.8	6.7	10.6	10.2	14.3		-5.8	6.1
	22.3	16.9	22.2	14.3	12.1		9.3	16.1
	8.1	8.9	9.0	6.9	6.9	% Profit Before Taxes/Total Assets	2.2	7.6
	2.6	2.4	3.0	1.8	3.0		-4.7	2.0
	87.4	41.8	15.1	13.6	10.7		23.5	25.6
	34.9	11.0	7.1	6.0	6.7	Sales/Net Fixed Assets	7.2	8.8
	9.4	4.4	4.5	3.2	3.9		3.7	4.6
	4.0	3.0	2.6	2.3	2.0		2.5	2.5
	2.5	2.2	2.0	1.7	1.7	Sales/Total Assets	1.8	1.9
	2.0	1.3	1.5	1.4	1.1		1.2	1.4
	.4	.6	1.2	2.0	1.8		1.2	1.2
	(21) 1.2	(72) 2.0	(86) 2.0	(42) 3.0	(35) 2.5	% Depr., Dep., Amort./Sales	(283) 2.7	(284) 2.6
	2.4	3.6	3.6	4.7	4.0		4.9	4.4
	3.3	1.2	.3				2.6	1.7
	(14) 5.7	(33) 2.8	(11) 1.8			% Officers', Directors' Owners' Comp/Sales	(88) 4.2	(83) 3.7
	6.8	4.3	2.1				7.7	6.7
7877M	**112372M**	**1077189M**	**4759510M**	**6523595M**	**14942814M**	Net Sales ($)	**18840159M**	**18632742M**
1203M	**37473M**	**446837M**	**2209453M**	**3454879M**	**8672514M**	Total Assets ($)	**10621910M**	**10113305M**

M = $ thousand MM = $ million

See Pages 9 through 22 for Explanation of Ratios and Data

Comparative Historical Data / Current Data Sorted by Sales

4/1/11-3/31/12 ALL	4/1/12-3/31/13 ALL	4/1/13-3/31/14 ALL	Type of Statement	0-1MM	1-3MM	3-5MM	5-10MM	10-25MM	25MM & OVER
77	63	74	Unqualified				3	10	61
68	54	48	Reviewed	1	3	3	7	17	17
34	31	30	Compiled		5	3	6	8	8
34	35	20	Tax Returns	3	4	7	4	1	1
160	161	145	Other		7	8	14	19	97
				37 (4/1-9/30/13)			280 (10/1/13-3/31/14)		
373	344	317	**NUMBER OF STATEMENTS**	4	19	21	34	55	184
%	%	%	**ASSETS**	%	%	%	%	%	%
7.3	8.5	9.5	Cash & Equivalents		23.0	12.5	9.7	9.9	7.5
23.9	24.0	23.0	Trade Receivables (net)		21.0	17.6	21.2	25.5	23.8
27.3	28.3	24.9	Inventory		20.6	20.5	37.4	30.9	21.8
3.1	3.3	3.2	All Other Current		.4	1.6	1.7	1.7	4.4
61.5	64.0	60.6	Total Current		65.0	52.1	70.0	68.1	57.4
26.8	24.1	27.4	Fixed Assets (net)		23.2	30.3	22.9	26.0	28.6
6.8	6.1	7.3	Intangibles (net)		9.4	10.4	5.1	1.4	8.8
5.0	5.8	4.6	All Other Non-Current		2.4	7.1	2.1	4.4	5.1
100.0	100.0	100.0	Total		100.0	100.0	100.0	100.0	100.0
			LIABILITIES						
10.5	9.8	8.9	Notes Payable-Short Term		9.0	7.8	7.1	11.9	8.4
3.1	2.8	2.9	Cur. Mat.-L.T.D.		2.8	2.5	2.1	4.1	2.7
15.6	14.7	16.1	Trade Payables		13.1	15.1	12.6	17.5	17.1
.2	.3	.2	Income Taxes Payable		.1	.2	.1	.2	.3
9.7	11.2	11.9	All Other Current		9.8	22.7	14.0	12.3	10.7
39.1	38.7	40.0	Total Current		34.7	48.2	35.9	46.0	39.1
15.1	13.9	14.6	Long-Term Debt		15.1	17.3	14.5	12.2	14.5
.8	1.1	.9	Deferred Taxes		.1	.0	.2	.5	1.4
9.8	7.1	5.6	All Other Non-Current		2.8	14.2	6.4	3.6	5.3
35.2	39.3	38.9	Net Worth		47.3	20.3	42.9	37.7	39.7
100.0	100.0	100.0	Total Liabilities & Net Worth		100.0	100.0	100.0	100.0	100.0
			INCOME DATA						
100.0	100.0	100.0	Net Sales		100.0	100.0	100.0	100.0	100.0
26.3	26.7	24.4	Gross Profit		36.4	37.4	37.4	24.3	18.6
20.6	21.0	18.3	Operating Expenses		28.7	35.2	30.2	18.5	12.8
5.6	5.7	6.0	Operating Profit		7.7	2.2	7.2	5.7	5.8
1.1	.9	1.2	All Other Expenses (net)		.2	.9	.5	.8	.9
4.5	4.8	4.9	Profit Before Taxes		7.4	1.3	6.7	4.9	4.9
			RATIOS						
2.5	2.9	2.7			4.2	4.4	4.6	3.1	2.3
1.6	1.8	1.6	Current		2.1	1.7	2.4	1.5	1.6
1.1	1.2	1.2			1.0	.7	1.8	1.0	1.2
1.3	1.4	1.4			2.7	2.0	1.7	1.4	1.2
.8	.9	.9	Quick		1.3	1.0	.9	.9	.8
.5	.5	.6			.6	.3	.5	.5	.6
30 12.2	**28** 13.0	**27** 13.3			**16** 23.1	**9** 40.2	**23** 16.2	**26** 14.2	**31** 11.6
44 8.3	**41** 8.8	**41** 9.0	Sales/Receivables		**30** 12.1	**30** 12.2	**37** 9.8	**39** 9.4	**41** 8.8
54 6.7	**55** 6.6	**56** 6.5			**47** 7.8	**57** 6.4	**47** 7.8	**55** 6.6	**57** 6.4
35 10.5	**30** 12.0	**28** 13.1			**18** 20.6	**11** 33.9	**59** 6.2	**33** 10.9	**26** 14.2
58 6.3	**60** 6.1	**52** 7.0	Cost of Sales/Inventory		**42** 8.6	**69** 5.3	**104** 3.5	**61** 6.0	**46** 8.0
107 3.4	**111** 3.3	**89** 4.1			**94** 3.9	**130** 2.8	**182** 2.0	**101** 3.6	**78** 4.7
19 19.3	**17** 22.0	**17** 21.3			**4** 83.8	**8** 46.0	**16** 23.0	**20** 18.4	**20** 18.7
34 10.7	**29** 12.7	**30** 12.2	Cost of Sales/Payables		**21** 17.3	**32** 11.5	**35** 10.4	**27** 13.4	**31** 11.6
49 7.5	**45** 8.2	**46** 7.9			**30** 12.0	**69** 5.3	**47** 7.8	**46** 7.9	**46** 7.9
5.2	4.6	5.0			4.1	3.2	2.7	5.0	5.5
9.5	8.4	9.0	Sales/Working Capital		11.6	8.0	5.7	9.1	9.9
38.7	25.1	35.4			88.1	-52.9	9.1	94.5	35.3
21.5	22.7	27.8			11.9	22.6	39.5	26.4	30.1
(339) 5.4	(308) 6.4	(285) 7.5	EBIT/Interest		(13) 5.7	(19) 3.2	(32) 8.7	(52) 7.9	(166) 7.9
1.6	2.0	2.3			2.7	1.3	1.3	2.6	2.8
9.3	9.3	13.3						24.2	13.7
(111) 3.4	(90) 3.4	(84) 4.9	Net Profit + Depr., Dep., Amort./Cur. Mat. L/T/D					(15) 6.5	(59) 5.5
1.7	1.7	1.5						.6	1.5
.3	.3	.3			.1	.3	.1	.2	.4
.8	.6	.8	Fixed/Worth		.4	1.1	.3	.6	.8
2.3	1.7	2.2			2.7	-39.8	1.4	1.5	2.5
.7	.6	.6			.4	.3	.5	.6	.7
1.9	1.6	1.7	Debt/Worth		.8	1.6	1.4	1.8	1.9
5.5	4.4	5.0			7.5	-50.6	3.3	3.6	6.0
48.7	47.8	47.5			96.1	37.1	57.1	63.4	46.6
(316) 23.1	(291) 24.7	(270) 24.8	% Profit Before Taxes/Tangible Net Worth		(15) 13.2	(15) 20.5	(33) 21.0	(49) 24.1	(154) 26.5
7.7	8.2	10.4			6.8	-.3	4.8	6.7	12.6
16.3	18.5	17.2			22.7	11.1	23.3	21.4	17.2
7.5	8.3	8.4	% Profit Before Taxes/Total Assets		8.1	4.7	9.8	9.0	8.5
1.8	2.0	2.7			3.0	-.3	2.2	2.4	3.2
20.2	25.2	21.7			38.8	40.9	61.1	31.8	14.2
8.3	9.2	7.6	Sales/Net Fixed Assets		10.8	6.8	12.8	10.5	7.2
4.2	4.9	4.4			4.7	3.9	3.9	4.9	4.4
2.6	2.8	2.7			2.9	2.3	2.7	3.0	2.6
1.9	2.0	2.0	Sales/Total Assets		2.3	1.9	1.9	2.3	1.9
1.4	1.4	1.4			1.6	1.2	1.3	1.5	1.4
1.2	1.1	1.2			1.2	.3	.5	1.0	1.3
(306) 2.4	(273) 2.1	(260) 2.2	% Depr., Dep., Amort./Sales		(16) 1.8	(18) 2.9	(22) 2.0	(50) 2.1	(152) 2.2
4.1	3.7	3.8			3.3	4.0	3.8	3.7	3.9
2.0	1.8	1.3					2.1	1.1	.6
(92) 4.0	(83) 2.9	(61) 2.8	% Officers', Directors' Owners' Comp/Sales				(15) 3.1	(17) 2.0	(13) 1.4
6.6	6.4	5.5					5.5	3.9	2.6
24670692M	25529191M	27423357M	Net Sales ($)	2772M	40762M	80870M	244659M	882327M	26171967M
13240888M	13818650M	14822359M	Total Assets ($)	7728M	27999M	56089M	146289M	463843M	14120411M

M = $ thousand MM = $ million

See Pages 9 through 22 for Explanation of Ratios and Data

Current Data Sorted by Assets							Comparative Historical Data	
						Type of Statement		
		2	2	2		Unqualified	4	5
		3	2			Reviewed	5	6
		2				Compiled	5	2
1	1					Tax Returns	3	3
	1	5	8	2	3	Other	11	12
	1 (4/1-9/30/13)		33 (10/1/13-3/31/14)				4/1/09-3/31/10	4/1/10-3/31/11
0-500M	500M-2MM	2-10MM	10-50MM	50-100MM	100-250MM		ALL	ALL
1	2	12	12	4	3	NUMBER OF STATEMENTS	28	28
%	%	%	%	%	%	**ASSETS**	%	%
		6.4	4.8			Cash & Equivalents	9.2	11.1
		28.2	15.3			Trade Receivables (net)	20.9	17.7
		33.7	28.2			Inventory	27.1	24.6
		8.0	8.5			All Other Current	9.1	8.0
		76.3	56.8			Total Current	66.3	61.4
		14.3	20.5			Fixed Assets (net)	21.3	27.8
		3.1	18.0			Intangibles (net)	4.4	3.5
		6.2	4.6			All Other Non-Current	8.1	7.3
		100.0	100.0			Total	100.0	100.0
						LIABILITIES		
		15.3	8.6			Notes Payable-Short Term	10.8	14.5
		1.4	5.6			Cur. Mat.-L.T.D.	4.4	3.3
		16.0	11.7			Trade Payables	12.5	12.2
		.1	.0			Income Taxes Payable	.0	.1
		14.6	10.7			All Other Current	16.1	16.5
		47.4	36.6			Total Current	43.7	46.6
		17.4	11.3			Long-Term Debt	16.0	18.2
		.0	.8			Deferred Taxes	.5	.2
		7.1	11.4			All Other Non-Current	19.4	24.1
		28.0	39.9			Net Worth	20.3	10.9
		100.0	100.0			Total Liabilities & Net Worth	100.0	100.0
						INCOME DATA		
		100.0	100.0			Net Sales	100.0	100.0
		28.6	25.0			Gross Profit	26.7	26.9
		21.3	16.0			Operating Expenses	24.2	21.4
		7.2	9.0			Operating Profit	2.5	5.5
		.8	1.5			All Other Expenses (net)	1.9	3.3
		6.4	7.5			Profit Before Taxes	.5	2.2
						RATIOS		
		2.3	2.2				2.6	2.1
		1.8	1.4			Current	1.5	1.5
		1.1	1.2				1.2	1.0
		1.3	1.0				1.3	1.6
		.6	.5			Quick	.7	.6
		.3	.4				.3	.2
		25 14.5	**31** 11.6				**26** 14.0	**14** 25.7
		37 9.8	**43** 8.4			Sales/Receivables	**46** 8.0	**45** 8.0
		54 6.7	**70** 5.2				**73** 5.0	**53** 6.9
		18 20.2	**94** 3.9				**13** 28.7	**15** 24.4
		104 3.5	**135** 2.7			Cost of Sales/Inventory	**67** 5.4	**84** 4.3
		166 2.2	**146** 2.5				**152** 2.4	**171** 2.1
		12 29.2	**28** 13.0				**20** 17.9	**18** 20.6
		31 11.6	**43** 8.4			Cost of Sales/Payables	**32** 11.3	**34** 10.7
		63 5.8	**69** 5.3				**48** 7.6	**58** 6.2
		5.0	3.9				3.8	4.9
		7.6	6.6			Sales/Working Capital	6.7	14.4
		34.7	12.4				27.8	-62.9
		26.1	15.8				7.0	12.9
		(10) 6.9	8.3			EBIT/Interest	(26) 3.1	(27) 5.1
		1.4	2.3				.7	.8
						Net Profit + Depr., Dep., Amort./Cur. Mat. L/T/D		
		.1	.4				.1	.5
		.4	.7			Fixed/Worth	.8	1.8
		2.8	1.7				-1.6	-2.8
		1.0	.7				1.3	1.4
		1.9	3.2			Debt/Worth	2.5	4.4
		8.4	3.9				-6.3	-16.3
		75.6	49.7				32.4	68.9
		(10) 32.9	(10) 36.3			% Profit Before Taxes/Tangible Net Worth	(19) 13.0	(18) 40.4
		13.8	22.2				6.3	11.3
		20.7	15.7				8.7	14.3
		9.5	9.6			% Profit Before Taxes/Total Assets	3.1	5.6
		3.2	2.0				-.7	-1.2
		69.8	13.6				56.2	9.5
		12.6	6.2			Sales/Net Fixed Assets	7.3	6.1
		7.5	3.5				2.3	2.7
		3.0	1.4				1.9	2.1
		1.9	1.2			Sales/Total Assets	1.3	1.3
		1.1	.9				.9	1.1
			.7				.9	2.0
			(11) 2.5			% Depr., Dep., Amort./Sales	(25) 2.5	(25) 3.1
			5.0				4.4	6.6
						% Officers', Directors' Owners' Comp/Sales		
1526M	6383M	110390M	390485M	289404M	573088M	Net Sales ($)	777324M	1268876M
268M	2345M	46681M	345013M	242333M	496303M	Total Assets ($)	614568M	978452M

M = $ thousand MM = $ million

See Pages 9 through 22 for Explanation of Ratios and Data

Comparative Historical Data / Current Data Sorted by Sales

4/1/11-3/31/12 ALL	4/1/12-3/31/13 ALL	4/1/13-3/31/14 ALL	Type of Statement	0-1MM	1-3MM	3-5MM	5-10MM	10-25MM	25MM & OVER
8	5	6	Unqualified		1		1	2	2
11	5	5	Reviewed			1	1	2	1
4	3	2	Compiled				1	1	
9	8	2	Tax Returns		2				
13	23	19	Other			3	1	3	12
					1 (4/1-9/30/13)		33 (10/1/13-3/31/14)		
45	44	34	NUMBER OF STATEMENTS		3	4	4	8	15
%	%	%	**ASSETS**	%	%	%	%	%	%
10.7	8.9	6.4	Cash & Equivalents	DATA NOT AVAILABLE					6.4
19.2	16.3	19.0	Trade Receivables (net)						14.8
27.0	29.8	32.9	Inventory						31.0
6.1	3.0	7.5	All Other Current						9.3
62.9	58.0	65.8	Total Current						61.5
22.9	22.6	19.0	Fixed Assets (net)						21.1
7.5	10.6	10.4	Intangibles (net)						15.0
6.6	8.9	4.7	All Other Non-Current						2.4
100.0	100.0	100.0	Total						100.0
			LIABILITIES						
9.7	8.1	13.7	Notes Payable-Short Term						9.8
1.9	1.7	3.0	Cur. Mat.-L.T.D.						3.8
11.6	9.4	12.3	Trade Payables						10.7
.2	.2	.2	Income Taxes Payable						.3
15.9	11.8	11.6	All Other Current						12.7
39.3	31.3	40.7	Total Current						37.2
18.4	19.8	27.7	Long-Term Debt						12.3
.6	.5	.7	Deferred Taxes						1.7
15.5	9.3	14.4	All Other Non-Current						19.3
26.2	39.1	16.4	Net Worth						29.5
100.0	100.0	100.0	Total Liabilties & Net Worth						100.0
			INCOME DATA						
100.0	100.0	100.0	Net Sales						100.0
27.9	30.4	26.1	Gross Profit						22.8
20.5	23.8	19.0	Operating Expenses						15.4
7.4	6.7	7.1	Operating Profit						7.3
2.0	1.8	1.9	All Other Expenses (net)						2.9
5.4	4.8	5.2	Profit Before Taxes						4.4
			RATIOS						
3.5	3.0	2.4	Current						3.4
1.7	1.8	1.6							1.5
1.3	1.5	1.3							1.2
1.6	1.5	1.1	Quick						1.1
1.0	.8	.5							.6
.4	.5	.4							.4
23 15.6	**27** 13.7	**26** 13.9	Sales/Receivables						**30** 12.0
39 9.3	**40** 9.2	**41** 8.9							**43** 8.4
58 6.3	**54** 6.8	**53** 6.9							**72** 5.1
19 19.1	**42** 8.7	**57** 6.4	Cost of Sales/Inventory						**85** 4.3
81 4.5	**114** 3.2	**118** 3.1							**130** 2.8
192 1.9	**182** 2.0	**152** 2.4							**166** 2.2
14 26.1	**17** 21.7	**15** 24.9	Cost of Sales/Payables						**17** 21.0
25 14.6	**32** 11.4	**35** 10.5							**44** 8.3
41 9.0	**49** 7.5	**55** 6.6							**59** 6.2
3.2	3.5	4.3	Sales/Working Capital						3.7
6.3	5.7	6.6							6.4
22.1	8.7	12.2							11.0
19.1	17.6	15.7	EBIT/Interest						15.1
(39) 3.3	(41) 6.8	(31) 3.9							(14) 4.6
.9	.5	1.3							.7
			Net Profit + Depr., Dep., Amort./Cur. Mat. L/T/D						
.2	.2	.4	Fixed/Worth						.4
.9	.7	.7							.7
NM	2.8	NM							1.8
.7	.5	1.2	Debt/Worth						.5
2.7	1.3	3.0							3.0
-525.3	5.7	NM							4.0
40.6	26.9	55.0	% Profit Before Taxes/Tangible Net Worth						43.7
(33) 19.8	(35) 12.8	(26) 32.0							(12) 22.1
2.8	5.3	10.3							-2.0
13.8	13.1	15.1	% Profit Before Taxes/Total Assets						12.8
7.2	5.9	6.8							3.7
-.4	-1.8	1.4							-1.1
19.4	13.5	16.2	Sales/Net Fixed Assets						12.6
8.2	7.4	8.5							5.5
4.3	4.1	5.4							3.2
2.4	2.0	1.9	Sales/Total Assets						1.4
1.4	1.2	1.3							1.2
.8	.8	1.0							.9
.9	1.6	1.0	% Depr., Dep., Amort./Sales						.9
(40) 2.5	(36) 3.2	(27) 3.1							(14) 2.9
4.7	4.7	4.6							5.0
1.2	1.5		% Officers', Directors' Owners' Comp/Sales						
(13) 2.3	(11) 3.2								
6.3	7.3								
1594870M	1484542M	1371276M	Net Sales ($)		5169M	17601M	31552M	132935M	1184019M
1441646M	1485829M	1132943M	Total Assets ($)		3239M	11870M	16680M	83547M	1017607M

M = $ thousand MM = $ million

See Pages 9 through 22 for Explanation of Ratios and Data

Current Data Sorted by Assets							Comparative Historical Data	
	20 (4/1-9/30/13)		97 (10/1/13-3/31/14)			**Type of Statement**		
		3	8	4	5	Unqualified	24	29
		15	8			Reviewed	21	22
	5	6	2		3	Compiled	4	8
	1	4				Tax Returns	10	9
1	5	18	18	4	7	Other	46	61
0-500M	**500M-2MM**	**2-10MM**	**10-50MM**	**50-100MM**	**100-250MM**		**4/1/09-3/31/10 ALL**	**4/1/10-3/31/11 ALL**
1	11	46	36	8	15	**NUMBER OF STATEMENTS**	105	129
%	%	%	%	%	%	**ASSETS**	%	%
	10.9	8.9	5.8		2.6	Cash & Equivalents	7.4	9.1
	20.7	21.8	16.7		15.5	Trade Receivables (net)	20.3	18.2
	25.1	37.8	38.9		29.7	Inventory	36.3	34.8
	1.0	2.2	2.4		3.0	All Other Current	2.4	2.7
	57.8	70.6	63.8		50.9	Total Current	66.4	64.8
	27.3	20.6	24.1		22.6	Fixed Assets (net)	24.7	23.8
	7.0	3.8	6.9		23.4	Intangibles (net)	4.2	6.4
	8.0	5.0	5.3		3.1	All Other Non-Current	4.6	5.0
	100.0	100.0	100.0		100.0	Total	100.0	100.0
						LIABILITIES		
	5.6	10.5	10.7		4.2	Notes Payable-Short Term	12.5	8.9
	10.6	4.2	4.2		4.2	Cur. Mat.-L.T.D.	3.7	4.1
	20.6	11.6	9.5		8.4	Trade Payables	10.4	11.1
	.0	.3	.1		.1	Income Taxes Payable	.6	.3
	19.7	9.5	11.1		6.0	All Other Current	8.9	9.1
	56.6	36.2	35.8		22.9	Total Current	36.0	33.5
	19.2	15.8	13.1		23.1	Long-Term Debt	15.8	15.8
	.1	.6	.8		1.4	Deferred Taxes	.9	.6
	12.1	3.5	8.6		9.4	All Other Non-Current	4.2	6.8
	12.1	43.9	41.8		43.2	Net Worth	43.1	43.2
	100.0	100.0	100.0		100.0	Total Liabilties & Net Worth	100.0	100.0
						INCOME DATA		
	100.0	100.0	100.0		100.0	Net Sales	100.0	100.0
	46.7	36.0	26.2		19.1	Gross Profit	26.1	30.5
	35.7	28.2	20.0		12.0	Operating Expenses	18.9	22.4
	11.0	7.8	6.1		7.1	Operating Profit	7.1	8.0
	1.0	.5	.8		3.6	All Other Expenses (net)	1.6	1.8
	10.0	7.3	5.3		3.5	Profit Before Taxes	5.5	6.2
						RATIOS		
	3.1	4.3	2.3		3.7		3.1	3.1
	1.3	2.3	1.7		2.6	Current	1.9	1.9
	.5	1.4	1.3		1.4		1.3	1.3
	2.0	2.2	.9		1.5		1.3	1.4
	.9	.9	.5		.7	Quick	.7	.7
	.3	.5	.4		.6		.5	.5
	17 21.4	**33** 10.9	**31** 11.7		**33** 11.2		**32** 11.6	**25** 14.5
	39 9.3	**46** 8.0	**46** 7.9		**50** 7.3	Sales/Receivables	**42** 8.7	**44** 8.2
	50 7.3	**60** 6.1	**54** 6.7		**63** 5.8		**55** 6.7	**58** 6.3
	16 22.9	**70** 5.2	**79** 4.6		**76** 4.8		**62** 5.9	**68** 5.4
	38 9.7	**126** 2.9	**135** 2.7		**111** 3.3	Cost of Sales/Inventory	**107** 3.4	**117** 3.1
	78 4.7	**174** 2.1	**215** 1.7		**159** 2.3		**169** 2.2	**167** 2.2
	17 22.1	**17** 21.9	**23** 15.9		**24** 15.0		**14** 26.1	**19** 18.8
	41 8.8	**30** 12.0	**36** 10.2		**31** 11.8	Cost of Sales/Payables	**25** 14.5	**32** 11.6
	70 5.2	**51** 7.2	**42** 8.6		**39** 9.3		**38** 9.6	**48** 7.7
	5.2	2.6	3.4		3.1		2.9	3.0
	18.3	5.1	4.8		4.5	Sales/Working Capital	5.4	6.0
	-14.8	11.2	9.5		7.9		12.7	12.8
		26.4	11.6		17.0		11.8	11.6
		(42) 6.7	(33) 4.9		(14) 3.2	EBIT/Interest	(96) 4.1	(108) 4.0
		2.6	1.1		.1		1.8	1.9
		6.9	3.3				6.1	4.4
		(11) 2.7	(17) 2.0			Net Profit + Depr., Dep., Amort./Cur. Mat. L/T/D	(25) 3.0	(31) 2.3
		1.6	.8				1.4	.7
	.3	.1	.2		.6		.1	.1
	1.1	.3	.6		1.0	Fixed/Worth	.6	.6
	-.7	1.0	1.5		-.4		1.5	1.5
	.5	.4	.8		.9		.6	.6
	2.1	1.2	1.9		2.9	Debt/Worth	1.6	1.5
	-8.4	3.0	4.0		-2.8		3.7	3.4
		65.7	39.5		37.3		44.8	34.1
		(42) 20.7	(33) 14.2		(10) 23.2	% Profit Before Taxes/Tangible Net Worth	(98) 23.3	(116) 19.0
		4.8	.9		10.6		8.5	7.3
	32.8	16.8	12.3		13.1		16.1	14.0
	18.2	8.2	7.5		7.8	% Profit Before Taxes/Total Assets	7.6	6.4
	9.5	3.9	1.4		-4.6		2.4	1.5
	90.9	61.0	17.1		13.2		24.7	24.3
	30.7	9.9	5.8		6.3	Sales/Net Fixed Assets	8.2	7.6
	3.8	4.3	3.0		3.5		3.4	3.7
	3.6	2.2	1.5		1.6		2.1	2.0
	2.2	1.7	1.3		1.1	Sales/Total Assets	1.5	1.5
	1.4	1.2	1.1		.8		1.1	1.0
		.6	2.0		1.6		1.2	1.2
		(35) 1.7	(33) 3.5		(11) 3.7	% Depr., Dep., Amort./Sales	(94) 2.4	(114) 2.7
		3.7	4.7		6.7		4.0	4.1
		1.9					2.7	1.9
		(14) 3.2				% Officers', Directors' Owners' Comp/Sales	(22) 4.5	(37) 4.0
		7.3					9.6	6.0
3294M	**28894M**	**423955M**	**974620M**	**706763M**	**2548720M**	Net Sales ($)	**4582138M**	**4413145M**
440M	**11943M**	**250504M**	**770640M**	**597020M**	**2132521M**	Total Assets ($)	**3126932M**	**2996453M**

M = $ thousand MM = $ million

See Pages 9 through 22 for Explanation of Ratios and Data

Comparative Historical Data				Current Data Sorted by Sales					
			Type of Statement						
22	19	20	Unqualified					8	12
26	35	23	Reviewed		1	1	9	7	5
9	5	16	Compiled	1	3	1	4	2	5
7	6	5	Tax Returns		1	3		1	
48	53	53	Other		3	4	13	16	17
4/1/11-3/31/12	**4/1/12-3/31/13**	**4/1/13-3/31/14**		**20 (4/1-9/30/13)**			**97 (10/1/13-3/31/14)**		
ALL	**ALL**	**ALL**		**0-1MM**	**1-3MM**	**3-5MM**	**5-10MM**	**10-25MM**	**25MM & OVER**
112	118	117	**NUMBER OF STATEMENTS**	1	8	9	26	34	39
%	%	%	**ASSETS**	%	%	%	%	%	%
7.0	8.2	7.1	Cash & Equivalents				10.9	4.6	4.9
21.8	21.0	19.5	Trade Receivables (net)				19.4	22.5	17.1
34.9	36.3	35.5	Inventory				39.4	37.7	34.3
3.4	2.0	2.4	All Other Current				1.6	3.3	2.6
67.0	67.4	64.4	Total Current				71.3	68.1	58.9
21.8	21.2	22.1	Fixed Assets (net)				16.0	25.2	20.4
7.0	7.7	8.6	Intangibles (net)				6.0	3.5	16.1
4.1	3.6	4.9	All Other Non-Current				6.7	3.1	4.6
100.0	100.0	100.0	Total				100.0	100.0	100.0
			LIABILITIES						
10.9	11.3	9.5	Notes Payable-Short Term				8.1	13.8	9.2
4.0	4.1	4.6	Cur. Mat.-L.T.D.				2.3	5.3	3.9
11.7	10.5	11.1	Trade Payables				12.7	11.5	9.5
.2	.2	.2	Income Taxes Payable				.5	.2	.1
8.3	8.0	11.0	All Other Current				6.4	9.6	8.8
35.1	34.1	36.5	Total Current				29.9	40.4	31.5
11.8	13.2	15.7	Long-Term Debt				14.4	12.5	16.1
1.1	.9	.7	Deferred Taxes				.0	1.4	.7
6.7	6.1	8.1	All Other Non-Current				4.6	6.0	9.5
45.2	45.7	39.1	Net Worth				51.1	39.7	42.1
100.0	100.0	100.0	Total Liabilties & Net Worth				100.0	100.0	100.0
			INCOME DATA						
100.0	100.0	100.0	Net Sales				100.0	100.0	100.0
30.0	30.6	31.1	Gross Profit				34.1	26.4	23.8
21.2	21.1	23.9	Operating Expenses				28.5	20.1	15.9
8.8	9.5	7.2	Operating Profit				5.6	6.3	7.9
1.3	1.5	1.1	All Other Expenses (net)				.8	.2	2.2
7.4	7.9	6.1	Profit Before Taxes				4.8	6.1	5.7
			RATIOS						
3.1	3.6	3.0					4.4	2.8	2.7
1.9	2.0	1.9	Current				2.6	1.6	1.9
1.4	1.4	1.3					1.6	1.3	1.3
1.7	1.6	1.3					2.2	.9	1.3
.7	.7	.7	Quick				.9	.6	.7
.5	.5	.5					.5	.4	.5
32 11.3	**32** 11.3	**33** 11.1					**24** 14.9	**39** 9.3	**37** 9.8
45 8.1	**47** 7.7	**47** 7.8	Sales/Receivables				**37** 9.8	**47** 7.8	**50** 7.3
61 6.0	**63** 5.8	**57** 6.4					**53** 6.9	**60** 6.1	**63** 5.8
66 5.5	**72** 5.1	**70** 5.2					**65** 5.6	**78** 4.7	**78** 4.7
118 3.1	**114** 3.2	**114** 3.2	Cost of Sales/Inventory				**135** 2.7	**114** 3.2	**126** 2.9
182 2.0	**192** 1.9	**192** 1.9					**192** 1.9	**159** 2.3	**192** 1.9
16 23.0	**18** 20.1	**20** 17.9					**17** 21.9	**17** 21.9	**24** 15.5
34 10.8	**28** 13.0	**33** 10.9	Cost of Sales/Payables				**26** 14.3	**35** 10.3	**34** 10.8
45 8.2	**46** 8.0	**48** 7.6					**53** 6.9	**40** 9.1	**47** 7.8
3.1	2.9	3.1					2.5	3.4	3.3
5.0	5.0	5.2	Sales/Working Capital				4.0	6.2	4.8
9.2	10.5	10.8					7.9	15.1	8.7
28.1	20.9	19.3					34.1	19.0	22.2
(96) 5.2	(105) 6.9	(106) 5.3	EBIT/Interest				(25) 5.2	(31) 6.2	(36) 4.2
2.0	2.4	1.8					1.5	3.6	.9
5.9	5.2	4.1						3.8	4.1
(29) 1.6	(33) 2.1	(36) 2.4	Net Profit + Depr., Dep., Amort./Cur. Mat. L/T/D					(14) 1.9	(14) 2.6
.8	1.3	1.3						1.2	1.3
.2	.2	.2					.0	.2	.3
.4	.4	.6	Fixed/Worth				.3	.6	.9
1.2	1.4	1.7					.7	1.5	3.2
.6	.6	.6					.4	.5	1.0
1.5	1.4	1.7	Debt/Worth				1.0	1.6	2.8
2.9	3.5	6.6					2.3	4.1	22.2
42.7	42.6	45.7					68.4	33.4	42.7
(104) 25.4	(108) 20.9	(98) 19.9	% Profit Before Taxes/Tangible Net Worth				21.9	(30) 16.5	(31) 23.5
10.1	8.3	7.0					1.3	8.8	9.4
18.8	16.2	13.7					17.2	13.5	12.4
8.2	7.9	8.6	% Profit Before Taxes/Total Assets				7.5	8.6	7.8
2.8	2.8	1.6					.7	4.3	-.2
31.0	23.9	31.3					217.0	21.3	13.5
8.1	8.6	6.8	Sales/Net Fixed Assets				18.0	5.8	6.5
4.5	4.0	3.9					5.2	3.3	3.9
2.2	1.9	1.9					2.4	1.9	1.5
1.5	1.5	1.4	Sales/Total Assets				1.6	1.5	1.3
1.1	1.1	1.1					1.1	1.2	1.0
.9	1.0	1.0					.3	1.5	1.6
(95) 2.1	(99) 2.6	(92) 3.1	% Depr., Dep., Amort./Sales				(21) 1.0	(30) 3.6	(31) 3.3
3.7	4.2	4.6					3.2	4.7	4.4
1.9	1.8	1.6							
(25) 3.1	(23) 3.4	(22) 3.0	% Officers', Directors' Owners' Comp/Sales						
5.1	4.0	5.9							
4941404M	**5815469M**	**4686246M**	Net Sales ($)	**764M**	**15553M**	**35087M**	**184122M**	**583052M**	**3867668M**
3435303M	**4228404M**	**3763068M**	Total Assets ($)	**1069M**	**11365M**	**20996M**	**134306M**	**402444M**	**3192888M**

M = $ thousand MM = $ million

See Pages 9 through 22 for Explanation of Ratios and Data

	Current Data Sorted by Assets						Comparative Historical Data	
Type of Statement								
Unqualified	2		2	10	1	3	35	29
Reviewed		2	21	16			34	48
Compiled		2	13	2			20	19
Tax Returns	1	5	6	1			18	13
Other	3	7	24	41	16	12	92	87
	28 (4/1-9/30/13)		162 (10/1/13-3/31/14)				4/1/09-3/31/10	4/1/10-3/31/11
	0-500M	500M-2MM	2-10MM	10-50MM	50-100MM	100-250MM	ALL	ALL
NUMBER OF STATEMENTS	6	16	66	70	17	15	199	196
ASSETS	%	%	%	%	%	%	%	%
Cash & Equivalents		17.1	8.5	10.1	4.5	7.7	9.9	10.8
Trade Receivables (net)		22.2	23.2	17.5	13.8	14.0	18.9	20.1
Inventory		38.8	34.6	35.0	21.7	22.7	33.2	30.9
All Other Current		.8	1.6	2.9	4.8	14.3	3.9	4.2
Total Current		78.9	67.9	65.5	44.9	58.8	65.9	66.1
Fixed Assets (net)		19.0	24.4	20.7	21.6	15.6	23.9	22.9
Intangibles (net)		.1	3.7	9.1	27.5	22.6	6.3	7.2
All Other Non-Current		1.9	3.9	4.8	6.0	3.0	3.9	3.9
Total		100.0	100.0	100.0	100.0	100.0	100.0	100.0
LIABILITIES								
Notes Payable-Short Term		16.3	9.0	7.5	4.9	5.9	9.0	8.6
Cur. Mat.-L.T.D.		2.0	3.6	3.8	5.7	1.0	4.3	3.7
Trade Payables		12.2	11.3	9.6	7.7	9.0	9.4	10.2
Income Taxes Payable		.0	.3	.2	.3	.2	.3	.3
All Other Current		11.9	7.3	8.1	4.4	11.7	8.3	9.1
Total Current		42.4	31.5	29.1	23.0	27.7	31.4	31.9
Long-Term Debt		11.9	20.3	12.0	21.3	22.1	16.3	13.6
Deferred Taxes		.0	.4	1.3	1.9	2.4	.8	1.0
All Other Non-Current		8.8	4.6	4.8	10.4	3.4	7.3	7.0
Net Worth		36.8	43.2	52.8	43.3	44.4	44.3	46.5
Total Liabilties & Net Worth		100.0	100.0	100.0	100.0	100.0	100.0	100.0
INCOME DATA								
Net Sales		100.0	100.0	100.0	100.0	100.0	100.0	100.0
Gross Profit		40.5	35.9	30.3	28.1	27.3	31.4	31.1
Operating Expenses		37.8	29.1	19.5	21.4	21.5	23.9	22.7
Operating Profit		2.6	6.9	10.8	6.7	5.8	7.5	8.3
All Other Expenses (net)		.9	1.3	1.7	4.8	1.6	1.7	1.9
Profit Before Taxes		1.7	5.6	9.1	1.9	4.2	5.8	6.4
RATIOS								
Current		3.5	4.3	4.5	3.4	3.2	4.1	3.9
		1.6	2.1	2.6	2.2	2.5	2.3	2.2
		1.2	1.5	1.6	1.3	1.9	1.6	1.5
Quick		2.1	1.9	2.0	1.2	1.8	1.9	1.9
		.9	.9	1.0	.6	.9	.9	1.0
		.3	.6	.4	.4	.6	.4	.5
Sales/Receivables		**15** 24.1	**33** 10.9	**31** 11.7	**43** 8.4	**42** 8.6	**29** 12.8	**31** 11.7
		31 11.6	**48** 7.6	**42** 8.6	**49** 7.5	**56** 6.5	**41** 8.8	**44** 8.4
		57 6.4	**58** 6.3	**55** 6.6	**76** 4.8	**60** 6.1	**54** 6.7	**58** 6.3
Cost of Sales/Inventory		**31** 11.8	**49** 7.4	**89** 4.1	**48** 7.6	**65** 5.6	**63** 5.8	**58** 6.2
		81 4.5	**114** 3.2	**118** 3.1	**114** 3.2	**122** 3.0	**105** 3.5	**110** 3.3
		159 2.3	**182** 2.0	**166** 2.2	**174** 2.1	**159** 2.3	**178** 2.1	**157** 2.3
Cost of Sales/Payables		**3** 106.9	**18** 20.8	**21** 17.0	**32** 11.4	**19** 19.0	**15** 24.0	**16** 22.6
		36 10.2	**27** 13.5	**28** 13.2	**49** 7.4	**40** 9.1	**25** 14.6	**29** 12.8
		63 5.8	**48** 7.6	**49** 7.5	**65** 5.6	**72** 5.1	**41** 8.9	**46** 7.9
Sales/Working Capital		4.6	3.1	2.3	2.7	2.7	2.8	2.8
		9.7	5.6	3.9	5.0	3.7	4.3	4.5
		14.7	10.0	7.9	9.4	4.6	8.2	9.2
EBIT/Interest		18.1	22.8	27.5	2.8	17.3	12.0	13.2
		(12) 2.2	(59) 8.0	(63) 9.2	(13) 1.5	(13) 4.6	(185) 4.6	(175) 4.9
		-.2	2.1	1.9	.0	.9	1.9	1.9
Net Profit + Depr., Dep., Amort./Cur. Mat. L/T/D			12.6	7.3			6.2	9.5
			(13) 2.6	(26) 3.3			(63) 2.6	(70) 2.6
			1.2	1.3			1.5	1.4
Fixed/Worth		.0	.2	.1	.2	.1	.2	.2
		.4	.6	.4	1.2	.6	.6	.5
		1.2	1.2	1.2	-.9	-2.8	1.6	1.5
Debt/Worth		.7	.6	.4	.6	.8	.6	.5
		1.9	1.4	.9	3.4	1.9	1.3	1.3
		5.8	3.6	2.9	-3.9	-8.7	3.7	3.6
% Profit Before Taxes/Tangible Net Worth		48.4	49.9	31.8	15.7	42.6	33.3	40.2
		(15) 17.5	(59) 22.7	(64) 19.8	(11) 9.2	(10) 21.3	(176) 19.7	(177) 17.8
		-6.4	6.4	5.3	-9.8	8.9	7.2	7.1
% Profit Before Taxes/Total Assets		22.7	18.9	16.8	6.8	11.5	15.8	15.3
		6.2	9.4	8.2	1.9	5.5	8.9	7.7
		-2.6	2.1	2.2	-3.8	-.5	2.1	2.2
Sales/Net Fixed Assets		407.7	28.3	21.1	11.2	29.2	17.0	19.2
		36.2	7.3	8.6	6.7	5.2	6.6	7.6
		8.6	4.5	3.9	2.7	3.5	3.7	3.8
Sales/Total Assets		3.6	2.5	1.7	1.0	1.3	2.1	2.0
		2.3	1.7	1.3	.8	.8	1.4	1.5
		1.7	1.3	.9	.6	.7	1.0	1.0
% Depr., Dep., Amort./Sales		.1	1.1	1.4	2.0		1.2	1.5
		(10) .7	(56) 2.6	(63) 2.2	(15) 5.4		(164) 2.9	(170) 2.9
		3.3	4.6	3.9	9.9		5.2	4.7
% Officers', Directors' Owners' Comp/Sales		4.5	2.6	1.8			1.7	1.8
		(10) 5.8	(30) 4.5	(14) 3.4			(65) 5.0	(67) 4.0
		11.3	7.9	4.5			8.9	7.4
Net Sales ($)	9680M	49926M	661050M	2030676M	1077704M	2384273M	6134648M	5429056M
Total Assets ($)	1670M	18516M	354931M	1488588M	1247343M	2410661M	5114060M	4563828M

M = $ thousand MM = $ million

See Pages 9 through 22 for Explanation of Ratios and Data

Comparative Historical Data / Current Data Sorted by Sales

4/1/11-3/31/12 ALL	4/1/12-3/31/13 ALL	4/1/13-3/31/14 ALL		0-1MM	1-3MM	3-5MM	5-10MM	10-25MM	25MM & OVER
			Type of Statement						
33	20	18	Unqualified	2				8	8
37	30	39	Reviewed		2	4	6	17	10
26	22	17	Compiled		3	3	6	3	2
16	18	13	Tax Returns		2	4	5	1	1
93	94	103	Other	3	6	4	15	27	48
					28 (4/1-9/30/13)		162 (10/1/13-3/31/14)		
205	184	190	**NUMBER OF STATEMENTS**	5	13	15	32	56	69
%	%	%	**ASSETS**	%	%	%	%	%	%
10.4	10.1	9.5	Cash & Equivalents		10.2	12.4	12.4	9.0	8.3
20.7	19.1	18.9	Trade Receivables (net)		19.2	18.7	21.7	19.7	18.0
31.8	32.5	32.6	Inventory		42.2	27.3	33.1	32.5	32.1
3.8	4.5	3.8	All Other Current		.1	1.8	2.5	2.3	5.5
66.6	66.2	64.8	Total Current		71.7	60.1	69.8	63.4	64.0
21.5	21.4	21.6	Fixed Assets (net)		12.7	34.2	19.7	24.5	17.4
7.4	8.1	8.9	Intangibles (net)		4.3	.4	6.9	7.1	14.7
4.4	4.4	4.7	All Other Non-Current		11.3	5.2	3.7	5.0	4.0
100.0	100.0	100.0	Total		100.0	100.0	100.0	100.0	100.0
			LIABILITIES						
7.6	8.3	8.6	Notes Payable-Short Term		15.2	14.0	5.4	9.4	5.8
4.4	3.7	3.4	Cur. Mat.-L.T.D.		2.2	3.9	3.2	4.1	3.3
9.4	9.3	10.6	Trade Payables		21.3	10.8	9.9	9.3	10.3
.2	.3	.2	Income Taxes Payable		.0	.0	.0	.4	.2
7.5	7.2	8.3	All Other Current		13.5	7.6	8.0	6.7	9.3
29.1	28.7	31.1	Total Current		52.2	36.3	26.5	29.9	29.0
16.2	16.3	17.6	Long-Term Debt		8.9	46.6	15.2	15.7	16.8
.8	.8	1.0	Deferred Taxes		.0	.0	.6	1.0	1.6
8.0	8.8	7.4	All Other Non-Current		14.6	23.4	4.8	6.8	3.8
45.9	45.4	42.9	Net Worth		24.2	-6.3	52.8	46.5	48.8
100.0	100.0	100.0	Total Liabilties & Net Worth		100.0	100.0	100.0	100.0	100.0
			INCOME DATA						
100.0	100.0	100.0	Net Sales		100.0	100.0	100.0	100.0	100.0
33.0	32.3	32.5	Gross Profit		33.6	37.8	35.6	35.4	26.8
24.0	24.1	24.7	Operating Expenses		34.4	30.7	29.7	26.7	17.9
9.0	8.2	7.8	Operating Profit		-.8	7.1	5.9	8.7	8.9
1.1	1.6	1.7	All Other Expenses (net)		1.9	.5	1.5	1.7	2.1
7.9	6.6	6.1	Profit Before Taxes		-2.7	6.6	4.4	7.0	6.8
			RATIOS						
4.1	4.7	4.1			2.4	2.3	5.5	4.4	3.7
2.3	2.4	2.2	Current		1.5	1.9	2.6	2.2	2.3
1.6	1.5	1.5			1.1	1.4	1.7	1.3	1.6
2.0	1.8	1.8			1.4	1.9	3.8	1.9	1.6
1.0	1.0	.9	Quick		.8	.8	1.0	.9	.9
.6	.5	.4				.4	.6	.4	.5
33 11.2	**30** 12.3	**31** 11.6			**6** 62.6	**23** 16.1	**32** 11.5	**33** 11.1	**35** 10.3
46 8.0	**45** 8.2	**46** 8.0	Sales/Receivables		**36** 10.0	**50** 7.3	**46** 8.0	**43** 8.4	**49** 7.5
62 5.9	**58** 6.3	**57** 6.4			**72** 5.1	**57** 6.4	**59** 6.2	**55** 6.6	**58** 6.3
65 5.6	**66** 5.5	**64** 5.7			**21** 17.8	**34** 10.8	**65** 5.6	**85** 4.3	**70** 5.2
104 3.5	**114** 3.2	**111** 3.3	Cost of Sales/Inventory		**118** 3.1	**69** 5.3	**126** 2.9	**111** 3.3	**114** 3.2
174 2.1	**174** 2.1	**174** 2.1			**192** 1.9	**174** 2.1	**182** 2.0	**152** 2.4	**159** 2.3
18 20.8	**17** 20.9	**18** 20.0			**18** 20.4	**17** 21.6	**15** 23.6	**20** 18.6	**20** 18.0
29 12.8	**28** 13.1	**31** 11.7	Cost of Sales/Payables		**34** 10.7	**36** 10.1	**24** 15.1	**31** 11.9	**31** 11.6
43 8.5	**46** 7.9	**53** 6.9			**78** 4.7	**62** 5.9	**52** 7.0	**49** 7.5	**53** 6.9
2.8	2.7	2.7			3.2	3.7	3.1	2.6	2.8
4.3	4.3	4.8	Sales/Working Capital		15.7	7.7	4.4	4.9	4.2
8.0	8.6	10.2			48.0	11.7	8.9	16.3	7.2
24.6	19.5	20.4			3.2	7.8	19.8	21.8	31.6
(190) 8.3	(165) 6.5	(165) 6.7	EBIT/Interest		(11) .0	(13) 2.7	(28) 8.5	(52) 7.8	(59) 5.6
2.3	1.8	1.5			-20.9	1.4	1.9	1.9	1.4
5.9	11.7	8.2						7.1	10.0
(78) 3.2	(55) 3.2	(48) 3.0	Net Profit + Depr., Dep., Amort./Cur. Mat. L/T/D					(19) 3.2	(23) 4.0
1.3	1.7	1.3						1.6	1.2
.2	.2	.1			.0	.2	.2	.2	.1
.5	.6	.5	Fixed/Worth		.3	1.2	.6	.5	.4
1.4	1.2	1.6			5.0	4.2	1.1	2.0	1.8
.5	.6	.5			1.4	1.5	.3	.6	.5
1.1	1.1	1.4	Debt/Worth		3.5	4.5	1.0	.9	1.5
3.8	4.1	4.3			10.2	7.2	3.0	3.2	4.9
52.3	39.9	40.6			114.3	58.6	35.3	44.1	36.6
(182) 23.3	(160) 19.9	(163) 19.9	% Profit Before Taxes/Tangible Net Worth		(11) -4.1	(12) 42.7	(29) 22.0	(50) 18.6	(56) 21.0
10.8	8.7	5.2			-42.8	3.8	8.7	1.9	5.7
21.7	16.5	16.8			11.2	23.7	17.7	17.1	16.4
10.4	8.9	7.5	% Profit Before Taxes/Total Assets		-2.0	5.8	11.4	7.5	7.7
3.6	2.2	1.1			-26.8	2.2	2.8	1.6	.8
24.0	26.8	29.1			486.8	20.4	35.4	24.6	27.5
8.7	8.5	8.1	Sales/Net Fixed Assets		109.8	5.8	11.5	7.1	9.1
4.4	4.1	4.1			7.3	2.7	4.5	4.4	3.9
2.1	2.2	2.1			3.5	2.4	2.5	2.0	2.0
1.5	1.4	1.4	Sales/Total Assets		2.0	1.7	1.6	1.4	1.2
1.1	1.0	1.0			1.2	1.2	1.3	.9	.8
1.4	1.2	1.1				1.0	.7	1.4	.9
(176) 2.7	(151) 2.6	(158) 2.3	% Depr., Dep., Amort./Sales			(13) 2.9	(26) 2.5	(49) 2.3	(59) 2.0
4.5	4.1	4.5				6.6	4.5	4.2	3.6
2.2	1.5	2.7					4.2	2.5	1.4
(63) 4.5	(52) 3.8	(55) 4.5	% Officers', Directors' Owners' Comp/Sales				(15) 5.2	(18) 3.7	(10) 2.5
6.5	8.4	6.8					8.3	7.5	4.5
7690945M	6070938M	6213309M	Net Sales ($)	2224M	26491M	62685M	226885M	888494M	5006530M
6481197M	5473810M	5521709M	Total Assets ($)	11926M	19819M	49597M	155524M	766192M	4518651M

M = $ thousand MM = $ million

See Pages 9 through 22 for Explanation of Ratios and Data

Current Data Sorted by Assets							Comparative Historical Data	
						Type of Statement		
		1	5		3	Unqualified	15	10
		2	1	1		Reviewed	5	5
		2				Compiled	5	1
		2				Tax Returns	3	2
	1		7	3	1	Other	17	21
	7 (4/1-9/30/13)		22 (10/1/13-3/31/14)				4/1/09-3/31/10	4/1/10-3/31/11
0-500M	500M-2MM	2-10MM	10-50MM	50-100MM	100-250MM		ALL	ALL
	1	7	13	4	4	**NUMBER OF STATEMENTS**	45	39
%	%	%	%	%	%	**ASSETS**	%	%
DATA NOT AVAILABLE			13.5			Cash & Equivalents	9.6	11.1
			22.1			Trade Receivables (net)	19.9	20.5
			21.9			Inventory	25.4	25.2
			11.5			All Other Current	4.1	5.1
			69.0			Total Current	59.0	61.9
			19.4			Fixed Assets (net)	25.0	25.5
			6.0			Intangibles (net)	8.7	3.3
			5.5			All Other Non-Current	7.3	9.4
			100.0			Total	100.0	100.0
						LIABILITIES		
			10.4			Notes Payable-Short Term	6.9	5.5
			4.6			Cur. Mat.-L.T.D.	3.3	3.6
			8.5			Trade Payables	9.3	10.3
			.6			Income Taxes Payable	.4	.5
			17.5			All Other Current	10.9	10.3
			41.6			Total Current	30.8	30.2
			6.6			Long-Term Debt	12.4	9.8
			1.7			Deferred Taxes	1.1	1.4
			2.7			All Other Non-Current	7.2	7.3
			47.4			Net Worth	48.5	51.3
			100.0			Total Liabilties & Net Worth	100.0	100.0
						INCOME DATA		
			100.0			Net Sales	100.0	100.0
			30.4			Gross Profit	32.3	30.3
			19.9			Operating Expenses	24.0	23.0
			10.5			Operating Profit	8.3	7.3
			.4			All Other Expenses (net)	1.3	.2
			10.1			Profit Before Taxes	7.0	7.1
						RATIOS		
			3.1				3.8	3.5
			1.7			Current	2.1	2.0
			1.3				1.2	1.2
			1.8				1.6	2.0
			1.1			Quick	1.0	1.2
			.5				.5	.6
			39 9.4				**29** 12.4	**30** 12.2
			48 7.6			Sales/Receivables	**38** 9.5	**46** 7.9
			76 4.8				**63** 5.8	**56** 6.5
			54 6.8				**30** 12.1	**35** 10.3
			76 4.8			Cost of Sales/Inventory	**77** 4.7	**65** 5.6
			118 3.1				**138** 2.6	**152** 2.4
			21 17.8				**16** 23.4	**17** 21.5
			26 14.1			Cost of Sales/Payables	**27** 13.3	**32** 11.3
			42 8.6				**54** 6.8	**51** 7.2
			2.9				3.2	2.3
			4.6			Sales/Working Capital	6.0	5.3
			16.9				12.5	12.6
			62.5				38.7	38.4
			(12) 10.1			EBIT/Interest	(42) 9.8	(36) 11.3
			2.6				2.0	2.4
								12.5
						Net Profit + Depr., Dep., Amort./Cur. Mat. L/T/D		(10) 5.4
								1.9
			.2				.3	.2
			.5			Fixed/Worth	.6	.5
			.8				1.4	1.0
			.7				.3	.4
			1.3			Debt/Worth	1.7	.9
			2.9				3.3	2.1
			58.5				51.0	34.4
			35.1			% Profit Before Taxes/Tangible Net Worth	(42) 19.4	18.7
			13.9				8.6	6.7
			22.4				17.8	20.2
			9.8			% Profit Before Taxes/Total Assets	6.9	9.8
			4.3				2.9	1.8
			13.9				14.6	16.0
			6.0			Sales/Net Fixed Assets	6.3	7.7
			4.5				3.9	3.1
			1.9				2.2	2.0
			1.3			Sales/Total Assets	1.3	1.4
			.8				.9	.9
			1.3				1.2	1.3
			(12) 1.5			% Depr., Dep., Amort./Sales	(38) 2.4	(35) 2.2
			3.8				3.9	3.5
						% Officers', Directors' Owners' Comp/Sales		
	2938M	63783M	396300M	426044M	578861M	Net Sales ($)	2151704M	1499422M
	1270M	28536M	308022M	289936M	445180M	Total Assets ($)	1857200M	1290032M

M = $ thousand MM = $ million

See Pages 9 through 22 for Explanation of Ratios and Data

Comparative Historical Data | **Current Data Sorted by Sales**

4/1/11-3/31/12 ALL	4/1/12-3/31/13 ALL	4/1/13-3/31/14 ALL	Type of Statement	0-1MM	1-3MM	3-5MM	5-10MM	10-25MM	25MM & OVER
9	11	9	Unqualified					2	7
4	5	4	Reviewed			1		1	2
1	2	2	Compiled			1	1		
2		2	Tax Returns			1	1		
25	14	12	Other		1		1	4	6
				7 (4/1-9/30/13)			22 (10/1/13-3/31/14)		
41	32	29	NUMBER OF STATEMENTS		1	3	3	7	15
%	%	%	**ASSETS**	%	%	%	%	%	%
8.3	10.4	11.4	Cash & Equivalents	DATA NOT AVAILABLE					12.2
21.4	19.1	20.7	Trade Receivables (net)						23.0
30.4	23.3	25.8	Inventory						24.4
5.6	4.7	7.6	All Other Current						7.1
65.7	57.5	65.5	Total Current						66.7
24.3	28.6	23.4	Fixed Assets (net)						26.0
3.3	7.0	4.1	Intangibles (net)						3.1
6.7	6.9	7.0	All Other Non-Current						4.2
100.0	100.0	100.0	Total						100.0
			LIABILITIES						
8.9	5.9	7.5	Notes Payable-Short Term						6.5
2.4	2.8	3.1	Cur. Mat.-L.T.D.						1.4
12.5	8.1	9.2	Trade Payables						8.8
.4	.3	.4	Income Taxes Payable						.6
8.5	11.7	14.2	All Other Current						18.3
32.8	28.7	34.3	Total Current						35.6
11.1	13.6	7.5	Long-Term Debt						7.6
1.1	1.9	1.3	Deferred Taxes						2.2
5.1	6.4	4.0	All Other Non-Current						4.1
49.9	49.3	52.9	Net Worth						50.5
100.0	100.0	100.0	Total Liabilties & Net Worth						100.0
			INCOME DATA						
100.0	100.0	100.0	Net Sales						100.0
28.2	29.1	27.8	Gross Profit						23.1
20.4	19.6	20.5	Operating Expenses						16.2
7.8	9.5	7.3	Operating Profit						6.9
.9	.8	.3	All Other Expenses (net)						.4
6.9	8.7	7.0	Profit Before Taxes						6.5
			RATIOS						
3.4	3.9	3.8							3.6
2.0	2.1	2.4	Current						2.4
1.5	1.4	1.4							1.2
1.7	2.7	2.3							2.0
1.1	1.1	1.3	Quick						1.1
.4	.5	.6							.7
35 10.3	**31** 11.8	**35** 10.5							**40** 9.1
48 7.6	**43** 8.4	**47** 7.7	Sales/Receivables						**48** 7.6
60 6.1	**58** 6.3	**74** 4.9							**74** 4.9
54 6.8	**34** 10.7	**54** 6.8							**53** 6.9
85 4.3	**66** 5.5	**79** 4.6	Cost of Sales/Inventory						**73** 5.0
140 2.6	**111** 3.3	**126** 2.9							**99** 3.7
27 13.5	**19** 19.7	**16** 22.7							**15** 24.3
36 10.1	**27** 13.6	**22** 16.9	Cost of Sales/Payables						**21** 17.1
49 7.5	**41** 8.8	**39** 9.4							**37** 9.9
2.8	3.2	2.6							2.6
4.6	5.0	5.0	Sales/Working Capital						5.3
10.7	11.6	13.3							25.0
32.2	51.9	50.3							68.0
(34) 8.5	(30) 12.9	(27) 7.7	EBIT/Interest						12.6
2.8	3.8	2.5							2.0
			Net Profit + Depr., Dep., Amort./Cur. Mat. L/T/D						
.2	.3	.2							.2
.5	.5	.5	Fixed/Worth						.6
.9	1.2	.9							1.1
.5	.5	.4							.4
1.1	1.0	.8	Debt/Worth						1.5
1.8	2.2	2.1							1.8
33.2	40.4	39.2							35.1
(40) 22.6	(30) 23.9	18.1	% Profit Before Taxes/Tangible Net Worth						18.1
12.3	11.5	6.6							7.9
17.8	17.8	15.3							16.2
11.9	8.9	5.2	% Profit Before Taxes/Total Assets						8.9
3.7	3.0	3.3							3.2
15.5	12.6	15.0							14.1
8.3	4.8	6.7	Sales/Net Fixed Assets						6.1
4.3	3.1	4.0							3.9
2.2	2.0	1.9							1.9
1.6	1.5	1.6	Sales/Total Assets						1.6
1.0	1.0	.9							1.2
1.2	1.1	1.4							1.3
(38) 2.4	(31) 2.4	(24) 2.0	% Depr., Dep., Amort./Sales					(13)	1.9
3.5	4.5	4.0							3.8
			% Officers', Directors' Owners' Comp/Sales						
1935639M	**1609822M**	**1467926M**	Net Sales ($)		**2938M**	**10652M**	**21780M**	**137885M**	**1294671M**
1774817M	**1199420M**	**1072944M**	Total Assets ($)		**1270M**	**11301M**	**20428M**	**128812M**	**911133M**

M = $ thousand MM = $ million

See Pages 9 through 22 for Explanation of Ratios and Data

Current Data Sorted by Assets							Comparative Historical Data	
						Type of Statement		
		2	11	9	7	Unqualified	20	17
	1	8	5			Reviewed	12	10
	3	6	1	2		Compiled	11	7
1	4	6				Tax Returns	6	10
1	1	4	8	2	5	Other	41	37
10 (4/1-9/30/13)			77 (10/1/13-3/31/14)				**4/1/09-3/31/10 ALL**	**4/1/10-3/31/11 ALL**
0-500M	**500M-2MM**	**2-10MM**	**10-50MM**	**50-100MM**	**100-250MM**			
2	9	26	25	13	12	**NUMBER OF STATEMENTS**	90	81
%	%	%	%	%	%	**ASSETS**	%	%
		18.5	12.4	8.9	12.0	Cash & Equivalents	11.8	11.5
		22.1	18.4	15.6	12.7	Trade Receivables (net)	20.0	20.0
		13.3	5.1	7.9	13.8	Inventory	11.6	14.9
		6.4	12.5	11.3	9.8	All Other Current	11.4	8.3
		60.3	48.4	43.8	48.2	Total Current	54.7	54.7
		30.1	40.7	43.4	31.9	Fixed Assets (net)	36.7	34.9
		4.2	4.0	6.2	12.3	Intangibles (net)	2.5	3.9
		5.4	6.9	6.7	7.6	All Other Non-Current	6.0	6.5
		100.0	100.0	100.0	100.0	Total	100.0	100.0
						LIABILITIES		
		4.4	4.5	3.8	9.1	Notes Payable-Short Term	8.5	10.2
		3.5	4.3	4.3	2.2	Cur. Mat.-L.T.D.	2.9	2.9
		12.9	12.5	10.0	7.3	Trade Payables	11.1	13.6
		.8	.4	.5	.0	Income Taxes Payable	.4	.2
		22.3	18.7	11.3	9.1	All Other Current	13.3	11.9
		43.9	40.4	29.8	27.7	Total Current	36.1	38.9
		18.6	17.3	24.5	20.7	Long-Term Debt	21.1	21.0
		.5	1.5	.7	1.2	Deferred Taxes	1.0	1.6
		4.3	4.3	8.5	1.0	All Other Non-Current	3.0	5.8
		32.7	36.6	36.6	49.4	Net Worth	38.8	32.7
		100.0	100.0	100.0	100.0	Total Liabilties & Net Worth	100.0	100.0
						INCOME DATA		
		100.0	100.0	100.0	100.0	Net Sales	100.0	100.0
		30.2	21.3	20.3	16.0	Gross Profit	25.2	26.9
		26.1	18.0	16.1	11.0	Operating Expenses	20.7	23.4
		4.1	3.3	4.2	5.0	Operating Profit	4.5	3.5
		.5	.8	.1	2.7	All Other Expenses (net)	.9	.5
		3.6	2.5	4.1	2.3	Profit Before Taxes	3.6	3.0
						RATIOS		
		2.0	2.2	2.1	2.4		2.4	2.2
		1.5	1.2	1.5	2.1	Current	1.5	1.5
		1.0	.9	1.0	1.1		1.1	1.1
		1.5	1.1	1.1	1.6		1.5	1.4
		1.0	.9	.6	1.1	Quick	.9	1.0
		.5	.5	.5	.5		.4	.4
		9 42.9	**11** 32.8	**11** 33.2	**17** 21.2		**16** 23.5	**18** 20.5
		39 9.4	**41** 8.8	**45** 8.1	**31** 11.8	Sales/Receivables	**34** 10.7	**33** 11.0
		53 6.9	**51** 7.1	**54** 6.8	**46** 7.9		**47** 7.7	**54** 6.7
		0 UND	**0** UND	**0** UND	**1** 311.8		**1** 476.5	**1** 696.4
		11 34.7	**4** 94.4	**8** 48.0	**7** 54.1	Cost of Sales/Inventory	**5** 75.7	**17** 20.9
		39 9.4	**13** 28.0	**20** 18.5	**51** 7.2		**45** 8.2	**79** 4.6
		12 31.6	**19** 18.9	**18** 20.2	**16** 23.5		**12** 30.9	**14** 25.5
		24 15.0	**29** 12.7	**32** 11.3	**23** 16.2	Cost of Sales/Payables	**24** 15.2	**27** 13.3
		38 9.6	**48** 7.6	**42** 8.7	**34** 10.7		**39** 9.5	**44** 8.3
		6.8	7.4	4.7	4.7		5.8	5.7
		16.0	24.7	9.7	5.8	Sales/Working Capital	10.4	10.6
		NM	-57.2	NM	30.6		53.0	117.1
		29.0	17.5	25.2	34.0		12.9	11.5
		(24) 7.1	(21) 6.0	(12) 5.7	12.0	EBIT/Interest	(83) 5.2	(72) 3.0
		1.6	1.8	1.5	1.8		.8	1.1
							9.2	3.9
						Net Profit + Depr., Dep., Amort./Cur. Mat. L/T/D	(30) 2.7	(23) 2.0
							.9	.8
		.5	.6	.8	.4		.5	.6
		1.0	1.1	1.2	.5	Fixed/Worth	.8	1.3
		NM	3.9	2.7	2.3		1.9	2.5
		1.0	.8	1.0	.5		.7	.9
		2.4	1.4	1.9	1.1	Debt/Worth	1.6	1.8
		NM	3.8	3.2	2.7		3.1	5.1
		54.3	31.6	37.1	37.3		43.8	48.0
		(20) 35.3	(21) 16.2	(11) 14.2	(11) 11.2	% Profit Before Taxes/Tangible Net Worth	(82) 16.3	(69) 11.5
		19.0	2.0	2.3	8.2		1.3	1.7
		19.6	14.3	11.2	21.8		15.4	13.6
		11.6	7.0	5.0	7.9	% Profit Before Taxes/Total Assets	5.7	3.8
		1.3	.3	1.0	2.3		-.3	.3
		64.3	8.8	4.9	7.8		13.7	18.2
		9.4	3.8	3.3	4.3	Sales/Net Fixed Assets	5.6	6.0
		3.3	2.7	2.5	2.0		2.6	2.7
		3.3	2.1	1.7	1.7		2.5	2.4
		2.4	1.7	1.5	1.2	Sales/Total Assets	1.7	1.7
		1.5	1.1	1.2	1.0		1.2	1.1
		1.5	1.3	1.9	1.6		1.2	1.2
		(19) 2.0	(21) 3.1	(12) 2.9	(11) 3.0	% Depr., Dep., Amort./Sales	(81) 2.4	(72) 2.4
		3.8	4.5	6.6	4.4		3.6	4.5
							1.1	2.1
						% Officers', Directors' Owners' Comp/Sales	(18) 2.7	(23) 3.9
							4.1	9.2
1908M	**32274M**	**319488M**	**1097812M**	**1279162M**	**2282091M**	Net Sales ($)	**5654797M**	**4624380M**
454M	**9435M**	**139808M**	**634220M**	**917494M**	**1808930M**	Total Assets ($)	**3796277M**	**2963922M**

M = $ thousand MM = $ million

See Pages 9 through 22 for Explanation of Ratios and Data

Comparative Historical Data				Current Data Sorted by Sales					
			Type of Statement						
22	18	29	Unqualified					6	23
13	10	14	Reviewed				5	5	4
11	7	12	Compiled		3		1	6	2
9	10	11	Tax Returns	1	3	3	2	2	
40	47	21	Other	1	1	1	2	3	13
4/1/11-3/31/12 ALL	4/1/12-3/31/13 ALL	4/1/13-3/31/14 ALL		10 (4/1-9/30/13)			77 (10/1/13-3/31/14)		
				0-1MM	1-3MM	3-5MM	5-10MM	10-25MM	25MM & OVER
95	92	87	**NUMBER OF STATEMENTS**	2	7	4	10	22	42
%	%	%	**ASSETS**	%	%	%	%	%	%
11.2	10.9	13.9	Cash & Equivalents				32.7	11.2	11.9
18.3	18.1	19.2	Trade Receivables (net)				10.1	24.3	17.9
12.3	9.6	10.7	Inventory				3.9	11.0	8.5
9.2	9.0	9.3	All Other Current				8.5	6.3	11.8
51.0	47.6	53.0	Total Current				55.2	52.8	50.1
36.7	39.3	34.1	Fixed Assets (net)				40.3	34.9	36.8
3.1	3.8	5.1	Intangibles (net)				2.1	5.2	6.2
9.2	9.3	7.8	All Other Non-Current				2.4	7.1	7.0
100.0	100.0	100.0	Total				100.0	100.0	100.0
			LIABILITIES						
6.9	5.6	8.9	Notes Payable-Short Term				3.7	4.4	5.9
4.9	3.4	4.0	Cur. Mat.-L.T.D.				3.8	3.3	4.1
10.8	11.3	11.6	Trade Payables				10.7	14.6	10.7
.2	.2	.4	Income Taxes Payable				.0	1.1	.3
18.0	17.8	16.7	All Other Current				24.7	20.4	13.0
40.9	38.3	41.6	Total Current				42.9	43.9	34.0
17.2	22.1	18.6	Long-Term Debt				16.2	17.8	20.0
1.7	.7	.8	Deferred Taxes				.1	.9	1.2
4.5	4.5	4.2	All Other Non-Current				.6	5.3	2.8
35.7	34.3	34.8	Net Worth				40.2	32.2	42.0
100.0	100.0	100.0	Total Liabilities & Net Worth				100.0	100.0	100.0
			INCOME DATA						
100.0	100.0	100.0	Net Sales				100.0	100.0	100.0
25.6	27.5	26.1	Gross Profit				36.4	22.1	20.4
22.3	22.5	22.2	Operating Expenses				30.5	18.9	15.3
3.3	5.0	3.9	Operating Profit				6.0	3.2	5.1
.9	.5	.8	All Other Expenses (net)				.3	.5	1.0
2.5	4.5	3.1	Profit Before Taxes				5.6	2.7	4.1
			RATIOS						
2.0	2.5	2.2					2.0	2.1	2.3
1.5	1.5	1.5	Current				1.4	1.5	1.6
.9	.9	1.0					.8	1.0	1.1
1.4	1.7	1.4					1.5	1.5	1.3
.8	.8	.9	Quick				.9	1.0	.9
.4	.5	.5					.6	.5	.5
12 30.1	14 25.8	10 35.0					5 80.3	12 30.6	18 20.8
33 11.0	32 11.3	38 9.5	Sales/Receivables				7 54.4	47 7.7	40 9.1
45 8.1	50 7.3	51 7.1					17 21.3	54 6.7	49 7.4
0 UND	0 999.8	0 UND					0 UND	0 UND	0 UND
4 99.0	5 78.2	5 72.7	Cost of Sales/Inventory				0 UND	7 55.3	4 98.7
60 6.1	28 13.0	38 9.6					22 16.5	38 9.6	21 17.3
16 23.5	13 28.1	16 22.5					13 28.5	12 31.2	18 20.3
25 14.4	28 13.1	25 14.8	Cost of Sales/Payables				22 16.3	25 14.5	25 14.4
40 9.1	40 9.1	39 9.3					34 10.8	41 9.0	38 9.5
5.9	6.7	5.9					6.3	7.2	5.5
11.6	13.0	15.9	Sales/Working Capital				25.6	16.8	10.3
-45.5	-43.2	245.6					-66.8	NM	39.1
11.3	20.5	22.6						19.8	23.7
(87) 5.0	(84) 6.4	(78) 7.2	EBIT/Interest					(21) 6.3	(37) 8.8
.4	2.0	1.9						1.2	2.5
5.1	3.4	9.1							17.0
(27) 1.5	(19) 2.3	(23) 5.9	Net Profit + Depr., Dep., Amort./Cur. Mat. L/T/D						(16) 7.3
.5	1.1	1.4							1.7
.5	.5	.5					.4	.7	.4
1.2	1.1	1.1	Fixed/Worth				1.4	1.2	1.0
2.0	3.2	2.5					NM	1.9	2.3
.7	.6	.8					.6	1.2	.8
1.7	1.5	1.9	Debt/Worth				1.3	2.4	1.4
4.5	5.8	4.3					NM	4.2	2.9
43.0	47.3	38.8						44.1	36.6
(81) 17.2	(76) 18.2	(71) 22.5	% Profit Before Taxes/Tangible Net Worth					(18) 22.9	(37) 15.5
1.8	5.7	8.4						2.0	8.3
13.6	19.7	14.9					40.8	18.9	13.6
6.5	6.9	7.5	% Profit Before Taxes/Total Assets				18.8	7.5	8.1
-.2	1.5	1.2					1.8	.3	2.6
15.6	16.1	17.3					144.5	13.1	7.6
4.6	4.1	5.1	Sales/Net Fixed Assets				8.5	6.3	4.2
2.9	2.5	2.9					2.9	3.2	2.6
2.4	3.0	2.8					3.6	3.3	1.9
1.7	1.7	1.7	Sales/Total Assets				2.6	2.1	1.6
1.1	1.2	1.2					1.5	1.5	1.2
1.2	1.3	1.4						1.4	1.6
(84) 2.9	(83) 3.0	(70) 2.6	% Depr., Dep., Amort./Sales					(18) 1.9	(37) 2.9
4.7	4.2	4.5						3.3	4.3
2.2	1.2	1.0							
(19) 3.9	(24) 2.4	(18) 2.2	% Officers', Directors' Owners' Comp/Sales						
8.2	3.1	6.5							
4649975M	4518971M	5012735M	Net Sales ($)	1908M	13783M	17816M	73086M	405368M	4500774M
3241609M	3201607M	3510341M	Total Assets ($)	454M	11374M	16919M	41214M	287674M	3152706M

M = $ thousand MM = $ million

See Pages 9 through 22 for Explanation of Ratios and Data

Current Data Sorted by Assets / Comparative Historical Data

0-500M	500M-2MM	2-10MM	10-50MM	50-100MM	100-250MM		4/1/09-3/31/10 ALL	4/1/10-3/31/11 ALL
						Type of Statement		
		3	4	6	2	Unqualified	16	15
	1	3	2	2		Reviewed	5	6
1	2	9	2			Compiled	6	6
	3	3				Tax Returns	7	12
	6	11	9	1	2	Other	30	31
	14 (4/1-9/30/13)		58 (10/1/13-3/31/14)					
1	12	29	17	9	4	**NUMBER OF STATEMENTS**	64	70
%	%	%	%	%	%	**ASSETS**	%	%
	9.4	14.2	17.5			Cash & Equivalents	9.5	11.3
	7.9	13.4	10.2			Trade Receivables (net)	10.8	11.0
	46.4	34.7	35.6			Inventory	32.3	29.6
	9.9	3.3	3.8			All Other Current	5.0	5.2
	73.6	65.5	67.2			Total Current	57.6	57.0
	19.6	26.9	19.3			Fixed Assets (net)	33.0	29.9
	1.6	4.0	7.1			Intangibles (net)	4.4	7.8
	5.2	3.6	6.3			All Other Non-Current	5.0	5.3
	100.0	100.0	100.0			Total	100.0	100.0
						LIABILITIES		
	13.1	5.9	4.6			Notes Payable-Short Term	12.3	14.9
	1.5	5.5	1.1			Cur. Mat.-L.T.D.	2.3	2.9
	22.4	17.0	9.9			Trade Payables	10.9	13.6
	.0	.1	.0			Income Taxes Payable	.4	.1
	49.3	12.3	21.9			All Other Current	12.4	12.4
	86.4	40.7	37.5			Total Current	38.2	43.9
	25.8	19.8	12.8			Long-Term Debt	18.5	30.2
	.0	.4	.0			Deferred Taxes	.1	.4
	6.9	5.1	2.9			All Other Non-Current	7.0	11.7
	-19.1	33.9	46.8			Net Worth	36.2	13.9
	100.0	100.0	100.0			Total Liabilties & Net Worth	100.0	100.0
						INCOME DATA		
	100.0	100.0	100.0			Net Sales	100.0	100.0
	35.6	23.5	19.3			Gross Profit	19.9	23.8
	33.0	21.9	13.8			Operating Expenses	23.4	21.8
	2.6	1.6	5.5			Operating Profit	-3.5	2.0
	1.6	.8	.2			All Other Expenses (net)	1.2	2.1
	1.0	.9	5.3			Profit Before Taxes	-4.7	-.1
						RATIOS		
	1.9	2.8	2.9				3.1	2.5
	1.0	1.8	2.1			Current	1.5	1.4
	.7	1.2	1.2				1.1	1.0
	.7	1.5	1.3				1.2	.9
	.2	.5	.7			Quick	.6	.6
	.1	.4	.4				.2	.2
	1 471.3	**6** 56.6	**2** 218.0				**8** 46.6	**9** 40.7
	6 60.1	**13** 27.3	**11** 32.3			Sales/Receivables	**16** 22.9	**16** 22.6
	37 9.8	**34** 10.8	**35** 10.4				**38** 9.5	**30** 12.0
	29 12.4	**36** 10.1	**28** 13.2				**34** 10.9	**38** 9.6
	64 5.7	**57** 6.4	**53** 6.9			Cost of Sales/Inventory	**86** 4.2	**76** 4.8
	135 2.7	**81** 4.5	**91** 4.0				**185** 2.0	**123** 3.0
	6 62.0	**16** 22.5	**10** 37.8				**15** 23.6	**13** 27.9
	39 9.4	**33** 10.9	**18** 20.1			Cost of Sales/Payables	**23** 15.6	**23** 15.7
	96 3.8	**42** 8.7	**23** 16.0				**37** 9.9	**34** 10.7
	9.0	5.5	4.9				3.0	5.0
	NM	10.3	9.6			Sales/Working Capital	9.5	13.2
	-7.7	28.9	25.5				57.9	-108.5
	38.3	10.7	139.7				2.5	5.6
	10.4	(27) 5.4	(14) 19.1			EBIT/Interest	(55) -.9	(62) 1.3
	1.4	1.4	3.5				-6.0	-.9
							4.8	4.2
						Net Profit + Depr., Dep., Amort./Cur. Mat. L/T/D	(13) 1.7	(12) 1.2
							-4.9	-.3
	.2	.4	.1				.4	.5
	1.5	1.2	.5			Fixed/Worth	1.0	1.4
	-.8	3.2	1.2				6.7	-2.4
	1.0	.7	.4				.7	1.0
	35.3	3.4	1.0			Debt/Worth	1.7	3.0
	-2.7	8.3	3.2				13.3	-6.6
		72.9	43.1				19.1	24.3
		(25) 34.2	(15) 21.2			% Profit Before Taxes/Tangible Net Worth	(52) -3.8	(49) 7.9
		1.7	6.8				-39.2	-5.9
	24.9	18.6	22.3				5.5	6.1
	13.4	12.1	10.4			% Profit Before Taxes/Total Assets	-2.7	.8
	2.2	.4	4.3				-19.7	-7.2
	64.0	37.8	47.5				11.4	15.3
	34.1	8.5	13.9			Sales/Net Fixed Assets	4.2	6.0
	4.2	5.4	10.1				2.4	3.3
	3.5	3.9	3.4				2.3	2.4
	2.6	2.8	2.3			Sales/Total Assets	1.3	1.6
	1.2	1.6	1.8				1.0	1.1
		.6	.6				1.4	1.1
		(26) 1.4	(15) 1.3			% Depr., Dep., Amort./Sales	(58) 2.5	(59) 2.6
		3.0	2.0				4.9	3.9
							1.3	1.6
						% Officers', Directors' Owners' Comp/Sales	(18) 2.7	(18) 2.5
							4.0	7.3
174M	35069M	483556M	1211133M	1284817M	821628M	Net Sales ($)	1981851M	2306371M
74M	12006M	164112M	423197M	582512M	726465M	Total Assets ($)	1688944M	1811469M

M = $ thousand MM = $ million

See Pages 9 through 22 for Explanation of Ratios and Data

Comparative Historical Data				Current Data Sorted by Sales					
			Type of Statement						
19	8	15	Unqualified				1		14
12	15	8	Reviewed		1		1	2	4
6	11	14	Compiled	1	1		3	6	3
9	11	6	Tax Returns	1	2		2	1	
22	44	29	Other	1	2	3	5	3	15
4/1/11-3/31/12 ALL	**4/1/12-3/31/13 ALL**	**4/1/13-3/31/14 ALL**		**14 (4/1-9/30/13)**			**58 (10/1/13-3/31/14)**		
				0-1MM	**1-3MM**	**3-5MM**	**5-10MM**	**10-25MM**	**25MM & OVER**
68	89	72	**NUMBER OF STATEMENTS**	3	6	3	12	12	36
%	%	%	**ASSETS**	%	%	%	%	%	%
12.9	12.3	13.4	Cash & Equivalents				9.2	19.0	12.3
10.7	11.8	11.0	Trade Receivables (net)				14.3	14.3	10.5
35.7	32.5	36.4	Inventory				36.0	28.7	37.2
3.4	4.6	4.8	All Other Current				4.5	3.6	3.7
62.6	61.1	65.7	Total Current				64.0	65.6	63.6
26.1	27.4	23.6	Fixed Assets (net)				31.0	30.3	20.0
5.8	5.0	6.2	Intangibles (net)				.6	.2	11.6
5.5	6.4	4.5	All Other Non-Current				4.4	4.0	4.8
100.0	100.0	100.0	Total				100.0	100.0	100.0
			LIABILITIES						
10.8	9.5	6.9	Notes Payable-Short Term				6.0	3.8	6.6
3.3	3.9	3.4	Cur. Mat.-L.T.D.				8.4	1.2	3.4
11.8	13.4	14.6	Trade Payables				17.5	18.3	12.5
.1	.0	.1	Income Taxes Payable				.0	.2	.1
14.6	19.9	27.0	All Other Current				7.0	24.5	16.3
40.7	46.8	51.9	Total Current				38.9	48.0	38.8
31.5	22.2	19.1	Long-Term Debt				29.6	12.9	15.6
.3	.3	.3	Deferred Taxes				.2	.4	.4
8.7	8.7	6.9	All Other Non-Current				6.6	5.8	8.3
18.8	22.0	21.8	Net Worth				24.7	33.0	36.9
100.0	100.0	100.0	Total Liabilties & Net Worth				100.0	100.0	100.0
			INCOME DATA						
100.0	100.0	100.0	Net Sales				100.0	100.0	100.0
21.3	22.2	23.4	Gross Profit				30.4	20.3	18.8
18.2	18.6	20.2	Operating Expenses				29.9	14.9	13.6
3.1	3.6	3.2	Operating Profit				.4	5.4	5.2
1.3	1.3	1.0	All Other Expenses (net)				1.1	.4	.9
1.9	2.3	2.2	Profit Before Taxes				-.7	5.0	4.3
			RATIOS						
2.6	2.5	2.6					3.2	1.9	2.8
1.6	1.4	1.6	Current				2.1	1.6	1.6
1.2	.9	1.0					.9	1.2	1.1
1.1	1.0	1.2					1.2	1.5	1.2
.6	.6	.5	Quick				.8	.6	.6
.3	.2	.2					.4	.3	.4
8 43.1	**5** 67.1	**3** 128.7					**8** 46.0	**9** 39.6	**2** 195.0
12 30.3	**13** 27.3	**12** 30.0	Sales/Receivables				**31** 11.9	**14** 25.2	**11** 32.1
23 16.2	**26** 14.0	**33** 11.0					**46** 8.0	**36** 10.1	**20** 18.5
36 10.1	**30** 12.2	**34** 10.6					**29** 12.4	**8** 48.5	**36** 10.2
58 6.3	**64** 5.7	**57** 6.4	Cost of Sales/Inventory				**64** 5.7	**39** 9.4	**53** 6.9
99 3.7	**111** 3.3	**91** 4.0					**114** 3.2	**78** 4.7	**89** 4.1
10 36.4	**11** 31.8	**14** 26.0					**15** 23.7	**16** 23.4	**10** 37.2
20 17.9	**22** 16.3	**22** 16.5	Cost of Sales/Payables				**34** 10.7	**32** 11.5	**19** 18.8
31 11.9	**36** 10.2	**36** 10.2					**50** 7.3	**38** 9.5	**29** 12.6
6.3	5.6	6.0					4.2	9.1	6.0
11.8	14.6	10.6	Sales/Working Capital				7.9	12.0	10.8
36.3	-39.1	-165.2					NM	32.0	77.3
15.1	15.0	31.6					21.4	135.1	34.2
(61) 4.4	(84) 5.0	(65) 6.2	EBIT/Interest				3.4	8.2	(31) 6.8
.9	.9	1.3					-3.3	4.2	1.4
10.1	17.1	14.6							
(18) 5.1	(18) 7.0	(15) 5.8	Net Profit + Depr., Dep., Amort./Cur. Mat. L/T/D						
1.3	2.9	.3							
.3	.4	.4					.5	.6	.3
.9	1.3	1.1	Fixed/Worth				1.9	1.1	.6
-5.1	-6.4	NM					3.2	2.4	-2.9
.6	.9	.7					1.0	1.0	.6
1.9	3.0	2.6	Debt/Worth				3.6	2.0	2.4
-22.2	-19.6	NM					11.0	5.2	-14.2
35.0	55.0	66.3					62.5	86.0	64.6
(50) 14.5	(63) 27.9	(54) 26.1	% Profit Before Taxes/Tangible Net Worth				(10) 12.6	(11) 34.2	(26) 26.1
3.5	8.7	6.6					-40.2	18.9	7.0
11.7	15.8	18.7					18.0	23.0	24.3
4.6	6.5	10.5	% Profit Before Taxes/Total Assets				6.2	12.5	10.7
.1	-.3	1.4					-11.6	6.8	3.0
27.3	23.8	37.9					16.6	17.3	48.4
9.9	10.4	10.7	Sales/Net Fixed Assets				6.4	8.8	13.3
5.0	5.0	5.7					3.5	6.1	8.4
3.3	3.2	3.7					3.2	3.7	3.8
2.1	2.2	2.4	Sales/Total Assets				1.9	2.8	2.6
1.5	1.7	1.7					1.1	2.2	1.9
.9	.9	.8					1.0	.9	.6
(59) 1.7	(76) 1.6	(62) 1.6	% Depr., Dep., Amort./Sales				(10) 2.5	1.4	(31) 1.3
2.7	3.1	2.8					3.6	2.8	2.3
1.8	1.5	1.2							
(16) 4.1	(22) 3.0	(15) 3.3	% Officers', Directors' Owners' Comp/Sales						
7.2	5.0	6.4							
3177149M	3979155M	3836377M	Net Sales ($)	1210M	11436M	9735M	86854M	198539M	3528603M
1838561M	1905205M	1908366M	Total Assets ($)	1907M	5218M	6453M	51823M	80289M	1762676M

M = $ thousand MM = $ million

See Pages 9 through 22 for Explanation of Ratios and Data

Current Data Sorted by Assets							Comparative Historical Data	
						Type of Statement		
			2		1	Unqualified	2	3
	2	5	1			Reviewed	3	3
		2			1	Compiled	5	6
	4	4				Tax Returns	13	10
1	5	8	4	1	1	Other	16	14
	3 (4/1-9/30/13)		39 (10/1/13-3/31/14)				4/1/09-3/31/10	4/1/10-3/31/11
0-500M	500M-2MM	2-10MM	10-50MM	50-100MM	100-250MM		ALL	ALL
1	11	19	7	1	3	**NUMBER OF STATEMENTS**	39	36
%	%	%	%	%	%	**ASSETS**	%	%
	24.6	11.8				Cash & Equivalents	9.6	9.1
	16.8	15.9				Trade Receivables (net)	14.9	16.3
	40.6	50.7				Inventory	44.7	40.9
	1.1	3.3				All Other Current	1.9	4.8
	83.2	81.7				Total Current	71.1	71.1
	10.2	10.2				Fixed Assets (net)	15.2	16.6
	2.1	4.2				Intangibles (net)	10.1	6.1
	4.5	3.8				All Other Non-Current	3.6	6.2
	100.0	100.0				Total	100.0	100.0
						LIABILITIES		
	11.1	23.0				Notes Payable-Short Term	16.7	10.6
	17.4	1.4				Cur. Mat.-L.T.D.	3.7	2.3
	24.0	14.6				Trade Payables	12.6	13.4
	.0	.0				Income Taxes Payable	.1	.2
	14.1	5.2				All Other Current	13.3	10.0
	66.7	44.2				Total Current	46.4	36.6
	10.1	8.3				Long-Term Debt	23.1	18.6
	.0	.0				Deferred Taxes	.0	.1
	26.4	13.3				All Other Non-Current	6.2	13.0
	-3.2	34.2				Net Worth	24.2	31.8
	100.0	100.0				Total Liabilties & Net Worth	100.0	100.0
						INCOME DATA		
	100.0	100.0				Net Sales	100.0	100.0
	43.5	32.4				Gross Profit	32.9	32.1
	38.3	24.6				Operating Expenses	30.2	28.7
	5.1	7.8				Operating Profit	2.7	3.4
	-.5	1.0				All Other Expenses (net)	3.1	.7
	5.6	6.9				Profit Before Taxes	-.4	2.6
						RATIOS		
	4.9	3.9					3.1	4.1
	2.0	2.0				Current	1.4	1.8
	1.2	1.5					1.0	1.3
	2.9	1.7					1.1	1.3
	1.3	.7				Quick	.3	.6
	.3	.2					.2	.3
	2 157.8	**6** 60.6					**11** 32.2	**5** 76.4
	15 24.3	**16** 23.3				Sales/Receivables	**22** 16.9	**28** 12.8
	29 12.7	**28** 13.0					**38** 9.6	**38** 9.6
	36 10.2	**73** 5.0					**62** 5.9	**61** 6.0
	66 5.5	**99** 3.7				Cost of Sales/Inventory	**116** 3.1	**90** 4.1
	122 3.0	**174** 2.1					**220** 1.7	**135** 2.7
	11 33.0	**6** 57.6					**18** 20.8	**11** 33.0
	35 10.3	**25** 14.8				Cost of Sales/Payables	**28** 12.9	**23** 15.9
	64 5.7	**50** 7.3					**59** 6.2	**44** 8.4
	5.0	3.4					4.0	3.7
	7.4	6.3				Sales/Working Capital	8.5	9.7
	25.2	13.6					58.0	19.2
	163.5	29.3					8.2	7.8
	(10) 9.2	(15) 14.3				EBIT/Interest	(36) 2.4	(33) 2.3
	-1.5	2.1					-1.1	.6
						Net Profit + Depr., Dep., Amort./Cur. Mat. L/T/D		
	.0	.0					.2	.1
	.2	.3				Fixed/Worth	.5	.5
	1.2	1.3					-1.3	NM
	.3	.4					.9	.9
	3.6	1.6				Debt/Worth	3.4	2.8
	-129.8	2.9					-9.4	NM
		104.1					56.2	34.9
		(16) 49.5				% Profit Before Taxes/Tangible Net Worth	(28) 16.7	(27) 5.9
		15.6					-1.4	-11.3
	48.7	33.5					10.2	11.9
	18.0	12.4				% Profit Before Taxes/Total Assets	4.0	2.7
	-2.5	1.2					-8.1	-2.6
	999.8	146.5					51.9	75.8
	114.6	41.1				Sales/Net Fixed Assets	18.8	31.9
	21.8	16.5					9.5	8.5
	4.5	3.8					2.9	3.6
	4.0	2.7				Sales/Total Assets	1.8	2.2
	2.9	1.8					1.3	1.5
		.2					1.0	.6
		(15) .5				% Depr., Dep., Amort./Sales	(25) 1.6	(25) 1.4
		2.1					4.9	4.6
							1.8	2.2
						% Officers', Directors' Owners' Comp/Sales	(17) 3.9	(14) 3.6
							8.9	9.0
641M	48232M	260794M	321585M	117630M	827938M	Net Sales ($)	1332209M	977340M
199M	12745M	97688M	143590M	65088M	508357M	Total Assets ($)	726940M	488229M

M = $ thousand MM = $ million

See Pages 9 through 22 for Explanation of Ratios and Data

Comparative Historical Data				Current Data Sorted by Sales					
			Type of Statement						
6	5	3	Unqualified						3
4	4	8	Reviewed			2	1	4	1
4	2	3	Compiled				1	1	1
13	9	8	Tax Returns		2	1	5		
18	19	20	Other	1	2	1	3	7	6
4/1/11-3/31/12 ALL	**4/1/12-3/31/13 ALL**	**4/1/13-3/31/14 ALL**			**3 (4/1-9/30/13)**			**39 (10/1/13-3/31/14)**	
				0-1MM	**1-3MM**	**3-5MM**	**5-10MM**	**10-25MM**	**25MM & OVER**
45	39	42	**NUMBER OF STATEMENTS**	1	4	4	10	12	11
%	%	%	**ASSETS**	%	%	%	%	%	%
9.9	9.8	13.4	Cash & Equivalents				21.4	9.3	6.2
19.3	18.7	20.1	Trade Receivables (net)				17.7	19.9	24.3
40.6	45.0	42.9	Inventory				44.1	50.4	35.3
1.9	3.7	2.4	All Other Current				.2	1.6	2.3
71.8	77.2	78.9	Total Current				83.5	81.2	68.1
17.2	14.8	10.6	Fixed Assets (net)				11.3	9.1	12.5
5.6	4.7	6.5	Intangibles (net)				1.5	6.3	15.5
5.4	3.3	3.9	All Other Non-Current				3.7	3.4	3.9
100.0	100.0	100.0	Total				100.0	100.0	100.0
			LIABILITIES						
17.4	16.8	15.1	Notes Payable-Short Term				11.6	18.5	6.9
2.0	1.2	5.5	Cur. Mat.-L.T.D.				17.1	1.5	1.3
14.3	17.0	18.6	Trade Payables				19.8	16.6	17.7
.1	.4	.0	Income Taxes Payable				.0	.0	.1
10.8	7.3	8.9	All Other Current				12.3	3.9	9.4
44.6	42.6	48.2	Total Current				60.8	40.5	35.5
13.3	11.5	8.5	Long-Term Debt				7.7	8.7	8.2
.1	.4	.4	Deferred Taxes				.0	.0	1.4
16.1	9.1	14.8	All Other Non-Current				23.0	7.2	3.6
26.0	36.3	28.1	Net Worth				8.5	43.6	51.3
100.0	100.0	100.0	Total Liabilties & Net Worth				100.0	100.0	100.0
			INCOME DATA						
100.0	100.0	100.0	Net Sales				100.0	100.0	100.0
33.3	35.0	32.8	Gross Profit				40.8	31.0	25.8
29.0	26.3	26.4	Operating Expenses				32.6	24.3	19.9
4.4	8.8	6.5	Operating Profit				8.2	6.7	5.9
1.8	1.0	.5	All Other Expenses (net)				-.9	1.1	.8
2.6	7.8	5.9	Profit Before Taxes				9.1	5.6	5.1
			RATIOS						
3.9	2.7	3.5					5.1	3.2	2.8
1.8	1.9	1.9	Current				3.5	1.6	1.9
1.2	1.4	1.5					1.8	1.5	1.6
1.7	1.3	1.7					3.0	1.6	1.4
.7	.7	.8	Quick				1.6	.8	.8
.3	.3	.4					.3	.4	.6
11 33.9	**3** 118.5	**7** 55.3					**6** 64.6	**11** 34.1	**39** 9.4
26 14.2	**26** 14.1	**25** 14.7	Sales/Receivables				**16** 22.4	**19** 19.6	**41** 8.9
50 7.3	**39** 9.3	**41** 9.0					**26** 14.3	**41** 9.0	**47** 7.7
53 6.9	**72** 5.1	**60** 6.1					**53** 6.9	**60** 6.1	**61** 6.0
91 4.0	**96** 3.8	**94** 3.9	Cost of Sales/Inventory				**74** 4.9	**99** 3.7	**94** 3.9
146 2.5	**130** 2.8	**122** 3.0					**96** 3.8	**135** 2.7	**99** 3.7
12 31.2	**12** 30.5	**16** 22.8					**12** 31.6	**7** 49.8	**33** 11.0
26 13.9	**31** 11.7	**36** 10.1	Cost of Sales/Payables				**27** 13.7	**29** 12.6	**43** 8.5
47 7.8	**50** 7.3	**51** 7.2					**38** 9.6	**52** 7.0	**51** 7.2
3.8	5.0	4.9					5.2	3.1	5.2
8.0	8.3	7.4	Sales/Working Capital				6.2	10.3	7.4
18.7	12.3	14.0					12.3	14.8	10.6
15.9	42.0	36.1							42.9
(43) 3.6	(35) 6.6	(37) 14.0	EBIT/Interest						14.0
1.1	3.5	2.1							5.8
			Net Profit + Depr., Dep., Amort./Cur. Mat. L/T/D						
.1	.1	.0					.0	.0	.1
.4	.4	.3	Fixed/Worth				.1	.3	.4
2.8	1.6	.9					.6	3.2	.7
.6	1.2	.6					.2	.5	.7
2.5	1.9	1.7	Debt/Worth				1.1	1.6	1.6
6.8	5.7	13.1					3.8	12.6	4.7
56.0	98.9	107.1						111.1	110.2
(35) 12.7	(33) 35.9	(35) 54.7	% Profit Before Taxes/Tangible Net Worth					(10) 63.3	(10) 50.7
2.0	13.7	20.9						21.7	21.4
19.2	40.2	28.6					43.7	32.9	26.4
5.4	13.7	13.8	% Profit Before Taxes/Total Assets				20.9	12.3	15.3
-.2	5.0	3.0					.3	3.2	7.8
89.6	124.3	168.9					999.8	136.3	25.9
20.9	29.0	28.3	Sales/Net Fixed Assets				143.6	50.8	16.7
9.0	17.0	15.4					16.0	17.0	12.5
2.9	3.5	3.9					4.6	4.1	2.6
2.2	2.7	2.8	Sales/Total Assets				3.5	2.8	2.2
1.6	1.8	1.9					2.9	1.8	1.7
.4	.3	.4						.2	1.2
(34) .9	(29) .5	(29) 1.0	% Depr., Dep., Amort./Sales					(10) .4	(10) 2.0
2.9	1.2	2.4						2.1	2.9
2.7	2.6	1.3							
(18) 3.5	(10) 4.1	(12) 2.8	% Officers', Directors' Owners' Comp/Sales						
8.2	7.5	4.8							
1286394M	1297717M	1576820M	Net Sales ($)	641M	8475M	16188M	63811M	220552M	1267153M
689143M	606113M	827667M	Total Assets ($)	199M	5300M	5849M	17831M	81453M	717035M

M = $ thousand MM = $ million

See Pages 9 through 22 for Explanation of Ratios and Data

Current Data Sorted by Assets							Comparative Historical Data	
						Type of Statement		
		2	3	2	1	Unqualified	9	9
	1	4	5			Reviewed	7	12
	3	2	1			Compiled	6	7
1	2	5	1			Tax Returns	10	11
1	6	11	3	3	1	Other	32	21
6 (4/1-9/30/13)			52 (10/1/13-3/31/14)				4/1/09-3/31/10	4/1/10-3/31/11
0-500M	500M-2MM	2-10MM	10-50MM	50-100MM	100-250MM		ALL	ALL
2	12	24	13	5	2	**NUMBER OF STATEMENTS**	64	60
%	%	%	%	%	%	**ASSETS**	%	%
	17.1	8.6	10.5			Cash & Equivalents	8.1	12.8
	21.3	17.0	27.7			Trade Receivables (net)	17.7	22.6
	36.0	37.1	26.2			Inventory	35.0	38.7
	.7	2.9	1.9			All Other Current	4.6	2.2
	75.1	65.6	66.3			Total Current	65.4	76.4
	19.2	26.9	22.1			Fixed Assets (net)	20.7	16.2
	.0	3.5	7.4			Intangibles (net)	7.6	3.1
	5.7	4.0	4.2			All Other Non-Current	6.3	4.3
	100.0	100.0	100.0			Total	100.0	100.0
						LIABILITIES		
	10.2	9.2	10.2			Notes Payable-Short Term	15.5	18.2
	1.1	3.7	2.0			Cur. Mat.-L.T.D.	5.4	1.6
	14.7	17.0	13.7			Trade Payables	13.9	15.0
	.0	.0	.4			Income Taxes Payable	.5	.1
	10.4	12.1	14.3			All Other Current	10.4	14.0
	36.5	42.0	40.5			Total Current	45.7	48.9
	5.3	21.1	14.0			Long-Term Debt	19.5	12.0
	.0	.1	.8			Deferred Taxes	.1	.5
	13.4	2.3	10.8			All Other Non-Current	10.8	6.2
	44.8	34.5	33.9			Net Worth	23.7	32.5
	100.0	100.0	100.0			Total Liabilties & Net Worth	100.0	100.0
						INCOME DATA		
	100.0	100.0	100.0			Net Sales	100.0	100.0
	39.8	31.5	23.3			Gross Profit	31.0	29.5
	36.4	25.0	18.3			Operating Expenses	30.2	25.0
	3.4	6.6	5.0			Operating Profit	.8	4.5
	1.5	.3	.2			All Other Expenses (net)	1.4	.3
	1.9	6.3	4.9			Profit Before Taxes	-.6	4.2
						RATIOS		
	3.6	3.1	2.4				2.7	2.3
	2.5	1.5	1.5			Current	1.5	1.6
	1.7	1.2	1.3				1.0	1.2
	2.2	1.2	1.5				1.1	1.2
	1.3	.8	.8			Quick	.7	.7
	.2	.3	.6				.4	.3
	6 63.0	**11** 32.0	**34** 10.8				**16** 23.4	**14** 25.6
	16 23.2	**20** 18.1	**54** 6.8			Sales/Receivables	**30** 12.3	**37** 9.9
	36 10.0	**45** 8.2	**66** 5.5				**50** 7.3	**51** 7.2
	0 UND	**39** 9.3	**35** 10.5				**27** 13.6	**41** 8.8
	39 9.4	**89** 4.1	**46** 8.0			Cost of Sales/Inventory	**80** 4.6	**61** 6.0
	140 2.6	**135** 2.7	**87** 4.2				**128** 2.9	**133** 2.7
	7 51.6	**15** 23.7	**17** 21.4				**12** 29.5	**14** 26.5
	21 17.4	**31** 11.8	**27** 13.4			Cost of Sales/Payables	**26** 14.0	**26** 14.1
	34 10.6	**50** 7.3	**44** 8.3				**43** 8.4	**43** 8.4
	5.9	4.4	4.1				3.8	4.8
	6.9	11.1	8.8			Sales/Working Capital	11.1	7.6
	14.9	28.9	18.8				85.6	29.1
	18.9	18.8	16.8				6.1	7.7
	(10) 8.4	(21) 10.5	(12) 9.3			EBIT/Interest	(56) 1.8	(51) 2.7
	.1	3.3	1.5				-1.3	.9
							4.3	12.3
						Net Profit + Depr., Dep., Amort./Cur. Mat. L/T/D	(15) 2.1	(12) 3.7
							.4	1.4
	.1	.5	.3				.2	.1
	.2	.9	.6			Fixed/Worth	.7	.4
	4.7	4.0	7.2				3.6	1.4
	.5	.8	.8				1.0	1.1
	1.3	2.3	2.2			Debt/Worth	2.5	2.2
	5.5	9.3	18.1				12.9	7.4
	54.0	73.6	101.2				56.6	63.5
	(11) 11.7	(20) 30.7	(11) 33.2			% Profit Before Taxes/Tangible Net Worth	(52) 8.6	(55) 20.8
	-3.8	9.2	.2				-21.4	2.1
	15.3	19.6	11.6				9.3	12.7
	4.7	10.6	7.6			% Profit Before Taxes/Total Assets	1.7	5.0
	-2.8	3.1	-.9				-9.5	.7
	202.6	26.0	20.2				35.2	69.9
	56.5	8.2	8.2			Sales/Net Fixed Assets	12.8	21.8
	13.4	4.5	5.6				5.9	7.3
	5.3	3.2	2.6				3.2	3.2
	3.8	2.2	2.3			Sales/Total Assets	2.0	2.3
	2.7	1.5	1.5				1.1	1.7
		.8	1.3				1.0	.7
		(20) 1.4	(12) 1.7			% Depr., Dep., Amort./Sales	(51) 1.5	(48) 1.1
		2.8	2.3				3.6	2.2
							2.1	1.0
						% Officers', Directors' Owners' Comp/Sales	(12) 6.7	(20) 2.5
							15.1	9.6
780M	68965M	291913M	546836M	360433M	527841M	Net Sales ($)	3654711M	2803995M
449M	17137M	118282M	271449M	334989M	265348M	Total Assets ($)	2044056M	1270869M

M = $ thousand MM = $ million

See Pages 9 through 22 for Explanation of Ratios and Data

Comparative Historical Data | **Current Data Sorted by Sales**

4/1/11-3/31/12 ALL	4/1/12-3/31/13 ALL	4/1/13-3/31/14 ALL	Type of Statement	0-1MM	1-3MM	3-5MM	5-10MM	10-25MM	25MM & OVER
12	6	8	Unqualified					1	7
12	6	10	Reviewed				3	1	6
6	7	6	Compiled		1	1	2	2	
16	14	9	Tax Returns	1		3	3	2	
27	29	25	Other	1		4	8	6	6
				6 (4/1-9/30/13)			52 (10/1/13-3/31/14)		
73	62	58	NUMBER OF STATEMENTS	2	1	8	16	12	19
%	%	%	ASSETS	%	%	%	%	%	%
8.8	9.3	13.4	Cash & Equivalents				9.7	17.3	13.3
23.6	21.6	19.2	Trade Receivables (net)				20.8	23.6	21.4
36.5	39.8	31.9	Inventory				32.2	30.7	26.0
3.8	1.5	1.9	All Other Current				.8	1.4	2.0
72.7	72.1	66.4	Total Current				63.5	73.0	62.8
16.7	18.9	23.5	Fixed Assets (net)				31.2	18.1	20.9
4.9	4.4	5.7	Intangibles (net)				.1	4.7	12.3
5.7	4.6	4.4	All Other Non-Current				5.3	4.2	4.0
100.0	100.0	100.0	Total				100.0	100.0	100.0
			LIABILITIES						
24.5	17.3	9.3	Notes Payable-Short Term				5.0	9.3	11.1
1.8	2.1	2.6	Cur. Mat.-L.T.D.				3.4	2.2	2.8
16.7	12.6	13.9	Trade Payables				13.8	13.1	13.2
.3	.2	.2	Income Taxes Payable				.0	.0	.6
12.7	9.0	12.9	All Other Current				13.1	19.5	12.0
56.1	41.1	39.0	Total Current				35.4	44.1	39.7
14.0	13.5	15.2	Long-Term Debt				15.8	12.3	13.0
.3	.4	.3	Deferred Taxes				.0	.0	.8
5.7	6.0	7.1	All Other Non-Current				9.5	7.6	6.4
23.9	39.0	38.4	Net Worth				39.4	36.0	40.1
100.0	100.0	100.0	Total Liabilties & Net Worth				100.0	100.0	100.0
			INCOME DATA						
100.0	100.0	100.0	Net Sales				100.0	100.0	100.0
31.2	28.6	32.5	Gross Profit				34.5	36.8	20.7
28.1	24.4	26.1	Operating Expenses				29.1	30.3	14.9
3.1	4.2	6.4	Operating Profit				5.4	6.5	5.8
1.0	.6	.8	All Other Expenses (net)				.7	.2	.5
2.1	3.6	5.6	Profit Before Taxes				4.7	6.3	5.3
			RATIOS						
2.6	2.9	3.1					3.6	2.7	2.6
1.6	1.7	1.8	Current				2.3	1.5	1.4
1.1	1.4	1.3					1.3	1.4	1.1
1.1	1.6	1.7					2.4	1.3	1.7
(72) .6	(61) .7	.9	Quick				1.4	1.0	.8
.3	.4	.5					.2	.6	.6
15 25.0	**18** 20.4	**13** 28.8					**11** 32.0	**16** 22.2	**20** 18.1
32 11.5	**29** 12.6	**32** 11.5	Sales/Receivables				**19** 19.1	**38** 9.5	**41** 9.0
54 6.7	**49** 7.4	**50** 7.3					**39** 9.3	**78** 4.7	**54** 6.7
40 9.1	**46** 8.0	**33** 11.1					**22** 16.6	**41** 9.0	**31** 11.7
69 5.3	**76** 4.8	**64** 5.7	Cost of Sales/Inventory				**40** 9.2	**76** 4.8	**46** 8.0
126 2.9	**135** 2.7	**107** 3.4					**118** 3.1	**111** 3.3	**76** 4.8
20 18.1	**12** 30.5	**13** 27.7					**10** 38.0	**17** 21.0	**13** 27.6
30 12.2	**24** 15.3	**26** 14.3	Cost of Sales/Payables				**19** 19.0	**33** 10.9	**22** 16.5
46 7.9	**37** 9.9	**42** 8.7					**40** 9.1	**58** 6.3	**36** 10.1
4.9	5.0	4.7					5.8	4.4	5.4
10.3	9.4	7.8	Sales/Working Capital				8.5	6.8	10.1
34.2	16.0	17.4					22.1	12.0	60.8
14.9	9.8	18.3					18.5	25.9	14.2
(64) 3.5	(55) 4.5	(51) 9.5	EBIT/Interest				(15) 8.9	16.4	(17) 6.7
1.2	1.2	2.8					2.0	4.8	2.8
22.5									
(13) 5.0			Net Profit + Depr., Dep., Amort./Cur. Mat. L/T/D						
2.9									
.1	.1	.2					.2	.2	.3
.4	.5	.8	Fixed/Worth				.8	.5	.8
1.9	1.2	2.8					4.0	1.2	1.6
.9	.6	.7					.5	.8	.8
2.2	2.0	1.6	Debt/Worth				1.6	1.9	2.1
18.9	7.0	9.9					7.1	9.3	16.0
57.9	48.9	77.6					96.0	91.3	76.4
(57) 23.3	(53) 13.7	(51) 29.0	% Profit Before Taxes/Tangible Net Worth				(15) 19.1	40.4	(16) 32.3
3.1	1.8	4.3					1.3	26.4	8.9
15.2	13.0	18.4					22.4	19.4	17.7
5.5	6.1	8.7	% Profit Before Taxes/Total Assets				8.7	14.1	8.6
.2	.4	1.0					-.9	7.3	2.3
67.3	45.7	45.7					57.4	39.4	36.6
21.5	14.6	9.1	Sales/Net Fixed Assets				8.2	9.3	9.1
6.9	7.5	5.2					5.7	5.0	5.3
3.3	3.5	3.2					4.9	3.1	2.9
2.5	2.5	2.4	Sales/Total Assets				3.2	1.9	2.3
1.7	1.7	1.5					1.9	1.5	1.5
.7	.4	.7					.7		1.1
(52) 1.3	(51) 1.3	(48) 1.5	% Depr., Dep., Amort./Sales				(13) .8		(18) 1.5
2.2	1.7	2.6					3.2		2.4
1.2	1.3	1.0							
(26) 3.0	(19) 3.2	(16) 3.4	% Officers', Directors' Owners' Comp/Sales						
6.0	8.2	5.7							
2396650M	1936714M	1796768M	Net Sales ($)	780M	1533M	30209M	117165M	189894M	1457187M
1304879M	962942M	1007654M	Total Assets ($)	449M	619M	20710M	42519M	145337M	798020M

M = $ thousand MM = $ million

See Pages 9 through 22 for Explanation of Ratios and Data

Current Data Sorted by Assets							Comparative Historical Data	
						Type of Statement		
		1	7	2	2	Unqualified	20	20
	2	16	3			Reviewed	32	36
4	9	7				Compiled	38	39
19	17	7				Tax Returns	46	56
5	7	17	13	3	3	Other	66	76
16 (4/1-9/30/13)			128 (10/1/13-3/31/14)				4/1/09-3/31/10 ALL	4/1/10-3/31/11 ALL
0-500M	**500M-2MM**	**2-10MM**	**10-50MM**	**50-100MM**	**100-250MM**			
28	35	48	23	5	5	**NUMBER OF STATEMENTS**	202	227
%	%	%	%	%	%	**ASSETS**	%	%
19.3	8.1	7.8	8.7			Cash & Equivalents	9.4	9.1
14.2	33.8	27.8	23.7			Trade Receivables (net)	22.0	24.6
15.3	18.4	27.8	20.4			Inventory	23.3	20.9
4.3	3.5	4.2	2.4			All Other Current	1.9	2.0
53.1	63.8	67.6	55.2			Total Current	56.6	56.7
35.8	25.6	22.6	31.6			Fixed Assets (net)	32.1	30.8
1.3	1.0	3.3	8.0			Intangibles (net)	3.5	4.4
9.8	9.6	6.5	5.2			All Other Non-Current	7.8	8.1
100.0	100.0	100.0	100.0			Total	100.0	100.0
						LIABILITIES		
47.7	10.9	12.0	9.7			Notes Payable-Short Term	17.5	17.7
3.0	4.5	4.1	2.7			Cur. Mat.-L.T.D.	4.6	4.4
12.6	21.9	18.3	11.4			Trade Payables	14.0	15.2
.0	.1	.3	.1			Income Taxes Payable	.1	.1
19.2	16.9	16.9	10.6			All Other Current	14.8	15.4
82.4	54.2	51.5	34.5			Total Current	51.1	52.7
27.2	20.5	19.0	11.8			Long-Term Debt	20.2	20.5
.1	.2	.3	.8			Deferred Taxes	.6	.3
22.8	14.4	9.3	14.8			All Other Non-Current	11.7	10.0
-32.3	10.7	19.9	38.1			Net Worth	16.4	16.5
100.0	100.0	100.0	100.0			Total Liabilties & Net Worth	100.0	100.0
						INCOME DATA		
100.0	100.0	100.0	100.0			Net Sales	100.0	100.0
47.5	32.4	29.1	26.6			Gross Profit	31.2	33.2
41.8	29.2	25.6	21.6			Operating Expenses	32.7	32.2
5.7	3.3	3.6	5.0			Operating Profit	-1.5	1.0
.9	.6	1.1	1.5			All Other Expenses (net)	1.0	1.1
4.9	2.7	2.5	3.5			Profit Before Taxes	-2.5	-.1
						RATIOS		
1.8	1.6	2.7	3.2				2.5	2.3
.8	1.2	1.6	1.7			Current	1.2	1.3
.3	.8	1.0	1.1				.7	.7
1.6	1.2	1.4	1.7				1.3	1.4
.5	.7	.7	.9			Quick	.7	.8
.2	.4	.4	.5				.3	.4
0 UND	**19** 19.5	**19** 18.9	**22** 16.5				**17** 21.0	**18** 20.7
0 UND	**34** 10.7	**27** 13.3	**34** 10.7			Sales/Receivables	**31** 12.0	**32** 11.3
16 23.1	**50** 7.3	**48** 7.6	**55** 6.6				**46** 8.0	**52** 7.1
0 UND	**9** 40.2	**21** 17.5	**31** 11.6				**24** 15.5	**20** 18.3
9 40.6	**21** 17.1	**44** 8.3	**44** 8.3			Cost of Sales/Inventory	**39** 9.4	**36** 10.0
34 10.7	**48** 7.6	**78** 4.7	**62** 5.9				**76** 4.8	**61** 5.9
0 UND	**13** 27.3	**12** 31.0	**15** 24.4				**9** 42.2	**11** 33.4
13 28.1	**27** 13.7	**27** 13.4	**20** 18.6			Cost of Sales/Payables	**21** 17.4	**24** 15.3
25 14.4	**62** 5.9	**45** 8.2	**39** 9.3				**41** 9.0	**45** 8.1
19.7	10.6	5.3	5.7				7.3	7.4
-70.4	73.3	14.4	11.6			Sales/Working Capital	28.3	19.8
-11.8	-27.8	UND	52.4				-17.5	-17.7
12.3	10.8	20.8	9.7				3.5	5.5
(24) 5.4	(28) 6.1	(45) 2.9	(21) 3.1			EBIT/Interest	(183) .8	(202) 1.7
1.7	1.3	1.3	-.1				-3.1	-1.0
		8.8					5.3	3.4
		(10) 2.8				Net Profit + Depr., Dep., Amort./Cur. Mat. L/T/D	(36) .7	(36) 1.5
		1.5					-.1	-.1
.4	.4	.3	.4				.4	.5
16.8	1.3	1.0	1.0			Fixed/Worth	1.3	1.2
-.7	6.5	-1.7	25.9				-3.9	-4.6
1.1	1.4	.8	.3				.8	.9
90.5	3.3	3.9	1.7			Debt/Worth	2.7	2.9
-2.6	12.2	-10.8	52.8				-10.3	-8.7
180.8	110.0	45.3	40.1				16.0	34.0
(16) 69.4	(27) 30.9	(35) 27.3	(18) 16.6			% Profit Before Taxes/Tangible Net Worth	(142) 1.8	(163) 7.0
15.6	2.0	5.6	2.9				-26.9	-9.7
46.3	19.0	17.3	13.0				5.6	9.3
18.8	9.6	5.6	5.0			% Profit Before Taxes/Total Assets	-1.1	1.7
3.0	.1	.3	-2.6				-10.0	-8.3
58.4	37.2	37.7	23.1				24.1	26.9
25.5	20.0	18.1	7.1			Sales/Net Fixed Assets	9.8	9.0
8.4	5.2	7.3	4.1				4.7	4.5
9.0	4.4	3.6	2.8				3.5	3.7
5.5	3.5	2.8	2.3			Sales/Total Assets	2.4	2.4
4.4	1.8	2.0	1.6				1.6	1.6
.9	.6	.8	1.5				1.2	1.1
(19) 1.7	(28) 1.2	(43) 1.5	(19) 2.1			% Depr., Dep., Amort./Sales	(170) 2.3	(188) 2.1
2.3	2.6	2.0	3.2				4.0	3.9
3.7	1.2	1.2					1.9	1.9
(22) 4.9	(23) 2.8	(22) 1.7				% Officers', Directors' Owners' Comp/Sales	(100) 3.5	(108) 3.6
8.3	6.8	3.1					7.6	7.0
36324M	133183M	658070M	1184582M	861253M	1147709M	Net Sales ($)	4307628M	7546906M
6408M	40607M	216987M	545859M	369308M	1037820M	Total Assets ($)	1760586M	2918765M

M = $ thousand MM = $ million

See Pages 9 through 22 for Explanation of Ratios and Data

Comparative Historical Data				Current Data Sorted by Sales					
			Type of Statement						
16	7	12	Unqualified					1	11
39	27	21	Reviewed		1		4	13	3
42	27	20	Compiled	1	8	2	6	3	
53	47	43	Tax Returns	11	16	7	8	1	
68	59	48	Other	2	7	4	7	8	20
4/1/11-3/31/12	**4/1/12-3/31/13**	**4/1/13-3/31/14**			**16 (4/1-9/30/13)**			**128 (10/1/13-3/31/14)**	
ALL	**ALL**	**ALL**		**0-1MM**	**1-3MM**	**3-5MM**	**5-10MM**	**10-25MM**	**25MM & OVER**
218	167	144	**NUMBER OF STATEMENTS**	14	32	13	25	26	34
%	%	%	**ASSETS**	%	%	%	%	%	%
9.8	10.0	10.0	Cash & Equivalents	19.0	13.1	11.2	4.9	8.2	8.2
24.7	26.4	25.3	Trade Receivables (net)	5.8	23.9	26.1	37.7	25.7	24.9
21.8	20.1	21.6	Inventory	10.5	18.6	16.5	27.5	28.1	21.5
2.2	3.0	3.6	All Other Current	8.9	3.3	5.3	4.4	1.1	2.4
58.5	59.5	60.5	Total Current	44.2	58.9	59.1	74.4	63.1	56.9
29.2	28.4	27.0	Fixed Assets (net)	46.9	27.5	32.5	15.9	29.3	22.5
3.6	4.5	4.9	Intangibles (net)	.0	2.1	.1	3.5	.7	15.8
8.7	7.5	7.6	All Other Non-Current	8.9	11.5	8.3	6.1	6.9	4.8
100.0	100.0	100.0	Total	100.0	100.0	100.0	100.0	100.0	100.0
			LIABILITIES						
14.3	13.3	18.0	Notes Payable-Short Term	75.7	15.8	5.7	8.2	16.4	9.5
4.2	4.1	3.6	Cur. Mat.-L.T.D.	2.5	4.9	5.9	3.8	1.8	3.1
14.7	15.8	16.3	Trade Payables	12.0	17.1	16.5	24.9	14.2	12.4
.2	.1	.1	Income Taxes Payable	.0	.0	.0	.7	.0	.1
19.3	15.0	15.6	All Other Current	19.6	19.0	15.3	16.8	15.4	10.2
52.7	48.2	53.6	Total Current	109.7	56.8	43.5	54.4	47.8	35.4
20.9	20.5	21.6	Long-Term Debt	26.2	24.4	36.7	12.8	17.0	21.3
.3	.2	.5	Deferred Taxes	.0	.1	.0	.4	.3	1.6
11.2	21.6	14.2	All Other Non-Current	15.2	25.0	9.1	6.5	12.0	12.9
14.9	9.4	10.1	Net Worth	-50.9	-6.3	10.7	25.9	22.9	28.9
100.0	100.0	100.0	Total Liabilties & Net Worth	100.0	100.0	100.0	100.0	100.0	100.0
			INCOME DATA						
100.0	100.0	100.0	Net Sales	100.0	100.0	100.0	100.0	100.0	100.0
33.1	35.1	32.8	Gross Profit	51.1	39.4	36.5	30.1	25.0	25.7
31.5	31.8	28.2	Operating Expenses	43.6	36.3	35.3	25.7	21.5	18.5
1.6	3.3	4.6	Operating Profit	7.5	3.0	1.3	4.4	3.5	7.2
.9	1.2	1.2	All Other Expenses (net)	1.3	.7	.8	.8	.8	2.5
.7	2.1	3.4	Profit Before Taxes	6.2	2.3	.5	3.6	2.7	4.7
			RATIOS						
2.8	2.4	2.4		1.0	1.8	3.9	2.8	2.6	2.8
1.5	1.4	1.5	Current	.6	.9	1.5	1.5	1.7	1.9
.7	.8	.8		.2	.8	1.1	1.0	.9	1.2
1.6	1.5	1.4		.9	1.1	2.0	1.3	1.6	1.6
.8	.8	.7	Quick	.2	.7	1.0	.7	.9	.9
.3	.4	.4		.1	.4	.4	.5	.4	.6
15 24.3	**15** 23.6	**15** 24.3		**0** UND	**4** 103.6	**12** 31.4	**24** 15.0	**18** 20.3	**25** 14.8
29 12.4	**29** 12.5	**28** 12.9	Sales/Receivables	**0** UND	**18** 19.8	**34** 10.7	**41** 8.9	**24** 15.3	**34** 10.7
47 7.8	**49** 7.5	**48** 7.6		**14** 25.7	**44** 8.3	**60** 6.1	**55** 6.6	**40** 9.2	**50** 7.3
17 21.6	**14** 26.3	**12** 31.7		**0** UND	**5** 72.5	**6** 58.7	**8** 46.0	**26** 14.2	**29** 12.8
35 10.3	**35** 10.5	**34** 10.8	Cost of Sales/Inventory	**10** 37.8	**20** 18.4	**21** 17.1	**28** 12.9	**48** 7.6	**43** 8.5
60 6.1	**54** 6.8	**58** 6.3		**54** 6.8	**44** 8.3	**54** 6.8	**104** 3.5	**76** 4.8	**59** 6.2
9 40.1	**13** 27.2	**12** 30.0		**0** UND	**5** 71.2	**13** 28.8	**17** 21.2	**8** 45.5	**14** 27.0
21 17.8	**25** 14.8	**22** 16.8	Cost of Sales/Payables	**15** 24.2	**20** 18.0	**18** 19.8	**35** 10.3	**17** 22.0	**23** 15.6
39 9.4	**44** 8.3	**42** 8.6		**45** 8.1	**49** 7.5	**73** 5.0	**54** 6.7	**28** 12.9	**36** 10.0
6.4	7.6	7.9		NM	13.5	5.9	4.8	6.6	5.4
15.7	17.7	19.7	Sales/Working Capital	-22.7	UND	15.7	16.8	18.3	11.0
-22.4	-29.0	-44.9		-6.5	-18.4	NM	283.6	-66.8	26.7
7.7	8.2	12.8		17.1	9.5	26.1	24.0	15.4	11.1
(187) 2.3	(142) 2.3	(128) 3.5	EBIT/Interest	6.6	(24) 3.8	(12) 3.4	(21) 5.8	(25) 2.8	(32) 3.3
-.8	.3	1.3		1.4	1.1	-.2	1.3	-.5	1.5
5.8	5.0	7.0							5.3
(29) 2.7	(33) 2.7	(22) 3.8	Net Profit + Depr., Dep., Amort./Cur. Mat. L/T/D						(10) 3.8
1.3	1.1	1.5							2.0
.4	.4	.4		1.6	.4	.6	.2	.4	.4
1.1	1.7	1.4	Fixed/Worth	-7.0	1.6	2.2	.8	1.4	1.2
-6.8	-1.9	-1.3		-1.0	-.7	-.7	3.6	-2.6	-1.2
.7	.9	1.0		2.1	1.2	1.3	1.2	.6	.7
2.1	4.7	3.2	Debt/Worth	-14.4	3.2	5.9	3.0	1.5	2.8
-18.7	-7.9	-8.1		-2.8	-3.9	-7.0	12.1	-11.8	-5.5
37.5	52.9	65.0			75.2		110.1	34.1	42.2
(157) 11.6	(116) 22.8	(101) 27.3	% Profit Before Taxes/Tangible Net Worth		(23) 24.5		(21) 38.5	(19) 16.5	(23) 30.1
-4.9	3.3	5.9			2.0		.2	-1.9	8.2
12.9	14.7	19.8		55.5	27.8	16.1	26.2	20.0	14.9
3.9	4.2	7.2	% Profit Before Taxes/Total Assets	16.2	7.4	9.6	6.5	6.7	5.9
-5.1	-1.2	.8		3.2	.0	-1.9	.0	-1.3	2.5
33.5	37.9	36.0		38.3	50.4	26.4	48.9	41.7	24.2
11.9	13.6	16.1	Sales/Net Fixed Assets	10.1	19.8	9.1	21.0	15.7	11.4
4.8	5.6	6.4		5.6	6.3	3.7	12.1	5.9	5.9
4.0	4.2	4.4		6.5	6.1	3.8	4.2	4.4	3.0
2.6	2.9	2.9	Sales/Total Assets	4.8	4.1	2.2	2.9	2.9	2.3
1.8	1.9	1.9		2.6	2.1	1.8	2.1	2.5	1.6
1.0	1.0	.9		.9	.9	.6	.8	.6	1.2
(185) 1.7	(136) 1.8	(117) 1.6	% Depr., Dep., Amort./Sales	(10) 1.5	(25) 1.8	(11) 2.9	(18) 1.2	(25) 1.2	(28) 1.8
3.3	2.8	2.7		2.3	2.5	4.3	1.7	2.0	3.5
2.1	1.7	1.3			2.0		1.0	1.2	
(103) 4.1	(77) 3.6	(69) 2.9	% Officers', Directors' Owners' Comp/Sales		(26) 4.1		(13) 2.2	(11) 1.4	
7.7	6.4	6.9			5.6		10.7	1.7	
3668932M	4767142M	4021121M	Net Sales ($)	8547M	65940M	53472M	179331M	428911M	3284920M
1738148M	1758829M	2216989M	Total Assets ($)	2443M	21201M	23169M	64372M	165652M	1940152M

M = $ thousand MM = $ million

See Pages 9 through 22 for Explanation of Ratios and Data

Current Data Sorted by Assets							Comparative Historical Data	
						Type of Statement		
		2	8	1	4	Unqualified	19	16
1	1	11	4			Reviewed	12	13
	1	4				Compiled	9	11
1		5				Tax Returns	7	8
	6	6	7	2	6	Other	33	34
14 (4/1-9/30/13)			56 (10/1/13-3/31/14)				4/1/09-3/31/10	4/1/10-3/31/11
0-500M	500M-2MM	2-10MM	10-50MM	50-100MM	100-250MM		ALL	ALL
2	8	28	19	3	10	**NUMBER OF STATEMENTS**	80	82
%	%	%	%	%	%	**ASSETS**	%	%
		11.9	4.7		5.8	Cash & Equivalents	9.5	8.3
		20.8	28.9		18.4	Trade Receivables (net)	24.2	23.6
		42.4	33.9		39.3	Inventory	32.3	31.8
		2.6	4.6		1.4	All Other Current	2.5	4.8
		77.7	72.2		64.9	Total Current	68.5	68.6
		17.8	21.6		19.3	Fixed Assets (net)	19.6	19.2
		.2	.3		8.0	Intangibles (net)	3.4	3.5
		4.3	6.0		7.8	All Other Non-Current	8.5	8.7
		100.0	100.0		100.0	Total	100.0	100.0
						LIABILITIES		
		10.2	9.5		6.8	Notes Payable-Short Term	10.8	10.1
		1.7	1.2		.7	Cur. Mat.-L.T.D.	3.3	2.7
		22.5	14.4		10.4	Trade Payables	14.0	16.8
		.2	.2		.2	Income Taxes Payable	.3	.5
		9.7	8.8		11.7	All Other Current	8.0	14.2
		44.3	34.2		29.9	Total Current	36.5	44.3
		8.6	11.0		8.5	Long-Term Debt	19.7	15.4
		.9	.2		.0	Deferred Taxes	.3	.4
		5.2	3.0		3.7	All Other Non-Current	5.4	5.3
		41.0	51.6		58.0	Net Worth	38.1	34.6
		100.0	100.0		100.0	Total Liabilties & Net Worth	100.0	100.0
						INCOME DATA		
		100.0	100.0		100.0	Net Sales	100.0	100.0
		24.7	21.3		24.9	Gross Profit	26.4	25.2
		21.3	17.5		19.7	Operating Expenses	23.9	24.3
		3.3	3.9		5.2	Operating Profit	2.5	.9
		.2	1.5		.4	All Other Expenses (net)	.7	1.1
		3.2	2.4		4.8	Profit Before Taxes	1.8	-.2
						RATIOS		
		3.0	3.6		4.3		4.1	3.4
		2.1	3.0		1.8	Current	2.2	1.7
		1.4	1.5		1.4		1.2	1.1
		1.6	1.8		1.7		2.1	1.5
		1.0	1.0		.9	Quick	1.1	.8
		.3	.7		.5		.5	.4
		10 36.9	**27** 13.6		**13** 27.5		**23** 16.1	**15** 24.3
		22 16.5	**41** 8.8		**34** 10.7	Sales/Receivables	**36** 10.2	**34** 10.9
		32 11.5	**48** 7.6		**41** 9.0		**46** 7.9	**46** 8.0
		35 10.5	**43** 8.5		**54** 6.8		**34** 10.6	**35** 10.5
		55 6.6	**57** 6.4		**89** 4.1	Cost of Sales/Inventory	**51** 7.2	**56** 6.5
		85 4.3	**101** 3.6		**114** 3.2		**91** 4.0	**96** 3.8
		17 22.1	**13** 28.8		**15** 24.3		**10** 35.3	**15** 24.6
		20 18.0	**22** 16.9		**23** 16.2	Cost of Sales/Payables	**22** 16.7	**24** 15.0
		35 10.3	**35** 10.4		**28** 12.9		**35** 10.6	**39** 9.4
		6.1	4.3		3.5		4.8	4.3
		9.7	6.2		8.5	Sales/Working Capital	8.4	9.6
		16.0	11.1		17.2		31.6	45.4
		15.5	30.3				11.5	13.7
		(24) 4.2	(15) 13.1			EBIT/Interest	(71) 2.5	(75) 2.6
		1.5	2.2				-.2	-.5
							4.2	10.4
						Net Profit + Depr., Dep., Amort./Cur. Mat. L/T/D	(14) 1.1	(13) 3.9
							-.2	-.8
		.1	.2		.2		.2	.2
		.3	.3		.3	Fixed/Worth	.4	.4
		.8	.7		NM		1.4	1.2
		.5	.3		.3		.4	.4
		1.1	1.0		.6	Debt/Worth	1.1	1.2
		2.3	2.6		NM		4.1	9.1
		61.8	40.6				40.1	37.5
		(25) 14.7	15.3			% Profit Before Taxes/Tangible Net Worth	(68) 8.7	(69) 9.7
		5.2	3.8				-10.0	-4.3
		30.4	15.9		17.2		14.1	12.6
		7.7	8.2		10.8	% Profit Before Taxes/Total Assets	3.7	3.6
		1.9	1.8		6.8		-4.0	-2.7
		57.3	16.4		23.5		32.3	43.6
		38.7	12.5		12.6	Sales/Net Fixed Assets	16.4	18.0
		17.5	8.0		6.4		9.4	8.4
		4.9	3.2		2.9		3.7	3.7
		3.7	2.2		2.2	Sales/Total Assets	2.8	2.6
		2.5	1.9		1.5		1.7	1.8
		.4	.6				.7	.6
		(25) .7	(18) .9			% Depr., Dep., Amort./Sales	(65) 1.1	(73) .9
		1.2	1.3				2.0	1.5
							1.4	1.6
						% Officers', Directors' Owners' Comp/Sales	(18) 3.0	(20) 3.4
							3.8	5.6
3396M	**42389M**	**554399M**	**1299049M**	**408987M**	**4023813M**	Net Sales ($)	**4166300M**	**4549430M**
953M	**11938M**	**147420M**	**485307M**	**255542M**	**1531895M**	Total Assets ($)	**1865964M**	**1927871M**

M = $ thousand MM = $ million

See Pages 9 through 22 for Explanation of Ratios and Data

Comparative Historical Data				Current Data Sorted by Sales					
			Type of Statement						
12	20	15	Unqualified					1	14
14	12	17	Reviewed		2		2	7	6
6	9	5	Compiled				3	2	
8	12	6	Tax Returns		1		1	3	1
22	37	27	Other		1	1	5	4	16
4/1/11-3/31/12 ALL	4/1/12-3/31/13 ALL	4/1/13-3/31/14 ALL		14 (4/1-9/30/13)			56 (10/1/13-3/31/14)		
				0-1MM	1-3MM	3-5MM	5-10MM	10-25MM	25MM & OVER
62	90	70	**NUMBER OF STATEMENTS**		4	1	11	17	37
%	%	%	**ASSETS**	%	%	%	%	%	%
8.1	9.6	9.6	Cash & Equivalents	DATA NOT AVAILABLE			11.2	14.1	6.8
24.2	22.3	23.3	Trade Receivables (net)				20.1	22.2	25.8
35.9	35.9	36.5	Inventory				34.2	43.3	35.5
2.5	3.6	2.7	All Other Current				1.3	2.7	3.4
70.7	71.3	72.1	Total Current				66.8	82.3	71.5
17.3	19.8	18.6	Fixed Assets (net)				22.8	12.3	20.5
3.0	3.0	1.9	Intangibles (net)				.3	.3	2.7
9.0	5.9	7.4	All Other Non-Current				10.1	5.1	5.3
100.0	100.0	100.0	Total				100.0	100.0	100.0
			LIABILITIES						
12.5	9.5	8.6	Notes Payable-Short Term				5.8	6.6	10.7
4.9	1.4	1.2	Cur. Mat.-L.T.D.				1.3	1.4	1.2
14.4	13.5	16.1	Trade Payables				12.0	19.3	17.4
.5	.2	.2	Income Taxes Payable				.1	.3	.2
17.8	21.3	10.3	All Other Current				8.6	8.9	10.7
50.1	45.9	36.4	Total Current				27.8	36.6	40.2
10.3	9.4	8.4	Long-Term Debt				16.0	4.4	8.6
.1	.2	.4	Deferred Taxes				1.7	.3	.1
7.0	4.3	5.8	All Other Non-Current				2.9	8.3	2.9
32.5	40.3	49.0	Net Worth				51.6	50.5	48.3
100.0	100.0	100.0	Total Liabilties & Net Worth				100.0	100.0	100.0
			INCOME DATA						
100.0	100.0	100.0	Net Sales				100.0	100.0	100.0
28.5	26.2	24.6	Gross Profit				27.6	26.8	21.0
26.1	22.5	21.0	Operating Expenses				26.2	23.6	16.5
2.5	3.8	3.6	Operating Profit				1.4	3.2	4.5
.6	.4	.6	All Other Expenses (net)				.6	1.4	.3
1.9	3.4	3.0	Profit Before Taxes				.8	1.8	4.2
			RATIOS						
3.0	3.7	3.6					3.9	3.8	3.4
1.7	2.2	2.4	Current				2.2	2.6	2.3
1.1	1.3	1.6					1.7	1.7	1.4
1.5	1.8	1.7					1.7	1.8	1.7
(61) .7	.9	1.1	Quick				1.2	1.1	1.0
.3	.5	.5					.3	.6	.6
14 26.3	17 20.9	18 19.9					9 40.5	19 19.1	24 15.5
33 11.2	31 11.9	29 12.4	Sales/Receivables				19 19.6	27 13.4	35 10.4
42 8.6	38 9.5	43 8.5					34 10.7	34 10.7	45 8.1
39 9.4	41 8.9	35 10.5					56 6.5	38 9.7	32 11.4
70 5.2	61 6.0	61 6.0	Cost of Sales/Inventory				76 4.8	53 6.9	57 6.4
104 3.5	85 4.3	101 3.6					87 4.2	104 3.5	99 3.7
13 27.1	11 32.0	14 25.9					13 27.1	16 22.9	15 24.8
24 15.2	20 18.1	20 18.0	Cost of Sales/Payables				18 20.2	20 18.4	22 16.5
35 10.3	32 11.5	34 10.6					34 10.7	38 9.7	35 10.5
4.4	5.1	4.5					6.1	4.4	4.4
10.4	8.3	7.7	Sales/Working Capital				8.6	9.0	6.5
45.9	20.6	14.1					11.6	12.1	18.3
8.7	37.1	21.1						36.5	34.5
(54) 2.5	(80) 7.8	(54) 9.0	EBIT/Interest					(13) 4.7	(30) 13.7
.0	1.6	2.1						1.6	3.4
35.1	34.7	7.2							
(12) 2.4	(19) 4.7	(14) 4.8	Net Profit + Depr., Dep., Amort./Cur. Mat. L/T/D						
.0	2.3	.6							
.2	.2	.2					.2	.1	.2
.4	.4	.3	Fixed/Worth				.3	.2	.3
1.1	.7	.7					.8	.5	.7
.5	.4	.4					.4	.4	.3
1.3	1.1	.9	Debt/Worth				1.0	1.0	.9
4.5	3.1	2.0					2.0	1.5	2.4
31.4	43.5	41.6					22.7	39.1	48.8
(51) 6.7	(81) 18.6	(64) 14.2	% Profit Before Taxes/Tangible Net Worth				5.5	(16) 9.9	(33) 18.1
.4	3.9	3.5					-2.2	3.7	6.0
11.9	20.0	17.2					8.8	16.9	20.9
2.8	8.3	8.5	% Profit Before Taxes/Total Assets				1.3	4.7	10.7
-1.6	1.4	1.7					-1.9	.9	4.3
69.1	42.3	47.1					38.9	63.1	21.7
19.3	17.8	18.8	Sales/Net Fixed Assets				23.3	46.5	13.7
9.0	8.7	9.1					7.6	15.3	9.3
3.6	3.6	4.0					4.1	4.6	3.6
2.5	2.8	3.0	Sales/Total Assets				3.2	3.3	2.7
1.8	2.1	2.0					2.0	2.5	1.9
.6	.5	.5						.4	.6
(48) 1.0	(71) .9	(59) .8	% Depr., Dep., Amort./Sales					(16) .7	(32) 1.0
1.5	1.3	1.3						1.3	1.3
2.9	2.0	1.9							
(22) 4.7	(24) 3.3	(14) 4.1	% Officers', Directors' Owners' Comp/Sales						
9.4	7.8	6.0							
3106679M	5915802M	6332033M	Net Sales ($)		6951M	4164M	80910M	311266M	5928742M
1362375M	2496489M	2433055M	Total Assets ($)		3822M	957M	32056M	111491M	2284729M

M = $ thousand MM = $ million

See Pages 9 through 22 for Explanation of Ratios and Data

Current Data Sorted by Assets | **Comparative Historical Data**

0-500M	500M-2MM	2-10MM	10-50MM	50-100MM	100-250MM	**Type of Statement**		
		1	2	1	1	Unqualified	9	7
		5	3			Reviewed	11	16
1	1		1	1		Compiled	7	7
2	2	5				Tax Returns	17	7
2	4	7	4	2	3	Other	31	33
12 (4/1-9/30/13)			36 (10/1/13-3/31/14)				4/1/09-3/31/10	4/1/10-3/31/11
0-500M	500M-2MM	2-10MM	10-50MM	50-100MM	100-250MM		ALL	ALL
5	7	18	10	4	4	**NUMBER OF STATEMENTS**	75	70
%	%	%	%	%	%	**ASSETS**	%	%
		12.1	5.0			Cash & Equivalents	6.5	8.5
		17.7	15.8			Trade Receivables (net)	17.9	18.9
		33.9	39.4			Inventory	39.5	36.3
		2.2	3.7			All Other Current	3.4	3.4
		65.9	63.9			Total Current	67.3	67.1
		26.4	15.5			Fixed Assets (net)	26.6	22.9
		.7	5.8			Intangibles (net)	1.0	2.6
		7.0	14.8			All Other Non-Current	5.1	7.4
		100.0	100.0			Total	100.0	100.0
						LIABILITIES		
		7.8	16.7			Notes Payable-Short Term	14.7	13.6
		2.2	.6			Cur. Mat.-L.T.D.	4.3	3.8
		10.1	12.3			Trade Payables	15.0	13.4
		.0	.0			Income Taxes Payable	.0	.1
		9.4	9.8			All Other Current	13.8	10.8
		29.4	39.4			Total Current	47.8	41.6
		19.7	11.5			Long-Term Debt	17.3	15.3
		.0	.2			Deferred Taxes	.1	.1
		2.4	2.0			All Other Non-Current	8.9	9.1
		48.5	46.8			Net Worth	25.9	33.9
		100.0	100.0			Total Liabilities & Net Worth	100.0	100.0
						INCOME DATA		
		100.0	100.0			Net Sales	100.0	100.0
		30.1	25.0			Gross Profit	31.7	32.3
		25.1	20.5			Operating Expenses	33.1	31.2
		5.1	4.5			Operating Profit	-1.4	1.1
		.0	.6			All Other Expenses (net)	.3	.5
		5.0	3.9			Profit Before Taxes	-1.7	.6
						RATIOS		
		4.4	5.4				3.2	3.5
		1.8	1.8			Current	1.7	1.7
		1.4	1.0				1.2	1.3
		1.6	1.1				1.4	1.5
		.9	.4			Quick	.6	(69) .7
		.6	.2				.2	.4
		6 60.0	9 40.9				9 38.6	11 32.1
		31 11.9	46 8.0			Sales/Receivables	30 12.0	29 12.5
		42 8.7	57 6.4				43 8.5	47 7.8
		37 9.9	72 5.1				47 7.8	43 8.5
		59 6.2	114 3.2			Cost of Sales/Inventory	82 4.5	87 4.2
		122 3.0	140 2.6				133 2.8	127 2.9
		7 49.7	18 20.3				14 27.0	14 25.9
		21 17.5	28 13.2			Cost of Sales/Payables	26 14.1	25 14.6
		34 10.8	53 6.9				39 9.4	40 9.2
		3.9	2.3				4.4	4.2
		8.4	8.7			Sales/Working Capital	8.4	8.0
		13.4	NM				18.3	26.1
		25.3	13.4				3.5	12.1
		(17) 3.9	5.8			EBIT/Interest	(70) .4	(66) 2.2
		.5	1.5				-4.1	-1.7
							1.9	2.9
						Net Profit + Depr., Dep., Amort./Cur. Mat. L/T/D	(12) .8	(13) 1.4
							-3.3	-.2
		.2	.1				.2	.2
		.4	.5			Fixed/Worth	.7	.5
		1.1	1.6				-43.6	1.6
		.8	.4				.7	.6
		1.3	2.3			Debt/Worth	1.8	1.4
		2.5	4.2				-18.3	5.1
		43.0					20.7	28.7
		21.2				% Profit Before Taxes/Tangible Net Worth	(55) .1	(58) 7.0
		1.2					-19.8	-7.0
		19.7	12.6				5.0	12.0
		8.0	6.6			% Profit Before Taxes/Total Assets	-1.7	3.0
		.4	1.0				-11.1	-4.2
		37.8	32.4				30.6	32.9
		9.8	11.2			Sales/Net Fixed Assets	11.0	10.7
		4.3	7.3				4.7	6.5
		3.3	2.0				3.1	3.2
		2.3	1.7			Sales/Total Assets	2.2	2.2
		1.5	1.0				1.5	1.7
		.4					.8	.8
		(15) .9				% Depr., Dep., Amort./Sales	(65) 2.1	(63) 1.6
		1.9					3.2	3.0
		2.1					2.2	2.1
		(10) 3.1				% Officers', Directors' Owners' Comp/Sales	(32) 4.6	(23) 3.9
		5.3					8.3	5.5
9253M	16411M	203495M	434626M	773563M	1308932M	Net Sales ($)	2819114M	3168527M
1814M	7640M	84881M	268077M	271919M	699080M	Total Assets ($)	1511608M	1680834M

M = $ thousand MM = $ million

See Pages 9 through 22 for Explanation of Ratios and Data

Comparative Historical Data / Current Data Sorted by Sales

4/1/11-3/31/12 ALL	4/1/12-3/31/13 ALL	4/1/13-3/31/14 ALL	Type of Statement	0-1MM	1-3MM	3-5MM	5-10MM	10-25MM	25MM & OVER
6	3	5	Unqualified					1	4
10	12	8	Reviewed		1	1		4	2
5	14	4	Compiled		1	1			2
18	18	9	Tax Returns		3	1	3	2	
27	27	22	Other	1	6	1	1	6	7
				12 (4/1-9/30/13)			36 (10/1/13-3/31/14)		
66	74	48	NUMBER OF STATEMENTS	1	11	4	4	13	15
%	%	%	**ASSETS**	%	%	%	%	%	%
11.2	9.8	8.3	Cash & Equivalents		8.5			13.2	5.8
19.8	20.1	15.6	Trade Receivables (net)		8.8			21.3	18.5
39.4	37.1	38.3	Inventory		34.2			34.7	38.4
1.7	2.2	3.7	All Other Current		.9			2.1	5.9
72.0	69.1	65.9	Total Current		52.4			71.2	68.6
18.9	20.4	21.9	Fixed Assets (net)		29.0			17.1	18.8
3.0	2.1	2.6	Intangibles (net)		2.1			.3	6.1
6.1	8.4	9.6	All Other Non-Current		16.5			11.3	6.5
100.0	100.0	100.0	Total		100.0			100.0	100.0
			LIABILITIES						
17.8	18.3	11.5	Notes Payable-Short Term		12.3			9.5	10.9
2.2	3.4	2.0	Cur. Mat.-L.T.D.		1.1			2.2	2.9
12.7	14.0	13.0	Trade Payables		11.2			9.8	17.6
.0	.0	.1	Income Taxes Payable		.0			.0	.4
26.4	19.2	11.0	All Other Current		14.2			12.8	8.0
59.1	55.0	37.6	Total Current		38.8			34.3	39.8
11.8	13.8	17.5	Long-Term Debt		29.9			10.1	13.4
.0	.0	.1	Deferred Taxes		.0			.2	.0
7.4	6.8	6.8	All Other Non-Current		4.0			1.9	15.5
21.6	24.3	38.0	Net Worth		27.3			53.5	31.3
100.0	100.0	100.0	Total Liabilties & Net Worth		100.0			100.0	100.0
			INCOME DATA						
100.0	100.0	100.0	Net Sales		100.0			100.0	100.0
36.8	34.8	31.2	Gross Profit		37.5			25.2	28.0
34.6	31.4	26.6	Operating Expenses		30.2			20.6	23.8
2.2	3.4	4.6	Operating Profit		7.3			4.7	4.3
.5	.2	.8	All Other Expenses (net)		2.2			.3	.9
1.7	3.2	3.8	Profit Before Taxes		5.1			4.4	3.4
			RATIOS						
3.3	2.6	2.9			3.0			5.1	3.0
1.6	1.6	1.8	Current		1.1			1.9	2.4
1.1	.9	1.3			.9			1.5	1.2
1.4	1.2	1.1			1.1			1.5	1.1
.7	.5	.7	Quick		.4			.9	.8
.3	.2	.2			.1			.6	.3
6 59.0	8 48.3	5 67.6			0 999.8			20 18.7	11 31.9
30 12.1	27 13.5	28 13.2	Sales/Receivables		6 62.6			38 9.6	38 9.5
43 8.5	41 8.9	45 8.2			32 11.5			55 6.6	50 7.3
47 7.8	40 9.2	43 8.4			32 11.5			36 10.0	68 5.4
91 4.0	73 5.0	79 4.6	Cost of Sales/Inventory		50 7.3			57 6.4	89 4.1
152 2.4	152 2.4	130 2.8			192 1.9			126 2.9	118 3.1
12 29.2	17 20.9	14 26.3			3 144.0			8 45.1	23 16.0
23 16.1	25 14.6	24 15.4	Cost of Sales/Payables		14 25.9			22 16.9	33 11.2
39 9.4	42 8.7	39 9.3			28 13.0			40 9.1	54 6.7
3.8	4.1	4.4			3.9			3.7	3.7
8.1	8.8	7.4	Sales/Working Capital		92.7			5.9	5.2
35.5	-39.6	19.6			-90.4			15.0	12.2
13.7	21.2	18.6			9.8			26.5	64.7
(62) 2.6	(66) 5.2	(45) 6.0	EBIT/Interest		(10) 3.7			7.2	(13) 9.4
.0	.0	1.1			.4			-.8	2.3
	8.7	6.8							
	(10) 4.1	(11) 3.2	Net Profit + Depr., Dep., Amort./Cur. Mat. L/T/D						
	1.6	1.7							
.2	.2	.2			.2			.1	.2
.4	.4	.4	Fixed/Worth		1.6			.2	.4
2.9	4.1	1.6			37.0			.5	1.8
.6	.9	.7			2.4			.5	.4
2.0	2.4	1.7	Debt/Worth		3.3			.8	2.5
26.3	13.0	3.2			74.0			1.9	5.3
60.5	48.7	38.8						42.9	26.4
(51) 6.7	(58) 18.6	(43) 14.8	% Profit Before Taxes/Tangible Net Worth					20.0	(12) 15.4
-4.6	4.0	2.9						-2.7	7.0
16.2	16.5	12.7			14.9			21.0	10.8
2.3	6.3	7.5	% Profit Before Taxes/Total Assets		8.0			8.2	7.0
-2.9	-.9	1.1			1.8			-1.0	1.6
54.1	36.8	39.0			48.4			47.3	20.3
20.4	16.7	13.3	Sales/Net Fixed Assets		11.0			15.1	12.0
6.9	9.0	6.9			2.7			6.6	7.6
3.5	3.5	2.8			5.4			3.4	2.5
2.2	2.2	2.1	Sales/Total Assets		2.1			2.2	1.9
1.6	1.5	1.5			1.2			1.6	1.4
.5	.5	.4						.2	.6
(55) 1.1	(63) 1.1	(42) .9	% Depr., Dep., Amort./Sales					(12) .4	(13) .9
1.7	2.1	1.6						1.7	1.4
1.9	1.8	1.9							
(26) 3.9	(31) 2.7	(20) 2.9	% Officers', Directors' Owners' Comp/Sales						
9.1	7.3	5.8							
2053636M	2531891M	2746280M	Net Sales ($)	987M	21468M	15068M	27081M	215015M	2466661M
958311M	1251502M	1333411M	Total Assets ($)	679M	12457M	7207M	10061M	114954M	1188053M

M = $ thousand MM = $ million

See Pages 9 through 22 for Explanation of Ratios and Data

	Current Data Sorted by Assets						Comparative Historical Data	
Type of Statement								
Unqualified			3	5	3	2	16	12
Reviewed		1	4	2			24	19
Compiled	1	4	8				12	10
Tax Returns	2	3	3	1			6	9
Other	2	7	13	8	4		56	42
	15 (4/1-9/30/13)		61 (10/1/13-3/31/14)				4/1/09-3/31/10	4/1/10-3/31/11
	0-500M	500M-2MM	2-10MM	10-50MM	50-100MM	100-250MM	ALL	ALL
NUMBER OF STATEMENTS	5	15	31	16	7	2	114	92
ASSETS	%	%	%	%	%	%	%	%
Cash & Equivalents		11.3	10.6	9.1			9.0	7.8
Trade Receivables (net)		27.8	29.8	24.1			24.6	27.2
Inventory		30.8	32.3	29.0			27.1	28.2
All Other Current		.6	1.5	2.4			2.5	2.4
Total Current		70.5	74.2	64.7			63.2	65.6
Fixed Assets (net)		20.6	20.5	26.8			24.1	22.8
Intangibles (net)		5.8	1.0	4.2			6.2	5.3
All Other Non-Current		3.1	4.4	4.4			6.5	6.2
Total		100.0	100.0	100.0			100.0	100.0
LIABILITIES								
Notes Payable-Short Term		10.1	8.1	7.3			12.1	10.5
Cur. Mat.-L.T.D.		2.3	1.9	2.4			3.1	5.2
Trade Payables		15.6	12.6	14.0			13.4	13.2
Income Taxes Payable		.0	.1	.2			.2	.1
All Other Current		13.1	17.2	11.0			11.6	12.2
Total Current		41.1	39.7	34.9			40.5	41.2
Long-Term Debt		11.4	11.4	13.7			18.1	17.5
Deferred Taxes		.0	.0	.1			.5	.2
All Other Non-Current		8.5	12.2	5.4			7.0	6.0
Net Worth		39.1	36.7	45.9			33.9	35.1
Total Liabilities & Net Worth		100.0	100.0	100.0			100.0	100.0
INCOME DATA								
Net Sales		100.0	100.0	100.0			100.0	100.0
Gross Profit		36.7	29.4	23.5			30.4	29.8
Operating Expenses		30.9	25.3	19.4			27.8	26.7
Operating Profit		5.8	4.1	4.1			2.6	3.1
All Other Expenses (net)		.4	.9	.8			1.4	.7
Profit Before Taxes		5.4	3.2	3.4			1.1	2.4
RATIOS								
Current		3.2	3.9	3.0			2.7	2.4
		1.6	1.8	1.8			1.7	1.8
		1.1	1.5	1.4			1.1	1.2
Quick		1.8	1.9	1.8			1.6	1.3
		.9	1.1	1.0			.8	.9
		.6	.7	.5			.5	.5
Sales/Receivables		**23** 15.6	**27** 13.7	**25** 14.5			**25** 14.4	**26** 13.8
		38 9.6	**35** 10.4	**36** 10.2			**37** 9.8	**41** 8.8
		61 6.0	**51** 7.2	**55** 6.6			**49** 7.4	**56** 6.5
Cost of Sales/Inventory		**36** 10.0	**39** 9.3	**42** 8.6			**31** 11.7	**32** 11.5
		49 7.5	**59** 6.2	**54** 6.7			**49** 7.4	**57** 6.4
		96 3.8	**104** 3.5	**91** 4.0			**102** 3.6	**92** 4.0
Cost of Sales/Payables		**13** 28.1	**13** 27.9	**21** 17.2			**14** 26.9	**14** 26.0
		26 14.2	**25** 14.5	**25** 14.7			**24** 15.0	**25** 14.5
		69 5.3	**38** 9.5	**43** 8.5			**40** 9.1	**40** 9.2
Sales/Working Capital		5.3	5.4	4.6			4.6	5.0
		7.9	7.3	6.6			10.0	10.2
		79.8	12.6	16.5			59.2	22.7
EBIT/Interest		12.4	21.1	16.5			12.6	11.4
		(11) 4.7	(28) 3.1	(14) 7.1			(104) 2.7	(81) 4.5
		2.6	-.6	2.7			-.2	.2
Net Profit + Depr., Dep., Amort./Cur. Mat. L/T/D							11.1	8.9
							(36) 1.6	(19) 2.9
							.8	.7
Fixed/Worth		.1	.2	.3			.3	.3
		.3	.3	.7			.6	.5
		4.9	1.1	1.8			4.9	1.7
Debt/Worth		.6	1.0	.7			.8	.8
		1.8	1.6	1.5			2.1	1.6
		5.7	4.4	3.5			12.0	5.0
% Profit Before Taxes/Tangible Net Worth		49.7	62.0	25.2			48.4	46.2
		(13) 21.9	(29) 26.3	(14) 11.3			(93) 15.5	(82) 18.0
		9.5	-2.0	4.5			-2.5	-.2
% Profit Before Taxes/Total Assets		21.3	19.0	11.9			12.7	12.8
		7.8	2.0	5.5			4.1	7.2
		6.3	-1.6	2.4			-2.7	-2.2
Sales/Net Fixed Assets		62.6	135.4	15.1			25.8	21.9
		19.4	22.0	6.9			11.3	12.4
		10.5	5.7	3.7			6.1	6.6
Sales/Total Assets		3.5	2.9	3.2			2.9	2.9
		2.5	2.4	2.1			2.2	2.1
		2.1	1.8	1.2			1.7	1.7
% Depr., Dep., Amort./Sales		.4	.5	1.3			.8	1.2
		(13) 1.4	(25) 1.0	(14) 2.1			(94) 1.9	(73) 1.7
		2.1	2.6	2.7			3.0	2.7
% Officers', Directors' Owners' Comp/Sales			1.6				1.7	1.8
			(14) 3.8				(34) 3.8	(35) 3.2
			5.7				8.2	5.7
Net Sales ($)	4709M	42812M	439674M	695253M	709050M	563329M	4773864M	2899945M
Total Assets ($)	1237M	16170M	162279M	338677M	451278M	339999M	2521370M	1521207M

M = $ thousand MM = $ million

See Pages 9 through 22 for Explanation of Ratios and Data

Comparative Historical Data				Current Data Sorted by Sales					
			Type of Statement						
19	14	13	Unqualified				1	4	8
13	18	7	Reviewed			1		4	2
9	9	13	Compiled	2		4	5	1	1
11	16	9	Tax Returns	2	4		2		1
41	31	34	Other	2	3	6	1	10	12
4/1/11-3/31/12 ALL	**4/1/12-3/31/13 ALL**	**4/1/13-3/31/14 ALL**		**15 (4/1-9/30/13)**			**61 (10/1/13-3/31/14)**		
				0-1MM	**1-3MM**	**3-5MM**	**5-10MM**	**10-25MM**	**25MM & OVER**
93	88	76	**NUMBER OF STATEMENTS**	6	7	11	9	19	24
%	%	%	**ASSETS**	%	%	%	%	%	%
9.1	10.5	9.3	Cash & Equivalents			8.9		10.3	7.9
24.2	26.6	26.8	Trade Receivables (net)			28.2		30.3	22.7
26.5	28.0	29.3	Inventory			30.8		30.8	28.5
2.9	1.7	1.6	All Other Current			.8		1.4	2.9
62.7	66.9	67.0	Total Current			68.6		72.9	62.0
20.1	21.5	21.7	Fixed Assets (net)			24.5		22.1	23.9
11.5	4.8	4.2	Intangibles (net)			2.7		1.4	8.3
5.8	6.9	7.1	All Other Non-Current			4.2		3.6	5.7
100.0	100.0	100.0	Total			100.0		100.0	100.0
			LIABILITIES						
11.6	8.8	7.5	Notes Payable-Short Term			9.3		6.8	5.5
4.5	4.1	2.5	Cur. Mat.-L.T.D.			2.4		1.5	1.7
13.6	13.0	13.4	Trade Payables			14.9		12.4	12.4
.3	.1	.1	Income Taxes Payable			.0		.0	.1
15.6	13.8	17.7	All Other Current			15.6		18.3	11.9
45.6	39.7	41.2	Total Current			42.3		39.0	31.7
14.8	11.5	15.0	Long-Term Debt			11.8		7.4	15.8
.3	.5	.4	Deferred Taxes			.0		.0	1.1
7.1	9.8	10.2	All Other Non-Current			7.8		12.0	10.9
32.2	38.5	33.1	Net Worth			38.1		41.7	40.5
100.0	100.0	100.0	Total Liabilties & Net Worth			100.0		100.0	100.0
			INCOME DATA						
100.0	100.0	100.0	Net Sales			100.0		100.0	100.0
31.5	31.9	29.1	Gross Profit			32.7		30.6	23.3
28.2	26.2	25.2	Operating Expenses			30.2		25.3	18.5
3.4	5.7	4.0	Operating Profit			2.5		5.3	4.8
1.2	1.3	.9	All Other Expenses (net)			.0		.8	1.2
2.1	4.4	3.1	Profit Before Taxes			2.5		4.5	3.6
			RATIOS						
2.2	2.7	3.1				3.2		2.5	3.0
1.8	1.9	1.8	Current			1.9		1.8	2.0
1.1	1.4	1.3				1.1		1.5	1.6
1.3	1.7	1.5				1.4		1.9	1.5
.9	.9	1.1	Quick			.9		1.2	1.1
.4	.6	.6				.6		.6	.6
26 13.8	**26** 14.3	**24** 14.9				**28** 13.0		**33** 10.9	**25** 14.8
41 9.0	**42** 8.7	**36** 10.0	Sales/Receivables			**33** 10.9		**46** 8.0	**36** 10.2
54 6.8	**56** 6.5	**54** 6.7				**47** 7.7		**72** 5.1	**51** 7.2
31 11.6	**39** 9.4	**41** 8.8				**36** 10.0		**41** 8.8	**43** 8.4
60 6.1	**54** 6.7	**54** 6.7	Cost of Sales/Inventory			**59** 6.2		**70** 5.2	**51** 7.1
99 3.7	**101** 3.6	**89** 4.1				**76** 4.8		**118** 3.1	**63** 5.8
16 22.6	**15** 24.0	**15** 24.7				**13** 28.6		**13** 27.9	**16** 23.5
28 13.2	**26** 14.2	**25** 14.4	Cost of Sales/Payables			**24** 15.3		**34** 10.7	**23** 16.2
48 7.6	**40** 9.1	**42** 8.6				**31** 11.7		**46** 8.0	**29** 12.6
5.2	5.2	5.3				4.9		4.5	5.5
8.8	9.0	7.3	Sales/Working Capital			6.7		6.9	8.2
39.6	14.1	14.6				79.8		10.0	13.1
15.0	26.6	14.5				6.9		47.2	15.2
(81) 3.6	(76) 5.0	(65) 5.3	EBIT/Interest			(10) 4.2		(17) 3.6	(23) 6.4
-.6	1.5	1.1				.7		1.6	1.0
4.1	5.9	7.6							
(21) 1.5	(21) 1.2	(13) 3.4	Net Profit + Depr., Dep., Amort./Cur. Mat. L/T/D						
.0	.2	.9							
.2	.2	.2				.3		.3	.3
.6	.5	.5	Fixed/Worth			.9		.5	.9
4.2	1.3	1.4				1.3		1.1	2.5
.8	.6	.8				.7		.8	1.1
2.0	1.4	1.6	Debt/Worth			1.6		1.3	1.7
16.3	3.6	5.8				4.5		3.7	37.9
62.2	45.5	52.6				22.3		55.3	40.0
(74) 20.8	(77) 17.6	(66) 14.7	% Profit Before Taxes/Tangible Net Worth			(10) 12.3		(18) 8.7	(20) 16.0
5.3	4.7	1.4				-3.3		2.7	-.3
15.2	18.1	17.0				9.8		18.4	13.0
5.6	7.5	6.0	% Profit Before Taxes/Total Assets			6.3		2.4	5.8
-2.8	1.4	.2				.1		.7	.2
29.5	33.0	52.2				39.9		64.7	42.0
15.1	11.9	12.9	Sales/Net Fixed Assets			17.5		8.7	8.2
7.5	6.7	5.1				5.2		3.9	5.1
3.1	3.1	3.1				4.2		2.9	3.4
2.1	2.3	2.3	Sales/Total Assets			2.6		2.3	2.1
1.5	1.6	1.6				1.9		1.4	1.7
.7	.7	.5						1.3	.6
(75) 1.6	(71) 1.4	(61) 1.6	% Depr., Dep., Amort./Sales					(14) 2.2	(21) 2.0
2.8	2.6	2.6						3.9	2.4
1.5	2.8	2.9							
(24) 3.3	(24) 4.4	(27) 4.9	% Officers', Directors' Owners' Comp/Sales						
5.9	8.5	6.4							
3471981M	**4186531M**	**2454827M**	Net Sales ($)	**3872M**	**14667M**	**43793M**	**66192M**	**307163M**	**2019140M**
1994228M	**2081227M**	**1309640M**	Total Assets ($)	**2081M**	**8068M**	**20210M**	**29848M**	**173124M**	**1076309M**

M = $ thousand MM = $ million

See Pages 9 through 22 for Explanation of Ratios and Data

Current Data Sorted by Assets							Comparative Historical Data	
						Type of Statement		
			4		1	Unqualified	5	4
	2	7	4	1		Reviewed	15	14
	3	4				Compiled	8	11
2	3					Tax Returns	5	6
2	5	10	2			Other	14	16
	13 (4/1-9/30/13)		37 (10/1/13-3/31/14)				4/1/09-3/31/10 ALL	4/1/10-3/31/11 ALL
0-500M	500M-2MM	2-10MM	10-50MM	50-100MM	100-250MM			
4	13	21	10	1	1	**NUMBER OF STATEMENTS**	47	51
%	%	%	%	%	%	**ASSETS**	%	%
	8.7	9.7	23.5			Cash & Equivalents	5.7	8.4
	29.7	29.2	18.5			Trade Receivables (net)	32.9	32.2
	30.4	22.9	19.0			Inventory	21.3	24.4
	1.3	3.6	1.0			All Other Current	5.1	2.8
	70.3	65.5	62.1			Total Current	65.0	67.8
	20.7	26.7	31.2			Fixed Assets (net)	28.0	25.5
	2.5	2.0	1.5			Intangibles (net)	1.7	1.2
	6.5	5.8	5.2			All Other Non-Current	5.2	5.5
	100.0	100.0	100.0			Total	100.0	100.0
						LIABILITIES		
	11.9	14.2	1.6			Notes Payable-Short Term	11.2	16.5
	4.2	2.5	2.8			Cur. Mat.-L.T.D.	3.6	2.7
	23.0	11.1	5.1			Trade Payables	16.3	14.3
	.0	.1	.2			Income Taxes Payable	.1	.1
	19.6	16.5	12.1			All Other Current	12.0	14.3
	58.7	44.4	21.7			Total Current	43.1	47.9
	15.1	12.3	10.6			Long-Term Debt	20.4	13.4
	.3	.9	.8			Deferred Taxes	.6	.6
	14.4	1.2	2.8			All Other Non-Current	3.7	3.6
	11.4	41.2	64.1			Net Worth	32.2	34.4
	100.0	100.0	100.0			Total Liabilties & Net Worth	100.0	100.0
						INCOME DATA		
	100.0	100.0	100.0			Net Sales	100.0	100.0
	27.9	29.5	31.7			Gross Profit	25.2	29.9
	26.0	24.9	24.5			Operating Expenses	23.0	27.1
	1.8	4.6	7.1			Operating Profit	2.2	2.8
	.8	.8	.4			All Other Expenses (net)	.8	.6
	1.1	3.8	6.7			Profit Before Taxes	1.4	2.2
						RATIOS		
	2.1	2.6	6.7				2.3	2.8
	1.2	1.8	3.3			Current	1.6	1.8
	.8	1.2	1.5				1.2	1.3
	1.4	1.8	5.1				1.3	1.7
	.4	1.1	2.3			Quick	.9	1.0
	.3	.6	.7				.6	.5
	14 26.4	**24** 15.1	**25** 14.6				**33** 11.0	**29** 12.7
	33 10.9	**36** 10.2	**31** 11.6			Sales/Receivables	**42** 8.6	**48** 7.6
	51 7.2	**79** 4.6	**63** 5.8				**61** 6.0	**65** 5.6
	31 11.8	**22** 16.7	**36** 10.0				**7** 51.8	**13** 29.0
	40 9.1	**40** 9.2	**51** 7.1			Cost of Sales/Inventory	**35** 10.5	**41** 8.8
	79 4.6	**72** 5.1	**81** 4.5				**77** 4.7	**104** 3.5
	20 18.4	**9** 41.4	**10** 37.6				**14** 25.9	**17** 22.1
	30 12.0	**20** 18.5	**12** 30.8			Cost of Sales/Payables	**22** 16.8	**25** 14.5
	52 7.0	**38** 9.7	**20** 18.4				**38** 9.6	**41** 8.8
	9.5	5.8	2.4				6.1	4.0
	21.4	8.4	4.0			Sales/Working Capital	11.4	7.1
	-22.9	24.5	15.9				34.9	16.0
	4.8	23.1					8.5	11.0
	(12) 2.7	(20) 7.6				EBIT/Interest	(43) 1.9	(45) 3.4
	-3.8	2.1					.1	-.3
							5.3	6.4
						Net Profit + Depr., Dep., Amort./Cur. Mat. L/T/D	(13) 3.6	(12) 2.6
							1.3	.1
	.3	.3	.2				.5	.3
	2.1	.6	.4			Fixed/Worth	.8	.5
	-2.5	1.0	1.0				2.0	1.3
	1.3	.5	.2				.8	.5
	4.8	.9	.5			Debt/Worth	2.2	1.5
	-10.7	3.3	1.2				6.5	4.6
		53.5	25.5				21.1	26.2
		(20) 23.6	14.1			% Profit Before Taxes/Tangible Net Worth	(42) 7.1	(46) 8.1
		10.4	1.0				-6.4	-2.8
	14.4	14.6	21.3				10.1	11.0
	2.1	7.4	8.6			% Profit Before Taxes/Total Assets	2.6	4.3
	-5.7	2.3	.2				-1.2	-1.9
	87.0	17.3	9.1				25.7	21.3
	13.6	9.8	5.5			Sales/Net Fixed Assets	12.2	12.7
	10.0	6.9	4.6				6.2	5.4
	4.5	2.9	2.0				3.3	3.2
	2.7	2.3	1.7			Sales/Total Assets	2.6	2.2
	2.5	2.1	1.4				1.9	1.6
	.4	1.3					.7	1.0
	(11) 1.2	(17) 1.9				% Depr., Dep., Amort./Sales	(42) 1.5	(46) 2.2
	2.1	2.3					3.2	3.1
							2.1	1.8
						% Officers', Directors' Owners' Comp/Sales	(18) 2.4	(23) 2.8
							6.4	5.2
7891M	54221M	218844M	280551M	89789M	266182M	Net Sales ($)	936923M	1064132M
884M	16957M	88851M	162758M	53649M	133012M	Total Assets ($)	448715M	538844M

M = $ thousand MM = $ million

See Pages 9 through 22 for Explanation of Ratios and Data

Comparative Historical Data			Type of Statement	Current Data Sorted by Sales					
8	4	5	Unqualified					2	3
15	12	14	Reviewed			2	3	5	4
12	6	7	Compiled		1	2	3	1	
9	10	5	Tax Returns	1	2	1	1		
22	16	19	Other		3	5	4	6	1
4/1/11-3/31/12 ALL	4/1/12-3/31/13 ALL	4/1/13-3/31/14 ALL		13 (4/1-9/30/13)			37 (10/1/13-3/31/14)		
				0-1MM	1-3MM	3-5MM	5-10MM	10-25MM	25MM & OVER
66	48	50	NUMBER OF STATEMENTS	1	6	10	11	14	8
%	%	%	ASSETS	%	%	%	%	%	%
10.8	9.9	12.2	Cash & Equivalents			6.1	9.6	14.9	
30.3	33.1	24.9	Trade Receivables (net)			29.9	28.6	23.6	
21.2	20.7	24.1	Inventory			26.3	24.9	28.2	
4.3	2.9	2.4	All Other Current			2.3	4.1	1.7	
66.6	66.6	63.6	Total Current			64.6	67.2	68.5	
25.9	24.1	26.6	Fixed Assets (net)			27.4	25.2	23.7	
2.3	3.5	1.9	Intangibles (net)			1.9	3.2	1.2	
5.1	5.9	7.9	All Other Non-Current			6.1	4.3	6.5	
100.0	100.0	100.0	Total			100.0	100.0	100.0	
			LIABILITIES						
16.6	13.9	12.3	Notes Payable-Short Term			18.9	15.7	8.4	
3.6	3.9	3.7	Cur. Mat.-L.T.D.			3.2	6.0	.8	
17.7	16.2	13.6	Trade Payables			28.3	17.9	6.8	
.2	.0	.2	Income Taxes Payable			.6	.2	.1	
18.3	13.0	15.8	All Other Current			18.8	13.0	18.4	
56.4	47.0	45.6	Total Current			69.9	52.9	34.5	
15.8	17.4	13.5	Long-Term Debt			11.8	17.5	4.5	
.6	.4	.7	Deferred Taxes			.1	1.6	.4	
5.8	6.8	9.2	All Other Non-Current			8.9	1.9	.9	
21.3	28.2	31.0	Net Worth			9.3	26.2	59.7	
100.0	100.0	100.0	Total Liabilties & Net Worth			100.0	100.0	100.0	
			INCOME DATA						
100.0	100.0	100.0	Net Sales			100.0	100.0	100.0	
28.7	28.0	30.4	Gross Profit			34.1	21.7	31.4	
26.1	26.4	26.0	Operating Expenses			32.7	18.9	25.9	
2.6	1.5	4.3	Operating Profit			1.4	2.8	5.5	
.7	.6	.7	All Other Expenses (net)			.8	1.0	.3	
1.9	.9	3.7	Profit Before Taxes			.7	1.8	5.2	
			RATIOS						
2.6	2.4	2.8				1.6	2.1	3.9	
1.5	1.5	1.7	Current			1.0	1.4	2.4	
1.0	1.0	.9				.6	1.2	1.1	
1.7	1.9	1.8				1.0	1.1	2.3	
.9	.9	1.0	Quick			.4	1.0	1.3	
.4	.4	.4				.3	.6	.6	
22 16.4	25 14.6	22 16.7				18 20.3	22 16.5	25 14.8	
45 8.2	42 8.6	32 11.4	Sales/Receivables			37 9.8	36 10.2	30 12.1	
64 5.7	68 5.4	55 6.6				54 6.7	81 4.5	56 6.5	
13 28.4	17 21.0	26 14.2				17 22.0	24 14.9	33 11.2	
35 10.3	37 9.9	41 9.0	Cost of Sales/Inventory			39 9.3	41 8.9	53 6.9	
69 5.3	70 5.2	70 5.2				94 3.9	69 5.3	99 3.7	
20 18.1	16 22.9	10 36.3				22 16.6	20 18.5	9 42.0	
29 12.6	26 13.8	20 18.5	Cost of Sales/Payables			40 9.1	28 12.9	11 34.7	
45 8.1	45 8.2	34 10.8				55 6.6	54 6.7	22 16.4	
4.8	5.1	5.3				8.8	5.9	4.4	
9.0	12.4	10.8	Sales/Working Capital			NM	14.0	7.1	
-261.1	154.6	-62.6				-14.5	31.8	NM	
9.7	11.3	17.1				8.4	10.2	66.3	
(60) 3.1	(44) 1.8	(44) 4.6	EBIT/Interest			3.7	3.6	(11) 13.5	
.3	-1.4	.7				-2.0	2.0	-2.3	
13.8		7.2							
(14) 2.8		(10) 3.6	Net Profit + Depr., Dep., Amort./Cur. Mat. L/T/D						
1.4		.3							
.4	.3	.3				.8	.5	.2	
.9	.7	.6	Fixed/Worth			2.4	.7	.3	
5.7	2.0	2.9				-1.5	2.8	.5	
.9	.8	.5				1.2	.7	.3	
2.6	2.1	1.3	Debt/Worth			6.6	1.7	.5	
12.1	11.6	6.4				-4.2	12.8	2.2	
42.8	28.9	46.2					40.3	47.1	
(51) 12.7	(40) 10.7	(43) 21.8	% Profit Before Taxes/Tangible Net Worth				(10) 18.5	23.0	
1.5	-7.1	2.5					9.0	-2.1	
11.1	9.8	19.9				19.9	12.2	23.7	
4.1	1.8	7.2	% Profit Before Taxes/Total Assets			4.1	6.8	10.2	
-1.7	-5.1	.7				-4.4	2.1	-.9	
21.0	40.6	19.5				49.8	15.7	18.7	
12.0	13.9	10.8	Sales/Net Fixed Assets			12.1	9.3	13.6	
5.7	5.4	5.6				8.3	7.8	6.6	
3.2	3.3	3.1				5.2	2.8	3.3	
2.2	2.4	2.4	Sales/Total Assets			2.8	2.3	2.3	
1.7	1.8	1.9				2.5	2.1	1.8	
.9	1.0	1.1						1.3	
(53) 2.1	(40) 1.7	(42) 1.8	% Depr., Dep., Amort./Sales					(11) 1.7	
2.7	2.4	2.6						2.7	
1.5	3.2	1.7							
(30) 2.3	(18) 5.3	(21) 3.2	% Officers', Directors' Owners' Comp/Sales						
5.3	6.7	6.4							
1447764M	826146M	917478M	Net Sales ($)	890M	11390M	40568M	78300M	226048M	560282M
795296M	390402M	456111M	Total Assets ($)	143M	5771M	16831M	31749M	106261M	295356M

M = $ thousand MM = $ million

See Pages 9 through 22 for Explanation of Ratios and Data

Current Data Sorted by Assets | **Comparative Historical Data**

0-500M	500M-2MM	2-10MM	10-50MM	50-100MM	100-250MM	Type of Statement	4/1/09-3/31/10 ALL	4/1/10-3/31/11 ALL
			1	1		Unqualified	1	2
	1	6	2	1		Reviewed	6	8
1	2	1				Compiled	4	5
1	7	2				Tax Returns	5	6
2	6	5	2			Other	12	11
3 (4/1-9/30/13)			38 (10/1/13-3/31/14)					
4	16	14	5	2		NUMBER OF STATEMENTS	28	32
%	%	%	%	%	%	**ASSETS**	%	%
	14.3	13.2			DATA NOT AVAILABLE	Cash & Equivalents	13.4	9.5
	40.2	30.6				Trade Receivables (net)	36.7	33.8
	10.5	22.7				Inventory	15.7	20.0
	.9	2.2				All Other Current	6.0	3.5
	65.8	68.7				Total Current	71.9	66.9
	13.5	26.8				Fixed Assets (net)	22.1	24.7
	4.5	1.2				Intangibles (net)	2.1	3.3
	16.1	3.2				All Other Non-Current	4.0	5.2
	100.0	100.0				Total	100.0	100.0
						LIABILITIES		
	12.8	8.8				Notes Payable-Short Term	14.2	17.4
	1.0	2.4				Cur. Mat.-L.T.D.	4.2	1.7
	19.0	13.3				Trade Payables	14.2	17.2
	.0	.1				Income Taxes Payable	.9	.0
	19.5	18.4				All Other Current	20.9	19.5
	52.3	42.9				Total Current	54.4	55.8
	9.3	14.8				Long-Term Debt	11.2	12.4
	.0	.3				Deferred Taxes	.3	.3
	3.0	3.0				All Other Non-Current	13.9	16.0
	35.4	39.0				Net Worth	20.2	15.6
	100.0	100.0				Total Liabilties & Net Worth	100.0	100.0
						INCOME DATA		
	100.0	100.0				Net Sales	100.0	100.0
	37.4	29.6				Gross Profit	28.8	30.0
	30.2	25.5				Operating Expenses	28.1	30.0
	7.1	4.0				Operating Profit	.7	.0
	.3	.2				All Other Expenses (net)	.0	1.0
	6.8	3.8				Profit Before Taxes	.7	-1.0
						RATIOS		
	1.9	2.5					2.9	3.0
	1.1	1.7				Current	1.5	1.9
	.8	1.1					1.0	1.0
	1.8	1.8					2.1	2.2
	.9	1.1				Quick	1.1	.9
	.6	.6					.6	.7
	29 12.8	**16** 23.4					**27** 13.5	**33** 10.9
	38 9.5	**30** 12.1				Sales/Receivables	**47** 7.8	**46** 8.0
	64 5.7	**57** 6.4					**58** 6.3	**73** 5.0
	0 UND	**10** 37.3					**7** 50.7	**13** 27.4
	6 57.6	**30** 12.0				Cost of Sales/Inventory	**17** 21.8	**35** 10.5
	43 8.5	**61** 6.0					**35** 10.5	**70** 5.2
	16 22.9	**17** 21.8					**12** 29.5	**20** 18.3
	28 13.0	**24** 15.2				Cost of Sales/Payables	**18** 20.4	**28** 13.2
	40 9.1	**41** 8.9					**35** 10.3	**48** 7.6
	9.7	5.4					4.7	4.6
	112.4	7.4				Sales/Working Capital	20.4	8.1
	-20.1	58.8					NM	-387.7
	16.0	94.9					15.6	14.9
	(12) 7.1	(12) 12.2				EBIT/Interest	(26) 2.4	(30) 1.9
	.8	2.2					-.5	-1.7
						Net Profit + Depr., Dep., Amort./Cur. Mat. L/T/D		
	.1	.3					.2	.3
	.5	.6				Fixed/Worth	.8	1.0
	3.7	2.6					-6.7	13.0
	.4	.7					.6	.6
	3.0	1.4				Debt/Worth	2.5	1.6
	29.3	5.1					-20.4	61.2
	81.7	32.7					33.0	32.2
	(13) 26.2	(13) 14.5				% Profit Before Taxes/Tangible Net Worth	(19) 10.0	(26) 6.3
	-49.2	3.8					-3.3	-28.2
	35.8	9.1					18.6	12.7
	10.2	4.5				% Profit Before Taxes/Total Assets	1.7	1.6
	2.5	1.2					-4.3	-9.9
	67.8	21.2					33.3	26.1
	31.7	13.6				Sales/Net Fixed Assets	10.1	10.5
	17.6	5.1					8.7	6.9
	5.7	3.3					3.2	3.2
	3.1	2.9				Sales/Total Assets	2.7	2.5
	2.0	1.9					1.9	1.6
		1.2					.9	.8
		(13) 1.3				% Depr., Dep., Amort./Sales	(24) 1.8	(30) 2.1
		1.8					2.8	3.3
	3.0						2.4	1.9
	(11) 4.8					% Officers', Directors' Owners' Comp/Sales	(17) 5.7	(14) 3.9
	8.7						10.4	8.0
2207M	64715M	139644M	186629M	90400M		Net Sales ($)	369666M	393696M
847M	18490M	59972M	82247M	107266M		Total Assets ($)	169475M	235237M

M = $ thousand MM = $ million

See Pages 9 through 22 for Explanation of Ratios and Data

Comparative Historical Data | **Current Data Sorted by Sales**

						Type of Statement							
			2		2	Unqualified							2
	12		12		10	Reviewed					4	3	3
	2		5		4	Compiled	1		1		2		
	10		7		10	Tax Returns	1	4	2		1	2	
	16		13		15	Other	3	1	3		3	3	2
							3 (4/1-9/30/13)			38 (10/1/13-3/31/14)			
	4/1/11-3/31/12 ALL		4/1/12-3/31/13 ALL		4/1/13-3/31/14 ALL		0-1MM	1-3MM	3-5MM		5-10MM	10-25MM	25MM & OVER
	40		39		41	NUMBER OF STATEMENTS	5	5	6		10	8	7
	%		%		%	**ASSETS**	%	%	%		%	%	%
	7.0		11.9		12.8	Cash & Equivalents					10.1		
	36.1		31.0		33.2	Trade Receivables (net)					39.1		
	15.8		21.2		17.4	Inventory					13.2		
	3.2		4.1		1.7	All Other Current					1.9		
	62.1		68.2		65.2	Total Current					64.3		
	28.4		20.8		20.5	Fixed Assets (net)					27.3		
	4.0		3.2		5.0	Intangibles (net)					.1		
	5.5		7.8		9.3	All Other Non-Current					8.2		
	100.0		100.0		100.0	Total					100.0		
						LIABILITIES							
	14.6		15.9		10.6	Notes Payable-Short Term					7.2		
	3.1		2.6		2.4	Cur. Mat.-L.T.D.					2.3		
	16.0		12.8		14.8	Trade Payables					15.2		
	.0		.4		.0	Income Taxes Payable					.0		
	11.7		13.9		15.5	All Other Current					16.6		
	45.5		45.6		43.3	Total Current					41.2		
	12.1		13.1		13.9	Long-Term Debt					13.6		
	.3		.2		.4	Deferred Taxes					.4		
	20.1		4.7		7.5	All Other Non-Current					2.0		
	22.0		36.0		34.9	Net Worth					42.8		
	100.0		100.0		100.0	Total Liabilties & Net Worth					100.0		
						INCOME DATA							
	100.0		100.0		100.0	Net Sales					100.0		
	29.2		28.0		33.9	Gross Profit					34.8		
	28.4		25.7		28.8	Operating Expenses					27.9		
	.8		2.3		5.2	Operating Profit					6.9		
	.7		.4		.4	All Other Expenses (net)					.1		
	.1		1.9		4.8	Profit Before Taxes					6.7		
						RATIOS							
	2.4		4.6		2.6						3.2		
	1.4		1.6		1.6	Current					1.4		
	.9		1.0		1.1						1.0		
	1.6		2.9		1.6						1.9		
	.9		1.0		.9	Quick					.9		
	.7		.6		.7						.6		
32	11.4	21	17.3	26	14.0					27	13.6		
50	7.3	35	10.4	35	10.3	Sales/Receivables				46	8.0		
79	4.6	63	5.8	61	6.0					87	4.2		
8	46.3	10	35.7	5	68.6					0	UND		
21	17.6	36	10.1	24	15.2	Cost of Sales/Inventory				13	28.0		
48	7.6	61	6.0	52	7.0					45	8.1		
18	20.6	11	34.2	15	24.6					17	21.5		
30	12.3	18	20.6	25	14.8	Cost of Sales/Payables				27	13.4		
41	8.8	36	10.0	39	9.3					61	6.0		
	6.1		4.8		5.8						3.1		
	13.1		11.5		14.1	Sales/Working Capital					13.5		
	-61.8		179.0		112.4						NM		
	6.7		14.1		19.4								
(35)	2.2	(33)	2.3	(34)	6.9	EBIT/Interest							
	-.3		-2.5		2.0								
						Net Profit + Depr., Dep., Amort./Cur. Mat. L/T/D							
	.3		.2		.2						.2		
	.9		.4		.8	Fixed/Worth					.5		
	9.1		1.0		5.4						2.6		
	.7		.4		.6						.6		
	2.8		1.7		2.7	Debt/Worth					1.4		
	23.0		3.6		11.8						10.0		
	18.9		34.8		68.6						104.6		
(32)	11.7	(33)	13.1	(34)	14.8	% Profit Before Taxes/Tangible Net Worth					17.8		
	-1.5		-2.7		3.6						10.8		
	8.0		17.5		23.1						14.1		
	1.8		5.8		6.6	% Profit Before Taxes/Total Assets					7.3		
	-3.8		-4.5		1.1						3.7		
	28.8		32.1		31.7						30.0		
	12.4		18.5		17.1	Sales/Net Fixed Assets					11.5		
	5.9		9.2		8.6						4.6		
	3.1		3.6		3.5						3.4		
	2.6		3.0		2.9	Sales/Total Assets					2.8		
	1.7		2.0		1.8						1.4		
	.9		.8		.9								
(37)	1.6	(31)	1.1	(30)	1.2	% Depr., Dep., Amort./Sales							
	2.9		2.0		1.6								
	2.4		1.9		3.0								
(21)	5.7	(17)	5.1	(19)	5.4	% Officers', Directors' Owners' Comp/Sales							
	12.3		9.6		9.5								
	423758M		568213M		483595M	Net Sales ($)	3139M	10933M	24275M		68144M	100075M	277029M
	239427M		265333M		268822M	Total Assets ($)	1350M	5455M	6387M		36003M	30114M	189513M

M = $ thousand MM = $ million

See Pages 9 through 22 for Explanation of Ratios and Data

Current Data Sorted by Assets							Comparative Historical Data	
						Type of Statement		
	1		2		1	Unqualified	20	7
	1	5	4			Reviewed	17	14
2	2	1	1			Compiled	4	5
1	1	4				Tax Returns	2	2
1	5	4	4	2		Other	24	23
	5 (4/1-9/30/13)		37 (10/1/13-3/31/14)				4/1/09-3/31/10 ALL	4/1/10-3/31/11 ALL
0-500M	500M-2MM	2-10MM	10-50MM	50-100MM	100-250MM			
4	10	14	11	2	1	**NUMBER OF STATEMENTS**	67	51
%	%	%	%	%	%	**ASSETS**	%	%
	10.8	3.7	9.6			Cash & Equivalents	8.0	9.2
	32.5	36.3	28.2			Trade Receivables (net)	29.9	35.1
	21.3	29.9	20.2			Inventory	25.9	21.8
	6.6	1.4	1.2			All Other Current	3.9	3.8
	71.2	71.3	59.1			Total Current	67.6	69.9
	18.1	19.7	22.6			Fixed Assets (net)	20.4	17.4
	3.4	4.5	9.6			Intangibles (net)	6.5	7.9
	7.3	4.4	8.7			All Other Non-Current	5.5	4.9
	100.0	100.0	100.0			Total	100.0	100.0
						LIABILITIES		
	9.0	3.8	14.0			Notes Payable-Short Term	9.0	8.2
	4.8	2.7	1.9			Cur. Mat.-L.T.D.	4.1	2.6
	27.2	14.6	20.7			Trade Payables	15.5	18.0
	.0	.4	.2			Income Taxes Payable	.4	.3
	9.1	16.0	9.9			All Other Current	13.2	11.7
	50.1	37.5	46.7			Total Current	42.2	40.9
	8.0	14.3	17.7			Long-Term Debt	17.1	14.2
	.8	.2	.3			Deferred Taxes	.6	.5
	.3	1.8	4.9			All Other Non-Current	8.4	4.3
	40.8	46.2	30.4			Net Worth	31.7	40.2
	100.0	100.0	100.0			Total Liabilties & Net Worth	100.0	100.0
						INCOME DATA		
	100.0	100.0	100.0			Net Sales	100.0	100.0
	29.1	36.1	33.9			Gross Profit	31.3	30.6
	26.1	28.3	29.4			Operating Expenses	27.5	26.7
	3.0	7.8	4.4			Operating Profit	3.8	4.0
	-.1	.3	.6			All Other Expenses (net)	1.5	1.0
	3.0	7.5	3.9			Profit Before Taxes	2.3	3.0
						RATIOS		
	3.6	3.6	2.5				2.4	2.7
	1.5	2.0	1.3			Current	1.7	1.6
	.8	1.5	.9				1.3	1.3
	1.9	1.8	1.4				1.5	1.6
	.8	1.1	.9			Quick	.9	1.0
	.4	.8	.6				.7	.7
	20 18.5	**31** 11.6	**34** 10.6				**33** 11.0	**38** 9.6
	27 13.7	**46** 8.0	**39** 9.3			Sales/Receivables	**41** 8.8	**49** 7.4
	46 8.0	**65** 5.6	**59** 6.2				**53** 6.8	**64** 5.7
	12 30.3	**43** 8.4	**36** 10.0				**25** 14.3	**23** 15.8
	31 11.6	**60** 6.1	**58** 6.3			Cost of Sales/Inventory	**49** 7.5	**46** 7.9
	51 7.2	**78** 4.7	**76** 4.8				**84** 4.4	**73** 5.0
	21 17.5	**14** 25.4	**27** 13.4				**17** 21.8	**19** 19.4
	35 10.5	**24** 15.2	**49** 7.4			Cost of Sales/Payables	**30** 12.0	**33** 11.1
	51 7.2	**53** 6.9	**69** 5.3				**45** 8.1	**56** 6.5
	5.7	5.7	7.9				5.7	6.1
	15.1	7.8	19.5			Sales/Working Capital	10.0	9.7
	-34.6	14.4	-82.8				21.9	15.7
		141.4	11.9				11.8	23.1
		34.9	8.0			EBIT/Interest	(62) 3.3	(44) 5.1
		4.8	1.1				1.2	2.1
							5.5	11.2
						Net Profit + Depr., Dep., Amort./Cur. Mat. L/T/D	(27) 2.3	(18) 3.6
							.3	1.4
	.0	.2	.6				.3	.2
	.5	.4	.8			Fixed/Worth	.7	.5
	3.2	.6	-1.6				2.0	1.4
	.4	.5	1.3				.8	.8
	1.3	1.3	5.4			Debt/Worth	1.8	1.8
	6.2	3.7	-10.0				11.6	11.3
		62.2					43.3	49.3
		(13) 48.7				% Profit Before Taxes/Tangible Net Worth	(54) 18.8	(43) 20.2
		12.6					1.2	9.8
	18.8	28.0	21.8				13.3	10.9
	7.6	16.3	9.2			% Profit Before Taxes/Total Assets	4.1	5.5
	1.4	5.1	.1				-.3	2.2
	302.6	46.1	18.4				32.6	57.0
	40.5	20.2	11.3			Sales/Net Fixed Assets	14.0	21.2
	13.2	5.7	6.8				6.4	8.4
	4.5	3.7	2.8				3.3	3.2
	4.1	2.4	2.3			Sales/Total Assets	2.4	2.5
	3.0	1.9	1.5				1.7	1.8
		.6	.9				.7	.6
		(13) .7	1.3			% Depr., Dep., Amort./Sales	(58) 1.9	(44) 1.5
		2.0	2.7				2.6	2.3
							1.1	2.2
						% Officers', Directors' Owners' Comp/Sales	(15) 2.8	(14) 3.3
							4.4	4.2
5094M	49832M	226926M	449144M	236846M	133273M	Net Sales ($)	3958712M	2111698M
1708M	12754M	83956M	215614M	121503M	117463M	Total Assets ($)	1910115M	1099765M

M = $ thousand MM = $ million

See Pages 9 through 22 for Explanation of Ratios and Data

Comparative Historical Data | **Current Data Sorted by Sales**

	4/1/11-3/31/12 ALL		4/1/12-3/31/13 ALL		4/1/13-3/31/14 ALL	Type of Statement	0-1MM	1-3MM	3-5MM	5-10MM		10-25MM		25MM & OVER
	3		2		4	Unqualified			1					3
	14		9		10	Reviewed				1		5		4
	3		3		6	Compiled	1	1	1	1		1		1
	4		3		6	Tax Returns		1		2		3		
	20		22		16	Other		3	1	2		3		7
								5 (4/1-9/30/13)		37 (10/1/13-3/31/14)				
	44		39		42	NUMBER OF STATEMENTS	1	5	3	6		12		15
	%		%		%	**ASSETS**	%	%	%	%		%		%
	8.9		10.8		8.6	Cash & Equivalents						3.9		9.8
	27.0		30.1		29.3	Trade Receivables (net)						36.9		26.8
	32.1		27.3		23.9	Inventory						28.7		22.7
	2.5		4.6		2.7	All Other Current						1.5		1.4
	70.4		72.8		64.4	Total Current						71.0		60.6
	19.7		17.3		20.2	Fixed Assets (net)						19.6		18.1
	6.5		5.9		8.2	Intangibles (net)						4.3		14.5
	3.4		4.0		7.1	All Other Non-Current						5.1		6.8
	100.0		100.0		100.0	Total						100.0		100.0
						LIABILITIES								
	9.7		8.6		8.7	Notes Payable-Short Term						4.5		11.2
	2.4		2.4		3.3	Cur. Mat.-L.T.D.						2.5		2.7
	15.6		18.0		18.6	Trade Payables						14.1		19.7
	.2		.1		.2	Income Taxes Payable						.5		.2
	12.1		11.3		12.7	All Other Current						15.5		11.8
	40.0		40.2		43.4	Total Current						37.1		45.5
	12.7		13.5		14.6	Long-Term Debt						13.2		19.8
	.8		.5		.6	Deferred Taxes						.3		.9
	3.7		6.6		3.1	All Other Non-Current						1.9		3.8
	42.8		39.2		38.2	Net Worth						47.5		29.9
	100.0		100.0		100.0	Total Liabilties & Net Worth						100.0		100.0
						INCOME DATA								
	100.0		100.0		100.0	Net Sales						100.0		100.0
	34.0		33.8		34.0	Gross Profit						37.5		32.9
	30.0		27.8		29.8	Operating Expenses						30.7		28.5
	4.0		6.0		4.2	Operating Profit						6.8		4.4
	1.0		.5		.5	All Other Expenses (net)						.3		1.1
	3.0		5.5		3.6	Profit Before Taxes						6.5		3.4
						RATIOS								
	2.7		2.6		2.6							3.1		1.9
	1.7		1.7		1.6	Current						2.0		1.4
	1.3		1.4		1.0							1.4		.9
	1.7		1.7		1.4							1.8		1.2
	.9		1.0		.9	Quick						1.2		.8
	.6		.7		.6							.8		.6
32	11.3	29	12.8	24	15.3						37	9.8	31	11.6
42	8.6	45	8.1	37	9.8	Sales/Receivables					51	7.2	38	9.5
60	6.1	55	6.6	53	6.9						72	5.1	57	6.4
38	9.6	38	9.6	36	10.2						47	7.8	38	9.5
64	5.7	53	6.9	51	7.1	Cost of Sales/Inventory					61	6.0	58	6.3
99	3.7	83	4.4	68	5.4						81	4.5	76	4.8
18	19.8	18	20.4	15	24.4						14	25.5	24	14.9
30	12.2	29	12.5	33	11.0	Cost of Sales/Payables					21	17.1	41	8.9
46	8.0	51	7.2	53	6.9						53	6.9	62	5.9
	4.7		5.6		6.1							5.2		8.7
	7.9		8.8		11.5	Sales/Working Capital						6.9		14.5
	13.0		19.5		NM							13.6		-82.8
	18.0		28.5		35.6							104.0		17.1
(38)	6.9	(33)	6.4	(38)	7.3	EBIT/Interest						16.6	(14)	7.0
	1.1		3.9		-.1							3.9		.1
	3.2		5.7											
(12)	2.1	(11)	3.9			Net Profit + Depr., Dep., Amort./Cur. Mat. L/T/D								
	.2		1.4											
	.3		.2		.4							.2		.5
	.5		.4		.6	Fixed/Worth						.4		1.3
	1.1		1.1		4.2							.6		-.7
	.7		.7		.5							.5		1.3
	1.3		1.5		1.8	Debt/Worth						1.3		7.1
	4.2		4.7		12.9							2.7		-4.8
	44.9		63.5		57.8							58.9		81.7
(40)	25.0	(34)	29.0	(33)	35.4	% Profit Before Taxes/Tangible Net Worth					(11)	39.8	(10)	47.4
	5.7		9.8		-.4							6.2		-2.2
	12.8		23.8		22.6							22.0		24.1
	5.5		12.0		8.4	% Profit Before Taxes/Total Assets						10.6		9.3
	-.4		4.7		-1.0							4.0		.1
	41.7		78.9		54.6							66.3		19.9
	12.6		25.6		17.5	Sales/Net Fixed Assets						22.4		14.6
	7.0		7.6		8.3							5.4		8.9
	3.0		3.6		3.7							3.3		3.5
	2.3		2.7		2.7	Sales/Total Assets						2.3		2.5
	1.8		1.9		1.9							1.9		1.5
	.9		.7		.4							.6		.9
(37)	1.4	(29)	1.3	(35)	1.2	% Depr., Dep., Amort./Sales					(11)	.7	(13)	1.3
	2.5		2.6		2.1							2.4		2.1
	1.8				1.2									
(12)	2.7			(14)	3.1	% Officers', Directors' Owners' Comp/Sales								
	4.3				5.2									
	1250963M		1319814M		1101115M	Net Sales ($)	809M	9216M	12125M	38510M		177739M		862716M
	812096M		729890M		552998M	Total Assets ($)	464M	3181M	2964M	11535M		77330M		457524M

M = $ thousand MM = $ million

See Pages 9 through 22 for Explanation of Ratios and Data

Current Data Sorted by Assets | **Comparative Historical Data**

0-500M	500M-2MM	2-10MM	10-50MM	50-100MM	100-250MM	Type of Statement	4/1/09-3/31/10 ALL	4/1/10-3/31/11 ALL
			7	4	2	Unqualified	15	17
		14	4	1		Reviewed	19	26
	5	4				Compiled	12	12
2	6	6	1			Tax Returns	9	16
2	8	16	20	3	3	Other	46	41
	18 (4/1-9/30/13)		90 (10/1/13-3/31/14)					
4	19	40	32	8	5	NUMBER OF STATEMENTS	101	112
%	%	%	%	%	%	**ASSETS**	%	%
	12.4	12.3	6.4			Cash & Equivalents	7.7	9.9
	36.6	29.8	27.8			Trade Receivables (net)	27.3	29.9
	30.9	21.6	25.2			Inventory	23.7	21.9
	1.5	2.9	3.7			All Other Current	2.2	2.0
	81.4	66.6	63.1			Total Current	61.0	63.7
	11.7	24.8	22.8			Fixed Assets (net)	26.8	24.0
	3.4	3.8	5.4			Intangibles (net)	6.8	5.8
	3.5	4.8	8.7			All Other Non-Current	5.4	6.5
	100.0	100.0	100.0			Total	100.0	100.0
						LIABILITIES		
	20.0	10.1	15.2			Notes Payable-Short Term	14.8	16.7
	2.2	3.0	1.9			Cur. Mat.-L.T.D.	4.1	5.5
	24.1	12.0	12.9			Trade Payables	14.1	16.1
	.0	.4	.0			Income Taxes Payable	.1	.3
	9.4	13.4	14.1			All Other Current	11.4	9.8
	55.7	39.0	44.1			Total Current	44.6	48.4
	13.9	16.1	15.2			Long-Term Debt	19.4	13.9
	.0	.1	.6			Deferred Taxes	.3	.3
	12.7	10.2	3.3			All Other Non-Current	7.8	12.7
	17.7	34.6	36.8			Net Worth	27.9	24.8
	100.0	100.0	100.0			Total Liabilties & Net Worth	100.0	100.0
						INCOME DATA		
	100.0	100.0	100.0			Net Sales	100.0	100.0
	32.9	28.5	26.8			Gross Profit	26.9	29.4
	31.5	22.8	20.4			Operating Expenses	26.4	26.9
	1.3	5.7	6.5			Operating Profit	.5	2.5
	.5	.9	1.0			All Other Expenses (net)	1.7	1.1
	.8	4.8	5.5			Profit Before Taxes	-1.3	1.4
						RATIOS		
	2.0	3.4	1.9				2.6	2.3
	1.4	1.9	1.4			Current	1.6	1.5
	1.0	1.3	1.2				1.0	1.1
	1.3	2.5	1.2				1.5	1.6
	.9	1.2	.6			Quick	.8	.9
	.4	.6	.5				.5	.5
	25 14.6	27 13.6	39 9.3				30 12.2	30 12.3
	43 8.5	39 9.3	49 7.5			Sales/Receivables	40 9.0	45 8.2
	70 5.2	58 6.3	54 6.7				60 6.1	60 6.1
	21 17.7	9 39.4	39 9.3				22 16.6	14 25.3
	61 6.0	43 8.4	66 5.5			Cost of Sales/Inventory	50 7.4	45 8.1
	101 3.6	91 4.0	78 4.7				85 4.3	80 4.5
	24 14.9	13 27.2	21 17.4				14 25.5	15 24.7
	35 10.3	23 15.6	31 11.8			Cost of Sales/Payables	25 14.7	26 14.1
	59 6.2	36 10.2	38 9.6				39 9.4	44 8.2
	6.3	5.0	6.5				5.4	5.8
	8.6	6.7	11.5			Sales/Working Capital	10.2	11.2
	650.6	14.3	24.5				550.2	98.2
	11.9	17.2	24.1				7.4	8.2
	(17) 3.4	(35) 4.1	(30) 10.4			EBIT/Interest	(95) 1.3	(102) 2.4
	.4	2.0	1.9				-2.2	.7
							5.8	6.0
						Net Profit + Depr., Dep., Amort./Cur. Mat. L/T/D	(29) 1.7	(28) 2.5
							-.6	1.0
	.1	.2	.4				.3	.3
	.5	.7	.6			Fixed/Worth	1.0	.9
	-1.1	1.8	1.9				18.4	4.9
	1.0	.9	1.1				.8	1.0
	4.4	1.8	1.7			Debt/Worth	2.9	1.8
	-11.1	7.2	3.0				54.9	16.6
	116.4	74.1	49.6				28.4	36.3
	(14) 56.7	(32) 27.7	(29) 22.7			% Profit Before Taxes/Tangible Net Worth	(78) 5.6	(89) 14.1
	9.4	6.1	5.8				-31.0	2.1
	28.9	18.5	20.0				8.2	11.3
	5.6	6.4	7.9			% Profit Before Taxes/Total Assets	1.6	3.6
	-1.3	.4	2.9				-10.2	-.6
	115.3	47.0	20.9				25.4	30.4
	71.9	14.1	11.2			Sales/Net Fixed Assets	10.4	11.4
	17.4	4.1	6.2				4.6	5.8
	4.2	3.0	2.7				2.9	3.2
	3.0	2.4	1.9			Sales/Total Assets	2.1	2.3
	2.2	1.4	1.7				1.6	1.7
	.4	.8	.8				1.4	1.0
	(13) 1.4	(36) 1.5	1.2			% Depr., Dep., Amort./Sales	(90) 2.2	(97) 2.1
	1.6	3.2	2.0				3.8	3.2
	2.8	1.8					2.8	2.4
	(12) 4.9	(14) 4.7				% Officers', Directors' Owners' Comp/Sales	(34) 4.6	(41) 4.7
	6.8	8.0					7.2	6.2
11682M	81665M	432884M	1567334M	726441M	1254555M	Net Sales ($)	2826805M	2839297M
1444M	24516M	196351M	777168M	510860M	866017M	Total Assets ($)	1483178M	1531761M

M = $ thousand MM = $ million

See Pages 9 through 22 for Explanation of Ratios and Data

Comparative Historical Data				Current Data Sorted by Sales					
			Type of Statement						
20	17	13	Unqualified					1	12
20	18	19	Reviewed			2	4	9	4
11	16	9	Compiled		1	3	3	2	
6	13	15	Tax Returns		3	4	5	2	1
46	41	52	Other	1	1	8	10	7	25
					18 (4/1-9/30/13)		90 (10/1/13-3/31/14)		
4/1/11-3/31/12 ALL	4/1/12-3/31/13 ALL	4/1/13-3/31/14 ALL		0-1MM	1-3MM	3-5MM	5-10MM	10-25MM	25MM & OVER
103	105	108	**NUMBER OF STATEMENTS**	1	5	17	22	21	42
%	%	%	**ASSETS**	%	%	%	%	%	%
8.9	6.4	9.8	Cash & Equivalents			11.7	14.8	13.4	5.1
33.1	33.0	29.5	Trade Receivables (net)			27.7	26.2	37.0	27.2
22.0	27.0	23.9	Inventory			28.5	24.6	18.6	25.4
2.8	2.7	2.7	All Other Current			1.9	2.1	3.1	3.5
66.7	69.1	65.9	Total Current			69.8	67.6	72.2	61.2
22.1	21.5	22.1	Fixed Assets (net)			21.1	23.8	20.5	20.6
6.0	4.3	6.2	Intangibles (net)			4.7	3.2	3.1	10.5
5.2	5.1	5.8	All Other Non-Current			4.4	5.3	4.2	7.7
100.0	100.0	100.0	Total			100.0	100.0	100.0	100.0
			LIABILITIES						
12.0	11.4	13.4	Notes Payable-Short Term			13.6	11.9	10.2	14.0
3.2	3.4	2.3	Cur. Mat.-L.T.D.			1.8	4.2	2.5	1.8
16.6	14.7	14.0	Trade Payables			17.1	14.1	15.0	12.0
.2	.3	.2	Income Taxes Payable			.0	.1	.6	.0
10.6	12.1	12.2	All Other Current			8.4	12.1	15.6	12.7
42.6	41.8	42.0	Total Current			40.8	42.4	43.8	40.5
15.4	15.9	16.3	Long-Term Debt			16.0	19.9	11.6	16.0
.3	.2	.4	Deferred Taxes			.0	.2	.1	.8
8.5	8.0	9.2	All Other Non-Current			15.3	6.3	8.8	5.2
33.2	34.2	32.1	Net Worth			27.8	31.1	35.7	37.5
100.0	100.0	100.0	Total Liabilities & Net Worth			100.0	100.0	100.0	100.0
			INCOME DATA						
100.0	100.0	100.0	Net Sales			100.0	100.0	100.0	100.0
28.7	28.7	29.8	Gross Profit			36.6	31.0	28.4	26.5
24.3	24.1	24.6	Operating Expenses			31.0	27.1	21.2	19.8
4.4	4.6	5.2	Operating Profit			5.6	3.9	7.2	6.8
.9	1.1	1.0	All Other Expenses (net)			.3	.9	.9	1.2
3.5	3.5	4.2	Profit Before Taxes			5.3	3.0	6.3	5.5
			RATIOS						
2.5	2.6	2.5				2.9	3.0	3.3	2.1
1.7	1.6	1.6	Current			1.9	1.8	1.8	1.5
1.1	1.2	1.2				1.0	1.1	1.3	1.3
1.5	1.6	1.4				1.9	2.0	2.4	1.2
1.0	.9	1.0	Quick			1.0	1.0	1.3	.8
.6	.6	.6				.4	.5	.7	.5
34 10.6	31 11.6	33 11.2				13 28.2	17 20.9	33 11.0	41 8.8
47 7.8	47 7.7	47 7.8	Sales/Receivables			37 9.8	38 9.7	39 9.4	49 7.4
70 5.2	70 5.2	62 5.9				65 5.6	60 6.1	59 6.2	55 6.6
23 16.0	26 13.9	24 15.0				17 21.7	22 16.3	3 122.6	45 8.2
41 8.8	53 6.9	59 6.2	Cost of Sales/Inventory			78 4.7	55 6.6	23 15.9	69 5.3
79 4.6	81 4.5	89 4.1				107 3.4	79 4.6	76 4.8	87 4.2
18 20.4	14 25.2	16 22.7				13 27.2	16 23.1	13 27.6	20 18.0
31 11.9	29 12.8	29 12.7	Cost of Sales/Payables			27 13.4	27 13.7	27 13.4	31 11.9
47 7.7	43 8.5	41 9.0				57 6.4	34 10.6	42 8.7	38 9.5
6.2	5.9	5.4				4.6	5.3	5.6	5.7
9.0	9.8	8.8	Sales/Working Capital			6.6	8.3	8.8	9.6
24.8	20.2	25.7				367.7	NM	14.2	16.3
15.2	22.3	19.1				17.2	11.9	26.1	24.1
(94) 3.5	(98) 4.7	(97) 3.9	EBIT/Interest			(15) 3.4	(20) 3.9	(19) 8.9	(38) 9.6
1.2	1.4	1.9				.6	1.0	2.0	2.6
5.0	8.1	10.4							13.0
(22) 2.9	(32) 4.9	(25) 4.8	Net Profit + Depr., Dep., Amort./Cur. Mat. L/T/D						(15) 4.8
1.2	1.3	2.1							2.1
.2	.3	.3				.1	.1	.2	.4
.7	.6	.7	Fixed/Worth			1.0	.9	.5	.7
5.7	2.0	2.7				NM	2.0	1.5	8.3
.8	.8	1.0				1.0	.9	.9	1.0
1.9	1.8	1.9	Debt/Worth			4.4	2.1	1.8	1.7
14.5	8.1	19.8				NM	8.7	2.4	21.8
51.4	65.7	61.2				224.3	80.5	86.0	51.7
(82) 21.7	(92) 24.8	(87) 24.8	% Profit Before Taxes/Tangible Net Worth			(13) 15.2	(18) 35.4	(18) 34.4	(35) 23.5
3.4	5.0	5.9				2.6	6.0	6.0	6.5
15.4	17.9	19.2				20.6	23.0	25.0	19.1
5.2	6.4	6.1	% Profit Before Taxes/Total Assets			6.1	4.9	15.9	6.8
.9	1.0	1.8				.8	-.1	2.2	2.9
33.3	41.7	36.5				105.9	72.4	73.7	22.7
11.6	17.1	13.5	Sales/Net Fixed Assets			25.0	14.8	25.9	10.8
6.3	6.4	5.6				7.5	4.1	6.4	5.7
2.8	3.2	3.0				3.4	4.1	3.4	2.5
2.2	2.4	2.2	Sales/Total Assets			2.4	2.7	2.8	1.9
1.8	1.7	1.6				1.5	1.2	2.2	1.5
.9	.9	.8				.3	1.0	.7	.9
(86) 1.5	(93) 1.3	(96) 1.4	% Depr., Dep., Amort./Sales			(14) 1.5	(18) 1.5	(17) 1.2	(41) 1.3
3.0	2.2	2.4				1.8	3.4	3.0	2.1
1.8	2.2	2.1							
(28) 3.5	(40) 3.3	(34) 4.6	% Officers', Directors' Owners' Comp/Sales						
5.2	6.0	7.2							
3511574M	4279213M	4074561M	Net Sales ($)	582M	9247M	64572M	160581M	333614M	3505965M
1877367M	2234746M	2376356M	Total Assets ($)	440M	6731M	33652M	85348M	130625M	2119560M

M = $ thousand MM = $ million

See Pages 9 through 22 for Explanation of Ratios and Data

Current Data Sorted by Assets							Comparative Historical Data	
						Type of Statement		
		2	1			Unqualified	3	3
		4	1			Reviewed	11	9
	5	1				Compiled	7	7
1	2	1				Tax Returns	2	4
	3	6	7			Other	20	21
	5 (4/1-9/30/13)		29 (10/1/13-3/31/14)				**4/1/09-3/31/10**	**4/1/10-3/31/11**
0-500M	**500M-2MM**	**2-10MM**	**10-50MM**	**50-100MM**	**100-250MM**		**ALL**	**ALL**
1	10	14	9			**NUMBER OF STATEMENTS**	43	44
%	%	%	%	%	%	**ASSETS**	%	%
	13.9	11.6		DATA NOT AVAILABLE	DATA NOT AVAILABLE	Cash & Equivalents	12.3	10.4
	31.4	25.2				Trade Receivables (net)	22.2	27.2
	30.2	23.0				Inventory	25.7	27.1
	1.6	1.1				All Other Current	3.3	3.0
	77.1	60.8				Total Current	63.5	67.7
	11.6	28.9				Fixed Assets (net)	26.3	21.8
	.3	7.4				Intangibles (net)	4.9	4.6
	11.0	2.9				All Other Non-Current	5.4	5.8
	100.0	100.0				Total	100.0	100.0
						LIABILITIES		
	4.8	7.7				Notes Payable-Short Term	7.1	8.8
	1.2	3.9				Cur. Mat.-L.T.D.	3.4	2.1
	20.7	20.6				Trade Payables	18.9	16.5
	.1	.0				Income Taxes Payable	.1	.3
	9.3	5.5				All Other Current	8.3	10.9
	36.1	37.8				Total Current	37.9	38.6
	19.4	9.3				Long-Term Debt	15.0	10.6
	.0	.8				Deferred Taxes	.3	.8
	14.0	.3				All Other Non-Current	6.3	11.4
	30.5	51.9				Net Worth	40.4	38.5
	100.0	100.0				Total Liabilities & Net Worth	100.0	100.0
						INCOME DATA		
	100.0	100.0				Net Sales	100.0	100.0
	36.8	26.9				Gross Profit	33.5	30.2
	32.6	21.3				Operating Expenses	31.4	26.2
	4.2	5.6				Operating Profit	2.1	4.0
	.4	.8				All Other Expenses (net)	.1	.4
	3.7	4.7				Profit Before Taxes	2.0	3.6
						RATIOS		
	10.5	2.2				Current	3.2	3.2
	2.6	2.0					1.7	1.9
	1.4	.9					1.0	1.1
	4.9	1.5				Quick	2.1	2.0
	1.3	1.2					.8	1.1
	.9	.4					.4	.5
	17 22.1	**21** 17.2				Sales/Receivables	**16** 22.9	**17** 21.0
	25 14.5	**27** 13.3					**28** 13.2	**33** 11.0
	41 8.9	**33** 10.9					**43** 8.6	**44** 8.2
	27 13.3	**25** 14.6				Cost of Sales/Inventory	**27** 13.3	**26** 13.8
	49 7.5	**33** 11.0					**42** 8.7	**44** 8.3
	69 5.3	**43** 8.4					**79** 4.6	**61** 6.0
	0 UND	**24** 15.4				Cost of Sales/Payables	**16** 23.0	**16** 22.1
	32 11.5	**33** 11.1					**27** 13.6	**23** 15.6
	42 8.6	**41** 8.9					**49** 7.5	**38** 9.6
	5.9	7.6				Sales/Working Capital	5.2	5.1
	7.3	11.3					12.7	11.9
	56.0	-98.7					247.8	42.8
		49.0				EBIT/Interest	13.7	9.0
		(10) 18.5					(36) 3.5	(32) 2.9
		1.1					-.4	-.2
						Net Profit + Depr., Dep., Amort./Cur. Mat. L/T/D	5.4	6.3
							(15) 2.2	(10) 2.8
							1.5	.3
	.0	.3				Fixed/Worth	.2	.2
	.3	.5					.6	.5
	-.3	1.7					3.7	4.9
	.5	.4				Debt/Worth	.5	.5
	1.1	.8					1.4	1.4
	-7.9	3.2					11.6	19.8
		50.2				% Profit Before Taxes/Tangible Net Worth	57.7	44.3
		(13) 32.1					(37) 17.5	(34) 14.7
		.1					-2.8	4.5
	20.3	36.0				% Profit Before Taxes/Total Assets	16.0	12.6
	10.5	13.8					6.2	4.8
	-3.0	.0					-3.1	.3
	561.7	21.7				Sales/Net Fixed Assets	29.5	42.3
	45.1	11.7					14.3	17.7
	13.7	5.7					6.6	9.7
	6.8	4.0				Sales/Total Assets	4.0	4.1
	3.5	3.5					2.8	2.8
	2.2	2.2					2.0	2.2
		1.0				% Depr., Dep., Amort./Sales	1.0	.8
		(13) 1.6					(37) 1.5	(40) 1.2
		2.0					2.7	1.9
						% Officers', Directors' Owners' Comp/Sales	.8	.8
							(14) 1.7	(15) 2.9
							5.8	7.5
1135M	56917M	252246M	642252M			Net Sales ($)	1646937M	2360188M
65M	13536M	75778M	233600M			Total Assets ($)	574351M	905274M

M = $ thousand MM = $ million

See Pages 9 through 22 for Explanation of Ratios and Data

Comparative Historical Data				Current Data Sorted by Sales					
			Type of Statement						
4	3	3	Unqualified					1	2
5	8	5	Reviewed				1	3	1
8	4	6	Compiled		1	1	2	2	
3	3	4	Tax Returns		2		1		1
19	14	16	Other		2	1	2	4	7
4/1/11-3/31/12 ALL	**4/1/12-3/31/13 ALL**	**4/1/13-3/31/14 ALL**			**5 (4/1-9/30/13)**		**29 (10/1/13-3/31/14)**		
				0-1MM	**1-3MM**	**3-5MM**	**5-10MM**	**10-25MM**	**25MM & OVER**
39	32	34	**NUMBER OF STATEMENTS**		5	2	6	10	11
%	%	%	**ASSETS**	%	%	%	%	%	%
9.0	10.3	12.4	Cash & Equivalents	DATA NOT AVAILABLE				7.6	14.1
25.4	25.6	25.8	Trade Receivables (net)					24.0	26.6
30.1	31.1	28.2	Inventory					31.8	24.5
1.2	2.0	2.0	All Other Current					.9	3.8
65.8	68.9	68.4	Total Current					64.2	68.9
24.1	21.6	21.9	Fixed Assets (net)					30.7	23.6
4.6	4.4	3.2	Intangibles (net)					2.3	.0
5.5	5.1	6.6	All Other Non-Current					2.7	7.4
100.0	100.0	100.0	Total					100.0	100.0
			LIABILITIES						
8.2	4.6	7.0	Notes Payable-Short Term					13.8	3.2
1.7	3.7	2.7	Cur. Mat.-L.T.D.					4.8	2.0
19.9	15.7	18.8	Trade Payables					24.9	14.4
.2	.0	.1	Income Taxes Payable					.0	.0
13.2	10.3	7.6	All Other Current					9.2	8.5
43.1	34.3	36.2	Total Current					52.7	28.0
10.4	11.0	11.1	Long-Term Debt					6.3	4.6
.7	.1	.4	Deferred Taxes					.0	.3
10.9	11.9	9.4	All Other Non-Current					8.0	6.8
34.9	42.7	43.0	Net Worth					33.0	60.3
100.0	100.0	100.0	Total Liabilties & Net Worth					100.0	100.0
			INCOME DATA						
100.0	100.0	100.0	Net Sales					100.0	100.0
30.3	30.2	30.9	Gross Profit					26.9	30.8
29.5	25.4	26.4	Operating Expenses					23.3	26.0
.9	4.8	4.5	Operating Profit					3.5	4.8
.4	.4	.5	All Other Expenses (net)					.8	-.3
.4	4.5	4.0	Profit Before Taxes					2.7	5.1
			RATIOS						
2.7	3.3	2.7						2.1	2.8
1.6	2.2	2.2	Current					1.0	2.4
1.1	1.2	1.1						.8	2.2
1.6	1.6	1.5						1.3	2.0
.8	1.2	1.2	Quick					.5	1.3
.4	.6	.6						.3	.6
18 20.1	**13** 27.5	**21** 17.2						**18** 20.2	**23** 15.7
28 13.1	**25** 14.8	**27** 13.4	Sales/Receivables					**26** 14.0	**31** 11.9
42 8.6	**46** 8.0	**34** 10.7						**31** 11.6	**35** 10.4
26 14.1	**24** 15.0	**25** 14.6						**31** 11.7	**22** 16.5
42 8.7	**36** 10.0	**39** 9.4	Cost of Sales/Inventory					**40** 9.1	**30** 12.3
74 4.9	**58** 6.3	**60** 6.1						**54** 6.8	**42** 8.6
17 22.0	**14** 26.6	**17** 21.0						**30** 12.2	**17** 20.9
30 12.0	**21** 17.6	**29** 12.6	Cost of Sales/Payables					**38** 9.5	**20** 18.7
42 8.7	**35** 10.3	**40** 9.2						**41** 8.8	**27** 13.5
7.7	7.4	6.5						10.3	4.7
14.5	10.7	9.8	Sales/Working Capital					NM	9.5
76.7	61.0	119.4						-31.7	13.5
5.7	67.9	30.7							
(32) 2.7	(25) 3.3	(23) 2.6	EBIT/Interest						
-2.4	.9	-.7							
			Net Profit + Depr., Dep., Amort./Cur. Mat. L/T/D						
.2	.1	.2						.3	.2
.9	.3	.4	Fixed/Worth					1.0	.3
4.7	1.6	1.2						2.3	.9
.7	.5	.5						.7	.3
1.3	1.0	1.0	Debt/Worth					2.1	.7
12.5	3.4	3.2						4.2	1.1
29.9	55.4	46.6							48.0
(30) 8.9	(27) 26.0	(29) 19.9	% Profit Before Taxes/Tangible Net Worth						15.9
-5.7	.3	1.4							-1.6
10.4	35.6	30.0						27.2	37.4
2.4	7.4	7.8	% Profit Before Taxes/Total Assets					2.8	9.0
-6.7	.1	-1.2						-4.4	-1.1
51.1	115.3	41.8						24.7	39.2
19.6	26.5	17.1	Sales/Net Fixed Assets					9.5	23.4
8.2	9.2	8.1						7.1	6.2
4.3	4.7	4.8						4.2	4.6
3.4	3.2	3.4	Sales/Total Assets					3.5	2.7
2.1	2.4	2.2						2.1	2.4
.6	.5	.9						.9	.8
(34) .9	(26) .9	(28) 1.1	% Depr., Dep., Amort./Sales					1.1	1.0
1.4	1.7	1.9						1.7	1.5
.6	1.0	1.8							
(13) 3.1	(13) 3.6	(11) 2.9	% Officers', Directors' Owners' Comp/Sales						
5.3	5.6	4.6							
1475802M	**1385939M**	**952550M**	Net Sales ($)		**8834M**	**7916M**	**48290M**	**170722M**	**716788M**
597330M	**402556M**	**322979M**	Total Assets ($)		**5993M**	**3050M**	**11544M**	**59123M**	**243269M**

Current Data Sorted by Assets | **Comparative Historical Data**

2 (4/1-9/30/13) | 20 (10/1/13-3/31/14)

0-500M	500M-2MM	2-10MM	10-50MM	50-100MM	100-250MM	Type of Statement	4/1/09-3/31/10 ALL	4/1/10-3/31/11 ALL
		1	2			Unqualified	1	4
	1	4	2			Reviewed	7	8
	1	1				Compiled	2	2
						Tax Returns	1	3
1	2		4	2	1	Other	14	13
1	4	6	8	2	1	**NUMBER OF STATEMENTS**	25	30
%	%	%	%	%	%	**ASSETS**	%	%
						Cash & Equivalents	7.1	8.5
						Trade Receivables (net)	25.5	24.1
						Inventory	35.4	35.9
						All Other Current	3.0	1.8
						Total Current	71.0	70.3
						Fixed Assets (net)	17.1	14.3
						Intangibles (net)	7.0	11.1
						All Other Non-Current	4.9	4.4
						Total	100.0	100.0
						LIABILITIES		
						Notes Payable-Short Term	20.8	21.3
						Cur. Mat.-L.T.D.	2.0	1.5
						Trade Payables	19.2	17.7
						Income Taxes Payable	.1	.1
						All Other Current	12.2	13.1
						Total Current	54.4	53.6
						Long-Term Debt	12.5	14.1
						Deferred Taxes	.8	.9
						All Other Non-Current	5.9	7.1
						Net Worth	26.5	24.3
						Total Liabilties & Net Worth	100.0	100.0
						INCOME DATA		
						Net Sales	100.0	100.0
						Gross Profit	34.0	36.5
						Operating Expenses	32.3	34.5
						Operating Profit	1.7	2.0
						All Other Expenses (net)	2.0	3.2
						Profit Before Taxes	-.4	-1.3
						RATIOS		
						Current	2.1	2.5
							1.5	1.5
							1.1	1.1
						Quick	1.1	1.2
							.8	.8
							.3	.4
						Sales/Receivables	**25** 14.6	**18** 20.7
							34 10.6	**29** 12.6
							46 7.9	**57** 6.4
						Cost of Sales/Inventory	**55** 6.7	**53** 6.8
							70 5.2	**74** 5.0
							87 4.2	**99** 3.7
						Cost of Sales/Payables	**20** 18.5	**14** 26.8
							35 10.5	**31** 11.7
							42 8.6	**42** 8.7
						Sales/Working Capital	6.5	4.7
							12.2	15.3
							45.0	34.6
						EBIT/Interest	9.5	7.9
							(23) 2.3	(28) 2.0
							-3.5	.1
						Net Profit + Depr., Dep., Amort./Cur. Mat. L/T/D		
						Fixed/Worth	.3	.2
							.4	.7
							-25.5	-1.0
						Debt/Worth	.9	1.2
							2.9	3.4
							-59.0	-6.2
						% Profit Before Taxes/Tangible Net Worth	34.8	16.7
							(18) 3.6	(21) 6.3
							-19.5	-8.6
						% Profit Before Taxes/Total Assets	11.3	6.5
							1.3	1.1
							-10.6	-3.9
						Sales/Net Fixed Assets	48.3	55.3
							20.8	26.9
							12.0	11.1
						Sales/Total Assets	3.7	4.4
							2.8	3.0
							1.9	1.8
						% Depr., Dep., Amort./Sales	.8	.8
							(19) 1.3	(19) 1.3
							2.5	1.9
						% Officers', Directors' Owners' Comp/Sales	1.9	2.1
							(11) 4.2	(12) 2.8
							5.6	4.7
1202M	20706M	104925M	454581M	138660M	80357M	Net Sales ($)	983819M	1137634M
395M	4976M	29785M	205513M	111370M	123889M	Total Assets ($)	437196M	586914M

M = $ thousand MM = $ million

See Pages 9 through 22 for Explanation of Ratios and Data

Comparative Historical Data				Current Data Sorted by Sales					
			Type of Statement						
3	3	3	Unqualified				1	1	1
6	5	7	Reviewed			1	1	3	2
5	1	2	Compiled				1	1	
6	2		Tax Returns						
10	12	10	Other		2	1			7
4/1/11-3/31/12 ALL	4/1/12-3/31/13 ALL	4/1/13-3/31/14 ALL			2 (4/1-9/30/13)		20 (10/1/13-3/31/14)		
				0-1MM	1-3MM	3-5MM	5-10MM	10-25MM	25MM & OVER
30	23	22	**NUMBER OF STATEMENTS**		2	2	3	5	10
%	%	%	**ASSETS**	%	%	%	%	%	%
7.6	7.3	12.0	Cash & Equivalents	DATA NOT AVAILABLE					17.1
24.7	25.9	22.9	Trade Receivables (net)						19.7
36.0	36.2	29.9	Inventory						28.4
2.5	2.8	3.2	All Other Current						2.6
70.8	72.1	68.0	Total Current						67.8
17.1	18.6	19.6	Fixed Assets (net)						20.4
10.6	5.8	9.9	Intangibles (net)						8.2
1.5	3.4	2.5	All Other Non-Current						3.6
100.0	100.0	100.0	Total						100.0
			LIABILITIES						
12.1	14.5	10.7	Notes Payable-Short Term						5.2
2.1	2.1	1.6	Cur. Mat.-L.T.D.						1.6
18.6	15.3	13.7	Trade Payables						15.1
.1	.0	.1	Income Taxes Payable						.1
21.6	14.7	16.3	All Other Current						16.4
54.4	46.7	42.3	Total Current						38.4
18.0	13.6	8.7	Long-Term Debt						9.2
.5	.4	.7	Deferred Taxes						.4
7.8	10.3	8.5	All Other Non-Current						5.4
19.3	28.9	39.8	Net Worth						46.5
100.0	100.0	100.0	Total Liabilties & Net Worth						100.0
			INCOME DATA						
100.0	100.0	100.0	Net Sales						100.0
33.4	34.8	33.7	Gross Profit						33.1
30.4	31.6	30.4	Operating Expenses						29.3
3.0	3.2	3.3	Operating Profit						3.8
1.9	2.2	2.1	All Other Expenses (net)						1.9
1.1	1.1	1.2	Profit Before Taxes						1.9
			RATIOS						
2.7	2.3	2.5							2.7
1.5	1.5	1.7	Current						1.7
1.2	1.2	1.2							1.3
1.1	1.1	1.3							1.7
.7	.8	.8	Quick						1.1
.3	.5	.5							.5
21 17.7	15 25.1	22 16.9							12 29.4
30 12.1	27 13.5	30 12.2	Sales/Receivables						35 10.5
49 7.4	51 7.1	49 7.4							57 6.4
46 7.9	36 10.0	43 8.4							41 8.8
72 5.1	70 5.2	68 5.4	Cost of Sales/Inventory						68 5.4
111 3.3	118 3.1	101 3.6							96 3.8
18 20.0	20 18.7	16 23.5							19 19.4
34 10.8	22 16.4	26 14.2	Cost of Sales/Payables						32 11.3
54 6.8	46 7.9	43 8.4							49 7.4
6.1	6.5	4.6							4.4
11.4	8.8	8.5	Sales/Working Capital						8.1
30.1	18.4	24.6							19.8
7.2	4.4	30.9							
(27) 2.3	(19) 2.3	(20) 7.0	EBIT/Interest						
.0	1.5	1.4							
			Net Profit + Depr., Dep., Amort./Cur. Mat. L/T/D						
.2	.2	.2							.2
.7	.4	.6	Fixed/Worth						.7
-4.4	1.6	1.3							1.1
.9	.7	.6							.7
4.5	3.5	1.6	Debt/Worth						1.4
-28.9	6.8	6.1							5.2
18.5	30.9	30.8							
(22) 2.9	(20) 11.1	(19) 15.1	% Profit Before Taxes/Tangible Net Worth						
-4.0	.3	3.3							
7.5	9.1	8.5							8.5
1.8	2.5	4.2	% Profit Before Taxes/Total Assets						2.9
-1.9	.1	.6							.9
50.2	57.8	40.5							26.3
20.4	28.3	14.3	Sales/Net Fixed Assets						11.4
8.3	10.1	7.4							6.4
3.3	3.8	3.2							3.4
2.6	2.6	2.3	Sales/Total Assets						2.5
1.8	1.9	1.7							1.2
.7	.5	1.1							1.2
(22) 1.2	(16) 1.0	(18) 1.4	% Depr., Dep., Amort./Sales						1.4
1.8	1.8	2.5							2.9
2.2									
(12) 3.0			% Officers', Directors' Owners' Comp/Sales						
7.3									
1125622M	1125755M	800431M	Net Sales ($)		2901M	8339M	23739M	69737M	695715M
535594M	520823M	475928M	Total Assets ($)		1246M	2877M	15330M	41637M	414838M

M = $ thousand MM = $ million

See Pages 9 through 22 for Explanation of Ratios and Data

Current Data Sorted by Assets							Comparative Historical Data	
						Type of Statement		
		7	19	11	4	Unqualified	54	50
1	2	18	14			Reviewed	26	30
1	3	6	4	1		Compiled	23	17
5	8	6	2			Tax Returns	14	14
4	7	37	28	9	18	Other	80	79
32 (4/1-9/30/13)			183 (10/1/13-3/31/14)				4/1/09-3/31/10	4/1/10-3/31/11
0-500M	500M-2MM	2-10MM	10-50MM	50-100MM	100-250MM		ALL	ALL
11	20	74	67	21	22	**NUMBER OF STATEMENTS**	197	190
%	%	%	%	%	%	**ASSETS**	%	%
37.5	22.3	13.8	12.2	15.9	18.8	Cash & Equivalents	12.2	12.8
13.2	30.6	25.6	20.8	12.5	14.7	Trade Receivables (net)	23.7	23.5
18.9	25.2	29.0	21.6	13.2	13.7	Inventory	22.8	20.8
1.4	2.6	1.6	2.5	6.2	2.2	All Other Current	2.9	2.7
70.9	80.7	70.1	57.1	47.7	49.4	Total Current	61.5	59.7
15.1	13.9	18.6	26.5	18.7	14.0	Fixed Assets (net)	20.4	20.9
6.0	2.7	5.3	8.7	29.3	31.7	Intangibles (net)	11.7	13.1
8.0	2.7	6.1	7.7	4.2	4.9	All Other Non-Current	6.4	6.3
100.0	100.0	100.0	100.0	100.0	100.0	Total	100.0	100.0
						LIABILITIES		
7.5	14.9	8.9	4.9	1.7	.9	Notes Payable-Short Term	8.3	6.3
4.2	3.5	2.5	4.3	2.2	2.0	Cur. Mat.-L.T.D.	3.5	3.6
11.0	22.9	13.7	9.1	6.5	5.2	Trade Payables	10.7	11.1
.0	.3	.2	.2	.0	.4	Income Taxes Payable	.3	.2
20.5	7.0	8.4	8.8	8.7	10.6	All Other Current	10.4	10.3
43.2	48.6	33.7	27.3	19.0	19.2	Total Current	33.3	31.5
10.8	9.6	10.3	19.7	18.4	18.6	Long-Term Debt	13.6	14.2
.0	.0	.2	.5	2.2	2.2	Deferred Taxes	.9	.7
52.4	4.7	5.8	6.0	7.1	3.6	All Other Non-Current	8.1	8.8
-6.3	37.2	50.2	46.4	53.2	56.5	Net Worth	44.1	44.8
100.0	100.0	100.0	100.0	100.0	100.0	Total Liabilties & Net Worth	100.0	100.0
						INCOME DATA		
100.0	100.0	100.0	100.0	100.0	100.0	Net Sales	100.0	100.0
54.2	43.6	46.3	44.8	49.5	52.4	Gross Profit	46.0	45.2
55.8	37.6	37.8	35.3	47.9	39.8	Operating Expenses	37.4	37.3
-1.6	6.1	8.6	9.5	1.6	12.6	Operating Profit	8.6	7.9
.2	1.5	.3	1.5	3.7	4.3	All Other Expenses (net)	2.1	1.7
-1.7	4.5	8.2	8.0	-2.1	8.3	Profit Before Taxes	6.5	6.2
						RATIOS		
6.5	4.8	4.9	3.5	4.2	5.7		3.9	3.9
2.5	1.6	2.4	2.3	2.3	3.1	Current	2.1	2.0
1.0	1.2	1.2	1.4	1.5	2.0		1.2	1.2
5.5	2.2	2.5	2.2	2.5	3.9		2.2	2.4
1.0	1.3	1.2	1.2	1.4	2.1	Quick	1.1	1.2
.5	.6	.6	.7	.8	.9		.6	.6
0 UND	22 16.5	32 11.5	38 9.7	34 10.8	47 7.7		34 10.7	36 10.2
0 UND	43 8.4	44 8.3	49 7.5	46 7.9	51 7.2	Sales/Receivables	44 8.2	47 7.8
37 9.9	58 6.3	58 6.3	58 6.3	60 6.1	68 5.4		58 6.3	58 6.3
1 324.9	13 27.9	56 6.5	54 6.7	51 7.1	68 5.4		50 7.3	44 8.3
14 25.7	55 6.6	83 4.4	89 4.1	85 4.3	104 3.5	Cost of Sales/Inventory	90 4.1	77 4.7
48 7.6	94 3.9	159 2.3	146 2.5	130 2.8	130 2.8		134 2.7	120 3.0
0 UND	26 14.3	17 20.9	14 25.9	20 18.0	21 17.2		19 19.4	18 20.5
0 UND	32 11.4	29 12.6	32 11.5	39 9.4	30 12.0	Cost of Sales/Payables	32 11.5	32 11.4
53 6.9	57 6.4	50 7.3	53 6.9	83 4.4	45 8.1		49 7.5	55 6.7
22.8	3.8	3.6	3.4	2.1	2.0		3.2	3.2
42.2	6.4	6.1	4.8	5.1	3.1	Sales/Working Capital	6.4	6.3
116.5	23.7	18.0	11.8	9.1	5.4		19.7	16.1
	43.3	58.0	15.5	30.3	13.8		17.6	24.5
	(14) 7.2	(64) 11.4	(55) 7.6	(20) .3	(18) 3.9	EBIT/Interest	(169) 5.7	(168) 6.0
	4.1	2.4	1.2	-1.7	1.3		1.7	1.2
			4.2				6.3	13.6
			(26) 2.4			Net Profit + Depr., Dep., Amort./Cur. Mat. L/T/D	(67) 3.3	(52) 2.7
			1.2				1.6	1.3
.0	.1	.1	.3	.2	.3		.2	.2
.5	.3	.2	.7	.7	.4	Fixed/Worth	.5	.6
-.2	1.8	1.0	2.4	-9.8	-.7		2.3	3.0
.5	.7	.3	.4	.4	.2		.4	.5
-6.4	1.7	1.0	.9	1.9	1.2	Debt/Worth	1.5	1.4
-2.5	6.4	3.2	4.4	-18.3	-2.9		8.9	12.3
	90.9	59.5	45.8	18.7	36.0		45.1	49.7
	(18) 35.5	(67) 28.2	(54) 16.7	(15) 8.1	(14) 19.9	% Profit Before Taxes/Tangible Net Worth	(158) 22.2	(150) 27.2
	14.4	8.5	2.4	-16.5	-9.3		6.5	8.0
90.2	23.9	23.1	19.4	6.2	17.0		21.6	20.3
6.9	10.9	11.5	7.2	-1.9	5.2	% Profit Before Taxes/Total Assets	8.6	9.3
.0	4.1	4.0	.4	-9.0	1.0		1.6	1.1
UND	99.0	53.6	21.7	17.2	11.4		26.4	27.9
63.3	37.6	19.1	6.5	7.4	7.2	Sales/Net Fixed Assets	10.8	10.3
25.8	12.2	5.8	3.0	3.9	5.6		4.6	4.4
17.3	3.8	2.7	1.9	1.4	1.3		2.3	2.3
6.8	2.7	2.0	1.6	.8	.8	Sales/Total Assets	1.7	1.6
3.4	2.0	1.4	1.1	.6	.6		1.1	1.1
	.1	.6	1.4	2.4	2.6		1.1	1.1
	(13) .6	(58) 2.0	(60) 3.1	(16) 4.0	(18) 3.6	% Depr., Dep., Amort./Sales	(155) 2.3	(153) 2.6
	2.4	3.8	5.5	9.0	6.4		4.7	4.7
	5.5	3.4	1.4				2.6	2.4
	(11) 6.7	(28) 7.0	(13) 3.2			% Officers', Directors' Owners' Comp/Sales	(39) 5.9	(49) 4.4
	14.7	10.2	5.2				9.4	8.4
15907M	75871M	796034M	2286492M	1525512M	3291180M	Net Sales ($)	7804768M	7752169M
2338M	25558M	379798M	1579341M	1550856M	3586016M	Total Assets ($)	5993680M	6135205M

M = $ thousand MM = $ million

See Pages 9 through 22 for Explanation of Ratios and Data

	Comparative Historical Data			Current Data Sorted by Sales					
Type of Statement									
Unqualified	49	31	41				4	8	29
Reviewed	31	29	35		4	2	7	13	9
Compiled	14	13	15		3	3	1	4	4
Tax Returns	30	30	21	4	3	5	5	4	
Other	83	93	103	2	3	10	19	23	46
	4/1/11-3/31/12 ALL	**4/1/12-3/31/13 ALL**	**4/1/13-3/31/14 ALL**		**32 (4/1-9/30/13)**		**183 (10/1/13-3/31/14)**		
				0-1MM	**1-3MM**	**3-5MM**	**5-10MM**	**10-25MM**	**25MM & OVER**
NUMBER OF STATEMENTS	207	196	215	6	13	20	36	52	88
ASSETS	%	%	%	%	%	%	%	%	%
Cash & Equivalents	13.3	12.0	16.0		25.0	20.7	12.8	13.6	14.9
Trade Receivables (net)	22.4	23.4	21.6		17.7	26.9	24.9	23.9	18.6
Inventory	23.7	25.0	22.7		20.9	19.3	28.3	28.1	18.0
All Other Current	2.7	3.4	2.5		2.1	.9	2.1	2.1	3.5
Total Current	62.1	63.8	62.8		65.7	67.7	68.0	67.7	55.0
Fixed Assets (net)	21.8	21.0	20.0		17.8	19.8	18.3	25.0	18.8
Intangibles (net)	9.8	8.4	11.2		12.2	3.9	7.6	4.9	18.6
All Other Non-Current	6.2	6.8	6.0		4.3	8.5	6.1	2.5	7.5
Total	100.0	100.0	100.0		100.0	100.0	100.0	100.0	100.0
LIABILITIES									
Notes Payable-Short Term	6.5	8.1	6.6		5.2	14.3	9.6	6.8	3.7
Cur. Mat.-L.T.D.	2.6	3.2	3.2		4.5	4.2	1.6	2.7	3.7
Trade Payables	11.3	12.9	11.4		10.8	15.0	13.1	14.1	8.3
Income Taxes Payable	.1	.2	.2		.0	.3	.2	.1	.3
All Other Current	9.7	13.1	9.3		14.0	7.7	8.2	9.6	8.8
Total Current	30.3	37.5	30.7		34.6	41.5	32.7	33.3	24.7
Long-Term Debt	15.3	18.0	14.8		12.1	16.5	6.8	14.2	18.9
Deferred Taxes	.6	.5	.7		.0	.0	.2	.5	1.2
All Other Non-Current	9.0	7.2	8.0		18.1	6.8	7.9	2.7	6.2
Net Worth	44.8	36.8	45.9		35.2	35.2	52.4	49.4	48.9
Total Liabilties & Net Worth	100.0	100.0	100.0		100.0	100.0	100.0	100.0	100.0
INCOME DATA									
Net Sales	100.0	100.0	100.0		100.0	100.0	100.0	100.0	100.0
Gross Profit	46.8	47.0	46.9		47.7	51.2	47.2	41.2	48.4
Operating Expenses	38.7	39.6	39.1		43.7	40.3	40.9	34.0	39.0
Operating Profit	8.1	7.4	7.8		3.9	10.8	6.3	7.3	9.3
All Other Expenses (net)	1.7	1.5	1.5		2.4	.8	.4	.6	2.6
Profit Before Taxes	6.4	5.9	6.3		1.6	10.0	5.9	6.7	6.7
RATIOS									
Current	4.1	3.3	4.0		7.9	3.6	5.4	3.8	3.9
	2.2	2.0	2.4		4.0	1.6	2.3	2.7	2.3
	1.3	1.2	1.4		1.2	1.1	1.3	1.2	1.6
Quick	2.5	1.9	2.5		6.3	2.1	2.1	2.5	2.5
	1.2	1.1	1.3		1.3	1.2	1.2	1.3	1.3
	.7	.6	.7		.5	.7	.6	.7	.8
Sales/Receivables	**32** 11.5	**33** 11.0	**34** 10.7		**17** 20.9	**17** 21.7	**36** 10.1	**31** 11.7	**41** 8.9
	43 8.5	**44** 8.3	**46** 7.9		**42** 8.7	**47** 7.8	**45** 8.2	**44** 8.3	**50** 7.3
	54 6.8	**59** 6.2	**58** 6.3		**59** 6.2	**63** 5.8	**58** 6.3	**57** 6.4	**60** 6.1
Cost of Sales/Inventory	**51** 7.1	**54** 6.7	**51** 7.2		**36** 10.2	**19** 19.4	**52** 7.0	**55** 6.6	**55** 6.6
	79 4.6	**87** 4.2	**81** 4.5		**59** 6.2	**70** 5.2	**96** 3.8	**76** 4.8	**87** 4.2
	130 2.8	**140** 2.6	**135** 2.7		**130** 2.8	**107** 3.4	**203** 1.8	**130** 2.8	**140** 2.6
Cost of Sales/Payables	**22** 16.9	**16** 22.2	**17** 21.0		**0** UND	**20** 18.4	**18** 19.9	**13** 27.5	**20** 18.1
	33 10.9	**34** 10.6	**31** 11.8		**31** 11.8	**37** 9.8	**31** 11.9	**27** 13.3	**32** 11.5
	54 6.7	**56** 6.5	**53** 6.9		**38** 9.5	**60** 6.1	**61** 6.0	**51** 7.1	**54** 6.8
Sales/Working Capital	3.5	3.6	3.3		2.6	5.2	3.0	3.5	2.9
	5.9	6.1	5.5		5.5	11.6	5.2	5.1	4.5
	16.2	29.8	17.4		56.2	41.3	17.7	22.4	9.6
EBIT/Interest	20.7	27.1	36.4			68.9	41.9	53.6	17.0
	(165) 7.0	(169) 6.7	(177) 7.5			(16) 8.4	(30) 9.8	(44) 7.9	(77) 5.2
	1.5	1.6	1.3			1.6	3.4	1.0	.7
Net Profit + Depr., Dep., Amort./Cur. Mat. L/T/D	6.5	7.6	4.5					3.8	5.3
	(50) 2.2	(39) 3.4	(50) 2.1					(13) 1.5	(33) 2.3
	1.1	1.5	1.0					1.2	1.1
Fixed/Worth	.2	.2	.2		.1	.1	.1	.1	.3
	.6	.6	.5		.5	.4	.3	.4	.6
	2.0	1.9	2.4		2.3	3.2	1.0	2.1	-6.0
Debt/Worth	.4	.6	.4		.5	.7	.3	.3	.5
	1.5	1.7	1.4		1.7	1.9	.9	.9	1.3
	5.3	4.9	7.5		NM	6.5	2.4	4.6	-23.7
% Profit Before Taxes/Tangible Net Worth	58.9	47.9	54.3		32.3	123.1	53.4	59.5	38.0
	(171) 29.2	(165) 21.5	(173) 22.9		(10) 24.7	(17) 68.9	(32) 25.6	(47) 21.3	(64) 16.7
	6.3	8.6	5.5		-.6	18.5	4.1	6.1	2.6
% Profit Before Taxes/Total Assets	21.6	19.9	19.6		14.5	32.7	17.8	21.3	16.4
	9.8	8.9	7.7		6.9	21.0	9.8	8.0	5.5
	1.7	1.0	.8		-2.4	3.7	2.2	.6	.1
Sales/Net Fixed Assets	25.0	36.1	39.7		43.9	94.1	45.9	40.2	17.9
	12.4	12.6	12.8		14.0	28.4	14.6	13.9	7.7
	4.8	4.5	4.8		11.1	5.5	5.7	3.2	4.6
Sales/Total Assets	2.5	2.5	2.5		3.8	3.0	2.6	2.7	1.9
	1.7	1.7	1.7		2.0	2.2	1.8	1.8	1.3
	1.2	1.3	1.1		1.2	1.4	1.4	1.3	.8
% Depr., Dep., Amort./Sales	1.2	1.0	.9		.2	.4	.7	.7	1.6
	(164) 2.3	(149) 2.4	(170) 2.6		(10) 1.0	(13) 2.9	(29) 2.2	(42) 2.2	(75) 3.1
	4.3	4.1	4.9		2.7	5.2	3.9	5.6	5.4
% Officers', Directors' Owners' Comp/Sales	2.6	2.5	3.1			5.2	6.6	2.6	1.0
	(58) 5.4	(64) 5.2	(57) 5.5			(10) 7.4	(13) 7.9	(17) 5.4	(13) 3.2
	8.9	8.2	9.6			16.3	11.4	8.6	5.2
Net Sales ($)	**7617314M**	**5707289M**	**7990996M**	**3945M**	**26231M**	**82615M**	**275600M**	**870025M**	**6732580M**
Total Assets ($)	**6107644M**	**4345480M**	**7123907M**	**729M**	**16857M**	**43735M**	**173545M**	**567054M**	**6321987M**

M = $ thousand MM = $ million

See Pages 9 through 22 for Explanation of Ratios and Data

	Current Data Sorted by Assets						Comparative Historical Data	
Type of Statement								
Unqualified		1	4	13	4	5	24	29
Reviewed		2	15	10	1		31	28
Compiled		2	10	1			16	18
Tax Returns	3	6	3				22	16
Other	2	12	19	19	5	11	66	63
	23 (4/1-9/30/13)			125 (10/1/13-3/31/14)			4/1/09-3/31/10	4/1/10-3/31/11
	0-500M	**500M-2MM**	**2-10MM**	**10-50MM**	**50-100MM**	**100-250MM**	**ALL**	**ALL**
NUMBER OF STATEMENTS	5	23	51	43	10	16	159	154
ASSETS	%	%	%	%	%	%	%	%
Cash & Equivalents		20.6	9.0	12.7	5.7	8.3	11.0	10.9
Trade Receivables (net)		21.0	30.8	21.9	18.3	15.0	28.0	26.6
Inventory		34.4	26.0	24.8	20.5	15.6	24.1	24.6
All Other Current		1.5	2.3	2.4	2.4	2.9	3.0	3.2
Total Current		77.5	68.0	61.7	46.9	41.8	66.1	65.3
Fixed Assets (net)		12.3	20.7	21.5	12.6	11.5	20.5	19.5
Intangibles (net)		3.1	3.8	10.1	29.1	43.5	8.0	10.1
All Other Non-Current		7.1	7.5	6.7	11.4	3.1	5.3	5.1
Total		100.0	100.0	100.0	100.0	100.0	100.0	100.0
LIABILITIES								
Notes Payable-Short Term		9.4	15.3	8.7	7.9	1.5	8.4	9.6
Cur. Mat.-L.T.D.		.8	2.7	2.9	2.2	2.4	3.0	3.0
Trade Payables		18.0	12.0	9.2	7.6	6.3	14.0	11.5
Income Taxes Payable		.1	.1	.1	.4	.0	.2	.1
All Other Current		14.2	7.0	8.2	7.1	7.6	11.5	9.7
Total Current		42.5	37.0	29.0	25.2	17.8	37.1	33.9
Long-Term Debt		9.1	9.9	9.1	20.5	28.5	12.1	13.7
Deferred Taxes		.0	.5	.5	1.7	4.5	.5	.6
All Other Non-Current		27.4	3.5	7.1	8.9	6.9	6.5	8.3
Net Worth		21.0	49.1	54.3	43.7	42.3	43.7	43.6
Total Liabilties & Net Worth		100.0	100.0	100.0	100.0	100.0	100.0	100.0
INCOME DATA								
Net Sales		100.0	100.0	100.0	100.0	100.0	100.0	100.0
Gross Profit		43.6	42.7	46.4	39.3	44.5	43.3	44.6
Operating Expenses		43.5	35.1	38.0	37.0	34.7	35.9	36.7
Operating Profit		.1	7.6	8.4	2.3	9.7	7.4	7.9
All Other Expenses (net)		-.1	.1	.9	2.2	4.8	1.2	1.1
Profit Before Taxes		.2	7.5	7.5	.1	5.0	6.2	6.7
RATIOS								
		4.7	4.7	3.6	2.3	3.7	3.4	3.9
Current		2.4	2.2	2.0	1.8	2.2	2.1	2.3
		1.1	1.3	1.5	1.4	1.3	1.3	1.3
		2.6	2.8	2.3	1.4	1.8	2.2	2.3
Quick		.9	1.1	1.1	.9	1.1	1.1	1.1
		.5	.6	.6	.6	.7	.7	.7
		24 15.2	**37** 9.9	**39** 9.4	**41** 8.8	**42** 8.6	**34** 10.6	**35** 10.4
Sales/Receivables		**35** 10.4	**47** 7.8	**45** 8.2	**57** 6.4	**51** 7.1	**45** 8.1	**47** 7.7
		43 8.4	**63** 5.8	**59** 6.2	**74** 4.9	**63** 5.8	**63** 5.8	**57** 6.4
		28 13.1	**34** 10.7	**59** 6.2	**46** 8.0	**59** 6.2	**35** 10.4	**44** 8.3
Cost of Sales/Inventory		**76** 4.8	**72** 5.1	**99** 3.7	**101** 3.6	**104** 3.5	**70** 5.2	**73** 5.0
		228 1.6	**146** 2.5	**159** 2.3	**228** 1.6	**118** 3.1	**117** 3.1	**116** 3.1
		15 24.3	**16** 22.3	**21** 17.6	**28** 12.9	**26** 14.1	**18** 20.8	**17** 21.2
Cost of Sales/Payables		**21** 17.0	**26** 14.3	**38** 9.5	**37** 9.9	**36** 10.2	**31** 11.9	**28** 13.1
		68 5.4	**47** 7.7	**54** 6.7	**51** 7.2	**50** 7.3	**52** 7.0	**46** 8.0
		3.9	3.7	3.1	3.9	3.2	4.0	3.8
Sales/Working Capital		5.5	6.1	5.1	5.9	5.5	6.7	6.1
		21.4	18.4	9.2	9.2	14.8	18.3	17.6
		9.5	34.8	43.2		12.0	24.6	21.7
EBIT/Interest		(14) 2.2	(38) 10.5	(36) 14.8		2.2	(134) 6.3	(130) 5.9
		-.9	2.5	2.9		1.0	2.0	1.8
			4.9	21.5			13.7	14.3
Net Profit + Depr., Dep., Amort./Cur. Mat. L/T/D			(10) 2.9	(14) 6.2			(41) 4.5	(30) 3.6
			1.3	2.3			1.5	2.7
		.0	.1	.3	.3	.4	.2	.2
Fixed/Worth		.2	.3	.5	.7	-.6	.5	.5
		1.2	.8	.8	-.9	-.1	1.4	1.9
		.3	.2	.4	.8	.8	.4	.5
Debt/Worth		.7	.7	.9	2.3	-3.4	1.2	1.4
		-116.6	1.9	1.8	-6.0	-1.7	4.7	5.4
		43.6	50.0	32.6			50.1	48.3
% Profit Before Taxes/Tangible Net Worth		(17) 11.9	(46) 23.9	(39) 20.6			(136) 25.0	(126) 26.0
		-4.3	7.5	4.4			7.3	8.9
		26.6	24.3	19.8	12.2	7.9	23.9	22.7
% Profit Before Taxes/Total Assets		7.7	9.3	8.2	3.4	4.3	9.8	8.8
		-2.0	2.7	2.2	-5.9	.1	1.5	1.9
		498.8	64.7	20.1	13.5	25.5	28.5	30.8
Sales/Net Fixed Assets		52.4	14.4	7.3	10.3	11.4	12.3	12.7
		15.4	4.5	4.6	7.1	6.3	5.5	5.8
		3.1	2.8	2.0	1.3	1.5	2.9	2.7
Sales/Total Assets		2.2	2.0	1.5	1.1	.9	2.1	1.9
		1.5	1.5	1.1	1.0	.6	1.5	1.4
		.4	.6	1.3			1.0	1.1
% Depr., Dep., Amort./Sales		(11) .8	(44) 1.4	(37) 2.9			(132) 1.9	(120) 1.9
		2.1	3.0	5.8			3.6	3.5
		3.5	1.6				2.6	3.7
% Officers', Directors' Owners' Comp/Sales		(11) 6.5	(16) 3.3				(51) 4.4	(39) 6.4
		10.6	5.8				9.9	10.0
Net Sales ($)	**6445M**	**60187M**	**538670M**	**1425398M**	**779743M**	**2830826M**	**6258573M**	**5302568M**
Total Assets ($)	**1555M**	**26442M**	**249663M**	**978727M**	**679505M**	**2808318M**	**4374966M**	**3848382M**

M = $ thousand MM = $ million

See Pages 9 through 22 for Explanation of Ratios and Data

Comparative Historical Data | **Current Data Sorted by Sales**

4/1/11-3/31/12 ALL	4/1/12-3/31/13 ALL	4/1/13-3/31/14 ALL	Type of Statement	0-1MM	1-3MM	3-5MM	5-10MM	10-25MM	25MM & OVER
33	24	27	Unqualified		1	1	4	6	15
22	20	28	Reviewed			4	6	11	7
13	12	13	Compiled		3	2	3	3	2
28	11	12	Tax Returns	2	5	1	2	2	
66	64	68	Other	2	8	4	13	7	34
				23 (4/1-9/30/13)			125 (10/1/13-3/31/14)		
162	131	148	**NUMBER OF STATEMENTS**	4	17	12	28	29	58
%	%	%	**ASSETS**	%	%	%	%	%	%
10.5	9.4	11.6	Cash & Equivalents		16.7	13.0	9.8	10.9	10.7
27.0	25.8	24.6	Trade Receivables (net)		21.9	22.8	29.5	29.3	20.8
26.3	24.8	25.1	Inventory		29.8	26.1	28.1	24.8	22.1
3.0	2.5	2.2	All Other Current		.6	3.5	.4	4.4	2.3
66.9	62.5	63.5	Total Current		69.1	65.4	67.7	69.4	55.8
17.4	19.1	18.1	Fixed Assets (net)		17.9	19.3	16.1	23.8	16.3
10.2	11.7	11.5	Intangibles (net)		6.5	8.5	5.4	2.9	20.7
5.6	6.7	7.0	All Other Non-Current		6.6	6.7	10.8	3.9	7.2
100.0	100.0	100.0	Total		100.0	100.0	100.0	100.0	100.0
			LIABILITIES						
11.3	11.8	10.3	Notes Payable-Short Term		11.6	3.9	21.5	9.1	6.6
2.6	3.9	2.3	Cur. Mat.-L.T.D.		.4	2.6	2.1	4.2	2.0
11.0	11.5	11.5	Trade Payables		16.8	15.4	12.9	11.4	8.6
.4	.3	.1	Income Taxes Payable		.1	.4	.0	.1	.1
12.3	7.8	9.4	All Other Current		11.0	14.1	9.9	7.0	8.2
37.5	35.3	33.6	Total Current		39.9	36.5	46.5	31.7	25.4
11.0	12.4	12.0	Long-Term Debt		9.1	13.7	9.4	9.0	15.9
.5	.6	.9	Deferred Taxes		.0	.5	.1	.8	1.8
8.1	7.2	10.5	All Other Non-Current		41.9	4.2	4.6	2.7	8.1
42.9	44.5	43.0	Net Worth		9.1	45.0	39.4	55.8	48.8
100.0	100.0	100.0	Total Liabilties & Net Worth		100.0	100.0	100.0	100.0	100.0
			INCOME DATA						
100.0	100.0	100.0	Net Sales		100.0	100.0	100.0	100.0	100.0
45.6	44.7	44.4	Gross Profit		41.6	50.4	43.0	47.8	43.0
38.8	36.3	38.0	Operating Expenses		41.5	40.6	38.3	42.3	33.1
6.8	8.4	6.4	Operating Profit		.1	9.8	4.7	5.4	9.9
1.0	1.2	1.0	All Other Expenses (net)		.2	-1.1	-.1	.5	2.3
5.8	7.2	5.5	Profit Before Taxes		-.1	11.0	4.8	4.9	7.6
			RATIOS						
3.6	3.4	3.8			5.8	4.7	4.5	3.4	3.8
2.2	1.9	2.1	Current		1.6	2.0	2.1	2.2	2.1
1.3	1.2	1.4			.9	1.1	1.0	1.6	1.5
2.3	1.9	2.5			2.9	2.4	2.7	2.2	2.1
1.0	1.0	1.1	Quick		.7	1.2	1.0	1.1	1.2
.6	.6	.6			.5	.5	.6	.6	.7
36 10.2	35 10.4	37 9.8			23 15.7	27 13.3	41 9.0	38 9.6	39 9.4
45 8.2	46 8.0	45 8.2	Sales/Receivables		33 11.2	40 9.2	51 7.2	43 8.5	47 7.7
57 6.4	57 6.4	60 6.1			42 8.6	49 7.5	81 4.5	63 5.8	59 6.2
43 8.5	42 8.6	49 7.5			12 30.1	31 11.7	51 7.1	34 10.8	54 6.7
81 4.5	79 4.6	85 4.3	Cost of Sales/Inventory		69 5.3	62 5.9	91 4.0	81 4.5	89 4.1
140 2.6	135 2.7	146 2.5			159 2.3	126 2.9	166 2.2	166 2.2	130 2.8
14 25.8	16 22.2	19 19.1			13 28.2	19 19.1	17 21.9	21 17.8	21 17.2
30 12.1	30 12.0	33 10.9	Cost of Sales/Payables		20 18.0	24 15.4	36 10.2	36 10.1	35 10.5
52 7.0	49 7.5	54 6.8			74 4.9	66 5.5	69 5.3	76 4.8	48 7.6
3.5	4.2	3.4			3.8	3.5	3.0	3.9	3.4
5.9	6.4	5.5	Sales/Working Capital		5.3	8.9	5.9	5.8	5.2
16.7	22.3	13.6			-220.5	NM	-102.5	8.8	11.0
20.5	25.4	26.7			29.6		23.9	23.2	35.9
(138) 6.6	(114) 6.3	(117) 6.8	EBIT/Interest		(11) 5.3		(22) 4.8	(25) 11.6	(49) 9.4
1.9	1.4	1.5			1.1		2.2	1.6	1.6
13.5	7.4	11.9						4.9	18.7
(40) 4.6	(39) 2.5	(36) 4.4	Net Profit + Depr., Dep., Amort./Cur. Mat. L/T/D					(11) 4.3	(19) 7.2
1.0	.4	1.4						.9	3.2
.2	.2	.2			.0	.1	.1	.2	.3
.4	.5	.4	Fixed/Worth		.2	.6	.4	.4	.6
1.6	1.8	1.2			1.0	NM	1.2	.8	-3.3
.5	.6	.4			.3	.2	.2	.3	.6
1.2	1.0	1.0	Debt/Worth		1.1	1.0	.9	.9	1.1
9.1	5.9	3.6			-9.8	NM	5.5	1.6	-43.7
51.1	53.2	41.8			33.9		35.3	44.4	42.0
(129) 23.6	(109) 24.1	(118) 20.1	% Profit Before Taxes/Tangible Net Worth		(12) 6.9		(23) 18.4	(28) 27.7	(43) 21.2
6.7	4.0	4.4			-4.0		5.0	2.7	12.2
22.5	22.6	18.5			22.5	45.7	11.2	23.3	19.0
8.5	8.6	7.5	% Profit Before Taxes/Total Assets		8.1	7.4	5.7	11.6	7.6
1.2	.9	1.3			-6.1	1.8	.9	1.5	1.8
49.6	30.8	35.7			681.7	143.5	74.2	22.9	25.9
15.3	12.2	12.7	Sales/Net Fixed Assets		34.6	32.6	14.0	8.1	10.1
6.7	5.4	5.5			9.9	4.0	4.8	4.4	5.6
2.7	2.6	2.5			3.1	3.2	2.6	2.8	1.9
1.8	1.9	1.7	Sales/Total Assets		2.0	2.1	1.9	1.9	1.5
1.3	1.3	1.1			1.4	1.1	1.3	1.3	1.0
.8	1.0	.8			.2		.7	.8	1.5
(114) 1.7	(110) 1.9	(110) 1.9	% Depr., Dep., Amort./Sales		(12) .7		(21) 1.4	(28) 1.8	(41) 2.2
3.3	3.5	3.8			.9		3.7	4.7	4.1
2.7	1.9	1.6							
(56) 4.9	(32) 4.6	(36) 3.7	% Officers', Directors' Owners' Comp/Sales						
8.8	6.8	6.5							
5182787M	**5411544M**	**5641269M**	Net Sales ($)	**3140M**	**31527M**	**49168M**	**198565M**	**441325M**	**4917544M**
4423387M	**4030122M**	**4744210M**	Total Assets ($)	**3891M**	**16302M**	**39732M**	**135756M**	**287787M**	**4260742M**

M = $ thousand MM = $ million

See Pages 9 through 22 for Explanation of Ratios and Data

Current Data Sorted by Assets / Comparative Historical Data

0-500M	500M-2MM	2-10MM	10-50MM	50-100MM	100-250MM		4/1/09-3/31/10 ALL	4/1/10-3/31/11 ALL
						Type of Statement		
			2		4	Unqualified	9	5
		2	3	1		Reviewed	6	8
1	1	1				Compiled	1	4
1	4	1				Tax Returns	5	8
1	7	3	6	2	4	Other	20	20
	8 (4/1-9/30/13)		36 (10/1/13-3/31/14)					
3	12	7	11	3	8	**NUMBER OF STATEMENTS**	41	45
%	%	%	%	%	%	**ASSETS**	%	%
	16.4		9.3			Cash & Equivalents	6.8	8.6
	22.7		18.2			Trade Receivables (net)	22.0	26.0
	23.4		27.1			Inventory	27.0	18.7
	2.7		1.4			All Other Current	2.7	2.2
	65.1		56.0			Total Current	58.4	55.6
	16.0		25.8			Fixed Assets (net)	20.1	25.4
	4.1		5.9			Intangibles (net)	16.3	14.6
	14.8		12.3			All Other Non-Current	5.3	4.3
	100.0		100.0			Total	100.0	100.0
						LIABILITIES		
	16.5		8.9			Notes Payable-Short Term	10.4	10.4
	1.6		4.2			Cur. Mat.-L.T.D.	2.6	3.7
	16.0		12.9			Trade Payables	9.1	13.3
	.0		.1			Income Taxes Payable	.3	.2
	12.3		9.0			All Other Current	10.7	9.8
	46.4		35.1			Total Current	33.2	37.5
	14.8		12.9			Long-Term Debt	13.7	18.7
	.0		.9			Deferred Taxes	.5	1.2
	6.7		2.3			All Other Non-Current	2.8	3.2
	32.0		48.7			Net Worth	49.7	39.4
	100.0		100.0			Total Liabilties & Net Worth	100.0	100.0
						INCOME DATA		
	100.0		100.0			Net Sales	100.0	100.0
	48.6		50.7			Gross Profit	45.5	44.2
	46.2		49.8			Operating Expenses	40.9	39.9
	2.4		1.0			Operating Profit	4.6	4.3
	.6		.7			All Other Expenses (net)	1.4	1.4
	1.7		.3			Profit Before Taxes	3.2	2.9
						RATIOS		
	2.0		1.8				2.7	2.6
	1.5		1.4			Current	1.7	1.7
	.9		1.1				1.4	1.2
	1.4		1.0				1.4	1.7
	1.1		.6			Quick	.8	1.0
	.4		.3				.6	.7
	0 UND		**30** 12.0				**30** 12.3	**37** 9.9
	30 12.3		**46** 8.0			Sales/Receivables	**41** 8.9	**43** 8.4
	38 9.7		**65** 5.6				**50** 7.2	**49** 7.4
	1 623.5		**104** 3.5				**59** 6.2	**20** 18.6
	33 11.2		**126** 2.9			Cost of Sales/Inventory	**98** 3.7	**64** 5.7
	126 2.9		**182** 2.0				**142** 2.6	**118** 3.1
	20 18.5		**31** 11.8				**16** 23.0	**17** 21.1
	35 10.5		**64** 5.7			Cost of Sales/Payables	**30** 12.2	**30** 12.0
	52 7.0		**96** 3.8				**58** 6.3	**52** 7.0
	7.2		4.7				6.2	5.7
	21.5		9.1			Sales/Working Capital	8.1	12.0
	NM		76.3				14.3	24.5
	13.2						11.9	15.7
	(11) 7.9					EBIT/Interest	(38) 4.8	(42) 7.2
	2.0						1.2	1.3
							4.1	7.0
						Net Profit + Depr., Dep., Amort./Cur. Mat. L/T/D	(14) 2.2	(12) 3.3
							1.5	.5
	.2		.3				.2	.3
	.3		.8			Fixed/Worth	.6	.9
	NM		1.1				1.2	2.0
	1.2		.4				.8	.9
	1.6		1.9			Debt/Worth	1.2	1.7
	NM		3.1				3.3	5.5
			19.7				55.5	74.1
			8.2			% Profit Before Taxes/Tangible Net Worth	(37) 24.5	(39) 34.6
			-4.2				5.9	8.7
	19.4		6.9				17.6	16.8
	9.7		4.4			% Profit Before Taxes/Total Assets	7.5	8.4
	2.9		-.9				.8	-.8
	59.8		30.9				26.0	36.1
	30.9		5.0			Sales/Net Fixed Assets	11.4	9.5
	19.0		2.5				5.2	3.9
	3.9		1.8				2.8	3.2
	3.3		1.2			Sales/Total Assets	1.9	1.9
	3.0		.9				1.1	1.4
			1.2				.9	1.0
			2.1			% Depr., Dep., Amort./Sales	(33) 2.5	(34) 2.3
			5.0				3.9	4.1
						% Officers', Directors' Owners' Comp/Sales		
2878M	**55855M**	**100925M**	**358611M**	**183043M**	**1454578M**	Net Sales ($)	**2551656M**	**2470934M**
1028M	**15963M**	**32880M**	**255679M**	**177415M**	**1166093M**	Total Assets ($)	**1806568M**	**1774173M**

M = $ thousand MM = $ million

See Pages 9 through 22 for Explanation of Ratios and Data

Comparative Historical Data / Current Data Sorted by Sales

4/1/11-3/31/12 ALL	4/1/12-3/31/13 ALL	4/1/13-3/31/14 ALL	Type of Statement	0-1MM	1-3MM	3-5MM	5-10MM	10-25MM	25MM & OVER
9	4	6	Unqualified					1	5
9	6	6	Reviewed					2	4
4	2	3	Compiled	1			1	1	
6	9	6	Tax Returns		1	4		1	
22	27	23	Other	1	1	5	1	6	9
					8 (4/1-9/30/13)		36 (10/1/13-3/31/14)		
50	48	44	NUMBER OF STATEMENTS	2	2	9	2	11	18
%	%	%	**ASSETS**	%	%	%	%	%	%
10.5	16.2	12.5	Cash & Equivalents					8.9	9.4
23.2	24.2	20.7	Trade Receivables (net)					27.6	18.3
24.4	22.0	22.9	Inventory					23.8	21.7
2.4	2.9	3.8	All Other Current					1.6	1.7
60.5	65.3	60.0	Total Current					61.9	51.1
20.4	17.5	19.8	Fixed Assets (net)					25.5	20.8
14.0	10.8	10.9	Intangibles (net)					2.9	20.9
5.1	6.4	9.3	All Other Non-Current					9.7	7.3
100.0	100.0	100.0	Total					100.0	100.0
			LIABILITIES						
9.5	9.2	10.7	Notes Payable-Short Term					9.7	9.2
2.3	2.8	2.8	Cur. Mat.-L.T.D.					3.7	2.9
9.8	12.0	12.0	Trade Payables					14.5	9.2
.4	.1	.1	Income Taxes Payable					.2	.0
10.0	14.0	12.1	All Other Current					8.2	11.3
31.9	38.1	37.7	Total Current					36.3	32.6
11.5	19.3	16.7	Long-Term Debt					8.5	17.6
1.3	.6	.9	Deferred Taxes					1.2	1.4
3.8	4.9	4.0	All Other Non-Current					1.6	4.3
51.5	37.1	40.7	Net Worth					52.3	44.2
100.0	100.0	100.0	Total Liabilties & Net Worth					100.0	100.0
			INCOME DATA						
100.0	100.0	100.0	Net Sales					100.0	100.0
49.1	50.3	49.7	Gross Profit					43.3	50.9
42.7	40.9	43.8	Operating Expenses					39.9	43.8
6.4	9.4	5.9	Operating Profit					3.4	7.1
1.0	.9	.9	All Other Expenses (net)					-.2	1.8
5.4	8.5	4.9	Profit Before Taxes					3.6	5.3
			RATIOS						
3.6	3.5	3.2						3.3	3.1
1.9	1.6	1.4	Current					1.5	1.4
1.4	1.1	1.1						1.1	1.1
1.7	1.9	1.3						1.4	1.3
1.2	1.0	.8	Quick					.9	.7
.6	.6	.6						.5	.6
35 10.5	**29** 12.8	**28** 12.9						**26** 14.3	**38** 9.7
41 8.9	**40** 9.1	**39** 9.3	Sales/Receivables					**41** 8.9	**49** 7.4
50 7.3	**49** 7.5	**48** 7.6						**47** 7.8	**59** 6.2
60 6.1	**13** 27.9	**29** 12.6						**13** 28.9	**83** 4.4
114 3.2	**79** 4.6	**104** 3.5	Cost of Sales/Inventory					**99** 3.7	**118** 3.1
159 2.3	**130** 2.8	**146** 2.5						**152** 2.4	**159** 2.3
19 18.8	**10** 35.3	**12** 29.4						**23** 15.8	**13** 28.6
30 12.0	**30** 12.3	**31** 11.7	Cost of Sales/Payables					**36** 10.2	**31** 11.7
45 8.1	**61** 6.0	**56** 6.5						**64** 5.7	**48** 7.6
4.0	5.2	5.1						5.2	3.4
6.6	7.7	12.4	Sales/Working Capital					12.8	10.4
14.5	66.8	75.3						70.1	40.2
42.6	27.2	12.3							12.4
(46) 8.4	(41) 6.4	(38) 7.8	EBIT/Interest						(17) 8.7
2.1	3.5	1.7							5.1
11.9	22.1	6.5							
(19) 6.7	(10) 2.0	(12) 2.1	Net Profit + Depr., Dep., Amort./Cur. Mat. L/T/D						
2.4	1.2	1.1							
.2	.1	.2						.2	.4
.5	.7	.7	Fixed/Worth					.5	1.0
1.5	3.0	1.6						1.0	NM
.5	.6	.7						.3	1.4
1.4	1.7	1.9	Debt/Worth					1.6	2.4
3.3	29.6	4.1						2.1	NM
61.6	64.8	25.8						19.7	28.3
(45) 25.5	(40) 24.4	(35) 15.6	% Profit Before Taxes/Tangible Net Worth					8.2	(14) 15.6
7.0	3.9	6.7						-4.2	-11.3
18.0	25.9	15.4						8.5	13.6
9.9	10.2	5.9	% Profit Before Taxes/Total Assets					4.4	6.4
2.8	1.7	2.8						-.9	3.0
21.3	47.4	34.0						24.5	15.3
11.3	15.7	13.2	Sales/Net Fixed Assets					12.4	7.8
5.0	9.2	5.0						5.0	3.3
2.4	3.8	3.2						5.0	1.7
1.8	2.4	1.9	Sales/Total Assets					2.4	1.3
1.3	1.4	1.2						1.2	1.0
1.5	.8	1.1							1.1
(37) 2.2	(36) 1.5	(33) 1.6	% Depr., Dep., Amort./Sales						(13) 2.0
3.6	2.4	2.6							3.1
4.7	3.1	2.8							
(15) 6.6	(21) 6.3	(13) 7.4	% Officers', Directors' Owners' Comp/Sales						
9.0	9.7	11.3							
2184071M	2014360M	2155890M	Net Sales ($)	1287M	2682M	38765M	10654M	166858M	1935644M
1896241M	1472625M	1649058M	Total Assets ($)	640M	957M	15447M	3206M	82743M	1546065M

M = $ thousand MM = $ million

See Pages 9 through 22 for Explanation of Ratios and Data

Current Data Sorted by Assets							Comparative Historical Data	
						Type of Statement		
			1		3	Unqualified	14	7
		2	2			Reviewed	3	5
1		3				Compiled	4	4
	4					Tax Returns	3	2
1		2	7	1	2	Other	12	16
	4 (4/1-9/30/13)		25 (10/1/13-3/31/14)				4/1/09-3/31/10	4/1/10-3/31/11
0-500M	500M-2MM	2-10MM	10-50MM	50-100MM	100-250MM		ALL	ALL
2	4	7	10	1	5	NUMBER OF STATEMENTS	36	34
%	%	%	%	%	%	**ASSETS**	%	%
			9.4			Cash & Equivalents	7.8	7.2
			17.9			Trade Receivables (net)	23.2	24.2
			21.9			Inventory	21.5	24.0
			2.4			All Other Current	3.8	2.7
			51.6			Total Current	56.3	58.1
			8.3			Fixed Assets (net)	21.6	20.2
			33.9			Intangibles (net)	14.0	13.4
			6.2			All Other Non-Current	8.1	8.3
			100.0			Total	100.0	100.0
						LIABILITIES		
			4.5			Notes Payable-Short Term	8.0	6.6
			3.4			Cur. Mat.-L.T.D.	3.7	3.4
			13.1			Trade Payables	16.3	18.4
			.0			Income Taxes Payable	.4	.1
			7.6			All Other Current	9.6	8.2
			28.7			Total Current	38.0	36.6
			8.5			Long-Term Debt	14.7	16.7
			.0			Deferred Taxes	.5	.9
			8.1			All Other Non-Current	7.9	4.6
			54.7			Net Worth	38.8	41.2
			100.0			Total Liabilities & Net Worth	100.0	100.0
						INCOME DATA		
			100.0			Net Sales	100.0	100.0
			47.8			Gross Profit	44.9	43.0
			33.3			Operating Expenses	38.4	34.9
			14.5			Operating Profit	6.5	8.0
			1.1			All Other Expenses (net)	1.3	1.5
			13.4			Profit Before Taxes	5.1	6.5
						RATIOS		
			2.2				2.7	2.5
			1.7			Current	1.4	1.6
			1.4				1.1	1.2
			1.7				1.3	1.4
			1.1			Quick	.8	.8
			.9				.5	.6
			29 12.4				**30** 12.1	**33** 11.2
			41 9.0			Sales/Receivables	**39** 9.5	**43** 8.6
			54 6.8				**45** 8.1	**49** 7.5
			36 10.0				**34** 10.8	**31** 11.8
			64 5.7			Cost of Sales/Inventory	**81** 4.5	**76** 4.8
			140 2.6				**126** 2.9	**136** 2.7
			15 24.3				**25** 14.9	**26** 14.0
			44 8.3			Cost of Sales/Payables	**41** 8.9	**60** 6.1
			74 4.9				**67** 5.5	**80** 4.5
			4.8				4.6	4.3
			7.2			Sales/Working Capital	12.1	9.6
			12.0				67.5	26.0
			25.4				15.9	12.9
			14.7			EBIT/Interest	(35) 2.5	(32) 4.8
			6.5				1.0	1.5
							8.8	6.7
						Net Profit + Depr., Dep., Amort./Cur. Mat. L/T/D	(13) 3.1	(12) 2.5
							.6	1.2
			.2				.3	.3
			.5			Fixed/Worth	.7	.6
			.6				4.0	2.9
			1.3				.7	.6
			2.4			Debt/Worth	1.8	1.5
			4.4				16.3	15.9
							38.1	38.8
						% Profit Before Taxes/Tangible Net Worth	(29) 10.4	(27) 18.0
							-1.0	6.4
			16.7				12.9	11.8
			11.1			% Profit Before Taxes/Total Assets	4.0	8.0
			6.9				.1	2.4
			44.3				34.9	48.0
			20.9			Sales/Net Fixed Assets	12.7	15.9
			13.0				5.1	6.2
			2.0				3.1	2.7
			1.5			Sales/Total Assets	1.6	1.9
			.6				.9	1.2
							1.2	.7
						% Depr., Dep., Amort./Sales	(28) 2.0	(25) 2.2
							3.0	3.3
								3.1
						% Officers', Directors' Owners' Comp/Sales		(11) 4.9
								6.3
2723M	12295M	70530M	291537M	111444M	1040529M	Net Sales ($)	1769103M	2131627M
727M	4776M	28536M	212631M	97288M	834864M	Total Assets ($)	1339203M	1413330M

M = $ thousand MM = $ million

See Pages 9 through 22 for Explanation of Ratios and Data

Comparative Historical Data				Current Data Sorted by Sales					
			Type of Statement						
5	10	4	Unqualified						4
3		4	Reviewed				1	3	
2	4	4	Compiled		1		2	1	
4		4	Tax Returns	1	1	1	1		
10	15	13	Other	1		1	1	4	6
4/1/11-3/31/12 ALL	**4/1/12-3/31/13 ALL**	**4/1/13-3/31/14 ALL**		**4 (4/1-9/30/13)**			**25 (10/1/13-3/31/14)**		
				0-1MM	**1-3MM**	**3-5MM**	**5-10MM**	**10-25MM**	**25MM & OVER**
24	29	29	**NUMBER OF STATEMENTS**	2	2	2	5	8	10
%	%	%	**ASSETS**	%	%	%	%	%	%
8.3	10.4	8.3	Cash & Equivalents						9.6
24.6	18.1	21.7	Trade Receivables (net)						19.6
22.4	24.8	26.2	Inventory						24.3
4.0	4.1	3.8	All Other Current						3.8
59.3	57.3	60.0	Total Current						57.3
19.3	16.7	19.3	Fixed Assets (net)						19.8
15.0	17.2	15.7	Intangibles (net)						14.9
6.5	8.8	4.9	All Other Non-Current						8.0
100.0	100.0	100.0	Total						100.0
			LIABILITIES						
6.5	6.6	7.7	Notes Payable-Short Term						5.4
5.7	5.5	3.2	Cur. Mat.-L.T.D.						3.7
13.9	12.3	15.0	Trade Payables						16.3
.3	.4	.0	Income Taxes Payable						.0
6.6	6.6	6.7	All Other Current						5.1
33.0	31.4	32.6	Total Current						30.5
14.9	18.0	17.3	Long-Term Debt						15.2
.5	.4	.2	Deferred Taxes						.5
10.8	4.4	9.7	All Other Non-Current						11.4
40.9	45.8	40.3	Net Worth						42.4
100.0	100.0	100.0	Total Liabilties & Net Worth						100.0
			INCOME DATA						
100.0	100.0	100.0	Net Sales						100.0
48.6	50.4	46.5	Gross Profit						40.8
39.6	37.2	37.3	Operating Expenses						29.8
9.1	13.1	9.2	Operating Profit						10.9
1.9	1.5	1.1	All Other Expenses (net)						1.8
7.1	11.7	8.1	Profit Before Taxes						9.1
			RATIOS						
2.6	2.9	2.4							2.3
1.9	1.8	1.8	Current						2.0
1.3	1.4	1.3							1.6
1.9	1.9	1.4							1.7
.9	.9	1.0	Quick						.8
.6	.5	.6							.6
36 10.0	**26** 14.3	**31** 11.8							**36** 10.1
45 8.1	**38** 9.5	**40** 9.1	Sales/Receivables						**45** 8.1
51 7.1	**47** 7.8	**51** 7.2							**56** 6.5
32 11.4	**44** 8.3	**35** 10.5							**29** 12.7
111 3.3	**101** 3.6	**118** 3.1	Cost of Sales/Inventory						**159** 2.3
146 2.5	**146** 2.5	**166** 2.2							**174** 2.1
27 13.7	**17** 22.0	**22** 16.8							**33** 11.1
53 6.9	**38** 9.6	**45** 8.1	Cost of Sales/Payables						**56** 6.5
85 4.3	**72** 5.1	**79** 4.6							**85** 4.3
3.7	4.1	5.0							4.2
5.9	7.4	6.9	Sales/Working Capital						5.1
21.3	17.4	10.2							7.1
31.3	26.3	38.2							55.7
(21) 7.7	(27) 16.1	(28) 11.4	EBIT/Interest						12.9
1.6	4.7	3.4							3.5
	15.2								
	(12) 4.8		Net Profit + Depr., Dep., Amort./Cur. Mat. L/T/D						
	1.1								
.4	.2	.1							.2
.7	.5	.5	Fixed/Worth						.6
NM	14.9	1.4							NM
.8	.8	1.0							.9
2.1	1.7	2.1	Debt/Worth						1.4
NM	130.9	4.7							NM
54.5	71.9	71.2							
(18) 22.3	(23) 34.2	(23) 31.3	% Profit Before Taxes/Tangible Net Worth						
1.3	16.2	15.9							
14.1	19.0	16.9							20.6
9.0	14.5	10.2	% Profit Before Taxes/Total Assets						9.5
2.4	6.2	4.2							4.0
18.6	26.9	40.8							20.1
10.2	15.8	17.6	Sales/Net Fixed Assets						11.3
6.1	8.9	5.5							4.0
2.4	2.6	2.6							1.9
1.5	2.0	1.7	Sales/Total Assets						1.5
1.1	.9	1.2							1.0
1.7	1.4	.9							
(19) 2.3	(24) 2.1	(24) 1.9	% Depr., Dep., Amort./Sales						
5.0	3.5	3.2							
	1.7	2.6							
	(10) 3.9	(10) 3.9	% Officers', Directors' Owners' Comp/Sales						
	6.9	7.4							
1449680M	**1608174M**	**1529058M**	Net Sales ($)	**1565M**	**3144M**	**8182M**	**39892M**	**138683M**	**1337592M**
1073286M	**1322458M**	**1178822M**	Total Assets ($)	**876M**	**1280M**	**3993M**	**17012M**	**127054M**	**1028607M**

M = $ thousand MM = $ million

See Pages 9 through 22 for Explanation of Ratios and Data

Current Data Sorted by Assets							Comparative Historical Data	
						Type of Statement		
		1		1		Unqualified	2	3
		2	2			Reviewed	2	2
	4					Compiled	5	4
6	3	1	1			Tax Returns	17	21
3	3	2			2	Other	19	10
9 (4/1-9/30/13)		22 (10/1/13-3/31/14)					**4/1/09-3/31/10 ALL**	**4/1/10-3/31/11 ALL**
0-500M	**500M-2MM**	**2-10MM**	**10-50MM**	**50-100MM**	**100-250MM**			
9	10	6	3	1	2	**NUMBER OF STATEMENTS**	45	40
%	%	%	%	%	%	**ASSETS**	%	%
	14.4					Cash & Equivalents	13.7	15.1
	39.0					Trade Receivables (net)	27.0	23.6
	7.2					Inventory	7.1	4.2
	1.0					All Other Current	3.9	3.1
	61.6					Total Current	51.6	46.0
	31.6					Fixed Assets (net)	29.2	35.2
	1.6					Intangibles (net)	7.5	10.4
	5.2					All Other Non-Current	11.7	8.4
	100.0					Total	100.0	100.0
						LIABILITIES		
	7.4					Notes Payable-Short Term	12.9	12.4
	7.7					Cur. Mat.-L.T.D.	4.8	8.0
	12.3					Trade Payables	8.7	13.4
	1.0					Income Taxes Payable	.4	.4
	11.4					All Other Current	10.4	12.1
	39.8					Total Current	37.3	46.3
	31.7					Long-Term Debt	27.4	25.1
	.4					Deferred Taxes	.4	.5
	2.6					All Other Non-Current	3.2	6.0
	25.5					Net Worth	31.7	22.1
	100.0					Total Liabilties & Net Worth	100.0	100.0
						INCOME DATA		
	100.0					Net Sales	100.0	100.0
						Gross Profit		
	94.2					Operating Expenses	93.7	95.6
	5.8					Operating Profit	6.3	4.4
	3.7					All Other Expenses (net)	.9	1.7
	2.1					Profit Before Taxes	5.5	2.6
						RATIOS		
	2.8						3.4	2.2
	1.8					Current	1.5	1.1
	.8						.8	.5
	2.2						2.6	1.7
	1.4					Quick	1.1	.9
	.7						.6	.5
	0 UND						**1** 309.9	**0** UND
	36 10.1					Sales/Receivables	**35** 10.5	**33** 10.9
	38 9.7						**40** 9.0	**41** 9.0
						Cost of Sales/Inventory		
						Cost of Sales/Payables		
	8.8						8.2	14.1
	14.4					Sales/Working Capital	31.2	74.5
	-36.5						-56.3	-12.7
							24.2	9.8
						EBIT/Interest	(37) 5.0	(30) 3.5
							1.7	.6
						Net Profit + Depr., Dep., Amort./Cur. Mat. L/T/D		
	.4						.3	.6
	.7					Fixed/Worth	1.0	3.0
	NM						UND	NM
	.8						.4	.8
	1.6					Debt/Worth	3.7	6.7
	NM						UND	-5.9
							109.6	172.8
						% Profit Before Taxes/Tangible Net Worth	(35) 52.2	(29) 43.1
							19.7	17.8
	10.0						36.1	30.8
	6.6					% Profit Before Taxes/Total Assets	12.9	11.5
	1.1						3.0	.5
	52.4						51.7	40.0
	23.1					Sales/Net Fixed Assets	18.2	16.7
	9.2						6.5	6.1
	5.6						5.5	5.2
	4.3					Sales/Total Assets	3.6	3.9
	3.3						2.2	2.5
							1.2	1.1
						% Depr., Dep., Amort./Sales	(31) 1.8	(29) 2.0
							3.6	3.3
							5.0	4.1
						% Officers', Directors' Owners' Comp/Sales	(30) 8.6	(24) 6.5
							13.5	10.3
8747M	**48514M**	**58662M**	**66557M**	**320411M**	**253392M**	Net Sales ($)	**421439M**	**709382M**
1338M	**11513M**	**25636M**	**57033M**	**84538M**	**276778M**	Total Assets ($)	**270208M**	**464337M**

M = $ thousand MM = $ million

See Pages 9 through 22 for Explanation of Ratios and Data

Comparative Historical Data / Current Data Sorted by Sales

4/1/11-3/31/12 ALL	4/1/12-3/31/13 ALL	4/1/13-3/31/14 ALL	Type of Statement	0-1MM	1-3MM	3-5MM	5-10MM	10-25MM	25MM & OVER
1	1	2	Unqualified				1		1
2	2	4	Reviewed		1	1			2
7	4	4	Compiled		2	2			
19	11	11	Tax Returns	6	1		1	3	
17	14	10	Other	1	2	2	1	2	2
				9 (4/1-9/30/13)			22 (10/1/13-3/31/14)		
46	32	31	NUMBER OF STATEMENTS	7	6	5	3	5	5
%	%	%	**ASSETS**	%	%	%	%	%	%
16.5	12.6	10.3	Cash & Equivalents						
25.7	29.7	32.4	Trade Receivables (net)						
4.6	5.2	4.9	Inventory						
1.5	1.1	1.1	All Other Current						
48.2	48.6	48.6	Total Current						
30.5	36.1	27.6	Fixed Assets (net)						
14.4	12.5	7.9	Intangibles (net)						
7.0	2.7	15.9	All Other Non-Current						
100.0	100.0	100.0	Total						
			LIABILITIES						
15.5	17.4	12.3	Notes Payable-Short Term						
5.0	4.0	3.4	Cur. Mat.-L.T.D.						
11.8	9.2	9.4	Trade Payables						
.0	.0	.3	Income Taxes Payable						
13.8	11.7	11.8	All Other Current						
46.1	42.2	37.3	Total Current						
24.2	31.3	24.0	Long-Term Debt						
.1	.7	.4	Deferred Taxes						
2.8	10.2	5.4	All Other Non-Current						
26.9	15.5	32.9	Net Worth						
100.0	100.0	100.0	Total Liabilities & Net Worth						
			INCOME DATA						
100.0	100.0	100.0	Net Sales						
			Gross Profit						
88.8	90.6	93.5	Operating Expenses						
11.2	9.4	6.5	Operating Profit						
3.7	3.0	2.0	All Other Expenses (net)						
7.4	6.4	4.5	Profit Before Taxes						
			RATIOS						
1.6	2.4	2.3	Current						
1.1	1.2	1.4							
.5	.6	.7							
1.4	2.1	2.0	Quick						
.8	1.1	.9							
.4	.5	.7							
0 UND	**0** UND	**28** 13.2	Sales/Receivables						
33 11.0	**37** 9.9	**36** 10.0							
42 8.7	**42** 8.6	**41** 8.8							
			Cost of Sales/Inventory						
			Cost of Sales/Payables						
19.1	8.2	11.0	Sales/Working Capital						
NM	28.5	27.4							
-14.4	-27.3	-40.3							
15.5	13.4	12.8	EBIT/Interest						
(39) 7.4	(22) 3.6	(20) 4.1							
1.8	.9	.7							
			Net Profit + Depr., Dep., Amort./Cur. Mat. L/T/D						
.6	.4	.1	Fixed/Worth						
3.1	1.8	.9							
-.8	-.6	-14.3							
.8	.6	.7	Debt/Worth						
5.3	3.9	1.8							
-4.0	-4.0	-51.3							
109.6	71.6	47.2	% Profit Before Taxes/Tangible Net Worth						
(28) 39.3	(21) 37.1	(23) 15.1							
19.5	4.9	6.4							
38.5	46.1	16.5	% Profit Before Taxes/Total Assets						
13.5	10.1	7.3							
1.4	.6	.4							
36.6	24.6	46.2	Sales/Net Fixed Assets						
14.9	16.8	20.2							
10.1	10.0	6.8							
5.1	5.5	5.3	Sales/Total Assets						
4.1	4.0	3.8							
2.1	2.6	1.3							
1.2	.7	1.2	% Depr., Dep., Amort./Sales						
(37) 2.0	(24) 1.7	(24) 2.2							
3.6	4.1	4.1							
3.1	4.4	3.3	% Officers', Directors' Owners' Comp/Sales						
(30) 5.5	(21) 8.2	(16) 8.5							
11.1	11.2	9.5							
460587M	**666080M**	**756283M**	Net Sales ($)	**3738M**	**11927M**	**20112M**	**28058M**	**63516M**	**628932M**
250615M	**409851M**	**456836M**	Total Assets ($)	**2169M**	**4025M**	**7634M**	**12272M**	**33079M**	**397657M**

M = $ thousand MM = $ million

See Pages 9 through 22 for Explanation of Ratios and Data

Current Data Sorted by Assets / Comparative Historical Data

0-500M	500M-2MM	2-10MM	10-50MM	50-100MM	100-250MM		4/1/09-3/31/10 ALL	4/1/10-3/31/11 ALL
						Type of Statement		
1		3	5			Unqualified	39	23
	1	12	1			Reviewed	42	43
1	3	6	2			Compiled	24	17
5	8	15	2			Tax Returns	44	31
5	11	21	13	4	1	Other	70	68
23 (4/1-9/30/13)		97 (10/1/13-3/31/14)						
12	23	57	23	4	1	**NUMBER OF STATEMENTS**	219	182
%	%	%	%	%	%	**ASSETS**	%	%
19.6	13.3	8.1	11.9			Cash & Equivalents	9.3	10.3
17.3	31.0	26.4	25.4			Trade Receivables (net)	26.2	27.1
30.1	35.5	36.3	35.9			Inventory	37.3	34.8
.2	1.1	3.1	4.2			All Other Current	1.3	1.8
67.2	80.8	73.9	77.5			Total Current	74.1	74.0
25.5	10.3	16.4	11.9			Fixed Assets (net)	17.2	16.1
4.9	.9	4.8	4.9			Intangibles (net)	1.8	3.5
2.4	7.9	4.9	5.7			All Other Non-Current	6.9	6.5
100.0	100.0	100.0	100.0			Total	100.0	100.0
						LIABILITIES		
8.2	26.8	14.0	17.9			Notes Payable-Short Term	17.9	13.4
.6	2.8	2.6	1.0			Cur. Mat.-L.T.D.	3.3	2.2
23.7	20.8	15.6	18.5			Trade Payables	16.4	16.2
.0	.0	.2	.2			Income Taxes Payable	.1	.2
1.9	23.5	7.9	8.3			All Other Current	10.9	11.3
34.5	73.8	40.4	46.0			Total Current	48.6	43.3
28.1	10.7	10.3	7.6			Long-Term Debt	10.8	11.4
.0	.0	.1	.1			Deferred Taxes	.2	.4
18.8	6.8	8.1	8.2			All Other Non-Current	5.9	5.3
18.6	8.6	41.1	38.0			Net Worth	34.5	39.7
100.0	100.0	100.0	100.0			Total Liabilties & Net Worth	100.0	100.0
						INCOME DATA		
100.0	100.0	100.0	100.0			Net Sales	100.0	100.0
42.2	35.5	34.6	36.2			Gross Profit	33.7	36.2
36.0	34.7	29.3	29.7			Operating Expenses	30.6	31.6
6.2	.8	5.4	6.6			Operating Profit	3.1	4.6
1.2	1.3	.4	2.1			All Other Expenses (net)	1.1	.8
4.9	-.5	4.9	4.5			Profit Before Taxes	1.9	3.8
						RATIOS		
12.0	2.1	3.3	2.6				3.0	3.0
3.5	1.5	2.1	1.7			Current	1.7	1.7
1.2	1.0	1.3	1.4				1.1	1.2
2.7	1.4	1.5	1.6				1.5	1.5
1.4	.7	.8	.9			Quick	.8	.9
.5	.3	.5	.4				.4	.5
0 UND	**23** 15.7	**22** 16.9	**24** 15.2				**31** 11.8	**27** 13.3
8 43.8	**37** 9.9	**42** 8.6	**52** 7.0			Sales/Receivables	**48** 7.6	**46** 8.0
33 11.1	**68** 5.4	**59** 6.2	**69** 5.3				**69** 5.3	**73** 5.0
1 401.2	**17** 21.9	**30** 12.1	**54** 6.8				**35** 10.3	**33** 10.9
30 12.1	**46** 7.9	**96** 3.8	**76** 4.8			Cost of Sales/Inventory	**91** 4.0	**91** 4.0
85 4.3	**166** 2.2	**203** 1.8	**152** 2.4				**203** 1.8	**182** 2.0
0 UND	**20** 17.9	**19** 19.2	**25** 14.6				**15** 24.1	**16** 22.8
17 21.8	**29** 12.7	**31** 11.7	**44** 8.3			Cost of Sales/Payables	**30** 12.0	**33** 10.9
43 8.5	**54** 6.7	**60** 6.1	**65** 5.6				**61** 6.0	**68** 5.4
4.6	6.2	3.3	3.7				3.5	3.5
14.0	11.7	5.8	6.5			Sales/Working Capital	6.7	7.8
756.0	961.2	16.0	11.6				26.4	17.8
	4.1	24.7	29.6				7.8	12.1
	(19) .5	(50) 5.5	(18) 3.5			EBIT/Interest	(192) 2.3	(158) 4.2
	-3.2	2.3	1.9				.5	1.6
							5.5	8.8
						Net Profit + Depr., Dep., Amort./Cur. Mat. L/T/D	(34) 1.7	(39) 2.8
							.2	1.1
.1	.1	.1	.1				.1	.1
.5	.2	.3	.3			Fixed/Worth	.3	.3
NM	1.2	1.2	.7				1.0	1.0
.5	1.7	.6	.7				.7	.7
1.4	3.3	1.6	1.7			Debt/Worth	1.7	1.8
NM	38.8	4.2	3.1				5.5	3.6
	44.4	47.3	35.0				34.5	42.4
	(18) 4.7	(49) 18.8	(20) 17.7			% Profit Before Taxes/Tangible Net Worth	(194) 9.6	(164) 14.2
	-66.7	5.9	6.0				.4	4.0
22.8	8.9	16.4	15.0				11.4	13.7
5.6	.9	9.6	4.8			% Profit Before Taxes/Total Assets	3.1	5.5
.1	-7.7	2.3	.8				-1.5	1.2
UND	166.6	58.7	40.6				78.6	61.2
30.0	48.1	22.9	19.6			Sales/Net Fixed Assets	22.5	23.8
7.5	21.1	9.8	10.0				8.0	8.3
8.3	4.0	3.0	2.4				2.8	2.8
4.1	3.0	2.0	1.8			Sales/Total Assets	1.9	2.0
1.9	2.1	1.4	1.5				1.2	1.3
	.3	.3	.8				.5	.5
	(18) .5	(44) .7	(19) 1.1			% Depr., Dep., Amort./Sales	(186) 1.2	(139) 1.1
	2.3	1.3	1.6				2.6	2.6
	2.7	2.8	1.3				1.4	2.0
	(18) 5.6	(35) 3.8	(10) 3.6			% Officers', Directors' Owners' Comp/Sales	(109) 3.5	(84) 3.8
	8.7	5.8	8.3				5.6	6.9
15224M	77318M	560901M	1017846M	332050M	452855M	Net Sales ($)	4218610M	4401633M
3061M	27041M	254421M	518308M	271965M	219584M	Total Assets ($)	2418386M	2659225M

M = $ thousand MM = $ million

See Pages 9 through 22 for Explanation of Ratios and Data

Comparative Historical Data

Type of Statement		4/1/11-3/31/12 ALL		4/1/12-3/31/13 ALL		4/1/13-3/31/14 ALL
Unqualified		30		11		9
Reviewed		39		30		14
Compiled		34		19		12
Tax Returns		54		33		30
Other		86		59		55
NUMBER OF STATEMENTS		243		152		120
ASSETS		%		%		%
Cash & Equivalents		10.0		10.8		10.9
Trade Receivables (net)		26.0		27.6		25.7
Inventory		35.0		36.9		35.9
All Other Current		1.6		2.1		2.7
Total Current		72.6		77.4		75.2
Fixed Assets (net)		16.4		14.1		15.0
Intangibles (net)		3.1		2.9		4.4
All Other Non-Current		7.9		5.6		5.5
Total		100.0		100.0		100.0
LIABILITIES						
Notes Payable-Short Term		10.8		13.5		16.4
Cur. Mat.-L.T.D.		2.2		3.0		2.2
Trade Payables		18.1		17.0		17.7
Income Taxes Payable		.1		.2		.3
All Other Current		15.2		13.0		10.3
Total Current		46.4		46.7		46.8
Long-Term Debt		14.2		10.6		11.6
Deferred Taxes		.2		.2		.1
All Other Non-Current		6.8		6.1		8.7
Net Worth		32.4		36.4		32.9
Total Liabilties & Net Worth		100.0		100.0		100.0
INCOME DATA						
Net Sales		100.0		100.0		100.0
Gross Profit		34.6		36.4		36.4
Operating Expenses		30.2		32.1		31.7
Operating Profit		4.4		4.3		4.7
All Other Expenses (net)		.8		.7		1.0
Profit Before Taxes		3.6		3.5		3.7
RATIOS						
Current		3.2		3.0		3.1
		1.9		2.0		1.9
		1.2		1.3		1.2
Quick		1.5		1.6		1.6
		.8		.9		.8
		.5		.5		.5
Sales/Receivables	**24**	15.5	**26**	13.9	**19**	18.9
	38	9.6	**41**	8.8	**42**	8.6
	54	6.8	**62**	5.9	**62**	5.9
Cost of Sales/Inventory	**30**	12.0	**40**	9.2	**30**	12.2
	78	4.7	**87**	4.2	**79**	4.6
	159	2.3	**182**	2.0	**166**	2.2
Cost of Sales/Payables	**16**	22.3	**18**	20.4	**20**	17.9
	34	10.7	**36**	10.1	**36**	10.2
	61	6.0	**56**	6.5	**59**	6.2
Sales/Working Capital		4.0		3.6		3.7
		8.3		6.7		6.6
		27.1		16.0		25.1
EBIT/Interest		18.6		15.5		15.3
	(198)	4.9	(128)	3.7	(100)	4.4
		1.4		1.3		1.0
Net Profit + Depr., Dep., Amort./Cur. Mat. L/T/D		10.8		13.6		9.0
	(36)	3.8	(14)	2.4	(17)	3.5
		1.2		.5		1.7
Fixed/Worth		.1		.1		.1
		.3		.3		.3
		1.0		1.0		1.2
Debt/Worth		.6		.7		.7
		1.8		1.6		1.8
		5.4		3.8		5.9
% Profit Before Taxes/Tangible Net Worth		42.0		39.7		45.2
	(213)	15.9	(134)	13.5	(100)	18.5
		3.8		2.9		2.1
% Profit Before Taxes/Total Assets		16.3		12.1		15.2
		6.9		5.2		5.9
		.5		.7		.4
Sales/Net Fixed Assets		79.2		96.2		65.3
		24.0		27.8		24.3
		10.6		13.6		10.1
Sales/Total Assets		3.4		3.3		3.3
		2.2		2.3		2.1
		1.5		1.5		1.5
% Depr., Dep., Amort./Sales		.5		.4		.4
	(177)	1.0	(109)	.9	(92)	.8
		2.3		2.1		1.8
% Officers', Directors' Owners' Comp/Sales		2.0		2.4		2.8
	(119)	3.9	(74)	4.0	(71)	4.5
		7.2		7.0		7.4
Net Sales ($)		**4694075M**		**3511118M**		**2456194M**
Total Assets ($)		**2516032M**		**1788607M**		**1294380M**

Current Data Sorted by Sales

23 (4/1-9/30/13) — 97 (10/1/13-3/31/14)

Type of Statement		0-1MM		1-3MM		3-5MM		5-10MM		10-25MM		25MM & OVER
Unqualified				1		1		2		3		2
Reviewed						3		6		4		1
Compiled		1		3		1		2		2		3
Tax Returns		4		6		5		7		7		1
Other		4		6		7		10		11		17
NUMBER OF STATEMENTS		9		16		17		27		27		24
ASSETS		%		%		%		%		%		%
Cash & Equivalents				13.1		10.4		8.7		9.3		13.0
Trade Receivables (net)				30.5		23.1		23.7		31.1		26.0
Inventory				32.9		30.6		41.7		31.9		34.0
All Other Current				.3		3.2		3.7		1.8		4.0
Total Current				76.8		67.3		77.8		74.2		76.9
Fixed Assets (net)				15.8		17.4		14.5		15.6		12.8
Intangibles (net)				.9		4.3		3.1		5.4		6.3
All Other Non-Current				6.6		11.0		4.6		4.8		4.0
Total				100.0		100.0		100.0		100.0		100.0
LIABILITIES												
Notes Payable-Short Term				25.8		8.8		16.7		15.9		16.0
Cur. Mat.-L.T.D.				1.3		4.9		2.7		1.8		1.1
Trade Payables				25.4		16.0		14.1		17.3		20.6
Income Taxes Payable				.0		.4		.2		.2		.5
All Other Current				3.2		22.8		9.7		8.5		6.9
Total Current				55.7		53.0		43.4		43.6		45.2
Long-Term Debt				10.8		17.4		14.6		3.4		7.3
Deferred Taxes				.0		.0		.0		.2		.1
All Other Non-Current				5.4		5.9		9.2		5.6		7.7
Net Worth				28.0		23.7		32.7		47.3		39.6
Total Liabilties & Net Worth				100.0		100.0		100.0		100.0		100.0
INCOME DATA												
Net Sales				100.0		100.0		100.0		100.0		100.0
Gross Profit				36.5		34.7		37.3		35.3		35.1
Operating Expenses				35.6		32.4		31.7		28.2		30.7
Operating Profit				1.0		2.3		5.6		7.1		4.4
All Other Expenses (net)				.9		.1		.6		1.2		1.7
Profit Before Taxes				.1		2.2		5.0		5.8		2.7
RATIOS												
Current				2.9		2.7		4.5		2.7		2.7
				1.6		2.0		1.9		1.9		1.6
				1.0		1.0		1.3		1.3		1.1
Quick				1.9		1.5		1.3		1.6		1.8
				.7		.7		.8		.9		.7
				.4		.4		.3		.5		.5
Sales/Receivables			**11**	32.3	**19**	19.6	**15**	23.7	**30**	12.3	**13**	28.8
			36	10.2	**38**	9.6	**38**	9.5	**54**	6.8	**45**	8.1
			68	5.4	**52**	7.0	**62**	5.9	**61**	6.0	**69**	5.3
Cost of Sales/Inventory			**16**	23.3	**13**	28.2	**36**	10.2	**27**	13.5	**37**	9.9
			35	10.3	**81**	4.5	**122**	3.0	**94**	3.9	**66**	5.5
			122	3.0	**166**	2.2	**228**	1.6	**114**	3.2	**152**	2.4
Cost of Sales/Payables			**18**	20.5	**20**	18.4	**21**	17.8	**18**	20.5	**26**	14.0
			37	9.9	**29**	12.7	**37**	9.8	**29**	12.8	**41**	9.0
			78	4.7	**55**	6.6	**51**	7.1	**61**	6.0	**73**	5.0
Sales/Working Capital				6.1		4.0		3.1		3.7		4.0
				8.3		11.7		5.5		6.3		7.5
				833.9		503.4		14.1		17.8		753.3
EBIT/Interest				8.5		6.2		18.3		35.4		58.5
			(13)	1.1	(16)	3.9	(21)	5.0	(24)	5.8	(20)	4.1
				-.4		.5		2.1		3.2		-1.7
Net Profit + Depr., Dep., Amort./Cur. Mat. L/T/D												
Fixed/Worth				.1		.0		.1		.1		.1
				.3		.3		.3		.3		.3
				7.6		1.5		2.3		.8		1.1
Debt/Worth				1.4		.5		.6		.6		.7
				2.3		2.7		2.0		1.0		1.7
				32.2		25.8		15.5		2.5		5.2
% Profit Before Taxes/Tangible Net Worth				60.1		39.5		37.2		62.7		40.7
			(13)	3.4	(14)	23.3	(22)	15.5	(24)	22.7	(20)	17.7
				-38.3		3.0		9.7		6.3		-1.7
% Profit Before Taxes/Total Assets				21.0		9.7		14.8		23.2		17.6
				1.0		3.1		9.6		10.7		5.1
				-1.7		-3.2		2.7		2.6		-1.8
Sales/Net Fixed Assets				182.1		159.7		63.6		37.6		73.3
				40.5		35.5		22.9		19.6		21.2
				19.1		13.0		9.2		9.7		13.4
Sales/Total Assets				4.1		4.0		2.6		3.1		2.9
				3.2		2.0		1.9		2.3		2.0
				2.1		1.3		1.4		1.7		1.5
% Depr., Dep., Amort./Sales				.3		.3		.2		.5		.7
			(12)	.6	(14)	.8	(18)	.6	(23)	1.1	(19)	1.0
				2.0		3.7		1.2		1.8		1.7
% Officers', Directors' Owners' Comp/Sales				3.3		2.2		2.8		2.8		1.0
			(13)	6.8	(13)	3.9	(15)	4.5	(15)	3.4	(11)	3.6
				11.1		9.0		7.1		4.9		8.0
Net Sales ($)		**4317M**		**34970M**		**70315M**		**181844M**		**412329M**		**1752419M**
Total Assets ($)		**6944M**		**14303M**		**39167M**		**101989M**		**196044M**		**935933M**

M = $ thousand **MM = $ million**

See Pages 9 through 22 for Explanation of Ratios and Data

Current Data Sorted by Assets							Comparative Historical Data	
						Type of Statement		
		6	15	3	2	Unqualified	34	40
		8	6			Reviewed	31	25
1	4	11	1		1	Compiled	14	17
1	8	5	2			Tax Returns	23	22
3	17	22	25	6	6	Other	94	88
	26 (4/1-9/30/13)		127 (10/1/13-3/31/14)				4/1/09-3/31/10	4/1/10-3/31/11
0-500M	**500M-2MM**	**2-10MM**	**10-50MM**	**50-100MM**	**100-250MM**		**ALL**	**ALL**
5	29	52	49	9	9	**NUMBER OF STATEMENTS**	196	192
%	%	%	%	%	%	**ASSETS**	%	%
	18.4	11.2	6.9			Cash & Equivalents	8.0	9.1
	15.7	18.4	21.0			Trade Receivables (net)	21.9	21.7
	45.4	39.9	38.5			Inventory	33.4	37.0
	1.5	2.7	4.0			All Other Current	3.2	3.5
	81.0	72.2	70.4			Total Current	66.5	71.3
	10.2	15.6	15.4			Fixed Assets (net)	16.4	14.0
	1.3	7.3	9.1			Intangibles (net)	10.5	8.9
	7.5	4.8	5.2			All Other Non-Current	6.6	5.8
	100.0	100.0	100.0			Total	100.0	100.0
						LIABILITIES		
	17.2	9.8	11.2			Notes Payable-Short Term	15.6	12.4
	2.5	2.5	3.8			Cur. Mat.-L.T.D.	2.7	3.5
	12.4	11.1	12.8			Trade Payables	12.0	13.0
	.1	.1	.1			Income Taxes Payable	.2	.2
	12.9	11.2	8.9			All Other Current	10.3	10.4
	45.1	34.7	36.9			Total Current	40.8	39.5
	11.5	12.5	11.1			Long-Term Debt	18.2	12.3
	.2	.2	.3			Deferred Taxes	.4	.5
	7.6	6.5	8.2			All Other Non-Current	8.9	11.6
	35.7	46.1	43.6			Net Worth	31.7	36.1
	100.0	100.0	100.0			Total Liabilties & Net Worth	100.0	100.0
						INCOME DATA		
	100.0	100.0	100.0			Net Sales	100.0	100.0
	42.4	35.1	37.2			Gross Profit	38.0	37.8
	35.1	27.9	29.3			Operating Expenses	33.9	31.9
	7.4	7.3	7.9			Operating Profit	4.1	5.9
	1.3	1.4	1.6			All Other Expenses (net)	2.6	1.6
	6.1	5.9	6.3			Profit Before Taxes	1.4	4.3
						RATIOS		
	3.9	5.1	3.9				3.3	3.7
	1.9	2.6	1.9			Current	1.7	1.9
	1.0	1.4	1.3				1.2	1.3
	2.7	3.0	1.8				1.5	1.6
	.6	.9	.7			Quick	.8	.8
	.4	.4	.5				.4	.4
	10 37.4	**16** 23.1	**34** 10.7				**24** 15.4	**26** 14.1
	16 22.3	**29** 12.4	**41** 8.8			Sales/Receivables	**41** 9.0	**40** 9.2
	34 10.7	**50** 7.3	**58** 6.3				**58** 6.3	**57** 6.4
	61 6.0	**74** 4.9	**81** 4.5				**65** 5.6	**69** 5.3
	94 3.9	**111** 3.3	**130** 2.8			Cost of Sales/Inventory	**98** 3.7	**109** 3.4
	152 2.4	**192** 1.9	**174** 2.1				**146** 2.5	**156** 2.3
	5 72.8	**14** 26.5	**19** 19.5				**14** 26.4	**16** 22.5
	30 12.1	**23** 16.1	**29** 12.4			Cost of Sales/Payables	**29** 12.5	**29** 12.4
	41 8.9	**42** 8.7	**45** 8.2				**45** 8.1	**48** 7.6
	3.7	3.0	3.4				3.7	3.4
	6.0	5.1	6.4			Sales/Working Capital	6.4	5.7
	329.6	13.1	10.9				21.6	14.3
	19.4	18.6	29.0				9.6	16.4
	(24) 3.6	(44) 4.9	(44) 7.1			EBIT/Interest	(176) 2.3	(166) 4.6
	.6	2.4	1.6				-.2	1.4
			8.3				3.9	11.1
			(14) 2.6			Net Profit + Depr., Dep., Amort./Cur. Mat. L/T/D	(38) 1.7	(38) 2.6
			1.6				.0	.8
	.1	.1	.1				.1	.1
	.2	.3	.3			Fixed/Worth	.4	.3
	.8	1.3	1.1				NM	3.6
	.4	.4	.7				.6	.4
	1.7	1.2	1.8			Debt/Worth	1.9	1.5
	6.7	3.5	6.1				-63.2	17.8
	58.9	48.1	54.9				33.3	43.5
	(25) 23.3	(45) 21.2	(44) 12.5			% Profit Before Taxes/Tangible Net Worth	(146) 12.7	(151) 20.0
	-.8	8.7	3.7				-2.9	8.6
	26.7	19.0	17.5				11.4	15.7
	9.7	9.8	6.5			% Profit Before Taxes/Total Assets	3.6	7.4
	-.9	2.1	1.1				-3.0	1.7
	88.4	52.3	49.7				49.3	54.3
	43.4	22.0	18.3			Sales/Net Fixed Assets	15.8	19.3
	13.3	7.8	6.8				7.4	9.0
	3.6	2.7	2.2				2.5	2.4
	2.9	1.8	1.8			Sales/Total Assets	1.7	1.9
	2.3	1.3	1.3				1.3	1.3
	.4	.8	.9				1.0	.9
	(22) 1.1	(44) 1.2	(41) 1.4			% Depr., Dep., Amort./Sales	(138) 2.1	(142) 1.8
	1.7	2.3	3.2				3.4	3.2
	2.7	1.7					2.3	2.0
	(15) 6.7	(19) 2.7				% Officers', Directors' Owners' Comp/Sales	(42) 4.5	(52) 4.3
	8.5	7.0					7.7	7.4
4438M	**92168M**	**558104M**	**2073661M**	**961000M**	**1694685M**	Net Sales ($)	**7755975M**	**6875019M**
1200M	**31397M**	**271262M**	**1145086M**	**655535M**	**1543613M**	Total Assets ($)	**5458449M**	**4975927M**

M = $ thousand MM = $ million

See Pages 9 through 22 for Explanation of Ratios and Data

Comparative Historical Data / Current Data Sorted by Sales

4/1/11-3/31/12 ALL	4/1/12-3/31/13 ALL	4/1/13-3/31/14 ALL	Type of Statement	0-1MM	1-3MM	3-5MM	5-10MM	10-25MM	25MM & OVER
40	28	26	Unqualified		1		2	5	18
26	22	14	Reviewed		1		5	7	1
16	11	18	Compiled	1	3	1	6	6	1
30	15	16	Tax Returns	1	4	4	3	3	1
88	79	79	Other	3	13	6	10	14	33
				26 (4/1-9/30/13)			127 (10/1/13-3/31/14)		
200	155	153	NUMBER OF STATEMENTS	5	22	11	26	35	54
%	%	%	**ASSETS**	%	%	%	%	%	%
8.4	8.2	11.3	Cash & Equivalents		16.2	19.8	12.2	11.9	7.6
21.5	19.4	18.3	Trade Receivables (net)		15.3	15.3	18.4	19.5	20.8
38.1	39.4	38.0	Inventory		41.7	37.7	40.2	40.5	35.2
3.6	3.6	3.0	All Other Current		1.0	.0	4.7	1.9	4.2
71.7	70.6	70.6	Total Current		74.2	72.8	75.5	73.7	67.8
14.7	14.7	14.4	Fixed Assets (net)		15.1	14.6	13.5	14.1	11.8
8.7	8.7	8.4	Intangibles (net)		1.2	10.7	4.8	7.7	13.6
4.8	6.0	6.5	All Other Non-Current		9.5	1.8	6.2	4.5	6.8
100.0	100.0	100.0	Total		100.0	100.0	100.0	100.0	100.0
			LIABILITIES						
12.8	16.3	10.9	Notes Payable-Short Term		19.1	9.0	10.2	7.7	9.2
3.5	2.6	2.7	Cur. Mat.-L.T.D.		2.3	.4	4.2	3.0	2.5
12.6	15.8	11.8	Trade Payables		11.6	6.2	13.9	12.3	12.5
.3	.2	.1	Income Taxes Payable		.1	.0	.0	.1	.1
10.7	9.5	13.4	All Other Current		22.6	4.4	10.9	7.6	9.9
40.0	44.5	38.8	Total Current		55.7	20.0	39.1	30.8	34.3
15.4	13.5	12.4	Long-Term Debt		13.8	15.2	11.7	13.8	10.0
.4	.4	.6	Deferred Taxes		.2	.1	.0	.2	1.2
8.9	11.5	8.2	All Other Non-Current		8.0	8.2	6.0	4.3	11.7
35.3	30.2	40.0	Net Worth		22.3	56.5	43.1	51.0	42.8
100.0	100.0	100.0	Total Liabilties & Net Worth		100.0	100.0	100.0	100.0	100.0
			INCOME DATA						
100.0	100.0	100.0	Net Sales		100.0	100.0	100.0	100.0	100.0
37.4	38.2	37.9	Gross Profit		42.0	42.5	35.8	36.3	35.7
32.4	32.8	30.9	Operating Expenses		36.7	33.0	29.8	27.0	29.6
5.1	5.4	7.0	Operating Profit		5.4	9.5	6.0	9.3	6.1
1.2	1.0	1.7	All Other Expenses (net)		1.4	1.2	1.0	1.3	2.0
3.9	4.4	5.3	Profit Before Taxes		4.0	8.3	5.0	8.0	4.1
			RATIOS						
3.7	3.4	4.1	Current		3.8	16.2	5.7	4.5	3.2
1.9	1.9	2.1			1.4	5.1	2.0	2.5	1.9
1.3	1.2	1.4			.9	2.6	1.1	1.6	1.5
1.6	1.3	2.1	Quick		1.5	8.5	3.2	2.6	1.4
.8	.7	.8			.6	2.4	.7	.8	.8
.4	.4	.5			.4	.5	.3	.5	.5
23 15.8	**16** 23.1	**17** 21.6	Sales/Receivables		**10** 36.4	**13** 27.2	**11** 34.4	**22** 16.3	**30** 12.3
40 9.2	**33** 10.9	**36** 10.1			**23** 16.0	**22** 16.5	**31** 11.7	**38** 9.7	**42** 8.6
58 6.3	**54** 6.8	**49** 7.4			**38** 9.6	**47** 7.8	**50** 7.3	**49** 7.4	**58** 6.3
73 5.0	**73** 5.0	**70** 5.2	Cost of Sales/Inventory		**68** 5.4	**47** 7.7	**60** 6.1	**78** 4.7	**73** 5.0
107 3.4	**107** 3.4	**111** 3.3			**122** 3.0	**107** 3.4	**94** 3.9	**114** 3.2	**111** 3.3
166 2.2	**159** 2.3	**166** 2.2			**203** 1.8	**122** 3.0	**215** 1.7	**159** 2.3	**140** 2.6
14 25.8	**14** 25.6	**15** 24.6	Cost of Sales/Payables		**4** 97.5	**6** 65.0	**11** 32.1	**18** 20.4	**18** 19.9
27 13.3	**28** 13.2	**26** 13.8			**32** 11.4	**14** 25.2	**26** 14.0	**26** 13.8	**27** 13.7
50 7.3	**52** 7.0	**42** 8.7			**53** 6.9	**30** 12.0	**40** 9.1	**43** 8.5	**43** 8.4
3.2	3.8	3.2	Sales/Working Capital		3.8	2.9	2.6	3.6	3.3
5.9	6.3	5.7			9.9	4.3	5.7	5.0	6.3
12.8	17.6	11.8			-46.0	7.5	117.9	11.1	9.1
16.5	19.9	20.9	EBIT/Interest		14.7		24.5	20.0	35.0
(179) 3.9	(135) 5.2	(131) 5.0			(17) 1.6		(23) 6.5	(31) 5.8	(51) 7.8
1.3	1.4	1.5			-1.3		2.2	2.4	1.5
7.4	7.0	8.3	Net Profit + Depr., Dep., Amort./Cur. Mat. L/T/D						8.4
(40) 2.5	(29) 1.7	(31) 2.3							(16) 2.4
1.0	.9	1.5							1.5
.1	.1	.1	Fixed/Worth		.1	.1	.1	.1	.1
.3	.3	.3			.7	.2	.3	.2	.2
2.3	2.0	1.4			-2.2	.7	1.3	1.0	1.1
.6	.6	.5	Debt/Worth		.5	.3	.4	.4	.6
1.7	1.7	1.6			2.0	.9	1.6	1.0	2.0
22.6	27.9	5.9			-10.3	4.0	5.0	3.6	9.2
45.5	54.3	52.9	% Profit Before Taxes/Tangible Net Worth		57.5	58.7	34.6	58.3	56.6
(157) 22.1	(120) 23.1	(130) 19.0			(16) 17.0	(10) 26.8	(22) 17.7	(32) 24.1	(46) 19.3
8.0	8.2	5.3			-3.9	10.4	4.1	5.4	6.3
15.9	20.2	18.2	% Profit Before Taxes/Total Assets		26.6	25.8	12.7	24.8	14.8
5.8	9.0	7.3			3.7	10.5	6.6	11.5	6.7
.4	1.4	.9			-6.1	3.7	-.9	2.7	.8
78.8	65.4	54.7	Sales/Net Fixed Assets		113.1	135.6	45.2	56.3	49.1
21.0	19.7	20.7			19.3	39.0	30.9	19.5	19.7
7.9	8.0	7.7			6.4	12.2	5.8	7.6	8.5
2.7	2.9	2.7	Sales/Total Assets		3.0	3.1	3.1	2.9	2.2
1.8	2.0	1.8			2.4	1.9	1.8	1.9	1.8
1.3	1.3	1.3			1.1	1.2	1.3	1.5	1.4
.8	.7	.8	% Depr., Dep., Amort./Sales		.7		.8	.4	.9
(155) 1.6	(120) 1.5	(123) 1.4			(15) 1.3		(19) 1.5	(32) 1.0	(44) 1.4
3.2	2.6	2.5			3.1		2.3	2.3	2.8
2.3	2.0	1.9	% Officers', Directors' Owners' Comp/Sales				1.9		
(60) 4.9	(42) 4.9	(38) 5.4					(13) 2.7		
8.3	7.7	7.4					6.8		
5602895M	4388286M	5384056M	Net Sales ($)	2287M	40217M	42780M	176246M	572196M	4550330M
4109772M	2757472M	3648093M	Total Assets ($)	13870M	27293M	26419M	106877M	299368M	3174266M

M = $ thousand MM = $ million

See Pages 9 through 22 for Explanation of Ratios and Data

Current Data Sorted by Assets							Comparative Historical Data	
						Type of Statement		
		2	3	1	3	Unqualified	16	9
		6	4			Reviewed	14	23
	2	2	1			Compiled	3	4
1	2	1				Tax Returns	7	4
	3	6	7	2	4	Other	21	29
	13 (4/1-9/30/13)		37 (10/1/13-3/31/14)				4/1/09-3/31/10 ALL	4/1/10-3/31/11 ALL
0-500M	500M-2MM	2-10MM	10-50MM	50-100MM	100-250MM			
1	7	17	15	3	7	**NUMBER OF STATEMENTS**	61	69
%	%	%	%	%	%	**ASSETS**	%	%
		7.9	17.0			Cash & Equivalents	9.9	9.3
		31.6	28.6			Trade Receivables (net)	26.4	27.9
		38.7	33.8			Inventory	29.9	32.8
		1.0	3.8			All Other Current	3.4	2.5
		79.2	83.2			Total Current	69.6	72.6
		13.7	11.3			Fixed Assets (net)	14.2	14.4
		3.0	.7			Intangibles (net)	7.8	6.2
		4.1	4.8			All Other Non-Current	8.4	6.7
		100.0	100.0			Total	100.0	100.0
						LIABILITIES		
		12.5	11.6			Notes Payable-Short Term	11.7	22.3
		1.4	.5			Cur. Mat.-L.T.D.	2.2	2.7
		14.8	11.9			Trade Payables	14.5	17.1
		.2	.4			Income Taxes Payable	.3	.1
		9.4	9.8			All Other Current	10.1	8.6
		38.4	34.1			Total Current	38.8	50.8
		13.8	4.9			Long-Term Debt	10.8	11.9
		.5	.3			Deferred Taxes	.3	.4
		4.2	4.4			All Other Non-Current	6.2	5.0
		43.1	56.3			Net Worth	43.9	31.8
		100.0	100.0			Total Liabilties & Net Worth	100.0	100.0
						INCOME DATA		
		100.0	100.0			Net Sales	100.0	100.0
		36.6	33.0			Gross Profit	39.3	35.5
		32.9	29.6			Operating Expenses	34.1	31.7
		3.7	3.4			Operating Profit	5.1	3.8
		.5	-.3			All Other Expenses (net)	1.7	1.1
		3.3	3.8			Profit Before Taxes	3.4	2.8
						RATIOS		
		3.3	8.9				3.2	2.6
		1.9	2.4			Current	2.0	1.6
		1.5	1.6				1.3	1.2
		1.6	5.7				1.9	1.3
		1.2	1.3			Quick	.9	.7
		.7	.7				.6	.5
		33 11.0	38 9.7				28 13.0	38 9.7
		36 10.0	79 4.6			Sales/Receivables	51 7.1	51 7.1
		74 4.9	87 4.2				65 5.6	69 5.3
		54 6.8	79 4.6				54 6.7	49 7.5
		122 3.0	111 3.3			Cost of Sales/Inventory	91 4.0	104 3.5
		174 2.1	182 2.0				126 2.9	159 2.3
		18 20.3	11 32.3				15 24.1	18 20.8
		30 12.1	34 10.6			Cost of Sales/Payables	36 10.0	36 10.2
		52 7.0	64 5.7				57 6.4	70 5.2
		3.4	2.1				3.5	4.1
		6.2	2.7			Sales/Working Capital	6.3	8.1
		8.1	7.2				12.6	18.5
		28.4	78.2				18.3	14.2
		(15) 5.1	(12) 36.6			EBIT/Interest	(56) 6.8	(61) 4.3
		2.1	.9				1.7	1.0
							11.7	10.4
						Net Profit + Depr., Dep., Amort./Cur. Mat. L/T/D	(17) 4.5	(10) 5.7
							2.2	2.3
		.1	.1				.1	.1
		.2	.1			Fixed/Worth	.3	.3
		.6	.3				1.1	1.2
		.4	.1				.6	.6
		1.1	1.1			Debt/Worth	1.7	1.7
		5.7	2.5				10.3	10.8
		30.2	53.3				62.9	38.2
		(15) 17.8	(14) 10.6			% Profit Before Taxes/Tangible Net Worth	(55) 35.8	(55) 18.8
		6.8	-1.7				4.2	3.1
		16.2	17.3				23.1	13.4
		7.7	5.6			% Profit Before Taxes/Total Assets	7.3	6.9
		1.4	-1.5				1.1	.3
		49.7	78.7				81.1	69.2
		22.1	20.1			Sales/Net Fixed Assets	26.3	26.7
		8.5	6.8				8.2	9.0
		2.7	2.0				2.6	2.5
		2.0	1.4			Sales/Total Assets	2.0	1.9
		1.4	1.1				1.4	1.4
		.5	.5				.7	.7
		(14) 1.5	(12) 1.3			% Depr., Dep., Amort./Sales	(45) 1.4	(57) 1.8
		2.9	3.2				3.1	3.1
							1.6	1.5
						% Officers', Directors' Owners' Comp/Sales	(22) 3.0	(13) 3.1
							5.6	4.4
765M	23628M	213004M	591224M	232652M	1577446M	Net Sales ($)	2875534M	2367920M
174M	8839M	104134M	345437M	174786M	1032276M	Total Assets ($)	1852373M	1579525M

M = $ thousand MM = $ million

See Pages 9 through 22 for Explanation of Ratios and Data

Comparative Historical Data / Current Data Sorted by Sales

4/1/11-3/31/12 ALL	4/1/12-3/31/13 ALL	4/1/13-3/31/14 ALL		0-1MM	1-3MM	3-5MM	5-10MM	10-25MM	25MM & OVER
			Type of Statement						
10	8	9	Unqualified					2	7
13	11	10	Reviewed				1	8	1
1	6	5	Compiled			2	1	1	1
1	7	4	Tax Returns	1	1	2			
29	25	22	Other		1	2	2	8	9
				13 (4/1-9/30/13)			37 (10/1/13-3/31/14)		
54	57	50	**NUMBER OF STATEMENTS**	1	2	6	4	19	18
%	%	%	**ASSETS**	%	%	%	%	%	%
6.9	8.3	11.1	Cash & Equivalents					8.8	11.4
26.8	29.7	29.1	Trade Receivables (net)					32.7	30.8
31.4	33.7	33.0	Inventory					38.4	23.5
3.3	2.6	2.8	All Other Current					1.4	4.8
68.4	74.4	76.1	Total Current					81.3	70.5
18.0	14.2	11.9	Fixed Assets (net)					11.5	9.3
9.1	5.9	5.2	Intangibles (net)					2.7	10.7
4.5	5.6	6.9	All Other Non-Current					4.5	9.4
100.0	100.0	100.0	Total					100.0	100.0
			LIABILITIES						
9.3	15.2	15.5	Notes Payable-Short Term					11.0	13.2
4.4	1.7	.9	Cur. Mat.-L.T.D.					1.3	.9
14.7	16.1	13.3	Trade Payables					13.4	14.0
.4	.2	.5	Income Taxes Payable					.4	.9
8.4	9.2	9.5	All Other Current					9.3	10.8
37.2	42.4	39.6	Total Current					35.4	39.8
19.3	9.6	11.1	Long-Term Debt					5.9	11.3
.4	.2	.5	Deferred Taxes					.7	.6
6.9	8.2	6.5	All Other Non-Current					4.4	8.2
36.2	39.5	42.3	Net Worth					53.6	40.1
100.0	100.0	100.0	Total Liabilities & Net Worth					100.0	100.0
			INCOME DATA						
100.0	100.0	100.0	Net Sales					100.0	100.0
37.7	35.5	36.5	Gross Profit					37.2	33.5
31.9	31.7	31.5	Operating Expenses					32.2	25.5
5.8	3.9	5.0	Operating Profit					4.9	8.0
1.1	.7	.6	All Other Expenses (net)					.1	.8
4.7	3.1	4.4	Profit Before Taxes					4.9	7.1
			RATIOS						
3.5	3.9	3.7						6.3	2.5
2.2	1.8	1.9	Current					2.4	1.9
1.3	1.3	1.4						1.6	1.4
2.1	2.1	2.0						3.9	1.8
1.0	.8	1.1	Quick					1.2	.9
.5	.6	.6						.8	.7
35 10.3	**38** 9.7	**33** 11.1						**33** 10.9	**46** 7.9
52 7.0	**49** 7.4	**52** 7.0	Sales/Receivables					**52** 7.0	**74** 4.9
78 4.7	**89** 4.1	**81** 4.5						**79** 4.6	**87** 4.2
73 5.0	**61** 6.0	**50** 7.3						**61** 6.0	**47** 7.7
101 3.6	**104** 3.5	**94** 3.9	Cost of Sales/Inventory					**122** 3.0	**66** 5.5
130 2.8	**152** 2.4	**159** 2.3						**174** 2.1	**104** 3.5
19 19.6	**21** 17.2	**13** 27.3						**14** 26.9	**23** 16.0
43 8.5	**36** 10.0	**33** 11.2	Cost of Sales/Payables					**30** 12.1	**40** 9.1
73 5.0	**54** 6.7	**54** 6.8						**51** 7.1	**61** 6.0
3.7	3.0	2.3						2.3	3.9
5.7	7.1	5.6	Sales/Working Capital					5.3	5.6
10.2	14.9	10.0						7.7	19.2
24.7	21.1	28.0						88.4	36.6
(44) 4.0	(50) 3.6	(44) 7.5	EBIT/Interest					(17) 10.0	(17) 11.6
.5	1.1	1.7						2.4	1.6
	5.0	25.9							
	(11) 4.0	(11) 8.0	Net Profit + Depr., Dep., Amort./Cur. Mat. L/T/D						
	2.2	4.0							
.1	.1	.1						.1	.1
.3	.3	.2	Fixed/Worth					.2	.3
UND	2.0	.8						.5	-1.7
.5	.7	.3						.2	1.1
1.8	2.4	1.4	Debt/Worth					1.1	2.2
UND	8.9	7.9						2.5	-18.6
56.1	57.6	40.0						27.3	76.3
(41) 23.6	(46) 15.0	(41) 16.7	% Profit Before Taxes/Tangible Net Worth					(18) 17.2	(13) 38.2
2.7	.0	1.3						4.1	9.5
18.2	15.1	16.8						16.5	18.5
6.7	5.8	8.4	% Profit Before Taxes/Total Assets					8.4	9.7
-.7	.0	.4						2.2	3.9
60.7	86.0	56.1						49.5	61.1
20.4	17.9	30.4	Sales/Net Fixed Assets					22.6	34.1
5.8	7.8	9.0						10.9	12.6
2.5	2.7	2.6						2.6	2.2
1.8	1.9	1.7	Sales/Total Assets					2.0	1.5
1.2	1.4	1.3						1.4	1.2
.7	.5	.5						.5	.5
(39) 1.5	(42) 1.5	(38) 1.2	% Depr., Dep., Amort./Sales					(17) 1.4	(14) 1.3
3.1	2.4	2.7						2.3	3.2
2.1	3.3	2.1							
(10) 4.7	(18) 5.0	(11) 3.3	% Officers', Directors' Owners' Comp/Sales						
7.6	6.6	5.2							
1905650M	2253683M	2638719M	Net Sales ($)	765M	2628M	22357M	25652M	293808M	2293509M
1531357M	1641085M	1665646M	Total Assets ($)	174M	2018M	11794M	29142M	165567M	1456951M

M = $ thousand MM = $ million

See Pages 9 through 22 for Explanation of Ratios and Data

	Current Data Sorted by Assets						Comparative Historical Data	
Type of Statement								
Unqualified			1	5	3		20	21
Reviewed		4	26	12	1		42	54
Compiled	3	13	11	2			31	26
Tax Returns	16	18	13	1			33	38
Other	17	22	23	27	1	2	85	80
	32 (4/1-9/30/13)		189 (10/1/13-3/31/14)				4/1/09-3/31/10	4/1/10-3/31/11
	0-500M	500M-2MM	2-10MM	10-50MM	50-100MM	100-250MM	ALL	ALL
NUMBER OF STATEMENTS	36	57	74	47	5	2	211	219
ASSETS	%	%	%	%	%	%	%	%
Cash & Equivalents	17.7	11.6	11.7	11.2			9.7	10.2
Trade Receivables (net)	28.7	33.7	31.6	29.4			30.4	30.5
Inventory	14.7	17.0	20.4	23.8			17.2	16.9
All Other Current	4.2	2.6	4.1	3.8			3.6	3.6
Total Current	65.3	65.0	67.9	68.3			60.8	61.2
Fixed Assets (net)	23.5	23.4	22.4	21.6			25.8	26.8
Intangibles (net)	5.5	5.5	4.4	4.3			5.6	4.9
All Other Non-Current	5.7	6.0	5.3	5.8			7.8	7.1
Total	100.0	100.0	100.0	100.0			100.0	100.0
LIABILITIES								
Notes Payable-Short Term	32.9	12.4	7.2	11.9			12.4	11.9
Cur. Mat.-L.T.D.	6.2	3.9	2.9	2.3			4.5	4.2
Trade Payables	15.4	14.7	15.1	14.6			13.5	15.6
Income Taxes Payable	.0	.2	.1	.0			.2	.1
All Other Current	22.6	16.7	17.7	12.7			12.0	12.7
Total Current	77.2	47.9	43.0	41.6			42.6	44.5
Long-Term Debt	23.9	21.5	14.3	17.3			19.8	19.9
Deferred Taxes	.0	.0	.4	.1			.5	.5
All Other Non-Current	26.9	6.5	7.1	14.4			7.3	9.3
Net Worth	-28.1	24.0	35.2	26.6			29.7	25.8
Total Liabilties & Net Worth	100.0	100.0	100.0	100.0			100.0	100.0
INCOME DATA								
Net Sales	100.0	100.0	100.0	100.0			100.0	100.0
Gross Profit	60.0	48.4	37.7	31.8			40.2	39.0
Operating Expenses	55.9	40.7	33.7	26.4			37.7	35.2
Operating Profit	4.1	7.7	4.1	5.4			2.5	3.8
All Other Expenses (net)	.2	.8	.2	.9			1.2	1.2
Profit Before Taxes	3.9	7.0	3.8	4.5			1.4	2.6
RATIOS								
Current	3.0	2.5	2.6	2.6			2.5	2.2
	1.5	1.5	1.7	1.5			1.6	1.5
	.5	1.1	1.2	1.2			1.1	1.1
Quick	1.9	1.7	1.9	1.8			1.7	1.4
	.8	.9	1.1	.8			1.0	1.0
	.3	.6	.6	.6			.6	.6
Sales/Receivables	**14** 25.2	**30** 12.1	**32** 11.5	**34** 10.6			**27** 13.3	**31** 11.6
	24 15.1	**41** 8.8	**44** 8.3	**54** 6.8			**42** 8.6	**48** 7.6
	38 9.7	**53** 6.9	**57** 6.4	**72** 5.1			**63** 5.8	**68** 5.3
Cost of Sales/Inventory	**0** UND	**13** 28.5	**19** 19.2	**34** 10.7			**16** 22.6	**13** 27.4
	27 13.7	**32** 11.3	**42** 8.6	**60** 6.1			**39** 9.5	**38** 9.6
	54 6.8	**73** 5.0	**63** 5.8	**104** 3.5			**68** 5.4	**63** 5.8
Cost of Sales/Payables	**16** 22.7	**17** 21.4	**19** 18.9	**23** 15.7			**18** 20.1	**17** 21.7
	23 16.1	**30** 12.0	**27** 13.7	**35** 10.4			**29** 12.6	**30** 12.1
	46 7.9	**54** 6.7	**47** 7.8	**59** 6.2			**48** 7.5	**51** 7.2
Sales/Working Capital	8.5	6.9	4.9	4.8			5.6	5.8
	19.2	13.0	10.1	8.1			11.1	11.4
	-8.0	129.1	22.9	21.4			70.6	79.6
EBIT/Interest	16.1	23.7	20.3	18.8			8.5	11.4
	(26) 2.2	(52) 7.9	(67) 6.1	(43) 3.3			(187) 2.9	(196) 2.9
	.7	2.4	2.6	1.5			-.9	.5
Net Profit + Depr., Dep., Amort./Cur. Mat. L/T/D			8.0				4.6	7.2
			(19) 3.0				(41) 2.0	(58) 3.2
			1.9				-.6	1.0
Fixed/Worth	.4	.2	.2	.2			.3	.3
	-9.5	.8	.5	.7			.8	.8
	-.4	10.2	2.4	5.9			5.4	2.4
Debt/Worth	1.0	.8	.7	.8			.8	.9
	-18.0	2.2	1.7	2.5			1.9	2.0
	-1.8	NM	5.1	27.3			9.8	6.7
% Profit Before Taxes/Tangible Net Worth	89.2	105.8	54.6	45.6			35.9	34.6
	(15) 25.0	(43) 40.5	(62) 22.9	(39) 19.1			(167) 12.3	(179) 14.2
	-.7	18.7	7.2	6.6			-1.0	-.3
% Profit Before Taxes/Total Assets	45.8	23.4	19.3	15.0			13.7	14.5
	6.9	12.5	8.6	5.4			4.0	4.5
	.1	5.7	3.4	.0			-4.9	-.9
Sales/Net Fixed Assets	72.3	36.2	30.1	26.4			27.8	24.8
	19.4	17.7	16.9	12.5			11.1	11.5
	11.0	9.1	7.0	4.9			5.6	6.3
Sales/Total Assets	5.5	3.7	3.3	2.5			3.1	3.1
	4.4	2.9	2.5	1.9			2.3	2.3
	2.9	2.3	2.0	1.6			1.6	1.8
% Depr., Dep., Amort./Sales	.9	1.1	1.0	1.0			1.1	1.1
	(20) 2.0	(36) 1.8	(65) 1.6	(41) 1.4			(168) 2.2	(185) 2.1
	3.6	3.2	3.1	2.7			3.5	3.5
% Officers', Directors' Owners' Comp/Sales	5.1	2.7	1.5	1.2			2.6	2.1
	(22) 8.2	(35) 4.2	(30) 3.0	(11) 2.3			(78) 4.4	(95) 4.8
	10.6	6.6	5.3	4.1			7.9	8.0
Net Sales ($)	38365M	204079M	911950M	1925103M	637069M	467168M	4402482M	4393402M
Total Assets ($)	9662M	67165M	342994M	974899M	307070M	333421M	2495686M	2220856M

M = $ thousand MM = $ million

See Pages 9 through 22 for Explanation of Ratios and Data

Comparative Historical Data

Current Data Sorted by Sales

			Type of Statement						
18	11	9	Unqualified					1	8
51	50	43	Reviewed			8	7	17	11
30	29	29	Compiled	2	5	7	7	6	2
46	54	48	Tax Returns	8	18	8	9	5	
80	73	92	Other	13	14	12	6	19	28
4/1/11-3/31/12	4/1/12-3/31/13	4/1/13-3/31/14		32 (4/1-9/30/13)			189 (10/1/13-3/31/14)		
ALL	ALL	ALL		0-1MM	1-3MM	3-5MM	5-10MM	10-25MM	25MM & OVER
225	217	221	NUMBER OF STATEMENTS	23	37	35	29	48	49
%	%	%	ASSETS	%	%	%	%	%	%
10.4	12.8	12.3	Cash & Equivalents	14.9	14.0	14.8	13.0	9.5	10.3
31.7	30.8	31.0	Trade Receivables (net)	20.5	33.9	32.7	35.8	30.3	30.5
17.1	18.6	19.3	Inventory	13.8	15.4	17.1	18.6	22.0	24.0
4.3	2.3	3.8	All Other Current	2.1	3.4	4.2	5.3	3.1	4.4
63.5	64.6	66.4	Total Current	51.2	66.8	68.8	72.7	64.9	69.3
24.5	23.9	22.6	Fixed Assets (net)	29.1	25.4	20.4	19.5	23.1	20.3
4.7	5.0	5.4	Intangibles (net)	12.2	3.4	4.2	3.8	5.8	5.1
7.3	6.5	5.6	All Other Non-Current	7.5	4.4	6.6	4.0	6.2	5.4
100.0	100.0	100.0	Total	100.0	100.0	100.0	100.0	100.0	100.0
			LIABILITIES						
12.9	14.2	13.6	Notes Payable-Short Term	34.9	21.0	6.3	7.4	10.8	9.9
4.0	4.6	3.6	Cur. Mat.-L.T.D.	3.3	6.9	3.0	3.5	3.1	2.2
15.5	18.8	15.0	Trade Payables	8.9	17.4	12.8	14.6	17.9	14.9
.1	.2	.1	Income Taxes Payable	.1	.0	.3	.1	.0	.2
14.8	15.7	17.1	All Other Current	14.3	22.9	18.2	15.3	17.5	14.2
47.2	53.6	49.4	Total Current	61.4	68.2	40.4	40.9	49.2	41.4
21.2	20.0	18.7	Long-Term Debt	37.7	20.5	13.4	14.4	16.9	16.2
.4	.2	.2	Deferred Taxes	.0	.0	.5	.1	.2	.3
8.8	11.0	11.6	All Other Non-Current	8.7	26.4	5.5	2.9	8.6	14.2
22.3	15.2	20.1	Net Worth	-7.9	-15.1	40.2	41.7	25.1	27.8
100.0	100.0	100.0	Total Liabilties & Net Worth	100.0	100.0	100.0	100.0	100.0	100.0
			INCOME DATA						
100.0	100.0	100.0	Net Sales	100.0	100.0	100.0	100.0	100.0	100.0
40.6	42.1	42.5	Gross Profit	65.3	51.1	43.4	38.9	37.6	31.6
37.1	38.7	37.2	Operating Expenses	56.6	46.6	37.4	35.7	33.6	25.5
3.5	3.4	5.2	Operating Profit	8.7	4.5	6.0	3.2	4.0	6.1
.9	1.1	.6	All Other Expenses (net)	.7	.8	-.2	-.1	.9	1.0
2.6	2.4	4.7	Profit Before Taxes	7.9	3.7	6.2	3.2	3.1	5.1
			RATIOS						
2.2	2.4	2.5		3.5	2.3	3.4	3.7	2.1	2.5
1.5	1.4	1.6	Current	1.6	1.4	1.8	1.8	1.4	1.5
1.0	.9	1.1		.6	.6	1.2	1.2	1.0	1.3
1.5	1.5	1.8		2.2	1.7	2.1	2.4	1.2	1.6
.9	.9	.9	Quick	.8	.9	1.3	1.1	.9	.9
.6	.5	.6		.4	.4	.8	.8	.6	.6
27 13.5	**27** 13.7	**27** 13.3		**9** 42.7	**20** 18.6	**33** 11.1	**33** 11.2	**32** 11.3	**33** 10.9
47 7.8	**42** 8.7	**42** 8.6	Sales/Receivables	**25** 14.5	**37** 9.9	**42** 8.6	**40** 9.1	**42** 8.6	**54** 6.7
63 5.8	**59** 6.2	**57** 6.4		**45** 8.2	**54** 6.8	**56** 6.5	**54** 6.8	**56** 6.5	**72** 5.1
9 38.5	**11** 33.1	**18** 19.8		**0** UND	**8** 45.4	**14** 25.7	**23** 16.1	**25** 14.6	**32** 11.4
35 10.4	**38** 9.5	**42** 8.6	Cost of Sales/Inventory	**52** 7.0	**22** 16.7	**36** 10.0	**38** 9.6	**43** 8.4	**57** 6.4
60 6.1	**74** 4.9	**72** 5.1		**89** 4.1	**49** 7.4	**72** 5.1	**52** 7.0	**73** 5.0	**83** 4.4
19 19.7	**17** 21.3	**19** 19.2		**15** 23.9	**18** 20.5	**12** 30.9	**16** 22.6	**22** 16.9	**23** 16.2
30 12.0	**30** 12.2	**29** 12.6	Cost of Sales/Payables	**21** 17.5	**36** 10.0	**25** 14.5	**29** 12.7	**28** 12.9	**33** 11.2
50 7.3	**52** 7.0	**51** 7.1		**37** 9.9	**56** 6.5	**43** 8.4	**42** 8.7	**59** 6.2	**54** 6.8
7.0	6.4	6.2		7.9	8.3	5.0	4.7	8.1	5.5
12.3	13.8	10.8	Sales/Working Capital	19.5	18.9	8.9	9.5	15.3	9.3
352.0	-146.7	56.3		-9.5	-9.6	28.9	33.9	NM	16.6
13.1	12.5	19.8		19.4	9.9	47.0	17.0	15.1	27.2
(199) 4.2	(186) 3.4	(195) 5.6	EBIT/Interest	(16) 3.3	(33) 3.1	(29) 13.2	(25) 5.3	(46) 5.9	(46) 4.2
1.4	.6	1.7		1.3	.9	2.8	2.2	2.5	1.4
7.8	6.9	6.8						11.6	15.1
(41) 2.9	(37) 4.3	(38) 2.7	Net Profit + Depr., Dep., Amort./Cur. Mat. L/T/D					(10) 3.1	(16) 3.2
.8	1.8	1.2						1.9	.3
.3	.2	.2		.3	.5	.2	.2	.3	.2
.8	.8	.8	Fixed/Worth	-2.5	1.5	.4	.5	1.1	.8
5.4	10.2	23.9		-1.5	-.8	1.2	1.8	NM	4.5
.9	.9	.8		.6	1.2	.7	.6	1.0	.8
2.4	2.9	2.6	Debt/Worth	-38.0	7.0	1.3	1.8	2.8	2.6
14.4	NM	-40.3		-3.1	-2.3	3.4	5.4	-30.4	21.0
44.7	59.5	63.5		111.5	73.1	67.3	61.8	63.4	48.9
(176) 20.3	(163) 16.7	(163) 26.1	% Profit Before Taxes/Tangible Net Worth	(11) 85.9	(20) 31.6	(29) 29.0	(28) 20.0	(35) 31.1	(40) 22.5
4.8	1.2	8.1		16.7	-.4	18.6	5.0	12.8	6.0
16.3	17.0	20.1		58.1	22.1	22.2	18.1	19.0	17.1
6.0	4.2	8.4	% Profit Before Taxes/Total Assets	14.3	6.8	12.5	6.5	6.6	5.7
.7	-1.1	1.9		2.7	.2	7.2	1.8	3.8	.6
29.0	34.4	33.2		74.0	24.9	38.9	37.0	30.2	27.0
13.7	14.4	16.3	Sales/Net Fixed Assets	15.0	14.9	23.9	15.6	18.0	15.0
6.1	6.9	7.1		6.6	6.5	9.6	10.1	5.7	6.6
3.5	3.7	3.5		5.2	4.5	3.2	3.8	3.7	2.6
2.5	2.5	2.6	Sales/Total Assets	2.8	3.3	2.6	2.8	2.4	2.0
1.8	1.8	1.9		2.1	2.6	2.0	2.3	1.9	1.6
1.0	.7	1.0		.3	1.4	1.0	.7	.9	1.0
(187) 1.8	(171) 1.7	(168) 1.7	% Depr., Dep., Amort./Sales	(14) 3.0	(22) 2.0	(24) 2.2	(23) 1.7	(40) 1.4	(45) 1.6
2.9	3.2	3.2		6.1	2.9	4.0	3.3	2.3	2.9
2.4	2.3	1.8		5.4	3.8	1.5	2.3	1.1	.4
(97) 4.3	(98) 4.5	(101) 4.3	% Officers', Directors' Owners' Comp/Sales	(10) 8.0	(26) 6.1	(18) 3.9	(16) 3.9	(18) 2.0	(13) 1.2
6.8	8.6	7.8		10.7	8.7	8.1	5.6	4.6	3.1
3916430M	3330947M	4183734M	Net Sales ($)	15107M	68723M	143020M	214847M	746192M	2995845M
2090630M	1647022M	2035211M	Total Assets ($)	6661M	24330M	66391M	79720M	333167M	1524942M

M = $ thousand MM = $ million

See Pages 9 through 22 for Explanation of Ratios and Data

Current Data Sorted by Assets							Comparative Historical Data	
						Type of Statement		
		1	1	2	4	Unqualified	11	10
	2	11	5			Reviewed	19	19
	1	6				Compiled	14	8
2	6	2				Tax Returns	6	7
	3	8	9	2	6	Other	33	43
	14 (4/1-9/30/13)		57 (10/1/13-3/31/14)				4/1/09-3/31/10 ALL	4/1/10-3/31/11 ALL
0-500M	500M-2MM	2-10MM	10-50MM	50-100MM	100-250MM			
2	12	28	15	4	10	**NUMBER OF STATEMENTS**	83	87
%	%	%	%	%	%	**ASSETS**	%	%
	18.7	13.7	10.9		7.0	Cash & Equivalents	10.4	9.1
	33.3	26.8	20.1		16.2	Trade Receivables (net)	24.4	26.9
	31.5	28.2	21.6		12.5	Inventory	22.8	24.3
	.3	2.7	4.7		2.1	All Other Current	2.9	3.0
	83.8	71.4	57.2		37.8	Total Current	60.5	63.3
	13.4	19.0	21.8		14.5	Fixed Assets (net)	25.2	21.7
	.0	2.2	15.8		29.2	Intangibles (net)	7.8	9.1
	2.8	7.4	5.2		18.4	All Other Non-Current	6.4	5.9
	100.0	100.0	100.0		100.0	Total	100.0	100.0
						LIABILITIES		
	10.9	10.3	9.6		.7	Notes Payable-Short Term	7.5	8.8
	.9	2.7	3.2		1.9	Cur. Mat.-L.T.D.	4.3	3.5
	15.1	12.1	9.2		4.9	Trade Payables	12.4	13.8
	.4	.5	.0		.2	Income Taxes Payable	.2	.4
	12.0	10.8	6.4		5.6	All Other Current	7.3	9.7
	39.4	36.3	28.4		13.3	Total Current	31.7	36.1
	11.2	10.9	16.8		25.9	Long-Term Debt	13.2	12.8
	.5	.5	1.3		2.2	Deferred Taxes	.9	.9
	4.2	4.3	12.9		15.1	All Other Non-Current	6.9	4.7
	44.8	48.0	40.5		43.5	Net Worth	47.4	45.5
	100.0	100.0	100.0		100.0	Total Liabilties & Net Worth	100.0	100.0
						INCOME DATA		
	100.0	100.0	100.0		100.0	Net Sales	100.0	100.0
	37.9	32.6	29.6		33.7	Gross Profit	30.7	32.2
	34.8	25.9	21.6		23.2	Operating Expenses	26.8	24.8
	3.1	6.7	8.0		10.5	Operating Profit	3.9	7.4
	1.2	.5	2.4		2.9	All Other Expenses (net)	.7	1.2
	1.9	6.2	5.6		7.6	Profit Before Taxes	3.2	6.2
						RATIOS		
	7.2	3.0	5.6		3.2		3.5	2.6
	3.5	1.9	3.3		2.6	Current	2.0	1.8
	1.2	1.3	1.5		1.7		1.3	1.3
	6.0	2.1	3.2		2.0		2.1	1.6
	1.4	1.1	1.8		1.3	Quick	1.2	1.0
	.7	.6	.6		1.0		.7	.7
	28 13.2	**34** 10.6	**36** 10.0		**39** 9.4		**38** 9.7	**39** 9.5
	43 8.4	**42** 8.7	**43** 8.5		**48** 7.6	Sales/Receivables	**43** 8.5	**46** 7.9
	52 7.0	**50** 7.3	**49** 7.5		**59** 6.2		**54** 6.8	**56** 6.5
	30 12.3	**33** 11.1	**49** 7.4		**51** 7.2		**39** 9.3	**43** 8.4
	59 6.2	**58** 6.3	**70** 5.2		**70** 5.2	Cost of Sales/Inventory	**61** 6.0	**69** 5.3
	89 4.1	**104** 3.5	**87** 4.2		**83** 4.4		**90** 4.0	**95** 3.9
	15 24.4	**20** 18.7	**19** 19.6		**24** 14.9		**19** 18.8	**19** 18.9
	25 14.5	**23** 15.7	**24** 15.4		**26** 14.1	Cost of Sales/Payables	**28** 13.0	**31** 11.7
	31 11.6	**34** 10.6	**34** 10.6		**30** 12.2		**44** 8.4	**44** 8.4
	3.0	4.5	3.1		3.9		3.7	4.3
	5.4	7.1	5.0		5.1	Sales/Working Capital	6.3	7.8
	25.6	17.2	13.5		10.0		16.9	17.5
		47.7	18.7				8.3	17.6
		(25) 13.8	(13) 2.8			EBIT/Interest	(70) 3.6	(74) 8.1
		6.7	1.8				.9	3.5
							2.8	9.2
						Net Profit + Depr., Dep., Amort./Cur. Mat. L/T/D	(20) 1.4	(17) 2.2
							.3	1.1
	.1	.1	.3		.3		.3	.3
	.4	.3	1.2		-12.0	Fixed/Worth	.6	.6
	1.4	.9	-27.1		-.5		1.3	1.3
	.2	.4	.5		.3		.5	.7
	1.8	1.1	2.1		-64.6	Debt/Worth	1.4	1.4
	5.5	2.0	-149.2		-2.5		3.0	4.7
	45.9	73.4	30.6				34.6	57.3
	(11) 17.8	(26) 34.9	(11) 21.4			% Profit Before Taxes/Tangible Net Worth	(74) 8.5	(73) 27.8
	4.1	16.8	1.7				.1	10.8
	22.6	26.0	13.1		15.9		11.1	18.4
	9.3	17.0	5.7		6.4	% Profit Before Taxes/Total Assets	3.6	9.7
	-4.1	7.8	1.4		-.7		.2	4.5
	139.0	37.4	18.7		15.5		18.3	25.0
	24.0	16.2	11.0		5.2	Sales/Net Fixed Assets	7.9	9.8
	16.3	7.3	6.4		4.3		3.9	5.3
	4.3	3.1	2.1		1.0		2.4	2.5
	2.4	2.1	1.6		.8	Sales/Total Assets	1.7	1.8
	2.0	1.8	1.2		.7		1.3	1.5
		.4	.7				1.0	.9
		(25) 1.1	1.3			% Depr., Dep., Amort./Sales	(69) 2.6	(74) 2.0
		2.4	3.0				4.0	3.1
		2.7					2.6	2.6
		(12) 4.5				% Officers', Directors' Owners' Comp/Sales	(28) 4.8	(27) 5.5
		6.2					8.2	10.2
4391M	43242M	345940M	498706M	356680M	1419010M	Net Sales ($)	2769891M	3504613M
810M	15544M	148040M	306517M	309327M	1576660M	Total Assets ($)	2051638M	2348505M

M = $ thousand MM = $ million

See Pages 9 through 22 for Explanation of Ratios and Data

Comparative Historical Data | **Current Data Sorted by Sales**

4/1/11-3/31/12 ALL	4/1/12-3/31/13 ALL	4/1/13-3/31/14 ALL		0-1MM	1-3MM	3-5MM	5-10MM	10-25MM	25MM & OVER
			Type of Statement						
10	8	8	Unqualified				1		7
13	11	18	Reviewed		1	3	3	8	3
10	9	7	Compiled			2	2	2	1
13	11	10	Tax Returns		3	4	2	1	
38	34	28	Other	1		2	3	9	13
				14 (4/1-9/30/13)		57 (10/1/13-3/31/14)			
84	73	71	**NUMBER OF STATEMENTS**	1	4	11	11	20	24
%	%	%	**ASSETS**	%	%	%	%	%	%
8.5	9.8	13.0	Cash & Equivalents			13.0	12.7	10.9	12.4
26.0	26.8	24.6	Trade Receivables (net)			33.0	22.7	24.0	21.6
25.6	25.8	23.9	Inventory			31.8	34.4	24.4	17.4
1.6	1.5	2.9	All Other Current			3.8	1.2	1.6	4.8
61.8	64.0	64.4	Total Current			81.6	71.1	60.8	56.3
20.2	21.6	18.3	Fixed Assets (net)			14.7	20.5	21.4	14.1
11.6	8.1	10.1	Intangibles (net)			1.3	.5	9.6	20.4
6.4	6.4	7.2	All Other Non-Current			2.4	8.0	8.1	9.3
100.0	100.0	100.0	Total			100.0	100.0	100.0	100.0
			LIABILITIES						
8.7	9.6	8.0	Notes Payable-Short Term			11.6	13.1	7.4	5.7
2.9	3.7	2.5	Cur. Mat.-L.T.D.			1.6	3.2	3.3	1.5
12.8	12.6	10.9	Trade Payables			12.3	12.8	10.2	8.6
.3	.3	.3	Income Taxes Payable			.9	.0	.3	.2
9.8	8.6	9.6	All Other Current			17.0	4.8	10.2	7.7
34.5	34.8	31.3	Total Current			43.3	33.9	31.4	23.7
11.8	14.6	14.0	Long-Term Debt			16.8	10.6	10.7	17.7
.9	.9	1.0	Deferred Taxes			.6	.7	.9	1.7
8.9	7.6	9.2	All Other Non-Current			9.2	1.8	7.8	14.9
43.9	42.1	44.4	Net Worth			30.1	52.9	49.2	42.0
100.0	100.0	100.0	Total Liabilties & Net Worth			100.0	100.0	100.0	100.0
			INCOME DATA						
100.0	100.0	100.0	Net Sales			100.0	100.0	100.0	100.0
32.0	33.3	32.8	Gross Profit			36.3	37.9	32.2	28.8
25.0	24.7	26.0	Operating Expenses			31.9	31.0	23.3	19.9
7.0	8.6	6.8	Operating Profit			4.4	6.9	8.9	8.9
1.1	1.2	1.5	All Other Expenses (net)			.6	1.0	1.3	2.4
5.9	7.3	5.3	Profit Before Taxes			3.8	5.9	7.5	6.5
			RATIOS						
3.0	3.5	4.6				6.0	4.6	4.4	4.1
1.9	2.0	2.1	Current			1.9	1.8	2.1	2.7
1.3	1.3	1.4				1.1	1.6	1.3	1.8
1.7	2.2	2.4				3.5	2.3	2.4	2.3
1.1	1.3	1.3	Quick			.8	.8	1.2	1.6
.7	.6	.7				.5	.5	.7	1.0
38 9.7	32 11.3	36 10.2				36 10.1	29 12.5	34 10.6	41 8.9
45 8.2	45 8.1	43 8.4	Sales/Receivables			45 8.2	43 8.5	39 9.3	48 7.6
54 6.8	54 6.7	53 6.9				53 6.9	47 7.8	47 7.7	60 6.1
39 9.3	33 10.9	41 9.0				28 12.9	46 8.0	45 8.1	42 8.6
64 5.7	61 6.0	63 5.8	Cost of Sales/Inventory			78 4.7	101 3.6	63 5.8	64 5.7
104 3.5	107 3.4	83 4.4				140 2.6	203 1.8	81 4.5	74 4.9
17 21.3	19 19.3	20 18.3				18 20.3	22 16.4	19 19.3	22 16.3
25 14.4	26 14.3	25 14.4	Cost of Sales/Payables			28 13.1	29 12.8	23 15.8	26 14.3
46 7.9	36 10.2	34 10.6				32 11.4	57 6.4	30 12.3	36 10.1
4.6	4.5	3.2				3.1	3.2	4.6	3.0
7.0	7.3	6.2	Sales/Working Capital			6.4	5.0	8.2	5.1
15.8	20.7	13.5				19.0	9.8	17.5	8.8
22.1	39.2	41.5					27.1	51.8	45.3
(73) 8.6	(68) 8.9	(60) 6.7	EBIT/Interest				12.5	(17) 10.5	(19) 3.6
1.6	3.0	1.4					1.4	4.1	.9
7.0	7.3	13.5							
(19) 2.7	(19) 3.9	(11) 4.7	Net Profit + Depr., Dep., Amort./Cur. Mat. L/T/D						
.7	1.7	1.7							
.2	.2	.2				.1	.1	.1	.3
.5	.6	.4	Fixed/Worth			1.2	.3	.4	.8
2.1	1.5	2.4				22.9	.4	1.3	-1.1
.6	.6	.4				.2	.5	.4	.4
1.9	1.9	1.5	Debt/Worth			5.0	1.1	1.2	4.5
6.3	4.2	7.6				182.2	1.6	2.4	-4.6
49.5	63.6	57.1					54.9	38.0	78.0
(68) 28.3	(62) 38.2	(56) 26.4	% Profit Before Taxes/Tangible Net Worth				11.7	(17) 25.1	(14) 33.1
6.6	12.7	11.1					1.7	13.5	16.1
17.1	20.0	20.8				24.7	23.2	22.9	17.7
11.1	13.3	9.5	% Profit Before Taxes/Total Assets			14.5	9.2	12.7	6.8
2.4	3.4	2.2				-6.1	.7	7.3	.1
21.7	24.9	26.9				88.5	79.0	36.7	17.8
10.9	16.2	13.9	Sales/Net Fixed Assets			22.0	13.9	12.0	11.2
6.0	6.1	6.4				10.7	6.8	6.4	5.2
2.5	3.0	2.7				3.4	2.8	2.7	2.2
1.9	1.9	1.8	Sales/Total Assets			2.2	1.8	1.9	1.2
1.5	1.6	1.2				2.0	1.4	1.6	.8
1.0	.9	.7					.6	.3	.8
(73) 2.0	(64) 1.3	(58) 1.4	% Depr., Dep., Amort./Sales				(10) 1.4	(18) 1.3	(17) 1.6
3.2	2.5	2.8					3.3	2.7	2.5
2.1	2.8	3.5							
(28) 5.1	(27) 4.9	(23) 5.8	% Officers', Directors' Owners' Comp/Sales						
7.1	7.2	7.7							
3320488M	2946556M	2667969M	Net Sales ($)	794M	8026M	45216M	83922M	302694M	2227317M
2463753M	2092654M	2356898M	Total Assets ($)	909M	2351M	21416M	51342M	173291M	2107589M

M = $ thousand MM = $ million

See Pages 9 through 22 for Explanation of Ratios and Data

Current Data Sorted by Assets							Comparative Historical Data	
						Type of Statement		
			3			Unqualified	9	11
		3	1			Reviewed	2	2
	1	1				Compiled	5	4
	1	1				Tax Returns	3	2
1		3	7	2	1	Other	13	10
	5 (4/1-9/30/13)		20 (10/1/13-3/31/14)				**4/1/09-3/31/10**	**4/1/10-3/31/11**
0-500M	**500M-2MM**	**2-10MM**	**10-50MM**	**50-100MM**	**100-250MM**		**ALL**	**ALL**
1	2	8	11	2	1	**NUMBER OF STATEMENTS**	32	29
%	%	%	%	%	%	**ASSETS**	%	%
			9.8			Cash & Equivalents	13.9	10.5
			18.8			Trade Receivables (net)	16.3	19.5
			47.3			Inventory	34.9	35.6
			3.2			All Other Current	3.5	2.5
			79.1			Total Current	68.6	68.1
			12.5			Fixed Assets (net)	20.6	19.2
			2.3			Intangibles (net)	4.1	3.9
			6.1			All Other Non-Current	6.7	8.8
			100.0			Total	100.0	100.0
						LIABILITIES		
			3.5			Notes Payable-Short Term	9.7	11.6
			1.0			Cur. Mat.-L.T.D.	1.4	3.3
			13.6			Trade Payables	10.4	10.1
			.8			Income Taxes Payable	.2	.4
			9.9			All Other Current	6.3	8.8
			28.7			Total Current	28.1	34.3
			1.5			Long-Term Debt	16.4	24.4
			.3			Deferred Taxes	.3	.1
			6.1			All Other Non-Current	7.3	8.5
			63.4			Net Worth	48.0	32.6
			100.0			Total Liabilties & Net Worth	100.0	100.0
						INCOME DATA		
			100.0			Net Sales	100.0	100.0
			28.9			Gross Profit	38.2	41.7
			25.7			Operating Expenses	33.2	36.6
			3.2			Operating Profit	5.0	5.1
			.5			All Other Expenses (net)	1.4	1.6
			2.7			Profit Before Taxes	3.6	3.6
						RATIOS		
			6.4				6.3	4.0
			2.9			Current	2.6	2.1
			2.0				1.5	1.2
			2.2				1.8	1.7
			1.0			Quick	1.1	.8
			.8				.6	.6
			45 8.2				**27** 13.8	**29** 12.5
			57 6.4			Sales/Receivables	**38** 9.7	**48** 7.7
			59 6.2				**53** 6.8	**53** 6.9
			152 2.4				**92** 4.0	**97** 3.8
			203 1.8			Cost of Sales/Inventory	**123** 3.0	**140** 2.6
			215 1.7				**184** 2.0	**209** 1.7
			16 23.5				**12** 30.2	**18** 20.3
			45 8.1			Cost of Sales/Payables	**21** 17.7	**37** 9.8
			111 3.3				**58** 6.3	**56** 6.5
			1.8				2.4	2.5
			2.3			Sales/Working Capital	3.6	4.0
			4.9				7.3	13.8
							15.2	14.0
						EBIT/Interest	(26) 3.4	(26) 2.6
							.5	1.2
								18.4
						Net Profit + Depr., Dep., Amort./Cur. Mat. L/T/D		(11) 1.8
								.7
			.1				.1	.2
			.1			Fixed/Worth	.4	.8
			.3				1.5	-1.1
			.2				.2	.4
			.5			Debt/Worth	.8	1.7
			1.0				3.6	-7.6
			11.9				19.2	21.5
			1.9			% Profit Before Taxes/Tangible Net Worth	(27) 10.8	(18) 8.4
			-1.7				.9	1.9
			10.9				13.4	12.9
			1.3			% Profit Before Taxes/Total Assets	7.3	4.7
			-.8				.1	.7
			18.2				26.1	21.6
			13.6			Sales/Net Fixed Assets	8.1	8.0
			9.8				5.3	5.5
			1.7				1.9	2.1
			1.4			Sales/Total Assets	1.6	1.7
			1.2				1.0	1.1
							.7	.7
						% Depr., Dep., Amort./Sales	(28) 2.0	(26) 1.8
							3.0	3.2
						% Officers', Directors' Owners' Comp/Sales		
789M	**6535M**	**106285M**	**358719M**	**211093M**	**112714M**	Net Sales ($)	**1584082M**	**1759549M**
210M	**2131M**	**48655M**	**282413M**	**144687M**	**122729M**	Total Assets ($)	**1074835M**	**1116276M**

M = $ thousand MM = $ million

See Pages 9 through 22 for Explanation of Ratios and Data

Comparative Historical Data				Current Data Sorted by Sales					
			Type of Statement						
7	2	3	Unqualified					1	2
1	2	4	Reviewed					2	2
2	2	2	Compiled			1	1		
4	5	2	Tax Returns		1			1	
11	9	14	Other	1			2	2	9
4/1/11-3/31/12 ALL	**4/1/12-3/31/13 ALL**	**4/1/13-3/31/14 ALL**		5 (4/1-9/30/13)			20 (10/1/13-3/31/14)		
				0-1MM	**1-3MM**	**3-5MM**	**5-10MM**	**10-25MM**	**25MM & OVER**
25	20	25	**NUMBER OF STATEMENTS**	1	1	1	3	6	13
%	%	%	**ASSETS**	%	%	%	%	%	%
11.7	13.4	11.3	Cash & Equivalents						4.7
17.7	16.7	19.3	Trade Receivables (net)						18.6
38.4	37.5	41.9	Inventory						45.5
2.6	1.8	2.1	All Other Current						1.4
70.5	69.4	74.6	Total Current						70.2
17.2	16.8	14.0	Fixed Assets (net)						14.8
3.6	1.8	3.0	Intangibles (net)						5.5
8.7	12.0	8.4	All Other Non-Current						9.6
100.0	100.0	100.0	Total						100.0
			LIABILITIES						
11.6	3.7	5.8	Notes Payable-Short Term						4.3
2.3	2.3	1.9	Cur. Mat.-L.T.D.						1.7
8.1	7.6	11.5	Trade Payables						12.8
.2	.1	.4	Income Taxes Payable						.3
9.4	13.7	7.1	All Other Current						9.0
31.5	27.4	26.6	Total Current						28.2
14.3	11.9	8.9	Long-Term Debt						5.0
.1	.2	.1	Deferred Taxes						.2
4.6	6.9	4.4	All Other Non-Current						6.9
49.5	53.6	59.9	Net Worth						59.6
100.0	100.0	100.0	Total Liabilties & Net Worth						100.0
			INCOME DATA						
100.0	100.0	100.0	Net Sales						100.0
36.8	42.0	35.6	Gross Profit						32.4
32.1	34.0	30.0	Operating Expenses						28.6
4.7	8.0	5.6	Operating Profit						3.9
1.1	.3	.0	All Other Expenses (net)						.2
3.6	7.7	5.6	Profit Before Taxes						3.6
			RATIOS						
3.9	8.1	6.7							4.6
2.3	2.9	2.9	Current						2.7
1.9	1.6	1.9							2.0
1.8	2.4	2.6							1.7
1.0	1.3	1.0	Quick						.9
.6	.7	.7							.6
27 13.3	**15** 24.2	**27** 13.5							**44** 8.3
38 9.6	**34** 10.8	**44** 8.3	Sales/Receivables						**49** 7.5
57 6.4	**61** 6.0	**57** 6.4							**57** 6.4
99 3.7	**96** 3.8	**101** 3.6							**130** 2.8
146 2.5	**146** 2.5	**152** 2.4	Cost of Sales/Inventory						**159** 2.3
174 2.1	**192** 1.9	**192** 1.9							**215** 1.7
15 24.3	**11** 34.7	**15** 24.2							**18** 20.8
23 16.1	**21** 17.1	**32** 11.5	Cost of Sales/Payables						**34** 10.8
36 10.0	**41** 8.9	**52** 7.0							**58** 6.3
2.4	2.1	2.2							2.3
4.2	4.8	4.2	Sales/Working Capital						4.3
7.3	6.7	5.9							5.6
9.8	37.3	31.4							37.4
(19) 4.4	(15) 10.5	(18) 10.6	EBIT/Interest						(11) 13.4
.9	2.3	.2							.1
			Net Profit + Depr., Dep., Amort./Cur. Mat. L/T/D						
.1	.1	.1							.1
.3	.3	.2	Fixed/Worth						.2
1.3	.8	.4							.4
.3	.4	.4							.4
.7	.8	.5	Debt/Worth						.7
6.0	2.5	1.4							1.3
23.8	41.6	27.4							19.7
(22) 6.6	21.3	11.9	% Profit Before Taxes/Tangible Net Worth						6.7
.6	4.7	-.2							-.5
13.9	16.1	15.3							11.2
5.4	8.6	9.9	% Profit Before Taxes/Total Assets						4.8
.1	2.8	-.2							-.2
30.0	44.9	51.9							16.1
14.7	10.3	13.9	Sales/Net Fixed Assets						11.3
6.2	4.3	6.6							5.6
2.2	2.6	2.5							1.8
1.4	1.4	1.6	Sales/Total Assets						1.4
1.2	1.0	1.2							1.2
.5	1.0	.5							.7
(20) .9	(16) 1.7	(20) 1.0	% Depr., Dep., Amort./Sales						(12) 1.9
2.6	2.9	3.6							5.3
			% Officers', Directors' Owners' Comp/Sales						
1134364M	**944658M**	**796135M**	Net Sales ($)	**789M**	**2244M**	**4291M**	**22139M**	**95694M**	**670978M**
757148M	**825296M**	**600825M**	Total Assets ($)	**210M**	**846M**	**1285M**	**13784M**	**75138M**	**509562M**

M = $ thousand MM = $ million

See Pages 9 through 22 for Explanation of Ratios and Data

Current Data Sorted by Assets							Comparative Historical Data	
						Type of Statement		
	2	18	32	14	13	Unqualified	97	87
1	8	45	21		1	Reviewed	90	101
4	15	23	4	1		Compiled	43	62
27	48	32	4			Tax Returns	100	96
17	52	73	49	11	12	Other	257	244
86 (4/1-9/30/13)		441 (10/1/13-3/31/14)					4/1/09-3/31/10	4/1/10-3/31/11
0-500M	500M-2MM	2-10MM	10-50MM	50-100MM	100-250MM		ALL	ALL
49	125	191	110	26	26	**NUMBER OF STATEMENTS**	587	590
%	%	%	%	%	%	**ASSETS**	%	%
14.8	14.8	10.1	6.3	7.6	9.6	Cash & Equivalents	9.8	10.1
20.9	25.9	25.0	23.3	17.1	19.2	Trade Receivables (net)	23.4	25.5
26.8	28.0	28.1	28.1	20.2	17.1	Inventory	26.7	28.0
3.5	2.1	2.0	1.2	2.3	4.4	All Other Current	3.4	2.2
66.0	70.8	65.3	59.0	47.2	50.3	Total Current	63.4	65.7
18.3	19.3	22.4	26.0	25.1	16.4	Fixed Assets (net)	23.8	21.6
6.4	2.7	4.8	11.0	21.5	20.9	Intangibles (net)	6.6	6.4
9.5	7.2	7.5	4.0	6.3	12.4	All Other Non-Current	6.2	6.3
100.0	100.0	100.0	100.0	100.0	100.0	Total	100.0	100.0
						LIABILITIES		
24.8	11.9	9.1	10.2	6.2	4.1	Notes Payable-Short Term	12.4	13.0
5.0	1.7	4.0	3.5	2.3	2.7	Cur. Mat.-L.T.D.	4.1	3.0
14.1	16.3	14.8	14.0	9.1	8.2	Trade Payables	14.8	15.0
.1	.2	.3	.1	.0	.5	Income Taxes Payable	.2	.3
14.1	9.3	10.7	11.1	7.9	9.7	All Other Current	12.5	10.5
58.1	39.2	39.0	39.0	25.5	25.2	Total Current	44.1	41.7
23.0	15.0	15.7	15.1	23.7	18.9	Long-Term Debt	17.6	16.1
.0	.1	.2	1.3	1.5	1.4	Deferred Taxes	.4	.4
19.1	7.3	5.2	5.7	7.2	11.4	All Other Non-Current	8.0	7.9
-.2	38.4	39.9	38.9	42.0	43.0	Net Worth	30.0	33.9
100.0	100.0	100.0	100.0	100.0	100.0	Total Liabilities & Net Worth	100.0	100.0
						INCOME DATA		
100.0	100.0	100.0	100.0	100.0	100.0	Net Sales	100.0	100.0
50.9	42.4	35.7	29.8	30.2	38.5	Gross Profit	34.2	35.0
43.6	34.9	29.8	24.3	22.8	29.9	Operating Expenses	30.4	29.7
7.3	7.5	5.9	5.5	7.4	8.6	Operating Profit	3.8	5.3
.6	.5	.8	1.0	3.3	.9	All Other Expenses (net)	1.8	1.2
6.7	7.0	5.1	4.6	4.1	7.7	Profit Before Taxes	2.0	4.1
						RATIOS		
5.8	4.0	3.0	2.6	3.1	2.8		3.1	2.8
2.4	2.0	1.8	1.6	1.7	1.8	Current	1.7	1.8
.9	1.2	1.1	1.2	1.4	1.6		1.1	1.2
2.8	2.1	1.8	1.2	1.4	1.7		1.7	1.6
1.0	1.0	.9	.8	1.1	1.1	Quick	.8	.9
.3	.6	.5	.5	.7	.8		.5	.5
0 UND	16 22.2	27 13.7	32 11.3	33 11.0	45 8.1		27 13.3	27 13.4
17 21.4	29 12.4	41 8.8	43 8.5	42 8.6	55 6.6	Sales/Receivables	43 8.6	44 8.3
29 12.7	51 7.1	53 6.9	56 6.5	56 6.5	68 5.4		58 6.3	58 6.3
6 63.0	12 31.7	39 9.4	50 7.3	42 8.7	52 7.0		38 9.7	35 10.4
43 8.5	50 7.3	70 5.2	76 4.8	74 4.9	78 4.7	Cost of Sales/Inventory	76 4.8	70 5.2
96 3.8	107 3.4	111 3.3	111 3.3	130 2.8	96 3.8		123 3.0	113 3.2
2 213.3	13 28.5	18 19.8	23 16.1	17 21.8	21 17.2		17 21.2	18 20.8
17 21.5	29 12.4	31 11.6	34 10.8	29 12.4	32 11.5	Cost of Sales/Payables	30 12.4	30 12.0
41 8.8	54 6.7	49 7.4	54 6.7	39 9.4	43 8.4		52 7.0	49 7.4
6.1	4.2	4.2	4.5	3.6	3.9		4.1	4.4
12.9	7.3	8.6	8.7	7.8	6.5	Sales/Working Capital	8.3	8.5
-46.5	31.8	44.3	25.6	11.4	8.4		61.9	28.6
30.3	38.8	24.9	16.8	8.6	29.9		9.9	12.3
(31) 3.5	(103) 7.9	(160) 6.3	(102) 4.8	(22) 3.3	(21) 6.4	EBIT/Interest	(519) 2.7	(514) 3.9
1.3	2.5	1.6	1.4	1.1	2.5		.0	1.1
		12.1	4.4		10.1		5.7	6.3
		(25) 3.7	(35) 2.5		(11) 2.8	Net Profit + Depr., Dep., Amort./Cur. Mat. L/T/D	(129) 2.4	(138) 2.7
		.7	1.5		.9		.6	.9
.1	.1	.2	.3	.5	.3		.2	.2
.4	.4	.5	.9	1.4	1.0	Fixed/Worth	.7	.6
-.5	1.6	1.8	2.8	-1.2	-.8		3.3	2.3
.4	.4	.6	.9	1.1	.8		.7	.7
3.2	2.0	1.5	2.3	2.3	3.6	Debt/Worth	2.0	1.7
-4.2	8.4	5.0	6.5	-8.9	-6.6		14.8	8.0
83.3	76.0	42.9	52.3	28.2	44.5		38.6	52.7
(30) 46.0	(105) 40.2	(164) 21.9	(93) 21.2	(19) 14.0	(19) 20.7	% Profit Before Taxes/Tangible Net Worth	(467) 15.9	(486) 18.9
9.3	8.9	6.1	5.3	1.7	12.5		1.7	3.4
37.6	25.5	18.6	14.3	8.5	13.0		12.1	17.0
23.8	12.7	8.3	6.4	4.6	7.1	% Profit Before Taxes/Total Assets	4.4	6.4
2.7	1.3	1.4	1.1	.5	2.6		-2.5	.6
127.3	70.3	36.6	20.9	15.2	14.0		29.7	34.9
40.3	17.9	13.2	7.5	6.4	8.8	Sales/Net Fixed Assets	10.2	14.2
10.2	8.5	5.2	4.0	3.1	5.8		4.5	5.4
6.3	3.9	2.6	2.3	2.0	1.6		2.6	2.9
4.1	2.8	2.1	1.7	1.3	1.3	Sales/Total Assets	1.9	2.0
2.5	1.8	1.6	1.2	.9	.9		1.2	1.4
.5	.5	.8	.9	1.7	1.2		1.0	.9
(22) .9	(84) 1.3	(157) 1.7	(104) 2.1	(21) 2.4	(18) 2.1	% Depr., Dep., Amort./Sales	(465) 2.3	(478) 1.8
3.1	2.7	3.4	3.8	4.8	3.3		4.4	3.6
5.2	2.4	1.8	.6				1.6	2.2
(26) 7.7	(68) 3.8	(73) 2.8	(16) 2.2			% Officers', Directors' Owners' Comp/Sales	(171) 3.5	(195) 3.8
12.8	6.4	4.5	4.6				6.8	7.1
55811M	409785M	2018110M	4324369M	2579888M	5355050M	Net Sales ($)	16106926M	15716564M
13034M	141033M	913655M	2377250M	1754644M	4098624M	Total Assets ($)	10297634M	9576502M

M = $ thousand MM = $ million

See Pages 9 through 22 for Explanation of Ratios and Data

Comparative Historical Data				Current Data Sorted by Sales					
			Type of Statement						
78	50	79	Unqualified			4	5	22	48
103	84	76	Reviewed		7	5	19	30	15
65	52	47	Compiled	3	7	12	14	8	3
131	107	111	Tax Returns	17	42	20	21	9	2
228	233	214	Other	13	33	28	33	48	59
4/1/11-3/31/12 ALL	**4/1/12-3/31/13 ALL**	**4/1/13-3/31/14 ALL**		**86 (4/1-9/30/13)**			**441 (10/1/13-3/31/14)**		
				0-1MM	**1-3MM**	**3-5MM**	**5-10MM**	**10-25MM**	**25MM & OVER**
605	526	527	**NUMBER OF STATEMENTS**	33	89	69	92	117	127
%	%	%	**ASSETS**	%	%	%	%	%	%
9.9	10.9	10.7	Cash & Equivalents	12.4	15.3	13.6	10.2	8.8	7.6
26.2	25.6	23.8	Trade Receivables (net)	15.6	23.2	24.9	23.4	26.1	24.0
27.1	27.3	27.0	Inventory	26.8	25.3	24.2	29.8	29.9	25.1
2.6	2.7	2.1	All Other Current	2.7	2.5	1.9	2.4	1.8	2.1
65.8	66.5	63.7	Total Current	57.5	66.3	64.6	65.8	66.6	58.7
21.1	20.7	21.9	Fixed Assets (net)	26.0	19.4	23.5	21.7	21.3	22.2
6.0	5.7	7.4	Intangibles (net)	9.1	4.1	3.5	4.2	7.5	13.4
7.1	7.1	7.1	All Other Non-Current	7.5	10.1	8.4	8.3	4.5	5.6
100.0	100.0	100.0	Total	100.0	100.0	100.0	100.0	100.0	100.0
			LIABILITIES						
12.0	11.1	11.1	Notes Payable-Short Term	19.1	12.5	15.8	10.7	7.7	8.8
2.7	3.1	3.3	Cur. Mat.-L.T.D.	6.0	1.5	3.1	4.0	4.0	2.8
15.1	15.7	14.3	Trade Payables	11.6	13.3	14.8	14.3	16.2	13.8
.3	.3	.2	Income Taxes Payable	.0	.1	.1	.4	.1	.3
11.4	11.8	10.6	All Other Current	11.2	9.1	10.8	9.4	12.1	10.7
41.6	42.0	39.5	Total Current	47.9	36.5	44.6	38.8	40.1	36.5
17.4	15.7	16.6	Long-Term Debt	26.7	18.9	16.6	13.1	16.2	15.5
.5	.3	.5	Deferred Taxes	.0	.0	.1	.3	1.0	.9
9.1	8.7	7.5	All Other Non-Current	31.8	6.6	3.9	7.7	4.2	6.7
31.5	33.3	35.9	Net Worth	-6.4	38.0	34.8	40.2	38.5	40.4
100.0	100.0	100.0	Total Liabilties & Net Worth	100.0	100.0	100.0	100.0	100.0	100.0
			INCOME DATA						
100.0	100.0	100.0	Net Sales	100.0	100.0	100.0	100.0	100.0	100.0
35.3	37.3	37.3	Gross Profit	55.2	47.9	40.3	34.5	32.1	30.6
29.5	30.9	30.8	Operating Expenses	45.0	39.4	33.9	29.5	27.3	23.5
5.8	6.5	6.6	Operating Profit	10.2	8.5	6.4	5.0	4.9	7.1
.7	.8	.9	All Other Expenses (net)	2.4	.5	.3	.9	.6	1.4
5.1	5.6	5.7	Profit Before Taxes	7.8	8.0	6.1	4.1	4.3	5.7
			RATIOS						
2.9	3.1	3.2		10.5	4.5	3.8	3.2	3.0	2.7
1.8	1.7	1.8	Current	2.7	2.3	1.4	1.9	1.8	1.6
1.2	1.2	1.2		1.2	1.2	1.0	1.1	1.2	1.3
1.6	1.7	1.7		3.4	2.7	2.0	1.8	1.6	1.4
.9	.9	.9	Quick	1.3	1.0	.9	.9	.9	.9
.5	.5	.5		.2	.6	.5	.5	.5	.6
26 13.8	**24** 15.2	**24** 15.1		**0** UND	**16** 22.2	**18** 20.6	**23** 15.8	**30** 12.1	**32** 11.4
41 8.9	**39** 9.3	**39** 9.3	Sales/Receivables	**17** 21.8	**30** 12.1	**36** 10.1	**38** 9.5	**42** 8.7	**46** 8.0
56 6.5	**54** 6.7	**54** 6.7		**46** 8.0	**59** 6.2	**53** 6.9	**50** 7.3	**54** 6.7	**56** 6.5
33 11.1	**32** 11.4	**36** 10.1		**10** 38.3	**5** 68.2	**18** 20.3	**39** 9.4	**43** 8.5	**42** 8.6
62 5.9	**68** 5.4	**65** 5.6	Cost of Sales/Inventory	**55** 6.6	**57** 6.4	**51** 7.1	**70** 5.2	**79** 4.6	**72** 5.1
111 3.3	**118** 3.1	**107** 3.4		**243** 1.5	**126** 2.9	**87** 4.2	**111** 3.3	**114** 3.2	**96** 3.8
15 23.7	**16** 23.5	**17** 21.0		**4** 87.9	**12** 29.4	**16** 22.5	**17** 21.0	**20** 18.7	**21** 17.3
29 12.4	**30** 12.2	**30** 12.0	Cost of Sales/Payables	**16** 23.5	**28** 12.9	**29** 12.7	**31** 11.7	**33** 11.2	**31** 11.9
47 7.7	**54** 6.7	**50** 7.3		**54** 6.8	**63** 5.8	**49** 7.5	**47** 7.7	**49** 7.5	**45** 8.1
4.4	4.5	4.3		3.1	4.0	4.5	4.4	4.4	4.9
8.1	8.9	8.2	Sales/Working Capital	6.5	7.1	15.6	8.3	7.7	8.3
26.6	28.6	33.1		UND	34.2	999.8	46.9	17.3	18.6
18.5	20.8	20.6		11.5	30.9	16.3	31.5	22.2	18.9
(506) 5.3	(441) 5.4	(439) 6.0	EBIT/Interest	(19) 2.8	(68) 6.8	(59) 7.5	(79) 6.2	(101) 5.2	(113) 5.9
1.8	1.6	1.5		-.8	2.5	1.7	1.2	1.5	1.7
9.7	7.6	6.3						12.1	5.1
(127) 3.4	(91) 3.5	(89) 3.0	Net Profit + Depr., Dep., Amort./Cur. Mat. L/T/D					(25) 2.4	(44) 3.3
1.6	1.8	1.2						.6	2.1
.2	.2	.2		.2	.1	.1	.2	.2	.3
.5	.5	.6	Fixed/Worth	.8	.4	.6	.6	.5	.8
2.3	2.2	2.5		-.4	1.8	2.5	1.5	2.0	3.1
.6	.7	.6		.5	.4	.6	.5	.6	.9
1.7	1.9	1.9	Debt/Worth	6.6	1.6	2.1	1.5	1.7	2.7
6.7	7.4	9.7		-2.7	11.1	10.0	7.7	5.3	7.4
58.1	60.0	56.0		83.3	68.5	83.9	38.4	41.0	54.2
(496) 25.7	(425) 25.5	(430) 26.5	% Profit Before Taxes/Tangible Net Worth	(21) 41.6	(69) 37.1	(59) 42.1	(78) 18.7	(98) 17.8	(105) 28.2
6.9	6.8	6.7		7.8	10.7	6.6	3.8	4.5	9.2
20.8	20.4	20.0		33.7	30.1	23.4	18.8	16.2	18.3
8.2	8.5	8.2	% Profit Before Taxes/Total Assets	10.6	12.5	8.6	6.5	7.8	7.2
1.7	1.7	1.4		-.4	3.8	1.2	.4	1.1	2.4
50.8	48.9	39.8		53.0	67.4	55.1	39.8	37.6	25.5
14.2	14.0	12.9	Sales/Net Fixed Assets	11.8	15.8	14.5	13.7	13.2	9.9
6.1	6.2	5.6		6.4	6.8	6.3	5.5	5.0	5.5
3.1	3.2	3.0		4.3	3.5	3.7	3.2	2.8	2.5
2.2	2.1	2.1	Sales/Total Assets	2.3	2.5	2.3	2.1	2.1	1.8
1.5	1.5	1.4		1.0	1.5	1.7	1.6	1.5	1.3
.8	.7	.8		.9	.5	.8	.6	.9	.8
(458) 1.7	(405) 1.5	(406) 1.7	% Depr., Dep., Amort./Sales	(14) 2.8	(56) 1.7	(50) 1.5	(79) 1.4	(95) 1.7	(112) 1.8
3.4	3.0	3.4		5.7	3.5	3.6	3.2	3.3	3.5
2.2	2.1	2.1		6.9	2.9	2.1	1.9	1.5	.6
(210) 4.4	(177) 3.4	(183) 3.7	% Officers', Directors' Owners' Comp/Sales	(13) 10.1	(48) 5.8	(40) 3.9	(35) 2.9	(37) 2.4	(10) .9
7.5	6.1	6.4		15.5	9.0	6.1	4.0	5.0	2.2
17792885M	**12768419M**	**14743013M**	Net Sales ($)	**17366M**	**172129M**	**281005M**	**676160M**	**1810246M**	**11786107M**
9712352M	**7282367M**	**9298240M**	Total Assets ($)	**11505M**	**100217M**	**139298M**	**362049M**	**1200187M**	**7484984M**

M = $ thousand MM = $ million

See Pages 9 through 22 for Explanation of Ratios and Data

WHOLESALE TRADE

Current Data Sorted by Assets							Comparative Historical Data	
						Type of Statement		
		9	11	8	12	Unqualified	48	41
	3	35	45	6	4	Reviewed	57	80
2	13	13	10	1		Compiled	51	54
4	28	24	3			Tax Returns	74	81
8	25	50	40	13	14	Other	148	153
	46 (4/1-9/30/13)		335 (10/1/13-3/31/14)				4/1/09-3/31/10	4/1/10-3/31/11
0-500M	500M-2MM	2-10MM	10-50MM	50-100MM	100-250MM		ALL	ALL
14	69	131	109	28	30	NUMBER OF STATEMENTS	378	409
%	%	%	%	%	%	**ASSETS**	%	%
16.1	11.3	12.1	10.0	8.0	8.6	Cash & Equivalents	12.2	11.4
19.7	17.4	18.3	16.5	15.6	12.8	Trade Receivables (net)	16.8	17.0
30.4	48.1	46.8	43.1	39.2	40.6	Inventory	41.5	41.9
1.4	1.2	2.4	4.0	2.7	3.4	All Other Current	3.0	3.1
67.5	78.0	79.6	73.6	65.5	65.5	Total Current	73.5	73.3
17.7	11.3	13.3	18.2	24.1	23.3	Fixed Assets (net)	16.2	17.5
4.8	2.3	2.1	2.8	5.4	2.7	Intangibles (net)	3.5	3.8
9.9	8.4	5.0	5.4	5.0	8.5	All Other Non-Current	6.8	5.4
100.0	100.0	100.0	100.0	100.0	100.0	Total	100.0	100.0
						LIABILITIES		
28.5	16.1	24.4	28.4	28.1	31.1	Notes Payable-Short Term	26.4	24.7
.2	2.8	2.7	2.5	2.9	4.5	Cur. Mat.-L.T.D.	3.4	2.4
13.0	16.8	15.9	12.0	11.8	6.0	Trade Payables	12.4	15.3
.0	.0	.1	.1	.0	.3	Income Taxes Payable	.1	.2
44.4	15.0	9.8	10.2	11.8	10.3	All Other Current	10.6	11.5
86.2	50.7	52.9	53.2	54.7	52.2	Total Current	52.9	54.2
4.6	18.2	10.6	11.0	11.6	20.5	Long-Term Debt	12.3	11.1
.0	.0	.3	.4	.8	1.1	Deferred Taxes	.4	.5
6.2	7.9	7.3	3.2	2.6	1.4	All Other Non-Current	4.7	5.5
3.0	23.1	29.0	32.1	30.5	24.8	Net Worth	29.6	28.8
100.0	100.0	100.0	100.0	100.0	100.0	Total Liabilties & Net Worth	100.0	100.0
						INCOME DATA		
100.0	100.0	100.0	100.0	100.0	100.0	Net Sales	100.0	100.0
40.9	25.8	23.9	20.2	21.7	16.4	Gross Profit	25.3	25.5
36.1	22.0	21.0	15.7	17.0	13.2	Operating Expenses	22.8	22.3
4.8	3.8	2.9	4.4	4.7	3.2	Operating Profit	2.5	3.2
.2	1.1	.3	.2	.6	.7	All Other Expenses (net)	.8	.5
4.5	2.7	2.6	4.3	4.1	2.5	Profit Before Taxes	1.7	2.8
						RATIOS		
6.9	3.3	2.0	1.7	1.3	1.4		2.1	1.9
1.4	1.6	1.5	1.3	1.1	1.2	Current	1.4	1.3
.3	1.0	1.2	1.1	1.0	1.0		1.1	1.1
4.3	1.2	.9	.8	.9	.5		1.0	.8
(13) 1.2	.5	.5	.4	.3	.4	Quick	(377) .5	.5
.2	.2	.3	.2	.2	.2		.2	.3
0 UND	0 UND	6 58.7	8 46.0	11 32.4	10 36.0		5 66.6	6 59.1
6 64.2	9 40.9	16 22.9	14 26.7	19 19.6	19 19.1	Sales/Receivables	16 23.0	16 22.2
25 14.7	29 12.4	30 12.0	26 14.3	28 12.9	27 13.6		32 11.3	30 12.3
0 UND	29 12.6	39 9.3	42 8.6	43 8.5	54 6.8		31 11.9	32 11.4
9 41.0	54 6.8	69 5.3	59 6.2	60 6.1	74 4.9	Cost of Sales/Inventory	62 5.9	64 5.7
126 2.9	89 4.1	114 3.2	83 4.4	104 3.5	89 4.1		107 3.4	99 3.7
0 UND	1 562.5	5 80.9	7 48.7	7 51.6	7 50.5		3 113.5	5 80.5
0 UND	14 26.6	16 22.3	11 34.1	11 31.9	11 32.3	Cost of Sales/Payables	13 27.7	15 24.5
16 22.8	38 9.7	31 11.7	19 19.2	17 21.0	15 25.1		30 12.3	37 9.8
6.8	6.1	6.9	10.2	10.2	14.0		7.4	8.0
107.3	15.1	13.4	19.3	38.8	23.4	Sales/Working Capital	15.9	17.3
-5.7	95.7	33.3	50.6	NM	219.3		89.1	98.3
	18.1	10.1	11.8	8.9	5.5		5.5	8.0
	(54) 6.0	(113) 4.3	(101) 6.2	(24) 4.4	(26) 3.7	EBIT/Interest	(325) 2.2	(359) 3.6
	.9	1.2	3.3	2.4	2.3		1.1	1.6
		18.0	8.9		4.2		4.9	5.8
		(22) 3.7	(20) 2.5		(12) 1.5	Net Profit + Depr., Dep., Amort./Cur. Mat. L/T/D	(62) 1.6	(69) 1.7
		1.4	1.6		1.0		.8	1.0
.0	.0	.1	.2	.4	.3		.1	.1
.4	.2	.3	.4	1.2	1.2	Fixed/Worth	.4	.5
-12.0	.7	1.6	1.0	2.2	2.5		1.7	2.0
.3	.7	1.1	1.4	1.9	2.9		1.1	1.3
4.6	2.3	2.8	2.9	4.4	4.5	Debt/Worth	2.8	2.9
-6.7	30.3	7.1	5.3	8.1	8.4		11.7	9.0
	77.8	47.7	49.1	65.6	43.3		34.9	43.4
	(56) 43.6	(115) 21.4	(105) 28.5	(27) 30.9	30.8	% Profit Before Taxes/Tangible Net Worth	(329) 13.8	(355) 21.7
	8.2	6.6	16.1	16.3	19.4		3.5	7.2
36.2	25.9	12.8	11.8	11.1	7.7		8.5	10.6
5.9	8.8	5.9	7.2	5.4	5.4	% Profit Before Taxes/Total Assets	3.0	5.5
2.8	1.0	.9	3.5	2.4	2.4		.4	1.4
UND	340.9	160.9	73.0	42.4	57.6		121.6	111.5
167.0	111.1	53.0	30.0	12.3	12.3	Sales/Net Fixed Assets	32.7	35.2
12.7	35.6	15.7	10.7	4.1	4.7		9.4	10.8
11.7	6.3	4.5	4.1	3.2	3.1		4.3	4.3
4.0	4.2	2.9	3.0	2.5	2.5	Sales/Total Assets	2.8	2.9
1.9	2.5	2.0	2.0	1.6	1.6		1.7	1.8
	.1	.2	.3	.4	.2		.3	.3
	(39) .5	(99) .4	(104) .6	(24) .8	(24) 1.0	% Depr., Dep., Amort./Sales	(285) .9	(325) .7
	1.1	1.2	1.6	2.7	1.6		2.1	1.9
	1.0	.6	.3				.8	.7
	(37) 2.2	(48) 1.6	(27) 1.0			% Officers', Directors' Owners' Comp/Sales	(134) 1.6	(155) 1.7
	5.0	3.2	2.1				4.0	4.1
26341M	421090M	2600705M	7569855M	4715002M	11335043M	Net Sales ($)	18952473M	20071196M
3216M	78693M	696288M	2561407M	1893443M	4664318M	Total Assets ($)	7569302M	7976447M

M = $ thousand MM = $ million

See Pages 9 through 22 for Explanation of Ratios and Data

Comparative Historical Data				Current Data Sorted by Sales					
			Type of Statement						
49	40	40	Unqualified		1		1	5	33
83	81	93	Reviewed		1	2	7	24	59
39	32	39	Compiled	2	4	6	7	6	14
81	93	59	Tax Returns	3	8	12	16	13	7
165	160	150	Other	7	12	9	17	31	74
					46 (4/1-9/30/13)		335 (10/1/13-3/31/14)		
4/1/11-3/31/12 ALL	4/1/12-3/31/13 ALL	4/1/13-3/31/14 ALL		0-1MM	1-3MM	3-5MM	5-10MM	10-25MM	25MM & OVER
417	406	381	**NUMBER OF STATEMENTS**	12	26	29	48	79	187
%	%	%	**ASSETS**	%	%	%	%	%	%
10.5	11.1	10.9	Cash & Equivalents	10.8	14.8	11.9	11.8	10.6	10.1
19.0	19.0	17.0	Trade Receivables (net)	11.3	19.1	20.6	16.3	18.8	16.1
45.0	43.5	44.3	Inventory	30.0	31.2	44.6	48.9	48.0	44.3
2.6	2.9	2.7	All Other Current	1.3	.7	3.1	2.2	2.4	3.3
77.1	76.6	75.0	Total Current	53.5	65.8	80.2	79.2	79.8	73.8
14.6	14.7	16.1	Fixed Assets (net)	30.3	22.7	10.2	10.1	13.3	17.9
3.3	3.1	2.7	Intangibles (net)	5.9	2.4	3.1	3.8	2.4	2.4
5.0	5.6	6.2	All Other Non-Current	10.3	9.1	6.6	6.9	4.5	6.0
100.0	100.0	100.0	Total	100.0	100.0	100.0	100.0	100.0	100.0
			LIABILITIES						
26.6	24.2	25.0	Notes Payable-Short Term	9.9	21.1	17.5	21.3	22.7	29.6
2.8	2.7	2.7	Cur. Mat.-L.T.D.	.4	3.1	2.7	3.0	3.2	2.6
16.1	14.9	13.7	Trade Payables	22.9	10.3	11.2	16.5	15.5	12.6
.2	.1	.1	Income Taxes Payable	.0	.1	.0	.2	.1	.1
9.0	9.6	12.3	All Other Current	50.0	20.2	9.0	7.5	12.9	10.3
54.7	51.5	53.9	Total Current	83.2	54.8	40.3	48.4	54.3	55.2
9.6	10.2	12.7	Long-Term Debt	17.3	19.5	15.9	15.5	9.1	11.8
.4	.4	.4	Deferred Taxes	.0	.0	.0	.2	.4	.5
3.6	6.6	5.4	All Other Non-Current	13.4	6.2	13.7	7.0	5.6	3.0
31.7	31.2	27.6	Net Worth	-13.9	19.6	30.0	28.9	30.6	29.5
100.0	100.0	100.0	Total Liabilties & Net Worth	100.0	100.0	100.0	100.0	100.0	100.0
			INCOME DATA						
100.0	100.0	100.0	Net Sales	100.0	100.0	100.0	100.0	100.0	100.0
23.6	23.9	23.0	Gross Profit	48.1	40.2	31.9	26.1	21.5	17.5
20.1	20.1	19.3	Operating Expenses	39.2	36.2	27.7	22.2	17.9	14.2
3.5	3.8	3.7	Operating Profit	8.9	4.0	4.2	3.9	3.5	3.3
.2	.2	.5	All Other Expenses (net)	3.4	2.6	.6	.1	.2	.2
3.4	3.6	3.3	Profit Before Taxes	5.5	1.5	3.6	3.8	3.4	3.1
			RATIOS						
2.0	2.3	2.0		3.2	3.6	4.5	2.3	2.6	1.6
1.3	1.4	1.3	Current	.9	1.4	1.9	1.6	1.4	1.3
1.1	1.1	1.1		.2	.8	1.3	1.2	1.2	1.1
.9	1.0	.9		1.7	1.5	2.1	1.0	1.0	.7
.5	.5	(380) .5	Quick	.4	.6	.9	(47) .5	.5	.4
.2	.3	.2		.1	.1	.3	.3	.2	.2
7 50.2	**6** 57.4	**6** 59.3		**0** UND	**0** UND	**1** 564.2	**4** 92.0	**3** 113.0	**8** 44.1
16 23.1	**16** 23.3	**15** 24.6	Sales/Receivables	**4** 83.7	**23** 16.1	**15** 24.6	**15** 24.0	**16** 23.1	**15** 24.8
32 11.4	**31** 11.7	**27** 13.4		**30** 12.3	**48** 7.6	**45** 8.2	**34** 10.7	**31** 11.6	**24** 15.5
37 9.9	**34** 10.8	**38** 9.7		**10** 35.1	**16** 23.3	**41** 8.9	**30** 12.3	**32** 11.5	**41** 9.0
64 5.7	**65** 5.6	**61** 6.0	Cost of Sales/Inventory	**130** 2.8	**66** 5.5	**68** 5.4	**81** 4.5	**57** 6.4	**59** 6.2
104 3.5	**101** 3.6	**94** 3.9		**365** 1.0	**146** 2.5	**135** 2.7	**118** 3.1	**94** 3.9	**83** 4.4
5 66.4	**5** 69.1	**5** 75.4		**0** UND	**0** UND	**3** 139.2	**4** 96.4	**5** 80.9	**7** 54.4
14 26.1	**12** 29.9	**12** 29.4	Cost of Sales/Payables	**15** 24.9	**13** 27.9	**17** 22.0	**24** 15.3	**10** 34.9	**12** 31.2
33 10.9	**31** 11.7	**27** 13.7		**146** 2.5	**66** 5.5	**34** 10.8	**47** 7.7	**25** 14.4	**17** 21.0
8.2	7.5	8.1		3.2	5.8	4.1	6.5	7.0	11.9
17.3	16.2	17.6	Sales/Working Capital	NM	35.8	8.3	10.9	15.3	24.7
71.9	47.0	53.1		-2.9	-24.7	16.9	29.8	45.6	54.6
13.7	10.7	10.7			8.1	14.4	16.7	9.4	11.0
(361) 4.7	(358) 4.3	(324) 4.6	EBIT/Interest		(19) 1.1	(22) 5.2	(42) 4.3	(71) 4.5	(167) 5.3
2.2	2.2	2.0			.5	1.2	1.0	1.7	3.0
13.4	6.7	7.3						23.1	8.2
(71) 2.7	(70) 2.8	(66) 2.5	Net Profit + Depr., Dep., Amort./Cur. Mat. L/T/D					(11) 3.6	(44) 1.9
1.3	1.2	1.3						.8	1.4
.1	.1	.1		.0	.2	.0	.0	.1	.2
.4	.3	.4	Fixed/Worth	.2	.8	.2	.1	.3	.5
1.3	1.3	1.6		UND	-8.3	2.2	.9	1.7	1.4
1.2	1.1	1.1		2.3	.5	.5	.9	1.0	1.6
2.7	2.7	3.1	Debt/Worth	22.3	5.2	1.5	1.9	2.6	3.3
7.0	6.7	7.3		-3.5	-19.7	7.6	8.1	7.1	5.8
47.0	52.7	52.0			92.2	61.8	66.5	49.8	46.9
(370) 22.7	(369) 25.2	(342) 27.1	% Profit Before Taxes/Tangible Net Worth		(17) 25.0	(25) 27.2	(42) 29.5	(69) 19.7	(181) 29.2
11.1	10.9	12.5			1.7	6.2	6.3	7.6	16.2
12.1	15.3	12.9		15.7	25.9	31.4	18.2	13.9	11.3
5.5	5.9	6.5	% Profit Before Taxes/Total Assets	4.5	4.4	7.7	8.5	6.1	6.7
2.4	2.5	2.2		-.3	-1.2	1.6	.5	1.7	3.0
123.9	177.0	141.5		UND	117.1	229.8	383.0	174.1	108.5
40.9	45.5	40.5	Sales/Net Fixed Assets	34.1	29.5	67.7	69.3	40.2	31.6
14.5	14.2	11.8		2.1	8.4	20.9	25.4	14.5	11.0
4.4	4.2	4.4		2.5	3.4	4.6	4.6	4.7	4.4
3.0	3.0	2.9	Sales/Total Assets	1.4	2.4	2.8	2.9	3.0	3.1
2.0	2.2	2.0		.7	1.3	1.8	1.7	2.3	2.2
.3	.2	.2			.2	.1	.3	.2	.2
(318) .6	(307) .6	(293) .5	% Depr., Dep., Amort./Sales		(18) 1.2	(17) .9	(30) .5	(60) .5	(165) .4
1.6	1.6	1.5			3.4	1.6	1.1	1.2	1.5
.6	.7	.5			2.8	1.7	.6	.8	.3
(156) 1.6	(155) 1.8	(130) 1.5	% Officers', Directors' Owners' Comp/Sales		(10) 5.2	(13) 2.8	(25) 2.2	(31) 1.4	(49) .6
3.4	4.0	3.3			7.1	7.0	4.0	3.1	1.6
25519297M	32625850M	26668036M	Net Sales ($)	4744M	56759M	113482M	341457M	1281526M	24870068M
9523370M	8787868M	9897365M	Total Assets ($)	6585M	34320M	66469M	137400M	533430M	9119161M

M = $ thousand MM = $ million

See Pages 9 through 22 for Explanation of Ratios and Data

Current Data Sorted by Assets / Comparative Historical Data

	Current Data Sorted by Assets													**Comparative Historical Data**		
												Type of Statement				
	1				7		24		9		11	Unqualified		66		54
			4		47		38		5			Reviewed		110		132
	2		11		48		11				1	Compiled		85		79
	19		47		31		2					Tax Returns		63		82
	7		31		68		80		18		14	Other		197		199
	85 (4/1-9/30/13)				451 (10/1/13-3/31/14)									4/1/09-3/31/10		4/1/10-3/31/11
	0-500M		**500M-2MM**		**2-10MM**		**10-50MM**		**50-100MM**		**100-250MM**			**ALL**		**ALL**
	29		93		201		155		32		26	**NUMBER OF STATEMENTS**		521		546
	%		%		%		%		%		%	**ASSETS**		%		%
	17.9		9.6		6.0		5.7		6.9		4.4	Cash & Equivalents		7.0		6.7
	22.1		21.3		23.9		19.9		21.0		17.5	Trade Receivables (net)		22.9		23.5
	37.8		51.1		51.1		50.5		38.2		33.5	Inventory		47.8		48.3
	1.4		1.7		2.0		2.4		1.7		3.1	All Other Current		2.5		2.7
	79.2		83.7		83.0		78.5		67.9		58.5	Total Current		80.2		81.2
	13.7		10.1		10.0		11.1		13.8		19.3	Fixed Assets (net)		11.6		10.2
	2.3		4.1		2.5		6.1		12.9		17.3	Intangibles (net)		4.1		4.2
	5.2		2.1		4.4		4.3		5.4		5.0	All Other Non-Current		4.1		4.4
	100.0		100.0		100.0		100.0		100.0		100.0	Total		100.0		100.0
												LIABILITIES				
	9.0		8.6		14.7		16.1		7.3		6.9	Notes Payable-Short Term		19.4		16.2
	5.4		1.2		2.0		1.9		3.4		2.3	Cur. Mat.-L.T.D.		2.3		2.0
	19.6		21.0		21.3		21.3		21.2		17.3	Trade Payables		19.6		20.1
	.0		.1		.1		.1		.1		.3	Income Taxes Payable		.2		.2
	19.8		11.1		5.8		6.2		6.4		5.5	All Other Current		6.9		7.0
	53.8		42.1		44.0		45.6		38.4		32.3	Total Current		48.5		45.5
	14.3		16.2		10.7		8.3		17.6		25.3	Long-Term Debt		9.4		9.4
	.0		.1		.2		.3		.9		1.9	Deferred Taxes		.2		.2
	2.5		9.6		6.1		3.7		3.1		5.0	All Other Non-Current		7.1		6.2
	29.4		32.0		39.0		42.1		40.1		35.4	Net Worth		34.7		38.8
	100.0		100.0		100.0		100.0		100.0		100.0	Total Liabilties & Net Worth		100.0		100.0
												INCOME DATA				
	100.0		100.0		100.0		100.0		100.0		100.0	Net Sales		100.0		100.0
	40.4		34.9		30.2		28.5		32.9		28.7	Gross Profit		31.2		31.3
	35.0		31.4		26.7		23.8		25.7		22.7	Operating Expenses		28.5		27.2
	5.4		3.5		3.5		4.6		7.2		6.1	Operating Profit		2.8		4.1
	.9		.3		.3		.3		.8		2.2	All Other Expenses (net)		1.0		.5
	4.4		3.1		3.2		4.4		6.4		3.9	Profit Before Taxes		1.7		3.5
												RATIOS				
	8.7		3.9		2.9		2.8		2.5		2.3			2.9		2.9
	2.2		2.1		1.9		1.7		1.8		1.8	Current		1.7		1.8
	.8		1.3		1.4		1.3		1.4		1.3			1.2		1.3
	3.3		1.2		1.1		1.0		.9		1.1			1.1		1.1
	1.2		.7		.6		.5		.6		.7	Quick		.6	(545)	.6
	.4		.4		.4		.3		.4		.4			.4		.4
3	126.4	**12**	31.0	**21**	17.5	**24**	14.9	**27**	13.4	**29**	12.8		**23**	16.0	**22**	16.3
20	18.3	**24**	14.9	**30**	12.3	**32**	11.4	**35**	10.5	**40**	9.2	Sales/Receivables	**34**	10.8	**34**	10.7
27	13.7	**38**	9.7	**41**	9.0	**41**	8.8	**46**	7.9	**56**	6.5		**46**	8.0	**47**	7.7
29	12.5	**51**	7.2	**63**	5.8	**76**	4.8	**74**	4.9	**55**	6.6		**69**	5.3	**64**	5.7
52	7.0	**104**	3.5	**101**	3.6	**126**	2.9	**122**	3.0	**101**	3.6	Cost of Sales/Inventory	**109**	3.4	**112**	3.3
99	3.7	**174**	2.1	**159**	2.3	**192**	1.9	**174**	2.1	**192**	1.9		**178**	2.0	**170**	2.2
0	UND	**17**	21.2	**22**	16.8	**27**	13.5	**31**	11.6	**25**	14.6		**21**	17.6	**22**	16.8
6	58.3	**33**	11.2	**36**	10.1	**46**	7.9	**43**	8.5	**47**	7.7	Cost of Sales/Payables	**36**	10.1	**38**	9.6
33	10.9	**49**	7.4	**54**	6.8	**68**	5.4	**68**	5.4	**76**	4.8		**61**	6.0	**61**	6.0
	4.4		4.1		4.1		3.9		4.0		4.0			4.0		4.1
	11.4		6.1		7.2		6.9		6.6		6.7	Sales/Working Capital		6.8		6.6
	-65.8		14.7		15.0		12.2		10.2		12.6			15.8		13.6
	25.1		30.5		17.4		21.2		34.0		8.2			8.7		14.1
(18)	3.8	(75)	6.3	(179)	4.7	(141)	6.7	(28)	14.0	(25)	4.5	EBIT/Interest	(471)	3.3	(485)	4.4
	-.8		1.7		2.0		2.5		3.2		1.8			1.1		1.8
					6.3		5.9				6.6			7.3		7.7
				(27)	2.7	(42)	2.8			(12)	2.3	Net Profit + Depr., Dep., Amort./Cur. Mat. L/T/D	(128)	2.7	(121)	2.7
					1.1		1.8				1.4			1.0		1.2
	.0		.0		.1		.1		.1		.3			.1		.1
	.1		.2		.2		.2		.7		.6	Fixed/Worth		.2		.2
	NM		1.2		.5		.7		NM		-20.2			.7		.7
	.2		.7		.7		.8		.9		1.1			.9		.8
	1.0		1.8		1.7		1.9		2.0		3.6	Debt/Worth		2.0		1.8
	-5.2		16.5		4.0		4.3		NM		-107.7			5.5		4.9
	47.1		45.1		35.7		36.7		58.9		44.5			28.0		37.9
(20)	24.2	(74)	14.4	(183)	16.5	(146)	17.2	(24)	30.7	(19)	19.5	% Profit Before Taxes/Tangible Net Worth	(452)	11.9	(493)	17.0
	-.2		5.3		5.3		7.7		16.1		8.1			2.1		5.2
	41.1		14.9		12.7		12.5		16.5		9.6			9.7		12.4
	12.4		5.4		5.4		6.6		10.3		6.0	% Profit Before Taxes/Total Assets		3.7		5.9
	-.8		2.0		1.9		2.4		4.5		2.1			.3		1.6
	153.5		324.0		148.9		81.7		61.6		48.7			89.3		95.3
	53.9		76.3		47.6		37.0		28.6		17.8	Sales/Net Fixed Assets		39.3		42.1
	23.0		23.2		22.7		14.4		8.1		4.8			16.3		19.6
	6.0		3.8		3.3		2.5		2.7		2.3			2.9		3.1
	3.7		2.9		2.6		1.9		2.1		1.7	Sales/Total Assets		2.3		2.3
	2.5		2.0		2.0		1.6		1.3		1.0			1.6		1.7
	.1		.3		.3		.3		.4		.7			.4		.4
(18)	.6	(61)	.6	(150)	.7	(132)	.6	(24)	1.1	(21)	1.1	% Depr., Dep., Amort./Sales	(427)	.8	(433)	.7
	1.6		1.2		1.0		1.1		1.8		3.2			1.4		1.3
	3.6		1.8		1.3		.6							1.6		1.3
(16)	7.6	(52)	3.5	(85)	2.4	(33)	1.1					% Officers', Directors' Owners' Comp/Sales	(201)	2.8	(199)	2.3
	11.4		6.0		4.4		2.3							5.4		4.0
	40379M		**350231M**		**2762815M**		**7516178M**		**4775246M**		**6795979M**	Net Sales ($)		**15288872M**		**18337050M**
	8865M		**110340M**		**1020800M**		**3386555M**		**2345388M**		**3913416M**	Total Assets ($)		**7696110M**		**8998468M**

M = $ thousand MM = $ million

See Pages 9 through 22 for Explanation of Ratios and Data

Comparative Historical Data / Current Data Sorted by Sales

4/1/11-3/31/12 ALL	4/1/12-3/31/13 ALL	4/1/13-3/31/14 ALL	Type of Statement	0-1MM	1-3MM	3-5MM	5-10MM	10-25MM	25MM & OVER
56	51	52	Unqualified	1				11	40
106	104	94	Reviewed		1	4	10	34	45
74	82	73	Compiled	1	5	5	24	31	7
121	76	99	Tax Returns	10	34	18	23	9	5
210	197	218	Other	3	19	16	28	47	105
					85 (4/1-9/30/13)			451 (10/1/13-3/31/14)	
567	510	536	**NUMBER OF STATEMENTS**	15	59	43	85	132	202
%	%	%	**ASSETS**	%	%	%	%	%	%
6.5	6.6	7.2	Cash & Equivalents	13.3	11.9	8.9	6.3	6.8	5.5
24.0	22.4	21.7	Trade Receivables (net)	14.8	19.2	19.8	25.3	22.8	21.2
48.8	48.5	48.6	Inventory	39.1	49.1	48.8	50.8	49.6	47.5
2.5	2.5	2.1	All Other Current	.6	1.2	5.3	1.2	1.9	2.3
81.7	80.1	79.6	Total Current	67.8	81.3	82.8	83.6	81.0	76.6
10.2	10.5	11.2	Fixed Assets (net)	23.7	11.1	10.4	10.4	9.7	11.9
3.8	4.9	5.1	Intangibles (net)	3.0	5.3	4.1	1.8	4.3	7.4
4.4	4.6	4.1	All Other Non-Current	6.2	2.3	2.8	4.1	4.9	4.1
100.0	100.0	100.0	Total	100.0	100.0	100.0	100.0	100.0	100.0
			LIABILITIES						
14.5	14.6	12.9	Notes Payable-Short Term	7.2	8.1	14.4	13.3	13.9	13.7
1.9	2.4	2.1	Cur. Mat.-L.T.D.	9.0	1.8	2.3	1.8	1.9	2.0
21.1	20.9	21.0	Trade Payables	5.7	18.7	19.6	20.5	21.9	22.7
.2	.1	.1	Income Taxes Payable	.0	.1	.0	.1	.2	.1
8.0	7.6	7.6	All Other Current	24.0	12.7	4.5	7.8	5.6	6.8
45.7	45.7	43.8	Total Current	45.9	41.4	40.9	43.4	43.5	45.2
10.3	10.8	12.3	Long-Term Debt	21.1	17.9	14.9	12.2	9.4	11.4
.2	.3	.3	Deferred Taxes	.0	.0	.3	.2	.2	.5
5.7	6.9	5.6	All Other Non-Current	4.2	10.9	5.1	7.1	5.9	3.5
38.2	36.4	38.0	Net Worth	28.9	29.7	38.8	37.1	41.1	39.4
100.0	100.0	100.0	Total Liabilties & Net Worth	100.0	100.0	100.0	100.0	100.0	100.0
			INCOME DATA						
100.0	100.0	100.0	Net Sales	100.0	100.0	100.0	100.0	100.0	100.0
30.6	30.8	31.2	Gross Profit	38.4	43.4	34.4	30.1	29.2	28.1
26.7	26.4	26.9	Operating Expenses	35.4	38.8	30.6	26.3	25.5	23.1
3.9	4.4	4.3	Operating Profit	3.0	4.6	3.8	3.8	3.7	4.9
.4	.6	.5	All Other Expenses (net)	1.1	.6	-.2	.4	.4	.6
3.4	3.8	3.8	Profit Before Taxes	1.9	4.0	4.0	3.4	3.3	4.4
			RATIOS						
2.9	3.0	3.1		13.8	4.6	3.4	2.8	3.2	2.4
1.8	1.8	1.9	Current	2.7	2.5	2.1	2.0	1.8	1.7
1.3	1.3	1.3		.6	1.2	1.3	1.4	1.3	1.3
1.1	1.1	1.1		2.7	1.4	1.2	1.2	1.1	1.0
(566) .6	.6	.6	Quick	1.2	.8	.6	.7	.6	.6
.4	.4	.4		.1	.3	.4	.4	.4	.3
23 15.6	**23** 16.2	**20** 18.5		**4** 84.2	**12** 29.6	**12** 30.3	**21** 17.4	**21** 17.1	**24** 15.4
33 11.1	**31** 11.8	**30** 12.1	Sales/Receivables	**26** 14.1	**25** 14.8	**26** 14.3	**32** 11.4	**31** 11.8	**31** 11.6
45 8.2	**42** 8.6	**41** 8.9		**36** 10.0	**37** 9.8	**38** 9.5	**47** 7.8	**40** 9.1	**42** 8.7
64 5.7	**64** 5.7	**63** 5.8		**46** 8.0	**46** 8.0	**66** 5.5	**63** 5.8	**63** 5.8	**64** 5.7
104 3.5	**104** 3.5	**107** 3.4	Cost of Sales/Inventory	**87** 4.2	**118** 3.1	**114** 3.2	**107** 3.4	**104** 3.5	**107** 3.4
159 2.3	**166** 2.2	**174** 2.1		**281** 1.3	**203** 1.8	**140** 2.6	**166** 2.2	**174** 2.1	**166** 2.2
21 17.1	**20** 18.5	**21** 17.6		**0** UND	**13** 29.0	**20** 18.2	**21** 17.4	**23** 15.9	**24** 15.2
40 9.1	**39** 9.4	**38** 9.6	Cost of Sales/Payables	**3** 114.2	**30** 12.0	**40** 9.2	**37** 9.9	**37** 9.9	**43** 8.5
64 5.7	**60** 6.1	**60** 6.1		**36** 10.0	**57** 6.4	**51** 7.1	**50** 7.3	**60** 6.1	**66** 5.5
4.1	4.1	4.1		2.1	3.9	5.1	3.7	3.9	4.7
6.8	7.2	7.0	Sales/Working Capital	5.8	5.5	6.6	6.5	6.6	7.7
14.8	16.7	14.5		-12.4	20.4	11.2	13.9	14.0	16.3
17.7	18.2	21.0		2.7	26.0	41.5	19.3	11.9	22.0
(505) 5.9	(446) 4.9	(466) 5.5	EBIT/Interest	(10) -.5	(46) 6.3	(38) 4.3	(75) 4.9	(110) 3.7	(187) 8.2
2.0	1.8	2.1		-26.3	1.6	1.6	1.8	2.1	2.7
6.8	5.7	6.6						5.5	7.3
(112) 2.7	(110) 2.5	(96) 2.7	Net Profit + Depr., Dep., Amort./Cur. Mat. L/T/D					(24) 2.0	(57) 2.9
1.2	1.1	1.4						1.0	1.8
.1	.1	.1		.1	.0	.0	.0	.1	.1
.2	.2	.2	Fixed/Worth	.2	.2	.2	.2	.2	.3
.7	.7	.8		-2.1	18.0	.7	.5	.6	.9
.8	.7	.8		.3	.6	.6	.7	.7	.9
1.8	1.9	1.8	Debt/Worth	1.0	1.7	1.6	1.6	1.8	2.0
4.4	5.0	5.7		-5.9	-40.6	5.7	2.9	4.3	5.8
41.0	39.4	38.1		25.6	48.0	38.1	35.7	29.3	45.7
(508) 17.6	(445) 18.8	(466) 17.5	% Profit Before Taxes/Tangible Net Worth	(11) -6.0	(42) 19.5	(36) 14.1	(76) 14.7	(120) 14.6	(181) 22.0
5.0	7.0	7.2		-42.9	10.6	4.8	4.8	4.9	11.7
13.4	14.3	13.0		12.1	14.8	18.8	13.5	12.1	13.4
6.5	6.2	6.2	% Profit Before Taxes/Total Assets	-.2	7.3	4.8	5.0	5.3	7.2
1.6	1.7	2.2		-6.7	1.8	2.3	1.6	1.7	3.3
119.7	96.8	108.4		51.8	319.6	200.1	257.1	104.0	80.0
45.8	44.8	43.1	Sales/Net Fixed Assets	20.3	73.3	39.9	55.3	47.6	33.6
19.3	20.0	18.3		14.2	23.3	15.8	24.7	20.0	14.0
3.2	3.2	3.1		3.1	3.6	3.3	3.5	3.1	3.0
2.4	2.4	2.4	Sales/Total Assets	2.0	2.3	2.7	2.7	2.3	2.3
1.8	1.8	1.7		.7	1.6	2.1	1.9	1.7	1.7
.3	.3	.3		1.1	.3	.3	.2	.4	.3
(432) .7	(400) .7	(406) .7	% Depr., Dep., Amort./Sales	(10) 1.6	(37) .7	(27) 1.0	(59) .5	(106) .7	(167) .7
1.2	1.2	1.3		2.8	1.3	1.6	.9	1.2	1.2
1.4	1.2	1.2			1.6	2.8	1.0	1.2	.7
(222) 2.7	(177) 2.5	(190) 2.5	% Officers', Directors' Owners' Comp/Sales		(36) 4.3	(22) 4.9	(41) 2.2	(45) 2.1	(37) 1.2
6.0	5.1	5.0			8.7	8.2	4.4	3.5	2.4
23028525M	19878541M	22240828M	Net Sales ($)	8932M	109502M	173341M	627702M	2177791M	19143560M
10068790M	9874365M	10785364M	Total Assets ($)	8980M	53765M	68562M	274551M	1023627M	9355879M

M = $ thousand MM = $ million

See Pages 9 through 22 for Explanation of Ratios and Data

Current Data Sorted by Assets							Comparative Historical Data	
						Type of Statement		
		1	5	7	4	Unqualified	23	21
	2	16	17	1		Reviewed	26	38
1	6	19	8			Compiled	30	26
4	4	8	1			Tax Returns	10	18
2	5	12	26	4	8	Other	49	55
19 (4/1-9/30/13)		142 (10/1/13-3/31/14)					4/1/09-3/31/10	4/1/10-3/31/11
0-500M	500M-2MM	2-10MM	10-50MM	50-100MM	100-250MM		ALL	ALL
7	17	56	57	12	12	**NUMBER OF STATEMENTS**	138	158
%	%	%	%	%	%	**ASSETS**	%	%
	8.9	6.5	4.6	1.1	5.6	Cash & Equivalents	5.9	6.6
	23.9	25.4	25.7	30.1	16.6	Trade Receivables (net)	26.0	28.6
	50.5	46.7	45.5	49.6	54.6	Inventory	41.4	42.6
	.6	1.8	1.4	.4	1.3	All Other Current	2.7	2.6
	83.9	80.4	77.3	81.3	78.1	Total Current	76.0	80.4
	8.1	12.4	16.0	6.3	11.2	Fixed Assets (net)	16.9	13.8
	.8	1.1	1.3	5.9	4.4	Intangibles (net)	2.9	2.0
	7.3	6.0	5.4	6.6	6.3	All Other Non-Current	4.2	3.7
	100.0	100.0	100.0	100.0	100.0	Total	100.0	100.0
						LIABILITIES		
	13.0	11.0	15.7	25.9	7.6	Notes Payable-Short Term	12.6	12.6
	1.3	1.6	1.8	1.9	.9	Cur. Mat.-L.T.D.	2.5	2.0
	28.7	35.3	28.8	28.5	30.6	Trade Payables	32.1	35.1
	.0	.1	.1	.2	.3	Income Taxes Payable	.3	.2
	14.0	7.2	5.0	7.4	12.6	All Other Current	8.1	9.9
	57.1	55.2	51.4	64.0	52.0	Total Current	55.5	59.8
	9.3	8.5	6.7	3.0	23.3	Long-Term Debt	11.3	9.0
	.1	.3	.5	.2	.7	Deferred Taxes	.2	.2
	5.7	3.4	2.4	4.0	.2	All Other Non-Current	3.8	5.0
	27.9	32.7	39.0	28.8	23.8	Net Worth	29.1	26.0
	100.0	100.0	100.0	100.0	100.0	Total Liabilties & Net Worth	100.0	100.0
						INCOME DATA		
	100.0	100.0	100.0	100.0	100.0	Net Sales	100.0	100.0
	22.0	22.3	22.2	14.6	17.1	Gross Profit	24.1	22.8
	21.7	20.7	19.1	14.4	13.7	Operating Expenses	22.6	20.2
	.3	1.6	3.0	.2	3.3	Operating Profit	1.5	2.7
	-1.0	-.3	.2	.5	-1.2	All Other Expenses (net)	.0	.0
	1.3	1.9	2.9	-.4	4.5	Profit Before Taxes	1.5	2.7
						RATIOS		
	2.2	1.9	2.2	1.6	2.7		1.8	1.9
	1.5	1.5	1.4	1.2	1.5	Current	1.4	1.4
	1.1	1.2	1.2	1.0	1.1		1.1	1.1
	.9	.8	.9	.7	.8		.8	.8
	.4	.5	.5	.4	.5	Quick	.6	.6
	.3	.3	.4	.3	.3		.4	.4
	8 43.1	18 20.1	24 15.1	31 11.9	12 29.8		20 18.0	21 17.5
	22 16.9	28 12.9	30 12.2	40 9.2	25 14.8	Sales/Receivables	34 10.7	34 10.9
	32 11.4	45 8.1	39 9.4	54 6.8	38 9.6		44 8.3	50 7.4
	38 9.6	56 6.5	61 6.0	63 5.8	69 5.3		53 6.9	48 7.6
	65 5.6	73 5.0	78 4.7	68 5.4	83 4.4	Cost of Sales/Inventory	71 5.1	68 5.4
	104 3.5	101 3.6	114 3.2	122 3.0	111 3.3		96 3.8	93 3.9
	21 17.4	40 9.2	22 16.4	23 15.7	18 20.3		32 11.5	36 10.2
	35 10.5	58 6.3	49 7.5	45 8.1	47 7.8	Cost of Sales/Payables	52 7.0	52 7.0
	48 7.6	69 5.3	69 5.3	60 6.1	94 3.9		71 5.1	74 5.0
	7.2	7.4	5.4	8.5	6.6		7.2	7.5
	13.8	10.4	10.2	14.8	8.0	Sales/Working Capital	14.1	12.7
	45.1	25.7	31.7	188.4	68.7		77.1	41.8
	14.3	12.2	27.8	15.9	22.3		10.9	11.4
	(13) 6.5	(54) 6.5	(52) 8.7	4.6	14.7	EBIT/Interest	(132) 4.1	(144) 5.7
	-1.9	1.8	3.9	.5	9.7		1.8	2.5
		4.3	14.4				9.8	11.1
		(12) 2.6	(20) 4.9			Net Profit + Depr., Dep., Amort./Cur. Mat. L/T/D	(40) 2.6	(40) 5.8
		.0	2.6				.8	1.8
	.1	.1	.2	.2	.4		.2	.1
	.2	.3	.4	.2	.9	Fixed/Worth	.5	.4
	.4	.9	.7	.9	NM		1.4	1.1
	1.5	1.3	.8	1.3	1.7		1.4	1.3
	3.6	2.3	2.1	3.9	8.3	Debt/Worth	2.5	2.7
	7.9	5.0	3.3	7.5	NM		5.8	6.1
	53.7	25.9	36.2	29.8			30.4	37.7
	(16) 26.9	(55) 14.4	(55) 17.7	(11) 13.9		% Profit Before Taxes/Tangible Net Worth	(127) 13.5	(142) 24.4
	1.4	5.1	11.3	-8.8			6.4	10.7
	10.0	7.8	13.2	8.2	11.3		8.8	11.8
	6.4	5.1	6.5	5.6	7.1	% Profit Before Taxes/Total Assets	4.1	6.9
	-1.2	1.2	3.6	-1.2	3.8		1.7	2.1
	147.8	135.4	47.2	89.0	88.2		62.1	100.6
	75.6	31.9	21.9	48.2	51.7	Sales/Net Fixed Assets	25.8	39.0
	55.5	15.8	9.6	33.9	11.4		9.9	15.9
	4.6	3.7	3.6	3.5	3.5		3.5	3.9
	3.6	3.1	2.7	2.7	2.4	Sales/Total Assets	2.8	2.9
	2.6	2.2	2.0	2.0	2.0		2.1	2.2
	.1	.3	.5		.1		.5	.4
	(11) .6	(45) .9	(54) 1.0		(11) .3	% Depr., Dep., Amort./Sales	(123) .9	(136) .7
	.8	1.4	1.3		1.2		1.6	1.3
	1.8	.6	.6				.8	.7
	(10) 2.1	(19) 1.2	(11) .7			% Officers', Directors' Owners' Comp/Sales	(52) 1.4	(57) 1.6
	4.1	1.4	.9				3.2	3.0
13566M	83489M	1019857M	4123561M	2637933M	5267298M	Net Sales ($)	10654643M	14164374M
2125M	21990M	337650M	1492594M	953249M	1830656M	Total Assets ($)	4191399M	5193459M

M = $ thousand MM = $ million

See Pages 9 through 22 for Explanation of Ratios and Data

Comparative Historical Data / Current Data Sorted by Sales

	4/1/11-3/31/12 ALL		4/1/12-3/31/13 ALL		4/1/13-3/31/14 ALL	Type of Statement		0-1MM		1-3MM		3-5MM		5-10MM		10-25MM		25MM & OVER
	21		19		17	Unqualified										1		16
	31		34		36	Reviewed						2		2		10		22
	22		20		34	Compiled				2		4		3		15		10
	33		31		17	Tax Returns		2		2		3		2		5		3
	60		62		57	Other		1		1		3		7		6		39
										19 (4/1-9/30/13)				142 (10/1/13-3/31/14)				
	167		166		161	NUMBER OF STATEMENTS		3		5		12		14		37		90
	%		%		%	ASSETS		%		%		%		%		%		%
	5.6		5.6		6.1	Cash & Equivalents						9.9		9.8		6.4		4.8
	27.4		25.3		25.7	Trade Receivables (net)						18.5		23.6		26.4		26.0
	46.3		45.7		46.2	Inventory						43.7		46.6		44.0		48.3
	1.7		1.5		1.4	All Other Current						.5		.6		1.6		1.5
	80.9		78.1		79.4	Total Current						72.6		80.5		78.4		80.6
	12.3		13.3		12.4	Fixed Assets (net)						13.8		10.4		14.8		12.1
	1.7		2.5		2.2	Intangibles (net)						.2		.8		1.3		2.4
	5.1		6.1		6.0	All Other Non-Current						13.4		8.2		5.4		4.9
	100.0		100.0		100.0	Total						100.0		100.0		100.0		100.0
						LIABILITIES												
	13.0		14.0		13.6	Notes Payable-Short Term						16.8		7.3		11.3		16.0
	1.9		2.0		1.6	Cur. Mat.-L.T.D.						.4		2.1		2.4		1.4
	31.5		31.3		31.0	Trade Payables						19.0		31.9		35.8		30.4
	.3		.1		.1	Income Taxes Payable						.0		.2		.1		.1
	9.3		9.9		8.9	All Other Current						26.6		8.6		3.1		6.9
	56.0		57.3		55.2	Total Current						62.8		50.1		52.6		54.7
	12.2		10.3		8.8	Long-Term Debt						8.1		11.2		10.3		7.4
	.3		.3		.3	Deferred Taxes						.1		.0		.4		.4
	4.3		5.3		2.9	All Other Non-Current						4.0		2.2		4.4		2.2
	27.2		26.9		32.7	Net Worth						25.0		36.4		32.3		35.3
	100.0		100.0		100.0	Total Liabilties & Net Worth						100.0		100.0		100.0		100.0
						INCOME DATA												
	100.0		100.0		100.0	Net Sales						100.0		100.0		100.0		100.0
	22.8		22.1		21.3	Gross Profit						25.5		24.7		21.2		20.2
	20.1		19.8		19.2	Operating Expenses						23.8		23.4		19.6		17.6
	2.7		2.3		2.1	Operating Profit						1.7		1.3		1.7		2.5
	.1		.0		-.2	All Other Expenses (net)						-.1		-2.0		.1		-.1
	2.6		2.3		2.3	Profit Before Taxes						1.8		3.3		1.5		2.6
						RATIOS												
	1.9		2.0		2.0							2.0		2.0		1.9		2.1
	1.5		1.4		1.5	Current						1.1		1.7		1.4		1.4
	1.2		1.1		1.2							1.0		1.3		1.2		1.1
	.8		.7		.8							.6		.9		.8		.8
(166)	.6		.5		.5	Quick						.4		.7		.5		.5
	.4		.4		.4							.2		.3		.4		.3
20	18.1	15	23.6	19	19.7						0	UND	18	20.7	18	20.1	22	16.7
31	11.8	29	12.7	29	12.5	Sales/Receivables					20	18.7	27	13.7	29	12.5	30	12.1
45	8.1	40	9.1	43	8.4						29	12.7	44	8.3	45	8.1	42	8.6
52	7.0	49	7.5	57	6.4						28	13.0	54	6.8	56	6.5	62	5.9
76	4.8	74	4.9	73	5.0	Cost of Sales/Inventory					63	5.8	79	4.6	69	5.3	73	5.0
104	3.5	104	3.5	104	3.5						107	3.4	126	2.9	96	3.8	101	3.6
30	12.2	27	13.5	28	13.2						0	UND	34	10.8	40	9.1	23	16.0
49	7.4	44	8.3	49	7.5	Cost of Sales/Payables					30	12.0	49	7.4	58	6.3	47	7.7
70	5.2	63	5.8	68	5.4						43	8.4	81	4.5	69	5.3	65	5.6
	7.0		7.3		7.0							16.4		7.1		7.6		6.6
	12.9		12.9		11.1	Sales/Working Capital						31.4		9.4		10.5		10.0
	25.8		35.9		32.1							UND		14.4		25.6		32.4
	13.0		14.2		18.6							20.2		20.0		9.6		26.6
(147)	5.5	(149)	6.4	(148)	7.5	EBIT/Interest					(10)	4.9	(12)	6.4	(35)	3.6	(85)	9.3
	2.7		2.2		2.7							-5.1		3.1		1.7		4.1
	12.3		15.4		10.6											3.7		21.5
(42)	4.0	(32)	4.5	(47)	4.1	Net Profit + Depr., Dep., Amort./Cur. Mat. L/T/D									(12)	1.9	(32)	5.2
	1.9		2.0		1.5											.8		3.5
	.1		.1		.1							.1		.1		.1		.1
	.3		.4		.4	Fixed/Worth						.3		.2		.4		.4
	.9		1.0		.8							1.6		.6		.9		.8
	1.3		1.2		1.0							1.5		.9		1.4		.9
	2.5		2.7		2.4	Debt/Worth						4.2		2.3		2.2		2.3
	5.2		6.9		4.8							12.8		3.8		4.7		4.7
	39.3		35.6		36.2							87.3		52.4		18.6		37.8
(152)	23.8	(146)	21.0	(151)	17.6	% Profit Before Taxes/Tangible Net Worth					(11)	42.9		23.7	(36)	13.7	(84)	20.4
	12.3		10.4		8.0							1.8		6.7		3.3		11.2
	11.5		11.1		10.1							11.4		9.5		6.8		11.6
	5.8		5.6		6.2	% Profit Before Taxes/Total Assets						9.2		6.6		4.1		6.6
	2.8		1.9		2.3							-1.7		2.6		1.2		3.6
	108.2		95.6		90.5							262.0		81.5		74.9		81.8
	36.6		41.1		33.1	Sales/Net Fixed Assets						68.5		35.1		31.4		30.5
	15.6		16.9		17.0							28.7		20.6		12.2		16.6
	4.1		4.0		3.8							5.8		3.8		3.8		3.7
	3.0		3.0		3.0	Sales/Total Assets						3.1		2.9		3.0		2.8
	2.2		2.3		2.1							2.4		2.0		2.0		2.1
	.3		.3		.4									.4		.5		.4
(142)	.7	(144)	.6	(133)	.8	% Depr., Dep., Amort./Sales							(12)	.7	(32)	.9	(80)	.8
	1.3		1.1		1.2									1.2		1.7		1.1
	.7		.7		.7											.6		.6
(63)	1.4	(51)	1.3	(46)	1.2	% Officers', Directors' Owners' Comp/Sales									(16)	1.1	(14)	.8
	2.7		2.2		1.9											1.4		1.1
	15061456M		12598790M		13145704M	Net Sales ($)		1261M		9960M		46408M		96205M		637572M		12354298M
	5382219M		4431325M		4638264M	Total Assets ($)		3672M		3187M		18580M		40192M		254619M		4318014M

M = $ thousand MM = $ million

See Pages 9 through 22 for Explanation of Ratios and Data

Current Data Sorted by Assets / Comparative Historical Data

0-500M	500M-2MM	2-10MM	10-50MM	50-100MM	100-250MM	Type of Statement	4/1/09-3/31/10 ALL	4/1/10-3/31/11 ALL
			1	2		Unqualified	7	6
		3	2			Reviewed	15	9
1	3	8	1			Compiled	12	10
2	5	4				Tax Returns	12	14
1	8	6	3	1	1	Other	14	9
	10 (4/1-9/30/13)		42 (10/1/13-3/31/14)					
4	16	21	7	3	1	NUMBER OF STATEMENTS	60	48
%	%	%	%	%	%	**ASSETS**	%	%
	11.9	8.3				Cash & Equivalents	7.2	6.5
	21.0	12.2				Trade Receivables (net)	21.9	20.0
	43.1	50.0				Inventory	46.6	44.3
	.6	4.0				All Other Current	3.2	2.1
	76.7	74.4				Total Current	78.9	72.9
	15.1	18.8				Fixed Assets (net)	13.4	15.4
	5.8	4.1				Intangibles (net)	2.9	4.4
	2.4	2.7				All Other Non-Current	4.8	7.4
	100.0	100.0				Total	100.0	100.0
						LIABILITIES		
	7.7	11.3				Notes Payable-Short Term	15.5	13.1
	1.6	2.9				Cur. Mat.-L.T.D.	3.6	4.8
	14.1	6.2				Trade Payables	16.0	19.4
	.0	.1				Income Taxes Payable	.1	.4
	4.3	12.7				All Other Current	9.2	5.4
	27.7	33.2				Total Current	44.5	43.1
	9.5	8.2				Long-Term Debt	7.9	11.6
	.0	.3				Deferred Taxes	.2	.2
	4.7	10.1				All Other Non-Current	8.7	3.1
	58.1	48.1				Net Worth	38.6	42.0
	100.0	100.0				Total Liabilties & Net Worth	100.0	100.0
						INCOME DATA		
	100.0	100.0				Net Sales	100.0	100.0
	32.8	32.6				Gross Profit	35.3	33.3
	29.7	28.5				Operating Expenses	32.7	30.1
	3.1	4.0				Operating Profit	2.6	3.3
	.8	.0				All Other Expenses (net)	.7	.0
	2.3	4.1				Profit Before Taxes	1.9	3.3
						RATIOS		
	7.8	6.2					2.7	3.1
	3.1	2.7				Current	1.6	1.7
	1.7	1.8					1.3	1.4
	1.9	1.8					1.2	1.3
	1.2	.5				Quick	.6	.6
	.5	.1					.3	.4
	2 151.6	**1** 516.9					**14** 25.7	**8** 48.4
	17 21.9	**8** 44.5				Sales/Receivables	**30** 12.1	**24** 14.9
	26 14.3	**26** 14.1					**40** 9.0	**40** 9.1
	30 12.3	**69** 5.3					**56** 6.5	**34** 10.6
	64 5.7	**101** 3.6				Cost of Sales/Inventory	**102** 3.6	**91** 4.0
	101 3.6	**166** 2.2					**164** 2.2	**137** 2.7
	8 47.5	**3** 132.9					**7** 50.2	**9** 41.4
	19 18.8	**7** 55.8				Cost of Sales/Payables	**25** 14.5	**23** 15.7
	33 11.1	**25** 14.7					**61** 6.0	**50** 7.2
	4.4	3.0					3.9	4.4
	8.8	5.6				Sales/Working Capital	7.2	9.0
	12.8	9.5					15.3	18.1
	31.7	20.7					13.8	23.9
	(12) 8.2	(17) 4.9				EBIT/Interest	(53) 3.7	(45) 7.2
	2.0	2.5					2.3	2.4
							7.1	11.4
						Net Profit + Depr., Dep., Amort./Cur. Mat. L/T/D	(18) 2.3	(13) 3.6
							1.1	1.4
	.0	.2					.1	.1
	.2	.4				Fixed/Worth	.2	.2
	.4	.8					.8	.5
	.5	.2					.8	.6
	.9	1.5				Debt/Worth	2.0	1.1
	1.4	3.5					3.2	2.5
	26.9	25.1					24.9	43.2
	15.6	(20) 16.2				% Profit Before Taxes/Tangible Net Worth	(53) 13.4	(45) 21.9
	5.4	6.9					5.3	8.3
	13.9	17.7					11.2	14.4
	8.0	6.5				% Profit Before Taxes/Total Assets	4.7	9.0
	2.5	1.8					1.9	3.3
	121.4	26.6					93.2	138.6
	42.6	15.6				Sales/Net Fixed Assets	34.7	37.1
	22.8	9.2					11.1	11.4
	5.3	3.0					3.4	3.8
	3.7	2.5				Sales/Total Assets	2.5	2.7
	2.3	1.5					1.8	1.8
	.4	.5					.4	.5
	(10) .7	(19) 1.2				% Depr., Dep., Amort./Sales	(51) .9	(38) .9
	1.3	2.4					2.1	1.9
	2.3	1.0					1.7	1.9
	(10) 3.8	(11) 3.5				% Officers', Directors' Owners' Comp/Sales	(28) 5.4	(21) 5.0
	5.6	4.4					9.0	10.0
4207M	75384M	213323M	437438M	573619M	395101M	Net Sales ($)	1684532M	1541179M
755M	20326M	89308M	161924M	241555M	210170M	Total Assets ($)	728861M	586463M

M = $ thousand MM = $ million

See Pages 9 through 22 for Explanation of Ratios and Data

Comparative Historical Data				Current Data Sorted by Sales					
			Type of Statement						
4	1	3	Unqualified						3
9	6	5	Reviewed				3	1	1
11	15	13	Compiled		2	3	5	2	1
14	11	11	Tax Returns	2	3		6		
14	17	20	Other		3	4	4	4	5
4/1/11-3/31/12 ALL	**4/1/12-3/31/13 ALL**	**4/1/13-3/31/14 ALL**			**10 (4/1-9/30/13)**		**42 (10/1/13-3/31/14)**		
				0-1MM	**1-3MM**	**3-5MM**	**5-10MM**	**10-25MM**	**25MM & OVER**
52	50	52	**NUMBER OF STATEMENTS**	2	8	7	18	7	10
%	%	%	**ASSETS**	%	%	%	%	%	%
9.9	10.3	9.9	Cash & Equivalents				6.2		2.0
19.3	16.9	16.6	Trade Receivables (net)				15.9		24.9
43.9	43.6	43.3	Inventory				51.2		38.4
.6	2.2	2.3	All Other Current				.9		2.3
73.7	73.1	72.1	Total Current				74.2		67.5
14.7	14.5	17.2	Fixed Assets (net)				17.6		16.3
7.3	6.7	7.4	Intangibles (net)				6.3		9.0
4.4	5.7	3.3	All Other Non-Current				1.9		7.2
100.0	100.0	100.0	Total				100.0		100.0
			LIABILITIES						
13.4	13.0	12.6	Notes Payable-Short Term				9.3		18.8
2.2	4.7	2.7	Cur. Mat.-L.T.D.				1.5		2.4
14.6	12.6	11.7	Trade Payables				11.4		16.4
.4	.4	.1	Income Taxes Payable				.0		.0
5.7	6.0	9.0	All Other Current				6.9		7.9
36.3	36.7	36.0	Total Current				29.1		45.6
10.2	8.7	11.6	Long-Term Debt				9.2		10.4
.2	.3	.1	Deferred Taxes				.2		.0
4.8	6.9	6.5	All Other Non-Current				5.4		1.6
48.4	47.4	45.7	Net Worth				56.1		42.4
100.0	100.0	100.0	Total Liabilties & Net Worth				100.0		100.0
			INCOME DATA						
100.0	100.0	100.0	Net Sales				100.0		100.0
34.5	32.4	33.0	Gross Profit				30.8		26.1
30.2	29.3	29.6	Operating Expenses				27.8		23.7
4.3	3.0	3.4	Operating Profit				3.1		2.5
.5	.4	.5	All Other Expenses (net)				-.1		1.1
3.8	2.6	3.0	Profit Before Taxes				3.2		1.4
			RATIOS						
4.4	4.2	4.2					4.5		2.6
2.2	1.9	2.3	Current				2.9		1.4
1.5	1.4	1.3					1.9		1.0
2.0	1.7	1.5					1.3		.9
.8	.8	.7	Quick				.7		.5
.4	.3	.3					.4		.3
6 64.1	**5** 77.5	**3** 120.7					**2** 180.1		**25** 14.8
22 16.5	**18** 20.1	**15** 24.1	Sales/Receivables				**14** 25.3		**33** 11.1
33 11.2	**33** 11.2	**30** 12.3					**24** 15.2		**54** 6.7
50 7.3	**41** 9.0	**41** 9.0					**59** 6.2		**28** 13.2
85 4.3	**76** 4.8	**76** 4.8	Cost of Sales/Inventory				**76** 4.8		**101** 3.6
122 3.0	**159** 2.3	**159** 2.3					**140** 2.6		**174** 2.1
4 102.1	**4** 88.3	**3** 104.8					**5** 74.2		**2** 218.1
20 18.3	**15** 24.7	**11** 32.5	Cost of Sales/Payables				**10** 38.2		**38** 9.5
42 8.7	**39** 9.4	**33** 11.1					**30** 12.2		**54** 6.7
4.8	4.7	3.6					4.2		4.3
7.8	8.0	8.1	Sales/Working Capital				8.5		10.7
15.8	16.1	19.1					10.6		NM
42.6	21.8	16.4					21.4		40.3
(45) 9.1	(45) 7.1	(43) 5.5	EBIT/Interest				(13) 8.1		4.5
4.0	3.3	2.0					3.4		.5
11.4	10.3								
(10) 4.3	(12) 4.3		Net Profit + Depr., Dep., Amort./Cur. Mat. L/T/D						
1.9	1.4								
.1	.1	.1					.1		.1
.3	.3	.3	Fixed/Worth				.2		.5
.5	.9	.8					.5		3.5
.4	.6	.6					.3		.5
1.2	1.3	1.3	Debt/Worth				1.0		2.5
2.6	2.3	3.6					2.2		22.7
52.1	40.4	25.7					24.3		
(48) 26.7	(46) 22.2	(47) 15.5	% Profit Before Taxes/Tangible Net Worth				17.8		
12.7	9.4	6.3					9.7		
20.9	16.0	13.9					17.6		9.9
11.5	9.1	7.2	% Profit Before Taxes/Total Assets				8.2		5.8
3.3	2.6	1.7					3.2		-1.1
125.8	80.6	77.6					51.0		93.5
28.7	22.4	23.3	Sales/Net Fixed Assets				23.3		21.1
14.5	13.9	10.7					14.9		9.4
4.1	4.0	4.2					5.0		3.0
3.2	2.7	2.7	Sales/Total Assets				3.4		2.2
2.2	2.1	1.9					2.3		1.8
.4	.5	.5					.5		
(42) .9	(41) .7	(40) .9	% Depr., Dep., Amort./Sales				(15) .9		
1.4	2.0	1.9					1.5		
1.7	2.3	2.2					2.2		
(27) 4.5	(23) 4.4	(24) 3.7	% Officers', Directors' Owners' Comp/Sales				(12) 3.7		
7.8	7.4	5.2					4.6		
1430978M	**1505319M**	**1699072M**	Net Sales ($)	**1115M**	**16141M**	**27063M**	**133359M**	**124493M**	**1396901M**
525845M	**601235M**	**724038M**	Total Assets ($)	**441M**	**12430M**	**13884M**	**49197M**	**45778M**	**602308M**

M = $ thousand MM = $ million

See Pages 9 through 22 for Explanation of Ratios and Data

Current Data Sorted by Assets							Comparative Historical Data	
						Type of Statement		
1	3	5	15	3	2	Unqualified	33	22
1	13	48	17	2		Reviewed	77	88
2	7	14	3			Compiled	29	40
9	19	10				Tax Returns	41	47
5	15	40	34	4	3	Other	97	121
32 (4/1-9/30/13)		243 (10/1/13-3/31/14)					4/1/09-3/31/10 ALL	4/1/10-3/31/11 ALL
0-500M	**500M-2MM**	**2-10MM**	**10-50MM**	**50-100MM**	**100-250MM**			
18	57	117	69	9	5	**NUMBER OF STATEMENTS**	277	318
%	%	%	%	%	%	**ASSETS**	%	%
21.6	12.1	7.5	7.8			Cash & Equivalents	10.4	9.6
26.0	28.6	40.8	34.5			Trade Receivables (net)	33.5	35.2
28.4	34.1	29.0	31.7			Inventory	30.2	30.5
2.7	2.9	3.6	4.6			All Other Current	3.6	3.7
78.8	77.6	80.9	78.7			Total Current	77.8	79.0
8.9	10.2	10.5	9.9			Fixed Assets (net)	12.2	11.6
4.7	2.8	3.5	7.1			Intangibles (net)	3.9	3.5
7.6	9.3	5.0	4.3			All Other Non-Current	6.1	5.8
100.0	100.0	100.0	100.0			Total	100.0	100.0
						LIABILITIES		
25.1	12.7	15.5	11.8			Notes Payable-Short Term	16.5	15.1
.0	4.0	1.5	3.4			Cur. Mat.-L.T.D.	2.1	2.0
26.5	23.2	19.8	16.9			Trade Payables	18.6	20.3
.1	.1	.3	.1			Income Taxes Payable	.2	.3
22.0	16.4	14.3	18.9			All Other Current	13.0	16.1
73.7	56.4	51.4	51.2			Total Current	50.4	53.8
7.4	8.7	6.8	9.6			Long-Term Debt	8.3	7.1
.0	.1	.1	.1			Deferred Taxes	.2	.1
18.6	6.1	4.5	4.8			All Other Non-Current	6.9	6.3
.2	28.7	37.2	34.3			Net Worth	34.2	32.7
100.0	100.0	100.0	100.0			Total Liabilties & Net Worth	100.0	100.0
						INCOME DATA		
100.0	100.0	100.0	100.0			Net Sales	100.0	100.0
36.8	28.3	25.6	28.1			Gross Profit	29.0	29.3
32.0	26.9	22.2	24.5			Operating Expenses	27.9	26.7
4.8	1.3	3.4	3.7			Operating Profit	1.1	2.6
.2	.4	.3	.3			All Other Expenses (net)	.7	.4
4.5	.9	3.1	3.3			Profit Before Taxes	.4	2.2
						RATIOS		
3.0	2.7	2.3	1.9				2.8	2.3
1.1	1.8	1.6	1.6			Current	1.6	1.5
.7	.9	1.2	1.2				1.1	1.1
1.9	1.4	1.3	1.1				1.6	1.3
.5	.7	.9	.9			Quick	(276) .9	.9
.2	.3	.6	.5				.5	.5
0 UND	**14** 26.9	**25** 14.8	**30** 12.3				**22** 16.6	**21** 17.2
18 20.3	**23** 15.7	**41** 8.8	**45** 8.2			Sales/Receivables	**36** 10.0	**39** 9.3
44 8.3	**37** 9.8	**58** 6.3	**57** 6.4				**53** 6.9	**58** 6.2
0 UND	**1** 340.5	**12** 30.2	**19** 19.4				**13** 28.9	**13** 28.4
24 15.5	**37** 9.8	**29** 12.7	**43** 8.5			Cost of Sales/Inventory	**36** 10.2	**36** 10.1
104 3.5	**126** 2.9	**89** 4.1	**126** 2.9				**103** 3.5	**108** 3.4
0 UND	**7** 49.2	**11** 32.4	**13** 27.1				**12** 30.7	**12** 29.7
22 16.8	**20** 18.4	**23** 16.0	**24** 15.5			Cost of Sales/Payables	**22** 16.3	**25** 14.3
41 8.9	**41** 9.0	**41** 8.8	**48** 7.6				**41** 8.9	**44** 8.2
7.1	5.6	6.8	6.8				5.5	6.7
NM	18.1	11.8	10.5			Sales/Working Capital	11.5	12.3
-14.3	-68.7	27.2	22.5				43.8	41.8
20.1	20.1	18.5	28.4				9.1	14.7
(12) 8.3	(45) 2.1	(106) 7.8	(62) 9.8			EBIT/Interest	(245) 2.4	(265) 3.9
-8.6	.7	2.4	2.6				-.1	1.3
		9.0	15.1				6.8	9.1
		(15) 5.1	(21) 3.6			Net Profit + Depr., Dep., Amort./Cur. Mat. L/T/D	(42) 2.5	(38) 2.6
		1.4	1.8				.3	.2
.0	.0	.1	.1				.1	.1
.5	.2	.2	.3			Fixed/Worth	.3	.3
-1.3	1.0	.5	.7				1.1	.8
2.3	.7	1.0	1.1				.8	.9
70.0	1.7	2.0	2.1			Debt/Worth	2.1	1.9
-3.2	59.0	4.4	5.1				7.1	7.8
184.2	39.2	46.3	54.3				35.3	42.4
(11) 87.7	(44) 8.6	(105) 22.7	(63) 30.8			% Profit Before Taxes/Tangible Net Worth	(238) 10.5	(283) 16.9
28.0	1.4	5.8	11.5				-2.7	2.7
32.0	13.2	16.2	15.9				10.0	14.4
10.4	2.3	6.2	8.6			% Profit Before Taxes/Total Assets	3.2	5.2
-6.2	-1.7	1.9	2.2				-1.8	.6
UND	381.3	173.3	110.2				114.3	154.5
613.8	102.3	62.2	52.6			Sales/Net Fixed Assets	48.3	55.5
59.3	21.9	28.1	19.2				20.2	22.0
8.7	5.4	4.2	3.7				4.4	4.5
5.5	3.5	3.2	2.7			Sales/Total Assets	3.1	3.1
2.3	2.2	2.5	1.9				2.2	2.2
	.1	.2	.3				.3	.3
	(38) .3	(94) .4	(58) .5			% Depr., Dep., Amort./Sales	(231) .5	(243) .5
	1.0	.7	.8				1.1	.9
	2.1	1.1					1.4	1.1
	(31) 3.3	(29) 1.9				% Officers', Directors' Owners' Comp/Sales	(100) 2.6	(108) 2.4
	5.6	3.9					5.5	4.3
29736M	**270621M**	**2054360M**	**3829169M**	**1679249M**	**1413686M**	Net Sales ($)	**6983518M**	**7281046M**
4980M	**67002M**	**606811M**	**1343983M**	**586367M**	**583917M**	Total Assets ($)	**2450873M**	**2713631M**

M = $ thousand MM = $ million

See Pages 9 through 22 for Explanation of Ratios and Data

Comparative Historical Data / **Current Data Sorted by Sales**

4/1/11-3/31/12 ALL	4/1/12-3/31/13 ALL	4/1/13-3/31/14 ALL	Type of Statement	0-1MM	1-3MM	3-5MM	5-10MM	10-25MM	25MM & OVER
28	19	29	Unqualified		2		2	5	20
79	76	81	Reviewed	2	1	8	14	25	31
37	36	26	Compiled	2	4	1	7	10	2
63	52	38	Tax Returns	2	14	7	7	8	
117	112	101	Other	4	8	4	15	23	47
				32 (4/1-9/30/13)			243 (10/1/13-3/31/14)		
324	295	275	NUMBER OF STATEMENTS	10	29	20	45	71	100
%	%	%	**ASSETS**	%	%	%	%	%	%
9.4	10.2	9.3	Cash & Equivalents	19.2	14.8	14.2	10.2	6.9	7.1
35.9	34.3	35.5	Trade Receivables (net)	15.3	19.7	28.2	31.9	41.9	40.7
32.5	33.0	31.1	Inventory	40.1	42.3	30.1	29.4	30.1	28.7
3.8	3.7	3.7	All Other Current	4.5	2.2	2.4	2.6	4.4	4.3
81.6	81.2	79.6	Total Current	79.0	78.9	75.0	74.1	83.2	80.7
9.4	9.6	10.2	Fixed Assets (net)	11.6	10.1	15.2	12.0	8.3	9.6
2.8	3.3	4.3	Intangibles (net)	7.2	5.8	.5	3.7	3.3	5.4
6.2	6.0	5.9	All Other Non-Current	2.3	5.2	9.3	10.2	5.1	4.3
100.0	100.0	100.0	Total	100.0	100.0	100.0	100.0	100.0	100.0
			LIABILITIES						
14.8	14.3	14.8	Notes Payable-Short Term	10.2	24.8	9.5	13.4	15.9	13.3
1.3	1.4	2.4	Cur. Mat.-L.T.D.	5.3	4.8	1.3	1.8	.7	3.1
20.5	18.6	20.1	Trade Payables	17.1	18.6	22.2	22.7	21.0	18.5
.2	.2	.2	Income Taxes Payable	.0	.1	.4	.3	.2	.2
15.0	16.4	16.5	All Other Current	11.5	22.7	11.8	11.6	18.2	17.2
51.7	50.9	54.0	Total Current	44.2	71.0	45.3	49.8	56.1	52.3
6.6	7.1	8.2	Long-Term Debt	4.2	15.5	9.4	7.9	4.9	8.7
.1	.1	.1	Deferred Taxes	.0	.0	.1	.1	.1	.1
6.2	6.3	5.9	All Other Non-Current	26.1	7.5	10.8	3.9	4.8	4.2
35.4	35.7	31.7	Net Worth	25.4	6.0	34.4	38.4	34.1	34.7
100.0	100.0	100.0	Total Liabilties & Net Worth	100.0	100.0	100.0	100.0	100.0	100.0
			INCOME DATA						
100.0	100.0	100.0	Net Sales	100.0	100.0	100.0	100.0	100.0	100.0
28.0	28.4	27.5	Gross Profit	47.1	34.8	25.9	25.9	26.7	25.0
24.9	24.9	24.4	Operating Expenses	39.2	32.8	22.6	23.2	24.3	21.4
3.1	3.4	3.1	Operating Profit	7.9	2.0	3.3	2.7	2.4	3.5
.4	.3	.3	All Other Expenses (net)	.6	1.2	.4	.0	.3	.2
2.7	3.1	2.8	Profit Before Taxes	7.4	.8	2.9	2.7	2.1	3.3
			RATIOS						
2.5	2.6	2.2		5.7	2.8	3.4	2.5	1.8	1.9
1.6	1.6	1.5	Current	2.0	.9	2.2	1.4	1.4	1.6
1.2	1.2	1.1		1.0	.8	1.4	1.1	1.2	1.2
1.4	1.3	1.3		3.2	.9	2.5	1.3	1.3	1.3
1.0	.9	.9	Quick	.6	.5	.8	.8	.9	.9
.5	.5	.5		.3	.2	.5	.5	.5	.7
21 17.2	**20** 18.4	**20** 18.2		**0** UND	**0** UND	**16** 22.2	**18** 20.5	**25** 14.6	**31** 11.7
37 9.9	**40** 9.1	**36** 10.0	Sales/Receivables	**41** 8.8	**15** 24.4	**23** 16.1	**28** 12.9	**41** 9.0	**47** 7.8
51 7.1	**53** 6.9	**55** 6.6		**70** 5.2	**45** 8.2	**36** 10.0	**41** 8.9	**61** 6.0	**56** 6.5
14 27.0	**13** 28.6	**12** 29.6		**44** 8.3	**0** UND	**6** 64.2	**10** 37.9	**12** 30.7	**16** 23.4
38 9.7	**36** 10.0	**35** 10.4	Cost of Sales/Inventory	**261** 1.4	**68** 5.4	**68** 5.4	**37** 9.9	**29** 12.7	**30** 12.0
104 3.5	**114** 3.2	**111** 3.3		**912** .4	**130** 2.8	**126** 2.9	**79** 4.6	**122** 3.0	**99** 3.7
12 29.7	**13** 27.9	**11** 32.4		**0** UND	**0** UND	**6** 57.2	**14** 27.0	**10** 35.5	**14** 26.7
22 16.6	**23** 16.2	**23** 15.8	Cost of Sales/Payables	**40** 9.2	**17** 21.1	**21** 17.3	**23** 15.8	**26** 14.2	**23** 15.7
41 9.0	**40** 9.1	**41** 8.9		**182** 2.0	**49** 7.5	**39** 9.3	**36** 10.2	**49** 7.4	**35** 10.4
6.9	5.5	6.7		1.2	5.4	5.0	5.9	6.7	7.6
12.2	11.2	11.9	Sales/Working Capital	2.8	-258.0	8.2	14.6	13.0	11.9
34.3	33.3	34.8		NM	-10.6	21.4	83.9	24.8	25.7
17.0	21.1	21.0			18.0	21.7	15.4	19.7	28.5
(272) 4.7	(246) 6.0	(237) 6.1	EBIT/Interest		(24) 1.2	(17) 3.1	(38) 5.7	(64) 5.7	(89) 11.5
1.9	2.1	1.8			-1.0	1.7	1.9	2.2	3.1
10.5	14.0	9.6						36.8	9.5
(48) 3.7	(44) 4.3	(48) 4.4	Net Profit + Depr., Dep., Amort./Cur. Mat. L/T/D					(11) 6.5	(30) 4.0
1.4	1.3	1.4						3.0	1.3
.1	.0	.1		.0	.0	.1	.1	.0	.1
.2	.2	.2	Fixed/Worth	.0	.2	.4	.3	.2	.2
.6	.7	.8		.9	-.2	1.5	.6	.7	.6
.8	.8	1.0		.7	.9	.5	.8	1.2	1.0
2.0	2.0	2.1	Debt/Worth	3.5	123.0	2.5	1.3	2.1	1.9
6.0	6.1	7.0		-20.7	-3.7	6.1	4.8	4.8	6.0
52.1	56.3	49.9			87.7	49.6	40.9	38.7	57.1
(289) 19.2	(263) 21.6	(234) 25.4	% Profit Before Taxes/Tangible Net Worth		(15) 10.6	(19) 13.5	(40) 21.8	(64) 19.5	(89) 33.4
6.0	6.8	6.5			.2	6.1	4.9	5.0	14.6
14.9	15.5	15.8		24.0	17.9	15.7	16.2	11.4	16.8
6.0	6.4	6.2	% Profit Before Taxes/Total Assets	3.5	.1	5.7	6.0	4.5	9.5
1.5	1.8	1.4		.6	-8.3	2.0	1.5	1.6	3.6
188.6	222.0	174.5		UND	840.9	264.0	130.0	211.8	129.1
69.0	69.8	63.8	Sales/Net Fixed Assets	UND	191.9	54.1	41.3	78.9	60.7
27.9	28.0	24.3		6.7	25.1	13.4	22.6	32.1	27.7
4.7	4.5	4.4		2.5	5.3	5.3	4.8	4.4	4.2
3.4	3.1	3.2	Sales/Total Assets	.8	2.7	3.0	3.5	3.2	3.3
2.3	2.1	2.2		.6	1.9	2.1	2.7	2.1	2.3
.2	.3	.2			.2	.2	.2	.2	.2
(240) .4	(206) .5	(209) .4	% Depr., Dep., Amort./Sales		(15) .4	(13) .5	(35) .4	(57) .4	(86) .4
.8	.9	.8			1.6	1.4	.9	.7	.8
1.2	1.5	1.2			2.1	1.0	2.2	1.0	.8
(125) 2.6	(121) 2.7	(79) 2.6	% Officers', Directors' Owners' Comp/Sales		(15) 3.7	(12) 1.9	(13) 3.0	(25) 1.8	(12) 1.4
4.8	4.9	4.8			6.2	4.4	4.8	4.1	2.4
9498329M	9267129M	9276821M	Net Sales ($)	4886M	54612M	74450M	354801M	1180398M	7607674M
3204854M	3302373M	3193060M	Total Assets ($)	5359M	22530M	27121M	110054M	427039M	2600957M

M = $ thousand MM = $ million

See Pages 9 through 22 for Explanation of Ratios and Data

Current Data Sorted by Assets							Comparative Historical Data	
Type of Statement								
Unqualified			6	16	6	5	36	46
Reviewed		2	52	31	1		79	91
Compiled	1	7	16	4			41	37
Tax Returns	11	24	17	2			41	36
Other	8	17	40	45	8	6	106	109
	49 (4/1-9/30/13)			276 (10/1/13-3/31/14)			4/1/09-3/31/10 ALL	4/1/10-3/31/11 ALL
	0-500M	500M-2MM	2-10MM	10-50MM	50-100MM	100-250MM		
NUMBER OF STATEMENTS	20	50	131	98	15	11	303	319
ASSETS	%	%	%	%	%	%	%	%
Cash & Equivalents	11.0	17.5	7.9	7.1	5.0	5.6	8.5	8.5
Trade Receivables (net)	24.3	27.2	27.0	27.3	22.9	27.1	28.0	26.4
Inventory	30.3	37.7	46.6	43.5	41.3	28.1	39.7	41.4
All Other Current	1.9	1.7	2.9	3.4	4.2	2.7	3.6	3.7
Total Current	67.5	84.1	84.4	81.3	73.4	63.5	79.7	80.0
Fixed Assets (net)	19.6	7.1	8.3	7.4	6.3	8.8	9.7	9.7
Intangibles (net)	.2	1.0	2.6	4.5	14.0	26.5	3.8	4.4
All Other Non-Current	12.7	7.8	4.8	6.7	6.3	1.2	6.8	5.9
Total	100.0	100.0	100.0	100.0	100.0	100.0	100.0	100.0
LIABILITIES								
Notes Payable-Short Term	17.0	7.3	18.1	15.5	12.0	7.9	18.7	17.3
Cur. Mat.-L.T.D.	10.3	2.0	1.2	.9	2.0	3.6	2.6	2.6
Trade Payables	23.5	19.8	19.6	15.8	14.6	15.5	18.3	19.0
Income Taxes Payable	.0	.1	.2	.2	.2	.4	.3	.2
All Other Current	7.0	9.3	10.1	9.5	9.7	12.5	11.2	9.9
Total Current	57.8	38.4	49.2	41.8	38.6	39.9	51.1	48.9
Long-Term Debt	23.4	10.4	6.6	5.2	15.3	13.4	8.6	8.2
Deferred Taxes	.0	.0	.1	.4	.5	2.1	.2	.2
All Other Non-Current	31.0	9.3	5.2	7.3	14.2	1.3	6.2	6.0
Net Worth	-12.2	41.9	38.9	45.3	31.3	43.2	34.0	36.6
Total Liabilties & Net Worth	100.0	100.0	100.0	100.0	100.0	100.0	100.0	100.0
INCOME DATA								
Net Sales	100.0	100.0	100.0	100.0	100.0	100.0	100.0	100.0
Gross Profit	42.2	33.8	32.8	33.2	30.8	29.5	31.6	33.1
Operating Expenses	38.7	30.8	28.6	27.5	24.1	24.1	29.2	30.0
Operating Profit	3.5	3.1	4.3	5.7	6.7	5.5	2.4	3.1
All Other Expenses (net)	.4	.5	.7	.7	1.9	2.0	1.1	1.0
Profit Before Taxes	3.1	2.6	3.6	5.1	4.8	3.5	1.3	2.1
RATIOS								
Current	2.6	4.0	2.7	3.3	3.2	2.5	2.5	2.9
	1.1	2.4	1.8	2.0	2.0	1.7	1.7	1.8
	.7	1.6	1.3	1.4	1.4	1.3	1.2	1.2
Quick	1.2	2.3	1.1	1.5	1.3	1.3	1.3	1.3
	.5	1.2	.7	.7	.9	.8	.7	.7
	.1	.7	.5	.5	.4	.5	.4	.4
Sales/Receivables	**0** UND	**12** 31.2	**23** 16.0	**29** 12.6	**31** 11.7	**34** 10.6	**25** 14.4	**24** 15.3
	10 35.2	**31** 11.9	**33** 11.1	**40** 9.2	**42** 8.6	**45** 8.1	**39** 9.4	**39** 9.4
	37 9.8	**49** 7.4	**49** 7.5	**56** 6.5	**54** 6.8	**63** 5.8	**58** 6.3	**56** 6.5
Cost of Sales/Inventory	**10** 35.9	**19** 19.6	**50** 7.3	**68** 5.4	**79** 4.6	**26** 14.2	**49** 7.4	**55** 6.6
	27 13.5	**73** 5.0	**91** 4.0	**96** 3.8	**118** 3.1	**78** 4.7	**81** 4.5	**90** 4.0
	114 3.2	**140** 2.6	**159** 2.3	**146** 2.5	**135** 2.7	**146** 2.5	**147** 2.5	**147** 2.5
Cost of Sales/Payables	**0** 775.0	**7** 50.8	**18** 19.9	**14** 25.3	**14** 27.0	**16** 22.6	**15** 24.2	**16** 22.5
	19 19.4	**23** 16.2	**31** 11.6	**29** 12.4	**34** 10.6	**41** 8.9	**29** 12.8	**30** 12.3
	49 7.4	**53** 6.9	**55** 6.6	**54** 6.7	**51** 7.2	**68** 5.4	**58** 6.3	**57** 6.4
Sales/Working Capital	11.4	3.3	4.1	4.2	4.2	5.8	4.4	4.0
	177.5	6.6	7.2	6.2	6.5	7.2	7.4	7.6
	-14.1	13.5	18.9	11.3	9.5	12.0	18.8	17.5
EBIT/Interest	15.0	17.8	20.6	30.3	37.6	41.2	7.4	12.1
	(11) 5.9	(35) 2.7	(120) 4.0	(86) 6.8	(13) 9.6	5.3	(270) 2.8	(274) 3.7
	2.5	-2.8	1.9	3.4	3.6	3.7	.8	1.3
Net Profit + Depr., Dep., Amort./Cur. Mat. L/T/D			9.2	61.2			6.1	11.3
			(17) 3.4	(21) 10.0			(44) 1.8	(56) 3.3
			1.1	3.1			.1	.8
Fixed/Worth	.0	.0	.1	.1	.1	.2	.1	.1
	1.3	.1	.1	.2	.2	.5	.2	.2
	-.7	.3	.5	.3	42.2	-.1	.7	.7
Debt/Worth	1.4	.6	.7	.7	1.0	1.0	.8	.7
	8.1	1.4	1.7	1.5	1.6	2.4	1.9	1.7
	-16.7	5.0	4.5	3.8	131.9	-3.6	4.6	6.5
% Profit Before Taxes/Tangible Net Worth	160.8	49.8	45.9	46.0	45.3		30.9	39.8
	(13) 63.3	(45) 15.9	(120) 15.4	(92) 28.3	(12) 24.5		(258) 8.3	(279) 14.7
	20.3	-1.0	4.4	10.1	13.0		1.0	1.7
% Profit Before Taxes/Total Assets	38.3	13.9	14.6	16.7	17.8	11.7	10.5	12.5
	13.3	4.0	5.9	7.8	7.1	5.8	2.8	4.5
	-2.0	-1.2	1.6	4.0	3.7	2.7	-.2	.4
Sales/Net Fixed Assets	UND	335.4	171.1	118.4	129.5	150.8	104.9	115.3
	70.5	100.3	63.1	47.4	52.2	38.4	46.4	52.1
	11.7	35.3	31.2	25.4	28.0	21.8	22.1	21.9
Sales/Total Assets	7.0	4.1	3.7	3.1	2.7	2.7	3.4	3.2
	4.0	3.0	2.6	2.3	1.9	1.8	2.3	2.3
	2.8	2.0	1.8	1.8	1.5	1.3	1.7	1.7
% Depr., Dep., Amort./Sales	.5	.1	.3	.2	.2		.3	.3
	(10) .6	(32) .3	(98) .5	(84) .6	(10) .3		(229) .6	(249) .6
	4.3	.7	1.1	.9	1.2		1.1	1.1
% Officers', Directors' Owners' Comp/Sales	2.6	1.4	1.1	.7			1.3	1.1
	(11) 5.1	(29) 3.7	(50) 2.3	(28) 1.5			(141) 2.3	(123) 2.1
	10.0	7.6	4.4	2.1			4.2	5.3
Net Sales ($)	**26946M**	**191513M**	**1848392M**	**5429044M**	**2387691M**	**2873374M**	**9285708M**	**10694806M**
Total Assets ($)	**5853M**	**57398M**	**660384M**	**2286688M**	**1110859M**	**1556374M**	**4710449M**	**5400466M**

M = $ thousand MM = $ million

See Pages 9 through 22 for Explanation of Ratios and Data

Comparative Historical Data				Current Data Sorted by Sales					
			Type of Statement						
42	33	33	Unqualified				1	7	25
81	72	86	Reviewed		1	3	16	36	30
41	25	28	Compiled		1	6	8	9	4
54	52	54	Tax Returns	8	14	12	15	3	2
121	152	124	Other	5	10	6	17	27	59
4/1/11-3/31/12 ALL	4/1/12-3/31/13 ALL	4/1/13-3/31/14 ALL		49 (4/1-9/30/13)			276 (10/1/13-3/31/14)		
				0-1MM	1-3MM	3-5MM	5-10MM	10-25MM	25MM & OVER
339	334	325	**NUMBER OF STATEMENTS**	13	26	27	57	82	120
%	%	%	**ASSETS**	%	%	%	%	%	%
7.4	7.0	9.1	Cash & Equivalents	8.7	9.8	12.9	12.3	9.2	6.6
27.5	26.0	26.8	Trade Receivables (net)	15.4	29.7	31.0	24.3	26.6	27.7
42.6	42.4	42.4	Inventory	49.0	33.2	37.9	45.1	43.1	43.0
2.7	3.9	2.8	All Other Current	3.1	.7	2.3	1.2	3.9	3.5
80.2	79.4	81.2	Total Current	76.1	73.4	84.2	82.9	82.7	80.8
9.4	9.9	8.4	Fixed Assets (net)	13.7	14.3	6.3	9.5	7.6	7.2
4.4	4.8	4.1	Intangibles (net)	1.5	.5	.1	3.0	3.1	7.3
6.0	6.0	6.3	All Other Non-Current	8.7	11.9	9.4	4.6	6.5	4.7
100.0	100.0	100.0	Total	100.0	100.0	100.0	100.0	100.0	100.0
			LIABILITIES						
16.3	15.6	14.9	Notes Payable-Short Term	21.4	10.9	6.5	15.2	17.6	15.1
1.8	2.4	1.9	Cur. Mat.-L.T.D.	14.6	.8	3.5	.7	1.1	1.5
18.3	17.7	18.4	Trade Payables	18.1	20.0	16.3	19.9	16.6	19.0
.2	.1	.2	Income Taxes Payable	.0	.0	.3	.1	.1	.2
8.6	9.3	9.6	All Other Current	2.3	7.6	5.6	9.9	11.5	10.4
45.1	45.3	45.0	Total Current	56.3	39.3	32.3	45.8	46.9	46.3
9.7	7.8	8.4	Long-Term Debt	29.5	14.4	8.8	7.6	5.0	7.5
.2	.2	.2	Deferred Taxes	.0	.0	.0	.0	.2	.5
6.2	6.5	8.3	All Other Non-Current	10.1	28.3	6.8	8.6	7.8	4.4
38.9	40.3	37.9	Net Worth	4.1	17.9	52.2	38.0	40.1	41.2
100.0	100.0	100.0	Total Liabilties & Net Worth	100.0	100.0	100.0	100.0	100.0	100.0
			INCOME DATA						
100.0	100.0	100.0	Net Sales	100.0	100.0	100.0	100.0	100.0	100.0
32.2	33.4	33.5	Gross Profit	43.6	40.7	33.8	31.7	34.3	31.0
28.4	29.2	28.8	Operating Expenses	38.6	38.4	30.5	26.2	30.2	25.7
3.8	4.2	4.6	Operating Profit	5.1	2.2	3.3	5.6	4.1	5.3
.7	.5	.7	All Other Expenses (net)	1.1	.6	.1	1.2	.6	.7
3.1	3.7	3.9	Profit Before Taxes	3.9	1.7	3.2	4.4	3.5	4.6
			RATIOS						
3.0	3.2	3.1		3.0	3.6	4.5	3.0	3.1	2.6
1.8	1.8	1.9	Current	1.3	2.2	2.8	1.9	1.8	1.8
1.3	1.3	1.3		.9	1.4	1.7	1.3	1.3	1.3
1.4	1.3	1.4		.9	1.9	2.4	1.2	1.6	1.3
.8	.7	.8	Quick	.3	1.0	1.8	.8	.7	.7
.4	.4	.5		.1	.7	.8	.5	.5	.4
25 14.8	**20** 17.9	**23** 16.0		**0** UND	**14** 25.7	**22** 16.6	**20** 18.5	**23** 16.0	**28** 13.0
39 9.4	**37** 9.8	**35** 10.5	Sales/Receivables	**10** 34.8	**32** 11.5	**33** 11.2	**31** 11.8	**33** 10.9	**39** 9.4
57 6.4	**54** 6.8	**52** 7.0		**59** 6.2	**49** 7.4	**60** 6.1	**49** 7.4	**55** 6.6	**53** 6.9
54 6.7	**54** 6.7	**51** 7.1		**60** 6.1	**11** 31.9	**16** 22.9	**53** 6.9	**54** 6.8	**58** 6.3
96 3.8	**94** 3.9	**87** 4.2	Cost of Sales/Inventory	**166** 2.2	**61** 6.0	**72** 5.1	**96** 3.8	**89** 4.1	**87** 4.2
159 2.3	**166** 2.2	**146** 2.5		**406** .9	**159** 2.3	**182** 2.0	**166** 2.2	**166** 2.2	**130** 2.8
13 27.3	**16** 22.4	**14** 25.6		**0** UND	**8** 46.9	**11** 33.9	**18** 20.5	**14** 26.6	**16** 22.5
31 11.8	**29** 12.4	**30** 12.3	Cost of Sales/Payables	**8** 47.0	**40** 9.2	**21** 17.5	**36** 10.1	**29** 12.8	**31** 11.9
56 6.5	**54** 6.8	**54** 6.7		**46** 8.0	**61** 6.0	**45** 8.2	**65** 5.6	**47** 7.8	**51** 7.2
3.9	3.8	4.2		2.3	3.3	3.4	3.7	4.0	4.9
7.0	7.3	7.2	Sales/Working Capital	8.0	9.0	5.7	6.8	7.1	7.6
16.9	19.0	15.9		UND	22.3	8.4	20.3	16.7	14.3
10.3	17.1	21.2			7.6	16.5	25.4	18.2	35.1
(298) 3.5	(277) 4.6	(276) 5.5	EBIT/Interest		(17) 4.0	(19) 2.7	(51) 5.8	(74) 3.4	(107) 8.2
1.6	1.8	2.2			-3.3	-1.3	2.3	1.6	4.1
13.3	15.2	11.0							40.5
(52) 4.3	(44) 6.4	(45) 5.4	Net Profit + Depr., Dep., Amort./Cur. Mat. L/T/D						(25) 6.3
1.8	2.0	1.6							2.7
.1	.0	.0		.0	.0	.0	.0	.1	.1
.2	.2	.2	Fixed/Worth	.8	.1	.0	.2	.2	.2
.6	.6	.5		-.3	1.6	.4	.5	.4	.5
.6	.6	.7		1.2	.7	.3	.9	.7	.7
1.9	1.5	1.7	Debt/Worth	8.4	1.6	.7	1.9	1.9	1.6
5.9	4.9	4.9		-22.2	8.0	1.9	3.8	5.0	4.6
39.8	44.7	49.0			69.5	25.8	63.8	36.7	49.9
(299) 16.6	(295) 18.5	(289) 21.0	% Profit Before Taxes/Tangible Net Worth		(22) 27.8	(25) 9.2	(51) 13.7	(75) 15.5	(107) 29.4
4.4	6.0	6.3			.5	.3	5.6	3.1	12.8
11.4	14.9	15.6		28.9	14.8	14.5	15.2	14.3	16.7
4.9	6.4	7.3	% Profit Before Taxes/Total Assets	5.0	7.4	4.0	5.1	5.6	8.3
1.2	1.6	2.1		-2.5	-8.3	-.7	2.1	1.0	4.4
129.9	152.4	171.3		UND	319.8	999.8	233.5	160.6	125.8
52.8	51.9	58.5	Sales/Net Fixed Assets	39.1	81.1	146.8	69.1	58.5	49.5
21.1	23.0	28.2		6.0	13.6	44.5	21.9	30.9	28.5
3.3	3.4	3.5		3.2	4.3	4.6	3.4	3.7	3.4
2.3	2.4	2.6	Sales/Total Assets	1.4	3.0	2.5	2.5	2.4	2.7
1.7	1.7	1.8		1.0	1.8	1.6	1.6	1.7	1.9
.3	.3	.2			.3	.1	.2	.3	.2
(259) .5	(251) .5	(241) .5	% Depr., Dep., Amort./Sales		(16) .6	(18) .4	(38) .4	(63) .5	(99) .6
1.0	1.0	1.0			.8	1.1	1.2	1.0	.9
1.0	1.2	1.1			1.4	2.6	1.2	1.0	.6
(139) 2.1	(124) 2.5	(121) 2.3	% Officers', Directors' Owners' Comp/Sales		(14) 4.4	(18) 5.0	(25) 2.3	(29) 1.8	(29) 1.2
4.6	5.6	5.2			6.4	10.8	4.4	3.6	2.7
10202716M	**11694835M**	**12756960M**	Net Sales ($)	**6853M**	**48463M**	**111226M**	**426712M**	**1356756M**	**10806950M**
5137657M	**5611254M**	**5677556M**	Total Assets ($)	**5864M**	**21009M**	**42329M**	**211208M**	**670925M**	**4726221M**

M = $ thousand MM = $ million

See Pages 9 through 22 for Explanation of Ratios and Data

Current Data Sorted by Assets / Comparative Historical Data

0-500M	500M-2MM	2-10MM	10-50MM	50-100MM	100-250MM		4/1/09-3/31/10 ALL	4/1/10-3/31/11 ALL
						Type of Statement		
	1	13	38	12	4	Unqualified	110	111
	6	71	49	3	1	Reviewed	216	223
2	25	58	8			Compiled	115	118
13	36	37	3			Tax Returns	98	93
8	46	85	66	22	10	Other	305	273
94 (4/1-9/30/13)			523 (10/1/13-3/31/14)					
23	114	264	164	37	15	**NUMBER OF STATEMENTS**	844	818
%	%	%	%	%	%	**ASSETS**	%	%
24.2	9.8	6.5	4.3	3.5	2.4	Cash & Equivalents	7.7	6.8
20.1	39.8	31.9	28.9	30.3	23.8	Trade Receivables (net)	29.1	29.4
30.5	30.7	37.5	39.4	36.9	30.0	Inventory	33.3	35.3
.9	1.2	2.4	2.2	2.2	4.2	All Other Current	3.5	2.5
75.6	81.4	78.3	74.9	72.9	60.3	Total Current	73.6	74.0
16.8	11.2	13.5	16.7	15.9	23.1	Fixed Assets (net)	17.6	16.9
1.1	1.9	2.5	2.3	4.6	7.4	Intangibles (net)	2.2	2.4
6.5	5.5	5.7	6.1	6.6	9.2	All Other Non-Current	6.7	6.6
100.0	100.0	100.0	100.0	100.0	100.0	Total	100.0	100.0
						LIABILITIES		
18.5	17.4	18.5	21.3	20.6	10.3	Notes Payable-Short Term	19.6	19.1
4.1	1.5	1.7	2.4	2.4	2.4	Cur. Mat.-L.T.D.	2.5	2.1
22.9	19.9	14.1	11.7	13.1	13.2	Trade Payables	12.7	13.7
.0	.1	.2	.1	.1	.8	Income Taxes Payable	.2	.2
17.7	14.3	8.0	7.6	6.8	7.3	All Other Current	8.3	9.1
63.1	53.2	42.3	43.1	42.9	33.9	Total Current	43.3	44.3
18.3	8.8	8.5	8.2	7.8	20.7	Long-Term Debt	10.4	10.5
.0	.0	.1	.3	.1	1.2	Deferred Taxes	.3	.2
12.6	5.8	6.0	4.4	3.5	1.1	All Other Non-Current	6.5	6.1
6.0	32.2	43.0	44.0	45.7	43.0	Net Worth	39.5	38.9
100.0	100.0	100.0	100.0	100.0	100.0	Total Liabilties & Net Worth	100.0	100.0
						INCOME DATA		
100.0	100.0	100.0	100.0	100.0	100.0	Net Sales	100.0	100.0
30.7	23.6	21.3	19.8	19.0	20.8	Gross Profit	21.9	22.0
29.0	20.8	18.5	16.6	15.5	18.0	Operating Expenses	22.4	21.2
1.7	2.8	2.8	3.2	3.5	2.8	Operating Profit	-.5	.8
-.2	.1	.1	.2	.4	.6	All Other Expenses (net)	.6	.4
1.9	2.7	2.7	3.0	3.0	2.2	Profit Before Taxes	-1.1	.4
						RATIOS		
2.6	2.6	3.1	2.8	3.2	2.8		3.2	3.1
1.4	1.7	1.9	1.6	1.9	2.1	Current	1.8	1.7
.7	1.3	1.3	1.3	1.3	1.1		1.2	1.2
1.5	1.7	1.7	1.2	1.3	1.3		1.6	1.4
.8	1.0	.9	.7	.8	.7	Quick	.8	.8
.2	.6	.5	.5	.5	.5		.5	.5
0 UND	**18** 20.4	**21** 17.2	**24** 15.2	**29** 12.8	**25** 14.5		**23** 16.1	**23** 15.9
11 33.8	**32** 11.3	**29** 12.4	**32** 11.3	**31** 11.7	**38** 9.6	Sales/Receivables	**34** 10.8	**33** 11.1
23 16.0	**44** 8.3	**41** 8.9	**41** 8.8	**42** 8.7	**41** 8.9		**47** 7.7	**45** 8.1
3 112.6	**14** 26.2	**27** 13.5	**44** 8.3	**41** 9.0	**41** 8.9		**30** 12.3	**31** 11.9
15 23.8	**34** 10.6	**49** 7.4	**62** 5.9	**57** 6.4	**46** 8.0	Cost of Sales/Inventory	**54** 6.8	**55** 6.6
46 7.9	**69** 5.3	**85** 4.3	**89** 4.1	**81** 4.5	**83** 4.4		**84** 4.3	**88** 4.2
1 502.0	**8** 48.6	**7** 55.8	**8** 43.5	**10** 37.9	**9** 39.3		**9** 41.7	**9** 41.1
21 17.2	**20** 18.3	**14** 25.8	**14** 25.5	**15** 24.5	**19** 19.1	Cost of Sales/Payables	**16** 22.7	**16** 22.2
35 10.5	**36** 10.1	**25** 14.8	**23** 16.0	**26** 14.0	**32** 11.4		**26** 14.0	**28** 13.1
7.6	7.5	6.2	5.7	5.7	5.3		5.1	5.6
29.9	11.9	9.1	10.2	8.8	8.6	Sales/Working Capital	9.9	10.1
-81.7	26.3	22.6	17.2	19.8	66.3		25.6	24.7
8.3	18.3	16.7	13.8	16.6	17.5		3.8	6.0
(17) 3.5	(102) 6.5	(245) 5.2	(154) 5.7	(35) 5.2	8.8	EBIT/Interest	(769) 1.0	(741) 1.9
.2	2.8	1.8	2.9	3.0	1.5		-2.7	-.5
		9.5	10.9	10.4			3.3	5.1
		(34) 2.6	(57) 3.8	(13) 7.0		Net Profit + Depr., Dep., Amort./Cur. Mat. L/T/D	(179) .8	(169) 1.9
		1.4	1.9	1.7			-.9	-.1
.0	.0	.1	.2	.1	.4		.1	.1
.3	.1	.2	.4	.3	.6	Fixed/Worth	.3	.3
10.9	.9	.7	.7	.7	.9		.9	.9
.9	.8	.6	.6	.6	.6		.6	.6
3.3	1.8	1.4	1.5	1.3	2.1	Debt/Worth	1.4	1.5
78.3	4.4	3.3	3.1	3.3	4.8		4.0	4.0
197.1	46.5	32.3	30.0	24.1	27.6		12.6	18.9
(18) 43.9	(98) 23.0	(243) 16.6	(160) 17.5	(36) 14.5	14.2	% Profit Before Taxes/Tangible Net Worth	(764) .8	(734) 4.6
.6	6.0	4.6	8.2	10.4	9.5		-15.1	-5.0
34.9	14.0	14.1	11.6	10.6	11.5		4.7	7.0
11.6	7.8	6.0	7.6	6.6	7.3	% Profit Before Taxes/Total Assets	.1	1.6
-1.2	2.3	1.9	3.3	3.0	.9		-7.2	-3.3
UND	341.3	130.5	60.4	64.6	19.6		76.4	89.9
181.8	132.2	41.2	21.0	28.9	14.9	Sales/Net Fixed Assets	24.8	29.7
20.2	31.3	13.6	10.0	8.9	7.6		8.2	9.2
9.0	5.4	4.5	3.7	3.7	3.4		3.7	3.9
5.5	4.0	3.2	2.8	2.8	2.9	Sales/Total Assets	2.7	2.8
2.9	2.9	2.5	2.1	2.0	1.9		1.9	2.0
.2	.1	.3	.3	.3	.6		.4	.4
(12) .8	(78) .3	(210) .6	(157) .6	(34) .7	(13) 1.0	% Depr., Dep., Amort./Sales	(723) .9	(705) .9
3.6	.7	1.1	1.3	1.6	1.2		1.9	1.6
2.3	1.7	1.0	.6				1.4	1.0
(14) 3.6	(60) 2.8	(111) 1.9	(46) 1.4			% Officers', Directors' Owners' Comp/Sales	(308) 2.6	(313) 1.9
7.4	4.3	3.2	3.1				4.8	4.0
46674M	620924M	4576130M	10653885M	7938134M	7176734M	Net Sales ($)	30402572M	30065106M
7659M	139594M	1270751M	3479827M	2623245M	2453127M	Total Assets ($)	11183799M	10695050M

M = $ thousand MM = $ million

See Pages 9 through 22 for Explanation of Ratios and Data

Comparative Historical Data				Current Data Sorted by Sales					
			Type of Statement						
97	80	68	Unqualified		1		1	14	52
166	157	130	Reviewed			4	13	49	64
116	88	93	Compiled	2	5	12	28	32	14
88	89	89	Tax Returns	3	18	14	25	26	3
283	254	237	Other	5	15	17	37	53	110
4/1/11-3/31/12	4/1/12-3/31/13	4/1/13-3/31/14		94 (4/1-9/30/13)			523 (10/1/13-3/31/14)		
ALL	ALL	ALL		0-1MM	1-3MM	3-5MM	5-10MM	10-25MM	25MM & OVER
750	668	617	**NUMBER OF STATEMENTS**	10	39	47	104	174	243
%	%	%	**ASSETS**	%	%	%	%	%	%
6.6	5.6	6.9	Cash & Equivalents	15.4	16.9	12.8	8.7	4.9	4.4
30.6	32.3	31.8	Trade Receivables (net)	8.7	25.7	35.2	33.5	32.2	32.2
35.2	35.7	36.2	Inventory	25.9	31.1	30.8	34.7	37.8	38.1
2.4	2.5	2.1	All Other Current	.7	1.5	.9	2.4	2.3	2.2
74.9	76.2	77.1	Total Current	50.7	75.1	79.7	79.3	77.2	76.9
15.7	15.4	14.5	Fixed Assets (net)	40.2	15.6	10.3	13.6	14.2	14.6
2.4	2.1	2.5	Intangibles (net)	2.0	3.2	3.5	1.3	2.3	2.9
6.9	6.3	5.9	All Other Non-Current	7.2	6.1	6.6	5.8	6.2	5.6
100.0	100.0	100.0	Total	100.0	100.0	100.0	100.0	100.0	100.0
			LIABILITIES						
20.4	20.1	18.9	Notes Payable-Short Term	7.5	13.5	17.5	17.5	18.8	21.3
2.3	1.9	2.0	Cur. Mat.-L.T.D.	4.3	1.9	1.5	2.3	2.1	1.8
14.2	14.2	14.8	Trade Payables	12.9	18.7	20.9	15.1	14.0	13.4
.1	.1	.1	Income Taxes Payable	.0	.0	.2	.1	.1	.2
8.0	7.7	9.3	All Other Current	6.5	15.5	12.7	11.6	7.6	8.0
45.0	44.1	45.1	Total Current	31.2	49.7	52.9	46.7	42.5	44.7
9.3	10.1	9.1	Long-Term Debt	29.4	17.8	6.9	9.7	8.9	7.1
.2	.1	.2	Deferred Taxes	.0	.0	.0	.1	.2	.3
8.3	6.8	5.5	All Other Non-Current	6.9	11.4	6.8	4.6	6.6	3.9
37.2	38.9	40.1	Net Worth	32.6	21.1	33.4	39.0	41.7	44.0
100.0	100.0	100.0	Total Liabilties & Net Worth	100.0	100.0	100.0	100.0	100.0	100.0
			INCOME DATA						
100.0	100.0	100.0	Net Sales	100.0	100.0	100.0	100.0	100.0	100.0
21.9	21.2	21.5	Gross Profit	41.9	28.0	24.9	24.3	20.8	18.3
20.8	19.3	18.6	Operating Expenses	39.5	24.6	22.4	21.3	18.0	15.3
1.1	2.0	2.9	Operating Profit	2.4	3.4	2.5	3.0	2.8	3.0
.3	.3	.2	All Other Expenses (net)	.1	-.1	.2	.1	.2	.2
.8	1.7	2.8	Profit Before Taxes	2.3	3.5	2.2	2.9	2.7	2.8
			RATIOS						
2.9	2.9	2.9		4.6	2.9	3.1	2.7	3.1	2.7
1.7	1.7	1.8	Current	2.1	2.0	1.7	1.8	1.8	1.7
1.2	1.3	1.3		1.3	1.2	1.2	1.3	1.3	1.3
1.4	1.5	1.5		2.3	1.9	1.8	1.8	1.6	1.3
.8	.8	.8	Quick	1.1	.8	.9	1.0	.9	.8
.5	.5	.5		.2	.5	.5	.5	.5	.5
23 15.6	**23** 15.8	**21** 17.1		**0** UND	**17** 21.8	**21** 17.5	**18** 20.6	**22** 16.3	**24** 15.5
34 10.7	**34** 10.8	**31** 11.8	Sales/Receivables	**9** 39.0	**26** 14.0	**39** 9.3	**31** 11.6	**30** 12.2	**31** 11.6
46 8.0	**46** 8.0	**42** 8.7		**21** 17.2	**43** 8.4	**60** 6.1	**43** 8.4	**41** 9.0	**40** 9.1
31 11.9	**29** 12.7	**27** 13.4		**7** 52.5	**15** 23.8	**14** 26.9	**21** 17.0	**26** 13.8	**34** 10.8
53 6.9	**54** 6.8	**51** 7.1	Cost of Sales/Inventory	**73** 5.0	**51** 7.1	**39** 9.3	**47** 7.7	**52** 7.0	**52** 7.0
87 4.2	**87** 4.2	**83** 4.4		**166** 2.2	**85** 4.3	**85** 4.3	**85** 4.3	**85** 4.3	**78** 4.7
9 39.2	**9** 41.6	**8** 46.0		**7** 52.8	**8** 47.6	**9** 39.9	**5** 70.7	**8** 43.4	**8** 43.7
16 22.3	**16** 22.6	**16** 23.5	Cost of Sales/Payables	**21** 17.6	**22** 16.3	**26** 14.3	**16** 23.2	**15** 24.3	**14** 25.6
29 12.4	**28** 12.9	**26** 14.0		**87** 4.2	**39** 9.4	**48** 7.6	**31** 11.9	**25** 14.8	**22** 16.5
5.6	5.9	6.2		2.5	4.6	5.7	6.7	6.2	6.3
10.3	10.1	10.5	Sales/Working Capital	6.3	7.4	11.9	11.1	9.6	10.9
25.1	21.6	24.1		NM	57.0	36.6	25.6	20.7	24.2
6.8	10.4	16.5			23.1	12.0	14.6	17.8	15.2
(675) 2.2	(612) 3.8	(568) 5.6	EBIT/Interest		(31) 4.1	(40) 4.7	(96) 4.9	(166) 5.7	(227) 6.3
.4	1.1	2.3			.9	2.0	2.1	1.8	2.9
5.5	6.8	10.5						9.2	11.6
(148) 1.8	(149) 3.1	(117) 4.1	Net Profit + Depr., Dep., Amort./Cur. Mat. L/T/D					(23) 2.3	(80) 4.5
.3	1.1	1.7						1.5	2.1
.1	.1	.1		.0	.0	.1	.1	.1	.1
.3	.3	.3	Fixed/Worth	1.6	.1	.2	.2	.3	.3
.9	.8	.7		NM	2.2	1.2	.8	.9	.6
.6	.6	.6		1.1	.6	.8	.6	.6	.6
1.5	1.6	1.5	Debt/Worth	2.0	1.5	1.9	1.8	1.5	1.5
3.8	4.0	3.5		NM	21.6	11.5	3.5	3.4	3.3
19.2	26.4	33.5			52.3	37.1	39.2	32.3	30.9
(677) 5.8	(613) 10.8	(570) 17.7	% Profit Before Taxes/Tangible Net Worth		(31) 21.3	(39) 14.8	(96) 18.7	(159) 17.5	(237) 17.4
-1.2	2.2	6.8			-1.0	6.0	4.1	5.2	9.3
7.8	9.8	13.2		12.0	22.5	12.0	13.5	14.4	12.3
2.2	4.4	7.2	% Profit Before Taxes/Total Assets	5.6	8.2	5.7	6.6	6.7	7.7
-1.1	.4	2.4		-3.3	-.7	1.8	2.1	1.9	3.0
102.5	107.5	136.1		UND	726.3	152.6	267.1	119.8	89.9
31.3	32.1	39.5	Sales/Net Fixed Assets	1.7	88.1	49.1	56.4	36.2	32.0
11.4	10.4	12.9		1.0	17.2	22.4	13.6	11.7	12.9
4.0	4.2	4.4		2.4	4.3	4.6	4.8	4.4	4.4
2.9	3.0	3.2	Sales/Total Assets	1.2	3.1	3.1	3.4	3.2	3.3
2.1	2.1	2.4		.6	2.0	2.2	2.4	2.5	2.4
.4	.3	.3			.3	.2	.2	.3	.3
(630) .8	(558) .7	(504) .6	% Depr., Dep., Amort./Sales		(23) .8	(37) .4	(70) .4	(146) .6	(221) .5
1.3	1.2	1.1			3.4	.9	1.1	1.3	1.0
.9	1.0	1.1			3.0	1.7	1.5	.9	.7
(269) 2.0	(239) 2.1	(233) 2.0	% Officers', Directors' Owners' Comp/Sales		(19) 4.5	(24) 2.7	(63) 2.3	(68) 1.8	(57) 1.4
4.1	3.6	3.8			7.8	3.9	4.0	2.9	2.4
32080213M	31882551M	31012481M	Net Sales ($)	6061M	80079M	187161M	751716M	2895036M	27092428M
11199019M	11299478M	9974203M	Total Assets ($)	6058M	34037M	75059M	245106M	1009201M	8604742M

M = $ thousand MM = $ million

See Pages 9 through 22 for Explanation of Ratios and Data

Current Data Sorted by Assets / Comparative Historical Data

0-500M	500M-2MM	2-10MM	10-50MM	50-100MM	100-250MM	Type of Statement	4/1/09-3/31/10 ALL	4/1/10-3/31/11 ALL
		3	9	2	4	Unqualified	23	30
	3	26	21	1		Reviewed	66	59
1	5	15	1		1	Compiled	39	38
5	14	16	2			Tax Returns	62	39
9	20	43	21	3	4	Other	104	101
31 (4/1-9/30/13)		198 (10/1/13-3/31/14)						
15	42	103	54	6	9	NUMBER OF STATEMENTS	294	267
%	%	%	%	%	%	**ASSETS**	%	%
14.6	9.5	7.9	7.0			Cash & Equivalents	6.6	8.0
21.5	27.0	24.5	24.8			Trade Receivables (net)	23.4	23.9
24.6	35.7	42.0	33.3			Inventory	35.2	34.0
.1	1.1	2.3	1.3			All Other Current	3.0	2.3
60.8	73.3	76.7	66.4			Total Current	68.2	68.2
23.8	19.5	16.7	22.3			Fixed Assets (net)	23.0	22.9
1.2	1.1	2.3	4.9			Intangibles (net)	2.9	3.0
14.2	6.2	4.2	6.5			All Other Non-Current	6.0	6.0
100.0	100.0	100.0	100.0			Total	100.0	100.0
						LIABILITIES		
40.8	10.1	11.8	14.7			Notes Payable-Short Term	12.6	14.5
.4	1.0	2.4	3.1			Cur. Mat.-L.T.D.	3.3	3.0
12.3	19.6	22.9	17.2			Trade Payables	21.9	24.2
.1	.0	.1	.1			Income Taxes Payable	.1	.1
10.2	19.5	6.4	8.1			All Other Current	8.5	9.1
63.7	50.2	43.6	43.3			Total Current	46.5	50.9
28.8	13.0	8.0	11.4			Long-Term Debt	18.1	12.0
.0	.0	.4	.5			Deferred Taxes	.4	.3
10.9	10.5	6.8	6.9			All Other Non-Current	7.4	6.7
-3.4	26.3	41.1	37.9			Net Worth	27.7	30.1
100.0	100.0	100.0	100.0			Total Liabilties & Net Worth	100.0	100.0
						INCOME DATA		
100.0	100.0	100.0	100.0			Net Sales	100.0	100.0
50.7	36.3	29.1	27.9			Gross Profit	30.9	30.9
47.2	34.2	24.6	23.8			Operating Expenses	31.9	30.1
3.5	2.1	4.5	4.2			Operating Profit	-1.0	.7
1.2	.5	.3	.8			All Other Expenses (net)	.8	.5
2.3	1.6	4.1	3.4			Profit Before Taxes	-1.7	.2
						RATIOS		
12.6	3.8	2.8	3.0				2.7	2.6
1.0	1.8	1.7	1.7			Current	1.6	1.6
.6	1.1	1.3	1.3				1.1	1.0
5.9	2.1	1.3	1.6				1.3	1.3
.5	.8	.7	.8			Quick	.6	.6
.2	.4	.4	.4				.4	.4
0 UND	**14** 25.3	**24** 15.5	**27** 13.3				**24** 15.1	**23** 15.5
11 32.7	**33** 10.9	**34** 10.7	**45** 8.1			Sales/Receivables	**37** 9.8	**38** 9.6
31 11.7	**45** 8.1	**53** 6.9	**57** 6.4				**54** 6.8	**52** 7.0
0 UND	**33** 11.0	**54** 6.8	**46** 8.0				**40** 9.1	**34** 10.9
13 28.9	**66** 5.5	**96** 3.8	**61** 6.0			Cost of Sales/Inventory	**83** 4.4	**73** 5.0
126 2.9	**130** 2.8	**166** 2.2	**135** 2.7				**148** 2.5	**148** 2.5
0 UND	**13** 27.2	**23** 16.2	**20** 18.7				**19** 19.0	**22** 16.3
4 86.6	**25** 14.6	**48** 7.6	**41** 8.8			Cost of Sales/Payables	**35** 10.4	**41** 8.8
40 9.1	**54** 6.8	**79** 4.6	**62** 5.9				**67** 5.4	**71** 5.1
7.0	4.5	3.6	4.5				4.2	4.5
UND	8.3	7.2	7.8			Sales/Working Capital	8.8	8.9
-21.8	NM	15.8	20.4				36.6	130.5
	17.1	19.3	17.5				3.4	4.9
	(32) 3.9	(92) 5.7	(49) 4.2			EBIT/Interest	(264) .8	(224) 1.3
	1.1	2.9	2.3				-3.3	-1.8
		8.1				Net Profit + Depr., Dep.,	2.6	4.2
		(23) 3.7				Amort./Cur. Mat. L/T/D	(58) .6	(43) 1.3
		2.5					-.4	.3
.0	.1	.1	.1				.2	.1
1.0	.5	.3	.6			Fixed/Worth	.6	.6
-1.6	2.9	.8	1.3				2.5	2.2
.1	.5	.8	.6				.9	.7
19.1	3.1	1.6	1.6			Debt/Worth	2.2	1.9
-3.6	10.6	2.8	4.6				8.1	6.2
	42.6	31.5	28.4			% Profit Before Taxes/Tangible	14.6	17.5
	(34) 16.7	(97) 16.2	(47) 13.5			Net Worth	(240) 1.2	(223) 3.2
	3.6	7.8	8.2				-13.8	-8.3
27.8	14.1	11.8	9.6			% Profit Before Taxes/Total	4.3	6.1
10.5	2.9	6.3	4.9			Assets	-.3	.7
-7.2	.3	2.9	3.0				-8.5	-4.4
UND	108.3	81.1	51.8				44.6	43.7
71.4	18.9	20.9	14.6			Sales/Net Fixed Assets	15.4	15.1
10.4	9.1	8.3	4.5				4.8	4.8
9.1	3.5	2.9	2.4				2.8	2.9
5.3	2.4	2.2	2.0			Sales/Total Assets	1.9	1.9
1.5	1.9	1.5	1.5				1.3	1.4
	.3	.4	.7				.7	.7
	(26) 1.0	(87) .9	(48) 1.2			% Depr., Dep., Amort./Sales	(239) 1.7	(223) 1.8
	2.8	1.7	3.4				3.6	4.1
	2.4	1.4	.4			% Officers', Directors'	2.0	1.8
	(22) 4.0	(44) 2.1	(18) 1.3			Owners' Comp/Sales	(129) 3.3	(95) 3.2
	5.7	3.9	1.7				5.0	5.0
15295M	152971M	1191365M	2106788M	641275M	1855414M	Net Sales ($)	4938246M	4587004M
3874M	55872M	524342M	1045831M	405451M	1506684M	Total Assets ($)	2742055M	2778464M

M = $ thousand MM = $ million

See Pages 9 through 22 for Explanation of Ratios and Data

Comparative Historical Data				Current Data Sorted by Sales					
			Type of Statement						
18	17	18	Unqualified				1	4	13
64	46	51	Reviewed		1	2	9	23	16
35	31	23	Compiled	1	3	3	6	8	2
59	45	37	Tax Returns	3	10	7	10	5	2
100	97	100	Other	5	17	11	17	26	24
					31 (4/1-9/30/13)		198 (10/1/13-3/31/14)		
4/1/11-3/31/12 ALL	**4/1/12-3/31/13 ALL**	**4/1/13-3/31/14 ALL**		**0-1MM**	**1-3MM**	**3-5MM**	**5-10MM**	**10-25MM**	**25MM & OVER**
276	236	229	**NUMBER OF STATEMENTS**	9	31	23	43	66	57
%	%	%	**ASSETS**	%	%	%	%	%	%
7.4	8.8	8.1	Cash & Equivalents		11.6	8.7	7.3	8.2	6.1
24.5	25.5	24.3	Trade Receivables (net)		20.6	23.6	23.8	26.8	25.9
35.2	36.4	36.5	Inventory		35.5	36.5	47.8	37.5	29.5
2.2	2.1	1.9	All Other Current		3.1	.7	.6	1.9	2.8
69.4	72.9	70.8	Total Current		70.9	69.4	79.5	74.5	64.2
21.2	19.3	20.0	Fixed Assets (net)		20.2	23.4	14.2	18.4	22.7
2.9	2.4	3.3	Intangibles (net)		.9	1.9	1.6	3.4	6.7
6.5	5.4	5.9	All Other Non-Current		8.0	5.3	4.7	3.7	6.4
100.0	100.0	100.0	Total		100.0	100.0	100.0	100.0	100.0
			LIABILITIES						
13.6	13.8	13.8	Notes Payable-Short Term		10.1	10.3	11.7	12.3	12.7
3.1	2.5	2.2	Cur. Mat.-L.T.D.		.9	1.9	2.5	2.3	3.0
22.6	22.0	19.4	Trade Payables		17.6	16.8	22.7	23.8	16.1
.2	.1	.1	Income Taxes Payable		.0	.0	.1	.1	.1
9.0	10.0	9.7	All Other Current		18.4	8.7	8.7	7.8	8.7
48.5	48.5	45.1	Total Current		47.0	37.6	45.7	46.3	40.7
12.9	11.0	11.3	Long-Term Debt		16.5	9.6	7.0	7.2	11.6
.3	.3	.4	Deferred Taxes		.0	.5	.3	.5	.4
9.7	8.0	8.3	All Other Non-Current		12.4	8.8	6.8	7.3	6.6
28.5	32.3	34.9	Net Worth		24.1	43.5	40.2	38.7	40.6
100.0	100.0	100.0	Total Liabilties & Net Worth		100.0	100.0	100.0	100.0	100.0
			INCOME DATA						
100.0	100.0	100.0	Net Sales		100.0	100.0	100.0	100.0	100.0
31.7	31.4	31.6	Gross Profit		34.6	34.7	29.3	28.7	28.6
29.5	28.1	27.5	Operating Expenses		33.3	30.2	24.7	24.4	23.7
2.2	3.2	4.1	Operating Profit		1.4	4.5	4.6	4.3	4.9
.3	.7	.6	All Other Expenses (net)		.3	.7	.4	.6	.5
1.8	2.6	3.6	Profit Before Taxes		1.0	3.8	4.2	3.7	4.4
			RATIOS						
2.7	2.6	3.2			7.5	3.7	3.3	2.3	3.1
1.5	1.6	1.7	Current		2.1	1.9	1.7	1.7	1.5
1.1	1.2	1.2			1.0	1.3	1.3	1.2	1.3
1.2	1.4	1.5			2.2	2.2	.9	1.6	1.5
.6	.7	.7	Quick		.7	.8	.6	.7	1.0
.4	.4	.4			.2	.4	.4	.4	.4
24 15.3	**22** 16.8	**21** 17.3			**13** 27.8	**15** 24.8	**19** 19.0	**24** 15.1	**29** 12.8
37 9.9	**36** 10.1	**35** 10.4	Sales/Receivables		**29** 12.4	**34** 10.7	**35** 10.4	**34** 10.7	**46** 8.0
55 6.6	**53** 6.9	**53** 6.9			**47** 7.8	**50** 7.3	**48** 7.6	**54** 6.7	**57** 6.4
35 10.4	**36** 10.1	**41** 9.0			**41** 9.0	**35** 10.3	**54** 6.7	**38** 9.7	**43** 8.4
69 5.3	**79** 4.6	**81** 4.5	Cost of Sales/Inventory		**111** 3.3	**94** 3.9	**114** 3.2	**70** 5.2	**62** 5.9
146 2.5	**135** 2.7	**146** 2.5			**215** 1.7	**130** 2.8	**192** 1.9	**122** 3.0	**135** 2.7
22 16.3	**21** 17.5	**18** 20.3			**11** 33.5	**17** 21.7	**20** 18.5	**22** 16.3	**20** 18.1
41 8.9	**36** 10.1	**37** 9.8	Cost of Sales/Payables		**29** 12.8	**29** 12.4	**54** 6.7	**46** 7.9	**33** 10.9
74 4.9	**68** 5.4	**65** 5.6			**60** 6.1	**63** 5.8	**78** 4.7	**81** 4.5	**58** 6.3
4.2	4.6	4.1			2.4	3.3	4.2	4.6	4.5
8.3	8.2	8.0	Sales/Working Capital		7.1	6.9	7.0	9.6	8.0
33.0	25.4	21.1			-215.4	25.7	15.7	21.5	17.1
7.5	10.1	18.2			3.1	23.1	25.2	17.7	25.8
(239) 2.3	(201) 3.5	(196) 5.1	EBIT/Interest		(22) 1.5	(20) 6.1	(37) 5.9	(59) 6.6	(52) 5.0
.3	1.4	2.1			-.4	1.3	3.1	2.9	2.8
4.5	9.0	10.1					16.1	8.1	
(42) 2.1	(43) 3.2	(36) 4.3	Net Profit + Depr., Dep., Amort./Cur. Mat. L/T/D				(10) 5.0	(14) 3.5	
.5	1.5	2.5					2.9	2.3	
.1	.1	.1			.0	.2	.0	.2	.1
.5	.4	.5	Fixed/Worth		1.0	.4	.3	.5	.7
2.1	1.7	1.2			7.6	1.2	.6	1.0	1.9
.8	.8	.6			.4	.4	.9	.6	.7
2.0	2.0	1.7	Debt/Worth		3.0	1.4	1.4	1.7	1.8
9.0	6.1	4.2			22.9	6.3	2.7	3.6	3.5
23.3	31.0	34.5			31.7	35.3	42.6	34.7	36.0
(224) 8.1	(199) 14.0	(200) 15.8	% Profit Before Taxes/Tangible Net Worth		(24) 12.8	(21) 6.9	(41) 23.0	(59) 16.4	(52) 15.2
.7	3.8	7.1			1.5	2.1	8.4	10.7	9.3
8.1	9.9	11.7			11.7	15.0	18.1	10.2	11.0
2.5	4.5	5.7	% Profit Before Taxes/Total Assets		1.5	3.0	9.6	6.4	5.2
-1.2	.9	2.4			-2.2	1.1	2.8	3.4	3.3
56.1	62.3	67.7			148.8	46.0	155.1	59.3	53.8
17.1	21.0	17.9	Sales/Net Fixed Assets		14.0	12.0	23.6	16.9	17.5
5.1	7.3	7.3			5.7	7.9	12.8	8.7	4.0
2.8	3.1	3.0			2.3	3.4	3.2	2.9	2.6
2.0	2.2	2.2	Sales/Total Assets		1.8	2.5	2.2	2.3	2.0
1.4	1.6	1.5			1.2	1.5	1.7	1.8	1.4
.6	.5	.5			.4	.7	.4	.4	.6
(216) 1.5	(190) 1.0	(176) 1.1	% Depr., Dep., Amort./Sales		(19) 1.6	(14) 2.0	(32) .9	(59) .9	(49) 1.1
3.3	2.9	2.3			4.2	2.7	1.7	1.9	3.5
2.1	1.9	1.3			2.3	1.7	1.7	1.2	.4
(104) 3.6	(97) 3.3	(93) 2.4	% Officers', Directors' Owners' Comp/Sales		(18) 4.0	(11) 2.7	(22) 2.5	(24) 1.6	(14) 1.1
6.4	5.9	5.0			7.1	6.6	3.5	5.1	1.9
4975916M	**4808963M**	**5963108M**	Net Sales ($)	**4408M**	**66325M**	**88277M**	**308212M**	**1031078M**	**4464808M**
2954900M	**2465393M**	**3542054M**	Total Assets ($)	**2210M**	**44574M**	**52637M**	**168736M**	**486143M**	**2787754M**

M = $ thousand MM = $ million

See Pages 9 through 22 for Explanation of Ratios and Data

Current Data Sorted by Assets / Comparative Historical Data

0-500M	500M-2MM	2-10MM	10-50MM	50-100MM	100-250MM	Type of Statement	4/1/09-3/31/10 ALL	4/1/10-3/31/11 ALL
1		1	5		3	Unqualified	18	20
1	1	12	11	1		Reviewed	33	42
1	6	5	3		1	Compiled	23	29
	9	10	1			Tax Returns	23	23
1	6	13	20	3	2	Other	46	53
14 (4/1-9/30/13)			103 (10/1/13-3/31/14)					
4	22	41	40	4	6	NUMBER OF STATEMENTS	143	167
%	%	%	%	%	%	**ASSETS**	%	%
	15.1	6.3	7.8			Cash & Equivalents	9.2	9.4
	32.8	34.6	32.2			Trade Receivables (net)	30.0	32.9
	34.7	43.6	39.4			Inventory	34.1	34.7
	2.0	1.4	2.7			All Other Current	4.3	3.2
	84.5	85.9	82.0			Total Current	77.6	80.2
	9.7	7.9	13.0			Fixed Assets (net)	13.2	13.0
	1.0	1.8	2.1			Intangibles (net)	3.1	2.3
	4.7	4.4	2.8			All Other Non-Current	6.1	4.6
	100.0	100.0	100.0			Total	100.0	100.0
						LIABILITIES		
	12.0	13.8	15.2			Notes Payable-Short Term	13.9	12.0
	2.3	.8	1.8			Cur. Mat.-L.T.D.	2.7	2.2
	21.6	23.1	22.7			Trade Payables	19.5	20.6
	.0	.0	.0			Income Taxes Payable	.1	.1
	8.9	6.6	8.0			All Other Current	7.7	7.5
	44.9	44.3	47.7			Total Current	43.9	42.5
	11.9	3.7	4.1			Long-Term Debt	12.0	11.0
	.0	.0	.2			Deferred Taxes	.4	.4
	12.0	5.5	3.6			All Other Non-Current	5.0	4.9
	31.2	46.5	44.4			Net Worth	38.7	41.2
	100.0	100.0	100.0			Total Liabilties & Net Worth	100.0	100.0
						INCOME DATA		
	100.0	100.0	100.0			Net Sales	100.0	100.0
	26.8	23.0	22.7			Gross Profit	26.7	25.5
	24.9	20.0	20.6			Operating Expenses	25.0	23.6
	1.9	2.9	2.1			Operating Profit	1.6	1.9
	-.2	-.4	.0			All Other Expenses (net)	.2	.2
	2.1	3.3	2.1			Profit Before Taxes	1.5	1.7
						RATIOS		
	2.9	2.9	2.5				3.2	3.0
	1.7	2.1	1.6			Current	1.7	1.9
	1.4	1.6	1.3				1.3	1.4
	1.8	1.7	1.3				1.8	1.7
	1.2	.9	.8			Quick	.8	(166) 1.0
	.6	.5	.5				.5	.7
	25 14.5	**23** 16.2	**33** 11.2				**27** 13.4	**26** 14.3
	37 9.9	**40** 9.1	**41** 8.8			Sales/Receivables	**36** 10.0	**41** 9.0
	47 7.8	**57** 6.4	**48** 7.6				**54** 6.7	**59** 6.2
	25 14.6	**42** 8.6	**49** 7.4				**37** 9.9	**42** 8.6
	56 6.5	**72** 5.1	**72** 5.1			Cost of Sales/Inventory	**58** 6.3	**59** 6.2
	79 4.6	**94** 3.9	**94** 3.9				**84** 4.4	**79** 4.6
	14 25.9	**16** 22.9	**24** 15.1				**16** 22.4	**20** 18.0
	27 13.3	**37** 9.8	**39** 9.4			Cost of Sales/Payables	**32** 11.5	**32** 11.4
	45 8.2	**49** 7.4	**47** 7.7				**50** 7.4	**49** 7.5
	4.8	4.8	5.8				5.1	4.7
	9.3	7.0	9.7			Sales/Working Capital	9.2	7.9
	16.7	11.7	16.6				21.0	17.7
	27.9	30.4	18.7				10.7	11.6
	(21) 2.9	(35) 8.6	(37) 7.0			EBIT/Interest	(133) 3.4	(149) 4.4
	.9	2.6	3.0				.6	1.2
			5.7				6.5	6.2
			(11) 2.2			Net Profit + Depr., Dep., Amort./Cur. Mat. L/T/D	(23) 2.5	(28) 2.2
			.9				.9	.7
	.0	.1	.1				.1	.1
	.3	.1	.3			Fixed/Worth	.3	.2
	1.0	.3	.6				.8	.7
	1.4	.7	.7				.7	.6
	2.9	1.1	1.5			Debt/Worth	1.8	1.5
	8.2	2.4	2.3				4.6	3.8
	60.2	39.6	37.7				38.9	30.5
	(20) 15.6	(40) 17.6	17.5			% Profit Before Taxes/Tangible Net Worth	(133) 13.0	(153) 11.9
	1.5	2.4	4.2				1.4	3.7
	21.7	13.5	12.7				11.6	10.9
	3.9	6.2	8.4			% Profit Before Taxes/Total Assets	3.7	3.9
	.0	1.4	2.1				-.3	.5
	411.1	117.5	64.5				61.8	80.9
	72.4	52.0	22.6			Sales/Net Fixed Assets	33.9	37.2
	17.8	22.9	16.7				16.4	16.0
	4.2	3.7	3.2				3.6	3.5
	3.7	3.1	2.6			Sales/Total Assets	2.7	2.9
	2.4	2.4	2.3				2.1	2.2
	.2	.3	.5				.5	.5
	(15) .8	(31) .6	(36) .7			% Depr., Dep., Amort./Sales	(117) .8	(141) .7
	1.2	1.1	1.2				1.4	1.5
	1.6	1.0					1.3	1.3
	(11) 3.3	(21) 2.4				% Officers', Directors' Owners' Comp/Sales	(57) 2.9	(61) 3.2
	6.1	3.3					4.8	5.2
12946M	100865M	612391M	2433452M	629503M	2145381M	Net Sales ($)	5643477M	5903390M
1201M	29323M	195579M	887570M	303143M	930361M	Total Assets ($)	2085012M	2313158M

M = $ thousand MM = $ million

See Pages 9 through 22 for Explanation of Ratios and Data

Comparative Historical Data / Current Data Sorted by Sales

4/1/11-3/31/12 ALL	4/1/12-3/31/13 ALL	4/1/13-3/31/14 ALL	Type of Statement	0-1MM	1-3MM	3-5MM	5-10MM	10-25MM	25MM & OVER
17	18	10	Unqualified			1	1		8
36	32	26	Reviewed		1	1	2	7	15
21	18	16	Compiled		2		7	3	4
26	26	20	Tax Returns		5	3	5	5	2
57	36	45	Other	1	2	4	6	6	26
				14 (4/1-9/30/13)			103 (10/1/13-3/31/14)		
157	130	117	NUMBER OF STATEMENTS	1	10	9	21	21	55
%	%	%	**ASSETS**	%	%	%	%	%	%
7.8	8.3	8.5	Cash & Equivalents		17.0		9.1	6.0	7.6
34.1	33.2	32.0	Trade Receivables (net)		21.2		33.5	34.8	32.5
34.5	36.5	38.4	Inventory		44.8		36.2	41.3	37.3
2.1	3.0	2.8	All Other Current		1.5		1.7	1.3	2.8
78.5	80.9	81.7	Total Current		84.4		80.5	83.4	80.2
12.8	12.0	11.3	Fixed Assets (net)		11.3		12.1	9.1	12.0
3.6	2.8	3.1	Intangibles (net)		.4		1.5	2.4	4.7
5.1	4.2	4.0	All Other Non-Current		3.9		6.0	5.1	3.1
100.0	100.0	100.0	Total		100.0		100.0	100.0	100.0
			LIABILITIES						
11.0	13.9	13.0	Notes Payable-Short Term		10.4		8.9	15.0	14.9
1.4	2.5	1.6	Cur. Mat.-L.T.D.		2.4		1.3	.6	2.1
21.8	21.4	21.7	Trade Payables		21.2		24.0	18.2	23.0
.1	.2	.0	Income Taxes Payable		.0		.0	.0	.0
8.8	7.8	7.7	All Other Current		7.9		8.8	8.7	7.1
43.1	45.9	44.1	Total Current		41.8		42.9	42.6	47.1
9.9	7.6	6.4	Long-Term Debt		4.8		6.1	5.1	5.4
.3	.2	.3	Deferred Taxes		.0		.0	.0	.5
5.2	6.0	6.1	All Other Non-Current		14.1		7.7	3.6	3.5
41.5	40.3	43.2	Net Worth		39.2		43.2	48.7	43.4
100.0	100.0	100.0	Total Liabilties & Net Worth		100.0		100.0	100.0	100.0
			INCOME DATA						
100.0	100.0	100.0	Net Sales		100.0		100.0	100.0	100.0
25.0	25.0	23.8	Gross Profit		27.1		24.0	22.3	22.7
21.6	22.0	21.2	Operating Expenses		26.7		22.3	19.1	20.3
3.4	3.0	2.6	Operating Profit		.4		1.7	3.3	2.4
-.1	.1	-.1	All Other Expenses (net)		-.7		-.4	.1	-.1
3.5	2.9	2.7	Profit Before Taxes		1.1		2.1	3.2	2.4
			RATIOS						
2.8	3.0	2.8			3.1		2.8	3.1	2.6
1.9	1.7	1.8	Current		1.8		2.0	1.9	1.7
1.3	1.3	1.4			1.6		1.5	1.4	1.3
1.5	1.5	1.6			1.4		1.7	1.7	1.5
(156) 1.0	.8	.9	Quick		1.0		.9	.9	.8
.6	.6	.6			.7		.5	.5	.6
29 12.6	25 14.6	26 14.1			19 19.1		21 17.2	21 17.4	32 11.4
43 8.5	38 9.5	40 9.2	Sales/Receivables		33 10.9		42 8.6	36 10.2	41 8.9
56 6.5	55 6.6	50 7.3			54 6.8		58 6.3	52 7.0	49 7.4
40 9.2	37 9.9	41 8.8			50 7.3		29 12.8	43 8.4	43 8.5
58 6.3	58 6.3	62 5.9	Cost of Sales/Inventory		69 5.3		49 7.4	63 5.8	62 5.9
76 4.8	89 4.1	91 4.0			135 2.7		81 4.5	83 4.4	85 4.3
22 16.7	18 20.4	20 18.0			0 UND		18 20.3	12 30.9	24 15.2
32 11.3	30 12.2	37 9.8	Cost of Sales/Payables		38 9.5		37 9.8	25 14.5	39 9.3
55 6.6	50 7.3	48 7.6			122 3.0		53 6.9	42 8.7	48 7.6
5.4	5.4	5.1			3.9		4.8	5.8	5.7
7.8	8.5	8.3	Sales/Working Capital		5.5		7.0	8.3	9.0
15.6	18.7	14.9			11.3		17.6	13.9	16.8
17.8	27.3	26.3					28.0	37.8	22.7
(144) 6.0	(119) 7.0	(104) 7.4	EBIT/Interest				(18) 5.1	(20) 13.6	(50) 7.0
2.1	1.8	2.5					1.3	3.6	3.0
15.2	8.1	4.4							4.8
(28) 3.8	(30) 3.1	(19) 2.4	Net Profit + Depr., Dep., Amort./Cur. Mat. L/T/D						(14) 2.6
1.7	1.5	.9							.9
.1	.1	.1			.0		.1	.0	.1
.3	.2	.2	Fixed/Worth		.2		.2	.1	.3
.5	.7	.6			.6		.7	.2	.7
.7	.6	.7			1.0		.5	.7	.7
1.6	1.6	1.5	Debt/Worth		1.8		1.1	.9	1.6
3.8	4.4	3.6			4.2		7.4	2.2	3.4
41.9	47.2	38.9					57.5	39.3	38.4
(145) 22.2	(121) 22.9	(112) 18.1	% Profit Before Taxes/Tangible Net Worth				(20) 12.1	20.8	(53) 18.1
8.8	6.6	4.6					1.1	8.4	7.9
13.3	15.5	12.9			18.0		16.8	26.6	12.2
7.7	7.7	7.0	% Profit Before Taxes/Total Assets		1.0		5.0	6.7	7.6
1.6	1.3	1.8			-.8		.6	3.4	2.5
64.9	93.3	108.6			UND		123.6	145.6	64.8
32.1	34.7	33.2	Sales/Net Fixed Assets		16.8		54.6	59.8	23.6
16.9	17.2	16.3			13.2		22.9	30.0	15.7
3.6	3.6	3.6			4.1		3.9	4.4	3.3
2.7	2.8	2.8	Sales/Total Assets		2.3		3.2	3.3	2.7
2.3	2.2	2.3			1.4		2.5	2.5	2.3
.4	.4	.4					.4	.3	.5
(134) .7	(100) .7	(90) .7	% Depr., Dep., Amort./Sales				(16) .7	(15) .5	(46) .7
1.0	1.2	1.2					1.1	1.0	1.2
1.4	1.8	1.0					1.2		1.5
(55) 2.4	(43) 3.4	(43) 2.4	% Officers', Directors' Owners' Comp/Sales				(13) 2.4		(11) 2.4
5.3	6.1	4.7					4.0		5.2
7279592M	6216501M	5934538M	Net Sales ($)	826M	22417M	39037M	152777M	346819M	5372662M
2896547M	2397841M	2347177M	Total Assets ($)	333M	12198M	14594M	53388M	117830M	2148834M

M = $ thousand MM = $ million

See Pages 9 through 22 for Explanation of Ratios and Data

Current Data Sorted by Assets							Comparative Historical Data	
						Type of Statement		
	1	6	5	4	3	Unqualified	34	36
1	6	28	14	1		Reviewed	75	68
2	11	20	3			Compiled	38	51
11	25	14	1	1		Tax Returns	42	56
3	22	45	13	6	1	Other	114	114
	34 (4/1-9/30/13)		213 (10/1/13-3/31/14)				4/1/09-3/31/10 ALL	4/1/10-3/31/11 ALL
0-500M	**500M-2MM**	**2-10MM**	**10-50MM**	**50-100MM**	**100-250MM**			
17	65	113	36	12	4	**NUMBER OF STATEMENTS**	303	325
%	%	%	%	%	%	**ASSETS**	%	%
19.8	11.5	7.3	5.8	7.8		Cash & Equivalents	8.9	10.0
23.2	34.1	33.9	31.8	29.1		Trade Receivables (net)	29.4	30.7
23.3	32.9	37.0	33.2	41.0		Inventory	31.6	33.5
9.8	1.7	2.1	2.5	2.4		All Other Current	2.5	3.0
76.0	80.2	80.2	73.3	80.2		Total Current	72.4	77.2
12.9	12.8	12.3	14.7	14.8		Fixed Assets (net)	19.2	14.8
2.3	1.1	2.5	6.0	1.6		Intangibles (net)	3.0	3.2
8.9	5.9	5.0	6.0	3.4		All Other Non-Current	5.3	4.9
100.0	100.0	100.0	100.0	100.0		Total	100.0	100.0
						LIABILITIES		
14.9	13.7	17.2	16.3	20.1		Notes Payable-Short Term	14.4	16.5
2.3	2.1	1.7	1.9	1.3		Cur. Mat.-L.T.D.	2.8	2.3
10.4	19.0	21.6	16.6	15.7		Trade Payables	15.7	18.2
.0	.2	.2	.1	.1		Income Taxes Payable	.1	.1
21.6	8.5	8.0	6.0	6.9		All Other Current	7.3	8.0
49.2	43.5	48.7	40.8	44.0		Total Current	40.3	45.1
18.9	10.8	6.8	10.7	8.3		Long-Term Debt	12.5	9.1
.0	.1	.2	.0	.6		Deferred Taxes	.2	.2
23.1	5.8	6.4	3.8	3.5		All Other Non-Current	5.9	7.3
8.8	39.9	37.8	44.7	43.6		Net Worth	41.0	38.2
100.0	100.0	100.0	100.0	100.0		Total Liabilities & Net Worth	100.0	100.0
						INCOME DATA		
100.0	100.0	100.0	100.0	100.0		Net Sales	100.0	100.0
33.4	30.7	26.5	23.9	26.3		Gross Profit	28.2	28.4
32.7	26.7	23.2	19.7	23.5		Operating Expenses	26.5	26.6
.7	4.1	3.3	4.3	2.8		Operating Profit	1.7	1.8
.5	.2	.3	.4	.3		All Other Expenses (net)	.5	.3
.3	3.8	3.1	3.9	2.5		Profit Before Taxes	1.2	1.5
						RATIOS		
3.3	2.9	2.7	3.0	3.3			3.2	3.3
2.4	2.1	1.7	1.7	1.8		Current	1.9	1.8
.9	1.4	1.2	1.3	1.4			1.3	1.3
2.5	1.7	1.3	1.5	1.3			1.7	1.7
.9	1.1	.8	.8	.7		Quick	1.0	.9
.4	.6	.5	.6	.5			.6	.6
0 UND	**25** 14.5	**26** 13.9	**36** 10.0	**28** 13.1			**26** 14.2	**24** 15.2
13 27.5	**37** 9.8	**40** 9.1	**46** 7.9	**33** 11.1		Sales/Receivables	**37** 9.9	**40** 9.1
30 12.2	**54** 6.8	**51** 7.1	**58** 6.3	**49** 7.5			**54** 6.7	**57** 6.4
0 UND	**23** 16.2	**37** 9.8	**44** 8.3	**38** 9.6			**31** 11.9	**31** 11.9
3 115.1	**49** 7.4	**54** 6.7	**65** 5.6	**87** 4.2		Cost of Sales/Inventory	**57** 6.4	**60** 6.0
69 5.3	**94** 3.9	**94** 3.9	**99** 3.7	**104** 3.5			**91** 4.0	**99** 3.7
0 UND	**12** 31.6	**18** 20.3	**18** 20.4	**14** 25.2			**13** 29.2	**15** 24.9
11 34.1	**21** 17.2	**29** 12.4	**28** 13.2	**22** 16.5		Cost of Sales/Payables	**24** 15.5	**27** 13.5
20 17.9	**45** 8.1	**49** 7.5	**36** 10.1	**43** 8.4			**38** 9.5	**46** 7.9
7.9	4.6	5.8	4.5	4.9			5.0	4.6
21.9	9.1	9.7	8.2	9.1		Sales/Working Capital	8.3	8.6
-75.5	19.9	20.4	14.9	12.9			16.5	17.1
11.5	22.4	18.4	20.4	18.1			7.1	11.3
(10) 5.3	(54) 5.0	(106) 8.4	(34) 9.0	(11) 6.0		EBIT/Interest	(271) 1.8	(282) 3.4
-.2	1.9	1.9	3.5	1.3			-.6	.8
		15.5					4.5	5.4
		(18) 2.9				Net Profit + Depr., Dep., Amort./Cur. Mat. L/T/D	(62) 1.7	(43) 1.8
		1.3					.0	.7
.0	.0	.1	.1	.1			.1	.1
.1	.2	.3	.3	.3		Fixed/Worth	.4	.3
NM	.5	.7	.7	.8			1.2	.9
.4	.6	.8	.6	.5			.6	.6
4.5	1.5	1.7	2.0	1.7		Debt/Worth	1.6	1.5
-8.5	3.4	4.2	3.1	3.8			3.6	3.7
97.4	56.4	48.2	34.6	37.7			23.4	28.8
(11) 64.0	(57) 23.5	(102) 25.1	(35) 21.3	16.4		% Profit Before Taxes/Tangible Net Worth	(274) 7.4	(289) 10.7
8.3	6.5	8.7	12.5	3.2			-5.9	.6
41.0	22.7	15.0	12.4	15.0			9.4	11.3
12.9	9.0	9.1	7.8	10.4		% Profit Before Taxes/Total Assets	2.6	3.9
-3.9	2.2	2.5	3.0	1.3			-3.0	-1.1
UND	149.4	96.0	53.9	33.5			55.1	90.4
94.7	44.3	36.5	28.5	23.9		Sales/Net Fixed Assets	21.7	32.3
42.8	17.6	17.6	10.6	15.0			7.9	12.8
11.2	4.0	3.8	2.9	3.3			3.5	3.4
4.4	3.3	3.0	2.4	2.8		Sales/Total Assets	2.5	2.6
3.3	2.6	2.1	1.7	2.5			1.7	1.8
	.2	.4	.5	.5			.5	.5
	(45) .6	(94) .7	(32) .7	(11) 1.0		% Depr., Dep., Amort./Sales	(252) 1.1	(258) .8
	1.2	1.2	1.0	1.3			2.3	1.7
2.0	2.4	1.3					2.1	1.9
(10) 4.8	(32) 3.6	(40) 2.1				% Officers', Directors' Owners' Comp/Sales	(126) 3.6	(127) 3.3
11.0	5.6	4.6					6.5	5.9
30587M	**271008M**	**1638960M**	**1983640M**	**2270104M**	**688402M**	Net Sales ($)	**8156121M**	**7729226M**
4507M	**79468M**	**555090M**	**782808M**	**804475M**	**556033M**	Total Assets ($)	**3640964M**	**3162869M**

M = $ thousand MM = $ million

See Pages 9 through 22 for Explanation of Ratios and Data

Comparative Historical Data | Current Data Sorted by Sales

	Comparative Historical Data			Current Data Sorted by Sales					
Type of Statement									
Unqualified	29	19	19		1	1	1	4	12
Reviewed	58	59	50		2		12	20	16
Compiled	48	38	36	2	3	5	12	12	2
Tax Returns	82	56	52	6	10	14	13	6	3
Other	99	114	90	4	6	11	19	26	24
	4/1/11-3/31/12	4/1/12-3/31/13	4/1/13-3/31/14	34 (4/1-9/30/13)		213 (10/1/13-3/31/14)			
	ALL	ALL	ALL	0-1MM	1-3MM	3-5MM	5-10MM	10-25MM	25MM & OVER
NUMBER OF STATEMENTS	316	286	247	12	22	31	57	68	57
ASSETS	%	%	%	%	%	%	%	%	%
Cash & Equivalents	8.7	8.5	9.1	10.0	14.4	13.0	7.9	8.5	6.4
Trade Receivables (net)	32.7	32.2	32.4	21.2	25.1	33.2	36.0	30.8	35.4
Inventory	32.3	35.1	34.3	23.4	34.0	33.9	36.5	35.0	34.1
All Other Current	2.2	3.4	2.6	12.4	1.4	1.9	1.5	2.7	2.2
Total Current	75.9	79.2	78.3	67.1	75.0	82.0	81.9	77.0	78.1
Fixed Assets (net)	15.5	13.9	13.1	18.9	14.9	12.7	9.0	15.2	12.9
Intangibles (net)	2.9	2.4	3.0	3.2	.0	1.6	2.5	2.6	6.1
All Other Non-Current	5.7	4.5	5.5	10.9	10.1	3.8	6.6	5.2	3.0
Total	100.0	100.0	100.0	100.0	100.0	100.0	100.0	100.0	100.0
LIABILITIES									
Notes Payable-Short Term	15.5	15.9	16.1	12.5	12.3	14.4	18.6	13.8	19.3
Cur. Mat.-L.T.D.	2.1	2.4	1.8	2.6	2.1	2.2	1.4	2.0	1.7
Trade Payables	19.0	16.7	18.9	5.6	20.8	22.5	19.5	18.9	18.3
Income Taxes Payable	.1	.1	.1	.0	.0	.4	.0	.2	.1
All Other Current	8.1	9.5	8.8	21.5	7.5	15.1	7.6	6.7	6.7
Total Current	44.8	44.5	45.7	42.2	42.8	54.5	47.2	41.6	46.1
Long-Term Debt	9.5	10.1	9.8	25.8	17.3	7.4	6.7	8.2	9.8
Deferred Taxes	.2	.2	.2	.1	.0	.1	.1	.3	.4
All Other Non-Current	7.5	6.3	6.8	4.9	15.6	5.6	8.4	4.8	5.3
Net Worth	38.0	38.9	37.5	27.1	24.3	32.3	37.6	45.1	38.5
Total Liabilties & Net Worth	100.0	100.0	100.0	100.0	100.0	100.0	100.0	100.0	100.0
INCOME DATA									
Net Sales	100.0	100.0	100.0	100.0	100.0	100.0	100.0	100.0	100.0
Gross Profit	28.0	27.8	27.8	39.4	31.5	29.0	28.1	26.7	24.1
Operating Expenses	25.6	24.5	24.2	39.1	28.5	25.2	24.5	22.9	20.4
Operating Profit	2.4	3.3	3.5	.4	3.0	3.9	3.7	3.8	3.7
All Other Expenses (net)	.3	.3	.3	.8	-.1	.4	.4	.2	.3
Profit Before Taxes	2.1	3.0	3.2	-.5	3.1	3.4	3.2	3.6	3.4
RATIOS									
Current	3.1	3.0	2.8	3.5	3.1	2.6	2.9	3.8	2.7
	1.7	1.8	1.9	2.4	2.1	1.7	1.7	1.9	1.7
	1.2	1.3	1.3	.9	1.0	1.3	1.3	1.3	1.3
Quick	1.5	1.6	1.6	2.8	1.5	1.4	1.6	1.8	1.5
	.9	.9	.9	.9	.9	.8	.9	.9	.9
	.6	.6	.5	.1	.5	.6	.5	.6	.6
Sales/Receivables	**29** 12.8	**26** 14.0	**26** 13.9	**0** UND	**17** 21.9	**27** 13.6	**22** 16.5	**26** 14.3	**32** 11.5
	41 9.0	**41** 8.9	**40** 9.2	**18** 20.0	**31** 11.6	**36** 10.0	**44** 8.3	**35** 10.4	**42** 8.7
	61 6.0	**56** 6.5	**53** 6.9	**57** 6.4	**47** 7.7	**54** 6.8	**62** 5.9	**47** 7.7	**54** 6.7
Cost of Sales/Inventory	**29** 12.5	**31** 11.9	**30** 12.1	**0** UND	**19** 19.2	**13** 28.2	**32** 11.3	**37** 9.8	**35** 10.3
	59 6.2	**62** 5.9	**54** 6.7	**42** 8.7	**51** 7.2	**59** 6.2	**59** 6.2	**54** 6.8	**54** 6.8
	91 4.0	**94** 3.9	**94** 3.9	**146** 2.5	**130** 2.8	**96** 3.8	**101** 3.6	**91** 4.0	**87** 4.2
Cost of Sales/Payables	**16** 23.1	**12** 29.2	**15** 24.1	**0** UND	**12** 29.2	**15** 23.6	**14** 25.3	**15** 23.8	**17** 21.1
	27 13.4	**24** 15.3	**26** 13.8	**6** 57.8	**23** 16.0	**34** 10.7	**29** 12.8	**28** 13.2	**26** 14.2
	46 8.0	**41** 8.8	**45** 8.2	**20** 18.3	**83** 4.4	**46** 7.9	**47** 7.7	**44** 8.3	**36** 10.1
Sales/Working Capital	4.8	4.8	5.5	3.3	3.9	6.1	6.1	5.5	5.6
	9.2	8.6	9.3	6.7	9.8	11.5	9.1	9.4	9.3
	24.1	17.9	18.8	NM	NM	28.7	14.8	17.3	17.7
EBIT/Interest	11.2	12.8	18.0		7.2	27.5	17.4	16.5	18.9
	(268) 3.6	(247) 5.2	(219) 6.3		(17) 3.7	(26) 12.0	(53) 6.7	(64) 7.0	(53) 9.6
	1.1	2.0	2.3		-.4	3.1	1.7	3.0	2.6
Net Profit + Depr., Dep., Amort./Cur. Mat. L/T/D	5.5	7.1	11.6					11.5	15.6
	(38) 2.2	(42) 3.3	(35) 3.3					(13) 2.1	(13) 4.2
	1.2	1.1	1.4					1.1	1.5
Fixed/Worth	.1	.1	.1	.0	.0	.2	.1	.1	.1
	.3	.2	.2	.1	.1	.3	.2	.3	.3
	1.0	.7	.8	10.2	1.8	.9	.4	.7	1.0
Debt/Worth	.6	.8	.7	.4	.5	.6	.9	.6	.7
	1.6	1.8	1.7	1.5	2.3	1.7	1.7	1.5	2.1
	5.1	3.6	4.3	NM	NM	7.7	3.7	2.7	5.1
% Profit Before Taxes/Tangible Net Worth	31.6	40.4	49.0		72.7	67.5	50.3	42.3	37.7
	(282) 11.6	(269) 17.3	(219) 25.0		(17) 21.1	(25) 32.3	(52) 23.3	(64) 23.2	(52) 28.9
	1.0	6.8	8.4		2.3	8.2	7.8	5.9	13.4
% Profit Before Taxes/Total Assets	12.1	12.7	15.8	20.1	21.5	28.4	13.4	14.4	15.3
	5.0	6.2	8.8	8.9	7.0	9.0	6.9	9.1	8.9
	.1	1.9	2.5	-21.3	-3.1	3.7	2.3	2.4	3.0
Sales/Net Fixed Assets	103.6	102.0	105.0	UND	269.9	57.4	136.0	86.5	95.0
	34.0	33.7	36.2	52.1	61.5	31.7	48.5	28.8	32.1
	11.7	16.9	17.4	5.7	18.0	17.4	24.9	13.8	14.1
Sales/Total Assets	3.5	3.6	3.8	3.7	5.0	4.1	3.7	3.7	3.8
	2.6	2.8	3.0	2.1	3.0	3.3	2.8	3.1	2.8
	1.9	2.1	2.1	1.2	1.8	2.6	2.1	1.9	2.3
% Depr., Dep., Amort./Sales	.4	.4	.4		.3	.2	.3	.4	.4
	(246) .8	(231) .7	(190) .7		(16) .8	(20) .6	(41) .7	(58) .7	(50) .6
	1.7	1.2	1.1		2.0	1.0	1.1	1.2	1.0
% Officers', Directors' Owners' Comp/Sales	1.6	1.5	1.4		3.1	2.5	1.6	1.3	1.2
	(137) 2.9	(122) 2.8	(92) 3.0		(12) 3.8	(15) 4.2	(22) 3.1	(29) 1.8	(10) 2.4
	5.5	5.5	5.7		8.3	6.9	5.7	2.8	7.8
Net Sales ($)	8570912M	8686649M	6882701M	9318M	42170M	126531M	415435M	1069233M	5220014M
Total Assets ($)	3660749M	3616132M	2782381M	5256M	16544M	41086M	162491M	419362M	2137642M

M = $ thousand MM = $ million

See Pages 9 through 22 for Explanation of Ratios and Data

	Current Data Sorted by Assets						Comparative Historical Data	
Type of Statement								
Unqualified				3	2		8	7
Reviewed			1	2			18	20
Compiled	1		2				5	6
Tax Returns	3	7					14	14
Other	3	5	10	10		1	11	16
		12 (4/1-9/30/13)		38 (10/1/13-3/31/14)			4/1/09-3/31/10 ALL	4/1/10-3/31/11 ALL
	0-500M	500M-2MM	2-10MM	10-50MM	50-100MM	100-250MM		
NUMBER OF STATEMENTS	7	12	13	15	2	1	56	63
ASSETS	%	%	%	%	%	%	%	%
Cash & Equivalents		25.3	16.0	5.9			13.5	11.8
Trade Receivables (net)		24.5	28.4	28.7			26.6	30.1
Inventory		33.6	32.8	46.0			33.3	33.6
All Other Current		.1	8.4	2.2			1.4	1.3
Total Current		83.6	85.6	82.8			74.9	76.8
Fixed Assets (net)		9.0	5.6	5.4			13.6	12.7
Intangibles (net)		5.4	2.0	5.6			6.0	5.1
All Other Non-Current		2.1	6.9	6.3			5.6	5.4
Total		100.0	100.0	100.0			100.0	100.0
LIABILITIES								
Notes Payable-Short Term		5.9	7.1	17.8			9.5	12.4
Cur. Mat.-L.T.D.		.2	3.5	.4			3.1	2.0
Trade Payables		16.9	25.8	22.6			25.2	23.5
Income Taxes Payable		.6	.1	.4			.4	.3
All Other Current		8.5	16.8	12.1			11.2	7.8
Total Current		32.1	53.2	53.3			49.4	45.9
Long-Term Debt		5.9	3.1	7.1			7.3	10.9
Deferred Taxes		.0	.0	.0			.1	.1
All Other Non-Current		23.2	4.2	9.5			4.8	2.3
Net Worth		38.8	39.5	30.1			38.5	40.9
Total Liabilties & Net Worth		100.0	100.0	100.0			100.0	100.0
INCOME DATA								
Net Sales		100.0	100.0	100.0			100.0	100.0
Gross Profit		36.9	26.9	27.5			29.1	29.2
Operating Expenses		33.5	22.5	24.2			25.8	23.6
Operating Profit		3.5	4.4	3.3			3.3	5.6
All Other Expenses (net)		-.3	.2	1.6			.2	.6
Profit Before Taxes		3.8	4.2	1.8			3.1	5.0
RATIOS								
Current		8.8	3.4	2.0			2.4	2.7
		3.0	2.2	1.6			1.6	1.7
		1.6	1.0	1.2			1.1	1.2
Quick		6.5	1.8	.9			1.4	1.5
		1.4	.9	.7			.8	.9
		.6	.5	.4			.5	.6
Sales/Receivables		**9** 39.2	**14** 26.5	**26** 13.8			**16** 22.5	**19** 19.4
		24 15.4	**32** 11.5	**41** 9.0			**32** 11.6	**34** 10.7
		29 12.7	**46** 7.9	**61** 6.0			**46** 7.9	**50** 7.3
Cost of Sales/Inventory		**10** 36.7	**19** 19.3	**62** 5.9			**25** 14.8	**29** 12.8
		26 14.1	**49** 7.5	**99** 3.7			**46** 7.9	**51** 7.1
		51 7.1	**96** 3.8	**130** 2.8			**93** 3.9	**93** 3.9
Cost of Sales/Payables		**0** UND	**7** 53.3	**17** 21.5			**17** 21.2	**13** 27.4
		10 35.8	**27** 13.3	**50** 7.3			**37** 9.8	**31** 11.7
		37 9.9	**55** 6.6	**78** 4.7			**66** 5.6	**55** 6.6
Sales/Working Capital		4.7	5.8	4.7			6.1	5.6
		6.2	7.2	8.6			14.0	9.9
		20.9	NM	12.4			106.9	35.5
EBIT/Interest				19.0			22.8	34.1
				6.8			(51) 7.0	(54) 6.7
				1.7			2.7	3.4
Net Profit + Depr., Dep., Amort./Cur. Mat. L/T/D							13.4	90.8
							(17) 3.3	(14) 10.9
							.7	2.8
Fixed/Worth		.0	.0	.0			.1	.0
		.1	.1	.2			.3	.2
		.9	.3	.4			.9	1.0
Debt/Worth		.3	.5	1.1			.7	.7
		1.0	1.2	3.9			2.6	1.5
		27.1	11.9	16.3			6.3	4.1
% Profit Before Taxes/Tangible Net Worth		87.0	91.8	41.1			50.4	63.9
		(10) 33.7	(12) 26.5	(14) 16.6			(49) 22.1	(57) 27.7
		12.7	5.9	8.0			11.4	9.3
% Profit Before Taxes/Total Assets		23.2	17.7	6.7			14.2	23.1
		15.9	8.0	3.8			6.1	8.6
		4.5	.8	1.9			2.8	2.8
Sales/Net Fixed Assets		UND	832.7	302.1			184.0	312.4
		89.0	174.5	108.6			57.5	63.6
		25.9	48.9	19.5			18.0	23.9
Sales/Total Assets		7.4	4.6	2.9			4.0	4.2
		3.7	3.0	2.1			2.9	2.9
		3.2	2.6	1.5			2.1	1.8
% Depr., Dep., Amort./Sales				.1			.2	.4
				(11) .3			(45) .8	(42) .7
				.5			2.0	1.2
% Officers', Directors' Owners' Comp/Sales							.9	.9
							(25) 2.7	(25) 1.8
							4.5	4.1
Net Sales ($)	16644M	67085M	245164M	1075411M	130118M	138064M	1440546M	1375532M
Total Assets ($)	1911M	12057M	61810M	420961M	118948M	191316M	655047M	417589M

M = $ thousand MM = $ million

See Pages 9 through 22 for Explanation of Ratios and Data

Comparative Historical Data				Current Data Sorted by Sales					
			Type of Statement						
6	4	5	Unqualified						5
16	10	3	Reviewed					1	2
5	3	3	Compiled		1			2	
18	16	10	Tax Returns		3	4	2	1	
20	22	29	Other	1	5	1	4	6	12
				12 (4/1-9/30/13)			38 (10/1/13-3/31/14)		
4/1/11-3/31/12 ALL	4/1/12-3/31/13 ALL	4/1/13-3/31/14 ALL		0-1MM	1-3MM	3-5MM	5-10MM	10-25MM	25MM & OVER
65	55	50	**NUMBER OF STATEMENTS**	1	9	5	6	10	19
%	%	%	**ASSETS**	%	%	%	%	%	%
7.7	11.8	14.5	Cash & Equivalents					14.1	6.6
33.5	29.7	27.9	Trade Receivables (net)					25.8	26.0
35.1	34.1	36.4	Inventory					41.2	40.5
1.1	4.6	3.7	All Other Current					1.9	7.4
77.4	80.1	82.5	Total Current					83.0	80.4
11.2	11.6	6.3	Fixed Assets (net)					5.6	5.0
4.9	4.5	6.1	Intangibles (net)					2.7	11.2
6.5	3.8	5.1	All Other Non-Current					8.7	3.4
100.0	100.0	100.0	Total					100.0	100.0
			LIABILITIES						
12.1	11.0	12.6	Notes Payable-Short Term					16.1	13.3
1.9	3.5	1.2	Cur. Mat.-L.T.D.					1.7	2.3
24.8	19.0	21.8	Trade Payables					24.6	20.4
.2	.2	.3	Income Taxes Payable					.1	.3
8.7	11.0	13.3	All Other Current					9.5	16.7
47.7	44.7	49.1	Total Current					52.0	53.1
10.7	6.3	7.2	Long-Term Debt					4.8	8.3
.1	.0	.0	Deferred Taxes					.0	.1
3.3	5.1	10.8	All Other Non-Current					7.8	10.1
38.3	43.9	32.8	Net Worth					35.5	28.3
100.0	100.0	100.0	Total Liabilties & Net Worth					100.0	100.0
			INCOME DATA						
100.0	100.0	100.0	Net Sales					100.0	100.0
27.8	33.1	32.8	Gross Profit					25.8	28.1
24.3	26.9	28.0	Operating Expenses					23.3	23.9
3.5	6.2	4.7	Operating Profit					2.5	4.2
.6	.5	1.1	All Other Expenses (net)					.4	2.2
2.9	5.7	3.7	Profit Before Taxes					2.1	2.0
			RATIOS						
2.7	3.1	2.8						2.2	2.4
1.8	1.9	1.9	Current					1.9	1.5
1.3	1.3	1.2						.9	1.2
1.6	1.7	1.7						1.2	1.1
.9	1.0	.9	Quick					.6	.7
.6	.5	.5						.4	.5
20 18.4	**27** 13.7	**17** 22.0						**0** UND	**23** 15.7
36 10.1	**40** 9.2	**30** 12.3	Sales/Receivables					**33** 10.9	**41** 9.0
47 7.7	**53** 6.9	**42** 8.6						**46** 8.0	**61** 6.0
27 13.7	**37** 9.8	**19** 19.2						**26** 13.8	**50** 7.3
55 6.6	**63** 5.8	**53** 6.9	Cost of Sales/Inventory					**47** 7.7	**99** 3.7
87 4.2	**96** 3.8	**114** 3.2						**96** 3.8	**130** 2.8
16 22.7	**12** 29.3	**8** 48.4						**12** 29.7	**12** 30.6
36 10.1	**30** 12.2	**26** 13.8	Cost of Sales/Payables					**26** 13.8	**38** 9.6
56 6.5	**53** 6.9	**59** 6.2						**64** 5.7	**69** 5.3
6.5	5.7	5.4						5.3	5.1
10.9	7.8	9.8	Sales/Working Capital					11.2	9.0
24.3	15.5	34.3						-31.9	16.1
37.0	42.9	24.1							39.7
(58) 7.1	(47) 6.8	(39) 9.6	EBIT/Interest						(18) 9.5
1.9	2.4	2.0							1.9
21.7									
(16) 10.0			Net Profit + Depr., Dep., Amort./Cur. Mat. L/T/D						
2.1									
.1	.0	.0						.0	.0
.2	.2	.1	Fixed/Worth					.0	.3
.9	.6	1.1						.3	1.3
.6	.5	.6						1.0	1.4
2.0	1.2	2.6	Debt/Worth					1.7	3.9
5.0	5.1	24.2						17.3	17.5
53.6	62.7	56.9						68.2	53.2
(58) 26.3	(50) 29.0	(41) 25.9	% Profit Before Taxes/Tangible Net Worth					21.0	(15) 20.2
6.2	10.3	9.0						5.4	10.5
23.3	23.2	18.7						14.0	10.8
7.9	9.5	6.7	% Profit Before Taxes/Total Assets					5.9	5.1
1.6	2.9	2.6						.7	2.1
192.7	188.3	732.3						UND	302.1
70.5	51.2	95.4	Sales/Net Fixed Assets					211.6	108.6
24.5	20.8	32.3						16.5	24.9
4.6	3.7	5.5						4.2	4.2
3.3	2.9	3.1	Sales/Total Assets					2.9	2.2
2.3	2.1	2.1						2.4	1.5
.3	.1	.1							.1
(46) .6	(43) .5	(26) .4	% Depr., Dep., Amort./Sales						(13) .3
1.2	1.2	1.1							.5
1.6	1.2	2.8							
(24) 2.7	(28) 3.6	(19) 4.5	% Officers', Directors' Owners' Comp/Sales						
4.6	5.0	7.5							
1496200M	1187398M	1672486M	Net Sales ($)	657M	17780M	18273M	48753M	166960M	1420063M
649500M	550021M	807003M	Total Assets ($)	65M	7495M	3080M	12879M	60472M	723012M

M = $ thousand MM = $ million

See Pages 9 through 22 for Explanation of Ratios and Data

Current Data Sorted by Assets							Comparative Historical Data	
						Type of Statement		
		4	11	2	1	Unqualified	19	21
	5	19	11	2		Reviewed	40	48
1	7	9				Compiled	23	27
4	9	9				Tax Returns	28	32
3	7	23	16	4	3	Other	70	58
	28 (4/1-9/30/13)		122 (10/1/13-3/31/14)				4/1/09-3/31/10	4/1/10-3/31/11
0-500M	500M-2MM	2-10MM	10-50MM	50-100MM	100-250MM		ALL	ALL
8	28	64	38	8	4	NUMBER OF STATEMENTS	180	186
%	%	%	%	%	%	**ASSETS**	%	%
	9.3	9.8	7.1			Cash & Equivalents	10.0	10.4
	31.1	31.1	27.9			Trade Receivables (net)	31.0	31.3
	30.0	25.1	28.3			Inventory	26.9	29.3
	.6	5.0	3.3			All Other Current	5.4	4.8
	71.1	71.0	66.6			Total Current	73.3	75.8
	14.1	12.7	16.3			Fixed Assets (net)	12.4	13.1
	8.4	8.5	10.0			Intangibles (net)	5.7	4.9
	6.4	7.9	7.1			All Other Non-Current	8.6	6.2
	100.0	100.0	100.0			Total	100.0	100.0
						LIABILITIES		
	9.7	9.7	7.9			Notes Payable-Short Term	12.0	10.6
	2.9	4.3	3.1			Cur. Mat.-L.T.D.	4.0	2.8
	25.0	17.8	17.6			Trade Payables	19.9	18.0
	.0	.1	.4			Income Taxes Payable	.2	.3
	12.0	17.4	13.8			All Other Current	16.0	14.2
	49.7	49.3	42.8			Total Current	52.1	45.8
	15.6	9.0	17.3			Long-Term Debt	10.7	12.3
	.2	.4	.5			Deferred Taxes	.3	.3
	5.5	4.9	3.5			All Other Non-Current	5.7	6.6
	29.0	36.4	35.9			Net Worth	31.3	35.0
	100.0	100.0	100.0			Total Liabilties & Net Worth	100.0	100.0
						INCOME DATA		
	100.0	100.0	100.0			Net Sales	100.0	100.0
	39.4	37.1	37.8			Gross Profit	39.5	40.0
	38.1	33.6	32.8			Operating Expenses	35.2	35.7
	1.3	3.5	5.0			Operating Profit	4.3	4.2
	.3	.4	.8			All Other Expenses (net)	.6	.1
	1.0	3.1	4.2			Profit Before Taxes	3.7	4.1
						RATIOS		
	2.6	2.1	2.2				2.2	2.4
	1.6	1.4	1.6			Current	1.4	1.7
	1.0	1.2	1.2				1.1	1.2
	1.2	1.3	1.4				1.3	1.5
	.9	.8	.7			Quick	(179) .8	.9
	.4	.5	.6				.5	.6
	17 22.0	**24** 15.2	**33** 11.2				**25** 14.7	**24** 15.4
	26 14.2	**36** 10.1	**38** 9.6			Sales/Receivables	**35** 10.5	**35** 10.5
	32 11.3	**49** 7.4	**51** 7.2				**46** 8.0	**47** 7.8
	13 29.0	**17** 21.5	**41** 8.8				**29** 12.7	**35** 10.4
	46 8.0	**47** 7.8	**68** 5.4			Cost of Sales/Inventory	**57** 6.4	**63** 5.8
	87 4.2	**73** 5.0	**94** 3.9				**90** 4.1	**89** 4.1
	18 20.5	**14** 26.2	**21** 17.8				**18** 20.3	**16** 22.5
	31 11.9	**30** 12.0	**31** 11.8			Cost of Sales/Payables	**33** 11.1	**30** 12.2
	55 6.6	**43** 8.4	**53** 6.9				**58** 6.3	**49** 7.5
	8.5	7.8	5.7				6.3	5.7
	17.7	13.7	10.8			Sales/Working Capital	12.8	10.5
	NM	37.7	28.2				82.7	27.4
	29.8	32.7	13.5				17.4	18.5
	(23) 8.1	(55) 5.8	(35) 8.8			EBIT/Interest	(158) 5.6	(159) 7.4
	1.3	2.4	2.1				1.8	2.5
		13.3	3.1				11.9	16.7
		(13) 4.6	(13) 1.9			Net Profit + Depr., Dep., Amort./Cur. Mat. L/T/D	(38) 3.8	(41) 3.2
		1.1	1.1				1.8	1.0
	.1	.1	.2				.1	.1
	.5	.3	.4			Fixed/Worth	.3	.2
	NM	1.7	1.6				2.4	1.3
	.8	.9	1.1				1.0	.8
	1.8	2.2	2.8			Debt/Worth	2.5	1.9
	NM	8.9	5.6				8.1	5.5
	80.2	46.3	49.6				47.2	50.2
	(21) 13.4	(53) 15.9	(33) 23.3			% Profit Before Taxes/Tangible Net Worth	(152) 24.0	(159) 21.6
	1.4	4.3	10.5				9.3	7.4
	15.4	12.8	13.4				15.0	16.3
	4.7	6.5	7.8			% Profit Before Taxes/Total Assets	7.2	6.6
	-.1	1.2	2.3				1.0	2.1
	87.6	117.5	51.0				90.6	97.5
	43.7	51.3	23.0			Sales/Net Fixed Assets	41.7	43.6
	19.7	15.9	11.0				16.1	16.7
	6.0	3.9	3.4				4.0	4.2
	3.9	3.0	2.3			Sales/Total Assets	2.9	3.0
	2.5	2.2	1.6				2.2	2.1
	.4	.3	.5				.5	.4
	(23) .8	(48) .7	(33) .9			% Depr., Dep., Amort./Sales	(139) 1.0	(149) .8
	2.2	2.5	2.0				2.3	2.1
	3.4	1.4					1.4	2.2
	(10) 5.1	(29) 2.2				% Officers', Directors' Owners' Comp/Sales	(77) 2.9	(68) 4.2
	7.3	4.8					7.7	7.0
14197M	142210M	994260M	1995495M	1284612M	842305M	Net Sales ($)	4578564M	5082971M
1868M	33940M	322945M	804028M	584758M	534751M	Total Assets ($)	2073318M	2372363M

M = $ thousand MM = $ million

See Pages 9 through 22 for Explanation of Ratios and Data

Comparative Historical Data / Current Data Sorted by Sales

4/1/11-3/31/12 ALL	4/1/12-3/31/13 ALL	4/1/13-3/31/14 ALL	Type of Statement	0-1MM	1-3MM	3-5MM	5-10MM	10-25MM	25MM & OVER
15	10	18	Unqualified					6	12
44	38	37	Reviewed		1	2	7	15	12
29	24	17	Compiled		4	1	6	5	1
23	20	22	Tax Returns	4		6	6	5	1
65	69	56	Other	1	6	4	7	12	26
				28 (4/1-9/30/13)			122 (10/1/13-3/31/14)		
176	161	150	**NUMBER OF STATEMENTS**	5	11	13	26	43	52
%	%	%	**ASSETS**	%	%	%	%	%	%
12.1	11.8	10.4	Cash & Equivalents		5.0	6.4	13.4	11.0	10.1
30.1	28.8	29.2	Trade Receivables (net)		20.3	27.5	29.5	30.3	32.0
27.2	26.3	27.6	Inventory		32.7	27.6	27.4	27.5	26.2
3.8	3.5	3.3	All Other Current		.3	.7	4.0	5.1	3.1
73.2	70.3	70.6	Total Current		58.3	62.2	74.2	74.0	71.4
12.6	13.4	13.3	Fixed Assets (net)		15.1	13.9	15.0	12.4	11.1
6.5	7.8	8.8	Intangibles (net)		13.7	19.5	4.5	6.9	9.2
7.7	8.4	7.4	All Other Non-Current		12.9	4.4	6.3	6.7	8.4
100.0	100.0	100.0	Total		100.0	100.0	100.0	100.0	100.0
			LIABILITIES						
12.6	12.3	9.0	Notes Payable-Short Term		4.2	7.8	9.2	11.2	7.0
3.3	3.7	3.4	Cur. Mat.-L.T.D.		7.8	1.4	2.6	4.4	2.7
18.7	16.6	18.2	Trade Payables		17.3	14.2	24.2	17.5	18.2
.2	.2	.2	Income Taxes Payable		.0	.0	.2	.1	.3
13.2	14.2	15.1	All Other Current		9.5	13.6	16.5	14.4	16.8
48.0	46.9	45.9	Total Current		38.7	37.0	52.6	47.5	45.0
10.4	12.9	12.4	Long-Term Debt		20.8	16.6	10.4	8.1	13.1
.4	.4	.4	Deferred Taxes		.0	.2	.6	.4	.4
5.5	5.1	5.8	All Other Non-Current		6.2	12.2	4.2	3.9	3.4
35.6	34.8	35.5	Net Worth		34.3	34.0	32.2	40.1	38.0
100.0	100.0	100.0	Total Liabilties & Net Worth		100.0	100.0	100.0	100.0	100.0
			INCOME DATA						
100.0	100.0	100.0	Net Sales		100.0	100.0	100.0	100.0	100.0
38.2	40.1	37.5	Gross Profit		41.3	48.9	39.0	35.2	33.6
34.2	34.7	33.9	Operating Expenses		37.1	46.1	37.3	31.7	29.0
4.0	5.4	3.6	Operating Profit		4.2	2.9	1.7	3.5	4.6
.2	.4	.5	All Other Expenses (net)		.6	1.0	-.4	.7	.3
3.8	5.0	3.1	Profit Before Taxes		3.6	1.9	2.1	2.8	4.2
			RATIOS						
2.6	2.3	2.5	Current		3.5	2.3	2.1	2.2	2.5
1.6	1.6	1.6			1.5	1.8	1.4	1.6	1.6
1.3	1.2	1.2			.3	1.1	1.2	1.2	1.2
1.5	1.5	1.4	Quick		2.1	1.4	1.2	1.3	1.5
.9	.9	.9			.5	1.1	.8	.9	.9
.6	.5	.5			.1	.6	.6	.5	.6
23 15.6	**25** 14.4	**23** 15.9	Sales/Receivables		**8** 45.6	**24** 15.5	**21** 17.6	**24** 15.4	**33** 11.1
33 11.2	**35** 10.5	**35** 10.4			**13** 28.6	**30** 12.0	**30** 12.1	**37** 9.8	**38** 9.6
42 8.7	**43** 8.5	**47** 7.8			**25** 14.4	**47** 7.8	**41** 8.9	**49** 7.5	**51** 7.2
26 14.1	**28** 13.0	**26** 14.2	Cost of Sales/Inventory		**0** UND	**28** 13.1	**22** 16.4	**24** 14.9	**36** 10.2
55 6.6	**58** 6.3	**54** 6.8			**49** 7.5	**81** 4.5	**56** 6.5	**49** 7.4	**54** 6.7
83 4.4	**85** 4.3	**81** 4.5			**114** 3.2	**107** 3.4	**76** 4.8	**83** 4.4	**79** 4.6
14 25.6	**12** 29.4	**15** 24.5	Cost of Sales/Payables		**18** 20.4	**17** 21.1	**21** 17.3	**13** 27.7	**15** 24.2
28 13.2	**28** 13.2	**30** 12.2			**39** 9.4	**25** 14.8	**40** 9.2	**26** 13.9	**29** 12.5
46 8.0	**45** 8.1	**45** 8.2			**76** 4.8	**57** 6.4	**48** 7.6	**44** 8.3	**43** 8.4
6.1	6.2	6.6	Sales/Working Capital		4.4	6.9	8.7	7.1	5.7
11.0	11.5	12.5			19.9	16.7	15.7	12.3	10.8
27.9	30.9	29.8			-8.4	NM	46.1	23.1	24.7
24.3	34.3	31.2	EBIT/Interest			31.2	25.1	24.3	50.5
(155) 8.8	(144) 10.0	(129) 8.2				9.4	(21) 4.2	(36) 5.7	(48) 10.9
2.5	2.3	2.1				1.5	1.1	1.9	3.8
10.7	50.9	8.7	Net Profit + Depr., Dep., Amort./Cur. Mat. L/T/D					18.0	3.8
(39) 2.5	(35) 7.3	(35) 2.6						(11) 4.4	(15) 1.9
1.2	2.3	1.1						1.5	1.1
.1	.1	.1	Fixed/Worth		.0	.2	.1	.1	.1
.2	.3	.3			.1	.7	.4	.2	.3
.8	1.4	1.6			-2.9	-.5	2.6	.7	.9
.8	.8	.8	Debt/Worth		.4	.9	1.1	.8	.7
1.7	2.0	2.0			1.6	4.6	2.3	1.8	2.2
4.6	8.4	8.0			-12.8	-6.2	6.5	8.2	5.1
47.8	58.9	51.9	% Profit Before Taxes/Tangible Net Worth				53.6	34.0	55.1
(153) 20.3	(135) 22.5	(125) 17.9					(22) 12.7	(38) 13.8	(46) 29.2
8.4	9.9	4.5					-2.3	3.5	11.4
18.2	18.0	14.4	% Profit Before Taxes/Total Assets		9.6	13.8	13.8	14.4	14.4
8.3	9.7	6.5			4.9	2.8	3.8	4.5	8.8
2.3	2.6	1.2			.6	.6	-.2	1.3	4.8
118.0	110.8	94.8	Sales/Net Fixed Assets		UND	138.7	119.0	104.8	93.9
41.3	33.4	41.6			67.4	38.4	41.5	51.7	33.1
15.2	13.5	15.0			13.6	12.9	16.0	15.6	14.2
4.3	3.9	3.9	Sales/Total Assets		3.8	3.7	5.0	4.3	3.8
3.2	2.8	2.9			2.1	2.8	3.4	3.0	2.9
2.1	2.0	2.0			1.2	1.8	2.2	2.0	2.0
.3	.4	.4	% Depr., Dep., Amort./Sales				.3	.3	.4
(134) .7	(122) 1.1	(118) .8					(21) .7	(32) .9	(44) .8
2.1	2.3	2.3					2.0	2.6	1.9
1.7	1.9	1.7	% Officers', Directors' Owners' Comp/Sales				1.7	1.5	.9
(65) 4.5	(48) 3.6	(49) 3.8					(11) 4.1	(14) 2.0	(11) 2.8
8.7	5.6	6.9					6.1	5.5	6.7
4527715M	4829204M	5273079M	Net Sales ($)	3713M	20575M	54250M	191389M	730957M	4272195M
1977803M	2069208M	2282290M	Total Assets ($)	1265M	17302M	21847M	76994M	274119M	1890763M

M = $ thousand MM = $ million

See Pages 9 through 22 for Explanation of Ratios and Data

Current Data Sorted by Assets | **Comparative Historical Data**

0-500M	500M-2MM	2-10MM	10-50MM	50-100MM	100-250MM		4/1/09-3/31/10 ALL	4/1/10-3/31/11 ALL
						Type of Statement		
		5	16	7	5	Unqualified	54	48
	1	18	10			Reviewed	42	53
	9	12	1			Compiled	19	25
8	10	11	1			Tax Returns	30	40
4	30	49	39	8	13	Other	108	119
32 (4/1-9/30/13)		225 (10/1/13-3/31/14)						
12	50	95	67	15	18	NUMBER OF STATEMENTS	253	285
%	%	%	%	%	%	**ASSETS**	%	%
21.7	15.7	18.7	8.3	10.0	4.7	Cash & Equivalents	15.5	14.3
35.5	38.5	42.5	44.2	39.8	37.4	Trade Receivables (net)	41.0	42.3
19.8	25.6	22.7	23.7	14.8	22.9	Inventory	19.6	20.2
.1	2.7	3.8	3.7	5.0	3.8	All Other Current	3.8	3.6
77.2	82.5	87.8	80.0	69.5	68.8	Total Current	79.9	80.4
12.0	7.3	6.2	5.5	5.7	4.4	Fixed Assets (net)	8.2	8.0
2.0	2.3	2.5	9.4	15.7	20.2	Intangibles (net)	5.7	5.2
8.8	7.8	3.5	5.0	9.1	6.6	All Other Non-Current	6.2	6.4
100.0	100.0	100.0	100.0	100.0	100.0	Total	100.0	100.0
						LIABILITIES		
14.3	11.6	9.9	14.5	8.4	10.7	Notes Payable-Short Term	14.2	13.9
5.6	1.1	2.0	1.2	1.9	.4	Cur. Mat.-L.T.D.	2.2	1.9
45.7	28.2	27.3	27.0	36.0	34.2	Trade Payables	27.2	28.9
.2	.1	.1	.1	1.0	.3	Income Taxes Payable	.2	.3
16.8	12.2	13.2	14.1	12.0	9.5	All Other Current	12.8	13.6
82.6	53.2	52.5	56.9	59.3	55.1	Total Current	56.6	58.7
15.2	6.7	6.6	4.4	3.2	7.6	Long-Term Debt	6.5	6.2
.0	.0	.1	.1	.0	1.8	Deferred Taxes	.2	.2
10.0	7.1	4.4	3.6	6.6	1.8	All Other Non-Current	7.6	6.4
-7.8	33.0	36.4	35.1	30.9	33.7	Net Worth	29.1	28.5
100.0	100.0	100.0	100.0	100.0	100.0	Total Liabilties & Net Worth	100.0	100.0
						INCOME DATA		
100.0	100.0	100.0	100.0	100.0	100.0	Net Sales	100.0	100.0
44.1	29.2	28.8	26.1	28.6	17.9	Gross Profit	28.8	29.1
40.4	25.6	25.1	21.8	25.8	15.8	Operating Expenses	25.7	24.8
3.8	3.6	3.7	4.3	2.8	2.1	Operating Profit	3.2	4.3
-1.5	.2	.3	.5	1.0	.7	All Other Expenses (net)	.4	.4
5.2	3.4	3.4	3.8	1.9	1.4	Profit Before Taxes	2.7	3.9
						RATIOS		
3.0	2.8	2.8	1.8	1.4	1.6		2.1	2.0
1.1	1.5	1.6	1.4	1.3	1.2	Current	1.4	1.3
.8	1.1	1.2	1.2	1.1	.9		1.1	1.1
2.4	2.2	1.9	1.3	1.3	1.0		1.5	1.4
.7	1.0	1.1	.9	.9	.8	Quick	1.0	1.0
.4	.7	.8	.6	.7	.5		.7	.7
11 33.2	**17** 21.5	**26** 13.8	**38** 9.6	**44** 8.3	**29** 12.8		**25** 14.5	**26** 13.9
20 18.6	**29** 12.7	**39** 9.3	**51** 7.1	**56** 6.5	**47** 7.7	Sales/Receivables	**42** 8.7	**42** 8.7
42 8.7	**46** 8.0	**54** 6.7	**64** 5.7	**74** 4.9	**68** 5.4		**63** 5.8	**63** 5.8
0 UND	**6** 57.2	**3** 119.9	**7** 55.3	**0** UND	**1** 433.1		**2** 215.9	**3** 113.6
22 16.9	**19** 19.7	**20** 17.9	**38** 9.7	**16** 23.4	**22** 16.6	Cost of Sales/Inventory	**18** 20.0	**21** 17.4
55 6.6	**49** 7.5	**50** 7.3	**69** 5.3	**65** 5.6	**46** 7.9		**48** 7.5	**52** 7.1
23 15.8	**13** 28.5	**16** 23.3	**24** 15.5	**36** 10.0	**24** 15.2		**17** 21.2	**20** 18.5
54 6.7	**25** 14.7	**29** 12.5	**40** 9.1	**55** 6.6	**38** 9.5	Cost of Sales/Payables	**33** 11.0	**37** 9.9
73 5.0	**38** 9.6	**56** 6.5	**54** 6.7	**101** 3.6	**87** 4.2		**54** 6.8	**58** 6.3
9.1	8.2	6.3	6.3	11.4	12.2		7.5	8.6
NM	16.0	12.8	13.4	15.7	21.2	Sales/Working Capital	16.9	18.5
-34.7	116.4	25.6	29.2	39.5	-43.5		50.3	53.2
	56.7	49.8	47.4	18.3	19.5		22.1	22.6
	(33) 11.8	(62) 9.0	(53) 8.7	(11) 8.8	(16) 9.4	EBIT/Interest	(213) 5.5	(234) 7.4
	2.3	1.4	2.9	2.4	.5		1.5	2.8
		4.8	41.7				20.0	20.3
		(10) 1.0	(10) 9.9			Net Profit + Depr., Dep., Amort./Cur. Mat. L/T/D	(44) 3.2	(43) 5.7
		-.7	2.0				1.2	3.0
.0	.0	.0	.0	.1	.0		.1	.0
.2	.1	.1	.1	.3	.3	Fixed/Worth	.2	.1
1.0	.7	.4	.4	-1.7	-.2		.7	.7
.7	.9	.6	1.4	1.8	1.5		1.0	1.1
4.6	2.0	1.8	2.2	4.9	7.6	Debt/Worth	2.7	3.0
-5.5	8.8	5.4	4.6	-20.5	-5.1		7.7	7.8
	84.9	63.3	63.0	37.8	49.6		54.4	67.1
	(43) 41.3	(81) 31.7	(60) 41.6	(11) 24.0	(12) 19.6	% Profit Before Taxes/Tangible Net Worth	(218) 21.4	(240) 32.9
	21.6	8.1	13.9	10.7	13.1		4.2	10.3
37.7	31.4	21.5	17.0	8.0	10.4		14.8	18.2
11.7	10.6	11.4	8.5	4.2	7.1	% Profit Before Taxes/Total Assets	5.8	8.3
6.1	1.9	1.4	2.3	1.0	-.2		.8	1.7
UND	589.7	491.9	252.5	278.7	384.4		314.1	366.7
88.1	139.9	135.3	102.0	58.0	160.5	Sales/Net Fixed Assets	103.3	106.5
27.4	43.0	50.9	31.3	23.7	41.4		36.6	35.9
8.6	6.5	5.1	4.0	3.7	4.7		4.9	4.9
4.5	4.6	3.9	2.8	2.9	2.7	Sales/Total Assets	3.3	3.4
3.8	3.3	2.6	1.9	1.4	1.8		2.3	2.3
	.1	.1	.2	.1	.1		.1	.1
	(30) .3	(55) .3	(59) .3	(11) .2	(12) .3	% Depr., Dep., Amort./Sales	(182) .5	(192) .4
	.8	.8	.9	.6	1.4		1.1	.8
	1.2	1.4	.3				1.0	.9
	(21) 1.9	(31) 2.2	(11) .9			% Officers', Directors' Owners' Comp/Sales	(68) 2.4	(95) 2.4
	4.3	3.6	1.9				5.4	4.2
16731M	351888M	1968356M	4762820M	2893262M	11324885M	Net Sales ($)	13948886M	16386918M
2867M	64698M	488909M	1607986M	1117931M	3288141M	Total Assets ($)	4985789M	5281680M

M = $ thousand MM = $ million

See Pages 9 through 22 for Explanation of Ratios and Data

Comparative Historical Data / Current Data Sorted by Sales

4/1/11-3/31/12 ALL	4/1/12-3/31/13 ALL	4/1/13-3/31/14 ALL		0-1MM	1-3MM	3-5MM	5-10MM	10-25MM	25MM & OVER
			Type of Statement						
50	34	33	Unqualified			1		1	31
38	29	29	Reviewed				2	10	17
21	14	22	Compiled		3	1	5	9	4
29	37	30	Tax Returns	4	4	3	7	9	3
116	123	143	Other	2	9	7	19	37	69
				32 (4/1-9/30/13)			225 (10/1/13-3/31/14)		
254	237	257	**NUMBER OF STATEMENTS**	6	16	12	33	66	124
%	%	%	**ASSETS**	%	%	%	%	%	%
14.0	14.8	14.1	Cash & Equivalents		20.9	14.8	16.8	19.4	9.5
41.8	43.0	41.3	Trade Receivables (net)		33.1	35.9	35.0	39.3	46.0
22.1	18.9	23.0	Inventory		16.7	26.8	27.0	24.5	21.5
3.1	3.0	3.5	All Other Current		4.8	2.2	2.7	2.3	4.3
81.1	79.6	81.8	Total Current		75.5	79.7	81.6	85.5	81.4
7.8	8.2	6.3	Fixed Assets (net)		12.9	6.4	9.4	6.3	4.6
5.7	5.2	6.3	Intangibles (net)		.4	5.7	2.3	5.0	9.0
5.4	6.9	5.5	All Other Non-Current		11.1	8.2	6.6	3.2	5.0
100.0	100.0	100.0	Total		100.0	100.0	100.0	100.0	100.0
			LIABILITIES						
14.0	11.2	11.6	Notes Payable-Short Term		8.8	9.2	12.7	9.6	12.7
2.0	1.9	1.7	Cur. Mat.-L.T.D.		.3	5.6	1.8	1.6	1.1
28.5	27.5	29.3	Trade Payables		19.0	54.9	21.6	27.5	31.5
.4	.2	.2	Income Taxes Payable		.2	.0	.1	.1	.2
15.1	14.2	13.1	All Other Current		18.5	16.0	8.5	12.6	13.7
59.9	55.0	55.8	Total Current		46.7	85.8	44.7	51.3	59.3
7.9	7.2	6.3	Long-Term Debt		9.9	17.5	5.4	5.5	5.4
.2	.3	.2	Deferred Taxes		.0	.0	.0	.2	.3
5.2	5.9	4.9	All Other Non-Current		11.8	8.0	6.4	4.7	3.3
26.8	31.6	32.8	Net Worth		31.6	-11.3	43.4	38.3	31.8
100.0	100.0	100.0	Total Liabilties & Net Worth		100.0	100.0	100.0	100.0	100.0
			INCOME DATA						
100.0	100.0	100.0	Net Sales		100.0	100.0	100.0	100.0	100.0
29.5	31.5	28.1	Gross Profit		48.1	34.2	35.7	30.1	21.3
25.1	26.1	24.4	Operating Expenses		44.4	35.1	29.6	25.5	18.1
4.4	5.3	3.7	Operating Profit		3.7	-.8	6.1	4.7	3.2
.5	.4	.3	All Other Expenses (net)		-.2	.4	.0	.3	.6
3.9	4.9	3.4	Profit Before Taxes		4.0	-1.3	6.1	4.4	2.6
			RATIOS						
2.0	2.1	2.2			4.3	1.7	3.6	2.7	1.7
1.4	1.4	1.5	Current		1.5	1.3	1.9	1.7	1.3
1.1	1.1	1.1			.9	.8	1.2	1.2	1.1
1.4	1.5	1.5			3.3	1.2	2.7	1.7	1.3
1.0	1.1	1.0	Quick		1.3	.6	1.0	1.1	.9
.6	.7	.7			.6	.3	.7	.8	.7
29 12.8	**31** 11.9	**26** 14.0			**14** 26.0	**22** 16.3	**21** 17.0	**20** 18.3	**34** 10.7
42 8.6	**46** 8.0	**42** 8.7	Sales/Receivables		**42** 8.7	**29** 12.8	**34** 10.6	**38** 9.7	**48** 7.6
60 6.1	**68** 5.4	**61** 6.0			**64** 5.7	**40** 9.1	**65** 5.6	**51** 7.1	**62** 5.9
3 111.9	**2** 216.4	**4** 82.0			**0** UND	**5** 72.8	**7** 51.0	**5** 73.4	**3** 145.6
22 16.8	**20** 18.1	**23** 16.1	Cost of Sales/Inventory		**21** 17.5	**47** 7.8	**32** 11.4	**21** 17.1	**21** 17.3
54 6.8	**51** 7.1	**57** 6.4			**51** 7.1	**69** 5.3	**62** 5.9	**55** 6.6	**56** 6.5
19 18.8	**22** 16.8	**20** 18.1			**19** 19.0	**24** 15.5	**17** 21.5	**14** 26.5	**22** 16.8
34 10.6	**36** 10.0	**33** 10.9	Cost of Sales/Payables		**30** 12.0	**30** 12.1	**31** 11.6	**29** 12.7	**36** 10.0
54 6.8	**64** 5.7	**56** 6.5			**61** 6.0	**89** 4.1	**56** 6.5	**55** 6.6	**61** 6.0
7.9	8.0	7.6			4.0	7.7	5.7	6.2	9.9
17.4	15.3	14.5	Sales/Working Capital		8.4	17.9	11.4	12.9	16.3
56.7	41.5	41.0			-64.6	-105.2	26.3	32.6	40.5
25.0	32.9	42.3					57.6	57.9	39.6
(212) 8.5	(187) 7.6	(181) 9.3	EBIT/Interest				(21) 20.7	(47) 9.3	(94) 9.7
2.4	2.5	2.2					1.3	1.8	2.7
18.0	37.8	16.1							22.7
(38) 3.6	(31) 17.2	(25) 2.7	Net Profit + Depr., Dep., Amort./Cur. Mat. L/T/D						(16) 5.4
1.2	1.4	.5							.9
.1	.0	.0			.1	.0	.0	.0	.0
.2	.2	.1	Fixed/Worth		.4	.2	.1	.1	.1
1.0	.7	.5			1.5	-.5	.4	.8	.4
1.3	1.1	1.0			.4	1.4	.5	.7	1.4
2.8	2.5	2.1	Debt/Worth		2.1	NM	1.4	1.7	2.5
10.8	6.8	6.9			6.1	-3.8	3.9	8.8	6.9
66.7	74.1	64.8			134.1		68.3	69.3	61.8
(207) 36.4	(199) 35.0	(214) 33.9	% Profit Before Taxes/Tangible Net Worth		(14) 30.5		(31) 39.1	(55) 33.3	(104) 35.8
12.4	12.6	13.1			-5.1		15.0	8.8	13.2
18.4	21.3	19.5			37.1	7.1	33.7	21.8	16.7
9.8	10.0	8.7	% Profit Before Taxes/Total Assets		9.0	2.2	17.7	9.3	8.0
2.7	2.1	1.8			-4.5	-9.1	2.5	2.3	1.9
313.9	349.2	365.3			95.0	552.0	326.3	521.6	347.0
86.8	91.2	117.0	Sales/Net Fixed Assets		35.8	118.9	75.0	136.4	138.6
32.6	32.8	36.6			19.6	23.7	20.1	47.7	44.9
5.0	4.8	5.0			4.9	5.9	4.8	5.9	4.8
3.6	3.5	3.7	Sales/Total Assets		3.8	3.3	3.6	4.0	3.5
2.2	2.2	2.4			1.9	2.5	2.0	2.6	2.4
.1	.2	.1				.2	.1	.1	.1
(175) .3	(164) .4	(171) .3	% Depr., Dep., Amort./Sales			(10) .4	(20) .6	(34) .5	(98) .3
.9	1.0	.9				1.2	1.7	1.2	.6
.9	1.5	1.0					1.1	1.4	.4
(69) 2.4	(64) 2.5	(74) 2.0	% Officers', Directors' Owners' Comp/Sales				(14) 2.0	(24) 2.4	(19) 1.0
4.4	5.7	4.2					2.3	3.8	1.7
16676147M	18177872M	21317942M	Net Sales ($)	3719M	31819M	46923M	231617M	1031573M	19972291M
5380922M	6192164M	6570532M	Total Assets ($)	2221M	10879M	15490M	79123M	406224M	6056595M

M = $ thousand MM = $ million

See Pages 9 through 22 for Explanation of Ratios and Data

Current Data Sorted by Assets							Comparative Historical Data	
						Type of Statement		
		5	9		3	Unqualified	27	19
1	6	30	15	1		Reviewed	55	59
2	10	18	3			Compiled	37	38
8	24	9	1			Tax Returns	33	42
1	23	46	15	4	2	Other	80	87
43 (4/1-9/30/13)		193 (10/1/13-3/31/14)					4/1/09-3/31/10	4/1/10-3/31/11
0-500M	**500M-2MM**	**2-10MM**	**10-50MM**	**50-100MM**	**100-250MM**		**ALL**	**ALL**
12	63	108	43	5	5	**NUMBER OF STATEMENTS**	232	245
%	%	%	%	%	%	**ASSETS**	%	%
25.9	12.9	9.1	7.0			Cash & Equivalents	9.8	9.3
24.4	31.7	29.7	29.2			Trade Receivables (net)	30.0	32.0
29.8	33.5	38.4	31.9			Inventory	32.6	31.6
3.5	.9	2.5	6.1			All Other Current	3.6	2.5
83.6	79.0	79.7	74.2			Total Current	75.9	75.4
8.0	13.5	12.5	14.9			Fixed Assets (net)	14.2	14.4
1.6	.5	2.5	5.6			Intangibles (net)	5.1	4.8
6.8	6.9	5.3	5.3			All Other Non-Current	4.8	5.3
100.0	100.0	100.0	100.0			Total	100.0	100.0
						LIABILITIES		
9.5	9.1	13.1	12.0			Notes Payable-Short Term	13.7	13.6
.0	1.9	1.7	2.0			Cur. Mat.-L.T.D.	2.7	3.3
21.4	23.9	22.6	21.5			Trade Payables	17.3	19.3
.2	.0	.1	.3			Income Taxes Payable	.1	.1
7.5	17.6	11.4	13.1			All Other Current	11.6	10.9
38.6	52.6	49.0	48.8			Total Current	45.4	47.1
8.4	10.9	6.1	10.5			Long-Term Debt	12.1	10.2
.0	.2	.4	.3			Deferred Taxes	.4	.4
13.5	3.2	6.2	6.8			All Other Non-Current	5.1	6.5
39.5	33.2	38.3	33.6			Net Worth	37.0	35.7
100.0	100.0	100.0	100.0			Total Liabilties & Net Worth	100.0	100.0
						INCOME DATA		
100.0	100.0	100.0	100.0			Net Sales	100.0	100.0
32.5	31.1	28.3	28.8			Gross Profit	30.4	30.7
27.1	25.9	24.9	22.2			Operating Expenses	27.2	26.3
5.4	5.2	3.4	6.6			Operating Profit	3.2	4.4
.0	.0	-.3	1.7			All Other Expenses (net)	.7	.4
5.4	5.2	3.7	4.9			Profit Before Taxes	2.4	4.0
						RATIOS		
6.0	3.3	2.5	2.1				3.1	2.5
3.4	1.6	1.7	1.5			Current	1.8	1.6
.9	1.1	1.2	1.2				1.2	1.2
4.3	1.7	1.4	1.0				1.6	1.4
1.1	.9	.8	.7			Quick	.9	.8
.5	.5	.4	.5				.5	.6
4 93.5	**15** 23.9	**24** 14.9	**26** 13.9				**24** 14.9	**26** 14.2
19 19.0	**30** 12.3	**38** 9.7	**41** 8.8			Sales/Receivables	**37** 9.8	**39** 9.5
27 13.6	**47** 7.8	**51** 7.1	**59** 6.2				**54** 6.8	**55** 6.7
7 55.5	**16** 22.3	**40** 9.1	**26** 14.1				**30** 12.1	**28** 13.0
24 15.1	**54** 6.8	**72** 5.1	**63** 5.8			Cost of Sales/Inventory	**60** 6.1	**57** 6.4
111 3.3	**114** 3.2	**122** 3.0	**99** 3.7				**99** 3.7	**99** 3.7
2 182.3	**14** 27.0	**21** 17.5	**19** 19.1				**14** 26.2	**16** 23.1
16 23.3	**29** 12.5	**34** 10.6	**27** 13.4			Cost of Sales/Payables	**28** 13.3	**27** 13.4
26 14.3	**44** 8.3	**56** 6.5	**58** 6.3				**46** 8.0	**50** 7.2
3.4	4.9	5.6	6.4				5.1	5.6
7.9	12.6	9.7	10.5			Sales/Working Capital	8.7	9.8
NM	80.7	19.2	22.2				23.8	31.8
	28.1	18.5	21.7				9.3	13.2
	(49) 9.3	(92) 6.0	(40) 5.6			EBIT/Interest	(198) 2.5	(217) 4.2
	2.8	2.5	2.8				.6	1.7
		12.8	15.8				6.6	9.4
		(21) 4.1	(10) 2.7			Net Profit + Depr., Dep., Amort./Cur. Mat. L/T/D	(40) 1.9	(43) 2.7
		1.2	1.2				1.1	1.1
.0	.0	.1	.1				.1	.1
.2	.2	.3	.2			Fixed/Worth	.2	.3
NM	.7	.7	1.1				1.1	1.1
.3	.7	.8	1.2				.6	.7
1.5	1.7	1.9	2.2			Debt/Worth	1.8	2.1
NM	3.9	4.2	4.9				5.4	6.6
	59.7	41.9	53.2				40.9	48.9
	(59) 36.4	(99) 19.8	(39) 23.7			% Profit Before Taxes/Tangible Net Worth	(201) 12.7	(211) 19.2
	4.9	6.7	12.2				1.1	4.7
29.0	22.7	12.8	14.4				12.6	14.7
19.0	10.4	6.2	6.8			% Profit Before Taxes/Total Assets	3.6	5.6
7.5	2.4	2.0	2.7				-.8	1.4
UND	517.3	91.9	201.3				105.9	144.3
290.5	67.2	32.9	42.9			Sales/Net Fixed Assets	34.5	49.3
24.1	23.8	16.2	12.7				13.2	12.7
6.3	4.8	3.5	3.0				3.7	3.7
4.8	3.4	2.6	2.3			Sales/Total Assets	2.8	2.8
2.4	2.4	2.0	1.5				1.9	1.9
	.2	.3	.2				.4	.4
	(36) .7	(93) .6	(32) .6			% Depr., Dep., Amort./Sales	(187) .8	(179) .8
	1.8	1.1	1.5				1.5	1.6
	2.5	1.3	.8				1.6	1.8
	(30) 4.0	(39) 2.5	(10) 3.8			% Officers', Directors' Owners' Comp/Sales	(91) 3.5	(99) 3.0
	8.6	4.7	5.8				6.7	6.0
16978M	**328430M**	**1417529M**	**2209583M**	**549414M**	**1455884M**	Net Sales ($)	**7168031M**	**6677472M**
3624M	**79316M**	**503057M**	**898540M**	**349176M**	**834565M**	Total Assets ($)	**3330617M**	**3138695M**

M = $ thousand MM = $ million

See Pages 9 through 22 for Explanation of Ratios and Data

Comparative Historical Data / Current Data Sorted by Sales

	4/1/11-3/31/12 ALL		4/1/12-3/31/13 ALL		4/1/13-3/31/14 ALL	Type of Statement		0-1MM		1-3MM		3-5MM		5-10MM		10-25MM		25MM & OVER
	29		18		17	Unqualified								2		4		11
	62		60		53	Reviewed				1		3		11		16		22
	42		30		33	Compiled		1		2		9		11		7		3
	55		46		42	Tax Returns		6		10		11		9		5		1
	82		88		91	Other		1		9		13		23		23		22
										43 (4/1-9/30/13)				193 (10/1/13-3/31/14)				
	270		242		236	NUMBER OF STATEMENTS		8		22		36		56		55		59
	%		%		%	ASSETS		%		%		%		%		%		%
	10.5		8.5		10.3	Cash & Equivalents				20.9		9.7		10.0		10.7		7.1
	30.5		30.7		29.5	Trade Receivables (net)				19.8		28.6		31.3		32.4		31.3
	33.8		36.6		34.9	Inventory				37.8		38.0		36.3		32.4		32.1
	2.7		2.8		2.8	All Other Current				1.2		1.0		2.2		2.5		5.1
	77.5		78.7		77.5	Total Current				79.6		77.3		79.8		77.9		75.6
	12.3		12.8		13.0	Fixed Assets (net)				12.6		15.9		11.9		14.1		10.3
	4.3		3.7		3.9	Intangibles (net)				.2		.7		2.1		3.8		9.1
	5.9		4.9		5.7	All Other Non-Current				7.5		6.0		6.3		4.1		5.0
	100.0		100.0		100.0	Total				100.0		100.0		100.0		100.0		100.0
						LIABILITIES												
	13.6		13.4		11.4	Notes Payable-Short Term				6.7		8.4		14.5		11.2		11.9
	2.9		2.4		1.7	Cur. Mat.-L.T.D.				.4		1.4		2.8		2.0		1.5
	20.6		21.4		22.2	Trade Payables				22.3		24.2		22.9		21.9		22.7
	.2		.2		.1	Income Taxes Payable				.0		.1		.0		.1		.2
	12.0		11.6		13.5	All Other Current				30.7		9.3		11.9		10.0		15.8
	49.3		48.9		48.9	Total Current				60.2		43.4		52.1		45.3		52.0
	9.4		10.5		8.8	Long-Term Debt				6.0		10.6		9.0		6.4		7.8
	.3		.2		.3	Deferred Taxes				.0		.1		.3		.6		.3
	6.9		4.1		5.9	All Other Non-Current				5.9		4.3		3.1		6.5		6.4
	34.0		36.3		36.1	Net Worth				28.0		41.6		35.4		41.2		33.6
	100.0		100.0		100.0	Total Liabilties & Net Worth				100.0		100.0		100.0		100.0		100.0
						INCOME DATA												
	100.0		100.0		100.0	Net Sales				100.0		100.0		100.0		100.0		100.0
	29.6		28.8		29.6	Gross Profit				37.5		33.9		28.0		28.2		25.7
	25.4		24.1		24.7	Operating Expenses				30.5		28.4		24.3		25.5		19.9
	4.2		4.7		4.9	Operating Profit				7.0		5.5		3.8		2.7		5.7
	.2		.1		.3	All Other Expenses (net)				.1		.2		.5		-.5		.8
	4.0		4.6		4.6	Profit Before Taxes				6.9		5.3		3.2		3.2		4.9
						RATIOS												
	2.6		2.5		2.5					5.9		3.4		2.2		2.5		2.0
	1.7		1.6		1.6	Current				1.9		1.9		1.5		1.8		1.5
	1.2		1.2		1.2					.9		1.0		1.2		1.3		1.2
	1.4		1.2		1.4					2.5		1.7		1.4		1.4		1.1
	.9		.8		.9	Quick				.8		.8		.9		.9		.8
	.6		.5		.5					.3		.5		.4		.6		.6
22	16.9	**25**	14.7	**22**	16.3				**0**	UND	**13**	27.8	**23**	15.8	**24**	15.0	**29**	12.6
39	9.4	**34**	10.6	**35**	10.3	Sales/Receivables			**19**	19.0	**30**	12.2	**42**	8.7	**35**	10.5	**40**	9.1
51	7.2	**50**	7.3	**51**	7.1				**32**	11.3	**64**	5.7	**52**	7.0	**44**	8.3	**56**	6.5
26	13.8	**33**	11.1	**29**	12.8				**22**	16.8	**30**	12.2	**23**	15.7	**28**	13.1	**37**	9.9
58	6.3	**63**	5.8	**60**	6.1	Cost of Sales/Inventory			**48**	7.6	**66**	5.5	**70**	5.2	**57**	6.4	**63**	5.8
99	3.7	**107**	3.4	**114**	3.2				**203**	1.8	**126**	2.9	**122**	3.0	**83**	4.4	**89**	4.1
15	24.5	**19**	18.9	**18**	20.5				**3**	110.7	**19**	19.0	**17**	21.4	**23**	15.8	**19**	19.0
31	11.7	**33**	11.2	**30**	12.1	Cost of Sales/Payables			**29**	12.5	**32**	11.4	**40**	9.2	**32**	11.4	**27**	13.6
51	7.2	**53**	6.9	**52**	7.0				**41**	8.8	**70**	5.2	**54**	6.8	**43**	8.5	**54**	6.8
	5.7		5.7		5.5					3.9		4.1		6.1		5.7		6.5
	10.3		10.0		10.3	Sales/Working Capital				6.7		7.9		12.2		10.4		10.9
	25.2		26.4		25.2					NM		677.0		25.3		18.8		23.9
	20.7		19.7		21.9					100.4		21.5		20.9		18.6		20.1
(238)	5.8	(216)	6.1	(196)	6.6	EBIT/Interest			(16)	9.9	(24)	6.2	(49)	5.6	(47)	6.0	(54)	6.7
	1.7		2.3		2.8					3.2		1.5		1.9		3.9		3.1
	14.9		7.5		8.4									8.6		10.3		7.8
(47)	4.6	(43)	4.3	(38)	3.6	Net Profit + Depr., Dep., Amort./Cur. Mat. L/T/D							(10)	1.0	(15)	4.8	(11)	3.9
	1.1		1.3		1.2									-.1		2.2		2.1
	.1		.1		.1					.0		.0		.1		.1		.1
	.2		.3		.2	Fixed/Worth				.1		.2		.2		.3		.3
	.9		1.0		.8					.7		1.2		.6		.8		1.2
	.8		.9		.9					.5		.4		1.0		.9		1.5
	2.1		1.9		2.0	Debt/Worth				1.4		1.2		2.5		1.7		2.4
	4.8		5.1		4.4					6.7		4.7		4.5		2.4		9.4
	63.8		53.0		51.0					69.2		43.4		66.7		35.8		63.3
(239)	26.0	(215)	24.3	(212)	25.8	% Profit Before Taxes/Tangible Net Worth			(20)	31.6	(33)	23.7	(52)	29.8	(50)	17.7	(51)	26.1
	4.6		9.9		7.9					18.2		4.8		4.4		7.6		13.3
	17.3		17.7		18.2					26.4		18.6		18.2		12.9		15.4
	7.2		7.3		7.4	% Profit Before Taxes/Total Assets				14.6		6.9		6.4		7.2		6.8
	1.2		2.9		2.4					4.0		2.1		1.4		2.7		2.7
	146.0		109.4		150.9					999.8		183.4		104.2		100.7		177.4
	52.7		43.8		42.0	Sales/Net Fixed Assets				59.6		50.2		39.5		32.4		50.7
	17.2		15.4		16.4					13.3		11.7		18.5		13.1		19.0
	3.9		3.6		3.8					4.8		4.0		3.8		3.9		3.9
	2.8		2.8		2.7	Sales/Total Assets				2.8		2.5		2.6		3.0		2.9
	2.0		2.1		1.9					1.7		1.9		1.9		2.2		1.9
	.3		.3		.3					.1		.4		.2		.3		.3
(210)	.6	(192)	.6	(176)	.7	% Depr., Dep., Amort./Sales			(13)	.7	(20)	.8	(44)	.6	(49)	.6	(45)	.6
	1.1		1.3		1.2					2.7		3.1		1.1		1.2		1.0
	1.6		1.5		1.3					3.0		.9		2.4		1.3		.4
(109)	3.0	(102)	2.7	(89)	3.2	% Officers', Directors' Owners' Comp/Sales			(10)	4.9	(15)	3.2	(23)	3.5	(23)	2.6	(15)	1.0
	6.1		6.1		6.1					14.3		8.5		6.7		5.6		3.9
	9635094M		7055690M		5977818M	Net Sales ($)		5638M		42780M		139461M		411930M		797519M		4580490M
	3805022M		2681009M		2668278M	Total Assets ($)		5307M		20578M		99392M		176389M		314013M		2052599M

M = $ thousand MM = $ million

See Pages 9 through 22 for Explanation of Ratios and Data

Current Data Sorted by Assets | **Comparative Historical Data**

0-500M	500M-2MM	2-10MM	10-50MM	50-100MM	100-250MM		4/1/09-3/31/10 ALL	4/1/10-3/31/11 ALL
						Type of Statement		
	1	11	31	8	6	Unqualified	54	58
	2	27	19	1		Reviewed	63	62
6	11	29	6	1		Compiled	53	63
12	28	17				Tax Returns	64	73
17	27	78	48	13	10	Other	165	176
	53 (4/1-9/30/13)		356 (10/1/13-3/31/14)					
35	69	162	104	23	16	**NUMBER OF STATEMENTS**	399	432
%	%	%	%	%	%	**ASSETS**	%	%
25.7	14.5	9.2	8.3	5.3	7.6	Cash & Equivalents	10.4	10.4
25.5	32.4	34.1	31.6	21.1	27.4	Trade Receivables (net)	32.8	32.1
29.6	28.0	29.9	28.2	19.8	24.8	Inventory	27.6	26.1
4.2	1.8	2.6	2.2	3.1	2.7	All Other Current	2.8	2.9
85.0	76.7	75.8	70.3	49.4	62.6	Total Current	73.6	71.5
9.9	11.7	12.8	13.8	19.5	11.5	Fixed Assets (net)	14.8	14.0
1.6	4.2	5.4	9.9	29.0	21.1	Intangibles (net)	7.0	8.2
3.6	7.4	6.0	6.0	2.1	4.8	All Other Non-Current	4.7	6.3
100.0	100.0	100.0	100.0	100.0	100.0	Total	100.0	100.0
						LIABILITIES		
21.5	14.7	14.3	13.8	12.4	7.2	Notes Payable-Short Term	14.4	13.6
1.0	2.7	3.1	3.1	1.8	1.7	Cur. Mat.-L.T.D.	3.2	3.1
16.7	23.1	25.2	16.4	12.9	12.1	Trade Payables	21.2	21.0
.6	.0	.2	.2	.2	.0	Income Taxes Payable	.2	.2
28.6	8.8	8.6	10.4	9.4	12.1	All Other Current	9.7	10.5
68.4	49.3	51.4	43.9	36.8	33.1	Total Current	48.6	48.4
5.7	12.5	8.7	11.0	24.4	17.1	Long-Term Debt	12.1	12.3
.0	.0	.1	.5	.9	1.7	Deferred Taxes	.2	.4
6.2	5.0	3.5	4.6	5.9	2.3	All Other Non-Current	5.5	5.3
19.7	33.1	36.3	39.9	32.0	45.8	Net Worth	33.5	33.6
100.0	100.0	100.0	100.0	100.0	100.0	Total Liabilties & Net Worth	100.0	100.0
						INCOME DATA		
100.0	100.0	100.0	100.0	100.0	100.0	Net Sales	100.0	100.0
46.5	42.2	39.2	36.9	42.0	39.0	Gross Profit	39.9	41.2
41.4	36.7	34.0	30.4	34.4	36.6	Operating Expenses	34.1	34.9
5.1	5.5	5.3	6.5	7.6	2.4	Operating Profit	5.9	6.2
.6	.3	.2	1.0	2.1	.9	All Other Expenses (net)	.7	.8
4.5	5.2	5.1	5.5	5.5	1.5	Profit Before Taxes	5.1	5.4
						RATIOS		
3.5	3.0	2.5	2.7	1.9	3.2		2.4	2.6
1.4	1.7	1.5	1.5	1.6	1.9	Current	1.5	1.6
1.1	1.1	1.1	1.2	1.1	1.2		1.2	1.1
2.3	1.7	1.3	1.6	1.1	1.8		1.5	1.5
.9	1.0	.8	.9	.8	1.0	Quick	.9	.9
.3	.5	.5	.5	.5	.7		.6	.5
0 UND	**21** 17.8	**31** 11.8	**32** 11.4	**17** 21.7	**37** 9.9		**30** 12.4	**28** 13.1
18 20.5	**31** 11.9	**42** 8.6	**42** 8.6	**42** 8.6	**46** 8.0	Sales/Receivables	**42** 8.7	**41** 8.9
29 12.6	**51** 7.1	**63** 5.8	**66** 5.5	**57** 6.4	**59** 6.2		**57** 6.4	**56** 6.6
1 269.5	**21** 17.3	**33** 10.9	**33** 11.1	**42** 8.6	**46** 7.9		**28** 13.1	**30** 12.3
22 16.9	**46** 8.0	**60** 6.1	**56** 6.5	**70** 5.2	**58** 6.3	Cost of Sales/Inventory	**52** 7.0	**51** 7.1
72 5.1	**91** 4.0	**111** 3.3	**107** 3.4	**130** 2.8	**152** 2.4		**96** 3.8	**99** 3.7
0 UND	**15** 25.1	**30** 12.0	**17** 21.3	**22** 16.7	**17** 21.9		**20** 18.5	**21** 17.1
12 30.8	**32** 11.5	**51** 7.2	**36** 10.2	**33** 10.9	**35** 10.5	Cost of Sales/Payables	**40** 9.2	**38** 9.7
43 8.5	**62** 5.9	**81** 4.5	**63** 5.8	**50** 7.3	**59** 6.2		**67** 5.5	**63** 5.8
9.4	5.6	5.3	4.8	7.0	2.8		6.0	5.8
28.4	15.1	11.2	10.7	11.4	8.0	Sales/Working Capital	11.3	12.4
109.6	59.0	56.9	22.9	50.7	20.9		33.9	54.9
32.9	20.3	20.2	32.2	12.9	54.0		21.6	30.7
(22) 5.6	(59) 4.9	(132) 5.9	(91) 9.0	(21) 6.3	(15) 4.3	EBIT/Interest	(348) 6.1	(373) 5.6
2.3	.5	2.4	3.1	2.8	1.4		2.0	2.0
		10.0	21.1				12.2	12.6
		(18) 5.5	(23) 7.7			Net Profit + Depr., Dep., Amort./Cur. Mat. L/T/D	(72) 4.2	(72) 4.8
		.9	2.5				1.8	1.8
.0	.0	.1	.1	.2	.1		.1	.1
.3	.3	.3	.3	1.6	.4	Fixed/Worth	.3	.4
2.3	1.2	1.1	1.9	-.1	NM		1.5	1.7
.6	.8	.8	.8	1.1	.7		.9	.8
3.3	2.5	2.2	2.0	14.8	3.5	Debt/Worth	2.1	2.2
-155.7	8.7	7.6	4.9	-1.4	NM		8.2	13.7
124.3	62.1	68.9	50.8	20.2	34.9		65.1	68.8
(26) 62.6	(56) 16.7	(142) 30.0	(86) 28.8	(12) 9.1	(12) 23.8	% Profit Before Taxes/Tangible Net Worth	(332) 30.7	(363) 29.9
19.6	1.9	9.1	11.9	1.0	6.0		11.2	11.4
61.4	22.0	19.0	16.6	8.5	13.4		20.6	21.5
26.9	7.3	8.6	9.3	5.3	5.4	% Profit Before Taxes/Total Assets	9.6	9.0
3.6	.1	2.4	3.2	1.1	.7		2.6	2.0
870.0	331.1	109.6	98.8	66.1	57.7		134.2	146.0
112.7	50.2	44.9	28.5	18.1	18.9	Sales/Net Fixed Assets	33.0	35.0
24.1	23.2	16.7	9.9	5.9	15.7		11.0	12.0
8.6	5.0	3.5	3.3	2.7	2.6		3.8	3.9
4.9	3.2	2.6	2.1	1.5	1.9	Sales/Total Assets	2.7	2.8
3.1	2.3	1.8	1.5	.5	1.2		1.8	1.8
.1	.2	.3	.3	.6			.3	.3
(15) .2	(42) .5	(120) .6	(90) .8	(14) 1.6		% Depr., Dep., Amort./Sales	(298) .8	(312) .8
.7	1.6	1.8	2.7	4.9			1.8	1.9
3.0	2.4	1.5	1.2				1.9	1.7
(17) 8.9	(44) 3.8	(56) 3.4	(16) 1.6			% Officers', Directors' Owners' Comp/Sales	(144) 3.6	(153) 3.4
16.8	7.0	5.5	2.5				6.9	6.0
59455M	292463M	2086515M	4977910M	2759631M	4599715M	Net Sales ($)	15516500M	15521468M
10311M	83779M	791316M	2134126M	1629120M	2351066M	Total Assets ($)	6612639M	7333154M

M = $ thousand MM = $ million

See Pages 9 through 22 for Explanation of Ratios and Data

Comparative Historical Data				Current Data Sorted by Sales					
			Type of Statement						
66	44	57	Unqualified			1	4	7	45
66	58	49	Reviewed		2	2	5	21	19
59	55	53	Compiled	4	5	8	13	15	8
80	62	57	Tax Returns	3	14	13	18	7	2
182	192	193	Other	12	19	18	34	46	64
					53 (4/1-9/30/13)		356 (10/1/13-3/31/14)		
4/1/11-3/31/12 ALL	**4/1/12-3/31/13 ALL**	**4/1/13-3/31/14 ALL**		**0-1MM**	**1-3MM**	**3-5MM**	**5-10MM**	**10-25MM**	**25MM & OVER**
453	411	409	**NUMBER OF STATEMENTS**	19	40	42	74	96	138
%	%	%	**ASSETS**	%	%	%	%	%	%
10.1	11.0	11.0	Cash & Equivalents	20.0	17.2	16.8	9.7	9.4	7.9
32.9	32.1	31.5	Trade Receivables (net)	15.2	29.3	29.9	35.2	34.5	30.8
28.1	27.5	28.4	Inventory	26.7	26.2	27.4	29.6	29.4	28.2
2.5	2.6	2.5	All Other Current	5.2	1.6	2.9	1.5	2.8	2.7
73.6	73.3	73.3	Total Current	67.2	74.3	77.0	76.0	76.0	69.5
13.1	13.4	12.9	Fixed Assets (net)	15.4	12.8	15.0	11.0	11.9	13.8
6.9	7.1	8.0	Intangibles (net)	6.4	3.5	4.4	5.7	7.8	11.9
6.4	6.2	5.8	All Other Non-Current	11.0	9.4	3.6	7.3	4.3	4.9
100.0	100.0	100.0	Total	100.0	100.0	100.0	100.0	100.0	100.0
			LIABILITIES						
12.9	13.4	14.5	Notes Payable-Short Term	16.1	17.4	15.7	16.1	12.5	13.6
2.8	3.2	2.7	Cur. Mat.-L.T.D.	1.6	3.0	2.3	3.8	2.3	2.6
22.9	21.4	20.7	Trade Payables	5.0	20.4	17.2	25.3	26.5	17.4
.2	.1	.2	Income Taxes Payable	1.0	.0	.0	.1	.3	.1
9.0	10.2	11.0	All Other Current	33.5	7.9	11.7	8.8	9.7	10.7
47.8	48.3	49.0	Total Current	57.2	48.7	47.0	54.1	51.3	44.4
12.4	12.9	10.9	Long-Term Debt	12.6	10.9	12.0	8.9	8.9	12.8
.4	.4	.3	Deferred Taxes	.0	.0	.1	.0	.1	.7
6.4	6.0	4.3	All Other Non-Current	7.1	4.7	6.6	2.9	3.9	4.3
33.0	32.5	35.4	Net Worth	23.1	35.7	34.3	34.0	35.7	37.9
100.0	100.0	100.0	Total Liabilties & Net Worth	100.0	100.0	100.0	100.0	100.0	100.0
			INCOME DATA						
100.0	100.0	100.0	Net Sales	100.0	100.0	100.0	100.0	100.0	100.0
39.7	41.2	39.9	Gross Profit	59.7	46.1	42.0	42.4	36.6	35.7
33.9	35.4	34.3	Operating Expenses	51.2	39.2	36.0	37.2	32.8	29.5
5.8	5.8	5.6	Operating Profit	8.5	6.9	6.0	5.2	3.8	6.2
.7	1.0	.6	All Other Expenses (net)	.7	.6	-.1	.1	.9	.8
5.2	4.8	5.1	Profit Before Taxes	7.9	6.3	6.1	5.2	2.9	5.4
			RATIOS						
2.5	2.5	2.7		5.9	3.0	4.2	2.0	2.5	2.4
1.5	1.6	1.5	Current	2.0	1.6	1.8	1.3	1.5	1.5
1.1	1.2	1.1		1.1	1.0	1.2	1.1	1.1	1.2
1.5	1.5	1.5		3.3	1.9	2.8	1.3	1.4	1.5
.9	(410) .9	.9	Quick	1.1	1.0	1.1	.8	.9	.8
.6	.6	.5		.3	.5	.5	.5	.5	.6
30 12.3	**27** 13.3	**28** 13.2		**0** UND	**8** 44.3	**17** 22.1	**29** 12.8	**32** 11.5	**29** 12.5
42 8.7	**40** 9.1	**39** 9.3	Sales/Receivables	**18** 20.5	**34** 10.8	**31** 11.9	**39** 9.3	**46** 7.9	**38** 9.5
58 6.3	**60** 6.1	**59** 6.2		**42** 8.6	**68** 5.4	**52** 7.0	**70** 5.2	**63** 5.8	**57** 6.4
29 12.4	**28** 13.0	**30** 12.2		**0** UND	**15** 24.5	**16** 22.2	**33** 11.2	**31** 11.6	**37** 9.8
55 6.6	**56** 6.5	**56** 6.5	Cost of Sales/Inventory	**61** 6.0	**54** 6.8	**45** 8.2	**59** 6.2	**58** 6.3	**55** 6.6
107 3.4	**104** 3.5	**101** 3.6		**96** 3.8	**146** 2.5	**99** 3.7	**99** 3.7	**101** 3.6	**101** 3.6
23 15.7	**20** 18.5	**19** 19.5		**0** UND	**12** 30.9	**9** 42.3	**26** 13.9	**33** 11.1	**16** 22.8
41 8.9	**40** 9.1	**40** 9.2	Cost of Sales/Payables	**6** 60.8	**36** 10.1	**29** 12.4	**53** 6.9	**51** 7.2	**33** 11.2
74 4.9	**70** 5.2	**69** 5.3		**56** 6.5	**94** 3.9	**54** 6.7	**79** 4.6	**78** 4.7	**57** 6.4
5.8	5.3	5.3		3.5	3.5	4.8	5.6	5.7	5.5
10.8	10.0	12.1	Sales/Working Capital	9.4	12.6	10.6	15.7	11.2	11.9
35.4	30.0	41.4		677.0	UND	33.8	56.9	48.6	28.7
23.4	18.6	22.8		17.5	15.5	26.4	14.9	21.8	31.2
(377) 6.4	(348) 5.7	(340) 6.4	EBIT/Interest	(11) 6.6	(29) 4.9	(33) 4.4	(61) 5.0	(83) 6.0	(123) 10.2
1.8	1.6	2.2		2.5	.2	1.7	2.1	2.0	3.7
13.0	12.4	16.8						14.9	25.7
(74) 3.7	(57) 4.4	(54) 6.9	Net Profit + Depr., Dep., Amort./Cur. Mat. L/T/D					(14) 8.0	(32) 7.2
1.3	1.7	2.1						2.6	2.6
.1	.1	.1		.0	.0	.1	.1	.1	.1
.4	.3	.3	Fixed/Worth	.3	.1	.5	.3	.3	.3
2.2	1.6	1.6		2.3	1.6	1.3	1.1	1.3	2.1
.9	.9	.8		.2	.6	.7	.8	.8	.9
2.5	2.3	2.2	Debt/Worth	2.5	1.2	2.3	2.8	2.4	2.2
12.9	9.1	8.3		6.6	3.8	20.3	6.0	13.5	12.1
71.2	65.1	60.8		77.7	66.4	74.7	72.1	52.3	56.1
(370) 28.6	(335) 27.7	(334) 27.9	% Profit Before Taxes/Tangible Net Worth	(15) 36.3	(32) 30.5	(34) 20.1	(63) 30.0	(81) 23.6	(109) 30.0
9.4	5.1	9.3		20.0	9.9	3.8	7.1	8.0	11.4
19.5	19.8	19.5		51.0	34.2	34.1	17.2	15.6	19.4
8.3	6.9	8.3	% Profit Before Taxes/Total Assets	19.9	9.7	10.0	7.8	7.9	8.4
1.8	.9	1.9		-.1	.5	1.5	2.0	.9	3.7
145.5	128.7	131.6		188.8	439.2	242.5	177.2	89.5	96.6
41.4	42.4	43.4	Sales/Net Fixed Assets	24.1	49.3	43.4	67.6	35.4	30.4
13.4	13.8	14.6		11.7	21.1	12.0	20.2	17.1	12.1
3.9	3.8	3.8		4.6	4.6	5.4	3.8	3.6	3.6
2.7	2.8	2.6	Sales/Total Assets	2.9	2.4	3.0	2.7	2.5	2.6
1.8	1.7	1.6		1.0	1.4	1.9	1.7	1.6	1.6
.3	.3	.3			.2	.3	.2	.4	.3
(325) .9	(279) .7	(289) .7	% Depr., Dep., Amort./Sales		(22) .6	(28) .7	(48) .4	(78) .8	(108) .7
2.0	2.0	1.9			3.6	1.9	.8	1.8	1.9
1.8	2.0	1.5			2.2	2.7	2.1	1.4	1.1
(163) 3.9	(140) 3.6	(133) 3.4	% Officers', Directors' Owners' Comp/Sales		(20) 6.1	(19) 4.1	(32) 3.0	(34) 2.7	(19) 1.5
7.1	6.6	6.5			8.6	5.5	6.6	5.5	2.9
18408578M	**17051327M**	**14775689M**	Net Sales ($)	**12670M**	**81466M**	**166479M**	**549895M**	**1521791M**	**12443388M**
8237052M	**8050110M**	**6999718M**	Total Assets ($)	**12870M**	**48405M**	**65494M**	**252329M**	**792569M**	**5828051M**

M = $ thousand MM = $ million

See Pages 9 through 22 for Explanation of Ratios and Data

Current Data Sorted by Assets | **Comparative Historical Data**

0-500M	500M-2MM	2-10MM	10-50MM	50-100MM	100-250MM	Type of Statement	4/1/09-3/31/10 ALL	4/1/10-3/31/11 ALL
			1			Unqualified	2	7
	2	4				Reviewed	5	8
		5				Compiled	5	9
2	2	2				Tax Returns	3	5
1		6	2		1	Other	12	12
	3 (4/1-9/30/13)		25 (10/1/13-3/31/14)					
3	4	17	3		1	**NUMBER OF STATEMENTS**	27	41
%	%	%	%	%	%	**ASSETS**	%	%
		3.9		DATA NOT AVAILABLE		Cash & Equivalents	3.4	9.6
		36.1				Trade Receivables (net)	30.9	33.0
		41.4				Inventory	37.5	34.5
		1.1				All Other Current	3.8	2.4
		82.5				Total Current	75.7	79.4
		7.0				Fixed Assets (net)	6.3	7.3
		5.6				Intangibles (net)	11.8	8.8
		4.8				All Other Non-Current	6.2	4.5
		100.0				Total	100.0	100.0
						LIABILITIES		
		16.1				Notes Payable-Short Term	17.6	13.8
		.6				Cur. Mat.-L.T.D.	1.5	1.7
		29.4				Trade Payables	28.0	31.3
		.0				Income Taxes Payable	.1	.1
		3.4				All Other Current	7.8	6.5
		49.6				Total Current	55.0	53.3
		6.8				Long-Term Debt	6.7	9.2
		.0				Deferred Taxes	.5	.0
		7.6				All Other Non-Current	4.1	3.4
		36.1				Net Worth	33.7	34.1
		100.0				Total Liabilties & Net Worth	100.0	100.0
						INCOME DATA		
		100.0				Net Sales	100.0	100.0
		35.0				Gross Profit	40.2	38.0
		32.7				Operating Expenses	37.4	33.9
		2.3				Operating Profit	2.8	4.2
		-.2				All Other Expenses (net)	1.1	1.0
		2.5				Profit Before Taxes	1.7	3.2
						RATIOS		
		2.3					1.9	2.0
		1.8				Current	1.3	1.5
		1.2					1.1	1.1
		1.0					.9	1.0
		.8				Quick	.6	.8
		.6					.4	.5
		32 11.4					32 11.3	33 11.2
		41 8.9				Sales/Receivables	41 8.9	39 9.4
		60 6.1					49 7.4	57 6.5
		47 7.8					50 7.3	44 8.3
		111 3.3				Cost of Sales/Inventory	90 4.1	83 4.4
		152 2.4					175 2.1	158 2.3
		33 11.0					40 9.1	36 10.3
		62 5.9				Cost of Sales/Payables	56 6.5	50 7.3
		78 4.7					80 4.5	72 5.0
		5.0					8.1	5.6
		8.0				Sales/Working Capital	12.8	12.7
		28.2					50.3	30.6
		16.7					15.3	18.7
		(15) 4.9				EBIT/Interest	7.6	(35) 8.4
		1.6					1.0	2.7
								8.3
						Net Profit + Depr., Dep., Amort./Cur. Mat. L/T/D		(16) 3.9
								1.9
		.1					.1	.1
		.1				Fixed/Worth	.2	.2
		.3					.7	.4
		1.4					1.8	1.2
		1.9				Debt/Worth	2.7	2.2
		5.0					12.6	8.3
		30.9					73.9	53.8
		(16) 15.3				% Profit Before Taxes/Tangible Net Worth	(22) 25.9	(36) 36.9
		2.3					2.5	10.3
		11.5					14.5	15.9
		4.1				% Profit Before Taxes/Total Assets	5.8	7.0
		.9					.1	2.4
		340.0					148.1	197.4
		84.7				Sales/Net Fixed Assets	63.8	54.7
		34.1					22.5	21.3
		3.6					3.8	3.9
		2.8				Sales/Total Assets	2.5	2.6
		1.9					1.4	1.8
		.1					.3	.3
		(10) .3				% Depr., Dep., Amort./Sales	(19) .6	(35) .7
		.5					1.2	1.0
							1.6	.9
						% Officers', Directors' Owners' Comp/Sales	(11) 4.0	(16) 2.1
							5.4	3.2
1247M	12071M	231982M	173275M		92338M	Net Sales ($)	1163852M	1586022M
364M	4688M	71026M	59401M		244505M	Total Assets ($)	601041M	715742M

M = $ thousand MM = $ million

See Pages 9 through 22 for Explanation of Ratios and Data

Comparative Historical Data				Current Data Sorted by Sales					
			Type of Statement						
6	3	1	Unqualified						1
7	9	6	Reviewed	1		1	1	2	1
4	8	5	Compiled			1	3	1	
7	4	6	Tax Returns	2	1	1	1	1	
19	20	10	Other	1			1	6	2
				3 (4/1-9/30/13)			25 (10/1/13-3/31/14)		
4/1/11-3/31/12 ALL	4/1/12-3/31/13 ALL	4/1/13-3/31/14 ALL		0-1MM	1-3MM	3-5MM	5-10MM	10-25MM	25MM & OVER
43	44	28	**NUMBER OF STATEMENTS**	4	1	3	6	10	4
%	%	%	**ASSETS**	%	%	%	%	%	%
5.1	10.1	5.9	Cash & Equivalents					3.1	
30.7	30.7	32.2	Trade Receivables (net)					27.9	
41.9	35.7	41.7	Inventory					43.1	
2.8	1.8	.8	All Other Current					.7	
80.6	78.3	80.6	Total Current					74.9	
8.4	10.6	9.5	Fixed Assets (net)					16.7	
6.2	5.7	4.2	Intangibles (net)					3.3	
4.8	5.4	5.8	All Other Non-Current					5.1	
100.0	100.0	100.0	Total					100.0	
			LIABILITIES						
15.9	14.6	17.0	Notes Payable-Short Term					17.0	
1.4	1.5	.6	Cur. Mat.-L.T.D.					.6	
26.8	26.1	26.8	Trade Payables					24.1	
.1	1.3	.0	Income Taxes Payable					.0	
8.4	5.7	5.8	All Other Current					6.5	
52.6	49.2	50.2	Total Current					48.2	
9.1	5.8	14.8	Long-Term Debt					30.3	
.0	.1	.0	Deferred Taxes					.0	
1.4	5.7	5.9	All Other Non-Current					1.4	
36.9	39.2	29.1	Net Worth					20.0	
100.0	100.0	100.0	Total Liabilities & Net Worth					100.0	
			INCOME DATA						
100.0	100.0	100.0	Net Sales					100.0	
39.4	42.7	40.8	Gross Profit					38.5	
33.9	37.1	36.3	Operating Expenses					35.0	
5.5	5.6	4.6	Operating Profit					3.5	
.5	.1	.3	All Other Expenses (net)					1.2	
5.0	5.5	4.3	Profit Before Taxes					2.3	
			RATIOS						
2.2	3.0	2.0						2.0	
1.5	1.5	1.7	Current					1.7	
1.2	1.1	1.3						1.1	
1.1	1.5	1.0						.9	
.7	.9	.8	Quick					.7	
.4	.5	.5						.4	
34 10.8	**33** 10.9	**32** 11.4						**27** 13.4	
41 8.9	**41** 8.8	**42** 8.7	Sales/Receivables					**42** 8.7	
52 7.0	**54** 6.7	**64** 5.7						**51** 7.2	
47 7.8	**41** 8.8	**51** 7.1						**46** 8.0	
107 3.4	**89** 4.1	**114** 3.2	Cost of Sales/Inventory					**89** 4.1	
174 2.1	**174** 2.1	**159** 2.3						**135** 2.7	
32 11.4	**30** 12.0	**33** 11.0						**33** 11.0	
44 8.3	**63** 5.8	**63** 5.8	Cost of Sales/Payables					**49** 7.4	
78 4.7	**99** 3.7	**104** 3.5						**76** 4.8	
5.0	4.1	5.0						7.2	
9.6	9.0	9.0	Sales/Working Capital					9.5	
21.4	33.0	14.2						283.2	
22.0	30.5	23.6							
(39) 8.5	(37) 5.1	(23) 7.2	EBIT/Interest						
2.6	1.5	2.2							
11.3	6.5								
(13) 3.3	(10) 4.3		Net Profit + Depr., Dep., Amort./Cur. Mat. L/T/D						
2.1	.8								
.1	.1	.0						.0	
.2	.2	.2	Fixed/Worth					.2	
.4	.6	.3						.6	
1.1	.7	1.5						1.2	
2.0	2.0	2.1	Debt/Worth					1.7	
4.1	5.6	5.2						6.1	
56.0	45.2	36.7							
(40) 32.2	(43) 21.0	(26) 19.2	% Profit Before Taxes/Tangible Net Worth						
7.7	2.9	7.3							
23.6	18.6	12.3						17.8	
10.1	4.8	5.4	% Profit Before Taxes/Total Assets					3.2	
1.1	.8	1.0						-2.4	
198.5	123.0	395.2						338.3	
56.7	42.8	68.9	Sales/Net Fixed Assets					75.8	
19.2	12.2	31.8						7.7	
3.8	3.3	3.6						3.5	
2.6	2.4	2.6	Sales/Total Assets					3.1	
1.8	1.7	1.8						2.0	
.2	.2	.1							
(33) .6	(34) .6	(18) .4	% Depr., Dep., Amort./Sales						
1.4	1.7	.7							
.8	1.6	2.1							
(15) 1.5	(20) 2.9	(11) 3.9	% Officers', Directors' Owners' Comp/Sales						
2.9	5.4	5.9							
1265508M	**908900M**	**510913M**	Net Sales ($)	**2153M**	**1397M**	**13315M**	**45402M**	**144916M**	**303730M**
466216M	**465927M**	**379984M**	Total Assets ($)	**1063M**	**743M**	**7815M**	**16987M**	**57587M**	**295789M**

M = $ thousand MM = $ million

See Pages 9 through 22 for Explanation of Ratios and Data

Current Data Sorted by Assets							Comparative Historical Data	
						Type of Statement		
		3	7			Unqualified	12	12
	1	14	1			Reviewed	19	27
1	3	6				Compiled	17	10
2	17	4				Tax Returns	21	18
2	5	15	10	5	2	Other	45	42
	15 (4/1-9/30/13)		83 (10/1/13-3/31/14)				4/1/09-3/31/10 ALL	4/1/10-3/31/11 ALL
0-500M	500M-2MM	2-10MM	10-50MM	50-100MM	100-250MM			
5	26	42	18	5	2	NUMBER OF STATEMENTS	114	109
%	%	%	%	%	%	**ASSETS**	%	%
	6.6	11.3	3.1			Cash & Equivalents	7.1	10.4
	30.4	34.7	27.3			Trade Receivables (net)	32.9	35.0
	37.3	36.3	37.8			Inventory	31.1	28.4
	1.0	3.7	4.8			All Other Current	3.5	3.1
	75.4	86.0	73.1			Total Current	74.7	76.8
	14.6	5.2	7.1			Fixed Assets (net)	13.0	10.7
	2.1	3.9	14.5			Intangibles (net)	6.0	6.6
	8.0	4.9	5.4			All Other Non-Current	6.3	5.9
	100.0	100.0	100.0			Total	100.0	100.0
						LIABILITIES		
	14.7	14.7	11.8			Notes Payable-Short Term	17.2	13.8
	4.3	1.1	2.0			Cur. Mat.-L.T.D.	2.4	1.6
	22.9	25.4	18.9			Trade Payables	20.2	21.2
	.0	1.2	.1			Income Taxes Payable	.1	.2
	8.4	9.0	14.2			All Other Current	9.3	10.4
	50.3	51.3	47.1			Total Current	49.2	47.1
	12.1	3.8	15.2			Long-Term Debt	10.9	8.7
	.0	.3	.0			Deferred Taxes	.1	.2
	1.5	5.3	7.4			All Other Non-Current	6.3	10.0
	36.0	39.3	30.2			Net Worth	33.4	34.0
	100.0	100.0	100.0			Total Liabilties & Net Worth	100.0	100.0
						INCOME DATA		
	100.0	100.0	100.0			Net Sales	100.0	100.0
	42.3	29.3	32.7			Gross Profit	33.7	34.2
	38.9	25.9	26.2			Operating Expenses	29.9	29.9
	3.4	3.4	6.5			Operating Profit	3.8	4.3
	.1	.2	1.2			All Other Expenses (net)	.6	.5
	3.3	3.2	5.3			Profit Before Taxes	3.2	3.8
						RATIOS		
	2.4	2.3	2.2				2.6	2.6
	1.5	1.6	1.6			Current	1.5	1.6
	1.0	1.3	1.3				1.2	1.2
	1.1	1.2	1.0				1.3	1.5
	.7	.9	.6			Quick	.8	.9
	.5	.6	.5				.5	.6
	23 16.1	**31** 11.9	**29** 12.6				**30** 12.3	**26** 14.1
	31 11.8	**40** 9.2	**37** 9.9			Sales/Receivables	**42** 8.8	**39** 9.3
	42 8.7	**60** 6.1	**47** 7.8				**58** 6.2	**56** 6.5
	8 43.2	**17** 21.4	**59** 6.2				**21** 17.2	**22** 16.2
	68 5.4	**64** 5.7	**70** 5.2			Cost of Sales/Inventory	**61** 6.0	**58** 6.3
	140 2.6	**130** 2.8	**130** 2.8				**118** 3.1	**95** 3.8
	19 19.3	**24** 14.9	**22** 16.7				**18** 20.5	**20** 18.5
	38 9.6	**40** 9.1	**34** 10.7			Cost of Sales/Payables	**32** 11.2	**36** 10.3
	59 6.2	**65** 5.6	**61** 6.0				**57** 6.4	**58** 6.3
	5.0	5.0	5.2				5.6	5.7
	13.6	9.2	7.9			Sales/Working Capital	11.6	9.1
	195.9	17.3	25.1				25.3	23.1
	13.1	48.3	11.8				12.3	24.2
	(23) 5.4	(38) 15.2	(17) 6.0			EBIT/Interest	(100) 4.4	(98) 6.5
	1.6	4.1	2.2				1.2	2.4
							7.2	8.1
						Net Profit + Depr., Dep., Amort./Cur. Mat. L/T/D	(25) 3.5	(19) 3.2
							.4	2.4
	.0	.0	.2				.1	.1
	.2	.1	.3			Fixed/Worth	.3	.3
	1.3	.4	-.6				1.3	.8
	.9	1.0	1.4				1.2	.8
	1.7	2.1	3.8			Debt/Worth	2.3	1.9
	4.8	4.5	-7.1				12.5	8.2
	63.0	45.8	25.6				49.9	58.6
	(24) 17.9	(39) 21.6	(13) 17.5			% Profit Before Taxes/Tangible Net Worth	(95) 23.0	(91) 23.5
	1.8	11.2	3.9				5.6	8.9
	23.3	15.2	13.4				14.9	16.8
	7.7	6.6	5.8			% Profit Before Taxes/Total Assets	6.8	6.7
	1.4	4.0	1.9				1.0	2.1
	301.4	367.1	51.6				120.6	131.6
	57.3	102.3	37.9			Sales/Net Fixed Assets	38.3	51.1
	17.7	34.0	20.8				15.3	21.4
	4.9	3.6	3.3				3.6	3.7
	3.3	2.8	2.3			Sales/Total Assets	2.6	2.9
	1.9	2.1	1.4				1.9	2.0
	.3	.1	.4				.3	.2
	(18) .8	(31) .3	(16) .7			% Depr., Dep., Amort./Sales	(91) .6	(85) .5
	1.9	.8	1.3				1.7	1.3
	2.4	1.6					1.3	1.4
	(15) 3.8	(21) 3.1				% Officers', Directors' Owners' Comp/Sales	(52) 3.1	(45) 3.4
	6.1	6.7					5.0	5.0
4871M	122631M	533268M	940891M	427004M	273908M	Net Sales ($)	3049980M	3029967M
1041M	31939M	184041M	389181M	293741M	265868M	Total Assets ($)	1434509M	1270706M

M = $ thousand MM = $ million

See Pages 9 through 22 for Explanation of Ratios and Data

Comparative Historical Data							Current Data Sorted by Sales									
						Type of Statement										
	18		8		10	Unqualified						1		2		7
	24		16		16	Reviewed				1		7		6		2
	12		9		10	Compiled	1			2		4		3		
	18		20		23	Tax Returns	1	7		7		5		2		1
	44		37		39	Other	2	1		5		7		9		15
							15 (4/1-9/30/13)				83 (10/1/13-3/31/14)					
	4/1/11-3/31/12 ALL		4/1/12-3/31/13 ALL		4/1/13-3/31/14 ALL		0-1MM	1-3MM		3-5MM		5-10MM		10-25MM		25MM & OVER
	116		90		98	**NUMBER OF STATEMENTS**	4	8		15		24		22		25
	%		%		%	**ASSETS**	%	%		%		%		%		%
	10.0		8.9		9.4	Cash & Equivalents				3.5		7.9		12.8		5.7
	36.1		34.9		30.2	Trade Receivables (net)				31.1		32.6		31.7		30.0
	30.8		35.0		35.5	Inventory				54.5		33.0		27.0		36.0
	3.0		1.8		2.9	All Other Current				.6		2.5		6.9		1.9
	79.8		80.6		78.0	Total Current				89.7		76.0		78.3		73.6
	8.9		8.5		8.2	Fixed Assets (net)				7.5		8.8		8.6		7.7
	4.6		4.8		7.2	Intangibles (net)				1.3		8.9		7.5		11.8
	6.6		6.0		6.6	All Other Non-Current				1.6		6.3		5.6		7.0
	100.0		100.0		100.0	Total				100.0		100.0		100.0		100.0
						LIABILITIES										
	14.2		17.1		12.8	Notes Payable-Short Term				19.5		14.6		11.9		11.8
	2.4		1.8		2.5	Cur. Mat.-L.T.D.				5.2		.7		2.6		1.8
	21.7		24.9		22.7	Trade Payables				26.8		21.6		22.2		22.8
	.1		.3		.5	Income Taxes Payable				.0		.7		1.5		.1
	12.5		9.3		9.8	All Other Current				6.7		8.6		14.4		10.0
	50.9		53.3		48.2	Total Current				58.2		46.3		52.7		46.4
	7.2		8.5		9.7	Long-Term Debt				6.1		7.9		6.8		10.8
	.2		.1		.2	Deferred Taxes				.0		.1		.5		.1
	7.0		4.4		4.6	All Other Non-Current				7.9		3.7		4.6		4.6
	34.8		33.7		37.3	Net Worth				27.7		42.0		35.5		38.1
	100.0		100.0		100.0	Total Liabilties & Net Worth				100.0		100.0		100.0		100.0
						INCOME DATA										
	100.0		100.0		100.0	Net Sales				100.0		100.0		100.0		100.0
	32.9		32.0		35.5	Gross Profit				41.1		32.7		32.2		29.5
	29.3		27.2		31.2	Operating Expenses				36.4		29.6		26.8		25.7
	3.6		4.8		4.3	Operating Profit				4.7		3.1		5.5		3.8
	.6		.5		.4	All Other Expenses (net)				-.3		.0		.8		.8
	3.0		4.2		3.9	Profit Before Taxes				5.0		3.1		4.7		2.9
						RATIOS										
	2.3		2.4		2.3					2.1		2.1		2.0		2.3
	1.6		1.7		1.6	Current				1.5		1.6		1.6		1.6
	1.2		1.2		1.2					1.2		1.2		1.2		1.3
	1.5		1.5		1.1					1.0		1.4		1.1		1.1
	.9		.9		.8	Quick				.6		.8		.9		.8
	.5		.5		.5					.4		.5		.5		.5
30	12.0	**23**	16.1	**28**	13.0				**30**	12.2	**22**	16.6	**19**	19.7	**30**	12.0
41	9.0	**38**	9.5	**36**	10.0	Sales/Receivables			**38**	9.6	**35**	10.3	**35**	10.3	**37**	9.9
57	6.4	**56**	6.5	**55**	6.6				**56**	6.5	**55**	6.6	**55**	6.6	**48**	7.6
16	22.2	**24**	15.4	**24**	15.3				**63**	5.8	**16**	23.2	**17**	21.7	**56**	6.5
60	6.1	**59**	6.2	**66**	5.5	Cost of Sales/Inventory			**135**	2.7	**65**	5.6	**52**	7.0	**72**	5.1
114	3.2	**122**	3.0	**130**	2.8				**215**	1.7	**135**	2.7	**78**	4.7	**118**	3.1
18	20.5	**21**	17.5	**23**	15.7				**36**	10.1	**20**	18.2	**17**	21.1	**25**	14.4
34	10.7	**38**	9.7	**38**	9.6	Cost of Sales/Payables			**54**	6.8	**38**	9.5	**32**	11.3	**35**	10.4
64	5.7	**59**	6.2	**63**	5.8				**79**	4.6	**60**	6.1	**47**	7.7	**63**	5.8
	5.7		5.6		5.0					4.7		5.7		5.6		6.4
	9.7		8.8		9.6	Sales/Working Capital				10.9		10.5		14.1		8.1
	24.2		27.1		23.0					28.5		29.9		21.2		18.7
	17.0		16.3		21.8					15.9		28.3		46.3		18.5
(100)	5.0	(79)	6.0	(87)	8.6	EBIT/Interest				10.3	(22)	13.8	(20)	8.6	(23)	5.7
	2.0		2.1		2.9					2.3		5.3		3.5		2.9
	9.9		5.1		11.0											
(21)	2.3	(18)	2.0	(17)	4.2	Net Profit + Depr., Dep., Amort./Cur. Mat. L/T/D										
	.6		.4		.3											
	.1		.1		.0					.0		.0		.1		.1
	.2		.2		.2	Fixed/Worth				.2		.2		.2		.2
	.6		.6		.6					1.5		.8		.6		.5
	.9		.9		1.0					1.6		.9		1.1		1.1
	2.0		2.2		2.0	Debt/Worth				3.0		2.1		2.8		1.5
	6.0		5.2		5.7					10.2		5.2		6.6		6.7
	49.9		51.7		46.2					59.2		53.3		56.9		30.1
(103)	21.2	(79)	22.4	(85)	20.2	% Profit Before Taxes/Tangible Net Worth			(12)	31.2	(22)	14.4	(19)	30.4	(21)	23.4
	5.5		6.3		6.7					7.8		6.9		13.7		7.6
	14.2		19.3		14.5					23.6		14.9		16.2		12.6
	5.5		6.9		6.2	% Profit Before Taxes/Total Assets				8.8		6.6		8.1		5.7
	1.8		1.9		2.7					1.7		3.9		4.1		2.7
	190.3		120.5		175.2					244.9		394.0		210.6		71.2
	54.4		63.1		54.4	Sales/Net Fixed Assets				73.6		42.3		67.5		44.6
	22.3		22.8		21.6					47.4		20.8		19.6		20.4
	3.7		4.1		3.8					3.4		4.5		4.2		3.3
	2.8		2.9		2.8	Sales/Total Assets				2.7		2.6		3.2		2.4
	2.0		2.0		1.8					1.8		2.0		2.2		1.6
	.3		.3		.3					.3		.1		.2		.4
(90)	.6	(61)	.7	(71)	.6	% Depr., Dep., Amort./Sales			(10)	.4	(19)	.8	(16)	.4	(21)	.7
	1.2		1.2		1.1					1.3		1.1		.9		1.2
	2.2		1.9		2.2							1.7		2.5		
(45)	4.7	(42)	3.1	(40)	3.8	% Officers', Directors' Owners' Comp/Sales					(13)	3.1	(10)	3.9		
	8.7		7.1		6.4							4.9		6.6		
	3323840M		**2257892M**		**2302573M**	Net Sales ($)	**2019M**	**14885M**		**62488M**		**167815M**		**344454M**		**1710912M**
	1290912M		**1081655M**		**1165811M**	Total Assets ($)	**1040M**	**7662M**		**24676M**		**74653M**		**155054M**		**902726M**

Current Data Sorted by Assets							Comparative Historical Data	
Type of Statement								
Unqualified		1	8	50	16	13	119	128
Reviewed		5	62	47	8	2	148	168
Compiled	4	24	50	19		1	100	95
Tax Returns	4	26	34	3			59	80
Other	5	26	69	102	33	24	266	250
	90 (4/1-9/30/13)			546 (10/1/13-3/31/14)			4/1/09-3/31/10	4/1/10-3/31/11
	0-500M	500M-2MM	2-10MM	10-50MM	50-100MM	100-250MM	ALL	ALL
NUMBER OF STATEMENTS	13	82	223	221	57	40	692	721
ASSETS	%	%	%	%	%	%	%	%
Cash & Equivalents	21.5	9.5	7.4	7.3	3.1	5.5	8.9	8.1
Trade Receivables (net)	24.7	36.0	32.8	28.0	25.9	22.2	28.4	30.0
Inventory	18.8	35.9	41.1	45.2	46.7	45.3	38.1	39.9
All Other Current	1.6	1.1	1.4	1.5	1.4	3.5	2.5	2.3
Total Current	66.6	82.5	82.8	81.9	77.1	76.5	77.9	80.3
Fixed Assets (net)	27.0	12.7	11.1	12.7	14.1	13.7	15.1	12.5
Intangibles (net)	.5	1.8	1.9	2.1	4.7	5.4	2.6	2.6
All Other Non-Current	5.9	3.0	4.2	3.3	4.1	4.4	4.5	4.5
Total	100.0	100.0	100.0	100.0	100.0	100.0	100.0	100.0
LIABILITIES								
Notes Payable-Short Term	15.2	18.3	21.4	22.0	19.3	13.7	18.2	18.4
Cur. Mat.-L.T.D.	3.1	2.5	1.4	2.2	1.5	1.0	3.1	2.3
Trade Payables	16.2	23.8	20.3	18.1	16.6	14.8	18.4	21.1
Income Taxes Payable	.2	.0	.1	.1	.2	.2	.2	.2
All Other Current	16.8	3.8	5.0	5.7	6.6	4.0	6.4	5.9
Total Current	51.5	48.3	48.2	48.1	44.2	33.7	46.3	47.9
Long-Term Debt	12.0	10.8	7.1	8.0	13.0	16.6	9.8	8.3
Deferred Taxes	.0	.1	.1	.3	.7	.4	.4	.3
All Other Non-Current	4.7	4.7	3.7	5.0	3.8	3.3	5.5	5.8
Net Worth	31.8	36.1	40.9	38.7	38.4	46.0	38.0	37.8
Total Liabilties & Net Worth	100.0	100.0	100.0	100.0	100.0	100.0	100.0	100.0
INCOME DATA								
Net Sales	100.0	100.0	100.0	100.0	100.0	100.0	100.0	100.0
Gross Profit	29.3	23.4	20.6	16.6	14.3	13.7	19.6	19.5
Operating Expenses	25.4	20.6	17.2	13.1	10.5	8.7	18.1	15.8
Operating Profit	3.9	2.8	3.4	3.5	3.8	5.0	1.5	3.7
All Other Expenses (net)	-.1	1.1	.3	.6	.7	1.3	.8	.7
Profit Before Taxes	4.0	1.7	3.1	2.9	3.2	3.6	.7	3.0
RATIOS								
Current	3.9	4.0	3.3	2.8	3.7	4.4	3.1	2.9
	1.7	1.7	1.7	1.6	1.9	2.5	1.7	1.7
	.8	1.1	1.2	1.2	1.1	1.6	1.2	1.2
Quick	2.5	1.8	1.5	1.3	1.3	1.6	1.4	1.3
	1.4	1.0	.8	.6	.7	.9	.8	.8
	.6	.6	.5	.4	.4	.5	.5	.5
Sales/Receivables	**0** UND	**20** 17.9	**27** 13.3	**32** 11.3	**33** 11.0	**33** 11.0	**31** 11.9	**31** 11.7
	23 15.6	**33** 11.0	**38** 9.5	**40** 9.1	**41** 9.0	**38** 9.6	**39** 9.3	**42** 8.7
	34 10.6	**43** 8.4	**54** 6.7	**51** 7.2	**46** 7.9	**47** 7.8	**52** 7.0	**52** 7.1
Cost of Sales/Inventory	**0** UND	**20** 18.1	**34** 10.7	**54** 6.8	**57** 6.4	**57** 6.4	**39** 9.5	**40** 9.1
	8 45.7	**40** 9.1	**63** 5.8	**83** 4.4	**94** 3.9	**94** 3.9	**70** 5.2	**74** 4.9
	46 8.0	**79** 4.6	**104** 3.5	**130** 2.8	**122** 3.0	**135** 2.7	**113** 3.2	**121** 3.0
Cost of Sales/Payables	**0** UND	**9** 41.7	**15** 24.2	**17** 21.2	**17** 20.9	**16** 22.4	**15** 24.2	**18** 20.3
	2 151.6	**24** 14.9	**29** 12.6	**30** 12.1	**24** 15.2	**28** 13.2	**27** 13.4	**31** 11.8
	32 11.4	**41** 8.9	**49** 7.4	**41** 8.8	**40** 9.1	**40** 9.2	**44** 8.3	**49** 7.5
Sales/Working Capital	9.2	6.2	4.6	4.1	3.7	3.6	4.0	4.2
	16.3	13.8	10.2	8.1	5.9	5.1	8.3	8.5
	NM	53.6	24.0	19.8	30.3	9.7	21.0	21.4
EBIT/Interest	68.7	10.8	15.7	14.6	18.2	12.7	8.8	12.9
	(11) 18.3	(71) 3.3	(207) 5.2	(203) 4.5	(54) 4.7	(36) 6.2	(629) 2.3	(652) 4.7
	3.0	-.1	1.8	1.5	1.9	2.4	-.7	1.8
Net Profit + Depr., Dep., Amort./Cur. Mat. L/T/D			7.3	9.3	14.6	10.4	6.3	10.3
			(22) 3.3	(54) 4.4	(16) 5.5	(14) 4.5	(161) 1.9	(154) 3.2
			1.6	1.2	.9	1.9	.3	1.2
Fixed/Worth	.0	.0	.0	.1	.1	.1	.1	.0
	.5	.2	.2	.2	.4	.3	.3	.2
	1.7	1.0	.5	.7	.9	.7	.8	.7
Debt/Worth	.4	.7	.6	.8	.9	.4	.7	.7
	2.1	1.8	2.0	2.0	2.0	1.5	1.7	1.9
	13.1	10.4	4.5	4.1	4.5	4.4	4.6	4.3
% Profit Before Taxes/Tangible Net Worth	76.7	43.0	36.0	30.8	33.5	36.7	28.1	39.6
	(11) 30.4	(72) 12.0	(212) 17.2	(208) 16.3	(54) 17.8	(36) 15.0	(627) 8.7	(653) 16.7
	5.7	-1.3	4.6	6.2	6.9	6.3	-5.3	5.4
% Profit Before Taxes/Total Assets	50.2	12.8	12.5	10.4	9.1	10.8	10.0	12.0
	24.9	3.6	5.5	5.1	4.7	6.5	2.8	5.8
	4.1	-.8	1.5	1.2	1.4	2.7	-3.3	1.5
Sales/Net Fixed Assets	UND	459.3	397.1	133.5	92.5	215.1	142.7	209.9
	55.9	68.1	57.5	29.0	19.1	24.6	28.4	40.2
	25.5	24.6	15.9	11.8	10.1	6.7	9.0	11.6
Sales/Total Assets	19.5	5.6	3.8	2.9	2.9	2.6	3.2	3.3
	6.0	4.0	2.8	2.3	2.2	2.1	2.4	2.4
	3.4	2.5	2.1	1.7	1.6	1.5	1.7	1.8
% Depr., Dep., Amort./Sales		.1	.2	.3	.4	.2	.3	.3
		(54) .6	(166) .6	(196) .7	(50) .6	(36) .6	(575) .9	(575) .8
		1.2	1.4	1.2	1.6	1.9	1.8	1.5
% Officers', Directors' Owners' Comp/Sales		1.7	1.1	.5			1.3	1.1
		(43) 2.9	(111) 2.2	(60) 1.3			(249) 2.3	(267) 2.1
		5.3	3.7	2.6			4.7	4.3
Net Sales ($)	**44351M**	**456495M**	**3499485M**	**12506675M**	**9957285M**	**13597423M**	**38713803M**	**39300877M**
Total Assets ($)	**4445M**	**105370M**	**1117377M**	**5140747M**	**4147319M**	**6231367M**	**16272173M**	**17072856M**

M = $ thousand MM = $ million

See Pages 9 through 22 for Explanation of Ratios and Data

Comparative Historical Data				Current Data Sorted by Sales					
			Type of Statement						
115	83	88	Unqualified				2	7	79
166	126	124	Reviewed		3	2	11	50	58
86	70	98	Compiled	3	7	11	29	29	19
90	65	67	Tax Returns	1	14	3	24	20	5
294	293	259	Other	1	12	13	29	57	147
					90 (4/1-9/30/13)		546 (10/1/13-3/31/14)		
4/1/11-3/31/12 ALL	**4/1/12-3/31/13 ALL**	**4/1/13-3/31/14 ALL**		**0-1MM**	**1-3MM**	**3-5MM**	**5-10MM**	**10-25MM**	**25MM & OVER**
751	637	636	**NUMBER OF STATEMENTS**	5	36	29	95	163	308
%	%	%	**ASSETS**	%	%	%	%	%	%
7.1	7.4	7.4	Cash & Equivalents		11.5	6.5	10.3	7.4	5.9
31.8	29.4	30.1	Trade Receivables (net)		25.4	31.6	29.7	32.7	29.6
40.8	41.3	42.2	Inventory		36.1	41.7	40.7	39.6	45.1
2.1	1.8	1.5	All Other Current		.6	.9	1.8	1.3	1.7
81.8	79.8	81.2	Total Current		73.5	80.7	82.5	81.0	82.2
11.8	13.2	12.6	Fixed Assets (net)		19.9	12.7	11.1	12.3	12.1
2.6	2.3	2.4	Intangibles (net)		1.5	.2	1.5	3.2	2.5
3.8	4.8	3.8	All Other Non-Current		5.1	6.3	4.8	3.5	3.2
100.0	100.0	100.0	Total		100.0	100.0	100.0	100.0	100.0
			LIABILITIES						
19.3	20.3	20.4	Notes Payable-Short Term		14.1	24.2	18.7	21.3	21.1
2.5	2.1	1.8	Cur. Mat.-L.T.D.		1.7	1.8	3.1	1.3	1.7
20.4	18.3	19.2	Trade Payables		12.6	23.7	19.5	20.7	18.8
.1	.2	.1	Income Taxes Payable		.0	.0	.0	.1	.1
6.3	6.0	5.4	All Other Current		6.0	4.4	4.7	5.3	5.8
48.7	46.8	47.0	Total Current		34.3	54.1	46.1	48.8	47.5
8.5	9.8	9.1	Long-Term Debt		12.9	9.3	9.8	7.4	9.3
.3	.3	.2	Deferred Taxes		.1	.0	.2	.1	.3
5.0	4.5	4.3	All Other Non-Current		5.8	5.1	4.2	4.5	3.7
37.5	38.6	39.4	Net Worth		46.9	31.5	39.6	39.2	39.2
100.0	100.0	100.0	Total Liabilties & Net Worth		100.0	100.0	100.0	100.0	100.0
			INCOME DATA						
100.0	100.0	100.0	Net Sales		100.0	100.0	100.0	100.0	100.0
18.7	18.9	18.8	Gross Profit		32.4	26.0	23.6	19.8	14.3
14.2	15.1	15.3	Operating Expenses		29.3	24.3	19.6	16.3	10.9
4.5	3.9	3.5	Operating Profit		3.1	1.7	4.1	3.5	3.4
.6	.7	.6	All Other Expenses (net)		1.0	.3	.5	.5	.5
3.8	3.2	2.9	Profit Before Taxes		2.1	1.4	3.6	3.0	2.8
			RATIOS						
2.9	3.1	3.3			10.2	3.1	4.5	2.7	3.0
1.7	1.7	1.7	Current		3.6	1.2	1.8	1.6	1.7
1.2	1.2	1.2			1.4	1.0	1.3	1.2	1.2
1.4	1.4	1.5			3.8	1.0	2.1	1.5	1.3
.8	.8	.8	Quick		1.5	.6	.9	.8	.7
.5	.5	.5			.9	.5	.4	.5	.5
30 12.3	28 13.2	29 12.4			27 13.6	27 13.3	21 17.0	29 12.6	31 11.8
40 9.2	36 10.1	39 9.4	Sales/Receivables		37 9.8	39 9.4	37 9.8	39 9.4	39 9.4
50 7.3	47 7.7	50 7.3			56 6.5	54 6.7	51 7.2	52 7.0	49 7.5
36 10.0	35 10.4	37 9.9			29 12.6	26 14.3	29 12.5	34 10.8	45 8.2
70 5.2	74 4.9	73 5.0	Cost of Sales/Inventory		74 4.9	66 5.5	60 6.1	66 5.5	76 4.8
107 3.4	114 3.2	114 3.2			203 1.8	146 2.5	114 3.2	114 3.2	111 3.3
15 24.5	13 28.2	16 23.5			5 75.4	15 25.0	14 25.7	15 24.3	17 21.9
28 13.0	25 14.4	29 12.8	Cost of Sales/Payables		22 16.3	38 9.5	28 12.9	29 12.5	28 13.0
45 8.2	40 9.1	43 8.5			45 8.2	56 6.5	55 6.6	46 7.9	40 9.2
4.8	4.5	4.4			2.3	5.5	4.0	4.5	4.4
9.2	9.1	8.9	Sales/Working Capital		7.0	15.2	8.8	10.5	8.3
21.6	22.6	23.7			21.4	-141.7	22.1	27.5	21.1
17.5	12.9	15.1			14.5	6.4	15.1	16.0	14.8
(684) 6.6	(574) 5.0	(582) 4.7	EBIT/Interest		(29) 3.5	(26) 2.3	(87) 5.2	(153) 4.6	(285) 5.1
2.4	1.9	1.7			.2	-.9	1.6	1.8	2.0
15.0	10.9	8.5						7.7	10.0
(149) 4.9	(115) 3.9	(113) 4.1	Net Profit + Depr., Dep., Amort./Cur. Mat. L/T/D					(20) 4.8	(80) 4.5
1.9	1.7	1.6						1.6	1.8
.0	.0	.0			.0	.0	.0	.0	.1
.2	.2	.2	Fixed/Worth		.3	.2	.2	.2	.2
.7	.7	.7			1.3	1.2	.8	.6	.7
.8	.7	.7			.2	1.1	.5	.7	.8
1.9	1.8	2.0	Debt/Worth		1.2	1.9	2.1	2.0	2.0
4.7	4.9	4.6			4.1	8.4	7.6	5.1	4.1
48.6	37.0	33.7			39.1	28.0	39.8	37.0	32.8
(696) 22.6	(583) 17.9	(593) 16.7	% Profit Before Taxes/Tangible Net Worth		(34) 9.6	(25) 2.3	(85) 17.3	(152) 17.2	(293) 17.4
8.6	7.5	4.5			-3.8	-6.1	2.6	6.0	7.5
14.8	12.4	11.6			11.9	6.6	15.7	13.0	10.3
7.3	5.8	5.3	% Profit Before Taxes/Total Assets		5.9	1.1	5.3	5.1	5.6
2.6	1.9	1.2			-1.3	-3.4	.6	1.6	2.0
266.0	215.6	225.6			177.0	110.9	223.9	344.6	226.4
43.7	35.2	38.3	Sales/Net Fixed Assets		24.5	57.8	57.5	42.3	33.0
15.0	13.6	12.6			5.5	28.5	15.9	12.6	12.2
3.6	3.7	3.6			3.6	4.1	4.0	3.9	3.2
2.7	2.6	2.5	Sales/Total Assets		2.3	3.0	2.6	2.7	2.5
2.0	1.9	1.9			1.5	1.8	2.0	1.9	1.9
.2	.2	.2			.4	.2	.3	.2	.2
(589) .6	(510) .6	(507) .7	% Depr., Dep., Amort./Sales		(25) .9	(21) .4	(68) .8	(123) .7	(269) .6
1.2	1.2	1.4			2.8	1.2	1.6	1.5	1.1
.9	.9	.9			2.7	1.9	1.7	.7	.5
(273) 1.8	(221) 2.0	(228) 1.9	% Officers', Directors' Owners' Comp/Sales		(18) 5.3	(13) 3.3	(54) 2.9	(76) 1.6	(66) 1.0
4.1	4.4	4.0			7.6	5.5	5.0	3.0	2.0
49372292M	44383274M	40061714M	Net Sales ($)	2134M	78709M	115597M	701963M	2719988M	36443323M
19572441M	17410632M	16746625M	Total Assets ($)	5048M	51557M	47741M	300534M	1188726M	15153019M

M = $ thousand MM = $ million

See Pages 9 through 22 for Explanation of Ratios and Data

Current Data Sorted by Assets							Comparative Historical Data	
						Type of Statement		
	1		4	2	2	Unqualified	10	7
	1	2	5			Reviewed	14	11
	4	2	1			Compiled	5	7
2	5	2				Tax Returns	7	4
	4	6	4	2	2	Other	20	33
	4 (4/1-9/30/13)		47 (10/1/13-3/31/14)				4/1/09-3/31/10	4/1/10-3/31/11
0-500M	500M-2MM	2-10MM	10-50MM	50-100MM	100-250MM		ALL	ALL
2	15	12	14	4	4	NUMBER OF STATEMENTS	56	62
%	%	%	%	%	%	**ASSETS**	%	%
	22.9	14.1	5.8			Cash & Equivalents	14.5	12.7
	21.1	35.3	31.0			Trade Receivables (net)	29.2	30.5
	19.2	20.6	32.0			Inventory	24.0	22.5
	3.2	2.2	5.5			All Other Current	5.7	3.5
	66.4	72.2	74.2			Total Current	73.4	69.3
	18.6	22.8	17.5			Fixed Assets (net)	16.5	19.6
	4.5	3.0	2.1			Intangibles (net)	2.5	2.1
	10.5	2.0	6.1			All Other Non-Current	7.6	9.0
	100.0	100.0	100.0			Total	100.0	100.0
						LIABILITIES		
	12.3	16.9	13.5			Notes Payable-Short Term	14.5	12.4
	1.6	1.2	1.1			Cur. Mat.-L.T.D.	3.5	4.9
	17.2	24.3	20.6			Trade Payables	16.0	19.3
	.0	.3	.1			Income Taxes Payable	.5	.1
	12.9	4.5	8.9			All Other Current	11.3	8.6
	44.0	47.3	44.1			Total Current	45.8	45.4
	16.8	9.1	5.2			Long-Term Debt	14.9	11.2
	.0	.0	.6			Deferred Taxes	.0	.2
	5.9	.7	.6			All Other Non-Current	3.5	4.3
	33.2	42.9	49.5			Net Worth	35.7	39.0
	100.0	100.0	100.0			Total Liabilties & Net Worth	100.0	100.0
						INCOME DATA		
	100.0	100.0	100.0			Net Sales	100.0	100.0
	23.6	20.1	11.1			Gross Profit	18.6	21.7
	19.8	14.2	7.5			Operating Expenses	13.0	17.1
	3.8	5.9	3.6			Operating Profit	5.6	4.6
	-.3	-.3	.1			All Other Expenses (net)	1.7	.5
	4.1	6.2	3.5			Profit Before Taxes	3.9	4.2
						RATIOS		
	3.8	2.8	2.9				3.0	3.2
	1.5	1.4	1.7			Current	1.7	1.7
	.8	1.0	1.3				1.1	1.0
	3.4	2.0	1.7				1.7	1.6
	.9	1.1	1.0			Quick	1.0	1.0
	.4	.6	.6				.6	.6
	4 81.2	**23** 15.8	**26** 14.0				**19** 18.8	**23** 15.9
	18 20.7	**59** 6.2	**35** 10.3			Sales/Receivables	**33** 11.1	**36** 10.1
	43 8.5	**72** 5.1	**47** 7.7				**46** 8.0	**47** 7.7
	0 UND	**0** UND	**18** 20.3				**0** UND	**0** UND
	17 21.9	**41** 8.8	**40** 9.1			Cost of Sales/Inventory	**35** 10.5	**35** 10.3
	54 6.7	**79** 4.6	**72** 5.1				**72** 5.0	**72** 5.1
	1 466.0	**23** 15.8	**11** 32.6				**8** 44.1	**15** 23.7
	23 16.1	**40** 9.1	**22** 16.4			Cost of Sales/Payables	**22** 16.8	**24** 15.0
	81 4.5	**59** 6.2	**32** 11.4				**35** 10.3	**42** 8.8
	5.9	5.3	5.7				4.9	5.7
	35.3	12.1	8.2			Sales/Working Capital	10.8	9.6
	-25.8	NM	38.4				43.0	313.8
	9.4	81.0	52.0				20.8	25.1
	(11) 4.5	(10) 8.3	20.8			EBIT/Interest	(52) 6.4	(53) 8.2
	1.2	1.9	2.6				1.6	1.0
							10.0	17.0
						Net Profit + Depr., Dep., Amort./Cur. Mat. L/T/D	(13) 2.3	(13) 3.1
							-.7	.3
	.0	.1	.1				.0	.0
	.6	.7	.4			Fixed/Worth	.3	.2
	1.6	1.9	.8				1.4	1.1
	.3	.5	.6				.7	.4
	3.6	2.0	1.0			Debt/Worth	1.9	1.4
	30.6	5.9	1.9				8.3	5.6
	123.0	35.3	38.0				37.9	43.3
	(13) 49.6	(10) 16.3	22.5			% Profit Before Taxes/Tangible Net Worth	(48) 19.2	(56) 22.2
	9.7	6.3	8.9				4.3	5.1
	13.8	21.0	18.0				15.6	20.0
	9.5	7.3	13.3			% Profit Before Taxes/Total Assets	7.0	11.1
	3.1	2.5	2.1				1.4	.1
	UND	270.9	54.9				543.9	477.5
	81.5	15.4	29.6			Sales/Net Fixed Assets	45.0	39.6
	9.3	5.9	9.6				9.4	6.5
	7.3	3.3	4.3				4.7	4.2
	2.7	2.5	3.3			Sales/Total Assets	2.9	2.8
	1.9	1.8	2.0				1.6	1.4
	.3	.5	.2				.1	.1
	(10) 2.8	(10) 2.2	(13) .6			% Depr., Dep., Amort./Sales	(40) .9	(46) .8
	4.8	3.9	1.4				4.3	2.7
							.8	1.1
						% Officers', Directors' Owners' Comp/Sales	(17) 1.5	(15) 3.5
							3.1	5.5
1830M	**88015M**	**171566M**	**1342188M**	**1149159M**	**1455741M**	Net Sales ($)	**3936119M**	**3953463M**
337M	**15270M**	**63468M**	**368290M**	**314889M**	**559124M**	Total Assets ($)	**1533598M**	**1743237M**

M = $ thousand MM = $ million

See Pages 9 through 22 for Explanation of Ratios and Data

Comparative Historical Data / Current Data Sorted by Sales

		4/1/11-3/31/12 ALL		4/1/12-3/31/13 ALL		4/1/13-3/31/14 ALL	0-1MM	1-3MM	3-5MM	5-10MM	10-25MM		25MM & OVER
Type of Statement													
Unqualified		8		8		9					1		8
Reviewed		15		8		8				1	1		6
Compiled		4		5		7		2	2				3
Tax Returns		7		6		9	1	5	1	2			
Other		24		21		18	1	1	2	3	3		8
							4 (4/1-9/30/13)			47 (10/1/13-3/31/14)			
NUMBER OF STATEMENTS		58		48		51	2	8	5	6	5		25
ASSETS		%		%		%	%	%	%	%	%		%
Cash & Equivalents		18.0		19.6		15.2							9.9
Trade Receivables (net)		33.5		32.4		27.4							29.6
Inventory		21.1		22.0		25.9							29.3
All Other Current		2.8		2.0		3.8							5.0
Total Current		75.4		75.9		72.3							73.8
Fixed Assets (net)		16.7		12.5		17.7							18.2
Intangibles (net)		1.2		1.4		3.7							3.2
All Other Non-Current		6.7		10.2		6.4							4.8
Total		100.0		100.0		100.0							100.0
LIABILITIES													
Notes Payable-Short Term		8.1		13.0		12.9							12.6
Cur. Mat.-L.T.D.		2.1		1.2		2.5							4.0
Trade Payables		24.3		18.4		20.9							21.5
Income Taxes Payable		.1		.1		.1							.0
All Other Current		8.2		13.2		15.1							10.7
Total Current		42.8		45.9		51.5							48.9
Long-Term Debt		10.7		7.0		9.3							5.2
Deferred Taxes		.0		.1		.2							.3
All Other Non-Current		3.4		6.4		2.5							1.3
Net Worth		43.1		40.5		36.6							44.3
Total Liabilities & Net Worth		100.0		100.0		100.0							100.0
INCOME DATA													
Net Sales		100.0		100.0		100.0							100.0
Gross Profit		14.0		15.9		17.5							9.7
Operating Expenses		9.0		10.9		13.1							6.2
Operating Profit		5.0		4.9		4.3							3.5
All Other Expenses (net)		.5		.1		-.1							.1
Profit Before Taxes		4.4		4.9		4.4							3.4
RATIOS													
Current		3.1		3.1		3.2							3.0
		1.9		1.8		1.5							1.3
		1.1		1.1		1.0							1.1
Quick		1.8		2.2		1.7							1.7
		1.1		1.1		.9							.9
		.7		.5		.5							.6
Sales/Receivables	16	22.3	24	15.3	14	26.5						26	14.0
	33	11.2	35	10.4	35	10.5						36	10.1
	46	7.9	48	7.6	51	7.1						51	7.2
Cost of Sales/Inventory	0	UND	0	UND	5	66.4						11	33.6
	19	19.1	24	15.3	36	10.0						37	9.9
	50	7.3	70	5.2	73	5.0						73	5.0
Cost of Sales/Payables	15	24.5	9	40.2	13	28.7						12	29.4
	24	15.2	22	16.3	25	14.4						22	16.3
	35	10.5	33	11.2	51	7.1						32	11.4
Sales/Working Capital		6.1		6.2		5.7							5.6
		18.0		11.0		15.0							25.9
		88.7		73.0		230.7							92.5
EBIT/Interest		38.9		39.1		33.7							44.9
	(49)	12.6	(39)	10.8	(42)	8.9						(24)	12.1
		4.6		1.6		2.1							2.3
Net Profit + Depr., Dep., Amort./Cur. Mat. L/T/D													
Fixed/Worth		.0		.0		.1							.1
		.2		.1		.4							.3
		1.2		.6		1.1							1.0
Debt/Worth		.6		.6		.5							.6
		1.3		1.3		1.2							1.1
		4.1		3.7		7.1							4.9
% Profit Before Taxes/Tangible Net Worth		63.4		59.0		48.1							41.3
	(54)	33.9	(42)	22.9	(45)	19.6						(24)	17.8
		16.7		4.9		7.2							7.5
% Profit Before Taxes/Total Assets		26.1		29.4		18.1							19.4
		13.8		10.5		8.6							8.6
		4.9		1.4		3.0							2.2
Sales/Net Fixed Assets		999.8		999.8		354.0							201.2
		58.0		64.7		33.4							47.2
		9.4		11.3		8.8							9.2
Sales/Total Assets		5.9		5.5		4.2							4.9
		3.9		3.0		2.8							3.3
		2.4		2.1		1.9							2.0
% Depr., Dep., Amort./Sales		.1		.1		.2							.2
	(45)	.6	(34)	.6	(41)	.7						(22)	.6
		1.9		1.9		2.5							1.8
% Officers', Directors' Owners' Comp/Sales		.7		.8		1.2							
	(18)	1.7	(17)	1.7	(12)	2.2							
		3.5		3.2		4.3							
Net Sales ($)		7358392M		4085876M		4208499M	1350M	15050M	18548M	42606M	65173M		4065772M
Total Assets ($)		1805562M		1074991M		1321378M	837M	7821M	6883M	22814M	21532M		1261491M

M = $ thousand MM = $ million

See Pages 9 through 22 for Explanation of Ratios and Data

Current Data Sorted by Assets							Comparative Historical Data	
						Type of Statement		
1	1	11	33	16	15	Unqualified	61	70
1	8	59	51	3		Reviewed	147	144
4	18	46	3	1		Compiled	90	90
25	38	32	7			Tax Returns	86	110
10	43	61	80	14	15	Other	219	232
	102 (4/1-9/30/13)		494 (10/1/13-3/31/14)				**4/1/09-3/31/10 ALL**	**4/1/10-3/31/11 ALL**
0-500M	**500M-2MM**	**2-10MM**	**10-50MM**	**50-100MM**	**100-250MM**			
41	108	209	174	34	30	**NUMBER OF STATEMENTS**	603	646
%	%	%	%	%	%	**ASSETS**	%	%
18.9	14.2	9.9	6.6	8.1	7.5	Cash & Equivalents	9.1	9.0
30.5	28.9	36.8	35.5	34.4	37.8	Trade Receivables (net)	34.9	36.5
23.6	33.4	33.3	34.0	27.2	28.9	Inventory	33.7	32.8
4.0	2.5	2.2	3.1	3.1	5.4	All Other Current	2.5	2.7
77.0	79.0	82.2	79.1	72.7	79.6	Total Current	80.2	80.9
8.3	12.2	10.2	11.3	11.5	9.5	Fixed Assets (net)	11.2	10.2
4.2	3.1	2.9	5.4	11.0	7.7	Intangibles (net)	3.3	3.2
10.6	5.7	4.7	4.1	4.7	3.2	All Other Non-Current	5.3	5.6
100.0	100.0	100.0	100.0	100.0	100.0	Total	100.0	100.0
						LIABILITIES		
18.6	14.7	12.5	13.3	9.1	8.1	Notes Payable-Short Term	14.3	13.4
3.1	1.3	1.5	2.3	1.2	.5	Cur. Mat.-L.T.D.	2.4	1.7
17.9	23.2	23.8	21.0	17.0	16.4	Trade Payables	21.1	21.9
.8	.2	.2	.2	.1	.1	Income Taxes Payable	.1	.2
17.6	10.5	8.0	9.1	9.2	11.3	All Other Current	8.4	8.6
58.1	49.9	46.0	45.9	36.7	36.4	Total Current	46.2	45.8
11.7	7.1	8.3	6.6	8.3	8.1	Long-Term Debt	7.9	7.8
.0	.1	.2	.4	.5	.5	Deferred Taxes	.2	.2
11.5	8.6	4.4	4.6	4.6	1.3	All Other Non-Current	5.1	4.6
18.7	34.2	41.1	42.6	49.8	53.7	Net Worth	40.7	41.5
100.0	100.0	100.0	100.0	100.0	100.0	Total Liabilties & Net Worth	100.0	100.0
						INCOME DATA		
100.0	100.0	100.0	100.0	100.0	100.0	Net Sales	100.0	100.0
40.5	35.2	29.9	25.7	24.5	21.7	Gross Profit	29.5	29.0
34.6	32.6	25.1	20.0	22.0	17.6	Operating Expenses	26.6	25.2
5.9	2.5	4.8	5.7	2.4	4.1	Operating Profit	2.9	3.8
1.2	.2	.3	.3	.1	.2	All Other Expenses (net)	.4	.4
4.7	2.3	4.5	5.5	2.4	3.9	Profit Before Taxes	2.5	3.4
						RATIOS		
2.8	2.7	2.8	2.6	3.2	3.1		2.8	2.8
1.5	1.7	1.8	1.7	2.0	2.2	Current	1.8	1.8
.9	1.1	1.4	1.3	1.5	1.7		1.3	1.3
1.5	1.4	1.5	1.5	2.0	1.8		1.6	1.7
.9	.9	1.0	.9	1.2	1.4	Quick	.9	1.0
.5	.5	.6	.7	.8	.8		.6	.7
0 UND	**16** 22.2	**33** 11.2	**39** 9.3	**44** 8.3	**49** 7.5		**35** 10.3	**36** 10.1
28 13.2	**31** 11.7	**43** 8.5	**51** 7.2	**58** 6.3	**54** 6.7	Sales/Receivables	**47** 7.8	**48** 7.5
53 6.9	**43** 8.4	**55** 6.6	**61** 6.0	**63** 5.8	**69** 5.3		**59** 6.1	**61** 6.0
0 UND	**16** 22.9	**31** 11.7	**41** 9.0	**42** 8.6	**27** 13.4		**36** 10.2	**31** 11.7
19 18.9	**49** 7.5	**57** 6.4	**61** 6.0	**50** 7.3	**57** 6.4	Cost of Sales/Inventory	**60** 6.1	**59** 6.2
60 6.1	**107** 3.4	**99** 3.7	**104** 3.5	**79** 4.6	**99** 3.7		**105** 3.5	**97** 3.8
0 UND	**19** 19.6	**24** 14.9	**24** 15.5	**29** 12.4	**20** 18.2		**23** 15.7	**23** 15.6
23 16.1	**36** 10.2	**38** 9.7	**36** 10.2	**36** 10.2	**31** 11.8	Cost of Sales/Payables	**36** 10.2	**37** 10.0
45 8.1	**52** 7.0	**53** 6.9	**47** 7.7	**47** 7.8	**38** 9.5		**50** 7.3	**52** 7.0
6.0	5.7	4.6	4.6	4.0	3.8		4.9	4.8
17.2	12.5	7.8	7.9	6.2	6.4	Sales/Working Capital	7.8	7.9
-106.5	66.1	15.6	15.6	11.9	8.1		16.0	14.8
11.4	27.3	35.9	28.3	30.0	159.2		12.9	19.9
(29) 3.4	(75) 7.6	(178) 7.0	(158) 11.2	(30) 6.8	(26) 18.3	EBIT/Interest	(536) 3.7	(554) 6.0
-.8	1.4	2.3	4.8	2.5	7.0		1.0	2.0
		11.2	22.6				6.4	10.2
		(36) 3.5	(48) 5.1			Net Profit + Depr., Dep., Amort./Cur. Mat. L/T/D	(128) 2.5	(129) 3.8
		1.2	2.3				.9	1.6
.0	.0	.1	.1	.1	.1		.1	.1
.1	.2	.2	.2	.2	.2	Fixed/Worth	.2	.2
3.4	.8	.5	.5	.6	.3		.5	.5
.9	.6	.7	.8	.7	.5		.6	.7
8.7	1.8	1.6	1.6	1.4	1.1	Debt/Worth	1.6	1.5
-19.0	15.8	3.6	3.4	3.9	1.9		3.6	3.5
380.1	59.8	44.7	51.4	21.0	30.9		30.8	39.4
(30) 42.6	(89) 26.8	(197) 21.1	(163) 28.0	(30) 15.6	19.0	% Profit Before Taxes/Tangible Net Worth	(556) 10.5	(594) 16.7
1.7	2.0	6.5	9.4	9.2	13.0		.7	4.0
33.4	19.6	16.5	18.3	11.1	12.3		11.2	14.0
13.7	7.1	7.4	9.0	5.5	8.2	% Profit Before Taxes/Total Assets	3.7	5.9
-.2	1.1	1.8	4.5	2.9	5.2		.1	1.6
UND	208.3	141.9	78.3	68.9	73.7		114.0	148.5
244.2	54.8	55.8	38.5	26.5	36.8	Sales/Net Fixed Assets	43.4	50.4
48.6	23.6	20.8	15.1	10.2	17.7		17.7	19.1
6.7	4.8	3.6	3.2	3.2	2.9		3.5	3.4
4.0	3.5	2.9	2.6	2.2	2.3	Sales/Total Assets	2.7	2.7
2.6	2.4	2.2	1.9	1.6	1.9		2.0	2.1
.1	.2	.3	.3	.3	.3		.4	.3
(18) .8	(64) .5	(160) .5	(155) .5	(29) .5	(27) .5	% Depr., Dep., Amort./Sales	(485) .6	(499) .6
2.5	1.1	.8	.9	1.3	.8		1.2	1.1
2.5	2.5	1.6	.6				1.8	1.6
(21) 6.8	(58) 5.0	(98) 2.5	(36) 1.2			% Officers', Directors' Owners' Comp/Sales	(239) 3.5	(264) 3.3
12.7	8.8	4.7	2.1				7.4	6.3
53501M	**505272M**	**3142701M**	**10275730M**	**5469184M**	**10913184M**	Net Sales ($)	**27561436M**	**28651042M**
11607M	**124586M**	**1030852M**	**3942884M**	**2419800M**	**4517761M**	Total Assets ($)	**10855210M**	**11329911M**

M = $ thousand MM = $ million

See Pages 9 through 22 for Explanation of Ratios and Data

Comparative Historical Data / Current Data Sorted by Sales

4/1/11-3/31/12 ALL	4/1/12-3/31/13 ALL	4/1/13-3/31/14 ALL	Type of Statement	0-1MM	1-3MM	3-5MM	5-10MM	10-25MM	25MM & OVER
65	53	77	Unqualified	1			2	11	63
161	137	122	Reviewed	1	5	4	11	49	52
95	62	72	Compiled	2	8	7	24	25	6
134	109	102	Tax Returns	15	27	20	20	13	7
229	250	223	Other	5	23	16	29	44	106
				102 (4/1-9/30/13)			494 (10/1/13-3/31/14)		
684	611	596	NUMBER OF STATEMENTS	24	63	47	86	142	234
%	%	%	**ASSETS**	%	%	%	%	%	%
10.0	9.9	10.1	Cash & Equivalents	17.6	15.5	13.3	10.6	9.3	7.5
36.0	36.5	34.5	Trade Receivables (net)	26.4	24.6	27.6	35.6	37.1	37.3
32.7	32.9	32.3	Inventory	33.1	28.8	33.6	35.2	31.9	32.0
3.0	2.6	2.8	All Other Current	7.6	3.0	1.2	1.2	2.7	3.3
81.6	81.9	79.7	Total Current	84.8	71.9	75.8	82.6	81.1	80.1
9.5	9.6	10.8	Fixed Assets (net)	7.8	15.0	12.8	9.0	11.3	9.9
3.6	3.7	4.5	Intangibles (net)	3.4	4.9	5.1	3.2	2.8	5.8
5.3	4.8	5.0	All Other Non-Current	4.0	8.2	6.3	5.2	4.8	4.1
100.0	100.0	100.0	Total	100.0	100.0	100.0	100.0	100.0	100.0
			LIABILITIES						
14.1	13.4	13.2	Notes Payable-Short Term	13.3	15.2	16.2	13.4	11.1	13.1
1.7	1.8	1.8	Cur. Mat.-L.T.D.	3.9	2.1	.9	1.9	1.2	1.9
23.0	23.0	21.7	Trade Payables	15.3	18.7	18.4	23.8	23.5	21.9
.2	.2	.2	Income Taxes Payable	.0	.7	.1	.1	.2	.2
9.2	8.5	9.7	All Other Current	16.2	12.3	8.6	7.9	8.4	9.9
48.2	46.8	46.5	Total Current	48.7	49.0	44.3	47.2	44.4	47.0
6.8	8.4	7.8	Long-Term Debt	9.8	10.9	12.4	8.7	7.3	5.9
.2	.1	.3	Deferred Taxes	.0	.0	.1	.1	.4	.3
5.5	5.1	5.6	All Other Non-Current	25.6	11.2	2.8	2.5	4.8	4.1
39.2	39.6	39.9	Net Worth	15.9	28.9	40.5	41.5	43.0	42.6
100.0	100.0	100.0	Total Liabilties & Net Worth	100.0	100.0	100.0	100.0	100.0	100.0
			INCOME DATA						
100.0	100.0	100.0	Net Sales	100.0	100.0	100.0	100.0	100.0	100.0
29.9	29.3	29.6	Gross Profit	47.5	40.7	36.4	31.3	29.0	23.2
25.3	24.2	25.1	Operating Expenses	43.8	33.7	32.6	26.7	24.9	18.8
4.6	5.1	4.6	Operating Profit	3.7	6.9	3.8	4.6	4.1	4.5
.3	.4	.3	All Other Expenses (net)	1.5	.7	.6	.3	.1	.2
4.4	4.7	4.3	Profit Before Taxes	2.2	6.3	3.1	4.3	4.0	4.3
			RATIOS						
2.8	2.9	2.8		4.2	2.8	3.8	2.9	2.8	2.5
1.8	1.9	1.8	Current	2.6	1.7	1.7	1.9	1.8	1.7
1.3	1.3	1.3		1.2	1.0	1.1	1.3	1.4	1.3
1.6	1.6	1.5		2.4	1.7	1.5	1.5	1.7	1.5
1.0	1.0	1.0	Quick	.9	.9	.9	1.0	1.0	.9
.6	.7	.6		.4	.5	.5	.6	.7	.7
33 11.2	**32** 11.4	**32** 11.5		**17** 21.8	**12** 30.1	**17** 20.9	**31** 11.7	**33** 11.0	**39** 9.3
46 7.9	**45** 8.1	**45** 8.2	Sales/Receivables	**40** 9.1	**28** 13.2	**41** 8.9	**39** 9.4	**47** 7.8	**51** 7.2
60 6.1	**57** 6.4	**58** 6.3		**85** 4.3	**40** 9.2	**56** 6.5	**52** 7.0	**59** 6.2	**60** 6.1
29 12.8	**29** 12.7	**29** 12.5		**7** 55.4	**5** 72.1	**8** 43.9	**26** 14.3	**31** 11.7	**36** 10.2
59 6.2	**54** 6.8	**55** 6.6	Cost of Sales/Inventory	**83** 4.4	**47** 7.7	**55** 6.6	**62** 5.9	**55** 6.6	**52** 7.0
99 3.7	**85** 4.3	**99** 3.7		**228** 1.6	**107** 3.4	**159** 2.3	**111** 3.3	**101** 3.6	**78** 4.7
24 15.4	**23** 16.0	**22** 16.4		**12** 31.7	**11** 34.2	**5** 67.5	**23** 15.6	**24** 15.1	**23** 15.9
37 9.9	**34** 10.6	**35** 10.3	Cost of Sales/Payables	**39** 9.3	**31** 11.8	**37** 9.8	**38** 9.6	**38** 9.7	**33** 11.0
54 6.8	**51** 7.1	**49** 7.4		**83** 4.4	**56** 6.5	**53** 6.9	**53** 6.9	**54** 6.7	**44** 8.3
5.0	5.0	4.9		1.5	5.4	4.2	4.6	4.5	5.4
8.1	8.4	8.0	Sales/Working Capital	4.9	11.3	8.4	8.0	7.7	8.4
17.9	16.5	18.2		11.5	261.8	62.4	16.3	14.1	17.4
26.2	36.5	29.5		9.0	17.5	22.6	46.3	31.9	31.5
(569) 8.9	(499) 10.7	(496) 8.0	EBIT/Interest	(16) 1.7	(43) 6.8	(35) 3.6	(74) 8.0	(117) 7.0	(211) 12.3
2.7	3.9	2.8		-1.8	1.9	1.0	1.4	2.8	5.3
12.7	11.7	14.0					30.8	13.5	13.5
(113) 3.8	(99) 4.2	(104) 4.4	Net Profit + Depr., Dep., Amort./Cur. Mat. L/T/D				(10) 2.4	(28) 4.9	(64) 4.7
1.4	1.8	1.9					.3	1.4	2.2
.0	.0	.1		.0	.0	.0	.0	.1	.1
.2	.2	.2	Fixed/Worth	.1	.2	.2	.1	.2	.2
.5	.5	.6		UND	4.4	1.1	.4	.5	.5
.7	.7	.7		.5	.7	.4	.6	.8	.8
1.5	1.5	1.6	Debt/Worth	7.2	3.8	1.7	1.6	1.3	1.6
4.2	3.9	4.0		-8.0	47.7	15.0	3.8	2.7	3.6
50.3	50.9	46.2		35.5	93.8	57.4	47.7	38.3	45.0
(620) 23.5	(556) 25.5	(539) 23.0	% Profit Before Taxes/Tangible Net Worth	(16) 3.4	(48) 49.3	(39) 23.4	(81) 20.8	(136) 19.4	(219) 23.3
8.7	10.1	7.5		-14.3	8.8	1.9	3.3	6.4	11.3
16.9	19.0	17.3		10.8	29.2	19.8	21.2	15.1	15.5
8.0	9.6	7.8	% Profit Before Taxes/Total Assets	1.3	13.6	7.8	7.3	7.3	8.3
2.6	3.7	2.3		-5.8	1.8	.4	1.4	2.1	4.6
162.1	176.5	127.6		UND	266.0	140.0	164.4	128.0	96.8
59.9	63.7	48.6	Sales/Net Fixed Assets	102.7	53.0	43.4	62.7	38.4	46.7
21.4	23.0	19.0		25.7	16.8	19.0	20.7	18.3	19.0
3.7	3.8	3.6		3.3	5.0	4.0	4.0	3.6	3.4
2.8	2.9	2.8	Sales/Total Assets	1.8	3.1	2.9	3.0	2.8	2.8
2.1	2.2	2.0		.9	2.0	2.0	2.2	2.0	2.2
.2	.2	.3		.8	.3	.3	.2	.3	.3
(513) .5	(470) .5	(453) .5	% Depr., Dep., Amort./Sales	(11) .9	(40) .6	(25) .8	(64) .4	(111) .5	(202) .5
1.0	.9	.9		3.0	1.5	1.5	.8	.9	.8
1.6	1.6	1.6		3.3	3.5	2.4	2.1	1.5	.6
(261) 3.1	(238) 3.1	(219) 2.9	% Officers', Directors' Owners' Comp/Sales	(10) 7.0	(34) 7.7	(25) 4.1	(52) 3.6	(51) 2.2	(47) 1.1
5.8	5.9	5.6		13.2	11.0	7.5	5.7	3.5	2.4
28580191M	29344547M	30359572M	Net Sales ($)	13406M	125364M	189816M	633871M	2355095M	27042020M
11313771M	10861667M	12047490M	Total Assets ($)	10459M	55640M	79822M	250572M	987013M	10663984M

M = $ thousand MM = $ million

See Pages 9 through 22 for Explanation of Ratios and Data

Current Data Sorted by Assets							Comparative Historical Data	
						Type of Statement		
		2	3	8	5	Unqualified	19	21
	2	14	6			Reviewed	25	34
1	6	9	3			Compiled	18	19
1	5	7				Tax Returns	22	20
1	6	14	25	9	4	Other	61	59
	20 (4/1-9/30/13)		111 (10/1/13-3/31/14)				**4/1/09-3/31/10 ALL**	**4/1/10-3/31/11 ALL**
0-500M	**500M-2MM**	**2-10MM**	**10-50MM**	**50-100MM**	**100-250MM**			
3	19	46	37	17	9	**NUMBER OF STATEMENTS**	145	153
%	%	%	%	%	%	**ASSETS**	%	%
	10.7	11.2	8.7	5.5		Cash & Equivalents	9.9	9.4
	29.0	30.6	26.3	31.3		Trade Receivables (net)	31.4	27.7
	42.2	44.7	44.8	38.6		Inventory	40.6	43.5
	5.4	1.8	2.0	2.6		All Other Current	2.4	2.5
	87.3	88.3	81.8	77.9		Total Current	84.2	83.1
	4.6	6.3	7.8	9.6		Fixed Assets (net)	8.9	9.1
	.6	1.8	6.9	10.6		Intangibles (net)	3.0	2.9
	7.5	3.6	3.5	2.0		All Other Non-Current	3.9	4.8
	100.0	100.0	100.0	100.0		Total	100.0	100.0
						LIABILITIES		
	20.6	9.2	14.2	9.8		Notes Payable-Short Term	16.5	14.8
	1.3	1.7	.5	3.3		Cur. Mat.-L.T.D.	2.0	1.8
	30.9	23.8	22.3	22.0		Trade Payables	23.4	24.3
	.1	.2	.0	.1		Income Taxes Payable	.2	.1
	10.3	9.5	9.5	11.4		All Other Current	9.4	11.4
	63.2	44.5	46.5	46.6		Total Current	51.6	52.4
	6.4	3.8	4.5	4.5		Long-Term Debt	6.1	7.3
	.1	.1	.1	.0		Deferred Taxes	.0	.1
	12.3	5.4	4.8	8.2		All Other Non-Current	6.7	6.1
	18.1	46.2	44.2	40.7		Net Worth	35.6	34.1
	100.0	100.0	100.0	100.0		Total Liabilties & Net Worth	100.0	100.0
						INCOME DATA		
	100.0	100.0	100.0	100.0		Net Sales	100.0	100.0
	25.3	24.3	20.3	17.9		Gross Profit	23.5	24.5
	23.6	20.5	17.3	13.0		Operating Expenses	21.6	22.1
	1.8	3.8	3.0	4.9		Operating Profit	1.9	2.3
	.1	.0	.3	.9		All Other Expenses (net)	.4	.2
	1.6	3.8	2.6	4.0		Profit Before Taxes	1.5	2.1
						RATIOS		
	2.2	3.6	2.8	2.2			2.6	2.5
	1.6	1.8	1.8	1.7		Current	1.6	1.7
	1.1	1.5	1.3	1.3			1.2	1.3
	1.0	1.8	1.2	1.1			1.5	1.2
	.6	.9	.7	.8		Quick	.8	.8
	.3	.5	.5	.5			.6	.4
	11 33.1	**23** 15.7	**19** 19.5	**23** 15.7			**23** 15.9	**20** 18.6
	28 13.1	**32** 11.4	**31** 11.8	**30** 12.3		Sales/Receivables	**31** 11.9	**30** 12.4
	55 6.6	**47** 7.8	**61** 6.0	**57** 6.4			**49** 7.5	**45** 8.1
	19 19.5	**37** 9.8	**55** 6.6	**29** 12.8			**39** 9.3	**41** 9.0
	48 7.6	**62** 5.9	**76** 4.8	**49** 7.5		Cost of Sales/Inventory	**62** 5.9	**67** 5.4
	126 2.9	**114** 3.2	**111** 3.3	**76** 4.8			**96** 3.8	**102** 3.6
	19 19.3	**15** 25.0	**16** 23.3	**18** 20.8			**17** 21.9	**16** 22.4
	30 12.0	**31** 11.8	**26** 14.0	**31** 11.6		Cost of Sales/Payables	**31** 11.7	**30** 12.2
	51 7.1	**54** 6.8	**44** 8.3	**44** 8.3			**46** 7.9	**50** 7.4
	5.3	4.9	5.3	7.2			5.5	5.4
	15.6	8.0	7.0	10.7		Sales/Working Capital	9.7	10.7
	49.2	15.3	16.6	14.8			20.7	21.2
	32.0	24.1	17.1	16.6			14.1	17.3
	(14) 4.4	(42) 8.9	(34) 8.1	(15) 7.7		EBIT/Interest	(133) 4.0	(136) 4.3
	2.4	2.2	1.7	3.1			.5	1.2
							54.2	37.8
						Net Profit + Depr., Dep., Amort./Cur. Mat. L/T/D	(22) 2.8	(26) 6.2
							.0	1.1
	.0	.0	.0	.1			.0	.1
	.1	.1	.1	.3		Fixed/Worth	.2	.2
	.4	.2	.5	.7			.4	.4
	1.0	.5	.6	1.0			.8	.8
	2.4	1.4	1.2	1.4		Debt/Worth	1.9	1.7
	39.0	2.2	3.6	7.8			5.0	4.1
	62.9	34.7	29.9	40.8			31.1	31.8
	(15) 24.0	(44) 20.1	(32) 14.8	(14) 32.2		% Profit Before Taxes/Tangible Net Worth	(129) 11.6	(135) 20.0
	16.2	5.3	4.6	21.4			2.2	5.0
	15.3	15.1	11.8	16.8			10.0	13.5
	7.0	6.5	5.9	11.2		% Profit Before Taxes/Total Assets	3.7	5.9
	2.7	1.6	1.7	4.0			-.8	.9
	999.8	548.1	184.5	206.8			223.7	164.7
	106.1	123.2	93.4	38.9		Sales/Net Fixed Assets	68.7	61.3
	35.7	33.7	27.1	28.7			29.9	26.9
	7.5	4.4	3.4	4.4			4.3	4.1
	4.2	3.1	2.5	3.1		Sales/Total Assets	2.9	3.1
	2.8	2.4	2.0	2.2			2.2	2.5
		.2	.2	.1			.2	.2
		(34) .3	(27) .3	(12) .5		% Depr., Dep., Amort./Sales	(103) .4	(125) .4
		.7	.5	1.0			.8	.9
		.8					1.0	.8
		(17) 1.9				% Officers', Directors' Owners' Comp/Sales	(47) 2.0	(54) 1.7
		4.5					3.6	3.6
8765M	126309M	797645M	2148058M	3834084M	2881341M	Net Sales ($)	8335990M	10406296M
705M	24252M	234694M	798351M	1135915M	1249731M	Total Assets ($)	2608827M	2944652M

M = $ thousand MM = $ million

See Pages 9 through 22 for Explanation of Ratios and Data

Comparative Historical Data				Current Data Sorted by Sales					
			Type of Statement						
13	18	18	Unqualified					1	17
31	18	22	Reviewed				7	8	7
22	13	19	Compiled	1		1	10	4	3
15	22	13	Tax Returns		2	3	3	5	
74	65	59	Other	1	1	3	3	12	39
4/1/11-3/31/12 ALL	**4/1/12-3/31/13 ALL**	**4/1/13-3/31/14 ALL**		**20 (4/1-9/30/13)**			**111 (10/1/13-3/31/14)**		
				0-1MM	**1-3MM**	**3-5MM**	**5-10MM**	**10-25MM**	**25MM & OVER**
155	136	131	**NUMBER OF STATEMENTS**	2	3	7	23	30	66
%	%	%	**ASSETS**	%	%	%	%	%	%
10.4	9.2	9.7	Cash & Equivalents				13.8	11.9	7.3
30.2	29.0	28.6	Trade Receivables (net)				26.8	29.9	28.1
40.6	41.9	42.6	Inventory				38.2	45.4	43.9
2.1	2.5	2.5	All Other Current				2.4	1.8	2.4
83.4	82.6	83.5	Total Current				81.3	88.9	81.7
8.1	8.9	7.2	Fixed Assets (net)				7.9	3.9	9.2
4.5	3.5	5.0	Intangibles (net)				2.0	2.9	6.8
4.1	4.9	4.3	All Other Non-Current				8.8	4.2	2.3
100.0	100.0	100.0	Total				100.0	100.0	100.0
			LIABILITIES						
14.6	15.8	12.8	Notes Payable-Short Term				6.9	11.1	12.5
1.6	1.3	1.4	Cur. Mat.-L.T.D.				1.2	1.3	1.6
25.5	22.5	24.0	Trade Payables				26.6	25.0	21.9
.0	.2	.1	Income Taxes Payable				.4	.1	.1
7.8	11.9	12.3	All Other Current				27.8	7.1	10.5
49.5	51.6	50.7	Total Current				62.9	44.5	46.5
5.5	5.7	5.2	Long-Term Debt				5.7	2.6	6.0
.1	.1	.1	Deferred Taxes				.2	.0	.1
7.6	6.5	6.9	All Other Non-Current				4.5	3.8	4.9
37.4	36.1	37.1	Net Worth				26.6	49.1	42.5
100.0	100.0	100.0	Total Liabilties & Net Worth				100.0	100.0	100.0
			INCOME DATA						
100.0	100.0	100.0	Net Sales				100.0	100.0	100.0
24.0	23.1	22.7	Gross Profit				27.5	21.7	19.5
20.6	19.5	19.5	Operating Expenses				23.8	17.8	16.4
3.4	3.6	3.2	Operating Profit				3.7	3.9	3.1
.1	.2	.3	All Other Expenses (net)				.2	-.2	.6
3.2	3.4	2.9	Profit Before Taxes				3.5	4.1	2.5
			RATIOS						
2.6	2.4	2.7					3.1	4.9	2.4
1.7	1.7	1.8	Current				1.7	1.8	1.8
1.3	1.2	1.3					1.3	1.5	1.3
1.3	1.2	1.2					1.1	2.8	1.1
.8	.7	.7	Quick				.7	.9	.7
.5	.5	.5					.5	.5	.5
21 17.6	**18** 20.4	**22** 16.7					**20** 18.7	**22** 16.9	**22** 16.7
34 10.8	**30** 12.0	**32** 11.5	Sales/Receivables				**35** 10.3	**30** 12.0	**30** 12.0
52 7.0	**49** 7.4	**54** 6.8					**49** 7.4	**56** 6.5	**54** 6.7
43 8.4	**32** 11.5	**42** 8.7					**19** 19.5	**27** 13.4	**45** 8.1
69 5.3	**68** 5.4	**68** 5.4	Cost of Sales/Inventory				**57** 6.4	**72** 5.1	**68** 5.4
101 3.6	**104** 3.5	**111** 3.3					**122** 3.0	**130** 2.8	**94** 3.9
20 18.7	**13** 27.5	**16** 23.1					**19** 19.3	**10** 37.4	**16** 23.5
34 10.6	**30** 12.2	**29** 12.6	Cost of Sales/Payables				**34** 10.6	**27** 13.3	**26** 13.9
53 6.9	**43** 8.5	**48** 7.6					**53** 6.9	**42** 8.7	**43** 8.4
5.5	5.4	5.3					5.2	4.8	5.8
9.3	9.8	8.1	Sales/Working Capital				8.2	8.2	8.1
19.7	26.0	18.7					17.7	20.1	17.3
15.8	26.0	20.8					21.0	28.5	16.4
(134) 5.0	(117) 6.2	(114) 7.7	EBIT/Interest				(18) 6.4	(26) 10.0	(61) 7.7
1.8	3.4	2.3					1.6	3.2	2.2
20.3	14.3	9.4							10.9
(18) 3.5	(21) 7.4	(21) 4.5	Net Profit + Depr., Dep., Amort./Cur. Mat. L/T/D						(12) 5.7
1.8	1.9	1.9							2.8
.0	.0	.0					.0	.0	.1
.2	.1	.1	Fixed/Worth				.1	.1	.2
.7	.7	.4					.4	.1	.5
.8	.9	.8					.7	.3	.8
1.7	1.9	1.5	Debt/Worth				1.5	1.4	1.3
7.2	4.9	3.9					3.9	2.3	3.8
45.1	50.0	38.8					41.2	34.5	38.9
(135) 18.3	(123) 25.6	(114) 22.9	% Profit Before Taxes/Tangible Net Worth				(21) 18.4	(29) 23.5	(59) 21.9
6.7	11.0	8.8					3.6	9.6	9.1
13.4	16.3	13.5					12.5	17.1	13.1
6.0	6.9	6.7	% Profit Before Taxes/Total Assets				6.0	7.2	7.5
2.2	3.2	2.2					1.6	3.9	2.7
228.6	283.7	275.5					914.4	999.8	175.9
88.9	92.5	96.5	Sales/Net Fixed Assets				106.1	128.7	71.9
26.9	27.8	31.4					26.8	49.9	19.5
3.8	4.1	4.2					4.2	4.4	3.9
3.0	3.1	2.9	Sales/Total Assets				3.1	3.1	2.8
2.3	2.3	2.3					2.3	2.4	2.3
.2	.1	.2					.3	.1	.2
(117) .4	(98) .3	(89) .3	% Depr., Dep., Amort./Sales				(15) .6	(18) .2	(53) .3
.8	.6	.8					1.1	.5	.8
.7	.7	.7						.6	
(55) 1.7	(41) 1.9	(33) 1.5	% Officers', Directors' Owners' Comp/Sales					(12) 1.4	
4.3	5.7	3.5						2.1	
9502043M	9045295M	9796202M	Net Sales ($)	955M	6028M	29156M	167389M	521319M	9071355M
3095231M	2992333M	3443648M	Total Assets ($)	788M	2128M	12702M	60505M	200348M	3167177M

M = $ thousand MM = $ million

See Pages 9 through 22 for Explanation of Ratios and Data

Current Data Sorted by Assets							Comparative Historical Data	
						Type of Statement		
		5	22	8	1	Unqualified	59	64
1	4	41	24			Reviewed	92	97
3	14	33	4			Compiled	47	51
5	30	20	2			Tax Returns	40	52
8	41	60	60	8	11	Other	175	154
	66 (4/1-9/30/13)		339 (10/1/13-3/31/14)				4/1/09-3/31/10 ALL	4/1/10-3/31/11 ALL
0-500M	500M-2MM	2-10MM	10-50MM	50-100MM	100-250MM			
17	89	159	112	16	12	**NUMBER OF STATEMENTS**	413	418
%	%	%	%	%	%	**ASSETS**	%	%
23.2	16.8	11.8	9.0	6.3	12.4	Cash & Equivalents	10.5	10.1
23.6	30.5	33.0	34.7	34.0	30.4	Trade Receivables (net)	33.2	34.9
35.5	34.6	33.4	34.5	32.2	31.8	Inventory	34.1	34.3
4.1	1.4	2.1	2.8	4.7	2.8	All Other Current	3.3	3.0
86.5	83.1	80.3	81.1	77.1	77.3	Total Current	81.0	82.2
7.1	8.0	9.0	8.2	6.0	9.2	Fixed Assets (net)	8.2	8.2
3.4	3.0	4.7	5.5	10.0	10.0	Intangibles (net)	5.1	4.5
3.0	5.8	6.0	5.2	6.8	3.4	All Other Non-Current	5.6	5.0
100.0	100.0	100.0	100.0	100.0	100.0	Total	100.0	100.0
						LIABILITIES		
24.7	10.9	13.0	13.8	12.5	12.7	Notes Payable-Short Term	14.6	13.4
1.0	1.2	1.3	2.2	1.3	3.5	Cur. Mat.-L.T.D.	1.9	1.5
35.3	20.8	22.4	25.9	25.3	20.9	Trade Payables	24.1	24.3
.0	.1	.3	.1	.6	.1	Income Taxes Payable	.2	.2
14.0	11.3	6.7	12.3	9.9	10.5	All Other Current	9.0	10.1
75.1	44.4	43.7	54.3	49.6	47.7	Total Current	49.7	49.6
10.4	7.8	6.7	6.1	7.0	7.4	Long-Term Debt	7.8	7.9
.0	.0	.2	.1	.0	1.7	Deferred Taxes	.2	.2
23.3	9.4	3.8	6.7	5.3	2.3	All Other Non-Current	6.2	5.5
-8.8	38.5	45.6	32.8	38.0	41.0	Net Worth	36.1	36.9
100.0	100.0	100.0	100.0	100.0	100.0	Total Liabilties & Net Worth	100.0	100.0
						INCOME DATA		
100.0	100.0	100.0	100.0	100.0	100.0	Net Sales	100.0	100.0
37.9	35.6	31.5	24.7	19.5	25.6	Gross Profit	28.3	28.2
29.8	30.7	26.2	20.2	13.4	21.8	Operating Expenses	25.9	23.8
8.0	4.9	5.2	4.5	6.1	3.7	Operating Profit	2.4	4.3
-.2	.2	.2	.9	.9	3.2	All Other Expenses (net)	.5	.4
8.2	4.7	5.0	3.6	5.2	.5	Profit Before Taxes	1.9	3.9
						RATIOS		
3.4	3.9	3.0	2.2	2.4	2.6		2.6	2.6
1.2	2.0	1.8	1.5	1.4	1.8	Current	1.6	1.7
.7	1.4	1.3	1.2	1.1	1.0		1.2	1.2
2.5	2.0	1.7	1.4	1.2	1.4		1.5	1.5
.7	1.2	1.0	.8	.8	.8	Quick	.8	(417) .9
.4	.6	.6	.5	.4	.6		.5	.6
0 UND	**16** 23.1	**28** 13.0	**32** 11.3	**23** 16.0	**42** 8.6		**31** 12.0	**34** 10.8
12 30.9	**31** 11.8	**40** 9.1	**47** 7.8	**47** 7.7	**45** 8.1	Sales/Receivables	**43** 8.6	**45** 8.2
30 12.3	**47** 7.7	**55** 6.6	**61** 6.0	**63** 5.8	**59** 6.2		**60** 6.1	**56** 6.5
12 29.6	**26** 13.9	**27** 13.6	**38** 9.6	**25** 14.4	**46** 8.0		**28** 12.8	**34** 10.8
21 17.6	**46** 7.9	**57** 6.4	**62** 5.9	**45** 8.2	**91** 4.0	Cost of Sales/Inventory	**55** 6.7	**57** 6.4
41 8.8	**99** 3.7	**89** 4.1	**99** 3.7	**62** 5.9	**130** 2.8		**104** 3.5	**94** 3.9
1 556.9	**12** 31.4	**18** 19.8	**27** 13.4	**24** 15.1	**31** 11.6		**22** 16.6	**22** 16.4
13 27.8	**31** 11.7	**33** 10.9	**43** 8.4	**31** 11.7	**45** 8.1	Cost of Sales/Payables	**38** 9.6	**36** 10.1
46 7.9	**53** 6.9	**53** 6.9	**57** 6.4	**47** 7.7	**58** 6.3		**59** 6.2	**58** 6.3
7.4	5.1	4.9	5.7	6.9	3.0		5.0	5.0
193.5	9.0	8.6	10.1	15.4	7.8	Sales/Working Capital	10.4	9.6
-27.2	18.0	17.8	24.0	25.9	NM		24.5	21.0
	19.5	26.3	27.2	42.9	57.4		16.5	22.8
	(55) 6.6	(131) 8.2	(101) 7.1	(14) 19.7	8.4	EBIT/Interest	(360) 3.7	(355) 6.3
	1.5	2.4	2.2	3.2	.0		1.2	2.1
		15.8	9.5				14.5	23.5
		(14) 2.6	(26) 3.9			Net Profit + Depr., Dep., Amort./Cur. Mat. L/T/D	(79) 2.3	(76) 5.3
		1.4	2.4				.8	1.3
.0	.0	.0	.1	.0	.1		.0	.0
.3	.1	.1	.2	.1	.6	Fixed/Worth	.2	.1
-5.6	.4	.4	1.2	.6	-1.9		.6	.6
.5	.5	.7	1.0	1.1	.7		.9	.8
2.8	1.3	1.5	2.0	1.9	2.4	Debt/Worth	2.2	1.8
-3.9	4.0	2.8	6.9	18.1	-121.9		5.4	4.5
123.3	59.6	48.9	44.1	82.3			35.1	50.7
(11) 27.6	(80) 26.8	(152) 23.2	(96) 23.5	(13) 31.9		% Profit Before Taxes/Tangible Net Worth	(359) 15.3	(372) 21.7
17.3	4.4	5.4	10.3	9.9			1.9	6.5
34.8	26.1	18.1	14.4	16.9	10.0		12.8	16.3
15.9	9.9	8.2	6.7	10.9	3.1	% Profit Before Taxes/Total Assets	4.2	7.2
8.2	1.4	2.0	2.1	4.9	-3.1		.3	1.9
UND	382.2	255.8	141.8	183.2	80.4		176.8	242.4
298.1	102.2	74.1	63.4	73.7	30.6	Sales/Net Fixed Assets	62.6	65.2
38.2	25.7	25.8	28.1	18.8	14.8		24.2	26.8
8.5	5.0	3.8	3.5	4.5	3.6		3.7	3.8
4.3	3.3	2.9	2.6	2.7	1.8	Sales/Total Assets	2.8	2.8
3.7	2.2	2.1	1.8	1.5	1.1		1.9	2.1
	.1	.2	.2	.2	.2		.2	.2
	(53) .4	(116) .4	(100) .4	(15) .4	(10) .8	% Depr., Dep., Amort./Sales	(306) .5	(330) .4
	1.0	.9	.9	.7	1.7		1.1	.9
	2.2	1.4	.7				1.8	1.3
	(48) 3.9	(59) 2.8	(14) 1.9			% Officers', Directors' Owners' Comp/Sales	(120) 3.0	(145) 2.7
	6.9	5.5	4.7				6.0	5.1
38020M	413189M	2580921M	6804664M	3479027M	3783357M	Net Sales ($)	19489850M	21243650M
4958M	107557M	809345M	2428032M	1141677M	1699317M	Total Assets ($)	7508373M	7626780M

M = $ thousand MM = $ million

See Pages 9 through 22 for Explanation of Ratios and Data

Comparative Historical Data / Current Data Sorted by Sales

Comparative Historical Data				Current Data Sorted by Sales					
			Type of Statement						
60	35	36	Unqualified				1	5	30
86	60	70	Reviewed	1		4	8	32	25
33	41	54	Compiled	1	4	7	19	17	6
61	54	57	Tax Returns	1	13	12	17	12	2
186	177	188	Other	4	14	30	21	37	82
					66 (4/1-9/30/13)		339 (10/1/13-3/31/14)		
4/1/11-3/31/12 ALL	4/1/12-3/31/13 ALL	4/1/13-3/31/14 ALL		0-1MM	1-3MM	3-5MM	5-10MM	10-25MM	25MM & OVER
426	367	405	**NUMBER OF STATEMENTS**	7	31	53	66	103	145
%	%	%	**ASSETS**	%	%	%	%	%	%
9.4	10.7	12.4	Cash & Equivalents		20.2	14.1	12.5	12.6	9.8
35.2	34.9	32.5	Trade Receivables (net)		20.8	30.8	32.1	32.3	36.1
34.7	33.1	34.0	Inventory		28.6	32.9	34.4	34.0	34.9
2.2	2.8	2.3	All Other Current		2.8	1.1	1.8	2.3	3.1
81.5	81.5	81.2	Total Current		72.3	79.0	80.8	81.2	83.9
8.2	9.0	8.4	Fixed Assets (net)		11.1	8.7	10.0	8.3	7.2
4.6	3.7	4.9	Intangibles (net)		6.8	6.4	3.9	4.4	4.7
5.8	5.7	5.6	All Other Non-Current		9.8	5.9	5.3	6.1	4.1
100.0	100.0	100.0	Total		100.0	100.0	100.0	100.0	100.0
			LIABILITIES						
15.8	14.6	13.2	Notes Payable-Short Term		9.2	11.0	13.7	12.3	13.2
1.4	1.4	1.6	Cur. Mat.-L.T.D.		2.3	1.1	1.0	1.5	2.0
24.8	23.8	23.6	Trade Payables		16.1	21.5	21.7	22.0	27.3
.4	.2	.2	Income Taxes Payable		.3	.3	.4	.1	.2
8.1	9.7	9.8	All Other Current		7.5	6.7	10.0	9.8	10.7
50.5	49.6	48.4	Total Current		35.4	40.6	46.8	45.7	53.3
7.7	7.5	7.0	Long-Term Debt		13.0	10.2	7.8	4.8	6.0
.2	.3	.2	Deferred Taxes		.0	.0	.0	.3	.2
7.0	6.7	6.6	All Other Non-Current		9.6	12.1	4.2	6.7	4.1
34.7	35.8	37.8	Net Worth		41.9	37.1	41.1	42.5	36.4
100.0	100.0	100.0	Total Liabilities & Net Worth		100.0	100.0	100.0	100.0	100.0
			INCOME DATA						
100.0	100.0	100.0	Net Sales		100.0	100.0	100.0	100.0	100.0
28.4	29.4	30.1	Gross Profit		42.6	39.7	33.7	27.5	23.1
23.7	25.2	25.1	Operating Expenses		35.4	33.5	28.3	23.1	18.9
4.7	4.2	5.1	Operating Profit		7.1	6.2	5.4	4.4	4.2
.4	.2	.5	All Other Expenses (net)		.0	.2	.4	.2	.9
4.3	4.0	4.6	Profit Before Taxes		7.1	6.0	5.0	4.2	3.3
			RATIOS						
2.5	2.8	2.9			5.2	3.5	3.3	3.0	2.2
1.7	1.8	1.7	Current		3.1	1.9	1.8	1.8	1.6
1.3	1.3	1.3			1.2	1.4	1.3	1.3	1.3
1.5	1.6	1.7			3.4	2.1	1.9	1.8	1.3
1.0	.9	1.0	Quick		1.7	1.2	1.0	1.1	.8
.6	.6	.6			.6	.7	.6	.6	.6
28 12.9	**29** 12.7	**26** 14.1			**11** 33.2	**26** 13.8	**22** 16.8	**26** 14.1	**30** 12.2
40 9.2	**41** 8.8	**41** 9.0	Sales/Receivables		**30** 12.1	**43** 8.4	**35** 10.4	**40** 9.2	**44** 8.3
54 6.7	**56** 6.5	**55** 6.6			**52** 7.0	**65** 5.6	**53** 6.9	**54** 6.8	**59** 6.2
29 12.4	**30** 12.3	**29** 12.7			**21** 17.6	**29** 12.5	**25** 14.6	**26** 13.8	**31** 11.6
56 6.5	**53** 6.9	**55** 6.6	Cost of Sales/Inventory		**56** 6.5	**63** 5.8	**44** 8.3	**60** 6.1	**53** 6.9
94 3.9	**91** 4.0	**96** 3.8			**101** 3.6	**126** 2.9	**114** 3.2	**83** 4.4	**91** 4.0
18 20.0	**19** 19.5	**18** 20.2			**6** 58.5	**18** 20.5	**13** 27.1	**16** 22.4	**27** 13.7
34 10.8	**33** 11.1	**33** 10.9	Cost of Sales/Payables		**32** 11.5	**33** 10.9	**32** 11.5	**31** 11.6	**38** 9.6
56 6.5	**55** 6.6	**54** 6.7			**63** 5.8	**69** 5.3	**53** 6.9	**53** 6.9	**53** 6.9
5.4	5.6	5.2			3.7	3.7	5.8	5.0	6.4
10.7	9.2	9.9	Sales/Working Capital		6.1	6.9	11.1	10.2	10.9
21.5	19.6	19.8			21.1	12.0	22.2	18.7	23.4
28.4	24.2	26.8			16.4	16.4	18.1	23.8	34.0
(357) 6.6	(295) 9.1	(319) 8.1	EBIT/Interest		(13) 5.4	(37) 6.8	(50) 6.1	(82) 6.4	(133) 10.7
2.3	2.7	2.3			1.7	2.1	1.6	2.0	3.3
17.0	20.7	12.7						17.4	14.4
(59) 4.6	(53) 5.3	(49) 3.3	Net Profit + Depr., Dep., Amort./Cur. Mat. L/T/D					(16) 3.4	(29) 4.0
1.4	1.6	1.7						1.7	2.3
.0	.1	.0			.0	.0	.0	.0	.1
.1	.2	.1	Fixed/Worth		.2	.1	.1	.1	.2
.5	.6	.5			1.8	.4	.5	.4	.9
.9	.8	.7			.3	.7	.5	.8	1.0
2.0	1.6	1.6	Debt/Worth		1.1	1.2	1.5	1.5	1.8
4.9	5.2	4.2			11.1	4.5	3.7	3.3	5.0
58.0	54.2	49.9			58.7	53.6	48.0	52.9	47.6
(374) 23.5	(320) 24.1	(360) 24.4	% Profit Before Taxes/Tangible Net Worth		(26) 30.1	(47) 20.5	(61) 22.1	(98) 24.7	(125) 25.7
7.4	7.9	7.4			6.3	4.3	6.1	4.2	11.9
18.7	17.5	18.6			19.2	21.0	21.8	18.4	15.7
8.3	8.4	8.4	% Profit Before Taxes/Total Assets		10.6	8.5	9.4	6.3	8.3
2.4	2.2	1.8			2.9	2.1	1.5	1.3	2.6
226.1	226.5	254.2			214.5	340.5	254.1	271.5	178.2
71.5	54.3	74.1	Sales/Net Fixed Assets		43.5	68.7	94.6	72.6	71.3
28.9	25.3	27.0			19.1	23.8	23.7	27.0	31.5
4.0	4.0	4.2			4.1	3.7	4.8	4.1	4.2
2.9	3.0	2.9	Sales/Total Assets		1.9	2.9	2.8	3.1	3.0
2.2	2.2	2.0			1.5	1.9	1.9	2.1	2.1
.2	.2	.2			.2	.3	.1	.2	.2
(314) .4	(280) .4	(299) .4	% Depr., Dep., Amort./Sales		(19) .9	(26) .7	(47) .3	(80) .5	(126) .4
.8	.9	.9			1.9	1.1	.9	1.0	.8
1.1	1.4	1.4			4.1	3.0	1.7	1.1	.5
(155) 2.8	(119) 3.3	(129) 3.2	% Officers', Directors' Owners' Comp/Sales		(13) 6.8	(24) 4.3	(30) 3.0	(37) 2.2	(22) 1.1
5.0	6.0	6.2			7.2	9.2	6.0	5.6	3.0
19177116M	18174315M	17099178M	Net Sales ($)	3808M	59029M	204334M	493731M	1667089M	14671187M
7152074M	6328596M	6190886M	Total Assets ($)	1893M	30393M	111543M	194070M	685477M	5167510M

M = $ thousand MM = $ million

See Pages 9 through 22 for Explanation of Ratios and Data

Current Data Sorted by Assets | **Comparative Historical Data**

0-500M	500M-2MM	2-10MM	10-50MM	50-100MM	100-250MM		4/1/09-3/31/10 ALL	4/1/10-3/31/11 ALL
						Type of Statement		
		4	10	5	2	Unqualified	43	29
	4	38	19			Reviewed	80	86
2	9	20	3			Compiled	44	48
5	12	22	1			Tax Returns	61	55
5	17	45	34	3	4	Other	117	118
	40 (4/1-9/30/13)		224 (10/1/13-3/31/14)					
12	42	129	67	8	6	**NUMBER OF STATEMENTS**	345	336
%	%	%	%	%	%	**ASSETS**	%	%
21.8	9.1	8.2	7.0			Cash & Equivalents	7.9	7.9
23.0	26.8	29.1	26.1			Trade Receivables (net)	27.1	29.1
35.3	44.6	45.4	42.9			Inventory	42.9	43.5
.7	2.2	1.1	1.8			All Other Current	3.0	2.1
80.8	82.7	83.8	77.8			Total Current	80.8	82.6
17.3	9.3	9.7	11.0			Fixed Assets (net)	11.4	10.3
.3	3.8	2.1	6.8			Intangibles (net)	2.9	2.4
1.7	4.2	4.4	4.4			All Other Non-Current	4.9	4.7
100.0	100.0	100.0	100.0			Total	100.0	100.0
						LIABILITIES		
9.2	16.7	14.4	15.2			Notes Payable-Short Term	17.2	16.7
11.1	1.8	1.8	2.2			Cur. Mat.-L.T.D.	2.8	2.1
21.4	21.8	19.3	15.7			Trade Payables	17.4	18.6
.0	.0	.1	.1			Income Taxes Payable	.2	.1
41.8	7.8	5.3	6.9			All Other Current	7.6	6.9
83.5	48.1	40.9	40.2			Total Current	45.1	44.4
70.8	14.8	7.1	9.1			Long-Term Debt	9.2	8.8
.0	.0	.2	.6			Deferred Taxes	.2	.2
.1	10.2	7.9	3.4			All Other Non-Current	5.0	5.8
-54.4	26.9	43.9	46.7			Net Worth	40.6	40.8
100.0	100.0	100.0	100.0			Total Liabilties & Net Worth	100.0	100.0
						INCOME DATA		
100.0	100.0	100.0	100.0			Net Sales	100.0	100.0
39.1	33.2	32.4	29.6			Gross Profit	31.2	31.9
34.6	29.1	28.3	23.8			Operating Expenses	29.2	28.9
4.5	4.1	4.0	5.9			Operating Profit	2.1	3.0
.3	.6	.3	.5			All Other Expenses (net)	.4	.5
4.2	3.5	3.8	5.4			Profit Before Taxes	1.7	2.5
						RATIOS		
2.2	3.6	3.7	3.8				3.3	3.5
1.2	1.8	2.2	2.1			Current	2.0	2.0
.8	1.4	1.5	1.3				1.3	1.3
1.5	1.5	1.6	1.4				1.5	1.6
.5	.8	.8	.9			Quick	(344) .7	.8
.2	.4	.5	.5				.5	.5
1 456.5	21 17.4	30 12.0	30 12.2				29 12.8	30 12.0
21 17.2	31 11.6	39 9.3	41 8.9			Sales/Receivables	38 9.5	40 9.1
41 8.9	42 8.6	49 7.5	55 6.6				50 7.2	54 6.8
5 71.5	51 7.1	58 6.3	79 4.6				55 6.7	54 6.8
43 8.4	91 4.0	96 3.8	99 3.7			Cost of Sales/Inventory	95 3.8	96 3.8
203 1.8	159 2.3	152 2.4	152 2.4				142 2.6	148 2.5
0 UND	18 20.5	20 18.2	20 17.9				18 20.0	20 17.9
29 12.6	30 12.3	33 11.0	31 11.6			Cost of Sales/Payables	32 11.3	34 10.8
76 4.8	46 7.9	49 7.4	45 8.1				48 7.6	50 7.3
6.1	4.3	3.7	3.5				4.3	4.1
47.1	7.6	5.9	6.1			Sales/Working Capital	6.4	6.5
-24.0	17.0	10.6	13.4				14.3	12.6
19.0	20.9	28.9	23.7				9.6	11.9
(10) 3.7	(37) 7.0	(112) 5.5	(62) 10.7			EBIT/Interest	(303) 2.8	(290) 3.4
2.2	2.3	1.9	3.4				.9	1.2
		4.1	33.0				6.7	4.3
		(28) 1.5	(20) 4.6			Net Profit + Depr., Dep., Amort./Cur. Mat. L/T/D	(82) 2.6	(72) 1.8
		.3	1.9				.7	.4
.0	.0	.1	.1				.1	.1
.4	.2	.2	.2			Fixed/Worth	.2	.2
-.7	1.1	.5	.9				.6	.6
1.5	.5	.5	.6				.6	.5
NM	1.9	1.2	1.3			Debt/Worth	1.4	1.5
-2.1	7.8	3.1	3.8				4.0	3.7
	39.8	36.3	36.5				25.5	30.9
	(33) 21.6	(120) 15.6	(59) 24.7			% Profit Before Taxes/Tangible Net Worth	(316) 8.2	(305) 11.1
	4.6	5.8	8.0				-.2	1.8
49.3	14.9	15.6	19.1				11.2	11.9
7.7	7.4	5.6	7.9			% Profit Before Taxes/Total Assets	3.3	3.8
2.5	2.4	1.7	3.0				-.4	.2
UND	186.2	94.3	76.3				84.2	94.8
49.7	55.7	49.0	41.3			Sales/Net Fixed Assets	36.4	40.7
25.4	26.1	18.3	20.8				16.7	18.2
5.9	4.2	3.2	2.9				3.2	3.1
4.1	2.7	2.6	2.2			Sales/Total Assets	2.4	2.4
1.5	2.1	1.8	1.6				1.8	1.8
	.1	.3	.3				.4	.3
	(29) .4	(112) .5	(61) .5			% Depr., Dep., Amort./Sales	(292) .7	(295) .6
	1.0	1.1	.9				1.3	1.1
	2.1	1.8	.9				2.0	1.8
	(24) 4.2	(66) 3.0	(12) 1.1			% Officers', Directors' Owners' Comp/Sales	(152) 3.9	(156) 3.6
	8.5	4.8	2.8				6.8	6.5
11212M	173799M	1655087M	3382733M	971035M	964571M	Net Sales ($)	9170963M	7595038M
3242M	51557M	645344M	1530610M	504538M	812981M	Total Assets ($)	4230835M	3298176M

M = $ thousand MM = $ million

See Pages 9 through 22 for Explanation of Ratios and Data

Comparative Historical Data / Current Data Sorted by Sales

	4/1/11-3/31/12 ALL	4/1/12-3/31/13 ALL	4/1/13-3/31/14 ALL	0-1MM	1-3MM	3-5MM	5-10MM	10-25MM	25MM & OVER
Type of Statement									
Unqualified	33	18	21				2	4	15
Reviewed	87	66	61	1	2	3	7	29	19
Compiled	45	35	34	1	6	5	11	8	3
Tax Returns	56	49	40	4	6	8	11	9	2
Other	115	95	108	4	12	6	15	29	42
				40 (4/1-9/30/13)			224 (10/1/13-3/31/14)		
NUMBER OF STATEMENTS	336	263	264	10	26	22	46	79	81
ASSETS	%	%	%	%	%	%	%	%	%
Cash & Equivalents	8.2	7.8	8.5	25.6	10.7	6.8	12.0	6.3	6.3
Trade Receivables (net)	28.9	28.4	27.1	13.7	22.0	22.5	25.3	33.0	27.1
Inventory	42.7	44.1	43.7	35.6	43.7	45.5	47.6	43.5	42.2
All Other Current	2.2	1.8	1.5	1.2	2.6	.6	1.8	.8	1.9
Total Current	82.0	82.0	80.9	76.1	79.0	75.4	86.7	83.7	77.5
Fixed Assets (net)	10.6	9.9	10.7	19.4	10.8	13.2	8.0	9.2	11.8
Intangibles (net)	2.3	3.7	4.2	.2	4.0	5.3	2.0	4.0	6.0
All Other Non-Current	5.0	4.5	4.3	4.3	6.1	6.1	3.3	3.2	4.7
Total	100.0	100.0	100.0	100.0	100.0	100.0	100.0	100.0	100.0
LIABILITIES									
Notes Payable-Short Term	17.2	16.0	14.2	16.3	14.5	9.6	12.0	17.3	13.2
Cur. Mat.-L.T.D.	2.2	2.2	2.3	11.4	2.4	3.6	1.4	1.8	2.0
Trade Payables	18.8	18.8	18.6	11.4	19.8	18.1	20.9	20.2	16.6
Income Taxes Payable	.1	.3	.1	.0	.0	.1	.1	.1	.2
All Other Current	7.8	6.7	7.8	6.2	23.1	7.7	5.9	4.9	7.0
Total Current	46.1	43.9	43.0	45.3	59.8	39.1	40.2	44.2	38.9
Long-Term Debt	9.8	10.2	12.7	62.2	22.3	18.2	7.8	6.6	10.7
Deferred Taxes	.2	.2	.2	.0	.0	.0	.2	.4	.3
All Other Non-Current	5.4	6.5	6.5	.1	8.3	15.6	11.6	4.5	3.4
Net Worth	38.5	39.2	37.5	-7.6	9.7	27.1	40.3	44.3	46.7
Total Liabilties & Net Worth	100.0	100.0	100.0	100.0	100.0	100.0	100.0	100.0	100.0
INCOME DATA									
Net Sales	100.0	100.0	100.0	100.0	100.0	100.0	100.0	100.0	100.0
Gross Profit	31.4	31.6	31.9	41.2	37.0	33.6	34.6	30.4	28.6
Operating Expenses	27.6	27.3	27.4	37.3	31.1	29.7	29.7	26.8	23.5
Operating Profit	3.8	4.3	4.5	3.9	5.9	3.8	4.9	3.6	5.1
All Other Expenses (net)	.4	.3	.4	1.6	-.1	.8	.2	.4	.5
Profit Before Taxes	3.4	3.9	4.1	2.3	6.0	3.0	4.6	3.2	4.7
RATIOS									
Current	3.1	3.5	3.6	4.7	7.7	3.2	3.4	3.7	3.6
	2.0	2.1	2.1	1.4	1.9	2.1	2.3	2.0	2.2
	1.3	1.3	1.4	1.1	.9	1.3	1.5	1.3	1.4
Quick	1.4	1.4	1.5	1.4	2.0	1.4	1.7	1.6	1.7
	.8	.9	.8	.6	.8	.8	.9	.8	.9
	.5	.5	.5	.3	.3	.5	.5	.6	.6
Sales/Receivables	**29** 12.6	**29** 12.6	**29** 12.8	**0** UND	**21** 17.3	**23** 16.1	**25** 14.4	**33** 11.0	**29** 12.4
	39 9.3	**40** 9.2	**39** 9.3	**24** 15.2	**35** 10.3	**38** 9.7	**32** 11.4	**42** 8.7	**41** 8.9
	52 7.0	**51** 7.1	**49** 7.4	**49** 7.5	**43** 8.4	**54** 6.7	**42** 8.7	**51** 7.1	**53** 6.9
Cost of Sales/Inventory	**52** 7.0	**58** 6.3	**55** 6.6	**0** UND	**48** 7.6	**72** 5.1	**72** 5.1	**48** 7.6	**61** 6.0
	96 3.8	**101** 3.6	**96** 3.8	**203** 1.8	**104** 3.5	**118** 3.1	**111** 3.3	**89** 4.1	**91** 4.0
	152 2.4	**152** 2.4	**152** 2.4	**365** 1.0	**174** 2.1	**192** 1.9	**174** 2.1	**135** 2.7	**135** 2.7
Cost of Sales/Payables	**19** 19.7	**18** 19.9	**20** 18.0	**0** UND	**8** 47.5	**25** 14.8	**17** 21.3	**22** 16.8	**23** 16.1
	33 11.0	**33** 11.1	**32** 11.4	**38** 9.5	**29** 12.4	**34** 10.8	**29** 12.6	**31** 11.8	**33** 11.2
	50 7.3	**55** 6.6	**47** 7.7	**69** 5.3	**49** 7.4	**46** 7.9	**59** 6.2	**45** 8.1	**43** 8.4
Sales/Working Capital	4.0	3.9	3.7	2.6	2.5	4.0	3.4	4.3	3.8
	7.4	6.3	6.1	10.5	5.3	5.9	5.2	6.5	6.1
	14.1	14.1	12.9	42.6	-98.4	12.2	9.2	13.0	11.3
EBIT/Interest	10.5	20.7	23.7		30.4	10.7	30.7	32.3	24.0
	(284) 3.6	(234) 5.4	(234) 6.3		(21) 9.2	(21) 5.5	(38) 6.8	(72) 5.5	(74) 8.6
	1.7	1.8	2.4		1.8	2.5	2.4	2.2	2.9
Net Profit + Depr., Dep., Amort./Cur. Mat. L/T/D	12.6	13.1	12.4					5.4	28.4
	(66) 3.3	(60) 3.5	(52) 2.9					(21) 2.5	(23) 5.3
	1.5	1.7	.8					1.0	1.0
Fixed/Worth	.1	.1	.1	.0	.0	.1	.1	.1	.1
	.2	.2	.2	.2	.2	.6	.1	.2	.2
	.6	.7	.7	.9	NM	NM	.4	.5	.9
Debt/Worth	.6	.6	.6	.9	.2	1.0	.6	.6	.5
	1.8	1.7	1.4	4.4	1.6	2.0	1.2	1.4	1.3
	4.1	4.0	4.2	NM	-5.6	NM	3.5	3.5	3.5
% Profit Before Taxes/Tangible Net Worth	36.3	36.3	36.4		37.9	36.1	60.6	33.4	36.4
	(302) 15.4	(230) 18.1	(227) 20.4		(18) 21.7	(17) 17.3	(41) 29.1	(73) 15.7	(70) 21.5
	4.8	5.2	6.1		1.5	4.6	4.5	8.3	5.7
% Profit Before Taxes/Total Assets	13.9	15.8	15.9	13.7	25.8	13.2	18.0	15.7	18.3
	5.0	6.3	6.5	3.8	7.6	5.0	7.5	5.4	7.0
	1.4	1.7	2.1	-19.9	1.2	.9	1.9	2.5	2.8
Sales/Net Fixed Assets	103.0	117.8	95.0	UND	251.2	69.0	131.0	95.1	81.5
	42.4	44.7	46.8	60.5	36.2	32.5	57.7	51.9	41.3
	18.4	18.5	17.8	3.9	19.2	9.4	27.3	18.5	13.8
Sales/Total Assets	3.2	3.1	3.2	4.0	3.7	2.8	3.2	3.7	3.0
	2.5	2.5	2.5	1.6	2.4	2.2	2.5	2.7	2.4
	1.9	1.9	1.8	1.3	1.5	1.5	1.8	2.0	1.8
% Depr., Dep., Amort./Sales	.3	.3	.3		.1	.4	.3	.3	.2
	(273) .5	(209) .5	(217) .5		(20) .4	(20) 1.0	(37) .5	(66) .5	(72) .5
	1.1	1.0	1.0		1.0	2.0	1.0	1.0	.8
% Officers', Directors' Owners' Comp/Sales	1.7	1.9	1.7		1.8		2.1	1.8	.8
	(141) 3.5	(108) 3.7	(111) 3.0		(15) 6.0		(26) 3.1	(38) 3.0	(18) 2.0
	6.4	6.7	5.7		10.5		5.5	3.8	2.9
Net Sales ($)	**7896090M**	**7367490M**	**7158437M**	**5907M**	**56115M**	**88755M**	**333977M**	**1253591M**	**5420092M**
Total Assets ($)	**3646144M**	**3289929M**	**3548272M**	**3597M**	**30590M**	**49631M**	**153182M**	**540140M**	**2771132M**

M = $ thousand MM = $ million

See Pages 9 through 22 for Explanation of Ratios and Data

	Current Data Sorted by Assets						Comparative Historical Data	
Type of Statement								
Unqualified			4	19	9	4	42	29
Reviewed	1	6	42	36			102	106
Compiled	1	20	30	5			59	60
Tax Returns	12	20	17	1			60	64
Other	4	9	47	38	9	4	137	118
	62 (4/1-9/30/13)			276 (10/1/13-3/31/14)			4/1/09-3/31/10	4/1/10-3/31/11
	0-500M	500M-2MM	2-10MM	10-50MM	50-100MM	100-250MM	ALL	ALL
NUMBER OF STATEMENTS	18	55	140	99	18	8	400	377
ASSETS	%	%	%	%	%	%	%	%
Cash & Equivalents	11.5	11.8	8.5	5.9	5.8		7.6	7.6
Trade Receivables (net)	25.4	27.5	29.8	30.4	26.1		30.3	31.6
Inventory	40.2	36.3	42.2	42.8	34.9		40.5	38.7
All Other Current	.4	3.2	2.2	2.5	3.8		2.7	2.2
Total Current	77.5	78.8	82.7	81.5	70.6		81.1	80.2
Fixed Assets (net)	13.0	10.9	10.1	12.3	13.4		11.5	12.1
Intangibles (net)	6.8	4.0	1.8	1.9	5.7		1.8	2.1
All Other Non-Current	2.7	6.3	5.5	4.3	10.4		5.6	5.7
Total	100.0	100.0	100.0	100.0	100.0		100.0	100.0
LIABILITIES								
Notes Payable-Short Term	23.8	8.6	14.2	17.4	14.8		17.4	15.2
Cur. Mat.-L.T.D.	.5	1.8	1.3	1.0	1.6		2.1	2.1
Trade Payables	29.5	19.2	19.6	17.6	17.2		19.1	19.1
Income Taxes Payable	.0	.7	.3	.2	.2		.2	.2
All Other Current	9.1	7.2	7.4	7.9	8.1		8.6	7.9
Total Current	62.9	37.6	42.7	44.0	41.7		47.3	44.5
Long-Term Debt	13.7	10.5	6.2	7.3	12.9		8.4	9.1
Deferred Taxes	.0	.2	.2	.5	1.9		.3	.3
All Other Non-Current	44.3	3.6	5.4	3.4	7.2		5.0	6.2
Net Worth	-21.0	48.1	45.4	44.8	36.3		39.0	40.0
Total Liabilties & Net Worth	100.0	100.0	100.0	100.0	100.0		100.0	100.0
INCOME DATA								
Net Sales	100.0	100.0	100.0	100.0	100.0		100.0	100.0
Gross Profit	34.4	35.7	27.7	27.9	27.1		30.2	30.4
Operating Expenses	30.3	31.7	24.1	24.2	22.5		29.1	28.2
Operating Profit	4.1	4.0	3.6	3.7	4.6		1.1	2.2
All Other Expenses (net)	1.5	-.1	-.1	.4	.4		.4	.2
Profit Before Taxes	2.5	4.1	3.7	3.3	4.3		.7	2.0
RATIOS								
Current	2.8	2.9	3.2	2.7	3.1		2.6	2.8
	1.4	2.3	2.0	1.9	1.7		1.8	1.9
	1.0	1.7	1.4	1.4	1.1		1.3	1.4
Quick	1.2	1.4	1.5	1.3	1.3		1.4	1.5
	.7	.9	.8	.8	.8		.8	.9
	.4	.6	.5	.5	.5		.5	.6
Sales/Receivables	**6** 58.0	**19** 18.8	**29** 12.6	**36** 10.1	**33** 10.9		**31** 11.6	**34** 10.8
	32 11.3	**29** 12.7	**36** 10.1	**42** 8.6	**37** 9.9		**41** 8.9	**43** 8.6
	43 8.4	**42** 8.7	**46** 8.0	**51** 7.2	**46** 8.0		**52** 7.0	**54** 6.8
Cost of Sales/Inventory	**16** 23.2	**32** 11.4	**51** 7.1	**60** 6.1	**63** 5.8		**52** 7.0	**50** 7.2
	72 5.1	**56** 6.5	**79** 4.6	**81** 4.5	**76** 4.8		**81** 4.5	**81** 4.5
	111 3.3	**107** 3.4	**104** 3.5	**122** 3.0	**94** 3.9		**121** 3.0	**114** 3.2
Cost of Sales/Payables	**15** 24.8	**18** 20.4	**22** 16.9	**25** 14.8	**33** 11.0		**22** 16.6	**24** 15.3
	44 8.3	**33** 10.9	**32** 11.3	**30** 12.0	**36** 10.0		**32** 11.4	**33** 11.1
	65 5.6	**53** 6.9	**47** 7.8	**40** 9.1	**43** 8.5		**46** 7.9	**51** 7.2
Sales/Working Capital	5.0	5.6	4.2	4.6	4.3		4.8	4.5
	12.5	7.1	7.2	7.4	8.0		7.9	7.3
	NM	11.8	13.4	11.8	33.0		16.7	12.7
EBIT/Interest	4.5	23.3	29.2	21.6	12.1		9.8	11.0
	(15) 1.6	(45) 7.9	(130) 7.3	(93) 8.0	(16) 5.8		(361) 2.4	(335) 3.5
	-3.0	1.5	2.7	3.7	2.1		-.3	1.2
Net Profit + Depr., Dep., Amort./Cur. Mat. L/T/D			28.6	9.9	27.5		7.0	8.1
			(34) 5.9	(30) 5.6	(10) 5.6		(98) 2.2	(94) 2.8
			1.1	2.6	1.2		.4	.9
Fixed/Worth	.0	.1	.1	.1	.2		.1	.1
	.3	.2	.2	.2	.4		.2	.2
	-.8	.8	.4	.5	.8		.6	.5
Debt/Worth	.7	.5	.6	.8	1.1		.7	.6
	5.5	.8	1.2	1.3	1.9		1.5	1.4
	-3.4	3.1	2.6	2.6	5.6		3.4	3.0
% Profit Before Taxes/Tangible Net Worth	69.2	62.3	41.0	35.4	22.5		19.3	21.1
	(11) 14.6	(51) 26.7	(134) 17.3	(98) 18.1	(16) 15.0		(360) 6.4	(340) 9.0
	3.3	7.2	3.7	10.4	9.7		-4.1	2.0
% Profit Before Taxes/Total Assets	13.4	28.5	15.7	12.2	9.3		8.4	8.9
	2.1	7.1	7.4	7.5	5.7		2.4	3.8
	-9.1	1.6	2.0	3.9	2.1		-3.2	.7
Sales/Net Fixed Assets	UND	94.3	100.4	56.1	48.5		70.9	74.8
	70.8	39.4	45.7	32.3	23.4		37.0	34.0
	32.6	20.7	24.4	16.0	13.5		16.1	15.1
Sales/Total Assets	5.0	4.1	3.4	3.1	3.1		3.3	3.2
	3.1	3.2	2.7	2.6	2.3		2.6	2.5
	2.7	2.4	2.1	2.1	1.7		2.0	2.0
% Depr., Dep., Amort./Sales	.2	.3	.3	.4	.4		.4	.4
	(12) .4	(45) .7	(115) .5	(93) .6	(17) .6		(339) .7	(329) .7
	.7	1.2	.7	.8	1.2		1.2	1.1
% Officers', Directors' Owners' Comp/Sales		3.1	1.6	1.1			1.5	1.5
		(30) 4.7	(69) 2.8	(35) 1.7			(162) 3.1	(157) 3.4
		9.5	4.3	3.5			6.3	6.4
Net Sales ($)	23288M	241833M	2073525M	5959029M	2775573M	2249078M	11497174M	11539742M
Total Assets ($)	4986M	74381M	733541M	2215545M	1211688M	1186504M	4840325M	4803773M

M = $ thousand MM = $ million

See Pages 9 through 22 for Explanation of Ratios and Data

Comparative Historical Data / Current Data Sorted by Sales

4/1/11-3/31/12 ALL	4/1/12-3/31/13 ALL	4/1/13-3/31/14 ALL		0-1MM	1-3MM	3-5MM	5-10MM	10-25MM	25MM & OVER
			Type of Statement						
38	41	36	Unqualified					3	33
92	86	85	Reviewed	1	2	1	16	31	34
64	61	56	Compiled		11	9	15	15	6
62	49	50	Tax Returns	5	14	8	14	8	1
134	129	111	Other	2	5	7	9	30	58
					62 (4/1-9/30/13)		276 (10/1/13-3/31/14)		
390	366	338	**NUMBER OF STATEMENTS**	8	32	25	54	87	132
%	%	%	**ASSETS**	%	%	%	%	%	%
7.1	7.1	8.1	Cash & Equivalents		9.0	8.1	13.1	7.6	5.9
31.1	29.7	29.1	Trade Receivables (net)		22.1	29.2	27.5	30.4	31.4
40.1	41.0	40.7	Inventory		39.8	35.5	40.4	42.9	41.0
2.2	2.3	2.5	All Other Current		2.2	2.5	3.4	2.1	2.5
80.5	80.1	80.4	Total Current		73.1	75.3	84.5	83.0	80.8
11.2	11.5	11.2	Fixed Assets (net)		10.6	16.2	8.1	11.4	10.9
3.3	3.0	3.2	Intangibles (net)		6.8	5.2	1.0	1.3	3.5
4.9	5.4	5.3	All Other Non-Current		9.5	3.3	6.3	4.4	4.8
100.0	100.0	100.0	Total		100.0	100.0	100.0	100.0	100.0
			LIABILITIES						
15.2	14.5	14.6	Notes Payable-Short Term		14.3	9.9	10.1	15.2	15.8
2.1	1.8	1.3	Cur. Mat.-L.T.D.		1.4	2.8	1.1	1.2	1.2
19.2	19.6	19.2	Trade Payables		19.3	19.0	21.1	19.3	18.7
.2	.2	.3	Income Taxes Payable		.3	.1	.7	.3	.2
8.2	8.1	7.6	All Other Current		8.0	7.2	6.2	8.4	7.9
44.8	44.1	43.0	Total Current		43.3	39.1	39.1	44.4	43.7
8.0	8.2	8.3	Long-Term Debt		14.4	10.9	7.1	6.1	7.8
.3	.4	.4	Deferred Taxes		.1	.0	.2	.3	.8
5.5	4.9	6.6	All Other Non-Current		14.6	19.5	6.2	3.9	4.1
41.4	42.4	41.6	Net Worth		27.6	30.5	47.4	45.3	43.6
100.0	100.0	100.0	Total Liabilties & Net Worth		100.0	100.0	100.0	100.0	100.0
			INCOME DATA						
100.0	100.0	100.0	Net Sales		100.0	100.0	100.0	100.0	100.0
29.5	28.6	29.4	Gross Profit		36.2	32.7	28.9	27.9	27.4
26.7	25.4	25.6	Operating Expenses		32.5	28.6	25.1	24.6	23.5
2.8	3.3	3.8	Operating Profit		3.6	4.1	3.8	3.3	3.9
.2	.1	.2	All Other Expenses (net)		.4	.0	.0	-.1	.4
2.7	3.1	3.6	Profit Before Taxes		3.2	4.1	3.8	3.4	3.5
			RATIOS						
2.9	3.0	3.0			3.0	2.7	3.7	2.9	2.8
1.8	1.9	2.0	Current		2.0	2.1	2.5	1.9	1.9
1.3	1.4	1.4			1.0	1.7	1.5	1.4	1.5
1.5	1.5	1.3			.9	1.3	1.9	1.3	1.3
.8	.8	.9	Quick		.7	.8	.9	.8	.9
.5	.5	.6			.5	.6	.6	.5	.6
31 11.9	**30** 12.0	**29** 12.6			**20** 17.9	**26** 14.0	**23** 15.6	**30** 12.2	**34** 10.7
41 9.0	**39** 9.4	**38** 9.7	Sales/Receivables		**35** 10.4	**35** 10.5	**30** 12.1	**36** 10.0	**41** 8.8
53 6.9	**49** 7.4	**47** 7.7			**45** 8.1	**55** 6.6	**42** 8.7	**47** 7.8	**51** 7.2
49 7.5	**50** 7.3	**49** 7.4			**41** 8.8	**49** 7.4	**37** 9.9	**52** 7.0	**52** 7.0
79 4.6	**81** 4.5	**78** 4.7	Cost of Sales/Inventory		**94** 3.9	**79** 4.6	**61** 6.0	**87** 4.2	**78** 4.7
118 3.1	**111** 3.3	**104** 3.5			**159** 2.3	**130** 2.8	**94** 3.9	**114** 3.2	**101** 3.6
23 15.8	**22** 16.7	**23** 15.9			**18** 20.0	**13** 28.2	**22** 16.6	**20** 17.9	**25** 14.4
33 11.2	**32** 11.5	**33** 11.1	Cost of Sales/Payables		**48** 7.6	**31** 11.8	**33** 11.2	**32** 11.4	**33** 11.2
49 7.5	**43** 8.4	**46** 7.9			**59** 6.2	**51** 7.1	**43** 8.5	**48** 7.6	**41** 9.0
4.6	4.5	4.7			4.4	5.0	4.8	4.7	4.7
7.4	7.1	7.4	Sales/Working Capital		7.6	6.1	7.0	7.7	7.5
14.3	13.9	12.9			NM	9.0	13.9	12.8	12.0
14.5	14.6	21.5			9.8	22.0	35.9	27.4	20.5
(348) 4.7	(329) 5.5	(307) 6.6	EBIT/Interest		(29) 3.3	(24) 3.5	(43) 7.3	(82) 6.3	(123) 8.8
1.7	1.9	2.5			1.0	1.3	2.2	2.7	4.4
9.0	10.2	21.2					6.2	16.9	26.9
(88) 3.4	(87) 3.5	(83) 5.6	Net Profit + Depr., Dep., Amort./Cur. Mat. L/T/D				(11) 3.4	(22) 7.5	(46) 5.8
1.4	1.5	1.9					.2	1.9	2.6
.1	.1	.1			.1	.1	.0	.1	.1
.2	.2	.2	Fixed/Worth		.3	.2	.1	.2	.2
.5	.5	.5			1.4	.6	.4	.4	.5
.7	.6	.6			.7	.7	.4	.6	.8
1.5	1.3	1.3	Debt/Worth		3.0	1.1	.9	1.3	1.3
3.6	3.0	2.8			32.4	2.3	2.7	2.7	2.7
31.9	30.3	40.3			47.4	55.4	44.6	40.8	37.7
(358) 13.3	(343) 14.3	(315) 17.6	% Profit Before Taxes/Tangible Net Worth		(25) 14.6	(23) 13.5	(50) 19.2	(86) 16.6	(125) 20.4
4.6	4.4	7.3			4.5	3.6	6.0	3.7	10.6
11.4	12.0	14.3			10.5	20.8	21.9	15.4	12.5
5.4	5.5	7.1	% Profit Before Taxes/Total Assets		3.7	5.1	7.1	5.8	7.9
1.4	1.6	2.3			-.3	.8	1.9	2.0	4.1
89.7	86.7	84.9			95.8	145.5	118.7	93.0	59.8
37.8	38.0	38.8	Sales/Net Fixed Assets		38.6	25.7	65.7	37.7	33.8
15.3	15.4	18.6			16.9	11.0	35.0	17.2	18.0
3.3	3.3	3.4			3.1	3.1	3.9	3.4	3.2
2.6	2.6	2.7	Sales/Total Assets		2.4	2.4	3.3	2.7	2.8
1.9	2.0	2.1			1.3	1.6	2.3	2.2	2.1
.3	.3	.3			.3	.2	.3	.3	.4
(318) .6	(305) .6	(288) .5	% Depr., Dep., Amort./Sales		(23) .7	(20) .4	(44) .5	(75) .5	(120) .6
1.1	.9	.9			1.7	1.2	.9	.8	.8
1.5	1.4	1.6			3.1	3.9	2.2	1.3	1.0
(167) 2.6	(137) 2.9	(143) 2.9	% Officers', Directors' Owners' Comp/Sales		(16) 4.5	(17) 5.5	(29) 2.9	(38) 2.5	(40) 1.7
4.7	4.9	5.0			8.8	9.2	4.8	3.6	3.1
11612219M	**13106605M**	**13322326M**	Net Sales ($)	**4896M**	**65332M**	**98577M**	**394540M**	**1472000M**	**11286981M**
5212181M	**5713646M**	**5426645M**	Total Assets ($)	**1670M**	**35499M**	**45004M**	**144059M**	**582207M**	**4618206M**

M = $ thousand MM = $ million

See Pages 9 through 22 for Explanation of Ratios and Data

Current Data Sorted by Assets / Comparative Historical Data

	Current Data Sorted by Assets						Comparative Historical Data	
Type of Statement								
Unqualified			1	16	4	1	38	35
Reviewed		9	37	27	1		77	79
Compiled	1	12	21	5			39	42
Tax Returns	8	15	14	3			31	31
Other	2	13	30	38	8	4	77	79
	46 (4/1-9/30/13)			224 (10/1/13-3/31/14)			4/1/09-3/31/10 ALL	4/1/10-3/31/11 ALL
	0-500M	500M-2MM	2-10MM	10-50MM	50-100MM	100-250MM		
NUMBER OF STATEMENTS	11	49	103	89	13	5	262	266
ASSETS	%	%	%	%	%	%	%	%
Cash & Equivalents	10.0	13.2	6.3	5.8	6.3		7.3	7.4
Trade Receivables (net)	39.8	34.9	43.5	31.2	29.5		36.5	37.1
Inventory	10.0	31.6	34.4	42.0	42.7		36.9	35.7
All Other Current	4.5	3.5	1.8	2.9	3.4		2.6	2.4
Total Current	64.2	83.2	85.9	81.9	82.0		83.4	82.5
Fixed Assets (net)	18.0	7.9	8.2	9.7	9.0		9.6	8.7
Intangibles (net)	5.5	1.9	2.5	3.5	1.8		2.3	3.4
All Other Non-Current	12.3	7.0	3.4	4.9	7.3		4.7	5.3
Total	100.0	100.0	100.0	100.0	100.0		100.0	100.0
LIABILITIES								
Notes Payable-Short Term	15.9	12.3	15.3	18.1	10.5		15.5	15.0
Cur. Mat.-L.T.D.	1.1	1.3	1.1	1.6	.4		1.9	1.7
Trade Payables	37.2	23.4	25.4	17.4	19.6		22.6	22.7
Income Taxes Payable	.0	.2	.3	.2	.2		.2	.3
All Other Current	9.7	13.3	10.4	8.1	6.5		11.4	11.2
Total Current	64.0	50.6	52.4	45.5	37.2		51.6	51.0
Long-Term Debt	16.0	8.2	4.8	5.4	12.6		5.7	6.4
Deferred Taxes	.0	.1	.2	.3	.2		.2	.3
All Other Non-Current	2.1	2.9	6.0	4.8	2.2		5.2	4.1
Net Worth	17.8	38.2	36.6	44.1	47.8		37.3	38.2
Total Liabilties & Net Worth	100.0	100.0	100.0	100.0	100.0		100.0	100.0
INCOME DATA								
Net Sales	100.0	100.0	100.0	100.0	100.0		100.0	100.0
Gross Profit	34.6	30.1	27.6	26.0	22.6		27.4	27.4
Operating Expenses	29.3	26.4	25.3	23.5	19.8		25.3	24.9
Operating Profit	5.3	3.8	2.2	2.5	2.8		2.0	2.5
All Other Expenses (net)	.2	-.1	-.1	-.3	-.3		.0	.2
Profit Before Taxes	5.1	3.8	2.4	2.8	3.1		2.0	2.3
RATIOS								
Current	2.7	3.1	2.3	2.5	4.5		2.4	2.5
	1.2	1.7	1.7	1.8	2.8		1.6	1.6
	.6	1.1	1.3	1.3	1.4		1.2	1.3
Quick	2.0	1.9	1.3	1.3	1.7		1.3	1.3
	(10) 1.1	1.0	1.0	.7	1.1		.8	.9
	.5	.6	.6	.5	.7		.5	.6
Sales/Receivables	**0** UND	**23** 16.0	**34** 10.6	**31** 11.6	**35** 10.5		**33** 11.0	**34** 10.7
	22 16.7	**35** 10.3	**46** 8.0	**40** 9.1	**44** 8.3		**43** 8.5	**46** 7.9
	51 7.2	**49** 7.5	**64** 5.7	**54** 6.8	**46** 8.0		**57** 6.5	**58** 6.3
Cost of Sales/Inventory	**0** UND	**14** 25.2	**16** 23.1	**60** 6.1	**64** 5.7		**30** 12.2	**32** 11.5
	0 UND	**45** 8.1	**58** 6.3	**91** 4.0	**85** 4.3		**77** 4.8	**70** 5.2
	38 9.7	**89** 4.1	**104** 3.5	**114** 3.2	**94** 3.9		**109** 3.3	**102** 3.6
Cost of Sales/Payables	**0** UND	**19** 19.5	**24** 15.0	**19** 19.1	**17** 21.1		**20** 18.2	**21** 17.1
	19 19.3	**31** 11.8	**38** 9.7	**27** 13.6	**34** 10.8		**33** 11.0	**37** 9.9
	48 7.6	**46** 8.0	**56** 6.5	**43** 8.5	**41** 8.8		**55** 6.6	**58** 6.3
Sales/Working Capital	8.7	6.0	5.3	4.5	4.2		5.4	5.0
	74.6	10.7	9.1	7.4	4.9		8.8	8.7
	-23.6	105.9	20.1	14.8	13.8		18.5	17.3
EBIT/Interest		15.3	20.1	21.7			13.3	16.5
		(43) 7.4	(96) 6.6	(84) 6.9			(241) 4.3	(241) 4.3
		1.6	2.4	2.7			1.1	1.9
Net Profit + Depr., Dep., Amort./Cur. Mat. L/T/D			6.6	34.7			9.0	11.6
			(18) 3.3	(24) 3.7			(60) 2.9	(72) 3.4
			2.5	1.8			.4	1.5
Fixed/Worth	.0	.0	.1	.1	.1		.1	.1
	1.0	.2	.2	.1	.2		.2	.2
	-.5	.7	.6	.4	.3		.6	.6
Debt/Worth	.9	.7	.8	.7	.5		.8	.7
	2.5	1.7	2.1	1.5	1.2		1.7	1.7
	-3.4	5.7	4.5	3.2	2.9		4.3	4.9
% Profit Before Taxes/Tangible Net Worth		49.4	41.5	26.3	23.6		28.4	34.4
		(42) 21.7	(94) 18.1	(85) 15.4	17.7		(242) 12.1	(238) 15.1
		8.6	5.3	7.7	9.7		2.9	3.6
% Profit Before Taxes/Total Assets	56.0	16.6	13.4	11.5	11.1		9.8	12.2
	26.2	7.2	5.3	6.4	9.3		4.0	5.4
	11.2	1.9	1.7	2.6	2.4		.3	1.0
Sales/Net Fixed Assets	UND	198.3	121.6	96.6	81.6		121.8	128.7
	129.3	79.6	58.1	48.2	39.2		49.1	51.3
	35.7	35.5	23.5	20.6	24.4		22.6	23.9
Sales/Total Assets	12.5	4.8	3.9	3.2	3.2		3.5	3.3
	6.4	3.2	3.1	2.5	2.6		2.7	2.7
	4.5	2.4	2.3	2.1	2.2		2.2	2.2
% Depr., Dep., Amort./Sales		.2	.2	.3	.3		.3	.3
		(37) .4	(90) .5	(78) .4	(12) .5		(232) .6	(226) .5
		.9	.8	.8	.7		.9	1.0
% Officers', Directors' Owners' Comp/Sales		2.6	1.4	1.0			1.5	1.3
		(27) 4.2	(45) 2.6	(21) 1.7			(83) 2.9	(96) 3.0
		9.2	4.9	4.3			5.9	5.8
Net Sales ($)	26778M	210921M	1570905M	5043755M	2547858M	2239676M	9568577M	11397319M
Total Assets ($)	3045M	59993M	509179M	1914872M	987781M	823786M	3642777M	4744338M

M = $ thousand MM = $ million

See Pages 9 through 22 for Explanation of Ratios and Data

Comparative Historical Data | **Current Data Sorted by Sales**

4/1/11-3/31/12 ALL	4/1/12-3/31/13 ALL	4/1/13-3/31/14 ALL		0-1MM	1-3MM	3-5MM	5-10MM	10-25MM	25MM & OVER
			Type of Statement						
34	21	22	Unqualified					1	21
75	59	74	Reviewed		1	7	7	28	31
38	34	39	Compiled		4	5	10	15	5
37	40	40	Tax Returns	2	12	7	7	8	4
96	94	95	Other	2	5	7	11	23	47
				46 (4/1-9/30/13)			224 (10/1/13-3/31/14)		
280	248	270	**NUMBER OF STATEMENTS**	4	22	26	35	75	108
%	%	%	**ASSETS**	%	%	%	%	%	%
7.5	7.6	7.6	Cash & Equivalents		9.6	10.5	11.8	5.1	5.8
36.1	36.4	36.6	Trade Receivables (net)		31.4	32.6	37.8	43.4	34.1
35.6	36.5	35.6	Inventory		32.2	34.3	33.1	34.7	39.3
3.3	2.3	2.6	All Other Current		4.1	1.6	2.7	2.5	2.7
82.5	82.8	82.5	Total Current		77.3	78.9	85.4	85.6	81.8
9.3	8.7	9.2	Fixed Assets (net)		9.9	10.9	7.7	8.6	9.1
2.8	3.2	3.2	Intangibles (net)		3.5	2.3	3.6	2.0	4.3
5.4	5.4	5.0	All Other Non-Current		9.3	7.9	3.3	3.8	4.8
100.0	100.0	100.0	Total		100.0	100.0	100.0	100.0	100.0
			LIABILITIES						
16.4	17.3	15.3	Notes Payable-Short Term		12.0	15.0	14.0	14.7	16.9
1.6	1.0	1.3	Cur. Mat.-L.T.D.		.9	.7	1.7	1.3	1.3
22.0	21.5	22.4	Trade Payables		28.4	23.9	25.2	25.3	18.6
.2	.3	.2	Income Taxes Payable		.2	.3	.3	.3	.2
12.1	10.5	9.9	All Other Current		15.8	9.1	11.4	9.9	8.5
52.3	50.6	49.1	Total Current		57.3	49.0	52.6	51.5	45.5
7.2	6.5	6.9	Long-Term Debt		12.5	6.9	9.3	4.1	7.1
.3	.1	.2	Deferred Taxes		.0	.1	.1	.2	.3
4.6	4.6	4.6	All Other Non-Current		2.1	3.8	4.5	8.5	2.8
35.6	38.2	39.2	Net Worth		28.1	40.2	33.5	35.7	44.3
100.0	100.0	100.0	Total Liabilties & Net Worth		100.0	100.0	100.0	100.0	100.0
			INCOME DATA						
100.0	100.0	100.0	Net Sales		100.0	100.0	100.0	100.0	100.0
27.9	28.8	27.7	Gross Profit		34.2	32.5	27.3	26.9	25.6
24.9	26.0	24.9	Operating Expenses		30.1	28.6	26.1	24.5	22.8
3.0	2.8	2.9	Operating Profit		4.2	3.9	1.2	2.5	2.8
.1	.0	-.1	All Other Expenses (net)		.1	.1	-.8	.0	-.2
2.9	2.8	3.0	Profit Before Taxes		4.1	3.8	2.0	2.4	3.0
			RATIOS						
2.4	2.6	2.6			3.5	2.8	2.3	2.3	2.6
1.6	1.7	1.7	Current		1.6	2.1	1.8	1.7	1.7
1.2	1.2	1.3			1.0	1.0	1.3	1.3	1.3
1.3	1.3	1.4			2.2	1.6	1.4	1.3	1.3
.9	.9	(269) .9	Quick		.8	1.0	(34) 1.0	.9	.8
.5	.5	.5			.5	.5	.6	.6	.5
30 12.3	**29** 12.7	**31** 11.9			**12** 30.3	**26** 14.0	**30** 12.1	**34** 10.8	**31** 11.6
41 8.9	**42** 8.6	**41** 9.0	Sales/Receivables		**23** 15.8	**35** 10.3	**39** 9.3	**47** 7.7	**41** 9.0
58 6.3	**58** 6.3	**56** 6.5			**54** 6.8	**45** 8.1	**57** 6.4	**65** 5.6	**53** 6.9
27 13.7	**19** 19.6	**20** 18.2			**0** UND	**19** 19.5	**16** 23.1	**16** 23.1	**48** 7.6
72 5.1	**76** 4.8	**69** 5.3	Cost of Sales/Inventory		**64** 5.7	**55** 6.6	**45** 8.1	**62** 5.9	**79** 4.6
104 3.5	**111** 3.3	**107** 3.4			**122** 3.0	**111** 3.3	**96** 3.8	**111** 3.3	**104** 3.5
20 18.5	**18** 20.8	**20** 18.7			**16** 23.3	**24** 15.2	**26** 14.0	**22** 16.7	**19** 19.4
32 11.5	**32** 11.4	**31** 11.7	Cost of Sales/Payables		**29** 12.5	**31** 11.6	**36** 10.1	**38** 9.7	**28** 12.9
51 7.2	**51** 7.2	**48** 7.6			**58** 6.3	**56** 6.5	**49** 7.5	**64** 5.7	**40** 9.1
5.3	5.1	5.1			5.4	4.0	5.2	5.3	4.8
9.4	8.8	8.9	Sales/Working Capital		11.5	9.5	9.1	9.3	7.6
24.1	21.1	19.7			NM	-111.7	20.3	20.1	16.2
19.6	18.6	20.2			17.2	28.0	28.6	16.9	27.5
(252) 6.0	(221) 6.8	(246) 7.1	EBIT/Interest		(19) 7.4	(23) 9.0	(31) 7.2	(70) 5.2	(100) 8.1
2.1	2.0	2.7			2.9	2.6	1.9	2.2	3.1
10.6	14.7	12.6						9.1	31.1
(56) 3.8	(53) 4.4	(55) 4.0	Net Profit + Depr., Dep., Amort./Cur. Mat. L/T/D					(13) 3.6	(30) 7.1
1.8	1.2	2.6						2.9	3.0
.1	.1	.1			.0	.1	.1	.1	.1
.2	.2	.2	Fixed/Worth		.2	.3	.2	.2	.2
.6	.5	.5			-21.5	1.0	.5	.6	.4
.8	.8	.8			.8	.6	.8	.9	.7
1.8	1.8	1.8	Debt/Worth		2.1	1.6	1.9	2.3	1.5
5.3	4.8	3.9			-300.6	11.1	6.2	5.2	3.2
37.4	40.0	35.4			33.2	45.6	50.6	42.5	26.4
(247) 17.1	(228) 15.4	(243) 17.6	% Profit Before Taxes/Tangible Net Worth		(16) 23.1	(22) 15.1	(28) 19.3	(70) 17.4	(103) 16.2
7.0	5.1	7.1			10.4	4.7	5.8	4.7	8.5
14.9	12.6	13.4			19.6	17.7	15.2	12.3	12.3
6.1	6.1	6.9	% Profit Before Taxes/Total Assets		7.9	7.0	6.1	4.9	7.4
2.1	1.4	2.3			3.0	2.6	1.6	1.2	3.1
146.2	148.1	133.5			265.8	97.3	182.5	130.8	95.9
50.6	57.4	57.7	Sales/Net Fixed Assets		104.5	42.7	75.3	67.0	47.8
23.3	23.0	26.0			28.6	26.8	34.6	23.5	23.9
3.5	3.6	3.8			4.7	4.9	4.5	3.9	3.3
2.8	2.8	2.9	Sales/Total Assets		2.9	3.1	3.2	3.0	2.7
2.3	2.2	2.2			1.7	2.1	2.3	2.3	2.3
.3	.2	.2			.1	.6	.3	.2	.3
(232) .5	(204) .5	(227) .5	% Depr., Dep., Amort./Sales		(20) .3	(19) .8	(25) .6	(67) .5	(94) .4
1.0	.9	.8			.7	1.2	1.0	.8	.8
1.5	1.7	1.6			3.4	2.3	1.9	1.3	1.0
(95) 3.3	(91) 2.8	(103) 2.9	% Officers', Directors' Owners' Comp/Sales		(16) 5.3	(13) 4.2	(16) 2.9	(34) 2.5	(22) 1.8
5.6	5.0	6.7			11.9	5.3	4.8	4.8	5.6
12085370M	9847966M	11639893M	Net Sales ($)	2499M	49591M	102049M	259494M	1241554M	9984706M
4699750M	3902405M	4298656M	Total Assets ($)	1707M	20327M	36995M	85965M	451158M	3702504M

M = $ thousand MM = $ million

See Pages 9 through 22 for Explanation of Ratios and Data

Current Data Sorted by Assets							Comparative Historical Data	
Type of Statement								
Unqualified			1	10	1		11	9
Reviewed		2	11	7			18	16
Compiled		4	5	2			12	10
Tax Returns		4					5	7
Other		4	6	6	2		26	22
		10 (4/1-9/30/13)		55 (10/1/13-3/31/14)				
	0-500M	500M-2MM	2-10MM	10-50MM	50-100MM	100-250MM	4/1/09-3/31/10 ALL	4/1/10-3/31/11 ALL
NUMBER OF STATEMENTS		14	23	25	3		72	64
ASSETS	%	%	%	%	%	%	%	%
Cash & Equivalents	DATA NOT AVAILABLE	8.8	7.2	6.2		DATA NOT AVAILABLE	11.7	11.5
Trade Receivables (net)		27.7	24.7	22.7			26.4	27.3
Inventory		42.8	35.0	43.3			38.5	36.0
All Other Current		.1	2.2	2.1			3.4	3.8
Total Current		79.4	69.1	74.3			80.0	78.6
Fixed Assets (net)		6.5	22.7	12.8			11.2	10.2
Intangibles (net)		9.4	3.3	7.0			4.7	5.0
All Other Non-Current		4.7	4.9	5.9			4.1	6.2
Total		100.0	100.0	100.0			100.0	100.0
LIABILITIES								
Notes Payable-Short Term		10.3	10.1	9.4			13.3	10.5
Cur. Mat.-L.T.D.		3.6	3.1	1.9			2.2	3.0
Trade Payables		15.6	18.0	16.7			18.5	18.7
Income Taxes Payable		.2	.1	.1			.1	.4
All Other Current		8.3	7.6	7.1			8.4	8.6
Total Current		37.9	38.9	35.1			42.5	41.3
Long-Term Debt		13.5	11.3	12.5			7.8	8.2
Deferred Taxes		.0	.5	.2			.2	.2
All Other Non-Current		5.1	2.3	11.1			6.7	5.6
Net Worth		43.5	47.0	41.1			42.7	44.8
Total Liabilties & Net Worth		100.0	100.0	100.0			100.0	100.0
INCOME DATA								
Net Sales		100.0	100.0	100.0			100.0	100.0
Gross Profit		30.4	28.4	27.0			28.7	30.0
Operating Expenses		30.0	24.6	22.1			25.0	25.9
Operating Profit		.5	3.8	4.9			3.7	4.1
All Other Expenses (net)		-.6	.2	.8			.3	.2
Profit Before Taxes		1.0	3.6	4.1			3.4	3.8
RATIOS								
Current		3.6	2.6	2.8			3.1	3.3
		2.0	1.7	2.2			2.0	1.8
		1.3	1.3	1.8			1.4	1.4
Quick		1.6	1.3	1.5			1.4	1.4
		1.0	.8	.9			.9	1.0
		.6	.5	.6			.6	.6
Sales/Receivables		**26** 14.0	**24** 14.9	**24** 15.1			**24** 15.1	**23** 16.0
		30 12.1	**32** 11.5	**33** 10.9			**34** 10.8	**31** 11.7
		54 6.8	**42** 8.7	**51** 7.1			**40** 9.0	**40** 9.1
Cost of Sales/Inventory		**42** 8.7	**37** 9.9	**48** 7.6			**44** 8.2	**26** 14.2
		78 4.7	**68** 5.4	**96** 3.8			**75** 4.8	**75** 4.9
		140 2.6	**91** 4.0	**166** 2.2			**124** 2.9	**123** 3.0
Cost of Sales/Payables		**13** 29.1	**22** 16.9	**16** 22.8			**17** 21.8	**17** 21.5
		28 12.9	**38** 9.7	**29** 12.4			**31** 11.8	**32** 11.6
		50 7.3	**47** 7.7	**42** 8.7			**48** 7.6	**44** 8.3
Sales/Working Capital		3.8	5.3	2.9			4.3	4.8
		5.3	9.8	6.3			6.7	7.7
		27.7	17.5	8.3			11.8	17.1
EBIT/Interest		19.7	8.0	18.7			12.6	31.6
		(12) 5.1	(17) 4.7	(23) 9.3			(64) 5.5	(54) 9.0
		-1.6	3.2	4.4			2.7	3.8
Net Profit + Depr., Dep., Amort./Cur. Mat. L/T/D							6.6	6.5
							(16) 5.2	(17) 2.8
							2.8	1.7
Fixed/Worth		.1	.1	.1			.1	.1
		.1	.5	.3			.2	.2
		.4	.9	1.2			.5	.6
Debt/Worth		.8	.8	.8			.5	.5
		1.8	1.3	1.2			1.2	1.2
		8.3	2.0	6.6			3.2	3.3
% Profit Before Taxes/Tangible Net Worth		24.8	29.3	49.6			26.9	38.7
		(13) 5.4	15.0	(21) 25.2			(64) 13.9	(57) 16.9
		-19.0	8.6	8.9			4.7	9.6
% Profit Before Taxes/Total Assets		7.2	12.9	17.5			11.4	14.8
		3.3	7.7	12.8			5.8	8.6
		-3.7	2.9	4.3			2.1	3.8
Sales/Net Fixed Assets		67.7	34.1	80.2			73.0	106.1
		41.6	16.9	24.9			38.2	36.6
		29.8	7.9	14.3			16.6	20.1
Sales/Total Assets		4.1	3.4	2.8			3.3	3.5
		2.7	2.7	2.2			2.6	2.6
		1.6	2.0	1.6			1.9	2.2
% Depr., Dep., Amort./Sales		.3	.6	.3			.5	.4
		(11) .4	(22) 1.2	(23) 1.0			(58) .8	(53) .8
		.5	1.9	1.2			1.3	1.1
% Officers', Directors' Owners' Comp/Sales		3.6					1.6	2.4
		(12) 5.0					(14) 2.5	(20) 3.4
		5.8					4.4	5.1
Net Sales ($)		54025M	359035M	1187027M	381474M		2200014M	1688555M
Total Assets ($)		18783M	135097M	548085M	248836M		939613M	667377M

M = $ thousand MM = $ million

See Pages 9 through 22 for Explanation of Ratios and Data

Comparative Historical Data				Current Data Sorted by Sales					
			Type of Statement						
13	7	12	Unqualified					2	10
21	14	20	Reviewed		1	1	3	7	8
12	11	11	Compiled		1		5	4	1
18	8	4	Tax Returns		3	1			
19	26	18	Other	1	1	3	1	4	8
4/1/11-3/31/12 ALL	**4/1/12-3/31/13 ALL**	**4/1/13-3/31/14 ALL**		**10 (4/1-9/30/13)**			**55 (10/1/13-3/31/14)**		
				0-1MM	**1-3MM**	**3-5MM**	**5-10MM**	**10-25MM**	**25MM & OVER**
83	66	65	**NUMBER OF STATEMENTS**	1	6	5	9	17	27
%	%	%	**ASSETS**	%	%	%	%	%	%
9.8	6.9	7.5	Cash & Equivalents					11.0	6.1
26.2	24.6	24.3	Trade Receivables (net)					21.8	24.2
38.4	44.0	40.1	Inventory					35.9	43.6
2.7	2.7	1.6	All Other Current					2.7	1.6
77.2	78.1	73.5	Total Current					71.4	75.4
12.9	13.1	15.1	Fixed Assets (net)					19.1	12.6
3.8	4.4	6.3	Intangibles (net)					5.6	5.3
6.1	4.4	5.1	All Other Non-Current					3.9	6.6
100.0	100.0	100.0	Total					100.0	100.0
			LIABILITIES						
13.6	12.5	10.0	Notes Payable-Short Term					8.0	10.7
3.0	2.2	2.7	Cur. Mat.-L.T.D.					2.7	2.0
16.9	17.2	16.6	Trade Payables					14.2	18.8
.3	.0	.1	Income Taxes Payable					.1	.1
7.3	8.3	7.4	All Other Current					7.2	8.4
41.1	40.2	36.8	Total Current					32.2	39.9
8.0	12.2	12.6	Long-Term Debt					11.4	12.3
.4	.4	.2	Deferred Taxes					.6	.2
3.8	6.2	6.4	All Other Non-Current					4.0	9.4
46.7	40.9	43.9	Net Worth					51.8	38.3
100.0	100.0	100.0	Total Liabilties & Net Worth					100.0	100.0
			INCOME DATA						
100.0	100.0	100.0	Net Sales					100.0	100.0
28.3	26.8	28.1	Gross Profit					29.9	23.9
24.8	23.3	24.6	Operating Expenses					27.5	18.2
3.5	3.6	3.5	Operating Profit					2.4	5.7
.2	-.1	.3	All Other Expenses (net)					.7	.2
3.3	3.6	3.2	Profit Before Taxes					1.6	5.5
			RATIOS						
3.3	3.2	2.9						4.2	2.5
2.1	2.0	2.0	Current					2.3	1.9
1.3	1.4	1.4						1.5	1.7
1.5	1.1	1.4						2.8	1.1
.8	.7	.8	Quick					1.0	.7
.6	.5	.6						.6	.6
21 17.5	**22** 16.9	**24** 14.9						**22** 16.7	**24** 15.0
32 11.5	**31** 11.9	**32** 11.4	Sales/Receivables					**30** 12.3	**33** 10.9
45 8.2	**40** 9.1	**45** 8.2						**43** 8.4	**45** 8.1
40 9.1	**58** 6.3	**46** 8.0						**39** 9.3	**51** 7.2
72 5.1	**87** 4.2	**85** 4.3	Cost of Sales/Inventory					**87** 4.2	**81** 4.5
111 3.3	**135** 2.7	**135** 2.7						**135** 2.7	**140** 2.6
15 23.9	**18** 19.8	**18** 19.9						**16** 23.0	**17** 21.7
26 14.3	**27** 13.4	**31** 11.7	Cost of Sales/Payables					**24** 15.4	**31** 11.7
38 9.5	**39** 9.4	**46** 8.0						**42** 8.7	**45** 8.2
4.0	4.1	3.9						3.2	4.5
7.3	7.1	7.1	Sales/Working Capital					6.4	7.6
19.6	13.7	13.4						16.5	9.7
26.7	33.3	17.0						12.5	19.5
(70) 7.5	(59) 9.6	(54) 6.5	EBIT/Interest					(13) 4.7	(24) 8.7
3.1	3.4	3.3						1.9	3.9
9.6	7.1	7.1							
(15) 3.6	(12) 3.1	(19) 4.1	Net Profit + Depr., Dep., Amort./Cur. Mat. L/T/D						
2.3	1.4	1.1							
.1	.1	.1						.1	.1
.2	.3	.3	Fixed/Worth					.3	.4
.5	.8	.8						1.0	.8
.5	.6	.8						.4	1.0
1.1	1.3	1.3	Debt/Worth					1.0	1.5
2.7	3.2	3.7						2.1	5.0
37.5	35.7	36.1						32.1	49.9
(76) 16.3	(60) 20.4	(60) 17.1	% Profit Before Taxes/Tangible Net Worth					(16) 13.9	(24) 24.1
6.3	5.7	7.1						6.5	11.6
16.1	15.4	14.0						12.8	18.0
7.3	8.6	7.7	% Profit Before Taxes/Total Assets					7.5	12.8
3.3	3.1	2.9						2.6	4.7
95.4	61.2	58.3						46.7	79.8
32.7	28.8	24.9	Sales/Net Fixed Assets					27.7	23.2
17.6	17.5	11.5						7.4	11.4
3.7	3.2	3.2						3.4	3.2
2.8	2.5	2.4	Sales/Total Assets					2.4	2.4
2.0	2.1	1.7						1.8	1.8
.4	.4	.3						.5	.3
(65) .8	(53) .7	(59) .9	% Depr., Dep., Amort./Sales					1.0	(24) .9
1.1	1.1	1.5						1.7	1.2
1.9	2.8	1.9							
(29) 2.8	(20) 3.8	(26) 3.9	% Officers', Directors' Owners' Comp/Sales						
3.9	5.4	5.8							
2330948M	**2286580M**	**1981561M**	Net Sales ($)	**631M**	**12926M**	**20463M**	**68589M**	**291979M**	**1586973M**
970830M	**984687M**	**950801M**	Total Assets ($)	**687M**	**6651M**	**11813M**	**28986M**	**168684M**	**733980M**

M = $ thousand MM = $ million

See Pages 9 through 22 for Explanation of Ratios and Data

Current Data Sorted by Assets							Comparative Historical Data	
						Type of Statement		
1		10	32	22	25	Unqualified	124	113
	5	51	49	11	3	Reviewed	127	140
	11	46	12	1		Compiled	75	63
8	17	25	4			Tax Returns	59	69
10	32	73	57	23	29	Other	227	215
	83 (4/1-9/30/13)		474 (10/1/13-3/31/14)				**4/1/09-3/31/10**	**4/1/10-3/31/11**
0-500M	**500M-2MM**	**2-10MM**	**10-50MM**	**50-100MM**	**100-250MM**		**ALL**	**ALL**
19	65	205	154	57	57	**NUMBER OF STATEMENTS**	612	600
%	%	%	%	%	%	**ASSETS**	%	%
18.5	10.8	9.9	6.6	3.5	2.7	Cash & Equivalents	7.3	7.6
30.1	23.9	20.3	13.5	11.6	14.2	Trade Receivables (net)	17.0	18.4
25.9	36.9	46.0	48.9	45.8	52.3	Inventory	46.9	47.4
1.0	1.9	2.0	2.3	3.5	1.5	All Other Current	1.9	1.8
75.5	73.5	78.3	71.3	64.4	70.6	Total Current	73.2	75.2
16.1	16.1	16.6	21.2	31.6	22.8	Fixed Assets (net)	20.0	18.0
3.8	3.3	2.2	3.1	1.0	1.1	Intangibles (net)	1.9	2.1
4.6	7.1	2.9	4.5	3.0	5.5	All Other Non-Current	4.9	4.7
100.0	100.0	100.0	100.0	100.0	100.0	Total	100.0	100.0
						LIABILITIES		
20.7	18.1	25.5	27.6	30.1	30.0	Notes Payable-Short Term	23.8	24.0
1.8	2.6	3.1	4.2	3.6	4.2	Cur. Mat.-L.T.D.	4.5	4.2
14.3	19.4	12.0	8.9	6.3	7.5	Trade Payables	11.0	12.5
.0	.4	.4	.5	.4	.9	Income Taxes Payable	.3	.4
11.5	10.6	6.1	6.2	6.6	6.3	All Other Current	9.0	7.6
48.3	50.9	47.2	47.4	47.0	48.9	Total Current	48.6	48.8
8.4	16.4	11.3	13.2	19.2	11.5	Long-Term Debt	13.1	11.0
.5	.2	.4	1.4	1.9	2.0	Deferred Taxes	.7	.7
.1	4.7	4.3	1.9	2.8	1.8	All Other Non-Current	3.6	4.5
42.6	27.8	36.8	36.2	29.1	35.9	Net Worth	34.0	34.9
100.0	100.0	100.0	100.0	100.0	100.0	Total Liabilties & Net Worth	100.0	100.0
						INCOME DATA		
100.0	100.0	100.0	100.0	100.0	100.0	Net Sales	100.0	100.0
30.7	33.3	27.9	27.1	22.5	23.6	Gross Profit	28.3	27.5
27.4	27.9	24.0	21.2	18.0	18.6	Operating Expenses	26.5	24.1
3.3	5.3	3.9	5.9	4.5	5.0	Operating Profit	1.9	3.5
.0	.8	.1	.6	1.1	.5	All Other Expenses (net)	1.1	.9
3.3	4.6	3.8	5.3	3.4	4.4	Profit Before Taxes	.7	2.6
						RATIOS		
3.5	2.2	2.3	2.2	2.0	2.0		2.3	2.1
1.5	1.5	1.6	1.4	1.3	1.4	Current	1.5	1.5
1.1	1.2	1.3	1.2	1.1	1.2		1.2	1.2
2.1	1.4	1.1	.8	.6	.5		.9	.9
1.3	.7	.6	.4	.3	.3	Quick	.4	.5
.4	.3	.3	.2	.2	.2		.2	.3
6 57.5	11 32.8	21 17.5	21 17.7	23 15.7	27 13.7		20 18.3	22 16.8
26 14.0	31 11.8	32 11.5	31 11.6	34 10.7	37 9.9	Sales/Receivables	33 11.0	36 10.2
43 8.5	46 7.9	46 7.9	45 8.1	45 8.2	54 6.8		48 7.6	51 7.2
0 UND	21 17.4	53 6.9	81 4.5	85 4.3	122 3.0		67 5.5	64 5.7
3 141.8	60 6.1	114 3.2	152 2.4	166 2.2	182 2.0	Cost of Sales/Inventory	156 2.3	134 2.7
76 4.8	126 2.9	203 1.8	243 1.5	281 1.3	281 1.3		253 1.4	224 1.6
0 UND	9 39.7	9 41.4	10 36.6	10 36.3	13 27.6		10 35.9	12 31.1
11 31.8	27 13.6	21 17.3	18 20.1	22 16.9	23 15.6	Cost of Sales/Payables	20 18.0	24 15.1
35 10.4	60 6.1	40 9.2	35 10.5	36 10.2	33 11.2		41 8.9	46 8.0
8.7	6.2	4.5	3.7	3.9	4.2		3.5	3.8
20.0	12.4	6.7	6.6	7.7	5.6	Sales/Working Capital	6.8	6.9
82.4	30.6	13.1	14.5	15.8	9.1		17.8	17.1
47.0	12.2	13.3	11.3	8.0	12.8		4.1	7.9
(13) 9.9	(51) 4.6	(188) 5.2	(149) 4.6	3.9	6.9	EBIT/Interest	(567) 1.7	(565) 2.9
-.3	1.5	2.0	2.1	2.3	3.3		.3	1.3
		11.0	4.4	6.2			5.1	8.0
		(31) 3.4	(31) 2.2	(16) 2.4		Net Profit + Depr., Dep., Amort./Cur. Mat. L/T/D	(119) 1.7	(123) 3.1
		1.5	1.1	.9			.5	1.0
.0	.1	.1	.1	.2	.1		.1	.1
.3	.3	.3	.3	1.1	.3	Fixed/Worth	.4	.3
1.0	1.2	1.0	1.3	1.9	1.3		1.2	1.1
.5	1.2	.9	1.1	1.6	1.1		1.0	1.0
1.3	2.5	1.9	2.1	2.6	2.2	Debt/Worth	2.1	1.9
5.9	11.1	4.1	3.9	4.1	3.0		4.4	3.9
128.8	78.1	39.8	31.5	27.1	24.4		17.8	24.0
(18) 59.1	(55) 30.4	(191) 18.7	(147) 19.4	(54) 15.8	(55) 15.2	% Profit Before Taxes/Tangible Net Worth	(568) 5.6	(549) 9.5
-7.8	7.7	6.6	8.7	7.6	12.8		-3.6	2.5
47.2	25.2	11.5	10.4	7.8	7.9		5.6	8.2
22.2	7.1	5.7	5.0	3.7	5.5	% Profit Before Taxes/Total Assets	1.6	3.5
-2.8	1.2	2.3	2.1	2.1	3.5		-1.7	.6
UND	165.9	60.3	42.9	18.5	33.6		39.8	49.7
50.1	35.2	24.2	19.3	5.9	13.2	Sales/Net Fixed Assets	16.5	20.9
16.5	13.8	9.3	4.8	2.0	2.7		5.2	6.4
5.7	4.9	2.6	1.9	1.4	1.6		2.2	2.4
4.3	2.6	1.9	1.4	1.2	1.2	Sales/Total Assets	1.4	1.6
2.4	1.7	1.4	1.0	.9	1.0		1.0	1.1
	.5	.6	.7	1.1	.4		.7	.7
	(32) 1.0	(147) 1.0	(109) 2.2	(37) 4.7	(20) .8	% Depr., Dep., Amort./Sales	(421) 1.5	(405) 1.3
	2.5	3.3	7.0	9.4	2.7		4.7	4.7
	2.0	1.6	1.0				1.5	1.5
	(33) 3.9	(83) 2.5	(31) 1.7			% Officers', Directors' Owners' Comp/Sales	(183) 2.9	(168) 2.6
	6.3	4.3	2.5				5.8	4.5
27641M	273819M	2105538M	5020182M	5058778M	11477061M	Net Sales ($)	23930316M	24733078M
5219M	84578M	1086203M	3478120M	4044393M	8974759M	Total Assets ($)	18153636M	17334370M

M = $ thousand MM = $ million

See Pages 9 through 22 for Explanation of Ratios and Data

Comparative Historical Data				Current Data Sorted by Sales					
			Type of Statement						
103	85	90	Unqualified		1		3	19	67
140	108	119	Reviewed		1	7	25	45	41
72	78	70	Compiled	1	6	7	27	20	9
95	62	54	Tax Returns	6	10	7	15	15	1
229	213	224	Other	6	17	19	44	50	88
				83 (4/1-9/30/13)			474 (10/1/13-3/31/14)		
4/1/11-3/31/12 ALL	**4/1/12-3/31/13 ALL**	**4/1/13-3/31/14 ALL**		**0-1MM**	**1-3MM**	**3-5MM**	**5-10MM**	**10-25MM**	**25MM & OVER**
639	546	557	**NUMBER OF STATEMENTS**	13	35	40	114	149	206
%	%	%	**ASSETS**	%	%	%	%	%	%
9.4	9.6	8.0	Cash & Equivalents	23.5	10.1	13.2	8.7	8.2	5.2
19.7	18.6	17.6	Trade Receivables (net)	19.9	22.9	24.8	18.7	18.0	14.4
45.0	46.3	45.7	Inventory	25.4	35.8	32.4	44.8	48.1	49.9
2.2	1.5	2.1	All Other Current	.3	.8	2.7	2.0	2.7	2.1
76.4	76.1	73.5	Total Current	69.2	69.5	73.1	74.3	76.9	71.6
17.2	17.7	20.0	Fixed Assets (net)	17.7	21.3	22.7	18.6	16.6	22.5
2.0	2.2	2.4	Intangibles (net)	1.0	5.1	1.8	2.6	3.0	1.6
4.4	4.0	4.1	All Other Non-Current	12.1	4.1	2.4	4.5	3.5	4.2
100.0	100.0	100.0	Total	100.0	100.0	100.0	100.0	100.0	100.0
			LIABILITIES						
22.2	25.1	26.0	Notes Payable-Short Term	17.1	22.3	18.7	24.2	25.7	29.8
3.3	3.7	3.5	Cur. Mat.-L.T.D.	1.2	1.9	6.1	4.1	2.9	3.4
13.8	12.8	11.0	Trade Payables	14.9	14.6	15.5	10.9	11.7	8.9
.4	.4	.5	Income Taxes Payable	.0	.4	.5	.3	.4	.6
9.4	8.4	6.9	All Other Current	19.1	8.4	6.3	7.1	6.1	6.5
49.0	50.4	47.9	Total Current	52.3	47.5	47.1	46.7	46.8	49.2
10.9	12.0	13.1	Long-Term Debt	6.0	22.5	14.9	13.8	10.5	13.3
.7	.8	1.0	Deferred Taxes	.0	.4	.4	.5	.7	1.6
4.2	3.8	3.1	All Other Non-Current	6.5	4.3	4.9	3.5	2.9	2.3
35.2	33.0	34.9	Net Worth	35.2	25.3	32.6	35.6	39.1	33.6
100.0	100.0	100.0	Total Liabilties & Net Worth	100.0	100.0	100.0	100.0	100.0	100.0
			INCOME DATA						
100.0	100.0	100.0	Net Sales	100.0	100.0	100.0	100.0	100.0	100.0
27.3	27.0	27.4	Gross Profit	38.6	37.9	35.7	30.1	25.9	22.9
22.5	21.7	22.6	Operating Expenses	32.1	34.1	31.1	25.6	20.7	18.2
4.8	5.3	4.8	Operating Profit	6.5	3.8	4.6	4.5	5.2	4.7
.5	.4	.5	All Other Expenses (net)	1.9	.2	.1	.3	.5	.6
4.3	4.9	4.3	Profit Before Taxes	4.6	3.6	4.5	4.2	4.7	4.1
			RATIOS						
2.3	2.3	2.2		2.3	3.5	2.2	2.4	2.2	2.0
1.5	1.4	1.5	Current	1.4	1.7	1.5	1.5	1.6	1.4
1.2	1.2	1.2		1.0	1.1	1.1	1.2	1.3	1.2
1.0	1.1	1.0		2.0	2.1	1.3	1.1	1.1	.7
(638) .5	(545) .5	.5	Quick	1.2	.8	.8	.5	.5	.3
.3	.2	.2		.3	.4	.4	.2	.3	.2
20 17.9	**19** 18.9	**21** 17.5		**0** UND	**22** 16.6	**17** 21.3	**20** 18.0	**19** 19.0	**24** 15.5
34 10.7	**32** 11.5	**32** 11.5	Sales/Receivables	**31** 11.7	**35** 10.5	**38** 9.5	**32** 11.5	**29** 12.5	**33** 11.1
47 7.8	**45** 8.1	**46** 7.9		**54** 6.8	**51** 7.1	**59** 6.2	**49** 7.5	**42** 8.6	**45** 8.1
53 6.9	**53** 6.9	**56** 6.5		**0** UND	**15** 23.7	**28** 13.1	**36** 10.2	**61** 6.0	**89** 4.1
118 3.1	**130** 2.8	**122** 3.0	Cost of Sales/Inventory	**0** UND	**79** 4.6	**91** 4.0	**107** 3.4	**130** 2.8	**152** 2.4
203 1.8	**228** 1.6	**228** 1.6		**91** 4.0	**215** 1.7	**146** 2.5	**215** 1.7	**228** 1.6	**243** 1.5
11 33.3	**10** 37.3	**10** 37.0		**0** UND	**5** 80.1	**13** 28.9	**7** 52.2	**8** 43.9	**12** 30.2
26 14.0	**22** 16.9	**21** 17.1	Cost of Sales/Payables	**14** 26.7	**35** 10.4	**32** 11.3	**21** 17.4	**17** 21.4	**23** 15.7
45 8.1	**43** 8.4	**38** 9.6		**72** 5.1	**72** 5.1	**63** 5.8	**38** 9.7	**33** 10.9	**37** 9.9
4.2	4.2	4.3		8.1	3.7	4.3	4.5	4.2	4.1
7.5	7.3	7.2	Sales/Working Capital	23.2	8.7	11.3	7.6	6.8	6.6
17.1	21.4	16.8		UND	28.8	27.6	19.5	13.3	13.6
12.3	11.9	12.2			9.1	11.0	11.4	15.5	12.4
(579) 4.8	(482) 5.2	(515) 4.9	EBIT/Interest		(27) 2.0	(35) 3.4	(105) 4.4	(140) 5.1	(202) 5.3
2.0	2.2	2.1			.1	1.5	1.8	2.5	2.6
12.8	10.2	6.6					18.3	4.4	8.2
(102) 2.9	(91) 3.5	(90) 2.6	Net Profit + Depr., Dep., Amort./Cur. Mat. L/T/D				(16) 2.5	(21) 1.6	(47) 3.2
1.1	1.4	1.0					.9	.8	1.5
.1	.1	.1		.0	.0	.1	.1	.1	.2
.3	.3	.3	Fixed/Worth	.2	.5	.4	.3	.3	.4
1.0	1.3	1.3		2.5	1.3	1.7	1.4	1.0	1.4
1.0	1.1	1.1		1.0	1.1	1.1	.8	1.0	1.4
2.0	2.3	2.2	Debt/Worth	1.5	2.0	2.7	2.3	1.6	2.3
3.8	4.4	4.1		9.6	14.8	5.7	4.9	3.3	3.8
37.5	38.0	34.9		125.8	56.4	61.5	48.9	36.0	27.7
(597) 18.9	(502) 19.3	(520) 18.6	% Profit Before Taxes/Tangible Net Worth	42.9	(27) 17.2	(37) 28.7	(102) 18.7	(144) 20.1	(197) 17.2
8.0	9.2	8.0		-3.2	.9	3.9	7.6	6.7	10.4
11.9	13.1	10.9		32.2	22.2	14.3	12.6	11.4	9.4
6.0	5.9	5.5	% Profit Before Taxes/Total Assets	4.9	6.1	6.0	5.3	5.9	5.0
2.5	2.4	2.3		-1.4	.2	1.0	2.2	2.6	2.6
79.5	65.0	50.5		UND	224.4	63.5	57.8	60.3	36.8
24.7	24.0	21.3	Sales/Net Fixed Assets	21.2	22.5	23.0	26.7	28.2	15.6
7.6	6.6	5.7		7.2	4.5	5.4	8.0	9.4	3.3
2.6	2.6	2.3		5.0	3.1	2.6	2.8	2.5	1.9
1.8	1.6	1.6	Sales/Total Assets	2.2	1.9	1.9	1.9	1.8	1.4
1.3	1.2	1.1		.7	1.2	1.3	1.2	1.2	1.1
.6	.5	.6			.5	.5	.6	.4	.7
(394) 1.2	(339) 1.2	(353) 1.2	% Depr., Dep., Amort./Sales		(17) 2.4	(23) 1.4	(81) 1.2	(103) .9	(124) 1.3
3.7	4.2	4.9			6.7	6.0	4.5	4.6	5.0
1.6	1.3	1.5			3.4	2.2	1.4	1.1	.9
(204) 2.7	(162) 2.3	(160) 2.5	% Officers', Directors' Owners' Comp/Sales		(15) 6.0	(19) 3.9	(46) 2.0	(51) 2.5	(26) 1.5
4.9	4.3	4.5			7.2	5.8	3.8	4.3	2.0
26421580M	**23748041M**	**23963019M**	Net Sales ($)	**7286M**	**65867M**	**161699M**	**824601M**	**2340209M**	**20563357M**
16876933M	**16342411M**	**17673272M**	Total Assets ($)	**5393M**	**40707M**	**97556M**	**547768M**	**1547478M**	**15434370M**

M = $ thousand MM = $ million

See Pages 9 through 22 for Explanation of Ratios and Data

Current Data Sorted by Assets / Comparative Historical Data

Type of Statement	0-500M	500M-2MM	2-10MM	10-50MM	50-100MM	100-250MM	4/1/09-3/31/10 ALL	4/1/10-3/31/11 ALL
Unqualified			5	18	13	7	43	39
Reviewed		3	28	27	2		72	81
Compiled		7	19	16	1		51	62
Tax Returns	5	16	20	11			43	41
Other	2	9	48	47	21	9	93	103
	58 (4/1-9/30/13)			276 (10/1/13-3/31/14)				
NUMBER OF STATEMENTS	7	35	120	119	37	16	302	326
ASSETS	%	%	%	%	%	%	%	%
Cash & Equivalents		8.7	8.2	4.8	6.0	4.3	6.5	7.0
Trade Receivables (net)		15.9	13.2	12.8	8.3	5.9	14.3	14.1
Inventory		54.2	62.0	65.1	67.3	67.4	57.9	60.4
All Other Current		4.7	1.0	2.3	2.5	2.0	2.0	2.3
Total Current		83.5	84.5	84.9	84.1	79.8	80.7	83.8
Fixed Assets (net)		10.6	9.9	10.3	9.3	13.1	12.9	11.3
Intangibles (net)		1.0	2.1	1.7	4.1	3.3	1.7	1.3
All Other Non-Current		4.9	3.5	3.0	2.6	3.8	4.7	3.7
Total		100.0	100.0	100.0	100.0	100.0	100.0	100.0
LIABILITIES								
Notes Payable-Short Term		23.2	25.3	30.7	24.9	32.2	26.8	25.6
Cur. Mat.-L.T.D.		.8	1.2	2.0	1.7	1.0	2.1	1.8
Trade Payables		17.1	18.0	16.1	16.3	9.4	17.0	16.4
Income Taxes Payable		.0	.3	.3	.1	.2	.2	.1
All Other Current		14.1	7.7	10.3	13.5	15.6	7.1	9.2
Total Current		55.3	52.4	59.5	56.7	58.3	53.3	53.2
Long-Term Debt		8.9	7.1	6.1	7.8	10.0	8.2	7.6
Deferred Taxes		.0	.3	.4	.5	.0	.4	.2
All Other Non-Current		7.1	3.9	2.9	1.7	.6	4.2	3.8
Net Worth		28.8	36.4	31.1	33.3	31.1	34.0	35.2
Total Liabilties & Net Worth		100.0	100.0	100.0	100.0	100.0	100.0	100.0
INCOME DATA								
Net Sales		100.0	100.0	100.0	100.0	100.0	100.0	100.0
Gross Profit		30.9	22.1	18.7	16.3	13.9	22.7	23.6
Operating Expenses		30.0	19.0	15.1	12.2	10.1	20.2	20.6
Operating Profit		.9	3.1	3.6	4.1	3.8	2.5	3.0
All Other Expenses (net)		-.2	-.1	.0	.2	-.1	.4	.3
Profit Before Taxes		1.1	3.2	3.6	3.9	3.9	2.1	2.7
RATIOS								
Current		3.2	2.6	1.7	1.9	1.5	2.2	2.1
		1.9	1.5	1.4	1.4	1.4	1.5	1.5
		1.1	1.2	1.2	1.2	1.2	1.2	1.3
Quick		1.0	.8	.5	.4	.3	.8	.7
		.5	.4	.2	.2	.1	.3	.3
		.2	.1	.1	.1	.0	.1	.1
Sales/Receivables		**8** 47.3	**7** 52.9	**5** 67.8	**4** 95.9	**1** 379.3	**7** 50.9	**7** 52.3
		23 15.7	**17** 21.5	**11** 33.8	**5** 69.2	**4** 85.6	**16** 22.9	**16** 23.4
		41 8.8	**31** 11.9	**35** 10.5	**18** 20.0	**14** 26.9	**35** 10.4	**36** 10.2
Cost of Sales/Inventory		**64** 5.7	**83** 4.4	**96** 3.8	**104** 3.5	**101** 3.6	**78** 4.7	**86** 4.2
		135 2.7	**135** 2.7	**130** 2.8	**126** 2.9	**118** 3.1	**119** 3.1	**125** 2.9
		166 2.2	**182** 2.0	**192** 1.9	**166** 2.2	**174** 2.1	**184** 2.0	**176** 2.1
Cost of Sales/Payables		**2** 165.7	**9** 39.5	**7** 51.4	**4** 87.6	**4** 84.2	**9** 39.1	**7** 52.9
		26 14.2	**22** 16.5	**15** 23.6	**21** 17.6	**7** 49.8	**24** 14.9	**23** 15.7
		73 5.0	**47** 7.7	**45** 8.1	**50** 7.3	**20** 17.9	**53** 6.9	**47** 7.8
Sales/Working Capital		3.8	4.1	6.0	5.1	8.9	5.0	4.9
		7.6	8.3	8.7	9.9	10.3	8.5	8.2
		45.9	13.7	14.2	13.5	12.8	15.3	14.3
EBIT/Interest		12.0	14.2	15.2	26.8	26.5	8.1	11.0
		(32) 4.1	(111) 5.8	(115) 6.4	(36) 12.6	(15) 11.5	(287) 3.0	(313) 3.8
		-1.8	2.9	3.1	7.8	8.1	1.1	1.7
Net Profit + Depr., Dep., Amort./Cur. Mat. L/T/D			7.4	17.1			6.1	7.1
			(28) 4.4	(35) 5.9			(86) 3.4	(75) 3.4
			2.7	2.5			1.1	1.6
Fixed/Worth		.0	.1	.1	.1	.2	.1	.1
		.2	.2	.2	.2	.3	.2	.2
		3.2	.4	.5	.5	.6	.6	.5
Debt/Worth		.7	.8	1.3	1.7	2.3	1.0	1.0
		1.9	2.2	2.8	2.2	2.8	2.1	2.2
		43.4	5.4	4.8	3.6	3.3	4.6	3.9
% Profit Before Taxes/Tangible Net Worth		38.6	34.7	37.4	39.1	41.1	28.5	30.5
		(27) 9.6	(113) 18.1	(114) 21.8	(36) 28.5	33.9	(285) 13.5	(310) 14.6
		3.0	8.0	14.5	22.3	24.7	1.7	5.7
% Profit Before Taxes/Total Assets		12.2	11.1	10.3	12.4	11.6	9.2	10.0
		5.0	4.8	6.1	8.7	8.5	3.7	4.1
		-3.6	2.4	3.6	5.6	5.1	.3	1.5
Sales/Net Fixed Assets		383.9	93.3	68.9	64.3	55.4	66.6	76.4
		44.4	38.9	38.7	35.3	29.5	31.2	35.0
		21.5	16.7	15.1	16.5	14.9	13.4	14.6
Sales/Total Assets		3.7	2.9	2.8	2.6	2.7	2.9	3.0
		2.2	2.2	2.1	2.2	2.2	2.2	2.3
		1.5	1.6	1.6	1.7	1.9	1.6	1.7
% Depr., Dep., Amort./Sales		.5	.3	.4	.3	.3	.4	.4
		(23) .8	(94) .7	(108) .6	(31) .5	(13) .5	(253) .8	(261) .7
		2.0	1.4	.9	.7	.6	1.6	1.3
% Officers', Directors' Owners' Comp/Sales		1.0	1.0	.5			.9	1.0
		(22) 2.3	(58) 1.6	(36) 1.0			(115) 1.9	(140) 1.8
		5.2	3.9	2.2			4.0	3.5
Net Sales ($)	16831M	114877M	1481361M	6412631M	5931393M	5408190M	11774119M	12841619M
Total Assets ($)	2452M	38977M	633506M	2862683M	2727431M	2477731M	5588385M	5805152M

M = $ thousand MM = $ million

See Pages 9 through 22 for Explanation of Ratios and Data

Comparative Historical Data / Current Data Sorted by Sales

			Type of Statement						
47	39	43	Unqualified				2	7	34
74	60	60	Reviewed		2	3	11	20	24
61	51	43	Compiled	1	3	6	5	13	15
42	48	52	Tax Returns	1	13	8	7	14	9
99	133	136	Other	2	6	11	18	23	76
4/1/11-3/31/12 ALL	4/1/12-3/31/13 ALL	4/1/13-3/31/14 ALL		58 (4/1-9/30/13)			276 (10/1/13-3/31/14)		
				0-1MM	1-3MM	3-5MM	5-10MM	10-25MM	25MM & OVER
323	331	334	NUMBER OF STATEMENTS	4	24	28	43	77	158
%	%	%	ASSETS	%	%	%	%	%	%
7.2	7.7	6.9	Cash & Equivalents		9.3	10.8	10.3	6.0	5.5
15.4	12.6	12.9	Trade Receivables (net)		16.6	17.2	13.5	12.3	11.6
59.1	62.6	62.5	Inventory		55.0	55.2	57.4	64.8	65.5
1.8	1.9	2.0	All Other Current		3.4	.3	.6	1.6	2.3
83.4	84.8	84.4	Total Current		84.3	83.5	81.8	84.7	85.0
11.4	9.6	10.1	Fixed Assets (net)		8.7	10.6	11.8	10.4	9.8
1.5	1.9	2.2	Intangibles (net)		.3	4.6	1.6	1.9	2.3
3.7	3.7	3.3	All Other Non-Current		6.8	1.3	4.8	3.1	3.0
100.0	100.0	100.0	Total		100.0	100.0	100.0	100.0	100.0
			LIABILITIES						
22.8	23.2	27.2	Notes Payable-Short Term		22.5	17.6	24.9	28.6	29.0
1.8	1.9	1.5	Cur. Mat.-L.T.D.		.8	1.2	1.1	2.5	1.3
17.3	17.8	16.4	Trade Payables		14.1	18.0	15.9	19.6	15.2
.2	.2	.2	Income Taxes Payable		.0	.0	.2	.2	.3
9.8	9.7	11.4	All Other Current		31.4	6.3	6.1	8.0	12.3
51.9	52.8	56.7	Total Current		68.8	43.1	48.2	59.0	58.1
7.4	7.5	7.2	Long-Term Debt		8.1	10.5	7.5	7.8	6.2
.3	.3	.3	Deferred Taxes		.0	.1	.3	.5	.3
4.2	3.2	3.5	All Other Non-Current		1.2	13.0	2.8	2.2	2.6
36.2	36.2	32.3	Net Worth		21.9	33.2	41.3	30.5	32.8
100.0	100.0	100.0	Total Liabilties & Net Worth		100.0	100.0	100.0	100.0	100.0
			INCOME DATA						
100.0	100.0	100.0	Net Sales		100.0	100.0	100.0	100.0	100.0
22.2	21.4	20.9	Gross Profit		32.1	25.4	22.7	20.6	17.5
18.7	18.0	17.8	Operating Expenses		32.4	23.1	20.1	17.5	13.6
3.5	3.4	3.2	Operating Profit		-.3	2.3	2.6	3.1	3.9
.2	-.1	-.1	All Other Expenses (net)		-.1	.6	-.2	-.3	.0
3.3	3.5	3.2	Profit Before Taxes		-.2	1.8	2.7	3.3	3.9
			RATIOS						
2.2	2.2	2.0			3.2	4.2	2.9	1.7	1.8
1.5	1.5	1.4	Current		1.8	2.3	1.9	1.4	1.4
1.3	1.3	1.2			.9	1.2	1.2	1.2	1.2
.8	.7	.7			.9	1.3	1.1	.6	.5
.4	.3	.3	Quick		.3	.5	.5	.2	.2
.2	.1	.1			.1	.2	.2	.1	.1
7 52.3	**6** 65.8	**5** 70.2			**9** 42.7	**10** 36.9	**9** 41.8	**5** 71.1	**4** 93.9
16 23.2	**13** 28.5	**13** 27.3	Sales/Receivables		**22** 16.3	**19** 19.4	**18** 20.7	**15** 25.1	**9** 40.3
35 10.3	**29** 12.5	**32** 11.5			**42** 8.6	**40** 9.2	**32** 11.5	**31** 11.9	**24** 15.0
81 4.5	**87** 4.2	**87** 4.2			**99** 3.7	**45** 8.1	**78** 4.7	**99** 3.7	**89** 4.1
114 3.2	**126** 2.9	**130** 2.8	Cost of Sales/Inventory		**152** 2.4	**114** 3.2	**146** 2.5	**146** 2.5	**118** 3.1
166 2.2	**182** 2.0	**182** 2.0			**281** 1.3	**228** 1.6	**203** 1.8	**192** 1.9	**166** 2.2
8 44.2	**7** 49.1	**6** 56.9			**2** 176.6	**8** 45.4	**8** 46.8	**9** 39.4	**6** 66.1
22 16.4	**20** 18.1	**18** 20.6	Cost of Sales/Payables		**27** 13.3	**22** 16.3	**23** 16.1	**18** 20.7	**15** 24.0
53 6.9	**54** 6.8	**47** 7.8			**76** 4.8	**54** 6.7	**41** 8.9	**52** 7.0	**43** 8.5
5.4	5.0	5.4			3.5	3.4	4.0	5.8	6.0
9.2	8.4	8.8	Sales/Working Capital		5.9	7.0	6.6	9.0	9.5
14.1	14.0	14.6			NM	16.2	13.1	14.7	14.2
16.3	19.1	16.3			9.0	8.0	12.1	18.3	18.4
(307) 4.9	(318) 7.0	(315) 7.2	EBIT/Interest		(21) 3.5	(25) 3.1	(38) 5.6	(74) 6.0	(153) 9.2
2.3	2.7	3.1			-3.8	.9	2.7	2.8	4.7
9.4	8.3	8.1					6.5	7.7	16.1
(80) 4.1	(85) 3.8	(71) 4.7	Net Profit + Depr., Dep., Amort./Cur. Mat. L/T/D				(10) 3.8	(15) 4.7	(43) 5.3
1.7	1.8	2.7					2.7	1.3	3.0
.1	.1	.1			.0	.0	.1	.1	.1
.2	.2	.2	Fixed/Worth		.1	.2	.2	.2	.2
.5	.5	.5			.4	.7	.5	.6	.5
1.1	1.0	1.1			.7	.8	.6	1.5	1.4
2.1	2.1	2.5	Debt/Worth		1.9	2.0	1.1	2.9	2.5
3.7	4.4	4.3			8.9	12.8	6.0	6.2	3.6
34.9	39.7	37.6			42.0	32.0	23.1	36.9	39.8
(309) 20.4	(316) 24.3	(312) 22.7	% Profit Before Taxes/Tangible Net Worth		(20) 12.7	(24) 5.3	(41) 13.9	(72) 20.8	(153) 27.8
9.1	11.1	12.3			-1.1	1.6	6.3	12.9	16.9
11.7	13.0	11.2			10.5	9.6	9.5	10.1	11.8
6.2	6.9	6.1	% Profit Before Taxes/Total Assets		4.6	3.2	4.2	5.2	7.8
2.6	2.9	3.1			-6.6	.7	2.0	2.6	4.5
89.2	98.2	80.9			866.7	106.0	67.9	111.2	66.7
39.9	41.3	39.5	Sales/Net Fixed Assets		42.8	42.2	26.3	54.9	36.8
16.8	17.0	17.2			12.4	21.2	11.8	25.4	18.9
3.0	2.9	2.9			3.0	4.2	2.5	2.8	2.9
2.3	2.3	2.2	Sales/Total Assets		2.0	2.0	2.2	2.1	2.3
1.8	1.7	1.6			1.1	1.4	1.5	1.6	1.9
.3	.3	.3			.6	.5	.5	.3	.3
(264) .6	(275) .6	(271) .6	% Depr., Dep., Amort./Sales		(13) .9	(18) .9	(35) .9	(63) .6	(139) .5
1.0	1.0	1.0			3.0	1.6	1.8	1.0	.8
.7	.6	.8			.9	1.2	.9	.8	.6
(133) 1.6	(130) 1.7	(125) 1.5	% Officers', Directors' Owners' Comp/Sales		(12) 3.5	(17) 1.9	(20) 1.7	(37) 1.4	(36) 1.1
3.8	3.5	3.8			6.5	3.2	4.9	2.7	3.1
15361886M	18115895M	19365283M	Net Sales ($)	2710M	44035M	110793M	328986M	1319726M	17559033M
6479591M	7571143M	8742780M	Total Assets ($)	2263M	26344M	58445M	175534M	683626M	7796568M

M = $ thousand MM = $ million

See Pages 9 through 22 for Explanation of Ratios and Data

Current Data Sorted by Assets							Comparative Historical Data	
						Type of Statement		
	1	26	63	20	26	Unqualified	175	164
	23	167	100	8		Reviewed	284	307
7	56	98	11		1	Compiled	204	210
19	92	97	5	1		Tax Returns	145	187
15	72	172	160	24	34	Other	436	481
237 (4/1-9/30/13)		1,061 (10/1/13-3/31/14)					4/1/09-3/31/10 ALL	4/1/10-3/31/11 ALL
0-500M	**500M-2MM**	**2-10MM**	**10-50MM**	**50-100MM**	**100-250MM**			
41	244	560	339	53	61	**NUMBER OF STATEMENTS**	1244	1349
%	%	%	%	%	%	**ASSETS**	%	%
16.8	12.8	10.1	7.9	5.2	5.1	Cash & Equivalents	8.4	9.4
22.9	33.1	31.9	26.6	23.7	20.1	Trade Receivables (net)	27.8	30.7
31.1	34.8	35.7	35.2	35.4	34.9	Inventory	34.9	34.0
4.4	2.1	2.2	3.1	3.4	3.4	All Other Current	3.2	2.5
75.2	82.8	80.0	72.8	67.7	63.5	Total Current	74.4	76.6
15.7	10.3	12.3	17.1	17.3	20.4	Fixed Assets (net)	16.8	14.9
5.2	2.3	2.3	3.7	7.0	11.6	Intangibles (net)	3.2	3.0
3.9	4.6	5.4	6.3	7.9	4.4	All Other Non-Current	5.5	5.5
100.0	100.0	100.0	100.0	100.0	100.0	Total	100.0	100.0
						LIABILITIES		
17.7	13.8	13.1	15.4	16.2	13.5	Notes Payable-Short Term	15.9	15.3
2.0	2.2	2.4	3.0	2.6	3.5	Cur. Mat.-L.T.D.	3.3	2.9
20.3	23.4	19.0	15.7	14.2	11.7	Trade Payables	16.8	19.0
.0	.1	.2	.3	.3	.2	Income Taxes Payable	.2	.2
17.7	10.1	11.5	11.6	10.9	11.6	All Other Current	9.4	10.7
57.6	49.6	46.3	46.0	44.3	40.6	Total Current	45.6	48.1
12.4	11.4	8.9	8.0	13.8	12.8	Long-Term Debt	10.7	9.7
.0	.1	.3	.8	.8	1.6	Deferred Taxes	.4	.4
5.3	4.8	4.4	4.5	4.2	6.6	All Other Non-Current	4.6	4.7
24.6	34.2	40.1	40.6	36.9	38.4	Net Worth	38.6	37.1
100.0	100.0	100.0	100.0	100.0	100.0	Total Liabilties & Net Worth	100.0	100.0
						INCOME DATA		
100.0	100.0	100.0	100.0	100.0	100.0	Net Sales	100.0	100.0
34.8	32.3	29.5	27.8	26.1	28.5	Gross Profit	31.0	31.1
29.3	28.7	25.6	22.4	21.4	21.1	Operating Expenses	28.8	27.5
5.5	3.6	3.9	5.3	4.7	7.4	Operating Profit	2.2	3.6
.1	.0	.2	.3	.3	1.7	All Other Expenses (net)	.7	.4
5.4	3.6	3.7	5.0	4.3	5.7	Profit Before Taxes	1.5	3.2
						RATIOS		
4.4	2.7	2.8	2.2	1.9	2.4		2.7	2.6
1.6	1.8	1.7	1.5	1.5	1.5	Current	1.7	1.6
1.0	1.3	1.3	1.2	1.2	1.2		1.2	1.2
1.8	1.5	1.5	1.1	1.2	1.1		1.4	1.4
.9	.9	.9	.7	.7	.7	Quick	.8	.9
.3	.6	.6	.5	.4	.3		.5	.5
0 UND	**22** 16.7	**29** 12.4	**33** 11.1	**38** 9.6	**34** 10.8		**29** 12.6	**33** 11.1
20 18.5	**33** 11.2	**41** 8.9	**42** 8.6	**45** 8.1	**48** 7.6	Sales/Receivables	**40** 9.1	**43** 8.4
36 10.0	**46** 8.0	**54** 6.8	**56** 6.5	**55** 6.6	**55** 6.6		**53** 6.9	**56** 6.5
4 84.5	**24** 15.5	**32** 11.5	**47** 7.8	**53** 6.9	**54** 6.8		**37** 9.8	**39** 9.4
39 9.3	**54** 6.8	**64** 5.7	**76** 4.8	**70** 5.2	**91** 4.0	Cost of Sales/Inventory	**72** 5.1	**71** 5.2
61 6.0	**99** 3.7	**118** 3.1	**135** 2.7	**114** 3.2	**166** 2.2		**135** 2.7	**121** 3.0
0 UND	**15** 24.3	**15** 24.3	**17** 21.0	**23** 16.0	**21** 17.0		**16** 22.5	**19** 18.9
15 23.7	**34** 10.6	**31** 11.9	**29** 12.5	**31** 11.9	**29** 12.4	Cost of Sales/Payables	**30** 12.3	**33** 11.2
57 6.4	**52** 7.0	**49** 7.4	**46** 8.0	**46** 8.0	**45** 8.1		**47** 7.7	**51** 7.1
7.5	5.6	4.7	4.6	5.6	4.0		4.5	4.7
22.4	10.8	8.3	8.3	8.0	7.6	Sales/Working Capital	8.2	8.6
-664.0	22.2	17.5	20.9	21.1	22.0		22.7	22.4
38.0	23.6	24.7	29.6	32.7	33.6		9.2	17.3
(21) 5.7	(200) 6.3	(489) 6.4	(311) 9.1	(49) 6.7	(57) 7.4	EBIT/Interest	(1125) 2.3	(1195) 4.8
1.5	2.0	2.2	3.7	2.4	2.7		.3	1.8
	7.4	10.7	16.2	7.7	33.4		8.7	8.3
	(22) 3.6	(103) 3.8	(90) 3.5	(16) 2.9	(13) 10.3	Net Profit + Depr., Dep., Amort./Cur. Mat. L/T/D	(304) 2.3	(291) 3.0
	1.5	1.8	1.8	1.6	1.3		.7	1.2
.0	.0	.1	.1	.1	.2		.1	.1
.2	.2	.2	.3	.5	.6	Fixed/Worth	.3	.3
2.7	.8	.7	1.0	1.9	2.3		1.0	.9
.8	.7	.7	.8	1.3	1.4		.7	.8
2.0	1.7	1.6	1.7	2.5	2.0	Debt/Worth	1.7	1.8
158.1	4.5	3.8	3.3	5.7	7.4		4.3	4.1
124.7	52.5	41.8	40.6	38.0	46.9		25.0	38.2
(32) 71.6	(210) 19.6	(525) 19.5	(322) 22.1	(48) 24.0	(50) 28.4	% Profit Before Taxes/Tangible Net Worth	(1139) 7.9	(1231) 16.5
32.1	7.1	6.7	10.4	10.6	13.3		-1.7	4.8
43.9	19.3	15.6	14.7	13.4	12.7		9.3	13.4
16.3	6.9	6.4	7.5	6.2	6.2	% Profit Before Taxes/Total Assets	2.6	5.7
1.1	1.9	2.3	3.4	3.3	3.3		-1.2	1.4
932.7	201.7	108.5	57.9	50.8	36.3		67.9	86.5
107.1	68.3	37.2	23.2	15.6	14.6	Sales/Net Fixed Assets	26.0	30.2
17.4	25.5	15.3	8.1	6.3	4.5		8.6	10.9
6.9	4.4	3.5	2.7	2.6	2.2		3.3	3.2
4.0	3.3	2.7	2.0	1.9	1.5	Sales/Total Assets	2.3	2.4
2.6	2.4	1.9	1.5	1.3	.9		1.5	1.6
.3	.3	.3	.4	.5	.5		.5	.4
(25) .6	(166) .6	(436) .7	(291) .9	(40) 1.4	(43) 1.0	% Depr., Dep., Amort./Sales	(997) 1.0	(1060) .9
1.7	1.2	1.4	2.3	4.9	2.4		2.6	2.4
2.4	2.3	1.5	.7				1.8	2.0
(24) 6.0	(150) 4.1	(249) 3.3	(54) 1.8			% Officers', Directors' Owners' Comp/Sales	(429) 3.7	(491) 3.9
10.8	6.9	5.6	3.2				6.5	6.8
85278M	**1108114M**	**7404636M**	**16290724M**	**7033469M**	**14382790M**	Net Sales ($)	**34660009M**	**37292081M**
12478M	**304829M**	**2777883M**	**7558577M**	**3538598M**	**8853905M**	Total Assets ($)	**19367366M**	**19321970M**

M = $ thousand MM = $ million

See Pages 9 through 22 for Explanation of Ratios and Data

Comparative Historical Data / Current Data Sorted by Sales

	4/1/11-3/31/12 ALL	4/1/12-3/31/13 ALL	4/1/13-3/31/14 ALL	0-1MM	1-3MM	3-5MM	5-10MM	10-25MM	25MM & OVER
Type of Statement									
Unqualified	148	122	136			1	5	22	108
Reviewed	322	290	298		9	12	50	124	103
Compiled	203	177	173	6	17	22	54	53	21
Tax Returns	222	185	214	9	38	43	72	44	8
Other	482	476	477	11	31	34	85	130	186
					237 (4/1-9/30/13)		1,061 (10/1/13-3/31/14)		
NUMBER OF STATEMENTS	1377	1250	1298	26	95	112	266	373	426
ASSETS	%	%	%	%	%	%	%	%	%
Cash & Equivalents	9.3	9.5	9.8	17.5	9.6	12.4	10.6	11.7	6.6
Trade Receivables (net)	31.1	30.4	29.6	16.0	24.2	29.3	31.7	32.0	28.3
Inventory	35.1	35.3	35.2	32.0	38.5	37.7	36.0	33.7	34.9
All Other Current	2.5	2.7	2.6	4.4	4.8	1.8	1.8	2.2	3.1
Total Current	78.0	77.9	77.2	70.0	77.1	81.2	80.0	79.6	72.9
Fixed Assets (net)	13.6	13.8	13.9	17.3	13.3	10.4	12.4	12.6	16.8
Intangibles (net)	3.1	3.1	3.4	9.9	3.6	1.7	1.7	3.0	4.8
All Other Non-Current	5.3	5.3	5.5	2.8	6.0	6.6	5.9	4.9	5.5
Total	100.0	100.0	100.0	100.0	100.0	100.0	100.0	100.0	100.0
LIABILITIES									
Notes Payable-Short Term	14.4	14.1	14.1	12.8	13.5	15.3	13.8	12.1	16.0
Cur. Mat.-L.T.D.	2.8	2.7	2.6	1.5	2.1	2.5	2.6	2.5	2.7
Trade Payables	19.7	19.0	18.5	21.6	16.7	20.9	21.4	18.5	16.2
Income Taxes Payable	.3	.3	.2	.0	.2	.0	.1	.3	.2
All Other Current	11.0	11.8	11.4	19.6	9.5	10.6	11.7	11.5	11.4
Total Current	48.1	47.8	46.8	55.4	42.1	49.3	49.8	44.9	46.6
Long-Term Debt	9.4	9.5	9.6	12.3	19.8	7.9	10.4	7.2	9.4
Deferred Taxes	.5	.5	.5	.0	.0	.1	.2	.5	.9
All Other Non-Current	4.8	4.2	4.6	7.0	8.1	5.5	4.0	3.6	4.7
Net Worth	37.2	37.9	38.4	25.3	30.0	37.3	35.7	43.7	38.5
Total Liabilties & Net Worth	100.0	100.0	100.0	100.0	100.0	100.0	100.0	100.0	100.0
INCOME DATA									
Net Sales	100.0	100.0	100.0	100.0	100.0	100.0	100.0	100.0	100.0
Gross Profit	30.4	29.9	29.5	38.9	37.7	33.2	29.8	29.7	25.9
Operating Expenses	25.9	25.0	25.1	35.1	33.0	29.7	26.3	24.8	21.0
Operating Profit	4.5	4.9	4.5	3.7	4.8	3.5	3.4	4.9	4.9
All Other Expenses (net)	.4	.2	.3	.3	.5	.0	.1	.2	.4
Profit Before Taxes	4.1	4.6	4.2	3.5	4.3	3.5	3.3	4.7	4.5
RATIOS									
Current	2.5	2.6	2.5	4.1	3.8	2.7	2.6	2.6	2.2
	1.6	1.6	1.6	1.5	2.1	1.7	1.6	1.8	1.5
	1.2	1.3	1.3	1.1	1.3	1.3	1.2	1.3	1.2
Quick	1.4	1.4	1.4	1.4	1.6	1.5	1.4	1.6	1.2
	.8	.8	.8	.9	.8	.8	.9	.9	.7
	.5	.5	.5	.2	.4	.5	.5	.6	.5
Sales/Receivables	**31** 11.8	**28** 13.1	**28** 13.0	**1** 299.3	**21** 17.5	**23** 16.0	**26** 14.1	**30** 12.2	**33** 10.9
	42 8.6	**40** 9.1	**41** 9.0	**14** 25.9	**36** 10.1	**32** 11.4	**40** 9.1	**41** 9.0	**43** 8.5
	54 6.7	**52** 7.0	**53** 6.9	**42** 8.7	**56** 6.5	**47** 7.8	**54** 6.8	**53** 6.9	**54** 6.8
Cost of Sales/Inventory	**36** 10.2	**33** 10.9	**35** 10.5	**7** 51.3	**44** 8.3	**29** 12.7	**26** 13.8	**32** 11.4	**41** 8.9
	66 5.5	**64** 5.7	**65** 5.6	**56** 6.5	**101** 3.6	**66** 5.5	**59** 6.2	**64** 5.7	**66** 5.5
	118 3.1	**118** 3.1	**118** 3.1	**203** 1.8	**174** 2.1	**135** 2.7	**118** 3.1	**118** 3.1	**111** 3.3
Cost of Sales/Payables	**18** 20.0	**17** 22.0	**16** 22.6	**7** 53.5	**13** 28.6	**14** 25.8	**15** 23.6	**16** 23.5	**18** 20.2
	32 11.4	**30** 12.3	**30** 12.0	**47** 7.8	**33** 11.0	**33** 11.0	**34** 10.8	**28** 13.1	**29** 12.4
	50 7.3	**47** 7.7	**49** 7.5	**99** 3.7	**64** 5.7	**54** 6.8	**57** 6.4	**47** 7.7	**41** 8.8
Sales/Working Capital	5.0	5.0	4.8	2.1	3.7	5.7	4.7	4.6	5.6
	9.0	9.0	8.9	7.9	6.1	10.5	9.6	8.3	9.1
	19.9	19.5	19.8	NM	14.2	20.6	21.6	16.3	22.1
EBIT/Interest	21.9	26.0	25.6	18.8	12.5	14.2	23.6	31.9	28.7
	(1198) 7.0	(1087) 7.9	(1127) 7.2	(15) 2.8	(73) 4.0	(88) 4.9	(233) 4.5	(325) 9.9	(393) 9.1
	2.4	2.7	2.4	-4.6	1.4	1.2	1.6	3.6	3.1
Net Profit + Depr., Dep., Amort./Cur. Mat. L/T/D	11.3	11.4	11.6			7.2	6.9	16.9	15.3
	(247) 3.8	(248) 3.9	(244) 3.7			(12) 1.9	(38) 3.6	(76) 5.1	(112) 3.5
	1.6	1.5	1.8			1.1	1.4	2.3	1.8
Fixed/Worth	.1	.1	.1	.0	.0	.0	.1	.1	.1
	.2	.3	.2	.1	.2	.2	.2	.2	.4
	.8	.9	.9	36.1	4.0	.7	.8	.6	1.0
Debt/Worth	.8	.8	.8	.7	.6	.8	.8	.7	.9
	1.9	1.7	1.7	3.7	1.9	1.7	1.8	1.4	1.9
	4.1	4.2	4.1	-5.9	23.0	3.3	4.5	2.9	4.2
% Profit Before Taxes/Tangible Net Worth	47.0	49.2	44.4	84.6	45.9	52.7	39.9	43.5	46.4
	(1250) 23.8	(1125) 23.3	(1187) 22.0	(19) 41.4	(74) 18.8	(102) 14.6	(239) 15.6	(356) 24.1	(397) 24.2
	9.0	9.1	8.3	-.5	5.0	4.1	4.3	9.4	11.7
% Profit Before Taxes/Total Assets	15.9	16.6	16.0	28.6	18.1	17.8	12.9	17.6	14.7
	7.5	8.1	7.0	10.2	6.8	5.6	5.3	8.2	7.6
	2.7	2.8	2.7	-2.3	1.0	1.2	1.1	3.6	3.5
Sales/Net Fixed Assets	100.3	95.1	96.2	UND	162.2	223.2	138.7	96.3	60.2
	36.4	34.6	33.8	51.1	40.0	55.3	41.0	38.5	24.0
	13.0	13.2	12.6	9.8	12.5	17.0	15.3	15.8	9.0
Sales/Total Assets	3.4	3.5	3.4	3.0	3.2	3.9	3.7	3.6	3.1
	2.5	2.6	2.5	2.3	2.2	2.8	2.7	2.7	2.3
	1.8	1.8	1.8	1.3	1.4	2.0	1.9	1.9	1.7
% Depr., Dep., Amort./Sales	.4	.3	.4	.5	.4	.3	.3	.4	.4
	(1042) .8	(960) .7	(1001) .7	(14) .8	(67) .8	(74) .7	(199) .7	(295) .6	(352) .9
	1.9	1.7	1.6	3.0	2.2	1.4	1.4	1.4	2.3
% Officers', Directors' Owners' Comp/Sales	2.0	1.8	1.7		2.2	2.9	1.7	1.6	.8
	(526) 3.8	(439) 3.7	(483) 3.3		(50) 4.9	(66) 4.6	(140) 3.0	(154) 3.5	(64) 1.4
	6.3	6.3	6.2		8.3	7.4	5.8	5.9	3.0
Net Sales ($)	**42715264M**	**46618504M**	**46305011M**	**17671M**	**196604M**	**443506M**	**1938474M**	**5827068M**	**37881688M**
Total Assets ($)	**20805060M**	**22131109M**	**23046270M**	**15030M**	**112421M**	**202941M**	**890399M**	**2733084M**	**19092395M**

M = $ thousand MM = $ million

See Pages 9 through 22 for Explanation of Ratios and Data

Current Data Sorted by Assets							Comparative Historical Data	
						Type of Statement		
	1	10	29	5	4	Unqualified	72	54
3	15	64	41	1	2	Reviewed	132	161
4	21	66	8	1	1	Compiled	99	94
11	32	34	1			Tax Returns	56	68
5	30	86	65	14	8	Other	194	213
	108 (4/1-9/30/13)		454 (10/1/13-3/31/14)				4/1/09-3/31/10 ALL	4/1/10-3/31/11 ALL
0-500M	**500M-2MM**	**2-10MM**	**10-50MM**	**50-100MM**	**100-250MM**			
23	99	260	144	21	15	**NUMBER OF STATEMENTS**	553	590
%	%	%	%	%	%	**ASSETS**	%	%
25.7	9.7	7.7	6.4	2.6	4.3	Cash & Equivalents	8.2	7.7
33.7	35.0	32.1	28.1	25.6	25.8	Trade Receivables (net)	30.4	33.1
19.5	35.1	38.8	37.5	31.8	28.3	Inventory	37.1	36.1
4.8	1.2	1.2	1.9	2.6	3.2	All Other Current	2.5	2.1
83.7	81.0	79.8	73.9	62.7	61.7	Total Current	78.2	78.9
13.2	12.3	11.4	13.9	21.0	16.3	Fixed Assets (net)	12.4	11.6
.1	1.3	3.9	5.2	9.4	18.8	Intangibles (net)	4.0	4.1
3.1	5.4	5.0	7.0	6.9	3.2	All Other Non-Current	5.5	5.4
100.0	100.0	100.0	100.0	100.0	100.0	Total	100.0	100.0
						LIABILITIES		
13.0	10.7	12.2	13.1	15.3	7.1	Notes Payable-Short Term	16.0	14.3
2.9	2.8	2.3	1.5	1.8	2.1	Cur. Mat.-L.T.D.	2.8	2.5
16.5	20.4	19.0	16.5	11.4	11.4	Trade Payables	18.3	21.5
.0	.1	.2	.2	.2	.1	Income Taxes Payable	.2	.3
23.2	9.7	6.5	7.4	6.1	6.7	All Other Current	7.1	8.2
55.7	43.7	40.2	38.7	34.8	27.4	Total Current	44.4	46.8
13.1	7.2	6.8	10.2	12.2	22.4	Long-Term Debt	9.2	8.6
.0	.1	.2	.3	1.4	.9	Deferred Taxes	.2	.3
3.6	5.1	6.5	5.7	5.7	11.7	All Other Non-Current	4.7	4.7
27.5	43.9	46.2	45.2	45.9	37.7	Net Worth	41.5	39.7
100.0	100.0	100.0	100.0	100.0	100.0	Total Liabilties & Net Worth	100.0	100.0
						INCOME DATA		
100.0	100.0	100.0	100.0	100.0	100.0	Net Sales	100.0	100.0
35.4	31.0	29.5	29.0	29.8	27.0	Gross Profit	31.1	31.1
30.6	27.1	25.0	22.5	22.3	20.8	Operating Expenses	27.8	26.9
4.8	3.8	4.5	6.5	7.5	6.2	Operating Profit	3.3	4.2
.5	.0	.2	.4	.6	1.6	All Other Expenses (net)	.6	.5
4.3	3.9	4.3	6.1	6.9	4.6	Profit Before Taxes	2.7	3.7
						RATIOS		
3.8	3.2	3.6	3.2	3.1	4.3		3.2	2.8
2.4	2.0	2.0	1.8	2.2	2.4	Current	1.8	1.7
1.5	1.3	1.3	1.4	1.4	1.7		1.3	1.3
3.3	1.8	1.8	1.6	1.2	1.7		1.6	1.5
1.9	1.1	1.0	.8	.7	1.2	Quick	.9	.9
1.0	.7	.6	.5	.6	.8		.5	.6
9 39.1	**27** 13.4	**31** 11.9	**34** 10.6	**37** 9.8	**46** 7.9		**31** 11.7	**35** 10.6
29 12.5	**34** 10.8	**39** 9.4	**43** 8.5	**47** 7.8	**49** 7.4	Sales/Receivables	**40** 9.2	**44** 8.4
46 7.9	**45** 8.2	**48** 7.6	**52** 7.0	**51** 7.1	**57** 6.4		**50** 7.3	**52** 7.0
4 81.2	**25** 14.4	**39** 9.3	**50** 7.3	**63** 5.8	**45** 8.2		**37** 10.0	**38** 9.5
24 15.0	**52** 7.0	**66** 5.5	**78** 4.7	**73** 5.0	**78** 4.7	Cost of Sales/Inventory	**67** 5.4	**67** 5.5
73 5.0	**81** 4.5	**122** 3.0	**130** 2.8	**107** 3.4	**146** 2.5		**121** 3.0	**116** 3.1
0 UND	**17** 21.6	**18** 20.5	**22** 16.6	**22** 16.3	**24** 15.0		**19** 19.2	**23** 16.0
12 30.2	**29** 12.7	**29** 12.8	**30** 12.1	**33** 11.2	**29** 12.4	Cost of Sales/Payables	**30** 12.1	**34** 10.6
54 6.8	**41** 8.9	**47** 7.8	**44** 8.3	**45** 8.2	**38** 9.6		**46** 7.9	**54** 6.8
4.0	5.3	4.3	4.1	3.9	3.3		4.4	4.9
7.3	8.8	7.8	6.9	6.7	5.0	Sales/Working Capital	8.1	8.6
20.2	27.1	18.3	13.4	13.2	8.4		18.2	18.4
34.3	26.0	24.1	40.7	20.0	35.7		13.0	19.0
(16) 7.3	(82) 8.6	(225) 7.1	(135) 14.2	9.6	(13) 8.6	EBIT/Interest	(504) 3.7	(535) 6.3
4.6	2.2	2.3	4.6	6.4	2.6		1.2	2.1
	4.1	11.4	20.6				8.2	10.9
	(12) 2.0	(51) 2.5	(41) 5.3			Net Profit + Depr., Dep., Amort./Cur. Mat. L/T/D	(138) 2.9	(138) 3.4
	.8	1.0	2.3				1.0	1.5
.0	.1	.1	.1	.1	.3		.1	.1
.3	.2	.2	.2	.6	1.3	Fixed/Worth	.3	.2
1.7	.7	.6	.8	1.2	-.2		.7	.7
.4	.5	.4	.6	.8	.6		.6	.6
1.3	1.3	1.4	1.3	1.7	1.8	Debt/Worth	1.6	1.6
8.8	3.3	3.2	2.9	5.5	-3.1		4.0	4.2
96.9	43.2	41.9	48.4	62.1			30.2	43.2
(19) 33.1	(91) 20.9	(239) 18.3	(134) 27.5	(20) 33.7		% Profit Before Taxes/Tangible Net Worth	(491) 13.9	(523) 21.6
13.8	8.1	7.7	15.7	16.3			2.8	8.0
29.3	17.1	17.1	16.6	15.5	11.3		11.8	15.2
14.0	7.9	7.9	10.3	8.5	10.2	% Profit Before Taxes/Total Assets	5.2	8.1
2.5	2.0	2.3	6.0	6.1	7.0		.5	2.3
UND	199.8	116.3	59.6	52.2	43.8		93.6	92.7
220.9	49.0	46.0	32.5	16.2	16.4	Sales/Net Fixed Assets	36.1	34.6
17.3	21.4	16.8	12.4	6.7	8.8		15.3	15.5
6.9	4.6	3.7	2.9	2.4	2.5		3.4	3.5
4.3	3.4	2.8	2.2	1.9	2.1	Sales/Total Assets	2.6	2.6
2.2	2.6	2.1	1.6	1.5	1.4		1.8	1.9
.1	.2	.2	.4	.6			.4	.4
(10) .5	(68) .5	(214) .6	(128) .7	.9		% Depr., Dep., Amort./Sales	(445) .8	(475) .8
1.3	1.4	1.0	1.3	2.7			1.5	1.4
3.1	3.2	1.6	.6				1.9	1.7
(10) 6.1	(60) 5.3	(121) 2.9	(22) 1.7			% Officers', Directors' Owners' Comp/Sales	(198) 3.4	(208) 3.3
8.3	7.8	5.8	4.4				6.6	6.7
43384M	451669M	3621816M	7350776M	2713439M	4114494M	Net Sales ($)	15164013M	16106702M
6491M	127681M	1291104M	3242347M	1452989M	2210873M	Total Assets ($)	6270446M	6975289M

M = $ thousand MM = $ million

See Pages 9 through 22 for Explanation of Ratios and Data

Comparative Historical Data				Current Data Sorted by Sales					
			Type of Statement						
71	47	49	Unqualified			2	1	10	36
146	105	126	Reviewed		5	5	32	43	41
97	91	101	Compiled	2	5	12	27	43	12
88	79	78	Tax Returns	3	23	11	18	21	2
194	217	208	Other	6	12	14	33	62	81
4/1/11-3/31/12	**4/1/12-3/31/13**	**4/1/13-3/31/14**			**108 (4/1-9/30/13)**		**454 (10/1/13-3/31/14)**		
ALL	**ALL**	**ALL**		**0-1MM**	**1-3MM**	**3-5MM**	**5-10MM**	**10-25MM**	**25MM & OVER**
596	539	562	**NUMBER OF STATEMENTS**	11	45	44	111	179	172
%	%	%	**ASSETS**	%	%	%	%	%	%
8.0	7.7	8.2	Cash & Equivalents	14.6	18.0	9.3	8.2	7.5	5.6
32.7	31.4	31.2	Trade Receivables (net)	34.3	24.9	31.0	31.5	32.8	30.9
36.9	37.3	36.5	Inventory	22.4	32.3	37.4	37.1	38.2	36.1
1.9	1.9	1.6	All Other Current	5.7	.7	2.2	1.4	1.2	2.0
79.5	78.4	77.5	Total Current	76.9	75.8	79.9	78.1	79.8	74.6
11.3	11.5	12.7	Fixed Assets (net)	18.6	16.4	12.0	12.5	10.5	14.0
4.2	4.3	4.2	Intangibles (net)	.2	2.6	1.7	3.5	4.4	5.9
4.9	5.8	5.5	All Other Non-Current	4.3	5.2	6.4	5.9	5.3	5.5
100.0	100.0	100.0	Total	100.0	100.0	100.0	100.0	100.0	100.0
			LIABILITIES						
14.0	14.5	12.2	Notes Payable-Short Term	21.5	9.2	8.7	12.0	11.9	13.7
2.1	2.1	2.2	Cur. Mat.-L.T.D.	4.5	3.6	2.7	2.1	2.4	1.5
20.2	19.0	18.0	Trade Payables	16.1	16.5	19.3	18.6	18.3	17.6
.3	.2	.1	Income Taxes Payable	.0	.1	.1	.1	.2	.2
7.5	7.6	7.9	All Other Current	10.1	7.1	6.9	9.4	7.6	7.7
44.0	43.4	40.5	Total Current	52.2	36.5	37.7	42.1	40.4	40.6
8.2	7.6	8.6	Long-Term Debt	16.6	12.4	8.4	5.2	8.1	9.9
.2	.2	.3	Deferred Taxes	.0	.0	.2	.3	.2	.4
4.9	6.7	6.0	All Other Non-Current	7.5	3.1	8.0	7.1	6.7	4.9
42.6	42.1	44.5	Net Worth	23.7	48.0	45.7	45.3	44.5	44.2
100.0	100.0	100.0	Total Liabilties & Net Worth	100.0	100.0	100.0	100.0	100.0	100.0
			INCOME DATA						
100.0	100.0	100.0	Net Sales	100.0	100.0	100.0	100.0	100.0	100.0
30.0	29.6	29.8	Gross Profit	36.6	38.6	31.5	30.3	29.3	27.0
25.0	24.6	24.8	Operating Expenses	33.7	31.0	27.8	26.0	24.3	21.5
5.0	5.0	5.1	Operating Profit	2.9	7.6	3.7	4.3	5.0	5.5
.3	.3	.3	All Other Expenses (net)	.5	.8	.1	.0	.4	.3
4.7	4.7	4.8	Profit Before Taxes	2.4	6.8	3.7	4.3	4.6	5.3
			RATIOS						
3.1	3.3	3.5		2.8	4.1	4.3	3.7	3.8	3.0
1.8	1.9	2.0	Current	2.0	2.3	2.3	2.1	1.9	1.8
1.3	1.3	1.3		.7	1.2	1.6	1.3	1.3	1.4
1.6	1.6	1.7		1.9	2.2	2.0	1.6	1.9	1.5
1.0	.9	1.0	Quick	1.4	1.1	1.3	1.0	1.0	.9
.6	.6	.6		.7	.6	.7	.6	.6	.6
32 11.4	**31** 11.8	**31** 11.8		**26** 13.8	**24** 15.4	**28** 13.1	**30** 12.3	**31** 11.6	**34** 10.6
42 8.7	**39** 9.3	**40** 9.2	Sales/Receivables	**46** 8.0	**31** 11.9	**37** 9.9	**38** 9.7	**40** 9.2	**43** 8.5
51 7.2	**49** 7.4	**49** 7.4		**81** 4.5	**41** 9.0	**45** 8.2	**46** 7.9	**49** 7.4	**51** 7.1
36 10.0	**38** 9.6	**38** 9.5		**20** 18.2	**22** 16.6	**35** 10.3	**38** 9.5	**38** 9.5	**42** 8.6
65 5.6	**64** 5.7	**66** 5.5	Cost of Sales/Inventory	**61** 6.0	**64** 5.7	**73** 5.0	**68** 5.4	**63** 5.8	**69** 5.3
107 3.4	**111** 3.3	**118** 3.1		**118** 3.1	**130** 2.8	**130** 2.8	**118** 3.1	**122** 3.0	**104** 3.5
21 17.4	**17** 21.6	**18** 20.0		**1** 280.0	**13** 28.1	**18** 20.5	**16** 22.7	**17** 21.3	**21** 17.1
31 11.6	**29** 12.7	**29** 12.5	Cost of Sales/Payables	**41** 8.9	**31** 11.6	**31** 11.9	**30** 12.0	**26** 13.8	**30** 12.2
48 7.6	**45** 8.1	**45** 8.2		**83** 4.4	**49** 7.5	**45** 8.2	**47** 7.8	**43** 8.5	**43** 8.5
4.7	4.9	4.3		3.4	4.6	4.2	4.1	4.1	4.6
8.3	8.2	7.8	Sales/Working Capital	4.0	8.5	7.1	8.0	7.9	7.7
16.6	19.1	16.5		-23.4	35.8	11.3	21.7	16.7	13.6
23.4	30.3	27.9			23.8	20.1	35.8	30.9	31.2
(524) 7.0	(482) 9.1	(492) 9.1	EBIT/Interest		(33) 9.5	(37) 7.4	(92) 6.2	(163) 8.5	(159) 11.9
2.4	3.2	3.2			2.1	1.4	1.4	2.9	5.6
9.8	12.8	10.8					9.5	8.4	29.1
(144) 3.7	(105) 4.6	(116) 3.8	Net Profit + Depr., Dep., Amort./Cur. Mat. L/T/D				(21) 2.1	(34) 3.1	(50) 5.1
1.6	2.1	1.6					.8	1.7	2.4
.1	.1	.1		.0	.0	.1	.1	.1	.1
.2	.2	.2	Fixed/Worth	.4	.2	.2	.2	.2	.2
.6	.7	.8		-.5	1.2	.8	.8	.7	.8
.6	.6	.5		.5	.3	.5	.3	.4	.6
1.5	1.5	1.4	Debt/Worth	8.8	.9	1.3	1.3	1.4	1.4
3.4	4.1	3.4		-4.9	3.0	2.7	3.2	3.6	3.3
49.8	50.3	44.9			47.0	37.9	42.8	46.6	47.6
(536) 23.6	(489) 25.4	(512) 22.4	% Profit Before Taxes/Tangible Net Worth		(40) 18.0	(40) 18.0	(102) 18.1	(162) 22.1	(160) 27.1
8.4	12.0	10.7			6.4	5.8	5.6	10.2	16.3
19.5	18.8	16.8		19.1	18.3	14.6	19.5	17.3	16.5
9.0	9.6	9.0	% Profit Before Taxes/Total Assets	12.7	7.7	7.0	6.9	9.2	9.9
2.7	3.9	3.0		.0	2.7	1.0	1.5	2.9	6.0
121.2	119.3	97.2		UND	121.2	235.9	137.7	108.9	69.6
41.7	41.1	37.8	Sales/Net Fixed Assets	391.0	34.4	33.0	37.2	46.6	33.7
15.3	16.0	15.5		7.0	15.8	19.8	14.4	17.3	12.4
3.7	3.8	3.6		2.4	4.3	3.6	3.9	3.8	3.1
2.7	2.8	2.6	Sales/Total Assets	2.0	2.7	2.8	2.7	2.8	2.4
2.0	2.0	2.0		1.5	1.7	2.2	1.9	2.1	1.9
.4	.3	.3			.2	.3	.2	.3	.4
(467) .6	(422) .7	(450) .7	% Depr., Dep., Amort./Sales		(28) .5	(30) .9	(89) .6	(147) .6	(153) .7
1.2	1.2	1.2			2.3	1.5	1.2	1.0	1.3
1.8	1.6	1.8			3.9	2.9	2.3	1.3	.5
(228) 3.3	(205) 3.4	(216) 3.6	% Officers', Directors' Owners' Comp/Sales		(28) 7.0	(22) 6.5	(52) 3.8	(85) 2.9	(27) 1.5
6.1	6.0	7.0			8.8	8.6	6.2	5.8	3.5
19329029M	**18913241M**	**18295578M**	Net Sales ($)	**4621M**	**99175M**	**182454M**	**828275M**	**2845854M**	**14335199M**
8286910M	**8279251M**	**8331485M**	Total Assets ($)	**3629M**	**71121M**	**73104M**	**347926M**	**1239561M**	**6596144M**

M = $ thousand MM = $ million

See Pages 9 through 22 for Explanation of Ratios and Data

Current Data Sorted by Assets							Comparative Historical Data	
						Type of Statement		
		1	4	3	2	Unqualified	17	13
1	6	30	10			Reviewed	45	41
1	9	17	2			Compiled	41	38
5	15	7				Tax Returns	26	33
6	17	29	17		2	Other	62	63
43 (4/1-9/30/13)		141 (10/1/13-3/31/14)					4/1/09-3/31/10 ALL	4/1/10-3/31/11 ALL
0-500M	500M-2MM	2-10MM	10-50MM	50-100MM	100-250MM			
13	47	84	33	3	4	**NUMBER OF STATEMENTS**	191	188
%	%	%	%	%	%	**ASSETS**	%	%
14.3	7.8	9.3	11.6			Cash & Equivalents	6.9	8.3
19.7	28.9	34.4	28.8			Trade Receivables (net)	30.9	30.7
35.5	38.1	30.1	31.2			Inventory	33.3	31.7
.0	2.9	2.6	1.9			All Other Current	3.7	3.5
69.5	77.8	76.4	73.4			Total Current	74.9	74.2
15.1	13.8	12.6	13.6			Fixed Assets (net)	13.3	12.1
5.7	4.3	4.7	5.2			Intangibles (net)	5.0	6.4
9.7	4.2	6.2	7.8			All Other Non-Current	6.8	7.3
100.0	100.0	100.0	100.0			Total	100.0	100.0
						LIABILITIES		
13.8	10.3	11.5	14.0			Notes Payable-Short Term	15.3	14.3
5.5	1.9	2.1	2.2			Cur. Mat.-L.T.D.	2.7	2.2
23.2	26.0	18.9	18.7			Trade Payables	20.2	20.9
.2	.0	.1	.2			Income Taxes Payable	.2	.3
15.4	23.4	12.6	9.3			All Other Current	13.1	12.6
58.1	61.6	45.3	44.4			Total Current	51.5	50.2
28.5	9.0	10.4	8.6			Long-Term Debt	13.5	10.0
.0	.0	.1	.3			Deferred Taxes	.2	.1
12.1	3.9	8.3	3.1			All Other Non-Current	6.1	6.9
1.3	25.5	35.9	43.7			Net Worth	28.7	32.8
100.0	100.0	100.0	100.0			Total Liabilties & Net Worth	100.0	100.0
						INCOME DATA		
100.0	100.0	100.0	100.0			Net Sales	100.0	100.0
36.8	33.6	32.0	30.1			Gross Profit	31.6	33.1
36.1	31.3	28.4	26.2			Operating Expenses	29.7	30.3
.7	2.3	3.6	3.9			Operating Profit	1.9	2.8
.4	.0	.0	-.5			All Other Expenses (net)	.4	.1
.3	2.2	3.7	4.4			Profit Before Taxes	1.5	2.7
						RATIOS		
2.5	2.0	2.5	2.5				2.6	2.3
1.2	1.3	1.7	1.6			Current	1.5	1.5
.8	1.0	1.3	1.2				1.1	1.1
1.0	1.0	1.7	1.4				1.2	1.3
.6	.6	.9	.9			Quick	.8	.8
.4	.4	.6	.6				.5	.5
0 UND	20 18.7	28 13.0	26 13.9				23 15.9	23 15.6
12 30.7	28 13.0	38 9.7	35 10.3			Sales/Receivables	34 10.9	35 10.4
30 12.1	40 9.2	50 7.3	54 6.8				46 8.0	47 7.7
7 49.1	36 10.2	31 11.7	33 10.9				31 11.6	29 12.8
41 8.8	60 6.1	53 6.9	68 5.4			Cost of Sales/Inventory	52 7.0	51 7.2
152 2.4	81 4.5	79 4.6	101 3.6				79 4.6	89 4.1
0 UND	17 21.2	16 22.3	16 22.3				16 23.1	16 23.1
10 37.0	38 9.7	31 11.6	27 13.7			Cost of Sales/Payables	28 13.3	30 12.3
49 7.4	53 6.9	48 7.6	49 7.4				43 8.4	50 7.3
5.5	8.3	6.0	6.0				6.6	6.5
71.1	23.2	8.8	8.2			Sales/Working Capital	14.3	12.8
-181.2	-739.0	21.7	26.5				73.3	54.0
15.2	18.1	13.9	96.4				9.1	10.5
(10) .2	(42) 7.3	(78) 4.6	(29) 9.1			EBIT/Interest	(170) 2.9	(169) 3.1
-21.0	1.4	2.4	3.3				.9	1.3
		4.9	15.9				7.3	8.0
		(18) 2.0	(10) 6.1			Net Profit + Depr., Dep., Amort./Cur. Mat. L/T/D	(41) 2.1	(28) 2.2
		1.2	1.7				1.2	1.1
.1	.1	.1	.1				.1	.1
7.8	.4	.2	.2			Fixed/Worth	.4	.3
-.8	3.4	.7	.7				2.4	2.0
.6	1.0	.8	.7				.9	1.0
UND	2.7	1.7	1.6			Debt/Worth	2.6	2.5
-3.1	-16.8	5.1	3.1				23.6	14.9
	59.0	41.9	53.6				32.3	29.6
	(34) 29.7	(79) 21.6	(31) 23.4			% Profit Before Taxes/Tangible Net Worth	(151) 17.8	(151) 12.8
	11.2	7.1	10.4				3.3	3.0
31.8	16.0	12.1	20.7				10.7	11.9
5.7	6.5	5.0	9.8			% Profit Before Taxes/Total Assets	4.8	4.9
-25.2	1.1	2.2	3.8				-.4	.8
999.8	118.0	94.2	61.0				106.0	95.7
26.4	40.7	34.6	26.9			Sales/Net Fixed Assets	46.1	41.3
17.3	17.4	16.3	9.2				19.5	19.1
10.3	4.5	3.7	3.8				4.2	4.1
6.2	3.7	3.0	2.8			Sales/Total Assets	3.2	3.1
2.3	2.5	2.3	1.7				2.4	2.2
	.5	.4	.4				.3	.4
	(31) .7	(67) .8	(27) .7			% Depr., Dep., Amort./Sales	(160) .7	(154) .7
	1.3	1.3	1.1				1.4	1.3
	1.9	1.8					1.8	2.3
	(30) 3.5	(43) 2.8				% Officers', Directors' Owners' Comp/Sales	(86) 4.1	(98) 4.5
	5.0	3.7					7.1	7.8
22270M	206324M	1158961M	1979679M	324615M	1978456M	Net Sales ($)	6607243M	4929956M
3459M	56178M	388513M	646309M	215704M	612769M	Total Assets ($)	2039301M	1660990M

M = $ thousand MM = $ million

See Pages 9 through 22 for Explanation of Ratios and Data

Comparative Historical Data / Current Data Sorted by Sales

	4/1/11-3/31/12 ALL		4/1/12-3/31/13 ALL		4/1/13-3/31/14 ALL		0-1MM		1-3MM		3-5MM		5-10MM		10-25MM		25MM & OVER
						Type of Statement											
	14		13		10	Unqualified									1		9
	46		44		47	Reviewed			2		2		11		20		12
	46		28		29	Compiled			3		3		8		13		2
	38		25		27	Tax Returns	1		8		8		6		4		
	63		59		71	Other	4		8		10		17		14		18
									43 (4/1-9/30/13)				141 (10/1/13-3/31/14)				
	207		169		184	**NUMBER OF STATEMENTS**	5		21		23		42		52		41
	%		%		%	**ASSETS**	%		%		%		%		%		%
	8.5		9.5		9.5	Cash & Equivalents			6.1		6.0		13.1		8.8		10.9
	31.5		29.8		30.9	Trade Receivables (net)			25.1		32.5		28.4		34.9		32.5
	31.4		30.7		32.5	Inventory			41.6		33.9		29.4		33.0		29.1
	3.1		3.5		2.4	All Other Current			4.9		1.3		2.5		2.1		2.4
	74.5		73.5		75.4	Total Current			77.7		73.7		73.4		78.8		74.9
	13.2		13.0		13.1	Fixed Assets (net)			15.5		16.0		13.6		12.3		11.2
	5.7		7.0		5.1	Intangibles (net)			5.4		3.5		6.0		2.9		6.8
	6.6		6.6		6.4	All Other Non-Current			1.5		6.8		7.0		5.9		7.0
	100.0		100.0		100.0	Total			100.0		100.0		100.0		100.0		100.0
						LIABILITIES											
	15.7		11.1		11.7	Notes Payable-Short Term			14.8		7.5		8.4		15.0		12.5
	2.5		2.6		2.4	Cur. Mat.-L.T.D.			3.0		2.1		2.2		2.0		2.6
	19.8		17.3		20.9	Trade Payables			21.4		27.4		21.2		19.8		19.0
	.3		.2		.1	Income Taxes Payable			.1		.0		.0		.2		.2
	10.8		12.5		14.9	All Other Current			23.8		21.2		16.9		12.0		9.4
	49.1		43.7		49.9	Total Current			63.2		58.2		48.6		49.1		43.6
	9.5		12.8		11.3	Long-Term Debt			23.3		10.1		13.6		7.6		9.5
	.1		.2		.1	Deferred Taxes			.0		.0		.0		.1		.2
	5.0		5.2		6.4	All Other Non-Current			2.7		4.0		6.7		9.7		3.7
	36.2		38.0		32.3	Net Worth			10.8		27.7		31.1		33.5		42.9
	100.0		100.0		100.0	Total Liabilties & Net Worth			100.0		100.0		100.0		100.0		100.0
						INCOME DATA											
	100.0		100.0		100.0	Net Sales			100.0		100.0		100.0		100.0		100.0
	31.3		31.7		32.4	Gross Profit			35.3		34.8		33.9		30.7		28.6
	29.0		28.2		29.3	Operating Expenses			33.8		31.3		30.5		27.8		24.4
	2.3		3.6		3.2	Operating Profit			1.5		3.4		3.4		2.9		4.2
	.0		.1		.0	All Other Expenses (net)			.5		-.3		.2		-.2		-.3
	2.3		3.5		3.2	Profit Before Taxes			1.0		3.7		3.2		3.1		4.5
						RATIOS											
	2.5		2.7		2.4				2.1		2.1		2.7		2.4		2.5
	1.5		1.7		1.6	Current			1.2		1.5		1.5		1.6		1.8
	1.1		1.3		1.2				.8		1.0		1.2		1.2		1.4
	1.3		1.3		1.4				.8		1.4		1.5		1.6		1.4
	.7		.8		.8	Quick			.6		.7		.8		.8		1.0
	.5		.5		.5				.3		.4		.5		.6		.6
25	14.5	24	15.0	24	15.2			13	28.9	20	18.2	19	19.3	29	12.4	29	12.7
36	10.0	34	10.7	33	10.9	Sales/Receivables		27	13.3	31	11.8	30	12.1	36	10.1	40	9.1
49	7.5	46	7.9	47	7.7			36	10.0	49	7.4	47	7.7	48	7.6	51	7.2
29	12.4	33	11.0	31	11.7			24	15.0	36	10.0	31	11.9	31	11.7	29	12.6
48	7.6	50	7.3	56	6.5	Cost of Sales/Inventory		51	7.1	63	5.8	61	6.0	50	7.3	52	7.0
85	4.3	85	4.3	87	4.2			111	3.3	83	4.4	81	4.5	87	4.2	87	4.2
16	22.7	15	23.6	16	22.3			2	215.8	17	21.5	17	21.4	17	22.0	17	21.6
28	13.2	24	15.2	31	11.9	Cost of Sales/Payables		26	14.2	43	8.5	33	11.1	31	11.8	26	13.8
45	8.2	42	8.7	48	7.6			60	6.1	66	5.5	56	6.5	42	8.6	45	8.1
	7.1		6.0		6.3				5.0		7.0		6.1		6.5		6.4
	12.9		9.4		9.7	Sales/Working Capital			23.2		12.2		9.9		9.8		8.9
	50.0		24.1		33.3				-179.0		-999.8		31.0		23.7		18.8
	10.2		17.2		16.7				9.7		29.0		15.6		13.1		35.3
(179)	4.4	(153)	6.0	(165)	5.9	EBIT/Interest		(17)	3.9	(22)	13.1	(40)	3.2	(49)	4.9	(35)	6.9
	1.2		1.8		2.2				.2		2.3		1.7		2.5		3.0
	5.1		6.0		7.5										6.9		7.3
(42)	2.2	(42)	2.1	(39)	3.4	Net Profit + Depr., Dep., Amort./Cur. Mat. L/T/D								(13)	2.1	(16)	5.3
	.9		.7		1.6										1.7		1.8
	.1		.1		.1				.1		.1		.2		.1		.1
	.3		.3		.3	Fixed/Worth			1.8		.4		.4		.2		.2
	1.0		1.0		1.2				UND		1.2		5.8		.7		.7
	.9		.7		.8				1.0		.9		1.0		.8		.6
	2.0		2.2		1.9	Debt/Worth			5.5		2.6		2.4		1.6		1.7
	6.0		4.9		7.4				-3.4		25.2		NM		4.3		3.7
	33.6		37.3		51.9				117.5		74.6		70.9		41.9		46.0
(179)	13.3	(146)	19.4	(158)	23.3	% Profit Before Taxes/Tangible Net Worth		(15)	30.4	(19)	33.6	(32)	24.4	(51)	21.6	(37)	23.2
	2.5		6.3		8.5				7.6		13.1		13.1		5.7		12.9
	10.1		13.5		14.9				11.9		17.8		11.1		13.4		19.0
	4.3		5.6		5.9	% Profit Before Taxes/Total Assets			5.0		8.5		4.5		4.8		9.3
	.3		1.9		2.1				-4.3		1.2		2.0		2.1		4.2
	95.8		89.7		97.0				311.6		95.7		223.0		111.6		72.9
	40.6		38.8		34.5	Sales/Net Fixed Assets			34.5		37.1		26.1		39.7		31.6
	14.7		17.4		15.2				18.2		14.1		13.2		18.2		14.6
	4.2		3.9		4.0				5.7		3.9		3.9		3.8		4.3
	3.0		3.0		3.1	Sales/Total Assets			3.3		3.0		3.0		3.2		3.2
	2.3		2.2		2.2				1.8		2.5		2.2		2.4		1.9
	.4		.4		.4				.6		.4		.6		.3		.4
(159)	.7	(138)	.6	(139)	.7	% Depr., Dep., Amort./Sales		(13)	.7	(16)	.8	(29)	1.2	(44)	.7	(35)	.7
	1.3		1.2		1.3				1.4		1.3		1.9		1.1		1.2
	2.2		2.2		1.9						1.9		1.5		1.8		1.5
(93)	4.2	(81)	3.5	(89)	3.0	% Officers', Directors' Owners' Comp/Sales				(17)	3.3	(26)	2.7	(27)	3.0	(10)	2.6
	6.6		5.4		4.6						4.8		4.6		3.9		7.4
	6468353M		5973625M		5670305M	Net Sales ($)	2759M		41786M		88991M		307287M		815257M		4414225M
	2319714M		1938201M		1922932M	Total Assets ($)	1205M		13916M		34089M		123641M		286425M		1463656M

M = $ thousand MM = $ million

See Pages 9 through 22 for Explanation of Ratios and Data

Current Data Sorted by Assets							Comparative Historical Data	
	1	3	12	3	4	**Type of Statement** Unqualified	31	34
	2	17	21	2		Reviewed	27	45
	3	8	5		1	Compiled	21	33
3	10	12	1			Tax Returns	20	27
4	15	30	26	6	6	Other	92	65
27 (4/1-9/30/13)		168 (10/1/13-3/31/14)					4/1/09-3/31/10	4/1/10-3/31/11
0-500M	**500M-2MM**	**2-10MM**	**10-50MM**	**50-100MM**	**100-250MM**		**ALL**	**ALL**
7	31	70	65	11	11	**NUMBER OF STATEMENTS**	191	204
%	%	%	%	%	%	**ASSETS**	%	%
	15.2	9.7	6.3	2.2	1.7	Cash & Equivalents	7.8	9.3
	26.6	22.1	20.2	18.7	13.6	Trade Receivables (net)	22.2	22.4
	42.7	41.5	47.3	37.5	39.0	Inventory	42.6	42.9
	4.6	2.4	1.6	3.1	2.0	All Other Current	3.0	4.0
	89.0	75.7	75.5	61.5	56.4	Total Current	75.6	78.6
	7.5	13.2	15.3	17.1	27.8	Fixed Assets (net)	15.4	13.5
	1.0	4.8	5.3	15.0	11.1	Intangibles (net)	2.6	3.1
	2.5	6.4	3.9	6.4	4.7	All Other Non-Current	6.4	4.7
	100.0	100.0	100.0	100.0	100.0	Total	100.0	100.0
						LIABILITIES		
	12.3	9.2	19.0	13.3	16.5	Notes Payable-Short Term	19.7	15.1
	2.2	3.5	2.1	2.1	4.5	Cur. Mat.-L.T.D.	3.2	3.4
	19.1	18.4	14.9	10.6	8.5	Trade Payables	15.8	14.9
	.0	.1	.1	.4	.5	Income Taxes Payable	.1	.1
	12.2	8.1	8.6	6.4	5.5	All Other Current	11.0	11.4
	45.7	39.4	44.7	32.7	35.3	Total Current	49.9	44.9
	9.9	9.2	9.9	28.0	17.9	Long-Term Debt	9.2	8.3
	.0	.2	.4	4.2	2.7	Deferred Taxes	.1	.2
	8.2	6.8	4.1	4.5	6.3	All Other Non-Current	5.9	6.8
	36.2	44.4	40.9	30.5	37.7	Net Worth	34.9	39.8
	100.0	100.0	100.0	100.0	100.0	Total Liabilties & Net Worth	100.0	100.0
						INCOME DATA		
	100.0	100.0	100.0	100.0	100.0	Net Sales	100.0	100.0
	27.9	28.4	29.0	33.3	30.7	Gross Profit	29.2	30.5
	24.8	23.3	22.5	24.5	23.1	Operating Expenses	25.3	24.9
	3.1	5.1	6.6	8.8	7.6	Operating Profit	3.9	5.6
	1.2	.7	.7	3.7	1.9	All Other Expenses (net)	.9	1.1
	1.9	4.4	5.9	5.1	5.7	Profit Before Taxes	3.0	4.5
						RATIOS		
	4.6	3.5	2.7	2.5	2.5		2.7	3.2
	1.9	2.4	1.5	1.8	1.5	Current	1.5	1.9
	1.2	1.3	1.2	1.2	1.1		1.2	1.2
	2.1	1.4	1.0	.8	.9		1.0	1.2
	1.0	.8	.5	.6	.6	Quick	.6	.7
	.4	.4	.3	.5	.2		.3	.3
	13 28.7	**17** 21.6	**30** 12.1	**35** 10.5	**33** 11.0		**20** 18.6	**16** 23.1
	23 16.1	**29** 12.5	**41** 8.8	**38** 9.7	**39** 9.3	Sales/Receivables	**34** 10.8	**32** 11.3
	40 9.1	**42** 8.7	**58** 6.3	**46** 8.0	**62** 5.9		**55** 6.6	**52** 7.0
	20 18.1	**41** 9.0	**58** 6.3	**56** 6.5	**99** 3.7		**43** 8.5	**40** 9.0
	78 4.7	**76** 4.8	**146** 2.5	**101** 3.6	**182** 2.0	Cost of Sales/Inventory	**99** 3.7	**88** 4.1
	174 2.1	**140** 2.6	**243** 1.5	**146** 2.5	**203** 1.8		**199** 1.8	**174** 2.1
	17 21.7	**18** 19.8	**18** 19.8	**20** 18.6	**22** 16.6		**16** 23.5	**18** 20.8
	27 13.7	**30** 12.2	**38** 9.7	**38** 9.6	**44** 8.3	Cost of Sales/Payables	**30** 12.0	**29** 12.7
	48 7.6	**43** 8.4	**65** 5.6	**45** 8.1	**61** 6.0		**50** 7.3	**46** 8.0
	2.6	3.8	3.0	3.4	2.5		4.2	3.7
	8.4	7.0	6.1	7.2	7.6	Sales/Working Capital	7.5	6.5
	19.7	17.8	15.1	23.4	17.0		40.3	18.9
	13.5	26.3	10.2	38.5	10.3		10.2	20.7
	(25) 4.3	(59) 8.1	(59) 5.0	(10) 6.3	4.5	EBIT/Interest	(171) 3.2	(179) 5.7
	-1.1	1.9	2.3	1.4	1.9		1.1	1.5
			8.5				7.4	13.1
			(14) 3.9			Net Profit + Depr., Dep., Amort./Cur. Mat. L/T/D	(33) 2.8	(42) 4.5
			2.4				1.3	.9
	.0	.0	.0	.1	.2		.1	.0
	.2	.2	.1	1.0	.4	Fixed/Worth	.3	.2
	.5	.7	.8	-.9	2.3		1.0	.7
	.7	.5	.8	2.2	1.6		.8	.6
	2.3	1.3	2.2	3.8	2.6	Debt/Worth	2.0	1.5
	5.8	3.0	3.8	-5.1	5.5		4.1	4.0
	25.0	53.6	44.3		45.5		33.1	42.6
	(29) 11.1	(63) 31.9	(61) 19.3		(10) 24.7	% Profit Before Taxes/Tangible Net Worth	(167) 14.7	(189) 18.6
	1.3	6.3	9.8		7.7		3.4	5.2
	10.0	21.8	14.3	11.8	9.6		12.7	15.6
	2.4	10.7	7.2	6.2	4.9	% Profit Before Taxes/Total Assets	3.7	7.5
	-.6	1.6	3.0	.7	2.3		.3	1.9
	490.2	158.2	154.5	54.1	27.4		113.9	122.0
	91.1	47.0	46.9	16.7	13.3	Sales/Net Fixed Assets	30.1	37.7
	27.8	15.1	6.2	6.6	1.3		9.9	11.7
	4.4	3.3	2.2	2.7	1.3		3.2	3.2
	2.5	2.4	1.6	.9	1.1	Sales/Total Assets	2.1	2.3
	1.8	1.7	1.0	.7	.9		1.3	1.4
	.3	.3	.2	.7			.3	.3
	(17) .7	(53) .5	(57) .5	(10) 1.5		% Depr., Dep., Amort./Sales	(154) .7	(161) .7
	1.6	1.7	1.8	5.7			1.4	1.7
	2.0	1.2	.9				1.9	2.1
	(20) 4.8	(31) 3.3	(18) 2.1			% Officers', Directors' Owners' Comp/Sales	(56) 3.3	(60) 4.4
	8.8	5.6	3.6				7.5	7.1
6511M	112085M	910706M	2253530M	1337872M	1894463M	Net Sales ($)	5394444M	5486799M
1621M	39472M	339421M	1418659M	832158M	1652147M	Total Assets ($)	3235022M	2914793M

M = $ thousand MM = $ million

See Pages 9 through 22 for Explanation of Ratios and Data

Comparative Historical Data / Current Data Sorted by Sales

4/1/11-3/31/12 ALL	4/1/12-3/31/13 ALL	4/1/13-3/31/14 ALL		0-1MM	1-3MM	3-5MM	5-10MM	10-25MM	25MM & OVER
			Type of Statement						
27	32	23	Unqualified				3	5	15
38	35	42	Reviewed		1	2	3	21	15
22	16	17	Compiled		1	4	4	3	5
41	25	26	Tax Returns	1	7	6	5	5	2
79	72	87	Other	5	8	9	10	21	34
				27 (4/1-9/30/13)			168 (10/1/13-3/31/14)		
207	180	195	**NUMBER OF STATEMENTS**	6	17	21	25	55	71
%	%	%	**ASSETS**	%	%	%	%	%	%
10.0	8.2	9.0	Cash & Equivalents		9.2	13.0	13.6	5.9	7.3
22.5	20.7	21.6	Trade Receivables (net)		19.2	24.5	20.8	22.6	21.6
44.4	45.6	42.8	Inventory		39.0	41.8	32.2	48.9	43.1
2.7	3.3	2.4	All Other Current		6.0	2.4	.7	2.9	1.9
79.6	77.8	75.8	Total Current		73.3	81.7	67.3	80.4	74.0
11.2	14.5	13.9	Fixed Assets (net)		11.2	12.0	19.7	11.7	15.2
3.2	2.8	5.1	Intangibles (net)		8.3	1.1	7.6	4.2	5.8
6.0	4.9	5.2	All Other Non-Current		7.2	5.2	5.4	3.7	5.0
100.0	100.0	100.0	Total		100.0	100.0	100.0	100.0	100.0
			LIABILITIES						
15.4	15.9	14.0	Notes Payable-Short Term		16.3	12.8	10.0	13.3	16.4
2.0	2.6	2.8	Cur. Mat.-L.T.D.		3.9	1.9	4.1	2.2	2.9
16.5	16.3	16.1	Trade Payables		10.9	18.6	18.2	15.5	16.8
.1	.1	.1	Income Taxes Payable		.3	.0	.0	.1	.2
11.6	8.8	9.3	All Other Current		4.1	14.8	4.6	10.7	7.8
45.6	43.7	42.2	Total Current		35.5	48.0	37.0	41.8	44.1
9.9	13.6	11.1	Long-Term Debt		11.3	7.3	17.0	9.2	11.9
.1	.3	.6	Deferred Taxes		.0	.0	.0	.3	1.4
6.2	5.3	5.7	All Other Non-Current		16.0	4.6	3.9	6.0	3.8
38.2	37.1	40.4	Net Worth		37.2	40.1	42.2	42.8	38.9
100.0	100.0	100.0	Total Liabilties & Net Worth		100.0	100.0	100.0	100.0	100.0
			INCOME DATA						
100.0	100.0	100.0	Net Sales		100.0	100.0	100.0	100.0	100.0
29.8	31.3	29.5	Gross Profit		41.9	27.9	31.2	28.7	26.1
23.7	24.6	24.1	Operating Expenses		36.7	25.7	24.3	22.5	19.7
6.1	6.7	5.5	Operating Profit		5.2	2.2	7.0	6.2	6.4
.7	.7	1.0	All Other Expenses (net)		.8	1.9	1.0	.1	1.5
5.4	6.0	4.4	Profit Before Taxes		4.4	.3	6.0	6.1	4.9
			RATIOS						
3.1	3.2	3.1			8.0	2.9	3.2	3.4	2.5
1.9	1.9	1.8	Current		2.2	1.9	1.8	2.1	1.4
1.3	1.3	1.2			1.0	1.1	1.2	1.4	1.2
1.2	1.2	1.3			1.6	1.3	1.7	1.4	1.0
.7	.7	.6	Quick		.5	.8	.7	.7	.6
.4	.4	.4			.2	.3	.4	.3	.4
19 18.9	**21** 17.0	**21** 17.3			**0** UND	**17** 21.5	**19** 18.9	**24** 15.3	**27** 13.3
36 10.1	**32** 11.5	**35** 10.4	Sales/Receivables		**21** 17.3	**35** 10.5	**30** 12.3	**40** 9.2	**38** 9.5
51 7.2	**47** 7.8	**50** 7.3			**39** 9.3	**48** 7.6	**38** 9.6	**58** 6.3	**50** 7.3
44 8.3	**41** 9.0	**45** 8.2			**3** 129.0	**14** 26.2	**30** 12.3	**56** 6.5	**54** 6.7
99 3.7	**101** 3.6	**99** 3.7	Cost of Sales/Inventory		**91** 4.0	**87** 4.2	**64** 5.7	**114** 3.2	**101** 3.6
166 2.2	**192** 1.9	**182** 2.0			**203** 1.8	**182** 2.0	**114** 3.2	**192** 1.9	**182** 2.0
19 19.6	**18** 19.8	**18** 19.9			**3** 126.1	**18** 20.1	**16** 23.2	**18** 19.9	**20** 18.0
32 11.4	**30** 12.1	**33** 11.2	Cost of Sales/Payables		**26** 13.9	**33** 11.1	**30** 12.3	**33** 10.9	**38** 9.7
47 7.8	**42** 8.7	**51** 7.1			**47** 7.7	**49** 7.5	**42** 8.6	**45** 8.1	**58** 6.3
3.9	3.4	3.7			2.2	3.4	5.3	3.1	4.4
6.9	6.2	7.1	Sales/Working Capital		4.2	7.4	8.6	5.9	8.9
18.2	16.2	19.6			-277.1	21.9	28.9	10.1	17.9
26.9	19.2	14.8			11.6	14.7	11.4	15.3	19.3
(180) 7.6	(161) 6.8	(168) 5.9	EBIT/Interest		(16) 6.1	(16) 4.2	(22) 5.5	(48) 6.7	(64) 5.3
2.8	2.3	2.0			1.8	-3.2	2.1	3.8	1.8
13.3	14.5	4.1						7.2	3.6
(35) 5.0	(32) 4.4	(31) 1.9	Net Profit + Depr., Dep., Amort./Cur. Mat. L/T/D					(13) 3.1	(14) 2.0
2.9	1.5	.4						.0	.9
.0	.0	.0			.0	.1	.0	.0	.0
.2	.2	.2	Fixed/Worth		.2	.2	.2	.1	.2
.5	.6	.9			.5	.7	2.4	.6	1.3
.7	.7	.8			.4	.5	.8	.7	.9
1.5	1.7	2.0	Debt/Worth		2.0	2.0	2.3	1.7	2.6
3.8	3.4	4.2			11.1	5.2	6.0	3.2	5.5
53.4	53.1	49.2			57.7	13.9	76.4	59.6	47.8
(191) 24.7	(166) 24.6	(177) 20.5	% Profit Before Taxes/Tangible Net Worth		(15) 15.5	(20) 6.8	(22) 29.0	(50) 33.0	(64) 25.4
9.7	9.3	6.5			4.8	-3.9	3.1	11.2	8.9
18.7	19.7	14.6			17.8	7.5	19.6	19.5	14.5
8.9	8.7	6.5	% Profit Before Taxes/Total Assets		4.6	1.1	11.0	11.1	6.2
2.6	2.8	1.4			1.5	-4.9	1.9	3.6	2.1
202.7	133.3	174.4			745.0	105.2	224.7	117.2	147.5
48.3	41.8	46.2	Sales/Net Fixed Assets		36.6	44.3	32.0	47.3	46.9
14.0	10.0	10.0			9.2	13.4	8.2	17.6	7.7
3.4	3.4	3.0			3.0	2.5	3.3	3.1	3.0
2.3	2.0	2.0	Sales/Total Assets		2.2	2.2	2.0	1.9	2.0
1.5	1.3	1.3			.9	1.7	1.6	1.4	1.1
.3	.2	.3			.3	.3	.5	.3	.2
(151) .7	(145) .7	(147) .6	% Depr., Dep., Amort./Sales		(10) 1.6	(16) .4	(16) 1.6	(41) .5	(63) .5
1.8	1.9	1.8			3.1	1.2	4.0	1.9	1.7
1.7	2.0	1.6				2.6	1.5	1.6	.6
(76) 4.8	(65) 4.2	(74) 3.4	% Officers', Directors' Owners' Comp/Sales			(17) 7.2	(12) 3.9	(20) 3.4	(16) 1.2
7.9	7.4	7.0				9.4	6.6	4.6	2.0
7005784M	**6621993M**	**6515167M**	Net Sales ($)	**3071M**	**31903M**	**79288M**	**182026M**	**863978M**	**5354901M**
3762554M	**4075915M**	**4283478M**	Total Assets ($)	**4166M**	**34144M**	**40335M**	**98900M**	**565968M**	**3539965M**

M = $ thousand MM = $ million

See Pages 9 through 22 for Explanation of Ratios and Data

Current Data Sorted by Assets							Comparative Historical Data	
						Type of Statement		
		7	16	9	4	Unqualified	62	41
	4	39	14	2	1	Reviewed	92	78
6	17	19	1	1	1	Compiled	42	46
10	33	28	4			Tax Returns	71	80
5	23	62	45	9	9	Other	155	169
62 (4/1-9/30/13)			307 (10/1/13-3/31/14)				4/1/09-3/31/10	4/1/10-3/31/11
0-500M	500M-2MM	2-10MM	10-50MM	50-100MM	100-250MM		ALL	ALL
21	77	155	80	21	15	**NUMBER OF STATEMENTS**	422	414
%	%	%	%	%	%	**ASSETS**	%	%
16.0	10.8	8.1	8.2	6.8	5.3	Cash & Equivalents	9.4	9.6
10.8	18.6	24.1	27.3	23.7	34.9	Trade Receivables (net)	26.9	26.0
40.5	49.3	46.3	41.2	40.8	32.5	Inventory	40.8	41.6
1.4	1.5	2.9	4.0	2.2	3.7	All Other Current	2.3	2.2
68.6	80.2	81.4	80.7	73.4	76.4	Total Current	79.4	79.5
17.5	9.1	10.0	8.3	10.5	8.3	Fixed Assets (net)	10.0	9.2
2.5	5.2	3.5	6.2	12.1	10.8	Intangibles (net)	5.4	5.3
11.4	5.5	5.1	4.8	4.0	4.5	All Other Non-Current	5.1	5.9
100.0	100.0	100.0	100.0	100.0	100.0	Total	100.0	100.0
						LIABILITIES		
17.3	12.8	15.8	17.9	17.6	17.5	Notes Payable-Short Term	18.7	16.0
1.7	1.3	1.4	1.8	.9	.8	Cur. Mat.-L.T.D.	2.2	2.0
10.7	19.8	21.7	22.9	16.7	18.1	Trade Payables	20.3	20.1
.0	.0	.1	.1	.2	.6	Income Taxes Payable	.2	.2
15.2	11.3	10.3	11.4	6.6	9.4	All Other Current	9.7	11.2
44.9	45.2	49.4	54.1	42.0	46.4	Total Current	51.1	49.5
15.1	15.1	7.5	7.8	11.1	20.8	Long-Term Debt	10.3	8.2
.0	.0	.2	.1	.6	1.8	Deferred Taxes	.2	.2
9.1	10.0	7.1	6.4	5.3	3.1	All Other Non-Current	7.1	6.8
30.9	29.7	35.8	31.6	41.0	27.9	Net Worth	31.3	35.3
100.0	100.0	100.0	100.0	100.0	100.0	Total Liabilties & Net Worth	100.0	100.0
						INCOME DATA		
100.0	100.0	100.0	100.0	100.0	100.0	Net Sales	100.0	100.0
43.3	40.2	31.6	30.1	27.4	22.9	Gross Profit	31.9	31.8
38.9	36.5	27.5	24.9	21.0	16.8	Operating Expenses	28.3	27.5
4.4	3.7	4.1	5.3	6.4	6.0	Operating Profit	3.7	4.2
-.1	.0	.8	1.5	1.0	1.5	All Other Expenses (net)	1.0	.5
4.6	3.7	3.3	3.8	5.4	4.5	Profit Before Taxes	2.7	3.7
						RATIOS		
8.0	4.8	3.0	2.2	3.2	3.4		2.8	2.8
2.5	1.8	1.7	1.4	1.9	2.0	Current	1.6	1.6
.6	1.2	1.2	1.2	1.3	1.1		1.2	1.2
2.5	1.4	1.2	1.0	1.2	2.2		1.3	1.2
.5	.6	.7	.6	.7	1.1	Quick	.7	.7
.2	.4	.4	.4	.4	.5		.4	.4
0 UND	3 113.5	17 21.0	27 13.7	18 20.1	33 11.2		19 19.1	19 19.0
1 310.0	19 19.3	30 12.3	42 8.6	34 10.7	63 5.8	Sales/Receivables	37 9.8	33 10.9
21 17.8	36 10.2	46 7.9	69 5.3	63 5.8	73 5.0		59 6.2	59 6.2
0 UND	49 7.4	61 6.0	65 5.6	72 5.1	61 6.0		52 7.0	51 7.1
29 12.7	101 3.6	104 3.5	111 3.3	91 4.0	73 5.0	Cost of Sales/Inventory	89 4.1	100 3.7
107 3.4	192 1.9	166 2.2	159 2.3	126 2.9	111 3.3		142 2.6	153 2.4
0 UND	9 40.0	17 21.7	25 14.8	15 24.0	16 22.7		14 26.2	15 24.5
1 656.6	26 14.3	35 10.5	46 8.0	26 14.1	27 13.5	Cost of Sales/Payables	31 11.8	35 10.3
20 18.2	54 6.7	68 5.4	78 4.7	41 8.8	42 8.6		55 6.7	59 6.2
7.1	4.5	4.1	5.0	3.2	2.8		4.3	4.4
16.8	7.9	8.6	7.9	6.2	6.8	Sales/Working Capital	8.7	8.4
-75.0	24.7	24.4	15.9	14.5	67.0		33.1	22.2
26.5	16.4	15.7	18.1	44.9	55.2		12.6	15.1
(15) 7.9	(65) 7.3	(142) 4.4	(76) 4.4	(19) 14.3	(14) 6.8	EBIT/Interest	(386) 3.3	(368) 4.2
-1.0	1.8	1.6	1.6	2.6	1.0		1.2	1.5
		5.6	17.8				9.4	13.2
		(24) 2.4	(20) 5.5			Net Profit + Depr., Dep., Amort./Cur. Mat. L/T/D	(72) 2.9	(62) 3.3
		1.4	1.3				.7	1.2
.0	.1	.1	.0	.1	.2		.0	.0
.1	.2	.2	.2	.3	.4	Fixed/Worth	.2	.2
NM	10.3	.8	.5	1.0	-.4		.9	.7
.5	.8	.7	1.0	.9	.8		.7	.7
1.2	2.0	2.2	2.6	1.6	2.1	Debt/Worth	2.2	2.2
-10.9	NM	5.7	5.1	18.6	-9.1		8.9	6.0
175.0	66.6	49.1	43.3	52.5	32.5		48.1	48.7
(15) 60.2	(58) 22.9	(137) 18.4	(68) 20.0	(18) 23.9	(10) 22.4	% Profit Before Taxes/Tangible Net Worth	(359) 19.7	(362) 20.2
11.9	7.7	5.7	3.6	18.1	3.5		4.1	5.1
60.5	20.7	13.4	14.3	19.7	10.5		15.5	14.8
19.7	7.5	5.3	3.8	7.5	8.2	% Profit Before Taxes/Total Assets	5.5	6.3
-.2	1.2	1.5	.6	3.0	.2		.6	1.1
UND	164.2	143.7	109.2	86.9	89.7		173.5	139.2
74.5	55.2	52.2	47.2	28.7	32.5	Sales/Net Fixed Assets	56.9	50.6
30.8	24.4	19.1	22.9	11.4	10.6		18.4	20.6
6.3	3.9	3.2	2.7	2.6	3.6		3.3	3.4
3.9	2.9	2.4	1.9	1.9	2.2	Sales/Total Assets	2.3	2.3
2.9	2.0	1.8	1.3	1.3	1.4		1.7	1.6
	.3	.3	.3	.2	.2		.3	.3
	(52) .7	(122) .6	(66) .6	(19) .4	.3	% Depr., Dep., Amort./Sales	(305) .6	(303) .6
	1.1	1.1	1.4	1.9	2.0		1.3	1.2
1.7	2.0	1.2	.8				1.6	1.6
(13) 4.9	(45) 3.3	(65) 2.3	(18) 1.6			% Officers', Directors' Owners' Comp/Sales	(158) 3.4	(168) 3.2
6.3	5.7	3.8	2.6				5.9	5.6
29436M	289680M	2083372M	3842170M	3248131M	6958561M	Net Sales ($)	19238299M	15476778M
6299M	86485M	781511M	1835723M	1441525M	2518883M	Total Assets ($)	7647073M	7270866M

M = $ thousand MM = $ million

See Pages 9 through 22 for Explanation of Ratios and Data

Comparative Historical Data

Current Data Sorted by Sales

4/1/11-3/31/12 ALL	4/1/12-3/31/13 ALL	4/1/13-3/31/14 ALL	Type of Statement	0-1MM	1-3MM	3-5MM	5-10MM	10-25MM	25MM & OVER
49	37	36	Unqualified				3	7	26
87	73	60	Reviewed		1	3	9	31	16
46	52	45	Compiled	4	13	7	7	5	9
75	68	75	Tax Returns	8	19	13	14	16	5
150	135	153	Other	1	19	13	24	39	57
				62 (4/1-9/30/13)			307 (10/1/13-3/31/14)		
407	365	369	**NUMBER OF STATEMENTS**	13	52	36	57	98	113
%	%	%	**ASSETS**	%	%	%	%	%	%
9.9	10.0	9.0	Cash & Equivalents	13.2	10.1	11.7	7.3	8.1	8.6
25.5	24.5	23.3	Trade Receivables (net)	2.9	15.8	16.2	22.7	26.8	28.6
43.0	44.4	44.6	Inventory	64.7	45.5	47.4	46.5	42.4	42.0
2.6	2.9	2.8	All Other Current	2.1	1.3	1.2	2.2	3.8	3.4
80.9	81.8	79.6	Total Current	82.9	72.7	76.5	78.6	81.1	82.6
9.1	9.1	9.8	Fixed Assets (net)	9.2	11.5	14.5	11.5	9.5	7.1
4.6	4.9	5.2	Intangibles (net)	.3	8.2	1.8	4.4	3.9	6.9
5.3	4.2	5.4	All Other Non-Current	7.5	7.6	7.2	5.5	5.4	3.4
100.0	100.0	100.0	Total	100.0	100.0	100.0	100.0	100.0	100.0
			LIABILITIES						
15.8	15.7	15.9	Notes Payable-Short Term	18.7	11.4	18.4	12.5	18.4	16.4
1.7	1.9	1.4	Cur. Mat.-L.T.D.	3.1	1.3	1.1	1.1	1.9	1.2
20.3	21.8	20.5	Trade Payables	5.9	14.2	18.6	19.4	24.0	23.2
.2	.2	.1	Income Taxes Payable	.0	.0	.0	.0	.1	.2
9.9	10.6	10.8	All Other Current	15.6	10.0	8.3	11.8	11.9	10.0
48.0	50.2	48.8	Total Current	43.2	36.9	46.4	44.8	56.3	51.0
8.3	8.6	10.3	Long-Term Debt	17.1	16.3	11.7	7.3	8.9	9.2
.2	.2	.2	Deferred Taxes	.0	.0	.0	.1	.3	.4
7.5	7.4	7.4	All Other Non-Current	11.6	11.7	7.6	9.0	6.2	5.1
36.0	33.6	33.3	Net Worth	28.0	35.1	34.3	38.8	28.3	34.4
100.0	100.0	100.0	Total Liabilities & Net Worth	100.0	100.0	100.0	100.0	100.0	100.0
			INCOME DATA						
100.0	100.0	100.0	Net Sales	100.0	100.0	100.0	100.0	100.0	100.0
31.6	30.5	33.2	Gross Profit	47.1	44.5	37.0	32.8	33.8	24.7
27.5	26.8	28.6	Operating Expenses	45.5	39.6	33.0	29.7	28.3	20.1
4.1	3.8	4.5	Operating Profit	1.6	4.8	4.0	3.1	5.5	4.7
.4	.8	.8	All Other Expenses (net)	-1.5	.4	.5	1.0	1.0	.9
3.7	2.9	3.7	Profit Before Taxes	3.1	4.4	3.5	2.1	4.5	3.7
			RATIOS						
3.0	3.3	3.0		15.7	6.1	4.7	3.0	2.3	2.8
1.8	1.7	1.7	Current	2.5	2.3	1.8	1.9	1.4	1.5
1.2	1.2	1.2		1.4	1.2	1.1	1.2	1.1	1.2
1.3	1.3	1.2		1.5	1.7	1.6	1.2	1.0	1.2
.7	.7	.6	Quick	.2	.6	.6	.7	.6	.7
.4	.4	.4		.1	.3	.1	.4	.4	.4
20 18.7	**18** 20.6	**14** 26.1		**0** UND	**3** 116.8	**1** 396.0	**19** 19.0	**17** 20.9	**23** 15.6
33 10.9	**33** 11.0	**30** 12.3	Sales/Receivables	**0** UND	**18** 20.1	**17** 21.9	**29** 12.6	**35** 10.5	**37** 9.8
55 6.6	**54** 6.8	**50** 7.3		**5** 78.4	**38** 9.5	**41** 9.0	**44** 8.3	**54** 6.8	**63** 5.8
53 6.9	**53** 6.9	**57** 6.4		**42** 8.7	**51** 7.2	**53** 6.9	**58** 6.3	**50** 7.3	**61** 6.0
96 3.8	**104** 3.5	**101** 3.6	Cost of Sales/Inventory	**166** 2.2	**104** 3.5	**130** 2.8	**107** 3.4	**101** 3.6	**83** 4.4
159 2.3	**166** 2.2	**159** 2.3		**304** 1.2	**215** 1.7	**192** 1.9	**192** 1.9	**159** 2.3	**122** 3.0
15 24.0	**14** 26.8	**15** 25.1		**0** UND	**3** 104.5	**13** 27.8	**22** 16.4	**16** 23.5	**18** 20.4
32 11.4	**32** 11.4	**31** 11.8	Cost of Sales/Payables	**0** UND	**21** 17.6	**38** 9.7	**32** 11.5	**36** 10.2	**31** 11.6
60 6.1	**65** 5.6	**64** 5.7		**5** 72.7	**61** 6.0	**70** 5.2	**55** 6.6	**70** 5.2	**60** 6.1
4.2	4.2	4.4		4.0	3.0	4.0	4.2	4.8	4.9
7.4	7.6	8.2	Sales/Working Capital	6.8	6.9	7.4	7.4	9.9	7.9
15.9	20.9	21.4		14.0	25.9	53.9	18.8	39.3	17.2
18.7	16.8	18.1			20.3	11.4	15.6	16.0	36.0
(342) 4.9	(318) 4.2	(331) 5.2	EBIT/Interest		(43) 4.3	(30) 4.0	(54) 3.3	(89) 6.7	(106) 6.7
1.7	1.3	1.6			2.0	2.1	.7	2.2	1.9
10.0	6.7	10.3						18.0	22.3
(61) 3.4	(60) 2.2	(59) 3.8	Net Profit + Depr., Dep., Amort./Cur. Mat. L/T/D					(15) 1.8	(28) 6.7
1.1	1.0	1.3						1.0	2.5
.0	.0	.1		.0	.0	.1	.1	.1	.1
.2	.2	.2	Fixed/Worth	.4	.2	.3	.2	.2	.2
.6	.8	1.0		NM	2.8	1.7	.6	1.0	.6
.7	.7	.8		.7	.7	.8	.6	.9	.9
1.9	2.1	2.2	Debt/Worth	1.8	1.8	2.1	1.7	2.7	2.4
5.9	8.7	9.3		-13.2	NM	6.5	5.9	8.8	9.4
49.2	47.4	52.5			68.4	55.4	32.3	69.3	47.5
(352) 22.2	(304) 18.8	(306) 21.0	% Profit Before Taxes/Tangible Net Worth		(39) 25.3	(30) 13.1	(50) 9.8	(83) 25.2	(95) 24.1
6.7	4.9	5.9			10.3	7.7	.0	10.6	5.5
15.6	14.0	15.4		65.0	21.6	13.5	9.8	16.6	15.1
6.7	6.0	6.1	% Profit Before Taxes/Total Assets	12.5	9.5	6.5	3.6	6.9	5.8
1.4	.7	1.4		-8.0	2.0	2.4	-.7	1.9	1.6
173.7	171.6	139.9		UND	199.2	113.9	129.2	122.3	132.7
55.4	52.1	50.4	Sales/Net Fixed Assets	74.5	45.0	51.2	41.3	50.2	55.9
20.1	20.4	20.9		8.2	21.0	12.2	16.4	18.8	25.4
3.3	3.4	3.4		4.3	3.5	3.5	3.4	3.2	3.3
2.3	2.3	2.4	Sales/Total Assets	2.8	2.7	2.2	2.3	2.4	2.4
1.6	1.6	1.7		1.3	1.6	1.6	1.7	1.8	1.7
.3	.3	.3			.6	.3	.2	.4	.1
(285) .6	(269) .6	(283) .6	% Depr., Dep., Amort./Sales		(31) .9	(23) 1.0	(43) .6	(80) .6	(99) .4
1.2	1.2	1.3			1.6	1.1	.9	1.3	1.3
1.5	1.2	1.3			2.2	2.5	1.3	1.2	.7
(156) 3.3	(148) 2.8	(143) 2.5	% Officers', Directors' Owners' Comp/Sales		(30) 3.6	(18) 4.5	(27) 2.2	(39) 1.9	(22) 1.2
5.7	5.1	5.0			5.7	6.7	5.0	3.3	2.2
13889962M	**14195723M**	**16451350M**	Net Sales ($)	**8774M**	**103526M**	**145405M**	**412003M**	**1559442M**	**14222200M**
6358108M	**5776698M**	**6670426M**	Total Assets ($)	**4316M**	**50949M**	**68817M**	**195477M**	**767990M**	**5582877M**

M = $ thousand MM = $ million

See Pages 9 through 22 for Explanation of Ratios and Data

Current Data Sorted by Assets							Comparative Historical Data	
						Type of Statement		
		1	9	1	3	Unqualified	14	23
	4	10	14			Reviewed	23	32
1	2	16	1			Compiled	15	28
5	12	12	2			Tax Returns	26	29
1	14	26	18	5	9	Other	60	53
21 (4/1-9/30/13)		145 (10/1/13-3/31/14)					4/1/09-3/31/10 ALL	4/1/10-3/31/11 ALL
0-500M	500M-2MM	2-10MM	10-50MM	50-100MM	100-250MM			
7	32	65	44	6	12	**NUMBER OF STATEMENTS**	138	165
%	%	%	%	%	%	**ASSETS**	%	%
	12.5	11.9	8.8		5.2	Cash & Equivalents	9.5	8.7
	21.5	22.3	25.0		25.1	Trade Receivables (net)	26.2	27.8
	46.8	44.8	45.0		33.0	Inventory	39.7	38.8
	1.8	1.9	1.6		1.6	All Other Current	3.0	4.2
	82.6	80.9	80.4		64.9	Total Current	78.4	79.5
	8.3	6.2	8.1		13.0	Fixed Assets (net)	12.0	10.1
	.8	5.3	5.4		19.6	Intangibles (net)	3.2	4.1
	8.3	7.6	6.0		2.5	All Other Non-Current	6.5	6.3
	100.0	100.0	100.0		100.0	Total	100.0	100.0
						LIABILITIES		
	18.7	17.2	15.4		5.5	Notes Payable-Short Term	16.1	17.1
	.9	1.4	1.2		2.9	Cur. Mat.-L.T.D.	2.6	2.3
	20.4	23.7	18.9		13.8	Trade Payables	16.8	19.0
	.0	.1	.1		.5	Income Taxes Payable	.3	.1
	8.3	5.9	8.1		5.9	All Other Current	6.9	9.4
	48.3	48.2	43.6		28.5	Total Current	42.7	47.9
	17.3	5.4	5.4		25.5	Long-Term Debt	7.9	7.4
	.0	.0	.1		2.7	Deferred Taxes	.1	.1
	9.9	7.9	6.6		5.8	All Other Non-Current	7.6	9.2
	24.6	38.6	44.3		37.4	Net Worth	41.7	35.4
	100.0	100.0	100.0		100.0	Total Liabilties & Net Worth	100.0	100.0
						INCOME DATA		
	100.0	100.0	100.0		100.0	Net Sales	100.0	100.0
	39.6	32.6	30.6		35.4	Gross Profit	34.7	33.6
	36.6	28.8	24.3		28.9	Operating Expenses	30.7	28.9
	3.0	3.7	6.3		6.5	Operating Profit	4.0	4.7
	.9	.4	.5		1.1	All Other Expenses (net)	.6	.7
	2.1	3.3	5.8		5.4	Profit Before Taxes	3.5	4.0
						RATIOS		
	4.5	2.5	2.9		3.8		3.0	3.1
	1.9	1.8	1.7		2.5	Current	1.9	1.7
	1.1	1.2	1.4		1.8		1.3	1.2
	1.5	1.1	1.3		2.3		1.5	1.3
	.7	.8	.7		1.2	Quick	.9	.8
	.4	.3	.5		.6		.4	.4
	10 37.2	11 32.9	22 16.4		29 12.6		18 20.5	14 26.7
	24 15.2	22 16.5	39 9.4		42 8.7	Sales/Receivables	36 10.0	35 10.6
	39 9.4	46 7.9	64 5.7		81 4.5		57 6.4	54 6.8
	35 10.4	47 7.7	66 5.5		56 6.5		44 8.3	40 9.1
	101 3.6	99 3.7	104 3.5		118 3.1	Cost of Sales/Inventory	101 3.6	97 3.8
	182 2.0	166 2.2	174 2.1		192 1.9		168 2.2	161 2.3
	11 34.3	18 19.8	21 17.4		25 14.5		16 23.0	13 28.5
	22 16.5	31 11.8	32 11.3		32 11.4	Cost of Sales/Payables	31 11.8	31 11.6
	54 6.8	61 6.0	56 6.5		49 7.5		51 7.2	64 5.7
	4.2	4.1	3.8		3.1		4.0	4.0
	9.4	7.9	6.1		5.1	Sales/Working Capital	6.9	8.7
	55.0	18.3	13.3		10.4		14.7	24.8
	13.5	16.0	57.4		9.3		18.7	16.4
	(27) 4.1	(57) 4.6	(42) 10.5		(10) 3.1	EBIT/Interest	(122) 5.3	(139) 4.8
	1.5	2.1	3.2		1.4		1.7	2.1
							3.7	6.8
						Net Profit + Depr., Dep., Amort./Cur. Mat. L/T/D	(16) 1.8	(23) 3.5
							1.4	1.2
	.0	.0	.0		.1		.0	.0
	.2	.1	.1		.5	Fixed/Worth	.1	.2
	.7	.3	.3		-.8		.6	.7
	.8	.8	.9		.9		.7	.9
	2.7	1.5	1.6		3.3	Debt/Worth	1.3	2.0
	NM	4.7	2.6		-6.6		3.4	6.6
	105.4	64.9	56.9				43.8	60.2
	(24) 39.2	(58) 17.2	(41) 28.0			% Profit Before Taxes/Tangible Net Worth	(127) 22.7	(142) 22.6
	6.0	6.8	10.8				3.7	7.4
	24.8	16.2	19.0		14.5		16.7	17.6
	6.7	6.0	9.9		6.8	% Profit Before Taxes/Total Assets	7.6	6.5
	.6	1.1	3.2		3.7		1.1	2.3
	368.5	213.8	167.8		49.7		229.2	247.2
	84.4	88.6	51.3		20.6	Sales/Net Fixed Assets	47.1	55.8
	52.6	33.0	17.9		12.0		14.6	15.1
	4.4	4.0	3.0		2.3		3.2	3.5
	3.3	2.2	2.1		1.8	Sales/Total Assets	2.2	2.3
	1.9	1.6	1.6		1.2		1.4	1.5
	.2	.2	.1		1.1		.4	.2
	(19) .3	(47) .4	(38) .5		(10) 1.5	% Depr., Dep., Amort./Sales	(88) .9	(115) .6
	.5	.9	1.1		2.1		1.6	1.5
	2.0	1.3					1.9	1.4
	(22) 3.1	(24) 2.5				% Officers', Directors' Owners' Comp/Sales	(56) 3.9	(65) 2.7
	6.7	3.8					7.5	5.2
13248M	142772M	783980M	2340130M	848391M	3207895M	Net Sales ($)	5319086M	6457695M
1863M	35034M	284944M	1045612M	393419M	1791794M	Total Assets ($)	2607094M	3275644M

M = $ thousand MM = $ million

See Pages 9 through 22 for Explanation of Ratios and Data

Comparative Historical Data				Current Data Sorted by Sales					
			Type of Statement						
18	22	14	Unqualified					2	12
26	18	28	Reviewed		1	4	2	9	12
18	17	20	Compiled		3	1	9	6	1
25	35	31	Tax Returns	4	8	4	5	7	3
59	64	73	Other	1	7	8	8	17	32
					21 (4/1-9/30/13)		145 (10/1/13-3/31/14)		
4/1/11-3/31/12 ALL	4/1/12-3/31/13 ALL	4/1/13-3/31/14 ALL		0-1MM	1-3MM	3-5MM	5-10MM	10-25MM	25MM & OVER
146	156	166	**NUMBER OF STATEMENTS**	5	19	17	24	41	60
%	%	%	**ASSETS**	%	%	%	%	%	%
8.9	10.3	11.8	Cash & Equivalents		17.8	8.3	10.6	13.0	8.6
27.5	27.3	22.5	Trade Receivables (net)		18.4	15.9	20.9	24.8	26.4
42.1	40.1	43.3	Inventory		43.1	52.9	47.8	41.6	41.9
4.1	3.9	1.8	All Other Current		.3	2.5	1.4	2.2	2.0
82.7	81.6	79.4	Total Current		79.6	79.7	80.7	81.6	78.9
8.6	8.0	8.5	Fixed Assets (net)		2.6	7.2	6.7	8.3	9.7
3.7	4.9	5.2	Intangibles (net)		7.0	1.0	5.3	2.8	7.8
5.0	5.5	6.9	All Other Non-Current		10.7	12.1	7.3	7.3	3.6
100.0	100.0	100.0	Total		100.0	100.0	100.0	100.0	100.0
			LIABILITIES						
17.5	16.2	16.9	Notes Payable-Short Term		28.2	20.0	16.9	13.4	14.8
2.5	1.4	1.3	Cur. Mat.-L.T.D.		1.2	.8	1.1	1.5	1.5
20.2	22.5	21.7	Trade Payables		21.4	18.9	17.2	30.4	18.7
.2	.2	.1	Income Taxes Payable		.0	.1	.0	.1	.2
7.6	9.0	6.8	All Other Current		4.2	8.5	7.0	7.0	7.2
47.9	49.2	46.8	Total Current		55.0	48.3	42.3	52.3	42.3
7.6	8.2	9.5	Long-Term Debt		17.4	11.0	5.5	4.4	10.0
.0	.0	.2	Deferred Taxes		.0	.0	.0	.1	.6
9.4	7.7	9.7	All Other Non-Current		8.6	9.3	6.0	8.0	6.0
35.1	34.8	33.7	Net Worth		19.0	31.4	46.2	35.2	41.1
100.0	100.0	100.0	Total Liabilties & Net Worth		100.0	100.0	100.0	100.0	100.0
			INCOME DATA						
100.0	100.0	100.0	Net Sales		100.0	100.0	100.0	100.0	100.0
32.9	31.7	33.2	Gross Profit		39.2	33.9	37.3	29.9	30.7
28.7	27.9	28.8	Operating Expenses		39.4	33.2	32.3	25.7	24.1
4.3	3.8	4.4	Operating Profit		-.2	.8	5.0	4.1	6.7
.7	.4	.6	All Other Expenses (net)		.1	.5	.9	.1	.6
3.6	3.4	3.8	Profit Before Taxes		-.2	.3	4.1	4.0	6.1
			RATIOS						
2.9	2.8	2.8			5.5	3.9	3.5	2.5	2.7
1.8	1.6	1.8	Current		1.5	1.7	2.0	1.6	1.8
1.3	1.2	1.2			1.0	1.3	1.3	1.2	1.4
1.3	1.2	1.3			1.7	1.2	1.8	1.0	1.3
.8	.8	.8	Quick		.6	.4	.8	.8	.7
.4	.4	.4			.4	.2	.3	.4	.5
17 20.9	**15** 24.1	**14** 25.6			**5** 72.1	**10** 37.5	**7** 55.0	**14** 26.7	**21** 17.7
35 10.5	**38** 9.7	**28** 12.9	Sales/Receivables		**28** 13.2	**22** 16.8	**20** 18.1	**23** 16.1	**36** 10.0
60 6.1	**68** 5.4	**54** 6.8			**48** 7.6	**36** 10.0	**47** 7.7	**53** 6.9	**66** 5.5
43 8.4	**38** 9.5	**49** 7.4			**64** 5.7	**81** 4.5	**51** 7.2	**42** 8.7	**62** 5.9
104 3.5	**96** 3.8	**101** 3.6	Cost of Sales/Inventory		**152** 2.4	**122** 3.0	**118** 3.1	**89** 4.1	**99** 3.7
182 2.0	**159** 2.3	**166** 2.2			**215** 1.7	**215** 1.7	**182** 2.0	**122** 3.0	**146** 2.5
16 22.9	**22** 16.8	**20** 18.6			**9** 41.1	**4** 102.5	**10** 37.0	**20** 18.3	**23** 15.8
32 11.3	**38** 9.6	**29** 12.5	Cost of Sales/Payables		**33** 11.2	**29** 12.7	**27** 13.4	**31** 11.8	**32** 11.4
54 6.7	**59** 6.2	**55** 6.6			**79** 4.6	**63** 5.8	**68** 5.4	**61** 6.0	**46** 7.9
4.1	4.5	4.3			3.0	3.2	3.4	5.1	4.4
7.3	7.9	7.4	Sales/Working Capital		10.2	6.4	7.8	7.9	7.2
14.5	17.6	18.8			137.4	25.9	15.0	29.7	13.1
15.5	16.9	17.0			12.5	6.3	13.1	26.3	41.3
(125) 4.4	(132) 4.5	(146) 5.4	EBIT/Interest		(16) 2.5	(16) 3.0	(20) 4.1	(36) 10.3	(55) 8.9
1.5	1.3	2.2			-4.7	1.6	3.0	2.2	2.3
7.6	49.9	15.5							11.1
(13) 2.1	(18) 17.8	(22) 6.4	Net Profit + Depr., Dep., Amort./Cur. Mat. L/T/D						(13) 6.2
.7	3.0	2.0							1.9
.0	.0	.0			.0	.0	.0	.0	.0
.1	.1	.1	Fixed/Worth		.1	.2	.1	.2	.2
.6	.6	.5			-.5	.3	.6	.4	.6
.8	1.1	.9			.7	1.0	.5	.9	1.0
1.8	2.2	1.8	Debt/Worth		6.9	1.5	1.2	1.9	1.7
4.6	5.2	6.2			-7.0	4.8	2.9	6.1	4.3
50.2	62.2	63.8			131.8	38.5	51.0	99.6	60.3
(128) 22.0	(141) 25.8	(141) 30.6	% Profit Before Taxes/Tangible Net Worth		(11) 22.4	(15) 8.9	(22) 26.8	(38) 25.8	(53) 37.3
7.9	4.1	9.5			3.8	2.4	11.5	8.3	11.5
16.7	17.7	19.1			25.0	7.5	22.3	18.3	22.2
6.5	6.2	8.1	% Profit Before Taxes/Total Assets		3.4	3.8	10.1	8.3	9.9
1.5	1.0	1.4			-14.6	1.4	3.3	2.0	3.7
339.2	319.3	198.8			999.8	87.9	153.7	180.6	141.9
72.2	74.1	68.9	Sales/Net Fixed Assets		181.6	55.9	46.9	93.2	43.0
21.1	23.9	27.4			69.4	29.1	24.3	33.8	15.7
3.6	3.4	3.7			3.5	3.4	4.0	5.8	3.3
2.4	2.3	2.3	Sales/Total Assets		2.0	2.0	2.3	2.4	2.2
1.5	1.7	1.6			1.2	1.3	1.6	2.0	1.7
.2	.2	.2				.2	.3	.2	.2
(101) .5	(113) .5	(122) .5	% Depr., Dep., Amort./Sales			(14) .3	(16) .5	(31) .3	(51) .7
1.1	1.1	1.1				1.0	1.0	.9	1.7
1.0	1.2	1.4			2.1	2.5	1.2	1.3	.5
(55) 2.3	(53) 2.6	(61) 2.6	% Officers', Directors' Owners' Comp/Sales		(11) 3.1	(10) 3.7	(10) 2.1	(17) 1.8	(10) 1.1
3.9	4.5	4.8			8.3	7.5	3.2	3.9	4.6
5738641M	6709699M	7336416M	Net Sales ($)	2403M	39040M	65994M	167247M	632010M	6429722M
2647523M	3491660M	3552666M	Total Assets ($)	2802M	22281M	36947M	77466M	253071M	3160099M

M = $ thousand MM = $ million

See Pages 9 through 22 for Explanation of Ratios and Data

	Current Data Sorted by Assets						Comparative Historical Data	
Type of Statement								
Unqualified	1		7	23	4	6	39	42
Reviewed	2	2	37	34	2		81	92
Compiled	5	11	29	9	1	1	51	67
Tax Returns	15	34	32	2			75	87
Other	10	42	63	66	8	16	173	207
	64 (4/1-9/30/13)			398 (10/1/13-3/31/14)			4/1/09-3/31/10	4/1/10-3/31/11
	0-500M	500M-2MM	2-10MM	10-50MM	50-100MM	100-250MM	ALL	ALL
NUMBER OF STATEMENTS	33	89	168	134	15	23	419	495
ASSETS	%	%	%	%	%	%	%	%
Cash & Equivalents	23.8	17.2	10.5	7.1	3.1	7.5	10.9	9.5
Trade Receivables (net)	16.8	21.3	26.8	30.5	30.7	23.4	24.0	25.3
Inventory	10.5	18.5	19.8	20.8	25.7	18.6	17.7	21.0
All Other Current	4.0	2.7	2.4	3.0	1.6	2.0	3.8	2.7
Total Current	55.0	59.7	59.5	61.3	61.1	51.5	56.3	58.5
Fixed Assets (net)	28.7	27.4	31.1	31.7	27.0	26.6	33.7	30.5
Intangibles (net)	3.9	3.9	3.2	2.0	5.8	16.1	3.4	3.9
All Other Non-Current	12.1	9.0	6.2	5.0	6.0	5.8	6.6	7.1
Total	100.0	100.0	100.0	100.0	100.0	100.0	100.0	100.0
LIABILITIES								
Notes Payable-Short Term	9.8	9.3	12.1	15.9	13.8	13.0	11.3	11.3
Cur. Mat.-L.T.D.	9.8	5.7	3.3	4.7	2.5	2.1	4.2	4.1
Trade Payables	10.2	14.8	17.5	14.8	19.1	13.1	14.8	16.6
Income Taxes Payable	.0	.0	.1	.0	.0	.3	.3	.2
All Other Current	19.9	7.1	5.5	5.6	4.3	3.8	7.5	8.7
Total Current	49.8	37.0	38.6	41.0	39.8	32.3	38.1	40.9
Long-Term Debt	36.9	24.5	17.9	15.4	12.3	15.0	16.4	15.9
Deferred Taxes	.0	.1	.1	.6	.0	1.1	.4	.4
All Other Non-Current	5.3	4.9	5.2	2.9	5.0	3.7	6.2	6.9
Net Worth	7.9	33.6	38.1	40.1	43.0	47.9	38.9	35.9
Total Liabilties & Net Worth	100.0	100.0	100.0	100.0	100.0	100.0	100.0	100.0
INCOME DATA								
Net Sales	100.0	100.0	100.0	100.0	100.0	100.0	100.0	100.0
Gross Profit	30.7	29.9	22.4	15.0	10.1	10.7	24.7	24.1
Operating Expenses	28.2	25.7	20.2	12.2	9.2	7.7	22.7	19.5
Operating Profit	2.5	4.2	2.2	2.8	.9	3.0	2.1	4.6
All Other Expenses (net)	.3	.2	.2	.9	.5	.8	.6	.3
Profit Before Taxes	2.2	4.0	1.9	1.9	.4	2.2	1.5	4.3
RATIOS								
Current	2.5	4.8	3.0	2.1	3.2	2.5	3.0	2.7
	1.4	1.8	1.5	1.4	1.5	1.9	1.6	1.5
	.6	1.1	1.0	1.1	1.0	1.1	1.0	1.0
Quick	2.1	3.6	1.8	1.4	1.5	1.6	2.0	1.6
	.8	1.0	.9	.8	.8	1.1	(418) .9	.9
	.4	.4	.4	.5	.6	.7	.5	.5
Sales/Receivables	0 UND	1 274.6	12 30.1	23 15.9	29 12.5	26 14.2	16 23.1	11 34.5
	2 208.3	12 30.9	24 15.0	32 11.3	36 10.0	32 11.5	32 11.3	27 13.5
	15 24.0	28 13.2	38 9.6	43 8.4	49 7.5	43 8.5	48 7.6	40 9.0
Cost of Sales/Inventory	0 UND	4 99.8	6 57.0	12 30.7	15 23.6	15 23.6	8 43.5	7 54.9
	5 67.9	12 31.6	22 16.8	26 13.8	31 11.6	27 13.3	26 14.1	21 17.8
	13 28.7	24 15.2	49 7.4	44 8.3	62 5.9	45 8.2	53 6.9	42 8.6
Cost of Sales/Payables	0 UND	1 455.2	6 59.9	9 39.5	19 19.3	13 28.5	10 36.8	7 53.0
	1 296.0	9 39.4	17 21.2	17 21.1	25 14.6	20 18.0	22 16.9	18 20.7
	21 17.3	24 15.3	38 9.7	30 12.2	30 12.1	26 14.0	41 9.0	32 11.4
Sales/Working Capital	24.8	8.2	9.0	9.4	7.1	7.5	6.7	8.8
	82.9	21.0	21.2	20.3	13.3	13.6	14.4	21.8
	-62.5	267.3	436.4	94.0	283.2	31.2	999.8	999.8
EBIT/Interest	10.1	17.2	12.1	7.6	7.1	7.9	11.9	21.1
	(21) 2.0	(73) 4.9	(148) 3.0	(129) 2.6	(13) 1.7	(22) 4.8	(376) 3.4	(441) 7.3
	-16.3	1.3	.5	1.1	-1.2	.4	-.3	2.7
Net Profit + Depr., Dep., Amort./Cur. Mat. L/T/D			7.5	5.2			2.9	8.9
			(23) 2.0	(35) 1.8			(62) 1.2	(84) 2.7
			.3	.9			-.1	1.0
Fixed/Worth	.1	.1	.2	.3	.4	.5	.3	.3
	.7	.7	.8	.9	.6	.7	.8	.8
	UND	4.6	2.1	1.8	2.6	1.4	2.5	2.1
Debt/Worth	.5	.5	.6	.8	.5	.8	.5	.7
	2.8	1.9	1.9	2.0	1.5	1.6	1.6	1.6
	-13.6	NM	6.1	4.1	4.2	3.2	4.7	6.0
% Profit Before Taxes/Tangible Net Worth	126.8	72.6	39.6	20.2	10.3	24.3	32.5	56.3
	(23) 33.7	(67) 25.7	(146) 15.3	(129) 6.6	(14) 3.3	(19) 9.2	(367) 12.1	(428) 28.3
	-9.5	5.5	.2	.6	-10.7	-1.9	-3.8	10.9
% Profit Before Taxes/Total Assets	54.4	24.3	12.4	7.3	5.3	8.5	12.3	20.2
	11.6	6.8	3.7	2.1	1.0	3.5	4.2	10.0
	-3.9	.6	-.4	.2	-4.0	-2.0	-2.8	3.3
Sales/Net Fixed Assets	311.7	98.7	38.9	32.7	32.6	19.0	24.6	37.9
	25.3	26.1	14.3	11.8	12.1	11.0	9.0	13.5
	15.2	8.6	5.4	4.7	5.6	5.6	3.8	5.8
Sales/Total Assets	21.2	6.8	5.3	4.4	3.4	3.0	3.6	5.1
	8.0	4.3	3.2	3.1	2.6	2.7	2.4	3.3
	4.0	2.6	2.1	1.9	2.2	1.8	1.6	2.2
% Depr., Dep., Amort./Sales	.5	.5	.8	.5	1.3	1.3	1.1	.8
	(17) 1.2	(59) 1.7	(139) 1.7	(129) 1.4	(14) 1.6	(14) 1.7	(357) 2.8	(408) 1.7
	3.0	3.2	3.0	3.0	3.2	2.2	5.1	3.3
% Officers', Directors' Owners' Comp/Sales	3.4	1.1	.7	.6			1.2	.7
	(13) 4.3	(50) 2.6	(75) 1.5	(33) 1.0			(163) 2.7	(185) 1.8
	9.3	4.0	2.7	1.7			4.6	3.6
Net Sales ($)	115010M	567976M	3373687M	10346507M	3070917M	9632695M	15348257M	30927431M
Total Assets ($)	9467M	109638M	843718M	2969943M	1065981M	3537816M	6942041M	9240525M

M = $ thousand MM = $ million

See Pages 9 through 22 for Explanation of Ratios and Data

Comparative Historical Data | Current Data Sorted by Sales

4/1/11-3/31/12 ALL	4/1/12-3/31/13 ALL	4/1/13-3/31/14 ALL	Type of Statement	0-1MM	1-3MM	3-5MM	5-10MM	10-25MM	25MM & OVER
37	27	41	Unqualified	1			1	7	32
97	90	77	Reviewed		4	2	5	27	39
57	63	56	Compiled	2	4	5	12	18	15
89	79	83	Tax Returns	4	16	10	33	13	7
205	200	205	Other	2	20	14	23	42	104
					64 (4/1-9/30/13)		398 (10/1/13-3/31/14)		
485	459	462	**NUMBER OF STATEMENTS**	9	44	31	74	107	197
%	%	%	**ASSETS**	%	%	%	%	%	%
11.6	10.0	11.3	Cash & Equivalents		18.4	17.3	12.9	10.5	8.1
24.5	24.8	26.0	Trade Receivables (net)		13.9	18.2	17.9	25.3	34.0
20.8	19.8	19.3	Inventory		10.9	14.7	19.9	20.8	21.5
2.9	2.6	2.7	All Other Current		3.1	3.9	2.8	2.0	2.8
59.8	57.3	59.4	Total Current		46.3	54.1	53.5	58.7	66.4
29.4	31.6	30.1	Fixed Assets (net)		33.3	35.5	32.6	34.9	24.6
3.9	3.8	3.7	Intangibles (net)		6.5	5.4	3.8	2.5	3.6
6.9	7.3	6.8	All Other Non-Current		13.9	5.0	10.1	3.9	5.4
100.0	100.0	100.0	Total		100.0	100.0	100.0	100.0	100.0
			LIABILITIES						
12.1	10.6	12.6	Notes Payable-Short Term		5.1	8.8	9.2	13.1	15.9
3.7	4.3	4.6	Cur. Mat.-L.T.D.		5.3	9.6	4.4	5.5	3.3
16.4	16.7	15.5	Trade Payables		9.7	13.8	13.6	14.3	18.9
.2	.2	.1	Income Taxes Payable		.0	.0	.1	.0	.1
9.2	9.0	6.7	All Other Current		12.7	4.7	7.5	3.9	6.0
41.7	40.7	39.5	Total Current		32.8	36.9	34.9	36.9	44.1
17.1	16.7	19.5	Long-Term Debt		31.1	32.2	28.6	16.6	13.1
.4	.4	.3	Deferred Taxes		.0	.0	.1	.3	.4
6.3	6.9	4.4	All Other Non-Current		11.2	5.1	2.9	4.0	3.6
34.5	35.3	36.3	Net Worth		24.9	25.7	33.5	42.3	38.8
100.0	100.0	100.0	Total Liabilties & Net Worth		100.0	100.0	100.0	100.0	100.0
			INCOME DATA						
100.0	100.0	100.0	Net Sales		100.0	100.0	100.0	100.0	100.0
21.4	20.2	21.3	Gross Profit		45.0	32.7	28.0	18.8	11.9
17.4	17.6	18.5	Operating Expenses		37.3	28.0	26.0	16.8	10.3
4.0	2.6	2.8	Operating Profit		7.7	4.6	2.0	2.0	1.6
.4	.5	.5	All Other Expenses (net)		1.7	.3	.2	.3	.4
3.6	2.0	2.3	Profit Before Taxes		6.0	4.4	1.8	1.7	1.2
			RATIOS						
2.7	2.7	2.7			3.0	3.3	3.6	3.3	2.4
1.5	1.5	1.5	Current		1.7	1.6	1.4	1.5	1.5
1.0	1.0	1.0			.6	.9	.9	1.0	1.2
1.7	1.7	1.8			2.8	1.4	1.9	2.1	1.5
1.0	.9	.9	Quick		.8	.9	.7	.9	.9
.5	.4	.5			.4	.4	.4	.4	.6
8 47.2	**9** 40.6	**11** 33.8			**0** UND	**0** 999.8	**2** 170.8	**12** 29.2	**22** 16.4
21 17.3	**24** 15.4	**26** 13.9	Sales/Receivables		**6** 65.7	**22** 16.8	**16** 23.5	**24** 15.4	**31** 11.6
33 10.9	**34** 10.8	**38** 9.6			**43** 8.5	**32** 11.5	**29** 12.7	**37** 9.9	**41** 8.9
5 74.0	**6** 57.1	**7** 54.6			**0** UND	**0** UND	**5** 70.5	**11** 33.9	**9** 40.5
16 22.8	**20** 18.0	**19** 18.8	Cost of Sales/Inventory		**10** 35.6	**9** 42.3	**18** 19.8	**22** 16.8	**22** 16.3
36 10.2	**42** 8.7	**39** 9.4			**36** 10.0	**36** 10.1	**42** 8.6	**52** 7.0	**38** 9.7
5 79.0	**5** 68.3	**5** 68.5			**0** UND	**0** 999.8	**3** 130.7	**6** 57.6	**8** 47.8
14 26.8	**14** 26.8	**16** 22.8	Cost of Sales/Payables		**17** 21.0	**12** 29.6	**11** 34.0	**17** 21.0	**17** 21.2
28 13.2	**27** 13.3	**30** 12.2			**56** 6.5	**41** 8.9	**36** 10.1	**32** 11.4	**28** 12.9
10.5	9.2	9.3			6.7	8.1	9.4	8.8	9.8
27.2	24.2	20.9	Sales/Working Capital		32.9	16.3	30.5	26.9	19.6
342.4	-319.3	233.5			-11.0	-94.0	-92.3	507.1	59.8
21.9	13.9	9.4			11.3	28.5	8.2	12.8	8.2
(439) 7.6	(407) 4.6	(406) 3.0	EBIT/Interest		(33) 1.9	(26) 7.4	(64) 2.4	(95) 3.3	(182) 2.9
2.4	1.0	.5			-.8	1.5	.7	.5	.7
12.3	7.6	6.7						7.3	5.9
(71) 3.7	(83) 2.7	(70) 1.9	Net Profit + Depr., Dep., Amort./Cur. Mat. L/T/D					(18) 1.9	(41) 1.6
1.8	.9	1.1						.8	1.1
.3	.3	.3			.3	.2	.1	.3	.3
.8	.9	.8	Fixed/Worth		.9	1.3	.8	.9	.6
2.2	2.9	2.2			88.3	4.3	5.0	2.2	1.4
.7	.7	.6			.6	.4	.5	.6	.8
2.0	1.9	1.8	Debt/Worth		3.5	1.3	2.5	1.5	1.8
6.1	5.9	5.7			-19.8	UND	10.4	3.4	4.4
61.3	41.7	33.8			66.7	84.3	49.6	29.9	25.8
(422) 29.0	(388) 16.4	(398) 10.9	% Profit Before Taxes/Tangible Net Worth		(32) 15.6	(24) 31.6	(57) 18.7	(95) 12.2	(183) 8.6
10.8	2.5	.9			-1.4	7.3	1.1	.2	.5
20.6	14.0	12.2			20.4	28.6	19.9	11.7	8.4
9.5	5.1	3.5	% Profit Before Taxes/Total Assets		2.0	8.2	4.2	3.0	2.6
2.5	.4	-.3			-2.0	.5	.0	-.8	.0
54.7	52.7	45.2			28.4	57.2	80.8	27.9	47.3
17.2	14.0	15.5	Sales/Net Fixed Assets		11.7	18.2	16.7	12.0	17.4
7.3	6.0	6.0			3.8	4.1	5.2	5.2	9.5
6.7	5.7	5.5			4.4	6.5	5.9	5.3	5.5
4.1	3.6	3.3	Sales/Total Assets		2.2	3.1	3.7	3.1	3.7
2.6	2.3	2.2			1.3	2.1	2.3	2.0	2.6
.6	.7	.6			1.1	.9	.9	.8	.5
(372) 1.3	(365) 1.5	(372) 1.6	% Depr., Dep., Amort./Sales		(31) 2.6	(23) 2.5	(50) 2.0	(92) 2.0	(172) 1.3
2.6	2.8	3.0			4.6	4.7	3.8	3.2	2.2
.7	.7	.8			3.6	1.7	1.2	.8	.5
(174) 1.5	(177) 1.8	(173) 1.7	% Officers', Directors' Owners' Comp/Sales		(15) 5.4	(11) 2.9	(47) 2.4	(45) 1.4	(52) .8
3.0	3.2	3.2			9.0	6.9	3.5	2.3	1.4
32960833M	27599449M	27106792M	Net Sales ($)	4565M	86656M	124722M	534704M	1797532M	24558613M
8209477M	7962358M	8536563M	Total Assets ($)	3037M	81377M	46486M	180136M	664291M	7561236M

M = $ thousand MM = $ million

See Pages 9 through 22 for Explanation of Ratios and Data

Current Data Sorted by Assets							Comparative Historical Data	
						Type of Statement		
			3	3	4	Unqualified	16	12
	1	14	15	3		Reviewed	57	44
	5	21	2			Compiled	30	30
3	17	27	6			Tax Returns	48	51
3	15	28	13	3	3	Other	62	56
	26 (4/1-9/30/13)		163 (10/1/13-3/31/14)				4/1/09-3/31/10 ALL	4/1/10-3/31/11 ALL
0-500M	500M-2MM	2-10MM	10-50MM	50-100MM	100-250MM			
6	38	90	39	9	7	**NUMBER OF STATEMENTS**	213	193
%	%	%	%	%	%	**ASSETS**	%	%
	16.3	9.1	7.5			Cash & Equivalents	9.7	11.1
	20.4	27.2	31.6			Trade Receivables (net)	28.4	26.2
	50.7	50.1	45.9			Inventory	47.5	47.6
	1.9	2.4	3.6			All Other Current	1.6	2.0
	89.3	88.8	88.7			Total Current	87.2	87.0
	3.3	5.2	6.1			Fixed Assets (net)	5.5	5.9
	2.9	.8	2.5			Intangibles (net)	1.5	2.1
	4.5	5.2	2.8			All Other Non-Current	5.8	5.0
	100.0	100.0	100.0			Total	100.0	100.0
						LIABILITIES		
	11.7	11.3	11.9			Notes Payable-Short Term	17.2	14.0
	1.4	.9	5.0			Cur. Mat.-L.T.D.	1.5	1.4
	21.8	30.3	34.4			Trade Payables	25.7	26.1
	.1	.0	.2			Income Taxes Payable	.2	.2
	5.7	5.6	10.2			All Other Current	8.4	8.6
	40.5	48.1	61.7			Total Current	52.9	50.3
	4.9	3.9	3.1			Long-Term Debt	5.7	5.2
	.0	.1	.0			Deferred Taxes	.1	.2
	16.0	9.2	3.2			All Other Non-Current	7.7	6.3
	38.5	38.7	31.9			Net Worth	33.7	37.9
	100.0	100.0	100.0			Total Liabilties & Net Worth	100.0	100.0
						INCOME DATA		
	100.0	100.0	100.0			Net Sales	100.0	100.0
	27.4	24.7	20.1			Gross Profit	25.3	27.2
	22.4	20.9	17.1			Operating Expenses	22.3	23.8
	5.0	3.8	3.0			Operating Profit	3.0	3.4
	.9	.4	.6			All Other Expenses (net)	.9	.6
	4.1	3.4	2.4			Profit Before Taxes	2.1	2.8
						RATIOS		
	5.4	3.2	2.2				2.5	3.0
	2.5	1.8	1.3			Current	1.6	1.8
	1.3	1.3	1.0				1.3	1.2
	2.8	1.3	.9				1.1	1.4
	1.2	.8	.6			Quick	.7	.7
	.2	.4	.4				.4	.4
	1 513.5	**14** 26.4	**28** 13.2				**11** 34.3	**8** 45.2
	13 27.7	**39** 9.4	**53** 6.9			Sales/Receivables	**48** 7.7	**33** 11.1
	41 9.0	**66** 5.5	**79** 4.6				**77** 4.7	**64** 5.7
	29 12.6	**41** 8.9	**42** 8.7				**45** 8.1	**37** 9.8
	79 4.6	**85** 4.3	**83** 4.4			Cost of Sales/Inventory	**108** 3.4	**92** 4.0
	152 2.4	**215** 1.7	**152** 2.4				**213** 1.7	**173** 2.1
	3 113.5	**15** 24.3	**18** 20.5				**13** 28.6	**12** 29.4
	18 19.8	**59** 6.2	**68** 5.4			Cost of Sales/Payables	**45** 8.2	**38** 9.6
	61 6.0	**118** 3.1	**96** 3.8				**89** 4.1	**83** 4.4
	4.9	3.8	4.1				3.0	3.9
	9.3	6.4	9.9			Sales/Working Capital	6.3	6.9
	22.8	15.9	68.1				18.0	29.1
	36.6	15.3	22.7				9.2	19.5
	(31) 5.0	(77) 4.5	(36) 3.5			EBIT/Interest	(175) 2.9	(153) 5.5
	2.2	1.8	1.6				1.3	1.8
							52.7	17.3
						Net Profit + Depr., Dep., Amort./Cur. Mat. L/T/D	(14) 6.4	(15) 8.3
							.1	.8
	.0	.0	.0				.0	.0
	.0	.0	.1			Fixed/Worth	.1	.1
	.2	.2	.5				.2	.2
	.4	.7	1.1				.9	.7
	1.8	1.8	3.0			Debt/Worth	2.1	1.7
	17.6	4.3	18.2				5.4	5.5
	82.1	39.7	55.8				36.0	48.9
	(33) 31.3	(87) 12.9	(37) 20.2			% Profit Before Taxes/Tangible Net Worth	(196) 11.5	(176) 17.6
	5.2	2.1	6.6				2.3	4.0
	24.5	11.7	12.4				11.5	15.9
	7.1	4.2	3.6			% Profit Before Taxes/Total Assets	2.9	5.2
	1.8	.7	1.5				.6	1.0
	UND	999.8	632.6				721.5	999.8
	167.1	280.8	138.3			Sales/Net Fixed Assets	126.9	134.1
	66.6	48.9	33.8				36.4	38.8
	5.3	3.5	2.7				3.2	4.0
	3.2	2.3	2.2			Sales/Total Assets	2.0	2.4
	2.1	1.3	1.5				1.2	1.5
	.0	.0	.1				.1	.1
	(14) .3	(55) .1	(30) .2			% Depr., Dep., Amort./Sales	(159) .2	(118) .4
	.6	.5	.9				.7	.9
	2.3	1.1	.5				1.4	1.3
	(25) 3.4	(64) 2.2	(19) 1.1			% Officers', Directors' Owners' Comp/Sales	(127) 2.8	(109) 2.8
	4.8	3.7	3.3				5.1	5.7
2536M	296198M	1754060M	2383812M	2325514M	8626952M	Net Sales ($)	21525980M	20440338M
1484M	43068M	475969M	845787M	723069M	1088250M	Total Assets ($)	3793394M	2563995M

M = $ thousand MM = $ million

See Pages 9 through 22 for Explanation of Ratios and Data

Comparative Historical Data | Current Data Sorted by Sales

4/1/11-3/31/12 ALL	4/1/12-3/31/13 ALL	4/1/13-3/31/14 ALL	Type of Statement	0-1MM	1-3MM	3-5MM	5-10MM	10-25MM	25MM & OVER
11	6	10	Unqualified						10
49	25	33	Reviewed	1			4	10	18
25	18	28	Compiled		2	5	6	11	4
69	59	53	Tax Returns	4	6	9	12	16	6
51	55	65	Other	4	8	7	15	11	20
				26 (4/1-9/30/13)		163 (10/1/13-3/31/14)			
205	163	189	NUMBER OF STATEMENTS	9	16	21	37	48	58
%	%	%	**ASSETS**	%	%	%	%	%	%
11.1	12.3	11.0	Cash & Equivalents		16.2	7.4	10.6	8.7	12.7
24.4	23.5	25.5	Trade Receivables (net)		15.9	15.8	33.7	28.1	25.4
46.7	47.3	49.0	Inventory		58.5	61.8	43.3	47.9	45.6
3.7	2.2	2.6	All Other Current		1.4	2.6	1.4	2.8	3.8
85.9	85.4	88.0	Total Current		92.0	87.7	89.0	87.5	87.5
6.4	5.5	5.7	Fixed Assets (net)		4.6	3.3	2.8	7.6	5.9
2.5	2.6	2.0	Intangibles (net)		.4	3.5	1.9	.5	3.4
5.1	6.6	4.3	All Other Non-Current		3.0	5.5	6.3	4.4	3.2
100.0	100.0	100.0	Total		100.0	100.0	100.0	100.0	100.0
			LIABILITIES						
12.2	10.7	11.2	Notes Payable-Short Term		12.4	10.8	12.0	11.8	10.0
1.6	1.1	2.1	Cur. Mat.-L.T.D.		.4	.5	.7	1.2	4.8
25.9	29.7	29.0	Trade Payables		28.6	24.0	34.1	30.0	27.2
.1	.1	.1	Income Taxes Payable		.0	.0	.1	.1	.3
6.0	8.2	7.4	All Other Current		11.3	2.0	5.0	5.2	12.7
45.8	49.8	49.9	Total Current		52.7	37.2	51.8	48.2	55.1
6.8	5.6	4.8	Long-Term Debt		5.1	4.3	3.1	6.0	4.5
.1	.1	.0	Deferred Taxes		.0	.0	.0	.1	.0
9.4	11.7	10.3	All Other Non-Current		20.3	13.4	8.5	8.2	4.4
37.8	32.8	35.0	Net Worth		21.9	45.1	36.5	37.5	36.0
100.0	100.0	100.0	Total Liabilties & Net Worth		100.0	100.0	100.0	100.0	100.0
			INCOME DATA						
100.0	100.0	100.0	Net Sales		100.0	100.0	100.0	100.0	100.0
29.2	29.0	25.4	Gross Profit		36.7	31.2	26.2	21.2	19.4
25.3	24.3	21.6	Operating Expenses		31.9	24.9	22.7	17.4	16.6
4.0	4.6	3.8	Operating Profit		4.8	6.2	3.5	3.8	2.9
.3	.7	.7	All Other Expenses (net)		1.0	1.1	.4	.6	.5
3.6	4.0	3.1	Profit Before Taxes		3.8	5.1	3.1	3.3	2.3
			RATIOS						
3.1	3.2	3.3			7.2	6.2	2.8	3.2	2.3
2.0	1.7	1.8	Current		1.8	3.1	1.6	1.8	1.5
1.3	1.1	1.2			1.1	1.4	1.2	1.3	1.1
1.3	1.5	1.3			2.0	1.7	1.7	1.3	1.2
.8	.7	.7	Quick		.7	.4	.8	.8	.6
.4	.4	.4			.2	.1	.4	.4	.4
10 38.2	**8** 43.8	**8** 47.1			**2** 242.4	**5** 71.6	**25** 14.4	**9** 41.0	**4** 99.1
34 10.6	**30** 12.1	**36** 10.0	Sales/Receivables		**26** 14.1	**27** 13.4	**43** 8.5	**38** 9.5	**35** 10.5
61 6.0	**53** 6.9	**65** 5.6			**43** 8.5	**48** 7.6	**104** 3.5	**64** 5.7	**65** 5.6
41 8.9	**32** 11.4	**41** 9.0			**89** 4.1	**66** 5.5	**42** 8.6	**29** 12.4	**22** 16.9
96 3.8	**91** 4.0	**85** 4.3	Cost of Sales/Inventory		**159** 2.3	**152** 2.4	**85** 4.3	**72** 5.1	**74** 4.9
203 1.8	**203** 1.8	**192** 1.9			**281** 1.3	**304** 1.2	**243** 1.5	**140** 2.6	**140** 2.6
11 33.4	**12** 31.2	**12** 31.3			**12** 30.8	**3** 142.1	**18** 20.6	**19** 19.7	**5** 80.4
38 9.5	**45** 8.1	**49** 7.4	Cost of Sales/Payables		**48** 7.6	**58** 6.3	**70** 5.2	**49** 7.5	**34** 10.8
85 4.3	**104** 3.5	**107** 3.4			**152** 2.4	**104** 3.5	**166** 2.2	**74** 4.9	**89** 4.1
3.4	3.9	4.0			2.3	2.3	4.0	4.5	5.0
7.2	8.0	7.1	Sales/Working Capital		5.6	5.7	6.0	7.3	15.9
17.4	40.8	22.5			24.3	13.4	12.8	19.2	67.2
20.2	18.2	18.2			31.6	21.8	14.8	17.1	21.5
(163) 6.2	(126) 5.9	(163) 4.0	EBIT/Interest		(14) 3.5	(19) 4.7	(30) 3.7	(39) 6.0	(55) 3.2
2.5	2.2	1.6			.6	2.2	2.0	1.8	1.6
15.4	16.3	6.8							
(13) 5.4	(10) 3.8	(15) .7	Net Profit + Depr., Dep., Amort./Cur. Mat. L/T/D						
1.6	.6	.0							
.0	.0	.0			.0	.0	.0	.0	.0
.1	.1	.1	Fixed/Worth		.1	.0	.0	.0	.2
.3	.4	.3			.6	.2	.1	.2	.6
.6	.9	.7			.8	.4	.7	.7	.8
1.8	2.9	2.0	Debt/Worth		7.2	1.8	2.6	1.7	2.0
5.3	10.6	7.6			501.0	14.4	4.5	6.3	6.9
47.2	54.1	53.5			134.2	144.0	33.2	57.2	45.4
(187) 20.7	(144) 20.4	(173) 15.5	% Profit Before Taxes/Tangible Net Worth		(13) 34.6	(20) 19.3	(35) 10.5	(46) 16.2	(52) 16.6
6.7	5.2	3.6			2.5	3.0	3.4	4.9	6.1
16.8	14.1	12.6			21.7	15.5	12.5	14.9	12.8
7.0	5.0	4.3	% Profit Before Taxes/Total Assets		3.8	5.0	3.2	6.2	3.7
1.7	1.6	.9			.1	1.0	.7	1.2	.6
999.8	795.2	999.8			UND	UND	UND	999.8	649.6
134.0	139.0	155.1	Sales/Net Fixed Assets		97.5	155.1	178.6	282.0	142.9
36.4	32.8	39.1			31.4	45.4	52.8	42.6	33.6
4.0	3.7	3.5			3.1	3.8	3.3	3.7	8.1
2.3	2.4	2.4	Sales/Total Assets		2.3	1.9	1.9	2.8	2.6
1.4	1.3	1.5			1.5	1.1	1.1	2.0	1.8
.1	.1	.0				.2	.0	.0	.0
(127) .3	(97) .3	(113) .2	% Depr., Dep., Amort./Sales			(10) .3	(21) .2	(31) .1	(42) .1
.9	.7	.7				.8	.4	.7	.4
1.3	1.1	1.0			2.6	2.3	1.9	1.2	.3
(119) 2.8	(98) 2.5	(114) 2.4	% Officers', Directors' Owners' Comp/Sales		(15) 4.2	(12) 3.7	(25) 2.8	(36) 2.2	(22) .6
5.2	5.0	4.2			6.6	4.8	3.6	4.5	1.4
7503010M	13306259M	15389072M	Net Sales ($)	4273M	36186M	80817M	283047M	719741M	14265008M
2207821M	2133802M	3177627M	Total Assets ($)	7418M	19901M	55846M	170097M	306243M	2618122M

M = $ thousand MM = $ million

See Pages 9 through 22 for Explanation of Ratios and Data

Current Data Sorted by Assets							Comparative Historical Data	
						Type of Statement		
2	1	15	22	8	5	Unqualified	63	52
	9	59	31	3		Reviewed	102	110
7	32	49	8	1		Compiled	97	98
45	126	93	6			Tax Returns	212	222
41	109	123	56	10	8	Other	251	275
	104 (4/1-9/30/13)		765 (10/1/13-3/31/14)				4/1/09-3/31/10 ALL	4/1/10-3/31/11 ALL
0-500M	500M-2MM	2-10MM	10-50MM	50-100MM	100-250MM			
95	277	339	123	22	13	**NUMBER OF STATEMENTS**	725	757
%	%	%	%	%	%	**ASSETS**	%	%
21.7	13.7	9.8	8.3	3.4	3.9	Cash & Equivalents	11.1	12.1
24.0	28.6	28.0	29.1	21.9	23.4	Trade Receivables (net)	30.9	29.4
30.0	36.0	40.4	39.4	43.5	39.9	Inventory	34.7	34.7
3.4	1.2	2.2	1.9	3.9	4.2	All Other Current	2.9	2.5
79.1	79.4	80.4	78.7	72.7	71.3	Total Current	79.6	78.6
10.7	11.3	10.6	9.9	5.4	8.7	Fixed Assets (net)	10.9	11.2
4.4	2.9	3.4	6.6	15.7	16.8	Intangibles (net)	4.1	4.6
5.7	6.4	5.6	4.8	6.2	3.2	All Other Non-Current	5.4	5.6
100.0	100.0	100.0	100.0	100.0	100.0	Total	100.0	100.0
						LIABILITIES		
16.4	14.1	12.9	14.2	18.1	10.6	Notes Payable-Short Term	16.4	15.0
2.3	2.2	1.5	1.6	1.3	.6	Cur. Mat.-L.T.D.	2.5	1.9
20.4	22.5	20.4	20.5	16.4	18.1	Trade Payables	22.0	21.6
.1	.1	.1	.3	.5	.2	Income Taxes Payable	.1	.2
16.9	7.9	8.9	8.9	7.2	12.2	All Other Current	9.9	8.3
56.2	46.8	43.8	45.6	43.5	41.7	Total Current	51.0	47.0
21.9	10.4	7.2	7.3	14.7	16.8	Long-Term Debt	10.3	10.6
.0	.0	.1	.1	1.4	2.1	Deferred Taxes	.1	.1
10.2	10.3	5.6	9.8	12.8	9.7	All Other Non-Current	6.6	7.3
11.7	32.5	43.2	37.3	27.7	29.8	Net Worth	32.0	35.0
100.0	100.0	100.0	100.0	100.0	100.0	Total Liabilties & Net Worth	100.0	100.0
						INCOME DATA		
100.0	100.0	100.0	100.0	100.0	100.0	Net Sales	100.0	100.0
38.2	34.9	30.0	25.9	24.1	26.5	Gross Profit	32.0	32.7
33.9	30.2	25.5	21.5	17.9	21.2	Operating Expenses	28.5	28.3
4.3	4.7	4.5	4.4	6.2	5.3	Operating Profit	3.5	4.4
.6	.3	.2	.2	.8	1.7	All Other Expenses (net)	.7	.6
3.8	4.4	4.2	4.3	5.4	3.5	Profit Before Taxes	2.8	3.8
						RATIOS		
3.5	3.4	3.1	2.9	2.8	2.9		2.8	3.1
1.7	1.9	1.9	1.7	1.5	2.0	Current	1.7	1.7
1.1	1.2	1.4	1.2	1.2	1.1		1.1	1.2
2.0	1.7	1.5	1.2	1.0	1.1		1.4	1.6
.9	1.0	.9	.8	.6	.6	Quick	.8	.9
.5	.5	.5	.5	.4	.4		.5	.5
0 999.8	**15** 24.6	**23** 16.0	**30** 12.1	**23** 16.1	**25** 14.5		**23** 15.8	**22** 16.9
14 26.3	**28** 13.0	**35** 10.4	**39** 9.3	**40** 9.1	**41** 8.9	Sales/Receivables	**37** 9.9	**37** 9.7
36 10.0	**46** 8.0	**54** 6.7	**56** 6.5	**49** 7.5	**47** 7.8		**54** 6.8	**54** 6.7
1 278.2	**27** 13.3	**39** 9.3	**45** 8.1	**43** 8.5	**33** 11.0		**26** 14.0	**27** 13.7
37 9.9	**54** 6.7	**74** 4.9	**76** 4.8	**99** 3.7	**96** 3.8	Cost of Sales/Inventory	**64** 5.7	**62** 5.9
104 3.5	**118** 3.1	**130** 2.8	**126** 2.9	**182** 2.0	**159** 2.3		**119** 3.1	**123** 3.0
2 233.3	**9** 40.6	**16** 23.0	**20** 18.1	**21** 17.2	**23** 15.6		**15** 25.0	**15** 24.7
21 17.7	**29** 12.5	**31** 11.6	**32** 11.3	**29** 12.7	**38** 9.5	Cost of Sales/Payables	**31** 11.8	**31** 11.9
49 7.5	**51** 7.1	**56** 6.5	**50** 7.3	**54** 6.7	**59** 6.2		**54** 6.8	**55** 6.6
5.0	4.8	4.3	4.4	4.9	4.0		5.1	4.8
20.5	9.9	7.4	7.5	9.2	5.9	Sales/Working Capital	9.9	8.8
108.1	34.9	13.6	17.7	24.8	22.0		34.9	26.6
20.2	19.4	21.8	31.2	30.4	16.5		12.8	17.3
(56) 4.3	(222) 6.2	(287) 8.0	(115) 6.9	(21) 6.4	(12) 10.7	EBIT/Interest	(638) 4.3	(646) 4.9
.9	1.7	2.6	3.1	2.4	4.1		1.2	1.7
		18.9	57.8				6.5	15.1
		(26) 3.5	(20) 8.6			Net Profit + Depr., Dep., Amort./Cur. Mat. L/T/D	(98) 2.9	(92) 4.8
		2.1	2.3				.7	1.5
.0	.0	.0	.0	.1	.2		.0	.0
.1	.2	.1	.2	.3	.5	Fixed/Worth	.2	.2
5.4	1.1	.4	.5	-1.7	-.5		1.1	.8
.7	.8	.6	.7	1.1	.7		.8	.7
2.7	2.0	1.4	1.9	3.6	5.3	Debt/Worth	2.1	1.8
-6.2	10.9	4.0	4.0	-10.1	-4.2		8.9	7.1
80.2	70.0	51.8	41.1	56.4			54.2	54.8
(63) 40.6	(230) 31.6	(319) 20.3	(114) 19.7	(16) 38.1		% Profit Before Taxes/Tangible Net Worth	(609) 19.3	(640) 23.8
12.7	10.2	7.6	9.5	15.1			2.9	7.1
28.5	22.2	16.9	14.5	20.2	12.0		15.5	18.4
12.1	9.7	7.6	7.1	9.2	6.7	% Profit Before Taxes/Total Assets	5.5	7.6
1.7	2.1	2.4	3.2	3.7	4.4		.4	1.4
UND	410.1	256.8	157.1	135.1	181.1		233.1	251.7
240.3	61.3	63.8	47.2	82.9	41.5	Sales/Net Fixed Assets	61.4	58.6
29.0	20.1	19.7	20.3	27.0	9.7		18.5	19.2
6.2	4.6	3.5	3.4	3.4	2.9		4.0	4.0
3.6	3.3	2.7	2.3	1.7	1.9	Sales/Total Assets	2.7	2.7
2.3	2.2	1.9	1.7	1.7	1.3		1.9	1.8
.4	.3	.2	.3	.3	.2		.2	.2
(34) .8	(140) .7	(235) .5	(100) .5	(16) .7	(12) .8	% Depr., Dep., Amort./Sales	(522) .6	(525) .6
1.9	1.5	1.0	1.2	1.4	1.3		1.3	1.3
2.7	2.3	1.3	.3				2.0	1.6
(37) 6.1	(168) 3.8	(158) 2.4	(29) 1.5			% Officers', Directors' Owners' Comp/Sales	(329) 3.8	(358) 3.3
9.8	6.1	4.5	3.6				6.7	5.8
126324M	**1154419M**	**4539854M**	**5987967M**	**3806445M**	**4350461M**	Net Sales ($)	**16563935M**	**17088766M**
26806M	**322114M**	**1618540M**	**2381481M**	**1528648M**	**1871634M**	Total Assets ($)	**6687697M**	**6862419M**

M = $ thousand MM = $ million

See Pages 9 through 22 for Explanation of Ratios and Data

Comparative Historical Data				Current Data Sorted by Sales					
			Type of Statement						
65	51	53	Unqualified	2			3	9	39
114	101	102	Reviewed		3	4	23	38	34
112	88	97	Compiled	2	16	8	29	29	13
296	269	270	Tax Returns	28	67	47	76	43	9
307	334	347	Other	28	60	52	64	70	73
4/1/11-3/31/12 ALL	4/1/12-3/31/13 ALL	4/1/13-3/31/14 ALL		104 (4/1-9/30/13)			765 (10/1/13-3/31/14)		
				0-1MM	1-3MM	3-5MM	5-10MM	10-25MM	25MM & OVER
894	843	869	**NUMBER OF STATEMENTS**	60	146	111	195	189	168
%	%	%	**ASSETS**	%	%	%	%	%	%
11.5	11.1	11.9	Cash & Equivalents	18.1	13.5	14.5	12.0	11.2	7.1
28.8	27.9	27.7	Trade Receivables (net)	24.4	22.9	29.2	29.3	27.7	30.1
36.5	37.7	37.8	Inventory	29.2	37.6	35.7	39.0	39.1	39.5
2.2	1.8	2.0	All Other Current	4.1	1.1	2.1	1.1	2.7	2.3
79.0	78.5	79.4	Total Current	75.8	75.1	81.5	81.5	80.6	79.1
10.2	10.7	10.6	Fixed Assets (net)	12.4	14.7	8.6	9.6	10.7	8.7
4.2	4.3	4.3	Intangibles (net)	3.6	4.9	3.7	3.0	3.0	7.5
6.6	6.6	5.7	All Other Non-Current	8.1	5.2	6.3	6.0	5.6	4.7
100.0	100.0	100.0	Total	100.0	100.0	100.0	100.0	100.0	100.0
			LIABILITIES						
14.5	14.1	13.9	Notes Payable-Short Term	13.4	15.7	13.2	13.6	13.9	13.6
2.1	2.0	1.8	Cur. Mat.-L.T.D.	1.6	2.4	2.7	1.8	1.0	1.7
20.8	21.9	21.0	Trade Payables	19.7	18.3	22.2	23.4	19.7	21.4
.1	.1	.2	Income Taxes Payable	.0	.1	.2	.2	.2	.2
10.0	10.7	9.5	All Other Current	17.2	7.7	11.7	6.8	9.2	10.0
47.6	48.7	46.3	Total Current	51.9	44.2	50.0	45.9	44.0	47.0
10.6	10.5	10.2	Long-Term Debt	21.4	15.0	10.0	7.6	7.1	8.4
.2	.1	.1	Deferred Taxes	.0	.0	.1	.0	.1	.4
8.1	8.4	8.4	All Other Non-Current	11.7	13.4	8.4	5.1	4.5	11.2
33.5	32.3	34.9	Net Worth	14.9	27.4	31.4	41.3	44.3	33.0
100.0	100.0	100.0	Total Liabilties & Net Worth	100.0	100.0	100.0	100.0	100.0	100.0
			INCOME DATA						
100.0	100.0	100.0	Net Sales	100.0	100.0	100.0	100.0	100.0	100.0
31.8	32.0	31.7	Gross Profit	43.8	39.4	34.0	30.7	28.1	24.2
27.6	27.5	27.1	Operating Expenses	37.3	35.9	29.6	25.8	23.6	19.5
4.2	4.6	4.6	Operating Profit	6.5	3.5	4.3	4.9	4.4	4.7
.5	.5	.3	All Other Expenses (net)	.7	.5	.1	.4	.1	.3
3.7	4.1	4.2	Profit Before Taxes	5.8	3.0	4.3	4.5	4.3	4.4
			RATIOS						
3.0	3.0	3.2		4.0	4.2	3.6	3.0	3.2	2.6
1.8	1.8	1.8	Current	1.7	1.9	1.9	1.9	1.9	1.7
1.2	1.2	1.3		1.0	1.2	1.2	1.3	1.3	1.2
1.6	1.6	1.6		2.0	2.0	1.7	1.6	1.6	1.2
(893) .9	.8	.9	Quick	1.1	.9	1.0	.9	.8	.8
.5	.5	.5		.5	.4	.5	.6	.5	.5
21 17.3	18 19.9	19 19.6		3 142.0	13 28.2	16 23.4	19 19.6	21 17.7	27 13.7
35 10.4	33 10.9	33 11.0	Sales/Receivables	19 19.2	29 12.4	32 11.3	33 10.9	33 10.9	37 9.9
51 7.1	51 7.2	49 7.4		59 6.2	49 7.4	52 7.0	51 7.2	45 8.1	47 7.7
26 13.8	29 12.4	33 11.2		0 UND	34 10.8	25 14.5	33 11.2	33 11.0	36 10.1
64 5.7	69 5.3	65 5.6	Cost of Sales/Inventory	54 6.7	87 4.2	62 5.9	66 5.5	63 5.8	63 5.8
122 3.0	122 3.0	122 3.0		146 2.5	182 2.0	135 2.7	114 3.2	118 3.1	114 3.2
13 27.1	15 23.8	14 25.4		0 UND	11 34.2	10 35.6	14 26.9	17 21.7	17 21.2
29 12.4	29 12.4	30 12.3	Cost of Sales/Payables	29 12.4	29 12.6	32 11.3	34 10.6	27 13.6	30 12.1
53 6.9	53 6.9	54 6.8		79 4.6	52 7.0	58 6.3	60 6.1	49 7.4	49 7.5
4.9	4.7	4.5		2.9	3.7	3.9	4.8	4.5	5.6
9.5	8.9	8.6	Sales/Working Capital	7.7	7.1	9.5	8.1	8.1	9.7
26.5	34.4	23.1		460.3	48.7	33.6	20.3	17.1	20.8
20.0	22.2	21.7		25.3	11.5	26.0	25.4	21.8	34.5
(737) 5.0	(696) 6.5	(713) 6.9	EBIT/Interest	(35) 3.3	(111) 3.7	(93) 7.7	(148) 7.2	(170) 8.7	(156) 8.6
1.8	1.9	2.4		.3	1.3	2.2	2.5	2.8	3.4
13.8	14.5	30.0					3.4	19.6	39.5
(79) 3.6	(71) 4.5	(68) 5.4	Net Profit + Depr., Dep., Amort./Cur. Mat. L/T/D				(13) 2.3	(15) 11.8	(31) 12.2
1.6	1.8	2.2					1.2	3.5	2.9
.0	.0	.0		.0	.0	.0	.0	.0	.1
.2	.2	.2	Fixed/Worth	.0	.3	.2	.1	.1	.2
.7	.9	.7		1.2	7.0	.6	.4	.4	.6
.8	.7	.7		.7	.6	.7	.7	.6	.9
1.9	2.0	1.7	Debt/Worth	1.7	2.5	2.1	1.5	1.2	2.1
6.4	8.1	5.8		-215.0	74.4	14.0	4.3	3.6	5.3
59.1	61.0	57.3		79.1	52.5	67.8	62.5	51.1	54.9
(774) 24.7	(710) 27.8	(751) 24.9	% Profit Before Taxes/Tangible Net Worth	(43) 36.7	(114) 24.0	(89) 25.1	(176) 20.2	(181) 26.0	(148) 25.4
7.4	9.2	9.5		5.3	8.8	5.6	9.4	6.8	13.1
18.5	20.4	18.7		21.3	15.6	24.2	19.4	18.4	18.0
7.1	8.8	8.5	% Profit Before Taxes/Total Assets	11.0	6.8	11.2	8.5	7.8	8.6
1.6	2.3	2.6		-.2	1.7	1.7	3.3	2.3	4.0
315.0	329.8	320.0		UND	281.6	999.8	450.3	210.3	176.4
69.4	59.2	63.6	Sales/Net Fixed Assets	207.3	39.4	67.3	80.5	58.4	64.2
21.9	21.3	21.5		14.0	10.4	26.7	24.8	22.7	25.5
4.1	4.0	3.9		3.5	3.5	4.1	4.4	3.8	4.0
2.8	2.8	2.8	Sales/Total Assets	2.2	2.5	3.1	2.9	2.8	3.0
1.9	2.0	1.9		1.2	1.5	2.1	2.2	2.1	2.0
.2	.2	.2		.5	.4	.2	.2	.2	.2
(582) .6	(561) .5	(537) .6	% Depr., Dep., Amort./Sales	(16) 1.1	(78) .9	(57) .6	(116) .5	(137) .6	(133) .5
1.3	1.2	1.2		2.5	2.2	1.1	1.2	1.0	1.1
1.9	1.6	1.6		3.9	3.0	1.9	1.8	1.3	.3
(433) 3.7	(397) 3.0	(395) 3.1	% Officers', Directors' Owners' Comp/Sales	(19) 7.6	(83) 5.0	(58) 3.1	(117) 2.8	(87) 2.4	(31) .9
6.5	6.2	5.6		14.1	8.0	5.8	4.9	4.3	1.7
22069415M	20149274M	19965470M	Net Sales ($)	33030M	286138M	422876M	1370999M	2936809M	14915618M
8478246M	7492567M	7749223M	Total Assets ($)	19509M	145630M	169353M	550901M	1179719M	5684111M

M = $ thousand MM = $ million

See Pages 9 through 22 for Explanation of Ratios and Data

Current Data Sorted by Assets / Comparative Historical Data

						Type of Statement		
			5	2	2	Unqualified	17	18
	2	9	6	1		Reviewed	24	24
	3	6				Compiled	18	12
3	8	3	3			Tax Returns	28	14
3	6	11	11	3	4	Other	39	38
	13 (4/1-9/30/13)		78 (10/1/13-3/31/14)				4/1/09-3/31/10	4/1/10-3/31/11
0-500M	**500M-2MM**	**2-10MM**	**10-50MM**	**50-100MM**	**100-250MM**		**ALL**	**ALL**
6	19	29	25	6	6	**NUMBER OF STATEMENTS**	126	106
%	%	%	%	%	%	**ASSETS**	%	%
	5.2	5.1	8.3			Cash & Equivalents	7.7	7.8
	35.7	42.3	38.2			Trade Receivables (net)	39.9	41.1
	30.2	30.4	25.8			Inventory	27.3	26.5
	.9	.9	3.8			All Other Current	2.3	3.4
	72.0	78.7	76.2			Total Current	77.1	78.9
	15.6	13.1	13.5			Fixed Assets (net)	12.9	11.9
	.9	.9	3.6			Intangibles (net)	3.7	3.0
	11.4	7.3	6.7			All Other Non-Current	6.3	6.2
	100.0	100.0	100.0			Total	100.0	100.0
						LIABILITIES		
	20.5	16.5	12.8			Notes Payable-Short Term	18.1	20.3
	.7	2.3	1.9			Cur. Mat.-L.T.D.	2.2	1.9
	26.4	24.9	21.8			Trade Payables	23.5	25.3
	.0	.1	.1			Income Taxes Payable	.1	.1
	3.5	5.6	5.7			All Other Current	9.0	9.8
	51.0	49.3	42.4			Total Current	52.8	57.4
	12.0	13.1	12.3			Long-Term Debt	13.6	9.5
	.0	.1	.3			Deferred Taxes	.1	.1
	5.7	3.2	2.9			All Other Non-Current	6.3	9.3
	31.4	34.3	42.1			Net Worth	27.2	23.7
	100.0	100.0	100.0			Total Liabilities & Net Worth	100.0	100.0
						INCOME DATA		
	100.0	100.0	100.0			Net Sales	100.0	100.0
	30.8	23.1	19.9			Gross Profit	21.8	20.9
	27.2	19.7	17.1			Operating Expenses	19.9	18.7
	3.6	3.5	2.8			Operating Profit	2.0	2.2
	.4	.5	.3			All Other Expenses (net)	.5	.3
	3.2	3.0	2.5			Profit Before Taxes	1.4	1.9
						RATIOS		
	2.4	2.4	3.3				2.7	2.3
	1.5	1.7	1.6			Current	1.6	1.4
	.9	1.2	1.3				1.1	1.1
	1.4	1.4	1.6				1.5	1.3
	.8	.9	1.1			Quick	1.0	.9
	.5	.6	.6				.6	.6
	23 16.1	**26** 14.0	**34** 10.7				**29** 12.6	**29** 12.4
	31 11.7	**38** 9.6	**38** 9.6			Sales/Receivables	**40** 9.2	**39** 9.4
	43 8.4	**57** 6.4	**45** 8.1				**52** 7.0	**48** 7.7
	18 20.2	**14** 26.4	**17** 21.4				**15** 23.9	**13** 27.1
	32 11.5	**32** 11.3	**28** 13.0			Cost of Sales/Inventory	**35** 10.4	**32** 11.3
	70 5.2	**99** 3.7	**62** 5.9				**58** 6.3	**53** 6.9
	19 19.2	**17** 21.1	**17** 21.5				**15** 24.4	**16** 23.0
	33 11.2	**34** 10.6	**27** 13.5			Cost of Sales/Payables	**26** 14.3	**25** 14.4
	46 7.9	**53** 6.9	**37** 9.9				**43** 8.5	**39** 9.4
	9.9	6.6	4.6				6.8	7.7
	13.3	11.5	7.9			Sales/Working Capital	12.0	15.4
	-74.7	36.5	23.8				45.1	82.5
	8.1	20.7	31.9				11.6	11.0
	(18) 3.5	4.1	(24) 8.0			EBIT/Interest	(113) 3.0	(95) 3.9
	1.0	1.7	2.4				1.1	1.5
							4.0	6.9
						Net Profit + Depr., Dep., Amort./Cur. Mat. L/T/D	(20) 1.9	(15) 3.4
							-.2	1.9
	.1	.0	.0				.1	.0
	.2	.2	.2			Fixed/Worth	.2	.2
	1.0	1.3	1.0				1.3	.8
	1.3	.8	.5				.8	1.1
	2.0	2.0	1.8			Debt/Worth	2.3	2.8
	4.4	4.0	3.5				8.9	9.7
	74.4	43.4	22.3				35.1	35.4
	(17) 17.7	(28) 14.8	(22) 15.2			% Profit Before Taxes/Tangible Net Worth	(110) 14.6	(92) 18.3
	.4	3.7	5.9				1.5	6.4
	19.1	10.5	10.4				11.5	11.2
	3.9	4.0	6.4			% Profit Before Taxes/Total Assets	3.4	4.2
	.0	1.4	1.9				.4	1.4
	88.7	267.6	605.4				288.6	398.3
	40.8	57.3	53.6			Sales/Net Fixed Assets	77.2	82.3
	20.1	11.2	17.1				14.9	22.6
	5.3	5.1	3.8				4.7	5.1
	4.4	3.3	2.7			Sales/Total Assets	3.3	3.6
	3.0	2.2	2.2				2.6	2.8
	.3	.2	.1				.2	.1
	(16) .6	(23) .3	(21) .4			% Depr., Dep., Amort./Sales	(98) .4	(88) .3
	1.2	1.2	1.3				.9	.8
	2.1	1.1					1.3	1.0
	(15) 2.7	(13) 2.4				% Officers', Directors' Owners' Comp/Sales	(56) 2.5	(44) 1.9
	3.5	3.8					5.3	6.2
9568M	105063M	548410M	1805235M	1164682M	2428396M	Net Sales ($)	7797035M	8356629M
1594M	24391M	139915M	523227M	427803M	946006M	Total Assets ($)	2260557M	2516631M

M = $ thousand MM = $ million

See Pages 9 through 22 for Explanation of Ratios and Data

Comparative Historical Data | Current Data Sorted by Sales

4/1/11-3/31/12 ALL		4/1/12-3/31/13 ALL		4/1/13-3/31/14 ALL		Type of Statement	0-1MM		1-3MM		3-5MM		5-10MM		10-25MM		25MM & OVER
	19		8		9	Unqualified												9
	22		16		18	Reviewed						2		3		3		10
	18		13		9	Compiled						2		3		3		1
	22		33		17	Tax Returns		1		3		3		5		2		3
	46		42		38	Other		1		3		3		6		6		19
							13 (4/1-9/30/13)				78 (10/1/13-3/31/14)							
	127		112		91	**NUMBER OF STATEMENTS**		2		6		10		17		14		42
	%		%		%	**ASSETS**		%		%		%		%		%		%
	9.7		11.1		7.2	Cash & Equivalents						5.1		5.1		11.2		5.9
	40.3		37.0		38.2	Trade Receivables (net)						33.5		32.7		37.4		43.3
	24.3		25.2		29.0	Inventory						33.4		32.3		24.3		29.6
	3.4		2.9		1.9	All Other Current						.0		.5		1.1		3.4
	77.7		76.3		76.3	Total Current						72.1		70.6		74.0		82.2
	13.6		14.8		13.6	Fixed Assets (net)						13.7		23.0		13.6		9.9
	3.3		3.0		2.5	Intangibles (net)						.6		.7		.9		3.5
	5.3		5.9		7.5	All Other Non-Current						13.6		5.7		11.5		4.5
	100.0		100.0		100.0	Total						100.0		100.0		100.0		100.0
						LIABILITIES												
	17.7		16.4		17.1	Notes Payable-Short Term						15.1		19.3		12.3		16.3
	2.1		2.1		1.9	Cur. Mat.-L.T.D.						1.0		2.9		1.2		1.5
	23.4		25.3		23.6	Trade Payables						19.7		24.7		19.8		27.1
	.1		.0		.1	Income Taxes Payable						.0		.1		.0		.1
	10.7		8.2		5.4	All Other Current						4.5		4.4		3.3		6.2
	54.0		52.1		48.1	Total Current						40.4		51.3		36.5		51.2
	11.4		12.3		12.0	Long-Term Debt						8.9		22.7		10.5		8.2
	.3		.1		.3	Deferred Taxes						.0		.0		.0		.5
	4.5		4.7		3.6	All Other Non-Current						8.8		2.2		1.6		4.0
	30.0		30.8		36.1	Net Worth						41.8		23.7		51.4		36.1
	100.0		100.0		100.0	Total Liabilities & Net Worth						100.0		100.0		100.0		100.0
						INCOME DATA												
	100.0		100.0		100.0	Net Sales						100.0		100.0		100.0		100.0
	21.8		26.4		23.9	Gross Profit						37.7		28.8		24.3		16.2
	20.1		23.4		20.4	Operating Expenses						34.8		23.0		22.1		13.7
	1.7		3.0		3.5	Operating Profit						2.9		5.8		2.3		2.4
	.5		.0		.4	All Other Expenses (net)						.6		.8		.2		.2
	1.2		3.0		3.1	Profit Before Taxes						2.3		5.0		2.1		2.2
						RATIOS												
	2.7		2.5		2.5							3.6		2.4		4.4		2.4
	1.5		1.6		1.6	Current						1.6		1.4		1.9		1.6
	1.1		1.2		1.2							.9		1.1		1.5		1.2
	1.5		1.6		1.5							1.5		1.2		2.0		1.4
	1.0		1.0		1.0	Quick						.8		.9		1.4		1.0
	.7		.7		.6							.5		.4		.7		.6
28	13.1	**27**	13.7	**27**	13.6						**26**	14.3	**20**	18.5	**27**	13.4	**31**	11.7
38	9.6	**34**	10.7	**37**	9.8	Sales/Receivables					**30**	12.0	**39**	9.4	**35**	10.4	**38**	9.6
46	7.9	**45**	8.1	**47**	7.8						**48**	7.6	**57**	6.4	**50**	7.3	**47**	7.7
10	37.2	**10**	35.0	**18**	20.5						**17**	22.0	**13**	28.5	**21**	17.2	**17**	21.1
27	13.6	**29**	12.6	**35**	10.3	Cost of Sales/Inventory					**55**	6.6	**39**	9.4	**28**	12.9	**35**	10.4
49	7.5	**53**	6.9	**72**	5.1						**111**	3.3	**94**	3.9	**104**	3.5	**68**	5.4
13	27.7	**15**	25.0	**19**	19.7						**18**	20.8	**16**	22.5	**16**	23.5	**19**	19.6
25	14.7	**27**	13.7	**29**	12.6	Cost of Sales/Payables					**35**	10.4	**49**	7.4	**29**	12.7	**26**	14.1
38	9.5	**43**	8.4	**45**	8.2						**49**	7.4	**58**	6.3	**44**	8.3	**40**	9.1
	7.4		7.1		6.3							6.2		4.6		3.6		6.5
	16.2		14.6		11.2	Sales/Working Capital						12.7		20.0		10.1		10.7
	55.1		50.4		32.3							-64.9		58.7		12.9		25.0
	15.5		19.3		17.8							4.7		30.9		20.7		22.7
(115)	4.5	(99)	5.3	(84)	4.3	EBIT/Interest						2.4		4.9	(13)	4.8	(39)	5.5
	1.4		1.8		1.8							.9		1.5		2.2		2.3
	9.7		8.5		10.5													13.9
(18)	2.4	(16)	3.2	(18)	3.7	Net Profit + Depr., Dep., Amort./Cur. Mat. L/T/D											(12)	4.4
	1.0		1.2		1.0													2.1
	.0		.1		.0							.1		.1		.0		.0
	.2		.3		.2	Fixed/Worth						.2		.7		.1		.2
	1.0		1.0		1.0							1.5		3.1		.4		.7
	.9		.9		.8							.7		1.4		.3		1.0
	2.7		1.7		2.0	Debt/Worth						1.6		3.0		1.2		2.2
	7.6		6.2		4.0							3.6		12.1		1.9		4.2
	34.2		38.8		34.1							67.9		83.0		17.5		29.1
(112)	14.7	(94)	17.1	(82)	15.2	% Profit Before Taxes/Tangible Net Worth						9.5	(15)	19.8		12.2	(38)	15.2
	4.3		5.9		4.0							.0		6.3		4.0		3.7
	10.5		17.5		10.6							10.8		12.4		8.7		10.6
	4.6		5.8		4.5	% Profit Before Taxes/Total Assets						3.3		4.0		4.2		4.8
	.6		1.5		1.5							.0		2.1		1.3		1.6
	375.2		201.2		199.3							71.6		117.1		251.5		605.2
	61.1		56.8		53.6	Sales/Net Fixed Assets						38.4		21.6		42.7		65.1
	19.9		17.5		20.1							27.2		7.1		12.6		30.4
	5.0		5.3		4.8							4.4		5.2		3.9		4.9
	3.8		3.8		3.3	Sales/Total Assets						3.3		3.1		2.8		3.3
	2.7		2.7		2.4							2.6		1.9		1.9		2.5
	.1		.2		.2									.3		.2		.1
(93)	.3	(85)	.4	(76)	.4	% Depr., Dep., Amort./Sales							(14)	1.0	(12)	.3	(35)	.3
	.7		1.0		1.2									1.7		1.1		.8
	1.1		1.3		1.3									2.1				
(59)	2.5	(59)	2.8	(37)	2.6	% Officers', Directors' Owners' Comp/Sales							(10)	3.0				
	4.9		4.8		3.5									6.2				
	7877149M		7266004M		6061354M	Net Sales ($)		1003M		13076M		42618M		120111M		227568M		5656978M
	2374732M		2278196M		2062936M	Total Assets ($)		247M		2946M		16248M		48530M		93090M		1901875M

M = $ thousand **MM = $ million**

See Pages 9 through 22 for Explanation of Ratios and Data

Current Data Sorted by Assets							Comparative Historical Data	
						Type of Statement		
		1	3	2		Unqualified	9	9
	3	25	6	2		Reviewed	47	40
1	6	4	1			Compiled	22	27
5	4	4	1			Tax Returns	12	15
3	9	13	13	1	2	Other	47	48
16 (4/1-9/30/13)			93 (10/1/13-3/31/14)				4/1/09-3/31/10 ALL	4/1/10-3/31/11 ALL
0-500M	**500M-2MM**	**2-10MM**	**10-50MM**	**50-100MM**	**100-250MM**			
9	22	47	24	5	2	**NUMBER OF STATEMENTS**	137	139
%	%	%	%	%	%	**ASSETS**	%	%
	15.3	10.0	5.7			Cash & Equivalents	7.4	8.6
	34.1	33.6	33.3			Trade Receivables (net)	37.2	36.6
	30.1	29.1	31.3			Inventory	28.7	26.0
	.9	4.8	4.5			All Other Current	3.9	4.4
	80.4	77.6	74.9			Total Current	77.1	75.6
	5.7	11.6	13.8			Fixed Assets (net)	11.6	11.8
	5.7	4.0	8.7			Intangibles (net)	6.4	6.1
	8.2	6.9	2.6			All Other Non-Current	4.9	6.5
	100.0	100.0	100.0			Total	100.0	100.0
						LIABILITIES		
	13.1	12.7	13.9			Notes Payable-Short Term	17.8	16.0
	.3	1.3	1.0			Cur. Mat.-L.T.D.	3.5	3.0
	28.8	22.5	18.2			Trade Payables	26.5	25.8
	.0	.2	.2			Income Taxes Payable	.2	.1
	10.5	8.2	11.9			All Other Current	9.7	11.7
	52.7	44.9	45.2			Total Current	57.6	56.6
	5.7	7.1	11.5			Long-Term Debt	9.9	8.4
	.2	.3	.6			Deferred Taxes	.3	.3
	7.2	4.2	6.8			All Other Non-Current	5.9	8.6
	34.2	43.5	35.9			Net Worth	26.3	26.2
	100.0	100.0	100.0			Total Liabilties & Net Worth	100.0	100.0
						INCOME DATA		
	100.0	100.0	100.0			Net Sales	100.0	100.0
	35.2	32.3	37.5			Gross Profit	32.6	32.0
	33.4	30.9	33.1			Operating Expenses	31.0	30.0
	1.7	1.5	4.5			Operating Profit	1.6	2.0
	-.1	.0	1.1			All Other Expenses (net)	.6	.5
	1.8	1.5	3.3			Profit Before Taxes	1.0	1.5
						RATIOS		
	2.2	2.8	3.6				2.0	2.4
	1.6	1.6	1.7			Current	1.5	1.5
	1.2	1.3	1.1				1.0	1.0
	1.7	1.7	1.6				1.2	1.5
	.9	1.0	.9			Quick	.7	.9
	.5	.6	.6				.6	.5
	21 17.5	**26** 13.8	**29** 12.7				**27** 13.7	**28** 13.2
	27 13.4	**34** 10.7	**37** 9.9			Sales/Receivables	**38** 9.5	**37** 9.8
	38 9.7	**45** 8.1	**64** 5.7				**47** 7.8	**48** 7.6
	15 24.3	**21** 17.2	**28** 13.2				**16** 22.6	**16** 22.4
	64 5.7	**32** 11.3	**65** 5.6			Cost of Sales/Inventory	**43** 8.5	**33** 10.9
	99 3.7	**114** 3.2	**111** 3.3				**83** 4.4	**79** 4.6
	23 15.8	**23** 15.7	**20** 18.3				**20** 18.5	**22** 16.2
	29 12.8	**30** 12.0	**30** 12.3			Cost of Sales/Payables	**34** 10.9	**35** 10.5
	54 6.8	**46** 7.9	**45** 8.1				**49** 7.4	**51** 7.2
	8.7	6.7	5.7				7.4	7.4
	14.3	10.5	9.8			Sales/Working Capital	14.2	13.9
	92.5	32.1	30.6				251.0	207.3
	26.1	10.3	9.0				5.6	9.4
	(17) 3.8	(40) 4.8	(21) 4.0			EBIT/Interest	(121) 2.7	(130) 3.3
	-2.3	1.2	1.8				-.2	.9
							3.7	5.3
						Net Profit + Depr., Dep., Amort./Cur. Mat. L/T/D	(41) 2.0	(35) 1.9
							.6	.9
	.0	.0	.1				.1	.1
	.2	.2	.4			Fixed/Worth	.4	.3
	.5	.5	2.3				2.4	.9
	1.3	.6	.7				1.1	1.1
	2.1	1.6	1.8			Debt/Worth	2.8	2.6
	4.5	3.2	22.1				23.5	13.2
	41.8	20.4	54.0				31.4	35.6
	(20) 11.2	(44) 7.5	(20) 20.4			% Profit Before Taxes/Tangible Net Worth	(106) 11.4	(112) 15.4
	2.5	.7	6.0				-.1	1.5
	11.2	9.9	14.4				10.0	9.9
	3.0	2.6	4.7			% Profit Before Taxes/Total Assets	2.7	3.6
	-6.2	.5	2.1				-1.8	.1
	485.6	192.8	84.6				165.6	152.9
	81.6	63.3	37.7			Sales/Net Fixed Assets	43.4	56.0
	50.2	19.6	17.2				18.1	18.5
	5.1	4.7	4.0				4.8	4.8
	4.1	3.6	2.8			Sales/Total Assets	3.4	3.5
	2.7	2.2	2.0				2.3	2.2
	.2	.2	.3				.4	.3
	(13) .4	(37) .6	(20) 1.1			% Depr., Dep., Amort./Sales	(106) .7	(114) .6
	.8	1.1	1.6				1.3	1.1
	1.8	1.1					1.3	1.4
	(14) 4.0	(21) 2.3				% Officers', Directors' Owners' Comp/Sales	(61) 3.3	(64) 3.1
	9.2	4.0					6.3	5.2
12077M	107552M	834939M	1308283M	981890M	918284M	Net Sales ($)	4692606M	6403806M
2049M	26537M	237214M	445051M	360573M	345972M	Total Assets ($)	1515748M	1979770M

M = $ thousand MM = $ million

See Pages 9 through 22 for Explanation of Ratios and Data

Comparative Historical Data / Current Data Sorted by Sales

	4/1/11-3/31/12 ALL	4/1/12-3/31/13 ALL	4/1/13-3/31/14 ALL	0-1MM	1-3MM	3-5MM	5-10MM	10-25MM	25MM & OVER
Type of Statement									
Unqualified	10	6	6						6
Reviewed	36	38	36		1		7	18	10
Compiled	19	11	12		3	1	4	1	3
Tax Returns	23	22	14	2	3	2	3	2	2
Other	53	38	41	2	4	2	9	8	16
					16 (4/1-9/30/13)		93 (10/1/13-3/31/14)		
NUMBER OF STATEMENTS	141	115	109	4	11	5	23	29	37
ASSETS	%	%	%	%	%	%	%	%	%
Cash & Equivalents	8.7	8.2	10.4		16.1		10.0	9.1	8.1
Trade Receivables (net)	34.8	35.9	33.0		20.3		29.9	36.4	34.5
Inventory	27.9	28.5	30.4		36.2		35.5	27.1	29.3
All Other Current	4.1	3.6	3.7		1.9		1.5	5.9	4.8
Total Current	75.5	76.2	77.6		74.5		76.9	78.5	76.7
Fixed Assets (net)	11.0	12.3	11.3		10.9		12.0	9.8	12.5
Intangibles (net)	6.6	5.6	5.3		4.4		5.2	5.8	6.5
All Other Non-Current	6.8	6.0	5.8		10.1		5.9	5.9	4.3
Total	100.0	100.0	100.0		100.0		100.0	100.0	100.0
LIABILITIES									
Notes Payable-Short Term	14.2	15.2	12.9		14.5		13.4	17.0	12.0
Cur. Mat.-L.T.D.	2.8	1.4	1.1		2.3		1.1	1.3	.8
Trade Payables	25.3	26.0	21.4		18.7		19.2	23.3	21.4
Income Taxes Payable	.1	.2	.1		.0		.0	.2	.2
All Other Current	12.3	9.5	10.2		8.2		11.9	9.9	12.1
Total Current	54.8	52.3	45.7		43.8		45.5	51.8	46.5
Long-Term Debt	11.1	8.6	8.3		8.6		7.7	5.1	10.8
Deferred Taxes	.3	.4	.3		.0		.7	.1	.5
All Other Non-Current	7.4	4.8	7.0		13.1		8.1	2.2	7.0
Net Worth	26.4	33.9	38.6		34.5		38.1	40.8	35.2
Total Liabilties & Net Worth	100.0	100.0	100.0		100.0		100.0	100.0	100.0
INCOME DATA									
Net Sales	100.0	100.0	100.0		100.0		100.0	100.0	100.0
Gross Profit	33.3	32.4	35.1		43.3		36.1	31.6	33.2
Operating Expenses	30.7	30.0	32.4		41.6		35.6	30.1	28.7
Operating Profit	2.6	2.4	2.7		1.7		.5	1.5	4.5
All Other Expenses (net)	.6	.1	.2		.4		-.3	.2	.6
Profit Before Taxes	2.0	2.3	2.4		1.4		.8	1.4	3.9
RATIOS									
Current	2.4	2.3	2.8		7.3		2.7	2.0	2.9
	1.5	1.5	1.7		1.5		1.8	1.6	1.7
	1.0	1.1	1.2		1.2		1.3	1.1	1.1
Quick	1.5	1.4	1.8		4.2		1.6	1.2	1.7
	.8	.8	.9		.7		.9	.9	.9
	.5	.5	.6		.4		.6	.5	.7
Sales/Receivables	27 13.7	26 13.9	24 15.1		17 21.9		26 13.8	23 16.1	26 14.2
	35 10.4	38 9.7	32 11.4		28 13.1		31 11.6	36 10.1	33 11.0
	47 7.7	49 7.4	46 8.0		35 10.4		52 7.0	48 7.6	50 7.3
Cost of Sales/Inventory	17 22.0	17 21.3	22 16.8		46 7.9		22 16.5	21 17.0	21 17.3
	42 8.7	37 9.8	45 8.2		76 4.8		68 5.4	31 11.8	41 8.8
	99 3.7	91 4.0	101 3.6		126 2.9		174 2.1	54 6.8	96 3.8
Cost of Sales/Payables	21 17.6	20 18.5	20 18.5		17 21.1		23 15.8	23 16.1	20 18.5
	33 11.2	31 11.7	28 13.0		23 15.6		33 11.1	27 13.3	28 12.9
	48 7.6	48 7.6	46 8.0		59 6.2		46 7.9	51 7.2	43 8.5
Sales/Working Capital	7.4	7.6	6.7		4.6		3.6	9.1	6.6
	14.2	14.8	10.9		10.2		9.0	12.7	14.4
	141.0	41.7	28.6		22.7		27.3	44.1	33.4
EBIT/Interest	8.1	10.4	11.7				22.4	13.1	9.6
	(122) 3.2	(100) 4.7	(89) 4.0				(19) 2.6	(27) 4.0	(31) 5.3
	.8	1.6	1.4				-.2	1.2	2.1
Net Profit + Depr., Dep., Amort./Cur. Mat. L/T/D	8.0	8.0	7.1						
	(25) 3.4	(22) 2.5	(14) 2.1						
	1.5	1.7	1.7						
Fixed/Worth	.0	.1	.0		.0		.0	.0	.1
	.3	.3	.2		.1		.3	.2	.3
	2.3	1.0	.7		-91.0		.5	.4	1.6
Debt/Worth	1.0	.9	.8		1.3		.8	.9	.8
	2.5	2.1	1.7		2.4		1.6	1.8	1.7
	NM	7.3	4.7		-168.0		6.5	4.1	8.0
% Profit Before Taxes/Tangible Net Worth	34.8	38.4	30.1				36.3	24.8	50.1
	(106) 12.9	(99) 14.9	(96) 10.6				(21) 3.6	(27) 7.9	(32) 20.4
	1.4	2.4	2.0				-3.4	.6	7.5
% Profit Before Taxes/Total Assets	10.6	12.6	13.1		11.1		11.5	12.0	15.8
	3.8	4.7	3.8		5.0		1.3	2.9	4.5
	-.2	1.1	.6		-6.6		-2.2	.4	2.4
Sales/Net Fixed Assets	259.3	248.2	239.9		645.3		432.3	180.4	126.5
	57.0	47.8	63.3		52.8		80.3	56.1	39.0
	19.8	16.4	22.4		23.8		27.5	31.7	16.0
Sales/Total Assets	4.9	4.7	4.8		5.2		4.6	4.7	4.7
	3.4	3.5	3.6		3.1		3.0	3.5	3.8
	2.2	2.3	2.2		1.6		1.7	2.4	2.3
% Depr., Dep., Amort./Sales	.3	.3	.2				.2	.2	.4
	(101) .7	(90) .7	(79) .6				(15) .6	(23) .6	(30) .6
	1.3	1.5	1.1				2.1	.9	1.5
% Officers', Directors' Owners' Comp/Sales	1.9	1.8	1.5				1.9	1.1	
	(71) 3.3	(58) 3.6	(45) 3.4				(14) 3.2	(12) 1.6	
	5.7	5.6	5.5				4.9	4.4	
Net Sales ($)	4417027M	4431966M	4163025M	1940M	22086M	17680M	160604M	453686M	3507029M
Total Assets ($)	1617236M	1514994M	1417396M	708M	10346M	3319M	71268M	144247M	1187508M

M = $ thousand MM = $ million

See Pages 9 through 22 for Explanation of Ratios and Data

Current Data Sorted by Assets							Comparative Historical Data	
						Type of Statement		
		2	7	2	2	Unqualified	25	26
1	4	27	19	2		Reviewed	65	69
1	7	13				Compiled	35	35
3	6	12	1			Tax Returns	28	24
1	14	16	15	2	4	Other	67	53
	28 (4/1-9/30/13)		133 (10/1/13-3/31/14)				4/1/09-3/31/10	4/1/10-3/31/11
0-500M	500M-2MM	2-10MM	10-50MM	50-100MM	100-250MM		ALL	ALL
6	31	70	42	6	6	NUMBER OF STATEMENTS	220	207
%	%	%	%	%	%	**ASSETS**	%	%
	8.2	5.2	4.0			Cash & Equivalents	7.0	6.5
	38.6	39.6	31.1			Trade Receivables (net)	36.1	37.7
	34.6	32.3	33.5			Inventory	30.0	33.4
	1.9	2.0	1.8			All Other Current	3.4	2.8
	83.3	79.1	70.4			Total Current	76.6	80.4
	11.0	11.8	17.4			Fixed Assets (net)	14.4	12.0
	1.5	3.0	7.0			Intangibles (net)	3.9	2.7
	4.2	6.0	5.2			All Other Non-Current	5.2	4.8
	100.0	100.0	100.0			Total	100.0	100.0
						LIABILITIES		
	12.6	16.2	20.8			Notes Payable-Short Term	16.5	16.7
	3.0	2.6	2.1			Cur. Mat.-L.T.D.	2.4	1.7
	30.1	25.2	20.1			Trade Payables	24.4	24.1
	.0	.0	.0			Income Taxes Payable	.2	.2
	8.8	7.6	7.1			All Other Current	7.8	7.1
	54.4	51.7	50.3			Total Current	51.3	49.7
	11.0	9.3	7.7			Long-Term Debt	10.0	8.0
	.1	.3	.4			Deferred Taxes	.3	.3
	1.2	3.4	6.0			All Other Non-Current	5.0	4.8
	33.3	35.2	35.6			Net Worth	33.5	37.1
	100.0	100.0	100.0			Total Liabilities & Net Worth	100.0	100.0
						INCOME DATA		
	100.0	100.0	100.0			Net Sales	100.0	100.0
	29.1	21.9	23.3			Gross Profit	23.9	23.5
	26.9	19.3	21.0			Operating Expenses	21.7	21.1
	2.2	2.6	2.4			Operating Profit	2.2	2.5
	-.1	.1	.5			All Other Expenses (net)	.5	.3
	2.2	2.5	1.9			Profit Before Taxes	1.6	2.1
						RATIOS		
	2.9	2.1	1.9				2.3	2.6
	1.6	1.5	1.6			Current	1.5	1.6
	1.1	1.2	1.1				1.1	1.2
	1.4	1.2	1.2				1.4	1.4
	.8	.8	.8			Quick	.8	.9
	.5	.6	.4				.6	.6
	25 14.5	**29** 12.7	**29** 12.7				**28** 13.2	**29** 12.8
	30 12.1	**34** 10.8	**37** 9.9			Sales/Receivables	**35** 10.4	**35** 10.4
	34 10.7	**44** 8.3	**48** 7.6				**45** 8.2	**44** 8.4
	27 13.6	**29** 12.6	**34** 10.7				**26** 14.2	**32** 11.4
	41 8.9	**40** 9.1	**50** 7.3			Cost of Sales/Inventory	**39** 9.5	**41** 8.8
	51 7.2	**60** 6.1	**83** 4.4				**61** 6.0	**61** 6.0
	23 15.9	**17** 21.8	**17** 21.1				**17** 21.5	**17** 22.0
	32 11.5	**26** 14.3	**24** 15.1			Cost of Sales/Payables	**28** 13.2	**28** 12.9
	47 7.7	**36** 10.0	**31** 11.6				**46** 7.9	**44** 8.3
	8.4	8.1	10.0				8.0	7.2
	15.2	14.6	13.8			Sales/Working Capital	13.9	12.8
	67.7	57.1	41.5				47.0	31.7
	13.7	21.7	16.9				10.1	11.4
	(27) 6.0	(63) 6.5	(40) 5.2			EBIT/Interest	(203) 3.3	(185) 4.1
	.2	2.2	2.7				1.2	1.6
		11.3	11.5				5.2	7.6
		(12) 3.5	(11) 3.5			Net Profit + Depr., Dep., Amort./Cur. Mat. L/T/D	(55) 1.9	(53) 3.3
		.7	2.0				.3	1.0
	.0	.1	.2				.1	.1
	.2	.2	.4			Fixed/Worth	.3	.2
	.8	.8	1.0				1.0	.8
	.5	1.1	1.1				1.0	.8
	2.5	1.9	2.0			Debt/Worth	2.2	1.9
	7.3	5.3	5.1				5.9	4.2
	75.3	43.7	34.1				32.9	34.0
	(27) 27.5	(62) 17.2	(38) 22.3			% Profit Before Taxes/Tangible Net Worth	(196) 14.7	(188) 15.2
	5.6	7.5	8.7				3.1	3.5
	20.1	12.9	13.2				10.1	9.5
	4.8	6.0	6.0			% Profit Before Taxes/Total Assets	3.5	4.8
	-.3	2.2	2.3				.4	1.1
	666.0	256.3	76.8				143.2	173.9
	94.9	67.8	24.8			Sales/Net Fixed Assets	47.2	58.5
	33.2	17.8	10.1				16.3	17.0
	5.5	5.0	4.2				4.5	4.5
	4.4	3.6	3.1			Sales/Total Assets	3.5	3.5
	3.8	2.8	2.2				2.5	2.7
	.3	.2	.4				.3	.3
	(21) .5	(57) .4	(39) .6			% Depr., Dep., Amort./Sales	(182) .6	(165) .6
	.9	.9	1.0				1.3	1.0
	2.6	1.2	.6				1.2	1.3
	(19) 4.0	(37) 2.0	(14) 1.3			% Officers', Directors' Owners' Comp/Sales	(98) 2.5	(92) 2.3
	6.6	4.2	2.3				4.0	4.6
9867M	178330M	1341564M	2614551M	1144612M	3154246M	Net Sales ($)	12497523M	10299975M
2079M	39120M	347240M	855090M	462461M	954859M	Total Assets ($)	3641056M	2926728M

M = $ thousand MM = $ million

See Pages 9 through 22 for Explanation of Ratios and Data

Comparative Historical Data				Current Data Sorted by Sales					
			Type of Statement						
20	15	13	Unqualified					4	9
70	56	53	Reviewed		1	1	4	18	29
32	22	21	Compiled	1	1	1	5	9	4
23	17	22	Tax Returns	2	3	3	5	7	2
62	58	52	Other		1	8	8	10	25
				28 (4/1-9/30/13)			133 (10/1/13-3/31/14)		
4/1/11-3/31/12 ALL	4/1/12-3/31/13 ALL	4/1/13-3/31/14 ALL		0-1MM	1-3MM	3-5MM	5-10MM	10-25MM	25MM & OVER
207	168	161	**NUMBER OF STATEMENTS**	3	6	13	22	48	69
%	%	%	**ASSETS**	%	%	%	%	%	%
6.6	6.3	5.6	Cash & Equivalents			7.0	7.0	5.1	4.6
38.2	36.9	35.7	Trade Receivables (net)			29.8	39.2	36.3	36.5
31.4	33.2	32.6	Inventory			28.3	34.1	33.3	31.8
2.6	1.9	2.3	All Other Current			2.4	2.0	2.1	1.9
78.7	78.4	76.2	Total Current			67.4	82.3	76.8	74.8
13.0	13.2	14.0	Fixed Assets (net)			11.8	13.5	15.4	13.8
3.0	3.3	4.3	Intangibles (net)			3.9	1.2	3.6	6.2
5.3	5.0	5.5	All Other Non-Current			16.9	3.0	4.2	5.2
100.0	100.0	100.0	Total			100.0	100.0	100.0	100.0
			LIABILITIES						
16.5	15.9	15.5	Notes Payable-Short Term			10.0	15.2	16.2	17.4
1.8	3.1	2.8	Cur. Mat.-L.T.D.			3.0	3.6	3.6	2.3
25.2	23.8	24.9	Trade Payables			24.9	31.7	23.0	23.2
.1	.2	.0	Income Taxes Payable			.0	.1	.0	.1
6.7	6.5	9.4	All Other Current			20.6	4.9	7.3	7.9
50.3	49.3	52.6	Total Current			58.5	55.5	50.0	50.9
8.4	9.3	10.0	Long-Term Debt			12.0	11.6	10.5	8.8
.4	.3	.5	Deferred Taxes			.3	.1	.4	.8
4.6	5.0	3.7	All Other Non-Current			.0	1.6	4.6	4.2
36.3	36.1	33.2	Net Worth			29.3	31.3	34.5	35.4
100.0	100.0	100.0	Total Liabilties & Net Worth			100.0	100.0	100.0	100.0
			INCOME DATA						
100.0	100.0	100.0	Net Sales			100.0	100.0	100.0	100.0
23.6	24.5	23.9	Gross Profit			27.1	30.2	22.9	21.7
21.3	22.2	21.3	Operating Expenses			25.9	26.5	20.7	18.8
2.3	2.3	2.5	Operating Profit			1.1	3.7	2.1	2.9
.1	.4	.2	All Other Expenses (net)			.3	.3	.3	.1
2.2	1.9	2.3	Profit Before Taxes			.8	3.5	1.8	2.8
			RATIOS						
2.4	2.3	2.3				2.4	2.5	2.5	2.0
1.6	1.5	1.6	Current			1.6	1.5	1.6	1.5
1.2	1.2	1.1				.8	1.0	1.1	1.1
1.3	1.4	1.2				1.1	1.4	1.3	1.2
.8	.8	.8	Quick			.8	.8	.8	.8
.6	.6	.6				.5	.5	.6	.6
29 12.5	**28** 13.0	**28** 13.0				**12** 30.1	**27** 13.3	**29** 12.8	**28** 13.0
36 10.2	**36** 10.2	**33** 10.9	Sales/Receivables			**31** 11.6	**32** 11.5	**33** 11.0	**37** 9.9
46 8.0	**44** 8.3	**44** 8.3				**42** 8.6	**40** 9.1	**43** 8.4	**47** 7.8
27 13.3	**31** 11.6	**29** 12.4				**19** 19.5	**34** 10.8	**30** 12.2	**30** 12.0
43 8.5	**42** 8.6	**43** 8.4	Cost of Sales/Inventory			**28** 13.1	**46** 8.0	**42** 8.6	**42** 8.6
59 6.2	**62** 5.9	**58** 6.3				**46** 8.0	**58** 6.3	**64** 5.7	**57** 6.4
18 20.3	**17** 21.0	**17** 21.1				**6** 62.9	**24** 15.1	**15** 24.2	**18** 19.9
25 14.7	**27** 13.7	**26** 14.1	Cost of Sales/Payables			**30** 12.2	**37** 9.8	**23** 15.8	**25** 14.4
41 8.9	**43** 8.5	**37** 9.8				**45** 8.1	**57** 6.4	**35** 10.5	**31** 11.8
8.0	7.5	7.8				8.2	8.8	6.7	9.4
13.4	14.0	14.4	Sales/Working Capital			17.8	14.9	14.5	14.4
31.9	30.2	51.4				-141.5	NM	68.1	43.8
15.5	12.0	17.5				12.0	25.1	16.1	18.2
(188) 5.2	(149) 5.2	(145) 5.9	EBIT/Interest			(11) 6.0	(21) 3.4	(44) 6.6	(63) 5.2
1.8	1.6	2.1				-3.3	1.5	1.9	2.8
7.8	17.0	10.5							5.8
(44) 4.2	(41) 5.4	(35) 3.4	Net Profit + Depr., Dep., Amort./Cur. Mat. L/T/D						(23) 3.4
1.7	1.8	1.1							2.0
.1	.1	.1				.0	.1	.1	.1
.3	.3	.3	Fixed/Worth			.1	.5	.3	.4
.8	1.0	.9				2.3	1.8	1.7	.9
.9	1.0	1.1				.8	.7	.8	1.1
2.0	1.8	2.0	Debt/Worth			1.8	2.9	1.9	2.1
4.8	4.4	5.8				94.6	10.8	7.2	5.4
37.2	38.4	44.9				99.1	90.5	36.6	50.7
(187) 15.8	(147) 18.0	(140) 20.5	% Profit Before Taxes/Tangible Net Worth			(11) 14.0	(19) 27.9	(40) 13.7	(62) 23.9
5.3	4.9	7.9				-7.4	11.0	6.2	11.7
10.9	11.9	13.3				27.3	27.3	12.0	13.2
5.2	5.7	5.9	% Profit Before Taxes/Total Assets			4.8	6.0	4.7	7.3
1.2	1.3	2.0				-3.9	1.3	1.9	2.5
165.7	177.2	159.8				832.9	679.5	132.0	91.8
57.9	59.0	59.2	Sales/Net Fixed Assets			65.9	92.4	50.8	51.6
15.0	16.0	15.6				28.9	13.9	11.7	15.4
4.6	4.7	4.8				5.4	5.0	5.1	4.4
3.6	3.6	3.6	Sales/Total Assets			4.9	4.1	3.6	3.5
2.6	2.6	2.6				2.1	2.8	2.7	2.6
.2	.2	.2					.4	.3	.2
(179) .5	(132) .5	(132) .5	% Depr., Dep., Amort./Sales				(15) .6	(40) .4	(62) .5
1.1	1.2	1.0					1.1	.8	1.0
1.2	1.2	1.3					2.1	1.3	.6
(97) 2.3	(72) 2.1	(75) 2.5	% Officers', Directors' Owners' Comp/Sales				(13) 4.3	(28) 2.1	(22) 1.3
4.0	4.8	4.5					6.3	4.1	2.5
11588936M	11026776M	8443170M	Net Sales ($)	1420M	13293M	50001M	163642M	738829M	7475985M
3621908M	3411610M	2660849M	Total Assets ($)	725M	3721M	16486M	47784M	254837M	2337296M

M = $ thousand MM = $ million

See Pages 9 through 22 for Explanation of Ratios and Data

	Current Data Sorted by Assets						Comparative Historical Data	
Type of Statement								
Unqualified			8	23	2	9	55	58
Reviewed		2	15	17			56	44
Compiled		7	12	5		1	19	20
Tax Returns	9	15	15		1		38	36
Other	4	15	33	40	15	13	97	106
	50 (4/1-9/30/13)			211 (10/1/13-3/31/14)			4/1/09-3/31/10	4/1/10-3/31/11
	0-500M	500M-2MM	2-10MM	10-50MM	50-100MM	100-250MM	ALL	ALL
NUMBER OF STATEMENTS	13	39	83	85	18	23	265	264
ASSETS	%	%	%	%	%	%	%	%
Cash & Equivalents	26.2	16.1	15.8	9.4	13.7	8.1	10.6	10.9
Trade Receivables (net)	18.9	27.0	27.9	30.1	28.9	35.6	29.4	30.7
Inventory	36.1	31.0	29.2	35.6	23.0	20.7	32.1	32.1
All Other Current	.9	.8	4.7	2.5	6.3	4.0	3.6	2.8
Total Current	82.1	74.9	77.6	77.6	71.9	68.5	75.7	76.5
Fixed Assets (net)	10.0	11.6	10.2	9.8	8.2	9.1	10.0	10.0
Intangibles (net)	2.7	4.5	5.2	7.1	15.0	18.6	8.5	9.3
All Other Non-Current	5.9	9.1	7.0	5.5	4.9	3.8	5.8	4.2
Total	100.0	100.0	100.0	100.0	100.0	100.0	100.0	100.0
LIABILITIES								
Notes Payable-Short Term	15.6	13.8	11.7	10.9	7.6	9.9	13.3	12.5
Cur. Mat.-L.T.D.	.0	1.0	2.3	1.5	1.9	1.4	2.4	1.6
Trade Payables	17.1	32.1	18.9	24.3	19.6	25.0	22.8	25.6
Income Taxes Payable	.0	.2	.1	.2	.3	.0	.2	.2
All Other Current	24.5	8.3	12.1	10.6	11.8	14.3	10.4	8.9
Total Current	57.3	55.4	45.1	47.4	41.2	50.6	49.1	48.8
Long-Term Debt	10.8	5.7	7.7	13.4	12.5	13.1	8.3	7.8
Deferred Taxes	.0	.0	.2	.5	.6	1.7	.3	.3
All Other Non-Current	14.3	7.5	7.7	6.5	2.0	7.2	7.5	6.4
Net Worth	18.3	31.4	39.4	32.3	43.8	27.4	34.8	36.6
Total Liabilties & Net Worth	100.0	100.0	100.0	100.0	100.0	100.0	100.0	100.0
INCOME DATA								
Net Sales	100.0	100.0	100.0	100.0	100.0	100.0	100.0	100.0
Gross Profit	41.6	31.6	34.3	30.8	40.7	24.3	31.7	31.8
Operating Expenses	35.9	27.5	27.6	24.0	30.9	19.8	26.8	26.3
Operating Profit	5.7	4.1	6.7	6.8	9.8	4.5	5.0	5.5
All Other Expenses (net)	.1	.2	.2	2.0	1.2	3.5	.8	1.0
Profit Before Taxes	5.6	3.9	6.4	4.8	8.6	1.0	4.1	4.5
RATIOS								
Current	6.2	2.3	3.8	2.4	3.7	1.8	2.3	2.3
	2.5	1.6	1.7	1.7	1.8	1.4	1.5	1.6
	.9	1.0	1.2	1.3	1.2	1.1	1.2	1.2
Quick	4.1	1.4	2.0	1.2	2.5	1.1	1.2	1.4
	1.2	.9	1.0	.8	.9	.9	.8	.8
	.2	.5	.6	.6	.6	.8	.5	.5
Sales/Receivables	**0** UND	**14** 27.0	**17** 21.7	**27** 13.3	**31** 11.8	**28** 12.9	**25** 14.7	**26** 14.0
	5 70.0	**29** 12.4	**33** 10.9	**39** 9.4	**46** 7.9	**43** 8.4	**38** 9.6	**37** 9.9
	18 20.8	**39** 9.3	**51** 7.2	**52** 7.0	**72** 5.1	**63** 5.8	**51** 7.2	**53** 6.9
Cost of Sales/Inventory	**12** 31.2	**18** 20.8	**22** 16.6	**32** 11.5	**46** 7.9	**13** 28.7	**28** 13.3	**27** 13.3
	30 12.2	**36** 10.1	**61** 6.0	**66** 5.5	**83** 4.4	**24** 14.9	**61** 6.0	**58** 6.3
	94 3.9	**81** 4.5	**104** 3.5	**122** 3.0	**130** 2.8	**63** 5.8	**119** 3.1	**107** 3.4
Cost of Sales/Payables	**0** UND	**23** 16.0	**10** 36.3	**18** 20.0	**26** 14.2	**29** 12.7	**20** 18.2	**22** 16.9
	3 131.9	**35** 10.3	**26** 14.0	**41** 9.0	**43** 8.4	**38** 9.5	**34** 10.6	**36** 10.0
	36 10.0	**72** 5.1	**54** 6.8	**65** 5.6	**99** 3.7	**45** 8.1	**59** 6.2	**60** 6.1
Sales/Working Capital	6.3	5.9	5.0	5.3	3.3	7.4	6.1	6.1
	12.6	20.0	9.7	9.4	7.5	21.0	11.6	11.0
	NM	-165.4	33.2	19.0	46.0	87.7	26.5	29.4
EBIT/Interest		31.3	64.8	34.7	31.3	8.8	18.6	26.0
		(26) 4.1	(63) 13.6	(75) 9.9	(17) 12.1	(17) 5.0	(227) 5.8	(214) 6.2
		1.0	2.6	2.7	4.0	1.7	2.2	2.3
Net Profit + Depr., Dep., Amort./Cur. Mat. L/T/D				12.7			11.3	16.4
				(19) 2.9			(49) 3.5	(42) 2.6
				.5			1.0	1.1
Fixed/Worth	.0	.0	.0	.0	.1	.2	.0	.0
	.0	.1	.2	.1	.1	.6	.2	.2
	1.2	1.7	.5	.7	.8	-2.3	.9	.9
Debt/Worth	.3	1.0	.6	.8	.8	2.2	1.0	.9
	4.6	2.0	1.4	2.1	2.5	5.5	2.3	2.1
	-2.8	20.6	6.4	4.9	5.4	-25.9	5.4	7.7
% Profit Before Taxes/Tangible Net Worth		63.7	80.0	69.9	105.4	49.8	62.5	61.2
		(31) 30.1	(76) 37.9	(76) 31.3	(16) 39.9	(16) 14.6	(233) 27.3	(222) 26.8
		5.6	9.7	17.5	10.9	5.5	11.1	10.2
% Profit Before Taxes/Total Assets	82.5	22.7	22.9	18.6	21.0	7.2	16.4	19.1
	19.0	9.1	11.1	10.3	7.1	3.8	6.8	7.4
	-27.8	.4	3.2	2.9	3.1	-.4	2.5	2.2
Sales/Net Fixed Assets	UND	UND	439.0	202.7	123.3	152.0	275.0	236.5
	UND	89.3	62.4	71.9	32.9	32.3	66.5	80.9
	77.8	18.2	27.2	15.9	15.6	16.5	19.4	23.8
Sales/Total Assets	9.7	5.5	4.3	3.7	3.1	4.7	4.0	4.2
	8.6	3.4	2.8	2.6	1.9	2.4	2.8	3.0
	4.2	2.2	2.0	1.9	1.1	1.4	1.9	1.8
% Depr., Dep., Amort./Sales		.2	.2	.1	.2	.1	.2	.2
		(22) .6	(58) .5	(76) .4	(13) .7	(15) .2	(176) .5	(192) .4
		1.4	1.1	1.1	1.5	.6	1.5	1.0
% Officers', Directors' Owners' Comp/Sales		1.3	1.0	.6			1.0	1.0
		(24) 3.2	(34) 1.6	(29) 1.2			(95) 2.2	(99) 2.1
		4.6	3.6	3.0			4.3	3.7
Net Sales ($)	22170M	200518M	1322706M	5455130M	2777725M	11171184M	17515127M	16373464M
Total Assets ($)	2563M	48731M	421013M	1996087M	1356610M	3455617M	6158936M	6527525M

M = $ thousand MM = $ million

See Pages 9 through 22 for Explanation of Ratios and Data

Comparative Historical Data / Current Data Sorted by Sales

4/1/11-3/31/12 ALL	4/1/12-3/31/13 ALL	4/1/13-3/31/14 ALL		0-1MM	1-3MM	3-5MM	5-10MM	10-25MM	25MM & OVER
			Type of Statement						
45	43	42	Unqualified					8	34
46	43	34	Reviewed	1		2	6	6	19
30	21	25	Compiled		3	3	6	8	5
55	41	40	Tax Returns	3	8	9	8	10	2
130	140	120	Other	3	7	4	11	26	69
				50 (4/1-9/30/13)			211 (10/1/13-3/31/14)		
306	288	261	**NUMBER OF STATEMENTS**	7	18	18	31	58	129
%	%	%	**ASSETS**	%	%	%	%	%	%
10.3	10.4	13.5	Cash & Equivalents		16.9	14.3	16.2	15.7	11.0
31.2	30.1	28.8	Trade Receivables (net)		18.1	25.4	29.0	26.6	32.7
31.5	33.2	30.7	Inventory		33.5	35.2	23.7	30.4	31.3
3.2	2.8	3.2	All Other Current		2.8	.9	4.7	4.1	3.1
76.2	76.4	76.2	Total Current		71.3	75.8	73.6	76.8	78.1
9.7	8.9	10.0	Fixed Assets (net)		8.1	11.9	11.5	10.5	8.3
8.0	8.2	7.4	Intangibles (net)		10.1	.7	4.6	6.4	9.2
6.2	6.5	6.3	All Other Non-Current		10.5	11.6	10.4	6.3	4.4
100.0	100.0	100.0	Total		100.0	100.0	100.0	100.0	100.0
			LIABILITIES						
12.2	13.8	11.5	Notes Payable-Short Term		18.7	21.7	10.6	8.3	10.6
1.6	1.8	1.6	Cur. Mat.-L.T.D.		1.1	.6	.9	2.1	1.7
22.8	25.5	23.1	Trade Payables		19.6	27.1	22.0	19.7	25.1
.2	.1	.1	Income Taxes Payable		.8	.0	.0	.2	.1
10.5	9.7	11.8	All Other Current		17.6	10.6	16.0	11.6	10.3
47.3	50.9	48.2	Total Current		57.8	60.1	49.5	41.9	47.9
7.7	9.7	10.2	Long-Term Debt		8.7	2.0	9.1	7.5	13.1
.3	.3	.4	Deferred Taxes		.0	.0	.1	.2	.7
9.7	6.0	7.2	All Other Non-Current		9.2	13.0	7.2	6.6	5.8
34.9	33.2	34.1	Net Worth		24.3	24.9	34.1	43.8	32.5
100.0	100.0	100.0	Total Liabilties & Net Worth		100.0	100.0	100.0	100.0	100.0
			INCOME DATA						
100.0	100.0	100.0	Net Sales		100.0	100.0	100.0	100.0	100.0
31.0	30.9	32.7	Gross Profit		43.9	32.5	29.9	36.2	28.9
25.8	25.4	26.4	Operating Expenses		36.7	29.9	25.1	28.9	22.4
5.2	5.5	6.3	Operating Profit		7.2	2.5	4.8	7.3	6.5
.9	.7	1.1	All Other Expenses (net)		-.1	1.0	.5	.0	2.1
4.3	4.7	5.1	Profit Before Taxes		7.3	1.6	4.3	7.3	4.4
			RATIOS						
2.7	2.4	2.7			4.8	2.0	3.3	3.8	2.4
1.7	1.6	1.7	Current		2.0	1.4	1.7	1.8	1.6
1.2	1.2	1.2			.6	.9	1.1	1.3	1.2
1.4	1.3	1.5			2.4	1.1	1.8	2.0	1.2
.9	.8	.9	Quick		.9	.7	1.0	1.0	.9
.6	.6	.6			.2	.4	.5	.6	.6
24 15.5	21 17.0	23 15.8			4 87.1	1 724.8	19 19.6	16 22.8	28 12.9
36 10.1	35 10.5	34 10.7	Sales/Receivables		22 16.3	30 12.1	33 11.0	32 11.4	39 9.4
50 7.3	51 7.2	49 7.4			48 7.6	40 9.1	52 7.0	51 7.1	52 7.0
20 18.3	21 17.1	22 16.3			18 19.8	18 20.3	18 20.8	22 16.6	24 14.9
51 7.1	51 7.1	59 6.2	Cost of Sales/Inventory		73 5.0	30 12.3	41 8.9	65 5.6	59 6.2
114 3.2	107 3.4	104 3.5			192 1.9	111 3.3	87 4.2	130 2.8	94 3.9
18 20.3	19 18.8	16 22.2			1 461.1	19 19.7	9 40.1	12 30.0	21 17.0
33 11.0	33 11.0	33 11.0	Cost of Sales/Payables		35 10.5	29 12.6	23 16.0	26 13.8	36 10.1
58 6.3	57 6.4	58 6.3			85 4.3	42 8.7	54 6.7	61 6.0	56 6.5
5.8	6.4	5.3			4.3	7.1	4.4	5.3	5.6
10.7	12.0	10.7	Sales/Working Capital		12.5	24.1	9.7	9.1	10.5
30.6	33.5	33.9			-19.1	-18.3	65.5	20.4	30.6
27.0	25.1	33.1			30.8	18.9	74.6	73.3	34.0
(246) 6.8	(236) 7.9	(201) 8.5	EBIT/Interest		(11) 3.9	(13) 4.2	(24) 4.5	(42) 13.1	(109) 9.9
2.4	2.7	2.5			1.4	-3.3	1.6	4.0	3.6
20.4	16.7	20.0							66.5
(54) 5.1	(49) 3.0	(38) 3.0	Net Profit + Depr., Dep., Amort./Cur. Mat. L/T/D						(26) 4.2
1.4	1.8	.9							2.1
.0	.0	.0			.0	.0	.0	.0	.0
.2	.2	.2	Fixed/Worth		.1	.1	.1	.1	.2
.8	.9	.8			-1.3	.8	.3	.5	.8
.9	1.0	.8			.4	1.0	.7	.6	.9
1.9	2.0	2.1	Debt/Worth		3.7	1.5	2.0	1.8	2.5
7.4	6.9	7.5			-3.4	NM	8.5	4.3	7.6
65.4	76.9	76.3			91.6	65.5	57.0	97.8	77.4
(263) 29.6	(239) 33.7	(224) 32.5	% Profit Before Taxes/Tangible Net Worth		(12) 49.2	(14) 16.7	(27) 23.3	(54) 38.4	(112) 31.3
10.9	12.5	12.2			13.3	-2.1	5.6	19.0	14.6
19.0	21.4	20.9			31.2	30.5	16.3	29.6	18.2
8.3	8.5	9.1	% Profit Before Taxes/Total Assets		14.6	4.7	6.6	14.1	7.8
2.2	3.0	2.5			.6	-4.1	2.3	3.3	2.9
324.2	384.2	292.2			UND	UND	805.6	318.3	211.2
75.8	84.2	67.9	Sales/Net Fixed Assets		80.5	62.5	66.2	62.8	68.0
27.6	26.2	20.3			26.8	16.5	16.8	24.1	23.2
4.4	4.5	4.2			6.9	6.9	4.0	4.1	4.1
3.0	3.1	2.8	Sales/Total Assets		2.3	3.5	3.0	2.8	2.9
1.9	2.0	1.9			1.4	2.0	1.9	2.0	1.9
.1	.1	.2			.4		.2	.2	.1
(219) .4	(202) .4	(187) .4	% Depr., Dep., Amort./Sales		(10) .6		(20) .8	(40) .5	(105) .3
1.0	1.1	1.0			2.3		1.5	1.6	.9
1.0	.8	1.0				1.4	1.1	.7	.6
(108) 2.5	(100) 1.8	(99) 2.0	% Officers', Directors' Owners' Comp/Sales			(11) 3.6	(12) 2.0	(22) 1.5	(41) 1.2
4.3	3.5	4.1				7.7	3.2	3.6	2.6
19365564M	20814686M	20949433M	Net Sales ($)	3999M	32965M	69047M	221251M	940138M	19682033M
7549348M	8026928M	7280621M	Total Assets ($)	3980M	17432M	23693M	104336M	392321M	6738859M

M = $ thousand MM = $ million

See Pages 9 through 22 for Explanation of Ratios and Data

Current Data Sorted by Assets							Comparative Historical Data	
						Type of Statement		
		1	10	3	4	Unqualified	22	13
	6	18	14			Reviewed	44	61
2	6	15	1			Compiled	24	30
10	20	16	1			Tax Returns	37	38
5	13	20	15	1	2	Other	48	66
32 (4/1-9/30/13)		151 (10/1/13-3/31/14)					4/1/09-3/31/10 ALL	4/1/10-3/31/11 ALL
0-500M	500M-2MM	2-10MM	10-50MM	50-100MM	100-250MM			
17	45	70	41	4	6	**NUMBER OF STATEMENTS**	175	208
%	%	%	%	%	%	**ASSETS**	%	%
27.6	11.5	10.6	7.7			Cash & Equivalents	9.9	8.9
26.2	26.4	30.6	29.3			Trade Receivables (net)	29.8	28.3
26.7	42.7	43.4	42.3			Inventory	41.2	40.2
3.9	1.9	1.8	1.6			All Other Current	3.5	4.3
84.5	82.4	86.5	81.0			Total Current	84.4	81.7
8.1	4.5	5.6	8.5			Fixed Assets (net)	6.6	8.4
2.9	4.9	2.0	6.2			Intangibles (net)	3.4	4.3
4.6	8.1	5.9	4.3			All Other Non-Current	5.6	5.7
100.0	100.0	100.0	100.0			Total	100.0	100.0
						LIABILITIES		
25.8	13.6	15.8	16.9			Notes Payable-Short Term	17.6	15.6
4.3	.7	.7	.6			Cur. Mat.-L.T.D.	3.1	2.8
37.1	22.4	24.0	15.7			Trade Payables	20.1	21.3
.1	.0	.0	.2			Income Taxes Payable	.1	.2
3.1	4.8	10.0	9.8			All Other Current	9.3	7.4
70.5	41.6	50.6	43.3			Total Current	50.2	47.3
29.6	6.4	4.3	4.5			Long-Term Debt	7.6	8.7
.0	.0	.2	.3			Deferred Taxes	.2	.1
5.9	8.8	5.1	4.6			All Other Non-Current	8.8	7.5
-6.1	43.2	39.8	47.3			Net Worth	33.2	36.3
100.0	100.0	100.0	100.0			Total Liabilties & Net Worth	100.0	100.0
						INCOME DATA		
100.0	100.0	100.0	100.0			Net Sales	100.0	100.0
40.5	31.8	30.9	30.1			Gross Profit	31.7	31.1
34.4	28.5	26.5	23.9			Operating Expenses	27.9	26.7
6.1	3.3	4.4	6.2			Operating Profit	3.8	4.4
.2	.6	.6	.6			All Other Expenses (net)	.7	.5
5.9	2.7	3.8	5.6			Profit Before Taxes	3.0	3.9
						RATIOS		
3.7	5.1	3.3	3.2				3.0	3.2
1.4	2.2	1.8	1.8			Current	1.7	1.7
1.0	1.2	1.3	1.3				1.2	1.2
3.2	3.0	1.9	1.4				1.4	1.4
1.0	.9	.6	.9			Quick	.8	.7
.3	.4	.4	.6				.4	.4
0 UND	**14** 26.5	**21** 17.1	**27** 13.7				**26** 14.2	**19** 18.8
12 30.8	**29** 12.5	**33** 11.1	**54** 6.8			Sales/Receivables	**40** 9.1	**37** 9.9
35 10.5	**45** 8.1	**66** 5.5	**73** 5.0				**62** 5.9	**58** 6.3
0 UND	**18** 20.0	**33** 10.9	**79** 4.6				**48** 7.5	**37** 9.8
12 29.4	**70** 5.2	**107** 3.4	**122** 3.0			Cost of Sales/Inventory	**94** 3.9	**86** 4.2
89 4.1	**166** 2.2	**152** 2.4	**174** 2.1				**147** 2.5	**135** 2.7
7 55.7	**10** 37.6	**18** 20.8	**20** 18.7				**18** 20.8	**16** 22.6
22 16.7	**29** 12.4	**40** 9.2	**36** 10.0			Cost of Sales/Payables	**34** 10.9	**31** 11.8
94 3.9	**51** 7.2	**66** 5.5	**55** 6.6				**53** 6.9	**57** 6.4
5.0	4.0	3.7	3.1				3.9	4.2
13.7	6.9	7.9	5.7			Sales/Working Capital	7.1	7.9
NM	34.5	19.8	10.9				16.5	24.6
41.4	25.1	22.9	31.1				13.4	19.7
(12) 3.1	(33) 10.1	(58) 5.4	(38) 8.6			EBIT/Interest	(151) 2.8	(184) 5.0
.7	2.2	2.4	2.3				1.3	1.9
							2.6	14.0
						Net Profit + Depr., Dep., Amort./Cur. Mat. L/T/D	(19) 1.7	(22) 3.0
							-.3	1.0
.0	.0	.0	.0				.0	.0
.0	.1	.1	.1			Fixed/Worth	.1	.1
NM	.3	.3	.4				.4	.5
.6	.3	.5	.7				.8	.9
2.1	1.5	1.5	1.3			Debt/Worth	2.0	1.9
-7.5	7.9	4.2	3.1				4.7	4.7
124.8	55.2	41.8	42.3				39.8	47.3
(10) 47.2	(41) 17.5	(64) 15.7	(39) 19.3			% Profit Before Taxes/Tangible Net Worth	(153) 15.3	(181) 22.3
19.1	4.6	6.8	7.3				2.3	10.2
46.4	17.8	13.3	14.6				13.5	17.3
14.8	8.1	4.9	8.3			% Profit Before Taxes/Total Assets	4.3	7.7
.0	1.5	2.6	2.5				.8	2.2
UND	999.8	717.3	99.8				440.0	433.3
907.0	151.6	83.6	45.3			Sales/Net Fixed Assets	76.9	108.4
32.3	40.5	32.1	16.7				32.0	29.3
6.7	4.4	3.5	2.4				3.2	3.5
4.3	2.9	2.5	1.9			Sales/Total Assets	2.2	2.4
2.9	2.0	1.9	1.5				1.7	1.8
	.2	.1	.1				.2	.1
	(22) .3	(50) .3	(36) .4			% Depr., Dep., Amort./Sales	(129) .4	(136) .4
	.4	.7	.8				1.0	.8
3.0	2.2	1.3	1.2				1.6	1.3
(13) 6.9	(31) 4.5	(35) 2.4	(15) 2.0			% Officers', Directors' Owners' Comp/Sales	(89) 3.4	(97) 2.5
13.9	7.9	5.9	5.9				7.0	6.3
19429M	179049M	1003168M	1829903M	647650M	1495871M	Net Sales ($)	4640146M	4965890M
4462M	51708M	342425M	975935M	273649M	775344M	Total Assets ($)	1971063M	1994236M

M = $ thousand MM = $ million

See Pages 9 through 22 for Explanation of Ratios and Data

Comparative Historical Data				Current Data Sorted by Sales					
			Type of Statement						
18	15	18	Unqualified					1	17
57	46	38	Reviewed	1	2	3	5	20	7
27	20	24	Compiled	2	2	4	8	5	3
47	59	47	Tax Returns	8	15	4	11	6	3
58	66	56	Other	3	8	6	7	16	16
					32 (4/1-9/30/13)			151 (10/1/13-3/31/14)	
4/1/11-3/31/12 ALL	**4/1/12-3/31/13 ALL**	**4/1/13-3/31/14 ALL**		**0-1MM**	**1-3MM**	**3-5MM**	**5-10MM**	**10-25MM**	**25MM & OVER**
207	206	183	**NUMBER OF STATEMENTS**	14	27	17	31	48	46
%	%	%	**ASSETS**	%	%	%	%	%	%
10.0	11.8	11.5	Cash & Equivalents	26.2	13.3	10.6	11.7	8.5	9.2
28.3	28.4	28.5	Trade Receivables (net)	17.7	29.3	27.7	33.1	26.3	30.9
41.6	41.2	41.2	Inventory	30.0	42.3	45.5	35.0	49.5	37.9
4.0	2.5	2.0	All Other Current	5.2	.1	2.1	3.0	2.0	1.3
83.9	83.9	83.2	Total Current	79.1	85.0	85.9	82.9	86.2	79.3
6.9	7.0	6.4	Fixed Assets (net)	2.7	7.9	3.6	6.7	6.2	7.9
3.3	2.8	4.6	Intangibles (net)	5.5	2.8	3.9	3.3	2.7	8.5
5.8	6.3	5.8	All Other Non-Current	12.7	4.2	6.5	7.2	4.9	4.3
100.0	100.0	100.0	Total	100.0	100.0	100.0	100.0	100.0	100.0
			LIABILITIES						
16.4	14.5	16.8	Notes Payable-Short Term	28.6	14.2	14.0	18.8	14.2	16.9
1.7	1.8	1.1	Cur. Mat.-L.T.D.	.0	3.3	.6	1.0	.6	.7
24.5	26.1	22.9	Trade Payables	28.8	23.5	15.7	27.4	24.3	18.8
.3	.1	.1	Income Taxes Payable	.0	.1	.0	.0	.0	.3
9.0	8.7	7.9	All Other Current	2.9	2.0	7.4	11.0	7.9	10.7
51.8	51.2	48.6	Total Current	60.4	43.1	37.8	58.3	47.1	47.4
8.6	9.3	7.6	Long-Term Debt	11.7	14.5	8.4	8.0	3.7	5.7
.1	.2	.2	Deferred Taxes	.0	.0	.0	.2	.4	.1
6.4	6.1	6.1	All Other Non-Current	6.4	13.5	3.0	6.4	4.5	4.4
33.1	33.2	37.5	Net Worth	21.5	28.9	50.7	27.2	44.3	42.4
100.0	100.0	100.0	Total Liabilties & Net Worth	100.0	100.0	100.0	100.0	100.0	100.0
			INCOME DATA						
100.0	100.0	100.0	Net Sales	100.0	100.0	100.0	100.0	100.0	100.0
30.8	29.1	31.6	Gross Profit	42.3	37.3	30.8	25.4	33.5	27.6
26.2	24.8	26.9	Operating Expenses	39.8	31.4	27.0	20.9	28.9	22.2
4.6	4.3	4.7	Operating Profit	2.5	5.8	3.8	4.5	4.6	5.3
.4	.5	.6	All Other Expenses (net)	.3	.8	.5	.6	.6	.7
4.2	3.7	4.1	Profit Before Taxes	2.3	5.0	3.3	3.9	4.0	4.6
			RATIOS						
3.1	3.3	3.5		4.4	3.7	6.1	2.7	3.4	2.4
1.7	1.6	1.8	Current	2.7	2.3	2.1	1.5	1.8	1.6
1.2	1.2	1.2		1.0	1.4	1.4	1.0	1.3	1.2
1.2	1.4	1.9		2.8	3.4	4.0	1.6	1.3	1.4
.7	.8	.8	Quick	.9	1.0	.9	.9	.6	.8
.5	.5	.4		.4	.4	.4	.3	.4	.6
17 21.4	**17** 21.0	**18** 19.9		**0** UND	**13** 28.3	**27** 13.3	**18** 20.0	**15** 24.8	**24** 15.1
36 10.1	**36** 10.0	**35** 10.5	Sales/Receivables	**16** 23.3	**34** 10.6	**37** 9.8	**29** 12.5	**30** 12.3	**50** 7.3
57 6.4	**60** 6.1	**57** 6.4		**49** 7.4	**78** 4.7	**47** 7.7	**66** 5.5	**47** 7.7	**63** 5.8
40 9.2	**35** 10.5	**36** 10.2		**0** UND	**8** 44.1	**61** 6.0	**14** 26.5	**79** 4.6	**56** 6.5
83 4.4	**85** 4.3	**101** 3.6	Cost of Sales/Inventory	**70** 5.2	**122** 3.0	**91** 4.0	**50** 7.3	**130** 2.8	**99** 3.7
146 2.5	**152** 2.4	**146** 2.5		**159** 2.3	**182** 2.0	**159** 2.3	**118** 3.1	**192** 1.9	**126** 2.9
15 25.1	**16** 22.3	**17** 21.4		**0** UND	**8** 44.5	**8** 48.3	**16** 22.5	**20** 18.7	**22** 16.7
36 10.2	**36** 10.1	**36** 10.0	Cost of Sales/Payables	**24** 15.0	**42** 8.6	**23** 16.1	**35** 10.3	**41** 8.9	**34** 10.7
65 5.6	**68** 5.4	**61** 6.0		**118** 3.1	**70** 5.2	**47** 7.7	**51** 7.1	**69** 5.3	**47** 7.8
4.2	4.0	3.9		2.1	3.6	3.4	5.7	3.5	4.8
8.5	10.0	7.7	Sales/Working Capital	8.8	6.0	4.4	13.2	6.4	8.6
21.9	21.4	20.6		-309.5	12.9	13.1	403.8	17.2	20.8
16.6	18.5	27.1			20.4	64.3	22.6	21.9	40.9
(175) 5.3	(157) 5.1	(151) 6.4	EBIT/Interest		(20) 9.8	(12) 4.3	(26) 6.4	(43) 4.7	(41) 9.9
2.4	2.0	2.1			1.9	2.9	2.4	1.6	2.7
18.5	4.7	20.3							26.9
(23) 6.7	(16) 2.5	(18) 4.5	Net Profit + Depr., Dep., Amort./Cur. Mat. L/T/D						(11) 9.8
2.1	.8	2.2							3.0
.0	.0	.0		.0	.0	.0	.0	.0	.0
.1	.1	.1	Fixed/Worth	.0	.1	.0	.1	.1	.2
.4	.3	.4		.0	.3	.2	1.5	.3	.7
.9	.8	.6		.3	.5	.2	.5	.6	.9
2.0	1.9	1.5	Debt/Worth	1.1	1.8	.7	2.6	1.4	1.7
6.1	5.2	4.5		-11.1	4.3	2.3	13.6	3.8	4.5
54.2	48.5	47.9			59.8	27.2	76.5	34.9	44.3
(176) 24.7	(183) 21.3	(161) 17.9	% Profit Before Taxes/Tangible Net Worth		(24) 28.1	(15) 14.0	(26) 17.6	(46) 15.3	(41) 20.9
9.3	6.3	7.2			8.4	6.6	7.3	5.4	11.2
17.5	17.2	15.4		29.0	26.8	18.2	17.5	14.9	14.5
7.3	6.6	6.5	% Profit Before Taxes/Total Assets	7.3	8.3	6.7	4.9	5.1	8.4
2.1	2.3	2.2		-3.6	1.4	3.4	2.6	1.7	3.0
583.9	691.9	540.2		UND	355.1	UND	434.8	297.1	139.3
118.1	115.3	80.4	Sales/Net Fixed Assets	UND	51.3	372.6	125.4	73.4	47.4
39.1	31.4	25.1		117.7	21.3	55.5	27.2	31.2	16.8
3.6	4.0	3.6		4.4	4.3	3.3	4.4	3.2	2.8
2.6	2.5	2.5	Sales/Total Assets	2.5	2.3	2.8	3.6	2.4	2.3
1.9	1.8	1.8		1.4	1.5	1.8	2.1	1.8	1.8
.1	.1	.1			.2		.1	.1	.1
(131) .3	(126) .4	(121) .4	% Depr., Dep., Amort./Sales		(18) .3		(17) .3	(36) .4	(40) .5
.7	.8	.8			.8		.9	.7	.9
1.5	1.4	1.6		5.9	2.8	2.6	1.1	1.1	1.2
(104) 2.8	(105) 3.0	(96) 3.3	% Officers', Directors' Owners' Comp/Sales	(10) 8.5	(21) 4.5	(10) 5.3	(16) 2.4	(21) 2.1	(18) 1.9
5.7	6.4	6.6		13.5	7.4	7.0	5.6	4.1	5.9
5089224M	**5744508M**	**5175070M**	Net Sales ($)	**9730M**	**56093M**	**64735M**	**230578M**	**763611M**	**4050323M**
2120985M	**2445264M**	**2423523M**	Total Assets ($)	**5258M**	**27530M**	**28241M**	**86826M**	**368356M**	**1907312M**

M = $ thousand MM = $ million

See Pages 9 through 22 for Explanation of Ratios and Data

	Current Data Sorted by Assets						Comparative Historical Data	
Type of Statement								
Unqualified		2	4	10	6	4	34	33
Reviewed		4	22	13	1		52	47
Compiled	1	1	8				11	15
Tax Returns	2	7	4				17	21
Other	4	9	20	21	3		46	65
	20 (4/1-9/30/13)		126 (10/1/13-3/31/14)				4/1/09-3/31/10 ALL	4/1/10-3/31/11 ALL
	0-500M	500M-2MM	2-10MM	10-50MM	50-100MM	100-250MM		
NUMBER OF STATEMENTS	7	23	58	44	10	4	160	181
ASSETS	%	%	%	%	%	%	%	%
Cash & Equivalents		10.5	11.4	5.2	1.7		11.3	7.9
Trade Receivables (net)		24.5	29.5	30.6	27.8		29.8	31.3
Inventory		49.2	41.3	42.0	49.8		36.3	39.4
All Other Current		3.6	4.9	3.0	2.0		4.4	5.0
Total Current		87.9	87.0	80.8	81.2		81.8	83.6
Fixed Assets (net)		6.7	6.2	5.4	9.5		8.9	7.6
Intangibles (net)		1.2	2.9	9.4	5.6		3.0	4.2
All Other Non-Current		4.3	3.8	4.3	3.7		6.3	4.6
Total		100.0	100.0	100.0	100.0		100.0	100.0
LIABILITIES								
Notes Payable-Short Term		10.4	17.8	20.3	24.8		16.7	16.6
Cur. Mat.-L.T.D.		2.5	.6	.9	1.3		1.8	2.1
Trade Payables		30.1	21.0	16.4	15.0		16.7	17.5
Income Taxes Payable		.0	.0	.1	.0		.1	.4
All Other Current		15.5	9.4	8.7	7.8		10.8	14.9
Total Current		58.4	48.7	46.4	49.0		46.2	51.5
Long-Term Debt		8.4	2.8	7.2	11.4		5.4	4.4
Deferred Taxes		.0	.0	.0	.0		.1	.2
All Other Non-Current		7.8	7.1	7.2	4.5		6.6	12.2
Net Worth		25.4	41.4	39.1	35.0		41.6	31.7
Total Liabilties & Net Worth		100.0	100.0	100.0	100.0		100.0	100.0
INCOME DATA								
Net Sales		100.0	100.0	100.0	100.0		100.0	100.0
Gross Profit		33.4	31.9	33.8	27.3		33.5	31.8
Operating Expenses		33.1	28.5	26.9	22.9		29.2	27.0
Operating Profit		.3	3.3	6.9	4.4		4.3	4.8
All Other Expenses (net)		1.8	.8	1.0	.7		.6	.8
Profit Before Taxes		-1.5	2.5	6.0	3.7		3.7	4.0
RATIOS								
Current		4.2	4.8	2.3	3.1		4.3	3.2
		1.4	1.9	1.7	1.6		1.9	1.8
		.9	1.4	1.4	1.2		1.3	1.3
Quick		1.4	1.7	1.2	1.1		1.8	1.5
		.6	.9	.7	.5		.9	.8
		.1	.5	.5	.3		.4	.5
Sales/Receivables		8 44.2	28 13.0	29 12.5	26 13.8		25 14.6	25 14.5
		32 11.4	45 8.2	45 8.2	40 9.1		43 8.5	45 8.1
		54 6.8	68 5.4	74 4.9	56 6.5		63 5.8	65 5.6
Cost of Sales/Inventory		45 8.2	47 7.7	63 5.8	76 4.8		41 8.9	43 8.5
		114 3.2	107 3.4	104 3.5	114 3.2		88 4.2	104 3.5
		146 2.5	166 2.2	174 2.1	166 2.2		138 2.6	156 2.3
Cost of Sales/Payables		23 16.0	14 26.0	16 22.5	21 17.4		12 31.0	11 32.7
		45 8.2	40 9.1	29 12.6	31 11.7		26 14.0	29 12.4
		81 4.5	73 5.0	51 7.1	37 9.8		54 6.8	55 6.6
Sales/Working Capital		3.6	3.3	3.8	4.5		3.8	3.7
		8.2	5.5	5.7	6.9		6.9	7.1
		-35.8	11.4	12.3	15.0		14.9	18.3
EBIT/Interest		11.8	11.1	24.2	21.1		18.3	18.3
		(19) 1.5	(47) 4.5	(39) 6.0	9.1		(137) 5.8	(147) 6.4
		-5.8	1.6	2.0	1.2		1.6	1.9
Net Profit + Depr., Dep., Amort./Cur. Mat. L/T/D							17.5	33.4
							(19) 7.0	(26) 7.0
							1.7	4.2
Fixed/Worth		.0	.0	.0	.1		.0	.0
		.1	.1	.1	.3		.1	.1
		-4.4	.3	.4	.6		.3	.4
Debt/Worth		.5	.4	.7	1.2		.4	.6
		2.9	1.5	2.4	1.9		1.1	1.5
		-10.2	2.8	6.0	5.9		3.5	5.2
% Profit Before Taxes/Tangible Net Worth		29.8	51.2	54.4			37.9	54.2
		(17) 9.7	(55) 14.8	(38) 34.1			(146) 15.5	(158) 25.3
		-8.0	1.9	11.8			3.0	7.3
% Profit Before Taxes/Total Assets		8.9	15.3	20.4	17.2		16.5	18.9
		.8	5.6	9.6	9.1		6.6	8.7
		-15.9	.6	4.5	.4		1.1	1.7
Sales/Net Fixed Assets		999.8	382.6	304.7	149.0		200.2	313.0
		69.1	71.3	73.3	38.3		61.0	91.2
		28.0	28.0	21.7	13.5		23.4	27.6
Sales/Total Assets		3.8	2.9	3.0	2.5		3.2	3.2
		3.0	2.1	2.1	2.4		2.4	2.2
		2.3	1.5	1.5	1.6		1.7	1.7
% Depr., Dep., Amort./Sales		.3	.1	.2	.2		.3	.2
		(11) .6	(44) .4	(33) .7	.6		(124) .5	(126) .4
		1.3	.8	1.2	2.5		1.0	1.3
% Officers', Directors' Owners' Comp/Sales		1.5	1.9	1.1			1.5	1.2
		(11) 2.7	(20) 2.7	(10) 2.2			(61) 3.3	(54) 2.5
		5.6	5.7	3.3			6.6	4.8
Net Sales ($)	30488M	82233M	657360M	2108167M	1493558M	1180235M	6017797M	6688652M
Total Assets ($)	2348M	29626M	293621M	996818M	673230M	590592M	2782683M	3141166M

M = $ thousand MM = $ million

See Pages 9 through 22 for Explanation of Ratios and Data

Comparative Historical Data / Current Data Sorted by Sales

4/1/11-3/31/12 ALL	4/1/12-3/31/13 ALL	4/1/13-3/31/14 ALL	Type of Statement	0-1MM	1-3MM	3-5MM	5-10MM	10-25MM	25MM & OVER
35	27	26	Unqualified				4	5	17
42	44	40	Reviewed		1	4	9	11	15
10	13	10	Compiled		1	2	3	4	
19	17	13	Tax Returns	1	4	5	2	1	
62	76	57	Other	2	3	4	13	16	19
				20 (4/1-9/30/13)			126 (10/1/13-3/31/14)		
168	177	146	NUMBER OF STATEMENTS	3	9	15	31	37	51
%	%	%	**ASSETS**	%	%	%	%	%	%
9.5	8.7	8.8	Cash & Equivalents			12.1	11.3	9.4	5.1
28.5	27.2	28.4	Trade Receivables (net)			21.5	28.3	28.9	30.6
41.9	40.7	42.9	Inventory			48.7	38.2	42.3	45.1
2.8	4.0	3.7	All Other Current			1.7	7.0	3.5	2.9
82.7	80.6	83.8	Total Current			84.0	84.7	84.1	83.7
7.6	8.3	6.9	Fixed Assets (net)			8.2	4.4	7.5	5.9
5.2	5.2	4.8	Intangibles (net)			1.5	5.0	4.7	6.5
4.5	5.8	4.4	All Other Non-Current			6.3	5.8	3.8	3.9
100.0	100.0	100.0	Total			100.0	100.0	100.0	100.0
			LIABILITIES						
17.9	16.0	18.1	Notes Payable-Short Term			8.9	20.6	17.2	20.5
1.6	1.3	2.0	Cur. Mat.-L.T.D.			.6	1.6	.6	1.0
17.5	19.1	20.1	Trade Payables			22.1	25.2	17.9	18.1
.3	.1	.0	Income Taxes Payable			.0	.0	.0	.0
10.9	10.8	10.5	All Other Current			9.9	14.2	8.7	9.4
48.2	47.2	50.8	Total Current			41.5	61.6	44.4	49.1
6.1	6.8	7.7	Long-Term Debt			1.7	3.3	8.1	6.9
.1	.1	.0	Deferred Taxes			.1	.0	.0	.0
7.3	8.9	6.9	All Other Non-Current			9.8	9.6	3.1	7.4
38.3	37.0	34.6	Net Worth			46.9	25.6	44.4	36.6
100.0	100.0	100.0	Total Liabilities & Net Worth			100.0	100.0	100.0	100.0
			INCOME DATA						
100.0	100.0	100.0	Net Sales			100.0	100.0	100.0	100.0
32.0	31.9	33.0	Gross Profit			36.6	32.6	34.1	30.1
27.5	27.8	28.6	Operating Expenses			37.2	31.9	27.0	24.0
4.6	4.1	4.4	Operating Profit			-.6	.7	7.1	6.1
.9	1.1	1.1	All Other Expenses (net)			.9	.6	2.1	.5
3.7	3.0	3.3	Profit Before Taxes			-1.5	.1	5.1	5.6
			RATIOS						
3.0	3.1	3.3				10.2	3.9	4.3	2.6
1.9	1.8	1.9	Current			3.3	1.9	1.9	1.7
1.3	1.3	1.3				1.4	1.3	1.4	1.4
1.4	1.5	1.4				6.0	1.5	1.7	1.1
.8	.7	.8	Quick			.9	.8	.8	.7
.5	.5	.5				.4	.3	.5	.5
22 16.9	**22** 16.6	**24** 15.4				**20** 18.6	**8** 45.3	**29** 12.7	**28** 12.9
42 8.6	**40** 9.1	**39** 9.3	Sales/Receivables			**36** 10.1	**41** 9.0	**37** 9.8	**44** 8.3
61 6.0	**62** 5.9	**69** 5.3				**57** 6.4	**73** 5.0	**62** 5.9	**72** 5.1
56 6.5	**49** 7.4	**54** 6.7				**45** 8.2	**54** 6.8	**43** 8.4	**62** 5.9
104 3.5	**96** 3.8	**104** 3.5	Cost of Sales/Inventory			**130** 2.8	**81** 4.5	**118** 3.1	**104** 3.5
152 2.4	**159** 2.3	**159** 2.3				**281** 1.3	**122** 3.0	**166** 2.2	**146** 2.5
14 26.8	**13** 28.7	**17** 21.4				**14** 26.5	**11** 34.1	**14** 25.5	**21** 17.0
30 12.2	**29** 12.5	**33** 10.9	Cost of Sales/Payables			**41** 8.8	**40** 9.1	**40** 9.2	**29** 12.5
51 7.1	**54** 6.8	**58** 6.3				**81** 4.5	**74** 4.9	**55** 6.6	**43** 8.5
3.8	3.5	3.7				1.3	3.8	3.7	4.0
6.7	6.9	6.3	Sales/Working Capital			4.4	6.3	6.3	6.9
14.3	13.5	16.4				24.4	34.5	15.3	13.0
20.1	16.3	13.3				16.2	5.5	12.0	27.8
(143) 4.7	(153) 4.3	(123) 5.1	EBIT/Interest			(10) 2.7	(25) 2.0	(30) 5.7	(47) 10.0
1.4	1.2	1.3				-.5	-1.5	1.7	2.7
23.2	31.3	33.6							22.7
(22) 3.8	(15) 5.8	(14) 5.6	Net Profit + Depr., Dep., Amort./Cur. Mat. L/T/D						(11) 4.8
.9	-.1	.6							1.3
.0	.0	.0				.0	.0	.0	.0
.1	.1	.1	Fixed/Worth			.1	.1	.1	.1
.7	.7	.4				.4	1.2	.3	.4
.5	.6	.6				.1	.4	.4	.8
1.6	1.6	1.8	Debt/Worth			.7	1.6	1.8	2.4
5.6	6.7	5.8				7.7	10.1	3.4	5.7
44.9	48.7	48.2				15.9	38.7	56.5	65.1
(146) 20.4	(153) 19.0	(127) 22.2	% Profit Before Taxes/Tangible Net Worth			(13) 5.6	(26) 11.7	(34) 31.0	(46) 33.0
5.0	2.9	6.8				-9.2	-.7	15.8	11.8
15.6	15.0	16.7				6.8	15.1	19.4	19.5
8.3	5.8	6.8	% Profit Before Taxes/Total Assets			.5	3.6	7.4	9.9
1.3	.5	.6				-6.0	-2.8	4.6	4.6
257.3	217.5	277.0				116.8	446.8	160.9	257.7
79.5	60.2	67.4	Sales/Net Fixed Assets			47.3	140.5	62.8	74.4
20.4	22.3	24.1				24.3	31.3	20.6	24.0
3.2	3.2	3.1				3.3	3.5	3.1	2.9
2.3	2.2	2.3	Sales/Total Assets			2.3	2.4	2.3	2.3
1.7	1.5	1.6				1.0	1.5	1.7	1.7
.2	.2	.2				.2	.1	.3	.2
(120) .5	(126) .5	(106) .5	% Depr., Dep., Amort./Sales			(10) .6	(18) .3	(30) .5	(41) .4
1.1	1.2	1.0				1.0	.8	1.2	1.1
1.3	1.2	1.7					1.6		1.0
(55) 2.2	(53) 2.4	(44) 2.6	% Officers', Directors' Owners' Comp/Sales				(10) 4.2		(11) 2.3
4.0	5.6	4.9					8.7		3.8
6895797M	7838365M	5552041M	Net Sales ($)	2156M	19805M	51055M	229136M	613382M	4636507M
3441203M	4013647M	2586235M	Total Assets ($)	1302M	11077M	33006M	108038M	297604M	2135208M

M = $ thousand MM = $ million

See Pages 9 through 22 for Explanation of Ratios and Data

	Current Data Sorted by Assets						Comparative Historical Data	
Type of Statement								
Unqualified		2	4	21	6	2	47	49
Reviewed	1	5	41	19	1	1	57	65
Compiled	4	10	14	2			11	17
Tax Returns	4	20	16	1			43	25
Other	7	20	33	25	14	6	60	104
	25 (4/1-9/30/13)		254 (10/1/13-3/31/14)				4/1/09-3/31/10	4/1/10-3/31/11
	0-500M	500M-2MM	2-10MM	10-50MM	50-100MM	100-250MM	ALL	ALL
NUMBER OF STATEMENTS	16	57	108	68	21	9	218	260
ASSETS	%	%	%	%	%	%	%	%
Cash & Equivalents	8.3	13.6	14.7	7.1	3.4		12.2	10.8
Trade Receivables (net)	26.3	30.4	33.7	28.3	30.7		33.3	30.5
Inventory	40.0	38.9	34.3	40.0	36.3		33.0	35.1
All Other Current	7.8	2.4	5.1	6.5	7.4		5.1	5.8
Total Current	82.5	85.2	87.8	81.9	77.8		83.6	82.2
Fixed Assets (net)	9.5	6.0	5.3	5.5	8.0		7.2	7.5
Intangibles (net)	.1	1.7	1.8	6.8	10.8		3.7	3.8
All Other Non-Current	8.0	7.2	5.1	5.8	3.4		5.5	6.5
Total	100.0	100.0	100.0	100.0	100.0		100.0	100.0
LIABILITIES								
Notes Payable-Short Term	21.0	12.0	18.8	19.0	28.0		20.6	20.5
Cur. Mat.-L.T.D.	12.7	.8	.5	.8	3.3		2.0	2.4
Trade Payables	23.4	24.2	25.2	21.9	17.5		22.0	21.8
Income Taxes Payable	.0	.1	.1	.2	.1		.1	.2
All Other Current	24.4	9.0	5.5	10.2	6.2		8.9	11.2
Total Current	81.5	46.0	50.1	52.1	55.1		53.6	56.1
Long-Term Debt	7.4	6.3	3.4	4.0	6.7		5.0	6.1
Deferred Taxes	.0	.0	.0	.3	.1		.2	.2
All Other Non-Current	4.7	12.2	4.4	4.2	5.9		10.1	9.2
Net Worth	6.4	35.6	42.0	39.4	32.2		31.1	28.3
Total Liabilties & Net Worth	100.0	100.0	100.0	100.0	100.0		100.0	100.0
INCOME DATA								
Net Sales	100.0	100.0	100.0	100.0	100.0		100.0	100.0
Gross Profit	40.3	31.3	31.3	31.5	31.9		31.7	32.1
Operating Expenses	37.5	27.1	25.5	26.2	24.5		27.0	27.2
Operating Profit	2.8	4.2	5.7	5.3	7.4		4.7	4.9
All Other Expenses (net)	1.1	.4	.3	.8	1.1		1.2	.9
Profit Before Taxes	1.7	3.8	5.4	4.5	6.3		3.5	4.0
RATIOS								
Current	1.7	3.2	3.2	2.5	1.9		2.8	2.6
	1.5	1.8	1.8	1.5	1.4		1.7	1.5
	.6	1.3	1.3	1.2	1.2		1.2	1.2
Quick	1.3	1.5	1.7	1.1	1.0		1.6	1.2
	.5	.9	.9	.7	.6		.8	(259) .7
	.2	.6	.5	.4	.4		.6	.5
Sales/Receivables	**0** 771.7	**11** 33.4	**26** 14.3	**13** 29.0	**32** 11.5		**22** 16.2	**19** 19.3
	19 19.5	**26** 13.9	**37** 9.9	**39** 9.3	**63** 5.8		**41** 8.8	**41** 8.8
	39 9.3	**59** 6.2	**70** 5.2	**58** 6.3	**89** 4.1		**63** 5.8	**60** 6.1
Cost of Sales/Inventory	**23** 15.6	**27** 13.6	**27** 13.6	**43** 8.5	**83** 4.4		**30** 12.1	**33** 11.1
	42 8.6	**61** 6.0	**60** 6.1	**78** 4.7	**107** 3.4		**57** 6.4	**65** 5.6
	73 5.0	**111** 3.3	**135** 2.7	**118** 3.1	**122** 3.0		**91** 4.0	**111** 3.3
Cost of Sales/Payables	**2** 152.7	**12** 30.0	**19** 19.7	**17** 21.5	**27** 13.6		**15** 24.4	**18** 20.6
	27 13.5	**30** 12.3	**38** 9.6	**35** 10.5	**50** 7.3		**31** 11.9	**33** 11.2
	41 8.8	**47** 7.7	**65** 5.6	**59** 6.2	**62** 5.9		**57** 6.4	**56** 6.5
Sales/Working Capital	7.0	4.5	4.1	4.6	5.2		5.2	5.7
	17.2	9.7	7.5	11.1	7.4		8.9	9.8
	-53.4	20.7	21.9	25.0	26.2		24.4	31.9
EBIT/Interest	4.6	18.7	20.6	18.4	25.7		15.2	14.9
	(10) 1.7	(47) 7.5	(85) 6.8	(62) 5.8	6.3		(188) 4.4	(213) 4.2
	-5.5	2.6	2.6	2.0	2.1		1.8	1.7
Net Profit + Depr., Dep., Amort./Cur. Mat. L/T/D				14.8			22.4	19.4
				(13) 8.5			(28) 2.7	(36) 3.5
				1.9			.3	.7
Fixed/Worth	.0	.0	.0	.1	.0		.0	.0
	.0	.1	.0	.1	.7		.1	.1
	NM	.3	.2	.3	NM		.4	.6
Debt/Worth	1.4	.9	.5	.9	1.1		.7	.9
	2.4	1.6	1.7	2.0	2.5		1.9	2.4
	-16.8	5.1	5.9	5.6	NM		5.7	8.1
% Profit Before Taxes/Tangible Net Worth	110.0	42.9	66.5	72.1	76.3		62.8	61.1
	(11) 60.3	(49) 19.9	(106) 31.8	(59) 27.8	(16) 36.0		(191) 27.0	(215) 29.2
	21.0	8.7	12.2	7.5	11.0		8.4	7.7
% Profit Before Taxes/Total Assets	24.1	17.1	22.8	20.7	21.5		20.4	19.1
	11.5	5.8	9.9	8.6	6.8		7.8	7.0
	-19.0	3.4	3.0	1.7	2.7		1.7	1.9
Sales/Net Fixed Assets	UND	UND	500.9	308.8	272.2		438.7	279.8
	UND	184.0	144.2	95.5	56.2		114.8	85.8
	50.8	61.5	46.6	38.9	20.4		40.9	34.1
Sales/Total Assets	7.7	4.7	3.7	3.9	2.5		3.9	3.8
	3.9	3.7	2.6	2.9	2.2		2.8	2.7
	2.6	2.4	1.9	1.7	1.4		1.9	1.9
% Depr., Dep., Amort./Sales		.1	.1	.2	.2		.2	.2
		(33) .3	(66) .3	(49) .4	(18) .6		(143) .4	(165) .4
		.5	.6	.6	1.3		.8	.8
% Officers', Directors' Owners' Comp/Sales		1.8	1.3	.8			1.0	1.2
		(30) 2.7	(50) 2.8	(26) 2.1			(107) 2.5	(85) 2.4
		7.4	4.0	3.2			5.0	4.0
Net Sales ($)	28188M	301531M	1524661M	4322333M	3061537M	3333211M	9115726M	12760262M
Total Assets ($)	4652M	77532M	499667M	1533953M	1508064M	1502108M	3625124M	5853432M

M = $ thousand MM = $ million

See Pages 9 through 22 for Explanation of Ratios and Data

Comparative Historical Data				Current Data Sorted by Sales					
			Type of Statement						
50	36	35	Unqualified			2	1	2	30
62	74	68	Reviewed	1	1	1	15	22	28
21	19	30	Compiled	1	4	7	9	7	2
33	45	41	Tax Returns	2	7	10	17	4	1
113	98	105	Other	4	8	14	15	18	46
				25 (4/1-9/30/13)		254 (10/1/13-3/31/14)			
4/1/11-3/31/12 ALL	4/1/12-3/31/13 ALL	4/1/13-3/31/14 ALL		0-1MM	1-3MM	3-5MM	5-10MM	10-25MM	25MM & OVER
279	272	279	**NUMBER OF STATEMENTS**	8	20	34	57	53	107
%	%	%	**ASSETS**	%	%	%	%	%	%
8.6	10.5	11.0	Cash & Equivalents		10.6	16.9	15.1	15.1	5.4
31.1	32.2	30.8	Trade Receivables (net)		21.6	34.1	27.3	34.1	31.8
38.1	36.2	37.3	Inventory		45.5	35.2	39.3	31.2	38.1
6.1	6.0	5.2	All Other Current		4.0	2.0	3.0	8.2	5.9
83.9	84.8	84.2	Total Current		81.8	88.2	84.6	88.6	81.1
6.7	6.2	5.9	Fixed Assets (net)		8.2	3.7	6.8	4.9	5.9
2.6	3.4	4.2	Intangibles (net)		2.7	1.1	1.2	2.1	8.4
6.8	5.6	5.6	All Other Non-Current		7.3	7.0	7.4	4.5	4.5
100.0	100.0	100.0	Total		100.0	100.0	100.0	100.0	100.0
			LIABILITIES						
18.9	18.8	18.0	Notes Payable-Short Term		15.3	9.9	21.4	15.9	19.6
1.6	1.3	1.6	Cur. Mat.-L.T.D.		4.5	1.2	1.9	.6	1.4
21.2	26.1	23.3	Trade Payables		18.8	26.1	21.4	27.1	23.1
.1	.3	.1	Income Taxes Payable		.0	.1	.1	.2	.1
10.1	11.1	8.6	All Other Current		19.5	6.2	5.8	6.1	9.2
52.0	57.7	51.6	Total Current		58.0	43.4	50.5	49.9	53.3
6.4	4.9	5.3	Long-Term Debt		11.6	4.0	3.9	2.4	6.0
.1	.1	.2	Deferred Taxes		.0	.0	.0	.1	.5
7.0	6.3	6.5	All Other Non-Current		5.4	15.9	6.1	3.4	5.3
34.5	31.0	36.5	Net Worth		25.0	36.6	39.5	44.2	34.8
100.0	100.0	100.0	Total Liabilties & Net Worth		100.0	100.0	100.0	100.0	100.0
			INCOME DATA						
100.0	100.0	100.0	Net Sales		100.0	100.0	100.0	100.0	100.0
33.2	31.5	32.0	Gross Profit		33.7	34.8	32.5	28.2	31.1
28.4	26.6	26.9	Operating Expenses		31.1	29.7	26.8	23.4	25.7
4.8	4.9	5.2	Operating Profit		2.6	5.1	5.6	4.8	5.4
1.3	.9	.6	All Other Expenses (net)		.7	.3	.6	.0	1.0
3.5	4.0	4.5	Profit Before Taxes		1.9	4.8	5.0	4.8	4.4
			RATIOS						
2.7	2.6	2.7			2.7	4.4	2.8	3.1	2.3
1.7	1.5	1.6	Current		1.7	1.9	1.8	1.6	1.5
1.3	1.1	1.2			1.1	1.4	1.2	1.3	1.2
1.3	1.3	1.4			1.2	2.5	1.5	1.6	1.1
.8	.7	.8	Quick		.8	1.1	.9	.9	.7
.5	.4	.5			.3	.7	.5	.6	.4
21 17.3	**16** 23.4	**16** 23.3			**5** 72.4	**23** 15.7	**14** 26.4	**18** 20.8	**20** 17.9
41 8.8	**38** 9.5	**36** 10.0	Sales/Receivables		**22** 16.4	**45** 8.2	**34** 10.7	**33** 11.1	**40** 9.2
59 6.2	**61** 6.0	**63** 5.8			**62** 5.9	**76** 4.8	**59** 6.2	**62** 5.9	**61** 6.0
39 9.4	**30** 12.3	**34** 10.8			**45** 8.1	**42** 8.6	**35** 10.3	**19** 19.2	**41** 8.9
73 5.0	**68** 5.4	**70** 5.2	Cost of Sales/Inventory		**85** 4.3	**83** 4.4	**73** 5.0	**37** 9.9	**78** 4.7
122 3.0	**111** 3.3	**122** 3.0			**192** 1.9	**135** 2.7	**130** 2.8	**81** 4.5	**114** 3.2
14 26.9	**17** 21.3	**17** 21.2			**14** 26.4	**17** 21.2	**11** 34.1	**19** 19.6	**22** 16.7
34 10.8	**32** 11.3	**36** 10.0	Cost of Sales/Payables		**32** 11.4	**50** 7.3	**27** 13.4	**37** 9.8	**37** 9.8
56 6.5	**57** 6.4	**59** 6.2			**41** 8.8	**76** 4.8	**53** 6.9	**60** 6.1	**59** 6.2
4.9	5.1	4.6			3.6	3.4	4.6	4.3	5.6
9.1	11.0	8.7	Sales/Working Capital		8.5	5.9	8.4	9.0	11.6
20.4	32.0	23.9			51.2	13.7	27.4	26.9	25.6
17.2	19.8	18.2			8.9	19.9	19.1	34.0	15.5
(238) 3.7	(222) 4.7	(233) 6.3	EBIT/Interest		(16) 2.6	(25) 5.2	(44) 7.0	(44) 8.0	(99) 6.3
1.4	1.5	2.0			.7	2.1	2.0	3.0	2.0
22.0	6.9	15.1							20.7
(32) 5.6	(26) 2.5	(35) 4.0	Net Profit + Depr., Dep., Amort./Cur. Mat. L/T/D						(25) 3.6
1.1	.1	.9							.8
.0	.0	.0			.0	.0	.0	.0	.0
.1	.1	.1	Fixed/Worth		.1	.0	.1	.1	.2
.4	.5	.4			1.2	.2	.4	.2	1.0
.8	.9	.8			1.0	.5	.7	.5	1.0
1.8	2.3	2.0	Debt/Worth		2.4	1.1	1.6	1.6	2.4
4.8	8.1	7.9			21.2	6.7	7.3	3.5	14.9
61.5	72.1	63.2			22.3	38.0	60.3	61.4	79.7
(245) 23.3	(237) 30.3	(246) 31.3	% Profit Before Taxes/Tangible Net Worth		(16) 18.3	(29) 26.9	(55) 31.7	(52) 30.2	(88) 39.8
5.2	8.5	9.6			9.6	9.0	8.9	11.4	10.6
18.1	21.5	21.7			9.5	15.0	23.0	24.6	21.7
6.0	8.8	7.5	% Profit Before Taxes/Total Assets		5.5	5.5	8.4	9.8	8.8
.9	1.4	2.4			.1	2.3	3.2	3.4	2.0
435.7	922.3	478.2			UND	UND	633.3	475.6	322.3
111.2	141.1	123.6	Sales/Net Fixed Assets		198.6	175.6	132.7	139.9	97.4
35.3	40.4	39.2			51.5	35.3	33.7	48.1	36.6
3.9	4.4	4.0			4.5	3.1	4.0	5.2	4.0
2.7	3.0	2.7	Sales/Total Assets		2.4	2.1	2.8	2.9	2.9
1.9	2.0	1.9			1.3	1.7	2.2	2.1	1.9
.1	.1	.1				.2	.2	.1	.1
(181) .3	(170) .3	(179) .3	% Depr., Dep., Amort./Sales			(16) .3	(39) .3	(34) .3	(79) .4
.8	.8	.7				.5	.9	.5	.8
1.3	1.2	1.3			1.2	2.6	1.6	.7	.9
(111) 3.0	(102) 2.5	(121) 2.7	% Officers', Directors' Owners' Comp/Sales		(11) 3.9	(16) 4.3	(32) 2.8	(25) 1.9	(36) 2.0
5.4	6.4	4.6			8.9	8.0	4.5	3.5	3.2
11517104M	**11491329M**	**12571461M**	Net Sales ($)	**3984M**	**40665M**	**136596M**	**413561M**	**815141M**	**11161514M**
4688692M	**4514233M**	**5125976M**	Total Assets ($)	**2075M**	**20388M**	**63139M**	**170748M**	**303792M**	**4565834M**

M = $ thousand MM = $ million

See Pages 9 through 22 for Explanation of Ratios and Data

Current Data Sorted by Assets							Comparative Historical Data	
						Type of Statement		
	2	1	7	4	3	Unqualified	18	17
	2	12	8			Reviewed	31	35
	2	6		1		Compiled	11	11
2	2	5				Tax Returns	7	10
2	5	13	16	4	2	Other	35	37
	11 (4/1-9/30/13)		88 (10/1/13-3/31/14)				4/1/09-3/31/10 ALL	4/1/10-3/31/11 ALL
0-500M	**500M-2MM**	**2-10MM**	**10-50MM**	**50-100MM**	**100-250MM**			
4	13	37	31	9	5	**NUMBER OF STATEMENTS**	102	110
%	%	%	%	%	%	**ASSETS**	%	%
	12.8	7.9	8.5			Cash & Equivalents	11.9	10.1
	30.2	30.7	28.3			Trade Receivables (net)	32.7	29.0
	45.0	40.1	39.8			Inventory	35.9	43.0
	.5	2.4	4.6			All Other Current	4.1	4.5
	88.4	81.0	81.2			Total Current	84.5	86.7
	4.0	4.8	7.0			Fixed Assets (net)	6.6	6.2
	2.2	5.4	3.5			Intangibles (net)	4.2	2.2
	5.3	8.8	8.3			All Other Non-Current	4.7	4.9
	100.0	100.0	100.0			Total	100.0	100.0
						LIABILITIES		
	7.4	13.3	19.0			Notes Payable-Short Term	16.4	17.1
	1.5	.4	1.4			Cur. Mat.-L.T.D.	1.6	1.2
	26.6	27.0	27.1			Trade Payables	17.5	22.0
	.0	.2	.1			Income Taxes Payable	.3	.2
	13.9	11.8	9.7			All Other Current	11.8	8.8
	49.4	52.7	57.3			Total Current	47.7	49.3
	5.2	2.6	3.5			Long-Term Debt	5.3	5.5
	.3	.0	.0			Deferred Taxes	.2	.2
	2.6	5.1	4.2			All Other Non-Current	5.6	6.4
	42.5	39.6	35.0			Net Worth	41.1	38.6
	100.0	100.0	100.0			Total Liabilities & Net Worth	100.0	100.0
						INCOME DATA		
	100.0	100.0	100.0			Net Sales	100.0	100.0
	30.4	27.9	32.4			Gross Profit	31.6	32.8
	27.8	27.1	28.9			Operating Expenses	27.8	28.3
	2.6	.8	3.5			Operating Profit	3.8	4.4
	.0	.5	.5			All Other Expenses (net)	.4	.6
	2.6	.4	2.9			Profit Before Taxes	3.4	3.9
						RATIOS		
	2.5	2.3	1.8				2.9	3.1
	2.0	1.4	1.4			Current	1.8	1.8
	1.2	1.1	1.1				1.4	1.3
	1.3	1.2	1.1				1.8	1.4
	1.1	.8	.7			Quick	1.0	.8
	.6	.4	.4				.5	.4
	8 45.7	**18** 20.1	**38** 9.6				**33** 11.0	**22** 16.8
	37 9.9	**35** 10.3	**49** 7.4			Sales/Receivables	**50** 7.3	**44** 8.3
	47 7.7	**59** 6.2	**60** 6.1				**69** 5.3	**61** 6.0
	30 12.0	**27** 13.3	**49** 7.4				**44** 8.3	**58** 6.3
	79 4.6	**94** 3.9	**83** 4.4			Cost of Sales/Inventory	**91** 4.0	**92** 4.0
	114 3.2	**159** 2.3	**159** 2.3				**142** 2.6	**153** 2.4
	16 22.9	**12** 29.2	**29** 12.8				**11** 31.9	**16** 22.7
	26 14.1	**32** 11.3	**59** 6.2			Cost of Sales/Payables	**30** 12.4	**38** 9.6
	59 6.2	**68** 5.4	**87** 4.2				**55** 6.7	**74** 4.9
	4.0	4.4	5.2				3.8	3.8
	10.3	18.4	10.3			Sales/Working Capital	6.2	7.4
	30.1	73.3	34.0				15.1	16.1
		12.1	13.9				11.2	17.0
		(34) 5.4	(25) 4.1			EBIT/Interest	(88) 4.1	(96) 6.2
		-1.1	2.1				1.5	1.8
							12.2	21.8
						Net Profit + Depr., Dep., Amort./Cur. Mat. L/T/D	(20) 5.3	(18) 5.7
							2.3	1.5
	.0	.0	.0				.0	.0
	.0	.1	.1			Fixed/Worth	.1	.1
	.2	.5	.7				.4	.2
	.7	.8	.9				.6	.7
	1.1	1.9	2.0			Debt/Worth	1.4	1.5
	7.4	7.7	5.8				4.2	4.5
	52.6	39.5	38.5				32.5	53.1
	(12) 19.2	(32) 23.6	(27) 12.2			% Profit Before Taxes/Tangible Net Worth	(92) 16.6	(102) 19.8
	4.1	1.9	7.5				4.1	6.2
	24.6	14.5	12.4				14.3	17.1
	3.9	6.6	6.1			% Profit Before Taxes/Total Assets	5.0	7.6
	1.4	-2.7	2.1				.6	1.8
	UND	657.2	137.3				209.5	199.3
	502.2	250.7	60.1			Sales/Net Fixed Assets	63.9	60.6
	83.7	59.8	27.9				29.1	27.0
	5.9	4.0	3.1				3.1	3.3
	3.7	2.5	2.2			Sales/Total Assets	2.3	2.4
	1.9	1.9	1.8				1.7	1.9
		.1	.2				.2	.3
		(26) .2	(26) .4			% Depr., Dep., Amort./Sales	(81) .5	(78) .6
		.7	.9				1.1	1.0
		1.1					1.3	1.0
		(19) 3.0				% Officers', Directors' Owners' Comp/Sales	(34) 2.4	(31) 2.1
		4.7					5.3	5.9
15002M	**69671M**	**630435M**	**1695613M**	**1418963M**	**972908M**	Net Sales ($)	**4569900M**	**4738392M**
1586M	**15589M**	**203567M**	**674869M**	**661205M**	**682947M**	Total Assets ($)	**2469810M**	**2151027M**

M = $ thousand MM = $ million

See Pages 9 through 22 for Explanation of Ratios and Data

Comparative Historical Data				Current Data Sorted by Sales					
			Type of Statement						
25	17	17	Unqualified		2			2	13
31	28	22	Reviewed			2	2	8	10
10	7	9	Compiled		1		4	2	2
11	14	9	Tax Returns	1	2	1	2	3	
35	35	42	Other		3	4	5	8	22
				11 (4/1-9/30/13)			88 (10/1/13-3/31/14)		
4/1/11-3/31/12 ALL	**4/1/12-3/31/13 ALL**	**4/1/13-3/31/14 ALL**		**0-1MM**	**1-3MM**	**3-5MM**	**5-10MM**	**10-25MM**	**25MM & OVER**
112	101	99	**NUMBER OF STATEMENTS**	1	8	7	13	23	47
%	%	%	**ASSETS**	%	%	%	%	%	%
9.9	9.7	10.4	Cash & Equivalents				10.9	6.9	11.9
28.4	27.6	27.0	Trade Receivables (net)				21.2	33.7	28.3
42.6	42.9	40.1	Inventory				53.8	41.8	34.7
2.9	4.0	3.4	All Other Current				3.1	2.7	4.8
83.8	84.2	80.9	Total Current				89.1	85.1	79.7
6.3	5.6	6.3	Fixed Assets (net)				2.0	7.7	6.2
4.2	4.9	5.2	Intangibles (net)				1.9	.8	6.5
5.7	5.3	7.6	All Other Non-Current				7.0	6.3	7.6
100.0	100.0	100.0	Total				100.0	100.0	100.0
			LIABILITIES						
18.6	12.6	13.2	Notes Payable-Short Term				8.5	19.3	12.8
1.2	.7	1.1	Cur. Mat.-L.T.D.				.0	.5	1.5
20.1	23.5	24.9	Trade Payables				27.3	27.8	25.4
.1	.2	.1	Income Taxes Payable				.0	.2	.1
9.7	11.7	11.6	All Other Current				11.2	11.2	11.1
49.8	48.6	50.9	Total Current				47.0	59.1	50.8
5.4	6.5	5.8	Long-Term Debt				3.9	1.5	4.9
.2	.0	.1	Deferred Taxes				.0	.0	.2
6.1	7.4	8.5	All Other Non-Current				.5	4.2	12.9
38.5	37.4	34.7	Net Worth				48.6	35.3	31.2
100.0	100.0	100.0	Total Liabilties & Net Worth				100.0	100.0	100.0
			INCOME DATA						
100.0	100.0	100.0	Net Sales				100.0	100.0	100.0
33.2	33.3	31.3	Gross Profit				29.6	30.8	30.9
29.6	29.2	28.2	Operating Expenses				25.9	29.4	25.8
3.6	4.2	3.1	Operating Profit				3.7	1.3	5.1
1.0	.8	.8	All Other Expenses (net)				-.4	.6	1.2
2.6	3.4	2.4	Profit Before Taxes				4.1	.7	3.9
			RATIOS						
3.1	3.0	2.4					5.6	2.0	2.3
1.7	1.7	1.6	Current				2.0	1.2	1.6
1.2	1.2	1.1					1.2	1.1	1.2
1.6	1.4	1.2					1.2	1.1	1.2
.8	.8	.8	Quick				.8	.7	.8
.5	.4	.5					.5	.5	.5
27 13.7	**23** 15.9	**18** 20.3					**5** 77.2	**29** 12.8	**21** 17.6
46 7.9	**40** 9.1	**41** 8.9	Sales/Receivables				**34** 10.8	**42** 8.6	**46** 7.9
58 6.3	**57** 6.4	**57** 6.4					**46** 7.9	**62** 5.9	**57** 6.4
61 6.0	**52** 7.0	**41** 8.9					**78** 4.7	**41** 8.9	**39** 9.3
107 3.4	**94** 3.9	**89** 4.1	Cost of Sales/Inventory				**94** 3.9	**118** 3.1	**83** 4.4
166 2.2	**166** 2.2	**152** 2.4					**152** 2.4	**152** 2.4	**146** 2.5
12 30.7	**15** 24.9	**15** 25.1					**14** 25.2	**18** 20.6	**9** 38.7
39 9.4	**35** 10.5	**33** 11.1	Cost of Sales/Payables				**31** 11.7	**39** 9.4	**33** 11.1
72 5.1	**79** 4.6	**76** 4.8					**66** 5.5	**72** 5.1	**76** 4.8
3.9	3.8	4.0					3.4	5.2	4.2
8.0	8.4	10.3	Sales/Working Capital				7.6	18.4	9.7
18.8	20.8	36.1					75.4	45.8	24.4
13.2	14.8	12.4					241.3	7.1	19.8
(98) 3.9	(85) 5.2	(84) 5.2	EBIT/Interest				(10) 4.3	(21) 4.8	(41) 8.0
1.5	1.8	1.3					1.7	-3.2	2.5
4.3	26.1	10.0							
(15) 1.0	(12) 5.0	(12) 2.7	Net Profit + Depr., Dep., Amort./Cur. Mat. L/T/D						
-1.8	.0	1.1							
.0	.0	.0					.0	.0	.0
.1	.1	.1	Fixed/Worth				.0	.1	.1
.3	.3	.5					.1	.5	.3
.8	.8	.9					.4	.9	.9
2.0	1.6	1.7	Debt/Worth				.8	2.1	1.7
5.0	4.2	5.9					8.2	5.2	5.4
43.0	47.6	39.4					48.0	38.1	49.7
(102) 15.4	(91) 22.0	(85) 23.2	% Profit Before Taxes/Tangible Net Worth				(12) 20.3	(20) 21.0	(41) 27.4
6.8	6.2	7.6					.9	-1.8	11.3
12.7	17.9	15.2					25.9	13.8	15.5
5.8	6.5	6.9	% Profit Before Taxes/Total Assets				8.9	6.1	8.2
1.9	1.6	1.9					.3	-3.7	4.2
175.0	245.2	345.8					863.8	572.8	180.8
68.3	85.0	95.0	Sales/Net Fixed Assets				330.6	100.6	60.1
25.3	28.5	27.9					82.4	21.1	23.4
3.2	3.3	3.6					3.5	3.6	3.7
2.3	2.4	2.3	Sales/Total Assets				2.7	2.0	2.3
1.7	1.7	1.7					2.3	1.8	1.7
.2	.2	.1						.2	.2
(87) .5	(77) .4	(71) .3	% Depr., Dep., Amort./Sales					(17) .5	(35) .4
1.0	.8	1.0						1.2	1.3
1.2	1.0	1.1						2.3	1.0
(36) 2.3	(32) 2.5	(32) 3.1	% Officers', Directors' Owners' Comp/Sales					(10) 3.3	(12) 1.2
6.2	6.0	4.4						4.7	3.9
5291758M	**5974696M**	**4802592M**	Net Sales ($)	**693M**	**16301M**	**28754M**	**99455M**	**409083M**	**4248306M**
2662070M	**2574938M**	**2239763M**	Total Assets ($)	**413M**	**10104M**	**17883M**	**47073M**	**176311M**	**1987979M**

M = $ thousand MM = $ million

See Pages 9 through 22 for Explanation of Ratios and Data

Current Data Sorted by Assets | **Comparative Historical Data**

	0-500M	500M-2MM	2-10MM	10-50MM	50-100MM	100-250MM	4/1/09-3/31/10 ALL	4/1/10-3/31/11 ALL
Type of Statement								
Unqualified		2	4	22	11	22	82	79
Reviewed	1	3	32	29	1		86	78
Compiled	9	13	31	4			67	64
Tax Returns	18	28	42	4			85	94
Other	3	22	63	37	9	14	136	168
	77 (4/1-9/30/13)		347 (10/1/13-3/31/14)					
NUMBER OF STATEMENTS	31	68	172	96	21	36	456	483
	%	%	%	%	%	%	%	%
ASSETS								
Cash & Equivalents	14.6	11.3	8.0	7.6	8.2	6.8	8.9	8.3
Trade Receivables (net)	12.6	33.3	34.9	26.8	29.3	26.5	30.1	29.7
Inventory	30.2	31.3	31.2	29.3	23.2	29.7	30.5	32.3
All Other Current	4.4	3.1	2.5	3.4	2.6	3.8	3.4	3.5
Total Current	61.8	79.0	76.6	67.2	63.3	66.9	72.9	73.8
Fixed Assets (net)	24.9	10.4	15.6	20.6	25.2	21.3	18.7	17.5
Intangibles (net)	8.7	2.9	3.5	6.1	4.8	5.6	3.1	2.8
All Other Non-Current	4.6	7.7	4.4	6.2	6.7	6.2	5.3	5.9
Total	100.0	100.0	100.0	100.0	100.0	100.0	100.0	100.0
LIABILITIES								
Notes Payable-Short Term	8.9	9.6	11.8	14.5	10.3	10.4	13.6	12.7
Cur. Mat.-L.T.D.	1.1	1.2	1.2	2.1	2.9	1.4	3.0	1.9
Trade Payables	19.6	30.9	26.1	19.7	22.6	22.9	24.0	24.3
Income Taxes Payable	1.0	.0	.1	.1	.2	.5	.3	.2
All Other Current	13.9	8.5	6.9	6.4	8.9	8.5	9.6	9.6
Total Current	44.5	50.2	46.0	42.8	44.9	43.7	50.4	48.6
Long-Term Debt	10.4	12.0	10.0	11.6	23.3	16.3	12.7	11.6
Deferred Taxes	.0	.0	.1	.4	.8	.9	.3	.3
All Other Non-Current	12.5	10.5	6.2	4.0	9.4	3.9	4.9	5.9
Net Worth	32.6	27.3	37.7	41.1	21.7	35.2	31.7	33.6
Total Liabilties & Net Worth	100.0	100.0	100.0	100.0	100.0	100.0	100.0	100.0
INCOME DATA								
Net Sales	100.0	100.0	100.0	100.0	100.0	100.0	100.0	100.0
Gross Profit	29.0	20.8	18.6	16.4	19.7	12.8	19.0	18.5
Operating Expenses	25.6	18.2	16.6	13.2	16.7	10.6	17.0	16.5
Operating Profit	3.4	2.6	2.0	3.2	3.0	2.2	2.0	2.0
All Other Expenses (net)	.9	-.1	.1	.1	1.2	.2	.3	.3
Profit Before Taxes	2.5	2.6	1.9	3.1	1.8	2.0	1.7	1.7
RATIOS								
Current	5.0	3.6	2.5	2.5	2.0	2.0	2.3	2.4
	2.0	1.7	1.7	1.5	1.3	1.5	1.5	1.5
	.8	1.2	1.3	1.1	1.1	1.1	1.1	1.2
Quick	1.7	1.8	1.5	1.3	1.2	1.1	1.3	1.3
	.6	.9	.8	.8	.9	.7	.8	(482) .8
	.3	.5	.6	.5	.5	.5	.5	.5
Sales/Receivables	**0** UND	**10** 38.4	**19** 19.6	**13** 28.8	**17** 21.1	**12** 31.2	**12** 30.2	**11** 31.8
	2 211.4	**20** 18.2	**27** 13.4	**23** 15.6	**29** 12.6	**18** 19.9	**23** 15.7	**23** 15.9
	20 18.7	**29** 12.7	**38** 9.5	**30** 12.1	**38** 9.7	**26** 13.8	**34** 10.7	**33** 10.9
Cost of Sales/Inventory	**14** 26.0	**10** 36.0	**15** 23.9	**16** 23.5	**18** 19.9	**16** 23.2	**15** 24.5	**15** 23.7
	27 13.6	**19** 19.3	**31** 11.8	**28** 13.2	**23** 15.8	**25** 14.5	**26** 14.1	**26** 13.8
	36 10.2	**36** 10.2	**51** 7.1	**44** 8.3	**51** 7.2	**33** 11.1	**44** 8.4	**44** 8.2
Cost of Sales/Payables	**0** UND	**8** 47.4	**13** 28.4	**10** 35.8	**14** 25.2	**14** 26.3	**10** 35.6	**10** 36.0
	10 38.2	**18** 20.3	**22** 16.5	**18** 20.4	**25** 14.6	**17** 21.8	**18** 19.8	**19** 19.4
	23 16.1	**29** 12.8	**39** 9.4	**29** 12.8	**39** 9.3	**22** 16.4	**32** 11.5	**31** 11.7
Sales/Working Capital	10.2	10.9	8.7	10.8	15.4	13.3	10.0	10.2
	31.3	20.4	14.4	16.2	39.5	22.7	22.4	22.1
	-239.7	78.3	41.0	76.3	84.1	80.1	72.9	65.0
EBIT/Interest	38.1	23.5	12.4	18.2	14.7	12.0	12.8	12.5
	(16) 11.3	(54) 6.8	(149) 5.6	(86) 8.6	(20) 5.5	(34) 4.3	(400) 4.6	(414) 4.1
	2.1	2.2	2.5	3.5	2.6	2.7	1.9	1.6
Net Profit + Depr., Dep., Amort./Cur. Mat. L/T/D			6.5	11.2	21.2	18.2	8.9	10.6
			(25) 3.1	(33) 4.9	(11) 3.4	(15) 4.3	(98) 3.2	(107) 3.9
			1.4	2.5	1.8	2.8	1.5	1.9
Fixed/Worth	.1	.0	.1	.2	.3	.2	.1	.1
	.6	.3	.3	.5	.9	.9	.4	.4
	72.0	5.1	1.0	1.6	1.9	1.4	1.5	1.4
Debt/Worth	.4	.8	.9	.8	1.0	1.3	1.1	.9
	3.5	2.7	2.1	1.9	3.1	2.6	2.4	2.4
	81.0	102.2	4.9	5.5	5.2	5.8	6.0	5.2
% Profit Before Taxes/Tangible Net Worth	116.6	95.5	34.5	37.9	24.7	25.3	42.2	36.6
	(25) 48.3	(52) 42.4	(158) 19.2	(86) 24.8	(19) 18.0	(33) 19.2	(407) 22.0	(437) 19.2
	1.9	12.3	9.1	11.4	8.8	12.0	8.3	5.8
% Profit Before Taxes/Total Assets	26.9	25.0	11.5	14.4	12.3	8.4	13.4	11.4
	12.6	8.8	5.9	7.4	5.1	4.7	6.1	5.3
	.0	3.6	2.0	3.4	2.3	2.6	2.0	1.5
Sales/Net Fixed Assets	267.3	999.8	305.9	65.7	54.7	147.5	153.8	171.9
	45.4	99.7	62.9	32.1	17.6	31.3	47.5	51.0
	13.5	42.2	15.4	14.3	6.8	13.4	14.8	17.0
Sales/Total Assets	7.6	9.4	6.3	6.3	6.2	6.6	6.9	7.2
	5.4	6.5	4.6	4.3	3.2	5.0	4.7	5.1
	3.1	4.5	3.0	2.7	1.7	3.6	3.0	3.1
% Depr., Dep., Amort./Sales	.3	.2	.1	.3	.5	.3	.2	.2
	(21) 1.0	(35) .4	(136) .4	(89) .5	(19) .6	(30) .5	(371) .5	(399) .5
	2.4	1.1	1.0	.8	1.4	1.0	1.0	.9
% Officers', Directors' Owners' Comp/Sales	1.4	.6	.6	.4			.6	.6
	(16) 2.6	(30) 1.6	(84) 1.0	(25) .8			(169) 1.4	(190) 1.1
	7.7	3.2	2.4	1.6			3.2	2.6
Net Sales ($)	56193M	580628M	4105150M	10629917M	6011628M	30729541M	49142349M	63463342M
Total Assets ($)	9135M	80189M	850404M	2200863M	1356559M	5779421M	10066495M	11282507M

M = $ thousand MM = $ million

See Pages 9 through 22 for Explanation of Ratios and Data

Comparative Historical Data				Current Data Sorted by Sales					
			Type of Statement						
85	66	61	Unqualified			2		3	56
87	84	66	Reviewed		1	1	2	15	47
69	63	57	Compiled	3	5	2	12	21	14
121	91	92	Tax Returns	8	13	8	20	34	9
176	149	148	Other		9	7	13	33	86
				77 (4/1-9/30/13)			347 (10/1/13-3/31/14)		
4/1/11-3/31/12 ALL	4/1/12-3/31/13 ALL	4/1/13-3/31/14 ALL		0-1MM	1-3MM	3-5MM	5-10MM	10-25MM	25MM & OVER
538	453	424	**NUMBER OF STATEMENTS**	11	28	20	47	106	212
%	%	%	**ASSETS**	%	%	%	%	%	%
9.0	8.9	8.8	Cash & Equivalents	24.8	7.2	11.7	7.4	10.4	7.5
30.9	30.0	30.2	Trade Receivables (net)	9.5	20.3	28.9	30.5	33.9	30.8
32.1	32.8	30.2	Inventory	22.7	26.4	26.9	28.5	32.5	30.6
2.7	2.8	3.0	All Other Current	.0	4.8	4.3	2.8	1.7	3.6
74.7	74.4	72.3	Total Current	57.0	58.7	71.8	69.3	78.5	72.5
15.8	16.4	17.5	Fixed Assets (net)	30.0	24.0	15.1	18.0	13.8	18.0
3.9	3.3	4.6	Intangibles (net)	8.5	7.1	.7	5.9	3.8	4.5
5.6	6.0	5.6	All Other Non-Current	4.6	10.1	12.4	6.8	3.8	5.0
100.0	100.0	100.0	Total	100.0	100.0	100.0	100.0	100.0	100.0
			LIABILITIES						
12.6	13.9	11.6	Notes Payable-Short Term	8.1	12.8	4.2	7.5	11.3	13.4
2.0	1.6	1.5	Cur. Mat.-L.T.D.	.0	1.8	.2	1.4	1.0	1.9
24.8	24.0	24.5	Trade Payables	21.5	17.4	23.6	29.3	26.5	23.6
.2	.2	.2	Income Taxes Payable	.0	1.2	.0	.0	.1	.2
8.5	7.5	7.8	All Other Current	3.8	14.9	14.8	6.4	7.2	7.0
48.2	47.1	45.6	Total Current	33.4	48.1	42.9	44.7	46.1	46.1
12.2	11.3	11.9	Long-Term Debt	8.1	14.2	18.6	14.6	8.2	12.4
.3	.3	.3	Deferred Taxes	.0	.0	.0	.0	.1	.5
5.0	5.7	6.8	All Other Non-Current	11.3	11.3	13.9	10.7	6.7	4.5
34.4	35.5	35.4	Net Worth	47.2	26.4	24.6	30.0	38.9	36.5
100.0	100.0	100.0	Total Liabilities & Net Worth	100.0	100.0	100.0	100.0	100.0	100.0
			INCOME DATA						
100.0	100.0	100.0	Net Sales	100.0	100.0	100.0	100.0	100.0	100.0
18.1	18.4	18.8	Gross Profit	33.7	32.2	31.5	21.4	18.0	14.8
15.6	16.1	16.2	Operating Expenses	31.1	27.7	27.1	18.9	15.9	12.5
2.5	2.3	2.5	Operating Profit	2.6	4.5	4.5	2.4	2.0	2.4
.2	.0	.2	All Other Expenses (net)	1.9	.9	.2	.0	.0	.2
2.3	2.3	2.3	Profit Before Taxes	.7	3.6	4.2	2.5	2.1	2.2
			RATIOS						
2.4	2.4	2.5		7.6	2.8	5.4	2.5	2.8	2.3
1.5	1.6	1.6	Current	1.6	1.7	2.3	1.7	1.8	1.6
1.2	1.2	1.1		.9	.6	1.2	1.2	1.2	1.1
1.3	1.2	1.4		4.2	1.3	2.4	1.5	1.7	1.2
.8	(452) .8	.8	Quick	.9	.6	1.1	.9	.8	.8
.5	.5	.5		.4	.3	.6	.6	.6	.5
12 29.5	**12** 29.8	**12** 29.4		**0** UND	**0** 799.1	**14** 26.0	**8** 45.8	**18** 20.5	**12** 29.2
23 15.7	**22** 16.3	**24** 15.5	Sales/Receivables	**0** 833.0	**24** 15.3	**24** 15.1	**24** 15.5	**25** 14.4	**23** 15.7
32 11.4	**33** 11.2	**32** 11.4		**18** 19.8	**33** 11.0	**35** 10.5	**32** 11.4	**35** 10.5	**30** 12.3
14 25.7	**15** 24.4	**15** 25.0		**14** 26.0	**4** 101.0	**10** 37.1	**14** 26.0	**15** 25.1	**15** 23.9
25 14.6	**27** 13.4	**26** 13.8	Cost of Sales/Inventory	**28** 13.0	**30** 12.1	**28** 13.0	**20** 17.9	**31** 11.6	**25** 14.5
43 8.4	**47** 7.8	**43** 8.4		**42** 8.7	**64** 5.7	**64** 5.7	**44** 8.3	**51** 7.2	**39** 9.4
10 36.0	**10** 36.7	**10** 36.0		**4** 95.0	**0** UND	**10** 35.1	**14** 25.7	**11** 34.6	**11** 34.2
18 20.2	**18** 20.0	**20** 18.7	Cost of Sales/Payables	**10** 35.8	**15** 23.7	**24** 15.1	**21** 17.0	**21** 17.2	**19** 19.3
30 12.0	**30** 12.0	**31** 11.7		**41** 8.8	**43** 8.4	**48** 7.6	**39** 9.4	**39** 9.4	**27** 13.4
11.0	10.4	10.1		6.9	8.9	6.3	8.1	8.7	11.8
21.7	19.8	17.6	Sales/Working Capital	24.6	22.4	15.4	14.8	13.3	21.2
62.6	53.6	66.2		-239.7	-16.6	32.7	34.3	44.5	66.1
14.4	16.9	15.8			29.4	30.1	11.4	14.6	16.2
(459) 4.8	(389) 5.8	(359) 5.8	EBIT/Interest		(21) 5.8	(16) 10.4	(40) 5.1	(87) 5.0	(192) 6.6
1.9	2.2	2.6			1.7	2.4	2.7	1.5	3.3
9.9	8.0	9.2						6.7	11.2
(107) 3.9	(100) 3.5	(88) 3.8	Net Profit + Depr., Dep., Amort./Cur. Mat. L/T/D					(15) 2.7	(68) 4.0
1.7	1.7	2.2						1.2	2.2
.1	.1	.1		.0	.3	.0	.0	.0	.1
.3	.3	.4	Fixed/Worth	.6	.6	.3	.3	.3	.4
1.4	1.4	1.6		72.0	5.2	5.1	2.0	1.0	1.4
1.0	.9	.9		.2	1.2	.7	1.2	.8	.9
2.5	2.3	2.3	Debt/Worth	2.0	3.3	4.7	2.7	1.8	2.2
5.3	4.9	5.7		81.0	29.0	12.1	21.5	4.9	5.1
40.7	40.9	42.1		79.3	82.1	110.0	42.9	37.4	35.9
(487) 21.1	(409) 22.8	(373) 21.3	% Profit Before Taxes/Tangible Net Worth	(10) 8.3	(22) 48.5	(17) 49.2	(38) 19.9	(93) 19.4	(193) 21.3
7.2	8.9	10.5		-14.0	8.7	27.0	9.3	7.0	11.9
13.1	14.4	14.2		14.8	23.3	26.1	14.7	14.6	13.3
6.0	6.2	6.5	% Profit Before Taxes/Total Assets	.0	9.7	11.8	5.9	5.8	6.8
2.0	2.4	2.7		-4.2	2.7	4.8	3.1	1.5	3.1
205.5	218.4	200.6		UND	81.5	722.8	690.4	327.5	147.2
66.2	61.9	53.0	Sales/Net Fixed Assets	28.6	37.7	51.7	59.0	63.5	47.6
19.2	19.4	16.1		6.2	9.2	17.5	15.9	17.1	16.6
7.4	7.0	6.7		6.0	5.8	5.4	7.4	6.7	6.9
5.0	4.9	4.8	Sales/Total Assets	3.1	4.1	4.4	4.4	4.7	5.2
3.3	3.2	3.1		2.5	2.1	2.5	2.4	3.2	3.4
.2	.2	.2			.5	.2	.2	.2	.2
(427) .4	(353) .4	(330) .5	% Depr., Dep., Amort./Sales		(17) 1.3	(13) .7	(29) .8	(81) .4	(183) .5
.9	.9	1.0			1.8	1.4	1.6	.9	.8
.7	.6	.6			1.2		1.1	.6	.3
(210) 1.3	(179) 1.3	(161) 1.1	% Officers', Directors' Owners' Comp/Sales		(14) 2.3		(21) 1.9	(55) 1.0	(59) .8
2.9	2.7	2.4			4.8		3.8	2.3	1.6
67867483M	**51044602M**	**52113057M**	Net Sales ($)	**6713M**	**56835M**	**79817M**	**343713M**	**1777342M**	**49848637M**
12321834M	**10227065M**	**10276571M**	Total Assets ($)	**2043M**	**23393M**	**25730M**	**113717M**	**461130M**	**9650558M**

M = $ thousand MM = $ million

See Pages 9 through 22 for Explanation of Ratios and Data

Current Data Sorted by Assets							Comparative Historical Data	
						Type of Statement		
		5	10	1	2	Unqualified	29	33
		11	7			Reviewed	27	25
	2	17	6			Compiled	21	15
4	8	13	1			Tax Returns	19	23
1	6	21	13	6	5	Other	59	55
	20 (4/1-9/30/13)		119 (10/1/13-3/31/14)				4/1/09-3/31/10 ALL	4/1/10-3/31/11 ALL
0-500M	500M-2MM	2-10MM	10-50MM	50-100MM	100-250MM			
5	16	67	37	7	7	**NUMBER OF STATEMENTS**	155	151
%	%	%	%	%	%	**ASSETS**	%	%
	10.6	8.1	7.7			Cash & Equivalents	6.9	7.1
	36.2	37.2	28.8			Trade Receivables (net)	33.4	32.2
	26.8	29.1	36.1			Inventory	30.5	32.6
	7.2	1.4	4.1			All Other Current	2.9	2.5
	80.8	75.8	76.8			Total Current	73.7	74.5
	14.4	16.2	15.3			Fixed Assets (net)	17.1	16.0
	.9	3.9	2.9			Intangibles (net)	4.7	5.7
	3.8	4.1	5.0			All Other Non-Current	4.5	3.8
	100.0	100.0	100.0			Total	100.0	100.0
						LIABILITIES		
	8.9	13.9	21.6			Notes Payable-Short Term	17.1	18.2
	.9	2.3	2.1			Cur. Mat.-L.T.D.	2.3	2.6
	31.4	26.7	21.5			Trade Payables	22.2	25.2
	.0	.1	.2			Income Taxes Payable	.2	.1
	17.8	7.6	8.2			All Other Current	7.6	6.8
	59.1	50.6	53.6			Total Current	49.4	52.8
	12.8	9.2	7.7			Long-Term Debt	12.6	10.3
	.0	.2	.1			Deferred Taxes	.2	.2
	13.3	5.0	4.7			All Other Non-Current	4.5	5.8
	14.8	35.0	34.0			Net Worth	33.3	30.8
	100.0	100.0	100.0			Total Liabilities & Net Worth	100.0	100.0
						INCOME DATA		
	100.0	100.0	100.0			Net Sales	100.0	100.0
	18.0	15.1	12.6			Gross Profit	18.3	18.3
	15.0	13.1	10.9			Operating Expenses	15.5	16.1
	3.0	2.0	1.6			Operating Profit	2.8	2.1
	.5	.2	.4			All Other Expenses (net)	.6	.3
	2.5	1.8	1.3			Profit Before Taxes	2.2	1.8
						RATIOS		
	2.2	2.4	2.2				2.1	2.0
	1.7	1.5	1.4			Current	1.4	1.4
	1.2	1.1	1.1				1.2	1.1
	1.7	1.5	1.2				1.2	1.2
	.8	.9	.6			Quick	.7	.7
	.5	.6	.4				.5	.4
	15 23.6	**18** 20.0	**18** 20.2				**18** 19.8	**17** 21.1
	21 17.3	**26** 13.8	**26** 14.1			Sales/Receivables	**27** 13.4	**27** 13.7
	42 8.7	**36** 10.0	**33** 10.9				**36** 10.1	**36** 10.2
	6 61.6	**14** 25.6	**21** 17.1				**19** 18.8	**19** 19.1
	16 22.9	**29** 12.4	**33** 11.2			Cost of Sales/Inventory	**29** 12.4	**31** 11.6
	58 6.3	**51** 7.2	**56** 6.5				**54** 6.8	**64** 5.7
	15 23.8	**12** 29.9	**13** 29.1				**11** 31.9	**12** 30.6
	23 15.9	**23** 15.6	**21** 17.7			Cost of Sales/Payables	**21** 17.7	**20** 18.0
	51 7.1	**41** 8.8	**31** 11.7				**30** 12.0	**34** 10.6
	11.3	9.0	11.1				9.6	9.4
	14.8	16.7	19.7			Sales/Working Capital	19.1	21.4
	33.4	51.9	37.5				65.0	63.2
	21.1	16.9	18.0				8.4	9.3
	(14) 4.6	(61) 5.9	(33) 6.7			EBIT/Interest	(144) 3.7	(140) 3.2
	2.0	2.3	2.6				1.8	1.9
							8.2	6.7
						Net Profit + Depr., Dep., Amort./Cur. Mat. L/T/D	(35) 2.6	(37) 2.3
							1.7	1.1
	.0	.0	.1				.1	.1
	.1	.3	.3			Fixed/Worth	.5	.5
	2.1	1.2	.9				1.6	2.0
	1.2	.7	1.2				1.0	1.5
	4.6	2.7	2.6			Debt/Worth	2.9	3.2
	10.6	8.1	6.2				5.7	9.9
	63.0	41.7	54.0				52.0	36.6
	(15) 31.3	(57) 20.3	(36) 26.0			% Profit Before Taxes/Tangible Net Worth	(138) 22.1	(127) 23.4
	17.7	7.7	10.9				6.5	10.3
	19.6	13.5	13.9				12.7	10.8
	10.0	5.9	7.1			% Profit Before Taxes/Total Assets	6.0	4.7
	1.8	1.8	2.7				1.9	1.9
	UND	475.5	629.1				184.7	280.0
	189.4	72.1	63.8			Sales/Net Fixed Assets	34.3	42.9
	37.0	12.9	15.0				15.1	16.2
	9.1	6.9	5.4				6.3	5.8
	6.3	4.2	4.5			Sales/Total Assets	4.2	3.9
	2.3	2.6	2.9				2.4	2.5
		.1	.1				.2	.2
		(53) .4	(31) .4			% Depr., Dep., Amort./Sales	(126) .6	(123) .5
		1.6	.9				1.1	1.1
		.7	.4				1.2	.6
		(29) 1.3	(13) .9			% Officers', Directors' Owners' Comp/Sales	(48) 1.9	(54) 1.6
		1.9	2.8				2.9	3.3
12631M	136358M	1535368M	4072295M	1619552M	5234256M	Net Sales ($)	16552126M	14610582M
1333M	20871M	335034M	852083M	445502M	1076224M	Total Assets ($)	3614234M	3506782M

M = $ thousand MM = $ million

See Pages 9 through 22 for Explanation of Ratios and Data

Comparative Historical Data				Current Data Sorted by Sales					
			Type of Statement						
28	21	18	Unqualified		1			2	15
31	24	18	Reviewed				1	5	12
17	12	25	Compiled			1	3	10	11
16	24	26	Tax Returns		5	2	9	6	4
77	72	52	Other		2	2	7	9	32
4/1/11-3/31/12 ALL	**4/1/12-3/31/13 ALL**	**4/1/13-3/31/14 ALL**			**20 (4/1-9/30/13)**		**119 (10/1/13-3/31/14)**		
				0-1MM	**1-3MM**	**3-5MM**	**5-10MM**	**10-25MM**	**25MM & OVER**
169	153	139	**NUMBER OF STATEMENTS**		8	5	20	32	74
%	%	%	**ASSETS**	%	%	%	%	%	%
6.4	8.2	7.7	Cash & Equivalents	D			9.5	10.5	5.7
34.5	32.5	33.7	Trade Receivables (net)	A			34.0	34.1	34.2
30.2	32.6	32.4	Inventory	T			28.7	27.7	35.9
2.9	2.7	3.0	All Other Current	A			3.5	1.6	3.8
74.0	76.0	76.7	Total Current				75.6	73.8	79.7
16.3	15.3	15.5	Fixed Assets (net)	N			15.9	20.6	12.1
5.1	4.3	3.5	Intangibles (net)	O			2.6	3.2	3.1
4.6	4.5	4.3	All Other Non-Current	T			5.9	2.4	5.1
100.0	100.0	100.0	Total				100.0	100.0	100.0
			LIABILITIES	A					
17.2	18.8	16.1	Notes Payable-Short Term	V			14.0	10.1	21.3
3.0	1.8	2.0	Cur. Mat.-L.T.D.	A			2.9	2.7	1.5
26.3	27.9	27.6	Trade Payables	I			34.8	26.0	22.5
.1	.2	.1	Income Taxes Payable	L			.0	.0	.2
7.2	7.4	8.8	All Other Current	A			4.9	8.6	8.2
53.9	56.0	54.7	Total Current	B			56.5	47.5	53.8
9.2	10.6	9.8	Long-Term Debt	L			10.6	10.1	7.4
.2	.1	.2	Deferred Taxes	E			.2	.0	.1
5.8	5.8	6.8	All Other Non-Current				4.8	4.8	4.8
30.9	27.5	28.6	Net Worth				28.0	37.6	33.9
100.0	100.0	100.0	Total Liabilities & Net Worth				100.0	100.0	100.0
			INCOME DATA						
100.0	100.0	100.0	Net Sales				100.0	100.0	100.0
16.7	15.1	14.6	Gross Profit				16.2	16.2	11.6
14.3	13.3	12.8	Operating Expenses				15.9	14.1	9.4
2.4	1.8	1.9	Operating Profit				.3	2.0	2.2
.5	.0	.2	All Other Expenses (net)				-.9	.6	.2
2.0	1.7	1.6	Profit Before Taxes				1.2	1.5	2.0
			RATIOS						
2.2	2.2	2.2					1.9	2.6	2.2
1.4	1.4	1.5	Current				1.3	1.7	1.4
1.1	1.1	1.1					.9	1.2	1.2
1.2	1.2	1.3					1.5	1.7	1.2
.7	.7	.8	Quick				.7	1.0	.7
.5	.4	.5					.3	.7	.5
18 19.9	**16** 22.9	**18** 20.5					**16** 22.8	**20** 18.7	**18** 20.5
26 13.8	**24** 15.4	**24** 15.0	Sales/Receivables				**24** 14.9	**28** 13.0	**24** 15.0
36 10.0	**37** 9.9	**35** 10.3					**70** 5.2	**36** 10.0	**31** 11.6
16 23.4	**15** 23.7	**14** 25.6					**21** 17.2	**13** 27.7	**20** 17.9
27 13.7	**29** 12.8	**30** 12.1	Cost of Sales/Inventory				**41** 8.9	**27** 13.6	**29** 12.4
46 8.0	**51** 7.1	**52** 7.0					**56** 6.5	**58** 6.3	**51** 7.2
13 28.8	**12** 30.0	**14** 26.5					**28** 13.1	**13** 27.9	**11** 34.6
21 17.6	**24** 15.5	**21** 17.6	Cost of Sales/Payables				**43** 8.5	**22** 16.7	**18** 20.7
34 10.8	**35** 10.3	**34** 10.8					**74** 4.9	**43** 8.5	**27** 13.7
9.5	10.7	10.9					11.0	8.7	12.5
20.6	20.5	18.7	Sales/Working Capital				15.4	16.9	22.1
112.4	80.0	49.0					NM	43.8	44.5
9.7	14.0	14.9					10.4	19.1	19.7
(157) 3.1	(133) 6.1	(125) 5.9	EBIT/Interest				(16) 6.3	(29) 5.4	(69) 6.4
1.6	1.8	2.2					1.6	1.9	3.2
7.2	6.4	6.8							6.7
(37) 2.2	(27) 1.8	(23) 2.7	Net Profit + Depr., Dep., Amort./Cur. Mat. L/T/D						(16) 2.8
.9	.6	.4							2.1
.1	.0	.1					.0	.1	.1
.4	.5	.3	Fixed/Worth				.2	.4	.3
1.5	2.4	1.1					2.4	2.7	.9
1.2	1.3	1.2					1.6	.7	1.2
3.2	3.2	2.8	Debt/Worth				5.1	1.7	2.4
9.0	12.4	7.5					9.9	7.6	6.2
36.9	56.8	47.5					36.0	42.2	52.8
(145) 19.1	(127) 20.7	(123) 24.3	% Profit Before Taxes/Tangible Net Worth				(19) 25.9	(28) 13.5	(68) 26.6
8.2	5.7	8.8					3.5	5.0	12.8
10.2	14.3	13.7					13.2	16.3	14.6
4.2	6.3	6.0	% Profit Before Taxes/Total Assets				4.6	4.4	8.0
1.5	1.4	1.8					.8	1.3	2.9
295.7	363.7	475.5					UND	209.2	458.3
53.9	62.0	69.1	Sales/Net Fixed Assets				93.0	59.5	73.3
13.4	16.9	15.6					13.4	6.9	20.7
6.8	6.8	6.8					5.3	8.1	6.8
4.3	4.5	4.5	Sales/Total Assets				2.7	4.2	4.7
2.6	2.8	2.8					2.0	2.9	3.7
.1	.1	.1					.4	.1	.1
(133) .5	(112) .4	(110) .4	% Depr., Dep., Amort./Sales				(12) 1.1	(28) .4	(62) .3
1.3	.9	1.2					2.7	2.6	.6
.6	.7	.7					1.3	.5	.5
(52) 1.1	(50) 1.6	(57) 1.3	% Officers', Directors' Owners' Comp/Sales				(11) 2.9	(14) .9	(24) .9
2.9	3.1	3.1					4.0	1.6	2.1
16944269M	**13753847M**	**12610460M**	Net Sales ($)		**17485M**	**18348M**	**143414M**	**568013M**	**11863200M**
3650203M	**3134700M**	**2731047M**	Total Assets ($)		**13759M**	**4968M**	**56317M**	**179668M**	**2476335M**

M = $ thousand **MM = $ million**

See Pages 9 through 22 for Explanation of Ratios and Data

Current Data Sorted by Assets							Comparative Historical Data	
						Type of Statement		
		3	6	2	3	Unqualified	24	20
	3	10	4			Reviewed	23	21
	2	5	5		1	Compiled	15	12
1	5	3				Tax Returns	7	10
1	1	12	12	4	6	Other	30	30
	22 (4/1-9/30/13)		67 (10/1/13-3/31/14)				**4/1/09-3/31/10**	**4/1/10-3/31/11**
0-500M	**500M-2MM**	**2-10MM**	**10-50MM**	**50-100MM**	**100-250MM**		**ALL**	**ALL**
2	11	33	27	6	10	**NUMBER OF STATEMENTS**	99	93
%	%	%	%	%	%	**ASSETS**	%	%
	14.3	9.1	9.1		6.2	Cash & Equivalents	9.0	10.0
	42.4	36.9	32.7		22.5	Trade Receivables (net)	35.0	34.0
	17.6	22.6	22.1		27.2	Inventory	24.0	23.8
	3.3	1.9	5.7		2.7	All Other Current	3.1	3.5
	77.6	70.5	69.5		58.6	Total Current	71.1	71.3
	20.9	21.4	23.1		36.6	Fixed Assets (net)	20.3	20.9
	.3	2.1	4.8		1.3	Intangibles (net)	3.0	3.5
	1.2	5.9	2.5		3.4	All Other Non-Current	5.6	4.3
	100.0	100.0	100.0		100.0	Total	100.0	100.0
						LIABILITIES		
	8.3	10.2	13.8		11.8	Notes Payable-Short Term	15.7	15.4
	1.3	3.2	2.1		3.1	Cur. Mat.-L.T.D.	2.7	3.7
	46.0	34.0	34.6		18.1	Trade Payables	30.2	31.0
	.1	.1	.0		.3	Income Taxes Payable	.2	.1
	8.2	9.6	6.1		10.4	All Other Current	8.5	10.5
	63.8	57.1	56.6		43.8	Total Current	57.3	60.6
	13.4	10.3	9.4		29.8	Long-Term Debt	10.9	11.8
	.6	.2	.7		.2	Deferred Taxes	.3	.3
	1.3	8.1	2.5		1.6	All Other Non-Current	5.1	4.9
	20.9	24.3	30.9		24.7	Net Worth	26.4	22.5
	100.0	100.0	100.0		100.0	Total Liabilties & Net Worth	100.0	100.0
						INCOME DATA		
	100.0	100.0	100.0		100.0	Net Sales	100.0	100.0
	23.8	19.2	15.6		18.4	Gross Profit	19.8	19.7
	21.6	18.5	14.0		15.5	Operating Expenses	16.8	16.7
	2.2	.8	1.5		2.9	Operating Profit	3.0	3.0
	.0	.2	-.1		1.2	All Other Expenses (net)	.5	.4
	2.1	.6	1.7		1.7	Profit Before Taxes	2.6	2.6
						RATIOS		
	1.5	1.5	1.4		1.5		1.7	1.7
	1.3	1.3	1.1		1.3	Current	1.3	1.3
	.9	1.1	1.0		1.1		1.1	1.0
	1.2	1.2	.9		1.1		1.1	1.1
	.9	.8	.7		.8	Quick	.8	.8
	.5	.5	.5		.5		.6	.5
	14 26.8	**17** 21.5	**16** 22.6		**18** 19.9		**18** 20.3	**19** 19.6
	15 23.7	**26** 13.9	**25** 14.8		**23** 15.9	Sales/Receivables	**27** 13.6	**25** 14.6
	18 20.3	**39** 9.3	**32** 11.5		**31** 11.8		**37** 9.9	**33** 11.2
	0 UND	**12** 30.1	**9** 41.7		**2** 169.7		**9** 41.9	**9** 39.4
	12 30.1	**19** 19.7	**13** 28.3		**13** 27.2	Cost of Sales/Inventory	**15** 23.7	**21** 17.7
	20 18.7	**29** 12.4	**32** 11.5		**60** 6.1		**48** 7.6	**35** 10.3
	14 25.2	**19** 19.7	**17** 21.3		**4** 95.8		**14** 26.6	**15** 23.6
	17 21.5	**29** 12.8	**26** 13.8		**22** 16.6	Cost of Sales/Payables	**25** 14.7	**25** 14.7
	20 18.3	**36** 10.0	**32** 11.3		**78** 4.7		**37** 9.9	**35** 10.4
	29.0	11.4	21.4		10.6		12.6	15.3
	49.3	28.5	87.7		30.7	Sales/Working Capital	29.7	34.8
	-182.9	94.2	999.8		NM		236.7	-353.9
	18.6	27.5	13.6		6.0		15.0	22.7
	(10) 4.5	(27) 3.7	(24) 6.6		3.9	EBIT/Interest	(89) 6.0	(80) 5.6
	.8	1.2	3.4		.0		2.2	1.5
							8.0	5.0
						Net Profit + Depr., Dep., Amort./Cur. Mat. L/T/D	(26) 3.5	(25) 3.0
							2.0	1.6
	.2	.0	.2		.6		.0	.1
	.5	.7	1.0		1.4	Fixed/Worth	.7	.8
	7.7	2.6	2.4		3.8		2.1	1.9
	1.2	1.8	1.1		1.7		1.0	1.2
	3.3	3.0	4.1		2.3	Debt/Worth	2.7	2.7
	44.8	9.7	8.3		12.1		6.4	6.8
	15.2	41.6	70.6				50.6	48.6
	(10) 5.3	(27) 15.0	(25) 18.7			% Profit Before Taxes/Tangible Net Worth	(85) 24.5	(80) 21.2
	-18.3	3.0	12.4				8.5	8.4
	3.8	9.4	9.1		4.9		13.8	14.9
	1.8	6.2	6.8		2.5	% Profit Before Taxes/Total Assets	7.4	7.0
	-.1	.2	3.0		-1.7		1.9	1.4
	362.1	427.8	93.7		17.0		377.3	225.9
	43.2	51.0	40.4		11.0	Sales/Net Fixed Assets	29.1	29.9
	16.8	8.8	11.8		6.3		11.5	12.8
	18.1	6.7	8.0		5.3		6.1	7.0
	9.3	4.2	5.4		3.9	Sales/Total Assets	4.3	4.4
	7.2	2.4	3.0		2.9		2.8	3.0
		.4	.2				.4	.4
		(24) 1.5	(26) .4			% Depr., Dep., Amort./Sales	(78) .8	(72) .9
		3.3	1.3				2.0	2.0
		.7					.9	.6
		(16) 1.2				% Officers', Directors' Owners' Comp/Sales	(34) 2.1	(34) 1.6
		1.7					4.6	2.3
14102M	**122084M**	**817900M**	**3819569M**	**1163270M**	**7560705M**	Net Sales ($)	**11366407M**	**10090059M**
558M	**12628M**	**170255M**	**647649M**	**341911M**	**1880069M**	Total Assets ($)	**2453572M**	**2433724M**

M = $ thousand MM = $ million

See Pages 9 through 22 for Explanation of Ratios and Data

Comparative Historical Data				Current Data Sorted by Sales					
			Type of Statement						
17	24	14	Unqualified					1	13
33	13	17	Reviewed			1	1	6	9
10	14	13	Compiled				3	1	9
16	9	9	Tax Returns				2	5	2
30	26	36	Other		1	1	3	6	25
4/1/11-3/31/12 ALL	**4/1/12-3/31/13 ALL**	**4/1/13-3/31/14 ALL**			**22 (4/1-9/30/13)**		**67 (10/1/13-3/31/14)**		
				0-1MM	**1-3MM**	**3-5MM**	**5-10MM**	**10-25MM**	**25MM & OVER**
106	86	89	**NUMBER OF STATEMENTS**		1	2	9	19	58
%	%	%	**ASSETS**	%	%	%	%	%	%
11.6	8.3	10.1	Cash & Equivalents	D				11.5	9.0
33.8	34.6	33.9	Trade Receivables (net)	A				33.8	35.4
22.1	21.3	22.1	Inventory	T				18.9	22.5
2.4	3.4	3.5	All Other Current	A				1.9	3.9
69.9	67.6	69.6	Total Current					66.1	70.8
21.0	22.4	23.5	Fixed Assets (net)	N				28.5	22.0
4.3	3.6	3.2	Intangibles (net)	O				.2	4.5
4.7	6.4	3.7	All Other Non-Current	T				5.2	2.7
100.0	100.0	100.0	Total					100.0	100.0
			LIABILITIES	A					
12.8	12.9	10.4	Notes Payable-Short Term	V				11.5	10.2
2.8	2.4	2.5	Cur. Mat.-L.T.D.	A				3.6	2.3
32.6	29.0	32.7	Trade Payables	I				31.5	34.1
.1	.1	.1	Income Taxes Payable	L				.3	.1
8.1	11.0	8.0	All Other Current	A				3.8	8.3
56.4	55.3	53.7	Total Current	B				50.7	55.0
11.0	13.2	12.8	Long-Term Debt	L				16.0	11.2
.5	.2	.4	Deferred Taxes	E				.2	.5
5.5	4.1	4.1	All Other Non-Current					6.0	2.9
26.6	27.2	28.9	Net Worth					27.2	30.4
100.0	100.0	100.0	Total Liabilities & Net Worth					100.0	100.0
			INCOME DATA						
100.0	100.0	100.0	Net Sales					100.0	100.0
19.1	17.5	18.5	Gross Profit					21.0	16.8
16.8	15.0	16.8	Operating Expenses					20.1	14.6
2.4	2.5	1.7	Operating Profit					.9	2.2
.6	.5	.2	All Other Expenses (net)					.3	.1
1.7	2.0	1.6	Profit Before Taxes					.6	2.1
			RATIOS						
1.6	1.6	1.6						1.5	1.6
1.3	1.2	1.3	Current					1.3	1.3
1.0	1.0	1.0						1.1	1.0
1.1	1.1	1.2						1.4	1.1
.8	.8	.8	Quick					.9	.8
.5	.6	.6						.6	.6
18 20.3	**17** 21.1	**16** 22.4						**10** 36.3	**18** 19.9
26 14.3	**23** 15.9	**24** 15.4	Sales/Receivables					**18** 20.4	**25** 14.4
31 11.6	**30** 12.2	**32** 11.4						**30** 12.0	**32** 11.3
8 45.5	**4** 86.1	**8** 46.1						**0** 999.8	**7** 50.3
18 20.6	**16** 22.2	**18** 20.4	Cost of Sales/Inventory					**18** 20.4	**13** 27.5
30 12.0	**34** 10.6	**35** 10.5						**35** 10.5	**34** 10.8
16 23.4	**12** 29.4	**16** 22.7						**15** 23.9	**20** 18.6
25 14.5	**20** 18.7	**26** 14.2	Cost of Sales/Payables					**18** 20.6	**29** 12.8
35 10.3	**34** 10.8	**35** 10.3						**24** 15.4	**36** 10.2
17.2	17.9	13.3						23.1	14.5
35.1	39.3	34.1	Sales/Working Capital					30.3	37.2
-451.3	999.8	392.2						245.5	654.2
18.8	16.8	18.6						16.5	25.1
(93) 5.0	(78) 4.2	(78) 4.8	EBIT/Interest					(16) 3.3	(50) 6.6
1.8	1.1	1.5						-.4	2.9
3.8	10.9	14.9							14.9
(27) 2.7	(16) 3.3	(19) 5.0	Net Profit + Depr., Dep., Amort./Cur. Mat. L/T/D						(15) 5.0
1.1	2.0	2.0							2.0
.2	.2	.2						.4	.2
.7	.7	.7	Fixed/Worth					.8	.8
2.6	3.3	2.5						2.4	2.4
1.3	1.3	1.2						1.2	1.2
3.0	3.7	3.0	Debt/Worth					3.0	3.0
16.4	11.8	8.6						8.8	7.1
44.2	46.4	39.7						43.4	41.6
(87) 16.7	(76) 20.2	(78) 15.3	% Profit Before Taxes/Tangible Net Worth					(18) 10.8	(51) 16.5
3.2	3.1	5.8						-1.8	9.3
10.6	10.8	9.0						9.1	9.0
4.5	5.6	5.0	% Profit Before Taxes/Total Assets					3.6	6.3
1.1	.5	.8						-.2	2.2
293.8	109.2	143.2						371.9	97.3
33.5	33.2	26.8	Sales/Net Fixed Assets					26.8	28.8
14.3	12.2	10.8						7.2	11.1
7.2	7.6	7.3						11.5	6.9
5.0	5.1	4.5	Sales/Total Assets					5.7	4.7
3.3	3.3	3.0						2.9	3.5
.2	.3	.2						.2	.2
(93) .7	(69) .7	(73) .7	% Depr., Dep., Amort./Sales					(14) 1.1	(51) .6
1.8	1.8	1.8						2.9	1.4
.7	.7	.6						1.3	.2
(38) 1.6	(28) 1.5	(33) 1.3	% Officers', Directors' Owners' Comp/Sales					(11) 1.6	(19) .8
2.5	2.1	1.9						2.5	1.3
11846811M	15361470M	13497630M	Net Sales ($)		1829M	9213M	57837M	302839M	13125912M
2296741M	3204891M	3053070M	Total Assets ($)		471M	2951M	21185M	71257M	2957206M

M = $ thousand MM = $ million

See Pages 9 through 22 for Explanation of Ratios and Data

Current Data Sorted by Assets							Comparative Historical Data	
						Type of Statement		
			4	1	3	Unqualified	9	14
	1	7	5			Reviewed	13	11
3	2	2	2			Compiled	7	8
	2	2				Tax Returns	7	9
	3	8	4	1		Other	20	28
	13 (4/1-9/30/13)		37 (10/1/13-3/31/14)				4/1/09-3/31/10	4/1/10-3/31/11
0-500M	500M-2MM	2-10MM	10-50MM	50-100MM	100-250MM		ALL	ALL
3	8	19	15	2	3	NUMBER OF STATEMENTS	56	70
%	%	%	%	%	%	**ASSETS**	%	%
		6.2	8.1			Cash & Equivalents	6.5	7.6
		53.3	33.3			Trade Receivables (net)	39.9	36.8
		18.8	12.6			Inventory	20.2	23.2
		.9	6.0			All Other Current	4.9	2.7
		79.2	60.0			Total Current	71.5	70.3
		8.2	29.7			Fixed Assets (net)	18.1	20.6
		2.3	1.5			Intangibles (net)	2.0	3.0
		10.3	8.7			All Other Non-Current	8.5	6.1
		100.0	100.0			Total	100.0	100.0
						LIABILITIES		
		21.9	5.2			Notes Payable-Short Term	16.3	17.3
		1.0	1.5			Cur. Mat.-L.T.D.	2.9	4.7
		29.4	33.2			Trade Payables	26.7	26.0
		.1	.3			Income Taxes Payable	.2	.1
		6.6	9.4			All Other Current	8.3	7.9
		59.0	49.7			Total Current	54.4	56.0
		4.3	9.2			Long-Term Debt	10.4	12.5
		.0	.4			Deferred Taxes	.3	.4
		3.7	3.7			All Other Non-Current	3.8	3.8
		33.0	37.0			Net Worth	31.1	27.3
		100.0	100.0			Total Liabilities & Net Worth	100.0	100.0
						INCOME DATA		
		100.0	100.0			Net Sales	100.0	100.0
		10.1	12.3			Gross Profit	13.9	16.6
		8.7	12.1			Operating Expenses	11.8	14.6
		1.4	.2			Operating Profit	2.1	2.1
		.0	-.5			All Other Expenses (net)	.2	.6
		1.4	.7			Profit Before Taxes	1.9	1.5
						RATIOS		
		1.7	1.5				2.2	2.1
		1.3	1.1			Current	1.3	1.4
		1.1	1.0				1.0	1.0
		1.2	1.0				1.3	1.3
		1.1	.8			Quick	.8	.8
		.7	.6				.5	.5
		16 22.3	15 23.7				13 29.0	15 23.7
		24 15.5	18 19.9			Sales/Receivables	20 18.2	23 16.0
		30 12.0	23 16.1				29 12.7	30 12.2
		3 138.9	4 94.1				5 71.8	7 51.9
		5 74.1	7 52.5			Cost of Sales/Inventory	10 37.0	13 28.0
		18 19.8	24 15.5				25 14.8	32 11.3
		9 39.0	10 36.7				10 35.0	10 38.3
		13 28.9	18 19.9			Cost of Sales/Payables	14 25.9	16 22.4
		20 17.9	52 7.0				24 15.4	30 12.0
		27.6	21.5				14.5	13.6
		37.9	62.1			Sales/Working Capital	37.0	32.2
		109.9	-198.2				271.7	247.8
		33.0	16.1				22.6	14.6
		(17) 9.1	(14) 4.7			EBIT/Interest	(49) 6.3	(63) 2.8
		3.3	1.5				1.2	.6
						Net Profit + Depr., Dep., Amort./Cur. Mat. L/T/D		
		.0	.1				.0	.1
		.0	1.2			Fixed/Worth	.4	.5
		.3	1.8				1.8	1.8
		1.1	1.2				.9	1.0
		2.5	1.9			Debt/Worth	3.1	2.7
		5.9	3.3				6.8	6.8
		76.9	27.2				57.6	38.2
		(18) 26.2	10.9			% Profit Before Taxes/Tangible Net Worth	(49) 33.6	(61) 16.4
		10.2	-.3				10.8	.0
		13.0	9.1				19.3	14.3
		9.8	3.2			% Profit Before Taxes/Total Assets	9.0	5.5
		2.9	-.1				1.3	-.9
		999.8	106.6				736.2	352.7
		597.3	45.3			Sales/Net Fixed Assets	64.0	48.5
		87.4	10.7				16.4	12.2
		11.4	9.2				10.5	9.1
		8.2	6.4			Sales/Total Assets	7.0	6.2
		5.2	1.4				4.7	2.9
		.0	.3				.0	.2
		(13) .2	.7			% Depr., Dep., Amort./Sales	(44) .2	(54) .5
		.8	1.1				1.1	1.2
							.3	.4
						% Officers', Directors' Owners' Comp/Sales	(18) 1.1	(11) 1.9
							3.2	3.3
11462M	112051M	851737M	2023801M	653254M	1456359M	Net Sales ($)	6366833M	7285664M
871M	11931M	99437M	303131M	132747M	461685M	Total Assets ($)	1358847M	1844891M

M = $ thousand MM = $ million

See Pages 9 through 22 for Explanation of Ratios and Data

Comparative Historical Data / Current Data Sorted by Sales

4/1/11-3/31/12 ALL	4/1/12-3/31/13 ALL	4/1/13-3/31/14 ALL	Type of Statement	0-1MM	1-3MM	3-5MM	5-10MM	10-25MM	25MM & OVER
6	5	8	Unqualified						8
14	11	13	Reviewed			1		3	9
9	4	9	Compiled	1	1		1	3	3
15	6	4	Tax Returns				1	2	1
22	24	16	Other				3	4	9
				13 (4/1-9/30/13)			37 (10/1/13-3/31/14)		
66	50	50	NUMBER OF STATEMENTS	1	1	1	5	12	30
%	%	%	ASSETS	%	%	%	%	%	%
8.1	6.3	7.2	Cash & Equivalents					8.0	5.7
41.5	40.0	44.3	Trade Receivables (net)					40.9	47.6
19.4	22.2	18.3	Inventory					15.7	16.9
2.0	4.5	3.8	All Other Current					6.1	2.1
71.0	73.1	73.6	Total Current					70.6	72.3
17.5	18.7	17.6	Fixed Assets (net)					14.9	19.2
3.0	2.5	1.3	Intangibles (net)					3.6	.8
8.5	5.7	7.4	All Other Non-Current					10.9	7.7
100.0	100.0	100.0	Total					100.0	100.0
			LIABILITIES						
17.2	15.0	15.8	Notes Payable-Short Term					24.2	10.5
2.5	2.5	2.5	Cur. Mat.-L.T.D.					2.1	1.9
30.5	26.4	28.7	Trade Payables					24.4	29.2
.4	.0	.2	Income Taxes Payable					.0	.2
6.0	6.7	7.8	All Other Current					7.3	7.7
56.6	50.7	55.0	Total Current					57.9	49.6
9.5	13.7	10.3	Long-Term Debt					8.1	8.7
.1	.0	.2	Deferred Taxes					.0	.4
5.8	4.6	7.2	All Other Non-Current					3.5	6.0
28.1	31.0	27.3	Net Worth					30.5	35.4
100.0	100.0	100.0	Total Liabilties & Net Worth					100.0	100.0
			INCOME DATA						
100.0	100.0	100.0	Net Sales					100.0	100.0
15.7	16.2	12.7	Gross Profit					10.1	11.6
13.6	14.3	11.7	Operating Expenses					9.8	10.0
2.2	1.9	1.0	Operating Profit					.3	1.6
.0	.4	-.1	All Other Expenses (net)					-.8	.2
2.1	1.5	1.1	Profit Before Taxes					1.0	1.4
			RATIOS						
1.7	2.4	1.9						1.5	2.0
1.3	1.5	1.4	Current					1.2	1.4
1.0	1.2	1.1						1.0	1.0
1.3	1.5	1.2						1.1	1.3
.9	.9	1.0	Quick					.9	1.0
.6	.5	.6						.7	.7
13 27.3	**15** 23.8	**14** 26.0						**19** 19.5	**14** 26.0
22 16.9	**19** 19.3	**20** 18.3	Sales/Receivables					**21** 17.1	**19** 19.5
29 12.7	**29** 12.8	**29** 12.6						**30** 12.1	**29** 12.8
3 111.6	**3** 116.9	**2** 186.4						**4** 85.1	**3** 128.8
10 34.9	**11** 34.5	**7** 50.9	Cost of Sales/Inventory					**8** 46.5	**7** 55.6
19 19.3	**37** 9.9	**22** 16.9						**24** 15.1	**15** 25.1
9 39.8	**9** 39.8	**9** 41.3						**5** 70.4	**9** 39.5
17 22.0	**16** 23.5	**14** 27.0	Cost of Sales/Payables					**18** 20.1	**13** 29.0
24 15.0	**24** 15.2	**21** 17.6						**25** 14.5	**19** 19.7
23.4	15.7	19.3						24.1	21.1
47.8	26.4	37.3	Sales/Working Capital					43.4	38.8
388.7	91.6	183.4						NM	250.6
21.6	20.5	17.8						17.6	30.0
(58) 4.5	(45) 5.7	(45) 4.9	EBIT/Interest					(11) 4.8	(27) 5.3
1.8	2.0	2.0						1.8	3.0
		11.3							
		(11) 2.4	Net Profit + Depr., Dep., Amort./Cur. Mat. L/T/D						
		.7							
.1	.0	.0						.0	.0
.4	.2	.2	Fixed/Worth					.3	.3
1.2	1.6	.9						.7	1.4
1.4	1.0	1.2						2.0	1.1
3.3	1.9	2.2	Debt/Worth					2.3	2.1
7.1	5.9	4.0						4.8	3.3
62.4	58.0	54.8						73.5	36.6
(58) 25.8	(45) 23.4	(47) 22.3	% Profit Before Taxes/Tangible Net Worth					(11) 38.2	21.8
13.0	9.6	5.5						1.2	9.5
15.3	13.5	17.3						20.7	13.8
6.8	6.5	5.8	% Profit Before Taxes/Total Assets					7.8	7.2
1.8	2.2	1.4						.9	2.0
334.3	999.8	999.8						340.1	999.8
88.4	98.7	125.0	Sales/Net Fixed Assets					93.2	142.1
25.5	17.6	21.1						23.9	16.2
9.5	8.8	10.6						10.2	11.8
6.9	6.3	6.4	Sales/Total Assets					6.3	7.0
4.8	4.3	4.6						2.0	5.3
.1	.1	.1						.2	.0
(50) .3	(34) .4	(38) .3	% Depr., Dep., Amort./Sales					(10) .4	(23) .3
.8	1.1	1.0						.8	1.1
.7	.6	.4							
(23) 1.5	(15) 1.6	(13) .6	% Officers', Directors' Owners' Comp/Sales						
3.9	3.4	2.1							
4916230M	5463836M	5108664M	Net Sales ($)	763M	2675M	4599M	39646M	233650M	4827331M
866572M	1251686M	1009802M	Total Assets ($)	141M	437M	967M	9041M	69151M	930065M

M = $ thousand MM = $ million

See Pages 9 through 22 for Explanation of Ratios and Data

Current Data Sorted by Assets | Comparative Historical Data

0-500M	500M-2MM	2-10MM	10-50MM	50-100MM	100-250MM	Type of Statement	4/1/09-3/31/10 ALL	4/1/10-3/31/11 ALL
			2	3	4	Unqualified	11	7
	1	5	8	1		Reviewed	20	24
	1	7				Compiled	17	10
2	5	2	1			Tax Returns	13	12
1	4	11	9	1	2	Other	16	25
	16 (4/1-9/30/13)		54 (10/1/13-3/31/14)					
3	11	25	20	5	6	**NUMBER OF STATEMENTS**	77	78
%	%	%	%	%	%	**ASSETS**	%	%
	9.2	9.4	6.9			Cash & Equivalents	6.6	6.9
	34.2	25.5	28.6			Trade Receivables (net)	27.3	28.3
	27.4	38.7	39.7			Inventory	33.7	34.0
	4.1	1.8	1.3			All Other Current	3.0	2.2
	74.9	75.4	76.4			Total Current	70.7	71.4
	14.6	17.9	14.7			Fixed Assets (net)	21.2	21.2
	5.1	2.1	3.7			Intangibles (net)	3.2	2.5
	5.3	4.6	5.2			All Other Non-Current	4.9	4.8
	100.0	100.0	100.0			Total	100.0	100.0
						LIABILITIES		
	15.4	17.7	20.0			Notes Payable-Short Term	18.2	14.1
	4.0	1.6	1.1			Cur. Mat.-L.T.D.	2.0	1.8
	28.9	19.2	20.1			Trade Payables	18.8	21.4
	.1	.0	.0			Income Taxes Payable	.2	.2
	2.9	5.3	5.6			All Other Current	8.8	6.9
	51.3	43.9	46.8			Total Current	47.9	44.5
	9.0	8.3	4.1			Long-Term Debt	12.5	13.9
	.0	.0	.3			Deferred Taxes	.2	.0
	11.5	9.9	1.4			All Other Non-Current	6.5	5.5
	28.2	37.9	47.3			Net Worth	32.8	36.0
	100.0	100.0	100.0			Total Liabilities & Net Worth	100.0	100.0
						INCOME DATA		
	100.0	100.0	100.0			Net Sales	100.0	100.0
	32.1	23.4	20.0			Gross Profit	23.1	24.6
	30.5	21.1	17.0			Operating Expenses	20.8	21.9
	1.6	2.3	3.0			Operating Profit	2.3	2.7
	.3	.3	.2			All Other Expenses (net)	.5	.8
	1.3	2.1	2.8			Profit Before Taxes	1.8	1.9
						RATIOS		
	2.8	3.1	3.9				2.6	2.1
	1.4	1.6	1.3			Current	1.6	1.5
	1.1	1.2	1.2				1.2	1.2
	1.7	1.4	2.1				1.2	1.1
	1.0	.7	.6			Quick	.8	.8
	.4	.5	.5				.5	.5
	5 69.1	**19** 19.3	**20** 17.9				**17** 21.3	**18** 20.6
	17 21.5	**28** 13.1	**29** 12.7			Sales/Receivables	**27** 13.7	**26** 13.8
	43 8.5	**33** 10.9	**38** 9.6				**37** 9.9	**38** 9.5
	5 68.9	**34** 10.7	**25** 14.4				**25** 14.8	**25** 14.4
	9 39.9	**53** 6.9	**60** 6.1			Cost of Sales/Inventory	**46** 7.9	**47** 7.8
	45 8.2	**65** 5.6	**85** 4.3				**66** 5.5	**65** 5.6
	5 68.6	**14** 26.6	**11** 32.9				**10** 36.8	**13** 28.2
	17 21.4	**23** 15.9	**21** 17.4			Cost of Sales/Payables	**22** 16.9	**24** 15.5
	49 7.4	**31** 11.8	**49** 7.4				**37** 9.8	**48** 7.6
	17.9	7.4	7.5				8.4	9.5
	33.3	12.3	20.1			Sales/Working Capital	16.7	18.3
	89.3	24.2	24.3				41.7	29.5
		13.2	43.3				9.6	9.5
		(24) 4.5	(19) 7.9			EBIT/Interest	(74) 4.0	(76) 4.0
		1.6	3.0				1.3	1.5
							15.1	5.4
						Net Profit + Depr., Dep., Amort./Cur. Mat. L/T/D	(17) 3.2	(18) 2.6
							1.0	1.4
	.0	.2	.1				.1	.2
	.3	.5	.3			Fixed/Worth	.4	.5
	7.3	.9	.6				1.3	1.3
	.5	.7	.3				.9	.9
	2.9	1.7	1.8			Debt/Worth	1.9	1.7
	208.7	4.2	3.2				4.9	3.9
		28.6	39.1				34.8	38.1
		(22) 17.0	17.9			% Profit Before Taxes/Tangible Net Worth	(68) 17.5	(69) 19.0
		9.6	10.4				5.7	5.4
	29.7	12.4	12.9				12.1	13.5
	11.8	6.3	6.6			% Profit Before Taxes/Total Assets	6.3	5.4
	.5	2.8	3.5				.9	1.3
	999.8	75.4	95.1				106.9	88.7
	107.2	29.4	35.9			Sales/Net Fixed Assets	30.1	29.7
	18.7	10.5	16.7				9.3	8.2
	11.1	4.7	4.7				4.6	4.5
	6.3	3.5	2.9			Sales/Total Assets	3.3	3.6
	3.2	2.7	2.4				2.4	2.4
		.3	.3				.2	.3
		(20) 1.1	(17) .6			% Depr., Dep., Amort./Sales	(67) .6	(69) .9
		2.0	1.6				1.6	2.0
		1.1	.3				1.1	.8
		(16) 1.9	(10) 1.0			% Officers', Directors' Owners' Comp/Sales	(45) 2.2	(37) 1.5
		3.4	2.8				4.8	2.8
3455M	93677M	372182M	1673214M	1110511M	2244978M	Net Sales ($)	2902395M	3282551M
924M	11018M	108161M	433250M	342061M	888427M	Total Assets ($)	894387M	942002M

M = $ thousand MM = $ million

See Pages 9 through 22 for Explanation of Ratios and Data

Comparative Historical Data										Current Data Sorted by Sales			
						Type of Statement							
	8		5		9	Unqualified							9
	23		20		15	Reviewed					4		11
	14		13		8	Compiled		1			7		
	12		7		10	Tax Returns	1	2	2	2	2		1
	27		29		28	Other		3		6	6		13
							16 (4/1-9/30/13)			54 (10/1/13-3/31/14)			
	4/1/11-3/31/12 ALL		**4/1/12-3/31/13 ALL**		**4/1/13-3/31/14 ALL**		**0-1MM**	**1-3MM**	**3-5MM**	**5-10MM**	**10-25MM**		**25MM & OVER**
	84		74		70	**NUMBER OF STATEMENTS**	1	6	2	8	19		34
	%		%		%	**ASSETS**	%	%	%	%	%		%
	8.4		7.3		8.2	Cash & Equivalents					9.4		6.8
	28.7		29.3		28.0	Trade Receivables (net)					26.5		29.0
	34.8		35.4		35.6	Inventory					34.0		36.4
	2.5		2.8		2.1	All Other Current					3.4		1.8
	74.4		74.8		73.9	Total Current					73.4		74.1
	15.8		15.0		16.4	Fixed Assets (net)					20.7		16.4
	5.2		6.2		5.1	Intangibles (net)					1.6		4.4
	4.6		4.0		4.6	All Other Non-Current					4.4		5.2
	100.0		100.0		100.0	Total					100.0		100.0
						LIABILITIES							
	14.1		18.5		16.6	Notes Payable-Short Term					16.7		16.5
	1.7		1.3		2.0	Cur. Mat.-L.T.D.					2.1		1.7
	24.0		22.9		21.2	Trade Payables					22.0		20.4
	.2		.1		.1	Income Taxes Payable					.0		.1
	7.8		6.2		6.0	All Other Current					6.7		7.2
	47.7		49.0		45.8	Total Current					47.6		45.9
	11.2		6.9		12.9	Long-Term Debt					9.4		14.6
	.1		.4		.3	Deferred Taxes					.0		.5
	7.7		5.2		6.3	All Other Non-Current					4.1		2.0
	33.2		38.4		34.8	Net Worth					38.9		36.9
	100.0		100.0		100.0	Total Liabilities & Net Worth					100.0		100.0
						INCOME DATA							
	100.0		100.0		100.0	Net Sales					100.0		100.0
	22.3		19.8		23.1	Gross Profit					24.8		19.5
	19.5		16.4		20.3	Operating Expenses					22.5		15.5
	2.7		3.5		2.9	Operating Profit					2.3		3.9
	.4		.5		.2	All Other Expenses (net)					.0		.1
	2.4		3.0		2.6	Profit Before Taxes					2.3		3.8
						RATIOS							
	2.1		2.2		2.8						2.8		2.9
	1.5		1.5		1.5	Current					1.5		1.3
	1.2		1.1		1.2						1.2		1.2
	1.2		1.0		1.5						1.4		1.6
	.7		.7		.7	Quick					.7		.6
	.5		.5		.5						.5		.5
18	20.7	**21**	17.6	**19**	19.1					**11**	34.0	**24**	15.2
27	13.6	**28**	13.1	**28**	13.1	Sales/Receivables				**20**	18.2	**30**	12.1
36	10.0	**36**	10.0	**35**	10.5					**30**	12.0	**38**	9.6
24	14.9	**25**	14.5	**26**	14.1					**24**	15.5	**32**	11.5
40	9.2	**43**	8.5	**48**	7.6	Cost of Sales/Inventory				**36**	10.2	**51**	7.1
64	5.7	**61**	6.0	**69**	5.3					**60**	6.1	**70**	5.2
11	33.0	**12**	30.0	**12**	29.2					**12**	29.9	**15**	24.1
23	16.2	**23**	15.7	**21**	17.5	Cost of Sales/Payables				**20**	17.9	**21**	17.6
45	8.1	**35**	10.5	**38**	9.5					**26**	14.1	**40**	9.1
	10.1		9.0		8.0						12.3		6.9
	18.1		16.9		16.9	Sales/Working Capital					23.5		20.1
	42.3		50.6		34.0						55.1		26.7
	20.4		18.1		20.3						13.2		35.9
(75)	6.2	(68)	7.4	(64)	6.4	EBIT/Interest					5.4	(33)	13.3
	2.7		3.8		3.0						3.1		5.3
	19.8		26.1		6.0								7.0
(18)	3.6	(18)	3.7	(17)	3.8	Net Profit + Depr., Dep., Amort./Cur. Mat. L/T/D						(11)	4.3
	1.8		1.3		1.5								2.3
	.1		.1		.1						.2		.0
	.4		.4		.4	Fixed/Worth					.5		.4
	1.0		1.0		.9						.9		.8
	1.2		1.0		.8						.6		.6
	2.5		2.1		1.8	Debt/Worth					1.4		1.7
	4.4		4.5		5.1						3.3		3.5
	43.4		44.4		43.2						45.9		42.9
(75)	28.5	(67)	26.4	(62)	21.0	% Profit Before Taxes/Tangible Net Worth				(16)	19.8	(32)	23.9
	9.0		13.8		10.1						10.7		13.9
	15.2		14.6		13.3						13.6		13.7
	8.3		8.0		8.0	% Profit Before Taxes/Total Assets					8.5		8.6
	2.3		3.3		3.6						4.5		6.2
	198.9		161.0		111.1						79.5		154.9
	52.6		56.8		38.9	Sales/Net Fixed Assets					52.4		35.8
	12.4		16.4		12.2						11.2		7.9
	5.0		5.2		4.8						5.7		4.5
	3.7		3.4		3.2	Sales/Total Assets					4.6		2.9
	2.5		2.4		2.6						3.2		2.3
	.2		.2		.3						.3		.3
(67)	.6	(60)	.6	(53)	.8	% Depr., Dep., Amort./Sales				(17)	1.2	(27)	.6
	1.6		1.4		1.9						2.3		1.8
	.6		.6		.8						1.1		.3
(43)	1.3	(40)	1.5	(35)	1.4	% Officers', Directors' Owners' Comp/Sales				(11)	1.8	(14)	.7
	2.8		2.9		2.7						3.7		2.3
	4141686M		**4816274M**		**5498017M**	Net Sales ($)	**885M**	**11174M**	**8251M**	**64940M**	**296600M**		**5116167M**
	1299692M		**1689312M**		**1783841M**	Total Assets ($)	**169M**	**3656M**	**1950M**	**23024M**	**73075M**		**1681967M**

M = $ thousand MM = $ million

See Pages 9 through 22 for Explanation of Ratios and Data

	Current Data Sorted by Assets						Comparative Historical Data	
Type of Statement								
Unqualified			4	13	6	2	35	32
Reviewed	1	2	28	13			62	64
Compiled		5	12	1	1		30	23
Tax Returns	5	9	14	1			35	37
Other	1	17	37	37	16	5	95	88
	41 (4/1-9/30/13)			189 (10/1/13-3/31/14)			4/1/09-3/31/10 ALL	4/1/10-3/31/11 ALL
	0-500M	**500M-2MM**	**2-10MM**	**10-50MM**	**50-100MM**	**100-250MM**		
NUMBER OF STATEMENTS	7	33	95	65	23	7	257	244
ASSETS	%	%	%	%	%	%	%	%
Cash & Equivalents		16.3	9.1	4.7	2.4		6.2	7.4
Trade Receivables (net)		38.4	39.5	31.6	29.0		35.3	34.8
Inventory		23.2	34.5	42.7	48.3		35.0	32.7
All Other Current		1.8	1.4	2.6	1.6		2.0	2.6
Total Current		79.7	84.5	81.5	81.3		78.5	77.6
Fixed Assets (net)		13.2	10.1	10.3	13.8		14.0	14.5
Intangibles (net)		.4	1.3	4.7	2.4		2.9	2.9
All Other Non-Current		6.7	4.1	3.5	2.5		4.6	5.0
Total		100.0	100.0	100.0	100.0		100.0	100.0
LIABILITIES								
Notes Payable-Short Term		9.2	17.5	28.5	36.1		22.1	21.2
Cur. Mat.-L.T.D.		.4	2.0	1.4	.6		3.1	1.7
Trade Payables		31.2	29.2	20.5	17.5		23.7	25.1
Income Taxes Payable		.1	.1	.1	.1		.1	.2
All Other Current		8.2	6.6	6.9	4.0		6.2	7.0
Total Current		49.2	55.3	57.5	58.2		55.1	55.2
Long-Term Debt		12.9	6.4	10.1	6.9		9.8	7.5
Deferred Taxes		.0	.1	.3	.0		.2	.2
All Other Non-Current		6.5	5.0	2.8	3.8		5.5	5.6
Net Worth		31.4	33.2	29.3	31.0		29.4	31.5
Total Liabilities & Net Worth		100.0	100.0	100.0	100.0		100.0	100.0
INCOME DATA								
Net Sales		100.0	100.0	100.0	100.0		100.0	100.0
Gross Profit		17.7	12.9	11.9	14.9		14.5	14.4
Operating Expenses		15.5	10.9	8.9	12.2		12.5	12.5
Operating Profit		2.2	2.0	3.0	2.7		2.0	2.0
All Other Expenses (net)		.2	.3	.6	.3		.5	.4
Profit Before Taxes		2.0	1.8	2.4	2.4		1.5	1.5
RATIOS								
Current		3.0	2.3	1.7	1.5		1.8	1.9
		1.7	1.5	1.3	1.4		1.4	1.4
		1.1	1.1	1.2	1.2		1.1	1.1
Quick		2.1	1.4	.8	.7		1.1	1.1
		1.0	.8	.6	.5		.7	.7
		.7	.5	.5	.4		.5	.5
Sales/Receivables		14 25.7	24 15.0	27 13.4	30 12.3		23 15.8	21 17.0
		27 13.3	30 12.2	33 11.1	32 11.3		29 12.4	30 12.0
		33 11.0	38 9.5	41 8.8	41 9.0		39 9.4	39 9.3
Cost of Sales/Inventory		2 217.5	10 36.5	26 13.8	51 7.1		16 22.7	12 31.3
		11 33.1	29 12.4	60 6.1	63 5.8		39 9.5	34 10.8
		36 10.0	62 5.9	94 3.9	96 3.8		58 6.3	65 5.6
Cost of Sales/Payables		10 37.5	16 23.5	12 31.3	14 26.4		13 27.8	12 29.6
		28 13.1	23 15.8	22 16.7	26 14.0		22 16.3	23 16.1
		41 8.9	34 10.6	35 10.4	33 11.1		33 11.0	34 10.7
Sales/Working Capital		9.4	9.7	8.3	6.7		10.3	10.3
		21.9	16.5	14.7	14.8		17.5	19.2
		298.9	57.8	30.8	36.2		56.4	70.0
EBIT/Interest		20.1	19.8	8.9	12.9		7.8	10.2
		(26) 3.8	(84) 6.6	(62) 4.3	5.0		(243) 3.1	(219) 4.4
		.9	1.8	2.1	2.3		1.3	1.8
Net Profit + Depr., Dep., Amort./Cur. Mat. L/T/D			41.0	8.3			7.5	10.2
			(12) 9.1	(15) 3.0			(64) 3.9	(53) 4.3
			3.0	1.3			1.0	1.7
Fixed/Worth		.0	.0	.0	.0		.0	.0
		.2	.2	.2	.1		.3	.3
		.9	.8	.9	.9		1.0	1.0
Debt/Worth		.8	1.1	1.7	1.9		1.4	1.2
		3.3	2.1	3.0	2.7		2.9	2.6
		8.1	4.9	5.9	4.0		7.7	6.0
% Profit Before Taxes/Tangible Net Worth		73.2	38.2	36.4	41.5		39.3	44.8
		(30) 23.4	(87) 18.4	(60) 26.7	19.8		(232) 15.3	(221) 21.6
		2.9	7.0	9.3	6.9		4.5	7.5
% Profit Before Taxes/Total Assets		24.8	15.2	11.9	13.4		10.4	11.6
		6.2	6.0	6.0	4.4		3.8	4.3
		.9	1.4	1.9	.9		.9	1.7
Sales/Net Fixed Assets		297.8	516.9	621.1	924.6		385.6	422.9
		104.8	93.4	113.1	164.5		79.9	88.1
		25.7	33.1	20.3	11.2		20.8	17.7
Sales/Total Assets		7.3	6.2	4.5	3.8		5.3	5.6
		5.9	4.1	3.1	3.0		4.1	3.9
		3.5	3.4	2.2	2.1		2.7	2.8
% Depr., Dep., Amort./Sales		.1	.1	.1	.0		.1	.1
		(19) .3	(70) .3	(57) .2	(21) .2		(212) .4	(191) .4
		.9	.6	.9	.9		.9	1.0
% Officers', Directors' Owners' Comp/Sales		1.4	.9				.8	.8
		(17) 2.1	(45) 1.5				(110) 1.3	(105) 1.5
		4.9	2.3				2.4	2.7
Net Sales ($)	50743M	234126M	2240701M	5134645M	5077746M	2451290M	15630556M	16377187M
Total Assets ($)	1862M	35857M	488764M	1613876M	1624600M	1042838M	5174124M	4964324M

M = $ thousand MM = $ million

See Pages 9 through 22 for Explanation of Ratios and Data

Comparative Historical Data				Current Data Sorted by Sales					
			Type of Statement						
35	36	25	Unqualified					4	21
56	41	44	Reviewed			2	1	19	22
30	34	19	Compiled		1		4	8	6
46	32	29	Tax Returns		3	5	5	9	7
102	105	113	Other		6	3	10	27	67
4/1/11-3/31/12 ALL	4/1/12-3/31/13 ALL	4/1/13-3/31/14 ALL		41 (4/1-9/30/13)			189 (10/1/13-3/31/14)		
				0-1MM	1-3MM	3-5MM	5-10MM	10-25MM	25MM & OVER
269	248	230	**NUMBER OF STATEMENTS**		10	10	20	67	123
%	%	%	**ASSETS**	%	%	%	%	%	%
9.5	7.1	8.4	Cash & Equivalents	DATA NOT AVAILABLE	12.7	16.4	13.7	10.1	5.5
32.3	31.4	34.9	Trade Receivables (net)		31.2	29.0	31.3	40.6	33.1
34.7	39.6	36.3	Inventory		28.3	23.0	26.2	33.4	41.3
3.1	2.9	2.0	All Other Current		.2	1.0	1.7	2.0	2.3
79.6	81.0	81.5	Total Current		72.5	69.4	72.9	86.1	82.1
13.7	12.0	11.8	Fixed Assets (net)		16.9	23.1	19.4	8.4	11.1
1.7	1.8	2.3	Intangibles (net)		.4	.8	.1	2.1	3.1
5.0	5.2	4.3	All Other Non-Current		10.2	6.7	7.7	3.4	3.6
100.0	100.0	100.0	Total		100.0	100.0	100.0	100.0	100.0
			LIABILITIES						
20.2	25.3	21.7	Notes Payable-Short Term		15.8	10.0	6.6	16.9	28.2
1.9	1.5	1.4	Cur. Mat.-L.T.D.		.4	.0	2.1	1.5	1.5
24.1	22.7	25.0	Trade Payables		30.5	16.4	30.6	28.9	22.2
.2	.1	.1	Income Taxes Payable		.6	.0	.0	.0	.1
6.4	7.0	6.9	All Other Current		4.6	14.2	6.2	8.1	5.9
52.7	56.6	55.1	Total Current		51.8	40.7	45.6	55.4	57.9
8.0	7.7	9.9	Long-Term Debt		35.5	15.6	23.7	3.4	8.6
.2	.1	.1	Deferred Taxes		.0	.0	.1	.1	.2
5.9	6.0	4.6	All Other Non-Current		9.1	3.6	5.5	6.9	2.9
33.2	29.6	30.3	Net Worth		3.6	40.0	25.1	34.1	30.4
100.0	100.0	100.0	Total Liabilties & Net Worth		100.0	100.0	100.0	100.0	100.0
			INCOME DATA						
100.0	100.0	100.0	Net Sales		100.0	100.0	100.0	100.0	100.0
14.2	12.8	13.5	Gross Profit		19.6	20.8	17.1	13.1	12.0
11.6	10.4	11.2	Operating Expenses		17.4	17.8	15.5	11.1	9.4
2.7	2.5	2.3	Operating Profit		2.2	3.0	1.6	2.0	2.6
.3	.3	.4	All Other Expenses (net)		.5	.0	.5	.2	.4
2.4	2.1	2.0	Profit Before Taxes		1.7	3.0	1.1	1.8	2.1
			RATIOS						
2.0	2.0	2.2			3.1	5.1	2.8	2.4	1.8
1.4	1.4	1.4	Current		1.5	2.4	1.8	1.5	1.4
1.2	1.1	1.1			.7	.9	.9	1.2	1.2
1.2	1.1	1.1			1.2	2.1	2.0	1.5	.9
.7	.6	.7	Quick		.7	1.0	.8	.8	.6
.5	.4	.5			.5	.7	.5	.5	.5
20 18.2	**23** 15.9	**24** 14.9			**2** 224.6	**0** UND	**10** 38.0	**26** 14.2	**26** 14.3
29 12.4	**30** 12.3	**30** 12.2	Sales/Receivables		**29** 12.6	**28** 12.9	**23** 16.0	**31** 11.7	**30** 12.0
37 9.9	**38** 9.7	**38** 9.5			**56** 6.5	**34** 10.7	**30** 12.0	**41** 8.9	**39** 9.3
12 29.3	**21** 17.5	**14** 26.9			**0** UND	**0** UND	**2** 176.9	**8** 46.2	**22** 16.6
35 10.3	**47** 7.7	**37** 9.9	Cost of Sales/Inventory		**38** 9.7	**5** 67.5	**20** 18.5	**29** 12.8	**51** 7.1
64 5.7	**81** 4.5	**69** 5.3			**81** 4.5	**66** 5.5	**39** 9.4	**69** 5.3	**76** 4.8
12 31.4	**12** 31.7	**14** 26.1			**33** 10.9	**0** UND	**12** 30.7	**15** 23.8	**14** 26.4
23 16.2	**22** 16.9	**23** 15.8	Cost of Sales/Payables		**42** 8.7	**8** 46.9	**16** 22.2	**24** 15.3	**23** 16.0
33 10.9	**33** 11.0	**36** 10.2			**60** 6.1	**33** 10.9	**39** 9.3	**37** 9.9	**31** 11.6
9.4	8.6	9.0			3.4	4.2	9.6	10.3	9.0
16.5	17.3	16.5	Sales/Working Capital		12.5	72.9	20.5	16.5	16.1
39.8	59.1	50.5			-81.5	-81.0	-81.5	41.9	44.2
12.9	10.2	14.7					10.1	18.2	12.3
(243) 4.8	(223) 3.9	(207) 4.6	EBIT/Interest				(18) 3.8	(57) 4.7	(117) 4.6
2.3	1.7	1.8					1.0	1.6	2.2
11.7	9.3	17.3							28.9
(49) 4.3	(44) 4.4	(33) 3.9	Net Profit + Depr., Dep., Amort./Cur. Mat. L/T/D						(25) 3.9
1.8	1.7	1.8							2.0
.0	.0	.0			.0	.0	.1	.0	.0
.2	.2	.2	Fixed/Worth		.1	.4	.6	.2	.2
.8	.9	.8			NM	2.0	1.6	.7	.8
1.2	1.3	1.2			.8	.4	1.2	1.1	1.6
2.6	2.8	2.9	Debt/Worth		3.7	1.2	2.6	2.5	2.9
5.8	6.2	5.8			NM	6.4	6.3	5.3	5.6
47.1	45.3	41.0					41.1	39.1	38.9
(254) 21.8	(232) 21.8	(211) 22.7	% Profit Before Taxes/Tangible Net Worth				(16) 15.8	(62) 16.7	(116) 25.9
9.1	9.1	7.4					2.4	4.3	9.8
12.0	12.9	13.7			17.6	29.4	12.1	14.9	13.1
6.2	5.2	6.0	% Profit Before Taxes/Total Assets		5.7	18.4	5.1	5.9	6.0
2.4	1.8	1.6			1.4	2.0	.5	1.0	2.1
617.5	534.6	519.1			343.1	248.9	297.3	509.1	811.1
85.4	107.2	104.2	Sales/Net Fixed Assets		32.8	50.8	85.9	101.3	154.0
20.7	23.4	25.2			23.9	18.3	15.7	40.6	21.0
5.5	5.3	6.0			5.8	6.9	7.5	6.0	5.0
4.0	3.7	3.9	Sales/Total Assets		3.3	5.5	5.1	4.1	3.6
2.7	2.5	2.5			1.9	2.9	3.4	3.3	2.4
.1	.1	.1					.1	.1	.1
(195) .4	(182) .3	(175) .3	% Depr., Dep., Amort./Sales				(13) .3	(50) .2	(100) .2
.9	.8	.7					1.0	.4	.9
.7	.8	.8					1.3	.9	.2
(107) 1.4	(87) 1.4	(79) 1.6	% Officers', Directors' Owners' Comp/Sales				(12) 1.8	(35) 1.4	(23) .8
2.6	2.3	2.6					2.9	2.0	2.6
17214139M	16868784M	15189251M	Net Sales ($)		22741M	38842M	152826M	1136108M	13838734M
5515326M	5656388M	4807797M	Total Assets ($)		7221M	9109M	33911M	299802M	4457754M

M = $ thousand MM = $ million

See Pages 9 through 22 for Explanation of Ratios and Data

Current Data Sorted by Assets | **Comparative Historical Data**

Type of Statement	0-500M	500M-2MM	2-10MM	10-50MM	50-100MM	100-250MM	4/1/09-3/31/10 ALL	4/1/10-3/31/11 ALL
Unqualified		1	4	14	2	4	32	32
Reviewed		1	22	7			52	49
Compiled	1	4	21	2			45	46
Tax Returns	4	18	12	2			20	27
Other		11	28	18	7	10	69	73
	28 (4/1-9/30/13)			165 (10/1/13-3/31/14)				
NUMBER OF STATEMENTS	5	35	87	43	9	14	218	227
ASSETS	%	%	%	%	%	%	%	%
Cash & Equivalents		10.4	9.2	7.1		4.0	8.4	7.3
Trade Receivables (net)		39.7	44.3	37.5		34.9	37.0	37.8
Inventory		22.6	24.2	27.8		33.5	25.7	27.1
All Other Current		.9	1.1	1.5		1.6	2.8	2.4
Total Current		73.7	78.8	74.0		74.0	73.9	74.5
Fixed Assets (net)		15.5	15.6	17.5		15.2	17.3	16.9
Intangibles (net)		7.1	2.0	3.4		8.0	4.9	4.2
All Other Non-Current		3.7	3.5	5.1		2.8	4.0	4.4
Total		100.0	100.0	100.0		100.0	100.0	100.0
LIABILITIES								
Notes Payable-Short Term		12.8	16.2	21.6		13.8	17.4	15.9
Cur. Mat.-L.T.D.		1.8	2.4	1.3		1.3	1.8	2.9
Trade Payables		26.2	23.7	18.3		26.3	18.7	21.0
Income Taxes Payable		.0	.0	.0		.0	.2	.1
All Other Current		5.0	5.9	7.4		5.8	7.6	7.3
Total Current		45.9	48.3	48.6		47.2	45.7	47.3
Long-Term Debt		20.0	10.9	9.7		18.0	11.7	10.3
Deferred Taxes		.0	.1	.2		.9	.1	.2
All Other Non-Current		8.7	4.7	6.3		3.1	9.8	6.8
Net Worth		25.4	36.0	35.2		30.9	32.7	35.5
Total Liabilties & Net Worth		100.0	100.0	100.0		100.0	100.0	100.0
INCOME DATA								
Net Sales		100.0	100.0	100.0		100.0	100.0	100.0
Gross Profit		17.2	13.0	11.1		8.5	16.5	14.5
Operating Expenses		15.4	11.5	9.9		7.3	13.9	12.5
Operating Profit		1.8	1.5	1.1		1.2	2.6	2.1
All Other Expenses (net)		.4	.2	.3		.7	.3	.4
Profit Before Taxes		1.4	1.3	.9		.5	2.3	1.7
RATIOS								
Current		3.3	2.2	2.6		2.3	2.8	2.4
		1.6	1.5	1.4		1.4	1.6	1.6
		1.1	1.2	1.2		1.1	1.2	1.2
Quick		2.6	1.6	1.9		1.4	1.6	1.6
		1.0	1.1	.9		.8	.9	.9
		.6	.7	.6		.4	.6	.6
Sales/Receivables		**12** 29.9	**17** 21.1	**15** 23.8		**16** 23.2	**15** 24.8	**15** 25.0
		18 20.1	**24** 15.1	**21** 17.0		**20** 18.5	**21** 17.5	**21** 17.5
		30 12.1	**33** 11.2	**29** 12.8		**22** 16.4	**29** 12.8	**28** 12.8
Cost of Sales/Inventory		**4** 84.5	**7** 52.3	**10** 38.3		**17** 20.9	**8** 43.6	**8** 43.7
		13 28.6	**17** 20.9	**18** 20.3		**21** 17.4	**18** 20.4	**18** 19.9
		21 17.4	**29** 12.6	**31** 11.6		**30** 12.1	**31** 11.6	**31** 11.9
Cost of Sales/Payables		**9** 40.8	**7** 50.1	**8** 47.0		**14** 26.5	**7** 49.4	**7** 51.7
		18 19.9	**15** 25.0	**12** 31.0		**16** 22.9	**12** 31.0	**13** 28.0
		25 14.8	**22** 16.9	**17** 21.9		**20** 18.7	**18** 20.0	**20** 18.4
Sales/Working Capital		15.7	13.0	12.4		14.7	11.2	11.6
		26.1	22.7	21.8		34.2	23.2	23.3
		135.4	60.2	85.8		54.9	68.2	57.6
EBIT/Interest		14.7	14.5	10.8		21.0	16.5	15.7
		(31) 4.8	(83) 5.1	(41) 3.6		(13) 4.2	(195) 5.2	(199) 5.0
		1.9	1.8	1.7		2.9	2.0	1.9
Net Profit + Depr., Dep., Amort./Cur. Mat. L/T/D			16.9				15.5	14.4
			(14) 2.6				(39) 4.7	(39) 5.1
			1.6				1.5	1.4
Fixed/Worth		.1	.1	.1		.5	.1	.1
		.7	.3	.4		.7	.4	.4
		2.6	1.0	.8		1.1	1.7	1.0
Debt/Worth		1.4	.9	.9		2.2	.8	1.0
		2.7	2.0	2.4		2.8	2.2	2.1
		10.6	4.3	4.7		7.5	7.1	4.6
% Profit Before Taxes/Tangible Net Worth		79.8	42.4	28.2		42.8	55.1	43.3
		(29) 27.3	(80) 24.4	(38) 14.1		(13) 32.6	(188) 27.9	(203) 23.3
		5.0	5.0	6.3		12.7	12.3	7.1
% Profit Before Taxes/Total Assets		15.7	13.9	9.2		8.4	18.2	15.3
		6.9	7.0	4.8		4.8	8.2	6.9
		2.4	1.7	1.9		3.0	2.5	2.0
Sales/Net Fixed Assets		294.8	396.5	225.8		109.8	234.6	315.3
		94.8	92.6	68.8		42.9	67.9	70.4
		28.9	16.7	13.1		19.1	15.6	16.3
Sales/Total Assets		9.6	8.2	8.3		7.6	8.1	8.7
		6.7	6.2	5.1		6.2	5.6	5.8
		5.6	4.5	3.6		5.1	3.7	4.0
% Depr., Dep., Amort./Sales		.1	.1	.2		.1	.1	.1
		(22) .5	(67) .3	(40) .3		.2	(176) .4	(180) .5
		1.0	1.0	.9		.8	.8	1.0
% Officers', Directors' Owners' Comp/Sales		.7	.6	.2			.7	.5
		(26) 1.5	(47) 1.0	(10) .9			(86) 1.6	(94) 1.1
		3.3	1.9	1.9			3.0	2.5
Net Sales ($)	18682M	337658M	3105890M	5579623M	3702244M	13484815M	20612883M	23073269M
Total Assets ($)	1496M	45851M	418485M	963345M	575025M	2175170M	3994373M	4178882M

M = $ thousand MM = $ million

See Pages 9 through 22 for Explanation of Ratios and Data

Comparative Historical Data | Current Data Sorted by Sales

4/1/11-3/31/12 ALL	4/1/12-3/31/13 ALL	4/1/13-3/31/14 ALL		0-1MM	1-3MM	3-5MM	5-10MM	10-25MM	25MM & OVER
			Type of Statement						
25	14	25	Unqualified				1		24
42	23	30	Reviewed					8	22
38	38	28	Compiled		1	1	4	10	12
26	24	36	Tax Returns		5	1	13	11	6
92	100	74	Other		2	3	4	15	50
				28 (4/1-9/30/13)			165 (10/1/13-3/31/14)		
223	199	193	**NUMBER OF STATEMENTS**		8	5	22	44	114
%	%	%	**ASSETS**	%	%	%	%	%	%
7.0	7.3	8.4	Cash & Equivalents	DATA NOT AVAILABLE			15.5	9.5	7.0
39.2	38.8	40.0	Trade Receivables (net)				33.8	39.1	42.9
26.7	26.8	26.3	Inventory				16.7	27.0	28.3
2.6	1.7	1.2	All Other Current				.1	.7	1.5
75.4	74.5	75.9	Total Current				66.2	76.3	79.7
15.4	16.6	16.6	Fixed Assets (net)				18.1	16.4	14.0
5.1	3.8	3.6	Intangibles (net)				12.0	2.8	2.7
4.1	5.2	3.8	All Other Non-Current				3.7	4.4	3.6
100.0	100.0	100.0	Total				100.0	100.0	100.0
			LIABILITIES						
18.7	18.3	17.3	Notes Payable-Short Term				11.0	13.2	20.1
2.1	2.4	2.0	Cur. Mat.-L.T.D.				1.7	2.6	1.7
24.3	22.5	22.7	Trade Payables				24.2	21.7	23.1
.1	.0	.0	Income Taxes Payable				.0	.0	.0
6.5	7.2	6.5	All Other Current				2.5	6.2	7.0
51.7	50.4	48.6	Total Current				39.4	43.9	52.0
12.3	10.6	13.0	Long-Term Debt				17.4	15.6	9.4
.3	.2	.2	Deferred Taxes				.0	.0	.3
6.6	9.9	6.3	All Other Non-Current				14.8	4.3	4.8
29.1	28.9	31.9	Net Worth				28.3	36.2	33.6
100.0	100.0	100.0	Total Liabilties & Net Worth				100.0	100.0	100.0
			INCOME DATA						
100.0	100.0	100.0	Net Sales				100.0	100.0	100.0
13.8	14.4	13.0	Gross Profit				17.4	14.7	9.9
11.8	12.6	11.6	Operating Expenses				16.4	12.9	8.6
2.0	1.8	1.4	Operating Profit				1.1	1.8	1.3
.3	.4	.3	All Other Expenses (net)				.3	.2	.3
1.7	1.4	1.0	Profit Before Taxes				.8	1.6	1.0
			RATIOS						
2.1	2.3	2.3	Current				3.3	2.8	2.2
1.4	1.5	1.5					1.7	1.7	1.4
1.1	1.1	1.2					1.3	1.1	1.2
1.3	1.5	1.6	Quick				3.2	2.4	1.4
.9	.9	1.0					1.4	1.0	.9
.6	.6	.6					.8	.6	.6
15 23.8	**15** 24.9	**16** 23.5	Sales/Receivables				**11** 33.4	**17** 22.0	**16** 22.9
20 17.9	**20** 17.9	**21** 17.4					**23** 15.7	**22** 16.8	**21** 17.7
28 12.9	**28** 13.1	**30** 12.2					**32** 11.3	**33** 11.2	**28** 13.2
8 48.0	**9** 41.6	**8** 46.5	Cost of Sales/Inventory				**3** 106.0	**8** 43.1	**9** 42.7
17 21.2	**17** 21.9	**18** 20.5					**12** 29.4	**20** 17.9	**17** 20.9
29 12.8	**29** 12.8	**29** 12.5					**26** 14.0	**30** 12.0	**27** 13.3
9 41.0	**8** 46.4	**8** 47.8	Cost of Sales/Payables				**6** 63.9	**7** 55.3	**8** 45.2
15 25.1	**13** 27.1	**14** 25.6					**21** 17.7	**14** 25.8	**14** 26.8
21 17.3	**19** 18.9	**21** 17.3					**32** 11.4	**22** 16.3	**18** 20.2
14.8	13.7	13.8	Sales/Working Capital				9.9	11.6	15.5
26.8	24.6	24.1					24.6	18.3	25.6
83.4	74.5	65.9					88.5	73.3	62.5
12.9	11.7	13.3	EBIT/Interest				25.2	9.3	15.2
(201) 4.4	(183) 5.0	(181) 4.2					(18) 4.4	(41) 3.9	(110) 4.7
1.7	1.9	1.9					-.1	1.8	2.2
8.1	10.6	13.5	Net Profit + Depr., Dep., Amort./Cur. Mat. L/T/D						14.9
(40) 3.8	(37) 3.0	(28) 2.6							(23) 2.7
1.8	1.1	1.1							1.2
.1	.1	.1	Fixed/Worth				.3	.0	.1
.4	.4	.4					.7	.4	.4
1.5	1.0	1.1					2.1	1.3	.8
1.3	1.1	1.2	Debt/Worth				1.2	.9	1.3
2.7	2.2	2.4					2.0	2.4	2.4
7.2	6.0	5.8					7.0	8.5	4.7
47.7	42.0	42.3	% Profit Before Taxes/Tangible Net Worth				70.9	44.8	41.5
(192) 23.3	(174) 21.6	(169) 22.9					(18) 28.1	(39) 21.8	(103) 22.4
7.8	9.3	8.6					-16.1	3.9	9.0
13.8	13.5	12.2	% Profit Before Taxes/Total Assets				21.5	11.3	10.2
5.5	6.4	5.7					7.7	5.5	5.2
2.1	2.1	2.0					-1.6	2.0	2.4
383.4	279.1	301.9	Sales/Net Fixed Assets				175.2	401.0	330.3
82.6	70.1	82.0					44.7	88.9	84.5
21.1	16.7	19.4					20.8	17.1	21.5
9.1	9.1	8.3	Sales/Total Assets				7.9	7.2	8.9
6.1	6.0	6.2					6.1	5.6	6.6
4.2	4.1	4.4					3.3	4.5	4.7
.1	.1	.1	% Depr., Dep., Amort./Sales				.2	.1	.1
(174) .3	(159) .4	(157) .3					(18) .8	(29) .5	(101) .3
.8	.8	.9					1.5	1.1	.7
.5	.7	.6	% Officers', Directors' Owners' Comp/Sales				1.1	.7	.4
(92) 1.1	(75) 1.1	(88) 1.2					(17) 1.7	(27) 1.1	(38) .7
2.0	2.1	2.1					2.2	2.5	1.4
26195256M	**24957736M**	**26228912M**	Net Sales ($)		**18592M**	**20003M**	**151214M**	**713066M**	**25326037M**
4281613M	**4330288M**	**4179372M**	Total Assets ($)		**6981M**	**6901M**	**31712M**	**134330M**	**3999448M**

M = $ thousand MM = $ million

See Pages 9 through 22 for Explanation of Ratios and Data

Current Data Sorted by Assets							Comparative Historical Data	
						Type of Statement		
	2	5	21	5	8	Unqualified	42	40
	1	35	31	1		Reviewed	76	72
4	16	47	12	3		Compiled	76	63
5	17	16	3			Tax Returns	43	39
3	16	61	39	8	5	Other	101	106
	106 (4/1-9/30/13)		258 (10/1/13-3/31/14)				4/1/09-3/31/10	4/1/10-3/31/11
0-500M	500M-2MM	2-10MM	10-50MM	50-100MM	100-250MM		ALL	ALL
12	52	164	106	17	13	NUMBER OF STATEMENTS	338	320
%	%	%	%	%	%	**ASSETS**	%	%
25.5	13.8	12.4	12.6	9.1	6.9	Cash & Equivalents	11.3	10.7
21.3	35.4	46.0	36.2	24.2	25.0	Trade Receivables (net)	41.2	40.0
11.8	11.8	11.2	11.7	13.3	8.7	Inventory	9.5	11.6
6.3	3.2	6.1	5.3	1.3	3.5	All Other Current	5.3	4.4
64.9	64.2	75.7	65.8	47.9	44.1	Total Current	67.3	66.8
28.8	22.1	15.7	23.2	37.1	36.9	Fixed Assets (net)	22.0	23.9
1.2	1.7	2.3	4.6	4.6	7.6	Intangibles (net)	2.7	3.2
5.1	12.0	6.4	6.4	10.5	11.4	All Other Non-Current	8.0	6.1
100.0	100.0	100.0	100.0	100.0	100.0	Total	100.0	100.0
						LIABILITIES		
9.9	9.9	8.1	6.5	5.7	4.9	Notes Payable-Short Term	9.3	8.0
6.5	.8	1.8	2.4	2.7	2.8	Cur. Mat.-L.T.D.	2.5	2.3
32.9	31.7	37.8	28.7	19.8	21.2	Trade Payables	31.8	31.3
.0	.2	.1	.3	.9	.1	Income Taxes Payable	.2	.2
33.8	7.9	9.1	11.2	7.4	7.5	All Other Current	8.9	9.3
83.0	50.5	56.9	49.1	36.4	36.6	Total Current	52.5	51.1
23.9	14.0	5.9	11.2	19.2	19.4	Long-Term Debt	12.6	12.2
.0	.0	.2	.5	.9	1.9	Deferred Taxes	.3	.4
10.5	5.0	4.5	2.9	1.4	3.3	All Other Non-Current	3.8	3.8
-17.4	30.5	32.5	36.3	42.1	38.8	Net Worth	30.8	32.5
100.0	100.0	100.0	100.0	100.0	100.0	Total Liabilities & Net Worth	100.0	100.0
						INCOME DATA		
100.0	100.0	100.0	100.0	100.0	100.0	Net Sales	100.0	100.0
18.7	15.9	20.5	24.1	23.7	24.9	Gross Profit	19.1	20.3
18.7	14.8	17.4	18.8	14.5	12.3	Operating Expenses	16.3	16.2
.0	1.1	3.2	5.3	9.2	12.6	Operating Profit	2.9	4.1
.5	.1	.3	.2	.4	.9	All Other Expenses (net)	.2	.3
-.5	1.0	2.9	5.1	8.8	11.7	Profit Before Taxes	2.7	3.8
						RATIOS		
18.2	2.1	1.9	1.8	1.8	1.5		1.9	1.8
1.3	1.3	1.3	1.3	1.3	1.2	Current	1.3	1.3
.4	.9	1.0	1.1	1.2	1.1		1.0	1.0
12.5	1.4	1.5	1.5	1.4	1.2		1.4	1.4
1.2	1.1	1.0	1.0	1.0	.8	Quick	1.0	1.0
.2	.7	.7	.7	.7	.7		.7	.7
0 UND	**9** 39.5	**21** 17.1	**24** 15.2	**26** 14.2	**24** 15.2		**21** 17.7	**23** 16.2
1 438.9	**20** 18.1	**29** 12.6	**30** 12.0	**28** 13.1	**28** 13.0	Sales/Receivables	**29** 12.6	**29** 12.7
19 18.8	**34** 10.7	**39** 9.4	**41** 8.8	**39** 9.3	**38** 9.7		**37** 9.7	**37** 9.8
0 UND	**0** UND	**2** 205.2	**4** 89.2	**6** 65.9	**6** 59.4		**2** 199.3	**3** 138.3
0 UND	**4** 92.3	**5** 72.7	**7** 50.6	**8** 44.5	**11** 32.4	Cost of Sales/Inventory	**6** 61.8	**6** 56.9
4 90.3	**19** 19.7	**11** 32.1	**21** 17.5	**36** 10.1	**27** 13.7		**11** 34.3	**15** 24.5
0 UND	**8** 47.8	**18** 20.5	**18** 20.2	**16** 22.5	**19** 19.0		**15** 24.3	**17** 21.6
3 112.5	**23** 15.6	**28** 12.9	**27** 13.3	**26** 13.8	**27** 13.4	Cost of Sales/Payables	**25** 14.8	**27** 13.3
23 16.0	**41** 8.8	**40** 9.1	**54** 6.7	**52** 7.0	**65** 5.6		**37** 9.8	**41** 9.0
20.5	18.6	13.6	11.4	12.8	15.4		14.7	13.7
259.7	52.1	38.8	28.9	26.0	30.8	Sales/Working Capital	35.3	34.8
-6.8	-182.7	225.3	155.1	60.6	93.4		725.5	228.6
	14.9	46.1	39.0	25.3	23.4		16.2	21.6
	(41) 4.2	(147) 12.2	(94) 10.3	10.4	(11) 8.2	EBIT/Interest	(298) 6.1	(282) 6.9
	1.5	2.2	3.9	4.1	2.5		1.7	2.7
		7.1	6.6				8.8	7.7
		(27) 3.2	(33) 3.3			Net Profit + Depr., Dep., Amort./Cur. Mat. L/T/D	(82) 3.0	(86) 3.4
		1.5	1.5				1.4	2.2
.0	.3	.1	.2	.7	.5		.2	.2
1.2	.5	.5	.6	1.0	1.1	Fixed/Worth	.6	.7
-.3	1.5	1.3	1.7	1.8	2.6		1.8	1.6
.8	.9	1.0	1.0	.9	.9		1.0	1.1
8.4	2.6	2.7	2.2	1.7	1.5	Debt/Worth	2.4	2.3
-2.2	8.0	7.0	4.5	2.3	6.0		6.0	5.2
	45.0	62.5	45.8	43.7	67.8		50.1	52.3
	(45) 12.5	(151) 26.9	(96) 23.6	(16) 23.5	(11) 28.2	% Profit Before Taxes/Tangible Net Worth	(303) 20.3	(292) 26.6
	3.4	9.1	13.0	9.6	17.8		5.1	8.1
24.1	11.0	16.0	14.3	17.5	20.5		15.2	14.9
4.5	3.0	8.2	7.8	12.3	10.6	% Profit Before Taxes/Total Assets	5.0	6.8
-28.6	.0	1.5	3.2	3.5	3.9		1.4	1.9
UND	144.5	159.8	72.8	13.6	18.8		161.0	119.1
361.0	49.5	43.0	20.1	9.4	12.2	Sales/Net Fixed Assets	34.9	28.4
9.7	18.1	17.0	7.4	5.9	1.6		10.2	9.1
14.6	9.0	7.8	5.8	4.4	4.8		7.5	7.3
8.2	5.9	5.9	3.7	3.1	2.9	Sales/Total Assets	5.3	5.3
3.5	4.0	3.8	2.0	1.8	.9		3.0	2.6
	.2	.2	.3	.7	.8		.2	.3
	(43) .4	(131) .5	(94) .6	1.2	(11) 1.1	% Depr., Dep., Amort./Sales	(278) .7	(269) .6
	.8	1.1	1.8	1.9	6.5		1.6	1.7
	1.1	.9	.6				.8	.7
	(31) 2.1	(67) 1.8	(20) .8			% Officers', Directors' Owners' Comp/Sales	(125) 1.7	(121) 1.4
	3.1	3.3	1.9				3.1	2.6
65448M	467628M	4760246M	8804697M	3715849M	5962797M	Net Sales ($)	21831021M	19768438M
3702M	66368M	812921M	2311611M	1192163M	1975953M	Total Assets ($)	5676819M	5522450M

M = $ thousand MM = $ million

See Pages 9 through 22 for Explanation of Ratios and Data

Comparative Historical Data / Current Data Sorted by Sales

Type of Statement	4/1/11-3/31/12 ALL	4/1/12-3/31/13 ALL	4/1/13-3/31/14 ALL	0-1MM	1-3MM	3-5MM	5-10MM	10-25MM	25MM & OVER
Unqualified	39	31	41		1		1	6	33
Reviewed	82	63	68			1	2	19	46
Compiled	72	74	82	2	5	5	13	24	33
Tax Returns	52	46	41		5	3	6	18	9
Other	112	131	132	2	3	7	18	29	73
					106 (4/1-9/30/13)		258 (10/1/13-3/31/14)		
NUMBER OF STATEMENTS	357	345	364	4	14	16	40	96	194
ASSETS	%	%	%	%	%	%	%	%	%
Cash & Equivalents	11.4	13.5	12.7		22.5	13.4	17.9	13.8	10.4
Trade Receivables (net)	40.8	41.1	39.0		19.0	21.8	34.7	43.2	41.4
Inventory	9.8	9.5	11.5		11.1	13.8	10.6	9.8	12.0
All Other Current	5.3	5.1	5.2		8.5	19.8	5.9	4.0	3.9
Total Current	67.4	69.2	68.4		61.1	68.7	69.0	70.9	67.7
Fixed Assets (net)	22.2	21.7	21.0		32.9	19.3	22.0	18.3	21.0
Intangibles (net)	3.5	2.9	3.1		1.0	1.5	1.2	2.6	4.1
All Other Non-Current	7.0	6.3	7.5		5.0	10.5	7.7	8.2	7.2
Total	100.0	100.0	100.0		100.0	100.0	100.0	100.0	100.0
LIABILITIES									
Notes Payable-Short Term	8.8	9.5	7.7		8.9	13.2	5.6	8.2	7.0
Cur. Mat.-L.T.D.	2.3	2.4	2.1		8.2	.3	1.5	1.9	2.0
Trade Payables	32.0	31.2	32.7		28.9	28.4	29.2	34.4	33.4
Income Taxes Payable	.2	.2	.2		.1	.2	.2	.1	.2
All Other Current	9.3	9.4	10.2		15.7	16.0	17.5	8.3	8.8
Total Current	52.6	52.7	52.9		61.8	58.1	54.0	53.0	51.4
Long-Term Debt	13.2	10.6	10.3		28.4	10.9	9.6	8.6	9.8
Deferred Taxes	.5	.4	.3		.1	.1	.2	.2	.5
All Other Non-Current	3.7	4.1	4.1		.0	6.0	3.9	4.6	3.7
Net Worth	30.1	32.2	32.4		9.8	24.8	32.2	33.7	34.5
Total Liabilities & Net Worth	100.0	100.0	100.0		100.0	100.0	100.0	100.0	100.0
INCOME DATA									
Net Sales	100.0	100.0	100.0		100.0	100.0	100.0	100.0	100.0
Gross Profit	20.6	22.4	21.1		31.1	50.5	25.4	20.9	17.2
Operating Expenses	16.3	18.9	17.1		28.7	45.7	21.0	16.7	13.3
Operating Profit	4.3	3.5	4.0		2.4	4.9	4.3	4.2	3.9
All Other Expenses (net)	.3	.0	.3		1.2	1.6	.2	.1	.2
Profit Before Taxes	4.0	3.5	3.7		1.2	3.2	4.1	4.1	3.7
RATIOS									
Current	1.8	1.9	1.9		2.9	1.8	2.8	2.1	1.7
	1.2	1.3	1.3		1.2	1.1	1.4	1.3	1.3
	1.0	1.0	1.0		.5	.9	1.0	1.0	1.1
Quick	1.4	1.6	1.5		1.6	1.0	1.7	1.7	1.4
	1.0	1.0	1.0		.8	.7	1.1	1.0	1.1
	.7	.7	.7		.2	.5	.8	.8	.8
Sales/Receivables	**21** 17.2	**21** 17.0	**21** 17.8		**0** UND	**8** 44.3	**15** 24.3	**19** 19.0	**23** 15.9
	28 13.1	**29** 12.7	**28** 13.1		**21** 17.0	**41** 8.9	**30** 12.2	**29** 12.6	**28** 13.1
	38 9.7	**39** 9.3	**39** 9.3		**37** 9.8	**182** 2.0	**51** 7.1	**41** 8.9	**36** 10.2
Cost of Sales/Inventory	**1** 259.2	**1** 269.2	**2** 165.9		**0** UND	**0** UND	**0** UND	**1** 403.5	**4** 95.3
	6 63.3	**6** 65.6	**6** 60.4		**0** UND	**33** 11.2	**6** 58.2	**4** 85.4	**6** 58.3
	12 30.0	**13** 28.8	**15** 24.1		**38** 9.7	**89** 4.1	**20** 18.6	**13** 27.5	**12** 29.7
Cost of Sales/Payables	**15** 24.2	**15** 24.4	**17** 22.1		**0** UND	**10** 38.0	**10** 35.5	**14** 26.8	**18** 20.3
	26 14.3	**28** 13.2	**27** 13.4		**21** 17.2	**146** 2.5	**26** 14.1	**30** 12.0	**25** 14.6
	39 9.3	**42** 8.7	**42** 8.6		**65** 5.6	**2000** .1	**50** 7.3	**42** 8.6	**37** 9.8
Sales/Working Capital	15.7	13.4	12.6		3.3	3.1	6.2	12.6	16.4
	40.1	30.4	36.5		20.6	11.4	21.5	42.7	38.1
	702.6	386.7	272.5		-13.4	NM	194.2	-566.7	147.3
EBIT/Interest	21.5	28.0	28.0		6.1	16.2	12.0	35.1	35.6
	(315) 7.3	(298) 9.0	(319) 8.8		(13) 2.9	(13) 3.9	(30) 6.3	(84) 12.2	(176) 11.8
	2.6	2.4	2.6		-1.3	1.1	1.6	2.5	3.1
Net Profit + Depr., Dep., Amort./Cur. Mat. L/T/D	7.2	7.2	7.5					15.6	7.3
	(89) 2.8	(66) 3.4	(78) 3.3					(14) 3.7	(59) 3.1
	1.6	1.5	1.5					2.1	1.5
Fixed/Worth	.2	.2	.2		.3	.2	.1	.2	.2
	.6	.6	.6		1.0	.4	.5	.6	.7
	1.8	1.5	1.6		-1.2	1.3	.7	1.6	1.7
Debt/Worth	1.1	1.0	1.0		.7	1.2	.9	.9	1.1
	2.5	2.1	2.3		4.4	4.1	1.6	3.1	2.2
	7.3	6.5	7.0		-6.5	10.6	3.3	7.3	6.0
% Profit Before Taxes/Tangible Net Worth	54.5	54.5	52.1		23.5	26.4	27.6	78.5	53.7
	(310) 22.4	(300) 22.5	(326) 23.9		(10) 6.7	(14) 15.1	(37) 16.8	(87) 28.9	(176) 26.4
	8.4	8.5	8.5		-2.2	1.7	.4	9.7	11.9
% Profit Before Taxes/Total Assets	14.5	15.5	14.9		5.3	8.1	11.9	18.4	15.9
	6.7	7.6	7.4		2.7	1.6	5.4	8.7	8.4
	1.8	2.0	2.0		-8.7	.2	-1.5	2.1	3.0
Sales/Net Fixed Assets	165.9	127.3	121.6		34.8	18.0	116.7	125.2	137.6
	35.1	32.8	30.8		7.9	10.7	20.1	53.0	31.3
	10.3	10.4	10.9		4.9	7.7	7.1	17.6	12.2
Sales/Total Assets	7.7	7.2	7.2		6.7	3.1	5.8	7.8	7.3
	5.2	5.0	5.1		2.6	1.2	4.2	5.9	5.1
	2.6	2.9	2.7		.8	.4	2.0	3.9	3.2
% Depr., Dep., Amort./Sales	.2	.2	.2		.5	.6	.2	.2	.2
	(300) .7	(283) .6	(302) .6		(13) 1.0	(13) 1.3	(32) .6	(75) .6	(167) .6
	1.6	1.4	1.3		3.1	2.6	1.7	1.2	1.1
% Officers', Directors' Owners' Comp/Sales	.8	.7	.8				1.4	1.1	.6
	(140) 1.4	(127) 1.4	(129) 1.8				(17) 2.2	(48) 1.8	(51) 1.1
	2.3	2.5	3.0				2.7	2.7	2.8
Net Sales ($)	20856734M	23428178M	23776665M	1967M	27322M	60093M	291291M	1631034M	21764958M
Total Assets ($)	5905495M	6271267M	6362718M	1369M	24271M	106432M	167842M	503038M	5559766M

M = $ thousand MM = $ million

See Pages 9 through 22 for Explanation of Ratios and Data

Current Data Sorted by Assets							Comparative Historical Data	
						Type of Statement		
	1	9	29	12	10	Unqualified	80	80
	3	48	28	2		Reviewed	100	107
12	22	30	7	1		Compiled	49	63
14	24	40	1			Tax Returns	66	69
16	29	42	61	19	6	Other	157	165
107 (4/1-9/30/13)			359 (10/1/13-3/31/14)				4/1/09-3/31/10	4/1/10-3/31/11
0-500M	**500M-2MM**	**2-10MM**	**10-50MM**	**50-100MM**	**100-250MM**		**ALL**	**ALL**
42	79	169	126	34	16	**NUMBER OF STATEMENTS**	452	484
%	%	%	%	%	%	**ASSETS**	%	%
19.4	8.5	9.7	7.3	9.0	6.8	Cash & Equivalents	7.9	8.1
13.9	35.9	32.4	27.9	26.6	25.3	Trade Receivables (net)	30.2	30.9
23.2	23.7	31.0	33.8	26.2	30.4	Inventory	30.9	31.8
.5	2.4	2.0	2.8	1.9	1.9	All Other Current	3.1	3.2
56.9	70.5	75.0	71.8	63.8	64.4	Total Current	72.0	73.9
32.7	20.3	15.8	16.8	20.2	14.2	Fixed Assets (net)	17.8	16.4
3.5	2.8	4.1	5.7	10.5	18.9	Intangibles (net)	4.8	4.7
6.8	6.4	5.1	5.7	5.5	2.5	All Other Non-Current	5.4	5.0
100.0	100.0	100.0	100.0	100.0	100.0	Total	100.0	100.0
						LIABILITIES		
14.9	13.8	11.3	15.6	12.6	11.4	Notes Payable-Short Term	15.8	15.7
.0	1.3	1.9	1.3	2.0	1.0	Cur. Mat.-L.T.D.	2.8	2.2
10.3	28.9	26.6	20.3	16.1	17.6	Trade Payables	22.8	25.6
.0	.0	.1	.1	.1	.1	Income Taxes Payable	.3	.2
5.8	9.2	6.2	9.3	9.1	13.1	All Other Current	9.0	8.1
31.0	53.3	46.1	46.7	40.0	43.1	Total Current	50.7	51.8
16.4	15.2	11.9	8.5	12.0	13.3	Long-Term Debt	12.3	10.8
.0	.0	.3	.2	1.4	1.0	Deferred Taxes	.3	.3
15.5	6.6	5.9	4.5	3.8	3.4	All Other Non-Current	4.5	4.4
37.1	25.0	35.9	40.2	42.8	39.2	Net Worth	32.2	32.8
100.0	100.0	100.0	100.0	100.0	100.0	Total Liabilties & Net Worth	100.0	100.0
						INCOME DATA		
100.0	100.0	100.0	100.0	100.0	100.0	Net Sales	100.0	100.0
43.9	27.1	22.7	21.6	21.9	22.2	Gross Profit	23.5	22.4
38.5	23.8	20.3	17.9	17.2	15.6	Operating Expenses	19.9	18.8
5.4	3.2	2.4	3.7	4.7	6.6	Operating Profit	3.6	3.6
.4	1.0	.2	.2	.4	.8	All Other Expenses (net)	.4	.3
5.1	2.2	2.2	3.5	4.3	5.8	Profit Before Taxes	3.2	3.2
						RATIOS		
5.2	2.2	2.4	2.0	2.4	2.5		2.1	2.1
3.1	1.6	1.6	1.5	1.5	1.5	Current	1.5	1.4
1.6	1.1	1.2	1.2	1.2	1.2		1.1	1.1
3.2	1.5	1.3	1.2	1.8	1.0		1.1	1.1
(41) 2.1	1.0	.9	.8	.8	.7	Quick	.8	.7
.7	.7	.6	.5	.5	.5		.5	.5
0 UND	16 23.3	20 18.3	22 16.8	22 16.7	22 16.4		19 19.1	20 18.3
0 UND	27 13.7	26 13.9	30 12.3	29 12.8	27 13.3	Sales/Receivables	27 13.3	28 13.0
16 22.6	35 10.5	37 9.8	37 9.8	37 9.9	34 10.6		38 9.6	38 9.5
5 70.0	9 38.8	18 20.5	20 18.4	23 15.6	15 24.4		19 19.5	19 19.4
7 50.7	18 20.0	33 11.2	41 8.9	39 9.4	46 7.9	Cost of Sales/Inventory	37 9.9	36 10.2
38 9.5	38 9.5	60 6.1	81 4.5	73 5.0	81 4.5		62 5.9	68 5.3
0 UND	13 28.5	16 23.3	15 24.4	14 25.6	10 36.9		15 24.7	14 25.5
0 UND	25 14.7	26 13.9	25 14.5	23 15.8	19 19.3	Cost of Sales/Payables	24 15.2	26 14.1
21 17.1	42 8.6	43 8.4	37 9.9	33 10.9	30 12.1		38 9.7	45 8.1
12.2	12.5	9.6	7.2	7.0	9.4		8.9	8.9
39.9	23.7	16.6	13.3	13.6	16.0	Sales/Working Capital	17.6	17.8
78.9	105.5	37.6	35.3	34.1	39.6		69.6	64.6
40.8	12.8	20.2	20.2	19.6	49.8		16.4	14.8
(22) 10.8	(69) 6.2	(150) 6.0	(115) 5.9	(30) 8.2	(15) 5.3	EBIT/Interest	(416) 5.2	(431) 5.6
5.7	2.3	2.2	2.6	2.4	2.3		2.0	2.3
		14.7	14.6	19.7			9.6	9.5
		(30) 5.2	(39) 3.6	(12) 6.1		Net Profit + Depr., Dep., Amort./Cur. Mat. L/T/D	(112) 4.0	(111) 3.3
		1.9	1.9	2.8			1.8	1.8
.1	.1	.1	.1	.2	.4		.1	.1
.7	.4	.3	.3	.6	1.2	Fixed/Worth	.4	.4
NM	2.6	1.0	1.0	1.6	3.2		1.7	1.5
.1	.9	1.0	.8	1.0	1.7		1.0	1.0
.5	2.4	2.1	2.3	1.9	2.9	Debt/Worth	2.4	2.6
NM	23.1	5.6	4.1	10.0	34.4		6.4	6.8
93.1	48.8	48.3	43.0	46.9	39.5		45.3	51.9
(32) 54.0	(63) 27.7	(152) 19.0	(116) 19.3	(30) 20.5	(13) 23.0	% Profit Before Taxes/Tangible Net Worth	(397) 25.1	(434) 23.8
29.7	14.1	7.8	9.5	13.2	12.1		11.1	9.5
50.9	16.8	11.3	11.8	16.1	9.4		14.9	15.2
28.8	7.5	5.1	5.9	7.6	4.5	% Profit Before Taxes/Total Assets	7.2	6.8
9.9	2.5	1.8	2.5	2.9	3.0		2.5	2.6
197.6	278.5	243.3	199.6	87.1	133.7		162.0	232.2
29.1	57.8	56.3	40.8	17.6	22.7	Sales/Net Fixed Assets	39.5	47.7
10.6	17.1	15.8	9.2	6.9	11.9		11.6	13.8
10.0	6.7	5.7	4.5	4.6	5.4		5.4	5.4
7.2	4.4	4.0	3.0	2.6	3.3	Sales/Total Assets	3.5	3.5
4.7	3.1	2.6	2.0	1.7	1.3		2.4	2.4
.2	.3	.2	.2	.2	.3		.2	.2
(29) .6	(49) 1.0	(137) .6	(108) .4	(29) .8	(13) .7	% Depr., Dep., Amort./Sales	(364) .7	(371) .6
1.4	2.0	1.6	1.2	1.4	1.9		1.6	1.5
3.3	1.3	.8	.6				.8	1.1
(14) 5.2	(34) 2.1	(86) 1.6	(34) .9			% Officers', Directors' Owners' Comp/Sales	(170) 1.8	(182) 2.0
8.0	4.0	3.1	2.8				3.7	3.5
84121M	513042M	3599832M	9802760M	7996497M	8565746M	Net Sales ($)	34063970M	33925884M
11513M	92989M	824506M	2693176M	2411520M	2471018M	Total Assets ($)	9107496M	8948939M

M = $ thousand MM = $ million

See Pages 9 through 22 for Explanation of Ratios and Data

Comparative Historical Data / Current Data Sorted by Sales

4/1/11-3/31/12 ALL	4/1/12-3/31/13 ALL	4/1/13-3/31/14 ALL	Type of Statement	0-1MM	1-3MM	3-5MM	5-10MM	10-25MM	25MM & OVER
67	69	61	Unqualified		1		2	6	52
104	78	81	Reviewed	1		1	8	28	43
66	46	72	Compiled	2	19	6	11	15	19
88	74	79	Tax Returns	5	9	8	23	24	10
159	181	173	Other	6	13	17	15	33	89
				107 (4/1-9/30/13)			359 (10/1/13-3/31/14)		
484	448	466	NUMBER OF STATEMENTS	14	42	32	59	106	213
%	%	%	**ASSETS**	%	%	%	%	%	%
8.3	8.2	9.6	Cash & Equivalents	24.3	12.1	12.7	10.6	8.3	7.9
29.4	28.9	29.4	Trade Receivables (net)	6.1	16.1	27.1	29.6	35.1	31.1
32.0	32.8	29.4	Inventory	21.9	18.8	26.0	27.9	29.5	32.9
2.9	3.1	2.1	All Other Current	.2	2.1	3.3	.5	2.4	2.4
72.6	73.1	70.6	Total Current	52.6	49.1	69.1	68.5	75.4	74.4
16.7	15.7	18.6	Fixed Assets (net)	21.7	41.3	18.2	22.1	14.0	15.4
5.3	5.3	5.2	Intangibles (net)	8.6	4.0	6.2	3.7	5.7	5.3
5.4	6.0	5.6	All Other Non-Current	17.1	5.6	6.5	5.7	5.0	4.9
100.0	100.0	100.0	Total	100.0	100.0	100.0	100.0	100.0	100.0
			LIABILITIES						
12.6	14.7	13.3	Notes Payable-Short Term	23.4	16.8	10.2	8.0	12.4	14.4
2.6	2.3	1.5	Cur. Mat.-L.T.D.	.3	.3	.9	1.9	1.7	1.6
24.8	23.0	22.7	Trade Payables	7.2	14.9	19.2	24.0	30.2	21.8
.2	.1	.1	Income Taxes Payable	.0	.0	.0	.1	.0	.1
8.3	8.0	8.0	All Other Current	2.7	9.1	8.1	5.6	7.8	8.8
48.7	48.1	46.6	Total Current	33.6	41.0	38.5	39.6	52.1	46.7
11.8	11.4	12.0	Long-Term Debt	17.5	23.1	10.5	16.7	10.6	9.1
.4	.3	.3	Deferred Taxes	.0	.0	.0	.0	.1	.5
5.7	5.8	6.2	All Other Non-Current	45.7	6.0	8.5	9.2	3.9	3.7
33.4	34.5	35.9	Net Worth	3.2	29.9	42.5	34.5	33.3	40.0
100.0	100.0	100.0	Total Liabilties & Net Worth	100.0	100.0	100.0	100.0	100.0	100.0
			INCOME DATA						
100.0	100.0	100.0	Net Sales	100.0	100.0	100.0	100.0	100.0	100.0
23.3	22.5	25.0	Gross Profit	46.2	44.0	31.9	25.6	24.1	19.0
19.7	18.8	21.5	Operating Expenses	38.6	39.9	27.4	22.4	21.3	15.7
3.6	3.7	3.5	Operating Profit	7.6	4.1	4.5	3.2	2.8	3.3
.7	.3	.4	All Other Expenses (net)	5.2	.5	.1	.1	.3	.2
2.9	3.4	3.1	Profit Before Taxes	2.4	3.6	4.4	3.1	2.5	3.1
			RATIOS						
2.3	2.4	2.5		8.7	3.1	4.0	3.1	2.2	2.4
1.5	1.5	1.6	Current	2.4	1.9	2.0	1.8	1.5	1.5
1.1	1.1	1.2		1.5	1.0	1.4	1.3	1.2	1.2
1.2	1.2	1.5		5.6	2.3	2.8	1.7	1.1	1.3
.8	(447) .7	(465) .9	Quick	1.2	(41) 1.0	1.1	1.0	.8	.8
.5	.5	.6		.2	.6	.7	.7	.6	.6
18 19.8	**19** 19.7	**18** 20.0		**0** UND	**0** UND	**12** 29.7	**21** 17.8	**19** 19.4	**21** 17.1
27 13.6	**28** 13.2	**26** 13.8	Sales/Receivables	**7** 49.5	**10** 35.4	**24** 15.4	**29** 12.5	**27** 13.7	**27** 13.4
37 9.9	**37** 9.9	**35** 10.3		**37** 9.9	**34** 10.8	**39** 9.4	**37** 9.8	**41** 8.9	**35** 10.5
19 19.4	**18** 20.6	**15** 24.1		**0** UND	**6** 60.4	**13** 28.6	**15** 23.6	**16** 22.3	**18** 20.3
37 9.8	**38** 9.6	**32** 11.5	Cost of Sales/Inventory	**65** 5.6	**12** 29.3	**30** 12.0	**37** 9.9	**33** 11.2	**33** 11.0
70 5.2	**78** 4.7	**62** 5.9		**192** 1.9	**43** 8.5	**46** 8.0	**68** 5.4	**62** 5.9	**65** 5.6
15 25.0	**14** 26.9	**14** 27.0		**6** 63.8	**0** UND	**6** 62.1	**15** 23.9	**19** 19.5	**14** 27.0
26 14.1	**24** 14.9	**24** 15.4	Cost of Sales/Payables	**16** 22.8	**8** 43.6	**22** 16.5	**29** 12.6	**28** 13.1	**23** 15.7
41 9.0	**42** 8.6	**37** 9.8		**50** 7.3	**31** 11.6	**46** 8.0	**46** 7.9	**48** 7.6	**33** 11.2
8.4	7.9	9.1		3.1	18.8	8.1	6.0	9.6	9.2
16.1	15.2	16.8	Sales/Working Capital	10.9	64.4	15.4	15.0	17.5	15.6
54.1	55.4	46.1		NM	216.8	57.0	29.8	46.2	33.9
15.9	17.4	19.1			19.5	15.7	12.1	20.7	21.7
(429) 5.4	(396) 5.9	(401) 6.4	EBIT/Interest		(27) 6.5	(26) 8.1	(51) 5.4	(95) 4.2	(193) 7.4
2.0	2.4	2.4			1.7	3.5	2.3	1.3	2.9
10.8	13.5	14.6					14.9	11.1	15.1
(98) 4.3	(91) 4.1	(89) 4.8	Net Profit + Depr., Dep., Amort./Cur. Mat. L/T/D				(10) 6.9	(22) 2.8	(57) 4.7
2.1	2.1	2.1					4.4	1.6	2.4
.1	.1	.1		.1	.4	.1	.1	.1	.1
.4	.3	.4	Fixed/Worth	.6	.8	.3	.4	.3	.3
1.5	1.3	1.4		-1.4	-4.6	1.9	1.9	1.5	1.0
.9	1.0	.9		.4	.2	.8	.9	1.1	.9
2.4	2.4	2.2	Debt/Worth	5.0	1.8	1.8	1.9	2.9	2.1
6.6	6.6	5.8		-3.0	-15.7	6.1	5.7	8.6	4.3
44.8	56.6	48.9			88.9	57.0	53.3	45.2	46.3
(424) 24.6	(397) 26.2	(406) 22.5	% Profit Before Taxes/Tangible Net Worth		(29) 34.4	(26) 37.7	(52) 18.5	(92) 15.4	(198) 21.1
9.0	10.1	10.8			9.3	27.1	8.8	4.8	11.9
15.0	15.4	15.3		23.1	45.1	27.3	16.4	9.4	13.4
6.9	7.4	6.8	% Profit Before Taxes/Total Assets	9.2	17.7	15.6	4.7	4.6	6.9
2.2	2.7	2.5		-9.8	2.3	5.3	1.7	1.2	3.4
221.3	276.2	200.4		UND	61.6	209.2	121.2	213.5	224.5
45.4	53.5	41.5	Sales/Net Fixed Assets	17.0	18.8	55.4	27.9	61.0	46.3
12.7	14.2	12.7		7.2	5.8	13.8	11.4	17.2	12.9
5.5	5.2	6.0		3.9	7.9	6.5	5.5	6.4	5.5
3.6	3.5	3.9	Sales/Total Assets	2.2	4.8	3.8	3.4	4.1	3.8
2.4	2.3	2.4		1.3	2.4	2.7	1.9	2.6	2.5
.2	.1	.2			.3	.5	.4	.1	.2
(366) .6	(338) .5	(365) .6	% Depr., Dep., Amort./Sales		(31) .8	(19) 1.3	(41) 1.4	(86) .5	(180) .4
1.6	1.3	1.5			1.8	2.0	3.1	1.4	1.0
1.0	.9	.8			2.9	1.0	1.4	.8	.6
(192) 2.0	(174) 1.8	(177) 1.6	% Officers', Directors' Owners' Comp/Sales		(12) 4.5	(11) 2.0	(33) 2.2	(49) 1.4	(66) 1.1
3.7	3.3	3.5			6.5	4.3	3.8	3.2	2.1
28249868M	**30941312M**	**30561998M**	Net Sales ($)	**8066M**	**88974M**	**123621M**	**428751M**	**1761292M**	**28151294M**
7856923M	**8780151M**	**8504722M**	Total Assets ($)	**8047M**	**27274M**	**37564M**	**172649M**	**630620M**	**7628568M**

M = $ thousand MM = $ million

See Pages 9 through 22 for Explanation of Ratios and Data

	Current Data Sorted by Assets						Comparative Historical Data	
Type of Statement								
Unqualified	2	3	38	78	28	27	171	185
Reviewed		4	43	22	1		65	69
Compiled		5	5	3			11	18
Tax Returns	3	11	4	3			19	26
Other	3	3	22	22	13	15	50	74
	190 (4/1-9/30/13)			168 (10/1/13-3/31/14)			4/1/09-3/31/10 ALL	4/1/10-3/31/11 ALL
	0-500M	500M-2MM	2-10MM	10-50MM	50-100MM	100-250MM		
NUMBER OF STATEMENTS	8	26	112	128	42	42	316	372
ASSETS	%	%	%	%	%	%	%	%
Cash & Equivalents		16.1	18.5	12.4	8.3	8.5	10.1	10.1
Trade Receivables (net)		23.8	19.0	15.8	15.7	16.9	19.2	19.0
Inventory		28.5	25.7	34.5	36.1	33.9	34.4	35.2
All Other Current		4.1	5.9	4.6	6.5	9.1	4.9	7.1
Total Current		72.5	69.1	67.4	66.5	68.4	68.7	71.4
Fixed Assets (net)		18.7	26.3	27.5	25.5	23.0	23.8	21.7
Intangibles (net)		.8	1.2	.5	1.3	.5	.4	.8
All Other Non-Current		8.0	3.4	4.7	6.7	8.1	7.1	6.1
Total		100.0	100.0	100.0	100.0	100.0	100.0	100.0
LIABILITIES								
Notes Payable-Short Term		3.2	7.6	10.9	13.3	12.1	13.6	17.2
Cur. Mat.-L.T.D.		2.2	1.2	2.0	1.4	1.2	2.2	1.9
Trade Payables		22.7	23.1	22.0	20.2	20.6	19.2	19.2
Income Taxes Payable		.1	.2	.3	.2	.2	.4	.3
All Other Current		8.8	10.7	10.7	10.9	14.3	11.8	12.2
Total Current		37.0	42.8	45.9	46.1	48.3	47.2	50.8
Long-Term Debt		19.0	7.8	10.1	9.2	10.4	11.6	9.5
Deferred Taxes		.5	2.4	2.0	1.8	2.0	1.3	1.2
All Other Non-Current		3.2	1.2	1.6	1.3	2.8	2.1	3.7
Net Worth		40.3	45.7	40.3	41.6	36.4	37.8	34.8
Total Liabilties & Net Worth		100.0	100.0	100.0	100.0	100.0	100.0	100.0
INCOME DATA								
Net Sales		100.0	100.0	100.0	100.0	100.0	100.0	100.0
Gross Profit		18.2	9.5	7.2	9.1	7.0	10.6	12.0
Operating Expenses		14.9	7.1	5.5	7.4	5.0	7.7	8.8
Operating Profit		3.3	2.4	1.6	1.7	2.0	3.0	3.2
All Other Expenses (net)		.0	-.1	.0	-.2	.3	-.1	-.1
Profit Before Taxes		3.3	2.5	1.6	1.9	1.7	3.1	3.2
RATIOS								
Current		3.4	2.3	1.8	1.8	1.6	1.9	1.8
		2.1	1.6	1.4	1.4	1.3	1.4	1.3
		1.3	1.2	1.2	1.2	1.2	1.2	1.1
Quick		2.2	1.3	1.0	.8	.7	1.0	1.0
		(25) 1.1	.9	.5	.5	.5	(315) .6	(371) .5
		.6	.5	.3	.2	.3	.3	.2
Sales/Receivables		4 101.4	5 74.9	7 49.5	7 50.8	7 50.9	6 60.6	7 48.7
		20 18.2	11 32.3	14 25.9	15 25.1	17 21.3	13 27.3	17 22.0
		35 10.5	23 15.7	24 14.9	27 13.7	29 12.8	28 13.1	31 11.6
Cost of Sales/Inventory		4 101.5	8 43.4	17 22.0	23 15.8	16 22.4	16 22.4	22 16.7
		36 10.1	21 17.5	44 8.3	48 7.6	47 7.8	37 9.9	44 8.2
		78 4.7	52 7.0	79 4.6	87 4.2	63 5.8	67 5.5	87 4.2
Cost of Sales/Payables		2 184.6	5 67.3	8 47.3	11 33.5	7 49.4	6 60.6	7 54.7
		6 58.7	16 23.2	19 19.7	17 21.3	21 17.0	16 22.4	18 20.5
		37 9.8	36 10.1	48 7.6	39 9.4	30 12.0	30 12.3	37 9.8
Sales/Working Capital		6.9	9.2	10.7	12.1	13.6	10.5	9.5
		15.5	17.6	17.6	19.4	17.6	19.4	16.4
		59.3	48.9	29.0	30.3	25.8	37.4	32.1
EBIT/Interest		10.6	9.8	11.5	10.7	11.6	13.6	16.9
		(18) 4.4	(100) 4.4	(119) 4.6	4.0	(41) 3.4	(295) 5.5	(349) 6.6
		1.1	1.8	1.9	2.2	2.0	2.7	2.9
Net Profit + Depr., Dep., Amort./Cur. Mat. L/T/D			4.4	5.7	6.7	13.8	9.9	8.8
			(29) 2.4	(50) 3.7	(19) 2.3	(19) 4.4	(107) 5.9	(133) 4.8
			1.4	1.6	1.5	2.5	2.8	2.5
Fixed/Worth		.0	.2	.4	.4	.3	.3	.3
		.4	.6	.7	.6	.6	.6	.6
		1.3	1.0	1.0	.9	1.1	1.0	.9
Debt/Worth		.4	.6	.9	.8	1.0	1.0	1.1
		.7	1.4	1.7	1.8	2.1	1.7	2.0
		8.1	2.3	2.6	2.7	3.2	3.4	3.7
% Profit Before Taxes/Tangible Net Worth		38.1	21.7	22.4	17.2	17.8	37.1	31.8
		(23) 9.7	10.4	13.6	9.6	13.4	(309) 23.2	(362) 22.1
		.0	2.4	4.6	3.8	8.7	10.1	11.3
% Profit Before Taxes/Total Assets		17.1	9.8	9.1	6.8	9.2	14.4	12.3
		5.8	3.1	4.7	4.2	3.9	7.8	7.0
		.3	1.3	1.6	1.6	1.7	3.3	3.2
Sales/Net Fixed Assets		171.4	40.2	19.7	26.2	42.7	32.3	35.7
		32.8	15.5	10.9	14.5	16.0	15.6	14.9
		10.9	8.5	7.4	7.6	8.7	9.3	8.3
Sales/Total Assets		9.5	5.6	4.4	4.4	4.8	4.9	4.3
		3.6	3.8	3.0	3.1	3.3	3.4	2.9
		2.5	2.6	2.1	2.3	2.4	2.5	1.9
% Depr., Dep., Amort./Sales		.2	.5	.6	.6	.3	.4	.5
		(21) .5	(106) .8	(121) 1.0	(40) .9	(40) .8	(294) .8	(334) .9
		1.5	1.2	1.5	1.6	1.2	1.2	1.3
% Officers', Directors' Owners' Comp/Sales		.9	.3	.1			.3	.7
		(11) 2.7	(23) 1.1	(12) .3			(55) .8	(63) 1.4
		4.5	2.1	.7			2.4	2.4
Net Sales ($)	32893M	204309M	3139173M	10236846M	11114522M	28055578M	39026495M	37795281M
Total Assets ($)	1605M	34798M	678984M	2762595M	2998633M	6817207M	10341080M	12328064M

M = $ thousand MM = $ million

See Pages 9 through 22 for Explanation of Ratios and Data

Comparative Historical Data				Current Data Sorted by Sales					
			Type of Statement						
177	162	176	Unqualified	2	1		4	22	147
81	79	70	Reviewed	1		1	9	22	37
19	17	13	Compiled		1	2	2	5	3
20	19	21	Tax Returns		3	2	7	6	3
66	75	78	Other	1	2	1	3	15	56
4/1/11-3/31/12 ALL	**4/1/12-3/31/13 ALL**	**4/1/13-3/31/14 ALL**		**190 (4/1-9/30/13)**			**168 (10/1/13-3/31/14)**		
				0-1MM	**1-3MM**	**3-5MM**	**5-10MM**	**10-25MM**	**25MM & OVER**
363	352	358	**NUMBER OF STATEMENTS**	4	7	6	25	70	246
%	%	%	**ASSETS**	%	%	%	%	%	%
9.6	10.5	13.9	Cash & Equivalents				20.8	17.1	12.3
16.6	16.4	17.7	Trade Receivables (net)				19.4	16.9	17.7
36.3	36.5	30.9	Inventory				27.5	29.3	31.8
9.7	8.0	5.7	All Other Current				5.7	4.6	6.0
72.2	71.3	68.2	Total Current				73.4	68.0	67.9
21.5	22.9	25.7	Fixed Assets (net)				18.9	25.6	26.4
1.0	.7	.8	Intangibles (net)				2.8	1.2	.5
5.4	5.1	5.3	All Other Non-Current				5.0	5.2	5.2
100.0	100.0	100.0	Total				100.0	100.0	100.0
			LIABILITIES						
20.9	15.5	9.8	Notes Payable-Short Term				7.9	8.6	10.5
1.6	1.7	1.9	Cur. Mat.-L.T.D.				1.3	1.6	1.6
18.6	21.3	22.5	Trade Payables				25.0	23.2	22.2
.2	.3	.2	Income Taxes Payable				.0	.2	.3
10.6	11.6	11.3	All Other Current				11.3	9.7	11.4
51.9	50.5	45.7	Total Current				45.5	43.4	45.9
9.1	9.1	10.3	Long-Term Debt				9.1	11.3	9.0
1.4	1.7	2.0	Deferred Taxes				.5	1.8	2.3
3.0	2.2	1.7	All Other Non-Current				3.0	1.7	1.6
34.6	36.6	40.3	Net Worth				41.9	41.9	41.1
100.0	100.0	100.0	Total Liabilities & Net Worth				100.0	100.0	100.0
			INCOME DATA						
100.0	100.0	100.0	Net Sales				100.0	100.0	100.0
11.0	9.7	9.0	Gross Profit				15.9	10.4	6.9
7.9	7.1	7.0	Operating Expenses				11.2	8.5	5.3
3.1	2.6	2.0	Operating Profit				4.7	2.0	1.7
.3	.1	.0	All Other Expenses (net)				-.5	.0	.0
2.8	2.6	2.0	Profit Before Taxes				5.3	1.9	1.7
			RATIOS						
1.7	1.8	2.0					2.8	2.6	1.8
1.3	1.4	1.4	Current				1.7	1.5	1.4
1.2	1.2	1.2					1.2	1.1	1.2
.8	.9	1.1					1.9	1.3	1.0
(351) .4	(357) .5	.7	Quick				.9	.8	.6
.2	.2	.3					.5	.5	.3
6 56.3	**6** 63.0	**6** 59.1					**5** 78.9	**5** 73.5	**7** 54.3
14 26.5	**12** 31.0	**13** 28.1	Sales/Receivables				**18** 20.7	**11** 31.9	**13** 28.1
27 13.7	**28** 12.9	**26** 14.2					**36** 10.0	**25** 14.4	**24** 15.2
19 19.3	**21** 17.4	**13** 27.9					**19** 19.1	**9** 42.9	**13** 27.2
47 7.7	**43** 8.4	**35** 10.3	Cost of Sales/Inventory				**40** 9.1	**42** 8.6	**33** 11.0
85 4.3	**85** 4.3	**64** 5.7					**81** 4.5	**74** 4.9	**61** 6.0
5 66.9	**7** 53.9	**6** 57.0					**3** 142.1	**5** 73.3	**8** 47.1
17 22.0	**19** 19.3	**18** 20.4	Cost of Sales/Payables				**35** 10.3	**22** 16.6	**17** 21.9
34 10.7	**40** 9.1	**37** 9.8					**66** 5.5	**61** 6.0	**35** 10.5
10.5	10.3	10.7					5.6	7.2	12.0
18.3	17.8	17.7	Sales/Working Capital				10.8	16.5	19.2
29.4	32.2	34.2					34.4	55.2	31.1
8.4	10.8	10.9					14.3	7.9	11.6
(343) 4.1	(334) 4.9	(325) 4.2	EBIT/Interest				(17) 3.4	(62) 3.1	(234) 4.8
2.3	2.1	1.9					1.2	1.4	2.0
8.1	6.6	5.8						3.8	6.4
(133) 4.5	(125) 3.9	(120) 3.0	Net Profit + Depr., Dep., Amort./Cur. Mat. L/T/D					(17) 2.0	(97) 3.6
2.4	2.2	1.7						1.4	1.8
.3	.4	.3					.1	.3	.4
.6	.6	.6	Fixed/Worth				.5	.7	.6
.9	1.0	1.0					1.2	1.0	1.0
1.2	1.1	.8					.3	.6	.8
2.2	2.0	1.7	Debt/Worth				1.8	1.4	1.7
3.4	3.4	2.7					6.8	2.8	2.6
29.2	26.1	21.3					32.3	17.7	21.8
(357) 17.9	(344) 17.0	(351) 12.1	% Profit Before Taxes/Tangible Net Worth				(24) 6.5	(68) 8.7	13.2
9.4	6.9	3.5					-.7	2.0	4.9
10.2	10.0	9.6					11.7	8.1	9.4
5.5	5.3	4.3	% Profit Before Taxes/Total Assets				3.2	2.7	4.7
2.3	1.9	1.4					-.1	1.0	1.7
32.8	31.7	35.5					65.2	35.7	31.9
14.9	14.9	13.8	Sales/Net Fixed Assets				20.7	14.9	13.5
9.6	9.5	8.2					9.6	7.4	8.3
4.6	4.4	4.9					4.2	5.0	5.0
3.1	3.2	3.4	Sales/Total Assets				2.9	3.2	3.6
2.1	2.1	2.3					1.4	2.0	2.5
.4	.5	.5					.5	.6	.5
(337) .8	(325) .8	(333) .9	% Depr., Dep., Amort./Sales				(22) 1.1	(66) .9	(231) .9
1.3	1.2	1.3					1.8	1.4	1.3
.5	.4	.3						.2	.3
(54) 1.1	(52) .8	(53) .9	% Officers', Directors' Owners' Comp/Sales					(17) .7	(21) .5
2.4	2.2	2.3						2.2	1.3
43505409M	**43690567M**	**52783321M**	Net Sales ($)	**1721M**	**14738M**	**23179M**	**183410M**	**1235740M**	**51324533M**
12960663M	**12783027M**	**13293822M**	Total Assets ($)	**1023M**	**12212M**	**12452M**	**76932M**	**470233M**	**12720970M**

M = $ thousand MM = $ million

See Pages 9 through 22 for Explanation of Ratios and Data

Current Data Sorted by Assets							Comparative Historical Data	
						Type of Statement		
		3	5	2	5	Unqualified	22	25
	1	6	7	4	1	Reviewed	27	20
1	3	3				Compiled	14	23
1	4	10	3			Tax Returns	15	17
2	6	12	8	4	8	Other	33	29
26 (4/1-9/30/13)		73 (10/1/13-3/31/14)					4/1/09-3/31/10	4/1/10-3/31/11
0-500M	**500M-2MM**	**2-10MM**	**10-50MM**	**50-100MM**	**100-250MM**		**ALL**	**ALL**
4	14	34	23	10	14	**NUMBER OF STATEMENTS**	111	114
%	%	%	%	%	%	**ASSETS**	%	%
	17.1	14.9	9.4	5.9	5.1	Cash & Equivalents	9.7	12.6
	38.9	31.2	27.5	34.5	22.4	Trade Receivables (net)	37.5	34.1
	25.9	26.9	31.2	37.7	39.6	Inventory	29.7	27.8
	6.6	4.8	4.7	6.5	4.2	All Other Current	5.0	6.1
	88.6	77.8	72.8	84.5	71.3	Total Current	81.8	80.6
	8.2	10.0	16.8	10.3	18.6	Fixed Assets (net)	12.9	13.4
	.1	3.6	6.9	1.3	3.1	Intangibles (net)	.8	2.2
	3.1	8.5	3.5	3.9	7.0	All Other Non-Current	4.6	3.8
	100.0	100.0	100.0	100.0	100.0	Total	100.0	100.0
						LIABILITIES		
	14.5	11.7	11.8	28.6	22.1	Notes Payable-Short Term	19.8	13.4
	2.5	1.9	1.0	1.7	1.0	Cur. Mat.-L.T.D.	1.0	1.8
	30.6	24.0	29.5	27.5	11.2	Trade Payables	22.6	26.3
	.0	.2	.5	.5	.0	Income Taxes Payable	.2	.1
	11.5	9.2	10.8	8.2	13.8	All Other Current	13.1	12.4
	59.1	47.1	53.6	66.4	48.1	Total Current	56.7	54.1
	3.1	2.6	8.4	9.4	9.8	Long-Term Debt	6.8	5.9
	.0	.3	.0	.0	1.0	Deferred Taxes	.2	.2
	5.6	3.5	1.9	5.1	4.4	All Other Non-Current	2.8	5.1
	32.3	46.5	36.0	19.1	36.7	Net Worth	33.4	34.7
	100.0	100.0	100.0	100.0	100.0	Total Liabilties & Net Worth	100.0	100.0
						INCOME DATA		
	100.0	100.0	100.0	100.0	100.0	Net Sales	100.0	100.0
	21.6	14.4	18.4	11.4	17.4	Gross Profit	16.4	17.1
	18.3	13.9	15.6	9.3	12.3	Operating Expenses	12.4	13.0
	3.2	.5	2.8	2.0	5.2	Operating Profit	4.0	4.0
	.5	-.2	.2	.5	.0	All Other Expenses (net)	.8	1.2
	2.8	.7	2.6	1.6	5.2	Profit Before Taxes	3.2	2.9
						RATIOS		
	2.9	2.5	2.1	1.6	2.2		1.9	2.0
	1.9	1.4	1.3	1.1	1.4	Current	1.3	1.5
	1.0	1.1	1.1	1.0	1.2		1.1	1.1
	1.7	1.8	1.2	.9	.9		1.2	1.3
	.9	.9	.7	.5	.6	Quick	.8	.8
	.6	.6	.3	.3	.5		.5	.5
	10 35.6	**12** 29.5	**25** 14.6	**22** 16.3	**21** 17.1		**23** 15.8	**17** 21.9
	24 15.4	**33** 11.0	**35** 10.3	**31** 11.7	**38** 9.6	Sales/Receivables	**37** 9.9	**35** 10.5
	52 7.0	**51** 7.1	**64** 5.7	**64** 5.7	**45** 8.2		**59** 6.2	**50** 7.3
	6 62.4	**6** 64.7	**33** 11.0	**29** 12.6	**30** 12.3		**3** 140.5	**3** 117.3
	9 38.5	**28** 13.2	**65** 5.6	**72** 5.1	**69** 5.3	Cost of Sales/Inventory	**33** 11.2	**39** 9.2
	140 2.6	**55** 6.6	**118** 3.1	**89** 4.1	**182** 2.0		**86** 4.2	**93** 3.9
	8 47.2	**3** 113.8	**24** 15.3	**9** 42.3	**14** 25.9		**9** 40.8	**12** 29.8
	15 23.7	**21** 17.2	**37** 9.9	**15** 23.8	**22** 16.6	Cost of Sales/Payables	**27** 13.5	**24** 15.1
	63 5.8	**51** 7.1	**69** 5.3	**68** 5.4	**34** 10.7		**49** 7.5	**55** 6.7
	6.7	6.5	5.7	8.8	8.1		7.8	7.0
	16.3	16.7	10.9	26.4	13.8	Sales/Working Capital	16.1	13.2
	NM	43.6	34.7	103.4	28.1		37.9	34.0
	248.0	14.9	41.0	12.0	18.0		24.8	18.3
	(10) 19.3	(31) 6.0	(22) 7.2	3.9	(13) 4.3	EBIT/Interest	(105) 6.2	(107) 6.5
	2.6	1.0	1.9	1.5	1.4		1.7	1.7
							9.5	16.5
						Net Profit + Depr., Dep., Amort./Cur. Mat. L/T/D	(19) 4.5	(16) 3.5
							1.8	.2
	.0	.0	.1	.0	.1		.0	.0
	.1	.1	.4	.3	.5	Fixed/Worth	.2	.3
	.8	.5	1.2	18.7	1.4		.8	.9
	.5	.4	1.4	2.2	.7		1.2	1.0
	2.8	1.7	1.9	6.7	1.8	Debt/Worth	2.4	2.6
	27.4	5.0	4.4	162.8	11.5		4.9	5.4
	104.5	54.3	33.2		29.7		60.7	51.2
	(12) 49.0	(32) 15.2	(22) 17.5		19.4	% Profit Before Taxes/Tangible Net Worth	(104) 25.1	(108) 19.2
	6.3	.3	6.3		9.4		7.6	4.6
	31.6	12.5	11.1	6.9	11.8		15.2	12.3
	5.8	5.6	3.1	2.9	4.9	% Profit Before Taxes/Total Assets	7.8	6.4
	2.2	.3	2.0	.3	2.3		1.5	1.3
	UND	999.8	212.5	280.0	123.5		574.0	341.8
	383.8	168.5	11.8	40.5	23.2	Sales/Net Fixed Assets	38.6	32.8
	18.9	15.6	6.0	21.1	7.1		11.5	10.6
	9.7	4.8	3.1	3.6	3.8		4.6	4.5
	4.1	3.6	1.9	2.6	1.9	Sales/Total Assets	3.0	2.9
	2.0	1.9	1.6	2.0	1.5		1.9	1.8
		.0	.3		.1		.3	.1
		(23) .7	(17) 1.3		(10) .5	% Depr., Dep., Amort./Sales	(82) .8	(91) .7
		1.3	2.2		2.4		1.6	1.4
			.6				.6	.7
			(10) 2.0			% Officers', Directors' Owners' Comp/Sales	(31) 1.5	(29) 1.7
			3.4				2.4	3.5
12546M	**102113M**	**696424M**	**1255853M**	**2312555M**	**5791940M**	Net Sales ($)	**6705988M**	**8827823M**
856M	**18512M**	**163863M**	**505492M**	**770178M**	**2116180M**	Total Assets ($)	**2501937M**	**3310686M**

M = $ thousand MM = $ million

See Pages 9 through 22 for Explanation of Ratios and Data

Comparative Historical Data				Current Data Sorted by Sales					
			Type of Statement						
21	17	15	Unqualified			1	1	1	12
25	21	19	Reviewed			1		5	13
15	15	7	Compiled		2		1	3	1
20	14	18	Tax Returns	1	1	4	3	5	4
33	50	40	Other	1	1	4	4	8	22
				26 (4/1-9/30/13)			73 (10/1/13-3/31/14)		
4/1/11-3/31/12 ALL	**4/1/12-3/31/13 ALL**	**4/1/13-3/31/14 ALL**		**0-1MM**	**1-3MM**	**3-5MM**	**5-10MM**	**10-25MM**	**25MM & OVER**
114	117	99	**NUMBER OF STATEMENTS**	2	4	10	9	22	52
%	%	%	**ASSETS**	%	%	%	%	%	%
7.7	8.9	11.7	Cash & Equivalents			15.0		12.2	9.7
32.5	31.0	30.3	Trade Receivables (net)			29.1		33.7	28.7
30.6	31.1	31.1	Inventory			15.5		25.7	36.0
6.1	5.4	4.9	All Other Current			10.7		2.8	4.6
76.9	76.4	78.0	Total Current			70.4		74.5	79.1
12.5	15.4	12.7	Fixed Assets (net)			15.3		12.8	12.9
4.0	2.4	3.4	Intangibles (net)			6.0		2.9	3.6
6.6	5.8	5.8	All Other Non-Current			8.3		9.8	4.5
100.0	100.0	100.0	Total			100.0		100.0	100.0
			LIABILITIES						
16.5	13.9	15.6	Notes Payable-Short Term			7.5		14.0	17.2
1.5	1.9	1.5	Cur. Mat.-L.T.D.			3.5		2.6	1.1
26.2	25.3	27.5	Trade Payables			33.8		29.5	23.8
.1	.3	.3	Income Taxes Payable			.0		.2	.4
13.7	11.5	10.5	All Other Current			17.0		4.0	12.3
58.0	52.8	55.4	Total Current			61.8		50.2	54.8
7.2	7.9	5.6	Long-Term Debt			.4		4.8	7.6
.2	.2	.3	Deferred Taxes			.0		.0	.5
2.7	4.3	3.6	All Other Non-Current			6.3		2.4	3.6
32.0	34.8	35.2	Net Worth			31.5		42.5	33.5
100.0	100.0	100.0	Total Liabilties & Net Worth			100.0		100.0	100.0
			INCOME DATA						
100.0	100.0	100.0	Net Sales			100.0		100.0	100.0
15.4	16.6	16.9	Gross Profit			23.4		14.5	13.8
11.5	12.5	14.8	Operating Expenses			25.2		11.3	10.7
3.9	4.1	2.1	Operating Profit			-1.7		3.2	3.1
.7	.9	.1	All Other Expenses (net)			-.7		.3	.3
3.2	3.2	2.1	Profit Before Taxes			-1.0		3.0	2.9
			RATIOS						
1.8	2.1	2.4				4.2		1.9	2.1
1.3	1.4	1.4	Current			1.1		1.4	1.3
1.1	1.1	1.1				1.0		1.1	1.1
1.1	1.2	1.3				2.6		1.3	1.1
.7	(116) .7	.8	Quick			.8		.9	.7
.3	.4	.5				.3		.6	.4
16 23.2	**15** 23.7	**20** 18.5				**19** 18.9		**14** 26.3	**21** 17.8
30 12.0	**31** 11.9	**30** 12.0	Sales/Receivables			**58** 6.3		**30** 12.1	**32** 11.5
47 7.7	**54** 6.7	**50** 7.3				**74** 4.9		**42** 8.6	**43** 8.4
6 56.6	**9** 39.1	**11** 32.2				**7** 51.2		**6** 59.3	**25** 14.6
39 9.3	**42** 8.6	**40** 9.1	Cost of Sales/Inventory			**30** 12.2		**25** 14.5	**57** 6.4
94 3.9	**94** 3.9	**101** 3.6				**74** 4.9		**53** 6.9	**111** 3.3
12 29.9	**9** 41.9	**9** 41.6				**20** 18.5		**9** 42.3	**10** 38.1
24 15.3	**21** 17.0	**24** 15.0	Cost of Sales/Payables			**56** 6.5		**25** 14.4	**24** 15.4
47 7.8	**43** 8.5	**57** 6.4				**85** 4.3		**49** 7.4	**57** 6.4
9.5	7.2	7.0				4.0		7.9	8.2
21.7	18.3	15.8	Sales/Working Capital			10.4		29.8	15.3
66.9	56.0	46.6				NM		51.7	44.1
19.0	32.6	19.0						18.4	20.2
(101) 5.9	(102) 7.2	(89) 5.5	EBIT/Interest					(20) 10.5	(50) 5.4
1.9	1.6	1.8						3.5	1.8
11.8	7.5	5.2							5.2
(22) 5.2	(19) 2.9	(14) 2.4	Net Profit + Depr., Dep., Amort./Cur. Mat. L/T/D						(14) 2.4
1.3	1.2	1.4							1.4
.1	.0	.0				.0		.0	.0
.3	.4	.2	Fixed/Worth			.1		.1	.4
.8	1.2	.8				.9		1.0	1.1
1.2	1.0	.7				.6		.7	1.4
2.8	2.6	2.0	Debt/Worth			6.1		1.7	2.3
6.8	7.2	7.4				27.4		3.6	8.7
45.1	44.2	47.8						55.6	37.9
(106) 23.9	(106) 20.8	(92) 17.1	% Profit Before Taxes/Tangible Net Worth					(20) 20.0	(50) 16.1
14.3	8.0	5.0						12.3	7.5
11.3	12.8	11.7				7.9		15.3	11.1
6.6	6.5	5.0	% Profit Before Taxes/Total Assets			3.5		9.6	3.4
2.1	1.7	1.5				-2.9		4.1	1.5
263.0	479.5	999.8				UND		UND	277.8
42.0	34.6	62.1	Sales/Net Fixed Assets			27.0		168.5	50.7
12.3	11.8	11.6				3.0		14.1	10.8
4.7	5.2	4.6				3.6		5.0	4.3
2.9	3.0	2.7	Sales/Total Assets			1.5		4.0	2.5
1.9	1.7	1.8				.6		2.4	1.8
.1	.1	.1						.1	.1
(88) .6	(85) .5	(68) .7	% Depr., Dep., Amort./Sales					(14) .6	(40) .3
1.4	1.3	1.4						1.6	1.3
.4	.5	.5							.5
(28) 1.0	(26) 1.0	(28) 1.6	% Officers', Directors' Owners' Comp/Sales						(15) 1.4
2.3	1.8	4.1							2.8
12620120M	**11425750M**	**10171431M**	Net Sales ($)	**553M**	**7688M**	**39952M**	**62227M**	**346846M**	**9714165M**
4598363M	**4378367M**	**3575081M**	Total Assets ($)	**2616M**	**4598M**	**58421M**	**17632M**	**111692M**	**3380122M**

M = $ thousand MM = $ million

See Pages 9 through 22 for Explanation of Ratios and Data

Current Data Sorted by Assets							Comparative Historical Data	
						Type of Statement		
		5	8	4	3	Unqualified	26	26
	1	12	10	1		Reviewed	33	33
2	4	10	1			Compiled	16	22
3	12	6	1			Tax Returns	26	22
2	11	21	16		4	Other	63	62
19 (4/1-9/30/13)			118 (10/1/13-3/31/14)				4/1/09-3/31/10	4/1/10-3/31/11
0-500M	500M-2MM	2-10MM	10-50MM	50-100MM	100-250MM		ALL	ALL
7	28	54	36	5	7	**NUMBER OF STATEMENTS**	164	165
%	%	%	%	%	%	**ASSETS**	%	%
	18.7	5.2	7.6			Cash & Equivalents	8.3	9.3
	38.6	42.8	37.8			Trade Receivables (net)	40.2	39.9
	27.4	34.4	34.5			Inventory	28.4	29.7
	2.6	3.1	1.6			All Other Current	1.9	1.8
	87.4	85.5	81.5			Total Current	78.8	80.7
	8.7	9.4	12.5			Fixed Assets (net)	11.1	11.7
	.1	1.8	3.2			Intangibles (net)	3.2	2.6
	3.8	3.3	2.8			All Other Non-Current	6.9	5.0
	100.0	100.0	100.0			Total	100.0	100.0
						LIABILITIES		
	17.5	17.6	20.4			Notes Payable-Short Term	17.4	15.2
	1.5	2.8	1.0			Cur. Mat.-L.T.D.	1.6	1.4
	25.0	28.4	25.2			Trade Payables	28.0	28.0
	.2	.8	.0			Income Taxes Payable	.2	.2
	6.4	7.8	5.6			All Other Current	6.4	8.2
	50.6	57.3	52.3			Total Current	53.6	53.0
	4.3	4.2	7.5			Long-Term Debt	9.3	7.4
	.1	.4	.2			Deferred Taxes	.3	.2
	4.7	2.8	4.1			All Other Non-Current	6.3	4.2
	40.4	35.2	36.0			Net Worth	30.5	35.1
	100.0	100.0	100.0			Total Liabilities & Net Worth	100.0	100.0
						INCOME DATA		
	100.0	100.0	100.0			Net Sales	100.0	100.0
	25.8	20.6	15.7			Gross Profit	21.5	23.3
	20.3	16.7	11.4			Operating Expenses	18.1	19.4
	5.5	3.9	4.3			Operating Profit	3.4	3.8
	.2	.0	.6			All Other Expenses (net)	.6	.4
	5.2	3.9	3.7			Profit Before Taxes	2.8	3.5
						RATIOS		
	3.5	1.9	2.3				2.4	2.5
	1.7	1.6	1.6			Current	1.5	1.5
	1.1	1.3	1.2				1.1	1.1
	2.3	1.4	1.3				1.4	1.5
	1.0	.8	.9			Quick	.9	.9
	.6	.6	.7				.6	.6
	23 16.0	**29** 12.4	**37** 9.9				**35** 10.6	**31** 11.6
	40 9.2	**40** 9.1	**43** 8.5			Sales/Receivables	**44** 8.3	**44** 8.3
	51 7.1	**51** 7.1	**61** 6.0				**58** 6.3	**56** 6.5
	13 27.3	**24** 15.3	**29** 12.4				**17** 21.4	**22** 16.6
	28 13.1	**52** 7.0	**60** 6.1			Cost of Sales/Inventory	**47** 7.8	**45** 8.2
	81 4.5	**85** 4.3	**83** 4.4				**75** 4.9	**76** 4.8
	12 29.4	**21** 17.4	**22** 16.4				**21** 17.6	**23** 15.6
	27 13.6	**40** 9.1	**32** 11.4			Cost of Sales/Payables	**37** 9.8	**36** 10.0
	40 9.1	**49** 7.5	**62** 5.9				**55** 6.7	**51** 7.1
	4.9	6.3	5.3				6.2	5.9
	15.4	10.7	9.8			Sales/Working Capital	12.7	11.9
	50.6	20.3	26.3				40.6	35.4
	30.8	17.2	11.3				16.1	26.8
	(20) 5.7	(43) 6.1	(32) 4.7			EBIT/Interest	(146) 6.0	(143) 6.4
	2.4	2.3	2.7				1.6	2.6
							5.3	13.1
						Net Profit + Depr., Dep., Amort./Cur. Mat. L/T/D	(32) 2.5	(31) 4.4
							1.1	2.1
	.0	.0	.0				.0	.0
	.0	.1	.1			Fixed/Worth	.2	.1
	.8	.4	.7				1.0	.6
	.5	.9	.8				1.1	.8
	1.2	2.1	2.0			Debt/Worth	2.6	2.0
	8.3	3.9	7.5				7.3	5.6
	62.6	55.3	43.0				53.6	47.3
	(24) 23.1	(53) 34.7	(34) 23.1			% Profit Before Taxes/Tangible Net Worth	(146) 27.4	(151) 23.2
	10.9	9.7	14.8				5.8	9.3
	21.8	16.0	13.9				15.3	16.3
	8.6	7.9	6.9			% Profit Before Taxes/Total Assets	6.0	6.9
	3.3	3.4	2.8				1.2	3.0
	999.8	999.8	544.4				548.2	499.0
	210.3	77.6	88.6			Sales/Net Fixed Assets	85.4	62.3
	33.6	25.4	23.3				14.5	14.9
	5.5	4.4	3.4				3.9	4.2
	3.5	3.4	2.8			Sales/Total Assets	2.9	3.0
	2.6	2.5	2.1				2.2	2.3
	.1	.1	.1				.1	.2
	(14) .5	(33) .8	(31) .2			% Depr., Dep., Amort./Sales	(111) .7	(120) .7
	1.3	1.4	.8				2.0	1.7
	2.1	1.1	.2				.6	.8
	(15) 3.8	(25) 1.4	(11) .5			% Officers', Directors' Owners' Comp/Sales	(67) 1.7	(72) 2.2
	4.9	2.7	.8				4.5	4.3
13496M	142938M	997098M	2156160M	1023604M	3633537M	Net Sales ($)	6745514M	8300926M
2245M	35578M	275597M	804604M	332556M	1167236M	Total Assets ($)	2361354M	2776305M

M = $ thousand MM = $ million

See Pages 9 through 22 for Explanation of Ratios and Data

Comparative Historical Data				Current Data Sorted by Sales					
			Type of Statement						
27	21	20	Unqualified					7	13
30	28	24	Reviewed			1	2	7	14
25	19	17	Compiled	1	1	4	4	6	1
38	22	22	Tax Returns	2	4	2	8	2	4
64	65	54	Other		4	6	8	13	23
4/1/11-3/31/12 ALL	4/1/12-3/31/13 ALL	4/1/13-3/31/14 ALL		19 (4/1-9/30/13)			118 (10/1/13-3/31/14)		
				0-1MM	1-3MM	3-5MM	5-10MM	10-25MM	25MM & OVER
184	155	137	**NUMBER OF STATEMENTS**	3	9	13	22	35	55
%	%	%	**ASSETS**	%	%	%	%	%	%
9.5	9.6	8.8	Cash & Equivalents			13.8	12.0	5.7	6.5
37.1	37.6	40.3	Trade Receivables (net)			41.9	35.6	42.7	41.7
30.3	31.7	32.1	Inventory			26.1	35.9	30.6	34.5
2.2	2.4	2.3	All Other Current			6.4	2.2	1.8	1.6
79.1	81.4	83.6	Total Current			88.2	85.7	80.8	84.3
12.1	11.7	10.2	Fixed Assets (net)			5.7	9.5	12.6	10.1
3.0	2.6	2.1	Intangibles (net)			.3	2.0	2.7	2.5
5.8	4.3	4.2	All Other Non-Current			5.8	2.8	3.9	3.1
100.0	100.0	100.0	Total			100.0	100.0	100.0	100.0
			LIABILITIES						
16.3	19.5	18.6	Notes Payable-Short Term			21.4	15.3	16.1	20.5
1.2	1.4	1.9	Cur. Mat.-L.T.D.			1.7	2.2	1.4	2.4
25.5	23.8	26.1	Trade Payables			19.1	26.0	25.8	29.7
.3	.1	.4	Income Taxes Payable			3.2	.1	.0	.1
7.4	7.1	7.1	All Other Current			4.3	5.6	6.6	7.0
50.6	51.9	54.1	Total Current			49.7	49.2	49.9	59.7
8.2	7.2	6.0	Long-Term Debt			2.8	5.0	6.6	7.0
.2	.2	.2	Deferred Taxes			.1	.2	.4	.3
7.2	8.9	3.5	All Other Non-Current			2.2	7.7	1.7	3.2
33.8	31.7	36.2	Net Worth			45.2	37.9	41.4	29.8
100.0	100.0	100.0	Total Liabilities & Net Worth			100.0	100.0	100.0	100.0
			INCOME DATA						
100.0	100.0	100.0	Net Sales			100.0	100.0	100.0	100.0
21.9	21.1	19.9	Gross Profit			30.4	22.6	20.9	14.9
18.2	16.9	15.6	Operating Expenses			24.8	19.2	16.0	10.9
3.8	4.3	4.4	Operating Profit			5.6	3.4	4.9	4.1
.4	.5	.2	All Other Expenses (net)			-1.5	.4	.4	.5
3.3	3.7	4.2	Profit Before Taxes			7.1	3.1	4.5	3.6
			RATIOS						
2.3	2.6	2.3				6.0	2.4	1.9	2.3
1.5	1.5	1.6	Current			1.5	1.6	1.6	1.5
1.1	1.1	1.2				1.1	1.3	1.3	1.1
1.5	1.4	1.4				4.0	1.4	1.5	1.2
.9	.9	.9	Quick			1.3	.8	1.0	.8
.6	.6	.6				.7	.5	.6	.6
29 12.8	**32** 11.4	**31** 11.7				**23** 16.1	**24** 15.1	**30** 12.2	**37** 9.9
41 8.8	**40** 9.1	**41** 8.8	Sales/Receivables			**51** 7.1	**30** 12.1	**45** 8.2	**44** 8.3
51 7.2	**49** 7.5	**52** 7.0				**68** 5.4	**41** 8.8	**55** 6.6	**53** 6.9
22 16.9	**24** 15.4	**23** 16.1				**6** 60.1	**20** 18.3	**22** 16.8	**28** 13.0
42 8.7	**49** 7.5	**47** 7.8	Cost of Sales/Inventory			**35** 10.4	**63** 5.8	**38** 9.7	**51** 7.1
68 5.4	**78** 4.7	**81** 4.5				**91** 4.0	**83** 4.4	**81** 4.5	**73** 5.0
19 19.2	**18** 20.0	**21** 17.4				**14** 25.9	**18** 20.2	**24** 15.3	**24** 15.5
34 10.7	**29** 12.8	**34** 10.8	Cost of Sales/Payables			**25** 14.6	**36** 10.2	**35** 10.3	**34** 10.7
46 7.9	**43** 8.5	**47** 7.7				**41** 9.0	**45** 8.1	**49** 7.5	**49** 7.4
6.7	6.3	6.1				4.0	6.2	6.3	6.4
12.6	12.5	11.2	Sales/Working Capital			6.3	9.9	10.3	16.0
39.4	37.5	35.3				49.3	28.4	40.4	31.8
22.2	15.1	15.0					13.7	15.0	16.8
(153) 6.6	(133) 6.2	(112) 6.3	EBIT/Interest				(18) 4.9	(27) 6.2	(49) 6.9
2.9	1.8	2.7					3.5	2.3	3.6
16.0	9.2	24.2							29.1
(35) 3.1	(24) 3.3	(23) 3.2	Net Profit + Depr., Dep., Amort./Cur. Mat. L/T/D						(13) 4.0
1.4	1.4	1.7							1.6
.0	.0	.0				.0	.0	.0	.0
.1	.2	.1	Fixed/Worth			.0	.2	.2	.1
.6	1.0	.5				.7	.7	.5	.4
.8	1.0	.8				.3	.7	.7	1.2
2.4	2.4	1.9	Debt/Worth			2.5	1.5	1.8	2.7
6.1	6.3	5.0				3.6	5.0	4.9	6.4
50.6	57.0	51.9				69.5	44.2	71.9	46.3
(170) 21.8	(140) 32.0	(128) 25.3	% Profit Before Taxes/Tangible Net Worth			10.2	(19) 21.6	24.9	(52) 36.0
10.5	9.9	14.5				.4	10.2	9.3	18.9
15.1	16.5	15.9				27.1	18.6	25.0	13.8
7.4	8.3	7.6	% Profit Before Taxes/Total Assets			6.8	6.6	6.9	9.1
2.7	2.2	3.4				-.2	4.1	2.3	4.3
665.7	850.4	999.8				999.8	844.7	999.8	999.8
118.0	118.1	126.8	Sales/Net Fixed Assets			279.8	122.1	61.3	135.4
16.8	15.9	27.2				27.7	24.9	18.0	34.1
4.3	4.0	4.3				3.8	4.9	4.4	3.7
3.2	3.2	3.2	Sales/Total Assets			3.0	3.5	3.4	3.2
2.4	2.3	2.4				2.1	2.8	2.3	2.6
.1	.1	.1					.1	.2	.0
(135) .5	(110) .5	(91) .4	% Depr., Dep., Amort./Sales				(15) .7	(20) .7	(46) .2
1.3	1.4	1.3					1.5	1.5	.8
1.0	1.0	.8					2.0	.7	.3
(70) 2.1	(57) 2.7	(53) 2.0	% Officers', Directors' Owners' Comp/Sales				(15) 3.1	(15) 1.3	(15) .6
5.2	5.2	3.9					7.5	2.2	1.4
10527957M	8701203M	7966833M	Net Sales ($)	2189M	17731M	52855M	159190M	584926M	7149942M
3316305M	3023341M	2617816M	Total Assets ($)	2084M	5518M	19762M	45973M	208761M	2335718M

M = $ thousand MM = $ million

See Pages 9 through 22 for Explanation of Ratios and Data

Current Data Sorted by Assets | **Comparative Historical Data**

	0-500M	500M-2MM	2-10MM	10-50MM	50-100MM	100-250MM	4/1/09-3/31/10 ALL	4/1/10-3/31/11 ALL
Type of Statement								
Unqualified		1	8	27	12	13	73	62
Reviewed		5	40	32	3	1	89	82
Compiled	2	9	29	4		1	47	57
Tax Returns	5	33	33	2			53	63
Other	2	20	66	69	14	12	152	173
	75 (4/1-9/30/13)			368 (10/1/13-3/31/14)				
NUMBER OF STATEMENTS	9	68	176	134	29	27	414	437
ASSETS	%	%	%	%	%	%	%	%
Cash & Equivalents		11.4	11.0	8.1	8.0	4.3	10.2	7.8
Trade Receivables (net)		39.5	37.8	32.9	29.8	31.9	34.0	36.3
Inventory		31.3	32.1	33.2	24.4	27.5	29.1	30.4
All Other Current		1.6	1.4	2.7	4.1	1.8	2.8	2.5
Total Current		83.8	82.3	77.0	66.4	65.5	76.0	77.1
Fixed Assets (net)		10.5	9.9	14.5	20.2	24.4	15.1	13.5
Intangibles (net)		1.6	3.0	4.7	6.9	7.1	3.9	4.5
All Other Non-Current		4.0	4.8	3.8	6.5	2.9	5.0	4.9
Total		100.0	100.0	100.0	100.0	100.0	100.0	100.0
LIABILITIES								
Notes Payable-Short Term		11.7	15.4	15.2	8.8	8.8	14.1	13.6
Cur. Mat.-L.T.D.		3.2	1.4	1.0	1.6	3.0	2.2	2.0
Trade Payables		27.0	26.0	22.3	18.2	19.3	22.3	24.5
Income Taxes Payable		.3	.1	.1	.1	.2	.3	.2
All Other Current		7.8	6.3	7.0	7.8	15.2	8.5	6.9
Total Current		50.0	49.1	45.6	36.4	46.5	47.3	47.2
Long-Term Debt		10.3	6.7	9.0	12.5	15.6	9.6	9.3
Deferred Taxes		.0	.1	.5	.3	.6	.4	.4
All Other Non-Current		5.8	3.1	4.6	7.1	4.0	3.0	4.3
Net Worth		33.9	40.9	40.4	43.8	33.3	39.7	38.8
Total Liabilties & Net Worth		100.0	100.0	100.0	100.0	100.0	100.0	100.0
INCOME DATA								
Net Sales		100.0	100.0	100.0	100.0	100.0	100.0	100.0
Gross Profit		28.6	26.2	19.9	19.6	26.6	26.4	26.1
Operating Expenses		25.1	21.3	15.4	14.9	23.1	21.9	21.7
Operating Profit		3.6	4.9	4.5	4.7	3.5	4.4	4.4
All Other Expenses (net)		.1	.0	.3	.2	.4	.4	.4
Profit Before Taxes		3.5	4.9	4.2	4.5	3.1	4.1	4.0
RATIOS								
Current		3.3	2.6	2.7	4.0	2.2	2.5	2.5
		1.6	1.7	1.7	1.9	1.3	1.6	1.7
		1.2	1.2	1.3	1.3	1.1	1.2	1.3
Quick		1.5	1.8	1.5	1.9	1.1	1.6	1.4
		1.0	.9	1.0	1.2	.8	1.0	.9
		.7	.6	.6	.7	.6	.6	.6
Sales/Receivables		27 13.7	29 12.4	33 11.2	36 10.1	35 10.3	32 11.4	32 11.3
		35 10.5	38 9.5	40 9.1	43 8.4	41 8.8	41 8.8	41 8.9
		47 7.7	51 7.2	48 7.6	49 7.4	50 7.3	53 6.9	52 7.0
Cost of Sales/Inventory		14 26.5	23 15.6	29 12.6	24 15.2	32 11.5	26 14.0	26 13.9
		36 10.2	46 7.9	51 7.1	42 8.7	52 7.0	48 7.6	48 7.6
		87 4.2	76 4.8	83 4.4	69 5.3	85 4.3	82 4.4	77 4.7
Cost of Sales/Payables		18 20.2	23 16.1	19 18.9	20 18.0	20 18.0	23 16.1	23 15.8
		33 11.1	36 10.2	31 11.6	28 12.9	30 12.2	33 11.0	35 10.5
		45 8.2	53 6.9	44 8.3	41 9.0	37 9.9	48 7.6	49 7.4
Sales/Working Capital		5.2	5.7	5.4	4.1	6.4	6.1	6.5
		12.4	9.8	9.1	10.1	10.2	10.5	10.5
		29.4	22.8	17.8	23.8	85.1	21.3	21.3
EBIT/Interest		24.7	38.7	25.6	16.9	13.7	16.3	23.8
		(58) 5.2	(149) 8.8	(120) 12.1	(26) 7.8	(24) 5.2	(369) 4.8	(381) 7.9
		1.8	3.3	4.1	4.1	1.2	2.1	2.6
Net Profit + Depr., Dep., Amort./Cur. Mat. L/T/D			5.7	19.3		14.7	9.0	12.5
			(28) 2.0	(30) 9.7		(10) 2.4	(95) 3.2	(96) 4.7
			1.1	4.5		1.2	1.4	2.5
Fixed/Worth		.0	.0	.0	.0	.2	.0	.0
		.1	.1	.3	.4	.8	.2	.2
		.8	.6	.7	1.2	1.3	.9	.7
Debt/Worth		.9	.7	.8	.6	1.4	.8	.8
		1.7	1.9	1.5	1.6	3.0	1.8	1.8
		6.7	4.5	3.1	3.5	6.1	3.9	4.2
% Profit Before Taxes/Tangible Net Worth		62.6	56.2	42.0	61.7	40.0	49.2	48.5
		(61) 21.8	(166) 26.2	(124) 25.7	(26) 19.1	(24) 16.4	(387) 24.7	(400) 25.2
		5.8	11.7	13.9	8.3	4.6	8.4	11.3
% Profit Before Taxes/Total Assets		22.3	19.9	16.8	13.1	11.0	17.1	16.7
		6.2	11.9	9.7	7.2	4.6	7.2	8.5
		1.7	3.1	4.8	3.9	.4	2.3	2.9
Sales/Net Fixed Assets		999.8	378.1	178.2	328.8	205.4	189.2	286.2
		114.0	70.3	40.8	15.9	10.9	40.7	50.5
		31.8	17.6	13.2	5.4	3.4	11.7	13.7
Sales/Total Assets		5.3	4.2	3.8	3.5	3.4	3.8	4.0
		3.4	3.1	3.0	2.5	2.0	2.8	3.0
		2.4	2.4	2.0	1.4	1.5	2.1	2.2
% Depr., Dep., Amort./Sales		.2	.2	.1	.3	.1	.3	.2
		(37) .6	(129) .5	(111) .5	(24) 1.3	(23) .9	(323) .8	(333) .6
		1.3	1.2	1.6	2.2	2.1	2.0	1.6
% Officers', Directors' Owners' Comp/Sales		2.1	1.9	.5			1.6	1.4
		(45) 4.4	(86) 2.9	(23) 1.0			(148) 3.3	(161) 2.6
		8.4	5.0	2.7			6.0	5.2
Net Sales ($)	10377M	347802M	2892605M	8531264M	5808078M	14221177M	21351752M	19694343M
Total Assets ($)	2202M	86318M	858633M	2815118M	2074471M	3962865M	7775832M	7127929M

M = $ thousand MM = $ million

See Pages 9 through 22 for Explanation of Ratios and Data

Comparative Historical Data				Current Data Sorted by Sales					
			Type of Statement						
83	55	61	Unqualified		1		1	10	49
94	87	81	Reviewed			4	14	18	45
61	41	45	Compiled	1	1	5	13	16	9
62	63	73	Tax Returns	5	16	4	27	18	3
167	186	183	Other	2	9	6	21	46	99
4/1/11-3/31/12 ALL	4/1/12-3/31/13 ALL	4/1/13-3/31/14 ALL		75 (4/1-9/30/13)			368 (10/1/13-3/31/14)		
				0-1MM	1-3MM	3-5MM	5-10MM	10-25MM	25MM & OVER
467	432	443	**NUMBER OF STATEMENTS**	8	27	19	76	108	205
%	%	%	**ASSETS**	%	%	%	%	%	%
8.4	9.5	9.8	Cash & Equivalents		10.3	12.0	11.5	10.3	8.1
35.6	35.6	35.7	Trade Receivables (net)		29.9	32.8	38.9	37.1	35.3
31.8	30.6	31.1	Inventory		32.7	32.6	28.1	33.6	31.1
2.6	2.0	2.1	All Other Current		2.8	1.5	.9	1.7	2.6
78.4	77.7	78.7	Total Current		75.7	79.0	79.5	82.7	77.0
12.6	13.2	13.0	Fixed Assets (net)		10.2	13.1	13.0	10.6	14.7
4.4	4.1	3.8	Intangibles (net)		5.3	1.6	3.0	3.0	4.4
4.5	5.0	4.5	All Other Non-Current		8.7	6.3	4.5	3.7	3.9
100.0	100.0	100.0	Total		100.0	100.0	100.0	100.0	100.0
			LIABILITIES						
14.5	14.9	14.2	Notes Payable-Short Term		22.0	15.0	11.4	16.9	12.9
1.7	1.5	1.6	Cur. Mat.-L.T.D.		3.3	2.0	1.6	1.7	1.3
23.8	22.9	24.2	Trade Payables		16.9	25.8	25.0	26.2	23.7
.2	.2	.1	Income Taxes Payable		.2	.0	.2	.1	.1
9.0	9.4	7.5	All Other Current		8.8	3.2	6.6	8.0	7.6
49.2	48.9	47.6	Total Current		51.2	46.0	44.9	52.9	45.6
8.0	8.4	8.9	Long-Term Debt		17.2	9.7	8.9	6.5	9.2
.3	.4	.3	Deferred Taxes		.0	.0	.1	.2	.4
5.1	5.5	4.2	All Other Non-Current		9.5	2.6	3.5	4.1	4.0
37.4	36.8	39.0	Net Worth		22.1	41.6	42.7	36.4	40.7
100.0	100.0	100.0	Total Liabilties & Net Worth		100.0	100.0	100.0	100.0	100.0
			INCOME DATA						
100.0	100.0	100.0	Net Sales		100.0	100.0	100.0	100.0	100.0
23.8	24.6	24.7	Gross Profit		33.3	31.1	30.3	23.6	20.1
19.1	20.2	20.1	Operating Expenses		29.5	26.5	25.0	19.4	15.8
4.8	4.4	4.6	Operating Profit		3.7	4.6	5.3	4.3	4.3
.3	.5	.2	All Other Expenses (net)		.6	.6	.1	.0	.2
4.4	3.9	4.4	Profit Before Taxes		3.1	3.9	5.3	4.3	4.1
			RATIOS						
2.5	2.6	2.7			4.2	3.2	3.3	2.2	2.6
1.6	1.7	1.7	Current		1.7	1.8	1.9	1.6	1.7
1.2	1.2	1.2			1.1	1.2	1.3	1.2	1.3
1.4	1.6	1.6			1.8	1.5	1.9	1.6	1.5
.9	.9	1.0	Quick		.9	.9	1.0	.9	1.0
.6	.6	.6			.3	.7	.7	.5	.6
30 12.0	30 12.0	30 12.1			4 95.4	24 15.3	30 12.1	30 12.1	31 11.7
40 9.1	38 9.5	39 9.4	Sales/Receivables		47 7.8	38 9.5	38 9.5	38 9.5	40 9.2
50 7.3	49 7.4	49 7.5			78 4.7	58 6.3	54 6.7	49 7.5	47 7.7
26 14.2	26 14.2	24 15.1			7 50.6	26 13.8	20 18.7	23 15.6	26 13.9
48 7.6	46 7.9	45 8.1	Cost of Sales/Inventory		91 4.0	54 6.7	42 8.6	53 6.9	44 8.3
78 4.7	70 5.2	78 4.7			152 2.4	114 3.2	74 4.9	78 4.7	70 5.2
20 17.9	18 20.5	21 17.8			7 51.8	21 17.4	20 18.5	24 15.2	20 18.0
31 11.9	29 12.8	33 11.1	Cost of Sales/Payables		30 12.0	48 7.6	36 10.1	34 10.7	30 12.0
46 7.9	43 8.5	47 7.8			55 6.6	68 5.4	54 6.7	50 7.3	41 8.9
6.1	6.1	5.5			3.4	3.1	5.1	6.5	5.6
10.8	10.9	9.9	Sales/Working Capital		9.1	10.7	9.7	9.9	10.1
22.7	27.2	23.5			31.8	39.0	21.1	23.7	23.4
23.0	23.7	26.4			5.7	8.9	38.8	33.9	25.6
(394) 8.3	(368) 7.6	(382) 8.2	EBIT/Interest		(23) 3.1	(16) 3.3	(63) 7.1	(95) 8.8	(182) 11.4
2.9	2.6	3.3			.5	.5	2.7	3.5	4.1
13.5	11.8	12.9					6.4	18.0	18.4
(102) 5.0	(72) 4.0	(83) 5.0	Net Profit + Depr., Dep., Amort./Cur. Mat. L/T/D				(18) 1.7	(15) 4.3	(47) 7.2
2.2	1.7	1.7					.7	1.4	2.9
.0	.0	.0			.0	.0	.1	.0	.0
.2	.2	.2	Fixed/Worth		.1	.1	.2	.2	.2
.7	.8	.7			-.7	1.4	.7	.6	.8
.8	.8	.8			1.0	.4	.6	.7	.8
1.8	1.8	1.8	Debt/Worth		3.1	1.6	1.5	2.2	1.6
4.8	5.0	4.1			-16.0	5.3	3.6	5.3	3.7
50.3	56.4	49.5			54.0	31.3	60.4	57.4	44.4
(432) 28.3	(392) 27.0	(408) 24.7	% Profit Before Taxes/Tangible Net Worth		(20) 10.4	(18) 16.8	(73) 19.2	(99) 26.3	(191) 26.3
11.5	10.2	10.4			2.8	2.1	6.6	17.5	13.1
17.9	19.1	18.3			22.8	17.1	23.9	19.6	16.5
8.0	8.5	9.4	% Profit Before Taxes/Total Assets		3.1	3.7	9.0	11.8	9.5
3.5	2.9	3.0			-2.0	.8	2.4	3.8	4.2
351.7	418.4	388.9			999.8	UND	172.1	439.6	435.2
57.7	61.4	54.1	Sales/Net Fixed Assets		52.5	34.5	44.3	69.2	53.3
13.9	14.2	13.5			21.0	16.1	13.4	16.3	11.4
4.1	4.3	4.1			3.2	3.7	4.1	4.4	4.1
3.1	3.1	3.0	Sales/Total Assets		2.3	2.5	2.9	3.2	3.2
2.2	2.2	2.1			1.3	2.0	2.3	2.3	2.2
.2	.1	.2			.3	.3	.3	.2	.1
(342) .5	(317) .5	(327) .5	% Depr., Dep., Amort./Sales		(13) .5	(12) .7	(51) .7	(76) .6	(172) .5
1.3	1.5	1.5			3.7	1.0	1.5	1.5	1.5
1.4	1.2	1.5			2.7		1.9	1.5	.8
(160) 2.6	(154) 2.5	(165) 2.9	% Officers', Directors' Owners' Comp/Sales		(14) 3.8		(49) 3.7	(46) 2.8	(42) 1.6
5.0	5.2	5.8			6.6		7.7	4.6	2.9
34817167M	34741844M	31811303M	Net Sales ($)	4533M	54360M	69755M	564598M	1762518M	29355539M
10394383M	9382179M	9799607M	Total Assets ($)	4899M	29960M	32356M	225047M	625189M	8882156M

M = $ thousand MM = $ million

See Pages 9 through 22 for Explanation of Ratios and Data

Current Data Sorted by Assets							Comparative Historical Data	
						Type of Statement		
	2	3	16	7	11	Unqualified	56	67
2	3	18	22	3		Reviewed	96	104
4	6	15	4			Compiled	63	69
4	5	9	6			Tax Returns	38	49
1	10	33	26	10	6	Other	98	104
	64 (4/1-9/30/13)		162 (10/1/13-3/31/14)				4/1/09-3/31/10 ALL	4/1/10-3/31/11 ALL
0-500M	500M-2MM	2-10MM	10-50MM	50-100MM	100-250MM			
11	26	78	74	20	17	**NUMBER OF STATEMENTS**	351	393
%	%	%	%	%	%	**ASSETS**	%	%
9.7	11.8	9.4	8.1	3.8	6.1	Cash & Equivalents	10.8	9.7
15.4	32.5	38.3	32.4	28.0	29.0	Trade Receivables (net)	28.6	30.8
22.6	15.3	15.5	13.3	12.2	25.7	Inventory	14.0	14.4
2.5	6.6	2.8	2.9	5.7	2.0	All Other Current	2.6	3.4
50.3	66.3	66.0	56.6	49.7	62.8	Total Current	56.1	58.3
27.9	24.6	22.8	31.6	40.9	28.5	Fixed Assets (net)	32.0	30.1
7.0	1.6	4.6	4.4	2.3	5.3	Intangibles (net)	4.1	3.7
14.9	7.5	6.6	7.4	7.1	3.4	All Other Non-Current	7.9	7.8
100.0	100.0	100.0	100.0	100.0	100.0	Total	100.0	100.0
						LIABILITIES		
5.6	6.5	11.6	11.0	9.7	11.1	Notes Payable-Short Term	9.0	10.3
3.6	3.0	3.1	3.0	3.1	3.7	Cur. Mat.-L.T.D.	3.8	3.3
15.7	21.9	27.2	21.5	16.5	19.0	Trade Payables	24.0	25.9
.0	.2	.2	.1	.0	.7	Income Taxes Payable	.2	.3
7.4	13.5	7.1	7.3	9.1	5.5	All Other Current	9.6	9.1
32.4	45.0	49.2	42.9	38.4	40.0	Total Current	46.6	48.9
13.6	14.7	9.6	15.1	18.3	21.9	Long-Term Debt	19.1	15.9
.0	.0	.8	1.5	1.7	1.2	Deferred Taxes	.6	.6
21.8	10.2	3.3	4.5	2.5	10.1	All Other Non-Current	2.8	3.8
32.4	30.1	37.1	36.0	39.1	26.8	Net Worth	30.8	30.8
100.0	100.0	100.0	100.0	100.0	100.0	Total Liabilties & Net Worth	100.0	100.0
						INCOME DATA		
100.0	100.0	100.0	100.0	100.0	100.0	Net Sales	100.0	100.0
21.7	23.5	9.6	10.8	15.3	10.1	Gross Profit	12.2	11.8
21.1	18.9	8.7	8.8	11.9	7.7	Operating Expenses	10.8	10.3
.7	4.6	.9	2.0	3.3	2.4	Operating Profit	1.4	1.5
-.4	1.8	.1	-.1	.3	.7	All Other Expenses (net)	.0	.0
1.0	2.7	.8	2.1	3.0	1.7	Profit Before Taxes	1.4	1.5
						RATIOS		
4.3	2.9	1.8	1.7	2.1	2.0		1.7	1.6
2.3	1.6	1.3	1.2	1.4	1.7	Current	1.2	1.2
.8	.9	1.0	1.0	1.0	1.2		.9	.9
3.3	2.1	1.4	1.2	1.5	1.1		1.2	1.2
1.0	1.3	.9	.9	.9	.8	Quick	.8	.8
.4	.4	.6	.7	.6	.7		.6	.6
1 278.0	**7** 49.4	**10** 37.9	**12** 31.4	**11** 33.2	**7** 53.3		**8** 45.3	**8** 45.3
7 55.4	**17** 22.0	**15** 25.1	**16** 23.4	**26** 13.9	**15** 24.4	Sales/Receivables	**15** 24.2	**15** 24.0
10 35.8	**28** 12.9	**24** 14.9	**23** 15.8	**32** 11.5	**31** 11.7		**25** 14.7	**26** 14.0
3 113.7	**1** 486.8	**3** 127.3	**2** 151.0	**4** 103.0	**8** 44.8		**3** 113.4	**3** 120.9
9 40.1	**9** 39.1	**7** 54.9	**6** 58.6	**5** 67.3	**14** 26.0	Cost of Sales/Inventory	**7** 51.7	**7** 50.7
17 21.8	**19** 19.4	**11** 33.9	**15** 24.6	**22** 16.6	**20** 18.3		**15** 23.6	**15** 23.8
0 UND	**9** 41.5	**8** 48.0	**8** 44.8	**7** 53.1	**7** 55.6		**10** 36.5	**9** 39.7
7 50.0	**13** 27.9	**10** 36.8	**10** 36.8	**14** 25.8	**9** 38.9	Cost of Sales/Payables	**13** 27.4	**13** 27.6
15 24.4	**24** 14.9	**15** 23.6	**14** 25.6	**18** 20.6	**19** 18.8		**20** 18.3	**18** 20.4
20.5	12.7	28.4	25.3	14.0	16.9		24.3	24.5
33.5	25.4	66.9	74.2	56.5	32.3	Sales/Working Capital	70.6	73.4
-89.8	-684.0	UND	NM	820.3	118.7		-172.6	-257.7
	10.4	8.1	18.5	38.0	6.7		8.0	8.4
	(21) 4.9	(70) 3.1	(71) 5.2	(19) 6.7	4.4	EBIT/Interest	(329) 3.0	(351) 2.9
	.2	.6	2.2	4.8	2.8		1.5	1.5
		3.7	4.6				5.5	4.1
		(12) 1.9	(24) 2.1			Net Profit + Depr., Dep., Amort./Cur. Mat. L/T/D	(108) 2.4	(112) 2.1
		1.0	1.4				1.4	1.2
.3	.1	.2	.4	.7	.4		.5	.5
.7	.6	.7	1.0	1.3	.7	Fixed/Worth	1.2	1.0
27.3	3.6	1.6	2.2	2.4	2.9		2.7	2.3
1.1	.5	.9	1.3	.7	2.6		1.3	1.3
2.5	1.7	1.9	2.3	2.2	3.8	Debt/Worth	2.6	2.5
73.0	5.3	6.4	4.5	4.1	8.4		6.9	5.9
	34.6	33.2	36.0	33.0	54.4		37.7	30.7
	(22) 17.4	(73) 13.7	(69) 21.6	21.0	(15) 25.3	% Profit Before Taxes/Tangible Net Worth	(317) 16.6	(358) 13.9
	7.9	-.7	6.3	10.6	17.5		4.6	4.4
24.5	12.6	8.8	10.3	9.7	11.8		8.7	7.9
7.1	6.2	3.5	5.8	7.2	4.7	% Profit Before Taxes/Total Assets	4.2	3.5
2.1	-.5	-.3	2.0	2.1	3.5		1.1	1.1
119.3	159.9	279.7	76.3	29.2	366.1		58.6	81.8
23.1	47.7	43.9	26.4	18.1	30.2	Sales/Net Fixed Assets	24.4	29.2
18.5	10.4	22.9	10.0	9.2	9.3		9.8	11.1
17.6	8.7	12.2	10.8	7.9	15.2		9.0	9.9
7.4	6.9	8.4	6.7	6.0	5.1	Sales/Total Assets	6.1	6.5
6.4	2.6	5.8	4.2	3.8	3.4		3.6	4.3
	.2	.2	.2	.5	.1		.5	.4
	(22) .6	(64) .4	(70) .7	(19) .8	.3	% Depr., Dep., Amort./Sales	(318) .8	(345) .7
	2.4	.7	1.2	1.5	1.1		1.4	1.1
	.3	.3	.2				.3	.3
	(12) .9	(33) .5	(16) .3			% Officers', Directors' Owners' Comp/Sales	(114) .6	(133) .4
	1.9	.9	1.0				1.3	1.0
28747M	**231868M**	**4281075M**	**13884462M**	**9139997M**	**25199521M**	Net Sales ($)	**43368505M**	**62359123M**
2761M	**30622M**	**423509M**	**1725898M**	**1475781M**	**3079778M**	Total Assets ($)	**7795804M**	**8765040M**

M = $ thousand MM = $ million

See Pages 9 through 22 for Explanation of Ratios and Data

Comparative Historical Data | Current Data Sorted by Sales

			Type of Statement						
54	43	39	Unqualified		1	1	1	2	34
88	62	48	Reviewed	2	1		1	5	39
74	43	29	Compiled		2	2	3	6	16
41	33	24	Tax Returns	1	2	1	4	4	12
98	92	86	Other	3	3	3	4	10	63
4/1/11-3/31/12	4/1/12-3/31/13	4/1/13-3/31/14		64 (4/1-9/30/13)			162 (10/1/13-3/31/14)		
ALL	ALL	ALL		0-1MM	1-3MM	3-5MM	5-10MM	10-25MM	25MM & OVER
355	273	226	NUMBER OF STATEMENTS	6	9	7	13	27	164
%	%	%	ASSETS	%	%	%	%	%	%
9.2	9.7	8.5	Cash & Equivalents				10.1	8.0	8.5
33.0	34.1	33.0	Trade Receivables (net)				27.0	35.9	35.4
14.3	14.9	15.6	Inventory				24.6	20.9	14.5
2.2	3.3	3.4	All Other Current				4.5	1.3	3.3
58.7	61.9	60.5	Total Current				66.2	66.1	61.7
29.2	28.1	28.1	Fixed Assets (net)				24.4	23.6	28.2
3.4	2.8	4.2	Intangibles (net)				2.3	2.2	3.7
8.7	7.1	7.2	All Other Non-Current				7.1	8.2	6.4
100.0	100.0	100.0	Total				100.0	100.0	100.0
			LIABILITIES						
12.6	13.0	10.3	Notes Payable-Short Term				7.9	14.5	10.8
3.5	3.3	3.1	Cur. Mat.-L.T.D.				2.6	1.2	3.3
26.9	25.1	22.6	Trade Payables				16.6	20.9	24.6
.1	.1	.2	Income Taxes Payable				.2	.2	.2
7.4	8.7	8.0	All Other Current				9.0	7.1	7.0
50.5	50.3	44.2	Total Current				36.2	44.0	45.8
15.4	14.3	13.9	Long-Term Debt				17.9	6.1	14.0
.7	.7	1.0	Deferred Taxes				.0	.8	1.3
4.3	5.3	5.8	All Other Non-Current				8.7	8.6	3.9
29.1	29.6	35.1	Net Worth				37.2	40.5	35.0
100.0	100.0	100.0	Total Liabilties & Net Worth				100.0	100.0	100.0
			INCOME DATA						
100.0	100.0	100.0	Net Sales				100.0	100.0	100.0
10.6	11.7	12.7	Gross Profit				17.7	15.8	8.1
9.7	10.5	10.7	Operating Expenses				14.9	12.8	6.9
1.0	1.1	2.0	Operating Profit				2.9	2.9	1.3
.0	.1	.3	All Other Expenses (net)				.6	.0	-.1
.9	1.1	1.7	Profit Before Taxes				2.3	3.0	1.3
			RATIOS						
1.6	1.9	2.0	Current				3.1	3.1	1.9
1.2	1.3	1.4					1.5	1.3	1.4
.9	1.0	1.0					1.1	1.0	1.0
1.1	1.3	1.4	Quick				2.1	2.1	1.3
.9	.9	.9					1.3	1.1	.9
.6	.6	.6					.5	.5	.7
9 41.3	9 41.2	9 38.9	Sales/Receivables				6 64.4	15 24.7	9 42.3
15 23.6	16 23.4	15 24.0					18 19.8	23 16.2	14 25.6
26 14.3	24 15.4	26 14.0					30 12.3	36 10.1	23 15.6
3 123.1	3 134.5	3 118.6	Cost of Sales/Inventory				6 58.5	7 53.4	3 131.4
7 53.0	6 59.0	7 52.9					13 28.0	10 36.0	6 61.5
13 27.4	13 27.2	15 24.5					18 20.5	30 12.0	12 29.4
9 41.8	8 45.3	8 46.5	Cost of Sales/Payables				1 248.8	8 46.4	8 46.2
12 29.9	11 33.5	11 34.7					11 32.5	12 29.6	10 37.3
17 21.4	16 22.3	17 21.6					17 21.0	30 12.0	15 24.5
31.3	23.2	20.4	Sales/Working Capital				14.1	13.7	25.1
92.1	59.4	60.9					28.9	29.5	65.9
-154.0	UND	UND					NM	141.1	999.8
8.2	8.2	12.3	EBIT/Interest				5.9	10.5	13.3
(326) 3.0	(253) 3.6	(205) 4.7					(10) 4.2	(25) 3.8	(154) 4.7
1.2	1.5	1.7					.5	-.1	1.8
4.5	4.6	3.9	Net Profit + Depr., Dep., Amort./Cur. Mat. L/T/D						3.4
(104) 2.1	(84) 2.3	(51) 2.1							(46) 2.0
1.2	1.6	1.3							1.3
.5	.3	.3	Fixed/Worth				.2	.1	.4
1.0	.9	.8					.5	.6	.9
2.1	2.1	2.2					2.0	1.6	2.2
1.2	1.2	1.1	Debt/Worth				.8	.9	1.1
2.6	2.4	2.3					1.8	1.8	2.4
6.3	6.3	5.6					5.2	3.2	5.6
32.4	36.0	34.5	% Profit Before Taxes/Tangible Net Worth				26.3	25.5	36.5
(321) 14.6	(247) 17.0	(208) 20.6					(12) 13.1	(26) 15.4	(155) 20.6
3.2	5.1	5.9					4.3	-2.3	5.8
8.0	9.1	10.2	% Profit Before Taxes/Total Assets				7.9	13.7	10.0
3.6	4.1	5.4					6.6	6.2	4.7
.5	.9	1.4					.8	-.4	1.5
80.5	87.4	111.6	Sales/Net Fixed Assets				172.2	82.0	117.2
33.4	36.4	30.8					74.9	38.0	33.7
12.5	13.9	12.9					10.8	15.1	14.4
10.4	10.9	11.6	Sales/Total Assets				9.4	8.6	12.4
7.1	7.8	7.4					6.9	6.0	7.9
4.3	4.7	4.2					4.2	2.3	5.0
.3	.3	.3	% Depr., Dep., Amort./Sales				.3	.3	.2
(313) .6	(245) .5	(201) .5					(11) .5	(23) .7	(149) .5
1.1	1.0	1.1					1.3	1.2	.9
.2	.2	.2	% Officers', Directors' Owners' Comp/Sales					.4	.2
(111) .5	(94) .4	(71) .6						(15) .8	(43) .4
1.0	.9	1.0						.9	.8
62555320M	54155116M	52765670M	Net Sales ($)	2596M	18001M	25336M	96509M	451896M	52171332M
8223721M	6670197M	6738349M	Total Assets ($)	3260M	14118M	5589M	84400M	131221M	6499761M

M = $ thousand MM = $ million

See Pages 9 through 22 for Explanation of Ratios and Data

Current Data Sorted by Assets | **Comparative Historical Data**

0-500M	500M-2MM	2-10MM	10-50MM	50-100MM	100-250MM	Type of Statement	4/1/09-3/31/10 ALL	4/1/10-3/31/11 ALL
	2	7	44	23	19	Unqualified	107	98
	4	68	87	7		Reviewed	184	171
1	22	50	20	1		Compiled	107	111
6	23	26	8			Tax Returns	59	55
8	13	71	108	26	20	Other	250	242
177 (4/1-9/30/13)		487 (10/1/13-3/31/14)						
15	64	222	267	57	39	NUMBER OF STATEMENTS	707	677
%	%	%	%	%	%	**ASSETS**	%	%
22.3	13.0	13.3	7.9	6.8	4.3	Cash & Equivalents	11.5	10.8
30.6	37.7	39.0	33.3	35.4	27.2	Trade Receivables (net)	31.8	33.2
22.5	15.6	12.8	13.4	13.1	20.4	Inventory	13.9	15.3
1.0	1.1	2.8	3.3	3.3	4.2	All Other Current	3.7	3.4
76.4	67.4	67.8	57.8	58.6	56.0	Total Current	60.8	62.7
13.9	19.6	20.1	28.4	29.1	27.2	Fixed Assets (net)	27.8	25.5
4.5	2.8	4.6	5.2	4.2	10.3	Intangibles (net)	3.8	3.6
5.1	10.2	7.4	8.5	8.1	6.4	All Other Non-Current	7.6	8.2
100.0	100.0	100.0	100.0	100.0	100.0	Total	100.0	100.0
						LIABILITIES		
4.1	12.8	10.5	11.7	11.7	11.9	Notes Payable-Short Term	9.4	12.0
.6	4.1	2.9	2.9	4.0	1.8	Cur. Mat.-L.T.D.	3.0	2.6
30.9	28.4	28.2	27.5	25.6	19.9	Trade Payables	27.0	28.1
.0	.2	.1	.2	.8	.4	Income Taxes Payable	.2	.2
29.3	9.0	8.9	5.9	6.8	6.5	All Other Current	8.0	7.2
64.9	54.5	50.6	48.3	48.8	40.5	Total Current	47.7	50.2
27.8	11.1	10.2	14.6	14.5	19.7	Long-Term Debt	16.7	13.6
.0	.3	.5	.9	.9	1.1	Deferred Taxes	.5	.6
5.2	7.4	3.5	4.0	3.5	5.1	All Other Non-Current	3.4	3.6
2.1	26.8	35.1	32.2	32.2	33.6	Net Worth	31.7	31.9
100.0	100.0	100.0	100.0	100.0	100.0	Total Liabilties & Net Worth	100.0	100.0
						INCOME DATA		
100.0	100.0	100.0	100.0	100.0	100.0	Net Sales	100.0	100.0
17.3	12.2	9.9	9.1	7.5	6.6	Gross Profit	11.5	10.6
15.1	11.4	8.4	7.6	6.6	5.3	Operating Expenses	10.2	9.5
2.2	.8	1.5	1.5	.8	1.4	Operating Profit	1.3	1.1
.2	.0	-.2	.0	.0	.1	All Other Expenses (net)	-.1	.0
2.1	.9	1.8	1.5	.8	1.3	Profit Before Taxes	1.4	1.1
						RATIOS		
3.4	2.0	2.0	1.5	1.4	2.0		1.6	1.6
1.0	1.4	1.3	1.1	1.1	1.3	Current	1.2	1.2
.7	1.0	1.0	.9	1.0	1.1		1.0	1.0
3.4	1.6	1.4	1.1	1.1	1.0		1.2	1.2
.6	1.0	1.0	.8	.8	.8	Quick	.9	.9
.5	.6	.7	.6	.7	.5		.6	.6
1 317.9	**8** 46.3	**9** 39.4	**7** 48.9	**10** 37.3	**6** 60.5		**9** 42.9	**8** 43.9
5 74.7	**16** 23.3	**17** 21.7	**14** 25.6	**16** 22.3	**13** 27.9	Sales/Receivables	**16** 23.1	**16** 22.4
16 22.6	**26** 14.1	**27** 13.4	**27** 13.7	**27** 13.5	**26** 13.9		**28** 13.1	**29** 12.7
0 UND	**1** 391.6	**1** 425.5	**2** 200.6	**3** 121.9	**3** 108.4		**2** 165.3	**2** 148.5
8 43.0	**6** 63.6	**5** 68.8	**5** 76.7	**5** 70.7	**7** 52.0	Cost of Sales/Inventory	**6** 56.9	**7** 54.4
16 22.5	**16** 22.2	**12** 29.5	**12** 30.2	**10** 36.7	**13** 27.1		**15** 25.2	**16** 23.4
0 999.8	**7** 53.6	**7** 49.9	**9** 42.2	**8** 46.1	**7** 52.4		**10** 36.8	**10** 36.9
9 39.2	**10** 36.6	**11** 33.0	**11** 32.1	**12** 31.5	**10** 36.8	Cost of Sales/Payables	**14** 26.5	**13** 27.3
21 17.3	**17** 21.0	**17** 21.0	**19** 19.3	**15** 23.8	**15** 24.4		**21** 17.6	**20** 18.0
22.1	18.6	17.8	33.4	49.5	17.7		22.5	21.8
-517.2	58.0	55.9	111.5	142.2	50.8	Sales/Working Capital	67.8	63.6
-98.3	505.8	920.3	-274.3	-766.2	136.8		-999.8	-415.1
	9.4	15.8	12.8	13.8	6.8		9.8	10.4
	(57) 4.1	(192) 5.3	(258) 5.4	(56) 4.4	(36) 4.4	EBIT/Interest	(657) 3.5	(614) 3.8
	1.2	2.1	2.4	1.4	1.4		1.7	1.7
		4.1	5.9	7.7			5.9	6.5
		(41) 2.3	(93) 3.0	(25) 2.2		Net Profit + Depr., Dep., Amort./Cur. Mat. L/T/D	(208) 2.5	(185) 2.7
		1.4	1.7	1.1			1.3	1.5
.1	.1	.2	.4	.5	.4		.3	.3
.5	.5	.6	1.0	1.1	1.1	Fixed/Worth	.9	.8
-.2	1.9	1.3	2.2	2.0	4.5		2.3	1.8
1.0	1.0	1.1	1.3	1.5	2.0		1.3	1.2
3.8	3.5	2.0	2.8	2.7	3.3	Debt/Worth	2.5	2.5
-3.6	5.9	4.6	6.4	5.4	8.7		6.3	5.6
	35.4	36.1	36.9	29.7	57.0		37.4	31.9
	(54) 17.4	(200) 16.4	(245) 18.6	(55) 13.7	(35) 22.8	% Profit Before Taxes/Tangible Net Worth	(645) 17.3	(625) 15.8
	3.8	5.0	7.9	2.9	4.2		5.3	6.4
38.3	9.2	10.7	9.7	6.6	9.4		10.0	8.5
18.0	4.2	4.3	5.5	3.5	4.7	% Profit Before Taxes/Total Assets	4.5	4.2
-4.7	.8	1.5	2.1	.6	1.0		1.3	1.4
586.3	247.3	207.3	82.4	68.2	277.9		85.7	94.6
196.7	72.1	59.1	32.3	30.3	23.1	Sales/Net Fixed Assets	29.9	35.8
57.3	23.2	21.1	14.8	14.0	12.3		11.9	14.0
27.2	13.4	13.3	12.0	11.8	10.4		9.7	10.2
13.5	8.1	8.0	7.5	8.2	6.4	Sales/Total Assets	6.1	6.7
5.7	5.1	4.9	4.3	4.5	3.4		3.9	4.1
	.1	.1	.3	.2	.1		.3	.3
	(52) .4	(192) .3	(255) .5	(56) .5	(30) .6	% Depr., Dep., Amort./Sales	(620) .7	(593) .6
	1.1	.7	1.0	.7	1.1		1.2	1.1
	.4	.3	.2				.2	.2
	(37) 1.0	(74) .6	(65) .4			% Officers', Directors' Owners' Comp/Sales	(222) .5	(186) .5
	2.2	1.2	.6				1.4	1.1
84276M	876034M	12602865M	52997985M	37171434M	48136709M	Net Sales ($)	123954917M	116925557M
4341M	84266M	1262147M	6099679M	4001984M	6323189M	Total Assets ($)	18554210M	16981003M

M = $ thousand MM = $ million

See Pages 9 through 22 for Explanation of Ratios and Data

Comparative Historical Data				Current Data Sorted by Sales					
			Type of Statement						
104	95	95	Unqualified		1		2	1	91
179	162	166	Reviewed			1	3	13	149
106	95	94	Compiled		3	2	9	25	55
62	56	63	Tax Returns		3	3	18	16	23
253	271	246	Other	2	6	5	11	31	191
4/1/11-3/31/12	**4/1/12-3/31/13**	**4/1/13-3/31/14**		**177 (4/1-9/30/13)**			**487 (10/1/13-3/31/14)**		
ALL	**ALL**	**ALL**		**0-1MM**	**1-3MM**	**3-5MM**	**5-10MM**	**10-25MM**	**25MM & OVER**
704	679	664	**NUMBER OF STATEMENTS**	2	13	11	43	86	509
%	%	%	**ASSETS**	%	%	%	%	%	%
10.3	10.5	10.2	Cash & Equivalents		7.1	18.3	13.3	12.2	9.5
35.4	33.5	35.4	Trade Receivables (net)		14.4	27.6	31.5	35.7	36.4
15.3	14.7	14.0	Inventory		23.9	26.3	19.0	14.1	12.9
3.1	3.5	2.9	All Other Current		1.1	1.1	1.0	2.2	3.3
64.1	62.1	62.5	Total Current		46.5	73.3	64.9	64.2	62.1
23.9	25.7	24.5	Fixed Assets (net)		22.1	14.7	25.6	21.5	25.2
4.1	4.3	5.0	Intangibles (net)		12.9	5.7	4.5	3.9	5.0
7.8	7.9	8.1	All Other Non-Current		18.4	6.2	5.0	10.4	7.7
100.0	100.0	100.0	Total		100.0	100.0	100.0	100.0	100.0
			LIABILITIES						
11.6	11.8	11.2	Notes Payable-Short Term		7.8	2.9	9.8	12.5	11.4
2.8	3.1	3.0	Cur. Mat.-L.T.D.		2.1	4.5	2.3	2.2	3.2
30.4	26.1	27.3	Trade Payables		15.8	28.8	25.1	21.6	28.8
.2	.1	.2	Income Taxes Payable		.5	.2	.2	.1	.2
7.5	7.5	7.9	All Other Current		14.0	12.6	11.3	9.4	7.1
52.5	48.6	49.6	Total Current		40.2	49.0	48.8	45.9	50.6
12.8	13.3	13.4	Long-Term Debt		23.9	19.2	15.6	12.3	12.8
.5	.6	.7	Deferred Taxes		.5	.5	.3	.5	.8
3.2	4.1	4.2	All Other Non-Current		.4	10.0	8.6	5.5	3.6
31.0	33.3	32.0	Net Worth		34.9	21.3	26.7	35.8	32.2
100.0	100.0	100.0	Total Liabilties & Net Worth		100.0	100.0	100.0	100.0	100.0
			INCOME DATA						
100.0	100.0	100.0	Net Sales		100.0	100.0	100.0	100.0	100.0
9.4	8.9	9.6	Gross Profit		46.9	16.9	22.6	13.3	6.7
8.3	7.8	8.2	Operating Expenses		35.5	16.0	18.6	11.5	5.8
1.2	1.1	1.4	Operating Profit		11.4	.9	4.0	1.8	.8
.0	-.2	-.1	All Other Expenses (net)		-.8	.2	.1	-.3	-.1
1.1	1.2	1.5	Profit Before Taxes		12.2	.7	3.8	2.1	.9
			RATIOS						
1.6	1.7	1.7			2.3	4.2	2.3	2.1	1.6
1.2	1.2	1.2	Current		1.0	1.6	1.7	1.4	1.2
1.0	1.0	1.0			.7	1.1	1.0	1.1	1.0
1.2	1.2	1.3			.6	3.5	1.7	1.5	1.2
.8	.9	.9	Quick		.5	.8	1.0	1.1	.9
.6	.6	.6			.3	.3	.4	.7	.6
8 45.6	**7** 53.7	**8** 46.1			**16** 23.3	**4** 99.7	**12** 31.7	**12** 29.2	**7** 51.2
16 23.3	**13** 27.4	**15** 23.9	Sales/Receivables		**26** 14.3	**16** 22.6	**26** 14.1	**22** 16.3	**13** 27.3
26 13.9	**23** 15.7	**27** 13.7			**41** 8.9	**28** 12.9	**42** 8.7	**35** 10.5	**24** 15.4
2 196.0	**2** 237.1	**1** 254.0			**18** 20.5	**9** 39.5	**2** 154.2	**3** 145.5	**1** 270.4
6 64.7	**5** 71.2	**5** 70.7	Cost of Sales/Inventory		**49** 7.4	**18** 20.1	**10** 35.1	**6** 58.4	**5** 79.4
13 28.3	**13** 28.4	**12** 29.6			**130** 2.8	**44** 8.3	**38** 9.6	**20** 18.3	**10** 37.7
9 41.5	**7** 53.8	**8** 47.4			**14** 26.2	**6** 58.6	**8** 46.7	**8** 43.0	**8** 48.1
12 29.7	**10** 35.3	**11** 32.5	Cost of Sales/Payables		**64** 5.7	**13** 29.0	**13** 28.7	**16** 22.7	**11** 34.5
19 19.4	**16** 22.9	**18** 20.8			**96** 3.8	**27** 13.4	**35** 10.3	**23** 16.1	**15** 24.0
25.6	27.5	23.6			7.6	12.7	9.8	15.1	36.3
92.7	91.5	76.4	Sales/Working Capital		428.8	23.6	22.5	28.4	99.7
-577.5	-465.6	-869.0			-13.8	149.6	-230.3	206.1	-839.2
12.8	11.8	12.5			18.3		14.1	11.3	12.8
(639) 4.5	(616) 4.6	(607) 5.1	EBIT/Interest		(11) 9.9		(36) 4.3	(78) 5.2	(473) 5.1
1.9	1.8	2.1			.8		1.0	2.6	2.2
7.2	6.2	5.7						3.5	5.9
(173) 3.3	(193) 2.7	(176) 2.4	Net Profit + Depr., Dep., Amort./Cur. Mat. L/T/D					(18) 2.1	(151) 2.7
1.8	1.5	1.5						1.3	1.5
.3	.3	.3			.2	.1	.1	.1	.3
.8	.8	.8	Fixed/Worth		.4	.3	.9	.4	.9
2.0	1.9	1.9			-31.8	6.6	1.7	1.6	2.0
1.3	1.2	1.3			.5	3.6	1.0	.9	1.4
2.6	2.3	2.5	Debt/Worth		2.0	5.5	2.3	1.8	2.6
6.0	5.9	5.9			-34.4	10.9	20.3	4.1	5.9
35.9	34.1	36.6					51.3	31.9	35.7
(636) 17.8	(620) 16.9	(598) 17.8	% Profit Before Taxes/Tangible Net Worth				(35) 23.0	(76) 16.8	(468) 17.9
6.2	6.4	6.4					6.3	5.1	6.7
9.4	9.0	9.7			19.6	8.7	16.4	12.4	8.9
4.9	4.7	4.9	% Profit Before Taxes/Total Assets		7.3	3.9	4.3	4.6	4.9
1.5	1.7	1.7			1.1	-3.4	-.7	2.2	1.7
146.1	129.6	133.6			26.7	586.3	124.1	198.2	120.1
45.2	43.0	38.8	Sales/Net Fixed Assets		12.8	57.2	26.5	55.5	40.3
16.9	16.2	16.1			3.0	7.9	10.1	12.8	18.1
12.5	12.6	12.6			3.3	12.0	7.5	9.5	13.4
7.7	8.1	7.7	Sales/Total Assets		1.5	3.8	4.6	5.7	8.6
4.5	4.9	4.5			.6	2.6	2.1	2.7	5.4
.2	.2	.2			.3		.5	.2	.2
(596) .5	(597) .5	(593) .4	% Depr., Dep., Amort./Sales		(10) 1.2		(30) 1.4	(76) .5	(470) .4
.9	.8	.9			3.1		3.2	1.1	.7
.2	.2	.2					1.0	.4	.2
(221) .5	(205) .5	(195) .5	% Officers', Directors' Owners' Comp/Sales				(23) 1.9	(40) .8	(122) .3
1.0	1.2	1.2					4.0	1.5	.6
162742751M	**158560521M**	**151869303M**	Net Sales ($)	**1653M**	**29866M**	**42058M**	**306377M**	**1503401M**	**149985948M**
19494075M	**18232947M**	**17775606M**	Total Assets ($)	**331M**	**36964M**	**10523M**	**138366M**	**404479M**	**17184943M**

M = $ thousand MM = $ million

See Pages 9 through 22 for Explanation of Ratios and Data

Current Data Sorted by Assets							Comparative Historical Data	
						Type of Statement		
		13	39	20	12	Unqualified	118	93
	3	35	37	3	2	Reviewed	106	119
	6	28	7	4		Compiled	52	45
2	6	6	2			Tax Returns	22	29
5	8	24	71	29	24	Other	195	192
37 (4/1-9/30/13)			349 (10/1/13-3/31/14)				4/1/09-3/31/10 ALL	4/1/10-3/31/11 ALL
0-500M	**500M-2MM**	**2-10MM**	**10-50MM**	**50-100MM**	**100-250MM**			
7	23	106	156	56	38	**NUMBER OF STATEMENTS**	493	478
%	%	%	%	%	%	**ASSETS**	%	%
	11.0	13.8	8.5	7.4	5.4	Cash & Equivalents	10.1	9.7
	12.0	8.0	8.6	6.9	4.6	Trade Receivables (net)	8.5	8.9
	40.0	29.1	18.5	12.4	12.3	Inventory	19.9	21.8
	1.1	1.7	1.9	2.7	2.2	All Other Current	2.3	2.1
	64.1	52.6	37.4	29.4	24.4	Total Current	40.8	42.5
	16.4	16.5	20.7	17.0	15.8	Fixed Assets (net)	19.9	18.6
	12.0	19.5	32.6	47.5	54.2	Intangibles (net)	29.3	30.1
	7.5	11.4	9.2	6.1	5.6	All Other Non-Current	10.0	8.9
	100.0	100.0	100.0	100.0	100.0	Total	100.0	100.0
						LIABILITIES		
	9.4	7.8	4.6	3.8	4.2	Notes Payable-Short Term	6.1	6.2
	2.4	2.9	3.3	2.0	1.7	Cur. Mat.-L.T.D.	3.4	3.8
	18.1	11.2	9.1	6.6	5.0	Trade Payables	8.9	10.0
	.1	.1	.4	.0	.1	Income Taxes Payable	.1	.1
	23.5	9.4	6.7	5.4	4.5	All Other Current	7.0	7.3
	53.4	31.5	24.0	17.8	15.5	Total Current	25.5	27.5
	20.9	13.6	24.3	33.8	33.4	Long-Term Debt	25.6	22.8
	.0	.3	.5	.3	.1	Deferred Taxes	.4	.4
	5.0	2.4	4.1	3.8	3.5	All Other Non-Current	5.6	5.4
	20.8	52.2	47.1	44.4	47.5	Net Worth	42.8	43.9
	100.0	100.0	100.0	100.0	100.0	Total Liabilties & Net Worth	100.0	100.0
						INCOME DATA		
	100.0	100.0	100.0	100.0	100.0	Net Sales	100.0	100.0
	25.3	25.8	26.0	25.0	25.1	Gross Profit	25.1	25.6
	24.5	22.1	21.2	19.7	19.8	Operating Expenses	20.5	20.9
	.8	3.7	4.8	5.3	5.4	Operating Profit	4.7	4.7
	.1	.1	.3	-.2	.3	All Other Expenses (net)	.4	.6
	.8	3.6	4.6	5.4	5.0	Profit Before Taxes	4.3	4.1
						RATIOS		
	2.7	3.4	2.4	2.3	2.0		2.8	2.7
	1.9	2.0	1.6	1.8	1.8	Current	1.6	1.6
	1.0	1.3	1.0	1.2	1.3		1.1	1.0
	.9	1.4	1.2	1.1	.8		1.2	1.2
	.5	.8	.6	.6	.5	Quick	.7	.6
	.2	.3	.3	.3	.4		.3	.3
	0 999.8	**1** 292.3	**2** 155.6	**3** 127.7	**3** 139.1		**1** 273.0	**2** 196.7
	2 167.6	**4** 85.2	**6** 58.3	**6** 64.2	**5** 69.1	Sales/Receivables	**4** 101.5	**5** 76.5
	16 23.5	**12** 29.7	**19** 19.5	**20** 18.4	**10** 36.7		**17** 21.3	**17** 21.4
	24 15.1	**26** 14.0	**23** 16.1	**23** 15.8	**24** 15.5		**19** 19.0	**22** 16.6
	33 11.1	**31** 11.7	**28** 13.1	**27** 13.7	**27** 13.5	Cost of Sales/Inventory	**23** 15.8	**26** 13.8
	65 5.6	**41** 8.9	**36** 10.1	**36** 10.2	**31** 11.8		**31** 11.6	**33** 11.1
	3 108.3	**6** 58.8	**8** 47.2	**10** 35.2	**5** 79.8		**6** 62.1	**6** 58.0
	12 29.5	**11** 34.2	**13** 28.7	**14** 26.6	**11** 33.2	Cost of Sales/Payables	**11** 32.8	**12** 30.2
	49 7.4	**16** 23.0	**20** 18.5	**21** 17.7	**17** 21.1		**16** 22.7	**18** 20.4
	16.0	9.6	12.3	11.8	20.8		13.1	12.9
	24.7	17.6	23.0	24.6	26.4	Sales/Working Capital	25.1	24.8
	UND	61.9	238.8	42.8	41.5		181.1	224.2
	29.4	35.1	21.7	17.2	18.3		14.1	16.4
	(17) 8.5	(89) 12.8	(146) 9.1	(50) 7.8	(37) 7.6	EBIT/Interest	(445) 6.3	(440) 6.6
	2.4	5.1	4.2	5.6	4.8		3.3	3.4
		4.4	9.8	30.4			8.7	8.5
		(13) 2.7	(27) 5.3	(15) 5.3		Net Profit + Depr., Dep., Amort./Cur. Mat. L/T/D	(94) 3.3	(95) 3.3
		1.2	2.6	2.2			1.9	1.5
	.2	.2	.5	.8	1.6		.3	.3
	.6	.4	1.3	-19.3	-1.0	Fixed/Worth	1.4	1.4
	-.2	1.7	-1.8	-.3	-.4		-1.1	-.8
	.6	.4	.9	2.0	3.1		.8	.8
	1.4	1.4	3.5	-144.4	-6.4	Debt/Worth	3.1	4.1
	-3.4	7.1	-7.5	-2.1	-1.8		-4.3	-4.0
	78.9	74.0	73.9	125.4	105.5		67.7	61.3
	(15) 44.2	(90) 30.8	(102) 40.5	(27) 45.2	(15) 56.0	% Profit Before Taxes/Tangible Net Worth	(312) 38.7	(300) 35.2
	8.4	16.2	23.8	26.0	14.5		20.9	20.2
	28.4	18.5	18.0	13.3	11.6		17.6	16.8
	9.5	12.0	11.7	9.8	8.8	% Profit Before Taxes/Total Assets	11.7	10.2
	3.0	5.0	5.8	6.3	6.6		6.6	5.6
	164.2	99.4	34.9	40.9	40.5		51.1	55.7
	36.4	39.8	20.5	21.1	12.2	Sales/Net Fixed Assets	22.5	25.7
	18.3	15.1	9.5	7.0	7.8		10.4	11.2
	7.5	5.4	3.7	2.5	2.4		4.5	4.5
	5.4	3.6	2.8	1.9	2.0	Sales/Total Assets	3.0	3.0
	2.7	2.6	2.1	1.6	1.3		2.2	2.2
	.7	.5	.7	.6	.7		.7	.6
	(13) 1.0	(83) .9	(141) 1.0	(53) 1.0	(31) 1.0	% Depr., Dep., Amort./Sales	(423) 1.0	(405) 1.0
	1.5	1.6	1.4	1.5	1.2		1.4	1.4
	1.4	1.2	.6				.8	.7
	(11) 2.2	(37) 1.9	(30) 1.7			% Officers', Directors' Owners' Comp/Sales	(135) 1.6	(134) 1.6
	6.5	4.8	3.4				2.9	2.8
15336M	**169952M**	**2440700M**	**10641305M**	**7927740M**	**11187033M**	Net Sales ($)	**36717361M**	**36195543M**
2915M	**30180M**	**630347M**	**3833971M**	**3929440M**	**5805932M**	Total Assets ($)	**14725305M**	**14526789M**

M = $ thousand MM = $ million

See Pages 9 through 22 for Explanation of Ratios and Data

Comparative Historical Data				Current Data Sorted by Sales					
			Type of Statement						
91	76	84	Unqualified					8	76
97	92	80	Reviewed				6	17	57
53	47	45	Compiled		1	3	2	18	21
28	24	16	Tax Returns		2	2	3	4	5
186	201	161	Other	3	7	1	2	16	132
4/1/11-3/31/12 ALL	**4/1/12-3/31/13 ALL**	**4/1/13-3/31/14 ALL**		**37 (4/1-9/30/13)**			**349 (10/1/13-3/31/14)**		
				0-1MM	**1-3MM**	**3-5MM**	**5-10MM**	**10-25MM**	**25MM & OVER**
455	440	386	**NUMBER OF STATEMENTS**	3	10	6	13	63	291
%	%	%	**ASSETS**	%	%	%	%	%	%
10.1	9.2	9.8	Cash & Equivalents		10.8		12.7	14.5	8.7
9.1	7.6	8.2	Trade Receivables (net)		15.2		9.1	7.7	7.8
22.8	22.0	21.5	Inventory		31.7		25.0	30.9	18.6
2.0	2.4	1.9	All Other Current		.4		.6	1.7	2.1
44.0	41.3	41.3	Total Current		58.1		47.3	54.7	37.2
18.6	18.6	18.0	Fixed Assets (net)		18.7		16.1	16.4	18.5
30.1	31.2	31.8	Intangibles (net)		14.3		31.5	18.6	36.2
7.3	8.9	8.8	All Other Non-Current		8.9		5.0	10.3	8.1
100.0	100.0	100.0	Total		100.0		100.0	100.0	100.0
			LIABILITIES						
6.0	6.3	5.6	Notes Payable-Short Term		1.4		15.6	8.1	4.8
3.8	3.0	2.8	Cur. Mat.-L.T.D.		.4		4.9	2.5	2.8
10.1	8.9	9.7	Trade Payables		17.6		9.7	11.3	8.6
.2	.2	.2	Income Taxes Payable		.0		.1	.1	.3
7.5	7.4	10.0	All Other Current		123.1		6.2	10.5	6.2
27.6	25.8	28.3	Total Current		142.5		36.5	32.4	22.6
22.0	24.1	23.3	Long-Term Debt		23.1		25.3	14.2	25.3
.4	.5	.3	Deferred Taxes		.0		.1	.3	.4
5.2	4.3	4.0	All Other Non-Current		2.3		2.3	2.5	3.4
44.8	45.4	44.1	Net Worth		-67.9		35.7	50.6	48.3
100.0	100.0	100.0	Total Liabilties & Net Worth		100.0		100.0	100.0	100.0
			INCOME DATA						
100.0	100.0	100.0	Net Sales		100.0		100.0	100.0	100.0
25.7	25.6	25.7	Gross Profit		33.1		23.7	25.9	25.4
21.2	21.1	21.5	Operating Expenses		36.0		19.5	22.0	20.7
4.5	4.5	4.2	Operating Profit		-2.9		4.2	3.9	4.7
.4	.3	.2	All Other Expenses (net)		3.4		.2	-.1	.1
4.0	4.1	4.1	Profit Before Taxes		-6.3		4.0	4.0	4.5
			RATIOS						
2.7	2.7	2.5	Current		1.8		2.7	3.5	2.3
1.6	1.7	1.7			.4		1.5	2.2	1.7
1.1	1.1	1.1			.3		.7	1.3	1.2
1.2	1.2	1.2	Quick		.3		1.4	1.3	1.2
.6	(438) .6	.6			.2		.6	.8	.6
.3	.3	.3			.1		.1	.3	.3
2 185.9	**2** 176.8	**2** 166.2	Sales/Receivables		**0** UND		**0** UND	**1** 431.1	**3** 143.3
5 78.0	**4** 83.9	**5** 70.0			**5** 66.4		**2** 167.6	**3** 139.2	**6** 66.0
18 20.5	**15** 25.1	**16** 22.9			**46** 8.0		**18** 19.8	**12** 30.1	**17** 21.9
23 16.2	**24** 15.3	**23** 15.6	Cost of Sales/Inventory		**31** 11.6		**21** 17.0	**26** 14.2	**23** 15.7
27 13.3	**29** 12.8	**29** 12.6			**41** 8.8		**27** 13.5	**31** 11.8	**28** 13.1
33 11.0	**35** 10.3	**37** 9.8			**79** 4.6		**33** 11.0	**43** 8.4	**35** 10.4
6 57.7	**6** 58.8	**7** 50.8	Cost of Sales/Payables		**0** UND		**4** 100.2	**4** 95.6	**8** 45.8
12 29.5	**11** 33.6	**12** 29.7			**36** 10.2		**10** 37.3	**10** 36.1	**13** 28.8
18 20.6	**17** 21.8	**19** 19.4			**60** 6.1		**15** 24.0	**15** 25.1	**19** 19.4
12.4	12.2	12.1	Sales/Working Capital		17.6		10.5	9.7	12.4
23.5	23.6	23.2			-3.4		30.2	16.5	23.7
95.0	83.6	96.5			-2.0		-23.3	86.4	70.3
16.0	18.7	21.4	EBIT/Interest				19.0	32.7	21.5
(411) 5.7	(390) 7.3	(342) 9.0					9.1	(50) 12.1	(269) 9.2
2.9	3.4	4.5					4.2	5.6	4.7
7.3	6.9	11.3	Net Profit + Depr., Dep., Amort./Cur. Mat. L/T/D						27.0
(88) 2.6	(82) 2.9	(63) 3.9							(52) 5.4
1.3	1.6	2.1							2.3
.3	.3	.3	Fixed/Worth		7.1		.3	.1	.4
1.1	1.1	1.4			-.2		2.0	.4	1.7
-1.3	-1.3	-1.0			-.1		-.1	2.2	-.8
.7	.8	.9	Debt/Worth		6.8		.7	.4	.9
3.4	3.1	3.7			-2.0		4.2	1.2	4.6
-4.0	-4.8	-4.9			-1.5		-1.9	7.2	-4.4
60.6	87.1	79.3	% Profit Before Taxes/Tangible Net Worth					93.7	78.0
(298) 32.7	(294) 38.1	(249) 40.1						(54) 38.7	(180) 41.7
17.7	18.6	19.8						19.0	22.5
16.2	16.9	17.1	% Profit Before Taxes/Total Assets		3.3		16.6	24.8	16.6
9.6	9.8	10.5			-16.5		14.2	10.7	10.9
4.8	5.3	5.7			-83.6		5.7	7.0	6.3
53.3	48.4	48.5	Sales/Net Fixed Assets		91.5		206.1	162.2	41.2
25.0	23.3	24.2			30.7		28.4	45.6	21.6
11.0	9.9	10.0			14.9		15.8	12.4	9.5
4.4	4.0	3.9	Sales/Total Assets		3.8		5.9	5.9	3.7
3.0	2.8	2.7			2.7		3.6	3.5	2.6
2.1	2.0	2.0			1.4		2.0	2.6	1.9
.6	.6	.7	% Depr., Dep., Amort./Sales					.5	.7
(395) .9	(382) 1.0	(322) 1.0						(47) 1.0	(258) 1.0
1.3	1.4	1.4						1.5	1.4
.8	.8	1.0	% Officers', Directors' Owners' Comp/Sales					1.2	.7
(129) 1.6	(107) 1.7	(86) 1.7						(20) 2.1	(54) 1.5
3.2	3.6	3.6						4.9	3.0
33941610M	**34462835M**	**32382066M**	Net Sales ($)	**2621M**	**19305M**	**26374M**	**94646M**	**1064002M**	**31175118M**
13655996M	**14579008M**	**14232785M**	Total Assets ($)	**1588M**	**32982M**	**12459M**	**31162M**	**316646M**	**13837948M**

M = $ thousand MM = $ million

See Pages 9 through 22 for Explanation of Ratios and Data

Current Data Sorted by Assets							Comparative Historical Data	
						Type of Statement		
	1	4	18	5	11	Unqualified	51	49
1		10	6	2		Reviewed	35	21
	3	10	3		2	Compiled	18	17
5	9	9				Tax Returns	17	29
3	8	16	26	7	16	Other	67	79
	36 (4/1-9/30/13)		139 (10/1/13-3/31/14)				4/1/09-3/31/10	4/1/10-3/31/11
0-500M	500M-2MM	2-10MM	10-50MM	50-100MM	100-250MM		ALL	ALL
9	21	49	53	14	29	NUMBER OF STATEMENTS	188	195
%	%	%	%	%	%	**ASSETS**	%	%
	11.1	9.9	9.3	4.5	5.7	Cash & Equivalents	6.5	5.4
	28.3	22.4	20.8	26.4	20.3	Trade Receivables (net)	21.7	23.7
	49.8	47.2	33.5	36.8	33.9	Inventory	41.5	42.2
	1.1	.7	4.7	4.6	2.3	All Other Current	2.7	2.7
	90.2	80.3	68.3	72.3	62.1	Total Current	72.4	73.9
	4.6	8.5	12.2	12.5	8.1	Fixed Assets (net)	11.2	10.1
	2.3	6.2	11.3	9.5	14.5	Intangibles (net)	9.9	9.4
	2.9	5.0	8.2	5.7	15.2	All Other Non-Current	6.5	6.6
	100.0	100.0	100.0	100.0	100.0	Total	100.0	100.0
						LIABILITIES		
	13.1	13.9	8.1	16.0	7.1	Notes Payable-Short Term	13.8	13.7
	2.9	1.0	1.1	2.0	3.4	Cur. Mat.-L.T.D.	1.6	2.6
	28.8	30.8	24.5	18.2	17.6	Trade Payables	23.1	25.6
	.1	.1	.2	.2	.1	Income Taxes Payable	.1	.1
	7.5	8.4	12.2	7.4	10.5	All Other Current	9.5	9.8
	52.4	54.2	46.0	43.8	38.7	Total Current	48.2	51.9
	4.6	5.8	12.7	9.9	16.4	Long-Term Debt	14.5	12.6
	.0	.4	.2	.5	.5	Deferred Taxes	.3	.2
	5.9	1.4	5.9	4.4	6.4	All Other Non-Current	4.0	4.4
	37.1	38.2	35.1	41.4	37.9	Net Worth	33.1	31.0
	100.0	100.0	100.0	100.0	100.0	Total Liabilties & Net Worth	100.0	100.0
						INCOME DATA		
	100.0	100.0	100.0	100.0	100.0	Net Sales	100.0	100.0
	28.4	29.5	24.9	22.8	24.0	Gross Profit	26.6	27.4
	24.3	25.2	20.5	20.8	20.1	Operating Expenses	23.2	23.7
	4.1	4.3	4.5	2.0	3.9	Operating Profit	3.4	3.7
	.1	.6	.9	-.4	.5	All Other Expenses (net)	.5	.6
	4.0	3.7	3.6	2.4	3.4	Profit Before Taxes	2.9	3.1
						RATIOS		
	2.5	2.0	2.4	2.6	2.5		2.1	2.2
	1.8	1.5	1.6	1.5	1.6	Current	1.5	1.5
	1.2	1.3	1.1	1.3	1.2		1.2	1.2
	1.0	1.1	1.0	.9	.9		.9	.9
	.8	.6	.7	.7	.6	Quick	.6	(194) .6
	.4	.3	.4	.6	.4		.4	.4
	5 70.5	**6** 65.8	**8** 47.8	**27** 13.7	**18** 19.9		**10** 35.2	**13** 28.2
	41 8.8	**30** 12.0	**29** 12.6	**37** 9.8	**34** 10.6	Sales/Receivables	**30** 12.4	**31** 11.7
	54 6.7	**48** 7.6	**41** 8.9	**54** 6.8	**49** 7.5		**44** 8.3	**47** 7.8
	38 9.5	**43** 8.5	**27** 13.6	**51** 7.2	**50** 7.3		**39** 9.4	**45** 8.1
	72 5.1	**78** 4.7	**51** 7.1	**57** 6.4	**56** 6.5	Cost of Sales/Inventory	**67** 5.5	**67** 5.5
	91 4.0	**118** 3.1	**83** 4.4	**85** 4.3	**79** 4.6		**102** 3.6	**110** 3.3
	5 67.9	**26** 14.0	**17** 21.5	**25** 14.8	**17** 20.9		**18** 20.3	**23** 16.1
	49 7.5	**46** 8.0	**31** 11.6	**27** 13.4	**36** 10.0	Cost of Sales/Payables	**32** 11.3	**38** 9.5
	69 5.3	**73** 5.0	**68** 5.4	**42** 8.6	**50** 7.3		**56** 6.5	**62** 5.9
	5.8	6.7	6.9	5.7	6.4		6.5	6.6
	9.8	10.6	14.4	12.1	11.5	Sales/Working Capital	11.3	12.7
	20.9	31.3	66.1	20.2	41.3		32.3	30.9
	25.4	45.8	21.0	21.3	26.4		18.9	18.8
	(18) 8.8	(43) 8.6	(42) 8.9	(12) 4.7	9.9	EBIT/Interest	(164) 5.9	(185) 6.4
	4.3	1.8	2.7	2.6	4.2		1.8	2.6
			11.2				7.5	11.4
			(12) 2.9			Net Profit + Depr., Dep., Amort./Cur. Mat. L/T/D	(41) 2.9	(42) 6.2
			.7				1.3	2.7
	.0	.0	.0	.2	.0		.1	.1
	.0	.1	.3	.4	.3	Fixed/Worth	.3	.3
	.4	.9	1.5	.7	17.2		1.9	2.1
	1.1	1.1	.8	.9	.9		1.0	1.2
	1.8	1.8	2.3	1.4	3.4	Debt/Worth	2.3	3.2
	6.3	7.1	9.9	5.0	73.1		20.2	29.3
	45.2	56.7	66.9	37.1	44.7		51.2	50.3
	31.4	(44) 24.2	(43) 21.7	(12) 12.7	(23) 31.9	% Profit Before Taxes/Tangible Net Worth	(148) 22.6	(153) 29.8
	10.5	8.2	10.4	3.0	8.9		5.5	10.7
	19.4	18.3	13.3	14.1	11.1		15.3	14.3
	8.8	6.4	6.6	2.7	7.5	% Profit Before Taxes/Total Assets	7.5	6.9
	4.5	1.4	2.8	1.4	3.0		2.0	3.0
	UND	281.7	249.9	62.7	133.3		154.2	196.6
	128.3	104.3	118.9	28.1	64.7	Sales/Net Fixed Assets	58.6	72.9
	41.2	34.7	14.8	13.5	22.1		22.6	20.8
	4.2	3.8	3.7	3.3	3.3		3.8	3.7
	3.0	2.8	2.8	3.0	2.6	Sales/Total Assets	3.0	2.8
	2.4	1.9	1.9	1.3	1.2		1.9	1.9
	.2	.2	.2	.4	.2		.3	.2
	(11) .4	(35) .3	(43) .5	.6	(24) .5	% Depr., Dep., Amort./Sales	(151) .6	(154) .5
	.9	.5	1.1	1.0	1.2		1.3	1.2
		1.6					1.2	2.3
		(17) 3.4				% Officers', Directors' Owners' Comp/Sales	(47) 2.1	(59) 3.5
		5.4					4.6	6.2
17794M	97911M	815919M	3678859M	2828346M	11323932M	Net Sales ($)	22779131M	24716295M
2731M	24706M	251875M	1270185M	987963M	5175691M	Total Assets ($)	8700126M	8971951M

M = $ thousand MM = $ million

See Pages 9 through 22 for Explanation of Ratios and Data

Comparative Historical Data | Current Data Sorted by Sales

4/1/11-3/31/12 ALL	4/1/12-3/31/13 ALL	4/1/13-3/31/14 ALL	Type of Statement	0-1MM	1-3MM	3-5MM	5-10MM	10-25MM	25MM & OVER
38	32	39	Unqualified			2	1	2	34
20	25	19	Reviewed				3	7	9
25	15	18	Compiled			2	1	8	7
28	25	23	Tax Returns	2	7		10	3	1
84	72	76	Other	1	5	7	4	11	48
				36 (4/1-9/30/13)			139 (10/1/13-3/31/14)		
195	169	175	NUMBER OF STATEMENTS	3	12	11	19	31	99
%	%	%	ASSETS	%	%	%	%	%	%
6.6	6.6	8.6	Cash & Equivalents		4.4	15.4	11.7	9.2	7.5
23.9	22.4	23.1	Trade Receivables (net)		33.3	22.4	24.2	23.6	21.5
39.5	41.9	40.6	Inventory		49.9	44.3	47.9	46.1	35.4
3.6	2.4	2.5	All Other Current		2.0	.3	.2	1.0	3.8
73.6	73.2	74.8	Total Current		89.6	82.4	84.0	79.9	68.2
10.9	10.7	9.2	Fixed Assets (net)		4.5	12.3	7.8	6.7	10.6
8.9	9.8	8.7	Intangibles (net)		1.9	2.8	5.3	8.2	11.3
6.6	6.3	7.3	All Other Non-Current		4.0	2.6	2.9	5.2	9.8
100.0	100.0	100.0	Total		100.0	100.0	100.0	100.0	100.0
			LIABILITIES						
12.3	12.7	10.8	Notes Payable-Short Term		9.6	11.8	6.3	13.9	9.7
2.1	2.1	1.7	Cur. Mat.-L.T.D.		3.2	2.5	.7	.5	2.0
25.7	25.1	27.5	Trade Payables		28.4	22.2	45.0	25.5	24.2
.2	.0	.1	Income Taxes Payable		.0	.0	.0	.3	.1
9.6	10.0	9.7	All Other Current		5.9	3.6	14.9	8.2	10.5
49.8	49.8	49.7	Total Current		47.0	40.0	67.0	48.3	46.6
13.1	13.2	10.0	Long-Term Debt		9.9	8.3	4.8	4.2	13.3
.2	.1	.3	Deferred Taxes		.0	.0	.0	.6	.4
7.0	5.0	4.7	All Other Non-Current		9.0	.8	5.5	4.5	4.7
29.9	31.8	35.2	Net Worth		34.1	50.9	22.8	42.4	35.1
100.0	100.0	100.0	Total Liabilties & Net Worth		100.0	100.0	100.0	100.0	100.0
			INCOME DATA						
100.0	100.0	100.0	Net Sales		100.0	100.0	100.0	100.0	100.0
27.0	27.3	26.5	Gross Profit		30.2	35.4	25.0	29.5	24.0
23.2	23.9	22.5	Operating Expenses		26.2	28.1	20.2	26.4	20.3
3.9	3.4	4.0	Operating Profit		4.0	7.4	4.9	3.1	3.7
.7	.6	.5	All Other Expenses (net)		.2	.2	.5	.9	.4
3.2	2.8	3.5	Profit Before Taxes		3.8	7.2	4.3	2.2	3.2
			RATIOS						
2.2	2.5	2.4			3.9	2.7	2.3	2.3	2.2
1.6	1.6	1.6	Current		1.9	2.0	1.9	1.6	1.5
1.2	1.2	1.2			1.2	1.7	1.1	1.4	1.1
1.0	1.0	1.0			1.5	1.3	1.1	1.1	.9
.6	.6	.6	Quick		.6	.8	.7	.7	.6
.4	.4	.4			.3	.6	.4	.4	.4
16 23.1	**9** 41.7	**9** 38.7			**16** 23.2	**2** 221.1	**4** 91.7	**11** 33.9	**9** 42.6
33 11.1	**30** 12.1	**33** 11.1	Sales/Receivables		**31** 11.9	**45** 8.2	**47** 7.8	**36** 10.0	**29** 12.4
49 7.5	**51** 7.2	**47** 7.7			**55** 6.6	**54** 6.8	**53** 6.9	**51** 7.2	**41** 8.9
45 8.2	**47** 7.7	**40** 9.1			**28** 12.9	**55** 6.6	**58** 6.3	**39** 9.4	**38** 9.5
69 5.3	**70** 5.2	**58** 6.3	Cost of Sales/Inventory		**56** 6.5	**81** 4.5	**91** 4.0	**78** 4.7	**54** 6.7
104 3.5	**99** 3.7	**91** 4.0			**107** 3.4	**243** 1.5	**126** 2.9	**118** 3.1	**72** 5.1
22 16.5	**21** 17.1	**19** 19.4			**8** 44.1	**4** 83.5	**21** 17.1	**25** 14.7	**19** 19.1
38 9.7	**38** 9.5	**36** 10.0	Cost of Sales/Payables		**26** 13.9	**41** 8.9	**68** 5.4	**46** 8.0	**34** 10.8
60 6.1	**65** 5.6	**65** 5.6			**79** 4.6	**78** 4.7	**101** 3.6	**65** 5.6	**52** 7.0
6.1	6.1	6.5			5.7	3.2	5.4	6.6	7.5
11.0	11.1	11.9	Sales/Working Capital		9.5	6.6	8.4	10.0	14.7
25.3	22.4	27.1			45.4	11.4	48.7	15.2	42.6
21.5	22.8	27.4				29.4	126.8	31.2	26.0
(172) 7.6	(152) 7.9	(148) 8.8	EBIT/Interest			(10) 9.9	(15) 9.6	(26) 7.2	(86) 9.1
1.9	2.2	2.7				3.8	2.2	1.5	2.7
17.7	4.3	8.4							6.8
(32) 5.5	(22) 3.3	(31) 2.9	Net Profit + Depr., Dep., Amort./Cur. Mat. L/T/D						(20) 3.3
1.9	1.9	1.0							1.3
.1	.0	.0			.0	.0	.0	.0	.1
.2	.3	.2	Fixed/Worth		.1	.1	.1	.1	.4
1.1	1.3	1.1			3.7	.8	1.5	.3	1.9
1.0	1.2	.9			.7	.5	1.0	.7	1.0
2.5	2.9	2.0	Debt/Worth		2.8	1.3	3.4	1.6	2.4
8.7	8.9	9.7			51.0	1.8	11.3	3.7	16.1
53.3	75.7	59.4			141.1	50.0	44.2	59.9	45.5
(162) 25.6	(142) 33.1	(150) 26.8	% Profit Before Taxes/Tangible Net Worth		60.5	32.5	(17) 22.1	(29) 26.4	(79) 22.9
8.1	9.2	8.8			24.9	6.4	10.9	3.0	8.3
14.3	15.1	13.9			22.0	26.3	18.1	18.5	13.0
6.8	7.9	7.2	% Profit Before Taxes/Total Assets		11.9	8.6	7.0	7.8	7.0
1.8	1.9	2.0			2.9	4.4	1.8	.4	2.2
199.1	184.8	246.6			886.0	378.1	UND	319.1	169.7
76.3	66.3	92.3	Sales/Net Fixed Assets		130.6	58.7	116.1	120.9	67.9
18.4	19.5	26.3			68.9	23.2	29.8	51.6	24.1
3.7	3.6	3.7			6.2	3.9	3.8	3.5	3.8
2.8	2.8	2.9	Sales/Total Assets		2.9	2.5	2.5	2.8	2.9
1.7	1.8	2.0			2.6	1.5	1.5	1.8	2.1
.3	.3	.2					.1	.2	.2
(133) .5	(130) .5	(129) .4	% Depr., Dep., Amort./Sales				(12) .3	(23) .3	(84) .5
1.1	1.1	.9					.7	1.5	.9
1.0	1.8	1.7						1.8	1.1
(58) 1.9	(45) 3.3	(41) 2.8	% Officers', Directors' Owners' Comp/Sales					(12) 3.1	(11) 3.6
3.5	6.7	5.8						6.9	6.0
23345179M	18360998M	18762761M	Net Sales ($)	1516M	21911M	41351M	141073M	486149M	18070761M
9174570M	6966698M	7713151M	Total Assets ($)	1483M	6574M	23302M	81220M	214820M	7385752M

M = $ thousand MM = $ million

See Pages 9 through 22 for Explanation of Ratios and Data

Current Data Sorted by Assets							Comparative Historical Data	
						Type of Statement		
	10	141	249	70	40	Unqualified	526	539
1	3	46	17	4	2	Reviewed	88	80
	5	20	10	1		Compiled	60	47
10	21	20	6			Tax Returns	30	38
3	23	50	48	9	8	Other	142	133
328 (4/1-9/30/13)			489 (10/1/13-3/31/14)				4/1/09-3/31/10	4/1/10-3/31/11
0-500M	**500M-2MM**	**2-10MM**	**10-50MM**	**50-100MM**	**100-250MM**		**ALL**	**ALL**
14	62	277	330	84	50	**NUMBER OF STATEMENTS**	846	837
%	%	%	%	%	%	**ASSETS**	%	%
14.4	11.1	10.6	8.9	8.7	9.4	Cash & Equivalents	7.7	6.9
18.3	19.2	21.3	19.0	16.8	14.0	Trade Receivables (net)	21.7	20.6
42.8	34.5	28.5	29.7	31.4	33.0	Inventory	30.9	31.8
.2	3.6	5.2	5.4	6.5	6.0	All Other Current	5.0	6.2
75.8	68.5	65.6	63.0	63.4	62.4	Total Current	65.4	65.5
13.8	19.5	21.1	22.9	21.5	23.3	Fixed Assets (net)	20.8	21.0
.4	1.1	.6	1.0	4.0	1.5	Intangibles (net)	.9	1.0
10.0	10.9	12.6	13.1	11.1	12.7	All Other Non-Current	12.9	12.5
100.0	100.0	100.0	100.0	100.0	100.0	Total	100.0	100.0
						LIABILITIES		
37.8	9.6	10.6	10.5	8.2	7.4	Notes Payable-Short Term	14.8	15.5
.0	3.1	1.4	2.0	1.5	1.3	Cur. Mat.-L.T.D.	1.7	2.1
8.9	18.1	19.0	22.7	27.0	24.9	Trade Payables	19.9	19.6
.0	.1	.4	.4	.5	.4	Income Taxes Payable	.3	.3
7.8	8.5	9.9	7.3	8.3	9.8	All Other Current	7.9	7.9
54.6	39.5	41.2	43.0	45.4	43.8	Total Current	44.6	45.4
4.7	11.2	5.8	7.2	10.6	10.6	Long-Term Debt	7.8	8.4
.0	.1	.5	.9	1.1	.7	Deferred Taxes	.4	.4
10.4	7.8	1.2	1.7	2.7	3.4	All Other Non-Current	2.2	2.0
30.2	41.4	51.2	47.3	40.3	41.6	Net Worth	44.9	43.8
100.0	100.0	100.0	100.0	100.0	100.0	Total Liabilties & Net Worth	100.0	100.0
						INCOME DATA		
100.0	100.0	100.0	100.0	100.0	100.0	Net Sales	100.0	100.0
35.4	23.0	15.9	12.4	10.6	10.1	Gross Profit	15.1	16.0
31.7	22.2	13.9	10.2	8.3	7.6	Operating Expenses	13.2	13.7
3.7	.8	2.0	2.2	2.3	2.5	Operating Profit	1.9	2.3
.3	-.7	-1.3	-1.5	-.9	-.5	All Other Expenses (net)	-.9	-.8
3.4	1.4	3.2	3.7	3.2	3.1	Profit Before Taxes	2.8	3.1
						RATIOS		
6.1	4.1	2.3	1.8	1.6	1.7		1.9	1.8
2.1	1.9	1.5	1.4	1.3	1.4	Current	1.4	1.4
1.2	1.2	1.2	1.2	1.2	1.2		1.2	1.2
4.5	1.7	1.2	.9	.8	.8		1.0	.9
.7	.8	.8	.7	.6	.6	Quick	.6	.6
.2	.4	.5	.4	.3	.2		.4	.4
0 UND	**8** 45.5	**14** 25.8	**16** 23.2	**14** 26.6	**11** 32.7		**17** 21.3	**17** 22.0
3 112.1	**17** 21.7	**25** 14.5	**24** 15.5	**19** 19.3	**16** 23.5	Sales/Receivables	**26** 13.9	**27** 13.5
14 26.6	**27** 13.3	**41** 8.9	**35** 10.3	**30** 12.1	**28** 12.9		**40** 9.2	**42** 8.7
5 68.6	**23** 15.9	**25** 14.8	**28** 12.9	**31** 11.9	**24** 15.1		**29** 12.7	**34** 10.7
31 11.6	**57** 6.4	**46** 7.9	**50** 7.3	**49** 7.4	**49** 7.4	Cost of Sales/Inventory	**49** 7.5	**57** 6.4
54 6.8	**94** 3.9	**73** 5.0	**78** 4.7	**89** 4.1	**91** 4.0		**81** 4.5	**90** 4.1
0 UND	**5** 78.8	**12** 30.1	**19** 19.2	**22** 16.5	**23** 15.8		**15** 24.0	**17** 21.3
0 UND	**19** 19.1	**25** 14.5	**31** 11.6	**32** 11.4	**35** 10.4	Cost of Sales/Payables	**26** 14.0	**29** 12.4
26 14.3	**33** 11.2	**43** 8.4	**59** 6.2	**64** 5.7	**54** 6.8		**47** 7.8	**51** 7.1
7.2	5.7	6.7	8.4	11.0	10.4		8.1	7.9
13.4	10.5	12.6	13.2	14.6	17.1	Sales/Working Capital	13.7	13.5
NM	38.1	23.8	23.7	23.6	24.3		24.8	22.5
13.5	15.1	29.4	22.4	16.8	10.4		13.5	15.9
(10) 3.5	(55) 3.9	(246) 8.6	(315) 9.8	(83) 9.1	6.2	EBIT/Interest	(793) 6.0	(791) 7.1
-.8	1.4	3.1	4.7	5.0	4.4		2.4	3.0
		9.2	10.6	9.6	9.1		10.9	10.7
		(87) 5.0	(173) 5.6	(47) 5.1	(32) 6.2	Net Profit + Depr., Dep., Amort./Cur. Mat. L/T/D	(384) 6.0	(379) 5.6
		2.6	3.2	3.1	3.8		3.0	3.4
.0	.1	.2	.3	.4	.4		.3	.3
.1	.3	.4	.5	.6	.6	Fixed/Worth	.4	.5
.5	.7	.7	.7	.8	.7		.7	.7
.2	.3	.4	.7	.9	.9		.6	.7
1.0	1.2	.9	1.1	1.6	1.5	Debt/Worth	1.2	1.3
2.0	4.9	2.0	2.0	2.9	2.3		2.3	2.6
55.0	27.2	24.0	23.6	25.1	18.9		25.9	24.2
(12) 15.8	(55) 8.0	(274) 12.7	(327) 16.4	(78) 19.0	(49) 16.6	% Profit Before Taxes/Tangible Net Worth	(818) 16.4	(812) 16.1
-8.5	1.8	6.0	10.7	13.6	12.7		6.6	8.1
23.6	9.5	11.9	11.5	10.1	9.3		11.5	10.1
11.4	3.8	6.8	7.3	7.0	6.5	% Profit Before Taxes/Total Assets	6.9	6.3
-3.6	.4	2.8	4.3	4.4	4.4		2.5	3.2
UND	74.6	25.3	17.0	16.6	15.4		22.8	19.3
362.6	19.9	12.5	11.2	12.2	12.8	Sales/Net Fixed Assets	13.2	11.8
24.6	8.0	8.2	7.6	8.0	8.6		8.7	7.6
10.6	4.9	3.3	3.2	3.3	3.3		3.3	3.0
4.8	3.1	2.5	2.3	2.4	2.5	Sales/Total Assets	2.5	2.2
2.2	2.1	1.9	1.8	1.9	2.0		1.9	1.6
	.5	.7	.8	.8	.7		.8	.8
	(44) 1.0	(263) 1.1	(324) 1.2	(81) 1.1	(49) 1.0	% Depr., Dep., Amort./Sales	(800) 1.1	(778) 1.3
	2.0	1.7	1.7	1.5	1.5		1.7	1.8
	1.0	1.1	.4				1.0	.9
	(28) 2.6	(47) 2.4	(19) 1.2			% Officers', Directors' Owners' Comp/Sales	(100) 2.0	(105) 2.1
	4.1	3.7	2.7				4.6	4.6
26701M	298945M	4442142M	20183689M	16199814M	21063977M	Net Sales ($)	54874862M	51029011M
3729M	82451M	1550315M	7657869M	5978658M	7490935M	Total Assets ($)	20463262M	22125447M

M = $ thousand MM = $ million

See Pages 9 through 22 for Explanation of Ratios and Data

Comparative Historical Data | **Current Data Sorted by Sales**

Type of Statement									
Unqualified	560	508	510		6	11	38	108	347
Reviewed	83	80	73		2	4	18	25	24
Compiled	57	49	36		2	1	8	13	12
Tax Returns	44	48	57	5	9	4	16	15	8
Other	142	138	141	1	8	11	17	43	61
					328 (4/1-9/30/13)		489 (10/1/13-3/31/14)		
	4/1/11-3/31/12 ALL	4/1/12-3/31/13 ALL	4/1/13-3/31/14 ALL	0-1MM	1-3MM	3-5MM	5-10MM	10-25MM	25MM & OVER
NUMBER OF STATEMENTS	886	823	817	6	27	31	97	204	452
ASSETS	%	%	%	%	%	%	%	%	%
Cash & Equivalents	7.0	7.6	9.7		14.8	11.7	10.6	9.1	9.5
Trade Receivables (net)	21.5	19.8	19.3		12.0	17.8	19.0	21.3	19.0
Inventory	32.8	32.3	30.3		43.9	29.7	29.7	28.7	30.3
All Other Current	6.7	6.5	5.2		1.0	2.3	7.1	5.0	5.5
Total Current	68.0	66.2	64.5		71.7	61.6	66.5	64.1	64.2
Fixed Assets (net)	19.2	20.5	21.8		19.1	23.5	20.2	21.7	22.1
Intangibles (net)	1.3	1.2	1.2		1.9	.1	.5	.9	1.6
All Other Non-Current	11.4	12.1	12.5		7.4	14.8	12.8	13.3	12.1
Total	100.0	100.0	100.0		100.0	100.0	100.0	100.0	100.0
LIABILITIES									
Notes Payable-Short Term	16.7	13.8	10.5		11.2	17.5	10.4	11.7	9.4
Cur. Mat.-L.T.D.	1.7	1.8	1.8		2.3	3.6	2.0	1.5	1.7
Trade Payables	20.6	22.0	21.4		16.1	14.3	15.3	20.1	24.3
Income Taxes Payable	.3	.3	.4		.1	.1	.4	.3	.4
All Other Current	8.1	8.4	8.5		5.3	9.5	9.0	8.8	8.5
Total Current	47.4	46.3	42.6		35.1	44.9	37.1	42.5	44.3
Long-Term Debt	7.3	7.9	7.5		10.3	9.9	7.8	6.1	7.9
Deferred Taxes	.4	.5	.7		.0	.5	.3	.6	.9
All Other Non-Current	2.1	2.4	2.3		1.2	1.4	5.3	1.0	2.1
Net Worth	42.7	42.9	46.8		53.5	43.2	49.5	49.7	44.8
Total Liabilties & Net Worth	100.0	100.0	100.0		100.0	100.0	100.0	100.0	100.0
INCOME DATA									
Net Sales	100.0	100.0	100.0		100.0	100.0	100.0	100.0	100.0
Gross Profit	15.2	14.5	14.5		24.6	23.5	19.2	16.1	11.0
Operating Expenses	12.8	12.0	12.4		22.9	24.0	17.2	13.6	8.9
Operating Profit	2.4	2.5	2.1		1.7	-.6	2.0	2.4	2.1
All Other Expenses (net)	-.6	-.9	-1.2		-.4	-1.4	-1.3	-1.4	-1.1
Profit Before Taxes	3.0	3.3	3.3		2.1	.9	3.4	3.8	3.3
RATIOS									
Current	1.8	1.8	2.0		4.7	3.9	2.9	2.0	1.7
	1.4	1.4	1.5		2.2	1.9	1.8	1.4	1.4
	1.2	1.2	1.2		1.4	1.2	1.3	1.2	1.2
Quick	.9	.9	1.1		2.1	1.6	1.5	1.1	.9
	(885) .6	.6	.7		.7	1.2	.7	.7	.7
	.3	.3	.4		.4	.5	.5	.4	.4
Sales/Receivables	15 24.2	13 27.8	13 27.1		7 55.4	13 29.0	14 26.1	15 23.8	13 27.5
	26 14.2	23 15.8	22 16.5		15 24.7	31 11.8	24 15.4	28 13.1	20 18.1
	40 9.2	35 10.4	35 10.4		27 13.4	41 8.9	38 9.5	44 8.3	31 11.8
Cost of Sales/Inventory	34 10.8	30 12.1	26 14.1		52 7.0	32 11.4	27 13.6	29 12.8	25 14.7
	55 6.6	51 7.2	48 7.6		85 4.3	54 6.7	48 7.6	52 7.0	43 8.4
	85 4.3	81 4.5	78 4.7		140 2.6	83 4.4	78 4.7	83 4.4	70 5.2
Cost of Sales/Payables	17 21.8	16 22.3	16 22.8		13 28.9	13 28.2	8 48.1	18 20.5	18 20.5
	28 12.9	29 12.7	28 13.0		21 17.1	22 16.9	21 17.5	34 10.8	28 12.9
	49 7.5	51 7.1	52 7.0		34 10.7	32 11.4	47 7.8	54 6.8	53 6.9
Sales/Working Capital	8.5	8.6	7.9		4.9	4.6	5.2	6.5	10.3
	14.6	14.6	13.3		6.3	10.3	8.5	11.8	15.0
	23.9	27.0	24.1		16.7	19.4	17.6	24.4	24.9
EBIT/Interest	13.6	16.8	21.3		14.8	10.6	26.5	28.2	19.8
	(831) 5.9	(767) 7.5	(759) 8.3		(21) 4.3	(27) 6.4	(88) 6.2	(184) 9.3	(435) 8.8
	3.0	3.9	3.9		1.4	.6	1.8	3.1	4.7
Net Profit + Depr., Dep., Amort./Cur. Mat. L/T/D	10.9	10.3	9.7				11.0	9.1	9.7
	(375) 5.9	(370) 5.3	(342) 5.4				(22) 5.9	(69) 5.0	(247) 5.5
	3.4	3.2	3.1				2.3	2.6	3.4
Fixed/Worth	.3	.3	.3		.1	.1	.2	.2	.3
	.4	.5	.5		.3	.3	.3	.4	.5
	.7	.7	.7		.7	.8	.6	.7	.7
Debt/Worth	.7	.7	.6		.2	.3	.4	.5	.8
	1.5	1.4	1.1		.9	.6	1.0	.9	1.2
	2.6	2.7	2.2		2.4	1.3	2.1	2.1	2.2
% Profit Before Taxes/Tangible Net Worth	24.9	27.0	23.7		21.4	14.7	24.8	23.9	23.7
	(862) 16.1	(799) 17.4	(795) 15.6		(24) 9.4	(27) 7.3	(95) 11.7	(203) 14.1	(441) 16.7
	8.1	10.1	8.4		1.5	-3.6	3.6	6.8	11.6
% Profit Before Taxes/Total Assets	9.9	11.1	11.3		10.5	7.2	12.7	11.5	10.9
	6.4	7.1	6.8		5.8	4.3	6.7	6.5	7.2
	3.1	4.1	3.5		-.5	-2.1	1.7	3.2	4.3
Sales/Net Fixed Assets	24.3	22.9	20.4		45.7	29.6	23.5	23.5	17.9
	14.1	13.7	12.2		15.7	13.1	12.4	10.5	12.6
	8.9	8.7	8.1		7.5	6.0	7.9	7.1	8.9
Sales/Total Assets	3.2	3.3	3.3		3.2	3.4	3.2	2.9	3.6
	2.4	2.5	2.4		2.3	2.1	2.4	2.3	2.6
	1.8	1.9	1.9		1.6	1.6	1.8	1.8	2.1
% Depr., Dep., Amort./Sales	.7	.7	.8		.5	.5	.8	.8	.8
	(813) 1.1	(764) 1.1	(767) 1.2		(20) .8	(27) 1.2	(89) 1.3	(189) 1.3	(441) 1.1
	1.6	1.5	1.7		1.8	2.5	2.2	2.0	1.5
% Officers', Directors' Owners' Comp/Sales	1.1	1.0	.8		2.7		.8	1.0	.4
	(102) 2.3	(89) 2.4	(103) 2.1		(10) 3.8		(28) 2.1	(33) 1.8	(26) 1.0
	3.3	3.7	3.7		13.5		3.6	3.7	2.7
Net Sales ($)	63799281M	65679530M	62215268M	2515M	57077M	127269M	700769M	3371094M	57956544M
Total Assets ($)	25560173M	25225144M	22763957M	1069M	27045M	75995M	328681M	1639075M	20692092M

M = $ thousand MM = $ million

See Pages 9 through 22 for Explanation of Ratios and Data

Current Data Sorted by Assets							Comparative Historical Data	
						Type of Statement		
			4	2		Unqualified	7	8
		6	3			Reviewed	11	11
	2	1	1			Compiled	9	7
2	1	4				Tax Returns	13	6
1	1	7	6	3		Other	28	25
	11 (4/1-9/30/13)		33 (10/1/13-3/31/14)				4/1/09-3/31/10 ALL	4/1/10-3/31/11 ALL
0-500M	**500M-2MM**	**2-10MM**	**10-50MM**	**50-100MM**	**100-250MM**			
3	4	18	14	5		**NUMBER OF STATEMENTS**	68	57
%	%	%	%	%	%	**ASSETS**	%	%
		12.4	4.5		D	Cash & Equivalents	10.0	7.8
		26.9	31.4		A	Trade Receivables (net)	26.5	26.0
		32.9	39.2		T	Inventory	33.1	34.1
		3.7	10.7		A	All Other Current	4.2	2.8
		76.0	85.9			Total Current	73.7	70.7
		12.2	7.5			Fixed Assets (net)	14.0	14.9
		6.9	2.8		N	Intangibles (net)	4.0	5.6
		4.9	3.9		O	All Other Non-Current	8.3	8.8
		100.0	100.0		T	Total	100.0	100.0
						LIABILITIES		
		3.5	13.1		A	Notes Payable-Short Term	9.5	10.1
		1.9	.6		V	Cur. Mat.-L.T.D.	4.6	2.3
		16.5	34.1		A	Trade Payables	28.7	28.9
		.0	.1		I	Income Taxes Payable	.1	.1
		20.2	9.5		L	All Other Current	12.5	8.5
		42.1	57.5		A	Total Current	55.5	49.8
		14.0	5.3		B	Long-Term Debt	11.6	12.4
		.1	.0		L	Deferred Taxes	.1	.1
		2.1	4.5		E	All Other Non-Current	4.6	4.5
		41.7	32.7			Net Worth	28.3	33.2
		100.0	100.0			Total Liabilties & Net Worth	100.0	100.0
						INCOME DATA		
		100.0	100.0			Net Sales	100.0	100.0
		39.4	23.6			Gross Profit	36.0	35.0
		35.5	20.1			Operating Expenses	32.3	31.4
		3.9	3.5			Operating Profit	3.7	3.6
		-.1	.6			All Other Expenses (net)	.5	1.2
		3.9	2.9			Profit Before Taxes	3.2	2.4
						RATIOS		
		3.8	2.1				2.3	2.4
		2.2	1.2			Current	1.3	1.5
		1.3	1.1				1.0	1.1
		1.8	.9				1.1	1.2
		1.1	.6			Quick	.6	.7
		.7	.5				.3	.4
		18 20.5	**26** 14.2				**17** 21.7	**20** 18.2
		30 12.1	**40** 9.1			Sales/Receivables	**34** 10.6	**35** 10.5
		37 9.9	**70** 5.2				**59** 6.2	**61** 6.0
		15 24.3	**45** 8.2				**18** 20.1	**32** 11.5
		79 4.6	**85** 4.3			Cost of Sales/Inventory	**74** 4.9	**69** 5.3
		215 1.7	**104** 3.5				**152** 2.4	**122** 3.0
		10 37.4	**23** 16.2				**28** 13.0	**21** 17.6
		24 15.5	**70** 5.2			Cost of Sales/Payables	**53** 6.8	**45** 8.1
		57 6.4	**107** 3.4				**88** 4.1	**90** 4.0
		3.5	6.9				3.9	5.6
		6.9	14.6			Sales/Working Capital	13.0	13.4
		NM	36.7				NM	114.8
		35.5	18.7				19.6	25.4
		(15) 3.0	(13) 9.2			EBIT/Interest	(54) 3.7	(52) 3.5
		1.1	1.7				1.2	1.3
						Net Profit + Depr., Dep., Amort./Cur. Mat. L/T/D		
		.0	.1				.1	.2
		.2	.2			Fixed/Worth	.5	.4
		1.0	.4				2.3	1.8
		.5	1.0				1.5	.9
		1.2	4.1			Debt/Worth	3.1	2.4
		13.2	5.3				17.1	7.1
		53.9	35.8				44.9	43.4
		(15) 12.8	(13) 12.7			% Profit Before Taxes/Tangible Net Worth	(56) 20.3	(48) 17.3
		-6.3	5.9				2.7	2.4
		28.0	12.1				14.2	11.8
		5.9	2.6			% Profit Before Taxes/Total Assets	3.5	4.6
		-2.8	1.4				.0	-.1
		82.0	190.3				102.0	83.3
		44.3	60.0			Sales/Net Fixed Assets	31.8	31.3
		13.5	33.7				14.4	11.4
		4.1	3.3				3.8	3.6
		3.2	2.4			Sales/Total Assets	2.4	2.6
		1.8	2.2				1.6	1.7
		.6	.2				.6	.4
		(14) 1.1	(13) .4			% Depr., Dep., Amort./Sales	(52) 1.1	(49) 1.0
		3.2	1.0				1.7	1.7
							1.8	2.3
						% Officers', Directors' Owners' Comp/Sales	(21) 2.6	(14) 3.9
							4.4	7.4
7270M	**18347M**	**230256M**	**809645M**	**769274M**		Net Sales ($)	**1771196M**	**1920452M**
1231M	**4976M**	**72411M**	**318489M**	**341008M**		Total Assets ($)	**710370M**	**761656M**

M = $ thousand MM = $ million

See Pages 9 through 22 for Explanation of Ratios and Data

Comparative Historical Data				Current Data Sorted by Sales					
			Type of Statement						
8	5	6	Unqualified					1	5
11	7	9	Reviewed				3	2	4
10	6	4	Compiled			1	1	1	1
13	3	7	Tax Returns	1		3	2		1
21	15	18	Other		2	1	2	5	8
4/1/11-3/31/12	**4/1/12-3/31/13**	**4/1/13-3/31/14**		**11 (4/1-9/30/13)**		**33 (10/1/13-3/31/14)**			
ALL	**ALL**	**ALL**		**0-1MM**	**1-3MM**	**3-5MM**	**5-10MM**	**10-25MM**	**25MM & OVER**
63	36	44	**NUMBER OF STATEMENTS**	1	2	5	8	9	19
%	%	%	**ASSETS**	%	%	%	%	%	%
6.8	9.1	9.0	Cash & Equivalents						5.6
27.9	23.9	27.5	Trade Receivables (net)						35.1
38.5	38.4	33.7	Inventory						37.6
2.7	1.9	5.6	All Other Current						6.5
75.9	73.2	75.9	Total Current						84.8
14.6	11.8	10.4	Fixed Assets (net)						8.0
4.1	5.4	4.5	Intangibles (net)						3.8
5.5	9.5	9.3	All Other Non-Current						3.4
100.0	100.0	100.0	Total						100.0
			LIABILITIES						
12.5	6.5	8.2	Notes Payable-Short Term						11.7
2.1	1.5	1.7	Cur. Mat.-L.T.D.						.5
32.7	39.0	28.8	Trade Payables						39.8
.1	1.0	.1	Income Taxes Payable						.3
7.7	9.3	12.6	All Other Current						14.1
55.1	57.2	51.5	Total Current						66.4
8.7	8.8	10.4	Long-Term Debt						7.4
.1	.1	.0	Deferred Taxes						.0
7.4	10.8	3.8	All Other Non-Current						4.2
28.7	23.1	34.3	Net Worth						22.1
100.0	100.0	100.0	Total Liabilties & Net Worth						100.0
			INCOME DATA						
100.0	100.0	100.0	Net Sales						100.0
38.9	34.8	35.8	Gross Profit						24.3
35.5	30.9	32.4	Operating Expenses						22.1
3.5	3.9	3.4	Operating Profit						2.2
.6	.4	.3	All Other Expenses (net)						.6
2.9	3.5	3.1	Profit Before Taxes						1.6
			RATIOS						
2.7	2.7	2.2							1.9
1.2	1.3	1.4	Current						1.1
1.0	1.1	1.0							1.0
1.0	1.1	1.2							.8
.6	.6	.7	Quick						.5
.4	.3	.4							.4
10 36.2	**15** 24.7	**16** 22.3							**23** 15.8
29 12.5	**30** 12.1	**30** 12.1	Sales/Receivables						**35** 10.3
52 7.0	**45** 8.1	**42** 8.6							**59** 6.2
37 9.9	**33** 11.0	**20** 18.3							**39** 9.4
83 4.4	**68** 5.4	**79** 4.6	Cost of Sales/Inventory						**81** 4.5
146 2.5	**130** 2.8	**135** 2.7							**101** 3.6
19 19.0	**13** 28.2	**13** 27.4							**16** 23.5
56 6.5	**64** 5.7	**53** 6.9	Cost of Sales/Payables						**70** 5.2
91 4.0	**114** 3.2	**104** 3.5							**111** 3.3
5.2	5.5	6.0							7.7
16.9	17.7	14.6	Sales/Working Capital						24.1
62.0	73.9	NM							126.8
15.0	18.6	27.7							17.1
(56) 4.5	(32) 4.9	(39) 3.0	EBIT/Interest						(18) 6.2
.7	.3	1.5							.9
			Net Profit + Depr., Dep., Amort./Cur. Mat. L/T/D						
.1	.1	.0							.1
.4	.3	.2	Fixed/Worth						.2
2.3	2.2	1.2							.8
1.1	.6	.7							1.0
2.5	2.8	2.8	Debt/Worth						5.0
24.1	52.3	10.3							313.0
54.2	61.8	47.6							42.9
(51) 19.3	(28) 22.9	(36) 12.7	% Profit Before Taxes/Tangible Net Worth						(15) 12.7
3.8	.1	.6							-4.3
12.0	21.3	16.9							13.0
3.9	3.0	3.5	% Profit Before Taxes/Total Assets						1.7
.0	-1.0	-.4							-.6
138.7	135.9	203.1							131.3
41.8	48.9	58.9	Sales/Net Fixed Assets						56.8
12.5	15.8	26.3							29.1
3.7	3.8	3.9							3.4
2.6	2.6	2.9	Sales/Total Assets						2.5
2.0	2.0	2.0							2.3
.4	.4	.3							.3
(47) .8	(32) .6	(34) .7	% Depr., Dep., Amort./Sales						(16) .5
1.6	1.4	1.5							1.1
2.2	1.7	2.0							
(20) 3.6	(10) 2.9	(14) 3.4	% Officers', Directors' Owners' Comp/Sales						
10.4	8.0	10.1							
2432435M	**2093351M**	**1834792M**	Net Sales ($)	**502M**	**5768M**	**18426M**	**65302M**	**126669M**	**1618125M**
975892M	**869190M**	**738115M**	Total Assets ($)	**374M**	**3622M**	**7145M**	**24751M**	**108249M**	**593974M**

M = $ thousand MM = $ million

See Pages 9 through 22 for Explanation of Ratios and Data

Current Data Sorted by Assets							Comparative Historical Data	
						Type of Statement		
1			4	2	1	Unqualified	14	9
	1	14	5			Reviewed	26	33
4	6	10	3			Compiled	27	25
4	14	14				Tax Returns	29	36
4	14	11	14	3	1	Other	47	36
	22 (4/1-9/30/13)		108 (10/1/13-3/31/14)				**4/1/09-3/31/10**	**4/1/10-3/31/11**
0-500M	**500M-2MM**	**2-10MM**	**10-50MM**	**50-100MM**	**100-250MM**		**ALL**	**ALL**
13	35	49	26	5	2	**NUMBER OF STATEMENTS**	143	139
%	%	%	%	%	%	**ASSETS**	%	%
27.9	9.2	10.9	11.7			Cash & Equivalents	8.7	7.7
17.2	27.0	23.6	21.4			Trade Receivables (net)	24.1	25.0
22.2	26.9	34.4	26.1			Inventory	29.2	26.1
7.4	3.7	1.5	4.9			All Other Current	3.1	4.1
74.7	66.8	70.5	64.2			Total Current	65.1	62.9
19.1	18.9	20.1	25.1			Fixed Assets (net)	24.5	25.2
6.0	2.3	4.0	2.7			Intangibles (net)	3.7	3.4
.3	12.1	5.4	8.1			All Other Non-Current	6.7	8.5
100.0	100.0	100.0	100.0			Total	100.0	100.0
						LIABILITIES		
10.5	11.3	14.0	9.1			Notes Payable-Short Term	12.6	15.0
.5	1.5	2.4	3.3			Cur. Mat.-L.T.D.	3.7	3.6
3.6	21.8	17.2	13.1			Trade Payables	16.2	20.6
.0	.1	.1	.2			Income Taxes Payable	.3	.3
18.3	7.5	5.5	5.7			All Other Current	5.8	8.6
33.0	42.1	39.1	31.4			Total Current	38.7	48.1
7.0	25.6	13.6	12.5			Long-Term Debt	18.1	18.7
.0	.0	.6	.6			Deferred Taxes	.1	.6
15.1	8.0	5.0	4.0			All Other Non-Current	9.5	12.5
45.0	24.2	41.7	51.5			Net Worth	33.6	20.2
100.0	100.0	100.0	100.0			Total Liabilties & Net Worth	100.0	100.0
						INCOME DATA		
100.0	100.0	100.0	100.0			Net Sales	100.0	100.0
44.3	38.6	33.8	29.2			Gross Profit	36.2	35.1
41.8	35.3	30.1	25.3			Operating Expenses	34.8	34.0
2.5	3.3	3.7	3.9			Operating Profit	1.5	1.0
.3	.6	.4	.8			All Other Expenses (net)	1.4	.8
2.2	2.7	3.3	3.1			Profit Before Taxes	.1	.3
						RATIOS		
20.5	4.2	3.4	4.4				3.4	2.5
5.0	2.1	2.0	2.3			Current	1.9	1.5
1.5	1.1	1.2	1.3				1.1	1.0
6.3	2.9	1.5	3.4				1.5	1.4
2.0	1.0	.9	1.0			Quick	.9	.8
.8	.4	.5	.3				.4	.4
0 UND	**18** 20.0	**12** 30.3	**14** 25.3				**12** 30.4	**9** 42.6
0 UND	**27** 13.5	**28** 13.1	**26** 14.3			Sales/Receivables	**29** 12.4	**26** 13.9
25 14.6	**42** 8.6	**40** 9.2	**36** 10.0				**40** 9.0	**46** 7.9
0 UND	**17** 21.0	**14** 25.4	**11** 33.7				**12** 31.4	**6** 59.0
13 27.7	**51** 7.1	**65** 5.6	**34** 10.7			Cost of Sales/Inventory	**48** 7.6	**48** 7.7
39 9.4	**174** 2.1	**182** 2.0	**192** 1.9				**156** 2.3	**121** 3.0
0 UND	**13** 29.0	**12** 29.5	**11** 33.6				**10** 38.1	**13** 29.0
0 UND	**28** 13.2	**28** 13.0	**27** 13.3			Cost of Sales/Payables	**23** 15.6	**31** 11.8
13 28.5	**81** 4.5	**49** 7.4	**38** 9.6				**45** 8.1	**56** 6.5
7.8	5.1	4.0	2.2				5.0	6.1
12.8	9.5	10.3	6.9			Sales/Working Capital	10.2	17.1
113.6	41.1	36.1	17.2				32.8	999.8
	10.1	20.5	16.4				7.1	8.1
	(33) 2.8	(43) 3.8	5.9			EBIT/Interest	(131) 1.8	(133) 1.8
	.9	1.9	1.9				.2	.2
							4.2	5.6
						Net Profit + Depr., Dep., Amort./Cur. Mat. L/T/D	(35) 1.7	(25) 2.2
							.9	.6
.0	.1	.1	.2				.2	.2
.2	.5	.3	.5			Fixed/Worth	.6	.6
1.4	4.2	1.4	.9				3.3	-19.0
.2	.9	.7	.4				.7	.9
.5	2.7	1.5	1.2			Debt/Worth	1.6	2.0
30.5	20.5	3.7	1.8				7.5	-28.0
104.7	41.5	32.2	18.4				27.4	31.6
(11) 53.1	(28) 19.5	(43) 19.2	(24) 9.1			% Profit Before Taxes/Tangible Net Worth	(116) 8.8	(101) 8.7
.0	-2.2	7.0	4.0				-.9	.2
97.7	11.9	14.7	8.8				10.1	7.6
32.0	4.6	4.9	3.9			% Profit Before Taxes/Total Assets	2.6	1.7
.0	-.6	2.4	1.1				-2.4	-1.8
UND	78.4	63.6	49.8				56.4	63.1
138.7	30.0	20.1	10.9			Sales/Net Fixed Assets	15.6	19.1
22.6	7.7	8.6	4.2				5.2	6.3
10.5	4.2	4.5	3.6				4.2	4.1
8.5	2.5	2.6	2.3			Sales/Total Assets	2.5	2.7
2.5	1.4	1.7	1.1				1.7	1.8
	.5	.4	.6				.7	.7
	(22) 1.0	(40) .8	(25) 1.3			% Depr., Dep., Amort./Sales	(126) 1.4	(124) 1.4
	3.5	2.4	2.3				3.5	2.9
	2.5	1.5					1.8	1.9
	(20) 4.6	(26) 3.5				% Officers', Directors' Owners' Comp/Sales	(59) 2.9	(70) 2.9
	9.5	5.1					6.4	4.8
18984M	**131961M**	**670963M**	**1365333M**	**646253M**	**490844M**	Net Sales ($)	**2864066M**	**2274555M**
2413M	**41252M**	**221125M**	**508142M**	**425110M**	**342112M**	Total Assets ($)	**1374721M**	**853644M**

M = $ thousand MM = $ million

See Pages 9 through 22 for Explanation of Ratios and Data

Comparative Historical Data				Current Data Sorted by Sales					
			Type of Statement						
7	7	8	Unqualified	1					7
26	12	20	Reviewed		1		7	8	4
25	24	23	Compiled	2	6	4	3	5	3
32	35	32	Tax Returns	3	10	4	10	4	1
52	48	47	Other	6	9	1	8	7	16
4/1/11-3/31/12 ALL	4/1/12-3/31/13 ALL	4/1/13-3/31/14 ALL		22 (4/1-9/30/13)			108 (10/1/13-3/31/14)		
				0-1MM	1-3MM	3-5MM	5-10MM	10-25MM	25MM & OVER
142	126	130	**NUMBER OF STATEMENTS**	12	26	9	28	24	31
%	%	%	**ASSETS**	%	%	%	%	%	%
9.7	9.1	11.8	Cash & Equivalents	10.1	14.8		12.6	12.8	8.6
25.3	24.7	23.5	Trade Receivables (net)	11.5	14.9		23.9	30.3	28.9
27.3	27.5	29.8	Inventory	23.1	36.0		33.0	32.8	22.6
2.5	3.6	3.4	All Other Current	8.0	3.3		1.2	1.6	4.6
64.9	64.9	68.5	Total Current	52.7	68.9		70.8	77.5	64.7
25.3	22.7	20.9	Fixed Assets (net)	30.4	20.7		18.9	15.0	24.4
2.4	2.9	3.6	Intangibles (net)	6.1	2.9		4.5	1.2	4.4
7.4	9.5	7.0	All Other Non-Current	10.7	7.6		5.9	6.3	6.4
100.0	100.0	100.0	Total	100.0	100.0		100.0	100.0	100.0
			LIABILITIES						
12.4	12.4	12.5	Notes Payable-Short Term	4.9	14.5		18.0	12.5	11.1
4.8	3.1	2.4	Cur. Mat.-L.T.D.	.4	3.1		2.1	.7	4.5
20.3	17.7	16.3	Trade Payables	5.9	14.4		18.4	18.5	19.0
.2	.1	.1	Income Taxes Payable	.0	.0		.2	.0	.4
5.1	9.2	7.3	All Other Current	10.8	10.0		7.3	5.2	5.3
42.9	42.4	38.6	Total Current	22.1	42.0		46.0	37.0	40.3
21.8	23.4	15.9	Long-Term Debt	26.4	17.1		23.4	5.4	12.1
.4	.3	.3	Deferred Taxes	.0	1.3		.3	.1	.1
7.6	5.0	6.6	All Other Non-Current	10.0	13.8		8.2	1.4	3.6
27.4	28.9	38.5	Net Worth	41.5	25.9		22.1	56.1	44.0
100.0	100.0	100.0	Total Liabilities & Net Worth	100.0	100.0		100.0	100.0	100.0
			INCOME DATA						
100.0	100.0	100.0	Net Sales	100.0	100.0		100.0	100.0	100.0
37.1	37.6	34.9	Gross Profit	54.7	36.9		33.4	28.2	28.4
35.0	33.7	31.3	Operating Expenses	52.0	32.2		29.3	24.8	25.7
2.1	3.9	3.5	Operating Profit	2.7	4.7		4.0	3.4	2.7
.8	.8	.6	All Other Expenses (net)	.6	1.5		.3	-.1	.7
1.3	3.1	2.9	Profit Before Taxes	2.1	3.2		3.7	3.5	2.0
			RATIOS						
3.1	3.0	4.0		7.8	5.0		2.9	4.2	2.3
1.6	1.9	2.1	Current	3.6	2.5		1.9	2.3	1.4
1.1	1.2	1.3		1.6	1.0		1.1	1.5	1.3
1.5	1.6	2.0		2.8	3.1		1.2	2.9	1.7
.8	.9	.9	Quick	1.0	.6		.7	1.1	1.0
.4	.4	.4		.4	.2		.5	.6	.6
8 48.1	**12** 30.8	**12** 29.3		**0** UND	**0** UND		**14** 25.6	**14** 26.4	**22** 16.9
27 13.5	**27** 13.6	**26** 13.9	Sales/Receivables	**17** 21.4	**25** 14.8		**25** 14.6	**26** 14.0	**30** 12.2
42 8.6	**41** 9.0	**38** 9.5		**44** 8.3	**42** 8.7		**38** 9.5	**42** 8.6	**38** 9.6
10 36.3	**11** 33.8	**13** 28.0		**20** 18.0	**0** UND		**19** 19.0	**16** 22.6	**10** 35.6
49 7.4	**47** 7.8	**43** 8.4	Cost of Sales/Inventory	**65** 5.6	**83** 4.4		**51** 7.1	**46** 8.0	**20** 18.2
135 2.7	**130** 2.8	**174** 2.1		**456** .8	**304** 1.2		**146** 2.5	**159** 2.3	**72** 5.1
11 33.0	**12** 29.4	**9** 38.7		**0** UND	**0** UND		**12** 29.5	**13** 28.1	**14** 25.2
30 12.2	**25** 14.5	**27** 13.3	Cost of Sales/Payables	**16** 23.0	**30** 12.1		**28** 13.2	**21** 17.2	**36** 10.2
50 7.3	**43** 8.5	**49** 7.5		**135** 2.7	**83** 4.4		**52** 7.0	**37** 9.8	**47** 7.8
5.6	4.7	4.5		3.0	2.5		4.3	3.3	6.8
12.5	10.7	9.8	Sales/Working Capital	4.5	11.7		10.5	7.8	11.2
168.1	41.6	29.9		33.3	NM		89.0	18.6	36.5
8.3	19.5	16.8			15.7		8.2	84.5	16.0
(123) 2.6	(115) 3.9	(116) 4.2	EBIT/Interest		(23) 2.7		(26) 2.6	(21) 13.3	(30) 7.9
.1	1.6	1.6			1.0		1.8	2.1	1.6
8.8	10.5	9.8							
(21) 2.6	(23) 3.3	(17) 4.1	Net Profit + Depr., Dep., Amort./Cur. Mat. L/T/D						
1.6	1.3	1.1							
.1	.2	.1		.0	.1		.2	.0	.2
.6	.5	.5	Fixed/Worth	.8	.8		.7	.2	.6
7.5	1.8	1.9		3.1	NM		3.7	.5	1.2
.7	.8	.5		.5	.9		1.1	.3	.9
1.7	1.4	1.5	Debt/Worth	2.5	1.7		3.1	.7	1.5
20.7	5.2	4.8		10.5	NM		NM	1.7	2.6
27.8	46.0	32.1		61.7	28.7		44.5	32.2	26.5
(109) 6.7	(108) 13.8	(112) 17.4	% Profit Before Taxes/Tangible Net Worth	12.0	(20) 6.2		(21) 19.7	(23) 16.5	(28) 12.5
-.1	3.4	4.5		-2.3	.1		6.2	5.6	5.3
9.8	14.4	14.1		6.1	14.3		13.2	19.6	12.4
2.3	4.0	4.8	% Profit Before Taxes/Total Assets	2.2	2.3		4.8	7.5	4.7
-3.3	1.4	.4		-.5	.0		1.0	2.9	1.2
70.3	74.1	80.8		130.1	97.4		71.9	110.7	39.8
16.9	16.4	19.4	Sales/Net Fixed Assets	12.9	17.3		22.7	43.7	13.5
5.5	6.4	7.7		2.3	4.9		8.9	5.1	7.8
4.4	4.3	4.3		2.7	2.9		3.9	5.8	3.9
2.6	2.6	2.5	Sales/Total Assets	1.3	1.7		2.6	3.0	3.1
1.7	1.3	1.4		.8	.9		1.8	1.4	1.7
.6	.5	.5			.8		.5	.3	.6
(118) 1.2	(108) 1.2	(98) 1.1	% Depr., Dep., Amort./Sales		(18) 1.7		(21) 1.1	(19) .5	(28) 1.2
2.5	2.7	2.5			2.6		3.0	1.4	1.8
1.6	1.8	1.3			3.5		1.3	1.3	
(60) 3.2	(65) 3.4	(56) 3.7	% Officers', Directors' Owners' Comp/Sales		(15) 4.7		(14) 3.1	(12) 2.1	
6.0	6.2	5.6			7.5		5.0	9.2	
2418084M	2602962M	3324338M	Net Sales ($)	6249M	59494M	34897M	190578M	414220M	2618900M
1139393M	1304892M	1540154M	Total Assets ($)	5013M	55653M	11369M	85389M	184819M	1197911M

M = $ thousand MM = $ million

See Pages 9 through 22 for Explanation of Ratios and Data

Current Data Sorted by Assets | **Comparative Historical Data**

Type of Statement	0-500M	500M-2MM	2-10MM	10-50MM	50-100MM	100-250MM	4/1/09-3/31/10 ALL	4/1/10-3/31/11 ALL
Unqualified			1	11	2	1	27	21
Reviewed		3	25	15	1		45	35
Compiled	1		3	3			22	17
Tax Returns	4	6	5				20	21
Other	1	10	14	10	1	7	37	36
	21 (4/1-9/30/13)			103 (10/1/13-3/31/14)				
NUMBER OF STATEMENTS	6	19	48	39	4	8	151	130
ASSETS	%	%	%	%	%	%	%	%
Cash & Equivalents		13.4	8.3	5.7			9.0	12.2
Trade Receivables (net)		22.7	31.4	31.1			32.0	29.0
Inventory		44.5	41.1	41.1			37.7	36.8
All Other Current		3.9	1.7	3.2			2.7	2.3
Total Current		84.5	82.4	81.1			81.5	80.3
Fixed Assets (net)		8.7	8.2	11.1			10.3	11.7
Intangibles (net)		.1	1.3	3.0			1.6	2.1
All Other Non-Current		6.7	8.0	4.9			6.6	5.9
Total		100.0	100.0	100.0			100.0	100.0
LIABILITIES								
Notes Payable-Short Term		10.9	20.0	31.1			18.4	15.5
Cur. Mat.-L.T.D.		1.3	1.7	1.0			2.0	1.4
Trade Payables		19.6	18.3	15.9			19.2	19.9
Income Taxes Payable		.0	.1	.1			.4	.3
All Other Current		11.4	10.4	6.1			8.4	7.4
Total Current		43.3	50.5	54.1			48.4	44.5
Long-Term Debt		9.5	3.7	7.4			7.2	8.8
Deferred Taxes		.0	.3	.2			.1	.2
All Other Non-Current		13.2	4.9	3.1			4.6	4.3
Net Worth		34.1	40.6	35.2			39.7	42.2
Total Liabilities & Net Worth		100.0	100.0	100.0			100.0	100.0
INCOME DATA								
Net Sales		100.0	100.0	100.0			100.0	100.0
Gross Profit		12.2	8.6	10.3			10.3	10.1
Operating Expenses		8.9	7.8	9.1			8.2	8.8
Operating Profit		3.3	.8	1.1			2.1	1.3
All Other Expenses (net)		.2	.0	.2			.0	.1
Profit Before Taxes		3.1	.9	.9			2.1	1.2
RATIOS								
Current		5.3	2.5	2.0			2.6	2.7
		1.8	1.8	1.4			1.7	1.8
		1.4	1.3	1.2			1.2	1.2
Quick		1.4	1.5	1.1			1.5	1.6
		.8	.9	.7			.8	(129) .9
		.5	.5	.5			.5	.6
Sales/Receivables		0 999.8	8 45.1	10 38.2			8 44.3	7 51.6
		8 46.8	12 30.0	14 25.4			14 25.7	12 29.3
		29 12.8	20 18.3	22 16.5			19 19.0	18 20.7
Cost of Sales/Inventory		14 26.5	13 27.5	10 36.2			11 32.6	10 35.3
		21 17.2	17 20.9	20 18.0			17 21.3	16 22.2
		91 4.0	25 14.4	34 10.6			29 12.7	29 12.8
Cost of Sales/Payables		1 385.3	3 118.6	4 89.6			3 126.1	3 113.7
		5 67.3	7 55.1	7 49.4			8 47.2	8 47.5
		18 19.9	16 22.2	13 27.7			14 26.2	14 25.8
Sales/Working Capital		5.7	13.9	18.8			14.6	16.1
		23.9	25.5	39.1			28.5	28.2
		35.8	44.6	71.5			64.2	53.2
EBIT/Interest		18.2	6.9	17.5			17.9	12.1
		(16) 7.4	(42) 3.7	3.8			(136) 5.9	(106) 4.7
		.5	1.9	1.6			2.6	2.0
Net Profit + Depr., Dep., Amort./Cur. Mat. L/T/D			17.0				15.8	15.8
			(10) 3.1				(35) 6.7	(29) 8.1
			2.0				2.9	2.6
Fixed/Worth		.0	.0	.1			.1	.1
		.1	.1	.2			.2	.2
		.6	.4	.6			.6	.5
Debt/Worth		.6	.7	1.0			.7	.6
		2.9	1.3	2.2			1.8	1.8
		7.9	2.9	4.9			4.3	3.9
% Profit Before Taxes/Tangible Net Worth		79.3	20.0	21.0			44.5	35.4
		(16) 30.7	(47) 9.9	(37) 14.4			(145) 20.2	(127) 18.5
		2.4	4.9	4.1			9.3	7.5
% Profit Before Taxes/Total Assets		27.8	7.4	9.2			14.3	13.9
		8.2	3.2	3.5			7.2	6.4
		-.3	1.9	.9			3.3	2.5
Sales/Net Fixed Assets		999.8	370.2	230.3			386.3	370.3
		152.1	186.3	125.7			130.4	113.0
		82.6	61.8	52.1			55.2	46.3
Sales/Total Assets		9.9	11.2	11.5			11.5	11.6
		6.0	8.4	8.1			8.4	8.6
		2.3	6.1	5.3			5.7	5.6
% Depr., Dep., Amort./Sales		.1	.0	.1			.1	.1
		(11) .1	(38) .1	(38) .2			(125) .2	(108) .2
		.5	.3	.4			.4	.4
% Officers', Directors' Owners' Comp/Sales			.4				.3	.3
			(22) .7				(68) .6	(55) .8
			1.9				1.3	1.3
Net Sales ($)	58191M	185138M	2005243M	6896672M	2486337M	6941321M	19811176M	17958672M
Total Assets ($)	1680M	25684M	230081M	878632M	279763M	1148194M	2973422M	2197317M

M = $ thousand MM = $ million

See Pages 9 through 22 for Explanation of Ratios and Data

Comparative Historical Data				Current Data Sorted by Sales					
			Type of Statement						
19	12	15	Unqualified						15
40	33	44	Reviewed				1	7	36
16	14	7	Compiled		1			3	3
19	21	15	Tax Returns	1	2		2	5	5
32	42	43	Other		3	4	3	7	26
4/1/11-3/31/12 ALL	**4/1/12-3/31/13 ALL**	**4/1/13-3/31/14 ALL**		**21 (4/1-9/30/13)**			**103 (10/1/13-3/31/14)**		
				0-1MM	**1-3MM**	**3-5MM**	**5-10MM**	**10-25MM**	**25MM & OVER**
126	122	124	**NUMBER OF STATEMENTS**	1	6	4	6	22	85
%	%	%	**ASSETS**	%	%	%	%	%	%
10.7	9.8	9.6	Cash & Equivalents					18.8	6.3
28.3	24.5	28.6	Trade Receivables (net)					24.5	32.0
37.4	40.8	40.5	Inventory					41.7	40.0
3.0	3.0	3.0	All Other Current					.4	3.1
79.3	78.1	81.7	Total Current					85.5	81.4
11.0	11.1	9.8	Fixed Assets (net)					8.5	10.5
1.2	1.5	1.8	Intangibles (net)					.3	2.0
8.5	9.4	6.6	All Other Non-Current					5.7	6.1
100.0	100.0	100.0	Total					100.0	100.0
			LIABILITIES						
18.9	17.2	21.3	Notes Payable-Short Term					17.1	25.2
1.3	2.1	1.3	Cur. Mat.-L.T.D.					1.2	1.5
18.9	17.5	20.4	Trade Payables					19.1	17.2
.1	.2	.2	Income Taxes Payable					.0	.2
8.1	7.5	11.8	All Other Current					17.1	5.9
47.3	44.5	55.0	Total Current					54.5	50.0
7.5	8.8	7.1	Long-Term Debt					3.5	7.6
.2	.2	.2	Deferred Taxes					.1	.3
3.7	6.6	5.0	All Other Non-Current					2.8	4.3
41.3	39.9	32.7	Net Worth					39.1	37.8
100.0	100.0	100.0	Total Liabilties & Net Worth					100.0	100.0
			INCOME DATA						
100.0	100.0	100.0	Net Sales					100.0	100.0
11.8	12.4	9.8	Gross Profit					11.8	7.7
9.8	10.2	8.4	Operating Expenses					9.8	6.9
2.0	2.2	1.4	Operating Profit					2.0	.9
.0	.2	.1	All Other Expenses (net)					.1	.1
2.0	2.0	1.2	Profit Before Taxes					2.0	.8
			RATIOS						
2.7	2.7	2.6						2.9	2.5
1.7	1.8	1.6	Current					1.5	1.6
1.3	1.3	1.3						1.2	1.3
1.3	1.4	1.4						1.5	1.3
(125) .8	.8	.7	Quick					.7	.8
.5	.4	.5						.4	.5
6 56.4	**5** 72.6	**7** 52.5						**1** 656.4	**9** 39.8
12 30.8	**10** 35.3	**12** 30.1	Sales/Receivables					**12** 29.7	**12** 29.2
17 20.9	**17** 21.7	**20** 18.5						**24** 15.5	**18** 19.9
11 34.2	**12** 29.4	**12** 30.8						**10** 38.3	**12** 30.6
16 22.5	**20** 18.2	**18** 20.5	Cost of Sales/Inventory					**22** 16.5	**16** 22.4
29 12.5	**32** 11.3	**31** 11.8						**48** 7.6	**27** 13.5
4 102.9	**3** 111.5	**3** 112.1						**2** 175.6	**4** 92.6
8 46.9	**7** 49.3	**7** 50.8	Cost of Sales/Payables					**9** 42.7	**7** 50.0
14 25.9	**15** 24.3	**14** 26.7						**21** 17.4	**13** 28.8
14.8	14.2	14.7						11.0	19.3
27.6	26.4	27.2	Sales/Working Capital					28.6	27.7
55.6	43.6	57.9						85.5	56.8
11.6	15.1	10.4						30.7	10.1
(108) 3.9	(102) 3.8	(110) 4.1	EBIT/Interest					(17) 6.9	(82) 4.0
1.9	1.1	1.8						1.8	1.8
15.0	13.0	21.8							21.5
(30) 5.0	(23) 4.3	(26) 7.5	Net Profit + Depr., Dep., Amort./Cur. Mat. L/T/D						(23) 7.9
2.1	1.3	2.6							2.7
.1	.1	.1						.0	.1
.2	.2	.2	Fixed/Worth					.2	.2
.5	.5	.5						.3	.5
.7	.6	.8						.5	.9
1.7	1.8	1.9	Debt/Worth					1.8	1.8
3.4	3.4	4.2						3.6	3.8
38.9	36.6	24.3						43.5	20.9
(125) 15.8	(115) 14.0	(114) 14.8	% Profit Before Taxes/Tangible Net Worth					(21) 12.6	(82) 14.8
6.0	1.7	4.8						2.6	5.3
12.7	12.3	9.9						23.4	9.0
4.9	5.5	3.6	% Profit Before Taxes/Total Assets					3.7	3.5
1.7	.5	1.1						.8	1.4
379.5	348.4	361.8						490.6	310.5
119.2	111.0	136.5	Sales/Net Fixed Assets					207.1	126.6
47.8	43.0	53.4						79.3	47.9
12.0	11.7	11.3						13.0	11.5
9.0	8.7	8.5	Sales/Total Assets					7.1	8.9
5.5	5.5	5.3						4.7	6.8
.1	.1	.1						.0	.1
(104) .2	(101) .2	(101) .2	% Depr., Dep., Amort./Sales					(17) .1	(78) .2
.4	.4	.4						.3	.4
.3	.3	.4						.5	.3
(54) .8	(38) .7	(40) .7	% Officers', Directors' Owners' Comp/Sales					(10) 1.5	(25) .6
1.3	1.9	2.2						3.3	1.0
17181542M	**16655151M**	**18572902M**	Net Sales ($)	**208M**	**13314M**	**15856M**	**41652M**	**365512M**	**18136360M**
2087268M	**2326876M**	**2564034M**	Total Assets ($)	**23M**	**7490M**	**5214M**	**11360M**	**82546M**	**2457401M**

M = $ thousand MM = $ million

See Pages 9 through 22 for Explanation of Ratios and Data

Current Data Sorted by Assets							Comparative Historical Data	
						Type of Statement		
	1	1	1	1		Unqualified	5	5
		3	3			Reviewed	11	9
		2	2			Compiled	13	7
	6	2				Tax Returns	6	9
1	6	7	5		1	Other	22	20
9 (4/1-9/30/13)		33 (10/1/13-3/31/14)					4/1/09-3/31/10	4/1/10-3/31/11
0-500M	**500M-2MM**	**2-10MM**	**10-50MM**	**50-100MM**	**100-250MM**		**ALL**	**ALL**
1	13	15	11	1	1	**NUMBER OF STATEMENTS**	57	50
%	%	%	%	%	%	**ASSETS**	%	%
	11.3	10.1	11.0			Cash & Equivalents	6.1	7.3
	35.0	27.3	24.0			Trade Receivables (net)	31.4	31.3
	35.5	38.6	34.5			Inventory	39.5	36.8
	5.5	.9	5.4			All Other Current	3.9	3.6
	87.3	77.0	74.8			Total Current	80.9	79.0
	10.2	10.9	11.5			Fixed Assets (net)	10.0	11.0
	1.1	4.7	7.8			Intangibles (net)	4.5	5.3
	1.3	7.5	5.9			All Other Non-Current	4.6	4.7
	100.0	100.0	100.0			Total	100.0	100.0
						LIABILITIES		
	8.1	12.8	2.4			Notes Payable-Short Term	15.5	14.9
	1.5	2.2	2.2			Cur. Mat.-L.T.D.	2.2	2.1
	43.6	34.1	21.0			Trade Payables	28.6	28.7
	.0	.0	.1			Income Taxes Payable	.1	.3
	3.3	3.6	4.8			All Other Current	4.4	5.6
	56.5	52.7	30.5			Total Current	50.8	51.6
	9.4	8.4	4.6			Long-Term Debt	14.8	13.0
	.0	.0	.5			Deferred Taxes	.3	.3
	8.9	7.8	10.0			All Other Non-Current	5.3	8.2
	25.1	31.1	54.5			Net Worth	28.8	26.8
	100.0	100.0	100.0			Total Liabilties & Net Worth	100.0	100.0
						INCOME DATA		
	100.0	100.0	100.0			Net Sales	100.0	100.0
	30.2	34.7	33.3			Gross Profit	31.8	32.2
	27.8	31.4	26.6			Operating Expenses	29.7	28.9
	2.4	3.3	6.6			Operating Profit	2.1	3.4
	.4	-.4	-.9			All Other Expenses (net)	.0	.5
	2.0	3.6	7.5			Profit Before Taxes	2.1	2.9
						RATIOS		
	2.5	2.2	4.5				2.5	2.6
	1.8	1.4	3.2			Current	1.6	1.7
	1.0	1.1	2.0				1.2	1.2
	1.6	1.0	2.7				1.4	1.3
	.8	.6	1.5			Quick	.7	.7
	.4	.5	.6				.5	.5
	27 13.7	**24** 15.0	**30** 12.3				**32** 11.6	**33** 10.9
	40 9.2	**33** 10.9	**37** 9.9			Sales/Receivables	**39** 9.5	**43** 8.5
	51 7.1	**45** 8.1	**56** 6.5				**52** 7.1	**59** 6.2
	26 14.0	**54** 6.8	**72** 5.1				**60** 6.1	**48** 7.6
	51 7.2	**79** 4.6	**89** 4.1			Cost of Sales/Inventory	**80** 4.6	**80** 4.5
	118 3.1	**107** 3.4	**203** 1.8				**127** 2.9	**112** 3.2
	28 13.1	**30** 12.1	**24** 15.2				**28** 13.0	**28** 13.2
	55 6.6	**51** 7.2	**42** 8.7			Cost of Sales/Payables	**57** 6.4	**52** 7.1
	166 2.2	**99** 3.7	**76** 4.8				**78** 4.7	**83** 4.4
	6.5	6.2	3.2				5.8	5.1
	11.1	11.9	3.7			Sales/Working Capital	8.5	10.6
	NM	31.7	9.6				19.3	33.3
	12.8	36.5					10.9	10.3
	(10) 7.1	(13) 6.9				EBIT/Interest	(49) 2.6	(46) 3.1
	4.5	1.7					.6	1.2
								25.6
						Net Profit + Depr., Dep., Amort./Cur. Mat. L/T/D		(10) 1.9
								.9
	.1	.1	.1				.1	.2
	.3	.3	.2			Fixed/Worth	.3	.5
	NM	1.2	.9				1.2	-3.7
	1.1	1.3	.3				1.4	1.0
	2.1	2.7	.4			Debt/Worth	3.4	3.7
	NM	5.0	2.5				10.2	-46.0
	38.2	62.2					49.8	34.6
	(10) 16.9	(13) 42.1				% Profit Before Taxes/Tangible Net Worth	(49) 14.9	(36) 12.9
	6.9	9.2					-.7	3.7
	8.9	20.4	18.7				10.2	10.4
	3.8	10.5	14.3			% Profit Before Taxes/Total Assets	4.0	5.1
	1.7	2.4	7.7				-1.6	.5
	153.2	97.0	63.3				78.8	82.2
	65.5	48.7	33.6			Sales/Net Fixed Assets	29.9	29.4
	26.0	17.1	11.9				16.1	17.0
	4.7	3.9	2.6				3.6	3.2
	2.7	3.0	2.0			Sales/Total Assets	2.3	2.5
	2.2	2.1	1.6				1.9	1.9
		.4					.5	.4
		(11) .6				% Depr., Dep., Amort./Sales	(44) .9	(37) .7
		1.2					1.7	1.6
	2.2						2.4	1.2
	(12) 3.1					% Officers', Directors' Owners' Comp/Sales	(23) 3.3	(25) 2.7
	4.6						5.2	4.5
909M	**52304M**	**201250M**	**484651M**	**166152M**	**265403M**	Net Sales ($)	**1414806M**	**1029163M**
428M	**15630M**	**62759M**	**231115M**	**50340M**	**246980M**	Total Assets ($)	**713208M**	**554749M**

M = $ thousand MM = $ million

See Pages 9 through 22 for Explanation of Ratios and Data

Comparative Historical Data / Current Data Sorted by Sales

4/1/11-3/31/12 ALL	4/1/12-3/31/13 ALL	4/1/13-3/31/14 ALL	Type of Statement	0-1MM	1-3MM	3-5MM	5-10MM	10-25MM	25MM & OVER
4	4	4	Unqualified			1		1	2
9	4	6	Reviewed				1	1	4
10	7	4	Compiled				2	1	1
9	8	8	Tax Returns			2	5	1	
13	16	20	Other	1	4	3	1	5	6
				9 (4/1-9/30/13)			33 (10/1/13-3/31/14)		
45	39	42	NUMBER OF STATEMENTS	1	4	6	9	9	13
%	%	%	**ASSETS**	%	%	%	%	%	%
5.6	8.7	10.2	Cash & Equivalents						13.2
28.9	27.6	28.4	Trade Receivables (net)						22.7
40.5	37.6	36.8	Inventory						34.2
3.4	3.0	3.6	All Other Current						3.9
78.5	76.9	78.9	Total Current						73.9
12.8	12.9	11.4	Fixed Assets (net)						9.7
5.0	5.4	4.9	Intangibles (net)						9.2
3.7	4.8	4.8	All Other Non-Current						7.2
100.0	100.0	100.0	Total						100.0
			LIABILITIES						
13.5	13.1	8.9	Notes Payable-Short Term						4.4
2.4	2.1	2.0	Cur. Mat.-L.T.D.						2.3
25.7	27.2	32.0	Trade Payables						21.0
.0	.2	.0	Income Taxes Payable						.1
6.8	5.7	3.7	All Other Current						6.2
48.4	48.3	46.6	Total Current						34.0
13.0	11.4	9.3	Long-Term Debt						8.1
.6	.5	.3	Deferred Taxes						1.1
7.1	8.6	8.6	All Other Non-Current						4.6
30.9	31.1	35.1	Net Worth						52.3
100.0	100.0	100.0	Total Liabilities & Net Worth						100.0
			INCOME DATA						
100.0	100.0	100.0	Net Sales						100.0
33.0	33.5	32.7	Gross Profit						37.4
29.0	28.6	28.8	Operating Expenses						30.8
4.1	5.0	3.9	Operating Profit						6.6
.0	1.0	-.2	All Other Expenses (net)						-.4
4.1	3.9	4.1	Profit Before Taxes						7.0
			RATIOS						
2.5	2.7	3.2							4.1
1.7	1.6	1.9	Current						3.2
1.3	1.2	1.2							1.5
1.2	1.2	1.5							1.9
.7	.8	.8	Quick						1.0
.5	.5	.5							.6
30 12.3	**27** 13.4	**27** 13.3							**27** 13.7
41 8.8	**36** 10.2	**36** 10.1	Sales/Receivables						**33** 10.9
51 7.2	**49** 7.4	**49** 7.5							**46** 8.0
52 7.0	**49** 7.4	**50** 7.3							**56** 6.5
96 3.8	**79** 4.6	**81** 4.5	Cost of Sales/Inventory						**83** 4.4
130 2.8	**122** 3.0	**118** 3.1							**159** 2.3
21 17.4	**28** 12.9	**28** 12.9							**19** 18.8
44 8.3	**37** 9.9	**49** 7.5	Cost of Sales/Payables						**41** 9.0
78 4.7	**81** 4.5	**99** 3.7							**68** 5.4
5.4	5.1	4.4							3.6
8.4	9.2	9.3	Sales/Working Capital						4.9
15.7	22.0	21.7							16.6
15.5	12.6	33.8							117.6
(42) 4.7	(33) 3.2	(35) 9.3	EBIT/Interest						(10) 21.9
2.5	2.7	3.9							3.6
14.2									
(11) 4.2			Net Profit + Depr., Dep., Amort./Cur. Mat. L/T/D						
1.5									
.2	.2	.1							.1
.4	.4	.3	Fixed/Worth						.2
3.4	1.7	1.5							1.0
.9	.9	.9							.4
2.7	2.4	2.1	Debt/Worth						.9
62.7	11.3	5.2							3.7
42.0	38.9	47.0							46.4
(35) 17.9	(31) 21.9	(35) 21.1	% Profit Before Taxes/Tangible Net Worth						(11) 23.9
8.3	12.7	9.9							11.5
13.1	10.0	16.1							18.9
7.3	7.1	7.8	% Profit Before Taxes/Total Assets						14.3
3.1	2.7	2.3							7.8
57.4	92.3	96.5							89.4
27.7	26.9	34.2	Sales/Net Fixed Assets						33.9
15.0	11.5	16.5							12.2
3.5	3.3	3.4							3.3
2.5	2.7	2.5	Sales/Total Assets						2.1
2.0	1.9	2.0							1.7
.4	.5	.6							
(34) .7	(33) 1.1	(29) .9	% Depr., Dep., Amort./Sales						
1.8	2.3	1.2							
2.0	1.0	1.5							
(17) 2.8	(19) 2.2	(21) 2.5	% Officers', Directors' Owners' Comp/Sales						
6.5	4.0	4.0							
1135935M	1540782M	1170669M	Net Sales ($)	909M	9674M	21248M	65189M	127735M	945914M
590121M	863890M	607252M	Total Assets ($)	428M	4326M	8688M	18013M	57689M	518108M

M = $ thousand MM = $ million

See Pages 9 through 22 for Explanation of Ratios and Data

Current Data Sorted by Assets							Comparative Historical Data	
						Type of Statement		
	1	10	22	7	6	Unqualified	55	53
	15	52	40	3		Reviewed	156	136
7	25	47	10	1	1	Compiled	102	105
50	79	81	6			Tax Returns	199	194
23	67	119	56	15	8	Other	269	259
97 (4/1-9/30/13)		654 (10/1/13-3/31/14)					4/1/09-3/31/10	4/1/10-3/31/11
0-500M	500M-2MM	2-10MM	10-50MM	50-100MM	100-250MM		ALL	ALL
80	187	309	134	26	15	**NUMBER OF STATEMENTS**	781	747
%	%	%	%	%	%	**ASSETS**	%	%
19.7	14.0	9.4	6.7	8.0	8.3	Cash & Equivalents	10.2	10.5
21.8	27.3	31.5	27.4	27.3	19.9	Trade Receivables (net)	30.8	29.2
32.5	35.1	34.7	38.6	31.2	19.9	Inventory	32.1	35.8
4.5	1.5	3.1	4.3	2.7	1.9	All Other Current	3.2	2.7
78.5	77.9	78.7	77.0	69.3	50.0	Total Current	76.2	78.2
12.3	12.3	10.8	12.0	10.1	17.6	Fixed Assets (net)	12.6	11.4
1.9	2.3	3.6	5.7	16.3	25.1	Intangibles (net)	4.8	4.9
7.3	7.5	6.9	5.3	4.4	7.2	All Other Non-Current	6.4	5.5
100.0	100.0	100.0	100.0	100.0	100.0	Total	100.0	100.0
						LIABILITIES		
19.4	11.5	12.5	17.3	15.9	10.9	Notes Payable-Short Term	15.5	15.8
1.7	3.2	1.4	1.7	3.7	2.8	Cur. Mat.-L.T.D.	2.8	2.4
23.0	21.8	24.7	20.2	16.8	15.6	Trade Payables	22.5	22.7
.0	.0	.1	.3	.8	.2	Income Taxes Payable	.2	.1
12.3	7.8	8.4	8.8	6.2	4.0	All Other Current	8.2	8.4
56.4	44.3	47.1	48.3	43.3	33.6	Total Current	49.2	49.3
23.0	13.7	9.4	6.8	8.5	18.0	Long-Term Debt	10.9	10.9
.0	.1	.1	.5	.9	.7	Deferred Taxes	.2	.2
11.1	13.1	6.4	5.9	1.8	5.8	All Other Non-Current	6.8	6.6
9.5	28.9	37.0	38.5	45.4	41.9	Net Worth	32.9	33.1
100.0	100.0	100.0	100.0	100.0	100.0	Total Liabilties & Net Worth	100.0	100.0
						INCOME DATA		
100.0	100.0	100.0	100.0	100.0	100.0	Net Sales	100.0	100.0
42.9	32.1	28.8	27.6	27.5	34.1	Gross Profit	31.6	32.7
38.0	28.0	24.8	22.9	21.3	26.1	Operating Expenses	27.5	28.3
5.0	4.2	3.9	4.8	6.3	8.0	Operating Profit	4.1	4.4
.5	.4	.2	.3	.4	.9	All Other Expenses (net)	.8	.6
4.5	3.8	3.8	4.4	5.8	7.1	Profit Before Taxes	3.3	3.8
						RATIOS		
6.9	3.8	2.8	2.0	2.3	2.3		2.6	2.8
2.3	2.0	1.7	1.5	1.5	1.5	Current	1.5	1.6
1.0	1.2	1.2	1.2	1.1	1.2		1.2	1.2
3.0	2.1	1.4	1.2	1.3	1.4		1.4	1.5
.9	1.0	.9	.7	.6	1.0	Quick	.8	.8
.3	.5	.5	.4	.5	.4		.5	.5
0 UND	**11** 33.1	**26** 14.3	**24** 15.4	**29** 12.5	**15** 25.1		**22** 16.7	**21** 17.5
9 40.1	**27** 13.3	**36** 10.0	**40** 9.2	**48** 7.6	**33** 11.1	Sales/Receivables	**36** 10.0	**36** 10.2
32 11.5	**41** 8.9	**53** 6.9	**52** 7.0	**59** 6.2	**47** 7.8		**53** 6.9	**51** 7.2
0 UND	**17** 22.0	**27** 13.6	**47** 7.8	**33** 11.0	**22** 16.9		**24** 15.2	**28** 13.0
29 12.7	**49** 7.4	**59** 6.2	**87** 4.2	**61** 6.0	**59** 6.2	Cost of Sales/Inventory	**56** 6.5	**63** 5.8
104 3.5	**101** 3.6	**114** 3.2	**140** 2.6	**101** 3.6	**111** 3.3		**108** 3.4	**116** 3.1
0 UND	**7** 51.2	**18** 20.3	**17** 21.1	**21** 17.5	**16** 22.2		**15** 24.6	**15** 24.8
14 27.0	**23** 15.8	**32** 11.4	**33** 11.2	**29** 12.7	**29** 12.5	Cost of Sales/Payables	**31** 11.8	**33** 11.1
41 9.0	**51** 7.1	**54** 6.7	**58** 6.3	**52** 7.0	**45** 8.1		**56** 6.6	**57** 6.4
6.0	5.0	4.8	5.1	5.5	6.5		5.4	5.1
13.1	9.3	9.4	9.1	9.0	9.1	Sales/Working Capital	11.6	11.0
-266.7	33.3	25.4	25.6	73.0	39.7		38.4	30.4
26.3	14.5	23.9	25.8	64.0	32.0		14.4	16.6
(47) 9.2	(140) 6.2	(259) 6.2	(124) 7.5	8.9	(13) 8.6	EBIT/Interest	(677) 4.3	(641) 5.4
2.8	1.9	2.1	2.4	3.0	2.8		1.4	2.0
	5.0	13.9	8.6				7.3	9.2
	(12) 1.8	(31) 4.5	(34) 3.0			Net Profit + Depr., Dep., Amort./Cur. Mat. L/T/D	(125) 2.6	(106) 3.3
	1.3	1.4	1.4				.8	1.4
.0	.0	.0	.1	.1	.2		.1	.0
.2	.1	.2	.2	.3	.9	Fixed/Worth	.3	.2
1.4	1.0	.6	.8	2.0	-.1		1.2	1.0
.6	.7	.7	1.1	.7	.9		.8	.8
2.3	1.9	2.0	2.2	1.9	2.5	Debt/Worth	2.2	2.1
291.3	9.2	5.7	4.9	18.3	-2.7		7.4	7.8
121.9	62.9	53.0	47.4	58.1	45.3		50.0	53.6
(62) 56.7	(155) 22.8	(275) 27.5	(128) 26.6	(22) 43.0	(10) 24.3	% Profit Before Taxes/Tangible Net Worth	(666) 20.0	(635) 21.8
18.5	8.7	8.9	11.4	14.0	18.2		5.1	8.1
53.0	19.7	18.6	16.6	19.2	15.2		16.2	16.8
22.3	8.4	7.2	7.7	9.4	10.0	% Profit Before Taxes/Total Assets	5.9	6.8
5.2	2.1	2.0	3.2	5.1	6.4		1.1	2.1
UND	453.0	223.2	125.7	63.7	113.4		177.8	257.7
176.4	77.4	63.8	43.3	34.6	65.0	Sales/Net Fixed Assets	53.7	63.4
30.3	22.7	22.4	13.4	13.6	7.4		16.7	19.8
9.4	5.0	4.1	3.1	2.8	2.3		4.2	4.1
4.4	3.3	2.7	2.2	2.2	1.6	Sales/Total Assets	2.8	2.8
2.8	2.4	1.8	1.6	1.6	1.1		1.9	1.8
.2	.2	.2	.2	.3			.3	.2
(30) .6	(109) .5	(228) .5	(112) .6	(22) .9		% Depr., Dep., Amort./Sales	(568) .6	(537) .5
1.3	1.4	1.1	1.3	1.7			1.5	1.4
2.1	1.7	1.0	.8				1.3	1.6
(47) 3.6	(110) 3.4	(158) 1.8	(53) 1.6			% Officers', Directors' Owners' Comp/Sales	(350) 2.9	(361) 2.9
8.5	6.4	3.9	3.1				5.2	5.2
132355M	899941M	4637708M	7366700M	4070063M	4723081M	Net Sales ($)	21871028M	21932786M
19565M	226129M	1442714M	2766973M	1704264M	2247725M	Total Assets ($)	8281865M	8350045M

M = $ thousand MM = $ million

See Pages 9 through 22 for Explanation of Ratios and Data

Comparative Historical Data				Current Data Sorted by Sales					
			Type of Statement						
52	40	46	Unqualified		1		4	8	33
146	108	110	Reviewed	2	1	7	16	45	39
111	104	91	Compiled	4	7	15	19	28	18
259	230	216	Tax Returns	23	48	34	61	37	13
292	262	288	Other	16	38	31	59	71	73
					97 (4/1-9/30/13)		654 (10/1/13-3/31/14)		
4/1/11-3/31/12 ALL	4/1/12-3/31/13 ALL	4/1/13-3/31/14 ALL		0-1MM	1-3MM	3-5MM	5-10MM	10-25MM	25MM & OVER
860	744	751	**NUMBER OF STATEMENTS**	45	95	87	159	189	176
%	%	%	**ASSETS**	%	%	%	%	%	%
10.5	11.0	11.1	Cash & Equivalents	17.9	15.8	12.3	11.7	8.0	8.9
28.9	27.6	28.3	Trade Receivables (net)	21.2	22.1	24.2	29.9	31.4	31.0
35.2	34.7	34.9	Inventory	28.9	35.4	36.6	33.9	37.1	33.7
1.9	2.4	3.0	All Other Current	5.2	2.6	1.8	2.2	2.9	4.2
76.4	75.8	77.3	Total Current	73.1	75.9	74.8	77.7	79.4	77.8
12.4	12.3	11.7	Fixed Assets (net)	16.1	12.3	14.1	11.7	10.8	9.9
5.1	4.9	4.3	Intangibles (net)	.9	3.3	4.5	3.2	3.5	7.7
6.1	7.0	6.7	All Other Non-Current	10.0	8.6	6.7	7.4	6.3	4.6
100.0	100.0	100.0	Total	100.0	100.0	100.0	100.0	100.0	100.0
			LIABILITIES						
14.4	15.9	13.9	Notes Payable-Short Term	16.9	12.9	13.5	9.9	16.1	15.2
2.2	1.8	2.0	Cur. Mat.-L.T.D.	2.0	3.5	2.5	1.7	1.6	1.7
22.8	22.6	22.6	Trade Payables	24.3	14.5	23.2	21.6	25.0	24.4
.1	.1	.1	Income Taxes Payable	.0	.0	.0	.1	.2	.3
9.1	8.3	8.6	All Other Current	6.6	13.1	6.4	8.4	8.3	8.2
48.7	48.7	47.2	Total Current	49.8	44.0	45.6	41.7	51.2	49.8
12.0	10.7	11.6	Long-Term Debt	25.6	17.3	19.1	9.6	7.9	7.1
.1	.1	.2	Deferred Taxes	.0	.0	.0	.1	.3	.4
8.4	9.1	8.3	All Other Non-Current	22.3	8.9	9.6	11.1	5.8	4.0
30.8	31.3	32.7	Net Worth	2.3	29.7	25.7	37.5	34.9	38.8
100.0	100.0	100.0	Total Liabilties & Net Worth	100.0	100.0	100.0	100.0	100.0	100.0
			INCOME DATA						
100.0	100.0	100.0	Net Sales	100.0	100.0	100.0	100.0	100.0	100.0
30.9	32.0	31.0	Gross Profit	50.2	41.7	31.2	31.3	26.6	24.5
26.7	27.2	26.6	Operating Expenses	45.1	36.2	27.2	27.2	23.1	19.5
4.2	4.7	4.4	Operating Profit	5.1	5.5	4.0	4.2	3.6	5.0
.5	.6	.3	All Other Expenses (net)	1.5	.4	.5	.1	.1	.3
3.7	4.1	4.1	Profit Before Taxes	3.6	5.1	3.5	4.1	3.5	4.7
			RATIOS						
2.8	3.1	3.1		22.8	4.7	3.6	3.4	2.3	2.3
1.6	1.6	1.7	Current	2.9	2.4	1.6	2.1	1.5	1.6
1.1	1.2	1.2		.9	1.4	1.1	1.3	1.2	1.1
1.5	1.5	1.6		8.2	2.6	1.7	2.1	1.2	1.2
.8	.8	.8	Quick	1.2	1.1	.8	1.0	.8	.8
.5	.5	.5		.4	.5	.5	.6	.5	.5
18 19.8	**18** 20.3	**18** 20.5		**0** UND	**4** 82.3	**11** 34.7	**23** 15.9	**24** 15.3	**22** 16.3
34 10.7	**33** 10.9	**33** 11.0	Sales/Receivables	**12** 30.2	**27** 13.3	**29** 12.8	**35** 10.4	**35** 10.3	**35** 10.4
51 7.2	**49** 7.5	**49** 7.4		**43** 8.4	**47** 7.7	**53** 6.9	**51** 7.1	**50** 7.3	**49** 7.4
26 14.0	**24** 15.5	**23** 16.1		**0** UND	**25** 14.6	**20** 18.0	**21** 17.0	**24** 15.3	**23** 16.1
59 6.2	**60** 6.1	**59** 6.2	Cost of Sales/Inventory	**79** 4.6	**76** 4.8	**72** 5.1	**62** 5.9	**55** 6.6	**54** 6.7
114 3.2	**111** 3.3	**114** 3.2		**228** 1.6	**146** 2.5	**135** 2.7	**111** 3.3	**111** 3.3	**101** 3.6
13 29.1	**14** 27.0	**13** 28.3		**0** UND	**5** 80.0	**9** 38.7	**13** 27.9	**19** 19.1	**17** 22.1
30 12.2	**29** 12.4	**29** 12.5	Cost of Sales/Payables	**12** 30.0	**24** 15.0	**38** 9.7	**30** 12.2	**30** 12.2	**29** 12.6
56 6.5	**54** 6.7	**52** 7.0		**46** 7.9	**47** 7.8	**70** 5.2	**57** 6.4	**49** 7.4	**47** 7.8
5.1	5.7	5.0		2.1	4.0	4.7	4.2	6.4	6.7
10.9	10.4	9.6	Sales/Working Capital	6.0	6.6	12.3	8.2	11.1	12.5
42.8	38.0	30.2		-32.6	26.9	36.8	22.0	32.5	31.5
19.9	18.6	23.0		29.5	17.3	15.9	18.8	23.4	34.5
(724) 5.3	(611) 5.3	(609) 6.7	EBIT/Interest	(22) 3.2	(63) 5.8	(73) 6.0	(126) 5.3	(167) 6.6	(158) 11.1
2.0	1.7	2.2		-.7	1.1	1.9	1.7	2.4	3.8
12.2	12.8	9.9					5.0	11.3	12.6
(85) 3.4	(76) 3.2	(85) 3.5	Net Profit + Depr., Dep., Amort./Cur. Mat. L/T/D				(12) 2.1	(31) 3.5	(35) 3.9
1.0	1.3	1.5					.3	1.2	2.9
.0	.0	.0		.0	.0	.0	.0	.1	.1
.2	.2	.2	Fixed/Worth	.2	.1	.3	.1	.2	.2
1.1	1.1	.8		UND	1.0	2.2	.8	.6	.7
.8	.8	.8		.4	.5	1.1	.5	.9	1.0
2.1	2.1	2.0	Debt/Worth	3.2	1.0	4.0	1.5	2.0	2.2
7.3	8.2	6.5		-3.1	5.1	10.6	6.5	5.7	5.2
59.0	57.9	56.9		81.3	66.7	64.1	54.2	51.7	57.2
(738) 23.8	(640) 27.7	(652) 28.4	% Profit Before Taxes/Tangible Net Worth	(30) 19.2	(79) 25.1	(71) 26.7	(140) 24.0	(171) 29.0	(161) 33.9
8.0	9.1	9.7		-11.6	6.4	8.7	5.8	11.1	16.3
18.3	19.4	20.3		38.8	25.2	17.6	18.9	18.3	19.4
6.9	7.9	8.3	% Profit Before Taxes/Total Assets	8.0	12.3	7.7	7.2	7.8	9.9
1.9	2.0	2.4		-7.7	1.1	1.8	1.4	2.5	5.1
258.5	239.5	280.0		UND	878.5	420.0	215.4	202.8	199.1
67.8	57.8	64.8	Sales/Net Fixed Assets	111.0	65.9	53.7	56.3	66.7	70.7
18.2	18.4	19.4		6.0	22.5	19.4	19.4	20.7	20.0
4.3	4.3	4.2		3.4	4.1	4.2	4.1	4.5	4.3
2.8	2.9	2.8	Sales/Total Assets	2.0	3.0	2.6	2.8	3.2	2.8
1.9	2.0	1.9		.9	1.8	1.9	1.9	1.9	2.1
.2	.2	.2		.7	.2	.3	.2	.2	.2
(600) .5	(530) .6	(510) .5	% Depr., Dep., Amort./Sales	(15) 2.7	(46) .5	(53) .8	(116) .6	(143) .5	(137) .4
1.2	1.2	1.3		8.7	2.0	1.5	1.3	1.1	1.1
1.4	1.4	1.2		4.9	3.0	1.4	1.6	1.0	.5
(448) 2.8	(343) 2.9	(376) 2.3	% Officers', Directors' Owners' Comp/Sales	(16) 7.5	(54) 5.0	(51) 2.7	(94) 2.5	(94) 1.7	(67) 1.1
5.4	5.9	5.0		10.9	9.2	5.7	4.8	2.6	2.9
24302522M	18693832M	21829848M	Net Sales ($)	19027M	187138M	345542M	1126265M	3099437M	17052439M
8969752M	7496725M	8407370M	Total Assets ($)	21091M	81723M	157620M	471389M	1254741M	6420806M

M = $ thousand MM = $ million

See Pages 9 through 22 for Explanation of Ratios and Data

Current Data Sorted by Assets							Comparative Historical Data	
			6	3		Type of Statement Unqualified	3	2
	1	2	1			Reviewed	3	5
1	1	3				Compiled	3	3
5	4	1				Tax Returns	6	12
3	7	10	3	1		Other	14	19
4 (4/1-9/30/13)			48 (10/1/13-3/31/14)				4/1/09-3/31/10 ALL	4/1/10-3/31/11 ALL
0-500M	500M-2MM	2-10MM	10-50MM	50-100MM	100-250MM			
9	13	16	10	4		NUMBER OF STATEMENTS	29	41
%	%	%	%	%	%	ASSETS	%	%
	14.1	7.1	9.4		DATA NOT AVAILABLE	Cash & Equivalents	15.5	16.9
	33.8	49.2	28.6			Trade Receivables (net)	33.1	34.1
	28.1	30.1	39.9			Inventory	28.8	25.3
	.3	1.4	4.7			All Other Current	3.5	4.8
	76.3	87.8	82.7			Total Current	80.9	81.1
	12.2	3.8	6.4			Fixed Assets (net)	9.6	10.0
	.5	1.4	8.3			Intangibles (net)	4.9	5.4
	11.0	7.1	2.6			All Other Non-Current	4.6	3.5
	100.0	100.0	100.0			Total	100.0	100.0
						LIABILITIES		
	19.1	9.0	8.0			Notes Payable-Short Term	11.8	10.2
	.2	1.1	1.1			Cur. Mat.-L.T.D.	3.4	7.0
	23.3	27.4	39.7			Trade Payables	23.6	25.3
	.5	.0	.0			Income Taxes Payable	.4	.3
	2.5	8.7	23.5			All Other Current	11.5	14.6
	45.6	46.2	72.3			Total Current	50.6	57.4
	10.5	13.5	9.3			Long-Term Debt	2.7	13.4
	.0	.0	.1			Deferred Taxes	.0	.0
	3.3	7.6	5.3			All Other Non-Current	5.4	2.8
	40.6	32.8	12.9			Net Worth	41.2	26.3
	100.0	100.0	100.0			Total Liabilties & Net Worth	100.0	100.0
						INCOME DATA		
	100.0	100.0	100.0			Net Sales	100.0	100.0
	34.0	25.4	26.6			Gross Profit	33.2	36.2
	29.1	20.5	22.5			Operating Expenses	30.5	31.0
	4.9	4.9	4.1			Operating Profit	2.7	5.3
	.3	-.1	.6			All Other Expenses (net)	.7	1.4
	4.6	5.0	3.5			Profit Before Taxes	2.0	3.8
						RATIOS		
	13.3	3.8	1.8				3.0	3.5
	1.5	2.0	1.3			Current	1.5	1.6
	1.0	1.3	1.2				1.2	1.0
	5.1	2.2	1.1				1.6	2.3
	1.0	1.1	.7			Quick	.8	1.0
	.6	.8	.2				.5	.5
	17 21.9	39 9.4	20 18.7				20 18.4	17 21.6
	24 14.9	43 8.5	33 10.9			Sales/Receivables	35 10.5	45 8.1
	36 10.0	70 5.2	54 6.7				49 7.5	56 6.5
	0 UND	6 58.7	31 11.8				12 31.6	5 68.8
	73 5.0	33 10.9	76 4.8			Cost of Sales/Inventory	56 6.5	36 10.0
	159 2.3	146 2.5	135 2.7				144 2.5	90 4.0
	10 35.5	20 18.2	20 18.6				11 32.8	14 26.3
	27 13.3	45 8.2	36 10.0			Cost of Sales/Payables	31 11.9	28 12.8
	51 7.2	72 5.1	53 6.9				49 7.4	48 7.6
	4.3	3.0	11.2				4.8	5.2
	23.8	5.8	16.6			Sales/Working Capital	11.2	10.7
	NM	34.5	26.9				68.2	58.8
	16.3	27.1					34.2	16.8
	(11) 6.3	(13) 12.8				EBIT/Interest	(24) 5.2	(34) 5.2
	3.1	2.6					-1.2	1.4
						Net Profit + Depr., Dep., Amort./Cur. Mat. L/T/D		
	.0	.0	.3				.1	.1
	.1	.1	.6			Fixed/Worth	.2	.2
	.2	.3	NM				.7	.8
	.8	.6	2.5				.7	.7
	1.8	2.0	3.0			Debt/Worth	1.9	1.4
	3.4	5.9	NM				5.2	6.6
	48.3	53.0					47.0	79.1
	18.4	(14) 33.0				% Profit Before Taxes/Tangible Net Worth	(25) 6.1	(37) 30.1
	10.9	15.6					-7.0	7.1
	13.2	18.2	15.9				14.2	30.7
	6.3	12.5	6.9			% Profit Before Taxes/Total Assets	3.6	9.4
	3.6	1.1	3.0				-2.7	1.9
	UND	575.3	138.9				211.3	243.5
	66.8	113.2	92.8			Sales/Net Fixed Assets	47.2	44.7
	19.2	77.7	27.0				20.1	24.1
	6.9	4.2	3.9				5.2	5.5
	2.5	2.4	3.0			Sales/Total Assets	3.2	3.2
	1.8	1.6	1.6				2.2	2.4
		.1					.4	.5
		(12) .3				% Depr., Dep., Amort./Sales	(18) 1.3	(29) .9
		.5					2.0	1.3
							.6	1.4
						% Officers', Directors' Owners' Comp/Sales	(11) 4.2	(19) 3.0
							5.3	6.5
15826M	73957M	284205M	801578M	1170013M		Net Sales ($)	601557M	1368426M
2069M	17014M	70226M	230469M	278766M		Total Assets ($)	179131M	423903M

M = $ thousand MM = $ million

See Pages 9 through 22 for Explanation of Ratios and Data

Comparative Historical Data				Current Data Sorted by Sales					
			Type of Statement						
8	8	9	Unqualified					1	8
19	4	4	Reviewed			1	1	1	1
6	3	5	Compiled		1	1	1	1	1
9	6	10	Tax Returns	1	4	3	1	1	
37	24	24	Other	1	6	4	3	5	5
4/1/11-3/31/12 ALL	4/1/12-3/31/13 ALL	4/1/13-3/31/14 ALL		4 (4/1-9/30/13)		48 (10/1/13-3/31/14)			
				0-1MM	1-3MM	3-5MM	5-10MM	10-25MM	25MM & OVER
79	45	52	**NUMBER OF STATEMENTS**	2	11	9	6	9	15
%	%	%	**ASSETS**	%	%	%	%	%	%
14.8	13.7	14.1	Cash & Equivalents		19.3				6.5
30.6	30.6	38.7	Trade Receivables (net)		31.2				46.7
24.3	26.3	28.1	Inventory		28.2				26.6
5.1	4.8	2.1	All Other Current		.1				3.5
74.8	75.4	82.8	Total Current		78.8				83.3
8.9	12.0	7.4	Fixed Assets (net)		8.8				7.1
6.9	5.0	3.1	Intangibles (net)		1.4				4.4
9.4	7.5	6.7	All Other Non-Current		10.9				5.2
100.0	100.0	100.0	Total		100.0				100.0
			LIABILITIES						
10.3	11.5	15.9	Notes Payable-Short Term		16.2				11.5
1.2	1.7	2.7	Cur. Mat.-L.T.D.		8.7				1.1
22.9	23.7	25.5	Trade Payables		17.0				25.7
.3	.1	.3	Income Taxes Payable		.0				.0
10.1	9.2	11.7	All Other Current		7.9				18.5
44.9	46.2	56.1	Total Current		49.8				56.8
8.8	17.8	15.1	Long-Term Debt		20.4				9.6
.1	.2	.0	Deferred Taxes		.0				.1
4.6	6.4	6.9	All Other Non-Current		8.3				3.6
41.6	29.4	21.9	Net Worth		21.5				29.9
100.0	100.0	100.0	Total Liabilties & Net Worth		100.0				100.0
			INCOME DATA						
100.0	100.0	100.0	Net Sales		100.0				100.0
31.1	35.3	27.5	Gross Profit		34.5				20.0
26.1	29.1	23.5	Operating Expenses		29.8				17.1
5.0	6.3	4.1	Operating Profit		4.7				2.9
.5	.4	.1	All Other Expenses (net)		-.4				.7
4.5	5.9	4.0	Profit Before Taxes		5.1				2.2
			RATIOS						
3.0	3.6	3.4			8.4				1.9
1.5	1.7	1.6	Current		1.5				1.4
1.1	1.2	1.2			.9				1.2
1.7	2.3	1.8			8.4				1.3
1.0	1.0	1.0	Quick		.5				1.0
.7	.6	.5			.4				.5
14 26.4	**26** 13.8	**20** 18.5			**11** 33.1				**23** 16.0
33 11.0	**38** 9.6	**38** 9.5	Sales/Receivables		**32** 11.5				**32** 11.3
52 7.0	**59** 6.2	**58** 6.3			**49** 7.4				**51** 7.2
1 285.6	**4** 97.2	**0** 930.9			**0** UND				**3** 138.1
35 10.4	**44** 8.3	**30** 12.2	Cost of Sales/Inventory		**73** 5.0				**13** 27.1
78 4.7	**85** 4.3	**111** 3.3			**152** 2.4				**85** 4.3
8 45.5	**10** 36.1	**10** 35.3			**14** 25.3				**10** 36.1
26 14.0	**30** 12.0	**28** 12.9	Cost of Sales/Payables		**29** 12.5				**20** 18.2
54 6.8	**63** 5.8	**52** 7.0			**51** 7.1				**41** 9.0
5.8	4.7	4.9			4.8				11.6
14.0	8.9	14.3	Sales/Working Capital		7.3				21.2
67.7	40.8	54.1			-19.0				35.2
59.1	32.6	16.1							15.9
(67) 13.1	(36) 10.6	(41) 5.8	EBIT/Interest						5.8
3.5	2.8	2.0							3.1
			Net Profit + Depr., Dep., Amort./Cur. Mat. L/T/D						
.1	.1	.0			.0				.0
.2	.2	.1	Fixed/Worth		.0				.4
.5	1.6	.6			.3				.7
.8	.6	1.1			.5				2.0
1.7	1.4	2.5	Debt/Worth		3.2				2.8
6.4	43.7	6.3			6.0				9.6
77.7	68.7	57.9							105.1
(70) 32.3	(36) 43.8	(45) 32.4	% Profit Before Taxes/Tangible Net Worth						19.4
10.5	15.2	14.3							13.5
24.7	27.8	16.4			14.4				10.6
11.9	12.0	9.1	% Profit Before Taxes/Total Assets		11.9				6.8
3.2	2.8	2.4			2.1				3.7
170.1	116.6	999.8			UND				391.0
83.1	55.1	113.3	Sales/Net Fixed Assets		UND				109.8
29.3	19.3	43.8			16.5				29.7
5.1	4.5	4.8			4.4				6.8
3.2	2.8	3.3	Sales/Total Assets		3.1				3.9
2.2	1.9	2.0			1.8				2.4
.2	.2	.2							.0
(57) .4	(28) .5	(33) .3	% Depr., Dep., Amort./Sales						(14) .2
.8	.9	.8							.5
1.3	1.9	1.2							
(32) 4.3	(14) 3.4	(23) 3.5	% Officers', Directors' Owners' Comp/Sales						
8.6	6.1	6.6							
3209762M	1737056M	2345579M	Net Sales ($)	1076M	18815M	34365M	41690M	151608M	2098025M
1335527M	836460M	598544M	Total Assets ($)	140M	9340M	16882M	9613M	68865M	493704M

M = $ thousand MM = $ million

See Pages 9 through 22 for Explanation of Ratios and Data

Current Data Sorted by Assets							Comparative Historical Data	
Type of Statement								
Unqualified			1	6	2	4	19	14
Reviewed	1	3	13	5	1		23	24
Compiled	6	7	14	1			29	25
Tax Returns	24	25	12				40	65
Other	7	27	27	13	7	1	64	69
	24 (4/1-9/30/13)		183 (10/1/13-3/31/14)				4/1/09-3/31/10 ALL	4/1/10-3/31/11 ALL
	0-500M	500M-2MM	2-10MM	10-50MM	50-100MM	100-250MM		
NUMBER OF STATEMENTS	38	62	67	25	10	5	175	197
ASSETS	%	%	%	%	%	%	%	%
Cash & Equivalents	28.1	18.0	9.7	10.8	8.3		12.2	15.1
Trade Receivables (net)	32.1	37.9	43.3	36.3	42.7		36.0	34.0
Inventory	16.0	26.0	28.4	24.6	9.8		25.2	25.4
All Other Current	4.0	3.8	1.9	7.4	4.7		5.1	3.3
Total Current	80.2	85.8	83.3	79.0	65.5		78.5	77.7
Fixed Assets (net)	5.2	8.9	8.1	8.9	9.9		10.7	10.8
Intangibles (net)	8.5	.7	2.5	5.9	18.9		2.3	3.5
All Other Non-Current	6.2	4.6	6.1	6.2	5.7		8.5	8.0
Total	100.0	100.0	100.0	100.0	100.0		100.0	100.0
LIABILITIES								
Notes Payable-Short Term	13.3	13.6	19.4	13.1	7.2		16.7	16.9
Cur. Mat.-L.T.D.	4.3	.9	1.8	1.7	1.6		3.8	2.6
Trade Payables	16.1	24.5	29.1	26.4	36.5		24.5	22.8
Income Taxes Payable	.1	.6	.2	.2	.0		.1	.1
All Other Current	12.7	10.8	7.6	11.3	6.3		10.5	11.8
Total Current	46.6	50.3	58.1	52.7	51.6		55.6	54.1
Long-Term Debt	5.5	7.1	4.9	5.9	20.2		8.8	8.9
Deferred Taxes	.0	.0	.1	.3	.0		.1	.1
All Other Non-Current	2.2	4.1	5.5	4.3	.3		4.6	7.6
Net Worth	45.7	38.5	31.4	36.8	27.9		31.0	29.2
Total Liabilties & Net Worth	100.0	100.0	100.0	100.0	100.0		100.0	100.0
INCOME DATA								
Net Sales	100.0	100.0	100.0	100.0	100.0		100.0	100.0
Gross Profit	31.3	30.7	22.5	21.6	42.9		26.4	26.5
Operating Expenses	24.3	25.5	18.0	18.2	39.0		22.7	22.2
Operating Profit	7.0	5.2	4.5	3.5	3.9		3.8	4.4
All Other Expenses (net)	.5	.1	.6	.1	3.0		.6	.4
Profit Before Taxes	6.5	5.1	3.9	3.4	.9		3.2	4.0
RATIOS								
Current	5.1	2.7	2.1	2.3	2.3		2.3	2.5
	2.1	2.0	1.4	1.6	1.2		1.5	1.6
	1.1	1.1	1.1	1.2	1.0		1.1	1.1
Quick	2.8	1.9	1.4	1.3	2.2		1.6	1.6
	1.6	1.3	(66) .8	.9	1.0		.9	1.0
	.7	.6	.6	.6	.6		.6	.5
Sales/Receivables	**0** UND	**15** 24.4	**24** 15.4	**21** 17.5	**30** 12.0		**14** 25.3	**11** 32.4
	14 25.5	**31** 11.9	**41** 8.8	**51** 7.2	**61** 6.0		**35** 10.5	**32** 11.3
	33 11.0	**56** 6.5	**57** 6.4	**66** 5.5	**96** 3.8		**59** 6.2	**54** 6.8
Cost of Sales/Inventory	**0** UND	**0** UND	**2** 150.4	**1** 360.9	**0** UND		**2** 240.2	**1** 343.6
	3 119.3	**13** 28.7	**33** 11.1	**28** 12.9	**3** 108.0		**28** 13.2	**27** 13.3
	29 12.8	**65** 5.6	**76** 4.8	**96** 3.8	**99** 3.7		**69** 5.3	**78** 4.7
Cost of Sales/Payables	**0** UND	**2** 232.4	**18** 20.6	**10** 37.1	**20** 18.5		**9** 39.4	**7** 53.7
	7 54.7	**28** 13.1	**36** 10.2	**27** 13.4	**74** 4.9		**25** 14.5	**24** 15.4
	37 9.9	**57** 6.4	**61** 6.0	**61** 6.0	**215** 1.7		**51** 7.1	**49** 7.4
Sales/Working Capital	9.7	5.7	7.7	5.8	8.0		6.5	6.1
	20.0	11.5	14.6	10.1	41.7		15.0	14.7
	230.5	139.8	54.2	38.4	NM		77.8	71.9
EBIT/Interest	70.0	60.4	35.7	20.8			13.5	16.4
	(22) 16.7	(41) 10.8	(58) 9.0	(19) 6.7			(145) 4.3	(159) 5.4
	3.1	2.8	2.5	4.1			1.8	2.0
Net Profit + Depr., Dep., Amort./Cur. Mat. L/T/D							4.3	10.1
							(20) 1.7	(24) 2.5
							.7	.6
Fixed/Worth	.0	.0	.0	.0	.0		.0	.0
	.0	.1	.1	.1	1.4		.2	.2
	.4	.6	.9	.5	-.2		.9	1.0
Debt/Worth	.4	.7	1.0	1.0	2.0		.9	1.0
	1.0	1.7	2.7	2.0	7.7		2.4	2.3
	NM	6.3	9.3	11.4	-8.4		6.2	8.5
% Profit Before Taxes/Tangible Net Worth	151.5	78.3	66.5	67.8			56.1	80.3
	(29) 90.0	(56) 50.4	(58) 36.7	(23) 37.0			(157) 18.9	(164) 33.0
	40.1	17.2	12.0	8.9			4.6	10.4
% Profit Before Taxes/Total Assets	63.2	31.2	22.2	15.3	8.5		14.9	24.6
	29.9	11.3	9.2	8.1	1.5		6.7	8.4
	11.5	4.3	2.2	3.0	-2.0		1.8	2.0
Sales/Net Fixed Assets	UND	999.8	584.7	999.8	999.8		420.0	706.1
	999.8	172.5	119.9	123.8	42.2		75.8	97.9
	95.9	48.1	36.8	21.9	6.6		18.5	27.0
Sales/Total Assets	10.3	5.3	5.8	5.4	5.5		6.1	6.5
	6.4	3.9	3.7	3.1	2.0		3.3	3.4
	3.8	2.4	2.6	1.3	.5		2.0	2.1
% Depr., Dep., Amort./Sales	.4	.1	.1	.1			.1	.1
	(10) .8	(36) .3	(47) .3	(20) .8			(125) .5	(127) .4
	2.2	.6	.6	2.0			1.1	1.1
% Officers', Directors' Owners' Comp/Sales	1.5	1.4	1.0				1.2	1.1
	(19) 3.0	(35) 3.7	(26) 1.7				(78) 2.4	(102) 2.2
	6.5	8.1	4.4				5.1	4.7
Net Sales ($)	87641M	352774M	1250267M	1919781M	2695752M	2656114M	12675131M	6164022M
Total Assets ($)	9948M	75894M	292699M	539406M	721160M	820233M	1977019M	1883801M

M = $ thousand MM = $ million

See Pages 9 through 22 for Explanation of Ratios and Data

Comparative Historical Data				Current Data Sorted by Sales					
			Type of Statement						
18	16	13	Unqualified					1	12
22	30	23	Reviewed		2		5	8	8
42	40	28	Compiled	1	5	5	3	10	4
51	65	61	Tax Returns	10	14	15	11	7	4
70	84	82	Other	3	13	10	15	18	23
4/1/11-3/31/12 ALL	4/1/12-3/31/13 ALL	4/1/13-3/31/14 ALL		24 (4/1-9/30/13)			183 (10/1/13-3/31/14)		
				0-1MM	1-3MM	3-5MM	5-10MM	10-25MM	25MM & OVER
203	235	207	NUMBER OF STATEMENTS	14	34	30	34	44	51
%	%	%	**ASSETS**	%	%	%	%	%	%
14.6	16.2	15.5	Cash & Equivalents	16.4	21.9	23.8	19.4	9.2	8.9
33.9	35.1	38.5	Trade Receivables (net)	35.8	27.1	32.9	36.6	46.8	44.4
24.3	26.6	24.0	Inventory	32.0	22.2	17.9	24.0	28.1	23.2
3.8	2.4	3.7	All Other Current	.0	8.2	3.4	3.0	2.0	3.9
76.5	80.3	81.8	Total Current	84.2	79.4	78.0	83.0	86.2	80.4
11.4	9.2	8.0	Fixed Assets (net)	5.0	10.5	9.2	8.3	6.9	7.3
3.1	3.0	4.6	Intangibles (net)	7.7	5.5	2.3	.8	2.7	8.8
8.9	7.5	5.5	All Other Non-Current	3.0	4.6	10.6	7.9	4.2	3.5
100.0	100.0	100.0	Total	100.0	100.0	100.0	100.0	100.0	100.0
			LIABILITIES						
13.1	16.0	15.0	Notes Payable-Short Term	16.1	11.5	11.2	18.2	16.1	16.2
3.5	2.8	1.9	Cur. Mat.-L.T.D.	6.9	.8	2.5	1.0	1.9	1.5
22.6	24.9	25.1	Trade Payables	15.3	15.6	21.0	25.6	34.0	28.7
.0	.1	.3	Income Taxes Payable	.0	1.1	.1	.1	.3	.2
10.9	12.1	9.9	All Other Current	6.9	13.7	15.1	7.0	9.1	7.9
50.1	55.9	52.3	Total Current	45.2	42.7	49.9	51.9	61.4	54.4
11.2	7.0	6.9	Long-Term Debt	7.1	11.6	4.6	3.7	4.1	9.7
.1	.1	.1	Deferred Taxes	.0	.0	.0	.1	.1	.1
5.7	4.9	4.0	All Other Non-Current	5.1	5.0	5.8	1.7	4.0	3.5
33.0	32.2	36.7	Net Worth	42.6	40.7	39.7	42.6	30.4	32.2
100.0	100.0	100.0	Total Liabilities & Net Worth	100.0	100.0	100.0	100.0	100.0	100.0
			INCOME DATA						
100.0	100.0	100.0	Net Sales	100.0	100.0	100.0	100.0	100.0	100.0
26.7	23.5	27.4	Gross Profit	36.2	40.8	28.5	29.1	20.6	20.2
22.3	18.9	22.4	Operating Expenses	27.9	33.8	23.7	24.0	16.3	16.9
4.4	4.7	5.0	Operating Profit	8.3	7.0	4.7	5.1	4.4	3.3
.4	.0	.5	All Other Expenses (net)	.6	1.1	.1	.1	.2	1.0
4.0	4.6	4.4	Profit Before Taxes	7.7	5.9	4.6	5.0	4.2	2.3
			RATIOS						
2.3	2.7	2.6	Current	6.3	3.3	2.7	3.0	2.1	2.1
1.6	1.5	1.7		2.0	2.1	1.9	1.8	1.4	1.6
1.1	1.1	1.1		1.1	1.1	1.2	1.0	1.1	1.1
1.6	1.6	1.9	Quick	5.0	2.5	2.2	2.1	1.3	1.4
1.0	.9	(206) 1.0		1.4	(33) 1.3	1.3	1.1	.8	.9
.6	.5	.6		.5	.5	.6	.7	.6	.6
12 30.8	**9** 41.2	**16** 22.2	Sales/Receivables	**0** UND	**6** 63.4	**5** 67.6	**24** 14.9	**22** 16.5	**17** 20.9
28 13.1	**28** 12.9	**33** 10.9		**30** 12.3	**25** 14.7	**21** 17.6	**41** 9.0	**40** 9.2	**41** 8.8
51 7.2	**45** 8.1	**57** 6.4		**79** 4.6	**43** 8.4	**58** 6.3	**63** 5.8	**54** 6.7	**64** 5.7
0 999.8	**0** 999.8	**0** UND	Cost of Sales/Inventory	**0** UND	**0** UND	**0** UND	**0** UND	**0** UND	**2** 241.4
21 17.4	**25** 14.6	**16** 23.0		**76** 4.8	**10** 36.2	**6** 64.3	**18** 20.6	**26** 14.1	**19** 19.5
70 5.2	**68** 5.4	**68** 5.4		**126** 2.9	**65** 5.6	**28** 12.9	**89** 4.1	**76** 4.8	**54** 6.8
8 45.6	**5** 71.6	**7** 54.7	Cost of Sales/Payables	**0** UND	**0** UND	**0** UND	**12** 30.7	**17** 21.2	**9** 39.8
25 14.5	**20** 18.3	**28** 13.1		**27** 13.4	**17** 21.4	**21** 17.5	**36** 10.0	**33** 11.1	**23** 16.1
49 7.4	**42** 8.7	**58** 6.3		**65** 5.6	**51** 7.1	**57** 6.4	**62** 5.9	**61** 6.0	**58** 6.3
7.4	8.2	6.7	Sales/Working Capital	3.2	5.7	5.7	6.4	8.2	8.1
16.6	16.1	14.6		7.4	11.3	14.5	13.1	18.3	18.7
60.8	94.0	75.2		57.2	NM	230.5	79.1	88.4	68.8
32.2	32.1	39.5	EBIT/Interest		59.8	49.9	96.3	45.5	20.3
(176) 6.5	(188) 8.8	(154) 7.3			(21) 10.8	(18) 13.6	(29) 11.0	(35) 12.1	(44) 6.5
2.4	2.2	2.5			4.0	2.4	1.8	1.8	2.9
11.3	27.6	14.8	Net Profit + Depr., Dep., Amort./Cur. Mat. L/T/D						26.0
(27) 3.3	(26) 11.0	(16) 4.0							(10) 4.0
2.1	3.0	1.5							1.8
.0	.0	.0	Fixed/Worth	.0	.0	.0	.0	.0	.0
.1	.1	.1		.0	.0	.1	.1	.1	.2
.9	.8	.8		.7	.7	.5	.7	.9	1.3
.9	.7	.8	Debt/Worth	.2	.7	.5	.4	1.2	1.2
1.7	2.3	2.0		2.7	2.0	1.1	1.3	2.8	2.2
6.6	11.8	9.0		NM	9.1	6.2	6.3	8.7	15.9
62.0	83.5	91.5	% Profit Before Taxes/Tangible Net Worth	90.0	141.4	105.7	73.0	111.1	65.2
(176) 27.2	(204) 34.3	(177) 44.7		(11) 36.0	(28) 55.3	(25) 51.5	(30) 37.6	(40) 46.2	(43) 28.1
6.6	11.8	13.8		10.6	19.1	13.7	3.6	17.1	12.2
20.5	27.0	28.0	% Profit Before Taxes/Total Assets	32.0	45.4	49.9	31.7	27.7	14.9
8.8	9.7	10.6		17.6	14.3	15.8	9.9	13.2	7.3
2.2	2.8	2.9		1.1	4.4	5.2	1.3	2.8	2.7
999.8	999.8	999.8	Sales/Net Fixed Assets	UND	UND	933.9	635.0	888.6	999.8
120.0	153.8	164.1		UND	158.1	147.1	189.1	144.4	122.7
34.3	36.2	36.8		21.2	36.2	52.0	39.4	62.8	26.7
7.0	7.6	6.2	Sales/Total Assets	4.9	6.3	7.7	4.9	7.2	6.9
3.9	4.2	3.9		2.8	3.7	4.5	3.4	4.4	4.6
2.3	2.4	2.4		1.6	1.9	2.4	2.3	2.7	2.5
.1	.1	.1	% Depr., Dep., Amort./Sales		.3	.1	.1	.1	.1
(126) .4	(138) .4	(123) .4			(16) .8	(17) .3	(24) .2	(27) .3	(34) .4
1.0	.9	1.0			2.0	.6	.6	.7	1.3
1.0	1.1	1.1	% Officers', Directors' Owners' Comp/Sales		3.2	1.3	1.4	.8	.3
(92) 2.2	(101) 2.2	(88) 2.6			(14) 5.7	(18) 2.3	(17) 2.5	(17) 1.8	(15) .6
4.9	4.2	5.5			13.0	5.7	5.8	3.7	1.5
7701262M	**13808063M**	**8962329M**	Net Sales ($)	**8142M**	**67478M**	**116450M**	**249004M**	**706025M**	**7815230M**
1871606M	**2609217M**	**2459340M**	Total Assets ($)	**3315M**	**27802M**	**33750M**	**110377M**	**195955M**	**2088141M**

M = $ thousand MM = $ million

See Pages 9 through 22 for Explanation of Ratios and Data

RETAIL TRADE

Current Data Sorted by Assets							Comparative Historical Data	
						Type of Statement		
1		12	48	15	7	Unqualified	115	87
	3	82	156	22	12	Reviewed	380	328
	11	43	29	1	1	Compiled	113	109
1	16	115	127	1	1	Tax Returns	335	290
3	29	577	747	59	33	Other	1747	1671
	101 (4/1-9/30/13)		2,051 (10/1/13-3/31/14)				4/1/09-3/31/10 ALL	4/1/10-3/31/11 ALL
0-500M	500M-2MM	2-10MM	10-50MM	50-100MM	100-250MM			
5	59	829	1107	98	54	NUMBER OF STATEMENTS	2690	2485
%	%	%	%	%	%	**ASSETS**	%	%
	11.5	11.0	12.6	11.8	11.6	Cash & Equivalents	12.3	12.2
	12.2	6.9	7.2	7.6	7.7	Trade Receivables (net)	7.7	7.3
	53.6	66.7	59.5	50.4	44.3	Inventory	54.7	57.7
	2.0	1.6	1.7	1.6	1.7	All Other Current	2.4	2.5
	79.4	86.2	81.0	71.5	65.4	Total Current	77.1	79.7
	7.2	7.1	10.0	15.6	21.0	Fixed Assets (net)	11.5	10.5
	2.8	2.1	3.0	5.2	5.7	Intangibles (net)	3.9	3.3
	10.7	4.6	6.0	7.7	7.8	All Other Non-Current	7.4	6.5
	100.0	100.0	100.0	100.0	100.0	Total	100.0	100.0
						LIABILITIES		
	33.0	56.5	53.6	40.7	35.2	Notes Payable-Short Term	46.0	48.8
	4.2	1.5	1.2	1.8	2.7	Cur. Mat.-L.T.D.	1.8	1.7
	10.0	3.7	3.8	4.8	10.0	Trade Payables	5.1	5.0
	.0	.1	.0	.1	.0	Income Taxes Payable	.1	.1
	12.2	9.5	10.1	10.5	9.8	All Other Current	11.0	9.9
	59.5	71.3	68.7	58.0	57.7	Total Current	63.9	65.5
	9.9	4.3	6.2	10.9	16.1	Long-Term Debt	9.3	7.9
	.0	.1	.1	.4	.6	Deferred Taxes	.1	.1
	8.1	3.8	2.7	4.1	1.7	All Other Non-Current	4.8	4.5
	22.5	20.5	22.3	26.6	23.9	Net Worth	21.9	22.0
	100.0	100.0	100.0	100.0	100.0	Total Liabilties & Net Worth	100.0	100.0
						INCOME DATA		
	100.0	100.0	100.0	100.0	100.0	Net Sales	100.0	100.0
	23.3	11.7	11.0	12.1	14.1	Gross Profit	14.0	13.1
	20.6	11.5	10.5	10.5	12.0	Operating Expenses	14.3	12.9
	2.7	.1	.4	1.6	2.1	Operating Profit	-.3	.3
	.3	-1.2	-1.4	-.7	-.5	All Other Expenses (net)	-.9	-1.0
	2.4	1.3	1.8	2.3	2.6	Profit Before Taxes	.6	1.3
						RATIOS		
	2.4	1.3	1.3	1.3	1.3		1.4	1.4
	1.4	1.2	1.2	1.2	1.1	Current	1.2	1.2
	1.1	1.1	1.1	1.1	1.0		1.1	1.1
	1.0	.3	.4	.4	.4		.4	.4
	.3	(827) .2	.3	.3	.3	Quick	(2688) .3	(2478) .3
	.1	.1	.2	.2	.2		.2	.2
	2 163.3	**3** 121.6	**4** 94.2	**4** 81.9	**4** 87.3		**3** 114.4	**3** 118.5
	7 56.1	**5** 70.0	**6** 57.0	**7** 51.0	**11** 34.6	Sales/Receivables	**6** 63.5	**6** 64.4
	19 19.3	**9** 40.2	**10** 36.5	**15** 24.9	**16** 23.5		**10** 36.1	**10** 37.4
	35 10.5	**61** 6.0	**58** 6.3	**57** 6.4	**57** 6.4		**51** 7.2	**54** 6.8
	74 4.9	**81** 4.5	**73** 5.0	**72** 5.1	**66** 5.5	Cost of Sales/Inventory	**66** 5.6	**68** 5.4
	107 3.4	**104** 3.5	**91** 4.0	**87** 4.2	**85** 4.3		**85** 4.3	**87** 4.2
	1 431.4	**2** 237.0	**2** 191.6	**2** 154.8	**4** 93.0		**2** 165.4	**2** 163.2
	5 67.3	**3** 134.7	**3** 115.2	**4** 88.2	**6** 62.0	Cost of Sales/Payables	**4** 95.6	**4** 94.1
	11 32.1	**5** 73.1	**5** 67.1	**7** 50.1	**12** 29.2		**7** 56.0	**6** 57.6
	8.1	14.7	17.7	14.6	19.1		14.0	14.7
	16.1	24.4	29.5	28.4	34.0	Sales/Working Capital	26.8	26.9
	46.3	55.3	71.9	62.5	94.5		99.1	69.5
	11.0	10.3	25.3	18.5	18.4		6.3	9.8
	(39) 2.0	(507) 3.8	(695) 7.3	(72) 6.4	(45) 6.3	EBIT/Interest	(1830) 2.3	(1650) 3.4
	-.9	1.3	2.6	2.7	3.0		.8	1.5
		17.3	9.0	5.8	13.8		4.3	8.6
		(31) 5.0	(58) 2.7	(14) 2.9	(12) 6.4	Net Profit + Depr., Dep., Amort./Cur. Mat. L/T/D	(157) 1.8	(154) 3.0
		2.2	1.2	1.0	2.1		.5	1.2
	.1	.1	.1	.3	.4		.1	.1
	.2	.3	.4	.7	1.0	Fixed/Worth	.4	.4
	.6	.7	1.0	1.6	2.1		1.8	1.2
	1.0	2.5	2.6	2.8	2.7		2.1	2.2
	3.7	4.5	4.5	4.8	4.3	Debt/Worth	4.3	4.2
	30.9	10.7	9.4	9.0	9.9		12.6	10.7
	72.4	42.2	53.2	52.3	73.6		34.5	43.7
	(45) 17.8	(742) 20.1	(1033) 29.8	(93) 26.6	(53) 33.7	% Profit Before Taxes/Tangible Net Worth	(2283) 14.3	(2174) 22.1
	-.9	5.4	14.7	16.3	16.3		1.0	7.0
	14.7	7.7	9.2	10.3	8.4		6.9	8.2
	3.6	3.6	5.3	5.5	4.8	% Profit Before Taxes/Total Assets	2.7	4.2
	-1.5	.8	2.5	2.8	2.9		-.4	1.1
	404.1	203.1	144.0	71.7	57.5		130.2	158.9
	106.2	96.2	62.0	28.6	12.8	Sales/Net Fixed Assets	57.4	65.1
	36.6	40.3	23.6	9.9	7.4		23.2	26.4
	4.5	4.2	4.1	3.4	3.4		4.3	4.3
	3.3	3.4	3.3	3.0	2.8	Sales/Total Assets	3.4	3.5
	2.4	2.8	2.7	2.3	2.1		2.6	2.7
	.2	.1	.1	.1	.2		.2	.1
	(37) .4	(671) .2	(970) .2	(90) .3	(45) .4	% Depr., Dep., Amort./Sales	(2319) .3	(2099) .3
	.6	.4	.4	.7	.8		.6	.5
	.8	.3	.2	.1	.1		.3	.3
	(29) 1.8	(481) .6	(633) .4	(37) .3	(14) .1	% Officers', Directors' Owners' Comp/Sales	(1541) .6	(1468) .6
	2.8	1.1	.7	.6	.6		1.2	1.2
7377M	**361238M**	**18744489M**	**75511534M**	**20168595M**	**22297003M**	Net Sales ($)	**107537821M**	**112010036M**
1392M	**79085M**	**5283027M**	**22246473M**	**6840905M**	**8449295M**	Total Assets ($)	**34551873M**	**34185159M**

M = $ thousand MM = $ million

See Pages 9 through 22 for Explanation of Ratios and Data

Comparative Historical Data | Current Data Sorted by Sales

			Type of Statement						
91	81	83	Unqualified	1			1	12	69
334	285	275	Reviewed		1	6	9	36	223
120	93	85	Compiled	2	6	3	6	29	39
306	287	261	Tax Returns	2	6	11	14	53	175
1689	1376	1448	Other	1	14	23	59	333	1018
4/1/11-3/31/12 ALL	4/1/12-3/31/13 ALL	4/1/13-3/31/14 ALL		101 (4/1-9/30/13)		2,051 (10/1/13-3/31/14)			
				0-1MM	1-3MM	3-5MM	5-10MM	10-25MM	25MM & OVER
2540	2122	2152	NUMBER OF STATEMENTS	6	27	43	89	463	1524
%	%	%	ASSETS	%	%	%	%	%	%
13.3	12.4	11.9	Cash & Equivalents		13.3	12.1	10.7	10.5	12.4
7.8	7.3	7.3	Trade Receivables (net)		23.2	6.3	9.7	5.8	7.3
57.1	59.5	61.2	Inventory		34.9	59.8	61.5	66.9	60.1
2.5	2.4	1.7	All Other Current		.6	3.6	2.6	1.5	1.7
80.6	81.6	82.1	Total Current		71.9	81.8	84.5	84.7	81.6
9.6	9.7	9.4	Fixed Assets (net)		17.4	11.4	7.7	7.8	9.6
3.3	3.2	2.8	Intangibles (net)		3.3	2.2	1.2	2.4	3.1
6.5	5.5	5.7	All Other Non-Current		7.4	4.7	6.6	5.1	5.7
100.0	100.0	100.0	Total		100.0	100.0	100.0	100.0	100.0
			LIABILITIES						
47.9	49.6	53.0	Notes Payable-Short Term		33.6	42.0	46.7	56.0	53.3
1.7	1.7	1.5	Cur. Mat.-L.T.D.		5.3	1.4	2.2	1.5	1.3
5.0	4.5	4.1	Trade Payables		8.4	4.6	6.4	4.2	3.9
.1	.1	.1	Income Taxes Payable		.0	.6	.1	.1	.0
10.4	10.6	10.0	All Other Current		13.6	13.1	9.3	9.5	10.0
65.0	66.5	68.6	Total Current		61.0	61.7	64.7	71.2	68.5
7.3	7.6	6.1	Long-Term Debt		19.2	7.3	7.0	4.7	6.2
.1	.2	.1	Deferred Taxes		.7	.0	.1	.1	.1
4.1	3.9	3.3	All Other Non-Current		7.1	8.3	5.7	3.5	2.9
23.4	21.9	21.8	Net Worth		12.2	22.7	22.4	20.6	22.3
100.0	100.0	100.0	Total Liabilities & Net Worth		100.0	100.0	100.0	100.0	100.0
			INCOME DATA						
100.0	100.0	100.0	Net Sales		100.0	100.0	100.0	100.0	100.0
12.5	12.3	11.8	Gross Profit		34.1	19.5	14.8	11.5	10.9
12.1	11.9	11.3	Operating Expenses		27.6	18.9	14.5	11.6	10.4
.4	.4	.5	Operating Profit		6.5	.6	.4	-.1	.5
-1.1	-1.1	-1.2	All Other Expenses (net)		.8	-.4	-.9	-1.3	-1.3
1.5	1.5	1.7	Profit Before Taxes		5.6	1.0	1.2	1.2	1.8
			RATIOS						
1.4	1.4	1.3			2.1	2.0	1.5	1.3	1.3
1.2	1.2	1.2	Current		1.2	1.3	1.2	1.2	1.2
1.1	1.1	1.1			1.0	1.0	1.1	1.1	1.1
.4	.4	.4			1.9	.6	.4	.3	.4
(2539) .3	(2120) .3	(2150) .3	Quick		.4	.2	.3	(462) .2	(1523) .3
.2	.2	.2			.2	.1	.1	.1	.2
3 112.0	3 120.5	3 106.5			2 168.5	2 199.0	3 139.8	3 122.3	4 99.1
6 61.7	6 61.3	6 61.0	Sales/Receivables		20 18.3	7 54.0	6 57.2	5 70.0	6 59.4
10 37.4	11 34.4	10 36.3			49 7.4	15 24.2	19 19.1	9 40.5	10 36.7
48 7.6	54 6.7	59 6.2			8 48.0	66 5.5	79 4.6	72 5.1	56 6.5
64 5.7	70 5.2	74 4.9	Cost of Sales/Inventory		74 4.9	101 3.6	122 3.0	89 4.1	70 5.2
83 4.4	91 4.0	96 3.8			192 1.9	192 1.9	146 2.5	111 3.3	87 4.2
2 166.6	2 177.6	2 202.4			2 176.8	2 224.2	2 171.4	2 219.5	2 196.0
4 97.2	4 104.0	3 117.4	Cost of Sales/Payables		7 55.4	6 65.5	5 67.8	3 128.2	3 117.9
6 59.3	6 61.5	5 66.5			19 18.8	11 32.1	14 25.5	6 64.4	5 70.9
14.9	15.1	16.3			4.0	7.5	6.8	14.2	18.3
25.8	25.9	27.4	Sales/Working Capital		12.2	12.5	15.5	23.3	29.7
61.0	55.9	65.7			39.9	465.3	36.4	51.1	71.3
11.9	12.1	18.6			14.9	8.1	5.6	9.3	23.8
(1654) 4.4	(1414) 4.1	(1361) 5.5	EBIT/Interest		(17) 1.8	(29) 2.5	(56) 2.6	(291) 3.3	(965) 6.9
1.9	1.7	2.0			-.3	.1	.8	1.3	2.6
5.7	9.9	10.2						19.4	9.3
(131) 2.3	(115) 2.8	(115) 4.1	Net Profit + Depr., Dep., Amort./Cur. Mat. L/T/D					(17) 3.6	(90) 4.4
1.0	1.0	1.3						1.7	1.2
.1	.1	.1			.1	.1	.1	.1	.1
.3	.3	.3	Fixed/Worth		.4	.3	.2	.3	.4
1.0	1.1	1.0			-3.4	.8	.8	.8	1.0
2.2	2.4	2.5			1.4	1.3	2.1	2.8	2.6
3.9	4.4	4.5	Debt/Worth		4.6	5.0	4.1	4.8	4.5
9.2	10.3	9.9			-10.2	23.6	7.3	10.3	9.6
47.4	47.8	49.5			51.2	23.2	26.1	36.5	55.1
(2285) 24.7	(1912) 24.8	(1968) 26.4	% Profit Before Taxes/Tangible Net Worth		(20) 15.4	(35) 8.2	(79) 9.1	(417) 17.0	(1414) 30.5
9.4	9.7	10.6			-23.4	-8.4	1.0	4.7	14.8
9.3	8.5	8.8			22.4	5.9	4.9	6.6	9.5
4.9	4.5	4.7	% Profit Before Taxes/Total Assets		1.7	1.5	1.7	3.0	5.4
1.7	1.3	1.6			-2.6	-1.8	-.4	.5	2.5
186.5	170.8	167.3			114.9	145.4	147.3	199.3	158.1
77.7	67.8	70.4	Sales/Net Fixed Assets		29.6	40.7	66.5	91.7	67.2
29.7	26.7	26.0			12.3	19.8	21.9	32.9	26.3
4.6	4.2	4.1			2.5	3.5	3.2	3.7	4.3
3.7	3.4	3.3	Sales/Total Assets		1.3	2.4	2.3	3.1	3.5
2.9	2.7	2.7			.4	1.5	1.6	2.5	2.8
.1	.1	.1			.5	.2	.2	.1	.1
(2142) .2	(1803) .2	(1815) .2	% Depr., Dep., Amort./Sales		(20) 1.0	(30) .4	(62) .3	(370) .2	(1329) .2
.4	.4	.4			2.9	.9	.6	.4	.4
.3	.3	.3				1.2	.5	.3	.2
(1407) .5	(1182) .5	(1196) .5	% Officers', Directors' Owners' Comp/Sales			(19) 1.9	(43) 1.1	(269) .6	(858) .4
1.1	1.0	.9				2.6	1.7	1.0	.8
135375142M	129476642M	137090236M	Net Sales ($)	3743M	57173M	178008M	687058M	8301100M	127863154M
39294867M	39740159M	42900177M	Total Assets ($)	7865M	83814M	111803M	390093M	3050383M	39256219M

M = $ thousand MM = $ million

See Pages 9 through 22 for Explanation of Ratios and Data

Current Data Sorted by Assets							Comparative Historical Data	
						Type of Statement		
1	1	3	6	3	2	Unqualified	25	14
	2	11	4			Reviewed	35	34
8	19	23	2	1		Compiled	99	105
41	91	46	3	1	1	Tax Returns	235	236
17	48	89	27	5	2	Other	147	157
36 (4/1-9/30/13)		421 (10/1/13-3/31/14)					4/1/09-3/31/10	4/1/10-3/31/11
0-500M	500M-2MM	2-10MM	10-50MM	50-100MM	100-250MM		ALL	ALL
67	161	172	42	10	5	NUMBER OF STATEMENTS	541	546
%	%	%	%	%	%	**ASSETS**	%	%
15.2	10.4	7.2	7.6	7.7		Cash & Equivalents	8.3	7.8
5.7	8.4	21.2	25.3	34.9		Trade Receivables (net)	15.1	13.3
61.5	62.3	51.3	44.1	28.1		Inventory	57.5	59.4
1.4	1.5	2.4	1.2	4.5		All Other Current	2.6	2.2
83.8	82.5	82.2	78.1	75.2		Total Current	83.6	82.7
9.4	9.8	9.8	10.8	7.9		Fixed Assets (net)	10.2	10.7
.7	.8	1.2	1.8	2.7		Intangibles (net)	1.2	1.1
6.2	6.9	6.8	9.3	14.2		All Other Non-Current	5.0	5.5
100.0	100.0	100.0	100.0	100.0		Total	100.0	100.0
						LIABILITIES		
28.6	32.7	37.4	40.1	32.7		Notes Payable-Short Term	39.8	35.4
3.2	2.0	.7	2.7	.4		Cur. Mat.-L.T.D.	3.6	3.4
8.0	5.9	5.9	3.1	3.0		Trade Payables	5.2	6.2
.0	.1	.1	.0	.0		Income Taxes Payable	.1	.1
11.5	12.9	11.6	15.6	7.7		All Other Current	12.7	12.3
51.3	53.6	55.6	61.6	43.7		Total Current	61.3	57.5
16.6	10.7	8.1	6.4	17.5		Long-Term Debt	11.8	12.0
.0	.0	.1	.1	.1		Deferred Taxes	.1	.0
10.0	9.8	7.7	3.6	18.0		All Other Non-Current	11.3	11.8
22.1	25.9	28.5	28.3	20.6		Net Worth	15.6	18.7
100.0	100.0	100.0	100.0	100.0		Total Liabilties & Net Worth	100.0	100.0
						INCOME DATA		
100.0	100.0	100.0	100.0	100.0		Net Sales	100.0	100.0
23.6	19.4	19.8	21.2	27.4		Gross Profit	20.2	20.4
20.0	17.2	17.6	18.6	26.3		Operating Expenses	18.6	18.1
3.7	2.2	2.3	2.6	1.1		Operating Profit	1.6	2.3
.5	.2	.4	-.5	1.1		All Other Expenses (net)	.8	.5
3.2	2.0	1.8	3.1	.0		Profit Before Taxes	.8	1.8
						RATIOS		
5.7	3.0	2.5	1.5	3.7			2.4	2.5
1.9	1.6	1.4	1.3	1.5		Current	1.4	1.4
1.1	1.1	1.1	1.1	1.0			1.1	1.1
1.3	.8	1.1	1.1	1.6			.7	.8
.3	(160) .3	.3	.3	1.1		Quick	(538) .3	(538) .3
.1	.1	.1	.1	.6			.1	.1
0 UND	**0** UND	**1** 279.1	**3** 107.6	**1** 400.3			**0** UND	**0** UND
0 UND	**2** 181.0	**7** 53.6	**9** 39.4	**68** 5.4		Sales/Receivables	**3** 119.8	**3** 127.4
2 223.5	**8** 43.1	**22** 16.5	**126** 2.9	**261** 1.4			**15** 25.1	**11** 34.5
28 12.9	**41** 8.8	**41** 8.9	**43** 8.4	**41** 8.8			**43** 8.5	**43** 8.4
62 5.9	**68** 5.4	**62** 5.9	**59** 6.2	**57** 6.4		Cost of Sales/Inventory	**65** 5.6	**63** 5.8
94 3.9	**101** 3.6	**94** 3.9	**81** 4.5	**107** 3.4			**100** 3.6	**97** 3.8
0 UND	**0** UND	**1** 398.2	**1** 471.6	**3** 113.9			**0** UND	**0** UND
0 UND	**2** 166.8	**3** 107.9	**3** 133.0	**7** 52.3		Cost of Sales/Payables	**2** 181.9	**2** 154.2
4 100.6	**9** 42.8	**10** 37.8	**7** 55.7	**14** 26.3			**7** 52.0	**7** 49.5
5.8	6.7	5.5	8.3	2.9			6.7	7.3
14.3	17.3	15.3	19.1	6.1		Sales/Working Capital	15.9	15.9
72.4	61.1	41.6	74.4	-758.2			102.0	58.2
11.7	7.0	6.8	10.2	4.3			4.9	5.6
(51) 4.0	(125) 2.7	(146) 3.1	(33) 3.5	1.7		EBIT/Interest	(472) 2.1	(476) 2.6
1.1	1.0	1.2	2.0	-.3			.7	1.1
							6.4	9.9
						Net Profit + Depr., Dep., Amort./Cur. Mat. L/T/D	(21) 3.4	(16) 2.8
							.5	.5
.0	.0	.0	.1	.1			.0	.0
.0	.2	.2	.3	.3		Fixed/Worth	.3	.2
.7	1.5	.8	.9	.9			4.0	2.2
.8	.8	1.4	1.9	2.3			1.4	1.4
2.7	3.0	2.7	3.1	4.0		Debt/Worth	4.1	3.9
-16.8	60.5	6.4	5.4	6.1			189.5	40.4
75.1	51.5	41.1	52.2				39.4	52.4
(49) 43.0	(125) 18.9	(153) 18.8	(40) 26.4			% Profit Before Taxes/Tangible Net Worth	(414) 17.7	(428) 23.0
17.0	1.6	3.7	10.3				2.8	6.3
33.6	14.7	10.5	10.6	7.1			9.1	12.3
13.5	5.4	4.5	5.8	1.1		% Profit Before Taxes/Total Assets	3.9	4.8
1.5	.0	.5	2.2	-4.2			-.8	.2
UND	756.5	239.0	166.7	80.9			463.8	462.2
285.3	191.3	83.9	40.7	41.3		Sales/Net Fixed Assets	90.7	96.9
52.8	32.7	27.3	19.8	23.1			26.1	27.2
8.1	5.8	5.3	4.7	3.0			5.3	5.8
5.1	4.0	3.6	3.0	1.9		Sales/Total Assets	3.6	4.0
3.0	2.6	1.5	1.1	.9			2.1	2.3
.1	.1	.1	.1				.1	.1
(29) .3	(97) .2	(113) .2	(38) .3			% Depr., Dep., Amort./Sales	(372) .3	(362) .3
.8	.6	.4	.7				.7	.6
1.0	.8	.7	.4				.9	.8
(36) 2.4	(91) 1.6	(88) 1.2	(14) .8			% Officers', Directors' Owners' Comp/Sales	(294) 1.8	(292) 1.7
3.8	2.9	2.3	2.3				3.2	3.2
114813M	872351M	2958321M	2434526M	1408676M	2179408M	Net Sales ($)	9299312M	7376818M
18805M	185788M	818125M	832547M	724149M	646936M	Total Assets ($)	2945039M	2351532M

M = $ thousand MM = $ million

See Pages 9 through 22 for Explanation of Ratios and Data

Comparative Historical Data | **Current Data Sorted by Sales**

4/1/11-3/31/12	4/1/12-3/31/13	4/1/13-3/31/14		0-1MM	1-3MM	3-5MM	5-10MM	10-25MM	25MM & OVER
			Type of Statement						
22	24	16	Unqualified		2			3	11
39	32	17	Reviewed	1			1	8	7
93	58	53	Compiled	5	11	9	13	7	8
226	216	183	Tax Returns	16	55	34	30	37	11
169	165	188	Other	14	25	17	34	46	52
4/1/11-3/31/12 ALL	4/1/12-3/31/13 ALL	4/1/13-3/31/14 ALL		36 (4/1-9/30/13)			421 (10/1/13-3/31/14)		
				0-1MM	1-3MM	3-5MM	5-10MM	10-25MM	25MM & OVER
549	495	457	**NUMBER OF STATEMENTS**	36	93	60	78	101	89
%	%	%	**ASSETS**	%	%	%	%	%	%
8.3	7.8	9.5	Cash & Equivalents	13.9	10.5	10.0	8.6	7.6	9.3
14.9	14.5	15.2	Trade Receivables (net)	10.5	12.7	16.3	12.8	19.1	16.6
57.1	56.4	55.5	Inventory	48.7	58.0	51.7	59.0	54.0	56.7
2.5	2.8	1.9	All Other Current	3.6	1.6	2.6	.9	2.0	1.6
82.8	81.4	82.0	Total Current	76.8	82.8	80.6	81.3	82.7	84.2
9.6	11.0	9.7	Fixed Assets (net)	13.1	10.2	10.3	9.2	9.9	7.7
1.4	1.0	1.1	Intangibles (net)	1.3	.9	.1	2.0	.7	1.5
6.2	6.6	7.1	All Other Non-Current	8.8	6.2	9.0	7.4	6.6	6.5
100.0	100.0	100.0	Total	100.0	100.0	100.0	100.0	100.0	100.0
			LIABILITIES						
33.8	34.7	34.6	Notes Payable-Short Term	20.8	35.8	29.5	34.5	33.3	43.9
1.9	2.7	1.7	Cur. Mat.-L.T.D.	2.5	1.4	.9	2.0	2.0	1.6
5.8	5.6	6.1	Trade Payables	9.1	4.5	6.9	5.6	6.9	5.3
.1	.1	.1	Income Taxes Payable	.0	.0	.1	.0	.1	.0
15.6	13.9	12.3	All Other Current	14.3	10.9	13.0	16.9	11.2	9.5
57.2	56.9	54.6	Total Current	46.8	52.7	50.4	59.0	53.5	60.2
12.7	13.7	10.4	Long-Term Debt	21.0	8.3	12.3	11.4	9.2	7.3
.0	.0	.0	Deferred Taxes	.0	.0	.0	.1	.1	.1
10.8	9.4	8.6	All Other Non-Current	21.1	7.7	11.1	8.3	7.1	4.6
19.3	19.9	26.4	Net Worth	11.1	31.3	26.2	21.2	30.0	27.9
100.0	100.0	100.0	Total Liabilties & Net Worth	100.0	100.0	100.0	100.0	100.0	100.0
			INCOME DATA						
100.0	100.0	100.0	Net Sales	100.0	100.0	100.0	100.0	100.0	100.0
21.3	19.3	20.5	Gross Profit	36.7	21.6	21.7	20.3	17.8	15.6
18.6	17.2	18.0	Operating Expenses	31.0	19.1	19.3	18.1	14.9	14.3
2.6	2.1	2.5	Operating Profit	5.6	2.5	2.3	2.2	2.9	1.2
.7	.4	.3	All Other Expenses (net)	1.9	.8	-.2	.4	.1	-.5
1.9	1.7	2.2	Profit Before Taxes	3.7	1.7	2.5	1.8	2.7	1.7
			RATIOS						
2.7	2.3	2.6		6.5	4.7	4.6	2.1	2.4	1.6
1.5	1.5	1.5	Current	1.9	1.7	1.6	1.3	1.5	1.3
1.1	1.1	1.1		1.0	1.2	1.0	1.1	1.1	1.1
1.0	.9	1.0		1.4	1.6	1.8	.8	.9	.7
(545) .3	(492) .2	(456) .3	Quick	.4	.3	.4	(77) .2	.4	.3
.1	.1	.1		.1	.1	.1	.1	.2	.2
0 UND	0 UND	0 UND		0 UND	0 UND	0 UND	0 UND	1 509.3	2 199.2
3 113.9	3 123.5	4 97.6	Sales/Receivables	1 615.0	1 332.8	4 83.9	1 257.2	7 52.1	5 76.7
14 26.3	11 33.0	14 27.0		30 12.0	12 30.9	19 19.0	10 37.4	19 19.7	13 29.1
45 8.1	41 8.9	41 9.0		50 7.3	62 5.9	39 9.3	41 8.8	33 11.0	41 9.0
66 5.5	62 5.9	64 5.7	Cost of Sales/Inventory	99 3.7	85 4.3	68 5.4	64 5.7	52 7.0	55 6.6
104 3.5	91 4.0	94 3.9		243 1.5	118 3.1	96 3.8	96 3.8	74 4.9	70 5.2
0 UND	0 UND	0 UND		0 UND	0 UND	0 UND	1 553.6	1 607.9	1 378.7
2 153.2	2 156.9	2 147.7	Cost of Sales/Payables	0 UND	2 206.1	2 189.5	4 95.5	3 136.2	2 157.1
9 41.0	8 48.5	8 43.7		11 33.7	6 56.3	9 41.6	10 37.1	8 44.1	6 59.8
5.4	7.0	5.9		3.2	4.8	4.6	7.4	8.9	10.5
13.6	17.5	15.6	Sales/Working Capital	4.3	10.3	10.2	15.0	18.2	22.4
56.7	56.4	54.6		NM	32.0	410.7	51.3	49.3	65.5
6.6	6.5	7.5		9.6	7.0	6.3	6.3	10.1	11.7
(464) 2.8	(436) 2.4	(368) 2.9	EBIT/Interest	(24) 2.4	(73) 2.1	(47) 2.7	(71) 2.4	(81) 3.4	(72) 3.9
1.2	1.1	1.1		.6	.8	1.1	1.1	1.8	1.9
21.7	3.9	19.3							25.7
(26) 8.7	(18) .8	(22) 4.3	Net Profit + Depr., Dep., Amort./Cur. Mat. L/T/D						(11) 3.4
1.3	.1	.3							.0
.0	.0	.0		.0	.0	.0	.1	.0	.1
.2	.2	.2	Fixed/Worth	.2	.1	.1	.3	.1	.3
1.0	1.1	.9		6.0	.7	1.6	1.5	.9	.8
1.2	1.4	1.1		1.1	.5	.6	2.0	1.2	1.9
3.4	3.2	3.0	Debt/Worth	4.9	2.0	2.9	4.7	2.6	3.1
12.2	13.7	10.5		-7.6	18.8	NM	54.9	5.5	7.5
51.9	48.0	51.5		73.5	40.4	65.1	47.7	51.0	53.9
(463) 22.3	(414) 21.4	(380) 21.9	% Profit Before Taxes/Tangible Net Worth	(25) 20.0	(72) 19.2	(45) 16.6	(66) 17.4	(90) 23.3	(82) 27.6
7.4	5.2	4.0		1.0	2.6	2.0	.7	8.9	10.1
11.7	12.3	14.2		20.0	18.3	14.3	9.6	15.2	12.4
5.3	5.0	5.7	% Profit Before Taxes/Total Assets	3.8	4.5	5.8	3.5	7.4	7.0
.6	.4	.5		-1.0	-.1	.3	.2	1.7	1.8
618.1	541.5	488.8		UND	909.2	999.8	312.2	523.9	240.6
121.8	120.1	111.8	Sales/Net Fixed Assets	73.4	141.9	148.8	82.4	120.3	96.1
32.1	30.1	29.5		8.8	24.2	21.0	32.8	40.7	34.4
5.5	5.9	5.4		3.5	4.8	5.2	5.3	6.4	6.1
3.6	3.9	3.7	Sales/Total Assets	1.8	3.1	3.3	3.6	4.5	4.6
2.0	2.2	2.1		.4	1.9	1.9	2.0	2.8	3.0
.1	.1	.1		.7	.1	.2	.1	.0	.1
(322) .3	(317) .3	(288) .2	% Depr., Dep., Amort./Sales	(15) 1.1	(48) .3	(29) .3	(58) .3	(69) .2	(69) .2
.6	.6	.6		3.6	.8	.6	.6	.4	.4
.8	.6	.7		1.6	1.1	.8	1.0	.6	.4
(284) 1.7	(260) 1.4	(232) 1.5	% Officers', Directors' Owners' Comp/Sales	(12) 5.6	(55) 2.6	(38) 1.9	(36) 1.4	(54) 1.1	(37) .8
2.9	2.8	2.8		10.9	3.7	3.1	2.1	2.0	2.2
8124826M	8971116M	9968095M	Net Sales ($)	18925M	191831M	230154M	556497M	1527164M	7443524M
2949996M	2872246M	3226350M	Total Assets ($)	21300M	91809M	95711M	227010M	477967M	2312553M

M = $ thousand MM = $ million

See Pages 9 through 22 for Explanation of Ratios and Data

Current Data Sorted by Assets							Comparative Historical Data	
						Type of Statement		
	2		4	3		Unqualified	12	10
	2	14	20	1		Reviewed	42	54
4	18	25	8			Compiled	108	90
6	16	24	7			Tax Returns	81	105
1	14	77	43	7	2	Other	154	100
24 (4/1-9/30/13)		274 (10/1/13-3/31/14)					4/1/09-3/31/10	4/1/10-3/31/11
0-500M	500M-2MM	2-10MM	10-50MM	50-100MM	100-250MM		ALL	ALL
11	52	140	82	11	2	**NUMBER OF STATEMENTS**	397	359
%	%	%	%	%	%	**ASSETS**	%	%
26.2	12.0	9.5	11.3	10.4		Cash & Equivalents	9.0	8.3
2.3	3.0	3.1	3.5	3.7		Trade Receivables (net)	2.9	3.2
41.4	65.5	76.1	69.5	65.8		Inventory	71.3	72.0
.1	1.7	1.2	.5	5.7		All Other Current	.7	.5
70.1	82.2	89.9	84.8	85.6		Total Current	84.0	84.0
21.8	13.5	6.1	9.8	4.8		Fixed Assets (net)	10.8	10.8
2.0	1.9	2.0	3.8	7.5		Intangibles (net)	3.1	3.0
6.2	2.4	2.1	1.5	2.0		All Other Non-Current	2.1	2.2
100.0	100.0	100.0	100.0	100.0		Total	100.0	100.0
						LIABILITIES		
27.2	39.6	51.2	51.4	50.1		Notes Payable-Short Term	45.8	46.4
4.4	1.2	1.4	1.3	.2		Cur. Mat.-L.T.D.	3.2	2.5
12.0	3.6	5.4	3.1	3.1		Trade Payables	6.3	6.6
.7	.0	.1	.2	.0		Income Taxes Payable	.1	.1
32.5	13.7	9.0	7.0	10.2		All Other Current	8.0	8.3
76.9	58.0	67.0	62.9	63.7		Total Current	63.4	63.8
18.6	9.3	3.7	5.7	7.1		Long-Term Debt	9.7	8.3
.0	.0	.0	.1	.0		Deferred Taxes	.0	.0
9.9	6.3	4.8	3.4	6.9		All Other Non-Current	4.5	6.3
-5.4	26.4	24.5	27.9	22.3		Net Worth	22.3	21.6
100.0	100.0	100.0	100.0	100.0		Total Liabilties & Net Worth	100.0	100.0
						INCOME DATA		
100.0	100.0	100.0	100.0	100.0		Net Sales	100.0	100.0
28.9	26.6	21.0	20.4	16.5		Gross Profit	21.4	20.8
26.3	25.6	17.4	15.9	12.2		Operating Expenses	20.9	18.7
2.6	1.0	3.6	4.5	4.2		Operating Profit	.4	2.1
.4	.9	.4	.4	.3		All Other Expenses (net)	1.3	.9
2.2	.1	3.2	4.1	3.9		Profit Before Taxes	-.8	1.2
						RATIOS		
3.7	2.2	1.5	1.5	1.8			1.6	1.6
.9	1.3	1.3	1.3	1.2		Current	1.3	1.3
.6	1.1	1.2	1.2	1.1			1.1	1.1
.9	.8	.3	.4	.3			.3	.3
.2	.2	.1	(81) .2	.2		Quick	.1	.1
.1	.1	.1	.1	.1			.1	.1
0 UND	0 UND	1 652.0	1 307.2	0 999.8			0 999.8	0 999.8
0 UND	1 636.4	2 207.9	3 126.3	1 414.4		Sales/Receivables	2 172.9	2 185.6
1 296.4	3 137.1	7 56.0	5 70.2	3 134.4			6 64.8	5 67.1
0 UND	104 3.5	118 3.1	114 3.2	94 3.9			109 3.4	104 3.5
41 9.0	146 2.5	152 2.4	140 2.6	101 3.6		Cost of Sales/Inventory	148 2.5	140 2.6
81 4.5	203 1.8	192 1.9	174 2.1	122 3.0			210 1.7	181 2.0
0 UND	0 UND	1 279.9	2 240.8	2 155.7			1 319.8	1 262.5
0 UND	2 171.5	4 82.2	4 92.9	4 100.7		Cost of Sales/Payables	4 100.8	4 95.9
1 323.0	6 58.5	11 34.3	9 42.5	7 50.7			11 34.1	10 35.8
14.5	4.8	6.7	7.7	9.3			6.3	7.3
-139.3	11.2	11.5	12.0	14.2		Sales/Working Capital	12.5	13.2
-10.5	61.9	19.3	17.2	30.5			30.0	32.9
	4.6	6.3	9.8				2.7	3.5
	(50) 2.2	(134) 3.3	(78) 4.2			EBIT/Interest	(377) 1.1	(343) 1.8
	1.0	2.0	2.8				.1	1.0
							4.8	3.7
						Net Profit + Depr., Dep., Amort./Cur. Mat. L/T/D	(19) 1.4	(19) 1.2
							.0	-8.5
.4	.1	.0	.1	.1			.1	.1
-1.3	.3	.2	.2	.6		Fixed/Worth	.3	.3
-.2	1.1	.6	.6	1.2			1.5	1.5
1.9	1.3	2.1	2.1	2.5			1.9	1.8
-4.7	3.4	3.6	3.4	4.1		Debt/Worth	3.8	3.8
-2.6	16.2	7.1	5.5	20.7			11.3	12.3
	53.7	57.4	60.0				23.2	35.3
	(43) 18.8	(125) 25.6	(77) 37.9			% Profit Before Taxes/Tangible Net Worth	(332) 5.0	(297) 13.8
	3.3	12.0	19.5				-9.9	1.6
23.2	10.1	11.8	12.4	15.6			4.5	7.1
3.8	3.5	6.1	7.5	8.6		% Profit Before Taxes/Total Assets	.4	3.0
-13.3	-.9	2.5	4.9	5.9			-3.9	.0
841.0	161.2	238.6	153.7	224.2			132.9	138.3
42.5	47.5	77.9	58.0	86.9		Sales/Net Fixed Assets	42.3	49.5
22.2	11.1	31.6	16.9	42.0			13.6	20.0
7.2	3.1	3.0	2.8	3.8			2.9	3.0
3.3	2.3	2.3	2.2	2.9		Sales/Total Assets	2.2	2.4
1.5	1.7	1.8	1.8	2.1			1.6	1.9
	.3	.2	.2	.1			.3	.2
	(36) .7	(110) .3	(60) .3	(10) .2		% Depr., Dep., Amort./Sales	(300) .5	(288) .4
	1.8	.5	.7	.4			1.2	1.0
	1.5	.7	.5				.9	.9
	(33) 2.4	(86) 1.4	(40) 1.0			% Officers', Directors' Owners' Comp/Sales	(228) 1.8	(213) 1.6
	4.3	2.4	1.8				3.2	2.9
11866M	170829M	1870961M	3476545M	2347165M	1024899M	Net Sales ($)	5583622M	5371833M
2798M	67975M	759236M	1534280M	798282M	431345M	Total Assets ($)	2440040M	2275240M

M = $ thousand MM = $ million

See Pages 9 through 22 for Explanation of Ratios and Data

Comparative Historical Data				Current Data Sorted by Sales					
			Type of Statement						
14	8	9	Unqualified	1	1				7
35	34	37	Reviewed			1	7	13	16
65	51	55	Compiled	4	11	7	13	15	5
65	57	53	Tax Returns	4	10	7	12	12	8
116	95	144	Other	3	8	9	20	47	57
4/1/11-3/31/12	4/1/12-3/31/13	4/1/13-3/31/14			24 (4/1-9/30/13)		274 (10/1/13-3/31/14)		
ALL	ALL	ALL		0-1MM	1-3MM	3-5MM	5-10MM	10-25MM	25MM & OVER
295	245	298	**NUMBER OF STATEMENTS**	12	30	24	52	87	93
%	%	%	**ASSETS**	%	%	%	%	%	%
8.7	9.8	11.0	Cash & Equivalents	22.3	9.0	14.2	9.9	9.1	11.9
3.2	2.7	3.2	Trade Receivables (net)	1.0	2.1	4.8	3.5	3.1	3.3
71.4	70.5	70.6	Inventory	38.7	70.7	67.0	75.6	73.8	70.0
.9	1.1	1.2	All Other Current	.5	2.4	.5	.4	1.4	1.5
84.2	84.0	86.1	Total Current	62.4	84.1	86.5	89.4	87.3	86.7
10.4	10.3	9.0	Fixed Assets (net)	30.2	11.0	8.9	6.6	8.1	7.8
3.1	3.2	2.8	Intangibles (net)	2.7	1.3	1.8	1.7	3.0	4.0
2.3	2.4	2.1	All Other Non-Current	4.7	3.6	2.8	2.3	1.6	1.5
100.0	100.0	100.0	Total	100.0	100.0	100.0	100.0	100.0	100.0
			LIABILITIES						
47.4	46.9	48.3	Notes Payable-Short Term	22.5	40.8	42.5	52.4	48.4	53.1
2.4	1.9	1.4	Cur. Mat.-L.T.D.	4.6	1.6	3.4	.3	2.1	.3
5.6	6.0	4.6	Trade Payables	11.7	1.9	8.5	2.7	6.0	3.3
.1	.1	.1	Income Taxes Payable	.0	.3	.0	.0	.1	.2
7.6	8.0	10.2	All Other Current	42.6	10.5	12.8	9.9	8.4	7.0
63.0	62.9	64.5	Total Current	81.5	55.0	67.2	65.4	65.0	63.9
8.9	7.9	5.9	Long-Term Debt	15.8	14.9	4.2	4.3	3.7	5.2
.1	.0	.1	Deferred Taxes	.0	.0	.0	.1	.0	.2
6.5	4.5	4.9	All Other Non-Current	.1	10.6	5.8	5.4	4.1	3.9
21.5	24.7	24.6	Net Worth	2.6	19.6	22.9	24.7	27.3	26.9
100.0	100.0	100.0	Total Liabilties & Net Worth	100.0	100.0	100.0	100.0	100.0	100.0
			INCOME DATA						
100.0	100.0	100.0	Net Sales	100.0	100.0	100.0	100.0	100.0	100.0
20.8	20.9	21.9	Gross Profit	32.2	27.2	24.1	21.1	21.6	19.1
18.8	18.7	18.5	Operating Expenses	37.2	24.9	21.1	17.5	17.7	14.8
2.1	2.2	3.4	Operating Profit	-5.0	2.3	3.0	3.5	3.9	4.3
.8	.3	.5	All Other Expenses (net)	2.9	1.0	-.2	.6	.3	.3
1.3	1.9	2.9	Profit Before Taxes	-7.9	1.3	3.2	3.0	3.6	4.0
			RATIOS						
1.6	1.5	1.6		1.3	6.6	2.1	1.6	1.5	1.6
1.3	1.3	1.3	Current	.8	1.3	1.3	1.4	1.3	1.3
1.1	1.2	1.2		.5	1.1	1.1	1.2	1.2	1.2
.3	.3	.3		.6	1.8	.4	.3	.3	.4
.1	.1	(297) .2	Quick	.2	.1	.2	.2	.1	(92) .2
.1	.1	.1		.0	.1	.1	.1	.1	.1
0 841.0	**0** 979.9	**0** 909.0		**0** UND	**0** UND	**0** UND	**0** 832.9	**1** 499.5	**1** 566.7
2 191.1	**2** 178.7	**2** 204.4	Sales/Receivables	**0** UND	**0** 902.3	**2** 188.8	**2** 170.8	**2** 200.9	**2** 169.6
6 61.9	**5** 69.9	**5** 69.8		**1** 302.1	**4** 83.4	**7** 52.8	**8** 45.5	**5** 68.8	**5** 73.7
104 3.5	**111** 3.3	**107** 3.4		**0** UND	**126** 2.9	**111** 3.3	**126** 2.9	**122** 3.0	**96** 3.8
140 2.6	**146** 2.5	**146** 2.5	Cost of Sales/Inventory	**61** 6.0	**174** 2.1	**146** 2.5	**174** 2.1	**146** 2.5	**126** 2.9
182 2.0	**182** 2.0	**182** 2.0		**304** 1.2	**243** 1.5	**228** 1.6	**215** 1.7	**192** 1.9	**152** 2.4
1 264.5	**2** 229.9	**1** 353.0		**0** UND	**0** UND	**1** 525.2	**0** UND	**2** 163.6	**2** 238.3
4 93.2	**4** 86.8	**4** 95.1	Cost of Sales/Payables	**0** UND	**2** 153.9	**5** 73.7	**3** 126.7	**5** 75.5	**4** 100.7
10 37.1	**11** 34.4	**9** 41.9		**11** 33.2	**7** 50.8	**22** 16.3	**9** 40.3	**9** 40.1	**8** 46.7
7.1	7.3	6.8		27.3	3.0	4.8	6.1	8.0	8.9
12.1	12.2	11.9	Sales/Working Capital	-12.0	9.3	12.8	9.9	11.8	12.7
24.1	21.1	23.1		-3.2	28.4	25.2	16.0	23.1	21.6
4.4	6.0	7.2		.0	6.3	5.4	5.0	7.1	11.2
(277) 2.2	(232) 2.7	(282) 3.5	EBIT/Interest	(10) -2.4	2.9	(22) 2.4	(50) 2.8	(82) 3.5	(88) 5.6
1.2	1.3	2.0		-21.3	.8	1.6	1.7	2.2	2.9
17.4	17.2	25.5							
(27) 7.0	(16) 6.5	(18) 8.3	Net Profit + Depr., Dep., Amort./Cur. Mat. L/T/D						
1.1	3.2	4.2							
.1	.1	.1		.7	.0	.1	.0	.1	.1
.2	.2	.2	Fixed/Worth	-1.2	.4	.2	.2	.2	.2
1.0	1.1	.7		-.6	NM	2.1	.4	.7	.6
1.9	2.0	1.9		.8	1.9	1.3	2.1	1.9	2.0
3.8	3.5	3.6	Debt/Worth	-9.2	6.0	3.7	3.6	3.6	3.3
10.6	7.1	8.4		-3.2	NM	17.4	5.5	7.1	6.1
37.5	46.9	58.7			62.6	65.4	49.5	51.3	72.1
(248) 17.8	(218) 23.7	(260) 29.9	% Profit Before Taxes/Tangible Net Worth		(23) 21.2	(21) 24.7	(48) 25.3	(79) 24.2	(85) 42.6
4.9	7.4	12.8			2.7	7.6	8.4	13.6	22.3
8.4	10.2	12.3		7.5	8.3	11.9	10.9	11.6	16.3
3.7	4.7	6.3	% Profit Before Taxes/Total Assets	-9.4	3.3	5.2	4.0	6.4	8.3
.6	1.0	2.6		-20.9	-1.3	1.8	2.0	3.6	5.1
175.6	186.1	194.4		641.4	298.3	179.6	219.6	144.6	209.2
60.5	57.8	66.7	Sales/Net Fixed Assets	15.4	45.5	82.2	60.8	70.6	75.0
17.2	14.4	22.7		1.6	14.7	16.5	32.7	22.2	25.4
2.9	2.9	3.0		3.3	2.5	2.7	2.8	2.9	3.1
2.4	2.3	2.3	Sales/Total Assets	1.4	1.8	2.3	2.2	2.3	2.7
1.8	1.8	1.8		.7	1.4	1.7	1.7	1.9	2.1
.2	.2	.2		.7	.2	.4	.2	.2	.2
(219) .4	(191) .3	(226) .4	% Depr., Dep., Amort./Sales	(10) 1.3	(18) .7	(16) .6	(42) .3	(68) .3	(72) .3
.8	.6	.6		6.2	2.0	.8	.6	.5	.5
.9	.9	.8			2.0	1.0	.8	.8	.5
(156) 1.6	(136) 1.5	(169) 1.5	% Officers', Directors' Owners' Comp/Sales		(19) 3.0	(16) 1.6	(31) 1.9	(55) 1.3	(45) .9
2.4	2.7	2.6			4.8	2.8	2.9	2.5	1.4
6075882M	**6067034M**	**8902265M**	Net Sales ($)	**6765M**	**62640M**	**95614M**	**371366M**	**1434404M**	**6931476M**
2465952M	**2446544M**	**3593916M**	Total Assets ($)	**7107M**	**36956M**	**46164M**	**174757M**	**664310M**	**2664622M**

M = $ thousand MM = $ million

See Pages 9 through 22 for Explanation of Ratios and Data

Current Data Sorted by Assets							Comparative Historical Data	
						Type of Statement		
			3	1	2	Unqualified	6	
		11	6			Reviewed	30	33
5	9	16	2			Compiled	53	44
9	20	15	1			Tax Returns	53	51
5	12	39	11	1	1	Other	91	86
19 (4/1-9/30/13)		150 (10/1/13-3/31/14)					4/1/09-3/31/10	4/1/10-3/31/11
0-500M	500M-2MM	2-10MM	10-50MM	50-100MM	100-250MM		ALL	ALL
19	41	81	23	2	3	**NUMBER OF STATEMENTS**	233	214
%	%	%	%	%	%	**ASSETS**	%	%
13.7	10.6	6.2	11.5			Cash & Equivalents	8.5	9.3
13.3	5.3	3.9	3.8			Trade Receivables (net)	5.0	5.0
53.5	65.9	71.3	49.0			Inventory	62.5	59.7
.1	.7	.9	3.8			All Other Current	1.4	1.6
80.6	82.5	82.3	68.0			Total Current	77.4	75.7
16.1	14.0	13.7	20.2			Fixed Assets (net)	16.8	18.4
.4	.3	1.4	4.5			Intangibles (net)	2.9	2.6
2.9	3.2	2.6	7.3			All Other Non-Current	2.8	3.4
100.0	100.0	100.0	100.0			Total	100.0	100.0
						LIABILITIES		
28.9	30.9	43.2	36.9			Notes Payable-Short Term	39.0	36.3
7.5	3.0	2.2	1.9			Cur. Mat.-L.T.D.	3.0	2.5
13.3	8.6	5.5	5.3			Trade Payables	5.9	6.5
.0	.1	.0	.2			Income Taxes Payable	.2	.2
14.5	15.5	11.0	7.6			All Other Current	11.1	10.3
64.2	58.0	61.9	51.9			Total Current	59.3	55.7
41.2	14.2	12.7	13.8			Long-Term Debt	16.2	16.5
.2	.0	.1	.4			Deferred Taxes	.1	.1
16.7	6.4	4.8	1.8			All Other Non-Current	5.0	6.6
-22.2	21.4	20.6	32.1			Net Worth	19.4	21.1
100.0	100.0	100.0	100.0			Total Liabilties & Net Worth	100.0	100.0
						INCOME DATA		
100.0	100.0	100.0	100.0			Net Sales	100.0	100.0
29.6	29.1	24.7	24.6			Gross Profit	26.2	28.4
26.9	25.5	21.5	20.1			Operating Expenses	25.2	25.5
2.7	3.6	3.2	4.6			Operating Profit	1.0	2.9
1.5	1.5	.6	1.4			All Other Expenses (net)	2.2	1.4
1.2	2.1	2.6	3.1			Profit Before Taxes	-1.2	1.5
						RATIOS		
5.1	2.7	1.4	1.4				1.7	1.9
1.7	1.5	1.3	1.3			Current	1.3	1.3
1.0	1.1	1.1	1.1				1.0	1.1
2.1	.8	.3	.4				.4	.5
.5	.2	(80) .1	.2			Quick	.2	.2
.1	.1	.1	.1				.1	.1
1 614.0	0 734.2	1 334.1	2 146.1				1 415.0	1 526.1
4 86.5	4 90.1	4 86.6	6 59.0			Sales/Receivables	5 73.8	5 70.5
14 25.3	12 31.0	8 46.7	13 28.9				12 29.8	13 28.1
26 13.8	94 3.9	140 2.6	107 3.4				103 3.5	116 3.1
76 4.8	174 2.1	192 1.9	182 2.0			Cost of Sales/Inventory	189 1.9	167 2.2
140 2.6	261 1.4	243 1.5	203 1.8				300 1.2	236 1.5
1 450.0	0 UND	2 180.6	4 96.2				1 440.8	1 312.8
10 36.6	3 137.1	5 68.3	7 48.8			Cost of Sales/Payables	5 71.4	7 56.0
20 18.3	17 21.7	9 40.4	17 21.5				15 24.5	19 19.2
8.0	4.4	7.1	5.2				4.8	5.2
13.7	8.3	10.7	8.9			Sales/Working Capital	9.4	9.7
UND	38.2	22.2	24.6				77.4	50.6
4.7	5.1	5.7	7.0				2.2	4.1
(17) 1.5	(39) 2.9	(77) 2.8	(22) 4.1			EBIT/Interest	(221) 1.0	(201) 1.6
-.6	1.6	1.6	2.3				-.3	.8
							1.6	3.4
						Net Profit + Depr., Dep., Amort./Cur. Mat. L/T/D	(30) .4	(20) 1.5
							-1.0	.8
.0	.1	.1	.2				.2	.1
.2	.3	.4	.7			Fixed/Worth	.8	.6
3.0	-2.5	1.5	.9				5.9	3.9
.7	1.0	2.1	2.0				1.7	1.5
1.1	2.6	4.0	3.2			Debt/Worth	4.8	3.8
-9.0	-18.9	17.4	4.6				36.4	22.3
35.5	29.1	51.3	36.4				18.5	33.8
(14) 10.2	(29) 13.4	(71) 20.0	17.4			% Profit Before Taxes/Tangible Net Worth	(186) 3.7	(173) 13.3
-14.8	7.1	8.3	10.5				-16.1	1.1
25.5	10.4	8.0	6.5				4.3	7.5
4.8	4.8	4.6	4.2			% Profit Before Taxes/Total Assets	.2	2.5
-7.8	1.5	1.4	2.7				-4.9	-1.0
146.6	124.0	93.8	68.3				69.4	75.6
91.8	40.5	40.5	15.9			Sales/Net Fixed Assets	20.9	22.2
28.6	11.2	9.1	3.9				6.4	6.0
8.6	2.7	2.5	1.7				2.5	2.5
4.8	2.0	1.8	1.5			Sales/Total Assets	1.7	1.8
2.4	1.5	1.4	1.2				1.1	1.2
.1	.2	.3	.3				.5	.5
(11) .7	(27) .6	(58) .6	(20) .6			% Depr., Dep., Amort./Sales	(189) .9	(161) .8
2.2	2.0	1.3	2.5				1.7	1.8
3.7	2.0	.6	.6				1.4	1.1
(10) 5.0	(26) 3.7	(46) 1.2	(11) .9			% Officers', Directors' Owners' Comp/Sales	(115) 2.6	(108) 2.3
6.2	5.2	2.6	1.3				4.7	4.1
24633M	106878M	700894M	853738M	259495M	657703M	Net Sales ($)	1955981M	1454600M
4801M	46744M	374941M	494468M	172940M	358716M	Total Assets ($)	1288789M	911798M

M = $ thousand MM = $ million

See Pages 9 through 22 for Explanation of Ratios and Data

Comparative Historical Data / Current Data Sorted by Sales

4/1/11-3/31/12 ALL	4/1/12-3/31/13 ALL	4/1/13-3/31/14 ALL	Type of Statement	0-1MM	1-3MM	3-5MM	5-10MM	10-25MM	25MM & OVER
3	3	6	Unqualified					1	5
30	19	17	Reviewed			4	6	1	6
39	35	32	Compiled	3	9	4	11	5	
53	63	45	Tax Returns	7	19	4	5	9	1
74	55	69	Other	4	10	10	23	16	6
				19 (4/1-9/30/13)			150 (10/1/13-3/31/14)		
199	175	169	**NUMBER OF STATEMENTS**	14	38	22	45	32	18
%	%	%	**ASSETS**	%	%	%	%	%	%
9.8	9.9	8.8	Cash & Equivalents	6.6	10.8	10.7	5.4	8.4	13.2
5.3	4.6	5.4	Trade Receivables (net)	6.8	4.8	5.4	7.6	2.8	4.7
60.3	63.5	64.1	Inventory	57.1	62.4	65.1	71.6	70.5	42.0
2.4	1.7	1.3	All Other Current	.0	.8	.7	1.0	2.2	3.2
77.7	79.7	79.6	Total Current	70.6	78.8	81.8	85.6	83.9	63.1
16.2	15.2	15.4	Fixed Assets (net)	24.7	16.5	13.7	11.4	12.2	23.7
2.2	1.6	1.5	Intangibles (net)	.6	.7	2.2	.9	2.4	3.3
3.9	3.5	3.4	All Other Non-Current	4.2	4.0	2.3	2.2	1.5	10.0
100.0	100.0	100.0	Total	100.0	100.0	100.0	100.0	100.0	100.0
			LIABILITIES						
39.1	36.1	37.3	Notes Payable-Short Term	41.5	29.2	33.3	40.7	45.2	33.8
2.9	3.6	3.0	Cur. Mat.-L.T.D.	8.8	4.0	.4	3.2	1.1	1.8
6.2	6.8	7.1	Trade Payables	11.3	6.5	6.9	8.0	5.6	6.2
.3	.1	.1	Income Taxes Payable	.0	.1	.0	.0	.1	.4
11.4	9.5	11.9	All Other Current	25.0	13.1	9.2	12.0	7.1	10.8
59.7	56.1	59.4	Total Current	86.7	52.8	49.8	63.8	59.2	53.1
14.9	16.2	16.6	Long-Term Debt	50.6	19.6	17.0	8.2	10.5	14.7
.1	.1	.1	Deferred Taxes	.0	.1	.1	.1	.1	.4
5.8	8.4	6.0	All Other Non-Current	20.1	6.6	2.6	6.6	2.7	2.4
19.5	19.2	17.9	Net Worth	-57.4	20.8	30.5	21.3	27.5	29.5
100.0	100.0	100.0	Total Liabilties & Net Worth	100.0	100.0	100.0	100.0	100.0	100.0
			INCOME DATA						
100.0	100.0	100.0	Net Sales	100.0	100.0	100.0	100.0	100.0	100.0
30.2	26.7	26.4	Gross Profit	37.8	29.7	27.9	23.1	22.5	23.4
26.5	23.4	22.9	Operating Expenses	34.0	25.6	24.5	20.5	18.6	19.8
3.7	3.3	3.5	Operating Profit	3.8	4.1	3.4	2.6	3.9	3.6
.9	1.0	1.0	All Other Expenses (net)	2.9	1.4	.5	.7	.8	.3
2.9	2.4	2.5	Profit Before Taxes	.8	2.6	2.9	1.9	3.1	3.2
			RATIOS						
1.8	2.0	1.7		1.8	3.0	2.9	1.5	1.4	1.4
1.3	1.4	1.3	Current	1.1	1.5	1.4	1.3	1.2	1.2
1.1	1.2	1.1		.6	1.1	1.2	1.1	1.2	1.1
.5	.4	.4		.6	.6	.8	.3	.3	.4
(174) .2	(168) .2	.2	Quick	.1	(37) .2	.3	.1	.1	.3
.1	.1	.1		.0	.1	.1	.1	.1	.1
1 321.8	1 707.3	1 319.8		0 UND	1 269.6	1 273.5	2 187.4	1 524.5	3 114.2
6 58.8	5 74.4	5 80.5	Sales/Receivables	4 88.2	4 89.9	7 55.9	4 86.2	3 130.3	5 67.0
15 24.9	12 30.7	12 31.0		12 29.6	11 32.3	16 23.1	14 26.3	10 36.5	13 28.6
107 3.4	107 3.4	111 3.3		41 9.0	70 5.2	159 2.3	140 2.6	126 2.9	66 5.5
174 2.1	166 2.2	174 2.1	Cost of Sales/Inventory	159 2.3	146 2.5	215 1.7	182 2.0	174 2.1	130 2.8
228 1.6	228 1.6	243 1.5		304 1.2	243 1.5	365 1.0	243 1.5	228 1.6	182 2.0
2 211.6	1 312.3	2 199.3		0 UND	0 UND	0 999.8	2 168.0	3 106.9	3 106.1
6 59.0	5 77.2	6 60.8	Cost of Sales/Payables	13 28.0	3 123.2	3 121.0	6 59.8	7 55.5	7 49.5
18 20.8	13 28.3	14 25.8		26 14.0	14 26.6	8 45.3	11 33.2	13 28.4	17 21.4
5.6	5.1	6.2		5.7	6.0	4.3	6.7	6.1	8.9
9.7	9.5	9.7	Sales/Working Capital	UND	9.9	7.2	10.3	10.1	18.2
56.8	21.7	25.9		-6.8	33.0	10.8	20.3	18.6	32.1
4.9	7.0	5.7		2.8	5.4	6.4	4.6	8.1	7.6
(187) 2.4	(168) 2.8	(160) 2.8	EBIT/Interest	(13) 1.8	(35) 2.1	(21) 2.5	(44) 2.5	(29) 4.3	4.9
1.2	1.2	1.5		-.6	1.1	1.4	1.5	2.4	2.5
6.8	8.0	4.2							
(24) 2.2	(18) 2.8	(13) 1.7	Net Profit + Depr., Dep., Amort./Cur. Mat. L/T/D						
.5	.9	.4							
.1	.1	.1		.1	.1	.1	.1	.1	.3
.5	.4	.5	Fixed/Worth	1.3	.5	.4	.2	.3	.7
3.6	2.5	1.9		-.2	-1.9	1.4	1.8	.9	1.9
1.5	1.5	1.6		1.0	1.1	1.0	1.9	2.1	1.9
3.6	3.4	3.2	Debt/Worth	2.6	2.6	2.1	3.9	3.2	3.5
21.7	10.1	12.1		-2.3	-16.9	9.8	27.2	5.6	5.0
38.1	38.0	37.8			37.4	30.0	41.7	48.4	36.6
(158) 15.9	(143) 15.9	(142) 18.6	% Profit Before Taxes/Tangible Net Worth		(26) 21.7	(19) 12.4	(39) 18.2	27.5	21.4
4.7	5.0	7.2			1.1	2.6	6.3	13.7	10.8
8.6	8.0	8.3		9.1	10.3	7.6	7.8	10.0	7.0
3.9	4.2	4.7	% Profit Before Taxes/Total Assets	5.0	4.3	4.8	3.4	5.6	4.8
.7	.9	1.4		-8.0	.2	.7	1.2	3.5	2.4
75.2	96.1	106.3		118.0	109.0	121.4	199.6	107.9	30.7
26.1	28.7	35.3	Sales/Net Fixed Assets	26.3	35.4	29.2	50.1	35.9	15.7
7.1	8.1	9.0		4.9	10.1	6.9	15.0	8.7	3.6
2.5	2.6	2.7		5.0	3.3	2.1	2.5	3.1	2.8
1.9	1.9	1.9	Sales/Total Assets	1.9	2.1	1.7	2.0	1.8	1.7
1.4	1.4	1.4		1.1	1.5	1.0	1.5	1.5	1.2
.4	.3	.3			.2	.3	.3	.2	.3
(146) .8	(134) .6	(121) .7	% Depr., Dep., Amort./Sales		(24) .7	(16) .6	(30) .6	(25) .5	(17) .8
1.5	1.5	1.8			2.0	1.2	1.4	1.9	2.2
1.2	.9	.7			2.7	.7	.7	.4	
(107) 2.5	(94) 1.8	(93) 1.8	% Officers', Directors' Owners' Comp/Sales		(27) 4.4	(12) 1.4	(25) 1.5	(18) .6	
5.0	4.1	4.3			5.5	2.4	2.6	1.4	
1836267M	1582774M	2603341M	Net Sales ($)	8308M	71201M	87507M	327395M	493304M	1615626M
1127930M	965921M	1452610M	Total Assets ($)	5959M	39613M	66346M	181272M	288891M	870529M

M = $ thousand MM = $ million

See Pages 9 through 22 for Explanation of Ratios and Data

Current Data Sorted by Assets / Comparative Historical Data

0-500M	500M-2MM	2-10MM	10-50MM	50-100MM	100-250MM	Type of Statement	4/1/09-3/31/10 ALL	4/1/10-3/31/11 ALL
1		1	17	11	2	Unqualified	40	48
	5	50	33	3	3	Reviewed	117	110
4	21	50	8		1	Compiled	133	115
15	49	52	4		1	Tax Returns	145	164
12	39	101	55	10	7	Other	214	224
77 (4/1-9/30/13)		478 (10/1/13-3/31/14)						
32	114	254	117	24	14	NUMBER OF STATEMENTS	649	661
%	%	%	%	%	%	**ASSETS**	%	%
18.3	8.7	9.1	7.5	4.7	8.1	Cash & Equivalents	7.8	8.9
9.3	7.3	6.4	10.5	9.6	11.7	Trade Receivables (net)	8.1	8.9
47.5	62.7	60.7	42.3	44.3	41.7	Inventory	56.5	54.4
.6	1.1	2.1	2.6	4.6	1.5	All Other Current	2.0	1.8
75.7	79.9	78.2	62.9	63.2	63.0	Total Current	74.3	73.9
17.8	12.2	11.9	22.2	21.1	25.9	Fixed Assets (net)	16.1	15.7
3.1	2.2	5.7	7.5	7.6	2.8	Intangibles (net)	4.4	4.9
3.4	5.7	4.2	7.4	8.0	8.3	All Other Non-Current	5.1	5.4
100.0	100.0	100.0	100.0	100.0	100.0	Total	100.0	100.0
						LIABILITIES		
23.3	27.2	31.6	28.0	33.2	29.9	Notes Payable-Short Term	33.0	31.3
2.4	3.4	2.3	4.5	3.4	3.3	Cur. Mat.-L.T.D.	4.4	4.1
17.0	13.3	10.7	8.3	5.4	5.2	Trade Payables	9.7	11.5
.4	.1	.1	.1	.1	.0	Income Taxes Payable	.0	.1
11.3	12.6	10.8	7.7	12.4	8.8	All Other Current	10.5	9.6
54.4	56.7	55.5	48.5	54.5	47.2	Total Current	57.7	56.5
16.8	11.1	9.4	13.7	14.2	26.8	Long-Term Debt	13.5	11.5
.0	.0	.1	.5	1.3	1.6	Deferred Taxes	.1	.2
9.5	9.1	2.9	3.7	1.6	2.9	All Other Non-Current	7.0	7.0
19.3	23.0	32.2	33.5	28.4	21.5	Net Worth	21.7	24.8
100.0	100.0	100.0	100.0	100.0	100.0	Total Liabilties & Net Worth	100.0	100.0
						INCOME DATA		
100.0	100.0	100.0	100.0	100.0	100.0	Net Sales	100.0	100.0
31.4	24.9	22.7	22.8	14.4	17.7	Gross Profit	23.6	23.7
28.9	23.0	20.3	18.5	12.2	15.8	Operating Expenses	23.3	22.2
2.6	1.9	2.4	4.3	2.2	1.8	Operating Profit	.3	1.5
.7	.6	-.1	.5	-.1	1.1	All Other Expenses (net)	.7	.4
1.9	1.3	2.5	3.8	2.4	.7	Profit Before Taxes	-.4	1.1
						RATIOS		
3.9	2.7	1.8	1.6	1.4	1.6		1.8	1.8
1.4	1.4	1.4	1.2	1.2	1.2	Current	1.3	1.3
.8	1.1	1.1	1.0	1.0	1.1		1.0	1.1
1.0	.7	.4	.6	.3	.6		.5	.6
.6	.2	.2	.4	.2	.4	Quick	(648) .2	(660) .2
.2	.1	.1	.2	.1	.3		.1	.1
0 UND	**0** 999.8	**2** 176.4	**5** 76.1	**6** 61.0	**11** 32.7		**2** 232.6	**2** 161.8
0 UND	**2** 166.8	**5** 72.6	**10** 35.1	**11** 34.7	**15** 23.8	Sales/Receivables	**6** 59.7	**7** 52.8
13 28.4	**9** 40.3	**11** 34.2	**21** 17.6	**17** 21.9	**36** 10.2		**17** 21.2	**18** 20.0
10 37.8	**73** 5.0	**76** 4.8	**51** 7.2	**56** 6.5	**60** 6.1		**70** 5.2	**64** 5.7
43 8.5	**107** 3.4	**111** 3.3	**78** 4.7	**78** 4.7	**73** 5.0	Cost of Sales/Inventory	**107** 3.4	**101** 3.6
104 3.5	**174** 2.1	**166** 2.2	**111** 3.3	**104** 3.5	**107** 3.4		**174** 2.1	**159** 2.3
0 UND	**2** 176.1	**5** 78.6	**6** 56.4	**3** 119.6	**6** 57.9		**4** 81.6	**5** 76.4
5 74.6	**9** 39.2	**10** 36.5	**11** 32.1	**9** 42.2	**10** 36.8	Cost of Sales/Payables	**11** 34.6	**12** 31.1
42 8.6	**25** 14.4	**20** 18.6	**19** 19.6	**13** 28.1	**17** 21.6		**22** 16.3	**24** 15.3
6.6	6.3	7.0	9.4	11.7	7.4		7.0	7.3
42.7	12.9	12.6	21.1	30.9	24.1	Sales/Working Capital	16.1	14.6
-45.3	82.4	34.3	78.2	168.7	46.8		117.8	78.4
9.3	6.6	9.1	13.1	9.3	5.7		3.1	5.5
(24) 4.0	(102) 2.7	(229) 3.2	(111) 6.0	(23) 6.4	(13) 3.7	EBIT/Interest	(581) 1.2	(604) 2.1
1.3	.7	1.5	2.9	3.7	2.3		-.5	.8
		3.8	4.7	4.8			2.2	2.7
		(23) 2.0	(25) 1.8	(11) 2.4		Net Profit + Depr., Dep., Amort./Cur. Mat. L/T/D	(68) 1.1	(75) 1.4
		.7	1.1	1.1			.1	.9
.1	.1	.1	.2	.2	.5		.2	.1
.9	.3	.3	.7	1.1	1.4	Fixed/Worth	.6	.5
-.8	NM	1.0	1.9	1.5	2.4		2.7	2.3
1.0	1.1	1.4	1.3	1.9	3.7		1.6	1.4
5.0	3.4	2.6	2.9	4.0	4.4	Debt/Worth	3.8	3.4
-13.3	NM	7.4	5.5	7.3	8.8		16.3	11.6
167.0	46.7	44.9	51.9	39.1	75.1		21.8	31.3
(21) 42.1	(86) 14.6	(221) 19.5	(111) 29.5	(23) 24.2	32.0	% Profit Before Taxes/Tangible Net Worth	(527) 4.8	(540) 12.5
15.2	3.4	3.8	17.1	20.5	9.4		-11.3	1.0
30.4	11.3	12.0	12.2	8.6	8.0		5.4	8.0
10.1	3.9	4.9	7.5	5.5	5.3	% Profit Before Taxes/Total Assets	.6	2.9
.4	-.4	1.0	3.2	3.0	2.4		-4.2	-.5
374.1	163.1	115.4	60.1	59.2	36.7		79.2	83.7
62.4	60.1	42.3	15.0	15.0	12.1	Sales/Net Fixed Assets	27.8	32.3
19.8	23.9	17.7	5.5	7.2	4.6		9.2	11.3
7.2	4.1	3.4	2.9	3.1	2.9		3.2	3.5
4.3	2.7	2.5	2.1	2.5	2.4	Sales/Total Assets	2.3	2.3
2.7	2.0	1.8	1.5	1.8	1.5		1.5	1.6
.2	.2	.3	.3	.3	.4		.4	.3
(21) .7	(81) .4	(207) .5	(107) .8	(22) .7	(12) 1.5	% Depr., Dep., Amort./Sales	(533) .8	(531) .7
2.0	1.0	1.0	2.3	2.1	3.0		1.8	1.6
3.0	1.1	.9	.4				1.1	1.0
(11) 4.3	(52) 1.9	(122) 1.6	(19) 1.3			% Officers', Directors' Owners' Comp/Sales	(291) 2.0	(299) 1.8
5.5	2.8	3.0	3.7				3.9	3.2
49553M	**479032M**	**3356226M**	**6451479M**	**4031869M**	**5146867M**	Net Sales ($)	**12626644M**	**16579016M**
8332M	**147577M**	**1235028M**	**2638937M**	**1650068M**	**2379633M**	Total Assets ($)	**5714390M**	**7365074M**

M = $ thousand MM = $ million

See Pages 9 through 22 for Explanation of Ratios and Data

Comparative Historical Data | Current Data Sorted by Sales

			Type of Statement						
46	42	32	Unqualified				1	2	29
93	92	94	Reviewed		3	4	10	38	39
106	96	84	Compiled	3	9	11	23	32	6
158	139	121	Tax Returns	14	20	22	31	27	7
230	210	224	Other	10	19	22	44	63	66
				77 (4/1-9/30/13)			478 (10/1/13-3/31/14)		
4/1/11-3/31/12 ALL	**4/1/12-3/31/13 ALL**	**4/1/13-3/31/14 ALL**		**0-1MM**	**1-3MM**	**3-5MM**	**5-10MM**	**10-25MM**	**25MM & OVER**
633	579	555	**NUMBER OF STATEMENTS**	27	51	59	109	162	147
%	%	%	**ASSETS**	%	%	%	%	%	%
9.2	9.6	9.0	Cash & Equivalents	18.5	9.1	7.4	8.7	8.7	8.5
8.5	8.1	7.9	Trade Receivables (net)	11.3	6.8	5.7	4.7	7.1	11.6
53.9	55.5	55.3	Inventory	38.0	60.7	67.4	65.7	54.5	44.9
1.7	1.5	2.0	All Other Current	.1	1.2	1.3	1.6	2.7	2.5
73.2	74.9	74.2	Total Current	68.0	77.9	81.7	80.7	73.0	67.4
15.9	14.3	15.2	Fixed Assets (net)	18.2	14.2	11.2	10.6	14.5	20.8
5.9	5.6	5.2	Intangibles (net)	3.2	3.7	3.4	4.4	7.6	4.9
5.1	5.2	5.4	All Other Non-Current	10.6	4.2	3.7	4.2	5.0	6.9
100.0	100.0	100.0	Total	100.0	100.0	100.0	100.0	100.0	100.0
			LIABILITIES						
29.1	29.0	29.5	Notes Payable-Short Term	22.0	28.7	31.6	31.1	29.3	29.2
3.5	3.8	3.1	Cur. Mat.-L.T.D.	.9	3.2	2.6	4.0	2.1	3.9
10.2	9.7	10.7	Trade Payables	11.1	13.2	11.9	11.6	10.5	9.0
.1	.1	.1	Income Taxes Payable	.6	.1	.0	.0	.1	.1
10.5	11.1	10.6	All Other Current	11.5	13.0	12.7	10.9	10.1	9.1
53.4	53.7	53.9	Total Current	46.1	58.2	58.8	57.7	52.0	51.3
13.2	12.7	11.7	Long-Term Debt	14.5	18.0	10.3	9.8	9.8	13.1
.2	.3	.2	Deferred Taxes	.0	.1	.0	.0	.1	.8
6.3	5.3	4.7	All Other Non-Current	12.9	5.7	11.9	3.0	2.7	3.4
26.9	28.1	29.4	Net Worth	26.5	18.1	18.9	29.6	35.4	31.4
100.0	100.0	100.0	Total Liabilities & Net Worth	100.0	100.0	100.0	100.0	100.0	100.0
			INCOME DATA						
100.0	100.0	100.0	Net Sales	100.0	100.0	100.0	100.0	100.0	100.0
24.2	23.0	23.2	Gross Profit	39.7	24.7	24.0	22.4	23.7	19.2
21.5	20.0	20.5	Operating Expenses	36.3	22.8	22.1	20.7	20.8	15.7
2.7	2.9	2.7	Operating Profit	3.4	1.9	1.9	1.8	2.9	3.5
.4	.2	.2	All Other Expenses (net)	1.5	.7	.3	.2	-.3	.3
2.3	2.7	2.5	Profit Before Taxes	1.8	1.3	1.6	1.6	3.2	3.2
			RATIOS						
1.9	2.0	1.9	Current	4.4	2.2	2.5	2.0	1.8	1.6
1.3	1.3	1.3		2.2	1.2	1.4	1.4	1.4	1.2
1.1	1.1	1.1		.9	1.1	1.1	1.1	1.1	1.1
.6	.6	.5	Quick	1.3	.6	.5	.4	.5	.6
(632) .3	.3	.3		.7	.2	.2	.2	.2	.4
.1	.1	.1		.2	.1	.1	.1	.1	.2
2 180.4	**2** 220.9	**2** 215.5	Sales/Receivables	**0** UND	**0** UND	**0** 999.8	**1** 316.0	**2** 208.8	**5** 69.1
7 53.6	**6** 60.6	**6** 62.6		**6** 60.5	**3** 143.3	**4** 91.5	**3** 128.8	**5** 70.1	**12** 31.3
17 21.5	**16** 23.3	**14** 25.8		**18** 20.6	**12** 29.2	**10** 38.1	**8** 46.6	**11** 33.3	**21** 17.5
68 5.4	**64** 5.7	**63** 5.8	Cost of Sales/Inventory	**3** 134.3	**66** 5.5	**91** 4.0	**83** 4.4	**68** 5.4	**51** 7.2
99 3.7	**94** 3.9	**96** 3.8		**104** 3.5	**152** 2.4	**146** 2.5	**140** 2.6	**94** 3.9	**68** 5.4
152 2.4	**140** 2.6	**152** 2.4		**215** 1.7	**203** 1.8	**192** 1.9	**182** 2.0	**135** 2.7	**89** 4.1
5 75.1	**5** 80.5	**5** 80.2	Cost of Sales/Payables	**0** UND	**2** 175.5	**2** 198.5	**4** 91.7	**6** 65.8	**6** 65.2
11 33.9	**10** 37.0	**10** 36.9		**5** 74.3	**9** 38.8	**9** 39.2	**10** 38.3	**10** 35.9	**10** 35.8
22 16.9	**18** 19.8	**20** 18.5		**42** 8.6	**28** 13.2	**26** 14.3	**20** 18.7	**18** 20.1	**18** 20.3
7.3	7.5	7.4	Sales/Working Capital	3.6	4.9	5.4	6.7	8.2	10.3
14.1	14.5	14.5		7.4	11.7	10.4	12.2	14.5	23.0
76.0	47.4	52.9		-12.8	56.8	30.5	43.7	54.8	62.3
7.6	8.7	9.3	EBIT/Interest	12.5	7.8	5.0	4.8	11.4	12.4
(571) 2.9	(522) 3.6	(502) 3.8		(17) 2.7	(48) 2.9	(54) 2.2	(93) 2.1	(152) 4.3	(138) 6.2
1.3	1.7	1.6		-2.8	.9	.9	1.0	2.0	3.2
5.3	6.5	4.1	Net Profit + Depr., Dep., Amort./Cur. Mat. L/T/D					4.1	5.4
(63) 2.4	(67) 1.9	(69) 1.8						(20) 2.1	(38) 1.7
1.2	1.2	.9						1.2	1.1
.1	.1	.1	Fixed/Worth	.0	.1	.1	.1	.1	.2
.5	.4	.4		.9	.6	.4	.2	.3	.6
2.6	2.1	1.7		-2.1	-8.1	4.6	2.0	1.2	1.8
1.5	1.4	1.3	Debt/Worth	.8	1.7	1.2	1.4	1.1	1.4
3.4	3.2	3.0		3.0	5.4	2.9	3.5	2.3	2.9
12.2	10.3	8.0		-17.7	-39.8	144.8	10.8	7.2	5.6
46.2	51.4	50.4	% Profit Before Taxes/Tangible Net Worth	61.5	49.9	43.1	31.0	48.6	55.1
(528) 19.5	(491) 22.9	(476) 23.1		(19) 13.5	(36) 16.6	(45) 15.9	(91) 14.8	(141) 22.2	(144) 31.5
5.4	9.3	7.4		.0	5.1	1.9	1.0	7.6	19.5
9.8	11.9	12.0	% Profit Before Taxes/Total Assets	20.3	10.3	8.3	8.6	12.7	13.9
4.2	5.2	5.4		3.6	4.0	2.5	2.7	6.0	7.9
.9	1.7	1.3		-7.9	.0	-.4	.1	2.2	3.9
100.6	115.7	106.0	Sales/Net Fixed Assets	291.3	98.7	164.1	148.0	106.0	68.6
35.2	40.0	37.3		49.5	36.4	60.5	53.8	39.8	20.0
10.6	13.1	11.6		15.5	12.9	23.0	20.9	11.9	8.0
3.5	3.7	3.6	Sales/Total Assets	3.3	3.3	3.3	3.5	3.5	3.8
2.4	2.5	2.5		1.9	2.3	2.4	2.3	2.6	2.7
1.7	1.8	1.8		1.2	1.6	1.6	1.8	1.8	2.0
.3	.3	.3	% Depr., Dep., Amort./Sales	.3	.2	.2	.3	.3	.3
(481) .7	(436) .6	(450) .6		(15) .8	(36) .7	(45) .4	(86) .5	(131) .6	(137) .7
1.5	1.2	1.4		2.3	2.2	.9	1.0	1.1	2.1
.8	.9	.9	% Officers', Directors' Owners' Comp/Sales		1.8	1.2	.9	1.0	.5
(288) 1.5	(244) 1.7	(210) 1.7			(19) 2.7	(27) 2.1	(58) 1.5	(74) 1.7	(26) .9
2.7	3.4	3.2			4.3	2.5	2.1	3.3	4.1
19616227M	20678411M	19515026M	Net Sales ($)	16930M	106556M	236137M	795057M	2503822M	15856524M
8396125M	7858188M	8059575M	Total Assets ($)	12724M	54362M	109402M	356943M	1095778M	6430366M

M = $ thousand MM = $ million

See Pages 9 through 22 for Explanation of Ratios and Data

Current Data Sorted by Assets							Comparative Historical Data	
						Type of Statement		
	1	2	10	2	5	Unqualified	20	18
	1	15	12			Reviewed	55	53
11	20	26	6			Compiled	77	78
48	60	24	5		1	Tax Returns	158	173
31	49	45	21	9	7	Other	116	144
45 (4/1-9/30/13)		366 (10/1/13-3/31/14)					4/1/09-3/31/10 ALL	4/1/10-3/31/11 ALL
0-500M	500M-2MM	2-10MM	10-50MM	50-100MM	100-250MM			
90	131	112	54	11	13	**NUMBER OF STATEMENTS**	426	466
%	%	%	%	%	%	**ASSETS**	%	%
17.2	9.4	8.9	6.3	9.3	3.4	Cash & Equivalents	7.5	8.8
11.4	13.0	18.4	14.9	15.7	13.2	Trade Receivables (net)	14.1	14.5
40.0	48.4	51.8	45.7	32.5	43.5	Inventory	46.2	47.4
1.6	.9	1.6	1.7	3.6	2.6	All Other Current	1.9	1.6
70.2	71.7	80.7	68.6	61.1	62.7	Total Current	69.7	72.3
16.0	19.1	11.5	19.0	24.5	22.7	Fixed Assets (net)	19.6	17.1
5.7	4.7	3.4	4.7	6.1	9.8	Intangibles (net)	4.6	4.2
8.1	4.5	4.4	7.6	8.3	4.8	All Other Non-Current	6.1	6.3
100.0	100.0	100.0	100.0	100.0	100.0	Total	100.0	100.0
						LIABILITIES		
14.5	8.5	13.6	18.7	11.7	8.6	Notes Payable-Short Term	12.1	9.7
2.4	2.7	2.8	2.5	1.7	1.9	Cur. Mat.-L.T.D.	3.0	2.8
16.2	18.2	22.1	17.8	15.3	19.0	Trade Payables	20.1	20.3
.3	.1	.2	.0	.0	.3	Income Taxes Payable	.1	.1
18.5	8.6	7.7	10.2	12.1	8.4	All Other Current	8.9	10.2
51.9	38.2	46.4	49.1	40.9	38.2	Total Current	44.2	43.1
20.3	18.2	12.6	11.1	19.4	21.5	Long-Term Debt	21.6	18.8
.0	.0	.1	.4	.1	1.6	Deferred Taxes	.1	.1
10.1	8.1	3.6	7.5	6.0	12.3	All Other Non-Current	7.1	9.2
17.7	35.4	37.3	32.0	33.6	26.4	Net Worth	27.0	28.8
100.0	100.0	100.0	100.0	100.0	100.0	Total Liabilties & Net Worth	100.0	100.0
						INCOME DATA		
100.0	100.0	100.0	100.0	100.0	100.0	Net Sales	100.0	100.0
45.1	39.0	31.3	29.3	28.6	35.6	Gross Profit	37.3	37.7
41.2	35.2	28.5	26.0	25.2	30.8	Operating Expenses	34.9	33.9
4.0	3.7	2.8	3.3	3.4	4.8	Operating Profit	2.4	3.8
.4	.3	.0	.5	.4	2.1	All Other Expenses (net)	.8	.9
3.5	3.4	2.7	2.9	3.1	2.8	Profit Before Taxes	1.6	2.9
						RATIOS		
5.8	3.8	2.9	2.3	6.6	2.2		3.3	3.4
1.9	2.1	1.6	1.3	1.5	1.7	Current	1.7	1.8
1.1	1.2	1.3	1.0	1.0	1.2		1.1	1.2
1.8	1.3	1.0	.7	1.8	.7		1.0	1.0
.7	.5	.6	.4	.7	.6	Quick	.5	.5
.3	.2	.3	.2	.3	.2		.3	.3
0 UND	**2** 153.2	**13** 28.8	**13** 27.1	**7** 50.7	**4** 92.9		**6** 60.4	**5** 68.7
7 54.1	**15** 23.8	**25** 14.4	**24** 15.0	**17** 21.7	**28** 12.9	Sales/Receivables	**20** 18.2	**19** 18.9
17 21.7	**27** 13.6	**34** 10.6	**37** 9.8	**63** 5.8	**47** 7.7		**33** 11.2	**31** 11.8
20 18.7	**47** 7.8	**63** 5.8	**58** 6.3	**42** 8.7	**69** 5.3		**55** 6.7	**52** 7.0
49 7.4	**91** 4.0	**99** 3.7	**114** 3.2	**81** 4.5	**111** 3.3	Cost of Sales/Inventory	**104** 3.5	**98** 3.7
130 2.8	**174** 2.1	**166** 2.2	**192** 1.9	**104** 3.5	**243** 1.5		**187** 2.0	**172** 2.1
0 UND	**7** 49.4	**21** 17.2	**18** 20.8	**17** 21.4	**31** 11.8		**21** 17.2	**18** 20.5
16 22.8	**30** 12.3	**40** 9.2	**40** 9.1	**27** 13.4	**58** 6.3	Cost of Sales/Payables	**37** 9.7	**35** 10.5
35 10.4	**51** 7.1	**60** 6.1	**69** 5.3	**40** 9.2	**69** 5.3		**59** 6.2	**59** 6.2
6.2	4.4	4.5	4.1	4.2	4.2		4.2	4.2
18.8	8.5	7.7	9.5	7.5	12.9	Sales/Working Capital	8.0	8.4
96.1	30.2	19.1	389.4	-114.0	19.3		39.4	37.0
13.1	13.6	11.8	11.3	41.3	20.5		6.1	11.8
(60) 2.7	(108) 4.5	(101) 4.8	(49) 3.8	(10) 6.0	5.7	EBIT/Interest	(381) 2.6	(403) 3.7
.5	1.9	2.2	1.8	.0	1.4		1.0	1.2
		8.8	3.9			Net Profit + Depr., Dep.,	4.8	4.7
		(22) 3.6	(11) 2.3			Amort./Cur. Mat. L/T/D	(62) 2.1	(72) 2.5
		1.4	.4				.6	.8
.0	.1	.1	.2	.4	.3		.1	.1
.3	.3	.2	.5	1.0	2.5	Fixed/Worth	.4	.3
3.9	1.9	.8	7.1	1.5	-2.6		3.3	1.9
.4	.8	1.0	1.2	1.5	.9		1.0	.8
1.8	2.1	2.1	2.9	2.5	3.5	Debt/Worth	2.3	1.8
-40.4	9.6	4.3	35.8	11.3	-21.5		13.8	9.0
72.1	51.9	31.4	36.9	24.9		% Profit Before Taxes/Tangible	30.8	39.8
(67) 29.6	(110) 18.4	(104) 17.1	(44) 17.6	(10) 13.0		Net Worth	(343) 11.4	(383) 17.2
-1.2	7.5	4.9	5.5	-17.0			.4	4.4
28.2	15.2	10.4	12.4	8.6	19.6	% Profit Before Taxes/Total	9.9	13.2
8.6	5.3	4.3	3.9	6.1	6.1	Assets	3.5	5.4
-1.2	1.8	1.8	1.1	-.1	2.0		-.2	.6
503.0	125.2	117.9	43.9	29.9	33.4		65.1	81.6
61.3	38.0	42.7	20.4	11.1	11.5	Sales/Net Fixed Assets	23.6	32.7
16.0	16.4	19.2	6.8	4.5	5.9		8.9	12.3
7.0	4.5	3.3	3.2	2.2	3.7		3.4	3.9
4.4	2.9	2.5	2.1	1.9	1.7	Sales/Total Assets	2.4	2.6
2.4	1.8	1.9	1.5	.9	1.2		1.7	1.8
.6	.4	.4	.4		.8		.6	.5
(48) .9	(89) .8	(81) .6	(51) .9		(10) 1.5	% Depr., Dep., Amort./Sales	(342) 1.1	(350) 1.0
1.9	1.4	1.2	1.7		3.0		1.8	1.8
3.5	2.1	1.1	.8			% Officers', Directors'	1.8	1.8
(41) 6.2	(79) 3.5	(61) 1.9	(16) 1.2			Owners' Comp/Sales	(222) 3.2	(240) 3.3
8.0	5.3	3.0	2.7				6.2	5.3
110539M	481131M	1557547M	3335315M	1955030M	4022197M	Net Sales ($)	7950722M	8602754M
24169M	144740M	515690M	1302785M	730911M	1843404M	Total Assets ($)	3851618M	4167823M

M = $ thousand MM = $ million

See Pages 9 through 22 for Explanation of Ratios and Data

Comparative Historical Data / Current Data Sorted by Sales

			Type of Statement						
27	19	20	Unqualified				2	4	14
63	32	28	Reviewed				5	11	12
79	53	63	Compiled	10	10	8	19	13	3
182	165	138	Tax Returns	28	51	21	25	5	8
152	145	162	Other	19	36	19	26	26	36
					45 (4/1-9/30/13)		366 (10/1/13-3/31/14)		
4/1/11-3/31/12 ALL	4/1/12-3/31/13 ALL	4/1/13-3/31/14 ALL		0-1MM	1-3MM	3-5MM	5-10MM	10-25MM	25MM & OVER
503	414	411	NUMBER OF STATEMENTS	57	97	48	77	59	73
%	%	%	ASSETS	%	%	%	%	%	%
9.2	10.6	10.4	Cash & Equivalents	18.5	10.9	7.4	9.7	9.0	7.1
14.5	14.8	14.5	Trade Receivables (net)	6.5	14.4	16.5	15.6	17.4	15.8
47.1	45.1	46.5	Inventory	36.1	47.2	51.7	50.6	49.2	44.2
1.7	1.5	1.5	All Other Current	2.1	.9	.7	1.0	1.7	2.4
72.5	72.0	72.8	Total Current	63.1	73.5	76.2	76.8	77.3	69.6
17.8	17.2	16.6	Fixed Assets (net)	21.7	16.5	14.8	15.1	11.2	19.8
3.7	4.6	4.8	Intangibles (net)	8.1	4.0	4.1	3.1	5.2	5.1
6.0	6.2	5.8	All Other Non-Current	7.0	6.0	4.9	5.0	6.3	5.5
100.0	100.0	100.0	Total	100.0	100.0	100.0	100.0	100.0	100.0
			LIABILITIES						
10.2	11.2	12.6	Notes Payable-Short Term	9.3	12.5	11.6	11.8	13.8	16.0
2.9	2.9	2.6	Cur. Mat.-L.T.D.	3.0	1.7	3.8	2.4	3.5	2.0
19.8	19.4	18.7	Trade Payables	13.7	15.6	17.2	23.0	21.4	21.1
.1	.1	.2	Income Taxes Payable	.2	.2	.1	.1	.2	.1
10.8	9.8	10.8	All Other Current	22.8	9.3	6.7	9.4	8.8	9.3
43.8	43.5	44.9	Total Current	48.9	39.4	39.4	46.8	47.8	48.6
17.8	20.9	16.3	Long-Term Debt	27.6	16.5	18.7	11.8	10.8	15.0
.2	.2	.1	Deferred Taxes	.0	.0	.0	.1	.3	.5
8.6	8.7	7.3	All Other Non-Current	8.8	10.3	7.2	4.4	5.6	6.6
29.7	26.7	31.3	Net Worth	14.7	33.8	34.6	36.9	35.5	29.3
100.0	100.0	100.0	Total Liabilties & Net Worth	100.0	100.0	100.0	100.0	100.0	100.0
			INCOME DATA						
100.0	100.0	100.0	Net Sales	100.0	100.0	100.0	100.0	100.0	100.0
37.3	37.0	36.6	Gross Profit	48.9	39.4	35.8	35.4	31.1	29.4
33.3	33.2	33.1	Operating Expenses	44.1	35.7	32.3	33.0	27.6	25.9
4.0	3.9	3.5	Operating Profit	4.8	3.6	3.4	2.4	3.4	3.5
.7	.7	.3	All Other Expenses (net)	1.1	.2	.3	-.3	.6	.5
3.3	3.2	3.1	Profit Before Taxes	3.7	3.5	3.1	2.7	2.9	3.0
			RATIOS						
3.4	3.4	3.3		6.9	4.2	3.3	2.9	2.7	2.0
1.8	1.9	1.7	Current	2.2	2.4	2.1	1.5	1.7	1.4
1.2	1.2	1.2		1.1	1.3	1.4	1.2	1.2	1.0
1.0	1.2	1.2		3.4	1.4	1.3	1.0	.9	.7
.5	.6	.5	Quick	.7	.6	.6	.5	.5	.4
.3	.3	.3		.1	.3	.2	.3	.3	.2
4 86.2	3 111.1	4 89.4		0 UND	4 103.7	6 60.7	4 98.7	11 32.5	10 37.8
17 21.5	15 24.8	17 20.9	Sales/Receivables	3 139.7	16 22.6	18 19.9	21 17.4	22 16.5	23 15.7
30 12.1	30 12.2	29 12.4		15 24.0	27 13.5	29 12.8	34 10.7	31 11.6	38 9.7
48 7.6	35 10.3	47 7.8		12 30.0	40 9.2	47 7.8	54 6.7	54 6.8	54 6.7
96 3.8	83 4.4	87 4.2	Cost of Sales/Inventory	79 4.6	85 4.3	85 4.3	85 4.3	89 4.1	83 4.4
166 2.2	159 2.3	166 2.2		182 2.0	192 1.9	174 2.1	140 2.6	174 2.1	152 2.4
16 22.3	13 28.7	12 31.4		0 UND	8 45.2	12 31.3	17 20.9	19 19.2	17 20.9
32 11.3	29 12.4	31 11.9	Cost of Sales/Payables	16 23.5	23 15.7	29 12.4	41 9.0	35 10.5	39 9.3
62 5.9	53 6.9	54 6.7		47 7.8	49 7.5	47 7.7	61 6.0	52 7.0	63 5.8
4.3	4.6	4.7		3.9	3.8	5.1	5.4	5.4	5.7
9.4	10.6	9.4	Sales/Working Capital	16.5	8.0	7.8	9.1	9.0	13.8
43.7	42.7	37.5		98.4	37.6	22.3	38.5	22.0	122.3
12.8	12.4	12.5		4.0	19.8	9.6	14.5	14.1	11.5
(421) 3.9	(338) 3.6	(341) 4.6	EBIT/Interest	(37) 1.9	(77) 4.6	(39) 5.6	(68) 6.3	(53) 3.4	(67) 5.7
1.4	1.4	1.6		-.4	1.0	1.3	2.4	1.7	2.1
4.9	7.0	6.7					8.6	9.9	5.9
(61) 2.6	(38) 2.8	(44) 3.0	Net Profit + Depr., Dep., Amort./Cur. Mat. L/T/D				(10) 3.6	(13) 2.8	(14) 2.9
.9	1.0	.8					1.5	.6	.6
.1	.1	.1		.0	.1	.1	.1	.1	.3
.4	.3	.3	Fixed/Worth	.2	.2	.3	.2	.2	.7
2.5	4.2	1.6		13.6	1.2	1.9	.9	1.2	10.8
.8	.6	.8		.3	.5	1.1	.9	.9	1.4
2.0	2.2	2.2	Debt/Worth	4.1	1.6	2.2	1.9	2.2	3.0
9.6	21.0	10.2		-9.0	9.4	13.5	3.7	6.3	39.0
42.4	45.3	42.8		73.6	44.0	63.1	39.0	37.1	37.8
(411) 19.6	(329) 18.4	(344) 18.5	% Profit Before Taxes/Tangible Net Worth	(41) 18.9	(80) 15.4	(42) 20.9	(70) 19.5	(52) 17.6	(59) 18.1
7.5	5.0	5.2		.2	3.0	5.4	7.7	5.1	7.1
14.3	15.2	14.4		14.5	19.2	12.8	14.7	14.3	11.4
6.1	5.1	4.9	% Profit Before Taxes/Total Assets	4.2	5.9	5.3	4.7	3.8	4.8
1.4	.9	1.5		-5.6	.3	1.4	2.2	1.7	1.9
87.1	110.0	112.8		UND	137.3	150.4	131.7	93.5	42.5
31.3	35.2	37.4	Sales/Net Fixed Assets	51.8	38.4	45.0	39.4	53.2	14.2
12.1	14.5	12.7		9.3	16.1	17.9	19.7	21.4	7.9
4.0	4.2	4.3		5.5	4.7	4.5	4.7	3.7	3.9
2.6	2.7	2.7	Sales/Total Assets	2.3	2.7	3.0	3.0	2.5	2.3
1.9	1.9	1.8		1.3	1.7	2.0	2.3	1.9	1.7
.4	.4	.4		.6	.5	.4	.5	.4	.4
(366) .9	(299) .8	(287) .8	% Depr., Dep., Amort./Sales	(26) 1.4	(63) .8	(35) .9	(54) .9	(47) .6	(62) 1.0
1.7	1.5	1.5		3.5	1.3	1.4	1.3	1.2	1.9
1.6	1.7	1.5		5.4	2.9	2.1	1.4	1.0	.5
(240) 2.8	(211) 3.2	(200) 2.8	% Officers', Directors' Owners' Comp/Sales	(26) 7.6	(53) 4.7	(30) 2.5	(43) 2.2	(30) 1.2	(18) 1.0
5.3	5.2	5.8		11.0	6.1	3.9	3.7	2.8	2.1
10354183M	7969397M	11461759M	Net Sales ($)	33984M	180310M	185738M	570281M	1002098M	9489348M
4202532M	3770305M	4561699M	Total Assets ($)	17486M	77136M	69200M	215595M	442731M	3739551M

M = $ thousand MM = $ million

See Pages 9 through 22 for Explanation of Ratios and Data

Current Data Sorted by Assets							Comparative Historical Data	
						Type of Statement		
			8	3	5	Unqualified	17	15
	6	20	15	3		Reviewed	33	46
7	9	12	9	1		Compiled	32	41
28	19	16	3			Tax Returns	49	50
11	15	18	20	4	2	Other	39	65
37 (4/1-9/30/13)			197 (10/1/13-3/31/14)				4/1/09-3/31/10 ALL	4/1/10-3/31/11 ALL
0-500M	**500M-2MM**	**2-10MM**	**10-50MM**	**50-100MM**	**100-250MM**			
46	49	66	55	11	7	**NUMBER OF STATEMENTS**	170	217
%	%	%	%	%	%	**ASSETS**	%	%
14.7	10.6	7.5	6.5	6.4		Cash & Equivalents	9.1	11.5
9.1	16.0	18.0	18.0	13.6		Trade Receivables (net)	18.7	16.3
34.2	38.6	41.4	42.7	45.0		Inventory	38.7	37.3
3.0	1.2	2.5	2.6	1.6		All Other Current	2.7	2.5
61.0	66.4	69.4	69.8	66.7		Total Current	69.3	67.7
18.9	20.8	21.0	22.5	25.9		Fixed Assets (net)	20.4	22.1
10.5	2.6	3.2	3.4	2.3		Intangibles (net)	4.2	4.4
9.6	10.2	6.4	4.4	5.1		All Other Non-Current	6.0	5.8
100.0	100.0	100.0	100.0	100.0		Total	100.0	100.0
						LIABILITIES		
20.1	6.5	10.8	8.8	12.4		Notes Payable-Short Term	9.8	8.2
3.2	3.7	1.4	1.8	2.0		Cur. Mat.-L.T.D.	3.1	3.2
41.5	25.8	24.6	30.8	30.5		Trade Payables	32.2	29.7
.0	.1	.1	.2	.0		Income Taxes Payable	.1	.1
12.2	11.9	8.0	7.5	9.5		All Other Current	7.2	11.0
77.1	48.0	44.8	49.1	54.5		Total Current	52.3	52.1
27.2	17.8	11.2	10.6	8.1		Long-Term Debt	17.4	16.5
.0	.0	.1	.5	.6		Deferred Taxes	.2	.1
8.6	5.6	4.2	2.6	2.6		All Other Non-Current	3.0	3.3
-12.9	28.6	39.7	37.2	34.2		Net Worth	27.1	28.0
100.0	100.0	100.0	100.0	100.0		Total Liabilities & Net Worth	100.0	100.0
						INCOME DATA		
100.0	100.0	100.0	100.0	100.0		Net Sales	100.0	100.0
44.3	38.3	31.9	28.2	28.9		Gross Profit	34.9	36.4
41.6	35.6	29.3	25.6	25.8		Operating Expenses	32.4	33.2
2.7	2.6	2.6	2.6	3.1		Operating Profit	2.5	3.2
.4	.3	.1	-.1	.1		All Other Expenses (net)	.2	.3
2.3	2.3	2.5	2.7	3.1		Profit Before Taxes	2.3	2.9
						RATIOS		
2.3	2.6	2.2	1.9	1.8			1.9	1.9
1.4	1.6	1.5	1.3	1.4		Current	1.4	1.4
.7	.9	1.2	1.1	.9			1.0	1.0
1.2	.9	.9	.7	.6			.9	.9
.3	.6	.6	.4	.4		Quick	(169) .5	(216) .5
.1	.3	.3	.3	.3			.3	.3
1 699.5	2 185.5	9 40.7	10 37.1	5 71.9			7 51.5	6 66.3
3 113.1	11 32.7	24 15.4	22 16.8	20 18.0		Sales/Receivables	18 20.8	15 24.7
9 42.3	28 13.0	31 11.6	32 11.3	27 13.4			33 11.1	32 11.4
18 20.7	34 10.7	47 7.7	54 6.7	51 7.1			45 8.1	44 8.4
37 9.9	62 5.9	73 5.0	72 5.1	81 4.5		Cost of Sales/Inventory	65 5.6	64 5.7
58 6.3	99 3.7	114 3.2	99 3.7	99 3.7			94 3.9	93 3.9
0 UND	22 16.6	27 13.3	39 9.4	30 12.2			35 10.4	29 12.4
30 12.0	35 10.4	43 8.4	49 7.4	38 9.5		Cost of Sales/Payables	49 7.4	48 7.6
62 5.9	53 6.9	60 6.1	63 5.8	61 6.0			66 5.5	67 5.4
11.7	7.1	6.1	8.5	9.4			9.3	8.2
26.9	19.9	10.9	20.0	17.1		Sales/Working Capital	15.6	18.4
-22.8	-51.0	32.5	45.7	-141.6			221.5	273.2
11.2	14.0	13.5	18.6	30.9			10.7	13.5
(29) 4.0	(39) 5.3	(62) 4.8	(51) 7.8	16.3		EBIT/Interest	(147) 4.1	(191) 4.6
-.4	.9	2.2	4.8	3.8			1.4	1.6
			8.7				5.0	9.1
			(23) 4.3			Net Profit + Depr., Dep., Amort./Cur. Mat. L/T/D	(37) 2.8	(37) 4.7
			2.0				1.8	2.8
.1	.1	.2	.2	.4			.2	.2
2.5	.5	.5	.6	1.2		Fixed/Worth	.6	.7
-.5	3.5	1.1	1.3	1.4			1.5	2.8
1.1	.7	.7	1.0	1.1			1.0	1.0
15.3	2.3	1.7	2.3	2.2		Debt/Worth	2.1	2.4
-3.6	15.1	4.2	3.2	3.8			5.3	9.8
170.8	56.4	24.0	31.0	29.5			35.8	34.1
(24) 44.9	(39) 20.0	(59) 13.5	(52) 21.3	(10) 20.5		% Profit Before Taxes/Tangible Net Worth	(144) 15.5	(176) 20.3
23.2	3.3	3.2	10.6	13.5			6.1	5.3
30.7	11.9	9.9	11.2	13.4			11.8	13.4
9.2	6.0	3.8	7.2	10.2		% Profit Before Taxes/Total Assets	5.1	6.0
-7.5	.5	1.2	3.3	3.2			.6	1.3
183.0	113.3	32.2	36.2	23.1			56.6	54.7
53.6	30.2	20.8	18.9	10.1		Sales/Net Fixed Assets	20.3	22.2
23.9	13.0	9.0	9.5	8.5			10.2	9.7
8.5	4.6	3.7	3.6	5.1			4.2	4.5
5.3	3.4	2.7	2.7	3.0		Sales/Total Assets	3.2	3.2
3.9	2.2	2.2	2.2	2.1			2.2	2.1
.3	.6	.6	.7	1.0			.7	.8
(29) .9	(37) 1.2	(59) 1.0	(52) 1.2	1.4		% Depr., Dep., Amort./Sales	(143) 1.2	(185) 1.3
1.8	2.0	1.4	1.9	2.1			1.8	1.8
3.7	1.6	1.0	.7				1.2	1.6
(24) 5.4	(22) 2.8	(31) 1.6	(18) 1.5			% Officers', Directors' Owners' Comp/Sales	(79) 3.0	(81) 2.8
8.6	5.9	3.1	3.3				6.3	5.6
59524M	202399M	965285M	3804121M	3190206M	3060760M	Net Sales ($)	6316932M	7269888M
10943M	58819M	326523M	1232231M	727637M	1301989M	Total Assets ($)	2256498M	2825544M

M = $ thousand MM = $ million

See Pages 9 through 22 for Explanation of Ratios and Data

Comparative Historical Data				Current Data Sorted by Sales					
			Type of Statement						
19	11	16	Unqualified						16
47	41	44	Reviewed		2	3	5	12	22
46	28	38	Compiled	2	8	2	7	10	9
52	61	66	Tax Returns	12	24	7	12	5	6
75	72	70	Other	5	13	5	14	8	25
4/1/11-3/31/12	**4/1/12-3/31/13**	**4/1/13-3/31/14**			**37 (4/1-9/30/13)**			**197 (10/1/13-3/31/14)**	
ALL	**ALL**	**ALL**		**0-1MM**	**1-3MM**	**3-5MM**	**5-10MM**	**10-25MM**	**25MM & OVER**
239	213	234	**NUMBER OF STATEMENTS**	19	47	17	38	35	78
%	%	%	**ASSETS**	%	%	%	%	%	%
9.9	9.5	9.4	Cash & Equivalents	16.4	10.1	9.5	12.7	6.1	7.1
15.7	16.1	15.4	Trade Receivables (net)	7.4	12.7	12.6	18.8	16.4	17.3
38.3	40.1	39.5	Inventory	22.9	36.4	43.7	39.7	43.9	42.5
2.3	2.4	2.3	All Other Current	.5	3.4	.9	3.2	2.6	1.7
66.3	68.1	66.5	Total Current	47.1	62.6	66.7	74.4	69.0	68.6
22.7	22.5	21.6	Fixed Assets (net)	27.1	22.9	13.9	16.2	23.8	22.7
4.8	3.2	4.5	Intangibles (net)	8.8	8.8	3.8	3.4	.8	3.2
6.2	6.3	7.4	All Other Non-Current	16.9	5.7	15.7	6.0	6.4	5.5
100.0	100.0	100.0	Total	100.0	100.0	100.0	100.0	100.0	100.0
			LIABILITIES						
7.1	7.0	11.0	Notes Payable-Short Term	40.7	4.5	13.8	5.5	12.1	9.4
2.4	2.3	2.4	Cur. Mat.-L.T.D.	.6	4.6	1.4	3.4	1.5	1.7
28.6	28.9	29.7	Trade Payables	48.5	26.8	24.1	31.3	23.6	30.1
.1	.1	.1	Income Taxes Payable	.0	.0	.1	.1	.2	.1
9.2	10.0	9.5	All Other Current	11.4	14.2	8.1	7.5	10.3	7.2
47.5	48.4	52.8	Total Current	101.2	50.1	47.4	47.9	47.7	48.5
17.8	16.2	16.0	Long-Term Debt	29.1	28.6	11.4	9.3	12.9	11.0
.2	.2	.2	Deferred Taxes	.0	.0	.0	.0	.1	.5
5.5	9.1	5.1	All Other Non-Current	4.1	8.4	7.5	6.8	2.5	3.2
29.1	26.0	25.9	Net Worth	-34.4	12.9	33.7	36.0	36.8	36.9
100.0	100.0	100.0	Total Liabilties & Net Worth	100.0	100.0	100.0	100.0	100.0	100.0
			INCOME DATA						
100.0	100.0	100.0	Net Sales	100.0	100.0	100.0	100.0	100.0	100.0
36.5	35.7	34.7	Gross Profit	43.2	43.7	36.4	33.5	32.2	28.5
33.0	32.1	32.0	Operating Expenses	41.3	40.5	33.4	31.6	29.4	25.5
3.5	3.6	2.7	Operating Profit	1.9	3.1	3.0	2.0	2.7	3.0
.5	.1	.1	All Other Expenses (net)	.4	.5	.4	.1	-.2	-.1
3.0	3.5	2.6	Profit Before Taxes	1.4	2.6	2.6	1.9	2.9	3.1
			RATIOS						
2.1	2.2	2.2		2.3	2.7	2.8	2.2	2.3	1.9
1.4	1.5	1.5	Current	1.4	1.7	1.5	1.8	1.3	1.4
1.1	1.0	1.0		.3	.8	.8	1.3	1.0	1.2
.8	1.0	.9		1.3	1.0	.8	1.1	.8	.7
(237) .6	(212) .6	.5	Quick	.2	.4	.3	.7	.4	.4
.3	.3	.3		.1	.1	.1	.4	.2	.3
5 75.7	**5** 72.3	**4** 82.1		**0** UND	**1** 430.0	**1** 457.1	**9** 41.1	**9** 40.2	**7** 48.8
14 26.7	**14** 25.7	**15** 24.9	Sales/Receivables	**4** 81.3	**5** 77.1	**8** 46.2	**22** 16.4	**22** 16.3	**20** 18.5
28 13.0	**29** 12.8	**28** 13.0		**9** 41.2	**17** 22.0	**27** 13.5	**29** 12.7	**35** 10.3	**29** 12.5
43 8.5	**38** 9.6	**40** 9.2		**9** 40.0	**28** 13.0	**33** 10.9	**39** 9.3	**54** 6.8	**51** 7.2
63 5.8	**62** 5.9	**63** 5.8	Cost of Sales/Inventory	**37** 9.8	**56** 6.5	**62** 5.9	**73** 5.0	**83** 4.4	**70** 5.2
94 3.9	**94** 3.9	**99** 3.7		**52** 7.0	**83** 4.4	**101** 3.6	**104** 3.5	**126** 2.9	**94** 3.9
29 12.8	**25** 14.7	**24** 15.1		**0** UND	**8** 47.6	**17** 21.5	**35** 10.4	**28** 12.9	**32** 11.3
46 8.0	**41** 9.0	**42** 8.7	Cost of Sales/Payables	**22** 16.8	**33** 11.2	**34** 10.8	**46** 8.0	**43** 8.4	**47** 7.7
69 5.3	**63** 5.8	**61** 6.0		**74** 4.9	**51** 7.1	**49** 7.5	**72** 5.1	**59** 6.2	**61** 6.0
8.1	8.2	8.1		10.7	8.8	6.1	6.1	8.0	8.4
17.3	15.5	17.2	Sales/Working Capital	30.0	17.3	23.1	10.0	20.3	17.7
73.2	226.4	236.2		-7.4	-29.9	-33.0	25.2	79.0	36.4
18.6	17.7	17.1		5.4	14.7	10.7	15.9	12.2	19.9
(207) 5.8	(192) 6.6	(199) 6.3	EBIT/Interest	(12) 3.0	(34) 5.1	(13) 6.6	(32) 5.0	3.3	(73) 8.8
1.9	1.9	2.2		-1.2	.4	.9	1.8	2.0	4.9
6.1	11.1	7.4							9.0
(42) 3.5	(34) 5.7	(42) 4.3	Net Profit + Depr., Dep., Amort./Cur. Mat. L/T/D						(30) 4.6
1.8	2.4	1.9							2.4
.2	.2	.2		.3	.1	.0	.2	.1	.2
.7	.6	.6	Fixed/Worth	-49.5	1.0	.2	.4	.7	.6
5.2	2.5	2.2		-.8	-1.0	3.0	.9	1.3	1.3
.9	.9	.8		.8	1.1	.5	.7	.7	1.0
2.2	2.7	2.3	Debt/Worth	-18.3	7.5	3.5	1.5	1.9	2.2
13.9	8.6	8.8		-3.1	-5.7	NM	3.6	4.8	3.8
46.8	46.9	37.7			122.2	57.4	24.8	24.7	34.7
(193) 22.5	(180) 22.7	(190) 19.7	% Profit Before Taxes/Tangible Net Worth		(31) 24.3	(13) 22.6	(32) 10.3	(33) 13.3	(73) 21.7
8.0	7.5	6.5			3.3	5.5	1.6	3.8	10.8
14.0	13.3	12.4		17.2	21.1	18.4	9.0	11.5	11.7
6.3	6.9	6.7	% Profit Before Taxes/Total Assets	8.2	6.2	9.8	4.1	5.4	8.1
1.6	1.6	1.5		-7.2	-3.7	.5	1.1	.8	4.3
48.5	53.5	54.9		99.3	124.1	655.6	54.9	29.5	38.7
23.7	21.3	22.9	Sales/Net Fixed Assets	37.3	32.6	35.1	20.8	16.6	20.6
9.8	11.8	9.7		9.5	11.5	15.2	13.1	8.5	9.3
4.2	4.9	4.6		6.5	5.5	6.0	4.5	3.8	3.9
3.1	3.6	3.1	Sales/Total Assets	4.8	3.9	3.0	3.1	2.7	3.0
2.2	2.3	2.2		2.7	2.2	2.3	2.3	2.0	2.3
.6	.6	.6		.4	.4	.3	.6	.8	.6
(192) 1.1	(173) 1.2	(195) 1.1	% Depr., Dep., Amort./Sales	(11) 1.0	(35) 1.1	(11) 1.1	(30) 1.0	(33) 1.2	(75) 1.1
1.7	1.7	1.7		2.7	2.4	1.7	1.6	1.7	1.7
1.3	1.3	1.0		7.3	1.8		1.1	.9	.7
(95) 2.8	(82) 2.8	(101) 2.2	% Officers', Directors' Owners' Comp/Sales	(11) 8.3	(20) 4.2		(23) 1.8	(11) 1.4	(27) 1.5
4.9	4.7	4.8		10.4	6.9		3.6	3.9	2.5
10599627M	**9828704M**	**11282295M**	Net Sales ($)	**11484M**	**84982M**	**66974M**	**272392M**	**572422M**	**10274041M**
3659627M	**3110786M**	**3658142M**	Total Assets ($)	**3212M**	**30255M**	**22887M**	**95003M**	**231042M**	**3275743M**

M = $ thousand MM = $ million

See Pages 9 through 22 for Explanation of Ratios and Data

Current Data Sorted by Assets | **Comparative Historical Data**

						Type of Statement		
1	2	7	19	9	10	Unqualified	70	47
1	11	32	29		1	Reviewed	105	79
4	29	35	8	2	1	Compiled	148	111
41	86	31	2		1	Tax Returns	176	157
25	54	62	36	9	10	Other	230	215
110 (4/1-9/30/13)			448 (10/1/13-3/31/14)				4/1/09-3/31/10 ALL	4/1/10-3/31/11 ALL
0-500M	500M-2MM	2-10MM	10-50MM	50-100MM	100-250MM			
72	182	167	94	20	23	NUMBER OF STATEMENTS	729	609
%	%	%	%	%	%	ASSETS	%	%
18.0	11.1	11.7	11.2	8.0	5.9	Cash & Equivalents	9.6	10.0
9.3	9.6	13.3	11.3	14.0	11.7	Trade Receivables (net)	11.8	12.3
50.8	51.2	44.6	36.6	33.8	27.3	Inventory	45.1	45.9
1.9	.9	1.7	1.5	3.1	2.2	All Other Current	2.2	2.0
79.9	72.8	71.3	60.6	59.0	47.0	Total Current	68.7	70.2
11.4	18.5	19.2	29.9	29.9	40.8	Fixed Assets (net)	22.2	21.0
2.9	2.3	3.3	3.5	9.1	3.4	Intangibles (net)	3.1	2.1
5.8	6.4	6.2	6.0	2.1	8.8	All Other Non-Current	6.0	6.7
100.0	100.0	100.0	100.0	100.0	100.0	Total	100.0	100.0
						LIABILITIES		
16.6	9.9	6.7	4.8	5.5	4.1	Notes Payable-Short Term	11.2	10.9
7.7	2.3	1.6	1.9	2.4	2.4	Cur. Mat.-L.T.D.	2.7	2.3
19.7	15.8	17.3	14.9	13.5	9.1	Trade Payables	18.4	17.7
.0	.2	.2	.1	.1	.0	Income Taxes Payable	.2	.2
20.5	17.2	18.6	20.4	14.7	12.8	All Other Current	19.8	19.0
64.5	45.3	44.4	42.1	36.2	28.4	Total Current	52.2	50.1
17.5	18.9	12.8	17.4	21.3	23.1	Long-Term Debt	15.0	15.8
.0	.0	.0	.2	.0	.4	Deferred Taxes	.1	.1
16.8	10.0	8.2	5.6	6.0	3.4	All Other Non-Current	7.1	9.1
1.1	25.7	34.6	34.8	36.5	44.7	Net Worth	25.6	24.9
100.0	100.0	100.0	100.0	100.0	100.0	Total Liabilties & Net Worth	100.0	100.0
						INCOME DATA		
100.0	100.0	100.0	100.0	100.0	100.0	Net Sales	100.0	100.0
44.8	44.8	41.8	43.5	45.5	46.0	Gross Profit	42.1	42.4
41.3	40.4	37.2	39.3	38.4	42.1	Operating Expenses	41.0	40.1
3.5	4.4	4.6	4.2	7.1	3.9	Operating Profit	1.1	2.3
.3	.7	.2	.2	-.3	.1	All Other Expenses (net)	.5	.4
3.2	3.8	4.3	4.0	7.4	3.7	Profit Before Taxes	.6	1.9
						RATIOS		
5.0	3.4	2.5	2.1	2.5	2.3		2.3	2.5
1.5	1.8	1.6	1.5	1.5	1.3	Current	1.4	1.5
1.0	1.1	1.1	1.2	1.2	1.1		1.0	1.1
1.6	1.1	.9	.9	1.1	1.0		.8	.9
(70) .5	.5	.4	.4	.5	.6	Quick	(724) .3	(608) .3
.1	.1	.1	.2	.1	.2		.1	.1
0 UND	0 UND	0 999.8	1 525.8	2 147.6	1 257.0		0 UND	0 999.8
0 UND	1 245.6	4 103.1	3 129.3	4 92.2	4 87.5	Sales/Receivables	3 118.6	3 113.2
7 51.5	16 22.6	23 15.9	12 29.5	27 13.3	63 5.8		20 18.4	20 18.4
28 13.0	58 6.3	51 7.2	58 6.3	89 4.1	87 4.2		59 6.2	62 5.9
76 4.8	118 3.1	104 3.5	99 3.7	114 3.2	122 3.0	Cost of Sales/Inventory	102 3.6	108 3.4
140 2.6	182 2.0	174 2.1	130 2.8	140 2.6	135 2.7		150 2.4	173 2.1
0 UND	14 26.2	18 20.2	20 18.0	23 16.1	25 14.7		17 21.1	16 22.7
12 29.4	28 13.0	31 11.7	32 11.4	40 9.2	39 9.3	Cost of Sales/Payables	33 11.2	32 11.5
32 11.3	44 8.3	50 7.3	46 7.9	59 6.2	61 6.0		53 6.9	51 7.1
8.0	4.8	5.3	7.2	4.7	4.3		6.6	5.4
18.8	8.8	12.6	12.4	12.1	14.6	Sales/Working Capital	16.5	12.5
NM	71.7	59.3	39.1	32.8	40.5		UND	66.6
11.8	18.0	33.4	23.7	43.2	11.0		7.1	13.4
(40) 3.7	(138) 3.7	(138) 6.6	(78) 5.1	(18) 8.7	(22) 3.5	EBIT/Interest	(611) 2.1	(499) 2.5
1.4	1.4	2.2	2.4	3.4	1.6		-.5	.6
		8.5	9.3				5.6	7.2
		(23) 3.1	(23) 5.0			Net Profit + Depr., Dep., Amort./Cur. Mat. L/T/D	(104) 2.1	(74) 2.7
		1.0	2.7				.4	.4
.0	.1	.1	.3	.4	.5		.2	.2
.3	.4	.4	.8	.7	1.0	Fixed/Worth	.8	.5
3.9	6.3	1.8	4.1	2.9	2.0		5.5	2.9
.5	.7	.9	.8	1.2	.8		1.0	.8
3.7	2.1	2.1	2.0	2.5	1.4	Debt/Worth	2.6	2.3
-11.1	41.7	5.7	7.2	8.2	3.0		21.3	10.1
130.7	52.9	45.0	49.1	85.2	20.8		32.7	42.1
(50) 47.5	(140) 17.2	(146) 20.8	(81) 27.2	(17) 31.2	(21) 12.4	% Profit Before Taxes/Tangible Net Worth	(572) 10.6	(497) 14.3
6.6	3.3	7.7	11.3	11.5	1.7		-.8	.7
41.0	14.8	16.4	15.5	17.8	10.6		9.4	13.3
9.5	6.4	7.1	7.0	11.1	4.5	% Profit Before Taxes/Total Assets	2.7	4.1
.5	1.2	2.2	3.0	5.8	1.5		-4.0	-.7
893.5	105.6	77.4	39.1	18.3	4.8		58.7	64.4
84.5	41.2	24.5	13.4	11.5	4.2	Sales/Net Fixed Assets	22.4	24.1
30.4	10.9	10.3	3.8	3.3	2.4		8.0	8.2
6.4	3.9	4.0	4.1	3.1	1.9		4.3	3.9
4.3	2.7	2.7	2.5	1.6	1.4	Sales/Total Assets	2.8	2.6
2.5	1.9	1.7	1.5	1.4	1.0		1.7	1.6
.3	.3	.3	.7	1.0	1.5		.5	.4
(33) .6	(126) .6	(129) .5	(86) 1.1	(19) 1.4	(17) 2.4	% Depr., Dep., Amort./Sales	(594) 1.0	(493) .9
1.4	1.3	1.0	1.8	1.8	3.2		1.7	1.6
2.6	1.8	1.0	.6				1.6	1.5
(37) 5.3	(105) 3.0	(70) 1.9	(18) 1.5			% Officers', Directors' Owners' Comp/Sales	(308) 3.0	(265) 3.0
7.5	5.3	3.6	2.6				5.4	5.3
86134M	612907M	2357711M	5757817M	3088036M	7043836M	Net Sales ($)	24075403M	17551637M
18422M	203593M	796655M	2079389M	1527401M	3792243M	Total Assets ($)	10598271M	8432478M

M = $ thousand MM = $ million

See Pages 9 through 22 for Explanation of Ratios and Data

Comparative Historical Data | **Current Data Sorted by Sales**

4/1/11-3/31/12 ALL	4/1/12-3/31/13 ALL	4/1/13-3/31/14 ALL		0-1MM	1-3MM	3-5MM	5-10MM	10-25MM	25MM & OVER
			Type of Statement						
37	46	48	Unqualified	1	2	1	1	8	35
91	73	74	Reviewed	1	7	6	10	19	31
122	87	79	Compiled	6	22	5	15	18	13
188	162	161	Tax Returns	23	59	35	29	13	2
232	206	196	Other	18	39	16	32	28	63
				110 (4/1-9/30/13)		448 (10/1/13-3/31/14)			
670	574	558	**NUMBER OF STATEMENTS**	49	129	63	87	86	144
%	%	%	**ASSETS**	%	%	%	%	%	%
10.8	11.6	11.9	Cash & Equivalents	14.3	11.6	12.1	11.6	13.7	10.2
12.0	10.9	11.2	Trade Receivables (net)	6.0	8.8	9.5	11.9	15.1	13.0
46.7	47.0	45.1	Inventory	47.0	50.0	52.3	46.8	41.0	38.3
2.0	1.9	1.5	All Other Current	1.0	.7	2.0	1.7	1.7	2.0
71.5	71.4	69.7	Total Current	68.3	71.1	75.8	71.9	71.6	63.6
19.4	20.2	21.0	Fixed Assets (net)	21.0	20.0	16.1	16.7	21.7	26.3
2.7	2.3	3.2	Intangibles (net)	3.8	2.2	2.3	4.0	2.2	4.3
6.5	6.1	6.2	All Other Non-Current	6.9	6.7	5.8	7.4	4.5	5.8
100.0	100.0	100.0	Total	100.0	100.0	100.0	100.0	100.0	100.0
			LIABILITIES						
10.5	9.3	8.6	Notes Payable-Short Term	14.8	12.6	6.3	7.9	7.4	4.8
2.4	2.5	2.7	Cur. Mat.-L.T.D.	8.2	3.3	1.4	2.3	1.5	1.9
17.4	17.1	16.2	Trade Payables	13.5	14.2	16.1	19.0	18.2	16.3
.2	.1	.1	Income Taxes Payable	.0	.2	.1	.1	.1	.2
17.9	19.0	18.3	All Other Current	17.0	14.8	20.3	19.8	18.2	20.1
48.5	48.0	46.0	Total Current	53.5	45.2	44.2	49.1	45.4	43.3
15.0	15.3	16.9	Long-Term Debt	23.3	21.9	16.9	15.0	11.1	14.9
.1	.1	.1	Deferred Taxes	.0	.0	.0	.0	.1	.2
8.9	9.0	9.2	All Other Non-Current	14.3	13.9	8.5	9.2	7.0	4.8
27.6	27.6	27.9	Net Worth	8.8	19.1	30.3	26.6	36.4	36.9
100.0	100.0	100.0	Total Liabilties & Net Worth	100.0	100.0	100.0	100.0	100.0	100.0
			INCOME DATA						
100.0	100.0	100.0	Net Sales	100.0	100.0	100.0	100.0	100.0	100.0
42.8	44.2	43.8	Gross Profit	51.3	45.7	43.7	41.7	39.2	43.6
39.8	40.0	39.4	Operating Expenses	46.3	40.3	40.3	37.7	35.5	39.2
3.0	4.2	4.4	Operating Profit	5.0	5.5	3.3	4.0	3.7	4.3
.4	.4	.4	All Other Expenses (net)	2.0	.5	.1	.3	.1	.0
2.6	3.9	4.0	Profit Before Taxes	3.0	5.0	3.2	3.7	3.6	4.3
			RATIOS						
2.7	2.7	2.7		6.0	3.4	3.4	2.5	2.4	2.1
1.6	1.6	1.6	Current	2.4	1.9	1.9	1.5	1.6	1.4
1.1	1.1	1.1		.9	1.1	1.2	1.0	1.1	1.1
1.0	1.0	1.0		2.1	1.3	1.1	.8	.9	1.0
(669) .4	(572) .4	(556) .4	Quick	.4	(127) .5	.4	.4	.5	.4
.1	.1	.2		.2	.1	.1	.2	.2	.2
0 UND	**0** UND	**0** UND		**0** UND	**0** UND	**0** UND	**0** UND	**1** 720.9	**1** 375.9
3 109.7	**3** 139.7	**3** 135.6	Sales/Receivables	**0** UND	**1** 363.2	**3** 135.1	**3** 143.7	**4** 101.5	**3** 107.8
20 18.5	**16** 22.3	**17** 21.7		**9** 41.6	**11** 33.9	**19** 19.6	**21** 17.5	**26** 13.8	**22** 16.8
63 5.8	**64** 5.7	**57** 6.4		**60** 6.1	**64** 5.7	**68** 5.4	**43** 8.4	**41** 8.8	**62** 5.9
107 3.4	**114** 3.2	**104** 3.5	Cost of Sales/Inventory	**140** 2.6	**118** 3.1	**126** 2.9	**104** 3.5	**96** 3.8	**96** 3.8
174 2.1	**166** 2.2	**152** 2.4		**261** 1.4	**203** 1.8	**166** 2.2	**166** 2.2	**146** 2.5	**126** 2.9
15 23.7	**18** 20.4	**16** 23.4		**0** UND	**11** 32.5	**15** 23.7	**17** 22.1	**19** 19.1	**20** 18.0
30 12.3	**32** 11.3	**30** 12.2	Cost of Sales/Payables	**7** 49.0	**28** 13.0	**31** 11.9	**30** 12.3	**31** 11.8	**32** 11.4
49 7.4	**51** 7.1	**46** 7.9		**38** 9.6	**47** 7.7	**46** 7.9	**44** 8.3	**46** 7.9	**47** 7.7
5.2	5.4	5.3		2.7	4.7	5.0	5.7	6.9	7.4
12.1	11.9	11.6	Sales/Working Capital	8.7	9.1	8.6	14.5	11.2	16.6
73.6	80.2	61.3		-73.9	54.3	40.3	-203.1	35.5	51.1
12.1	18.0	21.2		8.1	11.0	13.3	23.7	36.2	33.4
(541) 3.3	(472) 5.1	(434) 4.8	EBIT/Interest	(32) 3.5	(90) 3.3	(46) 3.3	(70) 5.9	(74) 7.2	(122) 8.0
1.1	1.9	1.8		.6	1.3	1.3	1.6	2.1	3.0
7.4	7.9	7.4					8.5		8.6
(70) 3.5	(62) 4.5	(64) 3.5	Net Profit + Depr., Dep., Amort./Cur. Mat. L/T/D				(11) 1.2		(32) 3.9
.8	2.1	1.6					.7		1.8
.1	.1	.1		.0	.1	.1	.1	.1	.3
.5	.6	.6	Fixed/Worth	.7	.4	.2	.8	.5	.7
2.6	2.3	3.0		32.8	4.5	2.1	8.0	1.6	2.0
.9	.9	.8		.5	.6	.8	.8	.9	.8
2.1	2.2	2.1	Debt/Worth	5.0	1.6	2.1	2.6	2.0	1.9
12.1	9.7	9.6		-19.3	53.1	6.6	45.5	4.3	4.8
43.2	50.1	53.7		76.7	58.9	47.0	78.9	43.4	57.1
(555) 17.9	(477) 20.7	(455) 20.8	% Profit Before Taxes/Tangible Net Worth	(34) 24.1	(99) 19.2	(51) 16.2	(67) 21.1	(79) 21.8	(125) 27.0
4.2	6.8	7.1		1.3	3.2	4.3	5.7	10.8	11.6
13.5	17.3	15.8		11.7	24.1	15.1	17.3	15.0	17.7
4.9	6.8	7.0	% Profit Before Taxes/Total Assets	4.6	7.1	6.0	7.1	6.6	8.6
.5	1.9	2.0		-3.6	1.2	1.1	1.4	2.6	3.3
77.7	79.6	89.1		423.0	85.1	135.8	117.1	101.1	40.0
27.1	22.3	25.4	Sales/Net Fixed Assets	36.5	28.9	51.9	38.5	22.9	15.9
9.8	8.7	8.2		6.7	8.7	10.5	11.9	5.1	4.8
4.1	4.2	4.2		3.5	4.0	4.2	3.9	4.3	4.3
2.7	2.7	2.7	Sales/Total Assets	2.2	2.6	2.8	2.9	2.8	2.8
1.7	1.7	1.7		1.0	1.7	2.0	2.0	1.9	1.6
.4	.4	.4		.2	.4	.3	.3	.3	.6
(500) .8	(441) .7	(410) .8	% Depr., Dep., Amort./Sales	(24) .6	(85) .7	(43) .4	(69) .5	(63) .7	(126) 1.1
1.4	1.3	1.5		2.7	1.4	1.2	1.1	1.1	1.7
1.4	1.4	1.4		2.6	2.1	1.4	1.5	.7	.6
(314) 2.8	(249) 2.7	(234) 2.6	% Officers', Directors' Owners' Comp/Sales	(23) 5.4	(74) 3.6	(35) 3.0	(47) 2.5	(30) 1.5	(25) 1.5
5.4	5.2	5.2		8.4	6.4	5.3	3.8	2.2	1.9
16637456M	**17780787M**	**18946441M**	Net Sales ($)	**27192M**	**247213M**	**252925M**	**612605M**	**1359606M**	**16446900M**
7699903M	**8452636M**	**8417703M**	Total Assets ($)	**22156M**	**122665M**	**120742M**	**249073M**	**592708M**	**7310359M**

M = $ thousand MM = $ million

See Pages 9 through 22 for Explanation of Ratios and Data

Current Data Sorted by Assets | **Comparative Historical Data**

0-500M	500M-2MM	2-10MM	10-50MM	50-100MM	100-250MM	Type of Statement	4/1/09-3/31/10 ALL	4/1/10-3/31/11 ALL
		1	3		1	Unqualified	9	10
1	4	19	6		1	Reviewed	52	49
3	9	13	2			Compiled	53	47
46	42	15	1			Tax Returns	121	107
13	30	25	9		2	Other	124	111
35 (4/1-9/30/13)		211 (10/1/13-3/31/14)						
63	85	73	21		4	NUMBER OF STATEMENTS	359	324
%	%	%	%	%	%	ASSETS	%	%
14.6	8.4	7.2	7.0	DATA NOT AVAILABLE		Cash & Equivalents	10.3	10.8
19.2	27.8	27.5	26.1			Trade Receivables (net)	21.1	22.8
35.9	37.2	36.3	36.9			Inventory	33.7	34.4
1.4	1.4	3.3	2.9			All Other Current	3.6	2.8
71.1	74.8	74.3	72.9			Total Current	68.8	70.9
14.5	12.4	15.1	19.2			Fixed Assets (net)	18.3	18.4
4.1	1.9	3.6	4.3			Intangibles (net)	4.2	3.2
10.2	10.9	7.1	3.6			All Other Non-Current	8.8	7.5
100.0	100.0	100.0	100.0			Total	100.0	100.0
						LIABILITIES		
20.7	9.3	11.2	11.7			Notes Payable-Short Term	15.2	15.8
5.1	.5	1.8	1.5			Cur. Mat.-L.T.D.	4.1	4.0
22.0	25.6	17.7	17.8			Trade Payables	19.4	19.9
.1	.0	.2	.1			Income Taxes Payable	.3	.1
18.0	18.2	17.9	19.0			All Other Current	17.7	21.2
65.8	53.6	48.7	50.2			Total Current	56.7	61.0
22.3	11.2	11.3	9.6			Long-Term Debt	14.7	11.5
.0	.0	.1	.4			Deferred Taxes	.1	.1
11.0	6.9	6.9	1.7			All Other Non-Current	9.5	8.2
.9	28.3	33.0	38.0			Net Worth	19.0	19.2
100.0	100.0	100.0	100.0			Total Liabilties & Net Worth	100.0	100.0
						INCOME DATA		
100.0	100.0	100.0	100.0			Net Sales	100.0	100.0
38.0	36.0	34.7	31.1			Gross Profit	37.5	36.1
35.3	33.2	31.6	28.7			Operating Expenses	37.6	34.5
2.8	2.9	3.0	2.4			Operating Profit	-.1	1.6
.2	-.3	.5	.3			All Other Expenses (net)	.6	.6
2.5	3.2	2.6	2.1			Profit Before Taxes	-.7	1.0
						RATIOS		
2.5	2.8	2.6	1.9				2.4	2.5
1.2	1.6	1.6	1.4			Current	1.4	1.3
.8	1.0	1.2	1.1				.9	.9
1.1	1.3	1.6	.9				1.2	1.2
.6	.8	.7	.6			Quick	(358) .6	.6
.3	.3	.3	.4				.2	.3
3 144.9	8 46.3	13 27.9	10 36.8				6 57.0	6 56.7
10 35.1	24 14.9	26 14.3	29 12.4			Sales/Receivables	20 18.5	21 17.5
25 14.5	40 9.1	47 7.7	39 9.4				32 11.3	39 9.4
14 26.0	24 15.3	30 12.2	32 11.5				24 15.4	23 16.2
33 11.2	49 7.5	54 6.8	68 5.4			Cost of Sales/Inventory	49 7.4	51 7.2
68 5.4	99 3.7	130 2.8	89 4.1				92 4.0	97 3.8
4 83.7	16 22.6	18 20.8	17 21.0				14 26.9	15 24.8
19 18.9	25 14.5	27 13.3	21 17.0			Cost of Sales/Payables	25 14.8	25 14.5
38 9.6	46 8.0	40 9.2	32 11.4				43 8.5	45 8.2
13.8	7.2	4.6	10.2				6.7	6.7
34.8	12.9	11.9	14.5			Sales/Working Capital	17.2	19.5
-51.8	-205.0	45.2	45.2				-50.2	-93.4
19.3	16.0	11.0	11.9				5.3	7.8
(41) 4.9	(62) 5.6	(64) 3.8	(19) 5.5			EBIT/Interest	(299) 1.0	(275) 2.1
.3	1.2	1.5	1.1				-4.1	-.5
		11.6					3.9	3.2
		(13) 2.2				Net Profit + Depr., Dep., Amort./Cur. Mat. L/T/D	(37) 1.7	(25) 2.0
		.5					-.2	.7
.2	.1	.1	.2				.2	.1
1.1	.3	.3	.5			Fixed/Worth	.6	.6
-.6	1.6	1.3	1.0				165.0	4.8
1.1	.8	.8	.8				.8	.8
5.0	2.6	1.8	1.9			Debt/Worth	2.4	2.3
-6.2	13.8	4.3	3.0				-70.7	UND
102.4	55.2	31.1	45.3				26.1	39.2
(41) 41.7	(70) 21.5	(61) 17.8	(19) 25.9			% Profit Before Taxes/Tangible Net Worth	(268) 5.6	(243) 9.7
.2	6.6	5.3	5.1				-12.7	-.9
29.1	18.9	11.6	13.3				8.6	10.6
10.7	8.3	5.9	9.8			% Profit Before Taxes/Total Assets	.9	2.7
-.5	1.1	1.6	.2				-9.3	-2.9
235.0	153.9	91.8	55.7				65.7	72.3
62.4	47.5	39.0	16.9			Sales/Net Fixed Assets	28.1	29.9
24.1	25.8	16.3	8.8				12.0	11.4
8.7	5.0	4.3	4.3				4.7	4.7
5.4	3.8	3.0	2.9			Sales/Total Assets	3.3	3.2
3.3	2.4	1.9	2.6				2.1	2.1
.3	.3	.3	.4				.4	.4
(36) .7	(58) .5	(58) .6	(20) .7			% Depr., Dep., Amort./Sales	(280) .9	(258) .7
1.6	.8	1.2	1.0				1.6	1.3
3.6	1.9	.9					2.1	1.6
(44) 5.1	(60) 2.9	(35) 2.3				% Officers', Directors' Owners' Comp/Sales	(193) 3.9	(191) 3.5
7.0	4.8	4.2					7.2	6.6
88493M	361869M	962926M	1182556M		862359M	Net Sales ($)	7966895M	5062112M
16689M	95731M	314975M	361908M		786892M	Total Assets ($)	2342391M	1543894M

M = $ thousand MM = $ million

See Pages 9 through 22 for Explanation of Ratios and Data

Comparative Historical Data / Current Data Sorted by Sales

4/1/11-3/31/12 ALL	4/1/12-3/31/13 ALL	4/1/13-3/31/14 ALL	Type of Statement	0-1MM	1-3MM	3-5MM	5-10MM	10-25MM	25MM & OVER
7	3	5	Unqualified					1	4
37	29	31	Reviewed		2	2	6	13	8
60	32	27	Compiled		9	5	2	9	2
146	112	104	Tax Returns	21	40	20	12	10	1
124	93	79	Other	5	19	13	13	16	13
				35 (4/1-9/30/13)			211 (10/1/13-3/31/14)		
374	269	246	NUMBER OF STATEMENTS	26	70	40	33	49	28
%	%	%	**ASSETS**	%	%	%	%	%	%
9.6	9.9	9.4	Cash & Equivalents	11.9	11.5	9.4	8.0	7.9	6.1
23.4	24.5	25.1	Trade Receivables (net)	13.6	20.9	22.4	32.7	32.9	27.1
36.4	34.7	36.4	Inventory	41.5	36.2	36.4	34.8	35.9	35.3
4.2	3.9	2.1	All Other Current	2.7	.6	1.0	3.0	4.0	2.9
73.6	72.9	73.0	Total Current	69.6	69.2	69.2	78.4	80.7	71.4
17.1	15.7	14.9	Fixed Assets (net)	10.1	17.1	15.7	12.3	11.3	22.1
2.8	3.0	3.1	Intangibles (net)	5.3	3.1	3.9	3.4	1.2	3.3
6.6	8.4	8.9	All Other Non-Current	15.0	10.6	11.2	5.9	6.8	3.1
100.0	100.0	100.0	Total	100.0	100.0	100.0	100.0	100.0	100.0
			LIABILITIES						
15.3	13.0	12.9	Notes Payable-Short Term	15.1	15.3	11.3	11.0	12.1	10.5
4.0	2.6	2.2	Cur. Mat.-L.T.D.	8.7	1.7	1.0	.5	2.0	1.0
18.8	20.4	21.4	Trade Payables	14.2	21.9	27.4	19.8	22.1	19.3
.2	.1	.1	Income Taxes Payable	.1	.0	.0	.1	.2	.1
15.4	17.2	18.0	All Other Current	13.8	15.9	16.4	24.8	18.4	20.4
53.7	53.2	54.5	Total Current	52.0	54.9	56.1	56.2	54.8	51.3
14.5	13.3	14.2	Long-Term Debt	28.4	18.2	13.5	8.9	6.9	11.2
.1	.1	.1	Deferred Taxes	.0	.0	.0	.0	.1	.3
10.9	10.0	7.5	All Other Non-Current	14.3	11.1	6.6	2.2	5.2	3.6
20.9	23.4	23.7	Net Worth	5.2	15.9	23.7	32.7	32.9	33.5
100.0	100.0	100.0	Total Liabilties & Net Worth	100.0	100.0	100.0	100.0	100.0	100.0
			INCOME DATA						
100.0	100.0	100.0	Net Sales	100.0	100.0	100.0	100.0	100.0	100.0
35.5	35.6	36.0	Gross Profit	44.3	38.2	36.9	35.7	29.1	33.9
34.4	32.6	33.1	Operating Expenses	40.5	34.3	34.0	34.3	27.0	31.1
1.1	3.0	2.9	Operating Profit	3.8	3.9	2.9	1.4	2.1	2.8
.4	.4	.3	All Other Expenses (net)	1.4	.0	-.2	.2	-.3	2.0
.8	2.6	2.6	Profit Before Taxes	2.4	3.9	3.1	1.1	2.4	.8
			RATIOS						
2.4	2.7	2.6		5.2	3.1	2.4	2.2	2.6	2.0
1.5	1.5	1.5	Current	1.2	1.6	1.5	1.4	1.5	1.4
1.0	1.1	1.0		.7	.9	.9	1.0	1.2	1.1
1.2	1.3	1.2		1.0	1.2	1.1	1.5	1.6	.9
.6	(268) .7	.7	Quick	.5	.8	.5	.7	.8	.6
.3	.4	.3		.2	.3	.2	.4	.4	.4
7 49.4	**7** 49.8	**8** 46.9		**1** 380.6	**4** 94.1	**6** 58.0	**13** 28.4	**21** 17.7	**10** 37.1
22 16.9	**20** 18.2	**23** 15.8	Sales/Receivables	**5** 73.2	**14** 26.9	**14** 25.5	**30** 12.1	**33** 11.0	**29** 12.6
37 9.8	**36** 10.0	**39** 9.3		**27** 13.5	**28** 13.0	**35** 10.5	**49** 7.4	**47** 7.7	**41** 8.8
26 14.2	**22** 16.9	**24** 14.9		**20** 17.9	**17** 22.1	**19** 19.0	**24** 15.3	**28** 13.2	**31** 11.9
51 7.2	**40** 9.1	**46** 7.9	Cost of Sales/Inventory	**69** 5.3	**36** 10.0	**49** 7.5	**38** 9.7	**46** 7.9	**66** 5.5
96 3.8	**85** 4.3	**104** 3.5		**215** 1.7	**99** 3.7	**122** 3.0	**87** 4.2	**68** 5.4	**99** 3.7
15 25.1	**13** 27.5	**15** 23.9		**1** 334.6	**11** 32.0	**14** 27.0	**17** 22.1	**18** 20.1	**20** 18.6
26 14.1	**27** 13.6	**24** 14.9	Cost of Sales/Payables	**27** 13.3	**21** 17.2	**25** 14.8	**24** 15.0	**29** 12.8	**24** 15.5
42 8.6	**42** 8.6	**41** 8.9		**76** 4.8	**34** 10.8	**46** 8.0	**46** 7.9	**40** 9.2	**53** 6.9
7.2	7.4	7.2		6.2	6.3	8.1	8.1	6.4	6.8
14.1	16.5	15.5	Sales/Working Capital	28.5	17.6	15.2	17.8	13.9	16.3
140.4	105.0	516.5		-28.6	-103.9	-698.6	-205.0	37.5	60.0
7.8	11.5	13.5		7.1	20.3	12.5	11.4	14.3	11.5
(303) 2.3	(213) 3.6	(190) 4.7	EBIT/Interest	(14) 1.0	(49) 6.5	(27) 4.5	(30) 2.3	(44) 6.5	(26) 4.6
-.1	.8	1.1		-7.0	1.4	1.4	-.6	2.6	-.7
4.6	16.3	6.7						17.6	
(28) 2.2	(29) 2.4	(27) 1.8	Net Profit + Depr., Dep., Amort./Cur. Mat. L/T/D					(10) 2.4	
.7	.8	.7						-.4	
.1	.1	.1		.0	.2	.1	.1	.1	.2
.4	.4	.5	Fixed/Worth	.5	.5	.5	.6	.2	.7
4.5	1.8	2.1		-.6	-3.3	1.7	2.0	.7	1.5
.9	.9	.9		1.1	1.0	.8	.9	.7	1.2
2.2	2.2	2.2	Debt/Worth	5.2	2.1	2.9	2.4	1.8	2.0
45.7	12.4	16.9		-2.8	-14.1	18.7	15.7	3.4	4.2
35.0	51.0	50.8		83.8	81.6	57.3	30.1	41.0	44.2
(284) 9.9	(213) 18.8	(195) 20.5	% Profit Before Taxes/Tangible Net Worth	(16) 24.1	(50) 33.0	(33) 20.8	(28) 9.0	(43) 19.5	(25) 19.6
.0	3.5	4.2		2.2	4.4	5.4	-1.1	11.7	-1.2
10.1	14.7	17.4		13.9	26.6	20.2	13.6	12.5	11.9
2.5	5.6	7.5	% Profit Before Taxes/Total Assets	3.7	12.9	7.2	2.3	7.6	7.6
-2.6	.1	.4		-5.9	1.5	1.3	-3.1	3.4	-1.1
96.3	115.6	128.5		UND	128.8	139.6	95.2	135.6	51.6
35.7	43.0	46.5	Sales/Net Fixed Assets	92.9	52.4	41.3	52.7	53.5	16.8
13.8	16.6	19.0		15.3	18.8	21.4	29.2	22.1	7.9
4.8	5.1	5.2		5.8	6.5	5.0	5.2	4.9	4.7
3.4	3.6	3.6	Sales/Total Assets	2.9	3.7	3.3	4.4	3.6	3.0
2.2	2.4	2.4		1.7	2.3	2.0	3.2	2.6	2.3
.4	.3	.3		.3	.3	.4	.4	.2	.4
(267) .7	(193) .6	(174) .6	% Depr., Dep., Amort./Sales	(14) .8	(45) .8	(28) .6	(21) .7	(41) .4	(25) .7
1.2	1.1	1.2		2.4	1.8	1.4	1.0	.7	1.0
1.7	1.4	1.8		4.6	2.3	2.1	1.7	.9	
(206) 3.1	(154) 2.9	(144) 3.4	% Officers', Directors' Owners' Comp/Sales	(16) 6.0	(50) 4.6	(25) 3.1	(19) 2.3	(27) 1.8	
6.1	5.5	5.6		11.1	6.8	3.9	3.8	3.6	
4879636M	3292573M	3458203M	Net Sales ($)	17228M	131826M	160381M	220015M	748558M	2180195M
1490193M	1088619M	1576195M	Total Assets ($)	14266M	46579M	56283M	67871M	229371M	1161825M

M = $ thousand MM = $ million

See Pages 9 through 22 for Explanation of Ratios and Data

Current Data Sorted by Assets							Comparative Historical Data	
						Type of Statement		
			1	1	2	Unqualified	12	14
		8	1			Reviewed	14	10
1	8	6				Compiled	28	24
22	21	13				Tax Returns	63	58
18	24	15	8	2	1	Other	69	60
21 (4/1-9/30/13)			131 (10/1/13-3/31/14)				4/1/09-3/31/10 ALL	4/1/10-3/31/11 ALL
0-500M	500M-2MM	2-10MM	10-50MM	50-100MM	100-250MM			
41	53	42	10	3	3	**NUMBER OF STATEMENTS**	186	166
%	%	%	%	%	%	**ASSETS**	%	%
12.4	11.9	8.8	11.6			Cash & Equivalents	13.0	12.7
13.5	14.7	9.5	7.9			Trade Receivables (net)	11.1	11.8
41.2	43.8	53.0	41.7			Inventory	44.5	43.4
3.5	1.3	2.6	1.8			All Other Current	3.0	2.9
70.6	71.7	74.0	62.9			Total Current	71.6	70.7
18.9	17.7	19.8	18.8			Fixed Assets (net)	16.7	16.7
2.5	3.4	1.2	14.2			Intangibles (net)	3.6	3.9
8.0	7.2	4.9	4.1			All Other Non-Current	8.2	8.6
100.0	100.0	100.0	100.0			Total	100.0	100.0
						LIABILITIES		
22.7	10.0	8.1	13.5			Notes Payable-Short Term	13.9	13.0
8.5	1.5	.8	1.8			Cur. Mat.-L.T.D.	2.9	2.0
17.6	17.0	14.2	10.6			Trade Payables	17.7	18.7
.0	.0	.0	.0			Income Taxes Payable	.2	.2
23.9	12.3	22.5	12.8			All Other Current	16.8	15.2
72.8	40.8	45.7	38.7			Total Current	51.4	49.0
18.9	18.6	15.1	14.3			Long-Term Debt	17.1	13.9
.0	.0	.1	.0			Deferred Taxes	.2	.1
16.3	11.9	5.3	29.0			All Other Non-Current	8.9	6.6
-8.0	28.8	33.8	18.1			Net Worth	22.4	30.4
100.0	100.0	100.0	100.0			Total Liabilties & Net Worth	100.0	100.0
						INCOME DATA		
100.0	100.0	100.0	100.0			Net Sales	100.0	100.0
43.8	41.6	46.9	43.0			Gross Profit	44.0	43.9
38.5	36.5	43.4	38.4			Operating Expenses	41.5	41.2
5.2	5.1	3.4	4.6			Operating Profit	2.6	2.7
.2	.9	.8	1.0			All Other Expenses (net)	.6	.5
5.0	4.2	2.6	3.6			Profit Before Taxes	1.9	2.2
						RATIOS		
3.3	3.5	3.2	2.0				2.8	2.9
1.4	1.9	2.3	1.5			Current	1.6	1.6
.6	1.3	1.1	1.1				1.0	1.0
1.5	1.4	.9	.9				1.1	1.1
.3	.5	.5	.3			Quick	.4	(165) .4
.1	.2	.1	.1				.1	.2
0 UND	**0** UND	**1** 688.9	**2** 232.4				**0** UND	**0** UND
2 196.3	**5** 68.5	**8** 47.1	**2** 177.7			Sales/Receivables	**6** 58.9	**7** 56.1
19 19.2	**26** 14.1	**25** 14.5	**37** 9.8				**23** 15.7	**22** 16.4
12 30.1	**44** 8.3	**94** 3.9	**118** 3.1				**63** 5.8	**49** 7.5
69 5.3	**101** 3.6	**166** 2.2	**152** 2.4			Cost of Sales/Inventory	**119** 3.1	**110** 3.3
140 2.6	**174** 2.1	**261** 1.4	**192** 1.9				**188** 1.9	**189** 1.9
5 68.0	**10** 36.8	**19** 19.5	**17** 21.3				**17** 21.5	**18** 20.8
19 18.8	**30** 12.2	**29** 12.6	**31** 11.9			Cost of Sales/Payables	**34** 10.8	**36** 10.3
45 8.2	**70** 5.2	**41** 9.0	**41** 8.8				**61** 6.0	**63** 5.8
6.2	5.0	4.1	4.3				5.0	4.7
21.3	10.2	6.4	16.3			Sales/Working Capital	11.4	10.1
-10.6	17.8	58.8	22.8				-119.1	NM
20.2	32.0	37.2					7.6	10.1
(27) 5.7	(42) 6.5	(33) 16.7				EBIT/Interest	(149) 2.8	(127) 4.1
1.6	1.3	2.8					.3	1.1
							17.3	32.2
						Net Profit + Depr., Dep., Amort./Cur. Mat. L/T/D	(21) 2.1	(19) 2.7
							.0	.8
.1	.1	.1	.1				.1	.1
1.0	.4	.6	1.0			Fixed/Worth	.6	.4
-.5	1.5	1.7	NM				UND	1.8
.7	.8	.6	1.1				.9	.7
10.1	2.3	1.8	2.1			Debt/Worth	2.4	2.3
-3.4	9.2	12.1	NM				-52.2	10.5
93.9	52.3	40.1					46.1	45.1
(23) 29.2	(45) 29.7	(36) 21.7				% Profit Before Taxes/Tangible Net Worth	(138) 14.7	(134) 15.9
3.1	2.5	5.7					1.2	2.3
32.2	17.9	13.8	15.2				15.4	13.4
10.0	7.7	6.5	6.3			% Profit Before Taxes/Total Assets	4.0	4.9
1.7	.7	2.3	-4.2				-2.6	.0
126.3	87.1	57.9	80.9				69.2	89.1
35.3	30.6	20.6	17.9			Sales/Net Fixed Assets	24.4	24.6
15.0	15.7	9.2	8.9				8.3	9.8
6.1	3.9	3.0	2.5				3.7	3.7
3.5	2.7	2.2	1.8			Sales/Total Assets	2.5	2.6
2.3	1.5	1.5	1.2				1.8	1.8
.4	.2	.5					.5	.5
(21) .8	(31) .6	(35) .9				% Depr., Dep., Amort./Sales	(137) 1.0	(117) 1.0
2.1	1.0	2.0					2.0	1.8
3.2	3.0	1.0					2.0	2.0
(19) 5.9	(28) 4.6	(21) 2.4				% Officers', Directors' Owners' Comp/Sales	(96) 4.6	(91) 4.1
8.0	7.3	6.3					7.4	7.6
44917M	184041M	401439M	411231M	405236M	1540911M	Net Sales ($)	5084226M	5569529M
12118M	61327M	180033M	208808M	171909M	520166M	Total Assets ($)	2198927M	2420665M

M = $ thousand MM = $ million

See Pages 9 through 22 for Explanation of Ratios and Data

Comparative Historical Data				Current Data Sorted by Sales					
			Type of Statement						
10	8	4	Unqualified						4
14	14	9	Reviewed	1			2	6	
27	24	15	Compiled	1	2	6	3	3	
81	68	56	Tax Returns	17	20	6	9	4	
81	56	68	Other	11	21	7	8	11	10
4/1/11-3/31/12 ALL	4/1/12-3/31/13 ALL	4/1/13-3/31/14 ALL		21 (4/1-9/30/13)			131 (10/1/13-3/31/14)		
				0-1MM	1-3MM	3-5MM	5-10MM	10-25MM	25MM & OVER
213	170	152	**NUMBER OF STATEMENTS**	30	43	19	22	24	14
%	%	%	**ASSETS**	%	%	%	%	%	%
12.9	13.7	11.8	Cash & Equivalents	12.5	7.4	15.1	16.9	6.9	19.5
11.1	8.0	12.0	Trade Receivables (net)	7.7	15.1	21.7	9.0	10.9	4.8
46.7	47.8	45.0	Inventory	36.1	48.5	39.6	52.5	51.7	37.7
2.0	1.7	2.4	All Other Current	2.8	2.2	.7	2.5	3.3	2.3
72.7	71.1	71.2	Total Current	59.2	73.3	77.0	80.9	72.8	64.3
17.4	19.6	18.9	Fixed Assets (net)	29.3	16.6	19.7	11.2	15.3	20.9
4.1	2.6	3.6	Intangibles (net)	4.2	3.1	1.3	.4	3.3	11.8
5.9	6.7	6.4	All Other Non-Current	7.3	7.0	2.0	7.4	8.5	3.0
100.0	100.0	100.0	Total	100.0	100.0	100.0	100.0	100.0	100.0
			LIABILITIES						
9.9	10.2	12.7	Notes Payable-Short Term	12.0	19.7	8.3	6.5	14.9	5.1
2.4	3.4	3.2	Cur. Mat.-L.T.D.	2.0	7.7	1.8	.9	.9	.7
18.9	16.3	16.3	Trade Payables	8.1	24.0	15.6	17.2	11.7	17.6
.1	.2	.0	Income Taxes Payable	.0	.0	.1	.1	.0	.1
13.3	15.6	18.4	All Other Current	18.8	15.6	14.8	18.3	27.4	15.8
44.5	45.7	50.6	Total Current	40.9	67.0	40.5	43.1	54.9	39.3
18.7	18.9	16.9	Long-Term Debt	37.2	13.2	15.2	8.7	9.7	12.0
.1	.1	.1	Deferred Taxes	.0	.0	.0	.0	.2	.3
12.8	11.3	12.3	All Other Non-Current	11.1	15.8	12.7	5.3	6.3	25.0
23.9	24.0	20.1	Net Worth	10.7	3.9	31.6	42.9	28.8	23.5
100.0	100.0	100.0	Total Liabilties & Net Worth	100.0	100.0	100.0	100.0	100.0	100.0
			INCOME DATA						
100.0	100.0	100.0	Net Sales	100.0	100.0	100.0	100.0	100.0	100.0
42.9	46.5	43.7	Gross Profit	48.3	43.0	38.7	44.0	44.1	41.5
39.3	42.8	39.2	Operating Expenses	40.8	39.2	34.2	40.5	40.2	39.2
3.7	3.6	4.5	Operating Profit	7.5	3.8	4.5	3.5	4.0	2.3
.5	.7	.7	All Other Expenses (net)	1.9	.3	.9	-.3	.6	1.0
3.1	2.9	3.8	Profit Before Taxes	5.7	3.6	3.6	3.8	3.3	1.2
			RATIOS						
3.0	3.2	3.2		8.7	3.5	4.1	2.9	2.9	2.3
1.9	1.8	1.8	Current	2.4	1.6	1.6	2.3	2.0	1.5
1.1	1.1	1.1		.7	.8	1.3	1.3	1.1	1.1
1.1	1.0	1.1		5.3	.9	1.7	.8	.9	.9
.5	(169) .4	.4	Quick	.8	.2	.6	.5	.3	.6
.2	.1	.1		.1	.1	.3	.3	.1	.2
0 UND	0 UND	0 UND		0 UND	0 UND	0 999.8	0 UND	1 267.4	0 UND
5 69.2	4 98.3	4 86.5	Sales/Receivables	1 449.1	5 68.5	11 33.7	1 381.7	10 35.2	2 177.7
20 17.9	14 26.1	22 16.5		14 25.5	19 19.7	42 8.7	27 13.6	26 14.1	6 59.7
53 6.9	53 6.9	47 7.7		41 8.9	34 10.6	18 20.5	47 7.7	89 4.1	65 5.6
107 3.4	126 2.9	107 3.4	Cost of Sales/Inventory	81 4.5	111 3.3	66 5.5	118 3.1	130 2.8	135 2.7
182 2.0	203 1.8	192 1.9		332 1.1	215 1.7	107 3.4	203 1.8	182 2.0	166 2.2
14 26.4	11 33.0	14 26.1		2 222.8	19 18.8	13 27.2	17 21.5	15 23.9	28 13.1
34 10.6	32 11.4	30 12.2	Cost of Sales/Payables	14 27.0	46 7.9	26 13.9	34 10.6	26 14.2	46 7.9
54 6.7	62 5.9	53 6.9		36 10.1	81 4.5	36 10.2	46 8.0	32 11.3	57 6.4
4.4	4.3	4.8		4.2	4.8	4.8	4.2	5.0	4.8
8.7	9.4	10.6	Sales/Working Capital	7.9	12.6	12.4	7.4	8.6	13.3
51.5	109.0	56.1		-10.8	-18.4	18.6	17.7	55.0	24.0
12.7	10.7	33.3		13.5	37.7	34.5	34.9	36.1	51.5
(171) 3.7	(124) 3.7	(114) 6.5	EBIT/Interest	(15) 2.6	(37) 6.1	(16) 14.0	(16) 14.6	(20) 11.4	(10) .2
1.1	1.0	1.4		-2.0	1.6	1.6	2.1	3.0	-13.1
16.7									
(12) 2.9			Net Profit + Depr., Dep., Amort./Cur. Mat. L/T/D						
1.3									
.1	.1	.1		.1	.1	.1	.1	.2	.4
.4	.5	.5	Fixed/Worth	1.0	.6	.4	.2	.6	1.0
2.8	UND	5.9		-1.3	-6.6	1.7	.5	1.4	4.3
.8	.7	.7		.6	.8	.7	.5	.7	1.0
2.1	2.1	2.3	Debt/Worth	6.1	3.3	2.2	1.0	1.9	3.0
19.5	UND	41.1		-6.2	-5.7	19.5	2.4	6.5	12.6
49.6	47.6	50.9		56.0	84.8	44.0	51.8	46.1	53.6
(167) 17.9	(129) 16.6	(118) 22.8	% Profit Before Taxes/Tangible Net Worth	(19) 21.7	(30) 32.7	(17) 16.6	(19) 23.1	(21) 21.9	(12) 11.5
3.1	4.3	3.7		2.9	2.9	4.7	2.7	15.3	-69.6
17.1	16.9	16.8		17.1	15.5	17.0	22.0	14.0	15.5
6.8	6.0	7.6	% Profit Before Taxes/Total Assets	7.3	9.3	5.6	7.8	8.5	-.9
.6	.5	.9		-1.5	.9	1.3	1.5	4.6	-8.2
85.1	86.7	70.4		64.1	129.3	66.3	103.6	126.8	27.0
29.6	24.2	25.0	Sales/Net Fixed Assets	20.3	28.4	37.4	37.6	20.6	15.4
9.9	9.3	11.7		5.3	15.4	15.1	19.8	9.8	9.2
3.8	3.7	3.8		3.3	4.9	4.4	4.0	3.3	3.1
2.6	2.6	2.6	Sales/Total Assets	2.0	2.7	3.1	3.4	2.9	2.3
1.9	1.7	1.6		.9	1.6	1.6	2.0	1.9	1.4
.4	.4	.4		.5	.4	.3	.2	.7	.9
(148) .9	(120) .9	(98) .8	% Depr., Dep., Amort./Sales	(18) 1.0	(24) .7	(14) .6	(13) .6	(19) .9	(10) 1.3
1.7	1.9	1.7		2.4	1.3	2.2	1.2	1.7	2.8
2.6	2.5	2.3		2.9	3.2	1.5	2.1		
(107) 4.7	(87) 4.3	(70) 4.6	% Officers', Directors' Owners' Comp/Sales	(13) 7.4	(21) 4.9	(13) 4.1	(13) 3.8		
8.4	7.8	7.4		13.3	7.2	8.3	4.8		
3967151M	4634242M	2987775M	Net Sales ($)	18970M	76835M	77953M	154124M	333233M	2326660M
1651641M	1936567M	1154361M	Total Assets ($)	17384M	36503M	34738M	50436M	140643M	874657M

M = $ thousand MM = $ million

See Pages 9 through 22 for Explanation of Ratios and Data

Current Data Sorted by Assets							Comparative Historical Data	
		1	5	3		**Type of Statement** Unqualified	5	6
	1	3	2	2		Reviewed	17	10
2	7	7				Compiled	23	31
7	20	5	1			Tax Returns	45	32
4	7	6	4	1	1	Other	42	41
16 (4/1-9/30/13)			73 (10/1/13-3/31/14)				4/1/09-3/31/10 ALL	4/1/10-3/31/11 ALL
0-500M	500M-2MM	2-10MM	10-50MM	50-100MM	100-250MM			
13	35	22	12	6	1	**NUMBER OF STATEMENTS**	132	120
%	%	%	%	%	%	**ASSETS**	%	%
18.3	16.1	9.6	11.1			Cash & Equivalents	10.9	10.7
13.0	13.2	15.6	14.4			Trade Receivables (net)	13.4	13.3
42.2	52.9	51.0	44.6			Inventory	45.1	49.2
1.6	2.0	.7	2.7			All Other Current	2.3	2.7
75.1	84.3	76.8	72.9			Total Current	71.7	75.9
20.7	10.3	16.8	16.7			Fixed Assets (net)	18.7	18.6
2.7	2.2	.1	5.8			Intangibles (net)	3.6	2.7
1.5	3.2	6.2	4.6			All Other Non-Current	6.0	2.8
100.0	100.0	100.0	100.0			Total	100.0	100.0
						LIABILITIES		
22.8	12.1	10.9	9.7			Notes Payable-Short Term	15.3	17.5
3.0	.4	.8	.6			Cur. Mat.-L.T.D.	4.1	3.0
23.6	25.1	14.0	18.7			Trade Payables	21.1	20.3
2.1	.0	.2	.0			Income Taxes Payable	.1	.1
10.4	15.7	12.8	23.3			All Other Current	16.8	15.9
61.8	53.5	38.7	52.3			Total Current	57.3	56.8
61.3	6.9	10.1	5.8			Long-Term Debt	16.0	11.1
.0	.0	.4	.2			Deferred Taxes	.1	.2
11.8	8.2	5.3	3.1			All Other Non-Current	8.2	6.8
-34.9	31.3	45.5	38.6			Net Worth	18.4	25.2
100.0	100.0	100.0	100.0			Total Liabilities & Net Worth	100.0	100.0
						INCOME DATA		
100.0	100.0	100.0	100.0			Net Sales	100.0	100.0
40.4	28.5	33.7	28.7			Gross Profit	33.5	32.1
35.5	26.1	29.2	26.0			Operating Expenses	32.1	30.9
4.9	2.4	4.6	2.8			Operating Profit	1.4	1.2
.7	-.1	-.5	-.2			All Other Expenses (net)	.4	.2
4.2	2.6	5.0	3.0			Profit Before Taxes	1.0	1.0
						RATIOS		
3.0	2.7	2.6	1.6				2.0	2.5
1.7	1.5	2.0	1.5			Current	1.4	1.4
.9	1.1	1.6	1.3				1.0	1.0
2.1	1.0	1.0	.7				.8	.9
.7	.6	.5	.5			Quick	.4	(118) .5
.2	.3	.3	.2				.2	.2
0 UND	**4** 102.8	**9** 40.4	**6** 61.1				**4** 85.4	**4** 86.5
7 55.4	**7** 51.8	**14** 25.7	**13** 27.2			Sales/Receivables	**10** 35.5	**10** 37.7
10 34.9	**22** 16.8	**39** 9.3	**31** 11.7				**20** 17.9	**21** 17.8
13 28.4	**61** 6.0	**57** 6.4	**59** 6.2				**46** 8.0	**55** 6.6
40 9.2	**73** 5.0	**85** 4.3	**76** 4.8			Cost of Sales/Inventory	**76** 4.8	**81** 4.5
87 4.2	**104** 3.5	**182** 2.0	**101** 3.6				**111** 3.3	**114** 3.2
0 UND	**13** 27.6	**10** 35.8	**23** 15.8				**16** 23.5	**13** 28.3
13 29.0	**36** 10.0	**22** 16.3	**31** 11.7			Cost of Sales/Payables	**30** 12.0	**23** 15.8
29 12.8	**55** 6.6	**38** 9.6	**45** 8.2				**55** 6.6	**53** 6.9
9.6	7.7	3.5	12.4				7.4	6.7
20.9	13.2	7.4	14.4			Sales/Working Capital	18.2	14.2
NM	29.1	11.9	19.5				810.3	105.9
27.9	12.8	57.1					8.9	9.2
(10) 6.6	(29) 3.8	(20) 5.8				EBIT/Interest	(117) 2.5	(100) 2.3
1.3	1.5	2.2					.4	.9
							12.2	17.9
						Net Profit + Depr., Dep., Amort./Cur. Mat. L/T/D	(25) 3.1	(20) 2.7
							1.1	.8
.1	.1	.1	.3				.2	.2
1.1	.3	.2	.5			Fixed/Worth	.6	.5
-.4	1.0	.5	7.4				5.0	1.6
2.1	.9	.5	1.0				1.3	1.0
4.9	2.3	1.3	1.7			Debt/Worth	3.0	2.5
-3.1	9.3	2.1	135.6				48.3	7.6
	52.2	32.9	51.7				37.2	27.1
	(32) 13.0	(21) 17.0	(10) 19.9			% Profit Before Taxes/Tangible Net Worth	(101) 13.5	(101) 9.7
	3.5	4.9	6.9				1.8	1.8
50.6	8.7	17.5	17.3				10.5	8.1
8.8	2.5	4.8	7.0			% Profit Before Taxes/Total Assets	2.6	2.6
-4.0	1.4	1.4	1.9				-1.1	-.6
168.7	159.3	52.4	61.9				73.9	62.4
26.5	82.0	32.2	25.7			Sales/Net Fixed Assets	27.1	28.3
14.6	28.9	9.1	13.9				11.8	12.9
6.4	4.4	3.8	3.5				4.3	4.3
4.3	3.4	2.8	3.1			Sales/Total Assets	3.1	3.1
3.5	2.8	2.2	2.9				2.3	2.2
	.2	.4	.5				.4	.3
	(22) .5	(18) .5	(10) 1.0			% Depr., Dep., Amort./Sales	(102) .8	(99) .7
	1.6	1.1	1.4				1.3	1.2
3.1	1.8	1.3					1.4	1.6
(10) 5.0	(19) 2.5	(11) 1.6				% Officers', Directors' Owners' Comp/Sales	(61) 2.8	(49) 2.6
8.6	3.9	3.3					4.9	4.3
17354M	157542M	293581M	719723M	822236M	292369M	Net Sales ($)	2669531M	3341086M
3548M	42075M	100465M	241371M	450601M	126388M	Total Assets ($)	939433M	1249544M

M = $ thousand MM = $ million

See Pages 9 through 22 for Explanation of Ratios and Data

Comparative Historical Data				Current Data Sorted by Sales					
			Type of Statement						
11	3	9	Unqualified					1	8
22	12	8	Reviewed			1	1		6
22	20	16	Compiled	1	3	3	3	5	1
42	39	33	Tax Returns	4	12	5	9	1	2
34	34	23	Other	3	3	3	5	3	6
4/1/11-3/31/12	**4/1/12-3/31/13**	**4/1/13-3/31/14**		**16 (4/1-9/30/13)**			**73 (10/1/13-3/31/14)**		
ALL	**ALL**	**ALL**		**0-1MM**	**1-3MM**	**3-5MM**	**5-10MM**	**10-25MM**	**25MM & OVER**
131	108	89	**NUMBER OF STATEMENTS**	8	18	12	18	10	23
%	%	%	**ASSETS**	%	%	%	%	%	%
9.6	14.2	14.0	Cash & Equivalents		15.7	12.3	13.0	13.8	13.2
13.6	13.5	13.5	Trade Receivables (net)		15.1	11.5	16.9	17.1	11.5
50.0	49.2	48.4	Inventory		42.5	59.5	53.7	50.3	43.5
1.8	2.0	1.8	All Other Current		1.5	3.8	1.0	.2	2.4
75.0	78.9	77.6	Total Current		74.9	87.1	84.6	81.4	70.6
15.4	14.9	14.9	Fixed Assets (net)		20.4	4.0	10.8	10.2	16.7
3.5	3.1	3.7	Intangibles (net)		2.6	3.0	1.7	.1	9.2
6.1	3.1	3.8	All Other Non-Current		2.0	5.9	2.9	8.4	3.5
100.0	100.0	100.0	Total		100.0	100.0	100.0	100.0	100.0
			LIABILITIES						
15.9	13.6	12.5	Notes Payable-Short Term		11.7	15.2	9.1	14.0	7.3
3.0	1.3	1.0	Cur. Mat.-L.T.D.		.4	.8	.4	.9	.7
20.3	19.7	20.1	Trade Payables		26.7	26.9	24.2	12.2	16.8
.1	.3	.4	Income Taxes Payable		.8	.0	.0	.0	.2
15.5	15.9	14.9	All Other Current		7.0	11.9	22.4	8.7	19.7
54.9	50.8	48.8	Total Current		46.6	54.7	56.1	35.8	44.7
15.0	12.0	17.4	Long-Term Debt		47.8	5.3	5.8	5.9	13.3
.2	.1	.2	Deferred Taxes		.0	.0	.1	.9	.1
9.7	7.0	7.1	All Other Non-Current		5.1	11.2	2.6	11.8	3.1
20.3	30.1	26.6	Net Worth		.4	28.8	35.4	45.6	38.7
100.0	100.0	100.0	Total Liabilities & Net Worth		100.0	100.0	100.0	100.0	100.0
			INCOME DATA						
100.0	100.0	100.0	Net Sales		100.0	100.0	100.0	100.0	100.0
34.3	33.5	33.0	Gross Profit		35.4	30.3	27.2	26.9	33.7
32.7	31.0	29.3	Operating Expenses		31.3	26.4	25.4	23.8	29.7
1.7	2.4	3.7	Operating Profit		4.2	3.9	1.8	3.1	4.0
.5	.3	.0	All Other Expenses (net)		.3	.5	-.1	-.3	.2
1.2	2.1	3.7	Profit Before Taxes		3.8	3.4	1.9	3.3	3.8
			RATIOS						
2.4	2.4	2.7			3.0	2.5	2.2	4.8	2.0
1.5	1.6	1.6	Current		1.9	1.6	1.6	2.2	1.5
1.1	1.2	1.3			1.2	1.2	1.2	1.7	1.3
.7	.9	1.1			1.7	.8	.9	1.5	1.1
.4	.5	.6	Quick		.6	.4	.4	.8	.5
.2	.3	.3			.3	.1	.2	.6	.3
5 67.9	**4** 84.8	**5** 76.1			**5** 77.2	**3** 116.9	**4** 101.4	**8** 47.3	**6** 58.6
11 34.1	**10** 35.5	**9** 39.6	Sales/Receivables		**9** 42.0	**6** 62.9	**12** 31.0	**15** 24.1	**13** 28.1
21 17.3	**23** 15.9	**23** 15.8			**31** 11.7	**22** 16.4	**26** 13.8	**21** 17.5	**24** 15.2
53 6.9	**52** 7.0	**54** 6.7			**16** 22.5	**63** 5.8	**51** 7.1	**47** 7.7	**56** 6.5
85 4.3	**81** 4.5	**74** 4.9	Cost of Sales/Inventory		**74** 4.9	**85** 4.3	**66** 5.5	**69** 5.3	**79** 4.6
122 3.0	**111** 3.3	**104** 3.5			**104** 3.5	**122** 3.0	**114** 3.2	**91** 4.0	**104** 3.5
17 21.6	**11** 32.9	**12** 31.5			**14** 25.7	**8** 43.6	**12** 31.5	**7** 55.0	**23** 16.2
29 12.7	**28** 13.0	**28** 13.1	Cost of Sales/Payables		**33** 11.0	**44** 8.3	**33** 11.2	**12** 29.3	**33** 11.0
49 7.5	**41** 8.9	**47** 7.7			**60** 6.1	**58** 6.3	**47** 7.7	**23** 16.2	**39** 9.4
6.2	6.7	6.0			5.4	6.0	7.4	5.2	6.0
13.9	12.6	11.4	Sales/Working Capital		11.2	11.2	10.3	9.3	13.7
63.6	35.4	23.7			149.2	27.1	37.1	14.5	20.5
9.3	18.1	16.8			23.5		25.2		36.5
(112) 2.8	(87) 4.1	(75) 5.0	EBIT/Interest		(16) 5.0		(17) 3.3		(19) 5.4
-.4	1.4	1.8			2.0		1.3		3.1
21.6	22.8	33.6							
(16) 6.0	(16) 4.0	(10) 5.5	Net Profit + Depr., Dep., Amort./Cur. Mat. L/T/D						
.3	.8	2.9							
.1	.1	.1			.1	.0	.2	.1	.2
.4	.3	.4	Fixed/Worth		.9	.2	.3	.2	.4
2.1	1.5	1.1			-76.0	.3	1.0	.7	1.3
1.1	1.1	.9			.7	1.3	1.1	.3	.8
2.8	2.1	1.9	Debt/Worth		3.2	2.9	1.5	1.1	1.7
17.8	8.5	9.2			-135.0	6.8	9.2	4.1	14.8
28.6	52.0	48.9			52.8	82.6	20.4	39.6	44.6
(104) 11.1	(92) 20.0	(75) 17.1	% Profit Before Taxes/Tangible Net Worth		(13) 28.5	(11) 48.3	(17) 4.4	19.8	(19) 18.5
-2.4	5.8	4.4			11.3	13.5	.5	13.1	5.5
9.0	15.1	12.7			20.8	15.8	3.2	11.0	12.5
3.0	5.9	4.8	% Profit Before Taxes/Total Assets		8.0	7.9	1.6	7.5	6.8
-2.6	1.0	1.2			1.9	1.7	.2	2.9	1.6
92.5	165.0	118.4			152.2	999.8	69.4	220.0	45.6
32.4	40.5	36.5	Sales/Net Fixed Assets		33.0	114.1	41.5	53.1	28.9
13.8	12.4	18.2			15.1	67.2	26.4	23.0	11.3
4.1	4.3	4.1			4.5	5.3	4.3	6.1	3.6
3.2	3.3	3.3	Sales/Total Assets		3.4	3.4	3.4	3.4	3.1
2.1	2.4	2.4			2.5	2.7	3.0	2.3	2.3
.3	.4	.4			.3		.6		.4
(98) .7	(74) .6	(62) .7	% Depr., Dep., Amort./Sales		(12) 1.0		(13) 1.0		(19) .9
1.3	1.2	1.2			2.0		2.1		1.4
1.7	1.3	1.5			2.9		1.3		
(64) 3.0	(50) 3.0	(42) 2.7	% Officers', Directors' Owners' Comp/Sales		(12) 4.4		(10) 1.6		
4.3	4.1	4.8			5.8		2.5		
3085870M	2422459M	2302805M	Net Sales ($)	4959M	36510M	44222M	128609M	130196M	1958309M
1232219M	980762M	964448M	Total Assets ($)	5285M	15048M	15272M	40342M	40143M	848358M

M = $ thousand MM = $ million

See Pages 9 through 22 for Explanation of Ratios and Data

Current Data Sorted by Assets / Comparative Historical Data

0-500M	500M-2MM	2-10MM	10-50MM	50-100MM	100-250MM		4/1/09-3/31/10 ALL	4/1/10-3/31/11 ALL
						Type of Statement		
		3	5	4	3	Unqualified	27	25
	1	8	7			Reviewed	39	36
3	12	15	1	1		Compiled	41	38
27	30	18				Tax Returns	78	86
19	34	43	17	3	2	Other	119	117
33 (4/1-9/30/13)			223 (10/1/13-3/31/14)					
49	77	87	30	8	5	**NUMBER OF STATEMENTS**	304	302
%	%	%	%	%	%	**ASSETS**	%	%
26.2	17.8	14.7	11.1			Cash & Equivalents	14.1	14.8
16.6	20.8	26.0	26.4			Trade Receivables (net)	26.5	24.8
28.4	32.2	32.3	30.3			Inventory	30.3	29.7
3.1	2.5	3.4	4.3			All Other Current	2.9	3.6
74.2	73.4	76.5	72.1			Total Current	73.7	73.1
14.6	12.4	12.3	15.2			Fixed Assets (net)	15.2	14.0
4.6	6.7	3.5	2.5			Intangibles (net)	4.3	5.6
6.5	7.6	7.7	10.1			All Other Non-Current	6.7	7.3
100.0	100.0	100.0	100.0			Total	100.0	100.0
						LIABILITIES		
23.5	11.1	6.6	9.5			Notes Payable-Short Term	13.0	11.3
3.8	1.7	1.7	1.2			Cur. Mat.-L.T.D.	3.1	2.0
23.3	23.4	29.5	33.8			Trade Payables	26.0	24.7
.1	.2	.3	.0			Income Taxes Payable	.4	.2
14.7	10.5	12.2	6.6			All Other Current	14.5	16.6
65.4	46.9	50.3	51.1			Total Current	57.1	54.8
14.4	9.0	8.8	5.8			Long-Term Debt	14.0	10.7
.0	.0	.2	.3			Deferred Taxes	.1	.1
12.5	7.7	6.2	11.8			All Other Non-Current	6.7	5.7
7.7	36.5	34.5	31.1			Net Worth	22.1	28.7
100.0	100.0	100.0	100.0			Total Liabilities & Net Worth	100.0	100.0
						INCOME DATA		
100.0	100.0	100.0	100.0			Net Sales	100.0	100.0
41.8	36.8	32.9	30.0			Gross Profit	36.2	37.2
34.4	33.5	28.5	25.7			Operating Expenses	32.6	33.3
7.4	3.2	4.4	4.3			Operating Profit	3.6	3.9
.5	-.1	.4	.1			All Other Expenses (net)	.4	.2
6.9	3.4	4.0	4.2			Profit Before Taxes	3.2	3.7
						RATIOS		
2.6	2.9	2.6	2.1				2.3	2.6
1.2	1.7	1.5	1.3			Current	1.3	1.5
.7	1.2	1.2	1.1				1.0	1.1
1.4	1.6	1.5	.9				1.2	1.3
.7	.9	.9	.7			Quick	.7	.8
.3	.4	.4	.5				.3	.4
0 UND	**2** 194.2	**6** 60.3	**11** 32.6				**7** 51.4	**5** 70.6
6 62.9	**15** 24.3	**22** 16.9	**26** 14.2			Sales/Receivables	**24** 15.0	**24** 15.4
15 24.5	**31** 11.8	**39** 9.3	**43** 8.5				**46** 7.9	**42** 8.6
0 UND	**14** 25.9	**15** 24.9	**22** 16.3				**12** 30.4	**12** 31.4
15 24.6	**39** 9.3	**34** 10.6	**34** 10.7			Cost of Sales/Inventory	**41** 8.9	**39** 9.4
85 4.3	**76** 4.8	**83** 4.4	**79** 4.6				**85** 4.3	**78** 4.7
0 UND	**11** 32.5	**14** 26.4	**30** 12.2				**18** 20.3	**14** 25.4
20 18.1	**26** 13.8	**29** 12.6	**41** 8.9			Cost of Sales/Payables	**36** 10.1	**33** 11.1
32 11.5	**55** 6.6	**58** 6.3	**72** 5.1				**58** 6.3	**53** 6.9
13.8	7.5	9.2	7.1				7.8	6.8
35.2	13.8	20.4	18.5			Sales/Working Capital	20.3	16.3
-30.2	37.7	61.9	295.1				UND	116.7
42.0	25.0	30.0	26.3				16.1	24.4
(30) 6.5	(56) 10.4	(67) 9.6	(23) 5.5			EBIT/Interest	(253) 5.0	(243) 6.3
1.6	4.0	3.4	2.2				1.5	1.2
		14.5					9.6	12.1
		(13) 1.4				Net Profit + Depr., Dep., Amort./Cur. Mat. L/T/D	(37) 2.4	(35) 3.0
		.5					1.1	.8
.0	.0	.1	.1				.1	.1
.3	.2	.3	.4			Fixed/Worth	.5	.3
-1.4	1.3	1.5	1.1				2.4	1.2
1.2	.8	.9	1.1				1.1	.8
3.8	2.1	2.7	2.6			Debt/Worth	2.8	2.3
-4.1	10.1	8.4	6.1				21.5	9.0
237.5	71.9	68.7	53.6				74.0	71.0
(30) 88.4	(60) 28.1	(79) 31.5	(26) 20.2			% Profit Before Taxes/Tangible Net Worth	(243) 27.8	(246) 31.5
31.9	8.5	13.6	6.5				6.7	4.9
66.4	21.5	16.6	17.5				17.8	24.5
20.2	10.8	9.6	8.8			% Profit Before Taxes/Total Assets	7.7	9.2
2.2	1.4	4.0	2.5				.9	.9
UND	538.8	137.4	91.8				142.5	139.3
78.4	56.8	44.7	31.9			Sales/Net Fixed Assets	40.1	45.3
32.0	20.9	25.1	18.9				14.3	16.4
10.8	5.2	5.0	4.5				4.7	5.2
5.2	3.9	3.9	3.2			Sales/Total Assets	3.4	3.5
3.4	2.6	3.0	2.2				2.5	2.5
.2	.2	.3	.4				.3	.4
(20) .5	(42) .7	(60) .6	(23) .8			% Depr., Dep., Amort./Sales	(210) .7	(196) .7
1.3	1.5	1.7	2.1				1.4	1.6
2.1	2.0	.6					1.5	1.6
(27) 3.7	(45) 3.6	(38) 1.4				% Officers', Directors' Owners' Comp/Sales	(124) 3.7	(142) 3.9
8.2	7.2	3.6					6.5	7.6
68927M	**422833M**	**1701338M**	**2371061M**	**1620644M**	**4100065M**	Net Sales ($)	**12135202M**	**13467344M**
11286M	**90476M**	**391668M**	**689085M**	**564262M**	**1016912M**	Total Assets ($)	**3627706M**	**3798246M**

M = $ thousand MM = $ million

See Pages 9 through 22 for Explanation of Ratios and Data

Comparative Historical Data / Current Data Sorted by Sales

4/1/11-3/31/12 ALL	4/1/12-3/31/13 ALL	4/1/13-3/31/14 ALL	Type of Statement	0-1MM	1-3MM	3-5MM	5-10MM	10-25MM	25MM & OVER
25	16	15	Unqualified				1		14
38	26	16	Reviewed				1	4	11
30	29	32	Compiled	3	5	5	4	10	5
86	95	75	Tax Returns	16	19	14	15	6	5
144	117	118	Other	9	21	10	19	29	30
				33 (4/1-9/30/13)			223 (10/1/13-3/31/14)		
323	283	256	NUMBER OF STATEMENTS	28	45	29	40	49	65
%	%	%	ASSETS	%	%	%	%	%	%
14.8	15.2	17.1	Cash & Equivalents	18.6	26.1	16.8	18.6	13.6	12.2
27.0	26.0	22.6	Trade Receivables (net)	18.2	16.2	19.1	26.0	24.6	26.9
28.6	30.3	30.9	Inventory	28.8	26.6	27.6	32.0	34.2	33.0
2.8	3.1	3.3	All Other Current	4.2	3.1	1.7	2.5	4.3	3.6
73.2	74.7	73.9	Total Current	69.8	72.0	65.1	79.1	76.6	75.6
14.8	13.1	13.4	Fixed Assets (net)	19.6	13.2	15.9	9.7	12.1	12.8
4.5	5.1	4.8	Intangibles (net)	5.7	6.9	6.9	4.6	3.7	3.1
7.4	7.0	7.9	All Other Non-Current	4.8	7.8	12.1	6.6	7.6	8.5
100.0	100.0	100.0	Total	100.0	100.0	100.0	100.0	100.0	100.0
			LIABILITIES						
12.4	10.6	11.5	Notes Payable-Short Term	17.6	16.7	12.2	11.5	7.5	7.9
1.9	2.1	2.0	Cur. Mat.-L.T.D.	4.4	1.6	4.0	1.4	1.6	1.0
27.8	27.8	26.9	Trade Payables	15.2	27.0	23.5	21.2	27.8	36.1
.1	.1	.2	Income Taxes Payable	.0	.1	.3	.1	.5	.0
13.2	12.7	11.7	All Other Current	15.2	9.7	11.4	13.7	13.6	9.2
55.4	53.2	52.2	Total Current	52.3	55.1	51.4	47.9	51.0	54.2
9.7	12.2	10.0	Long-Term Debt	14.2	14.9	12.5	5.5	9.1	7.2
.2	.1	.1	Deferred Taxes	.0	.0	.1	.0	.3	.2
7.6	5.4	8.6	All Other Non-Current	21.9	5.5	11.8	7.6	5.2	6.9
27.1	29.0	29.0	Net Worth	11.5	24.5	24.2	38.9	34.5	31.5
100.0	100.0	100.0	Total Liabilties & Net Worth	100.0	100.0	100.0	100.0	100.0	100.0
			INCOME DATA						
100.0	100.0	100.0	Net Sales	100.0	100.0	100.0	100.0	100.0	100.0
35.6	35.8	35.5	Gross Profit	41.2	42.6	43.8	37.5	33.7	24.4
32.1	32.1	30.8	Operating Expenses	31.1	39.0	37.8	33.0	29.9	21.3
3.5	3.7	4.6	Operating Profit	10.0	3.6	6.0	4.5	3.9	3.0
.3	.1	.2	All Other Expenses (net)	1.2	.1	.5	.1	.0	-.1
3.2	3.6	4.4	Profit Before Taxes	8.9	3.5	5.5	4.4	3.8	3.2
			RATIOS						
2.4	2.3	2.5		5.7	2.7	2.0	2.7	2.1	2.2
1.4	1.4	1.5	Current	1.6	1.5	1.5	1.7	1.5	1.3
1.0	1.1	1.1		1.0	.9	.9	1.2	1.2	1.1
1.3	1.4	1.5		2.9	1.5	1.3	1.7	1.4	1.0
(322) .8	(282) .8	.8	Quick	1.0	.9	.8	.9	.7	.7
.4	.4	.4		.3	.5	.3	.5	.4	.4
5 66.7	6 65.6	3 107.9		0 UND	2 155.6	0 UND	9 40.0	4 98.5	6 59.5
24 15.4	25 14.8	15 23.7	Sales/Receivables	2 232.0	10 36.4	17 21.9	22 16.8	17 22.0	22 16.5
46 7.9	41 8.9	34 10.8		29 12.6	20 18.0	33 11.1	37 9.8	35 10.3	44 8.3
10 35.4	13 27.2	11 32.3		0 UND	2 164.4	19 19.2	5 81.0	13 27.9	17 20.9
33 10.9	33 11.0	33 10.9	Cost of Sales/Inventory	33 10.9	30 12.2	50 7.3	33 10.9	34 10.6	29 12.5
70 5.2	78 4.7	78 4.7		130 2.8	94 3.9	96 3.8	87 4.2	64 5.7	65 5.6
17 21.9	15 23.8	13 28.5		0 UND	10 36.7	11 32.0	12 29.7	13 27.6	21 17.7
33 10.9	34 10.7	29 12.5	Cost of Sales/Payables	8 48.0	31 11.9	27 13.6	22 16.9	29 12.6	41 9.0
58 6.3	59 6.2	57 6.4		32 11.4	65 5.6	69 5.3	52 7.0	57 6.4	58 6.3
7.9	7.9	8.6		5.4	7.4	9.8	7.7	9.6	11.7
17.8	18.3	19.0	Sales/Working Capital	11.7	17.9	20.3	14.1	17.8	24.8
556.0	85.0	229.1		UND	-88.9	-58.6	22.8	49.5	199.2
28.9	27.2	26.6		44.0	16.2	34.8	22.5	23.5	42.9
(261) 6.4	(222) 7.7	(187) 7.8	EBIT/Interest	(13) 5.3	(30) 6.5	(24) 11.1	(31) 9.5	(38) 10.3	(51) 8.5
2.1	1.8	2.5		1.3	1.1	3.6	4.0	3.8	2.3
11.9	8.6	17.7							16.3
(34) 3.5	(30) 3.4	(24) 5.3	Net Profit + Depr., Dep., Amort./Cur. Mat. L/T/D						(12) 5.9
1.0	1.0	1.4							1.0
.1	.1	.1		.0	.0	.1	.1	.0	.1
.4	.3	.3	Fixed/Worth	.6	.3	.7	.2	.2	.4
1.3	1.4	1.7		-1.2	2.7	-6.5	.6	1.0	1.6
.9	.8	.9		1.4	.9	1.5	.8	1.0	.9
2.9	2.7	2.6	Debt/Worth	3.0	2.3	3.5	1.6	2.0	3.6
11.2	12.3	15.1		-4.5	-14.9	-18.1	6.4	15.1	6.7
67.2	75.8	79.1		183.2	71.3	194.8	70.7	81.1	57.2
(265) 28.7	(232) 29.4	(205) 31.9	% Profit Before Taxes/Tangible Net Worth	(17) 81.7	(32) 33.3	(20) 47.8	(36) 31.2	(42) 36.8	(58) 27.8
8.7	6.7	11.6		13.5	-2.1	22.1	12.9	9.8	11.6
18.2	22.2	21.5		69.6	25.1	20.5	22.9	27.6	16.0
8.6	8.1	9.9	% Profit Before Taxes/Total Assets	18.4	8.1	11.2	9.9	10.2	9.5
2.2	1.0	2.8		2.1	-.7	2.3	4.0	4.0	3.6
169.9	184.4	248.8		UND	919.8	290.9	165.4	454.7	114.2
45.0	50.8	47.5	Sales/Net Fixed Assets	70.6	50.8	34.6	64.2	70.5	36.5
16.7	19.2	23.2		12.8	19.1	9.8	29.2	23.5	24.2
5.5	5.1	5.3		8.4	5.3	5.1	5.0	6.0	5.4
3.7	3.7	3.9	Sales/Total Assets	3.4	3.9	3.4	3.9	4.3	4.0
2.5	2.4	2.8		2.0	2.6	2.2	2.7	3.6	3.0
.2	.2	.3		.4	.3	.7	.2	.2	.3
(223) .6	(192) .5	(155) .7	% Depr., Dep., Amort./Sales	(10) .8	(23) .6	(15) 1.2	(24) .5	(34) .7	(49) .6
1.3	1.2	1.8		2.5	1.2	2.3	1.6	2.0	1.6
1.3	1.4	1.3		1.7	2.8	1.7	1.1	.7	.4
(146) 3.5	(126) 2.7	(118) 2.9	% Officers', Directors' Owners' Comp/Sales	(13) 6.2	(24) 3.7	(19) 3.7	(19) 2.6	(23) 1.5	(20) 1.3
6.9	6.0	6.1		9.1	6.1	7.9	6.5	4.0	2.6
15098987M	11532634M	10284868M	Net Sales ($)	16584M	91884M	117992M	286141M	798159M	8974108M
4013029M	3389098M	2763689M	Total Assets ($)	8665M	26202M	40472M	111484M	218053M	2358813M

M = $ thousand MM = $ million

See Pages 9 through 22 for Explanation of Ratios and Data

	Current Data Sorted by Assets						Comparative Historical Data	
Type of Statement								
Unqualified			5	10	6	3	33	40
Reviewed		7	28	16			102	81
Compiled	1	19	26	6		1	75	76
Tax Returns	7	18	10	1		1	45	43
Other	3	12	24	20	2	3	102	115
	30 (4/1-9/30/13)			199 (10/1/13-3/31/14)			4/1/09-3/31/10 ALL	4/1/10-3/31/11 ALL
	0-500M	500M-2MM	2-10MM	10-50MM	50-100MM	100-250MM		
NUMBER OF STATEMENTS	11	56	93	53	8	8	357	355
ASSETS	%	%	%	%	%	%	%	%
Cash & Equivalents	23.5	12.2	7.9	4.2			7.6	8.3
Trade Receivables (net)	5.3	21.0	26.1	22.5			21.8	20.9
Inventory	39.4	44.6	39.3	30.8			33.3	36.9
All Other Current	3.5	1.4	1.0	3.4			2.3	2.3
Total Current	71.7	79.2	74.4	60.9			65.1	68.4
Fixed Assets (net)	21.2	12.6	17.0	28.1			22.8	21.5
Intangibles (net)	.3	1.2	.9	2.8			2.2	2.5
All Other Non-Current	6.7	7.0	7.8	8.2			10.0	7.6
Total	100.0	100.0	100.0	100.0			100.0	100.0
LIABILITIES								
Notes Payable-Short Term	24.4	12.3	10.8	12.2			12.6	17.2
Cur. Mat.-L.T.D.	2.4	1.1	2.7	3.2			3.2	2.9
Trade Payables	26.3	12.8	17.3	11.3			12.7	11.9
Income Taxes Payable	.0	.0	.2	.1			.1	.1
All Other Current	21.1	7.7	6.9	6.6			6.0	7.7
Total Current	74.2	33.9	37.8	33.5			34.6	39.8
Long-Term Debt	16.8	15.3	11.7	13.5			16.0	14.0
Deferred Taxes	.0	.0	.3	.7			.3	.3
All Other Non-Current	5.7	12.3	5.4	6.3			5.8	5.7
Net Worth	3.4	38.5	44.8	46.0			43.3	40.1
Total Liabilties & Net Worth	100.0	100.0	100.0	100.0			100.0	100.0
INCOME DATA								
Net Sales	100.0	100.0	100.0	100.0			100.0	100.0
Gross Profit	34.8	32.2	27.1	26.8			28.5	26.2
Operating Expenses	34.1	29.9	25.6	23.9			29.5	26.2
Operating Profit	.7	2.3	1.5	2.9			-1.0	.0
All Other Expenses (net)	.6	.1	-.1	.3			.0	.0
Profit Before Taxes	.0	2.2	1.6	2.6			-1.1	.1
RATIOS								
Current	7.0	5.2	3.3	3.3			3.5	3.5
	1.3	2.7	2.1	2.0			2.1	1.9
	.8	1.8	1.5	1.4			1.3	1.2
Quick	1.8	1.9	1.4	1.5			1.6	1.6
	.7	1.2	.9	.7			.9	.7
	.1	.6	.6	.5			.5	.4
Sales/Receivables	0 UND	10 34.9	19 19.2	25 14.5			23 15.8	16 22.9
	1 281.0	24 15.2	32 11.5	35 10.5			34 10.8	30 12.2
	6 65.8	41 8.8	45 8.1	43 8.4			47 7.8	43 8.5
Cost of Sales/Inventory	17 21.9	42 8.7	47 7.7	48 7.6			49 7.4	47 7.8
	46 8.0	87 4.2	70 5.2	65 5.6			70 5.3	68 5.4
	79 4.6	135 2.7	96 3.8	79 4.6			101 3.6	97 3.8
Cost of Sales/Payables	0 UND	10 36.0	17 21.5	15 24.5			14 25.9	11 34.7
	24 15.0	19 19.7	25 14.5	24 15.3			22 16.6	20 17.9
	45 8.1	31 11.6	37 9.8	32 11.5			35 10.5	31 11.8
Sales/Working Capital	7.2	4.3	5.3	4.8			4.5	4.8
	39.3	6.7	7.9	7.7			7.0	8.6
	-42.6	11.2	12.5	16.0			16.4	28.0
EBIT/Interest		18.5	11.9	13.5			3.0	4.7
		(49) 4.4	(86) 3.5	(51) 5.5			(323) .8	(307) 1.4
		.9	1.6	2.0			-2.8	-.7
Net Profit + Depr., Dep., Amort./Cur. Mat. L/T/D			5.6	7.4			3.2	3.2
			(27) 2.6	(14) 2.8			(85) 1.2	(79) 1.4
			1.3	1.6			-.4	.0
Fixed/Worth	.1	.1	.1	.3			.2	.2
	.8	.3	.3	.6			.5	.5
	-6.7	1.2	.7	1.0			1.2	1.2
Debt/Worth	.4	.6	.5	.5			.4	.6
	4.0	1.2	1.0	1.2			1.2	1.5
	-13.3	5.7	2.8	2.8			3.6	4.9
% Profit Before Taxes/Tangible Net Worth		45.8	16.1	18.6			7.0	17.1
		(48) 15.7	(89) 8.0	(52) 10.7			(319) -.7	(316) 3.7
		3.3	2.9	4.4			-13.3	-5.2
% Profit Before Taxes/Total Assets	12.3	16.9	7.5	9.4			3.1	5.8
	7.8	3.9	3.4	5.6			-.5	1.4
	.0	.1	.9	1.5			-6.9	-2.7
Sales/Net Fixed Assets	105.6	97.4	37.6	18.6			24.9	38.4
	37.1	24.7	19.8	9.6			11.0	15.1
	11.3	12.3	11.1	5.1			6.0	6.7
Sales/Total Assets	7.1	3.4	3.4	2.8			2.9	3.2
	5.0	2.7	2.8	2.3			2.2	2.5
	3.6	2.1	2.1	1.8			1.6	1.8
% Depr., Dep., Amort./Sales		.5	.5	.8			1.0	.6
		(44) .7	(87) .8	(51) 1.1			(318) 1.5	(310) 1.2
		1.2	1.3	1.6			2.4	2.0
% Officers', Directors' Owners' Comp/Sales		1.6	1.0	.5			1.5	.8
		(31) 3.0	(45) 1.7	(14) 1.7			(156) 2.8	(176) 2.0
		5.9	2.9	2.8			4.4	4.2
Net Sales ($)	12175M	217339M	1243251M	2767946M	1314499M	2870825M	8133858M	9548637M
Total Assets ($)	2609M	68698M	442911M	1214454M	564495M	1253425M	3971953M	4166891M

Comparative Historical Data				Current Data Sorted by Sales					
			Type of Statement						
35	34	24	Unqualified					3	21
80	55	51	Reviewed		3	1	13	16	18
63	51	53	Compiled	1	11	8	14	12	7
45	45	37	Tax Returns	4	11	6	7	6	3
106	84	64	Other	3	4	6	14	17	20
				30 (4/1-9/30/13)			199 (10/1/13-3/31/14)		
4/1/11-3/31/12 ALL	**4/1/12-3/31/13 ALL**	**4/1/13-3/31/14 ALL**		**0-1MM**	**1-3MM**	**3-5MM**	**5-10MM**	**10-25MM**	**25MM & OVER**
329	269	229	**NUMBER OF STATEMENTS**	8	29	21	48	54	69
%	%	%	**ASSETS**	%	%	%	%	%	%
7.6	7.3	8.8	Cash & Equivalents		12.9	6.1	11.4	9.5	4.4
21.0	22.1	22.4	Trade Receivables (net)		14.6	19.8	29.0	22.0	23.9
38.5	37.6	38.4	Inventory		43.1	47.1	35.3	38.8	34.8
2.1	1.8	1.8	All Other Current		1.4	.7	1.1	1.0	2.8
69.2	68.8	71.4	Total Current		72.1	73.7	76.8	71.3	65.9
21.1	21.4	19.6	Fixed Assets (net)		18.6	17.0	13.6	21.2	23.8
1.8	1.8	1.6	Intangibles (net)		.2	1.8	1.3	1.3	2.5
7.9	8.0	7.5	All Other Non-Current		9.1	7.6	8.3	6.2	7.7
100.0	100.0	100.0	Total		100.0	100.0	100.0	100.0	100.0
			LIABILITIES						
18.1	11.9	12.0	Notes Payable-Short Term		13.9	7.0	9.5	9.0	13.1
2.8	3.3	2.4	Cur. Mat.-L.T.D.		1.3	1.6	3.4	2.2	2.4
12.4	14.4	15.0	Trade Payables		13.7	16.5	16.5	16.3	12.9
.0	.1	.1	Income Taxes Payable		.0	.0	.1	.1	.2
9.5	7.6	7.7	All Other Current		8.2	7.8	7.5	6.4	7.0
42.8	37.3	37.2	Total Current		37.1	32.9	37.1	34.1	35.6
12.9	17.0	13.5	Long-Term Debt		19.0	14.6	12.8	13.3	10.0
.4	.4	.3	Deferred Taxes		.0	.0	.3	.4	.6
6.0	7.8	7.2	All Other Non-Current		14.8	11.8	7.0	4.0	5.7
37.9	37.5	41.8	Net Worth		29.1	40.8	42.8	48.2	48.2
100.0	100.0	100.0	Total Liabilties & Net Worth		100.0	100.0	100.0	100.0	100.0
			INCOME DATA						
100.0	100.0	100.0	Net Sales		100.0	100.0	100.0	100.0	100.0
26.7	30.3	28.7	Gross Profit		33.7	31.8	29.7	26.0	26.8
26.2	28.3	26.6	Operating Expenses		32.4	29.1	27.8	24.3	23.9
.5	2.1	2.1	Operating Profit		1.3	2.7	1.9	1.7	2.9
.0	.0	.1	All Other Expenses (net)		.0	.2	-.1	.1	-.1
.5	2.1	2.0	Profit Before Taxes		1.3	2.5	1.9	1.6	3.0
			RATIOS						
3.0	3.3	3.5			4.9	4.1	3.5	3.5	2.9
1.8	2.1	2.1	Current		2.0	2.2	2.5	2.2	2.0
1.2	1.5	1.4			1.3	1.6	1.4	1.6	1.4
1.4	1.5	1.5			1.8	1.5	1.6	1.8	1.3
.7	.8	.8	Quick		.7	.8	.9	.8	.8
.4	.5	.6			.3	.5	.7	.6	.5
15 24.9	**18** 20.5	**16** 23.0			**3** 122.5	**12** 31.0	**20** 18.1	**15** 24.3	**23** 15.9
31 11.6	**30** 12.1	**29** 12.8	Sales/Receivables		**17** 21.6	**23** 15.6	**34** 10.7	**28** 13.1	**30** 12.1
45 8.2	**45** 8.1	**43** 8.5			**41** 8.9	**42** 8.7	**53** 6.9	**41** 9.0	**45** 8.2
47 7.8	**51** 7.2	**46** 7.9			**45** 8.1	**83** 4.4	**45** 8.2	**45** 8.2	**47** 7.8
70 5.2	**76** 4.8	**72** 5.1	Cost of Sales/Inventory		**107** 3.4	**101** 3.6	**69** 5.3	**68** 5.4	**63** 5.8
104 3.5	**114** 3.2	**101** 3.6			**152** 2.4	**130** 2.8	**99** 3.7	**89** 4.1	**81** 4.5
13 28.6	**16** 23.2	**14** 26.0			**0** UND	**15** 25.0	**13** 27.6	**17** 21.3	**15** 24.5
23 16.2	**25** 14.5	**24** 15.4	Cost of Sales/Payables		**17** 21.2	**27** 13.3	**25** 14.5	**24** 15.0	**21** 17.8
36 10.2	**36** 10.0	**35** 10.5			**35** 10.4	**57** 6.4	**38** 9.5	**35** 10.3	**33** 11.1
5.1	4.8	4.8			3.7	4.5	4.5	5.2	5.6
7.9	7.4	7.8	Sales/Working Capital		6.7	6.7	7.1	8.2	8.5
25.2	12.7	12.8			25.9	11.1	14.8	12.5	12.7
4.6	10.9	13.3			17.3	10.1	15.3	10.8	14.7
(277) 1.8	(244) 3.3	(209) 4.5	EBIT/Interest		(26) 2.8	(20) 3.9	(40) 2.9	(50) 3.4	(67) 7.4
.4	1.3	1.8			.3	1.3	1.2	1.8	3.8
4.7	4.3	5.7					2.9	7.7	7.3
(68) 1.7	(55) 2.2	(49) 2.6	Net Profit + Depr., Dep., Amort./Cur. Mat. L/T/D				(12) 1.8	(16) 2.3	(20) 4.3
.6	.8	1.7					.8	1.8	2.2
.2	.2	.2			.2	.1	.1	.1	.3
.4	.5	.4	Fixed/Worth		.5	.6	.2	.4	.5
1.2	1.4	1.0			1.9	2.1	.6	.9	.8
.6	.6	.5			.6	.6	.5	.5	.5
1.5	1.3	1.2	Debt/Worth		2.1	1.6	1.0	1.0	1.0
4.2	4.2	3.4			7.1	15.2	3.6	2.7	2.1
14.6	19.8	21.4			61.9	34.6	20.0	14.6	21.1
(302) 3.9	(236) 8.2	(212) 10.0	% Profit Before Taxes/Tangible Net Worth		(25) 9.4	(18) 9.6	(45) 7.2	(53) 8.0	(67) 12.8
-1.2	2.1	3.9			.2	2.6	1.8	2.8	9.0
5.2	8.7	9.4			9.8	10.6	9.4	7.8	9.9
1.7	4.0	4.4	% Profit Before Taxes/Total Assets		3.4	3.1	3.4	3.2	6.9
-.8	.7	1.3			-2.1	.6	.4	1.4	3.7
44.6	38.2	35.2			30.5	78.4	54.0	33.1	22.7
16.7	15.0	16.4	Sales/Net Fixed Assets		13.0	23.2	26.9	15.3	12.2
6.7	6.7	9.5			9.9	12.9	12.8	9.0	6.4
3.4	3.1	3.3			3.0	3.1	3.3	3.7	3.1
2.5	2.4	2.7	Sales/Total Assets		2.1	2.7	2.7	2.8	2.6
1.7	1.8	2.0			1.5	2.3	2.0	1.9	2.1
.5	.6	.5			.6	.3	.5	.6	.7
(287) 1.0	(236) 1.0	(202) .9	% Depr., Dep., Amort./Sales		(24) .9	(19) .5	(39) .7	(51) .9	(65) 1.0
1.8	1.7	1.3			1.5	1.3	1.4	1.4	1.3
1.0	1.2	1.1			1.6	1.4	1.6	.7	.6
(156) 2.1	(117) 2.7	(102) 2.0	% Officers', Directors' Owners' Comp/Sales		(16) 3.9	(10) 2.3	(26) 2.6	(25) 1.3	(19) 1.8
3.8	3.8	4.7			7.4	4.5	3.7	2.5	3.1
8561943M	**8026751M**	**8426035M**	Net Sales ($)	**5362M**	**53483M**	**84786M**	**343212M**	**900152M**	**7039040M**
3681920M	**3591642M**	**3546592M**	Total Assets ($)	**2602M**	**25585M**	**35681M**	**146721M**	**382982M**	**2953021M**

M = $ thousand **MM = $ million**

See Pages 9 through 22 for Explanation of Ratios and Data

	Current Data Sorted by Assets						**Comparative Historical Data**	
Type of Statement								
Unqualified				1			4	1
Reviewed							5	1
Compiled	3	1	4	1			9	6
Tax Returns	3	7	1				10	16
Other	1	2	1	1			6	7
	2 (4/1-9/30/13)		24 (10/1/13-3/31/14)				4/1/09-3/31/10	4/1/10-3/31/11
	0-500M	500M-2MM	2-10MM	10-50MM	50-100MM	100-250MM	ALL	ALL
NUMBER OF STATEMENTS	7	10	6	3			34	31
ASSETS	%	%	%	%	%	%	%	%
Cash & Equivalents		8.4			DATA NOT AVAILABLE	DATA NOT AVAILABLE	7.7	8.6
Trade Receivables (net)		18.0					21.2	27.8
Inventory		40.9					38.8	37.6
All Other Current		1.7					2.9	1.1
Total Current		69.0					70.6	75.1
Fixed Assets (net)		15.5					18.1	17.1
Intangibles (net)		3.5					5.1	3.0
All Other Non-Current		12.0					6.2	4.7
Total		100.0					100.0	100.0
LIABILITIES								
Notes Payable-Short Term		11.0					12.7	11.6
Cur. Mat.-L.T.D.		.4					3.9	3.5
Trade Payables		19.3					17.0	29.1
Income Taxes Payable		.0					.2	.0
All Other Current		4.7					8.5	9.1
Total Current		35.5					42.3	53.4
Long-Term Debt		17.9					27.9	24.9
Deferred Taxes		.0					.3	.1
All Other Non-Current		13.7					3.0	9.9
Net Worth		32.8					26.6	11.7
Total Liabilties & Net Worth		100.0					100.0	100.0
INCOME DATA								
Net Sales		100.0					100.0	100.0
Gross Profit		37.1					34.4	35.7
Operating Expenses		33.8					36.6	34.1
Operating Profit		3.3					-2.2	1.7
All Other Expenses (net)		.0					.3	1.4
Profit Before Taxes		3.3					-2.5	.2
RATIOS								
Current		6.1					2.4	2.9
		2.1					1.8	1.9
		1.5					1.3	1.1
Quick		2.1					1.1	1.7
		.6					.7	1.0
		.4					.3	.4
Sales/Receivables		**10** 36.8					**15** 24.3	**16** 22.5
		19 18.9					**26** 14.2	**34** 10.8
		30 12.1					**44** 8.3	**53** 6.9
Cost of Sales/Inventory		**31** 11.6					**53** 6.9	**35** 10.4
		73 5.0					**79** 4.6	**56** 6.5
		140 2.6					**122** 3.0	**116** 3.1
Cost of Sales/Payables		**5** 75.6					**17** 21.3	**30** 12.4
		22 16.7					**33** 11.1	**41** 9.0
		55 6.6					**57** 6.4	**59** 6.2
Sales/Working Capital		4.3					4.9	4.7
		10.8					9.2	8.1
		85.4					21.2	35.9
EBIT/Interest							4.1	6.0
							(32) .8	(28) 1.6
							-4.0	-1.8
Net Profit + Depr., Dep., Amort./Cur. Mat. L/T/D								
Fixed/Worth		.2					.1	.1
		.8					.4	.4
		NM					3.4	UND
Debt/Worth		.5					.8	1.2
		4.1					2.0	2.5
		NM					7.1	UND
% Profit Before Taxes/Tangible Net Worth							13.6	23.2
							(27) .6	(24) 2.5
							-14.2	-14.7
% Profit Before Taxes/Total Assets		21.4					2.2	7.2
		6.9					-.6	1.2
		.4					-12.1	-8.1
Sales/Net Fixed Assets		87.2					72.6	73.6
		29.7					22.4	25.7
		7.6					9.9	14.1
Sales/Total Assets		4.1					3.4	3.5
		3.4					2.5	2.7
		2.2					1.9	2.1
% Depr., Dep., Amort./Sales							.8	.6
							(30) 1.4	(25) 1.3
							2.2	2.0
% Officers', Directors' Owners' Comp/Sales							1.8	.7
							(20) 2.9	(22) 2.3
							5.9	6.8
Net Sales ($)	8057M	28398M	45223M	114102M			263109M	180603M
Total Assets ($)	2302M	8813M	22663M	46637M			120147M	83122M

M = $ thousand MM = $ million

See Pages 9 through 22 for Explanation of Ratios and Data

Comparative Historical Data				Current Data Sorted by Sales					
			Type of Statement						
	1	1	Unqualified					1	
2			Reviewed						
9	7	9	Compiled	2	3		2	1	1
22	19	11	Tax Returns	2	6	1	2		
4	16	5	Other		3	1			1
				2 (4/1-9/30/13)		24 (10/1/13-3/31/14)			
4/1/11-3/31/12 ALL	4/1/12-3/31/13 ALL	4/1/13-3/31/14 ALL		0-1MM	1-3MM	3-5MM	5-10MM	10-25MM	25MM & OVER
37	43	26	**NUMBER OF STATEMENTS**	4	12	2	4	2	2
%	%	%	**ASSETS**	%	%	%	%	%	%
7.3	12.1	10.8	Cash & Equivalents		7.3				
25.7	20.9	18.8	Trade Receivables (net)		13.5				
38.9	33.2	37.7	Inventory		43.7				
1.8	10.5	1.1	All Other Current		.4				
73.7	76.7	68.4	Total Current		64.9				
13.2	10.7	17.5	Fixed Assets (net)		22.0				
4.3	4.1	4.4	Intangibles (net)		5.8				
8.8	8.5	9.7	All Other Non-Current		7.3				
100.0	100.0	100.0	Total		100.0				
			LIABILITIES						
10.1	14.5	7.2	Notes Payable-Short Term		8.9				
3.8	3.8	1.1	Cur. Mat.-L.T.D.		.7				
24.8	24.5	21.5	Trade Payables		25.6				
.1	.0	.0	Income Taxes Payable		.0				
7.1	5.7	11.4	All Other Current		13.9				
45.9	48.6	41.3	Total Current		49.1				
37.8	20.1	18.7	Long-Term Debt		15.7				
.0	.4	.0	Deferred Taxes		.0				
3.9	6.4	9.7	All Other Non-Current		8.7				
12.4	24.5	30.3	Net Worth		26.4				
100.0	100.0	100.0	Total Liabilties & Net Worth		100.0				
			INCOME DATA						
100.0	100.0	100.0	Net Sales		100.0				
34.0	38.3	36.9	Gross Profit		39.2				
31.2	35.9	33.5	Operating Expenses		36.1				
2.7	2.3	3.3	Operating Profit		3.1				
.6	.5	-.2	All Other Expenses (net)		-.1				
2.2	1.9	3.6	Profit Before Taxes		3.1				
			RATIOS						
2.5	3.0	3.6			2.4				
1.9	2.0	1.9	Current		1.7				
1.4	1.1	1.1			.9				
1.4	1.5	1.7			.6				
.7	.8	.7	Quick		.5				
.5	.4	.4			.1				
19 19.1	**13** 29.0	**9** 42.0			**0** UND				
30 12.1	**22** 16.4	**24** 15.2	Sales/Receivables		**10** 35.0				
43 8.4	**32** 11.5	**38** 9.5			**27** 13.6				
42 8.6	**20** 18.2	**36** 10.1			**35** 10.4				
62 5.9	**56** 6.5	**73** 5.0	Cost of Sales/Inventory		**91** 4.0				
99 3.7	**83** 4.4	**122** 3.0			**135** 2.7				
20 18.0	**18** 20.0	**7** 50.5			**8** 43.8				
33 11.1	**32** 11.3	**32** 11.4	Cost of Sales/Payables		**38** 9.5				
54 6.7	**48** 7.6	**60** 6.1			**87** 4.2				
6.2	5.9	5.1			4.2				
8.6	10.8	10.5	Sales/Working Capital		13.8				
17.5	62.4	95.6			-40.8				
11.4	9.6	16.5							
(33) 4.4	(30) 4.5	(17) 8.6	EBIT/Interest						
1.1	2.0	1.7							
			Net Profit + Depr., Dep., Amort./Cur. Mat. L/T/D						
.2	.1	.2			.8				
.6	.3	.8	Fixed/Worth		29.2				
-.9	2.2	-17.6			-1.3				
1.1	.9	.9			.8				
4.0	3.6	3.8	Debt/Worth		88.2				
-7.4	48.3	-129.9			-8.1				
57.3	129.8	54.5							
(25) 18.1	(33) 23.2	(19) 15.6	% Profit Before Taxes/Tangible Net Worth						
3.2	5.3	4.2							
15.8	17.2	17.2			10.0				
5.7	7.5	6.1	% Profit Before Taxes/Total Assets		2.0				
.4	.9	.7			-1.6				
86.7	216.7	87.2			74.1				
51.1	69.9	32.7	Sales/Net Fixed Assets		20.4				
22.9	34.5	7.9			6.8				
3.7	4.7	3.9			3.7				
2.7	3.2	3.1	Sales/Total Assets		2.9				
2.3	2.7	2.2			1.8				
.3	.3	.6							
(27) .7	(21) .9	(21) .9	% Depr., Dep., Amort./Sales						
1.1	1.4	1.6							
1.2	1.8	1.8							
(27) 3.2	(27) 6.5	(16) 3.7	% Officers', Directors' Owners' Comp/Sales						
7.7	7.6	6.4							
174561M	**212091M**	**195780M**	Net Sales ($)	**3287M**	**21829M**	**8470M**	**27180M**	**39845M**	**95169M**
59309M	**105646M**	**80415M**	Total Assets ($)	**1310M**	**11149M**	**2202M**	**10996M**	**29503M**	**25255M**

M = $ thousand MM = $ million

See Pages 9 through 22 for Explanation of Ratios and Data

Current Data Sorted by Assets							Comparative Historical Data	
						Type of Statement		
2	1	3	4	2	1	Unqualified	6	10
1	3	17	5	2		Reviewed	48	33
4	34	20	4			Compiled	64	88
20	68	16	1		1	Tax Returns	121	134
9	37	21	12	1	2	Other	98	104
	29 (4/1-9/30/13)		262 (10/1/13-3/31/14)				4/1/09-3/31/10	4/1/10-3/31/11
0-500M	500M-2MM	2-10MM	10-50MM	50-100MM	100-250MM		ALL	ALL
36	143	77	26	5	4	**NUMBER OF STATEMENTS**	337	369
%	%	%	%	%	%	**ASSETS**	%	%
12.1	7.7	7.3	7.1			Cash & Equivalents	7.2	6.8
12.2	7.7	13.5	10.2			Trade Receivables (net)	10.0	8.5
51.8	54.7	47.6	46.6			Inventory	51.0	53.1
1.3	1.0	1.5	1.3			All Other Current	1.7	2.1
77.4	71.0	69.9	65.2			Total Current	69.9	70.4
7.0	11.2	16.9	26.4			Fixed Assets (net)	15.3	15.0
1.7	3.4	3.4	1.2			Intangibles (net)	3.9	2.7
13.9	14.4	9.8	7.2			All Other Non-Current	10.9	11.8
100.0	100.0	100.0	100.0			Total	100.0	100.0
						LIABILITIES		
15.4	6.6	9.1	7.8			Notes Payable-Short Term	8.9	8.4
4.4	2.2	2.5	4.7			Cur. Mat.-L.T.D.	3.5	2.8
14.8	11.0	11.5	11.6			Trade Payables	12.0	12.9
.0	.1	.1	.2			Income Taxes Payable	.2	.1
7.6	8.1	6.1	6.8			All Other Current	6.5	6.9
42.2	28.0	29.3	31.1			Total Current	30.9	31.2
23.9	19.8	18.2	17.7			Long-Term Debt	22.7	21.0
.0	.1	.5	.3			Deferred Taxes	.1	.1
9.8	7.0	7.7	3.4			All Other Non-Current	9.5	11.5
24.2	45.2	44.2	47.5			Net Worth	36.7	36.1
100.0	100.0	100.0	100.0			Total Liabilities & Net Worth	100.0	100.0
						INCOME DATA		
100.0	100.0	100.0	100.0			Net Sales	100.0	100.0
42.0	39.5	35.1	39.6			Gross Profit	38.9	38.0
37.4	36.3	32.3	35.6			Operating Expenses	37.2	36.4
4.6	3.2	2.8	3.9			Operating Profit	1.7	1.6
-.2	-.5	.2	.5			All Other Expenses (net)	.0	-.2
4.8	3.7	2.5	3.5			Profit Before Taxes	1.8	1.8
						RATIOS		
7.8	5.5	4.3	3.6				4.9	4.5
2.8	3.3	2.6	2.4			Current	2.8	2.8
1.1	1.9	1.8	1.4				1.6	1.6
1.7	1.2	1.2	1.2				1.1	1.0
.5	(141) .6	.7	.4			Quick	.5	.5
.3	.3	.3	.2				.2	.2
3 132.2	**2** 158.7	**5** 69.0	**3** 130.7				**5** 78.7	**4** 98.1
10 37.6	**8** 43.8	**12** 30.4	**14** 26.6			Sales/Receivables	**10** 36.7	**8** 45.6
19 19.6	**19** 19.1	**29** 12.6	**31** 11.6				**20** 18.0	**18** 19.9
74 4.9	**99** 3.7	**89** 4.1	**107** 3.4				**95** 3.8	**100** 3.6
111 3.3	**135** 2.7	**130** 2.8	**140** 2.6			Cost of Sales/Inventory	**141** 2.6	**141** 2.6
203 1.8	**182** 2.0	**182** 2.0	**182** 2.0				**200** 1.8	**187** 1.9
9 42.0	**8** 46.7	**17** 22.1	**16** 22.5				**14** 26.6	**15** 24.2
20 18.0	**20** 18.0	**25** 14.8	**27** 13.4			Cost of Sales/Payables	**24** 15.4	**26** 13.9
42 8.6	**38** 9.6	**36** 10.2	**53** 6.9				**37** 9.8	**43** 8.4
4.0	3.5	3.6	3.3				3.7	3.7
7.0	5.3	5.4	5.9			Sales/Working Capital	5.5	5.4
26.0	7.7	8.3	13.1				9.2	10.1
7.7	17.4	14.2	16.1				6.7	6.6
(23) 3.8	(119) 5.1	(70) 6.5	(25) 5.1			EBIT/Interest	(295) 2.6	(336) 3.0
1.8	1.8	1.7	2.2				.5	1.0
	3.8	5.4					4.2	5.5
	(15) 1.2	(14) 2.1				Net Profit + Depr., Dep., Amort./Cur. Mat. L/T/D	(50) 1.6	(44) 1.6
	.4	1.0					.5	.4
.0	.1	.1	.1				.1	.1
.1	.2	.3	.6			Fixed/Worth	.3	.3
1.0	.6	.8	1.3				1.6	1.1
.4	.3	.6	.6				.6	.6
1.4	1.0	1.1	1.0			Debt/Worth	1.7	1.5
NM	5.1	3.0	2.4				7.3	5.6
58.7	41.9	23.9	24.0				26.9	23.9
(27) 17.4	(127) 17.1	(71) 12.1	15.0			% Profit Before Taxes/Tangible Net Worth	(280) 11.0	(311) 11.2
4.9	4.3	2.4	6.7				1.9	2.1
28.1	15.3	9.1	10.8				9.9	9.9
11.1	6.4	4.8	7.1			% Profit Before Taxes/Total Assets	4.1	4.1
3.0	1.1	1.1	2.7				-.5	.0
689.9	93.4	62.4	30.4				56.5	64.1
150.2	38.0	22.4	10.1			Sales/Net Fixed Assets	24.4	25.3
24.2	17.8	7.3	4.2				9.7	9.8
4.8	3.1	2.7	2.5				2.9	2.8
3.2	2.4	2.2	1.9			Sales/Total Assets	2.2	2.3
1.8	1.7	1.6	1.7				1.7	1.7
.2	.4	.5	.7				.6	.7
(15) .6	(99) .8	(62) 1.0	(25) 1.3			% Depr., Dep., Amort./Sales	(270) 1.3	(283) 1.2
1.9	1.5	1.9	2.0				2.2	2.1
2.6	2.5	1.0					1.9	1.6
(13) 4.1	(86) 4.1	(36) 3.1				% Officers', Directors' Owners' Comp/Sales	(201) 3.5	(220) 3.4
7.0	5.2	5.4					5.6	5.6
38713M	381428M	814119M	1032542M	535704M	1999083M	Net Sales ($)	3234499M	3274629M
11215M	155533M	339626M	520231M	294346M	785818M	Total Assets ($)	1496318M	1464549M

M = $ thousand MM = $ million

See Pages 9 through 22 for Explanation of Ratios and Data

Comparative Historical Data / Current Data Sorted by Sales

4/1/11-3/31/12 ALL	4/1/12-3/31/13 ALL	4/1/13-3/31/14 ALL		0-1MM	1-3MM	3-5MM	5-10MM	10-25MM	25MM & OVER
			Type of Statement						
8	9	13	Unqualified	1	1	1	2	2	6
35	41	28	Reviewed		2	2	8	6	10
79	62	62	Compiled	1	26	11	11	11	2
135	136	106	Tax Returns	21	52	14	14	4	1
107	75	82	Other	13	23	16	9	7	14
					29 (4/1-9/30/13)		262 (10/1/13-3/31/14)		
364	323	291	**NUMBER OF STATEMENTS**	36	104	44	44	30	33
%	%	%	**ASSETS**	%	%	%	%	%	%
7.1	8.4	8.1	Cash & Equivalents	8.2	7.8	8.7	7.9	9.0	7.7
9.7	10.9	9.9	Trade Receivables (net)	6.5	8.7	8.4	13.3	13.2	12.1
52.2	52.0	51.4	Inventory	54.4	54.2	53.4	45.4	49.2	46.6
2.2	1.4	1.2	All Other Current	1.1	1.0	1.0	1.2	1.5	1.9
71.1	72.7	70.7	Total Current	70.1	71.8	71.5	67.9	72.9	68.3
14.8	14.8	14.1	Fixed Assets (net)	14.6	11.2	10.6	15.7	17.8	22.0
3.7	2.4	3.0	Intangibles (net)	2.2	3.3	3.8	4.0	1.3	2.1
10.4	10.1	12.2	All Other Non-Current	13.0	13.7	14.0	12.4	8.0	7.6
100.0	100.0	100.0	Total	100.0	100.0	100.0	100.0	100.0	100.0
			LIABILITIES						
7.9	9.2	8.7	Notes Payable-Short Term	11.8	7.2	6.8	12.0	8.6	7.9
2.4	2.6	2.8	Cur. Mat.-L.T.D.	5.0	2.2	2.6	1.9	3.2	3.0
12.3	11.6	11.6	Trade Payables	9.7	10.5	9.5	17.4	10.9	13.0
.1	.1	.1	Income Taxes Payable	.0	.1	.1	.1	.1	.1
7.5	6.9	7.4	All Other Current	10.1	7.7	6.5	5.3	6.7	8.4
30.2	30.4	30.5	Total Current	36.6	27.6	25.5	36.6	29.6	32.4
19.8	20.1	19.4	Long-Term Debt	41.3	18.4	14.0	18.5	15.4	10.5
.1	.1	.2	Deferred Taxes	.5	.0	.2	.2	.4	.1
12.0	9.9	7.3	All Other Non-Current	10.2	7.2	7.0	8.7	5.2	5.0
37.8	39.5	42.6	Net Worth	11.5	46.7	53.4	35.9	49.4	52.0
100.0	100.0	100.0	Total Liabilties & Net Worth	100.0	100.0	100.0	100.0	100.0	100.0
			INCOME DATA						
100.0	100.0	100.0	Net Sales	100.0	100.0	100.0	100.0	100.0	100.0
38.1	36.6	38.6	Gross Profit	44.2	39.5	37.2	35.5	36.4	37.2
36.3	34.2	35.3	Operating Expenses	40.9	36.2	32.9	33.1	33.3	34.3
1.8	2.4	3.3	Operating Profit	3.3	3.3	4.2	2.4	3.1	2.9
-.2	-.1	-.2	All Other Expenses (net)	.1	-.5	-.2	.2	.1	.1
2.0	2.5	3.4	Profit Before Taxes	3.3	3.9	4.5	2.2	3.0	2.8
			RATIOS						
5.3	4.9	5.0		12.1	5.6	5.5	3.3	4.4	3.9
3.0	2.9	2.9	Current	3.2	3.5	3.5	2.2	3.0	2.1
1.8	1.8	1.7		1.3	1.9	1.9	1.5	1.7	1.4
1.1	1.3	1.3		1.7	1.3	2.1	1.0	1.5	1.2
(363) .5	(322) .6	(289) .6	Quick	(35) .4	.6	.7	(43) .7	.8	.4
.2	.3	.3		.3	.3	.3	.3	.2	.2
4 98.7	**4** 81.4	**4** 97.3		**3** 135.6	**4** 82.5	**2** 148.9	**4** 89.7	**4** 91.7	**2** 155.9
9 41.2	**11** 33.6	**10** 37.3	Sales/Receivables	**9** 41.2	**9** 40.0	**8** 44.6	**12** 30.9	**12** 31.4	**13** 27.5
18 20.0	**26** 14.2	**21** 17.5		**19** 19.5	**20** 18.7	**19** 19.2	**27** 13.6	**26** 14.2	**34** 10.6
99 3.7	**85** 4.3	**96** 3.8		**122** 3.0	**104** 3.5	**96** 3.8	**73** 5.0	**76** 4.8	**89** 4.1
140 2.6	**130** 2.8	**130** 2.8	Cost of Sales/Inventory	**215** 1.7	**135** 2.7	**114** 3.2	**114** 3.2	**114** 3.2	**130** 2.8
192 1.9	**182** 2.0	**182** 2.0		**332** 1.1	**182** 2.0	**152** 2.4	**152** 2.4	**192** 1.9	**174** 2.1
13 27.2	**12** 30.3	**11** 31.8		**3** 114.0	**10** 36.8	**6** 59.3	**17** 22.0	**16** 22.2	**18** 20.7
25 14.6	**22** 16.7	**23** 15.9	Cost of Sales/Payables	**21** 17.3	**21** 17.8	**20** 18.4	**29** 12.8	**22** 16.3	**26** 13.9
39 9.4	**37** 9.8	**38** 9.6		**52** 7.0	**37** 9.9	**32** 11.5	**45** 8.2	**34** 10.8	**40** 9.2
3.7	3.7	3.5		2.4	3.5	3.4	5.2	4.0	4.3
5.1	5.2	5.4	Sales/Working Capital	3.2	5.3	5.4	6.6	5.3	7.9
9.1	9.0	9.9		16.9	7.5	7.9	15.2	10.7	13.3
9.1	11.0	14.4		5.2	17.8	33.5	8.8	15.3	19.7
(318) 2.9	(276) 3.8	(245) 5.0	EBIT/Interest	(26) 2.5	(83) 5.5	(38) 6.4	(39) 2.8	(28) 7.2	(31) 5.8
1.0	1.3	1.8		1.2	1.8	1.8	1.0	2.4	4.4
10.6	3.7	4.0			8.6				
(39) 2.4	(38) 1.5	(38) 1.6	Net Profit + Depr., Dep., Amort./Cur. Mat. L/T/D		(10) 2.5				
.6	.6	.8			.8				
.1	.1	.1		.1	.0	.0	.1	.1	.1
.3	.3	.2	Fixed/Worth	.3	.1	.1	.4	.2	.5
1.0	1.0	.8		-.8	.5	.5	1.6	.8	.8
.5	.5	.4		.5	.3	.3	.7	.6	.4
1.4	1.1	1.1	Debt/Worth	3.8	.9	.9	1.9	1.0	.9
5.5	3.5	4.1		-7.7	4.1	2.3	4.4	2.3	2.1
28.3	31.6	34.1		24.9	45.5	34.3	33.8	24.7	22.6
(306) 10.7	(285) 13.4	(259) 14.2	% Profit Before Taxes/Tangible Net Worth	(24) 9.8	(91) 18.3	(42) 17.8	(40) 12.0	10.3	(32) 15.0
2.3	3.8	3.9		2.1	5.4	3.9	1.7	3.5	8.3
10.3	11.9	13.6		12.0	15.9	15.3	9.0	12.4	10.3
3.8	4.9	6.0	% Profit Before Taxes/Total Assets	3.9	7.6	6.6	4.8	5.8	7.3
.2	1.2	1.5		.6	2.9	2.1	.5	1.6	4.0
71.7	90.7	95.9		139.1	129.1	107.1	110.7	75.1	34.7
28.6	27.5	32.5	Sales/Net Fixed Assets	26.3	46.0	43.2	30.4	17.1	15.3
11.3	10.2	11.3		9.6	15.8	16.7	7.4	8.9	6.2
2.9	3.1	3.1		2.5	3.2	3.1	3.3	3.5	2.8
2.3	2.3	2.3	Sales/Total Assets	1.5	2.4	2.5	2.4	2.3	2.4
1.7	1.7	1.7		1.1	1.7	2.1	1.9	1.7	1.9
.5	.4	.5		.7	.4	.3	.5	.5	.7
(272) 1.0	(246) .9	(208) .9	% Depr., Dep., Amort./Sales	(15) 1.5	(72) .8	(30) .8	(37) 1.1	(24) .9	(30) 1.2
1.8	1.6	1.7		2.7	1.5	1.6	2.1	1.4	1.5
2.0	1.6	2.0		2.5	2.6	1.8	1.5	1.6	.4
(205) 3.2	(192) 3.6	(146) 3.8	% Officers', Directors' Owners' Comp/Sales	(17) 4.7	(59) 4.0	(24) 4.2	(24) 3.4	(12) 3.2	(10) 1.1
5.4	5.5	5.2		6.9	5.2	4.9	6.3	4.4	4.0
4804597M	4910343M	4801589M	Net Sales ($)	23697M	204407M	174776M	305134M	474651M	3618924M
2290433M	2323592M	2106769M	Total Assets ($)	19486M	97785M	77236M	137575M	220418M	1554269M

M = $ thousand MM = $ million

See Pages 9 through 22 for Explanation of Ratios and Data

Current Data Sorted by Assets							Comparative Historical Data	
						Type of Statement		
		7	14	9	1	Unqualified	37	38
3	11	53	24	1	1	Reviewed	94	89
12	23	40	7			Compiled	74	65
43	64	43	3			Tax Returns	135	153
17	43	74	29	6	5	Other	143	134
59 (4/1-9/30/13)			474 (10/1/13-3/31/14)				4/1/09-3/31/10 ALL	4/1/10-3/31/11 ALL
0-500M	500M-2MM	2-10MM	10-50MM	50-100MM	100-250MM			
75	141	217	77	16	7	**NUMBER OF STATEMENTS**	483	479
%	%	%	%	%	%	**ASSETS**	%	%
15.9	10.0	7.3	8.1	2.6		Cash & Equivalents	8.9	8.7
23.8	25.9	30.2	25.5	25.3		Trade Receivables (net)	25.1	25.2
32.7	37.7	34.5	31.2	29.3		Inventory	33.0	34.0
1.6	1.8	1.8	1.4	.6		All Other Current	2.4	2.3
74.1	75.4	73.8	66.2	57.8		Total Current	69.5	70.2
15.3	14.3	17.1	23.4	28.9		Fixed Assets (net)	19.0	19.1
3.3	3.3	2.6	3.5	3.6		Intangibles (net)	3.4	3.1
7.3	7.0	6.5	6.9	9.7		All Other Non-Current	8.1	7.6
100.0	100.0	100.0	100.0	100.0		Total	100.0	100.0
						LIABILITIES		
18.7	11.6	11.9	11.3	9.0		Notes Payable-Short Term	14.1	13.2
2.5	1.6	2.1	2.4	2.4		Cur. Mat.-L.T.D.	3.5	3.4
26.0	21.1	18.1	13.2	9.7		Trade Payables	17.6	18.5
.8	.1	.1	.1	.1		Income Taxes Payable	.1	.1
19.6	12.3	9.8	8.3	8.7		All Other Current	11.3	11.1
67.6	46.8	42.1	35.3	29.9		Total Current	46.6	46.3
13.7	17.6	11.9	11.2	11.2		Long-Term Debt	17.2	15.6
.0	.1	.2	.9	.4		Deferred Taxes	.3	.2
12.8	10.5	4.0	6.5	5.7		All Other Non-Current	8.7	8.9
5.8	25.1	41.8	46.0	52.9		Net Worth	27.3	29.1
100.0	100.0	100.0	100.0	100.0		Total Liabilties & Net Worth	100.0	100.0
						INCOME DATA		
100.0	100.0	100.0	100.0	100.0		Net Sales	100.0	100.0
39.8	31.2	27.8	27.0	21.9		Gross Profit	30.7	31.0
35.0	28.1	25.0	24.0	19.1		Operating Expenses	30.6	30.6
4.9	3.2	2.8	3.1	2.8		Operating Profit	.1	.4
.8	.3	-.1	.3	-.2		All Other Expenses (net)	.4	.2
4.1	2.9	2.9	2.8	3.0		Profit Before Taxes	-.3	.2
						RATIOS		
3.2	2.8	3.1	3.3	3.3			3.1	3.1
1.3	1.8	1.7	1.9	2.1		Current	1.7	1.8
.8	1.3	1.4	1.4	1.4			1.1	1.2
1.6	1.3	1.7	1.7	1.8			1.5	1.4
.7	.9	.9	.9	1.2		Quick	(482) .8	.8
.3	.5	.5	.6	.5			.4	.4
0 UND	16 23.4	23 16.1	24 15.3	36 10.0			19 19.5	19 19.5
12 31.1	27 13.7	36 10.1	40 9.2	42 8.6		Sales/Receivables	31 11.8	31 11.7
34 10.7	41 8.9	54 6.8	52 7.0	48 7.6			44 8.3	45 8.1
7 54.0	23 15.6	36 10.0	40 9.2	45 8.1			32 11.2	32 11.4
29 12.6	62 5.9	63 5.8	65 5.6	52 7.0		Cost of Sales/Inventory	61 6.0	64 5.7
81 4.5	114 3.2	91 4.0	99 3.7	81 4.5			101 3.6	102 3.6
0 UND	14 26.1	17 21.2	15 23.8	13 27.4			15 25.2	14 26.3
25 14.5	28 13.0	26 14.0	24 15.0	19 19.7		Cost of Sales/Payables	25 14.4	28 13.2
54 6.7	46 8.0	43 8.5	40 9.2	23 15.7			42 8.6	47 7.8
8.0	5.6	5.2	5.3	5.3			4.9	5.1
24.1	10.4	8.5	8.1	7.9		Sales/Working Capital	9.5	8.7
-39.9	30.2	16.4	13.8	16.5			39.5	43.6
14.0	12.9	18.3	12.9	30.9			5.9	6.4
(47) 2.6	(115) 4.7	(194) 4.8	(70) 5.9	9.5		EBIT/Interest	(415) 1.6	(424) 1.8
.6	1.9	2.1	2.2	3.8			-1.6	-.6
	10.8	8.2	5.4				3.1	4.8
	(12) 3.3	(37) 3.3	(24) 2.5			Net Profit + Depr., Dep., Amort./Cur. Mat. L/T/D	(73) 1.7	(74) 2.0
	1.2	1.7	1.5				.0	.4
.0	.1	.1	.2	.3			.1	.1
.6	.3	.3	.5	.5		Fixed/Worth	.4	.5
6.4	4.1	.8	.9	.8			2.0	1.8
1.0	.8	.6	.6	.3			.7	.7
4.6	2.7	1.6	1.2	1.2		Debt/Worth	1.9	1.7
-11.4	16.3	3.2	2.5	2.4			13.9	8.6
83.6	72.3	37.1	27.1	32.9			23.9	18.2
(53) 27.6	(112) 26.4	(198) 16.7	(72) 13.7	9.7		% Profit Before Taxes/Tangible Net Worth	(388) 4.7	(394) 4.9
4.2	6.9	5.6	5.1	6.2			-8.7	-4.7
29.3	16.6	12.9	9.6	10.5			7.7	7.7
4.6	7.6	5.4	5.4	6.0		% Profit Before Taxes/Total Assets	1.4	1.6
-1.5	2.5	2.0	1.9	2.8			-7.1	-3.2
UND	131.4	58.7	26.1	28.9			56.9	64.8
52.6	34.6	25.5	11.9	8.0		Sales/Net Fixed Assets	23.1	22.3
25.1	15.7	10.7	6.3	3.9			9.7	9.1
6.7	4.3	3.6	2.8	2.9			3.7	3.8
4.1	3.0	2.8	2.3	2.0		Sales/Total Assets	2.7	2.7
3.1	2.1	2.1	1.7	1.6			1.8	1.8
.5	.3	.4	.7	.6			.6	.6
(35) .7	(95) .6	(182) .7	(71) 1.0	1.5		% Depr., Dep., Amort./Sales	(399) 1.2	(366) 1.1
1.3	1.2	1.3	1.5	1.8			2.2	2.1
2.6	2.1	1.2	.7				1.9	1.8
(46) 3.8	(77) 3.1	(93) 1.9	(24) 1.3			% Officers', Directors' Owners' Comp/Sales	(224) 3.2	(237) 3.2
6.5	5.4	3.7	2.4				6.1	6.0
96555M	527103M	2883779M	3578904M	2506566M	2198271M	Net Sales ($)	8998197M	9257751M
20682M	157993M	1018488M	1541204M	1094174M	1066550M	Total Assets ($)	4110696M	4379547M

M = $ thousand MM = $ million

See Pages 9 through 22 for Explanation of Ratios and Data

Comparative Historical Data / Current Data Sorted by Sales

	4/1/11-3/31/12 ALL	4/1/12-3/31/13 ALL	4/1/13-3/31/14 ALL	0-1MM	1-3MM	3-5MM	5-10MM	10-25MM	25MM & OVER
Type of Statement									
Unqualified	31	32	31				1	9	21
Reviewed	105	90	93	2	3	9	17	37	25
Compiled	68	70	82	7	14	10	21	24	6
Tax Returns	140	182	153	22	54	25	29	18	5
Other	172	173	174	11	27	17	34	44	41
				59 (4/1-9/30/13)			474 (10/1/13-3/31/14)		
NUMBER OF STATEMENTS	516	547	533	42	98	61	102	132	98
ASSETS	%	%	%	%	%	%	%	%	%
Cash & Equivalents	9.0	9.8	9.2	16.7	9.4	11.9	8.3	7.9	6.5
Trade Receivables (net)	27.1	26.5	27.3	17.5	22.8	29.1	31.3	29.1	28.0
Inventory	32.7	31.6	34.4	39.9	35.8	33.4	31.9	35.3	32.7
All Other Current	2.8	2.1	1.7	1.7	1.9	1.4	2.1	1.6	1.3
Total Current	71.7	70.0	72.5	75.9	69.8	75.8	73.7	74.0	68.5
Fixed Assets (net)	17.2	19.1	17.5	15.7	18.1	15.2	17.5	16.3	20.8
Intangibles (net)	3.6	3.3	3.1	1.7	5.1	2.0	2.5	2.9	3.4
All Other Non-Current	7.6	7.6	6.8	6.7	7.0	7.1	6.3	6.8	7.3
Total	100.0	100.0	100.0	100.0	100.0	100.0	100.0	100.0	100.0
LIABILITIES									
Notes Payable-Short Term	12.8	13.0	12.5	17.6	13.1	12.4	11.4	12.2	11.5
Cur. Mat.-L.T.D.	3.1	2.9	2.1	1.9	2.6	1.3	2.1	2.1	2.0
Trade Payables	18.3	18.7	19.0	18.3	21.5	21.5	20.0	18.9	14.6
Income Taxes Payable	.1	.1	.2	.8	.4	.2	.1	.1	.1
All Other Current	10.6	9.5	11.6	17.6	14.7	12.9	10.6	8.7	9.9
Total Current	44.9	44.2	45.4	56.1	52.3	48.3	44.2	42.0	38.1
Long-Term Debt	15.0	13.8	13.6	12.6	19.2	19.8	13.6	9.2	10.2
Deferred Taxes	.2	.1	.2	.0	.1	.0	.2	.4	.5
All Other Non-Current	8.4	8.4	7.4	9.6	13.6	5.3	6.6	4.7	5.8
Net Worth	31.6	33.6	33.4	21.7	14.7	26.6	35.3	43.7	45.4
Total Liabilties & Net Worth	100.0	100.0	100.0	100.0	100.0	100.0	100.0	100.0	100.0
INCOME DATA									
Net Sales	100.0	100.0	100.0	100.0	100.0	100.0	100.0	100.0	100.0
Gross Profit	31.9	31.0	30.1	43.4	35.6	29.2	27.5	26.9	26.2
Operating Expenses	29.7	28.2	26.8	35.4	32.5	26.5	25.3	24.0	23.0
Operating Profit	2.2	2.8	3.2	8.0	3.1	2.8	2.2	2.9	3.2
All Other Expenses (net)	.3	.2	.2	.9	.7	-.2	.1	.0	.1
Profit Before Taxes	1.9	2.6	3.0	7.0	2.3	2.9	2.2	2.9	3.2
RATIOS									
Current	3.3	2.9	3.0	5.5	3.6	2.8	3.0	2.8	3.0
	1.9	1.8	1.8	1.7	1.9	1.6	1.7	1.7	1.9
	1.2	1.2	1.3	1.0	1.0	1.3	1.3	1.4	1.4
Quick	1.6	1.6	1.6	2.2	1.6	1.4	1.7	1.7	1.5
	.9	.8	.9	.8	.8	.9	1.0	.8	.9
	.5	.5	.5	.2	.3	.5	.6	.5	.6
Sales/Receivables	**19** 19.2	**17** 21.9	**19** 19.6	**0** UND	**7** 49.4	**19** 19.4	**24** 15.4	**21** 17.4	**25** 14.8
	34 10.6	**32** 11.5	**31** 11.8	**15** 25.1	**22** 16.7	**29** 12.8	**38** 9.7	**34** 10.8	**37** 9.8
	52 7.0	**47** 7.8	**49** 7.4	**54** 6.7	**41** 8.8	**45** 8.1	**54** 6.8	**50** 7.3	**49** 7.4
Cost of Sales/Inventory	**29** 12.5	**28** 13.0	**29** 12.7	**23** 16.0	**17** 21.9	**18** 20.8	**23** 16.2	**34** 10.8	**41** 8.8
	62 5.9	**55** 6.6	**60** 6.1	**81** 4.5	**63** 5.8	**46** 8.0	**59** 6.2	**60** 6.1	**59** 6.2
	104 3.5	**89** 4.1	**96** 3.8	**166** 2.2	**118** 3.1	**107** 3.4	**91** 4.0	**85** 4.3	**87** 4.2
Cost of Sales/Payables	**16** 22.3	**14** 25.2	**15** 23.8	**0** UND	**13** 28.7	**16** 23.1	**18** 20.4	**15** 23.8	**16** 23.1
	30 12.0	**26** 13.9	**25** 14.4	**22** 16.4	**30** 12.0	**26** 14.3	**28** 13.2	**24** 15.0	**24** 15.3
	48 7.6	**45** 8.2	**44** 8.3	**55** 6.6	**54** 6.7	**44** 8.3	**45** 8.2	**41** 9.0	**37** 9.8
Sales/Working Capital	5.0	5.7	5.6	3.5	5.8	5.4	5.1	5.8	6.2
	8.4	10.1	9.4	8.2	10.6	10.3	9.2	9.3	8.5
	26.9	36.0	22.6	-136.9	174.6	25.5	24.7	16.4	15.8
EBIT/Interest	8.8	10.1	17.0	9.0	12.1	12.4	17.3	20.7	24.4
	(437) 2.6	(464) 3.4	(449) 4.9	(23) 2.2	(75) 3.8	(53) 4.5	(89) 4.2	(116) 4.9	(93) 7.9
	.7	.9	2.1	1.0	1.1	2.4	1.5	2.4	2.8
Net Profit + Depr., Dep., Amort./Cur. Mat. L/T/D	4.7	9.0	7.8				3.5	17.9	7.1
	(76) 2.4	(75) 2.6	(78) 3.0				(17) 1.7	(26) 4.4	(25) 2.5
	.8	1.0	1.6				1.2	2.3	1.6
Fixed/Worth	.1	.1	.1	.0	.1	.1	.1	.1	.2
	.4	.4	.4	.4	.6	.5	.4	.3	.4
	1.5	1.6	1.2	2.9	-4.0	1.9	1.4	.7	.8
Debt/Worth	.6	.6	.6	.9	.7	.7	.6	.7	.5
	1.7	1.7	1.7	2.4	3.0	1.9	1.8	1.5	1.5
	7.2	6.3	5.4	UND	-8.6	8.8	5.5	2.7	2.7
% Profit Before Taxes/Tangible Net Worth	29.7	39.3	42.8	82.3	52.7	64.5	37.9	37.8	38.0
	(428) 8.8	(462) 14.8	(457) 17.4	(34) 24.7	(68) 22.5	(53) 21.9	(85) 17.6	(125) 16.5	(92) 15.1
	1.2	2.5	5.4	.0	4.9	5.6	4.6	6.3	6.1
% Profit Before Taxes/Total Assets	10.5	14.7	13.9	24.3	15.7	12.6	13.3	14.1	11.2
	3.4	4.8	6.1	7.0	6.3	6.4	4.7	6.1	6.7
	-.2	.5	1.8	-.1	.4	2.8	1.5	2.2	2.6
Sales/Net Fixed Assets	78.6	73.3	79.1	UND	119.9	96.0	97.9	60.3	42.9
	24.6	25.3	27.0	44.0	26.8	35.1	25.8	27.1	16.2
	10.3	8.9	9.5	7.7	12.3	15.6	8.7	12.7	7.7
Sales/Total Assets	3.7	4.0	4.0	3.7	5.0	4.3	3.9	4.0	3.3
	2.6	2.8	2.8	2.5	2.7	3.1	2.7	3.1	2.6
	1.9	1.9	2.0	1.3	2.0	2.0	2.1	2.2	1.9
% Depr., Dep., Amort./Sales	.5	.5	.4	.2	.4	.4	.3	.4	.6
	(381) 1.0	(422) 1.0	(406) .8	(18) .9	(65) .9	(40) .6	(84) .7	(110) .8	(89) .9
	1.9	1.9	1.4	2.2	1.5	1.2	1.5	1.2	1.5
% Officers', Directors' Owners' Comp/Sales	1.6	1.4	1.4	3.4	2.6	1.8	1.6	.8	.9
	(232) 3.1	(257) 2.8	(241) 2.7	(17) 4.3	(60) 3.7	(35) 2.8	(52) 2.8	(54) 1.5	(23) 1.3
	5.8	4.8	4.3	10.0	6.7	4.3	4.3	2.5	2.5
Net Sales ($)	9513052M	10033465M	11791178M	22787M	193426M	242916M	712639M	2191442M	8427968M
Total Assets ($)	4430298M	4395557M	4899091M	13685M	76896M	103262M	284170M	849505M	3571573M

M = $ thousand MM = $ million

See Pages 9 through 22 for Explanation of Ratios and Data

Current Data Sorted by Assets / Comparative Historical Data

0-500M	500M-2MM	2-10MM	10-50MM	50-100MM	100-250MM		4/1/09-3/31/10 ALL	4/1/10-3/31/11 ALL
						Type of Statement		
			2	1	1	Unqualified	3	4
		4	6			Reviewed	17	13
3	7	12	1			Compiled	26	21
8	9	5	1		1	Tax Returns	35	37
3	3	5	3	3	1	Other	22	33
	9 (4/1-9/30/13)		70 (10/1/13-3/31/14)					
14	19	26	13	4	3	**NUMBER OF STATEMENTS**	103	108
%	%	%	%	%	%	**ASSETS**	%	%
10.8	5.4	11.1	5.7			Cash & Equivalents	6.9	8.5
8.2	14.3	8.0	15.7			Trade Receivables (net)	12.0	11.5
61.4	61.7	65.2	61.7			Inventory	59.2	57.4
.4	1.2	1.0	2.4			All Other Current	1.0	1.5
80.7	82.6	85.3	85.5			Total Current	79.1	78.9
14.7	14.1	12.2	11.2			Fixed Assets (net)	14.8	14.9
1.0	.7	.6	.8			Intangibles (net)	1.5	2.5
3.2	2.5	1.9	2.6			All Other Non-Current	4.6	3.7
100.0	100.0	100.0	100.0			Total	100.0	100.0
						LIABILITIES		
7.9	17.6	25.6	32.9			Notes Payable-Short Term	19.0	23.7
2.3	3.5	1.2	1.0			Cur. Mat.-L.T.D.	3.5	2.1
19.7	32.8	18.0	16.2			Trade Payables	21.9	21.4
.1	.0	.1	.0			Income Taxes Payable	.1	.1
11.7	7.8	11.2	8.1			All Other Current	11.1	11.5
41.6	61.7	56.1	58.3			Total Current	55.6	58.7
24.6	17.3	6.2	6.9			Long-Term Debt	13.3	11.8
.0	.0	.1	.2			Deferred Taxes	.1	.2
3.3	4.9	1.6	1.7			All Other Non-Current	5.9	5.5
30.4	16.1	35.9	32.9			Net Worth	25.1	23.7
100.0	100.0	100.0	100.0			Total Liabilities & Net Worth	100.0	100.0
						INCOME DATA		
100.0	100.0	100.0	100.0			Net Sales	100.0	100.0
36.5	31.4	23.6	23.6			Gross Profit	28.6	27.6
35.6	30.2	20.4	20.2			Operating Expenses	28.3	26.3
1.0	1.1	3.2	3.4			Operating Profit	.4	1.3
-.2	.8	-.2	.0			All Other Expenses (net)	.7	.3
1.2	.3	3.4	3.5			Profit Before Taxes	-.3	1.0
						RATIOS		
6.4	1.9	2.2	1.8				2.3	1.9
2.1	1.6	1.4	1.5			Current	1.5	1.4
1.3	1.0	1.3	1.2				1.1	1.1
.8	.5	.6	.6				.5	.6
.3	.2	.3	.3			Quick	.2	.3
.2	.1	.1	.1				.1	.1
0 UND	**4** 100.4	**5** 79.9	**8** 48.0				**5** 77.3	**5** 78.7
3 108.4	**9** 42.2	**8** 47.5	**16** 22.3			Sales/Receivables	**11** 32.7	**11** 32.0
12 29.2	**36** 10.2	**17** 20.9	**27** 13.5				**26** 14.3	**25** 14.5
19 19.3	**56** 6.5	**89** 4.1	**79** 4.6				**79** 4.6	**63** 5.8
96 3.8	**130** 2.8	**146** 2.5	**114** 3.2			Cost of Sales/Inventory	**126** 2.9	**121** 3.0
215 1.7	**215** 1.7	**215** 1.7	**146** 2.5				**201** 1.8	**179** 2.0
1 243.4	**18** 20.0	**7** 51.5	**5** 67.3				**12** 29.3	**12** 31.7
19 18.9	**58** 6.3	**23** 15.6	**21** 17.7			Cost of Sales/Payables	**38** 9.5	**33** 10.9
68 5.4	**107** 3.4	**44** 8.3	**56** 6.5				**70** 5.2	**65** 5.6
5.1	7.4	5.2	6.0				5.8	6.0
11.2	10.7	8.7	9.5			Sales/Working Capital	10.1	11.7
83.3	-267.5	13.0	19.2				18.5	28.6
	9.8	29.5	12.1				4.4	8.2
	(18) 3.0	(24) 7.0	9.5			EBIT/Interest	(98) 2.1	(97) 3.0
	.9	3.9	3.9				1.1	1.0
							5.5	5.3
						Net Profit + Depr., Dep., Amort./Cur. Mat. L/T/D	(15) 2.9	(17) 2.8
							1.1	1.0
.0	.1	.1	.1				.1	.1
.2	.8	.3	.2			Fixed/Worth	.4	.3
1.9	-3.1	.5	.6				1.8	1.3
.5	2.0	.8	1.7				1.3	1.3
2.1	4.1	2.3	2.5			Debt/Worth	2.9	2.9
NM	-35.3	4.1	3.1				12.0	10.0
43.5	56.4	42.1	38.3				21.4	31.2
(11) 17.4	(13) 12.0	18.2	21.5			% Profit Before Taxes/Tangible Net Worth	(86) 9.7	(91) 14.2
1.4	6.1	10.2	10.9				2.2	2.7
13.2	7.3	9.6	10.2				4.9	8.8
3.6	2.4	6.6	9.3			% Profit Before Taxes/Total Assets	2.4	2.8
.2	.3	2.5	3.3				.1	.0
UND	158.2	103.2	128.3				78.6	68.6
50.5	25.7	47.3	40.8			Sales/Net Fixed Assets	33.3	29.4
17.8	18.3	9.3	16.8				11.6	11.9
7.0	4.1	3.2	3.1				3.2	3.3
4.0	2.6	2.1	2.7			Sales/Total Assets	2.3	2.4
2.3	2.1	1.7	2.3				1.6	1.7
	.4	.3					.5	.4
	(14) .6	(18) .6				% Depr., Dep., Amort./Sales	(87) .9	(74) 1.1
	1.1	1.4					1.9	2.2
	1.8	.7					1.2	.9
	(14) 3.8	(13) 1.2				% Officers', Directors' Owners' Comp/Sales	(53) 2.3	(45) 2.5
	7.7	3.1					5.6	5.4
12523M	71377M	264568M	762602M	598529M	871757M	Net Sales ($)	1505132M	2254456M
3011M	20530M	116332M	286887M	314652M	467662M	Total Assets ($)	734842M	882786M

M = $ thousand MM = $ million

See Pages 9 through 22 for Explanation of Ratios and Data

Comparative Historical Data | **Current Data Sorted by Sales**

4/1/11-3/31/12 ALL	4/1/12-3/31/13 ALL	4/1/13-3/31/14 ALL		0-1MM	1-3MM	3-5MM	5-10MM	10-25MM	25MM & OVER
			Type of Statement						
2	8	4	Unqualified						4
16	19	10	Reviewed				1	4	5
22	24	23	Compiled	3	3	1	9	5	2
44	36	24	Tax Returns	6	8	3	2	4	1
34	23	18	Other	3	5	2	1		7
				9 (4/1-9/30/13)			70 (10/1/13-3/31/14)		
118	110	79	**NUMBER OF STATEMENTS**	12	16	6	13	13	19
%	%	%	**ASSETS**	%	%	%	%	%	%
7.4	7.6	8.0	Cash & Equivalents	8.8	5.7		6.4	12.6	4.5
10.7	9.9	10.7	Trade Receivables (net)	10.5	4.3		18.1	9.4	11.4
58.9	62.3	62.9	Inventory	64.2	70.5		58.2	63.0	65.2
1.3	1.5	1.1	All Other Current	.0	.5		2.3	.9	1.7
78.3	81.3	82.8	Total Current	83.6	81.0		85.1	85.9	82.9
14.9	12.9	13.1	Fixed Assets (net)	13.0	16.5		13.9	9.6	10.4
2.0	1.2	1.6	Intangibles (net)	1.2	.0		.0	1.2	4.2
4.7	4.6	2.5	All Other Non-Current	2.2	2.2		1.0	3.4	2.5
100.0	100.0	100.0	Total	100.0	100.0		100.0	100.0	100.0
			LIABILITIES						
20.6	21.0	20.6	Notes Payable-Short Term	10.7	17.4		29.9	15.0	27.0
2.3	2.9	1.9	Cur. Mat.-L.T.D.	2.7	.5		1.8	1.6	1.2
20.3	21.7	22.4	Trade Payables	19.4	32.1		20.2	20.7	20.5
.1	.1	.1	Income Taxes Payable	.1	.0		.0	.0	.0
11.3	9.8	9.6	All Other Current	12.4	4.4		8.4	17.7	8.5
54.5	55.5	54.7	Total Current	45.3	54.4		60.2	55.1	57.2
11.8	17.0	12.5	Long-Term Debt	22.5	20.2		9.3	5.7	5.5
.1	.1	.1	Deferred Taxes	.0	.0		.0	.2	.1
8.4	5.5	2.6	All Other Non-Current	4.5	1.3		6.1	.1	1.2
25.1	22.0	30.1	Net Worth	27.7	24.1		24.4	38.9	35.9
100.0	100.0	100.0	Total Liabilties & Net Worth	100.0	100.0		100.0	100.0	100.0
			INCOME DATA						
100.0	100.0	100.0	Net Sales	100.0	100.0		100.0	100.0	100.0
31.3	26.5	27.6	Gross Profit	39.1	30.8		28.0	24.5	20.4
28.1	25.4	25.2	Operating Expenses	38.1	29.0		24.4	21.6	17.1
3.2	1.1	2.4	Operating Profit	1.1	1.8		3.6	2.9	3.3
.4	-.2	.0	All Other Expenses (net)	-.1	.8		-.3	-.1	-.4
2.7	1.2	2.4	Profit Before Taxes	1.1	1.0		3.9	3.0	3.7
			RATIOS						
2.1	2.1	2.1	Current	2.8	3.2		2.0	2.4	1.6
1.5	1.5	1.5		1.9	1.5		1.4	1.5	1.4
1.1	1.2	1.2		1.7	1.0		1.1	1.3	1.2
.5	.6	.6	Quick	.6	.4		.8	.8	.4
.3	.2	.3		.3	.1		.4	.4	.3
.1	.1	.1		.2	.1		.1	.2	.1
4 101.2	**4** 100.1	**4** 100.4	Sales/Receivables	**0** UND	**3** 131.7		**6** 57.6	**2** 157.9	**7** 50.7
9 38.9	**8** 43.8	**9** 40.9		**11** 31.8	**5** 68.0		**9** 40.0	**6** 61.4	**13** 28.9
22 16.3	**22** 16.7	**17** 21.3		**22** 16.9	**10** 36.8		**36** 10.1	**15** 23.6	**25** 14.8
72 5.1	**79** 4.6	**81** 4.5	Cost of Sales/Inventory	**44** 8.3	**89** 4.1		**72** 5.1	**64** 5.7	**91** 4.0
130 2.8	**126** 2.9	**140** 2.6		**203** 1.8	**159** 2.3		**182** 2.0	**104** 3.5	**140** 2.6
192 1.9	**192** 1.9	**192** 1.9		**261** 1.4	**243** 1.5		**215** 1.7	**159** 2.3	**146** 2.5
8 44.6	**8** 43.1	**9** 39.4	Cost of Sales/Payables	**3** 144.4	**9** 40.1		**7** 53.1	**11** 33.9	**8** 45.7
27 13.4	**28** 12.9	**26** 14.1		**45** 8.2	**31** 11.6		**23** 15.8	**25** 14.8	**39** 9.3
72 5.1	**73** 5.0	**78** 4.7		**83** 4.4	**135** 2.7		**91** 4.0	**49** 7.4	**54** 6.8
5.2	5.7	5.8	Sales/Working Capital	3.1	4.1		8.7	5.1	7.0
10.2	9.9	9.5		7.7	29.9		9.7	7.7	9.5
30.8	18.8	19.7		14.1	NM		21.2	14.1	19.7
12.3	16.7	13.1	EBIT/Interest		7.5		22.5	27.3	21.8
(111) 3.6	(96) 4.6	(71) 6.2			(14) 2.5		7.5	9.6	10.7
1.4	1.4	2.3			1.4		2.9	5.0	5.8
8.5	12.7	11.5	Net Profit + Depr., Dep., Amort./Cur. Mat. L/T/D						
(18) 4.7	(17) 4.8	(10) 2.9							
1.9	2.2	1.6							
.1	.1	.1	Fixed/Worth	.0	.2		.0	.0	.1
.4	.2	.3		.1	.7		.3	.2	.2
1.7	1.1	1.0		.5	-4.0		1.0	.3	.5
1.3	1.8	1.2	Debt/Worth	.6	.9		1.8	.7	1.5
2.5	2.8	2.5		2.3	5.3		3.4	2.2	2.5
7.7	6.8	4.7		8.6	-39.4		6.1	3.5	3.2
36.3	47.1	41.1	% Profit Before Taxes/Tangible Net Worth	44.2	21.1		71.1	35.2	39.8
(100) 13.8	(96) 18.3	(70) 19.5		(10) 6.4	(11) 12.0		41.0	(12) 15.9	30.9
5.3	4.5	9.1		-1.1	4.0		13.1	7.7	17.9
9.3	10.1	9.8	% Profit Before Taxes/Total Assets	10.3	7.1		13.8	11.3	10.6
3.9	6.2	6.4		1.6	2.5		9.8	6.8	9.3
.9	.5	1.7		-2.2	1.0		3.4	3.5	6.3
80.2	86.3	123.0	Sales/Net Fixed Assets	UND	130.4		209.0	140.2	70.8
33.2	46.1	40.9		114.5	23.9		40.9	69.7	40.8
13.5	18.2	17.3		13.9	8.0		14.0	32.1	18.7
3.4	3.4	3.4	Sales/Total Assets	5.3	4.0		3.8	3.4	3.1
2.4	2.5	2.5		2.4	2.5		2.1	2.5	2.5
1.7	1.8	2.0		1.7	1.6		1.7	2.0	2.1
.5	.3	.4	% Depr., Dep., Amort./Sales		.5			.1	.5
(78) .8	(80) .6	(53) .6			(10) .9			(10) .5	(16) .6
1.5	1.2	1.0			1.4			1.2	.8
1.2	1.3	1.1	% Officers', Directors' Owners' Comp/Sales		2.0				
(62) 2.7	(49) 2.4	(38) 2.9			(12) 4.0				
4.2	5.1	5.1			6.1				
2679471M	2654262M	2581356M	Net Sales ($)	7487M	30791M	22119M	97603M	184750M	2238606M
1077845M	1109117M	1209074M	Total Assets ($)	3492M	20261M	9115M	46967M	76180M	1053059M

M = $ thousand MM = $ million

See Pages 9 through 22 for Explanation of Ratios and Data

Current Data Sorted by Assets							Comparative Historical Data	
						Type of Statement		
		3	6	2	2	Unqualified	17	11
	6	12	12	2		Reviewed	33	35
2	22	14	2			Compiled	48	59
24	22	9				Tax Returns	60	77
10	30	26	10	5	4	Other	64	65
49 (4/1-9/30/13)			176 (10/1/13-3/31/14)				4/1/09-3/31/10	4/1/10-3/31/11
0-500M	500M-2MM	2-10MM	10-50MM	50-100MM	100-250MM		ALL	ALL
36	80	64	30	9	6	**NUMBER OF STATEMENTS**	222	247
%	%	%	%	%	%	**ASSETS**	%	%
13.3	9.1	6.9	7.5			Cash & Equivalents	7.7	7.9
9.2	11.2	13.0	9.1			Trade Receivables (net)	11.3	11.5
37.0	39.3	40.2	38.4			Inventory	37.9	38.9
3.1	2.4	3.9	1.6			All Other Current	1.8	1.7
62.7	61.9	64.0	56.6			Total Current	58.7	60.0
28.4	27.9	25.8	37.2			Fixed Assets (net)	32.4	29.6
1.4	3.5	1.9	1.0			Intangibles (net)	2.9	3.7
7.5	6.8	8.3	5.2			All Other Non-Current	6.1	6.6
100.0	100.0	100.0	100.0			Total	100.0	100.0
						LIABILITIES		
15.4	14.4	8.8	8.7			Notes Payable-Short Term	14.5	15.2
5.5	3.3	3.6	2.8			Cur. Mat.-L.T.D.	4.7	4.2
18.0	14.1	13.8	15.3			Trade Payables	16.6	15.2
.1	.0	.1	.1			Income Taxes Payable	.1	.3
15.4	9.7	8.5	7.0			All Other Current	14.8	13.0
54.4	41.6	34.7	33.9			Total Current	50.8	47.9
26.4	23.4	15.4	18.4			Long-Term Debt	21.3	23.7
.0	.1	.4	.4			Deferred Taxes	.4	.4
7.9	9.6	9.5	5.7			All Other Non-Current	7.3	7.0
11.4	25.3	40.0	41.6			Net Worth	20.2	21.0
100.0	100.0	100.0	100.0			Total Liabilities & Net Worth	100.0	100.0
						INCOME DATA		
100.0	100.0	100.0	100.0			Net Sales	100.0	100.0
42.3	37.5	31.5	33.8			Gross Profit	37.8	39.9
41.4	34.9	27.4	30.4			Operating Expenses	36.8	37.4
1.0	2.7	4.1	3.5			Operating Profit	.9	2.5
-.2	.6	.2	.1			All Other Expenses (net)	.7	1.0
1.2	2.0	3.8	3.4			Profit Before Taxes	.2	1.6
						RATIOS		
2.7	3.4	4.3	2.4				2.3	2.7
1.3	1.7	1.9	1.6			Current	1.4	1.4
.8	.9	1.2	1.1				.9	.9
1.3	1.2	1.2	1.2				.8	.9
.4	.5	.8	.4			Quick	.4	.4
.1	.1	.3	.1				.1	.1
0 UND	0 852.3	1 398.4	2 195.4				2 166.8	2 222.0
3 139.9	5 68.9	12 30.5	6 65.0			Sales/Receivables	9 41.7	10 35.6
13 27.2	24 15.4	37 9.9	25 14.4				24 15.0	28 13.2
31 11.9	49 7.5	54 6.7	65 5.6				44 8.4	43 8.4
49 7.5	81 4.5	85 4.3	91 4.0			Cost of Sales/Inventory	72 5.1	83 4.4
81 4.5	122 3.0	122 3.0	122 3.0				128 2.8	150 2.4
0 UND	4 88.4	9 38.7	18 20.4				9 41.3	9 42.5
16 22.5	22 16.5	23 15.8	31 11.7			Cost of Sales/Payables	23 15.8	27 13.8
41 9.0	43 8.5	38 9.5	65 5.6				51 7.2	53 6.9
11.2	5.4	4.5	5.1				7.1	5.9
29.2	13.7	8.9	13.5			Sales/Working Capital	15.6	17.1
-19.3	-67.8	21.1	39.2				-64.6	-45.0
11.5	11.3	23.1	11.9				5.7	5.2
(27) 2.9	(77) 3.3	(58) 5.1	(25) 4.1			EBIT/Interest	(206) 1.8	(225) 1.8
-.1	.6	2.5	2.0				.1	.0
	4.0	5.1	5.4				5.7	6.8
	(12) 2.3	(10) 2.3	(12) 3.1			Net Profit + Depr., Dep., Amort./Cur. Mat. L/T/D	(37) 2.9	(42) 2.8
	.6	.6	1.1				.4	.9
.4	.2	.2	.5				.4	.3
1.4	.9	.6	1.0			Fixed/Worth	1.2	1.0
-.6	22.1	1.5	2.3				14.9	7.4
.8	.9	.8	.7				.9	.9
4.5	2.1	1.4	2.1			Debt/Worth	2.2	2.9
-6.9	NM	3.0	3.3				38.0	43.2
76.2	47.2	42.8	46.3				25.2	37.5
(24) 17.9	(60) 15.0	(59) 22.1	(29) 19.9			% Profit Before Taxes/Tangible Net Worth	(173) 8.4	(194) 11.5
2.5	.9	7.9	10.0				-4.1	-3.7
14.8	15.9	18.8	12.8				8.3	10.7
5.6	3.7	6.9	8.2			% Profit Before Taxes/Total Assets	1.6	2.5
-3.1	-2.6	2.5	3.4				-2.2	-2.9
98.1	55.0	52.5	11.0				25.0	31.4
25.3	13.5	12.7	6.4			Sales/Net Fixed Assets	10.1	11.1
9.7	5.8	5.0	4.3				4.7	4.5
6.4	4.0	3.4	2.8				3.6	3.5
4.1	2.9	2.6	2.1			Sales/Total Assets	2.4	2.3
2.5	1.8	1.6	1.6				1.7	1.6
.9	.7	.5	.9				1.0	1.0
(22) 1.4	(61) 1.5	(54) 1.1	(29) 1.5			% Depr., Dep., Amort./Sales	(195) 1.8	(202) 1.7
3.6	3.3	2.7	3.0				3.6	3.4
2.2	2.3	1.1					1.5	2.4
(19) 4.1	(47) 3.7	(24) 1.9				% Officers', Directors' Owners' Comp/Sales	(114) 3.3	(120) 4.2
9.7	6.5	4.1					6.2	7.1
47524M	297194M	684292M	1306927M	901870M	2750481M	Net Sales ($)	3348207M	3829889M
10386M	93321M	272143M	573503M	612785M	838490M	Total Assets ($)	1429329M	1568762M

M = $ thousand MM = $ million

See Pages 9 through 22 for Explanation of Ratios and Data

Comparative Historical Data | Current Data Sorted by Sales

4/1/11-3/31/12 ALL	4/1/12-3/31/13 ALL	4/1/13-3/31/14 ALL	Type of Statement	0-1MM	1-3MM	3-5MM	5-10MM	10-25MM	25MM & OVER
13	11	13	Unqualified			1		4	8
34	28	32	Reviewed		1	2	8	10	11
52	42	40	Compiled	2	11	10	9	7	1
72	58	55	Tax Returns	10	27	10	6	2	
59	78	85	Other	7	18	10	19	13	18
				49 (4/1-9/30/13)		176 (10/1/13-3/31/14)			
230	217	225	NUMBER OF STATEMENTS	19	57	33	42	36	38
%	%	%	**ASSETS**	%	%	%	%	%	%
7.6	9.7	8.6	Cash & Equivalents	13.4	10.4	6.9	10.1	5.9	5.7
11.2	11.0	11.3	Trade Receivables (net)	7.4	7.0	15.2	14.8	13.4	10.7
40.6	38.2	39.2	Inventory	38.5	36.5	36.8	46.2	35.8	41.4
1.2	1.8	3.2	All Other Current	.5	2.7	.6	4.5	5.8	3.7
60.7	60.7	62.3	Total Current	59.8	56.6	59.5	75.5	60.8	61.6
30.3	29.1	28.1	Fixed Assets (net)	31.0	32.6	31.0	18.1	26.1	30.4
3.2	2.7	2.4	Intangibles (net)	1.4	4.6	1.8	.6	1.9	2.8
5.9	7.5	7.1	All Other Non-Current	7.7	6.2	7.7	5.8	11.2	5.2
100.0	100.0	100.0	Total	100.0	100.0	100.0	100.0	100.0	100.0
			LIABILITIES						
15.9	14.5	11.8	Notes Payable-Short Term	16.4	14.6	12.9	10.2	10.2	7.6
4.5	3.4	3.5	Cur. Mat.-L.T.D.	6.2	3.9	5.1	2.9	2.4	2.1
16.7	18.8	15.9	Trade Payables	14.2	11.8	15.3	14.8	19.2	21.8
.2	.2	.1	Income Taxes Payable	.0	.0	.1	.1	.1	.4
10.4	11.4	9.8	All Other Current	13.1	13.5	6.7	7.9	8.6	8.6
47.7	48.3	41.2	Total Current	49.8	43.8	40.1	35.8	40.4	40.4
22.9	20.2	20.6	Long-Term Debt	19.1	34.7	23.3	11.4	8.0	20.1
.3	.2	.3	Deferred Taxes	.0	.1	.1	.4	.5	.8
9.1	5.8	8.7	All Other Non-Current	7.2	10.8	5.7	13.1	6.6	6.1
19.9	25.5	29.2	Net Worth	23.8	10.5	30.9	39.4	44.5	32.6
100.0	100.0	100.0	Total Liabilties & Net Worth	100.0	100.0	100.0	100.0	100.0	100.0
			INCOME DATA						
100.0	100.0	100.0	Net Sales	100.0	100.0	100.0	100.0	100.0	100.0
37.4	35.4	35.6	Gross Profit	46.5	40.7	36.6	28.6	30.8	33.9
35.5	32.3	32.7	Operating Expenses	45.0	38.7	33.2	25.2	27.3	30.4
1.8	3.0	2.9	Operating Profit	1.6	2.0	3.4	3.4	3.5	3.5
.7	.5	.4	All Other Expenses (net)	-.1	.8	.1	.3	.1	.5
1.1	2.5	2.6	Profit Before Taxes	1.6	1.3	3.3	3.1	3.4	3.0
			RATIOS						
2.5	2.4	3.1		2.5	3.9	2.2	6.2	2.5	2.4
1.4	1.4	1.7	Current	1.7	1.5	1.6	2.2	1.5	1.6
.9	.9	1.0		.9	.9	1.1	1.5	1.0	1.1
.9	1.0	1.2		2.2	1.2	1.0	1.5	1.1	.7
.3	(216) .4	.5	Quick	.6	.4	.6	.9	.5	.4
.1	.1	.1		.1	.1	.2	.3	.1	.1
1 265.8	1 267.0	1 469.8		0 UND	0 UND	2 149.6	0 935.0	3 143.0	1 274.1
10 36.7	9 39.7	7 56.0	Sales/Receivables	6 63.4	3 110.9	13 28.1	4 85.1	9 39.4	7 50.9
23 15.8	24 15.2	25 14.5		20 18.7	17 21.1	29 12.8	35 10.3	42 8.7	26 13.8
37 9.8	43 8.5	49 7.4		45 8.1	38 9.6	38 9.7	54 6.8	56 6.5	54 6.7
81 4.5	73 5.0	79 4.6	Cost of Sales/Inventory	68 5.4	79 4.6	94 3.9	76 4.8	65 5.6	96 3.8
140 2.6	135 2.7	118 3.1		166 2.2	122 3.0	135 2.7	94 3.9	118 3.1	140 2.6
9 39.6	10 35.3	9 38.6		0 UND	2 167.5	17 22.0	4 98.4	11 31.9	24 15.1
28 13.0	24 15.4	26 14.3	Cost of Sales/Payables	20 18.5	16 22.6	31 11.7	18 20.1	30 12.2	36 10.1
51 7.1	49 7.5	47 7.7		46 8.0	43 8.5	48 7.6	31 11.8	59 6.2	70 5.2
6.8	6.5	5.5		7.3	5.3	5.7	4.4	5.9	5.1
16.5	16.7	13.0	Sales/Working Capital	14.9	19.4	15.7	8.5	11.3	12.7
-104.0	-134.4	132.6		-20.7	-21.0	NM	18.0	NM	42.6
7.4	9.7	16.0		11.5	6.4	15.8	25.4	26.1	22.4
(216) 2.4	(192) 3.3	(202) 4.3	EBIT/Interest	(12) 5.3	(53) 1.4	(31) 2.9	(39) 5.4	(32) 9.2	(35) 5.8
.7	1.0	1.2		.0	.2	1.6	3.0	1.9	2.4
4.8	5.3	5.5							7.3
(39) 1.9	(34) 2.5	(38) 3.2	Net Profit + Depr., Dep., Amort./Cur. Mat. L/T/D						(13) 5.1
1.1	1.0	1.0							2.8
.4	.3	.3		.2	.5	.4	.1	.3	.5
1.1	1.0	.9	Fixed/Worth	.9	2.5	1.0	.3	.7	1.1
48.4	4.6	3.1		-22.8	-1.8	2.2	1.0	1.2	2.6
1.1	.8	.9		.4	1.1	.9	.8	.6	1.1
2.4	2.4	2.0	Debt/Worth	3.7	6.1	2.0	1.2	1.6	2.1
165.9	12.1	10.3		-31.8	-5.6	4.8	5.1	2.5	5.0
32.7	35.5	42.2		79.4	32.5	50.3	48.8	28.6	44.3
(175) 14.1	(175) 16.8	(184) 18.0	% Profit Before Taxes/Tangible Net Worth	(14) 15.2	(35) 15.5	(30) 14.2	(38) 28.1	(33) 19.6	(34) 20.9
2.3	4.0	5.9		2.7	-.2	4.5	6.5	6.9	11.5
9.9	13.2	14.3		16.5	11.3	13.6	22.5	15.5	12.0
3.4	5.4	6.0	% Profit Before Taxes/Total Assets	9.8	1.9	2.9	7.6	8.3	7.7
-.6	.1	.7		-4.1	-4.1	1.3	2.1	2.4	3.6
31.4	33.0	48.9		102.0	40.7	34.0	129.9	47.3	19.5
12.8	11.9	12.3	Sales/Net Fixed Assets	19.0	13.6	8.5	33.0	10.4	9.9
4.8	5.1	5.0		3.9	4.2	4.7	11.1	4.6	4.7
3.8	3.6	3.9		4.1	4.1	3.5	4.3	3.1	3.1
2.6	2.5	2.6	Sales/Total Assets	2.4	2.5	2.7	3.6	2.3	2.4
1.7	1.8	1.7		1.3	1.7	1.4	2.8	1.5	1.9
.7	.8	.7			1.1	.6	.2	.6	.9
(201) 1.5	(181) 1.3	(179) 1.3	% Depr., Dep., Amort./Sales		(43) 1.7	(26) 1.3	(35) .7	(31) 1.1	(35) 1.2
3.1	3.0	3.0			3.8	3.9	2.0	2.9	2.0
1.9	1.8	1.7			2.4	1.7	1.7		
(107) 3.3	(98) 3.2	(92) 3.3	% Officers', Directors' Owners' Comp/Sales		(37) 4.5	(16) 3.3	(20) 2.8		
5.5	6.3	6.0			6.6	4.9	4.4		
3699336M	3702273M	5988288M	Net Sales ($)	10462M	106801M	130820M	305152M	589228M	4845825M
1681243M	1757539M	2400628M	Total Assets ($)	4991M	44639M	60106M	98177M	334951M	1857764M

M = $ thousand MM = $ million

See Pages 9 through 22 for Explanation of Ratios and Data

	Current Data Sorted by Assets						Comparative Historical Data	
Type of Statement								
Unqualified			6	22	12	24	75	85
Reviewed	1	12	27	40	4	1	93	69
Compiled	9	67	55	12	1	2	161	150
Tax Returns	47	143	49	4			242	232
Other	15	85	95	50	18	34	287	270
	140 (4/1-9/30/13)		695 (10/1/13-3/31/14)				4/1/09-3/31/10	4/1/10-3/31/11
	0-500M	500M-2MM	2-10MM	10-50MM	50-100MM	100-250MM	ALL	ALL
NUMBER OF STATEMENTS	72	307	232	128	35	61	858	806
ASSETS	%	%	%	%	%	%	%	%
Cash & Equivalents	15.8	16.5	15.8	14.0	14.3	7.1	14.0	12.8
Trade Receivables (net)	2.5	2.7	3.7	4.1	6.9	4.3	3.8	4.0
Inventory	50.8	38.4	25.4	24.5	19.1	22.0	30.9	30.4
All Other Current	2.2	2.0	3.3	3.2	3.9	3.0	2.9	3.7
Total Current	71.3	59.6	48.1	45.7	44.2	36.3	51.6	50.9
Fixed Assets (net)	18.7	25.8	34.0	40.8	36.2	45.8	33.5	33.0
Intangibles (net)	5.5	5.2	6.1	4.8	8.9	8.8	5.6	6.1
All Other Non-Current	4.5	9.3	11.7	8.7	10.7	9.1	9.3	10.0
Total	100.0	100.0	100.0	100.0	100.0	100.0	100.0	100.0
LIABILITIES								
Notes Payable-Short Term	10.0	3.9	2.3	2.4	1.0	2.8	5.0	4.6
Cur. Mat.-L.T.D.	1.4	3.4	3.8	3.3	1.8	2.7	3.9	4.4
Trade Payables	15.4	19.8	19.9	17.0	14.7	15.1	19.2	18.2
Income Taxes Payable	.2	.1	.2	.2	.2	.4	.1	.1
All Other Current	18.4	12.9	9.9	8.6	10.4	12.1	10.4	10.6
Total Current	45.4	40.1	36.2	31.4	28.0	33.2	38.6	37.9
Long-Term Debt	14.1	23.3	23.8	23.6	15.1	22.8	24.3	23.7
Deferred Taxes	.0	.0	.2	.2	.9	1.0	.2	.2
All Other Non-Current	15.2	11.1	5.6	5.1	4.6	11.5	8.3	9.2
Net Worth	25.3	25.5	34.3	39.7	51.3	31.6	28.5	28.9
Total Liabilties & Net Worth	100.0	100.0	100.0	100.0	100.0	100.0	100.0	100.0
INCOME DATA								
Net Sales	100.0	100.0	100.0	100.0	100.0	100.0	100.0	100.0
Gross Profit	27.3	26.2	27.1	27.3	23.5	29.4	26.6	26.3
Operating Expenses	25.9	25.0	25.6	25.6	21.8	27.5	24.9	24.9
Operating Profit	1.4	1.2	1.6	1.6	1.7	2.0	1.7	1.4
All Other Expenses (net)	-.7	-.4	-.4	-.3	.2	.0	-.3	-.2
Profit Before Taxes	2.1	1.6	2.0	1.9	1.5	1.9	2.0	1.6
RATIOS								
	10.7	3.8	2.6	2.2	1.8	1.5	2.6	2.5
Current	2.9	2.0	1.5	1.4	1.3	1.0	1.4	1.4
	1.1	1.1	.8	1.0	1.0	.9	.9	.9
	2.7	1.4	1.1	1.0	.9	.5	1.0	.9
Quick	(69) .8	(304) .5	.4	.5	.5	.3	(855) .4	(803) .4
	.2	.1	.2	.2	.3	.2	.2	.2
	0 UND	0 UND	0 999.8	1 378.7	1 436.3	2 180.0	0 999.8	0 999.8
Sales/Receivables	0 UND	0 999.8	1 544.8	2 159.9	3 110.6	3 105.2	1 307.2	1 310.3
	1 512.1	2 240.8	2 155.1	5 81.1	6 57.6	5 67.5	3 122.0	3 106.9
	18 20.7	18 20.0	16 22.8	20 18.5	19 19.7	23 16.0	17 20.9	18 20.7
Cost of Sales/Inventory	30 12.0	25 14.8	22 16.4	27 13.7	22 16.7	28 12.9	24 15.0	25 14.5
	48 7.6	34 10.6	34 10.6	34 10.6	29 12.7	34 10.7	34 10.8	35 10.6
	0 UND	5 80.9	10 38.1	12 29.8	12 30.1	16 23.5	7 50.5	8 48.2
Cost of Sales/Payables	5 78.5	10 35.8	16 23.1	18 19.8	16 23.1	18 19.9	14 26.5	14 27.0
	12 30.9	19 19.5	24 14.9	26 14.3	24 15.4	27 13.4	22 16.5	22 16.9
	11.4	14.2	14.9	14.3	18.7	34.3	16.7	16.6
Sales/Working Capital	23.3	28.6	38.0	35.0	35.0	959.8	40.8	40.7
	125.5	211.2	-47.6	-999.8	-999.8	-85.7	-204.5	-243.4
	15.5	19.6	16.9	11.4	33.3	9.8	12.9	12.1
EBIT/Interest	(42) 5.1	(213) 4.1	(191) 4.6	(119) 4.1	(32) 10.7	4.9	(717) 4.6	(684) 3.5
	.3	.4	1.5	2.0	3.4	2.3	1.6	1.2
		4.9	6.6	7.9	10.6	5.9	6.8	5.7
Net Profit + Depr., Dep., Amort./Cur. Mat. L/T/D		(10) 2.2	(34) 3.2	(44) 2.8	(14) 6.5	(13) 3.7	(150) 2.8	(125) 2.1
		.3	1.8	1.8	2.2	3.0	1.3	1.1
	.1	.3	.3	.6	.4	1.1	.4	.4
Fixed/Worth	.4	.8	1.1	1.3	1.0	1.8	1.3	1.2
	5.2	19.9	13.3	3.0	1.8	38.3	15.3	15.2
	.4	.5	.6	.8	.6	1.0	.8	.8
Debt/Worth	1.6	2.0	1.9	1.4	1.0	2.4	2.3	2.3
	96.6	194.0	27.4	6.1	3.5	81.9	64.9	48.9
	81.2	64.4	46.3	31.6	25.3	40.5	55.2	51.9
% Profit Before Taxes/Tangible Net Worth	(55) 27.5	(232) 28.0	(181) 24.4	(116) 13.9	(32) 13.3	(47) 20.6	(657) 23.1	(618) 20.0
	10.6	8.8	6.9	5.3	6.0	10.2	9.0	5.8
	26.7	21.1	16.2	10.4	11.7	10.8	16.9	13.9
% Profit Before Taxes/Total Assets	12.6	8.2	6.2	5.1	6.4	7.2	7.6	5.5
	-.4	-.3	1.2	1.6	1.1	3.3	2.0	.6
	292.8	94.6	46.3	22.2	23.4	12.6	47.2	47.0
Sales/Net Fixed Assets	78.4	34.7	18.4	10.8	14.3	8.8	19.5	18.8
	26.0	16.0	8.1	6.8	7.2	6.3	8.6	8.5
	11.5	10.0	7.0	5.6	5.1	4.6	7.7	7.4
Sales/Total Assets	8.2	7.0	5.0	4.3	4.3	4.1	5.5	5.0
	5.3	4.9	3.5	2.9	3.0	2.7	3.7	3.6
	.2	.3	.6	.8	.9	1.2	.6	.6
% Depr., Dep., Amort./Sales	(48) .5	(242) .8	(209) 1.0	(124) 1.1	(30) 1.2	(30) 1.5	(727) 1.0	(683) 1.0
	.9	1.4	1.8	1.9	1.5	1.9	1.5	1.6
	1.2	.8	.5	.3			.6	.7
% Officers', Directors' Owners' Comp/Sales	(38) 2.4	(141) 1.3	(76) .9	(29) .6			(322) 1.2	(292) 1.2
	4.1	2.4	2.2	1.7			2.5	2.3
Net Sales ($)	198013M	2656427M	5974860M	12450562M	10880083M	38780818M	70072922M	68768480M
Total Assets ($)	20943M	359422M	1145541M	2745839M	2527161M	9692587M	15304591M	15281343M

M = $ thousand MM = $ million

See Pages 9 through 22 for Explanation of Ratios and Data

Comparative Historical Data / Current Data Sorted by Sales

4/1/11-3/31/12 ALL	4/1/12-3/31/13 ALL	4/1/13-3/31/14 ALL	Type of Statement	0-1MM	1-3MM	3-5MM	5-10MM	10-25MM	25MM & OVER
83	55	64	Unqualified				1	5	58
89	74	85	Reviewed		1	4	9	9	62
177	130	146	Compiled	3	6	18	30	45	44
314	228	243	Tax Returns	17	29	27	85	63	22
299	283	297	Other	4	23	18	46	71	135
				140 (4/1-9/30/13)			695 (10/1/13-3/31/14)		
962	770	835	**NUMBER OF STATEMENTS**	24	59	67	171	193	321
%	%	%	**ASSETS**	%	%	%	%	%	%
14.5	15.1	15.1	Cash & Equivalents	13.6	14.7	16.4	15.8	16.8	13.5
3.3	3.5	3.5	Trade Receivables (net)	1.7	2.7	1.2	2.9	2.9	4.9
31.6	31.8	31.7	Inventory	41.9	42.7	31.6	36.1	33.6	25.5
3.1	2.5	2.7	All Other Current	.2	1.9	3.7	1.5	3.5	2.9
52.4	52.9	53.0	Total Current	57.4	62.0	52.9	56.3	56.8	46.9
31.6	30.9	31.7	Fixed Assets (net)	30.5	25.9	32.5	27.4	27.5	37.5
6.3	5.6	5.9	Intangibles (net)	10.6	6.3	5.0	5.2	5.8	6.0
9.6	10.5	9.5	All Other Non-Current	1.5	5.8	9.6	11.2	9.9	9.7
100.0	100.0	100.0	Total	100.0	100.0	100.0	100.0	100.0	100.0
			LIABILITIES						
4.2	2.7	3.6	Notes Payable-Short Term	10.3	10.5	3.6	4.0	2.6	2.1
3.3	3.1	3.2	Cur. Mat.-L.T.D.	.5	2.0	2.2	3.8	3.5	3.4
18.7	17.6	18.5	Trade Payables	11.9	7.9	15.8	17.4	23.3	19.1
.1	.1	.2	Income Taxes Payable	.0	.2	.1	.0	.2	.3
10.5	10.7	11.7	All Other Current	16.5	18.5	14.4	10.3	12.9	9.6
36.7	34.2	37.1	Total Current	39.3	39.2	36.0	35.5	42.5	34.5
21.9	22.2	22.3	Long-Term Debt	24.1	20.4	30.1	23.2	20.0	21.8
.3	.2	.2	Deferred Taxes	.0	.0	.0	.1	.1	.4
9.8	9.4	8.8	All Other Non-Current	18.8	12.6	7.6	11.5	7.7	6.7
31.3	34.0	31.6	Net Worth	17.8	27.8	26.2	29.7	29.7	36.6
100.0	100.0	100.0	Total Liabilities & Net Worth	100.0	100.0	100.0	100.0	100.0	100.0
			INCOME DATA						
100.0	100.0	100.0	Net Sales	100.0	100.0	100.0	100.0	100.0	100.0
26.1	26.2	26.8	Gross Profit	30.5	30.4	30.0	24.9	26.4	26.5
25.0	24.7	25.4	Operating Expenses	30.3	28.3	28.5	23.5	25.1	24.9
1.1	1.5	1.5	Operating Profit	.2	2.1	1.5	1.4	1.3	1.6
-.3	-.4	-.4	All Other Expenses (net)	-1.5	-.4	-.1	-.3	-.5	-.3
1.4	1.9	1.8	Profit Before Taxes	1.7	2.5	1.6	1.7	1.8	1.8
			RATIOS						
2.9	3.1	3.0		16.8	8.9	6.7	3.7	2.6	2.1
1.5	1.7	1.6	Current	6.2	2.9	2.3	2.1	1.4	1.4
.9	1.0	.9		.8	.9	.9	1.2	.8	.9
1.0	1.2	1.1		3.2	3.7	1.9	1.5	.8	.9
(961) .4	(765) .5	(829) .4	Quick	(23) .9	(57) .8	(66) .6	(170) .6	(192) .3	.4
.2	.2	.2		.2	.2	.1	.1	.1	.2
0 UND	**0** UND	**0** UND		**0** UND	**0** UND	**0** UND	**0** UND	**0** UND	**1** 505.8
1 438.4	**1** 483.6	**1** 461.4	Sales/Receivables	**0** UND	**0** UND	**0** UND	**1** 595.1	**0** 749.1	**2** 170.1
3 128.8	**3** 132.4	**3** 128.3		**0** UND	**3** 120.5	**1** 498.3	**2** 198.8	**2** 223.0	**5** 80.5
18 20.1	**18** 20.0	**18** 20.2		**29** 12.5	**28** 13.1	**21** 17.0	**19** 19.7	**17** 22.0	**18** 20.5
25 14.7	**26** 14.0	**25** 14.6	Cost of Sales/Inventory	**60** 6.1	**40** 9.2	**26** 13.9	**25** 14.7	**22** 16.6	**24** 15.3
35 10.5	**35** 10.3	**34** 10.6		**122** 3.0	**79** 4.6	**38** 9.7	**36** 10.2	**29** 12.5	**33** 11.1
8 47.4	**7** 51.3	**7** 51.1		**0** UND	**0** UND	**3** 131.1	**6** 57.4	**8** 47.6	**12** 31.1
14 26.2	**14** 26.5	**14** 25.9	Cost of Sales/Payables	**0** UND	**4** 102.4	**8** 43.7	**11** 34.4	**14** 25.6	**17** 21.1
22 16.4	**22** 16.9	**22** 16.4		**14** 27.0	**12** 30.7	**20** 18.0	**18** 20.7	**22** 16.7	**25** 14.7
14.5	13.4	14.7		4.2	7.0	10.0	14.4	19.4	17.4
37.5	29.3	34.3	Sales/Working Capital	10.1	14.2	20.1	25.4	49.8	45.3
-273.7	742.9	-252.4		NM	-297.4	-76.7	89.8	-112.8	-178.0
13.3	15.8	15.9		3.1	10.8	10.6	18.7	21.3	14.7
(792) 4.2	(604) 5.3	(658) 4.6	EBIT/Interest	(13) 1.5	(39) 4.3	(48) 1.6	(123) 4.6	(143) 6.0	(292) 5.4
1.3	1.6	1.3		-1.5	.2	.0	.3	1.0	2.2
5.1	5.8	7.0						12.7	6.9
(137) 2.6	(105) 2.7	(115) 3.2	Net Profit + Depr., Dep., Amort./Cur. Mat. L/T/D					(17) 4.2	(86) 3.3
1.3	1.5	1.9						1.9	2.1
.4	.3	.4		.0	.1	.3	.3	.3	.5
1.1	.9	1.0	Fixed/Worth	.7	1.1	1.1	.7	.9	1.2
6.6	3.8	6.1		26.3	-24.0	8.3	19.9	10.8	4.3
.8	.6	.6		.6	.2	.5	.4	.7	.8
2.1	1.7	1.7	Debt/Worth	1.8	1.8	1.8	1.6	2.5	1.6
18.1	8.5	18.8		NM	-32.6	66.9	-32.9	20.3	7.4
52.0	46.8	46.8		86.2	41.7	51.9	46.9	63.4	40.5
(763) 20.9	(636) 22.2	(663) 22.5	% Profit Before Taxes/Tangible Net Worth	(18) 13.8	(43) 19.3	(52) 18.8	(128) 26.7	(151) 30.3	(271) 20.9
6.6	8.5	7.6		-13.2	5.0	-1.4	7.7	7.4	8.9
14.3	16.1	16.5		20.4	18.0	15.8	21.5	20.2	13.0
6.6	7.5	7.1	% Profit Before Taxes/Total Assets	5.5	6.7	5.2	8.9	7.3	6.9
1.0	2.2	1.0		-5.2	1.2	-2.4	.0	.9	1.8
56.5	58.1	56.7		184.0	178.5	66.6	74.6	95.9	28.3
20.0	20.4	20.8	Sales/Net Fixed Assets	12.3	28.4	20.8	30.8	31.3	13.3
9.2	8.9	8.7		4.0	7.3	7.7	13.0	14.5	7.5
7.7	7.5	7.8		6.9	7.3	7.0	8.7	10.6	6.6
5.2	5.2	5.4	Sales/Total Assets	3.1	4.2	5.3	6.4	7.0	4.8
3.6	3.4	3.6		1.3	2.3	3.3	4.1	4.3	3.5
.5	.5	.5		.4	.4	.5	.3	.4	.7
(817) .9	(611) .9	(683) .9	% Depr., Dep., Amort./Sales	(14) .7	(43) 1.2	(57) 1.0	(135) .8	(160) .8	(274) 1.1
1.6	1.5	1.6		1.9	2.1	1.9	1.5	1.3	1.7
.7	.7	.6		2.4	1.8	.9	.9	.5	.4
(401) 1.4	(298) 1.3	(298) 1.2	% Officers', Directors' Owners' Comp/Sales	(15) 3.4	(23) 3.4	(29) 1.3	(80) 1.2	(73) .9	(78) .8
2.6	2.3	2.5		4.9	6.2	1.8	2.0	2.6	1.4
65908125M	63151391M	70940763M	Net Sales ($)	14656M	117432M	267412M	1268864M	3052261M	66220138M
15170543M	14403094M	16491493M	Total Assets ($)	7636M	46427M	68756M	275336M	580762M	15512576M

M = $ thousand MM = $ million

See Pages 9 through 22 for Explanation of Ratios and Data

Current Data Sorted by Assets							Comparative Historical Data	
Type of Statement								
Unqualified				1	1	2	9	8
Reviewed	1	2	3	5	1		15	10
Compiled	8	3	3	2			30	31
Tax Returns	75	31	6	1		1	184	151
Other	23	20	14	6	3	2	70	87
	15 (4/1-9/30/13)			199 (10/1/13-3/31/14)			4/1/09-3/31/10	4/1/10-3/31/11
	0-500M	**500M-2MM**	**2-10MM**	**10-50MM**	**50-100MM**	**100-250MM**	**ALL**	**ALL**
NUMBER OF STATEMENTS	107	56	26	15	5	5	308	287
ASSETS	%	%	%	%	%	%	%	%
Cash & Equivalents	21.8	14.6	9.3	9.1			11.7	12.9
Trade Receivables (net)	2.3	2.5	3.1	6.6			2.8	3.8
Inventory	46.9	17.8	16.1	17.4			29.2	26.0
All Other Current	1.6	1.8	1.8	.4			1.5	1.5
Total Current	72.6	36.7	30.2	33.5			45.2	44.2
Fixed Assets (net)	14.3	51.0	55.8	55.0			40.1	41.2
Intangibles (net)	9.6	7.1	6.0	5.4			8.2	7.6
All Other Non-Current	3.5	5.2	8.0	6.1			6.5	7.0
Total	100.0	100.0	100.0	100.0			100.0	100.0
LIABILITIES								
Notes Payable-Short Term	5.9	6.4	2.3	3.0			6.5	5.0
Cur. Mat.-L.T.D.	2.2	2.2	4.7	3.0			2.5	2.7
Trade Payables	10.2	8.6	11.9	17.7			11.0	10.7
Income Taxes Payable	.0	.0	.3	.0			.1	.1
All Other Current	8.1	12.6	8.0	10.1			12.2	12.0
Total Current	26.4	29.8	27.2	33.8			32.3	30.4
Long-Term Debt	21.6	42.4	33.3	30.9			35.8	33.5
Deferred Taxes	1.0	.4	.0	1.5			.2	.3
All Other Non-Current	16.5	4.2	8.7	3.9			9.5	11.3
Net Worth	34.6	23.3	30.7	29.9			22.2	24.6
Total Liabilties & Net Worth	100.0	100.0	100.0	100.0			100.0	100.0
INCOME DATA								
Net Sales	100.0	100.0	100.0	100.0			100.0	100.0
Gross Profit	21.4	19.4	16.9	14.4			20.2	21.4
Operating Expenses	20.4	16.8	14.8	14.8			18.6	19.8
Operating Profit	1.0	2.6	2.1	-.4			1.6	1.6
All Other Expenses (net)	-1.3	-.2	-1.2	-1.1			-.5	-.3
Profit Before Taxes	2.3	2.8	3.3	.7			2.2	1.9
RATIOS								
Current	11.9	3.1	1.7	1.2			4.9	5.3
	4.6	1.5	1.1	1.0			1.7	1.8
	1.8	.6	.8	.6			.9	.9
Quick	2.6	1.0	.6	.7			1.8	1.9
	(105) 1.2	.4	.4	.4			(307) .5	(285) .6
	.4	.2	.2	.2			.2	.2
Sales/Receivables	0 UND	0 UND	0 999.8	2 191.1			0 UND	0 UND
	0 UND	0 UND	2 233.1	3 130.0			0 UND	0 UND
	0 UND	1 572.5	3 112.8	4 87.7			2 230.3	2 180.1
Cost of Sales/Inventory	10 35.4	9 41.3	8 44.4	8 46.2			10 37.2	9 40.0
	20 18.0	15 24.7	10 35.4	12 29.8			18 20.1	16 23.4
	33 11.1	33 10.9	16 22.2	19 19.5			35 10.3	28 13.1
Cost of Sales/Payables	0 UND	0 UND	4 89.9	8 46.6			0 UND	0 UND
	0 UND	4 97.9	7 49.3	13 28.8			4 103.2	2 180.3
	4 82.4	11 31.9	13 27.1	16 23.0			13 29.0	10 37.4
Sales/Working Capital	10.2	11.9	31.8	104.0			14.5	15.2
	20.8	76.1	255.5	-999.8			42.6	38.0
	46.9	-29.1	-107.5	-25.1			-256.6	-240.1
EBIT/Interest	19.8	6.5	13.3	15.9			6.6	7.1
	(48) 5.4	(45) 2.3	(23) 3.0	(14) 3.4			(233) 2.7	(217) 2.7
	1.2	1.0	2.1	.7			1.1	1.1
Net Profit + Depr., Dep., Amort./Cur. Mat. L/T/D							4.2	3.7
							(20) 2.0	(19) 2.2
							1.4	1.1
Fixed/Worth	.0	.6	1.1	1.0			.3	.4
	.1	5.2	3.6	2.1			2.1	1.8
	1.4	-8.0	NM	7.3			195.4	46.0
Debt/Worth	.3	1.0	.8	1.1			1.1	.9
	1.2	7.0	4.6	2.2			3.9	3.9
	22.2	-12.9	NM	6.9			-66.7	-27.0
% Profit Before Taxes/Tangible Net Worth	106.0	116.0	67.7	29.4			75.3	54.0
	(82) 30.0	(38) 23.3	(20) 28.9	(12) 14.6			(224) 29.8	(208) 25.8
	2.7	6.1	11.7	5.0			11.3	5.7
% Profit Before Taxes/Total Assets	33.9	11.5	12.5	7.9			15.2	16.6
	12.0	4.5	5.7	4.4			6.4	6.1
	.0	.8	3.2	-.3			.7	.4
Sales/Net Fixed Assets	UND	25.7	13.9	17.2			71.1	93.8
	307.1	6.4	7.9	9.3			15.3	16.0
	40.4	2.8	4.3	7.9			4.8	5.1
Sales/Total Assets	16.5	6.3	7.0	6.4			9.1	9.6
	9.2	3.2	4.9	5.2			4.4	4.8
	5.0	1.7	2.7	4.3			2.4	2.7
% Depr., Dep., Amort./Sales	.3	.6	.7	.8			.5	.5
	(50) .6	(49) 1.4	(23) 1.2	1.0			(223) 1.1	(208) 1.1
	1.3	2.4	1.5	1.2			2.0	1.9
% Officers', Directors' Owners' Comp/Sales	1.3	.9					.8	.7
	(58) 2.3	(23) 1.6					(149) 1.7	(130) 1.7
	3.6	2.4					3.6	3.5
Net Sales ($)	257628M	241325M	791461M	1887904M	1541183M	6188680M	14852356M	10555281M
Total Assets ($)	21721M	54702M	132764M	334337M	400364M	857009M	3010621M	1966001M

M = $ thousand MM = $ million

See Pages 9 through 22 for Explanation of Ratios and Data

Comparative Historical Data				Current Data Sorted by Sales					
			Type of Statement						
9	13	4	Unqualified						4
15	14	12	Reviewed			1	2	1	8
25	34	16	Compiled	3	6	1	2		4
189	133	114	Tax Returns	36	37	18	14	6	3
88	92	68	Other	6	19	10	9	6	18
4/1/11-3/31/12 ALL	4/1/12-3/31/13 ALL	4/1/13-3/31/14 ALL		15 (4/1-9/30/13)			199 (10/1/13-3/31/14)		
				0-1MM	1-3MM	3-5MM	5-10MM	10-25MM	25MM & OVER
326	286	214	**NUMBER OF STATEMENTS**	45	62	30	27	13	37
%	%	%	**ASSETS**	%	%	%	%	%	%
13.1	14.2	16.8	Cash & Equivalents	19.8	17.5	21.0	15.9	19.0	8.4
3.2	3.5	2.7	Trade Receivables (net)	1.0	1.3	2.0	5.1	6.3	4.9
29.7	27.8	31.9	Inventory	40.9	35.5	33.8	29.3	23.5	18.5
.8	1.7	1.6	All Other Current	1.1	2.5	.6	2.0	1.0	1.4
46.8	47.2	53.0	Total Current	62.7	56.8	57.4	52.3	49.7	33.2
38.1	39.5	34.2	Fixed Assets (net)	21.7	30.3	25.3	36.8	47.2	56.6
8.9	6.2	7.9	Intangibles (net)	12.5	9.3	10.2	3.4	1.2	3.7
6.3	7.1	4.9	All Other Non-Current	3.1	3.6	7.0	7.5	1.8	6.5
100.0	100.0	100.0	Total	100.0	100.0	100.0	100.0	100.0	100.0
			LIABILITIES						
5.2	4.5	5.1	Notes Payable-Short Term	1.7	5.6	5.7	8.6	16.5	1.4
2.6	3.3	2.6	Cur. Mat.-L.T.D.	2.1	2.9	2.1	.4	3.5	4.4
10.0	10.4	10.6	Trade Payables	5.1	8.0	5.1	18.0	21.9	16.7
.1	.1	.1	Income Taxes Payable	.0	.0	.0	.1	.0	.2
13.8	10.8	9.3	All Other Current	9.8	9.1	11.0	10.8	2.9	9.0
31.7	29.0	27.7	Total Current	18.7	25.5	23.9	37.8	44.8	31.8
31.7	32.0	30.0	Long-Term Debt	22.2	37.4	28.8	27.6	20.0	33.3
.2	.3	.8	Deferred Taxes	2.3	.0	.3	.4	.0	1.1
12.8	10.2	10.8	All Other Non-Current	27.9	5.8	5.0	12.6	4.7	4.1
23.6	28.5	30.7	Net Worth	29.0	31.2	42.0	21.6	30.5	29.7
100.0	100.0	100.0	Total Liabilties & Net Worth	100.0	100.0	100.0	100.0	100.0	100.0
			INCOME DATA						
100.0	100.0	100.0	Net Sales	100.0	100.0	100.0	100.0	100.0	100.0
18.1	19.1	19.5	Gross Profit	29.3	21.3	13.2	17.4	13.9	13.2
17.3	17.8	18.0	Operating Expenses	28.1	19.1	11.3	15.8	13.2	12.7
.9	1.3	1.5	Operating Profit	1.1	2.2	2.0	1.6	.7	.5
-.5	-.5	-.9	All Other Expenses (net)	-1.5	-1.3	-.5	-.2	-.5	-.6
1.3	1.8	2.4	Profit Before Taxes	2.7	3.5	2.4	1.8	1.2	1.1
			RATIOS						
5.0	5.5	7.1		17.1	7.1	8.6	3.7	2.2	1.4
1.9	1.6	2.0	Current	7.3	2.2	3.3	1.6	1.3	1.1
.9	.9	.9		2.0	.9	1.1	1.1	.7	.8
1.6	1.6	1.7		3.0	2.4	2.3	1.2	1.3	.7
(323) .6	(284) .6	(212) .6	Quick	(44) 1.1	(61) .6	1.2	.8	.6	.4
.2	.2	.2		.3	.3	.1	.2	.2	.2
0 UND	0 UND	0 UND		0 UND	0 UND	0 UND	0 UND	0 960.2	1 280.1
0 UND	0 UND	0 UND	Sales/Receivables	0 UND	0 UND	0 UND	0 907.4	1 547.9	2 169.6
1 291.2	2 193.5	2 201.7		0 UND	0 UND	1 620.8	3 134.5	2 179.3	3 109.7
9 42.4	7 51.3	9 40.4		21 17.7	12 30.3	8 48.3	8 43.1	4 82.9	7 51.8
16 23.3	12 30.6	14 26.0	Cost of Sales/Inventory	35 10.5	21 17.4	10 37.9	10 36.0	6 56.9	11 34.7
31 11.9	29 12.7	29 12.4		52 7.0	34 10.8	15 24.3	14 26.0	8 46.5	13 28.7
0 UND	0 UND	0 UND		0 UND	0 UND	0 UND	0 999.8	3 109.6	7 49.6
3 125.2	3 109.2	3 112.4	Cost of Sales/Payables	0 UND	2 236.1	0 801.9	6 61.7	6 60.2	11 34.0
9 39.6	11 34.4	11 33.9		3 118.1	11 33.9	3 113.5	16 23.2	8 45.1	14 25.5
16.6	15.3	13.1		6.0	10.2	19.4	17.3	82.1	76.4
41.4	49.7	37.2	Sales/Working Capital	11.8	23.7	35.5	47.3	121.9	273.6
-313.2	-275.4	-468.9		18.4	-468.9	NM	263.2	-117.2	-80.1
7.3	8.1	10.7		6.1	10.9	13.3	16.8		11.4
(218) 2.6	(206) 2.9	(140) 3.9	EBIT/Interest	(15) 2.1	(46) 3.2	(17) 3.7	(19) 5.1		(35) 4.4
1.1	1.3	1.4		.6	1.1	1.4	1.9		2.0
6.2	6.3								
(14) 2.2	(26) 2.5		Net Profit + Depr., Dep., Amort./Cur. Mat. L/T/D						
1.2	1.2								
.3	.4	.1		.0	.0	.1	.1	.5	1.1
1.7	1.7	1.0	Fixed/Worth	.1	.5	.3	1.2	1.4	2.6
-37.1	17.9	18.1		225.6	NM	NM	31.4	19.3	12.8
.8	.7	.6		.2	.5	.3	1.6	.6	.9
3.6	2.5	2.0	Debt/Worth	2.0	2.0	1.1	2.2	6.9	2.6
-19.0	127.2	NM		-3.7	-203.0	-6.8	43.5	37.3	49.2
49.7	43.6	68.7		49.7	138.9	45.1	87.8	51.6	31.9
(235) 20.8	(217) 19.9	(161) 25.6	% Profit Before Taxes/Tangible Net Worth	(30) 25.5	(46) 44.5	(22) 23.4	(22) 25.2	(11) 29.9	(30) 18.5
5.2	6.4	7.0		2.3	16.1	-.8	1.5	3.3	11.2
15.3	13.7	19.9		22.4	34.2	17.8	22.7	13.9	8.3
6.1	5.5	6.5	% Profit Before Taxes/Total Assets	6.4	9.5	5.0	5.3	5.9	5.1
.0	1.1	1.0		-.7	2.2	.6	.0	.1	2.7
106.6	90.9	369.6		UND	715.9	500.8	134.5	142.5	15.2
21.0	16.5	27.3	Sales/Net Fixed Assets	131.0	40.2	139.0	25.1	15.5	9.1
5.7	7.2	7.3		9.5	4.7	9.1	10.5	5.3	7.9
11.1	10.0	10.8		6.5	11.4	18.4	13.2	33.9	7.6
5.4	5.6	6.1	Sales/Total Assets	3.9	5.8	10.6	7.3	10.7	6.0
2.8	3.2	3.1		2.4	2.6	4.0	5.1	4.5	4.5
.6	.5	.5		1.2	.6	.2	.3	.2	.6
(233) 1.0	(214) .8	(143) 1.0	% Depr., Dep., Amort./Sales	(20) 1.6	(40) 1.3	(20) .4	(22) .7	(10) .7	(31) 1.0
1.7	1.4	1.8		2.3	2.3	.9	1.6	1.2	1.2
.6	.7	1.0		2.1	1.3	.7			
(144) 1.2	(123) 1.7	(93) 2.1	% Officers', Directors' Owners' Comp/Sales	(24) 3.2	(33) 2.1	(17) 1.5			
2.9	3.5	3.2		6.7	3.1	2.4			
11935161M	18736218M	10908181M	Net Sales ($)	29336M	106893M	117078M	182122M	183713M	10289039M
2113628M	3277713M	1800897M	Total Assets ($)	10585M	30148M	20647M	30555M	39769M	1669193M

M = $ thousand MM = $ million

See Pages 9 through 22 for Explanation of Ratios and Data

Current Data Sorted by Assets							Comparative Historical Data	
						Type of Statement		
						Unqualified	1	1
			1			Reviewed	4	3
2	2	4				Compiled	11	7
12	12			1	1	Tax Returns	23	19
7	4	5	2	1		Other	27	18
8 (4/1-9/30/13)		46 (10/1/13-3/31/14)					4/1/09-3/31/10	4/1/10-3/31/11
0-500M	**500M-2MM**	**2-10MM**	**10-50MM**	**50-100MM**	**100-250MM**		**ALL**	**ALL**
21	18	9	3	2	1	**NUMBER OF STATEMENTS**	66	48
%	%	%	%	%	%	**ASSETS**	%	%
24.5	19.0					Cash & Equivalents	11.9	18.1
4.1	3.6					Trade Receivables (net)	7.4	7.3
21.4	17.2					Inventory	21.8	18.1
.3	1.1					All Other Current	1.6	1.2
50.3	40.9					Total Current	42.8	44.6
42.0	43.8					Fixed Assets (net)	38.7	39.1
3.7	9.0					Intangibles (net)	11.0	5.2
4.0	6.4					All Other Non-Current	7.5	11.1
100.0	100.0					Total	100.0	100.0
						LIABILITIES		
6.6	7.6					Notes Payable-Short Term	7.5	10.7
2.3	3.4					Cur. Mat.-L.T.D.	3.0	5.7
23.9	14.4					Trade Payables	16.6	13.2
.0	.0					Income Taxes Payable	.1	.1
10.3	7.6					All Other Current	14.0	6.1
43.0	32.9					Total Current	41.2	35.9
26.5	24.8					Long-Term Debt	29.3	35.1
.0	.0					Deferred Taxes	.0	.0
30.8	19.7					All Other Non-Current	15.9	10.8
-.3	22.6					Net Worth	13.6	18.1
100.0	100.0					Total Liabilities & Net Worth	100.0	100.0
						INCOME DATA		
100.0	100.0					Net Sales	100.0	100.0
40.8	36.3					Gross Profit	35.2	37.6
37.8	32.0					Operating Expenses	31.9	33.3
3.0	4.3					Operating Profit	3.3	4.3
.7	1.0					All Other Expenses (net)	.6	.9
2.3	3.3					Profit Before Taxes	2.7	3.4
						RATIOS		
9.4	2.9						2.4	3.6
1.9	1.6					Current	1.3	1.6
.5	.6						.7	.7
7.9	1.8						1.1	2.6
1.2	.8					Quick	(65) .5	.6
.2	.3						.1	.3
0 UND	**0** UND						**0** UND	**0** UND
0 UND	**1** 502.5					Sales/Receivables	**1** 382.9	**2** 158.0
2 227.2	**6** 66.3						**8** 47.7	**10** 37.4
6 59.0	**8** 44.1						**6** 59.7	**5** 71.2
17 21.0	**13** 28.4					Cost of Sales/Inventory	**20** 18.2	**14** 25.3
38 9.5	**32** 11.5						**32** 11.5	**34** 10.9
0 UND	**0** UND						**2** 187.7	**0** UND
8 44.5	**17** 21.2					Cost of Sales/Payables	**16** 23.5	**9** 40.0
40 9.1	**34** 10.8						**28** 13.0	**22** 16.8
8.1	15.1						16.8	15.1
46.8	32.9					Sales/Working Capital	69.6	38.9
-20.2	-32.5						-48.5	-40.3
17.4	11.4						8.5	13.2
(12) 5.8	(16) 2.0					EBIT/Interest	(52) 3.1	(36) 3.5
-1.2	.1						.2	1.4
						Net Profit + Depr., Dep., Amort./Cur. Mat. L/T/D		
.2	.6						.5	.4
2.1	5.9					Fixed/Worth	1.8	1.9
-.9	-1.2						-3.2	NM
.3	.7						1.2	1.0
2.3	8.1					Debt/Worth	4.5	2.9
-2.2	-5.3						-5.0	NM
105.7	79.8						82.7	74.9
(12) 50.9	(11) 23.2					% Profit Before Taxes/Tangible Net Worth	(45) 21.0	(36) 32.6
21.6	-4.2						-6.0	7.8
40.9	18.7						19.0	21.3
13.6	2.7					% Profit Before Taxes/Total Assets	7.5	9.5
-23.2	-3.2						-3.3	1.5
48.3	28.9						61.1	75.6
17.9	10.9					Sales/Net Fixed Assets	16.3	12.4
5.6	4.3						5.2	3.7
9.4	5.5						8.8	7.7
5.9	3.2					Sales/Total Assets	4.6	4.0
3.2	2.1						2.3	2.3
.4	.6						.6	.7
(17) 1.2	(15) 2.0					% Depr., Dep., Amort./Sales	(50) 1.6	(39) 2.0
4.5	2.9						3.3	3.0
1.9	1.3						1.3	.8
(13) 3.7	(12) 3.0					% Officers', Directors' Owners' Comp/Sales	(36) 3.2	(26) 3.3
6.6	5.7						6.9	5.8
34322M	82091M	130032M	105847M	644664M	169035M	Net Sales ($)	1144166M	524442M
5701M	20770M	29019M	58563M	119862M	239631M	Total Assets ($)	342653M	124766M

M = $ thousand MM = $ million

See Pages 9 through 22 for Explanation of Ratios and Data

Comparative Historical Data				Current Data Sorted by Sales					
			Type of Statement						
1			Unqualified						
2	2	1	Reviewed						1
10	5	8	Compiled		2	1	2	2	1
27	29	26	Tax Returns	4	13	4	2	1	2
15	20	19	Other	4	4	4		5	2
4/1/11-3/31/12 ALL	4/1/12-3/31/13 ALL	4/1/13-3/31/14 ALL		8 (4/1-9/30/13)		46 (10/1/13-3/31/14)			
				0-1MM	1-3MM	3-5MM	5-10MM	10-25MM	25MM & OVER
55	56	54	**NUMBER OF STATEMENTS**	8	19	9	4	8	6
%	%	%	**ASSETS**	%	%	%	%	%	%
9.2	15.1	22.6	Cash & Equivalents		27.3				
9.7	10.6	5.3	Trade Receivables (net)		4.4				
16.8	19.1	16.8	Inventory		15.5				
1.5	1.1	1.2	All Other Current		.9				
37.3	45.9	45.8	Total Current		48.1				
49.5	35.0	42.0	Fixed Assets (net)		39.2				
3.9	10.2	6.1	Intangibles (net)		8.6				
9.2	8.8	6.1	All Other Non-Current		4.1				
100.0	100.0	100.0	Total		100.0				
			LIABILITIES						
14.6	10.7	9.1	Notes Payable-Short Term		10.9				
2.8	1.8	2.6	Cur. Mat.-L.T.D.		3.6				
8.5	9.8	17.9	Trade Payables		10.7				
.0	.2	.1	Income Taxes Payable		.0				
9.3	7.4	8.9	All Other Current		8.4				
35.2	29.9	38.6	Total Current		33.7				
38.8	26.3	25.2	Long-Term Debt		40.9				
.0	.0	.0	Deferred Taxes		.0				
16.1	26.8	20.4	All Other Non-Current		16.0				
10.0	17.0	15.8	Net Worth		9.5				
100.0	100.0	100.0	Total Liabilities & Net Worth		100.0				
			INCOME DATA						
100.0	100.0	100.0	Net Sales		100.0				
32.9	33.5	39.0	Gross Profit		41.5				
29.3	30.8	35.5	Operating Expenses		36.3				
3.6	2.7	3.4	Operating Profit		5.2				
1.0	.2	.6	All Other Expenses (net)		1.2				
2.6	2.5	2.8	Profit Before Taxes		4.0				
			RATIOS						
2.3	5.9	4.6			8.5				
1.3	2.1	1.5	Current		2.3				
.7	.9	.6			.5				
1.6	2.4	3.4			6.3				
.8	1.2	.8	Quick		1.1				
.2	.3	.3			.4				
0 UND	0 UND	0 UND			0 UND				
2 242.3	1 250.1	0 878.5	Sales/Receivables		0 UND				
13 28.2	16 23.0	4 81.2			2 151.5				
8 48.6	7 49.7	8 45.8			9 40.6				
13 27.9	15 24.3	17 21.8	Cost of Sales/Inventory		16 22.2				
26 14.0	29 12.4	34 10.8			40 9.1				
0 UND	0 UND	0 UND			0 UND				
8 43.7	6 62.4	12 31.4	Cost of Sales/Payables		8 44.5				
19 19.7	18 20.1	40 9.2			31 11.6				
16.7	14.7	10.3			7.0				
71.6	28.8	41.3	Sales/Working Capital		22.0				
-55.8	UND	-20.1			-19.8				
6.7	12.1	13.0			24.3				
(49) 3.0	(39) 3.5	(42) 2.8	EBIT/Interest		(15) 6.0				
1.7	1.3	.0			-.4				
			Net Profit + Depr., Dep., Amort./Cur. Mat. L/T/D						
.8	.2	.5			.7				
2.1	1.6	2.4	Fixed/Worth		6.0				
-88.1	-16.6	-1.1			-.8				
1.3	.8	.7			.7				
4.0	4.1	3.7	Debt/Worth		9.1				
-121.4	-28.8	-4.2			-2.7				
62.5	134.8	75.3			146.8				
(39) 23.8	(41) 57.5	(36) 28.0	% Profit Before Taxes/Tangible Net Worth		(10) 50.9				
10.5	5.7	6.5			32.0				
15.5	22.7	25.5			40.9				
4.8	8.9	7.3	% Profit Before Taxes/Total Assets		11.0				
1.7	-.2	-3.2			-7.7				
21.1	183.6	35.4			37.0				
10.5	15.5	9.8	Sales/Net Fixed Assets		12.9				
3.6	6.8	4.8			4.6				
6.3	7.0	7.6			6.2				
4.1	4.6	3.9	Sales/Total Assets		3.3				
2.6	2.4	2.4			2.2				
.5	.8	.7			.7				
(50) 1.5	(39) 2.0	(44) 1.6	% Depr., Dep., Amort./Sales		(17) 2.2				
2.4	3.3	3.3			3.3				
1.3	.9	1.5			2.2				
(38) 3.1	(30) 1.7	(30) 2.5	% Officers', Directors' Owners' Comp/Sales		(14) 4.2				
5.6	3.8	5.6			6.7				
597199M	1642900M	1165991M	Net Sales ($)	4660M	35314M	32649M	30644M	127959M	934765M
159525M	481719M	473546M	Total Assets ($)	2061M	14381M	8148M	6076M	36964M	405916M

M = $ thousand MM = $ million

See Pages 9 through 22 for Explanation of Ratios and Data

Current Data Sorted by Assets							Comparative Historical Data	
						Type of Statement		
						Unqualified	2	3
		5				Reviewed	4	3
	5	3	1			Compiled	12	12
6	3	2				Tax Returns	16	5
4	4	1	3	1	1	Other	10	5
4 (4/1-9/30/13)			35 (10/1/13-3/31/14)				4/1/09-3/31/10	4/1/10-3/31/11
0-500M	500M-2MM	2-10MM	10-50MM	50-100MM	100-250MM		ALL	ALL
10	12	11	4	1	1	**NUMBER OF STATEMENTS**	44	28
%	%	%	%	%	%	**ASSETS**	%	%
19.7	7.3	15.3				Cash & Equivalents	17.0	16.6
8.5	12.6	16.6				Trade Receivables (net)	19.0	13.7
21.7	25.7	19.0				Inventory	17.2	14.4
.1	2.0	2.1				All Other Current	.9	2.1
50.0	47.7	53.0				Total Current	54.0	46.8
41.1	37.4	27.2				Fixed Assets (net)	34.0	33.5
7.0	8.4	6.3				Intangibles (net)	5.3	8.5
2.0	6.5	13.4				All Other Non-Current	6.7	11.2
100.0	100.0	100.0				Total	100.0	100.0
						LIABILITIES		
16.4	3.6	10.2				Notes Payable-Short Term	6.1	7.8
4.3	.8	1.4				Cur. Mat.-L.T.D.	5.7	6.4
10.3	28.7	20.1				Trade Payables	29.5	27.3
.0	.9	.3				Income Taxes Payable	.6	.1
21.8	40.0	16.7				All Other Current	11.9	8.8
52.8	73.9	48.7				Total Current	53.8	50.4
13.2	25.1	13.5				Long-Term Debt	16.4	32.0
.0	.2	.0				Deferred Taxes	.0	.1
38.7	11.0	7.9				All Other Non-Current	6.9	3.8
-4.7	-10.2	30.0				Net Worth	22.8	13.6
100.0	100.0	100.0				Total Liabilties & Net Worth	100.0	100.0
						INCOME DATA		
100.0	100.0	100.0				Net Sales	100.0	100.0
43.9	27.4	30.2				Gross Profit	29.2	26.7
42.3	25.1	27.6				Operating Expenses	26.9	23.9
1.5	2.3	2.7				Operating Profit	2.3	2.8
.1	1.3	-.3				All Other Expenses (net)	.2	.4
1.4	1.0	3.0				Profit Before Taxes	2.1	2.3
						RATIOS		
5.8	1.3	1.8					2.2	1.4
2.1	1.1	1.4				Current	1.1	.9
.3	.4	.5					.6	.7
4.0	.9	1.1					2.0	1.1
1.0	(10) .4	.8				Quick	(43) .9	.5
.3	.2	.2					.3	.2
0 UND	**0** UND	**0** 999.8					**0** UND	**0** UND
0 UND	**0** UND	**1** 724.5				Sales/Receivables	**3** 135.5	**1** 653.3
4 85.2	**7** 49.7	**30** 12.1					**27** 13.3	**29** 12.7
3 142.9	**6** 64.8	**7** 49.2					**4** 83.7	**3** 112.1
18 20.5	**16** 23.2	**16** 22.2				Cost of Sales/Inventory	**8** 44.9	**10** 37.0
30 12.1	**27** 13.7	**19** 18.8					**22** 16.9	**17** 21.3
0 UND	**3** 119.9	**7** 50.7					**3** 106.8	**9** 40.6
3 105.2	**20** 18.5	**13** 27.8				Cost of Sales/Payables	**18** 20.4	**25** 14.8
16 23.5	**28** 12.9	**27** 13.7					**40** 9.1	**43** 8.5
10.2	50.1	20.0					17.4	49.9
NM	162.4	55.4				Sales/Working Capital	127.2	-207.6
-22.1	-22.8	-16.3					-24.0	-25.7
							5.7	15.5
						EBIT/Interest	(29) 3.4	(23) 4.4
							.7	2.1
						Net Profit + Depr., Dep., Amort./Cur. Mat. L/T/D		
.2	.6	.2					.3	.2
NM	6.7	.6				Fixed/Worth	1.4	1.2
-.9	-.6	5.1					15.6	3.1
.3	1.2	.6					.8	1.2
NM	6.5	3.7				Debt/Worth	2.6	4.1
-2.0	-5.5	12.2					NM	36.2
							92.4	59.4
						% Profit Before Taxes/Tangible Net Worth	(33) 29.5	(22) 28.1
							11.7	11.0
23.3	17.9	34.1					15.5	21.3
10.6	5.4	4.8				% Profit Before Taxes/Total Assets	8.8	6.1
-3.8	1.6	2.3					3.3	2.8
45.7	91.8	96.0					76.9	84.6
17.7	38.8	23.8				Sales/Net Fixed Assets	26.6	19.4
8.2	3.7	13.1					6.3	5.7
8.0	12.5	8.2					9.3	7.9
6.3	8.1	5.9				Sales/Total Assets	4.5	4.6
4.4	2.6	4.3					2.6	2.6
							.5	.3
						% Depr., Dep., Amort./Sales	(39) 1.1	(24) 1.1
							2.5	2.0
							1.2	1.6
						% Officers', Directors' Owners' Comp/Sales	(21) 2.1	(13) 2.7
							4.1	4.2
14200M	**108973M**	**361059M**	**190164M**	**121679M**	**336457M**	Net Sales ($)	**1145425M**	**875468M**
2313M	**13820M**	**47416M**	**55541M**	**65179M**	**189427M**	Total Assets ($)	**299020M**	**229310M**

M = $ thousand MM = $ million

See Pages 9 through 22 for Explanation of Ratios and Data

Comparative Historical Data / Current Data Sorted by Sales

			Type of Statement						
	2		Unqualified						
3	2	5	Reviewed					2	3
7	4	9	Compiled	1	1		1	4	2
10	5	11	Tax Returns	3	1	2	1	4	
11	16	14	Other	3	2	2	1	1	5
					4 (4/1-9/30/13)			35 (10/1/13-3/31/14)	
4/1/11-3/31/12 ALL	4/1/12-3/31/13 ALL	4/1/13-3/31/14 ALL		0-1MM	1-3MM	3-5MM	5-10MM	10-25MM	25MM & OVER
31	29	39	NUMBER OF STATEMENTS	7	4	4	3	11	10
%	%	%	**ASSETS**	%	%	%	%	%	%
11.3	17.5	15.2	Cash & Equivalents					13.5	21.9
15.5	15.5	11.9	Trade Receivables (net)					16.0	10.6
14.9	22.1	20.2	Inventory					27.6	12.4
2.2	3.1	1.3	All Other Current					1.9	1.7
43.9	58.3	48.6	Total Current					59.0	46.6
39.0	30.7	34.2	Fixed Assets (net)					27.4	24.8
10.9	1.7	9.6	Intangibles (net)					5.2	15.0
6.2	9.3	7.5	All Other Non-Current					8.4	13.6
100.0	100.0	100.0	Total					100.0	100.0
			LIABILITIES						
4.9	20.3	8.2	Notes Payable-Short Term					9.6	.8
3.2	2.5	1.9	Cur. Mat.-L.T.D.					1.1	.8
26.2	26.9	18.9	Trade Payables					30.3	14.8
.2	.0	.4	Income Taxes Payable					1.3	.2
19.2	18.8	23.4	All Other Current					14.3	12.3
53.6	68.6	52.9	Total Current					56.6	28.9
35.4	17.2	19.7	Long-Term Debt					12.5	23.4
.3	.8	.1	Deferred Taxes					.0	.0
12.3	8.2	16.8	All Other Non-Current					12.0	5.1
-1.5	5.2	10.6	Net Worth					18.9	42.6
100.0	100.0	100.0	Total Liabilities & Net Worth					100.0	100.0
			INCOME DATA						
100.0	100.0	100.0	Net Sales					100.0	100.0
29.1	28.0	33.5	Gross Profit					26.0	30.9
27.3	26.2	30.7	Operating Expenses					24.4	25.7
1.8	1.8	2.9	Operating Profit					1.7	5.1
.3	.4	.4	All Other Expenses (net)					.2	-.2
1.5	1.4	2.4	Profit Before Taxes					1.5	5.3
			RATIOS						
1.5	1.7	2.1						1.7	2.1
.7	1.1	1.3	Current					1.1	1.5
.4	.8	.5						.8	1.4
1.2	1.1	1.4						.9	1.7
(29) .5	.7	(37) .8	Quick					.4	1.0
.1	.1	.2						.1	.6
0 UND	**0** UND	**0** UND						**0** UND	**0** 941.7
1 463.7	**3** 139.4	**1** 724.5	Sales/Receivables					**1** 346.0	**1** 342.4
22 16.7	**29** 12.8	**14** 26.3						**14** 26.3	**30** 12.1
6 65.2	**9** 39.3	**7** 49.2						**7** 49.2	**6** 63.2
11 32.5	**17** 21.2	**17** 21.4	Cost of Sales/Inventory					**16** 22.2	**15** 25.1
20 18.3	**32** 11.4	**24** 15.5						**19** 19.4	**22** 16.8
6 56.4	**8** 45.3	**6** 58.9						**8** 48.5	**9** 41.0
18 20.5	**21** 17.7	**14** 27.0	Cost of Sales/Payables					**13** 27.8	**18** 20.7
27 13.6	**32** 11.5	**27** 13.7						**28** 13.1	**26** 13.9
33.1	22.5	20.0						38.9	17.2
-89.6	114.8	70.9	Sales/Working Capital					131.1	29.7
-22.8	-59.2	-27.5						-55.1	71.2
15.7	13.1	15.2							
(23) 4.0	(24) 4.0	(28) 4.9	EBIT/Interest						
.0	1.7	2.4							
			Net Profit + Depr., Dep., Amort./Cur. Mat. L/T/D						
.5	.1	.4						.5	.3
5.8	.6	1.9	Fixed/Worth					1.9	.6
-1.0	NM	-1.4						-1.4	-1.1
1.8	1.2	.8						1.1	.7
37.6	3.4	5.2	Debt/Worth					9.1	1.2
-2.7	-9.8	-4.5						-12.4	-4.1
98.0	84.6	61.4							
(16) 26.2	(21) 29.0	(25) 29.0	% Profit Before Taxes/Tangible Net Worth						
7.3	8.5	7.4							
20.8	18.2	22.3						22.3	29.5
7.3	8.2	8.9	% Profit Before Taxes/Total Assets					11.4	17.6
-2.5	1.9	2.5						2.3	5.8
87.2	131.0	50.4						65.0	105.6
14.4	28.5	24.1	Sales/Net Fixed Assets					43.2	16.0
6.1	7.7	10.1						19.5	12.3
8.2	8.0	8.5						12.4	6.1
4.5	5.6	5.8	Sales/Total Assets					8.2	4.0
3.3	2.8	3.3						5.9	2.1
.4	.3	.5							
(25) 1.1	(20) .9	(29) .9	% Depr., Dep., Amort./Sales						
2.9	2.4	1.7							
1.3	.5	1.0							
(10) 4.3	(12) 2.6	(22) 3.0	% Officers', Directors' Owners' Comp/Sales						
7.1	3.7	6.9							
735936M	735003M	1132532M	Net Sales ($)	4583M	8720M	14080M	26731M	189921M	888497M
138609M	299646M	373696M	Total Assets ($)	1730M	3039M	5363M	3171M	25023M	335370M

M = $ thousand MM = $ million

See Pages 9 through 22 for Explanation of Ratios and Data

Current Data Sorted by Assets							Comparative Historical Data	
						Type of Statement		
					1	Unqualified	2	1
			1			Reviewed		
3	3					Compiled	2	2
19	8	5				Tax Returns	36	22
10	6	7				Other	9	10
	4 (4/1-9/30/13)		59 (10/1/13-3/31/14)				**4/1/09-3/31/10**	**4/1/10-3/31/11**
0-500M	**500M-2MM**	**2-10MM**	**10-50MM**	**50-100MM**	**100-250MM**		**ALL**	**ALL**
32	17	12	1		1	**NUMBER OF STATEMENTS**	49	35
%	%	%	%	%	%	**ASSETS**	%	%
13.4	15.2	12.8		DATA NOT AVAILABLE		Cash & Equivalents	7.9	11.4
2.1	6.8	3.5				Trade Receivables (net)	5.7	1.7
5.6	6.2	6.6				Inventory	5.2	4.4
2.3	2.8	1.1				All Other Current	1.6	13.5
23.4	30.9	24.0				Total Current	20.4	31.1
35.7	45.2	51.2				Fixed Assets (net)	41.2	44.9
19.8	15.3	16.1				Intangibles (net)	22.0	12.6
20.9	8.6	8.7				All Other Non-Current	16.4	11.5
100.0	100.0	100.0				Total	100.0	100.0
						LIABILITIES		
9.1	5.4	5.1				Notes Payable-Short Term	2.7	5.6
7.5	2.2	2.9				Cur. Mat.-L.T.D.	2.8	3.7
7.8	6.5	9.1				Trade Payables	10.1	7.3
.0	.0	.1				Income Taxes Payable	.1	.0
20.3	4.1	12.1				All Other Current	28.5	25.9
44.7	18.2	29.4				Total Current	44.3	42.5
25.7	35.9	38.3				Long-Term Debt	50.9	44.0
.0	.0	.0				Deferred Taxes	.1	.0
20.9	12.0	6.2				All Other Non-Current	24.3	10.7
8.8	34.0	26.2				Net Worth	-19.6	2.8
100.0	100.0	100.0				Total Liabilties & Net Worth	100.0	100.0
						INCOME DATA		
100.0	100.0	100.0				Net Sales	100.0	100.0
55.0	52.3	51.3				Gross Profit	57.7	57.0
47.8	43.8	44.7				Operating Expenses	54.4	52.1
7.2	8.5	6.6				Operating Profit	3.3	4.9
.8	2.3	.9				All Other Expenses (net)	2.0	1.3
6.4	6.2	5.7				Profit Before Taxes	1.4	3.6
						RATIOS		
3.8	5.8	1.4					1.1	2.1
1.1	2.0	.8				Current	.5	.6
.3	.8	.2					.2	.3
3.5	3.8	.8					.7	.8
(31) .7	1.1	.5				Quick	.3	.3
.1	.5	.2					.1	.1
0 UND	0 UND	0 UND					0 UND	0 UND
0 UND	0 UND	0 UND				Sales/Receivables	0 UND	0 UND
0 UND	15 23.9	8 46.7					3 129.4	0 UND
0 UND	4 97.8	3 129.7					3 123.8	2 149.4
4 83.3	9 40.2	12 31.0				Cost of Sales/Inventory	6 63.7	5 70.2
10 35.2	14 25.6	32 11.3					10 34.9	10 37.0
0 UND	0 UND	11 33.5					0 UND	3 110.4
3 105.8	4 93.9	21 17.1				Cost of Sales/Payables	15 23.8	22 16.8
18 20.7	30 12.2	48 7.6					33 10.9	26 13.9
19.8	8.6	16.6					137.2	20.3
244.4	17.7	-113.5				Sales/Working Capital	-31.0	-41.2
-16.2	-125.2	-14.6					-7.6	-14.2
13.5	10.9	47.5					4.8	10.2
(23) 9.0	(14) 6.1	(11) 9.1				EBIT/Interest	(40) 1.7	(25) 3.4
1.2	2.2	2.1					.8	1.4
						Net Profit + Depr., Dep., Amort./Cur. Mat. L/T/D		
.7	1.0	.7					1.0	.9
6.0	78.1	5.7				Fixed/Worth	-4.1	UND
-.4	-4.3	-3.6					-.3	-.8
.8	1.0	.8					6.0	1.8
7.0	135.8	6.0				Debt/Worth	-5.0	UND
-3.3	-10.0	-4.9					-1.6	-2.3
197.7							87.3	146.7
(20) 77.1						% Profit Before Taxes/Tangible Net Worth	(15) 28.7	(18) 45.7
22.4							2.6	10.8
53.5	22.2	30.4					28.8	31.4
15.7	15.3	12.1				% Profit Before Taxes/Total Assets	5.6	10.1
1.3	6.4	4.0					-.7	3.8
37.5	8.5	9.9					18.2	24.4
16.7	5.7	5.3				Sales/Net Fixed Assets	7.9	6.7
5.7	2.4	3.8					4.1	4.5
7.1	3.9	3.3					4.2	6.1
4.8	2.4	2.5				Sales/Total Assets	2.5	3.3
2.7	1.3	2.2					1.6	1.9
1.0		1.7					1.5	1.3
(22) 2.0		(10) 3.2				% Depr., Dep., Amort./Sales	(37) 5.0	(30) 2.9
3.8		4.5					7.9	5.1
2.3							2.7	3.4
(13) 5.2						% Officers', Directors' Owners' Comp/Sales	(14) 4.2	(13) 6.8
7.2							6.4	13.4
32897M	52327M	149690M	20469M		36527M	Net Sales ($)	3176672M	121272M
7781M	17822M	53411M	24083M		100401M	Total Assets ($)	457986M	45558M

M = $ thousand MM = $ million

See Pages 9 through 22 for Explanation of Ratios and Data

Comparative Historical Data

Current Data Sorted by Sales

			Type of Statement						
	1	1	Unqualified						1
1		1	Reviewed					1	
6	4	6	Compiled	1	4	1			
44	38	32	Tax Returns	11	11	1	6	3	
22	19	23	Other	8	7	1	2	5	
4/1/11-3/31/12 ALL	4/1/12-3/31/13 ALL	4/1/13-3/31/14 ALL		4 (4/1-9/30/13)		59 (10/1/13-3/31/14)			
				0-1MM	1-3MM	3-5MM	5-10MM	10-25MM	25MM & OVER
73	62	63	NUMBER OF STATEMENTS	20	22	3	8	9	1
%	%	%	**ASSETS**	%	%	%	%	%	%
13.4	17.0	13.4	Cash & Equivalents	13.4	12.9				
4.8	4.5	3.6	Trade Receivables (net)	2.8	1.1				
6.1	6.0	5.8	Inventory	4.9	7.7				
10.0	7.8	2.1	All Other Current	1.0	4.4				
34.3	35.2	24.9	Total Current	22.1	26.1				
45.0	42.3	41.0	Fixed Assets (net)	39.9	37.3				
12.7	12.3	19.0	Intangibles (net)	20.2	18.4				
8.0	10.1	15.1	All Other Non-Current	17.8	18.1				
100.0	100.0	100.0	Total	100.0	100.0				
			LIABILITIES						
8.5	4.6	7.0	Notes Payable-Short Term	8.9	6.8				
3.0	4.0	5.0	Cur. Mat.-L.T.D.	1.8	9.7				
9.2	9.4	7.5	Trade Payables	6.9	5.9				
.0	.0	.0	Income Taxes Payable	.1	.0				
30.8	20.8	13.8	All Other Current	19.2	13.9				
51.4	38.8	33.3	Total Current	36.9	36.3				
28.5	33.7	31.3	Long-Term Debt	32.2	28.0				
.0	.0	.0	Deferred Taxes	.0	.0				
19.7	10.1	15.0	All Other Non-Current	23.4	13.7				
.5	17.4	20.4	Net Worth	7.5	22.0				
100.0	100.0	100.0	Total Liabilties & Net Worth	100.0	100.0				
			INCOME DATA						
100.0	100.0	100.0	Net Sales	100.0	100.0				
55.4	56.1	53.7	Gross Profit	56.3	51.8				
50.0	48.6	46.2	Operating Expenses	50.8	42.7				
5.4	7.5	7.5	Operating Profit	5.5	9.1				
.5	.4	1.3	All Other Expenses (net)	1.1	.9				
4.9	7.1	6.2	Profit Before Taxes	4.4	8.2				
			RATIOS						
2.3	2.3	3.8		5.5	4.3				
.9	1.2	1.2	Current	1.7	.9				
.4	.5	.5		.6	.4				
1.4	1.4	3.1		5.5	3.6				
.4	.6	(62) .7	Quick	(19) 1.5	.3				
.1	.2	.2		.2	.1				
0 UND	0 UND	0 UND		0 UND	0 UND				
0 UND	0 UND	0 UND	Sales/Receivables	0 UND	0 UND				
2 187.3	2 184.3	3 108.3		0 UND	0 UND				
3 116.7	4 83.1	2 147.5		0 UND	2 164.9				
7 52.2	8 43.1	7 49.4	Cost of Sales/Inventory	5 80.8	6 58.2				
14 25.6	18 20.7	15 24.5		18 20.3	14 25.2				
0 UND	4 84.7	0 UND		0 UND	0 UND				
7 54.1	20 18.1	7 53.1	Cost of Sales/Payables	1 379.0	4 95.8				
29 12.7	35 10.3	26 14.0		23 15.9	10 35.0				
17.8	15.7	14.5		12.3	20.2				
-297.5	90.3	122.7	Sales/Working Capital	61.3	NM				
-14.8	-16.2	-21.9		-41.0	-17.1				
19.4	29.2	12.3		10.1	24.3				
(50) 4.4	(45) 10.0	(50) 7.2	EBIT/Interest	(13) 7.1	(18) 9.3				
1.2	3.0	2.0		.7	2.9				
			Net Profit + Depr., Dep., Amort./Cur. Mat. L/T/D						
.8	.8	.7		1.0	.6				
14.0	3.1	8.9	Fixed/Worth	44.5	1.6				
-.7	-1.6	-1.5		-.5	-1.7				
.8	.8	.9		1.2	.4				
14.4	7.3	9.6	Debt/Worth	52.4	1.9				
-2.3	-4.8	-4.6		-3.2	-4.6				
89.1	199.2	131.2		116.2	340.7				
(37) 39.7	(38) 73.7	(37) 50.3	% Profit Before Taxes/Tangible Net Worth	(11) 33.3	(14) 64.8				
14.1	21.4	19.0		23.6	20.0				
29.1	34.1	31.2		16.5	53.8				
13.2	19.3	13.9	% Profit Before Taxes/Total Assets	10.9	21.3				
1.3	2.5	3.0		.0	11.7				
15.7	13.4	22.5		21.2	41.6				
8.5	7.8	8.4	Sales/Net Fixed Assets	5.4	15.6				
4.8	4.5	3.9		2.4	4.5				
4.9	4.1	5.2		5.4	7.6				
3.2	2.7	3.0	Sales/Total Assets	2.5	4.8				
2.1	1.8	2.1		1.3	2.3				
1.5	1.7	1.4		1.6	.9				
(55) 2.6	(48) 3.0	(43) 2.4	% Depr., Dep., Amort./Sales	(12) 2.6	(15) 2.0				
5.3	5.2	4.4		8.2	3.1				
1.9	2.0	2.1							
(24) 5.8	(28) 3.9	(24) 3.2	% Officers', Directors' Owners' Comp/Sales						
9.2	5.9	6.7							
1735729M	235085M	291910M	Net Sales ($)	12731M	32003M	11868M	50266M	148515M	36527M
190847M	95609M	203498M	Total Assets ($)	6224M	9300M	3703M	16108M	67762M	100401M

M = $ thousand MM = $ million

See Pages 9 through 22 for Explanation of Ratios and Data

Current Data Sorted by Assets							Comparative Historical Data	
						Type of Statement		
		1	1	1		Unqualified	6	3
	1					Reviewed		2
1		2	1			Compiled	13	12
2	2	2				Tax Returns	21	11
1	1	5	2			Other	6	11
6 (4/1-9/30/13)		17 (10/1/13-3/31/14)					4/1/09-3/31/10	4/1/10-3/31/11
0-500M	500M-2MM	2-10MM	10-50MM	50-100MM	100-250MM		ALL	ALL
4	4	10	4	1		**NUMBER OF STATEMENTS**	46	39
%	%	%	%	%	%	**ASSETS**	%	%
		10.6			DATA NOT AVAILABLE	Cash & Equivalents	17.6	15.2
		10.8				Trade Receivables (net)	9.2	7.7
		30.9				Inventory	16.4	24.1
		1.5				All Other Current	2.3	1.5
		53.8				Total Current	45.4	48.6
		35.0				Fixed Assets (net)	36.5	35.1
		8.4				Intangibles (net)	4.1	3.9
		2.8				All Other Non-Current	13.9	12.4
		100.0				Total	100.0	100.0
						LIABILITIES		
		12.5				Notes Payable-Short Term	3.4	10.1
		3.4				Cur. Mat.-L.T.D.	3.0	2.3
		16.9				Trade Payables	9.5	10.3
		.0				Income Taxes Payable	.4	.1
		4.4				All Other Current	16.7	11.2
		37.2				Total Current	33.1	34.1
		17.7				Long-Term Debt	36.4	24.8
		.4				Deferred Taxes	.1	.1
		11.3				All Other Non-Current	13.2	8.0
		33.4				Net Worth	17.2	33.1
		100.0				Total Liabilities & Net Worth	100.0	100.0
						INCOME DATA		
		100.0				Net Sales	100.0	100.0
		34.8				Gross Profit	54.5	50.8
		32.3				Operating Expenses	49.1	46.7
		2.6				Operating Profit	5.4	4.1
		.7				All Other Expenses (net)	1.7	.5
		1.9				Profit Before Taxes	3.8	3.7
						RATIOS		
		2.4					4.3	3.0
		1.4				Current	1.6	1.5
		1.1					.6	1.2
		.6					2.3	1.6
		.4				Quick	.7	.7
		.2					.2	.2
		1 439.7					0 UND	0 UND
		4 88.0				Sales/Receivables	1 595.6	0 999.8
		30 12.3					12 30.4	18 20.8
		43 8.5					9 40.3	22 16.4
		68 5.4				Cost of Sales/Inventory	35 10.5	49 7.4
		114 3.2					68 5.4	88 4.1
		16 22.6					0 UND	1 464.7
		27 13.6				Cost of Sales/Payables	13 27.6	14 26.7
		49 7.4					31 11.9	31 11.6
		7.4					5.9	9.5
		13.9				Sales/Working Capital	18.6	16.2
		62.1					-17.1	56.0
							8.9	11.8
						EBIT/Interest	(35) 3.8	(32) 3.2
							1.3	.8
						Net Profit + Depr., Dep., Amort./Cur. Mat. L/T/D		
		.7					.3	.4
		1.0				Fixed/Worth	.9	1.0
		2.2					-2.9	4.4
		.9					.6	.6
		3.6				Debt/Worth	2.4	1.6
		8.6					-5.3	7.7
							47.9	54.9
						% Profit Before Taxes/Tangible Net Worth	(30) 26.6	(31) 25.4
							2.8	-1.0
		9.6					20.4	25.7
		2.5				% Profit Before Taxes/Total Assets	7.7	8.4
		-.8					.7	-.5
		15.1					17.8	19.7
		8.9				Sales/Net Fixed Assets	5.8	8.3
		3.3					3.9	4.6
		3.6					3.9	4.9
		2.1				Sales/Total Assets	2.5	2.7
		1.4					1.6	1.9
		.5					1.1	.5
		2.0				% Depr., Dep., Amort./Sales	(35) 2.0	(31) 1.8
		4.0					4.8	4.3
							3.0	1.5
						% Officers', Directors' Owners' Comp/Sales	(18) 5.2	(19) 2.8
							7.3	6.2
4100M	12444M	145283M	158845M	121794M		Net Sales ($)	714404M	1157013M
1263M	3148M	65116M	74114M	54076M		Total Assets ($)	358976M	384287M

M = $ thousand MM = $ million

See Pages 9 through 22 for Explanation of Ratios and Data

Comparative Historical Data / Current Data Sorted by Sales

4/1/11-3/31/12 ALL	4/1/12-3/31/13 ALL	4/1/13-3/31/14 ALL	Type of Statement	0-1MM	1-3MM	3-5MM	5-10MM	10-25MM	25MM & OVER
1		3	Unqualified				1		2
1	3	1	Reviewed			1			
10	4	4	Compiled		1		1	2	
11	8	6	Tax Returns	2	2			1	1
13	7	9	Other	1	1		1	3	3
				6 (4/1-9/30/13)			17 (10/1/13-3/31/14)		
36	22	23	NUMBER OF STATEMENTS	3	4	1	3	6	6
%	%	%	ASSETS	%	%	%	%	%	%
20.5	23.3	12.7	Cash & Equivalents						
7.3	8.7	14.7	Trade Receivables (net)						
19.5	27.5	25.9	Inventory						
1.0	1.5	2.4	All Other Current						
48.3	60.9	55.7	Total Current						
33.6	25.1	31.8	Fixed Assets (net)						
5.5	4.9	9.1	Intangibles (net)						
12.5	9.0	3.4	All Other Non-Current						
100.0	100.0	100.0	Total						
			LIABILITIES						
11.8	12.9	11.7	Notes Payable-Short Term						
3.2	2.6	3.7	Cur. Mat.-L.T.D.						
11.4	11.2	12.3	Trade Payables						
.2	.0	.0	Income Taxes Payable						
9.9	9.6	6.9	All Other Current						
36.5	36.2	34.6	Total Current						
32.5	34.3	22.6	Long-Term Debt						
.1	.3	.2	Deferred Taxes						
7.3	11.1	9.4	All Other Non-Current						
23.5	18.1	33.2	Net Worth						
100.0	100.0	100.0	Total Liabilties & Net Worth						
			INCOME DATA						
100.0	100.0	100.0	Net Sales						
50.2	54.4	42.7	Gross Profit						
46.2	47.6	37.1	Operating Expenses						
3.9	6.8	5.6	Operating Profit						
1.6	2.6	.9	All Other Expenses (net)						
2.3	4.3	4.7	Profit Before Taxes						
			RATIOS						
2.9	4.9	2.9							
1.3	2.2	1.5	Current						
.7	1.0	1.1							
1.3	2.9	1.1							
.6	.9	.6	Quick						
.3	.2	.4							
0 UND	0 UND	2 213.7							
1 425.3	7 48.9	14 26.4	Sales/Receivables						
14 26.6	12 29.8	35 10.3							
8 45.9	24 14.9	28 13.1							
33 11.0	48 7.6	54 6.7	Cost of Sales/Inventory						
68 5.4	114 3.2	91 4.0							
0 UND	1 290.0	12 29.4							
16 22.5	18 19.9	24 15.0	Cost of Sales/Payables						
30 12.3	36 10.0	35 10.5							
8.3	3.0	7.5							
19.9	17.8	10.4	Sales/Working Capital						
-17.5	101.2	56.6							
13.9	9.4	13.4							
(26) 1.5	(18) 4.6	(19) 6.9	EBIT/Interest						
-.3	.8	1.4							
			Net Profit + Depr., Dep., Amort./Cur. Mat. L/T/D						
.5	.2	.4							
1.2	.8	1.1	Fixed/Worth						
-2.2	-.9	9.6							
.8	.5	.6							
1.5	1.2	2.3	Debt/Worth						
-5.1	-4.4	14.9							
51.6	32.2	76.8							
(25) 20.0	(13) 18.3	(18) 24.0	% Profit Before Taxes/Tangible Net Worth						
-5.4	8.1	4.3							
20.0	22.8	17.7							
4.3	10.2	8.1	% Profit Before Taxes/Total Assets						
-3.8	1.6	1.0							
50.0	27.9	17.3							
8.4	9.4	8.6	Sales/Net Fixed Assets						
4.2	5.1	4.5							
4.1	4.5	4.1							
2.8	2.4	2.4	Sales/Total Assets						
1.8	1.5	1.6							
.7	.8	.9							
(23) 2.1	(17) 2.0	(21) 2.2	% Depr., Dep., Amort./Sales						
3.6	3.7	4.3							
1.4									
(19) 5.3			% Officers', Directors' Owners' Comp/Sales						
6.9									
392679M	98848M	442466M	Net Sales ($)	2363M	9334M	4847M	22652M	83426M	319844M
146455M	53541M	197717M	Total Assets ($)	864M	2809M	738M	18453M	42593M	132260M

M = $ thousand MM = $ million

See Pages 9 through 22 for Explanation of Ratios and Data

Current Data Sorted by Assets							Comparative Historical Data	
						Type of Statement		
		1	2	1	1	Unqualified	20	14
	4	4	1			Reviewed	26	9
11	7	1				Compiled	22	23
67	36	3			3	Tax Returns	124	93
31	24	17	4	2	3	Other	63	86
22 (4/1-9/30/13)			201 (10/1/13-3/31/14)				4/1/09-3/31/10	4/1/10-3/31/11
0-500M	**500M-2MM**	**2-10MM**	**10-50MM**	**50-100MM**	**100-250MM**		**ALL**	**ALL**
109	71	26	7	3	7	**NUMBER OF STATEMENTS**	255	225
%	%	%	%	%	%	**ASSETS**	%	%
24.9	15.1	14.2				Cash & Equivalents	15.5	14.4
3.1	9.2	14.8				Trade Receivables (net)	7.2	8.6
15.7	18.7	24.6				Inventory	18.4	16.0
1.6	2.3	3.1				All Other Current	2.5	2.5
45.2	45.4	56.8				Total Current	43.6	41.5
34.7	38.7	32.7				Fixed Assets (net)	36.5	38.9
13.6	8.4	3.6				Intangibles (net)	12.2	12.3
6.3	7.5	6.9				All Other Non-Current	7.7	7.3
100.0	100.0	100.0				Total	100.0	100.0
						LIABILITIES		
11.1	6.8	7.2				Notes Payable-Short Term	7.6	7.4
4.7	3.1	5.8				Cur. Mat.-L.T.D.	4.8	3.9
16.9	12.1	20.9				Trade Payables	11.7	12.4
.3	.1	.2				Income Taxes Payable	.1	.2
24.7	11.4	12.7				All Other Current	15.2	15.9
57.5	33.4	46.7				Total Current	39.4	39.8
21.3	29.4	27.7				Long-Term Debt	29.1	28.3
.0	.1	.2				Deferred Taxes	.1	.1
20.3	7.2	8.2				All Other Non-Current	8.3	12.5
.9	29.9	17.1				Net Worth	23.2	19.2
100.0	100.0	100.0				Total Liabilties & Net Worth	100.0	100.0
						INCOME DATA		
100.0	100.0	100.0				Net Sales	100.0	100.0
54.8	46.6	43.5				Gross Profit	46.6	48.4
50.8	42.5	37.2				Operating Expenses	42.8	43.6
4.0	4.1	6.3				Operating Profit	3.8	4.8
.0	.7	1.3				All Other Expenses (net)	.8	1.0
3.9	3.4	5.0				Profit Before Taxes	3.0	3.8
						RATIOS		
3.7	3.3	1.9					2.7	3.0
1.1	1.5	1.2				Current	1.3	1.3
.3	.8	.7					.7	.6
2.0	1.6	1.2					1.7	1.7
.7	(70) .7	.6				Quick	.6	.7
.2	.3	.4					.2	.2
0 UND	**0** UND	**0** UND					**0** UND	**0** UND
0 UND	**0** 931.8	**5** 74.6				Sales/Receivables	**0** UND	**0** 999.8
0 999.8	**13** 27.8	**25** 14.8					**6** 58.1	**9** 39.0
2 216.7	**10** 37.4	**9** 40.5					**7** 51.4	**7** 54.9
9 40.8	**22** 16.3	**25** 14.5				Cost of Sales/Inventory	**17** 20.9	**15** 23.8
24 15.3	**46** 8.0	**78** 4.7					**47** 7.7	**39** 9.5
0 UND	**0** UND	**12** 29.6					**0** UND	**0** UND
4 96.8	**13** 29.1	**22** 16.3				Cost of Sales/Payables	**15** 24.3	**14** 26.3
23 16.1	**33** 11.0	**49** 7.5					**32** 11.4	**31** 11.9
17.7	11.2	7.5					12.8	12.7
324.2	28.5	63.8				Sales/Working Capital	32.9	54.4
-16.5	-36.9	-39.7					-38.7	-31.0
26.2	8.2	14.0					13.9	13.2
(62) 7.8	(53) 3.1	(24) 6.6				EBIT/Interest	(200) 3.7	(182) 5.1
2.0	1.3	2.1					1.1	1.8
							5.0	4.3
						Net Profit + Depr., Dep., Amort./Cur. Mat. L/T/D	(33) 1.6	(22) 2.8
							.8	1.8
.4	.4	.3					.5	.6
1.7	1.3	1.1				Fixed/Worth	1.4	1.9
-1.5	6.3	3.7					-4.6	-2.7
.6	1.1	1.3					.8	.9
5.8	1.9	2.3				Debt/Worth	2.8	4.1
-3.2	10.9	6.2					-5.1	-5.1
148.9	61.2	69.8					75.3	124.4
(69) 72.7	(56) 26.7	(23) 20.5				% Profit Before Taxes/Tangible Net Worth	(171) 30.0	(152) 41.1
23.9	3.4	8.7					10.5	14.9
49.4	19.0	15.7					24.4	27.5
17.3	6.3	8.4				% Profit Before Taxes/Total Assets	9.0	10.1
2.5	1.0	2.6					.7	2.6
72.4	26.0	51.5					32.8	33.6
25.3	11.6	13.0				Sales/Net Fixed Assets	11.9	11.5
8.6	4.3	5.3					5.0	5.1
10.5	5.3	5.3					5.5	5.8
5.7	3.0	2.8				Sales/Total Assets	3.4	3.3
3.2	2.1	1.5					2.0	2.3
.6	1.1	.3					.9	.9
(68) 1.5	(57) 2.3	(23) 1.3				% Depr., Dep., Amort./Sales	(208) 1.8	(172) 1.8
3.1	4.6	2.4					3.5	3.9
3.3	1.9	.5					.9	1.9
(59) 5.4	(38) 3.8	(10) .9				% Officers', Directors' Owners' Comp/Sales	(116) 3.3	(106) 3.3
9.9	7.8	2.7					5.7	6.8
143642M	**278041M**	**442134M**	**302093M**	**302648M**	**6836928M**	Net Sales ($)	**8919875M**	**4106904M**
23619M	**75478M**	**118444M**	**112313M**	**168677M**	**1180718M**	Total Assets ($)	**2455672M**	**1620071M**

M = $ thousand MM = $ million

See Pages 9 through 22 for Explanation of Ratios and Data

Comparative Historical Data				Current Data Sorted by Sales					
			Type of Statement						
8	2	5	Unqualified					2	3
16	7	9	Reviewed		1	1	3	4	
26	19	19	Compiled	6	6	3	1	3	
115	132	109	Tax Returns	36	46	12	11	1	3
67	63	81	Other	22	19	11	8	8	13
					22 (4/1-9/30/13)		201 (10/1/13-3/31/14)		
4/1/11-3/31/12 ALL	4/1/12-3/31/13 ALL	4/1/13-3/31/14 ALL		0-1MM	1-3MM	3-5MM	5-10MM	10-25MM	25MM & OVER
232	223	223	**NUMBER OF STATEMENTS**	64	72	27	23	18	19
%	%	%	**ASSETS**	%	%	%	%	%	%
13.5	17.8	20.2	Cash & Equivalents	20.2	20.4	22.7	20.6	15.9	19.8
6.3	5.9	6.6	Trade Receivables (net)	1.9	6.2	8.8	11.4	9.9	11.8
20.1	19.3	17.5	Inventory	11.9	16.8	19.1	30.1	20.6	18.6
3.2	2.3	2.1	All Other Current	2.3	.9	3.9	3.3	3.1	1.9
43.0	45.2	46.5	Total Current	36.2	44.2	54.4	65.5	49.6	52.1
37.5	38.7	36.2	Fixed Assets (net)	41.7	35.4	30.6	28.6	34.0	39.8
10.0	7.6	10.5	Intangibles (net)	14.9	13.1	7.8	1.6	6.8	3.8
9.4	8.5	6.8	All Other Non-Current	7.1	7.3	7.2	4.2	9.6	4.3
100.0	100.0	100.0	Total	100.0	100.0	100.0	100.0	100.0	100.0
			LIABILITIES						
7.7	8.2	9.0	Notes Payable-Short Term	10.6	4.0	15.3	15.8	6.2	7.8
4.1	3.0	4.1	Cur. Mat.-L.T.D.	6.6	3.1	1.8	1.5	7.6	2.5
13.8	11.4	15.8	Trade Payables	11.2	10.9	23.6	29.6	17.2	20.7
.2	.2	.2	Income Taxes Payable	.4	.1	.0	.1	.2	.1
21.1	16.1	18.9	All Other Current	29.8	15.4	9.9	11.5	13.8	21.9
46.9	39.0	47.9	Total Current	58.5	33.5	50.6	58.4	45.0	52.9
26.6	24.5	24.5	Long-Term Debt	31.6	22.7	16.8	17.6	30.2	20.7
.1	.1	.1	Deferred Taxes	.0	.0	.1	.0	.7	.4
17.3	18.1	16.5	All Other Non-Current	17.0	17.5	1.7	17.3	3.9	43.5
9.1	18.4	11.0	Net Worth	-7.1	26.3	30.8	6.6	20.2	-17.5
100.0	100.0	100.0	Total Liabilities & Net Worth	100.0	100.0	100.0	100.0	100.0	100.0
			INCOME DATA						
100.0	100.0	100.0	Net Sales	100.0	100.0	100.0	100.0	100.0	100.0
45.9	47.0	50.5	Gross Profit	58.4	53.4	44.5	39.1	44.9	40.4
43.0	42.8	46.3	Operating Expenses	53.8	48.5	40.5	35.7	41.1	39.0
2.9	4.1	4.2	Operating Profit	4.6	4.9	4.0	3.4	3.8	1.4
.6	.4	.5	All Other Expenses (net)	.8	.3	.2	.0	.9	.7
2.4	3.8	3.7	Profit Before Taxes	3.8	4.6	3.8	3.4	2.9	.6
			RATIOS						
2.7	2.9	2.6		2.7	4.4	2.0	2.4	2.0	2.1
1.3	1.5	1.3	Current	1.0	1.6	1.5	1.4	1.2	1.2
.5	.7	.6		.3	.5	.6	.8	.6	.7
1.4	1.7	1.6		1.9	2.6	1.2	1.5	1.2	1.4
(230) .4	(222) .7	(222) .7	Quick	.6	.7	.9	(22) .4	.5	1.0
.1	.2	.2		.1	.3	.4	.2	.2	.3
0 UND	0 UND	0 UND		0 UND	0 UND	0 UND	0 UND	0 UND	0 999.8
0 UND	0 UND	0 UND	Sales/Receivables	0 UND	0 UND	0 931.8	1 285.7	4 84.4	4 97.0
5 72.5	4 85.2	4 97.0		0 UND	3 139.2	21 17.5	4 83.7	19 19.7	22 16.7
6 65.2	6 61.6	5 71.7		0 UND	2 153.7	10 37.8	17 21.1	7 54.8	10 38.1
16 22.2	15 23.7	17 21.7	Cost of Sales/Inventory	12 29.9	12 31.0	24 15.3	25 14.8	29 12.8	17 21.3
53 6.9	41 8.9	33 11.2		24 14.9	33 11.0	33 11.2	42 8.6	46 7.9	54 6.8
4 98.5	0 UND	0 UND		0 UND	0 UND	5 70.7	9 39.4	13 28.8	15 23.6
15 23.6	11 32.4	13 27.5	Cost of Sales/Payables	2 224.0	3 116.3	20 18.6	23 15.7	27 13.6	31 11.6
34 10.8	28 13.2	34 10.6		26 14.1	21 17.1	47 7.8	60 6.1	40 9.2	57 6.4
12.6	10.9	12.3		21.1	10.5	12.3	8.8	14.2	8.5
49.0	44.7	67.4	Sales/Working Capital	473.0	60.4	21.5	42.2	123.7	85.4
-17.2	-44.9	-25.9		-12.3	-32.0	-27.2	-58.5	-30.9	-27.2
12.8	14.6	16.0		22.5	24.7	11.6	16.0	9.0	18.2
(177) 4.1	(155) 6.6	(154) 5.5	EBIT/Interest	(39) 4.5	(44) 6.3	(20) 5.1	(18) 6.0	(16) 7.0	(17) 3.9
.6	1.5	1.6		1.1	2.7	1.6	-3.0	1.9	-.5
18.0	4.1	4.6							
(17) 6.6	(11) 2.2	(10) 2.2	Net Profit + Depr., Dep., Amort./Cur. Mat. L/T/D						
1.5	1.4	1.3							
.4	.4	.4		.5	.4	.2	.2	.3	.5
1.6	1.4	1.3	Fixed/Worth	2.2	1.6	.8	.7	1.1	1.5
-2.4	-6.2	-7.5		-1.0	53.6	4.2	2.0	NM	-1.3
.9	.6	.9		.4	1.0	1.0	.9	.7	1.1
3.5	2.4	2.4	Debt/Worth	4.5	3.7	1.9	1.8	2.0	2.3
-4.3	-9.5	-7.9		-2.2	-13.9	7.9	4.6	NM	-2.7
59.3	94.2	95.7		100.9	106.4	97.2	79.9	72.0	53.9
(147) 21.9	(156) 37.2	(160) 41.4	% Profit Before Taxes/Tangible Net Worth	(38) 64.5	(52) 55.6	(22) 37.5	(20) 26.8	(14) 20.0	(14) 14.0
6.3	10.5	9.5		13.6	15.7	4.9	7.5	5.4	-6.5
21.5	31.4	26.2		45.8	39.2	21.0	20.5	18.4	17.8
7.8	12.1	11.5	% Profit Before Taxes/Total Assets	10.7	15.8	11.4	10.7	7.8	7.9
-1.4	1.9	1.9		-1.1	5.2	1.9	1.0	2.7	-1.5
41.3	34.2	44.3		43.3	56.8	49.6	55.7	29.9	22.5
12.0	10.9	16.0	Sales/Net Fixed Assets	11.3	17.4	16.1	23.4	9.2	12.5
4.9	4.9	5.4		3.5	4.9	6.2	15.6	5.6	5.8
5.3	5.9	7.1		7.8	7.7	7.2	6.9	6.8	6.7
3.3	3.6	3.8	Sales/Total Assets	3.7	3.7	4.0	5.6	3.4	3.5
2.3	2.1	2.4		2.0	2.4	2.5	3.1	1.8	2.4
.8	.8	.7		.7	.8	1.0	.5	.5	.4
(176) 1.9	(169) 1.8	(161) 1.9	% Depr., Dep., Amort./Sales	(41) 2.3	(53) 2.0	(20) 2.2	(16) .9	(16) 1.9	(15) 1.9
4.3	3.4	3.5		4.5	3.9	3.5	1.4	3.3	2.3
1.8	1.9	2.1		2.6	3.4	2.4	1.6		
(101) 3.7	(105) 3.9	(108) 4.6	% Officers', Directors' Owners' Comp/Sales	(31) 6.4	(37) 4.9	(13) 3.2	(17) 3.3		
6.2	7.1	8.1		12.0	7.8	10.6	6.6		
4825525M	2335787M	8305486M	Net Sales ($)	37226M	123205M	107726M	157553M	286918M	7592858M
1339671M	822299M	1679249M	Total Assets ($)	15559M	39414M	32018M	37829M	141480M	1412949M

M = $ thousand MM = $ million

See Pages 9 through 22 for Explanation of Ratios and Data

	Current Data Sorted by Assets						Comparative Historical Data	
Type of Statement								
Unqualified		2	1	3	1	2	15	11
Reviewed		3	15	5			20	24
Compiled	6	18	21	2		2	60	48
Tax Returns	87	68	28			4	224	211
Other	31	36	21	13	4	3	57	70
	49 (4/1-9/30/13)		327 (10/1/13-3/31/14)				4/1/09-3/31/10	4/1/10-3/31/11
	0-500M	500M-2MM	2-10MM	10-50MM	50-100MM	100-250MM	ALL	ALL
NUMBER OF STATEMENTS	124	127	86	23	5	11	376	364
ASSETS	%	%	%	%	%	%	%	%
Cash & Equivalents	14.5	13.0	15.2	7.1		3.7	11.4	12.5
Trade Receivables (net)	1.4	1.5	1.8	5.6		4.6	1.7	1.6
Inventory	49.8	51.0	45.7	41.7		57.7	46.8	47.1
All Other Current	1.4	1.7	.8	1.3		4.7	2.0	2.2
Total Current	67.1	67.1	63.5	55.7		70.7	61.9	63.4
Fixed Assets (net)	13.9	14.4	19.7	17.7		13.0	17.6	18.0
Intangibles (net)	13.1	13.1	10.0	15.7		14.5	15.0	13.4
All Other Non-Current	6.0	5.4	6.8	10.9		1.8	5.5	5.2
Total	100.0	100.0	100.0	100.0		100.0	100.0	100.0
LIABILITIES								
Notes Payable-Short Term	6.8	6.3	11.0	5.5		6.7	6.6	7.6
Cur. Mat.-L.T.D.	2.5	2.2	2.2	7.3		1.4	3.0	2.8
Trade Payables	13.9	18.5	21.6	17.0		17.7	14.6	16.1
Income Taxes Payable	.2	.1	.1	.3		.0	.1	.1
All Other Current	18.4	7.8	6.5	9.4		3.7	10.3	9.4
Total Current	41.7	34.9	41.5	39.5		29.4	34.6	36.1
Long-Term Debt	22.7	15.9	19.1	18.6		16.3	23.6	22.6
Deferred Taxes	.2	.0	.0	.2		.0	.0	.0
All Other Non-Current	15.5	11.3	7.9	4.2		1.6	12.5	14.6
Net Worth	20.0	37.9	31.5	37.5		52.6	29.3	26.7
Total Liabilties & Net Worth	100.0	100.0	100.0	100.0		100.0	100.0	100.0
INCOME DATA								
Net Sales	100.0	100.0	100.0	100.0		100.0	100.0	100.0
Gross Profit	26.8	22.6	22.9	25.9		21.8	23.0	24.0
Operating Expenses	24.8	19.6	19.2	21.2		19.7	21.2	22.2
Operating Profit	2.0	3.0	3.7	4.7		2.1	1.9	1.9
All Other Expenses (net)	-.2	-.1	.5	1.0		-.2	-.5	-.1
Profit Before Taxes	2.2	3.2	3.2	3.7		2.2	2.3	2.0
RATIOS								
Current	10.0	7.8	2.3	2.0		32.4	5.3	4.7
	2.2	2.4	1.5	1.5		2.3	2.1	2.0
	1.0	1.4	1.1	1.1		1.3	1.2	1.2
Quick	1.1	1.2	.7	.6		1.3	1.2	1.0
	(122) .4	.5	(85) .4	.2		.3	(370) .4	(360) .3
	.1	.1	.1	.1		.1	.1	.1
Sales/Receivables	**0** UND	**0** UND	**0** UND	**0** 999.8		**0** UND	**0** UND	**0** UND
	0 UND	**0** UND	**0** UND	**3** 138.0		**1** 516.8	**0** UND	**0** UND
	0 UND	**0** 999.8	**1** 286.4	**8** 48.1		**3** 127.8	**1** 552.4	**0** 999.8
Cost of Sales/Inventory	**24** 15.2	**47** 7.8	**41** 8.8	**50** 7.3		**54** 6.7	**40** 9.2	**37** 10.0
	42 8.6	**70** 5.2	**59** 6.2	**61** 6.0		**65** 5.6	**63** 5.8	**61** 6.0
	78 4.7	**104** 3.5	**94** 3.9	**135** 2.7		**99** 3.7	**88** 4.1	**93** 3.9
Cost of Sales/Payables	**0** UND	**0** UND	**7** 49.9	**14** 25.9		**0** UND	**0** UND	**0** UND
	1 609.0	**23** 16.1	**32** 11.3	**27** 13.5		**15** 24.7	**12** 30.1	**17** 21.0
	21 17.2	**41** 8.8	**45** 8.1	**55** 6.6		**41** 9.0	**33** 11.0	**34** 10.7
Sales/Working Capital	7.7	4.9	7.5	6.1		6.3	5.8	6.5
	17.0	8.8	16.9	19.6		10.1	12.1	12.6
	UND	24.2	69.7	107.9		39.5	32.9	48.1
EBIT/Interest	9.9	15.0	15.8	12.6			8.0	9.3
	(74) 4.1	(84) 4.4	(71) 6.0	4.8			(276) 3.2	(275) 3.2
	.5	1.5	1.8	3.7			1.1	1.1
Net Profit + Depr., Dep., Amort./Cur. Mat. L/T/D			2.8				7.5	5.1
			(10) 1.6				(21) 2.2	(14) 1.7
			.9				1.0	.4
Fixed/Worth	.0	.1	.1	.2		.0	.1	.1
	.4	.3	.6	.6		.3	.9	.9
	-2.8	-16.2	14.9	18.0		1.2	-1.7	-1.2
Debt/Worth	.6	.5	1.1	1.5		.1	.8	.9
	4.6	1.8	2.8	2.5		2.1	3.8	4.3
	-5.0	-13.0	-45.0	52.7		5.5	-7.4	-5.6
% Profit Before Taxes/Tangible Net Worth	61.7	50.0	69.5	94.7		50.0	63.5	50.2
	(77) 37.2	(91) 17.6	(64) 31.6	(18) 33.0		31.6	(249) 22.7	(233) 23.1
	7.0	7.4	7.0	7.8		10.8	9.3	7.9
% Profit Before Taxes/Total Assets	25.9	16.4	19.8	11.3		10.7	14.1	13.3
	9.1	6.4	6.7	5.8		8.3	6.1	5.9
	-.9	1.7	1.4	2.6		5.0	.8	.6
Sales/Net Fixed Assets	774.5	186.1	156.7	50.4		999.8	127.8	150.9
	94.1	46.2	37.2	28.0		38.1	37.1	39.7
	24.5	16.3	9.3	10.6		20.9	11.6	11.9
Sales/Total Assets	6.8	4.5	4.6	3.4		5.6	4.8	5.3
	4.9	3.3	3.1	2.4		3.8	3.1	3.3
	3.5	2.0	1.9	1.6		2.8	2.1	2.3
% Depr., Dep., Amort./Sales	.4	.3	.2	.5			.4	.3
	(65) .7	(82) .6	(70) .5	(21) .8			(261) .8	(255) .7
	1.4	1.5	.9	1.2			1.9	1.7
% Officers', Directors' Owners' Comp/Sales	1.8	1.7	.7				1.3	1.5
	(69) 3.2	(59) 3.1	(37) 1.9				(199) 2.5	(197) 2.7
	6.1	4.5	2.8				4.1	4.6
Net Sales ($)	158709M	440139M	1081676M	1215411M	679948M	8630977M	4940075M	9465836M
Total Assets ($)	32702M	127359M	338734M	506717M	358052M	2076168M	1589747M	2163357M

M = $ thousand MM = $ million

See Pages 9 through 22 for Explanation of Ratios and Data

Comparative Historical Data				Current Data Sorted by Sales					
			Type of Statement						
14	13	9	Unqualified		2			1	6
27	25	23	Reviewed			3	4	11	5
43	52	49	Compiled	3	11	5	11	13	6
231	192	187	Tax Returns	38	89	24	20	12	4
92	113	108	Other	22	25	14	13	14	20
4/1/11-3/31/12 ALL	**4/1/12-3/31/13 ALL**	**4/1/13-3/31/14 ALL**		**49 (4/1-9/30/13)**			**327 (10/1/13-3/31/14)**		
				0-1MM	**1-3MM**	**3-5MM**	**5-10MM**	**10-25MM**	**25MM & OVER**
407	395	376	**NUMBER OF STATEMENTS**	63	127	46	48	51	41
%	%	%	**ASSETS**	%	%	%	%	%	%
11.7	12.2	13.3	Cash & Equivalents	9.0	13.7	14.9	17.9	16.6	7.2
1.5	1.6	1.9	Trade Receivables (net)	1.8	1.1	1.4	1.8	1.7	5.5
48.7	46.4	49.0	Inventory	48.0	48.4	48.2	54.0	49.1	47.2
1.5	2.2	1.5	All Other Current	1.4	.9	3.7	.8	1.2	2.3
63.5	62.4	65.6	Total Current	60.2	64.0	68.2	74.5	68.6	62.1
18.0	17.3	15.6	Fixed Assets (net)	14.5	16.9	14.4	14.3	16.1	15.5
13.8	15.6	12.6	Intangibles (net)	17.5	12.8	11.6	8.5	7.9	15.9
4.7	4.7	6.2	All Other Non-Current	7.8	6.2	5.8	2.7	7.4	6.5
100.0	100.0	100.0	Total	100.0	100.0	100.0	100.0	100.0	100.0
			LIABILITIES						
6.1	6.6	7.8	Notes Payable-Short Term	9.2	5.3	5.2	10.5	11.7	8.1
2.4	2.3	2.6	Cur. Mat.-L.T.D.	1.8	2.9	2.0	1.5	2.6	4.7
17.9	15.1	17.5	Trade Payables	7.5	14.4	21.3	23.7	27.2	18.8
.1	.0	.1	Income Taxes Payable	.1	.2	.1	.1	.1	.2
9.7	11.5	11.0	All Other Current	16.9	13.8	4.6	8.0	8.2	7.3
36.3	35.5	38.9	Total Current	35.5	36.6	33.2	43.7	49.7	39.0
23.2	22.2	18.9	Long-Term Debt	30.7	18.6	19.7	18.4	8.4	14.7
.0	.0	.1	Deferred Taxes	.0	.2	.0	.0	.0	.2
18.1	13.7	11.1	All Other Non-Current	14.0	17.3	3.8	8.1	7.7	3.7
22.4	28.5	30.9	Net Worth	19.9	27.3	43.3	29.8	34.3	42.5
100.0	100.0	100.0	Total Liabilities & Net Worth	100.0	100.0	100.0	100.0	100.0	100.0
			INCOME DATA						
100.0	100.0	100.0	Net Sales	100.0	100.0	100.0	100.0	100.0	100.0
23.7	25.0	24.2	Gross Profit	27.0	25.0	23.1	21.4	23.3	23.1
22.7	21.7	21.3	Operating Expenses	25.5	21.9	20.0	18.2	20.1	19.5
1.0	3.4	2.9	Operating Profit	1.5	3.2	3.1	3.2	3.2	3.6
-.2	.2	.1	All Other Expenses (net)	-.1	-.1	.4	.0	.2	.5
1.2	3.2	2.9	Profit Before Taxes	1.6	3.3	2.7	3.2	3.0	3.1
			RATIOS						
5.1	5.9	4.6		15.0	10.3	4.5	2.8	1.8	2.0
2.1	1.9	1.8	Current	2.3	2.5	2.1	1.7	1.4	1.5
1.2	1.2	1.1		1.0	1.2	1.3	1.3	1.1	1.2
1.0	1.0	1.1		1.3	1.3	1.3	1.0	.6	.6
(403) .4	(390) .3	(373) .4	Quick	(61) .3	.4	(45) .5	.5	.4	.3
.1	.1	.1		.1	.1	.1	.1	.1	.1
0 UND	**0** UND	**0** UND		**0** UND	**0** UND	**0** UND	**0** UND	**0** UND	**0** 999.8
0 UND	**0** UND	**0** UND	Sales/Receivables	**0** UND	**0** UND	**0** UND	**0** UND	**0** 999.8	**2** 158.4
0 999.8	**0** 999.8	**1** 484.9		**0** UND	**0** UND	**1** 368.6	**1** 256.7	**1** 265.6	**8** 45.5
44 8.3	**39** 9.3	**38** 9.6		**34** 10.7	**35** 10.3	**36** 10.0	**42** 8.6	**41** 8.8	**43** 8.5
66 5.5	**60** 6.1	**60** 6.1	Cost of Sales/Inventory	**72** 5.1	**55** 6.6	**63** 5.8	**60** 6.1	**54** 6.8	**61** 6.0
96 3.8	**91** 4.0	**94** 3.9		**118** 3.1	**91** 4.0	**83** 4.4	**91** 4.0	**81** 4.5	**114** 3.2
0 UND	**0** UND	**0** UND		**0** UND	**0** UND	**4** 92.5	**6** 57.4	**12** 30.0	**10** 37.3
17 21.3	**12** 29.3	**15** 25.0	Cost of Sales/Payables	**0** UND	**3** 140.6	**25** 14.4	**36** 10.2	**33** 10.9	**25** 14.7
40 9.1	**35** 10.5	**38** 9.5		**16** 23.4	**33** 11.0	**42** 8.6	**43** 8.4	**45** 8.2	**39** 9.4
5.6	6.4	6.2		4.6	5.8	5.4	6.6	12.0	6.9
11.9	13.3	13.5	Sales/Working Capital	14.3	11.4	9.1	14.0	21.7	17.6
40.3	56.6	75.4		UND	125.5	42.8	24.2	123.8	38.7
8.4	14.1	13.6		5.3	13.0	16.7	16.3	22.8	13.1
(288) 3.1	(290) 4.6	(264) 4.5	EBIT/Interest	(36) 1.5	(78) 4.3	(35) 4.3	(38) 5.3	(43) 7.4	(34) 4.7
1.1	1.7	1.6		.1	1.4	.8	1.8	3.4	3.8
5.7	3.8	2.9							
(17) 2.0	(18) 2.2	(29) 1.7	Net Profit + Depr., Dep., Amort./Cur. Mat. L/T/D						
1.4	1.5	.8							
.1	.1	.1		.0	.0	.0	.1	.1	.2
.8	.7	.4	Fixed/Worth	.5	.5	.2	.3	.4	.6
-1.7	-1.5	NM		-8.8	-1.1	NM	7.3	1.8	1.8
1.1	.9	.8		.8	.5	.5	1.0	.9	1.5
5.6	3.9	2.8	Debt/Worth	7.3	4.2	1.4	2.5	2.5	2.5
-6.0	-7.0	-15.2		-5.1	-4.1	NM	-19.7	7.6	10.3
50.8	61.9	57.4		59.8	55.1	41.6	76.3	65.9	61.9
(254) 20.0	(257) 25.7	(265) 27.7	% Profit Before Taxes/Tangible Net Worth	(39) 23.2	(80) 28.7	(35) 19.3	(35) 29.1	(41) 34.0	(35) 31.6
6.9	11.2	7.5		2.1	7.9	2.5	9.6	7.0	10.8
12.1	16.9	18.7		18.9	18.7	19.7	20.3	20.0	11.2
4.9	7.5	7.3	% Profit Before Taxes/Total Assets	3.9	8.6	7.2	6.0	9.6	6.6
.3	1.8	1.4		-2.8	1.7	.9	1.7	2.0	4.2
127.3	181.7	215.7		804.0	506.0	194.8	172.5	173.5	58.8
36.8	42.1	44.8	Sales/Net Fixed Assets	79.7	46.2	63.2	51.8	37.6	36.4
11.4	12.5	16.4		14.6	16.4	19.1	20.7	17.2	13.0
4.7	5.1	5.1		5.4	5.4	4.8	5.3	5.2	3.8
3.2	3.3	3.6	Sales/Total Assets	3.4	3.7	3.8	3.6	4.0	3.1
2.1	2.1	2.3		1.5	2.4	1.8	2.7	2.3	2.3
.3	.3	.3		.5	.5	.3	.2	.2	.5
(282) .8	(253) .8	(248) .6	% Depr., Dep., Amort./Sales	(25) 1.1	(81) 1.0	(31) .8	(35) .4	(43) .4	(33) .7
1.7	1.5	1.3		2.7	2.0	1.0	.6	.9	1.1
1.5	1.5	1.5		1.7	1.9	.9	1.7	.6	
(217) 2.5	(206) 2.7	(175) 2.6	% Officers', Directors' Owners' Comp/Sales	(31) 3.2	(70) 3.3	(22) 2.2	(23) 2.6	(20) 1.5	
4.7	4.4	4.3		5.7	5.9	3.3	3.2	2.1	
5571192M	**6397633M**	**12206860M**	Net Sales ($)	**41265M**	**230493M**	**171680M**	**331233M**	**783754M**	**10648435M**
1906791M	**2176456M**	**3439732M**	Total Assets ($)	**18742M**	**80732M**	**64838M**	**99714M**	**262241M**	**2913465M**

M = $ thousand MM = $ million

See Pages 9 through 22 for Explanation of Ratios and Data

Current Data Sorted by Assets							Comparative Historical Data	
1	2	2	9	3	4	**Type of Statement** Unqualified	19	29
2	10	15	4			Reviewed	32	35
15	29	27	5	1		Compiled	73	69
62	111	30				Tax Returns	160	146
13	60	33	25	3	9	Other	114	118
56 (4/1-9/30/13)			419 (10/1/13-3/31/14)				4/1/09-3/31/10 ALL	4/1/10-3/31/11 ALL
0-500M	**500M-2MM**	**2-10MM**	**10-50MM**	**50-100MM**	**100-250MM**			
93	212	107	43	7	13	**NUMBER OF STATEMENTS**	398	397
%	%	%	%	%	%	**ASSETS**	%	%
21.1	15.3	12.5	13.0		7.7	Cash & Equivalents	11.9	10.6
13.9	21.0	30.5	29.4		19.3	Trade Receivables (net)	24.8	25.0
42.7	32.8	24.4	23.5		22.4	Inventory	32.6	34.1
.7	2.1	1.5	2.9		1.5	All Other Current	1.4	2.0
78.4	71.3	68.9	68.8		50.9	Total Current	70.7	71.8
14.1	12.5	14.9	11.8		10.4	Fixed Assets (net)	12.4	12.7
3.1	8.5	7.9	13.7		35.9	Intangibles (net)	7.6	8.3
4.4	7.7	8.3	5.7		2.8	All Other Non-Current	9.4	7.2
100.0	100.0	100.0	100.0		100.0	Total	100.0	100.0
						LIABILITIES		
8.7	6.9	9.4	7.8		4.4	Notes Payable-Short Term	11.2	9.4
2.0	2.2	2.8	4.1		1.4	Cur. Mat.-L.T.D.	3.4	4.0
23.7	23.8	26.6	21.8		20.5	Trade Payables	27.0	24.8
.0	.1	.2	.0		.2	Income Taxes Payable	.1	.1
13.3	7.1	8.3	10.5		5.9	All Other Current	9.1	9.4
47.6	40.1	47.2	44.2		32.4	Total Current	50.9	47.7
16.4	19.3	14.4	10.6		25.0	Long-Term Debt	15.1	15.3
.0	.0	.0	.3		.5	Deferred Taxes	.1	.1
15.0	7.2	4.8	3.3		9.9	All Other Non-Current	5.7	5.6
20.9	33.4	33.6	41.5		32.1	Net Worth	28.2	31.3
100.0	100.0	100.0	100.0		100.0	Total Liabilities & Net Worth	100.0	100.0
						INCOME DATA		
100.0	100.0	100.0	100.0		100.0	Net Sales	100.0	100.0
26.3	28.6	30.8	31.2		27.7	Gross Profit	26.8	26.0
25.4	25.8	26.0	22.5		24.1	Operating Expenses	23.7	23.5
.9	2.9	4.7	8.7		3.6	Operating Profit	3.1	2.4
-.1	-.1	.4	.4		1.5	All Other Expenses (net)	.2	.2
1.0	3.0	4.4	8.3		2.1	Profit Before Taxes	2.9	2.2
						RATIOS		
5.3	3.6	2.0	2.8		2.8		2.6	2.6
2.1	2.0	1.5	1.6		1.8	Current	1.6	1.6
1.2	1.3	1.1	1.1		1.2		1.1	1.1
2.0	1.8	1.3	1.8		1.8		1.4	1.3
1.0	1.0	.8	1.0		1.0	Quick	.8	(395) .8
.4	.5	.6	.7		.6		.5	.5
0 UND	**4** 89.4	**15** 24.1	**21** 17.7		**18** 20.5		**8** 46.2	**9** 42.2
4 102.9	**13** 28.1	**26** 14.2	**27** 13.7		**22** 16.3	Sales/Receivables	**19** 18.7	**19** 19.3
16 22.9	**21** 17.4	**36** 10.1	**38** 9.5		**38** 9.6		**28** 12.8	**29** 12.8
16 22.8	**20** 18.3	**18** 20.8	**20** 18.2		**15** 23.9		**20** 18.0	**21** 17.5
28 13.2	**31** 11.6	**32** 11.5	**31** 11.6		**22** 16.9	Cost of Sales/Inventory	**31** 11.9	**32** 11.3
42 8.7	**44** 8.3	**48** 7.6	**65** 5.6		**64** 5.7		**45** 8.1	**47** 7.8
1 584.8	**10** 36.4	**18** 19.9	**17** 21.3		**20** 18.7		**13** 27.1	**13** 28.7
15 23.7	**19** 19.5	**31** 11.9	**27** 13.3		**31** 11.9	Cost of Sales/Payables	**23** 15.6	**23** 16.0
27 13.7	**31** 11.6	**42** 8.7	**38** 9.5		**43** 8.5		**41** 8.9	**36** 10.1
9.6	9.1	9.0	7.4		8.1		10.3	10.2
18.2	14.7	18.4	15.3		11.9	Sales/Working Capital	20.8	18.6
75.0	35.3	57.3	51.9		32.3		111.4	82.7
18.8	19.1	21.0	57.0		36.1		18.5	17.3
(48) 3.7	(144) 4.8	(85) 4.8	(36) 12.5		5.6	EBIT/Interest	(319) 4.9	(317) 4.3
-1.3	1.1	1.4	2.5		2.0		1.4	1.3
		16.8					4.6	4.3
		(13) 2.2				Net Profit + Depr., Dep., Amort./Cur. Mat. L/T/D	(45) 1.4	(48) 1.3
		.8					.7	.3
.1	.1	.1	.1		.6		.1	.1
.4	.3	.4	.5		-.4	Fixed/Worth	.4	.4
UND	-22.3	1.6	4.4		-.1		3.9	3.0
.6	.5	.8	.7		2.1		.9	.9
2.0	1.8	2.4	1.9		-6.0	Debt/Worth	2.8	2.7
-24.5	-39.7	10.3	47.2		-1.8		44.6	27.5
123.2	78.0	88.5	63.2				88.1	82.8
(67) 41.6	(155) 26.4	(86) 30.2	(33) 47.7			% Profit Before Taxes/Tangible Net Worth	(305) 33.5	(314) 27.1
-1.3	5.6	6.1	25.2				10.6	4.2
45.7	25.2	23.9	34.3		8.8		22.6	19.9
11.9	8.2	7.2	14.2		5.5	% Profit Before Taxes/Total Assets	9.3	7.8
-4.2	.9	1.0	8.7		3.2		1.3	.5
449.1	239.9	138.4	168.4		94.9		180.2	200.1
108.5	76.4	48.3	45.3		34.2	Sales/Net Fixed Assets	58.0	59.5
30.4	27.7	15.8	20.5		18.2		25.3	23.9
11.3	6.6	5.4	4.8		3.9		6.5	6.8
6.9	4.8	3.8	3.7		2.5	Sales/Total Assets	4.6	4.6
4.7	3.7	3.0	2.6		1.3		3.5	3.4
.1	.1	.2	.3				.2	.2
(56) .4	(132) .4	(75) .7	(36) .8			% Depr., Dep., Amort./Sales	(288) .6	(275) .5
.7	1.1	1.3	1.7				1.1	1.0
2.5	2.3	1.3					1.5	1.7
(49) 4.1	(141) 3.4	(51) 2.1				% Officers', Directors' Owners' Comp/Sales	(218) 2.8	(188) 3.1
6.3	6.0	3.6					4.3	5.7
236486M	1241767M	1774933M	3213008M	1444638M	6615945M	Net Sales ($)	8741307M	13061035M
28811M	233202M	426314M	965569M	513502M	2328891M	Total Assets ($)	2596477M	3912816M

M = $ thousand MM = $ million

See Pages 9 through 22 for Explanation of Ratios and Data

Comparative Historical Data				Current Data Sorted by Sales					
			Type of Statement						
27	19	21	Unqualified	1		1	2	1	16
30	30	31	Reviewed		2	2	6	13	8
73	51	77	Compiled	2	16	8	23	19	9
206	170	203	Tax Returns	8	49	61	54	29	2
95	140	143	Other	3	27	24	23	27	39
4/1/11-3/31/12	**4/1/12-3/31/13**	**4/1/13-3/31/14**		**56 (4/1-9/30/13)**		**419 (10/1/13-3/31/14)**			
ALL	**ALL**	**ALL**		**0-1MM**	**1-3MM**	**3-5MM**	**5-10MM**	**10-25MM**	**25MM & OVER**
431	410	475	**NUMBER OF STATEMENTS**	14	94	96	108	89	74
%	%	%	**ASSETS**	%	%	%	%	%	%
13.4	14.1	15.2	Cash & Equivalents	14.9	17.3	15.8	16.2	14.5	11.3
23.4	24.0	22.5	Trade Receivables (net)	5.9	16.3	17.2	22.1	30.8	31.0
33.5	32.4	31.6	Inventory	35.6	37.2	36.2	30.9	27.5	23.5
1.8	2.0	1.8	All Other Current	.4	.6	2.6	1.0	2.9	2.2
72.1	72.6	71.1	Total Current	56.8	71.3	71.8	70.3	75.8	68.0
11.4	12.1	13.3	Fixed Assets (net)	32.5	14.0	13.3	12.9	11.6	11.2
9.6	8.1	8.8	Intangibles (net)	2.9	9.0	8.1	7.9	5.8	15.4
7.0	7.2	6.9	All Other Non-Current	7.8	5.6	6.9	8.9	6.7	5.4
100.0	100.0	100.0	Total	100.0	100.0	100.0	100.0	100.0	100.0
			LIABILITIES						
10.9	7.3	7.7	Notes Payable-Short Term	6.7	10.2	5.3	6.0	10.1	7.6
2.8	3.8	2.5	Cur. Mat.-L.T.D.	.0	1.3	3.3	2.3	2.8	3.3
25.0	25.0	24.1	Trade Payables	13.5	18.4	24.5	23.6	31.2	24.8
.2	.1	.1	Income Taxes Payable	.0	.0	.0	.2	.0	.1
9.2	7.7	9.0	All Other Current	13.4	8.8	8.0	10.1	8.3	8.5
48.0	44.0	43.3	Total Current	33.7	38.8	41.2	42.3	52.3	44.4
16.7	16.9	16.9	Long-Term Debt	25.2	22.1	24.1	13.5	9.7	13.0
.1	.0	.1	Deferred Taxes	.0	.0	.0	.0	.1	.3
6.0	6.2	7.9	All Other Non-Current	20.6	13.2	7.7	6.7	4.7	4.4
29.3	32.9	31.8	Net Worth	20.5	25.9	26.9	37.5	33.2	37.9
100.0	100.0	100.0	Total Liabilties & Net Worth	100.0	100.0	100.0	100.0	100.0	100.0
			INCOME DATA						
100.0	100.0	100.0	Net Sales	100.0	100.0	100.0	100.0	100.0	100.0
26.1	27.5	28.8	Gross Profit	45.7	27.3	27.2	30.9	28.2	27.0
23.2	24.2	25.3	Operating Expenses	51.7	24.6	24.2	27.4	24.2	21.1
2.9	3.3	3.4	Operating Profit	-6.0	2.8	3.0	3.5	4.0	5.9
.1	.1	.1	All Other Expenses (net)	.8	.2	.0	-.3	.1	.4
2.8	3.2	3.4	Profit Before Taxes	-6.9	2.5	3.0	3.8	3.8	5.5
			RATIOS						
3.0	3.2	3.4		7.5	5.0	4.6	3.4	2.0	2.7
1.7	1.8	1.8	Current	2.7	2.2	2.0	1.9	1.5	1.6
1.2	1.2	1.2		1.1	1.5	1.3	1.2	1.1	1.1
1.6	1.6	1.7		1.6	1.9	1.8	1.9	1.3	1.6
(430) .9	.9	.9	Quick	1.0	1.2	.9	1.0	.8	1.0
.5	.5	.5		.4	.5	.5	.5	.6	.6
7 55.9	7 50.2	5 72.6		0 UND	0 UND	2 210.5	5 78.3	14 27.0	20 18.7
17 21.4	17 21.7	16 22.4	Sales/Receivables	0 UND	13 28.0	12 31.6	14 25.9	20 18.5	26 14.3
27 13.6	27 13.7	26 13.8		18 20.5	20 18.2	19 19.0	23 15.6	34 10.8	35 10.3
19 19.1	19 19.1	18 20.1		0 UND	24 15.4	21 17.5	18 20.5	15 24.3	16 23.2
31 11.9	31 11.9	30 12.0	Cost of Sales/Inventory	83 4.4	34 10.8	33 11.2	30 12.1	26 14.2	25 14.4
44 8.3	45 8.2	47 7.8		159 2.3	51 7.2	45 8.2	40 9.2	41 9.0	52 7.0
11 32.9	12 29.9	12 29.4		17 21.1	4 85.2	7 53.9	10 35.5	17 20.9	19 19.0
21 17.6	21 17.7	22 16.8	Cost of Sales/Payables	46 8.0	17 21.4	17 22.0	20 18.3	28 13.2	29 12.8
34 10.8	35 10.4	35 10.4		59 6.2	28 12.9	30 12.2	35 10.5	37 9.8	39 9.4
9.8	9.4	9.1		4.6	7.5	9.9	9.5	12.7	8.8
18.8	15.9	16.0	Sales/Working Capital	7.4	12.6	14.3	18.2	23.5	15.9
56.1	53.6	51.0		NM	28.5	38.9	54.1	59.4	58.5
19.3	21.8	21.8			6.2	12.4	28.1	22.5	60.8
(318) 4.5	(301) 7.2	(333) 5.2	EBIT/Interest		(50) 2.3	(65) 3.2	(80) 7.5	(69) 5.2	(64) 12.0
1.5	1.7	1.2			-1.1	.9	1.7	2.2	2.0
4.8	18.5	11.0						3.6	15.0
(27) 1.1	(27) 2.6	(36) 2.1	Net Profit + Depr., Dep., Amort./Cur. Mat. L/T/D					(10) 1.9	(15) 3.2
.3	.8	.2						.0	.0
.1	.1	.1		.4	.1	.1	.1	.1	.1
.4	.3	.4	Fixed/Worth	UND	.4	.6	.2	.3	.5
5.1	3.2	149.0		-2.9	-1.9	-.9	1.1	.9	-7.7
.8	.7	.7		.3	.6	.7	.5	.8	.7
3.1	2.2	2.1	Debt/Worth	UND	1.9	2.6	1.7	2.3	2.6
-69.7	52.0	-93.3		-5.3	-7.8	-10.8	17.7	7.4	-66.4
83.8	92.5	80.5			69.7	76.8	81.8	100.3	96.5
(321) 32.7	(317) 36.4	(351) 32.5	% Profit Before Taxes/Tangible Net Worth		(65) 35.0	(66) 26.2	(86) 29.9	(71) 30.1	(55) 50.0
5.4	9.4	7.1			10.4	2.8	6.3	6.2	21.9
22.0	26.4	26.9		7.8	24.3	25.0	29.5	26.6	33.8
8.2	11.1	9.5	% Profit Before Taxes/Total Assets	-4.5	9.4	9.5	8.2	10.5	11.0
1.2	1.7	1.0		-34.4	-.9	.2	2.3	2.6	4.1
305.2	267.7	213.9		41.2	234.8	244.8	342.3	157.8	157.5
78.7	71.8	64.5	Sales/Net Fixed Assets	13.8	58.8	78.6	91.6	71.7	44.0
28.5	26.5	23.0		3.7	22.5	26.8	30.6	23.1	20.8
7.0	7.0	6.5		4.9	6.5	6.8	6.7	7.5	5.3
4.8	4.8	4.7	Sales/Total Assets	2.3	4.5	4.6	4.9	5.3	3.7
3.4	3.4	3.3		.8	3.2	3.5	3.6	3.7	2.7
.2	.2	.2		.6	.2	.2	.1	.1	.3
(283) .5	(262) .5	(314) .5	% Depr., Dep., Amort./Sales	(10) 2.6	(52) .6	(55) .4	(72) .3	(68) .5	(57) .8
1.1	1.0	1.1		10.2	1.1	1.1	.8	1.0	1.5
1.6	1.9	2.0			2.4	2.6	2.1	1.6	.4
(235) 3.0	(221) 3.1	(247) 3.2	% Officers', Directors' Owners' Comp/Sales		(51) 4.6	(61) 3.8	(72) 3.2	(48) 2.2	(12) 1.1
5.6	5.1	5.6			6.2	6.0	4.9	3.3	2.9
11292037M	11559485M	14526777M	Net Sales ($)	8439M	191972M	381132M	769419M	1360280M	11815535M
3326681M	3008065M	4496289M	Total Assets ($)	8783M	50541M	85352M	179460M	349200M	3822953M

M = $ thousand MM = $ million

See Pages 9 through 22 for Explanation of Ratios and Data

Current Data Sorted by Assets							Comparative Historical Data	
						Type of Statement		
		2	2	3	3	Unqualified	10	7
	1	5	2			Reviewed	5	4
	5	8	1			Compiled	12	5
8	6	4	1			Tax Returns	20	25
4	15	12	2	6	1	Other	25	28
7 (4/1-9/30/13)			84 (10/1/13-3/31/14)				4/1/09-3/31/10 ALL	4/1/10-3/31/11 ALL
0-500M	500M-2MM	2-10MM	10-50MM	50-100MM	100-250MM			
12	27	31	8	9	4	NUMBER OF STATEMENTS	72	69
%	%	%	%	%	%	**ASSETS**	%	%
13.4	10.8	13.6				Cash & Equivalents	12.6	14.4
.0	8.1	12.9				Trade Receivables (net)	13.1	11.5
67.1	60.4	44.5				Inventory	44.4	41.4
2.3	.3	1.6				All Other Current	3.4	3.0
82.9	79.7	72.5				Total Current	73.5	70.4
3.7	13.0	11.2				Fixed Assets (net)	16.9	16.7
1.8	2.7	2.5				Intangibles (net)	3.8	9.0
11.6	4.6	13.7				All Other Non-Current	5.8	3.9
100.0	100.0	100.0				Total	100.0	100.0
						LIABILITIES		
4.1	6.7	9.5				Notes Payable-Short Term	11.0	11.5
2.6	1.5	2.2				Cur. Mat.-L.T.D.	2.2	3.5
4.8	10.6	20.3				Trade Payables	19.9	20.2
.0	.0	.0				Income Taxes Payable	.1	.2
14.6	16.4	6.1				All Other Current	12.4	7.5
26.1	35.2	38.2				Total Current	45.7	42.9
44.9	16.6	12.2				Long-Term Debt	14.3	14.0
.0	.0	.0				Deferred Taxes	.2	.1
27.7	14.9	2.8				All Other Non-Current	8.1	6.4
1.4	33.3	46.9				Net Worth	31.7	36.5
100.0	100.0	100.0				Total Liabilities & Net Worth	100.0	100.0
						INCOME DATA		
100.0	100.0	100.0				Net Sales	100.0	100.0
49.4	43.6	48.4				Gross Profit	47.7	47.7
45.5	38.7	39.3				Operating Expenses	43.5	41.0
3.9	4.9	9.1				Operating Profit	4.1	6.7
.6	.3	-.1				All Other Expenses (net)	.8	1.0
3.3	4.6	9.2				Profit Before Taxes	3.3	5.7
						RATIOS		
23.9	11.7	5.0					4.1	3.4
4.4	3.0	1.8				Current	1.7	1.9
1.6	1.9	1.2					1.1	1.1
1.5	1.3	1.6					1.3	1.2
.8	.4	.7				Quick	.6	.5
.2	.1	.3					.2	.2
0 UND	**0** UND	**0** 999.8					**0** UND	**1** 391.1
0 UND	**0** UND	**13** 27.4				Sales/Receivables	**7** 54.1	**10** 35.3
0 UND	**13** 27.9	**31** 11.7					**32** 11.3	**30** 12.1
58 6.3	**65** 5.6	**66** 5.5					**68** 5.3	**69** 5.3
140 2.6	**146** 2.5	**135** 2.7				Cost of Sales/Inventory	**112** 3.3	**112** 3.3
243 1.5	**281** 1.3	**215** 1.7					**165** 2.2	**176** 2.1
0 UND	**0** UND	**20** 18.5					**26** 14.2	**15** 24.1
0 UND	**20** 18.5	**46** 7.9				Cost of Sales/Payables	**34** 10.7	**32** 11.5
0 UND	**61** 6.0	**96** 3.8					**56** 6.5	**68** 5.3
3.0	3.1	3.2					4.0	4.5
5.3	5.2	8.0				Sales/Working Capital	9.9	9.8
33.7	12.7	32.3					56.0	77.3
	15.1	34.4					10.9	20.1
	(18) 6.3	(25) 13.8				EBIT/Interest	(53) 3.2	(48) 4.8
	3.2	4.5					-.4	.6
								24.4
						Net Profit + Depr., Dep., Amort./Cur. Mat. L/T/D		(10) 5.2
								1.9
.0	.0	.0					.0	.0
.1	.0	.2				Fixed/Worth	.3	.3
.3	1.3	.8					1.3	3.5
.3	.5	.4					.6	.5
1.5	1.6	1.2				Debt/Worth	1.6	1.8
UND	7.1	2.3					8.2	25.6
238.5	78.2	73.0					54.3	87.3
(10) 21.7	(22) 37.5	(29) 46.3				% Profit Before Taxes/Tangible Net Worth	(57) 16.7	(53) 29.6
9.9	11.4	12.1					.5	7.7
20.7	38.1	36.0					19.9	24.2
8.5	7.0	17.2				% Profit Before Taxes/Total Assets	5.3	7.5
2.9	1.9	4.7					-4.2	.4
UND	407.1	149.3					179.8	273.2
137.4	93.5	40.2				Sales/Net Fixed Assets	44.0	31.9
43.9	17.3	14.0					7.0	9.0
9.6	4.2	3.0					3.5	3.6
2.8	2.6	2.2				Sales/Total Assets	2.7	2.5
2.5	1.6	1.9					1.9	1.5
	.1	.4					.2	.3
	(13) .3	(23) .6				% Depr., Dep., Amort./Sales	(46) 1.3	(45) 1.5
	2.2	1.7					3.2	3.0
	1.8	1.3					1.3	1.3
	(14) 3.5	(13) 2.6				% Officers', Directors' Owners' Comp/Sales	(26) 3.4	(28) 2.4
	5.8	5.6					7.7	5.1
16430M	105344M	368228M	382074M	663107M	1012686M	Net Sales ($)	1714207M	1663577M
2303M	29831M	147534M	214696M	691970M	606793M	Total Assets ($)	765714M	932739M

M = $ thousand MM = $ million

See Pages 9 through 22 for Explanation of Ratios and Data

Comparative Historical Data / Current Data Sorted by Sales

4/1/11-3/31/12 ALL	4/1/12-3/31/13 ALL	4/1/13-3/31/14 ALL		0-1MM	1-3MM	3-5MM	5-10MM	10-25MM	25MM & OVER
			Type of Statement						
5	8	10	Unqualified				1	1	8
4	4	8	Reviewed				1	5	2
11	5	14	Compiled		4	1	3	5	1
32	38	19	Tax Returns	10	2	1	4	2	
31	37	40	Other	4	8	3	8	8	9
				7 (4/1-9/30/13)			84 (10/1/13-3/31/14)		
83	92	91	**NUMBER OF STATEMENTS**	14	14	5	17	21	20
%	%	%	**ASSETS**	%	%	%	%	%	%
12.9	12.8	11.4	Cash & Equivalents	10.1	7.9		13.4	16.8	7.9
10.8	11.7	9.7	Trade Receivables (net)	.1	6.1		17.8	10.5	13.2
47.9	44.1	48.1	Inventory	67.2	64.8		38.1	49.8	25.0
2.5	1.9	2.5	All Other Current	2.0	.3		1.5	1.4	7.1
74.2	70.4	71.7	Total Current	79.4	79.1		70.9	78.5	53.2
14.8	13.4	11.1	Fixed Assets (net)	11.0	7.0		15.3	11.2	11.7
6.9	4.8	8.2	Intangibles (net)	1.7	3.4		3.8	.7	28.6
4.2	11.5	9.0	All Other Non-Current	7.9	10.5		10.0	9.6	6.5
100.0	100.0	100.0	Total	100.0	100.0		100.0	100.0	100.0
			LIABILITIES						
10.4	6.0	6.8	Notes Payable-Short Term	2.7	8.8		8.6	10.2	4.5
1.9	2.7	2.0	Cur. Mat.-L.T.D.	3.1	1.1		1.9	2.2	2.1
17.3	13.4	13.4	Trade Payables	4.4	4.6		20.8	22.2	11.4
.1	.0	.0	Income Taxes Payable	.0	.0		.0	.0	.1
8.4	8.0	12.3	All Other Current	14.5	27.7		5.6	5.4	15.3
38.0	30.1	34.5	Total Current	24.7	42.2		37.0	39.9	33.4
11.3	17.5	18.5	Long-Term Debt	49.2	17.5		13.6	9.3	14.6
.2	.2	.5	Deferred Taxes	.0	.0		.0	.0	2.5
8.4	18.1	10.6	All Other Non-Current	22.5	11.9		10.6	3.6	7.1
42.1	34.1	35.9	Net Worth	3.6	28.4		38.8	47.2	42.4
100.0	100.0	100.0	Total Liabilties & Net Worth	100.0	100.0		100.0	100.0	100.0
			INCOME DATA						
100.0	100.0	100.0	Net Sales	100.0	100.0		100.0	100.0	100.0
42.0	49.0	47.3	Gross Profit	50.4	47.2		51.5	41.3	50.0
35.8	39.9	40.6	Operating Expenses	44.6	45.2		43.5	33.4	42.8
6.2	9.1	6.7	Operating Profit	5.8	1.9		8.0	7.8	7.2
.5	.1	.6	All Other Expenses (net)	1.2	-.2		-.1	.0	2.1
5.7	9.0	6.1	Profit Before Taxes	4.6	2.1		8.0	7.8	5.1
			RATIOS						
4.5	4.8	5.0		14.1	13.6		5.8	3.0	2.2
2.1	2.4	2.2	Current	3.5	3.4		2.1	2.2	1.6
1.4	1.5	1.3		1.8	1.4		1.0	1.3	1.1
1.2	1.5	1.3		1.2	1.0		2.9	.9	1.0
.6	(91) .8	.6	Quick	.4	.4		1.2	.5	.6
.3	.5	.2		.2	.1		.3	.2	.3
0 UND	**0** UND	**0** UND		**0** UND	**0** UND		**0** 999.8	**0** UND	**4** 82.5
5 67.1	**5** 68.8	**5** 73.1	Sales/Receivables	**0** UND	**0** UND		**28** 13.1	**7** 50.9	**28** 13.1
28 13.0	**20** 18.5	**31** 11.9		**0** UND	**9** 42.2		**33** 11.1	**29** 12.4	**50** 7.3
61 6.0	**57** 6.4	**66** 5.5		**114** 3.2	**126** 2.9		**56** 6.5	**45** 8.2	**81** 4.5
122 3.0	**91** 4.0	**140** 2.6	Cost of Sales/Inventory	**215** 1.7	**228** 1.6		**130** 2.8	**89** 4.1	**126** 2.9
182 2.0	**146** 2.5	**228** 1.6		**332** 1.1	**281** 1.3		**159** 2.3	**215** 1.7	**174** 2.1
11 33.4	**12** 29.5	**0** UND		**0** UND	**0** UND		**20** 18.5	**19** 19.2	**35** 10.4
33 10.9	**26** 14.0	**33** 11.0	Cost of Sales/Payables	**0** UND	**0** UND		**33** 11.0	**47** 7.8	**45** 8.2
64 5.7	**47** 7.7	**66** 5.5		**0** UND	**45** 8.2		**101** 3.6	**76** 4.8	**64** 5.7
3.4	4.7	3.3		2.2	3.0		3.1	4.6	5.2
7.3	8.9	6.2	Sales/Working Capital	4.0	3.7		7.9	9.0	8.5
25.4	24.3	24.2		5.6	22.5		NM	28.3	35.2
34.5	28.0	27.1					26.7	38.5	38.7
(53) 4.1	(47) 3.7	(68) 7.0	EBIT/Interest				(13) 10.1	(18) 18.0	4.2
.1	1.2	2.6					3.0	4.4	1.0
	14.6		Net Profit + Depr., Dep.,						
	(11) 2.6		Amort./Cur. Mat. L/T/D						
	.9								
.0	.0	.0		.0	.0		.0	.0	.1
.3	.2	.2	Fixed/Worth	.1	.1		.2	.1	.7
.9	1.2	1.2		UND	NM		1.4	.6	-.4
.5	.3	.6		.5	.5		.3	.6	.8
1.1	1.2	1.6	Debt/Worth	1.6	1.7		2.1	1.2	3.4
6.6	3.6	8.8		UND	NM		10.9	1.9	-3.7
80.2	99.5	77.5	% Profit Before Taxes/Tangible	163.4	42.3		69.7	109.4	84.5
(74) 26.4	(79) 31.0	(75) 39.7	Net Worth	(11) 25.8	(11) 17.6		(15) 46.3	59.0	(13) 51.0
5.7	6.3	9.7		7.7	5.7		10.9	10.1	2.7
24.5	39.9	26.0	% Profit Before Taxes/Total	24.0	17.1		37.3	40.1	13.6
9.6	16.4	7.9	Assets	6.9	6.2		18.0	17.1	7.5
1.1	2.9	2.7		1.3	1.8		4.0	3.6	-.7
118.8	999.8	174.8		UND	254.2		546.9	339.0	38.5
35.8	86.5	45.3	Sales/Net Fixed Assets	104.0	72.6		56.3	49.6	22.8
12.4	11.8	15.5		30.0	27.0		18.6	9.7	8.7
3.5	4.3	3.2		3.6	3.3		3.9	5.5	1.9
2.8	2.9	2.2	Sales/Total Assets	2.5	2.3		2.7	2.5	1.7
1.8	2.0	1.7		1.3	1.6		2.0	2.0	.7
.4	.3	.4					.6	.3	1.4
(55) 1.0	(48) .9	(55) 1.1	% Depr., Dep., Amort./Sales				(12) 1.0	(13) .5	(14) 2.0
2.2	1.7	2.4					2.2	1.9	3.2
1.4	1.6	1.4	% Officers', Directors'						
(36) 2.5	(43) 5.3	(36) 3.5	Owners' Comp/Sales						
7.0	8.4	6.6							
1753518M	2271617M	2547869M	Net Sales ($)	7476M	27347M	18860M	125338M	322114M	2046734M
921832M	919254M	1693127M	Total Assets ($)	5459M	13461M	9084M	47168M	115146M	1502809M

M = $ thousand MM = $ million

See Pages 9 through 22 for Explanation of Ratios and Data

Current Data Sorted by Assets							Comparative Historical Data	
						Type of Statement		
			2			Unqualified	2	3
		1	1			Reviewed	2	3
		2	1			Compiled	5	4
13	4					Tax Returns	22	25
2	2	6	2	2		Other	21	10
3 (4/1-9/30/13)		35 (10/1/13-3/31/14)					4/1/09-3/31/10 ALL	4/1/10-3/31/11 ALL
0-500M	500M-2MM	2-10MM	10-50MM	50-100MM	100-250MM			
15	6	9	6	2		**NUMBER OF STATEMENTS**	52	45
%	%	%	%	%	%	**ASSETS**	%	%
23.7					DATA NOT AVAILABLE	Cash & Equivalents	13.4	14.4
7.8						Trade Receivables (net)	9.1	12.9
21.4						Inventory	26.3	28.1
.0						All Other Current	2.5	1.8
52.9						Total Current	51.3	57.2
29.5						Fixed Assets (net)	25.7	25.0
16.7						Intangibles (net)	10.3	11.9
.9						All Other Non-Current	12.6	5.9
100.0						Total	100.0	100.0
						LIABILITIES		
9.8						Notes Payable-Short Term	5.8	8.5
.9						Cur. Mat.-L.T.D.	7.1	5.5
9.2						Trade Payables	19.9	18.0
.0						Income Taxes Payable	.0	.2
5.1						All Other Current	21.8	11.9
24.9						Total Current	54.7	44.1
8.1						Long-Term Debt	17.3	24.1
.0						Deferred Taxes	.1	.0
.2						All Other Non-Current	8.6	9.8
66.7						Net Worth	19.3	22.0
100.0						Total Liabilties & Net Worth	100.0	100.0
						INCOME DATA		
100.0						Net Sales	100.0	100.0
59.9						Gross Profit	58.5	61.2
52.4						Operating Expenses	52.9	54.9
7.6						Operating Profit	5.6	6.3
.6						All Other Expenses (net)	.5	.6
7.0						Profit Before Taxes	5.1	5.7
						RATIOS		
7.0							2.2	2.4
2.5						Current	1.3	1.4
1.1							.9	.9
5.8							.8	1.1
2.1						Quick	.4	.6
.2							.1	.3
0 UND							**0** UND	**0** UND
0 UND						Sales/Receivables	**1** 404.6	**10** 35.1
6 66.1							**16** 23.2	**20** 18.3
8 46.4							**35** 10.5	**52** 7.1
48 7.6						Cost of Sales/Inventory	**90** 4.0	**80** 4.6
72 5.1							**183** 2.0	**117** 3.1
0 UND							**21** 17.4	**22** 16.7
7 51.3						Cost of Sales/Payables	**46** 8.0	**41** 9.0
29 12.5							**122** 3.0	**61** 6.0
5.9							12.6	12.4
46.8						Sales/Working Capital	30.3	22.3
380.7							-38.8	-50.9
							27.6	20.7
						EBIT/Interest	(36) 4.4	(35) 6.8
							2.3	2.5
						Net Profit + Depr., Dep., Amort./Cur. Mat. L/T/D		
.1							.3	.3
.9						Fixed/Worth	.8	.7
1.4							NM	-2.6
.1							.8	.7
.4						Debt/Worth	3.3	2.3
11.2							-11.6	-7.5
146.6							145.1	110.9
(12) 47.9						% Profit Before Taxes/Tangible Net Worth	(38) 66.4	(32) 56.7
12.9							30.5	19.7
55.1							30.0	36.6
20.8						% Profit Before Taxes/Total Assets	9.3	13.0
.0							1.6	4.5
197.5							69.5	43.8
20.8						Sales/Net Fixed Assets	13.2	17.0
11.7							5.5	8.4
7.1							3.8	5.0
4.7						Sales/Total Assets	2.5	3.4
2.5							1.7	2.4
							.5	.6
						% Depr., Dep., Amort./Sales	(30) 1.2	(39) 1.6
							2.7	3.1
4.4							2.7	2.1
(10) 7.6						% Officers', Directors' Owners' Comp/Sales	(23) 6.9	(18) 6.0
19.6							12.3	11.1
17525M	11983M	75346M	431605M	384819M		Net Sales ($)	727408M	925626M
3378M	4800M	35494M	153278M	130343M		Total Assets ($)	248819M	367736M

M = $ thousand MM = $ million

See Pages 9 through 22 for Explanation of Ratios and Data

Comparative Historical Data				Current Data Sorted by Sales					
			Type of Statement						
3	1	2	Unqualified						2
4	4	2	Reviewed				1	1	
8	8	3	Compiled				1	1	1
29	12	17	Tax Returns	7	9	1			
16	23	14	Other	3	1	2	3	1	4
4/1/11-3/31/12	**4/1/12-3/31/13**	**4/1/13-3/31/14**		**3 (4/1-9/30/13)**			**35 (10/1/13-3/31/14)**		
ALL	**ALL**	**ALL**		**0-1MM**	**1-3MM**	**3-5MM**	**5-10MM**	**10-25MM**	**25MM & OVER**
60	48	38	**NUMBER OF STATEMENTS**	10	10	3	5	3	7
%	%	%	**ASSETS**	%	%	%	%	%	%
16.7	18.8	16.3	Cash & Equivalents	38.4	9.4				
10.1	10.0	9.1	Trade Receivables (net)	5.1	8.5				
26.6	27.4	25.6	Inventory	21.5	27.4				
2.4	1.0	1.7	All Other Current	.0	.4				
55.8	57.3	52.8	Total Current	65.0	45.6				
23.3	20.5	27.3	Fixed Assets (net)	20.7	30.6				
12.8	10.3	13.8	Intangibles (net)	14.0	17.7				
8.1	12.0	6.1	All Other Non-Current	.3	6.0				
100.0	100.0	100.0	Total	100.0	100.0				
			LIABILITIES						
4.4	8.2	11.3	Notes Payable-Short Term	11.4	8.3				
4.5	3.3	3.6	Cur. Mat.-L.T.D.	1.0	3.8				
12.3	18.1	17.0	Trade Payables	5.9	14.8				
.0	.1	.0	Income Taxes Payable	.0	.0				
13.6	7.8	7.2	All Other Current	7.1	3.7				
34.9	37.6	39.0	Total Current	25.4	30.6				
23.7	24.2	14.9	Long-Term Debt	4.9	29.4				
.2	.3	.0	Deferred Taxes	.0	.0				
16.0	6.4	4.5	All Other Non-Current	.0	.4				
25.2	31.5	41.6	Net Worth	69.6	39.6				
100.0	100.0	100.0	Total Liabilties & Net Worth	100.0	100.0				
			INCOME DATA						
100.0	100.0	100.0	Net Sales	100.0	100.0				
58.1	56.1	58.6	Gross Profit	63.8	56.7				
52.0	51.1	50.9	Operating Expenses	50.4	52.0				
6.1	5.0	7.8	Operating Profit	13.5	4.7				
.3	.7	.3	All Other Expenses (net)	.9	-.5				
5.8	4.3	7.4	Profit Before Taxes	12.5	5.2				
			RATIOS						
3.8	2.8	2.9		6.8	3.6				
1.4	1.5	1.2	Current	5.0	1.2				
1.0	1.0	.8		1.0	1.0				
1.7	1.2	1.6		5.9	2.9				
.7	.8	.4	Quick	3.2	.5				
.3	.4	.2		.2	.1				
0 UND	0 UND	0 UND		0 UND	0 UND				
2 169.5	5 80.2	3 122.5	Sales/Receivables	0 UND	2 234.7				
18 20.7	24 15.5	17 21.3		3 104.4	7 53.0				
40 9.1	33 11.1	24 15.5		0 UND	19 19.7				
74 4.9	76 4.8	70 5.2	Cost of Sales/Inventory	51 7.1	60 6.1				
122 3.0	146 2.5	122 3.0		79 4.6	140 2.6				
0 UND	0 UND	0 UND		0 UND	0 UND				
19 19.3	40 9.1	36 10.1	Cost of Sales/Payables	4 90.2	31 11.8				
66 5.5	101 3.6	96 3.8		29 12.8	54 6.7				
7.4	11.3	6.6		4.1	6.2				
21.3	25.4	50.7	Sales/Working Capital	6.3	95.0				
-148.9	324.3	-22.9		UND	NM				
17.9	19.0	31.3							
(43) 7.0	(35) 6.0	(30) 5.8	EBIT/Interest						
1.2	1.2	1.3							
			Net Profit + Depr., Dep., Amort./Cur. Mat. L/T/D						
.1	.1	.3		.0	.8				
.8	.6	1.1	Fixed/Worth	.1	2.3				
-5.6	1.8	-5.5		1.1	-.2				
.5	.5	.5		.1	.7				
1.8	1.4	2.1	Debt/Worth	.3	3.2				
-6.4	4.9	-12.6		NM	-2.9				
84.6	77.0	125.9							
(41) 44.3	(40) 36.8	(26) 32.8	% Profit Before Taxes/Tangible Net Worth						
14.5	11.9	11.4							
34.2	27.9	29.0		44.8	28.1				
13.0	12.2	10.0	% Profit Before Taxes/Total Assets	17.9	9.3				
4.2	2.2	1.2		7.6	.2				
89.7	54.5	36.5		UND	37.5				
24.6	18.6	15.7	Sales/Net Fixed Assets	76.4	16.4				
10.9	9.8	9.1		16.4	9.0				
5.0	4.7	4.2		6.0	5.7				
3.5	3.3	2.7	Sales/Total Assets	3.2	3.5				
2.1	2.2	2.2		2.0	1.8				
.8	.6	.6							
(43) 1.4	(33) 1.5	(26) 1.5	% Depr., Dep., Amort./Sales						
2.6	2.6	2.2							
1.9	1.5	3.3							
(27) 7.4	(17) 4.8	(19) 5.4	% Officers', Directors' Owners' Comp/Sales						
15.3	11.9	11.4							
1140518M	933822M	921278M	Net Sales ($)	6117M	17024M	9771M	45105M	44164M	799097M
591636M	394585M	327293M	Total Assets ($)	4265M	6623M	2590M	19799M	21404M	272612M

M = $ thousand MM = $ million

See Pages 9 through 22 for Explanation of Ratios and Data

Current Data Sorted by Assets / Comparative Historical Data

0-500M	500M-2MM	2-10MM	10-50MM	50-100MM	100-250MM		4/1/09-3/31/10 ALL	4/1/10-3/31/11 ALL
						Type of Statement		
		1	2	2		Unqualified	5	5
	1	3				Reviewed	2	1
3	1	2			1	Compiled	3	6
5	7	4	1			Tax Returns	14	10
7	5	8	4	1	1	Other	16	16
8 (4/1-9/30/13)			51 (10/1/13-3/31/14)					
15	14	18	7	3	2	NUMBER OF STATEMENTS	40	38
%	%	%	%	%	%	**ASSETS**	%	%
25.4	18.9	17.4				Cash & Equivalents	13.3	17.5
2.8	18.4	18.2				Trade Receivables (net)	12.5	12.2
39.9	29.7	40.3				Inventory	27.5	27.1
6.9	3.6	3.5				All Other Current	7.0	5.6
74.9	70.6	79.4				Total Current	60.3	62.4
14.1	15.5	11.3				Fixed Assets (net)	20.7	19.2
5.2	6.5	5.7				Intangibles (net)	9.2	9.8
5.7	7.4	3.6				All Other Non-Current	9.8	8.6
100.0	100.0	100.0				Total	100.0	100.0
						LIABILITIES		
9.3	11.1	9.4				Notes Payable-Short Term	9.2	8.8
1.7	1.7	1.2				Cur. Mat.-L.T.D.	5.5	3.8
3.7	19.5	29.0				Trade Payables	23.7	17.7
.0	.1	.5				Income Taxes Payable	.0	.1
18.0	7.9	15.3				All Other Current	15.8	13.2
32.6	40.4	55.4				Total Current	54.3	43.6
15.9	10.5	8.7				Long-Term Debt	21.1	34.1
.0	.0	.0				Deferred Taxes	.0	.2
.0	5.4	1.4				All Other Non-Current	17.3	11.1
51.5	43.8	34.4				Net Worth	7.3	11.1
100.0	100.0	100.0				Total Liabilties & Net Worth	100.0	100.0
						INCOME DATA		
100.0	100.0	100.0				Net Sales	100.0	100.0
51.6	42.8	36.1				Gross Profit	54.7	52.1
39.3	38.8	26.9				Operating Expenses	48.7	47.6
12.3	4.0	9.2				Operating Profit	6.1	4.6
.1	.2	.2				All Other Expenses (net)	1.2	.2
12.2	3.8	8.9				Profit Before Taxes	4.9	4.4
						RATIOS		
15.1	3.7	3.6					3.0	2.9
2.5	1.7	2.0				Current	1.5	1.8
1.1	.9	1.0					.9	1.0
3.4	1.4	1.8					1.5	1.8
1.4	1.1	.8				Quick	.5	(37) .7
.1	.7	.4					.1	.1
0 UND	**0** UND	**0** UND					**0** UND	**0** 999.8
0 UND	**1** 638.5	**3** 117.0				Sales/Receivables	**3** 136.8	**5** 70.7
1 676.8	**29** 12.7	**40** 9.1					**17** 21.0	**23** 15.8
0 UND	**16** 22.6	**33** 11.1					**26** 13.9	**26** 14.2
54 6.8	**43** 8.5	**58** 6.3				Cost of Sales/Inventory	**59** 6.2	**51** 7.1
94 3.9	**78** 4.7	**94** 3.9					**104** 3.5	**84** 4.4
0 UND	**6** 63.5	**16** 22.9					**4** 103.1	**10** 35.0
0 UND	**17** 21.5	**40** 9.2				Cost of Sales/Payables	**24** 15.2	**31** 11.7
14 26.5	**48** 7.6	**69** 5.3					**60** 6.1	**52** 7.0
6.1	7.7	5.0					11.2	5.7
20.7	20.1	14.5				Sales/Working Capital	27.2	14.2
40.4	-112.2	NM					-48.1	NM
	85.0	32.4					20.0	9.4
	(11) 4.5	(14) 19.7				EBIT/Interest	(30) 3.6	(29) 3.3
	.5	1.8					1.2	1.5
						Net Profit + Depr., Dep., Amort./Cur. Mat. L/T/D		
.0	.0	.0					.2	.2
.0	.2	.3				Fixed/Worth	1.0	.7
.7	.9	NM					-.5	-.3
.1	.4	.5					.9	.5
1.0	1.2	1.7				Debt/Worth	2.5	3.2
3.6	6.9	NM					-2.3	-2.7
294.0	76.2	100.3					105.3	89.1
(13) 70.0	(12) 31.0	(14) 77.6				% Profit Before Taxes/Tangible Net Worth	(25) 45.0	(23) 27.0
39.0	4.6	33.0					18.7	8.4
140.7	49.3	51.2					32.7	35.0
50.0	19.2	21.0				% Profit Before Taxes/Total Assets	16.8	11.5
16.8	-.2	3.2					.6	1.6
UND	UND	999.8					104.0	74.5
236.0	89.9	92.6				Sales/Net Fixed Assets	25.9	21.7
23.6	14.5	19.9					10.5	12.9
8.6	7.6	5.2					7.1	5.5
5.1	3.5	4.7				Sales/Total Assets	4.0	3.8
2.6	2.7	3.0					2.4	2.2
	.1	.0					.5	.6
	(10) .6	(14) .5				% Depr., Dep., Amort./Sales	(26) 1.0	(26) 1.2
	2.0	.9					2.3	1.7
							2.7	2.7
						% Officers', Directors' Owners' Comp/Sales	(14) 9.8	(14) 9.3
							14.6	19.5
22086M	73439M	463470M	450791M	862544M	738241M	Net Sales ($)	1355877M	1581069M
3946M	15763M	106828M	188750M	269952M	328243M	Total Assets ($)	444400M	541408M

M = $ thousand MM = $ million

See Pages 9 through 22 for Explanation of Ratios and Data

Comparative Historical Data | **Current Data Sorted by Sales**

4/1/11-3/31/12 ALL	4/1/12-3/31/13 ALL	4/1/13-3/31/14 ALL	Type of Statement	0-1MM	1-3MM	3-5MM	5-10MM	10-25MM	25MM & OVER
4	3	5	Unqualified					1	4
5	4	4	Reviewed				2	1	1
2	6	7	Compiled	2	2			1	2
16	20	17	Tax Returns	4	3	3	3	2	2
28	24	26	Other	2	5	2	1	6	10
				8 (4/1-9/30/13)		51 (10/1/13-3/31/14)			
55	57	59	**NUMBER OF STATEMENTS**	8	10	5	6	11	19
%	%	%	**ASSETS**	%	%	%	%	%	%
15.2	14.8	17.7	Cash & Equivalents		18.7			18.5	9.8
18.0	9.6	12.0	Trade Receivables (net)		9.4			30.1	6.2
31.8	30.5	37.4	Inventory		41.0			28.1	45.3
3.3	2.2	4.2	All Other Current		3.4			3.7	2.8
68.3	57.1	71.3	Total Current		72.5			80.3	64.1
14.1	22.4	15.2	Fixed Assets (net)		12.4			9.0	18.2
4.8	9.2	7.5	Intangibles (net)		10.8			6.9	10.9
12.8	11.3	6.0	All Other Non-Current		4.3			3.7	6.8
100.0	100.0	100.0	Total		100.0			100.0	100.0
			LIABILITIES						
10.7	9.2	8.9	Notes Payable-Short Term		16.9			8.2	7.5
3.3	2.1	1.8	Cur. Mat.-L.T.D.		1.1			1.4	2.4
25.2	19.5	17.8	Trade Payables		7.6			27.7	23.4
.0	2.4	.3	Income Taxes Payable		.0			.1	.5
10.8	10.3	13.8	All Other Current		11.6			5.8	19.8
50.0	43.6	42.6	Total Current		37.1			43.1	53.6
16.2	23.9	13.0	Long-Term Debt		6.6			4.1	17.5
.0	.3	.2	Deferred Taxes		.0			.1	.7
15.2	14.0	3.2	All Other Non-Current		.0			1.6	5.2
18.6	18.3	40.9	Net Worth		56.3			51.1	23.1
100.0	100.0	100.0	Total Liabilties & Net Worth		100.0			100.0	100.0
			INCOME DATA						
100.0	100.0	100.0	Net Sales		100.0			100.0	100.0
44.4	49.5	42.8	Gross Profit		41.3			31.5	38.8
38.2	44.0	34.6	Operating Expenses		32.2			21.0	33.6
6.2	5.5	8.2	Operating Profit		9.2			10.5	5.2
.3	.7	.4	All Other Expenses (net)		.3			.3	.9
5.8	4.9	7.8	Profit Before Taxes		8.9			10.2	4.3
			RATIOS						
2.9	2.4	3.9			23.9			4.9	2.0
1.5	1.6	1.7	Current		1.5			2.1	1.3
.8	.7	1.1			1.1			1.2	.7
1.4	1.1	1.5			1.8			3.1	.6
(54) .6	.5	.8	Quick		.8			1.4	.3
.3	.2	.3			.1			.8	.2
0 999.8	0 UND	0 UND			0 UND			0 999.8	2 215.4
16 23.3	1 311.1	2 176.8	Sales/Receivables		0 UND			26 14.2	5 69.4
34 10.7	22 16.7	20 17.9			1 576.8			42 8.6	14 26.0
32 11.3	23 16.0	25 14.4			38 9.6			23 16.2	52 7.0
54 6.7	62 5.9	56 6.5	Cost of Sales/Inventory		60 6.1			26 13.8	74 4.9
99 3.7	122 3.0	101 3.6			87 4.2			78 4.7	114 3.2
16 22.7	13 29.0	9 39.9			0 UND			14 25.7	17 21.0
40 9.1	35 10.3	18 20.2	Cost of Sales/Payables		4 98.9			18 20.0	42 8.6
79 4.6	64 5.7	50 7.3			37 9.8			63 5.8	57 6.4
7.1	8.8	6.1			6.5			5.0	6.7
19.0	16.1	19.5	Sales/Working Capital		14.4			15.8	21.7
-46.3	-37.5	62.3			NM			41.6	-18.5
22.4	16.8	39.5							28.8
(43) 8.6	(47) 6.1	(41) 14.4	EBIT/Interest						(16) 13.1
1.1	1.6	2.1							2.0
	30.2		Net Profit + Depr., Dep.,						
	(10) 4.9		Amort./Cur. Mat. L/T/D						
	2.2								
.2	.1	.0			.0			.0	.1
.7	1.2	.3	Fixed/Worth		.2			.2	.8
-1.4	-1.5	.9			.9			.7	-.5
1.1	1.1	.4			.2			.2	1.1
3.7	3.1	1.4	Debt/Worth		1.2			1.0	2.2
-9.4	-4.4	4.2			3.4			6.9	-3.4
98.3	95.2	81.5	% Profit Before Taxes/Tangible					152.0	71.7
(35) 55.6	(36) 29.0	(48) 50.1	Net Worth					(10) 66.7	(13) 18.3
24.6	3.2	17.1						19.0	10.8
37.3	24.5	51.2	% Profit Before Taxes/Total		47.2			68.0	32.7
13.9	9.6	19.1	Assets		19.6			15.0	10.0
1.2	1.1	2.8			13.8			2.8	1.6
155.3	85.1	999.8			UND			999.8	140.1
50.9	24.0	57.1	Sales/Net Fixed Assets		73.7			248.5	29.5
18.2	6.9	15.6			14.5			46.4	10.6
5.1	5.1	5.6			6.3			5.7	5.1
3.4	3.0	3.5	Sales/Total Assets		4.2			3.5	3.2
2.4	2.0	2.2			2.6			3.2	1.8
.3	.3	.1							.3
(40) .7	(43) 1.1	(36) .6	% Depr., Dep., Amort./Sales						(13) .6
1.2	2.1	1.6							2.9
1.2	1.3	1.4	% Officers', Directors'						
(18) 3.9	(25) 3.0	(24) 3.3	Owners' Comp/Sales						
7.3	6.6	5.6							
1585889M	1604321M	2610571M	Net Sales ($)	3725M	21216M	20183M	40570M	170469M	2354408M
627998M	778072M	913482M	Total Assets ($)	1465M	6226M	5165M	12049M	48283M	840294M

M = $ thousand MM = $ million

See Pages 9 through 22 for Explanation of Ratios and Data

Current Data Sorted by Assets							Comparative Historical Data	
						Type of Statement		
		2	1	1	2	Unqualified	4	3
		6				Reviewed	2	4
1	4	4				Compiled	5	8
12	9	7	1			Tax Returns	9	13
6	7	6	4	1		Other	11	25
	9 (4/1-9/30/13)		65 (10/1/13-3/31/14)				4/1/09-3/31/10 ALL	4/1/10-3/31/11 ALL
0-500M	500M-2MM	2-10MM	10-50MM	50-100MM	100-250MM			
19	20	25	6	2	2	**NUMBER OF STATEMENTS**	31	53
%	%	%	%	%	%	**ASSETS**	%	%
26.0	10.5	5.8				Cash & Equivalents	8.6	15.8
12.1	23.2	27.2				Trade Receivables (net)	32.5	20.6
25.8	28.3	24.9				Inventory	22.8	22.8
.4	.7	1.5				All Other Current	6.2	2.8
64.4	62.7	59.5				Total Current	70.1	61.9
13.1	19.4	24.0				Fixed Assets (net)	18.8	20.9
5.8	7.1	4.7				Intangibles (net)	5.2	13.2
16.7	10.8	11.8				All Other Non-Current	5.9	4.0
100.0	100.0	100.0				Total	100.0	100.0
						LIABILITIES		
44.5	9.9	11.2				Notes Payable-Short Term	7.9	15.8
.7	3.5	4.8				Cur. Mat.-L.T.D.	3.9	4.2
15.3	15.9	23.6				Trade Payables	29.2	19.1
.1	.0	.0				Income Taxes Payable	1.5	1.3
4.9	7.8	11.4				All Other Current	17.4	14.7
65.4	37.1	50.9				Total Current	59.8	55.1
22.5	18.9	15.0				Long-Term Debt	17.1	20.2
.0	.0	.1				Deferred Taxes	.3	.7
21.0	19.3	3.7				All Other Non-Current	6.0	3.7
-8.9	24.7	30.3				Net Worth	16.8	20.3
100.0	100.0	100.0				Total Liabilties & Net Worth	100.0	100.0
						INCOME DATA		
100.0	100.0	100.0				Net Sales	100.0	100.0
53.3	55.2	46.9				Gross Profit	52.9	52.6
50.9	48.2	43.2				Operating Expenses	47.6	47.2
2.4	6.9	3.8				Operating Profit	5.2	5.4
.4	.9	.6				All Other Expenses (net)	1.6	1.5
2.0	6.0	3.2				Profit Before Taxes	3.7	3.9
						RATIOS		
6.0	2.2	2.3					2.3	2.5
1.5	1.8	1.3				Current	1.4	1.5
.3	1.1	1.1					1.0	.8
3.8	1.4	1.1					1.2	1.5
.7	.8	.8				Quick	(30) .8	.9
.1	.5	.4					.5	.4
0 UND	**6** 61.8	**5** 75.6					**15** 24.3	**0** UND
0 UND	**33** 11.1	**45** 8.1				Sales/Receivables	**52** 7.0	**24** 15.0
28 13.1	**46** 7.9	**65** 5.6					**61** 5.9	**45** 8.1
0 UND	**18** 20.5	**28** 13.0					**14** 26.6	**19** 19.5
18 20.0	**59** 6.2	**54** 6.7				Cost of Sales/Inventory	**43** 8.5	**40** 9.2
83 4.4	**126** 2.9	**118** 3.1					**63** 5.8	**80** 4.6
0 UND	**0** UND	**33** 10.9					**26** 14.1	**12** 30.9
0 UND	**17** 21.2	**63** 5.8				Cost of Sales/Payables	**50** 7.3	**37** 9.9
34 10.7	**87** 4.2	**104** 3.5					**99** 3.7	**68** 5.3
6.5	4.7	9.5					7.9	6.5
26.6	12.7	16.8				Sales/Working Capital	17.4	20.0
-18.9	390.3	135.6					-135.8	-39.0
24.3	17.2	24.9					14.9	13.6
(12) 13.0	(15) 2.6	(23) 4.0				EBIT/Interest	(25) 4.1	(43) 4.5
-4.3	-1.1	1.6					1.7	.9
						Net Profit + Depr., Dep., Amort./Cur. Mat. L/T/D		
.0	.1	.4					.2	.2
.3	.6	.8				Fixed/Worth	.9	.8
-.4	-1.3	2.3					-3.0	NM
.1	.8	.9					1.3	.9
1.7	2.5	2.0				Debt/Worth	4.3	2.1
-1.5	-13.6	11.1					-13.8	-4.2
133.1	97.4	45.7					95.8	76.1
(12) 51.5	(14) 19.0	(21) 14.4				% Profit Before Taxes/Tangible Net Worth	(21) 36.5	(38) 24.6
33.3	4.4	2.9					13.4	.6
47.1	34.5	13.7					23.3	26.4
31.6	7.4	7.0				% Profit Before Taxes/Total Assets	8.9	7.4
-7.2	1.5	1.1					.4	-.9
999.8	78.6	31.2					82.3	113.6
87.8	27.1	14.6				Sales/Net Fixed Assets	26.6	24.4
40.0	11.0	4.8					13.3	8.4
11.1	4.0	3.8					4.5	5.7
6.8	2.7	2.5				Sales/Total Assets	3.4	3.5
2.4	1.6	1.6					2.0	1.8
	.3	.6					.6	.6
	(12) 2.0	(20) 2.1				% Depr., Dep., Amort./Sales	(23) 1.2	(37) 1.5
	4.0	4.0					5.8	3.3
2.2	2.7	1.1					3.7	3.0
(13) 5.3	(12) 5.9	(10) 2.9				% Officers', Directors' Owners' Comp/Sales	(16) 5.7	(25) 5.0
13.4	10.1	4.4					11.9	10.6
29988M	**66057M**	**339474M**	**371150M**	**178001M**	**481552M**	Net Sales ($)	**1066570M**	**1085754M**
4686M	**23287M**	**121918M**	**159376M**	**123020M**	**340335M**	Total Assets ($)	**405311M**	**766636M**

M = $ thousand MM = $ million

See Pages 9 through 22 for Explanation of Ratios and Data

Comparative Historical Data				Current Data Sorted by Sales					
			Type of Statement						
4	4	6	Unqualified					2	4
3	5	6	Reviewed				4	1	1
7	2	9	Compiled		1	2	4	2	
17	29	29	Tax Returns	6	10	5	1	5	2
28	24	24	Other	2	7	4	4	3	4
4/1/11-3/31/12 ALL	**4/1/12-3/31/13 ALL**	**4/1/13-3/31/14 ALL**		9 (4/1-9/30/13)		65 (10/1/13-3/31/14)			
				0-1MM	**1-3MM**	**3-5MM**	**5-10MM**	**10-25MM**	**25MM & OVER**
59	64	74	**NUMBER OF STATEMENTS**	8	18	11	13	13	11
%	%	%	**ASSETS**	%	%	%	%	%	%
11.5	17.3	12.6	Cash & Equivalents		21.8	19.5	3.6	6.7	8.5
30.3	23.5	20.6	Trade Receivables (net)		21.4	18.2	28.1	30.0	14.4
22.6	23.9	25.6	Inventory		19.3	31.8	22.0	21.5	31.0
1.1	2.6	1.6	All Other Current		.0	1.5	1.0	3.1	4.4
65.6	67.2	60.4	Total Current		62.5	71.0	54.8	61.3	58.2
20.1	20.4	18.5	Fixed Assets (net)		21.4	10.0	25.9	23.6	10.2
9.0	6.4	9.1	Intangibles (net)		3.8	7.4	5.1	7.0	25.3
5.3	6.0	12.1	All Other Non-Current		12.3	11.7	14.3	8.2	6.3
100.0	100.0	100.0	Total		100.0	100.0	100.0	100.0	100.0
			LIABILITIES						
9.4	16.1	18.4	Notes Payable-Short Term		36.2	18.0	11.0	11.7	5.7
3.7	2.4	3.3	Cur. Mat.-L.T.D.		3.2	2.2	4.6	4.4	3.4
19.6	23.4	18.1	Trade Payables		15.6	15.6	19.7	24.1	22.0
.1	.1	.0	Income Taxes Payable		.1	.0	.0	.0	.1
7.0	7.9	8.8	All Other Current		5.4	10.4	6.5	14.8	14.6
39.9	49.9	48.6	Total Current		60.4	46.2	41.8	55.0	45.8
27.6	13.9	18.1	Long-Term Debt		29.0	17.9	11.8	11.8	18.8
.3	.1	.1	Deferred Taxes		.0	.0	.2	.0	.3
7.5	6.0	12.8	All Other Non-Current		12.7	7.3	10.4	4.7	7.3
24.8	30.1	20.4	Net Worth		-2.2	28.5	35.7	28.4	27.8
100.0	100.0	100.0	Total Liabilties & Net Worth		100.0	100.0	100.0	100.0	100.0
			INCOME DATA						
100.0	100.0	100.0	Net Sales		100.0	100.0	100.0	100.0	100.0
53.3	54.1	50.7	Gross Profit		54.8	54.8	51.5	43.3	40.3
45.5	46.1	46.3	Operating Expenses		48.8	47.4	46.4	40.7	36.5
7.8	8.0	4.4	Operating Profit		6.0	7.5	5.1	2.6	3.8
1.2	1.0	1.0	All Other Expenses (net)		1.1	.7	.3	1.0	2.6
6.6	7.0	3.3	Profit Before Taxes		4.9	6.8	4.8	1.6	1.2
			RATIOS						
4.0	2.7	2.4	Current		6.0	3.6	2.3	2.0	2.2
2.2	1.5	1.5			1.7	1.9	1.4	1.3	1.6
1.3	.9	.9			.8	1.2	1.1	1.1	.9
2.6	1.8	1.4	Quick		4.4	1.8	1.4	1.2	1.0
1.3	.8	.9			1.0	.9	1.0	.9	.6
.7	.4	.4			.4	.7	.4	.5	.2
5 68.3	**0** UND	**0** UND	Sales/Receivables		**0** UND	**0** UND	**27** 13.5	**23** 15.9	**5** 72.0
39 9.4	**26** 13.9	**30** 12.2			**21** 17.6	**21** 17.1	**47** 7.7	**43** 8.5	**22** 16.8
58 6.3	**48** 7.6	**49** 7.5			**41** 8.9	**47** 7.7	**99** 3.7	**54** 6.8	**54** 6.7
7 55.3	**19** 19.3	**17** 20.9	Cost of Sales/Inventory		**0** UND	**14** 26.1	**36** 10.1	**15** 23.6	**20** 18.1
38 9.5	**46** 7.9	**54** 6.8			**21** 17.0	**55** 6.6	**60** 6.1	**54** 6.7	**74** 4.9
79 4.6	**78** 4.7	**111** 3.3			**101** 3.6	**130** 2.8	**114** 3.2	**83** 4.4	**126** 2.9
10 36.9	**3** 109.3	**7** 49.1	Cost of Sales/Payables		**0** UND	**0** UND	**32** 11.3	**21** 17.4	**35** 10.4
35 10.3	**49** 7.5	**40** 9.2			**15** 24.5	**9** 41.8	**69** 5.3	**50** 7.3	**46** 7.9
74 4.9	**94** 3.9	**89** 4.1			**64** 5.7	**111** 3.3	**107** 3.4	**89** 4.1	**72** 5.1
6.2	7.7	6.4	Sales/Working Capital		5.9	6.5	6.5	7.8	6.6
10.2	16.4	16.2			41.0	12.5	15.7	16.4	10.9
38.9	-44.8	-215.8			-26.9	23.6	105.6	135.6	-39.6
38.7	31.4	19.8	EBIT/Interest		19.0			18.2	
(50) 9.8	(42) 7.4	(58) 3.3			(14) 3.2			1.9	
1.8	2.0	1.1			-.4			.4	
			Net Profit + Depr., Dep., Amort./Cur. Mat. L/T/D						
.2	.2	.2	Fixed/Worth		.0	.0	.2	.3	.8
.7	.7	.7			.5	.5	.5	.7	-1.8
-1.3	2.9	-1.4			UND	-.4	1.8	2.2	-.1
.8	.6	.8	Debt/Worth		.9	.9	.6	.8	2.2
1.9	2.1	2.1			7.5	1.9	.9	1.2	-13.0
-10.7	30.6	-12.1			-16.6	-4.3	3.3	46.5	-4.2
77.7	103.4	53.4	% Profit Before Taxes/Tangible Net Worth		56.0		46.7	42.0	
(42) 42.5	(52) 49.5	(52) 21.3			(13) 35.3		(12) 19.0	(11) 9.3	
14.5	16.3	4.4			11.4		11.8	-2.0	
29.8	36.4	24.6	% Profit Before Taxes/Total Assets		32.4	65.7	16.3	12.9	8.9
17.7	15.0	8.3			15.9	33.4	10.2	2.7	1.7
2.9	3.7	.8			1.3	2.0	3.3	-2.5	-4.9
78.5	111.8	90.3	Sales/Net Fixed Assets		828.2	136.8	27.1	38.9	95.0
24.2	26.8	28.4			70.2	44.3	8.0	14.6	65.5
9.3	7.1	8.0			4.6	24.6	3.7	7.3	21.2
4.9	4.8	4.4	Sales/Total Assets		7.0	9.5	4.0	3.8	5.2
3.2	3.6	2.8			3.0	3.4	2.4	3.1	1.8
2.1	2.0	1.6			1.6	2.6	1.4	2.0	1.1
.3	.5	.5	% Depr., Dep., Amort./Sales		.2			.5	.4
(38) 1.0	(39) 1.2	(50) 2.0			(10) 2.8			(11) 2.0	(10) .8
2.9	3.5	4.1			4.4			4.6	3.6
2.1	2.1	2.2	% Officers', Directors' Owners' Comp/Sales		3.1				
(23) 5.5	(30) 5.7	(36) 4.7			(12) 6.8				
8.3	10.2	10.1			10.1				
981311M	**1153079M**	**1466222M**	Net Sales ($)	**4321M**	**33011M**	**39237M**	**96411M**	**198644M**	**1094598M**
506678M	**646744M**	**772622M**	Total Assets ($)	**1799M**	**14564M**	**10745M**	**49546M**	**77654M**	**618314M**

M = $ thousand MM = $ million

See Pages 9 through 22 for Explanation of Ratios and Data

Current Data Sorted by Assets							Comparative Historical Data	
Type of Statement								
Unqualified	1	2	6	37	10	21	93	93
Reviewed	1	16	43	44	8		122	109
Compiled	28	38	46	20	2	1	175	201
Tax Returns	190	192	78	11		2	603	513
Other	73	118	132	80	31	30	322	390
	169 (4/1-9/30/13)			1,092 (10/1/13-3/31/14)			4/1/09-3/31/10 ALL	4/1/10-3/31/11 ALL
	0-500M	500M-2MM	2-10MM	10-50MM	50-100MM	100-250MM		
NUMBER OF STATEMENTS	293	366	305	192	51	54	1315	1306
ASSETS	%	%	%	%	%	%	%	%
Cash & Equivalents	20.4	11.9	9.9	11.3	12.3	7.2	12.0	11.7
Trade Receivables (net)	4.5	4.7	5.7	8.5	9.4	6.8	5.4	5.9
Inventory	40.3	14.7	11.8	12.8	9.4	10.7	20.8	20.2
All Other Current	2.5	1.6	1.4	2.5	1.6	1.3	2.0	1.8
Total Current	67.7	32.8	28.7	35.0	32.8	26.0	40.3	39.6
Fixed Assets (net)	16.3	52.0	57.5	51.3	56.1	62.0	44.6	45.6
Intangibles (net)	10.1	7.9	6.0	5.4	5.5	5.8	7.4	7.1
All Other Non-Current	5.9	7.2	7.7	8.3	5.5	6.2	7.7	7.7
Total	100.0	100.0	100.0	100.0	100.0	100.0	100.0	100.0
LIABILITIES								
Notes Payable-Short Term	6.0	1.9	1.6	2.6	4.2	3.8	4.4	3.8
Cur. Mat.-L.T.D.	2.0	2.9	3.4	4.3	3.7	3.5	2.9	3.8
Trade Payables	20.0	9.9	13.1	18.0	15.4	13.5	15.8	15.7
Income Taxes Payable	.1	.4	.0	.0	.2	.2	.1	.1
All Other Current	19.0	10.2	8.2	7.1	7.9	7.1	10.8	9.4
Total Current	47.0	25.5	26.3	32.0	31.5	28.1	34.0	32.8
Long-Term Debt	19.9	43.6	43.0	27.8	30.8	32.4	35.9	36.9
Deferred Taxes	.0	.0	.3	1.1	.7	.7	.3	.2
All Other Non-Current	14.6	8.2	5.6	2.8	4.2	3.9	10.9	10.0
Net Worth	18.5	22.7	24.8	36.3	32.9	34.9	18.9	20.1
Total Liabilties & Net Worth	100.0	100.0	100.0	100.0	100.0	100.0	100.0	100.0
INCOME DATA								
Net Sales	100.0	100.0	100.0	100.0	100.0	100.0	100.0	100.0
Gross Profit	13.4	12.2	12.2	10.9	8.6	9.7	13.5	12.8
Operating Expenses	12.9	10.8	10.6	9.8	7.3	8.6	12.7	11.7
Operating Profit	.5	1.4	1.6	1.1	1.3	1.2	.8	1.1
All Other Expenses (net)	-.8	.3	.3	.1	.2	.1	.1	.1
Profit Before Taxes	1.3	1.2	1.3	1.0	1.1	1.0	.8	1.0
RATIOS								
Current	8.1	3.6	2.4	1.6	1.7	1.2	2.5	2.8
	2.1	1.7	1.2	1.1	1.1	.9	1.3	1.3
	1.0	.8	.7	.8	.7	.6	.8	.8
Quick	2.5	1.6	1.4	.9	1.1	.7	1.1	1.1
	(291) .7	.7	(294) .7	(191) .6	.6	.4	(1313) .5	(1300) .5
	.2	.2	.3	.3	.4	.3	.2	.2
Sales/Receivables	**0** UND	**0** UND	**0** UND	**1** 339.4	**2** 215.4	**2** 199.2	**0** UND	**0** UND
	0 UND	**0** UND	**1** 522.8	**3** 123.3	**4** 101.8	**3** 110.4	**1** 478.2	**1** 420.9
	0 932.0	**2** 182.6	**4** 95.3	**6** 60.4	**7** 55.6	**4** 81.4	**3** 105.5	**4** 101.1
Cost of Sales/Inventory	**5** 69.6	**5** 77.3	**4** 83.5	**5** 79.3	**3** 105.4	**4** 97.5	**6** 65.3	**5** 67.4
	9 40.4	**8** 48.1	**7** 51.6	**7** 50.6	**5** 68.4	**6** 63.4	**9** 40.0	**9** 42.6
	16 23.3	**12** 30.6	**10** 36.2	**11** 34.2	**9** 41.4	**10** 36.0	**14** 26.1	**13** 28.9
Cost of Sales/Payables	**0** UND	**0** UND	**2** 214.1	**7** 54.6	**6** 63.2	**6** 62.6	**1** 406.0	**1** 488.7
	2 189.2	**3** 115.7	**5** 69.0	**10** 36.4	**9** 39.9	**10** 36.3	**6** 59.1	**6** 61.2
	7 52.1	**8** 45.8	**10** 35.1	**12** 29.4	**11** 31.9	**13** 28.9	**12** 29.3	**12** 30.2
Sales/Working Capital	24.0	28.1	37.1	55.6	35.3	131.5	32.2	34.8
	52.5	71.2	130.1	347.9	219.3	-216.2	109.2	115.6
	UND	-155.5	-88.8	-105.4	-57.4	-64.6	-77.9	-81.6
EBIT/Interest	10.1	4.7	6.3	11.1	8.0	13.8	4.7	5.3
	(103) 4.3	(288) 1.9	(277) 2.4	(183) 3.9	(49) 3.8	(52) 4.9	(1006) 2.0	(1023) 2.2
	1.2	1.0	1.1	1.6	1.6	2.2	.9	1.0
Net Profit + Depr., Dep., Amort./Cur. Mat. L/T/D		6.8	6.5	6.4	7.3	8.6	3.4	3.9
		(16) 1.8	(31) 3.1	(56) 2.4	(16) 1.5	(18) 3.3	(150) 2.0	(144) 1.9
		.7	1.6	1.4	1.0	1.7	1.3	1.2
Fixed/Worth	.0	.8	1.3	.9	1.5	1.3	.7	.7
	.3	4.4	3.0	1.7	2.3	2.2	2.7	2.9
	UND	-6.9	49.5	3.7	4.1	4.2	-15.3	-21.8
Debt/Worth	.3	1.2	1.4	1.0	1.4	1.1	1.3	1.4
	2.3	5.7	3.7	2.1	3.0	1.9	4.1	4.2
	-7.3	-11.9	57.6	5.1	7.8	6.0	-19.4	-28.6
% Profit Before Taxes/Tangible Net Worth	90.9	54.5	35.9	27.4	29.1	26.8	47.8	47.4
	(199) 34.8	(247) 21.2	(235) 13.9	(173) 12.8	(44) 16.9	(47) 16.8	(943) 20.9	(937) 20.6
	7.8	5.6	2.5	4.1	11.0	10.7	4.9	5.6
% Profit Before Taxes/Total Assets	27.1	12.7	8.6	8.0	8.9	9.0	10.9	11.4
	10.0	4.2	3.3	4.3	5.0	6.2	3.9	4.6
	1.3	.3	.3	.9	1.8	3.6	.0	.2
Sales/Net Fixed Assets	UND	66.6	27.9	26.5	18.8	11.2	84.6	81.0
	264.3	8.8	8.4	12.7	10.6	7.6	13.6	14.2
	61.5	4.0	3.5	6.6	6.1	5.9	4.9	5.1
Sales/Total Assets	25.7	11.2	8.9	10.1	8.8	7.4	12.2	12.7
	16.8	5.0	5.0	6.6	5.5	5.3	5.9	6.2
	9.3	3.0	2.5	4.2	3.9	4.2	3.1	3.4
% Depr., Dep., Amort./Sales	.1	.4	.5	.5	.6	.6	.5	.5
	(143) .3	(291) 1.0	(251) .8	(183) .8	(48) .9	(33) .9	(1037) 1.0	(1041) 1.0
	.7	1.6	1.4	1.4	1.3	1.1	1.8	1.6
% Officers', Directors' Owners' Comp/Sales	.5	.4	.2	.1	.1		.4	.4
	(156) .9	(170) .8	(115) .5	(45) .3	(10) .2		(572) .8	(531) .7
	1.9	1.3	.9	.4	1.1		1.6	1.4
Net Sales ($)	1223799M	3059575M	9679215M	32625563M	24180434M	63256916M	84856215M	95228672M
Total Assets ($)	73435M	413576M	1391962M	4343600M	3669069M	8830449M	15791819M	16105062M

M = $ thousand MM = $ million

See Pages 9 through 22 for Explanation of Ratios and Data

Comparative Historical Data				Current Data Sorted by Sales					
			Type of Statement						
101	77	77	Unqualified		1	1	2	1	72
109	101	112	Reviewed	5	3	6	9	13	76
193	194	135	Compiled	4	21	17	22	21	50
660	536	473	Tax Returns	24	93	111	140	68	37
518	495	464	Other	13	48	44	88	67	204
4/1/11-3/31/12	4/1/12-3/31/13	4/1/13-3/31/14		169 (4/1-9/30/13)			1,092 (10/1/13-3/31/14)		
ALL	ALL	ALL		0-1MM	1-3MM	3-5MM	5-10MM	10-25MM	25MM & OVER
1581	1403	1261	**NUMBER OF STATEMENTS**	46	166	179	261	170	439
%	%	%	**ASSETS**	%	%	%	%	%	%
12.4	12.7	13.1	Cash & Equivalents	13.2	12.7	11.3	15.0	14.5	12.3
5.8	6.0	5.8	Trade Receivables (net)	2.6	3.5	2.4	3.9	6.0	9.4
21.0	19.5	19.3	Inventory	21.1	26.0	26.3	18.2	16.7	15.3
1.7	2.0	1.8	All Other Current	1.1	1.1	2.4	1.5	2.5	2.0
40.8	40.1	40.0	Total Current	38.1	43.2	42.4	38.5	39.7	39.0
44.1	45.4	45.5	Fixed Assets (net)	43.2	41.7	42.8	45.5	45.0	48.5
7.9	6.7	7.4	Intangibles (net)	13.4	8.0	8.5	8.4	7.1	5.6
7.2	7.7	7.1	All Other Non-Current	5.3	7.0	6.3	7.6	8.2	7.0
100.0	100.0	100.0	Total	100.0	100.0	100.0	100.0	100.0	100.0
			LIABILITIES						
4.6	4.2	3.1	Notes Payable-Short Term	2.9	4.0	2.9	2.9	2.4	3.1
3.2	3.4	3.1	Cur. Mat.-L.T.D.	2.7	2.3	2.2	3.1	3.4	3.6
16.4	14.0	14.6	Trade Payables	7.1	8.1	12.7	12.3	15.6	19.7
.1	.1	.2	Income Taxes Payable	.0	.0	.1	.5	.1	.1
10.8	11.6	11.1	All Other Current	10.7	12.0	13.1	14.5	8.6	8.8
35.1	33.3	32.0	Total Current	23.3	26.5	30.9	33.4	30.1	35.4
36.5	35.8	34.6	Long-Term Debt	41.6	39.1	37.0	39.9	36.6	27.2
.2	.2	.3	Deferred Taxes	.0	.0	.0	.0	.1	.8
11.2	8.4	7.9	All Other Non-Current	14.1	11.2	7.1	12.3	8.4	3.5
17.0	22.3	25.2	Net Worth	20.9	23.2	24.9	14.4	24.8	33.1
100.0	100.0	100.0	Total Liabilities & Net Worth	100.0	100.0	100.0	100.0	100.0	100.0
			INCOME DATA						
100.0	100.0	100.0	Net Sales	100.0	100.0	100.0	100.0	100.0	100.0
11.9	11.5	12.0	Gross Profit	31.3	16.3	11.6	11.6	10.3	9.5
11.0	10.6	10.9	Operating Expenses	27.8	15.0	10.5	10.2	9.1	8.7
.9	.9	1.2	Operating Profit	3.5	1.3	1.2	1.4	1.2	.8
.1	.0	.0	All Other Expenses (net)	-.8	-.1	.2	.2	.0	-.1
.8	.8	1.2	Profit Before Taxes	4.3	1.4	1.0	1.2	1.2	.8
			RATIOS						
2.9	2.6	2.9		11.2	7.4	5.1	3.6	3.2	1.7
1.3	1.3	1.4	Current	2.2	2.2	1.6	1.8	1.5	1.1
.8	.8	.8		.7	.7	.7	.8	.8	.8
1.3	1.3	1.5		3.1	2.3	1.7	1.7	1.9	1.0
(1573) .6	(1397) .6	(1247) .6	Quick	.4	.6	.4	(259) .7	(160) .9	(437) .6
.2	.3	.3		.1	.2	.1	.3	.4	.3
0 UND	0 UND	0 UND		0 UND	0 UND	0 UND	0 UND	0 UND	1 377.6
1 695.1	1 577.5	1 641.6	Sales/Receivables	0 UND	0 UND	0 UND	0 UND	1 532.9	3 127.2
3 107.4	3 106.2	3 104.3		0 UND	0 999.8	1 439.8	1 264.6	4 97.3	5 67.4
5 78.4	4 81.4	5 80.4		15 25.1	9 41.8	6 61.0	4 82.6	4 98.7	4 85.1
8 48.5	7 50.4	7 48.9	Cost of Sales/Inventory	38 9.7	12 29.2	9 41.3	7 55.0	5 74.9	7 53.5
12 31.0	12 31.3	11 32.3		64 5.7	21 17.4	14 26.5	10 36.7	8 45.6	10 38.2
1 572.4	1 713.5	1 434.8		0 UND	0 UND	0 UND	0 999.8	1 316.4	5 70.7
5 71.1	5 72.0	5 71.0	Cost of Sales/Payables	0 UND	0 900.3	3 131.9	3 119.9	4 89.6	9 39.6
11 32.9	10 35.9	10 35.0		20 18.0	7 53.5	7 49.7	8 47.2	8 46.2	12 30.8
35.0	35.5	31.8		6.0	19.8	26.9	32.8	41.1	50.8
105.2	115.7	102.1	Sales/Working Capital	16.9	42.8	66.8	77.1	96.6	296.8
-106.5	-102.0	-120.5		-16.2	-61.1	-101.7	-180.0	-270.7	-103.8
5.2	6.6	7.3		3.1	3.6	4.2	5.2	8.9	11.1
(1189) 2.2	(1068) 2.6	(952) 2.7	EBIT/Interest	(23) 1.3	(99) 1.9	(113) 1.9	(176) 2.3	(133) 3.3	(408) 4.0
1.0	1.1	1.2		-.4	.7	1.1	1.2	1.1	1.6
3.2	4.1	6.5					1.3	7.0	6.4
(141) 2.0	(133) 2.4	(137) 2.7	Net Profit + Depr., Dep., Amort./Cur. Mat. L/T/D				(10) 1.0	(14) 3.8	(109) 2.9
1.2	1.1	1.3					.4	1.4	1.5
.7	.7	.6		.2	.2	.1	.6	.5	.9
2.7	2.4	2.2	Fixed/Worth	3.6	2.8	2.0	4.0	2.3	1.9
-13.9	-826.0	34.4		-12.6	UND	15.9	-4.0	-5.9	4.3
1.2	1.2	1.0		1.1	.6	.8	.9	.9	1.1
4.6	3.4	3.3	Debt/Worth	5.0	4.1	4.0	7.8	3.2	2.5
-14.7	-50.5	-999.8		-16.0	-25.0	-48.1	-6.7	-12.3	7.4
46.5	49.2	44.3		74.8	52.7	54.6	66.6	58.4	31.3
(1109) 20.7	(1032) 21.2	(945) 18.0	% Profit Before Taxes/Tangible Net Worth	(30) 3.8	(121) 21.8	(133) 21.2	(166) 23.1	(120) 22.7	(375) 14.7
6.8	6.1	4.8		-7.0	2.8	4.1	6.7	6.2	5.6
11.5	11.9	12.0		13.8	14.4	12.6	15.7	17.0	9.0
4.5	5.1	4.7	% Profit Before Taxes/Total Assets	2.6	3.8	3.9	5.3	7.0	4.9
.2	.5	.8		-1.4	-.6	1.0	.9	.8	1.4
125.6	97.8	97.2		137.7	200.2	621.7	210.3	113.1	33.9
17.0	15.5	15.3	Sales/Net Fixed Assets	5.6	17.2	9.2	16.2	18.9	14.9
5.7	5.5	5.5		.7	2.8	4.1	4.6	6.3	7.9
14.6	12.9	13.2		4.1	13.1	17.1	14.6	16.6	11.2
7.2	6.6	6.8	Sales/Total Assets	1.9	4.8	5.4	7.1	8.8	7.5
3.8	3.7	3.6		.5	2.0	3.0	3.3	4.5	5.0
.4	.4	.4		1.2	.4	.4	.4	.3	.5
(1217) .8	(1074) .8	(949) .8	% Depr., Dep., Amort./Sales	(26) 3.9	(122) 1.0	(118) 1.0	(181) .8	(121) .6	(381) .7
1.3	1.3	1.4		9.3	2.1	1.7	1.4	1.1	1.1
.4	.3	.3		2.0	.8	.4	.5	.3	.1
(611) .6	(519) .6	(504) .7	% Officers', Directors' Owners' Comp/Sales	(12) 3.7	(66) 1.5	(90) .8	(141) .7	(76) .7	(119) .3
1.3	1.3	1.3		5.2	2.4	1.2	1.2	1.2	.5
131303005M	126480340M	134025502M	Net Sales ($)	29269M	333634M	718813M	1825971M	2572136M	128545679M
20530752M	18582426M	18722091M	Total Assets ($)	39886M	124937M	177623M	431637M	455678M	17492330M

M = $ thousand MM = $ million

See Pages 9 through 22 for Explanation of Ratios and Data

Current Data Sorted by Assets							Comparative Historical Data	
						Type of Statement		
	1		5	3	2	Unqualified	25	22
		3	6			Reviewed	31	27
4	9	8	3			Compiled	44	44
17	24	8				Tax Returns	67	51
14	12	10	10	7	5	Other	107	101
21 (4/1-9/30/13)		130 (10/1/13-3/31/14)					4/1/09-3/31/10	4/1/10-3/31/11
0-500M	500M-2MM	2-10MM	10-50MM	50-100MM	100-250MM		ALL	ALL
35	46	29	24	10	7	NUMBER OF STATEMENTS	274	245
%	%	%	%	%	%	**ASSETS**	%	%
26.3	17.0	12.2	9.5	6.0		Cash & Equivalents	11.5	10.7
9.3	13.9	4.1	12.6	17.9		Trade Receivables (net)	9.8	10.6
35.3	14.7	10.7	10.9	14.7		Inventory	14.2	14.4
1.7	1.4	1.0	3.1	3.2		All Other Current	2.9	4.8
72.6	47.0	28.0	36.1	41.8		Total Current	38.4	40.6
15.4	36.0	50.9	50.7	46.4		Fixed Assets (net)	46.3	46.3
4.9	6.2	8.8	4.8	6.8		Intangibles (net)	6.8	5.5
7.1	10.8	12.2	8.4	5.0		All Other Non-Current	8.5	7.6
100.0	100.0	100.0	100.0	100.0		Total	100.0	100.0
						LIABILITIES		
8.0	3.9	1.8	2.3	10.9		Notes Payable-Short Term	4.3	3.9
3.3	2.1	2.8	3.5	1.8		Cur. Mat.-L.T.D.	4.0	3.2
37.2	18.8	9.2	20.3	17.8		Trade Payables	14.3	17.8
.0	.0	.1	.2	.1		Income Taxes Payable	.1	.1
22.0	6.9	3.2	6.7	3.8		All Other Current	9.7	8.3
70.5	31.7	17.0	33.0	34.3		Total Current	32.3	33.3
6.2	26.4	45.5	23.1	24.0		Long-Term Debt	35.5	33.9
.0	.0	.4	.7	.5		Deferred Taxes	.7	.3
11.5	4.5	4.7	3.5	2.7		All Other Non-Current	7.1	6.4
11.7	37.4	32.3	39.8	38.5		Net Worth	24.3	26.2
100.0	100.0	100.0	100.0	100.0		Total Liabilties & Net Worth	100.0	100.0
						INCOME DATA		
100.0	100.0	100.0	100.0	100.0		Net Sales	100.0	100.0
13.1	15.0	14.0	7.5	9.7		Gross Profit	14.1	12.7
12.8	13.6	11.9	6.7	8.3		Operating Expenses	12.4	11.1
.4	1.5	2.2	.8	1.4		Operating Profit	1.7	1.6
-.6	.2	.9	-.1	.1		All Other Expenses (net)	.3	.4
.9	1.2	1.3	.9	1.3		Profit Before Taxes	1.3	1.2
						RATIOS		
5.4	2.9	4.0	1.4	1.6			2.2	2.4
1.6	1.3	1.7	1.1	1.3		Current	1.2	1.3
.5	.8	1.0	.9	1.0			.7	.9
2.9	1.6	1.7	.8	1.1			1.3	1.2
.8	.8	.9	.6	.7		Quick	.6	(243) .7
.2	.3	.5	.3	.5			.3	.4
0 UND	0 UND	0 UND	1 330.8	4 100.8			0 734.2	0 UND
1 637.5	0 999.8	0 999.8	3 141.3	5 72.6		Sales/Receivables	3 137.8	3 123.8
2 199.1	7 49.3	3 132.7	6 60.5	11 34.5			7 51.6	7 51.9
4 89.8	3 139.2	3 122.8	2 157.5	4 84.4			5 75.6	4 95.6
6 58.1	6 57.3	6 60.6	5 66.5	6 62.2		Cost of Sales/Inventory	8 46.7	7 51.3
8 46.3	12 29.3	11 33.4	7 53.0	12 29.4			12 29.8	11 33.0
1 257.0	4 89.7	1 636.2	4 92.6	7 54.8			2 198.4	2 186.4
3 110.6	8 45.9	4 93.7	9 42.8	10 34.9		Cost of Sales/Payables	9 41.6	9 39.4
10 36.2	15 24.5	9 42.3	11 34.7	12 29.5			14 26.4	13 27.1
34.3	31.3	35.1	127.5	37.6			30.4	30.2
121.6	86.8	50.8	585.1	65.6		Sales/Working Capital	132.1	93.5
-40.6	-153.1	618.0	-798.8	999.8			-73.6	-171.3
14.3	14.7	14.7	12.7	28.8			5.8	7.3
(14) 2.2	(32) 2.5	(27) 5.7	5.9	6.5		EBIT/Interest	(243) 2.6	(209) 2.6
.2	1.2	1.6	3.5	4.8			1.1	1.5
							3.6	4.8
						Net Profit + Depr., Dep., Amort./Cur. Mat. L/T/D	(39) 2.2	(37) 3.1
							1.5	1.2
.0	.1	.6	1.0	.9			.9	.7
.6	1.2	1.7	1.1	1.2		Fixed/Worth	2.1	1.7
-.5	4.5	NM	8.7	10.8			21.9	7.6
.2	.9	.7	.8	.6			1.4	1.3
8.1	2.2	1.5	1.7	1.8		Debt/Worth	3.0	2.6
-2.8	6.9	-11.4	9.9	16.9			34.6	12.7
44.2	48.0	32.3	25.7				39.6	34.1
(19) 28.0	(41) 23.5	(21) 13.8	(21) 16.6			% Profit Before Taxes/Tangible Net Worth	(217) 16.0	(200) 17.9
16.8	1.9	6.2	9.4				4.3	5.9
27.0	14.8	12.9	7.2	11.9			8.7	9.6
12.3	4.3	7.8	5.4	6.6		% Profit Before Taxes/Total Assets	3.9	4.6
.7	.6	1.9	3.1	4.5			.0	1.3
999.8	163.8	21.5	32.1	43.6			40.3	44.5
339.7	60.0	10.0	17.0	11.9		Sales/Net Fixed Assets	10.9	13.0
79.4	6.8	5.6	8.8	7.5			5.7	5.5
40.2	16.3	7.5	15.3	9.6			9.5	10.4
21.6	5.9	5.0	8.2	5.8		Sales/Total Assets	5.4	6.0
14.0	3.7	2.8	5.5	4.5			3.1	3.3
.1	.2	.5	.3				.6	.4
(22) .4	(38) .6	(27) .9	(23) .6			% Depr., Dep., Amort./Sales	(218) 1.0	(191) .8
.5	1.5	1.9	.9				1.6	1.4
.4	.6	.2					.4	.3
(25) .5	(24) 1.3	(10) .7				% Officers', Directors' Owners' Comp/Sales	(99) .8	(88) .6
3.1	2.0	1.3					2.0	1.2
167885M	440130M	693641M	6518485M	5578728M	8794539M	Net Sales ($)	27193363M	32673472M
7663M	48953M	126543M	602370M	724412M	1166069M	Total Assets ($)	5501208M	5639583M

M = $ thousand MM = $ million

See Pages 9 through 22 for Explanation of Ratios and Data

Comparative Historical Data				Current Data Sorted by Sales					
			Type of Statement						
14	13	11	Unqualified		1				10
22	24	9	Reviewed					1	8
31	23	24	Compiled		3	1	3	10	7
53	46	49	Tax Returns	2	6	14	14	12	1
72	67	58	Other		8	8	8	8	26
4/1/11-3/31/12 ALL	**4/1/12-3/31/13 ALL**	**4/1/13-3/31/14 ALL**		**21 (4/1-9/30/13)**			**130 (10/1/13-3/31/14)**		
				0-1MM	**1-3MM**	**3-5MM**	**5-10MM**	**10-25MM**	**25MM & OVER**
192	173	151	**NUMBER OF STATEMENTS**	2	18	23	25	31	52
%	%	%	**ASSETS**	%	%	%	%	%	%
10.8	14.2	15.8	Cash & Equivalents		18.3	18.2	21.2	16.2	10.5
13.6	12.6	10.9	Trade Receivables (net)		3.7	11.3	13.2	8.9	13.3
16.2	14.0	18.0	Inventory		24.6	25.5	21.4	14.7	12.4
3.7	4.0	1.8	All Other Current		2.3	.6	1.3	1.8	2.4
44.2	44.9	46.4	Total Current		48.8	55.4	57.0	41.5	38.6
43.7	40.5	37.7	Fixed Assets (net)		45.8	25.3	28.2	35.8	46.2
6.1	6.7	6.7	Intangibles (net)		3.5	2.7	7.6	9.4	7.9
6.0	7.9	9.2	All Other Non-Current		1.9	16.6	7.2	13.2	7.2
100.0	100.0	100.0	Total		100.0	100.0	100.0	100.0	100.0
			LIABILITIES						
4.7	4.7	4.7	Notes Payable-Short Term		.9	8.7	3.0	5.1	5.0
3.0	3.5	2.7	Cur. Mat.-L.T.D.		6.5	1.2	1.2	3.4	2.6
18.5	17.3	21.3	Trade Payables		21.7	30.8	20.6	17.8	20.0
.2	.0	.1	Income Taxes Payable		.0	.0	.0	.0	.1
7.5	8.9	9.5	All Other Current		15.6	4.8	19.1	5.0	6.1
33.8	34.4	38.3	Total Current		44.7	45.5	43.9	31.3	33.8
31.4	23.0	24.7	Long-Term Debt		31.9	20.1	23.2	29.5	21.9
.4	.4	.2	Deferred Taxes		.0	.0	.0	.1	.6
6.3	6.7	6.0	All Other Non-Current		10.6	13.9	2.7	4.4	3.8
28.1	35.6	30.7	Net Worth		12.8	20.6	30.2	34.6	39.9
100.0	100.0	100.0	Total Liabilties & Net Worth		100.0	100.0	100.0	100.0	100.0
			INCOME DATA						
100.0	100.0	100.0	Net Sales		100.0	100.0	100.0	100.0	100.0
11.0	13.5	12.6	Gross Profit		20.4	15.3	14.5	10.8	8.0
10.1	12.3	11.4	Operating Expenses		18.5	14.1	13.6	9.4	7.0
.9	1.1	1.2	Operating Profit		1.9	1.2	.9	1.5	1.0
.0	.1	.1	All Other Expenses (net)		.3	.3	.2	.1	-.1
.9	1.0	1.1	Profit Before Taxes		1.6	.9	.7	1.4	1.1
			RATIOS						
2.4	2.2	2.2			3.7	4.4	5.2	2.6	1.5
1.3	1.3	1.3	Current		.7	1.2	1.9	1.6	1.1
.8	.8	.8			.4	.7	1.2	.8	.9
1.3	1.4	1.3			2.1	1.8	3.6	1.2	1.0
.7	.7	.7	Quick		.1	.7	1.0	.8	.6
.3	.4	.3			.0	.3	.4	.5	.4
1 604.2	1 602.1	0 UND			0 UND	0 UND	0 UND	0 UND	1 330.8
3 104.3	3 113.1	2 238.1	Sales/Receivables		0 UND	1 486.4	0 999.8	2 226.1	3 129.5
8 45.8	7 49.9	5 81.0			1 308.9	3 116.1	8 46.2	3 105.7	6 57.5
4 98.5	3 115.1	3 119.5			7 55.2	5 69.2	3 125.6	3 138.3	3 138.9
7 51.1	6 64.9	6 59.5	Cost of Sales/Inventory		10 36.8	7 53.7	5 75.6	4 83.7	5 69.1
11 32.4	9 40.1	9 40.3			16 23.2	10 35.3	7 52.0	9 39.8	7 49.0
3 130.3	4 98.0	3 118.2			1 317.3	2 167.4	2 199.9	2 229.3	4 82.8
8 44.4	7 50.2	7 52.7	Cost of Sales/Payables		4 90.3	10 36.2	5 68.2	6 64.9	9 40.9
13 27.1	11 32.1	12 31.3			25 14.7	19 19.2	9 40.7	10 34.8	11 32.8
29.7	34.4	40.0			25.1	32.0	27.1	43.4	51.4
109.1	98.1	115.8	Sales/Working Capital		-140.5	79.9	53.3	108.7	300.6
-128.0	-168.8	-153.5			-27.6	-71.3	178.8	-104.1	-436.3
8.1	14.0	13.4			12.7	6.6	5.9	15.8	17.9
(158) 2.5	(140) 4.4	(114) 4.5	EBIT/Interest		(12) 1.6	(14) 2.1	(15) 1.8	(21) 2.8	(51) 7.2
1.1	1.4	1.7			1.0	.7	1.4	1.8	3.8
5.4	7.6	2.7							5.4
(32) 3.8	(29) 2.5	(14) 1.9	Net Profit + Depr., Dep., Amort./Cur. Mat. L/T/D						(10) 2.1
2.1	1.6	1.8							1.9
.6	.5	.4			.4	.1	.0	.3	1.0
1.6	1.3	1.2	Fixed/Worth		17.3	2.3	.5	.9	1.2
7.2	3.4	11.4			-.6	-.5	3.2	3.4	2.5
1.2	.8	.7			.3	.5	.5	1.0	.8
2.5	1.8	2.0	Debt/Worth		16.9	6.8	1.9	1.6	1.7
14.8	6.5	44.3			-3.8	-8.3	7.3	3.7	5.6
28.6	36.7	38.1			47.4	37.6	43.2	53.2	38.0
(154) 15.4	(146) 22.4	(116) 19.6	% Profit Before Taxes/Tangible Net Worth		(10) 21.7	(15) 22.9	(21) 18.4	(24) 18.4	(45) 19.4
6.7	9.0	10.6			-1.2	3.3	2.8	7.3	11.0
8.6	14.2	13.4			28.7	12.8	13.7	14.8	10.4
3.8	7.1	6.5	% Profit Before Taxes/Total Assets		4.3	3.5	4.7	9.9	6.6
.6	2.1	1.7			.6	-2.2	.8	2.7	4.0
56.4	89.5	157.8			149.1	798.6	999.8	133.9	50.8
15.7	21.1	27.3	Sales/Net Fixed Assets		11.7	99.8	98.4	33.0	15.2
6.8	7.7	8.2			2.6	11.0	10.3	9.4	7.9
11.9	14.4	17.8			19.5	21.6	20.5	19.1	15.3
7.0	8.1	7.9	Sales/Total Assets		4.4	7.6	8.6	7.9	7.9
4.0	4.1	4.7			1.9	4.4	4.4	4.7	5.2
.3	.3	.2			.3	.4	.1	.2	.3
(157) .7	(144) .6	(124) .6	% Depr., Dep., Amort./Sales		(16) .6	(15) .5	(19) .4	(27) .8	(46) .6
1.2	1.2	1.2			1.9	1.6	1.3	1.2	1.1
.3	.2	.4			.7	.4	.4	.5	.1
(83) .6	(75) .5	(64) .7	% Officers', Directors' Owners' Comp/Sales		(11) 2.7	(17) .5	(11) .6	(13) .9	(10) .3
1.2	1.2	1.9			5.4	1.9	1.3	2.0	.7
23831117M	31233070M	22193408M	Net Sales ($)	1747M	36442M	91403M	178857M	489730M	21395229M
3497159M	4435352M	2676010M	Total Assets ($)	169M	11173M	19106M	31602M	73209M	2540751M

M = $ thousand MM = $ million

See Pages 9 through 22 for Explanation of Ratios and Data

Current Data Sorted by Assets							Comparative Historical Data	
						Type of Statement		
1		1		1	1	Unqualified	4	2
		1	2			Reviewed	7	9
3	4	2				Compiled	10	13
6	9	2				Tax Returns	15	11
2	18	3	4		3	Other	18	24
11 (4/1-9/30/13)			52 (10/1/13-3/31/14)				4/1/09-3/31/10 ALL	4/1/10-3/31/11 ALL
0-500M	500M-2MM	2-10MM	10-50MM	50-100MM	100-250MM			
12	31	9	6	1	4	**NUMBER OF STATEMENTS**	54	59
%	%	%	%	%	%	**ASSETS**	%	%
15.9	13.7					Cash & Equivalents	12.4	13.5
2.8	7.5					Trade Receivables (net)	6.4	7.6
63.0	44.4					Inventory	50.1	45.1
3.4	.2					All Other Current	2.6	1.9
85.2	65.8					Total Current	71.5	68.1
4.3	9.0					Fixed Assets (net)	17.4	15.7
4.6	6.5					Intangibles (net)	3.0	3.0
5.9	18.7					All Other Non-Current	8.1	13.2
100.0	100.0					Total	100.0	100.0
						LIABILITIES		
26.1	6.1					Notes Payable-Short Term	8.4	9.1
.6	.9					Cur. Mat.-L.T.D.	3.0	2.0
13.6	20.3					Trade Payables	23.6	22.0
.1	.0					Income Taxes Payable	.2	.1
13.4	11.5					All Other Current	13.8	15.1
53.8	38.7					Total Current	49.0	48.3
5.9	11.8					Long-Term Debt	15.1	9.3
.0	.0					Deferred Taxes	.1	.0
2.4	10.4					All Other Non-Current	2.9	5.5
37.9	39.1					Net Worth	32.8	37.0
100.0	100.0					Total Liabilities & Net Worth	100.0	100.0
						INCOME DATA		
100.0	100.0					Net Sales	100.0	100.0
46.2	53.5					Gross Profit	44.6	51.0
41.9	47.8					Operating Expenses	42.6	45.0
4.3	5.7					Operating Profit	1.9	6.0
.3	.2					All Other Expenses (net)	.5	.5
4.0	5.5					Profit Before Taxes	1.4	5.5
						RATIOS		
4.3	3.2						3.0	3.0
2.0	2.1					Current	1.7	1.9
1.1	1.1						1.1	1.1
.9	1.1						.8	1.2
.4	.4					Quick	.3	.3
.1	.1						.1	.1
0 UND	**0** UND						**0** UND	**0** UND
0 UND	**0** 977.0					Sales/Receivables	**3** 118.0	**1** 262.0
2 147.5	**5** 69.7						**12** 30.0	**15** 24.9
81 4.5	**107** 3.4						**83** 4.4	**114** 3.2
140 2.6	**159** 2.3					Cost of Sales/Inventory	**143** 2.5	**148** 2.5
261 1.4	**261** 1.4						**229** 1.6	**225** 1.6
5 76.2	**27** 13.3						**32** 11.2	**34** 10.6
23 15.6	**63** 5.8					Cost of Sales/Payables	**49** 7.5	**60** 6.1
45 8.2	**107** 3.4						**89** 4.1	**147** 2.5
4.7	4.0						4.3	4.2
9.3	7.8					Sales/Working Capital	9.0	7.2
NM	23.1						35.6	43.9
	17.6						6.1	21.6
	(21) 7.9					EBIT/Interest	(45) 3.0	(42) 4.9
	1.8						-.6	.7
						Net Profit + Depr., Dep., Amort./Cur. Mat. L/T/D		
.1	.0						.1	.1
.1	.1					Fixed/Worth	.5	.4
UND	.4						UND	2.2
.4	.4						.7	.4
.9	1.1					Debt/Worth	1.4	1.0
UND	5.0						UND	14.8
63.4	66.2						24.5	59.0
(10) 34.5	(28) 27.0					% Profit Before Taxes/Tangible Net Worth	(41) 13.0	(47) 15.9
6.1	7.3						.6	5.9
34.8	21.4						9.8	15.2
7.0	10.2					% Profit Before Taxes/Total Assets	4.4	6.1
.9	3.2						-4.6	.8
116.1	269.3						53.3	64.0
78.4	38.0					Sales/Net Fixed Assets	17.8	27.6
47.0	16.8						7.4	10.1
4.4	3.1						3.2	3.1
3.5	2.2					Sales/Total Assets	2.3	2.0
1.8	1.3						1.5	1.3
	.4						.4	.3
	(20) .4					% Depr., Dep., Amort./Sales	(43) .7	(43) .9
	.9						1.9	1.6
							1.9	3.4
						% Officers', Directors' Owners' Comp/Sales	(21) 5.0	(23) 6.6
							7.7	11.3
11165M	79471M	84796M	339729M	113202M	1078228M	Net Sales ($)	2597531M	1234385M
3608M	32306M	35863M	121651M	85980M	726143M	Total Assets ($)	1084817M	641330M

M = $ thousand MM = $ million

See Pages 9 through 22 for Explanation of Ratios and Data

Comparative Historical Data / Current Data Sorted by Sales

4/1/11-3/31/12 ALL	4/1/12-3/31/13 ALL	4/1/13-3/31/14 ALL	Type of Statement	0-1MM	1-3MM	3-5MM	5-10MM	10-25MM	25MM & OVER
3	1	4	Unqualified	1					3
7	7	3	Reviewed			1		1	1
10	4	9	Compiled	3	4		2		
18	15	17	Tax Returns	9	7			1	
25	30	30	Other	1	16	2	2	2	7
					11 (4/1-9/30/13)		52 (10/1/13-3/31/14)		
63	57	63	**NUMBER OF STATEMENTS**	14	27	3	4	4	11
%	%	%	**ASSETS**	%	%	%	%	%	%
11.3	16.2	14.2	Cash & Equivalents	9.5	16.5				19.4
7.4	8.1	7.3	Trade Receivables (net)	4.7	6.1				4.9
49.8	49.6	46.2	Inventory	48.5	47.9				38.8
1.9	.9	1.6	All Other Current	.8	1.7				3.5
70.3	74.8	69.2	Total Current	63.5	72.1				66.7
14.6	11.8	10.6	Fixed Assets (net)	11.4	8.6				16.4
2.8	2.1	6.3	Intangibles (net)	13.8	2.4				8.8
12.3	11.3	13.9	All Other Non-Current	11.2	16.9				8.2
100.0	100.0	100.0	Total	100.0	100.0				100.0
			LIABILITIES						
15.9	11.2	11.7	Notes Payable-Short Term	11.6	14.1				2.6
2.0	1.1	1.1	Cur. Mat.-L.T.D.	.7	.4				3.1
21.1	16.6	19.7	Trade Payables	11.7	20.7				17.9
.1	.1	.1	Income Taxes Payable	.1	.0				.3
14.2	6.4	11.3	All Other Current	15.2	9.2				11.4
53.3	35.4	43.8	Total Current	39.3	44.4				35.2
11.1	8.3	9.9	Long-Term Debt	12.7	9.8				7.1
.1	.1	.2	Deferred Taxes	.0	.0				1.0
3.9	6.6	7.3	All Other Non-Current	7.2	9.2				8.0
31.7	49.6	38.8	Net Worth	40.8	36.6				48.7
100.0	100.0	100.0	Total Liabilities & Net Worth	100.0	100.0				100.0
			INCOME DATA						
100.0	100.0	100.0	Net Sales	100.0	100.0				100.0
48.3	49.7	49.6	Gross Profit	49.4	53.4				47.7
43.7	43.4	43.8	Operating Expenses	43.4	45.7				44.3
4.6	6.3	5.7	Operating Profit	6.0	7.8				3.4
.8	.3	.7	All Other Expenses (net)	1.0	.5				1.1
3.8	6.0	5.1	Profit Before Taxes	5.0	7.3				2.3
			RATIOS						
2.7	3.6	3.1	Current	6.1	3.3				2.4
1.6	2.4	2.0		1.8	2.1				1.6
1.0	1.6	1.2		.8	1.9				1.4
.7	1.4	1.0	Quick	1.0	1.0				1.1
.3	.5	.4		.2	.5				.6
.1	.3	.1		.0	.3				.3
0 UND	0 UND	0 UND	Sales/Receivables	0 UND	0 UND				0 UND
1 451.5	1 435.0	1 282.2		0 UND	1 490.3				5 80.8
11 33.9	11 34.4	6 58.5		2 187.9	3 126.6				35 10.4
114 3.2	104 3.5	99 3.7	Cost of Sales/Inventory	91 4.0	99 3.7				91 4.0
152 2.4	159 2.3	146 2.5		174 2.1	166 2.2				140 2.6
203 1.8	228 1.6	228 1.6		730 .5	228 1.6				174 2.1
26 13.8	26 14.0	25 14.5	Cost of Sales/Payables	0 UND	27 13.3				40 9.1
58 6.3	50 7.3	55 6.6		11 33.1	65 5.6				63 5.8
114 3.2	79 4.6	101 3.6		64 5.7	122 3.0				94 3.9
4.8	3.7	4.6	Sales/Working Capital	3.6	4.0				4.6
9.2	6.5	7.9		11.9	6.2				8.4
-639.6	10.8	20.2		-11.3	10.9				12.7
9.1	14.3	19.1	EBIT/Interest	6.5	23.8				
(46) 2.9	(38) 5.3	(46) 7.4		(10) 3.8	(16) 7.9				
.6	1.7	.9		1.1	1.1				
			Net Profit + Depr., Dep., Amort./Cur. Mat. L/T/D						
.1	.0	.1	Fixed/Worth	.1	.0				.1
.3	.2	.2		.3	.1				.4
1.5	.5	.7		UND	.4				.7
.5	.5	.5	Debt/Worth	.2	.4				.7
1.5	.9	1.1		1.8	.8				1.3
14.5	2.0	5.0		UND	4.4				2.1
36.5	62.9	51.8	% Profit Before Taxes/Tangible Net Worth	50.0	79.9				44.4
(49) 10.9	(52) 12.8	(55) 21.4		(11) 18.6	(24) 18.4				(10) 19.4
1.2	5.7	5.2		6.0	7.3				-14.3
12.6	20.2	20.1	% Profit Before Taxes/Total Assets	11.1	28.6				16.1
4.4	7.8	8.1		4.2	10.6				6.2
-.4	2.3	.2		-.5	3.8				-5.8
110.4	285.3	111.0	Sales/Net Fixed Assets	85.7	209.6				34.7
34.2	45.5	37.7		37.5	38.0				12.8
10.1	11.2	12.8		4.6	16.8				8.2
3.0	3.2	3.4	Sales/Total Assets	3.5	3.4				3.0
2.2	2.3	2.3		1.2	2.3				1.7
1.4	1.6	1.4		.5	1.7				1.5
.4	.4	.3	% Depr., Dep., Amort./Sales		.3				
(47) 1.0	(39) .8	(44) .4			(20) .4				
1.9	1.4	1.1			.8				
3.3	3.4	3.3	% Officers', Directors' Owners' Comp/Sales						
(19) 8.4	(20) 7.2	(20) 5.8							
11.4	11.8	9.6							
1372409M	987095M	1706591M	Net Sales ($)	8312M	53125M	13187M	28286M	62619M	1541062M
693014M	620978M	1005551M	Total Assets ($)	7972M	27204M	5567M	9846M	22413M	932549M

M = $ thousand MM = $ million

See Pages 9 through 22 for Explanation of Ratios and Data

Current Data Sorted by Assets							Comparative Historical Data	
						Type of Statement		
		3	4	2	4	Unqualified	16	14
		9	5			Reviewed	11	11
1	2	2				Compiled	9	14
14	5	3				Tax Returns	38	25
11	21	11	9	6	9	Other	35	35
16 (4/1-9/30/13)		105 (10/1/13-3/31/14)					4/1/09-3/31/10 ALL	4/1/10-3/31/11 ALL
0-500M	500M-2MM	2-10MM	10-50MM	50-100MM	100-250MM			
26	28	28	18	8	13	**NUMBER OF STATEMENTS**	109	99
%	%	%	%	%	%	**ASSETS**	%	%
24.6	26.1	16.8	13.8		15.9	Cash & Equivalents	14.5	16.5
2.6	7.3	16.2	7.3		1.7	Trade Receivables (net)	4.9	8.9
51.3	34.9	40.1	36.5		29.7	Inventory	41.3	38.8
.7	.4	1.0	4.4		4.1	All Other Current	5.5	5.3
79.2	68.6	74.1	62.0		51.4	Total Current	66.3	69.5
11.0	14.9	14.6	25.1		29.8	Fixed Assets (net)	23.9	19.0
3.9	3.2	.5	4.1		13.4	Intangibles (net)	3.9	4.2
5.9	13.3	10.9	8.7		5.4	All Other Non-Current	5.9	7.3
100.0	100.0	100.0	100.0		100.0	Total	100.0	100.0
						LIABILITIES		
21.2	2.1	7.5	4.4		1.4	Notes Payable-Short Term	8.8	12.6
1.5	.6	1.8	.4		1.2	Cur. Mat.-L.T.D.	4.8	4.2
7.4	14.8	18.2	20.0		15.8	Trade Payables	13.7	18.9
.1	.0	.2	.1		.0	Income Taxes Payable	.1	.3
11.4	8.8	6.5	11.2		18.0	All Other Current	15.1	13.4
41.7	26.3	34.3	36.0		36.3	Total Current	42.6	49.3
10.9	10.8	12.2	7.8		6.2	Long-Term Debt	15.9	12.1
.0	.0	.0	.3		1.4	Deferred Taxes	.5	.3
17.7	16.3	6.0	14.8		8.5	All Other Non-Current	8.0	8.8
29.8	46.5	47.6	41.1		47.6	Net Worth	33.0	29.5
100.0	100.0	100.0	100.0		100.0	Total Liabilties & Net Worth	100.0	100.0
						INCOME DATA		
100.0	100.0	100.0	100.0		100.0	Net Sales	100.0	100.0
49.7	50.9	45.3	47.9		41.8	Gross Profit	46.4	46.4
43.1	41.5	38.3	47.1		42.7	Operating Expenses	44.8	41.5
6.6	9.5	7.0	.8		-.9	Operating Profit	1.6	4.9
.4	.4	.7	-.2		1.1	All Other Expenses (net)	.9	1.0
6.1	9.0	6.3	1.0		-2.0	Profit Before Taxes	.7	3.9
						RATIOS		
7.1	78.5	4.5	2.8		1.9		3.6	3.0
3.1	4.0	2.5	1.9		1.6	Current	1.7	1.7
1.1	1.4	1.4	1.2		1.0		1.1	1.0
2.8	37.5	1.7	1.1		.8		1.0	1.2
.8	1.9	.8	.5		.5	Quick	.4	(98) .5
.2	.3	.4	.2		.2		.2	.1
0 UND	**0** UND	**0** UND	**0** UND		**0** 741.1		**0** UND	**0** UND
0 UND	**0** UND	**15** 24.3	**2** 156.3		**2** 178.0	Sales/Receivables	**0** 999.8	**1** 446.5
0 UND	**5** 80.3	**38** 9.6	**8** 44.6		**4** 98.1		**4** 94.9	**9** 39.4
37 9.8	**46** 8.0	**38** 9.5	**60** 6.1		**46** 8.0		**50** 7.2	**49** 7.5
104 3.5	**140** 2.6	**89** 4.1	**96** 3.8		**61** 6.0	Cost of Sales/Inventory	**84** 4.3	**86** 4.3
152 2.4	**243** 1.5	**182** 2.0	**140** 2.6		**101** 3.6		**148** 2.5	**141** 2.6
0 UND	**0** UND	**19** 19.0	**26** 14.0		**20** 18.4		**8** 43.6	**16** 22.9
1 509.9	**9** 41.3	**40** 9.2	**41** 9.0		**38** 9.7	Cost of Sales/Payables	**22** 17.0	**36** 10.0
24 15.4	**65** 5.6	**65** 5.6	**69** 5.3		**66** 5.5		**53** 6.9	**61** 6.0
4.1	2.0	3.5	6.0		9.4		5.6	5.5
13.4	5.0	7.5	11.6		12.9	Sales/Working Capital	12.4	13.1
61.0	13.1	25.4	23.1		NM		58.2	136.1
24.8	48.8	30.0	48.9		30.3		8.8	18.6
(17) 5.0	(15) 11.3	(26) 8.1	(13) 10.7		(12) -2.5	EBIT/Interest	(81) 1.4	(81) 4.4
1.3	1.9	2.2	.1		-43.2		-5.1	1.2
							22.3	12.7
						Net Profit + Depr., Dep., Amort./Cur. Mat. L/T/D	(14) 1.9	(13) 4.1
							-.3	1.3
.0	.1	.1	.1		.5		.2	.1
.2	.2	.2	.8		.7	Fixed/Worth	.6	.5
-2.6	.8	.4	1.6		NM		2.0	1.6
.4	.1	.4	.9		.8		.5	.5
1.2	.9	1.0	2.0		.8	Debt/Worth	1.5	1.6
-9.1	3.6	1.7	3.2		NM		8.0	14.2
200.3	82.9	53.5	39.0		14.0		33.5	69.2
(18) 40.1	(24) 26.5	(26) 22.3	19.2		(10) 1.7	% Profit Before Taxes/Tangible Net Worth	(90) 12.0	(79) 25.0
-1.0	3.9	2.5	-.7		-43.7		-7.2	4.8
44.0	27.5	30.6	12.8		6.0		13.8	22.0
15.4	8.9	10.5	5.0		-1.4	% Profit Before Taxes/Total Assets	3.2	11.3
-.2	2.4	1.9	-.4		-17.7		-6.9	.9
UND	40.1	71.7	71.2		11.7		44.9	82.4
78.9	26.2	26.4	16.1		9.4	Sales/Net Fixed Assets	15.1	16.7
24.7	9.2	16.2	7.2		7.7		7.3	9.1
5.7	3.1	3.8	3.9		3.3		3.9	4.2
3.9	1.7	2.9	2.9		2.6	Sales/Total Assets	2.8	2.9
2.5	1.2	2.0	2.0		2.2		2.1	2.2
.2	.2	.3	.6				.6	.5
(13) .4	(13) .4	(23) .6	(16) 2.2			% Depr., Dep., Amort./Sales	(80) 1.5	(72) 1.3
1.0	1.2	1.2	3.7				2.6	2.5
7.6	.5	1.1					1.8	1.8
(11) 9.1	(11) 2.9	(14) 1.8				% Officers', Directors' Owners' Comp/Sales	(43) 4.0	(38) 3.6
11.1	8.1	3.9					6.1	7.1
22283M	**97118M**	**443355M**	**1219589M**	**1661903M**	**5067860M**	Net Sales ($)	**8363772M**	**6814175M**
5116M	**34831M**	**142788M**	**422558M**	**582407M**	**2002564M**	Total Assets ($)	**3128948M**	**2403813M**

M = $ thousand MM = $ million

See Pages 9 through 22 for Explanation of Ratios and Data

Comparative Historical Data / Current Data Sorted by Sales

Type of Statement	4/1/11-3/31/12 ALL	4/1/12-3/31/13 ALL	4/1/13-3/31/14 ALL	0-1MM	1-3MM	3-5MM	5-10MM	10-25MM	25MM & OVER
Unqualified	19	12	13			1		2	10
Reviewed	10	7	14				3	2	9
Compiled	16	16	5	1	1	1		2	
Tax Returns	39	28	22	13	5	1		3	
Other	52	45	67	11	17	1	6	8	24
				16 (4/1-9/30/13)		105 (10/1/13-3/31/14)			
NUMBER OF STATEMENTS	136	108	121	25	23	4	9	17	43
ASSETS	%	%	%	%	%	%	%	%	%
Cash & Equivalents	17.0	18.7	19.7	22.6	26.9			24.2	14.1
Trade Receivables (net)	6.0	5.7	7.4	4.5	5.1			13.9	4.9
Inventory	42.6	42.6	39.6	48.5	38.7			33.8	37.5
All Other Current	2.7	2.5	1.8	.5	.5			.4	3.7
Total Current	68.3	69.4	68.5	76.1	71.3			72.2	60.2
Fixed Assets (net)	20.2	17.1	17.7	12.8	13.3			12.6	26.3
Intangibles (net)	3.0	3.5	4.6	4.5	2.3			.2	8.4
All Other Non-Current	8.4	9.9	9.2	6.6	13.1			15.0	5.2
Total	100.0	100.0	100.0	100.0	100.0			100.0	100.0
LIABILITIES									
Notes Payable-Short Term	6.3	7.1	8.0	15.5	9.2			7.3	3.9
Cur. Mat.-L.T.D.	2.3	1.7	1.1	.9	1.2			.8	1.3
Trade Payables	18.3	18.3	14.9	8.0	12.4			15.2	18.7
Income Taxes Payable	.2	.1	.1	.0	.0			.0	.2
All Other Current	16.9	11.6	10.6	8.5	8.5			6.3	13.8
Total Current	44.0	38.7	34.7	33.0	31.4			29.6	38.0
Long-Term Debt	14.1	11.4	10.8	16.3	3.9			12.5	9.2
Deferred Taxes	.1	.2	.2	.0	.0			.0	.6
All Other Non-Current	15.3	11.6	12.6	22.0	10.4			8.3	8.3
Net Worth	26.5	38.0	41.7	28.8	54.4			49.6	44.0
Total Liabilties & Net Worth	100.0	100.0	100.0	100.0	100.0			100.0	100.0
INCOME DATA									
Net Sales	100.0	100.0	100.0	100.0	100.0			100.0	100.0
Gross Profit	48.1	45.0	47.9	52.3	53.0			41.6	46.8
Operating Expenses	44.4	41.0	42.7	47.1	41.0			37.4	45.4
Operating Profit	3.7	3.9	5.2	5.2	12.0			4.2	1.4
All Other Expenses (net)	.3	.4	.5	1.0	-.1			.0	.7
Profit Before Taxes	3.3	3.6	4.7	4.3	12.0			4.2	.7
RATIOS									
Current	4.9	4.8	4.4	9.0	9.6			5.0	2.1
	1.8	1.8	2.1	4.0	2.7			4.3	1.7
	1.2	1.2	1.2	2.1	1.4			1.5	1.2
Quick	1.5	1.4	2.3	4.4	3.7			2.7	.8
	(135) .6	.4	.7	1.1	1.3			1.4	.5
	.2	.1	.2	.2	.3			.5	.2
Sales/Receivables	0 UND	0 UND	0 UND	0 UND	0 UND			0 UND	0 825.1
	0 UND	0 UND	1 385.5	0 UND	0 UND			5 76.9	2 176.9
	5 72.4	4 88.6	6 59.6	0 UND	2 189.9			34 10.7	5 77.2
Cost of Sales/Inventory	54 6.7	49 7.4	51 7.2	62 5.9	44 8.3			24 15.0	54 6.8
	101 3.6	87 4.2	96 3.8	140 2.6	114 3.2			79 4.6	85 4.3
	174 2.1	182 2.0	159 2.3	332 1.1	192 1.9			140 2.6	135 2.7
Cost of Sales/Payables	7 49.4	3 139.7	4 82.7	0 UND	0 UND			6 63.0	27 13.7
	33 11.0	31 11.8	30 12.2	0 UND	5 73.9			30 12.0	38 9.7
	58 6.3	49 7.4	63 5.8	35 10.3	94 3.9			48 7.6	66 5.5
Sales/Working Capital	5.2	4.7	4.4	2.5	2.6			4.7	8.2
	9.7	11.1	8.7	4.6	6.3			7.5	13.2
	45.1	50.4	34.8	27.7	57.5			57.3	41.1
EBIT/Interest	16.9	19.7	27.6	14.3	96.8			20.0	35.8
	(86) 4.1	(65) 3.0	(88) 5.9	(14) 4.3	(14) 30.8			(15) 6.0	(33) 6.4
	1.2	-1.9	.2	1.3	1.7			1.0	-5.4
Net Profit + Depr., Dep., Amort./Cur. Mat. L/T/D			33.4						
			(10) 5.6						
			.2						
Fixed/Worth	.2	.1	.1	.0	.1			.0	.3
	.6	.5	.4	.1	.2			.2	.8
	4.7	1.4	1.2	-2.6	.5			.6	1.8
Debt/Worth	.7	.5	.5	.2	.3			.3	.8
	1.5	1.3	1.3	1.0	.9			1.4	1.4
	48.7	7.7	4.4	-9.0	2.4			2.4	3.9
% Profit Before Taxes/Tangible Net Worth	49.9	58.6	51.2	43.7	114.7			73.8	33.0
	(106) 18.4	(90) 19.0	(102) 18.3	(17) 10.9	(22) 49.5			(16) 22.7	(38) 8.9
	3.1	2.3	1.4	-1.7	5.3			.1	-10.4
% Profit Before Taxes/Total Assets	18.3	17.3	22.6	24.2	46.4			44.6	11.6
	6.0	6.7	7.1	7.7	13.2			6.2	4.3
	.1	-3.6	.0	-1.5	6.1			.1	-7.2
Sales/Net Fixed Assets	74.8	120.4	80.9	UND	34.0			162.6	24.1
	16.6	21.7	22.5	92.1	26.4			22.5	11.5
	9.5	10.4	10.1	14.8	16.2			15.0	7.9
Sales/Total Assets	4.3	4.2	3.9	4.0	5.3			4.9	3.8
	2.9	3.1	2.9	2.5	1.9			3.0	3.1
	2.0	1.8	1.8	1.1	1.5			2.3	2.3
% Depr., Dep., Amort./Sales	.4	.2	.3	.2				.2	.7
	(94) 1.1	(72) .7	(76) .9	(13) .4				(13) 1.1	(31) 1.8
	2.1	2.3	2.3	1.0				2.0	3.1
% Officers', Directors' Owners' Comp/Sales	2.5	2.1	1.2						.8
	(62) 4.6	(50) 3.6	(41) 3.2						(11) 1.1
	6.6	5.9	7.9						3.3
Net Sales ($)	7550109M	8549091M	8512108M	15957M	45344M	15577M	68499M	243642M	8123089M
Total Assets ($)	2605585M	3420194M	3190264M	9972M	23799M	7013M	27206M	93801M	3028473M

M = $ thousand MM = $ million

See Pages 9 through 22 for Explanation of Ratios and Data

Current Data Sorted by Assets							Comparative Historical Data	
						Type of Statement		
	1	1	4	3	2	Unqualified	11	10
		4	5			Reviewed	20	9
1	2	4	1			Compiled	13	13
15	19	3	1			Tax Returns	24	25
3	10	10	2	3	2	Other	30	35
	10 (4/1-9/30/13)		86 (10/1/13-3/31/14)				4/1/09-3/31/10	4/1/10-3/31/11
0-500M	500M-2MM	2-10MM	10-50MM	50-100MM	100-250MM		ALL	ALL
19	32	22	13	6	4	**NUMBER OF STATEMENTS**	98	92
%	%	%	%	%	%	**ASSETS**	%	%
8.2	15.5	10.0	20.8			Cash & Equivalents	14.8	11.9
.3	7.8	7.6	3.4			Trade Receivables (net)	8.2	7.3
70.1	54.3	48.2	36.3			Inventory	46.5	54.1
3.3	.9	1.4	2.0			All Other Current	2.4	2.4
81.9	78.5	67.2	62.4			Total Current	71.9	75.7
5.2	11.8	23.4	32.5			Fixed Assets (net)	17.2	17.1
6.7	1.8	3.4	2.4			Intangibles (net)	3.3	2.3
6.3	8.0	6.0	2.7			All Other Non-Current	7.6	4.9
100.0	100.0	100.0	100.0			Total	100.0	100.0
						LIABILITIES		
10.2	9.6	3.7	2.2			Notes Payable-Short Term	7.4	8.8
3.4	.8	6.9	2.4			Cur. Mat.-L.T.D.	2.9	3.5
28.7	24.9	20.0	12.3			Trade Payables	16.3	22.0
.0	.0	.2	.2			Income Taxes Payable	.3	.3
5.5	7.4	10.8	13.1			All Other Current	13.4	9.2
47.8	42.7	41.6	30.2			Total Current	40.3	43.6
16.0	5.1	16.2	8.4			Long-Term Debt	14.3	10.8
.0	.0	.1	.1			Deferred Taxes	.1	.1
11.6	21.1	17.3	11.1			All Other Non-Current	6.2	6.4
24.6	31.1	24.9	50.2			Net Worth	39.2	39.1
100.0	100.0	100.0	100.0			Total Liabilties & Net Worth	100.0	100.0
						INCOME DATA		
100.0	100.0	100.0	100.0			Net Sales	100.0	100.0
36.5	43.4	48.8	47.6			Gross Profit	44.0	42.3
33.3	39.6	43.0	39.9			Operating Expenses	40.9	38.3
3.3	3.8	5.8	7.7			Operating Profit	3.1	4.0
.1	.2	1.6	.3			All Other Expenses (net)	.2	.2
3.2	3.6	4.2	7.4			Profit Before Taxes	2.8	3.8
						RATIOS		
3.0	4.3	2.7	3.4				4.3	3.2
1.8	1.6	2.1	1.6			Current	2.0	2.0
1.1	1.2	1.3	1.2				1.2	1.3
.9	1.8	.6	1.5				1.2	1.1
.0	.3	.3	.5			Quick	.6	.3
.0	.1	.1	.3				.2	.1
0 UND	**0** UND	**0** UND	**0** UND				**0** UND	**0** UND
0 UND	**0** UND	**1** 378.4	**0** UND			Sales/Receivables	**0** 973.0	**1** 325.1
0 UND	**4** 87.9	**3** 139.7	**3** 111.6				**13** 28.1	**6** 58.7
49 7.4	**47** 7.7	**111** 3.4	**57** 6.4				**73** 5.0	**72** 5.1
107 3.4	**135** 2.7	**159** 2.3	**107** 3.4			Cost of Sales/Inventory	**109** 3.4	**120** 3.1
152 2.4	**203** 1.8	**261** 1.4	**146** 2.5				**179** 2.0	**210** 1.7
3 109.4	**10** 38.3	**24** 15.4	**17** 22.0				**11** 32.7	**17** 22.0
29 12.8	**49** 7.5	**44** 8.3	**29** 12.4			Cost of Sales/Payables	**34** 10.8	**41** 9.0
45 8.1	**83** 4.4	**78** 4.7	**48** 7.6				**53** 6.9	**69** 5.3
5.3	4.4	4.9	6.6				4.3	4.0
7.6	11.6	9.3	10.7			Sales/Working Capital	9.0	8.9
157.2	32.6	21.7	26.2				29.8	30.8
3.7	26.0	10.0					12.7	20.2
(10) -.3	(18) 9.9	(19) 4.2				EBIT/Interest	(73) 4.0	(71) 6.0
-5.3	-1.1	1.3					1.2	1.4
							8.3	10.4
						Net Profit + Depr., Dep., Amort./Cur. Mat. L/T/D	(12) 1.5	(13) 2.2
							-3.9	.3
.0	.0	.2	.2				.1	.1
.1	.3	.7	.8			Fixed/Worth	.4	.3
1.0	.8	1.5	1.6				1.1	1.4
1.0	.8	.9	.4				.5	.5
5.4	1.6	1.6	1.5			Debt/Worth	1.2	1.5
-21.3	5.0	NM	2.8				5.4	5.2
103.0	61.6	64.1	82.8				58.0	50.6
(13) 5.7	(26) 33.3	(17) 27.8	27.2			% Profit Before Taxes/Tangible Net Worth	(84) 15.2	(82) 22.5
-12.8	1.9	3.4	10.0				4.0	3.7
25.5	26.3	25.8	21.8				16.7	19.4
2.1	7.2	4.8	11.5			% Profit Before Taxes/Total Assets	5.4	7.5
-7.2	-2.0	.6	4.2				.7	1.2
UND	140.4	42.2	24.8				114.0	92.8
193.2	50.8	20.5	12.5			Sales/Net Fixed Assets	21.1	24.9
73.1	17.9	8.2	4.1				10.5	10.2
6.5	3.9	3.7	3.6				4.2	4.4
4.3	2.5	2.8	2.7			Sales/Total Assets	2.8	2.6
2.3	2.0	1.8	1.8				1.7	1.7
	.2	.5	1.4				.5	.4
	(23) .7	(13) .7	(12) 1.9			% Depr., Dep., Amort./Sales	(68) 1.1	(67) .7
	1.2	1.9	4.0				1.6	1.5
2.0	1.7	.7					1.3	1.1
(10) 3.9	(22) 4.5	(10) 1.7				% Officers', Directors' Owners' Comp/Sales	(37) 3.8	(30) 2.6
6.4	6.6	5.4					6.7	5.6
22756M	144173M	285487M	884296M	804263M	2022441M	Net Sales ($)	3894911M	5987829M
4709M	38519M	95530M	310679M	413559M	625266M	Total Assets ($)	1358963M	2138977M

M = $ thousand MM = $ million

See Pages 9 through 22 for Explanation of Ratios and Data

Comparative Historical Data | Current Data Sorted by Sales

4/1/11-3/31/12 ALL	4/1/12-3/31/13 ALL	4/1/13-3/31/14 ALL	Type of Statement	0-1MM	1-3MM	3-5MM	5-10MM	10-25MM	25MM & OVER
11	7	11	Unqualified		1			1	9
14	10	9	Reviewed		1		1	2	5
15	17	8	Compiled		1	1	4		2
35	24	38	Tax Returns	8	17	6	4	2	1
29	42	30	Other	6	4	2	5	5	8
				10 (4/1-9/30/13)			86 (10/1/13-3/31/14)		
104	100	96	**NUMBER OF STATEMENTS**	14	24	9	14	10	25
%	%	%	**ASSETS**	%	%	%	%	%	%
15.2	16.2	13.0	Cash & Equivalents	8.9	5.6		18.6	10.4	18.3
5.9	6.6	5.5	Trade Receivables (net)	2.2	1.2		5.3	.9	6.9
50.9	49.8	52.2	Inventory	60.4	65.1		54.9	50.5	37.1
2.4	1.6	1.9	All Other Current	5.1	.8		1.4	1.6	2.0
74.4	74.2	72.5	Total Current	76.7	72.7		80.2	63.5	64.3
15.8	14.1	16.5	Fixed Assets (net)	10.4	13.5		17.5	25.5	22.9
2.0	2.7	4.8	Intangibles (net)	5.2	5.6		.0	4.6	8.3
7.8	9.0	6.2	All Other Non-Current	7.7	8.3		2.3	6.4	4.5
100.0	100.0	100.0	Total	100.0	100.0		100.0	100.0	100.0
			LIABILITIES						
8.4	7.6	6.9	Notes Payable-Short Term	9.0	8.4		4.3	8.5	3.1
2.3	1.2	3.1	Cur. Mat.-L.T.D.	3.6	2.5		8.4	1.9	1.9
20.7	23.9	22.4	Trade Payables	11.9	32.6		26.1	18.6	16.1
.2	.1	.2	Income Taxes Payable	.1	.0		.3	.1	.4
10.3	14.7	8.5	All Other Current	8.3	5.0		12.7	9.8	9.6
41.9	47.5	41.1	Total Current	32.9	48.6		51.7	38.9	31.0
10.2	11.9	11.4	Long-Term Debt	23.2	11.8		10.2	7.2	10.5
.1	.2	.1	Deferred Taxes	.0	.0		.0	.2	.2
9.5	12.0	15.3	All Other Non-Current	20.9	20.2		24.9	7.2	7.7
38.3	28.4	32.1	Net Worth	23.1	19.4		13.2	46.5	50.6
100.0	100.0	100.0	Total Liabilties & Net Worth	100.0	100.0		100.0	100.0	100.0
			INCOME DATA						
100.0	100.0	100.0	Net Sales	100.0	100.0		100.0	100.0	100.0
42.6	44.2	43.6	Gross Profit	40.4	39.6		53.6	43.1	45.0
38.1	40.3	38.6	Operating Expenses	36.9	36.3		47.5	38.2	37.4
4.4	3.9	5.0	Operating Profit	3.4	3.3		6.1	4.9	7.6
.2	.5	.6	All Other Expenses (net)	.9	1.0		.8	.4	.5
4.3	3.4	4.4	Profit Before Taxes	2.5	2.3		5.3	4.5	7.2
			RATIOS						
3.1	3.0	3.2		6.7	3.6		3.3	2.4	3.5
2.0	1.7	1.7	Current	2.3	1.3		1.8	1.7	1.9
1.2	1.3	1.2		1.5	1.1		1.0	1.1	1.3
1.2	1.1	1.0		1.5	.4		.7	.5	1.6
(103) .4	.4	.3	Quick	.2	.2		.3	.3	.7
.1	.1	.1		.0	.0		.1	.1	.2
0 UND	0 UND	0 UND		0 UND	0 UND		0 UND	0 UND	0 UND
1 329.4	1 657.0	0 UND	Sales/Receivables	0 UND	0 UND		0 UND	1 619.9	1 718.9
6 57.9	7 52.0	3 123.8		1 243.5	0 999.8		1 288.9	2 210.8	5 77.7
81 4.5	68 5.4	64 5.7		104 3.5	74 4.9		96 3.8	69 5.3	56 6.5
114 3.2	107 3.4	122 3.0	Cost of Sales/Inventory	166 2.2	140 2.6		166 2.2	101 3.6	104 3.5
166 2.2	152 2.4	166 2.2		304 1.2	228 1.6		182 2.0	135 2.7	126 2.9
14 25.3	24 15.2	18 20.0		0 UND	4 86.3		36 10.0	16 22.5	19 19.1
39 9.3	49 7.5	39 9.3	Cost of Sales/Payables	24 14.9	45 8.2		57 6.4	32 11.3	35 10.3
66 5.5	74 4.9	65 5.6		68 5.4	81 4.5		104 3.5	47 7.8	49 7.5
4.6	6.0	5.0		3.7	4.8		5.1	8.5	6.4
9.0	11.1	10.5	Sales/Working Capital	5.2	16.4		9.3	15.8	12.9
27.1	26.7	32.3		7.5	128.6		401.5	NM	22.7
21.2	29.1	14.4		3.5	11.1		14.4		57.4
(80) 5.3	(78) 6.4	(63) 4.3	EBIT/Interest	(11) -.9	(13) 4.5		(11) 4.3		(17) 12.0
1.5	1.8	.8		-4.0	-.3		3.3		2.8
9.8	5.8	5.4							
(13) 2.2	(13) 3.4	(10) 2.7	Net Profit + Depr., Dep., Amort./Cur. Mat. L/T/D						
.8	1.2	.7							
.1	.1	.1		.0	.0		.1	.3	.2
.3	.4	.4	Fixed/Worth	.5	.2		.6	.6	.7
1.2	.9	1.4		NM	1.3		-2.1	.9	1.5
.5	.7	.9		.6	1.1		.9	.9	.4
1.5	1.6	1.9	Debt/Worth	29.6	2.6		2.3	1.5	1.7
5.3	4.7	6.7		-6.6	-16.0		-5.1	1.9	4.0
60.1	59.4	71.5			33.9		59.9	68.0	96.2
(91) 24.9	(83) 28.5	(77) 28.1	% Profit Before Taxes/Tangible Net Worth		(16) 8.4		(10) 45.9	18.2	(23) 30.9
4.8	8.3	3.0			-16.4		25.5	2.2	13.0
21.9	19.6	22.5		32.9	15.0		26.7	35.1	29.4
8.6	9.3	7.1	% Profit Before Taxes/Total Assets	.2	2.8		10.6	8.9	11.5
1.8	1.3	-.2		-8.6	-6.8		1.4	.4	5.4
95.3	94.2	166.5		UND	478.1		67.9	45.8	42.0
28.5	29.3	28.2	Sales/Net Fixed Assets	43.2	73.8		28.2	25.0	16.7
13.6	16.0	12.1		13.8	13.5		17.8	8.2	7.7
4.2	4.0	4.0		3.4	4.7		3.9	6.2	3.8
2.9	3.2	2.7	Sales/Total Assets	2.0	2.6		3.0	3.5	2.7
1.8	2.2	2.0		1.2	1.9		2.5	2.6	2.2
.4	.4	.4			.3				.8
(81) .8	(71) .9	(64) .8	% Depr., Dep., Amort./Sales		(15) .7				(22) 1.7
1.5	1.6	2.0			2.5				2.4
1.0	1.4	1.3			1.9				
(49) 3.0	(39) 3.0	(48) 3.7	% Officers', Directors' Owners' Comp/Sales		(17) 3.7				
6.1	6.6	6.1			8.7				
5267788M	5198131M	4163416M	Net Sales ($)	8324M	45186M	36330M	101865M	168444M	3803267M
2078061M	2148585M	1488262M	Total Assets ($)	8400M	27307M	12299M	36579M	61194M	1342483M

M = $ thousand MM = $ million

See Pages 9 through 22 for Explanation of Ratios and Data

Current Data Sorted by Assets							Comparative Historical Data	
						Type of Statement		
					1	Unqualified	4	5
		1	2			Reviewed	6	8
3		3	1			Compiled	3	9
3	6	4	1			Tax Returns	35	25
3	5	9	3		1	Other	22	26
	6 (4/1-9/30/13)		40 (10/1/13-3/31/14)				**4/1/09-3/31/10 ALL**	**4/1/10-3/31/11 ALL**
0-500M	**500M-2MM**	**2-10MM**	**10-50MM**	**50-100MM**	**100-250MM**			
9	11	17	7		2	**NUMBER OF STATEMENTS**	70	73
%	%	%	%	%	%	**ASSETS**	%	%
	18.0	16.0		DATA NOT AVAILABLE		Cash & Equivalents	12.0	11.3
	3.0	11.6				Trade Receivables (net)	11.0	12.7
	41.9	40.3				Inventory	48.1	45.2
	.9	2.5				All Other Current	2.4	1.7
	63.8	70.5				Total Current	73.4	71.0
	31.2	21.6				Fixed Assets (net)	14.7	17.8
	1.7	1.1				Intangibles (net)	4.3	3.5
	3.4	6.7				All Other Non-Current	7.6	7.8
	100.0	100.0				Total	100.0	100.0
						LIABILITIES		
	18.4	8.1				Notes Payable-Short Term	14.1	6.4
	.8	1.4				Cur. Mat.-L.T.D.	2.6	3.1
	13.0	15.7				Trade Payables	24.3	18.2
	2.0	.4				Income Taxes Payable	.3	.4
	18.2	12.6				All Other Current	8.7	9.3
	52.4	38.3				Total Current	50.1	37.5
	15.5	13.9				Long-Term Debt	13.3	22.1
	.0	.1				Deferred Taxes	.3	.3
	19.6	6.4				All Other Non-Current	10.5	12.1
	12.5	41.3				Net Worth	25.8	28.1
	100.0	100.0				Total Liabilties & Net Worth	100.0	100.0
						INCOME DATA		
	100.0	100.0				Net Sales	100.0	100.0
	52.3	44.7				Gross Profit	48.0	46.8
	49.6	40.0				Operating Expenses	45.7	42.4
	2.7	4.7				Operating Profit	2.4	4.4
	.0	-.8				All Other Expenses (net)	.7	.9
	2.7	5.5				Profit Before Taxes	1.6	3.5
						RATIOS		
	1.9	4.2					3.4	4.7
	1.5	1.4				Current	1.7	1.9
	.7	1.1					.9	1.2
	.7	1.2					.9	1.3
	.4	.4				Quick	(69) .4	.5
	.1	.2					.1	.2
	0 UND	**0** UND					**0** UND	**0** UND
	0 UND	**4** 83.8				Sales/Receivables	**2** 152.9	**3** 104.7
	5 75.1	**34** 10.6					**20** 18.6	**23** 15.6
	60 6.1	**78** 4.7					**61** 6.0	**72** 5.1
	87 4.2	**114** 3.2				Cost of Sales/Inventory	**124** 2.9	**114** 3.2
	159 2.3	**152** 2.4					**268** 1.4	**182** 2.0
	10 35.9	**21** 17.8					**11** 33.0	**8** 44.3
	16 22.3	**37** 9.9				Cost of Sales/Payables	**38** 9.5	**41** 9.0
	54 6.8	**78** 4.7					**76** 4.8	**67** 5.5
	9.3	4.3					3.6	4.3
	15.3	7.8				Sales/Working Capital	8.5	7.6
	-18.5	NM					-82.0	27.3
	8.9	11.5					10.1	16.3
	(10) 3.7	(12) 4.2				EBIT/Interest	(53) 3.1	(54) 5.4
	1.3	1.2					-.6	.3
						Net Profit + Depr., Dep., Amort./Cur. Mat. L/T/D		
	.4	.1					.1	.1
	1.1	.4				Fixed/Worth	.4	.5
	-1.5	1.4					NM	NM
	.5	.7					.5	.6
	1.8	1.5				Debt/Worth	2.2	2.4
	-6.7	3.2					NM	NM
		68.2					57.2	47.3
		14.6				% Profit Before Taxes/Tangible Net Worth	(53) 20.0	(55) 23.0
		4.0					-4.7	9.2
	10.9	22.4					24.6	19.4
	1.9	5.5				% Profit Before Taxes/Total Assets	6.5	7.8
	.7	1.4					-3.6	.0
	38.1	43.8					103.1	89.9
	17.1	18.8				Sales/Net Fixed Assets	30.9	22.7
	4.7	8.0					11.8	8.1
	3.7	3.1					4.1	3.8
	3.1	2.6				Sales/Total Assets	2.4	2.5
	2.4	1.6					1.7	1.7
		.7					.4	.3
		(13) 1.1				% Depr., Dep., Amort./Sales	(52) .7	(52) 1.2
		2.3					1.9	2.3
							1.9	2.3
						% Officers', Directors' Owners' Comp/Sales	(30) 5.0	(31) 3.4
							10.3	6.8
7404M	33785M	162496M	422910M		771355M	Net Sales ($)	916192M	1408739M
2431M	12022M	67634M	166345M		394973M	Total Assets ($)	526226M	834658M

M = $ thousand MM = $ million

See Pages 9 through 22 for Explanation of Ratios and Data

Comparative Historical Data				Current Data Sorted by Sales					
10	5	1	**Type of Statement** Unqualified						1
6	4	3	Reviewed				1	1	1
10	9	7	Compiled	1	2	1	1	1	1
30	40	14	Tax Returns	3	5	2	2	1	1
24	23	21	Other	2	3	1	7	4	4
					6 (4/1-9/30/13)		40 (10/1/13-3/31/14)		
4/1/11-3/31/12 ALL	**4/1/12-3/31/13 ALL**	**4/1/13-3/31/14 ALL**		**0-1MM**	**1-3MM**	**3-5MM**	**5-10MM**	**10-25MM**	**25MM & OVER**
80	81	46	**NUMBER OF STATEMENTS**	6	10	4	11	7	8
%	%	%	**ASSETS**	%	%	%	%	%	%
13.9	12.3	15.3	Cash & Equivalents		20.5		11.9		
9.0	15.3	8.4	Trade Receivables (net)		4.7		15.1		
44.3	43.7	42.4	Inventory		46.4		51.2		
2.9	2.1	2.1	All Other Current		2.2		3.9		
70.0	73.5	68.3	Total Current		73.8		82.1		
15.5	16.0	22.0	Fixed Assets (net)		19.0		15.4		
4.4	2.4	4.2	Intangibles (net)		2.6		.9		
10.1	8.1	5.5	All Other Non-Current		4.6		1.6		
100.0	100.0	100.0	Total		100.0		100.0		
			LIABILITIES						
8.5	8.0	11.5	Notes Payable-Short Term		18.1		15.2		
2.0	2.3	2.4	Cur. Mat.-L.T.D.		.6		.1		
17.9	18.3	15.4	Trade Payables		9.4		19.0		
.4	.4	1.2	Income Taxes Payable		.1		.6		
10.1	11.1	14.1	All Other Current		17.0		10.9		
38.8	40.1	44.6	Total Current		45.3		45.8		
14.5	12.8	16.4	Long-Term Debt		5.5		10.0		
.2	.3	.4	Deferred Taxes		.0		.1		
14.4	11.4	10.8	All Other Non-Current		18.2		6.6		
32.1	35.5	27.7	Net Worth		31.0		37.6		
100.0	100.0	100.0	Total Liabilties & Net Worth		100.0		100.0		
			INCOME DATA						
100.0	100.0	100.0	Net Sales		100.0		100.0		
46.6	42.5	47.7	Gross Profit		50.5		40.9		
42.8	38.8	44.8	Operating Expenses		49.1		39.3		
3.8	3.6	2.9	Operating Profit		1.4		1.6		
.9	.2	-.1	All Other Expenses (net)		-.6		-1.9		
2.8	3.4	3.0	Profit Before Taxes		2.0		3.5		
			RATIOS						
3.6	4.4	3.0			2.7		4.5		
1.9	2.1	1.5	Current		1.8		2.0		
1.1	1.1	1.0			1.4		1.1		
1.4	1.4	.8			.7		.9		
.6	.8	.4	Quick		.5		.5		
.1	.2	.2			.3		.2		
0 UND	**0** UND	**0** UND			**0** UND		**1** 260.8		
2 182.6	**4** 84.8	**3** 135.8	Sales/Receivables		**0** UND		**10** 35.8		
13 27.4	**33** 11.2	**10** 35.3			**7** 49.9		**43** 8.5		
55 6.6	**42** 8.7	**69** 5.3			**61** 6.0		**99** 3.7		
99 3.7	**118** 3.1	**111** 3.3	Cost of Sales/Inventory		**78** 4.7		**114** 3.2		
174 2.1	**215** 1.7	**166** 2.2			**159** 2.3		**146** 2.5		
11 32.2	**7** 56.0	**11** 34.1			**0** UND		**20** 18.2		
30 12.1	**34** 10.7	**29** 12.4	Cost of Sales/Payables		**15** 24.6		**53** 6.9		
58 6.3	**63** 5.8	**70** 5.2			**35** 10.4		**74** 4.9		
5.8	3.9	5.4			6.7		3.7		
9.9	8.9	11.3	Sales/Working Capital		12.2		6.7		
38.7	36.9	NM			22.5		41.9		
19.9	28.0	17.1							
(62) 7.2	(59) 5.9	(36) 4.9	EBIT/Interest						
1.5	1.5	1.1							
			Net Profit + Depr., Dep., Amort./Cur. Mat. L/T/D						
.1	.1	.1			.0		.1		
.4	.2	.8	Fixed/Worth		.6		.3		
2.2	.9	18.7			NM		.9		
.8	.6	.6			.4		.8		
1.8	1.8	1.6	Debt/Worth		1.0		1.5		
10.8	5.3	32.9			NM		3.4		
66.1	53.9	56.7					66.7		
(64) 24.4	(70) 20.5	(36) 15.7	% Profit Before Taxes/Tangible Net Worth				(10) 14.1		
6.2	5.0	2.3					4.0		
18.9	18.0	15.2			13.3		14.9		
7.8	6.1	5.5	% Profit Before Taxes/Total Assets		3.7		5.5		
1.1	1.2	.6			.4		1.6		
128.0	246.5	47.0			589.9		41.9		
31.4	32.6	17.9	Sales/Net Fixed Assets		62.1		20.9		
11.7	11.0	7.9			8.0		12.2		
3.9	3.4	3.4			3.8		3.5		
2.7	2.6	2.9	Sales/Total Assets		3.5		2.9		
2.0	1.7	1.8			2.9		2.2		
.5	.6	.5							
(54) 1.1	(52) 1.1	(33) 1.3	% Depr., Dep., Amort./Sales						
2.1	2.9	2.8							
1.7	2.4	2.3							
(31) 4.8	(36) 5.6	(21) 3.7	% Officers', Directors' Owners' Comp/Sales						
6.6	8.6	7.2							
2193684M	**2265716M**	**1397950M**	Net Sales ($)	**3217M**	**17234M**	**16764M**	**79804M**	**100047M**	**1180884M**
1116168M	**1029097M**	**643405M**	Total Assets ($)	**2334M**	**6133M**	**9852M**	**31311M**	**43467M**	**550308M**

M = $ thousand MM = $ million

See Pages 9 through 22 for Explanation of Ratios and Data

Current Data Sorted by Assets							Comparative Historical Data	
						Type of Statement		
	1	1	7	4		Unqualified	19	9
1	2	13	1			Reviewed	19	25
	12	5	3			Compiled	22	17
30	22	6				Tax Returns	54	52
15	19	19	6	3		Other	55	56
29 (4/1-9/30/13)			141 (10/1/13-3/31/14)				4/1/09-3/31/10 ALL	4/1/10-3/31/11 ALL
0-500M	**500M-2MM**	**2-10MM**	**10-50MM**	**50-100MM**	**100-250MM**			
46	56	44	17	7		**NUMBER OF STATEMENTS**	169	159
%	%	%	%	%	%	**ASSETS**	%	%
18.0	19.1	10.6	7.9		DATA NOT AVAILABLE	Cash & Equivalents	11.1	10.4
10.8	9.6	16.3	8.3			Trade Receivables (net)	10.9	10.9
47.4	44.6	41.6	41.0			Inventory	44.2	47.7
1.2	.4	1.5	3.7			All Other Current	2.0	2.3
77.5	73.7	69.9	60.9			Total Current	68.2	71.3
12.5	15.7	18.0	23.6			Fixed Assets (net)	19.9	17.3
4.4	2.6	5.4	9.6			Intangibles (net)	5.0	5.1
5.6	8.0	6.7	5.9			All Other Non-Current	6.8	6.2
100.0	100.0	100.0	100.0			Total	100.0	100.0
						LIABILITIES		
15.8	11.1	10.6	12.1			Notes Payable-Short Term	13.6	11.7
5.3	1.7	3.0	1.7			Cur. Mat.-L.T.D.	3.5	2.7
26.1	19.0	19.1	11.6			Trade Payables	19.1	21.3
.0	.1	.1	.0			Income Taxes Payable	.1	.1
17.2	14.3	10.0	11.0			All Other Current	9.4	8.7
64.4	46.2	42.8	36.4			Total Current	45.7	44.6
22.7	18.1	10.3	12.6			Long-Term Debt	17.8	12.4
.0	.0	.1	.0			Deferred Taxes	.1	.1
4.2	4.0	2.5	6.5			All Other Non-Current	12.7	8.8
8.6	31.7	44.4	44.4			Net Worth	23.6	34.2
100.0	100.0	100.0	100.0			Total Liabilties & Net Worth	100.0	100.0
						INCOME DATA		
100.0	100.0	100.0	100.0			Net Sales	100.0	100.0
44.6	45.7	42.2	53.0			Gross Profit	46.2	47.7
42.5	40.7	37.0	43.6			Operating Expenses	42.7	42.9
2.1	5.0	5.2	9.4			Operating Profit	3.6	4.8
.0	.8	.4	.8			All Other Expenses (net)	1.2	.9
2.1	4.2	4.8	8.6			Profit Before Taxes	2.4	3.9
						RATIOS		
3.4	2.9	2.7	2.7				2.5	2.9
1.9	1.7	2.1	1.8			Current	1.7	1.8
.9	1.2	1.3	1.1				1.1	1.1
1.3	1.2	1.2	.9				1.1	1.0
.5	.5	.6	.3			Quick	(168) .4	.4
.1	.2	.3	.1				.1	.1
0 UND	0 UND	0 999.8	1 663.1				0 UND	0 UND
0 UND	2 191.5	20 18.0	1 285.0			Sales/Receivables	4 94.4	3 128.3
14 25.6	18 20.1	43 8.4	24 15.0				29 12.8	26 14.2
14 25.2	45 8.1	64 5.7	99 3.7				74 4.9	73 5.0
81 4.5	122 3.0	96 3.8	182 2.0			Cost of Sales/Inventory	120 3.0	132 2.8
174 2.1	182 2.0	152 2.4	281 1.3				200 1.8	204 1.8
0 UND	11 34.6	21 17.1	29 12.8				17 21.5	20 18.5
20 18.2	35 10.5	36 10.2	55 6.6			Cost of Sales/Payables	42 8.8	44 8.3
61 6.0	55 6.6	70 5.2	89 4.1				75 4.9	85 4.3
6.1	4.8	4.8	3.8				4.7	5.0
15.1	11.4	8.4	8.6			Sales/Working Capital	10.1	8.6
-86.2	39.4	25.7	58.7				64.2	43.5
19.4	15.5	39.4	16.6				8.9	13.7
(31) 4.0	(40) 5.0	(36) 5.6	7.0			EBIT/Interest	(136) 3.3	(131) 3.3
-1.8	1.0	1.3	3.5				.6	1.0
							11.2	16.8
						Net Profit + Depr., Dep., Amort./Cur. Mat. L/T/D	(19) 2.7	(14) 4.0
							1.1	1.3
.0	.0	.1	.2				.1	.1
.2	.4	.4	.5			Fixed/Worth	.5	.4
2.6	1.3	1.1	2.4				9.9	1.9
.5	.7	.5	.6				.7	.7
1.5	2.0	1.2	1.4			Debt/Worth	2.3	2.0
-40.7	11.8	4.1	5.4				45.9	10.8
76.9	70.6	64.7	55.2				45.7	53.9
(34) 30.6	(46) 19.2	(40) 27.6	(15) 26.1			% Profit Before Taxes/Tangible Net Worth	(130) 15.5	(131) 18.6
2.1	1.9	4.3	17.2				1.2	4.4
30.4	18.9	25.3	16.5				16.5	15.4
10.4	10.4	8.8	9.4			% Profit Before Taxes/Total Assets	5.5	4.6
-5.4	.9	1.2	4.8				-1.3	.6
UND	207.7	48.9	22.1				86.9	81.5
51.3	27.8	22.2	10.7			Sales/Net Fixed Assets	21.7	21.5
26.1	10.0	10.7	6.5				8.0	9.9
6.1	4.0	3.7	2.5				3.5	3.6
4.0	2.8	2.4	1.6			Sales/Total Assets	2.4	2.6
2.9	1.9	1.9	1.2				1.6	1.7
.2	.3	.4	1.1				.4	.5
(23) .4	(34) .6	(39) .6	(15) 2.0			% Depr., Dep., Amort./Sales	(122) 1.0	(111) 1.0
1.3	1.8	1.3	3.0				2.1	2.3
3.6	2.9	1.4					2.4	2.1
(23) 4.8	(35) 4.5	(17) 1.9				% Officers', Directors' Owners' Comp/Sales	(90) 4.0	(80) 3.7
7.1	7.4	4.8					6.5	5.8
53141M	190424M	611016M	741472M	860376M		Net Sales ($)	3789332M	2988057M
11894M	61920M	223336M	382272M	479208M		Total Assets ($)	1544098M	1405791M

M = $ thousand MM = $ million

See Pages 9 through 22 for Explanation of Ratios and Data

Comparative Historical Data				Current Data Sorted by Sales					
			Type of Statement						
9	6	13	Unqualified		1		1		11
19	13	17	Reviewed		2	1	2	10	2
22	24	20	Compiled		4	4	5	5	2
57	51	58	Tax Returns	20	24	6	7	1	
75	58	62	Other	10	14	9	10	10	9
					29 (4/1-9/30/13)		141 (10/1/13-3/31/14)		
4/1/11-3/31/12 ALL	**4/1/12-3/31/13 ALL**	**4/1/13-3/31/14 ALL**		**0-1MM**	**1-3MM**	**3-5MM**	**5-10MM**	**10-25MM**	**25MM & OVER**
182	152	170	**NUMBER OF STATEMENTS**	30	45	20	25	26	24
%	%	%	**ASSETS**	%	%	%	%	%	%
11.0	13.3	14.9	Cash & Equivalents	19.0	13.3	15.7	22.1	11.1	9.1
8.9	9.4	11.8	Trade Receivables (net)	4.9	13.5	9.9	13.6	16.6	11.4
47.3	47.2	43.9	Inventory	46.8	46.9	43.0	38.8	42.3	42.4
1.9	1.9	1.3	All Other Current	1.8	.4	.4	1.5	1.3	2.8
69.2	71.7	71.9	Total Current	72.5	74.1	69.0	76.1	71.3	65.6
19.7	15.7	16.9	Fixed Assets (net)	15.7	14.7	15.7	18.3	14.7	24.2
3.6	4.1	4.7	Intangibles (net)	6.0	3.0	4.7	1.7	7.7	6.1
7.5	8.5	6.6	All Other Non-Current	5.8	8.2	10.6	3.9	6.3	4.1
100.0	100.0	100.0	Total	100.0	100.0	100.0	100.0	100.0	100.0
			LIABILITIES						
12.4	12.8	12.1	Notes Payable-Short Term	21.5	10.1	11.0	9.6	13.2	6.6
1.9	2.6	3.1	Cur. Mat.-L.T.D.	6.9	2.3	.9	1.1	.9	6.0
18.1	15.6	20.0	Trade Payables	16.3	24.1	18.9	21.2	19.3	17.6
.1	.2	.1	Income Taxes Payable	.0	.2	.0	.0	.2	.0
10.9	13.2	13.4	All Other Current	24.9	10.1	12.5	8.9	15.1	8.6
43.4	44.3	48.7	Total Current	69.7	46.7	43.4	40.8	48.7	38.9
15.0	15.0	17.1	Long-Term Debt	38.6	13.3	20.9	9.6	6.5	13.1
.0	.0	.0	Deferred Taxes	.0	.0	.0	.0	.2	.0
7.1	7.1	3.8	All Other Non-Current	7.6	2.5	4.0	1.4	2.4	5.5
34.5	33.7	30.4	Net Worth	-15.9	37.4	31.8	48.1	42.3	42.5
100.0	100.0	100.0	Total Liabilties & Net Worth	100.0	100.0	100.0	100.0	100.0	100.0
			INCOME DATA						
100.0	100.0	100.0	Net Sales	100.0	100.0	100.0	100.0	100.0	100.0
48.1	48.8	45.1	Gross Profit	49.5	44.2	45.4	44.3	40.0	47.1
42.8	42.1	40.4	Operating Expenses	47.3	39.3	42.5	38.9	35.1	39.5
5.3	6.7	4.7	Operating Profit	2.2	5.0	2.9	5.3	4.9	7.6
1.3	.9	.5	All Other Expenses (net)	1.2	.4	-.1	.4	.3	.4
4.0	5.8	4.2	Profit Before Taxes	1.1	4.6	3.0	5.0	4.6	7.2
			RATIOS						
3.5	4.1	2.9		4.0	3.3	2.5	3.2	2.4	2.5
1.8	2.1	1.8	Current	1.8	1.9	1.7	2.2	1.8	2.0
1.2	1.1	1.1		.8	1.1	1.1	1.4	1.0	1.3
1.2	1.4	1.1		1.1	1.2	1.0	2.2	.9	.9
.4	.5	(169) .5	Quick	.3	.5	.5	.9	.5	(23) .6
.1	.1	.2		.1	.2	.2	.3	.2	.1
0 UND	0 UND	0 UND		0 UND	0 UND	0 UND	0 999.8	0 769.6	0 UND
1 257.6	1 257.6	2 211.5	Sales/Receivables	0 UND	6 62.7	1 317.4	6 58.9	23 16.0	1 321.0
25 14.4	15 24.5	25 14.6		9 42.5	28 13.0	16 22.9	33 11.2	42 8.6	14 25.5
72 5.1	62 5.9	49 7.5		38 9.6	47 7.8	41 8.9	16 22.2	83 4.4	63 5.8
135 2.7	140 2.6	104 3.5	Cost of Sales/Inventory	182 2.0	91 4.0	91 4.0	64 5.7	96 3.8	130 2.8
228 1.6	261 1.4	182 2.0		304 1.2	174 2.1	166 2.2	159 2.3	215 1.7	192 1.9
17 21.1	11 34.2	12 31.1		0 UND	9 41.4	9 41.1	17 22.1	22 16.3	28 13.2
35 10.3	31 11.8	33 10.9	Cost of Sales/Payables	16 22.9	34 10.8	35 10.5	27 13.3	35 10.4	45 8.1
73 5.0	63 5.8	68 5.4		57 6.4	65 5.6	52 7.0	57 6.4	72 5.1	76 4.8
4.4	4.5	5.1		4.0	4.8	5.8	5.5	5.5	4.0
8.8	8.9	10.0	Sales/Working Capital	8.9	7.7	14.7	8.8	11.7	8.6
38.8	44.6	43.7		-28.1	90.4	37.8	32.9	313.9	25.5
16.0	18.9	19.9		16.5	14.8	30.2	37.2	24.5	44.1
(139) 3.3	(117) 5.2	(131) 5.6	EBIT/Interest	(23) 1.7	(32) 6.9	(16) 2.5	(16) 8.6	(22) 7.0	(22) 7.2
1.3	2.0	1.3		-3.7	1.4	.9	2.0	1.9	2.4
44.5		7.2							
(12) 2.9		(16) 2.8	Net Profit + Depr., Dep., Amort./Cur. Mat. L/T/D						
1.3		.4							
.1	.1	.1		.0	.1	.0	.0	.2	.2
.4	.3	.4	Fixed/Worth	.4	.3	.7	.2	.4	.5
2.5	2.7	1.4		NM	1.5	1.9	.6	2.5	1.7
.5	.5	.5		.9	.4	.5	.6	.6	.6
1.6	1.7	1.5	Debt/Worth	2.3	1.5	2.8	.9	1.3	1.3
8.8	15.6	12.6		-2.4	10.6	14.3	2.8	12.6	2.9
44.9	67.1	62.8		73.3	57.7	57.0	65.9	65.7	92.4
(148) 20.3	(121) 28.6	(142) 25.1	% Profit Before Taxes/Tangible Net Worth	(19) 15.7	(37) 22.5	(17) 15.1	(24) 27.4	(23) 33.5	(22) 26.8
5.9	8.9	4.4		-17.6	4.9	-2.1	7.3	12.2	8.0
18.7	24.0	20.9		20.5	21.3	14.3	35.8	20.5	24.8
5.6	11.3	9.7	% Profit Before Taxes/Total Assets	4.9	11.1	5.5	12.4	9.5	9.7
1.1	2.4	1.0		-9.4	1.2	.0	3.0	3.4	1.4
68.1	107.0	128.2		UND	122.9	284.8	388.0	49.4	37.9
22.6	29.5	27.6	Sales/Net Fixed Assets	43.4	31.2	32.3	40.8	21.7	18.4
8.6	9.2	10.7		8.7	12.5	11.5	15.5	10.7	7.9
3.6	3.8	4.2		4.9	3.9	4.5	5.4	3.7	3.8
2.4	2.4	2.8	Sales/Total Assets	2.5	3.2	2.8	3.2	2.3	2.4
1.5	1.6	1.9		1.3	1.9	2.2	2.2	1.8	1.6
.4	.3	.3		.4	.2	.3	.2	.3	.6
(126) .9	(105) .9	(117) .7	% Depr., Dep., Amort./Sales	(14) 1.0	(30) .5	(12) .8	(17) .4	(23) .6	(21) 1.2
2.1	2.3	2.0		4.8	1.6	2.0	1.5	1.0	2.3
2.2	2.5	2.4		3.5	3.6	2.8	1.9	1.2	
(88) 3.9	(69) 3.9	(79) 4.3	% Officers', Directors' Owners' Comp/Sales	(18) 5.7	(23) 4.8	(12) 3.8	(11) 4.0	(11) 1.5	
6.5	7.8	6.8		11.4	6.7	6.3	7.1	3.3	
2141128M	**2161226M**	**2456429M**	Net Sales ($)	**15314M**	**88202M**	**74744M**	**175969M**	**383691M**	**1718509M**
1121345M	**1038915M**	**1158630M**	Total Assets ($)	**8032M**	**37834M**	**35945M**	**76366M**	**169597M**	**830856M**

M = $ thousand MM = $ million

See Pages 9 through 22 for Explanation of Ratios and Data

	Current Data Sorted by Assets						Comparative Historical Data	
Type of Statement								
Unqualified				5	2	1	4	8
Reviewed			4	3			8	15
Compiled		3	6	1			17	9
Tax Returns	5	17	3	1			31	37
Other	2	4	14	4	3		38	26
		11 (4/1-9/30/13)		67 (10/1/13-3/31/14)			4/1/09-3/31/10	4/1/10-3/31/11
	0-500M	500M-2MM	2-10MM	10-50MM	50-100MM	100-250MM	ALL	ALL
NUMBER OF STATEMENTS	7	24	27	14	5	1	98	95
ASSETS	%	%	%	%	%	%	%	%
Cash & Equivalents		6.3	9.7	14.9			11.0	10.0
Trade Receivables (net)		5.8	3.3	3.1			5.3	4.1
Inventory		64.8	59.1	50.5			58.7	58.4
All Other Current		.3	1.2	1.5			2.3	1.8
Total Current		77.2	73.3	69.9			77.3	74.3
Fixed Assets (net)		14.0	17.5	21.7			13.1	14.7
Intangibles (net)		1.9	3.1	7.0			3.5	3.1
All Other Non-Current		6.9	6.0	1.3			6.2	7.8
Total		100.0	100.0	100.0			100.0	100.0
LIABILITIES								
Notes Payable-Short Term		9.6	5.1	8.3			10.1	9.2
Cur. Mat.-L.T.D.		2.3	1.5	1.0			3.9	1.3
Trade Payables		25.8	23.5	25.0			18.6	20.8
Income Taxes Payable		.0	.1	.1			.2	.0
All Other Current		12.6	14.9	11.5			21.5	8.2
Total Current		50.2	45.1	46.0			54.3	39.6
Long-Term Debt		16.5	6.4	4.0			12.1	13.1
Deferred Taxes		.0	.3	.6			.0	.1
All Other Non-Current		9.7	10.2	2.7			2.5	11.0
Net Worth		23.6	38.0	46.8			31.0	36.2
Total Liabilties & Net Worth		100.0	100.0	100.0			100.0	100.0
INCOME DATA								
Net Sales		100.0	100.0	100.0			100.0	100.0
Gross Profit		38.7	46.3	44.4			45.0	42.3
Operating Expenses		36.2	41.7	38.8			41.9	38.0
Operating Profit		2.6	4.6	5.6			3.1	4.3
All Other Expenses (net)		.7	.1	.3			1.5	.6
Profit Before Taxes		1.9	4.5	5.3			1.6	3.7
RATIOS								
		3.9	4.1	2.4			3.0	3.4
Current		1.7	2.0	1.6			1.8	2.1
		1.1	1.3	1.1			1.2	1.5
		.5	.7	.6			.8	.7
Quick		.2	.2	.4			.2	.3
		.0	.1	.1			.0	.0
		0 UND	**0** UND	**0** UND			**0** UND	**0** UND
Sales/Receivables		**3** 133.4	**1** 682.9	**1** 296.8			**0** 999.8	**1** 544.2
		12 31.2	**6** 65.3	**4** 91.0			**6** 56.5	**5** 76.8
		126 2.9	**107** 3.4	**87** 4.2			**88** 4.2	**95** 3.8
Cost of Sales/Inventory		**146** 2.5	**152** 2.4	**114** 3.2			**163** 2.2	**144** 2.5
		192 1.9	**243** 1.5	**203** 1.8			**255** 1.4	**213** 1.7
		27 13.4	**31** 11.7	**36** 10.0			**15** 24.6	**27** 13.4
Cost of Sales/Payables		**52** 7.0	**55** 6.6	**51** 7.1			**40** 9.2	**42** 8.8
		96 3.8	**73** 5.0	**70** 5.2			**75** 4.9	**59** 6.1
		4.3	4.1	5.5			3.6	3.9
Sales/Working Capital		10.2	6.8	10.7			8.3	7.4
		64.4	18.9	62.0			24.2	18.4
		9.2	17.7	79.9			23.3	12.8
EBIT/Interest		(22) 3.6	(22) 7.9	(13) 30.5			(76) 4.2	(77) 2.9
		1.8	2.6	5.4			.6	1.3
							3.9	9.4
Net Profit + Depr., Dep., Amort./Cur. Mat. L/T/D							(13) 2.1	(13) 2.7
							1.2	.8
		.1	.1	.3			.1	.1
Fixed/Worth		.4	.3	.5			.3	.3
		4.4	.8	1.2			1.2	2.0
		.8	.5	.8			.5	.7
Debt/Worth		3.2	1.2	1.5			1.6	1.7
		26.3	3.6	2.2			6.9	5.6
		37.9	41.4	55.6			36.8	36.7
% Profit Before Taxes/Tangible Net Worth		(20) 10.7	(24) 16.6	33.2			(79) 16.7	(82) 20.7
		3.8	5.6	20.4			.2	7.3
		11.4	21.0	21.2			17.6	17.6
% Profit Before Taxes/Total Assets		3.7	6.1	11.3			5.5	6.7
		2.1	1.9	6.9			-1.6	2.1
		63.2	38.2	22.5			93.7	71.4
Sales/Net Fixed Assets		19.6	22.6	14.7			25.6	29.4
		14.1	12.1	9.4			11.6	11.3
		3.2	3.0	3.3			3.4	3.5
Sales/Total Assets		2.8	2.4	2.7			2.4	2.4
		1.9	2.0	2.0			1.7	1.9
		.3	.6	.5			.4	.6
% Depr., Dep., Amort./Sales		(21) .7	(22) .8	1.0			(73) .7	(76) .9
		1.5	1.2	2.2			1.5	1.8
		1.6	1.8				2.1	2.1
% Officers', Directors' Owners' Comp/Sales		(16) 3.2	(12) 2.2				(56) 4.1	(51) 3.6
		7.6	4.4				7.9	6.6
Net Sales ($)	6809M	71668M	337518M	871640M	795862M	190789M	2235573M	2311244M
Total Assets ($)	2220M	24512M	133825M	318025M	381418M	100153M	1011578M	1238903M

M = $ thousand MM = $ million

See Pages 9 through 22 for Explanation of Ratios and Data

Comparative Historical Data				Current Data Sorted by Sales					
			Type of Statement						
3	5	8	Unqualified					1	7
18	15	7	Reviewed					3	4
11	10	10	Compiled		3		1	5	1
34	26	26	Tax Returns	7	8	6	3	1	1
34	34	27	Other		2	3	9	5	8
				11 (4/1-9/30/13)			67 (10/1/13-3/31/14)		
4/1/11-3/31/12 ALL	**4/1/12-3/31/13 ALL**	**4/1/13-3/31/14 ALL**		**0-1MM**	**1-3MM**	**3-5MM**	**5-10MM**	**10-25MM**	**25MM & OVER**
100	90	78	**NUMBER OF STATEMENTS**	7	13	9	13	15	21
%	%	%	**ASSETS**	%	%	%	%	%	%
10.7	12.9	9.5	Cash & Equivalents		9.1		4.3	15.0	12.4
3.6	3.3	4.1	Trade Receivables (net)		4.5		2.9	1.7	4.0
60.8	56.7	59.0	Inventory		60.0		65.8	52.0	52.7
.8	2.3	1.1	All Other Current		.3		1.9	.9	2.0
76.0	75.3	73.7	Total Current		73.9		74.9	69.6	71.1
15.3	15.2	17.5	Fixed Assets (net)		18.3		15.0	18.3	19.9
3.0	2.7	4.0	Intangibles (net)		3.7		3.2	3.3	6.6
5.7	6.9	4.8	All Other Non-Current		4.1		6.9	8.8	2.4
100.0	100.0	100.0	Total		100.0		100.0	100.0	100.0
			LIABILITIES						
9.7	9.2	7.8	Notes Payable-Short Term		6.2		8.2	3.6	8.5
1.3	2.0	1.5	Cur. Mat.-L.T.D.		.6		3.7	1.0	.9
22.8	26.1	25.3	Trade Payables		35.4		22.7	28.9	21.9
.1	.2	.1	Income Taxes Payable		.0		.0	.1	.1
14.0	10.8	12.6	All Other Current		4.0		6.8	9.5	9.3
47.9	48.2	47.3	Total Current		46.3		41.4	43.1	40.7
11.1	12.5	10.9	Long-Term Debt		19.9		13.0	4.4	7.6
.1	.1	.3	Deferred Taxes		.0		.0	.5	.6
7.0	7.8	9.2	All Other Non-Current		15.4		11.7	3.4	5.7
34.0	31.4	32.4	Net Worth		18.5		33.9	48.6	45.4
100.0	100.0	100.0	Total Liabilties & Net Worth		100.0		100.0	100.0	100.0
			INCOME DATA						
100.0	100.0	100.0	Net Sales		100.0		100.0	100.0	100.0
42.2	41.7	41.8	Gross Profit		41.8		43.4	47.7	42.4
37.8	36.1	37.7	Operating Expenses		37.7		40.7	40.6	37.3
4.4	5.5	4.1	Operating Profit		4.1		2.7	7.1	5.1
.3	.6	.4	All Other Expenses (net)		.5		.1	.0	.6
4.1	4.9	3.7	Profit Before Taxes		3.7		2.6	7.2	4.5
			RATIOS						
3.6	3.3	3.1			4.0		3.5	2.3	2.5
1.9	1.8	1.7	Current		1.6		1.8	1.7	1.8
1.2	1.1	1.2			1.0		1.4	1.2	1.5
.6	.8	.5			.7		.5	.7	.6
.2	.3	.2	Quick		.3		.2	.3	.3
.1	.1	.1			.1		.0	.1	.1
0 UND	**0** UND	**0** UND			**0** UND		**0** UND	**0** UND	**0** UND
0 999.8	**1** 561.7	**1** 476.3	Sales/Receivables		**0** UND		**0** 999.8	**1** 652.6	**1** 288.4
5 73.3	**5** 70.1	**7** 50.6			**11** 32.9		**6** 61.6	**5** 67.2	**5** 79.4
89 4.1	**73** 5.0	**107** 3.4			**126** 2.9		**65** 5.6	**111** 3.3	**101** 3.6
140 2.6	**135** 2.7	**135** 2.7	Cost of Sales/Inventory		**146** 2.5		**192** 1.9	**135** 2.7	**114** 3.2
215 1.7	**203** 1.8	**192** 1.9			**174** 2.1		**228** 1.6	**215** 1.7	**203** 1.8
26 14.1	**28** 13.2	**30** 12.0			**7** 52.0		**23** 15.8	**55** 6.6	**27** 13.5
44 8.3	**48** 7.6	**52** 7.0	Cost of Sales/Payables		**85** 4.3		**47** 7.7	**70** 5.2	**50** 7.3
72 5.1	**79** 4.6	**83** 4.4			**146** 2.5		**65** 5.6	**85** 4.3	**72** 5.1
4.2	4.4	5.1			5.2		5.2	5.7	5.9
7.3	8.6	8.3	Sales/Working Capital		8.9		7.7	12.8	7.8
20.6	67.2	43.3			NM		24.8	21.3	13.9
16.3	22.7	31.3			23.4		12.4	20.6	83.8
(85) 5.5	(71) 6.2	(66) 5.3	EBIT/Interest		(10) 3.4		(12) 6.9	(10) 11.0	23.6
1.9	2.3	2.4			.8		3.3	3.2	2.7
	20.8	7.5							
	(13) 5.1	(11) 4.0	Net Profit + Depr., Dep., Amort./Cur. Mat. L/T/D						
	1.8	2.2							
.1	.1	.2			.3		.1	.2	.3
.3	.4	.5	Fixed/Worth		3.1		.5	.3	.5
1.3	1.3	2.4			-2.8		NM	.8	1.2
.5	.7	.7			1.6		.8	.5	.7
1.4	1.8	1.6	Debt/Worth		8.4		1.8	1.0	1.5
7.5	13.6	9.7			-16.4		NM	2.2	2.9
47.2	47.9	47.3					41.3	42.0	51.8
(85) 17.0	(73) 24.3	(64) 20.7	% Profit Before Taxes/Tangible Net Worth				(10) 11.4	33.5	(19) 24.3
5.0	7.2	5.9					5.8	9.2	11.6
15.0	16.8	16.9			19.4		13.7	22.4	20.0
7.1	8.3	6.0	% Profit Before Taxes/Total Assets		4.0		7.1	12.0	10.0
1.6	1.9	1.9			-1.0		2.8	2.3	3.7
83.5	129.8	40.5			88.5		49.1	31.4	23.0
24.3	24.2	18.3	Sales/Net Fixed Assets		15.6		33.1	15.1	12.9
14.8	12.5	11.7			6.5		16.0	12.0	10.6
3.7	3.7	3.2			3.1		4.3	3.0	3.2
2.7	2.7	2.6	Sales/Total Assets		2.6		2.8	2.3	2.6
2.0	2.1	1.9			2.1		2.3	2.0	2.0
.4	.3	.5			.6		.3	.6	.7
(75) .8	(63) .8	(66) .9	% Depr., Dep., Amort./Sales		(10) 1.1		(10) .7	(14) .8	1.1
1.5	1.6	1.5			1.6		1.2	1.2	2.1
2.0	1.5	1.5							
(55) 3.1	(43) 2.6	(39) 2.7	% Officers', Directors' Owners' Comp/Sales						
7.3	3.7	4.4							
2194306M	**2205909M**	**2274286M**	Net Sales ($)	**4729M**	**22309M**	**34641M**	**84766M**	**237296M**	**1890545M**
878213M	**837064M**	**960153M**	Total Assets ($)	**2929M**	**9572M**	**15518M**	**30434M**	**98503M**	**803197M**

M = $ thousand MM = $ million

See Pages 9 through 22 for Explanation of Ratios and Data

Current Data Sorted by Assets / Comparative Historical Data

Type of Statement	0-500M	500M-2MM	2-10MM	10-50MM	50-100MM	100-250MM	4/1/09-3/31/10 ALL	4/1/10-3/31/11 ALL
Unqualified			1	6	2	1	16	15
Reviewed		1	15	7			31	34
Compiled	2	25	29	1			56	64
Tax Returns	13	48	22	2		1	92	81
Other	9	12	29	23	7	3	81	74
		57 (4/1-9/30/13)		202 (10/1/13-3/31/14)				
NUMBER OF STATEMENTS	24	86	96	39	9	5	276	268
ASSETS	%	%	%	%	%	%	%	%
Cash & Equivalents	15.7	16.0	7.2	6.3			7.8	8.0
Trade Receivables (net)	3.3	2.6	9.4	6.6			7.4	6.3
Inventory	65.8	64.3	63.6	69.2			65.5	66.9
All Other Current	.6	1.8	3.0	.9			1.7	1.7
Total Current	85.4	84.7	83.1	83.0			82.4	82.9
Fixed Assets (net)	6.9	8.8	11.6	11.8			10.5	10.5
Intangibles (net)	2.1	1.6	.5	1.7			2.3	1.9
All Other Non-Current	5.6	4.9	4.8	3.6			4.9	4.6
Total	100.0	100.0	100.0	100.0			100.0	100.0
LIABILITIES								
Notes Payable-Short Term	14.7	8.6	7.5	11.1			14.5	14.8
Cur. Mat.-L.T.D.	2.5	1.1	1.7	1.2			2.4	2.4
Trade Payables	16.2	14.7	20.8	15.9			17.7	18.0
Income Taxes Payable	.2	.1	.1	.1			.2	.2
All Other Current	7.6	9.2	11.4	16.3			9.0	9.9
Total Current	41.1	33.7	41.4	44.7			43.8	45.2
Long-Term Debt	12.0	9.4	10.3	8.9			12.4	11.5
Deferred Taxes	.0	.0	.0	.1			.1	.2
All Other Non-Current	3.8	4.0	5.4	3.4			8.3	9.4
Net Worth	43.0	52.9	42.9	42.9			35.4	33.8
Total Liabilties & Net Worth	100.0	100.0	100.0	100.0			100.0	100.0
INCOME DATA								
Net Sales	100.0	100.0	100.0	100.0			100.0	100.0
Gross Profit	45.7	47.1	39.4	41.2			42.7	43.8
Operating Expenses	40.7	38.3	35.4	35.8			39.4	39.1
Operating Profit	5.0	8.7	4.0	5.4			3.3	4.7
All Other Expenses (net)	.3	.4	.8	.6			1.3	1.3
Profit Before Taxes	4.7	8.3	3.2	4.7			2.1	3.3
RATIOS								
Current	3.8	5.6	3.5	3.1			3.4	3.7
	2.2	3.1	2.1	2.0			2.0	2.0
	1.7	1.6	1.4	1.5			1.4	1.4
Quick	1.2	1.6	.9	.7			.6	.7
	.3	.6	.4	.2			.3	.2
	.2	.2	.1	.1			.1	.1
Sales/Receivables	**0** UND	**0** UND	**0** UND	**1** 273.6			**0** UND	**0** UND
	0 UND	**0** UND	**6** 61.6	**5** 81.0			**5** 68.2	**4** 102.0
	1 373.0	**5** 76.0	**24** 15.5	**20** 18.3			**18** 20.2	**15** 24.2
Cost of Sales/Inventory	**78** 4.7	**146** 2.5	**159** 2.3	**203** 1.8			**185** 2.0	**183** 2.0
	135 2.7	**215** 1.7	**281** 1.3	**281** 1.3			**308** 1.2	**291** 1.3
	261 1.4	**406** .9	**456** .8	**365** 1.0			**496** .7	**456** .8
Cost of Sales/Payables	**0** UND	**10** 37.8	**41** 8.8	**27** 13.6			**24** 14.9	**28** 13.2
	6 57.1	**35** 10.4	**66** 5.5	**52** 7.0			**54** 6.7	**56** 6.5
	40 9.1	**61** 6.0	**114** 3.2	**74** 4.9			**102** 3.6	**104** 3.5
Sales/Working Capital	3.5	2.6	2.1	3.1			2.0	2.3
	7.3	3.4	4.1	4.3			3.9	4.0
	15.3	6.2	6.8	8.4			8.4	8.3
EBIT/Interest	24.5	29.8	9.4	23.4			8.1	7.7
	(20) 12.3	(67) 8.4	(86) 2.6	11.1			(249) 2.8	(249) 3.1
	2.0	2.8	1.1	2.6			1.0	1.0
Net Profit + Depr., Dep., Amort./Cur. Mat. L/T/D			3.7	8.3			6.8	4.2
			(15) 1.7	(11) 3.9			(36) 1.4	(39) 1.6
			1.1	2.8			.7	.2
Fixed/Worth	.0	.0	.0	.1			.0	.1
	.0	.1	.2	.3			.2	.2
	.7	.3	.5	.6			.6	.6
Debt/Worth	.4	.3	.6	.5			.7	.7
	1.0	.6	1.3	1.3			1.8	1.6
	2.6	2.0	3.6	2.7			5.9	3.9
% Profit Before Taxes/Tangible Net Worth	67.0	58.3	24.1	38.9			20.7	25.9
	(22) 21.2	(82) 25.6	(89) 9.0	(36) 16.7			(237) 8.2	(235) 10.0
	7.4	6.9	1.5	8.9			1.7	1.4
% Profit Before Taxes/Total Assets	20.2	33.6	9.5	12.0			8.1	9.6
	13.7	9.4	2.6	6.6			2.8	3.6
	4.4	2.7	.2	2.8			-.2	.1
Sales/Net Fixed Assets	UND	330.8	98.1	25.2			68.2	63.6
	122.8	45.5	21.8	17.1			21.2	23.5
	26.7	15.7	9.1	10.4			8.5	10.5
Sales/Total Assets	4.6	2.6	2.2	2.1			2.0	2.2
	3.2	2.0	1.5	1.6			1.4	1.5
	2.0	1.4	1.0	1.4			1.0	1.0
% Depr., Dep., Amort./Sales	.1	.2	.3	.8			.5	.4
	(11) .4	(52) .6	(74) .9	(35) 1.0			(207) 1.1	(213) .9
	1.6	1.3	1.8	1.6			2.0	1.9
% Officers', Directors' Owners' Comp/Sales	3.0	4.1	1.8	1.2			2.7	2.6
	(18) 5.8	(50) 5.6	(47) 3.1	(14) 1.8			(124) 5.3	(140) 4.9
	11.3	7.9	5.0	2.4			9.3	8.4
Net Sales ($)	23457M	190798M	747632M	1616146M	1595187M	2434765M	4469390M	4919053M
Total Assets ($)	7320M	92098M	454440M	931987M	741466M	801879M	2776435M	2936651M

M = $ thousand MM = $ million

See Pages 9 through 22 for Explanation of Ratios and Data

Comparative Historical Data				Current Data Sorted by Sales					
			Type of Statement						
16	8	10	Unqualified			1		2	7
40	31	23	Reviewed		2	3	6	8	4
53	42	57	Compiled	4	26	12	9	4	2
78	111	86	Tax Returns	17	32	21	8	6	2
77	80	83	Other	12	10	10	8	13	30
				57 (4/1-9/30/13)			202 (10/1/13-3/31/14)		
4/1/11-3/31/12 ALL	**4/1/12-3/31/13 ALL**	**4/1/13-3/31/14 ALL**		**0-1MM**	**1-3MM**	**3-5MM**	**5-10MM**	**10-25MM**	**25MM & OVER**
264	272	259	**NUMBER OF STATEMENTS**	33	70	47	31	33	45
%	%	%	**ASSETS**	%	%	%	%	%	%
9.7	10.3	11.0	Cash & Equivalents	11.9	14.8	12.1	6.6	7.6	8.8
6.6	6.5	6.2	Trade Receivables (net)	6.3	2.9	4.9	9.8	9.8	7.4
64.1	64.6	64.4	Inventory	64.1	65.4	65.4	65.4	60.8	64.2
1.8	2.2	2.1	All Other Current	2.0	2.0	1.9	2.3	2.7	2.2
82.3	83.6	83.7	Total Current	84.3	85.0	84.3	84.1	80.9	82.6
9.6	9.4	10.2	Fixed Assets (net)	8.1	10.0	10.1	9.8	11.4	11.8
2.3	1.4	1.4	Intangibles (net)	1.0	2.0	.9	.3	.9	2.3
5.8	5.6	4.7	All Other Non-Current	6.6	3.0	4.8	5.9	6.8	3.3
100.0	100.0	100.0	Total	100.0	100.0	100.0	100.0	100.0	100.0
			LIABILITIES						
9.7	10.8	9.2	Notes Payable-Short Term	13.0	6.1	9.5	10.1	10.2	9.9
2.2	1.8	1.4	Cur. Mat.-L.T.D.	1.2	1.9	1.3	2.2	.7	1.1
16.4	19.5	17.6	Trade Payables	10.2	15.7	22.7	18.1	20.6	18.2
.2	.2	.1	Income Taxes Payable	.2	.0	.2	.1	.0	.1
8.8	10.6	11.2	All Other Current	5.5	9.7	11.2	13.4	11.1	16.5
37.3	42.9	39.7	Total Current	30.1	33.5	44.9	43.8	42.6	45.7
11.2	10.1	9.7	Long-Term Debt	14.0	9.7	12.2	6.9	8.3	7.1
.1	.0	.0	Deferred Taxes	.0	.0	.0	.1	.1	.0
7.1	6.3	4.6	All Other Non-Current	3.9	5.3	5.9	3.1	4.3	3.6
44.3	40.8	46.0	Net Worth	52.0	51.4	37.0	46.2	44.7	43.5
100.0	100.0	100.0	Total Liabilties & Net Worth	100.0	100.0	100.0	100.0	100.0	100.0
			INCOME DATA						
100.0	100.0	100.0	Net Sales	100.0	100.0	100.0	100.0	100.0	100.0
42.2	43.5	43.0	Gross Profit	46.5	47.9	42.7	37.5	38.3	40.1
35.8	37.2	37.0	Operating Expenses	40.0	39.7	37.4	33.2	34.6	34.7
6.4	6.2	5.9	Operating Profit	6.5	8.2	5.3	4.3	3.7	5.5
1.1	.9	.6	All Other Expenses (net)	.6	.6	.7	.6	.5	.3
5.3	5.3	5.4	Profit Before Taxes	5.9	7.7	4.5	3.7	3.3	5.1
			RATIOS						
4.4	3.5	4.2		8.0	5.9	3.5	3.1	3.0	3.3
2.3	2.0	2.3	Current	3.0	3.4	2.0	2.0	1.9	2.0
1.5	1.5	1.5		1.8	1.8	1.4	1.5	1.3	1.3
1.0	.8	1.0		1.3	1.9	.7	.9	.7	.9
(262) .3	(270) .3	.4	Quick	.4	.7	.4	.3	.4	.2
.1	.1	.1		.2	.1	.1	.0	.1	.1
0 UND	**0** UND	**0** UND		**0** UND	**0** UND	**0** UND	**0** UND	**1** 268.4	**1** 284.0
3 110.0	**3** 124.3	**2** 164.0	Sales/Receivables	**0** UND	**0** 999.8	**2** 211.0	**7** 54.8	**6** 61.0	**5** 80.8
14 26.2	**12** 30.7	**13** 27.6		**3** 142.0	**5** 70.8	**10** 36.5	**24** 15.2	**24** 15.0	**21** 17.6
140 2.6	**152** 2.4	**135** 2.7		**126** 2.9	**174** 2.1	**114** 3.2	**135** 2.7	**104** 3.5	**126** 2.9
243 1.5	**261** 1.4	**243** 1.5	Cost of Sales/Inventory	**281** 1.3	**261** 1.4	**215** 1.7	**261** 1.4	**228** 1.6	**215** 1.7
365 1.0	**406** .9	**365** 1.0		**521** .7	**521** .7	**406** .9	**332** 1.1	**332** 1.1	**332** 1.1
22 16.4	**26** 14.2	**23** 15.8		**0** UND	**17** 22.0	**31** 11.8	**40** 9.2	**37** 9.9	**24** 15.1
46 8.0	**62** 5.9	**52** 7.0	Cost of Sales/Payables	**24** 15.4	**40** 9.1	**57** 6.4	**53** 6.9	**56** 6.5	**60** 6.1
79 4.6	**107** 3.4	**81** 4.5		**72** 5.1	**76** 4.8	**114** 3.2	**76** 4.8	**96** 3.8	**74** 4.9
2.3	2.4	2.6		1.5	2.0	2.8	3.0	3.1	3.6
4.2	4.3	4.3	Sales/Working Capital	3.2	3.1	5.0	4.1	4.6	5.0
8.4	7.8	7.5		6.7	5.4	11.3	6.2	9.0	11.0
15.8	22.1	22.0		18.6	28.7	27.1	7.9	22.7	29.1
(232) 5.1	(240) 5.0	(225) 5.8	EBIT/Interest	(27) 5.3	(57) 5.7	(39) 5.2	(28) 2.6	(30) 6.9	(44) 10.5
1.5	2.3	1.9		1.9	1.5	1.3	1.9	1.5	4.1
11.6	6.4	7.8							43.6
(38) 2.3	(45) 2.1	(37) 3.0	Net Profit + Depr., Dep., Amort./Cur. Mat. L/T/D						(15) 4.4
.5	1.2	1.6							3.4
.0	.1	.0		.0	.0	.0	.0	.1	.1
.2	.2	.2	Fixed/Worth	.0	.1	.2	.1	.2	.2
.4	.4	.5		.6	.3	.8	.4	.4	.6
.5	.6	.4		.2	.3	.6	.4	.7	.5
1.2	1.4	1.2	Debt/Worth	1.1	.6	1.4	1.3	1.4	1.1
2.7	3.6	2.7		2.7	1.6	11.0	2.6	2.7	3.7
38.5	43.8	42.5		50.4	55.1	54.5	22.8	29.4	43.7
(244) 17.0	(250) 17.9	(239) 16.5	% Profit Before Taxes/Tangible Net Worth	(32) 16.6	(66) 15.6	(41) 18.6	(29) 9.5	10.0	(38) 18.6
3.7	6.6	4.7		3.9	4.5	6.0	3.2	.9	9.8
16.0	15.6	15.7		15.6	32.3	19.9	10.5	14.5	12.7
6.9	6.7	5.9	% Profit Before Taxes/Total Assets	6.5	6.8	4.2	3.5	4.4	8.6
1.5	2.0	1.2		1.1	1.3	1.1	1.1	.4	4.5
103.1	74.3	114.3		722.8	254.8	251.7	234.0	43.7	23.9
30.2	25.5	24.7	Sales/Net Fixed Assets	60.3	36.6	30.2	42.8	19.7	17.0
12.9	12.9	11.0		11.2	14.0	10.1	9.8	11.9	10.8
2.5	2.5	2.5		2.3	2.4	2.7	2.3	2.6	2.5
1.8	1.7	1.8	Sales/Total Assets	1.5	1.8	2.1	1.7	1.7	1.9
1.2	1.2	1.3		1.0	1.0	1.2	1.3	1.4	1.5
.3	.4	.3		.4	.2	.2	.3	.3	.7
(193) .8	(204) .7	(185) .9	% Depr., Dep., Amort./Sales	(15) .7	(47) .7	(32) .7	(23) .7	(28) .8	(40) 1.1
1.3	1.4	1.7		1.5	1.7	1.5	1.0	1.5	2.0
2.4	2.4	2.1		3.0	4.1	1.9	1.8	1.6	
(138) 4.8	(152) 4.8	(129) 4.2	% Officers', Directors' Owners' Comp/Sales	(18) 6.9	(38) 5.6	(31) 3.9	(17) 3.7	(16) 2.1	
7.5	7.7	7.0		11.0	8.0	6.5	5.2	2.9	
5462359M	**4832821M**	**6607985M**	Net Sales ($)	**22778M**	**133229M**	**188402M**	**234918M**	**515652M**	**5513006M**
2782612M	**2609450M**	**3029190M**	Total Assets ($)	**19168M**	**102607M**	**114714M**	**149965M**	**292539M**	**2350197M**

M = $ thousand MM = $ million

See Pages 9 through 22 for Explanation of Ratios and Data

Current Data Sorted by Assets							Comparative Historical Data	
						Type of Statement		
		3	5	2	1	Unqualified	20	19
	4	20	9			Reviewed	34	31
2	19	22	7	1		Compiled	65	51
43	52	26	1		1	Tax Returns	101	122
22	32	46	14	1	7	Other	125	129
50 (4/1-9/30/13)		290 (10/1/13-3/31/14)					4/1/09-3/31/10 ALL	4/1/10-3/31/11 ALL
0-500M	500M-2MM	2-10MM	10-50MM	50-100MM	100-250MM			
67	107	117	36	4	9	**NUMBER OF STATEMENTS**	345	352
%	%	%	%	%	%	**ASSETS**	%	%
18.5	13.5	10.2	7.9			Cash & Equivalents	9.6	9.6
4.1	4.9	4.8	3.0			Trade Receivables (net)	5.5	5.8
62.8	56.5	57.1	53.9			Inventory	58.0	56.7
.9	1.1	1.9	2.1			All Other Current	2.1	1.8
86.4	76.1	74.0	66.9			Total Current	75.2	73.9
9.5	14.7	17.0	22.3			Fixed Assets (net)	16.0	16.4
1.9	3.9	3.9	6.0			Intangibles (net)	4.5	4.4
2.2	5.4	5.1	4.8			All Other Non-Current	4.3	5.3
100.0	100.0	100.0	100.0			Total	100.0	100.0
						LIABILITIES		
10.7	9.4	9.3	7.7			Notes Payable-Short Term	12.8	12.1
1.7	1.6	1.6	2.1			Cur. Mat.-L.T.D.	3.8	3.1
20.6	21.3	24.6	20.3			Trade Payables	25.4	23.7
.1	.0	.1	.1			Income Taxes Payable	.2	.1
30.5	14.9	9.3	7.1			All Other Current	12.3	10.0
63.5	47.2	44.9	37.4			Total Current	54.6	49.0
12.2	11.9	10.2	15.8			Long-Term Debt	14.4	17.1
.0	.0	.0	.1			Deferred Taxes	.1	.1
13.6	7.5	6.0	3.3			All Other Non-Current	6.2	8.6
10.6	33.3	38.9	43.5			Net Worth	24.8	25.2
100.0	100.0	100.0	100.0			Total Liabilties & Net Worth	100.0	100.0
						INCOME DATA		
100.0	100.0	100.0	100.0			Net Sales	100.0	100.0
38.1	39.3	36.8	38.6			Gross Profit	36.9	37.6
34.9	35.8	33.4	32.7			Operating Expenses	34.8	34.5
3.2	3.5	3.4	5.9			Operating Profit	2.1	3.2
.8	.6	.7	.8			All Other Expenses (net)	.8	1.2
2.4	3.0	2.7	5.2			Profit Before Taxes	1.2	2.0
						RATIOS		
7.9	3.2	2.6	2.9				2.6	2.5
1.8	1.9	1.7	1.7			Current	1.5	1.6
1.1	1.2	1.2	1.1				1.1	1.1
1.5	1.0	.6	.6				.6	.7
(66) .3	.3	.2	.1			Quick	(343) .2	.2
.1	.1	.1	.1				.1	.1
0 UND	0 UND	0 UND	1 634.0				0 UND	0 UND
0 UND	0 999.8	1 359.1	2 192.1			Sales/Receivables	2 219.6	1 302.5
1 301.0	8 45.4	9 42.0	6 62.6				8 43.6	7 50.2
61 6.0	85 4.3	96 3.8	107 3.4				91 4.0	93 3.9
122 3.0	135 2.7	135 2.7	166 2.2			Cost of Sales/Inventory	144 2.5	140 2.6
192 1.9	203 1.8	203 1.8	243 1.5				209 1.7	201 1.8
0 UND	17 21.8	22 16.9	25 14.5				25 14.8	23 15.6
26 14.0	40 9.1	47 7.7	49 7.5			Cost of Sales/Payables	48 7.5	47 7.8
68 5.4	83 4.4	74 4.9	74 4.9				84 4.4	87 4.2
4.6	4.4	4.7	3.9				4.9	5.3
9.7	7.7	8.5	8.8			Sales/Working Capital	10.1	9.4
42.0	24.3	23.4	28.3				51.1	45.4
18.9	14.3	19.6	20.8				7.1	10.1
(42) 4.2	(80) 3.6	(101) 5.4	(33) 6.3			EBIT/Interest	(301) 2.1	(301) 3.2
.2	.8	1.8	4.0				.1	.7
		9.6					8.1	6.6
		(14) 5.1				Net Profit + Depr., Dep., Amort./Cur. Mat. L/T/D	(47) 1.6	(42) 2.5
		2.4					.3	.3
.0	.1	.1	.2				.1	.1
.1	.3	.3	.4			Fixed/Worth	.4	.4
16.0	1.2	1.1	2.3				6.3	2.9
.5	.6	.7	.6				1.0	1.1
4.6	1.8	1.5	1.6			Debt/Worth	2.9	2.7
-6.3	10.6	4.1	5.3				26.3	24.8
87.8	49.2	34.2	41.9				31.3	44.9
(45) 34.7	(90) 20.8	(106) 19.6	(34) 28.9			% Profit Before Taxes/Tangible Net Worth	(264) 12.7	(273) 19.0
5.8	3.6	5.6	14.4				-.3	4.3
24.9	13.8	13.3	12.7				9.3	12.6
8.0	5.0	6.4	7.5			% Profit Before Taxes/Total Assets	3.4	5.0
-2.8	.2	1.4	3.2				-2.3	-.3
UND	110.3	73.4	31.0				80.3	88.8
100.4	35.9	24.5	10.0			Sales/Net Fixed Assets	27.2	28.7
32.8	10.5	9.0	6.2				10.8	11.0
5.1	3.4	3.4	2.7				3.2	3.3
3.6	2.5	2.4	2.0			Sales/Total Assets	2.3	2.4
2.0	1.7	1.6	1.3				1.7	1.6
.3	.4	.4	.5				.4	.4
(27) .4	(70) .8	(88) .7	(33) 1.3			% Depr., Dep., Amort./Sales	(256) .8	(253) .8
1.4	1.7	1.6	2.4				1.7	1.7
4.0	2.0	.9	.6				1.8	1.6
(37) 5.5	(61) 3.0	(63) 1.8	(10) 1.1			% Officers', Directors' Owners' Comp/Sales	(166) 3.3	(168) 3.5
8.5	5.3	4.6	2.1				6.2	6.5
62371M	316583M	1305320M	1392374M	644894M	4884237M	Net Sales ($)	9031200M	6882605M
16547M	119255M	519695M	701046M	286553M	1485260M	Total Assets ($)	3416877M	2961101M

M = $ thousand MM = $ million

See Pages 9 through 22 for Explanation of Ratios and Data

Comparative Historical Data				Current Data Sorted by Sales					
			Type of Statement						
16	17	11	Unqualified				1	2	8
32	30	33	Reviewed	1	3	4	4	13	8
65	52	51	Compiled	1	12	8	8	14	8
146	126	123	Tax Returns	31	40	24	16	9	3
148	112	122	Other	22	26	15	23	15	21
				50 (4/1-9/30/13)			290 (10/1/13-3/31/14)		
4/1/11-3/31/12 ALL	**4/1/12-3/31/13 ALL**	**4/1/13-3/31/14 ALL**		**0-1MM**	**1-3MM**	**3-5MM**	**5-10MM**	**10-25MM**	**25MM & OVER**
407	337	340	**NUMBER OF STATEMENTS**	55	81	51	52	53	48
%	%	%	**ASSETS**	%	%	%	%	%	%
9.9	11.9	12.6	Cash & Equivalents	16.1	13.0	14.4	11.8	9.2	10.3
5.8	5.4	4.5	Trade Receivables (net)	4.4	3.1	6.0	4.5	6.3	3.7
58.2	59.1	57.8	Inventory	58.3	58.5	53.8	55.7	61.6	58.3
1.9	1.7	1.5	All Other Current	1.0	1.1	.7	2.5	2.5	1.2
75.9	78.2	76.4	Total Current	79.8	75.8	74.9	74.6	79.4	73.5
15.4	14.3	15.4	Fixed Assets (net)	12.8	17.6	15.4	16.2	12.3	17.3
3.4	3.0	3.7	Intangibles (net)	3.0	2.8	4.2	4.4	3.5	5.2
5.4	4.5	4.5	All Other Non-Current	4.4	3.9	5.5	4.9	4.8	4.0
100.0	100.0	100.0	Total	100.0	100.0	100.0	100.0	100.0	100.0
			LIABILITIES						
13.7	11.5	9.7	Notes Payable-Short Term	10.9	8.7	10.1	8.2	10.1	11.0
3.0	2.0	1.6	Cur. Mat.-L.T.D.	1.8	1.6	1.9	1.7	1.6	1.2
25.8	23.9	22.1	Trade Payables	17.3	19.5	26.8	21.5	26.6	22.8
.1	.1	.1	Income Taxes Payable	.1	.0	.1	.1	.1	.1
8.8	11.2	15.2	All Other Current	42.8	11.9	8.5	7.4	9.4	11.1
51.4	48.7	48.8	Total Current	73.0	41.8	47.4	38.8	47.9	46.2
15.1	13.5	11.9	Long-Term Debt	10.6	16.7	10.9	10.1	8.5	12.2
.1	.1	.0	Deferred Taxes	.0	.0	.0	.1	.0	.1
8.4	6.9	7.8	All Other Non-Current	20.3	6.5	5.5	6.5	2.4	5.6
25.0	30.8	31.4	Net Worth	-3.9	34.9	36.2	44.4	41.2	35.9
100.0	100.0	100.0	Total Liabilties & Net Worth	100.0	100.0	100.0	100.0	100.0	100.0
			INCOME DATA						
100.0	100.0	100.0	Net Sales	100.0	100.0	100.0	100.0	100.0	100.0
37.3	36.6	38.0	Gross Profit	40.3	40.4	37.4	36.9	35.0	36.7
34.0	33.3	34.5	Operating Expenses	38.9	36.4	33.7	33.4	30.6	32.4
3.4	3.3	3.5	Operating Profit	1.4	4.0	3.7	3.5	4.3	4.2
.8	.8	.7	All Other Expenses (net)	.9	1.0	.5	.5	.5	.5
2.5	2.5	2.9	Profit Before Taxes	.5	3.0	3.2	2.9	3.9	3.7
			RATIOS						
2.8	2.8	3.3		7.1	3.7	3.9	3.1	2.4	2.3
1.6	1.7	1.8	Current	1.7	1.9	1.5	2.1	1.6	1.6
1.1	1.2	1.2		.8	1.2	1.1	1.3	1.2	1.1
.6	.8	.9		1.4	.9	.9	1.1	.6	.6
(405) .2	(336) .3	(338) .2	Quick	(54) .3	.2	.3	.3	.2	(47) .1
.1	.1	.1		.1	.1	.1	.1	.1	.1
0 UND	**0** UND	**0** UND		**0** UND	**0** UND	**0** UND	**0** UND	**0** UND	**0** 882.9
1 343.1	**1** 411.4	**1** 578.3	Sales/Receivables	**0** UND	**0** UND	**2** 198.5	**1** 419.3	**2** 202.7	**2** 154.0
8 46.3	**8** 44.8	**6** 58.5		**4** 102.9	**4** 103.6	**8** 46.1	**13** 28.1	**9** 40.7	**7** 55.4
91 4.0	**87** 4.2	**91** 4.0		**91** 4.0	**111** 3.3	**56** 6.5	**89** 4.1	**89** 4.1	**91** 4.0
146 2.5	**135** 2.7	**130** 2.8	Cost of Sales/Inventory	**174** 2.1	**140** 2.6	**111** 3.3	**118** 3.1	**118** 3.1	**126** 2.9
203 1.8	**192** 1.9	**203** 1.8		**243** 1.5	**203** 1.8	**192** 1.9	**182** 2.0	**203** 1.8	**174** 2.1
25 14.4	**22** 16.9	**17** 22.0		**0** UND	**11** 33.0	**17** 21.9	**16** 22.7	**31** 11.9	**22** 16.6
53 6.9	**42** 8.6	**43** 8.5	Cost of Sales/Payables	**29** 12.8	**38** 9.6	**53** 6.9	**41** 8.9	**48** 7.6	**49** 7.5
87 4.2	**74** 4.9	**76** 4.8		**96** 3.8	**79** 4.6	**91** 4.0	**78** 4.7	**68** 5.4	**61** 6.0
4.8	5.0	4.6		3.8	3.8	5.1	4.7	5.2	6.4
9.7	9.1	8.6	Sales/Working Capital	9.2	7.5	10.0	7.1	10.5	12.2
42.7	24.1	29.4		-20.6	18.1	35.2	16.9	20.3	57.6
11.0	15.1	18.0		10.5	19.0	10.3	30.8	26.9	19.4
(349) 4.1	(268) 4.3	(267) 4.8	EBIT/Interest	(34) 3.2	(61) 3.3	(40) 3.1	(45) 8.0	(45) 6.4	(42) 6.1
1.0	1.3	1.3		-1.8	1.7	.1	2.4	1.9	.8
7.8	12.7	8.0							
(50) 3.4	(33) 5.2	(26) 3.0	Net Profit + Depr., Dep., Amort./Cur. Mat. L/T/D						
.8	1.8	1.4							
.1	.1	.1		.0	.1	.1	.1	.1	.2
.3	.3	.3	Fixed/Worth	.3	.3	.3	.2	.2	.7
2.4	1.9	1.5		-1.1	2.1	1.7	.6	.6	2.4
.9	.8	.7		.8	.6	.8	.6	.7	.7
2.5	2.2	1.9	Debt/Worth	5.1	1.9	2.2	1.2	1.5	3.0
13.7	9.5	7.7		-3.9	10.7	10.6	2.4	3.7	10.4
43.4	48.6	47.6		87.8	47.1	50.6	33.2	36.5	60.5
(326) 19.8	(279) 19.8	(285) 21.0	% Profit Before Taxes/Tangible Net Worth	(33) 23.3	(65) 14.3	(45) 11.3	(49) 19.7	(51) 21.8	(42) 31.0
4.1	5.1	5.5		7.7	1.9	1.4	6.2	8.8	6.1
13.1	14.9	14.9		17.2	15.5	12.1	12.5	15.8	15.8
5.4	5.3	5.9	% Profit Before Taxes/Total Assets	4.8	4.9	4.3	6.2	8.0	7.8
.1	.4	.8		-11.4	1.0	.6	1.7	1.8	1.1
104.1	126.9	104.3		UND	119.4	104.5	90.9	99.7	45.1
29.9	36.4	31.1	Sales/Net Fixed Assets	51.1	34.0	36.4	24.5	43.5	17.8
11.5	14.1	10.4		10.2	7.7	12.0	11.2	13.2	9.7
3.2	3.6	3.6		4.0	3.4	3.7	3.5	3.9	3.4
2.4	2.6	2.5	Sales/Total Assets	2.0	2.2	2.6	2.3	2.6	2.7
1.8	1.7	1.7		1.4	1.6	1.7	1.8	1.8	2.1
.4	.3	.4		.4	.4	.3	.5	.3	.4
(287) .9	(233) .7	(227) .8	% Depr., Dep., Amort./Sales	(22) .8	(51) .8	(38) .6	(35) .8	(40) .5	(41) 1.2
1.7	1.6	1.7		3.7	1.8	1.8	1.7	1.3	2.2
2.1	1.9	1.4		4.0	2.1	1.9	1.0	.8	1.1
(200) 3.5	(172) 3.6	(174) 3.0	% Officers', Directors' Owners' Comp/Sales	(24) 5.7	(52) 4.0	(33) 2.8	(26) 1.8	(24) 1.3	(15) 1.8
5.8	6.7	6.1		8.2	6.6	5.4	4.6	3.2	3.5
7337246M	**7346224M**	**8605779M**	Net Sales ($)	**30663M**	**156873M**	**196743M**	**391638M**	**809530M**	**7020332M**
3209893M	**2791591M**	**3128356M**	Total Assets ($)	**18450M**	**87715M**	**90985M**	**201845M**	**345420M**	**2383941M**

M = $ thousand MM = $ million

See Pages 9 through 22 for Explanation of Ratios and Data

Current Data Sorted by Assets							Comparative Historical Data	
						Type of Statement		
					3	Unqualified	6	8
			1			Reviewed	4	2
2	3				1	Compiled	4	7
7	7	4	1			Tax Returns	27	19
12	4	1	1	1	2	Other	19	26
4 (4/1-9/30/13)		46 (10/1/13-3/31/14)					4/1/09-3/31/10	4/1/10-3/31/11
0-500M	500M-2MM	2-10MM	10-50MM	50-100MM	100-250MM		ALL	ALL
21	14	5	3	1	6	**NUMBER OF STATEMENTS**	60	62
%	%	%	%	%	%	**ASSETS**	%	%
23.5	19.6					Cash & Equivalents	9.0	12.5
5.0	6.3					Trade Receivables (net)	6.7	7.9
53.0	56.2					Inventory	57.9	53.8
1.1	.8					All Other Current	2.1	1.9
82.6	82.9					Total Current	75.7	76.1
8.5	8.5					Fixed Assets (net)	14.0	13.6
3.2	6.9					Intangibles (net)	6.3	5.3
5.7	1.7					All Other Non-Current	4.0	5.0
100.0	100.0					Total	100.0	100.0
						LIABILITIES		
19.4	10.2					Notes Payable-Short Term	8.9	14.3
4.1	.5					Cur. Mat.-L.T.D.	2.0	1.9
25.2	9.4					Trade Payables	15.4	16.9
.3	.0					Income Taxes Payable	.1	.1
10.6	4.6					All Other Current	11.9	14.8
59.5	24.7					Total Current	38.2	48.0
20.0	7.7					Long-Term Debt	26.1	21.9
.0	.0					Deferred Taxes	.1	.2
19.7	5.3					All Other Non-Current	5.0	10.8
.7	62.4					Net Worth	30.6	19.1
100.0	100.0					Total Liabilties & Net Worth	100.0	100.0
						INCOME DATA		
100.0	100.0					Net Sales	100.0	100.0
46.5	43.7					Gross Profit	45.3	42.7
43.3	38.6					Operating Expenses	41.8	39.6
3.2	5.1					Operating Profit	3.5	3.1
1.1	-.1					All Other Expenses (net)	1.3	1.7
2.2	5.3					Profit Before Taxes	2.2	1.4
						RATIOS		
4.8	16.5						4.3	2.6
1.5	3.3					Current	2.2	1.8
1.0	1.7						1.4	1.3
1.5	4.1						1.1	.9
.5	1.2					Quick	(59) .3	.4
.3	.4						.2	.1
0 UND	0 UND						0 UND	0 UND
0 UND	1 325.3					Sales/Receivables	2 216.8	1 245.2
1 245.1	10 35.5						15 23.9	13 29.1
65 5.6	91 4.0						96 3.8	75 4.9
146 2.5	135 2.7					Cost of Sales/Inventory	168 2.2	107 3.4
228 1.6	174 2.1						243 1.5	199 1.8
0 UND	0 UND						23 15.9	15 24.0
56 6.5	9 40.8					Cost of Sales/Payables	37 9.8	35 10.5
85 4.3	36 10.0						57 6.5	56 6.5
3.6	3.7						3.1	6.3
9.9	6.1					Sales/Working Capital	5.9	9.2
NM	9.8						16.4	25.9
6.6							10.0	9.0
(14) 2.8						EBIT/Interest	(53) 3.2	(55) 2.4
.6							-.1	-.3
						Net Profit + Depr., Dep., Amort./Cur. Mat. L/T/D		
.2	.0						.1	.1
1.4	.1					Fixed/Worth	.3	.5
-.2	.7						2.0	-1.0
2.5	.2						.6	1.1
137.0	.5					Debt/Worth	2.3	3.9
-4.7	2.1						10.4	-6.2
371.4	56.7						71.2	69.9
(11) 94.7	(13) 24.7					% Profit Before Taxes/Tangible Net Worth	(50) 17.5	(42) 23.3
7.8	10.4						-5.2	3.5
20.4	22.5						12.2	14.2
5.7	9.8					% Profit Before Taxes/Total Assets	6.3	4.0
.5	3.2						-3.8	-2.4
620.3	370.1						112.9	124.3
87.8	77.8					Sales/Net Fixed Assets	31.7	32.2
16.3	31.1						9.7	11.0
4.4	4.0						3.0	4.7
3.4	3.2					Sales/Total Assets	2.1	2.5
1.9	1.6						1.5	1.9
.2							.5	.4
(10) .6						% Depr., Dep., Amort./Sales	(42) .8	(42) .9
1.1							2.7	2.1
	2.0						1.3	1.8
	(11) 4.2					% Officers', Directors' Owners' Comp/Sales	(31) 3.1	(26) 5.1
	5.6						6.5	8.9
14690M	42795M	130850M	414792M	78885M	2462694M	Net Sales ($)	1343624M	2375856M
4826M	13285M	34030M	64104M	58630M	1094000M	Total Assets ($)	779602M	984614M

M = $ thousand MM = $ million

See Pages 9 through 22 for Explanation of Ratios and Data

Comparative Historical Data				Current Data Sorted by Sales					
			Type of Statement						
5	3	3	Unqualified						3
3	3	1	Reviewed						1
10	3	6	Compiled	2	3				1
21	16	19	Tax Returns	6	5	2	2	2	2
22	25	21	Other	11	4			1	5
4/1/11-3/31/12 ALL	4/1/12-3/31/13 ALL	4/1/13-3/31/14 ALL		4 (4/1-9/30/13)		46 (10/1/13-3/31/14)			
				0-1MM	1-3MM	3-5MM	5-10MM	10-25MM	25MM & OVER
61	50	50	**NUMBER OF STATEMENTS**	19	12	2	2	3	12
%	%	%	**ASSETS**	%	%	%	%	%	%
15.3	15.3	18.1	Cash & Equivalents	21.2	26.5				8.1
5.2	5.6	5.9	Trade Receivables (net)	6.8	1.3				7.9
56.9	53.5	55.9	Inventory	53.0	53.0				58.4
1.6	2.1	1.5	All Other Current	1.0	.6				2.8
79.0	76.5	81.4	Total Current	82.1	81.4				77.3
11.0	12.7	10.5	Fixed Assets (net)	8.3	9.5				17.7
4.7	3.9	4.1	Intangibles (net)	3.2	7.9				3.0
5.2	6.9	4.0	All Other Non-Current	6.4	1.1				1.9
100.0	100.0	100.0	Total	100.0	100.0				100.0
			LIABILITIES						
15.9	12.8	13.3	Notes Payable-Short Term	21.1	10.1				8.8
2.8	1.3	2.4	Cur. Mat.-L.T.D.	2.6	3.2				1.8
16.2	18.4	19.4	Trade Payables	23.0	13.0				20.6
.2	.1	.2	Income Taxes Payable	.3	.0				.3
15.9	8.2	8.3	All Other Current	11.3	3.4				9.5
51.1	40.8	43.7	Total Current	58.3	29.7				41.0
17.4	14.8	12.8	Long-Term Debt	18.9	12.6				8.8
.0	.1	.0	Deferred Taxes	.0	.0				.2
9.5	11.6	12.4	All Other Non-Current	13.3	17.8				9.9
22.0	32.8	31.1	Net Worth	9.4	39.9				40.2
100.0	100.0	100.0	Total Liabilities & Net Worth	100.0	100.0				100.0
			INCOME DATA						
100.0	100.0	100.0	Net Sales	100.0	100.0				100.0
41.2	41.2	43.3	Gross Profit	47.7	46.0				39.7
37.3	36.7	39.1	Operating Expenses	45.7	38.5				35.2
3.9	4.5	4.2	Operating Profit	2.0	7.4				4.5
1.1	1.0	.6	All Other Expenses (net)	1.1	.0				.7
2.8	3.5	3.6	Profit Before Taxes	1.0	7.4				3.8
			RATIOS						
4.2	3.4	4.7		3.9	15.4				2.8
1.8	2.1	2.1	Current	1.7	4.0				2.0
1.2	1.4	1.4		.9	1.5				1.4
1.1	1.1	1.3		1.5	8.5				.7
(60) .4	.4	.6	Quick	.5	1.0				.5
.1	.2	.2		.3	.4				.1
0 UND	**0** UND	**0** UND		**0** UND	**0** UND				**0** UND
1 475.0	**1** 260.7	**0** 812.0	Sales/Receivables	**0** UND	**0** UND				**4** 92.0
9 39.5	**9** 42.0	**10** 37.9		**18** 20.6	**1** 320.3				**13** 28.8
66 5.5	**74** 4.9	**76** 4.8		**107** 3.4	**54** 6.7				**85** 4.3
118 3.1	**111** 3.3	**130** 2.8	Cost of Sales/Inventory	**166** 2.2	**135** 2.7				**130** 2.8
243 1.5	**203** 1.8	**192** 1.9		**243** 1.5	**174** 2.1				**215** 1.7
10 36.7	**19** 19.0	**4** 81.8		**2** 216.0	**0** UND				**23** 15.7
30 12.2	**38** 9.7	**41** 9.0	Cost of Sales/Payables	**60** 6.1	**6** 64.4				**51** 7.2
59 6.2	**47** 7.7	**61** 6.0		**104** 3.5	**40** 9.2				**59** 6.2
5.0	3.9	3.8		2.8	4.3				3.7
8.7	6.7	7.0	Sales/Working Capital	7.2	5.2				8.4
63.8	12.2	15.7		-189.0	11.5				18.9
16.8	15.2	26.6		4.7					59.6
(48) 3.9	(42) 4.4	(37) 4.0	EBIT/Interest	(12) 1.9					(11) 26.2
.5	-.2	1.1		-2.2					.7
			Net Profit + Depr., Dep., Amort./Cur. Mat. L/T/D						
.0	.0	.0		.0	.1				.1
.3	.2	.3	Fixed/Worth	.6	.4				.5
86.1	2.9	44.3		-.5	NM				.9
.6	.6	.4		.7	.1				1.0
2.4	2.2	1.5	Debt/Worth	18.3	1.1				1.4
-21.8	13.6	NM		-6.1	NM				4.2
61.9	51.8	87.7		242.9					83.0
(44) 24.7	(40) 26.4	(38) 28.5	% Profit Before Taxes/Tangible Net Worth	(11) 49.3					(11) 25.5
-.3	4.6	6.8		7.7					-.9
24.6	19.3	21.0		9.5	35.9				21.8
7.3	8.6	7.7	% Profit Before Taxes/Total Assets	4.0	17.9				11.6
-1.1	-.8	.5		-7.0	6.6				-1.0
329.0	237.3	338.8		490.5	307.8				121.0
40.3	39.3	71.8	Sales/Net Fixed Assets	87.8	71.8				17.9
12.8	10.3	16.5		16.7	26.4				6.0
4.3	3.9	4.2		3.6	4.3				4.3
2.8	2.5	2.9	Sales/Total Assets	2.0	3.2				2.3
1.8	1.7	1.8		1.7	1.8				1.8
.5	.3	.2							
(35) 1.0	(28) .8	(23) .6	% Depr., Dep., Amort./Sales						
2.1	1.5	1.6							
1.3	.9	1.8							
(33) 3.2	(20) 1.7	(27) 2.8	% Officers', Directors' Owners' Comp/Sales						
5.0	3.7	5.8							
1645932M	2037951M	3144706M	Net Sales ($)	10712M	24135M	6892M	14226M	41761M	3046980M
789432M	1089748M	1268875M	Total Assets ($)	4613M	8806M	1580M	3773M	15007M	1235096M

M = $ thousand MM = $ million

See Pages 9 through 22 for Explanation of Ratios and Data

Current Data Sorted by Assets							Comparative Historical Data	
						Type of Statement		
			1			Unqualified	6	4
	1	6	1			Reviewed	12	9
1	10	6				Compiled	20	21
7	11	6				Tax Returns	25	27
3	5	12	2	1	1	Other	12	34
11 (4/1-9/30/13)			63 (10/1/13-3/31/14)				4/1/09-3/31/10 ALL	4/1/10-3/31/11 ALL
0-500M	**500M-2MM**	**2-10MM**	**10-50MM**	**50-100MM**	**100-250MM**			
11	27	30	4	1	1	**NUMBER OF STATEMENTS**	75	95
%	%	%	%	%	%	**ASSETS**	%	%
19.8	7.4	6.5				Cash & Equivalents	6.3	6.0
4.9	6.8	13.2				Trade Receivables (net)	10.9	12.7
60.1	58.5	58.2				Inventory	62.2	57.9
.2	1.6	2.6				All Other Current	2.4	2.4
85.1	74.3	80.5				Total Current	81.8	79.0
10.2	20.4	11.3				Fixed Assets (net)	12.3	12.7
.0	.5	1.4				Intangibles (net)	1.9	2.4
4.7	4.9	6.8				All Other Non-Current	4.0	5.8
100.0	100.0	100.0				Total	100.0	100.0
						LIABILITIES		
26.0	12.7	17.3				Notes Payable-Short Term	17.2	16.7
2.6	6.2	6.9				Cur. Mat.-L.T.D.	2.8	2.4
17.2	23.9	18.0				Trade Payables	14.8	16.0
.1	.0	.0				Income Taxes Payable	.1	.1
11.5	7.5	6.1				All Other Current	7.5	10.9
57.3	50.3	48.3				Total Current	42.4	46.0
4.9	12.2	10.1				Long-Term Debt	12.0	14.8
.0	.0	.2				Deferred Taxes	.1	.1
25.4	18.6	5.3				All Other Non-Current	9.3	8.0
12.3	19.0	36.1				Net Worth	36.1	31.1
100.0	100.0	100.0				Total Liabilties & Net Worth	100.0	100.0
						INCOME DATA		
100.0	100.0	100.0				Net Sales	100.0	100.0
47.3	40.6	39.8				Gross Profit	43.5	43.8
51.8	39.4	37.6				Operating Expenses	42.0	40.2
-4.5	1.2	2.2				Operating Profit	1.5	3.6
-.1	.4	-.2				All Other Expenses (net)	.5	1.9
-4.4	.8	2.4				Profit Before Taxes	1.0	1.7
						RATIOS		
3.1	3.1	3.0					3.5	3.0
2.1	1.5	1.5				Current	1.9	1.7
1.7	1.0	1.1					1.3	1.2
2.7	.6	.7					.7	.6
.2	.3	.5				Quick	.3	.3
.1	.1	.1					.1	.1
0 UND	**3** 130.2	**5** 69.0					**2** 147.7	**2** 174.0
2 192.0	**6** 57.9	**20** 18.1				Sales/Receivables	**11** 32.2	**10** 37.9
7 55.6	**19** 19.2	**45** 8.1					**24** 15.5	**29** 12.4
91 4.0	**99** 3.7	**140** 2.6					**142** 2.6	**124** 2.9
228 1.6	**182** 2.0	**182** 2.0				Cost of Sales/Inventory	**227** 1.6	**196** 1.9
406 .9	**365** 1.0	**332** 1.1					**321** 1.1	**348** 1.0
0 UND	**22** 16.9	**23** 15.6					**16** 22.8	**22** 16.4
4 88.0	**63** 5.8	**51** 7.2				Cost of Sales/Payables	**36** 10.2	**39** 9.2
18 20.3	**130** 2.8	**135** 2.7					**55** 6.7	**68** 5.3
1.9	3.7	3.3					2.8	3.0
6.0	8.7	6.0				Sales/Working Capital	5.0	5.3
11.7	200.3	19.3					11.1	22.1
	4.6	9.2					5.3	5.2
	(24) 1.6	(29) 2.2				EBIT/Interest	(70) 1.5	(84) 2.1
	.3	-.3					.6	1.1
							29.6	5.3
						Net Profit + Depr., Dep., Amort./Cur. Mat. L/T/D	(15) 5.5	(11) 1.7
							.4	.7
.0	.1	.1					.1	.1
.1	.5	.2				Fixed/Worth	.2	.3
.8	-4.5	1.5					1.1	1.7
.6	1.2	.5					.9	1.0
3.0	2.6	1.6				Debt/Worth	2.1	2.6
28.5	-6.4	8.2					4.2	9.1
	25.8	20.8					19.2	34.3
	(20) 7.9	(25) 10.2				% Profit Before Taxes/Tangible Net Worth	(68) 4.4	(83) 10.6
	1.3	1.7					-3.6	.7
1.2	10.3	7.4					5.8	8.8
.4	1.6	2.6				% Profit Before Taxes/Total Assets	1.3	2.5
-18.3	-2.5	-.5					-1.7	.0
UND	225.4	92.7					87.6	96.7
64.0	16.6	21.8				Sales/Net Fixed Assets	26.1	26.7
19.8	5.3	11.0					12.1	9.6
4.2	3.3	2.3					2.7	2.6
1.7	2.1	1.6				Sales/Total Assets	1.8	1.7
1.3	1.3	1.4					1.3	1.3
	.3	.3					.5	.4
	(21) .5	(24) 1.1				% Depr., Dep., Amort./Sales	(63) 1.0	(64) .9
	3.0	3.3					2.1	2.1
	1.5	1.4					2.2	2.2
	(12) 3.5	(11) 1.8				% Officers', Directors' Owners' Comp/Sales	(38) 4.5	(44) 3.9
	7.8	5.4					8.2	7.5
8740M	**67882M**	**317331M**	**222383M**	**277357M**	**32125M**	Net Sales ($)	**1215551M**	**1104638M**
3298M	**28442M**	**167267M**	**86325M**	**85902M**	**107874M**	Total Assets ($)	**613180M**	**640896M**

M = $ thousand MM = $ million

See Pages 9 through 22 for Explanation of Ratios and Data

Comparative Historical Data / Current Data Sorted by Sales

Comparative Historical Data				Current Data Sorted by Sales					
			Type of Statement						
2	3	1	Unqualified						1
12	8	8	Reviewed		2		1	4	1
24	29	17	Compiled	3	6	3	3	2	
19	23	24	Tax Returns	5	7	7	4	1	
27	20	24	Other	1	5	3	5	6	4
				11 (4/1-9/30/13)			63 (10/1/13-3/31/14)		
4/1/11-3/31/12 ALL	**4/1/12-3/31/13 ALL**	**4/1/13-3/31/14 ALL**		**0-1MM**	**1-3MM**	**3-5MM**	**5-10MM**	**10-25MM**	**25MM & OVER**
84	83	74	**NUMBER OF STATEMENTS**	9	20	13	13	13	6
%	%	%	**ASSETS**	%	%	%	%	%	%
7.0	8.6	8.5	Cash & Equivalents		9.7	5.4	4.7	5.6	
12.5	10.0	11.7	Trade Receivables (net)		5.0	11.4	14.5	18.6	
56.4	58.3	55.6	Inventory		54.7	62.0	60.4	55.6	
2.1	1.9	2.3	All Other Current		2.4	3.0	2.1	2.4	
78.0	78.9	78.0	Total Current		71.9	81.8	81.7	82.3	
13.8	15.0	15.2	Fixed Assets (net)		22.4	10.8	8.6	11.0	
2.0	1.0	1.0	Intangibles (net)		.0	.9	1.2	1.9	
6.2	5.1	5.9	All Other Non-Current		5.7	6.4	8.5	4.8	
100.0	100.0	100.0	Total		100.0	100.0	100.0	100.0	
			LIABILITIES						
14.0	15.3	16.9	Notes Payable-Short Term		11.0	13.0	24.5	13.8	
5.0	3.8	5.9	Cur. Mat.-L.T.D.		7.5	4.2	5.0	8.5	
18.3	17.0	19.5	Trade Payables		17.0	30.0	21.1	15.0	
.1	.2	.0	Income Taxes Payable		.0	.0	.0	.0	
10.4	8.8	7.7	All Other Current		10.3	5.7	4.2	8.9	
47.8	45.0	50.1	Total Current		45.9	52.9	54.8	46.3	
13.1	11.7	9.8	Long-Term Debt		11.4	10.6	11.8	9.8	
.0	.1	.1	Deferred Taxes		.0	.0	.1	.3	
8.8	10.6	13.2	All Other Non-Current		21.5	17.2	3.4	4.8	
30.3	32.7	26.8	Net Worth		21.3	19.3	29.9	38.9	
100.0	100.0	100.0	Total Liabilties & Net Worth		100.0	100.0	100.0	100.0	
			INCOME DATA						
100.0	100.0	100.0	Net Sales		100.0	100.0	100.0	100.0	
43.8	42.5	41.8	Gross Profit		44.2	38.9	39.0	37.5	
41.7	40.9	40.4	Operating Expenses		41.7	41.4	35.3	36.4	
2.2	1.6	1.3	Operating Profit		2.6	-2.5	3.7	1.2	
.4	-.1	.2	All Other Expenses (net)		.7	-2.0	.7	.0	
1.7	1.6	1.1	Profit Before Taxes		1.9	-.6	2.9	1.1	
			RATIOS						
2.9	3.5	2.9			3.0	4.2	3.3	2.4	
1.6	1.8	1.6	Current		1.8	1.5	1.3	1.6	
1.1	1.3	1.1			1.2	1.0	1.2	1.3	
.6	.8	.7			.5	.9	.7	.6	
.3	.3	.3	Quick		.3	.2	.4	.5	
.2	.2	.1			.0	.1	.2	.2	
3 127.9	2 184.2	3 131.6			1 453.7	3 107.5	14 26.5	6 60.8	
12 31.2	8 44.4	12 29.3	Sales/Receivables		6 57.9	6 57.9	17 21.1	25 14.5	
25 14.4	20 18.5	25 14.5			15 24.8	28 12.9	65 5.6	46 8.0	
135 2.7	107 3.4	104 3.5			99 3.7	101 3.6	152 2.4	126 2.9	
192 1.9	174 2.1	182 2.0	Cost of Sales/Inventory		243 1.5	114 3.2	203 1.8	166 2.2	
281 1.3	281 1.3	332 1.1			406 .9	228 1.6	332 1.1	215 1.7	
24 15.0	17 21.0	18 20.5			14 25.7	21 17.4	29 12.5	18 20.6	
43 8.4	32 11.4	37 9.9	Cost of Sales/Payables		61 6.0	72 5.1	62 5.9	25 14.5	
72 5.1	68 5.4	111 3.3			140 2.6	140 2.6	111 3.3	85 4.3	
3.5	3.1	2.8			2.4	3.9	3.4	3.3	
6.7	5.8	6.8	Sales/Working Capital		5.8	7.4	12.8	5.1	
41.1	20.7	24.9			21.5	NM	25.5	18.0	
5.1	6.6	7.2			4.6	2.8	10.5	8.2	
(77) 2.0	(73) 3.3	(67) 2.0	EBIT/Interest		(17) 1.8	(12) .7	4.3	2.4	
.9	1.1	.3			.2	-2.1	1.5	.1	
2.4		2.1							
(12) 1.1		(10) .7	Net Profit + Depr., Dep., Amort./Cur. Mat. L/T/D						
.3		.3							
.1	.1	.0			.2	.0	.1	.0	
.3	.2	.3	Fixed/Worth		.7	.4	.4	.1	
3.2	1.2	1.8			8.4	-.9	1.2	.4	
1.0	.9	1.0			1.0	.7	.8	1.1	
2.2	1.7	2.1	Debt/Worth		3.4	2.1	2.6	1.6	
10.5	5.5	8.2			24.3	-4.7	17.0	3.3	
31.0	34.8	23.5			23.5		20.5	16.2	
(70) 9.7	(71) 13.2	(60) 7.9	% Profit Before Taxes/Tangible Net Worth		(16) 5.1		(11) 15.7	(12) 5.4	
-1.0	1.8	.9			1.6		9.1	1.0	
7.0	9.8	7.4			8.1	5.5	9.7	6.1	
1.9	3.1	2.1	% Profit Before Taxes/Total Assets		1.2	1.5	4.4	2.1	
-.6	.0	-1.9			-1.8	-3.6	1.9	-1.4	
88.6	99.9	108.9			38.9	376.8	111.2	84.3	
28.0	25.4	25.9	Sales/Net Fixed Assets		15.2	82.1	21.7	40.9	
11.6	11.6	10.1			4.7	11.5	12.0	19.4	
2.5	2.6	2.9			2.6	3.4	2.2	2.7	
1.9	2.2	1.7	Sales/Total Assets		1.6	2.4	1.4	2.1	
1.3	1.5	1.3			1.2	1.7	1.2	1.4	
.5	.4	.5			.5		.5	.2	
(63) .8	(64) 1.1	(55) 1.0	% Depr., Dep., Amort./Sales		(17) 1.0		(10) 1.7	(11) .9	
3.5	2.8	3.1			4.4		4.5	1.2	
1.6	1.5	1.6			2.9				
(36) 4.2	(41) 2.9	(31) 3.3	% Officers', Directors' Owners' Comp/Sales		(10) 4.6				
7.1	6.4	7.6			9.4				
1080787M	955278M	925818M	Net Sales ($)	3704M	32037M	50749M	85178M	192669M	561481M
559796M	393782M	479108M	Total Assets ($)	3420M	20387M	24073M	57545M	103836M	269847M

M = $ thousand MM = $ million

See Pages 9 through 22 for Explanation of Ratios and Data

Current Data Sorted by Assets							Comparative Historical Data	
			5	3		**Type of Statement** Unqualified	8	11
	1	1	2			Reviewed	4	8
1	5	1				Compiled	7	10
5	6	4				Tax Returns	22	17
4	3	6	3		4	Other	18	28
	11 (4/1-9/30/13)		43 (10/1/13-3/31/14)				4/1/09-3/31/10 ALL	4/1/10-3/31/11 ALL
0-500M	500M-2MM	2-10MM	10-50MM	50-100MM	100-250MM			
10	15	12	10	3	4	**NUMBER OF STATEMENTS**	59	74
%	%	%	%	%	%	**ASSETS**	%	%
25.5	11.7	18.6	12.2			Cash & Equivalents	14.0	10.6
6.0	11.0	7.2	4.2			Trade Receivables (net)	5.0	9.9
48.3	52.2	45.3	35.0			Inventory	50.7	46.0
.1	2.0	1.9	2.4			All Other Current	2.2	2.7
79.9	76.9	73.0	53.8			Total Current	71.9	69.1
13.0	13.3	12.3	38.4			Fixed Assets (net)	17.6	18.4
4.6	3.7	2.5	1.2			Intangibles (net)	2.8	3.4
2.5	6.0	12.2	6.6			All Other Non-Current	7.7	9.1
100.0	100.0	100.0	100.0			Total	100.0	100.0
						LIABILITIES		
37.8	14.5	16.0	7.4			Notes Payable-Short Term	14.8	18.7
7.6	.8	.8	.8			Cur. Mat.-L.T.D.	2.9	1.6
21.6	34.8	26.8	10.5			Trade Payables	22.0	23.5
.4	.0	.0	.1			Income Taxes Payable	.6	.6
14.4	11.1	4.1	10.5			All Other Current	14.7	12.0
81.7	61.2	47.7	29.4			Total Current	55.1	56.4
8.1	8.0	2.5	13.2			Long-Term Debt	17.6	12.2
.0	.0	.1	1.1			Deferred Taxes	.3	.1
8.5	17.2	4.4	2.4			All Other Non-Current	3.9	7.5
1.7	13.6	45.3	53.9			Net Worth	23.1	23.7
100.0	100.0	100.0	100.0			Total Liabilties & Net Worth	100.0	100.0
						INCOME DATA		
100.0	100.0	100.0	100.0			Net Sales	100.0	100.0
39.3	39.4	38.2	48.7			Gross Profit	41.3	40.1
37.5	38.3	33.6	45.1			Operating Expenses	37.9	38.2
1.8	1.1	4.6	3.5			Operating Profit	3.4	1.9
.1	.4	-1.3	.6			All Other Expenses (net)	.9	.8
1.7	.7	5.9	2.9			Profit Before Taxes	2.6	1.1
						RATIOS		
5.4	2.0	1.9	3.6				2.8	2.5
.9	1.2	1.6	2.8			Current	1.8	1.5
.7	.9	1.1	1.2				1.0	1.0
3.1	.5	.8	1.9				1.0	.9
.3	.3	.6	.5			Quick	.4	(73) .4
.1	.1	.1	.3				.2	.1
0 UND	**1** 325.0	**2** 227.3	**2** 229.5				**0** UND	**1** 679.0
1 635.5	**3** 121.8	**7** 55.6	**4** 85.2			Sales/Receivables	**3** 142.9	**3** 111.5
5 68.2	**29** 12.8	**14** 26.2	**14** 26.7				**17** 21.2	**20** 18.3
29 12.4	**70** 5.2	**51** 7.1	**72** 5.1				**92** 4.0	**67** 5.4
69 5.3	**107** 3.4	**76** 4.8	**126** 2.9			Cost of Sales/Inventory	**123** 3.0	**112** 3.2
146 2.5	**166** 2.2	**146** 2.5	**203** 1.8				**161** 2.3	**168** 2.2
0 UND	**47** 7.7	**21** 17.6	**24** 15.1				**21** 17.5	**24** 15.3
24 15.0	**78** 4.7	**72** 5.1	**38** 9.5			Cost of Sales/Payables	**47** 7.8	**57** 6.5
87 4.2	**111** 3.3	**104** 3.5	**69** 5.3				**79** 4.6	**82** 4.4
12.4	8.9	5.8	4.1				4.8	5.3
-90.5	19.9	8.0	5.5			Sales/Working Capital	9.0	12.4
-9.4	-37.1	49.2	17.7				474.7	120.9
	6.4	65.9					15.7	14.2
	(13) 1.6	(10) 24.5				EBIT/Interest	(46) 3.9	(59) 5.1
	-2.2	12.4					.7	-.8
						Net Profit + Depr., Dep., Amort./Cur. Mat. L/T/D		
.1	.1	.1	.2				.1	.1
-2.4	.7	.2	.4			Fixed/Worth	.4	.4
-.2	-5.4	.5	1.3				1.8	1.4
2.2	2.0	.7	.4				.5	.7
-14.0	4.7	1.2	.7			Debt/Worth	1.7	2.0
-4.1	-39.5	3.1	2.2				64.1	11.0
	24.6	51.7	17.4				38.9	46.9
	(10) 7.1	33.9	5.2			% Profit Before Taxes/Tangible Net Worth	(46) 9.3	(58) 14.7
	.0	9.3	.2				.8	.8
30.5	3.5	30.1	6.6				14.9	14.3
21.5	1.2	14.9	3.2			% Profit Before Taxes/Total Assets	3.2	4.2
-10.7	-5.0	4.3	.6				.2	-2.7
UND	102.0	101.1	27.9				139.7	110.0
25.7	50.7	36.4	6.0			Sales/Net Fixed Assets	20.8	24.8
16.7	9.0	16.0	1.3				8.7	7.6
7.1	3.6	3.4	2.2				3.3	3.3
4.5	2.8	2.5	2.0			Sales/Total Assets	2.5	2.5
2.3	2.0	2.0	1.1				1.7	1.7
	.3	.4					.7	.8
	(11) .7	(10) .6				% Depr., Dep., Amort./Sales	(39) 1.3	(55) 1.4
	.9	1.0					2.2	2.1
							2.8	1.8
						% Officers', Directors' Owners' Comp/Sales	(22) 4.6	(18) 3.5
							8.2	6.2
13417M	**61762M**	**130443M**	**347219M**	**231487M**	**1154475M**	Net Sales ($)	**1644900M**	**1690271M**
3042M	**19691M**	**46195M**	**205768M**	**181376M**	**564632M**	Total Assets ($)	**739325M**	**831403M**

M = $ thousand MM = $ million
See Pages 9 through 22 for Explanation of Ratios and Data

Comparative Historical Data				Current Data Sorted by Sales					
			Type of Statement						
8	5	8	Unqualified					2	6
3	5	4	Reviewed				1	2	1
9	8	7	Compiled		5	1	1		
21	18	15	Tax Returns	2	4	6	1	2	
17	19	20	Other	1	6		3	2	8
4/1/11-3/31/12	4/1/12-3/31/13	4/1/13-3/31/14		11 (4/1-9/30/13)			43 (10/1/13-3/31/14)		
ALL	ALL	ALL		0-1MM	1-3MM	3-5MM	5-10MM	10-25MM	25MM & OVER
58	55	54	**NUMBER OF STATEMENTS**	3	15	7	6	8	15
%	%	%	**ASSETS**	%	%	%	%	%	%
12.0	14.3	16.7	Cash & Equivalents		21.9				13.1
5.6	3.6	7.6	Trade Receivables (net)		7.6				6.6
50.0	44.2	43.4	Inventory		43.5				36.9
2.0	1.8	1.7	All Other Current		.3				3.4
69.6	63.9	69.3	Total Current		73.3				60.1
20.1	23.9	19.4	Fixed Assets (net)		15.9				26.8
4.4	2.8	3.9	Intangibles (net)		6.1				5.2
5.7	9.5	7.3	All Other Non-Current		4.6				7.8
100.0	100.0	100.0	Total		100.0				100.0
			LIABILITIES						
12.5	16.3	16.6	Notes Payable-Short Term		18.2				7.5
1.4	1.8	2.2	Cur. Mat.-L.T.D.		5.8				1.1
23.5	22.4	24.3	Trade Payables		30.3				18.3
.0	.2	.2	Income Taxes Payable		.2				.4
20.2	16.1	9.3	All Other Current		15.1				9.9
57.6	56.8	52.6	Total Current		69.6				37.3
6.6	12.0	9.3	Long-Term Debt		9.7				7.5
.1	.2	.2	Deferred Taxes		.0				.8
13.2	10.2	9.2	All Other Non-Current		7.1				6.3
22.5	20.8	28.7	Net Worth		13.6				48.0
100.0	100.0	100.0	Total Liabilties & Net Worth		100.0				100.0
			INCOME DATA						
100.0	100.0	100.0	Net Sales		100.0				100.0
44.1	46.1	41.8	Gross Profit		40.9				50.3
42.4	42.3	39.1	Operating Expenses		40.8				48.7
1.7	3.8	2.6	Operating Profit		.1				1.5
.3	.5	.0	All Other Expenses (net)		.2				.3
1.4	3.3	2.6	Profit Before Taxes		-.1				1.3
			RATIOS						
2.4	2.3	2.9			2.3				3.3
1.4	1.3	1.3	Current		.9				1.9
.9	.8	.9			.7				1.0
.8	.7	1.3			.6				1.7
.3	.2	.4	Quick		.4				.4
.1	.1	.2			.2				.2
1 321.3	**1** 513.4	**1** 347.9			**0** 999.8				**2** 234.2
4 101.4	**2** 154.8	**3** 107.9	Sales/Receivables		**2** 217.1				**3** 143.3
12 29.3	**7** 53.3	**11** 33.6			**19** 19.0				**9** 38.6
76 4.8	**79** 4.6	**63** 5.8			**68** 5.4				**76** 4.8
104 3.5	**111** 3.3	**107** 3.4	Cost of Sales/Inventory		**107** 3.4				**130** 2.8
166 2.2	**146** 2.5	**146** 2.5			**166** 2.2				**182** 2.0
22 16.6	**23** 15.9	**24** 15.1			**28** 13.0				**29** 12.5
46 8.0	**45** 8.1	**60** 6.1	Cost of Sales/Payables		**85** 4.3				**57** 6.4
96 3.8	**74** 4.9	**99** 3.7			**96** 3.8				**91** 4.0
5.5	6.0	5.5			10.4				4.9
12.8	17.1	13.1	Sales/Working Capital		-51.6				6.6
-68.0	-25.7	-41.4			-17.8				-999.8
10.6	20.5	21.2			2.1				10.9
(50) 2.2	(46) 5.9	(42) 3.1	EBIT/Interest		(11) -1.8				(11) .2
-1.4	1.2	-.9			-2.7				-7.1
			Net Profit + Depr., Dep., Amort./Cur. Mat. L/T/D						
.2	.2	.2			.1				.2
.5	.6	.5	Fixed/Worth		-8.4				.4
1.5	14.2	NM			-2.1				1.6
.8	.7	.7			1.5				.4
1.6	1.6	2.8	Debt/Worth		-39.5				1.1
11.0	62.8	NM			-7.8				5.3
33.0	63.3	38.1							8.8
(46) 7.2	(42) 12.3	(41) 10.1	% Profit Before Taxes/Tangible Net Worth						(13) 4.5
-5.5	2.1	2.1							-9.0
7.3	16.8	17.3			25.6				5.6
2.6	3.8	3.9	% Profit Before Taxes/Total Assets		-3.2				2.8
-3.6	-.2	-2.2			-10.5				-2.8
50.1	37.2	65.7			67.2				24.0
25.4	15.9	21.3	Sales/Net Fixed Assets		19.2				8.5
7.2	7.0	8.3			9.0				5.6
3.5	3.3	3.4			5.4				2.2
2.5	2.6	2.3	Sales/Total Assets		2.5				2.1
1.6	1.6	1.9			2.0				1.8
.6	.5	.6			.7				1.3
(46) 1.0	(50) 1.1	(42) 1.1	% Depr., Dep., Amort./Sales		(11) .9				(12) 1.6
1.5	1.7	1.7			1.5				3.3
2.3	1.7	1.8							
(19) 3.2	(21) 3.7	(21) 3.7	% Officers', Directors' Owners' Comp/Sales						
4.8	6.7	6.9							
1369696M	1216871M	1938803M	Net Sales ($)	1715M	29601M	29591M	46173M	121976M	1709747M
612418M	674954M	1020704M	Total Assets ($)	497M	11835M	11329M	31209M	95471M	870363M

M = $ thousand MM = $ million

See Pages 9 through 22 for Explanation of Ratios and Data

Current Data Sorted by Assets							Comparative Historical Data	
						Type of Statement		
			4	1	2	Unqualified	10	7
		1	2			Reviewed	9	7
		1				Compiled	9	5
2	2	3				Tax Returns	9	5
1	2	2	4	1		Other	16	7
4 (4/1-9/30/13)			24 (10/1/13-3/31/14)				4/1/09-3/31/10 ALL	4/1/10-3/31/11 ALL
0-500M	500M-2MM	2-10MM	10-50MM	50-100MM	100-250MM			
3	4	7	10	2	2	**NUMBER OF STATEMENTS**	53	31
%	%	%	%	%	%	**ASSETS**	%	%
			9.5			Cash & Equivalents	15.0	14.2
			2.8			Trade Receivables (net)	9.2	9.9
			44.7			Inventory	45.0	47.9
			4.2			All Other Current	1.7	1.8
			61.2			Total Current	71.0	73.8
			30.1			Fixed Assets (net)	21.6	17.1
			2.4			Intangibles (net)	2.4	1.7
			6.3			All Other Non-Current	5.0	7.4
			100.0			Total	100.0	100.0
						LIABILITIES		
			.6			Notes Payable-Short Term	10.3	9.3
			3.3			Cur. Mat.-L.T.D.	2.1	1.9
			12.9			Trade Payables	16.4	18.8
			.5			Income Taxes Payable	.5	.1
			13.0			All Other Current	7.9	8.7
			30.4			Total Current	37.2	38.8
			20.2			Long-Term Debt	14.5	12.2
			1.5			Deferred Taxes	.5	.3
			8.5			All Other Non-Current	9.3	6.0
			39.4			Net Worth	38.6	42.6
			100.0			Total Liabilties & Net Worth	100.0	100.0
						INCOME DATA		
			100.0			Net Sales	100.0	100.0
			35.3			Gross Profit	41.1	39.4
			36.8			Operating Expenses	35.9	34.0
			-1.5			Operating Profit	5.2	5.4
			.3			All Other Expenses (net)	2.5	.1
			-1.7			Profit Before Taxes	2.7	5.3
						RATIOS		
			5.6				3.1	2.9
			1.8			Current	2.1	1.9
			1.2				1.3	1.3
			1.2				1.2	1.2
			.4			Quick	.8	.6
			.1				.2	.2
			0 UND				0 UND	0 999.8
			2 200.0			Sales/Receivables	2 216.7	2 167.5
			12 31.0				15 24.1	15 24.3
			81 4.5				54 6.8	54 6.8
			130 2.8			Cost of Sales/Inventory	104 3.5	106 3.4
			174 2.1				155 2.4	136 2.7
			6 56.9				8 43.0	14 26.9
			36 10.1			Cost of Sales/Payables	26 14.2	36 10.1
			47 7.7				42 8.7	50 7.3
			3.2				5.4	3.8
			10.7			Sales/Working Capital	7.7	8.1
			36.6				19.3	17.7
			35.6				25.9	28.6
			-3.4			EBIT/Interest	(44) 5.3	(28) 4.3
			-5.9				1.8	1.4
							8.9	
						Net Profit + Depr., Dep., Amort./Cur. Mat. L/T/D	(18) 3.4	
							.1	
			.2				.1	.1
			1.3			Fixed/Worth	.4	.4
			-4.8				1.2	.8
			.3				.5	.6
			2.0			Debt/Worth	1.6	1.5
			-14.0				6.3	2.7
							41.6	46.1
						% Profit Before Taxes/Tangible Net Worth	(46) 17.5	(29) 17.4
							5.7	4.3
			6.2				16.6	20.2
			-2.4			% Profit Before Taxes/Total Assets	8.0	4.7
			-7.7				1.7	.9
			13.7				88.3	149.3
			8.7			Sales/Net Fixed Assets	24.3	28.7
			3.8				7.9	11.6
			2.9				4.2	4.2
			2.1			Sales/Total Assets	2.7	2.9
			1.4				1.8	1.8
			.5				.3	.5
			1.7			% Depr., Dep., Amort./Sales	(46) .9	(24) .7
			2.2				2.0	1.5
							1.8	.8
						% Officers', Directors' Owners' Comp/Sales	(24) 3.3	(10) 2.1
							5.5	5.7
2706M	19255M	77231M	701268M	279321M	1093611M	Net Sales ($)	3072976M	2501446M
633M	4740M	29813M	289758M	141989M	442080M	Total Assets ($)	1193591M	875007M

M = $ thousand MM = $ million

See Pages 9 through 22 for Explanation of Ratios and Data

Comparative Historical Data | Current Data Sorted by Sales

4/1/11-3/31/12 ALL	4/1/12-3/31/13 ALL	4/1/13-3/31/14 ALL	Type of Statement	0-1MM	1-3MM	3-5MM	5-10MM	10-25MM	25MM & OVER
				4 (4/1-9/30/13)			24 (10/1/13-3/31/14)		
4	7	7	Unqualified					1	6
6	6	3	Reviewed						3
5	5	1	Compiled			1			
8	5	7	Tax Returns	2	1	1	2	1	
8	5	10	Other		2		2	1	5
31	28	28	NUMBER OF STATEMENTS	2	3	2	4	3	14
%	%	%	**ASSETS**	%	%	%	%	%	%
20.7	18.3	15.1	Cash & Equivalents						8.5
5.7	2.3	3.9	Trade Receivables (net)						3.2
43.4	42.4	41.4	Inventory						48.3
1.4	2.0	5.0	All Other Current						4.6
71.3	65.0	65.4	Total Current						64.6
19.2	27.3	24.5	Fixed Assets (net)						27.9
2.4	1.3	2.4	Intangibles (net)						2.4
7.1	6.3	7.7	All Other Non-Current						5.1
100.0	100.0	100.0	Total						100.0
			LIABILITIES						
5.7	7.0	2.7	Notes Payable-Short Term						1.4
.7	1.3	2.4	Cur. Mat.-L.T.D.						2.6
16.9	16.4	14.2	Trade Payables						17.2
.3	.3	.6	Income Taxes Payable						.4
8.2	8.3	11.2	All Other Current						13.8
31.8	33.2	31.1	Total Current						35.4
12.5	15.9	21.3	Long-Term Debt						19.6
.2	1.0	1.2	Deferred Taxes						1.2
8.8	6.0	6.4	All Other Non-Current						7.2
46.7	43.8	40.1	Net Worth						36.5
100.0	100.0	100.0	Total Liabilties & Net Worth						100.0
			INCOME DATA						
100.0	100.0	100.0	Net Sales						100.0
36.6	38.9	41.9	Gross Profit						38.4
32.3	36.3	39.7	Operating Expenses						38.1
4.3	2.6	2.2	Operating Profit						.2
-.3	-.3	.2	All Other Expenses (net)						.0
4.6	2.9	2.0	Profit Before Taxes						.2
			RATIOS						
3.5	3.7	4.1							4.0
2.2	1.7	1.9	Current						1.5
1.5	1.3	1.2							1.2
1.5	1.2	1.3							.6
.7	.6	.5	Quick						.3
.3	.3	.1							.1
0 UND	0 UND	0 UND							0 UND
2 234.6	2 180.5	2 149.4	Sales/Receivables						2 200.0
9 39.2	6 56.4	9 40.8							12 31.2
43 8.4	42 8.6	66 5.5							99 3.7
79 4.6	89 4.1	114 3.2	Cost of Sales/Inventory						140 2.6
114 3.2	152 2.4	166 2.2							174 2.1
10 35.3	5 66.7	6 61.6							6 56.9
34 10.7	35 10.4	33 10.9	Cost of Sales/Payables						36 10.0
44 8.3	51 7.2	74 4.9							81 4.5
3.7	6.1	3.7							3.3
8.5	12.3	9.3	Sales/Working Capital						16.8
20.3	32.4	32.9							29.7
46.2	30.8	57.5							44.5
(25) 5.7	(22) 8.9	(22) 4.9	EBIT/Interest						.3
1.6	1.6	-4.0							-4.2
			Net Profit + Depr., Dep., Amort./Cur. Mat. L/T/D						
.1	.2	.2							.3
.3	.4	.6	Fixed/Worth						.7
1.2	1.5	2.8							NM
.4	.6	.5							.4
1.1	1.3	2.1	Debt/Worth						2.1
2.7	3.5	5.5							NM
43.5	55.0	49.5							28.2
(28) 20.2	(25) 21.1	(24) 17.2	% Profit Before Taxes/Tangible Net Worth						(11) 7.1
4.4	6.3	-2.0							-25.6
23.9	20.2	21.8							6.3
6.6	8.8	5.2	% Profit Before Taxes/Total Assets						2.0
2.1	1.5	-4.9							-7.1
90.6	77.5	59.4							13.7
29.0	15.3	10.9	Sales/Net Fixed Assets						9.4
11.9	4.5	4.2							5.9
4.2	5.1	4.7							3.0
2.8	2.9	2.3	Sales/Total Assets						2.2
1.9	1.5	1.4							1.9
.3	.5	.5							.5
(24) .7	(25) 1.2	(24) 1.3	% Depr., Dep., Amort./Sales						(13) 1.4
1.7	1.9	2.2							2.0
.8	1.2	1.3							
(12) 2.2	(11) 2.7	(10) 2.7	% Officers', Directors' Owners' Comp/Sales						
6.2	3.9	4.7							
1888654M	2177862M	2173392M	Net Sales ($)	1532M	5031M	7967M	31443M	36637M	2090782M
665974M	806812M	909013M	Total Assets ($)	438M	6366M	3914M	10164M	16473M	871658M

M = $ thousand MM = $ million

See Pages 9 through 22 for Explanation of Ratios and Data

Current Data Sorted by Assets							Comparative Historical Data	
Type of Statement								
Unqualified			1	1	4	1	20	15
Reviewed			8	9			19	18
Compiled		4	5				15	29
Tax Returns	18	13	6				61	52
Other	7	15	17	4	3	4	62	49
	12 (4/1-9/30/13)			108 (10/1/13-3/31/14)			4/1/09-3/31/10	4/1/10-3/31/11
	0-500M	500M-2MM	2-10MM	10-50MM	50-100MM	100-250MM	ALL	ALL
NUMBER OF STATEMENTS	25	32	37	14	7	5	177	163
ASSETS	%	%	%	%	%	%	%	%
Cash & Equivalents	20.6	8.2	8.9	5.3			12.3	11.1
Trade Receivables (net)	5.7	10.2	13.2	12.5			8.8	7.2
Inventory	44.4	48.4	45.4	54.6			43.9	48.4
All Other Current	.2	3.5	2.6	4.0			2.8	2.3
Total Current	70.8	70.4	70.1	76.3			67.8	69.0
Fixed Assets (net)	14.6	19.2	20.2	18.9			20.0	19.1
Intangibles (net)	4.3	1.5	3.2	1.5			6.1	5.0
All Other Non-Current	10.4	8.9	6.5	3.3			6.1	6.9
Total	100.0	100.0	100.0	100.0			100.0	100.0
LIABILITIES								
Notes Payable-Short Term	10.7	13.3	10.6	8.4			9.9	9.3
Cur. Mat.-L.T.D.	.5	3.9	1.4	1.9			2.6	2.9
Trade Payables	21.3	16.4	17.3	13.7			14.9	16.4
Income Taxes Payable	.0	.0	.3	.0			.1	.1
All Other Current	13.5	7.9	8.4	20.8			10.6	9.2
Total Current	46.1	41.5	38.1	44.9			38.2	37.8
Long-Term Debt	17.5	22.5	11.6	5.7			20.0	20.3
Deferred Taxes	.0	.0	.5	.1			.1	.2
All Other Non-Current	27.1	9.2	13.9	3.2			11.1	9.0
Net Worth	9.4	26.8	35.9	46.2			30.5	32.7
Total Liabilties & Net Worth	100.0	100.0	100.0	100.0			100.0	100.0
INCOME DATA								
Net Sales	100.0	100.0	100.0	100.0			100.0	100.0
Gross Profit	44.0	39.5	38.4	31.7			40.1	36.7
Operating Expenses	42.9	33.4	33.2	26.1			37.0	32.4
Operating Profit	1.1	6.1	5.2	5.6			3.1	4.4
All Other Expenses (net)	-.2	1.0	.6	.2			.8	.8
Profit Before Taxes	1.3	5.1	4.6	5.4			2.3	3.6
RATIOS								
	5.4	2.5	4.1	2.9			4.1	3.8
Current	2.4	1.6	2.3	1.9			2.1	1.8
	1.4	1.3	1.4	1.1			1.2	1.2
	1.3	.9	1.4	.8			1.2	1.0
Quick	.5	.3	.4	.5			(176) .4	(161) .4
	.3	.2	.1	.0			.1	.2
	0 UND	0 UND	1 266.5	0 999.8			0 UND	0 UND
Sales/Receivables	0 UND	0 840.3	8 48.2	1 561.9			2 184.8	2 153.7
	3 144.8	22 16.7	31 11.7	33 10.9			12 29.4	13 27.1
	24 15.5	43 8.4	32 11.3	54 6.7			36 10.2	51 7.2
Cost of Sales/Inventory	64 5.7	140 2.6	99 3.7	140 2.6			99 3.7	110 3.3
	135 2.7	203 1.8	203 1.8	166 2.2			181 2.0	164 2.2
	0 UND	11 34.3	17 21.7	11 32.3			6 56.4	7 48.8
Cost of Sales/Payables	14 26.3	23 16.1	35 10.3	24 15.1			23 15.7	27 13.5
	30 12.2	52 7.0	46 7.9	38 9.7			48 7.7	48 7.6
	5.7	5.1	3.3	5.2			4.5	4.1
Sales/Working Capital	11.9	10.5	8.3	7.2			8.0	10.3
	42.6	20.7	20.2	41.1			31.1	35.0
	10.8	11.8	15.8	27.4			15.9	10.7
EBIT/Interest	(13) 2.1	(28) 3.8	(31) 4.2	(13) 22.4			(144) 3.9	(136) 3.0
	-1.7	1.5	1.8	4.9			.6	1.2
							9.0	12.9
Net Profit + Depr., Dep., Amort./Cur. Mat. L/T/D							(25) 3.7	(17) 4.8
							2.2	2.4
	.0	.0	.2	.2			.1	.1
Fixed/Worth	.4	.6	.5	.5			.5	.6
	-1.3	2.2	4.1	.7			2.7	4.5
	.6	1.1	.6	.5			.7	.7
Debt/Worth	2.9	2.1	2.3	1.3			2.1	2.3
	-4.5	8.7	11.2	3.0			8.5	26.7
	71.7	76.7	41.9	64.3			50.9	58.2
% Profit Before Taxes/Tangible Net Worth	(17) 19.8	(28) 30.2	(31) 26.3	34.2			(143) 19.5	(130) 19.7
	4.9	3.5	5.1	12.7			4.4	4.1
	18.2	15.1	20.1	25.5			16.3	15.0
% Profit Before Taxes/Total Assets	3.7	4.9	5.0	11.8			6.1	5.2
	-9.8	1.3	2.3	6.6			-.9	.6
	231.5	364.9	76.1	29.4			56.2	83.2
Sales/Net Fixed Assets	70.1	40.9	23.5	23.1			21.4	21.6
	25.8	9.1	6.7	12.5			8.6	8.8
	7.4	4.2	3.5	3.6			3.8	3.8
Sales/Total Assets	4.7	2.4	2.1	2.7			2.5	2.6
	2.2	1.5	1.3	2.1			1.8	1.8
	.3	.3	.4	.6			.7	.6
% Depr., Dep., Amort./Sales	(17) 1.0	(17) .7	(33) .8	.7			(133) 1.2	(123) .9
	1.7	2.8	2.0	.9			2.0	1.9
	1.7	1.3	1.9				1.8	1.8
% Officers', Directors' Owners' Comp/Sales	(18) 6.4	(14) 4.4	(16) 2.5				(70) 3.9	(61) 3.8
	10.4	6.1	4.0				6.9	6.8
Net Sales ($)	30788M	105208M	472074M	863671M	1061303M	3005736M	8503183M	7323733M
Total Assets ($)	5605M	32872M	179378M	309117M	493316M	974291M	3142103M	2743407M

M = $ thousand MM = $ million

See Pages 9 through 22 for Explanation of Ratios and Data

Comparative Historical Data				Current Data Sorted by Sales					
			Type of Statement						
12	8	7	Unqualified					1	6
12	18	17	Reviewed				3	5	9
28	15	9	Compiled	2	1	1	3	2	
72	52	37	Tax Returns	13	13	3	4	4	
49	54	50	Other	6	10	6	7	9	12
4/1/11-3/31/12	4/1/12-3/31/13	4/1/13-3/31/14			12 (4/1-9/30/13)			108 (10/1/13-3/31/14)	
ALL	ALL	ALL		0-1MM	1-3MM	3-5MM	5-10MM	10-25MM	25MM & OVER
173	147	120	**NUMBER OF STATEMENTS**	21	24	10	17	21	27
%	%	%	**ASSETS**	%	%	%	%	%	%
12.3	12.3	10.5	Cash & Equivalents	22.0	7.9	6.6	8.8	10.1	6.6
9.0	7.3	9.8	Trade Receivables (net)	1.6	7.9	13.8	16.7	16.2	7.1
45.9	46.1	47.7	Inventory	42.1	47.5	56.7	44.9	44.7	53.1
3.1	3.0	2.3	All Other Current	3.1	2.1	.6	1.1	3.6	2.4
70.2	68.7	70.3	Total Current	68.9	65.4	77.5	71.5	74.5	69.2
19.6	21.4	19.1	Fixed Assets (net)	24.4	18.8	15.9	15.8	15.9	20.8
4.2	3.5	2.9	Intangibles (net)	1.9	4.3	5.7	.5	3.0	2.8
6.0	6.3	7.7	All Other Non-Current	5.0	11.5	.8	12.1	6.5	7.3
100.0	100.0	100.0	Total	100.0	100.0	100.0	100.0	100.0	100.0
			LIABILITIES						
12.6	10.9	10.8	Notes Payable-Short Term	8.7	11.3	14.6	9.9	14.7	8.2
2.4	1.9	1.9	Cur. Mat.-L.T.D.	.8	2.7	1.7	1.9	3.2	1.0
17.1	16.7	18.1	Trade Payables	9.5	8.3	20.6	40.5	17.5	18.8
.1	.1	.1	Income Taxes Payable	.0	.0	.0	.0	.4	.1
13.9	15.4	10.8	All Other Current	14.6	8.2	3.2	9.9	9.0	15.0
46.0	45.0	41.7	Total Current	33.6	30.5	40.1	62.2	44.9	43.1
15.1	19.5	15.5	Long-Term Debt	23.3	23.4	11.4	17.3	6.9	9.3
.2	.1	.3	Deferred Taxes	.0	.3	.0	.1	.4	.8
10.6	10.1	13.2	All Other Non-Current	21.6	20.3	17.7	11.7	8.1	3.9
28.1	25.3	29.3	Net Worth	21.7	25.4	30.8	8.8	39.7	43.0
100.0	100.0	100.0	Total Liabilties & Net Worth	100.0	100.0	100.0	100.0	100.0	100.0
			INCOME DATA						
100.0	100.0	100.0	Net Sales	100.0	100.0	100.0	100.0	100.0	100.0
39.7	40.9	38.9	Gross Profit	46.4	42.3	41.4	32.9	37.4	34.2
34.9	37.3	34.5	Operating Expenses	42.4	36.4	36.1	31.2	32.4	29.7
4.7	3.6	4.5	Operating Profit	4.1	5.9	5.3	1.7	5.0	4.5
.3	.6	.4	All Other Expenses (net)	.8	.8	1.0	-.4	.6	.0
4.5	3.0	4.1	Profit Before Taxes	3.3	5.2	4.2	2.1	4.4	4.6
			RATIOS						
3.8	4.6	3.6		5.4	6.0	2.6	3.2	4.6	2.4
1.8	2.0	2.0	Current	2.3	2.1	2.1	2.3	1.9	1.6
1.1	1.1	1.3		1.2	1.4	1.4	1.0	1.4	1.2
1.0	1.2	1.0		2.3	.8	1.0	.8	1.3	.6
(172) .4	.5	.4	Quick	.6	.4	.3	.4	.5	.3
.1	.1	.1		.3	.2	.2	.2	.2	.0
0 UND	0 UND	0 UND		0 UND	0 UND	1 634.7	0 999.8	1 266.5	0 UND
1 474.7	0 999.8	2 219.7	Sales/Receivables	0 UND	1 523.1	13 28.2	14 25.9	8 46.6	1 297.6
15 24.2	8 43.6	19 19.6		2 236.0	15 24.1	30 12.3	33 11.2	29 12.5	9 38.5
38 9.7	50 7.3	44 8.3		64 5.7	45 8.2	43 8.5	26 14.0	25 14.7	54 6.7
91 4.0	101 3.6	111 3.3	Cost of Sales/Inventory	140 2.6	130 2.8	96 3.8	81 4.5	81 4.5	118 3.1
159 2.3	166 2.2	174 2.1		215 1.7	174 2.1	215 1.7	203 1.8	159 2.3	152 2.4
4 86.2	5 73.3	12 31.2		0 UND	0 UND	25 14.8	14 26.0	11 33.7	21 17.2
18 20.0	23 15.8	25 14.6	Cost of Sales/Payables	11 34.5	14 26.1	36 10.0	38 9.6	26 14.1	31 11.7
42 8.6	46 7.9	45 8.1		36 10.2	38 9.5	54 6.8	59 6.2	44 8.3	47 7.7
4.5	4.8	4.8		2.6	4.8	4.8	4.6	3.6	5.9
11.4	10.1	9.9	Sales/Working Capital	7.5	10.0	10.1	18.0	8.5	10.2
38.6	64.7	22.5		38.3	18.0	13.0	NM	22.2	33.8
15.4	14.9	15.3		12.9	5.0		14.2	21.7	25.8
(139) 5.5	(112) 3.8	(97) 5.0	EBIT/Interest	(10) 2.0	(19) 2.8		(16) 2.9	(17) 5.2	(26) 13.7
1.6	1.0	1.7		-1.3	1.1		-1.3	2.0	5.5
7.3	17.8	11.2							
(22) 4.2	(18) 4.3	(16) 3.8	Net Profit + Depr., Dep., Amort./Cur. Mat. L/T/D						
1.8	1.6	1.3							
.1	.1	.1		.0	.2	.0	.1	.1	.3
.4	.5	.6	Fixed/Worth	1.1	.5	.6	1.2	.3	.6
3.4	3.4	1.9		-2.8	2.3	NM	NM	1.4	.8
.6	.7	.8		.7	1.1	1.2	.6	.5	.7
2.1	3.3	2.0	Debt/Worth	3.7	2.2	2.1	3.6	1.8	1.4
12.6	12.4	7.7		-49.1	8.7	NM	NM	5.1	3.6
56.8	51.7	47.6		43.4	34.9		73.6	43.1	57.7
(135) 24.7	(123) 22.5	(102) 28.7	% Profit Before Taxes/Tangible Net Worth	(15) 16.4	(20) 26.0		(13) 31.3	(19) 35.8	38.6
7.1	2.2	7.5		2.9	5.2		-1.9	8.0	13.7
20.2	16.9	19.7		15.1	18.4	19.9	5.9	22.8	23.5
8.9	6.2	6.7	% Profit Before Taxes/Total Assets	3.4	4.3	8.5	3.0	10.7	12.9
2.1	.0	1.7		-3.1	.2	2.6	-1.3	3.1	5.6
79.8	128.7	91.8		130.4	212.1	344.9	267.5	81.0	24.9
26.6	28.4	25.0	Sales/Net Fixed Assets	28.5	51.3	51.8	89.1	33.8	16.5
10.7	7.5	9.3		8.5	7.3	8.2	10.7	17.0	9.2
4.4	4.2	4.3		5.2	3.8	5.9	5.2	5.8	3.6
2.7	2.7	2.5	Sales/Total Assets	2.0	2.6	2.7	2.1	3.0	2.6
1.9	1.4	1.9		1.2	1.6	1.2	1.7	1.9	2.2
.5	.4	.4		.9	.1		.3	.4	.6
(134) .8	(109) 1.0	(89) .8	% Depr., Dep., Amort./Sales	(13) 1.8	(17) .5		(12) .9	(17) .8	(23) .8
1.7	2.0	1.6		3.8	1.5		2.9	1.8	1.0
1.8	2.2	1.8		7.5	1.6			1.4	
(83) 4.5	(69) 3.9	(51) 3.3	% Officers', Directors' Owners' Comp/Sales	(11) 9.9	(16) 4.0			(11) 2.2	
7.5	7.4	5.8		11.3	5.2			3.6	
6509668M	4173774M	5538780M	Net Sales ($)	11891M	43067M	36923M	120363M	310729M	5015807M
2360978M	1593858M	1994579M	Total Assets ($)	7631M	21281M	18028M	51336M	117932M	1778371M

M = $ thousand MM = $ million

See Pages 9 through 22 for Explanation of Ratios and Data

Current Data Sorted by Assets							Comparative Historical Data	
						Type of Statement		
		1				Unqualified	2	1
1		2	1			Reviewed	3	4
3	1	1				Compiled	7	11
15	6	2				Tax Returns	25	25
6	4	1	1	1		Other	15	12
10 (4/1-9/30/13)		36 (10/1/13-3/31/14)					4/1/09-3/31/10 ALL	4/1/10-3/31/11 ALL
0-500M	500M-2MM	2-10MM	10-50MM	50-100MM	100-250MM			
25	11	7	2	1		NUMBER OF STATEMENTS	52	53
%	%	%	%	%	%	**ASSETS**	%	%
19.9	10.6				DATA NOT AVAILABLE	Cash & Equivalents	11.7	15.1
8.9	16.0					Trade Receivables (net)	14.9	12.1
23.5	16.5					Inventory	20.6	27.6
3.8	.2					All Other Current	3.6	2.8
56.1	43.3					Total Current	50.8	57.7
28.4	29.8					Fixed Assets (net)	36.2	27.0
5.6	8.2					Intangibles (net)	6.8	6.6
9.9	18.7					All Other Non-Current	6.2	8.8
100.0	100.0					Total	100.0	100.0
						LIABILITIES		
16.0	5.8					Notes Payable-Short Term	10.8	10.2
5.5	1.2					Cur. Mat.-L.T.D.	4.7	4.8
10.7	25.8					Trade Payables	27.9	18.5
.0	.0					Income Taxes Payable	.1	.1
9.1	11.8					All Other Current	17.9	11.7
41.4	44.7					Total Current	61.3	45.4
25.7	9.9					Long-Term Debt	40.8	22.4
.0	.0					Deferred Taxes	.0	.0
19.9	23.7					All Other Non-Current	14.6	16.9
13.1	21.8					Net Worth	-16.6	15.3
100.0	100.0					Total Liabilties & Net Worth	100.0	100.0
						INCOME DATA		
100.0	100.0					Net Sales	100.0	100.0
57.1	58.7					Gross Profit	54.4	55.5
51.6	56.5					Operating Expenses	53.3	54.8
5.5	2.2					Operating Profit	1.1	.6
.6	.0					All Other Expenses (net)	.4	-.1
4.9	2.2					Profit Before Taxes	.7	.8
						RATIOS		
3.8	1.9						1.8	3.5
1.8	1.1					Current	1.2	1.1
.8	.7						.8	.7
1.8	1.3						.9	1.4
.7	.7					Quick	.5	.6
.4	.2						.3	.3
0 UND	**2** 184.9						**7** 49.4	**2** 161.6
1 317.0	**11** 33.4					Sales/Receivables	**13** 27.6	**10** 37.6
8 46.0	**25** 14.8						**22** 16.6	**22** 16.6
3 108.5	**2** 181.8						**22** 16.2	**24** 15.2
24 15.4	**8** 45.2					Cost of Sales/Inventory	**38** 9.6	**59** 6.2
68 5.4	**118** 3.1						**104** 3.5	**112** 3.3
0 UND	**26** 14.0						**9** 39.7	**16** 22.8
1 538.7	**47** 7.8					Cost of Sales/Payables	**42** 8.7	**41** 8.9
28 13.2	**91** 4.0						**66** 5.5	**78** 4.7
14.2	14.8						11.0	8.4
60.6	77.0					Sales/Working Capital	50.6	44.3
-49.8	-17.9						-25.7	-25.6
22.2							5.6	3.7
(20) 8.1						EBIT/Interest	(45) 1.4	(37) .8
3.5							-.4	-3.3
						Net Profit + Depr., Dep., Amort./Cur. Mat. L/T/D		
.2	.3						.6	.2
1.1	2.0					Fixed/Worth	7.2	1.4
-.9	-.8						-1.7	-1.5
.7	.4						3.1	.5
1.5	2.4					Debt/Worth	15.3	3.0
-3.9	-5.2						-3.5	-5.0
104.4							135.2	25.2
(17) 62.9						% Profit Before Taxes/Tangible Net Worth	(31) 28.9	(35) -1.6
25.4							2.6	-12.8
52.4	18.3						16.7	6.1
24.4	4.1					% Profit Before Taxes/Total Assets	1.6	.0
6.8	-20.4						-7.2	-6.2
95.8	37.0						29.7	98.2
30.1	20.1					Sales/Net Fixed Assets	13.2	15.5
15.5	7.1						3.3	6.5
7.7	4.4						4.7	5.6
5.4	3.3					Sales/Total Assets	2.7	3.4
3.5	2.4						1.7	2.3
.5							1.2	.5
(13) .8						% Depr., Dep., Amort./Sales	(40) 2.2	(45) 1.6
1.9							3.8	2.7
2.6							2.4	3.1
(12) 6.7						% Officers', Directors' Owners' Comp/Sales	(30) 5.4	(27) 6.0
7.5							7.2	9.2
40208M	38633M	104183M	39234M	101990M		Net Sales ($)	157394M	1065344M
6552M	10602M	35428M	23719M	99890M		Total Assets ($)	69580M	304262M

M = $ thousand MM = $ million

See Pages 9 through 22 for Explanation of Ratios and Data

Comparative Historical Data / Current Data Sorted by Sales

	4/1/11-3/31/12 ALL	4/1/12-3/31/13 ALL	4/1/13-3/31/14 ALL		0-1MM	1-3MM	3-5MM	5-10MM	10-25MM	25MM & OVER
Type of Statement										
Unqualified	1	1	1							1
Reviewed	2	2	4			1			2	1
Compiled	12	8	5		2	2		1		
Tax Returns	25	24	23		8	7	4	3	1	
Other	19	11	13		5	1	2	3	1	1
					10 (4/1-9/30/13)		36 (10/1/13-3/31/14)			
NUMBER OF STATEMENTS	59	46	46		15	11	6	7	4	3
ASSETS	%	%	%		%	%	%	%	%	%
Cash & Equivalents	12.3	13.2	16.2		17.8	14.5				
Trade Receivables (net)	11.4	17.0	10.8		4.0	17.0				
Inventory	23.0	22.9	21.7		23.1	22.1				
All Other Current	3.6	1.5	2.2		4.5	2.3				
Total Current	50.3	54.7	50.9		49.4	55.9				
Fixed Assets (net)	32.4	27.8	30.7		29.0	30.7				
Intangibles (net)	9.2	9.2	6.3		9.1	4.1				
All Other Non-Current	8.0	8.3	12.1		12.5	9.3				
Total	100.0	100.0	100.0		100.0	100.0				
LIABILITIES										
Notes Payable-Short Term	23.6	8.3	12.4		18.4	11.4				
Cur. Mat.-L.T.D.	4.3	4.1	4.5		6.4	3.2				
Trade Payables	20.3	18.8	14.8		4.8	18.5				
Income Taxes Payable	.2	.0	.1		.0	.0				
All Other Current	17.7	11.9	9.3		5.7	9.1				
Total Current	66.1	43.1	41.0		35.3	42.2				
Long-Term Debt	24.5	26.5	20.8		22.1	26.8				
Deferred Taxes	.1	.0	.0		.0	.0				
All Other Non-Current	13.0	16.3	17.1		32.6	15.0				
Net Worth	-3.7	14.2	21.1		10.0	16.0				
Total Liabilties & Net Worth	100.0	100.0	100.0		100.0	100.0				
INCOME DATA										
Net Sales	100.0	100.0	100.0		100.0	100.0				
Gross Profit	53.2	53.6	55.0		57.5	55.1				
Operating Expenses	51.2	49.6	50.8		50.2	51.6				
Operating Profit	2.0	3.9	4.2		7.4	3.6				
All Other Expenses (net)	.5	-.2	.5		.9	-.2				
Profit Before Taxes	1.5	4.2	3.7		6.5	3.8				
RATIOS										
Current	2.1	2.2	2.4		6.5	2.0				
	1.0	1.6	1.3		2.1	1.2				
	.6	.8	.9		.6	.9				
Quick	1.0	1.4	1.4		2.0	1.3				
	.5	.7	.7		.9	.7				
	.2	.3	.3		.4	.4				
Sales/Receivables	2 195.5	2 196.9	0 UND		0 UND	6 65.2				
	10 37.2	9 40.3	5 68.7		0 UND	11 33.4				
	17 22.1	24 15.2	17 21.2		3 117.7	23 15.6				
Cost of Sales/Inventory	20 18.5	13 28.9	4 101.4		2 168.0	3 121.0				
	39 9.3	49 7.5	39 9.4		23 16.2	23 16.2				
	74 4.9	83 4.4	79 4.6		61 6.0	89 4.1				
Cost of Sales/Payables	13 27.7	13 29.0	0 UND		0 UND	25 14.7				
	37 9.9	29 12.6	27 13.5		0 UND	36 10.1				
	51 7.1	43 8.5	48 7.6		22 16.6	47 7.8				
Sales/Working Capital	10.2	8.7	14.4		9.5	16.6				
	999.8	19.8	56.1		51.6	60.6				
	-19.3	-42.1	-64.9		-13.1	-75.1				
EBIT/Interest	3.3	11.5	21.8		22.3					
	(46) 1.7	(36) 5.2	(37) 7.5		(11) 8.0					
	-.1	1.6	1.4		1.3					
Net Profit + Depr., Dep., Amort./Cur. Mat. L/T/D										
Fixed/Worth	.8	.4	.4		.1	.3				
	10.9	1.5	1.1		1.7	1.5				
	-.5	-.6	-2.8		-.4	-1.2				
Debt/Worth	1.1	.8	.6		.4	.5				
	34.5	3.2	2.4		8.6	2.4				
	-2.7	-4.6	-9.2		-2.6	-3.1				
% Profit Before Taxes/Tangible Net Worth	28.4	50.4	88.7							
	(30) 9.6	(29) 15.5	(33) 43.1							
	.3	3.0	6.2							
% Profit Before Taxes/Total Assets	11.4	24.2	37.3		69.7	36.9				
	2.1	7.1	13.0		24.4	7.8				
	-3.2	1.7	.7		16.7	.2				
Sales/Net Fixed Assets	45.7	51.1	48.4		141.0	30.1				
	15.2	20.9	20.2		37.4	20.1				
	5.6	8.3	6.0		11.4	4.2				
Sales/Total Assets	5.0	5.7	6.0		6.6	5.4				
	3.5	3.8	3.8		4.4	3.3				
	1.9	2.1	2.6		2.7	2.4				
% Depr., Dep., Amort./Sales	.7	.4	.6							
	(47) 1.6	(38) 1.3	(31) 1.8							
	3.1	2.2	2.4							
% Officers', Directors' Owners' Comp/Sales	2.8	3.0	3.0							
	(25) 5.4	(25) 5.3	(23) 4.9							
	7.0	8.8	7.3							
Net Sales ($)	293571M	224818M	324248M		7601M	21465M	24121M	47376M	58410M	165275M
Total Assets ($)	124020M	91017M	176191M		2238M	5739M	3945M	16493M	29015M	118761M

M = $ thousand MM = $ million

See Pages 9 through 22 for Explanation of Ratios and Data

Current Data Sorted by Assets | **Comparative Historical Data**

0-500M	500M-2MM	2-10MM	10-50MM	50-100MM	100-250MM	Type of Statement	4/1/09-3/31/10 ALL	4/1/10-3/31/11 ALL
		1		1		Unqualified	7	6
	2	4	3			Reviewed	12	18
2	12	12				Compiled	24	17
4	8	7				Tax Returns	33	23
	10	9	2	1		Other	37	42
	20 (4/1-9/30/13)		58 (10/1/13-3/31/14)					
6	32	33	5	2		NUMBER OF STATEMENTS	113	106
%	%	%	%	%	%	**ASSETS**	%	%
	9.2	7.1			DATA NOT AVAILABLE	Cash & Equivalents	8.7	11.0
	35.7	36.9				Trade Receivables (net)	29.2	25.9
	33.9	25.3				Inventory	27.8	26.5
	2.0	3.2				All Other Current	3.1	4.2
	80.9	72.4				Total Current	68.8	67.5
	10.3	12.8				Fixed Assets (net)	17.4	13.7
	2.6	7.0				Intangibles (net)	5.8	9.3
	6.3	7.8				All Other Non-Current	8.0	9.4
	100.0	100.0				Total	100.0	100.0
						LIABILITIES		
	13.6	14.9				Notes Payable-Short Term	16.0	13.5
	2.0	3.5				Cur. Mat.-L.T.D.	3.4	4.2
	21.1	23.3				Trade Payables	22.4	22.7
	.0	.1				Income Taxes Payable	.1	.3
	11.8	9.2				All Other Current	10.5	11.3
	48.5	51.0				Total Current	52.4	52.0
	11.8	14.7				Long-Term Debt	14.2	14.6
	.0	.5				Deferred Taxes	.1	.1
	6.0	3.8				All Other Non-Current	5.2	6.8
	33.8	30.0				Net Worth	28.0	26.4
	100.0	100.0				Total Liabilties & Net Worth	100.0	100.0
						INCOME DATA		
	100.0	100.0				Net Sales	100.0	100.0
	39.6	34.4				Gross Profit	38.7	38.9
	36.4	32.0				Operating Expenses	37.3	36.7
	3.2	2.4				Operating Profit	1.3	2.2
	-.2	.4				All Other Expenses (net)	.3	.5
	3.3	2.0				Profit Before Taxes	1.0	1.7
						RATIOS		
	3.8	1.9					2.0	2.1
	1.7	1.4				Current	1.3	1.3
	1.1	1.2					1.0	1.0
	1.9	1.2					1.2	1.3
	1.0	.9				Quick	.8	.8
	.5	.6					.4	.4
	23 15.6	**24** 15.1					**21** 17.6	**12** 30.6
	33 11.1	**33** 11.0				Sales/Receivables	**29** 12.4	**29** 12.7
	40 9.2	**51** 7.1					**40** 9.1	**36** 10.1
	18 20.8	**16** 23.4					**16** 23.0	**18** 20.1
	55 6.6	**38** 9.7				Cost of Sales/Inventory	**39** 9.4	**40** 9.2
	94 3.9	**61** 6.0					**93** 3.9	**74** 4.9
	10 35.3	**22** 16.8					**20** 18.7	**18** 19.8
	26 14.1	**27** 13.6				Cost of Sales/Payables	**34** 10.8	**28** 13.1
	43 8.4	**47** 7.8					**49** 7.4	**49** 7.4
	5.8	7.1					9.7	9.1
	16.0	12.8				Sales/Working Capital	22.4	21.0
	48.7	40.0					-165.8	-122.3
	16.0	11.9					7.6	9.7
	(27) 6.2	(31) 2.8				EBIT/Interest	(104) 1.9	(97) 2.9
	2.4	1.3					.0	1.0
							5.7	6.2
						Net Profit + Depr., Dep., Amort./Cur. Mat. L/T/D	(18) 2.4	(15) 2.5
							-.6	1.3
	.1	.1					.2	.1
	.2	.3				Fixed/Worth	.7	.6
	.9	1.8					4.8	4.8
	.6	1.5					1.0	1.3
	2.0	2.9				Debt/Worth	2.6	2.6
	8.6	9.2					33.1	NM
	48.4	29.6					35.7	38.3
	(26) 22.5	(27) 6.2				% Profit Before Taxes/Tangible Net Worth	(87) 5.8	(80) 10.2
	6.6	2.0					-1.7	.3
	16.8	8.9					11.6	10.8
	5.9	3.2				% Profit Before Taxes/Total Assets	2.3	3.5
	3.7	.4					-1.8	-.2
	164.6	132.6					75.4	100.8
	60.4	41.7				Sales/Net Fixed Assets	35.2	35.7
	28.8	23.2					10.7	17.1
	5.7	5.2					4.8	4.9
	4.2	3.7				Sales/Total Assets	3.4	3.4
	2.5	2.4					2.2	2.3
	.2	.3					.5	.5
	(21) .7	(26) .7				% Depr., Dep., Amort./Sales	(91) 1.1	(79) 1.0
	1.3	1.1					2.2	1.5
	2.6	.7					1.8	1.4
	(20) 3.3	(19) 2.7				% Officers', Directors' Owners' Comp/Sales	(54) 3.3	(45) 4.1
	4.3	5.2					6.5	6.9
6239M	148912M	544063M	287210M	271853M		Net Sales ($)	2282500M	1645639M
1529M	34989M	145188M	63981M	135894M		Total Assets ($)	721321M	517817M

M = $ thousand MM = $ million

See Pages 9 through 22 for Explanation of Ratios and Data

Comparative Historical Data / Current Data Sorted by Sales

4/1/11-3/31/12 ALL	4/1/12-3/31/13 ALL	4/1/13-3/31/14 ALL	Type of Statement	0-1MM	1-3MM	3-5MM	5-10MM	10-25MM	25MM & OVER
4	4	2	Unqualified					1	1
16	11	9	Reviewed		1	2		3	3
21	23	26	Compiled	1	4	5	4	7	5
35	28	19	Tax Returns	3	2	3	7	4	
36	31	22	Other		6	3	3	4	6
					20 (4/1-9/30/13)		58 (10/1/13-3/31/14)		
112	97	78	NUMBER OF STATEMENTS	4	13	13	14	19	15
%	%	%	**ASSETS**	%	%	%	%	%	%
10.2	14.2	8.8	Cash & Equivalents		10.2	7.6	9.9	7.5	7.2
30.4	30.7	34.2	Trade Receivables (net)		24.3	36.7	39.1	38.2	39.3
26.9	25.7	28.9	Inventory		30.7	33.5	36.2	25.1	18.9
2.5	4.1	2.4	All Other Current		.3	1.9	3.7	3.2	2.8
70.0	74.7	74.3	Total Current		65.5	79.7	88.9	74.0	68.1
15.2	12.4	12.5	Fixed Assets (net)		19.7	11.3	6.3	11.2	16.0
7.5	7.1	6.2	Intangibles (net)		2.7	2.8	.8	8.5	9.3
7.4	5.7	7.0	All Other Non-Current		12.1	6.2	3.9	6.3	6.6
100.0	100.0	100.0	Total		100.0	100.0	100.0	100.0	100.0
			LIABILITIES						
16.7	12.6	13.4	Notes Payable-Short Term		7.9	8.3	20.2	14.1	14.0
4.2	3.7	2.9	Cur. Mat.-L.T.D.		1.4	1.3	4.7	3.0	3.3
18.7	21.5	22.0	Trade Payables		19.2	16.7	28.3	22.7	25.5
.1	.1	.1	Income Taxes Payable		.0	.0	.0	.1	.5
12.3	11.1	10.2	All Other Current		5.6	15.4	9.9	10.0	12.0
52.0	49.0	48.6	Total Current		34.1	41.8	63.2	49.9	55.2
16.6	11.9	13.9	Long-Term Debt		22.3	14.6	7.1	11.4	13.4
.2	.2	.3	Deferred Taxes		.0	.0	.0	.9	.5
8.8	6.1	5.0	All Other Non-Current		5.8	1.7	7.3	5.1	4.6
22.5	32.7	32.2	Net Worth		37.8	41.8	22.4	32.8	26.4
100.0	100.0	100.0	Total Liabilties & Net Worth		100.0	100.0	100.0	100.0	100.0
			INCOME DATA						
100.0	100.0	100.0	Net Sales		100.0	100.0	100.0	100.0	100.0
39.4	38.6	37.8	Gross Profit		44.1	42.6	32.4	32.2	36.2
36.2	34.8	34.7	Operating Expenses		38.0	37.8	32.7	29.4	34.2
3.1	3.8	3.1	Operating Profit		6.1	4.8	-.3	2.8	2.1
.4	-.2	.2	All Other Expenses (net)		1.1	.5	-.7	-.1	.2
2.7	4.0	2.8	Profit Before Taxes		5.0	4.3	.4	2.9	1.9
			RATIOS						
2.3	2.8	2.7			5.0	4.2	1.7	1.9	2.1
1.5	1.6	1.5	Current		2.4	1.9	1.5	1.4	1.2
1.0	1.2	1.1			1.2	1.2	1.2	1.3	.9
1.3	1.7	1.3			2.6	2.3	1.2	1.1	1.2
.8	.9	.9	Quick		1.0	1.3	.8	1.0	.8
.5	.6	.6			.7	.5	.5	.7	.6
19 18.8	**17** 21.1	**23** 16.2			**21** 17.2	**24** 15.2	**15** 24.4	**28** 13.2	**23** 15.6
30 12.1	**30** 12.0	**32** 11.3	Sales/Receivables		**32** 11.3	**34** 10.6	**31** 11.6	**33** 11.0	**28** 12.9
42 8.7	**40** 9.2	**40** 9.1			**43** 8.4	**49** 7.4	**41** 8.9	**51** 7.2	**34** 10.7
17 20.9	**12** 30.7	**18** 20.6			**13** 27.1	**21** 17.4	**2** 189.1	**26** 14.2	**10** 38.1
39 9.3	**37** 9.9	**41** 8.8	Cost of Sales/Inventory		**65** 5.6	**63** 5.8	**45** 8.1	**38** 9.7	**20** 17.9
76 4.8	**76** 4.8	**83** 4.4			**140** 2.6	**104** 3.5	**96** 3.8	**59** 6.2	**44** 8.3
11 32.5	**14** 25.2	**17** 21.2			**4** 101.6	**15** 24.5	**18** 20.4	**24** 15.5	**21** 17.7
25 14.6	**28** 13.2	**27** 13.3	Cost of Sales/Payables		**39** 9.4	**22** 16.7	**31** 11.9	**26** 14.2	**31** 11.8
35 10.3	**42** 8.7	**46** 7.9			**68** 5.4	**43** 8.5	**44** 8.3	**41** 9.0	**42** 8.6
8.0	6.4	6.7			4.1	4.6	9.6	11.6	11.2
17.3	14.6	14.6	Sales/Working Capital		5.7	10.3	18.4	12.9	44.8
129.0	53.3	46.3			41.8	50.0	44.0	22.8	-37.3
7.3	16.0	15.7			16.5	54.0	7.6	26.9	19.4
(99) 2.8	(86) 4.5	(69) 4.5	EBIT/Interest		(10) 4.3	(11) 6.2	(12) 3.3	4.6	(13) 5.9
.7	1.8	1.4			1.8	1.4	-4.1	2.2	1.7
4.4	8.5	14.5							
(19) 3.2	(11) 2.8	(14) 3.9	Net Profit + Depr., Dep., Amort./Cur. Mat. L/T/D						
.6	1.5	2.1							
.2	.1	.1			.1	.1	.1	.1	.2
.5	.4	.4	Fixed/Worth		.4	.2	.1	.4	2.0
UND	1.7	1.8			1.3	1.2	.8	.9	-.9
1.2	.9	.8			.6	.5	1.5	1.4	.6
2.5	2.1	2.6	Debt/Worth		1.3	1.4	2.6	2.7	5.8
UND	190.6	9.8			NM	6.1	6.2	6.6	-6.2
49.1	52.0	35.7			32.5	43.1	32.3	51.5	54.1
(84) 14.8	(74) 11.8	(62) 16.5	% Profit Before Taxes/Tangible Net Worth		(10) 17.9	(12) 12.7	(12) 6.2	(16) 23.6	(10) 15.0
1.0	3.7	3.3			-2.8	5.5	-40.9	7.1	3.1
12.0	14.2	14.3			13.9	21.7	11.4	16.5	14.1
3.9	5.1	5.0	% Profit Before Taxes/Total Assets		5.7	3.9	3.2	5.7	6.6
-.4	1.1	1.0			1.6	2.0	-8.3	2.6	.7
90.5	146.8	144.7			105.6	136.2	711.7	162.3	94.0
37.9	40.5	45.5	Sales/Net Fixed Assets		32.9	49.4	101.1	104.6	40.0
19.0	19.5	22.8			10.8	25.9	37.3	22.5	22.8
4.8	5.2	5.3			3.7	6.1	6.2	5.3	6.4
3.7	3.8	3.8	Sales/Total Assets		2.3	4.0	4.9	3.7	4.6
2.6	2.5	2.4			1.7	2.6	3.3	2.9	3.6
.4	.3	.3				.3		.2	.7
(86) .8	(76) .6	(58) .8	% Depr., Dep., Amort./Sales			(10) .8		(15) .5	(13) .8
1.7	1.3	1.2				1.3		1.1	1.1
2.6	1.9	2.2						1.6	
(52) 4.9	(46) 3.4	(45) 3.6	% Officers', Directors' Owners' Comp/Sales					(12) 3.0	
6.7	5.7	6.7						5.0	
1786758M	1688226M	1258277M	Net Sales ($)	1962M	26228M	53095M	98474M	265813M	812705M
650644M	604793M	381581M	Total Assets ($)	1114M	14271M	16608M	23243M	80072M	246273M

M = $ thousand MM = $ million

See Pages 9 through 22 for Explanation of Ratios and Data

Current Data Sorted by Assets | **Comparative Historical Data**

0-500M	500M-2MM	2-10MM	10-50MM	50-100MM	100-250MM	Type of Statement	4/1/09-3/31/10 ALL	4/1/10-3/31/11 ALL
			3	1	1	Unqualified	11	9
	1	1	5	1		Reviewed	8	23
6	8	3	2			Compiled	37	40
40	20	11				Tax Returns	100	98
19	18	17	11	1		Other	81	77
25 (4/1-9/30/13)		144 (10/1/13-3/31/14)						
65	47	32	21	3	1	NUMBER OF STATEMENTS	237	247
%	%	%	%	%	%	**ASSETS**	%	%
22.9	19.3	18.2	11.2			Cash & Equivalents	14.2	14.1
3.4	5.0	2.4	10.1			Trade Receivables (net)	5.8	6.3
42.2	48.9	39.1	34.9			Inventory	45.1	45.8
3.3	3.4	2.1	3.2			All Other Current	3.9	2.4
71.8	76.6	61.9	59.5			Total Current	68.9	68.6
12.2	18.6	28.7	27.2			Fixed Assets (net)	21.7	21.2
4.4	1.2	4.1	5.4			Intangibles (net)	2.9	3.4
11.5	3.6	5.3	8.0			All Other Non-Current	6.4	6.7
100.0	100.0	100.0	100.0			Total	100.0	100.0
						LIABILITIES		
13.9	12.3	4.8	7.5			Notes Payable-Short Term	17.2	10.2
2.0	.9	2.4	3.7			Cur. Mat.-L.T.D.	3.0	3.7
11.8	11.9	14.4	20.0			Trade Payables	17.4	22.0
.2	.1	.0	.1			Income Taxes Payable	.1	.1
10.8	6.1	13.0	8.9			All Other Current	11.7	12.3
38.8	31.4	34.6	40.2			Total Current	49.5	48.2
13.5	14.8	20.3	11.7			Long-Term Debt	18.5	20.7
.0	.0	.1	.2			Deferred Taxes	.1	.1
15.2	4.4	4.3	1.7			All Other Non-Current	12.7	9.2
32.5	49.4	40.7	46.2			Net Worth	19.3	21.7
100.0	100.0	100.0	100.0			Total Liabilties & Net Worth	100.0	100.0
						INCOME DATA		
100.0	100.0	100.0	100.0			Net Sales	100.0	100.0
48.2	48.5	50.9	47.9			Gross Profit	49.3	48.6
42.9	44.1	46.9	43.9			Operating Expenses	45.8	44.1
5.2	4.4	4.1	4.0			Operating Profit	3.5	4.6
1.0	.2	1.0	.2			All Other Expenses (net)	1.1	1.6
4.2	4.1	3.1	3.9			Profit Before Taxes	2.5	2.9
						RATIOS		
8.8	9.0	7.1	2.2				3.2	3.8
2.9	3.3	2.2	1.5			Current	1.7	1.8
1.2	1.5	.9	1.0				1.0	1.0
3.3	2.3	2.2	1.0				.9	1.2
(64) .9	1.0	.6	.5			Quick	.4	(243) .4
.2	.3	.2	.2				.1	.1
0 UND	0 UND	0 UND	3 125.7				0 UND	0 UND
0 UND	0 UND	0 999.8	7 52.3			Sales/Receivables	0 UND	0 999.8
1 345.0	5 69.1	4 85.6	20 18.3				4 99.7	5 74.3
34 10.8	60 6.1	64 5.7	54 6.7				70 5.2	55 6.7
96 3.8	126 2.9	118 3.1	94 3.9			Cost of Sales/Inventory	136 2.7	116 3.1
192 1.9	228 1.6	166 2.2	159 2.3				217 1.7	198 1.8
0 UND	0 759.6	10 35.0	35 10.4				9 39.0	8 45.8
11 34.0	19 18.8	32 11.4	50 7.3			Cost of Sales/Payables	35 10.4	31 11.7
49 7.4	46 8.0	68 5.4	72 5.1				74 4.9	80 4.6
3.9	3.3	3.8	6.0				5.0	5.0
9.1	6.4	9.5	14.8			Sales/Working Capital	10.6	10.5
26.2	17.2	-60.8	-373.6				NM	153.0
10.2	28.4	9.0	29.3				10.4	9.2
(46) 2.9	(39) 9.9	(26) 3.2	(17) 6.5			EBIT/Interest	(185) 3.2	(198) 2.6
.8	2.5	1.2	3.8				.4	.4
							3.8	16.1
						Net Profit + Depr., Dep., Amort./Cur. Mat. L/T/D	(19) 2.2	(17) 2.2
							-.2	1.0
.0	.0	.1	.3				.1	.1
.2	.2	.6	.5			Fixed/Worth	.6	.5
2.3	1.0	4.7	1.4				23.2	4.7
.2	.2	.3	.6				.8	.6
1.1	.8	1.5	1.6			Debt/Worth	2.3	2.4
NM	4.2	8.6	3.5				UND	60.9
53.3	41.5	29.6	41.2				50.3	53.0
(49) 25.8	(43) 19.2	(26) 14.5	(19) 22.3			% Profit Before Taxes/Tangible Net Worth	(178) 22.7	(192) 19.1
1.8	9.7	6.1	11.1				2.4	2.9
28.6	20.6	14.1	16.0				19.2	16.8
9.1	12.4	4.5	7.4			% Profit Before Taxes/Total Assets	5.1	5.1
-1.2	2.6	.8	5.1				-1.1	-1.1
820.9	123.7	65.5	31.2				76.3	96.7
36.5	29.6	15.4	11.7			Sales/Net Fixed Assets	22.1	24.8
17.9	14.5	2.6	5.9				8.1	8.0
4.3	3.8	3.8	3.6				3.7	3.9
2.8	2.7	2.3	2.5			Sales/Total Assets	2.4	2.5
2.1	1.8	1.1	1.7				1.6	1.5
.4	.4	.5	1.2				.5	.5
(33) .9	(32) .6	(26) 1.3	(18) 1.9			% Depr., Dep., Amort./Sales	(186) 1.3	(173) 1.2
1.6	1.0	3.3	2.8				2.4	2.7
3.2	1.8	1.0					2.1	2.1
(30) 6.1	(33) 3.8	(20) 2.9				% Officers', Directors' Owners' Comp/Sales	(101) 3.8	(117) 4.0
10.2	7.8	4.9					6.9	6.9
68081M	161793M	352650M	1350126M	331634M	380262M	Net Sales ($)	3921186M	4796041M
17321M	51575M	135038M	506961M	182782M	167221M	Total Assets ($)	1793172M	1851574M

M = $ thousand MM = $ million

See Pages 9 through 22 for Explanation of Ratios and Data

Comparative Historical Data / Current Data Sorted by Sales

4/1/11-3/31/12 ALL	4/1/12-3/31/13 ALL	4/1/13-3/31/14 ALL	Type of Statement	0-1MM	1-3MM	3-5MM	5-10MM	10-25MM	25MM & OVER
3	5	5	Unqualified						5
18	16	8	Reviewed			1	1	1	5
32	28	19	Compiled	7	4	3	2	1	2
96	78	71	Tax Returns	29	20	12	7	3	
87	80	66	Other	16	13	8	6	8	15
				25 (4/1-9/30/13)		144 (10/1/13-3/31/14)			
236	207	169	NUMBER OF STATEMENTS	52	37	24	16	13	27
%	%	%	**ASSETS**	%	%	%	%	%	%
15.3	18.1	19.2	Cash & Equivalents	20.5	18.8	26.5	19.9	16.5	11.7
7.4	3.8	4.4	Trade Receivables (net)	4.6	.5	5.8	5.9	3.1	7.9
41.8	40.1	42.2	Inventory	41.8	44.6	37.4	57.0	43.1	34.6
2.6	2.0	3.4	All Other Current	2.3	4.8	1.7	3.1	3.4	5.5
67.1	64.1	69.2	Total Current	69.2	68.7	71.4	85.9	66.1	59.8
21.1	25.2	19.6	Fixed Assets (net)	14.8	22.4	21.4	11.7	22.8	26.8
4.0	4.7	3.6	Intangibles (net)	5.5	1.4	1.9	.6	1.8	6.8
7.7	6.1	7.5	All Other Non-Current	10.4	7.5	5.3	1.9	9.4	6.6
100.0	100.0	100.0	Total	100.0	100.0	100.0	100.0	100.0	100.0
			LIABILITIES						
10.6	10.3	10.8	Notes Payable-Short Term	14.3	8.8	14.1	7.5	9.9	6.4
2.9	2.1	2.1	Cur. Mat.-L.T.D.	2.1	1.2	2.1	.3	2.5	4.0
16.8	15.0	13.6	Trade Payables	11.0	11.1	11.7	13.7	14.9	22.9
.1	.1	.1	Income Taxes Payable	.0	.4	.0	.1	.0	.1
9.0	8.6	10.0	All Other Current	10.9	4.1	7.9	17.6	11.9	12.5
39.3	36.1	36.5	Total Current	38.4	25.5	35.7	39.3	39.2	45.9
15.2	21.5	15.0	Long-Term Debt	14.6	20.8	16.3	3.3	21.4	10.3
.1	.0	.1	Deferred Taxes	.0	.0	.0	.0	.0	.8
11.6	8.9	8.3	All Other Non-Current	17.2	5.7	3.3	7.3	1.4	3.1
33.7	33.5	40.1	Net Worth	29.8	48.0	44.6	50.2	38.0	39.9
100.0	100.0	100.0	Total Liabilities & Net Worth	100.0	100.0	100.0	100.0	100.0	100.0
			INCOME DATA						
100.0	100.0	100.0	Net Sales	100.0	100.0	100.0	100.0	100.0	100.0
48.6	49.1	48.7	Gross Profit	52.4	47.4	48.3	45.0	47.5	46.1
44.1	43.3	44.1	Operating Expenses	46.0	42.7	43.9	43.5	43.8	42.9
4.5	5.8	4.6	Operating Profit	6.4	4.7	4.4	1.5	3.8	3.3
1.0	1.0	.7	All Other Expenses (net)	1.3	1.0	.1	-.1	.8	.3
3.4	4.8	3.9	Profit Before Taxes	5.2	3.7	4.3	1.6	3.0	3.0
			RATIOS						
4.4	4.5	7.0		7.2	15.4	3.5	7.5	6.1	2.0
2.0	1.9	2.6	Current	2.6	7.1	2.6	3.0	1.7	1.5
1.1	1.2	1.2		1.2	2.8	1.3	1.6	.7	.9
1.6	1.6	2.1		2.1	5.4	2.3	1.6	2.8	1.0
(235) .5	(205) .5	(168) .7	Quick	.8	(36) 1.1	1.3	.8	.3	.5
.2	.2	.2		.2	.3	.3	.4	.1	.2
0 UND	0 UND	0 UND		0 UND	0 UND	0 UND	0 UND	0 UND	1 564.7
0 UND	0 UND	0 UND	Sales/Receivables	0 UND	0 UND	1 466.5	0 999.8	0 861.8	4 92.3
7 50.5	3 109.4	5 66.5		9 42.9	0 UND	10 37.7	7 49.3	7 49.7	15 24.6
51 7.2	60 6.1	53 6.9		65 5.6	31 11.7	39 9.4	56 6.5	64 5.7	54 6.7
114 3.2	114 3.2	114 3.2	Cost of Sales/Inventory	174 2.1	94 3.9	85 4.3	114 3.2	79 4.6	78 4.7
203 1.8	192 1.9	182 2.0		243 1.5	243 1.5	146 2.5	135 2.7	159 2.3	126 2.9
4 92.8	5 76.9	4 93.3		0 UND	0 UND	5 78.1	2 163.2	4 96.8	31 11.6
28 13.0	25 14.4	24 15.2	Cost of Sales/Payables	22 16.3	14 25.9	17 21.4	23 15.8	52 7.0	49 7.4
66 5.5	57 6.4	57 6.4		61 6.0	37 9.9	52 7.0	41 9.0	69 5.3	74 4.9
4.5	4.4	3.9		3.4	3.1	4.9	4.2	6.0	6.6
9.6	9.2	8.3	Sales/Working Capital	6.7	5.5	6.6	8.9	14.2	15.4
98.2	40.2	25.0		33.1	17.5	19.9	16.9	-21.5	-54.4
13.3	16.4	14.7		8.2	14.5	26.5		14.0	21.4
(186) 3.5	(170) 4.6	(132) 4.4	EBIT/Interest	(37) 2.0	(29) 4.2	(23) 9.9		(11) 6.5	(23) 5.0
1.0	2.0	1.4		.7	1.8	1.9		1.8	2.0
6.2	11.2	12.5							
(11) 1.3	(11) 3.3	(11) 2.4	Net Profit + Depr., Dep., Amort./Cur. Mat. L/T/D						
.1	1.2	-6.8							
.1	.1	.1		.1	.0	.1	.0	.1	.3
.5	.5	.3	Fixed/Worth	.3	.2	.3	.2	.4	.6
3.6	4.1	1.7		9.9	1.5	.8	.5	2.1	1.8
.4	.5	.3		.2	.2	.3	.1	.3	.6
2.0	2.4	1.1	Debt/Worth	2.1	.6	1.1	.9	2.4	1.9
13.8	17.9	7.5		-14.1	4.0	4.9	3.6	8.3	4.4
45.3	62.4	43.9		45.0	47.0	46.0	16.5	62.5	40.1
(188) 19.4	(165) 24.9	(140) 19.1	% Profit Before Taxes/Tangible Net Worth	(38) 19.5	(33) 25.8	(22) 26.3	(14) 13.9	(11) 17.5	(22) 20.0
4.7	7.2	5.8		1.9	.7	12.8	5.2	5.7	9.7
19.1	17.9	19.6		24.1	25.2	22.3	13.4	24.6	14.1
5.5	7.8	8.6	% Profit Before Taxes/Total Assets	7.3	10.4	14.5	7.9	9.7	6.5
-.1	2.1	1.1		-.7	.0	4.5	1.7	.9	3.3
103.8	60.0	109.8		110.5	195.6	61.5	244.9	73.6	31.3
23.0	19.5	26.2	Sales/Net Fixed Assets	26.7	34.3	21.6	88.1	24.4	16.3
8.9	5.9	10.4		13.1	9.6	9.4	31.6	8.0	6.1
4.2	3.7	3.8		3.1	4.1	3.9	4.5	4.4	3.7
2.5	2.3	2.5	Sales/Total Assets	2.3	2.5	3.0	3.7	3.2	2.8
1.6	1.3	1.9		1.5	1.7	1.6	2.7	1.8	2.0
.6	.5	.5		.8	.4	.4	.2	.2	1.0
(162) 1.3	(160) 1.0	(111) .9	% Depr., Dep., Amort./Sales	(28) 1.0	(22) .9	(19) .7	(10) .5	(11) .8	(21) 2.1
2.6	2.3	2.1		2.2	1.5	2.0	.7	3.2	2.8
1.8	1.7	1.9		3.5	2.8	2.0	1.7		
(122) 3.5	(109) 4.2	(86) 4.3	% Officers', Directors' Owners' Comp/Sales	(25) 6.3	(21) 4.5	(19) 3.8	(12) 3.1		
6.5	6.4	9.4		10.3	7.1	9.5	11.8		
3705441M	2355609M	2644546M	Net Sales ($)	29031M	63920M	92986M	115812M	187391M	2155406M
1567554M	1057531M	1060898M	Total Assets ($)	17080M	33475M	41706M	34858M	78022M	855757M

M = $ thousand MM = $ million

See Pages 9 through 22 for Explanation of Ratios and Data

Current Data Sorted by Assets							Comparative Historical Data	
Type of Statement								
Unqualified			1	6	1	1	10	7
Reviewed			1	1			10	13
Compiled	1	5	1	1			10	11
Tax Returns	10	13	8				33	38
Other	8	12	7	4			20	27
	22 (4/1-9/30/13)		59 (10/1/13-3/31/14)				4/1/09-3/31/10	4/1/10-3/31/11
	0-500M	500M-2MM	2-10MM	10-50MM	50-100MM	100-250MM	ALL	ALL
NUMBER OF STATEMENTS	19	30	18	12	1	1	83	96
ASSETS	%	%	%	%	%	%	%	%
Cash & Equivalents	25.5	18.8	9.3	11.6			14.5	16.0
Trade Receivables (net)	1.9	10.3	13.6	8.9			13.2	16.4
Inventory	29.0	34.4	32.2	16.8			35.4	29.0
All Other Current	1.9	5.2	8.6	2.2			5.4	5.7
Total Current	58.3	68.8	63.7	39.5			68.5	67.1
Fixed Assets (net)	25.1	16.5	13.3	42.1			21.3	21.6
Intangibles (net)	8.7	4.4	5.2	6.4			3.0	5.0
All Other Non-Current	7.8	10.3	17.8	12.0			7.2	6.3
Total	100.0	100.0	100.0	100.0			100.0	100.0
LIABILITIES								
Notes Payable-Short Term	7.6	5.4	9.1	9.4			15.4	15.3
Cur. Mat.-L.T.D.	2.4	.3	1.3	1.7			4.9	4.0
Trade Payables	3.7	8.2	11.1	5.1			6.7	6.4
Income Taxes Payable	.1	.1	.1	.4			.1	.4
All Other Current	17.9	16.7	6.6	4.6			13.4	15.9
Total Current	31.8	30.7	28.1	21.2			40.4	42.0
Long-Term Debt	39.5	9.5	13.8	18.8			12.1	10.6
Deferred Taxes	.0	.0	.0	.7			.0	.0
All Other Non-Current	14.0	3.3	7.0	4.8			5.4	5.3
Net Worth	14.7	56.6	51.1	54.5			42.1	42.0
Total Liabilties & Net Worth	100.0	100.0	100.0	100.0			100.0	100.0
INCOME DATA								
Net Sales	100.0	100.0	100.0	100.0			100.0	100.0
Gross Profit	59.3	56.6	57.1	58.0			58.7	59.6
Operating Expenses	55.4	53.6	50.2	49.4			52.7	52.9
Operating Profit	3.9	3.1	6.9	8.5			6.0	6.7
All Other Expenses (net)	-.3	.2	2.3	1.3			.6	.7
Profit Before Taxes	4.2	2.9	4.6	7.2			5.3	6.0
RATIOS								
Current	7.0	10.1	14.2	3.2			5.7	6.4
	1.9	3.5	3.6	1.9			2.1	2.4
	.7	1.2	1.0	1.3			1.4	1.4
Quick	3.7	2.3	2.8	2.4			2.2	3.0
	1.3	1.2	.8	1.0			.8	1.2
	.2	.5	.3	.3			.3	.5
Sales/Receivables	**0** UND	**0** UND	**0** UND	**0** UND			**0** UND	**0** UND
	0 UND	**0** UND	**2** 154.8	**4** 92.7			**3** 113.7	**2** 190.1
	0 UND	**19** 18.8	**85** 4.3	**15** 24.0			**45** 8.1	**68** 5.4
Cost of Sales/Inventory	**18** 20.7	**11** 32.6	**52** 7.0	**25** 14.6			**46** 8.0	**27** 13.3
	41 9.0	**51** 7.1	**192** 1.9	**61** 6.0			**124** 2.9	**95** 3.9
	89 4.1	**159** 2.3	**243** 1.5	**152** 2.4			**254** 1.4	**179** 2.0
Cost of Sales/Payables	**0** UND	**0** UND	**4** 101.6	**12** 30.4			**0** UND	**2** 178.7
	1 321.0	**3** 108.1	**13** 28.5	**17** 21.1			**14** 25.9	**13** 27.1
	6 62.3	**22** 16.4	**38** 9.6	**23** 15.7			**36** 10.1	**34** 10.7
Sales/Working Capital	5.5	4.0	1.7	4.6			2.6	3.1
	19.9	9.4	3.1	9.9			6.2	8.7
	-128.1	45.3	NM	49.3			22.6	23.4
EBIT/Interest	27.0	254.8	40.3	22.2			31.8	41.3
	(10) 16.8	(17) 15.5	(16) 7.9	(11) 3.3			(64) 6.0	(72) 8.2
	4.2	1.8	1.3	1.9			1.2	1.4
Net Profit + Depr., Dep., Amort./Cur. Mat. L/T/D								
Fixed/Worth	.2	.0	.0	.4			.0	.1
	.7	.2	.2	1.1			.2	.3
	-2.4	.7	.6	1.4			1.0	.9
Debt/Worth	.8	.2	.5	.4			.3	.3
	2.1	.5	1.0	.9			.9	.8
	-6.3	3.3	2.2	2.1			2.7	3.0
% Profit Before Taxes/Tangible Net Worth	80.7	62.0	29.5	54.2			49.3	54.8
	(13) 37.0	(26) 17.4	10.3	(11) 18.9			(72) 20.1	(85) 30.1
	13.8	1.9	4.9	3.6			4.6	8.7
% Profit Before Taxes/Total Assets	34.7	32.7	15.7	33.3			28.6	31.6
	17.6	6.7	5.3	9.7			9.5	11.6
	2.2	1.3	2.3	2.1			1.8	2.8
Sales/Net Fixed Assets	80.5	334.7	88.9	40.9			118.6	110.8
	35.7	51.1	27.0	6.8			24.4	29.1
	14.8	19.1	9.9	2.1			10.4	10.9
Sales/Total Assets	9.6	5.6	2.9	3.8			4.5	5.5
	5.4	3.3	1.6	1.7			2.0	2.4
	3.3	1.6	1.1	.9			1.2	1.4
% Depr., Dep., Amort./Sales	.5	.2	.5	1.2			.3	.4
	(13) .8	(20) .5	(14) 1.4	(11) 2.1			(64) 1.0	(74) 1.0
	1.2	1.0	1.9	4.1			2.0	1.8
% Officers', Directors' Owners' Comp/Sales	1.9	1.1					1.2	1.2
	(14) 5.1	(15) 4.3					(43) 3.4	(42) 2.6
	8.0	6.7					7.0	6.0
Net Sales ($)	29927M	143944M	175323M	545358M	77823M	436478M	813923M	895251M
Total Assets ($)	4580M	31987M	75552M	257858M	53494M	153284M	471343M	397257M

M = $ thousand MM = $ million

See Pages 9 through 22 for Explanation of Ratios and Data

Comparative Historical Data | **Current Data Sorted by Sales**

4/1/11-3/31/12 ALL	4/1/12-3/31/13 ALL	4/1/13-3/31/14 ALL		0-1MM	1-3MM	3-5MM	5-10MM	10-25MM	25MM & OVER
			Type of Statement						
9	10	9	Unqualified				1	1	7
3	3	2	Reviewed						2
10	9	8	Compiled	1	3	1	3		
36	31	31	Tax Returns	5	17	3	4	2	
27	33	31	Other	3	9	5	5	6	3
				22 (4/1-9/30/13)			59 (10/1/13-3/31/14)		
85	86	81	**NUMBER OF STATEMENTS**	9	29	9	13	9	12
%	%	%	**ASSETS**	%	%	%	%	%	%
15.8	19.5	16.9	Cash & Equivalents		20.2		13.3		12.2
13.1	13.7	8.7	Trade Receivables (net)		6.1		18.3		2.6
32.5	32.0	29.8	Inventory		28.0		29.7		18.7
4.3	3.0	5.0	All Other Current		5.7		5.9		3.9
65.7	68.2	60.5	Total Current		60.1		67.2		37.5
22.8	20.9	22.0	Fixed Assets (net)		17.6		11.2		42.3
4.0	1.8	5.8	Intangibles (net)		8.8		2.0		6.3
7.5	9.1	11.8	All Other Non-Current		13.4		19.7		13.9
100.0	100.0	100.0	Total		100.0		100.0		100.0
			LIABILITIES						
16.2	13.6	7.5	Notes Payable-Short Term		9.2		5.5		6.9
2.0	2.0	1.2	Cur. Mat.-L.T.D.		1.2		1.3		1.9
6.9	6.8	7.9	Trade Payables		6.6		7.5		12.0
.3	.0	.1	Income Taxes Payable		.2		.4		.0
16.9	20.3	12.9	All Other Current		10.4		13.9		7.9
42.3	42.7	29.6	Total Current		27.5		28.6		28.7
11.6	13.4	18.9	Long-Term Debt		33.6		11.7		14.2
.0	.0	.1	Deferred Taxes		.0		.0		.6
11.1	7.0	6.8	All Other Non-Current		8.2		1.9		4.2
35.0	36.8	44.5	Net Worth		30.6		57.7		52.4
100.0	100.0	100.0	Total Liabilties & Net Worth		100.0		100.0		100.0
			INCOME DATA						
100.0	100.0	100.0	Net Sales		100.0		100.0		100.0
58.9	59.9	57.2	Gross Profit		55.7		63.0		55.9
52.0	52.4	52.3	Operating Expenses		51.4		51.8		49.4
6.9	7.5	5.0	Operating Profit		4.3		11.3		6.5
.5	.2	.7	All Other Expenses (net)		1.0		2.1		.5
6.3	7.3	4.2	Profit Before Taxes		3.3		9.2		5.9
			RATIOS						
5.7	6.0	7.2			8.6		8.8		2.0
2.1	2.7	2.5	Current		2.8		3.3		1.5
1.1	1.2	1.2			1.2		1.4		.9
2.1	3.1	2.5			4.2		2.8		1.2
(84) .9	1.0	1.1	Quick		1.3		1.0		.3
.3	.3	.3			.3		.6		.2
0 UND	0 UND	0 UND			0 UND		0 UND		0 UND
3 116.3	2 180.8	0 886.0	Sales/Receivables		0 UND		16 23.2		2 221.4
20 18.0	46 8.0	10 35.7			3 106.0		130 2.8		7 50.1
28 13.0	29 12.7	21 17.7			14 25.2		43 8.5		20 17.9
81 4.5	96 3.8	69 5.3	Cost of Sales/Inventory		50 7.3		130 2.8		27 13.4
243 1.5	228 1.6	182 2.0			203 1.8		215 1.7		94 3.9
0 UND	0 UND	0 UND			0 UND		3 112.8		13 28.1
9 42.8	6 60.0	6 62.3	Cost of Sales/Payables		3 105.5		8 43.1		21 17.0
45 8.1	56 6.5	24 15.2			34 10.7		26 14.3		32 11.4
3.4	3.2	3.8			3.9		1.8		9.0
13.2	7.4	11.7	Sales/Working Capital		12.0		6.5		41.3
68.5	71.2	68.5			64.3		13.9		NM
36.3	29.6	32.6			25.7		43.5		35.5
(65) 11.8	(69) 7.3	(56) 10.4	EBIT/Interest		(20) 7.3		(11) 21.4		(11) 9.6
4.4	2.1	2.0			1.2		3.0		2.9
			Net Profit + Depr., Dep., Amort./Cur. Mat. L/T/D						
.1	.1	.1			.1		.0		.8
.4	.3	.3	Fixed/Worth		.2		.1		1.2
1.0	1.2	1.2			7.0		.5		1.4
.5	.4	.3			.4		.2		.4
1.0	.9	.9	Debt/Worth		1.2		.7		.9
4.5	4.0	3.3			NM		1.7		2.1
65.7	54.1	51.6			47.0		74.9		92.0
(74) 29.3	(74) 26.5	(69) 19.7	% Profit Before Taxes/Tangible Net Worth		(22) 21.0		26.8		(10) 16.9
8.3	6.3	3.9			1.6		6.3		3.5
35.3	31.4	26.4			27.0		40.1		39.4
13.4	14.5	8.7	% Profit Before Taxes/Total Assets		6.7		15.7		9.9
5.5	2.8	1.8			.8		3.5		3.2
121.4	115.8	99.9			123.7		120.4		34.2
30.7	28.7	35.7	Sales/Net Fixed Assets		35.7		37.7		7.5
11.6	11.4	10.0			13.7		11.8		2.5
5.3	4.7	5.3			5.5		3.7		4.3
2.6	2.3	2.9	Sales/Total Assets		2.6		2.2		2.6
1.4	1.2	1.5			1.6		1.1		1.5
.3	.3	.4			.3		.3		1.1
(64) .9	(56) .9	(60) 1.0	% Depr., Dep., Amort./Sales		(21) .6		(11) 1.3		(11) 1.4
2.1	2.2	1.5			1.1		1.7		3.5
1.7	2.2	1.2			3.4				
(43) 4.0	(34) 3.7	(39) 4.7	% Officers', Directors' Owners' Comp/Sales		(17) 5.4				
5.2	6.0	6.8			7.9				
1162034M	996038M	1408853M	Net Sales ($)	4788M	57044M	35984M	97661M	135642M	1077734M
456222M	468321M	576755M	Total Assets ($)	6267M	24525M	11876M	59991M	45514M	428582M

M = $ thousand MM = $ million

See Pages 9 through 22 for Explanation of Ratios and Data

Current Data Sorted by Assets							Comparative Historical Data	
						Type of Statement		
		1	1	1		Unqualified	6	4
		2				Reviewed	8	3
3	4	1	1			Compiled	10	9
22	5	6	1			Tax Returns	28	27
5	12	7	5			Other	19	21
10 (4/1-9/30/13)			67 (10/1/13-3/31/14)				4/1/09-3/31/10	4/1/10-3/31/11
0-500M	500M-2MM	2-10MM	10-50MM	50-100MM	100-250MM		ALL	ALL
30	21	17	8	1		**NUMBER OF STATEMENTS**	71	64
%	%	%	%	%	%	**ASSETS**	%	%
17.5	15.0	8.7			D	Cash & Equivalents	9.7	7.6
4.8	9.1	6.4			A	Trade Receivables (net)	7.7	6.2
49.7	39.4	50.6			T	Inventory	46.5	46.3
.1	.6	1.2			A	All Other Current	2.2	3.4
72.2	64.1	66.9				Total Current	66.2	63.5
16.5	21.1	28.4			N	Fixed Assets (net)	23.7	24.8
2.0	6.2	2.6			O	Intangibles (net)	4.8	6.2
9.3	8.5	2.1			T	All Other Non-Current	5.4	5.4
100.0	100.0	100.0				Total	100.0	100.0
					A	**LIABILITIES**		
15.6	10.8	5.6			V	Notes Payable-Short Term	13.3	17.5
2.0	.7	1.0			A	Cur. Mat.-L.T.D.	1.5	6.7
17.2	10.8	25.1			I	Trade Payables	17.2	17.4
.1	.0	.4			L	Income Taxes Payable	.1	.1
17.9	17.5	10.2			A	All Other Current	9.3	10.3
52.7	39.9	42.2			B	Total Current	41.4	52.0
20.8	13.2	25.1			L	Long-Term Debt	24.3	16.2
.0	.0	.0			E	Deferred Taxes	.1	.1
8.3	4.7	2.5				All Other Non-Current	6.9	11.7
18.2	42.2	30.2				Net Worth	27.3	19.9
100.0	100.0	100.0				Total Liabilties & Net Worth	100.0	100.0
						INCOME DATA		
100.0	100.0	100.0				Net Sales	100.0	100.0
45.3	36.1	36.9				Gross Profit	36.7	42.5
43.2	29.2	34.0				Operating Expenses	34.2	38.7
2.1	6.9	2.9				Operating Profit	2.5	3.8
.4	.1	1.3				All Other Expenses (net)	.7	.5
1.7	6.8	1.6				Profit Before Taxes	1.9	3.3
						RATIOS		
3.5	4.7	2.7					2.9	3.1
1.8	1.8	1.7				Current	1.6	1.7
.9	1.0	1.0					1.1	.9
.7	1.7	.7					.8	.7
(29) .3	.7	.4				Quick	(70) .4	.3
.1	.3	.1					.1	.0
0 UND	**0** UND	**0** 946.0					**0** UND	**0** UND
0 UND	**4** 102.7	**3** 128.9				Sales/Receivables	**1** 601.5	**0** UND
2 177.3	**13** 28.1	**6** 56.5					**8** 46.9	**7** 52.1
48 7.6	**36** 10.1	**47** 7.8					**48** 7.6	**44** 8.3
65 5.6	**53** 6.9	**65** 5.6				Cost of Sales/Inventory	**62** 5.9	**61** 6.0
91 4.0	**74** 4.9	**79** 4.6					**95** 3.8	**109** 3.3
0 UND	**4** 85.0	**18** 20.0					**12** 30.8	**7** 52.5
13 27.2	**12** 31.2	**24** 15.0				Cost of Sales/Payables	**24** 14.9	**23** 15.8
37 9.8	**19** 18.8	**59** 6.2					**41** 8.9	**36** 10.2
7.7	6.6	8.6					8.6	10.0
14.9	17.3	22.0				Sales/Working Capital	15.6	16.8
-47.7	NM	NM					125.8	-180.0
11.6	155.0	49.9					16.2	13.3
(21) 3.6	(18) 20.1	(15) 10.4				EBIT/Interest	(65) 4.0	(55) 7.0
-.4	4.0	4.2					.9	1.2
						Net Profit + Depr., Dep., Amort./Cur. Mat. L/T/D		
.1	.2	.4					.2	.3
.6	.4	.8				Fixed/Worth	.8	1.0
-1.8	4.4	3.1					4.0	NM
.4	.5	1.2					1.1	1.1
2.8	1.3	2.5				Debt/Worth	2.9	2.1
-7.4	16.5	5.0					10.9	NM
157.2	112.7	53.2					61.4	65.8
(21) 51.6	(18) 37.8	(15) 40.9				% Profit Before Taxes/Tangible Net Worth	(58) 33.5	(48) 32.7
8.5	17.3	15.1					9.1	12.0
28.7	27.5	23.7					18.8	20.7
7.1	16.1	8.5				% Profit Before Taxes/Total Assets	9.6	8.7
-2.7	8.8	4.0					-.1	.9
257.6	55.4	42.4					66.6	58.0
51.2	27.6	19.5				Sales/Net Fixed Assets	26.3	28.6
17.4	11.4	14.9					8.1	9.0
6.6	5.5	6.2					5.1	6.3
4.8	3.3	4.1				Sales/Total Assets	3.5	4.1
2.7	2.3	2.6					2.3	2.2
.3	.5	.6					.4	.5
(19) .8	(17) .7	(13) 1.2				% Depr., Dep., Amort./Sales	(52) 1.0	(46) 1.0
1.1	1.9	2.4					1.7	1.8
3.4		.6					2.3	2.1
(18) 6.1		(10) 1.0				% Officers', Directors' Owners' Comp/Sales	(31) 3.6	(26) 3.3
8.2		2.7					6.4	6.6
38702M	112855M	401780M	383355M	281283M		Net Sales ($)	1951133M	1375586M
8622M	26770M	82210M	167274M	77734M		Total Assets ($)	689655M	544913M

M = $ thousand MM = $ million

See Pages 9 through 22 for Explanation of Ratios and Data

Comparative Historical Data / Current Data Sorted by Sales

4/1/11-3/31/12 ALL	4/1/12-3/31/13 ALL	4/1/13-3/31/14 ALL		0-1MM	1-3MM	3-5MM	5-10MM	10-25MM	25MM & OVER
			Type of Statement						
3	3	3	Unqualified					1	2
11	8	2	Reviewed				1	1	
6	4	9	Compiled	1	1	1	4	1	1
26	19	34	Tax Returns	11	13	1	5	1	3
26	26	29	Other	2	8	3	5	4	7
				10 (4/1-9/30/13)		67 (10/1/13-3/31/14)			
72	60	77	**NUMBER OF STATEMENTS**	14	22	5	15	8	13
%	%	%	**ASSETS**	%	%	%	%	%	%
13.1	13.6	13.3	Cash & Equivalents	14.1	18.2		9.4		4.4
9.3	8.6	6.5	Trade Receivables (net)	2.2	5.8		9.2		8.6
40.5	44.7	44.9	Inventory	48.9	43.8		46.3		46.8
2.0	1.4	.7	All Other Current	.0	.2		.9		2.5
64.8	68.2	65.4	Total Current	65.2	68.1		65.7		62.2
24.2	23.7	22.7	Fixed Assets (net)	19.5	20.4		24.7		28.8
4.5	4.7	5.2	Intangibles (net)	3.2	4.3		1.8		7.0
6.5	3.3	6.6	All Other Non-Current	12.1	7.2		7.8		2.0
100.0	100.0	100.0	Total	100.0	100.0		100.0		100.0
			LIABILITIES						
8.2	9.8	10.8	Notes Payable-Short Term	8.1	16.4		8.9		5.9
3.3	2.2	1.5	Cur. Mat.-L.T.D.	1.5	1.9		1.3		1.4
12.6	13.9	17.1	Trade Payables	10.9	17.5		14.6		28.7
.1	.2	.1	Income Taxes Payable	.2	.0		.0		.1
10.2	14.6	14.9	All Other Current	10.5	26.5		8.0		9.5
34.3	40.7	44.3	Total Current	31.2	62.3		32.9		45.6
21.0	15.0	20.0	Long-Term Debt	23.1	26.1		19.7		16.7
.1	.2	.1	Deferred Taxes	.0	.0		.0		.5
6.1	4.8	5.8	All Other Non-Current	7.6	8.2		3.4		5.6
38.4	39.3	29.7	Net Worth	38.1	3.5		44.0		31.7
100.0	100.0	100.0	Total Liabilties & Net Worth	100.0	100.0		100.0		100.0
			INCOME DATA						
100.0	100.0	100.0	Net Sales	100.0	100.0		100.0		100.0
41.7	38.8	40.1	Gross Profit	44.7	45.8		33.9		33.0
37.8	32.6	36.1	Operating Expenses	46.3	41.1		26.9		30.3
4.0	6.2	4.0	Operating Profit	-1.6	4.7		7.0		2.7
.5	.4	.6	All Other Expenses (net)	2.3	.4		.0		.0
3.5	5.8	3.4	Profit Before Taxes	-3.8	4.3		6.9		2.7
			RATIOS						
4.2	4.2	3.1		6.8	3.5		3.8		1.9
1.8	1.7	1.7	Current	1.9	1.3		1.8		1.4
1.3	1.2	1.0		1.3	.7		1.4		1.0
1.6	1.4	.9		.4	1.0		1.1		.4
.6	(58) .5	(76) .4	Quick	.2	(21) .4		.7		.3
.2	.2	.1		.0	.2		.2		.1
0 UND	0 999.8	0 UND		0 UND	0 UND		0 892.2		0 999.8
2 219.3	2 217.9	1 277.2	Sales/Receivables	0 UND	0 UND		4 86.9		2 191.6
9 40.0	16 22.5	7 49.4		8 48.5	4 84.8		16 23.2		8 47.8
45 8.2	43 8.4	45 8.1		52 7.0	48 7.6		34 10.7		44 8.3
61 6.0	62 5.9	62 5.9	Cost of Sales/Inventory	96 3.8	65 5.6		65 5.6		48 7.6
87 4.2	83 4.4	87 4.2		192 1.9	76 4.8		72 5.1		61 6.0
4 88.8	9 41.4	7 55.1		0 UND	5 75.7		9 42.7		17 21.8
15 23.9	17 21.2	19 19.5	Cost of Sales/Payables	6 65.3	17 22.0		15 25.1		35 10.3
39 9.3	31 11.6	38 9.6		54 6.7	35 10.4		26 13.9		41 9.0
7.1	6.0	8.4		4.6	10.7		5.5		11.7
13.8	15.2	17.3	Sales/Working Capital	13.4	79.1		12.6		33.1
35.2	37.1	NM		47.1	-18.6		26.5		NM
12.2	37.3	27.5			16.0		105.0		33.4
(55) 3.4	(53) 12.4	(63) 7.0	EBIT/Interest		(18) 5.0		(13) 14.9		7.6
.9	3.9	3.3			-.6		4.0		3.8
7.8	20.1								
(12) 4.4	(11) 13.6		Net Profit + Depr., Dep., Amort./Cur. Mat. L/T/D						
.8	2.2								
.1	.1	.2		.0	.3		.2		.6
.5	.5	.7	Fixed/Worth	.2	317.0		.4		1.0
3.6	1.6	6.9		UND	-.8		2.5		2.3
.5	.8	.7		.3	1.2		.5		1.5
1.4	1.8	2.2	Debt/Worth	.7	526.0		1.6		2.1
9.4	5.3	199.5		UND	-4.3		2.5		5.9
52.2	73.5	83.4		68.4	814.7		71.8		75.7
(60) 21.7	(52) 36.0	(61) 40.9	% Profit Before Taxes/Tangible Net Worth	(11) 14.8	(12) 56.8		(14) 43.4		(12) 38.1
5.1	13.1	14.2		6.6	13.7		22.9		9.6
20.3	29.2	25.0		14.9	25.4		34.2		20.3
7.4	16.1	10.8	% Profit Before Taxes/Total Assets	6.0	14.1		13.1		8.5
.4	7.7	2.8		-5.7	-3.8		8.0		4.0
53.0	59.6	68.2		UND	93.6		59.3		44.4
24.5	23.8	26.0	Sales/Net Fixed Assets	64.0	26.3		27.6		19.5
9.2	8.2	11.9		10.0	11.6		13.7		7.6
4.2	5.1	5.7		5.7	5.8		5.8		6.8
3.4	3.6	3.9	Sales/Total Assets	2.3	4.3		4.1		4.0
2.3	2.6	2.4		1.6	2.7		2.8		3.4
.6	.5	.5			.4		.5		.5
(55) 1.1	(51) .9	(58) 1.0	% Depr., Dep., Amort./Sales		(17) 1.1		(11) .6		(12) 1.1
1.8	1.7	1.9			2.3		1.2		2.0
1.8	2.4	1.2			1.5				
(34) 3.3	(30) 3.2	(37) 3.4	% Officers', Directors' Owners' Comp/Sales		(13) 5.5				
7.6	5.9	6.2			6.1				
1686372M	2858916M	1217975M	Net Sales ($)	8681M	38034M	19155M	113422M	145214M	893469M
745051M	719332M	362610M	Total Assets ($)	5203M	10047M	6138M	34999M	80366M	225857M

M = $ thousand MM = $ million

See Pages 9 through 22 for Explanation of Ratios and Data

Current Data Sorted by Assets / Comparative Historical Data

	0-500M	500M-2MM	2-10MM	10-50MM	50-100MM	100-250MM	4/1/09-3/31/10 ALL	4/1/10-3/31/11 ALL
Type of Statement								
Unqualified				3		2	4	2
Reviewed			2	5	1	1	7	9
Compiled	1	1	3	2			6	1
Tax Returns	6	8	5				12	18
Other	2	5	7	6	2	1	16	17
	13 (4/1-9/30/13)			50 (10/1/13-3/31/14)				
NUMBER OF STATEMENTS	9	14	17	16	3	4	45	47
ASSETS	%	%	%	%	%	%	%	%
Cash & Equivalents		21.2	14.5	13.4			16.3	12.1
Trade Receivables (net)		15.6	10.6	5.0			8.8	9.0
Inventory		36.6	58.3	49.7			49.2	53.2
All Other Current		1.0	.3	14.0			1.2	1.6
Total Current		74.4	83.7	82.2			75.5	76.0
Fixed Assets (net)		14.4	8.7	7.8			14.1	15.6
Intangibles (net)		2.9	.2	4.4			2.3	2.3
All Other Non-Current		8.3	7.3	5.6			8.1	6.1
Total		100.0	100.0	100.0			100.0	100.0
LIABILITIES								
Notes Payable-Short Term		7.7	6.0	19.1			13.5	16.6
Cur. Mat.-L.T.D.		.7	.3	1.3			.9	1.9
Trade Payables		12.0	22.0	9.1			9.3	17.7
Income Taxes Payable		.0	.0	.0			.3	.0
All Other Current		5.4	6.4	17.7			9.8	13.5
Total Current		25.8	34.7	47.2			33.7	49.6
Long-Term Debt		10.1	7.8	3.2			12.8	5.9
Deferred Taxes		.0	.0	.2			.0	.0
All Other Non-Current		17.0	19.7	7.8			9.5	9.7
Net Worth		47.1	37.9	41.5			43.9	34.7
Total Liabilities & Net Worth		100.0	100.0	100.0			100.0	100.0
INCOME DATA								
Net Sales		100.0	100.0	100.0			100.0	100.0
Gross Profit		48.5	43.1	33.9			42.1	46.5
Operating Expenses		43.6	37.0	25.5			36.1	39.8
Operating Profit		4.9	6.1	8.4			6.0	6.7
All Other Expenses (net)		-.2	.2	1.9			1.6	2.7
Profit Before Taxes		5.1	5.8	6.5			4.4	4.0
RATIOS								
Current		8.7	5.1	3.3			5.0	5.2
		4.2	2.7	1.9			2.4	1.6
		1.4	1.4	1.4			1.4	.9
Quick		4.1	1.2	.8			2.1	1.1
		1.5	.5	.4			.6	.4
		.5	.2	.1			.2	.1
Sales/Receivables		3 129.1	0 UND	0 UND			0 UND	0 UND
		12 29.7	7 52.1	6 58.3			13 27.6	6 58.4
		39 9.4	39 9.4	25 14.4			49 7.4	40 9.0
Cost of Sales/Inventory		1 284.9	53 6.9	72 5.1			69 5.3	80 4.5
		87 4.2	228 1.6	261 1.4			247 1.5	209 1.7
		215 1.7	456 .8	730 .5			655 .6	795 .5
Cost of Sales/Payables		0 UND	18 20.2	9 40.6			2 167.1	8 48.2
		21 17.7	55 6.6	40 9.2			25 14.5	42 8.6
		70 5.2	152 2.4	61 6.0			77 4.8	105 3.5
Sales/Working Capital		1.8	1.7	.7			1.5	1.1
		4.4	3.1	2.6			4.3	6.4
		NM	7.8	6.1			20.0	-15.9
EBIT/Interest		15.8	46.3	19.8			14.2	15.7
		(11) 1.3	(13) 7.2	(14) 3.8			(35) 4.1	(37) 4.0
		-1.1	1.3	.9			1.6	.8
Net Profit + Depr., Dep., Amort./Cur. Mat. L/T/D								
Fixed/Worth		.0	.1	.0			.0	.1
		.1	.1	.0			.2	.4
		.7	.4	1.4			2.0	4.7
Debt/Worth		.1	.7	.5			.4	.4
		1.2	2.0	1.1			1.6	2.3
		3.7	4.4	3.5			6.8	49.5
% Profit Before Taxes/Tangible Net Worth		60.5	43.5	19.8			49.2	77.0
		(12) 3.7	(15) 33.6	(13) 14.1			(41) 14.7	(39) 17.4
		-1.4	.6	1.6			4.6	.5
% Profit Before Taxes/Total Assets		32.0	21.2	12.6			11.0	19.7
		1.8	10.8	4.9			5.8	6.4
		-.5	.2	-.6			.6	-.3
Sales/Net Fixed Assets		422.3	55.3	404.7			98.0	84.2
		22.1	32.8	67.7			22.0	24.2
		13.4	13.7	7.7			9.5	7.8
Sales/Total Assets		3.8	2.1	1.5			2.5	4.5
		1.6	1.4	.9			1.6	1.2
		1.3	1.0	.5			.5	.5
% Depr., Dep., Amort./Sales		.2	.2	.1			.2	.3
		(10) 1.2	(12) .3	(11) .3			(28) 1.2	(33) .7
		1.6	1.2	.8			1.9	1.6
% Officers', Directors' Owners' Comp/Sales		.7	2.4				2.0	2.6
		(10) 5.3	(10) 3.2				(25) 3.2	(29) 6.0
		10.4	20.0				7.5	10.1
Net Sales ($)	8487M	43070M	122026M	323710M	641130M	543569M	870265M	557806M
Total Assets ($)	1764M	16008M	76770M	322780M	238143M	802442M	689616M	687830M

M = $ thousand MM = $ million

See Pages 9 through 22 for Explanation of Ratios and Data

Comparative Historical Data | **Current Data Sorted by Sales**

4/1/11-3/31/12 ALL	4/1/12-3/31/13 ALL	4/1/13-3/31/14 ALL		0-1MM	1-3MM	3-5MM	5-10MM	10-25MM	25MM & OVER
			Type of Statement						
3	2	5	Unqualified		1			2	2
6	10	9	Reviewed		2		1	2	4
4	9	7	Compiled			3	1	2	1
17	21	19	Tax Returns	6	6	1	3	3	
20	28	23	Other	3	5	4	4	2	5
				13 (4/1-9/30/13)			50 (10/1/13-3/31/14)		
50	70	63	**NUMBER OF STATEMENTS**	9	14	8	9	11	12
%	%	%	**ASSETS**	%	%	%	%	%	%
16.0	18.1	16.1	Cash & Equivalents		20.2			25.4	15.1
9.9	7.3	8.6	Trade Receivables (net)		10.6			5.7	6.9
49.0	49.4	46.6	Inventory		45.5			44.8	36.5
3.1	3.7	4.9	All Other Current		2.0			3.0	14.9
78.0	78.5	76.3	Total Current		78.3			78.8	73.3
10.3	10.2	12.5	Fixed Assets (net)		9.6			8.4	17.6
2.0	2.6	2.4	Intangibles (net)		.3			6.5	.7
9.7	8.7	8.8	All Other Non-Current		11.9			6.3	8.4
100.0	100.0	100.0	Total		100.0			100.0	100.0
			LIABILITIES						
14.5	11.7	13.9	Notes Payable-Short Term		7.6			13.6	12.0
.7	1.5	1.9	Cur. Mat.-L.T.D.		1.5			2.0	5.6
14.2	14.2	13.9	Trade Payables		15.0			22.4	12.4
.0	.0	.0	Income Taxes Payable		.1			.0	.0
9.8	16.9	12.3	All Other Current		8.9			18.3	23.1
39.3	44.3	42.1	Total Current		33.1			56.3	53.1
9.3	9.6	6.6	Long-Term Debt		6.1			3.7	9.1
.0	.1	.2	Deferred Taxes		.0			.4	.5
29.1	13.1	16.1	All Other Non-Current		20.8			8.2	5.5
22.2	32.9	35.1	Net Worth		39.9			31.5	31.9
100.0	100.0	100.0	Total Liabilities & Net Worth		100.0			100.0	100.0
			INCOME DATA						
100.0	100.0	100.0	Net Sales		100.0			100.0	100.0
46.2	47.8	42.9	Gross Profit		51.0			29.6	32.5
35.9	41.3	35.9	Operating Expenses		46.1			25.1	28.0
10.3	6.5	6.9	Operating Profit		4.9			4.4	4.5
1.7	.1	.7	All Other Expenses (net)		.9			1.1	.6
8.6	6.4	6.2	Profit Before Taxes		4.0			3.4	3.9
			RATIOS						
5.0	4.4	5.3			8.3			2.6	2.3
2.2	2.0	1.9	Current		3.6			1.4	1.8
1.3	1.3	1.3			1.3			1.1	1.2
1.0	1.5	1.3			4.1			1.0	.7
.5	.5	.5	Quick		.6			.5	.2
.2	.2	.1			.2			.1	.1
0 UND	0 UND	0 UND			2 160.1			0 UND	1 295.3
10 36.2	9 39.6	6 61.7	Sales/Receivables		20 18.1			2 172.8	6 57.7
45 8.1	34 10.7	28 12.9			50 7.3			11 33.6	33 11.0
89 4.1	81 4.5	41 8.9			0 UND			21 17.1	56 6.5
203 1.8	215 1.7	174 2.1	Cost of Sales/Inventory		111 3.3			215 1.7	152 2.4
608 .6	521 .7	406 .9			1825 .2			281 1.3	406 .9
5 78.0	9 42.5	7 52.7			9 41.9			14 26.8	2 156.9
37 9.8	31 11.6	24 15.3	Cost of Sales/Payables		35 10.5			47 7.7	19 19.7
104 3.5	85 4.3	65 5.6			122 3.0			166 2.2	56 6.5
2.0	2.3	1.6			.6			4.4	2.2
4.8	4.3	4.4	Sales/Working Capital		2.0			8.0	4.0
15.7	10.8	12.8			NM			23.5	6.1
20.3	14.0	20.7			15.8				19.6
(38) 6.2	(47) 4.5	(51) 2.5	EBIT/Interest		(11) 1.3				(11) 2.0
1.6	.8	1.0			-1.1				.7
			Net Profit + Depr., Dep., Amort./Cur. Mat. L/T/D						
.1	.0	.0			.0			.0	.0
.2	.2	.1	Fixed/Worth		.0			.2	.5
5.4	.6	1.7			.3			1.7	1.6
.7	.4	.5			.3			1.1	.7
2.2	1.7	1.5	Debt/Worth		1.0			3.1	1.5
25.5	5.7	5.1			NM			5.1	4.7
65.6	57.9	42.0			13.2				43.3
(41) 20.0	(62) 20.1	(49) 14.8	% Profit Before Taxes/Tangible Net Worth		(11) .6				(10) 6.1
5.4	2.4	.4			-6.1				1.7
15.5	19.9	16.6			14.8			11.0	11.9
5.5	7.7	4.0	% Profit Before Taxes/Total Assets		1.0			6.9	1.4
1.1	.0	-.1			-2.1			.7	-.6
62.8	103.7	200.5			289.8			200.5	61.3
26.4	35.1	24.1	Sales/Net Fixed Assets		82.3			38.8	16.4
10.8	10.7	8.6			8.4			12.9	3.0
2.4	2.6	2.2			3.0			2.2	1.8
1.7	1.4	1.4	Sales/Total Assets		1.4			1.6	1.1
.6	.8	.7			.5			.9	.6
.2	.2	.2							.4
(31) .6	(44) .6	(47) .5	% Depr., Dep., Amort./Sales						(11) .7
1.4	1.3	1.4							2.3
2.1	3.3	2.0			1.1				
(34) 5.4	(38) 6.1	(35) 4.4	% Officers', Directors' Owners' Comp/Sales		(11) 4.8				
8.1	9.0	9.6			9.1				
495860M	824133M	1681992M	Net Sales ($)	3393M	25132M	33618M	63520M	162643M	1393686M
644637M	1127387M	1457907M	Total Assets ($)	4344M	62089M	25088M	52780M	133143M	1180463M

M = $ thousand MM = $ million

See Pages 9 through 22 for Explanation of Ratios and Data

Current Data Sorted by Assets / Comparative Historical Data

	0-500M	500M-2MM	2-10MM	10-50MM	50-100MM	100-250MM	4/1/09-3/31/10 ALL	4/1/10-3/31/11 ALL
Type of Statement								
Unqualified				1	1		6	5
Reviewed		1	3	3			15	10
Compiled	2	11	4	1			26	34
Tax Returns	2	12	6				28	24
Other		7	6	5			31	32
	10 (4/1-9/30/13)		55 (10/1/13-3/31/14)					
NUMBER OF STATEMENTS	4	31	19	10	1		106	105
	%	%	%	%	%	%	%	%
ASSETS								
Cash & Equivalents		15.3	14.6	5.1		DATA NOT AVAILABLE	8.9	13.9
Trade Receivables (net)		10.0	14.6	11.8			8.6	11.1
Inventory		53.3	38.5	27.8			49.7	40.6
All Other Current		2.7	4.1	1.0			4.9	3.6
Total Current		81.3	71.9	45.6			72.1	69.2
Fixed Assets (net)		11.3	17.0	28.1			18.1	18.8
Intangibles (net)		.2	1.6	.3			1.3	1.3
All Other Non-Current		7.3	9.5	26.0			8.5	10.7
Total		100.0	100.0	100.0			100.0	100.0
LIABILITIES								
Notes Payable-Short Term		38.8	29.4	15.9			37.6	29.3
Cur. Mat.-L.T.D.		1.7	.4	1.1			3.9	4.6
Trade Payables		4.5	5.0	2.0			5.3	5.6
Income Taxes Payable		.3	.1	.0			.1	.2
All Other Current		9.2	18.6	13.6			13.2	11.5
Total Current		54.5	53.5	32.5			60.1	51.3
Long-Term Debt		6.7	10.9	9.8			16.4	13.5
Deferred Taxes		.0	.0	.0			.0	.0
All Other Non-Current		3.4	2.6	8.9			9.0	13.8
Net Worth		35.4	33.0	48.8			14.4	21.4
Total Liabilties & Net Worth		100.0	100.0	100.0			100.0	100.0
INCOME DATA								
Net Sales		100.0	100.0	100.0			100.0	100.0
Gross Profit		25.2	21.8	31.8			27.7	28.5
Operating Expenses		21.4	19.9	28.7			26.4	25.8
Operating Profit		3.7	1.9	3.1			1.2	2.7
All Other Expenses (net)		.8	.4	.8			1.2	.2
Profit Before Taxes		3.0	1.5	2.4			.1	2.5
RATIOS								
Current		2.5	3.6	3.5			2.2	2.5
		1.4	1.3	1.9			1.3	1.6
		1.1	.9	1.0			.9	1.0
Quick		1.1	1.2	1.8			.6	1.1
		.4	.4	.6			(105) .2	.5
		.2	.1	.2			.1	.2
Sales/Receivables		0 UND	2 175.1	0 UND			0 UND	0 UND
		5 67.1	9 40.7	10 35.5			5 79.4	6 60.6
		27 13.6	72 5.1	83 4.4			20 18.5	29 12.8
Cost of Sales/Inventory		99 3.7	52 7.0	94 3.9			73 5.0	60 6.1
		146 2.5	114 3.2	122 3.0			159 2.3	117 3.1
		215 1.7	152 2.4	243 1.5			271 1.3	176 2.1
Cost of Sales/Payables		0 UND	2 151.7	1 338.8			0 UND	0 UND
		4 96.5	6 65.3	6 60.7			6 64.8	8 45.7
		14 26.5	24 15.2	30 12.1			18 20.4	21 17.6
Sales/Working Capital		3.5	3.5	2.6			4.1	3.5
		8.7	12.9	7.7			17.1	8.1
		30.0	-31.4	NM			-32.7	-595.5
EBIT/Interest		9.6	8.0				3.8	8.7
		(28) 2.2	(18) 2.5				(104) 1.3	(98) 2.7
		1.2	.5				-.5	.9
Net Profit + Depr., Dep., Amort./Cur. Mat. L/T/D							6.2	
							(11) 3.5	
							-3.2	
Fixed/Worth		.0	.1	.1			.2	.1
		.2	.9	.4			.7	.4
		.6	3.2	1.0			-4.4	1.6
Debt/Worth		.6	1.0	.3			1.8	.8
		1.9	1.8	1.5			4.4	2.4
		5.5	17.7	2.5			-23.2	8.4
% Profit Before Taxes/Tangible Net Worth		41.2	38.7	18.4			34.3	24.7
		(27) 10.8	(16) 10.6	5.9			(76) 10.0	(87) 11.4
		4.5	-1.5	-.4			-7.9	1.0
% Profit Before Taxes/Total Assets		14.0	6.0	8.4			7.0	8.8
		4.2	3.7	2.9			1.4	3.6
		1.0	-.4	-.3			-5.4	-.5
Sales/Net Fixed Assets		161.3	40.0	18.2			46.8	42.7
		27.7	23.0	6.4			14.3	14.6
		7.6	7.9	1.4			5.1	5.1
Sales/Total Assets		2.6	2.3	1.8			2.3	2.5
		1.9	2.0	.9			1.7	1.8
		1.4	.9	.3			1.1	1.0
% Depr., Dep., Amort./Sales		.3	.3				.6	.6
		(21) .4	(17) .8				(80) .9	(78) .9
		1.4	1.2				1.9	2.0
% Officers', Directors', Owners' Comp/Sales		2.1					1.3	1.7
		(17) 2.7					(43) 2.5	(42) 2.8
		4.4					4.3	5.5
Net Sales ($)	2772M	73735M	164456M	259971M	142468M		1333561M	2179177M
Total Assets ($)	1581M	38152M	93425M	222738M	85657M		682865M	990069M

M = $ thousand MM = $ million

See Pages 9 through 22 for Explanation of Ratios and Data

Comparative Historical Data				Current Data Sorted by Sales					
			Type of Statement						
4	3	2	Unqualified				1		1
7	8	7	Reviewed		2	1	1	2	1
26	22	18	Compiled	3	7	4	2	2	
26	18	20	Tax Returns	1	10	3	4	2	
25	23	18	Other		8	2	3	3	2
4/1/11-3/31/12 ALL	**4/1/12-3/31/13 ALL**	**4/1/13-3/31/14 ALL**			**10 (4/1-9/30/13)**		**55 (10/1/13-3/31/14)**		
				0-1MM	**1-3MM**	**3-5MM**	**5-10MM**	**10-25MM**	**25MM & OVER**
88	74	65	**NUMBER OF STATEMENTS**	4	27	10	11	9	4
%	%	%	**ASSETS**	%	%	%	%	%	%
10.7	14.7	13.0	Cash & Equivalents		11.3	18.0	16.9		
10.6	8.2	13.1	Trade Receivables (net)		11.0	10.8	18.8		
45.4	44.5	42.8	Inventory		51.7	45.5	33.5		
2.9	2.7	2.9	All Other Current		1.9	4.4	4.0		
69.6	70.1	71.8	Total Current		75.9	78.7	73.2		
20.1	18.7	16.3	Fixed Assets (net)		16.1	12.3	7.6		
1.5	1.0	.6	Intangibles (net)		1.0	.3	.2		
8.8	10.2	11.3	All Other Non-Current		6.9	8.7	19.0		
100.0	100.0	100.0	Total		100.0	100.0	100.0		
			LIABILITIES						
27.4	25.5	30.7	Notes Payable-Short Term		37.6	39.0	16.7		
3.1	3.6	1.2	Cur. Mat.-L.T.D.		1.9	.8	.6		
5.2	4.0	4.5	Trade Payables		2.8	6.4	5.8		
.0	.0	.2	Income Taxes Payable		.3	.2	.0		
12.5	14.9	12.2	All Other Current		13.5	8.2	10.8		
48.3	48.0	48.7	Total Current		56.1	54.7	34.0		
15.6	15.8	10.3	Long-Term Debt		11.0	5.0	14.1		
.0	.1	.0	Deferred Taxes		.0	.0	.0		
10.0	4.5	4.2	All Other Non-Current		4.8	.2	9.4		
26.1	31.7	36.8	Net Worth		28.1	40.0	42.5		
100.0	100.0	100.0	Total Liabilities & Net Worth		100.0	100.0	100.0		
			INCOME DATA						
100.0	100.0	100.0	Net Sales		100.0	100.0	100.0		
29.0	28.6	24.6	Gross Profit		24.0	24.0	27.4		
26.2	26.0	22.2	Operating Expenses		22.1	19.0	25.1		
2.8	2.6	2.4	Operating Profit		1.9	5.0	2.3		
1.1	.2	.7	All Other Expenses (net)		.9	.1	2.3		
1.6	2.5	1.7	Profit Before Taxes		1.0	4.9	-.1		
			RATIOS						
2.7	3.0	3.2			2.5	2.2	3.8		
1.4	1.4	1.4	Current		1.4	1.3	2.7		
.9	1.0	1.0			.8	1.1	1.6		
.9	1.3	1.2			.8	1.2	2.8		
.3	.3	.5	Quick		.4	.4	1.2		
.2	.1	.2			.1	.1	.5		
0 UND	**0** UND	**1** 495.3			**1** 402.7	**0** UND	**2** 189.6		
6 56.6	**5** 72.8	**7** 52.3	Sales/Receivables		**8** 48.3	**3** 125.0	**11** 34.3		
25 14.7	**24** 15.2	**37** 9.8			**35** 10.5	**30** 12.0	**83** 4.4		
94 3.9	**94** 3.9	**96** 3.8			**107** 3.4	**83** 4.4	**66** 5.5		
140 2.6	**146** 2.5	**126** 2.9	Cost of Sales/Inventory		**159** 2.3	**111** 3.3	**118** 3.1		
203 1.8	**215** 1.7	**203** 1.8			**243** 1.5	**152** 2.4	**203** 1.8		
1 549.0	**0** UND	**0** UND			**0** UND	**0** UND	**4** 95.3		
6 57.5	**4** 102.5	**4** 90.3	Cost of Sales/Payables		**3** 122.1	**3** 117.9	**6** 65.3		
23 15.7	**15** 23.6	**18** 20.8			**8** 47.9	**29** 12.5	**28** 13.1		
3.9	2.7	3.4			3.5	4.4	2.3		
8.3	9.6	8.7	Sales/Working Capital		7.7	13.5	3.5		
-40.0	NM	223.2			-11.4	49.8	12.9		
4.5	7.8	7.8			3.5		28.2		
(83) 2.4	(66) 2.3	(59) 2.2	EBIT/Interest		1.6		(10) 3.3		
.5	1.0	.8			.7		-.3		
			Net Profit + Depr., Dep., Amort./Cur. Mat. L/T/D						
.1	.1	.1			.0	.0	.0		
.5	.4	.3	Fixed/Worth		.3	.1	.1		
3.5	1.6	1.0			1.7	.9	.4		
1.1	1.1	.6			.8	1.0	.5		
2.8	2.5	1.8	Debt/Worth		2.8	1.9	1.0		
13.2	7.3	4.7			24.9	4.0	7.4		
40.0	27.8	19.3			16.5	77.3	43.6		
(70) 8.6	(66) 10.9	(57) 9.8	% Profit Before Taxes/Tangible Net Worth		(21) 7.4	12.2	(10) 8.3		
-.2	2.1	1.4			.0	10.2	1.1		
9.6	8.3	8.8			4.9	20.2	25.3		
3.1	3.9	3.3	% Profit Before Taxes/Total Assets		1.7	6.5	4.3		
-2.2	.1	-.3			-1.0	3.1	.0		
47.3	82.3	71.5			92.5	190.5	306.5		
13.5	13.1	17.6	Sales/Net Fixed Assets		18.6	23.0	30.1		
5.1	4.4	6.3			7.1	11.0	8.2		
2.5	2.4	2.4			2.5	2.4	2.7		
1.6	1.6	1.8	Sales/Total Assets		1.7	1.8	2.1		
1.0	.9	1.1			1.0	1.5	.6		
.5	.4	.3			.2				
(63) 1.4	(54) .8	(49) .6	% Depr., Dep., Amort./Sales		(20) .4				
2.5	1.9	2.1			1.8				
1.4	1.8	2.1			2.3				
(31) 2.9	(32) 3.0	(26) 2.9	% Officers', Directors' Owners' Comp/Sales		(13) 3.4				
6.1	4.3	4.3			5.5				
1114453M	**987255M**	**643402M**	Net Sales ($)	**2031M**	**51094M**	**35551M**	**79179M**	**145013M**	**330534M**
537216M	**567830M**	**441553M**	Total Assets ($)	**2919M**	**58460M**	**24583M**	**107821M**	**80189M**	**167581M**

M = $ thousand MM = $ million

See Pages 9 through 22 for Explanation of Ratios and Data

Current Data Sorted by Assets / Comparative Historical Data

0-500M	500M-2MM	2-10MM	10-50MM	50-100MM	100-250MM	Type of Statement	4/1/09-3/31/10 ALL	4/1/10-3/31/11 ALL
			1			Unqualified	1	3
		4	2			Reviewed	7	7
	3	5	1		1	Compiled	4	4
14	15	6				Tax Returns	33	30
9	4	4	2		1	Other	23	13
	13 (4/1-9/30/13)		59 (10/1/13-3/31/14)					
23	22	19	6		2	NUMBER OF STATEMENTS	68	57
%	%	%	%	%	%	**ASSETS**	%	%
19.3	11.0	11.8		DATA NOT AVAILABLE		Cash & Equivalents	10.0	10.0
11.1	17.5	10.5				Trade Receivables (net)	10.9	15.0
44.5	52.1	47.7				Inventory	39.7	38.8
1.0	.5	2.7				All Other Current	2.6	2.4
75.9	81.1	72.7				Total Current	63.2	66.1
8.5	9.4	17.8				Fixed Assets (net)	21.7	20.1
12.1	7.2	4.5				Intangibles (net)	5.2	4.2
3.5	2.2	4.9				All Other Non-Current	9.8	9.6
100.0	100.0	100.0				Total	100.0	100.0
						LIABILITIES		
4.0	17.8	10.9				Notes Payable-Short Term	12.1	12.8
2.2	2.1	3.7				Cur. Mat.-L.T.D.	2.5	3.0
17.7	17.3	17.2				Trade Payables	18.3	19.0
.0	.1	.1				Income Taxes Payable	.1	.4
6.2	15.0	8.3				All Other Current	10.1	14.0
30.1	52.1	40.2				Total Current	43.0	49.2
12.9	13.5	16.5				Long-Term Debt	19.7	18.8
.0	.0	.3				Deferred Taxes	.0	.0
17.0	12.9	8.5				All Other Non-Current	17.4	17.1
40.1	21.4	34.6				Net Worth	19.9	14.9
100.0	100.0	100.0				Total Liabilties & Net Worth	100.0	100.0
						INCOME DATA		
100.0	100.0	100.0				Net Sales	100.0	100.0
34.9	38.2	26.7				Gross Profit	35.5	35.8
31.2	34.7	22.7				Operating Expenses	35.6	33.3
3.7	3.4	4.0				Operating Profit	-.1	2.5
-.7	.3	.2				All Other Expenses (net)	.5	.9
4.4	3.2	3.8				Profit Before Taxes	-.6	1.6
						RATIOS		
12.8	2.9	3.1					2.9	2.2
3.5	1.7	1.7				Current	1.4	1.4
1.6	1.2	1.2					1.1	1.0
3.3	1.2	1.2					1.0	.9
1.1	.6	.4				Quick	.3	.4
.2	.3	.2					.1	.2
0 UND	0 UND	0 999.8					0 823.1	0 UND
1 243.7	11 34.0	3 132.4				Sales/Receivables	3 122.2	3 130.4
15 24.2	36 10.2	12 30.7					21 17.2	24 15.2
18 19.8	51 7.2	24 15.1					16 23.0	11 33.8
60 6.1	99 3.7	60 6.1				Cost of Sales/Inventory	42 8.8	40 9.2
87 4.2	182 2.0	94 3.9					134 2.7	117 3.1
0 UND	6 63.5	12 31.0					8 47.1	0 UND
9 42.7	27 13.6	18 20.0				Cost of Sales/Payables	21 17.5	19 19.3
28 13.2	60 6.1	28 13.1					57 6.3	53 6.9
5.8	4.4	6.9					6.7	7.1
10.7	8.1	10.1				Sales/Working Capital	19.1	30.3
49.2	46.9	108.0					106.9	-248.8
34.0	24.1	23.8					13.3	13.7
(13) 11.3	(18) 3.7	(17) 5.0				EBIT/Interest	(50) 3.3	(44) 4.2
2.4	.8	1.5					.2	1.2
						Net Profit + Depr., Dep., Amort./Cur. Mat. L/T/D		
.0	.1	.1					.2	.1
.1	.4	.4				Fixed/Worth	.7	.7
-1.8	1.7	1.7					14.5	-7.1
.4	1.0	.8					1.2	1.1
1.2	5.3	2.9				Debt/Worth	3.0	4.1
-35.4	20.4	7.3					UND	-13.3
88.8	93.7	75.4					71.5	57.5
(17) 54.9	(18) 66.0	(16) 16.4				% Profit Before Taxes/Tangible Net Worth	(52) 25.4	(40) 24.5
9.1	34.2	8.3					2.1	6.9
36.5	29.2	18.9					20.4	16.5
14.0	9.8	6.5				% Profit Before Taxes/Total Assets	3.2	5.4
-.4	.7	1.9					-4.8	.0
475.8	181.6	107.8					101.4	245.6
81.1	77.1	49.3				Sales/Net Fixed Assets	30.0	36.5
35.4	21.4	10.4					9.5	12.8
6.8	4.5	5.1					5.4	7.0
4.4	2.7	4.3				Sales/Total Assets	2.9	3.3
2.3	1.4	2.4					1.9	1.8
	.4	.3					.3	.4
	(15) .7	(16) .6				% Depr., Dep., Amort./Sales	(51) 1.0	(44) 1.1
	1.6	1.6					3.1	2.7
3.1	1.7						1.7	1.2
(11) 4.5	(16) 3.7					% Officers', Directors' Owners' Comp/Sales	(26) 3.8	(25) 4.5
6.8	5.1						7.2	6.9
24287M	108190M	411035M	404595M		1133557M	Net Sales ($)	2697543M	2717725M
5366M	22771M	94666M	136421M		371106M	Total Assets ($)	748514M	622411M

M = $ thousand MM = $ million

See Pages 9 through 22 for Explanation of Ratios and Data

Comparative Historical Data				Current Data Sorted by Sales					
			Type of Statement						
2	1	1	Unqualified						1
8	6	6	Reviewed					2	4
5	13	10	Compiled	1	1		2	3	3
51	31	35	Tax Returns	9	12	6	2	4	2
25	24	20	Other	5	7	2	2	1	3
				13 (4/1-9/30/13)			59 (10/1/13-3/31/14)		
4/1/11-3/31/12 ALL	4/1/12-3/31/13 ALL	4/1/13-3/31/14 ALL		0-1MM	1-3MM	3-5MM	5-10MM	10-25MM	25MM & OVER
91	75	72	**NUMBER OF STATEMENTS**	15	20	8	6	10	13
%	%	%	**ASSETS**	%	%	%	%	%	%
12.7	11.3	13.4	Cash & Equivalents	18.5	16.7			13.4	8.8
9.8	15.1	12.7	Trade Receivables (net)	12.2	13.3			12.8	4.1
45.6	45.0	47.0	Inventory	37.2	51.8			44.9	47.5
1.3	3.1	2.0	All Other Current	.4	.8			4.2	1.8
69.4	74.5	75.1	Total Current	68.2	82.6			75.3	62.3
19.2	14.1	12.1	Fixed Assets (net)	8.1	8.9			16.7	17.7
1.8	3.4	7.5	Intangibles (net)	19.8	5.7			4.2	4.6
9.6	7.9	5.3	All Other Non-Current	3.9	2.8			3.8	15.4
100.0	100.0	100.0	Total	100.0	100.0			100.0	100.0
			LIABILITIES						
9.6	14.3	11.1	Notes Payable-Short Term	5.7	8.0			20.1	13.0
2.9	3.9	2.4	Cur. Mat.-L.T.D.	4.2	1.0			6.3	1.1
16.9	20.4	17.1	Trade Payables	12.9	19.1			10.1	21.4
.0	.2	.0	Income Taxes Payable	.0	.0			.1	.0
15.8	11.6	9.8	All Other Current	3.0	15.8			9.7	6.2
45.3	50.4	40.5	Total Current	25.7	43.9			46.3	41.7
15.7	12.2	13.9	Long-Term Debt	13.1	13.6			13.4	11.8
.0	.2	.1	Deferred Taxes	.0	.0			.5	.0
8.2	8.3	11.7	All Other Non-Current	32.4	6.1			.4	.9
30.7	28.9	33.8	Net Worth	28.7	36.4			39.3	45.6
100.0	100.0	100.0	Total Liabilities & Net Worth	100.0	100.0			100.0	100.0
			INCOME DATA						
100.0	100.0	100.0	Net Sales	100.0	100.0			100.0	100.0
33.9	36.7	32.4	Gross Profit	38.3	38.6			26.9	18.7
31.2	32.3	28.5	Operating Expenses	35.4	34.4			21.9	15.7
2.7	4.4	4.0	Operating Profit	2.9	4.2			5.1	3.0
.2	.0	.0	All Other Expenses (net)	-.5	-.2			.5	.0
2.5	4.4	3.9	Profit Before Taxes	3.4	4.3			4.5	2.9
			RATIOS						
2.7	3.2	3.7		22.1	4.0			2.5	2.6
1.6	1.4	1.9	Current	3.7	2.5			1.7	1.2
1.1	.9	1.2		1.7	1.5			1.4	1.1
1.0	.9	1.5		3.5	1.5			1.2	.5
.4	.5	.6	Quick	1.5	.8			.3	.3
.1	.2	.2		.6	.2			.3	.2
0 UND	**1** 479.5	**0** UND		**0** UND	**0** UND			**0** UND	**1** 402.6
1 254.8	**4** 98.7	**3** 122.0	Sales/Receivables	**1** 243.7	**4** 90.9			**4** 101.9	**2** 175.4
9 39.8	**30** 12.2	**21** 17.8		**18** 19.8	**33** 11.2			**14** 25.5	**4** 89.5
24 15.0	**23** 15.8	**26** 14.0		**0** UND	**41** 9.0			**19** 18.9	**20** 18.5
57 6.4	**48** 7.6	**66** 5.5	Cost of Sales/Inventory	**73** 5.0	**78** 4.7			**46** 7.9	**31** 11.7
135 2.7	**126** 2.9	**140** 2.6		**243** 1.5	**174** 2.1			**101** 3.6	**89** 4.1
1 289.6	**9** 41.1	**6** 56.9		**0** UND	**7** 49.2			**4** 98.1	**13** 28.7
15 23.6	**21** 17.4	**19** 19.3	Cost of Sales/Payables	**9** 42.7	**28** 13.1			**13** 27.7	**17** 21.4
53 6.9	**56** 6.5	**37** 9.8		**24** 15.5	**52** 7.0			**25** 14.5	**28** 13.2
6.2	7.1	4.6		2.3	4.6			6.9	8.2
22.1	17.7	9.9	Sales/Working Capital	7.3	8.7			10.5	58.1
106.1	-139.3	52.5		53.6	31.1			NM	253.9
31.4	23.8	26.0			30.3			33.9	39.1
(68) 5.1	(62) 7.4	(55) 6.2	EBIT/Interest		(14) 13.0			4.9	(12) 23.1
1.9	2.2	1.6			-.1			1.5	6.3
	39.1								
	(11) 3.6		Net Profit + Depr., Dep., Amort./Cur. Mat. L/T/D						
	.5								
.0	.1	.1		.1	.0			.1	.1
.4	.4	.2	Fixed/Worth	.3	.1			.2	.5
2.7	1.1	1.7		-.3	.9			NM	1.0
.7	.9	.8		.8	.4			.8	.7
2.5	2.1	2.1	Debt/Worth	28.4	1.0			1.3	1.5
11.7	9.9	14.9		-6.0	10.9			NM	5.2
63.8	91.2	81.0			88.8				98.9
(77) 33.5	(65) 45.0	(59) 40.3	% Profit Before Taxes/Tangible Net Worth		(17) 45.1				30.0
5.9	17.1	8.9			7.2				11.5
21.4	29.8	23.2		26.2	41.5			13.1	18.1
9.2	13.8	9.1	% Profit Before Taxes/Total Assets	9.6	13.6			5.5	14.3
1.2	2.5	2.0		-.4	.5			1.4	7.1
277.9	217.6	146.3		123.1	868.8			250.6	92.0
36.8	56.8	57.4	Sales/Net Fixed Assets	58.6	90.6			27.8	49.3
10.4	16.0	19.0		18.9	24.3			9.2	19.2
6.4	6.1	5.4		3.6	5.6			5.2	8.2
2.9	3.8	3.2	Sales/Total Assets	2.3	3.7			2.7	4.8
1.9	2.4	2.2		1.0	1.9			2.5	2.5
.4	.2	.3			.1				.2
(50) 1.2	(50) .4	(47) .5	% Depr., Dep., Amort./Sales		(10) .6				.4
2.0	.9	1.4			1.1				.5
1.5	1.5	1.4			2.9				
(48) 3.4	(35) 3.1	(37) 4.2	% Officers', Directors' Owners' Comp/Sales		(14) 5.1				
6.9	6.1	6.0			6.3				
2074815M	827468M	2081664M	Net Sales ($)	8682M	34241M	30690M	50813M	162955M	1794283M
599395M	213188M	630330M	Total Assets ($)	4036M	11695M	11674M	19969M	66272M	516684M

M = $ thousand MM = $ million

See Pages 9 through 22 for Explanation of Ratios and Data

Current Data Sorted by Assets							Comparative Historical Data	
						Type of Statement		
		3	6	2	5	Unqualified	45	35
4	10	14	12			Reviewed	69	42
2	14	12	2			Compiled	82	82
54	58	24	1			Tax Returns	187	164
39	55	44	8	10	4	Other	205	182
	43 (4/1-9/30/13)			340 (10/1/13-3/31/14)			4/1/09-3/31/10	4/1/10-3/31/11
0-500M	500M-2MM	2-10MM	10-50MM	50-100MM	100-250MM		ALL	ALL
99	137	97	29	12	9	**NUMBER OF STATEMENTS**	588	505
%	%	%	%	%	%	**ASSETS**	%	%
18.1	12.1	10.5	8.3	10.8		Cash & Equivalents	11.7	11.2
9.9	13.3	12.5	15.5	9.7		Trade Receivables (net)	14.9	14.3
45.7	37.9	42.5	41.3	35.8		Inventory	37.3	38.1
1.4	2.0	6.1	7.0	3.3		All Other Current	2.7	3.0
75.2	65.3	71.6	72.1	59.5		Total Current	66.6	66.6
14.0	18.9	20.1	16.1	14.3		Fixed Assets (net)	20.2	21.7
5.6	6.3	3.4	6.8	18.2		Intangibles (net)	5.8	4.9
5.2	9.5	4.8	4.9	7.9		All Other Non-Current	7.3	6.9
100.0	100.0	100.0	100.0	100.0		Total	100.0	100.0
						LIABILITIES		
20.9	14.2	10.0	7.9	9.8		Notes Payable-Short Term	13.0	14.2
2.4	2.0	2.9	6.6	1.6		Cur. Mat.-L.T.D.	3.7	3.3
15.6	16.9	17.4	17.0	25.0		Trade Payables	18.6	17.4
.0	.1	.1	.2	.3		Income Taxes Payable	.2	.1
12.6	10.5	16.4	9.8	8.0		All Other Current	14.3	15.5
51.5	43.8	46.8	41.5	44.7		Total Current	49.9	50.5
23.3	16.0	13.4	7.3	22.8		Long-Term Debt	17.9	16.1
.0	.1	.1	.4	.0		Deferred Taxes	.3	.1
21.4	9.7	6.3	6.7	15.1		All Other Non-Current	9.3	9.6
3.8	30.5	33.4	44.0	17.4		Net Worth	22.5	23.7
100.0	100.0	100.0	100.0	100.0		Total Liabilties & Net Worth	100.0	100.0
						INCOME DATA		
100.0	100.0	100.0	100.0	100.0		Net Sales	100.0	100.0
48.7	42.5	34.9	36.8	39.8		Gross Profit	39.6	41.4
44.0	38.6	30.3	32.1	35.1		Operating Expenses	36.4	37.8
4.6	3.9	4.7	4.7	4.7		Operating Profit	3.2	3.6
.8	.7	.0	.3	1.2		All Other Expenses (net)	.9	1.2
3.8	3.2	4.7	4.5	3.6		Profit Before Taxes	2.2	2.4
						RATIOS		
4.8	2.9	3.1	2.9	2.8			2.6	2.7
2.1	1.8	1.9	1.6	1.3		Current	1.5	1.5
1.1	1.0	1.3	1.1	1.0			1.0	1.0
1.8	1.2	1.4	1.2	1.4			1.1	1.0
(97) .7	.5	.4	.6	.5		Quick	(587) .5	.5
.3	.2	.2	.1	.1			.2	.2
0 UND	**1** 564.7	**1** 560.7	**3** 137.5	**2** 228.0			**1** 507.0	**0** 999.8
0 828.0	**9** 42.6	**5** 66.6	**15** 24.3	**6** 59.0		Sales/Receivables	**10** 35.7	**10** 36.4
13 28.6	**26** 13.9	**28** 13.1	**33** 11.0	**28** 12.9			**36** 10.1	**33** 11.2
27 13.4	**30** 12.0	**33** 11.0	**41** 8.8	**37** 9.9			**28** 13.0	**30** 12.0
74 4.9	**79** 4.6	**85** 4.3	**79** 4.6	**118** 3.1		Cost of Sales/Inventory	**70** 5.2	**69** 5.3
140 2.6	**146** 2.5	**140** 2.6	**130** 2.8	**159** 2.3			**139** 2.6	**137** 2.7
0 UND	**9** 39.6	**8** 45.1	**10** 35.6	**23** 16.2			**12** 31.7	**8** 43.5
14 26.4	**29** 12.4	**24** 15.2	**31** 11.6	**46** 7.9		Cost of Sales/Payables	**29** 12.4	**28** 13.1
39 9.4	**61** 6.0	**45** 8.2	**54** 6.8	**65** 5.6			**57** 6.5	**56** 6.6
6.2	5.5	4.7	6.3	5.9			6.2	6.0
12.6	11.5	9.9	11.4	15.1		Sales/Working Capital	14.5	15.0
117.8	-121.7	30.1	49.0	754.7			-155.8	-168.1
11.9	12.7	21.2	57.3	62.8			9.5	10.1
(57) 3.3	(116) 4.5	(85) 7.8	(27) 15.7	8.7		EBIT/Interest	(507) 2.8	(414) 3.2
.3	1.1	1.9	4.4	1.8			.6	.7
		6.5					5.7	6.3
		(13) 4.0				Net Profit + Depr., Dep., Amort./Cur. Mat. L/T/D	(108) 2.3	(60) 2.1
		1.8					.6	.7
.0	.1	.1	.1	.2			.2	.1
.4	.5	.3	.4	NM		Fixed/Worth	.7	.6
-.5	3.3	1.0	1.0	-1.2			13.4	3.6
.5	.8	.8	.8	1.7			.9	.9
3.2	3.1	1.5	1.5	NM		Debt/Worth	2.8	2.4
-4.3	14.2	6.6	4.1	-7.2			100.8	19.6
81.1	63.6	51.6	54.8				53.3	50.1
(62) 38.8	(112) 26.7	(86) 27.4	(26) 20.6			% Profit Before Taxes/Tangible Net Worth	(452) 16.5	(403) 19.0
13.3	2.7	8.7	9.0				1.9	3.4
34.8	18.4	19.8	18.0	14.8			14.0	15.6
14.0	6.2	7.3	8.3	10.5		% Profit Before Taxes/Total Assets	4.8	5.5
.8	.5	2.0	5.0	2.5			-.7	-.4
722.0	99.1	131.4	72.4	32.8			80.1	106.3
54.8	28.0	30.3	30.7	18.9		Sales/Net Fixed Assets	21.9	26.4
19.2	11.2	7.9	11.9	11.5			7.1	7.9
6.7	4.1	3.9	4.2	3.8			4.0	4.2
3.6	2.9	2.5	3.0	1.9		Sales/Total Assets	2.7	2.7
2.5	2.0	1.7	2.1	1.7			1.7	1.8
.4	.3	.3	.4	1.0			.5	.4
(45) .8	(90) 1.0	(72) 1.1	(27) .9	1.2		% Depr., Dep., Amort./Sales	(447) 1.1	(374) 1.1
2.0	1.8	2.3	2.1	3.0			2.4	2.4
3.1	1.9	1.4	.2				1.8	1.6
(52) 5.2	(74) 3.9	(49) 2.1	(11) .9			% Officers', Directors' Owners' Comp/Sales	(238) 3.8	(232) 4.2
9.0	6.9	3.5	2.6				6.5	7.9
116708M	525679M	1399906M	1986962M	2152823M	2786184M	Net Sales ($)	14869721M	14317661M
26262M	151669M	426309M	689456M	892727M	1371319M	Total Assets ($)	7178099M	5435881M

M = $ thousand MM = $ million

See Pages 9 through 22 for Explanation of Ratios and Data

Comparative Historical Data				Current Data Sorted by Sales					
			Type of Statement						
35	24	16	Unqualified				1	1	14
50	36	40	Reviewed	2	8	4	5	9	12
56	41	30	Compiled	2	6	7	7	5	3
204	154	137	Tax Returns	39	42	20	20	11	5
178	157	160	Other	34	44	17	16	25	24
4/1/11-3/31/12 ALL	4/1/12-3/31/13 ALL	4/1/13-3/31/14 ALL		43 (4/1-9/30/13)			340 (10/1/13-3/31/14)		
				0-1MM	1-3MM	3-5MM	5-10MM	10-25MM	25MM & OVER
523	412	383	**NUMBER OF STATEMENTS**	77	100	48	49	51	58
%	%	%	**ASSETS**	%	%	%	%	%	%
11.8	11.6	13.0	Cash & Equivalents	16.1	11.8	14.1	13.6	12.1	10.1
13.5	14.3	12.1	Trade Receivables (net)	4.7	14.0	13.0	17.5	13.6	11.8
39.2	40.9	41.1	Inventory	42.4	39.1	39.4	43.4	41.3	41.9
2.6	2.7	3.6	All Other Current	1.4	2.6	3.6	1.9	8.5	5.3
67.0	69.5	69.7	Total Current	64.6	67.5	70.2	76.3	75.6	69.1
19.5	18.0	17.7	Fixed Assets (net)	20.1	19.5	18.2	14.8	14.2	16.5
7.4	4.8	6.0	Intangibles (net)	9.1	5.0	2.9	3.9	4.3	9.2
6.1	7.7	6.6	All Other Non-Current	6.1	8.0	8.8	4.9	6.0	5.3
100.0	100.0	100.0	Total	100.0	100.0	100.0	100.0	100.0	100.0
			LIABILITIES						
11.2	15.4	14.1	Notes Payable-Short Term	26.7	12.2	11.0	11.8	11.4	7.5
3.1	2.9	2.7	Cur. Mat.-L.T.D.	2.5	2.0	3.2	1.2	2.8	4.8
16.6	17.5	16.9	Trade Payables	10.7	18.2	15.4	20.8	19.8	18.1
.1	.1	.1	Income Taxes Payable	.0	.1	.1	.2	.0	.4
13.3	12.8	12.4	All Other Current	11.2	11.8	10.2	9.0	24.0	9.6
44.3	48.8	46.2	Total Current	51.2	44.3	39.8	42.9	58.1	40.5
18.4	15.9	17.0	Long-Term Debt	27.8	18.1	18.1	10.7	6.5	14.2
.1	.2	.1	Deferred Taxes	.0	.2	.1	.0	.0	.2
8.6	12.1	11.7	All Other Non-Current	27.4	9.4	7.7	7.1	3.2	9.6
28.6	22.9	25.0	Net Worth	-6.4	28.0	34.3	39.3	32.2	35.4
100.0	100.0	100.0	Total Liabilities & Net Worth	100.0	100.0	100.0	100.0	100.0	100.0
			INCOME DATA						
100.0	100.0	100.0	Net Sales	100.0	100.0	100.0	100.0	100.0	100.0
42.0	40.2	41.6	Gross Profit	52.1	45.6	39.6	36.4	33.0	34.6
37.7	36.0	37.2	Operating Expenses	47.5	41.1	34.6	32.7	28.4	30.6
4.4	4.2	4.4	Operating Profit	4.6	4.5	5.0	3.7	4.5	4.1
.7	.6	.5	All Other Expenses (net)	1.4	1.0	.0	-.6	-.2	.5
3.6	3.6	3.9	Profit Before Taxes	3.2	3.5	4.9	4.3	4.7	3.6
			RATIOS						
3.2	3.3	3.3		4.4	4.1	2.7	3.1	3.0	3.0
1.7	1.7	1.8	Current	1.9	1.6	2.0	2.4	1.7	1.6
1.0	1.1	1.1		1.0	.9	1.2	1.3	1.1	1.2
1.2	1.3	1.4		1.5	1.5	1.3	1.6	1.0	1.3
.5	(411) .5	(381) .5	Quick	(75) .5	.5	.5	.9	.4	.5
.2	.2	.2		.1	.2	.3	.3	.2	.1
0 UND	0 UND	0 999.8		0 UND	0 UND	1 529.2	1 708.5	1 461.4	1 407.1
8 46.9	9 38.9	5 68.8	Sales/Receivables	0 UND	9 42.7	10 37.2	9 40.9	8 48.3	7 54.7
26 14.3	27 13.3	24 15.3		7 52.7	27 13.7	27 13.7	25 14.8	29 12.6	22 16.6
30 12.1	31 11.7	32 11.5		42 8.6	40 9.2	29 12.7	29 12.6	26 14.3	28 13.2
76 4.8	81 4.5	79 4.6	Cost of Sales/Inventory	114 3.2	85 4.3	64 5.7	76 4.8	57 6.4	69 5.3
146 2.5	159 2.3	146 2.5		243 1.5	140 2.6	126 2.9	118 3.1	114 3.2	122 3.0
7 55.0	10 35.0	6 65.3		0 UND	9 38.8	5 69.2	6 64.6	10 35.6	8 45.3
28 13.2	28 13.2	24 14.9	Cost of Sales/Payables	18 19.8	24 14.9	23 15.8	29 12.8	21 17.6	28 12.9
55 6.6	56 6.5	51 7.2		48 7.6	69 5.3	46 7.9	42 8.6	54 6.8	49 7.4
5.7	5.1	5.4		4.8	4.9	5.4	5.4	6.9	6.3
13.9	10.9	11.1	Sales/Working Capital	8.8	13.3	8.9	9.0	19.1	14.1
198.1	91.8	70.5		-313.3	-82.9	35.6	34.3	58.5	29.6
12.2	15.4	16.0		8.4	9.2	18.5	28.3	42.8	37.4
(435) 3.9	(337) 4.9	(306) 5.4	EBIT/Interest	(51) 1.7	(73) 3.3	(40) 5.4	(44) 8.3	(44) 12.8	(54) 10.9
1.1	1.5	1.3		-.1	.6	1.9	3.3	2.5	2.7
6.9	4.4	9.5							11.9
(47) 2.4	(34) 2.3	(36) 5.0	Net Profit + Depr., Dep., Amort./Cur. Mat. L/T/D						(16) 5.2
.5	.9	2.0							2.8
.1	.1	.1		.1	.1	.1	.1	.1	.1
.6	.5	.4	Fixed/Worth	2.6	.7	.3	.3	.3	.6
4.3	2.5	3.0		-.4	15.3	1.3	.9	.7	1.5
.9	.9	.8		1.0	.8	.6	.8	.6	.9
2.6	2.1	2.2	Debt/Worth	9.1	3.7	1.7	1.5	1.4	1.9
24.0	18.8	24.5		-2.8	-79.9	4.8	4.6	3.9	10.8
58.8	57.0	61.1		81.0	69.0	61.3	53.8	65.8	46.6
(414) 24.4	(323) 26.6	(300) 28.7	% Profit Before Taxes/Tangible Net Worth	(45) 24.6	(74) 30.7	(43) 30.0	(46) 29.1	(45) 32.8	(47) 19.2
5.2	8.7	7.9		-.7	2.9	9.0	8.1	8.9	9.4
18.6	18.0	20.4		23.0	20.9	22.8	21.9	25.9	15.4
7.6	8.2	8.5	% Profit Before Taxes/Total Assets	7.2	8.5	10.8	9.7	9.4	8.5
.6	1.6	1.4		-2.6	.4	2.0	2.6	3.5	4.5
117.7	134.3	132.4		107.4	194.2	99.5	150.3	210.1	66.2
31.6	33.0	32.9	Sales/Net Fixed Assets	28.0	32.9	27.8	56.2	71.2	30.4
10.0	10.0	11.2		9.2	9.1	13.6	13.1	11.7	11.6
4.3	4.3	4.5		4.2	4.1	4.2	5.0	5.1	4.6
2.7	2.8	3.0	Sales/Total Assets	2.3	2.8	3.1	3.3	3.3	3.0
1.9	1.8	1.9		1.3	1.9	2.3	2.3	2.4	1.8
.4	.3	.4		.4	.4	.4	.3	.2	.4
(363) 1.0	(277) .9	(251) 1.0	% Depr., Dep., Amort./Sales	(35) 1.3	(62) 1.1	(34) .9	(33) .8	(36) 1.0	(51) 1.0
2.2	2.0	2.1		3.3	2.8	2.0	1.6	1.8	2.2
2.0	1.8	1.5		2.8	2.9	1.7	1.4	1.1	.5
(245) 3.8	(201) 3.6	(187) 3.2	% Officers', Directors' Owners' Comp/Sales	(32) 6.5	(54) 4.5	(32) 3.3	(26) 2.6	(26) 1.8	(17) 1.1
7.4	7.2	6.1		11.1	7.5	6.0	3.8	2.5	3.5
12319242M	9399372M	8968262M	Net Sales ($)	44859M	193606M	189654M	343637M	815201M	7381305M
5029236M	3638674M	3557742M	Total Assets ($)	30667M	89732M	71714M	115987M	324576M	2925066M

M = $ thousand MM = $ million

See Pages 9 through 22 for Explanation of Ratios and Data

Current Data Sorted by Assets							Comparative Historical Data	
						Type of Statement		
	1		6	4	4	Unqualified	13	20
		9	5			Reviewed	4	11
4	3	8				Compiled	4	8
17	19	12	2			Tax Returns	15	27
9	14	31	19	9	7	Other	46	49
16 (4/1-9/30/13)		167 (10/1/13-3/31/14)					4/1/09-3/31/10 ALL	4/1/10-3/31/11 ALL
0-500M	500M-2MM	2-10MM	10-50MM	50-100MM	100-250MM			
30	37	60	32	13	11	**NUMBER OF STATEMENTS**	82	115
%	%	%	%	%	%	**ASSETS**	%	%
30.6	25.9	14.7	12.6	22.0	21.1	Cash & Equivalents	16.9	20.0
5.7	7.2	9.6	7.7	8.9	10.9	Trade Receivables (net)	10.5	10.6
40.3	44.1	51.1	43.6	36.3	17.0	Inventory	36.3	36.3
2.1	1.5	2.1	6.2	5.0	3.8	All Other Current	4.9	4.9
78.7	78.7	77.5	70.2	72.2	52.9	Total Current	68.6	71.9
9.8	11.0	10.8	16.2	16.7	10.7	Fixed Assets (net)	15.4	12.5
3.9	4.9	7.4	5.5	5.9	32.8	Intangibles (net)	10.3	9.1
7.6	5.4	4.4	8.2	5.2	3.7	All Other Non-Current	5.7	6.5
100.0	100.0	100.0	100.0	100.0	100.0	Total	100.0	100.0
						LIABILITIES		
15.2	13.0	9.6	7.1	8.3	3.2	Notes Payable-Short Term	9.4	9.6
.6	1.9	.6	4.5	2.9	2.0	Cur. Mat.-L.T.D.	2.0	1.7
19.0	20.9	22.9	25.6	21.5	16.6	Trade Payables	22.1	25.1
.0	.2	.1	.0	.2	.1	Income Taxes Payable	.4	.3
14.4	10.2	11.1	11.9	14.5	8.0	All Other Current	13.6	10.5
49.2	46.2	44.3	49.1	47.5	30.0	Total Current	47.5	47.2
10.7	9.0	12.8	8.3	15.1	24.2	Long-Term Debt	11.8	9.6
.0	.0	.1	.2	.0	1.9	Deferred Taxes	.4	.4
10.7	7.6	6.2	12.7	4.7	2.5	All Other Non-Current	5.0	2.8
29.3	37.2	36.7	29.7	32.7	41.5	Net Worth	35.3	40.0
100.0	100.0	100.0	100.0	100.0	100.0	Total Liabilties & Net Worth	100.0	100.0
						INCOME DATA		
100.0	100.0	100.0	100.0	100.0	100.0	Net Sales	100.0	100.0
39.3	36.0	35.6	38.8	41.5	35.7	Gross Profit	39.2	37.7
33.9	31.5	31.3	36.3	39.9	31.1	Operating Expenses	34.8	34.4
5.4	4.5	4.4	2.5	1.6	4.6	Operating Profit	4.5	3.3
.2	.2	.1	.6	1.2	.2	All Other Expenses (net)	.8	.4
5.3	4.3	4.2	1.8	.4	4.5	Profit Before Taxes	3.6	2.9
						RATIOS		
6.4	3.0	3.0	2.8	1.9	2.9		2.3	2.5
1.8	1.9	1.8	1.6	1.5	1.7	Current	1.5	1.5
1.2	1.2	1.2	1.2	1.0	1.2		1.1	1.1
4.2	1.2	.8	1.0	1.0	1.6		1.1	1.1
1.2	.7	.5	.3	.4	1.2	Quick	.6	.5
.3	.2	.3	.1	.2	.4		.2	.3
0 UND	0 UND	1 643.5	0 999.8	4 94.0	4 84.3		0 999.8	0 999.8
0 UND	2 231.0	5 75.2	3 140.9	6 59.4	12 29.6	Sales/Receivables	3 117.9	3 134.8
2 209.8	7 49.9	12 31.6	17 21.8	15 23.7	57 6.4		14 25.7	14 26.4
1 307.9	6 60.6	46 8.0	40 9.1	13 27.4	17 21.9		30 12.3	17 21.5
33 11.2	44 8.3	78 4.7	101 3.6	94 3.9	69 5.3	Cost of Sales/Inventory	61 6.0	59 6.2
104 3.5	76 4.8	111 3.3	130 2.8	130 2.8	107 3.4		107 3.4	102 3.6
0 UND	6 62.2	14 26.3	24 14.9	28 13.2	37 9.9		20 18.0	20 18.7
1 339.2	22 16.6	31 11.6	39 9.3	41 8.9	55 6.6	Cost of Sales/Payables	34 10.7	35 10.3
31 11.8	36 10.1	56 6.5	65 5.6	87 4.2	58 6.3		53 6.9	56 6.5
8.2	7.7	5.6	6.2	5.1	3.1		7.7	7.2
16.6	13.5	11.5	11.0	13.0	8.9	Sales/Working Capital	17.3	15.9
152.1	78.0	30.1	29.3	NM	22.3		158.1	143.0
56.7	77.0	58.3	54.6		342.3		56.2	23.5
(17) 9.0	(23) 10.2	(51) 12.2	(25) 12.9		(10) 6.3	EBIT/Interest	(65) 9.3	(93) 7.6
-.4	.9	2.5	1.3		-3.0		1.7	1.5
							146.8	17.1
						Net Profit + Depr., Dep., Amort./Cur. Mat. L/T/D	(13) 25.1	(15) 8.3
							2.8	2.9
.0	.0	.0	.2	.1	.3		.1	.1
.0	.1	.1	.5	.8	.8	Fixed/Worth	.4	.3
1.7	.7	1.3	1.1	NM	-.2		2.1	1.5
.4	.8	.9	.8	.9	.5		.8	.9
2.2	1.7	1.7	2.1	2.5	2.3	Debt/Worth	1.9	2.2
36.8	4.3	4.2	5.5	NM	-2.5		7.9	8.1
137.6	92.9	69.2	68.3	48.7			76.4	75.7
(24) 36.3	(31) 52.5	(50) 39.5	(28) 31.3	(10) 14.8		% Profit Before Taxes/Tangible Net Worth	(70) 39.9	(96) 40.5
6.6	12.9	25.0	3.3	-1.4			15.6	11.8
73.3	41.8	25.6	20.0	14.8	18.3		27.2	30.4
16.2	18.1	13.3	13.1	6.7	6.9	% Profit Before Taxes/Total Assets	11.8	9.7
-1.5	1.2	4.7	-.2	-2.3	-.6		2.1	1.2
UND	578.7	338.4	48.8	44.0	27.8		110.0	241.0
339.3	122.6	83.2	22.0	23.3	15.5	Sales/Net Fixed Assets	31.3	45.4
46.2	36.7	24.8	13.2	10.5	11.2		16.3	20.0
10.3	7.2	4.8	3.6	3.6	2.0		5.5	5.4
6.3	5.4	3.6	2.8	2.7	1.6	Sales/Total Assets	3.4	3.4
3.3	3.2	2.4	1.9	2.0	1.1		2.4	2.2
.1	.1	.1	.5	.8			.5	.4
(11) .6	(20) .3	(34) .5	(31) 1.0	(12) 1.2		% Depr., Dep., Amort./Sales	(53) 1.2	(77) .9
3.1	.8	.8	2.2	1.8			2.5	2.1
3.0	1.4	.9					1.0	1.0
(17) 5.8	(17) 2.0	(20) 1.8				% Officers', Directors' Owners' Comp/Sales	(21) 2.6	(35) 2.0
9.1	5.4	3.4					7.6	4.6
63427M	234744M	925768M	2069158M	2585334M	3798189M	Net Sales ($)	6007468M	9475805M
7688M	42801M	258430M	694706M	918610M	2017903M	Total Assets ($)	2497632M	3439207M

M = $ thousand MM = $ million

See Pages 9 through 22 for Explanation of Ratios and Data

Comparative Historical Data / Current Data Sorted by Sales

					16 (4/1-9/30/13)		167 (10/1/13-3/31/14)		
4/1/11-3/31/12 ALL	4/1/12-3/31/13 ALL	4/1/13-3/31/14 ALL	**Type of Statement**	0-1MM	1-3MM	3-5MM	5-10MM	10-25MM	25MM & OVER
24	20	15	Unqualified			1			14
9	11	14	Reviewed			1	1	5	7
12	10	15	Compiled	1	1	2	5	3	3
20	54	50	Tax Returns	5	11	11	10	11	2
72	75	89	Other	8	5	4	15	21	36
137	170	183	**NUMBER OF STATEMENTS**	14	17	19	31	40	62
%	%	%	**ASSETS**	%	%	%	%	%	%
15.9	17.7	20.1	Cash & Equivalents	26.9	19.3	22.7	27.6	14.6	17.8
11.2	11.4	8.2	Trade Receivables (net)	3.7	6.4	7.2	10.6	7.8	9.0
39.8	39.0	43.5	Inventory	29.2	39.0	58.5	41.4	50.2	40.1
5.2	6.0	3.0	All Other Current	6.8	.0	.5	1.9	3.7	3.9
72.1	74.0	74.8	Total Current	66.5	64.8	88.8	81.4	76.3	70.8
11.1	11.9	12.0	Fixed Assets (net)	8.5	18.6	7.6	7.0	13.4	14.0
10.1	9.7	7.4	Intangibles (net)	16.3	6.5	1.4	7.7	4.0	9.6
6.7	4.4	5.8	All Other Non-Current	8.6	10.1	2.2	3.9	6.4	5.6
100.0	100.0	100.0	Total	100.0	100.0	100.0	100.0	100.0	100.0
			LIABILITIES						
9.7	10.4	10.3	Notes Payable-Short Term	13.1	9.1	13.4	12.7	11.6	7.0
2.5	2.8	1.8	Cur. Mat.-L.T.D.	4.5	.0	.7	.4	1.4	3.0
27.5	22.1	21.8	Trade Payables	7.5	24.5	16.2	22.5	26.1	23.0
.5	.2	.1	Income Taxes Payable	.0	.0	.0	.0	.3	.1
12.2	11.6	11.7	All Other Current	11.7	13.2	10.0	10.3	12.4	11.9
52.4	47.0	45.7	Total Current	36.7	46.8	40.3	45.9	51.8	45.0
11.6	14.1	11.8	Long-Term Debt	12.3	24.9	4.5	9.6	10.9	11.9
.2	.2	.2	Deferred Taxes	.1	.0	.0	.0	.0	.5
4.5	6.8	8.0	All Other Non-Current	23.0	2.0	11.7	7.8	7.3	5.7
31.3	31.9	34.3	Net Worth	27.7	26.3	43.5	36.7	30.0	36.9
100.0	100.0	100.0	Total Liabilties & Net Worth	100.0	100.0	100.0	100.0	100.0	100.0
			INCOME DATA						
100.0	100.0	100.0	Net Sales	100.0	100.0	100.0	100.0	100.0	100.0
37.2	36.0	37.3	Gross Profit	45.6	44.5	35.6	35.0	31.4	38.8
33.9	32.5	33.2	Operating Expenses	42.4	40.0	30.8	29.8	27.8	35.3
3.4	3.5	4.0	Operating Profit	3.2	4.5	4.8	5.2	3.6	3.6
.7	.5	.3	All Other Expenses (net)	.8	.2	-.1	.4	-.1	.6
2.7	3.0	3.7	Profit Before Taxes	2.3	4.2	4.9	4.8	3.8	3.0
			RATIOS						
2.3	2.6	3.0		14.3	3.9	6.7	3.0	2.8	2.6
1.5	1.5	1.7	Current	1.5	1.4	3.0	1.9	1.6	1.6
1.1	1.1	1.2		.8	.9	1.8	1.2	1.2	1.2
.9	1.1	1.2		7.4	1.5	2.0	1.3	.8	1.2
.4	(169) .6	.6	Quick	.9	.6	.8	.7	.5	.4
.2	.2	.2		.3	.2	.3	.3	.3	.2
0 757.2	0 999.8	0 999.8		0 UND	0 UND	0 UND	0 UND	0 996.2	1 256.4
3 111.5	5 80.6	3 125.2	Sales/Receivables	0 UND	0 UND	0 999.8	3 107.2	3 141.0	5 69.4
15 25.0	14 25.6	12 29.6		17 21.9	10 36.2	8 47.3	14 27.0	10 36.3	16 22.7
18 20.8	18 20.8	27 13.6		0 UND	5 76.7	29 12.7	14 25.7	31 11.6	37 9.8
59 6.2	62 5.9	68 5.4	Cost of Sales/Inventory	41 8.8	46 7.9	65 5.6	53 6.9	54 6.7	81 4.5
107 3.4	111 3.3	114 3.2		104 3.5	140 2.6	146 2.5	104 3.5	107 3.4	126 2.9
16 22.6	11 31.9	9 39.2		0 UND	4 94.9	0 UND	3 116.5	14 26.5	27 13.4
35 10.5	27 13.4	30 12.2	Cost of Sales/Payables	7 50.3	29 12.8	5 79.9	29 12.4	26 14.3	40 9.1
61 6.0	47 7.8	55 6.6		122 3.0	47 7.7	29 12.8	57 6.4	54 6.7	58 6.3
7.1	7.0	6.0		5.0	8.0	4.1	5.9	7.6	6.0
17.2	15.3	12.6	Sales/Working Capital	10.4	34.6	10.2	12.6	13.9	11.9
191.5	126.0	41.5		-26.1	-124.5	16.4	71.9	39.1	26.2
56.6	37.1	54.0			26.0	66.8	46.2	68.7	83.0
(108) 7.7	(130) 6.8	(134) 11.1	EBIT/Interest		(11) 6.8	(13) 8.5	(19) 6.5	(31) 14.5	(51) 12.9
.4	1.1	1.4			-3.0	-5.8	.6	3.1	2.3
26.7	18.3	9.5							5.1
(16) 1.6	(18) 6.0	(20) 3.0	Net Profit + Depr., Dep., Amort./Cur. Mat. L/T/D						(11) 3.7
-.7	2.4	-.9							-.4
.0	.0	.0		.0	.0	.0	.0	.0	.1
.2	.2	.2	Fixed/Worth	.7	.2	.0	.1	.3	.3
1.2	1.7	1.3		NM	NM	.1	.8	1.8	1.0
.9	.9	.8		1.5	.6	.3	1.0	.9	.8
2.2	2.0	1.9	Debt/Worth	2.6	1.8	.9	2.3	2.1	1.7
21.4	11.6	7.3		NM	-78.6	2.3	17.8	9.1	6.0
91.9	71.9	76.7		125.8	77.5	92.8	87.1	84.9	59.9
(106) 33.9	(137) 34.2	(149) 37.5	% Profit Before Taxes/Tangible Net Worth	(11) 20.8	(12) 37.2	(16) 38.6	(25) 45.3	(33) 58.3	(52) 27.9
10.5	7.1	12.9		-10.1	9.8	8.5	29.4	24.6	3.3
29.1	22.3	25.6		24.2	25.3	44.2	30.9	36.0	19.6
10.2	8.6	12.9	% Profit Before Taxes/Total Assets	5.5	16.0	18.4	12.7	17.5	10.8
-.2	1.0	.7		-3.0	.9	4.7	1.7	3.4	-.1
320.6	346.3	276.0		476.0	UND	UND	999.8	271.2	62.1
52.8	59.3	55.1	Sales/Net Fixed Assets	72.6	122.6	233.8	158.9	64.9	25.5
20.1	21.0	19.4		8.0	21.8	78.6	58.8	22.2	15.2
5.2	5.9	5.6		3.5	7.9	9.3	7.6	6.2	4.5
3.6	3.4	3.4	Sales/Total Assets	2.5	3.8	4.7	3.8	3.9	2.9
2.2	2.3	2.2		.9	2.4	2.5	2.8	2.8	2.0
.4	.3	.3					.1	.1	.6
(83) .7	(104) .8	(114) .7	% Depr., Dep., Amort./Sales				(16) .3	(24) .5	(53) 1.0
2.0	1.9	1.3					.5	1.3	1.8
.8	1.4	1.2				1.6	1.3	.7	
(35) 2.5	(53) 2.6	(59) 2.3	% Officers', Directors' Owners' Comp/Sales			(12) 2.7	(15) 2.2	(13) 1.6	
4.3	4.2	5.8				6.6	3.6	2.9	
9732498M	9201986M	9676620M	Net Sales ($)	7751M	27006M	79953M	230360M	614537M	8717013M
3371764M	3863562M	3940138M	Total Assets ($)	13584M	9885M	22338M	65506M	190778M	3638047M

M = $ thousand MM = $ million

See Pages 9 through 22 for Explanation of Ratios and Data

Current Data Sorted by Assets							Comparative Historical Data	
		1	10	1	3	Type of Statement Unqualified	31	31
		5	4	1		Reviewed	13	10
	3	6				Compiled	10	10
1	4					Tax Returns	12	9
1	5	18	17	3	9	Other	58	60
	8 (4/1-9/30/13)		84 (10/1/13-3/31/14)				4/1/09-3/31/10	4/1/10-3/31/11
0-500M	**500M-2MM**	**2-10MM**	**10-50MM**	**50-100MM**	**100-250MM**		ALL	ALL
2	12	30	31	5	12	**NUMBER OF STATEMENTS**	124	120
%	%	%	%	%	%	**ASSETS**	%	%
	8.3	15.2	15.6		7.1	Cash & Equivalents	13.3	16.5
	16.8	10.6	16.4		7.2	Trade Receivables (net)	12.8	11.1
	54.0	46.4	32.0		21.6	Inventory	37.0	38.1
	1.0	3.7	3.6		4.9	All Other Current	4.4	4.3
	80.1	75.8	67.5		40.8	Total Current	67.5	70.1
	8.8	11.3	12.0		12.7	Fixed Assets (net)	16.4	14.5
	2.9	7.1	15.3		38.6	Intangibles (net)	8.4	9.5
	8.2	5.9	5.1		8.0	All Other Non-Current	7.7	5.9
	100.0	100.0	100.0		100.0	Total	100.0	100.0
						LIABILITIES		
	34.0	10.8	3.8		3.0	Notes Payable-Short Term	10.0	10.4
	1.1	1.9	1.8		2.9	Cur. Mat.-L.T.D.	2.0	2.1
	26.6	24.8	20.1		9.3	Trade Payables	21.2	19.6
	.0	.1	.1		.1	Income Taxes Payable	.3	.3
	3.8	15.2	10.9		11.7	All Other Current	10.6	10.4
	65.5	52.8	36.7		27.0	Total Current	44.1	42.8
	10.4	8.5	6.8		24.9	Long-Term Debt	11.8	10.1
	.0	.0	.8		2.1	Deferred Taxes	.8	.6
	8.3	9.2	12.7		6.9	All Other Non-Current	15.0	7.9
	15.8	29.6	43.0		39.1	Net Worth	28.3	38.7
	100.0	100.0	100.0		100.0	Total Liabilities & Net Worth	100.0	100.0
						INCOME DATA		
	100.0	100.0	100.0		100.0	Net Sales	100.0	100.0
	30.4	40.6	42.5		52.5	Gross Profit	43.4	44.1
	33.2	39.5	35.9		45.6	Operating Expenses	39.3	39.1
	-2.8	1.0	6.6		6.9	Operating Profit	4.1	5.0
	.1	.4	1.2		4.4	All Other Expenses (net)	1.0	.9
	-2.9	.7	5.3		2.5	Profit Before Taxes	3.1	4.1
						RATIOS		
	2.7	2.1	3.3		1.9		2.8	2.9
	1.8	1.5	2.0		1.6	Current	1.7	1.6
	.9	1.1	1.1		1.2		1.1	1.1
	1.1	.9	1.4		.9		1.2	1.1
	.3	.5	.9		.3	Quick	.6	.6
	.1	.2	.5		.2		.2	.2
	2 210.5	**3** 114.3	**2** 218.6		**1** 427.7		**2** 171.4	**2** 182.1
	14 26.1	**7** 49.4	**11** 34.1		**6** 60.9	Sales/Receivables	**7** 55.9	**5** 78.3
	30 12.0	**18** 20.8	**35** 10.5		**28** 13.0		**21** 17.4	**20** 18.1
	30 12.0	**39** 9.3	**33** 10.9		**49** 7.5		**45** 8.0	**46** 7.9
	83 4.4	**94** 3.9	**64** 5.7		**94** 3.9	Cost of Sales/Inventory	**82** 4.5	**81** 4.5
	203 1.8	**122** 3.0	**146** 2.5		**182** 2.0		**124** 2.9	**128** 2.8
	11 34.3	**21** 17.1	**20** 17.9		**21** 17.0		**19** 19.4	**20** 18.6
	23 15.9	**35** 10.5	**29** 12.5		**35** 10.5	Cost of Sales/Payables	**35** 10.3	**35** 10.4
	63 5.8	**81** 4.5	**73** 5.0		**73** 5.0		**53** 6.9	**59** 6.2
	5.1	6.1	5.2		7.7		5.8	6.1
	8.9	12.3	9.0		10.1	Sales/Working Capital	11.6	12.1
	-46.2	43.0	32.9		31.7		76.7	75.3
	25.2	9.5	152.4		9.2		20.5	23.8
	(10) 1.2	(26) 3.4	(26) 14.5		(10) 2.3	EBIT/Interest	(102) 5.1	(99) 7.6
	-3.0	-1.3	1.6		-1.2		1.1	2.3
			33.2				20.4	24.4
			(10) 6.0			Net Profit + Depr., Dep., Amort./Cur. Mat. L/T/D	(26) 3.6	(23) 5.4
			.5				.9	1.7
	.1	.1	.1		.8		.1	.1
	.2	.4	.2		-.7	Fixed/Worth	.4	.4
	-2.4	NM	2.8		-.1		1.9	1.7
	.4	1.3	.4		1.8		.6	.5
	15.1	2.7	1.3		-4.3	Debt/Worth	1.7	2.0
	-4.9	NM	7.7		-2.5		7.5	9.0
		37.6	57.5				55.8	66.0
		(23) 11.8	(26) 39.4			% Profit Before Taxes/Tangible Net Worth	(98) 24.6	(97) 29.0
		-15.1	12.7				10.3	7.2
	22.0	11.5	22.5		26.5		17.4	16.1
	.3	5.5	10.2		5.8	% Profit Before Taxes/Total Assets	9.1	10.2
	-21.3	-1.9	2.6		1.3		1.3	2.5
	765.7	107.3	117.7		50.8		69.0	109.5
	51.9	40.2	47.1		19.2	Sales/Net Fixed Assets	28.6	31.7
	20.2	21.1	19.5		10.2		13.3	13.5
	5.5	5.0	3.8		2.2		4.8	4.1
	2.9	3.1	2.6		1.6	Sales/Total Assets	3.1	3.1
	1.9	2.2	1.7		1.0		1.9	2.1
	.1	.4	.4				.5	.4
	(10) .3	(24) .7	(25) .8			% Depr., Dep., Amort./Sales	(90) .8	(88) 1.0
	1.6	1.3	1.1				1.6	1.5
							1.1	2.0
						% Officers', Directors' Owners' Comp/Sales	(21) 3.0	(26) 3.2
							5.6	7.8
3762M	**50588M**	**613165M**	**2166661M**	**1249034M**	**3749151M**	Net Sales ($)	**11333065M**	**11359707M**
782M	**14693M**	**162557M**	**723449M**	**345284M**	**1962064M**	Total Assets ($)	**4602199M**	**3892078M**

M = $ thousand MM = $ million

See Pages 9 through 22 for Explanation of Ratios and Data

Comparative Historical Data / Current Data Sorted by Sales

4/1/11-3/31/12 ALL	4/1/12-3/31/13 ALL	4/1/13-3/31/14 ALL	Type of Statement	0-1MM	1-3MM	3-5MM	5-10MM	10-25MM	25MM & OVER
25	15	15	Unqualified						15
13	16	10	Reviewed				1	2	7
9	6	9	Compiled		1		3	3	2
11	14	5	Tax Returns		4	1			
46	56	53	Other		3	5	2	14	29
					8 (4/1-9/30/13)		84 (10/1/13-3/31/14)		
104	107	92	NUMBER OF STATEMENTS		8	6	6	19	53
%	%	%	ASSETS	%	%	%	%	%	%
12.9	14.6	13.8	Cash & Equivalents	DATA NOT AVAILABLE				11.9	15.3
13.2	11.0	12.3	Trade Receivables (net)					17.9	10.9
40.3	40.7	39.6	Inventory					35.2	35.2
3.5	3.7	3.4	All Other Current					3.9	4.1
69.9	70.0	69.1	Total Current					68.9	65.5
14.7	12.1	11.2	Fixed Assets (net)					14.0	10.8
7.8	11.1	13.8	Intangibles (net)					13.4	16.9
7.6	6.8	5.9	All Other Non-Current					3.7	6.8
100.0	100.0	100.0	Total					100.0	100.0
			LIABILITIES						
10.7	8.9	10.3	Notes Payable-Short Term					9.4	4.9
1.9	1.8	1.8	Cur. Mat.-L.T.D.					3.2	1.6
23.3	23.0	21.7	Trade Payables					23.5	19.6
.2	.1	.1	Income Taxes Payable					.0	.1
11.5	10.3	11.3	All Other Current					14.6	11.9
47.6	44.1	45.2	Total Current					50.8	38.2
11.0	10.3	9.9	Long-Term Debt					11.4	9.0
.5	.4	.5	Deferred Taxes					.6	.7
11.4	14.5	9.3	All Other Non-Current					15.5	7.4
29.5	30.7	35.1	Net Worth					21.7	44.6
100.0	100.0	100.0	Total Liabilties & Net Worth					100.0	100.0
			INCOME DATA						
100.0	100.0	100.0	Net Sales					100.0	100.0
42.9	40.1	40.7	Gross Profit					41.9	42.5
38.6	36.0	37.5	Operating Expenses					38.4	37.3
4.3	4.1	3.2	Operating Profit					3.6	5.2
.9	.9	1.2	All Other Expenses (net)					1.5	1.4
3.4	3.2	2.0	Profit Before Taxes					2.1	3.8
			RATIOS						
3.0	3.2	2.9						2.1	3.0
1.6	1.6	1.7	Current					1.4	1.7
1.0	1.1	1.1						1.0	1.2
1.1	1.1	1.0						1.0	1.0
(103) .5	.5	.6	Quick					.7	.7
.1	.2	.2						.2	.3
1 271.1	1 362.3	2 217.2						10 38.1	2 235.2
5 77.8	5 68.4	6 59.4	Sales/Receivables					18 20.8	5 75.4
23 15.9	18 20.2	27 13.5						31 11.6	25 14.8
40 9.1	39 9.3	39 9.4						17 21.2	44 8.3
78 4.7	81 4.5	79 4.6	Cost of Sales/Inventory					60 6.1	78 4.7
130 2.8	122 3.0	140 2.6						118 3.1	118 3.1
21 17.7	18 20.1	20 17.9						21 17.1	20 17.9
35 10.4	30 12.3	33 11.1	Cost of Sales/Payables					59 6.2	28 13.1
58 6.3	63 5.8	73 5.0						87 4.2	69 5.3
6.5	6.2	6.0						6.4	5.6
12.9	12.9	9.5	Sales/Working Capital					19.3	10.3
-320.0	114.9	40.3						150.0	35.7
28.8	40.7	17.1						9.3	40.8
(88) 5.6	(83) 7.5	(75) 4.1	EBIT/Interest					(17) 1.9	(41) 9.1
.1	.6	1.1						.8	2.1
24.4	34.1	22.6							
(15) 7.5	(12) 9.8	(13) 2.5	Net Profit + Depr., Dep., Amort./Cur. Mat. L/T/D						
.5	-.4	.9							
.1	.1	.1						.1	.1
.3	.3	.3	Fixed/Worth					.4	.5
3.2	-31.6	-4.5						-.5	7.1
.6	.7	.7						.9	.5
2.4	2.1	2.7	Debt/Worth					3.0	1.6
15.8	-54.9	-10.1						-3.4	20.4
56.3	68.8	50.8						39.3	53.8
(82) 26.1	(79) 35.1	(67) 16.5	% Profit Before Taxes/Tangible Net Worth					(12) 16.7	(41) 19.1
5.7	7.8	3.5						-1.1	5.0
21.1	20.1	15.3						9.6	23.3
10.2	8.3	5.8	% Profit Before Taxes/Total Assets					4.1	7.7
-1.2	-1.5	-1.0						-1.4	1.8
99.4	133.7	112.4						97.9	114.6
39.0	44.0	40.1	Sales/Net Fixed Assets					22.7	38.2
14.5	20.8	19.5						10.7	19.5
4.9	4.8	4.3						4.4	4.4
3.2	3.2	2.7	Sales/Total Assets					2.7	2.8
2.0	2.0	1.8						1.8	1.9
.4	.3	.4						.3	.4
(82) .9	(80) .6	(71) .8	% Depr., Dep., Amort./Sales					(18) .8	(39) .8
1.6	1.5	1.5						2.8	1.1
1.4	1.6	1.4							
(27) 2.5	(23) 3.0	(17) 2.9	% Officers', Directors' Owners' Comp/Sales						
5.6	5.8	9.3							
9170838M	8596306M	7832361M	Net Sales ($)		16606M	25489M	44028M	346928M	7399310M
3263416M	2982597M	3208829M	Total Assets ($)		7538M	12720M	14889M	141900M	3031782M

M = $ thousand MM = $ million

See Pages 9 through 22 for Explanation of Ratios and Data

Current Data Sorted by Assets							Comparative Historical Data	
						Type of Statement		
1			2	1		Unqualified	6	8
		5	3			Reviewed	14	17
	3	6	2			Compiled	15	17
7	11	2	1			Tax Returns	17	20
3	7	10	5	2	1	Other	39	32
9 (4/1-9/30/13)		63 (10/1/13-3/31/14)					4/1/09-3/31/10	4/1/10-3/31/11
0-500M	500M-2MM	2-10MM	10-50MM	50-100MM	100-250MM		ALL	ALL
11	21	23	13	3	1	NUMBER OF STATEMENTS	91	94
%	%	%	%	%	%	**ASSETS**	%	%
19.0	17.0	10.8	7.9			Cash & Equivalents	12.8	15.0
2.2	7.2	7.5	9.7			Trade Receivables (net)	9.0	7.6
29.3	15.4	23.9	13.1			Inventory	14.9	15.6
.3	.8	1.6	1.9			All Other Current	1.9	3.8
50.9	40.5	43.7	32.7			Total Current	38.6	41.9
30.5	40.5	41.8	45.7			Fixed Assets (net)	45.3	42.1
7.7	10.4	6.4	15.3			Intangibles (net)	10.1	8.2
11.0	8.6	8.1	6.3			All Other Non-Current	6.0	7.7
100.0	100.0	100.0	100.0			Total	100.0	100.0
						LIABILITIES		
12.3	8.2	3.0	4.2			Notes Payable-Short Term	7.2	8.7
12.6	6.4	7.0	8.0			Cur. Mat.-L.T.D.	8.5	6.3
14.2	15.1	13.2	15.5			Trade Payables	11.5	15.4
.0	.0	.0	.0			Income Taxes Payable	.1	.1
12.9	10.3	7.8	9.2			All Other Current	7.4	9.5
52.0	40.0	30.9	36.8			Total Current	34.7	40.0
52.2	44.3	29.2	23.7			Long-Term Debt	29.7	27.1
.0	.0	1.1	.7			Deferred Taxes	.3	.3
7.2	3.4	24.2	8.9			All Other Non-Current	10.6	9.0
-11.3	12.3	14.6	29.9			Net Worth	24.7	23.6
100.0	100.0	100.0	100.0			Total Liabilties & Net Worth	100.0	100.0
						INCOME DATA		
100.0	100.0	100.0	100.0			Net Sales	100.0	100.0
46.9	56.7	41.9	45.7			Gross Profit	45.4	44.8
49.2	50.4	41.8	43.0			Operating Expenses	41.4	41.2
-2.3	6.3	.1	2.7			Operating Profit	4.0	3.6
.7	-.2	.9	1.0			All Other Expenses (net)	.8	.2
-3.0	6.5	-.8	1.7			Profit Before Taxes	3.2	3.4
						RATIOS		
2.7	2.0	2.2	1.4				1.8	2.0
1.0	1.0	1.4	.8			Current	1.1	1.1
.4	.6	.9	.5				.6	.7
1.0	1.1	.8	1.0				1.2	1.1
.4	.5	.6	.4			Quick	(90) .5	.5
.1	.3	.4	.2				.2	.3
0 UND	1 282.7	4 88.8	5 77.8				0 999.8	0 867.5
0 UND	8 46.5	9 41.2	10 36.4			Sales/Receivables	3 106.3	4 86.5
1 274.7	12 31.3	14 26.5	32 11.5				12 30.0	13 28.5
9 39.5	18 19.9	24 15.0	27 13.3				14 25.9	15 23.9
16 22.2	29 12.6	46 7.9	35 10.3			Cost of Sales/Inventory	32 11.3	34 10.8
57 6.4	42 8.7	64 5.7	49 7.5				47 7.8	49 7.5
4 89.1	13 28.5	13 27.1	31 11.7				7 53.7	10 37.4
18 20.1	29 12.4	29 12.7	45 8.2			Cost of Sales/Payables	17 21.3	27 13.7
33 11.1	55 6.6	43 8.5	70 5.2				37 9.9	42 8.6
23.4	22.1	11.1	10.4				16.5	18.4
UND	999.8	42.7	-34.4			Sales/Working Capital	133.0	81.5
-7.8	-17.6	-52.3	-13.2				-20.7	-25.1
	8.0	3.3	12.7				6.1	7.3
	(19) 3.2	(21) 2.2	6.9			EBIT/Interest	(84) 2.3	(83) 2.5
	1.2	.4	.8				.8	.9
							2.7	5.6
						Net Profit + Depr., Dep., Amort./Cur. Mat. L/T/D	(13) 2.1	(16) 2.9
							1.4	1.2
1.1	.7	.6	1.0				1.0	.7
-2.5	2.4	2.1	3.4			Fixed/Worth	2.8	1.9
-.4	-1.2	22.7	-10.3				-13.3	-8.9
2.1	.7	2.1	1.2				1.3	.7
-5.4	6.8	2.6	4.1			Debt/Worth	4.4	3.4
-2.1	-2.8	-11.6	-15.3				-24.2	-19.1
	115.2	28.9					71.5	49.8
	(13) 82.5	(17) 11.3				% Profit Before Taxes/Tangible Net Worth	(66) 19.0	(69) 19.7
	6.4	4.2					.9	1.4
14.8	28.9	6.9	11.0				11.9	11.9
7.0	8.1	3.0	7.2			% Profit Before Taxes/Total Assets	3.6	5.4
-16.0	1.2	-4.1	1.1				-.8	-.1
151.0	14.2	10.8	8.8				12.4	15.7
24.2	9.6	7.1	4.6			Sales/Net Fixed Assets	6.4	7.3
13.2	4.0	5.0	3.3				3.6	4.1
9.8	5.0	3.6	3.1				4.1	4.0
5.6	3.7	2.6	2.1			Sales/Total Assets	2.8	2.9
1.9	1.8	1.5	1.6				1.7	2.0
	2.4	2.5	2.4				3.0	2.3
	(17) 5.1	(21) 4.3	4.1			% Depr., Dep., Amort./Sales	(68) 5.0	(76) 4.1
	7.6	6.6	5.7				6.6	6.3
	1.0	1.7					1.5	.9
	(12) 2.9	(10) 2.1				% Officers', Directors' Owners' Comp/Sales	(31) 3.2	(30) 3.0
	8.1	3.3					5.8	4.6
18661M	73579M	251886M	664639M	359766M	124995M	Net Sales ($)	1389197M	1573453M
2851M	21132M	95160M	290638M	194622M	118437M	Total Assets ($)	493798M	668006M

M = $ thousand MM = $ million

See Pages 9 through 22 for Explanation of Ratios and Data

Comparative Historical Data				Current Data Sorted by Sales					
			Type of Statement						
5	4	4	Unqualified	1					3
13	10	8	Reviewed				1	4	3
15	13	11	Compiled		2	1	4	2	2
25	22	21	Tax Returns	4	8	5	3		1
30	26	28	Other	2	5	4	6	2	9
4/1/11-3/31/12	**4/1/12-3/31/13**	**4/1/13-3/31/14**		**9 (4/1-9/30/13)**			**63 (10/1/13-3/31/14)**		
ALL	**ALL**	**ALL**		**0-1MM**	**1-3MM**	**3-5MM**	**5-10MM**	**10-25MM**	**25MM & OVER**
88	75	72	**NUMBER OF STATEMENTS**	7	15	10	14	8	18
%	%	%	**ASSETS**	%	%	%	%	%	%
14.5	12.2	13.1	Cash & Equivalents		14.9	21.3	10.7		7.7
6.6	8.1	6.8	Trade Receivables (net)		7.7	6.6	7.0		8.6
17.3	18.6	19.6	Inventory		18.1	23.4	23.3		15.4
3.9	4.1	1.2	All Other Current		1.0	.3	2.4		1.8
42.3	43.0	40.7	Total Current		41.7	51.7	43.4		33.5
39.0	40.7	40.2	Fixed Assets (net)		38.8	40.5	38.8		42.4
10.7	9.8	10.6	Intangibles (net)		12.7	3.4	8.6		16.8
8.0	6.5	8.5	All Other Non-Current		6.9	4.4	9.2		7.3
100.0	100.0	100.0	Total		100.0	100.0	100.0		100.0
			LIABILITIES						
7.4	7.5	6.0	Notes Payable-Short Term		6.3	8.2	2.3		3.4
8.1	6.2	7.7	Cur. Mat.-L.T.D.		4.2	7.3	7.0		7.1
16.5	13.7	14.0	Trade Payables		14.9	17.3	12.9		16.3
.0	.1	.0	Income Taxes Payable		.0	.1	.0		.0
9.5	11.2	9.7	All Other Current		10.9	20.8	7.7		9.7
41.5	38.6	37.4	Total Current		36.3	53.5	29.9		36.6
37.4	28.2	36.8	Long-Term Debt		41.3	31.7	40.9		24.2
.3	.7	.6	Deferred Taxes		.0	.0	.3		1.0
9.1	12.0	12.6	All Other Non-Current		2.3	37.1	9.5		12.4
11.7	20.5	12.6	Net Worth		20.1	-22.4	19.3		25.7
100.0	100.0	100.0	Total Liabilties & Net Worth		100.0	100.0	100.0		100.0
			INCOME DATA						
100.0	100.0	100.0	Net Sales		100.0	100.0	100.0		100.0
48.5	48.0	46.8	Gross Profit		56.6	47.0	42.2		39.7
45.0	44.1	44.7	Operating Expenses		54.7	45.1	41.6		37.0
3.5	3.9	2.2	Operating Profit		1.9	1.9	.5		2.7
.8	.7	.7	All Other Expenses (net)		-.3	1.8	-.2		1.3
2.7	3.2	1.5	Profit Before Taxes		2.1	.2	.7		1.4
			RATIOS						
2.0	1.8	2.0			2.6	2.1	2.1		1.1
1.1	1.1	1.0	Current		1.1	.8	1.7		1.0
.7	.7	.7			.6	.5	.9		.6
1.0	1.0	.9			2.3	.7	.9		.5
.5	.4	.5	Quick		.6	.5	.7		.4
.3	.3	.3			.4	.1	.4		.3
1 653.9	**1** 518.7	**1** 262.8			**0** UND	**2** 179.4	**3** 117.3		**5** 76.1
4 84.7	**6** 59.6	**7** 50.9	Sales/Receivables		**8** 47.4	**4** 85.4	**10** 37.1		**7** 49.3
12 29.2	**13** 28.1	**13** 27.3			**14** 26.7	**8** 46.1	**14** 26.5		**15** 23.6
22 16.6	**23** 15.6	**20** 18.6			**16** 23.2	**17** 21.0	**21** 17.1		**24** 15.3
35 10.5	**36** 10.1	**33** 11.1	Cost of Sales/Inventory		**31** 11.6	**26** 13.8	**33** 11.1		**35** 10.3
55 6.6	**52** 7.0	**49** 7.4			**58** 6.3	**44** 8.3	**61** 6.0		**46** 7.9
14 25.4	**11** 33.7	**13** 27.1			**7** 49.4	**6** 64.9	**9** 41.5		**28** 13.0
26 13.9	**26** 13.9	**29** 12.5	Cost of Sales/Payables		**26** 14.0	**19** 19.7	**30** 12.3		**42** 8.6
49 7.5	**39** 9.4	**45** 8.2			**66** 5.5	**33** 11.1	**44** 8.3		**54** 6.8
12.4	13.3	17.3			7.6	23.5	14.1		66.4
185.0	140.8	611.8	Sales/Working Capital		356.8	-514.5	19.1		-788.7
-21.0	-24.5	-24.5			-24.5	-12.7	-58.9		-18.4
9.3	7.2	6.9			6.3		8.6		9.7
(77) 2.0	(69) 2.8	(65) 2.5	EBIT/Interest		(14) 2.4		(11) 2.3		4.6
.2	.5	.9			-.6		1.9		1.6
3.9		3.4							
(10) 2.5		(15) 2.3	Net Profit + Depr., Dep., Amort./Cur. Mat. L/T/D						
.9		1.8							
.9	1.0	.8			.7	.5	.8		1.1
2.9	2.8	3.4	Fixed/Worth		2.4	2.4	2.9		8.2
-3.2	-1.4	-2.9			-.7	-1.3	-4.2		-4.4
1.1	1.1	1.3			.4	2.2	.6		1.3
4.5	3.9	8.2	Debt/Worth		22.3	10.9	5.4		14.9
-9.4	-5.5	-6.4			-3.1	-2.6	-9.5		-11.2
61.0	34.7	72.6							49.0
(62) 10.9	(46) 16.9	(44) 23.5	% Profit Before Taxes/Tangible Net Worth						(10) 29.7
-11.2	5.1	7.9							14.7
14.1	13.4	10.1			17.1	15.9	13.9		9.3
3.2	4.5	5.0	% Profit Before Taxes/Total Assets		2.0	1.1	5.3		6.1
-2.2	-1.5	-1.0			-5.6	-16.4	1.1		2.5
15.5	17.6	15.0			17.9	121.1	12.4		8.7
7.2	8.5	7.1	Sales/Net Fixed Assets		9.6	12.7	10.4		6.0
4.0	3.9	4.4			3.1	5.5	5.5		4.0
4.2	4.4	4.3			5.1	6.4	4.4		3.3
2.8	3.3	2.7	Sales/Total Assets		3.3	4.3	3.1		2.0
1.8	1.8	1.7			1.4	1.7	2.1		1.7
2.7	2.1	2.1			2.0		1.6		2.6
(72) 4.1	(59) 3.4	(63) 4.1	% Depr., Dep., Amort./Sales		(14) 6.4		(12) 3.1		(17) 4.3
7.4	5.4	6.3			8.7		5.0		5.8
1.1	1.0	1.6							
(40) 2.6	(34) 2.7	(29) 2.4	% Officers', Directors' Owners' Comp/Sales						
4.3	8.2	7.0							
1825455M	**1307231M**	**1493526M**	Net Sales ($)	**3363M**	**33486M**	**39178M**	**106055M**	**110553M**	**1200891M**
754046M	**463334M**	**722840M**	Total Assets ($)	**1500M**	**14565M**	**13208M**	**50280M**	**42105M**	**601182M**

M = $ thousand MM = $ million

See Pages 9 through 22 for Explanation of Ratios and Data

Current Data Sorted by Assets							Comparative Historical Data	
						Type of Statement		
		5	15	6	2	Unqualified	42	42
	5	45	17	1		Reviewed	120	100
3	12	27	3			Compiled	76	81
13	32	8	3			Tax Returns	72	57
2	19	20	14	1	6	Other	93	86
105 (4/1-9/30/13)			154 (10/1/13-3/31/14)				4/1/09-3/31/10	4/1/10-3/31/11
0-500M	500M-2MM	2-10MM	10-50MM	50-100MM	100-250MM		ALL	ALL
18	68	105	52	8	8	**NUMBER OF STATEMENTS**	403	366
%	%	%	%	%	%	**ASSETS**	%	%
25.8	16.3	14.3	10.8			Cash & Equivalents	15.9	13.4
15.8	34.2	35.5	26.2			Trade Receivables (net)	24.1	28.0
15.1	12.4	11.8	8.5			Inventory	11.2	12.2
1.1	2.1	2.3	3.7			All Other Current	3.7	2.9
57.9	65.1	63.9	49.1			Total Current	54.9	56.4
30.1	22.3	23.2	29.5			Fixed Assets (net)	29.2	28.5
2.2	3.9	6.5	13.1			Intangibles (net)	7.4	6.5
10.0	8.6	6.5	8.3			All Other Non-Current	8.4	8.5
100.0	100.0	100.0	100.0			Total	100.0	100.0
						LIABILITIES		
11.0	10.0	9.1	8.7			Notes Payable-Short Term	9.1	10.5
7.3	5.3	2.4	3.0			Cur. Mat.-L.T.D.	4.9	3.5
14.5	19.3	18.8	15.4			Trade Payables	16.8	17.8
.0	.2	.4	.1			Income Taxes Payable	.2	.2
16.8	19.0	17.7	11.7			All Other Current	17.3	14.4
49.6	53.8	48.4	38.9			Total Current	48.3	46.4
21.8	19.3	7.9	15.7			Long-Term Debt	17.8	17.0
.0	.1	.8	1.6			Deferred Taxes	.7	.8
6.5	7.5	2.5	4.3			All Other Non-Current	5.7	6.0
22.1	19.4	40.4	39.5			Net Worth	27.5	29.9
100.0	100.0	100.0	100.0			Total Liabilties & Net Worth	100.0	100.0
						INCOME DATA		
100.0	100.0	100.0	100.0			Net Sales	100.0	100.0
24.0	21.6	18.3	20.8			Gross Profit	23.3	20.8
18.6	19.2	15.7	17.5			Operating Expenses	20.5	18.8
5.4	2.4	2.6	3.3			Operating Profit	2.8	2.0
.7	-.5	.2	.1			All Other Expenses (net)	.2	.3
4.7	2.9	2.5	3.2			Profit Before Taxes	2.6	1.7
						RATIOS		
3.5	2.0	2.0	1.8				1.8	1.9
1.0	1.2	1.3	1.2			Current	1.2	1.2
.7	.8	1.0	.9				.8	.9
2.0	1.8	1.6	1.3				1.4	1.4
.9	.9	1.1	.9			Quick	.9	.8
.5	.5	.6	.5				.5	.6
0 UND	**14** 25.5	**13** 27.2	**16** 23.2				**9** 40.1	**12** 29.9
0 UND	**24** 15.5	**24** 15.2	**21** 17.0			Sales/Receivables	**19** 19.0	**22** 16.8
15 24.9	**38** 9.7	**34** 10.6	**31** 11.6				**31** 11.8	**35** 10.5
0 UND	**3** 128.5	**3** 143.0	**4** 103.8				**5** 76.6	**5** 71.4
4 100.2	**11** 33.7	**9** 39.6	**11** 34.2			Cost of Sales/Inventory	**11** 34.5	**11** 34.3
20 18.6	**17** 21.8	**18** 20.5	**20** 18.4				**22** 16.9	**22** 16.9
0 UND	**6** 64.4	**9** 42.3	**10** 36.9				**9** 42.5	**9** 38.7
1 476.0	**13** 28.0	**14** 26.5	**12** 29.8			Cost of Sales/Payables	**15** 24.2	**15** 23.9
16 22.3	**31** 11.8	**22** 16.5	**19** 19.0				**26** 13.8	**26** 14.1
22.6	11.5	13.0	18.0				15.5	13.6
NM	49.8	33.3	51.8			Sales/Working Capital	51.9	62.9
-37.9	-33.6	NM	-114.1				-53.3	-63.1
14.3	7.8	17.4	12.7				13.0	10.2
(14) 7.3	(59) 3.7	(90) 6.1	(50) 6.9			EBIT/Interest	(365) 3.9	(331) 2.9
1.6	1.5	2.6	2.7				1.5	1.2
		5.9	4.8				8.7	4.6
		(23) 2.9	(24) 2.6			Net Profit + Depr., Dep., Amort./Cur. Mat. L/T/D	(109) 3.3	(97) 2.2
		1.3	1.9				1.4	1.3
.0	.2	.2	.5				.4	.4
.6	2.4	.6	1.0			Fixed/Worth	1.2	1.1
NM	-1.9	1.7	7.6				6.2	4.5
.9	.9	.7	1.0				1.1	1.0
8.6	12.1	1.6	1.9			Debt/Worth	2.6	2.8
-22.3	-7.9	5.4	14.1				35.9	12.1
126.1	57.9	37.6	46.7				55.0	37.8
(13) 41.5	(39) 16.4	(93) 19.0	(44) 22.9			% Profit Before Taxes/Tangible Net Worth	(311) 22.3	(295) 17.1
-4.2	5.2	5.5	8.9				7.9	3.4
34.6	11.6	12.8	10.8				14.9	10.3
16.0	5.0	5.7	6.6			% Profit Before Taxes/Total Assets	6.1	4.4
.8	1.1	2.3	3.3				1.5	.5
UND	76.7	70.8	46.8				43.5	45.0
67.3	28.3	25.4	14.7			Sales/Net Fixed Assets	17.6	18.1
15.0	14.2	12.3	6.3				9.2	8.7
15.3	6.4	7.2	6.5				6.0	6.4
8.3	4.8	4.8	3.6			Sales/Total Assets	3.9	4.0
5.0	3.0	3.2	2.4				2.7	2.7
.9	.6	.4	.5				.8	.6
(11) 1.5	(49) 1.0	(93) 1.1	(48) 1.3			% Depr., Dep., Amort./Sales	(336) 1.4	(328) 1.3
4.3	1.7	2.1	2.9				2.7	2.4
	1.1	.6	.2				1.2	.9
	(40) 2.2	(56) 1.5	(14) .3			% Officers', Directors' Owners' Comp/Sales	(191) 2.2	(180) 1.8
	4.7	3.3	1.2				4.2	3.8
46364M	**446454M**	**2941249M**	**4887142M**	**2761712M**	**6003528M**	Net Sales ($)	**23181403M**	**25657530M**
5325M	**83659M**	**522998M**	**1146635M**	**532184M**	**1186665M**	Total Assets ($)	**5108904M**	**5701182M**

M = $ thousand MM = $ million

See Pages 9 through 22 for Explanation of Ratios and Data

Comparative Historical Data				Current Data Sorted by Sales					
			Type of Statement						
44	34	28	Unqualified		1		2	3	22
116	85	68	Reviewed			3	8	25	32
67	73	45	Compiled	1	3	3	7	11	20
75	67	56	Tax Returns	1	18	8	15	7	7
66	56	62	Other	3	6	5	8	11	29
4/1/11-3/31/12	**4/1/12-3/31/13**	**4/1/13-3/31/14**		**105 (4/1-9/30/13)**			**154 (10/1/13-3/31/14)**		
ALL	**ALL**	**ALL**		**0-1MM**	**1-3MM**	**3-5MM**	**5-10MM**	**10-25MM**	**25MM & OVER**
368	315	259	**NUMBER OF STATEMENTS**	5	28	19	40	57	110
%	%	%	**ASSETS**	%	%	%	%	%	%
13.2	14.7	14.6	Cash & Equivalents		17.5	23.0	15.7	14.4	12.7
30.6	28.6	31.6	Trade Receivables (net)		22.3	22.3	31.9	30.4	37.3
12.2	12.0	11.4	Inventory		14.4	13.4	12.8	12.4	9.5
3.6	3.3	2.4	All Other Current		3.7	1.3	2.2	2.2	2.6
59.6	58.6	60.0	Total Current		58.0	60.0	62.7	59.4	62.1
26.0	27.5	25.5	Fixed Assets (net)		31.0	19.6	24.0	24.7	23.4
6.9	5.9	6.9	Intangibles (net)		1.6	9.9	5.5	8.0	7.9
7.4	8.1	7.6	All Other Non-Current		9.5	10.4	7.8	7.8	6.5
100.0	100.0	100.0	Total		100.0	100.0	100.0	100.0	100.0
			LIABILITIES						
11.9	11.8	9.3	Notes Payable-Short Term		10.4	7.7	9.5	7.0	10.3
3.3	3.4	3.7	Cur. Mat.-L.T.D.		5.9	5.0	6.3	2.7	2.7
19.9	17.7	17.5	Trade Payables		14.5	15.0	18.7	15.9	19.8
.3	.0	.2	Income Taxes Payable		.4	.0	.5	.3	.1
13.5	15.0	16.5	All Other Current		6.1	32.8	19.5	19.3	13.3
48.8	47.9	47.3	Total Current		37.3	60.5	54.6	45.3	46.2
15.4	16.1	14.5	Long-Term Debt		20.6	21.2	12.3	11.7	11.8
.6	.6	.8	Deferred Taxes		.0	.0	1.2	.9	.9
7.3	8.5	4.6	All Other Non-Current		9.6	3.4	7.5	1.8	4.2
27.9	26.9	32.9	Net Worth		32.4	14.9	24.4	40.3	36.9
100.0	100.0	100.0	Total Liabilties & Net Worth		100.0	100.0	100.0	100.0	100.0
			INCOME DATA						
100.0	100.0	100.0	Net Sales		100.0	100.0	100.0	100.0	100.0
17.5	18.9	20.1	Gross Profit		29.4	20.8	21.0	22.9	13.9
16.0	17.1	17.2	Operating Expenses		26.8	18.7	17.1	18.9	12.4
1.5	1.7	2.9	Operating Profit		2.6	2.1	3.9	4.0	1.5
.0	.0	.0	All Other Expenses (net)		-.7	-.4	.1	.1	-.1
1.4	1.7	2.9	Profit Before Taxes		3.3	2.5	3.7	3.9	1.7
			RATIOS						
1.9	2.1	2.0			4.7	2.0	2.0	2.0	1.9
1.3	1.2	1.3	Current		1.8	.9	1.0	1.4	1.3
.9	.9	.9			.8	.7	.8	.9	1.0
1.4	1.5	1.5			3.3	1.2	1.4	1.5	1.6
.9	.9	1.0	Quick		1.1	.6	.8	.9	1.1
.6	.6	.6			.5	.4	.6	.6	.7
12 29.6	**10** 36.7	**13** 28.8			**7** 52.0	**6** 63.6	**16** 22.4	**13** 27.2	**13** 28.4
21 17.4	**20** 18.6	**23** 16.2	Sales/Receivables		**29** 12.6	**19** 19.7	**26** 14.2	**23** 16.0	**22** 16.5
31 11.7	**30** 12.3	**34** 10.6			**40** 9.2	**29** 12.5	**36** 10.0	**36** 10.2	**33** 11.2
3 108.1	**3** 106.3	**3** 136.4			**3** 106.0	**2** 164.2	**4** 91.2	**6** 65.1	**2** 182.4
9 41.5	**9** 40.8	**10** 38.1	Cost of Sales/Inventory		**14** 25.9	**14** 27.0	**12** 29.6	**11** 34.0	**6** 64.0
19 19.7	**18** 20.3	**19** 19.5			**26** 13.8	**38** 9.6	**21** 17.6	**21** 17.5	**15** 24.6
9 41.5	**7** 49.2	**7** 50.3			**1** 548.5	**1** 412.6	**7** 54.7	**9** 42.8	**9** 42.1
14 27.0	**11** 31.8	**12** 30.6	Cost of Sales/Payables		**15** 23.8	**12** 31.6	**21** 17.7	**14** 25.4	**12** 31.0
22 16.6	**19** 18.9	**23** 16.0			**30** 12.1	**28** 13.0	**31** 11.7	**26** 14.2	**16** 22.2
16.3	16.1	14.3			6.8	22.7	15.5	11.4	16.6
50.2	49.5	42.0	Sales/Working Capital		15.9	-213.5	236.0	24.6	42.3
-94.4	-76.5	-85.3			-60.3	-22.1	-28.2	-79.9	999.8
9.3	10.9	12.5			13.3	11.2	9.8	19.5	11.4
(333) 3.5	(286) 3.1	(229) 5.7	EBIT/Interest		(24) 6.3	(17) 2.5	(32) 5.2	(50) 6.7	(102) 5.5
1.3	1.0	2.4			2.2	1.6	1.9	2.9	2.6
5.8	5.4	5.3						4.0	5.6
(86) 2.7	(65) 1.7	(61) 2.7	Net Profit + Depr., Dep., Amort./Cur. Mat. L/T/D					(15) 2.9	(39) 2.7
1.7	1.2	1.6						1.3	1.8
.3	.3	.3			.1	.3	.3	.3	.3
.9	1.1	.9	Fixed/Worth		.8	-36.7	1.1	.7	.8
5.0	5.4	9.1			-14.6	-.7	-2.6	4.2	1.8
1.1	1.0	.9			.6	1.0	.8	.7	.9
2.6	2.6	2.4	Debt/Worth		1.9	-83.5	5.4	2.0	1.8
18.5	20.0	22.2			-41.6	-6.5	-10.4	13.1	7.7
33.1	34.5	43.8			60.6		50.6	57.4	36.2
(290) 15.7	(254) 14.1	(202) 19.3	% Profit Before Taxes/Tangible Net Worth		(20) 7.4		(25) 24.7	(48) 22.8	(97) 19.0
4.1	1.7	7.2			-1.5		13.8	10.5	6.1
9.5	10.0	12.2			16.6	18.8	18.0	13.2	10.3
4.2	4.0	5.9	% Profit Before Taxes/Total Assets		5.4	4.0	6.5	7.3	5.1
.8	.0	2.2			1.0	1.8	1.0	2.7	2.3
70.5	70.2	71.0			40.8	60.3	95.0	44.4	109.5
21.7	23.5	24.8	Sales/Net Fixed Assets		18.8	22.3	27.5	19.5	32.8
10.4	10.3	10.8			4.2	14.0	9.2	11.2	13.9
7.5	7.7	7.2			6.4	6.4	5.6	6.1	8.5
4.7	4.9	4.6	Sales/Total Assets		3.2	4.3	4.5	4.2	5.5
3.1	2.8	2.8			1.8	2.9	2.8	2.7	3.6
.5	.4	.5			1.0	.6	.7	.9	.3
(318) 1.0	(264) 1.0	(214) 1.1	% Depr., Dep., Amort./Sales		(22) 1.7	(14) 1.2	(30) 1.0	(48) 1.4	(96) .8
2.0	2.2	2.2			4.0	1.8	2.5	2.2	1.6
.9	.6	.6			3.1		1.0	.8	.3
(185) 1.7	(155) 1.6	(120) 1.5	% Officers', Directors' Owners' Comp/Sales		(17) 5.0		(21) 1.4	(33) 1.7	(43) .5
3.4	3.4	3.7			7.1		4.6	3.0	2.0
32031010M	27821024M	17086449M	Net Sales ($)	3112M	62106M	79101M	296116M	929756M	15716258M
5559108M	4406025M	3477466M	Total Assets ($)	5182M	25170M	19228M	101849M	285607M	3040430M

M = $ thousand MM = $ million

See Pages 9 through 22 for Explanation of Ratios and Data

Current Data Sorted by Assets							Comparative Historical Data	
1	1	2	5	4	8	**Type of Statement** Unqualified	23	28
	3	5	1	3		Reviewed	23	10
5	12	16	1	1		Compiled	23	32
35	48	23	3		2	Tax Returns	92	94
26	32	40	14	6	8	Other	92	105
37 (4/1-9/30/13)		268 (10/1/13-3/31/14)					4/1/09-3/31/10	4/1/10-3/31/11
0-500M	**500M-2MM**	**2-10MM**	**10-50MM**	**50-100MM**	**100-250MM**		ALL	ALL
67	96	86	24	14	18	**NUMBER OF STATEMENTS**	253	269
%	%	%	%	%	%	**ASSETS**	%	%
23.4	17.7	17.7	15.1	27.0	18.9	Cash & Equivalents	15.0	16.8
17.5	20.2	24.9	21.0	8.8	9.6	Trade Receivables (net)	21.6	19.8
23.5	32.3	28.5	27.4	25.8	24.1	Inventory	27.9	28.8
3.6	1.6	3.2	4.9	4.1	4.0	All Other Current	3.2	3.1
68.0	71.8	74.3	68.3	65.7	56.6	Total Current	67.7	68.5
19.8	16.3	12.2	13.3	19.1	21.2	Fixed Assets (net)	17.8	15.7
3.6	3.7	4.2	8.3	9.9	14.9	Intangibles (net)	6.9	7.1
8.7	8.2	9.3	10.1	5.3	7.3	All Other Non-Current	7.6	8.8
100.0	100.0	100.0	100.0	100.0	100.0	Total	100.0	100.0
						LIABILITIES		
24.8	14.9	9.5	10.9	3.5	5.9	Notes Payable-Short Term	14.2	12.3
3.6	2.9	2.8	1.5	2.9	3.0	Cur. Mat.-L.T.D.	3.4	3.9
18.2	19.7	19.0	11.1	13.0	12.2	Trade Payables	17.2	20.2
.1	.1	.0	.1	.3	.0	Income Taxes Payable	.2	.3
10.5	10.0	16.0	13.8	15.5	14.6	All Other Current	16.0	21.3
57.2	47.6	47.2	37.4	35.2	35.8	Total Current	51.0	58.0
18.1	17.3	9.9	9.5	18.1	18.2	Long-Term Debt	19.2	14.3
.0	.0	.2	1.1	.0	.0	Deferred Taxes	.1	.3
15.7	8.7	4.4	5.1	3.8	13.4	All Other Non-Current	6.1	9.0
9.0	26.4	38.3	46.9	42.8	32.6	Net Worth	23.6	18.4
100.0	100.0	100.0	100.0	100.0	100.0	Total Liabilties & Net Worth	100.0	100.0
						INCOME DATA		
100.0	100.0	100.0	100.0	100.0	100.0	Net Sales	100.0	100.0
49.4	42.2	42.4	38.4	54.2	43.7	Gross Profit	42.0	43.5
44.7	37.4	35.3	34.9	44.4	34.4	Operating Expenses	36.9	39.1
4.7	4.7	7.1	3.5	9.8	9.4	Operating Profit	5.1	4.5
.6	.4	.2	3.5	-.4	1.3	All Other Expenses (net)	1.0	.7
4.1	4.4	6.9	.0	10.1	8.1	Profit Before Taxes	4.1	3.8
						RATIOS		
4.6	3.2	3.1	3.0	2.7	2.0		2.7	2.2
1.8	1.5	1.6	2.0	1.9	1.4	Current	1.5	1.5
.8	1.0	1.0	1.4	1.3	1.1		1.0	.8
2.2	1.7	1.7	1.8	1.3	1.6		1.6	1.3
.8	.8	1.0	1.0	1.0	.8	Quick	(251) .8	.7
.3	.4	.5	.6	.7	.3		.3	.4
0 UND	**1** 649.2	**8** 45.3	**2** 166.0	**1** 264.7	**3** 133.3		**1** 343.1	**1** 636.6
1 245.0	**21** 17.8	**27** 13.6	**25** 14.7	**3** 121.1	**11** 32.4	Sales/Receivables	**15** 24.8	**14** 26.3
27 13.7	**34** 10.7	**47** 7.7	**55** 6.6	**25** 14.6	**24** 15.1		**39** 9.4	**40** 9.1
0 UND	**16** 22.9	**9** 42.5	**24** 15.3	**30** 12.1	**10** 35.7		**8** 45.4	**9** 41.2
19 19.0	**54** 6.8	**45** 8.1	**50** 7.3	**111** 3.3	**83** 4.4	Cost of Sales/Inventory	**40** 9.1	**47** 7.7
122 3.0	**94** 3.9	**94** 3.9	**159** 2.3	**152** 2.4	**135** 2.7		**92** 4.0	**109** 3.3
0 UND	**6** 58.2	**16** 23.3	**12** 30.5	**21** 17.1	**9** 42.4		**6** 58.2	**10** 38.2
4 96.4	**28** 13.1	**34** 10.8	**29** 12.4	**34** 10.8	**33** 10.9	Cost of Sales/Payables	**24** 15.5	**29** 12.6
46 8.0	**59** 6.2	**54** 6.8	**57** 6.4	**65** 5.6	**54** 6.8		**49** 7.5	**57** 6.4
5.2	6.7	4.8	4.1	4.5	9.7		6.7	7.3
15.7	16.4	13.1	7.9	11.5	13.0	Sales/Working Capital	21.2	17.5
-54.8	NM	173.6	27.3	45.9	113.0		-150.5	-63.5
21.3	25.0	79.9	60.4	48.0	130.7		18.5	21.4
(47) 6.7	(77) 4.1	(75) 16.7	(17) 5.1	(13) 26.2	(13) 17.1	EBIT/Interest	(201) 4.3	(212) 4.3
.0	1.1	3.3	-5.2	5.0	3.2		1.2	1.1
							13.9	11.9
						Net Profit + Depr., Dep., Amort./Cur. Mat. L/T/D	(21) 3.2	(26) 2.9
							1.2	1.0
.0	.0	.0	.1	.2	.3		.1	.1
.7	.3	.2	.1	.6	1.3	Fixed/Worth	.6	.5
-20.7	19.4	1.0	.8	2.7	-.8		44.8	14.9
.5	.7	.6	.5	.6	1.2		.8	1.0
3.0	3.3	1.7	1.2	1.2	4.1	Debt/Worth	3.8	3.5
-11.3	153.2	8.2	2.4	16.8	-4.5		UND	-25.5
115.5	97.3	76.0	62.0	266.5	110.4		102.9	97.0
(48) 50.8	(73) 53.5	(72) 42.5	(22) 25.9	(12) 35.3	(13) 49.7	% Profit Before Taxes/Tangible Net Worth	(190) 31.2	(196) 36.4
14.0	17.4	23.5	-5.5	21.2	29.0		9.5	8.9
49.0	24.9	31.9	22.1	33.5	34.3		28.1	24.7
17.6	7.1	16.3	6.3	14.5	19.4	% Profit Before Taxes/Total Assets	9.4	9.2
-2.2	.4	4.7	-8.8	6.6	6.3		.9	.2
999.8	244.4	227.7	87.2	46.8	77.3		115.5	187.7
50.0	46.9	62.2	35.4	20.0	20.0	Sales/Net Fixed Assets	33.3	44.5
22.2	13.0	18.3	11.8	9.9	7.3		11.6	15.6
8.0	5.0	4.3	3.5	3.8	4.4		5.5	5.0
4.2	3.4	3.0	2.3	2.2	2.3	Sales/Total Assets	3.1	3.2
2.6	2.3	1.9	1.5	1.3	1.9		2.0	2.0
.2	.5	.2	.8	.6	.7		.4	.4
(26) .9	(50) .8	(54) .5	(11) 1.1	(12) 1.0	(10) 1.2	% Depr., Dep., Amort./Sales	(162) 1.3	(175) 1.0
2.6	2.1	1.5	3.3	2.3	2.8		2.4	2.0
3.8	2.4	1.4					1.8	1.8
(31) 6.8	(56) 4.1	(43) 2.1				% Officers', Directors' Owners' Comp/Sales	(103) 3.7	(116) 3.6
9.4	5.9	4.3					7.5	9.2
97918M	**415949M**	**1227049M**	**1746079M**	**2864181M**	**8832964M**	Net Sales ($)	**11173401M**	**10219906M**
16053M	**106964M**	**347286M**	**670730M**	**952587M**	**3024418M**	Total Assets ($)	**4100067M**	**3882267M**

M = $ thousand MM = $ million

See Pages 9 through 22 for Explanation of Ratios and Data

Comparative Historical Data				Current Data Sorted by Sales					
			Type of Statement						
26	22	21	Unqualified	1		1	1		18
20	12	12	Reviewed		1		3	2	6
35	35	35	Compiled	4	7	3	9	10	2
133	108	111	Tax Returns	19	33	15	25	14	5
132	141	126	Other	17	25	14	24	13	33
4/1/11-3/31/12	**4/1/12-3/31/13**	**4/1/13-3/31/14**			**37 (4/1-9/30/13)**		**268 (10/1/13-3/31/14)**		
ALL	**ALL**	**ALL**		**0-1MM**	**1-3MM**	**3-5MM**	**5-10MM**	**10-25MM**	**25MM & OVER**
346	318	305	**NUMBER OF STATEMENTS**	41	66	33	62	39	64
%	%	%	**ASSETS**	%	%	%	%	%	%
18.1	18.0	19.2	Cash & Equivalents	16.9	19.2	20.5	19.6	16.2	21.6
21.5	21.2	19.9	Trade Receivables (net)	12.2	21.0	26.9	20.7	26.3	15.2
28.2	27.2	28.1	Inventory	25.6	23.7	31.5	35.4	27.7	25.9
3.6	3.1	3.0	All Other Current	5.9	2.2	1.0	1.4	2.4	5.0
71.3	69.4	70.2	Total Current	60.6	66.1	79.9	77.0	72.6	67.6
15.0	16.2	16.1	Fixed Assets (net)	25.0	19.4	10.2	12.6	12.8	15.5
5.2	4.9	5.1	Intangibles (net)	4.8	4.7	1.0	4.4	3.7	9.5
8.5	9.4	8.6	All Other Non-Current	9.6	9.8	8.9	6.1	10.9	7.4
100.0	100.0	100.0	Total	100.0	100.0	100.0	100.0	100.0	100.0
			LIABILITIES						
14.0	9.2	14.2	Notes Payable-Short Term	15.0	20.3	14.3	17.9	7.3	7.9
2.6	2.7	2.9	Cur. Mat.-L.T.D.	4.8	3.1	2.0	1.9	3.5	2.6
18.2	18.2	17.8	Trade Payables	14.3	18.1	22.2	18.8	18.3	16.0
.1	.1	.1	Income Taxes Payable	.1	.0	.0	.1	.0	.1
15.0	16.3	12.6	All Other Current	6.5	9.9	7.7	17.4	17.8	14.2
50.0	46.6	47.6	Total Current	40.8	51.3	46.2	56.2	46.9	40.8
13.1	15.2	14.9	Long-Term Debt	23.2	21.7	9.8	11.9	5.9	13.4
.2	.1	.1	Deferred Taxes	.0	.0	.0	.2	.0	.4
7.6	12.3	8.8	All Other Non-Current	11.2	16.1	9.4	4.9	2.7	6.9
29.2	25.9	28.7	Net Worth	24.8	10.9	34.6	26.8	44.6	38.5
100.0	100.0	100.0	Total Liabilties & Net Worth	100.0	100.0	100.0	100.0	100.0	100.0
			INCOME DATA						
100.0	100.0	100.0	Net Sales	100.0	100.0	100.0	100.0	100.0	100.0
43.9	44.2	44.2	Gross Profit	52.8	46.5	43.4	40.3	37.9	44.2
37.1	38.0	38.4	Operating Expenses	48.5	41.2	38.2	34.8	30.8	37.0
6.8	6.2	5.8	Operating Profit	4.3	5.3	5.2	5.5	7.1	7.2
.5	.3	.7	All Other Expenses (net)	.7	.8	.1	.1	1.4	.9
6.3	5.9	5.2	Profit Before Taxes	3.6	4.5	5.0	5.4	5.7	6.4
			RATIOS						
3.1	3.6	3.2		4.6	3.2	4.7	3.1	2.2	2.8
1.6	1.7	1.7	Current	2.2	1.3	1.8	1.7	1.6	1.7
1.0	1.0	1.0		1.1	.9	1.1	1.0	1.0	1.1
1.8	2.0	1.7		2.3	2.0	2.7	1.8	1.5	1.5
(345) .8	(317) .9	.9	Quick	.5	.9	.9	.8	1.0	.9
.4	.4	.5		.2	.4	.6	.3	.5	.5
1 310.5	**1** 345.0	**1** 618.6		**0** UND	**1** 471.6	**2** 152.3	**0** UND	**7** 52.4	**2** 225.5
19 19.5	**16** 23.0	**18** 19.9	Sales/Receivables	**1** 299.0	**22** 16.4	**27** 13.5	**19** 19.2	**24** 15.1	**10** 36.4
43 8.5	**38** 9.6	**36** 10.2		**29** 12.8	**36** 10.0	**47** 7.8	**38** 9.5	**45** 8.1	**27** 13.4
11 33.0	**7** 55.6	**11** 34.4		**16** 22.7	**0** UND	**13** 27.4	**10** 36.8	**8** 44.4	**18** 19.8
42 8.7	**41** 8.9	**45** 8.1	Cost of Sales/Inventory	**81** 4.5	**26** 14.0	**54** 6.8	**49** 7.4	**33** 10.9	**50** 7.3
101 3.6	**101** 3.6	**111** 3.3		**203** 1.8	**96** 3.8	**99** 3.7	**85** 4.3	**81** 4.5	**118** 3.1
5 69.6	**6** 58.0	**5** 69.8		**0** UND	**0** UND	**17** 21.1	**8** 48.0	**15** 24.8	**12** 31.2
26 13.9	**25** 14.8	**28** 13.2	Cost of Sales/Payables	**15** 24.9	**30** 12.0	**32** 11.3	**26** 14.3	**27** 13.5	**32** 11.3
54 6.7	**48** 7.6	**51** 7.1		**51** 7.1	**63** 5.8	**69** 5.3	**49** 7.5	**40** 9.2	**55** 6.6
5.9	5.6	5.5		4.2	7.6	4.1	5.9	5.8	6.1
16.0	14.2	13.2	Sales/Working Capital	6.9	21.6	10.1	13.1	16.2	14.3
-501.9	267.1	184.4		NM	-38.2	97.0	236.1	156.5	62.5
28.6	38.6	40.8		8.2	30.7	20.6	40.2	107.9	79.9
(265) 7.4	(233) 7.3	(242) 8.3	EBIT/Interest	(24) 1.8	(55) 3.4	(28) 5.5	(50) 8.9	(34) 36.9	(51) 17.1
1.6	2.2	1.3		-1.1	-.1	1.3	1.2	8.3	3.5
15.9	27.1	4.3							6.1
(31) 3.1	(20) 4.7	(22) 3.1	Net Profit + Depr., Dep., Amort./Cur. Mat. L/T/D						(11) 3.1
.6	1.6	.4							.1
.1	.0	.0		.0	.1	.0	.0	.0	.1
.3	.3	.3	Fixed/Worth	.7	.8	.2	.3	.2	.4
3.4	2.2	3.9		NM	-4.0	.9	NM	.8	2.1
.6	.6	.7		.3	1.0	.6	.6	.6	.6
2.4	2.1	2.2	Debt/Worth	1.3	6.5	2.3	2.1	1.2	2.0
155.2	12.1	23.0		-9.1	-7.3	10.8	NM	3.8	12.1
100.0	89.9	97.4		55.5	142.9	110.3	77.3	93.4	139.2
(266) 44.7	(252) 47.9	(240) 44.0	% Profit Before Taxes/Tangible Net Worth	(30) 25.4	(44) 42.6	(29) 54.8	(47) 49.5	(36) 45.6	(54) 43.6
14.0	14.8	18.0		4.0	15.3	9.6	20.5	34.7	23.9
35.1	37.8	33.6		28.1	38.0	32.1	36.3	38.0	29.9
11.8	13.0	12.3	% Profit Before Taxes/Total Assets	4.5	8.3	7.3	11.2	19.1	16.5
2.7	2.3	1.6		-3.3	-4.2	.9	1.7	9.6	4.9
237.6	251.8	227.9		194.8	227.5	366.3	442.9	337.9	140.1
51.0	55.8	45.0	Sales/Net Fixed Assets	31.0	37.3	93.7	72.2	58.9	35.5
15.1	16.3	13.5		4.4	11.2	26.8	22.6	22.8	12.1
5.4	5.3	4.9		3.2	5.4	5.2	5.2	4.6	5.8
3.1	3.4	3.2	Sales/Total Assets	2.3	3.1	3.5	3.7	3.6	3.0
2.0	1.9	2.1		1.5	2.1	2.2	2.8	2.6	1.8
.4	.3	.3		1.1	.2	.2	.3	.2	.3
(198) .9	(179) .9	(163) .8	% Depr., Dep., Amort./Sales	(21) 2.1	(30) .8	(15) .5	(33) .7	(24) .8	(40) .9
2.1	1.8	2.1		5.0	2.7	.8	2.1	1.3	1.6
1.8	1.8	1.7		4.8	3.0	3.1	1.7	.9	.4
(142) 3.4	(143) 3.5	(140) 3.7	% Officers', Directors' Owners' Comp/Sales	(17) 10.6	(32) 4.4	(20) 5.0	(39) 2.9	(22) 1.5	(10) 1.7
7.7	8.0	6.7		12.3	8.5	7.5	5.0	2.0	8.4
11563755M	**13635300M**	**15184140M**	Net Sales ($)	**21843M**	**129721M**	**131631M**	**438043M**	**611991M**	**13850911M**
5109397M	**5087809M**	**5118038M**	Total Assets ($)	**13599M**	**57566M**	**43447M**	**139575M**	**200694M**	**4663157M**

M = $ thousand MM = $ million

See Pages 9 through 22 for Explanation of Ratios and Data

TRANSPORTATION AND WAREHOUSING

Current Data Sorted by Assets							Comparative Historical Data	
						Type of Statement		
		1	4	1	3	Unqualified	13	11
		1	5			Reviewed	6	6
1						Compiled	1	5
4	1					Tax Returns	15	9
2	3	6	6	3	1	Other	31	39
8 (4/1-9/30/13)		34 (10/1/13-3/31/14)					4/1/09-3/31/10	4/1/10-3/31/11
0-500M	500M-2MM	2-10MM	10-50MM	50-100MM	100-250MM		ALL	ALL
7	4	8	15	4	4	NUMBER OF STATEMENTS	66	70
%	%	%	%	%	%	**ASSETS**	%	%
			9.2			Cash & Equivalents	12.5	12.5
			14.5			Trade Receivables (net)	16.7	18.1
			9.3			Inventory	6.4	5.6
			5.1			All Other Current	4.6	4.6
			38.1			Total Current	40.3	40.8
			51.4			Fixed Assets (net)	41.4	41.7
			3.8			Intangibles (net)	5.0	3.5
			6.7			All Other Non-Current	13.2	14.0
			100.0			Total	100.0	100.0
						LIABILITIES		
			3.4			Notes Payable-Short Term	7.9	4.3
			3.5			Cur. Mat.-L.T.D.	4.9	4.6
			11.2			Trade Payables	12.4	13.7
			.6			Income Taxes Payable	.1	.1
			11.3			All Other Current	14.5	13.7
			30.0			Total Current	39.8	36.5
			15.0			Long-Term Debt	27.7	29.5
			1.5			Deferred Taxes	.9	.7
			2.9			All Other Non-Current	5.3	4.2
			50.6			Net Worth	26.4	29.0
			100.0			Total Liabilties & Net Worth	100.0	100.0
						INCOME DATA		
			100.0			Net Sales	100.0	100.0
						Gross Profit		
			88.3			Operating Expenses	94.6	91.5
			11.7			Operating Profit	5.4	8.5
			1.2			All Other Expenses (net)	1.8	2.7
			10.5			Profit Before Taxes	3.6	5.8
						RATIOS		
			2.0				2.5	2.5
			1.4			Current	1.3	1.3
			.8				.7	.6
			1.4				1.7	1.8
			.8			Quick	.8	.8
			.3				.5	.4
			9 41.4				**10** 35.7	**9** 38.6
			20 18.6			Sales/Receivables	**23** 15.7	**24** 15.5
			33 11.2				**44** 8.2	**40** 9.0
						Cost of Sales/Inventory		
						Cost of Sales/Payables		
			5.3				6.0	6.9
			34.4			Sales/Working Capital	22.0	24.5
			-15.7				-17.1	-15.3
			11.3				8.0	16.9
			(13) 8.9			EBIT/Interest	(56) 3.3	(58) 3.9
			1.4				.4	1.3
							4.3	4.3
						Net Profit + Depr., Dep., Amort./Cur. Mat. L/T/D	(13) 2.0	(14) 1.7
							.9	.9
			.7				.9	.4
			1.3			Fixed/Worth	1.4	1.5
			1.5				6.0	4.2
			.5				.9	.7
			.7			Debt/Worth	3.1	2.5
			2.7				9.4	9.3
			25.7				45.1	44.8
			(14) 10.7			% Profit Before Taxes/Tangible Net Worth	(54) 23.7	(56) 26.5
			2.6				5.0	4.7
			13.4				13.3	19.0
			5.7			% Profit Before Taxes/Total Assets	5.2	8.7
			1.8				-1.2	.5
			11.0				19.7	23.6
			2.4			Sales/Net Fixed Assets	4.2	4.5
			1.1				1.8	1.6
			2.5				2.8	3.1
			1.1			Sales/Total Assets	1.8	1.7
			.8				1.0	.9
			1.4				1.2	1.2
			(13) 3.8			% Depr., Dep., Amort./Sales	(58) 4.1	(58) 3.6
			8.3				9.0	7.7
							1.5	1.4
						% Officers', Directors' Owners' Comp/Sales	(12) 3.7	(12) 2.0
							9.3	4.7
3913M	7233M	65142M	651486M	651066M	656699M	Net Sales ($)	2422050M	3720189M
1508M	3627M	45406M	395648M	350682M	557567M	Total Assets ($)	1443375M	2226601M

M = $ thousand   MM = $ million

See Pages 9 through 22 for Explanation of Ratios and Data

Comparative Historical Data				Current Data Sorted by Sales					
			Type of Statement						
14	12	9	Unqualified		1		1	3	4
8	5	6	Reviewed			1		4	1
3	3	1	Compiled	1					
5	8	5	Tax Returns	4			1		
24	23	21	Other	3	3	1	1	5	8
4/1/11-3/31/12	4/1/12-3/31/13	4/1/13-3/31/14		8 (4/1-9/30/13)			34 (10/1/13-3/31/14)		
ALL	ALL	ALL		0-1MM	1-3MM	3-5MM	5-10MM	10-25MM	25MM & OVER
54	51	42	**NUMBER OF STATEMENTS**	8	4	2	3	12	13
%	%	%	**ASSETS**	%	%	%	%	%	%
11.5	14.1	14.5	Cash & Equivalents					8.7	8.2
14.7	12.7	13.3	Trade Receivables (net)					9.1	20.2
7.2	6.1	10.2	Inventory					8.0	7.9
3.6	3.4	3.7	All Other Current					2.5	6.5
37.1	36.3	41.7	Total Current					28.3	42.8
51.5	50.2	47.2	Fixed Assets (net)					59.8	42.3
3.1	3.8	3.3	Intangibles (net)					4.4	5.6
8.4	9.7	7.7	All Other Non-Current					7.6	9.4
100.0	100.0	100.0	Total					100.0	100.0
			LIABILITIES						
7.5	4.7	4.2	Notes Payable-Short Term					1.4	3.6
4.1	2.9	6.1	Cur. Mat.-L.T.D.					3.8	5.2
10.1	14.0	9.3	Trade Payables					5.8	16.5
.1	1.4	.2	Income Taxes Payable					.1	.6
15.9	12.0	23.1	All Other Current					8.4	14.0
37.6	34.9	42.9	Total Current					19.4	40.0
36.6	36.9	40.7	Long-Term Debt					23.9	22.0
1.0	1.7	1.4	Deferred Taxes					1.9	2.4
3.9	10.2	4.8	All Other Non-Current					2.7	3.0
21.0	16.3	10.2	Net Worth					52.0	32.6
100.0	100.0	100.0	Total Liabilities & Net Worth					100.0	100.0
			INCOME DATA						
100.0	100.0	100.0	Net Sales					100.0	100.0
			Gross Profit						
89.6	87.4	88.4	Operating Expenses					93.0	96.7
10.4	12.6	11.6	Operating Profit					7.0	3.3
2.2	3.5	2.8	All Other Expenses (net)					1.5	1.3
8.2	9.1	8.8	Profit Before Taxes					5.6	1.9
			RATIOS						
2.4	2.2	2.8						2.8	1.5
1.5	1.3	1.4	Current					1.4	.9
.7	.7	.8						.9	.7
2.0	1.9	1.9						1.9	1.1
.8	.8	.8	Quick					.8	.6
.3	.4	.4						.3	.4
5 67.9	**2** 214.2	**5** 77.1						**8** 45.7	**17** 21.5
17 21.1	**12** 29.8	**19** 18.8	Sales/Receivables					**24** 15.4	**22** 16.5
27 13.5	**29** 12.5	**38** 9.7						**41** 8.9	**36** 10.1
			Cost of Sales/Inventory						
			Cost of Sales/Payables						
6.3	8.5	4.2						4.3	16.0
23.2	33.5	26.8	Sales/Working Capital					26.0	-53.1
-18.9	-26.3	-17.0						-41.8	-15.9
8.3	9.9	11.7						9.3	11.6
(49) 3.9	(41) 4.3	(33) 6.4	EBIT/Interest					(11) 3.7	(10) 4.8
1.5	1.7	.6						.6	-.4
4.8	3.4								
(10) 1.8	(12) 1.7		Net Profit + Depr., Dep., Amort./Cur. Mat. L/T/D						
1.1	1.4								
1.0	.8	.5						1.2	.4
1.4	2.4	1.3	Fixed/Worth					1.3	1.3
9.0	26.0	3.6						2.4	7.4
.9	1.1	.7						.5	.9
2.0	4.0	1.6	Debt/Worth					.9	2.2
14.3	999.8	12.1						2.5	12.8
43.6	60.5	48.3						34.8	37.3
(43) 22.0	(39) 26.1	(33) 17.0	% Profit Before Taxes/Tangible Net Worth					(11) 10.0	(11) 15.5
2.3	11.3	4.5						-2.1	4.3
17.2	18.1	17.0						14.9	7.2
5.3	5.4	6.0	% Profit Before Taxes/Total Assets					5.4	4.0
.9	1.2	-.5						-.5	-1.8
12.3	13.6	11.6						2.6	15.2
2.7	2.9	2.8	Sales/Net Fixed Assets					1.4	5.4
.8	1.1	1.1						.7	2.1
3.3	2.8	2.6						1.5	3.1
1.6	1.6	1.4	Sales/Total Assets					.8	2.2
.6	.8	.7						.6	1.4
1.6	1.4	1.6						4.0	1.3
(44) 4.1	(34) 4.2	(27) 4.2	% Depr., Dep., Amort./Sales					(10) 8.2	(12) 1.9
9.7	8.6	9.2						14.7	4.1
			% Officers', Directors' Owners' Comp/Sales						
2107080M	1814360M	2035539M	Net Sales ($)	3420M	7767M	9164M	19404M	196941M	1798843M
1394804M	953892M	1354438M	Total Assets ($)	2915M	39005M	15002M	6766M	359629M	931121M

M = $ thousand MM = $ million

See Pages 9 through 22 for Explanation of Ratios and Data

Current Data Sorted by Assets							Comparative Historical Data	
						Type of Statement		
	1	1	3		2	Unqualified	16	13
1		7	3	1		Reviewed	12	14
1	3	4	1			Compiled	11	9
3	7	4	2			Tax Returns	7	11
1	16	15	10	1	2	Other	45	47
	8 (4/1-9/30/13)		81 (10/1/13-3/31/14)				**4/1/09-3/31/10 ALL**	**4/1/10-3/31/11 ALL**
0-500M	**500M-2MM**	**2-10MM**	**10-50MM**	**50-100MM**	**100-250MM**			
6	27	31	19	2	4	**NUMBER OF STATEMENTS**	91	94
%	%	%	%	%	%	**ASSETS**	%	%
	15.1	8.6	10.6			Cash & Equivalents	9.9	10.8
	17.1	11.8	18.5			Trade Receivables (net)	15.1	16.0
	3.6	7.1	2.1			Inventory	8.5	7.0
	11.1	4.5	2.5			All Other Current	5.1	6.0
	47.0	32.0	33.7			Total Current	38.6	39.8
	48.2	49.6	49.6			Fixed Assets (net)	45.7	45.8
	.7	2.2	7.8			Intangibles (net)	4.6	4.8
	4.2	16.1	8.9			All Other Non-Current	11.1	9.6
	100.0	100.0	100.0			Total	100.0	100.0
						LIABILITIES		
	7.9	11.1	2.6			Notes Payable-Short Term	11.4	6.5
	6.0	4.8	3.2			Cur. Mat.-L.T.D.	6.2	5.8
	17.9	10.0	12.0			Trade Payables	13.6	10.5
	.0	.6	.0			Income Taxes Payable	.2	.4
	28.5	13.5	14.3			All Other Current	12.5	14.1
	60.2	40.0	32.1			Total Current	43.9	37.3
	40.9	37.5	26.2			Long-Term Debt	38.5	41.2
	.0	.3	.7			Deferred Taxes	.9	.9
	30.5	3.1	11.4			All Other Non-Current	7.1	15.1
	-31.6	19.1	29.6			Net Worth	9.5	5.5
	100.0	100.0	100.0			Total Liabilities & Net Worth	100.0	100.0
						INCOME DATA		
	100.0	100.0	100.0			Net Sales	100.0	100.0
						Gross Profit		
	89.1	86.4	89.8			Operating Expenses	98.7	93.3
	10.9	13.6	10.2			Operating Profit	1.3	6.7
	5.7	3.0	1.8			All Other Expenses (net)	2.8	4.0
	5.1	10.6	8.4			Profit Before Taxes	-1.5	2.6
						RATIOS		
	2.5	2.3	2.1				1.7	1.7
	.9	1.0	1.0			Current	1.0	1.1
	.3	.5	.3				.5	.6
	1.3	1.6	2.1				1.1	1.3
	.5	.7	.6			Quick	.6	.7
	.2	.2	.2				.2	.3
	4 101.2	**8** 47.1	**8** 44.1				**13** 27.4	**14** 26.4
	14 26.3	**18** 20.0	**29** 12.5			Sales/Receivables	**25** 14.4	**26** 14.3
	30 12.2	**38** 9.7	**57** 6.4				**43** 8.5	**42** 8.7
						Cost of Sales/Inventory		
						Cost of Sales/Payables		
	14.3	8.9	7.6				10.8	9.3
	-57.8	172.9	-999.8			Sales/Working Capital	256.1	118.0
	-3.9	-6.8	-6.2				-7.4	-11.5
	13.2	10.6	12.3				4.5	6.1
	(17) 3.7	(30) 4.6	(17) 2.6			EBIT/Interest	(79) .7	(86) 2.7
	-1.2	1.8	1.5				-.1	.2
							2.6	1.5
						Net Profit + Depr., Dep., Amort./Cur. Mat. L/T/D	(22) 1.2	(17) .6
							.4	.0
	.6	1.0	.6				.9	1.2
	5.2	2.6	1.3			Fixed/Worth	3.3	2.5
	-.4	36.7	6.3				-3.8	-2.7
	1.8	1.4	.7				1.3	1.1
	14.1	3.3	1.5			Debt/Worth	6.4	4.3
	-4.7	38.7	8.4				-9.2	-5.5
	112.3	94.1	30.8				30.3	40.2
	(16) 62.2	(24) 45.1	(16) 20.5			% Profit Before Taxes/Tangible Net Worth	(59) 5.3	(63) 13.3
	15.3	17.4	7.3				-8.3	.6
	19.4	21.9	12.1				7.2	11.8
	5.1	7.2	2.6			% Profit Before Taxes/Total Assets	-.9	3.2
	-6.4	3.4	1.4				-5.8	-2.9
	74.3	11.1	5.8				9.1	12.4
	10.0	3.2	2.2			Sales/Net Fixed Assets	3.1	3.7
	.4	1.1	1.5				1.5	1.4
	5.6	2.3	2.2				2.2	2.4
	1.8	1.4	1.3			Sales/Total Assets	1.4	1.4
	.4	.6	.6				.9	.8
	.3	1.5	2.2				2.1	2.5
	(17) 10.6	(22) 3.4	(17) 4.8			% Depr., Dep., Amort./Sales	(68) 5.2	(70) 5.3
	32.1	14.7	11.3				10.3	10.7
							1.8	1.8
						% Officers', Directors' Owners' Comp/Sales	(16) 2.9	(20) 2.9
							5.8	6.1
11146M	97891M	278156M	845557M	73762M	507830M	Net Sales ($)	2667953M	2667132M
1618M	30170M	167134M	487277M	156210M	492030M	Total Assets ($)	2309377M	2022992M

M = $ thousand MM = $ million

See Pages 9 through 22 for Explanation of Ratios and Data

Comparative Historical Data / Current Data Sorted by Sales

			Type of Statement						
8	12	7	Unqualified	1				1	5
6	9	12	Reviewed		1	2	1	7	1
12	16	9	Compiled		3	4	1	1	
10	10	16	Tax Returns	7	1	2	3	2	1
43	59	45	Other	9	4	4	9	10	9
4/1/11-3/31/12 ALL	**4/1/12-3/31/13 ALL**	**4/1/13-3/31/14 ALL**		**8 (4/1-9/30/13)**		**81 (10/1/13-3/31/14)**			
				0-1MM	**1-3MM**	**3-5MM**	**5-10MM**	**10-25MM**	**25MM & OVER**
79	106	89	**NUMBER OF STATEMENTS**	17	9	12	14	21	16
%	%	%	**ASSETS**	%	%	%	%	%	%
11.1	11.5	13.5	Cash & Equivalents	5.4		3.6	25.2	13.6	10.1
18.0	12.7	14.1	Trade Receivables (net)	2.6		8.0	21.1	20.9	19.9
7.5	8.5	4.3	Inventory	2.4		3.6	7.1	6.3	3.4
5.2	4.9	5.9	All Other Current	6.4		7.2	4.2	7.1	4.1
41.8	37.7	37.8	Total Current	16.8		22.3	57.6	47.9	37.4
43.2	48.6	49.2	Fixed Assets (net)	77.9		59.6	28.1	37.9	47.8
5.4	3.7	3.2	Intangibles (net)	.8		6.7	1.1	2.6	7.2
9.7	10.0	9.9	All Other Non-Current	4.5		11.4	13.1	11.6	7.6
100.0	100.0	100.0	Total	100.0		100.0	100.0	100.0	100.0
			LIABILITIES						
12.0	7.3	6.9	Notes Payable-Short Term	4.3		5.6	6.0	13.9	2.1
4.5	8.8	4.3	Cur. Mat.-L.T.D.	7.6		5.7	1.3	2.8	3.1
12.6	9.0	12.7	Trade Payables	.9		3.7	16.3	24.4	16.4
.3	.3	.2	Income Taxes Payable	.0		.1	.0	.7	.0
12.5	9.6	23.7	All Other Current	57.8		30.1	15.3	14.6	13.9
42.0	35.0	47.9	Total Current	70.6		45.2	38.9	56.3	35.4
40.0	43.9	38.1	Long-Term Debt	63.8		47.4	11.1	20.9	24.7
.5	.3	.5	Deferred Taxes	.0		.7	.9	.5	.7
9.6	8.5	12.9	All Other Non-Current	4.6		65.6	3.2	6.3	5.0
7.9	12.3	.6	Net Worth	-39.0		-59.0	46.0	16.0	34.3
100.0	100.0	100.0	Total Liabilities & Net Worth	100.0		100.0	100.0	100.0	100.0
			INCOME DATA						
100.0	100.0	100.0	Net Sales	100.0		100.0	100.0	100.0	100.0
			Gross Profit						
94.2	91.6	88.3	Operating Expenses	79.1		98.6	90.7	90.5	92.4
5.8	8.4	11.7	Operating Profit	20.9		1.4	9.3	9.5	7.6
2.9	3.8	3.7	All Other Expenses (net)	12.8		2.8	.3	1.1	1.5
3.0	4.6	8.0	Profit Before Taxes	8.1		-1.4	9.0	8.3	6.2
			RATIOS						
2.0	2.5	2.3		.7		2.1	3.1	2.0	1.9
1.3	1.3	1.0	Current	.4		.6	1.9	1.1	1.0
.7	.6	.4		.1		.1	.8	.7	.7
1.5	1.4	1.6		.4		1.4	3.0	1.7	1.4
.8	.7	.6	Quick	.2		.3	1.3	.8	.8
.4	.3	.2		.1		.1	.8	.3	.4
15 24.6	**7** 52.1	**5** 79.0		**0** UND		**2** 155.4	**11** 33.0	**9** 39.3	**18** 19.8
26 14.2	**20** 18.1	**18** 19.8	Sales/Receivables	**4** 84.3		**14** 25.9	**26** 13.8	**23** 15.9	**28** 12.9
38 9.5	**33** 11.2	**36** 10.0		**18** 20.6		**35** 10.4	**42** 8.7	**40** 9.1	**41** 8.9
			Cost of Sales/Inventory						
			Cost of Sales/Payables						
9.0	8.9	10.5		-41.2		15.5	9.7	8.5	10.9
30.1	36.9	-174.6	Sales/Working Capital	-4.5		-16.0	16.6	170.0	NM
-22.8	-10.1	-5.4		-.5		-2.4	-38.2	-14.5	-14.8
7.4	8.5	12.3				4.5	16.6	23.5	13.7
(67) 2.5	(90) 3.3	(73) 4.1	EBIT/Interest			(11) 2.0	(11) 8.8	(20) 8.7	(15) 2.9
.4	1.1	1.5				.2	4.1	2.2	1.6
6.1	7.5								
(15) 1.9	(12) 1.7		Net Profit + Depr., Dep., Amort./Cur. Mat. L/T/D						
1.0	.7								
.8	.7	.7		3.7		2.3	.1	.6	.7
2.9	2.2	2.6	Fixed/Worth	28.2		NM	.5	1.7	1.3
-3.6	-2.6	-5.3		-2.1		-.3	1.8	-2.6	6.3
1.5	1.1	1.0		3.2		2.3	.5	1.4	1.0
4.4	3.3	3.3	Debt/Worth	29.3		NM	.8	2.1	3.1
-6.8	-6.3	-23.5		-4.9		-1.5	5.8	-23.5	8.0
60.0	60.6	68.9		114.3			81.0	67.8	54.1
(51) 23.1	(71) 20.1	(66) 30.4	% Profit Before Taxes/Tangible Net Worth	(11) 40.2			(13) 31.0	(15) 36.5	(14) 20.3
6.8	6.4	13.1		-8.0			20.0	25.5	10.7
13.9	15.6	17.9		7.7		6.2	34.7	30.9	8.9
4.8	5.5	5.6	% Profit Before Taxes/Total Assets	2.8		2.0	14.4	15.2	3.9
-2.2	.3	1.8		-4.7		-8.8	8.6	3.6	2.1
23.6	11.3	19.4		1.4		6.5	UND	84.0	11.5
3.8	3.2	2.9	Sales/Net Fixed Assets	.4		1.5	37.0	6.6	2.3
1.4	1.7	.8		.2		.6	2.3	2.8	1.5
3.2	2.6	3.1		.8		2.0	5.8	4.6	2.9
1.8	1.5	1.3	Sales/Total Assets	.4		.9	3.2	2.2	1.5
.9	.8	.6		.2		.6	1.0	1.1	.9
1.4	2.3	1.6		2.5				1.2	1.8
(65) 3.7	(74) 4.0	(63) 4.1	% Depr., Dep., Amort./Sales	(10) 24.7				(18) 3.2	(13) 2.4
10.8	13.5	16.3		52.1				7.1	6.2
1.6	1.4	1.4							
(23) 3.5	(20) 2.2	(17) 3.2	% Officers', Directors' Owners' Comp/Sales						
4.9	4.3	5.7							
2113362M	3822876M	1814342M	Net Sales ($)	6522M	15639M	47116M	100913M	324595M	1319557M
1387984M	3232380M	1334439M	Total Assets ($)	20192M	21050M	75982M	91173M	245959M	880083M

M = $ thousand MM = $ million

See Pages 9 through 22 for Explanation of Ratios and Data

Current Data Sorted by Assets | **Comparative Historical Data**

0-500M	500M-2MM	2-10MM	10-50MM	50-100MM	100-250MM	**Type of Statement**	4/1/09-3/31/10 ALL	4/1/10-3/31/11 ALL
1	2		5	3	1	Unqualified	12	11
	1	1	2			Reviewed	5	4
2	1	3				Compiled	5	5
	3	6				Tax Returns	4	7
3	6	10	14	2	3	Other	25	25
	9 (4/1-9/30/13)		60 (10/1/13-3/31/14)					
6	13	20	21	5	4	**NUMBER OF STATEMENTS**	51	52
%	%	%	%	%	%	**ASSETS**	%	%
	21.4	14.6	10.5			Cash & Equivalents	8.3	10.7
	21.4	9.9	13.7			Trade Receivables (net)	13.2	12.7
	3.8	5.4	6.1			Inventory	6.3	6.3
	5.3	1.9	5.7			All Other Current	3.6	3.0
	51.9	31.8	36.1			Total Current	31.4	32.7
	39.4	44.9	48.2			Fixed Assets (net)	51.1	54.2
	1.5	4.9	4.6			Intangibles (net)	5.9	3.0
	7.2	18.4	11.1			All Other Non-Current	11.6	10.0
	100.0	100.0	100.0			Total	100.0	100.0
						LIABILITIES		
	8.2	4.3	2.8			Notes Payable-Short Term	8.3	10.7
	3.7	4.4	5.8			Cur. Mat.-L.T.D.	4.7	6.0
	17.8	14.4	5.5			Trade Payables	12.4	5.9
	.0	.1	.1			Income Taxes Payable	.2	.0
	17.0	10.1	14.6			All Other Current	14.1	6.2
	46.7	33.3	28.8			Total Current	39.7	28.9
	51.7	38.5	21.8			Long-Term Debt	40.1	40.7
	.1	.0	1.6			Deferred Taxes	.8	1.2
	23.2	7.1	7.7			All Other Non-Current	5.2	4.1
	-21.7	21.2	40.2			Net Worth	14.2	25.2
	100.0	100.0	100.0			Total Liabilties & Net Worth	100.0	100.0
						INCOME DATA		
	100.0	100.0	100.0			Net Sales	100.0	100.0
						Gross Profit		
	95.5	97.2	86.6			Operating Expenses	87.8	87.9
	4.5	2.8	13.4			Operating Profit	12.2	12.1
	4.0	1.4	3.4			All Other Expenses (net)	7.1	7.1
	.5	1.4	10.0			Profit Before Taxes	5.1	5.0
						RATIOS		
	1.8	3.5	3.3				1.6	3.2
	1.4	1.2	1.4			Current	.9	1.2
	.7	.9	.6				.5	.4
	1.7	3.4	2.6				1.0	2.3
	1.1	1.0	1.3			Quick	.6	.8
	.6	.5	.2				.3	.3
	3 105.8	4 100.2	4 85.6				0 999.8	0 UND
	19 19.5	17 22.1	27 13.3			Sales/Receivables	25 14.7	23 16.0
	32 11.4	35 10.5	44 8.3				44 8.3	40 9.1
						Cost of Sales/Inventory		
						Cost of Sales/Payables		
	8.9	11.1	6.1				12.6	8.6
	47.1	26.7	19.0			Sales/Working Capital	-56.8	20.1
	-43.0	-76.1	-7.4				-6.6	-11.1
		11.5	10.0				4.7	14.2
		(17) 2.0	(18) 3.5			EBIT/Interest	(39) 2.0	(41) 4.3
		-.4	.5				-.3	.0
							12.5	9.5
						Net Profit + Depr., Dep., Amort./Cur. Mat. L/T/D	(10) 2.7	(11) 2.8
							.4	2.2
	.4	.6	.8				.8	.6
	9.5	3.1	1.2			Fixed/Worth	2.3	1.6
	-.6	8.9	14.7				-6.5	19.2
	1.3	1.2	.5				1.3	.7
	16.4	5.3	1.2			Debt/Worth	3.6	2.1
	-2.2	9.5	19.9				-7.3	NM
		92.4	30.6				26.1	56.7
		(16) 4.0	(17) 21.1			% Profit Before Taxes/Tangible Net Worth	(35) 8.9	(39) 9.5
		-5.5	-.1				-4.8	1.8
	23.7	16.7	19.7				7.8	16.0
	2.9	1.0	5.6			% Profit Before Taxes/Total Assets	3.3	3.5
	-4.7	-4.1	.3				-3.0	-3.3
	72.9	9.4	5.9				12.4	8.7
	6.6	2.7	3.6			Sales/Net Fixed Assets	1.6	2.3
	1.2	2.2	1.0				.9	.9
	5.0	2.5	2.0				1.9	2.1
	2.7	1.4	1.5			Sales/Total Assets	1.0	1.1
	.8	.6	.7				.5	.6
		2.3	1.0				3.2	2.9
		(16) 7.0	(20) 5.7			% Depr., Dep., Amort./Sales	(42) 7.1	(41) 6.6
		10.5	11.8				12.3	18.5
								1.0
						% Officers', Directors' Owners' Comp/Sales		(12) 1.8
								8.9
3183M	56280M	150824M	748164M	662842M	775815M	Net Sales ($)	1194015M	1494587M
1140M	13571M	101570M	470554M	345309M	506502M	Total Assets ($)	936038M	1406432M

M = $ thousand MM = $ million

See Pages 9 through 22 for Explanation of Ratios and Data

Comparative Historical Data / Current Data Sorted by Sales

4/1/11-3/31/12 ALL	4/1/12-3/31/13 ALL	4/1/13-3/31/14 ALL		0-1MM	1-3MM	3-5MM	5-10MM	10-25MM	25MM & OVER
			Type of Statement						
10	5	12	Unqualified	1	2			2	7
3	5	4	Reviewed				1	2	1
6	6	6	Compiled	3	1		2		
1	10	9	Tax Returns	2	2		4	1	
28	33	38	Other	4	3	9	2	6	14
				9 (4/1-9/30/13)		60 (10/1/13-3/31/14)			
48	59	69	**NUMBER OF STATEMENTS**	10	8	9	9	11	22
%	%	%	**ASSETS**	%	%	%	%	%	%
13.0	17.6	14.8	Cash & Equivalents	9.2				20.0	14.7
12.3	14.0	15.2	Trade Receivables (net)	11.6				15.6	18.5
7.2	5.6	5.1	Inventory	.0				.3	8.6
7.3	3.3	3.9	All Other Current	1.4				7.5	3.5
39.8	40.4	39.0	Total Current	22.2				43.6	45.3
46.6	46.1	44.0	Fixed Assets (net)	59.5				48.1	37.2
2.0	2.6	4.7	Intangibles (net)	4.1				3.2	6.1
11.6	10.9	12.4	All Other Non-Current	14.1				5.1	11.5
100.0	100.0	100.0	Total	100.0				100.0	100.0
			LIABILITIES						
2.8	7.3	6.6	Notes Payable-Short Term	14.2				1.1	2.6
8.5	3.2	4.7	Cur. Mat.-L.T.D.	1.6				2.3	5.9
7.9	10.5	12.2	Trade Payables	6.3				21.6	13.0
.4	.6	.1	Income Taxes Payable	.0				.1	.3
20.7	16.4	12.1	All Other Current	2.5				7.2	16.9
40.2	38.1	35.8	Total Current	24.6				32.3	38.7
43.8	41.9	33.3	Long-Term Debt	49.3				20.5	15.1
.5	.5	.8	Deferred Taxes	.0				1.7	1.4
6.7	5.1	10.0	All Other Non-Current	28.3				4.9	4.5
8.8	14.4	20.2	Net Worth	-2.2				40.5	40.2
100.0	100.0	100.0	Total Liabilities & Net Worth	100.0				100.0	100.0
			INCOME DATA						
100.0	100.0	100.0	Net Sales	100.0				100.0	100.0
			Gross Profit						
91.5	89.2	93.0	Operating Expenses	98.1				91.7	91.6
8.5	10.8	7.0	Operating Profit	1.9				8.3	8.4
3.7	2.5	2.4	All Other Expenses (net)	7.4				-.4	2.4
4.8	8.3	4.6	Profit Before Taxes	-5.5				8.7	6.0
			RATIOS						
1.9	3.2	2.0		3.4				4.7	1.7
1.2	1.5	1.4	Current	1.5				2.1	1.3
.5	.8	.9		.4				.8	1.0
1.3	2.8	2.0		3.4				3.7	1.4
.6	1.1	1.0	Quick	1.4				2.1	1.0
.2	.5	.5		.3				.7	.5
2 205.6	4 104.1	4 86.9		0 UND				3 126.6	13 28.3
19 19.7	18 20.7	19 19.3	Sales/Receivables	6 63.9				15 23.8	31 11.9
31 11.8	40 9.2	43 8.5		33 11.2				36 10.2	52 7.0
			Cost of Sales/Inventory						
			Cost of Sales/Payables						
11.5	5.2	8.3		7.6				3.9	8.7
37.3	13.3	19.4	Sales/Working Capital	17.0				8.2	17.5
-9.9	-24.0	-53.5		-19.2				-122.0	162.1
10.2	11.0	13.7						19.9	12.8
(37) 3.9	(48) 4.1	(55) 3.5	EBIT/Interest					5.0	(17) 4.9
.8	.9	-.3						-6.6	1.9
			Net Profit + Depr., Dep., Amort./Cur. Mat. L/T/D						
.9	.6	.6		.4				.6	.5
1.6	2.1	1.3	Fixed/Worth	1.4				1.2	1.1
-3.4	-5.2	NM		-24.2				-2.1	1.8
.8	.9	.9		.8				.4	.9
5.6	3.3	2.5	Debt/Worth	1.3				.7	1.6
-7.9	-7.1	-25.4		-7.2				-8.1	5.5
53.5	69.8	41.0							34.2
(32) 22.4	(42) 33.9	(51) 15.9	% Profit Before Taxes/Tangible Net Worth						(20) 24.4
-.1	3.9	-3.9							5.1
16.6	21.1	20.0		22.4				29.0	18.6
5.4	10.2	4.2	% Profit Before Taxes/Total Assets	-1.9				4.2	5.7
-4.0	-.3	-3.0		-10.7				-4.7	1.6
17.5	13.9	10.6		17.3				6.3	14.1
2.9	5.6	3.2	Sales/Net Fixed Assets	1.0				3.1	4.4
1.1	1.7	1.9		.3				1.1	2.5
3.6	2.8	2.9		3.1				2.2	2.6
1.3	1.8	1.6	Sales/Total Assets	.7				1.2	1.7
.7	.9	.8		.2				.8	1.2
1.0	2.4	1.4						4.1	.8
(37) 3.8	(44) 5.0	(52) 6.4	% Depr., Dep., Amort./Sales					(10) 10.5	(16) 2.1
18.4	8.8	11.3						12.6	5.7
	2.1	2.9							
	(13) 3.7	(14) 5.0	% Officers', Directors' Owners' Comp/Sales						
	5.2	11.9							
2010661M	2090487M	2397108M	Net Sales ($)	4278M	15019M	34165M	62710M	192198M	2088738M
1071413M	1441210M	1438646M	Total Assets ($)	16050M	28697M	42073M	28344M	157073M	1166409M

M = $ thousand MM = $ million

See Pages 9 through 22 for Explanation of Ratios and Data

Current Data Sorted by Assets							Comparative Historical Data	
		1	3	1	6	**Type of Statement** Unqualified	22	21
		3	1		1	Reviewed	8	7
	1	1				Compiled	6	6
	1	1	1			Tax Returns	8	5
		3	11	1	7	Other	33	35
	4 (4/1-9/30/13)		39 (10/1/13-3/31/14)				4/1/09-3/31/10 ALL	4/1/10-3/31/11 ALL
0-500M	500M-2MM	2-10MM	10-50MM	50-100MM	100-250MM			
	2	9	16	2	14	**NUMBER OF STATEMENTS**	77	74
%	%	%	%	%	%	**ASSETS**	%	%
DATA NOT AVAILABLE			17.7		9.8	Cash & Equivalents	9.5	12.2
			13.9		10.4	Trade Receivables (net)	16.0	15.9
			2.0		1.2	Inventory	2.0	2.8
			1.7		2.1	All Other Current	3.5	3.4
			35.4		23.5	Total Current	30.9	34.2
			50.9		71.9	Fixed Assets (net)	52.3	53.9
			10.6		1.3	Intangibles (net)	2.9	2.0
			3.1		3.3	All Other Non-Current	13.9	9.9
			100.0		100.0	Total	100.0	100.0
						LIABILITIES		
			4.7		1.4	Notes Payable-Short Term	2.6	4.0
			2.2		.7	Cur. Mat.-L.T.D.	6.0	5.1
			11.6		5.4	Trade Payables	9.0	8.5
			.0		.9	Income Taxes Payable	.4	.2
			8.6		6.1	All Other Current	27.1	9.5
			27.0		14.5	Total Current	45.0	27.3
			16.8		10.5	Long-Term Debt	29.4	22.5
			2.6		9.5	Deferred Taxes	2.3	3.5
			11.7		7.5	All Other Non-Current	3.2	6.7
			41.8		58.0	Net Worth	20.2	39.9
			100.0		100.0	Total Liabilties & Net Worth	100.0	100.0
						INCOME DATA		
			100.0		100.0	Net Sales	100.0	100.0
						Gross Profit		
			82.2		84.2	Operating Expenses	88.9	86.1
			17.8		15.8	Operating Profit	11.1	13.9
			2.7		-.5	All Other Expenses (net)	2.0	1.0
			15.1		16.3	Profit Before Taxes	9.1	12.9
						RATIOS		
			2.0		2.3		2.3	2.1
			1.5		1.5	Current	1.1	1.4
			.9		1.0		.6	.7
			1.6		1.9		1.8	1.8
			1.1		1.3	Quick	.8	1.1
			.9		.7		.4	.6
			17 20.9		**33** 11.0		**15** 24.9	**23** 16.2
			41 8.8		**48** 7.6	Sales/Receivables	**38** 9.5	**40** 9.2
			64 5.7		**59** 6.2		**57** 6.4	**58** 6.3
						Cost of Sales/Inventory		
						Cost of Sales/Payables		
			4.8		3.5		6.2	5.4
			12.3		14.8	Sales/Working Capital	74.0	22.2
			NM		NM		-8.4	-23.1
			32.8		213.3		8.7	14.9
			(14) 15.2		36.3	EBIT/Interest	(69) 2.8	(63) 4.8
			3.4		12.0		1.2	2.6
							5.6	5.5
						Net Profit + Depr., Dep., Amort./Cur. Mat. L/T/D	(28) 1.9	(23) 1.8
							1.4	.7
			1.1		1.0		.8	.6
			1.5		1.3	Fixed/Worth	1.5	1.6
			5.3		1.6		4.7	3.1
			.7		.6		.6	.8
			1.4		.7	Debt/Worth	1.8	1.8
			10.5		.8		7.2	4.1
			60.3		25.3		32.0	50.3
			(13) 26.0		10.7	% Profit Before Taxes/Tangible Net Worth	(66) 15.2	(70) 21.5
			16.1		8.2		3.6	6.3
			20.5		13.3		12.8	14.5
			11.6		6.8	% Profit Before Taxes/Total Assets	6.3	7.9
			5.7		4.6		.8	3.4
			3.4		1.0		7.1	5.7
			1.1		.7	Sales/Net Fixed Assets	1.7	1.4
			.7		.5		.7	.6
			1.8		.7		2.4	2.0
			.7		.5	Sales/Total Assets	.9	.8
			.5		.4		.4	.4
			2.2		5.2		3.8	2.5
			(13) 5.7		(13) 8.3	% Depr., Dep., Amort./Sales	(70) 8.8	(63) 7.4
			10.7		10.5		11.6	11.4
						% Officers', Directors' Owners' Comp/Sales		
	12350M	64989M	646618M	194085M	2368468M	Net Sales ($)	2172616M	4421863M
	3538M	39768M	426681M	125644M	2505300M	Total Assets ($)	2766320M	2978835M

M = $ thousand MM = $ million

See Pages 9 through 22 for Explanation of Ratios and Data

Comparative Historical Data				Current Data Sorted by Sales					
Type of Statement									
Unqualified	17	10	11		1			1	9
Reviewed	12	10	5		1		2	1	1
Compiled	2	4	2		1		1		
Tax Returns	3	3	3				1	1	1
Other	28	26	22	1	2	1	4	3	11
	4/1/11-3/31/12 ALL	**4/1/12-3/31/13 ALL**	**4/1/13-3/31/14 ALL**	**4 (4/1-9/30/13)**			**39 (10/1/13-3/31/14)**		
				0-1MM	**1-3MM**	**3-5MM**	**5-10MM**	**10-25MM**	**25MM & OVER**
NUMBER OF STATEMENTS	62	53	43	1	5	1	8	6	22
	%	%	%	%	%	%	%	%	%
ASSETS									
Cash & Equivalents	12.7	12.6	15.8						14.1
Trade Receivables (net)	19.6	13.8	15.0						15.1
Inventory	3.1	2.5	1.5						1.7
All Other Current	3.5	6.4	1.8						2.2
Total Current	38.9	35.3	34.1						33.1
Fixed Assets (net)	49.0	56.8	58.3						58.9
Intangibles (net)	2.1	1.7	4.4						5.0
All Other Non-Current	9.9	6.2	3.2						3.0
Total	100.0	100.0	100.0						100.0
LIABILITIES									
Notes Payable-Short Term	4.5	3.9	4.0						.9
Cur. Mat.-L.T.D.	4.5	3.3	2.3						1.4
Trade Payables	8.1	6.7	9.1						11.3
Income Taxes Payable	.3	.3	.3						.6
All Other Current	14.7	6.0	8.7						9.1
Total Current	32.1	20.2	24.4						23.3
Long-Term Debt	17.6	20.4	13.6						11.3
Deferred Taxes	2.6	2.6	4.4						6.0
All Other Non-Current	7.2	6.4	10.3						11.8
Net Worth	40.5	50.5	47.3						47.5
Total Liabilities & Net Worth	100.0	100.0	100.0						100.0
INCOME DATA									
Net Sales	100.0	100.0	100.0						100.0
Gross Profit									
Operating Expenses	87.1	82.7	84.4						86.6
Operating Profit	12.9	17.3	15.6						13.4
All Other Expenses (net)	.5	2.3	1.4						-.1
Profit Before Taxes	12.4	15.0	14.2						13.5
RATIOS									
Current	2.3	3.1	2.3						1.9
	1.5	1.6	1.4						1.4
	.9	.9	1.0						1.0
Quick	1.9	2.4	1.8						1.7
	1.2	1.3	1.2						1.1
	.7	.6	.9						.9
Sales/Receivables	**25** 14.5	**21** 17.4	**23** 16.1						**31** 11.9
	39 9.3	**43** 8.4	**43** 8.4						**42** 8.6
	59 6.2	**62** 5.9	**60** 6.1						**59** 6.2
Cost of Sales/Inventory									
Cost of Sales/Payables									
Sales/Working Capital	4.2	3.3	4.5						5.3
	17.2	7.6	16.0						14.8
	-58.6	-55.2	391.8						199.9
EBIT/Interest	17.1	26.4	38.2						55.7
	(54) 7.4	(48) 11.7	(41) 15.7						30.7
	2.7	3.8	5.5						10.1
Net Profit + Depr., Dep., Amort./Cur. Mat. L/T/D	14.5	12.5	19.7						
	(30) 6.3	(20) 6.6	(14) 8.0						
	2.8	2.3	2.8						
Fixed/Worth	.6	.6	1.0						1.0
	1.2	1.2	1.3						1.3
	2.5	1.8	2.0						2.0
Debt/Worth	.7	.5	.6						.7
	1.5	.9	.8						.8
	2.9	2.7	2.5						1.8
% Profit Before Taxes/Tangible Net Worth	35.0	29.2	39.6						33.5
	(58) 22.1	(51) 17.8	(39) 21.9						(20) 17.7
	10.3	6.7	10.3						8.6
% Profit Before Taxes/Total Assets	14.3	14.6	14.9						14.1
	8.6	7.9	10.0						8.7
	1.9	3.3	4.4						4.6
Sales/Net Fixed Assets	7.4	3.8	5.3						5.3
	2.0	1.3	1.0						1.0
	.9	.6	.5						.5
Sales/Total Assets	2.3	1.8	2.3						2.6
	1.0	.7	.7						.7
	.5	.4	.4						.4
% Depr., Dep., Amort./Sales	3.1	5.0	2.1						1.4
	(52) 7.1	(45) 7.7	(39) 6.3						(21) 6.0
	9.5	11.2	10.5						9.2
% Officers', Directors' Owners' Comp/Sales									
Net Sales ($)	3119687M	2045323M	3286510M	670M	10962M	3493M	62858M	108303M	3100224M
Total Assets ($)	2631295M	2252936M	3100931M	4443M	67796M	3442M	55369M	193395M	2776486M

M = $ thousand MM = $ million

See Pages 9 through 22 for Explanation of Ratios and Data

Current Data Sorted by Assets							Comparative Historical Data	
						Type of Statement		
			7	1	8	Unqualified	7	6
		1				Reviewed	1	2
	1		2		2	Compiled	2	
		1				Tax Returns	2	6
2		3	1	3	2	Other	12	15
1 (4/1-9/30/13)			33 (10/1/13-3/31/14)				4/1/09-3/31/10 ALL	4/1/10-3/31/11 ALL
0-500M	**500M-2MM**	**2-10MM**	**10-50MM**	**50-100MM**	**100-250MM**			
2	1	5	10	4	12	**NUMBER OF STATEMENTS**	24	29
%	%	%	%	%	%	**ASSETS**	%	%
			16.0		16.0	Cash & Equivalents	12.2	16.8
			8.7		8.3	Trade Receivables (net)	18.2	13.2
			.2		1.8	Inventory	6.2	5.6
			.2		.5	All Other Current	2.7	7.6
			25.1		26.6	Total Current	39.3	43.3
			59.0		59.0	Fixed Assets (net)	43.5	47.6
			7.2		5.3	Intangibles (net)	2.7	1.1
			8.6		9.1	All Other Non-Current	14.5	8.0
			100.0		100.0	Total	100.0	100.0
						LIABILITIES		
			.8		.2	Notes Payable-Short Term	4.9	4.7
			3.4		4.7	Cur. Mat.-L.T.D.	8.8	6.9
			2.1		5.7	Trade Payables	14.2	7.8
			.0		.0	Income Taxes Payable	.1	.1
			11.3		10.1	All Other Current	10.0	11.8
			17.7		20.7	Total Current	38.0	31.3
			25.9		34.1	Long-Term Debt	37.2	34.5
			.5		.5	Deferred Taxes	1.4	1.6
			5.9		7.3	All Other Non-Current	5.2	7.0
			50.1		37.4	Net Worth	18.2	25.6
			100.0		100.0	Total Liabilties & Net Worth	100.0	100.0
						INCOME DATA		
			100.0		100.0	Net Sales	100.0	100.0
						Gross Profit		
			90.8		84.8	Operating Expenses	92.4	85.7
			9.2		15.2	Operating Profit	7.6	14.3
			12.3		1.6	All Other Expenses (net)	3.3	3.4
			-3.1		13.6	Profit Before Taxes	4.3	10.9
						RATIOS		
			2.2		1.9		1.8	1.8
			.8		1.4	Current	1.3	1.4
			.3		.9		.6	.8
			2.1		1.8		1.5	1.4
			.8		1.3	Quick	1.1	.7
			.3		.7		.3	.4
			0 UND		**19** 19.5		**18** 20.0	**0** UND
			4 101.0		**31** 11.7	Sales/Receivables	**33** 11.0	**18** 20.1
			22 16.5		**54** 6.8		**53** 7.0	**40** 9.2
						Cost of Sales/Inventory		
						Cost of Sales/Payables		
			8.7		6.9		8.1	6.7
			-275.5		14.7	Sales/Working Capital	32.2	18.0
			-.9		NM		-15.5	-37.8
					9.1		3.7	17.3
					3.6	EBIT/Interest	(23) 1.9	(25) 3.3
					-.3		1.3	1.4
						Net Profit + Depr., Dep., Amort./Cur. Mat. L/T/D		
			.6		.8		.2	.1
			1.6		2.4	Fixed/Worth	1.2	1.7
			2.6		3.5		2.5	2.7
			.5		.9		1.1	1.4
			1.0		2.6	Debt/Worth	1.6	2.0
			4.1		3.5		20.5	4.8
			59.2		32.5		27.5	57.8
			6.3		13.3	% Profit Before Taxes/Tangible Net Worth	(20) 7.4	(27) 21.4
			-5.3		-5.5		1.3	2.8
			25.0		7.1		12.7	17.3
			2.7		4.7	% Profit Before Taxes/Total Assets	2.6	5.5
			-2.2		-2.0		.4	1.2
			23.7		3.7		25.4	74.8
			.2		1.2	Sales/Net Fixed Assets	3.9	3.4
			.1		.3		1.1	1.0
			2.2		1.9		2.3	3.6
			.2		.6	Sales/Total Assets	1.2	1.1
			.1		.2		.7	.7
							1.5	1.5
						% Depr., Dep., Amort./Sales	(16) 4.8	(16) 4.8
							8.4	21.5
						% Officers', Directors' Owners' Comp/Sales		
3627M	3727M	54535M	403402M	195571M	1983035M	Net Sales ($)	1520333M	2790947M
738M	969M	24336M	263658M	342293M	2208405M	Total Assets ($)	1212218M	1919451M

M = $ thousand MM = $ million

See Pages 9 through 22 for Explanation of Ratios and Data

Comparative Historical Data				Current Data Sorted by Sales					
			Type of Statement						
7	4	16	Unqualified	1	2	1			12
1	1	1	Reviewed					1	
	2	5	Compiled			1	2		2
2	2	1	Tax Returns					1	
16	14	11	Other	1	2	2	3		3
4/1/11-3/31/12 ALL	4/1/12-3/31/13 ALL	4/1/13-3/31/14 ALL			1 (4/1-9/30/13)		33 (10/1/13-3/31/14)		
				0-1MM	1-3MM	3-5MM	5-10MM	10-25MM	25MM & OVER
26	23	34	**NUMBER OF STATEMENTS**	2	4	4	5	2	17
%	%	%	**ASSETS**	%	%	%	%	%	%
18.8	11.1	14.0	Cash & Equivalents						17.9
16.2	14.7	12.4	Trade Receivables (net)						11.6
5.2	4.3	2.8	Inventory						1.5
5.8	8.3	4.0	All Other Current						2.1
46.0	38.3	33.1	Total Current						33.1
41.8	50.8	51.9	Fixed Assets (net)						53.4
4.3	1.0	4.1	Intangibles (net)						5.4
7.8	9.9	10.9	All Other Non-Current						8.1
100.0	100.0	100.0	Total						100.0
			LIABILITIES						
3.0	1.5	2.3	Notes Payable-Short Term						.3
6.0	5.3	4.3	Cur. Mat.-L.T.D.						4.7
9.1	12.1	7.6	Trade Payables						5.3
.1	.1	.0	Income Taxes Payable						.0
11.9	6.3	9.8	All Other Current						14.1
30.1	25.3	24.0	Total Current						24.3
16.1	27.0	30.4	Long-Term Debt						35.0
.6	.8	.4	Deferred Taxes						.6
5.5	6.0	5.9	All Other Non-Current						6.8
47.6	40.8	39.4	Net Worth						33.2
100.0	100.0	100.0	Total Liabilities & Net Worth						100.0
			INCOME DATA						
100.0	100.0	100.0	Net Sales						100.0
			Gross Profit						
85.4	82.4	88.2	Operating Expenses						86.6
14.6	17.6	11.8	Operating Profit						13.4
.8	2.1	5.7	All Other Expenses (net)						2.3
13.9	15.5	6.1	Profit Before Taxes						11.1
			RATIOS						
2.7	3.3	1.9							1.9
1.3	2.0	1.3	Current						1.5
.9	1.0	.8							.9
2.0	2.8	1.6							1.8
.9	1.5	1.0	Quick						1.2
.5	.8	.4							.7
8 47.9	14 26.4	2 164.8							18 20.5
31 11.8	39 9.3	19 19.2	Sales/Receivables						30 12.1
49 7.5	74 4.9	49 7.5							50 7.3
			Cost of Sales/Inventory						
			Cost of Sales/Payables						
3.5	3.1	7.3							7.1
56.8	4.5	16.1	Sales/Working Capital						12.5
-49.6	-355.6	-12.9							-286.1
121.3	13.9	40.6							53.9
(21) 10.6	(20) 6.2	(29) 3.9	EBIT/Interest						(16) 3.6
2.3	1.8	.0							-.2
			Net Profit + Depr., Dep., Amort./Cur. Mat. L/T/D						
.2	.4	.5							.7
.8	1.2	1.5	Fixed/Worth						2.7
2.4	2.7	2.8							3.8
.5	.6	.8							1.0
1.4	1.5	1.7	Debt/Worth						3.1
2.5	4.2	3.5							4.1
82.0	38.1	35.8							44.9
29.8	(22) 22.2	(32) 14.1	% Profit Before Taxes/Tangible Net Worth						(16) 20.0
6.2	11.2	-3.9							-4.4
34.7	18.2	8.2							12.3
12.0	7.4	4.7	% Profit Before Taxes/Total Assets						4.8
3.7	3.0	-1.6							-1.8
48.2	26.6	15.3							9.1
9.0	2.0	1.9	Sales/Net Fixed Assets						2.5
1.2	.7	.2							.6
3.7	1.9	2.2							2.0
1.2	1.1	.6	Sales/Total Assets						.8
.7	.5	.2							.4
1.0	1.9	1.7							1.6
(18) 3.1	(14) 6.9	(24) 6.8	% Depr., Dep., Amort./Sales						(14) 5.7
7.1	19.2	19.5							9.3
			% Officers', Directors' Owners' Comp/Sales						
2416304M	1465342M	2643897M	Net Sales ($)	305M	7769M	13625M	37940M	35151M	2549107M
1579494M	1588969M	2840399M	Total Assets ($)	16462M	151382M	59779M	148673M	11106M	2452997M

M = $ thousand MM = $ million

See Pages 9 through 22 for Explanation of Ratios and Data

Current Data Sorted by Assets							Comparative Historical Data	
						Type of Statement		
		1	1	3	6	Unqualified	13	9
		1		1		Reviewed	3	2
		4				Compiled	1	2
	2	3				Tax Returns	2	1
1	1	5	8	3	6	Other	12	7
7 (4/1-9/30/13)			39 (10/1/13-3/31/14)				4/1/09-3/31/10 ALL	4/1/10-3/31/11 ALL
0-500M	500M-2MM	2-10MM	10-50MM	50-100MM	100-250MM			
1	3	14	9	7	12	NUMBER OF STATEMENTS	31	21
%	%	%	%	%	%	**ASSETS**	%	%
		9.0			7.6	Cash & Equivalents	12.6	12.1
		18.7			11.1	Trade Receivables (net)	12.9	11.7
		1.0			3.4	Inventory	1.9	.8
		4.0			2.3	All Other Current	5.6	3.4
		32.6			24.4	Total Current	33.0	28.0
		60.2			68.5	Fixed Assets (net)	55.0	64.6
		1.7			4.3	Intangibles (net)	2.5	2.7
		5.6			2.8	All Other Non-Current	9.5	4.7
		100.0			100.0	Total	100.0	100.0
						LIABILITIES		
		2.0			2.3	Notes Payable-Short Term	5.8	6.4
		3.9			6.7	Cur. Mat.-L.T.D.	6.3	3.8
		7.5			3.1	Trade Payables	7.4	5.1
		.0			.2	Income Taxes Payable	.1	1.0
		5.7			5.5	All Other Current	7.4	8.5
		19.1			17.8	Total Current	27.0	24.8
		21.2			27.3	Long-Term Debt	28.2	36.0
		.2			.8	Deferred Taxes	2.3	.0
		.4			6.1	All Other Non-Current	5.2	7.6
		59.0			48.0	Net Worth	37.3	31.5
		100.0			100.0	Total Liabilities & Net Worth	100.0	100.0
						INCOME DATA		
		100.0			100.0	Net Sales	100.0	100.0
						Gross Profit		
		76.1			84.2	Operating Expenses	86.8	85.8
		23.9			15.8	Operating Profit	13.2	14.2
		.4			-.3	All Other Expenses (net)	1.9	5.4
		23.5			16.0	Profit Before Taxes	11.3	8.7
						RATIOS		
		14.9			2.6		2.2	2.0
		2.2			2.0	Current	1.2	1.1
		1.0			.7		.7	.6
		14.7			2.0		1.8	1.8
		2.1			1.8	Quick	1.0	1.0
		1.0			.6		.2	.4
		20 17.9			**43** 8.5		**14** 25.6	**32** 11.6
		63 5.8			**51** 7.1	Sales/Receivables	**38** 9.7	**39** 9.3
		91 4.0			**76** 4.8		**55** 6.7	**54** 6.7
						Cost of Sales/Inventory		
						Cost of Sales/Payables		
		3.6			3.8		7.0	5.2
		12.2			8.0	Sales/Working Capital	38.2	58.3
		NM			-6.6		-9.2	-8.7
		142.9			15.0		5.1	13.5
		13.3			10.2	EBIT/Interest	(27) 1.8	(20) 3.0
		5.7			3.3		1.2	.4
						Net Profit + Depr., Dep., Amort./Cur. Mat. L/T/D		
		.7			1.3		1.1	1.2
		1.1			1.5	Fixed/Worth	1.6	2.0
		1.3			1.8		4.4	7.5
		.3			.6		.7	1.0
		.4			1.1	Debt/Worth	2.1	2.9
		1.8			1.3		6.2	8.7
		49.7			25.9		47.3	70.8
		(13) 23.6			(11) 11.8	% Profit Before Taxes/Tangible Net Worth	(29) 15.3	(18) 20.5
		9.2			9.1		2.1	-2.6
		29.6			17.8		9.1	14.2
		14.7			7.2	% Profit Before Taxes/Total Assets	3.4	4.8
		5.5			4.8		1.6	-1.2
		8.7			1.2		10.5	2.1
		2.1			.9	Sales/Net Fixed Assets	1.1	.7
		.3			.6		.5	.4
		2.2			.9		2.5	1.2
		1.3			.6	Sales/Total Assets	.5	.5
		.2			.4		.3	.3
		2.9					2.2	2.8
		(13) 6.8				% Depr., Dep., Amort./Sales	(24) 5.5	(17) 9.3
		30.5					11.5	17.1
						% Officers', Directors' Owners' Comp/Sales		
3157M	10751M	111394M	259610M	280271M	1829463M	Net Sales ($)	1469650M	921202M
340M	3933M	67773M	201341M	512171M	2303869M	Total Assets ($)	1993348M	1364144M

M = $ thousand MM = $ million

See Pages 9 through 22 for Explanation of Ratios and Data

Comparative Historical Data				Current Data Sorted by Sales					
14	13	11	Unqualified				1	1	9
7	4	2	Reviewed				1		1
1	7	4	Compiled			1	2		1
3	3	5	Tax Returns	1	1	2		1	
21	21	24	Other	1	4	3	1	6	9
4/1/11-3/31/12	4/1/12-3/31/13	4/1/13-3/31/14		7 (4/1-9/30/13)			39 (10/1/13-3/31/14)		
ALL	ALL	ALL		0-1MM	1-3MM	3-5MM	5-10MM	10-25MM	25MM & OVER
46	48	46	NUMBER OF STATEMENTS	2	5	6	5	8	20
%	%	%	ASSETS	%	%	%	%	%	%
11.6	10.1	9.9	Cash & Equivalents						9.4
15.8	12.7	14.7	Trade Receivables (net)						17.5
1.7	2.2	2.1	Inventory						2.4
3.2	2.6	2.6	All Other Current						2.4
32.2	27.6	29.3	Total Current						31.7
61.4	64.1	59.6	Fixed Assets (net)						53.4
2.4	2.0	3.3	Intangibles (net)						5.1
4.0	6.3	7.8	All Other Non-Current						9.8
100.0	100.0	100.0	Total						100.0
			LIABILITIES						
7.2	5.3	3.9	Notes Payable-Short Term						2.8
3.5	5.3	5.5	Cur. Mat.-L.T.D.						5.0
7.1	5.2	6.8	Trade Payables						6.7
.7	.3	.0	Income Taxes Payable						.1
8.7	8.0	5.6	All Other Current						6.2
27.2	24.1	21.9	Total Current						20.8
31.6	30.5	25.8	Long-Term Debt						25.9
1.6	.6	.5	Deferred Taxes						.9
7.2	2.7	3.3	All Other Non-Current						5.3
32.4	42.1	48.5	Net Worth						47.0
100.0	100.0	100.0	Total Liabilities & Net Worth						100.0
			INCOME DATA						
100.0	100.0	100.0	Net Sales						100.0
			Gross Profit						
88.6	86.1	83.3	Operating Expenses						85.3
11.4	13.9	16.7	Operating Profit						14.7
2.9	2.9	2.1	All Other Expenses (net)						.3
8.4	11.1	14.5	Profit Before Taxes						14.3
			RATIOS						
2.1	2.2	4.0							3.3
1.1	1.1	1.3	Current						2.1
.6	.5	.7							.8
1.8	1.9	2.6							2.3
.9	.9	1.2	Quick						1.9
.4	.4	.6							.7
25 14.6	19 19.2	21 17.1							42 8.6
43 8.5	38 9.5	49 7.4	Sales/Receivables						49 7.4
64 5.7	65 5.6	73 5.0							72 5.1
			Cost of Sales/Inventory						
			Cost of Sales/Payables						
5.4	7.5	3.6							3.2
69.6	84.3	15.1	Sales/Working Capital						8.0
-7.2	-5.6	-15.3							-23.4
11.3	11.2	18.4							32.8
(42) 4.2	(47) 3.9	(44) 8.0	EBIT/Interest						10.6
1.9	1.5	2.8							3.0
	12.1								
	(11) 3.5		Net Profit + Depr., Dep., Amort./Cur. Mat. L/T/D						
	1.6								
1.2	1.2	.7							.5
2.1	1.7	1.3	Fixed/Worth						1.4
4.3	3.7	2.1							1.8
1.0	.7	.4							.6
2.4	1.5	1.1	Debt/Worth						1.2
5.3	3.3	2.3							2.2
47.7	40.5	32.1							32.8
(41) 20.5	(44) 12.5	(42) 14.4	% Profit Before Taxes/Tangible Net Worth						(19) 18.6
5.4	2.5	8.4							10.0
15.5	14.7	16.8							16.6
6.2	5.5	7.2	% Profit Before Taxes/Total Assets						8.3
1.9	.7	3.6							4.8
4.1	4.3	4.9							5.9
1.8	1.0	1.4	Sales/Net Fixed Assets						1.1
.7	.5	.6							.7
2.2	2.0	1.6							1.2
1.0	.7	.8	Sales/Total Assets						.7
.6	.4	.4							.5
2.8	1.8	3.5							1.3
(35) 4.0	(42) 8.8	(35) 6.8	% Depr., Dep., Amort./Sales						(12) 4.7
10.4	17.4	15.2							9.1
		1.4							
		(11) 2.7	% Officers', Directors' Owners' Comp/Sales						
		5.1							
2844319M	3611771M	2494646M	Net Sales ($)	1589M	8523M	24092M	34445M	147913M	2278084M
2913838M	3230551M	3089427M	Total Assets ($)	6009M	27757M	31086M	96576M	201196M	2726803M

M = $ thousand MM = $ million

See Pages 9 through 22 for Explanation of Ratios and Data

Current Data Sorted by Assets							Comparative Historical Data	
						Type of Statement		
		3	9	4	4	Unqualified	23	18
		3	9	6	1	Reviewed	11	8
3	3	3	2			Compiled	11	14
4	4	1	4			Tax Returns	12	13
1	6	13	16	2	10	Other	70	59
16 (4/1-9/30/13)		95 (10/1/13-3/31/14)					4/1/09-3/31/10 ALL	4/1/10-3/31/11 ALL
0-500M	500M-2MM	2-10MM	10-50MM	50-100MM	100-250MM			
8	13	23	40	12	15	NUMBER OF STATEMENTS	127	112
%	%	%	%	%	%	**ASSETS**	%	%
	12.0	9.4	10.4	10.2	4.6	Cash & Equivalents	12.3	15.3
	25.5	20.5	14.2	8.0	8.9	Trade Receivables (net)	12.1	14.7
	.2	.6	1.0	2.1	1.7	Inventory	.9	1.4
	.9	1.8	1.4	2.9	3.5	All Other Current	3.8	4.4
	38.7	32.3	27.0	23.2	18.7	Total Current	29.1	35.8
	45.6	52.2	62.9	59.4	72.9	Fixed Assets (net)	61.4	56.6
	4.7	.7	1.7	3.0	1.9	Intangibles (net)	2.5	1.6
	11.1	14.8	8.4	14.4	6.5	All Other Non-Current	7.0	5.9
	100.0	100.0	100.0	100.0	100.0	Total	100.0	100.0
						LIABILITIES		
	9.8	5.0	2.8	1.2	4.5	Notes Payable-Short Term	3.0	3.4
	4.5	3.9	4.5	3.9	3.7	Cur. Mat.-L.T.D.	6.2	5.0
	4.9	5.7	7.4	4.6	5.9	Trade Payables	6.0	8.6
	.0	.1	.0	.0	.0	Income Taxes Payable	.2	.1
	5.8	7.4	8.1	3.0	5.8	All Other Current	10.3	9.5
	24.9	22.1	22.8	12.8	19.9	Total Current	25.6	26.6
	55.1	29.0	34.1	28.8	45.8	Long-Term Debt	37.3	33.8
	.0	.8	1.4	1.1	2.9	Deferred Taxes	1.3	1.5
	2.2	4.1	3.0	1.1	2.0	All Other Non-Current	4.5	4.7
	17.8	44.0	38.6	56.1	29.6	Net Worth	31.3	33.4
	100.0	100.0	100.0	100.0	100.0	Total Liabilties & Net Worth	100.0	100.0
						INCOME DATA		
	100.0	100.0	100.0	100.0	100.0	Net Sales	100.0	100.0
						Gross Profit		
	85.0	81.5	83.1	74.1	84.9	Operating Expenses	87.8	85.5
	15.0	18.5	16.9	25.9	15.1	Operating Profit	12.2	14.5
	4.7	3.9	4.6	3.1	5.3	All Other Expenses (net)	5.1	4.0
	10.3	14.5	12.3	22.7	9.8	Profit Before Taxes	7.0	10.5
						RATIOS		
	7.5	2.6	2.4	2.5	1.9		2.5	3.1
	1.5	1.7	1.3	1.7	1.4	Current	1.4	1.4
	.7	.8	.6	1.2	1.0		.6	.7
	7.5	2.1	2.0	1.9	1.6		2.1	2.5
	1.4	1.7	1.0	1.2	1.0	Quick	1.0	1.1
	.7	.6	.5	.8	.6		.4	.5
	0 UND	**19** 19.6	**16** 23.2	**24** 15.2	**32** 11.5		**5** 66.7	**12** 30.4
	31 11.8	**31** 11.6	**36** 10.2	**41** 8.8	**40** 9.2	Sales/Receivables	**30** 12.2	**31** 11.9
	59 6.2	**54** 6.7	**46** 7.9	**47** 7.8	**53** 6.9		**47** 7.7	**47** 7.8
						Cost of Sales/Inventory		
						Cost of Sales/Payables		
	3.9	7.0	6.2	3.5	7.8		5.6	5.4
	18.0	22.9	20.2	8.3	15.5	Sales/Working Capital	24.2	17.8
	-512.7	-23.7	-7.7	35.6	216.7		-9.5	-22.8
	83.6	20.2	29.1	35.2	5.2		7.9	14.7
	(10) 3.3	(22) 11.7	(31) 7.7	5.5	(14) 2.9	EBIT/Interest	(102) 2.9	(93) 5.1
	1.6	4.4	2.1	1.9	1.6		.4	2.2
							4.6	3.9
						Net Profit + Depr., Dep., Amort./Cur. Mat. L/T/D	(16) 3.3	(13) 1.3
							1.1	1.0
	.2	.3	.8	.6	1.6		1.0	.7
	1.0	1.6	1.7	1.3	2.1	Fixed/Worth	2.4	1.7
	NM	3.6	5.9	2.0	4.4		10.6	5.0
	.3	.5	.7	.4	1.3		.8	.7
	1.1	1.5	1.4	1.1	2.7	Debt/Worth	2.1	2.2
	-16.4	5.5	5.7	1.6	9.8		12.9	5.7
		112.5	28.0	27.4	31.2		49.0	46.8
		(22) 39.5	(37) 17.9	12.8	(14) 10.1	% Profit Before Taxes/Tangible Net Worth	(105) 16.4	(98) 23.3
		13.5	7.9	6.3	3.3		-1.6	11.8
	41.1	21.6	12.4	16.0	5.4		11.1	15.2
	14.9	12.8	7.4	7.2	2.9	% Profit Before Taxes/Total Assets	4.8	7.4
	-.1	7.6	1.6	2.3	1.1		-2.2	3.1
	17.1	9.9	3.6	2.3	1.1		3.6	7.5
	6.2	2.4	1.2	.9	.6	Sales/Net Fixed Assets	1.2	1.7
	1.0	1.3	.3	.6	.4		.6	.8
	4.4	2.0	1.5	1.0	.7		1.6	2.3
	2.0	1.2	.8	.6	.4	Sales/Total Assets	.9	1.1
	.8	.8	.3	.3	.4		.5	.6
	2.9	1.1	4.3	3.4			4.0	2.6
	(10) 6.3	(18) 3.8	(39) 6.9	(11) 8.4		% Depr., Dep., Amort./Sales	(97) 8.7	(88) 6.9
	23.7	11.1	23.0	9.5			18.4	12.8
							1.3	1.2
						% Officers', Directors' Owners' Comp/Sales	(17) 2.3	(21) 2.6
							12.2	5.1
4510M	43574M	210420M	781608M	682712M	1738313M	Net Sales ($)	4402210M	4646657M
2295M	15997M	125492M	858542M	891967M	2509335M	Total Assets ($)	5381805M	4760202M

M = $ thousand MM = $ million

See Pages 9 through 22 for Explanation of Ratios and Data

Comparative Historical Data | **Current Data Sorted by Sales**

	4/1/11-3/31/12 ALL	4/1/12-3/31/13 ALL	4/1/13-3/31/14 ALL	0-1MM	1-3MM	3-5MM	5-10MM	10-25MM	25MM & OVER
Type of Statement									
Unqualified	25	14	20				1	6	13
Reviewed	9	13	19		3	1	2	7	6
Compiled	16	13	11	3	4		1	1	2
Tax Returns	14	9	13	7	2	1	1	2	
Other	52	57	48	2	6	7	10	7	16
				16 (4/1-9/30/13)			95 (10/1/13-3/31/14)		
NUMBER OF STATEMENTS	116	106	111	12	15	9	15	23	37
ASSETS	%	%	%	%	%	%	%	%	%
Cash & Equivalents	15.6	13.9	10.9	20.2	8.4		9.5	11.4	10.5
Trade Receivables (net)	16.2	15.3	14.7	3.6	14.5		14.9	17.2	17.1
Inventory	1.2	.8	1.1	.8	.2		.7	1.7	1.4
All Other Current	3.5	2.1	2.0	1.7	.7		1.9	2.8	2.4
Total Current	36.5	32.1	28.7	26.2	23.8		27.0	33.1	31.4
Fixed Assets (net)	54.0	57.5	58.8	58.6	60.0		63.6	55.6	57.7
Intangibles (net)	2.2	3.8	2.0	1.8	.2		2.5	2.2	2.8
All Other Non-Current	7.3	6.6	10.6	13.4	15.9		6.9	9.1	8.0
Total	100.0	100.0	100.0	100.0	100.0		100.0	100.0	100.0
LIABILITIES									
Notes Payable-Short Term	3.7	2.3	3.9	5.1	5.2		3.3	2.7	2.9
Cur. Mat.-L.T.D.	6.3	4.4	5.2	14.6	3.0		6.7	4.4	3.9
Trade Payables	6.5	5.8	7.8	.3	1.1		8.2	8.3	8.0
Income Taxes Payable	.1	.1	.0	.0	.0		.0	.0	.0
All Other Current	9.1	5.1	6.5	4.1	2.2		7.0	4.8	8.7
Total Current	25.7	17.8	21.5	24.1	11.5		25.3	20.2	23.6
Long-Term Debt	31.0	36.0	44.4	115.2	46.1		38.6	30.6	29.6
Deferred Taxes	2.1	1.5	1.2	.0	.0		.4	2.6	1.8
All Other Non-Current	5.5	3.1	2.8	3.0	7.0		1.8	2.5	2.0
Net Worth	35.7	41.7	30.2	-42.2	35.5		33.9	44.1	43.0
Total Liabilties & Net Worth	100.0	100.0	100.0	100.0	100.0		100.0	100.0	100.0
INCOME DATA									
Net Sales	100.0	100.0	100.0	100.0	100.0		100.0	100.0	100.0
Gross Profit									
Operating Expenses	85.6	83.1	82.7	82.3	73.6		83.4	83.4	86.4
Operating Profit	14.4	16.9	17.3	17.7	26.4		16.6	16.6	13.6
All Other Expenses (net)	3.5	3.5	4.3	6.5	12.0		1.7	3.6	1.6
Profit Before Taxes	10.9	13.4	13.0	11.2	14.4		14.9	13.0	12.1
RATIOS									
	2.7	3.3	2.6	3.9	11.2		2.0	2.6	2.2
Current	1.4	1.7	1.5	.6	3.8		1.1	1.6	1.6
	.8	.9	.8	.1	.3		.4	.9	1.1
	2.4	3.0	2.1	3.4	11.2		1.9	2.1	1.9
Quick	1.1	1.5	1.2	.6	1.7		.7	1.2	1.3
	.7	.8	.7	.1	.3		.4	.8	.8
	17 21.1	**21** 17.1	**15** 25.1	**0** UND	**0** UND		**2** 230.7	**19** 19.6	**33** 11.0
Sales/Receivables	**38** 9.6	**34** 10.6	**35** 10.5	**0** UND	**31** 11.7		**43** 8.4	**30** 12.1	**41** 8.8
	52 7.0	**50** 7.3	**48** 7.6	**24** 15.2	**79** 4.6		**58** 6.3	**46** 7.9	**47** 7.8
Cost of Sales/Inventory									
Cost of Sales/Payables									
	5.1	4.8	6.1	3.8	3.8		6.1	4.1	7.5
Sales/Working Capital	14.2	11.0	16.1	-74.2	14.0		125.0	14.6	11.6
	-26.4	-63.1	-25.6	-2.1	-6.5		-16.2	-48.5	64.1
	12.9	18.1	17.4		42.1		14.0	13.3	25.4
EBIT/Interest	(100) 3.9	(91) 5.4	(96) 5.9		(10) 7.1		6.3	(20) 6.4	(36) 6.1
	1.5	2.3	1.9		3.0		3.4	.4	2.0
	4.6	38.0	13.9						40.2
Net Profit + Depr., Dep., Amort./Cur. Mat. L/T/D	(18) 1.9	(17) 6.1	(14) 4.1						(10) 4.1
	1.3	2.3	1.7						1.8
	.7	.6	.5	.7	.3		.9	.3	.8
Fixed/Worth	1.7	1.6	1.6	8.3	1.1		3.3	1.3	1.7
	3.7	4.2	5.0	-13.1	6.2		9.6	5.0	2.4
	.7	.5	.6	2.1	.3		.6	.6	.7
Debt/Worth	1.8	1.6	1.6	NM	1.1		3.3	.9	1.5
	4.9	4.9	5.7	-10.4	5.5		9.4	5.7	2.7
	40.4	53.5	43.7		55.0		83.2	49.9	30.1
% Profit Before Taxes/Tangible Net Worth	(100) 21.8	(99) 26.3	(97) 20.1		(13) 8.0		(14) 20.0	(21) 20.1	(35) 19.9
	4.2	11.3	7.0		1.2		7.9	9.5	6.4
	16.4	20.3	16.4	17.6	34.8		12.8	14.4	16.1
% Profit Before Taxes/Total Assets	5.9	9.1	7.7	6.7	7.6		9.8	6.6	7.4
	.5	2.8	1.9	-4.7	1.9		7.3	2.7	2.2
	6.8	5.1	5.4	5.2	10.4		3.9	9.9	3.5
Sales/Net Fixed Assets	1.5	1.7	1.5	1.1	2.2		2.0	2.1	1.5
	.8	.7	.6	.5	.2		.7	.9	.6
	1.9	1.9	1.6	1.7	1.2		1.4	1.6	1.9
Sales/Total Assets	.9	1.1	.9	.8	.8		1.0	1.2	.9
	.6	.5	.4	.3	.1		.5	.8	.5
	3.4	3.0	3.1	11.1	3.0		3.1	1.8	1.9
% Depr., Dep., Amort./Sales	(90) 7.2	(92) 6.4	(93) 7.3	(11) 24.6	(11) 24.8		(13) 9.4	(22) 5.2	(30) 5.8
	11.5	10.6	13.3	31.7	57.0		11.9	12.5	7.8
	1.5	1.1	1.9						
% Officers', Directors' Owners' Comp/Sales	(18) 3.4	(17) 2.3	(17) 3.4						
	9.3	5.0	9.6						
Net Sales ($)	5504884M	4668463M	3461137M	6443M	27265M	33575M	108370M	362315M	2923169M
Total Assets ($)	5665574M	5016507M	4403628M	22426M	102712M	129737M	206126M	558963M	3383664M

M = $ thousand MM = $ million

See Pages 9 through 22 for Explanation of Ratios and Data

Current Data Sorted by Assets | **Comparative Historical Data**

0-500M	500M-2MM	2-10MM	10-50MM	50-100MM	100-250MM		4/1/09-3/31/10 ALL	4/1/10-3/31/11 ALL
						Type of Statement		
1	2	7	25	19	9	Unqualified	63	58
2	15	51	38	3	1	Reviewed	173	153
21	46	72	9	2		Compiled	191	202
107	114	50	6	3		Tax Returns	274	267
60	106	148	68	23	11	Other	349	380
118 (4/1-9/30/13)			901 (10/1/13-3/31/14)					
191	283	328	146	50	21	**NUMBER OF STATEMENTS**	1050	1060
%	%	%	%	%	%	**ASSETS**	%	%
22.1	13.1	9.7	7.1	7.7	4.1	Cash & Equivalents	11.1	12.0
17.6	28.2	29.4	26.9	18.3	17.2	Trade Receivables (net)	25.3	28.2
1.4	1.8	2.2	3.0	.9	3.6	Inventory	2.1	1.7
4.5	2.6	4.2	3.1	3.3	3.6	All Other Current	4.4	4.1
45.6	45.7	45.4	40.1	30.1	28.6	Total Current	42.8	46.0
39.6	40.0	42.9	48.5	59.0	56.6	Fixed Assets (net)	43.5	41.0
4.4	4.3	3.5	4.0	4.7	3.8	Intangibles (net)	4.0	3.2
10.4	10.0	8.2	7.4	6.1	11.1	All Other Non-Current	9.7	9.8
100.0	100.0	100.0	100.0	100.0	100.0	Total	100.0	100.0
						LIABILITIES		
12.8	9.9	7.1	8.9	5.1	4.4	Notes Payable-Short Term	11.0	10.3
6.9	4.7	7.5	8.5	11.2	9.5	Cur. Mat.-L.T.D.	9.5	8.3
10.8	11.5	10.6	9.1	5.9	7.3	Trade Payables	10.5	10.9
.1	.2	.2	.2	.3	.0	Income Taxes Payable	.2	.2
16.9	9.2	7.9	6.7	5.7	7.0	All Other Current	10.6	11.0
47.5	35.5	33.3	33.4	28.1	28.4	Total Current	41.8	40.7
43.6	29.9	27.3	27.1	32.3	40.2	Long-Term Debt	30.2	28.6
.1	.2	.6	1.4	3.9	1.6	Deferred Taxes	.9	.8
16.8	6.1	4.2	2.3	3.3	2.3	All Other Non-Current	7.1	6.4
-7.9	28.4	34.6	35.8	32.5	27.5	Net Worth	20.1	23.4
100.0	100.0	100.0	100.0	100.0	100.0	Total Liabilties & Net Worth	100.0	100.0
						INCOME DATA		
100.0	100.0	100.0	100.0	100.0	100.0	Net Sales	100.0	100.0
						Gross Profit		
93.9	93.6	93.4	95.9	95.6	95.3	Operating Expenses	96.7	95.7
6.1	6.4	6.6	4.1	4.4	4.7	Operating Profit	3.3	4.3
.6	1.0	.9	.7	1.3	.8	All Other Expenses (net)	1.6	.9
5.5	5.4	5.7	3.4	3.1	3.9	Profit Before Taxes	1.6	3.4
						RATIOS		
3.6	2.9	2.6	1.6	1.6	1.3		2.1	2.2
1.0	1.3	1.3	1.2	1.1	1.1	Current	1.1	1.2
.4	.7	.8	.9	.8	.8		.6	.7
3.0	2.8	2.3	1.4	1.4	1.3		1.8	2.0
.9	1.1	1.1	1.0	1.0	.8	Quick	.9	(1059) 1.1
.3	.6	.7	.7	.7	.5		.5	.6
0 UND	**0** UND	**20** 18.3	**30** 12.2	**27** 13.5	**27** 13.5		**11** 31.8	**12** 29.3
0 UND	**25** 14.6	**35** 10.3	**41** 9.0	**37** 9.8	**35** 10.5	Sales/Receivables	**32** 11.6	**32** 11.5
19 19.0	**40** 9.2	**46** 7.9	**49** 7.4	**46** 7.9	**44** 8.3		**46** 8.0	**47** 7.7
						Cost of Sales/Inventory		
						Cost of Sales/Payables		
19.2	11.4	8.9	14.2	16.9	22.4		11.3	11.2
999.8	48.2	28.4	43.5	89.5	74.9	Sales/Working Capital	82.4	46.3
-19.8	-39.4	-42.0	-73.9	-34.7	-34.1		-16.6	-27.4
13.0	14.7	12.1	10.1	8.2	6.5		6.3	9.2
(124) 4.4	(223) 4.3	(293) 4.8	(143) 4.5	(47) 3.6	4.3	EBIT/Interest	(927) 1.9	(927) 3.2
.1	1.3	1.7	2.1	1.8	2.4		-.4	1.0
	5.6	3.4	2.6	2.3			2.3	2.5
	(13) 1.5	(57) 1.8	(53) 1.7	(20) 1.7		Net Profit + Depr., Dep., Amort./Cur. Mat. L/T/D	(188) 1.2	(177) 1.7
	.4	1.0	1.4	1.2			.7	1.1
.1	.3	.5	.9	1.2	1.6		.6	.5
1.4	1.3	1.5	1.6	1.9	2.1	Fixed/Worth	1.7	1.3
-2.1	30.2	3.9	2.7	3.5	3.5		25.5	6.6
.7	.8	.8	1.2	1.0	1.5		.9	.8
4.7	2.5	2.1	1.9	2.4	2.0	Debt/Worth	2.7	2.2
-3.5	67.6	7.5	4.0	4.5	6.8		UND	14.2
126.0	64.9	50.7	36.0	30.7	41.3		33.8	46.5
(119) 36.6	(219) 29.3	(283) 24.2	(135) 22.5	(45) 18.1	(19) 18.7	% Profit Before Taxes/Tangible Net Worth	(790) 10.6	(854) 18.9
9.0	7.8	7.2	7.9	5.1	11.4		-5.5	2.5
34.1	23.6	16.0	11.5	9.1	8.3		11.4	16.7
12.2	8.3	7.9	6.7	5.8	5.9	% Profit Before Taxes/Total Assets	2.7	6.1
.0	1.4	1.8	2.2	2.0	2.8		-5.8	.0
475.6	44.9	17.4	8.4	4.0	3.5		22.3	28.8
19.8	11.6	7.3	4.5	2.7	2.6	Sales/Net Fixed Assets	7.7	8.2
6.5	4.0	3.5	2.5	1.8	1.8		3.0	3.6
9.8	5.8	4.1	3.3	2.3	1.9		4.8	5.0
5.4	3.7	2.8	2.1	1.5	1.6	Sales/Total Assets	2.7	2.9
3.0	2.2	1.9	1.5	1.2	1.3		1.6	1.8
1.0	1.2	1.5	2.3	4.0			1.8	1.7
(87) 3.9	(184) 3.3	(271) 3.8	(138) 4.3	(28) 6.1		% Depr., Dep., Amort./Sales	(804) 5.0	(821) 3.9
8.0	7.5	6.4	7.2	8.3			8.9	7.6
2.6	1.7	1.4	.4				1.6	1.5
(78) 3.7	(128) 2.7	(116) 2.5	(29) 1.1			% Officers', Directors' Owners' Comp/Sales	(389) 3.4	(395) 3.0
7.2	5.4	4.2	3.2				6.2	5.4
314556M	1347960M	4243106M	8300075M	6904794M	6063448M	Net Sales ($)	24314987M	31202397M
43925M	305102M	1469706M	3308385M	3702912M	3560609M	Total Assets ($)	11173569M	10988437M

M = $ thousand MM = $ million

See Pages 9 through 22 for Explanation of Ratios and Data

Comparative Historical Data				Current Data Sorted by Sales					
			Type of Statement						
70	46	63	Unqualified			2	3	8	50
162	124	110	Reviewed	2	9	3	14	36	46
193	155	150	Compiled	10	21	18	38	47	16
305	268	280	Tax Returns	73	80	34	57	26	10
410	408	416	Other	51	69	37	70	88	101
4/1/11-3/31/12 ALL	4/1/12-3/31/13 ALL	4/1/13-3/31/14 ALL		118 (4/1-9/30/13)			901 (10/1/13-3/31/14)		
				0-1MM	1-3MM	3-5MM	5-10MM	10-25MM	25MM & OVER
1140	1001	1019	**NUMBER OF STATEMENTS**	136	179	94	182	205	223
%	%	%	**ASSETS**	%	%	%	%	%	%
12.2	13.2	12.4	Cash & Equivalents	17.5	15.3	13.4	13.0	10.5	7.7
28.0	25.5	25.7	Trade Receivables (net)	9.6	19.8	23.2	31.4	33.7	29.2
1.7	1.9	2.0	Inventory	.9	2.0	1.3	1.8	3.5	1.9
3.8	3.2	3.6	All Other Current	3.1	4.2	2.9	3.6	3.3	3.9
45.7	43.7	43.7	Total Current	31.1	41.3	40.8	49.9	51.0	42.7
41.6	43.8	43.3	Fixed Assets (net)	55.1	45.2	41.0	36.7	37.6	46.3
3.4	3.4	4.0	Intangibles (net)	4.1	3.6	5.8	4.6	3.1	4.0
9.3	9.1	9.0	All Other Non-Current	9.7	9.9	12.4	8.8	8.3	7.1
100.0	100.0	100.0	Total	100.0	100.0	100.0	100.0	100.0	100.0
			LIABILITIES						
10.5	8.5	9.0	Notes Payable-Short Term	11.1	8.0	9.2	9.7	9.2	7.8
7.5	7.5	7.0	Cur. Mat.-L.T.D.	6.6	6.4	4.1	6.0	7.7	9.0
11.5	11.0	10.4	Trade Payables	6.6	8.8	10.9	12.3	12.5	10.2
.2	.1	.2	Income Taxes Payable	.1	.0	.2	.1	.3	.3
10.9	9.7	9.7	All Other Current	12.6	11.6	11.4	7.6	8.2	8.7
40.5	36.9	36.2	Total Current	37.0	35.0	35.8	35.6	37.8	36.0
32.0	29.5	31.5	Long-Term Debt	44.0	39.7	31.3	29.5	23.4	26.6
.8	.6	.7	Deferred Taxes	.0	.2	.3	.3	1.0	1.7
6.9	6.9	6.7	All Other Non-Current	12.7	11.9	7.6	4.5	3.7	3.2
19.9	26.1	24.8	Net Worth	6.3	13.3	25.1	30.1	34.1	32.5
100.0	100.0	100.0	Total Liabilties & Net Worth	100.0	100.0	100.0	100.0	100.0	100.0
			INCOME DATA						
100.0	100.0	100.0	Net Sales	100.0	100.0	100.0	100.0	100.0	100.0
			Gross Profit						
94.4	93.9	94.1	Operating Expenses	81.7	94.3	96.6	97.1	95.9	96.2
5.6	6.1	5.9	Operating Profit	18.3	5.7	3.4	2.9	4.1	3.8
1.3	1.2	.8	All Other Expenses (net)	4.4	.5	.1	-.2	.2	.7
4.3	4.9	5.1	Profit Before Taxes	13.9	5.3	3.4	3.1	3.9	3.1
			RATIOS						
2.3	2.5	2.3		2.1	3.9	3.6	2.7	2.4	1.6
1.3	1.3	1.2	Current	.7	1.3	1.2	1.4	1.3	1.2
.7	.7	.7		.3	.5	.5	.8	.9	.9
2.0	2.2	2.0		2.0	3.6	3.5	2.4	2.0	1.4
(1139) 1.1	(1000) 1.1	1.1	Quick	.6	1.1	1.1	1.2	1.1	1.0
.6	.5	.6		.2	.4	.4	.7	.7	.7
6 60.2	**4** 95.9	**5** 75.8		**0** UND	**0** UND	**0** UND	**13** 27.8	**22** 16.7	**29** 12.8
29 12.4	**29** 12.6	**30** 12.0	Sales/Receivables	**0** UND	**13** 28.1	**24** 15.2	**31** 11.7	**35** 10.3	**39** 9.3
45 8.2	**43** 8.4	**43** 8.5		**25** 14.7	**36** 10.0	**40** 9.2	**43** 8.5	**46** 7.9	**47** 7.7
			Cost of Sales/Inventory						
			Cost of Sales/Payables						
12.9	11.6	12.5		18.3	11.1	11.0	9.9	10.8	16.2
42.7	47.6	48.5	Sales/Working Capital	-44.9	38.8	75.1	32.7	29.3	45.3
-30.5	-30.5	-36.3		-4.3	-26.8	-27.7	-75.9	-85.5	-73.3
11.1	13.0	11.7		10.3	11.1	15.0	11.2	15.2	10.9
(990) 4.1	(842) 4.5	(851) 4.3	EBIT/Interest	(77) 3.3	(136) 4.2	(79) 3.3	(161) 3.9	(184) 5.9	(214) 4.8
1.3	1.6	1.5		.3	1.0	1.0	1.7	1.5	2.4
3.9	2.8	3.0					3.1	3.8	2.8
(168) 1.9	(146) 1.8	(148) 1.7	Net Profit + Depr., Dep., Amort./Cur. Mat. L/T/D				(19) 1.4	(42) 2.0	(75) 1.7
1.2	1.2	1.2					1.1	1.1	1.3
.5	.5	.5		.6	.3	.6	.4	.4	.8
1.5	1.5	1.5	Fixed/Worth	2.7	1.7	1.6	1.2	1.4	1.5
6.7	6.3	7.1		-8.4	-28.6	NM	4.0	3.2	3.1
1.0	.8	.9		.7	.7	.7	.7	1.0	1.2
2.4	2.2	2.3	Debt/Worth	2.7	3.1	2.3	1.8	2.2	2.2
19.7	13.5	14.3		-6.0	-13.5	-141.4	8.3	7.6	4.6
57.2	58.0	54.8		75.9	104.8	40.3	49.3	65.4	38.0
(905) 23.8	(804) 25.0	(820) 25.0	% Profit Before Taxes/Tangible Net Worth	(93) 20.1	(128) 37.5	(70) 17.4	(152) 26.9	(178) 27.9	(199) 22.8
7.0	8.5	8.1		8.0	6.6	4.7	9.5	7.2	10.0
17.2	19.3	17.2		21.3	30.1	22.9	17.1	17.7	11.8
7.1	8.2	7.9	% Profit Before Taxes/Total Assets	8.0	10.3	6.5	7.8	9.0	6.7
.9	1.8	1.5		-.8	1.1	.1	2.2	1.7	2.5
32.7	27.9	30.9		32.0	32.3	39.8	43.1	40.8	12.6
9.2	7.9	7.8	Sales/Net Fixed Assets	3.6	9.1	9.2	12.6	9.2	5.2
3.6	3.3	3.2		.5	3.4	4.1	4.7	3.9	2.6
5.3	5.2	5.0		3.6	5.8	5.7	6.0	5.1	4.0
3.2	3.1	3.0	Sales/Total Assets	1.8	3.3	3.0	3.9	3.3	2.4
1.9	1.8	1.8		.4	2.1	2.1	2.3	2.2	1.6
1.4	1.5	1.6		4.6	1.9	1.7	1.3	1.1	1.6
(839) 3.7	(716) 3.7	(713) 3.9	% Depr., Dep., Amort./Sales	(78) 9.7	(114) 4.6	(61) 3.6	(124) 2.9	(166) 3.2	(170) 3.4
7.0	6.9	7.3		20.1	8.5	7.5	5.8	6.2	5.7
1.3	1.3	1.5		3.3	2.5	2.0	1.4	1.0	.6
(427) 2.6	(367) 2.4	(353) 2.9	% Officers', Directors' Owners' Comp/Sales	(35) 5.8	(79) 3.9	(46) 3.0	(81) 2.4	(76) 2.2	(36) 1.6
5.2	5.0	5.4		10.9	7.0	5.8	4.2	3.8	3.4
31015184M	**29683797M**	**27173939M**	Net Sales ($)	**63697M**	**344789M**	**373871M**	**1327642M**	**3194548M**	**21869392M**
12498040M	**11085312M**	**12390639M**	Total Assets ($)	**99845M**	**170787M**	**149865M**	**434906M**	**1181469M**	**10353767M**

M = $ thousand MM = $ million

See Pages 9 through 22 for Explanation of Ratios and Data

Current Data Sorted by Assets							Comparative Historical Data	
						Type of Statement		
	5	7	39	33	30	Unqualified	140	122
2	19	90	109	18	2	Reviewed	231	251
15	48	100	28	6	2	Compiled	214	245
78	77	53	5	3		Tax Returns	161	197
45	99	180	176	59	39	Other	463	533
	196 (4/1-9/30/13)		1,171 (10/1/13-3/31/14)				4/1/09-3/31/10 ALL	4/1/10-3/31/11 ALL
0-500M	500M-2MM	2-10MM	10-50MM	50-100MM	100-250MM			
140	248	430	357	119	73	**NUMBER OF STATEMENTS**	1209	1348
%	%	%	%	%	%	**ASSETS**	%	%
28.5	14.3	9.9	7.4	6.3	3.8	Cash & Equivalents	9.6	9.5
27.3	32.4	29.7	22.8	20.1	20.2	Trade Receivables (net)	26.8	29.2
1.2	2.1	1.3	1.0	1.6	3.1	Inventory	1.4	1.3
1.7	4.6	3.7	3.6	3.0	2.8	All Other Current	5.5	5.1
58.8	53.3	44.6	34.7	31.0	29.9	Total Current	43.3	45.2
29.0	34.0	44.6	56.7	59.6	59.6	Fixed Assets (net)	45.7	42.5
2.6	3.8	3.6	2.8	2.9	5.4	Intangibles (net)	2.8	2.8
9.7	8.9	7.2	5.8	6.4	5.2	All Other Non-Current	8.2	9.5
100.0	100.0	100.0	100.0	100.0	100.0	Total	100.0	100.0
						LIABILITIES		
18.9	10.7	6.6	5.1	5.3	4.0	Notes Payable-Short Term	10.5	8.9
7.6	5.7	8.3	10.7	9.5	8.6	Cur. Mat.-L.T.D.	10.2	9.0
16.8	11.3	9.2	6.8	6.1	6.8	Trade Payables	9.7	10.9
.0	.1	.1	.1	.1	.2	Income Taxes Payable	.1	.2
17.3	13.3	8.7	6.6	7.0	7.4	All Other Current	11.2	10.5
60.5	41.2	33.0	29.3	28.1	27.0	Total Current	41.8	39.5
35.2	28.0	27.7	31.5	36.2	34.2	Long-Term Debt	26.8	25.8
.0	.3	.7	2.1	2.7	3.7	Deferred Taxes	1.5	1.3
7.7	6.6	4.7	2.7	5.2	1.8	All Other Non-Current	5.1	5.2
-3.5	23.9	34.0	34.4	27.8	33.2	Net Worth	24.9	28.2
100.0	100.0	100.0	100.0	100.0	100.0	Total Liabilties & Net Worth	100.0	100.0
						INCOME DATA		
100.0	100.0	100.0	100.0	100.0	100.0	Net Sales	100.0	100.0
						Gross Profit		
96.7	94.2	94.2	95.0	95.7	95.4	Operating Expenses	96.6	94.8
3.3	5.8	5.8	5.0	4.3	4.6	Operating Profit	3.4	5.2
.3	.5	1.0	.7	.7	1.0	All Other Expenses (net)	1.5	1.2
3.0	5.3	4.8	4.2	3.6	3.6	Profit Before Taxes	1.9	3.9
						RATIOS		
2.8	3.3	2.3	1.7	1.6	1.6		1.9	1.9
1.3	1.4	1.3	1.2	1.1	1.1	Current	1.1	1.2
.5	.9	.9	.8	.8	.8		.7	.8
2.9	2.7	2.1	1.4	1.4	1.3		1.6	1.6
(138) 1.2	1.3	1.2	1.0	.9	1.0	Quick	(1207) .9	(1347) 1.0
.5	.7	.7	.7	.6	.7		.5	.6
0 UND	**2** 181.4	**20** 17.9	**29** 12.8	**30** 12.1	**36** 10.2		**21** 17.4	**21** 17.2
10 35.6	**25** 14.7	**31** 11.6	**37** 9.9	**38** 9.7	**41** 8.9	Sales/Receivables	**34** 10.8	**34** 10.7
27 13.5	**41** 8.9	**41** 8.9	**44** 8.3	**46** 8.0	**50** 7.3		**44** 8.4	**44** 8.3
						Cost of Sales/Inventory		
						Cost of Sales/Payables		
16.7	11.8	12.3	13.9	14.5	17.2		13.5	14.1
97.9	32.2	31.3	48.9	65.9	71.5	Sales/Working Capital	82.4	50.6
-36.4	-87.6	-64.0	-37.8	-24.2	-30.6		-17.4	-29.1
9.7	13.3	10.5	8.2	6.4	7.7		4.9	7.8
(91) 2.8	(195) 4.8	(387) 4.2	(345) 4.4	(116) 4.2	(72) 4.4	EBIT/Interest	(1078) 1.7	(1191) 3.1
-.7	1.1	1.9	2.3	2.3	2.0		-.3	1.3
	7.3	2.7	2.1	1.9	2.7		2.0	2.7
	(17) 3.8	(86) 1.7	(137) 1.5	(38) 1.4	(10) 1.9	Net Profit + Depr., Dep., Amort./Cur. Mat. L/T/D	(273) 1.2	(295) 1.5
	1.6	1.4	1.2	1.1	1.2		.8	1.0
.0	.2	.6	1.2	1.4	1.5		.7	.6
1.0	1.1	1.5	1.9	1.9	2.1	Fixed/Worth	1.7	1.5
-2.9	9.1	4.0	3.2	3.6	3.5		4.6	3.6
.8	1.0	.9	1.2	1.5	1.6		1.0	.9
6.0	2.8	2.2	2.2	2.3	2.1	Debt/Worth	2.5	2.2
-4.8	124.3	5.8	4.3	4.5	4.5		8.8	7.2
120.7	72.3	49.1	35.9	28.7	29.1		28.7	40.0
(90) 42.7	(190) 29.6	(371) 23.7	(329) 20.7	(111) 18.5	(68) 20.4	% Profit Before Taxes/Tangible Net Worth	(1004) 8.5	(1145) 17.9
14.3	5.8	6.4	10.0	8.6	10.5		-6.3	4.4
29.0	20.8	14.8	10.8	8.1	7.9		8.7	13.0
8.6	8.9	7.0	7.0	5.6	5.7	% Profit Before Taxes/Total Assets	2.2	5.7
-3.7	.3	2.1	3.0	2.7	2.6		-4.1	.8
UND	99.3	25.4	5.6	4.2	4.5		19.8	24.8
65.7	21.9	6.0	3.3	2.8	2.5	Sales/Net Fixed Assets	5.7	6.4
13.3	5.9	3.2	2.1	1.8	1.8		2.7	3.2
12.1	6.5	4.5	2.7	2.3	2.1		4.3	4.6
7.5	4.3	2.9	2.0	1.7	1.6	Sales/Total Assets	2.6	2.8
4.6	2.6	1.9	1.4	1.2	1.3		1.6	1.8
.3	.5	1.4	3.3	4.4	1.4		2.1	1.8
(67) 1.5	(153) 2.9	(358) 4.1	(345) 5.9	(88) 6.9	(12) 2.0	% Depr., Dep., Amort./Sales	(942) 5.7	(1021) 4.9
5.5	8.0	8.1	9.2	9.7	3.6		9.8	8.0
1.3	1.1	.9	.6	.5			1.5	1.1
(63) 2.5	(83) 2.2	(141) 1.7	(71) 1.1	(13) 1.1		% Officers', Directors' Owners' Comp/Sales	(353) 2.8	(417) 2.3
5.7	3.9	3.1	3.4	9.5			6.0	4.5
362873M	**1398230M**	**7343574M**	**19101190M**	**17342062M**	**20084467M**	Net Sales ($)	**49389067M**	**64588243M**
37144M	**286883M**	**2215884M**	**8763550M**	**8483532M**	**11457450M**	Total Assets ($)	**24328149M**	**27350905M**

M = $ thousand MM = $ million

See Pages 9 through 22 for Explanation of Ratios and Data

Comparative Historical Data | **Current Data Sorted by Sales**

			Type of Statement						
119	108	114	Unqualified		1	3	2	7	101
272	231	240	Reviewed	3	6	5	20	71	135
232	256	199	Compiled	16	14	21	37	67	44
199	221	216	Tax Returns	34	45	41	45	42	9
533	564	598	Other	39	48	34	79	127	271
4/1/11-3/31/12 ALL	**4/1/12-3/31/13 ALL**	**4/1/13-3/31/14 ALL**		**196 (4/1-9/30/13)**			**1,171 (10/1/13-3/31/14)**		
				0-1MM	**1-3MM**	**3-5MM**	**5-10MM**	**10-25MM**	**25MM & OVER**
1355	1380	1367	**NUMBER OF STATEMENTS**	92	114	104	183	314	560
%	%	%	**ASSETS**	%	%	%	%	%	%
9.9	10.9	11.3	Cash & Equivalents	21.3	17.5	14.0	12.8	11.0	7.6
29.8	28.0	26.8	Trade Receivables (net)	15.2	21.0	28.2	29.6	29.7	27.1
1.4	1.5	1.5	Inventory	.3	3.5	.9	1.6	1.2	1.5
4.2	4.4	3.5	All Other Current	1.8	2.9	5.3	3.5	2.9	3.9
45.3	44.9	43.1	Total Current	38.6	44.9	48.4	47.5	44.7	40.1
43.1	44.6	46.3	Fixed Assets (net)	50.9	42.3	41.2	39.9	44.8	50.3
3.3	3.3	3.3	Intangibles (net)	4.5	3.9	3.5	3.8	2.5	3.3
8.3	7.2	7.2	All Other Non-Current	6.0	8.9	6.9	8.8	7.9	6.2
100.0	100.0	100.0	Total	100.0	100.0	100.0	100.0	100.0	100.0
			LIABILITIES						
7.4	8.1	8.0	Notes Payable-Short Term	7.2	11.3	11.7	10.4	8.4	5.7
8.9	8.4	8.5	Cur. Mat.-L.T.D.	7.0	6.8	8.0	7.1	9.3	9.2
11.0	10.1	9.3	Trade Payables	12.2	10.1	9.4	10.8	9.1	8.4
.2	.2	.1	Income Taxes Payable	.1	.1	.0	.1	.1	.2
10.1	9.4	9.7	All Other Current	10.6	10.7	9.2	12.3	8.9	8.9
37.6	36.1	35.6	Total Current	37.1	39.0	38.3	40.7	35.7	32.4
27.0	28.9	30.6	Long-Term Debt	38.0	40.3	34.2	28.3	28.3	28.9
1.4	1.3	1.3	Deferred Taxes	.2	.0	.7	.4	1.0	2.2
6.2	6.0	4.7	All Other Non-Current	11.5	7.7	3.2	5.5	3.9	3.5
27.8	27.7	27.8	Net Worth	13.4	13.0	23.5	25.2	31.1	33.0
100.0	100.0	100.0	Total Liabilties & Net Worth	100.0	100.0	100.0	100.0	100.0	100.0
			INCOME DATA						
100.0	100.0	100.0	Net Sales	100.0	100.0	100.0	100.0	100.0	100.0
			Gross Profit						
95.2	94.2	94.9	Operating Expenses	80.8	92.3	95.4	97.0	95.9	96.3
4.8	5.8	5.1	Operating Profit	19.2	7.7	4.6	3.0	4.1	3.7
.9	.9	.8	All Other Expenses (net)	4.6	1.1	.6	.1	.5	.4
3.8	4.9	4.4	Profit Before Taxes	14.6	6.6	3.9	2.8	3.6	3.3
			RATIOS						
1.9	2.0	2.1		2.6	4.1	2.7	2.5	2.2	1.7
1.2	1.2	1.3	Current	1.0	1.7	1.3	1.3	1.3	1.2
.8	.8	.8		.3	.7	.7	.7	.9	.9
1.7	1.8	1.9		2.3	3.4	2.6	2.1	2.0	1.5
1.1	(1379) 1.1	(1365) 1.1	Quick	(91) 1.0	1.5	1.1	(182) 1.2	1.2	1.0
.6	.6	.7		.3	.6	.5	.7	.8	.7
21 17.6	**19** 19.1	**20** 18.7		**0** UND	**0** UND	**0** UND	**14** 25.3	**21** 17.1	**30** 12.0
33 10.9	**33** 11.2	**33** 11.2	Sales/Receivables	**0** UND	**13** 27.5	**24** 15.3	**29** 12.7	**31** 11.8	**37** 9.8
43 8.4	**42** 8.7	**42** 8.6		**36** 10.2	**33** 10.9	**40** 9.2	**42** 8.7	**41** 8.9	**44** 8.3
			Cost of Sales/Inventory						
			Cost of Sales/Payables						
14.2	14.0	13.3		8.0	8.6	12.4	13.9	14.1	14.5
50.8	43.8	43.2	Sales/Working Capital	UND	35.2	33.0	44.1	38.1	44.5
-38.5	-38.6	-42.1		-3.9	-35.1	-34.3	-40.4	-70.8	-50.5
9.9	9.9	9.2		8.7	8.2	9.8	12.4	10.0	8.4
(1205) 4.0	(1209) 4.2	(1206) 4.2	EBIT/Interest	(56) 3.1	(91) 3.0	(82) 2.6	(155) 3.7	(287) 4.5	(535) 4.5
1.7	1.8	1.8		.0	.5	.4	1.5	2.2	2.3
3.0	2.8	2.5				10.8	2.7	2.8	2.3
(296) 1.6	(274) 1.6	(289) 1.6	Net Profit + Depr., Dep., Amort./Cur. Mat. L/T/D			(10) 1.9	(28) 1.7	(61) 1.6	(185) 1.5
1.1	1.1	1.2				1.1	1.4	1.2	1.2
.6	.6	.7		.2	.2	.5	.4	.6	1.0
1.5	1.7	1.7	Fixed/Worth	1.8	1.8	1.9	1.6	1.6	1.7
4.0	4.0	4.1		UND	-93.0	17.1	6.7	3.4	3.1
1.0	1.0	1.1		.7	.7	1.0	1.1	1.1	1.2
2.4	2.2	2.3	Debt/Worth	3.7	3.6	3.2	2.5	2.2	2.2
7.9	7.5	6.8		-8.8	-11.8	109.1	31.8	5.9	4.5
46.6	47.7	45.2		72.2	64.9	58.4	57.7	52.9	34.4
(1154) 22.7	(1156) 24.1	(1159) 22.6	% Profit Before Taxes/Tangible Net Worth	(65) 28.0	(79) 22.3	(80) 17.6	(147) 25.8	(276) 27.1	(512) 20.7
8.1	10.9	8.5		7.7	3.2	1.8	8.2	8.1	10.3
14.2	15.3	13.1		15.1	19.0	18.6	16.8	16.0	10.0
7.0	7.7	6.9	% Profit Before Taxes/Total Assets	5.2	6.3	6.5	6.9	7.6	6.7
1.9	2.3	2.0		-.2	-1.6	-1.5	1.1	2.2	2.9
29.4	29.0	25.9		68.2	55.9	58.2	64.2	29.3	9.0
6.7	6.0	5.4	Sales/Net Fixed Assets	3.6	9.5	12.8	9.3	6.0	4.0
3.2	2.9	2.6		.4	3.7	3.7	3.8	2.9	2.3
4.9	4.8	4.7		3.7	5.8	7.3	5.9	4.9	3.4
3.0	2.8	2.6	Sales/Total Assets	1.1	3.7	3.7	3.7	3.1	2.2
1.9	1.7	1.6		.3	1.7	2.1	2.1	1.9	1.6
1.5	1.5	1.8		4.8	1.5	1.1	1.2	1.7	2.2
(1056) 4.1	(1049) 4.1	(1023) 4.9	% Depr., Dep., Amort./Sales	(59) 14.0	(70) 6.3	(63) 4.5	(132) 3.9	(256) 4.5	(443) 4.9
7.3	7.6	8.6		23.9	13.7	11.0	7.7	7.8	7.8
1.0	.9	.9		2.1	1.9	1.3	1.0	.8	.6
(395) 2.1	(381) 1.8	(375) 1.8	% Officers', Directors' Owners' Comp/Sales	(12) 4.6	(41) 2.8	(43) 2.9	(74) 1.8	(108) 1.7	(97) 1.1
4.5	4.3	4.0		8.7	5.7	6.3	3.0	3.0	3.8
66256595M	**69695655M**	**65632396M**	Net Sales ($)	**51481M**	**221257M**	**405074M**	**1359671M**	**4967556M**	**58627357M**
29274086M	**29536788M**	**31244443M**	Total Assets ($)	**101381M**	**166459M**	**295936M**	**626131M**	**2328615M**	**27725921M**

M = $ thousand MM = $ million

See Pages 9 through 22 for Explanation of Ratios and Data

Current Data Sorted by Assets							Comparative Historical Data	
						Type of Statement		
		1	7	8	4	Unqualified	19	19
	2	9	8	3	1	Reviewed	16	25
3	1	10	2	1		Compiled	16	19
2	3	6		1		Tax Returns	13	10
4	8	17	17	5	4	Other	36	50
21 (4/1-9/30/13)			106 (10/1/13-3/31/14)				4/1/09-3/31/10 ALL	4/1/10-3/31/11 ALL
0-500M	500M-2MM	2-10MM	10-50MM	50-100MM	100-250MM			
9	14	43	34	18	9	NUMBER OF STATEMENTS	100	123
%	%	%	%	%	%	**ASSETS**	%	%
	10.0	8.1	6.9	9.1		Cash & Equivalents	8.2	9.1
	33.6	32.7	24.5	20.6		Trade Receivables (net)	28.9	29.3
	.0	2.0	1.4	.6		Inventory	1.6	1.6
	4.7	5.3	3.9	4.0		All Other Current	3.5	5.3
	48.3	48.1	36.7	34.3		Total Current	42.2	45.2
	42.1	44.2	54.4	52.1		Fixed Assets (net)	47.6	46.0
	4.8	1.9	4.1	5.2		Intangibles (net)	2.4	1.9
	4.8	5.9	4.9	8.5		All Other Non-Current	7.8	6.9
	100.0	100.0	100.0	100.0		Total	100.0	100.0
						LIABILITIES		
	3.5	7.9	4.8	1.9		Notes Payable-Short Term	6.1	6.3
	3.7	7.0	8.5	6.0		Cur. Mat.-L.T.D.	9.3	9.5
	10.2	14.1	12.0	7.1		Trade Payables	8.4	11.4
	.0	.1	.2	.6		Income Taxes Payable	.1	.2
	13.4	10.3	5.5	11.1		All Other Current	11.9	10.4
	30.8	39.5	31.0	26.7		Total Current	35.8	37.8
	26.0	30.3	30.3	31.4		Long-Term Debt	26.6	27.2
	.0	.0	2.5	4.3		Deferred Taxes	1.5	1.5
	6.6	3.0	5.5	3.2		All Other Non-Current	3.4	5.4
	36.5	27.3	30.9	34.4		Net Worth	32.7	28.2
	100.0	100.0	100.0	100.0		Total Liabilties & Net Worth	100.0	100.0
						INCOME DATA		
	100.0	100.0	100.0	100.0		Net Sales	100.0	100.0
						Gross Profit		
	94.7	93.4	97.9	91.8		Operating Expenses	96.0	96.2
	5.3	6.6	2.1	8.2		Operating Profit	4.0	3.8
	.6	2.7	.4	.6		All Other Expenses (net)	2.8	1.8
	4.8	3.9	1.7	7.6		Profit Before Taxes	1.2	2.1
						RATIOS		
	4.1	1.6	2.2	1.8			1.9	2.1
	1.6	1.1	1.2	1.5		Current	1.2	1.2
	.8	.9	.9	.9			.8	.7
	4.1	1.5	1.7	1.7			1.7	1.7
	1.4	.9	1.0	1.2		Quick	1.0	1.1
	.8	.6	.7	.7			.6	.6
	0 UND	**21** 17.6	**31** 11.8	**31** 11.9			**31** 11.7	**26** 14.3
	34 10.6	**33** 11.1	**38** 9.5	**36** 10.0		Sales/Receivables	**37** 9.9	**38** 9.6
	43 8.5	**41** 8.8	**44** 8.3	**46** 8.0			**47** 7.7	**44** 8.3
						Cost of Sales/Inventory		
						Cost of Sales/Payables		
	10.2	15.0	12.2	11.9			14.2	11.8
	21.4	76.1	58.7	17.3		Sales/Working Capital	37.1	46.4
	-360.7	-53.8	-54.8	-52.9			-25.1	-20.3
	67.8	7.6	5.6	14.5			3.6	7.0
	(10) 4.9	(36) 3.7	2.8	4.9		EBIT/Interest	(89) 1.4	(109) 2.3
	2.1	1.8	1.0	1.1			-.2	.3
			1.7				2.2	2.1
			(15) 1.3			Net Profit + Depr., Dep., Amort./Cur. Mat. L/T/D	(29) 1.3	(30) 1.3
			1.0				.8	.7
	.3	1.0	1.3	1.2			.6	.5
	.7	1.5	2.4	1.7		Fixed/Worth	1.6	1.5
	4.5	4.2	5.2	NM			3.1	6.6
	.9	1.5	1.5	1.2			1.0	.8
	1.7	2.7	2.6	1.6		Debt/Worth	1.9	1.9
	13.6	15.4	6.5	NM			5.4	9.8
	54.5	41.1	30.0	21.6			19.7	25.0
	(13) 17.4	(39) 24.1	(32) 16.4	(14) 15.8		% Profit Before Taxes/Tangible Net Worth	(86) 6.4	(100) 13.0
	11.5	5.4	.3	14.6			-3.3	.7
	17.5	12.1	7.9	8.7			6.7	10.5
	7.9	4.7	4.1	6.6		% Profit Before Taxes/Total Assets	1.1	2.9
	1.0	1.6	.0	-.2			-2.7	-2.4
	45.1	19.2	6.1	6.6			14.5	16.6
	15.0	7.2	3.6	3.1		Sales/Net Fixed Assets	5.5	5.7
	1.8	3.1	2.9	1.7			2.4	3.1
	5.6	4.4	3.1	3.2			3.9	4.4
	2.9	3.5	2.2	1.4		Sales/Total Assets	2.2	2.7
	.6	1.9	1.8	1.2			1.5	1.8
	.4	.9	2.8	3.3			2.5	2.1
	(12) 1.3	(35) 4.5	(33) 5.0	(15) 5.4		% Depr., Dep., Amort./Sales	(73) 5.0	(91) 4.3
	10.2	7.5	7.0	12.4			8.3	7.4
							1.2	1.0
						% Officers', Directors' Owners' Comp/Sales	(30) 2.5	(27) 2.2
							6.2	4.4
13634M	66709M	615561M	2755727M	2473076M	2347043M	Net Sales ($)	5623594M	9222273M
2473M	18104M	194313M	827082M	1164321M	1525986M	Total Assets ($)	2974051M	4485492M

M = $ thousand MM = $ million

See Pages 9 through 22 for Explanation of Ratios and Data

Comparative Historical Data / Current Data Sorted by Sales

4/1/11-3/31/12 ALL	4/1/12-3/31/13 ALL	4/1/13-3/31/14 ALL	Type of Statement	0-1MM	1-3MM	3-5MM	5-10MM	10-25MM	25MM & OVER
14	20	20	Unqualified					3	17
14	17	23	Reviewed			3		6	14
15	16	17	Compiled	2	3		1	7	4
12	9	12	Tax Returns	2	1	2	2	5	
59	52	55	Other	6	3	1	7	13	25
				21 (4/1-9/30/13)			106 (10/1/13-3/31/14)		
114	114	127	NUMBER OF STATEMENTS	10	7	6	10	34	60
%	%	%	ASSETS	%	%	%	%	%	%
8.8	11.2	8.7	Cash & Equivalents	8.7			11.9	7.7	8.2
29.9	26.6	26.8	Trade Receivables (net)	11.4			34.4	35.9	24.4
.9	1.2	1.2	Inventory	.0			.0	2.5	1.1
6.1	4.5	5.0	All Other Current	.1			5.5	6.3	5.3
45.7	43.5	41.6	Total Current	20.2			51.9	52.2	39.0
45.1	44.7	48.3	Fixed Assets (net)	71.6			37.8	38.9	52.0
2.6	4.1	4.2	Intangibles (net)	3.7			3.0	4.0	3.8
6.6	7.6	5.9	All Other Non-Current	4.6			7.4	4.9	5.2
100.0	100.0	100.0	Total	100.0			100.0	100.0	100.0
			LIABILITIES						
6.2	6.0	6.3	Notes Payable-Short Term	6.3			5.0	8.0	4.4
7.9	8.6	7.1	Cur. Mat.-L.T.D.	5.7			5.1	5.7	8.1
10.2	9.6	11.5	Trade Payables	3.1			7.0	16.6	10.4
.1	.4	.2	Income Taxes Payable	.0			.0	.0	.3
15.8	9.9	9.7	All Other Current	9.1			5.5	10.6	10.6
40.2	34.5	34.8	Total Current	24.3			22.7	40.9	33.8
27.2	23.7	30.0	Long-Term Debt	44.6			31.7	24.6	29.6
1.2	1.7	1.3	Deferred Taxes	.0			.0	.1	2.6
5.3	9.9	5.5	All Other Non-Current	9.1			3.6	3.5	4.4
26.1	30.2	28.5	Net Worth	22.0			42.0	30.9	29.7
100.0	100.0	100.0	Total Liabilties & Net Worth	100.0			100.0	100.0	100.0
			INCOME DATA						
100.0	100.0	100.0	Net Sales	100.0			100.0	100.0	100.0
			Gross Profit						
92.5	95.2	94.8	Operating Expenses	73.4			88.9	97.1	97.4
7.5	4.8	5.2	Operating Profit	26.6			11.1	2.9	2.6
1.9	.4	1.2	All Other Expenses (net)	10.8			-1.0	.6	.4
5.6	4.4	4.1	Profit Before Taxes	15.8			12.1	2.3	2.2
			RATIOS						
2.0	1.9	1.9		1.5			3.5	2.2	1.7
1.3	1.1	1.1	Current	.2			2.0	1.1	1.2
.8	.8	.8		.1			1.2	.9	.9
1.8	1.7	1.6		1.5			3.4	1.9	1.6
(113) 1.0	1.0	1.1	Quick	.2			1.8	.9	1.1
.7	.7	.7		.1			1.1	.7	.7
23 16.1	22 16.3	23 15.6		0 UND			2 193.3	26 14.0	30 12.2
35 10.4	33 10.9	35 10.5	Sales/Receivables	8 46.6			29 12.8	35 10.3	36 10.0
42 8.7	39 9.3	41 8.8		41 8.9			48 7.6	42 8.7	44 8.3
			Cost of Sales/Inventory						
			Cost of Sales/Payables						
12.3	13.5	12.6		NM			10.4	12.4	12.6
38.8	74.6	63.5	Sales/Working Capital	-3.8			17.5	91.4	41.5
-37.8	-42.9	-43.9		-1.1			48.1	-66.3	-46.9
9.3	8.9	7.4						9.0	6.4
(99) 3.7	(96) 4.0	(113) 3.4	EBIT/Interest					(31) 4.2	(59) 3.2
1.7	2.3	1.6						2.1	1.0
1.8	4.1	2.3							2.2
(22) 1.4	(28) 1.9	(35) 1.4	Net Profit + Depr., Dep., Amort./Cur. Mat. L/T/D						(26) 1.4
.9	1.1	1.0							1.0
.6	.6	.9		.6			.4	.4	1.1
1.5	1.7	1.8	Fixed/Worth	5.3			1.1	1.5	1.8
3.2	3.1	4.7		87.9			1.5	3.6	3.5
.9	.9	1.3		1.3			.9	1.3	1.4
1.9	2.1	2.2	Debt/Worth	10.2			1.4	2.2	2.3
6.1	5.7	14.4		NM			1.7	9.0	12.8
41.0	48.3	34.4					96.0	37.9	27.1
(100) 17.4	(103) 22.8	(108) 16.6	% Profit Before Taxes/Tangible Net Worth				36.2	(31) 23.1	(50) 15.3
5.1	10.9	6.3					15.8	6.0	4.4
12.9	15.6	11.5		17.7			31.7	12.6	8.3
6.3	5.9	4.9	% Profit Before Taxes/Total Assets	6.3			11.3	5.1	4.8
.8	3.2	.9		1.4			5.3	1.8	-.1
17.6	35.9	17.2		UND			42.8	44.2	7.2
5.3	5.6	4.8	Sales/Net Fixed Assets	.5			8.7	7.9	3.7
3.0	3.0	2.5		.1			3.1	3.5	2.7
4.8	4.2	4.0		1.0			5.6	4.9	3.4
2.6	2.7	2.3	Sales/Total Assets	.4			3.3	3.4	2.2
1.7	1.7	1.6		.1			1.8	2.0	1.6
1.4	1.0	1.9						.5	2.8
(84) 3.8	(78) 4.2	(101) 4.7	% Depr., Dep., Amort./Sales					(27) 4.5	(48) 5.0
7.7	8.1	7.4						7.4	7.0
1.2	.8	.8							.9
(31) 2.9	(32) 1.4	(28) 1.2	% Officers', Directors' Owners' Comp/Sales						(10) .9
9.8	3.8	2.5							2.2
9625910M	10349542M	8271750M	Net Sales ($)	2962M	14236M	26516M	71080M	552528M	7604428M
3963253M	4444430M	3732279M	Total Assets ($)	15200M	2860M	13278M	79073M	211662M	3410206M

M = $ thousand MM = $ million

See Pages 9 through 22 for Explanation of Ratios and Data

Current Data Sorted by Assets							Comparative Historical Data	
						Type of Statement		
			3	3	2	Unqualified	8	14
	8	24	10			Reviewed	43	42
8	21	13	3			Compiled	39	42
14	17	8				Tax Returns	34	49
8	20	28	14	3	4	Other	64	66
15 (4/1-9/30/13)			196 (10/1/13-3/31/14)				4/1/09-3/31/10	4/1/10-3/31/11
0-500M	500M-2MM	2-10MM	10-50MM	50-100MM	100-250MM		ALL	ALL
30	66	73	30	6	6	**NUMBER OF STATEMENTS**	188	213
%	%	%	%	%	%	**ASSETS**	%	%
26.1	11.5	12.4	8.8			Cash & Equivalents	12.5	13.8
18.6	29.6	27.0	27.9			Trade Receivables (net)	30.0	29.8
.2	.4	1.1	3.6			Inventory	.5	1.5
4.8	3.9	3.8	3.1			All Other Current	5.5	4.4
49.6	45.4	44.2	43.4			Total Current	48.5	49.5
29.6	34.7	41.5	37.6			Fixed Assets (net)	33.9	34.4
8.6	5.3	3.3	5.9			Intangibles (net)	4.3	3.6
12.2	14.6	11.0	13.1			All Other Non-Current	13.4	12.5
100.0	100.0	100.0	100.0			Total	100.0	100.0
						LIABILITIES		
5.7	7.8	5.3	2.6			Notes Payable-Short Term	8.4	8.9
9.4	5.8	4.6	3.4			Cur. Mat.-L.T.D.	8.4	6.8
9.9	8.4	9.3	9.3			Trade Payables	10.3	10.6
.0	.0	.0	.1			Income Taxes Payable	.3	.2
22.6	14.3	7.8	11.2			All Other Current	16.7	14.9
47.6	36.3	27.1	26.7			Total Current	44.1	41.4
45.0	27.0	28.9	23.4			Long-Term Debt	26.0	24.3
.0	.5	.7	.7			Deferred Taxes	.3	.8
6.6	3.7	1.9	2.5			All Other Non-Current	8.1	9.8
.8	32.4	41.4	46.8			Net Worth	21.4	23.8
100.0	100.0	100.0	100.0			Total Liabilties & Net Worth	100.0	100.0
						INCOME DATA		
100.0	100.0	100.0	100.0			Net Sales	100.0	100.0
						Gross Profit		
92.3	90.0	87.1	87.7			Operating Expenses	97.2	92.1
7.7	10.0	12.9	12.3			Operating Profit	2.8	7.9
.2	2.1	3.9	1.7			All Other Expenses (net)	2.0	2.3
7.5	8.0	9.0	10.6			Profit Before Taxes	.7	5.6
						RATIOS		
3.0	2.5	2.7	2.4				2.9	2.5
1.5	1.3	1.6	1.6			Current	1.4	1.5
.6	.7	1.0	1.2				.7	.7
2.3	2.5	2.5	2.0				2.4	2.3
1.3	1.2	1.4	1.4			Quick	1.2	1.2
.6	.6	.8	1.0				.6	.7
0 UND	6 61.2	16 22.3	33 11.0				19 19.7	17 21.7
7 53.5	26 14.0	33 11.2	45 8.2			Sales/Receivables	38 9.7	35 10.3
24 15.3	46 7.9	51 7.1	58 6.3				57 6.4	53 6.9
						Cost of Sales/Inventory		
						Cost of Sales/Payables		
15.0	12.6	8.1	5.6				9.0	9.8
52.0	36.4	18.3	15.9			Sales/Working Capital	26.1	21.2
-52.2	-28.1	NM	32.7				-23.3	-28.8
54.8	15.8	14.8	34.9				7.8	13.8
(18) 17.7	(53) 5.2	(58) 4.6	(25) 6.3			EBIT/Interest	(158) 1.8	(178) 3.3
3.3	2.3	1.5	3.2				-2.0	1.1
		3.0				Net Profit + Depr., Dep.,	3.7	3.8
		(16) 1.8				Amort./Cur. Mat. L/T/D	(44) 1.7	(56) 1.7
		1.0					.1	1.0
.4	.3	.3	.3				.4	.4
69.3	.8	.9	.7			Fixed/Worth	.9	1.0
-.9	3.9	2.8	2.2				4.0	5.1
1.2	.9	.7	.8				.7	.7
UND	2.4	1.2	1.4			Debt/Worth	1.7	2.1
-5.3	8.8	4.2	3.3				10.1	9.9
429.9	47.8	45.3	44.6			% Profit Before Taxes/Tangible	30.3	50.2
(16) 110.7	(54) 16.3	(68) 17.8	17.3			Net Worth	(151) 7.0	(173) 17.6
37.8	5.7	4.7	7.0				-6.4	2.5
93.7	15.6	14.1	12.4			% Profit Before Taxes/Total	10.1	17.8
47.7	5.9	5.0	6.1			Assets	1.7	5.2
6.6	1.9	1.8	3.3				-5.3	.4
179.4	44.3	20.2	15.0				28.2	32.4
42.2	12.7	7.5	7.5			Sales/Net Fixed Assets	12.0	12.8
10.6	5.7	2.9	1.7				4.1	4.3
8.9	5.4	3.8	2.8				4.3	4.5
6.2	3.5	2.6	2.1			Sales/Total Assets	2.8	3.0
4.0	2.1	1.5	1.1				1.7	1.7
.5	.8	1.2	1.3				1.6	1.5
(14) 2.2	(45) 1.8	(66) 2.7	(27) 3.1			% Depr., Dep., Amort./Sales	(151) 2.9	(174) 2.7
3.2	4.7	5.5	4.5				4.8	4.5
1.7	2.1	1.1				% Officers', Directors'	2.2	2.2
(18) 4.2	(27) 3.8	(19) 3.7				Owners' Comp/Sales	(62) 4.9	(71) 4.7
7.1	5.1	9.9					9.0	9.3
46284M	295233M	788551M	1278003M	649783M	2352755M	Net Sales ($)	3010282M	5107332M
7207M	76632M	311411M	660748M	442532M	1148547M	Total Assets ($)	1258368M	1963830M

M = $ thousand MM = $ million

See Pages 9 through 22 for Explanation of Ratios and Data

Comparative Historical Data				Current Data Sorted by Sales					
			Type of Statement						
5	10	8	Unqualified						8
43	48	42	Reviewed		3	1	11	18	9
33	48	45	Compiled	6	9	9	13	7	1
50	34	39	Tax Returns	10	13	5	6	5	
86	79	77	Other	11	15	7	11	16	17
4/1/11-3/31/12 ALL	**4/1/12-3/31/13 ALL**	**4/1/13-3/31/14 ALL**		**15 (4/1-9/30/13)**			**196 (10/1/13-3/31/14)**		
				0-1MM	**1-3MM**	**3-5MM**	**5-10MM**	**10-25MM**	**25MM & OVER**
217	219	211	**NUMBER OF STATEMENTS**	27	40	22	41	46	35
%	%	%	**ASSETS**	%	%	%	%	%	%
12.8	15.1	13.1	Cash & Equivalents	14.9	16.4	12.0	12.6	13.6	8.5
27.4	29.0	26.6	Trade Receivables (net)	7.4	17.8	29.7	32.3	35.6	31.0
1.1	1.7	1.1	Inventory	.1	.6	.3	1.8	1.1	1.8
4.5	5.1	3.8	All Other Current	2.5	2.8	6.0	3.8	4.0	4.1
45.8	50.9	44.5	Total Current	24.8	37.6	48.0	50.5	54.3	45.5
33.1	33.1	37.6	Fixed Assets (net)	64.8	39.9	35.0	29.5	29.4	36.0
6.0	4.7	5.5	Intangibles (net)	5.4	7.9	2.7	4.9	3.1	8.1
15.1	11.2	12.4	All Other Non-Current	4.9	14.6	14.3	15.2	13.2	10.4
100.0	100.0	100.0	Total	100.0	100.0	100.0	100.0	100.0	100.0
			LIABILITIES						
9.8	11.1	6.1	Notes Payable-Short Term	2.9	5.3	7.8	5.2	6.8	8.8
5.9	5.9	5.5	Cur. Mat.-L.T.D.	4.5	9.2	2.9	7.2	3.6	4.4
9.9	9.5	9.1	Trade Payables	4.7	7.2	6.8	10.5	11.8	10.9
.1	.0	.1	Income Taxes Payable	.0	.0	.0	.1	.0	.3
18.4	10.5	12.5	All Other Current	8.8	15.2	14.1	15.4	10.4	11.0
44.2	37.2	33.4	Total Current	20.9	36.9	31.6	38.4	32.7	35.4
26.5	25.2	29.4	Long-Term Debt	52.9	34.3	35.9	26.9	19.0	18.4
.4	.4	.5	Deferred Taxes	.0	.2	1.2	.7	.4	.7
6.6	9.1	3.3	All Other Non-Current	6.0	3.3	4.2	3.7	1.2	3.0
22.2	28.1	33.4	Net Worth	20.4	25.2	27.1	30.3	46.8	42.5
100.0	100.0	100.0	Total Liabilties & Net Worth	100.0	100.0	100.0	100.0	100.0	100.0
			INCOME DATA						
100.0	100.0	100.0	Net Sales	100.0	100.0	100.0	100.0	100.0	100.0
			Gross Profit						
92.8	91.2	89.4	Operating Expenses	58.8	88.1	90.7	97.1	95.8	96.3
7.2	8.8	10.6	Operating Profit	41.2	11.9	9.3	2.9	4.2	3.7
2.2	1.8	2.3	All Other Expenses (net)	13.4	1.8	2.0	.0	.2	.1
5.0	7.0	8.3	Profit Before Taxes	27.7	10.1	7.3	2.8	4.0	3.6
			RATIOS						
2.2	2.7	2.4		2.6	3.5	3.2	2.2	2.7	1.7
1.3	1.5	1.4	Current	.6	1.5	1.6	1.5	1.6	1.3
.6	1.0	.8		.2	.6	.8	1.0	1.0	1.1
2.0	2.4	2.2		2.3	2.6	3.2	1.9	2.6	1.5
1.2	1.4	1.3	Quick	.6	1.3	1.5	1.4	1.4	1.2
.5	.8	.8		.2	.6	.7	.9	1.0	.8
5 74.8	**10** 35.5	**9** 40.9		**0** UND	**1** 439.2	**0** UND	**18** 20.1	**26** 14.2	**33** 10.9
31 11.6	**36** 10.2	**30** 12.3	Sales/Receivables	**0** UND	**16** 23.1	**27** 13.4	**30** 12.3	**34** 10.6	**44** 8.3
54 6.8	**53** 6.9	**47** 7.8		**2** 221.5	**49** 7.5	**49** 7.4	**46** 8.0	**51** 7.1	**57** 6.4
			Cost of Sales/Inventory						
			Cost of Sales/Payables						
9.1	7.5	10.4		13.9	7.3	11.6	10.1	8.5	11.6
30.9	18.3	25.5	Sales/Working Capital	-76.6	52.0	22.1	25.5	23.9	24.8
-30.0	586.5	-66.0		-3.0	-13.7	-92.4	NM	184.0	85.0
13.5	18.8	19.1		51.5	21.3	25.4	11.8	35.9	12.2
(175) 4.1	(177) 5.0	(166) 5.0	EBIT/Interest	(10) 6.9	(30) 5.1	(15) 13.2	(39) 3.8	(40) 4.9	(32) 3.6
1.5	2.1	2.3		5.9	2.4	3.2	1.6	1.9	2.7
7.3	5.4	4.3					2.0		13.1
(38) 2.9	(54) 3.1	(37) 2.0	Net Profit + Depr., Dep., Amort./Cur. Mat. L/T/D				(11) 1.7		(13) 4.6
1.6	1.4	1.4					1.6		2.1
.3	.3	.4		1.8	.5	.4	.3	.3	.4
.8	.7	1.0	Fixed/Worth	3.4	2.8	.8	.8	.5	.9
4.9	2.6	3.6		-750.0	-17.7	29.9	2.2	1.5	2.2
.7	.7	.8		1.3	1.2	.5	.7	.6	1.0
2.0	1.5	1.8	Debt/Worth	3.6	3.2	1.9	1.7	1.2	1.4
11.4	4.1	5.9		-18.3	-23.0	41.1	4.1	2.9	3.6
42.5	46.6	53.0		63.1	87.6	76.8	25.0	54.3	34.0
(173) 16.4	(188) 20.9	(179) 18.9	% Profit Before Taxes/Tangible Net Worth	(19) 28.8	(28) 30.7	(18) 44.2	(35) 8.4	(45) 22.4	(34) 10.7
3.6	7.7	6.3		10.1	10.2	10.6	3.9	6.9	5.5
18.2	19.2	17.8		19.2	38.0	34.6	13.3	16.6	9.0
5.9	8.1	6.1	% Profit Before Taxes/Total Assets	8.2	8.6	14.7	5.4	5.1	5.1
.8	2.2	2.2		3.5	2.6	3.6	1.5	1.8	2.8
38.3	33.9	33.0		42.1	23.1	46.3	46.5	47.0	17.4
14.7	13.3	9.9	Sales/Net Fixed Assets	.3	6.7	16.4	13.9	15.9	8.5
4.3	4.8	3.5		.1	4.5	4.4	5.6	6.8	3.0
4.7	4.2	4.6		6.3	4.3	6.1	5.1	4.6	3.0
3.0	2.9	2.9	Sales/Total Assets	.3	2.7	3.7	3.5	3.7	2.3
1.7	1.8	1.6		.1	1.6	2.1	2.0	2.3	1.4
.8	1.1	1.1		9.4	1.0	.8	1.0	.9	1.3
(178) 2.2	(168) 1.8	(161) 2.5	% Depr., Dep., Amort./Sales	(17) 17.1	(29) 3.5	(14) 1.5	(33) 1.8	(38) 1.8	(30) 2.0
4.1	3.8	5.1		23.8	7.1	4.3	3.2	4.0	4.5
1.8	1.9	1.6			1.9	3.1	1.9	.9	
(74) 3.5	(64) 4.2	(68) 3.6	% Officers', Directors' Owners' Comp/Sales		(20) 4.9	(10) 4.4	(16) 2.7	(13) 1.6	
5.9	6.9	6.7			6.3	10.1	9.2	5.0	
5662883M	**5818769M**	**5410609M**	Net Sales ($)	**11096M**	**77224M**	**89873M**	**277518M**	**711865M**	**4243033M**
2190943M	**2666713M**	**2647077M**	Total Assets ($)	**34093M**	**73933M**	**60808M**	**121143M**	**251428M**	**2105672M**

M = $ thousand MM = $ million

See Pages 9 through 22 for Explanation of Ratios and Data

Current Data Sorted by Assets							Comparative Historical Data	
						Type of Statement		
	1	3	7	9	3	Unqualified	7	12
2	3	21	23		1	Reviewed	49	69
4	15	26	6	3		Compiled	39	46
26	32	12				Tax Returns	60	67
20	28	48	21	8	4	Other	94	94
52 (4/1-9/30/13)			274 (10/1/13-3/31/14)				4/1/09-3/31/10 ALL	4/1/10-3/31/11 ALL
0-500M	500M-2MM	2-10MM	10-50MM	50-100MM	100-250MM			
52	79	110	57	20	8	**NUMBER OF STATEMENTS**	249	288
%	%	%	%	%	%	**ASSETS**	%	%
19.4	14.0	9.8	8.1	7.0		Cash & Equivalents	12.0	13.2
21.0	24.6	23.2	23.5	21.8		Trade Receivables (net)	23.1	24.6
2.3	1.0	1.7	2.1	1.4		Inventory	1.8	1.3
3.0	3.4	4.1	3.1	2.6		All Other Current	4.5	5.0
45.7	43.1	38.8	36.9	32.7		Total Current	41.3	44.1
37.7	46.1	49.8	51.8	54.0		Fixed Assets (net)	45.8	43.4
4.8	3.5	3.5	4.5	6.2		Intangibles (net)	2.7	4.1
11.8	7.3	8.0	6.8	7.1		All Other Non-Current	10.0	8.4
100.0	100.0	100.0	100.0	100.0		Total	100.0	100.0
						LIABILITIES		
13.8	10.8	6.7	2.3	4.4		Notes Payable-Short Term	6.9	10.1
5.4	11.3	8.9	9.4	9.3		Cur. Mat.-L.T.D.	9.6	8.9
6.0	9.7	9.6	9.9	7.4		Trade Payables	10.7	10.6
.0	.2	.2	.2	.1		Income Taxes Payable	.3	.2
15.7	13.5	5.9	5.3	7.8		All Other Current	7.7	10.3
40.9	45.4	31.3	27.3	29.0		Total Current	35.3	40.2
38.7	36.5	30.6	27.3	34.2		Long-Term Debt	33.8	29.6
.0	.3	1.2	1.1	1.2		Deferred Taxes	.5	.5
6.3	4.8	4.4	1.6	2.7		All Other Non-Current	4.7	5.0
14.1	12.9	32.5	42.8	32.9		Net Worth	25.7	24.8
100.0	100.0	100.0	100.0	100.0		Total Liabilties & Net Worth	100.0	100.0
						INCOME DATA		
100.0	100.0	100.0	100.0	100.0		Net Sales	100.0	100.0
						Gross Profit		
94.2	93.7	95.4	95.0	94.9		Operating Expenses	95.8	94.1
5.8	6.3	4.6	5.0	5.1		Operating Profit	4.2	5.9
.3	1.8	.1	.9	1.2		All Other Expenses (net)	1.2	.7
5.5	4.5	4.6	4.0	3.9		Profit Before Taxes	3.0	5.2
						RATIOS		
4.6	2.5	1.9	2.1	1.7			2.3	2.4
1.6	1.2	1.3	1.3	1.0		Current	1.2	1.3
.5	.5	.8	.9	.7			.6	.7
4.0	2.4	1.6	1.9	1.6			2.0	2.1
1.0	1.0	1.1	1.1	.8		Quick	1.0	1.2
.3	.4	.7	.7	.5			.5	.6
0 UND	**0** UND	**18** 20.7	**29** 12.7	**33** 11.1			**11** 32.5	**14** 26.7
9 41.6	**18** 20.7	**31** 11.7	**35** 10.3	**40** 9.2		Sales/Receivables	**26** 13.9	**32** 11.5
29 12.6	**38** 9.7	**45** 8.1	**49** 7.5	**52** 7.0			**43** 8.5	**47** 7.8
						Cost of Sales/Inventory		
						Cost of Sales/Payables		
12.3	11.7	12.6	10.7	12.9			12.4	11.2
49.4	92.4	31.0	26.7	NM		Sales/Working Capital	82.4	38.1
-20.9	-11.7	-32.4	-124.0	-14.2			-21.9	-22.6
16.4	16.5	11.1	11.2	6.1			7.8	11.0
(36) 6.2	(66) 6.1	(102) 4.1	(50) 6.5	(18) 3.3		EBIT/Interest	(218) 2.8	(253) 3.8
1.5	1.7	.8	3.2	1.0			.1	.9
		3.2	2.9				2.4	3.0
		(23) 1.6	(19) 2.3			Net Profit + Depr., Dep., Amort./Cur. Mat. L/T/D	(52) 1.6	(53) 1.9
		1.1	1.0				.8	.9
.3	.8	.8	.8	1.2			.6	.6
1.2	2.3	1.7	1.4	2.3		Fixed/Worth	1.4	1.6
-24.9	-4.0	3.9	2.6	4.2			8.0	5.4
.9	1.5	.9	.8	.9			.8	.7
6.1	4.1	1.9	1.5	2.3		Debt/Worth	2.3	2.2
-6.8	-8.4	5.3	4.4	3.9			20.8	13.8
109.5	81.1	50.1	34.1	41.3			45.0	60.8
(35) 70.4	(52) 32.5	(96) 26.4	(55) 21.6	(17) 24.8		% Profit Before Taxes/Tangible Net Worth	(195) 15.9	(232) 21.8
20.1	9.1	3.4	10.3	9.3			.0	2.3
40.6	19.4	16.4	13.4	10.8			17.6	23.0
12.8	10.5	7.6	8.6	7.1		% Profit Before Taxes/Total Assets	5.6	8.2
4.2	1.8	-.9	2.8	1.1			-2.3	.1
46.7	18.4	9.0	6.4	5.6			18.1	25.1
15.4	8.8	4.6	4.0	2.3		Sales/Net Fixed Assets	6.1	6.2
7.5	3.2	2.6	2.3	1.4			2.8	3.0
7.1	5.8	3.2	3.0	2.3			4.5	4.4
4.3	3.6	2.2	2.1	1.3		Sales/Total Assets	2.5	2.6
3.2	1.8	1.7	1.5	1.1			1.7	1.7
2.3	2.2	3.2	2.4	4.9			2.1	2.6
(29) 3.5	(53) 5.1	(95) 5.6	(53) 4.4	(15) 7.5		% Depr., Dep., Amort./Sales	(196) 5.1	(216) 5.8
9.4	10.9	9.0	6.5	9.1			10.3	9.9
1.8	2.6	.8					1.3	1.5
(17) 2.8	(38) 4.1	(35) 1.7				% Officers', Directors' Owners' Comp/Sales	(85) 3.1	(96) 3.4
5.8	5.6	3.8					6.3	6.5
85996M	380624M	1355195M	3015386M	2788324M	1766440M	Net Sales ($)	3796516M	5600418M
13835M	91288M	515964M	1289991M	1359478M	1184605M	Total Assets ($)	1646024M	2565694M

M = $ thousand MM = $ million

See Pages 9 through 22 for Explanation of Ratios and Data

Comparative Historical Data

Type of Statement	4/1/11-3/31/12 ALL	4/1/12-3/31/13 ALL	4/1/13-3/31/14 ALL
Unqualified	21	18	23
Reviewed	63	58	50
Compiled	55	39	54
Tax Returns	79	78	70
Other	93	99	129
NUMBER OF STATEMENTS	311	292	326
ASSETS	%	%	%
Cash & Equivalents	13.3	11.6	11.9
Trade Receivables (net)	25.9	21.4	23.0
Inventory	1.4	1.7	1.7
All Other Current	4.5	3.5	3.5
Total Current	45.2	38.2	40.0
Fixed Assets (net)	41.7	48.5	47.6
Intangibles (net)	5.0	3.5	4.1
All Other Non-Current	8.1	9.7	8.2
Total	100.0	100.0	100.0
LIABILITIES			
Notes Payable-Short Term	10.0	9.5	7.8
Cur. Mat.-L.T.D.	8.1	8.2	9.1
Trade Payables	11.0	9.0	8.9
Income Taxes Payable	.3	.1	.2
All Other Current	9.1	9.4	9.3
Total Current	38.5	36.3	35.2
Long-Term Debt	31.6	35.9	33.3
Deferred Taxes	.8	.7	.8
All Other Non-Current	6.2	5.0	4.2
Net Worth	23.0	22.1	26.4
Total Liabilities & Net Worth	100.0	100.0	100.0
INCOME DATA			
Net Sales	100.0	100.0	100.0
Gross Profit			
Operating Expenses	92.9	95.1	94.7
Operating Profit	7.1	4.9	5.3
All Other Expenses (net)	.4	.7	.8
Profit Before Taxes	6.7	4.2	4.5
RATIOS			
Current	2.3	2.1	2.1
	1.4	1.1	1.3
	.8	.6	.7
Quick	2.1	1.9	1.8
	(310) 1.2	1.0	1.1
	.6	.5	.5
Sales/Receivables	**9** 42.0	**6** 57.4	**11** 32.4
	31 11.9	**27** 13.4	**29** 12.5
	45 8.2	**42** 8.7	**44** 8.3
Cost of Sales/Inventory			
Cost of Sales/Payables			
Sales/Working Capital	11.2	14.4	11.9
	32.1	97.4	39.2
	-53.0	-20.1	-24.5
EBIT/Interest	13.2	10.9	11.6
	(277) 4.9	(260) 4.2	(280) 4.6
	1.5	1.0	1.6
Net Profit + Depr., Dep., Amort./Cur. Mat. L/T/D	3.3	3.2	2.9
	(49) 2.0	(61) 2.0	(59) 1.8
	1.4	1.4	1.1
Fixed/Worth	.6	.6	.8
	1.3	1.8	1.7
	7.0	17.0	6.4
Debt/Worth	.9	.8	1.0
	2.1	2.3	2.3
	23.8	110.2	11.9
% Profit Before Taxes/Tangible Net Worth	63.7	47.2	56.8
	(242) 28.5	(221) 23.0	(261) 27.7
	9.4	6.6	9.8
% Profit Before Taxes/Total Assets	22.5	17.7	17.5
	9.5	7.0	8.1
	2.0	-.6	1.5
Sales/Net Fixed Assets	31.7	15.1	14.2
	7.3	5.7	5.4
	3.7	2.9	2.8
Sales/Total Assets	5.0	4.7	4.2
	2.8	2.7	2.4
	1.8	1.6	1.6
% Depr., Dep., Amort./Sales	2.1	2.5	2.8
	(232) 4.6	(224) 5.0	(246) 5.0
	7.7	8.6	8.7
% Officers', Directors' Owners' Comp/Sales	1.1	1.4	1.0
	(106) 2.7	(103) 2.6	(103) 3.0
	6.2	5.2	5.3
Net Sales ($)	**6701946M**	**6700332M**	**9391965M**
Total Assets ($)	**3009222M**	**3469971M**	**4455161M**

Current Data Sorted by Sales

Type of Statement	0-1MM	1-3MM	3-5MM	5-10MM	10-25MM	25MM & OVER
Unqualified		1		1	2	19
Reviewed	1	5	4	3	16	21
Compiled	4	6	10	13	10	11
Tax Returns	19	17	13	18	3	
Other	11	20	19	22	24	33
	52 (4/1-9/30/13)			274 (10/1/13-3/31/14)		
NUMBER OF STATEMENTS	35	49	46	57	55	84
ASSETS	%	%	%	%	%	%
Cash & Equivalents	17.3	12.3	16.7	8.9	12.4	8.6
Trade Receivables (net)	14.8	22.2	22.1	21.9	26.2	25.9
Inventory	.5	.9	1.3	2.3	2.3	2.0
All Other Current	3.8	3.1	3.2	4.2	3.1	3.4
Total Current	36.4	38.6	43.3	37.3	44.0	39.9
Fixed Assets (net)	52.3	44.0	47.2	49.2	47.2	47.2
Intangibles (net)	2.3	6.0	1.7	4.6	4.1	4.8
All Other Non-Current	9.1	11.5	7.8	8.9	4.6	8.1
Total	100.0	100.0	100.0	100.0	100.0	100.0
LIABILITIES						
Notes Payable-Short Term	6.8	12.4	7.9	12.6	5.8	3.4
Cur. Mat.-L.T.D.	8.6	8.7	9.0	9.4	9.6	9.2
Trade Payables	3.3	10.5	4.5	9.7	10.4	11.2
Income Taxes Payable	.0	.4	.0	.0	.2	.3
All Other Current	13.7	12.1	7.3	11.6	7.4	6.6
Total Current	32.5	44.0	28.7	43.3	33.3	30.6
Long-Term Debt	42.4	38.7	34.7	35.7	25.8	28.9
Deferred Taxes	.0	.8	.4	1.0	.6	1.4
All Other Non-Current	8.6	4.1	6.1	5.6	1.7	2.2
Net Worth	16.5	12.4	30.1	14.4	38.6	37.0
Total Liabilities & Net Worth	100.0	100.0	100.0	100.0	100.0	100.0
INCOME DATA						
Net Sales	100.0	100.0	100.0	100.0	100.0	100.0
Gross Profit						
Operating Expenses	82.1	98.1	94.0	97.0	96.2	95.9
Operating Profit	17.9	1.9	6.0	3.0	3.8	4.1
All Other Expenses (net)	5.3	-.3	1.0	-.1	-.1	.6
Profit Before Taxes	12.6	2.2	5.0	3.1	3.9	3.5
RATIOS						
Current	5.5	2.0	3.7	1.9	2.0	1.9
	1.3	1.0	1.6	1.1	1.4	1.3
	.5	.3	.8	.6	.8	.9
Quick	2.6	1.6	3.5	1.7	1.7	1.6
	.9	.9	1.5	.9	1.1	1.2
	.4	.2	.6	.4	.7	.7
Sales/Receivables	**0** UND	**0** UND	**11** 32.7	**9** 42.7	**21** 17.5	**29** 12.8
	6 64.0	**18** 20.0	**27** 13.6	**22** 16.7	**33** 11.0	**35** 10.4
	39 9.3	**43** 8.4	**43** 8.4	**41** 9.0	**49** 7.4	**46** 7.9
Cost of Sales/Inventory						
Cost of Sales/Payables						
Sales/Working Capital	5.3	12.4	9.8	17.9	10.5	12.5
	51.5	666.5	19.2	110.5	30.8	31.5
	-6.1	-12.1	-33.4	-18.1	-26.1	-122.2
EBIT/Interest	14.0	17.5	15.7	9.7	11.0	10.9
	(22) 4.2	(40) 6.1	(41) 4.1	(53) 5.0	(48) 4.1	(76) 4.8
	2.2	1.0	1.9	.5	1.7	2.3
Net Profit + Depr., Dep., Amort./Cur. Mat. L/T/D					10.4	2.5
					(10) 2.4	(30) 1.6
					1.3	1.1
Fixed/Worth	.6	.5	.7	1.1	.5	.8
	3.3	1.9	1.3	1.9	1.6	1.5
	-9.5	-4.3	7.1	NM	2.7	3.1
Debt/Worth	1.1	1.2	.6	1.5	.9	.9
	4.9	4.0	2.5	2.5	1.7	2.1
	-8.1	-6.3	18.1	NM	5.1	5.2
% Profit Before Taxes/Tangible Net Worth	102.1	76.6	43.3	74.3	51.8	41.8
	(24) 65.6	(32) 26.1	(37) 21.5	(43) 34.8	(50) 27.1	(75) 25.7
	29.6	8.9	4.1	2.7	2.8	15.0
% Profit Before Taxes/Total Assets	31.6	18.3	18.4	20.0	18.3	13.2
	10.8	6.1	7.8	8.8	8.9	8.0
	5.1	-1.3	1.1	-2.8	.6	3.2
Sales/Net Fixed Assets	12.4	26.8	14.7	14.5	12.2	13.4
	4.6	9.2	5.1	5.6	5.0	4.4
	.8	3.1	2.5	3.8	2.6	2.7
Sales/Total Assets	3.5	5.4	4.6	5.6	4.2	3.5
	2.2	3.6	2.3	2.6	2.4	2.2
	.5	1.4	1.6	2.1	1.8	1.5
% Depr., Dep., Amort./Sales	4.3	3.3	3.2	2.8	2.8	2.2
	(25) 13.3	(28) 7.0	(34) 5.8	(45) 4.4	(46) 4.8	(68) 3.5
	31.4	12.9	10.9	6.9	8.1	6.4
% Officers', Directors' Owners' Comp/Sales		2.6	1.8	1.0	.8	.4
		(21) 4.1	(18) 3.6	(27) 2.1	(15) 1.3	(15) 1.0
		6.0	6.0	3.6	4.3	4.8
Net Sales ($)	**18593M**	**99199M**	**186196M**	**406517M**	**835995M**	**7845465M**
Total Assets ($)	**17218M**	**51499M**	**130492M**	**151157M**	**387278M**	**3717517M**

M = $ thousand MM = $ million

See Pages 9 through 22 for Explanation of Ratios and Data

	Current Data Sorted by Assets						Comparative Historical Data	
Type of Statement								
Unqualified		1	2	16	9	10	43	46
Reviewed	1	4	26	29	3	1	44	58
Compiled	6	11	26	12	2		28	31
Tax Returns	19	11	12	1			22	26
Other	7	16	40	44	21	12	85	86
	43 (4/1-9/30/13)		299 (10/1/13-3/31/14)				**4/1/09-3/31/10**	**4/1/10-3/31/11**
	0-500M	**500M-2MM**	**2-10MM**	**10-50MM**	**50-100MM**	**100-250MM**	**ALL**	**ALL**
NUMBER OF STATEMENTS	33	43	106	102	35	23	222	247
ASSETS	%	%	%	%	%	%	%	%
Cash & Equivalents	16.0	18.0	9.5	8.7	6.1	7.4	10.3	9.9
Trade Receivables (net)	26.7	27.9	27.8	20.8	16.4	17.1	23.5	26.8
Inventory	2.1	1.2	1.3	1.1	1.2	2.2	1.9	1.4
All Other Current	2.9	2.4	4.2	3.8	3.3	2.7	4.6	4.0
Total Current	47.8	49.5	42.7	34.4	26.9	29.5	40.2	42.1
Fixed Assets (net)	39.5	39.3	47.5	55.5	59.7	57.8	47.2	45.4
Intangibles (net)	1.6	2.1	2.8	4.8	6.9	5.4	4.1	4.2
All Other Non-Current	11.3	9.1	6.9	5.3	6.4	7.4	8.4	8.3
Total	100.0	100.0	100.0	100.0	100.0	100.0	100.0	100.0
LIABILITIES								
Notes Payable-Short Term	7.8	5.3	9.0	5.2	3.7	1.6	12.0	7.8
Cur. Mat.-L.T.D.	14.7	6.5	8.5	9.1	11.2	10.4	9.8	9.1
Trade Payables	18.3	7.3	9.8	5.8	5.5	7.4	8.2	9.7
Income Taxes Payable	.1	.4	.1	.1	.1	.1	.3	.2
All Other Current	16.0	7.7	7.6	7.9	6.1	5.8	10.9	8.6
Total Current	56.8	27.1	35.0	28.2	26.6	25.4	41.2	35.4
Long-Term Debt	51.8	30.1	28.5	30.6	30.9	35.3	27.1	26.4
Deferred Taxes	.0	.1	.9	1.5	4.5	1.9	1.8	2.0
All Other Non-Current	3.8	6.7	2.0	5.0	4.1	1.2	4.6	5.1
Net Worth	-12.4	36.0	33.5	34.7	33.9	36.2	25.3	31.0
Total Liabilities & Net Worth	100.0	100.0	100.0	100.0	100.0	100.0	100.0	100.0
INCOME DATA								
Net Sales	100.0	100.0	100.0	100.0	100.0	100.0	100.0	100.0
Gross Profit								
Operating Expenses	94.2	94.9	93.6	94.9	95.5	94.2	97.5	95.6
Operating Profit	5.8	5.1	6.4	5.1	4.5	5.8	2.5	4.4
All Other Expenses (net)	1.6	.2	1.0	.8	.9	1.1	1.0	.9
Profit Before Taxes	4.3	4.9	5.4	4.3	3.6	4.7	1.5	3.5
RATIOS								
Current	2.2	4.9	1.9	1.8	1.4	1.4	1.8	2.1
	.9	2.5	1.2	1.2	.9	1.0	1.1	1.2
	.3	1.0	.8	.9	.7	.8	.7	.7
Quick	2.1	4.9	1.7	1.5	1.3	1.3	1.6	1.8
	.7	2.0	1.1	1.0	.8	.9	.9	1.1
	.2	.9	.7	.8	.6	.5	.5	.6
Sales/Receivables	**0** UND	**3** 128.6	**17** 21.0	**28** 13.1	**29** 12.4	**26** 13.8	**20** 18.6	**26** 14.3
	0 UND	**21** 17.5	**31** 11.9	**35** 10.4	**36** 10.0	**36** 10.1	**34** 10.7	**36** 10.2
	20 17.9	**36** 10.0	**41** 8.8	**45** 8.2	**47** 7.7	**46** 8.0	**44** 8.4	**47** 7.8
Cost of Sales/Inventory								
Cost of Sales/Payables								
Sales/Working Capital	18.8	10.3	13.8	10.7	17.5	17.2	15.9	12.5
	-345.4	18.8	51.5	43.4	-87.2	999.8	98.7	48.2
	-16.4	505.2	-30.9	-54.2	-21.2	-29.1	-16.9	-26.4
EBIT/Interest	22.0	13.6	11.3	9.2	5.8	8.2	5.9	9.5
	(25) 1.8	(34) 2.2	(94) 4.4	(96) 4.0	3.4	(21) 4.8	(205) 2.3	(231) 3.9
	.7	-2.4	1.9	1.7	1.7	2.2	.4	1.4
Net Profit + Depr., Dep., Amort./Cur. Mat. L/T/D			4.0	2.1	3.1		2.5	3.0
			(26) 1.8	(40) 1.5	(17) 1.4		(74) 1.3	(85) 1.5
			1.2	1.1	1.0		.9	1.0
Fixed/Worth	.4	.3	.5	1.2	1.6	1.6	.7	.6
	-17.7	.9	1.5	1.8	2.3	1.9	1.8	1.6
	-.5	4.6	2.5	3.9	3.8	2.6	3.9	6.0
Debt/Worth	1.4	.5	1.0	1.2	1.6	1.5	1.1	1.0
	-85.0	1.4	1.9	2.0	2.1	2.0	2.6	2.4
	-3.1	8.9	5.2	4.5	4.2	6.2	7.4	11.5
% Profit Before Taxes/Tangible Net Worth	265.7	49.7	50.5	35.9	23.3	41.5	34.2	47.0
	(16) 82.2	(36) 19.7	(94) 24.3	(92) 21.6	(30) 14.6	(21) 22.7	(189) 13.5	(210) 21.4
	15.1	.9	8.2	10.2	4.4	14.1	-.4	6.2
% Profit Before Taxes/Total Assets	42.8	18.3	17.5	13.1	9.2	15.7	10.1	16.4
	3.2	5.3	7.9	6.3	5.8	5.9	3.6	6.4
	-.9	-4.7	2.0	1.9	1.6	2.9	-1.9	1.3
Sales/Net Fixed Assets	79.4	27.3	13.6	5.1	3.4	4.4	15.3	16.2
	28.1	9.6	5.4	3.1	2.4	2.3	5.5	5.4
	5.6	5.0	3.1	2.1	1.7	1.5	2.6	2.9
Sales/Total Assets	11.5	7.5	4.3	2.4	1.9	1.9	4.1	4.2
	6.7	3.8	2.8	1.7	1.6	1.4	2.5	2.5
	3.4	2.9	1.9	1.4	1.0	1.0	1.5	1.7
% Depr., Dep., Amort./Sales	.7	1.0	1.9	3.7	3.3		2.3	1.9
	(19) 3.3	(31) 3.1	(92) 4.7	(98) 6.4	(27) 7.5		(180) 5.2	(188) 4.0
	11.4	5.9	7.9	8.9	10.3		8.7	7.4
% Officers', Directors' Owners' Comp/Sales	2.3	1.4	1.0	.7			1.0	.9
	(19) 4.2	(14) 1.9	(37) 1.8	(14) 1.4			(68) 2.2	(78) 1.6
	5.7	4.1	2.7	3.3			5.0	4.9
Net Sales ($)	86208M	256108M	1595214M	5080289M	4046871M	11691266M	13484310M	13688524M
Total Assets ($)	8486M	54102M	525242M	2558131M	2416501M	3830089M	6123903M	7145822M

M = $ thousand MM = $ million

See Pages 9 through 22 for Explanation of Ratios and Data

Comparative Historical Data | **Current Data Sorted by Sales**

Type of Statement	4/1/11-3/31/12 ALL	4/1/12-3/31/13 ALL	4/1/13-3/31/14 ALL	0-1MM	1-3MM	3-5MM	5-10MM	10-25MM	25MM & OVER
Unqualified	38	42	38			1		4	33
Reviewed	53	64	64	1	1	2	5	22	33
Compiled	24	37	57	6	4	4	15	19	9
Tax Returns	31	32	43	8	9	6	7	13	
Other	112	119	140	4	14	3	13	28	78
				43 (4/1-9/30/13)			299 (10/1/13-3/31/14)		
NUMBER OF STATEMENTS	258	294	342	19	28	16	40	86	153
ASSETS	%	%	%	%	%	%	%	%	%
Cash & Equivalents	8.9	10.1	10.5	12.0	23.3	11.4	8.2	11.1	8.1
Trade Receivables (net)	25.4	25.2	23.7	14.0	15.2	24.2	23.7	29.6	23.2
Inventory	1.4	1.7	1.3	3.1	1.3	.7	1.1	1.2	1.3
All Other Current	4.5	4.0	3.5	1.6	2.1	3.9	4.7	3.8	3.5
Total Current	40.1	40.9	39.1	30.8	42.0	40.2	37.7	45.6	36.2
Fixed Assets (net)	47.4	47.9	50.0	56.4	46.0	50.5	49.8	44.1	53.3
Intangibles (net)	5.5	4.0	3.8	2.5	1.6	.7	5.7	2.9	4.6
All Other Non-Current	7.0	7.3	7.1	10.4	10.5	8.6	6.8	7.4	5.9
Total	100.0	100.0	100.0	100.0	100.0	100.0	100.0	100.0	100.0
LIABILITIES									
Notes Payable-Short Term	8.5	6.6	6.2	1.4	4.0	7.4	9.4	7.2	5.8
Cur. Mat.-L.T.D.	9.5	8.9	9.5	7.4	14.1	9.2	8.1	9.0	9.5
Trade Payables	10.0	9.1	8.5	3.8	9.0	15.6	9.1	9.5	7.5
Income Taxes Payable	.3	.1	.1	.1	.1	.0	.5	.1	.1
All Other Current	7.5	6.7	8.3	5.4	6.6	15.1	8.3	8.5	8.0
Total Current	35.8	31.5	32.6	18.2	33.8	47.3	35.5	34.4	30.9
Long-Term Debt	28.1	28.3	32.3	54.6	43.3	41.3	29.3	27.0	30.3
Deferred Taxes	1.8	1.7	1.3	.0	.4	.3	.4	1.0	2.3
All Other Non-Current	4.6	6.9	3.8	5.7	5.3	1.1	9.4	1.9	3.2
Net Worth	29.7	31.7	30.0	21.5	17.3	10.1	25.4	35.8	33.4
Total Liabilties & Net Worth	100.0	100.0	100.0	100.0	100.0	100.0	100.0	100.0	100.0
INCOME DATA									
Net Sales	100.0	100.0	100.0	100.0	100.0	100.0	100.0	100.0	100.0
Gross Profit									
Operating Expenses	95.3	93.8	94.4	75.4	90.2	97.0	98.7	96.2	95.2
Operating Profit	4.7	6.2	5.6	24.6	9.8	3.0	1.3	3.8	4.8
All Other Expenses (net)	.8	.8	.9	8.8	-.1	.3	.0	.7	.5
Profit Before Taxes	3.9	5.5	4.7	15.8	9.8	2.7	1.3	3.1	4.3
RATIOS									
Current	1.8	1.9	2.0	5.0	4.2	7.9	1.9	2.4	1.6
	1.1	1.2	1.2	.4	1.6	2.3	1.2	1.4	1.1
	.7	.8	.8	.3	.8	.5	.7	1.0	.8
Quick	1.6	1.7	1.7	5.0	2.4	7.8	1.7	2.3	1.4
	.9	1.1	1.0	.4	1.5	1.5	.9	1.3	1.0
	.6	.7	.7	.2	.6	.5	.6	.7	.7
Sales/Receivables	22 16.5	20 18.5	17 21.3	0 UND	0 UND	0 903.2	17 21.6	24 15.4	28 13.1
	35 10.4	33 11.1	31 11.7	0 UND	12 31.0	11 32.5	24 15.0	32 11.3	35 10.3
	45 8.2	42 8.6	41 8.8	16 22.4	29 12.5	31 11.9	36 10.0	41 8.8	45 8.1
Cost of Sales/Inventory									
Cost of Sales/Payables									
Sales/Working Capital	13.1	13.9	13.1	11.4	6.0	8.1	18.1	10.7	14.6
	68.5	44.4	52.6	-15.6	24.9	29.8	224.9	29.8	91.3
	-20.6	-33.5	-32.2	-6.3	-165.2	-14.9	-21.9	-317.2	-40.6
EBIT/Interest	10.0	9.4	10.0	8.7	16.5	10.4	10.9	11.4	9.1
	(241) 4.1	(271) 4.2	(305) 3.8	(11) .9	(23) 4.3	(14) 3.1	(37) 2.1	(74) 5.1	(146) 4.2
	1.8	1.9	1.5	.7	1.8	-1.1	-1.2	1.9	1.9
Net Profit + Depr., Dep., Amort./Cur. Mat. L/T/D	3.0	3.1	2.4					5.0	2.3
	(74) 1.6	(79) 1.5	(84) 1.7					(19) 1.8	(58) 1.5
	1.2	1.0	1.1					1.2	1.1
Fixed/Worth	.8	.7	.8	.4	.5	.7	1.3	.4	1.3
	1.9	1.6	1.8	4.3	2.4	2.3	3.1	1.3	1.8
	4.5	3.4	4.2	-4.0	-2.3	-3.3	NM	2.2	3.2
Debt/Worth	1.2	1.0	1.1	.3	.4	.7	1.3	.8	1.4
	2.2	2.1	2.0	3.4	2.7	2.4	3.9	1.9	2.0
	6.6	5.6	6.5	-13.9	-5.9	-8.3	NM	4.2	4.2
% Profit Before Taxes/Tangible Net Worth	51.0	48.3	44.9	82.2	50.9	38.2	109.6	49.8	33.9
	(219) 24.2	(255) 25.3	(289) 22.5	(13) 21.3	(19) 23.9	(11) 16.2	(30) 20.0	(80) 24.4	(136) 20.2
	9.6	9.4	8.3	-1.0	8.2	7.6	-1.5	8.4	10.8
% Profit Before Taxes/Total Assets	13.7	15.6	14.2	15.5	21.2	13.4	18.6	18.1	12.3
	6.4	6.6	6.1	.5	8.8	5.3	3.3	8.7	6.2
	2.0	2.1	1.7	-1.0	3.1	-3.1	-4.2	2.5	2.2
Sales/Net Fixed Assets	15.7	15.8	12.0	17.5	27.5	21.8	15.9	24.9	5.9
	4.4	4.8	4.1	2.5	7.2	8.1	7.3	5.8	3.2
	2.6	2.4	2.4	.2	1.9	2.5	3.2	3.1	2.1
Sales/Total Assets	3.9	4.2	4.2	4.4	5.9	8.4	5.1	5.2	2.8
	2.2	2.3	2.3	.7	3.1	3.3	3.2	2.9	1.8
	1.6	1.5	1.5	.2	1.1	1.6	2.1	1.9	1.4
% Depr., Dep., Amort./Sales	2.0	2.0	2.6	4.9	3.2	1.6	2.3	1.6	3.0
	(201) 4.8	(225) 4.8	(269) 5.2	(12) 18.3	(21) 6.4	(12) 5.8	(34) 4.6	(71) 4.4	(119) 5.8
	8.1	7.7	8.2	37.1	10.3	13.4	7.0	7.8	8.2
% Officers', Directors' Owners' Comp/Sales	.9	1.1	1.1		2.5		1.5	.9	.5
	(70) 2.2	(72) 2.3	(89) 1.9		(16) 4.1		(16) 2.2	(26) 1.5	(22) 1.2
	4.8	5.5	4.1		5.6		3.3	2.4	2.4
Net Sales ($)	16492263M	16579834M	22755956M	9468M	55954M	63506M	309051M	1366238M	20951739M
Total Assets ($)	8814484M	8728934M	9392551M	15910M	46765M	34226M	151170M	645550M	8498930M

M = $ thousand MM = $ million

See Pages 9 through 22 for Explanation of Ratios and Data

Current Data Sorted by Assets							Comparative Historical Data	
						Type of Statement		
	1		3	1		Unqualified	8	6
	1	2	2	2		Reviewed	6	6
	2	1	2	1		Compiled	7	6
10	2	4	1			Tax Returns	9	21
3	7	9	2	1		Other	22	28
	14 (4/1-9/30/13)		43 (10/1/13-3/31/14)				4/1/09-3/31/10 ALL	4/1/10-3/31/11 ALL
0-500M	**500M-2MM**	**2-10MM**	**10-50MM**	**50-100MM**	**100-250MM**			
13	13	16	10	5		**NUMBER OF STATEMENTS**	52	67
%	%	%	%	%	%	**ASSETS**	%	%
22.1	21.5	14.2	8.5		D A T A N O T A V A I L A B L E	Cash & Equivalents	20.9	16.1
20.6	15.8	9.1	16.5			Trade Receivables (net)	16.3	13.2
.7	.0	.3	.8			Inventory	.6	.3
10.6	6.1	8.2	10.3			All Other Current	11.3	9.0
54.0	43.4	31.7	36.2			Total Current	49.2	38.6
13.8	39.5	42.4	45.3			Fixed Assets (net)	31.3	35.2
12.5	10.9	6.5	9.9			Intangibles (net)	8.0	9.4
19.7	6.2	19.3	8.7			All Other Non-Current	11.5	16.9
100.0	100.0	100.0	100.0			Total	100.0	100.0
						LIABILITIES		
7.5	1.7	4.5	18.2			Notes Payable-Short Term	10.0	12.9
6.4	2.6	5.4	24.4			Cur. Mat.-L.T.D.	6.2	4.9
6.6	4.0	9.1	9.7			Trade Payables	12.2	10.2
.0	.0	.0	.0			Income Taxes Payable	.1	.2
71.6	40.7	6.4	9.4			All Other Current	23.2	21.4
92.2	49.0	25.5	61.7			Total Current	51.6	49.6
10.8	19.0	25.6	29.2			Long-Term Debt	19.4	21.8
.0	.5	.2	2.1			Deferred Taxes	1.1	.3
26.3	8.5	12.4	1.0			All Other Non-Current	9.0	19.2
-29.3	23.0	36.3	6.1			Net Worth	18.8	9.1
100.0	100.0	100.0	100.0			Total Liabilties & Net Worth	100.0	100.0
						INCOME DATA		
100.0	100.0	100.0	100.0			Net Sales	100.0	100.0
						Gross Profit		
83.0	90.7	88.8	83.1			Operating Expenses	88.8	89.2
17.0	9.3	11.2	16.9			Operating Profit	11.2	10.8
-.3	1.9	7.1	6.9			All Other Expenses (net)	3.9	4.4
17.3	7.4	4.1	10.0			Profit Before Taxes	7.3	6.4
						RATIOS		
1.9	3.1	5.0	1.1				1.9	2.3
1.0	1.0	1.2	.6			Current	1.1	.8
.2	.4	.5	.4				.5	.3
1.9	3.0	2.5	.9				1.6	1.6
.9	(12) 1.1	.9	.3			Quick	.7	.6
.2	.3	.3	.1				.3	.2
0 UND	**0** UND	**3** 116.4	**0** UND				**0** 744.1	**0** UND
0 UND	**8** 47.6	**7** 51.9	**15** 24.0			Sales/Receivables	**14** 26.7	**9** 38.8
34 10.8	**27** 13.4	**29** 12.7	**33** 10.9				**32** 11.3	**29** 12.5
						Cost of Sales/Inventory		
						Cost of Sales/Payables		
18.6	7.0	7.0	NM				11.3	8.3
-251.0	323.1	70.5	-15.0			Sales/Working Capital	76.4	-84.8
-14.5	-24.7	-6.4	-2.5				-13.0	-10.6
		27.1					18.3	13.5
		(14) 3.1				EBIT/Interest	(37) 5.9	(47) 5.8
		2.0					.8	1.2
							6.9	
						Net Profit + Depr., Dep., Amort./Cur. Mat. L/T/D	(10) 3.4	
							1.8	
.0	.2	.5	.4				.2	.5
.0	1.4	1.2	2.0			Fixed/Worth	1.5	2.3
-1.3	NM	7.2	-.6				-6.2	-3.0
.9	.5	.4	1.5				1.3	1.4
6.2	2.5	2.2	3.0			Debt/Worth	4.8	6.0
-1.5	NM	NM	-1.7				-14.7	-5.7
	106.3	47.8					86.8	71.0
	(10) 29.7	(12) 30.8				% Profit Before Taxes/Tangible Net Worth	(36) 50.4	(43) 18.8
	-8.4	6.6					15.5	7.2
21.9	24.8	13.9	20.8				30.0	17.5
9.7	8.7	7.9	6.6			% Profit Before Taxes/Total Assets	9.0	6.5
.9	-4.0	.5	1.8				1.4	-1.8
UND	164.8	10.0	17.4				78.5	63.6
UND	11.8	7.5	3.6			Sales/Net Fixed Assets	11.1	11.9
33.8	5.1	2.5	2.6				5.3	4.4
11.8	4.6	3.3	3.6				4.5	4.9
4.7	3.7	1.8	1.8			Sales/Total Assets	2.5	2.3
.8	2.1	1.2	.6				1.7	1.5
		2.8	1.9				3.1	3.2
		(11) 5.0	8.2			% Depr., Dep., Amort./Sales	(29) 5.9	(42) 5.9
		11.9	17.1				7.8	9.2
							1.0	1.8
						% Officers', Directors' Owners' Comp/Sales	(12) 4.0	(19) 4.2
							8.6	6.6
12871M	**58478M**	**162478M**	**467879M**	**324370M**		Net Sales ($)	**1251672M**	**763498M**
2441M	**14298M**	**82968M**	**249169M**	**396140M**		Total Assets ($)	**885993M**	**495230M**

M = $ thousand MM = $ million

See Pages 9 through 22 for Explanation of Ratios and Data

Comparative Historical Data				Current Data Sorted by Sales					
			Type of Statement						
4	5	5	Unqualified		1				4
4	10	7	Reviewed			1		4	2
6	7	6	Compiled		1	2		2	1
18	12	17	Tax Returns	6	7	2		2	
25	21	22	Other	4	3	3	6	2	4
4/1/11-3/31/12 ALL	4/1/12-3/31/13 ALL	4/1/13-3/31/14 ALL		14 (4/1-9/30/13)			43 (10/1/13-3/31/14)		
				0-1MM	1-3MM	3-5MM	5-10MM	10-25MM	25MM & OVER
57	55	57	**NUMBER OF STATEMENTS**	10	12	8	6	10	11
%	%	%	**ASSETS**	%	%	%	%	%	%
27.3	19.1	16.4	Cash & Equivalents	15.8	27.8			9.4	14.2
17.9	15.4	13.9	Trade Receivables (net)	18.0	20.0			6.7	14.8
2.8	.9	.4	Inventory	.0	.7			.6	.3
5.9	8.3	8.1	All Other Current	10.8	3.6			10.4	9.8
53.8	43.6	38.7	Total Current	44.5	52.2			27.1	39.2
28.7	23.6	35.4	Fixed Assets (net)	17.3	24.0			41.5	41.0
11.2	11.4	11.5	Intangibles (net)	11.2	5.9			15.6	12.1
6.2	21.4	14.4	All Other Non-Current	26.9	18.0			15.7	7.7
100.0	100.0	100.0	Total	100.0	100.0			100.0	100.0
			LIABILITIES						
5.1	16.0	7.1	Notes Payable-Short Term	4.3	11.8			11.2	5.4
5.0	4.9	11.1	Cur. Mat.-L.T.D.	.4	17.8			11.6	15.6
8.8	6.5	6.8	Trade Payables	2.1	6.4			9.6	9.3
.2	.1	.0	Income Taxes Payable	.0	.0			.0	.0
21.9	25.8	30.2	All Other Current	43.4	53.3			13.4	12.1
41.0	53.3	55.3	Total Current	50.2	89.3			45.8	42.4
26.1	20.4	20.1	Long-Term Debt	11.4	14.4			10.5	32.2
.1	.0	.5	Deferred Taxes	.0	.5			.3	1.9
9.2	7.0	11.8	All Other Non-Current	5.5	28.6			1.2	1.6
23.6	19.2	12.3	Net Worth	33.0	-32.8			42.2	22.0
100.0	100.0	100.0	Total Liabilities & Net Worth	100.0	100.0			100.0	100.0
			INCOME DATA						
100.0	100.0	100.0	Net Sales	100.0	100.0			100.0	100.0
			Gross Profit						
90.6	86.1	85.7	Operating Expenses	61.3	87.3			88.7	90.4
9.4	13.9	14.3	Operating Profit	38.7	12.7			11.3	9.6
3.8	5.9	3.8	All Other Expenses (net)	9.7	5.9			1.9	1.1
5.6	8.0	10.5	Profit Before Taxes	29.0	6.8			9.5	8.6
			RATIOS						
2.4	1.8	2.2		3.6	2.8			2.7	1.8
1.3	1.1	.9	Current	1.5	1.2			.5	.9
.7	.4	.4		.5	.1			.1	.5
2.3	1.7	1.9		3.2	2.8				1.8
1.0	.9	(56) .8	Quick	.9	1.1				.6
.4	.2	.2		.5	.1				.3
0 UND	0 999.8	0 UND		0 UND	0 UND			0 UND	2 165.6
13 28.6	7 52.3	6 63.4	Sales/Receivables	0 UND	6 56.5			5 70.0	7 50.2
36 10.0	31 11.7	24 15.1		521 .7	23 15.6			18 20.6	17 21.7
			Cost of Sales/Inventory						
			Cost of Sales/Payables						
9.0	8.5	8.6		.8	15.7			8.8	7.9
60.5	191.0	-225.8	Sales/Working Capital	15.1	NM			-51.8	-58.9
-20.3	-8.3	-6.8		-1.6	-7.0			-2.0	-13.0
12.9	11.7	14.3						35.0	
(43) 4.8	(34) 6.0	(40) 4.1	EBIT/Interest					5.6	
1.6	1.4	1.9						.9	
			Net Profit + Depr., Dep., Amort./Cur. Mat. L/T/D						
.4	.0	.3		.0	.0			.6	.5
2.3	1.0	1.6	Fixed/Worth	.0	2.0			1.5	1.9
-1.7	-7.0	-5.2		.4	-.5			NM	-.5
1.0	1.0	.6		.3	1.0			.8	.7
4.5	3.9	3.2	Debt/Worth	1.0	5.5			1.5	3.2
-6.7	-5.5	-6.7		-4.5	-1.7			NM	-2.3
66.9	78.2	60.7							
(36) 36.1	(36) 36.7	(38) 38.5	% Profit Before Taxes/Tangible Net Worth						
17.5	18.2	12.4							
21.3	23.1	21.0		39.0	19.4			21.8	28.4
9.0	6.9	8.4	% Profit Before Taxes/Total Assets	11.0	2.6			8.3	18.3
1.3	.7	1.7		.5	-.2			2.2	4.5
117.3	213.4	75.7		UND	736.8			38.3	10.2
14.9	28.8	9.1	Sales/Net Fixed Assets	UND	40.6			7.5	3.9
5.1	7.2	3.4		3.4	13.6			2.1	3.1
5.0	5.0	4.3		1.7	11.8			3.7	3.6
2.8	2.9	2.4	Sales/Total Assets	.3	4.4			2.1	2.4
1.6	1.3	1.2		.1	2.3			1.1	1.2
1.1	.5	2.4							
(38) 5.6	(33) 3.8	(35) 5.0	% Depr., Dep., Amort./Sales						
8.3	9.3	11.6							
2.6	2.5	2.0							
(20) 6.3	(19) 6.5	(17) 4.9	% Officers', Directors' Owners' Comp/Sales						
12.8	9.2	10.6							
888912M	865825M	1026076M	Net Sales ($)	2658M	23852M	32719M	44895M	171919M	750033M
520072M	651415M	745016M	Total Assets ($)	16689M	60909M	9821M	25834M	225259M	406504M

M = $ thousand MM = $ million
See Pages 9 through 22 for Explanation of Ratios and Data

Current Data Sorted by Assets							Comparative Historical Data	
		2	1	1		**Type of Statement** Unqualified	3	3
	2	6	2			Reviewed	1	5
1	3	3				Compiled	10	12
13	12	3				Tax Returns	14	19
4	6	13	1		1	Other	14	14
	5 (4/1-9/30/13)		69 (10/1/13-3/31/14)				4/1/09-3/31/10 ALL	4/1/10-3/31/11 ALL
0-500M	500M-2MM	2-10MM	10-50MM	50-100MM	100-250MM			
18	23	27	4	1	1	**NUMBER OF STATEMENTS**	42	53
%	%	%	%	%	%	**ASSETS**	%	%
16.2	14.7	13.9				Cash & Equivalents	9.9	12.8
6.9	10.2	19.3				Trade Receivables (net)	13.3	17.2
4.0	2.4	.6				Inventory	1.8	2.6
5.0	1.4	4.3				All Other Current	1.8	5.8
32.2	28.7	38.1				Total Current	26.7	38.3
55.3	58.9	50.2				Fixed Assets (net)	47.3	51.1
4.3	1.7	4.4				Intangibles (net)	14.1	5.3
8.2	10.7	7.3				All Other Non-Current	12.0	5.2
100.0	100.0	100.0				Total	100.0	100.0
						LIABILITIES		
10.2	12.2	4.7				Notes Payable-Short Term	6.6	8.1
8.9	12.5	12.6				Cur. Mat.-L.T.D.	10.1	12.2
2.4	4.2	9.4				Trade Payables	8.7	15.7
.2	.0	.1				Income Taxes Payable	.0	.3
47.2	7.1	9.1				All Other Current	9.1	8.0
68.9	35.9	35.9				Total Current	34.6	44.3
63.3	48.5	37.8				Long-Term Debt	42.3	50.6
.0	.1	.4				Deferred Taxes	.3	.4
19.4	6.2	2.9				All Other Non-Current	8.7	6.6
-51.6	9.3	23.0				Net Worth	14.2	-1.9
100.0	100.0	100.0				Total Liabilties & Net Worth	100.0	100.0
						INCOME DATA		
100.0	100.0	100.0				Net Sales	100.0	100.0
						Gross Profit		
91.9	96.4	95.4				Operating Expenses	97.3	96.3
8.1	3.6	4.6				Operating Profit	2.7	3.7
4.3	.7	.8				All Other Expenses (net)	1.7	1.4
3.8	2.9	3.9				Profit Before Taxes	1.0	2.2
						RATIOS		
2.0	1.4	2.1					2.2	2.0
.5	.8	1.0				Current	.8	1.2
.1	.4	.6					.3	.3
.9	1.4	1.8					2.2	1.8
.2	.7	.9				Quick	.7	.8
.1	.4	.5					.2	.3
0 UND	0 UND	11 34.6					0 UND	0 UND
0 UND	2 217.2	17 20.9				Sales/Receivables	12 31.1	8 48.3
7 51.0	15 24.4	27 13.4					36 10.2	25 14.6
						Cost of Sales/Inventory		
						Cost of Sales/Payables		
20.2	50.8	16.3					23.8	17.0
-25.2	-90.9	263.8				Sales/Working Capital	-65.6	145.9
-7.0	-26.1	-19.2					-9.7	-11.6
7.5	13.2	18.2					4.8	8.5
(14) 3.2	(19) 1.0	(26) 3.0				EBIT/Interest	(37) 1.5	(48) 2.8
.7	-1.3	.9					.0	.9
						Net Profit + Depr., Dep., Amort./Cur. Mat. L/T/D		
4.0	1.1	.8					1.3	.9
-21.0	3.3	2.4				Fixed/Worth	UND	3.6
-.3	-3.1	332.6					-1.6	-4.4
6.7	1.5	1.2					1.8	3.0
-7.0	5.0	2.4				Debt/Worth	UND	7.9
-2.4	-4.9	701.6					-3.3	-4.6
	191.3	75.0					66.8	80.5
	(14) 43.4	(21) 26.3				% Profit Before Taxes/Tangible Net Worth	(22) 13.8	(32) 28.1
	-3.8	3.7					-4.3	2.1
16.4	40.5	23.1					10.9	19.6
3.1	.6	7.5				% Profit Before Taxes/Total Assets	1.5	6.6
-7.0	-3.9	.0					-3.8	-.2
212.9	15.6	21.3					18.1	24.0
4.5	6.2	4.3				Sales/Net Fixed Assets	5.8	6.0
2.3	2.4	3.5					2.7	3.3
5.4	5.4	3.9					3.9	7.0
3.0	3.6	2.9				Sales/Total Assets	2.1	3.5
1.7	1.7	2.3					1.3	2.2
7.5	1.9	1.7					2.3	4.2
(10) 12.7	(18) 6.1	(25) 6.9				% Depr., Dep., Amort./Sales	(36) 7.6	(43) 6.8
16.8	13.4	9.0					13.0	11.2
3.7	2.8						3.1	3.5
(10) 5.7	(12) 4.8					% Officers', Directors' Owners' Comp/Sales	(20) 5.5	(27) 4.5
13.4	5.9						7.3	8.1
13113M	105310M	404196M	262969M	110943M	223419M	Net Sales ($)	389918M	552980M
4147M	23818M	118914M	74817M	53525M	112671M	Total Assets ($)	163926M	235594M

M = $ thousand MM = $ million

See Pages 9 through 22 for Explanation of Ratios and Data

Comparative Historical Data / Current Data Sorted by Sales

4/1/11-3/31/12 ALL	4/1/12-3/31/13 ALL	4/1/13-3/31/14 ALL	Type of Statement	0-1MM	1-3MM	3-5MM	5-10MM	10-25MM	25MM & OVER
1	2	4	Unqualified					1	3
7	8	10	Reviewed				2	7	1
9	6	7	Compiled	1	1		2	3	
17	19	28	Tax Returns	10	11		6	1	
28	31	25	Other	5	2	2	6	7	3
				5 (4/1-9/30/13)		69 (10/1/13-3/31/14)			
62	66	74	NUMBER OF STATEMENTS	16	14	2	16	19	7
%	%	%	**ASSETS**	%	%	%	%	%	%
12.7	13.9	14.2	Cash & Equivalents	12.0	19.5		14.8	9.8	
13.4	11.8	14.1	Trade Receivables (net)	4.5	8.2		14.0	19.7	
1.7	2.4	2.0	Inventory	.0	5.2		3.5	.9	
3.3	2.0	3.8	All Other Current	2.8	3.5		.6	4.9	
31.1	30.1	34.1	Total Current	19.3	36.4		32.8	35.4	
54.7	52.8	52.3	Fixed Assets (net)	65.2	48.9		62.6	49.4	
5.2	8.6	4.7	Intangibles (net)	4.1	1.0		1.5	6.7	
8.9	8.5	9.0	All Other Non-Current	11.5	13.7		3.1	8.6	
100.0	100.0	100.0	Total	100.0	100.0		100.0	100.0	
			LIABILITIES						
7.8	7.9	8.8	Notes Payable-Short Term	7.0	17.5		7.6	8.3	
13.7	13.1	11.3	Cur. Mat.-L.T.D.	6.8	12.0		12.4	14.5	
9.0	6.1	6.2	Trade Payables	1.3	2.3		4.0	11.6	
.1	.1	.1	Income Taxes Payable	.3	.0		.1	.0	
9.2	6.6	18.0	All Other Current	48.6	13.8		5.7	8.1	
39.9	33.7	44.5	Total Current	64.0	45.5		29.8	42.6	
43.9	44.0	46.7	Long-Term Debt	41.6	85.2		49.5	27.7	
.2	.7	.3	Deferred Taxes	.0	.0		.1	.5	
8.3	10.5	9.0	All Other Non-Current	21.7	7.3		5.6	1.7	
7.7	11.0	-.4	Net Worth	-27.3	-38.1		15.0	27.6	
100.0	100.0	100.0	Total Liabilities & Net Worth	100.0	100.0		100.0	100.0	
			INCOME DATA						
100.0	100.0	100.0	Net Sales	100.0	100.0		100.0	100.0	
			Gross Profit						
93.4	94.8	94.8	Operating Expenses	95.0	92.5		95.9	96.4	
6.6	5.2	5.2	Operating Profit	5.0	7.5		4.1	3.6	
2.4	1.1	1.8	All Other Expenses (net)	4.9	1.0		.8	.5	
4.3	4.1	3.4	Profit Before Taxes	.0	6.5		3.2	3.0	
			RATIOS						
1.5	2.0	1.7		4.3	2.0		1.4	1.5	
.7	.7	.9	Current	.5	.7		1.0	.7	
.3	.4	.4		.2	.0		.8	.4	
1.3	1.5	1.4		4.1	1.3		1.4	1.4	
.7	.7	.7	Quick	.3	.5		.9	.6	
.3	.3	.3		.1	.0		.7	.4	
0 999.8	0 UND	0 UND		0 UND	0 UND		0 UND	11 34.6	
13 28.6	15 24.4	11 33.9	Sales/Receivables	0 UND	0 UND		12 31.6	20 18.3	
23 15.9	25 14.8	24 15.0		9 39.1	3 135.1		21 17.1	27 13.4	
			Cost of Sales/Inventory						
			Cost of Sales/Payables						
27.0	40.1	21.4		69.9	17.8		31.0	21.4	
-41.5	-45.7	-114.0	Sales/Working Capital	-20.5	-32.4		NM	-45.3	
-8.7	-12.4	-11.8		-4.2	-11.0		-68.4	-10.5	
9.8	7.9	13.2		6.3	3.2		16.1	13.4	
(56) 4.8	(55) 3.4	(65) 2.1	EBIT/Interest	(12) 1.1	(12) 1.4		(15) 1.1	(18) 3.0	
1.2	1.5	.4		-.9	.4		-1.3	.5	
2.2	2.0		Net Profit + Depr., Dep.,						
(13) 1.5	(11) 1.1		Amort./Cur. Mat. L/T/D						
.9	1.0								
1.3	1.4	1.0		2.1	1.6		1.1	.9	
4.3	3.4	5.2	Fixed/Worth	-42.7	-1.9		4.9	1.9	
-5.7	-1.6	-2.8		-1.2	-.4		-11.6	13.0	
1.7	1.4	1.6		3.0	2.4		1.6	1.2	
6.7	7.4	6.7	Debt/Worth	-45.3	-3.5		7.5	1.7	
-9.4	-5.7	-4.7		-2.7	-2.8		-17.3	17.4	
102.5	86.9	126.0	% Profit Before Taxes/Tangible				143.8	70.9	
(40) 42.1	(40) 22.6	(44) 27.1	Net Worth				(11) 27.6	(15) 22.0	
16.3	8.8	7.0					6.9	.0	
22.9	19.4	23.8		8.6	21.1		18.8	32.0	
8.0	6.6	3.5	% Profit Before Taxes/Total Assets	.2	1.0		4.7	7.5	
.6	.8	-1.8		-27.6	-1.8		-2.1	.0	
11.4	16.3	22.1		4.5	141.0		7.3	24.2	
4.4	5.2	5.4	Sales/Net Fixed Assets	2.6	6.4		5.0	5.2	
3.1	2.8	3.3		1.2	2.4		3.8	3.5	
3.7	4.4	4.9		2.8	5.4		4.6	5.3	
2.8	2.9	3.1	Sales/Total Assets	1.7	3.5		3.5	3.0	
1.7	1.9	2.0		.8	2.0		2.6	2.6	
3.9	3.4	1.8		11.4			2.5	1.9	
(51) 7.2	(47) 7.5	(58) 7.3	% Depr., Dep., Amort./Sales	(10) 16.6			7.2	(16) 6.9	
9.8	9.7	11.6		20.1			11.2	8.0	
2.9	2.8	2.6	% Officers', Directors'		2.7				
(22) 4.6	(28) 4.2	(29) 4.3	Owners' Comp/Sales		(11) 5.6				
7.9	5.7	6.4			7.7				
993368M	858909M	1119950M	Net Sales ($)	6157M	23126M	7314M	112480M	306866M	664007M
436434M	446579M	387892M	Total Assets ($)	6684M	7693M	1730M	38821M	94157M	238807M

M = $ thousand MM = $ million

See Pages 9 through 22 for Explanation of Ratios and Data

Current Data Sorted by Assets							Comparative Historical Data	
						Type of Statement		
	1	1	5	3	2	Unqualified	15	17
	4	25	10		1	Reviewed	40	45
2	9	13	3			Compiled	31	36
7	13	10			1	Tax Returns	31	36
	4	17	11	5	4	Other	31	25
	50 (4/1-9/30/13)		101 (10/1/13-3/31/14)				4/1/09-3/31/10 ALL	4/1/10-3/31/11 ALL
0-500M	**500M-2MM**	**2-10MM**	**10-50MM**	**50-100MM**	**100-250MM**			
9	31	66	29	8	8	**NUMBER OF STATEMENTS**	148	159
%	%	%	%	%	%	**ASSETS**	%	%
	16.6	13.4	7.6			Cash & Equivalents	14.1	13.0
	9.5	13.2	10.8			Trade Receivables (net)	10.4	10.8
	1.3	2.5	2.9			Inventory	1.7	3.0
	2.0	3.1	2.6			All Other Current	2.1	3.0
	29.4	32.3	23.8			Total Current	28.3	29.9
	53.9	55.5	63.0			Fixed Assets (net)	59.5	57.6
	3.3	3.1	6.9			Intangibles (net)	4.3	3.5
	13.4	9.1	6.3			All Other Non-Current	8.0	9.0
	100.0	100.0	100.0			Total	100.0	100.0
						LIABILITIES		
	5.6	6.1	4.1			Notes Payable-Short Term	5.7	5.4
	16.5	12.2	9.4			Cur. Mat.-L.T.D.	12.1	12.4
	2.6	3.3	3.0			Trade Payables	2.9	4.5
	.0	.7	.4			Income Taxes Payable	.4	.2
	3.6	8.9	7.9			All Other Current	6.1	4.8
	28.4	31.2	24.8			Total Current	27.1	27.3
	35.9	36.4	30.6			Long-Term Debt	33.9	31.0
	.4	.7	1.5			Deferred Taxes	1.7	1.6
	10.2	3.3	7.2			All Other Non-Current	4.3	4.3
	25.1	28.3	35.9			Net Worth	32.9	35.8
	100.0	100.0	100.0			Total Liabilities & Net Worth	100.0	100.0
						INCOME DATA		
	100.0	100.0	100.0			Net Sales	100.0	100.0
						Gross Profit		
	97.4	96.2	95.6			Operating Expenses	91.8	92.5
	2.6	3.8	4.4			Operating Profit	8.2	7.5
	1.6	.5	.5			All Other Expenses (net)	1.7	1.5
	1.0	3.3	3.9			Profit Before Taxes	6.5	5.9
						RATIOS		
	2.7	2.2	2.3				2.1	2.1
	.7	1.1	.9			Current	1.0	1.1
	.2	.5	.5				.5	.5
	2.4	2.2	1.9				1.9	1.8
	.5	.8	.8			Quick	.9	.9
	.1	.3	.3				.4	.4
	0 UND	5 68.7	10 35.5				3 106.1	2 184.0
	6 57.6	24 15.3	21 17.0			Sales/Receivables	18 20.1	15 23.7
	24 14.9	39 9.4	43 8.5				34 10.8	35 10.3
						Cost of Sales/Inventory		
						Cost of Sales/Payables		
	5.3	11.1	9.6				10.0	9.4
	-31.5	119.9	-67.2			Sales/Working Capital	853.4	107.0
	-6.7	-10.0	-7.5				-10.1	-10.8
	4.8	8.1	6.2				7.6	8.3
	(30) 1.7	(63) 2.3	2.8			EBIT/Interest	(141) 3.7	(146) 3.4
	-.5	.9	1.5				2.0	1.4
		1.9	2.3				2.5	2.4
		(22) 1.4	(15) 1.4			Net Profit + Depr., Dep., Amort./Cur. Mat. L/T/D	(57) 1.9	(46) 1.7
		.9	.8				1.2	1.1
	.7	.8	1.3				1.1	.9
	2.5	1.8	2.3			Fixed/Worth	2.0	1.6
	15.0	-11.3	10.9				5.7	4.6
	.7	1.0	1.0				1.0	.8
	2.8	2.4	2.5			Debt/Worth	2.1	1.8
	26.4	-19.9	16.5				7.2	6.9
	39.7	34.0	42.2				50.4	46.5
	(25) 11.0	(48) 17.9	(26) 16.4			% Profit Before Taxes/Tangible Net Worth	(123) 26.8	(139) 22.7
	-5.6	7.8	3.0				13.0	12.4
	8.7	12.1	8.3				13.9	15.4
	2.4	3.6	4.2			% Profit Before Taxes/Total Assets	8.1	7.5
	-5.0	-.1	1.5				2.7	1.5
	5.6	6.6	3.1				4.9	5.4
	2.6	3.1	1.6			Sales/Net Fixed Assets	2.7	3.0
	1.7	1.7	1.2				1.6	1.8
	2.1	2.4	1.5				2.4	2.5
	1.3	1.7	1.2			Sales/Total Assets	1.6	1.6
	1.1	1.2	.9				1.1	1.2
	7.8	5.1	6.7				6.3	5.9
	(27) 12.0	(59) 9.5	9.9			% Depr., Dep., Amort./Sales	(134) 9.8	(142) 9.8
	15.1	12.5	14.4				13.3	14.6
	1.7	2.8	.4				2.1	1.3
	(15) 3.0	(30) 4.4	(14) 1.2			% Officers', Directors' Owners' Comp/Sales	(76) 3.9	(82) 4.3
	6.1	6.9	3.5				6.3	7.0
14981M	60251M	563154M	838805M	777435M	1796390M	Net Sales ($)	2983604M	3844294M
2412M	36275M	304852M	624374M	579988M	1143625M	Total Assets ($)	1872455M	2192502M

M = $ thousand MM = $ million

See Pages 9 through 22 for Explanation of Ratios and Data

Comparative Historical Data | Current Data Sorted by Sales

4/1/11-3/31/12 ALL	4/1/12-3/31/13 ALL	4/1/13-3/31/14 ALL	Type of Statement	0-1MM	1-3MM	3-5MM	5-10MM	10-25MM	25MM & OVER
16	16	12	Unqualified		1			4	7
53	47	40	Reviewed		4	5	14	13	4
31	37	27	Compiled	4	4	8	7	2	2
40	36	31	Tax Returns	7	13	5	2	3	1
32	34	41	Other	2	3	4	7	11	14
				50 (4/1-9/30/13)			101 (10/1/13-3/31/14)		
172	170	151	NUMBER OF STATEMENTS	13	25	22	30	33	28
%	%	%	**ASSETS**	%	%	%	%	%	%
14.2	15.1	13.5	Cash & Equivalents	21.2	14.9	14.0	14.8	11.4	9.1
12.0	10.4	11.6	Trade Receivables (net)	7.5	4.9	10.6	11.8	16.6	14.0
2.7	3.7	2.3	Inventory	.6	.8	2.8	1.5	2.8	4.6
2.7	3.2	2.9	All Other Current	2.4	1.3	1.4	3.3	2.5	5.7
31.6	32.3	30.3	Total Current	31.6	21.9	28.8	31.4	33.4	33.4
54.9	55.7	57.0	Fixed Assets (net)	60.8	59.9	54.8	61.0	54.6	53.0
4.6	4.0	4.0	Intangibles (net)	.4	5.6	3.1	1.4	4.8	6.6
8.9	8.0	8.8	All Other Non-Current	7.2	12.6	13.3	6.3	7.2	7.1
100.0	100.0	100.0	Total	100.0	100.0	100.0	100.0	100.0	100.0
			LIABILITIES						
6.6	7.5	5.4	Notes Payable-Short Term	5.5	4.3	8.8	5.9	4.2	4.6
12.1	12.7	13.0	Cur. Mat.-L.T.D.	14.6	21.3	12.2	13.2	10.0	8.6
4.0	3.4	3.2	Trade Payables	2.7	2.0	2.4	3.7	3.3	4.4
.2	.2	.5	Income Taxes Payable	.0	.0	.0	1.1	.6	.9
9.5	8.6	7.4	All Other Current	3.4	8.3	10.2	6.6	7.7	6.8
32.5	32.4	29.5	Total Current	26.2	35.9	33.6	30.4	25.8	25.3
33.3	32.1	33.6	Long-Term Debt	42.7	39.6	34.7	30.9	34.2	25.2
1.3	1.1	.9	Deferred Taxes	.0	.4	.6	1.2	1.0	1.5
5.4	4.6	7.1	All Other Non-Current	7.3	11.1	4.6	5.5	4.9	9.9
27.5	29.8	28.9	Net Worth	23.8	12.9	26.5	32.0	34.0	38.1
100.0	100.0	100.0	Total Liabilties & Net Worth	100.0	100.0	100.0	100.0	100.0	100.0
			INCOME DATA						
100.0	100.0	100.0	Net Sales	100.0	100.0	100.0	100.0	100.0	100.0
			Gross Profit						
94.3	94.7	96.0	Operating Expenses	89.4	96.8	98.3	96.0	95.5	97.2
5.7	5.3	4.0	Operating Profit	10.6	3.2	1.7	4.0	4.5	2.8
1.4	1.3	.9	All Other Expenses (net)	3.4	1.8	-.6	.7	.0	1.7
4.3	4.0	3.0	Profit Before Taxes	7.2	1.5	2.3	3.3	4.5	1.1
			RATIOS						
2.3	2.0	2.2		5.3	2.8	2.3	1.8	3.3	1.9
1.1	1.0	1.0	Current	.9	.5	.8	1.0	1.4	1.0
.5	.4	.5		.2	.2	.3	.6	.6	.9
2.0	1.6	2.1		5.1	2.6	2.2	1.5	3.1	1.5
.8	.8	.8	Quick	.9	.3	.7	.7	1.1	.9
.3	.3	.3		.1	.1	.3	.4	.5	.4
5 75.9	**1** 315.7	**3** 108.8		**0** UND	**0** UND	**3** 122.6	**4** 82.1	**15** 23.9	**16** 22.5
23 16.2	**18** 20.5	**21** 17.0	Sales/Receivables	**0** UND	**8** 45.2	**18** 20.1	**26** 13.8	**27** 13.7	**33** 11.0
38 9.5	**35** 10.4	**40** 9.1		**0** UND	**26** 13.9	**26** 14.0	**40** 9.1	**47** 7.7	**45** 8.2
			Cost of Sales/Inventory						
			Cost of Sales/Payables						
8.6	9.7	7.8		2.5	6.9	7.5	17.7	6.0	9.2
68.0	199.8	248.4	Sales/Working Capital	-57.9	-15.9	-28.1	NM	19.9	177.5
-9.2	-10.1	-9.4		-7.2	-3.7	-7.0	-10.5	-18.8	-64.3
7.1	5.3	6.6		7.7	3.6	7.1	6.8	12.4	4.1
(160) 2.7	(161) 2.6	(144) 2.5	EBIT/Interest	1.0	(23) 1.5	(21) 1.5	(28) 2.1	(32) 4.1	(27) 3.1
1.2	1.1	.9		-.3	-.7	-.7	.9	1.6	1.9
2.2	1.8	2.1					2.0	2.1	1.7
(56) 1.2	(57) 1.2	(51) 1.4	Net Profit + Depr., Dep., Amort./Cur. Mat. L/T/D				(16) 1.5	(13) 1.5	(14) 1.4
.9	.9	1.0					.9	1.0	1.1
1.0	.9	1.1		1.0	.8	1.0	1.1	1.1	.9
1.8	1.8	2.0	Fixed/Worth	2.0	10.6	1.8	1.8	2.1	1.6
14.6	8.4	19.1		13.8	-3.0	UND	12.7	7.7	2.5
.9	1.2	1.0		1.2	.7	1.0	.9	.9	1.4
2.2	2.0	2.1	Debt/Worth	2.8	10.3	7.2	1.9	2.5	1.7
25.9	13.1	23.1		17.1	-6.3	UND	14.6	14.4	3.6
42.6	40.1	36.3		63.8	29.6	75.5	29.6	58.3	16.8
(135) 17.1	(138) 16.5	(119) 14.8	% Profit Before Taxes/Tangible Net Worth	(11) 14.3	(14) 8.5	(18) 17.0	(24) 15.0	(29) 26.1	(23) 11.7
4.4	3.3	2.3		-5.2	-12.4	-.5	8.1	10.8	2.3
15.5	12.6	8.7		14.6	6.3	11.1	8.5	15.0	5.2
4.9	4.5	3.7	% Profit Before Taxes/Total Assets	.0	2.4	1.6	3.2	6.9	4.0
.6	.5	-.2		-2.7	-4.3	-3.1	-.4	2.2	.9
5.8	6.4	4.6		6.5	5.0	6.9	4.2	8.6	3.6
2.9	3.0	2.6	Sales/Net Fixed Assets	1.7	2.3	2.9	3.0	3.2	2.0
1.7	1.8	1.5		1.0	1.4	1.4	1.7	1.5	1.4
2.5	2.7	2.1		2.3	1.7	2.3	2.4	2.8	1.9
1.6	1.7	1.5	Sales/Total Assets	.9	1.3	1.6	1.7	1.6	1.2
1.2	1.1	1.0		.3	1.0	.8	1.2	1.1	.9
5.4	5.5	6.3		6.6	9.2	7.6	5.5	4.6	4.4
(148) 8.8	(150) 9.1	(133) 9.6	% Depr., Dep., Amort./Sales	(11) 10.2	(23) 12.8	(18) 11.1	(29) 9.5	(30) 8.4	(22) 7.3
13.1	12.8	13.5		20.2	14.7	19.4	11.5	12.6	10.7
2.0	1.7	1.3			2.9	1.9	2.6	1.9	.3
(78) 4.1	(88) 4.0	(68) 3.2	% Officers', Directors' Owners' Comp/Sales		(11) 4.2	(10) 3.2	(16) 4.4	(16) 3.6	(11) .6
7.5	7.0	5.3			6.4	7.5	6.4	5.9	1.2
2953307M	**3316610M**	**4051016M**	Net Sales ($)	**6921M**	**47847M**	**85237M**	**231367M**	**521451M**	**3158193M**
2391304M	**2508557M**	**2691526M**	Total Assets ($)	**8221M**	**38230M**	**72522M**	**142554M**	**355506M**	**2074493M**

M = $ thousand MM = $ million

See Pages 9 through 22 for Explanation of Ratios and Data

	Current Data Sorted by Assets						**Comparative Historical Data**	
Type of Statement								
Unqualified				3	2	1	5	11
Reviewed	1	1	9	8			21	27
Compiled	1	5	10	6		1	24	17
Tax Returns	5	15	9	1			22	34
Other	8	9	23	12	5	3	50	68
	32 (4/1-9/30/13)		106 (10/1/13-3/31/14)				4/1/09-3/31/10	4/1/10-3/31/11
	0-500M	**500M-2MM**	**2-10MM**	**10-50MM**	**50-100MM**	**100-250MM**	**ALL**	**ALL**
NUMBER OF STATEMENTS	15	30	51	30	7	5	122	157
ASSETS	%	%	%	%	%	%	%	%
Cash & Equivalents	26.6	11.0	8.9	8.9			10.7	9.3
Trade Receivables (net)	18.1	8.2	9.6	7.9			8.4	8.7
Inventory	.9	1.9	1.4	3.9			2.0	1.5
All Other Current	7.0	2.4	2.8	1.6			4.3	4.1
Total Current	52.5	23.4	22.6	22.3			25.4	23.6
Fixed Assets (net)	31.4	59.6	63.2	68.3			64.7	64.8
Intangibles (net)	5.3	5.5	5.2	2.7			2.4	2.8
All Other Non-Current	10.6	11.5	8.9	6.6			7.5	8.9
Total	100.0	100.0	100.0	100.0			100.0	100.0
LIABILITIES								
Notes Payable-Short Term	5.0	7.3	4.1	4.1			4.9	6.5
Cur. Mat.-L.T.D.	9.7	14.5	9.0	7.6			12.4	11.8
Trade Payables	10.6	8.2	5.7	4.3			5.1	5.1
Income Taxes Payable	.0	.0	.0	.0			.2	.3
All Other Current	27.5	11.9	4.7	4.4			8.5	7.8
Total Current	52.7	41.8	23.5	20.5			31.3	31.5
Long-Term Debt	56.2	59.5	42.2	37.5			49.2	47.7
Deferred Taxes	.0	.0	1.4	2.9			1.4	2.1
All Other Non-Current	22.5	4.4	4.0	6.4			7.1	7.1
Net Worth	-31.3	-5.8	28.9	32.6			11.0	11.6
Total Liabilties & Net Worth	100.0	100.0	100.0	100.0			100.0	100.0
INCOME DATA								
Net Sales	100.0	100.0	100.0	100.0			100.0	100.0
Gross Profit								
Operating Expenses	95.4	96.5	94.3	90.3			94.4	93.5
Operating Profit	4.6	3.5	5.7	9.7			5.6	6.5
All Other Expenses (net)	1.2	1.1	.8	3.4			1.9	2.2
Profit Before Taxes	3.3	2.4	4.9	6.3			3.7	4.3
RATIOS								
Current	6.5	1.7	1.6	1.6			1.6	1.5
	1.7	.6	.9	.9			.8	.7
	.8	.2	.3	.5			.4	.4
Quick	6.0	1.7	1.4	1.2			1.2	1.0
	1.6	.5	.7	.7			.6	.5
	.6	.2	.2	.4			.3	.3
Sales/Receivables	1 300.0	0 UND	3 111.1	11 31.8			5 75.8	5 69.2
	5 73.2	1 351.4	19 18.9	23 15.6			13 27.7	16 22.7
	14 25.4	17 21.6	31 11.7	38 9.7			27 13.4	25 14.3
Cost of Sales/Inventory								
Cost of Sales/Payables								
Sales/Working Capital	12.9	36.6	12.1	14.4			15.8	17.7
	24.6	-22.4	-83.5	-49.7			-41.0	-28.6
	-61.4	-8.7	-10.0	-10.2			-9.1	-7.4
EBIT/Interest	9.9	5.7	6.1	5.3			4.1	4.7
	(13) 5.7	(29) 2.1	(47) 2.7	(28) 3.2			(114) 2.5	(147) 2.2
	1.6	-.2	1.2	1.7			1.1	.9
Net Profit + Depr., Dep., Amort./Cur. Mat. L/T/D			1.7	1.4			2.2	1.8
			(11) 1.3	(12) .9			(34) 1.5	(48) 1.3
			1.1	.8			1.3	1.0
Fixed/Worth	.6	3.6	1.3	1.6			1.5	1.6
	-.8	-3.7	3.0	2.4			3.2	3.1
	-.2	-1.2	59.2	5.1			-5.0	-32.8
Debt/Worth	.8	4.4	.9	1.5			1.5	1.5
	-4.6	-7.3	3.2	2.5			4.4	3.3
	-2.1	-3.5	58.7	5.0			-7.2	-44.8
% Profit Before Taxes/Tangible Net Worth		70.1	38.0	26.5			34.3	32.8
		(13) 21.5	(39) 17.7	(27) 17.7			(84) 18.6	(115) 13.8
		5.5	1.9	13.0			5.7	.4
% Profit Before Taxes/Total Assets	52.6	11.8	11.2	7.8			10.6	10.8
	26.0	4.0	4.3	4.1			5.0	3.9
	.0	-2.2	1.1	2.2			.7	-.3
Sales/Net Fixed Assets	93.0	8.6	3.3	2.4			4.3	4.1
	29.8	4.3	1.8	1.3			2.2	2.1
	18.6	2.4	1.3	.8			1.3	1.4
Sales/Total Assets	14.7	4.3	2.0	1.5			2.4	2.4
	5.9	2.3	1.3	.9			1.4	1.5
	4.0	1.5	.9	.6			1.0	1.0
% Depr., Dep., Amort./Sales		4.0	7.3	7.1			5.7	6.7
		(21) 10.2	(38) 10.7	(28) 9.7			(108) 10.3	(131) 9.4
		17.2	15.9	13.5			15.1	14.0
% Officers', Directors' Owners' Comp/Sales	3.8	1.6	1.7				1.5	1.5
	(10) 5.9	(14) 3.2	(32) 3.1				(48) 2.8	(59) 2.7
	8.1	5.4	4.7				4.8	4.6
Net Sales ($)	28158M	96428M	359074M	558464M	432710M	668956M	1383072M	1844716M
Total Assets ($)	3938M	35210M	240025M	565608M	511759M	665101M	1157546M	1638653M

M = $ thousand MM = $ million

See Pages 9 through 22 for Explanation of Ratios and Data

Comparative Historical Data / Current Data Sorted by Sales

4/1/11-3/31/12 ALL	4/1/12-3/31/13 ALL	4/1/13-3/31/14 ALL	Type of Statement	0-1MM	1-3MM	3-5MM	5-10MM	10-25MM	25MM & OVER
8	7	6	Unqualified						6
20	26	19	Reviewed	1		6	5	7	
20	24	23	Compiled		5	4	5	7	2
42	38	30	Tax Returns	3	11	9	5	2	
62	62	60	Other	3	9	17	7	13	11
				32 (4/1-9/30/13)		106 (10/1/13-3/31/14)			
152	157	138	NUMBER OF STATEMENTS	7	25	36	22	29	19
%	%	%	ASSETS	%	%	%	%	%	%
13.6	11.3	11.1	Cash & Equivalents		17.7	7.3	8.1	12.9	9.7
8.7	9.0	9.7	Trade Receivables (net)		9.8	7.9	12.4	10.5	10.7
1.6	1.4	2.0	Inventory		.3	1.8	2.2	3.3	2.6
2.6	4.0	2.8	All Other Current		5.2	2.6	2.3	2.3	2.2
26.5	25.7	25.6	Total Current		32.9	19.6	25.0	29.0	25.1
59.5	62.8	59.7	Fixed Assets (net)		50.9	65.0	57.1	61.4	56.3
4.1	3.1	5.9	Intangibles (net)		4.8	5.3	6.7	2.7	13.4
9.9	8.4	8.8	All Other Non-Current		11.4	10.1	11.3	6.9	5.2
100.0	100.0	100.0	Total		100.0	100.0	100.0	100.0	100.0
			LIABILITIES						
10.7	4.2	4.9	Notes Payable-Short Term		2.3	3.6	11.6	4.6	4.1
14.8	12.9	9.9	Cur. Mat.-L.T.D.		10.4	10.8	9.3	9.4	8.0
5.8	5.8	6.2	Trade Payables		7.1	7.3	6.8	4.8	6.0
.2	.2	.0	Income Taxes Payable		.0	.0	.0	.1	.1
8.1	6.3	8.6	All Other Current		16.5	4.6	5.3	6.2	5.2
39.6	29.3	29.6	Total Current		36.2	26.3	33.1	25.0	23.4
52.0	47.8	45.9	Long-Term Debt		61.2	59.1	36.8	35.5	31.6
1.5	1.6	2.1	Deferred Taxes		.1	.8	2.0	2.0	7.9
10.6	10.6	7.0	All Other Non-Current		4.9	9.4	9.4	4.7	7.5
-3.7	10.5	15.3	Net Worth		-2.5	4.5	18.7	32.8	29.6
100.0	100.0	100.0	Total Liabilties & Net Worth		100.0	100.0	100.0	100.0	100.0
			INCOME DATA						
100.0	100.0	100.0	Net Sales		100.0	100.0	100.0	100.0	100.0
			Gross Profit						
94.4	92.9	93.9	Operating Expenses		95.4	93.2	94.3	93.8	94.3
5.6	7.1	6.1	Operating Profit		4.6	6.8	5.7	6.2	5.7
2.1	1.7	1.8	All Other Expenses (net)		3.8	1.1	1.0	1.0	3.2
3.5	5.4	4.3	Profit Before Taxes		.9	5.8	4.7	5.2	2.5
			RATIOS						
1.6	1.5	1.6			5.2	1.4	1.2	2.1	1.2
.9	.8	.9	Current		1.6	.7	.8	1.1	.8
.3	.3	.5			.4	.3	.3	.5	.6
1.2	1.3	1.5			3.9	1.1	1.1	1.7	1.1
.6	.6	.7	Quick		1.5	.5	.7	.7	.7
.2	.3	.3			.3	.2	.1	.5	.4
0 UND	4 102.4	3 144.4			0 UND	0 UND	6 65.8	11 33.4	22 16.3
11 32.0	11 32.3	16 23.0	Sales/Receivables		8 45.0	8 45.2	16 23.4	24 15.4	26 13.8
25 14.7	26 13.9	30 12.2			19 19.6	24 15.4	35 10.3	33 11.1	40 9.1
			Cost of Sales/Inventory						
			Cost of Sales/Payables						
20.2	22.8	14.8			11.9	43.0	39.6	9.7	31.0
-50.5	-36.9	-49.7	Sales/Working Capital		31.0	-28.2	-40.2	138.1	-19.5
-9.0	-8.3	-10.4			-11.1	-9.5	-9.8	-10.7	-9.7
5.1	5.7	6.0			3.4	6.0	15.8	6.7	5.0
(141) 2.2	(144) 2.4	(129) 2.7	EBIT/Interest		(23) 1.7	(32) 2.5	3.1	(27) 4.7	(18) 2.7
1.0	1.2	1.3			-.5	1.2	1.8	1.8	.8
1.7	1.8	1.6						1.8	1.8
(36) 1.4	(41) 1.2	(35) 1.2	Net Profit + Depr., Dep., Amort./Cur. Mat. L/T/D					(10) 1.1	(15) 1.4
1.0	.8	.9						.9	.9
1.4	1.9	1.6			1.9	1.7	1.9	1.1	1.6
3.1	4.3	3.7	Fixed/Worth		-137.9	5.2	5.0	2.2	2.5
-5.2	-66.4	-3.1			-.9	-2.7	-63.7	4.6	-6.5
1.4	1.7	1.6			2.6	1.3	2.4	1.0	1.8
4.3	4.2	3.8	Debt/Worth		-6.5	4.6	5.0	1.9	3.6
-8.0	-158.4	-6.4			-3.2	-4.6	-74.1	5.0	-9.1
28.5	54.3	36.0			43.0	38.0	98.8	32.5	24.0
(103) 12.0	(116) 20.6	(91) 19.2	% Profit Before Taxes/Tangible Net Worth		(11) 17.7	(23) 19.2	(15) 20.5	(25) 17.7	(12) 19.4
1.4	4.8	7.0			8.6	4.4	5.8	5.5	15.3
12.7	15.1	11.0			8.6	13.9	15.4	9.4	7.6
4.1	5.2	4.5	% Profit Before Taxes/Total Assets		3.1	4.7	5.5	7.0	4.5
-.2	1.3	.8			-2.4	1.4	1.8	2.0	-1.0
7.4	6.7	6.5			28.7	4.4	29.0	5.2	3.6
2.6	2.3	2.1	Sales/Net Fixed Assets		5.2	1.7	2.8	2.1	1.7
1.4	1.2	1.3			1.9	1.2	1.3	1.1	1.2
3.7	3.0	2.9			4.6	2.7	3.3	2.3	1.6
1.8	1.5	1.5	Sales/Total Assets		2.4	1.3	1.9	1.4	1.0
1.0	1.0	.9			1.3	.8	1.0	.8	.6
5.8	5.5	5.7			10.2	7.9	4.8	5.7	5.3
(117) 9.9	(126) 9.4	(104) 10.2	% Depr., Dep., Amort./Sales		(14) 16.8	(27) 10.9	(18) 9.8	(23) 7.7	(18) 8.6
14.2	13.2	15.3			22.1	17.2	10.4	14.1	14.2
1.5	1.4	1.7			3.4	1.4	1.8	1.7	
(63) 3.3	(71) 2.9	(64) 3.3	% Officers', Directors' Owners' Comp/Sales		(15) 4.6	(18) 2.8	(13) 4.0	(13) 2.9	
5.2	4.9	5.4			5.9	4.6	5.5	3.4	
1613802M	2448469M	2143790M	Net Sales ($)	3623M	50481M	138711M	169825M	445573M	1335577M
1146941M	1637274M	2021641M	Total Assets ($)	3748M	45318M	143832M	114701M	390437M	1323605M

M = $ thousand MM = $ million

See Pages 9 through 22 for Explanation of Ratios and Data

Current Data Sorted by Assets							Comparative Historical Data	
						Type of Statement		
		5	1	1		Unqualified	4	6
		3				Reviewed	2	2
	2	1				Compiled	4	7
5	2					Tax Returns	7	6
3	3	2	1			Other	11	15
	8 (4/1-9/30/13)		21 (10/1/13-3/31/14)				**4/1/09-3/31/10 ALL**	**4/1/10-3/31/11 ALL**
0-500M	**500M-2MM**	**2-10MM**	**10-50MM**	**50-100MM**	**100-250MM**			
8	7	11	2	1		**NUMBER OF STATEMENTS**	28	36
%	%	%	%	%	%	**ASSETS**	%	%
		15.3			**DATA NOT AVAILABLE**	Cash & Equivalents	14.6	15.9
		42.1				Trade Receivables (net)	30.0	27.7
		.0				Inventory	1.4	1.5
		3.9				All Other Current	4.3	1.8
		61.3				Total Current	50.3	46.9
		28.8				Fixed Assets (net)	43.8	38.8
		5.0				Intangibles (net)	1.2	3.6
		5.0				All Other Non-Current	4.7	10.8
		100.0				Total	100.0	100.0
						LIABILITIES		
		8.1				Notes Payable-Short Term	7.5	9.3
		1.7				Cur. Mat.-L.T.D.	14.1	6.1
		4.4				Trade Payables	8.6	10.6
		.0				Income Taxes Payable	.9	.7
		7.3				All Other Current	11.3	14.1
		21.5				Total Current	42.5	40.9
		2.7				Long-Term Debt	36.0	19.9
		.1				Deferred Taxes	.3	1.1
		3.6				All Other Non-Current	2.8	2.5
		72.0				Net Worth	18.4	35.6
		100.0				Total Liabilties & Net Worth	100.0	100.0
						INCOME DATA		
		100.0				Net Sales	100.0	100.0
						Gross Profit		
		102.4				Operating Expenses	92.7	89.6
		-2.4				Operating Profit	7.3	10.4
		-2.2				All Other Expenses (net)	1.9	2.0
		-.3				Profit Before Taxes	5.4	8.4
						RATIOS		
		11.3					4.8	3.3
		4.7				Current	2.1	1.7
		1.1					.6	.6
		11.3					4.7	3.3
		4.7				Quick	1.4	1.6
		1.1					.4	.5
		43 8.4					**0** UND	**0** UND
		55 6.6				Sales/Receivables	**32** 11.3	**38** 9.6
		101 3.6					**48** 7.5	**47** 7.8
						Cost of Sales/Inventory		
						Cost of Sales/Payables		
		2.7					5.9	8.1
		5.0				Sales/Working Capital	13.4	24.3
		149.2					-13.8	-14.5
							13.4	17.9
						EBIT/Interest	(22) 4.4	(28) 9.8
							1.2	1.4
						Net Profit + Depr., Dep., Amort./Cur. Mat. L/T/D		
		.2					.3	.4
		.3				Fixed/Worth	1.6	.8
		.8					-260.2	8.5
		.1					.5	.6
		.4				Debt/Worth	1.3	2.0
		.6					-294.6	19.6
		33.7					84.9	84.3
		8.7				% Profit Before Taxes/Tangible Net Worth	(20) 53.6	(30) 26.5
		-4.9					16.5	7.2
		20.9					53.7	32.9
		5.9				% Profit Before Taxes/Total Assets	14.7	14.0
		-3.8					.0	4.5
		17.8					28.4	27.8
		13.2				Sales/Net Fixed Assets	8.9	8.9
		5.3					4.1	4.2
		3.2					4.9	4.2
		2.3				Sales/Total Assets	3.5	3.1
		1.1					1.8	2.2
		1.7					1.4	1.4
		(10) 4.0				% Depr., Dep., Amort./Sales	(24) 4.4	(28) 3.0
		8.4					11.1	7.8
							1.5	3.2
						% Officers', Directors' Owners' Comp/Sales	(16) 4.1	(13) 4.7
							6.4	7.9
9775M	16186M	110337M	221282M	48556M		Net Sales ($)	332268M	441370M
1876M	7008M	43398M	59770M	84691M		Total Assets ($)	114373M	143415M

M = $ thousand MM = $ million

See Pages 9 through 22 for Explanation of Ratios and Data

Comparative Historical Data				Current Data Sorted by Sales					
			Type of Statement						
4	5	7	Unqualified		1	1		3	2
3	2	3	Reviewed				2	1	
3	3	3	Compiled	1	1			1	
5	3	7	Tax Returns	2	4	1			
15	9	9	Other	1	4	2	1		1
					8 (4/1-9/30/13)		21 (10/1/13-3/31/14)		
4/1/11-3/31/12 ALL	**4/1/12-3/31/13 ALL**	**4/1/13-3/31/14 ALL**		**0-1MM**	**1-3MM**	**3-5MM**	**5-10MM**	**10-25MM**	**25MM & OVER**
30	22	29	**NUMBER OF STATEMENTS**	4	10	4	3	5	3
%	%	%	**ASSETS**	%	%	%	%	%	%
17.4	10.7	15.8	Cash & Equivalents		12.3				
32.2	35.3	29.4	Trade Receivables (net)		25.2				
2.6	.3	1.1	Inventory		3.2				
2.6	4.0	5.3	All Other Current		5.3				
54.9	50.3	51.6	Total Current		46.0				
31.0	37.0	33.4	Fixed Assets (net)		46.4				
4.9	6.7	6.6	Intangibles (net)		4.7				
9.2	6.0	8.4	All Other Non-Current		2.9				
100.0	100.0	100.0	Total		100.0				
			LIABILITIES						
6.1	11.3	11.2	Notes Payable-Short Term		21.6				
6.0	7.5	3.6	Cur. Mat.-L.T.D.		.0				
7.3	12.2	10.0	Trade Payables		19.3				
.2	.0	.2	Income Taxes Payable		.5				
10.3	4.1	13.7	All Other Current		27.0				
29.8	35.0	38.7	Total Current		68.4				
19.7	27.5	16.2	Long-Term Debt		25.3				
.9	.0	.3	Deferred Taxes		.9				
.2	3.0	17.7	All Other Non-Current		32.2				
49.4	34.4	27.1	Net Worth		-26.8				
100.0	100.0	100.0	Total Liabilties & Net Worth		100.0				
			INCOME DATA						
100.0	100.0	100.0	Net Sales		100.0				
			Gross Profit						
91.0	93.5	94.8	Operating Expenses		96.2				
9.0	6.5	5.2	Operating Profit		3.8				
2.0	2.2	.2	All Other Expenses (net)		.8				
7.0	4.3	4.9	Profit Before Taxes		3.0				
			RATIOS						
5.6	2.7	9.2			4.8				
2.5	1.5	1.9	Current		1.1				
1.0	1.0	.8			.2				
5.3	2.5	9.0			3.7				
2.5	1.4	1.7	Quick		1.1				
.9	.8	.8			.1				
19 18.8	**33** 11.1	**0** UND			**0** UND				
45 8.2	**42** 8.6	**47** 7.8	Sales/Receivables		**26** 14.0				
58 6.3	**65** 5.6	**68** 5.4			**51** 7.1				
			Cost of Sales/Inventory						
			Cost of Sales/Payables						
5.7	5.4	3.2			4.6				
10.6	21.2	10.6	Sales/Working Capital		NM				
NM	-812.6	-50.3			-9.2				
23.6	10.9	17.0							
(20) 3.8	(20) 5.2	(19) 6.0	EBIT/Interest						
-1.1	-.8	2.4							
			Net Profit + Depr., Dep., Amort./Cur. Mat. L/T/D						
.3	.3	.2			.1				
.7	.9	.8	Fixed/Worth		NM				
3.1	4.0	NM			-.8				
.4	.7	.2			.3				
.8	1.5	.9	Debt/Worth		NM				
4.6	7.2	NM			-2.3				
49.2	34.1	51.5							
(26) 22.7	(19) 15.4	(22) 24.8	% Profit Before Taxes/Tangible Net Worth						
1.4	1.5	4.4							
29.2	14.2	22.4			31.9				
11.6	4.3	8.3	% Profit Before Taxes/Total Assets		7.0				
.6	.8	-.1			-4.9				
41.1	41.5	22.6			52.6				
9.5	10.9	11.9	Sales/Net Fixed Assets		16.1				
4.6	3.7	5.4			3.9				
5.3	3.8	3.5			15.5				
3.4	2.8	2.4	Sales/Total Assets		2.9				
1.8	1.8	1.3			1.7				
1.2	1.5	2.3							
(25) 2.7	(18) 4.5	(21) 5.4	% Depr., Dep., Amort./Sales						
7.7	7.9	8.3							
			% Officers', Directors' Owners' Comp/Sales						
400402M	250702M	406136M	Net Sales ($)	1085M	17791M	15548M	21442M	80432M	269838M
141890M	107873M	196743M	Total Assets ($)	1821M	7413M	9139M	8778M	25131M	144461M

M = $ thousand MM = $ million

See Pages 9 through 22 for Explanation of Ratios and Data

Current Data Sorted by Assets							Comparative Historical Data	
						Type of Statement		
		8	4		1	Unqualified	19	15
	1	10	4	2		Reviewed	18	22
1		5	1			Compiled	23	18
11	4	3	1			Tax Returns	14	22
1	3	21	10		4	Other	36	38
14 (4/1-9/30/13)		81 (10/1/13-3/31/14)					4/1/09-3/31/10	4/1/10-3/31/11
0-500M	500M-2MM	2-10MM	10-50MM	50-100MM	100-250MM		ALL	ALL
13	8	47	20	2	5	NUMBER OF STATEMENTS	110	115
%	%	%	%	%	%	**ASSETS**	%	%
22.4		13.5	12.0			Cash & Equivalents	12.7	12.6
16.2		21.7	20.1			Trade Receivables (net)	21.7	22.2
.8		.4	2.0			Inventory	.7	.9
1.6		2.4	4.5			All Other Current	4.0	5.1
40.9		38.1	38.5			Total Current	39.1	40.7
39.1		45.1	46.4			Fixed Assets (net)	40.7	40.4
9.8		7.0	7.7			Intangibles (net)	7.1	9.3
10.2		9.8	7.3			All Other Non-Current	13.1	9.6
100.0		100.0	100.0			Total	100.0	100.0
						LIABILITIES		
8.8		5.1	4.3			Notes Payable-Short Term	7.6	8.3
7.8		6.5	3.6			Cur. Mat.-L.T.D.	9.0	10.6
5.3		8.9	8.3			Trade Payables	8.5	7.5
.4		.4	.0			Income Taxes Payable	.2	.4
16.4		9.0	8.2			All Other Current	10.6	12.3
38.6		29.8	24.4			Total Current	35.9	39.1
41.0		25.1	28.0			Long-Term Debt	26.8	27.4
.0		.9	.6			Deferred Taxes	.5	.2
24.5		4.0	2.2			All Other Non-Current	4.2	6.4
-4.2		40.0	44.7			Net Worth	32.6	26.9
100.0		100.0	100.0			Total Liabilties & Net Worth	100.0	100.0
						INCOME DATA		
100.0		100.0	100.0			Net Sales	100.0	100.0
						Gross Profit		
96.7		91.3	88.7			Operating Expenses	94.9	94.5
3.3		8.7	11.3			Operating Profit	5.1	5.5
.6		.7	.5			All Other Expenses (net)	1.3	1.2
2.6		8.0	10.8			Profit Before Taxes	3.8	4.3
						RATIOS		
2.9		2.6	3.2				2.2	2.1
.5		1.3	1.6			Current	1.1	1.1
.4		.5	.8				.5	.5
2.6		2.3	3.2				2.1	1.9
.5		1.2	1.3			Quick	.9	1.0
.3		.4	.5				.4	.4
0 UND		4 91.3	26 14.2				4 93.6	2 158.2
1 377.3		28 13.1	35 10.4			Sales/Receivables	26 13.9	22 16.3
48 7.6		57 6.4	60 6.1				52 7.0	44 8.3
						Cost of Sales/Inventory		
						Cost of Sales/Payables		
21.5		7.6	5.5				8.9	12.4
-66.3		21.5	14.0			Sales/Working Capital	74.3	178.4
-10.5		-16.3	-65.5				-16.1	-15.6
		15.3	10.6				11.9	11.8
		(41) 6.5	(17) 4.2			EBIT/Interest	(99) 3.4	(97) 4.9
		2.4	1.6				1.3	1.1
							2.3	3.4
						Net Profit + Depr., Dep., Amort./Cur. Mat. L/T/D	(24) 1.7	(16) 2.0
							1.2	.7
.6		.7	.7				.5	.6
-3.8		1.3	1.4			Fixed/Worth	1.7	1.8
-.5		6.0	3.3				12.4	-7.6
.3		.6	.5				.8	1.1
-13.3		1.4	1.8			Debt/Worth	2.6	2.8
-1.9		7.3	3.6				157.5	-19.0
		82.3	73.8				58.7	84.4
		(39) 35.6	(19) 39.1			% Profit Before Taxes/Tangible Net Worth	(84) 27.0	(81) 41.6
		15.5	14.8				4.5	5.1
37.1		20.3	25.1				19.0	26.0
12.9		11.2	9.5			% Profit Before Taxes/Total Assets	6.9	7.8
-29.0		4.5	2.0				1.1	.1
182.6		14.3	16.1				16.8	30.8
10.1		4.8	3.0			Sales/Net Fixed Assets	8.4	9.6
5.7		2.1	1.1				3.1	3.5
9.4		3.3	2.6				3.5	4.7
3.2		1.9	1.6			Sales/Total Assets	2.4	2.9
2.3		1.2	.7				1.6	1.7
		2.6	1.4				2.3	2.1
		(41) 5.6	(18) 7.1			% Depr., Dep., Amort./Sales	(90) 4.7	(81) 4.6
		10.4	11.9				9.1	7.8
		.6					1.7	2.5
		(11) 1.4				% Officers', Directors' Owners' Comp/Sales	(36) 4.8	(37) 3.5
		4.2					12.4	6.3
13887M	33334M	580808M	940142M	119517M	810730M	Net Sales ($)	3163278M	2999859M
2641M	9264M	239280M	439167M	106917M	842078M	Total Assets ($)	1712174M	1489439M

M = $ thousand MM = $ million

See Pages 9 through 22 for Explanation of Ratios and Data

Comparative Historical Data | Current Data Sorted by Sales

			Type of Statement						
19	13	13	Unqualified		1		1	6	5
16	10	17	Reviewed		1		6	6	4
16	9	7	Compiled	1	1			5	
26	23	19	Tax Returns	6	5	4	3		1
53	67	39	Other	1	3	10	8	8	9
				14 (4/1-9/30/13)			81 (10/1/13-3/31/14)		
4/1/11-3/31/12 ALL	4/1/12-3/31/13 ALL	4/1/13-3/31/14 ALL		0-1MM	1-3MM	3-5MM	5-10MM	10-25MM	25MM & OVER
130	122	95	NUMBER OF STATEMENTS	8	11	14	18	25	19
%	%	%	ASSETS	%	%	%	%	%	%
14.9	14.2	14.5	Cash & Equivalents		21.4	13.2	11.3	13.3	14.3
20.4	24.4	20.7	Trade Receivables (net)		14.5	13.2	23.5	25.1	22.7
1.2	.7	.8	Inventory		.9	.1	.6	.7	1.8
3.7	4.0	2.6	All Other Current		.5	2.2	1.6	2.0	5.9
40.2	43.4	38.5	Total Current		37.3	28.7	36.9	41.1	44.7
42.2	39.6	44.4	Fixed Assets (net)		46.1	50.6	43.2	43.3	39.6
7.2	6.3	7.4	Intangibles (net)		9.7	6.2	7.0	10.0	4.6
10.5	10.8	9.6	All Other Non-Current		6.9	14.5	12.8	5.6	11.1
100.0	100.0	100.0	Total		100.0	100.0	100.0	100.0	100.0
			LIABILITIES						
8.2	8.2	5.3	Notes Payable-Short Term		1.4	2.8	4.8	7.4	3.8
7.6	6.5	5.7	Cur. Mat.-L.T.D.		7.1	9.0	5.4	4.4	5.8
9.4	11.1	9.1	Trade Payables		3.6	7.2	12.4	6.2	15.4
.2	.3	.2	Income Taxes Payable		.0	.4	.8	.0	.1
10.4	9.6	9.1	All Other Current		13.1	5.0	8.8	7.8	9.5
35.8	35.7	29.5	Total Current		25.2	24.3	32.2	25.8	34.5
29.9	25.8	30.1	Long-Term Debt		41.3	40.5	25.3	23.4	26.1
.7	.8	1.0	Deferred Taxes		.0	.5	.9	1.2	2.0
5.9	5.5	7.3	All Other Non-Current		10.8	8.5	4.7	3.3	3.5
27.7	32.2	32.2	Net Worth		22.6	26.1	36.9	46.3	33.9
100.0	100.0	100.0	Total Liabilities & Net Worth		100.0	100.0	100.0	100.0	100.0
			INCOME DATA						
100.0	100.0	100.0	Net Sales		100.0	100.0	100.0	100.0	100.0
			Gross Profit						
93.7	95.5	92.3	Operating Expenses		97.2	87.0	91.0	91.6	94.0
6.3	4.5	7.7	Operating Profit		2.8	13.0	9.0	8.4	6.0
.8	.3	.7	All Other Expenses (net)		1.2	.7	.6	.8	.7
5.5	4.2	7.0	Profit Before Taxes		1.6	12.3	8.4	7.6	5.3
			RATIOS						
2.3	2.2	2.4			4.6	2.3	2.1	3.1	1.6
1.2	1.2	1.3	Current		1.9	1.3	.8	1.7	1.2
.5	.7	.5			.3	.3	.5	.8	.6
2.1	2.1	2.3			4.2	2.3	2.0	3.1	1.3
1.0	1.1	1.1	Quick		1.9	1.2	.8	1.5	1.1
.5	.5	.5			.3	.2	.4	.7	.5
5 66.9	**7** 49.7	**9** 42.3			**7** 51.7	**0** UND	**13** 27.3	**24** 15.0	**26** 13.9
23 15.9	**30** 12.0	**30** 12.1	Sales/Receivables		**29** 12.7	**6** 57.6	**26** 13.9	**38** 9.5	**30** 12.0
42 8.7	**54** 6.8	**50** 7.3			**49** 7.5	**60** 6.1	**53** 6.9	**64** 5.7	**38** 9.5
			Cost of Sales/Inventory						
			Cost of Sales/Payables						
11.7	10.2	8.4			4.5	6.2	8.3	7.0	12.3
64.1	52.8	26.1	Sales/Working Capital		25.9	31.1	-28.4	13.8	29.7
-23.0	-29.7	-22.0			-19.2	-50.6	-11.7	-48.0	-28.7
15.6	19.6	10.6				8.9	13.6	16.8	9.7
(106) 4.7	(99) 5.7	(79) 4.9	EBIT/Interest			(13) 5.4	(16) 4.9	(21) 6.5	(17) 4.9
1.5	1.3	1.6				2.6	1.2	2.1	1.6
2.9	5.4	3.6							
(20) 1.8	(19) 2.4	(14) 1.8	Net Profit + Depr., Dep., Amort./Cur. Mat. L/T/D						
1.4	1.2	1.3							
.5	.5	.7			.5	.9	.5	.7	.5
1.6	1.3	1.5	Fixed/Worth		-11.6	2.2	1.0	1.3	1.5
-13.1	5.0	29.0			-2.9	-3.5	2.4	3.1	3.0
.9	.8	.6			.2	.6	.3	.6	1.3
3.0	1.9	2.2	Debt/Worth		-20.6	5.2	1.5	2.2	2.2
-20.8	11.1	73.6			-4.8	-10.3	4.5	4.1	3.8
90.5	71.3	82.8				212.4	52.4	84.1	69.1
(95) 38.6	(99) 28.0	(74) 38.4	% Profit Before Taxes/Tangible Net Worth			(10) 30.9	(15) 22.4	(23) 38.5	(17) 51.7
9.4	8.7	14.7				13.9	3.2	14.8	22.3
24.5	23.5	20.9			26.9	18.8	20.7	25.3	22.8
10.4	9.6	10.6	% Profit Before Taxes/Total Assets		5.1	11.2	8.2	11.8	10.8
2.3	.0	2.0			-28.3	8.2	1.4	2.3	2.0
25.3	46.2	14.3			10.1	9.6	24.1	13.3	34.2
6.8	7.7	4.8	Sales/Net Fixed Assets		3.4	3.6	4.6	4.7	9.7
2.6	3.2	1.9			1.1	1.2	1.9	2.3	1.9
5.1	5.0	3.4			2.8	2.1	3.4	3.0	4.7
2.7	2.5	1.9	Sales/Total Assets		1.6	1.5	1.9	1.8	2.8
1.6	1.6	1.2			1.0	.8	1.2	1.3	1.2
2.0	.8	2.5				2.7	2.1	2.6	.7
(99) 4.2	(93) 3.5	(79) 5.8	% Depr., Dep., Amort./Sales			(11) 7.7	(13) 5.9	(24) 5.6	(17) 2.6
9.1	7.2	10.7				16.0	12.3	10.1	7.3
1.3	1.8	.7							
(37) 2.8	(42) 3.4	(26) 2.8	% Officers', Directors' Owners' Comp/Sales						
6.6	6.7	5.8							
3879823M	**2645907M**	**2498418M**	Net Sales ($)	**4200M**	**18445M**	**59794M**	**142029M**	**379289M**	**1894661M**
2050079M	**1571226M**	**1639347M**	Total Assets ($)	**1425M**	**12526M**	**64792M**	**82280M**	**274536M**	**1203788M**

M = $ thousand MM = $ million

See Pages 9 through 22 for Explanation of Ratios and Data

Current Data Sorted by Assets							Comparative Historical Data	
			2	1	1	**Type of Statement** Unqualified	5	4
		1	2			Reviewed	1	4
	2	2				Compiled	3	4
4	1					Tax Returns	3	5
3	2	4	5		2	Other	15	13
	1 (4/1-9/30/13)		31 (10/1/13-3/31/14)				**4/1/09-3/31/10**	**4/1/10-3/31/11**
0-500M	**500M-2MM**	**2-10MM**	**10-50MM**	**50-100MM**	**100-250MM**		**ALL**	**ALL**
7	5	7	9	1	3	**NUMBER OF STATEMENTS**	27	30
%	%	%	%	%	%	**ASSETS**	%	%
						Cash & Equivalents	13.6	15.4
						Trade Receivables (net)	6.6	8.2
						Inventory	1.8	3.4
						All Other Current	2.0	3.2
						Total Current	24.1	30.1
						Fixed Assets (net)	56.5	50.7
						Intangibles (net)	8.6	10.1
						All Other Non-Current	10.8	9.2
						Total	100.0	100.0
						LIABILITIES		
						Notes Payable-Short Term	4.6	9.5
						Cur. Mat.-L.T.D.	5.6	4.1
						Trade Payables	4.1	5.4
						Income Taxes Payable	.0	.0
						All Other Current	23.9	9.8
						Total Current	38.2	29.0
						Long-Term Debt	55.2	44.7
						Deferred Taxes	.5	.3
						All Other Non-Current	19.8	4.9
						Net Worth	-13.7	21.1
						Total Liabilties & Net Worth	100.0	100.0
						INCOME DATA		
						Net Sales	100.0	100.0
						Gross Profit		
						Operating Expenses	89.7	85.9
						Operating Profit	10.3	14.1
						All Other Expenses (net)	5.1	2.9
						Profit Before Taxes	5.2	11.2
						RATIOS		
							2.4	2.0
						Current	.8	1.1
							.3	.7
							1.7	1.9
						Quick	.5	.9
							.2	.3
							0 UND	**0** UND
						Sales/Receivables	**1** 305.1	**4** 97.6
							12 31.0	**17** 20.9
						Cost of Sales/Inventory		
						Cost of Sales/Payables		
							12.5	9.4
						Sales/Working Capital	-48.2	293.4
							-6.2	-12.5
							4.3	8.1
						EBIT/Interest	(22) 2.5	(27) 3.6
							.4	1.5
						Net Profit + Depr., Dep., Amort./Cur. Mat. L/T/D		
							1.7	1.5
						Fixed/Worth	7.4	3.5
							-1.3	-4.5
							1.9	1.7
						Debt/Worth	11.9	3.9
							-3.2	-9.1
							37.2	77.3
						% Profit Before Taxes/Tangible Net Worth	(14) 10.4	(19) 24.6
							-20.6	12.2
							14.6	21.1
						% Profit Before Taxes/Total Assets	3.5	7.1
							-2.1	2.6
							5.0	5.8
						Sales/Net Fixed Assets	2.2	2.0
							1.2	1.4
							2.1	1.7
						Sales/Total Assets	1.0	1.0
							.7	.8
							4.0	3.9
						% Depr., Dep., Amort./Sales	(24) 6.3	(27) 6.2
							11.6	9.6
						% Officers', Directors' Owners' Comp/Sales		
6096M	**10437M**	**144145M**	**269589M**	**35978M**	**341623M**	Net Sales ($)	**339159M**	**458781M**
1222M	**6438M**	**41805M**	**200985M**	**57989M**	**566623M**	Total Assets ($)	**340968M**	**404383M**

M = $ thousand MM = $ million

See Pages 9 through 22 for Explanation of Ratios and Data

Comparative Historical Data				Current Data Sorted by Sales					
			Type of Statement						
5	3	4	Unqualified					1	3
2	1	3	Reviewed					1	2
4	1	4	Compiled	1	1	1	1		
7	6	5	Tax Returns	2	3				
14	14	16	Other	3	1	2		4	6
4/1/11-3/31/12 ALL	**4/1/12-3/31/13 ALL**	**4/1/13-3/31/14 ALL**		**1 (4/1-9/30/13)**			**31 (10/1/13-3/31/14)**		
				0-1MM	**1-3MM**	**3-5MM**	**5-10MM**	**10-25MM**	**25MM & OVER**
32	25	32	**NUMBER OF STATEMENTS**	6	5	3	1	6	11
%	%	%	**ASSETS**	%	%	%	%	%	%
19.0	16.9	9.6	Cash & Equivalents						8.6
6.4	5.1	6.8	Trade Receivables (net)						4.7
2.2	2.4	3.5	Inventory						1.2
2.5	4.2	6.0	All Other Current						.3
30.2	28.6	26.0	Total Current						14.8
48.7	50.1	52.6	Fixed Assets (net)						56.3
13.1	14.6	10.0	Intangibles (net)						20.2
8.0	6.7	11.3	All Other Non-Current						8.6
100.0	100.0	100.0	Total						100.0
			LIABILITIES						
7.8	3.3	9.3	Notes Payable-Short Term						2.6
6.4	4.9	3.9	Cur. Mat.-L.T.D.						2.3
5.1	4.3	10.7	Trade Payables						8.5
.3	.0	.0	Income Taxes Payable						.0
8.2	8.2	21.6	All Other Current						22.7
27.8	20.6	45.5	Total Current						36.1
47.9	51.8	52.0	Long-Term Debt						29.4
.5	1.2	.9	Deferred Taxes						2.5
6.8	10.4	33.8	All Other Non-Current						3.7
16.9	16.1	-32.1	Net Worth						28.3
100.0	100.0	100.0	Total Liabilties & Net Worth						100.0
			INCOME DATA						
100.0	100.0	100.0	Net Sales						100.0
			Gross Profit						
93.1	90.0	93.0	Operating Expenses						93.1
6.9	10.0	7.0	Operating Profit						6.9
1.5	1.9	5.3	All Other Expenses (net)						2.3
5.4	8.1	1.7	Profit Before Taxes						4.6
			RATIOS						
2.1	2.6	1.1							1.1
1.3	1.3	.5	Current						.3
.4	.5	.1							.1
1.8	2.1	.7							.8
1.1	1.1	.2	Quick						.2
.3	.3	.1							.1
0 UND	**0** UND	**0** UND							**1** 375.7
2 206.9	**3** 142.8	**1** 428.3	Sales/Receivables						**7** 54.4
10 36.1	**12** 30.3	**7** 48.7							**13** 27.5
			Cost of Sales/Inventory						
			Cost of Sales/Payables						
10.5	9.2	NM							67.5
26.4	31.3	-15.0	Sales/Working Capital						-10.7
-12.9	-27.1	-5.4							-3.5
4.4	9.5	4.3							
(27) 2.7	(24) 4.4	(27) 1.8	EBIT/Interest						
.8	1.7	.4							
			Net Profit + Depr., Dep., Amort./Cur. Mat. L/T/D						
.7	1.1	1.3							3.1
5.9	2.9	6.3	Fixed/Worth						5.4
-2.8	-4.5	-1.3							-1.1
.8	1.0	1.3							3.0
15.1	5.1	8.6	Debt/Worth						5.6
-3.9	-5.7	-3.2							-4.3
149.0	129.9	48.0							
(20) 43.2	(18) 58.8	(19) 11.2	% Profit Before Taxes/Tangible Net Worth						
6.9	10.3	-11.0							
21.0	19.6	5.8							6.6
3.8	8.5	1.5	% Profit Before Taxes/Total Assets						3.2
-.1	3.4	-2.4							.2
8.6	8.3	12.1							6.9
3.2	2.1	3.0	Sales/Net Fixed Assets						2.1
1.6	1.5	1.5							1.6
3.0	2.7	5.0							3.1
1.5	1.1	1.6	Sales/Total Assets						1.4
1.0	.9	.8							.6
3.9	3.3	2.1							
(25) 6.3	(17) 6.4	(26) 5.4	% Depr., Dep., Amort./Sales						
7.9	9.6	9.1							
3.4	1.4								
(15) 12.3	(11) 4.3		% Officers', Directors' Owners' Comp/Sales						
22.3	8.3								
324126M	**440738M**	**807868M**	Net Sales ($)	**3454M**	**7085M**	**9976M**	**7155M**	**96691M**	**683507M**
264459M	**565859M**	**875062M**	Total Assets ($)	**5006M**	**3808M**	**22931M**	**6531M**	**56362M**	**780424M**

M = $ thousand MM = $ million

See Pages 9 through 22 for Explanation of Ratios and Data

Current Data Sorted by Assets							Comparative Historical Data	
						Type of Statement		
		4	10	2	5	Unqualified	28	21
	1	6				Reviewed	16	10
		6				Compiled	7	6
6	3	5	1			Tax Returns	12	10
3	4	12	14		5	Other	55	43
16 (4/1-9/30/13)		71 (10/1/13-3/31/14)					4/1/09-3/31/10	4/1/10-3/31/11
0-500M	500M-2MM	2-10MM	10-50MM	50-100MM	100-250MM		ALL	ALL
9	8	33	25	2	10	NUMBER OF STATEMENTS	118	90
%	%	%	%	%	%	**ASSETS**	%	%
		12.6	4.5		6.3	Cash & Equivalents	10.9	10.7
		16.4	15.5		7.2	Trade Receivables (net)	15.1	16.5
		10.6	10.2		5.8	Inventory	7.7	7.3
		1.2	1.5		6.5	All Other Current	4.6	6.5
		40.8	31.7		25.8	Total Current	38.3	41.0
		48.8	52.3		56.1	Fixed Assets (net)	47.3	46.6
		2.9	11.2		2.8	Intangibles (net)	7.0	4.7
		7.5	4.8		15.2	All Other Non-Current	7.4	7.7
		100.0	100.0		100.0	Total	100.0	100.0
						LIABILITIES		
		4.9	5.6		.3	Notes Payable-Short Term	10.7	7.6
		4.2	3.3		1.3	Cur. Mat.-L.T.D.	3.4	3.6
		10.4	7.3		4.5	Trade Payables	9.5	7.7
		.0	.0		.0	Income Taxes Payable	.2	.1
		20.7	9.6		6.1	All Other Current	11.7	13.6
		40.1	25.9		12.3	Total Current	35.5	32.6
		25.1	24.0		22.2	Long-Term Debt	33.0	25.7
		.2	.3		.3	Deferred Taxes	.4	.3
		7.4	4.1		7.3	All Other Non-Current	8.9	10.6
		27.2	45.7		57.8	Net Worth	22.2	30.8
		100.0	100.0		100.0	Total Liabilties & Net Worth	100.0	100.0
						INCOME DATA		
		100.0	100.0		100.0	Net Sales	100.0	100.0
						Gross Profit		
		93.1	91.6		97.6	Operating Expenses	95.4	93.7
		6.9	8.4		2.4	Operating Profit	4.6	6.3
		1.2	1.8		2.7	All Other Expenses (net)	3.3	2.2
		5.7	6.6		-.2	Profit Before Taxes	1.3	4.1
						RATIOS		
		2.3	1.5		5.6		2.0	2.4
		1.0	1.0		3.5	Current	1.2	1.4
		.8	.7		1.7		.6	.9
		1.7	1.2		4.2		1.3	1.8
		.7	.7		1.3	Quick	.7	1.0
		.4	.4		.9		.4	.5
		7 52.1	**14** 27.0		**15** 25.0		**9** 39.1	**9** 39.6
		25 14.6	**28** 13.0		**32** 11.4	Sales/Receivables	**22** 16.9	**24** 15.4
		39 9.3	**43** 8.4		**48** 7.6		**39** 9.3	**53** 6.9
						Cost of Sales/Inventory		
						Cost of Sales/Payables		
		7.2	13.4		1.0		8.3	5.8
		67.0	273.9		3.7	Sales/Working Capital	30.3	16.4
		-23.6	-14.4		11.4		-16.1	-84.1
		15.3	8.3		14.8		7.8	9.4
		(32) 3.7	4.1		1.7	EBIT/Interest	(101) 2.1	(70) 3.5
		.5	1.7		-.6		-.8	.6
							8.7	29.4
						Net Profit + Depr., Dep., Amort./Cur. Mat. L/T/D	(20) 2.4	(10) 2.5
							.5	1.2
		.8	1.0		.7		.8	.6
		1.3	1.7		1.1	Fixed/Worth	1.7	1.3
		3.5	5.2		2.5		-9.5	3.8
		.9	.5		.2		.9	.7
		2.0	2.4		.6	Debt/Worth	2.7	1.6
		9.2	15.4		4.8		-16.2	5.6
		52.0	27.2				46.8	35.4
		(27) 23.7	(20) 9.8			% Profit Before Taxes/Tangible Net Worth	(84) 14.1	(74) 14.5
		6.7	-.1				-1.6	.5
		12.7	8.7		8.0		10.3	13.0
		5.9	5.3		1.4	% Profit Before Taxes/Total Assets	2.5	5.3
		-.4	.7		-1.1		-4.1	-.7
		10.0	9.5		6.6		13.1	12.6
		3.4	3.0		1.1	Sales/Net Fixed Assets	3.7	3.2
		1.7	.6		.2		1.3	1.1
		2.6	2.8		1.2		2.9	2.4
		2.2	1.3		.5	Sales/Total Assets	1.5	1.4
		.8	.5		.1		.7	.7
		2.0	1.3				1.6	1.5
		(29) 3.6	(23) 3.2			% Depr., Dep., Amort./Sales	(99) 3.9	(73) 4.7
		7.9	6.1				7.3	11.3
							1.6	1.5
						% Officers', Directors' Owners' Comp/Sales	(25) 2.7	(24) 2.1
							9.7	6.8
8997M	25406M	388437M	896313M	13226M	1317710M	Net Sales ($)	4543989M	2542585M
2369M	11002M	186538M	560468M	155399M	1612112M	Total Assets ($)	3542363M	2386134M

M = $ thousand MM = $ million

See Pages 9 through 22 for Explanation of Ratios and Data

Comparative Historical Data / Current Data Sorted by Sales

4/1/11-3/31/12 ALL	4/1/12-3/31/13 ALL	4/1/13-3/31/14 ALL	Type of Statement	0-1MM	1-3MM	3-5MM	5-10MM	10-25MM	25MM & OVER
17	21	21	Unqualified		3	2		9	7
12	6	7	Reviewed		1	1	3	2	
12	7	6	Compiled				3	2	1
17	6	15	Tax Returns	5	5	1	2	2	
45	45	38	Other	1	5	4	6	9	13
				16 (4/1-9/30/13)			71 (10/1/13-3/31/14)		
103	85	87	**NUMBER OF STATEMENTS**	6	14	8	14	24	21
%	%	%	**ASSETS**	%	%	%	%	%	%
14.3	11.8	11.1	Cash & Equivalents		11.1		11.9	10.0	8.7
14.8	15.0	15.6	Trade Receivables (net)		10.0		20.1	11.8	24.2
9.4	9.2	10.7	Inventory		5.0		12.0	8.6	12.5
2.4	2.7	1.7	All Other Current		1.2		1.6	1.6	3.4
40.9	38.7	39.2	Total Current		27.2		45.7	32.1	48.7
46.5	46.0	48.8	Fixed Assets (net)		61.5		47.6	53.2	34.7
5.5	6.6	4.7	Intangibles (net)		.4		3.1	8.6	6.0
7.1	8.7	7.4	All Other Non-Current		10.9		3.7	6.1	10.6
100.0	100.0	100.0	Total		100.0		100.0	100.0	100.0
			LIABILITIES						
4.8	6.4	4.8	Notes Payable-Short Term		3.1		8.1	1.9	5.8
3.9	4.7	2.9	Cur. Mat.-L.T.D.		1.8		3.4	3.4	3.5
9.5	10.0	9.5	Trade Payables		6.5		10.3	8.1	10.6
.2	.2	.0	Income Taxes Payable		.0		.0	.0	.0
10.7	12.8	13.6	All Other Current		9.6		14.5	17.6	14.7
29.0	34.0	30.9	Total Current		20.9		36.3	31.0	34.6
30.0	21.3	32.4	Long-Term Debt		28.6		27.6	24.5	22.6
.0	.2	.2	Deferred Taxes		.0		.3	.3	.3
8.5	6.7	5.6	All Other Non-Current		12.9		5.2	4.0	6.4
32.4	37.8	30.8	Net Worth		37.6		30.6	40.2	36.2
100.0	100.0	100.0	Total Liabilties & Net Worth		100.0		100.0	100.0	100.0
			INCOME DATA						
100.0	100.0	100.0	Net Sales		100.0		100.0	100.0	100.0
			Gross Profit						
91.7	94.7	92.5	Operating Expenses		89.0		93.5	91.4	95.5
8.3	5.3	7.5	Operating Profit		11.0		6.5	8.6	4.5
3.2	1.7	1.9	All Other Expenses (net)		.4		1.8	3.0	1.0
5.1	3.6	5.6	Profit Before Taxes		10.6		4.7	5.6	3.5
			RATIOS						
2.8	2.7	2.9			3.0		2.1	4.3	1.9
1.3	1.5	1.2	Current		1.2		1.0	1.8	1.7
.8	.9	.8			.5		.8	.8	1.0
2.0	1.8	2.2			2.6		1.7	2.9	1.6
.9	1.0	.9	Quick		1.0		.8	1.0	.9
.4	.5	.4			.3		.5	.5	.6
6 56.4	**10** 38.0	**10** 36.2			**0** UND		**14** 26.4	**15** 25.1	**22** 16.9
19 19.3	**24** 15.4	**23** 15.8	Sales/Receivables		**16** 23.0		**31** 11.6	**22** 16.6	**36** 10.1
45 8.2	**40** 9.2	**42** 8.6			**35** 10.5		**47** 7.7	**40** 9.2	**45** 8.1
			Cost of Sales/Inventory						
			Cost of Sales/Payables						
7.0	6.8	6.9			6.4		7.5	2.4	10.6
26.9	20.3	25.8	Sales/Working Capital		27.2		NM	20.1	15.1
-44.1	-69.6	-23.6			-12.2		-33.0	-18.7	NM
8.6	8.7	12.8			29.3		15.5	14.2	8.4
(84) 3.4	(71) 2.6	(77) 3.5	EBIT/Interest		(11) 2.0		(12) 4.9	3.5	(20) 3.6
.9	1.0	.9			-1.1		.7	1.1	1.4
3.8	5.3	8.8							
(12) 1.4	(14) 2.1	(11) 2.3	Net Profit + Depr., Dep., Amort./Cur. Mat. L/T/D						
.8	1.4	1.2							
.5	.7	.7			.5		.8	.8	.5
1.3	1.3	1.2	Fixed/Worth		1.1		2.1	1.3	1.1
6.3	4.9	3.6			NM		4.0	2.7	5.2
.6	.6	.6			.1		1.1	.5	.7
1.7	1.6	1.5	Debt/Worth		1.1		1.9	1.0	2.7
9.1	10.4	5.7			NM		7.5	2.8	11.1
41.9	37.4	46.3			13.4		48.5	47.9	32.6
(82) 15.6	(70) 18.2	(71) 13.6	% Profit Before Taxes/Tangible Net Worth		(11) 4.5		(12) 24.0	(20) 14.8	(18) 13.5
3.5	.0	.2			-.4		10.2	-.3	.8
11.9	12.3	11.9			14.4		15.8	9.3	9.0
5.1	4.6	5.3	% Profit Before Taxes/Total Assets		2.4		6.6	4.9	6.1
-.1	-.2	.0			-2.4		.4	.3	.7
19.7	14.6	11.3			11.0		16.1	5.8	11.1
3.5	4.0	4.0	Sales/Net Fixed Assets		.9		2.8	3.1	9.3
1.2	1.6	.9			.2		1.2	.5	3.8
3.0	2.7	2.9			3.1		2.8	2.3	3.6
1.6	1.6	1.8	Sales/Total Assets		.4		1.4	1.4	2.3
.6	.8	.6			.2		.8	.3	1.2
1.4	1.7	1.6					2.4	1.6	1.2
(87) 3.1	(71) 3.1	(72) 3.2	% Depr., Dep., Amort./Sales				(12) 3.6	(23) 3.9	(18) 2.1
8.3	7.5	7.7					7.2	8.9	3.5
1.5	1.7	1.3							
(33) 2.5	(16) 5.0	(15) 2.7	% Officers', Directors' Owners' Comp/Sales						
4.6	8.9	6.3							
2729236M	4400818M	2650089M	Net Sales ($)	2155M	22922M	29741M	98267M	382425M	2114579M
1912170M	2962326M	2527888M	Total Assets ($)	1374M	126773M	65740M	77637M	969134M	1287230M

M = $ thousand MM = $ million

See Pages 9 through 22 for Explanation of Ratios and Data

Current Data Sorted by Assets / Comparative Historical Data

0-500M	500M-2MM	2-10MM	10-50MM	50-100MM	100-250MM		4/1/09-3/31/10 ALL	4/1/10-3/31/11 ALL
						Type of Statement		
		8	7	2	3	Unqualified	15	19
1		6	4			Reviewed	12	21
2	5	8	2			Compiled	8	7
5	7	4				Tax Returns	11	10
3	12	21	9	2	3	Other	37	41
19 (4/1-9/30/13)		95 (10/1/13-3/31/14)						
11	24	47	22	4	6	**NUMBER OF STATEMENTS**	83	98
%	%	%	%	%	%	**ASSETS**	%	%
19.1	13.7	11.1	10.2			Cash & Equivalents	14.3	12.4
29.8	34.1	26.8	23.0			Trade Receivables (net)	18.0	22.1
22.7	21.9	22.8	13.3			Inventory	15.8	19.2
1.1	1.4	2.4	4.4			All Other Current	4.3	3.7
72.7	71.1	63.1	50.8			Total Current	52.4	57.4
11.7	17.1	23.9	33.3			Fixed Assets (net)	36.6	31.3
4.2	1.6	5.7	6.1			Intangibles (net)	4.9	3.7
11.4	10.2	7.3	9.8			All Other Non-Current	6.0	7.6
100.0	100.0	100.0	100.0			Total	100.0	100.0
						LIABILITIES		
3.6	8.0	7.3	7.6			Notes Payable-Short Term	7.3	7.7
.1	1.1	3.9	3.5			Cur. Mat.-L.T.D.	4.1	3.8
18.7	15.2	15.0	8.1			Trade Payables	9.3	12.8
1.1	.0	.2	.8			Income Taxes Payable	.1	.4
22.1	11.7	12.1	12.8			All Other Current	11.3	12.4
45.6	36.0	38.5	32.8			Total Current	32.2	37.0
6.8	18.1	18.9	26.4			Long-Term Debt	31.1	19.4
.0	.0	.2	.4			Deferred Taxes	.1	.4
16.6	6.3	2.5	9.0			All Other Non-Current	7.1	5.7
31.0	39.6	39.8	31.4			Net Worth	29.4	37.5
100.0	100.0	100.0	100.0			Total Liabilties & Net Worth	100.0	100.0
						INCOME DATA		
100.0	100.0	100.0	100.0			Net Sales	100.0	100.0
						Gross Profit		
93.3	91.1	90.7	92.3			Operating Expenses	92.7	92.3
6.7	8.9	9.3	7.7			Operating Profit	7.3	7.7
.3	1.0	1.7	2.6			All Other Expenses (net)	1.9	2.4
6.4	7.9	7.6	5.1			Profit Before Taxes	5.3	5.3
						RATIOS		
6.0	4.7	2.5	2.5				2.6	2.5
2.0	2.1	1.7	1.4			Current	1.7	1.6
.6	1.3	1.2	1.1				1.0	1.2
2.8	4.7	1.6	1.5				1.6	1.5
1.3	1.6	.9	1.0			Quick	1.0	1.0
.0	1.0	.6	.6				.6	.5
0 UND	**9** 39.7	**22** 16.9	**15** 24.1				**13** 28.9	**16** 22.7
17 21.6	**33** 11.1	**40** 9.1	**31** 11.6			Sales/Receivables	**24** 15.2	**36** 10.1
81 4.5	**73** 5.0	**66** 5.5	**52** 7.0				**48** 7.6	**55** 6.6
						Cost of Sales/Inventory		
						Cost of Sales/Payables		
3.2	5.3	4.4	6.5				6.1	5.0
10.9	10.9	11.7	15.6			Sales/Working Capital	13.8	10.1
-40.7	21.4	58.4	101.4				-297.7	37.2
	15.5	16.6	8.3				10.2	19.2
	(17) 9.2	(40) 5.8	(18) 3.6			EBIT/Interest	(73) 3.6	(82) 3.6
	6.3	1.7	1.5				1.8	1.8
							12.2	4.6
						Net Profit + Depr., Dep., Amort./Cur. Mat. L/T/D	(14) 3.2	(28) 2.3
							2.0	.8
.0	.0	.1	.2				.4	.3
.1	.3	.7	1.4			Fixed/Worth	1.3	.7
2.0	3.6	1.7	7.5				9.6	2.1
.8	.4	.9	1.3				.8	.8
5.8	1.4	1.7	2.7			Debt/Worth	2.4	1.7
18.6	7.7	4.5	17.8				32.9	4.2
311.9	123.9	65.3	93.0				52.6	49.8
(10) 52.2	(21) 41.3	(41) 26.0	(20) 34.7			% Profit Before Taxes/Tangible Net Worth	(69) 24.3	(87) 17.8
12.6	12.7	9.4	5.7				3.6	4.3
84.9	32.1	18.3	13.9				15.9	17.5
16.4	19.6	9.3	8.7			% Profit Before Taxes/Total Assets	5.4	6.6
3.9	7.5	2.9	1.5				1.0	1.1
539.0	328.0	65.1	91.2				24.9	26.0
58.3	44.3	14.0	6.8			Sales/Net Fixed Assets	6.3	8.9
24.5	7.2	7.3	1.7				1.8	3.8
9.1	3.8	3.3	3.2				3.3	2.9
3.0	3.0	2.2	1.3			Sales/Total Assets	1.7	2.0
2.2	2.2	1.5	.9				1.1	1.2
		.5	1.9				1.2	.9
		(36) 1.6	(19) 2.8			% Depr., Dep., Amort./Sales	(68) 2.3	(75) 1.8
		3.0	6.7				5.0	4.6
		1.6					2.1	1.6
		(16) 2.8				% Officers', Directors' Owners' Comp/Sales	(26) 4.1	(24) 4.4
		5.0					11.6	8.3
13359M	108974M	710944M	986088M	281075M	1349535M	Net Sales ($)	3003771M	3022265M
2836M	31467M	267573M	567453M	273801M	897025M	Total Assets ($)	2034493M	2108117M

M = $ thousand MM = $ million

See Pages 9 through 22 for Explanation of Ratios and Data

Comparative Historical Data

Current Data Sorted by Sales

4/1/11-3/31/12 ALL	4/1/12-3/31/13 ALL	4/1/13-3/31/14 ALL	Type of Statement	0-1MM	1-3MM	3-5MM	5-10MM	10-25MM	25MM & OVER
22	21	20	Unqualified					7	13
19	10	11	Reviewed	1			3	5	2
15	18	17	Compiled	2	4	3	3	4	1
16	14	16	Tax Returns	6	2	3	2	3	
40	45	50	Other	2	5	6	13	10	14
				19 (4/1-9/30/13)			95 (10/1/13-3/31/14)		
112	108	114	NUMBER OF STATEMENTS	11	11	12	21	29	30
%	%	%	**ASSETS**	%	%	%	%	%	%
13.1	10.7	11.7	Cash & Equivalents	26.4	6.9	8.6	8.4	14.5	9.1
22.0	21.5	27.4	Trade Receivables (net)	8.4	35.0	39.3	31.5	22.3	29.0
16.1	19.7	19.7	Inventory	22.8	17.0	27.8	23.7	22.2	11.2
3.2	4.5	2.5	All Other Current	.0	1.1	1.2	1.7	3.0	4.6
54.5	56.3	61.4	Total Current	57.6	60.0	77.0	65.3	61.9	53.9
29.8	29.9	24.2	Fixed Assets (net)	30.0	18.0	10.3	23.8	24.5	29.7
6.4	7.6	5.7	Intangibles (net)	.6	4.3	2.6	6.4	4.4	10.0
9.3	6.2	8.8	All Other Non-Current	11.9	17.7	10.1	4.5	9.2	6.4
100.0	100.0	100.0	Total	100.0	100.0	100.0	100.0	100.0	100.0
			LIABILITIES						
7.8	10.0	6.9	Notes Payable-Short Term	3.6	2.5	11.1	8.7	6.7	7.2
4.0	3.8	2.8	Cur. Mat.-L.T.D.	.5	.7	1.7	3.4	3.8	3.4
13.9	12.5	13.7	Trade Payables	5.7	21.5	13.8	11.7	16.8	12.0
.2	.2	.4	Income Taxes Payable	1.1	.0	.7	.0	.6	.1
12.8	15.0	13.0	All Other Current	8.0	18.3	17.7	8.3	11.2	15.9
38.7	41.4	36.8	Total Current	19.0	43.0	45.0	32.1	39.2	38.6
20.6	23.0	19.7	Long-Term Debt	19.4	26.9	6.3	18.6	21.1	21.7
.3	.3	.2	Deferred Taxes	.0	.0	.0	.1	.3	.6
4.6	6.0	6.2	All Other Non-Current	16.7	6.5	7.4	4.1	5.3	4.2
35.9	29.3	37.1	Net Worth	44.8	23.6	41.3	45.1	34.1	34.9
100.0	100.0	100.0	Total Liabilties & Net Worth	100.0	100.0	100.0	100.0	100.0	100.0
			INCOME DATA						
100.0	100.0	100.0	Net Sales	100.0	100.0	100.0	100.0	100.0	100.0
			Gross Profit						
91.5	91.9	91.3	Operating Expenses	88.2	94.0	85.7	89.3	92.5	94.0
8.5	8.1	8.7	Operating Profit	11.8	6.0	14.3	10.7	7.5	6.0
1.6	2.5	1.6	All Other Expenses (net)	2.8	-1.1	4.0	1.3	2.0	1.1
6.8	5.6	7.1	Profit Before Taxes	9.0	7.1	10.4	9.4	5.5	4.9
			RATIOS						
2.6	2.2	3.0		20.8	3.1	5.1	3.5	2.4	2.0
1.4	1.4	1.7	Current	4.0	1.5	1.6	2.0	1.8	1.5
.9	1.0	1.2		.1	1.3	1.1	1.4	1.1	1.1
1.6	1.3	1.8		11.2	2.3	5.1	2.2	1.7	1.4
(111) .8	.9	1.1	Quick	2.0	1.3	1.1	1.1	.9	1.0
.6	.5	.6		.0	.7	.6	.8	.6	.7
16 22.3	12 30.8	16 22.3		0 UND	17 21.8	22 16.9	23 15.9	18 20.2	20 18.5
32 11.3	26 14.1	36 10.0	Sales/Receivables	4 86.1	42 8.6	47 7.8	31 11.6	37 9.9	41 8.9
50 7.3	51 7.2	65 5.6		17 21.6	83 4.4	96 3.8	78 4.7	59 6.2	65 5.6
			Cost of Sales/Inventory						
			Cost of Sales/Payables						
6.1	6.5	4.5		1.7	6.4	3.3	4.4	5.1	7.8
12.9	21.6	11.2	Sales/Working Capital	3.6	14.5	12.9	8.3	11.4	14.2
-74.0	-150.3	41.7		-27.1	51.2	23.9	22.9	40.4	101.4
16.7	12.8	13.6					19.4	15.5	14.9
(96) 3.8	(89) 4.8	(90) 5.9	EBIT/Interest				(18) 8.3	(25) 5.9	(27) 5.9
1.1	1.4	2.2					2.4	1.6	2.5
4.1	3.7	3.5							4.3
(34) 2.1	(27) 1.8	(20) 1.7	Net Profit + Depr., Dep., Amort./Cur. Mat. L/T/D						(10) 1.7
1.2	.9	1.2							1.2
.3	.2	.1		.0	.0	.0	.1	.2	.5
1.0	1.1	.8	Fixed/Worth	.3	.9	.1	.3	.6	1.4
3.0	18.8	2.7		2.0	12.9	2.1	1.6	3.4	3.7
1.0	1.1	.9		.4	1.4	.4	.7	.9	1.4
2.2	2.4	2.2	Debt/Worth	1.3	2.6	2.5	1.3	2.9	2.5
8.8	89.8	6.5		5.8	44.3	5.7	3.1	18.6	6.5
64.2	60.4	77.2		40.5		107.3	71.8	133.2	73.9
(96) 28.8	(82) 27.0	(101) 35.8	% Profit Before Taxes/Tangible Net Worth	15.0		(11) 63.9	(18) 42.4	(26) 31.7	(26) 33.3
4.7	8.7	10.3		-5.5		19.8	10.3	12.2	2.7
22.7	18.3	22.2		10.4	27.5	26.3	44.4	17.4	16.2
8.0	7.4	10.0	% Profit Before Taxes/Total Assets	7.1	7.7	19.8	14.6	9.3	9.8
1.0	1.4	3.1		-5.2	3.9	14.3	1.6	3.0	2.0
36.6	61.8	79.1		92.7	469.3	446.1	84.6	69.6	69.8
10.0	10.9	17.1	Sales/Net Fixed Assets	24.5	23.7	38.3	14.9	13.8	9.2
3.0	3.2	4.1		.6	6.4	23.1	3.5	4.8	2.8
3.4	3.8	3.4		2.6	4.2	3.5	3.6	2.8	3.6
2.1	2.4	2.3	Sales/Total Assets	1.3	2.5	2.2	2.7	2.1	2.7
1.3	1.2	1.3		.2	2.3	1.4	1.6	1.2	1.1
1.1	.8	.9					.7	.7	1.3
(94) 1.8	(81) 1.9	(74) 2.3	% Depr., Dep., Amort./Sales				(12) 1.5	(22) 2.2	(23) 2.5
5.2	6.9	3.9					3.3	4.4	3.8
1.7	1.3	1.5							
(34) 3.4	(34) 2.6	(30) 2.8	% Officers', Directors' Owners' Comp/Sales						
5.3	5.2	4.3							
3156822M	3414504M	3449975M	Net Sales ($)	6058M	19446M	47829M	149541M	446864M	2780237M
2212729M	1753195M	2040155M	Total Assets ($)	11646M	10690M	23861M	97497M	293075M	1603386M

M = $ thousand MM = $ million

See Pages 9 through 22 for Explanation of Ratios and Data

Current Data Sorted by Assets							Comparative Historical Data	
						Type of Statement		
			3	2	2	Unqualified	4	2
1		1	3			Reviewed	2	6
	3	3	1			Compiled	2	4
	2	4				Tax Returns	1	2
1	3	5	11		2	Other	9	11
	5 (4/1-9/30/13)		42 (10/1/13-3/31/14)				4/1/09-3/31/10	4/1/10-3/31/11
0-500M	**500M-2MM**	**2-10MM**	**10-50MM**	**50-100MM**	**100-250MM**		**ALL**	**ALL**
2	8	13	18	2	4	**NUMBER OF STATEMENTS**	18	25
%	%	%	%	%	%	**ASSETS**	%	%
		19.3	7.1			Cash & Equivalents	9.1	12.0
		22.2	20.6			Trade Receivables (net)	20.8	32.2
		10.5	8.1			Inventory	9.6	4.7
		2.0	7.4			All Other Current	4.9	5.5
		53.8	43.2			Total Current	44.3	54.4
		29.1	45.9			Fixed Assets (net)	45.0	38.3
		2.4	3.6			Intangibles (net)	3.7	.4
		14.6	7.3			All Other Non-Current	6.9	6.9
		100.0	100.0			Total	100.0	100.0
						LIABILITIES		
		8.9	3.9			Notes Payable-Short Term	7.6	4.4
		3.9	6.3			Cur. Mat.-L.T.D.	2.1	3.4
		17.2	6.1			Trade Payables	7.1	11.2
		.8	.4			Income Taxes Payable	.4	.3
		4.1	7.2			All Other Current	11.6	11.9
		34.8	23.8			Total Current	28.8	31.2
		13.8	28.9			Long-Term Debt	23.7	19.2
		.0	1.1			Deferred Taxes	2.3	.7
		9.1	.5			All Other Non-Current	9.5	9.1
		42.2	45.6			Net Worth	35.7	39.9
		100.0	100.0			Total Liabilities & Net Worth	100.0	100.0
						INCOME DATA		
		100.0	100.0			Net Sales	100.0	100.0
						Gross Profit		
		83.7	84.7			Operating Expenses	89.0	89.3
		16.3	15.3			Operating Profit	11.0	10.7
		1.7	3.4			All Other Expenses (net)	4.7	2.5
		14.6	11.9			Profit Before Taxes	6.4	8.1
						RATIOS		
		3.7	2.3				2.3	3.7
		1.1	1.5			Current	1.5	1.6
		.7	1.3				.8	1.0
		2.8	1.5				1.5	3.3
		1.1	1.1			Quick	.9	1.3
		.5	.7				.5	.8
		6 66.3	**23** 16.1				**0** UND	**33** 11.1
		24 15.5	**40** 9.1			Sales/Receivables	**41** 8.8	**44** 8.4
		70 5.2	**61** 6.0				**58** 6.3	**73** 5.0
						Cost of Sales/Inventory		
						Cost of Sales/Payables		
		4.0	4.9				5.8	5.0
		74.0	11.0			Sales/Working Capital	9.6	13.6
		-19.2	32.9				-17.1	NM
		30.7	38.9				12.1	194.4
		(12) 9.6	(17) 4.7			EBIT/Interest	(16) 3.3	(22) 18.7
		-2.7	3.1				1.7	2.3
						Net Profit + Depr., Dep., Amort./Cur. Mat. L/T/D		
		.2	.5				.5	.4
		.8	1.3			Fixed/Worth	1.4	.9
		5.6	2.9				4.4	1.6
		.5	.4				.9	.2
		1.1	1.8			Debt/Worth	2.3	1.1
		17.4	2.9				5.6	5.7
		142.2	46.0				34.8	91.7
		(12) 38.1	(17) 28.3			% Profit Before Taxes/Tangible Net Worth	(16) 19.8	(23) 23.6
		2.4	13.6				7.0	10.6
		26.3	22.6				11.9	20.7
		17.0	8.0			% Profit Before Taxes/Total Assets	4.6	12.2
		-1.1	4.3				1.7	2.9
		78.0	7.4				8.8	30.0
		5.8	3.9			Sales/Net Fixed Assets	3.7	4.9
		4.1	2.4				1.0	2.7
		3.2	2.2				2.3	4.2
		1.9	1.8			Sales/Total Assets	1.4	1.9
		1.4	.9				.7	1.3
		1.3	2.9				2.8	.7
		(12) 3.7	(17) 4.8			% Depr., Dep., Amort./Sales	(16) 6.2	(21) 3.4
		7.9	8.3				11.3	8.1
						% Officers', Directors' Owners' Comp/Sales		
5650M	**23269M**	**154462M**	**656571M**	**127511M**	**1674644M**	Net Sales ($)	**1067846M**	**2125761M**
840M	**7594M**	**74029M**	**333621M**	**177766M**	**663139M**	Total Assets ($)	**835828M**	**877955M**

M = $ thousand MM = $ million

See Pages 9 through 22 for Explanation of Ratios and Data

Comparative Historical Data / Current Data Sorted by Sales

	4/1/11-3/31/12 ALL		4/1/12-3/31/13 ALL		4/1/13-3/31/14 ALL	Type of Statement	0-1MM	1-3MM	3-5MM	5-10MM		10-25MM		25MM & OVER
	4		3		7	Unqualified						1		6
	4		8		5	Reviewed		2		1		1		1
	4		8		7	Compiled	2			1		4		
	4		5		6	Tax Returns				3		2		1
	16		21		22	Other	2	2	3	4		3		8
							5 (4/1-9/30/13)			42 (10/1/13-3/31/14)				
	32		45		47	NUMBER OF STATEMENTS	4	4	3	9		11		16
	%		%		%	**ASSETS**	%	%	%	%		%		%
	15.9		14.0		15.2	Cash & Equivalents						14.7		7.4
	24.6		22.6		23.4	Trade Receivables (net)						21.5		27.4
	6.4		5.9		7.2	Inventory						9.4		11.4
	2.7		3.6		4.3	All Other Current						1.5		9.2
	49.6		46.1		50.1	Total Current						47.2		55.2
	41.3		43.4		38.0	Fixed Assets (net)						38.7		38.1
	2.8		3.1		2.4	Intangibles (net)						6.6		.3
	6.3		7.5		9.5	All Other Non-Current						7.5		6.4
	100.0		100.0		100.0	Total						100.0		100.0
						LIABILITIES								
	4.1		8.3		6.3	Notes Payable-Short Term						2.4		7.5
	3.2		7.1		4.5	Cur. Mat.-L.T.D.						4.4		4.5
	10.0		11.0		12.7	Trade Payables						10.9		13.0
	.1		.8		.7	Income Taxes Payable						1.2		1.0
	10.2		8.1		7.0	All Other Current						10.7		9.3
	27.6		35.4		31.2	Total Current						29.6		35.3
	21.2		22.4		18.2	Long-Term Debt						18.2		19.8
	.8		.7		.7	Deferred Taxes						.6		1.7
	6.6		7.5		3.5	All Other Non-Current						1.3		1.1
	43.8		34.1		46.3	Net Worth						50.3		42.0
	100.0		100.0		100.0	Total Liabilties & Net Worth						100.0		100.0
						INCOME DATA								
	100.0		100.0		100.0	Net Sales						100.0		100.0
						Gross Profit								
	87.8		87.0		82.4	Operating Expenses						90.2		91.9
	12.2		13.0		17.6	Operating Profit						9.8		8.1
	3.0		3.5		2.8	All Other Expenses (net)						2.8		2.0
	9.1		9.5		14.7	Profit Before Taxes						7.0		6.2
						RATIOS								
	2.9		2.1		3.3							4.1		2.2
	1.8		1.4		1.5	Current						1.6		1.5
	1.1		.9		1.0							1.0		1.0
	2.5		1.7		2.1							2.4		1.6
	1.3		1.1		1.2	Quick						1.3		.9
	.9		.6		.6							.9		.5
29	12.8	21	17.8	14	26.1						22	16.7	24	15.4
39	9.4	33	11.1	35	10.4	Sales/Receivables					31	11.7	36	10.0
50	7.3	64	5.7	58	6.3						73	5.0	55	6.6
						Cost of Sales/Inventory								
						Cost of Sales/Payables								
	4.3		4.9		4.2							4.6		4.6
	9.1		19.8		13.2	Sales/Working Capital						13.2		21.2
	65.5		-57.3		-141.5							-102.2		NM
	24.6		37.4		39.1									46.6
(26)	10.5	(35)	10.6	(41)	7.7	EBIT/Interest								3.9
	2.7		1.9		2.8									.8
					44.3									
				(12)	1.8	Net Profit + Depr., Dep., Amort./Cur. Mat. L/T/D								
					1.4									
	.5		.4		.3							.3		.5
	1.1		1.3		.8	Fixed/Worth						1.2		1.1
	2.2		3.6		2.4							7.8		2.0
	.4		.8		.4							.3		.5
	1.3		2.1		1.4	Debt/Worth						1.1		1.8
	4.2		7.7		2.9							30.7		2.8
	54.4		82.1		57.5									31.8
(29)	27.3	(41)	25.3	(44)	28.3	% Profit Before Taxes/Tangible Net Worth							(15)	18.7
	11.1		9.5		13.1									7.3
	17.9		28.6		26.4							23.7		15.8
	10.3		6.3		11.8	% Profit Before Taxes/Total Assets						5.6		5.3
	3.3		2.2		2.8							.7		-.3
	19.9		24.0		23.5							12.4		35.2
	4.2		4.7		4.9	Sales/Net Fixed Assets						4.6		4.2
	2.5		1.7		2.2							3.0		2.2
	3.2		3.1		3.2							2.4		3.1
	1.8		1.5		1.7	Sales/Total Assets						2.0		1.9
	1.0		1.0		.8							1.0		1.3
	.8		1.6		1.7							2.7		.7
(28)	3.2	(35)	5.2	(40)	4.6	% Depr., Dep., Amort./Sales						5.8	(15)	4.5
	6.2		9.5		8.4							8.6		5.3
					1.4									
				(11)	3.4	% Officers', Directors' Owners' Comp/Sales								
					11.2									
	3173336M		2837408M		2642107M	Net Sales ($)	2019M	9291M	10685M	56101M		181626M		2382385M
	1400026M		1000225M		1256989M	Total Assets ($)	2608M	32960M	19447M	45471M		189218M		967285M

M = $ thousand MM = $ million

See Pages 9 through 22 for Explanation of Ratios and Data

Current Data Sorted by Assets							Comparative Historical Data	
						Type of Statement		
	1		4	2	2	Unqualified	6	7
				1		Reviewed	1	1
	1	2				Compiled	2	4
1	1					Tax Returns	3	1
1		4	6	2	2	Other	8	11
	4 (4/1-9/30/13)		26 (10/1/13-3/31/14)				4/1/09-3/31/10	4/1/10-3/31/11
0-500M	500M-2MM	2-10MM	10-50MM	50-100MM	100-250MM		ALL	ALL
2	3	6	10	5	4	**NUMBER OF STATEMENTS**	20	24
%	%	%	%	%	%	**ASSETS**	%	%
			9.8			Cash & Equivalents	13.3	21.1
			16.0			Trade Receivables (net)	14.2	10.0
			1.0			Inventory	1.7	1.6
			4.6			All Other Current	5.5	1.6
			31.4			Total Current	34.7	34.2
			56.2			Fixed Assets (net)	56.4	55.6
			.2			Intangibles (net)	1.6	4.0
			12.2			All Other Non-Current	7.2	6.2
			100.0			Total	100.0	100.0
						LIABILITIES		
			.6			Notes Payable-Short Term	4.6	.7
			4.0			Cur. Mat.-L.T.D.	3.0	3.5
			8.7			Trade Payables	8.7	8.4
			.1			Income Taxes Payable	.1	.1
			9.5			All Other Current	18.1	9.7
			22.9			Total Current	34.5	22.4
			35.8			Long-Term Debt	43.8	36.2
			1.1			Deferred Taxes	.5	.6
			1.4			All Other Non-Current	3.1	6.4
			38.8			Net Worth	18.1	34.5
			100.0			Total Liabilties & Net Worth	100.0	100.0
						INCOME DATA		
			100.0			Net Sales	100.0	100.0
						Gross Profit		
			79.4			Operating Expenses	92.5	89.5
			20.6			Operating Profit	7.5	10.5
			8.1			All Other Expenses (net)	6.1	5.8
			12.6			Profit Before Taxes	1.5	4.6
						RATIOS		
			2.3			Current	2.3	2.7
			1.3				.9	1.5
			.7				.6	.8
			2.2			Quick	1.7	2.7
			1.2				.8	1.4
			.5				.4	.6
			8 43.7			Sales/Receivables	12 29.3	19 19.6
			31 11.9				37 9.9	33 11.0
			79 4.6				52 7.0	43 8.5
						Cost of Sales/Inventory		
						Cost of Sales/Payables		
			6.4			Sales/Working Capital	6.3	4.2
			14.1				-100.1	13.7
			-96.7				-6.0	-12.4
						EBIT/Interest	11.6	10.5
							(18) .3	(15) 4.9
							-2.2	.8
						Net Profit + Depr., Dep., Amort./Cur. Mat. L/T/D		
			.5			Fixed/Worth	.9	.6
			.9				1.6	1.7
			NM				8.2	-11.1
			.9			Debt/Worth	.6	.7
			2.0				1.3	1.0
			NM				17.7	-13.1
						% Profit Before Taxes/Tangible Net Worth	14.1	79.9
							(18) -3.1	(16) 13.5
							-17.3	4.0
			9.5			% Profit Before Taxes/Total Assets	6.2	14.6
			5.5				-.6	3.0
			1.9				-5.7	-1.1
			8.4			Sales/Net Fixed Assets	18.8	10.1
			2.7				1.9	1.5
			.2				.3	.4
			1.7			Sales/Total Assets	2.7	1.8
			.9				1.2	.9
			.2				.3	.2
						% Depr., Dep., Amort./Sales	1.4	2.7
							(14) 10.6	(19) 8.1
							26.7	20.0
						% Officers', Directors' Owners' Comp/Sales		
992M	14889M	66433M	276537M	128785M	309664M	Net Sales ($)	802045M	457858M
583M	2262M	33871M	244743M	360626M	581863M	Total Assets ($)	610959M	653050M

M = $ thousand MM = $ million

See Pages 9 through 22 for Explanation of Ratios and Data

Comparative Historical Data | Current Data Sorted by Sales

4/1/11-3/31/12 ALL	4/1/12-3/31/13 ALL	4/1/13-3/31/14 ALL		0-1MM	1-3MM	3-5MM	5-10MM	10-25MM	25MM & OVER
			Type of Statement						
11	6	9	Unqualified			3		3	3
1		1	Reviewed						1
5	4	3	Compiled	1			2		
5	2	2	Tax Returns	1				1	
9	8	15	Other	1	1	1	2	4	6
				4 (4/1-9/30/13)		26 (10/1/13-3/31/14)			
31	20	30	**NUMBER OF STATEMENTS**	3	1	4	4	8	10
%	%	%	**ASSETS**	%	%	%	%	%	%
14.3	8.8	10.4	Cash & Equivalents						7.8
9.9	10.0	19.7	Trade Receivables (net)						13.6
.4	.6	.9	Inventory						2.6
4.8	8.0	4.5	All Other Current						7.8
29.5	27.4	35.5	Total Current						31.8
57.0	56.6	50.3	Fixed Assets (net)						54.8
4.5	5.3	4.8	Intangibles (net)						8.1
9.0	10.7	9.3	All Other Non-Current						5.3
100.0	100.0	100.0	Total						100.0
			LIABILITIES						
2.3	2.8	2.8	Notes Payable-Short Term						3.0
3.3	3.6	2.2	Cur. Mat.-L.T.D.						1.9
4.4	6.2	12.3	Trade Payables						3.7
.0	.4	.2	Income Taxes Payable						.0
10.6	9.2	11.4	All Other Current						13.9
20.6	22.3	28.8	Total Current						22.5
35.1	49.6	26.8	Long-Term Debt						25.8
.5	.8	1.3	Deferred Taxes						1.3
5.2	19.8	4.6	All Other Non-Current						12.0
38.6	7.5	38.5	Net Worth						38.4
100.0	100.0	100.0	Total Liabilities & Net Worth						100.0
			INCOME DATA						
100.0	100.0	100.0	Net Sales						100.0
			Gross Profit						
81.1	79.4	83.9	Operating Expenses						84.9
18.9	20.6	16.1	Operating Profit						15.1
5.3	10.7	2.8	All Other Expenses (net)						2.7
13.7	9.8	13.3	Profit Before Taxes						12.4
			RATIOS						
2.7	2.4	2.8							3.7
1.4	1.5	1.8	Current						1.7
.7	.6	.9							1.3
2.7	1.8	2.7							3.3
.9	1.3	1.7	Quick						1.4
.4	.3	.6							.5
9 41.9	**13** 27.8	**19** 19.3							**19** 19.3
27 13.6	**27** 13.6	**30** 12.0	Sales/Receivables						**29** 12.7
46 7.9	**47** 7.8	**64** 5.7							**57** 6.4
			Cost of Sales/Inventory						
			Cost of Sales/Payables						
4.6	4.3	5.1							6.1
26.1	9.7	9.0	Sales/Working Capital						10.1
-15.5	-8.7	-103.4							50.3
8.4	17.0	17.9							
(24) 3.9	(15) 3.8	(26) 7.4	EBIT/Interest						
2.2	.8	2.1							
			Net Profit + Depr., Dep., Amort./Cur. Mat. L/T/D						
.9	.9	.8							.8
1.5	1.7	1.5	Fixed/Worth						2.3
5.2	-4.9	-133.5							NM
.3	.6	.5							1.0
.9	3.2	2.0	Debt/Worth						2.1
8.2	-7.7	-143.6							NM
53.7	50.3	33.8							
(25) 17.0	(12) 13.1	(22) 16.7	% Profit Before Taxes/Tangible Net Worth						
4.2	2.5	6.1							
12.5	17.6	9.5							12.9
5.3	2.3	4.6	% Profit Before Taxes/Total Assets						7.3
1.9	-1.2	2.6							3.2
4.2	4.7	8.0							5.1
1.6	1.3	2.4	Sales/Net Fixed Assets						1.1
.4	.2	.5							.7
2.0	1.9	1.7							2.3
1.0	.7	1.0	Sales/Total Assets						.6
.2	.2	.4							.5
3.5	4.5	2.8							3.9
(28) 8.2	(18) 7.6	(28) 6.1	% Depr., Dep., Amort./Sales						5.7
18.3	19.5	17.6							10.8
2.6									
(10) 7.1			% Officers', Directors' Owners' Comp/Sales						
31.9									
767577M	**1468538M**	**797300M**	Net Sales ($)	**1966M**	**2003M**	**14528M**	**24958M**	**118697M**	**635148M**
835633M	**1206196M**	**1223948M**	Total Assets ($)	**1211M**	**10156M**	**72954M**	**47340M**	**245970M**	**846317M**

M = $ thousand MM = $ million

See Pages 9 through 22 for Explanation of Ratios and Data

Current Data Sorted by Assets							Comparative Historical Data	
						Type of Statement		
		3	9	3	4	Unqualified	28	21
	1	8	8	2		Reviewed	11	14
	2					Compiled	6	3
1						Tax Returns	10	6
3	2	8	23	5	9	Other	45	53
12 (4/1-9/30/13)			79 (10/1/13-3/31/14)				**4/1/09-3/31/10 ALL**	**4/1/10-3/31/11 ALL**
0-500M	**500M-2MM**	**2-10MM**	**10-50MM**	**50-100MM**	**100-250MM**			
4	5	19	40	10	13	**NUMBER OF STATEMENTS**	100	97
%	%	%	%	%	%	**ASSETS**	%	%
		11.3	14.6	8.0	10.5	Cash & Equivalents	10.9	14.1
		30.0	19.0	14.7	21.1	Trade Receivables (net)	18.9	20.9
		2.3	2.4	3.6	.1	Inventory	1.5	1.7
		3.2	5.3	1.6	3.4	All Other Current	5.7	6.1
		46.9	41.3	27.9	35.0	Total Current	36.9	42.8
		40.6	42.6	51.6	49.5	Fixed Assets (net)	47.1	42.3
		4.9	8.5	9.9	8.6	Intangibles (net)	5.1	5.4
		7.6	7.7	10.6	6.8	All Other Non-Current	10.9	9.5
		100.0	100.0	100.0	100.0	Total	100.0	100.0
						LIABILITIES		
		4.0	6.1	1.5	.3	Notes Payable-Short Term	4.9	5.8
		7.7	3.5	4.5	3.0	Cur. Mat.-L.T.D.	8.0	4.0
		15.1	7.5	4.4	9.6	Trade Payables	9.7	11.1
		.0	.0	1.4	.0	Income Taxes Payable	.2	.6
		16.2	8.0	9.1	10.0	All Other Current	11.4	9.6
		43.0	25.1	20.8	22.8	Total Current	34.2	31.2
		22.6	15.9	31.3	52.7	Long-Term Debt	30.5	25.8
		.2	.4	3.8	1.6	Deferred Taxes	.7	.7
		4.9	5.2	3.8	10.7	All Other Non-Current	10.2	3.7
		29.4	53.5	40.4	12.2	Net Worth	24.3	38.6
		100.0	100.0	100.0	100.0	Total Liabilties & Net Worth	100.0	100.0
						INCOME DATA		
		100.0	100.0	100.0	100.0	Net Sales	100.0	100.0
						Gross Profit		
		90.3	87.1	88.3	84.7	Operating Expenses	88.0	87.2
		9.7	12.9	11.7	15.3	Operating Profit	12.0	12.8
		1.7	2.3	.1	3.9	All Other Expenses (net)	2.7	3.7
		8.1	10.6	11.7	11.4	Profit Before Taxes	9.3	9.1
						RATIOS		
		1.4	3.7	2.4	2.3		2.2	3.1
		1.1	1.6	1.4	1.7	Current	1.2	1.4
		1.0	1.0	.9	1.2		.7	.8
		1.3	3.3	2.1	2.1		1.8	2.6
		1.0	1.4	1.1	1.5	Quick	.9	1.1
		.6	.7	.8	1.1		.5	.7
		39 9.4	**28** 13.1	**39** 9.4	**40** 9.1		**25** 14.9	**27** 13.6
		43 8.5	**44** 8.3	**46** 7.9	**45** 8.2	Sales/Receivables	**39** 9.3	**41** 8.8
		47 7.7	**61** 6.0	**58** 6.3	**64** 5.7		**57** 6.4	**58** 6.3
						Cost of Sales/Inventory		
						Cost of Sales/Payables		
		16.4	4.1	5.0	5.5		6.5	5.0
		47.5	10.8	14.6	12.8	Sales/Working Capital	31.5	15.6
		-345.5	NM	-140.7	32.3		-10.6	-30.2
		11.2	48.8		8.9		11.2	23.9
		(18) 6.0	(34) 7.9		(12) 4.2	EBIT/Interest	(87) 3.7	(74) 6.3
		-1.3	3.2		.6		.8	1.9
			24.8				6.2	13.3
			(11) 2.8			Net Profit + Depr., Dep., Amort./Cur. Mat. L/T/D	(27) 3.2	(23) 4.9
			1.5				2.4	2.6
		.5	.3	1.5	1.0		.8	.5
		1.2	.8	2.2	1.5	Fixed/Worth	1.5	1.1
		2.9	1.7	NM	4.3		2.7	2.4
		.7	.6	1.3	.6		.7	.5
		2.2	1.2	2.4	1.2	Debt/Worth	1.8	1.6
		5.0	1.8	NM	4.8		4.6	4.3
		58.6	37.1		30.6		47.4	47.2
		(16) 31.6	(39) 20.3		(11) 23.0	% Profit Before Taxes/Tangible Net Worth	(83) 17.1	(86) 25.0
		-6.2	4.7		-1.5		3.2	4.9
		17.4	12.3	16.7	12.2		14.0	21.0
		7.9	7.2	10.2	6.9	% Profit Before Taxes/Total Assets	5.3	8.8
		-5.5	2.4	6.2	1.0		.2	1.8
		14.6	18.0	4.3	6.2		10.0	12.7
		5.5	3.5	1.9	1.3	Sales/Net Fixed Assets	2.7	3.5
		2.4	.8	1.0	.6		1.0	1.1
		3.9	2.5	1.4	2.5		2.0	2.6
		2.2	1.4	.9	.8	Sales/Total Assets	1.3	1.3
		1.3	.4	.7	.4		.6	.6
		2.3	1.4		2.4		3.1	3.1
		(18) 3.3	(38) 3.9		(11) 6.3	% Depr., Dep., Amort./Sales	(85) 5.8	(79) 6.6
		6.6	19.9		10.5		10.4	10.2
						% Officers', Directors' Owners' Comp/Sales		
8555M	**11424M**	**274126M**	**1499856M**	**809045M**	**2828234M**	Net Sales ($)	**4875476M**	**4175898M**
1201M	**7461M**	**115896M**	**947809M**	**703660M**	**1969147M**	Total Assets ($)	**3954039M**	**3177608M**

M = $ thousand MM = $ million

See Pages 9 through 22 for Explanation of Ratios and Data

Comparative Historical Data | **Current Data Sorted by Sales**

			Type of Statement						
22	14	19	Unqualified		1		5	2	11
16	12	19	Reviewed	1	1	1	3	8	5
6	7	2	Compiled		1	1			
9	5	1	Tax Returns		1				
41	43	50	Other	3	2	4	5	8	28
4/1/11-3/31/12 ALL	4/1/12-3/31/13 ALL	4/1/13-3/31/14 ALL		12 (4/1-9/30/13)			79 (10/1/13-3/31/14)		
				0-1MM	1-3MM	3-5MM	5-10MM	10-25MM	25MM & OVER
94	81	91	**NUMBER OF STATEMENTS**	4	6	6	13	18	44
%	%	%	**ASSETS**	%	%	%	%	%	%
14.0	17.5	12.5	Cash & Equivalents				11.2	14.6	10.7
19.5	19.9	20.6	Trade Receivables (net)				10.2	27.5	25.2
1.8	1.0	1.9	Inventory				.0	2.8	2.8
4.9	5.3	4.7	All Other Current				1.7	4.5	4.6
40.1	43.7	39.7	Total Current				23.1	49.4	43.3
44.6	42.0	44.7	Fixed Assets (net)				64.1	38.5	37.1
4.7	4.5	7.5	Intangibles (net)				5.1	5.4	10.6
10.6	9.8	8.1	All Other Non-Current				7.7	6.6	8.9
100.0	100.0	100.0	Total				100.0	100.0	100.0
			LIABILITIES						
5.1	6.1	4.8	Notes Payable-Short Term				1.4	2.7	3.2
4.0	5.1	4.5	Cur. Mat.-L.T.D.				8.0	3.6	4.2
9.5	11.9	9.0	Trade Payables				4.6	12.2	10.5
.4	.2	.2	Income Taxes Payable				.0	.0	.4
10.0	8.0	10.9	All Other Current				13.2	11.8	9.5
29.0	31.2	29.4	Total Current				27.1	30.3	27.8
25.6	27.2	25.3	Long-Term Debt				29.9	15.8	29.5
.8	.5	.9	Deferred Taxes				.3	.3	1.5
8.6	4.7	5.3	All Other Non-Current				4.8	6.5	5.8
36.0	36.5	39.1	Net Worth				37.8	47.0	35.4
100.0	100.0	100.0	Total Liabilties & Net Worth				100.0	100.0	100.0
			INCOME DATA						
100.0	100.0	100.0	Net Sales				100.0	100.0	100.0
			Gross Profit						
86.0	86.3	86.9	Operating Expenses				84.2	91.5	90.5
14.0	13.7	13.1	Operating Profit				15.8	8.5	9.5
1.8	1.9	2.8	All Other Expenses (net)				3.1	-.1	1.4
12.2	11.8	10.3	Profit Before Taxes				12.7	8.6	8.1
			RATIOS						
2.8	2.5	2.5					1.9	3.1	2.4
1.5	1.4	1.4	Current				1.0	1.5	1.5
.9	1.0	1.0					.6	1.1	1.2
2.4	2.0	2.0					1.6	2.8	2.1
1.2	1.4	1.2	Quick				.9	1.3	1.4
.7	.7	.7					.6	.8	.9
18 20.5	**18** 20.6	**28** 13.2					**16** 23.1	**42** 8.7	**38** 9.5
40 9.2	**42** 8.6	**42** 8.6	Sales/Receivables				**40** 9.1	**51** 7.2	**45** 8.1
53 6.9	**54** 6.8	**56** 6.5					**46** 8.0	**66** 5.5	**57** 6.4
			Cost of Sales/Inventory						
			Cost of Sales/Payables						
5.5	5.0	6.3					10.2	4.9	6.7
14.0	15.4	20.3	Sales/Working Capital				988.2	8.4	14.8
-68.7	NM	-131.4					-9.1	49.1	43.4
26.9	16.0	21.0					10.9	49.4	33.3
(77) 7.4	(65) 6.6	(80) 6.7	EBIT/Interest				4.2	(15) 9.9	(40) 6.8
2.8	2.6	2.4					.7	7.0	2.4
14.2	4.5	20.3							25.8
(22) 4.7	(13) 2.0	(24) 2.5	Net Profit + Depr., Dep., Amort./Cur. Mat. L/T/D						(14) 4.9
3.3	1.1	.9							1.4
.5	.4	.5					.9	.5	.3
1.1	1.1	1.2	Fixed/Worth				2.3	1.0	1.1
3.3	2.3	2.6					13.5	1.5	2.2
.6	.8	.7					.6	.7	.7
1.8	1.5	1.4	Debt/Worth				1.7	1.5	1.4
4.4	2.9	3.3					15.1	3.5	2.9
50.7	54.7	41.9					43.0	52.9	38.5
(80) 27.0	(73) 30.0	(81) 26.0	% Profit Before Taxes/Tangible Net Worth				(11) 19.5	(17) 29.6	(39) 26.7
16.1	13.5	5.6					4.7	19.5	6.3
22.4	23.0	16.5					9.8	17.9	16.3
9.9	9.9	7.7	% Profit Before Taxes/Total Assets				6.4	11.0	8.2
4.6	3.3	2.4					-.6	6.1	3.2
18.0	36.6	12.9					3.0	13.3	34.5
4.2	4.2	3.4	Sales/Net Fixed Assets				1.2	4.4	5.6
1.0	1.2	1.0					.4	1.9	1.4
2.9	3.1	2.6					1.4	2.5	2.9
1.4	1.4	1.4	Sales/Total Assets				.9	1.7	2.1
.7	.6	.6					.2	.8	.8
1.5	1.9	2.3					4.7	2.2	1.2
(83) 4.0	(69) 4.5	(82) 4.2	% Depr., Dep., Amort./Sales				9.6	(16) 3.4	(40) 3.5
10.2	8.7	10.5					28.2	6.9	6.8
1.5	1.0								
(16) 2.7	(15) 2.7		% Officers', Directors' Owners' Comp/Sales						
4.3	6.4								
4621317M	3509040M	5431240M	Net Sales ($)	1416M	11054M	24317M	103764M	307463M	4983226M
3126575M	2918106M	3745174M	Total Assets ($)	9216M	80612M	38202M	202346M	246579M	3168219M

M = $ thousand MM = $ million

See Pages 9 through 22 for Explanation of Ratios and Data

Current Data Sorted by Assets							Comparative Historical Data	
						Type of Statement		
		3	2	1	2	Unqualified	12	7
		2	4	1		Reviewed	7	11
4	5	7	1			Compiled	13	10
	3					Tax Returns	2	4
	3	5	11	3	7	Other	30	31
	15 (4/1-9/30/13)		49 (10/1/13-3/31/14)				**4/1/09-3/31/10**	**4/1/10-3/31/11**
0-500M	**500M-2MM**	**2-10MM**	**10-50MM**	**50-100MM**	**100-250MM**		**ALL**	**ALL**
4	11	17	18	5	9	**NUMBER OF STATEMENTS**	64	63
%	%	%	%	%	%	**ASSETS**	%	%
	9.7	10.4	8.4			Cash & Equivalents	12.3	12.1
	17.6	23.8	12.0			Trade Receivables (net)	16.4	16.5
	.0	.0	.4			Inventory	1.9	1.5
	4.3	3.6	2.9			All Other Current	1.7	3.5
	31.5	37.8	23.7			Total Current	32.3	33.6
	54.6	52.6	68.0			Fixed Assets (net)	54.1	56.2
	3.5	1.0	2.7			Intangibles (net)	2.1	2.1
	10.5	8.6	5.6			All Other Non-Current	11.5	8.1
	100.0	100.0	100.0			Total	100.0	100.0
						LIABILITIES		
	10.4	2.5	2.5			Notes Payable-Short Term	3.2	3.5
	7.0	2.9	3.4			Cur. Mat.-L.T.D.	5.1	4.0
	10.8	2.9	5.6			Trade Payables	5.7	5.8
	.0	.2	.3			Income Taxes Payable	.1	.1
	17.5	14.1	6.0			All Other Current	8.6	5.8
	45.7	22.6	17.8			Total Current	22.7	19.2
	55.4	34.7	36.6			Long-Term Debt	37.0	31.1
	.0	.8	2.2			Deferred Taxes	1.1	1.6
	.5	1.9	6.8			All Other Non-Current	3.0	2.2
	-1.6	40.0	36.6			Net Worth	36.2	45.9
	100.0	100.0	100.0			Total Liabilties & Net Worth	100.0	100.0
						INCOME DATA		
	100.0	100.0	100.0			Net Sales	100.0	100.0
						Gross Profit		
	75.1	77.1	81.1			Operating Expenses	84.4	86.0
	24.9	22.9	18.9			Operating Profit	15.6	14.0
	9.5	1.2	3.8			All Other Expenses (net)	3.0	2.6
	15.4	21.8	15.2			Profit Before Taxes	12.6	11.4
						RATIOS		
	.8	5.9	2.4				2.8	2.9
	.6	1.2	1.4			Current	1.4	1.5
	.1	.8	.9				.9	1.0
	.8	5.7	2.0				1.9	2.3
	.6	1.2	1.1			Quick	1.3	1.2
	.1	.6	.9				.8	.8
	0 UND	**0** UND	**23** 15.8				**21** 17.5	**22** 17.0
	5 80.9	**34** 10.6	**33** 11.0			Sales/Receivables	**38** 9.5	**44** 8.4
	66 5.5	**51** 7.1	**59** 6.2				**55** 6.6	**58** 6.3
						Cost of Sales/Inventory		
						Cost of Sales/Payables		
	-32.9	7.0	8.8				6.3	4.8
	-13.2	35.9	14.3			Sales/Working Capital	22.0	13.3
	-1.6	-84.9	-45.9				-51.0	-142.6
		9.1	29.2				9.8	9.6
		(11) 4.0	(17) 7.0			EBIT/Interest	(54) 3.7	(57) 2.8
		.8	3.3				1.8	1.3
							3.9	9.2
						Net Profit + Depr., Dep., Amort./Cur. Mat. L/T/D	(12) 2.1	(13) 2.3
							1.8	1.5
	1.4	.6	1.3				.7	.6
	4.0	1.1	1.8			Fixed/Worth	1.5	1.3
	-7.5	7.4	5.1				3.4	3.3
	1.4	.5	1.1				.8	.5
	11.1	1.7	1.5			Debt/Worth	1.6	1.0
	-8.5	8.6	6.3				4.8	3.2
		261.1	55.1				55.1	34.9
		(16) 32.1	(17) 27.5			% Profit Before Taxes/Tangible Net Worth	(57) 12.8	(59) 19.1
		7.7	11.4				3.1	2.1
	24.4	36.3	13.3				15.0	15.2
	8.2	11.0	7.7			% Profit Before Taxes/Total Assets	7.5	5.1
	-.8	.2	3.5				1.7	.8
	9.8	8.2	2.2				6.4	5.8
	3.1	2.5	1.5			Sales/Net Fixed Assets	1.6	1.7
	.3	1.1	1.2				.9	.9
	3.0	2.5	1.3				1.7	1.8
	1.8	1.6	1.0			Sales/Total Assets	.9	1.0
	.2	.9	.8				.6	.7
		2.9	4.1				2.2	3.5
		(15) 5.4	6.2			% Depr., Dep., Amort./Sales	(51) 5.8	(56) 7.1
		9.3	11.4				10.2	10.6
							1.6	1.4
						% Officers', Directors' Owners' Comp/Sales	(16) 8.1	(11) 3.3
							17.8	14.1
3382M	**17551M**	**145352M**	**529212M**	**227306M**	**1072077M**	Net Sales ($)	**2437926M**	**2128454M**
1161M	**11209M**	**83849M**	**484036M**	**328067M**	**1393048M**	Total Assets ($)	**2924423M**	**2678795M**

M = $ thousand MM = $ million

See Pages 9 through 22 for Explanation of Ratios and Data

Comparative Historical Data / Current Data Sorted by Sales

4/1/11-3/31/12 ALL	4/1/12-3/31/13 ALL	4/1/13-3/31/14 ALL	Type of Statement	0-1MM	1-3MM	3-5MM	5-10MM	10-25MM	25MM & OVER
14	10	8	Unqualified	1			1	1	5
7	10	7	Reviewed				2	3	2
6	8	17	Compiled	4	4	1	5	3	
12	14	3	Tax Returns		3				
34	37	29	Other	4	2		2	4	17
				15 (4/1-9/30/13)			49 (10/1/13-3/31/14)		
73	79	64	NUMBER OF STATEMENTS	9	9	1	10	11	24
%	%	%	**ASSETS**	%	%	%	%	%	%
15.2	11.5	9.5	Cash & Equivalents				13.7	6.4	8.2
20.1	17.8	15.7	Trade Receivables (net)				23.9	21.6	11.5
1.0	.3	.3	Inventory				.0	.2	.7
3.1	1.6	2.7	All Other Current				5.8	2.7	1.7
39.4	31.2	28.2	Total Current				43.4	30.9	22.1
50.3	61.3	61.5	Fixed Assets (net)				50.3	61.3	66.6
2.9	2.1	2.0	Intangibles (net)				1.7	3.1	1.6
7.4	5.4	8.3	All Other Non-Current				4.7	4.7	9.7
100.0	100.0	100.0	Total				100.0	100.0	100.0
			LIABILITIES						
3.8	3.1	4.4	Notes Payable-Short Term				1.0	1.9	2.8
3.8	4.3	3.9	Cur. Mat.-L.T.D.				3.5	4.6	3.5
6.1	7.3	5.1	Trade Payables				4.9	4.0	5.0
.0	.1	.2	Income Taxes Payable				.0	.5	.2
9.1	7.9	10.5	All Other Current				10.9	9.5	5.3
22.9	22.7	24.1	Total Current				20.4	20.5	16.8
29.8	33.1	45.5	Long-Term Debt				31.2	31.9	32.6
.9	.6	1.3	Deferred Taxes				.6	.9	2.9
5.2	6.2	3.4	All Other Non-Current				2.4	6.8	4.5
41.2	37.4	25.7	Net Worth				45.6	39.9	43.3
100.0	100.0	100.0	Total Liabilities & Net Worth				100.0	100.0	100.0
			INCOME DATA						
100.0	100.0	100.0	Net Sales				100.0	100.0	100.0
			Gross Profit						
80.6	84.9	80.5	Operating Expenses				88.9	83.5	82.0
19.4	15.1	19.5	Operating Profit				11.1	16.5	18.0
4.1	3.2	3.4	All Other Expenses (net)				-.7	.8	.8
15.3	11.9	16.1	Profit Before Taxes				11.9	15.7	17.2
			RATIOS						
4.0	2.8	2.2	Current				7.1	1.9	2.3
1.8	1.4	1.1					2.9	1.3	1.4
1.0	.7	.7					.8	1.1	1.0
3.5	2.5	1.9	Quick				7.1	1.7	2.0
1.5	1.4	1.0					2.9	1.3	1.0
.8	.7	.6					.6	1.1	.8
16 23.2	23 16.2	16 22.3	Sales/Receivables				0 UND	33 11.0	31 11.6
35 10.5	38 9.7	37 9.9					36 10.2	46 7.9	44 8.3
62 5.9	54 6.7	53 6.9					56 6.5	64 5.7	52 7.0
			Cost of Sales/Inventory						
			Cost of Sales/Payables						
4.2	6.7	9.2	Sales/Working Capital				6.2	11.4	8.3
13.1	22.0	43.0					9.6	35.9	16.1
UND	-20.1	-23.3					-98.6	74.9	-182.1
15.6	10.8	11.8	EBIT/Interest					10.3	36.9
(59) 3.8	(65) 5.1	(52) 5.9						(10) 4.1	(23) 6.2
1.5	1.4	2.9						2.8	3.1
8.2	8.8	6.5	Net Profit + Depr., Dep., Amort./Cur. Mat. L/T/D						
(13) 2.2	(10) 2.3	(10) 3.3							
1.6	1.4	1.7							
.6	1.0	1.1	Fixed/Worth				.5	1.1	1.2
1.4	1.8	1.7					.7	1.6	1.7
3.6	4.2	5.1					7.3	3.6	2.2
.5	.8	.8	Debt/Worth				.2	.8	1.0
1.4	1.5	1.6					1.0	1.6	1.4
5.4	4.8	8.0					8.1	3.5	2.0
61.8	40.8	53.8	% Profit Before Taxes/Tangible Net Worth					102.7	33.7
(64) 18.5	(71) 17.5	(56) 26.9						(10) 20.9	23.6
3.2	2.0	8.7						5.8	9.8
27.4	16.3	18.3	% Profit Before Taxes/Total Assets				32.1	13.1	16.2
6.8	7.1	8.1					14.1	7.3	7.6
1.5	.7	3.1					2.2	3.7	3.4
10.3	4.9	3.5	Sales/Net Fixed Assets				12.1	2.2	2.5
2.1	1.7	1.6					4.9	1.6	1.4
1.1	.8	.9					2.1	1.3	.9
2.6	1.7	1.9	Sales/Total Assets				3.0	1.3	1.3
1.2	1.1	1.1					2.1	1.2	.9
.7	.6	.6					1.4	.8	.6
2.5	3.1	3.7	% Depr., Dep., Amort./Sales					5.4	3.2
(60) 5.2	(60) 7.6	(53) 6.9						(10) 8.3	(18) 5.4
10.8	13.2	10.7						12.2	8.3
4.0	1.3	1.3	% Officers', Directors' Owners' Comp/Sales						
(11) 6.3	(15) 7.1	(11) 2.8							
12.3	14.3	8.3							
2366384M	2876741M	1994880M	Net Sales ($)	3349M	15591M	4435M	73694M	181099M	1716712M
2628858M	2976278M	2301370M	Total Assets ($)	33860M	10673M	4751M	42083M	175096M	2034907M

M = $ thousand MM = $ million

See Pages 9 through 22 for Explanation of Ratios and Data

Current Data Sorted by Assets							Comparative Historical Data	
						Type of Statement		
		1	6		4	Unqualified	8	8
		2	4	2		Reviewed	4	7
	1	5				Compiled	6	5
2	3	2				Tax Returns	4	4
1		6	9	1		Other	27	23
	9 (4/1-9/30/13)		40 (10/1/13-3/31/14)				4/1/09-3/31/10	4/1/10-3/31/11
0-500M	500M-2MM	2-10MM	10-50MM	50-100MM	100-250MM		ALL	ALL
3	4	16	19	3	4	**NUMBER OF STATEMENTS**	49	47
%	%	%	%	%	%	**ASSETS**	%	%
		19.6	13.2			Cash & Equivalents	12.2	9.1
		23.8	15.5			Trade Receivables (net)	17.9	21.2
		1.1	.6			Inventory	2.4	4.0
		2.9	2.9			All Other Current	6.0	4.8
		47.5	32.1			Total Current	38.5	39.1
		38.5	52.2			Fixed Assets (net)	48.9	50.2
		1.8	5.9			Intangibles (net)	3.2	4.2
		12.2	9.8			All Other Non-Current	9.4	6.6
		100.0	100.0			Total	100.0	100.0
						LIABILITIES		
		2.3	2.2			Notes Payable-Short Term	4.6	5.5
		5.8	4.8			Cur. Mat.-L.T.D.	3.9	4.4
		10.1	4.9			Trade Payables	10.3	11.7
		.0	.1			Income Taxes Payable	.3	.3
		9.6	12.6			All Other Current	9.7	8.4
		27.7	24.6			Total Current	28.7	30.4
		32.2	28.0			Long-Term Debt	27.2	31.4
		.0	1.9			Deferred Taxes	1.4	.6
		14.4	5.7			All Other Non-Current	5.1	14.4
		25.7	39.9			Net Worth	37.6	23.2
		100.0	100.0			Total Liabilties & Net Worth	100.0	100.0
						INCOME DATA		
		100.0	100.0			Net Sales	100.0	100.0
						Gross Profit		
		84.6	85.7			Operating Expenses	89.5	89.9
		15.4	14.3			Operating Profit	10.5	10.1
		1.2	.9			All Other Expenses (net)	4.7	3.4
		14.2	13.5			Profit Before Taxes	5.9	6.8
						RATIOS		
		6.1	2.7				2.8	2.5
		1.7	1.8			Current	1.4	1.6
		1.0	.6				.8	.8
		4.2	2.5				2.3	1.9
		1.4	1.3			Quick	1.0	1.0
		1.0	.5				.4	.6
		23 15.7	**35** 10.3				**23** 15.7	**16** 23.5
		46 8.0	**47** 7.8			Sales/Receivables	**38** 9.6	**35** 10.4
		66 5.5	**58** 6.3				**63** 5.8	**61** 6.0
						Cost of Sales/Inventory		
						Cost of Sales/Payables		
		4.0	4.6				4.7	5.9
		15.1	9.6			Sales/Working Capital	11.4	10.2
		484.3	-7.7				-26.2	-26.7
		28.7	42.3				25.6	9.7
		(14) 6.2	(17) 6.8			EBIT/Interest	(35) 2.9	(40) 2.2
		3.4	2.5				1.5	.8
							5.9	6.1
						Net Profit + Depr., Dep., Amort./Cur. Mat. L/T/D	(10) 3.6	(11) 1.7
							1.5	.9
		1.1	.8				.3	.9
		4.0	1.9			Fixed/Worth	1.5	2.1
		7.1	17.1				5.3	-18.8
		.9	.8				.8	1.0
		7.2	1.7			Debt/Worth	1.9	2.8
		88.8	20.6				9.9	-41.2
		211.0	91.9				42.4	43.7
		(14) 92.1	(16) 32.1			% Profit Before Taxes/Tangible Net Worth	(41) 21.5	(34) 14.9
		36.5	10.6				1.4	1.4
		27.0	17.0				19.8	19.0
		15.5	9.6			% Profit Before Taxes/Total Assets	4.8	3.9
		9.2	4.7				.1	-.1
		22.8	4.6				13.3	5.8
		5.1	1.8			Sales/Net Fixed Assets	2.4	2.6
		2.3	1.1				.9	1.2
		2.9	1.3				1.9	2.1
		1.7	1.0			Sales/Total Assets	.9	1.2
		1.2	.8				.5	.7
		.7	3.1				2.5	2.3
		(13) 2.8	(18) 5.9			% Depr., Dep., Amort./Sales	(39) 5.5	(38) 5.0
		4.8	8.5				16.0	15.3
							.9	
						% Officers', Directors' Owners' Comp/Sales	(12) 2.8	
							5.9	
21420M	12266M	158141M	548889M	84720M	515828M	Net Sales ($)	1732681M	1976337M
220M	4410M	84168M	472724M	210531M	547119M	Total Assets ($)	1677439M	1743365M

M = $ thousand MM = $ million

See Pages 9 through 22 for Explanation of Ratios and Data

Comparative Historical Data / Current Data Sorted by Sales

4/1/11-3/31/12 ALL	4/1/12-3/31/13 ALL	4/1/13-3/31/14 ALL	Type of Statement	0-1MM	1-3MM	3-5MM	5-10MM	10-25MM	25MM & OVER
8	8	11	Unqualified			1	1	1	8
7	5	8	Reviewed					5	3
4	4	6	Compiled	1		1	2	2	
8	6	7	Tax Returns	2	3		2		
19	18	17	Other				3	11	3
				9 (4/1-9/30/13)			40 (10/1/13-3/31/14)		
46	41	49	NUMBER OF STATEMENTS	3	3	2	8	19	14
%	%	%	**ASSETS**	%	%	%	%	%	%
17.9	9.6	17.6	Cash & Equivalents					19.8	12.1
14.4	19.8	17.3	Trade Receivables (net)					15.1	17.1
3.6	3.9	.9	Inventory					.7	1.5
4.6	3.5	3.6	All Other Current					2.7	3.6
40.4	36.7	39.4	Total Current					38.3	34.4
46.1	51.9	45.0	Fixed Assets (net)					46.5	52.9
1.9	2.3	4.1	Intangibles (net)					6.5	3.0
11.5	9.0	11.4	All Other Non-Current					8.7	9.8
100.0	100.0	100.0	Total					100.0	100.0
			LIABILITIES						
3.4	3.2	2.8	Notes Payable-Short Term					2.9	1.9
4.2	6.4	4.4	Cur. Mat.-L.T.D.					6.2	3.6
7.5	9.2	6.9	Trade Payables					5.4	6.3
.0	.1	.0	Income Taxes Payable					.0	.2
12.4	8.0	12.1	All Other Current					14.9	12.7
27.5	27.0	26.2	Total Current					29.4	24.7
33.1	33.6	32.8	Long-Term Debt					31.9	30.3
.2	.2	1.1	Deferred Taxes					1.1	2.3
7.4	5.9	8.7	All Other Non-Current					8.3	2.5
31.8	33.3	31.1	Net Worth					29.4	40.2
100.0	100.0	100.0	Total Liabilties & Net Worth					100.0	100.0
			INCOME DATA						
100.0	100.0	100.0	Net Sales					100.0	100.0
			Gross Profit						
86.9	84.7	85.9	Operating Expenses					77.4	89.1
13.1	15.3	14.1	Operating Profit					22.6	10.9
4.6	5.0	1.4	All Other Expenses (net)					3.0	.5
8.6	10.3	12.7	Profit Before Taxes					19.5	10.4
			RATIOS						
2.3	2.3	3.0						3.0	2.1
1.5	1.4	1.8	Current					2.0	1.6
1.0	.6	.9						.6	.9
2.1	2.0	2.5						2.8	1.6
1.2	1.1	1.3	Quick					1.5	1.3
.8	.5	.6						.5	.6
9 40.7	17 21.7	23 15.6						24 14.9	26 13.9
25 14.8	41 8.9	40 9.2	Sales/Receivables					47 7.8	36 10.2
47 7.8	64 5.7	56 6.5						70 5.2	54 6.7
			Cost of Sales/Inventory						
			Cost of Sales/Payables						
8.2	6.6	5.7						3.0	6.8
12.3	16.9	9.6	Sales/Working Capital					6.9	10.7
NM	-17.6	-286.7						-9.1	-79.8
11.0	18.7	19.3						21.8	16.3
(37) 4.9	(32) 3.1	(42) 5.1	EBIT/Interest					(16) 6.3	(12) 3.1
.8	1.6	2.2						3.0	1.9
4.3									
(10) 2.3			Net Profit + Depr., Dep., Amort./Cur. Mat. L/T/D						
.2									
.6	.6	.7						.8	.5
1.1	1.6	2.2	Fixed/Worth					2.2	1.8
3.9	17.8	12.1						17.8	3.4
.9	.8	.9						1.4	1.0
1.7	1.8	2.9	Debt/Worth					2.9	1.8
6.3	21.7	68.9						-72.4	4.4
43.0	111.2	107.0						166.6	51.0
(39) 20.5	(34) 20.4	(39) 37.5	% Profit Before Taxes/Tangible Net Worth					(14) 60.9	23.0
.2	8.0	13.6						17.1	10.6
17.5	17.3	17.8						25.9	18.2
6.4	6.1	9.9	% Profit Before Taxes/Total Assets					14.0	6.9
.0	1.4	3.5						4.9	2.8
22.6	13.6	14.8						5.0	23.3
3.3	2.2	3.3	Sales/Net Fixed Assets					2.0	1.9
.9	.9	1.3						1.1	1.0
3.0	2.8	2.0						1.8	1.8
1.3	1.3	1.2	Sales/Total Assets					1.0	1.2
.6	.6	.8						.8	.8
1.1	2.0	2.4						4.2	2.0
(39) 4.4	(33) 5.0	(41) 3.8	% Depr., Dep., Amort./Sales					(17) 6.1	(12) 3.7
11.1	8.5	6.5						11.1	5.4
1.9	1.6								
(16) 3.9	(11) 2.9		% Officers', Directors' Owners' Comp/Sales						
6.8	5.5								
1402934M	1337807M	1341264M	Net Sales ($)	1691M	6910M	6724M	55251M	280302M	990386M
1311389M	1535053M	1319172M	Total Assets ($)	1029M	4509M	7711M	38781M	339165M	927977M

M = $ thousand MM = $ million

See Pages 9 through 22 for Explanation of Ratios and Data

Current Data Sorted by Assets							Comparative Historical Data	
						Type of Statement		
		2	2	1	2	Unqualified	6	5
	2	4	1			Reviewed	6	3
4	5	5				Compiled	15	13
25	15	4				Tax Returns	60	71
8	12	7	4	2		Other	31	42
24 (4/1-9/30/13)			81 (10/1/13-3/31/14)				**4/1/09-3/31/10**	**4/1/10-3/31/11**
0-500M	**500M-2MM**	**2-10MM**	**10-50MM**	**50-100MM**	**100-250MM**		**ALL**	**ALL**
37	34	22	7	3	2	**NUMBER OF STATEMENTS**	118	134
%	%	%	%	%	%	**ASSETS**	%	%
20.7	14.1	20.0				Cash & Equivalents	12.6	13.2
17.4	10.6	14.8				Trade Receivables (net)	10.9	11.5
4.8	3.6	5.2				Inventory	7.0	6.8
2.8	4.1	3.5				All Other Current	2.9	4.4
45.8	32.3	43.6				Total Current	33.4	35.8
39.4	49.7	47.8				Fixed Assets (net)	47.5	46.7
6.8	9.5	3.6				Intangibles (net)	10.7	10.3
7.9	8.6	5.0				All Other Non-Current	8.4	7.1
100.0	100.0	100.0				Total	100.0	100.0
						LIABILITIES		
9.5	10.6	5.9				Notes Payable-Short Term	12.4	9.3
2.5	4.1	7.2				Cur. Mat.-L.T.D.	9.7	11.3
6.5	8.3	6.4				Trade Payables	7.6	6.7
.0	.4	.4				Income Taxes Payable	.3	.2
13.2	4.4	4.8				All Other Current	10.4	7.9
31.7	27.8	24.7				Total Current	40.5	35.4
41.0	45.1	29.6				Long-Term Debt	51.3	41.7
.0	.2	.5				Deferred Taxes	.3	.2
21.8	4.5	3.3				All Other Non-Current	12.5	11.8
5.4	22.3	42.0				Net Worth	-4.6	10.9
100.0	100.0	100.0				Total Liabilties & Net Worth	100.0	100.0
						INCOME DATA		
100.0	100.0	100.0				Net Sales	100.0	100.0
						Gross Profit		
93.0	90.7	91.3				Operating Expenses	93.1	93.8
7.0	9.3	8.7				Operating Profit	6.9	6.2
-.1	3.0	2.9				All Other Expenses (net)	3.1	1.1
7.1	6.4	5.8				Profit Before Taxes	3.8	5.1
						RATIOS		
4.1	2.6	3.7					1.9	2.0
2.0	1.3	1.4				Current	1.0	1.0
.8	.4	.8					.3	.5
3.8	2.6	3.0					1.7	1.6
1.5	.7	1.2				Quick	.6	.6
.6	.3	.7					.2	.3
0 UND	**0** UND	**9** 42.5					**0** UND	**0** UND
10 37.1	**9** 39.8	**26** 13.8				Sales/Receivables	**8** 48.3	**8** 43.5
21 17.3	**24** 15.0	**36** 10.2					**25** 14.9	**24** 15.3
						Cost of Sales/Inventory		
						Cost of Sales/Payables		
12.6	11.8	6.6					17.1	11.7
21.5	66.1	39.0				Sales/Working Capital	-807.8	UND
-209.7	-7.7	-28.3					-9.6	-24.1
12.9	14.5	20.2					5.6	7.5
(32) 3.9	(29) 3.0	(17) 6.5				EBIT/Interest	(103) 1.7	(111) 3.3
.8	1.3	3.5					.3	1.2
							16.7	
						Net Profit + Depr., Dep., Amort./Cur. Mat. L/T/D	(13) 1.7	
							1.0	
1.0	1.3	.4					1.0	.9
2.6	2.6	1.2				Fixed/Worth	4.8	2.8
-1.5	-6.0	5.8					-1.1	-1.6
.9	1.5	.5					1.7	1.1
7.8	3.6	1.6				Debt/Worth	9.9	5.2
-3.4	-13.1	5.9					-2.9	-4.0
99.9	81.6	47.1					100.0	73.2
(21) 63.5	(24) 22.8	(19) 20.8				% Profit Before Taxes/Tangible Net Worth	(71) 18.1	(81) 25.1
2.6	.4	5.9					-4.3	3.0
43.4	22.6	16.6					19.2	27.8
14.7	4.0	9.3				% Profit Before Taxes/Total Assets	4.6	7.2
.0	.4	4.1					-2.4	.5
30.6	17.1	17.5					19.3	19.6
13.1	5.4	4.2				Sales/Net Fixed Assets	6.0	6.3
6.4	2.2	2.1					3.0	3.4
6.8	3.6	3.0					4.2	4.6
4.9	2.3	1.7				Sales/Total Assets	2.4	2.9
3.3	1.4	1.3					1.5	1.9
1.4	2.4	4.7					2.9	2.2
(27) 3.4	(24) 5.3	(14) 6.1				% Depr., Dep., Amort./Sales	(87) 5.4	(91) 5.4
7.5	10.2	8.9					12.5	9.5
3.6	2.3						2.6	2.9
(23) 5.6	(20) 4.3					% Officers', Directors' Owners' Comp/Sales	(57) 5.4	(74) 4.5
10.7	6.9						9.4	7.9
44497M	**95033M**	**158716M**	**305856M**	**301587M**	**478358M**	Net Sales ($)	**879655M**	**1272914M**
9233M	**38148M**	**71329M**	**175786M**	**202047M**	**337856M**	Total Assets ($)	**534418M**	**695799M**

M = $ thousand MM = $ million

See Pages 9 through 22 for Explanation of Ratios and Data

Comparative Historical Data				Current Data Sorted by Sales					
			Type of Statement						
4	9	7	Unqualified				1	1	5
7	3	7	Reviewed		1	1	3	1	1
11	9	14	Compiled	3	4	2	4	1	
67	62	44	Tax Returns	14	21	7	2		
38	43	33	Other	6	11	5	6	2	3
4/1/11-3/31/12	**4/1/12-3/31/13**	**4/1/13-3/31/14**		**24 (4/1-9/30/13)**			**81 (10/1/13-3/31/14)**		
ALL	**ALL**	**ALL**		**0-1MM**	**1-3MM**	**3-5MM**	**5-10MM**	**10-25MM**	**25MM & OVER**
127	126	105	**NUMBER OF STATEMENTS**	23	37	15	16	5	9
%	%	%	**ASSETS**	%	%	%	%	%	%
16.9	15.1	17.5	Cash & Equivalents	16.6	15.6	22.3	15.3		
13.2	10.9	14.4	Trade Receivables (net)	16.0	11.6	10.5	17.2		
6.1	4.0	4.6	Inventory	3.0	5.5	4.1	4.7		
3.1	2.0	3.5	All Other Current	1.4	4.9	3.2	1.7		
39.4	32.0	39.9	Total Current	36.9	37.6	40.0	39.0		
42.1	48.6	44.4	Fixed Assets (net)	48.2	42.1	51.0	53.4		
8.4	7.6	8.0	Intangibles (net)	11.6	8.9	1.6	2.3		
10.2	11.8	7.7	All Other Non-Current	3.2	11.4	7.4	5.3		
100.0	100.0	100.0	Total	100.0	100.0	100.0	100.0		
			LIABILITIES						
10.2	8.5	8.7	Notes Payable-Short Term	12.2	9.0	10.0	2.1		
7.9	9.5	4.2	Cur. Mat.-L.T.D.	1.6	4.0	5.0	6.3		
9.3	6.5	7.1	Trade Payables	3.5	8.3	7.5	8.8		
.1	.1	.3	Income Taxes Payable	.0	.3	.2	.4		
8.7	7.3	8.5	All Other Current	5.9	12.1	2.9	6.5		
36.2	32.0	28.7	Total Current	23.2	33.6	25.6	24.1		
46.9	48.9	38.0	Long-Term Debt	44.1	42.7	34.4	38.3		
.2	.6	.2	Deferred Taxes	.0	.2	.7	.0		
7.9	13.8	11.0	All Other Non-Current	15.0	15.1	5.3	1.5		
8.8	4.8	22.1	Net Worth	17.6	8.3	33.9	36.2		
100.0	100.0	100.0	Total Liabilties & Net Worth	100.0	100.0	100.0	100.0		
			INCOME DATA						
100.0	100.0	100.0	Net Sales	100.0	100.0	100.0	100.0		
			Gross Profit						
93.5	94.1	91.9	Operating Expenses	78.9	96.0	95.0	97.0		
6.5	5.9	8.1	Operating Profit	21.1	4.0	5.0	3.0		
1.6	1.0	1.6	All Other Expenses (net)	7.5	.2	-.8	-.3		
4.9	5.0	6.5	Profit Before Taxes	13.7	3.9	5.8	3.3		
			RATIOS						
2.6	2.2	3.0		7.8	2.5	12.7	3.5		
1.0	1.0	1.5	Current	1.7	1.5	1.3	1.4		
.6	.5	.6		.5	.4	.5	1.0		
2.1	2.0	3.0		7.2	2.0	6.3	1.7		
.8	.7	1.1	Quick	1.4	.9	.8	1.2		
.3	.3	.4		.3	.4	.4	.8		
0 UND	**0** UND	**0** UND		**0** UND	**0** UND	**3** 120.5	**8** 46.5		
8 43.7	**8** 46.9	**14** 25.2	Sales/Receivables	**17** 21.6	**9** 40.7	**21** 17.5	**22** 16.5		
23 15.6	**24** 15.3	**29** 12.6		**31** 11.8	**19** 18.9	**32** 11.3	**35** 10.4		
			Cost of Sales/Inventory						
			Cost of Sales/Payables						
11.2	17.9	9.1		8.1	13.3	4.8	13.8		
341.0	242.1	35.7	Sales/Working Capital	19.0	53.9	34.7	39.0		
-30.6	-13.7	-19.2		-4.5	-16.0	-18.9	NM		
9.5	8.1	15.6		27.8	6.9	24.6	14.4		
(110) 3.2	(101) 1.9	(89) 4.1	EBIT/Interest	(16) 9.3	(33) 2.4	(13) 6.5	(14) 3.3		
.6	.5	1.3		2.7	.9	2.3	1.0		
		3.8							
		(11) 3.0	Net Profit + Depr., Dep., Amort./Cur. Mat. L/T/D						
		.5							
.7	.9	.7		.9	1.2	.4	.9		
2.6	2.9	2.2	Fixed/Worth	2.8	4.7	1.9	2.2		
-2.2	-2.5	-5.8		-2.8	-3.0	6.9	3.6		
1.1	1.1	1.0		.8	1.5	.5	.8		
5.1	3.9	3.4	Debt/Worth	6.4	10.5	1.6	2.6		
-4.6	-4.8	-13.1		-4.0	-8.2	8.1	3.8		
97.5	69.8	78.7		94.5	88.8	84.6	43.4		
(82) 29.9	(81) 21.2	(74) 22.0	% Profit Before Taxes/Tangible Net Worth	(14) 43.8	(21) 28.8	(12) 15.0	(15) 9.3		
6.2	2.4	5.1		.0	5.2	5.3	-6.0		
28.0	22.0	24.7		60.0	24.1	22.5	17.3		
7.1	5.3	7.7	% Profit Before Taxes/Total Assets	21.2	6.6	6.5	5.2		
-.5	-.7	.7		.1	.6	2.7	-.9		
24.3	18.9	22.0		23.7	26.7	17.4	14.3		
9.3	7.0	8.3	Sales/Net Fixed Assets	4.0	9.9	3.9	6.5		
3.7	3.1	2.9		1.0	5.4	2.6	2.3		
5.2	5.1	4.8		4.6	5.2	3.5	4.6		
2.9	3.2	2.5	Sales/Total Assets	2.1	3.5	1.7	3.1		
1.8	1.5	1.6		.6	2.1	1.4	1.9		
2.5	1.6	2.2		3.2	1.4	1.8			
(85) 5.1	(86) 4.5	(75) 5.1	% Depr., Dep., Amort./Sales	(16) 7.3	(29) 3.2	(12) 5.0			
8.6	9.2	8.2		11.9	8.1	5.6			
2.1	2.3	2.8		5.9	2.8	2.6			
(68) 4.2	(67) 5.0	(52) 4.3	% Officers', Directors' Owners' Comp/Sales	(11) 9.2	(23) 4.4	(10) 4.1			
8.1	9.2	7.9		14.3	7.1	5.9			
2632328M	1348616M	1384047M	Net Sales ($)	10849M	64531M	60009M	119224M	61388M	1068046M
858495M	864116M	834399M	Total Assets ($)	15071M	22838M	31916M	63588M	30446M	670540M

M = $ thousand MM = $ million

See Pages 9 through 22 for Explanation of Ratios and Data

Current Data Sorted by Assets							Comparative Historical Data	
			4		3	Type of Statement Unqualified	5	10
	4	2	5	2		Reviewed	15	15
2	3	4	1			Compiled	12	11
11	8	6				Tax Returns	23	15
9	11	12	9	2	2	Other	32	31
13 (4/1-9/30/13)			87 (10/1/13-3/31/14)				4/1/09-3/31/10 ALL	4/1/10-3/31/11 ALL
0-500M	500M-2MM	2-10MM	10-50MM	50-100MM	100-250MM			
22	26	24	19	4	5	NUMBER OF STATEMENTS	87	82
%	%	%	%	%	%	ASSETS	%	%
22.9	8.6	8.2	9.2			Cash & Equivalents	18.0	13.0
35.6	27.9	27.2	23.5			Trade Receivables (net)	18.3	18.5
4.7	5.4	9.5	13.6			Inventory	5.5	6.0
2.0	3.8	3.4	5.0			All Other Current	5.1	5.5
65.2	45.7	48.3	51.2			Total Current	46.8	42.9
18.6	36.6	40.6	40.3			Fixed Assets (net)	36.0	38.8
5.3	14.6	4.6	3.6			Intangibles (net)	8.2	8.4
11.0	3.1	6.6	4.8			All Other Non-Current	8.9	9.8
100.0	100.0	100.0	100.0			Total	100.0	100.0
						LIABILITIES		
15.5	11.0	2.5	6.3			Notes Payable-Short Term	6.0	12.5
7.7	2.9	6.7	8.4			Cur. Mat.-L.T.D.	7.9	3.5
16.7	8.4	14.7	11.6			Trade Payables	8.5	9.3
.0	.0	.0	.4			Income Taxes Payable	.0	.0
10.9	9.3	9.8	6.8			All Other Current	9.0	13.6
50.8	31.6	33.6	33.5			Total Current	31.5	38.8
32.5	22.8	32.5	22.5			Long-Term Debt	26.1	22.5
.0	.0	.0	1.1			Deferred Taxes	.1	.2
8.0	7.7	4.4	5.6			All Other Non-Current	9.3	6.8
8.8	37.9	29.5	37.2			Net Worth	33.0	31.7
100.0	100.0	100.0	100.0			Total Liabilities & Net Worth	100.0	100.0
						INCOME DATA		
100.0	100.0	100.0	100.0			Net Sales	100.0	100.0
						Gross Profit		
92.5	86.7	92.7	94.8			Operating Expenses	87.8	89.0
7.5	13.3	7.3	5.2			Operating Profit	12.2	11.0
1.6	2.7	.6	.8			All Other Expenses (net)	3.2	2.5
5.9	10.7	6.6	4.4			Profit Before Taxes	9.0	8.5
						RATIOS		
2.8	4.0	3.6	2.5				2.8	3.3
1.4	1.1	1.4	1.5			Current	1.5	1.4
.6	.6	.8	1.0				.8	.7
2.7	3.1	2.8	2.1				2.4	2.5
1.3	1.0	1.1	1.0			Quick	1.2	1.0
.3	.2	.5	.7				.6	.6
0 UND	**6** 58.0	**16** 23.1	**20** 18.7				**1** 293.0	**5** 74.4
16 23.1	**27** 13.6	**33** 10.9	**36** 10.0			Sales/Receivables	**22** 16.7	**26** 14.1
30 12.3	**50** 7.3	**47** 7.7	**53** 6.9				**41** 8.9	**44** 8.4
						Cost of Sales/Inventory		
						Cost of Sales/Payables		
7.1	6.6	6.2	6.0				5.9	5.3
49.9	86.0	26.0	17.3			Sales/Working Capital	24.4	19.4
-62.7	-8.1	-12.0	-734.2				-37.4	-19.4
17.7	17.3	11.6	7.2				15.3	16.5
(11) 4.1	(19) 6.9	(22) 5.4	(17) 5.2			EBIT/Interest	(67) 3.6	(63) 5.1
2.3	2.0	1.4	1.7				1.2	2.1
								2.8
						Net Profit + Depr., Dep., Amort./Cur. Mat. L/T/D		(13) 1.7
								1.3
.0	.2	.7	.6				.1	.3
.9	2.2	1.7	1.5			Fixed/Worth	1.0	1.2
-1.1	18.2	7.0	2.3				3.3	3.6
.5	.9	.9	.8				.5	.6
10.7	3.9	3.5	1.8			Debt/Worth	1.6	1.7
-3.6	24.1	65.0	5.4				8.8	5.3
199.1	93.5	84.3	45.8				58.3	51.6
(12) 45.1	(22) 37.2	(19) 36.9	(16) 23.9			% Profit Before Taxes/Tangible Net Worth	(69) 27.0	(68) 23.4
22.7	20.1	14.9	4.9				4.7	8.0
58.8	20.5	19.2	16.5				22.5	20.4
27.2	11.2	8.2	7.8			% Profit Before Taxes/Total Assets	7.4	6.4
13.0	1.6	1.5	1.1				.5	2.9
UND	64.7	23.3	21.7				82.3	48.1
87.2	9.2	5.0	3.8			Sales/Net Fixed Assets	8.7	5.7
45.5	2.2	1.8	2.2				2.0	2.0
11.8	4.7	3.5	3.6				3.0	3.4
6.3	2.3	1.8	1.7			Sales/Total Assets	1.8	1.8
3.0	1.0	.9	1.2				.9	.7
.8	.9	.7	1.7				1.0	1.5
(12) 1.0	(13) 3.5	(19) 3.9	(16) 4.5			% Depr., Dep., Amort./Sales	(61) 4.1	(61) 3.3
2.6	6.3	7.0	6.4				12.4	13.8
							1.7	1.7
						% Officers', Directors' Owners' Comp/Sales	(25) 2.8	(21) 3.7
							7.1	6.2
33715M	84200M	319861M	833592M	297664M	778797M	Net Sales ($)	1293595M	1443560M
4508M	28680M	119969M	379747M	264030M	744070M	Total Assets ($)	841924M	956031M

M = $ thousand MM = $ million

See Pages 9 through 22 for Explanation of Ratios and Data

Comparative Historical Data / Current Data Sorted by Sales

4/1/11-3/31/12 ALL	4/1/12-3/31/13 ALL	4/1/13-3/31/14 ALL		0-1MM	1-3MM	3-5MM	5-10MM	10-25MM	25MM & OVER
			Type of Statement						
7	5	7	Unqualified						7
18	13	13	Reviewed	1	1	1	2	3	5
11	12	10	Compiled		3	3	3	1	
34	27	25	Tax Returns	9	7	4	2	1	2
34	35	45	Other	9	6	4	8	8	10
				13 (4/1-9/30/13)			87 (10/1/13-3/31/14)		
104	92	100	**NUMBER OF STATEMENTS**	19	17	12	15	13	24
%	%	%	**ASSETS**	%	%	%	%	%	%
14.7	14.7	13.5	Cash & Equivalents	19.7	9.3	7.4	16.0	6.1	17.0
26.1	19.2	27.0	Trade Receivables (net)	28.8	26.4	25.9	24.3	28.0	27.4
5.1	4.9	7.5	Inventory	4.6	1.8	8.1	12.2	14.8	6.4
3.8	5.1	3.5	All Other Current	1.1	2.6	3.9	2.6	5.5	5.3
49.7	44.0	51.4	Total Current	54.2	40.2	45.3	55.2	54.4	56.1
35.0	37.4	34.9	Fixed Assets (net)	36.3	35.0	40.7	31.4	34.3	33.5
6.4	9.5	7.5	Intangibles (net)	7.6	10.8	9.5	6.8	6.2	5.3
8.9	9.1	6.1	All Other Non-Current	1.9	13.9	4.5	6.6	5.1	5.1
100.0	100.0	100.0	Total	100.0	100.0	100.0	100.0	100.0	100.0
			LIABILITIES						
9.1	6.7	8.3	Notes Payable-Short Term	9.0	19.4	4.8	7.0	5.0	4.1
3.4	4.7	6.2	Cur. Mat.-L.T.D.	5.4	7.5	9.1	4.2	7.8	5.0
14.3	10.6	12.1	Trade Payables	10.5	13.7	5.9	10.0	16.7	14.2
.1	.2	.2	Income Taxes Payable	.0	.1	.0	.0	.6	.3
9.6	7.7	9.0	All Other Current	12.9	5.4	10.1	10.2	4.9	9.6
36.4	30.1	35.8	Total Current	37.9	46.1	29.9	31.4	35.0	33.2
22.3	27.0	27.2	Long-Term Debt	16.6	59.1	21.5	25.2	19.4	21.1
.3	.3	.2	Deferred Taxes	.0	.0	.0	.0	.0	1.0
6.7	10.7	6.3	All Other Non-Current	11.3	2.1	11.6	5.0	4.4	4.4
34.4	31.9	30.5	Net Worth	34.3	-7.2	37.0	38.4	41.2	40.3
100.0	100.0	100.0	Total Liabilties & Net Worth	100.0	100.0	100.0	100.0	100.0	100.0
			INCOME DATA						
100.0	100.0	100.0	Net Sales	100.0	100.0	100.0	100.0	100.0	100.0
			Gross Profit						
90.2	91.0	91.1	Operating Expenses	82.5	90.9	93.7	95.2	92.4	93.6
9.8	9.0	8.9	Operating Profit	17.5	9.1	6.3	4.8	7.6	6.4
2.9	1.7	1.3	All Other Expenses (net)	5.2	.8	.1	.3	.8	.3
6.9	7.3	7.5	Profit Before Taxes	12.3	8.3	6.2	4.6	6.8	6.1
			RATIOS						
3.3	3.5	3.4		3.0	2.1	4.6	4.1	4.2	3.1
1.6	1.5	1.4	Current	.9	.8	2.1	1.2	1.4	1.5
.9	.9	.8		.2	.6	.7	.8	.9	1.1
2.7	2.8	2.8		3.0	2.1	3.8	3.6	2.5	2.9
1.3	1.2	1.0	Quick	.9	.8	1.4	1.0	1.0	1.3
.7	.5	.5		.2	.3	.2	.4	.7	.7
8 43.8	0 999.8	12 31.3		0 UND	9 39.2	11 32.5	7 55.4	24 15.3	18 20.5
34 10.8	24 15.0	29 12.5	Sales/Receivables	17 21.9	29 12.5	25 14.5	25 14.7	41 8.9	36 10.2
47 7.7	37 9.9	47 7.8		42 8.6	55 6.6	51 7.2	30 12.0	79 4.6	51 7.2
			Cost of Sales/Inventory						
			Cost of Sales/Payables						
7.3	8.9	6.3		3.6	18.0	5.8	5.8	4.5	5.0
15.1	28.6	27.9	Sales/Working Capital	-230.5	-64.8	34.0	27.7	13.8	20.9
-101.7	-78.0	-30.4		-7.2	-9.3	-10.3	-56.3	-160.1	105.2
17.4	27.7	16.4		32.8	6.9		33.4	12.1	53.9
(86) 6.4	(66) 9.8	(78) 5.3	EBIT/Interest	(10) 5.6	(15) 4.1		(11) 7.0	(11) 4.5	(22) 6.5
1.9	1.5	2.1		1.9	1.6		2.0	1.1	4.7
4.8	15.4	7.3							
(12) 2.5	(11) 4.1	(10) 1.8	Net Profit + Depr., Dep., Amort./Cur. Mat. L/T/D						
1.7	1.7	.9							
.1	.3	.3		.0	2.1	.2	.4	.3	.3
.9	.9	1.7	Fixed/Worth	2.0	16.6	2.0	.9	1.9	.8
3.4	4.1	17.2		-2.8	-.7	6.0	1.8	2.3	2.8
.5	.5	.8		.5	3.1	.6	.8	.4	.6
1.8	2.1	2.4	Debt/Worth	1.7	21.4	1.6	3.6	2.0	1.6
14.2	10.4	27.5		-5.9	-3.7	58.4	19.0	6.1	5.2
67.0	68.2	65.4		149.3	101.6	59.0	75.8	64.8	63.8
(86) 30.0	(76) 33.7	(78) 32.8	% Profit Before Taxes/Tangible Net Worth	(13) 31.2	(10) 63.4	(10) 18.8	(13) 30.6	(11) 29.9	(21) 29.8
7.3	11.4	15.5		19.8	39.5	7.5	7.9	21.3	11.9
20.8	24.9	23.9		28.4	27.6	17.5	32.3	20.3	18.5
6.9	9.4	10.5	% Profit Before Taxes/Total Assets	14.6	15.9	7.8	15.9	8.9	8.2
1.0	.5	2.5		1.3	3.0	1.7	2.6	.3	3.3
58.2	44.3	62.1		89.7	104.1	UND	81.1	21.9	38.5
11.1	10.6	10.6	Sales/Net Fixed Assets	29.2	13.2	4.1	24.5	3.3	8.7
2.2	2.2	2.5		1.7	2.3	1.6	4.6	2.2	3.0
5.4	5.0	4.7		6.0	5.9	3.7	6.1	2.9	4.3
2.4	2.5	2.2	Sales/Total Assets	2.2	2.7	1.8	4.0	1.6	2.2
1.0	1.1	1.1		.9	1.2	.8	1.6	1.0	1.1
.7	.9	.9		.9	1.2			.8	.9
(67) 3.5	(62) 3.4	(65) 3.3	% Depr., Dep., Amort./Sales	(10) 2.2	(11) 3.9			(10) 5.1	(17) 2.2
9.9	8.7	6.6		14.2	6.6			14.0	4.9
2.6	2.5	2.0			1.4				
(34) 5.6	(26) 3.7	(32) 4.4	% Officers', Directors' Owners' Comp/Sales		(10) 5.7				
11.4	7.2	9.9			9.6				
2114606M	2717237M	2347829M	Net Sales ($)	10936M	28944M	46888M	103303M	206999M	1950759M
1309243M	1398879M	1541004M	Total Assets ($)	9224M	16071M	35521M	40151M	174025M	1266012M

M = $ thousand MM = $ million

See Pages 9 through 22 for Explanation of Ratios and Data

Current Data Sorted by Assets							Comparative Historical Data	
						Type of Statement		
	1	5	21	6	10	Unqualified	43	59
3	9	36	34	1	1	Reviewed	70	78
8	24	30	9			Compiled	50	62
23	48	30	2			Tax Returns	56	90
14	52	79	70	11	13	Other	194	206
72 (4/1-9/30/13)		468 (10/1/13-3/31/14)					4/1/09-3/31/10	4/1/10-3/31/11
0-500M	500M-2MM	2-10MM	10-50MM	50-100MM	100-250MM		ALL	ALL
48	134	180	136	18	24	NUMBER OF STATEMENTS	413	495
%	%	%	%	%	%	**ASSETS**	%	%
26.8	17.2	11.7	9.0	4.8	8.4	Cash & Equivalents	13.5	14.2
33.6	46.0	50.2	48.5	38.0	39.9	Trade Receivables (net)	48.1	48.5
.1	.9	.9	.8	.3	.3	Inventory	.7	.8
2.2	3.9	4.8	6.2	14.0	5.3	All Other Current	7.1	5.4
62.7	68.1	67.7	64.6	57.1	54.0	Total Current	69.4	68.9
20.8	22.0	22.9	21.2	23.1	7.4	Fixed Assets (net)	17.4	17.2
4.0	2.9	2.3	5.8	11.6	32.4	Intangibles (net)	4.4	4.5
12.6	7.0	7.1	8.4	8.2	6.2	All Other Non-Current	8.8	9.5
100.0	100.0	100.0	100.0	100.0	100.0	Total	100.0	100.0
						LIABILITIES		
30.4	9.1	8.8	8.8	8.6	2.6	Notes Payable-Short Term	11.9	11.3
.9	2.2	2.6	3.0	4.6	1.4	Cur. Mat.-L.T.D.	3.2	3.2
25.5	26.9	28.5	26.6	16.7	23.2	Trade Payables	27.1	27.8
.0	.1	.1	.2	.5	.2	Income Taxes Payable	.1	.3
17.2	11.7	10.0	13.5	17.6	12.1	All Other Current	11.5	13.6
73.9	50.1	50.0	52.2	48.0	39.6	Total Current	53.8	56.1
13.6	16.9	13.0	13.1	21.4	23.7	Long-Term Debt	11.6	11.2
.0	.1	.1	.6	1.9	2.8	Deferred Taxes	.4	.3
1.0	4.1	2.8	4.6	6.0	4.0	All Other Non-Current	4.3	5.2
11.5	28.9	34.0	29.6	22.7	29.8	Net Worth	29.9	27.2
100.0	100.0	100.0	100.0	100.0	100.0	Total Liabilties & Net Worth	100.0	100.0
						INCOME DATA		
100.0	100.0	100.0	100.0	100.0	100.0	Net Sales	100.0	100.0
						Gross Profit		
93.9	91.4	93.6	94.6	96.8	96.1	Operating Expenses	96.4	94.7
6.1	8.6	6.4	5.4	3.2	3.9	Operating Profit	3.6	5.3
1.5	2.2	1.5	1.2	.1	2.2	All Other Expenses (net)	1.4	.9
4.6	6.4	4.8	4.2	3.1	1.7	Profit Before Taxes	2.1	4.4
						RATIOS		
3.2	2.0	2.1	1.7	1.5	1.6		2.1	1.9
1.3	1.4	1.3	1.2	1.3	1.5	Current	1.3	1.3
.4	.9	1.0	.9	.9	1.0		1.0	.9
3.2	1.9	2.0	1.5	1.5	1.5		1.8	1.7
1.3	1.3	1.3	1.1	1.0	1.3	Quick	1.2	1.2
.4	.7	.8	.8	.8	.9		.8	.8
0 UND	**11** 33.4	**28** 13.2	**34** 10.8	**34** 10.8	**41** 8.9		**28** 12.8	**25** 14.5
12 29.6	**31** 11.6	**38** 9.5	**42** 8.7	**47** 7.8	**46** 7.9	Sales/Receivables	**40** 9.1	**40** 9.2
32 11.3	**46** 8.0	**54** 6.8	**60** 6.1	**58** 6.3	**61** 6.0		**61** 6.0	**56** 6.5
						Cost of Sales/Inventory		
						Cost of Sales/Payables		
13.5	14.3	8.8	12.1	7.6	10.2		9.9	11.1
159.4	27.2	26.3	37.3	28.1	20.7	Sales/Working Capital	26.7	29.6
-26.6	-111.4	-359.5	-64.1	-82.7	79.6		-261.6	-133.4
35.2	31.2	28.4	31.5	15.8	13.2		17.0	25.8
(17) 9.6	(96) 7.0	(134) 6.3	(123) 6.8	5.7	(23) 4.3	EBIT/Interest	(321) 4.1	(378) 8.2
-.5	1.6	1.6	2.1	2.1	.7		.5	2.2
		3.5	12.5				19.5	10.1
		(19) 2.0	(40) 3.0			Net Profit + Depr., Dep., Amort./Cur. Mat. L/T/D	(65) 3.5	(87) 3.4
		1.4	1.2				.9	1.1
.0	.0	.1	.1	.4	.2		.1	.1
.9	.3	.5	.6	1.9	NM	Fixed/Worth	.3	.4
-1.7	3.1	1.9	3.0	-8.0	-.1		1.8	2.1
.4	1.0	.9	1.5	2.0	1.4		1.0	1.1
4.0	2.6	2.3	3.0	4.7	NM	Debt/Worth	2.6	2.8
-5.2	9.4	7.2	12.8	-178.6	-2.0		8.3	10.7
103.6	82.3	61.7	47.6	59.8	52.9		52.4	76.9
(31) 41.9	(112) 31.6	(162) 26.6	(117) 22.4	(13) 18.4	(12) 35.9	% Profit Before Taxes/Tangible Net Worth	(347) 18.1	(418) 33.9
8.4	10.2	4.0	8.4	3.3	17.8		2.0	10.0
76.6	25.1	20.0	13.8	12.3	8.9		15.8	21.2
11.9	11.3	6.2	6.0	6.0	3.7	% Profit Before Taxes/Total Assets	4.9	8.9
-2.3	2.3	1.2	1.6	.5	-.6		-1.3	1.8
UND	703.5	325.0	184.7	64.6	78.1		253.9	305.7
203.4	62.0	46.6	48.4	13.9	37.3	Sales/Net Fixed Assets	50.8	63.8
26.3	16.4	8.9	10.1	4.1	15.2		12.2	14.6
19.3	7.8	6.3	6.1	5.3	3.6		6.3	7.1
8.1	5.4	4.3	3.7	2.3	1.8	Sales/Total Assets	3.9	4.7
3.4	3.0	2.3	1.7	1.4	.8		2.0	2.5
.2	.2	.1	.3	.3	.6		.3	.2
(21) .7	(69) .5	(136) .5	(116) .7	(15) 1.3	(15) .9	% Depr., Dep., Amort./Sales	(283) .8	(352) .5
4.0	4.6	2.5	2.3	3.0	1.1		2.4	1.7
2.0	1.3	1.2	.7				1.3	1.4
(15) 3.8	(59) 2.1	(61) 2.1	(35) 1.6			% Officers', Directors' Owners' Comp/Sales	(125) 3.3	(155) 2.8
5.7	5.2	4.1	3.6				7.9	5.9
118773M	**849413M**	**3690461M**	**11716371M**	**3441013M**	**10270786M**	Net Sales ($)	**23691187M**	**28925914M**
10177M	**152360M**	**841112M**	**3097485M**	**1173972M**	**4147217M**	Total Assets ($)	**6538872M**	**8604907M**

M = $ thousand MM = $ million

See Pages 9 through 22 for Explanation of Ratios and Data

Comparative Historical Data				Current Data Sorted by Sales					
			Type of Statement						
51	36	43	Unqualified			1	1	6	35
87	73	84	Reviewed	3	2	4	7	23	45
76	62	71	Compiled	9	8	2	18	23	11
102	105	103	Tax Returns	20	20	14	22	18	9
252	267	239	Other	12	14	15	34	60	104
				72 (4/1-9/30/13)			468 (10/1/13-3/31/14)		
4/1/11-3/31/12 ALL	4/1/12-3/31/13 ALL	4/1/13-3/31/14 ALL		0-1MM	1-3MM	3-5MM	5-10MM	10-25MM	25MM & OVER
568	543	540	**NUMBER OF STATEMENTS**	44	44	36	82	130	204
%	%	%	**ASSETS**	%	%	%	%	%	%
12.8	15.3	13.4	Cash & Equivalents	14.8	22.9	18.7	16.2	13.4	8.9
50.1	45.2	46.4	Trade Receivables (net)	18.9	30.7	35.9	48.7	51.0	53.8
.8	.9	.8	Inventory	.0	.0	1.4	1.2	.7	.8
4.9	5.2	5.0	All Other Current	1.8	5.0	2.2	2.3	6.2	6.7
68.6	66.7	65.6	Total Current	35.6	58.5	58.3	68.4	71.3	70.1
15.9	18.3	21.4	Fixed Assets (net)	56.4	24.4	21.9	22.5	19.4	13.9
5.3	5.1	5.1	Intangibles (net)	2.5	3.0	4.3	2.1	2.8	9.0
10.2	9.9	7.9	All Other Non-Current	5.7	14.2	15.6	7.0	6.5	7.0
100.0	100.0	100.0	Total	100.0	100.0	100.0	100.0	100.0	100.0
			LIABILITIES						
9.4	9.8	10.5	Notes Payable-Short Term	9.3	21.1	11.3	7.7	11.9	8.6
2.9	2.9	2.5	Cur. Mat.-L.T.D.	1.9	1.8	3.6	2.2	2.4	2.7
26.2	27.8	26.8	Trade Payables	12.1	17.2	23.7	27.5	29.1	30.7
.2	.1	.1	Income Taxes Payable	.0	.0	.2	.2	.1	.2
12.6	11.0	12.3	All Other Current	10.2	16.9	15.0	8.7	11.0	13.6
51.4	51.6	52.2	Total Current	33.5	57.0	53.9	46.3	54.6	55.7
11.2	12.3	14.8	Long-Term Debt	38.5	16.0	9.8	16.0	12.5	11.3
.4	.3	.4	Deferred Taxes	.0	.1	.4	.2	.3	.7
4.9	4.8	3.6	All Other Non-Current	3.9	5.3	1.4	3.8	2.3	4.2
32.1	31.1	29.0	Net Worth	24.1	21.5	34.5	33.7	30.3	28.1
100.0	100.0	100.0	Total Liabilties & Net Worth	100.0	100.0	100.0	100.0	100.0	100.0
			INCOME DATA						
100.0	100.0	100.0	Net Sales	100.0	100.0	100.0	100.0	100.0	100.0
			Gross Profit						
94.4	94.0	93.6	Operating Expenses	70.6	92.4	93.7	95.2	95.4	96.9
5.6	6.0	6.4	Operating Profit	29.4	7.6	6.3	4.8	4.6	3.1
.9	1.0	1.6	All Other Expenses (net)	12.5	1.8	.2	.3	.2	.8
4.7	5.0	4.9	Profit Before Taxes	16.9	5.8	6.2	4.5	4.4	2.3
			RATIOS						
2.1	2.0	2.0		3.3	2.7	2.2	2.7	2.0	1.6
1.3	1.3	1.3	Current	.9	1.2	1.4	1.5	1.3	1.2
1.0	.9	.9		.3	.6	.7	1.0	1.0	.9
1.9	1.8	1.7		3.2	2.7	1.8	2.7	1.8	1.5
1.2	1.2	1.2	Quick	.9	1.1	1.3	1.5	1.3	1.1
.9	.8	.8		.3	.5	.7	.9	.8	.8
25 14.4	**23** 15.8	**24** 15.5		**0** UND	**0** UND	**5** 69.4	**19** 18.9	**29** 12.7	**31** 11.6
39 9.4	**35** 10.4	**38** 9.5	Sales/Receivables	**0** UND	**34** 10.8	**29** 12.7	**40** 9.2	**38** 9.5	**41** 8.8
53 6.9	**51** 7.1	**53** 6.9		**43** 8.5	**58** 6.3	**62** 5.9	**55** 6.6	**51** 7.2	**55** 6.6
			Cost of Sales/Inventory						
			Cost of Sales/Payables						
11.3	11.5	11.2		4.8	8.4	6.0	9.2	11.9	15.4
27.8	33.5	30.1	Sales/Working Capital	UND	30.7	25.2	20.4	25.2	41.7
-999.8	-151.7	-83.1		-4.7	-13.3	-46.7	NM	999.8	-110.9
24.9	34.0	28.9		6.0	19.8	70.0	22.1	23.3	34.9
(417) 7.8	(404) 8.9	(411) 6.7	EBIT/Interest	(12) 2.3	(31) 4.5	(19) 11.9	(61) 5.2	(105) 6.2	(183) 7.5
2.9	2.1	1.7		2.0	-.2	2.2	1.2	1.6	1.9
16.3	9.6	7.6					3.6	4.3	16.6
(94) 2.8	(94) 2.8	(80) 2.7	Net Profit + Depr., Dep., Amort./Cur. Mat. L/T/D				(10) 1.8	(14) 2.6	(52) 2.9
1.2	1.0	1.4					1.1	1.4	1.6
.0	.1	.1		.2	.0	.1	.0	.1	.1
.3	.4	.5	Fixed/Worth	2.3	.7	.3	.5	.4	.5
1.5	2.2	3.1		24.7	516.4	2.6	2.2	1.7	4.4
1.0	.9	1.0		.6	.9	.5	.8	1.0	1.5
2.4	2.3	2.9	Debt/Worth	2.1	3.2	2.6	2.4	2.2	3.6
7.9	10.1	13.7		248.5	757.7	NM	8.7	7.7	41.4
76.7	68.1	64.5		54.5	86.4	90.3	80.5	57.8	54.8
(494) 35.8	(446) 31.2	(447) 27.3	% Profit Before Taxes/Tangible Net Worth	(36) 17.1	(34) 41.8	(27) 24.7	(74) 30.7	(116) 29.4	(160) 24.9
13.8	10.4	7.8		5.6	.9	9.2	6.8	9.6	8.1
22.3	22.5	18.6		11.9	32.1	25.3	28.9	20.3	14.7
9.8	9.8	7.6	% Profit Before Taxes/Total Assets	3.8	6.2	11.0	13.0	7.8	5.7
3.2	2.0	1.2		.9	-4.0	4.4	.8	1.3	1.3
452.7	349.6	334.1		UND	748.9	257.7	396.0	269.0	316.9
88.5	73.1	52.6	Sales/Net Fixed Assets	2.3	37.9	27.6	44.3	62.9	67.1
17.4	13.4	11.1		.1	6.4	7.9	16.4	12.3	16.8
7.1	7.1	6.8		3.1	5.3	7.8	8.0	7.2	6.7
4.7	4.6	4.3	Sales/Total Assets	.6	2.7	3.7	5.5	4.8	4.5
2.6	2.3	2.1		.1	1.5	1.5	2.7	2.7	2.7
.1	.2	.2		7.5	.3	.5	.2	.2	.2
(374) .5	(373) .6	(372) .7	% Depr., Dep., Amort./Sales	(28) 20.1	(25) 3.5	(19) 1.1	(47) .5	(93) .5	(160) .5
1.6	1.6	2.4		25.5	5.1	3.1	1.8	1.8	1.3
1.4	1.1	1.2			2.8	1.6	1.5	.9	.8
(179) 2.4	(172) 2.3	(172) 2.1	% Officers', Directors' Owners' Comp/Sales		(21) 5.1	(18) 2.0	(23) 2.1	(54) 2.1	(50) 1.5
5.0	4.4	4.7			8.8	5.4	5.4	3.4	2.8
29495185M	**35668015M**	**30086817M**	Net Sales ($)	**17985M**	**86054M**	**138816M**	**591280M**	**2127913M**	**27124769M**
8957248M	**10557324M**	**9422323M**	Total Assets ($)	**50688M**	**60527M**	**155989M**	**196504M**	**773177M**	**8185438M**

M = $ thousand MM = $ million

See Pages 9 through 22 for Explanation of Ratios and Data

Current Data Sorted by Assets							Comparative Historical Data	
						Type of Statement		
	1		2	1	2	Unqualified	4	8
		4	4	2		Reviewed	15	9
2	2	1				Compiled	11	10
6	6	4				Tax Returns	13	10
4	10	11	2	1	1	Other	33	21
7 (4/1-9/30/13)			59 (10/1/13-3/31/14)				4/1/09-3/31/10	4/1/10-3/31/11
0-500M	500M-2MM	2-10MM	10-50MM	50-100MM	100-250MM		ALL	ALL
12	19	20	8	4	3	NUMBER OF STATEMENTS	76	58
%	%	%	%	%	%	**ASSETS**	%	%
23.5	15.7	9.0				Cash & Equivalents	12.4	12.2
21.8	39.8	33.1				Trade Receivables (net)	29.7	32.0
5.7	1.6	7.1				Inventory	11.4	8.4
1.0	.6	1.6				All Other Current	2.6	4.3
52.0	57.8	50.9				Total Current	56.1	56.8
23.2	22.4	28.0				Fixed Assets (net)	28.5	24.2
10.6	6.7	6.7				Intangibles (net)	4.8	7.4
14.1	13.1	14.4				All Other Non-Current	10.6	11.6
100.0	100.0	100.0				Total	100.0	100.0
						LIABILITIES		
24.1	9.9	9.7				Notes Payable-Short Term	16.9	8.8
5.0	5.4	3.2				Cur. Mat.-L.T.D.	4.3	2.3
13.5	23.2	16.3				Trade Payables	14.8	12.8
.0	.0	.1				Income Taxes Payable	.1	.1
11.8	14.0	15.3				All Other Current	13.7	13.5
54.5	52.6	44.6				Total Current	49.8	37.3
33.6	44.4	14.5				Long-Term Debt	14.9	17.4
.0	.0	.1				Deferred Taxes	.3	1.0
4.6	4.4	12.1				All Other Non-Current	2.9	8.0
7.4	-1.5	28.8				Net Worth	32.2	36.2
100.0	100.0	100.0				Total Liabilties & Net Worth	100.0	100.0
						INCOME DATA		
100.0	100.0	100.0				Net Sales	100.0	100.0
						Gross Profit		
95.3	89.7	91.9				Operating Expenses	90.6	91.1
4.7	10.3	8.1				Operating Profit	9.4	8.9
2.5	2.9	1.1				All Other Expenses (net)	2.4	2.0
2.2	7.4	7.0				Profit Before Taxes	7.0	6.9
						RATIOS		
14.6	2.0	3.0					2.6	3.9
.8	1.2	1.5				Current	1.4	1.7
.2	.4	.8					.9	1.0
13.5	2.0	2.6					2.4	2.6
.6	1.1	1.3				Quick	1.3	1.3
.1	.4	.7					.6	.5
0 UND	**4** 83.5	**29** 12.4					**29** 12.7	**24** 14.9
6 63.6	**28** 13.2	**45** 8.1				Sales/Receivables	**45** 8.0	**45** 8.1
35 10.5	**46** 8.0	**51** 7.1					**61** 6.0	**62** 5.9
						Cost of Sales/Inventory		
						Cost of Sales/Payables		
17.5	14.7	6.3					6.3	6.9
UND	38.1	17.2				Sales/Working Capital	15.5	14.5
-8.5	-9.0	-13.8					-51.0	NM
	51.9	30.9					21.0	19.4
	(14) 9.9	(18) 12.3				EBIT/Interest	(59) 5.0	(42) 5.2
	4.2	2.7					1.3	.1
							4.2	
						Net Profit + Depr., Dep., Amort./Cur. Mat. L/T/D	(12) 1.9	
							1.1	
.0	.2	.3					.3	.1
29.3	.8	1.3				Fixed/Worth	.8	.7
-3.2	-1.5	25.4					2.4	3.4
5.5	1.8	.8					.7	.8
NM	5.6	1.8				Debt/Worth	1.9	1.9
-9.2	-18.9	73.4					8.1	7.4
	240.5	74.8					56.6	65.6
	(13) 75.7	(16) 41.5				% Profit Before Taxes/Tangible Net Worth	(64) 27.5	(46) 19.2
	18.0	20.7					7.8	3.4
58.6	26.2	27.9					19.4	24.9
18.4	16.2	16.9				% Profit Before Taxes/Total Assets	8.0	6.5
-3.8	7.1	1.4					2.2	.4
UND	129.0	29.6					31.7	48.4
68.9	38.2	9.3				Sales/Net Fixed Assets	12.1	19.7
5.1	14.4	4.1					5.1	7.9
9.6	6.1	3.2					3.5	3.9
7.4	4.5	2.1				Sales/Total Assets	2.5	2.8
2.3	2.5	1.8					1.3	1.7
	.3	.7					.9	.6
	(14) 1.9	(19) 1.8				% Depr., Dep., Amort./Sales	(58) 2.1	(42) 1.6
	4.1	4.1					3.8	3.0
	3.2						1.8	1.8
	(12) 5.5					% Officers', Directors' Owners' Comp/Sales	(25) 4.6	(18) 3.9
	7.7						7.2	6.4
17729M	96121M	221903M	317858M	769469M	761496M	Net Sales ($)	1577275M	1495294M
3366M	21026M	88879M	186978M	260613M	545854M	Total Assets ($)	674622M	629658M

M = $ thousand MM = $ million

See Pages 9 through 22 for Explanation of Ratios and Data

Comparative Historical Data | **Current Data Sorted by Sales**

4/1/11-3/31/12 ALL	4/1/12-3/31/13 ALL	4/1/13-3/31/14 ALL	Type of Statement	0-1MM	1-3MM	3-5MM	5-10MM	10-25MM	25MM & OVER
9	5	6	Unqualified		1			1	4
14	8	10	Reviewed				3	3	4
10	7	5	Compiled	1	1	1	1	1	
17	21	16	Tax Returns	5	6	2	2	1	
26	35	29	Other	1	6	3	5	11	3
				7 (4/1-9/30/13)			59 (10/1/13-3/31/14)		
76	76	66	**NUMBER OF STATEMENTS**	7	14	6	11	17	11
%	%	%	**ASSETS**	%	%	%	%	%	%
17.1	17.0	13.4	Cash & Equivalents		23.7		20.5	7.1	7.9
31.3	28.3	30.0	Trade Receivables (net)		24.5		43.2	32.5	28.0
9.5	10.0	9.1	Inventory		1.5		3.3	11.7	23.2
2.2	3.0	1.5	All Other Current		1.0		.3	3.6	1.0
60.1	58.3	54.0	Total Current		50.7		67.4	54.9	60.2
24.5	28.2	26.1	Fixed Assets (net)		17.6		20.7	28.5	26.9
4.7	3.7	7.5	Intangibles (net)		14.1		1.6	4.4	4.0
10.8	9.9	12.3	All Other Non-Current		17.6		10.4	12.2	8.8
100.0	100.0	100.0	Total		100.0		100.0	100.0	100.0
			LIABILITIES						
5.9	9.7	12.9	Notes Payable-Short Term		10.7		13.0	11.4	11.2
3.4	4.0	4.0	Cur. Mat.-L.T.D.		4.8		.8	3.1	2.7
17.0	12.4	17.3	Trade Payables		14.8		19.4	19.6	15.2
.0	.2	.0	Income Taxes Payable		.0		.1	.1	.0
16.6	13.8	12.6	All Other Current		9.8		16.3	16.1	7.4
42.9	40.1	46.9	Total Current		40.0		49.6	50.2	36.5
19.0	21.4	26.8	Long-Term Debt		66.5		11.0	14.8	11.1
.1	.3	.1	Deferred Taxes		.0		.1	.1	.1
6.8	10.2	7.8	All Other Non-Current		5.8		3.9	11.3	4.0
31.2	28.0	18.4	Net Worth		-12.3		35.4	23.6	48.3
100.0	100.0	100.0	Total Liabilties & Net Worth		100.0		100.0	100.0	100.0
			INCOME DATA						
100.0	100.0	100.0	Net Sales		100.0		100.0	100.0	100.0
			Gross Profit						
89.1	90.3	92.9	Operating Expenses		88.2		95.4	96.1	95.3
10.9	9.7	7.1	Operating Profit		11.8		4.6	3.9	4.7
2.1	1.8	2.0	All Other Expenses (net)		2.9		.2	.9	.8
8.8	7.9	5.2	Profit Before Taxes		8.9		4.4	3.0	3.9
			RATIOS						
2.6	2.9	2.1			6.3		3.4	1.6	3.1
1.6	1.5	1.3	Current		1.3		2.1	1.3	1.6
1.1	.9	.7			.4		.8	.7	.9
2.4	2.2	2.0			5.9		3.1	1.3	2.3
1.4	1.0	1.0	Quick		1.1		2.1	.8	.8
.7	.5	.4			.2		.8	.4	.5
13 27.3	**21** 17.4	**19** 19.0			**0** UND		**26** 14.2	**24** 14.9	**34** 10.7
38 9.5	**38** 9.6	**33** 10.9	Sales/Receivables		**14** 25.8		**46** 7.9	**35** 10.3	**41** 9.0
58 6.3	**54** 6.8	**49** 7.5			**33** 11.1		**58** 6.3	**50** 7.3	**60** 6.1
			Cost of Sales/Inventory						
			Cost of Sales/Payables						
6.3	6.3	9.0			11.7		6.3	7.1	6.3
15.0	15.5	31.7	Sales/Working Capital		35.1		11.4	21.6	11.7
185.7	-85.4	-20.5			-8.4		-17.8	-32.9	-40.1
71.3	37.5	42.9						55.4	175.4
(55) 11.4	(58) 6.7	(52) 10.0	EBIT/Interest					8.9	(10) 15.5
2.2	1.4	1.5						1.2	.4
10.0	7.8								
(14) 3.1	(10) 2.1		Net Profit + Depr., Dep., Amort./Cur. Mat. L/T/D						
2.3	-.3								
.1	.1	.2			.0		.2	.4	.1
.5	.5	1.1	Fixed/Worth		21.7		.5	.7	.3
3.2	3.6	-27.5			-.5		-1.5	NM	1.9
.5	.6	1.3			2.4		.5	1.0	.4
1.6	1.7	3.9	Debt/Worth		NM		1.4	2.9	1.5
7.1	18.3	-35.4			-2.7		-25.8	NM	4.5
109.5	86.1	79.9						84.8	41.7
(65) 43.3	(63) 40.2	(48) 39.4	% Profit Before Taxes/Tangible Net Worth					(13) 37.2	14.6
13.5	14.0	9.2						7.3	2.6
34.9	31.5	25.2			33.5		31.1	24.9	17.9
12.2	11.5	13.4	% Profit Before Taxes/Total Assets		22.3		14.4	9.5	5.8
4.0	3.8	1.4			15.6		-.1	.6	.3
74.4	55.4	66.7			UND		129.0	38.7	59.9
22.1	11.2	16.0	Sales/Net Fixed Assets		28.7		38.2	9.6	10.8
7.1	5.3	4.3			13.1		6.7	3.8	3.6
4.4	3.9	4.9			8.2		6.7	5.4	3.4
2.9	2.7	2.6	Sales/Total Assets		3.8		3.4	2.1	2.4
1.8	1.8	1.7			2.4		2.0	1.2	1.5
.6	.9	.7						.7	
(53) 1.3	(56) 1.7	(49) 1.5	% Depr., Dep., Amort./Sales					(16) 1.2	
3.7	4.4	4.6						3.7	
1.7	2.8	2.5							
(25) 4.7	(26) 5.0	(27) 5.5	% Officers', Directors' Owners' Comp/Sales						
6.8	11.1	7.6							
1837238M	1495965M	2184576M	Net Sales ($)	3074M	29184M	24908M	76706M	242023M	1808681M
741149M	751235M	1106716M	Total Assets ($)	4668M	11251M	8265M	27212M	150236M	905084M

M = $ thousand MM = $ million

See Pages 9 through 22 for Explanation of Ratios and Data

Current Data Sorted by Assets							Comparative Historical Data	
						Type of Statement		
		3	5	1	3	Unqualified	23	15
	1	7	4			Reviewed	17	16
4	3	6	2		1	Compiled	15	13
13	10	4				Tax Returns	27	22
11	11	15	12	3	1	Other	48	62
10 (4/1-9/30/13)		110 (10/1/13-3/31/14)					4/1/09-3/31/10 ALL	4/1/10-3/31/11 ALL
0-500M	**500M-2MM**	**2-10MM**	**10-50MM**	**50-100MM**	**100-250MM**			
28	25	35	23	4	5	**NUMBER OF STATEMENTS**	130	128
%	%	%	%	%	%	**ASSETS**	%	%
21.8	16.9	14.6	16.6			Cash & Equivalents	16.0	15.3
19.8	24.1	37.4	34.8			Trade Receivables (net)	29.3	28.2
.4	2.5	3.8	1.9			Inventory	5.6	3.9
2.7	5.0	4.1	4.7			All Other Current	5.0	3.7
44.7	48.4	59.9	58.0			Total Current	56.0	51.2
37.8	36.5	33.2	36.5			Fixed Assets (net)	30.2	34.2
4.0	1.4	1.8	1.1			Intangibles (net)	6.4	6.9
13.3	13.7	5.1	4.3			All Other Non-Current	7.5	7.8
100.0	100.0	100.0	100.0			Total	100.0	100.0
						LIABILITIES		
7.5	11.4	12.2	6.0			Notes Payable-Short Term	6.5	8.2
7.8	4.2	3.7	2.6			Cur. Mat.-L.T.D.	4.9	4.8
13.1	16.7	23.0	18.2			Trade Payables	14.8	10.4
.0	.2	.1	.1			Income Taxes Payable	.2	.4
15.2	11.5	9.7	10.3			All Other Current	12.4	11.8
43.6	44.0	48.6	37.3			Total Current	38.7	35.5
18.3	18.3	23.5	20.8			Long-Term Debt	23.1	23.5
.6	.0	.0	1.3			Deferred Taxes	.4	.4
21.8	7.0	3.4	3.2			All Other Non-Current	7.7	8.2
15.7	30.7	24.4	37.4			Net Worth	30.1	32.4
100.0	100.0	100.0	100.0			Total Liabilities & Net Worth	100.0	100.0
						INCOME DATA		
100.0	100.0	100.0	100.0			Net Sales	100.0	100.0
						Gross Profit		
87.8	93.7	92.1	87.9			Operating Expenses	92.0	90.1
12.2	6.3	7.9	12.1			Operating Profit	8.0	9.9
1.5	.9	2.2	2.2			All Other Expenses (net)	1.6	2.1
10.7	5.4	5.7	9.9			Profit Before Taxes	6.4	7.8
						RATIOS		
3.2	2.9	1.5	2.0				2.7	2.5
1.0	1.5	1.0	1.5			Current	1.4	1.4
.5	.6	.8	1.2				.9	.9
3.2	2.6	1.4	1.8				2.3	2.1
.9	1.2	.9	1.2			Quick	1.2	1.2
.5	.5	.6	.9				.7	.6
0 UND	0 UND	13 27.4	27 13.5				16 23.1	5 78.8
4 85.5	24 15.0	32 11.3	40 9.1			Sales/Receivables	33 11.2	34 10.7
28 13.2	40 9.2	53 6.9	66 5.5				53 6.9	60 6.1
						Cost of Sales/Inventory		
						Cost of Sales/Payables		
22.9	6.7	13.7	6.2				7.8	7.2
NM	25.0	610.8	12.0			Sales/Working Capital	18.8	26.4
-7.6	-27.0	-21.5	66.6				-74.3	-161.5
31.1	14.2	10.0	33.1				17.0	22.4
(17) 12.6	(20) 7.9	(25) 4.0	(20) 6.4			EBIT/Interest	(94) 4.8	(102) 5.2
2.2	.9	1.0	3.3				1.6	1.7
							7.7	7.7
						Net Profit + Depr., Dep., Amort./Cur. Mat. L/T/D	(18) 3.2	(11) 3.8
							1.4	1.3
.3	.2	.1	.1				.2	.2
1.0	.8	1.4	.9			Fixed/Worth	.9	1.0
13.5	12.8	10.2	2.3				3.6	5.9
.5	.8	1.3	1.0				.6	.7
2.3	2.4	4.8	2.6			Debt/Worth	1.9	2.1
NM	42.7	101.9	4.2				42.1	17.6
128.8	111.0	79.6	62.9				67.7	62.6
(21) 33.3	(21) 31.1	(28) 39.4	34.1			% Profit Before Taxes/Tangible Net Worth	(101) 23.1	(102) 23.7
11.6	6.8	10.0	16.8				7.1	4.3
57.1	19.1	28.6	25.8				17.9	20.7
14.4	10.6	6.1	7.5			% Profit Before Taxes/Total Assets	8.7	9.5
4.0	-.4	.1	4.8				1.7	.9
539.3	53.9	214.8	96.9				66.5	64.3
31.6	10.3	22.7	8.8			Sales/Net Fixed Assets	13.9	11.2
4.8	5.6	2.9	1.4				3.7	3.3
10.2	5.2	5.8	4.1				4.8	4.3
4.2	2.9	2.9	2.1			Sales/Total Assets	2.5	2.4
1.9	1.9	1.7	.9				1.4	1.3
1.4	.2	.3	.4				.8	.8
(13) 7.1	(18) 1.3	(28) .7	(19) 2.3			% Depr., Dep., Amort./Sales	(91) 2.2	(86) 2.9
43.8	3.7	5.3	6.3				5.9	8.5
	1.0						1.9	1.6
	(10) 1.7					% Officers', Directors' Owners' Comp/Sales	(38) 4.0	(43) 3.3
	3.9						6.7	7.8
36211M	127066M	636449M	1317350M	587480M	1568079M	Net Sales ($)	4528771M	3794736M
5885M	33337M	172473M	519261M	260156M	749938M	Total Assets ($)	2196723M	1871289M

M = $ thousand MM = $ million

See Pages 9 through 22 for Explanation of Ratios and Data

Comparative Historical Data				Current Data Sorted by Sales					
			Type of Statement						
18	15	12	Unqualified		1			1	10
18	11	12	Reviewed	1	1		2	7	1
21	14	16	Compiled	2	3	2	4	3	2
25	27	27	Tax Returns	10	5	4	5	3	
54	59	53	Other	5	9	6	7	9	17
				10 (4/1-9/30/13)			110 (10/1/13-3/31/14)		
4/1/11-3/31/12 ALL	4/1/12-3/31/13 ALL	4/1/13-3/31/14 ALL		0-1MM	1-3MM	3-5MM	5-10MM	10-25MM	25MM & OVER
136	126	120	**NUMBER OF STATEMENTS**	18	19	12	18	23	30
%	%	%	**ASSETS**	%	%	%	%	%	%
17.1	15.9	17.3	Cash & Equivalents	14.5	24.9	17.8	15.7	15.2	16.6
32.1	34.9	29.2	Trade Receivables (net)	14.7	24.8	9.7	31.2	45.1	35.0
5.3	2.5	2.5	Inventory	.1	.5	3.0	4.3	1.7	4.6
4.0	5.1	4.0	All Other Current	2.9	4.5	5.3	1.8	4.0	5.2
58.5	58.3	53.0	Total Current	32.3	54.7	35.7	52.9	66.0	61.4
27.7	27.6	35.2	Fixed Assets (net)	51.1	25.7	53.1	39.8	26.7	28.3
5.9	3.4	3.0	Intangibles (net)	5.5	.9	.4	1.8	2.6	4.9
7.9	10.7	8.8	All Other Non-Current	10.8	18.8	10.8	5.5	4.7	5.5
100.0	100.0	100.0	Total	100.0	100.0	100.0	100.0	100.0	100.0
			LIABILITIES						
9.7	9.5	9.3	Notes Payable-Short Term	8.9	11.4	4.0	14.8	9.4	6.9
4.2	3.9	4.4	Cur. Mat.-L.T.D.	9.7	3.3	7.5	3.5	3.2	2.0
15.2	16.2	17.6	Trade Payables	8.9	10.0	11.5	22.4	27.8	19.5
.2	.2	.1	Income Taxes Payable	.0	.0	.4	.0	.1	.2
10.1	8.3	11.4	All Other Current	5.5	27.7	8.0	5.8	8.8	11.3
39.3	38.0	42.8	Total Current	33.0	52.4	31.3	46.6	49.2	39.9
19.3	20.2	20.3	Long-Term Debt	24.6	19.2	32.5	22.9	13.9	16.9
.4	.2	.5	Deferred Taxes	1.0	.0	.0	.0	.8	.7
6.9	7.4	8.3	All Other Non-Current	17.7	22.6	8.4	2.6	1.6	2.1
34.1	34.2	28.2	Net Worth	23.7	5.9	27.8	28.0	34.4	40.4
100.0	100.0	100.0	Total Liabilties & Net Worth	100.0	100.0	100.0	100.0	100.0	100.0
			INCOME DATA						
100.0	100.0	100.0	Net Sales	100.0	100.0	100.0	100.0	100.0	100.0
			Gross Profit						
91.1	91.1	90.4	Operating Expenses	75.6	95.0	96.8	94.1	93.4	89.5
8.9	8.9	9.6	Operating Profit	24.4	5.0	3.2	5.9	6.6	10.5
1.6	1.2	1.7	All Other Expenses (net)	6.6	.0	2.0	1.3	.6	.5
7.3	7.8	7.9	Profit Before Taxes	17.8	5.0	1.2	4.6	6.0	10.0
			RATIOS						
3.3	3.4	2.3		1.8	7.4	2.9	2.1	2.3	2.6
1.4	1.6	1.2	Current	.7	1.6	1.1	1.0	1.1	1.5
.9	1.0	.8		.5	.5	.5	.7	1.0	1.1
3.0	3.1	2.0		1.8	7.4	2.7	1.8	1.8	1.8
1.2	1.3	1.1	Quick	.7	1.2	.8	.9	1.0	1.2
.6	.8	.6		.5	.5	.3	.6	.8	.8
16 23.1	**14** 26.4	**5** 74.6		**0** UND	**0** UND	**0** UND	**0** UND	**30** 12.3	**26** 14.2
36 10.0	**29** 12.5	**31** 11.7	Sales/Receivables	**4** 87.7	**18** 20.3	**0** UND	**30** 12.0	**46** 7.9	**35** 10.3
55 6.6	**46** 7.9	**51** 7.2		**33** 11.0	**49** 7.4	**29** 12.8	**56** 6.5	**53** 6.9	**59** 6.2
			Cost of Sales/Inventory						
			Cost of Sales/Payables						
6.5	7.2	8.9		25.5	5.1	11.9	14.2	7.3	9.7
20.3	18.2	34.6	Sales/Working Capital	-29.9	25.8	UND	-250.4	76.8	14.9
-76.3	915.7	-31.3		-2.9	-13.0	-23.9	-20.2	-225.4	92.8
23.7	30.5	20.6		20.0	15.6	11.9	11.2	35.5	54.7
(102) 6.6	(88) 10.0	(89) 6.3	EBIT/Interest	(11) 6.5	(14) 10.0	(10) 4.1	(13) 1.0	(18) 6.4	(23) 9.8
1.8	1.6	2.1		2.0	1.2	1.1	-.2	2.3	4.5
7.6	10.8	9.2							
(24) 2.5	(14) 4.4	(14) 4.0	Net Profit + Depr., Dep., Amort./Cur. Mat. L/T/D						
1.5	1.9	1.9							
.1	.1	.2		.6	.0	.8	.2	.1	.3
.7	.6	.9	Fixed/Worth	1.8	.6	2.6	1.3	1.3	.5
4.1	2.0	3.8		29.9	-1.9	15.1	11.1	2.3	2.0
.7	.6	.7		1.0	.5	.7	1.1	.5	.9
2.1	1.9	2.6	Debt/Worth	3.4	3.4	2.4	3.3	4.2	2.1
11.1	5.2	15.3		NM	-3.9	43.6	14.1	19.6	3.6
86.6	82.1	72.5		107.0	132.3	438.2	52.6	84.5	63.9
(111) 28.0	(108) 40.2	(101) 33.3	% Profit Before Taxes/Tangible Net Worth	(14) 30.6	(13) 27.9	(11) 15.0	(15) 27.8	(21) 49.2	(27) 33.3
11.5	13.9	15.5		5.5	11.3	-19.7	.7	27.3	16.8
23.2	30.5	24.4		30.9	29.5	13.6	23.1	28.6	27.8
11.4	13.2	10.5	% Profit Before Taxes/Total Assets	10.0	14.0	4.2	6.7	11.8	14.8
2.1	1.2	2.4		2.8	2.4	-10.5	-2.3	3.0	5.9
81.4	132.7	85.8		32.1	181.7	29.1	151.4	225.4	65.0
22.4	17.2	12.4	Sales/Net Fixed Assets	3.8	43.2	6.6	10.7	33.5	16.4
5.4	5.9	3.2		.4	6.9	2.2	3.3	3.2	5.2
4.9	5.9	5.0		3.4	8.9	8.2	5.4	6.3	4.6
2.9	3.7	2.8	Sales/Total Assets	1.2	3.5	2.8	3.1	3.0	3.1
1.6	1.8	1.5		.3	1.8	1.3	1.9	1.5	1.6
.5	.6	.3		9.8	.2		.2	.3	.3
(99) 1.6	(89) 1.5	(83) 1.9	% Depr., Dep., Amort./Sales	(10) 21.8	(13) .7		(13) 1.5	(18) 1.4	(23) .9
4.2	3.9	6.3		67.8	6.7		5.2	5.7	3.3
2.2	1.0	1.2							
(49) 3.0	(41) 2.0	(33) 2.9	% Officers', Directors' Owners' Comp/Sales						
8.0	5.9	5.8							
5622159M	5319891M	4272635M	Net Sales ($)	7283M	35782M	47525M	132893M	372893M	3676259M
2203393M	2328408M	1741050M	Total Assets ($)	12289M	28433M	22800M	94216M	183387M	1399925M

M = $ thousand MM = $ million

See Pages 9 through 22 for Explanation of Ratios and Data

Current Data Sorted by Assets							Comparative Historical Data	
						Type of Statement		
			2	1	1	Unqualified	12	16
	4	11	4			Reviewed	15	17
1	5	3	2			Compiled	14	11
8	8	7				Tax Returns	21	16
8	6	13	6	1	4	Other	53	49
6 (4/1-9/30/13)		89 (10/1/13-3/31/14)					4/1/09-3/31/10 ALL	4/1/10-3/31/11 ALL
0-500M	500M-2MM	2-10MM	10-50MM	50-100MM	100-250MM			
17	23	34	14	2	5	**NUMBER OF STATEMENTS**	115	109
%	%	%	%	%	%	**ASSETS**	%	%
21.6	16.5	8.1	14.9			Cash & Equivalents	12.9	11.9
16.6	44.6	52.8	30.4			Trade Receivables (net)	34.3	35.7
.0	.0	.0	.6			Inventory	.7	1.3
4.9	4.2	2.2	10.0			All Other Current	5.1	5.7
43.0	65.4	63.1	56.0			Total Current	53.0	54.6
28.1	21.4	20.7	18.1			Fixed Assets (net)	26.9	24.1
12.7	6.6	7.5	18.8			Intangibles (net)	11.0	13.1
16.2	6.6	8.7	7.1			All Other Non-Current	9.1	8.2
100.0	100.0	100.0	100.0			Total	100.0	100.0
						LIABILITIES		
23.6	19.1	12.7	1.6			Notes Payable-Short Term	15.9	14.5
1.3	3.6	3.8	2.1			Cur. Mat.-L.T.D.	5.3	5.9
7.2	19.1	19.2	13.4			Trade Payables	11.5	12.3
.0	.5	.1	.2			Income Taxes Payable	.2	.3
17.9	8.9	9.7	17.4			All Other Current	14.5	11.0
50.0	51.3	45.5	34.8			Total Current	47.5	44.0
25.8	22.5	14.8	8.9			Long-Term Debt	21.2	23.1
.0	1.4	.3	1.2			Deferred Taxes	.6	.5
12.6	6.9	5.9	10.7			All Other Non-Current	5.6	5.7
11.6	17.9	33.4	44.4			Net Worth	25.1	26.6
100.0	100.0	100.0	100.0			Total Liabilties & Net Worth	100.0	100.0
						INCOME DATA		
100.0	100.0	100.0	100.0			Net Sales	100.0	100.0
						Gross Profit		
94.8	94.7	96.9	88.8			Operating Expenses	94.7	95.6
5.2	5.3	3.1	11.2			Operating Profit	5.3	4.4
1.3	1.5	.1	1.4			All Other Expenses (net)	2.8	2.2
3.9	3.8	3.0	9.8			Profit Before Taxes	2.6	2.2
						RATIOS		
3.9	2.9	2.2	2.4				2.0	2.1
1.2	1.7	1.5	1.7			Current	1.3	1.3
.5	1.1	.8	.9				.8	.8
3.7	2.7	2.1	2.3				1.7	1.9
1.2	1.6	1.4	1.5			Quick	1.0	1.2
.5	1.0	.8	.7				.7	.6
0 UND	**9** 42.5	**30** 12.3	**22** 16.4				**14** 25.8	**16** 22.6
6 64.0	**35** 10.4	**41** 9.0	**36** 10.0			Sales/Receivables	**31** 11.8	**32** 11.3
15 24.2	**54** 6.8	**51** 7.2	**53** 6.9				**42** 8.8	**43** 8.5
						Cost of Sales/Inventory		
						Cost of Sales/Payables		
28.1	11.3	11.9	9.1				15.7	13.7
193.0	18.9	22.1	13.6			Sales/Working Capital	51.8	49.8
-23.8	270.7	-43.1	-182.1				-47.8	-50.9
21.1	20.6	19.3	153.3				11.4	14.3
(13) 11.0	(18) 5.6	(31) 11.7	(12) 30.7			EBIT/Interest	(99) 4.5	(91) 4.3
1.0	.8	4.4	11.6				1.4	.9
							7.1	4.2
						Net Profit + Depr., Dep., Amort./Cur. Mat. L/T/D	(17) 2.8	(20) 1.1
							1.4	.0
.2	.0	.1	.2				.3	.3
1.3	.7	.4	.7			Fixed/Worth	1.2	1.1
NM	-32.4	3.8	-7.4				16.2	-3.3
1.6	1.0	.7	.6				1.2	1.0
4.7	4.4	2.3	1.7			Debt/Worth	3.3	3.3
-5.8	-35.4	17.1	-615.1				-57.6	-6.7
214.9	113.4	126.2	62.0				70.3	81.7
(12) 99.4	(17) 32.3	(28) 36.3	(10) 36.5			% Profit Before Taxes/Tangible Net Worth	(84) 28.7	(78) 20.1
9.9	5.8	11.7	15.6				5.3	9.0
34.4	26.1	25.1	34.9				17.4	18.2
22.5	11.8	10.6	8.8			% Profit Before Taxes/Total Assets	9.1	7.1
-.6	.4	3.9	5.1				1.4	.3
666.0	528.2	239.5	102.0				110.2	78.8
46.0	69.3	47.9	26.0			Sales/Net Fixed Assets	28.5	34.3
8.5	21.9	10.8	8.0				7.5	9.8
13.1	8.1	7.1	4.6				7.0	6.8
8.0	5.8	4.7	2.4			Sales/Total Assets	4.5	4.8
4.5	2.5	3.2	1.3				2.2	2.4
	.3	.3	.7				.7	.5
	(10) .9	(24) .9	(12) 1.2			% Depr., Dep., Amort./Sales	(78) 1.7	(82) 1.2
	4.2	1.7	5.0				3.8	2.7
3.1	2.6	1.6					2.8	1.7
(10) 3.8	(11) 3.9	(18) 2.2				% Officers', Directors' Owners' Comp/Sales	(44) 4.3	(40) 3.5
9.5	7.7	4.3					9.2	6.6
58345M	**171727M**	**722844M**	**765379M**	**617825M**	**1070439M**	Net Sales ($)	**5504625M**	**3777823M**
3917M	**30174M**	**156436M**	**314076M**	**166735M**	**866593M**	Total Assets ($)	**1354402M**	**1586222M**

M = $ thousand MM = $ million

See Pages 9 through 22 for Explanation of Ratios and Data

Comparative Historical Data / Current Data Sorted by Sales

4/1/11-3/31/12 ALL	4/1/12-3/31/13 ALL	4/1/13-3/31/14 ALL	Type of Statement	0-1MM	1-3MM	3-5MM	5-10MM	10-25MM	25MM & OVER
10	10	4	Unqualified					1	3
14	9	19	Reviewed			1	4	5	9
13	11	11	Compiled		1	1	2	5	2
32	30	23	Tax Returns	3	2	5	6	6	1
47	44	38	Other	5	4	3	3	8	15
				6 (4/1-9/30/13)		89 (10/1/13-3/31/14)			
116	104	95	NUMBER OF STATEMENTS	8	7	10	15	25	30
%	%	%	ASSETS	%	%	%	%	%	%
11.3	12.8	13.0	Cash & Equivalents			12.0	15.4	15.0	8.1
34.5	32.9	38.7	Trade Receivables (net)			41.0	39.3	49.8	38.3
1.3	1.5	.1	Inventory			.1	.0	.0	.3
5.5	5.4	4.2	All Other Current			4.5	2.0	3.1	5.7
52.6	52.6	56.0	Total Current			57.6	56.8	68.0	52.4
24.2	21.9	21.5	Fixed Assets (net)			22.8	25.5	16.4	17.1
11.8	16.4	12.9	Intangibles (net)			8.2	8.2	9.8	20.9
11.3	9.2	9.6	All Other Non-Current			11.3	9.5	5.8	9.7
100.0	100.0	100.0	Total			100.0	100.0	100.0	100.0
			LIABILITIES						
17.1	24.0	13.8	Notes Payable-Short Term			25.4	20.9	12.8	8.8
3.6	5.0	3.0	Cur. Mat.-L.T.D.			3.4	6.8	2.0	2.6
12.8	12.6	15.2	Trade Payables			15.3	10.2	19.6	17.6
.4	.2	.2	Income Taxes Payable			.0	.3	.4	.1
13.2	11.1	12.0	All Other Current			10.2	7.4	13.0	11.9
47.1	52.9	44.3	Total Current			54.4	45.5	47.8	41.1
18.1	23.0	19.5	Long-Term Debt			28.0	23.7	13.5	15.7
.6	.3	.9	Deferred Taxes			.0	.0	1.7	1.5
6.1	8.0	7.8	All Other Non-Current			.5	5.5	3.4	9.3
28.1	15.7	27.5	Net Worth			17.2	25.3	33.6	32.4
100.0	100.0	100.0	Total Liabilties & Net Worth			100.0	100.0	100.0	100.0
			INCOME DATA						
100.0	100.0	100.0	Net Sales			100.0	100.0	100.0	100.0
			Gross Profit						
94.5	94.3	94.7	Operating Expenses			95.4	96.4	95.1	94.1
5.5	5.7	5.3	Operating Profit			4.6	3.6	4.9	5.9
2.7	1.3	1.0	All Other Expenses (net)			.5	.3	.3	1.0
2.8	4.4	4.4	Profit Before Taxes			4.1	3.3	4.6	4.9
			RATIOS						
2.2	2.1	2.5				3.0	4.8	2.3	2.1
1.4	1.3	1.5	Current			1.6	1.7	1.6	1.1
.9	.8	.8				1.0	1.0	1.0	.8
1.9	2.0	2.4				2.8	4.8	2.3	2.1
1.1	1.3	1.4	Quick			1.6	1.7	1.5	1.1
.6	.6	.8				.9	1.0	.9	.8
11 32.9	**3** 114.5	**16** 23.5				**6** 62.2	**9** 40.6	**21** 17.0	**29** 12.5
32 11.3	**29** 12.7	**35** 10.5	Sales/Receivables			**36** 10.0	**39** 9.4	**39** 9.4	**35** 10.3
42 8.6	**40** 9.1	**46** 7.9				**72** 5.1	**55** 6.6	**46** 7.9	**43** 8.4
			Cost of Sales/Inventory						
			Cost of Sales/Payables						
12.8	14.4	11.8				10.3	7.4	13.1	10.7
31.6	34.7	29.4	Sales/Working Capital			25.4	14.1	21.4	84.3
-68.2	-47.4	-48.0				NM	-999.3	NM	-34.6
25.5	34.0	28.7					7.7	53.2	51.1
(101) 4.5	(88) 7.6	(80) 9.3	EBIT/Interest				(13) 4.8	(24) 14.1	(26) 14.0
.8	1.4	1.9					1.7	5.7	1.1
13.3	9.9	15.7							
(16) 3.1	(15) 2.1	(15) 2.9	Net Profit + Depr., Dep., Amort./Cur. Mat. L/T/D						
1.0	1.6	.4							
.2	.3	.1				.0	.2	.1	.2
1.0	1.1	.7	Fixed/Worth			2.4	.8	.3	1.4
-8.6	-.8	-9.5				NM	2.0	5.2	-.6
.9	.9	1.0				1.1	.7	.5	1.1
3.6	4.4	3.6	Debt/Worth			10.3	2.0	2.8	3.6
-21.6	-3.0	-11.7				NM	14.9	28.0	-2.9
117.1	109.3	109.1					143.5	143.3	62.0
(85) 44.9	(66) 47.7	(69) 44.2	% Profit Before Taxes/Tangible Net Worth				(13) 33.4	(20) 57.3	(18) 32.5
7.7	15.8	10.3					6.8	20.2	15.8
31.9	33.0	25.8				27.1	26.1	30.1	15.2
9.8	11.0	10.2	% Profit Before Taxes/Total Assets			9.9	7.3	16.7	9.6
.5	1.1	1.0				.5	2.9	6.1	1.3
115.8	101.7	222.3				682.3	227.5	309.4	106.6
37.6	36.9	43.9	Sales/Net Fixed Assets			32.2	56.8	60.8	25.9
8.2	9.6	9.4				15.2	6.6	25.9	9.0
7.4	7.1	7.2				8.4	6.0	8.0	6.1
4.9	4.6	4.5	Sales/Total Assets			3.9	4.3	6.0	3.5
2.2	2.2	2.2				2.2	2.4	3.6	1.5
.3	.6	.4					.2	.2	.4
(88) 1.1	(66) 1.5	(58) 1.1	% Depr., Dep., Amort./Sales				(10) .7	(16) .5	(21) 1.1
3.9	4.3	2.8					3.7	1.2	2.0
2.0	2.1	1.9					2.0	1.1	
(54) 3.8	(52) 3.5	(45) 2.9	% Officers', Directors' Owners' Comp/Sales				(11) 3.9	(15) 2.2	
6.9	7.3	5.7					7.1	3.8	
5622580M	4477106M	3406559M	Net Sales ($)	3429M	14626M	40240M	114046M	435990M	2798228M
1566591M	1532893M	1537931M	Total Assets ($)	1666M	2476M	11166M	34288M	118622M	1369713M

M = $ thousand MM = $ million

See Pages 9 through 22 for Explanation of Ratios and Data

Current Data Sorted by Assets							Comparative Historical Data	
						Type of Statement		
		5	12	3	6	Unqualified	33	32
1	4	37	23	5	1	Reviewed	59	59
4	17	16	2	1		Compiled	47	55
18	54	22	2		1	Tax Returns	111	90
9	43	34	32	10	1	Other	132	164
32 (4/1-9/30/13)		331 (10/1/13-3/31/14)					4/1/09-3/31/10 ALL	4/1/10-3/31/11 ALL
0-500M	500M-2MM	2-10MM	10-50MM	50-100MM	100-250MM			
32	118	114	71	19	9	NUMBER OF STATEMENTS	382	400
%	%	%	%	%	%	**ASSETS**	%	%
27.8	11.9	9.8	10.8	9.0		Cash & Equivalents	10.8	12.2
18.2	21.9	22.1	18.2	20.7		Trade Receivables (net)	18.1	19.5
.3	.9	2.4	3.6	2.6		Inventory	2.5	1.9
4.7	3.8	3.5	4.0	2.0		All Other Current	3.5	3.1
51.0	38.6	37.8	36.6	34.3		Total Current	34.9	36.7
28.7	46.8	49.1	46.3	40.9		Fixed Assets (net)	51.5	48.9
1.2	3.3	4.3	6.5	16.8		Intangibles (net)	4.4	5.0
19.1	11.4	8.8	10.6	8.1		All Other Non-Current	9.1	9.5
100.0	100.0	100.0	100.0	100.0		Total	100.0	100.0
						LIABILITIES		
54.8	6.6	4.6	4.6	4.7		Notes Payable-Short Term	8.4	7.6
2.7	4.0	4.6	5.1	4.0		Cur. Mat.-L.T.D.	5.7	4.0
15.1	10.3	8.8	8.9	22.0		Trade Payables	7.4	8.0
.0	.0	.1	.2	.0		Income Taxes Payable	.2	.1
22.2	10.1	8.8	8.3	7.8		All Other Current	9.1	13.7
94.8	31.1	26.9	27.1	38.4		Total Current	30.8	33.5
25.9	37.7	34.1	29.8	16.5		Long-Term Debt	38.4	35.9
.0	.0	.2	.9	.5		Deferred Taxes	.2	.2
2.0	9.1	5.5	4.7	4.9		All Other Non-Current	6.8	6.4
-22.7	22.0	33.3	37.5	39.8		Net Worth	23.9	24.0
100.0	100.0	100.0	100.0	100.0		Total Liabilities & Net Worth	100.0	100.0
						INCOME DATA		
100.0	100.0	100.0	100.0	100.0		Net Sales	100.0	100.0
						Gross Profit		
83.5	84.9	80.2	86.9	90.2		Operating Expenses	85.1	84.4
16.5	15.1	19.8	13.1	9.8		Operating Profit	14.9	15.6
3.0	5.1	6.8	3.7	1.3		All Other Expenses (net)	7.7	7.7
13.5	10.0	13.0	9.3	8.4		Profit Before Taxes	7.3	7.9
						RATIOS		
2.1	3.0	2.5	2.4	2.7			2.4	2.7
1.1	1.3	1.3	1.3	1.8		Current	1.2	1.2
.3	.7	.8	1.0	.6			.6	.6
1.5	2.7	2.2	2.1	2.6			2.0	2.5
.9	1.1	1.1	1.1	1.1		Quick	1.0	1.1
.3	.5	.7	.7	.3			.5	.4
0 UND	**0** UND	**9** 42.6	**17** 21.2	**36** 10.0			**0** UND	**3** 118.9
7 52.0	**21** 17.1	**37** 9.8	**41** 9.0	**52** 7.0		Sales/Receivables	**28** 13.0	**30** 12.2
29 12.6	**43** 8.5	**51** 7.1	**57** 6.4	**59** 6.2			**45** 8.1	**46** 7.9
						Cost of Sales/Inventory		
						Cost of Sales/Payables		
13.7	8.6	7.1	6.2	5.0			7.5	6.8
UND	31.7	28.3	24.4	14.0		Sales/Working Capital	41.4	36.4
-6.6	-27.9	-21.5	-103.3	-4.5			-12.9	-12.7
88.0	9.2	16.7	16.5	35.4			8.3	10.9
(19) 21.0	(85) 3.7	(90) 4.1	(62) 6.6	(17) 5.7		EBIT/Interest	(285) 2.9	(285) 3.5
2.4	1.8	2.4	2.5	3.0			1.0	1.4
		11.7	6.1			Net Profit + Depr., Dep.,	3.5	7.8
		(18) 2.8	(24) 2.4			Amort./Cur. Mat. L/T/D	(67) 2.0	(62) 3.3
		1.1	1.4				1.2	1.6
.2	.3	.6	.7	.6			.7	.6
.8	1.5	1.6	1.5	1.6		Fixed/Worth	2.1	1.7
-.5	-72.9	5.3	3.3	4.1			23.1	34.2
.7	.7	1.0	.8	.5			1.0	.8
2.6	2.3	2.4	2.4	3.2		Debt/Worth	2.9	2.5
-2.4	-22.2	6.0	5.8	4.3			278.2	115.5
217.3	44.9	51.9	52.9	36.0		% Profit Before Taxes/Tangible	42.5	51.3
(19) 104.0	(86) 25.2	(99) 24.3	(64) 26.5	(16) 20.7		Net Worth	(288) 16.3	(303) 17.5
25.9	7.8	9.3	9.6	15.6			5.3	5.8
72.0	18.1	12.4	15.3	11.9		% Profit Before Taxes/Total	11.2	13.9
26.6	8.2	6.7	7.6	6.9		Assets	4.7	5.4
5.1	1.3	3.1	3.1	3.4			-.1	.5
83.7	20.5	18.8	9.3	9.8			15.1	21.7
31.1	5.5	1.9	2.5	3.8		Sales/Net Fixed Assets	2.7	3.7
4.7	.9	.3	.9	.8			.5	.5
6.3	3.8	3.0	2.3	2.7			2.8	3.1
4.2	2.0	1.0	1.2	.9		Sales/Total Assets	1.1	1.3
2.0	.5	.3	.5	.5			.3	.4
.6	1.6	1.6	2.1	2.3			2.0	2.1
(20) 1.7	(96) 4.5	(99) 4.1	(66) 4.0	(17) 4.9		% Depr., Dep., Amort./Sales	(319) 5.1	(317) 5.1
4.8	12.1	10.9	7.3	8.5			12.2	12.7
	3.2	2.1				% Officers', Directors'	2.6	2.8
	(39) 5.2	(27) 3.4				Owners' Comp/Sales	(99) 5.0	(101) 4.7
	10.0	7.3					9.6	9.7
40895M	331882M	1112030M	2413421M	1851555M	2499028M	Net Sales ($)	7699245M	7788967M
8464M	140978M	566428M	1513293M	1353389M	1540543M	Total Assets ($)	4929404M	4485268M

M = $ thousand MM = $ million

See Pages 9 through 22 for Explanation of Ratios and Data

Comparative Historical Data / Current Data Sorted by Sales

Comparative Historical Data			Type of Statement	Current Data Sorted by Sales					
36	20	26	Unqualified				1	5	20
61	48	71	Reviewed	11	6	3	6	25	20
54	47	40	Compiled	12	18	5	1	1	3
130	97	97	Tax Returns	41	25	6	15	7	3
180	165	129	Other	19	31	18	20	10	31
4/1/11-3/31/12 ALL	4/1/12-3/31/13 ALL	4/1/13-3/31/14 ALL		32 (4/1-9/30/13)			331 (10/1/13-3/31/14)		
				0-1MM	1-3MM	3-5MM	5-10MM	10-25MM	25MM & OVER
461	377	363	**NUMBER OF STATEMENTS**	83	80	32	43	48	77
%	%	%	**ASSETS**	%	%	%	%	%	%
12.0	11.9	12.2	Cash & Equivalents	8.5	16.6	9.5	12.3	16.3	10.3
18.1	20.1	20.8	Trade Receivables (net)	5.6	16.7	30.2	29.8	26.3	29.2
2.8	2.3	2.5	Inventory	.4	.8	1.5	1.8	2.4	7.3
3.0	3.1	3.7	All Other Current	1.7	4.4	4.5	4.9	4.3	3.8
36.0	37.4	39.3	Total Current	16.2	38.6	45.7	48.7	49.2	50.7
48.9	46.7	45.3	Fixed Assets (net)	68.7	46.2	37.5	37.3	37.6	31.5
4.6	4.3	4.8	Intangibles (net)	4.2	2.9	3.2	4.0	4.9	8.4
10.6	11.6	10.7	All Other Non-Current	11.0	12.4	13.7	10.0	8.2	9.4
100.0	100.0	100.0	Total	100.0	100.0	100.0	100.0	100.0	100.0
			LIABILITIES						
6.8	8.4	10.0	Notes Payable-Short Term	20.0	7.5	4.3	8.9	4.6	8.4
4.3	3.7	4.3	Cur. Mat.-L.T.D.	3.3	4.2	7.8	5.9	3.9	3.3
8.4	10.2	10.6	Trade Payables	7.1	8.6	9.4	9.6	10.4	17.8
.2	.1	.1	Income Taxes Payable	.0	.0	.0	.0	.3	.1
11.7	12.9	10.2	All Other Current	4.6	11.5	14.6	11.9	14.1	9.7
31.5	35.3	35.2	Total Current	35.0	31.9	36.2	36.3	33.2	39.2
38.0	33.0	32.4	Long-Term Debt	60.0	31.5	31.2	23.4	21.6	16.0
.3	.3	.3	Deferred Taxes	.0	.0	.0	.1	.8	.8
7.0	7.5	6.2	All Other Non-Current	3.1	7.1	7.6	7.4	9.4	5.6
23.2	23.9	25.8	Net Worth	2.0	29.5	25.1	32.8	35.0	38.4
100.0	100.0	100.0	Total Liabilties & Net Worth	100.0	100.0	100.0	100.0	100.0	100.0
			INCOME DATA						
100.0	100.0	100.0	Net Sales	100.0	100.0	100.0	100.0	100.0	100.0
			Gross Profit						
83.7	85.4	84.1	Operating Expenses	65.3	83.8	89.6	91.8	93.0	92.6
16.3	14.6	15.9	Operating Profit	34.7	16.2	10.4	8.2	7.0	7.4
6.6	5.8	5.0	All Other Expenses (net)	14.0	5.6	2.2	.6	.6	.8
9.7	8.8	11.0	Profit Before Taxes	20.6	10.6	8.2	7.6	6.5	6.7
			RATIOS						
3.0	3.2	2.4		2.1	2.7	2.4	3.0	3.8	2.0
1.4	1.4	1.3	Current	.9	1.5	1.3	1.3	1.5	1.4
.7	.7	.8		.2	.5	.7	.8	1.0	1.1
2.7	2.4	2.1		1.5	2.0	2.3	2.7	3.5	1.7
1.1	1.2	1.1	Quick	.8	1.2	1.2	1.1	1.3	1.2
.6	.6	.6		.2	.4	.6	.7	.8	.8
0 937.9	1 264.7	5 79.8		0 UND	0 838.6	24 15.2	19 19.3	36 10.0	28 13.1
27 13.3	33 11.1	34 10.7	Sales/Receivables	0 UND	22 16.8	43 8.4	36 10.2	47 7.8	43 8.4
45 8.1	50 7.3	50 7.3		18 20.4	46 7.9	65 5.6	47 7.8	59 6.2	57 6.4
			Cost of Sales/Inventory						
			Cost of Sales/Payables						
6.1	7.1	7.7		13.8	6.9	7.6	8.5	5.2	7.8
28.0	25.3	29.5	Sales/Working Capital	-68.6	21.6	31.0	36.1	17.1	19.9
-20.3	-19.0	-24.7		-4.5	-18.7	-22.5	-33.6	-119.5	70.0
12.6	11.6	17.0		5.2	9.7	30.5	19.8	10.3	25.9
(331) 4.2	(286) 4.6	(281) 5.1	EBIT/Interest	(45) 2.7	(59) 3.3	(26) 5.7	(36) 6.2	(43) 6.1	(72) 11.5
1.7	1.5	2.3		1.7	1.4	2.5	2.9	2.5	3.9
5.5	6.4	10.9						11.4	13.8
(73) 3.0	(57) 2.7	(55) 2.8	Net Profit + Depr., Dep., Amort./Cur. Mat. L/T/D					(12) 3.5	(26) 2.7
1.4	1.7	1.4						2.3	1.7
.5	.6	.5		1.6	.4	.3	.4	.6	.5
1.6	1.5	1.5	Fixed/Worth	5.3	1.6	.9	1.2	.9	.8
14.1	7.1	6.1		-4.6	8.7	5.3	2.7	2.8	1.9
.8	.8	.9		1.7	.7	.6	.7	.8	.9
2.3	2.1	2.4	Debt/Worth	5.0	1.7	1.7	1.8	2.0	2.1
24.2	19.4	9.3		-6.0	15.8	6.9	4.3	5.6	5.6
45.3	42.7	53.9		44.1	58.1	42.2	53.8	45.6	76.4
(363) 20.0	(293) 19.9	(292) 25.9	% Profit Before Taxes/Tangible Net Worth	(54) 20.2	(63) 19.9	(26) 23.9	(38) 31.1	(40) 25.2	(71) 32.6
8.2	7.1	10.2		5.6	2.6	9.1	20.6	10.5	16.9
13.5	14.3	16.4		10.2	25.1	18.1	18.0	12.6	18.7
6.4	6.8	7.5	% Profit Before Taxes/Total Assets	5.1	7.1	10.2	10.1	6.7	9.7
1.4	1.0	3.1		1.0	1.0	4.7	5.3	4.0	5.2
18.8	20.4	20.3		1.3	19.9	25.4	21.6	19.8	34.4
3.9	4.0	4.4	Sales/Net Fixed Assets	.3	4.3	11.2	10.7	6.1	8.5
.5	.8	.8		.2	.8	2.1	1.7	2.2	2.8
3.2	3.3	3.2		.8	2.8	2.9	5.3	3.2	3.9
1.3	1.4	1.5	Sales/Total Assets	.3	1.3	2.1	3.1	2.3	2.3
.4	.5	.5		.1	.5	.9	1.1	.9	1.2
1.8	1.4	1.6		6.7	1.9	.9	1.4	1.3	1.3
(373) 4.7	(310) 3.9	(304) 4.1	% Depr., Dep., Amort./Sales	(69) 15.5	(67) 5.2	(25) 3.0	(35) 2.1	(44) 3.1	(64) 2.6
12.6	11.3	10.0		23.3	10.9	6.0	4.4	5.8	4.8
2.7	2.0	2.5		4.4	4.1	1.4	3.2	1.4	
(114) 4.9	(97) 4.2	(82) 4.4	% Officers', Directors' Owners' Comp/Sales	(11) 9.6	(26) 6.1	(10) 3.3	(15) 5.2	(14) 2.4	
8.9	9.2	8.5		14.2	10.2	4.3	9.7	3.1	
8974142M	8581328M	8248811M	Net Sales ($)	37739M	154822M	122496M	300475M	752880M	6880399M
6215535M	4950337M	5123095M	Total Assets ($)	147155M	289234M	139470M	170731M	630581M	3745924M

M = $ thousand MM = $ million

See Pages 9 through 22 for Explanation of Ratios and Data

Current Data Sorted by Assets							Comparative Historical Data	
						Type of Statement		
		3	8	1	3	Unqualified	29	26
	2	9	7			Reviewed	10	16
2	1	15	6	1	1	Compiled	19	25
2	7	3				Tax Returns	11	21
4	6	13	14	4	5	Other	45	58
22 (4/1-9/30/13)		95 (10/1/13-3/31/14)					4/1/09-3/31/10	4/1/10-3/31/11
0-500M	**500M-2MM**	**2-10MM**	**10-50MM**	**50-100MM**	**100-250MM**		**ALL**	**ALL**
8	16	43	35	6	9	**NUMBER OF STATEMENTS**	114	146
%	%	%	%	%	%	**ASSETS**	%	%
	14.0	8.6	8.2			Cash & Equivalents	10.2	9.4
	24.1	16.0	10.8			Trade Receivables (net)	12.2	13.4
	2.7	5.5	4.7			Inventory	4.3	4.8
	5.6	1.9	1.3			All Other Current	2.2	2.4
	46.3	32.0	24.9			Total Current	28.8	29.9
	35.5	60.0	61.1			Fixed Assets (net)	60.6	61.5
	7.8	1.7	4.1			Intangibles (net)	4.3	2.4
	10.4	6.3	9.9			All Other Non-Current	6.3	6.1
	100.0	100.0	100.0			Total	100.0	100.0
						LIABILITIES		
	7.3	5.6	6.3			Notes Payable-Short Term	6.6	5.1
	3.0	5.2	5.5			Cur. Mat.-L.T.D.	5.8	3.5
	26.2	7.4	3.9			Trade Payables	4.6	5.0
	.1	.1	.1			Income Taxes Payable	.2	.3
	17.9	6.9	4.6			All Other Current	12.1	8.7
	54.5	25.3	20.5			Total Current	29.4	22.7
	22.6	38.1	32.6			Long-Term Debt	36.9	39.1
	.0	.9	1.0			Deferred Taxes	.8	.9
	9.8	6.8	3.5			All Other Non-Current	7.2	9.1
	13.1	28.9	42.3			Net Worth	25.8	28.2
	100.0	100.0	100.0			Total Liabilties & Net Worth	100.0	100.0
						INCOME DATA		
	100.0	100.0	100.0			Net Sales	100.0	100.0
						Gross Profit		
	87.9	84.1	85.4			Operating Expenses	86.4	83.4
	12.1	15.9	14.6			Operating Profit	13.6	16.6
	2.7	6.4	2.5			All Other Expenses (net)	5.3	6.5
	9.4	9.5	12.0			Profit Before Taxes	8.3	10.0
						RATIOS		
	3.4	2.6	2.1				2.5	2.7
	1.3	1.0	1.2			Current	1.1	1.4
	.5	.6	.6				.5	.7
	3.2	2.1	1.9				2.1	2.3
	.8	.8	1.0			Quick	.9	1.1
	.4	.4	.6				.4	.5
	0 UND	18 20.4	24 15.2				17 21.8	14 25.8
	29 12.8	33 11.1	31 11.6			Sales/Receivables	29 12.5	32 11.5
	41 9.0	46 8.0	40 9.1				41 9.0	46 8.0
						Cost of Sales/Inventory		
						Cost of Sales/Payables		
	5.1	7.3	7.9				9.1	6.2
	37.6	508.8	27.3			Sales/Working Capital	40.7	26.5
	-5.8	-6.0	-19.2				-9.6	-18.4
	19.3	15.7	13.0				7.1	11.0
	(11) 5.9	(36) 5.3	(33) 4.6			EBIT/Interest	(96) 2.9	(114) 3.0
	3.0	1.7	1.7				1.2	1.5
							6.3	5.5
						Net Profit + Depr., Dep., Amort./Cur. Mat. L/T/D	(32) 2.1	(30) 2.8
							1.4	2.0
	.5	.7	1.0				1.0	.9
	4.5	2.5	1.9			Fixed/Worth	2.3	2.3
	-1.0	13.1	3.1				8.1	17.4
	.4	.7	.7				.9	.8
	5.8	2.7	1.9			Debt/Worth	2.2	2.9
	-2.5	25.4	6.3				11.0	22.9
	72.6	47.9	28.5				37.8	39.7
	(10) 54.0	(35) 25.5	(30) 17.5			% Profit Before Taxes/Tangible Net Worth	(98) 16.7	(121) 20.0
	33.6	2.6	7.8				6.2	9.7
	27.2	17.3	10.0				12.6	12.2
	9.3	6.5	6.4			% Profit Before Taxes/Total Assets	5.9	6.1
	2.6	.4	1.9				.6	.9
	22.7	6.5	2.3				6.0	5.9
	10.0	1.9	1.0			Sales/Net Fixed Assets	1.3	1.2
	3.1	.6	.6				.6	.6
	3.7	2.7	1.1				2.4	2.0
	2.7	1.1	.6			Sales/Total Assets	.8	.8
	1.2	.4	.5				.5	.4
	1.7	1.7	3.0				3.4	3.5
	(14) 2.3	(39) 7.8	(32) 7.8			% Depr., Dep., Amort./Sales	(101) 7.9	(132) 7.6
	13.2	14.7	12.9				11.0	13.6
		3.5					2.2	1.4
		(11) 4.1				% Officers', Directors' Owners' Comp/Sales	(20) 4.8	(27) 3.2
		13.0					7.0	9.3
6888M	57030M	391305M	1001651M	190580M	974785M	Net Sales ($)	2512483M	2351709M
1087M	20302M	234513M	788693M	392603M	1450526M	Total Assets ($)	3024988M	2939234M

M = $ thousand MM = $ million

See Pages 9 through 22 for Explanation of Ratios and Data

Comparative Historical Data				Current Data Sorted by Sales					
			Type of Statement						
22	11	15	Unqualified				1	7	7
18	22	18	Reviewed	1	2	1	9	4	1
23	24	26	Compiled	3	3	4	2	7	7
14	16	12	Tax Returns	6	2	4			
55	56	46	Other	5	6	7	12	6	10
4/1/11-3/31/12	**4/1/12-3/31/13**	**4/1/13-3/31/14**			**22 (4/1-9/30/13)**			**95 (10/1/13-3/31/14)**	
ALL	**ALL**	**ALL**		**0-1MM**	**1-3MM**	**3-5MM**	**5-10MM**	**10-25MM**	**25MM & OVER**
132	129	117	**NUMBER OF STATEMENTS**	15	13	16	24	24	25
%	%	%	**ASSETS**	%	%	%	%	%	%
9.0	10.9	12.8	Cash & Equivalents	19.4	21.6	11.8	6.8	11.7	12.0
16.3	16.9	15.1	Trade Receivables (net)	11.6	10.6	15.1	17.4	14.0	18.2
5.9	4.8	4.0	Inventory	7.7	.0	.8	4.4	2.6	6.8
2.3	2.8	2.0	All Other Current	.2	1.4	1.0	5.1	.5	2.6
33.5	35.2	33.9	Total Current	38.9	33.6	28.7	33.6	28.7	39.5
56.8	55.1	54.4	Fixed Assets (net)	43.5	51.7	57.6	59.6	60.0	49.9
3.8	3.5	4.6	Intangibles (net)	3.8	6.0	10.3	.9	1.9	6.7
5.9	6.2	7.2	All Other Non-Current	13.7	8.7	3.3	5.9	9.4	4.0
100.0	100.0	100.0	Total	100.0	100.0	100.0	100.0	100.0	100.0
			LIABILITIES						
8.4	7.2	5.8	Notes Payable-Short Term	12.6	2.5	6.9	7.4	1.4	5.4
5.3	5.3	6.1	Cur. Mat.-L.T.D.	13.4	4.5	6.8	7.7	3.4	3.0
6.6	6.6	8.4	Trade Payables	3.4	7.7	5.0	15.3	6.1	9.4
.1	.2	.1	Income Taxes Payable	.0	.4	.0	.2	.1	.1
9.3	7.0	8.3	All Other Current	11.1	17.7	12.1	4.3	4.5	6.8
29.5	26.3	28.6	Total Current	40.5	32.8	30.8	34.8	15.5	24.7
36.1	33.5	31.4	Long-Term Debt	46.6	39.7	29.0	31.4	28.0	22.7
.5	.5	1.1	Deferred Taxes	.0	.0	1.3	.5	.4	3.5
12.0	5.2	6.6	All Other Non-Current	.2	3.3	10.9	9.6	6.6	6.6
21.9	34.5	32.2	Net Worth	12.8	24.2	28.0	23.6	49.5	42.5
100.0	100.0	100.0	Total Liabilities & Net Worth	100.0	100.0	100.0	100.0	100.0	100.0
			INCOME DATA						
100.0	100.0	100.0	Net Sales	100.0	100.0	100.0	100.0	100.0	100.0
			Gross Profit						
87.4	84.6	84.4	Operating Expenses	68.9	71.9	88.0	89.1	87.5	90.6
12.6	15.4	15.6	Operating Profit	31.1	28.1	12.0	10.9	12.5	9.4
6.1	6.2	4.6	All Other Expenses (net)	12.8	6.5	5.8	4.0	1.3	1.7
6.6	9.2	11.0	Profit Before Taxes	18.3	21.6	6.3	6.9	11.3	7.7
			RATIOS						
2.1	2.7	2.7		2.0	3.2	2.3	1.7	2.7	2.8
1.3	1.5	1.2	Current	.8	2.0	.7	1.0	1.3	1.8
.6	.6	.6		.2	.3	.4	.6	.6	1.2
1.8	2.4	2.1		1.7	2.9	2.3	1.4	2.7	2.0
.9	1.2	.9	Quick	.6	1.6	.7	.8	1.1	1.5
.4	.5	.5		.1	.3	.3	.4	.6	.8
16 23.3	**22** 16.3	**18** 20.5		**0** UND	**0** UND	**18** 20.3	**24** 15.5	**24** 14.9	**26** 14.3
28 12.9	**33** 10.9	**33** 11.0	Sales/Receivables	**5** 77.0	**18** 20.7	**36** 10.0	**37** 9.8	**33** 11.0	**33** 10.9
47 7.8	**44** 8.3	**43** 8.5		**41** 8.9	**38** 9.5	**42** 8.6	**46** 7.9	**45** 8.2	**46** 7.9
			Cost of Sales/Inventory						
			Cost of Sales/Payables						
8.0	7.0	7.6		15.3	5.5	10.2	8.5	6.9	7.3
33.7	14.9	39.4	Sales/Working Capital	-30.3	59.5	-19.3	332.5	33.6	10.2
-12.3	-13.7	-11.1		-1.5	-3.9	-4.5	-17.5	-9.7	35.0
9.0	12.9	15.6		24.8		5.9	15.6	20.7	10.7
(107) 2.6	(103) 4.4	(99) 5.3	EBIT/Interest	(12) 4.0		(11) 2.4	(23) 4.4	(21) 7.3	(24) 6.1
1.0	1.4	1.7		.0		-.3	1.4	3.1	1.9
5.3	9.5	4.5							4.3
(22) 2.8	(27) 2.7	(24) 2.5	Net Profit + Depr., Dep., Amort./Cur. Mat. L/T/D						(10) 2.5
1.2	1.5	1.1							1.5
.7	.5	.7		.5	.5	.9	1.1	.6	.7
2.1	1.6	2.2	Fixed/Worth	7.6	3.1	4.8	2.5	1.7	1.5
40.3	4.7	12.2		-6.1	NM	-2.6	412.7	2.9	2.7
.8	.6	.7		1.7	1.2	.4	.6	.5	.7
2.3	1.8	2.1	Debt/Worth	12.2	2.7	5.5	3.5	1.4	1.5
-42.1	6.2	33.1		-6.0	NM	-5.5	637.7	2.3	6.4
41.6	35.5	41.3		70.1	273.8	69.8	50.4	41.3	19.8
(98) 18.6	(113) 13.8	(92) 18.4	% Profit Before Taxes/Tangible Net Worth	(10) 21.9	(10) 32.7	(10) 25.5	(19) 17.5	(23) 25.5	(20) 15.1
4.5	4.9	7.7		-12.1	12.6	-.8	8.7	13.5	7.7
11.8	12.4	14.6		8.5	14.7	19.8	17.7	21.0	12.5
4.2	5.4	6.9	% Profit Before Taxes/Total Assets	4.9	9.2	5.9	5.8	10.1	6.8
-.1	.4	1.3		.0	3.0	.3	1.0	5.1	2.0
8.3	8.3	9.1		202.5	12.3	10.1	7.6	7.7	18.8
1.6	1.5	1.8	Sales/Net Fixed Assets	2.0	1.0	1.4	1.5	2.6	2.1
.7	.7	.6		.2	.3	.7	.6	.7	.7
2.9	2.7	2.7		5.8	3.7	2.7	2.6	2.3	3.0
1.0	.9	.9	Sales/Total Assets	.4	.5	1.0	.8	1.0	1.1
.5	.5	.4		.1	.3	.6	.5	.5	.6
3.7	2.8	2.5		13.9		2.0	2.3	2.6	1.9
(111) 7.1	(117) 7.1	(97) 7.8	% Depr., Dep., Amort./Sales	(10) 22.6		(14) 8.3	(23) 7.2	(21) 7.3	(21) 5.2
11.6	11.6	13.7		30.4		13.3	16.6	9.2	8.9
2.6	2.2	2.0							
(28) 4.0	(24) 3.3	(23) 3.5	% Officers', Directors' Owners' Comp/Sales						
5.4	4.3	4.7							
2778271M	**2983711M**	**2622239M**	Net Sales ($)	**7606M**	**23190M**	**62651M**	**177811M**	**380454M**	**1970527M**
3266273M	**3112008M**	**2887724M**	Total Assets ($)	**28265M**	**59784M**	**147487M**	**243039M**	**519805M**	**1889344M**

M = $ thousand MM = $ million

See Pages 9 through 22 for Explanation of Ratios and Data

Current Data Sorted by Assets / Comparative Historical Data

0-500M	500M-2MM	2-10MM	10-50MM	50-100MM	100-250MM	Type of Statement	4/1/09-3/31/10 ALL	4/1/10-3/31/11 ALL
1	3	5	7	2	2	Unqualified	25	30
	5	11	6			Reviewed	38	28
		1	1	1		Compiled	6	6
	1	5				Tax Returns	9	11
1	5	5	7		2	Other	15	19
	36 (4/1-9/30/13)		35 (10/1/13-3/31/14)					
0-500M	500M-2MM	2-10MM	10-50MM	50-100MM	100-250MM		4/1/09-3/31/10 ALL	4/1/10-3/31/11 ALL
2	14	27	21	3	4	NUMBER OF STATEMENTS	93	94
%	%	%	%	%	%	ASSETS	%	%
	15.0	16.3	10.4			Cash & Equivalents	10.2	9.1
	17.7	16.1	13.8			Trade Receivables (net)	13.5	16.0
	12.5	19.7	20.4			Inventory	23.4	24.4
	6.0	5.7	8.7			All Other Current	6.1	7.2
	51.2	57.8	53.3			Total Current	53.3	56.7
	40.4	37.7	36.3			Fixed Assets (net)	37.2	34.4
	.6	.2	1.0			Intangibles (net)	.7	.6
	7.8	4.4	9.4			All Other Non-Current	8.8	8.4
	100.0	100.0	100.0			Total	100.0	100.0
						LIABILITIES		
	1.0	6.1	8.2			Notes Payable-Short Term	12.1	12.8
	.7	1.8	3.2			Cur. Mat.-L.T.D.	3.1	3.3
	14.5	13.6	16.5			Trade Payables	11.1	14.2
	.0	.0	.7			Income Taxes Payable	.4	.1
	4.5	13.3	6.9			All Other Current	10.1	11.1
	20.6	34.9	35.5			Total Current	36.8	41.6
	2.9	12.4	16.5			Long-Term Debt	15.4	16.8
	.9	1.5	1.2			Deferred Taxes	1.1	1.2
	3.2	2.0	3.7			All Other Non-Current	1.8	3.6
	72.4	49.2	43.1			Net Worth	44.9	36.8
	100.0	100.0	100.0			Total Liabilties & Net Worth	100.0	100.0
						INCOME DATA		
	100.0	100.0	100.0			Net Sales	100.0	100.0
						Gross Profit		
	98.8	95.6	95.4			Operating Expenses	90.6	94.8
	1.2	4.4	4.6			Operating Profit	9.4	5.2
	2.3	.3	-.8			All Other Expenses (net)	1.2	.7
	-1.2	4.2	5.4			Profit Before Taxes	8.3	4.5
						RATIOS		
	4.6	3.6	2.2				2.3	2.1
	2.4	1.5	1.4			Current	1.4	1.5
	1.6	1.1	1.2				1.0	1.1
	4.3	2.8	1.0				1.1	1.3
	2.0	1.0	.7			Quick	.6	.7
	.5	.3	.4				.3	.3
	2 185.9	3 116.8	7 53.6				4 85.4	9 42.1
	10 36.5	22 16.7	33 11.2			Sales/Receivables	17 22.0	20 18.3
	20 18.7	32 11.5	52 7.0				33 11.0	42 8.8
						Cost of Sales/Inventory		
						Cost of Sales/Payables		
	7.1	9.4	4.8				8.0	7.8
	13.0	17.8	12.8			Sales/Working Capital	18.7	17.4
	31.2	45.1	23.6				151.9	42.4
		7.3	14.4				11.4	10.9
		3.4	9.9			EBIT/Interest	(87) 5.0	(89) 4.0
		.9	3.1				2.5	1.8
			3.8				24.4	7.5
			(10) 1.0			Net Profit + Depr., Dep., Amort./Cur. Mat. L/T/D	(29) 6.0	(32) 3.5
			.3				3.1	1.4
	.2	.3	.4				.4	.4
	.4	.7	.6			Fixed/Worth	.8	.8
	.9	1.3	1.4				1.3	1.3
	.1	.4	.9				.6	.7
	.3	1.1	1.3			Debt/Worth	1.4	1.5
	.7	2.4	2.2				3.1	4.1
	17.0	17.0	28.1				34.7	24.3
	9.0	(25) 6.3	17.6			% Profit Before Taxes/Tangible Net Worth	(91) 21.1	(88) 15.7
	-2.2	-.1	7.3				10.2	6.5
	9.6	6.2	9.7				15.5	10.8
	5.0	3.6	5.7			% Profit Before Taxes/Total Assets	6.8	4.6
	-2.1	-.1	1.8				2.9	1.6
	151.8	22.9	19.7				21.4	23.2
	15.5	10.3	5.8			Sales/Net Fixed Assets	9.6	10.7
	1.5	3.0	1.5				1.5	3.1
	7.7	4.6	3.3				3.7	3.6
	3.6	2.8	1.5			Sales/Total Assets	1.8	2.3
	1.1	.9	.8				.8	1.0
	.4	.6	.7				.7	.6
	(13) 2.2	(25) 1.2	2.0			% Depr., Dep., Amort./Sales	(85) 1.6	(89) 1.2
	5.3	4.2	4.5				4.3	3.3
							.6	.4
						% Officers', Directors' Owners' Comp/Sales	(21) 2.0	(23) 1.5
							2.6	3.8
7320M	78035M	385524M	1113236M	507691M	2370403M	Net Sales ($)	2226041M	3498477M
568M	17743M	119571M	493412M	225189M	720967M	Total Assets ($)	1168421M	1380378M

M = $ thousand MM = $ million

See Pages 9 through 22 for Explanation of Ratios and Data

Comparative Historical Data

Current Data Sorted by Sales

4/1/11-3/31/12 ALL	4/1/12-3/31/13 ALL	4/1/13-3/31/14 ALL	Type of Statement	0-1MM	1-3MM	3-5MM	5-10MM	10-25MM	25MM & OVER
25	24	20	Unqualified	1			2	5	12
27	25	22	Reviewed		2	3	5	7	5
8	6	3	Compiled			1		1	1
11	5	6	Tax Returns	1			1	2	2
13	26	20	Other	3	4	2	2	5	4
				36 (4/1-9/30/13)			35 (10/1/13-3/31/14)		
84	86	71	NUMBER OF STATEMENTS	5	6	6	10	20	24
%	%	%	**ASSETS**	%	%	%	%	%	%
12.8	13.4	15.1	Cash & Equivalents				20.8	15.4	12.2
17.8	13.2	15.1	Trade Receivables (net)				17.2	17.3	18.6
20.9	21.8	19.7	Inventory				28.2	18.7	26.8
7.5	5.8	7.2	All Other Current				9.9	6.3	8.8
58.9	54.2	57.1	Total Current				76.0	57.6	66.5
34.3	34.3	35.1	Fixed Assets (net)				22.9	32.4	23.5
.4	.9	.5	Intangibles (net)				.1	.2	.5
6.3	10.6	7.3	All Other Non-Current				1.0	9.8	9.5
100.0	100.0	100.0	Total				100.0	100.0	100.0
			LIABILITIES						
13.0	8.9	6.7	Notes Payable-Short Term				5.6	4.8	10.8
2.3	3.6	2.0	Cur. Mat.-L.T.D.				2.6	2.7	2.0
11.9	13.3	15.4	Trade Payables				19.9	10.9	22.1
.3	.3	.3	Income Taxes Payable				1.2	.0	.4
11.0	11.0	9.8	All Other Current				14.0	10.1	9.6
38.5	37.1	34.2	Total Current				43.3	28.5	44.9
11.9	12.0	11.0	Long-Term Debt				9.7	14.3	9.1
.9	.8	1.3	Deferred Taxes				1.2	1.1	2.0
2.3	1.5	2.5	All Other Non-Current				2.5	5.6	.7
46.3	48.6	50.9	Net Worth				43.4	50.5	43.4
100.0	100.0	100.0	Total Liabilties & Net Worth				100.0	100.0	100.0
			INCOME DATA						
100.0	100.0	100.0	Net Sales				100.0	100.0	100.0
			Gross Profit						
94.4	93.0	95.2	Operating Expenses				100.1	97.3	93.9
5.6	7.0	4.8	Operating Profit				-.1	2.7	6.1
.4	.8	.3	All Other Expenses (net)				.1	-.6	-.5
5.2	6.2	4.5	Profit Before Taxes				-.2	3.3	6.6
			RATIOS						
2.8	2.3	3.1					9.2	3.7	1.7
1.6	1.4	1.6	Current				1.4	1.9	1.5
1.1	1.0	1.2					1.1	1.3	1.2
1.6	1.3	2.4					4.5	2.8	1.0
.8	.6	.7	Quick				.9	.9	.7
.3	.2	.3					.2	.4	.4
6 60.6	7 50.9	5 71.4					0 UND	4 102.1	7 55.8
17 21.7	18 20.3	17 21.7	Sales/Receivables				13 27.1	14 27.0	18 20.0
33 11.1	31 11.7	33 10.9					32 11.5	32 11.4	35 10.3
			Cost of Sales/Inventory						
			Cost of Sales/Payables						
7.2	8.0	7.2					4.2	7.0	12.9
17.4	19.0	14.8	Sales/Working Capital				19.8	13.9	18.2
89.8	NM	30.9					NM	39.7	24.9
13.5	16.4	16.0						12.6	18.7
(72) 5.5	(75) 6.6	(63) 5.6	EBIT/Interest					(19) 4.9	(23) 6.5
2.1	2.2	1.4						1.4	3.4
6.1	6.7	8.5							8.4
(19) 4.3	(26) 2.5	(18) 2.4	Net Profit + Depr., Dep., Amort./Cur. Mat. L/T/D						(11) 3.4
2.5	1.6	.8							1.1
.4	.3	.3					.2	.2	.3
.7	.7	.6	Fixed/Worth				.4	.6	.5
1.3	1.1	1.1					NM	1.2	.7
.5	.4	.4					.5	.3	.7
1.2	1.1	1.1	Debt/Worth				1.8	1.2	1.3
3.4	3.0	2.3					NM	2.0	2.4
34.9	27.5	20.7						23.6	21.8
(80) 15.3	(83) 16.8	(68) 11.5	% Profit Before Taxes/Tangible Net Worth					11.1	17.8
5.6	3.8	.4						.9	6.7
12.1	14.9	9.2					4.5	13.0	10.6
5.8	6.7	4.9	% Profit Before Taxes/Total Assets				.6	5.1	5.6
2.6	1.6	.1					-11.2	.7	3.0
30.9	20.1	25.3					73.0	48.6	32.6
11.7	9.3	10.3	Sales/Net Fixed Assets				14.2	11.3	15.1
3.0	3.5	1.9					5.6	2.9	7.8
4.7	3.6	4.5					4.1	7.2	4.4
2.6	2.1	2.5	Sales/Total Assets				2.5	3.7	3.0
1.1	1.1	.9					1.8	1.0	2.1
.5	.7	.7						.7	.4
(74) 1.3	(77) 1.3	(67) 1.5	% Depr., Dep., Amort./Sales					(19) 1.2	(23) .9
3.7	3.7	4.2						4.0	1.3
.3	.6	.3							
(19) 1.2	(21) 2.5	(18) 1.6	% Officers', Directors' Owners' Comp/Sales						
2.8	6.5	2.8							
7214189M	7192976M	4462209M	Net Sales ($)	2531M	9800M	22780M	73892M	334333M	4018873M
1263193M	1794489M	1577450M	Total Assets ($)	7671M	12184M	27146M	37817M	182707M	1309925M

M = $ thousand MM = $ million

See Pages 9 through 22 for Explanation of Ratios and Data

Current Data Sorted by Assets / Comparative Historical Data

						Type of Statement		
		3	4	1		Unqualified	7	6
1	3	8	5	2		Reviewed	25	23
1	2	6				Compiled	13	13
5	10	1	1			Tax Returns	18	23
6	13	18	6	4	3	Other	44	53
	11 (4/1-9/30/13)		92 (10/1/13-3/31/14)				4/1/09-3/31/10 ALL	4/1/10-3/31/11 ALL
0-500M	**500M-2MM**	**2-10MM**	**10-50MM**	**50-100MM**	**100-250MM**			
13	28	36	16	7	3	**NUMBER OF STATEMENTS**	107	118
%	%	%	%	%	%	**ASSETS**	%	%
30.8	6.7	8.8	18.4			Cash & Equivalents	9.8	10.5
18.2	25.1	23.8	24.7			Trade Receivables (net)	18.3	18.9
1.0	2.6	5.3	5.0			Inventory	3.7	6.8
2.8	1.7	2.6	2.5			All Other Current	3.5	3.9
52.9	36.1	40.5	50.6			Total Current	35.2	40.1
26.6	47.1	46.0	34.8			Fixed Assets (net)	49.3	47.6
2.6	9.5	9.6	6.9			Intangibles (net)	6.5	5.4
17.9	7.3	4.0	7.7			All Other Non-Current	8.9	6.9
100.0	100.0	100.0	100.0			Total	100.0	100.0
						LIABILITIES		
64.7	8.8	8.0	2.7			Notes Payable-Short Term	6.1	5.5
1.9	1.4	4.0	2.5			Cur. Mat.-L.T.D.	4.5	3.4
25.6	7.5	10.7	11.1			Trade Payables	6.1	7.9
.0	.1	.4	.0			Income Taxes Payable	.1	.0
39.8	6.0	6.2	7.1			All Other Current	6.3	7.0
131.9	23.9	29.3	23.4			Total Current	23.1	23.9
27.9	38.7	30.6	14.7			Long-Term Debt	41.6	39.5
.0	.0	.4	.1			Deferred Taxes	.2	.1
38.5	4.1	3.2	1.5			All Other Non-Current	8.0	5.1
-98.3	33.3	36.5	60.3			Net Worth	27.1	31.4
100.0	100.0	100.0	100.0			Total Liabilities & Net Worth	100.0	100.0
						INCOME DATA		
100.0	100.0	100.0	100.0			Net Sales	100.0	100.0
						Gross Profit		
94.5	78.0	84.8	84.4			Operating Expenses	83.4	82.2
5.5	22.0	15.2	15.6			Operating Profit	16.6	17.8
-.7	8.7	4.8	-1.7			All Other Expenses (net)	7.1	7.5
6.2	13.4	10.4	17.3			Profit Before Taxes	9.5	10.3
						RATIOS		
1.3	3.5	2.8	3.2				2.3	2.8
.6	2.1	1.4	2.2			Current	1.5	1.5
.2	.7	.9	1.2				.8	.9
.9	3.5	2.0	3.1				2.1	2.4
.6	2.1	1.2	1.7			Quick	1.1	1.0
.2	.6	.6	.9				.6	.6
0 UND	0 UND	18 20.4	33 11.2				5 76.6	0 UND
12 31.0	26 14.0	36 10.1	43 8.4			Sales/Receivables	38 9.7	32 11.4
17 21.7	55 6.6	53 6.9	66 5.5				52 7.1	50 7.3
						Cost of Sales/Inventory		
						Cost of Sales/Payables		
95.8	7.9	8.9	2.8				7.2	5.6
-21.8	21.2	24.8	7.6			Sales/Working Capital	17.6	13.5
-4.1	-34.7	-32.6	NM				-33.0	-70.5
	13.7	19.9	126.7				15.2	13.1
	(17) 4.5	(33) 3.3	(14) 34.5			EBIT/Interest	(79) 3.6	(83) 4.4
	1.7	1.4	8.9				1.1	1.3
							9.4	13.0
						Net Profit + Depr., Dep., Amort./Cur. Mat. L/T/D	(27) 5.1	(24) 3.5
							1.6	1.9
.0	.7	.4	.2				.6	.5
.9	1.5	2.0	.6			Fixed/Worth	1.6	1.4
-.2	4.2	5.2	1.6				12.2	8.9
.5	1.1	1.1	.4				.8	.7
UND	2.4	2.2	.7			Debt/Worth	2.4	2.2
-1.5	10.6	5.2	1.7				31.1	15.1
	86.3	39.3	82.5				59.6	45.3
	(23) 22.2	(30) 23.4	34.8			% Profit Before Taxes/Tangible Net Worth	(82) 25.5	(97) 16.9
	4.0	4.8	26.2				8.0	3.3
52.6	27.5	13.0	31.3				16.0	15.8
8.8	7.9	5.9	24.7			% Profit Before Taxes/Total Assets	5.1	5.7
-2.0	1.1	1.2	9.3				.4	.6
UND	25.0	19.7	33.0				11.4	17.7
22.9	3.3	5.2	5.2			Sales/Net Fixed Assets	3.3	3.2
13.4	.3	.9	1.8				.5	.5
15.0	4.3	3.7	2.7				2.7	2.7
5.7	1.2	1.8	1.3			Sales/Total Assets	1.3	1.3
2.7	.3	.5	.8				.4	.3
	2.8	1.0	1.2				2.6	1.9
	(16) 9.0	(34) 4.5	(15) 3.7			% Depr., Dep., Amort./Sales	(96) 5.3	(92) 4.2
	15.9	10.1	6.9				10.5	12.0
							2.0	1.9
						% Officers', Directors' Owners' Comp/Sales	(18) 4.6	(27) 4.6
							9.0	7.4
10671M	61515M	412679M	607804M	645079M	339329M	Net Sales ($)	2312895M	2468656M
2028M	31060M	191179M	294793M	415993M	565468M	Total Assets ($)	2118779M	1662112M

M = $ thousand MM = $ million

See Pages 9 through 22 for Explanation of Ratios and Data

Comparative Historical Data				Current Data Sorted by Sales					
			Type of Statement						
14	8	8	Unqualified	1		2		3	2
14	20	19	Reviewed	1	1	2	6	5	4
15	12	9	Compiled	3	1			4	1
25	32	17	Tax Returns	10	3	2		1	1
43	44	50	Other	14	7	5	5	7	12
4/1/11-3/31/12 ALL	**4/1/12-3/31/13 ALL**	**4/1/13-3/31/14 ALL**		**11 (4/1-9/30/13)**			**92 (10/1/13-3/31/14)**		
				0-1MM	**1-3MM**	**3-5MM**	**5-10MM**	**10-25MM**	**25MM & OVER**
111	116	103	**NUMBER OF STATEMENTS**	29	12	11	11	20	20
%	%	%	**ASSETS**	%	%	%	%	%	%
11.5	10.6	12.2	Cash & Equivalents	13.1	14.6	6.6	9.0	16.7	9.6
16.7	18.8	23.4	Trade Receivables (net)	4.4	27.2	38.7	31.4	20.1	39.3
3.4	4.8	4.2	Inventory	.5	.2	6.7	5.6	6.5	7.4
3.2	2.1	2.7	All Other Current	.5	2.7	4.8	1.2	3.1	5.0
34.8	36.3	42.5	Total Current	18.5	44.7	56.9	47.3	46.4	61.4
48.3	47.9	40.3	Fixed Assets (net)	61.1	40.5	33.9	34.8	35.7	21.1
7.8	6.6	9.6	Intangibles (net)	8.5	8.3	6.4	13.8	9.8	11.1
9.1	9.2	7.7	All Other Non-Current	11.9	6.5	2.9	4.0	8.1	6.5
100.0	100.0	100.0	Total	100.0	100.0	100.0	100.0	100.0	100.0
			LIABILITIES						
6.1	10.0	14.3	Notes Payable-Short Term	20.7	28.9	15.8	10.3	5.6	6.5
4.2	4.5	2.6	Cur. Mat.-L.T.D.	2.5	1.0	3.5	3.3	3.0	2.6
5.7	8.7	11.9	Trade Payables	11.2	3.4	10.6	13.1	9.1	20.8
.2	.2	.2	Income Taxes Payable	.0	.0	.0	.3	.6	.1
7.4	7.9	10.5	All Other Current	11.2	29.7	8.2	3.9	6.4	7.0
23.5	31.2	39.5	Total Current	45.7	63.0	38.1	30.9	24.7	36.9
36.9	39.9	30.3	Long-Term Debt	47.2	46.9	25.1	22.1	14.6	18.8
.3	.4	.3	Deferred Taxes	.0	.0	.7	.0	.8	.6
4.5	5.3	7.9	All Other Non-Current	20.2	1.1	4.7	2.5	3.0	3.8
34.7	23.2	21.9	Net Worth	-13.1	-11.1	31.4	44.5	56.9	39.9
100.0	100.0	100.0	Total Liabilties & Net Worth	100.0	100.0	100.0	100.0	100.0	100.0
			INCOME DATA						
100.0	100.0	100.0	Net Sales	100.0	100.0	100.0	100.0	100.0	100.0
			Gross Profit						
79.4	84.8	84.3	Operating Expenses	67.1	88.9	95.3	95.4	86.8	91.9
20.6	15.2	15.7	Operating Profit	32.9	11.1	4.7	4.6	13.2	8.1
7.0	6.7	4.1	All Other Expenses (net)	12.4	1.8	2.4	-.6	.3	.5
13.6	8.6	11.6	Profit Before Taxes	20.5	9.2	2.3	5.2	12.9	7.6
			RATIOS						
2.7	2.8	2.7		3.1	7.2	2.4	2.0	3.5	2.3
1.4	1.4	1.5	Current	1.0	1.0	1.5	1.4	2.0	1.9
.7	.7	.7		.3	.3	.8	1.1	1.1	1.0
2.4	2.1	2.3		2.4	7.2	2.4	2.0	3.0	1.8
1.2	1.1	1.2	Quick	.9	.9	1.0	1.3	1.8	1.4
.5	.5	.6		.3	.3	.6	.9	.7	.8
0 UND	**0** UND	**10** 37.5		**0** UND	**0** UND	**26** 14.2	**33** 11.0	**26** 14.1	**39** 9.3
34 10.8	**31** 11.6	**35** 10.4	Sales/Receivables	**0** UND	**13** 28.0	**35** 10.3	**47** 7.7	**40** 9.1	**48** 7.6
50 7.3	**47** 7.7	**54** 6.8		**14** 26.5	**60** 6.1	**63** 5.8	**57** 6.4	**53** 6.9	**73** 5.0
			Cost of Sales/Inventory						
			Cost of Sales/Payables						
7.0	8.0	7.4		7.5	14.2	11.2	9.8	5.1	6.0
22.0	27.3	16.5	Sales/Working Capital	-194.0	NM	14.0	27.4	9.8	8.6
-24.0	-18.6	-30.6		-8.3	-6.1	-30.6	122.8	62.3	NM
12.6	17.5	23.6		7.3			17.2	72.0	105.2
(83) 4.3	(83) 4.8	(79) 5.8	EBIT/Interest	(15) 2.9			3.6	(18) 16.9	(19) 20.7
2.0	2.0	2.0		.6			2.0	2.7	3.7
4.6	6.5	16.0	Net Profit + Depr., Dep.,						
(23) 2.1	(17) 2.9	(18) 3.1	Amort./Cur. Mat. L/T/D						
1.5	1.3	1.8							
.5	.6	.3		1.2	.2	.3	.1	.4	.2
1.6	1.9	1.2	Fixed/Worth	4.2	2.5	1.9	1.0	.6	.5
7.8	763.6	4.8		UND	-.6	2.8	3.2	1.7	7.6
.7	.9	.7		1.5	1.0	1.4	.6	.4	.6
2.0	2.6	2.1	Debt/Worth	3.8	137.5	2.1	2.6	.9	1.7
9.2	763.5	12.3		-38.2	-2.2	12.3	3.9	2.0	24.4
46.6	50.7	65.0		55.1			46.4	43.8	99.5
(92) 22.9	(88) 21.7	(84) 31.0	% Profit Before Taxes/Tangible Net Worth	(21) 17.6			(10) 27.9	32.1	(17) 39.6
4.6	7.3	8.7		3.7			2.5	16.8	17.2
16.5	18.4	23.6		13.3	36.6	27.7	15.5	26.7	34.0
6.9	6.7	8.2	% Profit Before Taxes/Total Assets	4.4	6.6	3.4	6.8	13.3	12.6
1.9	1.2	1.6		.6	.2	.3	.7	6.5	5.0
12.9	27.2	26.3		13.4	UND	48.4	65.3	20.3	48.5
2.9	4.4	6.1	Sales/Net Fixed Assets	.4	12.5	10.6	7.4	6.8	16.0
.4	.5	1.2		.2	1.2	1.2	1.5	2.0	5.0
2.6	3.4	4.1		2.1	6.4	5.1	4.1	2.9	4.4
1.0	1.4	1.4	Sales/Total Assets	.3	2.1	3.9	1.2	1.5	2.9
.3	.3	.7		.2	1.0	.7	.8	1.1	1.3
2.0	1.0	1.4		5.1				1.0	1.0
(94) 5.5	(98) 4.4	(78) 5.1	% Depr., Dep., Amort./Sales	(20) 12.5				4.1	(17) 1.5
11.7	12.4	9.9		19.1				7.6	3.6
3.9	3.0	3.3	% Officers', Directors'						
(26) 6.5	(34) 5.1	(23) 5.4	Owners' Comp/Sales						
13.1	7.1	10.2							
2116181M	**2716385M**	**2077077M**	Net Sales ($)	**14294M**	**20260M**	**45478M**	**78327M**	**321248M**	**1597470M**
2022744M	**1685133M**	**1500521M**	Total Assets ($)	**43832M**	**17321M**	**28881M**	**57455M**	**320879M**	**1032153M**

M = $ thousand MM = $ million

See Pages 9 through 22 for Explanation of Ratios and Data

INFORMATION

Current Data Sorted by Assets | Comparative Historical Data

0-500M	500M-2MM	2-10MM	10-50MM	50-100MM	100-250MM		4/1/09-3/31/10 ALL	4/1/10-3/31/11 ALL
						Type of Statement		
		1	3	2	2	Unqualified	20	11
1		1	3			Reviewed	6	9
	3	1				Compiled	1	5
	4	1				Tax Returns	17	14
1	2	5	7	2	4	Other	27	42
	12 (4/1-9/30/13)		31 (10/1/13-3/31/14)					
2	9	9	13	4	6	NUMBER OF STATEMENTS	71	81
%	%	%	%	%	%	**ASSETS**	%	%
			9.6			Cash & Equivalents	11.6	12.7
			16.5			Trade Receivables (net)	23.0	21.9
			2.5			Inventory	3.3	4.0
			8.8			All Other Current	2.8	3.1
			37.4			Total Current	40.7	41.8
			36.3			Fixed Assets (net)	28.1	29.2
			20.6			Intangibles (net)	19.8	18.4
			5.6			All Other Non-Current	11.4	10.6
			100.0			Total	100.0	100.0
						LIABILITIES		
			1.3			Notes Payable-Short Term	6.8	6.7
			6.7			Cur. Mat.-L.T.D.	4.3	4.3
			5.0			Trade Payables	9.6	8.8
			.2			Income Taxes Payable	.2	.1
			13.3			All Other Current	15.1	10.8
			26.5			Total Current	36.0	30.8
			25.4			Long-Term Debt	24.4	24.3
			.3			Deferred Taxes	.4	.4
			1.7			All Other Non-Current	17.6	6.8
			46.1			Net Worth	21.6	37.7
			100.0			Total Liabilties & Net Worth	100.0	100.0
						INCOME DATA		
			100.0			Net Sales	100.0	100.0
			51.2			Gross Profit	50.0	55.6
			50.1			Operating Expenses	46.9	49.7
			1.1			Operating Profit	3.1	5.9
			.0			All Other Expenses (net)	2.0	2.4
			1.1			Profit Before Taxes	1.1	3.5
						RATIOS		
			3.7				2.5	2.9
			1.2			Current	1.4	1.4
			.7				.8	.9
			2.1				1.9	2.3
			1.0			Quick	1.1	1.0
			.6				.7	.7
			35 10.5				33 11.2	30 12.3
			38 9.5			Sales/Receivables	39 9.5	37 9.9
			48 7.6				50 7.2	52 7.1
			5 72.2				0 UND	0 UND
			9 42.8			Cost of Sales/Inventory	6 66.3	9 42.7
			30 12.1				16 22.9	26 14.2
			8 47.2				10 37.0	11 33.2
			22 16.7			Cost of Sales/Payables	17 20.9	24 15.3
			62 5.9				44 8.4	55 6.6
			4.2				7.7	7.1
			35.3			Sales/Working Capital	31.5	22.4
			-22.5				-24.2	-35.4
			8.7				4.4	6.4
			(10) 3.4			EBIT/Interest	(57) 1.0	(66) 2.9
			-.8				-.9	-.1
								4.2
						Net Profit + Depr., Dep., Amort./Cur. Mat. L/T/D		(17) 2.0
								.5
			.6				.5	.3
			1.7			Fixed/Worth	2.9	1.2
			-6.8				-1.2	-4.9
			.6				.6	.5
			1.8			Debt/Worth	8.3	2.4
			-12.8				-2.8	-6.7
							25.6	49.2
						% Profit Before Taxes/Tangible Net Worth	(40) 9.3	(55) 13.6
							-7.6	-5.1
			10.1				8.1	12.3
			2.1			% Profit Before Taxes/Total Assets	1.9	5.0
			-2.5				-5.0	-2.5
			6.7				30.8	27.4
			4.3			Sales/Net Fixed Assets	7.4	6.7
			2.7				2.9	2.5
			2.3				2.6	2.6
			1.3			Sales/Total Assets	1.4	1.7
			1.0				1.0	.9
			2.6				1.0	1.1
			3.5			% Depr., Dep., Amort./Sales	(57) 3.2	(65) 3.0
			6.7				4.8	5.3
							2.1	2.3
						% Officers', Directors' Owners' Comp/Sales	(13) 3.3	(19) 7.3
							15.7	9.2
1766M	29411M	51563M	389213M	192782M	1013539M	Net Sales ($)	2236585M	2256780M
611M	9629M	43682M	296713M	259044M	953186M	Total Assets ($)	2043962M	2187744M

M = $ thousand MM = $ million

See Pages 9 through 22 for Explanation of Ratios and Data

Comparative Historical Data				Current Data Sorted by Sales					
			Type of Statement						
19	8	8	Unqualified					1	7
7	5	5	Reviewed		1		1	2	1
8	5	4	Compiled		2	1	1		
22	6	5	Tax Returns		3	1	1		
31	26	21	Other	2	1	3	3	2	10
4/1/11-3/31/12 ALL	**4/1/12-3/31/13 ALL**	**4/1/13-3/31/14 ALL**			**12 (4/1-9/30/13)**		**31 (10/1/13-3/31/14)**		
				0-1MM	**1-3MM**	**3-5MM**	**5-10MM**	**10-25MM**	**25MM & OVER**
87	50	43	**NUMBER OF STATEMENTS**	2	7	5	6	5	18
%	%	%	**ASSETS**	%	%	%	%	%	%
11.6	11.7	10.7	Cash & Equivalents						10.3
20.2	20.0	19.4	Trade Receivables (net)						14.5
2.8	2.2	1.8	Inventory						2.1
3.0	3.1	4.6	All Other Current						1.5
37.6	37.1	36.4	Total Current						28.4
32.0	31.9	35.9	Fixed Assets (net)						35.8
20.1	21.1	18.7	Intangibles (net)						26.2
10.3	9.9	8.9	All Other Non-Current						9.6
100.0	100.0	100.0	Total						100.0
			LIABILITIES						
5.5	2.9	4.1	Notes Payable-Short Term						1.3
4.4	8.4	9.8	Cur. Mat.-L.T.D.						6.4
7.4	8.2	10.9	Trade Payables						4.4
.0	.2	.2	Income Taxes Payable						.1
17.0	13.2	12.3	All Other Current						13.4
34.4	33.0	37.3	Total Current						25.6
24.4	28.9	28.2	Long-Term Debt						28.5
.5	.6	.6	Deferred Taxes						1.3
8.8	11.9	3.2	All Other Non-Current						5.2
32.0	25.5	30.7	Net Worth						39.3
100.0	100.0	100.0	Total Liabilities & Net Worth						100.0
			INCOME DATA						
100.0	100.0	100.0	Net Sales						100.0
51.2	51.3	54.8	Gross Profit						53.7
46.9	47.1	50.0	Operating Expenses						49.3
4.3	4.2	4.8	Operating Profit						4.3
1.8	2.2	2.0	All Other Expenses (net)						1.9
2.5	2.0	2.8	Profit Before Taxes						2.4
			RATIOS						
3.3	2.0	2.3							1.7
1.2	1.2	1.1	Current						1.0
.8	.8	.6							.6
2.4	1.9	1.8							1.4
1.0	1.0	.9	Quick						.8
.6	.6	.5							.5
27 13.3	**31** 11.7	**31** 11.8							**35** 10.5
36 10.2	**38** 9.6	**36** 10.0	Sales/Receivables						**38** 9.5
46 8.0	**48** 7.6	**48** 7.6							**44** 8.3
0 UND	**0** UND	**0** UND							**5** 74.2
8 46.4	**5** 66.7	**6** 56.8	Cost of Sales/Inventory						**9** 42.8
19 19.4	**14** 25.4	**16** 22.9							**20** 18.4
8 46.8	**11** 32.3	**11** 34.4							**16** 22.4
24 15.1	**26** 14.1	**31** 11.9	Cost of Sales/Payables						**24** 15.4
42 8.6	**54** 6.7	**68** 5.4							**56** 6.5
6.4	6.6	6.7							11.7
68.0	71.3	58.9	Sales/Working Capital						NM
-27.5	-32.5	-10.1							-10.7
6.7	5.7	6.2							4.1
(68) 2.3	(37) 2.8	(35) 2.6	EBIT/Interest						(13) 2.9
-.3	.7	-.5							-.9
3.3	4.2	4.1							
(14) 2.4	(13) 1.9	(17) 1.7	Net Profit + Depr., Dep., Amort./Cur. Mat. L/T/D						
.9	1.2	.5							
.4	.3	.4							.6
1.4	1.6	1.4	Fixed/Worth						37.4
-5.5	-1.7	-11.9							-2.8
.9	.9	.9							.9
2.8	4.2	2.7	Debt/Worth						52.6
-7.9	-4.2	-18.7							-6.2
45.7	18.9	34.9							54.5
(59) 6.8	(34) 10.1	(30) 11.9	% Profit Before Taxes/Tangible Net Worth						(10) 8.3
-7.8	.8	-2.0							-23.2
11.5	9.8	12.5							14.8
2.9	3.7	4.2	% Profit Before Taxes/Total Assets						3.7
-4.4	-1.8	-3.4							-4.6
25.2	20.9	9.5							6.1
5.0	4.6	4.6	Sales/Net Fixed Assets						3.9
2.5	2.4	2.3							2.4
2.9	2.1	2.4							2.0
1.6	1.2	1.4	Sales/Total Assets						1.3
.9	.7	1.0							.6
1.3	1.9	2.2							3.1
(66) 3.2	(39) 3.5	(38) 3.4	% Depr., Dep., Amort./Sales						(17) 4.0
5.2	5.2	5.8							5.0
2.0									
(24) 3.7			% Officers', Directors' Owners' Comp/Sales						
7.5									
2712710M	**1750369M**	**1678274M**	Net Sales ($)	**826M**	**15131M**	**19156M**	**41258M**	**81196M**	**1520707M**
2300819M	**1780143M**	**1562865M**	Total Assets ($)	**1926M**	**14327M**	**8991M**	**39065M**	**70274M**	**1428282M**

M = $ thousand MM = $ million

See Pages 9 through 22 for Explanation of Ratios and Data

Current Data Sorted by Assets							Comparative Historical Data	
						Type of Statement		
		5	6	2	2	Unqualified	17	21
		5	7			Reviewed	11	8
1	1	2	2			Compiled	9	16
1	4	1	1		1	Tax Returns	10	9
2	3	13	8	5	4	Other	58	54
9 (4/1-9/30/13)		67 (10/1/13-3/31/14)					**4/1/09-3/31/10 ALL**	**4/1/10-3/31/11 ALL**
0-500M	**500M-2MM**	**2-10MM**	**10-50MM**	**50-100MM**	**100-250MM**			
4	8	26	24	7	7	**NUMBER OF STATEMENTS**	105	108
%	%	%	%	%	%	**ASSETS**	%	%
		19.8	16.8			Cash & Equivalents	14.2	16.8
		28.1	19.8			Trade Receivables (net)	25.6	26.4
		5.4	3.9			Inventory	5.9	5.6
		2.9	1.6			All Other Current	4.6	4.3
		56.2	42.1			Total Current	50.3	53.1
		20.2	7.9			Fixed Assets (net)	14.8	15.2
		15.4	34.5			Intangibles (net)	25.8	22.5
		8.3	15.5			All Other Non-Current	9.1	9.2
		100.0	100.0			Total	100.0	100.0
						LIABILITIES		
		2.2	3.1			Notes Payable-Short Term	8.2	13.9
		2.8	1.7			Cur. Mat.-L.T.D.	6.8	4.9
		10.4	11.2			Trade Payables	12.9	10.2
		.0	1.0			Income Taxes Payable	.3	.2
		25.1	13.8			All Other Current	21.8	20.0
		40.6	30.7			Total Current	50.0	49.2
		17.0	7.6			Long-Term Debt	26.1	24.8
		.2	1.2			Deferred Taxes	.5	.1
		9.3	26.1			All Other Non-Current	19.1	15.1
		32.8	34.4			Net Worth	4.4	10.7
		100.0	100.0			Total Liabilties & Net Worth	100.0	100.0
						INCOME DATA		
		100.0	100.0			Net Sales	100.0	100.0
		48.5	50.8			Gross Profit	47.9	54.0
		41.3	43.8			Operating Expenses	44.4	48.9
		7.2	7.0			Operating Profit	3.5	5.1
		.5	.8			All Other Expenses (net)	3.4	2.0
		6.7	6.2			Profit Before Taxes	.0	3.1
						RATIOS		
		2.2	2.2				2.0	2.3
		1.3	1.3			Current	1.0	1.2
		1.0	1.0				.6	.7
		2.1	2.0				1.5	1.9
		1.2	1.1			Quick	.8	1.0
		.8	.6				.4	.5
		27 13.6	**28** 13.0				**28** 13.2	**27** 13.5
		36 10.1	**42** 8.6			Sales/Receivables	**39** 9.4	**41** 8.8
		64 5.7	**68** 5.4				**60** 6.0	**58** 6.3
		0 UND	**0** UND				**0** UND	**0** UND
		0 UND	**3** 110.9			Cost of Sales/Inventory	**5** 67.7	**3** 143.8
		22 16.7	**27** 13.3				**23** 15.6	**23** 15.5
		18 20.7	**17** 20.9				**15** 24.6	**12** 29.5
		26 13.8	**50** 7.3			Cost of Sales/Payables	**33** 11.0	**29** 12.6
		59 6.2	**126** 2.9				**84** 4.3	**54** 6.7
		5.4	7.2				8.3	6.4
		14.2	23.2			Sales/Working Capital	183.6	22.6
		-506.6	-102.6				-8.1	-11.4
		50.6	72.8				7.0	13.0
		(18) 6.4	(18) 13.1			EBIT/Interest	(89) 1.6	(89) 3.6
		1.4	.9				-.9	.6
							2.3	2.5
						Net Profit + Depr., Dep., Amort./Cur. Mat. L/T/D	(18) .6	(12) 2.1
							-3.8	.6
		.1	.2				.3	.2
		.7	NM			Fixed/Worth	49.0	NM
		-1.4	-.1				-.1	-.2
		.8	.8				1.8	1.3
		2.3	-27.5			Debt/Worth	-8.0	-15.7
		-5.3	-2.3				-1.8	-2.1
		90.4	67.2				55.7	70.9
		(18) 32.5	(11) 19.4			% Profit Before Taxes/Tangible Net Worth	(47) 10.1	(48) 18.8
		6.4	-14.6				-18.5	4.7
		19.4	21.7				9.7	16.0
		9.8	9.2			% Profit Before Taxes/Total Assets	2.0	6.0
		1.9	-1.5				-8.1	-1.6
		56.8	58.0				66.0	71.6
		18.8	17.8			Sales/Net Fixed Assets	20.8	25.2
		8.0	10.7				10.2	9.9
		2.8	2.0				3.0	3.0
		2.3	1.4			Sales/Total Assets	2.0	2.0
		1.7	1.1				1.0	1.3
		.8	1.0				.8	.8
		(21) 1.1	(14) 2.4			% Depr., Dep., Amort./Sales	(64) 1.4	(64) 1.6
		2.4	4.6				2.2	2.8
							2.6	2.5
						% Officers', Directors' Owners' Comp/Sales	(29) 5.2	(27) 5.3
							10.5	9.5
3509M	29608M	312218M	919061M	627439M	2260127M	Net Sales ($)	3000648M	4518879M
665M	7857M	143779M	604216M	540093M	1105554M	Total Assets ($)	3007780M	2833575M

M = $ thousand MM = $ million

See Pages 9 through 22 for Explanation of Ratios and Data

Comparative Historical Data				Current Data Sorted by Sales					
			Type of Statement						
21	9	15	Unqualified				2	4	9
13	12	12	Reviewed			1	2	4	5
13	10	6	Compiled		2	1	1	1	1
13	13	8	Tax Returns	1	2	2	1	1	1
53	41	35	Other	1	2	2	5	12	13
4/1/11-3/31/12 ALL	4/1/12-3/31/13 ALL	4/1/13-3/31/14 ALL		9 (4/1-9/30/13)			67 (10/1/13-3/31/14)		
				0-1MM	1-3MM	3-5MM	5-10MM	10-25MM	25MM & OVER
113	85	76	**NUMBER OF STATEMENTS**	2	6	6	11	22	29
%	%	%	**ASSETS**	%	%	%	%	%	%
16.0	17.5	17.0	Cash & Equivalents				28.5	17.8	11.9
26.3	22.0	25.1	Trade Receivables (net)				20.8	27.4	20.6
6.2	5.0	4.2	Inventory				4.0	3.7	3.4
4.2	4.1	3.3	All Other Current				2.5	2.2	4.7
52.8	48.5	49.6	Total Current				55.8	51.1	40.6
14.2	16.2	13.1	Fixed Assets (net)				16.0	16.8	10.3
22.6	20.5	24.8	Intangibles (net)				16.8	19.3	35.4
10.4	14.7	12.5	All Other Non-Current				11.5	12.8	13.7
100.0	100.0	100.0	Total				100.0	100.0	100.0
			LIABILITIES						
8.1	13.1	4.7	Notes Payable-Short Term				7.2	1.0	2.1
6.2	2.8	3.8	Cur. Mat.-L.T.D.				.6	3.2	6.5
14.3	13.6	12.0	Trade Payables				9.0	10.6	11.3
.2	.3	.5	Income Taxes Payable				.6	.2	.9
21.9	21.4	20.1	All Other Current				14.9	25.7	16.5
50.7	51.3	41.1	Total Current				32.4	40.8	37.3
17.9	23.3	23.0	Long-Term Debt				14.6	13.3	19.9
.4	.4	.5	Deferred Taxes				1.1	.2	.8
13.1	14.6	14.3	All Other Non-Current				14.7	10.8	20.8
17.8	10.4	21.1	Net Worth				37.2	34.9	21.2
100.0	100.0	100.0	Total Liabilties & Net Worth				100.0	100.0	100.0
			INCOME DATA						
100.0	100.0	100.0	Net Sales				100.0	100.0	100.0
50.3	49.8	50.9	Gross Profit				52.3	49.1	50.1
44.8	44.9	43.3	Operating Expenses				41.9	46.3	39.7
5.6	4.9	7.6	Operating Profit				10.4	2.8	10.4
1.7	.8	1.3	All Other Expenses (net)				-.1	.5	2.5
3.8	4.1	6.3	Profit Before Taxes				10.5	2.3	7.9
			RATIOS						
2.2	1.9	2.1					2.0	2.2	1.9
1.2	1.1	1.3	Current				1.5	1.1	1.1
.7	.7	.9					1.2	.7	.9
1.8	1.6	2.0					2.0	2.1	1.4
1.0	.9	1.0	Quick				1.3	.9	1.0
.6	.6	.6					.8	.6	.6
24 15.3	**19** 18.9	**26** 13.8					**21** 17.1	**26** 14.0	**29** 12.8
36 10.2	**33** 11.1	**37** 9.8	Sales/Receivables				**33** 11.0	**37** 9.8	**34** 10.6
60 6.1	**49** 7.4	**64** 5.7					**69** 5.3	**59** 6.2	**66** 5.5
0 UND	**0** UND	**0** UND					**0** UND	**0** UND	**0** UND
0 UND	**0** UND	**1** 698.4	Cost of Sales/Inventory				**0** UND	**3** 129.6	**3** 115.5
21 17.5	**23** 15.8	**20** 18.2					**27** 13.3	**28** 13.0	**20** 18.5
12 31.1	**14** 27.0	**18** 20.0					**20** 18.2	**17** 21.8	**14** 25.9
32 11.4	**30** 12.2	**35** 10.5	Cost of Sales/Payables				**43** 8.4	**28** 13.2	**41** 8.8
64 5.7	**68** 5.4	**68** 5.4					**130** 2.8	**70** 5.2	**70** 5.2
7.1	8.2	7.2					8.1	5.5	8.1
28.3	44.3	29.5	Sales/Working Capital				13.7	92.5	46.6
-14.6	-19.5	-57.8					44.4	-23.5	-93.5
17.0	22.9	21.8						69.4	31.0
(92) 3.4	(67) 6.4	(57) 6.3	EBIT/Interest					(15) 7.0	(24) 5.4
.5	1.1	1.4						1.2	1.4
2.9	3.2	23.5							
(15) 2.7	(12) 2.0	(13) 2.6	Net Profit + Depr., Dep., Amort./Cur. Mat. L/T/D						
-.6	1.2	.5							
.3	.2	.1					.1	.1	.7
2.0	1.3	1.4	Fixed/Worth				.6	.5	-.5
-.2	-.4	-.3					-1.4	-13.3	-.1
1.2	1.2	.9					.9	.5	2.3
16.7	21.1	14.9	Debt/Worth				1.7	2.2	-10.5
-2.2	-2.4	-2.5					-9.4	-5.3	-2.0
66.9	66.5	82.9						91.7	77.3
(60) 28.8	(48) 21.0	(41) 23.2	% Profit Before Taxes/Tangible Net Worth					(15) 15.2	(11) 58.1
6.3	-2.7	3.1						-14.6	7.9
16.1	15.4	19.4					48.0	18.8	22.5
6.1	4.9	9.1	% Profit Before Taxes/Total Assets				9.3	5.6	9.1
-.8	-1.2	.8					3.3	-1.6	1.5
70.7	74.4	67.5					129.3	32.0	56.7
27.4	21.6	25.1	Sales/Net Fixed Assets				24.8	16.6	22.3
11.1	9.4	10.7					4.9	8.8	12.6
3.0	3.1	2.8					2.8	2.8	2.3
2.0	1.9	1.9	Sales/Total Assets				2.1	2.1	1.4
1.2	1.2	1.2					.6	1.4	.8
.7	.9	.8						.8	.7
(71) 1.5	(62) 1.5	(48) 1.5	% Depr., Dep., Amort./Sales					(18) 1.8	(19) 1.5
2.6	3.4	3.9						4.0	3.8
3.6	3.5	2.6							
(28) 5.4	(22) 8.1	(18) 4.1	% Officers', Directors' Owners' Comp/Sales						
7.8	14.9	7.0							
3471385M	2692027M	4151962M	Net Sales ($)	1111M	9495M	24596M	84521M	352831M	3679408M
2597080M	2235853M	2402164M	Total Assets ($)	561M	3500M	17395M	66108M	219426M	2095174M

M = $ thousand MM = $ million

See Pages 9 through 22 for Explanation of Ratios and Data

	Current Data Sorted by Assets						Comparative Historical Data	
Type of Statement								
Unqualified		1	5	8	5	5	22	20
Reviewed		1	11	6	1		22	17
Compiled		3	3	1			2	7
Tax Returns	4	3	3				12	9
Other	1	6	9	13	5	5	41	40
	16 (4/1-9/30/13)		83 (10/1/13-3/31/14)				4/1/09-3/31/10	4/1/10-3/31/11
	0-500M	500M-2MM	2-10MM	10-50MM	50-100MM	100-250MM	ALL	ALL
NUMBER OF STATEMENTS	5	14	31	28	11	10	99	93
ASSETS	%	%	%	%	%	%	%	%
Cash & Equivalents		15.7	13.2	11.9	12.7	12.9	12.5	14.1
Trade Receivables (net)		26.2	20.5	19.1	16.3	17.7	22.2	21.8
Inventory		35.9	35.2	19.9	12.4	14.1	26.3	26.9
All Other Current		4.1	6.2	10.2	12.2	4.5	6.5	6.6
Total Current		81.9	75.1	61.1	53.6	49.2	67.6	69.4
Fixed Assets (net)		5.2	9.1	8.2	7.1	8.4	11.6	10.9
Intangibles (net)		3.1	7.6	15.3	30.4	36.4	13.6	11.2
All Other Non-Current		9.8	8.2	15.4	8.9	6.0	7.2	8.5
Total		100.0	100.0	100.0	100.0	100.0	100.0	100.0
LIABILITIES								
Notes Payable-Short Term		28.8	4.5	3.6	2.9	.5	8.2	6.1
Cur. Mat.-L.T.D.		1.9	1.4	3.1	1.7	2.8	2.6	4.1
Trade Payables		16.8	12.5	11.4	7.4	7.0	10.6	13.0
Income Taxes Payable		.0	.3	.6	.0	.2	.4	.4
All Other Current		22.1	11.0	23.4	17.1	16.8	13.4	14.8
Total Current		69.7	29.8	42.1	29.1	27.3	35.1	38.3
Long-Term Debt		5.6	7.3	5.4	12.8	40.5	16.0	9.9
Deferred Taxes		.0	.0	.9	.4	2.4	.4	.6
All Other Non-Current		13.4	13.3	7.6	20.5	4.0	12.6	17.8
Net Worth		11.2	49.6	44.0	37.2	25.8	35.9	33.4
Total Liabilties & Net Worth		100.0	100.0	100.0	100.0	100.0	100.0	100.0
INCOME DATA								
Net Sales		100.0	100.0	100.0	100.0	100.0	100.0	100.0
Gross Profit		63.9	53.3	52.8	52.6	55.7	53.0	53.2
Operating Expenses		56.6	49.0	46.1	51.4	44.9	50.2	49.6
Operating Profit		7.3	4.3	6.7	1.2	10.8	2.8	3.7
All Other Expenses (net)		.9	1.5	1.7	-.3	3.2	2.1	1.9
Profit Before Taxes		6.4	2.8	5.0	1.5	7.6	.7	1.7
RATIOS								
Current		2.9	3.8	3.5	3.4	2.1	3.2	3.4
		1.5	3.0	1.7	2.8	1.7	2.1	2.2
		.9	1.9	.8	1.0	1.4	1.3	1.3
Quick		1.9	2.2	1.7	2.1	1.3	1.8	1.7
		.5	1.2	.7	.7	1.0	.9	1.1
		.4	.8	.4	.6	.7	.5	.5
Sales/Receivables		**31** 11.7	**23** 16.0	**30** 12.0	**63** 5.8	**29** 12.5	**28** 13.2	**23** 15.7
		47 7.7	**41** 8.9	**48** 7.6	**70** 5.2	**59** 6.2	**49** 7.4	**50** 7.3
		81 4.5	**76** 4.8	**78** 4.7	**85** 4.3	**91** 4.0	**83** 4.4	**88** 4.2
Cost of Sales/Inventory		**55** 6.6	**104** 3.5	**79** 4.6	**96** 3.8	**63** 5.8	**63** 5.8	**58** 6.3
		159 2.3	**159** 2.3	**130** 2.8	**118** 3.1	**118** 3.1	**140** 2.6	**116** 3.1
		912 .4	**261** 1.4	**228** 1.6	**140** 2.6	**166** 2.2	**246** 1.5	**237** 1.5
Cost of Sales/Payables		**24** 15.3	**19** 19.6	**33** 11.0	**30** 12.2	**22** 16.9	**23** 15.6	**26** 14.0
		57 6.4	**53** 6.9	**54** 6.7	**50** 7.3	**53** 6.9	**47** 7.7	**47** 7.8
		146 2.5	**114** 3.2	**111** 3.3	**122** 3.0	**111** 3.3	**87** 4.2	**81** 4.5
Sales/Working Capital		3.7	2.0	2.2	1.0	3.5	2.6	2.3
		5.3	3.2	5.1	4.1	5.3	4.3	4.0
		-28.3	6.1	NM	-89.9	7.9	11.6	10.1
EBIT/Interest		20.3	35.0	34.4		47.3	8.1	11.6
		(11) 3.5	(23) 12.7	(24) 4.1		4.1	(86) 2.8	(72) 4.0
		.4	2.0	.2		2.0	-1.0	.4
Net Profit + Depr., Dep., Amort./Cur. Mat. L/T/D							15.3	13.5
							(20) 1.8	(14) 1.5
							.6	-.3
Fixed/Worth		.0	.0	.0	.2	.2	.1	.1
		.1	.1	.2	.4	NM	.3	.3
		NM	.6	.9	-3.3	-.1	1.6	1.3
Debt/Worth		1.0	.4	.6	1.2	.8	.5	.6
		2.2	.9	1.2	5.8	NM	1.7	1.4
		-6.1	2.1	10.3	-33.5	-1.9	34.6	24.6
% Profit Before Taxes/Tangible Net Worth		66.6	26.6	31.2			24.5	35.5
		(10) 13.6	(28) 10.1	(23) 12.5			(76) 6.2	(73) 9.4
		.8	2.2	2.0			-3.7	.0
% Profit Before Taxes/Total Assets		21.5	10.5	16.1	6.9	8.5	9.4	9.1
		4.8	5.7	3.5	3.5	6.3	2.4	3.5
		-.2	.2	-1.1	-2.8	3.3	-3.4	-2.5
Sales/Net Fixed Assets		469.9	120.2	68.9	43.6	35.6	55.2	75.9
		87.5	47.7	25.6	36.8	24.9	24.6	24.1
		30.4	8.5	11.7	8.6	9.0	8.2	10.0
Sales/Total Assets		3.0	2.1	1.4	1.2	1.2	1.8	2.1
		1.6	1.5	1.2	1.0	.8	1.4	1.5
		1.0	1.0	.8	.6	.7	1.0	.9
% Depr., Dep., Amort./Sales			.6	.5			.6	.6
			(18) .9	(21) 1.5			(71) 1.8	(63) 1.5
			2.1	3.4			2.9	2.5
% Officers', Directors' Owners' Comp/Sales							3.8	1.4
							(19) 5.0	(17) 2.9
							11.8	14.7
Net Sales ($)	5701M	36294M	275620M	787275M	744563M	1313718M	3031102M	2913090M
Total Assets ($)	1440M	17089M	182137M	678686M	814655M	1466685M	2670146M	2580931M

M = $ thousand MM = $ million

See Pages 9 through 22 for Explanation of Ratios and Data

Comparative Historical Data				Current Data Sorted by Sales					
			Type of Statement						
16	12	24	Unqualified		3		5	3	13
17	12	19	Reviewed	1	1	2	4	8	3
8	6	7	Compiled		2	1	1	2	1
10	12	10	Tax Returns	2	3	1	4		
44	39	39	Other	2	4	3	3	12	15
				16 (4/1-9/30/13)			83 (10/1/13-3/31/14)		
4/1/11-3/31/12 ALL	4/1/12-3/31/13 ALL	4/1/13-3/31/14 ALL		0-1MM	1-3MM	3-5MM	5-10MM	10-25MM	25MM & OVER
95	81	99	**NUMBER OF STATEMENTS**	5	13	7	17	25	32
%	%	%	**ASSETS**	%	%	%	%	%	%
12.9	12.7	13.3	Cash & Equivalents		13.4		13.9	8.5	14.3
22.6	23.9	19.8	Trade Receivables (net)		18.6		23.6	19.8	19.5
25.5	22.7	25.9	Inventory		29.8		29.3	25.7	18.3
5.6	4.4	7.6	All Other Current		5.5		9.0	11.3	6.4
66.6	63.6	66.6	Total Current		67.4		75.8	65.2	58.4
10.1	8.8	8.1	Fixed Assets (net)		6.1		10.1	8.0	7.9
14.5	14.3	15.1	Intangibles (net)		13.8		6.3	14.5	25.6
8.9	13.2	10.2	All Other Non-Current		12.7		7.9	12.2	8.1
100.0	100.0	100.0	Total		100.0		100.0	100.0	100.0
			LIABILITIES						
10.0	5.5	7.4	Notes Payable-Short Term		10.5		2.4	4.9	3.0
2.3	2.7	2.5	Cur. Mat.-L.T.D.		3.0		.6	3.4	2.1
12.2	12.7	11.4	Trade Payables		16.4		9.9	13.6	9.7
.3	.4	.3	Income Taxes Payable		.1		.2	.5	.4
14.0	21.3	19.9	All Other Current		15.8		27.1	17.1	18.7
38.7	42.7	41.6	Total Current		45.8		40.2	39.7	33.8
10.3	9.9	12.0	Long-Term Debt		14.3		6.0	3.4	20.0
.7	.7	.5	Deferred Taxes		.0		.5	.7	.9
11.8	7.8	14.7	All Other Non-Current		27.0		8.6	16.4	6.9
38.4	39.0	31.2	Net Worth		12.9		44.7	39.8	38.4
100.0	100.0	100.0	Total Liabilties & Net Worth		100.0		100.0	100.0	100.0
			INCOME DATA						
100.0	100.0	100.0	Net Sales		100.0		100.0	100.0	100.0
53.5	54.4	55.2	Gross Profit		51.5		52.7	50.9	56.3
47.0	48.0	49.9	Operating Expenses		51.3		46.1	46.5	49.3
6.5	6.4	5.4	Operating Profit		.2		6.5	4.4	7.0
.7	1.1	1.5	All Other Expenses (net)		2.2		1.1	1.2	1.3
5.8	5.2	3.9	Profit Before Taxes		-2.0		5.4	3.3	5.7
			RATIOS						
2.8	3.7	3.5			3.8		4.7	3.8	2.8
2.0	2.0	2.1	Current		1.5		3.1	2.1	1.7
1.3	1.1	1.2			1.0		2.0	1.1	1.1
1.5	1.8	1.6			2.0		2.5	1.6	1.6
1.0	1.3	.9	Quick		.6		1.2	.8	.7
.6	.5	.5			.4		.6	.3	.6
26 14.1	**35** 10.5	**29** 12.8			**28** 13.1		**22** 16.8	**30** 12.1	**33** 11.0
52 7.0	**57** 6.4	**47** 7.8	Sales/Receivables		**43** 8.5		**43** 8.5	**47** 7.8	**62** 5.9
79 4.6	**81** 4.5	**79** 4.6			**104** 3.5		**68** 5.4	**79** 4.6	**87** 4.2
62 5.9	**58** 6.3	**83** 4.4			**40** 9.2		**111** 3.3	**76** 4.8	**87** 4.2
135 2.7	**135** 2.7	**140** 2.6	Cost of Sales/Inventory		**159** 2.3		**159** 2.3	**182** 2.0	**118** 3.1
215 1.7	**203** 1.8	**228** 1.6			**521** .7		**203** 1.8	**243** 1.5	**159** 2.3
30 12.2	**26** 14.1	**24** 15.1			**2** 239.4		**19** 19.3	**30** 12.2	**30** 12.0
49 7.5	**54** 6.8	**51** 7.2	Cost of Sales/Payables		**76** 4.8		**44** 8.3	**76** 4.8	**45** 8.1
83 4.4	**94** 3.9	**111** 3.3			**152** 2.4		**63** 5.8	**114** 3.2	**118** 3.1
2.7	2.4	2.1			1.8		2.0	2.2	2.2
5.9	5.2	4.5	Sales/Working Capital		4.4		3.2	4.2	5.3
13.8	34.4	18.3			NM		7.4	17.4	26.1
31.8	14.8	25.2					82.6	29.4	31.4
(82) 5.7	(71) 3.2	(82) 4.7	EBIT/Interest				(13) 15.9	(21) 5.4	(29) 4.4
.7	.4	.6					1.0	.8	1.1
19.6	3.8	4.5							
(11) 4.4	(15) 2.0	(16) 2.2	Net Profit + Depr., Dep., Amort./Cur. Mat. L/T/D						
2.1	.3	.4							
.0	.0	.0			.0		.0	.0	.1
.2	.2	.2	Fixed/Worth		.0		.0	.2	.3
1.5	.9	.9			.5		.6	NM	-1.0
.6	.5	.6			1.2		.4	.7	.8
1.4	1.3	1.6	Debt/Worth		2.6		.6	1.1	3.6
60.8	19.1	306.5			-4.8		7.3	NM	-10.6
35.3	29.3	31.2					25.1	31.2	36.3
(72) 14.2	(63) 11.8	(75) 10.1	% Profit Before Taxes/Tangible Net Worth				(15) 9.8	(19) 14.0	(22) 10.8
2.8	2.9	1.0					5.0	6.5	1.3
13.5	11.2	10.5			10.2		13.0	11.6	9.3
5.7	4.2	4.1	% Profit Before Taxes/Total Assets		.3		5.7	4.1	4.6
-.2	-1.1	-.5			-21.2		.6	-.9	1.0
84.3	89.3	85.8			UND		116.3	103.0	43.4
29.5	30.9	36.8	Sales/Net Fixed Assets		148.1		47.7	36.9	26.4
11.0	12.8	13.0			25.3		12.2	9.0	12.5
2.0	2.2	1.8			2.1		2.2	1.7	1.3
1.4	1.4	1.3	Sales/Total Assets		1.3		1.5	1.3	1.1
1.0	.9	.8			.8		.8	1.0	.8
.5	.6	.6						.3	1.0
(59) 1.1	(49) 1.1	(60) 1.3	% Depr., Dep., Amort./Sales					(17) .7	(21) 1.8
2.2	2.3	2.6						3.0	2.8
2.3	2.8	1.6							
(16) 7.1	(19) 6.2	(20) 3.7	% Officers', Directors' Owners' Comp/Sales						
15.5	22.3	8.9							
3457874M	**2159508M**	**3163171M**	Net Sales ($)	**2638M**	**24595M**	**28421M**	**130690M**	**388622M**	**2588205M**
3354526M	**2133768M**	**3160692M**	Total Assets ($)	**2587M**	**26348M**	**18431M**	**128036M**	**376402M**	**2608888M**

M = $ thousand MM = $ million

See Pages 9 through 22 for Explanation of Ratios and Data

Current Data Sorted by Assets							Comparative Historical Data	
						Type of Statement		
		2	4	5	3	Unqualified	17	17
		6	2			Reviewed	9	11
1	1	1				Compiled	2	3
2		2				Tax Returns	3	6
1	3	8	4	1	2	Other	29	23
6 (4/1-9/30/13)			42 (10/1/13-3/31/14)				4/1/09-3/31/10	4/1/10-3/31/11
0-500M	500M-2MM	2-10MM	10-50MM	50-100MM	100-250MM		ALL	ALL
4	4	19	10	6	5	**NUMBER OF STATEMENTS**	60	60
%	%	%	%	%	%	**ASSETS**	%	%
		16.1	12.3			Cash & Equivalents	13.7	17.8
		21.1	23.3			Trade Receivables (net)	25.2	25.5
		16.3	13.6			Inventory	12.1	13.4
		1.4	3.3			All Other Current	5.2	5.7
		54.9	52.5			Total Current	56.2	62.3
		9.8	14.8			Fixed Assets (net)	16.4	13.3
		14.8	24.3			Intangibles (net)	19.7	17.2
		20.4	8.4			All Other Non-Current	7.7	7.2
		100.0	100.0			Total	100.0	100.0
						LIABILITIES		
		7.3	6.1			Notes Payable-Short Term	7.2	9.0
		.4	3.1			Cur. Mat.-L.T.D.	2.7	2.2
		11.8	10.0			Trade Payables	15.0	14.7
		.0	.0			Income Taxes Payable	.2	.8
		16.1	12.6			All Other Current	15.9	16.0
		35.6	31.8			Total Current	40.9	42.8
		2.7	31.1			Long-Term Debt	13.7	11.2
		.3	.7			Deferred Taxes	.8	.4
		17.0	7.7			All Other Non-Current	17.2	13.6
		44.4	28.8			Net Worth	27.5	32.0
		100.0	100.0			Total Liabilties & Net Worth	100.0	100.0
						INCOME DATA		
		100.0	100.0			Net Sales	100.0	100.0
		56.2	53.6			Gross Profit	52.0	55.5
		50.0	46.7			Operating Expenses	47.0	47.9
		6.3	6.8			Operating Profit	5.0	7.6
		.0	4.6			All Other Expenses (net)	3.0	2.5
		6.3	2.2			Profit Before Taxes	2.0	5.1
						RATIOS		
		3.8	2.5				2.1	2.5
		1.7	1.7			Current	1.4	1.4
		1.1	1.0				1.0	1.0
		2.2	1.8				1.5	1.6
		1.3	1.3			Quick	1.0	1.0
		.6	.9				.6	.6
		19 19.6	**24** 15.5				**32** 11.3	**26** 14.0
		29 12.7	**51** 7.1			Sales/Receivables	**44** 8.2	**41** 8.8
		56 6.5	**78** 4.7				**64** 5.7	**65** 5.6
		0 UND	**0** UND				**0** UND	**0** UND
		19 19.2	**10** 35.6			Cost of Sales/Inventory	**15** 25.1	**20** 18.2
		81 4.5	**126** 2.9				**77** 4.7	**88** 4.1
		15 23.9	**15** 25.1				**17** 22.1	**16** 22.8
		35 10.5	**34** 10.8			Cost of Sales/Payables	**42** 8.6	**45** 8.1
		63 5.8	**83** 4.4				**82** 4.5	**91** 4.0
		3.3	5.1				5.6	4.3
		9.5	20.9			Sales/Working Capital	16.6	15.8
		291.2	-142.8				-78.4	201.2
		77.1					8.9	22.1
		(13) 10.0				EBIT/Interest	(53) 3.2	(49) 5.1
		-.7					.2	.9
							6.8	5.4
						Net Profit + Depr., Dep., Amort./Cur. Mat. L/T/D	(12) 4.1	(14) 2.0
							1.1	.5
		.0	.2				.2	.1
		.3	1.5			Fixed/Worth	1.6	.6
		1.0	-.3				-.7	NM
		.4	.5				1.3	1.0
		1.7	3.5			Debt/Worth	6.5	6.3
		21.7	-2.0				-4.0	-9.3
		51.7					80.8	110.5
		(15) 20.4				% Profit Before Taxes/Tangible Net Worth	(37) 18.0	(41) 24.7
		13.5					-6.5	3.4
		24.0	15.3				15.2	19.6
		12.2	3.5			% Profit Before Taxes/Total Assets	5.2	6.8
		4.5	-2.9				-6.4	.3
		137.1	27.4				61.3	107.3
		41.6	14.4			Sales/Net Fixed Assets	19.9	27.7
		14.4	6.7				6.4	6.4
		2.5	2.3				2.7	2.9
		2.2	1.5			Sales/Total Assets	1.9	1.8
		1.2	1.2				1.1	1.0
		.4					.7	.7
		(12) .9				% Depr., Dep., Amort./Sales	(41) 1.9	(37) 1.5
		2.5					3.5	3.3
								2.6
						% Officers', Directors' Owners' Comp/Sales		(16) 3.6
								10.1
2890M	11703M	189533M	306036M	714234M	649863M	Net Sales ($)	1988380M	2331661M
842M	4618M	97323M	211667M	479539M	675153M	Total Assets ($)	1673610M	1986798M

M = $ thousand MM = $ million

See Pages 9 through 22 for Explanation of Ratios and Data

Comparative Historical Data / **Current Data Sorted by Sales**

			Type of Statement						
16	10	14	Unqualified					4	10
20	15	8	Reviewed				4	2	2
1	5	3	Compiled	1			1	1	
10	9	4	Tax Returns	1	1	1		1	
21	33	19	Other	1	4		3	5	6
				6 (4/1-9/30/13)			42 (10/1/13-3/31/14)		
4/1/11-3/31/12 ALL	4/1/12-3/31/13 ALL	4/1/13-3/31/14 ALL		0-1MM	1-3MM	3-5MM	5-10MM	10-25MM	25MM & OVER
68	72	48	NUMBER OF STATEMENTS	3	5	1	8	13	18
%	%	%	ASSETS	%	%	%	%	%	%
15.2	16.0	14.5	Cash & Equivalents					12.3	14.0
23.1	22.4	21.9	Trade Receivables (net)					21.0	21.4
14.6	16.1	13.6	Inventory					17.9	12.4
6.6	3.5	4.0	All Other Current					2.3	2.3
59.5	58.0	54.1	Total Current					53.5	50.0
16.3	13.7	15.2	Fixed Assets (net)					13.9	13.7
15.6	18.7	18.7	Intangibles (net)					12.9	28.8
8.6	9.5	12.0	All Other Non-Current					19.7	7.4
100.0	100.0	100.0	Total					100.0	100.0
			LIABILITIES						
6.5	6.0	6.8	Notes Payable-Short Term					5.1	2.3
5.4	3.9	1.7	Cur. Mat.-L.T.D.					1.2	2.9
12.9	12.5	10.4	Trade Payables					13.1	11.4
.1	1.0	.1	Income Taxes Payable					.1	.1
16.7	15.4	13.6	All Other Current					13.0	15.0
41.6	38.7	32.6	Total Current					32.5	31.7
15.4	20.9	21.9	Long-Term Debt					8.8	26.6
.3	.4	.5	Deferred Taxes					.6	.9
18.2	13.6	12.5	All Other Non-Current					11.6	10.0
24.5	26.3	32.6	Net Worth					46.5	30.8
100.0	100.0	100.0	Total Liabilties & Net Worth					100.0	100.0
			INCOME DATA						
100.0	100.0	100.0	Net Sales					100.0	100.0
54.7	53.7	51.8	Gross Profit					54.3	43.1
48.5	45.4	45.4	Operating Expenses					47.8	35.6
6.2	8.3	6.4	Operating Profit					6.5	7.5
2.6	2.2	1.8	All Other Expenses (net)					1.1	3.5
3.6	6.1	4.6	Profit Before Taxes					5.4	3.9
			RATIOS						
2.9	3.2	2.9						2.8	2.1
1.5	1.4	1.5	Current					1.4	1.2
.9	.9	1.0						1.1	1.0
1.9	2.0	1.8						2.0	1.5
.9	1.0	1.1	Quick					1.0	.9
.6	.4	.8						.6	.8
20 18.0	18 20.1	23 15.8						20 18.1	42 8.7
43 8.5	45 8.2	46 8.0	Sales/Receivables					32 11.4	49 7.4
66 5.5	66 5.5	60 6.1						57 6.4	72 5.1
0 UND	0 UND	0 UND						0 UND	0 UND
23 15.6	25 14.8	17 21.0	Cost of Sales/Inventory					40 9.2	19 19.4
94 3.9	96 3.8	72 5.1						111 3.3	68 5.4
26 14.2	19 19.6	15 23.7						29 12.7	17 21.2
47 7.7	34 10.8	33 11.2	Cost of Sales/Payables					38 9.6	31 11.8
89 4.1	79 4.6	61 6.0						68 5.4	60 6.1
4.0	3.8	3.8						5.5	5.2
12.5	12.6	11.9	Sales/Working Capital					10.9	37.1
-69.8	-48.4	UND						169.2	-143.1
15.1	18.9	23.9						72.6	7.2
(57) 5.2	(56) 6.5	(38) 3.2	EBIT/Interest					(10) 6.5	(14) 2.5
1.2	1.8	1.6						2.2	.3
4.5	9.0	40.9							
(10) 2.7	(11) 2.6	(11) 3.7	Net Profit + Depr., Dep., Amort./Cur. Mat. L/T/D						
1.1	.4	2.1							
.2	.1	.1						.1	.2
1.1	1.0	.7	Fixed/Worth					.5	2.1
-.4	-.4	-4.0						NM	-.2
1.2	.7	.7						.5	.7
5.4	3.9	2.4	Debt/Worth					1.7	6.2
-4.5	-3.8	-15.9						NM	-1.9
63.5	85.7	44.8						51.5	45.0
(44) 18.8	(46) 28.6	(33) 17.0	% Profit Before Taxes/Tangible Net Worth					(10) 14.2	(10) 10.5
6.4	11.0	2.1						11.1	.3
13.8	24.5	15.9						19.7	10.0
6.9	8.3	6.2	% Profit Before Taxes/Total Assets					8.7	3.4
.4	1.9	1.6						4.2	-.3
101.5	102.0	92.8						66.1	60.5
21.3	23.5	27.1	Sales/Net Fixed Assets					33.7	18.9
6.6	6.7	8.4						6.4	9.9
2.9	2.5	2.4						2.8	2.2
1.9	1.7	1.7	Sales/Total Assets					1.8	1.5
1.2	1.0	1.1						1.4	.7
.7	.8	.7						.4	.8
(47) 1.5	(44) 1.5	(31) 1.9	% Depr., Dep., Amort./Sales					(10) 1.5	(12) 2.4
3.0	2.7	4.2						7.2	4.4
2.7	2.1								
(22) 5.2	(21) 4.3		% Officers', Directors' Owners' Comp/Sales						
8.6	8.9								
2082172M	2995151M	1874259M	Net Sales ($)	1655M	10010M	3136M	58049M	190101M	1611308M
1713754M	2579221M	1469142M	Total Assets ($)	826M	7001M	5103M	30813M	121193M	1304206M

M = $ thousand MM = $ million

See Pages 9 through 22 for Explanation of Ratios and Data

Current Data Sorted by Assets / **Comparative Historical Data**

0-500M	500M-2MM	2-10MM	10-50MM	50-100MM	100-250MM		4/1/09-3/31/10 ALL	4/1/10-3/31/11 ALL
						Type of Statement		
		12	15	6	14	Unqualified	86	89
	1	4	4	1		Reviewed	17	14
2	2	4	3			Compiled	6	11
6	9	1				Tax Returns	15	21
5	10	38	67	18	43	Other	135	137
35 (4/1-9/30/13)		230 (10/1/13-3/31/14)						
13	22	59	89	25	57	**NUMBER OF STATEMENTS**	259	272
%	%	%	%	%	%	**ASSETS**	%	%
20.7	30.9	24.2	26.8	29.7	21.8	Cash & Equivalents	26.2	24.1
37.7	32.0	33.2	27.4	11.2	16.0	Trade Receivables (net)	24.2	24.9
.0	3.5	.9	2.6	.9	.4	Inventory	1.7	1.9
3.2	4.4	5.8	7.5	7.2	4.1	All Other Current	5.8	6.9
61.6	70.9	64.1	64.3	49.0	42.3	Total Current	57.8	57.8
5.0	10.4	13.2	11.9	13.1	6.1	Fixed Assets (net)	10.7	9.3
14.5	6.1	10.9	14.6	30.8	46.6	Intangibles (net)	22.1	24.4
18.9	12.7	11.7	9.3	7.2	5.0	All Other Non-Current	9.4	8.4
100.0	100.0	100.0	100.0	100.0	100.0	Total	100.0	100.0
						LIABILITIES		
11.5	7.5	8.8	4.0	.4	.4	Notes Payable-Short Term	6.5	5.1
4.0	.4	4.2	3.4	1.8	1.4	Cur. Mat.-L.T.D.	4.0	4.6
10.9	7.0	8.0	8.0	2.9	5.0	Trade Payables	5.9	9.4
.7	.0	.0	.6	.2	1.2	Income Taxes Payable	.7	1.0
17.2	21.4	36.7	35.1	30.4	22.9	All Other Current	31.8	30.6
44.4	36.3	57.8	51.2	35.6	30.9	Total Current	49.0	50.7
29.3	7.9	9.6	22.8	19.2	29.7	Long-Term Debt	16.8	16.8
.1	.0	.2	.6	1.0	2.2	Deferred Taxes	1.1	1.2
20.7	13.6	9.1	10.0	14.3	9.2	All Other Non-Current	9.5	11.3
5.4	42.2	23.2	15.4	29.9	28.1	Net Worth	23.7	19.9
100.0	100.0	100.0	100.0	100.0	100.0	Total Liabilities & Net Worth	100.0	100.0
						INCOME DATA		
100.0	100.0	100.0	100.0	100.0	100.0	Net Sales	100.0	100.0
						Gross Profit		
95.6	92.6	95.6	93.1	94.3	92.3	Operating Expenses	92.9	92.9
4.4	7.4	4.4	6.9	5.7	7.7	Operating Profit	7.1	7.1
.4	.9	.9	2.9	3.4	6.4	All Other Expenses (net)	3.8	3.7
4.0	6.6	3.5	4.0	2.3	1.3	Profit Before Taxes	3.4	3.4
						RATIOS		
4.6	5.8	2.2	2.7	2.8	2.3		2.4	2.0
2.6	2.5	1.2	1.3	1.2	1.2	Current	1.3	1.2
.5	1.0	.8	.8	.8	.8		.8	.8
4.6	5.0	2.0	2.3	2.4	1.9		2.1	1.6
2.1	2.2	.9	1.0	1.0	1.0	Quick	1.0	1.0
.5	.7	.6	.6	.6	.6		.6	.6
0 UND	**4** 91.1	**29** 12.7	**37** 9.8	**20** 18.2	**50** 7.3		**39** 9.5	**36** 10.1
27 13.7	**16** 22.6	**56** 6.5	**57** 6.4	**47** 7.7	**65** 5.6	Sales/Receivables	**59** 6.2	**56** 6.5
42 8.7	**69** 5.3	**76** 4.8	**85** 4.3	**62** 5.9	**85** 4.3		**80** 4.6	**77** 4.7
						Cost of Sales/Inventory		
						Cost of Sales/Payables		
8.1	5.6	5.6	3.9	4.0	3.3		4.5	5.5
16.7	10.7	31.9	13.2	9.4	16.0	Sales/Working Capital	15.1	18.5
-18.2	-978.7	-13.3	-16.4	-12.1	-8.5		-12.4	-17.3
	56.4	36.6	26.9	12.4	8.8		12.3	11.4
	(11) 20.5	(45) 9.2	(65) 4.2	(19) .9	(45) 1.7	EBIT/Interest	(190) 3.1	(201) 2.3
	-4.2	-.9	-2.2	-5.3	.1		-1.6	-1.3
			17.5				8.0	4.1
			(18) 2.4			Net Profit + Depr., Dep., Amort./Cur. Mat. L/T/D	(35) 2.8	(51) 1.3
			.7				-.3	.0
.0	.0	.1	.1	.3	.4		.2	.1
.1	.2	.5	.5	2.5	-.2	Fixed/Worth	.7	1.0
-.3	.7	-2.5	-.4	-.1	.0		-.2	-.1
.4	.2	1.2	1.0	2.0	1.3		.9	1.3
2.2	1.0	2.4	4.9	9.7	-2.7	Debt/Worth	5.2	8.7
-3.1	4.6	-9.3	-3.0	-2.1	-1.5		-2.7	-2.2
	133.2	78.6	72.3	104.4	25.1		74.3	97.5
	(19) 78.2	(42) 51.6	(56) 22.9	(14) 24.6	(21) 11.5	% Profit Before Taxes/Tangible Net Worth	(162) 21.2	(154) 25.9
	24.3	17.2	-1.3	-.7	-10.0		.9	2.5
52.2	63.1	23.7	19.5	14.8	6.2		16.3	16.0
13.7	27.9	14.1	5.2	4.5	2.1	% Profit Before Taxes/Total Assets	4.7	4.9
1.2	-3.8	-2.9	-5.9	-11.3	-4.7		-6.2	-4.8
UND	UND	88.5	63.0	35.4	34.7		48.2	53.7
709.3	68.4	38.9	26.3	12.2	20.2	Sales/Net Fixed Assets	19.7	27.5
138.4	28.1	12.4	9.8	5.2	8.2		11.3	14.0
8.5	6.0	3.0	2.1	1.2	.9		2.2	2.4
4.4	4.1	2.1	1.5	1.0	.6	Sales/Total Assets	1.2	1.4
3.2	2.4	1.5	1.1	.7	.5		.8	.7
		.7	.9	3.1	2.9		1.2	1.1
		(33) 1.8	(59) 1.8	(14) 5.3	(22) 4.9	% Depr., Dep., Amort./Sales	(142) 2.5	(139) 2.5
		4.3	3.7	7.4	6.9		4.7	4.6
	4.8		1.7				4.2	3.2
	(11) 9.4		(10) 7.4			% Officers', Directors' Owners' Comp/Sales	(28) 9.5	(37) 7.6
	10.3		17.8				15.1	12.6
19501M	96335M	663812M	3357434M	1676876M	6912132M	Net Sales ($)	12382776M	13201487M
3960M	23649M	295407M	2014469M	1745074M	9440373M	Total Assets ($)	14052707M	14279089M

M = $ thousand MM = $ million

See Pages 9 through 22 for Explanation of Ratios and Data

Comparative Historical Data				Current Data Sorted by Sales					
			Type of Statement						
55	73	47	Unqualified			1	2	16	28
21	15	10	Reviewed		1	1	2	1	5
8	6	11	Compiled		2	2	2	5	
26	25	16	Tax Returns	2	8	4	2		
185	192	181	Other	3	7	6	20	45	100
4/1/11-3/31/12 ALL	**4/1/12-3/31/13 ALL**	**4/1/13-3/31/14 ALL**		**35 (4/1-9/30/13)**			**230 (10/1/13-3/31/14)**		
				0-1MM	**1-3MM**	**3-5MM**	**5-10MM**	**10-25MM**	**25MM & OVER**
295	311	265	**NUMBER OF STATEMENTS**	5	18	14	28	67	133
%	%	%	**ASSETS**	%	%	%	%	%	%
25.6	22.7	25.5	Cash & Equivalents		19.1	27.8	25.5	28.2	25.2
25.8	22.9	25.6	Trade Receivables (net)		43.1	30.2	23.9	26.6	22.5
1.6	1.4	1.5	Inventory		.0	4.0	2.6	.5	1.9
5.6	6.4	5.9	All Other Current		2.6	6.8	6.7	6.8	5.8
58.7	53.4	58.5	Total Current		64.8	68.7	58.8	62.1	55.3
9.5	10.7	10.6	Fixed Assets (net)		5.8	12.8	17.5	12.9	8.7
24.0	27.8	21.5	Intangibles (net)		9.7	9.9	14.7	13.2	29.3
7.9	8.1	9.5	All Other Non-Current		19.7	8.6	9.0	11.9	6.7
100.0	100.0	100.0	Total		100.0	100.0	100.0	100.0	100.0
			LIABILITIES						
3.8	4.1	4.6	Notes Payable-Short Term		5.7	6.6	8.8	6.7	1.8
3.2	3.8	2.8	Cur. Mat.-L.T.D.		3.1	1.3	3.2	4.4	2.1
8.2	7.5	7.0	Trade Payables		8.8	7.9	7.4	5.1	7.4
.6	.5	.5	Income Taxes Payable		.5	.0	.0	.2	.8
28.5	27.7	30.4	All Other Current		24.9	42.4	19.2	32.0	32.2
44.3	43.6	45.2	Total Current		43.0	58.2	38.6	48.4	44.2
15.2	23.2	20.1	Long-Term Debt		24.6	12.3	14.3	11.4	26.2
1.1	1.3	.8	Deferred Taxes		.1	.1	.5	.6	1.2
12.7	11.5	10.9	All Other Non-Current		16.5	10.8	9.6	9.7	11.1
26.6	20.5	23.0	Net Worth		15.8	18.6	37.0	29.8	17.3
100.0	100.0	100.0	Total Liabilties & Net Worth		100.0	100.0	100.0	100.0	100.0
			INCOME DATA						
100.0	100.0	100.0	Net Sales		100.0	100.0	100.0	100.0	100.0
			Gross Profit						
91.0	93.2	93.7	Operating Expenses		94.0	99.0	91.6	93.4	93.7
9.0	6.8	6.3	Operating Profit		6.0	1.0	8.4	6.6	6.3
2.8	3.9	3.0	All Other Expenses (net)		1.2	5.1	1.1	1.9	4.0
6.1	2.9	3.3	Profit Before Taxes		4.8	-4.1	7.3	4.8	2.2
			RATIOS						
2.7	2.2	2.6			3.3	3.4	4.1	2.6	2.3
1.4	1.2	1.3	Current		1.8	1.1	1.6	1.4	1.2
.8	.8	.8			.7	.5	.8	.8	.8
2.4	1.9	2.3			3.3	3.2	3.6	2.1	1.9
1.2	1.1	1.0	Quick		1.6	.8	1.4	1.1	.9
.6	.7	.6			.6	.4	.7	.7	.6
34 10.6	**33** 10.9	**31** 11.9			**13** 27.6	**16** 23.5	**11** 33.9	**32** 11.5	**40** 9.1
58 6.3	**58** 6.3	**57** 6.4	Sales/Receivables		**49** 7.4	**59** 6.2	**29** 12.6	**57** 6.4	**61** 6.0
81 4.5	**83** 4.4	**79** 4.6			**89** 4.1	**107** 3.4	**61** 6.0	**79** 4.6	**81** 4.5
			Cost of Sales/Inventory						
			Cost of Sales/Payables						
3.9	5.3	4.2			6.6	3.9	5.9	3.5	4.0
13.2	16.7	15.8	Sales/Working Capital		15.6	59.0	15.0	8.0	27.2
-14.1	-17.4	-14.6			-19.5	-3.7	-20.0	-18.5	-11.4
22.7	20.7	20.6			15.3		32.6	34.1	14.3
(209) 3.9	(236) 3.1	(194) 4.1	EBIT/Interest		(12) 4.4		(18) 9.3	(48) 8.4	(104) 2.0
-.6	.0	-.6			.6		.0	-1.6	-.2
32.8	7.2	7.9							12.4
(47) 2.6	(48) 3.3	(39) 2.7	Net Profit + Depr., Dep., Amort./Cur. Mat. L/T/D						(28) 3.3
.7	-.5	.3							-5.6
.1	.2	.1			.0	.0	.1	.0	.2
1.0	3.1	.6	Fixed/Worth		.1	.3	.5	.3	-23.5
-.2	-.1	-.2			-.2	-.8	2.6	1.8	-.1
.9	1.3	1.0			.5	.4	1.0	.8	1.8
6.3	28.5	4.9	Debt/Worth		1.9	6.6	2.0	1.7	-24.9
-2.7	-1.9	-2.5			-4.0	-2.9	6.9	-5.6	-1.9
90.1	67.9	84.6			74.2		125.3	65.0	86.7
(171) 34.9	(159) 24.0	(161) 28.6	% Profit Before Taxes/Tangible Net Worth		(12) 16.5		(22) 93.8	(50) 29.7	(64) 19.3
5.4	5.9	4.7			-6.6		47.3	13.1	-8.5
18.3	14.3	21.1			31.7	56.7	39.5	23.0	12.8
5.6	4.3	5.7	% Profit Before Taxes/Total Assets		8.3	-5.1	18.1	8.6	3.4
-2.0	-2.8	-4.4			-3.3	-32.4	1.5	-2.8	-5.6
62.7	49.5	62.0			UND	186.2	70.2	87.3	41.8
30.6	21.9	26.4	Sales/Net Fixed Assets		151.0	77.1	31.5	22.5	22.9
13.2	11.0	11.2			30.4	9.1	13.1	8.0	9.3
2.5	2.3	2.4			4.5	4.1	4.6	2.2	1.8
1.3	1.2	1.5	Sales/Total Assets		3.7	2.0	2.2	1.5	1.1
.7	.6	.8			1.6	1.0	1.6	1.1	.6
.9	.9	1.0					.6	.9	1.1
(147) 1.8	(148) 2.2	(140) 2.2	% Depr., Dep., Amort./Sales				(14) 1.6	(38) 2.3	(75) 2.5
3.7	4.3	4.9					5.2	5.5	5.0
2.7	3.4	3.2			3.2				
(45) 4.3	(45) 7.6	(35) 9.8	% Officers', Directors' Owners' Comp/Sales		(10) 10.5				
10.2	14.5	14.9			15.0				
12715480M	**15002861M**	**12726090M**	Net Sales ($)	**2649M**	**38368M**	**53161M**	**201600M**	**1129256M**	**11301056M**
14419134M	**18939506M**	**13522932M**	Total Assets ($)	**1083M**	**17933M**	**41738M**	**116814M**	**930237M**	**12415127M**

M = $ thousand MM = $ million

See Pages 9 through 22 for Explanation of Ratios and Data

	Current Data Sorted by Assets						Comparative Historical Data	
Type of Statement								
Unqualified		1	3	8	7	4	16	17
Reviewed	1	1	3	7	2		19	30
Compiled	5	8	5	2		1	12	18
Tax Returns	18	18	8				32	34
Other	21	26	16	8	8	8	62	59
	26 (4/1-9/30/13)		163 (10/1/13-3/31/14)				4/1/09-3/31/10	4/1/10-3/31/11
	0-500M	500M-2MM	2-10MM	10-50MM	50-100MM	100-250MM	ALL	ALL
NUMBER OF STATEMENTS	45	54	35	25	17	13	141	158
ASSETS	%	%	%	%	%	%	%	%
Cash & Equivalents	38.7	16.3	10.6	13.2	5.6	5.7	16.9	19.1
Trade Receivables (net)	18.5	27.1	27.6	21.2	17.1	11.7	23.0	21.9
Inventory	1.5	5.4	4.8	.7	2.7	3.6	3.7	2.8
All Other Current	1.1	4.4	5.8	6.2	8.4	9.2	6.7	4.8
Total Current	59.8	53.2	48.9	41.3	33.7	30.2	50.3	48.7
Fixed Assets (net)	22.9	31.6	32.2	23.7	22.9	7.4	36.0	33.6
Intangibles (net)	1.6	3.2	9.3	16.2	30.6	42.4	4.8	8.4
All Other Non-Current	15.7	12.0	9.6	18.8	12.8	20.0	8.9	9.3
Total	100.0	100.0	100.0	100.0	100.0	100.0	100.0	100.0
LIABILITIES								
Notes Payable-Short Term	16.9	10.9	14.5	9.9	5.7	13.4	10.3	12.4
Cur. Mat.-L.T.D.	2.5	3.4	4.5	7.3	3.7	4.3	4.9	5.2
Trade Payables	9.8	8.5	14.8	8.0	8.4	3.1	9.3	8.8
Income Taxes Payable	1.8	.0	.7	.7	.2	.1	.4	.3
All Other Current	15.8	12.6	14.6	15.8	14.1	9.8	17.0	19.3
Total Current	46.8	35.4	49.1	41.7	32.2	30.7	41.9	45.9
Long-Term Debt	18.3	20.2	19.6	21.9	26.5	24.3	21.6	25.8
Deferred Taxes	.0	.2	.1	.8	.7	.6	.4	.4
All Other Non-Current	13.8	21.9	6.3	16.8	8.5	16.2	8.0	9.6
Net Worth	21.2	22.4	24.8	18.9	32.1	28.2	28.1	18.3
Total Liabilties & Net Worth	100.0	100.0	100.0	100.0	100.0	100.0	100.0	100.0
INCOME DATA								
Net Sales	100.0	100.0	100.0	100.0	100.0	100.0	100.0	100.0
Gross Profit								
Operating Expenses	90.5	88.1	92.0	89.8	89.5	97.8	91.1	90.5
Operating Profit	9.5	11.9	8.0	10.2	10.5	2.2	8.9	9.5
All Other Expenses (net)	2.8	2.7	2.7	4.0	3.5	4.8	2.2	3.3
Profit Before Taxes	6.7	9.2	5.3	6.2	6.9	-2.5	6.7	6.3
RATIOS								
Current	7.8	4.2	2.0	2.7	1.3	6.4	2.9	2.7
	1.5	1.7	1.5	.9	1.2	1.5	1.3	1.2
	.5	.6	.9	.6	.6	.6	.8	.7
Quick	6.8	3.5	1.5	2.1	1.0	2.7	2.4	2.4
	1.4	1.4	.9	.8	.7	1.1	.9	1.0
	.5	.5	.5	.4	.4	.3	.5	.5
Sales/Receivables	0 UND	0 UND	14 26.0	17 20.9	24 15.4	17 22.1	7 50.4	5 69.1
	0 UND	21 17.7	33 11.0	56 6.5	44 8.3	39 9.3	37 9.8	33 11.1
	35 10.5	49 7.4	54 6.7	73 5.0	94 3.9	152 2.4	64 5.7	58 6.3
Cost of Sales/Inventory								
Cost of Sales/Payables								
Sales/Working Capital	8.6	6.4	9.0	4.4	8.2	1.5	5.9	5.4
	32.7	16.7	19.7	-82.0	17.8	4.1	25.1	28.0
	-14.0	-27.1	-31.5	-3.8	-7.9	-16.5	-16.7	-16.5
EBIT/Interest	26.9	60.1	19.9	30.4	28.1	3.3	14.0	15.6
	(25) 7.0	(37) 12.6	(29) 4.2	(21) 7.9	(15) 7.9	(12) .3	(110) 4.3	(120) 4.5
	-3.3	1.3	.1	3.5	4.4	-2.5	-.1	1.0
Net Profit + Depr., Dep., Amort./Cur. Mat. L/T/D							4.5	5.3
							(21) 2.0	(21) 3.0
							.9	1.5
Fixed/Worth	.0	.2	.5	.2	.3	.0	.3	.2
	.5	.7	1.5	1.1	1.6	.1	.9	1.2
	-4.5	36.2	-2.0	-.6	-.3	-.5	5.7	47.2
Debt/Worth	.3	.5	.8	1.0	1.6	1.4	.6	.7
	1.6	1.7	2.4	4.7	4.1	-5.1	2.0	2.9
	-7.2	38.2	-7.4	-3.5	-4.0	-1.5	19.9	-61.8
% Profit Before Taxes/Tangible Net Worth	135.0	115.2	42.6	64.6	86.7		67.9	70.3
	(30) 76.9	(42) 38.9	(25) 17.6	(14) 32.9	(10) 36.1		(113) 21.1	(116) 26.3
	18.3	16.5	4.3	.0	8.5		2.2	4.4
% Profit Before Taxes/Total Assets	83.6	45.6	19.6	17.4	11.2	9.6	21.3	22.9
	35.4	17.5	7.1	11.0	5.2	-1.3	6.7	9.1
	3.5	1.5	-4.3	4.6	3.0	-5.2	-1.5	.0
Sales/Net Fixed Assets	401.9	72.4	36.0	534.6	104.8	UND	23.8	38.7
	64.1	16.0	12.0	15.5	7.0	186.2	7.2	10.5
	15.2	5.5	3.1	3.2	1.6	12.7	2.6	3.3
Sales/Total Assets	7.8	5.1	4.3	1.6	.9	.9	3.3	3.7
	4.8	3.4	2.1	1.3	.6	.6	1.9	2.1
	2.9	1.9	1.2	1.0	.4	.4	1.1	1.2
% Depr., Dep., Amort./Sales	.6	.5	1.3	2.5	4.9		2.1	1.1
	(27) 2.8	(25) 2.5	(29) 2.8	(12) 4.9	(12) 6.2		(90) 4.7	(108) 3.9
	4.8	5.2	14.1	7.8	14.7		10.1	7.6
% Officers', Directors' Owners' Comp/Sales	4.8	3.2	1.8				5.0	4.0
	(20) 6.8	(26) 7.3	(12) 3.2				(50) 8.3	(64) 7.1
	18.6	11.6	5.5				12.7	13.8
Net Sales ($)	58729M	217229M	456954M	753279M	1053872M	1444536M	2440448M	2849522M
Total Assets ($)	9562M	61832M	161616M	548769M	1220218M	2160771M	1998862M	2535649M

M = $ thousand MM = $ million

See Pages 9 through 22 for Explanation of Ratios and Data

Comparative Historical Data | **Current Data Sorted by Sales**

4/1/11-3/31/12 ALL	4/1/12-3/31/13 ALL	4/1/13-3/31/14 ALL		0-1MM	1-3MM	3-5MM	5-10MM	10-25MM	25MM & OVER
			Type of Statement						
19	13	23	Unqualified		1	2		7	13
21	19	14	Reviewed	1		1	1	7	4
26	20	21	Compiled	4	2	3	6	4	2
45	36	44	Tax Returns	18	8	9	5	4	
73	89	87	Other	17	14	13	10	8	25
					26 (4/1-9/30/13)		163 (10/1/13-3/31/14)		
184	177	189	**NUMBER OF STATEMENTS**	40	25	28	22	30	44
%	%	%	**ASSETS**	%	%	%	%	%	%
18.4	19.8	18.5	Cash & Equivalents	25.9	28.1	22.4	12.2	15.2	9.3
19.8	17.6	22.4	Trade Receivables (net)	12.3	27.7	21.4	34.6	24.6	21.5
3.0	3.3	3.4	Inventory	2.8	2.4	3.5	5.7	3.4	3.2
4.0	5.9	4.8	All Other Current	2.3	4.5	1.3	4.2	8.9	6.9
45.1	46.6	49.1	Total Current	43.3	62.7	48.6	56.8	52.1	40.9
32.6	28.7	26.2	Fixed Assets (net)	37.1	26.8	30.1	24.2	22.1	17.1
8.6	9.1	10.8	Intangibles (net)	5.4	1.4	4.6	6.6	14.5	24.7
13.7	15.6	13.9	All Other Non-Current	14.1	9.1	16.7	12.4	11.3	17.3
100.0	100.0	100.0	Total	100.0	100.0	100.0	100.0	100.0	100.0
			LIABILITIES						
12.5	13.7	12.6	Notes Payable-Short Term	9.5	16.2	13.3	25.7	6.8	10.2
5.4	8.2	4.0	Cur. Mat.-L.T.D.	4.8	1.6	3.1	1.4	7.7	3.9
11.0	9.1	9.5	Trade Payables	9.9	5.6	6.2	13.8	14.4	8.1
.2	.3	.7	Income Taxes Payable	2.0	.0	.2	.0	1.1	.2
22.2	18.8	14.1	All Other Current	11.3	18.2	15.0	11.4	12.2	16.5
51.3	50.1	40.9	Total Current	37.4	41.6	37.9	52.3	42.1	38.9
24.3	22.8	20.7	Long-Term Debt	29.6	16.1	17.2	13.4	21.2	20.7
.6	.5	.3	Deferred Taxes	.1	.3	.0	.1	.0	.9
11.9	12.3	14.8	All Other Non-Current	11.2	12.5	4.5	23.6	23.8	15.4
11.9	14.3	23.4	Net Worth	21.7	29.5	40.4	10.5	12.8	24.1
100.0	100.0	100.0	Total Liabilties & Net Worth	100.0	100.0	100.0	100.0	100.0	100.0
			INCOME DATA						
100.0	100.0	100.0	Net Sales	100.0	100.0	100.0	100.0	100.0	100.0
			Gross Profit						
91.0	89.6	90.4	Operating Expenses	83.7	91.4	90.2	92.9	91.2	94.4
9.0	10.4	9.6	Operating Profit	16.3	8.6	9.8	7.1	8.8	5.6
3.4	2.9	3.1	All Other Expenses (net)	8.4	.5	2.0	.1	1.3	3.3
5.6	7.4	6.5	Profit Before Taxes	7.9	8.2	7.8	7.1	7.5	2.3
			RATIOS						
2.9	2.7	3.1		7.0	9.5	3.8	2.5	2.2	1.9
1.3	1.3	1.4	Current	1.3	2.4	1.6	1.4	1.6	1.3
.5	.5	.6		.2	.5	.6	.8	.6	.8
2.5	2.0	2.5		6.4	5.7	3.1	1.7	1.6	1.5
1.0	.9	1.0	Quick	.9	2.4	1.6	1.0	.9	1.0
.4	.3	.4		.2	.5	.6	.4	.5	.6
1 676.6	0 821.1	0 UND		0 UND	0 UND	0 UND	10 35.4	22 16.3	21 17.0
24 15.5	26 13.9	28 12.9	Sales/Receivables	0 UND	21 17.5	20 18.4	35 10.5	45 8.1	41 8.8
54 6.8	46 7.9	56 6.5		31 11.8	54 6.7	40 9.1	68 5.4	61 6.0	78 4.7
			Cost of Sales/Inventory						
			Cost of Sales/Payables						
6.5	6.1	6.8		4.4	8.2	8.1	7.9	7.2	5.1
30.0	30.2	20.4	Sales/Working Capital	26.3	29.6	20.1	38.8	17.2	19.2
-11.5	-11.8	-14.4		-7.4	-13.4	-53.7	-50.3	-11.8	-26.1
17.5	20.5	25.8		8.0	57.4	54.0	94.8	24.8	16.9
(137) 4.9	(137) 5.3	(139) 6.3	EBIT/Interest	(19) -.5	(16) 7.8	(21) 12.6	(18) 3.4	(28) 10.1	(37) 4.6
.6	1.0	.7		-8.3	1.7	5.0	-.4	3.5	-.3
6.1	4.0	4.4							
(23) 3.7	(18) 1.4	(16) 3.0	Net Profit + Depr., Dep., Amort./Cur. Mat. L/T/D						
1.6	.4	.5							
.2	.1	.1		.1	.1	.2	.1	.4	.0
1.0	.9	.9	Fixed/Worth	.8	1.5	.6	1.1	2.2	.8
-31.3	-8.7	-3.7		UND	-3.6	1.7	-.4	-.4	-.9
.7	.6	.6		.4	.3	.5	.5	.8	1.5
2.5	2.7	2.7	Debt/Worth	2.0	2.9	1.3	2.9	NM	3.8
-11.5	-7.0	-6.2		UND	-14.7	3.3	-12.7	-3.7	-3.4
70.1	104.4	98.7		90.3	125.4	134.2	99.0	70.4	79.7
(128) 26.5	(121) 33.0	(126) 36.6	% Profit Before Taxes/Tangible Net Worth	(30) 18.3	(16) 71.9	(23) 88.8	(16) 35.3	(15) 35.3	(26) 19.0
8.7	8.6	10.1		-1.2	29.5	27.9	13.8	26.8	3.4
23.9	27.2	30.0		25.7	69.9	62.1	60.4	19.8	15.6
8.5	8.9	11.5	% Profit Before Taxes/Total Assets	5.9	33.9	30.1	11.6	12.5	4.9
-.3	-.6	.3		-5.6	7.9	6.4	.1	4.7	-4.9
53.8	79.3	105.4		92.2	250.1	76.1	61.7	39.8	999.8
13.4	13.5	17.5	Sales/Net Fixed Assets	15.2	18.3	22.1	27.0	14.7	46.6
3.4	4.0	5.2		1.3	6.4	5.5	11.0	4.2	3.7
4.3	3.4	4.6		3.5	6.7	5.4	5.7	4.5	1.8
2.1	1.9	2.3	Sales/Total Assets	2.2	3.8	3.5	3.5	1.5	.9
1.1	1.0	1.0		.3	2.1	2.0	2.0	1.0	.6
1.2	1.0	.8		2.3	.5	.5	.6	1.7	.7
(114) 3.3	(93) 3.3	(109) 3.2	% Depr., Dep., Amort./Sales	(26) 4.3	(13) 2.8	(14) 2.4	(13) 2.2	(21) 3.2	(22) 4.9
7.6	7.0	7.0		16.3	5.3	10.9	6.2	6.4	8.5
3.1	3.2	3.4			4.6	3.6	3.2		
(70) 5.5	(62) 6.4	(62) 6.3	% Officers', Directors' Owners' Comp/Sales		(13) 8.3	(17) 5.3	(10) 7.3		
8.3	10.9	12.1			10.6	14.5	14.2		
4530662M	3340948M	3984599M	Net Sales ($)	19990M	47798M	102436M	152020M	459705M	3202650M
3745746M	3406054M	4162768M	Total Assets ($)	25408M	14528M	109466M	56536M	399266M	3557564M

M = $ thousand MM = $ million

See Pages 9 through 22 for Explanation of Ratios and Data

Current Data Sorted by Assets / Comparative Historical Data

0-500M	500M-2MM	2-10MM	10-50MM	50-100MM	100-250MM	Type of Statement	4/1/09-3/31/10 ALL	4/1/10-3/31/11 ALL
		4	9	4	2	Unqualified	14	17
		5	6	1		Reviewed	14	5
2	2	10	3			Compiled	18	22
4	7	14	1	1		Tax Returns	21	32
2	13	16	18	6	5	Other	54	43
3 (4/1-9/30/13)		132 (10/1/13-3/31/14)						
8	22	49	37	12	7	**NUMBER OF STATEMENTS**	121	119
%	%	%	%	%	%	**ASSETS**	%	%
	13.9	12.2	11.0	5.2		Cash & Equivalents	9.8	13.0
	2.5	.8	1.6	2.0		Trade Receivables (net)	.8	2.5
	2.3	.9	1.1	.9		Inventory	1.2	1.4
	5.8	5.2	3.0	1.4		All Other Current	1.8	1.2
	24.5	19.2	16.6	9.5		Total Current	13.6	18.0
	64.7	72.9	71.2	71.3		Fixed Assets (net)	75.9	73.0
	6.5	3.6	4.1	11.9		Intangibles (net)	4.9	3.5
	4.3	4.3	8.1	7.3		All Other Non-Current	5.5	5.5
	100.0	100.0	100.0	100.0		Total	100.0	100.0
						LIABILITIES		
	1.6	2.4	.3	1.4		Notes Payable-Short Term	2.7	7.7
	4.8	5.2	5.9	2.8		Cur. Mat.-L.T.D.	6.6	5.0
	6.8	5.9	4.5	7.2		Trade Payables	8.0	7.5
	.0	.0	.1	2.0		Income Taxes Payable	.2	.0
	33.4	11.0	9.8	5.5		All Other Current	9.9	8.8
	46.6	24.4	20.6	18.8		Total Current	27.3	29.0
	39.9	49.3	45.7	34.0		Long-Term Debt	42.0	49.3
	.0	.0	.0	.0		Deferred Taxes	.1	.0
	4.5	9.8	12.9	6.2		All Other Non-Current	12.6	8.1
	9.0	16.5	20.8	41.1		Net Worth	17.9	13.7
	100.0	100.0	100.0	100.0		Total Liabilities & Net Worth	100.0	100.0
						INCOME DATA		
	100.0	100.0	100.0	100.0		Net Sales	100.0	100.0
						Gross Profit		
	90.7	83.4	86.9	91.9		Operating Expenses	86.6	88.6
	9.3	16.6	13.1	8.1		Operating Profit	13.4	11.4
	3.7	8.0	4.5	3.5		All Other Expenses (net)	7.2	6.2
	5.5	8.6	8.6	4.6		Profit Before Taxes	6.3	5.2
						RATIOS		
	2.0	1.8	1.1	.7			1.0	1.3
	.8	.7	.7	.6		Current	.5	.7
	.3	.3	.4	.4			.2	.3
	1.9	1.4	1.0	.6			.8	1.1
	.4	.5	.5	.4		Quick	.4	.5
	.2	.2	.3	.3			.1	.2
	0 UND	0 UND	0 UND	1 259.5			0 UND	0 UND
	0 UND	0 UND	3 126.4	6 60.9		Sales/Receivables	0 UND	0 UND
	4 84.6	1 339.7	7 52.1	8 44.1			3 129.9	3 123.3
						Cost of Sales/Inventory		
						Cost of Sales/Payables		
	10.7	18.9	39.5	-25.2			UND	52.1
	-69.1	-61.0	-25.5	-18.6		Sales/Working Capital	-17.3	-25.9
	-4.1	-7.6	-7.0	-11.2			-5.6	-7.3
	46.1	8.1	8.3	4.0			4.0	4.7
	(20) 3.7	(38) 3.7	(34) 4.1	(11) 1.9		EBIT/Interest	(93) 2.1	(97) 2.1
	1.9	1.7	2.1	1.2			1.4	.8
							15.5	9.6
						Net Profit + Depr., Dep., Amort./Cur. Mat. L/T/D	(17) 3.1	(12) 2.3
							1.4	1.0
	1.0	1.6	2.0	1.5			2.0	1.7
	3.2	3.9	3.0	2.4		Fixed/Worth	4.0	3.7
	-1.6	-45.3	12.1	5.1			-28.3	68.4
	.8	1.1	1.7	1.1			1.5	1.5
	4.9	3.8	2.6	1.9		Debt/Worth	3.5	3.5
	-2.3	-53.2	13.0	4.6			-30.0	133.0
	74.0	63.6	46.8	21.7			46.7	51.4
	(15) 30.0	(35) 14.1	(31) 29.1	(10) 16.3		% Profit Before Taxes/Tangible Net Worth	(89) 18.5	(93) 15.3
	12.5	4.2	11.4	-1.0			6.8	-1.3
	20.0	15.0	13.6	8.1			10.5	8.2
	7.8	5.8	9.1	4.5		% Profit Before Taxes/Total Assets	3.6	2.9
	2.3	1.5	2.8	1.2			1.2	-.7
	4.4	3.0	2.7	2.5			2.8	3.4
	2.7	1.0	1.1	1.4		Sales/Net Fixed Assets	1.1	1.1
	1.5	.5	.7	.9			.6	.6
	2.5	1.8	1.7	1.4			2.1	2.1
	1.6	.8	.8	1.1		Sales/Total Assets	1.0	.9
	1.1	.5	.5	.8			.5	.5
	2.8	4.6	4.5	4.8			4.3	4.4
	(17) 7.1	(47) 7.0	(36) 7.6	(11) 6.4		% Depr., Dep., Amort./Sales	(115) 6.5	(108) 7.3
	12.0	13.6	10.6	8.4			10.1	10.9
							1.4	1.6
						% Officers', Directors' Owners' Comp/Sales	(20) 2.9	(27) 3.6
							5.4	6.7
14793M	47730M	409560M	1219857M	948603M	758235M	Net Sales ($)	2637099M	1884436M
2753M	27169M	241085M	936768M	861619M	1128326M	Total Assets ($)	2579884M	2061277M

M = $ thousand MM = $ million

See Pages 9 through 22 for Explanation of Ratios and Data

Comparative Historical Data				Current Data Sorted by Sales					
			Type of Statement						
25	15	19	Unqualified		1		2	3	13
10	11	12	Reviewed		1		5	3	3
23	16	17	Compiled	2	6	6	1	2	
17	26	27	Tax Returns	6	12	1	2	3	3
54	75	60	Other	3	16	6	6	9	20
4/1/11-3/31/12	4/1/12-3/31/13	4/1/13-3/31/14		3 (4/1-9/30/13)			132 (10/1/13-3/31/14)		
ALL	ALL	ALL		0-1MM	1-3MM	3-5MM	5-10MM	10-25MM	25MM & OVER
129	143	135	**NUMBER OF STATEMENTS**	11	36	13	16	20	39
%	%	%	**ASSETS**	%	%	%	%	%	%
9.7	14.7	12.2	Cash & Equivalents	9.4	13.5	11.2	8.7	13.3	12.9
1.9	2.4	2.3	Trade Receivables (net)	.0	5.1	.4	.5	1.0	2.5
1.3	1.1	1.2	Inventory	2.5	.7	1.3	.6	1.0	1.5
2.6	3.5	3.8	All Other Current	.8	6.2	1.1	3.6	1.9	4.3
15.4	21.6	19.5	Total Current	12.7	25.6	14.0	13.4	17.2	21.3
71.9	68.6	67.9	Fixed Assets (net)	75.6	64.5	82.2	76.6	73.9	57.6
5.6	4.7	6.9	Intangibles (net)	4.2	6.5	1.9	4.5	1.8	13.4
7.2	5.1	5.7	All Other Non-Current	7.5	3.4	1.9	5.6	7.0	7.8
100.0	100.0	100.0	Total	100.0	100.0	100.0	100.0	100.0	100.0
			LIABILITIES						
4.8	2.4	1.9	Notes Payable-Short Term	6.6	2.4	.2	3.1	.1	1.0
4.7	4.2	5.0	Cur. Mat.-L.T.D.	3.2	4.6	3.8	5.0	9.1	4.2
5.3	6.5	6.6	Trade Payables	.2	8.0	4.9	4.8	4.9	9.3
.1	.1	.2	Income Taxes Payable	.0	.0	.0	.0	.2	.6
9.0	14.7	16.2	All Other Current	23.2	24.0	18.0	7.1	13.5	11.5
23.9	27.9	29.9	Total Current	33.2	39.0	26.9	20.1	27.9	26.6
47.9	43.8	43.4	Long-Term Debt	52.7	46.3	43.1	39.5	39.9	41.5
.0	.0	.1	Deferred Taxes	.0	.0	.0	.0	.0	.5
13.1	11.6	9.7	All Other Non-Current	.6	8.7	.2	3.5	11.3	18.3
15.1	16.7	16.9	Net Worth	13.5	6.0	29.8	36.9	21.0	13.1
100.0	100.0	100.0	Total Liabilties & Net Worth	100.0	100.0	100.0	100.0	100.0	100.0
			INCOME DATA						
100.0	100.0	100.0	Net Sales	100.0	100.0	100.0	100.0	100.0	100.0
			Gross Profit						
90.2	87.7	87.5	Operating Expenses	58.5	89.3	89.2	90.1	87.6	92.5
9.8	12.3	12.5	Operating Profit	41.5	10.7	10.8	9.9	12.4	7.5
6.2	5.0	5.3	All Other Expenses (net)	25.2	5.2	3.6	2.3	3.5	2.4
3.5	7.3	7.2	Profit Before Taxes	16.3	5.5	7.2	7.6	9.0	5.1
			RATIOS						
1.4	1.8	1.3		8.4	2.4	1.7	1.1	1.2	.9
.6	.8	.7	Current	.1	1.2	1.2	.6	.5	.7
.3	.4	.3		.0	.3	.5	.3	.3	.4
1.1	1.4	1.0		5.5	1.8	1.6	1.0	1.0	.7
.4	.6	.5	Quick	.1	.6	.8	.4	.4	.5
.2	.2	.2		.0	.2	.4	.2	.2	.3
0 UND	0 UND	0 UND		0 UND	0 UND	0 UND	0 UND	0 UND	1 326.9
0 999.8	1 657.4	1 478.6	Sales/Receivables	0 UND	1 520.1	0 UND	0 UND	0 UND	6 61.9
4 95.6	6 63.2	6 60.0		0 UND	6 65.0	1 291.8	5 72.6	5 78.3	7 50.3
			Cost of Sales/Inventory						
			Cost of Sales/Payables						
25.8	16.8	30.3		6.1	6.8	38.5	65.5	NM	-77.7
-17.8	-37.2	-25.5	Sales/Working Capital	-2.1	88.3	104.2	-33.8	-19.5	-19.4
-8.0	-9.0	-7.0		-.4	-7.4	-10.7	-7.3	-5.8	-9.8
4.3	6.8	8.8			10.5	9.7	7.2	9.4	6.9
(112) 2.2	(111) 2.5	(114) 3.6	EBIT/Interest		(27) 3.8	(12) 3.6	(14) 3.9	(19) 3.0	(36) 3.3
.7	1.2	1.7			2.1	1.0	1.1	1.8	1.4
4.0	2.8	3.5							12.1
(23) 1.7	(12) 1.9	(22) 1.7	Net Profit + Depr., Dep., Amort./Cur. Mat. L/T/D						(10) 3.6
1.0	1.7	1.2							2.5
1.8	1.7	1.6		1.2	1.4	1.3	1.1	2.5	1.7
4.7	4.4	3.5	Fixed/Worth	4.4	4.2	3.2	2.9	3.8	2.9
-10.0	-8.1	-10.6		-55.1	-1.3	11.8	5.8	NM	-1.9
1.5	1.3	1.3		2.1	1.4	.5	.4	2.1	1.3
4.3	5.0	3.6	Debt/Worth	6.6	4.5	3.2	2.7	4.7	2.2
-10.9	-12.8	-24.9		-36.8	-14.2	12.0	5.2	NM	-3.4
38.2	71.0	61.3			74.1	74.0	46.0	82.0	30.5
(86) 11.4	(98) 24.3	(96) 22.1	% Profit Before Taxes/Tangible Net Worth		(24) 29.8	(11) 15.1	(14) 21.1	(15) 45.4	(25) 21.1
-.1	8.0	8.2			7.1	3.6	2.4	11.4	3.9
9.2	17.0	14.8		6.5	20.2	12.6	14.5	15.4	16.7
3.6	5.1	6.5	% Profit Before Taxes/Total Assets	3.1	5.7	4.7	7.9	9.4	7.0
-1.3	.9	2.0		-.3	-.1	.6	.9	3.1	1.9
3.3	4.5	3.9		.7	6.9	3.0	2.2	3.2	5.4
1.2	1.7	1.5	Sales/Net Fixed Assets	.2	1.7	1.3	1.3	1.2	2.0
.6	.8	.8		.1	.7	.9	.9	.7	1.2
1.9	2.7	2.1		.7	2.7	2.5	1.6	1.8	2.8
.9	1.2	1.1	Sales/Total Assets	.1	1.3	1.1	1.1	.9	1.3
.5	.7	.6		.1	.6	.7	.7	.5	.8
4.3	3.6	4.6			1.8	4.1	5.3	4.6	4.4
(113) 6.8	(123) 6.7	(120) 6.4	% Depr., Dep., Amort./Sales		(28) 7.7	6.1	7.1	6.8	(35) 5.2
10.2	10.2	10.7			11.8	9.2	10.4	9.5	8.0
1.9	1.6	.9			3.4				
(29) 3.4	(22) 3.4	(24) 3.4	% Officers', Directors' Owners' Comp/Sales		(10) 4.1				
7.8	6.7	4.9			6.7				
2790964M	3460427M	3398778M	Net Sales ($)	4976M	70185M	49663M	121158M	308157M	2844639M
2720823M	2822539M	3197720M	Total Assets ($)	32110M	91118M	55512M	144487M	377602M	2496891M

M = $ thousand MM = $ million

See Pages 9 through 22 for Explanation of Ratios and Data

Current Data Sorted by Assets							Comparative Historical Data	
						Type of Statement		
			2			Unqualified		
	2	1	2			Reviewed	3	2
	1	2				Compiled	2	2
3	1					Tax Returns		9
3	2	7	4			Other	13	13
1 (4/1-9/30/13)		29 (10/1/13-3/31/14)					**4/1/09-3/31/10 ALL**	**4/1/10-3/31/11 ALL**
0-500M	**500M-2MM**	**2-10MM**	**10-50MM**	**50-100MM**	**100-250MM**			
6	6	10	8			**NUMBER OF STATEMENTS**	18	26
%	%	%	%	%	%	**ASSETS**	%	%
		11.2		DATA NOT AVAILABLE	DATA NOT AVAILABLE	Cash & Equivalents	13.5	23.4
		28.4				Trade Receivables (net)	24.1	20.7
		.4				Inventory	.6	2.4
		2.8				All Other Current	3.4	1.5
		42.8				Total Current	41.6	48.0
		45.3				Fixed Assets (net)	38.1	30.4
		4.2				Intangibles (net)	6.2	9.7
		7.6				All Other Non-Current	14.1	12.0
		100.0				Total	100.0	100.0
						LIABILITIES		
		29.6				Notes Payable-Short Term	16.0	10.6
		6.3				Cur. Mat.-L.T.D.	5.9	3.0
		14.0				Trade Payables	12.8	6.1
		.9				Income Taxes Payable	.2	.2
		6.9				All Other Current	12.6	13.4
		57.7				Total Current	47.5	33.4
		21.0				Long-Term Debt	23.8	24.1
		.2				Deferred Taxes	.7	.0
		.9				All Other Non-Current	20.9	14.3
		20.3				Net Worth	7.1	28.3
		100.0				Total Liabilties & Net Worth	100.0	100.0
						INCOME DATA		
		100.0				Net Sales	100.0	100.0
						Gross Profit		
		92.0				Operating Expenses	99.0	90.0
		8.0				Operating Profit	1.0	10.0
		4.8				All Other Expenses (net)	2.6	3.0
		3.2				Profit Before Taxes	-1.6	7.0
						RATIOS		
		2.0					1.6	4.4
		1.2				Current	1.2	1.2
		.4					.7	.7
		2.0					1.5	4.2
		1.1				Quick	.9	1.1
		.4					.6	.7
		24 15.0					**27** 13.6	**0** UND
		36 10.1				Sales/Receivables	**41** 8.9	**44** 8.4
		54 6.8					**74** 4.9	**72** 5.1
						Cost of Sales/Inventory		
						Cost of Sales/Payables		
		7.3					6.7	4.0
		50.2				Sales/Working Capital	32.3	25.1
		-11.2					-17.9	-44.7
							5.0	41.8
						EBIT/Interest	(16) 1.1	(22) 11.6
							-13.5	1.6
						Net Profit + Depr., Dep., Amort./Cur. Mat. L/T/D		
		.3					.8	.2
		2.1				Fixed/Worth	1.5	1.2
		5.7					NM	3.1
		.7					1.0	.5
		3.5				Debt/Worth	2.1	1.9
		7.6					NM	15.9
							47.0	178.2
						% Profit Before Taxes/Tangible Net Worth	(14) -17.2	(22) 45.6
							-47.5	7.9
		32.0					13.2	29.1
		5.9				% Profit Before Taxes/Total Assets	.8	9.3
		-2.1					-24.7	1.1
		23.9					27.5	72.8
		6.9				Sales/Net Fixed Assets	4.9	10.0
		2.7					3.4	2.8
		3.6					3.2	3.0
		2.5				Sales/Total Assets	1.9	2.0
		1.6					1.3	1.2
							2.5	3.5
						% Depr., Dep., Amort./Sales	(13) 4.4	(15) 6.1
							12.7	8.7
						% Officers', Directors' Owners' Comp/Sales		
13601M	38270M	139824M	233944M			Net Sales ($)	437719M	202496M
1426M	8664M	53484M	153901M			Total Assets ($)	315694M	129629M

M = $ thousand MM = $ million

See Pages 9 through 22 for Explanation of Ratios and Data

Comparative Historical Data				Current Data Sorted by Sales					
			Type of Statement						
2	1	2	Unqualified					1	1
3	3	5	Reviewed			1		1	3
4	4	3	Compiled				2	1	
9	6	4	Tax Returns	1	1	1	1		
12	7	16	Other	2	3	2	1	8	
				1 (4/1-9/30/13)			29 (10/1/13-3/31/14)		
4/1/11-3/31/12 ALL	**4/1/12-3/31/13 ALL**	**4/1/13-3/31/14 ALL**		**0-1MM**	**1-3MM**	**3-5MM**	**5-10MM**	**10-25MM**	**25MM & OVER**
30	21	30	**NUMBER OF STATEMENTS**	3	4	4	4	11	4
%	%	%	**ASSETS**	%	%	%	%	%	%
18.8	15.6	17.2	Cash & Equivalents					10.5	
19.2	20.5	24.8	Trade Receivables (net)					28.3	
3.0	2.2	3.9	Inventory					8.4	
.9	7.3	5.2	All Other Current					11.6	
41.9	45.5	51.0	Total Current					58.8	
38.2	34.8	35.6	Fixed Assets (net)					27.6	
7.9	8.9	7.9	Intangibles (net)					7.4	
12.0	10.8	5.5	All Other Non-Current					6.2	
100.0	100.0	100.0	Total					100.0	
			LIABILITIES						
13.3	8.6	17.2	Notes Payable-Short Term					26.4	
9.1	11.9	6.0	Cur. Mat.-L.T.D.					3.6	
11.1	10.1	8.7	Trade Payables					4.5	
5.2	.1	.7	Income Taxes Payable					1.2	
9.9	9.5	14.4	All Other Current					18.4	
48.5	40.2	47.1	Total Current					54.1	
35.0	26.6	22.1	Long-Term Debt					20.3	
.7	1.1	1.4	Deferred Taxes					2.1	
25.7	13.3	7.9	All Other Non-Current					6.0	
-9.9	18.8	21.5	Net Worth					17.5	
100.0	100.0	100.0	Total Liabilties & Net Worth					100.0	
			INCOME DATA						
100.0	100.0	100.0	Net Sales					100.0	
			Gross Profit						
90.7	86.0	94.5	Operating Expenses					97.1	
9.3	14.0	5.5	Operating Profit					2.9	
2.9	2.2	1.9	All Other Expenses (net)					.9	
6.4	11.9	3.6	Profit Before Taxes					2.1	
			RATIOS						
1.7	1.4	2.9						2.7	
1.0	1.1	1.4	Current					1.8	
.5	.6	.8						.9	
1.7	1.4	2.7						2.6	
.8	.8	1.3	Quick					1.8	
.4	.5	.4						.2	
0 UND	**0** UND	**17** 21.9						**26** 14.0	
30 12.1	**33** 10.9	**31** 11.8	Sales/Receivables					**44** 8.3	
51 7.2	**42** 8.6	**54** 6.8						**64** 5.7	
			Cost of Sales/Inventory						
			Cost of Sales/Payables						
10.1	10.9	7.8						5.0	
NM	53.8	22.5	Sales/Working Capital					9.9	
-20.6	-35.8	-26.4						-47.5	
11.0	27.3	41.7						59.6	
(26) 4.2	(20) 6.9	(28) 5.1	EBIT/Interest					16.2	
.1	2.7	-.2						-6.4	
			Net Profit + Depr., Dep., Amort./Cur. Mat. L/T/D						
.5	.4	.3						.1	
1.7	.8	1.0	Fixed/Worth					.8	
-1.0	2.4	-1.3						-.4	
1.3	.9	.6						.6	
3.5	2.0	3.5	Debt/Worth					1.5	
-2.3	6.9	-5.5						-2.3	
84.2	115.0	90.3							
(20) 36.0	(18) 57.1	(21) 20.1	% Profit Before Taxes/Tangible Net Worth						
-3.8	28.0	-6.6							
49.1	35.7	41.2						39.3	
14.9	15.3	7.6	% Profit Before Taxes/Total Assets					9.0	
-2.7	7.3	-1.4						-2.3	
56.9	18.9	40.5						29.0	
12.3	10.3	12.6	Sales/Net Fixed Assets					9.4	
2.9	4.8	4.9						3.6	
3.8	4.3	4.4						2.6	
2.5	2.8	3.1	Sales/Total Assets					1.3	
1.5	1.4	1.2						1.1	
1.9	2.8	1.8							
(22) 4.3	(15) 3.8	(21) 3.5	% Depr., Dep., Amort./Sales						
7.7	10.6	10.2							
4.4		5.2							
(17) 7.5		(10) 9.1	% Officers', Directors' Owners' Comp/Sales						
9.3		14.8							
362610M	**281932M**	**425639M**	Net Sales ($)	**1930M**	**8485M**	**17147M**	**28029M**	**182658M**	**187390M**
185887M	**182665M**	**217475M**	Total Assets ($)	**3342M**	**3522M**	**4280M**	**7920M**	**119545M**	**78866M**

M = $ thousand MM = $ million

See Pages 9 through 22 for Explanation of Ratios and Data

Current Data Sorted by Assets							Comparative Historical Data	
						Type of Statement		
			2	1	1	Unqualified	1	2
		3	1			Reviewed	4	7
	2	2				Compiled	6	2
5	2	1				Tax Returns	5	6
1	2	4	2		1	Other	12	13
	4 (4/1-9/30/13)		26 (10/1/13-3/31/14)				4/1/09-3/31/10 ALL	4/1/10-3/31/11 ALL
0-500M	500M-2MM	2-10MM	10-50MM	50-100MM	100-250MM			
6	6	10	5	1	2	**NUMBER OF STATEMENTS**	28	30
%	%	%	%	%	%	**ASSETS**	%	%
		14.4				Cash & Equivalents	15.7	17.1
		31.2				Trade Receivables (net)	25.5	29.3
		3.7				Inventory	5.8	3.2
		1.0				All Other Current	4.3	4.2
		50.3				Total Current	51.3	53.9
		32.3				Fixed Assets (net)	35.2	32.4
		8.1				Intangibles (net)	2.5	6.8
		9.2				All Other Non-Current	10.9	6.9
		100.0				Total	100.0	100.0
						LIABILITIES		
		5.0				Notes Payable-Short Term	13.7	9.7
		2.8				Cur. Mat.-L.T.D.	6.3	8.3
		16.6				Trade Payables	10.3	13.5
		.1				Income Taxes Payable	.4	.6
		12.4				All Other Current	9.2	12.0
		36.9				Total Current	40.0	44.1
		20.7				Long-Term Debt	18.4	16.2
		.0				Deferred Taxes	.7	.2
		2.8				All Other Non-Current	11.3	5.4
		39.6				Net Worth	29.6	34.1
		100.0				Total Liabilties & Net Worth	100.0	100.0
						INCOME DATA		
		100.0				Net Sales	100.0	100.0
						Gross Profit		
		93.5				Operating Expenses	94.8	95.7
		6.5				Operating Profit	5.2	4.3
		.1				All Other Expenses (net)	1.2	.7
		6.4				Profit Before Taxes	4.0	3.6
						RATIOS		
		3.3					3.2	2.0
		1.4				Current	1.3	1.2
		.8					.8	.7
		3.2					2.5	1.6
		1.2				Quick	1.2	1.0
		.7					.6	.6
		3 114.1					**28** 13.1	**36** 10.2
		40 9.1				Sales/Receivables	**39** 9.3	**54** 6.7
		57 6.4					**60** 6.1	**71** 5.1
						Cost of Sales/Inventory		
						Cost of Sales/Payables		
		10.4					7.1	5.9
		25.3				Sales/Working Capital	14.1	32.1
		-18.7					-18.0	-9.1
							8.3	19.7
						EBIT/Interest	(27) 2.8	(26) 4.0
							.8	-.7
						Net Profit + Depr., Dep., Amort./Cur. Mat. L/T/D		
		.2					.5	.4
		1.0				Fixed/Worth	1.3	.9
		NM					3.7	11.1
		.3					.5	.6
		1.5				Debt/Worth	2.2	3.9
		NM					17.3	61.5
							56.5	73.3
						% Profit Before Taxes/Tangible Net Worth	(24) 8.1	(24) 24.3
							-.7	1.3
		16.0					7.5	22.9
		5.5				% Profit Before Taxes/Total Assets	4.1	6.3
		3.5					-.4	-2.0
		23.9					30.8	24.5
		9.2				Sales/Net Fixed Assets	5.6	6.0
		5.3					2.7	3.1
		3.3					3.0	2.6
		2.7				Sales/Total Assets	2.2	1.9
		2.2					1.2	1.4
							1.9	2.1
						% Depr., Dep., Amort./Sales	(21) 4.3	(23) 5.8
							10.9	10.1
							2.2	6.0
						% Officers', Directors' Owners' Comp/Sales	(13) 4.7	(11) 6.7
							12.5	15.9
16593M	34281M	123180M	185670M	52220M	214998M	Net Sales ($)	717648M	583586M
1602M	9006M	52885M	123965M	55251M	380423M	Total Assets ($)	520012M	391512M

M = $ thousand MM = $ million

See Pages 9 through 22 for Explanation of Ratios and Data

Comparative Historical Data | **Current Data Sorted by Sales**

						Type of Statement						
	3		1		4	Unqualified						4
	4		3		4	Reviewed				2	2	
	3		5		4	Compiled			2		2	
	7		7		8	Tax Returns	1	2	3	1	1	
	17		13		10	Other		1		3	4	2
	4/1/11-3/31/12 ALL		4/1/12-3/31/13 ALL		4/1/13-3/31/14 ALL		4 (4/1-9/30/13)			26 (10/1/13-3/31/14)		
							0-1MM	1-3MM	3-5MM	5-10MM	10-25MM	25MM & OVER
	34		29		30	NUMBER OF STATEMENTS	1	3	5	6	9	6
	%		%		%	ASSETS	%	%	%	%	%	%
	12.2		15.5		19.3	Cash & Equivalents						
	23.8		23.2		21.1	Trade Receivables (net)						
	2.9		1.9		1.6	Inventory						
	2.7		2.0		2.4	All Other Current						
	41.7		42.7		44.4	Total Current						
	40.0		38.2		32.7	Fixed Assets (net)						
	3.9		7.4		13.6	Intangibles (net)						
	14.3		11.7		9.3	All Other Non-Current						
	100.0		100.0		100.0	Total						
						LIABILITIES						
	8.7		3.8		4.8	Notes Payable-Short Term						
	3.8		2.2		2.7	Cur. Mat.-L.T.D.						
	17.8		13.2		9.2	Trade Payables						
	.2		.3		.2	Income Taxes Payable						
	8.9		15.5		24.0	All Other Current						
	39.4		34.9		40.9	Total Current						
	26.4		32.9		24.4	Long-Term Debt						
	1.3		.2		.1	Deferred Taxes						
	6.3		11.9		8.2	All Other Non-Current						
	26.5		20.2		26.4	Net Worth						
	100.0		100.0		100.0	Total Liabilties & Net Worth						
						INCOME DATA						
	100.0		100.0		100.0	Net Sales						
						Gross Profit						
	89.3		89.7		95.2	Operating Expenses						
	10.7		10.3		4.8	Operating Profit						
	3.8		3.7		.2	All Other Expenses (net)						
	6.9		6.6		4.6	Profit Before Taxes						
						RATIOS						
	4.9		3.0		3.9							
	1.3		1.5		1.9	Current						
	.6		.8		.6							
	2.8		2.9		3.3							
	1.0		1.4		1.6	Quick						
	.5		.6		.6							
20	18.1	**4**	94.3	**0**	UND							
41	8.8	**44**	8.3	**37**	9.8	Sales/Receivables						
63	5.8	**68**	5.4	**57**	6.4							
						Cost of Sales/Inventory						
						Cost of Sales/Payables						
	7.6		6.8		5.5							
	45.0		14.8		20.2	Sales/Working Capital						
	-9.2		-32.7		-34.5							
	26.1		3.8		15.0							
(29)	5.6	(24)	1.8	(22)	6.5	EBIT/Interest						
	1.7		-.1		1.9							
						Net Profit + Depr., Dep., Amort./Cur. Mat. L/T/D						
	.4		.5		.3							
	1.5		3.7		1.1	Fixed/Worth						
	-18.6		-49.0		23.7							
	.6		1.1		.7							
	2.6		6.7		1.9	Debt/Worth						
	-25.3		-54.7		NM							
	56.3		102.6		75.0							
(25)	23.9	(21)	31.5	(23)	25.3	% Profit Before Taxes/Tangible Net Worth						
	6.6		.1		8.4							
	29.2		14.6		20.3							
	6.7		3.3		7.3	% Profit Before Taxes/Total Assets						
	.4		-.5		1.0							
	13.3		23.4		27.6							
	5.8		5.5		9.3	Sales/Net Fixed Assets						
	2.2		2.6		4.1							
	3.0		2.6		3.7							
	1.6		2.1		2.4	Sales/Total Assets						
	1.0		1.1		1.6							
	2.4		2.3		1.9							
(24)	4.4	(22)	3.9	(21)	3.6	% Depr., Dep., Amort./Sales						
	9.4		8.9		7.4							
	2.5											
(12)	6.9					% Officers', Directors' Owners' Comp/Sales						
	11.3											
	655647M		470387M		626942M	Net Sales ($)	331M	4276M	18576M	46228M	145412M	412119M
	431700M		401396M		623132M	Total Assets ($)	184M	704M	13434M	11506M	64070M	533234M

M = $ thousand MM = $ million

See Pages 9 through 22 for Explanation of Ratios and Data

Current Data Sorted by Assets							Comparative Historical Data	
						Type of Statement		
1	1	9	12			Unqualified	25	31
		4	4			Reviewed	5	9
2	5	3	1		1	Compiled	8	5
5	6	3				Tax Returns	12	15
3	7	11	11	6	3	Other	63	64
14 (4/1-9/30/13)		84 (10/1/13-3/31/14)					4/1/09-3/31/10 ALL	4/1/10-3/31/11 ALL
0-500M	500M-2MM	2-10MM	10-50MM	50-100MM	100-250MM			
11	19	30	28	6	4	**NUMBER OF STATEMENTS**	113	124
%	%	%	%	%	%	**ASSETS**	%	%
13.2	13.0	14.1	16.4			Cash & Equivalents	7.8	10.5
11.3	12.3	12.0	8.7			Trade Receivables (net)	12.4	9.4
.0	.2	.0	.3			Inventory	.2	.0
1.2	1.3	2.3	3.0			All Other Current	2.8	3.4
25.7	26.8	28.5	28.5			Total Current	23.1	23.3
32.4	27.6	25.5	21.8			Fixed Assets (net)	23.1	25.1
26.5	27.8	36.6	39.8			Intangibles (net)	42.4	40.8
15.4	17.9	9.5	9.9			All Other Non-Current	11.3	10.8
100.0	100.0	100.0	100.0			Total	100.0	100.0
						LIABILITIES		
9.1	2.6	1.1	1.6			Notes Payable-Short Term	7.9	2.7
23.0	9.5	6.1	3.3			Cur. Mat.-L.T.D.	6.9	9.9
23.6	5.6	2.3	2.5			Trade Payables	4.1	2.8
.0	.0	.1	.4			Income Taxes Payable	.0	.3
8.5	13.4	10.3	4.5			All Other Current	17.1	11.0
64.1	31.1	20.0	12.2			Total Current	36.0	26.7
59.4	48.2	27.0	23.2			Long-Term Debt	40.0	44.2
.0	.0	.4	1.4			Deferred Taxes	.6	.3
35.4	10.6	22.7	5.3			All Other Non-Current	15.9	15.9
-58.8	10.1	29.9	58.0			Net Worth	7.4	12.9
100.0	100.0	100.0	100.0			Total Liabilties & Net Worth	100.0	100.0
						INCOME DATA		
100.0	100.0	100.0	100.0			Net Sales	100.0	100.0
						Gross Profit		
98.1	93.0	93.9	86.9			Operating Expenses	91.5	88.5
1.9	7.0	6.1	13.1			Operating Profit	8.5	11.5
.6	1.3	.8	2.6			All Other Expenses (net)	10.9	7.4
1.3	5.7	5.3	10.5			Profit Before Taxes	-2.4	4.1
						RATIOS		
2.2	10.7	4.1	3.2				2.4	2.7
.9	.9	2.3	1.8			Current	1.3	1.2
.1	.4	1.3	1.0				.5	.5
2.2	10.7	3.9	3.1				2.2	2.3
.9	.9	2.0	1.4			Quick	1.1	1.0
.1	.3	1.1	.8				.5	.4
0 UND	**17** 22.1	**36** 10.2	**38** 9.6				**39** 9.4	**23** 15.7
15 24.4	**38** 9.6	**49** 7.5	**54** 6.7			Sales/Receivables	**55** 6.6	**45** 8.1
30 12.2	**56** 6.5	**60** 6.1	**66** 5.5				**67** 5.5	**59** 6.2
						Cost of Sales/Inventory		
						Cost of Sales/Payables		
16.2	3.8	4.0	3.8				5.6	6.3
-30.3	-61.6	7.7	6.7			Sales/Working Capital	15.9	23.9
-6.7	-4.2	18.9	-186.5				-5.3	-4.8
7.3	9.3	4.8	8.4				3.0	3.6
(10) 1.4	(14) 3.4	(26) 2.0	(22) 2.7			EBIT/Interest	(88) 1.0	(94) 1.5
-6.0	.2	.3	1.8				-.6	.4
							2.8	3.5
						Net Profit + Depr., Dep., Amort./Cur. Mat. L/T/D	(20) 1.0	(16) 1.1
							.1	.6
.7	.1	.5	.4				1.5	1.1
-.6	2.2	NM	2.0			Fixed/Worth	-.8	-1.2
-.2	-.3	-.4	-2.1				-.2	-.2
1.2	.7	.3	.3				5.5	1.6
-3.0	28.4	NM	4.2			Debt/Worth	-2.9	-3.3
-1.4	-1.6	-2.3	-5.5				-1.5	-1.5
	28.9	12.3	95.8				45.5	72.0
	(10) 9.7	(15) 3.9	(18) 16.6			% Profit Before Taxes/Tangible Net Worth	(37) 5.9	(48) 14.3
	-11.0	-9.1	8.4				-1.0	.2
54.6	15.2	6.9	11.3				3.9	8.9
3.3	6.7	3.1	5.0			% Profit Before Taxes/Total Assets	-.3	1.7
-20.9	-4.2	-2.7	2.4				-7.2	-1.7
16.2	14.8	7.9	6.4				8.4	8.6
7.3	5.3	3.3	2.5			Sales/Net Fixed Assets	3.2	3.7
5.8	1.9	2.2	1.8				1.8	1.8
3.9	1.3	1.0	.8				1.0	1.0
2.7	.9	.7	.5			Sales/Total Assets	.5	.6
1.3	.7	.5	.4				.4	.4
1.3	1.5	2.5	2.2				3.4	3.3
(10) 3.4	(15) 4.5	(27) 3.3	(26) 3.8			% Depr., Dep., Amort./Sales	(97) 6.3	(98) 6.1
4.8	6.9	9.8	5.1				10.0	10.1
							3.3	5.2
						% Officers', Directors' Owners' Comp/Sales	(20) 5.9	(25) 6.4
							8.4	9.6
8068M	24478M	120088M	400420M	152247M	296950M	Net Sales ($)	1852322M	1717165M
2718M	23004M	156157M	636350M	376074M	589340M	Total Assets ($)	3626548M	2991759M

M = $ thousand MM = $ million

See Pages 9 through 22 for Explanation of Ratios and Data

Comparative Historical Data				Current Data Sorted by Sales					
			Type of Statement						
24	16	23	Unqualified	1	3	4	8	5	2
9	11	8	Reviewed		2	2	2	2	
5	8	12	Compiled	7	1	2	1		1
15	22	14	Tax Returns	6	4	3	1		
45	53	41	Other	5	11	4	5	10	6
4/1/11-3/31/12 ALL	**4/1/12-3/31/13 ALL**	**4/1/13-3/31/14 ALL**		**14 (4/1-9/30/13)**			**84 (10/1/13-3/31/14)**		
				0-1MM	**1-3MM**	**3-5MM**	**5-10MM**	**10-25MM**	**25MM & OVER**
98	110	98	**NUMBER OF STATEMENTS**	19	21	15	17	17	9
%	%	%	**ASSETS**	%	%	%	%	%	%
10.0	10.6	13.9	Cash & Equivalents	12.5	12.8	12.5	15.2	15.9	
9.2	10.6	10.6	Trade Receivables (net)	8.2	11.7	12.3	12.2	10.0	
.2	.1	.2	Inventory	.0	.2	.0	.0	.5	
3.5	2.7	2.1	All Other Current	1.3	1.3	3.5	2.5	2.5	
22.8	23.9	26.8	Total Current	21.9	26.0	28.3	29.9	29.0	
24.5	25.0	24.2	Fixed Assets (net)	30.5	26.3	19.2	26.5	21.9	
43.0	40.1	37.6	Intangibles (net)	28.8	36.3	38.4	35.0	42.5	
9.7	11.1	11.4	All Other Non-Current	18.8	11.4	14.1	8.5	6.7	
100.0	100.0	100.0	Total	100.0	100.0	100.0	100.0	100.0	
			LIABILITIES						
7.0	4.6	2.4	Notes Payable-Short Term	5.6	2.2	3.1	1.0	1.1	
7.8	10.9	7.5	Cur. Mat.-L.T.D.	16.7	8.4	2.5	7.6	3.2	
3.3	2.7	5.2	Trade Payables	11.5	5.4	5.5	2.6	2.0	
.1	.1	.2	Income Taxes Payable	.0	.0	.2	.0	.7	
8.8	7.2	8.5	All Other Current	5.8	19.5	4.7	5.6	5.5	
27.0	25.5	23.8	Total Current	39.6	35.4	15.9	16.7	12.4	
40.7	38.8	34.1	Long-Term Debt	46.8	51.4	18.2	21.7	27.2	
.6	.8	.8	Deferred Taxes	.0	.0	.4	1.7	.7	
18.0	7.1	14.8	All Other Non-Current	30.1	10.3	9.9	2.2	23.3	
13.7	27.8	26.5	Net Worth	-16.5	2.8	55.5	57.6	36.3	
100.0	100.0	100.0	Total Liabilities & Net Worth	100.0	100.0	100.0	100.0	100.0	
			INCOME DATA						
100.0	100.0	100.0	Net Sales	100.0	100.0	100.0	100.0	100.0	
			Gross Profit						
88.6	87.6	90.5	Operating Expenses	95.0	94.7	89.5	94.2	82.5	
11.4	12.4	9.5	Operating Profit	5.0	5.3	10.5	5.8	17.5	
6.7	3.9	2.4	All Other Expenses (net)	1.0	1.5	.5	1.9	3.1	
4.7	8.5	7.2	Profit Before Taxes	4.0	3.9	10.1	3.9	14.4	
			RATIOS						
3.2	3.6	3.9		10.6	3.7	3.3	7.7	4.7	
1.8	2.0	1.7	Current	.9	1.3	1.4	1.8	2.2	
.7	.8	.8		.1	.3	.8	.9	1.1	
2.6	3.2	3.5		9.0	3.7	3.3	7.3	3.6	
1.3	1.6	1.3	Quick	.9	1.1	1.3	1.8	1.7	
.6	.7	.7		.1	.3	.6	.7	1.0	
27 13.5	**37** 9.8	**29** 12.4		**0** UND	**34** 10.7	**27** 13.6	**33** 11.0	**45** 8.1	
47 7.7	**50** 7.3	**47** 7.7	Sales/Receivables	**28** 12.9	**48** 7.6	**45** 8.2	**49** 7.5	**58** 6.3	
59 6.2	**60** 6.1	**63** 5.8		**45** 8.1	**58** 6.3	**73** 5.0	**63** 5.8	**68** 5.4	
			Cost of Sales/Inventory						
			Cost of Sales/Payables						
4.7	4.2	3.9		3.9	3.2	4.3	3.0	3.4	
11.6	8.2	10.2	Sales/Working Capital	-323.5	14.0	8.6	6.8	6.0	
-17.5	-44.6	-28.3		-9.8	-3.8	-30.3	NM	42.8	
6.0	9.7	7.1		6.8	7.5	8.9	5.4	11.9	
(86) 2.1	(94) 3.2	(81) 2.7	EBIT/Interest	(15) 1.9	(19) 2.5	(13) 3.9	(14) 1.5	(13) 3.2	
.5	1.3	.9		-.1	.3	1.5	-3.2	2.3	
	26.2	3.9							
	(13) 2.3	(10) 1.2	Net Profit + Depr., Dep., Amort./Cur. Mat. L/T/D						
	1.1	.9							
1.6	.6	.5		.1	.9	.3	.4	.4	
-1.4	6.4	4.4	Fixed/Worth	-2.9	-.9	3.9	1.0	-11.4	
-.2	-.3	-.4		-.2	-.2	-1.8	-.4	-.5	
2.0	.6	.4		.8	1.1	.3	.2	1.0	
-4.6	176.1	25.3	Debt/Worth	-5.0	-2.7	5.2	.4	-24.0	
-1.5	-1.6	-1.9		-1.4	-1.5	-7.1	-2.0	-2.2	
123.9	69.9	50.2					13.6		
(40) 23.5	(56) 22.8	(51) 12.3	% Profit Before Taxes/Tangible Net Worth				(11) 3.9		
5.1	2.8	.0					-9.1		
9.6	12.6	11.1		15.2	8.7	11.2	6.9	12.9	
3.4	4.7	4.6	% Profit Before Taxes/Total Assets	4.8	1.7	5.0	3.4	7.0	
-1.9	.1	.0		-4.2	-4.8	.1	-3.1	4.4	
7.2	7.5	8.4		14.8	7.5	9.0	7.2	5.8	
3.9	4.0	4.2	Sales/Net Fixed Assets	7.3	4.0	2.7	2.9	3.6	
1.9	2.3	2.2		3.9	2.2	1.5	1.8	2.3	
1.0	1.2	1.1		2.7	1.1	1.4	.9	.8	
.6	.7	.7	Sales/Total Assets	1.3	.8	.8	.6	.5	
.4	.4	.5		.7	.5	.3	.5	.4	
2.9	2.5	2.1		1.6	3.2	1.2	1.6	1.5	
(84) 5.0	(97) 4.5	(88) 3.7	% Depr., Dep., Amort./Sales	(14) 2.9	(20) 5.8	(13) 3.3	(16) 3.4	(16) 4.0	
8.6	7.9	6.3		4.8	9.1	6.8	6.9	5.0	
5.2	5.3	2.9							
(16) 7.2	(21) 8.0	(17) 7.7	% Officers', Directors' Owners' Comp/Sales						
11.7	13.4	10.9							
1296122M	**1536896M**	**1002251M**	Net Sales ($)	**10966M**	**41878M**	**55754M**	**119028M**	**298380M**	**476245M**
2205720M	**2493167M**	**1783643M**	Total Assets ($)	**11463M**	**59941M**	**100120M**	**201704M**	**563043M**	**847372M**

M = $ thousand MM = $ million

See Pages 9 through 22 for Explanation of Ratios and Data

Current Data Sorted by Assets							Comparative Historical Data	
						Type of Statement		
		11	17	6	4	Unqualified	40	47
		1	1	2		Reviewed	2	4
		1			1	Compiled	5	3
	4	2				Tax Returns	2	2
2	2	12	8	6	3	Other	32	31
	26 (4/1-9/30/13)		57 (10/1/13-3/31/14)				4/1/09-3/31/10	4/1/10-3/31/11
0-500M	500M-2MM	2-10MM	10-50MM	50-100MM	100-250MM		ALL	ALL
2	6	27	26	14	8	**NUMBER OF STATEMENTS**	81	87
%	%	%	%	%	%	**ASSETS**	%	%
		15.8	13.6	14.3		Cash & Equivalents	8.4	11.3
		8.8	9.9	9.0		Trade Receivables (net)	8.8	10.9
		.4	.4	.1		Inventory	.2	.5
		1.1	5.6	1.5		All Other Current	5.1	4.9
		26.1	29.4	24.8		Total Current	22.6	27.5
		46.3	38.9	25.0		Fixed Assets (net)	41.2	41.0
		15.3	16.5	26.8		Intangibles (net)	20.7	17.4
		12.3	15.1	23.4		All Other Non-Current	15.5	14.2
		100.0	100.0	100.0		Total	100.0	100.0
						LIABILITIES		
		3.6	3.6	.7		Notes Payable-Short Term	3.9	2.2
		2.0	3.7	6.1		Cur. Mat.-L.T.D.	5.2	3.5
		3.8	3.1	2.7		Trade Payables	4.3	4.8
		.0	.0	.4		Income Taxes Payable	.1	.1
		8.5	6.1	17.2		All Other Current	7.1	6.7
		17.9	16.5	27.0		Total Current	20.5	17.3
		24.9	24.0	18.7		Long-Term Debt	35.1	31.2
		.4	1.1	.5		Deferred Taxes	.6	.8
		5.8	8.8	9.8		All Other Non-Current	11.5	5.6
		51.0	49.6	44.0		Net Worth	32.3	45.2
		100.0	100.0	100.0		Total Liabilities & Net Worth	100.0	100.0
						INCOME DATA		
		100.0	100.0	100.0		Net Sales	100.0	100.0
						Gross Profit		
		90.3	90.8	80.5		Operating Expenses	98.0	92.6
		9.7	9.2	19.5		Operating Profit	2.0	7.4
		3.4	2.6	5.1		All Other Expenses (net)	4.6	3.3
		6.2	6.6	14.5		Profit Before Taxes	-2.6	4.1
						RATIOS		
		3.2	3.4	3.6			2.7	2.6
		1.5	1.7	1.2		Current	1.3	1.4
		.5	.8	.6			.5	.9
		3.0	2.8	2.0			2.2	2.2
		1.5	1.4	.9		Quick	1.0	1.2
		.4	.6	.4			.4	.7
		2 212.5	14 26.6	30 12.3			16 23.5	21 17.0
		8 44.0	41 8.8	51 7.1		Sales/Receivables	42 8.7	46 8.0
		56 6.5	69 5.3	66 5.5			61 6.0	67 5.5
						Cost of Sales/Inventory		
						Cost of Sales/Payables		
		2.8	3.4	3.0			4.7	4.4
		9.8	7.0	55.9		Sales/Working Capital	16.1	14.1
		-15.3	-30.8	-7.3			-8.1	-45.3
		8.4	12.6	10.8			3.9	7.1
		(18) 2.7	(20) 4.6	(10) 7.4		EBIT/Interest	(63) 1.3	(71) 3.1
		-7.7	.8	3.5			-4.1	-.7
								3.0
						Net Profit + Depr., Dep., Amort./Cur. Mat. L/T/D		(12) 2.7
								1.0
		.4	.7	.2			.7	.5
		1.2	1.1	1.4		Fixed/Worth	1.3	1.0
		17.2	2.5	5.5			-1.1	-2.6
		.3	.4	.9			.3	.2
		1.1	1.4	1.7		Debt/Worth	1.3	.9
		-26.7	3.5	NM			-2.6	-5.5
		13.2	29.0	47.4			10.7	17.8
		(20) -2.0	(21) 3.2	(11) 31.5		% Profit Before Taxes/Tangible Net Worth	(52) .8	(60) 3.6
		-19.1	-4.3	13.1			-16.1	-8.3
		10.2	16.4	12.4			3.8	9.0
		2.9	2.4	7.0		% Profit Before Taxes/Total Assets	.1	3.0
		-9.3	-.7	3.5			-8.3	-4.2
		7.6	3.9	10.0			3.4	3.8
		1.6	2.1	2.7		Sales/Net Fixed Assets	1.7	2.1
		.6	1.1	1.9			1.2	1.1
		.9	1.0	.9			1.0	.9
		.7	.8	.6		Sales/Total Assets	.6	.7
		.5	.5	.4			.4	.5
		4.1	6.1	4.5			5.8	5.5
		(24) 9.9	(23) 10.3	(11) 8.1		% Depr., Dep., Amort./Sales	(71) 10.0	(73) 8.7
		19.5	16.0	13.2			16.2	15.7
						% Officers', Directors' Owners' Comp/Sales		
3557M	11177M	126732M	543480M	662093M	1115374M	Net Sales ($)	1834048M	2479403M
536M	4420M	159972M	657776M	973287M	1669782M	Total Assets ($)	3218520M	3789133M

M = $ thousand MM = $ million

See Pages 9 through 22 for Explanation of Ratios and Data

Comparative Historical Data / Current Data Sorted by Sales

4/1/11-3/31/12 ALL	4/1/12-3/31/13 ALL	4/1/13-3/31/14 ALL	Type of Statement	0-1MM	1-3MM	3-5MM	5-10MM	10-25MM	25MM & OVER
35	39	38	Unqualified		3	6	4	12	13
4	5	4	Reviewed					2	2
4	3	2	Compiled			1			1
5	3	6	Tax Returns	1	5				
34	45	33	Other	3	8	4	3	5	10
				26 (4/1-9/30/13)			57 (10/1/13-3/31/14)		
82	95	83	NUMBER OF STATEMENTS	4	16	11	7	19	26
%	%	%	**ASSETS**	%	%	%	%	%	%
12.6	12.2	14.1	Cash & Equivalents		18.9	11.6		17.1	11.5
8.9	9.2	9.6	Trade Receivables (net)		8.3	6.6		11.3	12.6
.9	.6	1.0	Inventory		3.9	.0		.7	.3
4.7	3.5	4.0	All Other Current		7.2	.8		5.1	3.0
27.0	25.5	28.7	Total Current		38.3	19.1		34.4	27.3
39.6	38.1	34.3	Fixed Assets (net)		34.8	46.0		34.4	27.8
18.6	18.1	20.2	Intangibles (net)		9.9	17.7		14.6	27.9
14.7	18.3	16.8	All Other Non-Current		16.9	17.3		16.7	17.1
100.0	100.0	100.0	Total		100.0	100.0		100.0	100.0
			LIABILITIES						
3.6	5.4	4.0	Notes Payable-Short Term		8.6	1.7		6.1	.3
5.5	4.0	3.2	Cur. Mat.-L.T.D.		1.5	.8		3.7	5.1
5.5	4.8	4.2	Trade Payables		6.2	3.5		4.6	3.6
.1	.1	.1	Income Taxes Payable		.0	.0		.0	.2
5.7	8.3	10.1	All Other Current		12.7	13.4		6.9	13.3
20.2	22.7	21.6	Total Current		29.0	19.3		21.4	22.5
31.7	24.3	30.1	Long-Term Debt		28.0	25.2		25.8	39.0
.6	.6	.7	Deferred Taxes		.7	.0		.3	1.0
8.0	7.5	9.5	All Other Non-Current		7.7	9.5		7.3	13.9
39.4	44.9	38.1	Net Worth		34.7	46.0		45.2	23.6
100.0	100.0	100.0	Total Liabilities & Net Worth		100.0	100.0		100.0	100.0
			INCOME DATA						
100.0	100.0	100.0	Net Sales		100.0	100.0		100.0	100.0
			Gross Profit						
91.5	88.9	88.2	Operating Expenses		100.4	94.9		94.3	80.2
8.5	11.1	11.8	Operating Profit		-.4	5.1		5.7	19.8
3.1	3.0	3.3	All Other Expenses (net)		2.8	1.8		-.2	3.8
5.4	8.2	8.4	Profit Before Taxes		-3.2	3.3		5.9	16.0
			RATIOS						
3.5	2.8	2.7			9.7	1.9		2.8	2.3
1.5	1.5	1.6	Current		2.3	.8		1.9	1.4
.9	.7	.7			.4	.4		.8	.9
2.6	2.3	2.2			7.4	1.9		2.7	1.9
1.2	1.3	(82) 1.3	Quick		(15) .8	.8		1.7	1.3
.6	.5	.5			.2	.2		.6	.8
10 38.3	15 24.2	5 72.9			0 UND	4 101.6		17 20.9	46 8.0
42 8.7	32 11.4	40 9.2	Sales/Receivables		4 93.9	13 29.0		49 7.4	55 6.6
61 6.0	55 6.6	59 6.2			35 10.3	76 4.8		60 6.1	70 5.2
			Cost of Sales/Inventory						
			Cost of Sales/Payables						
4.2	4.8	3.6			1.7	8.5		3.5	5.2
9.7	11.3	11.5	Sales/Working Capital		10.7	-21.4		6.1	11.5
-24.9	-8.2	-15.3			-7.1	-9.4		-30.4	-43.1
10.0	11.8	10.7			10.7			5.5	12.8
(69) 3.1	(78) 4.7	(60) 4.4	EBIT/Interest		(11) 1.0			(18) 3.3	(20) 8.4
-.3	.9	1.0			-4.3			.1	4.1
12.8	6.4	6.5							
(10) 1.8	(15) 2.5	(13) 3.1	Net Profit + Depr., Dep., Amort./Cur. Mat. L/T/D						
1.2	1.4	1.3							
.6	.5	.4			.1	.4		.7	.3
1.1	1.0	1.4	Fixed/Worth		.7	2.3		.9	2.3
-1.7	-16.3	-7.1			NM	-23.7		2.1	-1.9
.3	.3	.4			.3	.3		.4	1.0
1.1	1.0	1.8	Debt/Worth		1.1	2.3		1.1	3.2
-4.3	-4.7	-5.5			-6.1	-26.7		3.4	-3.2
16.1	33.2	41.8			66.3			14.0	60.7
(54) 3.9	(68) 7.5	(58) 6.8	% Profit Before Taxes/Tangible Net Worth		(11) 7.2			(15) 2.1	(17) 31.5
-10.2	-3.0	-2.9			-19.2			-2.9	9.8
7.4	14.5	16.2			25.4	10.2		7.7	19.4
2.7	5.5	4.1	% Profit Before Taxes/Total Assets		1.8	2.9		1.6	9.7
-4.4	-.5	-.2			-10.0	-5.3		-.2	5.8
5.2	5.4	7.6			81.0	6.1		5.1	5.4
2.1	2.4	2.5	Sales/Net Fixed Assets		5.3	1.6		2.2	2.9
1.0	1.2	1.1			.7	.8		1.1	2.2
1.0	1.0	1.1			3.5	.9		1.0	1.4
.6	.7	.7	Sales/Total Assets		1.0	.7		.7	.7
.4	.5	.5			.5	.5		.5	.6
5.8	6.4	4.3			1.5	3.3		4.3	3.8
(69) 10.1	(79) 10.2	(67) 8.1	% Depr., Dep., Amort./Sales		(12) 13.9	(10) 8.7		6.5	(18) 7.5
15.6	14.7	16.0			29.0	18.5		13.5	10.5
3.2									
(11) 8.6			% Officers', Directors' Owners' Comp/Sales						
12.6									
2112190M	2905196M	2462413M	Net Sales ($)	2014M	32820M	44268M	49056M	295236M	2039019M
3406531M	4151386M	3465773M	Total Assets ($)	27007M	93800M	75902M	112733M	462132M	2694199M

M = $ thousand MM = $ million

See Pages 9 through 22 for Explanation of Ratios and Data

Current Data Sorted by Assets							Comparative Historical Data	
						Type of Statement		
		3	3		6	Unqualified	25	23
	1	1	1			Reviewed	6	5
	1		1			Compiled	5	7
1		1				Tax Returns	10	3
1	4	6	4		8	Other	21	25
6 (4/1-9/30/13)			36 (10/1/13-3/31/14)				4/1/09-3/31/10 ALL	4/1/10-3/31/11 ALL
0-500M	500M-2MM	2-10MM	10-50MM	50-100MM	100-250MM			
2	6	11	9		14	NUMBER OF STATEMENTS	67	63
%	%	%	%	%	%	**ASSETS**	%	%
		11.8		DATA NOT AVAILABLE	8.4	Cash & Equivalents	15.3	14.0
		17.2			11.5	Trade Receivables (net)	16.2	18.6
		.9			.2	Inventory	2.6	2.6
		5.0			2.3	All Other Current	3.7	2.8
		34.8			22.4	Total Current	37.8	38.0
		43.4			21.4	Fixed Assets (net)	35.6	39.3
		9.0			38.6	Intangibles (net)	18.2	15.4
		12.8			17.5	All Other Non-Current	8.4	7.3
		100.0			100.0	Total	100.0	100.0
						LIABILITIES		
		5.4			.0	Notes Payable-Short Term	5.8	5.4
		3.1			3.4	Cur. Mat.-L.T.D.	6.5	4.7
		7.2			5.0	Trade Payables	9.1	12.5
		.3			.1	Income Taxes Payable	.3	.1
		12.3			6.3	All Other Current	15.3	15.4
		28.3			14.9	Total Current	36.9	38.1
		45.0			100.1	Long-Term Debt	35.2	32.4
		.5			3.8	Deferred Taxes	.9	1.1
		7.3			42.5	All Other Non-Current	8.5	9.3
		19.0			-61.3	Net Worth	18.5	19.1
		100.0			100.0	Total Liabilties & Net Worth	100.0	100.0
						INCOME DATA		
		100.0			100.0	Net Sales	100.0	100.0
						Gross Profit		
		90.7			76.4	Operating Expenses	91.7	91.5
		9.3			23.6	Operating Profit	8.3	8.5
		4.0			6.9	All Other Expenses (net)	4.1	4.2
		5.4			16.8	Profit Before Taxes	4.2	4.3
						RATIOS		
		4.4			2.4		1.4	2.1
		.9			1.5	Current	.8	1.1
		.1			.6		.4	.5
		4.4			2.0		1.3	2.0
		.8			1.3	Quick	.6	.8
		.1			.5		.3	.4
		0 UND			24 15.0		8 46.9	10 36.6
		20 18.4			41 9.0	Sales/Receivables	21 17.4	26 13.8
		41 8.8			62 5.9		38 9.5	48 7.6
						Cost of Sales/Inventory		
						Cost of Sales/Payables		
		6.9			5.3		14.5	6.6
		-66.9			50.8	Sales/Working Capital	-24.7	127.5
		-5.5			-13.1		-7.8	-7.5
					6.8		11.5	11.5
					(13) 3.8	EBIT/Interest	(60) 3.4	(50) 3.1
					2.6		.9	1.1
						Net Profit + Depr., Dep., Amort./Cur. Mat. L/T/D		
		.2			NM		.3	.4
		2.7			-.9	Fixed/Worth	2.3	1.9
		-1.9			-.1		-1.3	-3.6
		1.5			NM		1.2	1.0
		2.8			-2.6	Debt/Worth	4.9	3.1
		-4.0			-1.6		-5.6	-6.0
							51.5	79.4
						% Profit Before Taxes/Tangible Net Worth	(39) 21.5	(44) 30.8
							7.6	9.4
		12.3			31.0		16.0	16.0
		6.2			8.5	% Profit Before Taxes/Total Assets	5.4	6.6
		1.0			5.5		.5	1.2
		112.9			29.4		36.2	20.6
		1.4			2.6	Sales/Net Fixed Assets	3.4	3.5
		.7			1.9		1.3	1.3
		4.3			1.3		2.8	2.7
		.9			.8	Sales/Total Assets	1.3	1.0
		.6			.5		.6	.6
							1.4	1.5
						% Depr., Dep., Amort./Sales	(52) 8.3	(40) 6.9
							17.7	17.6
							.6	
						% Officers', Directors' Owners' Comp/Sales	(12) 3.1	
							9.3	
4555M	19643M	196128M	374381M		2176751M	Net Sales ($)	2494963M	2596689M
699M	7089M	69451M	255629M		2608875M	Total Assets ($)	2648726M	2874178M

M = $ thousand MM = $ million

See Pages 9 through 22 for Explanation of Ratios and Data

Comparative Historical Data				Current Data Sorted by Sales					
Type of Statement									
Unqualified	18	16	12		1	1	1	2	7
Reviewed	3	4	3		1	1			1
Compiled	5	2	2				1		1
Tax Returns	8	2	2	1	1				
Other	25	29	23	1	3	2	2	1	14
	4/1/11-3/31/12 ALL	4/1/12-3/31/13 ALL	4/1/13-3/31/14 ALL	6 (4/1-9/30/13)		36 (10/1/13-3/31/14)			
				0-1MM	1-3MM	3-5MM	5-10MM	10-25MM	25MM & OVER
NUMBER OF STATEMENTS	59	53	42	2	6	4	4	3	23
ASSETS	%	%	%	%	%	%	%	%	%
Cash & Equivalents	13.0	11.8	11.2						12.1
Trade Receivables (net)	16.6	22.7	17.5						22.7
Inventory	3.5	4.1	.8						.9
All Other Current	2.3	4.4	4.1						5.8
Total Current	35.4	43.1	33.7						41.5
Fixed Assets (net)	34.2	28.0	36.5						19.6
Intangibles (net)	19.9	20.4	18.0						24.5
All Other Non-Current	10.5	8.5	11.9						14.4
Total	100.0	100.0	100.0						100.0
LIABILITIES									
Notes Payable-Short Term	7.9	13.2	3.0						4.0
Cur. Mat.-L.T.D.	3.4	4.6	2.5						2.4
Trade Payables	12.0	12.0	8.8						8.1
Income Taxes Payable	.3	.3	.1						.1
All Other Current	21.2	11.4	10.2						10.9
Total Current	44.8	41.4	24.6						25.4
Long-Term Debt	35.8	33.8	53.5						63.2
Deferred Taxes	1.1	.8	1.5						2.3
All Other Non-Current	12.6	14.7	18.9						30.2
Net Worth	5.7	9.3	1.4						-21.1
Total Liabilties & Net Worth	100.0	100.0	100.0						100.0
INCOME DATA									
Net Sales	100.0	100.0	100.0						100.0
Gross Profit									
Operating Expenses	89.1	89.2	86.2						82.3
Operating Profit	10.9	10.8	13.8						17.7
All Other Expenses (net)	3.9	2.9	3.8						4.3
Profit Before Taxes	7.0	7.9	10.0						13.4
RATIOS									
Current	2.0	1.9	2.3						2.4
	1.1	1.2	1.1						1.9
	.6	.6	.5						.7
Quick	2.0	1.6	1.9						2.3
	.8	.8	.9						1.2
	.4	.4	.4						.5
Sales/Receivables	**6** 57.8	**22** 16.8	**10** 36.8						**20** 17.9
	29 12.6	**39** 9.3	**32** 11.3						**46** 7.9
	59 6.2	**62** 5.9	**56** 6.5						**63** 5.8
Cost of Sales/Inventory									
Cost of Sales/Payables									
Sales/Working Capital	7.0	9.2	6.4						5.8
	55.4	29.1	66.2						14.8
	-11.8	-12.4	-11.1						-21.9
EBIT/Interest	21.5	15.3	11.9						10.8
	(42) 4.5	(47) 4.6	(34) 4.0						(18) 4.3
	1.6	1.7	2.0						2.7
Net Profit + Depr., Dep., Amort./Cur. Mat. L/T/D		19.3	29.3						
		(11) 6.4	(12) 4.3						
		1.7	1.9						
Fixed/Worth	.5	.3	.6						.4
	2.6	1.8	2.7						4.5
	-1.0	-1.3	-1.4						-.4
Debt/Worth	.7	1.1	.9						.9
	4.8	4.1	3.4						16.3
	-2.9	-3.1	-2.8						-2.0
% Profit Before Taxes/Tangible Net Worth	79.3	62.8	100.0						154.9
	(38) 26.9	(34) 35.9	(27) 30.7						(12) 66.9
	4.2	10.3	5.8						23.6
% Profit Before Taxes/Total Assets	21.4	23.1	32.1						46.2
	5.7	7.5	7.6						9.0
	-.1	2.1	2.5						5.5
Sales/Net Fixed Assets	27.8	30.0	30.5						44.5
	3.7	5.7	4.2						8.2
	1.5	2.1	1.6						2.3
Sales/Total Assets	2.4	2.6	3.0						3.2
	1.3	1.4	1.0						1.2
	.5	.6	.6						.5
% Depr., Dep., Amort./Sales	2.1	1.3	.9						.4
	(37) 8.5	(38) 3.9	(31) 5.9						(14) 1.7
	20.1	13.3	18.7						6.3
% Officers', Directors' Owners' Comp/Sales									
Net Sales ($)	2311920M	3262541M	2771458M	1475M	10263M	16581M	31381M	47954M	2663804M
Total Assets ($)	2485067M	3180890M	2941743M	906M	18412M	11301M	39803M	65681M	2805640M

M = $ thousand MM = $ million

See Pages 9 through 22 for Explanation of Ratios and Data

Current Data Sorted by Assets | **Comparative Historical Data**

0-500M	500M-2MM	2-10MM	10-50MM	50-100MM	100-250MM	**Type of Statement**	4/1/09-3/31/10 ALL	4/1/10-3/31/11 ALL
	7	14	40	21	21	Unqualified	169	143
	3	7	6			Reviewed	39	14
	3	6	5		2	Compiled	16	18
10	9	9	1			Tax Returns	36	23
4	10	26	31	10	8	Other	133	139
35 (4/1-9/30/13)		218 (10/1/13-3/31/14)						
0-500M	**500M-2MM**	**2-10MM**	**10-50MM**	**50-100MM**	**100-250MM**		**4/1/09-3/31/10 ALL**	**4/1/10-3/31/11 ALL**
14	32	62	83	31	31	**NUMBER OF STATEMENTS**	393	337
%	%	%	%	%	%	**ASSETS**	%	%
33.1	17.5	16.4	14.1	8.8	6.8	Cash & Equivalents	14.0	12.7
9.4	17.0	22.6	11.6	9.5	6.0	Trade Receivables (net)	17.0	16.8
4.4	3.5	4.0	1.9	1.2	1.6	Inventory	3.8	3.2
6.6	3.7	2.5	2.3	4.8	1.7	All Other Current	4.1	3.8
53.5	41.7	45.6	29.9	24.3	16.1	Total Current	39.0	36.6
20.1	39.5	34.8	50.9	51.0	42.7	Fixed Assets (net)	41.1	43.6
15.5	6.4	8.5	9.1	16.5	32.4	Intangibles (net)	10.4	9.8
10.9	12.5	11.2	10.1	8.2	8.8	All Other Non-Current	9.5	10.1
100.0	100.0	100.0	100.0	100.0	100.0	Total	100.0	100.0
						LIABILITIES		
19.0	22.5	8.9	3.0	2.9	.9	Notes Payable-Short Term	5.2	5.7
4.8	3.7	3.7	4.4	2.2	2.3	Cur. Mat.-L.T.D.	4.6	3.8
21.9	11.6	10.8	8.4	5.6	5.0	Trade Payables	10.4	10.9
.3	.1	.2	.5	.1	.2	Income Taxes Payable	.3	.4
12.1	8.9	12.9	10.6	12.7	5.7	All Other Current	11.5	11.4
58.2	46.8	36.5	26.9	23.5	14.0	Total Current	32.0	32.2
36.0	17.2	20.6	28.3	16.2	35.3	Long-Term Debt	22.9	25.1
.0	.5	.6	1.9	1.0	1.9	Deferred Taxes	1.2	1.1
1.6	4.4	8.7	11.9	8.3	7.4	All Other Non-Current	7.6	8.4
4.1	31.2	33.7	30.9	51.0	41.4	Net Worth	36.3	33.2
100.0	100.0	100.0	100.0	100.0	100.0	Total Liabilities & Net Worth	100.0	100.0
						INCOME DATA		
100.0	100.0	100.0	100.0	100.0	100.0	Net Sales	100.0	100.0
						Gross Profit		
96.3	83.5	92.8	88.9	93.3	87.5	Operating Expenses	91.6	91.3
3.7	16.5	7.2	11.1	6.7	12.5	Operating Profit	8.4	8.7
-.9	3.3	1.3	2.4	1.0	6.2	All Other Expenses (net)	1.8	2.2
4.6	13.2	5.9	8.6	5.8	6.2	Profit Before Taxes	6.6	6.5
						RATIOS		
4.2	2.5	2.2	2.4	1.8	2.5		2.1	2.1
1.5	1.3	1.4	1.2	1.3	1.2	Current	1.3	1.2
.5	.5	.7	.7	.7	.8		.8	.7
4.2	2.2	2.0	2.1	1.4	1.6		1.8	1.7
1.2	.9	1.3	1.0	.9	.9	Quick	.9	.9
.3	.4	.6	.5	.5	.7		.6	.5
0 UND	**0** UND	**15** 23.7	**17** 21.1	**23** 15.7	**23** 15.8		**17** 21.9	**19** 19.7
3 107.9	**11** 32.9	**30** 12.1	**31** 11.7	**33** 10.9	**34** 10.8	Sales/Receivables	**32** 11.3	**31** 11.7
11 33.1	**36** 10.1	**46** 7.9	**49** 7.5	**47** 7.8	**42** 8.6		**49** 7.4	**48** 7.6
						Cost of Sales/Inventory		
						Cost of Sales/Payables		
15.6	6.8	8.4	4.5	6.0	4.7		6.2	6.3
56.5	26.1	17.0	16.9	15.3	33.1	Sales/Working Capital	21.0	24.4
-19.2	-9.9	-41.3	-12.8	-13.0	-24.7		-23.4	-17.4
131.0	26.7	41.0	15.6	13.7	10.2		12.1	14.3
(11) 16.1	(23) 7.6	(55) 6.6	(81) 3.8	(30) 6.1	(27) 3.8	EBIT/Interest	(349) 4.1	(306) 4.6
1.0	2.9	1.0	1.2	-1.5	.7		1.5	1.1
		21.3	3.4				6.6	6.3
		(14) 2.2	(32) 2.5			Net Profit + Depr., Dep., Amort./Cur. Mat. L/T/D	(131) 3.4	(112) 3.4
		1.2	1.4				1.9	2.0
.1	.2	.3	.9	1.0	1.1		.6	.7
.2	1.0	1.0	2.0	1.3	3.7	Fixed/Worth	1.3	1.4
-.6	2.7	1.8	27.3	74.7	-.8		5.8	5.7
.3	.7	.7	.6	.6	.6		.7	.7
2.1	1.7	1.3	3.1	.9	3.7	Debt/Worth	1.8	1.9
-2.6	5.7	4.2	34.1	81.0	-2.4		10.9	14.1
	111.0	60.4	51.9	30.0	21.5		44.5	49.3
	(29) 16.0	(53) 23.1	(64) 15.1	(24) 10.1	(17) 8.4	% Profit Before Taxes/Tangible Net Worth	(310) 15.4	(268) 13.2
	1.2	3.5	1.9	-1.3	4.6		4.0	1.6
132.1	30.0	21.9	11.3	13.4	6.5		15.0	14.1
44.5	6.8	9.2	5.8	4.4	3.4	% Profit Before Taxes/Total Assets	5.7	5.9
-5.9	-.1	.4	.1	-1.2	-1.5		1.2	.5
554.8	76.6	33.5	7.1	3.9	4.8		18.1	18.3
67.3	13.1	9.0	1.0	1.2	1.1	Sales/Net Fixed Assets	3.2	2.5
34.7	1.2	1.5	.6	.6	.6		.8	.8
15.9	4.4	3.9	1.5	1.2	.8		2.6	2.6
10.5	2.5	2.4	.6	.7	.5	Sales/Total Assets	1.1	1.0
3.9	.6	.8	.4	.4	.3		.5	.5
	2.3	1.2	5.8	8.2			2.3	2.7
	(20) 6.0	(52) 4.9	(75) 16.4	(24) 14.1		% Depr., Dep., Amort./Sales	(311) 9.3	(262) 10.7
	14.3	12.0	21.8	25.8			20.3	20.8
	5.1	1.1					2.3	2.3
	(12) 7.2	(15) 3.3				% Officers', Directors' Owners' Comp/Sales	(64) 6.1	(48) 5.0
	14.1	7.2					11.3	8.5
30300M	109856M	788985M	1951800M	2261972M	3960340M	Net Sales ($)	14737964M	13141903M
3637M	39590M	333900M	1878044M	2337723M	5226285M	Total Assets ($)	14971540M	13392894M

M = $ thousand MM = $ million

See Pages 9 through 22 for Explanation of Ratios and Data

Comparative Historical Data				Current Data Sorted by Sales					
			Type of Statement						
154	98	103	Unqualified	4	10	4	15	27	43
17	23	16	Reviewed	1	1	1	3	7	3
18	13	16	Compiled	2	1	2	1	7	3
25	27	29	Tax Returns	3	12	7	4	3	
123	120	89	Other	1	8	8	20	19	33
4/1/11-3/31/12 ALL	4/1/12-3/31/13 ALL	4/1/13-3/31/14 ALL		35 (4/1-9/30/13)			218 (10/1/13-3/31/14)		
				0-1MM	1-3MM	3-5MM	5-10MM	10-25MM	25MM & OVER
337	281	253	**NUMBER OF STATEMENTS**	11	32	22	43	63	82
%	%	%	**ASSETS**	%	%	%	%	%	%
12.6	15.5	14.6	Cash & Equivalents	6.9	20.0	21.7	15.6	13.1	12.2
15.3	16.3	13.9	Trade Receivables (net)	4.3	7.4	17.7	9.7	18.7	15.3
3.6	2.9	2.6	Inventory	4.5	1.2	3.8	1.4	4.3	1.9
4.0	2.6	3.0	All Other Current	3.6	5.5	1.9	1.6	2.1	3.7
35.6	37.3	34.2	Total Current	19.4	34.2	45.1	28.4	38.1	33.2
43.0	42.9	42.8	Fixed Assets (net)	60.0	42.7	35.6	53.0	43.0	37.0
11.7	9.2	12.7	Intangibles (net)	15.7	8.6	6.5	7.3	7.5	22.4
9.8	10.6	10.3	All Other Non-Current	4.9	14.5	12.8	11.4	11.3	7.4
100.0	100.0	100.0	Total	100.0	100.0	100.0	100.0	100.0	100.0
			LIABILITIES						
5.5	7.2	7.5	Notes Payable-Short Term	9.5	22.8	9.7	5.8	5.6	3.0
4.2	4.6	3.6	Cur. Mat.-L.T.D.	3.9	3.5	4.5	4.2	4.4	2.5
10.3	10.9	9.4	Trade Payables	6.1	11.6	6.9	6.6	10.4	10.3
.4	.3	.3	Income Taxes Payable	.0	.2	.1	.6	.3	.2
12.6	14.1	10.7	All Other Current	6.4	8.1	9.3	8.7	11.5	13.1
33.0	37.3	31.5	Total Current	26.0	46.3	30.7	25.9	32.2	29.2
26.0	23.6	24.8	Long-Term Debt	29.8	29.5	19.8	32.6	22.2	21.5
1.1	1.1	1.2	Deferred Taxes	.4	.6	.7	2.3	1.1	1.2
8.2	12.5	8.6	All Other Non-Current	4.4	7.1	5.6	10.6	5.4	11.9
31.7	25.6	33.9	Net Worth	39.3	16.6	43.2	28.5	39.0	36.3
100.0	100.0	100.0	Total Liabilties & Net Worth	100.0	100.0	100.0	100.0	100.0	100.0
			INCOME DATA						
100.0	100.0	100.0	Net Sales	100.0	100.0	100.0	100.0	100.0	100.0
			Gross Profit						
91.1	91.7	90.0	Operating Expenses	70.0	88.5	92.3	86.7	91.9	92.9
8.9	8.3	10.0	Operating Profit	30.0	11.5	7.7	13.3	8.1	7.1
2.7	2.3	2.4	All Other Expenses (net)	8.8	1.1	1.1	3.2	.6	3.2
6.2	6.0	7.7	Profit Before Taxes	21.2	10.4	6.7	10.1	7.5	3.9
			RATIOS						
2.0	2.2	2.3		2.4	3.6	4.9	2.4	2.3	1.8
1.1	1.3	1.3	Current	1.4	1.4	2.2	1.3	1.3	1.2
.7	.6	.7		.5	.5	.7	.7	.7	.7
1.7	1.8	1.9		2.1	3.3	3.3	1.9	1.7	1.5
(336) .9	.9	1.0	Quick	1.0	1.2	2.0	1.1	1.0	.9
.5	.5	.5		.3	.4	.6	.5	.5	.6
16 23.5	16 23.1	13 27.1		0 UND	2 160.0	5 80.9	8 46.2	19 18.9	23 15.7
31 11.8	29 12.5	30 12.2	Sales/Receivables	2 152.0	21 17.7	27 13.5	29 12.6	31 11.7	33 10.9
49 7.5	51 7.1	43 8.5		33 11.2	34 10.6	49 7.4	36 10.0	48 7.6	51 7.2
			Cost of Sales/Inventory						
			Cost of Sales/Payables						
7.0	6.4	5.8		8.6	3.2	5.5	5.2	6.5	6.4
36.9	37.3	19.0	Sales/Working Capital	26.2	15.6	41.7	17.1	15.0	32.7
-14.1	-13.4	-16.2		-3.9	-9.4	-10.8	-42.2	-20.7	-15.3
14.2	12.6	17.4			18.8	46.9	10.7	42.0	15.8
(302) 4.3	(236) 4.3	(227) 5.5	EBIT/Interest		(27) 7.3	(20) 4.2	(39) 4.4	(57) 6.5	(77) 4.7
1.2	.9	1.2			1.7	.7	1.5	1.0	.7
7.6	8.3	5.3					3.6	6.2	20.3
(110) 3.0	(76) 2.9	(63) 2.5	Net Profit + Depr., Dep., Amort./Cur. Mat. L/T/D				(14) 2.5	(17) 2.6	(18) 3.6
1.7	1.4	1.5					1.5	1.4	1.2
.7	.5	.6		1.0	.2	.1	.8	.6	.9
1.4	1.4	1.4	Fixed/Worth	2.3	1.1	.7	1.6	1.2	1.8
15.5	NM	15.5		54.1	3.0	5.7	6.6	4.2	-1.8
.7	.6	.6		.3	.7	.5	.5	.6	.7
1.8	2.0	1.9	Debt/Worth	1.9	1.6	1.1	1.3	2.0	2.2
48.2	-88.6	29.2		56.6	NM	6.8	7.2	7.4	-4.7
44.3	49.5	56.4			66.6	199.4	54.6	53.7	35.9
(258) 14.7	(208) 19.0	(195) 16.4	% Profit Before Taxes/Tangible Net Worth		(24) 14.9	(20) 15.1	(36) 14.8	(52) 21.0	(54) 17.0
3.0	3.8	3.2			1.8	4.0	.5	3.8	1.9
13.1	14.9	13.8		12.4	20.8	41.5	12.7	21.3	12.2
5.5	5.3	5.4	% Profit Before Taxes/Total Assets	2.4	4.3	6.9	6.0	7.2	4.0
.5	-.4	-.1		-5.4	.0	-.2	.6	.2	-1.5
18.1	20.8	17.2		40.1	29.8	49.8	7.7	28.2	13.4
2.0	3.2	2.8	Sales/Net Fixed Assets	.6	2.1	6.9	1.1	3.3	3.7
.7	.9	.7		.2	.7	1.1	.6	.8	1.0
2.4	3.0	2.7		.9	3.9	3.6	2.4	3.2	2.1
.9	1.2	1.0	Sales/Total Assets	.5	1.1	2.3	.6	1.5	1.0
.5	.5	.4		.1	.4	.3	.4	.5	.5
3.1	2.7	3.2			2.7	3.4	7.1	1.9	2.9
(252) 12.2	(206) 9.6	(185) 10.7	% Depr., Dep., Amort./Sales		(25) 12.0	(15) 13.2	(38) 13.6	(53) 8.3	(46) 7.0
20.8	20.5	20.9			23.1	20.3	22.7	21.4	12.7
3.1	2.2	2.6			3.2			.9	
(50) 5.0	(57) 4.4	(41) 5.8	% Officers', Directors' Owners' Comp/Sales		(11) 8.7			(10) 1.2	
9.8	9.5	9.8			9.8			2.8	
12360356M	9928461M	9103253M	Net Sales ($)	5128M	63510M	89058M	321992M	1011044M	7612521M
13856382M	10311569M	9819179M	Total Assets ($)	11652M	124661M	118314M	548947M	1423377M	7592228M

M = $ thousand MM = $ million

See Pages 9 through 22 for Explanation of Ratios and Data

Current Data Sorted by Assets							Comparative Historical Data	
						Type of Statement		
		4	8	5	5	Unqualified	36	38
	1	5	2			Reviewed	13	14
3	1	6				Compiled	9	8
2	4	2				Tax Returns	25	23
2	3	23	15	6	5	Other	39	45
10 (4/1-9/30/13)			92 (10/1/13-3/31/14)				4/1/09-3/31/10	4/1/10-3/31/11
0-500M	500M-2MM	2-10MM	10-50MM	50-100MM	100-250MM		ALL	ALL
7	9	40	25	11	10	**NUMBER OF STATEMENTS**	122	128
%	%	%	%	%	%	**ASSETS**	%	%
		16.2	17.9	11.5	13.2	Cash & Equivalents	14.5	14.4
		22.8	21.3	11.8	11.0	Trade Receivables (net)	17.3	22.4
		15.4	11.5	8.9	4.7	Inventory	12.3	12.1
		7.5	4.3	4.1	2.1	All Other Current	4.6	4.1
		61.8	55.0	36.4	31.0	Total Current	48.7	53.0
		27.7	35.5	42.4	54.6	Fixed Assets (net)	33.2	29.8
		5.1	3.8	6.1	9.6	Intangibles (net)	11.0	9.2
		5.4	5.7	15.2	4.8	All Other Non-Current	7.1	8.0
		100.0	100.0	100.0	100.0	Total	100.0	100.0
						LIABILITIES		
		6.9	5.0	3.4	2.4	Notes Payable-Short Term	10.1	6.7
		2.5	2.8	1.0	2.3	Cur. Mat.-L.T.D.	4.8	3.9
		22.4	22.2	9.9	6.7	Trade Payables	15.9	19.6
		.3	.0	.0	.0	Income Taxes Payable	.1	.1
		12.5	8.8	9.3	6.6	All Other Current	11.8	10.1
		44.6	38.8	23.6	18.0	Total Current	42.7	40.3
		18.3	10.6	9.9	30.0	Long-Term Debt	19.5	22.2
		.3	.5	.6	.0	Deferred Taxes	.4	.6
		2.3	5.1	4.9	10.6	All Other Non-Current	8.2	9.3
		34.4	45.0	61.0	41.4	Net Worth	29.3	27.6
		100.0	100.0	100.0	100.0	Total Liabilties & Net Worth	100.0	100.0
						INCOME DATA		
		100.0	100.0	100.0	100.0	Net Sales	100.0	100.0
						Gross Profit		
		90.1	88.1	93.1	93.5	Operating Expenses	91.0	91.6
		9.9	11.9	6.9	6.5	Operating Profit	9.0	8.4
		1.9	.6	-.4	3.9	All Other Expenses (net)	1.3	2.2
		8.0	11.2	7.4	2.6	Profit Before Taxes	7.8	6.2
						RATIOS		
		2.2	3.4	2.8	4.9		2.1	2.4
		1.5	1.5	1.6	1.6	Current	1.2	1.3
		1.1	.9	1.3	.8		.8	.9
		2.0	2.6	2.8	4.0		1.4	1.8
		1.0	1.0	1.1	1.2	Quick	.8	.9
		.3	.5	.5	.7		.4	.6
		13 28.7	**10** 37.5	**22** 16.8	**26** 14.0		**8** 47.5	**14** 26.8
		26 13.8	**24** 15.2	**26** 14.3	**36** 10.0	Sales/Receivables	**25** 14.7	**33** 10.9
		59 6.2	**41** 8.9	**50** 7.3	**42** 8.6		**46** 8.0	**55** 6.6
						Cost of Sales/Inventory		
						Cost of Sales/Payables		
		6.5	3.9	4.2	1.7		8.1	7.3
		12.7	13.2	6.6	33.1	Sales/Working Capital	32.7	20.0
		51.8	-308.8	15.5	-33.1		-30.2	-41.2
		77.7	83.4		23.0		28.7	19.9
		(33) 9.2	(19) 15.5		4.1	EBIT/Interest	(104) 6.4	(108) 5.0
		2.6	5.0		-1.1		1.6	1.8
								28.0
						Net Profit + Depr., Dep., Amort./Cur. Mat. L/T/D		(15) 2.6
								1.0
		.3	.4	.4	.8		.4	.3
		.7	.8	1.0	1.8	Fixed/Worth	.9	1.0
		2.4	1.6	1.3	NM		37.5	5.4
		.7	.4	.1	.3		.7	.8
		1.6	1.1	.7	1.6	Debt/Worth	2.4	2.0
		23.2	7.0	1.6	NM		NM	16.1
		78.4	122.8	30.7			99.4	78.6
		(32) 36.7	(21) 29.7	18.8		% Profit Before Taxes/Tangible Net Worth	(92) 35.8	(103) 24.5
		14.0	14.6	-5.1			7.8	6.6
		24.4	31.6	22.0	8.8		26.8	18.5
		12.8	13.0	10.3	5.7	% Profit Before Taxes/Total Assets	10.5	8.1
		2.1	5.4	-3.0	-6.5		1.9	1.3
		33.4	44.1	2.6	5.6		41.9	51.4
		11.8	12.2	2.3	1.1	Sales/Net Fixed Assets	9.0	11.7
		5.5	1.6	1.1	.8		2.0	1.9
		3.7	4.9	1.1	1.2		4.0	4.0
		2.5	2.2	.9	.6	Sales/Total Assets	2.1	2.1
		1.5	.8	.6	.6		.9	.8
		.9	.5				.7	.7
		(28) 1.9	(23) 3.0			% Depr., Dep., Amort./Sales	(90) 2.9	(91) 2.9
		10.5	12.0				11.0	11.4
		.7					1.8	1.2
		(11) 1.9				% Officers', Directors' Owners' Comp/Sales	(36) 3.1	(33) 3.3
		4.5					7.6	6.2
8207M	67928M	508187M	1548793M	950729M	2054895M	Net Sales ($)	5795849M	5016317M
1745M	10037M	195975M	536449M	775545M	1656244M	Total Assets ($)	4028142M	4197576M

M = $ thousand MM = $ million

See Pages 9 through 22 for Explanation of Ratios and Data

Comparative Historical Data				Current Data Sorted by Sales					
			Type of Statement						
29	22	22	Unqualified		2	1	2	1	16
8	6	8	Reviewed				1	2	5
11	6	10	Compiled	4	1	1	1	2	1
20	10	8	Tax Returns	1	1	3		2	1
43	61	54	Other	2	3	2	15	11	21
4/1/11-3/31/12 ALL	**4/1/12-3/31/13 ALL**	**4/1/13-3/31/14 ALL**		**10 (4/1-9/30/13)**			**92 (10/1/13-3/31/14)**		
				0-1MM	**1-3MM**	**3-5MM**	**5-10MM**	**10-25MM**	**25MM & OVER**
111	105	102	**NUMBER OF STATEMENTS**	7	7	7	19	18	44
%	%	%	**ASSETS**	%	%	%	%	%	%
15.0	15.4	15.2	Cash & Equivalents				10.7	20.6	16.2
23.5	19.0	21.9	Trade Receivables (net)				21.8	27.5	19.5
10.8	12.3	12.6	Inventory				8.4	20.8	10.0
4.4	3.9	4.8	All Other Current				6.5	6.7	5.2
53.7	50.6	54.6	Total Current				47.3	75.6	50.9
28.9	33.1	33.7	Fixed Assets (net)				39.1	19.1	35.9
9.7	8.4	4.9	Intangibles (net)				3.1	1.3	6.3
7.7	7.9	6.8	All Other Non-Current				10.5	4.0	7.0
100.0	100.0	100.0	Total				100.0	100.0	100.0
			LIABILITIES						
7.6	6.5	9.4	Notes Payable-Short Term				8.4	5.1	4.6
4.2	3.7	2.4	Cur. Mat.-L.T.D.				1.7	1.2	2.8
21.0	15.8	18.5	Trade Payables				11.5	32.1	19.4
.0	.1	.1	Income Taxes Payable				.2	.4	.0
11.4	8.6	11.3	All Other Current				6.0	12.6	10.5
44.3	34.6	41.7	Total Current				28.0	51.5	37.3
22.0	17.6	19.2	Long-Term Debt				23.6	5.9	16.6
.6	.6	.3	Deferred Taxes				.2	.5	.4
6.1	11.5	4.9	All Other Non-Current				3.1	2.8	4.7
27.0	35.8	33.9	Net Worth				45.1	39.3	40.9
100.0	100.0	100.0	Total Liabilties & Net Worth				100.0	100.0	100.0
			INCOME DATA						
100.0	100.0	100.0	Net Sales				100.0	100.0	100.0
			Gross Profit						
94.9	92.8	90.6	Operating Expenses				88.5	96.3	91.6
5.1	7.2	9.4	Operating Profit				11.5	3.7	8.4
2.5	1.5	1.3	All Other Expenses (net)				3.5	-1.5	.8
2.6	5.7	8.1	Profit Before Taxes				8.0	5.2	7.7
			RATIOS						
2.0	3.9	2.8					3.3	4.2	2.4
1.3	1.7	1.5	Current				2.0	1.8	1.4
.9	1.1	.9					1.3	1.0	1.0
1.5	2.4	2.3					2.5	3.8	2.2
.9	1.1	1.0	Quick				1.5	1.4	1.0
.5	.6	.5					.5	.2	.5
15 24.2	**6** 60.0	**15** 24.4					**16** 22.7	**11** 34.7	**14** 25.6
31 11.9	**27** 13.4	**26** 14.0	Sales/Receivables				**36** 10.1	**25** 14.7	**26** 14.0
47 7.7	**43** 8.4	**47** 7.8					**69** 5.3	**46** 8.0	**41** 8.8
			Cost of Sales/Inventory						
			Cost of Sales/Payables						
7.3	6.4	5.2					5.6	7.3	5.1
23.1	17.8	13.3	Sales/Working Capital				8.1	12.1	15.9
-42.3	266.1	-492.5					24.7	NM	NM
19.9	33.0	55.2					39.0	149.8	54.8
(88) 3.6	(74) 6.2	(83) 7.7	EBIT/Interest				(13) 8.0	(17) 40.3	(37) 7.7
.8	2.9	2.2					1.2	3.0	3.3
19.4	23.3	6.1							
(16) 3.3	(10) 9.7	(15) 3.6	Net Profit + Depr., Dep., Amort./Cur. Mat. L/T/D						
-.1	1.4	.8							
.3	.4	.3					.4	.2	.4
1.1	.8	.8	Fixed/Worth				.7	.5	.9
-10.6	5.4	1.8					1.4	3.6	1.7
.7	.4	.5					.3	.3	.4
2.4	1.7	1.5	Debt/Worth				1.2	1.6	1.6
-27.1	11.3	6.7					2.4	42.1	6.2
40.5	76.4	73.0					44.9	80.2	85.0
(83) 16.0	(81) 29.9	(83) 27.1	% Profit Before Taxes/Tangible Net Worth				(16) 17.6	(15) 33.4	(37) 29.7
5.0	12.8	13.5					12.7	13.5	15.1
16.0	26.1	23.1					14.9	22.0	37.0
5.2	10.2	11.9	% Profit Before Taxes/Total Assets				12.3	12.9	12.2
-.5	3.5	2.2					2.0	1.6	5.1
45.3	44.6	35.7					11.0	144.6	39.9
13.7	13.0	10.3	Sales/Net Fixed Assets				5.4	20.9	10.1
2.2	3.0	1.7					1.0	11.5	1.7
4.0	4.4	4.4					2.5	5.2	4.8
2.2	2.5	2.3	Sales/Total Assets				1.7	3.6	2.3
.9	1.0	.9					.5	2.4	.8
.9	.6	.9					1.7	.8	.6
(82) 2.7	(68) 3.1	(70) 2.5	% Depr., Dep., Amort./Sales				(14) 5.3	(13) 1.4	(31) 2.9
10.9	10.3	10.6					17.0	2.2	8.5
1.2	.9	.7							
(26) 4.7	(18) 5.3	(23) 1.9	% Officers', Directors' Owners' Comp/Sales						
7.9	8.7	5.5							
5432677M	**3974367M**	**5138739M**	Net Sales ($)	**4605M**	**11378M**	**24585M**	**144861M**	**284343M**	**4668967M**
3132156M	**2695776M**	**3175995M**	Total Assets ($)	**7170M**	**24032M**	**22928M**	**236203M**	**108932M**	**2776730M**

M = $ thousand MM = $ million

See Pages 9 through 22 for Explanation of Ratios and Data

Current Data Sorted by Assets							Comparative Historical Data	
		1	3	3	3	Type of Statement Unqualified	6	12
	1	3	3			Reviewed	7	10
		2	1	1		Compiled	3	2
	1	3	1			Tax Returns	6	5
	2	16	18	1	6	Other	15	19
	2 (4/1-9/30/13)		67 (10/1/13-3/31/14)				4/1/09-3/31/10 ALL	4/1/10-3/31/11 ALL
0-500M	500M-2MM	2-10MM	10-50MM	50-100MM	100-250MM			
	4	25	26	5	9	NUMBER OF STATEMENTS	37	48
%	%	%	%	%	%	ASSETS	%	%
DATA NOT AVAILABLE		17.3	17.3			Cash & Equivalents	10.8	12.7
		32.0	24.9			Trade Receivables (net)	28.2	28.0
		13.3	13.7			Inventory	14.5	12.6
		5.8	6.2			All Other Current	5.4	9.4
		68.3	62.1			Total Current	58.9	62.8
		14.8	20.5			Fixed Assets (net)	16.9	19.2
		6.5	10.7			Intangibles (net)	12.1	11.9
		10.4	6.8			All Other Non-Current	12.0	6.1
		100.0	100.0			Total	100.0	100.0
						LIABILITIES		
		6.2	7.0			Notes Payable-Short Term	17.2	8.0
		1.7	.9			Cur. Mat.-L.T.D.	3.8	3.0
		30.3	26.2			Trade Payables	28.0	29.6
		.5	.1			Income Taxes Payable	.4	.6
		16.7	17.4			All Other Current	16.3	12.4
		55.4	51.6			Total Current	65.6	53.5
		8.7	12.8			Long-Term Debt	18.9	12.6
		.2	.0			Deferred Taxes	.4	1.1
		3.0	4.8			All Other Non-Current	7.0	5.9
		32.6	30.8			Net Worth	8.1	27.0
		100.0	100.0			Total Liabilties & Net Worth	100.0	100.0
						INCOME DATA		
		100.0	100.0			Net Sales	100.0	100.0
						Gross Profit		
		94.1	93.7			Operating Expenses	93.6	97.2
		5.9	6.3			Operating Profit	6.4	2.8
		.2	1.5			All Other Expenses (net)	2.8	1.4
		5.7	4.7			Profit Before Taxes	3.6	1.5
						RATIOS		
		2.3	1.6				1.7	1.7
		1.4	1.3			Current	1.0	1.2
		.9	.9				.6	.9
		1.5	1.1				.9	1.2
		.9	.7			Quick	.6	(47) .7
		.6	.6				.4	.5
		19 19.0	17 21.5				13 27.7	19 18.7
		33 11.2	28 12.9			Sales/Receivables	31 11.9	34 10.9
		41 8.8	47 7.7				51 7.1	46 7.9
						Cost of Sales/Inventory		
						Cost of Sales/Payables		
		9.3	8.5				10.7	6.3
		80.0	26.9			Sales/Working Capital	-152.5	34.2
		-28.7	-32.5				-9.8	-79.3
		44.6	68.8				16.7	36.3
		(20) 11.8	(21) 12.5			EBIT/Interest	(33) 5.3	(42) 6.3
		1.6	1.9				.6	2.5
						Net Profit + Depr., Dep., Amort./Cur. Mat. L/T/D		
		.2	.2				.3	.2
		.6	.8			Fixed/Worth	2.1	1.2
		NM	-1.2				-.4	-26.2
		.6	1.3				1.7	1.7
		2.3	3.4			Debt/Worth	-17.0	4.8
		NM	-14.3				-2.9	-28.0
		128.5	66.0				84.5	84.8
		(19) 53.1	(19) 43.9			% Profit Before Taxes/Tangible Net Worth	(18) 24.1	(34) 30.5
		17.7	13.1				11.2	-1.9
		37.9	16.0				18.2	17.9
		9.3	8.0			% Profit Before Taxes/Total Assets	6.5	6.6
		3.5	1.9				-.8	.0
		137.9	61.1				120.5	120.3
		55.7	33.9			Sales/Net Fixed Assets	36.7	44.0
		12.1	11.7				12.3	10.0
		6.0	3.9				5.9	5.2
		3.0	2.7			Sales/Total Assets	3.2	3.0
		2.2	1.7				1.7	1.1
		.2	.4				.5	.4
		(15) 1.5	(21) .7			% Depr., Dep., Amort./Sales	(27) .9	(33) .8
		2.1	2.3				2.8	3.5
								.7
						% Officers', Directors' Owners' Comp/Sales		(11) 3.0
								9.7
	65147M	561834M	1770370M	1086586M	3647301M	Net Sales ($)	2351557M	2520018M
	5135M	124235M	587956M	365409M	1610573M	Total Assets ($)	1316658M	1791794M

M = $ thousand MM = $ million

See Pages 9 through 22 for Explanation of Ratios and Data

Comparative Historical Data / Current Data Sorted by Sales

4/1/11-3/31/12 ALL	4/1/12-3/31/13 ALL	4/1/13-3/31/14 ALL	Type of Statement	0-1MM	1-3MM	3-5MM	5-10MM	10-25MM	25MM & OVER
16	11	10	Unqualified						10
4	9	7	Reviewed				1	2	4
3	6	4	Compiled		1	1		1	1
11	6	5	Tax Returns					3	2
30	45	43	Other		2	1	2	12	26
				2 (4/1-9/30/13)			67 (10/1/13-3/31/14)		
64	77	69	NUMBER OF STATEMENTS		3	2	3	18	43
%	%	%	**ASSETS**	%	%	%	%	%	%
21.0	17.1	16.6	Cash & Equivalents	DATA NOT AVAILABLE				16.6	17.8
23.1	28.1	26.6	Trade Receivables (net)					27.3	28.0
11.9	7.1	10.9	Inventory					13.7	10.2
6.3	5.5	6.8	All Other Current					7.9	7.4
62.3	57.7	61.0	Total Current					65.4	63.5
21.3	24.4	20.8	Fixed Assets (net)					23.2	16.7
7.6	8.3	10.1	Intangibles (net)					6.3	12.7
8.9	9.5	8.1	All Other Non-Current					5.1	7.1
100.0	100.0	100.0	Total					100.0	100.0
			LIABILITIES						
6.7	6.4	5.6	Notes Payable-Short Term					6.8	5.4
3.7	4.4	1.9	Cur. Mat.-L.T.D.					1.7	2.0
24.2	21.6	25.9	Trade Payables					18.7	31.0
.6	1.4	.3	Income Taxes Payable					.5	.2
20.2	16.4	16.7	All Other Current					23.0	15.3
55.4	50.2	50.3	Total Current					50.7	53.9
16.3	15.5	14.0	Long-Term Debt					16.2	11.9
.6	1.0	.3	Deferred Taxes					.3	.3
4.1	5.9	4.5	All Other Non-Current					4.3	5.2
23.6	27.4	30.8	Net Worth					28.5	28.7
100.0	100.0	100.0	Total Liabilties & Net Worth					100.0	100.0
			INCOME DATA						
100.0	100.0	100.0	Net Sales					100.0	100.0
			Gross Profit						
93.1	92.0	94.2	Operating Expenses					94.8	95.1
6.9	8.0	5.8	Operating Profit					5.2	4.9
2.5	1.5	1.1	All Other Expenses (net)					.7	.8
4.4	6.5	4.8	Profit Before Taxes					4.5	4.1
			RATIOS						
1.8	1.8	2.0						2.2	1.7
1.2	1.2	1.3	Current					1.3	1.1
.8	.8	.8						.9	.8
1.5	1.4	1.4						1.6	1.3
.8	.8	.9	Quick					.9	.8
.5	.6	.5						.5	.5
6 57.1	**17** 20.9	**18** 20.3						**29** 12.8	**17** 21.5
26 13.8	**30** 12.0	**30** 12.1	Sales/Receivables					**38** 9.5	**27** 13.5
53 6.9	**49** 7.4	**42** 8.7						**50** 7.3	**40** 9.1
			Cost of Sales/Inventory						
			Cost of Sales/Payables						
9.0	11.3	9.0						7.6	10.5
45.9	41.5	33.0	Sales/Working Capital					218.0	80.0
-56.1	-42.5	-37.0						-40.2	-34.7
37.1	34.4	44.1						16.9	51.9
(48) 7.1	(57) 7.7	(56) 10.8	EBIT/Interest					(14) 8.7	(36) 12.1
1.7	2.0	1.5						-1.1	1.8
6.0	7.3	7.4							
(11) 2.6	(17) 2.9	(11) 4.8	Net Profit + Depr., Dep., Amort./Cur. Mat. L/T/D						
.3	1.4	3.6							
.1	.2	.2						.3	.2
.5	1.1	1.0	Fixed/Worth					1.1	.9
3.1	8.0	-2.9						-1.7	-1.1
1.0	.9	1.2						1.0	1.3
2.5	3.5	3.3	Debt/Worth					3.5	3.3
32.5	65.0	-19.3						-20.5	-8.2
100.0	89.3	83.0						106.9	90.0
(51) 29.7	(60) 36.5	(51) 45.0	% Profit Before Taxes/Tangible Net Worth					(13) 36.2	(31) 60.2
5.4	11.6	18.1						14.5	26.7
28.1	25.7	22.0						19.1	25.8
10.9	10.8	8.1	% Profit Before Taxes/Total Assets					6.4	9.3
.8	3.3	2.4						.6	3.2
154.0	77.2	79.0						75.2	99.3
32.3	25.5	30.9	Sales/Net Fixed Assets					21.9	34.3
9.1	8.8	9.5						10.9	9.8
4.7	4.6	4.2						4.4	4.3
2.7	3.2	3.0	Sales/Total Assets					2.6	3.5
1.1	1.7	1.9						1.8	2.2
.3	.4	.4						.1	.4
(51) 1.0	(54) 1.0	(46) .9	% Depr., Dep., Amort./Sales					(12) 1.7	(29) .7
3.8	3.1	2.2						11.2	1.6
.7	.6	.8							
(11) 3.3	(14) 1.9	(17) 1.9	% Officers', Directors' Owners' Comp/Sales						
7.1	6.1	4.7							
4794711M	6364419M	7131238M	Net Sales ($)		8093M	6548M	20864M	282962M	6812771M
1867032M	2411258M	2693308M	Total Assets ($)		20826M	7584M	6957M	153580M	2504361M

M = $ thousand MM = $ million

See Pages 9 through 22 for Explanation of Ratios and Data

	Current Data Sorted by Assets						Comparative Historical Data	
Type of Statement								
Unqualified			8	11	3	7	40	33
Reviewed		2	10	5			15	13
Compiled	1	6	6	2			11	20
Tax Returns	4	13	5				17	24
Other	4	14	23	14	10	9	89	71
	16 (4/1-9/30/13)			141 (10/1/13-3/31/14)			4/1/09-3/31/10 ALL	4/1/10-3/31/11 ALL
	0-500M	500M-2MM	2-10MM	10-50MM	50-100MM	100-250MM		
NUMBER OF STATEMENTS	9	35	52	32	13	16	172	161
ASSETS	%	%	%	%	%	%	%	%
Cash & Equivalents		18.0	14.9	16.2	5.6	10.4	14.0	11.9
Trade Receivables (net)		31.2	36.0	28.4	15.8	12.5	24.9	28.6
Inventory		8.1	7.6	6.5	3.4	3.5	6.6	6.4
All Other Current		.7	5.8	6.3	2.2	1.7	5.5	4.4
Total Current		58.0	64.4	57.4	27.0	28.1	50.9	51.4
Fixed Assets (net)		30.3	21.9	24.4	36.6	34.0	29.0	29.7
Intangibles (net)		2.6	3.8	10.8	25.8	29.2	11.6	9.5
All Other Non-Current		9.1	9.9	7.4	10.7	8.6	8.5	9.4
Total		100.0	100.0	100.0	100.0	100.0	100.0	100.0
LIABILITIES								
Notes Payable-Short Term		22.4	9.4	1.9	3.7	1.3	9.4	11.2
Cur. Mat.-L.T.D.		1.5	3.2	4.1	1.7	1.9	3.9	3.9
Trade Payables		15.9	20.0	18.4	8.8	6.8	15.2	14.1
Income Taxes Payable		.0	.5	.2	.1	.0	.1	.4
All Other Current		15.9	12.8	18.6	9.9	12.5	18.3	13.2
Total Current		55.7	45.9	43.2	24.3	22.5	46.8	42.7
Long-Term Debt		24.1	12.7	32.2	24.2	30.0	22.5	23.3
Deferred Taxes		.0	.3	.4	.9	1.9	.7	.5
All Other Non-Current		6.6	13.1	13.3	9.2	7.8	7.0	8.5
Net Worth		13.6	28.0	11.0	41.4	37.7	23.0	24.9
Total Liabilties & Net Worth		100.0	100.0	100.0	100.0	100.0	100.0	100.0
INCOME DATA								
Net Sales		100.0	100.0	100.0	100.0	100.0	100.0	100.0
Gross Profit								
Operating Expenses		87.1	94.8	92.8	97.3	91.9	93.7	90.5
Operating Profit		12.9	5.2	7.2	2.7	8.1	6.3	9.5
All Other Expenses (net)		3.7	.5	3.1	3.0	3.4	1.9	3.7
Profit Before Taxes		9.2	4.7	4.1	-.3	4.8	4.4	5.8
RATIOS								
Current		2.9	3.2	2.4	2.1	2.3	1.7	2.2
		1.4	1.5	1.3	1.0	.9	1.1	1.3
		.9	.9	.8	.7	.6	.6	.7
Quick		2.9	2.7	1.5	1.5	1.9	1.4	1.8
		1.2	1.2	.9	.7	.7	.8	1.0
		.7	.8	.6	.6	.5	.5	.5
Sales/Receivables		**0** UND	**24** 15.5	**27** 13.7	**23** 16.1	**26** 14.3	**17** 21.4	**18** 20.1
		31 11.6	**44** 8.3	**42** 8.7	**56** 6.5	**38** 9.6	**38** 9.6	**39** 9.3
		60 6.1	**63** 5.8	**64** 5.7	**85** 4.3	**54** 6.7	**60** 6.1	**63** 5.8
Cost of Sales/Inventory								
Cost of Sales/Payables								
Sales/Working Capital		7.1	6.6	8.4	5.8	4.6	10.7	6.2
		27.4	18.2	24.1	60.2	-69.0	46.5	19.4
		-28.2	-70.4	-32.0	-22.0	-5.7	-13.4	-27.9
EBIT/Interest		42.4	42.4	33.6	3.7	10.9	13.9	19.7
		(25) 9.1	(41) 12.2	(28) 7.5	(11) .9	(14) 2.4	(141) 3.7	(139) 4.5
		.6	2.8	.9	-1.3	-.1	1.0	1.2
Net Profit + Depr., Dep., Amort./Cur. Mat. L/T/D				6.0			8.1	7.1
				(10) 1.7			(30) 3.3	(26) 2.5
				.8			1.1	1.4
Fixed/Worth		.2	.2	.2	1.0	.6	.3	.3
		.7	.4	1.0	2.8	1.7	1.4	1.2
		43.0	3.4	2.9	-.5	-1.8	-2.5	42.0
Debt/Worth		.5	.6	1.2	1.5	1.2	1.3	1.0
		2.6	1.4	2.8	2.6	4.9	4.1	2.7
		228.3	8.6	29.3	-5.6	-3.3	-5.4	134.1
% Profit Before Taxes/Tangible Net Worth		127.4	74.0	78.3		44.2	66.0	66.5
		(27) 54.4	(44) 42.2	(25) 14.3		(11) 37.9	(119) 26.0	(122) 25.7
		13.9	16.3	.8		27.6	8.3	4.3
% Profit Before Taxes/Total Assets		48.1	25.5	13.8	4.8	10.6	14.4	18.9
		22.6	12.0	4.4	-.6	4.0	6.4	7.6
		1.1	4.0	-.1	-7.4	-1.8	.9	.3
Sales/Net Fixed Assets		132.6	79.6	47.1	17.5	17.5	48.5	46.2
		22.0	16.9	23.7	4.7	3.4	14.8	14.6
		4.0	7.7	3.8	.7	.6	3.7	3.1
Sales/Total Assets		4.5	4.2	3.4	1.5	1.3	3.3	3.5
		2.7	3.2	1.9	.7	.6	2.0	1.9
		1.7	2.3	.9	.3	.3	1.0	.9
% Depr., Dep., Amort./Sales		.4	.5	.8			1.1	1.1
		(25) 1.7	(42) 1.8	(29) 1.7			(123) 2.3	(124) 2.5
		4.4	4.4	9.8			8.1	8.3
% Officers', Directors' Owners' Comp/Sales		2.5	.8				1.1	1.9
		(14) 3.6	(18) 2.2				(32) 4.6	(35) 4.5
		8.8	4.9				13.1	9.8
Net Sales ($)	**10730M**	**140649M**	**821172M**	**1697433M**	**740061M**	**2682692M**	**6157303M**	**6632604M**
Total Assets ($)	**2159M**	**43536M**	**244991M**	**845827M**	**890528M**	**2860170M**	**4221608M**	**4884092M**

M = $ thousand MM = $ million

See Pages 9 through 22 for Explanation of Ratios and Data

Comparative Historical Data | **Current Data Sorted by Sales**

4/1/11-3/31/12 ALL	4/1/12-3/31/13 ALL	4/1/13-3/31/14 ALL		0-1MM	1-3MM	3-5MM	5-10MM	10-25MM	25MM & OVER
			Type of Statement						
23	23	29	Unqualified		1		2	9	17
25	13	17	Reviewed			3	1	8	5
20	18	15	Compiled		3	2	3	5	2
9	24	22	Tax Returns	7	4	3	6	2	
73	68	74	Other	4	6	7	9	17	31
				16 (4/1-9/30/13)			141 (10/1/13-3/31/14)		
150	146	157	**NUMBER OF STATEMENTS**	11	14	15	21	41	55
%	%	%	**ASSETS**	%	%	%	%	%	%
12.6	18.7	17.2	Cash & Equivalents	28.4	28.6	18.4	13.9	18.3	12.2
28.2	28.6	28.1	Trade Receivables (net)	19.6	12.8	26.3	37.0	32.8	27.2
7.7	7.3	6.3	Inventory	.6	6.5	11.9	5.5	8.5	4.7
4.8	2.9	3.7	All Other Current	.1	1.2	4.3	1.1	4.3	5.5
53.4	57.4	55.4	Total Current	48.7	49.0	61.0	57.7	63.9	49.5
27.1	23.0	26.7	Fixed Assets (net)	48.1	36.9	26.2	24.6	22.0	24.4
8.8	8.9	9.1	Intangibles (net)	.4	4.7	4.3	4.9	6.5	16.9
10.7	10.7	8.8	All Other Non-Current	2.8	9.3	8.6	12.9	7.5	9.2
100.0	100.0	100.0	Total	100.0	100.0	100.0	100.0	100.0	100.0
			LIABILITIES						
7.6	7.8	9.1	Notes Payable-Short Term	.9	15.5	11.1	27.1	6.9	3.2
4.0	4.3	2.9	Cur. Mat.-L.T.D.	2.8	5.4	1.8	1.5	3.4	2.8
20.1	16.2	17.2	Trade Payables	17.4	19.1	8.6	29.7	12.7	17.7
.1	.3	.2	Income Taxes Payable	.0	.2	.0	.7	.3	.1
13.2	15.6	14.6	All Other Current	12.2	24.8	12.6	10.5	8.7	19.1
44.9	44.2	44.1	Total Current	33.3	65.1	34.2	69.5	32.0	43.0
17.2	23.9	24.4	Long-Term Debt	52.5	54.1	8.8	8.2	13.3	29.8
.5	.3	.5	Deferred Taxes	.0	.0	.1	.0	.6	.9
7.3	11.1	10.7	All Other Non-Current	3.6	15.5	7.5	3.2	14.8	11.7
30.1	20.5	20.3	Net Worth	10.5	-34.7	49.4	19.0	39.3	14.7
100.0	100.0	100.0	Total Liabilities & Net Worth	100.0	100.0	100.0	100.0	100.0	100.0
			INCOME DATA						
100.0	100.0	100.0	Net Sales	100.0	100.0	100.0	100.0	100.0	100.0
			Gross Profit						
91.6	92.7	92.0	Operating Expenses	69.2	90.0	96.3	93.3	95.2	93.0
8.4	7.3	8.0	Operating Profit	30.8	10.0	3.7	6.7	4.8	7.0
1.8	1.9	2.3	All Other Expenses (net)	9.9	3.8	.9	1.0	.6	2.5
6.6	5.4	5.7	Profit Before Taxes	20.9	6.2	2.8	5.6	4.2	4.5
			RATIOS						
2.2	2.5	2.7		3.5	2.8	3.7	1.9	4.5	1.7
1.2	1.3	1.4	Current	1.4	1.5	2.2	1.1	2.0	1.1
.7	.8	.9		.4	.3	1.1	.4	1.1	.8
1.8	2.3	2.3		3.5	2.7	3.3	1.8	3.7	1.5
.9	1.1	1.1	Quick	1.4	1.2	1.4	1.0	1.6	.9
.5	.6	.6		.4	.2	.9	.4	.8	.6
21 17.0	**20** 18.0	**19** 18.8		**0** UND	**0** UND	**0** UND	**21** 17.1	**26** 13.9	**25** 14.8
39 9.4	**37** 9.9	**40** 9.2	Sales/Receivables	**23** 15.7	**6** 58.2	**48** 7.6	**31** 11.6	**45** 8.2	**40** 9.2
59 6.2	**59** 6.2	**62** 5.9		**72** 5.1	**35** 10.5	**58** 6.3	**62** 5.9	**63** 5.8	**57** 6.4
			Cost of Sales/Inventory						
			Cost of Sales/Payables						
6.7	6.8	6.8		7.1	4.7	4.5	9.3	5.2	9.0
24.0	29.0	20.6	Sales/Working Capital	13.7	15.9	18.5	45.3	12.5	60.2
-17.6	-28.2	-30.6		-3.1	-4.2	105.1	-11.5	45.3	-25.8
14.5	20.7	30.3			43.5	88.1	28.5	51.4	16.6
(120) 5.2	(112) 3.8	(125) 6.8	EBIT/Interest		(12) 3.8	(11) 13.3	(16) 6.1	(32) 18.0	(49) 5.3
1.4	.6	.9			1.1	-.7	.4	2.3	.8
8.2	17.1	6.6							12.4
(26) 2.2	(14) 3.9	(21) 2.9	Net Profit + Depr., Dep., Amort./Cur. Mat. L/T/D						(10) 4.4
1.4	1.1	1.1							1.1
.2	.2	.2		.0	.2	.2	.1	.1	.3
1.1	.8	.8	Fixed/Worth	3.6	2.1	.5	.8	.3	1.3
5.0	50.4	6.5		-6.4	-.2	3.7	NM	1.9	-1.3
1.0	.8	.7		2.6	.5	.2	.3	.4	1.5
2.7	3.2	2.6	Debt/Worth	8.0	3.1	1.2	1.6	1.2	4.4
22.4	-32.0	29.4		-9.3	-2.5	9.7	NM	3.4	-5.2
63.7	81.4	77.1				50.0	115.4	71.9	72.1
(115) 25.9	(108) 27.9	(121) 38.5	% Profit Before Taxes/Tangible Net Worth			(14) 22.4	(16) 39.7	(37) 37.1	(38) 37.6
6.7	5.4	11.7				-23.8	3.7	13.8	12.0
16.2	21.8	25.3		30.0	39.1	48.1	35.0	31.2	12.7
6.7	5.7	8.1	% Profit Before Taxes/Total Assets	7.5	7.0	6.7	11.5	13.4	4.6
1.0	-1.9	.4		1.6	.5	-3.3	-.2	4.8	-.6
62.9	66.0	64.0		UND	41.0	26.8	141.7	70.9	47.1
19.2	24.3	17.3	Sales/Net Fixed Assets	2.1	5.8	10.8	39.6	17.3	18.4
4.4	5.1	4.8		.2	2.0	6.3	4.5	8.1	3.3
3.7	4.7	3.8		2.1	3.3	3.3	5.4	4.1	3.8
2.4	2.3	2.3	Sales/Total Assets	1.3	1.9	2.7	2.8	3.1	1.7
1.1	1.2	1.0		.2	1.2	2.4	2.1	1.7	.7
.7	.6	.7			1.7	.7	.3	.4	.8
(107) 2.2	(90) 1.7	(110) 1.9	% Depr., Dep., Amort./Sales		(10) 3.5	(10) 2.2	(16) .9	(34) 1.8	(34) 1.7
6.9	5.3	6.5			25.3	3.8	4.3	5.6	6.8
1.4	1.1	1.2						.8	
(29) 4.0	(30) 5.6	(43) 3.1	% Officers', Directors' Owners' Comp/Sales					(15) 1.9	
9.9	11.1	5.1						3.4	
6021005M	5989413M	6092737M	Net Sales ($)	5706M	27344M	62039M	148698M	645128M	5203822M
4164115M	4397128M	4887211M	Total Assets ($)	7172M	32806M	29487M	227122M	528091M	4062533M

M = $ thousand MM = $ million

See Pages 9 through 22 for Explanation of Ratios and Data

Current Data Sorted by Assets							Comparative Historical Data	
Type of Statement								
Unqualified			10	16	15	9	93	77
Reviewed		4	10	8			21	42
Compiled	2	6	9	3	1	2	20	22
Tax Returns	19	11	11				34	31
Other	16	29	44	45	10	18	149	152
	36 (4/1-9/30/13)			262 (10/1/13-3/31/14)			4/1/09-3/31/10	4/1/10-3/31/11
	0-500M	**500M-2MM**	**2-10MM**	**10-50MM**	**50-100MM**	**100-250MM**	**ALL**	**ALL**
NUMBER OF STATEMENTS	37	50	84	72	26	29	317	324
ASSETS	%	%	%	%	%	%	%	%
Cash & Equivalents	39.1	19.3	21.8	24.2	13.2	10.5	19.6	22.2
Trade Receivables (net)	15.7	31.9	36.0	21.8	13.1	12.4	26.7	27.1
Inventory	1.6	4.3	1.5	.5	.9	1.2	1.8	1.4
All Other Current	4.8	4.3	5.3	4.6	7.7	3.6	5.1	5.6
Total Current	61.1	59.8	64.6	51.1	34.8	27.6	53.2	56.3
Fixed Assets (net)	23.8	25.1	20.9	22.5	30.1	16.8	21.7	22.2
Intangibles (net)	6.9	8.2	8.0	16.4	27.7	46.4	14.3	12.5
All Other Non-Current	8.3	6.9	6.5	10.1	7.4	9.2	10.7	9.0
Total	100.0	100.0	100.0	100.0	100.0	100.0	100.0	100.0
LIABILITIES								
Notes Payable-Short Term	29.0	10.9	7.2	3.2	1.2	.6	13.1	7.1
Cur. Mat.-L.T.D.	3.1	7.6	3.3	3.4	3.8	1.5	3.9	4.8
Trade Payables	8.4	10.8	13.3	9.8	7.6	4.8	10.8	12.3
Income Taxes Payable	.1	.1	.2	.2	.2	.2	.4	.4
All Other Current	28.8	17.4	16.6	30.2	13.8	11.5	19.4	18.5
Total Current	69.3	46.7	40.8	46.7	26.6	18.7	47.6	43.1
Long-Term Debt	10.0	17.4	13.0	19.4	36.7	27.6	18.3	17.4
Deferred Taxes	.0	.0	.6	.8	2.0	2.6	.7	.6
All Other Non-Current	8.7	2.7	11.7	9.8	7.2	4.6	10.7	10.0
Net Worth	12.0	33.2	33.9	23.3	27.5	46.6	22.8	28.9
Total Liabilities & Net Worth	100.0	100.0	100.0	100.0	100.0	100.0	100.0	100.0
INCOME DATA								
Net Sales	100.0	100.0	100.0	100.0	100.0	100.0	100.0	100.0
Gross Profit								
Operating Expenses	92.8	91.8	91.2	93.4	88.7	92.2	92.9	92.5
Operating Profit	7.2	8.2	8.8	6.6	11.3	7.8	7.1	7.5
All Other Expenses (net)	.1	.9	1.4	2.6	5.2	6.9	2.4	1.8
Profit Before Taxes	7.2	7.3	7.4	3.9	6.0	1.0	4.6	5.7
RATIOS								
Current	3.9	2.6	2.5	2.7	2.1	2.4	2.1	3.2
	1.3	1.3	1.6	1.2	1.2	1.5	1.2	1.4
	.6	.7	1.1	.8	.7	1.0	.8	.8
Quick	3.2	2.0	2.4	2.7	1.6	1.9	1.9	2.9
	1.2	1.2	1.4	1.2	.9	1.2	(316) 1.0	1.2
	.5	.7	.8	.5	.6	.7	.7	.7
Sales/Receivables	0 UND	7 50.9	23 15.7	27 13.3	21 17.0	31 11.9	20 18.1	16 22.4
	0 UND	33 11.2	50 7.3	48 7.6	37 9.9	49 7.4	42 8.6	42 8.8
	22 16.8	55 6.6	70 5.2	73 5.0	53 6.9	72 5.1	60 6.0	63 5.8
Cost of Sales/Inventory								
Cost of Sales/Payables								
Sales/Working Capital	11.3	8.7	5.3	4.5	6.3	4.2	7.4	5.1
	111.5	20.6	11.5	13.6	17.6	7.0	27.1	16.3
	-17.9	-27.8	126.8	-18.7	-13.1	-656.3	-37.3	-31.1
EBIT/Interest	37.3	41.1	39.9	24.4	8.1	3.8	17.6	32.5
	(21) 25.2	(38) 5.9	(65) 8.9	(56) 2.8	(22) 2.5	(22) 1.6	(251) 3.7	(251) 5.6
	1.6	1.6	2.1	.6	-2.6	-.3	.4	.6
Net Profit + Depr., Dep., Amort./Cur. Mat. L/T/D			5.9	5.7	4.0		12.7	8.2
			(11) 1.9	(13) 3.9	(10) 3.0		(50) 2.8	(54) 2.2
			1.1	1.3	1.0		1.1	.9
Fixed/Worth	.0	.1	.2	.2	.5	.7	.2	.1
	.4	.5	.5	1.2	4.3	-2.2	1.0	.8
	NM	NM	1.9	-2.1	-.2	-.4	-3.3	-4.7
Debt/Worth	.3	.7	.7	.9	1.2	2.8	.9	.6
	1.4	1.8	2.2	3.6	5.2	-7.4	3.1	2.7
	-8.9	-29.3	14.3	-11.2	-2.9	-2.5	-10.2	-16.7
% Profit Before Taxes/Tangible Net Worth	276.1	97.0	89.1	65.1	24.4	44.4	67.1	75.8
	(25) 87.5	(36) 57.4	(69) 36.9	(51) 30.8	(15) 12.0	(12) 15.9	(215) 26.0	(230) 32.3
	37.2	15.1	10.5	-1.4	-6.5	-73.2	8.4	5.6
% Profit Before Taxes/Total Assets	85.5	44.4	24.8	15.4	9.3	6.2	18.1	27.0
	33.3	15.5	10.7	6.6	3.2	2.9	7.0	8.7
	6.1	3.5	2.7	-1.4	-2.0	-1.8	-1.8	.3
Sales/Net Fixed Assets	642.5	414.3	54.5	30.8	21.4	10.7	48.6	53.7
	42.0	24.9	22.4	13.4	6.7	6.0	14.4	15.7
	21.3	5.9	6.8	3.9	1.7	1.0	6.6	5.5
Sales/Total Assets	11.5	4.5	3.5	2.2	1.5	1.1	3.8	3.6
	5.4	3.2	2.5	1.4	.9	.4	1.9	2.0
	2.8	2.3	1.7	.8	.4	.3	1.1	1.1
% Depr., Dep., Amort./Sales	.2	.6	1.0	1.3	2.3	2.2	.9	1.0
	(15) 1.1	(26) 1.8	(57) 2.0	(57) 2.7	(21) 4.1	(12) 4.8	(204) 2.8	(221) 2.8
	2.3	6.7	4.4	11.5	18.9	11.1	6.3	5.8
% Officers', Directors' Owners' Comp/Sales	4.3	2.6	2.2				2.4	2.5
	(14) 11.8	(19) 6.3	(27) 3.4				(67) 4.8	(82) 6.1
	24.5	12.9	6.3				12.6	13.0
Net Sales ($)	65644M	215443M	1141181M	2700999M	1830811M	3601129M	11368362M	12886710M
Total Assets ($)	8661M	58763M	430077M	1829958M	1831754M	4779429M	8915552M	8863154M

M = $ thousand MM = $ million

See Pages 9 through 22 for Explanation of Ratios and Data

Comparative Historical Data | **Current Data Sorted by Sales**

	4/1/11-3/31/12 ALL	4/1/12-3/31/13 ALL	4/1/13-3/31/14 ALL	0-1MM	1-3MM	3-5MM	5-10MM	10-25MM	25MM & OVER
Type of Statement									
Unqualified	64	53	50				4	15	31
Reviewed	29	27	22		2	1	6	7	6
Compiled	22	16	23	2	2	5	4	6	4
Tax Returns	44	46	41	11	13	7	7	2	1
Other	158	151	162	9	17	18	16	38	64
				36 (4/1-9/30/13)		262 (10/1/13-3/31/14)			
NUMBER OF STATEMENTS	317	293	298	22	34	31	37	68	106
ASSETS	%	%	%	%	%	%	%	%	%
Cash & Equivalents	18.6	20.6	22.2	29.2	28.6	25.1	19.2	19.9	20.5
Trade Receivables (net)	28.2	26.9	25.1	11.7	20.3	22.1	38.0	29.9	22.6
Inventory	2.4	1.9	1.7	.3	4.6	2.8	3.4	.4	.9
All Other Current	5.2	5.1	4.9	3.1	1.7	6.5	3.2	6.3	5.6
Total Current	54.4	54.6	53.9	44.2	55.1	56.5	63.8	56.5	49.6
Fixed Assets (net)	23.7	24.0	22.7	35.1	31.3	22.8	21.7	23.3	17.4
Intangibles (net)	12.4	11.2	15.4	10.7	7.3	12.1	7.0	12.0	25.1
All Other Non-Current	9.5	10.3	8.0	9.9	6.3	8.6	7.5	8.3	7.9
Total	100.0	100.0	100.0	100.0	100.0	100.0	100.0	100.0	100.0
LIABILITIES									
Notes Payable-Short Term	7.0	9.8	8.4	13.3	28.4	7.6	6.6	6.5	3.0
Cur. Mat.-L.T.D.	3.1	3.9	3.9	1.8	8.1	5.8	3.6	3.4	2.8
Trade Payables	11.9	11.0	10.1	5.4	8.3	9.3	11.7	13.1	9.4
Income Taxes Payable	.5	.6	.2	.0	.3	.2	.1	.2	.2
All Other Current	18.3	20.0	20.8	34.2	19.8	18.6	13.6	18.7	22.8
Total Current	40.8	45.2	43.4	54.7	64.9	41.5	35.5	42.0	38.3
Long-Term Debt	17.8	15.1	18.4	23.8	18.1	12.8	13.4	14.3	23.4
Deferred Taxes	.7	.7	.8	.0	.0	.0	.8	.7	1.4
All Other Non-Current	10.6	11.6	8.2	10.2	6.1	2.4	9.1	8.0	10.2
Net Worth	30.1	27.5	29.2	11.3	11.0	43.3	41.2	35.0	26.7
Total Liabilties & Net Worth	100.0	100.0	100.0	100.0	100.0	100.0	100.0	100.0	100.0
INCOME DATA									
Net Sales	100.0	100.0	100.0	100.0	100.0	100.0	100.0	100.0	100.0
Gross Profit									
Operating Expenses	92.3	92.1	91.9	87.3	90.2	91.7	92.0	94.6	91.7
Operating Profit	7.7	7.9	8.1	12.7	9.8	8.3	8.0	5.4	8.3
All Other Expenses (net)	2.1	1.7	2.3	3.2	1.2	1.2	1.4	1.6	3.6
Profit Before Taxes	5.6	6.2	5.8	9.5	8.6	7.1	6.5	3.8	4.7
RATIOS									
Current	2.5	2.5	2.5	4.0	3.9	2.1	3.6	2.5	2.4
	1.3	1.4	1.4	1.4	1.0	1.3	1.8	1.3	1.6
	.9	.8	.9	.5	.4	.9	1.1	.8	1.0
Quick	2.0	2.3	2.2	3.6	3.6	1.7	3.2	2.4	2.0
	1.1	1.2	1.2	1.1	.9	1.1	1.4	1.2	1.3
	.7	.7	.7	.5	.3	.7	.9	.7	.8
Sales/Receivables	20 18.4	13 29.0	16 22.9	0 UND	0 UND	6 57.5	34 10.7	21 17.5	27 13.5
	38 9.7	38 9.7	41 8.9	4 88.8	9 39.2	24 15.4	51 7.2	44 8.3	48 7.6
	62 5.9	62 5.9	62 5.9	60 6.1	35 10.4	51 7.2	69 5.3	79 4.6	63 5.8
Cost of Sales/Inventory									
Cost of Sales/Payables									
Sales/Working Capital	7.0	6.5	5.3	3.9	11.9	7.2	7.1	5.5	4.3
	18.9	18.1	16.8	35.9	NM	20.8	12.4	14.1	10.6
	-31.9	-29.4	-55.7	-5.8	-8.6	-57.6	30.7	-17.9	-597.9
EBIT/Interest	29.9	17.6	28.0		42.8	41.1	35.8	32.9	12.9
	(257) 5.7	(229) 4.6	(224) 4.8		(27) 6.4	(22) 14.2	(30) 8.7	(54) 3.4	(82) 2.4
	1.2	.4	.9		.0	4.5	2.2	.0	.6
Net Profit + Depr., Dep., Amort./Cur. Mat. L/T/D	7.4	3.9	5.4					5.2	5.4
	(61) 2.3	(45) 2.5	(41) 3.7					(13) 3.8	(21) 3.7
	1.1	1.1	1.1					1.4	1.0
Fixed/Worth	.2	.2	.2	.0	.1	.1	.1	.2	.2
	.8	.7	.7	1.2	1.1	.6	.4	.6	1.8
	108.7	17.5	-4.2	NM	-2.2	2.8	1.8	4.4	-.5
Debt/Worth	.8	.8	.8	.8	.5	.7	.5	.9	1.0
	2.7	2.4	3.1	5.0	3.0	1.6	1.7	2.2	9.1
	-64.9	374.0	-9.9	-5.8	-4.7	69.7	8.6	8.7	-3.0
% Profit Before Taxes/Tangible Net Worth	86.1	77.4	90.8	90.8	97.7	103.4	94.5	100.5	57.3
	(236) 32.8	(221) 34.3	(208) 38.5	(15) 52.6	(20) 61.4	(24) 55.9	(31) 27.3	(57) 36.9	(61) 35.4
	8.6	7.9	10.2	19.0	-1.7	14.5	9.5	.0	7.1
% Profit Before Taxes/Total Assets	22.8	24.4	24.4	35.8	75.9	33.8	24.6	26.1	13.8
	8.0	7.8	8.2	7.8	9.8	16.0	10.5	9.6	5.8
	.4	-.4	.5	.1	.0	5.5	2.9	-1.8	-.3
Sales/Net Fixed Assets	66.7	60.4	51.3	591.8	146.5	159.8	77.4	51.9	31.3
	14.6	17.2	17.6	15.8	26.7	25.7	22.4	18.2	13.2
	5.0	5.5	5.9	1.8	7.8	8.2	6.3	6.2	4.4
Sales/Total Assets	3.7	3.8	3.5	3.1	8.9	4.5	3.8	3.3	2.5
	2.2	2.3	2.2	2.4	3.6	2.7	2.6	2.1	1.4
	1.1	1.1	1.0	.6	2.4	2.0	1.4	.9	.6
% Depr., Dep., Amort./Sales	1.1	.8	1.0	1.7	.5	.8	.6	1.2	.9
	(213) 2.8	(199) 2.4	(188) 2.4	(10) 5.6	(15) 1.8	(17) 2.2	(24) 2.9	(54) 2.5	(68) 2.3
	7.0	6.2	7.3	24.7	11.0	7.5	5.3	7.8	5.6
% Officers', Directors' Owners' Comp/Sales	2.9	2.8	2.5		3.3	2.7	2.2	.7	
	(76) 6.6	(78) 5.7	(69) 4.6		(15) 5.3	(13) 8.7	(14) 3.4	(15) 2.6	
	12.5	12.0	11.5		20.3	15.7	5.1	4.6	
Net Sales ($)	11334576M	9627535M	9555207M	11160M	71472M	117041M	270132M	1064297M	8021105M
Total Assets ($)	8556991M	7065875M	8938642M	15462M	42609M	118488M	149791M	1002984M	7609308M

M = $ thousand MM = $ million

See Pages 9 through 22 for Explanation of Ratios and Data

Current Data Sorted by Assets							Comparative Historical Data	
						Type of Statement		
		4	2	2	1	Unqualified	7	3
		1	2			Reviewed		1
1	1	3			1	Compiled	3	
1	1	2				Tax Returns	5	5
4	2	7	8	5	7	Other	15	21
5 (4/1-9/30/13)		50 (10/1/13-3/31/14)					4/1/09-3/31/10 ALL	4/1/10-3/31/11 ALL
0-500M	500M-2MM	2-10MM	10-50MM	50-100MM	100-250MM			
6	4	17	12	7	9	**NUMBER OF STATEMENTS**	30	30
%	%	%	%	%	%	**ASSETS**	%	%
		33.0	24.4			Cash & Equivalents	28.5	26.1
		36.0	15.0			Trade Receivables (net)	19.2	24.1
		.8	2.7			Inventory	3.3	1.2
		2.3	6.4			All Other Current	7.6	5.1
		72.1	48.4			Total Current	58.5	56.5
		7.1	13.6			Fixed Assets (net)	11.7	13.9
		8.4	15.2			Intangibles (net)	22.2	21.1
		12.4	22.8			All Other Non-Current	7.6	8.5
		100.0	100.0			Total	100.0	100.0
						LIABILITIES		
		5.6	1.3			Notes Payable-Short Term	26.0	1.7
		1.2	2.6			Cur. Mat.-L.T.D.	2.6	1.8
		8.8	15.0			Trade Payables	11.8	11.2
		1.6	.4			Income Taxes Payable	.2	.3
		14.3	36.1			All Other Current	22.5	32.4
		31.5	55.4			Total Current	63.1	47.3
		3.0	13.1			Long-Term Debt	24.0	10.7
		.0	.5			Deferred Taxes	.2	.6
		33.2	1.6			All Other Non-Current	8.7	4.6
		32.3	29.4			Net Worth	4.1	36.8
		100.0	100.0			Total Liabilities & Net Worth	100.0	100.0
						INCOME DATA		
		100.0	100.0			Net Sales	100.0	100.0
						Gross Profit		
		92.2	93.5			Operating Expenses	95.1	92.0
		7.8	6.5			Operating Profit	4.9	8.0
		-.5	2.5			All Other Expenses (net)	1.0	1.3
		8.3	4.0			Profit Before Taxes	3.9	6.7
						RATIOS		
		7.1	5.1				2.4	2.6
		2.8	1.5			Current	1.4	1.3
		1.3	.4				.9	.8
		6.5	3.4				2.4	2.3
		2.8	1.3			Quick	1.1	1.1
		1.1	.3				.7	.7
		0 UND	**0** UND				**3** 139.8	**6** 64.3
		45 8.2	**35** 10.4			Sales/Receivables	**23** 16.2	**40** 9.1
		78 4.7	**60** 6.1				**62** 5.9	**66** 5.6
						Cost of Sales/Inventory		
						Cost of Sales/Payables		
		4.0	3.3				8.1	5.8
		7.4	NM			Sales/Working Capital	15.9	39.7
		33.2	-2.4				-25.6	-15.4
							12.4	51.3
						EBIT/Interest	(22) 3.5	(19) 5.4
							-4.3	1.1
						Net Profit + Depr., Dep., Amort./Cur. Mat. L/T/D		
		.0	.1				.1	.2
		.1	.8			Fixed/Worth	1.5	.5
		1.1	-.2				-.4	-1.4
		.1	.2				1.8	.7
		1.0	2.6			Debt/Worth	13.3	2.9
		18.3	-4.0				-1.9	-10.0
		112.6					90.4	124.4
		(14) 50.9				% Profit Before Taxes/Tangible Net Worth	(16) 45.1	(21) 61.9
		22.1					17.1	9.2
		46.1	18.8				32.3	24.6
		29.1	-.2			% Profit Before Taxes/Total Assets	9.0	8.7
		-3.2	-20.1				-2.9	-1.0
		214.1	38.9				116.7	60.7
		80.4	25.9			Sales/Net Fixed Assets	32.9	36.6
		22.7	8.7				19.3	16.6
		4.3	2.0				6.0	3.3
		2.6	1.5			Sales/Total Assets	2.3	2.0
		1.7	.9				1.3	1.3
		.2	.5				.5	.4
		(11) .5	(10) 1.3			% Depr., Dep., Amort./Sales	(17) 1.4	(19) 1.7
		1.2	4.5				2.7	5.2
						% Officers', Directors' Owners' Comp/Sales		
11899M	30357M	185962M	364339M	687511M	1364716M	Net Sales ($)	1632322M	1651943M
823M	3288M	66626M	249705M	530864M	1440288M	Total Assets ($)	1130920M	1170826M

M = $ thousand MM = $ million

See Pages 9 through 22 for Explanation of Ratios and Data

Comparative Historical Data | **Current Data Sorted by Sales**

4/1/11-3/31/12 ALL	4/1/12-3/31/13 ALL	4/1/13-3/31/14 ALL	Type of Statement	0-1MM	1-3MM	3-5MM	5-10MM	10-25MM	25MM & OVER
10	6	9	Unqualified			1	1	2	5
1	3	3	Reviewed				1	2	
5	3	6	Compiled		1	3	1		1
5	8	4	Tax Returns	1		1	1	1	
26	25	33	Other	2	1	2	2	9	17
					5 (4/1-9/30/13)		50 (10/1/13-3/31/14)		
47	45	55	NUMBER OF STATEMENTS	3	2	7	6	14	23
%	%	%	**ASSETS**	%	%	%	%	%	%
19.6	22.7	28.9	Cash & Equivalents					35.8	20.7
22.8	25.1	24.3	Trade Receivables (net)					25.9	14.8
1.2	.5	1.1	Inventory					1.4	1.6
4.1	3.2	3.7	All Other Current					2.8	6.6
47.6	51.4	57.9	Total Current					65.9	43.7
18.8	16.2	8.9	Fixed Assets (net)					7.5	9.2
23.4	25.6	20.6	Intangibles (net)					7.9	36.5
10.3	6.7	12.7	All Other Non-Current					18.7	10.5
100.0	100.0	100.0	Total					100.0	100.0
			LIABILITIES						
7.1	4.5	9.9	Notes Payable-Short Term					3.4	.6
1.3	2.1	1.6	Cur. Mat.-L.T.D.					1.1	2.4
9.8	9.1	10.3	Trade Payables					11.5	14.3
.2	.1	.6	Income Taxes Payable					2.2	.0
20.4	26.4	26.2	All Other Current					15.8	31.4
38.8	42.1	48.5	Total Current					34.1	48.8
17.1	17.1	7.9	Long-Term Debt					3.4	16.0
1.2	.8	.2	Deferred Taxes					.0	.5
6.5	11.7	14.1	All Other Non-Current					.1	8.3
36.5	28.3	29.4	Net Worth					62.3	26.4
100.0	100.0	100.0	Total Liabilties & Net Worth					100.0	100.0
			INCOME DATA						
100.0	100.0	100.0	Net Sales					100.0	100.0
			Gross Profit						
88.3	91.4	97.1	Operating Expenses					88.8	101.3
11.7	8.6	2.9	Operating Profit					11.2	-1.3
3.4	3.1	1.8	All Other Expenses (net)					1.4	3.7
8.3	5.5	1.1	Profit Before Taxes					9.9	-5.0
			RATIOS						
2.2	3.4	3.5						7.5	2.3
1.1	1.6	1.4	Current					2.4	1.0
.7	.9	.7						1.3	.7
2.2	3.2	3.2						6.7	2.2
1.0	1.5	1.4	Quick					2.4	1.0
.5	.7	.6						1.2	.5
4 81.9	10 36.0	7 55.1						0 UND	7 50.6
29 12.5	41 8.8	32 11.3	Sales/Receivables					39 9.3	41 8.9
53 6.9	63 5.8	65 5.6						55 6.6	73 5.0
			Cost of Sales/Inventory						
			Cost of Sales/Payables						
6.9	5.0	4.7						4.3	5.0
149.8	14.1	12.7	Sales/Working Capital					7.4	182.4
-16.7	NM	-13.0						31.6	-7.9
14.0	14.3	21.1							3.6
(30) 4.9	(30) 3.3	(34) .2	EBIT/Interest						(19) -.4
.3	-1.4	-33.2							-25.0
			Net Profit + Depr., Dep., Amort./Cur. Mat. L/T/D						
.2	.1	.1						.0	.4
2.4	.7	.4	Fixed/Worth					.1	-.5
-.1	-.2	-.2						.3	-.1
.5	.5	.4						.1	3.0
11.1	3.5	3.0	Debt/Worth					.6	-4.7
-3.0	-2.5	-3.8						1.4	-1.9
86.4	119.4	63.0						81.9	
(27) 55.1	(28) 31.0	(36) 22.1	% Profit Before Taxes/Tangible Net Worth					(13) 43.6	
.1	-15.8	-33.6						1.1	
27.8	29.4	18.9						44.3	4.6
6.6	5.5	3.6	% Profit Before Taxes/Total Assets					20.2	-1.4
-.2	-8.1	-14.8						2.4	-22.1
71.8	60.1	150.7						360.5	37.9
30.4	28.7	37.9	Sales/Net Fixed Assets					84.3	23.2
8.8	12.1	17.5						21.7	10.6
3.8	3.8	4.0						5.4	1.8
1.7	2.1	1.8	Sales/Total Assets					2.5	1.3
1.1	1.0	1.0						1.8	.6
.6	.9	.2						.1	.8
(24) 2.0	(20) 1.7	(29) 1.0	% Depr., Dep., Amort./Sales					(10) .6	(10) 3.4
5.6	4.5	2.9						1.3	6.4
			% Officers', Directors' Owners' Comp/Sales						
2162163M	2471075M	2644784M	Net Sales ($)	1791M	3003M	26243M	45338M	230413M	2337996M
2256528M	1995419M	2291594M	Total Assets ($)	703M	302M	14041M	29663M	109530M	2137355M

M = $ thousand MM = $ million

See Pages 9 through 22 for Explanation of Ratios and Data

Current Data Sorted by Assets / Comparative Historical Data

0-500M	500M-2MM	2-10MM	10-50MM	50-100MM	100-250MM		4/1/09-3/31/10 ALL	4/1/10-3/31/11 ALL
						Type of Statement		
		3	3	3	2	Unqualified	12	9
	2	2				Reviewed	9	4
	1	1	1			Compiled	1	1
8	6	5				Tax Returns	16	12
9	11	9	13	3	5	Other	21	35
12 (4/1-9/30/13)		75 (10/1/13-3/31/14)						
17	20	20	17	6	7	**NUMBER OF STATEMENTS**	59	61
%	%	%	%	%	%	**ASSETS**	%	%
44.8	22.2	27.2	12.4			Cash & Equivalents	18.8	28.5
13.7	24.9	36.2	28.1			Trade Receivables (net)	34.4	27.4
2.4	4.7	3.2	3.3			Inventory	7.1	3.3
3.7	4.5	1.9	7.5			All Other Current	3.0	6.0
64.6	56.3	68.5	51.3			Total Current	63.3	65.2
12.9	24.4	13.9	15.9			Fixed Assets (net)	17.3	14.8
1.6	3.8	9.7	21.1			Intangibles (net)	9.5	11.5
21.1	15.6	7.9	11.7			All Other Non-Current	9.9	8.5
100.0	100.0	100.0	100.0			Total	100.0	100.0
						LIABILITIES		
35.8	7.9	7.1	6.4			Notes Payable-Short Term	13.9	10.6
.1	1.2	3.4	3.9			Cur. Mat.-L.T.D.	3.0	1.5
22.3	7.3	22.1	6.8			Trade Payables	14.6	17.3
.1	.1	.5	.3			Income Taxes Payable	.2	.4
35.0	10.5	31.7	28.0			All Other Current	20.1	19.3
93.3	26.9	64.8	45.5			Total Current	51.9	49.1
.1	16.7	9.5	32.3			Long-Term Debt	13.8	14.2
.0	.0	.2	.3			Deferred Taxes	.5	.7
8.3	13.0	11.0	18.3			All Other Non-Current	8.6	6.8
-1.7	43.4	14.4	3.6			Net Worth	25.2	29.2
100.0	100.0	100.0	100.0			Total Liabilities & Net Worth	100.0	100.0
						INCOME DATA		
100.0	100.0	100.0	100.0			Net Sales	100.0	100.0
						Gross Profit		
89.2	84.1	96.4	88.0			Operating Expenses	93.1	93.2
10.8	15.9	3.6	12.0			Operating Profit	6.9	6.8
.3	5.7	.6	2.3			All Other Expenses (net)	1.4	1.2
10.5	10.2	3.0	9.7			Profit Before Taxes	5.5	5.6
						RATIOS		
3.4	4.4	2.1	1.7				2.4	3.7
.6	2.6	1.3	1.2			Current	1.4	1.6
.4	1.2	.9	.8				1.0	.8
3.3	4.1	2.0	1.5				2.0	3.5
.6	2.4	1.3	1.0			Quick	1.2	1.5
.2	.9	.6	.7				.5	.6
0 UND	9 41.7	19 19.3	34 10.6				18 20.5	4 93.4
0 UND	23 16.2	32 11.5	52 7.0			Sales/Receivables	39 9.4	31 11.7
2 202.4	45 8.2	62 5.9	78 4.7				63 5.8	58 6.3
						Cost of Sales/Inventory		
						Cost of Sales/Payables		
15.9	7.0	7.4	8.9				5.5	5.2
-22.6	13.5	24.5	24.2			Sales/Working Capital	19.7	16.4
-8.5	36.2	NM	-17.9				117.3	-40.0
	133.4	33.0	17.8				12.4	25.2
	(10) 8.3	(13) 16.6	(13) 8.0			EBIT/Interest	(45) 3.6	(36) 7.1
	3.6	-.1	3.8				.4	1.8
						Net Profit + Depr., Dep., Amort./Cur. Mat. L/T/D		
.0	.1	.1	.6				.1	.1
.0	.4	.4	2.9			Fixed/Worth	.5	.4
1.9	4.9	3.2	-.4				1.7	-5.7
.5	.3	1.0	2.5				.9	.8
2.4	1.6	6.2	16.6			Debt/Worth	2.3	2.7
-2.4	7.5	NM	-2.2				19.5	-17.0
253.8	90.5	109.2	141.5				54.4	106.4
(10) 120.9	(17) 28.0	(15) 54.5	(10) 65.7			% Profit Before Taxes/Tangible Net Worth	(46) 22.7	(44) 56.9
26.6	9.1	9.5	42.1				.3	3.3
121.2	72.3	23.6	21.2				12.3	50.6
25.3	15.9	7.1	12.3			% Profit Before Taxes/Total Assets	6.7	12.2
-7.2	1.8	-2.4	3.4				-.8	1.3
UND	110.6	345.1	27.5				168.9	197.2
999.8	23.9	36.8	12.0			Sales/Net Fixed Assets	30.4	46.2
76.0	10.1	15.2	8.9				10.6	14.4
13.8	4.4	4.0	2.7				5.0	6.1
7.7	3.5	3.2	2.1			Sales/Total Assets	2.5	3.0
5.0	1.9	2.5	.9				1.3	1.4
	.6	.7	1.5				.4	.9
	(13) 1.4	(10) 1.0	(11) 1.9			% Depr., Dep., Amort./Sales	(37) 1.6	(32) 2.1
	7.5	2.9	2.9				3.1	3.9
							2.8	2.3
						% Officers', Directors' Owners' Comp/Sales	(19) 6.3	(15) 6.8
							22.6	9.6
27772M	81960M	297506M	644621M	435741M	970321M	Net Sales ($)	1737488M	1698987M
2718M	23869M	88607M	440289M	485771M	1152529M	Total Assets ($)	1541380M	1262831M

M = $ thousand MM = $ million

See Pages 9 through 22 for Explanation of Ratios and Data

Comparative Historical Data | **Current Data Sorted by Sales**

	4/1/11-3/31/12 ALL	4/1/12-3/31/13 ALL	4/1/13-3/31/14 ALL	0-1MM	1-3MM	3-5MM	5-10MM	10-25MM	25MM & OVER
Type of Statement									
Unqualified	13	20	11					4	7
Reviewed	6	8	4			1	1	2	
Compiled	2	3	3		1		1		1
Tax Returns	16	22	19	3	6	4	3	3	
Other	37	53	50	5	5	5	7	8	20
					12 (4/1-9/30/13)		75 (10/1/13-3/31/14)		
NUMBER OF STATEMENTS	74	106	87	8	12	10	12	17	28
ASSETS	%	%	%	%	%	%	%	%	%
Cash & Equivalents	22.2	28.2	24.4		32.1	20.8	26.4	26.6	13.2
Trade Receivables (net)	29.3	23.2	23.9		24.4	21.5	18.2	34.1	24.5
Inventory	3.9	2.0	3.2		2.6	6.6	5.5	2.2	2.9
All Other Current	5.6	3.7	4.2		5.3	1.8	7.5	1.5	3.7
Total Current	61.1	57.2	55.8		64.4	50.7	57.6	64.4	44.3
Fixed Assets (net)	17.6	18.6	16.5		21.9	17.4	10.3	13.4	15.8
Intangibles (net)	13.0	11.4	15.1		.0	10.2	4.4	18.4	30.2
All Other Non-Current	8.3	12.8	12.6		13.7	21.7	27.6	3.7	9.7
Total	100.0	100.0	100.0		100.0	100.0	100.0	100.0	100.0
LIABILITIES									
Notes Payable-Short Term	5.7	8.1	11.7		28.1	23.1	14.0	6.7	4.8
Cur. Mat.-L.T.D.	1.7	4.1	2.4		.2	1.4	.6	4.4	3.8
Trade Payables	17.8	8.5	13.0		7.4	4.8	11.9	20.7	6.0
Income Taxes Payable	.6	.4	.3		.1	.2	.0	.0	.8
All Other Current	23.4	15.9	23.6		10.0	6.9	20.0	30.8	22.4
Total Current	49.1	37.1	51.0		45.7	36.4	46.5	62.6	37.8
Long-Term Debt	20.4	16.8	19.1		3.0	22.0	5.7	11.3	38.7
Deferred Taxes	.5	.3	.4		.0	.0	.0	.1	1.0
All Other Non-Current	9.8	8.6	11.4		9.8	14.9	13.4	8.3	10.6
Net Worth	20.2	37.3	18.1		41.4	26.7	34.4	17.7	11.8
Total Liabilties & Net Worth	100.0	100.0	100.0		100.0	100.0	100.0	100.0	100.0
INCOME DATA									
Net Sales	100.0	100.0	100.0		100.0	100.0	100.0	100.0	100.0
Gross Profit									
Operating Expenses	87.8	88.0	88.8		89.7	93.1	95.2	92.8	86.8
Operating Profit	12.2	12.0	11.2		10.3	6.9	4.8	7.2	13.2
All Other Expenses (net)	1.7	2.6	2.6		.3	1.0	.2	1.5	3.1
Profit Before Taxes	10.5	9.4	8.6		10.0	6.0	4.6	5.7	10.1
RATIOS									
Current	3.4	3.8	2.5		4.2	6.2	5.4	2.1	1.9
	1.4	1.6	1.4		2.5	1.7	1.8	1.4	1.3
	.8	.9	.8		.5	.9	.7	.7	.9
Quick	2.8	3.3	2.5		4.2	4.7	4.1	2.0	1.6
	1.2	1.3	1.2		1.9	1.6	1.8	1.4	1.1
	.7	.7	.6		.1	.7	.5	.6	.8
Sales/Receivables	**19** 18.8	**0** UND	**6** 64.3		**0** UND	**0** UND	**1** 273.1	**20** 18.2	**28** 13.0
	47 7.7	**33** 10.9	**29** 12.6		**2** 203.5	**19** 19.7	**17** 22.1	**30** 12.1	**49** 7.5
	70 5.2	**59** 6.2	**52** 7.0		**43** 8.4	**50** 7.3	**41** 8.9	**61** 6.0	**79** 4.6
Cost of Sales/Inventory									
Cost of Sales/Payables									
Sales/Working Capital	5.3	5.8	8.0		7.2	8.9	5.6	10.8	7.0
	16.9	16.6	18.7		12.4	19.7	24.9	28.4	17.5
	-28.2	-40.0	-20.1		-46.5	UND	-17.8	-11.8	NM
EBIT/Interest	35.8	33.2	23.1					37.5	13.1
	(55) 7.5	(71) 10.0	(58) 6.8					(12) 11.4	(25) 6.0
	.3	2.5	2.3					3.9	2.8
Net Profit + Depr., Dep., Amort./Cur. Mat. L/T/D	5.3	4.6							
	(10) 3.4	(12) 3.1							
	.9	2.0							
Fixed/Worth	.1	.0	.1		.0	.1	.0	.1	.6
	.5	.7	.7		.2	2.7	.2	.5	3.9
	-2.1	6.8	-1.3		1.2	-.4	2.1	NM	-.1
Debt/Worth	.7	.6	1.0		.4	.6	.3	1.0	1.8
	3.5	1.9	4.7		.7	4.4	2.0	6.9	11.7
	-4.6	38.4	-3.6		2.6	-3.3	NM	-2.1	-1.7
% Profit Before Taxes/Tangible Net Worth	95.5	106.9	115.1		123.7			148.5	80.1
	(47) 28.6	(84) 47.2	(57) 54.5		(11) 87.8			(12) 69.4	(15) 43.6
	14.4	9.1	13.4		12.3			10.8	22.1
% Profit Before Taxes/Total Assets	49.1	43.8	28.0		77.5	83.3	42.8	26.5	21.2
	11.1	14.5	9.6		24.4	18.7	3.4	9.9	10.5
	-.1	.8	.6		-1.5	5.4	-2.7	3.7	3.1
Sales/Net Fixed Assets	115.5	285.1	114.4		774.6	143.9	999.8	563.4	43.9
	38.6	32.5	30.0		52.0	54.6	57.1	32.3	16.0
	10.8	9.6	10.6		10.1	13.8	12.0	13.9	8.7
Sales/Total Assets	4.1	3.9	4.4		7.4	12.5	5.2	5.1	2.5
	2.4	2.4	2.8		5.0	3.8	3.5	3.7	1.3
	1.3	1.3	1.5		3.5	2.4	2.5	2.4	.8
% Depr., Dep., Amort./Sales	.7	.6	.8						1.7
	(44) 1.4	(58) 2.0	(44) 2.0						(15) 2.2
	3.6	5.1	3.7						3.7
% Officers', Directors' Owners' Comp/Sales	3.7	4.0	2.7						
	(21) 6.5	(26) 9.9	(22) 4.5						
	12.1	19.4	10.0						
Net Sales ($)	**1565986M**	**2406144M**	**2457921M**	**1809M**	**18090M**	**40896M**	**83853M**	**273509M**	**2039764M**
Total Assets ($)	**1205443M**	**1844142M**	**2193783M**	**3696M**	**4507M**	**10373M**	**57788M**	**126950M**	**1990469M**

M = $ thousand MM = $ million

See Pages 9 through 22 for Explanation of Ratios and Data

FINANCE AND INSURANCE

	Current Data Sorted by Assets						Comparative Historical Data	
Type of Statement								
Unqualified			3	37	14	18	88	81
Reviewed			18	16	3	1	37	33
Compiled	1	3	9	7	1	1	25	24
Tax Returns	4	9	11	1	1		24	24
Other	4	11	48	60	30	28	88	98
	28 (4/1-9/30/13)		311 (10/1/13-3/31/14)				4/1/09-3/31/10	4/1/10-3/31/11
	0-500M	500M-2MM	2-10MM	10-50MM	50-100MM	100-250MM	ALL	ALL
NUMBER OF STATEMENTS	9	23	89	121	49	48	262	260
ASSETS	%	%	%	%	%	%	%	%
Cash & Equivalents		6.7	5.9	3.8	3.8	1.9	6.1	8.6
Trade Receivables (net)		45.7	56.8	58.4	56.6	58.6	46.0	43.0
Inventory		2.1	4.4	4.9	3.5	3.0	4.8	4.1
All Other Current		20.7	5.7	5.1	6.6	6.4	7.5	8.7
Total Current		75.2	72.9	72.2	70.5	69.9	64.4	64.4
Fixed Assets (net)		13.4	8.8	8.6	9.4	6.9	13.9	13.4
Intangibles (net)		.2	3.3	1.2	.5	5.1	1.6	1.3
All Other Non-Current		11.2	15.0	18.0	19.6	18.1	20.1	20.9
Total		100.0	100.0	100.0	100.0	100.0	100.0	100.0
LIABILITIES								
Notes Payable-Short Term		17.8	32.3	31.7	30.1	30.9	26.2	23.1
Cur. Mat.-L.T.D.		2.7	2.8	4.0	2.7	5.2	6.2	7.3
Trade Payables		7.5	2.0	2.2	2.1	2.5	3.8	3.2
Income Taxes Payable		.0	.0	.0	.0	.3	.2	.2
All Other Current		17.4	11.5	8.8	6.1	4.0	9.7	10.1
Total Current		45.3	48.6	46.8	41.1	42.8	46.1	43.9
Long-Term Debt		18.6	12.0	15.8	23.7	24.6	22.7	19.0
Deferred Taxes		.0	.3	.1	.4	1.4	.7	.7
All Other Non-Current		7.7	8.0	9.1	7.0	3.9	7.9	7.6
Net Worth		28.3	31.2	28.2	27.8	27.3	22.5	28.7
Total Liabilties & Net Worth		100.0	100.0	100.0	100.0	100.0	100.0	100.0
INCOME DATA								
Net Sales		100.0	100.0	100.0	100.0	100.0	100.0	100.0
Gross Profit								
Operating Expenses		74.3	69.6	71.8	71.0	62.8	74.1	71.1
Operating Profit		25.7	30.4	28.2	29.0	37.2	25.9	28.9
All Other Expenses (net)		5.6	12.2	10.6	9.6	12.7	12.7	11.7
Profit Before Taxes		20.1	18.2	17.7	19.4	24.6	13.2	17.2
RATIOS								
Current		4.2	2.6	2.5	5.4	4.2	2.4	2.9
		1.4	1.5	1.4	1.5	1.3	1.4	1.5
		.8	1.0	1.2	1.2	1.1	1.0	1.1
Quick		2.8	2.2	1.8	2.6	2.6	2.0	2.4
		.6	1.3	1.3	1.4	1.3	1.3	1.3
		.2	.5	.9	.4	.8	.2	.3
Sales/Receivables		**0** UND	**47** 7.8	**41** 8.9	**22** 16.8	**99** 3.7	**5** 76.4	**6** 65.4
		215 1.7	**608** .6	**521** .7	**608** .6	**730** .5	**252** 1.4	**178** 2.0
		608 .6	**1217** .3	**1217** .3	**1825** .2	**1825** .2	**1193** .3	**1025** .4
Cost of Sales/Inventory								
Cost of Sales/Payables								
Sales/Working Capital		.7	.5	.8	.5	.4	.7	.7
		2.0	1.6	1.5	1.4	1.2	2.0	2.0
		-571.4	NM	5.1	3.5	8.0	188.3	60.0
EBIT/Interest		22.0	7.3	4.7	5.2	4.7	5.8	7.2
		(17) 9.3	(62) 3.6	(91) 3.0	(37) 2.4	(35) 3.1	(177) 2.4	(171) 3.1
		1.8	2.3	1.7	1.8	2.5	1.4	1.6
Net Profit + Depr., Dep., Amort./Cur. Mat. L/T/D				10.0			2.0	5.3
				(12) 1.4			(15) .5	(18) .3
				.1			.1	.1
Fixed/Worth		.0	.0	.0	.0	.0	.0	.0
		.0	.0	.0	.0	.0	.1	.0
		.6	.2	.3	.2	.2	.7	.5
Debt/Worth		.6	.9	1.6	1.6	2.6	1.6	1.2
		2.4	2.5	2.9	3.2	4.0	3.5	3.4
		13.8	8.8	8.6	6.9	7.2	7.7	7.0
% Profit Before Taxes/Tangible Net Worth		64.2	31.6	38.7	32.8	38.2	30.8	38.9
		(20) 26.7	(76) 17.8	(117) 21.6	(48) 17.8	(47) 23.2	(237) 13.2	(237) 17.0
		11.4	8.1	6.6	9.4	13.2	4.0	5.7
% Profit Before Taxes/Total Assets		18.2	9.4	8.2	7.1	7.2	7.1	9.0
		7.8	5.1	4.5	4.3	4.7	3.0	4.2
		1.5	2.0	1.7	1.9	1.9	.6	1.3
Sales/Net Fixed Assets		UND	UND	187.1	323.5	81.9	235.9	264.0
		350.6	104.0	46.8	48.4	37.1	38.7	49.4
		9.2	25.1	11.1	18.7	5.2	7.0	6.5
Sales/Total Assets		1.3	.5	.8	.6	.3	.6	.7
		.6	.3	.3	.3	.2	.3	.3
		.3	.2	.2	.1	.1	.2	.2
% Depr., Dep., Amort./Sales			.3	.4	.5	.5	.4	.4
			(47) .7	(78) .8	(26) .9	(33) 1.1	(157) 1.1	(156) .9
			5.1	2.2	2.4	2.6	4.0	4.9
% Officers', Directors' Owners' Comp/Sales			4.5	1.6			3.8	2.3
			(15) 8.8	(17) 3.1			(43) 7.4	(37) 7.1
			18.3	10.4			19.3	15.7
Net Sales ($)	14393M	30500M	229088M	1473931M	1751915M	2167845M	5453004M	4167742M
Total Assets ($)	2677M	24828M	436304M	2806582M	3727892M	7781909M	9259504M	8469361M

M = $ thousand MM = $ million

See Pages 9 through 22 for Explanation of Ratios and Data

Comparative Historical Data / Current Data Sorted by Sales

4/1/11-3/31/12 ALL	4/1/12-3/31/13 ALL	4/1/13-3/31/14 ALL	Type of Statement	0-1MM	1-3MM	3-5MM	5-10MM	10-25MM	25MM & OVER
100	79	72	Unqualified	1	7	6	11	27	20
43	51	38	Reviewed	4	12	7	7	3	5
16	15	22	Compiled	3	10	1	4	2	2
30	30	26	Tax Returns	17	5	1	2		1
133	141	181	Other	28	32	18	29	34	40
				28 (4/1-9/30/13)		311 (10/1/13-3/31/14)			
322	316	339	NUMBER OF STATEMENTS	53	66	33	53	66	68
%	%	%	**ASSETS**	%	%	%	%	%	%
7.5	6.1	5.2	Cash & Equivalents	7.4	6.2	5.6	5.7	2.3	4.8
48.1	55.3	56.0	Trade Receivables (net)	53.3	51.5	64.4	58.7	60.7	51.6
6.0	5.2	4.0	Inventory	1.8	1.6	2.0	5.7	3.5	8.1
7.9	7.0	6.6	All Other Current	6.9	11.5	2.5	3.9	7.3	5.2
69.4	73.6	71.8	Total Current	69.4	70.8	74.5	74.0	73.7	69.7
9.4	10.3	9.2	Fixed Assets (net)	12.6	10.1	5.0	5.7	7.5	12.1
1.9	2.4	2.1	Intangibles (net)	.4	1.3	3.7	2.3	1.9	3.2
19.2	13.7	16.9	All Other Non-Current	17.5	17.7	16.8	17.9	16.8	14.9
100.0	100.0	100.0	Total	100.0	100.0	100.0	100.0	100.0	100.0
			LIABILITIES						
28.0	30.4	30.7	Notes Payable-Short Term	31.7	21.5	37.0	35.7	36.7	26.0
5.1	3.2	3.6	Cur. Mat.-L.T.D.	3.7	4.9	2.1	1.1	4.5	3.8
3.5	2.6	2.5	Trade Payables	1.8	2.8	1.3	1.3	3.2	3.6
.2	.1	.1	Income Taxes Payable	.0	.0	.0	.0	.2	.1
10.6	9.1	9.6	All Other Current	15.3	13.2	5.5	11.3	5.8	6.0
47.5	45.4	46.4	Total Current	52.6	42.4	46.0	49.3	50.4	39.5
16.5	16.1	17.3	Long-Term Debt	10.2	21.1	10.4	16.4	16.9	23.7
.6	.5	.4	Deferred Taxes	.8	.2	.0	.0	.4	1.0
8.0	8.3	8.0	All Other Non-Current	10.2	9.9	7.7	5.8	6.8	7.5
27.4	29.7	27.8	Net Worth	26.2	26.4	35.9	28.5	25.5	28.2
100.0	100.0	100.0	Total Liabilities & Net Worth	100.0	100.0	100.0	100.0	100.0	100.0
			INCOME DATA						
100.0	100.0	100.0	Net Sales	100.0	100.0	100.0	100.0	100.0	100.0
			Gross Profit						
68.4	69.9	70.3	Operating Expenses	63.8	66.4	69.4	68.9	74.7	76.4
31.6	30.1	29.7	Operating Profit	36.2	33.6	30.6	31.1	25.3	23.6
11.3	10.3	10.6	All Other Expenses (net)	13.7	13.1	12.2	11.3	8.3	6.8
20.3	19.8	19.1	Profit Before Taxes	22.5	20.5	18.4	19.8	17.0	16.7
			RATIOS						
3.0	2.7	2.9		2.6	3.5	3.5	2.6	2.2	5.4
1.5	1.5	1.4	Current	1.3	1.6	1.4	1.5	1.3	1.4
1.1	1.2	1.1		.6	1.1	1.3	1.2	1.1	1.2
2.3	2.1	2.2		2.2	2.7	1.9	2.4	1.6	2.5
1.3	1.3	1.3	Quick	1.1	1.4	1.4	1.4	1.2	1.3
.3	.8	.5		.3	.3	1.0	.6	.9	.5
14 25.2	33 11.1	30 12.2		0 UND	5 69.0	192 1.9	70 5.2	52 7.0	26 14.3
365 1.0	521 .7	521 .7	Sales/Receivables	912 .4	608 .6	730 .5	608 .6	365 1.0	365 1.0
1217 .3	1217 .3	1217 .3		1825 .2	1217 .3	1217 .3	1217 .3	1825 .2	730 .5
			Cost of Sales/Inventory						
			Cost of Sales/Payables						
.6	.7	.6		.3	.5	.8	.7	.7	1.1
1.5	1.4	1.5	Sales/Working Capital	.8	1.0	1.2	1.3	2.2	2.1
21.8	10.5	13.2		-4.0	NM	3.2	12.5	5.1	14.8
6.5	6.7	5.5		10.7	7.1	4.6	6.4	4.7	6.6
(232) 3.5	(236) 3.7	(246) 3.1	EBIT/Interest	(29) 4.5	(39) 3.6	(24) 2.7	(40) 3.4	(52) 2.5	(62) 3.1
1.9	2.0	1.9		2.1	2.3	1.8	1.9	1.4	2.3
2.3	3.9	13.5							
(29) .4	(22) .9	(25) 2.7	Net Profit + Depr., Dep., Amort./Cur. Mat. L/T/D						
.1	.1	.3							
.0	.0	.0		.0	.0	.0	.0	.0	.0
.0	.0	.0	Fixed/Worth	.0	.0	.0	.0	.0	.1
.3	.3	.2		.1	.2	.2	.2	.2	.7
1.6	1.4	1.4		.8	1.2	.9	1.3	2.1	1.8
3.4	3.3	3.0	Debt/Worth	2.7	3.0	2.5	2.6	5.4	2.9
7.3	7.1	8.2		11.0	10.2	5.3	6.9	8.6	5.3
48.8	44.8	37.3		34.5	34.0	34.4	42.0	34.0	45.8
(299) 23.7	(298) 23.9	(314) 19.9	% Profit Before Taxes/Tangible Net Worth	(47) 13.1	(56) 19.0	21.8	(49) 21.3	(63) 18.3	(66) 23.1
8.5	10.5	9.2		3.4	5.5	9.1	6.2	9.5	14.2
10.8	10.1	8.4		7.7	9.4	7.7	9.1	6.8	11.1
5.2	5.5	4.8	% Profit Before Taxes/Total Assets	2.9	5.1	4.4	5.3	3.4	6.5
1.8	2.4	1.9		.7	1.1	2.1	2.8	1.3	2.9
916.3	262.6	343.5		UND	389.0	UND	424.3	130.9	100.8
60.1	49.1	53.2	Sales/Net Fixed Assets	257.0	69.9	63.5	53.2	37.7	34.5
9.6	12.4	16.5		30.0	14.0	13.6	20.5	15.0	5.8
.7	.7	.6		.3	.4	.4	.7	.9	1.0
.3	.3	.3	Sales/Total Assets	.2	.3	.3	.3	.3	.5
.2	.2	.2		.1	.2	.2	.2	.1	.3
.3	.3	.4		.3	.4	.5	.3	.5	.5
(191) .8	(192) .8	(190) .8	% Depr., Dep., Amort./Sales	(16) 3.4	(37) .8	(21) .7	(34) .6	(38) 1.1	(44) .8
2.6	2.7	2.6		25.7	5.9	1.7	1.7	2.6	2.3
3.7	3.3	2.7			8.3		2.1		
(45) 10.8	(51) 8.2	(48) 6.3	% Officers', Directors' Owners' Comp/Sales		(10) 10.1		(10) 3.5		
19.1	17.4	15.9			19.1		5.3		
7142002M	5150822M	5667672M	Net Sales ($)	23528M	120588M	130845M	390603M	1036187M	3965921M
12020231M	10931759M	14780192M	Total Assets ($)	157319M	633343M	585394M	1551747M	4974271M	6878118M

M = $ thousand MM = $ million

See Pages 9 through 22 for Explanation of Ratios and Data

Current Data Sorted by Assets							Comparative Historical Data	
						Type of Statement		
		10	27	6	13	Unqualified	76	79
	1	10	5			Reviewed	23	25
1	13	18	5	1		Compiled	55	49
1	8	4		1		Tax Returns	21	15
6	28	37	30	10	11	Other	122	89
37 (4/1-9/30/13)			209 (10/1/13-3/31/14)				4/1/09-3/31/10	4/1/10-3/31/11
0-500M	**500M-2MM**	**2-10MM**	**10-50MM**	**50-100MM**	**100-250MM**		**ALL**	**ALL**
8	50	79	67	18	24	**NUMBER OF STATEMENTS**	297	257
%	%	%	%	%	%	**ASSETS**	%	%
	10.6	6.0	6.7	7.9	6.4	Cash & Equivalents	7.5	7.4
	71.0	71.9	69.7	66.3	65.3	Trade Receivables (net)	70.5	68.3
	1.0	.4	2.1	2.7	3.5	Inventory	1.4	.8
	1.6	3.0	6.4	8.9	4.6	All Other Current	4.9	6.0
	84.1	81.3	85.0	85.8	79.8	Total Current	84.3	82.5
	7.0	4.8	3.6	2.5	2.3	Fixed Assets (net)	4.4	4.7
	1.0	2.2	4.1	1.7	5.6	Intangibles (net)	2.4	2.1
	7.9	11.7	7.2	10.0	12.2	All Other Non-Current	8.9	10.6
	100.0	100.0	100.0	100.0	100.0	Total	100.0	100.0
						LIABILITIES		
	21.9	35.3	32.1	32.4	34.6	Notes Payable-Short Term	35.4	32.9
	1.2	1.6	1.9	.7	1.8	Cur. Mat.-L.T.D.	1.9	2.5
	1.8	1.5	1.6	.9	2.3	Trade Payables	2.0	2.0
	.0	.1	.1	.2	.1	Income Taxes Payable	.1	.1
	21.5	8.1	5.3	5.0	8.0	All Other Current	10.2	9.8
	46.5	46.6	40.9	39.2	46.8	Total Current	49.6	47.3
	9.1	6.0	10.3	6.0	11.7	Long-Term Debt	11.4	10.8
	.5	.0	.1	.0	1.8	Deferred Taxes	.0	.0
	18.3	15.8	13.3	12.3	13.3	All Other Non-Current	13.7	14.3
	25.7	31.5	35.4	42.5	26.4	Net Worth	25.3	27.5
	100.0	100.0	100.0	100.0	100.0	Total Liabilties & Net Worth	100.0	100.0
						INCOME DATA		
	100.0	100.0	100.0	100.0	100.0	Net Sales	100.0	100.0
						Gross Profit		
	80.1	76.0	72.4	62.5	77.1	Operating Expenses	74.7	72.9
	19.9	24.0	27.6	37.5	22.9	Operating Profit	25.3	27.1
	8.5	9.2	8.7	6.7	8.8	All Other Expenses (net)	12.3	11.2
	11.4	14.8	18.8	30.8	14.2	Profit Before Taxes	13.0	15.9
						RATIOS		
	4.3	2.6	4.4	31.9	2.9		2.7	3.2
	2.1	1.7	2.0	1.6	1.6	Current	1.6	1.7
	1.2	1.3	1.4	1.4	1.4		1.3	1.3
	4.3	2.6	4.1	31.9	2.0		2.6	2.9
	2.1	1.6	1.7	1.6	1.4	Quick	1.4	1.5
	1.2	1.3	1.3	1.1	1.2		1.2	1.3
	243 1.5	**332** 1.1	**261** 1.4	**70** 5.2	**304** 1.2		**276** 1.3	**165** 2.2
	521 .7	**730** .5	**730** .5	**521** .7	**730** .5	Sales/Receivables	**716** .5	**680** .5
	912 .4	**912** .4	**1217** .3	**1217** .3	**912** .4		**1207** .3	**1176** .3
						Cost of Sales/Inventory		
						Cost of Sales/Payables		
	.8	.7	.5	.4	.8		.7	.6
	1.3	1.4	1.0	1.4	1.6	Sales/Working Capital	1.3	1.3
	4.8	2.4	1.7	4.5	3.7		3.0	3.1
	5.7	5.0	7.3	6.6	4.6		4.9	5.3
	(45) 2.1	(68) 2.9	(54) 4.3	(12) 4.4	(20) 2.7	EBIT/Interest	(234) 2.7	(193) 2.8
	1.3	1.5	1.9	2.8	1.8		1.5	1.6
							36.0	8.8
						Net Profit + Depr., Dep., Amort./Cur. Mat. L/T/D	(21) 5.2	(19) 1.6
							1.5	.2
	.0	.0	.0	.0	.0		.0	.0
	.0	.1	.1	.0	.1	Fixed/Worth	.1	.1
	1.1	.3	.2	.1	.2		.3	.3
	1.2	1.3	1.0	.5	2.4		1.5	1.5
	3.7	2.7	2.3	2.0	3.9	Debt/Worth	3.9	3.5
	22.6	8.1	6.4	3.8	7.2		10.0	9.6
	40.4	48.8	47.1	52.2	36.1		47.2	49.7
	(39) 19.9	(74) 18.7	(64) 25.7	(17) 26.7	(22) 23.9	% Profit Before Taxes/Tangible Net Worth	(265) 20.6	(231) 21.5
	9.7	5.3	10.2	15.5	4.4		6.4	6.9
	10.8	9.7	10.9	14.3	7.9		9.6	10.5
	4.5	4.6	4.9	9.0	4.6	% Profit Before Taxes/Total Assets	4.3	4.6
	.9	1.4	2.3	5.2	1.2		1.4	1.5
	UND	315.0	88.6	999.8	104.2		138.5	186.0
	48.6	31.5	41.9	87.3	46.7	Sales/Net Fixed Assets	36.3	36.7
	10.6	13.2	8.4	27.8	20.9		13.4	13.2
	.8	.6	.5	1.2	.7		.7	.7
	.6	.4	.3	.4	.4	Sales/Total Assets	.4	.4
	.4	.3	.2	.2	.3		.2	.2
	1.0	.3	.5		.2		.5	.5
	(25) 1.6	(61) .8	(49) .9		(12) .9	% Depr., Dep., Amort./Sales	(190) 1.1	(169) 1.0
	3.3	1.3	1.7		2.3		2.1	2.2
	3.1	3.2	2.3				3.3	3.4
	(12) 7.6	(16) 7.6	(13) 3.5			% Officers', Directors' Owners' Comp/Sales	(68) 7.6	(52) 6.3
	18.2	20.9	10.6				15.8	15.1
1607M	52280M	245491M	4071899M	911808M	2118365M	Net Sales ($)	5943353M	4348672M
2733M	65089M	411270M	1604567M	1296123M	3837154M	Total Assets ($)	9528417M	8159287M

M = $ thousand MM = $ million

See Pages 9 through 22 for Explanation of Ratios and Data

Comparative Historical Data / Current Data Sorted by Sales

Comparative Historical Data			Type of Statement	Current Data Sorted by Sales					
71	75	56	Unqualified	2	9	3	12	10	20
35	20	16	Reviewed	3	5	4	3	1	
46	44	38	Compiled	13	16	4	3	1	1
18	26	14	Tax Returns	7	5	1			1
118	126	122	Other	32	30	16	16	10	18
4/1/11-3/31/12 ALL	4/1/12-3/31/13 ALL	4/1/13-3/31/14 ALL		37 (4/1-9/30/13)		209 (10/1/13-3/31/14)			
				0-1MM	1-3MM	3-5MM	5-10MM	10-25MM	25MM & OVER
288	291	246	NUMBER OF STATEMENTS	57	65	28	34	22	40
%	%	%	ASSETS	%	%	%	%	%	%
7.6	6.6	7.2	Cash & Equivalents	5.6	6.9	12.1	6.8	3.4	9.0
66.7	70.0	69.9	Trade Receivables (net)	72.2	74.2	64.5	72.0	74.3	59.4
2.1	2.5	1.6	Inventory	1.1	.2	.2	1.8	.6	6.1
4.3	3.9	4.5	All Other Current	3.6	4.1	.9	3.7	13.0	5.0
80.8	83.0	83.3	Total Current	82.5	85.5	77.7	84.3	91.3	79.4
5.3	4.4	4.4	Fixed Assets (net)	3.9	4.3	6.2	5.6	2.5	4.1
2.1	1.9	2.9	Intangibles (net)	2.1	1.2	2.2	4.5	1.5	6.8
11.8	10.7	9.4	All Other Non-Current	11.5	9.0	13.9	5.5	4.8	9.7
100.0	100.0	100.0	Total	100.0	100.0	100.0	100.0	100.0	100.0
			LIABILITIES						
34.1	33.0	31.6	Notes Payable-Short Term	32.0	32.0	26.9	30.0	41.6	29.7
2.3	1.8	1.5	Cur. Mat.-L.T.D.	1.4	1.5	1.2	2.8	.6	1.3
1.9	2.2	1.6	Trade Payables	.6	.4	4.9	2.1	1.1	2.5
.1	.1	.1	Income Taxes Payable	.1	.1	.0	.2	.0	.2
7.0	8.7	9.8	All Other Current	14.7	12.8	5.7	7.8	4.3	5.3
45.4	45.7	44.6	Total Current	48.8	46.7	38.7	42.9	47.5	38.9
9.9	9.7	8.2	Long-Term Debt	9.2	6.9	9.1	6.9	9.2	8.8
.1	.1	.3	Deferred Taxes	.3	.1	.0	.1	1.3	.4
13.6	15.1	15.5	All Other Non-Current	21.8	13.7	16.1	9.5	16.1	13.5
31.0	29.4	31.5	Net Worth	19.8	32.6	36.0	40.6	25.9	38.5
100.0	100.0	100.0	Total Liabilties & Net Worth	100.0	100.0	100.0	100.0	100.0	100.0
			INCOME DATA						
100.0	100.0	100.0	Net Sales	100.0	100.0	100.0	100.0	100.0	100.0
			Gross Profit						
71.4	71.1	74.8	Operating Expenses	75.2	74.7	71.6	71.6	69.1	82.5
28.6	28.9	25.2	Operating Profit	24.8	25.3	28.4	28.4	30.9	17.5
10.2	10.0	8.7	All Other Expenses (net)	11.3	9.0	10.2	5.4	10.1	5.6
18.4	19.0	16.5	Profit Before Taxes	13.5	16.3	18.2	23.0	20.8	11.9
			RATIOS						
2.8	3.6	3.8		3.0	4.1	3.6	4.3	4.2	4.0
1.7	1.7	1.7	Current	1.8	1.7	2.1	1.7	1.8	1.6
1.3	1.3	1.3		1.2	1.3	1.6	1.3	1.3	1.5
2.6	3.0	3.4		3.0	4.0	3.6	3.6	3.5	3.8
1.5	1.5	1.7	Quick	1.8	1.6	2.1	1.6	1.5	1.5
1.3	1.2	1.2		1.2	1.3	1.6	1.3	1.2	1.2
135 2.7	182 2.0	261 1.4		456 .8	365 1.0	76 4.8	304 1.2	406 .9	85 4.3
730 .5	730 .5	608 .6	Sales/Receivables	730 .5	730 .5	730 .5	608 .6	608 .6	281 1.3
1217 .3	1217 .3	1217 .3		1217 .3	1217 .3	1217 .3	1217 .3	912 .4	730 .5
			Cost of Sales/Inventory						
			Cost of Sales/Payables						
.7	.6	.6		.6	.6	.4	.7	.6	1.3
1.3	1.3	1.2	Sales/Working Capital	1.0	1.2	1.2	1.0	1.2	2.2
3.1	2.9	2.7		2.6	2.1	2.9	1.8	2.2	4.8
6.2	6.5	6.0		3.0	5.9	5.9	10.4	5.7	6.7
(218) 3.5	(223) 3.6	(206) 3.0	EBIT/Interest	(47) 2.1	(53) 3.2	(25) 4.0	(27) 5.5	(20) 4.3	(34) 2.8
1.8	1.9	1.7		1.2	1.7	1.6	2.2	2.0	2.0
24.8	22.2	7.1							
(27) 4.7	(24) 5.2	(16) 1.4	Net Profit + Depr., Dep., Amort./Cur. Mat. L/T/D						
.8	.7	.3							
.0	.0	.0		.0	.0	.0	.0	.0	.0
.0	.0	.1	Fixed/Worth	.0	.0	.0	.1	.1	.1
.3	.2	.3		1.4	.1	.4	.3	.2	.2
1.2	1.3	1.3		1.8	1.3	1.0	.7	2.1	.9
2.7	2.9	2.9	Debt/Worth	5.4	2.7	2.1	2.0	3.2	2.8
6.8	7.5	7.5		65.8	8.0	6.2	4.8	6.1	6.9
43.8	47.6	45.5		48.0	43.0	46.5	34.2	65.4	52.3
(262) 24.5	(266) 26.6	(224) 24.4	% Profit Before Taxes/Tangible Net Worth	(44) 25.1	(62) 16.0	21.3	(32) 23.1	30.6	(36) 30.2
9.6	10.7	9.0		7.5	7.3	6.8	11.6	22.4	13.1
11.7	11.0	10.5		8.1	8.9	8.5	13.3	14.6	11.9
5.7	6.0	5.1	% Profit Before Taxes/Total Assets	3.5	4.4	5.1	6.7	6.7	6.6
1.7	2.5	1.8		.5	1.5	2.7	2.3	3.2	2.2
205.8	239.8	173.6		UND	602.2	113.8	88.3	50.2	139.0
41.1	43.9	43.8	Sales/Net Fixed Assets	63.0	48.0	47.4	30.6	30.0	70.4
14.8	17.7	13.6		11.9	13.0	13.8	7.7	13.6	27.8
.7	.7	.7		.5	.7	.7	.8	.6	1.4
.4	.4	.4	Sales/Total Assets	.4	.4	.4	.4	.4	.8
.2	.2	.3		.3	.2	.2	.2	.3	.4
.4	.4	.5		1.0	.4	.3	.7	.6	.4
(192) .8	(179) .8	(158) .9	% Depr., Dep., Amort./Sales	(31) 1.5	(44) .8	(22) .5	(24) 1.0	(14) .8	(23) .9
1.9	1.7	1.7		3.7	1.4	1.8	2.2	1.6	1.3
2.9	2.7	2.8		3.0	3.3				
(41) 6.6	(53) 5.6	(46) 5.7	% Officers', Directors' Owners' Comp/Sales	(11) 11.8	(14) 6.8				
16.1	17.7	15.6		20.0	10.8				
5452118M	5931149M	7401450M	Net Sales ($)	30212M	112607M	107558M	255665M	342911M	6552497M
9954548M	11098782M	7216936M	Total Assets ($)	98018M	416561M	339019M	915383M	1092145M	4355810M

M = $ thousand MM = $ million

See Pages 9 through 22 for Explanation of Ratios and Data

Current Data Sorted by Assets							Comparative Historical Data	
						Type of Statement		
3	11	56	120	50	28	Unqualified	177	166
	1	1	2			Reviewed	6	7
2	1	1	3			Compiled	12	15
3	4	8	2			Tax Returns	27	20
48	16	21	41	9	12	Other	94	87
44 (4/1-9/30/13)		399 (10/1/13-3/31/14)					4/1/09-3/31/10	4/1/10-3/31/11
0-500M	**500M-2MM**	**2-10MM**	**10-50MM**	**50-100MM**	**100-250MM**		**ALL**	**ALL**
56	33	87	168	59	40	**NUMBER OF STATEMENTS**	316	295
%	%	%	%	%	%	**ASSETS**	%	%
62.4	36.2	23.0	16.1	13.4	10.9	Cash & Equivalents	14.1	13.0
6.3	6.7	15.3	6.3	11.1	11.2	Trade Receivables (net)	25.2	26.3
4.0	16.6	26.4	49.0	48.7	50.4	Inventory	13.5	14.5
2.0	10.2	6.2	4.7	2.8	4.9	All Other Current	17.4	13.5
74.7	69.7	70.9	76.2	76.0	77.3	Total Current	70.2	67.3
16.4	16.9	7.8	5.2	2.3	2.5	Fixed Assets (net)	7.5	8.2
.6	.2	.3	.8	3.2	2.7	Intangibles (net)	2.9	2.1
8.4	13.2	21.0	17.8	18.5	17.4	All Other Non-Current	19.5	22.4
100.0	100.0	100.0	100.0	100.0	100.0	Total	100.0	100.0
						LIABILITIES		
7.2	26.1	35.3	51.4	50.5	53.7	Notes Payable-Short Term	41.6	42.0
2.0	.9	.9	.7	1.8	.4	Cur. Mat.-L.T.D.	2.0	1.8
2.0	3.4	2.9	1.7	2.5	1.2	Trade Payables	4.4	4.1
.0	.0	.1	.2	.6	.6	Income Taxes Payable	.2	.1
8.8	5.5	6.4	6.3	5.6	11.0	All Other Current	7.6	7.0
20.0	36.0	45.6	60.3	60.9	67.0	Total Current	55.8	55.0
9.2	8.3	10.6	7.5	6.0	4.1	Long-Term Debt	10.5	11.8
.0	.0	.0	.2	.3	.3	Deferred Taxes	.2	.3
1.2	3.2	3.0	.8	.7	2.8	All Other Non-Current	4.3	4.0
69.6	52.6	40.8	31.3	32.0	25.9	Net Worth	29.3	28.9
100.0	100.0	100.0	100.0	100.0	100.0	Total Liabilties & Net Worth	100.0	100.0
						INCOME DATA		
100.0	100.0	100.0	100.0	100.0	100.0	Net Sales	100.0	100.0
						Gross Profit		
80.6	82.2	75.7	78.0	75.0	73.6	Operating Expenses	74.2	74.9
19.4	17.8	24.3	22.0	25.0	26.4	Operating Profit	25.8	25.1
2.0	1.9	9.3	8.5	7.9	5.2	All Other Expenses (net)	10.5	11.1
17.4	15.9	15.0	13.5	17.1	21.1	Profit Before Taxes	15.3	14.0
						RATIOS		
15.5	19.9	2.2	1.4	1.6	1.3		1.8	1.8
5.2	2.2	1.5	1.2	1.2	1.1	Current	1.2	1.1
2.3	1.3	1.2	1.1	1.1	1.1		1.0	1.0
15.4	13.3	1.6	.6	.9	.7		1.4	1.3
5.0	1.2	.7	.2	.2	.2	Quick	.8	(294) .9
2.1	.4	.3	.1	.1	.1		.1	.1
0 UND	**0** UND	**0** UND	**0** UND	**0** 999.8	**0** 864.2		**0** UND	**0** UND
0 UND	**1** 282.8	**8** 48.0	**3** 113.2	**4** 94.4	**6** 61.2	Sales/Receivables	**15** 23.7	**18** 20.7
3 137.5	**5** 69.5	**69** 5.3	**18** 20.6	**24** 15.2	**21** 17.0		**452** .8	**473** .8
						Cost of Sales/Inventory		
						Cost of Sales/Payables		
4.2	2.3	1.0	2.2	1.4	2.0		1.6	1.7
8.1	4.6	2.5	4.4	4.5	3.6	Sales/Working Capital	4.6	4.9
21.5	7.7	6.4	9.0	13.6	9.5		15.3	19.0
	11.1	8.2	5.9	6.2	6.7		6.5	7.1
	(10) 3.7	(58) 3.4	(144) 2.8	(44) 3.4	(28) 4.3	EBIT/Interest	(207) 3.2	(200) 3.0
	2.2	1.0	1.4	1.8	2.8		1.7	1.7
			34.1				13.1	13.7
			(23) 8.9			Net Profit + Depr., Dep., Amort./Cur. Mat. L/T/D	(20) 1.9	(24) 3.3
			.0				1.0	.6
.0	.0	.0	.0	.0	.0		.0	.0
.1	.1	.0	.1	.0	.0	Fixed/Worth	.1	.1
.4	.7	.2	.2	.1	.1		.2	.3
.1	.1	.8	1.4	1.8	2.4		1.4	1.4
.2	.8	1.4	3.0	3.1	4.3	Debt/Worth	4.0	3.9
.9	2.9	3.4	5.1	4.9	7.6		7.8	7.9
164.8	94.2	30.4	36.1	44.3	58.0		53.7	43.8
(55) 81.7	28.7	(86) 10.5	(165) 14.9	18.4	(38) 31.1	% Profit Before Taxes/Tangible Net Worth	(299) 21.1	(285) 16.0
15.1	5.0	.7	3.7	5.9	8.0		4.3	5.5
118.0	32.3	10.9	9.7	9.4	11.5		9.2	7.3
44.9	6.4	4.0	4.6	4.3	7.3	% Profit Before Taxes/Total Assets	4.4	3.7
9.0	2.7	.1	1.0	2.1	2.0		.8	.9
999.8	150.3	127.8	101.1	96.2	154.8		152.5	162.3
69.8	28.7	43.1	40.9	43.7	72.4	Sales/Net Fixed Assets	49.8	49.0
19.0	3.6	11.0	13.1	23.0	15.9		12.9	10.1
7.4	1.6	.8	.8	.6	.6		.7	.6
4.2	1.0	.6	.6	.5	.4	Sales/Total Assets	.4	.4
2.7	.6	.3	.3	.2	.1		.1	.1
.4	.4	.2	.3	.3	.4		.4	.4
(12) .6	(15) .7	(62) .6	(134) .7	(43) .8	(25) .7	% Depr., Dep., Amort./Sales	(191) .8	(184) .8
2.5	2.3	1.5	1.3	1.2	1.4		1.5	1.5
		4.7	4.5				3.2	2.5
		(14) 10.4	(18) 7.4			% Officers', Directors' Owners' Comp/Sales	(60) 6.5	(49) 6.1
		15.2	27.1				14.0	18.4
62248M	49807M	332945M	2971896M	2092234M	2615977M	Net Sales ($)	3996577M	3925121M
12706M	40223M	496995M	4391852M	4084197M	5957769M	Total Assets ($)	10197336M	10349510M

M = $ thousand MM = $ million

See Pages 9 through 22 for Explanation of Ratios and Data

Comparative Historical Data				Current Data Sorted by Sales					
			Type of Statement						
184	232	268	Unqualified	13	30	36	43	68	78
7	6	4	Reviewed	2	2				
11	6	7	Compiled	2	1	2			2
19	24	17	Tax Returns	11	3	1	2		
69	68	147	Other	37	43	13	11	20	23
4/1/11-3/31/12 ALL	**4/1/12-3/31/13 ALL**	**4/1/13-3/31/14 ALL**		**44 (4/1-9/30/13)**			**399 (10/1/13-3/31/14)**		
				0-1MM	**1-3MM**	**3-5MM**	**5-10MM**	**10-25MM**	**25MM & OVER**
290	336	443	**NUMBER OF STATEMENTS**	65	79	52	56	88	103
%	%	%	**ASSETS**	%	%	%	%	%	%
12.2	12.6	24.0	Cash & Equivalents	37.9	35.3	26.6	20.8	15.5	14.2
22.3	18.0	9.2	Trade Receivables (net)	11.9	12.2	12.9	6.1	8.2	5.8
25.0	33.3	36.5	Inventory	6.6	13.5	26.3	40.0	55.8	59.8
10.9	12.2	4.9	All Other Current	6.4	5.2	3.4	7.4	4.8	3.1
70.3	76.0	74.6	Total Current	62.7	66.3	69.2	74.3	84.3	82.9
6.5	6.1	7.4	Fixed Assets (net)	15.1	11.3	6.9	5.6	4.5	3.1
1.2	1.2	1.1	Intangibles (net)	.7	.2	.0	2.1	1.1	2.1
21.9	16.6	17.0	All Other Non-Current	21.5	22.2	23.9	18.0	10.1	11.9
100.0	100.0	100.0	Total	100.0	100.0	100.0	100.0	100.0	100.0
			LIABILITIES						
50.3	52.2	40.9	Notes Payable-Short Term	17.7	21.8	38.6	40.5	58.9	56.0
1.0	.9	1.0	Cur. Mat.-L.T.D.	4.0	.4	.4	.7	.6	.6
1.7	2.0	2.1	Trade Payables	.6	2.6	1.3	2.8	2.2	2.7
.2	.2	.2	Income Taxes Payable	.0	.0	.1	.2	.4	.5
6.8	7.9	6.9	All Other Current	8.0	6.3	4.4	5.9	7.2	8.3
59.9	63.2	51.2	Total Current	30.3	31.1	44.9	50.1	69.2	68.1
10.1	8.4	7.9	Long-Term Debt	18.9	11.4	9.0	8.4	3.9	.8
.2	.2	.1	Deferred Taxes	.0	.0	.0	.0	.3	.3
2.8	1.9	1.6	All Other Non-Current	3.3	1.5	1.1	3.4	.7	.7
27.1	26.3	39.2	Net Worth	47.5	56.0	44.9	38.0	25.9	30.2
100.0	100.0	100.0	Total Liabilities & Net Worth	100.0	100.0	100.0	100.0	100.0	100.0
			INCOME DATA						
100.0	100.0	100.0	Net Sales	100.0	100.0	100.0	100.0	100.0	100.0
			Gross Profit						
76.4	70.1	77.4	Operating Expenses	66.3	75.5	74.5	76.6	82.0	83.7
23.6	29.9	22.6	Operating Profit	33.7	24.5	25.5	23.4	18.0	16.3
10.8	8.7	7.0	All Other Expenses (net)	13.1	8.3	7.7	5.0	6.5	3.3
12.9	21.3	15.6	Profit Before Taxes	20.6	16.2	17.8	18.4	11.5	13.0
			RATIOS						
1.6	1.4	2.3		12.9	7.2	2.3	2.2	1.3	1.3
1.1	1.1	1.3	Current	1.8	2.7	1.4	1.5	1.2	1.2
1.0	1.1	1.1		1.1	1.2	1.1	1.2	1.1	1.1
1.1	1.1	1.6		8.7	6.9	2.0	1.2	.4	.4
.5	.2	.4	Quick	1.6	2.2	.8	.5	.2	.2
.1	.1	.2		.3	.5	.3	.2	.1	.1
0 UND	**0** UND	**0** UND		**0** UND	**0** UND	**0** UND	**0** UND	**0** 887.3	**0** 999.8
13 28.4	**6** 59.2	**3** 116.4	Sales/Receivables	**0** UND	**2** 174.8	**3** 108.0	**3** 135.6	**3** 110.0	**5** 77.5
456 .8	**74** 4.9	**17** 21.7		**17** 21.5	**16** 22.7	**41** 8.8	**19** 19.0	**16** 23.2	**13** 27.9
			Cost of Sales/Inventory						
			Cost of Sales/Payables						
1.9	2.2	2.0		1.3	1.7	1.2	1.5	2.6	3.2
4.7	4.3	4.4	Sales/Working Capital	4.1	4.9	2.4	2.4	4.4	6.1
13.3	9.5	9.8		24.2	15.0	7.6	5.1	8.0	14.6
5.2	10.3	6.7		9.9	8.0	9.7	7.3	6.2	6.1
(204) 2.6	(266) 4.6	(293) 3.3	EBIT/Interest	(19) 4.0	(28) 4.1	(40) 3.7	(47) 3.8	(76) 2.5	(83) 3.3
1.3	2.8	1.4		1.1	2.4	1.2	1.4	1.2	1.8
14.0	129.3	32.6						73.6	32.6
(20) 4.3	(26) 14.9	(34) 8.4	Net Profit + Depr., Dep., Amort./Cur. Mat. L/T/D					(13) 14.5	(10) 7.7
.7	3.8	.3						.6	3.1
.0	.0	.0		.0	.0	.0	.0	.0	.0
.1	.0	.1	Fixed/Worth	.1	.0	.0	.1	.1	.1
.2	.1	.2		.5	.3	.1	.3	.3	.1
1.6	2.0	.8		.3	.1	.6	1.1	2.4	1.9
4.8	4.8	2.4	Debt/Worth	.9	.7	1.2	1.7	3.6	3.1
9.7	8.7	4.7		4.0	2.9	3.8	4.2	5.8	5.4
30.8	66.2	49.4		93.3	81.7	28.1	32.3	39.3	56.4
(283) 13.4	(326) 36.8	(436) 20.1	% Profit Before Taxes/Tangible Net Worth	(62) 26.5	14.4	9.9	(54) 10.6	(86) 22.6	30.9
2.0	12.1	4.8		4.5	4.0	1.4	3.8	3.8	10.9
5.9	10.9	13.4		35.9	31.6	12.1	12.9	9.0	12.7
2.3	6.3	5.7	% Profit Before Taxes/Total Assets	4.9	5.7	4.3	5.3	4.4	7.7
.3	2.4	1.5		1.3	1.8	.4	1.0	.8	3.2
139.9	169.2	122.4		UND	500.5	124.7	96.4	107.6	89.3
47.5	64.4	44.6	Sales/Net Fixed Assets	35.0	62.6	37.6	27.9	42.6	48.8
11.7	17.6	13.2		4.8	18.6	11.1	7.6	11.5	27.3
.5	.6	1.0		2.9	3.5	.7	.8	.8	.9
.3	.4	.6	Sales/Total Assets	.6	1.0	.5	.5	.6	.7
.2	.2	.3		.1	.3	.2	.2	.4	.5
.4	.3	.3		.6	.3	.2	.3	.3	.3
(203) .7	(237) .5	(291) .7	% Depr., Dep., Amort./Sales	(22) 2.5	(35) .5	(36) .7	(43) .7	(74) .7	(81) .7
1.3	1.1	1.3		5.3	1.3	1.3	1.2	1.0	1.2
4.5	3.6	4.8		5.6				3.8	
(33) 9.2	(49) 5.9	(48) 8.9	% Officers', Directors' Owners' Comp/Sales	(10) 14.0				(10) 5.3	
15.1	11.8	18.4		34.6				20.5	
9888196M	13562448M	8125107M	Net Sales ($)	33682M	146030M	205848M	399944M	1454248M	5885355M
10686064M	14932998M	14983742M	Total Assets ($)	151083M	460341M	959182M	1414488M	3446547M	8552101M

M = $ thousand MM = $ million

See Pages 9 through 22 for Explanation of Ratios and Data

Current Data Sorted by Assets							Comparative Historical Data	
						Type of Statement		
4	2	12	41	14	29	Unqualified	134	118
	1	7	7	2	1	Reviewed	28	26
4	1	4	1			Compiled	14	19
1	6	10			2	Tax Returns	31	26
5	13	33	39	20	23	Other	122	109
	38 (4/1-9/30/13)		244 (10/1/13-3/31/14)				4/1/09-3/31/10	4/1/10-3/31/11
0-500M	500M-2MM	2-10MM	10-50MM	50-100MM	100-250MM		ALL	ALL
14	23	66	88	36	55	**NUMBER OF STATEMENTS**	329	298
%	%	%	%	%	%	**ASSETS**	%	%
19.4	21.6	15.2	7.6	5.9	4.7	Cash & Equivalents	10.7	11.4
25.7	28.8	50.7	55.6	63.5	53.1	Trade Receivables (net)	49.7	49.4
25.1	8.3	5.1	1.1	.7	.4	Inventory	3.3	2.8
10.6	10.1	8.9	11.4	6.1	10.2	All Other Current	7.5	9.6
80.9	68.9	79.9	75.8	76.3	68.4	Total Current	71.1	73.1
6.1	6.8	6.7	2.8	4.4	2.3	Fixed Assets (net)	8.4	8.3
.6	.2	2.8	2.4	2.8	5.2	Intangibles (net)	2.9	2.6
12.2	24.1	10.6	19.0	16.5	24.1	All Other Non-Current	17.5	16.0
100.0	100.0	100.0	100.0	100.0	100.0	Total	100.0	100.0
						LIABILITIES		
30.8	15.3	23.4	32.2	33.5	26.3	Notes Payable-Short Term	27.3	28.6
1.1	5.1	1.9	2.0	.5	2.8	Cur. Mat.-L.T.D.	4.3	3.1
2.8	6.4	3.3	1.8	5.7	5.0	Trade Payables	4.6	4.0
.0	.0	.1	.1	.0	.4	Income Taxes Payable	.2	.1
11.1	4.6	11.6	9.9	6.8	5.4	All Other Current	9.0	9.3
45.9	31.5	40.2	46.1	46.5	39.9	Total Current	45.3	45.2
6.7	10.8	9.7	14.6	20.4	27.4	Long-Term Debt	16.1	16.5
.0	.0	.0	.1	.0	1.0	Deferred Taxes	.3	.2
.4	35.5	7.8	7.2	8.0	5.0	All Other Non-Current	7.7	8.1
46.9	22.2	42.3	31.9	25.0	26.6	Net Worth	30.6	30.0
100.0	100.0	100.0	100.0	100.0	100.0	Total Liabilities & Net Worth	100.0	100.0
						INCOME DATA		
100.0	100.0	100.0	100.0	100.0	100.0	Net Sales	100.0	100.0
						Gross Profit		
90.1	77.7	78.6	65.7	63.9	60.1	Operating Expenses	73.7	71.5
9.9	22.3	21.4	34.3	36.1	39.9	Operating Profit	26.3	28.5
-.2	3.4	8.3	13.9	11.8	11.4	All Other Expenses (net)	9.8	11.7
10.1	18.9	13.1	20.4	24.4	28.5	Profit Before Taxes	16.5	16.7
						RATIOS		
9.1	15.9	5.0	2.7	3.1	4.4		3.1	3.0
2.1	4.9	2.4	1.5	1.5	1.4	Current	1.5	1.5
1.2	1.2	1.4	1.3	1.2	1.2		1.1	1.2
4.3	10.4	4.5	2.5	2.4	2.8		2.4	2.5
1.2	3.5	2.0	1.4	1.3	1.3	Quick	1.4	1.4
.5	.7	1.2	1.1	.8	.7		.8	.9
0 UND	**0** UND	**22** 16.5	**21** 17.1	**94** 3.9	**7** 49.0		**17** 21.6	**21** 17.1
41 8.8	**24** 15.3	**215** 1.7	**912** .4	**1217** .3	**1217** .3	Sales/Receivables	**526** .7	**609** .6
74 4.9	**228** 1.6	**1217** .3	**1825** .2	**2000** .1	**1825** .2		**1439** .3	**1552** .2
						Cost of Sales/Inventory		
						Cost of Sales/Payables		
1.3	1.4	.6	.5	.4	.3		.6	.5
3.1	4.2	1.4	.9	.7	.8	Sales/Working Capital	1.4	1.2
22.5	6.4	3.1	2.7	5.1	6.7		10.8	7.0
	9.2	11.3	4.3	5.3	10.0		5.7	5.1
	(13) 4.8	(49) 3.0	(54) 2.6	(21) 3.2	(29) 4.6	EBIT/Interest	(196) 2.5	(168) 3.0
	1.8	1.9	1.4	2.2	3.0		1.5	1.4
							5.5	7.9
						Net Profit + Depr., Dep., Amort./Cur. Mat. L/T/D	(26) 2.1	(10) 2.1
							.1	.3
.0	.0	.0	.0	.0	.0		.0	.0
.0	.1	.0	.0	.0	.0	Fixed/Worth	.0	.0
.2	1.4	.1	.1	.1	.1		.4	.3
.1	.4	.5	1.6	2.1	2.5		1.4	1.3
1.2	1.4	1.3	2.7	4.1	4.5	Debt/Worth	3.2	3.1
4.7	4.4	4.1	6.0	7.1	7.7		9.5	7.7
35.7	60.3	28.7	36.7	32.6	44.1		33.0	38.9
(12) 30.8	(18) 26.2	(61) 13.3	(84) 17.7	(34) 24.2	(51) 22.1	% Profit Before Taxes/Tangible Net Worth	(297) 15.1	(276) 15.8
7.0	10.1	3.9	5.8	11.6	6.3		4.8	4.6
31.6	35.8	11.1	8.3	6.0	7.9		7.7	8.0
7.7	13.2	4.2	3.3	4.3	3.5	% Profit Before Taxes/Total Assets	3.2	3.5
-.8	2.6	1.2	1.6	2.3	1.5		1.1	1.0
UND	UND	UND	730.1	563.5	650.3		258.2	603.2
64.0	148.4	83.7	71.7	87.2	64.4	Sales/Net Fixed Assets	45.0	47.7
21.3	30.7	16.2	15.9	17.3	30.2		11.3	10.1
3.0	3.8	1.2	.3	.3	.3		.6	.5
1.7	1.3	.4	.2	.2	.1	Sales/Total Assets	.3	.2
.3	.3	.2	.1	.1	.1		.2	.1
	.1	.3	.4	.4	.4		.5	.6
	(11) .8	(35) .9	(51) .8	(19) .7	(23) .8	% Depr., Dep., Amort./Sales	(185) 1.3	(148) 1.5
	1.5	2.0	1.8	1.7	4.3		3.0	3.4
		4.0					4.3	3.5
		(21) 10.1				% Officers', Directors' Owners' Comp/Sales	(64) 11.5	(60) 10.1
		22.5					20.0	15.9
10345M	48402M	335944M	751640M	717599M	2248789M	Net Sales ($)	5251124M	4150995M
3543M	27453M	337699M	2253170M	2511267M	9045371M	Total Assets ($)	11549976M	11932117M

M = $ thousand MM = $ million

See Pages 9 through 22 for Explanation of Ratios and Data

Comparative Historical Data							Current Data Sorted by Sales											
						Type of Statement												
	127		113		102	Unqualified		10		21		9		20		27		15
	34		18		18	Reviewed		4		5		4		1		2		2
	13		20		10	Compiled		4		2		1		2				1
	22		17		19	Tax Returns		6		3		2		5		3		
	98		131		133	Other		13		27		23		23		31		16
	4/1/11-3/31/12 ALL		**4/1/12-3/31/13 ALL**		**4/1/13-3/31/14 ALL**					**38 (4/1-9/30/13)**				**244 (10/1/13-3/31/14)**				
								0-1MM		**1-3MM**		**3-5MM**		**5-10MM**		**10-25MM**		**25MM & OVER**
	294		299		282	**NUMBER OF STATEMENTS**		37		58		39		51		63		34
	%		%		%	**ASSETS**		%		%		%		%		%		%
	10.8		10.1		10.3	Cash & Equivalents		9.7		15.1		9.7		8.1		7.8		11.6
	50.2		53.6		51.3	Trade Receivables (net)		47.4		40.3		47.1		62.7		58.6		48.8
	3.7		3.6		3.7	Inventory		9.0		4.3		1.8		3.4		1.7		2.9
	9.3		9.6		9.8	All Other Current		8.5		11.2		16.1		5.8		9.9		7.4
	74.0		76.9		75.1	Total Current		74.6		70.9		74.6		79.9		78.0		70.7
	7.8		7.3		4.3	Fixed Assets (net)		5.6		2.8		2.6		4.8		3.5		8.2
	2.8		2.1		2.8	Intangibles (net)		.1		1.3		2.0		3.0		3.7		7.4
	15.4		13.8		17.8	All Other Non-Current		19.7		25.0		20.8		12.3		14.8		13.8
	100.0		100.0		100.0	Total		100.0		100.0		100.0		100.0		100.0		100.0
						LIABILITIES												
	28.9		30.1		27.7	Notes Payable-Short Term		28.0		27.1		30.4		28.6		26.6		25.9
	3.1		2.4		2.1	Cur. Mat.-L.T.D.		4.8		1.2		.6		2.5		2.1		2.0
	3.9		4.2		3.7	Trade Payables		1.6		2.6		2.9		4.0		4.9		6.4
	.1		.1		.1	Income Taxes Payable		.0		.1		.0		.1		.3		.3
	8.5		8.1		8.7	All Other Current		6.7		7.2		8.7		13.9		6.5		9.4
	44.5		45.0		42.4	Total Current		41.3		38.2		42.7		49.1		40.3		44.1
	17.6		15.0		16.0	Long-Term Debt		9.0		15.8		13.0		14.5		23.8		15.5
	.3		.1		.2	Deferred Taxes		.0		.0		.0		.0		.2		1.7
	9.1		7.7		9.0	All Other Non-Current		6.6		7.7		17.3		11.0		6.2		6.5
	28.5		32.2		32.4	Net Worth		43.1		38.3		27.1		25.4		29.5		32.3
	100.0		100.0		100.0	Total Liabilties & Net Worth		100.0		100.0		100.0		100.0		100.0		100.0
						INCOME DATA												
	100.0		100.0		100.0	Net Sales		100.0		100.0		100.0		100.0		100.0		100.0
						Gross Profit												
	69.5		69.4		69.6	Operating Expenses		75.4		67.9		67.9		72.3		63.0		76.3
	30.5		30.6		30.4	Operating Profit		24.6		32.1		32.1		27.7		37.0		23.7
	12.3		9.7		10.3	All Other Expenses (net)		7.6		16.3		9.6		7.7		12.8		2.9
	18.2		20.9		20.2	Profit Before Taxes		17.0		15.8		22.5		20.1		24.3		20.8
						RATIOS												
	3.2		3.6		5.2			6.1		5.0		6.8		5.7		10.4		2.2
	1.6		1.6		1.6	Current		2.0		2.2		1.6		1.5		1.5		1.4
	1.2		1.3		1.3			1.1		1.4		1.3		1.2		1.2		1.1
	2.7		2.9		3.6			4.2		3.2		5.9		2.9		4.4		2.0
	1.4		1.4		1.4	Quick		1.8		1.6		1.4		1.4		1.5		1.3
	.9		1.0		1.0			.6		1.1		.6		1.1		1.2		.8
12	29.5	**32**	11.5	**17**	21.1		**14**	26.9	**0**	UND	**0**	UND	**85**	4.3	**37**	9.9	**26**	14.2
456	.8	**608**	.6	**456**	.8	Sales/Receivables	**730**	.5	**215**	1.7	**281**	1.3	**1217**	.3	**912**	.4	**182**	2.0
1217	.3	**1825**	.2	**1825**	.2		**1825**	.2	**1217**	.3	**1825**	.2	**1825**	.2	**1825**	.2	**1217**	.3
						Cost of Sales/Inventory												
						Cost of Sales/Payables												
	.5		.4		.4			.3		.4		.5		.3		.4		.9
	1.2		1.1		1.0	Sales/Working Capital		.9		1.0		.9		.9		.9		4.9
	7.3		4.2		4.5			3.5		2.5		3.7		3.1		3.3		12.3
	7.2		7.6		6.6			5.0		5.9		9.7		5.5		5.1		11.2
(172)	3.4	(174)	3.9	(173)	3.2	EBIT/Interest	(21)	2.0	(37)	3.0	(21)	2.6	(29)	3.7	(37)	3.2	(28)	5.7
	2.0		2.1		1.8			1.0		1.6		1.6		2.0		2.1		3.2
	3.8		8.7		3.1													
(16)	1.5	(15)	2.2	(14)	1.6	Net Profit + Depr., Dep., Amort./Cur. Mat. L/T/D												
	.1		.2		.6													
	.0		.0		.0			.0		.0		.0		.0		.0		.0
	.0		.0		.0	Fixed/Worth		.0		.0		.0		.0		.0		.0
	.2		.2		.1			.0		.1		.1		.1		.2		.3
	1.4		1.3		1.0			.4		.8		.9		1.3		2.0		1.9
	3.0		2.9		2.7	Debt/Worth		1.3		2.1		2.6		2.8		4.2		3.2
	8.1		6.2		5.9			4.5		4.6		9.6		7.3		6.7		6.2
	43.8		44.0		35.0			32.2		29.4		27.8		31.6		37.1		69.2
(270)	16.9	(279)	17.4	(260)	19.1	% Profit Before Taxes/Tangible Net Worth	(34)	6.6	(57)	11.9	(33)	12.3	(45)	17.7	(59)	24.1	(32)	43.2
	5.7		7.1		5.9			2.0		1.7		4.3		7.0		11.5		22.8
	10.0		10.7		9.6			9.6		6.8		7.8		9.5		8.3		13.3
	3.9		4.7		3.9	% Profit Before Taxes/Total Assets		2.1		3.2		3.4		4.5		4.2		8.7
	1.5		2.0		1.6			.4		.8		1.7		1.8		2.2		5.0
	526.5		653.0		768.8			UND		UND		UND		178.9		180.2		122.7
	69.1		64.8		74.6	Sales/Net Fixed Assets		UND		88.5		148.4		74.1		64.4		54.1
	13.0		13.1		18.2			25.1		14.8		37.8		16.6		16.7		12.1
	.9		.7		.7			.5		.4		.9		.5		.6		1.6
	.3		.3		.2	Sales/Total Assets		.2		.2		.2		.2		.2		.6
	.1		.1		.1			.1		.1		.1		.1		.1		.3
	.5		.4		.3			.7		.3		.3		.3		.4		.7
(152)	1.1	(162)	.8	(143)	.8	% Depr., Dep., Amort./Sales	(10)	1.3	(34)	.9	(15)	.5	(33)	.7	(34)	.7	(17)	1.6
	3.3		2.1		1.8			2.1		1.7		.8		2.0		1.8		5.5
	3.5		3.0		3.6					6.8								
(64)	6.6	(58)	7.8	(43)	7.8	% Officers', Directors' Owners' Comp/Sales			(17)	12.8								
	17.2		13.5		18.7					24.4								
	4364277M		**4178902M**		**4112719M**	Net Sales ($)		**18869M**		**107345M**		**155505M**		**370728M**		**957003M**		**2503269M**
	10730057M		**11536791M**		**14178503M**	Total Assets ($)		**110737M**		**856784M**		**1040512M**		**2368709M**		**5613684M**		**4188077M**

M = $ thousand MM = $ million

See Pages 9 through 22 for Explanation of Ratios and Data

Current Data Sorted by Assets							Comparative Historical Data	
Type of Statement								
Unqualified	3	1	14	17	8	3	105	87
Reviewed	1	1	1	1			5	1
Compiled	2		1	1			6	5
Tax Returns	5	2	1	1	1	1	21	13
Other	5	10	9	12	3	2	74	41
	13 (4/1-9/30/13)			93 (10/1/13-3/31/14)			4/1/09-3/31/10 ALL	4/1/10-3/31/11 ALL
	0-500M	500M-2MM	2-10MM	10-50MM	50-100MM	100-250MM		
NUMBER OF STATEMENTS	16	14	26	32	12	6	211	147
ASSETS	%	%	%	%	%	%	%	%
Cash & Equivalents	44.0	21.9	30.7	17.7	11.8		18.1	19.9
Trade Receivables (net)	3.8	11.3	15.2	16.7	1.5		26.3	13.3
Inventory	.0	12.3	9.1	14.4	15.2		9.8	13.0
All Other Current	3.9	17.7	17.2	20.8	11.4		15.6	23.6
Total Current	51.7	63.2	72.3	69.6	39.8		69.8	69.8
Fixed Assets (net)	18.9	14.9	7.7	5.5	.9		8.6	8.7
Intangibles (net)	10.2	4.4	2.1	5.4	20.8		1.8	2.5
All Other Non-Current	19.2	17.4	17.9	19.4	38.5		19.8	19.0
Total	100.0	100.0	100.0	100.0	100.0		100.0	100.0
LIABILITIES								
Notes Payable-Short Term	33.8	17.4	25.1	46.2	31.4		42.5	38.1
Cur. Mat.-L.T.D.	1.2	2.6	1.0	.3	10.3		2.2	1.6
Trade Payables	7.2	.4	2.0	1.7	1.3		3.9	3.7
Income Taxes Payable	.0	.8	.2	.0	.0		.1	.3
All Other Current	8.7	6.0	11.9	7.8	2.0		9.7	9.1
Total Current	50.8	27.2	40.2	56.1	44.9		58.4	52.9
Long-Term Debt	17.7	21.1	10.4	6.3	9.6		10.2	11.6
Deferred Taxes	.0	.0	.2	.6	.7		.1	.2
All Other Non-Current	.0	.0	5.3	.7	1.0		3.6	1.8
Net Worth	31.4	51.7	43.8	36.2	43.7		27.8	33.5
Total Liabilties & Net Worth	100.0	100.0	100.0	100.0	100.0		100.0	100.0
INCOME DATA								
Net Sales	100.0	100.0	100.0	100.0	100.0		100.0	100.0
Gross Profit								
Operating Expenses	80.4	69.5	82.9	75.7	73.4		79.6	80.2
Operating Profit	19.6	30.5	17.1	24.3	26.6		20.4	19.8
All Other Expenses (net)	1.9	2.6	4.6	2.2	5.0		8.3	6.4
Profit Before Taxes	17.7	27.9	12.5	22.1	21.6		12.1	13.4
RATIOS								
Current	5.9	12.2	4.0	1.5	1.4		2.0	1.9
	1.2	3.3	2.0	1.2	1.1		1.2	1.2
	.2	1.2	1.1	1.0	.4		1.0	1.1
Quick	5.9	10.3	4.0	1.4	.5		1.5	1.5
	1.0	2.0	1.5	.3	.3		.9	.3
	.2	.2	.5	.1	.1		.1	.1
Sales/Receivables	0 UND	0 UND	0 UND	0 UND	0 UND		0 UND	0 UND
	0 UND	0 UND	6 59.0	5 69.6	0 UND		13 28.2	4 84.3
	3 111.1	13 27.4	38 9.6	81 4.5	16 22.7		403 .9	33 11.2
Cost of Sales/Inventory								
Cost of Sales/Payables								
Sales/Working Capital	11.1	1.0	1.3	2.6	3.0		1.8	2.6
	NM	4.5	3.2	5.3	5.4		6.1	6.4
	-15.5	12.3	18.3	39.6	-2.0		269.0	18.6
EBIT/Interest			63.1	9.8			8.8	9.1
			(17) 5.6	(24) 4.1			(132) 3.3	(99) 3.6
			3.0	1.8			2.0	2.2
Net Profit + Depr., Dep., Amort./Cur. Mat. L/T/D								24.7
								(10) 2.4
								1.1
Fixed/Worth	.0	.0	.0	.0	.0		.0	.0
	.1	.1	.0	.0	.0		.1	.1
	NM	.4	.2	.3	NM		.4	.2
Debt/Worth	.1	.1	.5	1.4	.8		1.3	1.0
	1.0	1.0	1.4	3.5	4.6		3.3	3.4
	-10.7	8.2	5.2	6.4	NM		7.6	6.6
% Profit Before Taxes/Tangible Net Worth	262.5	219.7	34.2	75.5			57.7	51.3
	(11) 55.8	(13) 29.1	(25) 24.2	(30) 29.5			(193) 21.1	(142) 24.6
	.7	9.6	10.1	9.3			6.8	8.4
% Profit Before Taxes/Total Assets	133.2	38.5	14.7	11.8	7.7		11.6	12.6
	17.9	15.4	7.3	7.0	5.2		4.9	5.0
	.2	6.0	2.8	3.4	1.9		1.1	1.5
Sales/Net Fixed Assets	724.0	UND	106.3	221.6	124.6		257.2	223.5
	180.3	70.6	37.6	56.3	88.7		48.3	51.6
	36.0	3.6	10.0	17.3	50.9		14.9	15.0
Sales/Total Assets	13.4	1.5	1.3	.8	.6		1.5	1.0
	4.4	.8	.7	.7	.4		.5	.5
	1.9	.4	.5	.2	.2		.2	.2
% Depr., Dep., Amort./Sales		.3	.4	.3			.5	.4
		(10) .5	(17) .6	(20) .6			(138) .9	(98) .9
		1.1	1.6	1.2			1.7	1.5
% Officers', Directors' Owners' Comp/Sales							6.6	4.2
							(33) 14.9	(32) 10.5
							26.0	26.3
Net Sales ($)	23341M	23436M	176598M	492732M	351101M	329254M	3465399M	6818169M
Total Assets ($)	3866M	16918M	137021M	802064M	825135M	994041M	7080365M	4578036M

M = $ thousand MM = $ million

See Pages 9 through 22 for Explanation of Ratios and Data

Comparative Historical Data | **Current Data Sorted by Sales**

4/1/11-3/31/12 ALL	4/1/12-3/31/13 ALL	4/1/13-3/31/14 ALL	Type of Statement	0-1MM	1-3MM	3-5MM	5-10MM	10-25MM	25MM & OVER
147	135	46	Unqualified	2	7	6	7	15	9
4	3	4	Reviewed		4				
7	9	4	Compiled	2			2		
13	16	11	Tax Returns	4	5		1		1
38	39	41	Other	12	6	6	5	4	8
					13 (4/1-9/30/13)		93 (10/1/13-3/31/14)		
209	202	106	NUMBER OF STATEMENTS	20	22	12	15	19	18
%	%	%	ASSETS	%	%	%	%	%	%
14.6	18.6	24.3	Cash & Equivalents	30.2	27.0	28.7	28.8	18.0	14.6
10.9	12.5	13.0	Trade Receivables (net)	6.8	16.7	14.0	15.8	16.4	8.6
35.0	32.9	10.7	Inventory	3.3	4.8	11.8	14.4	12.7	20.4
12.4	13.3	16.0	All Other Current	11.0	17.0	22.9	9.2	19.8	17.5
73.0	77.2	64.0	Total Current	51.3	65.6	77.3	68.2	66.8	61.1
6.1	6.0	8.5	Fixed Assets (net)	14.1	11.3	10.7	6.0	5.5	3.0
2.1	2.8	6.6	Intangibles (net)	10.7	.7	.9	4.6	12.2	8.9
18.8	13.9	20.8	All Other Non-Current	24.0	22.4	11.0	21.2	15.4	27.0
100.0	100.0	100.0	Total	100.0	100.0	100.0	100.0	100.0	100.0
			LIABILITIES						
47.7	49.4	32.9	Notes Payable-Short Term	20.5	32.4	28.8	27.4	48.1	38.7
1.2	.8	2.0	Cur. Mat.-L.T.D.	1.3	2.3	.2	3.6	.3	4.2
3.8	3.2	2.3	Trade Payables	3.4	2.5	.6	2.8	1.4	2.6
.2	.2	.2	Income Taxes Payable	.2	.0	.0	.5	.3	.1
9.6	9.3	8.6	All Other Current	5.3	13.4	11.3	5.3	6.0	10.0
62.5	62.8	46.0	Total Current	30.8	50.6	40.9	39.7	56.1	55.5
8.1	7.8	12.4	Long-Term Debt	24.6	13.5	.2	13.6	11.9	4.8
.1	.2	.3	Deferred Taxes	.0	.0	.0	.0	1.4	.2
1.7	2.0	1.8	All Other Non-Current	1.3	.2	6.5	2.4	1.3	1.4
27.6	27.3	39.5	Net Worth	43.2	35.7	52.3	44.3	29.3	38.0
100.0	100.0	100.0	Total Liabilties & Net Worth	100.0	100.0	100.0	100.0	100.0	100.0
			INCOME DATA						
100.0	100.0	100.0	Net Sales	100.0	100.0	100.0	100.0	100.0	100.0
			Gross Profit						
82.7	78.6	76.3	Operating Expenses	62.4	68.0	83.8	84.2	82.9	83.1
17.3	21.4	23.7	Operating Profit	37.6	32.0	16.2	15.8	17.1	16.9
5.6	4.4	3.8	All Other Expenses (net)	9.0	3.7	-2.8	2.9	6.8	-.1
11.8	17.0	20.0	Profit Before Taxes	28.6	28.3	19.0	12.8	10.3	17.1
			RATIOS						
1.5	1.6	3.0		31.8	3.3	16.4	3.5	2.7	1.5
1.1	1.1	1.3	Current	1.4	1.7	2.0	1.6	1.2	1.1
1.0	1.1	1.0		.3	.5	1.1	1.2	1.0	.8
1.0	1.1	2.5		10.4	2.6	7.8	3.5	2.2	1.0
.2	.3	.9	Quick	.9	1.4	2.0	1.2	.3	.3
.1	.1	.2		.1	.2	.4	.7	.1	.1
0 UND	0 UND	0 UND		0 UND	0 UND	0 UND	0 UND	0 999.8	0 UND
4 90.9	3 119.6	2 161.2	Sales/Receivables	0 UND	2 236.4	0 UND	8 45.6	7 55.1	2 159.0
37 9.9	33 11.0	23 16.0		5 68.6	41 9.0	8 43.8	159 2.3	41 8.9	15 24.5
			Cost of Sales/Inventory						
			Cost of Sales/Payables						
2.2	2.5	1.9		.8	1.0	1.0	1.9	3.3	3.8
5.5	5.7	5.5	Sales/Working Capital	7.6	4.5	3.9	4.2	5.4	13.3
19.9	13.3	68.0		-15.5	-28.0	7.1	18.2	47.1	-57.3
7.9	8.5	15.8			29.9		27.5	5.5	12.8
(163) 2.6	(156) 4.0	(71) 4.2	EBIT/Interest		(13) 4.2		(10) 4.9	(17) 2.8	(16) 4.6
1.5	2.3	2.6			3.0		2.1	1.9	2.1
13.3	105.3								
(11) 2.3	(14) 14.7		Net Profit + Depr., Dep., Amort./Cur. Mat. L/T/D						
.9	4.0								
.0	.0	.0		.0	.0	.0	.0	.0	.0
.0	.1	.0	Fixed/Worth	.0	.0	.0	.1	.3	.0
.1	.2	.3		.4	.4	.4	.1	.6	.2
1.4	1.5	.6		.1	.3	.1	.7	3.0	1.1
4.6	4.9	2.1	Debt/Worth	1.2	1.1	1.3	1.6	6.5	3.1
8.5	8.7	7.7		UND	5.5	5.1	4.4	12.3	5.3
42.5	69.8	59.2		210.8	70.0	36.8	40.5	80.7	75.4
(201) 18.0	(194) 38.3	(94) 27.4	% Profit Before Taxes/Tangible Net Worth	(15) 29.1	(21) 19.0	(11) 26.1	29.3	(16) 29.6	(16) 45.2
3.6	16.6	9.8		11.7	7.7	10.3	6.1	16.5	17.3
7.9	15.4	15.2		39.7	21.4	14.0	14.6	10.4	15.1
3.0	6.9	7.8	% Profit Before Taxes/Total Assets	13.7	8.1	8.5	6.6	5.2	10.5
.5	2.6	3.3		1.8	4.1	5.8	1.8	3.6	2.5
107.4	134.9	191.2		UND	177.5	153.1	169.6	140.4	197.9
48.3	58.7	69.3	Sales/Net Fixed Assets	154.8	71.0	72.5	69.3	35.5	78.3
19.5	21.8	17.4		6.1	35.3	7.7	30.4	11.5	40.6
.6	.9	1.3		3.6	2.3	1.2	1.4	.7	1.1
.4	.5	.7	Sales/Total Assets	.5	.7	.7	.8	.6	.7
.2	.3	.3		.2	.2	.3	.7	.3	.5
.4	.3	.3			.3			.2	.0
(164) .8	(153) .5	(67) .5	% Depr., Dep., Amort./Sales		(16) .5			(13) .6	(11) .3
1.3	1.0	1.1			.9			2.6	.8
6.4	3.7	4.6							
(29) 11.7	(41) 8.5	(22) 7.0	% Officers', Directors' Owners' Comp/Sales						
27.6	23.9	11.4							
7869059M	3548042M	1396462M	Net Sales ($)	9327M	43822M	45330M	107630M	315569M	874784M
6650051M	7655735M	2779045M	Total Assets ($)	30033M	211738M	128688M	202233M	922733M	1283620M

M = $ thousand MM = $ million

See Pages 9 through 22 for Explanation of Ratios and Data

	Current Data Sorted by Assets						Comparative Historical Data	
Type of Statement								
Unqualified		4	10	20	4	5	42	54
Reviewed			3	1			3	2
Compiled		2	1				2	
Tax Returns	2	4	1				5	9
Other	3	7	17	17	9	13	46	36
	12 (4/1-9/30/13)		111 (10/1/13-3/31/14)				4/1/09-3/31/10	4/1/10-3/31/11
	0-500M	500M-2MM	2-10MM	10-50MM	50-100MM	100-250MM	ALL	ALL
NUMBER OF STATEMENTS	5	17	32	38	13	18	98	101
ASSETS	%	%	%	%	%	%	%	%
Cash & Equivalents		38.1	28.2	34.1	35.1	13.0	27.6	29.1
Trade Receivables (net)		20.3	20.0	18.1	19.4	14.8	15.9	19.9
Inventory		3.9	1.1	1.2	.2	.5	2.2	1.1
All Other Current		9.7	11.6	9.4	9.5	12.1	12.4	12.1
Total Current		72.1	60.9	62.9	64.2	40.4	58.0	62.2
Fixed Assets (net)		7.7	13.8	12.0	9.1	13.5	15.6	14.0
Intangibles (net)		7.1	11.5	11.4	6.2	40.1	17.6	14.9
All Other Non-Current		13.1	13.8	13.8	20.5	6.0	8.8	8.9
Total		100.0	100.0	100.0	100.0	100.0	100.0	100.0
LIABILITIES								
Notes Payable-Short Term		14.0	5.6	2.7	6.9	3.9	8.4	12.2
Cur. Mat.-L.T.D.		27.4	12.7	3.1	4.0	1.9	5.8	3.4
Trade Payables		14.3	9.1	17.2	8.1	7.6	15.3	13.8
Income Taxes Payable		.2	.0	.9	.0	.5	.5	.2
All Other Current		12.2	25.1	21.8	37.5	15.5	18.9	16.4
Total Current		68.0	52.5	45.7	56.5	29.4	48.9	46.1
Long-Term Debt		9.6	27.2	28.8	13.8	63.9	19.6	23.3
Deferred Taxes		.0	.2	.2	.5	1.1	.5	.3
All Other Non-Current		2.8	20.0	5.9	9.0	7.6	6.6	7.4
Net Worth		19.5	.1	19.4	20.1	-2.0	24.3	23.0
Total Liabilties & Net Worth		100.0	100.0	100.0	100.0	100.0	100.0	100.0
INCOME DATA								
Net Sales		100.0	100.0	100.0	100.0	100.0	100.0	100.0
Gross Profit								
Operating Expenses		83.6	87.6	87.2	83.7	90.1	90.2	88.2
Operating Profit		16.4	12.4	12.8	16.3	9.9	9.8	11.8
All Other Expenses (net)		1.5	1.2	1.8	.4	4.0	2.8	2.1
Profit Before Taxes		14.8	11.2	11.0	15.8	5.9	7.0	9.7
RATIOS								
Current		5.5	2.4	2.3	1.3	1.9	1.8	2.7
		1.5	1.2	1.2	1.0	1.4	1.2	1.5
		.9	.9	.9	.8	1.0	.8	1.1
Quick		3.5	2.3	2.2	1.2	1.5	1.5	2.3
		1.2	1.0	1.1	.9	.8	1.0	1.2
		.6	.6	.6	.7	.5	.5	.6
Sales/Receivables		0 UND	1 332.3	15 24.3	26 13.9	14 26.0	4 81.1	7 53.1
		0 999.8	30 12.3	39 9.4	42 8.7	22 16.8	21 17.4	31 11.8
		25 14.6	42 8.7	61 6.0	104 3.5	61 6.0	50 7.2	66 5.5
Cost of Sales/Inventory								
Cost of Sales/Payables								
Sales/Working Capital		2.6	4.8	3.8	6.2	5.0	5.3	3.6
		10.3	13.0	11.1	11.6	14.2	17.0	7.5
		NM	-42.2	-42.3	-26.0	NM	-29.0	64.1
EBIT/Interest		16.6	32.2	54.1		3.6	19.5	24.8
		(10) 4.3	(22) 6.9	(26) 4.4		(17) 2.6	(66) 3.3	(77) 5.5
		3.0	2.4	.8		.3	-.7	1.6
Net Profit + Depr., Dep., Amort./Cur. Mat. L/T/D							25.5	10.3
							(18) 4.7	(10) 4.0
							1.7	2.9
Fixed/Worth		.0	.2	.2	.2	.3	.1	.1
		.0	.9	.9	.3	-.3	.6	.5
		.4	-1.1	-10.6	-2.3	-.1	-1.0	-1.1
Debt/Worth		.4	1.2	1.0	3.1	3.3	1.1	.8
		1.7	9.5	8.5	11.0	-2.4	4.6	3.1
		6.3	-5.3	-48.7	-25.7	-1.5	-4.3	-5.4
% Profit Before Taxes/Tangible Net Worth		81.6	272.2	125.3			87.2	83.6
		(15) 50.0	(19) 49.2	(28) 50.6			(67) 34.0	(71) 43.4
		27.1	22.2	.6			1.9	6.2
% Profit Before Taxes/Total Assets		31.8	31.1	28.0	15.9	13.3	20.3	23.5
		15.8	17.2	5.2	11.4	5.2	5.4	10.7
		6.3	7.0	-.9	4.0	-1.2	-3.3	1.1
Sales/Net Fixed Assets		999.8	113.2	40.7	42.0	29.9	57.7	54.4
		86.8	28.7	23.4	15.7	24.3	15.9	23.0
		15.2	7.9	7.5	7.1	5.4	6.2	8.7
Sales/Total Assets		3.8	4.0	2.2	1.9	2.2	2.5	2.9
		1.5	1.9	1.2	1.3	1.1	1.3	1.4
		.9	1.0	.5	.6	.6	.6	.8
% Depr., Dep., Amort./Sales			.7	.8	.9		1.6	1.0
			(18) 1.1	(27) 1.8	(10) 2.3		(61) 3.1	(64) 2.9
			3.8	3.5	4.5		5.1	5.1
% Officers', Directors' Owners' Comp/Sales							2.1	2.2
							(22) 4.9	(15) 5.5
							10.1	10.2
Net Sales ($)	7935M	122409M	401341M	1630376M	1115514M	3784717M	4537676M	5309381M
Total Assets ($)	1213M	19790M	161354M	966740M	878753M	2847072M	4138907M	3948505M

M = $ thousand MM = $ million

See Pages 9 through 22 for Explanation of Ratios and Data

Comparative Historical Data				Current Data Sorted by Sales					
			Type of Statement						
48	39	43	Unqualified	1	2	3	6	13	18
4	4	4	Reviewed				1	2	1
3	5	3	Compiled	2			1		
5	11	7	Tax Returns	1	1	3	2		
50	66	66	Other	5	7	6	5	9	34
				12 (4/1-9/30/13)			111 (10/1/13-3/31/14)		
4/1/11-3/31/12 ALL	**4/1/12-3/31/13 ALL**	**4/1/13-3/31/14 ALL**		**0-1MM**	**1-3MM**	**3-5MM**	**5-10MM**	**10-25MM**	**25MM & OVER**
110	125	123	**NUMBER OF STATEMENTS**	9	10	12	15	24	53
%	%	%	**ASSETS**	%	%	%	%	%	%
32.6	33.4	31.3	Cash & Equivalents		36.5	40.6	31.9	36.8	24.2
17.7	22.0	17.8	Trade Receivables (net)		10.2	6.0	12.3	24.5	19.9
2.0	1.6	1.3	Inventory		.2	5.5	.9	1.4	.8
6.8	6.6	10.4	All Other Current		26.1	24.2	10.1	6.4	7.7
59.0	63.6	60.9	Total Current		73.0	76.4	55.2	69.1	52.7
14.3	13.5	12.1	Fixed Assets (net)		8.0	7.0	19.4	6.8	14.3
16.2	14.7	14.2	Intangibles (net)		5.2	12.8	13.4	9.4	19.0
10.5	8.1	12.8	All Other Non-Current		13.8	3.8	12.0	14.7	14.0
100.0	100.0	100.0	Total		100.0	100.0	100.0	100.0	100.0
			LIABILITIES						
8.4	5.6	5.6	Notes Payable-Short Term		2.0	6.4	6.1	3.7	4.7
3.0	3.8	9.1	Cur. Mat.-L.T.D.		44.7	1.6	1.3	15.3	4.2
10.5	12.1	11.7	Trade Payables		9.6	16.5	7.6	17.2	11.3
.4	.2	.4	Income Taxes Payable		.0	.1	.0	.1	.8
20.1	18.6	21.4	All Other Current		12.3	21.8	23.6	22.8	20.7
42.4	40.3	48.1	Total Current		68.6	46.5	38.6	59.2	41.7
27.5	31.4	28.2	Long-Term Debt		18.3	15.0	10.0	14.4	48.1
.4	.3	.3	Deferred Taxes		.4	.6	.5	.1	.4
6.8	5.9	10.1	All Other Non-Current		3.8	10.3	15.4	3.2	14.0
22.9	22.0	13.2	Net Worth		8.9	27.7	35.5	23.2	-4.3
100.0	100.0	100.0	Total Liabilities & Net Worth		100.0	100.0	100.0	100.0	100.0
			INCOME DATA						
100.0	100.0	100.0	Net Sales		100.0	100.0	100.0	100.0	100.0
			Gross Profit						
86.9	86.6	86.8	Operating Expenses		77.1	93.0	91.3	85.5	89.1
13.1	13.4	13.2	Operating Profit		22.9	7.0	8.7	14.5	10.9
2.4	3.1	1.8	All Other Expenses (net)		3.7	.5	1.0	1.3	2.3
10.7	10.3	11.4	Profit Before Taxes		19.3	6.5	7.7	13.1	8.7
			RATIOS						
2.6	3.4	2.4			53.4	4.1	2.5	2.8	1.9
1.5	1.7	1.3	Current		7.6	1.7	1.5	1.1	1.2
1.0	1.1	.9			1.0	1.0	.8	.9	.9
2.2	3.1	2.3			24.9	3.7	2.5	2.6	1.6
1.3	1.4	1.0	Quick		1.8	1.4	1.3	1.0	.9
.8	.9	.6			.5	.3	.3	.6	.7
6 66.2	**8** 43.4	**6** 65.5			**0** UND	**0** UND	**9** 41.7	**21** 17.3	**14** 26.3
24 14.9	**28** 13.2	**25** 14.6	Sales/Receivables		**0** UND	**7** 48.9	**39** 9.4	**43** 8.5	**27** 13.3
60 6.1	**60** 6.1	**50** 7.3			**23** 15.8	**32** 11.3	**70** 5.2	**70** 5.2	**55** 6.6
			Cost of Sales/Inventory						
			Cost of Sales/Payables						
4.3	3.5	4.4			2.1	3.3	3.1	4.1	6.3
11.1	7.6	11.1	Sales/Working Capital		6.1	11.5	6.0	12.2	32.5
76.8	80.9	-78.6			78.2	NM	-60.1	-17.9	-78.6
16.0	22.7	17.0						67.4	15.1
(70) 6.7	(86) 5.1	(85) 4.2	EBIT/Interest					(14) 14.2	(44) 3.9
2.5	1.5	1.9						-1.8	1.6
12.2	9.6	16.0							17.4
(20) 6.0	(15) 5.0	(19) 6.3	Net Profit + Depr., Dep., Amort./Cur. Mat. L/T/D						(14) 7.9
2.5	3.0	2.9							3.3
.1	.1	.2			.0	.1	.2	.1	.3
.4	.4	.6	Fixed/Worth		.2	.4	.8	.2	3.2
-52.6	-2.2	-1.1			NM	-.9	-2.5	NM	-.2
.8	.6	.9			.2	1.4	.9	.6	2.1
3.9	2.5	7.2	Debt/Worth		2.0	6.6	1.7	5.8	16.5
-18.5	-7.6	-9.6			NM	-11.3	-14.1	-71.7	-2.1
121.6	83.4	102.8					51.8	191.1	85.0
(81) 37.9	(88) 29.6	(82) 49.3	% Profit Before Taxes/Tangible Net Worth				(11) 38.6	(17) 39.5	(30) 49.6
8.8	3.1	14.7					1.9	6.6	16.3
25.5	27.9	27.1			51.0	12.8	25.9	28.1	25.4
8.9	9.3	10.9	% Profit Before Taxes/Total Assets		17.2	5.7	8.9	15.3	10.9
1.7	.7	2.2			5.8	-.3	.7	.8	3.5
62.1	57.3	63.6			104.4	178.1	42.5	60.7	38.4
25.3	26.7	24.5	Sales/Net Fixed Assets		51.4	28.0	9.3	39.7	24.0
8.7	7.1	8.9			10.6	12.9	4.4	12.3	8.4
2.7	3.3	2.6			3.8	3.6	2.1	2.5	2.8
1.5	1.5	1.5	Sales/Total Assets		1.5	1.7	1.0	1.4	1.8
.7	.8	.7			.9	.6	.4	.7	1.0
.7	1.1	.6					.6	.9	1.1
(73) 1.8	(74) 1.9	(72) 1.6	% Depr., Dep., Amort./Sales				(10) 2.7	(16) 1.3	(34) 2.0
3.9	3.8	3.5					4.1	3.7	3.5
2.7	2.1	5.3							
(15) 4.9	(22) 6.7	(27) 8.1	% Officers', Directors' Owners' Comp/Sales						
17.9	10.7	10.8							
7050844M	**7386141M**	**7062292M**	Net Sales ($)	**5006M**	**21242M**	**48605M**	**98240M**	**393824M**	**6495375M**
5380984M	**5422782M**	**4874922M**	Total Assets ($)	**12634M**	**79400M**	**87226M**	**140199M**	**412040M**	**4143423M**

M = $ thousand MM = $ million

See Pages 9 through 22 for Explanation of Ratios and Data

Current Data Sorted by Assets							Comparative Historical Data	
						Type of Statement		
3	6	10	12	4	6	Unqualified	124	94
1	1					Reviewed	9	5
1	2	1				Compiled	11	11
3	3	3				Tax Returns	19	10
2	5	3	11	10	14	Other	49	31
18 (4/1-9/30/13)		83 (10/1/13-3/31/14)					4/1/09-3/31/10	4/1/10-3/31/11
0-500M	**500M-2MM**	**2-10MM**	**10-50MM**	**50-100MM**	**100-250MM**		**ALL**	**ALL**
10	17	17	23	14	20	**NUMBER OF STATEMENTS**	212	151
%	%	%	%	%	%	**ASSETS**	%	%
60.4	46.2	25.5	17.5	19.4	16.0	Cash & Equivalents	47.5	45.2
15.8	13.0	29.2	15.6	13.3	13.3	Trade Receivables (net)	15.4	14.3
.3	.2	1.9	9.7	18.4	18.6	Inventory	1.2	.8
2.3	6.2	5.0	23.3	10.3	10.6	All Other Current	4.8	7.3
78.8	65.5	61.6	66.1	61.3	58.6	Total Current	69.0	67.5
5.8	18.2	19.6	6.2	9.4	3.4	Fixed Assets (net)	13.5	15.1
.0	3.8	8.2	7.5	7.1	16.9	Intangibles (net)	8.4	9.1
15.4	12.4	10.7	20.2	22.2	21.1	All Other Non-Current	9.1	8.3
100.0	100.0	100.0	100.0	100.0	100.0	Total	100.0	100.0
						LIABILITIES		
22.9	19.3	6.1	15.6	29.9	29.6	Notes Payable-Short Term	17.3	15.4
.6	4.1	1.1	2.5	.2	2.6	Cur. Mat.-L.T.D.	3.6	2.8
7.8	12.7	12.6	5.8	7.9	9.0	Trade Payables	10.3	12.3
.0	.0	.0	.0	.0	.9	Income Taxes Payable	.2	.2
26.3	6.1	24.3	17.1	11.7	11.2	All Other Current	11.0	12.7
57.5	42.2	44.2	41.0	49.7	53.3	Total Current	42.4	43.4
3.9	15.5	11.4	11.0	5.6	5.8	Long-Term Debt	11.4	8.0
.0	.0	.1	.3	.0	.0	Deferred Taxes	.1	.2
3.1	4.4	7.1	5.0	9.3	4.2	All Other Non-Current	7.7	10.7
35.4	37.8	37.2	42.6	35.3	36.6	Net Worth	38.3	37.6
100.0	100.0	100.0	100.0	100.0	100.0	Total Liabilties & Net Worth	100.0	100.0
						INCOME DATA		
100.0	100.0	100.0	100.0	100.0	100.0	Net Sales	100.0	100.0
						Gross Profit		
80.4	82.8	87.4	80.4	82.1	75.8	Operating Expenses	83.1	87.0
19.6	17.2	12.6	19.6	17.9	24.2	Operating Profit	16.9	13.0
3.1	3.3	4.9	10.0	2.8	3.3	All Other Expenses (net)	5.2	3.6
16.6	13.8	7.7	9.6	15.1	20.8	Profit Before Taxes	11.7	9.4
						RATIOS		
3.3	3.5	2.9	3.1	1.5	1.3		3.4	3.1
1.6	1.5	1.6	1.6	1.2	1.1	Current	1.6	1.5
.7	1.0	1.1	1.0	.9	.8		1.1	1.1
3.3	3.2	2.7	1.7	1.2	1.0		3.3	2.9
1.3	1.1	1.6	1.0	.5	.3	Quick	1.5	1.4
.7	.8	1.0	.3	.2	.1		1.1	.9
0 UND	**0** UND	**6** 63.7	**10** 34.8	**10** 35.4	**4** 87.2		**0** UND	**1** 719.0
0 UND	**3** 123.9	**53** 6.9	**20** 18.0	**33** 10.9	**21** 17.8	Sales/Receivables	**3** 114.1	**7** 51.2
4 88.3	**20** 18.5	**174** 2.1	**51** 7.1	**130** 2.8	**79** 4.6		**53** 6.9	**47** 7.8
						Cost of Sales/Inventory		
						Cost of Sales/Payables		
.5	5.9	2.3	1.0	2.3	3.5		1.6	2.0
3.8	10.3	6.5	3.4	5.4	9.8	Sales/Working Capital	4.1	4.7
-21.2	NM	146.7	14.2	-169.8	-4.4		18.5	24.9
	17.2	29.9	42.8	4.9	16.5		16.6	9.0
	(14) 3.5	(12) 4.4	(14) 10.3	(11) 3.6	(19) 4.1	EBIT/Interest	(154) 5.2	(110) 3.2
	.7	1.9	3.3	2.3	2.4		1.7	1.1
							9.9	5.7
						Net Profit + Depr., Dep., Amort./Cur. Mat. L/T/D	(33) 2.8	(21) 3.0
							1.0	1.3
.0	.1	.1	.0	.0	.0		.1	.1
.1	.6	.3	.1	.1	.0	Fixed/Worth	.3	.3
2.7	1.1	.7	.3	.5	.2		1.1	1.4
.5	1.2	.8	.5	1.3	2.0		.6	.7
1.7	2.2	1.3	2.1	2.6	3.9	Debt/Worth	1.8	2.2
NM	5.2	2.1	4.4	6.3	9.0		7.3	6.0
	79.5	53.6	21.5	38.9	37.0		44.8	40.1
	(16) 19.2	(15) 14.8	(22) 9.6	(13) 30.0	(17) 27.3	% Profit Before Taxes/Tangible Net Worth	(182) 20.6	(125) 11.1
	.8	3.5	2.2	17.9	12.5		6.3	2.7
30.8	50.8	18.2	7.4	14.9	11.7		16.9	13.3
10.9	3.1	5.1	3.5	6.2	5.3	% Profit Before Taxes/Total Assets	6.8	3.9
-3.6	.5	-.1	1.0	4.0	1.8		1.7	.5
UND	98.5	81.0	101.4	172.4	152.4		54.3	42.0
26.2	13.9	22.6	37.6	45.2	50.3	Sales/Net Fixed Assets	12.1	12.7
5.4	3.2	2.8	12.3	22.8	20.4		5.8	5.4
3.1	4.1	3.1	.9	1.0	.8		1.3	1.4
1.5	1.1	1.8	.4	.8	.6	Sales/Total Assets	.9	.9
.2	.9	.6	.1	.4	.3		.5	.6
	.4	.4	1.1		.3		.6	.8
	(12) 1.6	1.4	(16) 1.7		(14) 1.3	% Depr., Dep., Amort./Sales	(160) 1.8	(120) 1.7
	4.4	3.3	3.0		3.2		3.1	3.1
	4.3						7.0	8.8
	(11) 7.9					% Officers', Directors' Owners' Comp/Sales	(88) 12.2	(59) 13.9
	10.2						22.5	23.5
9007M	**38740M**	**318698M**	**485472M**	**762238M**	**1936099M**	Net Sales ($)	**4424124M**	**2175828M**
2794M	**18556M**	**90593M**	**652371M**	**1060707M**	**3129799M**	Total Assets ($)	**4543056M**	**2950025M**

M = $ thousand **MM = $ million**

See Pages 9 through 22 for Explanation of Ratios and Data

Comparative Historical Data | **Current Data Sorted by Sales**

4/1/11-3/31/12 ALL	4/1/12-3/31/13 ALL	4/1/13-3/31/14 ALL	Type of Statement	0-1MM	1-3MM	3-5MM	5-10MM	10-25MM	25MM & OVER
119	123	41	Unqualified	6	8	5	3	6	13
8	5	2	Reviewed				2		
8	10	4	Compiled	3					1
15	9	9	Tax Returns	3	1	2	3		
41	37	45	Other	4	6	2	3	6	24
				18 (4/1-9/30/13)			83 (10/1/13-3/31/14)		
191	184	101	NUMBER OF STATEMENTS	16	15	9	11	12	38
%	%	%	**ASSETS**	%	%	%	%	%	%
43.1	45.1	27.9	Cash & Equivalents	46.2	35.5		17.7	19.4	19.7
13.0	14.0	16.7	Trade Receivables (net)	11.9	11.3		38.5	27.4	10.3
3.3	2.6	8.8	Inventory	.2	.0		.1	10.9	19.9
10.0	10.3	10.9	All Other Current	2.6	24.3		6.7	4.3	11.6
69.4	71.9	64.4	Total Current	60.9	71.0		62.9	62.0	61.4
12.7	11.0	10.3	Fixed Assets (net)	17.7	11.4		5.8	7.7	8.9
9.0	6.3	8.1	Intangibles (net)	2.5	2.3		13.2	6.2	13.0
8.9	10.8	17.3	All Other Non-Current	18.9	15.3		18.1	24.2	16.7
100.0	100.0	100.0	Total	100.0	100.0		100.0	100.0	100.0
			LIABILITIES						
18.9	16.9	20.1	Notes Payable-Short Term	27.4	12.6		3.0	17.5	28.0
1.9	1.3	2.0	Cur. Mat.-L.T.D.	1.9	.4		3.4	1.1	1.5
12.5	11.7	9.2	Trade Payables	5.0	14.4		7.9	9.1	9.5
.2	.1	.2	Income Taxes Payable	.0	.0		.0	.1	.5
12.6	10.0	15.5	All Other Current	7.5	16.1		44.0	12.1	9.9
46.2	40.0	47.0	Total Current	41.8	43.4		58.3	40.0	49.4
7.3	7.8	9.4	Long-Term Debt	16.0	10.0		7.7	8.2	4.8
.2	.1	.1	Deferred Taxes	.0	.0		.1	.2	.2
9.2	12.3	5.5	All Other Non-Current	4.5	5.2		7.2	7.3	6.0
37.1	39.7	38.0	Net Worth	37.7	41.4		26.7	44.4	39.7
100.0	100.0	100.0	Total Liabilities & Net Worth	100.0	100.0		100.0	100.0	100.0
			INCOME DATA						
100.0	100.0	100.0	Net Sales	100.0	100.0		100.0	100.0	100.0
			Gross Profit						
86.8	83.9	81.3	Operating Expenses	73.7	72.7		88.7	82.3	83.9
13.2	16.1	18.7	Operating Profit	26.3	27.3		11.3	17.7	16.1
3.4	3.8	5.0	All Other Expenses (net)	8.7	8.6		9.7	2.7	2.7
9.8	12.3	13.7	Profit Before Taxes	17.6	18.7		1.7	15.0	13.4
			RATIOS						
3.1	3.6	2.3	Current	2.1	3.0		5.8	3.0	1.9
1.4	1.6	1.3		1.6	1.2		2.1	1.5	1.2
1.1	1.1	1.0		.5	1.0		.4	.6	1.0
2.7	3.0	1.8	Quick	2.1	1.5		5.8	2.9	1.2
1.2	1.5	1.0		1.4	1.1		1.3	.9	.5
.8	1.0	.3		.4	.5		.4	.4	.2
0 UND	**0** UND	**3** 140.8	Sales/Receivables	**0** UND	**3** 109.0		**18** 20.2	**12** 29.8	**4** 101.2
8 44.3	**7** 53.6	**18** 20.2		**0** UND	**17** 21.8		**42** 8.6	**31** 11.9	**21** 17.7
40 9.2	**36** 10.0	**61** 6.0		**3** 121.5	**27** 13.7		**228** 1.6	**166** 2.2	**54** 6.7
			Cost of Sales/Inventory						
			Cost of Sales/Payables						
1.7	1.3	2.4	Sales/Working Capital	1.0	.3		1.6	1.8	3.4
4.8	3.1	7.0		3.8	7.3		10.3	6.5	8.9
17.2	10.1	290.0		-7.6	29.5		-2.5	-26.2	189.9
12.5	8.3	16.3	EBIT/Interest	11.8	13.0			51.6	17.9
(146) 3.3	(133) 3.2	(76) 4.5		(10) 4.3	(11) 2.3			(10) 6.2	(34) 4.5
1.3	1.2	2.1		1.6	-1.0			3.6	2.1
6.1	5.7	7.0	Net Profit + Depr., Dep., Amort./Cur. Mat. L/T/D						8.9
(35) 1.8	(20) 1.6	(18) 2.7							(10) 5.1
.8	.9	.9							1.5
.0	.0	.0	Fixed/Worth	.0	.0		.0	.0	.0
.2	.2	.1		.1	.1		.1	.1	.1
.8	.7	.6		2.7	.8		.3	.4	.4
.8	.8	.9	Debt/Worth	.9	.8		.3	1.2	.9
2.4	2.2	2.2		2.2	1.4		1.7	1.5	2.5
7.1	6.5	4.6		3.0	2.9		-6.1	3.9	8.6
43.4	48.2	51.9	% Profit Before Taxes/Tangible Net Worth	55.6	22.6			64.5	44.0
(168) 17.7	(173) 15.7	(91) 19.3		(14) 6.9	6.6			20.5	(34) 30.0
3.2	2.4	6.0		3.7	-13.2			7.4	14.3
12.5	13.3	15.1	% Profit Before Taxes/Total Assets	14.6	9.7		19.7	16.0	15.8
3.6	3.9	5.1		2.0	3.6		5.1	6.7	6.3
.6	.7	1.4		.5	-1.6		-4.6	2.8	2.7
55.3	72.0	115.7	Sales/Net Fixed Assets	UND	39.0		468.8	107.4	105.5
14.3	15.3	36.8		14.1	13.0		116.4	34.1	43.6
5.1	5.3	8.8		2.2	2.9		37.6	9.7	17.3
1.2	1.2	1.6	Sales/Total Assets	1.4	1.1		5.1	2.4	1.1
.8	.7	.8		.7	.4		1.9	.8	.8
.5	.4	.3		.1	.1		.4	.2	.5
.7	.7	.7	% Depr., Dep., Amort./Sales		1.3			.5	.6
(152) 1.7	(139) 1.5	(71) 1.6			(12) 1.7			(10) 1.2	(26) 1.7
3.1	2.9	3.2			2.6			2.3	2.7
6.9	7.6	4.6	% Officers', Directors' Owners' Comp/Sales						
(65) 11.3	(67) 11.9	(24) 10.0							
21.4	25.3	20.9							
3692170M	3110982M	3550254M	Net Sales ($)	7008M	28360M	35193M	75550M	214574M	3189569M
5360380M	5328258M	4954820M	Total Assets ($)	21396M	149611M	190532M	113396M	675651M	3804234M

M = $ thousand MM = $ million

See Pages 9 through 22 for Explanation of Ratios and Data

Current Data Sorted by Assets							Comparative Historical Data	
						Type of Statement		
	3	3	10	3	3	Unqualified	31	25
		1			1	Reviewed	1	2
	1		1			Compiled	3	1
2	2	1		1		Tax Returns	6	8
1	1	6	2	2	2	Other	22	15
5 (4/1-9/30/13)			41 (10/1/13-3/31/14)				4/1/09-3/31/10 ALL	4/1/10-3/31/11 ALL
0-500M	500M-2MM	2-10MM	10-50MM	50-100MM	100-250MM			
3	7	11	13	6	6	**NUMBER OF STATEMENTS**	63	51
%	%	%	%	%	%	**ASSETS**	%	%
		15.7	37.6			Cash & Equivalents	30.7	33.5
		14.3	17.5			Trade Receivables (net)	16.5	14.2
		6.4	16.7			Inventory	2.9	4.2
		15.7	11.2			All Other Current	11.1	7.4
		52.2	83.0			Total Current	61.2	59.3
		14.3	6.2			Fixed Assets (net)	13.6	12.1
		14.2	1.0			Intangibles (net)	6.6	6.7
		19.3	9.8			All Other Non-Current	18.6	21.9
		100.0	100.0			Total	100.0	100.0
						LIABILITIES		
		18.2	7.5			Notes Payable-Short Term	8.8	16.4
		11.4	2.7			Cur. Mat.-L.T.D.	1.3	2.7
		4.4	16.8			Trade Payables	11.3	11.9
		.1	.7			Income Taxes Payable	.1	.0
		12.0	13.3			All Other Current	15.4	14.3
		46.1	40.9			Total Current	36.8	45.3
		22.8	8.5			Long-Term Debt	8.1	12.2
		.0	.1			Deferred Taxes	.6	.4
		4.1	2.8			All Other Non-Current	4.1	7.8
		27.0	47.7			Net Worth	50.4	34.3
		100.0	100.0			Total Liabilties & Net Worth	100.0	100.0
						INCOME DATA		
		100.0	100.0			Net Sales	100.0	100.0
						Gross Profit		
		79.4	82.6			Operating Expenses	81.8	87.2
		20.6	17.4			Operating Profit	18.2	12.8
		9.3	4.1			All Other Expenses (net)	3.3	1.9
		11.3	13.3			Profit Before Taxes	14.9	10.9
						RATIOS		
		2.2	4.9				2.9	3.2
		1.2	1.9			Current	1.9	1.5
		.2	1.4				1.1	1.1
		1.1	3.0				2.1	2.1
		.5	1.3			Quick	1.4	1.3
		.1	.4				.5	.6
		0 UND	**10** 34.8				**0** UND	**0** UND
		11 31.8	**41** 8.8			Sales/Receivables	**8** 44.5	**16** 22.5
		40 9.2	**304** 1.2				**81** 4.5	**42** 8.7
						Cost of Sales/Inventory		
						Cost of Sales/Payables		
		3.8	.8				2.4	3.2
		12.7	3.9			Sales/Working Capital	4.5	7.1
		-12.1	6.0				241.0	75.2
							57.6	39.0
						EBIT/Interest	(33) 15.6	(32) 6.6
							2.7	1.0
						Net Profit + Depr., Dep., Amort./Cur. Mat. L/T/D		
		.0	.0				.0	.0
		2.1	.1			Fixed/Worth	.1	.1
		-2.3	.3				.5	1.0
		1.4	.6				.5	.6
		4.7	1.1			Debt/Worth	1.2	1.7
		-16.4	2.9				3.1	3.9
			35.6				80.9	74.0
			13.5			% Profit Before Taxes/Tangible Net Worth	(59) 19.3	(44) 24.6
			5.9				2.0	.7
		15.5	13.4				31.9	36.7
		4.4	6.9			% Profit Before Taxes/Total Assets	6.5	6.5
		-.9	2.4				.5	.1
		137.3	98.8				356.2	136.9
		38.8	48.8			Sales/Net Fixed Assets	39.3	38.0
		2.4	22.8				17.5	14.0
		2.7	1.9				2.0	3.2
		1.4	1.2			Sales/Total Assets	1.0	1.7
		.2	.2				.3	.7
			.2				.6	.5
			(11) .5			% Depr., Dep., Amort./Sales	(35) .9	(36) .9
			.8				1.9	2.2
							3.3	3.4
						% Officers', Directors' Owners' Comp/Sales	(14) 7.3	(12) 10.3
							29.7	27.1
2078M	36214M	80928M	391338M	2432601M	531780M	Net Sales ($)	3077773M	1341641M
845M	8804M	57413M	320860M	410990M	947322M	Total Assets ($)	2654327M	1383849M

M = $ thousand MM = $ million

See Pages 9 through 22 for Explanation of Ratios and Data

Comparative Historical Data | **Current Data Sorted by Sales**

4/1/11-3/31/12 ALL	4/1/12-3/31/13 ALL	4/1/13-3/31/14 ALL	Type of Statement	0-1MM	1-3MM	3-5MM	5-10MM	10-25MM	25MM & OVER
32	28	22	Unqualified		3	3	5	2	9
2		2	Reviewed					1	1
3	3	2	Compiled			2			
13	10	6	Tax Returns	3	1		1		1
17	19	14	Other	3			4	4	3
				5 (4/1-9/30/13)			41 (10/1/13-3/31/14)		
67	60	46	NUMBER OF STATEMENTS	6	4	5	10	7	14
%	%	%	**ASSETS**	%	%	%	%	%	%
30.6	39.6	26.8	Cash & Equivalents				30.3		28.6
20.5	11.8	15.1	Trade Receivables (net)				4.0		17.3
5.4	3.7	7.2	Inventory				10.3		6.6
9.2	7.4	11.5	All Other Current				6.4		14.8
65.6	62.4	60.6	Total Current				50.9		67.3
13.1	13.8	12.7	Fixed Assets (net)				19.1		11.4
8.5	5.9	9.6	Intangibles (net)				9.0		11.1
12.8	17.9	17.1	All Other Non-Current				20.9		10.2
100.0	100.0	100.0	Total				100.0		100.0
			LIABILITIES						
13.4	7.0	12.3	Notes Payable-Short Term				12.1		2.8
4.6	3.0	4.6	Cur. Mat.-L.T.D.				1.8		3.3
10.7	13.8	8.6	Trade Payables				2.8		12.3
.1	.3	.3	Income Taxes Payable				.1		.5
20.6	15.3	13.8	All Other Current				15.8		23.8
49.4	39.2	39.6	Total Current				32.5		42.6
11.8	11.5	17.1	Long-Term Debt				22.9		16.6
.2	.1	.2	Deferred Taxes				.6		.1
8.0	11.0	4.6	All Other Non-Current				1.5		2.8
30.7	38.1	38.6	Net Worth				42.6		37.9
100.0	100.0	100.0	Total Liabilties & Net Worth				100.0		100.0
			INCOME DATA						
100.0	100.0	100.0	Net Sales				100.0		100.0
			Gross Profit						
83.5	84.0	78.5	Operating Expenses				76.6		86.9
16.5	16.0	21.5	Operating Profit				23.4		13.1
2.6	2.5	6.1	All Other Expenses (net)				3.9		1.7
13.9	13.5	15.4	Profit Before Taxes				19.5		11.4
			RATIOS						
2.5	3.2	3.5					2.9		2.4
1.5	1.8	1.8	Current				1.5		1.8
1.1	1.1	1.1					.6		1.1
2.2	2.6	2.8					2.7		1.7
1.2	1.5	1.1	Quick				1.0		1.1
.6	.6	.4					.3		.6
0 999.8	1 631.9	0 UND					0 UND		9 42.6
14 27.0	13 28.9	19 19.7	Sales/Receivables				2 147.8		23 15.8
64 5.7	41 8.8	72 5.1					48 7.6		64 5.7
			Cost of Sales/Inventory						
			Cost of Sales/Payables						
3.6	4.0	2.6					3.4		3.8
6.3	6.8	7.5	Sales/Working Capital				11.2		6.0
26.4	104.2	145.1					-9.9		NM
28.3	211.3	51.8							
(42) 6.6	(32) 8.4	(27) 7.1	EBIT/Interest						
2.9	3.1	3.1							
			Net Profit + Depr., Dep., Amort./Cur. Mat. L/T/D						
.0	.0	.0					.0		.1
.1	.1	.1	Fixed/Worth				.5		.2
1.3	1.3	5.9					NM		-8.2
.5	.6	.5					.5		.6
1.8	1.6	1.6	Debt/Worth				1.6		1.2
6.5	5.5	NM					NM		-12.9
78.4	93.1	47.8							79.9
(58) 23.6	(50) 18.9	(35) 17.5	% Profit Before Taxes/Tangible Net Worth						(10) 33.5
5.1	.0	7.9							8.8
31.3	61.4	25.2					103.1		27.9
10.1	7.8	8.4	% Profit Before Taxes/Total Assets				7.6		13.5
1.5	-.1	2.3					2.1		2.7
159.9	149.0	142.2					153.2		52.1
45.3	42.8	43.4	Sales/Net Fixed Assets				41.6		26.6
14.4	13.5	19.1					2.2		18.7
2.7	3.5	2.7					3.5		2.2
1.4	1.6	1.3	Sales/Total Assets				1.1		1.3
.7	1.0	.3					.3		.9
.5	.4	.4							.4
(47) 1.0	(41) .9	(32) .8	% Depr., Dep., Amort./Sales						(11) .8
2.2	2.2	2.0							1.7
2.6	3.9	7.3							
(12) 7.9	(13) 18.6	(11) 13.9	% Officers', Directors' Owners' Comp/Sales						
17.2	30.5	36.6							
1888499M	1858477M	3474939M	Net Sales ($)	3616M	7190M	20912M	70657M	96809M	3275755M
2090975M	1955004M	1746234M	Total Assets ($)	14780M	36152M	66992M	193558M	310295M	1124457M

M = $ thousand MM = $ million

See Pages 9 through 22 for Explanation of Ratios and Data

Current Data Sorted by Assets							Comparative Historical Data	
						Type of Statement		
	3	14	13	3	7	Unqualified	62	55
1	1		2			Reviewed	3	5
2				1		Compiled	4	2
4	6	2	1	1		Tax Returns	15	26
4	7	11	12	1	2	Other	32	51
16 (4/1-9/30/13)			82 (10/1/13-3/31/14)				4/1/09-3/31/10 ALL	4/1/10-3/31/11 ALL
0-500M	**500M-2MM**	**2-10MM**	**10-50MM**	**50-100MM**	**100-250MM**			
11	17	27	28	6	9	**NUMBER OF STATEMENTS**	116	139
%	%	%	%	%	%	**ASSETS**	%	%
44.7	31.5	31.0	37.3			Cash & Equivalents	33.2	38.0
7.1	19.2	14.3	19.3			Trade Receivables (net)	17.2	13.2
.0	.0	.2	1.9			Inventory	2.3	2.1
4.3	3.1	7.8	6.4			All Other Current	9.0	13.0
56.0	53.9	53.3	64.9			Total Current	61.7	66.3
31.2	13.3	13.1	11.7			Fixed Assets (net)	10.8	12.5
6.6	16.3	4.2	10.9			Intangibles (net)	6.7	5.0
6.2	16.4	29.4	12.5			All Other Non-Current	20.7	16.3
100.0	100.0	100.0	100.0			Total	100.0	100.0
						LIABILITIES		
20.2	3.5	2.5	1.7			Notes Payable-Short Term	9.8	6.7
.7	4.2	.3	2.3			Cur. Mat.-L.T.D.	2.9	1.9
2.7	9.8	10.8	16.3			Trade Payables	12.8	13.5
.0	.0	.0	.1			Income Taxes Payable	.4	.4
7.4	11.3	16.0	17.3			All Other Current	17.4	20.8
31.1	28.9	29.6	37.7			Total Current	43.3	43.3
11.3	11.8	8.5	12.1			Long-Term Debt	11.5	11.3
.0	.0	.0	.1			Deferred Taxes	.3	.0
8.8	4.9	6.4	6.0			All Other Non-Current	5.2	6.5
48.9	54.5	55.5	44.1			Net Worth	39.6	38.8
100.0	100.0	100.0	100.0			Total Liabilties & Net Worth	100.0	100.0
						INCOME DATA		
100.0	100.0	100.0	100.0			Net Sales	100.0	100.0
						Gross Profit		
86.4	88.1	86.8	83.3			Operating Expenses	83.4	87.2
13.6	11.9	13.2	16.7			Operating Profit	16.6	12.8
.3	3.3	-.8	2.1			All Other Expenses (net)	2.9	1.4
13.4	8.7	14.0	14.6			Profit Before Taxes	13.7	11.4
						RATIOS		
5.3	6.0	3.3	3.0				3.3	2.8
1.2	2.0	2.0	1.7			Current	1.7	1.7
.7	.4	1.2	1.2				1.0	1.1
5.3	6.0	3.3	2.5				2.9	2.4
1.2	2.0	1.4	1.6			Quick	1.4	1.5
.3	.4	.8	1.0				.6	.6
0 UND	0 UND	0 UND	7 49.5				0 UND	0 UND
0 UND	9 41.3	13 29.1	27 13.3			Sales/Receivables	15 23.7	10 37.4
0 UND	35 10.5	33 11.0	69 5.3				40 9.1	34 10.8
						Cost of Sales/Inventory		
						Cost of Sales/Payables		
14.9	5.6	5.0	2.9				3.1	2.5
42.2	23.2	11.4	8.5			Sales/Working Capital	7.9	9.5
-95.7	-90.4	69.5	59.1				NM	60.8
		138.8	340.1				32.9	53.7
		(14) 17.0	(20) 33.4			EBIT/Interest	(68) 10.6	(76) 6.7
		2.6	7.3				1.2	1.9
						Net Profit + Depr., Dep., Amort./Cur. Mat. L/T/D		
.0	.0	.0	.0				.0	.0
.3	.0	.0	.1			Fixed/Worth	.1	.1
-6.8	1.3	.1	.5				.6	.4
.2	.2	.4	.4				.4	.4
1.0	.6	.7	1.4			Debt/Worth	1.2	1.3
-12.0	5.9	1.3	4.2				10.2	7.4
	81.4	123.5	54.1				61.4	44.7
	(14) 15.7	(25) 29.2	(24) 18.6			% Profit Before Taxes/Tangible Net Worth	(93) 23.2	(118) 18.1
	-3.5	4.5	7.6				4.0	1.0
230.8	94.5	69.8	21.3				28.2	24.7
12.9	5.7	12.9	9.5			% Profit Before Taxes/Total Assets	8.6	5.9
.0	.4	2.1	3.5				.2	.5
UND	UND	601.6	276.6				391.5	737.1
56.8	129.4	68.4	55.9			Sales/Net Fixed Assets	67.9	83.8
7.0	21.9	23.6	22.2				22.9	25.3
11.4	7.8	3.7	2.9				3.9	5.6
6.7	4.5	2.2	1.7			Sales/Total Assets	1.5	1.9
1.9	.5	1.5	.5				.6	.6
		.2	.4				.3	.4
		(18) .4	(12) .8			% Depr., Dep., Amort./Sales	(73) .8	(84) .8
		1.1	1.1				2.3	1.9
							4.1	3.7
						% Officers', Directors' Owners' Comp/Sales	(22) 8.2	(33) 16.0
							27.3	23.3
20199M	96891M	367698M	1337920M	1344813M	1545980M	Net Sales ($)	5139257M	6257429M
1747M	20130M	143737M	610178M	419370M	1474239M	Total Assets ($)	3688502M	4036662M

M = $ thousand MM = $ million

See Pages 9 through 22 for Explanation of Ratios and Data

Comparative Historical Data | **Current Data Sorted by Sales**

			Type of Statement						
45	48	40	Unqualified	1	2	3	6	11	17
5	6	4	Reviewed	1	1	1			1
2	1	3	Compiled	2					1
20	18	14	Tax Returns	4	2	1	3	2	2
42	28	37	Other	7	3	2	6	6	13
4/1/11-3/31/12	**4/1/12-3/31/13**	**4/1/13-3/31/14**		**16 (4/1-9/30/13)**			**82 (10/1/13-3/31/14)**		
ALL	**ALL**	**ALL**		**0-1MM**	**1-3MM**	**3-5MM**	**5-10MM**	**10-25MM**	**25MM & OVER**
114	101	98	**NUMBER OF STATEMENTS**	15	8	7	15	19	34
%	%	%	**ASSETS**	%	%	%	%	%	%
34.3	38.3	35.7	Cash & Equivalents	37.5			23.5	42.2	37.4
15.1	15.6	14.7	Trade Receivables (net)	5.4			9.5	26.5	15.2
3.6	4.0	1.3	Inventory	.0			.5	1.5	2.5
9.5	7.9	6.2	All Other Current	1.3			8.6	7.0	6.5
62.5	65.8	57.9	Total Current	44.2			42.0	77.3	61.7
12.9	7.9	13.6	Fixed Assets (net)	30.8			12.2	6.1	12.3
5.0	5.3	9.6	Intangibles (net)	11.8			19.4	1.9	10.3
19.6	20.9	18.9	All Other Non-Current	13.2			26.3	14.8	15.7
100.0	100.0	100.0	Total	100.0			100.0	100.0	100.0
			LIABILITIES						
10.0	7.5	5.4	Notes Payable-Short Term	9.9			4.9	.9	5.1
1.4	1.9	1.6	Cur. Mat.-L.T.D.	1.1			.7	3.3	.9
12.1	12.6	11.4	Trade Payables	3.5			9.3	19.1	12.5
.6	.5	.1	Income Taxes Payable	.0			.0	.0	.1
17.7	19.1	15.2	All Other Current	6.2			17.7	18.4	20.1
41.9	41.7	33.7	Total Current	20.7			32.6	41.6	38.7
8.6	9.2	11.0	Long-Term Debt	18.0			17.0	5.4	7.6
.0	.0	.1	Deferred Taxes	.0			.0	.1	.3
7.3	7.1	6.6	All Other Non-Current	10.8			3.3	6.0	7.7
42.2	42.0	48.5	Net Worth	50.4			47.1	46.9	45.7
100.0	100.0	100.0	Total Liabilties & Net Worth	100.0			100.0	100.0	100.0
			INCOME DATA						
100.0	100.0	100.0	Net Sales	100.0			100.0	100.0	100.0
			Gross Profit						
84.5	83.5	85.1	Operating Expenses	79.6			83.1	88.8	88.1
15.5	16.5	14.9	Operating Profit	20.4			16.9	11.2	11.9
2.8	1.5	.9	All Other Expenses (net)	7.9			-.3	.1	-1.2
12.7	15.0	13.9	Profit Before Taxes	12.5			17.2	11.1	13.1
			RATIOS						
2.8	2.9	3.5		4.3			3.3	3.5	2.5
1.6	1.7	1.8	Current	1.2			1.2	2.0	1.7
1.0	1.2	1.1		.7			.3	1.5	1.3
2.5	2.5	3.4		4.3			2.3	3.4	2.4
1.4	1.5	1.5	Quick	1.2			1.2	1.8	1.6
.6	.7	.8		.7			.3	1.1	1.0
0 UND	**0** UND	**0** UND		**0** UND			**0** UND	**8** 48.3	**1** 339.7
9 40.9	**11** 32.4	**9** 39.0	Sales/Receivables	**0** UND			**9** 41.3	**18** 20.2	**17** 20.9
37 9.9	**39** 9.4	**35** 10.3		**26** 13.8			**39** 9.4	**33** 11.0	**34** 10.6
			Cost of Sales/Inventory						
			Cost of Sales/Payables						
4.3	3.2	4.1		5.4			6.9	4.6	3.4
12.1	9.1	11.3	Sales/Working Capital	41.4			11.1	12.7	8.5
348.2	38.0	89.5		-141.3			-12.9	27.2	39.5
40.9	51.3	68.4					76.6	50.3	221.4
(56) 8.2	(61) 9.9	(57) 16.5	EBIT/Interest				(10) 13.9	(10) 13.1	(23) 42.7
1.6	2.4	2.4					2.9	7.8	15.7
4.6									
(12) 1.7			Net Profit + Depr., Dep., Amort./Cur. Mat. L/T/D						
.3									
.0	.0	.0		.0			.0	.0	.0
.1	.0	.1	Fixed/Worth	.1			.2	.0	.1
.4	.1	.5		3.7			-24.1	.1	.7
.4	.5	.3		.3			.3	.4	.4
1.2	1.2	1.1	Debt/Worth	1.5			2.0	.7	1.4
4.5	4.2	4.0		8.5			-143.7	1.3	3.4
71.4	83.9	99.9		335.0			129.8	119.4	70.5
(96) 27.6	(94) 30.2	(84) 20.5	% Profit Before Taxes/Tangible Net Worth	(12) 30.3			(11) 76.4	(18) 17.2	(30) 23.3
5.9	4.1	6.9		1.8			5.0	6.7	13.1
48.2	35.7	41.3		172.6			76.8	69.8	25.6
9.9	11.2	9.8	% Profit Before Taxes/Total Assets	3.7			21.9	10.9	11.5
1.8	1.9	2.0		.0			1.1	3.2	5.8
UND	847.3	381.8		UND			169.7	609.3	310.9
85.7	85.8	59.9	Sales/Net Fixed Assets	56.8			30.5	83.6	51.6
20.4	24.0	22.5		1.4			21.9	54.4	21.9
5.1	3.8	4.6		6.7			4.0	7.5	4.0
1.9	2.0	2.2	Sales/Total Assets	1.4			2.2	3.5	2.5
.7	.8	.6		.4			1.1	1.8	.8
.5	.4	.3					.3	.1	.4
(63) .9	(60) .8	(50) .8	% Depr., Dep., Amort./Sales				(11) 1.1	(10) .4	(18) .8
2.2	1.3	1.5					1.8	1.0	1.1
2.9	6.3	6.6							
(22) 9.1	(26) 11.8	(15) 10.4	% Officers', Directors' Owners' Comp/Sales						
21.8	23.1	27.9							
4456691M	**3691351M**	**4713501M**	Net Sales ($)	**6677M**	**20482M**	**27714M**	**104488M**	**295739M**	**4258401M**
3188323M	**2773274M**	**2669401M**	Total Assets ($)	**21471M**	**63041M**	**115134M**	**201408M**	**124678M**	**2143669M**

M = $ thousand MM = $ million

See Pages 9 through 22 for Explanation of Ratios and Data

Current Data Sorted by Assets							Comparative Historical Data	
						Type of Statement		
	1	3	7	2	1	Unqualified	14	16
		1				Reviewed	2	4
	1		2			Compiled	2	5
1		2		1		Tax Returns	6	7
	2		4	1	1	Other	19	15
	4 (4/1-9/30/13)		26 (10/1/13-3/31/14)				4/1/09-3/31/10 ALL	4/1/10-3/31/11 ALL
0-500M	500M-2MM	2-10MM	10-50MM	50-100MM	100-250MM			
1	4	6	13	4	2	**NUMBER OF STATEMENTS**	43	47
%	%	%	%	%	%	**ASSETS**	%	%
			51.9			Cash & Equivalents	28.6	23.6
			17.7			Trade Receivables (net)	21.9	24.3
			4.3			Inventory	8.9	9.5
			6.8			All Other Current	9.1	10.3
			80.8			Total Current	68.5	67.8
			10.0			Fixed Assets (net)	22.5	15.3
			2.2			Intangibles (net)	1.7	2.9
			7.0			All Other Non-Current	7.2	14.0
			100.0			Total	100.0	100.0
						LIABILITIES		
			3.9			Notes Payable-Short Term	13.2	17.8
			4.8			Cur. Mat.-L.T.D.	1.6	1.3
			15.1			Trade Payables	8.5	9.8
			.2			Income Taxes Payable	.1	.2
			21.5			All Other Current	16.7	12.5
			45.6			Total Current	40.1	41.6
			4.7			Long-Term Debt	17.2	12.8
			.0			Deferred Taxes	.0	.2
			2.9			All Other Non-Current	4.1	4.7
			46.9			Net Worth	38.6	40.7
			100.0			Total Liabilties & Net Worth	100.0	100.0
						INCOME DATA		
			100.0			Net Sales	100.0	100.0
						Gross Profit		
			82.1			Operating Expenses	70.3	73.9
			17.9			Operating Profit	29.7	26.1
			2.4			All Other Expenses (net)	8.6	4.7
			15.5			Profit Before Taxes	21.0	21.4
						RATIOS		
			3.8				5.1	3.6
			1.8			Current	1.4	1.3
			1.3				1.0	1.1
			2.8				3.4	3.4
			1.4			Quick	1.0	1.1
			1.1				.5	.6
			9 42.8				**0** UND	**7** 56.0
			18 20.4			Sales/Receivables	**22** 16.9	**35** 10.5
			215 1.7				**66** 5.5	**94** 3.9
						Cost of Sales/Inventory		
						Cost of Sales/Payables		
			1.2				1.4	1.7
			2.5			Sales/Working Capital	7.1	6.4
			6.7				999.8	65.9
			151.5				16.5	32.0
			(10) 3.7			EBIT/Interest	(24) 7.8	(33) 7.0
			1.4				3.7	2.2
						Net Profit + Depr., Dep., Amort./Cur. Mat. L/T/D		
			.0				.0	.0
			.1			Fixed/Worth	.2	.1
			.3				1.0	.6
			.3				.5	.5
			1.6			Debt/Worth	2.4	1.7
			7.5				6.2	7.0
			52.4				50.2	61.7
			22.0			% Profit Before Taxes/Tangible Net Worth	(40) 24.1	(43) 29.4
			4.0				8.6	8.3
			21.8				17.4	23.9
			5.2			% Profit Before Taxes/Total Assets	9.5	8.6
			1.0				2.2	1.7
			75.1				590.4	626.3
			23.6			Sales/Net Fixed Assets	38.8	42.5
			14.5				.9	6.0
			1.7				2.9	2.8
			.5			Sales/Total Assets	.5	.8
			.4				.1	.2
			.5				.6	.4
			(11) 1.0			% Depr., Dep., Amort./Sales	(29) 1.6	(30) 1.2
			2.3				8.8	3.2
								.4
						% Officers', Directors' Owners' Comp/Sales		(10) 1.6
								12.9
440M	41017M	173129M	408272M	657843M	2564547M	Net Sales ($)	2411412M	1919101M
75M	6527M	36262M	333861M	292320M	341718M	Total Assets ($)	1137772M	1314870M

M = $ thousand MM = $ million

See Pages 9 through 22 for Explanation of Ratios and Data

Comparative Historical Data | Current Data Sorted by Sales

DATA NOT AVAILABLE (0-1MM and 1-3MM columns)

4/1/11-3/31/12 ALL	4/1/12-3/31/13 ALL	4/1/13-3/31/14 ALL		0-1MM	1-3MM	3-5MM	5-10MM	10-25MM	25MM & OVER
			Type of Statement						
17	11	14	Unqualified	1			1	8	4
1	2	1	Reviewed				1		
6	3	3	Compiled			1		1	1
5	4	4	Tax Returns	1				1	2
17	12	8	Other	1		1		1	5
				4 (4/1-9/30/13)		26 (10/1/13-3/31/14)			
46	32	30	**NUMBER OF STATEMENTS**	3		2	2	11	12
%	%	%	**ASSETS**	%	%	%	%	%	%
32.6	27.1	33.1	Cash & Equivalents					35.6	26.9
21.4	19.2	22.8	Trade Receivables (net)					19.4	32.7
7.0	9.3	9.3	Inventory					5.6	17.4
6.9	4.6	6.9	All Other Current					7.1	8.2
68.0	60.2	72.1	Total Current					67.7	85.1
17.5	17.1	13.4	Fixed Assets (net)					15.6	8.5
3.5	6.5	4.5	Intangibles (net)					8.5	.4
10.9	16.2	10.0	All Other Non-Current					8.1	6.0
100.0	100.0	100.0	Total					100.0	100.0
			LIABILITIES						
12.9	9.9	9.2	Notes Payable-Short Term					7.2	9.6
3.0	2.2	3.9	Cur. Mat.-L.T.D.					2.5	4.5
15.8	14.9	15.6	Trade Payables					14.1	22.9
.3	.0	.4	Income Taxes Payable					1.1	.0
10.4	7.8	17.3	All Other Current					16.3	11.4
42.4	34.8	46.3	Total Current					41.3	48.4
16.4	13.0	4.7	Long-Term Debt					2.5	4.7
1.2	.4	.6	Deferred Taxes					1.5	.0
3.3	4.9	3.9	All Other Non-Current					5.9	1.7
36.7	46.9	44.6	Net Worth					48.9	45.2
100.0	100.0	100.0	Total Liabilties & Net Worth					100.0	100.0
			INCOME DATA						
100.0	100.0	100.0	Net Sales					100.0	100.0
			Gross Profit						
82.0	78.5	83.1	Operating Expenses					83.7	95.2
18.0	21.5	16.9	Operating Profit					16.3	4.8
4.5	1.3	3.8	All Other Expenses (net)					.7	.4
13.5	20.2	13.0	Profit Before Taxes					15.5	4.5
			RATIOS						
3.2	4.3	3.4						3.8	3.6
1.9	1.8	1.6	Current					1.8	1.6
1.0	1.2	1.0						.9	1.3
2.5	2.3	2.0						2.0	3.3
1.5	1.3	1.1	Quick					1.0	1.3
.6	.7	.7						.7	.6
0 UND	**2** 172.6	**10** 36.4						**6** 60.0	**14** 25.9
38 9.5	**29** 12.8	**19** 18.9	Sales/Receivables					**18** 20.4	**23** 16.1
87 4.2	**47** 7.8	**39** 9.4						**33** 10.9	**39** 9.3
			Cost of Sales/Inventory						
			Cost of Sales/Payables						
1.6	1.5	2.3						2.5	4.7
5.7	4.6	6.7	Sales/Working Capital					7.7	21.8
143.1	34.2	41.2						-83.9	43.5
43.7	49.8	71.3							74.5
(33) 4.0	(27) 10.1	(25) 6.3	EBIT/Interest						9.7
1.6	3.5	2.1							2.4
			Net Profit + Depr., Dep., Amort./Cur. Mat. L/T/D						
.0	.1	.0						.0	.0
.2	.2	.1	Fixed/Worth					.1	.1
1.4	1.2	.4						.6	.3
.6	.4	.5						.2	.5
2.6	1.4	1.7	Debt/Worth					1.6	1.6
7.9	4.7	8.9						17.2	3.1
54.6	65.8	54.3						49.6	55.1
(42) 33.0	(31) 27.1	(29) 17.2	% Profit Before Taxes/Tangible Net Worth					(10) 19.6	32.9
8.5	9.7	7.0						13.8	3.6
19.8	32.1	16.4						14.8	19.4
7.0	8.9	6.7	% Profit Before Taxes/Total Assets					6.6	10.9
1.3	1.7	1.1						5.0	.6
448.5	113.9	526.2						85.2	999.8
24.9	30.1	35.1	Sales/Net Fixed Assets					22.6	135.0
6.5	4.3	12.2						13.1	22.3
3.4	3.1	6.3						4.2	8.0
.9	.8	1.7	Sales/Total Assets					.9	6.1
.3	.2	.4						.4	1.9
.5	.2	.2							
(29) 1.4	(23) 1.1	(23) 1.2	% Depr., Dep., Amort./Sales						
3.0	3.2	2.6							
.5									
(11) 2.0			% Officers', Directors' Owners' Comp/Sales						
6.2									
4248282M	5245982M	3845248M	Net Sales ($)	784M		8168M	16801M	190766M	3628729M
1231965M	1139219M	1010763M	Total Assets ($)	3071M		41884M	44833M	275436M	645539M

M = $ thousand MM = $ million

See Pages 9 through 22 for Explanation of Ratios and Data

Current Data Sorted by Assets							Comparative Historical Data	
						Type of Statement		
1	2	5	4	8	8	Unqualified	43	36
		3	3		1	Reviewed	13	7
1	2	4	2			Compiled	9	9
11	14	11	1			Tax Returns	26	39
11	16	32	35	11	7	Other	74	81
12 (4/1-9/30/13)			181 (10/1/13-3/31/14)				4/1/09-3/31/10	4/1/10-3/31/11
0-500M	**500M-2MM**	**2-10MM**	**10-50MM**	**50-100MM**	**100-250MM**		**ALL**	**ALL**
24	34	55	45	19	16	**NUMBER OF STATEMENTS**	165	172
%	%	%	%	%	%	**ASSETS**	%	%
38.1	18.4	11.6	13.8	8.2	20.1	Cash & Equivalents	14.6	15.4
5.9	8.4	17.2	32.9	36.9	29.3	Trade Receivables (net)	13.3	12.2
1.2	2.6	2.1	3.2	.2	1.9	Inventory	3.3	3.7
9.8	7.4	5.6	3.3	1.7	7.2	All Other Current	9.4	10.4
55.1	36.7	36.5	53.2	47.1	58.5	Total Current	40.6	41.7
20.9	37.3	38.1	16.4	13.3	15.7	Fixed Assets (net)	26.7	30.0
9.3	6.7	3.7	5.4	5.9	8.2	Intangibles (net)	2.5	5.9
14.7	19.2	21.8	25.0	33.8	17.6	All Other Non-Current	30.1	22.4
100.0	100.0	100.0	100.0	100.0	100.0	Total	100.0	100.0
						LIABILITIES		
11.6	8.3	11.6	20.8	19.4	25.0	Notes Payable-Short Term	14.8	12.0
.1	1.7	6.5	1.1	.9	5.3	Cur. Mat.-L.T.D.	1.9	2.7
6.8	7.1	4.7	2.5	7.2	2.6	Trade Payables	5.3	5.2
.2	.0	.2	.1	.0	.0	Income Taxes Payable	.1	.1
36.8	12.7	9.2	9.3	2.4	2.5	All Other Current	8.6	11.7
55.5	29.7	32.1	33.8	29.8	35.3	Total Current	30.7	31.8
9.7	21.4	27.1	14.3	19.3	26.4	Long-Term Debt	22.6	25.7
.0	.0	.4	.3	.0	.3	Deferred Taxes	.0	.1
7.9	6.9	8.0	3.4	.7	9.0	All Other Non-Current	4.9	3.8
27.0	42.1	32.4	48.1	50.2	29.0	Net Worth	41.8	38.6
100.0	100.0	100.0	100.0	100.0	100.0	Total Liabilties & Net Worth	100.0	100.0
						INCOME DATA		
100.0	100.0	100.0	100.0	100.0	100.0	Net Sales	100.0	100.0
						Gross Profit		
75.1	66.7	62.8	55.2	51.5	52.6	Operating Expenses	65.9	65.6
24.9	33.3	37.2	44.8	48.5	47.4	Operating Profit	34.1	34.4
2.9	5.3	16.0	11.4	17.2	26.6	All Other Expenses (net)	13.6	12.5
22.0	28.0	21.2	33.4	31.2	20.8	Profit Before Taxes	20.5	21.9
						RATIOS		
6.7	3.3	2.3	2.8	3.9	6.0		3.8	2.8
1.9	1.2	1.3	1.6	1.6	2.0	Current	1.4	1.3
.4	.3	.3	.8	.3	1.3		.5	.5
4.2	2.7	1.8	2.4	3.9	3.4		2.9	2.1
1.2	.8	.9	1.3	1.6	1.4	Quick	1.0	.8
.2	.3	.3	.6	.1	.6		.2	.2
0 UND	**0** UND	**0** UND	**0** 999.8	**0** UND	**14** 25.5		**0** UND	**0** UND
0 UND	**0** UND	**0** UND	**54** 6.8	**35** 10.3	**62** 5.9	Sales/Receivables	**2** 203.3	**1** 276.2
0 UND	**0** UND	**25** 14.8	**1825** .2	**2000** .1	**912** .4		**41** 9.0	**34** 10.6
						Cost of Sales/Inventory		
						Cost of Sales/Payables		
6.1	2.8	2.0	.3	.2	.2		2.0	2.0
58.7	31.6	193.8	1.7	2.3	.4	Sales/Working Capital	9.5	14.8
-19.8	-4.2	-5.7	-68.5	-1.9	5.9		-7.8	-10.5
	13.1	13.8	16.6				25.3	17.2
	(16) 7.9	(26) 3.9	(27) 5.9			EBIT/Interest	(84) 3.7	(100) 4.2
	2.3	.8	2.2				1.2	2.1
						Net Profit + Depr., Dep., Amort./Cur. Mat. L/T/D		
.0	.0	.0	.0	.0	.0		.0	.0
.1	1.1	.6	.0	.0	.0	Fixed/Worth	.1	.5
4.7	3.7	8.6	1.0	.2	NM		2.1	3.5
.2	.3	.9	.3	.6	1.8		.3	.5
1.8	1.5	2.4	1.5	1.4	5.6	Debt/Worth	1.7	1.7
-14.0	7.1	16.6	4.5	2.3	NM		8.1	11.1
682.0	53.7	50.1	29.3	9.6	13.3		37.9	49.5
(17) 111.9	(28) 19.9	(47) 18.8	(39) 11.6	(18) 5.1	(12) 8.8	% Profit Before Taxes/Tangible Net Worth	(143) 9.5	(144) 15.6
18.9	7.8	2.4	2.5	.8	4.0		1.3	3.0
197.4	23.7	10.3	10.2	5.2	4.6		11.1	19.8
70.7	6.3	3.1	5.1	3.0	2.4	% Profit Before Taxes/Total Assets	3.6	4.9
2.9	1.9	.3	1.6	.6	-.3		.6	1.4
UND	UND	999.8	UND	UND	UND		UND	724.1
123.6	10.0	17.8	53.3	UND	232.6	Sales/Net Fixed Assets	30.7	21.5
8.7	.2	.2	4.2	4.8	2.3		1.0	.6
18.7	2.1	1.1	.6	.2	.4		1.5	1.7
3.7	.6	.3	.1	.1	.1	Sales/Total Assets	.2	.4
.7	.1	.1	.1	.1	.1		.1	.1
.3	3.0	1.3	.6				.7	.9
(12) 1.0	(17) 9.3	(29) 7.1	(20) 1.3			% Depr., Dep., Amort./Sales	(89) 2.4	(101) 3.5
8.0	18.9	22.7	9.4				17.6	16.3
9.4							3.9	4.8
(12) 22.0						% Officers', Directors' Owners' Comp/Sales	(18) 9.6	(16) 10.4
41.2							22.9	25.3
47609M	46367M	354141M	2170879M	345389M	1120489M	Net Sales ($)	2739279M	4274657M
5498M	39994M	253665M	1125560M	1307414M	2521782M	Total Assets ($)	4794079M	4217115M

M = $ thousand MM = $ million

See Pages 9 through 22 for Explanation of Ratios and Data

Comparative Historical Data				Current Data Sorted by Sales					
			Type of Statement						
30	27	28	Unqualified		6	5	7	6	4
14	10	7	Reviewed	1	1		1	2	2
10	7	9	Compiled	4	3	1			1
46	29	37	Tax Returns	23	11	1	1		1
82	78	112	Other	34	23	17	13	15	10
4/1/11-3/31/12	4/1/12-3/31/13	4/1/13-3/31/14		12 (4/1-9/30/13)		181 (10/1/13-3/31/14)			
ALL	ALL	ALL		0-1MM	1-3MM	3-5MM	5-10MM	10-25MM	25MM & OVER
182	151	193	**NUMBER OF STATEMENTS**	62	44	24	22	23	18
%	%	%	**ASSETS**	%	%	%	%	%	%
20.2	15.5	17.0	Cash & Equivalents	14.0	19.2	11.6	19.9	17.3	24.8
14.9	17.2	20.9	Trade Receivables (net)	10.1	24.2	28.1	29.4	27.9	20.8
3.7	2.6	2.2	Inventory	.0	2.7	2.8	2.2	2.2	7.2
8.3	7.9	5.6	All Other Current	4.0	5.1	10.4	6.8	7.0	2.9
47.1	43.2	45.6	Total Current	28.1	51.3	52.9	58.3	54.4	55.7
23.6	24.6	26.5	Fixed Assets (net)	49.1	14.3	16.5	10.8	14.5	25.9
4.9	5.9	5.9	Intangibles (net)	6.0	2.5	4.3	13.8	2.5	11.1
24.4	26.3	22.0	All Other Non-Current	16.8	32.0	26.4	17.1	28.7	7.3
100.0	100.0	100.0	Total	100.0	100.0	100.0	100.0	100.0	100.0
			LIABILITIES						
11.4	13.9	15.0	Notes Payable-Short Term	11.8	18.3	16.4	19.3	16.0	10.0
3.3	2.1	2.9	Cur. Mat.-L.T.D.	4.3	.6	3.6	1.1	3.1	5.1
3.3	2.7	4.9	Trade Payables	.9	7.9	1.6	3.5	8.3	13.4
.2	.0	.1	Income Taxes Payable	.0	.0	.0	.3	.6	.0
15.0	10.6	12.0	All Other Current	11.8	13.9	7.5	10.0	13.3	15.3
33.2	29.3	35.0	Total Current	28.8	40.7	29.1	34.1	41.2	43.9
18.2	23.3	20.1	Long-Term Debt	29.9	13.3	22.3	8.0	16.8	19.1
.1	.1	.2	Deferred Taxes	.0	.0	.5	.0	1.0	.2
7.0	7.2	6.1	All Other Non-Current	5.1	6.1	8.3	4.5	11.0	1.9
41.6	40.2	38.6	Net Worth	36.2	40.0	39.7	53.4	30.0	34.8
100.0	100.0	100.0	Total Liabilties & Net Worth	100.0	100.0	100.0	100.0	100.0	100.0
			INCOME DATA						
100.0	100.0	100.0	Net Sales	100.0	100.0	100.0	100.0	100.0	100.0
			Gross Profit						
66.7	58.8	61.3	Operating Expenses	56.4	60.8	54.3	67.1	61.5	81.3
33.3	41.2	38.7	Operating Profit	43.6	39.2	45.7	32.9	38.5	18.7
11.8	12.3	12.4	All Other Expenses (net)	17.1	7.7	16.4	9.5	9.7	9.4
21.5	28.9	26.3	Profit Before Taxes	26.5	31.5	29.3	23.3	28.8	9.4
			RATIOS						
9.2	4.7	3.4		3.6	3.4	3.3	3.3	4.3	3.5
1.6	1.4	1.5	Current	.9	1.6	2.0	1.7	1.5	1.3
.5	.6	.5		.2	.5	1.3	1.0	.7	.8
5.7	2.5	2.4		3.3	2.5	2.0	3.3	1.9	3.0
1.1	(150) .9	1.2	Quick	.7	1.2	1.2	1.3	1.0	1.2
.1	.3	.3		.2	.3	.8	.2	.4	.5
0 UND	0 UND	0 UND		0 UND	0 UND	0 UND	0 999.8	2 180.0	4 93.8
0 860.7	0 UND	0 999.8	Sales/Receivables	0 UND	0 UND	7 53.7	47 7.8	24 14.9	30 12.2
36 10.2	46 7.9	81 4.5		0 UND	521 .7	2000 .1	304 1.2	78 4.7	66 5.5
			Cost of Sales/Inventory						
			Cost of Sales/Payables						
1.5	.8	.8		1.9	.6	.4	.2	.6	6.6
18.0	12.2	12.0	Sales/Working Capital	UND	6.1	2.3	4.1	23.2	21.1
-14.5	-17.6	-15.8		-1.4	-23.7	38.8	NM	-19.7	-23.2
21.5	15.7	12.4		7.2	17.7		20.7	11.1	87.2
(93) 4.8	(83) 5.3	(92) 5.6	EBIT/Interest	(24) 3.9	(23) 5.6		(13) 5.8	(12) 5.5	(11) 11.6
1.6	2.4	1.6		1.0	1.6		-1.9	.0	-.1
			Net Profit + Depr., Dep., Amort./Cur. Mat. L/T/D						
.0	.0	.0		.0	.0	.0	.0	.0	.2
.1	.1	.1	Fixed/Worth	1.9	.0	.0	.0	.1	.8
1.9	1.8	2.9		7.6	.1	1.5	.5	3.1	-6.6
.5	.5	.4		.7	.2	.7	.4	1.0	.9
1.7	1.8	1.7	Debt/Worth	2.5	1.0	1.9	1.2	2.6	6.7
8.4	7.5	10.2		12.4	4.1	5.1	3.7	39.7	-11.5
63.4	39.1	41.9		43.9	31.1	50.7	12.4	132.2	219.6
(160) 19.7	(130) 14.6	(161) 14.4	% Profit Before Taxes/Tangible Net Worth	(51) 14.5	(37) 13.6	(21) 15.0	(20) 8.8	(19) 26.0	(13) 40.9
2.4	5.5	3.2		1.8	3.5	3.6	3.8	9.7	-2.7
21.7	15.9	17.6		10.6	20.5	18.8	7.8	20.4	57.3
5.3	5.5	4.7	% Profit Before Taxes/Total Assets	3.0	6.3	3.7	4.0	7.4	8.2
.9	1.5	.9		.7	1.4	.8	1.3	.3	-.4
UND	UND	UND		400.9	UND	UND	UND	UND	341.7
32.4	47.3	56.1	Sales/Net Fixed Assets	.4	768.3	271.7	432.7	74.7	22.4
2.8	1.8	.7		.1	20.0	2.7	40.0	9.2	3.2
2.5	1.9	1.7		.4	1.1	2.3	1.7	3.6	5.3
.5	.3	.2	Sales/Total Assets	.1	.3	.1	.3	.5	2.2
.1	.1	.1		.1	.1	.1	.1	.1	.6
.5	.9	.7		5.2	.3			1.1	.2
(93) 1.6	(77) 2.8	(93) 2.9	% Depr., Dep., Amort./Sales	(37) 16.0	(15) .9			(12) 2.1	(12) 1.9
12.8	15.7	18.5		23.9	7.1			3.4	2.9
3.4	3.2	3.3			4.4				
(25) 10.1	(23) 10.9	(31) 11.3	% Officers', Directors' Owners' Comp/Sales		(10) 12.1				
27.3	26.6	17.7			29.1				
2320900M	1952489M	4084874M	Net Sales ($)	23210M	81938M	93733M	154423M	373713M	3357857M
3780000M	4496163M	5253913M	Total Assets ($)	178092M	554691M	757012M	1028034M	1540199M	1195885M

M = $ thousand MM = $ million

See Pages 9 through 22 for Explanation of Ratios and Data

Current Data Sorted by Assets							Comparative Historical Data	
						Type of Statement		
	1	5	11	9	8	Unqualified	36	33
		3	1	1	1	Reviewed	7	6
	1	1	1		4	Compiled	5	5
8	4	3	3	1		Tax Returns	29	21
9	14	25	24	9	11	Other	64	72
	17 (4/1-9/30/13)		141 (10/1/13-3/31/14)				4/1/09-3/31/10 ALL	4/1/10-3/31/11 ALL
0-500M	500M-2MM	2-10MM	10-50MM	50-100MM	100-250MM			
17	20	37	40	20	24	NUMBER OF STATEMENTS	141	137
%	%	%	%	%	%	**ASSETS**	%	%
46.1	21.3	23.7	29.3	25.6	24.1	Cash & Equivalents	25.8	24.0
2.2	16.7	14.0	15.7	15.4	7.9	Trade Receivables (net)	15.1	17.9
.2	.0	2.1	.1	1.0	2.5	Inventory	.6	1.5
8.2	5.6	8.5	4.2	12.0	3.9	All Other Current	9.8	10.5
56.6	43.6	48.2	49.2	53.9	38.3	Total Current	51.2	53.9
19.3	29.1	25.8	17.5	5.3	14.7	Fixed Assets (net)	19.4	18.0
9.7	19.5	7.0	8.1	16.8	19.5	Intangibles (net)	7.4	10.9
14.4	7.7	19.0	25.2	24.0	27.4	All Other Non-Current	21.9	17.2
100.0	100.0	100.0	100.0	100.0	100.0	Total	100.0	100.0
						LIABILITIES		
44.4	13.3	9.5	4.7	3.0	4.3	Notes Payable-Short Term	15.6	17.4
3.4	1.7	3.7	1.0	.6	.8	Cur. Mat.-L.T.D.	4.4	3.5
3.2	2.7	2.8	4.7	2.9	2.2	Trade Payables	4.5	6.2
.0	.0	.0	.0	.1	.0	Income Taxes Payable	.2	.3
37.5	30.4	11.9	9.0	9.2	5.2	All Other Current	19.8	16.2
88.5	48.1	27.9	19.4	15.8	12.5	Total Current	44.4	43.7
25.3	24.0	17.5	11.7	15.2	16.9	Long-Term Debt	25.7	20.1
.0	.0	.0	.5	.4	.0	Deferred Taxes	.3	.3
2.4	6.0	5.4	4.3	6.6	4.7	All Other Non-Current	8.3	3.6
-16.2	21.8	49.1	64.1	62.0	66.0	Net Worth	21.2	32.2
100.0	100.0	100.0	100.0	100.0	100.0	Total Liabilties & Net Worth	100.0	100.0
						INCOME DATA		
100.0	100.0	100.0	100.0	100.0	100.0	Net Sales	100.0	100.0
						Gross Profit		
70.1	71.1	70.2	69.7	52.6	47.9	Operating Expenses	75.6	70.2
29.9	28.9	29.8	30.3	47.4	52.1	Operating Profit	24.4	29.8
1.2	2.4	4.8	6.2	2.3	4.2	All Other Expenses (net)	6.2	6.0
28.8	26.5	25.0	24.1	45.1	47.8	Profit Before Taxes	18.2	23.8
						RATIOS		
5.0	5.1	4.4	7.2	14.7	9.3		4.2	4.7
1.2	.9	1.7	2.8	5.7	2.7	Current	1.9	1.9
.4	.5	.8	1.2	1.3	.7		.9	.9
5.0	3.5	3.8	6.4	7.6	5.8		3.6	3.6
1.1	.9	1.4	2.4	4.6	2.3	Quick	1.3	1.5
.3	.4	.2	.9	.9	.3		.5	.4
0 UND	0 UND	0 UND	0 UND	0 UND	0 UND		0 UND	0 UND
0 UND	0 UND	6 66.1	15 24.8	25 14.8	4 93.2	Sales/Receivables	2 177.8	7 48.7
0 UND	27 13.3	53 6.9	63 5.8	81 4.5	43 8.5		38 9.6	41 9.0
						Cost of Sales/Inventory		
						Cost of Sales/Payables		
18.9	9.2	3.0	1.8	1.0	1.3		3.3	3.2
108.6	-137.1	12.2	5.5	3.2	3.8	Sales/Working Capital	11.6	9.5
-48.3	-15.2	-63.0	280.7	8.8	-10.8		-16.9	-59.1
115.1	17.1	180.6	84.0	419.7	73.2		47.4	52.4
(11) 68.3	(11) 11.0	(21) 58.2	(23) 9.1	(13) 18.7	(18) 17.2	EBIT/Interest	(78) 7.4	(69) 9.4
4.0	4.8	1.1	.6	4.7	9.8		1.2	1.9
							19.3	9.3
						Net Profit + Depr., Dep., Amort./Cur. Mat. L/T/D	(10) 2.3	(11) 1.8
							.4	.2
.1	.1	.0	.0	.0	.0		.0	.0
.9	1.5	.2	.1	.1	.2	Fixed/Worth	.4	.2
-.5	-.4	2.2	.6	.9	3.6		14.7	3.4
.7	.5	.3	.1	.1	.1		.3	.3
2.7	2.3	1.2	.6	.2	.8	Debt/Worth	1.5	1.4
-3.5	-2.1	3.7	2.1	15.1	6.9		-154.2	15.8
999.8	234.9	122.3	111.2	155.1	58.3		84.7	124.4
(11) 398.9	(12) 51.2	(32) 31.0	(36) 14.9	(17) 89.4	(20) 11.5	% Profit Before Taxes/Tangible Net Worth	(105) 22.2	(112) 41.2
131.2	15.4	9.0	.7	4.6	6.9		2.1	10.6
703.1	70.4	51.2	30.7	64.5	12.5		42.1	53.2
193.1	24.0	11.4	10.1	9.5	7.5	% Profit Before Taxes/Total Assets	9.8	10.5
62.8	8.6	2.4	.2	4.1	5.1		.2	2.8
208.5	130.6	127.3	UND	341.0	UND		208.1	250.2
92.0	44.2	43.6	34.6	79.3	24.6	Sales/Net Fixed Assets	35.0	44.6
45.5	4.2	2.6	11.0	21.7	4.2		8.6	15.3
26.3	5.6	2.6	2.1	1.5	.6		3.4	3.7
16.2	3.0	1.1	.8	.7	.2	Sales/Total Assets	1.6	1.5
4.8	.9	.6	.1	.2	.1		.3	.3
		.6	.6		.8		.6	.6
		(22) 1.0	(22) 1.4		(13) 1.9	% Depr., Dep., Amort./Sales	(92) 1.5	(71) 1.8
		8.6	3.8		8.3		5.0	6.1
							9.4	7.2
						% Officers', Directors' Owners' Comp/Sales	(24) 18.7	(29) 11.8
							27.2	20.3
60528M	67121M	277451M	893398M	1868399M	2456202M	Net Sales ($)	3482531M	5087890M
3623M	18329M	187722M	962137M	1440225M	3841941M	Total Assets ($)	3519422M	4313200M

M = $ thousand MM = $ million

See Pages 9 through 22 for Explanation of Ratios and Data

Comparative Historical Data				Current Data Sorted by Sales					
			Type of Statement						
43	22	34	Unqualified		1	3	4	10	16
3	2	6	Reviewed		3			2	1
5	8	7	Compiled	1			3	2	1
25	23	19	Tax Returns	8	4	2	3	2	
73	70	92	Other	11	18	10	13	17	23
4/1/11-3/31/12	**4/1/12-3/31/13**	**4/1/13-3/31/14**		17 (4/1-9/30/13)			141 (10/1/13-3/31/14)		
ALL	**ALL**	**ALL**		**0-1MM**	**1-3MM**	**3-5MM**	**5-10MM**	**10-25MM**	**25MM & OVER**
149	125	158	**NUMBER OF STATEMENTS**	20	26	15	23	33	41
%	%	%	**ASSETS**	%	%	%	%	%	%
25.0	26.5	27.5	Cash & Equivalents	26.1	28.5	24.1	32.5	30.0	24.1
13.8	12.7	12.7	Trade Receivables (net)	.6	6.8	16.9	17.6	10.6	20.0
.9	2.8	1.0	Inventory	.1	.5	.4	2.7	.6	1.4
7.4	8.1	6.7	All Other Current	4.2	2.0	3.0	7.8	9.5	9.5
47.1	50.2	48.0	Total Current	31.0	37.8	44.4	60.5	50.7	55.0
22.8	24.8	19.2	Fixed Assets (net)	39.0	25.5	22.1	14.6	14.2	10.9
11.2	10.7	12.3	Intangibles (net)	6.9	14.1	13.1	6.6	6.9	20.9
19.0	14.3	20.6	All Other Non-Current	23.2	22.6	20.4	18.3	28.2	13.2
100.0	100.0	100.0	Total	100.0	100.0	100.0	100.0	100.0	100.0
			LIABILITIES						
20.3	12.7	10.9	Notes Payable-Short Term	5.6	14.7	29.4	24.9	1.4	4.2
3.6	1.6	1.9	Cur. Mat.-L.T.D.	1.4	2.0	.8	2.7	3.1	1.0
4.1	3.2	3.3	Trade Payables	.9	2.8	1.0	3.6	3.1	5.4
.0	.2	.0	Income Taxes Payable	.0	.0	.0	.0	.0	.0
17.8	15.4	14.9	All Other Current	27.4	11.5	14.9	16.2	13.8	11.1
45.9	33.1	31.0	Total Current	35.2	31.1	46.2	47.4	21.4	21.7
22.4	21.9	17.3	Long-Term Debt	21.9	10.4	38.0	18.0	13.8	14.3
.2	.3	.2	Deferred Taxes	.0	.0	.0	.0	.9	.0
7.1	4.6	4.9	All Other Non-Current	3.8	4.0	7.0	4.1	2.8	7.5
24.4	40.2	46.6	Net Worth	39.1	54.5	8.9	30.4	61.1	56.6
100.0	100.0	100.0	Total Liabilties & Net Worth	100.0	100.0	100.0	100.0	100.0	100.0
			INCOME DATA						
100.0	100.0	100.0	Net Sales	100.0	100.0	100.0	100.0	100.0	100.0
			Gross Profit						
69.5	72.8	64.6	Operating Expenses	47.4	69.5	67.9	74.6	59.3	67.2
30.5	27.2	35.4	Operating Profit	52.6	30.5	32.1	25.4	40.7	32.8
8.3	7.4	4.0	All Other Expenses (net)	11.1	4.5	5.5	1.1	5.0	.7
22.2	19.8	31.4	Profit Before Taxes	41.5	25.9	26.6	24.3	35.8	32.1
			RATIOS						
5.0	7.3	6.7		11.6	3.8	11.3	5.1	9.5	7.6
1.9	2.2	2.5	Current	1.5	1.2	1.5	2.5	3.0	2.7
.5	.9	.8		.3	.5	.6	.9	1.1	1.2
4.2	5.0	5.1		11.6	3.5	11.3	4.4	4.3	6.1
1.5	1.6	2.0	Quick	.9	.9	1.5	2.5	2.4	2.1
.3	.5	.6		.2	.5	.4	.6	.8	.8
0 UND	0 UND	0 UND		0 UND	0 UND	0 UND	0 UND	0 UND	4 103.8
6 63.1	4 93.5	4 89.7	Sales/Receivables	0 UND	0 UND	4 81.3	2 146.0	3 109.9	34 10.7
41 8.9	36 10.1	45 8.1		0 UND	38 9.7	41 9.0	53 6.9	24 15.3	76 4.8
			Cost of Sales/Inventory						
			Cost of Sales/Payables						
3.3	2.5	2.4		1.5	3.9	.9	3.8	2.1	3.0
10.4	8.6	8.7	Sales/Working Capital	35.5	86.4	20.0	8.9	7.1	4.6
-9.5	-38.0	-37.8		-2.5	-6.9	-15.7	-197.5	NM	50.4
63.3	31.1	122.9			79.6	25.8	148.1	496.8	220.9
(75) 10.0	(74) 7.5	(97) 17.1	EBIT/Interest		(16) 5.4	(10) 8.4	(17) 21.7	(19) 42.0	(29) 18.7
3.0	1.5	3.1			1.4	2.4	5.1	4.7	6.7
6.1		24.4							
(15) 2.1		(13) 4.3	Net Profit + Depr., Dep., Amort./Cur. Mat. L/T/D						
1.0		1.0							
.0	.0	.0		.0	.0	.0	.0	.0	.1
.2	.3	.2	Fixed/Worth	1.2	.2	8.8	.1	.1	.3
5.4	3.9	3.1		3.4	1.3	-.1	15.7	.3	1.8
.4	.3	.2		.4	.3	.2	.2	.1	.2
1.4	1.5	.9	Debt/Worth	1.1	.9	17.9	1.1	.4	1.7
51.8	9.0	8.2		10.4	2.6	-2.6	17.4	3.7	7.0
120.7	97.6	140.6		109.7	267.8		127.5	73.2	184.8
(117) 29.3	(103) 20.3	(128) 30.5	% Profit Before Taxes/Tangible Net Worth	(17) 10.9	(23) 21.8		(18) 60.1	(29) 10.4	(33) 134.2
4.9	3.9	7.2		2.6	2.7		15.4	6.8	29.7
47.5	42.9	58.4		24.1	61.1	110.9	67.6	29.9	98.6
9.6	6.9	12.4	% Profit Before Taxes/Total Assets	7.1	7.2	9.9	20.3	9.1	29.6
1.9	1.5	4.0		1.5	.9	3.6	4.8	5.2	8.5
206.2	108.4	199.6		UND	UND	142.3	300.2	UND	74.0
40.0	24.1	47.7	Sales/Net Fixed Assets	34.4	51.6	49.4	107.6	56.6	22.8
10.3	4.2	12.5		.1	3.0	2.1	46.9	18.5	13.1
3.0	2.8	2.9		1.0	3.6	3.4	5.6	2.2	2.4
1.3	1.1	1.0	Sales/Total Assets	.1	.8	.9	2.4	.5	1.3
.2	.2	.2		.1	.1	.2	1.0	.1	.7
.7	.8	.6			.8		.4	.4	.6
(88) 1.3	(71) 1.7	(83) 1.2	% Depr., Dep., Amort./Sales		(12) 2.8		(13) .8	(18) 1.1	(26) .9
6.9	6.9	3.3			25.5		1.5	2.1	2.3
5.0	4.2	6.0							
(27) 12.9	(24) 10.3	(25) 11.9	% Officers', Directors' Owners' Comp/Sales						
24.7	22.0	31.4							
4593758M	4149872M	5623099M	Net Sales ($)	9876M	47372M	57128M	171619M	556673M	4780431M
4713471M	4638921M	6453977M	Total Assets ($)	173912M	295048M	194891M	387674M	2114676M	3287776M

M = $ thousand MM = $ million

See Pages 9 through 22 for Explanation of Ratios and Data

Current Data Sorted by Assets							Comparative Historical Data	
						Type of Statement		
1	5	5	11	6	9	Unqualified	29	31
	1	1	2		1	Reviewed	4	8
2	1	2	2	2		Compiled	13	10
21	14	6			1	Tax Returns	36	31
16	17	19	8	5	9	Other	68	58
13 (4/1-9/30/13)			154 (10/1/13-3/31/14)				4/1/09-3/31/10 ALL	4/1/10-3/31/11 ALL
0-500M	500M-2MM	2-10MM	10-50MM	50-100MM	100-250MM			
40	38	33	23	13	20	NUMBER OF STATEMENTS	150	138
%	%	%	%	%	%	**ASSETS**	%	%
47.0	29.3	26.6	30.9	20.7	23.7	Cash & Equivalents	25.1	25.7
1.8	14.3	13.4	20.1	23.8	14.7	Trade Receivables (net)	15.4	17.3
2.6	.0	.0	1.0	.0	.1	Inventory	1.0	1.2
3.9	5.7	3.8	9.0	3.8	3.3	All Other Current	7.1	6.6
55.3	49.3	43.8	60.9	48.4	41.8	Total Current	48.7	50.7
19.7	19.9	25.5	6.7	4.1	8.5	Fixed Assets (net)	22.5	20.8
9.0	12.1	10.4	24.0	37.2	28.2	Intangibles (net)	15.0	10.3
16.0	18.7	20.3	8.3	10.4	21.4	All Other Non-Current	13.8	18.1
100.0	100.0	100.0	100.0	100.0	100.0	Total	100.0	100.0
						LIABILITIES		
16.7	8.6	4.1	7.5	1.1	.2	Notes Payable-Short Term	22.6	16.8
1.7	5.3	1.5	3.9	4.3	3.2	Cur. Mat.-L.T.D.	4.8	5.4
1.7	2.2	5.7	2.1	2.3	1.3	Trade Payables	4.7	4.1
.0	.0	.3	.0	.0	.8	Income Taxes Payable	.4	.3
19.5	17.7	15.7	16.6	16.9	24.4	All Other Current	18.5	18.9
39.6	33.9	27.3	30.1	24.6	30.0	Total Current	51.1	45.5
15.2	16.1	17.6	24.4	20.3	26.6	Long-Term Debt	23.3	24.8
.0	.0	.3	.0	.2	1.1	Deferred Taxes	.4	.3
10.2	18.3	9.1	7.7	17.0	3.2	All Other Non-Current	14.2	7.6
35.0	31.7	45.7	37.8	37.9	39.1	Net Worth	11.1	21.8
100.0	100.0	100.0	100.0	100.0	100.0	Total Liabilties & Net Worth	100.0	100.0
						INCOME DATA		
100.0	100.0	100.0	100.0	100.0	100.0	Net Sales	100.0	100.0
						Gross Profit		
79.8	82.3	82.8	71.4	66.5	70.1	Operating Expenses	79.1	77.8
20.2	17.7	17.2	28.6	33.5	29.9	Operating Profit	20.9	22.2
.8	1.9	3.1	3.1	3.5	6.7	All Other Expenses (net)	5.3	4.2
19.5	15.8	14.0	25.5	30.0	23.3	Profit Before Taxes	15.7	18.0
						RATIOS		
6.1	6.1	3.2	4.6	3.3	2.5		3.4	2.9
1.6	1.9	1.6	1.7	1.6	1.4	Current	1.4	1.4
.6	.5	.9	1.1	.9	1.0		.5	.6
6.1	4.6	3.0	3.6	2.9	2.4		2.9	2.7
1.4	1.4	1.2	1.6	1.5	1.3	Quick	1.1	.9
.3	.5	.9	.9	.8	.9		.4	.4
0 UND	**0** UND	**0** UND	**9** 41.7	**19** 19.7	**0** UND		**0** UND	**0** UND
0 UND	**0** UND	**4** 89.3	**31** 11.7	**69** 5.3	**26** 14.1	Sales/Receivables	**4** 88.6	**3** 114.6
0 UND	**15** 24.5	**37** 9.9	**63** 5.8	**130** 2.8	**72** 5.1		**50** 7.3	**65** 5.6
						Cost of Sales/Inventory		
						Cost of Sales/Payables		
7.4	8.2	5.9	3.5	2.6	5.1		5.3	6.7
48.7	36.1	20.8	8.8	9.6	14.2	Sales/Working Capital	39.2	60.6
-53.2	-25.4	-338.5	57.5	-19.5	NM		-15.3	-19.1
100.3	214.8	247.9	68.4		36.3		37.8	74.2
(14) 36.9	(20) 16.8	(21) 7.3	(17) 27.1		(13) 13.9	EBIT/Interest	(89) 5.2	(84) 15.1
11.2	4.3	1.5	20.4		1.3		2.0	3.2
							13.2	
						Net Profit + Depr., Dep., Amort./Cur. Mat. L/T/D	(12) 1.2	
							-.2	
.0	.0	.0	.0	.1	.0		.1	.0
.1	.3	.3	.4	2.6	.5	Fixed/Worth	.5	.4
1.4	80.1	1.7	-.8	-.1	-.2		-2.0	23.7
.2	.2	.6	.6	1.1	.4		.4	.6
.8	1.2	1.3	5.2	39.7	2.7	Debt/Worth	2.3	2.4
41.8	NM	3.5	-5.4	-1.9	-7.8		-3.0	-14.7
364.3	311.3	155.7	95.7		95.7		112.8	148.2
(31) 73.4	(29) 93.4	(28) 50.7	(15) 40.5		(12) 20.8	% Profit Before Taxes/Tangible Net Worth	(98) 44.2	(100) 62.3
21.1	9.2	23.1	13.5		13.0		6.4	10.9
208.5	85.8	43.6	49.7	49.2	34.5		52.1	71.9
67.3	27.1	13.7	16.9	17.8	16.6	% Profit Before Taxes/Total Assets	12.2	23.6
5.1	6.1	3.3	8.8	4.9	1.3		1.5	3.6
UND	259.0	234.9	144.3	61.2	55.8		118.5	177.9
142.6	104.0	39.6	42.9	27.8	35.5	Sales/Net Fixed Assets	36.0	38.4
24.6	21.2	3.2	14.9	24.7	17.1		12.8	14.7
13.0	7.2	3.3	2.8	1.5	1.5		5.7	5.8
6.4	3.8	2.0	2.1	.9	.9	Sales/Total Assets	2.1	2.6
2.7	1.5	.8	.7	.4	.4		.7	.9
.2	.4	.5	.8				.7	.5
(15) .3	(21) .7	(21) 1.9	(14) 1.3			% Depr., Dep., Amort./Sales	(92) 1.3	(78) 1.3
1.4	1.4	9.0	2.4				3.3	3.2
16.1	7.2						9.9	7.6
(24) 21.8	(15) 13.4					% Officers', Directors' Owners' Comp/Sales	(32) 16.0	(41) 17.0
32.9	28.3						28.4	25.9
43155M	200655M	291309M	877863M	796464M	3655175M	Net Sales ($)	4278754M	4343406M
7045M	39904M	129036M	497031M	935179M	3632443M	Total Assets ($)	3625264M	2538518M

M = $ thousand MM = $ million

See Pages 9 through 22 for Explanation of Ratios and Data

Comparative Historical Data / Current Data Sorted by Sales

Type of Statement	4/1/11-3/31/12 ALL	4/1/12-3/31/13 ALL	4/1/13-3/31/14 ALL	0-1MM	1-3MM	3-5MM	5-10MM	10-25MM	25MM & OVER
Unqualified	39	31	37	1		3	4	8	21
Reviewed	7	6	5			1	1	1	2
Compiled	13	12	9	1		3		2	3
Tax Returns	34	38	42	18	12	5	5	1	1
Other	81	71	74	13	19	6	5	12	19
				13 (4/1-9/30/13)			154 (10/1/13-3/31/14)		
NUMBER OF STATEMENTS	174	158	167	33	31	18	15	24	46
ASSETS	%	%	%	%	%	%	%	%	%
Cash & Equivalents	27.0	26.4	31.9	33.2	34.8	39.5	24.2	35.5	26.5
Trade Receivables (net)	16.8	13.0	12.7	2.7	8.3	8.3	12.9	17.0	22.3
Inventory	.9	1.3	.8	3.2	.0	.0	.0	.0	.6
All Other Current	6.4	7.1	4.9	7.5	5.3	2.8	2.3	4.6	4.7
Total Current	51.2	47.7	50.3	46.5	48.4	50.6	39.4	57.1	54.1
Fixed Assets (net)	20.1	17.6	16.6	22.3	28.8	8.3	27.0	8.9	8.0
Intangibles (net)	11.6	15.7	16.6	11.1	8.3	10.0	11.3	25.2	25.8
All Other Non-Current	17.0	18.9	16.6	20.0	14.6	31.1	22.2	8.7	12.1
Total	100.0	100.0	100.0	100.0	100.0	100.0	100.0	100.0	100.0
LIABILITIES									
Notes Payable-Short Term	13.5	14.1	7.9	14.3	12.6	4.3	8.4	5.0	3.0
Cur. Mat.-L.T.D.	2.7	3.2	3.2	2.5	3.1	1.0	6.2	2.4	3.9
Trade Payables	3.5	4.3	2.7	1.1	1.0	3.0	4.8	6.3	2.1
Income Taxes Payable	.4	.2	.2	.0	.0	.1	.0	.3	.4
All Other Current	21.6	19.7	18.3	13.2	14.9	22.3	29.3	12.3	22.3
Total Current	41.7	41.4	32.2	31.2	31.6	30.8	48.7	26.3	31.7
Long-Term Debt	19.3	18.7	18.9	24.7	16.2	16.8	11.5	6.8	26.1
Deferred Taxes	.3	.3	.2	.0	.0	.0	.0	.3	.5
All Other Non-Current	11.9	4.7	11.2	13.9	.1	18.4	35.6	3.3	10.0
Net Worth	26.9	34.9	37.5	30.3	52.1	33.9	4.2	63.2	31.7
Total Liabilities & Net Worth	100.0	100.0	100.0	100.0	100.0	100.0	100.0	100.0	100.0
INCOME DATA									
Net Sales	100.0	100.0	100.0	100.0	100.0	100.0	100.0	100.0	100.0
Gross Profit									
Operating Expenses	77.7	74.6	77.6	72.2	80.7	75.5	90.3	84.1	72.7
Operating Profit	22.3	25.4	22.4	27.8	19.3	24.5	9.7	15.9	27.3
All Other Expenses (net)	3.5	2.4	2.7	2.3	4.0	5.6	2.8	.5	2.1
Profit Before Taxes	18.8	23.0	19.7	25.5	15.3	18.9	6.8	15.4	25.1
RATIOS									
	4.6	3.0	3.7	6.1	3.1	25.9	3.5	3.4	2.8
Current	1.6	1.3	1.6	1.6	2.0	2.0	1.0	1.9	1.6
	.8	.6	.9	.2	.6	1.0	.6	1.3	1.1
	3.5	2.5	3.5	5.1	3.1	24.8	3.5	3.4	2.3
Quick	1.5	1.1	1.4	1.3	1.8	1.4	.9	1.6	1.5
	.6	.4	.8	.2	.4	.8	.6	1.0	1.0
	0 UND	**0** UND	**0** UND	**0** UND	**0** UND	**0** UND	**0** UND	**3** 108.6	**10** 35.5
Sales/Receivables	**10** 35.6	**3** 107.4	**2** 156.1	**0** UND	**0** UND	**0** UND	**6** 65.0	**13** 28.9	**36** 10.1
	49 7.5	**36** 10.0	**38** 9.6	**0** UND	**10** 35.4	**17** 21.6	**16** 22.8	**33** 11.2	**73** 5.0
Cost of Sales/Inventory									
Cost of Sales/Payables									
	5.2	6.6	5.5	3.4	8.2	5.0	18.1	6.9	4.8
Sales/Working Capital	14.5	28.8	19.2	22.2	59.6	31.1	-561.9	14.6	11.6
	-83.5	-30.3	-163.1	-7.5	-36.2	NM	-15.9	30.2	216.4
	60.2	64.7	84.4	35.3	229.3		235.5	465.8	38.4
EBIT/Interest	(109) 20.9	(90) 17.6	(94) 22.3	(16) 9.0	(11) 69.7		(10) 18.2	(16) 74.2	(33) 23.8
	3.2	6.7	3.4	1.9	1.2		3.5	7.2	4.3
Net Profit + Depr., Dep., Amort./Cur. Mat. L/T/D									
	.1	.0	.0	.0	.0	.0	.2	.1	.1
Fixed/Worth	.4	.3	.3	.1	.1	.0	1.7	.2	.5
	3.3	34.0	277.4	13.3	2.0	-13.6	14.3	1.3	-.2
	.5	.6	.4	.2	.1	.1	.6	.5	.9
Debt/Worth	1.4	1.6	1.7	1.0	.7	2.1	4.6	1.3	3.8
	NM	-10.2	-48.7	NM	8.5	-43.4	23.1	4.4	-3.1
	142.2	183.6	198.8	356.7	201.8	207.5	616.1	274.4	103.7
% Profit Before Taxes/Tangible Net Worth	(131) 59.3	(114) 68.1	(122) 57.0	(25) 67.4	(25) 42.0	(12) 22.5	(12) 52.2	(20) 167.7	(28) 37.7
	15.7	19.1	15.9	13.9	-4.4	10.1	28.6	51.4	16.8
	63.6	83.8	72.7	111.6	109.1	40.8	47.4	94.0	48.0
% Profit Before Taxes/Total Assets	26.9	35.0	23.8	20.5	29.8	10.3	21.9	34.5	22.2
	6.0	7.4	4.1	3.1	1.5	.0	5.3	9.6	4.4
	117.0	262.3	250.0	UND	250.0	UND	50.7	212.0	63.8
Sales/Net Fixed Assets	34.4	44.5	48.7	133.0	86.7	259.5	31.9	54.3	31.2
	12.7	14.5	16.2	7.3	10.0	22.0	14.7	21.9	20.6
	4.8	5.4	5.3	6.4	11.8	4.2	9.5	5.4	2.3
Sales/Total Assets	2.2	2.5	2.4	2.3	3.4	2.7	5.0	2.9	1.5
	1.1	1.0	.9	.5	1.1	.5	3.3	1.6	.8
	.6	.5	.4	.3	.2		.8	.5	.7
% Depr., Dep., Amort./Sales	(113) 1.1	(75) 1.1	(86) 1.0	(14) 1.5	(15) .4		(11) 1.3	(13) .8	(27) 1.1
	3.0	2.7	1.9	11.3	2.2		1.9	2.0	1.8
	12.3	10.2	12.3	15.1	9.8				
% Officers', Directors' Owners' Comp/Sales	(49) 19.3	(55) 16.8	(47) 19.3	(17) 18.9	(15) 22.7				
	30.7	27.9	28.8	26.4	34.8				
Net Sales ($)	6023785M	4700612M	5864621M	15418M	60167M	72111M	104364M	378662M	5233899M
Total Assets ($)	3511171M	3023712M	5240638M	19373M	54112M	199582M	28215M	267526M	4671830M

M = $ thousand MM = $ million

See Pages 9 through 22 for Explanation of Ratios and Data

Current Data Sorted by Assets | **Comparative Historical Data**

0-500M	500M-2MM	2-10MM	10-50MM	50-100MM	100-250MM	Type of Statement	4/1/09-3/31/10 ALL	4/1/10-3/31/11 ALL
	1	2	8	1	1	Unqualified	12	19
				1	1	Reviewed	1	1
	1		1			Compiled	6	2
		4	1			Tax Returns	3	7
2	2	5	5	3	1	Other	20	15
	7 (4/1-9/30/13)		33 (10/1/13-3/31/14)					
2	4	11	15	5	3	**NUMBER OF STATEMENTS**	42	44
%	%	%	%	%	%	**ASSETS**	%	%
		29.3	37.6			Cash & Equivalents	31.9	33.2
		7.3	8.3			Trade Receivables (net)	13.3	11.3
		.0	.0			Inventory	4.1	1.7
		3.6	.4			All Other Current	5.7	3.9
		40.3	46.4			Total Current	55.0	50.1
		35.9	17.4			Fixed Assets (net)	23.4	17.4
		9.6	15.2			Intangibles (net)	4.7	13.0
		14.2	21.1			All Other Non-Current	17.0	19.4
		100.0	100.0			Total	100.0	100.0
						LIABILITIES		
		.2	4.7			Notes Payable-Short Term	2.8	4.0
		4.0	.5			Cur. Mat.-L.T.D.	2.0	3.6
		5.7	11.0			Trade Payables	5.7	4.2
		.0	.2			Income Taxes Payable	1.0	1.0
		18.6	15.8			All Other Current	21.1	18.1
		28.5	32.2			Total Current	32.7	30.9
		17.6	9.6			Long-Term Debt	26.4	25.3
		1.8	.0			Deferred Taxes	.2	1.0
		.1	12.3			All Other Non-Current	5.6	6.1
		52.0	45.9			Net Worth	35.1	36.7
		100.0	100.0			Total Liabilties & Net Worth	100.0	100.0
						INCOME DATA		
		100.0	100.0			Net Sales	100.0	100.0
						Gross Profit		
		59.8	69.5			Operating Expenses	76.0	79.2
		40.2	30.5			Operating Profit	24.0	20.8
		11.1	9.2			All Other Expenses (net)	7.7	4.9
		29.2	21.3			Profit Before Taxes	16.3	16.0
						RATIOS		
		3.3	9.3				4.2	4.5
		1.9	1.0			Current	1.8	1.7
		.4	.6				1.0	1.0
		3.3	9.2				4.2	4.5
		1.9	.9			Quick	1.3	1.7
		.1	.6				.8	.7
		0 UND	0 UND				0 UND	0 UND
		0 UND	32 11.4			Sales/Receivables	30 12.1	23 15.9
		3 124.8	41 8.8				52 7.0	48 7.7
						Cost of Sales/Inventory		
						Cost of Sales/Payables		
		4.7	.5				2.0	2.2
		8.3	-41.0			Sales/Working Capital	7.6	6.2
		-11.9	-6.0				-830.0	-138.5
							12.4	117.5
						EBIT/Interest	(18) 7.0	(23) 7.9
							1.3	1.4
						Net Profit + Depr., Dep., Amort./Cur. Mat. L/T/D		
		.1	.0				.0	.0
		.9	.4			Fixed/Worth	.5	.2
		9.1	-.6				1.7	10.2
		.3	.6				.5	.5
		1.1	1.4			Debt/Worth	1.6	1.5
		8.1	-31.1				9.2	UND
		14.3	70.5				31.2	64.1
		(10) 8.2	(11) 22.8			% Profit Before Taxes/Tangible Net Worth	(35) 8.9	(34) 17.3
		-1.5	3.7				1.0	.6
		9.3	16.7				13.2	17.8
		3.8	10.7			% Profit Before Taxes/Total Assets	3.6	8.5
		.1	1.5				.2	.2
		UND	333.2				857.8	104.3
		4.3	65.7			Sales/Net Fixed Assets	23.0	28.1
		.2	5.5				1.6	6.1
		2.8	1.3				2.4	2.1
		.2	.5			Sales/Total Assets	.7	.7
		.1	.1				.2	.2
			.3				1.3	.8
			(11) 2.4			% Depr., Dep., Amort./Sales	(24) 2.3	(26) 1.3
			11.3				9.3	5.3
						% Officers', Directors' Owners' Comp/Sales		
2364M	13720M	71580M	355347M	141990M	148512M	Net Sales ($)	1011906M	1161967M
446M	4808M	55261M	383495M	291103M	385610M	Total Assets ($)	973511M	1262930M

M = $ thousand MM = $ million

See Pages 9 through 22 for Explanation of Ratios and Data

Comparative Historical Data				Current Data Sorted by Sales					
			Type of Statement						
14	13	13	Unqualified		2	2		4	5
1	1	2	Reviewed					1	1
1	2	2	Compiled			1	1		
7	3	5	Tax Returns	3			1	1	
21	20	18	Other	5	5	2		2	4
4/1/11-3/31/12	**4/1/12-3/31/13**	**4/1/13-3/31/14**		**7 (4/1-9/30/13)**		**33 (10/1/13-3/31/14)**			
ALL	**ALL**	**ALL**		**0-1MM**	**1-3MM**	**3-5MM**	**5-10MM**	**10-25MM**	**25MM & OVER**
44	39	40	**NUMBER OF STATEMENTS**	8	7	5	2	8	10
%	%	%	**ASSETS**	%	%	%	%	%	%
35.0	32.1	31.5	Cash & Equivalents						24.8
11.1	9.9	7.6	Trade Receivables (net)						11.8
1.6	.0	.0	Inventory						.0
6.4	7.1	4.8	All Other Current						1.0
54.2	49.1	43.8	Total Current						37.5
18.9	20.7	25.0	Fixed Assets (net)						7.2
7.8	9.3	12.7	Intangibles (net)						30.9
19.1	21.0	18.5	All Other Non-Current						24.3
100.0	100.0	100.0	Total						100.0
			LIABILITIES						
2.9	5.5	3.0	Notes Payable-Short Term						6.0
2.9	2.2	2.0	Cur. Mat.-L.T.D.						2.6
6.1	7.1	6.0	Trade Payables						19.7
.1	.1	.1	Income Taxes Payable						.2
13.7	10.9	15.6	All Other Current						15.3
25.7	25.8	26.7	Total Current						43.7
21.3	12.6	15.0	Long-Term Debt						6.4
.0	1.0	.5	Deferred Taxes						.0
6.8	4.1	6.4	All Other Non-Current						5.1
46.2	56.4	51.4	Net Worth						44.8
100.0	100.0	100.0	Total Liabilities & Net Worth						100.0
			INCOME DATA						
100.0	100.0	100.0	Net Sales						100.0
			Gross Profit						
76.2	65.4	65.9	Operating Expenses						86.1
23.8	34.6	34.1	Operating Profit						13.9
8.8	5.8	8.1	All Other Expenses (net)						3.1
15.0	28.8	25.9	Profit Before Taxes						10.8
			RATIOS						
6.4	6.8	4.3							1.4
2.5	2.3	1.5	Current						.8
1.0	.8	.6							.5
5.7	6.5	3.7							1.4
2.2	1.8	1.1	Quick						.7
.7	.5	.6							.5
0 UND	0 UND	0 UND							2 168.6
15 23.8	3 143.6	2 179.4	Sales/Receivables						35 10.5
45 8.2	35 10.4	38 9.6							43 8.4
			Cost of Sales/Inventory						
			Cost of Sales/Payables						
.8	1.2	2.9							16.1
5.4	5.8	17.8	Sales/Working Capital						-27.6
UND	-10.3	-6.0							-5.0
37.3	49.3	41.9							
(17) 6.0	(20) 5.6	(21) 12.5	EBIT/Interest						
-.9	2.6	3.0							
			Net Profit + Depr., Dep., Amort./Cur. Mat. L/T/D						
.0	.0	.0							.1
.1	.1	.4	Fixed/Worth						.3
1.2	1.0	2.2							-.2
.3	.3	.4							.7
.7	.7	1.0	Debt/Worth						NM
5.8	1.3	9.0							-2.4
29.1	57.8	45.0							
(38) 15.5	(35) 16.4	(33) 15.9	% Profit Before Taxes/Tangible Net Worth						
1.8	3.8	3.3							
14.3	15.9	16.0							20.8
7.4	7.7	6.4	% Profit Before Taxes/Total Assets						10.2
.1	2.4	1.0							1.4
127.8	UND	316.3							UND
24.1	33.3	19.0	Sales/Net Fixed Assets						29.6
4.7	2.1	.3							7.3
2.1	2.0	1.6							1.9
.6	.7	.6	Sales/Total Assets						.9
.2	.1	.1							.8
1.0	.9	.7							
(24) 1.9	(20) 3.7	(26) 4.1	% Depr., Dep., Amort./Sales						
6.7	7.7	14.4							
			% Officers', Directors' Owners' Comp/Sales						
754833M	639791M	733513M	Net Sales ($)	3955M	11558M	18868M	16394M	116266M	566472M
911823M	1075420M	1120723M	Total Assets ($)	43778M	97776M	80433M	4762M	390369M	503605M

M = $ thousand MM = $ million

See Pages 9 through 22 for Explanation of Ratios and Data

Current Data Sorted by Assets							Comparative Historical Data	
						Type of Statement		
	2	5	11	6	3	Unqualified	18	21
		1	3	1		Reviewed	2	3
1		3		1		Compiled	4	4
13	7	4	3	1		Tax Returns	20	19
7	8	8	16	8	6	Other	66	36
15 (4/1-9/30/13)		103 (10/1/13-3/31/14)					4/1/09-3/31/10	4/1/10-3/31/11
0-500M	500M-2MM	2-10MM	10-50MM	50-100MM	100-250MM		ALL	ALL
21	17	21	33	17	9	**NUMBER OF STATEMENTS**	110	83
%	%	%	%	%	%	**ASSETS**	%	%
45.5	22.0	15.7	27.2	26.8		Cash & Equivalents	16.6	22.6
8.8	16.9	16.1	15.0	3.7		Trade Receivables (net)	18.1	11.4
.2	.6	1.5	1.3	.6		Inventory	.8	.7
1.9	1.8	10.8	5.1	7.5		All Other Current	8.8	10.7
56.5	41.3	44.1	48.5	38.5		Total Current	44.4	45.5
8.2	20.8	28.3	8.0	6.0		Fixed Assets (net)	27.5	20.0
7.9	8.2	6.4	11.6	9.7		Intangibles (net)	3.8	4.7
27.4	29.7	21.2	31.9	45.7		All Other Non-Current	24.4	29.8
100.0	100.0	100.0	100.0	100.0		Total	100.0	100.0
						LIABILITIES		
40.7	14.6	12.2	7.4	3.7		Notes Payable-Short Term	20.3	19.7
.0	1.1	2.7	2.0	2.8		Cur. Mat.-L.T.D.	4.6	1.4
4.4	2.1	6.8	8.9	1.1		Trade Payables	3.0	3.1
.0	.1	.0	.2	.0		Income Taxes Payable	.1	.1
7.3	14.6	5.2	8.2	9.3		All Other Current	10.7	10.2
52.4	32.5	27.0	26.6	17.0		Total Current	38.7	34.6
5.4	26.2	25.7	31.6	20.3		Long-Term Debt	32.4	21.1
.0	.6	.0	.0	.0		Deferred Taxes	.2	.0
12.9	11.3	4.3	5.6	2.8		All Other Non-Current	5.3	7.4
29.4	29.4	43.0	36.3	59.8		Net Worth	23.4	36.9
100.0	100.0	100.0	100.0	100.0		Total Liabilties & Net Worth	100.0	100.0
						INCOME DATA		
100.0	100.0	100.0	100.0	100.0		Net Sales	100.0	100.0
						Gross Profit		
83.4	67.8	63.1	55.6	56.2		Operating Expenses	64.0	57.4
16.6	32.2	36.9	44.4	43.8		Operating Profit	36.0	42.6
-.1	5.9	6.0	12.4	11.8		All Other Expenses (net)	13.8	15.1
16.7	26.3	30.9	32.0	32.0		Profit Before Taxes	22.2	27.5
						RATIOS		
8.9	5.6	4.4	4.0	13.7			3.6	4.7
3.9	1.2	1.5	2.0	3.5		Current	1.5	1.7
.7	.2	.9	1.1	1.2			.5	.6
8.5	5.6	4.2	3.9	6.9			2.9	3.8
2.9	1.0	1.4	1.4	2.9		Quick	1.2	(82) 1.3
.7	.2	.3	.6	1.0			.4	.2
0 UND	0 UND	0 UND	0 UND	0 UND			0 UND	0 UND
0 UND	0 UND	19 19.2	18 20.7	0 UND		Sales/Receivables	0 UND	0 UND
3 114.7	22 16.4	51 7.1	52 7.0	69 5.3			52 7.0	25 14.7
						Cost of Sales/Inventory		
						Cost of Sales/Payables		
6.0	5.4	2.6	1.8	.2			.9	1.0
14.7	38.7	13.7	6.5	.5		Sales/Working Capital	10.3	6.4
-41.3	-5.6	-138.1	43.5	501.6			-6.9	-7.2
53.0	14.9	14.5	40.4	24.1			18.2	22.7
(10) 8.1	(12) 5.6	(14) 4.2	(14) 7.0	(12) 6.8		EBIT/Interest	(47) 4.2	(32) 6.1
.4	1.9	1.3	1.6	1.6			1.2	2.0
							25.0	
						Net Profit + Depr., Dep., Amort./Cur. Mat. L/T/D	(10) 1.7	
							.8	
.0	.0	.0	.0	.0			.0	.0
.0	.4	.3	.0	.0		Fixed/Worth	.1	.1
.3	UND	2.0	.3	.3			2.4	1.4
.1	.8	.6	.2	.1			.5	.3
.6	4.9	1.4	.8	.5		Debt/Worth	2.1	1.3
UND	UND	6.8	6.7	2.4			8.2	9.7
297.4	207.7	69.8	39.3	15.0			58.2	48.4
(16) 113.3	(13) 43.3	(19) 28.9	(28) 14.9	(15) 2.5		% Profit Before Taxes/Tangible Net Worth	(93) 12.5	(71) 16.4
16.0	18.4	5.1	4.8	-.5			3.0	4.7
162.3	39.9	17.0	13.7	7.1			19.3	16.6
32.7	18.8	8.5	5.0	1.1		% Profit Before Taxes/Total Assets	3.8	5.5
8.2	2.0	3.0	1.1	.2			.5	1.8
UND	UND	572.8	UND	UND			UND	UND
UND	50.7	14.8	177.0	62.9		Sales/Net Fixed Assets	40.3	39.1
38.1	12.7	1.0	25.3	2.1			.5	3.6
8.8	2.8	1.6	1.6	.2			1.3	1.5
4.1	2.3	.4	.2	.1		Sales/Total Assets	.3	.2
1.7	.5	.1	.1	.0			.1	.1
		.7	.3				1.0	.7
		(14) 2.4	(15) .6			% Depr., Dep., Amort./Sales	(55) 5.8	(37) 2.5
		15.1	1.1				22.9	19.8
							3.7	4.4
						% Officers', Directors' Owners' Comp/Sales	(13) 17.2	(12) 12.7
							22.6	17.9
13708M	35412M	124961M	952043M	276123M	893486M	Net Sales ($)	973144M	917200M
3442M	18322M	104120M	850313M	1312082M	1385403M	Total Assets ($)	3043527M	2560168M

M = $ thousand MM = $ million

See Pages 9 through 22 for Explanation of Ratios and Data

Comparative Historical Data				Current Data Sorted by Sales					
			Type of Statement						
30	27	27	Unqualified	2	5	2	4	7	7
2	6	5	Reviewed	2	1		1	1	
2	4	5	Compiled	2			2		1
22	20	28	Tax Returns	17	7	2	1		1
54	49	53	Other	15	11	6	6	7	8
				15 (4/1-9/30/13)			103 (10/1/13-3/31/14)		
4/1/11-3/31/12 ALL	4/1/12-3/31/13 ALL	4/1/13-3/31/14 ALL		0-1MM	1-3MM	3-5MM	5-10MM	10-25MM	25MM & OVER
110	106	118	**NUMBER OF STATEMENTS**	38	24	10	14	15	17
%	%	%	**ASSETS**	%	%	%	%	%	%
19.5	26.7	27.6	Cash & Equivalents	32.4	17.3	24.1	23.3	41.4	25.0
12.9	12.1	11.9	Trade Receivables (net)	14.5	4.4	3.0	10.2	12.1	23.2
1.2	2.4	1.0	Inventory	.3	.2	.0	1.3	1.6	3.8
7.7	4.6	5.2	All Other Current	7.1	1.8	5.3	2.4	1.4	11.0
41.4	45.8	45.7	Total Current	54.3	23.6	32.4	37.2	56.6	63.0
18.7	20.8	13.4	Fixed Assets (net)	13.4	21.1	17.5	10.5	4.2	10.4
7.6	4.2	9.1	Intangibles (net)	2.8	15.3	9.3	6.7	11.9	13.9
32.4	29.1	31.8	All Other Non-Current	29.5	39.9	40.8	45.6	27.3	12.6
100.0	100.0	100.0	Total	100.0	100.0	100.0	100.0	100.0	100.0
			LIABILITIES						
17.0	12.6	14.6	Notes Payable-Short Term	23.8	22.4	7.5	13.0	.0	1.5
4.7	4.7	1.7	Cur. Mat.-L.T.D.	.7	.8	5.4	.1	1.3	4.5
3.6	5.2	5.1	Trade Payables	1.7	5.0	4.6	1.4	6.8	14.5
.2	.3	.1	Income Taxes Payable	.0	.1	.0	.0	.1	.3
13.5	12.0	8.3	All Other Current	4.8	5.1	8.8	15.3	11.8	11.3
39.1	34.8	29.7	Total Current	31.1	33.2	26.3	29.8	20.1	32.1
25.5	22.2	22.2	Long-Term Debt	16.0	21.4	29.1	9.7	20.2	45.4
.3	.0	.2	Deferred Taxes	.0	.4	.0	.0	.0	.9
7.3	6.3	6.9	All Other Non-Current	6.4	9.1	9.2	12.9	1.7	3.2
27.8	36.8	41.0	Net Worth	46.6	35.9	35.4	47.6	57.9	18.5
100.0	100.0	100.0	Total Liabilties & Net Worth	100.0	100.0	100.0	100.0	100.0	100.0
			INCOME DATA						
100.0	100.0	100.0	Net Sales	100.0	100.0	100.0	100.0	100.0	100.0
			Gross Profit						
65.0	66.7	63.0	Operating Expenses	55.7	66.2	68.8	54.0	63.9	78.0
35.0	33.3	37.0	Operating Profit	44.3	33.8	31.2	46.0	36.1	22.0
12.2	9.1	8.2	All Other Expenses (net)	7.6	8.6	15.6	9.0	12.0	.5
22.8	24.2	28.8	Profit Before Taxes	36.7	25.2	15.6	37.0	24.1	21.5
			RATIOS						
4.6	5.1	5.8		12.1	4.8	3.6	4.4	6.8	3.4
1.8	1.9	2.0	Current	4.4	1.5	1.3	1.8	3.4	1.9
.6	.4	.9		.5	.3	.3	.7	1.4	1.4
3.9	4.0	5.0		12.1	3.8	3.6	4.1	6.8	2.4
1.4	1.6	1.6	Quick	3.3	1.1	.7	1.6	2.5	1.4
.3	.3	.5		.2	.2	.2	.7	1.2	1.0
0 UND	0 UND	0 UND		0 UND	0 UND	0 UND	0 UND	4 84.0	17 22.1
0 999.8	1 301.5	3 144.8	Sales/Receivables	0 UND	0 UND	1 576.8	0 UND	35 10.5	24 14.9
41 8.9	46 7.9	35 10.3		32 11.5	10 36.5	23 16.0	56 6.5	48 7.6	63 5.8
			Cost of Sales/Inventory						
			Cost of Sales/Payables						
2.1	1.3	1.5		.7	2.7	2.1	2.5	.5	2.2
8.0	10.7	10.2	Sales/Working Capital	6.0	37.7	24.2	12.0	3.3	12.9
-26.1	-5.6	-69.2		-8.3	-16.0	-4.9	-4.1	14.0	28.4
56.8	15.7	20.1		14.4	15.1			33.9	34.7
(56) 9.9	(53) 5.6	(68) 6.6	EBIT/Interest	(20) 6.2	(13) 6.7			(10) 4.1	(12) 4.9
3.2	3.2	1.8		2.3	1.9			.6	.3
			Net Profit + Depr., Dep., Amort./Cur. Mat. L/T/D						
.0	.0	.0		.0	.0	.0	.0	.0	.0
.1	.1	.0	Fixed/Worth	.0	.0	.5	.0	.0	.2
1.1	1.8	.7		.1	1.4	UND	.7	.3	-.2
.3	.4	.2		.1	.3	.6	.2	.2	.5
1.1	1.4	1.1	Debt/Worth	.5	2.0	9.7	1.7	.8	1.4
157.5	8.3	7.1		5.1	NM	UND	4.4	1.9	-2.7
65.0	75.8	61.1		101.0	81.2		56.6	47.1	48.5
(84) 15.1	(89) 13.8	(99) 17.5	% Profit Before Taxes/Tangible Net Worth	(34) 24.6	(18) 14.9		(12) 7.1	(14) 9.6	(12) 33.0
1.7	1.8	3.7		4.1	1.8		3.8	2.1	18.1
29.9	23.5	28.8		33.9	36.1	11.2	21.0	11.8	41.2
5.5	4.5	7.3	% Profit Before Taxes/Total Assets	8.1	6.7	2.9	6.1	5.0	12.2
.4	.8	1.2		1.8	2.0	-3.4	1.2	.2	4.1
UND	UND	UND		UND	UND	UND	UND	UND	288.2
67.2	43.7	94.8	Sales/Net Fixed Assets	UND	47.7	54.5	40.3	51.0	51.1
6.4	3.8	12.8		25.6	3.8	9.9	2.3	25.1	18.4
2.8	2.3	2.6		2.9	3.3	2.3	1.1	1.4	4.5
.5	.3	.5	Sales/Total Assets	.5	.7	.5	.1	.5	2.1
.1	.1	.1		.1	.1	.1	.1	.1	.8
.8	.8	.5		1.8	.8				.2
(47) 2.5	(50) 1.3	(49) 1.6	% Depr., Dep., Amort./Sales	(11) 4.0	(12) 3.2				(10) .6
10.8	10.2	4.6		19.0	11.7				2.6
1.6	6.1	2.8							
(22) 8.2	(17) 12.4	(24) 11.1	% Officers', Directors' Owners' Comp/Sales						
33.0	28.1	27.5							
1073363M	2013947M	2295733M	Net Sales ($)	16693M	46350M	39822M	97462M	233928M	1861478M
2990747M	3785105M	3673682M	Total Assets ($)	235961M	435145M	225959M	900227M	821567M	1054823M

M = $ thousand MM = $ million

See Pages 9 through 22 for Explanation of Ratios and Data

Current Data Sorted by Assets							Comparative Historical Data	
						Type of Statement		
		2	2	2	3	Unqualified	15	10
						Reviewed	3	2
						Compiled	2	5
						Tax Returns	4	2
1		2	1	3	4	Other	16	16
	4 (4/1-9/30/13)		16 (10/1/13-3/31/14)				**4/1/09-3/31/10**	**4/1/10-3/31/11**
0-500M	**500M-2MM**	**2-10MM**	**10-50MM**	**50-100MM**	**100-250MM**		**ALL**	**ALL**
1		4	3	5	7	**NUMBER OF STATEMENTS**	40	35
%	%	%	%	%	%	**ASSETS**	%	%
	D A T A N O T A V A I L A B L E					Cash & Equivalents	49.5	43.6
						Trade Receivables (net)	12.8	14.4
						Inventory	2.2	.2
						All Other Current	5.3	7.5
						Total Current	69.9	65.7
						Fixed Assets (net)	5.6	7.6
						Intangibles (net)	5.7	6.7
						All Other Non-Current	18.8	20.0
						Total	100.0	100.0
						LIABILITIES		
						Notes Payable-Short Term	6.7	3.8
						Cur. Mat.-L.T.D.	3.9	1.7
						Trade Payables	10.6	6.0
						Income Taxes Payable	.1	.2
						All Other Current	45.4	29.5
						Total Current	66.8	41.3
						Long-Term Debt	11.6	12.4
						Deferred Taxes	.1	.0
						All Other Non-Current	6.9	8.3
						Net Worth	14.6	38.0
						Total Liabilties & Net Worth	100.0	100.0
						INCOME DATA		
						Net Sales	100.0	100.0
						Gross Profit		
						Operating Expenses	90.0	86.1
						Operating Profit	10.0	13.9
						All Other Expenses (net)	3.2	3.6
						Profit Before Taxes	6.8	10.3
						RATIOS		
							2.2	4.3
						Current	1.2	1.5
							.9	1.0
							2.1	4.3
						Quick	1.1	1.5
							.7	.9
							0 857.8	**0** 999.8
						Sales/Receivables	**18** 20.0	**22** 16.4
							66 5.5	**133** 2.7
						Cost of Sales/Inventory		
						Cost of Sales/Payables		
							1.6	1.0
						Sales/Working Capital	7.8	5.5
							-5.5	-119.1
							29.1	60.0
						EBIT/Interest	(24) 6.7	(16) 18.6
							2.6	3.6
						Net Profit + Depr., Dep., Amort./Cur. Mat. L/T/D		
							.0	.0
						Fixed/Worth	.0	.0
							.8	.3
							1.3	.5
						Debt/Worth	4.8	2.2
							16.2	11.5
							42.6	55.8
						% Profit Before Taxes/Tangible Net Worth	(33) 14.4	(31) 15.2
							4.5	3.7
							11.7	18.2
						% Profit Before Taxes/Total Assets	3.4	5.1
							.6	.6
							UND	UND
						Sales/Net Fixed Assets	114.6	81.5
							31.9	19.7
							2.2	2.0
						Sales/Total Assets	.8	.9
							.2	.3
							.5	.5
						% Depr., Dep., Amort./Sales	(16) 1.6	(15) 1.6
							3.7	2.8
						% Officers', Directors' Owners' Comp/Sales		
1137M		**58062M**	**71135M**	**205075M**	**317502M**	Net Sales ($)	**1842034M**	**1986552M**
258M		**29826M**	**80215M**	**326965M**	**1297188M**	Total Assets ($)	**2182467M**	**2208299M**

M = $ thousand MM = $ million

See Pages 9 through 22 for Explanation of Ratios and Data

Comparative Historical Data / Current Data Sorted by Sales

4/1/11-3/31/12 ALL	4/1/12-3/31/13 ALL	4/1/13-3/31/14 ALL	Type of Statement	0-1MM	1-3MM	3-5MM	5-10MM	10-25MM	25MM & OVER
14	10	9	Unqualified				3	2	4
3	2		Reviewed						
3	1		Compiled						
6	7		Tax Returns						
16	19	11	Other		1	1		2	7
				4 (4/1-9/30/13)			16 (10/1/13-3/31/14)		
42	39	20	NUMBER OF STATEMENTS		1	1	3	4	11
%	%	%	**ASSETS**	%	%	%	%	%	%
40.6	35.6	46.8	Cash & Equivalents	DATA NOT AVAILABLE					58.6
9.2	8.2	4.0	Trade Receivables (net)						4.7
.0	.2	.0	Inventory						.0
7.2	5.5	12.4	All Other Current						17.8
57.1	49.5	63.2	Total Current						81.2
9.1	7.8	4.1	Fixed Assets (net)						3.1
10.8	8.5	8.8	Intangibles (net)						.0
23.0	34.2	24.0	All Other Non-Current						15.7
100.0	100.0	100.0	Total						100.0
			LIABILITIES						
8.6	8.8	1.7	Notes Payable-Short Term						.0
2.0	1.4	3.6	Cur. Mat.-L.T.D.						6.3
13.5	11.0	4.2	Trade Payables						6.6
.2	.3	1.1	Income Taxes Payable						.9
35.8	23.0	41.5	All Other Current						46.2
60.1	44.5	52.2	Total Current						60.1
12.3	7.1	7.9	Long-Term Debt						14.1
.2	.1	.4	Deferred Taxes						.2
6.4	10.1	12.3	All Other Non-Current						7.8
21.0	38.2	27.2	Net Worth						17.7
100.0	100.0	100.0	Total Liabilties & Net Worth						100.0
			INCOME DATA						
100.0	100.0	100.0	Net Sales						100.0
			Gross Profit						
88.1	84.1	92.0	Operating Expenses						89.3
11.9	15.9	8.0	Operating Profit						10.7
3.3	.4	.9	All Other Expenses (net)						4.4
8.6	15.5	7.1	Profit Before Taxes						6.3
			RATIOS						
2.1	2.4	2.4							2.4
1.1	1.2	1.3	Current						1.2
.7	.8	.9							.9
2.1	2.1	2.1							1.8
1.0	.9	.9	Quick						.9
.5	.3	.8							.9
0 762.1	0 UND	0 UND							0 UND
25 14.8	2 200.0	8 44.2	Sales/Receivables						11 33.6
53 6.9	63 5.8	45 8.2							54 6.8
			Cost of Sales/Inventory						
			Cost of Sales/Payables						
2.1	1.5	1.1							1.0
12.1	14.2	6.1	Sales/Working Capital						9.1
-3.3	-10.3	-19.0							-37.0
28.7	26.6								
(21) 7.2	(16) 13.8		EBIT/Interest						
2.0	6.4								
			Net Profit + Depr., Dep., Amort./Cur. Mat. L/T/D						
.0	.0	.0							.0
.0	.0	.0	Fixed/Worth						.0
1.6	.5	.4							.4
1.0	.4	1.0							1.1
4.7	3.2	2.9	Debt/Worth						3.4
NM	18.4	90.3							14.6
35.0	30.8	19.6							28.8
(32) 10.7	(33) 14.3	(16) 10.9	% Profit Before Taxes/Tangible Net Worth						(10) 11.1
.6	2.6	2.4							1.2
8.6	18.9	14.7							8.4
2.4	6.1	4.7	% Profit Before Taxes/Total Assets						1.3
.0	1.2	.2							.2
UND	UND	UND							UND
175.8	75.6	409.6	Sales/Net Fixed Assets						999.8
19.2	11.3	34.5							67.1
1.8	1.3	1.4							1.5
.5	.5	.5	Sales/Total Assets						.6
.3	.2	.2							.3
.4	.3								
(16) 2.0	(16) .8		% Depr., Dep., Amort./Sales						
4.0	1.9								
			% Officers', Directors' Owners' Comp/Sales						
1037459M	685818M	652911M	Net Sales ($)		1137M	4179M	19953M	46301M	581341M
1657329M	2321894M	1734452M	Total Assets ($)		258M	2684M	285339M	230742M	1215429M

M = $ thousand MM = $ million

See Pages 9 through 22 for Explanation of Ratios and Data

Current Data Sorted by Assets							Comparative Historical Data	
						Type of Statement		
		2	15	11	7	Unqualified	51	43
	1					Reviewed	1	
					1	Compiled	11	2
2	2					Tax Returns	1	4
1	3	2	9	9	12	Other	33	37
	9 (4/1-9/30/13)		68 (10/1/13-3/31/14)				4/1/09-3/31/10	4/1/10-3/31/11
0-500M	500M-2MM	2-10MM	10-50MM	50-100MM	100-250MM		ALL	ALL
3	6	4	24	20	20	**NUMBER OF STATEMENTS**	97	86
%	%	%	%	%	%	**ASSETS**	%	%
			52.2	49.5	41.1	Cash & Equivalents	43.0	47.1
			8.8	9.2	9.8	Trade Receivables (net)	16.3	12.8
			.1	.5	.3	Inventory	.4	.3
			10.3	9.2	5.1	All Other Current	5.4	7.5
			71.3	68.4	56.3	Total Current	65.1	67.6
			6.4	6.2	4.0	Fixed Assets (net)	15.6	12.5
			4.3	8.1	14.7	Intangibles (net)	7.3	5.6
			18.0	17.3	25.0	All Other Non-Current	12.0	14.2
			100.0	100.0	100.0	Total	100.0	100.0
						LIABILITIES		
			.2	4.2	2.1	Notes Payable-Short Term	3.7	.5
			.6	.3	.7	Cur. Mat.-L.T.D.	1.2	1.3
			13.4	15.1	15.7	Trade Payables	12.9	17.5
			.0	.5	.3	Income Taxes Payable	.2	.3
			29.8	23.3	19.6	All Other Current	26.2	24.7
			44.2	43.4	38.4	Total Current	44.2	44.3
			3.8	7.7	18.6	Long-Term Debt	10.3	12.7
			.1	.1	2.6	Deferred Taxes	.5	.7
			9.7	5.3	5.0	All Other Non-Current	6.1	6.6
			42.2	43.5	35.3	Net Worth	39.0	35.7
			100.0	100.0	100.0	Total Liabilities & Net Worth	100.0	100.0
						INCOME DATA		
			100.0	100.0	100.0	Net Sales	100.0	100.0
						Gross Profit		
			98.2	98.4	96.7	Operating Expenses	93.8	92.1
			1.8	1.6	3.3	Operating Profit	6.2	7.9
			.0	-.3	.3	All Other Expenses (net)	.4	2.1
			1.8	1.9	3.0	Profit Before Taxes	5.7	5.9
						RATIOS		
			3.1	3.1	2.2		3.3	2.4
			1.6	1.5	1.6	Current	1.6	1.4
			1.1	1.2	.9		1.0	1.1
			2.5	3.1	2.0		3.0	2.3
			1.4	1.4	1.3	Quick	1.5	1.3
			.9	.7	.7		.8	.9
			1 337.4	**5** 76.2	**2** 151.7		**5** 77.4	**2** 149.1
			11 33.8	**9** 42.2	**13** 28.0	Sales/Receivables	**18** 20.4	**15** 24.6
			26 14.3	**21** 17.0	**29** 12.7		**33** 10.9	**25** 14.9
						Cost of Sales/Inventory		
						Cost of Sales/Payables		
			2.7	6.1	6.3		5.2	5.8
			8.8	17.8	12.7	Sales/Working Capital	12.3	17.1
			78.0	34.3	-34.8		UND	77.5
			345.7				58.4	51.5
			(10) 113.7			EBIT/Interest	(53) 6.6	(40) 6.6
			25.4				1.9	1.4
							18.6	9.6
						Net Profit + Depr., Dep., Amort./Cur. Mat. L/T/D	(17) 4.0	(14) 5.8
							1.1	1.5
			.0	.0	.0		.0	.0
			.1	.1	.1	Fixed/Worth	.3	.2
			.3	.8	NM		1.4	1.6
			.8	.5	.6		.6	.7
			1.7	1.6	1.8	Debt/Worth	1.5	1.3
			2.8	3.9	NM		11.5	14.6
			45.4	23.6	18.5		38.3	42.6
			(23) 21.3	(16) 13.2	(15) 13.8	% Profit Before Taxes/Tangible Net Worth	(81) 15.9	(73) 13.0
			3.8	1.6	3.3		1.1	3.0
			10.8	8.9	11.9		13.8	15.8
			7.6	5.9	5.8	% Profit Before Taxes/Total Assets	6.1	5.1
			1.2	.6	-.6		.4	.6
			UND	251.3	UND		362.1	625.0
			75.8	43.3	189.0	Sales/Net Fixed Assets	43.6	71.3
			26.9	22.4	71.1		10.9	19.2
			4.4	4.7	3.9		4.2	4.6
			2.3	3.5	2.6	Sales/Total Assets	2.4	2.8
			1.1	1.7	1.3		1.0	1.4
			.3	.2	.1		.2	.2
			(11) .6	(16) .5	(12) .3	% Depr., Dep., Amort./Sales	(65) .8	(58) .5
			1.0	1.6	.8		2.8	1.8
							4.7	4.1
						% Officers', Directors' Owners' Comp/Sales	(11) 7.5	(10) 7.5
							14.2	10.2
6218M	19940M	71143M	2264172M	4848519M	8569545M	Net Sales ($)	12983816M	16200942M
740M	6943M	21743M	706617M	1443764M	3335586M	Total Assets ($)	4754326M	5300395M

M = $ thousand MM = $ million

See Pages 9 through 22 for Explanation of Ratios and Data

Comparative Historical Data | **Current Data Sorted by Sales**

			Type of Statement						
44	32	35	Unqualified			1	2	2	30
2	1	1	Reviewed				1		
2	1	1	Compiled						1
4	3	4	Tax Returns		3		1		
35	28	36	Other	2	3			3	28
				9 (4/1-9/30/13)			68 (10/1/13-3/31/14)		
4/1/11-3/31/12 ALL	4/1/12-3/31/13 ALL	4/1/13-3/31/14 ALL		0-1MM	1-3MM	3-5MM	5-10MM	10-25MM	25MM & OVER
87	65	77	NUMBER OF STATEMENTS	2	6	1	4	5	59
%	%	%	ASSETS	%	%	%	%	%	%
44.7	47.1	46.8	Cash & Equivalents						46.1
14.3	13.9	11.7	Trade Receivables (net)						11.2
.2	.1	.3	Inventory						.3
5.4	5.7	7.9	All Other Current						9.0
64.6	66.8	66.6	Total Current						66.6
12.6	9.3	7.7	Fixed Assets (net)						6.1
7.9	7.0	8.3	Intangibles (net)						7.9
15.0	16.9	17.3	All Other Non-Current						19.3
100.0	100.0	100.0	Total						100.0
			LIABILITIES						
3.1	5.0	5.5	Notes Payable-Short Term						2.2
1.3	2.2	1.0	Cur. Mat.-L.T.D.						.6
18.1	17.1	15.2	Trade Payables						16.7
.3	.7	.2	Income Taxes Payable						.3
23.9	24.9	23.1	All Other Current						23.7
46.7	49.9	45.0	Total Current						43.5
13.6	10.7	9.9	Long-Term Debt						9.4
.7	.5	.7	Deferred Taxes						.9
4.0	8.5	6.3	All Other Non-Current						5.8
35.0	30.3	38.1	Net Worth						40.4
100.0	100.0	100.0	Total Liabilties & Net Worth						100.0
			INCOME DATA						
100.0	100.0	100.0	Net Sales						100.0
			Gross Profit						
92.2	91.5	94.9	Operating Expenses						97.5
7.8	8.5	5.1	Operating Profit						2.5
2.3	1.6	.1	All Other Expenses (net)						-.2
5.5	7.0	5.0	Profit Before Taxes						2.7
			RATIOS						
2.4	2.3	2.4							2.4
1.4	1.4	1.5	Current						1.5
1.0	1.0	1.0							1.0
2.2	2.2	2.1							2.1
1.3	1.4	1.3	Quick						1.3
.9	.9	.7							.7
3 111.4	**3** 123.0	**2** 180.1							**3** 121.2
13 28.9	**11** 32.9	**11** 33.4	Sales/Receivables						**11** 34.2
33 10.9	**25** 14.7	**30** 12.0							**21** 17.5
			Cost of Sales/Inventory						
			Cost of Sales/Payables						
5.3	6.3	5.2							6.3
16.5	13.7	13.0	Sales/Working Capital						19.6
-336.1	-812.4	661.8							999.8
67.4	48.5	99.2							163.1
(48) 17.8	(24) 11.6	(31) 14.0	EBIT/Interest						(23) 26.0
3.6	4.2	1.7							1.7
30.6		7.8							9.6
(14) 9.1		(11) 5.5	Net Profit + Depr., Dep., Amort./Cur. Mat. L/T/D						(10) 6.1
1.6		1.5							-.6
.0	.0	.0							.0
.2	.1	.1	Fixed/Worth						.1
1.2	.5	.8							.5
.9	.6	.7							.6
1.9	1.8	1.7	Debt/Worth						1.7
11.1	6.7	5.6							4.2
53.2	39.4	43.7							40.6
(72) 15.7	(55) 15.0	(65) 15.1	% Profit Before Taxes/Tangible Net Worth						(50) 15.1
6.7	4.6	3.3							3.7
14.8	11.9	11.9							11.0
7.0	6.5	6.5	% Profit Before Taxes/Total Assets						6.8
2.0	1.4	1.4							1.2
730.0	999.8	UND							999.8
48.8	108.0	82.7	Sales/Net Fixed Assets						71.3
16.5	23.6	25.9							26.1
4.1	4.5	4.2							4.2
2.2	2.6	2.9	Sales/Total Assets						3.4
1.1	1.4	1.3							1.8
.2	.2	.2							.2
(53) 1.4	(39) .5	(46) .6	% Depr., Dep., Amort./Sales						(37) .4
3.8	1.8	1.5							1.0
			% Officers', Directors' Owners' Comp/Sales						
12816379M	**12579509M**	**15779537M**	Net Sales ($)	**1109M**	**10756M**	**3707M**	**31911M**	**79297M**	**15652757M**
4681531M	**4008851M**	**5515393M**	Total Assets ($)	**8671M**	**3996M**	**2060M**	**65066M**	**122029M**	**5313571M**

M = $ thousand MM = $ million

See Pages 9 through 22 for Explanation of Ratios and Data

Current Data Sorted by Assets							Comparative Historical Data	
						Type of Statement		
	1	2	1	8	9	Unqualified	32	20
		1				Reviewed	3	2
	2				1	Compiled	5	5
4	2		1			Tax Returns	3	7
1	3	7	13	8	14	Other	39	39
	0 (4/1-9/30/13)		78 (10/1/13-3/31/14)				4/1/09-3/31/10	4/1/10-3/31/11
0-500M	**500M-2MM**	**2-10MM**	**10-50MM**	**50-100MM**	**100-250MM**		**ALL**	**ALL**
5	8	10	15	16	24	**NUMBER OF STATEMENTS**	82	73
%	%	%	%	%	%	**ASSETS**	%	%
		54.8	45.7	65.4	49.2	Cash & Equivalents	44.8	49.5
		21.9	11.8	9.5	11.4	Trade Receivables (net)	13.8	15.7
		.0	.0	.0	.0	Inventory	.3	.0
		3.6	8.6	4.7	5.8	All Other Current	8.3	4.2
		80.3	66.1	79.7	66.3	Total Current	67.2	69.4
		3.3	5.9	1.8	2.0	Fixed Assets (net)	3.3	4.0
		1.3	7.0	4.7	2.0	Intangibles (net)	2.5	5.3
		15.1	21.0	13.8	29.7	All Other Non-Current	27.0	21.3
		100.0	100.0	100.0	100.0	Total	100.0	100.0
						LIABILITIES		
		.0	1.1	.2	2.7	Notes Payable-Short Term	4.2	3.8
		.9	1.6	.2	1.5	Cur. Mat.-L.T.D.	1.1	.7
		27.1	12.7	4.6	10.8	Trade Payables	13.6	10.6
		.1	.3	.3	.2	Income Taxes Payable	.2	.3
		25.8	37.7	46.3	33.2	All Other Current	33.6	35.6
		54.0	53.3	51.7	48.4	Total Current	52.7	51.0
		3.1	23.3	2.0	2.7	Long-Term Debt	4.0	5.0
		.0	.0	.0	.1	Deferred Taxes	.0	.1
		6.6	9.3	8.9	11.9	All Other Non-Current	9.0	6.7
		36.3	14.0	37.4	37.0	Net Worth	34.2	37.2
		100.0	100.0	100.0	100.0	Total Liabilities & Net Worth	100.0	100.0
						INCOME DATA		
		100.0	100.0	100.0	100.0	Net Sales	100.0	100.0
						Gross Profit		
		83.0	89.8	87.8	95.4	Operating Expenses	90.6	92.6
		17.0	10.2	12.2	4.6	Operating Profit	9.4	7.4
		-1.4	.8	-2.5	-3.6	All Other Expenses (net)	-1.1	-2.9
		18.4	9.3	14.6	8.2	Profit Before Taxes	10.6	10.2
						RATIOS		
		2.1	1.6	2.1	1.9		1.9	2.1
		1.5	1.2	1.6	1.4	Current	1.5	1.6
		1.1	.9	1.2	1.1		1.0	.9
		2.1	1.6	2.1	1.9		1.7	2.1
		1.3	1.1	1.6	1.3	Quick	1.3	1.5
		1.0	.7	1.1	.9		.7	.7
		0 UND	**0** 741.4	**8** 44.9	**24** 15.5		**2** 188.6	**7** 51.7
		24 15.1	**33** 11.2	**51** 7.2	**69** 5.3	Sales/Receivables	**39** 9.3	**65** 5.6
		111 3.3	**135** 2.7	**99** 3.7	**114** 3.2		**109** 3.3	**127** 2.9
						Cost of Sales/Inventory		
						Cost of Sales/Payables		
		1.1	1.1	.8	1.2		1.0	.8
		6.4	12.5	1.4	2.9	Sales/Working Capital	3.9	4.3
		64.7	-40.4	4.8	26.1		NM	-19.5
							17.6	26.8
						EBIT/Interest	(30) 3.6	(24) 11.9
							2.2	3.0
						Net Profit + Depr., Dep., Amort./Cur. Mat. L/T/D		
		.0	.0	.0	.0		.0	.0
		.0	.0	.0	.0	Fixed/Worth	.0	.0
		.3	.6	.1	.1		.2	.1
		1.0	1.1	1.0	.9		.8	.9
		1.9	3.2	1.4	1.7	Debt/Worth	2.0	1.6
		4.3	6.9	4.8	3.0		4.6	3.6
		99.9	63.9	21.2	17.2		20.7	16.4
		86.4	(13) 10.9	(14) 12.1	(22) 9.8	% Profit Before Taxes/Tangible Net Worth	(75) 9.8	(65) 7.9
		20.2	4.2	7.1	4.1		2.5	4.0
		34.1	18.2	8.4	6.1		7.0	7.9
		20.3	5.7	4.6	4.2	% Profit Before Taxes/Total Assets	3.3	3.3
		5.6	2.4	2.2	2.1		.4	1.2
		UND	UND	UND	512.5		UND	UND
		548.1	37.4	108.0	35.9	Sales/Net Fixed Assets	116.5	88.6
		39.8	11.6	17.9	26.5		21.7	27.6
		2.3	3.0	.6	.7		1.2	1.0
		1.3	.6	.4	.5	Sales/Total Assets	.5	.5
		.5	.3	.3	.3		.3	.3
					.2		.5	.4
					(11) .3	% Depr., Dep., Amort./Sales	(28) 1.0	(21) .9
					1.4		1.7	1.8
							5.7	1.9
						% Officers', Directors' Owners' Comp/Sales	(10) 9.9	(15) 9.3
							22.1	22.8
4587M	**13356M**	**81594M**	**385014M**	**561483M**	**2205182M**	Net Sales ($)	**2439278M**	**2273684M**
876M	**12227M**	**45313M**	**388630M**	**1189353M**	**4021605M**	Total Assets ($)	**5236832M**	**4794458M**

M = $ thousand MM = $ million

See Pages 9 through 22 for Explanation of Ratios and Data

Comparative Historical Data				Current Data Sorted by Sales					
			Type of Statement						
29	23	21	Unqualified		1	2	1	4	13
3	4	1	Reviewed				1		
4	5	3	Compiled	2					1
11	4	7	Tax Returns	4	2				1
37	38	46	Other	2	4	2	4	11	23
				0 (4/1-9/30/13)			78 (10/1/13-3/31/14)		
4/1/11-3/31/12 ALL	**4/1/12-3/31/13 ALL**	**4/1/13-3/31/14 ALL**		**0-1MM**	**1-3MM**	**3-5MM**	**5-10MM**	**10-25MM**	**25MM & OVER**
84	74	78	**NUMBER OF STATEMENTS**	8	7	4	6	15	38
%	%	%	**ASSETS**	%	%	%	%	%	%
47.2	44.9	49.5	Cash & Equivalents					44.9	52.8
10.9	14.0	12.0	Trade Receivables (net)					14.5	10.9
.0	.0	1.0	Inventory					.0	.0
7.0	7.0	6.0	All Other Current					4.8	6.8
65.1	65.9	68.5	Total Current					64.2	70.5
8.8	7.4	5.5	Fixed Assets (net)					4.5	2.9
3.8	4.8	4.6	Intangibles (net)					5.2	3.9
22.3	21.9	21.4	All Other Non-Current					26.1	22.7
100.0	100.0	100.0	Total					100.0	100.0
			LIABILITIES						
6.1	3.5	3.2	Notes Payable-Short Term					1.1	1.8
.8	.3	1.2	Cur. Mat.-L.T.D.					1.6	1.2
11.3	11.5	14.4	Trade Payables					13.6	9.0
1.5	.5	.2	Income Taxes Payable					.4	.1
31.5	32.3	33.7	All Other Current					28.3	39.6
51.2	48.1	52.6	Total Current					44.9	51.8
8.6	4.8	9.9	Long-Term Debt					5.0	10.4
.0	.1	.0	Deferred Taxes					.0	.1
8.7	9.9	14.8	All Other Non-Current					10.5	10.6
31.4	37.0	22.6	Net Worth					39.7	27.2
100.0	100.0	100.0	Total Liabilties & Net Worth					100.0	100.0
			INCOME DATA						
100.0	100.0	100.0	Net Sales					100.0	100.0
			Gross Profit						
95.2	91.1	90.9	Operating Expenses					87.7	94.1
4.8	8.9	9.1	Operating Profit					12.3	5.9
-.3	-1.7	-.9	All Other Expenses (net)					.2	-3.1
5.1	10.5	10.0	Profit Before Taxes					12.1	9.0
			RATIOS						
2.3	2.4	1.9						1.7	1.9
1.3	1.5	1.4	Current					1.2	1.4
1.0	.9	1.0						1.0	1.1
2.0	2.1	1.8						1.6	1.9
1.3	1.3	1.2	Quick					1.2	1.3
.8	.7	.8						.9	.8
1 623.2	0 UND	0 UND						7 54.8	1 270.6
39 9.3	46 7.9	37 9.9	Sales/Receivables					43 8.5	44 8.3
76 4.8	96 3.8	104 3.5						135 2.7	101 3.6
			Cost of Sales/Inventory						
			Cost of Sales/Payables						
1.7	1.4	1.2						1.2	1.1
5.9	6.3	4.6	Sales/Working Capital					4.8	3.0
NM	-11.5	NM						154.0	31.8
17.5	16.1	33.9							36.8
(33) 3.8	(24) 5.9	(28) 14.0	EBIT/Interest						(13) 19.6
-1.5	1.2	3.5							4.0
			Net Profit + Depr., Dep., Amort./Cur. Mat. L/T/D						
.0	.0	.0						.0	.0
.0	.0	.0	Fixed/Worth					.0	.0
.4	.5	.4						.4	.1
1.0	.9	1.1						1.1	.9
2.1	1.7	1.9	Debt/Worth					1.6	1.7
5.0	4.6	5.9						5.6	3.6
25.1	33.6	35.9						94.0	27.9
(75) 10.9	(65) 9.3	(65) 11.8	% Profit Before Taxes/Tangible Net Worth					(14) 12.5	(33) 11.1
-1.7	2.1	5.9						5.9	5.9
7.3	9.4	15.0						26.8	9.5
2.8	3.5	4.9	% Profit Before Taxes/Total Assets					5.7	4.5
-1.1	.6	2.1						1.9	2.5
UND	UND	UND						UND	796.7
47.3	34.7	44.1	Sales/Net Fixed Assets					67.8	35.9
14.2	14.1	18.5						11.6	23.8
1.4	1.4	1.3						.8	1.0
.6	.6	.5	Sales/Total Assets					.5	.5
.3	.3	.3						.3	.4
.4	.6	.3							.2
(44) 1.1	(36) 1.2	(35) 1.1	% Depr., Dep., Amort./Sales						(18) .8
1.5	2.2	1.7							1.5
8.6		2.4							
(14) 10.4		(12) 7.6	% Officers', Directors' Owners' Comp/Sales						
23.7		13.4							
3716824M	3362279M	3251216M	Net Sales ($)	4570M	13988M	15026M	45960M	278558M	2893114M
5483560M	4655972M	5658004M	Total Assets ($)	7060M	19678M	34051M	170282M	583467M	4843466M

M = $ thousand MM = $ million

See Pages 9 through 22 for Explanation of Ratios and Data

Current Data Sorted by Assets							Comparative Historical Data	
						Type of Statement		
		2	3	1	4	Unqualified	9	16
		1				Reviewed	2	1
2						Compiled	3	2
2	1				1	Tax Returns	8	5
	3	1	4	1		Other	17	18
	3 (4/1-9/30/13)		23 (10/1/13-3/31/14)				4/1/09-3/31/10	4/1/10-3/31/11
0-500M	500M-2MM	2-10MM	10-50MM	50-100MM	100-250MM		ALL	ALL
4	4	4	7	2	5	**NUMBER OF STATEMENTS**	39	42
%	%	%	%	%	%	**ASSETS**	%	%
						Cash & Equivalents	31.6	36.0
						Trade Receivables (net)	5.3	7.4
						Inventory	.3	.0
						All Other Current	5.5	10.7
						Total Current	42.8	54.2
						Fixed Assets (net)	24.1	15.2
						Intangibles (net)	13.9	12.3
						All Other Non-Current	19.3	18.4
						Total	100.0	100.0
						LIABILITIES		
						Notes Payable-Short Term	9.9	6.8
						Cur. Mat.-L.T.D.	2.1	2.9
						Trade Payables	5.6	9.7
						Income Taxes Payable	.6	.4
						All Other Current	13.3	21.1
						Total Current	31.5	40.9
						Long-Term Debt	24.1	12.5
						Deferred Taxes	.7	.8
						All Other Non-Current	13.3	12.1
						Net Worth	30.5	33.7
						Total Liabilities & Net Worth	100.0	100.0
						INCOME DATA		
						Net Sales	100.0	100.0
						Gross Profit		
						Operating Expenses	92.6	92.2
						Operating Profit	7.4	7.8
						All Other Expenses (net)	2.9	.9
						Profit Before Taxes	4.5	7.0
						RATIOS		
							4.3	3.5
						Current	1.5	1.6
							1.0	1.0
							2.6	2.9
						Quick	1.4	1.4
							.9	.6
							0 UND	0 UND
						Sales/Receivables	3 110.5	5 66.4
							14 27.0	16 23.3
						Cost of Sales/Inventory		
						Cost of Sales/Payables		
							6.7	5.1
						Sales/Working Capital	18.4	12.7
							368.1	NM
							37.1	33.3
						EBIT/Interest	(28) 5.3	(31) 6.6
							.4	1.4
						Net Profit + Depr., Dep., Amort./Cur. Mat. L/T/D		
							.2	.2
						Fixed/Worth	.9	.5
							-.6	18.2
							.6	.7
						Debt/Worth	1.8	2.4
							-7.3	77.8
							90.0	66.3
						% Profit Before Taxes/Tangible Net Worth	(28) 22.7	(33) 27.9
							-1.5	-.9
							32.9	24.4
						% Profit Before Taxes/Total Assets	6.3	6.7
							-1.5	.1
							56.0	108.6
						Sales/Net Fixed Assets	21.8	30.6
							7.0	10.5
							3.5	3.6
						Sales/Total Assets	2.3	1.9
							.8	1.0
							.7	.4
						% Depr., Dep., Amort./Sales	(27) 1.3	(34) 1.2
							3.5	2.1
						% Officers', Directors' Owners' Comp/Sales		
8387M	8313M	27164M	244566M	350701M	1213805M	Net Sales ($)	1172388M	2469121M
1107M	4573M	20755M	147517M	152328M	953233M	Total Assets ($)	880119M	862802M

M = $ thousand MM = $ million

See Pages 9 through 22 for Explanation of Ratios and Data

Comparative Historical Data				Current Data Sorted by Sales					
			Type of Statement						
13	9	10	Unqualified				1	3	6
2	1	1	Reviewed		1				
1	1	2	Compiled	1	1				
9	7	4	Tax Returns	1	1	1			1
18	13	9	Other		4	1	1		3
4/1/11-3/31/12 ALL	**4/1/12-3/31/13 ALL**	**4/1/13-3/31/14 ALL**		**3 (4/1-9/30/13)**		**23 (10/1/13-3/31/14)**			
				0-1MM	**1-3MM**	**3-5MM**	**5-10MM**	**10-25MM**	**25MM & OVER**
43	31	26	**NUMBER OF STATEMENTS**	2	7	2	2	3	10
%	%	%	**ASSETS**	%	%	%	%	%	%
34.2	34.6	29.1	Cash & Equivalents						35.9
6.9	9.0	11.0	Trade Receivables (net)						12.5
.0	.0	.0	Inventory						.0
12.3	9.5	5.8	All Other Current						3.1
53.5	53.1	45.9	Total Current						51.6
20.2	15.9	18.5	Fixed Assets (net)						10.8
8.2	7.0	9.4	Intangibles (net)						11.4
18.1	24.0	26.3	All Other Non-Current						26.2
100.0	100.0	100.0	Total						100.0
			LIABILITIES						
8.0	6.2	6.0	Notes Payable-Short Term						.0
1.7	.5	1.4	Cur. Mat.-L.T.D.						.1
9.1	7.7	9.9	Trade Payables						16.1
.7	.0	.3	Income Taxes Payable						.6
22.9	22.4	15.3	All Other Current						20.2
42.4	36.8	33.0	Total Current						36.9
17.8	11.5	11.9	Long-Term Debt						7.1
.2	.8	.4	Deferred Taxes						.7
7.2	4.0	7.1	All Other Non-Current						.3
32.4	46.9	47.6	Net Worth						55.0
100.0	100.0	100.0	Total Liabilties & Net Worth						100.0
			INCOME DATA						
100.0	100.0	100.0	Net Sales						100.0
			Gross Profit						
91.4	86.8	90.6	Operating Expenses						93.0
8.6	13.2	9.4	Operating Profit						7.0
1.2	.5	.0	All Other Expenses (net)						-2.2
7.5	12.7	9.4	Profit Before Taxes						9.1
			RATIOS						
2.7	4.3	3.1							2.3
1.5	1.9	1.5	Current						1.5
1.0	.8	.7							.7
2.4	3.8	2.8							2.2
1.3	1.9	1.5	Quick						1.3
.8	.8	.6							.7
0 UND	**0** UND	**0** UND							**6** 66.3
3 113.7	**1** 605.9	**11** 33.9	Sales/Receivables						**26** 13.8
22 16.8	**16** 22.7	**29** 12.8							**34** 10.7
			Cost of Sales/Inventory						
			Cost of Sales/Payables						
4.6	5.7	5.3							4.1
13.0	9.1	17.3	Sales/Working Capital						11.3
-999.8	-27.0	-25.8							-7.2
44.0	96.8	30.9							
(27) 6.3	(16) 18.6	(18) 4.5	EBIT/Interest						
1.9	5.2	.6							
			Net Profit + Depr., Dep., Amort./Cur. Mat. L/T/D						
.1	.0	.0							.0
.3	.2	.4	Fixed/Worth						.2
1.2	1.1	NM							1.5
.6	.4	.4							.5
2.0	1.1	1.2	Debt/Worth						1.0
19.9	11.5	NM							11.8
95.5	99.9	37.1							
(35) 20.3	(27) 41.6	(20) 26.0	% Profit Before Taxes/Tangible Net Worth						
5.5	17.4	16.4							
17.2	37.4	16.6							11.5
8.2	15.3	10.5	% Profit Before Taxes/Total Assets						10.5
-.3	7.9	1.7							2.4
166.0	297.5	59.6							41.3
31.3	35.7	26.3	Sales/Net Fixed Assets						20.3
10.9	16.5	12.7							10.8
4.2	4.0	4.2							4.0
1.9	2.1	1.4	Sales/Total Assets						.8
.6	.7	.6							.6
.6	.3	.3							
(30) 1.0	(21) .7	(19) 1.1	% Depr., Dep., Amort./Sales						
2.4	2.0	2.5							
			% Officers', Directors' Owners' Comp/Sales						
1138013M	918097M	1852936M	Net Sales ($)	1037M	15132M	8248M	15555M	58201M	1754763M
705972M	841554M	1279513M	Total Assets ($)	1923M	14191M	13369M	16249M	25256M	1208525M

M = $ thousand MM = $ million

See Pages 9 through 22 for Explanation of Ratios and Data

Current Data Sorted by Assets							Comparative Historical Data	
Type of Statement								
Unqualified			5	4	2	8	25	25
Reviewed								1
Compiled		1					3	4
Tax Returns	2		1				10	7
Other	1	2	3	8		5	19	23
	3 (4/1-9/30/13)		39 (10/1/13-3/31/14)				4/1/09-3/31/10 ALL	4/1/10-3/31/11 ALL
	0-500M	500M-2MM	2-10MM	10-50MM	50-100MM	100-250MM		
NUMBER OF STATEMENTS	3	3	9	12	2	13	57	60
ASSETS	%	%	%	%	%	%	%	%
Cash & Equivalents				50.3		45.9	48.5	51.1
Trade Receivables (net)				18.0		7.1	8.7	11.6
Inventory				.0		.1	.8	.6
All Other Current				12.6		1.5	5.0	5.8
Total Current				81.0		54.6	63.0	69.1
Fixed Assets (net)				4.4		2.7	3.8	5.7
Intangibles (net)				.5		.6	10.5	5.6
All Other Non-Current				14.2		42.1	22.7	19.7
Total				100.0		100.0	100.0	100.0
LIABILITIES								
Notes Payable-Short Term				4.9		.1	10.6	4.9
Cur. Mat.-L.T.D.				7.3		.3	2.0	.4
Trade Payables				12.1		15.1	10.2	12.3
Income Taxes Payable				.1		.3	.6	.1
All Other Current				30.0		24.0	28.2	31.0
Total Current				54.4		39.8	51.5	48.7
Long-Term Debt				1.5		1.6	5.4	7.0
Deferred Taxes				.0		.1	.7	.6
All Other Non-Current				9.8		25.9	13.0	6.4
Net Worth				34.3		32.7	29.4	37.4
Total Liabilties & Net Worth				100.0		100.0	100.0	100.0
INCOME DATA								
Net Sales				100.0		100.0	100.0	100.0
Gross Profit								
Operating Expenses				86.9		81.8	89.3	86.8
Operating Profit				13.1		18.2	10.7	13.2
All Other Expenses (net)				.1		2.7	.1	-.2
Profit Before Taxes				13.0		15.5	10.7	13.3
RATIOS								
Current				11.4		3.3	2.8	2.4
				1.8		1.2	1.5	1.5
				1.0		.8	.9	1.0
Quick				11.4		2.3	2.7	2.1
				1.8		1.1	1.4	1.4
				.6		.8	.7	.9
Sales/Receivables				0 UND		0 UND	0 UND	0 867.6
				31 11.7		56 6.5	7 50.6	15 24.7
				104 3.5		122 3.0	43 8.5	48 7.6
Cost of Sales/Inventory								
Cost of Sales/Payables								
Sales/Working Capital				.8		.8	1.7	1.7
				2.2		1.3	6.6	7.7
				91.9		-27.9	-20.7	97.1
EBIT/Interest							31.2	40.5
							(26) 7.8	(30) 9.7
							.4	2.0
Net Profit + Depr., Dep., Amort./Cur. Mat. L/T/D								
Fixed/Worth				.0		.0	.0	.0
				.0		.0	.0	.0
				NM		.2	.2	.3
Debt/Worth				.3		.7	.8	.9
				2.7		4.2	2.7	2.1
				NM		9.3	9.8	10.5
% Profit Before Taxes/Tangible Net Worth						18.3	53.1	41.9
						2.8	(48) 13.8	(53) 13.8
						-1.8	1.4	3.8
% Profit Before Taxes/Total Assets				22.1		8.1	18.5	11.5
				3.7		1.6	4.3	5.6
				.6		.0	.1	.6
Sales/Net Fixed Assets				UND		UND	UND	UND
				UND		34.6	164.0	254.3
				47.2		10.7	26.6	25.6
Sales/Total Assets				1.7		.5	2.3	2.6
				.6		.2	.7	.7
				.2		.1	.4	.3
% Depr., Dep., Amort./Sales							.3	.3
							(21) .9	(24) .6
							1.8	1.9
% Officers', Directors' Owners' Comp/Sales								2.5
								(10) 8.6
								18.6
Net Sales ($)	1300M	13439M	50101M	233178M	36091M	707548M	2398420M	3035917M
Total Assets ($)	339M	2789M	48376M	307555M	117636M	2061728M	3127302M	3831212M

M = $ thousand MM = $ million

See Pages 9 through 22 for Explanation of Ratios and Data

Comparative Historical Data | Current Data Sorted by Sales

			Type of Statement						
26	21	19	Unqualified		4	1	2	6	6
2	1		Reviewed						
1	1	1	Compiled				1		
4	5	3	Tax Returns	2		1			
29	17	19	Other	3		3	4	3	6
4/1/11-3/31/12	4/1/12-3/31/13	4/1/13-3/31/14		3 (4/1-9/30/13)		39 (10/1/13-3/31/14)			
ALL	ALL	ALL		0-1MM	1-3MM	3-5MM	5-10MM	10-25MM	25MM & OVER
62	45	42	NUMBER OF STATEMENTS	5	4	5	7	9	12
%	%	%	ASSETS	%	%	%	%	%	%
50.1	46.2	48.0	Cash & Equivalents						47.3
13.7	15.8	10.3	Trade Receivables (net)						21.2
.0	1.6	.0	Inventory						.1
4.9	3.7	4.7	All Other Current						1.6
68.7	67.3	63.0	Total Current						70.2
2.9	7.3	6.2	Fixed Assets (net)						7.3
5.8	6.1	.8	Intangibles (net)						.7
22.5	19.4	30.1	All Other Non-Current						21.8
100.0	100.0	100.0	Total						100.0
			LIABILITIES						
3.2	6.3	4.3	Notes Payable-Short Term						2.6
.7	.5	4.0	Cur. Mat.-L.T.D.						7.6
12.3	12.9	10.1	Trade Payables						27.1
.5	.2	.2	Income Taxes Payable						.3
29.4	26.8	27.3	All Other Current						21.6
46.1	46.8	45.9	Total Current						59.2
5.9	5.3	2.5	Long-Term Debt						2.0
.6	.4	.0	Deferred Taxes						.1
11.3	13.5	12.4	All Other Non-Current						15.2
36.1	34.1	39.2	Net Worth						23.6
100.0	100.0	100.0	Total Liabilities & Net Worth						100.0
			INCOME DATA						
100.0	100.0	100.0	Net Sales						100.0
			Gross Profit						
90.5	87.3	84.5	Operating Expenses						92.5
9.5	12.7	15.5	Operating Profit						7.5
-1.0	.2	.7	All Other Expenses (net)						1.3
10.5	12.5	14.8	Profit Before Taxes						6.2
			RATIOS						
2.7	2.6	4.3							2.4
1.4	1.3	1.2	Current						1.1
1.0	.9	.8							.8
2.5	2.4	4.2							2.3
1.3	1.2	1.2	Quick						1.1
.8	.8	.5							.8
0 835.8	0 845.5	0 UND							18 20.6
28 13.1	31 11.9	12 30.3	Sales/Receivables						99 3.7
81 4.5	101 3.6	96 3.8							140 2.6
			Cost of Sales/Inventory						
			Cost of Sales/Payables						
1.1	1.1	1.1							1.4
5.5	4.4	7.6	Sales/Working Capital						52.3
-61.4	-55.1	-18.1							-6.5
20.1	38.4	108.1							
(24) 4.4	(20) 6.5	(16) 20.1	EBIT/Interest						
-1.9	2.4	3.6							
			Net Profit + Depr., Dep., Amort./Cur. Mat. L/T/D						
.0	.0	.0							.0
.0	.0	.0	Fixed/Worth						.2
.2	.7	.2							NM
1.3	1.2	.4							1.1
2.6	2.9	2.7	Debt/Worth						4.8
6.4	14.0	9.7							NM
45.7	89.1	56.4							
(54) 14.4	(39) 14.4	(38) 11.5	% Profit Before Taxes/Tangible Net Worth						
-5.0	2.1	1.2							
11.2	11.6	13.5							9.0
3.4	4.2	3.7	% Profit Before Taxes/Total Assets						3.7
-2.7	.6	.3							-.7
UND	UND	UND							36.0
144.5	63.9	UND	Sales/Net Fixed Assets						28.7
33.5	18.1	31.4							6.7
1.4	1.3	1.7							1.7
.6	.6	.5	Sales/Total Assets						.6
.3	.2	.2							.2
.3	.5	.5							
(24) .9	(17) 1.1	(13) 1.7	% Depr., Dep., Amort./Sales						
1.9	2.4	2.8							
			% Officers', Directors' Owners' Comp/Sales						
1496171M	1650000M	1041657M	Net Sales ($)	2829M	9957M	17026M	51775M	167481M	792589M
2845834M	2633082M	2538423M	Total Assets ($)	6049M	128160M	93284M	294852M	616980M	1399098M

M = $ thousand MM = $ million

See Pages 9 through 22 for Explanation of Ratios and Data

Current Data Sorted by Assets | Comparative Historical Data

						Type of Statement		
3	2	21	30	8	18	Unqualified	107	119
3	15	32	18	1		Reviewed	92	93
12	26	34	4		1	Compiled	106	98
140	108	45	6	1	4	Tax Returns	262	255
53	65	72	46	18	21	Other	312	313
76 (4/1-9/30/13)		731 (10/1/13-3/31/14)					4/1/09-3/31/10	4/1/10-3/31/11
0-500M	500M-2MM	2-10MM	10-50MM	50-100MM	100-250MM		ALL	ALL
211	216	204	104	28	44	NUMBER OF STATEMENTS	879	878
%	%	%	%	%	%	ASSETS	%	%
36.7	22.1	29.7	33.3	39.0	26.1	Cash & Equivalents	29.7	28.3
8.3	12.1	20.8	22.3	18.8	13.7	Trade Receivables (net)	16.9	15.4
.2	.4	.4	.0	.0	.0	Inventory	.2	.3
6.1	3.8	5.6	7.3	11.5	6.0	All Other Current	6.4	6.0
51.2	38.4	56.5	62.9	69.3	45.7	Total Current	53.1	50.1
22.2	18.1	11.0	7.8	6.7	10.2	Fixed Assets (net)	13.1	15.4
14.6	29.0	20.4	15.4	12.8	26.1	Intangibles (net)	17.6	19.9
11.9	14.5	12.1	13.8	11.2	18.0	All Other Non-Current	16.1	14.7
100.0	100.0	100.0	100.0	100.0	100.0	Total	100.0	100.0
						LIABILITIES		
18.3	8.7	5.5	4.8	4.7	2.4	Notes Payable-Short Term	10.4	11.9
8.7	3.2	1.8	3.6	1.0	1.9	Cur. Mat.-L.T.D.	4.8	4.0
10.0	14.6	26.8	24.9	16.8	16.2	Trade Payables	19.1	18.6
.4	.0	.3	.5	.7	.2	Income Taxes Payable	.3	.1
22.5	11.8	13.8	22.5	20.6	21.3	All Other Current	20.0	18.7
59.9	38.3	48.1	56.3	43.8	42.0	Total Current	54.5	53.2
29.2	32.7	15.3	11.1	19.0	28.2	Long-Term Debt	19.5	22.0
.2	.1	.1	.2	1.0	.7	Deferred Taxes	.1	.3
9.2	8.4	7.9	4.9	4.2	5.4	All Other Non-Current	7.6	7.3
1.5	20.5	28.5	27.5	31.9	23.6	Net Worth	18.2	17.2
100.0	100.0	100.0	100.0	100.0	100.0	Total Liabilties & Net Worth	100.0	100.0
						INCOME DATA		
100.0	100.0	100.0	100.0	100.0	100.0	Net Sales	100.0	100.0
						Gross Profit		
84.7	86.2	86.5	87.7	85.6	89.5	Operating Expenses	88.1	89.1
15.3	13.8	13.5	12.3	14.4	10.5	Operating Profit	11.9	10.9
1.5	2.8	1.0	1.0	2.0	3.6	All Other Expenses (net)	2.3	2.0
13.8	11.0	12.6	11.3	12.5	7.0	Profit Before Taxes	9.5	8.9
						RATIOS		
2.7	2.1	1.9	1.4	2.3	1.3		1.7	1.7
1.0	1.0	1.1	1.2	1.3	1.0	Current	1.0	1.0
.3	.5	.8	1.0	1.1	.8		.6	.6
2.5	2.0	1.8	1.3	1.9	1.2		1.6	1.5
.8	1.0	1.1	1.1	1.1	.9	Quick	.9	.9
.2	.4	.6	.9	.9	.5		.4	.4
0 UND	**0** UND	**3** 126.8	**15** 23.7	**7** 49.6	**4** 102.2		**0** UND	**0** UND
0 UND	**2** 214.3	**33** 11.2	**57** 6.4	**35** 10.4	**31** 11.7	Sales/Receivables	**17** 21.6	**13** 27.9
4 89.1	**27** 13.7	**74** 4.9	**107** 3.4	**135** 2.7	**96** 3.8		**59** 6.2	**53** 6.9
						Cost of Sales/Inventory		
						Cost of Sales/Payables		
16.0	12.1	5.9	4.0	1.8	18.5		7.3	9.4
-359.7	201.7	23.1	12.7	7.4	-50.1	Sales/Working Capital	83.8	118.3
-11.0	-13.5	-20.4	-32.8	21.3	-10.8		-10.2	-11.1
43.8	20.8	37.9	51.7	62.0	16.8		25.5	21.7
(141) 10.0	(165) 5.7	(153) 9.0	(73) 15.7	(20) 23.2	(28) 7.0	EBIT/Interest	(624) 6.0	(624) 5.7
2.3	2.5	3.5	6.6	6.2	2.3		1.8	1.7
		34.9	4.0				8.0	9.6
		(17) 4.6	(23) 3.0			Net Profit + Depr., Dep., Amort./Cur. Mat. L/T/D	(98) 1.9	(96) 2.6
		2.3	1.2				.8	.7
.0	.1	.1	.1	.0	.1		.1	.1
.6	2.0	.5	.5	.2	4.1	Fixed/Worth	.6	.9
-1.0	-.4	-.8	10.4	.7	-.1		-.8	-.5
.7	1.8	1.5	2.0	1.0	1.9		1.3	1.5
6.3	586.7	6.9	5.5	3.3	49.6	Debt/Worth	6.2	8.4
-2.1	-2.2	-6.9	769.9	7.7	-2.1		-4.4	-3.3
429.6	167.9	132.6	91.8	115.4	86.5		119.7	114.1
(120) 137.0	(110) 73.0	(135) 50.7	(79) 41.5	(25) 33.6	(25) 29.1	% Profit Before Taxes/Tangible Net Worth	(567) 31.3	(527) 33.8
50.0	15.3	22.6	13.9	13.8	3.1		6.3	7.1
117.1	31.9	23.2	16.5	15.4	10.9		21.7	24.6
40.4	11.9	12.8	7.3	10.7	6.5	% Profit Before Taxes/Total Assets	7.1	7.7
6.7	3.3	4.5	2.4	3.6	.5		1.1	1.6
999.8	119.6	118.6	69.4	68.6	61.5		131.6	99.6
59.1	37.6	42.3	23.1	25.1	36.0	Sales/Net Fixed Assets	33.5	32.1
15.6	12.8	16.9	9.7	9.2	13.5		13.7	12.0
9.8	3.3	2.0	1.3	1.2	1.4		3.2	3.5
4.8	1.9	1.3	1.0	.8	.8	Sales/Total Assets	1.6	1.6
2.6	1.0	.8	.6	.6	.4		.8	.8
.4	.6	.6	.9	1.4	.4		.7	.7
(104) .8	(114) 1.4	(117) 1.1	(72) 1.5	(20) 2.0	(18) 1.4	% Depr., Dep., Amort./Sales	(495) 1.4	(525) 1.6
2.4	3.4	2.2	3.3	4.0	3.5		2.6	2.7
7.4	6.9	4.0	4.8				6.8	7.1
(143) 15.3	(120) 11.4	(88) 8.9	(17) 8.7			% Officers', Directors' Owners' Comp/Sales	(389) 13.4	(391) 13.7
24.6	20.3	16.4	12.9				22.5	21.6
246178M	**545892M**	**1670322M**	**2429020M**	**2455474M**	**8977647M**	Net Sales ($)	**10809436M**	**14802575M**
44610M	**227514M**	**1004946M**	**2401348M**	**2008896M**	**7089841M**	Total Assets ($)	**12505704M**	**13704714M**

M = $ thousand MM = $ million

See Pages 9 through 22 for Explanation of Ratios and Data

Comparative Historical Data				Current Data Sorted by Sales					
			Type of Statement						
102	71	82	Unqualified	3	8	7	10	20	34
81	79	69	Reviewed	5	10	14	17	12	11
95	91	77	Compiled	15	19	11	17	13	2
301	321	304	Tax Returns	126	103	32	22	13	8
318	315	275	Other	53	58	29	44	36	55
4/1/11-3/31/12 ALL	4/1/12-3/31/13 ALL	4/1/13-3/31/14 ALL		76 (4/1-9/30/13)		731 (10/1/13-3/31/14)			
				0-1MM	1-3MM	3-5MM	5-10MM	10-25MM	25MM & OVER
897	877	807	**NUMBER OF STATEMENTS**	202	198	93	110	94	110
%	%	%	**ASSETS**	%	%	%	%	%	%
29.7	30.2	30.1	Cash & Equivalents	26.6	27.9	33.3	30.3	35.0	33.1
15.9	14.4	14.9	Trade Receivables (net)	8.1	12.9	17.1	21.8	20.2	17.8
.1	.1	.2	Inventory	.2	.1	.0	.6	.8	.0
5.0	4.8	5.7	All Other Current	4.7	4.0	3.8	7.3	7.1	9.3
50.8	49.5	50.9	Total Current	39.5	45.0	54.2	60.1	63.2	60.2
14.7	16.0	15.2	Fixed Assets (net)	25.1	15.1	13.1	8.1	9.6	11.1
19.3	19.0	20.6	Intangibles (net)	23.7	26.5	17.3	15.4	14.1	17.7
15.2	15.4	13.2	All Other Non-Current	11.6	13.4	15.3	16.4	13.1	11.0
100.0	100.0	100.0	Total	100.0	100.0	100.0	100.0	100.0	100.0
			LIABILITIES						
11.5	10.5	9.4	Notes Payable-Short Term	11.8	13.6	10.6	6.6	5.6	2.3
3.3	4.8	4.2	Cur. Mat.-L.T.D.	7.4	4.4	2.7	2.2	2.9	2.2
18.7	17.6	18.0	Trade Payables	8.2	15.7	23.4	23.7	28.0	21.2
.2	.1	.3	Income Taxes Payable	.2	.3	.1	.2	.5	.5
17.7	17.7	17.3	All Other Current	14.9	15.7	15.1	16.8	18.9	25.6
51.5	50.7	49.2	Total Current	42.6	49.8	51.9	49.5	55.9	51.8
21.0	23.3	23.9	Long-Term Debt	36.3	31.3	13.0	13.5	8.3	20.6
.1	.1	.2	Deferred Taxes	.1	.1	.0	.4	.2	.5
8.3	8.3	7.7	All Other Non-Current	7.8	8.2	5.4	10.1	9.9	4.5
19.0	17.6	19.0	Net Worth	13.2	10.6	29.7	26.6	25.6	22.7
100.0	100.0	100.0	Total Liabilties & Net Worth	100.0	100.0	100.0	100.0	100.0	100.0
			INCOME DATA						
100.0	100.0	100.0	Net Sales	100.0	100.0	100.0	100.0	100.0	100.0
			Gross Profit						
88.2	87.3	86.2	Operating Expenses	79.0	87.6	88.9	88.2	90.3	89.3
11.8	12.7	13.8	Operating Profit	21.0	12.4	11.1	11.8	9.7	10.7
2.1	2.2	1.8	All Other Expenses (net)	4.5	1.3	.8	1.5	-.3	.8
9.7	10.5	12.0	Profit Before Taxes	16.5	11.2	10.3	10.3	10.0	9.9
			RATIOS						
1.7	1.9	2.0		2.9	1.9	1.8	2.0	1.7	1.4
1.0	1.1	1.1	Current	1.0	1.0	1.1	1.2	1.2	1.1
.6	.6	.6		.3	.5	.7	.9	1.0	.9
1.6	1.7	1.8		2.8	1.8	1.8	1.8	1.6	1.3
1.0	(876) 1.0	1.0	Quick	.8	1.0	1.1	1.1	1.0	1.0
.5	.5	.5		.2	.4	.6	.7	.8	.7
0 UND	0 UND	0 UND		0 UND	0 UND	0 999.8	1 383.0	5 73.0	10 38.3
13 28.8	7 56.0	8 45.8	Sales/Receivables	0 UND	2 214.3	15 24.6	27 13.5	31 11.9	34 10.7
51 7.1	47 7.7	53 6.9		4 89.3	39 9.4	62 5.9	72 5.1	73 5.0	96 3.8
			Cost of Sales/Inventory						
			Cost of Sales/Payables						
9.8	9.0	8.0		10.5	14.6	5.9	5.9	5.5	8.0
116.4	64.4	53.7	Sales/Working Capital	612.5	778.4	41.9	23.9	19.6	22.4
-12.3	-14.6	-14.2		-7.9	-12.9	-14.1	-39.3	-40.6	-22.9
24.3	32.0	34.5		15.9	23.6	54.2	37.0	61.9	45.4
(623) 7.0	(605) 8.1	(580) 9.0	EBIT/Interest	(132) 4.5	(155) 5.7	(69) 15.4	(76) 9.0	(70) 21.6	(78) 15.5
2.0	2.3	3.0		1.7	2.4	4.0	3.9	6.4	5.6
13.6	4.0	8.6					8.4	11.1	9.3
(84) 2.6	(59) 1.4	(65) 3.4	Net Profit + Depr., Dep., Amort./Cur. Mat. L/T/D				(10) 3.1	(13) 3.0	(27) 4.0
1.0	.7	1.3					1.8	.8	1.9
.1	.1	.1		.0	.1	.1	.1	.1	.2
.8	.6	.7	Fixed/Worth	.8	1.3	.6	.4	.4	.7
-.6	-1.1	-.8		-1.1	-.4	-1.1	-1.1	2.0	-1.4
1.4	1.3	1.4		.9	1.8	1.0	1.5	1.5	1.9
8.8	6.8	8.1	Debt/Worth	9.4	UND	5.0	6.1	4.7	5.3
-3.6	-4.4	-3.1		-1.6	-2.0	-7.1	-8.5	51.8	-8.7
133.6	159.5	167.8		295.5	211.2	140.3	155.3	132.5	110.6
(542) 40.5	(548) 49.8	(494) 59.9	% Profit Before Taxes/Tangible Net Worth	(111) 62.5	(100) 97.8	(61) 49.4	(74) 67.8	(73) 57.0	(75) 47.0
8.4	11.7	20.2		16.7	20.2	12.8	23.0	25.9	14.5
28.6	31.6	33.9		56.6	36.3	38.5	28.9	24.2	20.0
8.3	10.6	12.5	% Profit Before Taxes/Total Assets	12.4	13.8	15.2	12.6	13.8	8.2
1.8	2.5	3.3		2.4	3.1	4.0	3.9	3.7	3.3
152.5	171.1	134.8		782.3	124.1	157.8	149.8	101.3	59.2
38.6	39.7	38.3	Sales/Net Fixed Assets	32.0	43.7	51.2	50.9	34.7	24.5
14.7	13.9	13.1		7.8	15.8	13.5	23.2	16.1	10.3
3.6	4.0	3.5		4.7	4.0	4.0	3.3	2.4	1.9
1.7	1.8	1.7	Sales/Total Assets	1.5	2.2	2.0	1.7	1.4	1.1
.8	.9	.9		.6	1.1	1.1	.9	1.0	.7
.7	.5	.6		.8	.5	.6	.5	.5	.9
(500) 1.4	(481) 1.3	(445) 1.3	% Depr., Dep., Amort./Sales	(93) 2.1	(102) 1.1	(51) 1.4	(69) .8	(57) 1.2	(73) 1.6
2.5	2.6	3.0		9.3	2.6	2.5	1.4	2.0	3.2
7.7	6.9	6.3		8.5	6.7	5.1	4.4	2.2	1.2
(407) 14.3	(435) 13.1	(380) 11.9	% Officers', Directors' Owners' Comp/Sales	(113) 15.8	(122) 12.2	(46) 10.8	(52) 9.0	(26) 6.9	(21) 11.6
22.2	22.2	22.5		25.5	22.0	23.8	14.0	14.2	22.7
15961529M	14573227M	16324533M	Net Sales ($)	100012M	357286M	371276M	785081M	1426897M	13283981M
12782156M	12071825M	12777155M	Total Assets ($)	116103M	319496M	319804M	1035779M	1393873M	9592100M

M = $ thousand MM = $ million

See Pages 9 through 22 for Explanation of Ratios and Data

Current Data Sorted by Assets							Comparative Historical Data	
						Type of Statement		
		3	5	1		Unqualified	8	6
	1	1				Reviewed	4	
	1	1				Compiled	1	1
4	1	1				Tax Returns	4	7
1	4	4		2	2	Other	6	10
5 (4/1-9/30/13)			27 (10/1/13-3/31/14)				4/1/09-3/31/10 ALL	4/1/10-3/31/11 ALL
0-500M	500M-2MM	2-10MM	10-50MM	50-100MM	100-250MM			
5	7	10	5	3	2	**NUMBER OF STATEMENTS**	23	24
%	%	%	%	%	%	**ASSETS**	%	%
		30.3				Cash & Equivalents	29.2	29.4
		35.4				Trade Receivables (net)	16.6	23.2
		.0				Inventory	1.0	.0
		9.7				All Other Current	4.1	13.3
		75.4				Total Current	50.9	66.0
		18.6				Fixed Assets (net)	18.7	10.7
		.7				Intangibles (net)	13.5	11.3
		5.3				All Other Non-Current	16.9	12.1
		100.0				Total	100.0	100.0
						LIABILITIES		
		9.3				Notes Payable-Short Term	7.0	5.7
		2.4				Cur. Mat.-L.T.D.	1.5	3.2
		7.4				Trade Payables	4.9	5.8
		.0				Income Taxes Payable	.0	.0
		31.0				All Other Current	32.4	25.2
		50.1				Total Current	45.8	39.9
		6.0				Long-Term Debt	12.8	15.0
		.0				Deferred Taxes	.5	.6
		1.4				All Other Non-Current	19.4	5.3
		42.5				Net Worth	21.5	39.2
		100.0				Total Liabilities & Net Worth	100.0	100.0
						INCOME DATA		
		100.0				Net Sales	100.0	100.0
						Gross Profit		
		94.7				Operating Expenses	89.3	90.4
		5.3				Operating Profit	10.7	9.6
		.4				All Other Expenses (net)	6.8	1.7
		5.0				Profit Before Taxes	3.9	7.9
						RATIOS		
		11.3					2.2	3.8
		1.2				Current	1.2	1.7
		1.0					.6	1.1
		8.3					1.8	3.2
		1.1				Quick	1.0	1.4
		.8					.6	.7
		14 26.3					**0** UND	**0** UND
		29 12.4				Sales/Receivables	**19** 19.0	**27** 13.7
		48 7.6					**33** 11.1	**53** 6.9
						Cost of Sales/Inventory		
						Cost of Sales/Payables		
		7.3					9.9	5.9
		13.0				Sales/Working Capital	30.8	14.1
		NM					-6.1	83.6
							66.5	51.4
						EBIT/Interest	(16) 4.9	(16) 14.4
							1.9	1.9
								15.8
						Net Profit + Depr., Dep., Amort./Cur. Mat. L/T/D		(10) 5.5
								.6
		.1					.3	.1
		.4				Fixed/Worth	.6	.3
		1.2					-.2	.8
		.3					1.0	.5
		2.1				Debt/Worth	3.1	2.0
		5.0					-15.8	43.4
							141.0	80.6
						% Profit Before Taxes/Tangible Net Worth	(15) 19.9	(20) 28.3
							3.2	17.8
		10.5					26.8	34.1
		5.2				% Profit Before Taxes/Total Assets	8.0	11.7
		1.7					2.8	3.8
		78.6					111.4	122.1
		28.4				Sales/Net Fixed Assets	23.8	41.6
		9.4					13.7	12.0
		5.8					3.7	4.0
		3.6				Sales/Total Assets	2.0	2.4
		1.5					1.1	1.4
							1.2	.6
						% Depr., Dep., Amort./Sales	(15) 2.2	(16) 1.1
							3.3	1.7
								4.0
						% Officers', Directors' Owners' Comp/Sales		(10) 7.2
								15.7
15658M	18797M	169863M	137432M	150470M	512996M	Net Sales ($)	512492M	503401M
1376M	8198M	47024M	87737M	188232M	345709M	Total Assets ($)	379420M	267919M

M = $ thousand MM = $ million

See Pages 9 through 22 for Explanation of Ratios and Data

Comparative Historical Data | Current Data Sorted by Sales

4/1/11-3/31/12 ALL	4/1/12-3/31/13 ALL	4/1/13-3/31/14 ALL	Type of Statement	0-1MM	1-3MM	3-5MM	5-10MM	10-25MM	25MM & OVER
6	5	9	Unqualified				1	2	6
2	1	2	Reviewed				2		
2	5	2	Compiled		1		1		
9	13	6	Tax Returns	1	2	3			
16	11	13	Other	2	1	2	1	3	4
					5 (4/1-9/30/13)		27 (10/1/13-3/31/14)		
35	35	32	NUMBER OF STATEMENTS	3	4	5	5	5	10
%	%	%	**ASSETS**	%	%	%	%	%	%
17.8	32.9	32.7	Cash & Equivalents						24.6
31.0	29.9	20.5	Trade Receivables (net)						26.6
.3	2.1	.0	Inventory						.0
6.8	4.2	3.6	All Other Current						2.7
55.9	69.2	56.8	Total Current						53.9
13.5	11.8	18.8	Fixed Assets (net)						19.6
16.8	5.4	11.9	Intangibles (net)						13.0
13.7	13.4	12.6	All Other Non-Current						13.4
100.0	100.0	100.0	Total						100.0
			LIABILITIES						
7.1	10.0	8.4	Notes Payable-Short Term						6.2
1.8	1.8	1.4	Cur. Mat.-L.T.D.						2.6
10.7	9.9	7.7	Trade Payables						15.7
.8	.4	.1	Income Taxes Payable						.2
28.5	25.3	23.4	All Other Current						21.7
49.0	47.4	40.9	Total Current						46.4
13.7	12.9	12.7	Long-Term Debt						7.4
.6	.5	.0	Deferred Taxes						.0
12.8	7.7	2.5	All Other Non-Current						2.6
23.9	31.3	43.9	Net Worth						43.6
100.0	100.0	100.0	Total Liabilties & Net Worth						100.0
			INCOME DATA						
100.0	100.0	100.0	Net Sales						100.0
			Gross Profit						
85.4	85.3	86.9	Operating Expenses						91.3
14.6	14.7	13.1	Operating Profit						8.7
1.8	2.4	.7	All Other Expenses (net)						.0
12.8	12.3	12.3	Profit Before Taxes						8.7
			RATIOS						
2.5	4.3	2.6							2.3
1.3	1.9	1.6	Current						1.5
.6	1.2	1.0							.7
1.7	3.5	2.5							2.3
1.0	1.5	1.6	Quick						1.4
.3	1.0	.8							.7
0 UND	0 UND	0 UND							0 UND
25 14.8	16 23.4	14 26.4	Sales/Receivables						41 9.0
47 7.7	64 5.7	41 8.8							45 8.1
			Cost of Sales/Inventory						
			Cost of Sales/Payables						
5.5	4.6	6.4							5.9
22.2	10.2	14.2	Sales/Working Capital						11.0
-19.8	106.3	NM							-33.9
31.2	21.5	170.9							
(26) 7.9	(18) 8.1	(21) 31.1	EBIT/Interest						
2.5	2.1	5.2							
			Net Profit + Depr., Dep., Amort./Cur. Mat. L/T/D						
.1	.0	.1							.3
.6	.2	.5	Fixed/Worth						.5
-.4	.7	1.7							NM
.9	.6	.5							.6
4.5	1.9	1.8	Debt/Worth						1.6
-5.8	6.7	15.8							NM
119.3	119.1	140.4							
(23) 38.1	(31) 45.6	(28) 52.7	% Profit Before Taxes/Tangible Net Worth						
6.9	21.7	15.8							
34.3	51.1	32.6							18.4
8.8	15.8	11.0	% Profit Before Taxes/Total Assets						7.8
2.3	5.8	4.3							.0
598.5	999.8	122.8							20.5
63.7	54.1	21.0	Sales/Net Fixed Assets						12.4
14.8	18.4	6.6							9.1
4.8	4.9	5.6							4.6
1.8	2.6	2.8	Sales/Total Assets						2.5
.8	1.3	.9							1.3
.7	.2	1.0							
(13) 2.7	(19) .7	(22) 1.9	% Depr., Dep., Amort./Sales						
5.2	2.3	4.1							
2.0	2.6								
(15) 9.8	(17) 5.7		% Officers', Directors' Owners' Comp/Sales						
21.0	13.9								
481445M	430376M	1005216M	Net Sales ($)	1280M	8143M	20158M	39739M	85318M	850578M
558003M	336632M	678276M	Total Assets ($)	4189M	3156M	2710M	29503M	98065M	540653M

M = $ thousand MM = $ million

See Pages 9 through 22 for Explanation of Ratios and Data

Current Data Sorted by Assets | **Comparative Historical Data**

19 (4/1-9/30/13) 78 (10/1/13-3/31/14)

0-500M	500M-2MM	2-10MM	10-50MM	50-100MM	100-250MM	Type of Statement	4/1/09-3/31/10 ALL	4/1/10-3/31/11 ALL
	1	16	8	4	8	Unqualified	40	41
	1	1				Reviewed	2	4
		3		1	1	Compiled	4	5
4	6					Tax Returns	13	10
3	9	13	9	5	4	Other	40	48
7	17	33	17	10	13	NUMBER OF STATEMENTS	99	108
%	%	%	%	%	%	**ASSETS**	%	%
	35.5	38.5	19.3	42.1	30.6	Cash & Equivalents	27.5	28.9
	16.9	19.3	16.5	14.3	10.4	Trade Receivables (net)	17.3	14.9
	.7	.0	.5	.0	.0	Inventory	1.3	.1
	6.9	6.1	16.9	12.5	4.2	All Other Current	8.2	7.1
	60.0	63.9	53.2	69.0	45.2	Total Current	54.2	51.0
	20.9	16.1	6.7	7.5	7.5	Fixed Assets (net)	19.1	17.7
	12.6	11.3	19.9	8.1	29.7	Intangibles (net)	14.6	16.6
	6.5	8.7	20.3	15.4	17.6	All Other Non-Current	12.0	14.7
	100.0	100.0	100.0	100.0	100.0	Total	100.0	100.0
						LIABILITIES		
	7.3	1.2	6.5	6.9	.4	Notes Payable-Short Term	6.2	10.7
	4.5	1.8	1.7	1.4	2.2	Cur. Mat.-L.T.D.	3.9	2.8
	17.7	11.4	13.7	4.3	10.3	Trade Payables	11.9	14.1
	.5	1.3	3.2	.2	.7	Income Taxes Payable	.4	.5
	35.2	33.1	34.0	33.9	28.5	All Other Current	26.5	23.3
	65.1	48.7	59.0	46.6	42.2	Total Current	48.9	51.4
	14.0	10.3	4.4	13.2	14.9	Long-Term Debt	16.3	13.9
	.6	.3	1.7	.1	2.1	Deferred Taxes	.4	.8
	3.6	3.6	3.7	17.9	11.4	All Other Non-Current	10.7	10.0
	16.6	37.1	31.3	22.1	29.4	Net Worth	23.7	23.9
	100.0	100.0	100.0	100.0	100.0	Total Liabilties & Net Worth	100.0	100.0
						INCOME DATA		
	100.0	100.0	100.0	100.0	100.0	Net Sales	100.0	100.0
						Gross Profit		
	94.3	88.0	89.3	86.8	94.7	Operating Expenses	88.2	89.6
	5.7	12.0	10.7	13.2	5.3	Operating Profit	11.8	10.4
	.1	.7	1.0	1.3	1.9	All Other Expenses (net)	1.6	1.0
	5.6	11.3	9.7	11.9	3.4	Profit Before Taxes	10.2	9.4
						RATIOS		
	4.8	2.7	1.5	1.7	1.7		2.2	2.0
	1.5	1.2	.9	1.5	1.0	Current	1.2	1.1
	.5	1.1	.7	1.3	.8		.7	.7
	3.5	2.5	1.2	1.6	1.5		1.8	1.7
	1.5	1.1	.7	1.3	1.0	Quick	1.0	1.0
	.5	.9	.2	.9	.7		.6	.6
	0 UND	**5** 68.8	**5** 74.2	**8** 45.8	**13** 28.6		**1** 583.8	**1** 552.0
	10 37.0	**27** 13.7	**13** 28.9	**32** 11.5	**24** 15.1	Sales/Receivables	**17** 21.3	**17** 21.4
	26 13.9	**39** 9.4	**53** 6.9	**45** 8.2	**49** 7.5		**39** 9.4	**35** 10.5
						Cost of Sales/Inventory		
						Cost of Sales/Payables		
	7.3	6.1	6.4	1.6	5.1		5.9	7.4
	34.8	14.7	-27.8	3.9	22.3	Sales/Working Capital	29.0	39.1
	-22.1	66.7	-9.4	15.3	-25.6		-15.9	-17.5
	66.5	185.4	98.9				38.6	52.7
	(12) 8.9	(18) 16.5	(10) 4.8			EBIT/Interest	(77) 10.6	(75) 8.3
	4.5	5.8	1.6				2.0	1.8
							12.7	24.1
						Net Profit + Depr., Dep., Amort./Cur. Mat. L/T/D	(17) 2.5	(18) 3.7
							1.6	.9
	.1	.2	.1	.1	.1		.2	.1
	1.0	.4	.4	.9	-1.0	Fixed/Worth	1.0	.7
	-3.0	1.3	-.5	-.3	-.4		-2.0	-1.3
	.8	1.0	1.9	1.5	2.3		1.2	1.0
	2.1	3.4	5.9	12.9	-6.2	Debt/Worth	4.4	2.9
	-4.5	7.7	-4.1	-11.2	-3.2		-9.8	-4.8
		113.8	63.2				115.3	87.4
		(30) 67.2	(11) 31.5			% Profit Before Taxes/Tangible Net Worth	(68) 35.5	(73) 26.5
		37.4	17.4				7.9	6.3
	33.0	34.6	15.3	16.6	4.8		27.9	19.2
	10.6	16.4	10.0	5.6	2.5	% Profit Before Taxes/Total Assets	8.4	5.4
	-2.9	7.5	2.1	2.4	-1.8		2.2	1.3
	448.3	53.6	64.1	UND	33.7		50.5	84.7
	54.5	26.0	33.7	51.0	29.3	Sales/Net Fixed Assets	19.3	27.6
	22.0	12.2	21.0	6.1	6.6		9.4	7.8
	9.2	3.6	2.5	1.8	1.2		3.8	3.6
	4.9	2.0	1.4	1.0	1.0	Sales/Total Assets	1.8	1.7
	3.6	1.2	.8	.2	.6		.8	.9
		.9	.6				.8	.6
		(25) 1.8	(14) 1.0			% Depr., Dep., Amort./Sales	(72) 1.9	(74) 1.5
		2.5	2.1				2.9	3.1
							3.7	3.7
						% Officers', Directors' Owners' Comp/Sales	(20) 7.0	(11) 5.7
							10.2	7.1
7596M	149750M	357886M	1011783M	779924M	2378487M	Net Sales ($)	3667818M	4949379M
831M	18524M	146804M	428828M	698861M	2397617M	Total Assets ($)	2285801M	3822606M

M = $ thousand MM = $ million

See Pages 9 through 22 for Explanation of Ratios and Data

Comparative Historical Data / Current Data Sorted by Sales

4/1/11-3/31/12 ALL	4/1/12-3/31/13 ALL	4/1/13-3/31/14 ALL	Type of Statement	0-1MM	1-3MM	3-5MM	5-10MM	10-25MM	25MM & OVER
43	41	37	Unqualified	1	1	2	5	11	17
3	4	2	Reviewed			2			
4	7	5	Compiled				2	1	2
15	10	10	Tax Returns	2	2	3		1	2
41	47	43	Other	2	6	4	11	5	15
				19 (4/1-9/30/13)		78 (10/1/13-3/31/14)			
106	109	97	NUMBER OF STATEMENTS	5	9	11	18	18	36
%	%	%	**ASSETS**	%	%	%	%	%	%
29.1	27.8	33.5	Cash & Equivalents			40.8	42.0	25.0	27.6
18.6	13.3	15.3	Trade Receivables (net)			18.3	14.1	26.3	13.8
1.5	.9	.7	Inventory			1.1	.0	.0	.2
9.8	9.8	8.8	All Other Current			1.7	10.4	7.2	10.4
58.9	51.8	58.2	Total Current			62.0	66.5	58.5	52.0
15.5	16.6	13.5	Fixed Assets (net)			15.3	10.9	17.1	9.2
12.0	13.8	15.0	Intangibles (net)			15.3	10.6	9.8	23.8
13.6	17.8	13.2	All Other Non-Current			7.4	12.0	14.7	15.0
100.0	100.0	100.0	Total			100.0	100.0	100.0	100.0
			LIABILITIES						
11.2	5.3	11.8	Notes Payable-Short Term			11.4	.4	8.2	1.8
2.0	1.5	3.4	Cur. Mat.-L.T.D.			7.7	.7	.9	2.6
14.4	10.2	11.2	Trade Payables			16.5	5.8	10.4	16.8
.4	.5	1.2	Income Taxes Payable			1.6	.0	.8	1.7
31.8	27.3	32.0	All Other Current			41.1	42.6	22.9	33.9
59.8	44.8	59.6	Total Current			78.3	49.5	43.2	56.8
13.5	14.2	11.6	Long-Term Debt			8.6	6.6	10.3	11.4
.9	.8	.8	Deferred Taxes			1.1	.1	.4	1.6
11.5	11.7	8.9	All Other Non-Current			2.4	5.8	3.9	9.8
14.4	28.5	19.1	Net Worth			9.7	38.0	42.1	20.4
100.0	100.0	100.0	Total Liabilties & Net Worth			100.0	100.0	100.0	100.0
			INCOME DATA						
100.0	100.0	100.0	Net Sales			100.0	100.0	100.0	100.0
			Gross Profit						
90.6	91.6	89.7	Operating Expenses			84.0	90.8	90.7	92.7
9.4	8.4	10.3	Operating Profit			16.0	9.2	9.3	7.3
1.3	1.6	.8	All Other Expenses (net)			1.8	.1	.8	.7
8.1	6.8	9.4	Profit Before Taxes			14.2	9.1	8.4	6.6
			RATIOS						
1.9	2.2	1.8				1.1	3.7	2.4	1.6
1.2	1.2	1.2	Current			1.0	1.4	1.4	1.1
.9	.7	.8				.6	1.0	1.0	.7
1.7	1.6	1.7				1.1	3.3	1.9	1.5
1.1	1.0	1.1	Quick			.8	1.4	1.3	1.0
.5	.4	.6				.6	.3	.9	.4
1 340.6	1 576.9	0 745.4				3 115.3	3 134.1	8 46.5	7 53.4
15 23.7	14 25.7	18 20.5	Sales/Receivables			21 17.6	12 29.3	27 13.5	23 16.0
35 10.3	31 11.8	38 9.6				49 7.5	39 9.4	41 9.0	38 9.5
			Cost of Sales/Inventory						
			Cost of Sales/Payables						
6.1	6.1	5.7				14.8	6.2	6.3	5.2
25.0	22.9	22.3	Sales/Working Capital			-192.3	16.3	20.2	30.8
-37.1	-21.5	-23.7				-7.3	NM	NM	-21.6
42.2	36.4	43.6					185.4		29.5
(71) 6.7	(65) 9.1	(60) 7.7	EBIT/Interest				(10) 9.9		(26) 5.9
3.0	2.2	3.1					7.3		3.1
22.3	43.2	33.6							
(15) 3.3	(15) 4.1	(13) 3.2	Net Profit + Depr., Dep., Amort./Cur. Mat. L/T/D						
1.1	1.6	1.9							
.1	.0	.1				.2	.1	.1	.2
.6	.6	.5	Fixed/Worth			1.4	.4	.4	1.7
-3.1	3.5	-4.4				-.4	.9	2.0	-.3
1.1	1.0	1.2				4.4	1.0	.8	2.8
4.1	3.2	4.9	Debt/Worth			-8.5	2.4	1.5	37.8
-7.9	-346.6	-7.1				-4.0	6.7	8.5	-3.4
73.3	79.7	90.3					95.7	90.3	110.5
(72) 25.5	(81) 27.3	(67) 48.0	% Profit Before Taxes/Tangible Net Worth				(17) 48.0	(15) 72.4	(19) 25.2
7.1	5.0	12.4					8.2	27.2	11.5
19.6	19.9	30.7				22.0	31.0	36.4	12.2
7.7	6.2	10.1	% Profit Before Taxes/Total Assets			14.1	10.2	16.3	5.1
1.8	1.1	2.7				5.0	1.9	6.2	1.9
125.0	106.1	85.8				106.8	103.3	83.4	50.7
28.2	34.2	33.7	Sales/Net Fixed Assets			28.2	31.9	27.9	32.8
10.6	10.8	14.0				12.4	12.5	13.2	20.7
4.7	3.3	4.1				4.1	3.4	4.5	2.8
1.9	1.8	1.9	Sales/Total Assets			2.2	2.0	2.9	1.4
1.1	.9	1.1				1.1	1.4	1.1	.9
.7	.7	.6						1.3	.5
(80) 1.6	(69) 1.6	(62) 1.2	% Depr., Dep., Amort./Sales					(14) 2.1	(28) 1.1
2.9	3.3	2.3						2.9	1.9
2.7	2.5	4.4							
(16) 6.7	(17) 7.9	(16) 6.7	% Officers', Directors' Owners' Comp/Sales						
14.1	12.5	13.2							
4042694M	4732293M	4685426M	Net Sales ($)	2164M	16459M	44042M	125094M	293595M	4204072M
2449522M	3223098M	3691465M	Total Assets ($)	5393M	13928M	42435M	124743M	287997M	3216969M

M = $ thousand MM = $ million

See Pages 9 through 22 for Explanation of Ratios and Data

Current Data Sorted by Assets | **Comparative Historical Data**

0-500M	500M-2MM	2-10MM	10-50MM	50-100MM	100-250MM	Type of Statement	4/1/09-3/31/10 ALL	4/1/10-3/31/11 ALL
		2	8	4	4	Unqualified	10	21
	1		1			Reviewed	1	1
1	1	5	1	1		Compiled	7	3
6	4	3	1		1	Tax Returns	5	8
2	5	11	10	5	6	Other	23	23
12 (4/1-9/30/13)			71 (10/1/13-3/31/14)					
9	11	21	21	10	11	NUMBER OF STATEMENTS	46	56
%	%	%	%	%	%	**ASSETS**	%	%
	29.3	26.9	35.5	40.5	34.5	Cash & Equivalents	27.7	24.5
	21.6	27.7	30.6	21.2	11.4	Trade Receivables (net)	23.1	22.3
	.0	.0	.0	.0	.0	Inventory	.1	.3
	4.0	5.1	3.3	4.0	10.0	All Other Current	8.6	9.5
	55.0	59.6	69.4	65.7	55.9	Total Current	59.5	56.7
	23.2	11.5	5.5	7.3	7.0	Fixed Assets (net)	11.5	12.5
	1.9	13.1	7.1	7.8	21.4	Intangibles (net)	16.5	14.1
	20.0	15.7	18.1	19.2	15.7	All Other Non-Current	12.5	16.7
	100.0	100.0	100.0	100.0	100.0	Total	100.0	100.0
						LIABILITIES		
	8.1	11.8	4.2	.0	7.1	Notes Payable-Short Term	10.4	11.9
	.4	2.1	1.0	.3	1.2	Cur. Mat.-L.T.D.	1.9	2.9
	9.4	7.0	20.6	18.0	10.2	Trade Payables	12.8	9.6
	.2	.0	.2	.3	.6	Income Taxes Payable	.6	.3
	9.4	12.9	37.0	26.8	19.2	All Other Current	20.9	20.8
	27.5	33.9	62.9	45.3	38.4	Total Current	46.7	45.5
	11.5	9.0	6.4	3.9	13.3	Long-Term Debt	12.2	18.1
	.0	.0	.0	1.4	5.0	Deferred Taxes	.4	.8
	9.6	7.0	11.3	4.7	12.9	All Other Non-Current	10.4	15.2
	51.4	50.1	19.3	44.8	30.4	Net Worth	30.3	20.4
	100.0	100.0	100.0	100.0	100.0	Total Liabilties & Net Worth	100.0	100.0
						INCOME DATA		
	100.0	100.0	100.0	100.0	100.0	Net Sales	100.0	100.0
						Gross Profit		
	78.2	80.4	91.3	90.4	87.7	Operating Expenses	85.0	90.3
	21.8	19.6	8.7	9.6	12.3	Operating Profit	15.0	9.7
	4.2	2.6	.6	1.5	3.9	All Other Expenses (net)	1.8	.5
	17.6	17.0	8.1	8.1	8.4	Profit Before Taxes	13.1	9.2
						RATIOS		
	3.2	6.2	1.4	3.4	3.1		1.8	2.1
	1.6	2.0	1.1	1.6	1.7	Current	1.3	1.5
	1.1	.9	.8	.7	.9		.7	.8
	2.8	5.3	1.4	3.3	2.5		1.7	1.7
	1.6	1.9	1.1	1.5	1.2	Quick	1.2	1.1
	1.1	.6	.8	.7	.7		.5	.6
	0 UND	**0** UND	**26** 14.2	**11** 32.9	**0** UND		**8** 43.7	**4** 94.6
	7 54.1	**27** 13.7	**47** 7.8	**51** 7.2	**43** 8.5	Sales/Receivables	**35** 10.3	**24** 15.3
	37 9.9	**107** 3.4	**135** 2.7	**192** 1.9	**96** 3.8		**49** 7.5	**46** 7.9
						Cost of Sales/Inventory		
						Cost of Sales/Payables		
	7.9	4.0	6.1	1.4	.4		5.7	4.8
	16.1	10.5	26.1	7.2	10.4	Sales/Working Capital	16.9	14.1
	54.1	NM	-13.5	-10.0	-17.7		-24.1	-40.7
		39.0	100.6				54.4	41.0
		(13) 15.8	(10) 8.0			EBIT/Interest	(29) 3.8	(34) 10.0
		4.9	3.5				-5.1	1.2
						Net Profit + Depr., Dep., Amort./Cur. Mat. L/T/D		
	.0	.0	.0	.0	.0		.0	.1
	.2	.2	.1	.0	.3	Fixed/Worth	.3	.5
	1.2	.5	1.8	.2	-.3		NM	-.2
	.5	.4	2.1	.8	1.1		1.1	.8
	1.0	1.0	2.6	1.7	4.0	Debt/Worth	2.7	2.3
	2.3	6.0	28.0	2.6	-3.6		-7.4	-4.9
	131.5	68.3	105.6				81.1	80.8
	72.5	(19) 31.7	(18) 24.2			% Profit Before Taxes/Tangible Net Worth	(34) 35.6	(37) 37.5
	18.7	11.7	7.5				6.8	9.1
	116.5	32.0	14.2	10.8	13.9		20.4	29.9
	32.0	13.6	5.8	5.1	2.9	% Profit Before Taxes/Total Assets	7.5	11.1
	5.2	5.1	1.1	.6	-4.1		-.7	1.4
	90.0	UND	UND	UND	210.3		359.1	171.7
	42.9	58.6	75.6	101.1	29.6	Sales/Net Fixed Assets	33.9	36.8
	5.1	13.2	29.8	26.6	16.0		17.8	12.1
	5.6	3.4	2.1	3.1	1.8		3.8	4.0
	3.9	1.3	.9	.9	.6	Sales/Total Assets	1.7	1.5
	.8	.6	.4	.6	.2		.4	.6
			.4				.6	.8
			(10) 1.1			% Depr., Dep., Amort./Sales	(24) 1.4	(32) 1.7
			2.9				2.4	3.1
							5.3	4.3
						% Officers', Directors' Owners' Comp/Sales	(13) 7.6	(14) 6.1
							27.0	13.0
14216M	38250M	170273M	720213M	1084127M	2805806M	Net Sales ($)	1873209M	2292998M
2722M	12594M	97522M	520219M	631778M	2014874M	Total Assets ($)	1403162M	1841038M

M = $ thousand MM = $ million

See Pages 9 through 22 for Explanation of Ratios and Data

Comparative Historical Data				Current Data Sorted by Sales					
			Type of Statement						
23	29	18	Unqualified		2	1	1	3	11
2	5	2	Reviewed		1	1			
11	16	9	Compiled	2	3			2	2
9	14	15	Tax Returns	3	6	4			2
27	43	39	Other	1	4	4	9	7	14
4/1/11-3/31/12 ALL	4/1/12-3/31/13 ALL	4/1/13-3/31/14 ALL		12 (4/1-9/30/13)			71 (10/1/13-3/31/14)		
				0-1MM	1-3MM	3-5MM	5-10MM	10-25MM	25MM & OVER
72	107	83	**NUMBER OF STATEMENTS**	6	16	10	10	12	29
%	%	%	**ASSETS**	%	%	%	%	%	%
25.4	31.6	33.0	Cash & Equivalents		30.7	33.9	43.5	42.8	31.7
25.4	22.9	22.6	Trade Receivables (net)		28.9	24.2	17.7	16.9	23.4
.1	.4	.0	Inventory		.0	.0	.0	.0	.0
8.1	7.5	4.5	All Other Current		4.5	5.5	2.6	4.1	5.8
59.0	62.5	60.2	Total Current		64.1	63.6	63.9	63.8	60.9
13.2	9.9	10.8	Fixed Assets (net)		12.9	5.3	11.9	5.8	8.5
13.0	8.8	11.8	Intangibles (net)		15.3	8.0	8.3	11.5	12.8
14.8	18.8	17.3	All Other Non-Current		7.7	23.1	15.9	18.9	17.8
100.0	100.0	100.0	Total		100.0	100.0	100.0	100.0	100.0
			LIABILITIES						
5.5	8.8	8.5	Notes Payable-Short Term		19.8	8.2	4.9	1.1	4.0
3.0	3.3	1.2	Cur. Mat.-L.T.D.		1.2	1.7	.4	2.2	1.0
17.0	11.9	13.0	Trade Payables		7.2	7.3	7.3	14.0	19.6
.2	.8	.2	Income Taxes Payable		.0	.2	.3	.5	.2
31.8	23.3	20.2	All Other Current		12.5	24.7	24.5	22.2	23.5
57.4	48.1	43.1	Total Current		40.7	42.1	37.4	40.0	48.2
15.2	11.7	11.9	Long-Term Debt		19.4	4.2	1.4	17.0	7.4
.4	.4	.8	Deferred Taxes		.0	.0	.0	1.9	1.6
12.6	12.3	8.7	All Other Non-Current		5.6	1.1	4.7	3.4	15.3
14.3	27.6	35.5	Net Worth		34.3	52.5	56.5	37.7	27.5
100.0	100.0	100.0	Total Liabilties & Net Worth		100.0	100.0	100.0	100.0	100.0
			INCOME DATA						
100.0	100.0	100.0	Net Sales		100.0	100.0	100.0	100.0	100.0
			Gross Profit						
94.1	87.9	85.8	Operating Expenses		76.3	86.8	82.9	88.9	93.2
5.9	12.1	14.2	Operating Profit		23.7	13.2	17.1	11.1	6.8
.8	1.9	2.1	All Other Expenses (net)		2.7	.1	-.4	3.0	.7
5.1	10.2	12.1	Profit Before Taxes		21.0	13.0	17.4	8.1	6.0
			RATIOS						
1.9	2.4	3.0			7.8	4.3	3.7	3.2	2.2
1.2	1.2	1.4	Current		1.5	1.5	1.8	1.9	1.2
.8	.8	.8			.4	1.0	1.0	.4	.9
1.7	2.1	2.6			7.7	4.0	3.7	3.0	2.0
(71) 1.0	1.1	1.2	Quick		1.2	1.5	1.8	1.8	1.2
.6	.6	.7			.3	.8	.9	.4	.8
0 UND	0 UND	0 UND			0 UND	0 UND	1 697.3	0 UND	8 47.1
35 10.3	26 14.3	34 10.6	Sales/Receivables		8 46.9	31 11.8	27 13.6	44 8.3	34 10.6
60 6.1	60 6.1	83 4.4			608 .6	83 4.4	56 6.5	89 4.1	69 5.3
			Cost of Sales/Inventory						
			Cost of Sales/Payables						
6.1	5.6	4.6			.7	10.3	3.0	.8	6.1
31.0	18.9	13.5	Sales/Working Capital		7.5	31.2	10.1	6.8	16.0
-22.1	-23.5	-19.7			-14.6	NM	NM	-13.5	-18.2
37.4	53.7	95.6			128.0				106.9
(45) 13.8	(60) 11.6	(46) 18.5	EBIT/Interest		(11) 15.8				(16) 13.7
2.3	3.2	4.8			3.8				4.1
111.8									
(12) 14.3			Net Profit + Depr., Dep., Amort./Cur. Mat. L/T/D						
2.0									
.0	.0	.0			.0	.0	.0	.0	.0
.5	.1	.1	Fixed/Worth		.0	.2	.2	.0	.2
-1.1	1.4	1.2			2.8	.2	.7	.3	NM
1.5	.9	.7			.5	.5	.4	.6	1.7
4.7	3.4	2.1	Debt/Worth		2.0	.9	1.0	2.3	2.5
-8.6	22.2	14.9			19.0	2.8	2.0	7.5	NM
113.0	99.9	79.2			91.4	246.4	114.8	26.4	77.3
(49) 30.4	(84) 30.7	(68) 32.4	% Profit Before Taxes/Tangible Net Worth		(13) 31.7	88.8	26.1	(10) 6.4	(22) 40.5
2.9	5.0	10.1			10.3	18.9	10.2	-13.3	9.5
23.2	27.9	27.7			46.1	66.6	33.9	16.4	14.7
6.9	9.1	10.4	% Profit Before Taxes/Total Assets		15.2	35.7	11.5	2.9	9.9
.8	.3	3.1			3.6	6.6	4.8	-1.5	2.9
568.1	UND	570.6			UND	UND	UND	UND	122.2
46.8	97.8	57.2	Sales/Net Fixed Assets		UND	78.8	15.9	158.2	39.6
14.0	23.4	17.1			28.3	29.6	10.0	48.8	18.8
4.0	4.2	3.7			3.6	6.8	3.6	3.6	3.5
2.0	1.9	1.5	Sales/Total Assets		.7	3.8	1.7	.8	1.8
.8	.5	.5			.2	.9	.7	.2	.8
.4	.5	.3							.2
(37) 1.2	(48) .9	(37) 1.1	% Depr., Dep., Amort./Sales						(16) 1.2
3.6	2.3	2.5							2.7
4.0	2.4	3.4							
(17) 9.2	(25) 5.8	(26) 7.9	% Officers', Directors' Owners' Comp/Sales						
19.9	16.2	18.3							
3893751M	6732753M	4832885M	Net Sales ($)	3370M	30452M	41125M	70922M	211181M	4475835M
2321488M	3337697M	3279709M	Total Assets ($)	10787M	88627M	26601M	114598M	458271M	2580825M

M = $ thousand MM = $ million

See Pages 9 through 22 for Explanation of Ratios and Data

Current Data Sorted by Assets							Comparative Historical Data	
1		1	5	1	2	**Type of Statement** Unqualified	21	16
				1		Reviewed	3	2
1	1					Compiled	2	2
		2				Tax Returns	6	5
1	3	1	7	1	3	Other	26	31
4 (4/1-9/30/13)			27 (10/1/13-3/31/14)				**4/1/09-3/31/10**	**4/1/10-3/31/11**
0-500M	**500M-2MM**	**2-10MM**	**10-50MM**	**50-100MM**	**100-250MM**		**ALL**	**ALL**
3	4	4	12	3	5	**NUMBER OF STATEMENTS**	58	56
%	%	%	%	%	%	**ASSETS**	%	%
			39.0			Cash & Equivalents	20.1	32.2
			12.6			Trade Receivables (net)	13.3	11.1
			2.3			Inventory	1.8	1.1
			4.6			All Other Current	6.1	6.8
			58.5			Total Current	41.3	51.1
			13.1			Fixed Assets (net)	14.0	18.3
			9.1			Intangibles (net)	3.0	4.3
			19.2			All Other Non-Current	41.7	26.4
			100.0			Total	100.0	100.0
						LIABILITIES		
			7.2			Notes Payable-Short Term	7.6	12.8
			2.4			Cur. Mat.-L.T.D.	2.7	1.8
			6.3			Trade Payables	3.4	4.0
			.1			Income Taxes Payable	.1	.0
			5.6			All Other Current	11.7	8.7
			21.7			Total Current	25.5	27.3
			1.7			Long-Term Debt	13.5	20.5
			1.3			Deferred Taxes	.9	.6
			7.0			All Other Non-Current	3.2	5.2
			68.4			Net Worth	57.0	46.5
			100.0			Total Liabilties & Net Worth	100.0	100.0
						INCOME DATA		
			100.0			Net Sales	100.0	100.0
						Gross Profit		
			64.6			Operating Expenses	66.8	68.9
			35.4			Operating Profit	33.2	31.1
			5.3			All Other Expenses (net)	8.4	8.1
			30.1			Profit Before Taxes	24.8	23.0
						RATIOS		
			9.4				6.8	16.1
			3.8			Current	1.7	2.2
			1.3				.6	1.0
			9.3				4.9	13.7
			3.8			Quick	1.5	1.7
			1.0				.4	.6
			0 UND				**0** UND	**0** UND
			28 12.9			Sales/Receivables	**5** 73.3	**25** 14.4
			62 5.9				**44** 8.3	**48** 7.7
						Cost of Sales/Inventory		
						Cost of Sales/Payables		
			.4				1.7	1.8
			4.8			Sales/Working Capital	8.6	4.0
			58.2				-6.1	NM
							127.3	161.3
						EBIT/Interest	(29) 9.5	(29) 12.2
							2.4	1.6
						Net Profit + Depr., Dep., Amort./Cur. Mat. L/T/D		
			.0				.0	.0
			.0			Fixed/Worth	.1	.1
			.5				.7	1.2
			.1				.1	.1
			.8			Debt/Worth	.6	.7
			1.4				2.6	7.3
			43.9				41.5	102.7
			26.3			% Profit Before Taxes/Tangible Net Worth	(49) 13.5	(49) 11.7
			14.5				1.7	1.3
			22.8				30.2	40.7
			14.4			% Profit Before Taxes/Total Assets	7.4	6.1
			3.9				1.2	.5
			UND				UND	UND
			76.5			Sales/Net Fixed Assets	40.6	35.2
			16.2				7.4	6.0
			1.0				2.1	1.8
			.5			Sales/Total Assets	.4	.7
			.2				.1	.2
							.7	.5
						% Depr., Dep., Amort./Sales	(33) 1.2	(29) 1.3
							6.6	4.5
						% Officers', Directors' Owners' Comp/Sales		
8108M	20380M	5042M	241780M	209474M	374047M	Net Sales ($)	1282887M	2182649M
902M	4789M	18392M	286031M	179640M	804093M	Total Assets ($)	2631580M	1686805M

M = $ thousand MM = $ million

See Pages 9 through 22 for Explanation of Ratios and Data

Comparative Historical Data				Current Data Sorted by Sales					
			Type of Statement						
20	11	10	Unqualified		1	2	4	2	1
1		1	Reviewed					1	
3	1	2	Compiled	1	1				
3	4	2	Tax Returns	2					
19	19	16	Other	3	1	1	3	2	6
4/1/11-3/31/12 ALL	**4/1/12-3/31/13 ALL**	**4/1/13-3/31/14 ALL**			**4 (4/1-9/30/13)**			**27 (10/1/13-3/31/14)**	
				0-1MM	**1-3MM**	**3-5MM**	**5-10MM**	**10-25MM**	**25MM & OVER**
46	35	31	**NUMBER OF STATEMENTS**	6	3	3	7	5	7
%	%	%	**ASSETS**	%	%	%	%	%	%
24.4	35.0	27.2	Cash & Equivalents						
17.5	10.7	11.6	Trade Receivables (net)						
5.1	1.4	1.9	Inventory						
4.4	6.9	4.0	All Other Current						
51.4	54.1	44.7	Total Current						
19.2	16.0	30.3	Fixed Assets (net)						
6.0	3.6	5.6	Intangibles (net)						
23.3	26.3	19.4	All Other Non-Current						
100.0	100.0	100.0	Total						
			LIABILITIES						
12.2	16.0	6.7	Notes Payable-Short Term						
1.3	.4	3.5	Cur. Mat.-L.T.D.						
8.5	2.6	4.4	Trade Payables						
.0	.0	.1	Income Taxes Payable						
7.1	5.2	10.9	All Other Current						
29.0	24.3	25.6	Total Current						
13.7	12.2	19.7	Long-Term Debt						
.4	.8	1.5	Deferred Taxes						
6.8	2.1	3.4	All Other Non-Current						
50.1	60.6	49.8	Net Worth						
100.0	100.0	100.0	Total Liabilties & Net Worth						
			INCOME DATA						
100.0	100.0	100.0	Net Sales						
			Gross Profit						
63.9	59.7	65.3	Operating Expenses						
36.1	40.3	34.7	Operating Profit						
9.9	10.6	9.5	All Other Expenses (net)						
26.3	29.8	25.2	Profit Before Taxes						
			RATIOS						
10.8	7.4	3.9							
1.4	1.6	1.5	Current						
.7	.9	.7							
9.7	7.0	3.9							
1.2	1.5	1.1	Quick						
.5	.5	.4							
0 UND	**0** UND	**0** UND							
5 79.9	**0** UND	**2** 165.3	Sales/Receivables						
55 6.6	**43** 8.4	**35** 10.5							
			Cost of Sales/Inventory						
			Cost of Sales/Payables						
2.3	1.2	1.8							
6.1	4.0	14.4	Sales/Working Capital						
-38.8	-21.8	-10.1							
139.8	52.2	25.1							
(24) 10.3	(19) 4.0	(19) 5.8	EBIT/Interest						
2.0	1.7	2.4							
			Net Profit + Depr., Dep., Amort./Cur. Mat. L/T/D						
.0	.0	.0							
.1	.0	.1	Fixed/Worth						
1.2	.2	2.3							
.1	.1	.6							
1.5	.6	1.3	Debt/Worth						
2.8	1.8	3.6							
58.5	55.1	65.7							
(41) 8.2	(33) 9.1	(30) 23.5	% Profit Before Taxes/Tangible Net Worth						
4.1	1.9	10.5							
20.8	14.4	22.9							
5.7	4.4	6.9	% Profit Before Taxes/Total Assets						
1.8	1.4	2.6							
UND	UND	212.8							
38.7	109.0	45.4	Sales/Net Fixed Assets						
7.1	10.8	.4							
2.2	1.5	1.6							
.6	.3	.4	Sales/Total Assets						
.1	.1	.1							
.6	.7	.8							
(28) 1.3	(20) 1.8	(20) 1.6	% Depr., Dep., Amort./Sales						
8.4	7.7	21.0							
			% Officers', Directors' Owners' Comp/Sales						
2232379M	**2028773M**	**858831M**	Net Sales ($)	**2547M**	**5063M**	**10184M**	**47201M**	**97550M**	**696286M**
2387247M	**1853520M**	**1293847M**	Total Assets ($)	**36827M**	**12538M**	**3870M**	**303177M**	**263105M**	**674330M**

M = $ thousand MM = $ million

See Pages 9 through 22 for Explanation of Ratios and Data

	Current Data Sorted by Assets						Comparative Historical Data	
Type of Statement								
Unqualified		2	4	15	9	15	23	26
Reviewed		1	5	1		1	5	8
Compiled	1	2	1	3	1		14	14
Tax Returns		6	5	7			49	47
Other	3	9	15	21	8	6	86	66
		21 (4/1-9/30/13)		120 (10/1/13-3/31/14)			4/1/09-3/31/10 ALL	4/1/10-3/31/11 ALL
	0-500M	500M-2MM	2-10MM	10-50MM	50-100MM	100-250MM		
NUMBER OF STATEMENTS	4	20	30	47	18	22	177	161
ASSETS	%	%	%	%	%	%	%	%
Cash & Equivalents		13.5	11.9	18.6	16.7	9.4	16.1	17.0
Trade Receivables (net)		10.5	4.9	8.0	10.0	12.2	13.2	11.1
Inventory		.9	.2	.3	4.4	.1	1.6	1.5
All Other Current		.9	7.2	5.0	12.0	8.1	7.6	8.0
Total Current		25.9	24.2	32.0	43.1	29.8	38.6	37.7
Fixed Assets (net)		35.7	42.2	25.2	29.0	17.3	39.9	36.0
Intangibles (net)		8.3	4.5	9.5	2.8	13.5	3.3	6.3
All Other Non-Current		30.1	29.1	33.3	25.1	39.3	18.2	19.9
Total		100.0	100.0	100.0	100.0	100.0	100.0	100.0
LIABILITIES								
Notes Payable-Short Term		33.9	8.1	8.1	6.4	18.8	13.6	10.3
Cur. Mat.-L.T.D.		2.3	2.1	2.3	2.6	2.8	3.1	4.2
Trade Payables		5.7	2.7	2.1	4.1	2.7	2.7	4.6
Income Taxes Payable		.1	1.0	.1	.1	.0	.2	.1
All Other Current		17.5	13.5	7.1	7.2	10.5	7.8	9.4
Total Current		59.5	27.4	19.6	20.3	34.7	27.4	28.7
Long-Term Debt		25.3	32.7	31.5	19.4	19.0	37.4	30.4
Deferred Taxes		.2	.1	.6	.1	.0	.3	.1
All Other Non-Current		2.0	2.8	6.4	7.2	3.5	7.6	3.8
Net Worth		13.1	37.0	41.8	53.0	42.7	27.4	37.1
Total Liabilties & Net Worth		100.0	100.0	100.0	100.0	100.0	100.0	100.0
INCOME DATA								
Net Sales		100.0	100.0	100.0	100.0	100.0	100.0	100.0
Gross Profit								
Operating Expenses		64.7	60.4	61.3	58.9	67.6	64.6	65.7
Operating Profit		35.3	39.6	38.7	41.1	32.4	35.4	34.3
All Other Expenses (net)		14.0	8.1	14.2	12.3	17.0	18.0	14.5
Profit Before Taxes		21.2	31.5	24.5	28.8	15.4	17.4	19.8
RATIOS								
Current		1.9	2.0	6.7	6.4	1.7	3.5	3.5
		.8	.8	1.9	1.8	1.0	1.4	1.4
		.1	.3	1.0	1.2	.2	.4	.5
Quick		1.6	1.3	6.8	4.1	1.5	2.8	2.9
		.7	.6	(46) 1.5	1.3	.4	1.1	1.0
		.1	.2	.6	.4	.1	.2	.2
Sales/Receivables		**0** UND	**0** UND	**0** UND	**0** UND	**0** UND	**0** UND	**0** UND
		0 UND	**0** UND	**6** 65.6	**14** 26.2	**7** 55.8	**0** UND	**0** 999.8
		13 28.2	**6** 56.9	**62** 5.9	**79** 4.6	**53** 6.9	**41** 8.8	**38** 9.5
Cost of Sales/Inventory								
Cost of Sales/Payables								
Sales/Working Capital		9.5	6.9	1.2	.4	3.2	1.9	2.1
		-30.6	-49.2	3.8	4.3	NM	9.8	18.7
		-2.2	-2.6	-160.6	20.5	-2.8	-5.7	-7.2
EBIT/Interest			20.4	11.1		4.8	15.7	26.7
			(13) 4.7	(29) 4.1		(11) 3.2	(88) 5.1	(85) 5.0
			1.7	1.8		.3	1.3	1.6
Net Profit + Depr., Dep., Amort./Cur. Mat. L/T/D								
Fixed/Worth		.0	.1	.0	.0	.0	.0	.0
		1.1	2.0	.1	.1	.1	1.0	1.1
		NM	5.9	3.0	1.3	.7	8.0	6.4
Debt/Worth		.8	.5	.6	.1	.6	.7	.5
		2.7	2.6	2.7	1.2	2.3	3.2	2.3
		-7.5	13.3	8.0	8.1	11.4	19.4	13.9
% Profit Before Taxes/Tangible Net Worth		45.7	62.3	24.9	55.9	32.4	35.4	45.5
		(14) 19.3	(25) 18.6	(38) 9.6	9.9	(19) 14.5	(144) 13.4	(132) 16.4
		-9.5	6.4	.8	1.4	-1.4	.9	3.2
% Profit Before Taxes/Total Assets		13.4	15.7	9.3	13.9	7.9	9.0	14.9
		5.3	8.1	3.0	4.6	2.1	2.6	4.4
		-7.4	1.1	.6	.6	-.6	.0	.1
Sales/Net Fixed Assets		UND	92.4	UND	UND	250.7	72.4	86.2
		28.2	.9	26.3	65.1	33.5	4.3	7.1
		.3	.2	.2	.1	1.0	.2	.2
Sales/Total Assets		3.1	1.2	.6	.7	.5	.9	1.2
		.5	.2	.2	.1	.2	.2	.2
		.2	.1	.1	.1	.1	.1	.1
% Depr., Dep., Amort./Sales		.8	1.2	1.1		.5	2.7	1.8
		(12) 8.6	(19) 8.9	(29) 4.8		(11) 1.7	(105) 9.1	(97) 9.3
		18.3	19.6	34.0		12.8	22.2	18.8
% Officers', Directors' Owners' Comp/Sales							2.1	2.9
							(23) 10.9	(25) 7.8
							15.6	16.4
Net Sales ($)	10061M	46018M	103699M	505497M	719718M	2442487M	1562705M	2853546M
Total Assets ($)	807M	22393M	145088M	1295148M	1381378M	3472661M	4347235M	4221452M

M = $ thousand MM = $ million

See Pages 9 through 22 for Explanation of Ratios and Data

Comparative Historical Data				Current Data Sorted by Sales					
			Type of Statement						
26	31	45	Unqualified	4	7	5	6	7	16
11	6	8	Reviewed	2	3	1			2
9	8	8	Compiled	2		3	1	1	1
49	30	18	Tax Returns	11	2	1	3		1
78	72	62	Other	11	14	10	8	12	7
4/1/11-3/31/12 ALL	**4/1/12-3/31/13 ALL**	**4/1/13-3/31/14 ALL**		**21 (4/1-9/30/13)**			**120 (10/1/13-3/31/14)**		
				0-1MM	**1-3MM**	**3-5MM**	**5-10MM**	**10-25MM**	**25MM & OVER**
173	147	141	**NUMBER OF STATEMENTS**	30	26	20	18	20	27
%	%	%	**ASSETS**	%	%	%	%	%	%
17.1	13.4	15.4	Cash & Equivalents	9.7	17.7	14.5	19.6	11.3	20.4
13.7	13.4	9.1	Trade Receivables (net)	5.5	2.6	2.1	10.8	24.8	11.5
1.7	1.2	.9	Inventory	.0	.0	.2	.3	1.6	3.0
4.7	4.7	6.3	All Other Current	5.5	2.0	4.4	2.4	12.2	10.8
37.2	32.7	31.6	Total Current	20.7	22.3	21.2	33.1	49.8	45.7
32.3	26.9	29.5	Fixed Assets (net)	46.4	33.2	35.3	37.1	12.7	10.1
7.2	6.1	7.8	Intangibles (net)	1.5	6.3	11.3	5.5	11.9	12.0
23.4	34.3	31.2	All Other Non-Current	31.3	38.1	32.2	24.3	25.6	32.2
100.0	100.0	100.0	Total	100.0	100.0	100.0	100.0	100.0	100.0
			LIABILITIES						
11.2	10.5	13.0	Notes Payable-Short Term	11.5	4.6	30.7	14.0	10.0	11.2
3.4	2.8	2.4	Cur. Mat.-L.T.D.	2.4	1.2	3.6	.3	1.4	4.5
4.4	2.6	3.0	Trade Payables	.1	.8	2.7	2.2	7.3	5.9
.3	.1	.2	Income Taxes Payable	.3	.8	.0	.0	.1	.1
10.6	8.1	11.0	All Other Current	5.9	10.8	2.8	15.1	18.2	14.8
29.9	24.1	29.6	Total Current	20.2	18.3	39.8	31.7	37.1	36.4
27.0	30.1	27.6	Long-Term Debt	35.5	25.9	43.1	33.0	10.8	17.9
.1	.1	.3	Deferred Taxes	.0	.1	.0	.0	1.6	.0
5.4	10.2	5.2	All Other Non-Current	5.4	4.2	6.2	3.0	4.6	7.0
37.6	35.5	37.3	Net Worth	38.8	51.5	10.9	32.4	45.8	38.6
100.0	100.0	100.0	Total Liabilties & Net Worth	100.0	100.0	100.0	100.0	100.0	100.0
			INCOME DATA						
100.0	100.0	100.0	Net Sales	100.0	100.0	100.0	100.0	100.0	100.0
			Gross Profit						
61.8	58.4	62.5	Operating Expenses	42.0	59.6	61.3	79.2	69.2	72.7
38.2	41.6	37.5	Operating Profit	58.0	40.4	38.7	20.8	30.8	27.3
14.2	13.0	13.2	All Other Expenses (net)	22.4	9.5	19.7	11.1	6.2	8.2
23.9	28.6	24.4	Profit Before Taxes	35.6	31.0	19.0	9.7	24.5	19.1
			RATIOS						
3.7	5.5	3.3		6.9	14.1	3.7	2.8	5.3	2.1
1.2	1.2	1.2	Current	.8	1.8	1.2	1.2	1.3	1.2
.6	.4	.6		.1	.7	.5	.8	.9	.6
2.8	3.5	2.3		3.6	11.8	3.8	2.8	1.7	2.0
(172) .9	1.0	(140) 1.0	Quick	.5	1.3	(19) 1.0	1.1	1.0	.6
.2	.2	.3		.1	.5	.5	.7	.5	.2
0 UND	0 UND	0 UND		0 UND	0 UND	0 UND	0 UND	2 150.0	0 UND
0 UND	0 UND	1 334.7	Sales/Receivables	0 UND	0 UND	2 149.7	8 44.2	22 16.3	8 45.1
42 8.6	47 7.8	40 9.2		0 UND	1 252.5	36 10.1	74 4.9	60 6.1	58 6.3
			Cost of Sales/Inventory						
			Cost of Sales/Payables						
1.6	1.4	1.7		1.6	.7	.8	2.9	1.3	3.9
33.1	20.1	14.0	Sales/Working Capital	-64.7	4.5	21.1	12.6	6.2	24.5
-5.8	-6.0	-7.3		-.7	-11.6	-4.3	-15.3	NM	-6.2
12.3	13.3	11.1		15.0	7.1	4.6	5.1		25.2
(87) 5.6	(73) 6.6	(69) 4.1	EBIT/Interest	(10) 5.3	(10) 4.1	(11) 1.8	(11) 2.1		(19) 4.8
2.0	2.5	1.6		3.2	1.9	.3	-.5		2.6
			Net Profit + Depr., Dep., Amort./Cur. Mat. L/T/D						
.0	.0	.0		.0	.0	.0	.0	.0	.0
.6	.2	.2	Fixed/Worth	1.3	.3	.2	1.0	.1	.1
3.7	3.0	3.7		4.3	3.7	8.2	-34.1	.9	.5
.5	.4	.5		.2	.2	1.1	1.1	.2	.9
2.1	2.6	2.4	Debt/Worth	1.7	1.2	3.5	3.0	2.1	3.5
12.9	12.2	12.6		13.3	4.2	84.0	-28.1	23.9	9.5
34.6	40.7	50.0		30.8	19.0	26.6	25.6	95.3	173.1
(142) 13.6	(124) 15.6	(117) 14.5	% Profit Before Taxes/Tangible Net Worth	(26) 14.8	(23) 4.6	(16) 8.6	(12) 4.0	(16) 14.5	(24) 55.6
2.9	4.4	1.1		1.9	.8	-2.3	-1.2	8.6	20.1
11.8	13.6	12.2		11.9	8.9	8.0	5.5	14.0	30.6
4.3	4.5	4.5	% Profit Before Taxes/Total Assets	5.3	3.0	.6	1.7	7.1	9.8
1.0	1.4	.5		.8	.7	-.2	-1.7	2.7	2.8
170.3	UND	999.8		UND	UND	49.6	283.3	999.8	117.7
10.4	40.0	24.9	Sales/Net Fixed Assets	.3	34.4	1.7	19.4	51.5	42.2
.2	.3	.3		.2	.2	.2	.2	6.9	11.4
1.0	.7	.8		.3	.6	.2	1.3	1.2	2.0
.2	.2	.2	Sales/Total Assets	.2	.1	.1	.2	.5	.9
.1	.1	.1		.1	.1	.1	.1	.1	.4
1.1	.4	.8		10.6	5.7	1.4	1.1	.4	.2
(110) 8.1	(73) 4.2	(76) 6.0	% Depr., Dep., Amort./Sales	(16) 17.8	(10) 13.1	(12) 33.5	(10) 2.0	(13) .8	(15) .7
19.9	19.5	22.6		24.3	24.5	43.8	34.9	3.6	2.4
3.0	1.6	2.5							
(17) 11.6	(14) 5.4	(12) 9.9	% Officers', Directors' Owners' Comp/Sales						
25.2	17.9	19.0							
1977209M	2192395M	3827480M	Net Sales ($)	11604M	46882M	74142M	125686M	323434M	3245732M
5348360M	5028847M	6317475M	Total Assets ($)	106648M	573341M	813073M	774242M	1320009M	2730162M

M = $ thousand MM = $ million

See Pages 9 through 22 for Explanation of Ratios and Data

REAL ESTATE AND RENTAL AND LEASING

REAL ESTATE AND RENTAL AND LEASING

Current Data Sorted by Assets							Comparative Historical Data	
						Type of Statement		
3	47	128	61	16	21	Unqualified	308	334
4	10	26	9	6	4	Reviewed	70	53
13	48	73	29	1		Compiled	229	221
244	633	437	64	4	1	Tax Returns	1527	1436
84	304	346	116	15	23	Other	788	893
	147 (4/1-9/30/13)		2,623 (10/1/13-3/31/14)				4/1/09-3/31/10	4/1/10-3/31/11
0-500M	500M-2MM	2-10MM	10-50MM	50-100MM	100-250MM		ALL	ALL
348	1042	1010	279	42	49	**NUMBER OF STATEMENTS**	2922	2937
%	%	%	%	%	%	**ASSETS**	%	%
15.4	6.1	4.8	6.9	14.4	9.0	Cash & Equivalents	6.5	6.5
1.1	1.0	1.1	3.3	6.3	2.6	Trade Receivables (net)	2.0	1.8
1.1	.7	.8	1.3	2.4	.8	Inventory	1.6	1.3
1.9	1.7	1.4	2.4	5.3	4.2	All Other Current	1.5	2.1
19.4	9.4	8.1	13.9	28.3	16.6	Total Current	11.6	11.7
73.4	83.5	83.2	69.0	47.6	54.8	Fixed Assets (net)	78.6	79.2
1.4	1.4	1.8	1.8	5.2	2.6	Intangibles (net)	1.6	1.7
5.8	5.7	6.9	15.2	18.9	26.0	All Other Non-Current	8.2	7.4
100.0	100.0	100.0	100.0	100.0	100.0	Total	100.0	100.0
						LIABILITIES		
5.1	3.8	2.9	2.5	5.1	5.2	Notes Payable-Short Term	3.6	4.1
5.8	3.3	3.0	2.0	1.5	1.3	Cur. Mat.-L.T.D.	4.2	3.9
2.2	1.4	.7	2.3	4.3	3.7	Trade Payables	1.3	1.6
.0	.0	.0	.0	.0	.0	Income Taxes Payable	.0	.0
12.2	5.8	4.8	3.9	8.3	8.2	All Other Current	7.5	6.6
25.4	14.3	11.4	10.7	19.2	18.4	Total Current	16.5	16.1
68.7	73.9	68.3	59.8	43.9	56.5	Long-Term Debt	73.1	70.9
.1	.0	.1	.2	.2	.2	Deferred Taxes	.1	.0
5.2	3.2	4.1	4.2	8.8	2.6	All Other Non-Current	3.1	3.8
.6	8.6	16.1	25.0	28.0	22.2	Net Worth	7.3	9.1
100.0	100.0	100.0	100.0	100.0	100.0	Total Liabilties & Net Worth	100.0	100.0
						INCOME DATA		
100.0	100.0	100.0	100.0	100.0	100.0	Net Sales	100.0	100.0
						Gross Profit		
70.1	66.7	68.1	70.6	79.3	77.4	Operating Expenses	67.5	67.8
29.9	33.3	31.9	29.4	20.7	22.6	Operating Profit	32.5	32.2
15.0	19.8	21.4	17.6	8.8	13.6	All Other Expenses (net)	24.2	23.5
14.9	13.5	10.4	11.8	11.8	9.0	Profit Before Taxes	8.3	8.7
						RATIOS		
2.0	1.6	1.9	3.0	3.9	2.8		1.8	1.8
.7	.5	.6	1.1	1.7	1.3	Current	.6	.6
.2	.2	.2	.4	.5	.6		.1	.2
1.8	1.4	1.5	2.0	2.4	2.7		1.4	1.4
(347) .6	.4	(1009) .4	.9	1.2	.8	Quick	(2921) .4	(2935) .5
.1	.1	.1	.3	.3	.4		.1	.1
0 UND	0 UND	0 UND	0 UND	0 UND	0 UND		0 UND	0 UND
0 UND	0 UND	0 UND	1 610.5	4 103.3	4 86.9	Sales/Receivables	0 UND	0 UND
0 UND	0 UND	2 202.9	12 30.9	32 11.4	18 20.7		2 171.4	2 174.4
						Cost of Sales/Inventory		
						Cost of Sales/Payables		
9.9	12.3	8.5	2.7	1.7	3.6		10.5	9.1
-40.9	-9.9	-11.3	34.6	6.3	12.1	Sales/Working Capital	-11.1	-12.8
-3.9	-2.7	-2.6	-4.1	-11.0	-7.7		-2.6	-2.7
6.2	5.0	4.5	4.4	14.3	9.1		5.5	5.5
(158) 3.2	(456) 2.5	(447) 2.5	(135) 2.4	(25) 4.5	(31) 2.5	EBIT/Interest	(1054) 2.6	(1063) 2.5
1.7	1.2	1.1	1.1	1.4	1.1		1.1	1.1
	3.4	3.5					4.4	4.4
	(13) 2.2	(30) 2.1				Net Profit + Depr., Dep., Amort./Cur. Mat. L/T/D	(41) 2.1	(59) 1.6
	.9	1.5					.5	.5
1.5	2.2	2.1	1.2	.2	.5		2.1	2.0
6.7	6.2	5.0	3.2	1.4	2.5	Fixed/Worth	6.8	6.0
-9.9	-16.0	-26.6	30.9	6.9	17.8		-11.2	-14.6
1.0	1.6	1.5	1.2	.7	1.4		1.9	1.6
8.6	5.9	5.2	3.5	1.8	4.8	Debt/Worth	7.3	6.5
-9.1	-18.5	-29.3	44.5	22.7	18.3		-13.4	-16.1
64.5	29.9	23.2	23.5	24.5	20.9		27.8	26.7
(237) 15.9	(711) 9.8	(709) 6.6	(220) 5.7	(33) 5.6	(43) 7.0	% Profit Before Taxes/Tangible Net Worth	(1939) 7.0	(2002) 7.6
-.4	-1.0	-2.1	.3	1.3	-1.0		-3.2	-2.7
16.3	7.1	4.9	4.4	6.8	4.5		6.0	5.8
4.2	2.4	1.6	1.6	2.5	1.2	% Profit Before Taxes/Total Assets	1.3	1.5
-1.1	-.6	-.8	-.1	.4	-.1		-1.5	-1.3
1.7	.4	.3	.6	36.6	8.8		.5	.5
.4	.2	.2	.2	.6	.3	Sales/Net Fixed Assets	.2	.2
.2	.1	.1	.1	.2	.2		.1	.1
1.0	.3	.3	.3	.6	.4		.3	.3
.3	.2	.2	.2	.3	.1	Sales/Total Assets	.2	.2
.2	.1	.1	.1	.1	.1		.1	.1
8.6	12.9	14.2	10.2	1.7	2.2		11.0	11.6
(272) 17.6	(872) 19.3	(833) 21.8	(219) 19.5	(38) 8.7	(41) 12.5	% Depr., Dep., Amort./Sales	(2512) 18.8	(2457) 19.2
25.0	27.9	30.4	29.5	18.3	26.3		27.1	28.4
4.7	3.0	3.1	2.0				2.7	3.0
(30) 7.0	(70) 5.0	(96) 6.9	(23) 3.6			% Officers', Directors' Owners' Comp/Sales	(270) 5.3	(255) 5.6
10.4	12.1	12.7	9.0				11.0	10.7
84900M	468288M	1162407M	1828508M	2165804M	4441624M	Net Sales ($)	9240220M	7496952M
94651M	1216303M	4383094M	5636959M	2990863M	7789277M	Total Assets ($)	22183155M	20663249M

M = $ thousand MM = $ million

See Pages 9 through 22 for Explanation of Ratios and Data

Comparative Historical Data | **Current Data Sorted by Sales**

Type of Statement	4/1/11-3/31/12 ALL	4/1/12-3/31/13 ALL	4/1/13-3/31/14 ALL	0-1MM	1-3MM	3-5MM	5-10MM	10-25MM	25MM & OVER
Unqualified	367	272	276	159	36	12	23	23	23
Reviewed	76	64	59	28	11	6	3	5	6
Compiled	205	214	164	98	45	6	12	2	1
Tax Returns	1652	1655	1383	1156	184	23	16	1	3
Other	897	929	888	593	162	43	36	30	24
				147 (4/1-9/30/13)		2,623 (10/1/13-3/31/14)			
NUMBER OF STATEMENTS	3197	3134	2770	2034	438	90	90	61	57
ASSETS	%	%	%	%	%	%	%	%	%
Cash & Equivalents	6.5	7.1	7.0	6.0	7.3	11.2	14.3	13.0	16.8
Trade Receivables (net)	1.6	1.4	1.4	.5	1.5	3.7	5.9	7.3	13.8
Inventory	1.1	1.0	.9	.6	1.7	1.5	1.4	1.7	3.1
All Other Current	1.5	1.9	1.8	1.1	1.9	5.1	6.9	5.5	8.7
Total Current	10.8	11.4	11.0	8.1	12.4	21.4	28.5	27.6	42.4
Fixed Assets (net)	79.6	79.5	79.6	84.9	75.9	58.8	52.2	45.3	31.8
Intangibles (net)	1.8	1.7	1.7	1.3	2.5	2.3	2.6	2.3	5.3
All Other Non-Current	7.8	7.4	7.7	5.6	9.3	17.5	16.6	24.8	20.4
Total	100.0	100.0	100.0	100.0	100.0	100.0	100.0	100.0	100.0
LIABILITIES									
Notes Payable-Short Term	3.4	3.8	3.6	3.4	3.5	2.3	4.8	5.4	6.5
Cur. Mat.-L.T.D.	3.5	3.6	3.3	3.5	3.5	2.4	1.9	1.3	1.6
Trade Payables	1.5	1.1	1.4	.8	1.8	2.3	2.9	4.9	12.4
Income Taxes Payable	.1	.0	.0	.0	.0	.0	.0	.1	.0
All Other Current	7.1	7.2	6.1	5.7	6.3	7.3	8.6	5.1	14.8
Total Current	15.6	15.7	14.4	13.5	15.1	14.3	18.3	16.9	35.3
Long-Term Debt	70.5	71.0	69.0	69.9	77.3	66.3	49.2	39.7	38.7
Deferred Taxes	.0	.1	.1	.1	.1	.2	.3	.1	.3
All Other Non-Current	3.8	4.1	4.0	4.0	3.6	3.9	4.0	4.0	6.2
Net Worth	10.0	9.2	12.5	12.6	3.9	15.3	28.2	39.4	19.5
Total Liabilties & Net Worth	100.0	100.0	100.0	100.0	100.0	100.0	100.0	100.0	100.0
INCOME DATA									
Net Sales	100.0	100.0	100.0	100.0	100.0	100.0	100.0	100.0	100.0
Gross Profit									
Operating Expenses	67.1	66.4	68.4	66.9	68.8	69.9	79.3	82.7	87.4
Operating Profit	32.9	33.6	31.6	33.1	31.2	30.1	20.7	17.3	12.6
All Other Expenses (net)	22.5	21.4	19.3	21.7	15.4	12.7	8.8	7.8	3.1
Profit Before Taxes	10.3	12.2	12.3	11.5	15.9	17.4	11.9	9.5	9.6
RATIOS									
	1.8	1.9	2.0	1.6	2.5	3.1	5.2	5.1	2.4
Current	.6	.6	.7	.5	.8	1.4	2.0	1.5	1.3
	.2	.2	.2	.1	.2	.6	.7	.8	1.0
	1.5	1.5	1.6	1.4	1.9	2.5	3.7	4.8	1.4
Quick	(3195) .5	(3132) .4	(2768) .5	(2032) .4	.5	1.1	1.3	1.2	1.1
	.1	.1	.1	.1	.1	.4	.5	.6	.6
	0 UND	0 UND	0 UND	0 UND	0 UND	0 UND	0 UND	0 UND	0 UND
Sales/Receivables	0 UND	0 UND	0 UND	0 UND	0 UND	0 UND	1 250.4	10 35.2	13 27.2
	2 236.0	1 319.0	1 317.6	0 UND	3 105.1	7 51.0	22 16.3	37 9.9	38 9.6
Cost of Sales/Inventory									
Cost of Sales/Payables									
	9.3	8.3	7.9	10.9	7.0	2.9	2.3	2.6	5.0
Sales/Working Capital	-14.3	-13.3	-14.3	-9.5	-29.0	20.0	8.5	9.4	11.5
	-2.8	-2.7	-2.9	-2.5	-3.8	-12.5	-13.1	-31.0	105.9
	5.2	5.4	5.0	4.3	5.6	8.1	18.1	7.4	24.4
EBIT/Interest	(1197) 2.5	(1250) 2.7	(1252) 2.5	(814) 2.4	(249) 2.8	(52) 3.0	(56) 3.0	(39) 2.5	(42) 3.9
	1.0	1.3	1.2	1.0	1.4	2.2	1.7	1.3	1.0
	3.2	2.5	4.0	2.7	4.0				
Net Profit + Depr., Dep., Amort./Cur. Mat. L/T/D	(72) 1.4	(60) 1.4	(63) 2.2	(30) 2.1	(15) 1.8				
	.6	.7	1.5	.9	1.6				
	2.0	2.0	1.9	2.1	2.1	.5	.3	.2	.1
Fixed/Worth	5.8	5.8	5.1	5.5	7.1	3.7	2.2	1.0	.7
	-15.0	-14.8	-26.1	-29.0	-5.1	-86.8	26.5	4.4	9.9
	1.6	1.6	1.4	1.5	1.9	.5	.8	.7	1.2
Debt/Worth	6.2	6.3	5.3	5.4	8.4	4.1	2.7	1.9	3.5
	-17.5	-16.2	-27.8	-29.6	-7.4	-67.9	28.9	7.3	33.4
	26.7	27.6	29.8	25.5	40.8	44.0	34.7	28.2	72.8
% Profit Before Taxes/Tangible Net Worth	(2187) 7.7	(2133) 8.6	(1953) 8.4	(1442) 6.8	(277) 14.7	(64) 10.2	(70) 13.0	(55) 6.4	(45) 33.4
	-2.0	-1.1	-1.3	-2.2	2.9	2.7	2.3	.7	7.2
	6.0	6.5	6.6	5.6	8.0	10.0	13.4	9.1	18.6
% Profit Before Taxes/Total Assets	1.8	2.0	2.0	1.7	2.8	3.6	4.2	1.9	6.9
	-1.0	-.6	-.6	-1.0	.3	1.1	.3	.0	.7
	.4	.4	.4	.3	.7	4.6	17.9	35.0	96.2
Sales/Net Fixed Assets	.2	.2	.2	.2	.3	.5	.8	.9	11.4
	.1	.1	.1	.1	.2	.2	.3	.2	.9
	.3	.3	.3	.3	.5	.6	1.0	.8	2.1
Sales/Total Assets	.2	.2	.2	.2	.2	.3	.4	.3	1.1
	.1	.1	.1	.1	.1	.2	.2	.1	.4
	12.0	12.2	12.3	14.8	9.5	3.3	2.1	.7	.6
% Depr., Dep., Amort./Sales	(2683) 19.7	(2578) 19.4	(2275) 19.8	(1684) 21.8	(353) 16.9	(71) 10.8	(67) 8.7	(55) 7.2	(45) 1.5
	28.6	27.4	28.4	30.4	24.4	20.5	18.6	20.2	8.2
	3.0	3.0	3.2	4.1	2.1	2.8	3.1		
% Officers', Directors' Owners' Comp/Sales	(277) 6.4	(260) 6.4	(227) 6.3	(121) 7.3	(65) 4.4	(12) 4.6	(15) 5.0		
	12.1	11.3	11.5	14.7	9.8	7.1	13.0		
Net Sales ($)	8748060M	7561789M	10151531M	662366M	716624M	345792M	633284M	960641M	6832824M
Total Assets ($)	22233762M	20104317M	22111147M	4271217M	3576291M	1657200M	2646676M	4262978M	5696785M

M = $ thousand MM = $ million

See Pages 9 through 22 for Explanation of Ratios and Data

	Current Data Sorted by Assets						Comparative Historical Data	
Type of Statement								
Unqualified	2	18	66	71	13	29	222	203
Reviewed	3	38	130	73	13	8	263	314
Compiled	38	239	400	117	9	5	918	868
Tax Returns	627	2664	2175	195	5	10	5789	6072
Other	224	1154	1592	470	65	44	2498	3100
	281 (4/1-9/30/13)			10,216 (10/1/13-3/31/14)			4/1/09-3/31/10	4/1/10-3/31/11
	0-500M	500M-2MM	2-10MM	10-50MM	50-100MM	100-250MM	ALL	ALL
NUMBER OF STATEMENTS	894	4113	4363	926	105	96	9690	10557
ASSETS	%	%	%	%	%	%	%	%
Cash & Equivalents	12.3	4.4	4.3	5.3	6.3	5.9	4.7	4.8
Trade Receivables (net)	1.2	.7	.9	1.9	4.3	1.1	1.3	1.5
Inventory	.9	.3	.5	2.0	3.4	2.8	.9	.8
All Other Current	1.8	1.0	1.1	2.1	2.1	2.6	1.3	1.6
Total Current	16.2	6.4	6.8	11.3	16.0	12.4	8.2	8.6
Fixed Assets (net)	76.7	87.5	85.7	76.6	65.8	66.6	84.5	84.1
Intangibles (net)	2.2	1.7	2.2	2.6	3.1	4.1	1.7	1.7
All Other Non-Current	5.0	4.5	5.3	9.4	15.0	16.9	5.7	5.6
Total	100.0	100.0	100.0	100.0	100.0	100.0	100.0	100.0
LIABILITIES								
Notes Payable-Short Term	5.0	2.9	2.2	3.4	3.4	2.6	3.3	3.4
Cur. Mat.-L.T.D.	4.5	4.0	3.7	3.3	4.6	3.6	4.5	4.2
Trade Payables	1.6	.5	.5	2.0	2.2	1.6	1.0	.9
Income Taxes Payable	.1	.0	.0	.0	.0	.6	.0	.0
All Other Current	10.5	3.7	3.7	4.8	4.3	4.9	4.1	4.1
Total Current	21.7	11.1	10.1	13.6	14.5	13.3	12.9	12.6
Long-Term Debt	65.2	68.3	66.7	56.0	49.9	46.5	68.1	67.5
Deferred Taxes	.0	.0	.0	.1	.3	.6	.0	.0
All Other Non-Current	4.0	2.8	3.1	3.7	4.8	5.1	2.6	2.9
Net Worth	9.1	17.8	20.0	26.6	30.5	34.4	16.3	17.0
Total Liabilties & Net Worth	100.0	100.0	100.0	100.0	100.0	100.0	100.0	100.0
INCOME DATA								
Net Sales	100.0	100.0	100.0	100.0	100.0	100.0	100.0	100.0
Gross Profit								
Operating Expenses	50.1	46.1	48.5	56.2	67.3	66.0	49.2	48.9
Operating Profit	49.9	53.9	51.5	43.8	32.7	34.0	50.8	51.1
All Other Expenses (net)	19.0	25.7	25.4	20.4	15.7	15.5	29.7	29.0
Profit Before Taxes	30.9	28.2	26.1	23.5	17.0	18.5	21.1	22.0
RATIOS								
Current	1.9	1.6	1.7	2.3	2.6	2.2	1.7	1.8
	.6	.5	.6	.8	1.1	.7	.5	.6
	.2	.1	.2	.2	.3	.2	.1	.2
Quick	1.5	1.3	1.4	1.8	1.7	1.8	1.4	1.4
	.6	(4112) .4	(4362) .5	(924) .6	.6	.5	(9684) .4	(10552) .4
	.2	.1	.1	.1	.2	.2	.1	.1
Sales/Receivables	0 UND	0 UND	0 UND	0 UND	0 UND	0 UND	0 UND	0 UND
	0 UND	0 UND	0 UND	0 UND	5 69.1	6 62.3	0 UND	0 UND
	0 UND	0 UND	0 UND	9 42.9	27 13.3	21 17.6	0 UND	0 UND
Cost of Sales/Inventory								
Cost of Sales/Payables								
Sales/Working Capital	13.2	12.0	8.5	4.2	2.1	3.5	9.1	8.5
	-15.6	-7.3	-8.6	-22.1	64.8	-16.2	-9.5	-9.8
	-3.0	-2.4	-2.6	-2.4	-2.6	-3.5	-2.6	-2.7
EBIT/Interest	9.0	7.4	6.9	7.0	8.8	6.8	7.0	7.0
	(365) 5.4	(1401) 4.4	(1564) 4.2	(395) 4.0	(55) 3.3	(46) 3.1	(2779) 4.0	(3123) 4.1
	3.3	2.8	2.6	2.3	1.6	1.5	2.2	2.4
Net Profit + Depr., Dep., Amort./Cur. Mat. L/T/D		2.9	2.7	3.2	5.4	4.9	3.3	3.5
		(40) 1.9	(129) 1.9	(71) 2.0	(16) 2.9	(19) 1.9	(267) 1.6	(310) 1.8
		1.3	1.1	1.1	1.5	1.5	.8	1.0
Fixed/Worth	1.4	2.3	2.3	1.7	1.0	1.0	2.3	2.2
	3.9	4.9	4.9	3.3	2.6	2.3	5.6	5.1
	-40.6	52.6	55.0	18.7	9.5	6.6	118.2	94.9
Debt/Worth	1.0	1.7	1.7	1.2	1.2	.9	1.8	1.7
	3.4	4.4	4.4	3.1	2.4	2.5	5.3	4.8
	-25.0	64.1	59.2	21.7	9.6	7.0	164.1	125.6
% Profit Before Taxes/Tangible Net Worth	60.7	34.4	32.3	25.2	19.9	17.4	33.3	33.2
	(652) 22.6	(3185) 16.3	(3378) 14.6	(744) 11.4	(89) 8.5	(85) 8.3	(7378) 14.2	(8065) 14.6
	8.8	6.2	5.3	3.4	2.5	.5	3.1	3.9
% Profit Before Taxes/Total Assets	18.7	8.3	7.1	6.4	4.9	5.0	7.0	7.2
	7.4	4.1	3.6	3.1	2.5	2.0	3.0	3.2
	2.0	1.3	1.0	.8	.7	.1	.3	.5
Sales/Net Fixed Assets	.8	.2	.2	.3	.7	.7	.3	.3
	.3	.2	.2	.2	.2	.2	.2	.2
	.2	.1	.1	.1	.1	.1	.1	.1
Sales/Total Assets	.6	.2	.2	.2	.2	.2	.2	.2
	.2	.1	.1	.1	.2	.1	.1	.1
	.1	.1	.1	.1	.1	.1	.1	.1
% Depr., Dep., Amort./Sales	8.6	12.8	14.1	13.2	6.7	11.3	12.6	12.5
	(731) 15.1	(3668) 18.6	(3792) 19.7	(804) 19.9	(88) 18.2	(72) 18.6	(8784) 18.5	(9377) 18.5
	21.7	25.0	26.8	28.2	26.6	26.6	25.4	25.5
% Officers', Directors' Owners' Comp/Sales	4.7	3.1	2.0	1.4	1.3		2.4	2.4
	(61) 9.2	(185) 6.5	(226) 5.0	(90) 4.5	(11) 3.0		(584) 5.3	(640) 5.6
	17.6	13.6	10.7	8.8	8.7		11.8	12.4
Net Sales ($)	228018M	1102536M	3966247M	6881199M	3512581M	3767372M	19871403M	22771902M
Total Assets ($)	275855M	4901628M	18349596M	18375556M	7414915M	15325934M	56315124M	60456042M

M = $ thousand MM = $ million

See Pages 9 through 22 for Explanation of Ratios and Data

Comparative Historical Data / Current Data Sorted by Sales

4/1/11-3/31/12 ALL	4/1/12-3/31/13 ALL	4/1/13-3/31/14 ALL	Type of Statement	0-1MM	1-3MM	3-5MM	5-10MM	10-25MM	25MM & OVER
205	212	199	Unqualified	59	51	19	24	22	24
341	305	265	Reviewed	117	60	18	23	24	23
1011	889	808	Compiled	590	142	26	24	16	10
7234	6806	5676	Tax Returns	5094	480	60	15	14	13
3545	3648	3549	Other	2645	562	119	84	84	55
				281 (4/1-9/30/13)			10,216 (10/1/13-3/31/14)		
12336	11860	10497	NUMBER OF STATEMENTS	8505	1295	242	170	160	125
%	%	%	**ASSETS**	%	%	%	%	%	%
4.8	5.1	5.1	Cash & Equivalents	4.6	6.8	6.8	11.9	10.2	8.1
1.3	1.0	1.0	Trade Receivables (net)	.6	1.2	2.5	5.2	5.6	12.9
.8	.7	.6	Inventory	.1	.8	3.0	1.6	7.8	15.5
1.4	1.4	1.2	All Other Current	1.0	2.2	2.1	1.6	3.2	4.6
8.3	8.1	8.0	Total Current	6.2	10.9	14.4	20.4	26.8	41.1
84.5	84.8	84.5	Fixed Assets (net)	87.3	78.9	70.8	63.9	56.4	41.4
1.7	1.7	2.0	Intangibles (net)	1.8	2.9	3.5	2.4	4.6	5.6
5.5	5.4	5.5	All Other Non-Current	4.7	7.3	11.3	13.2	12.3	12.0
100.0	100.0	100.0	Total	100.0	100.0	100.0	100.0	100.0	100.0
			LIABILITIES						
2.8	3.0	2.9	Notes Payable-Short Term	2.7	3.1	4.0	3.8	4.4	7.4
3.9	4.0	3.9	Cur. Mat.-L.T.D.	3.9	4.0	3.7	3.3	5.2	3.4
.9	.8	.8	Trade Payables	.4	.9	2.8	2.9	4.9	14.3
.0	.0	.0	Income Taxes Payable	.0	.0	.0	.0	.4	.1
4.1	4.2	4.4	All Other Current	4.1	4.8	5.4	7.3	7.8	10.7
11.7	12.1	11.9	Total Current	11.0	12.7	15.8	17.4	22.7	35.9
67.5	67.2	65.9	Long-Term Debt	67.4	65.1	58.6	51.4	46.4	30.8
.0	.0	.0	Deferred Taxes	.0	.0	.1	.2	.4	.7
3.2	3.3	3.2	All Other Non-Current	2.7	4.3	6.0	4.7	6.1	7.4
17.5	17.4	19.0	Net Worth	18.9	17.8	19.5	26.4	24.4	25.2
100.0	100.0	100.0	Total Liabilities & Net Worth	100.0	100.0	100.0	100.0	100.0	100.0
			INCOME DATA						
100.0	100.0	100.0	Net Sales	100.0	100.0	100.0	100.0	100.0	100.0
			Gross Profit						
48.8	47.9	48.7	Operating Expenses	46.1	54.1	61.8	68.8	73.9	87.0
51.2	52.1	51.3	Operating Profit	53.9	45.9	38.2	31.2	26.1	13.0
28.7	27.0	24.4	All Other Expenses (net)	26.4	18.3	15.0	11.2	11.0	4.1
22.5	25.1	26.9	Profit Before Taxes	27.5	27.7	23.2	20.0	15.1	8.9
			RATIOS						
1.8	1.8	1.7		1.6	2.5	2.3	2.9	2.3	2.0
.6	.6	.6	Current	.5	.8	.9	1.2	1.2	1.2
.2	.2	.2		.1	.2	.2	.3	.4	.7
1.4	1.4	1.4		1.3	1.9	1.7	2.2	1.7	1.2
(12330) .4	(11859) .4	(10493) .5	Quick	(8504) .4	(1293) .6	(241) .6	.7	.6	.6
.1	.1	.1		.1	.2	.2	.2	.2	.2
0 UND	0 UND	0 UND		0 UND	0 UND	0 UND	0 UND	0 UND	3 112.5
0 UND	0 UND	0 UND	Sales/Receivables	0 UND	0 UND	0 UND	4 100.5	5 70.0	13 28.1
0 UND	0 UND	0 UND		0 UND	3 126.9	9 41.9	23 16.1	22 16.4	39 9.4
			Cost of Sales/Inventory						
			Cost of Sales/Payables						
8.7	8.2	8.9		11.1	5.6	4.5	5.8	4.1	6.1
-9.8	-8.8	-8.9	Sales/Working Capital	-7.3	-21.6	-52.6	142.5	43.8	22.4
-2.7	-2.5	-2.5		-2.3	-3.4	-3.9	-3.2	-5.3	-25.3
7.4	7.3	7.3		7.1	7.4	9.5	9.0	8.9	14.4
(3629) 4.3	(3782) 4.3	(3826) 4.3	EBIT/Interest	(2746) 4.4	(652) 4.3	(132) 4.5	(93) 3.9	(102) 3.3	(101) 4.8
2.4	2.6	2.6		2.7	2.5	2.6	2.1	1.6	1.6
3.6	3.2	3.0		2.7	2.5	3.6	3.1	4.0	5.5
(314) 1.9	(306) 1.9	(283) 2.0	Net Profit + Depr., Dep., Amort./Cur. Mat. L/T/D	(137) 1.9	(56) 1.9	(15) 1.8	(14) 1.6	(22) 2.1	(39) 3.1
1.0	1.0	1.2		1.2	1.1	.7	1.2	1.6	1.6
2.2	2.2	2.1		2.3	1.8	1.6	1.2	.8	.5
4.9	4.8	4.6	Fixed/Worth	4.8	4.6	3.6	2.7	2.5	1.5
64.3	63.3	50.5		41.7	-37.8	NM	15.4	11.0	7.2
1.7	1.6	1.6		1.6	1.3	1.2	1.1	1.1	1.3
4.6	4.4	4.2	Debt/Worth	4.2	4.5	4.2	2.9	3.0	3.1
79.2	85.8	60.7		48.3	-35.8	-154.2	22.4	16.7	13.0
31.7	33.2	33.4		32.2	42.1	45.1	38.3	35.8	34.5
(9492) 14.2	(9139) 15.1	(8133) 15.3	% Profit Before Taxes/Tangible Net Worth	(6655) 15.0	(935) 17.5	(180) 18.1	(135) 13.8	(127) 13.9	(101) 16.6
3.6	5.0	5.5		5.4	6.4	7.0	5.1	4.4	8.6
7.3	7.7	7.9		7.5	9.5	9.3	10.1	9.4	11.0
3.2	3.6	3.9	% Profit Before Taxes/Total Assets	3.7	5.1	4.8	4.6	3.7	5.0
.6	.9	1.2		1.0	1.8	1.4	1.5	.7	1.9
.3	.3	.3		.2	.4	.7	1.5	12.6	25.0
.2	.2	.2	Sales/Net Fixed Assets	.2	.2	.3	.3	.5	7.2
.1	.1	.1		.1	.1	.2	.2	.2	.7
.2	.2	.2		.2	.3	.4	.7	1.6	3.0
.1	.1	.1	Sales/Total Assets	.1	.2	.2	.3	.3	1.4
.1	.1	.1		.1	.1	.1	.1	.1	.4
13.0	12.9	13.0		13.8	11.4	9.1	7.2	1.6	.8
(10920) 18.8	(10405) 18.7	(9155) 18.9	% Depr., Dep., Amort./Sales	(7458) 19.4	(1121) 17.1	(199) 17.5	(133) 14.6	(137) 11.5	(107) 1.8
25.7	25.4	25.7		26.1	24.7	25.4	26.6	21.2	8.0
2.6	2.7	2.2		3.1	2.9	1.7	2.1	1.5	.3
(714) 5.6	(659) 5.9	(581) 5.6	% Officers', Directors' Owners' Comp/Sales	(322) 6.5	(131) 6.1	(39) 4.1	(33) 5.1	(28) 2.4	(28) .7
12.8	13.6	12.4		14.8	13.3	8.8	9.1	6.4	1.8
21949677M	20512138M	19457953M	Net Sales ($)	2687500M	2085703M	920283M	1174605M	2417448M	10172414M
71264094M	66940050M	64643484M	Total Assets ($)	19780873M	12912233M	5240844M	5957541M	10228174M	10523819M

M = $ thousand MM = $ million

See Pages 9 through 22 for Explanation of Ratios and Data

Current Data Sorted by Assets							Comparative Historical Data	
						Type of Statement		
	1	1	1	1	1	Unqualified	6	9
	1	7	9			Reviewed	19	19
1	18	20	6			Compiled	37	56
42	110	102	7			Tax Returns	216	296
27	73	85	14	5	2	Other	159	186
	18 (4/1-9/30/13)		516 (10/1/13-3/31/14)				4/1/09-3/31/10 ALL	4/1/10-3/31/11 ALL
0-500M	500M-2MM	2-10MM	10-50MM	50-100MM	100-250MM			
70	203	215	37	6	3	NUMBER OF STATEMENTS	437	566
%	%	%	%	%	%	**ASSETS**	%	%
23.1	5.8	4.0	5.7			Cash & Equivalents	7.0	6.6
3.3	1.2	.9	1.7			Trade Receivables (net)	1.8	1.1
.9	.5	.3	.2			Inventory	1.5	.9
2.8	.6	1.2	1.3			All Other Current	1.4	1.4
30.1	8.1	6.4	9.0			Total Current	11.7	10.1
55.8	84.8	84.2	84.0			Fixed Assets (net)	81.2	82.4
7.6	2.3	2.2	1.7			Intangibles (net)	2.0	2.9
6.6	4.7	7.3	5.3			All Other Non-Current	5.2	4.6
100.0	100.0	100.0	100.0			Total	100.0	100.0
						LIABILITIES		
8.1	3.6	3.9	3.4			Notes Payable-Short Term	3.5	3.8
2.5	4.0	3.2	1.6			Cur. Mat.-L.T.D.	3.5	3.9
1.7	.2	.5	.6			Trade Payables	1.3	1.0
.1	.0	.0	.1			Income Taxes Payable	.0	.0
23.1	4.0	4.3	3.0			All Other Current	6.3	8.9
35.5	11.8	11.8	8.8			Total Current	14.6	17.7
47.4	74.5	66.0	64.8			Long-Term Debt	68.7	73.1
.0	.0	.0	.3			Deferred Taxes	.0	.1
17.6	5.8	3.4	3.4			All Other Non-Current	2.8	4.7
-.6	8.0	18.8	22.6			Net Worth	13.9	4.5
100.0	100.0	100.0	100.0			Total Liabilties & Net Worth	100.0	100.0
						INCOME DATA		
100.0	100.0	100.0	100.0			Net Sales	100.0	100.0
						Gross Profit		
77.5	58.8	61.5	58.8			Operating Expenses	64.0	64.5
22.5	41.2	38.5	41.2			Operating Profit	36.0	35.5
6.8	18.3	19.9	18.8			All Other Expenses (net)	23.5	23.7
15.7	22.8	18.6	22.5			Profit Before Taxes	12.6	11.8
						RATIOS		
3.4	1.9	2.0	2.8				2.2	1.2
.8	.6	.5	.9			Current	.6	.5
.2	.2	.2	.3				.2	.2
2.8	1.7	1.6	1.9				1.7	1.0
(69) .7	.5	.5	.6			Quick	.5	(565) .4
.2	.2	.1	.3				.1	.1
0 UND	0 UND	0 UND	0 UND				0 UND	0 UND
0 UND	0 UND	0 UND	4 88.6			Sales/Receivables	0 UND	0 UND
0 UND	0 UND	0 999.8	17 21.3				3 120.0	0 UND
						Cost of Sales/Inventory		
						Cost of Sales/Payables		
25.4	11.4	11.1	4.4				11.8	44.3
-86.5	-14.5	-12.9	-55.2			Sales/Working Capital	-19.7	-8.6
-4.9	-3.9	-3.4	-3.0				-3.0	-3.1
8.3	6.0	4.4	6.8				5.0	4.5
(33) 4.6	(120) 3.4	(100) 3.1	(22) 3.5			EBIT/Interest	(166) 2.8	(204) 2.9
.4	2.4	2.0	2.2				1.7	1.6
							2.3	3.8
						Net Profit + Depr., Dep., Amort./Cur. Mat. L/T/D	(13) 1.4	(16) 2.4
							.7	1.2
.5	2.7	2.1	2.0				2.4	2.8
2.0	11.2	5.0	4.9			Fixed/Worth	6.6	10.7
-5.3	-9.7	-22.5	NM				-24.0	-7.7
.4	2.2	1.6	1.3				1.7	2.4
2.4	11.5	4.5	4.2			Debt/Worth	6.6	12.0
-6.8	-10.8	-23.6	NM				-26.4	-9.1
138.7	64.2	36.2	35.8				40.4	39.2
(48) 38.2	(127) 27.0	(153) 12.5	(28) 23.7			% Profit Before Taxes/Tangible Net Worth	(294) 15.6	(342) 15.0
9.7	10.6	2.2	9.2				1.2	.4
44.1	11.2	7.1	7.4				7.9	7.1
11.9	5.2	3.3	3.8			% Profit Before Taxes/Total Assets	2.7	2.4
1.1	1.8	.7	1.1				-.2	-.5
46.1	.5	.3	.3				.4	.4
4.1	.3	.2	.2			Sales/Net Fixed Assets	.2	.2
.5	.2	.1	.1				.2	.2
8.7	.4	.2	.2				.4	.3
1.5	.2	.2	.2			Sales/Total Assets	.2	.2
.4	.2	.1	.1				.1	.1
1.4	8.9	10.7	13.6				10.5	11.1
(42) 6.1	(164) 14.0	(179) 16.9	(30) 17.0			% Depr., Dep., Amort./Sales	(346) 15.4	(454) 16.8
13.0	21.5	23.0	22.1				22.9	22.9
2.8	3.0	2.5					3.7	2.9
(14) 4.8	(24) 6.5	(27) 5.2				% Officers', Directors' Owners' Comp/Sales	(60) 7.1	(63) 6.5
11.0	10.3	9.7					14.0	13.2
25773M	81268M	244480M	236752M	253505M	88330M	Net Sales ($)	1121534M	1357345M
15885M	244951M	842829M	763969M	354698M	632202M	Total Assets ($)	2662511M	3163383M

M = $ thousand MM = $ million

See Pages 9 through 22 for Explanation of Ratios and Data

Comparative Historical Data / Current Data Sorted by Sales

			Type of Statement						
12	5	5	Unqualified	2				2	1
8	19	17	Reviewed	5	2	7	3		
47	42	45	Compiled	25	16		1	2	1
305	350	261	Tax Returns	232	22	5	1	1	
237	229	206	Other	163	26	4	4	6	3
				18 (4/1-9/30/13)			516 (10/1/13-3/31/14)		
4/1/11-3/31/12 ALL	4/1/12-3/31/13 ALL	4/1/13-3/31/14 ALL		0-1MM	1-3MM	3-5MM	5-10MM	10-25MM	25MM & OVER
609	645	534	NUMBER OF STATEMENTS	427	66	16	9	11	5
%	%	%	ASSETS	%	%	%	%	%	%
6.3	8.4	7.3	Cash & Equivalents	6.8	11.6	4.8		4.0	
1.6	1.3	1.5	Trade Receivables (net)	.9	1.9	1.2		12.4	
.9	.6	.4	Inventory	.3	1.0	.1		1.1	
1.3	1.5	1.2	All Other Current	1.0	1.0	5.2		4.0	
10.2	11.8	10.4	Total Current	8.9	15.5	11.3		21.5	
81.4	80.7	80.5	Fixed Assets (net)	82.1	75.5	80.3		64.3	
2.2	2.1	3.0	Intangibles (net)	3.0	2.3	1.0		2.4	
6.2	5.4	6.1	All Other Non-Current	5.9	6.7	7.5		11.8	
100.0	100.0	100.0	Total	100.0	100.0	100.0		100.0	
			LIABILITIES						
4.1	3.1	4.3	Notes Payable-Short Term	4.2	4.2	8.2		3.1	
3.3	4.0	3.3	Cur. Mat.-L.T.D.	3.4	2.9	1.3		4.3	
1.1	1.1	.5	Trade Payables	.3	.8	.3		5.0	
.0	.0	.0	Income Taxes Payable	.0	.1	.0		.5	
7.4	6.4	6.5	All Other Current	6.9	5.4	2.7		7.4	
16.0	14.7	14.7	Total Current	14.9	13.4	12.5		20.3	
71.7	75.0	66.8	Long-Term Debt	68.4	61.7	63.4		60.5	
.0	.0	.0	Deferred Taxes	.0	.1	.8		.2	
4.1	4.0	6.2	All Other Non-Current	6.6	4.7	5.9		4.2	
8.2	6.3	12.3	Net Worth	10.1	20.1	17.4		14.8	
100.0	100.0	100.0	Total Liabilities & Net Worth	100.0	100.0	100.0		100.0	
			INCOME DATA						
100.0	100.0	100.0	Net Sales	100.0	100.0	100.0		100.0	
			Gross Profit						
62.8	61.9	62.5	Operating Expenses	61.0	66.2	71.0		71.2	
37.2	38.1	37.5	Operating Profit	39.0	33.8	29.0		28.8	
21.4	20.5	17.4	All Other Expenses (net)	19.0	11.3	16.7		11.9	
15.7	17.6	20.1	Profit Before Taxes	20.0	22.5	12.2		16.9	
			RATIOS						
1.7	2.2	2.1		1.8	3.7	5.8		2.7	
.6	.7	.6	Current	.5	1.3	1.1		1.5	
.2	.2	.2		.2	.4	.4		.3	
1.4	1.8	1.7		1.4	3.4	5.8		2.0	
.5	(644) .5	(533) .5	Quick	(426) .5	.9	.5		1.0	
.1	.2	.2		.1	.3	.2		.3	
0 UND	0 UND	0 UND		0 UND	0 UND	0 UND		0 UND	
0 UND	0 UND	0 UND	Sales/Receivables	0 UND	0 UND	4 85.2		9 41.7	
1 394.8	1 635.4	0 UND		0 UND	3 138.5	11 34.0		59 6.2	
			Cost of Sales/Inventory						
			Cost of Sales/Payables						
15.7	14.5	12.1		18.8	5.2	4.3		3.5	
-15.8	-19.1	-15.6	Sales/Working Capital	-12.8	28.8	NM		31.3	
-3.0	-3.5	-3.7		-3.3	-5.3	-7.3		-10.9	
5.8	5.8	5.7		4.9	10.3				
(246) 3.2	(261) 3.2	(279) 3.3	EBIT/Interest	(207) 3.3	(45) 4.1				
1.8	1.9	2.2		2.2	2.4				
3.7	3.1	4.1							
(12) 1.8	(14) 1.9	(12) 2.3	Net Profit + Depr., Dep., Amort./Cur. Mat. L/T/D						
.8	1.2	1.5							
2.3	2.2	1.9		2.1	1.4	1.7		.6	
7.4	7.9	5.8	Fixed/Worth	6.2	4.1	16.8		1.8	
-9.2	-7.0	-12.1		-12.1	-8.7	-16.8		-1.2	
1.7	1.8	1.4		1.7	.9	2.5		.9	
8.6	8.8	6.0	Debt/Worth	6.7	3.9	19.0		1.5	
-11.5	-7.9	-13.2		-13.1	-11.1	-19.5		-2.6	
37.1	47.1	49.2		48.7	63.4	37.0			
(391) 15.5	(398) 18.2	(361) 20.9	% Profit Before Taxes/Tangible Net Worth	(287) 18.8	(45) 28.0	(10) 13.7			
3.0	3.8	5.6		4.3	13.4	2.9			
8.8	10.0	10.0		9.6	15.4	5.0		15.9	
3.2	4.1	4.6	% Profit Before Taxes/Total Assets	4.1	8.3	2.2		6.6	
.2	.7	1.1		1.0	3.5	.6		.4	
.4	.5	.5		.4	1.3	.6		9.9	
.2	.3	.3	Sales/Net Fixed Assets	.2	.4	.3		.5	
.2	.2	.2		.2	.2	.2		.4	
.3	.4	.4		.3	.8	.4		2.5	
.2	.2	.2	Sales/Total Assets	.2	.3	.2		.3	
.1	.2	.1		.1	.2	.1		.2	
11.3	9.4	8.9		10.0	5.1	13.8			
(476) 17.1	(532) 14.1	(422) 14.7	% Depr., Dep., Amort./Sales	(328) 15.5	(58) 11.8	(14) 15.9			
23.8	22.3	21.9		22.4	19.7	22.9			
3.5	3.2	3.0		2.5	3.5				
(83) 5.3	(85) 5.1	(74) 5.5	% Officers', Directors' Owners' Comp/Sales	(51) 5.1	(16) 6.9				
10.0	9.9	10.0		10.0	17.5				
1395711M	769294M	930108M	Net Sales ($)	171778M	113701M	62499M	59012M	184792M	338326M
2877520M	2584211M	2854534M	Total Assets ($)	858651M	418411M	279944M	207798M	703794M	385936M

M = $ thousand MM = $ million

See Pages 9 through 22 for Explanation of Ratios and Data

Current Data Sorted by Assets							Comparative Historical Data	
						Type of Statement		
	6	21	27	5	9	Unqualified	99	73
1	7	20	14	2	2	Reviewed	100	83
13	45	83	19	2	1	Compiled	256	221
102	305	253	26	1	1	Tax Returns	1008	997
37	137	218	70	10	11	Other	607	609
	79 (4/1-9/30/13)		1,369 (10/1/13-3/31/14)				4/1/09-3/31/10	4/1/10-3/31/11
0-500M	500M-2MM	2-10MM	10-50MM	50-100MM	100-250MM		ALL	ALL
153	500	595	156	20	24	NUMBER OF STATEMENTS	2070	1983
%	%	%	%	%	%	**ASSETS**	%	%
12.2	5.3	5.6	4.6	6.0	5.7	Cash & Equivalents	5.7	6.4
1.8	1.4	1.4	2.7	4.9	3.4	Trade Receivables (net)	2.1	1.6
1.0	.6	1.1	1.6	1.9	2.8	Inventory	1.5	1.4
1.6	2.3	1.8	2.0	1.9	1.5	All Other Current	2.0	1.9
16.5	9.6	9.9	10.8	14.7	13.4	Total Current	11.2	11.4
73.4	82.5	81.7	75.7	63.0	73.0	Fixed Assets (net)	79.7	79.6
3.8	2.3	2.1	5.2	.5	2.8	Intangibles (net)	2.0	2.0
6.2	5.6	6.2	8.2	21.8	10.8	All Other Non-Current	7.1	7.1
100.0	100.0	100.0	100.0	100.0	100.0	Total	100.0	100.0
						LIABILITIES		
3.7	3.9	2.3	2.7	1.4	5.3	Notes Payable-Short Term	3.9	4.4
3.9	4.7	3.8	3.5	1.8	3.1	Cur. Mat.-L.T.D.	5.3	4.4
1.7	1.2	1.1	2.5	2.4	1.8	Trade Payables	1.3	1.2
.0	.1	.0	.0	.6	.0	Income Taxes Payable	.0	.0
12.1	4.4	4.7	5.1	4.1	3.0	All Other Current	5.2	5.3
21.5	14.3	11.9	13.8	10.4	13.3	Total Current	15.8	15.3
64.7	65.8	62.0	52.5	51.0	60.1	Long-Term Debt	64.7	61.2
.0	.0	.0	.2	1.2	.2	Deferred Taxes	.1	.0
10.3	5.6	5.7	3.9	8.5	3.9	All Other Non-Current	3.7	4.9
3.5	14.3	20.4	29.6	28.9	22.6	Net Worth	15.8	18.5
100.0	100.0	100.0	100.0	100.0	100.0	Total Liabilities & Net Worth	100.0	100.0
						INCOME DATA		
100.0	100.0	100.0	100.0	100.0	100.0	Net Sales	100.0	100.0
						Gross Profit		
59.4	51.5	49.9	57.7	80.7	70.0	Operating Expenses	53.6	53.2
40.6	48.5	50.1	42.3	19.3	30.0	Operating Profit	46.4	46.8
15.5	21.9	23.1	21.4	14.2	20.4	All Other Expenses (net)	25.2	25.5
25.1	26.6	27.1	21.0	5.2	9.5	Profit Before Taxes	21.3	21.2
						RATIOS		
2.3	2.0	2.2	2.2	4.3	1.9		2.2	2.1
.7	.5	.7	.8	1.0	1.3	Current	.6	.6
.2	.1	.2	.2	.2	.5		.2	.2
1.8	1.3	1.8	1.6	3.5	1.5		1.6	1.5
.6	.4	.5	(155) .4	.5	.8	Quick	(2068) .4	.4
.2	.1	.1	.1	.1	.3		.1	.1
0 UND	0 UND	0 UND	0 UND	0 UND	3 145.6		0 UND	0 UND
0 UND	0 UND	0 UND	1 316.1	4 100.0	12 30.0	Sales/Receivables	0 UND	0 UND
0 UND	0 UND	1 371.8	8 43.2	25 14.4	27 13.4		2 214.3	0 UND
						Cost of Sales/Inventory		
						Cost of Sales/Payables		
9.8	8.8	5.1	3.4	1.7	3.8		6.5	6.5
-31.3	-9.1	-10.5	-19.2	NM	22.1	Sales/Working Capital	-12.6	-11.0
-3.5	-2.4	-2.1	-2.1	-1.9	-7.1		-2.4	-2.6
7.2	8.3	6.8	6.0	3.1	7.9		7.6	7.9
(68) 4.0	(219) 4.1	(237) 4.4	(73) 3.9	(14) 1.8	(12) 3.4	EBIT/Interest	(756) 4.2	(695) 4.2
1.7	2.1	2.0	1.5	-.1	1.0		2.0	2.0
	15.2	2.6	2.3				2.8	2.9
	(10) 4.3	(24) 1.7	(16) 1.5			Net Profit + Depr., Dep., Amort./Cur. Mat. L/T/D	(77) 1.8	(66) 1.7
	1.0	.9	.8				1.0	.9
1.1	1.8	1.8	1.5	.6	1.5		1.8	1.7
3.7	4.5	4.5	3.2	4.0	2.6	Fixed/Worth	4.6	4.2
-156.3	-98.1	39.1	15.5	27.6	63.5		116.0	31.7
.9	1.3	1.3	1.0	.5	1.2		1.5	1.4
3.4	4.2	4.2	2.7	3.4	3.1	Debt/Worth	4.6	3.9
-10.1	-108.8	50.4	15.2	28.4	NM		198.6	46.5
56.2	38.1	28.1	18.9	11.0	19.1		33.3	30.8
(110) 20.9	(371) 16.5	(463) 14.3	(124) 9.2	(16) 5.0	(18) 9.1	% Profit Before Taxes/Tangible Net Worth	(1567) 14.6	(1543) 13.6
6.1	4.8	4.3	1.7	-1.1	.4		3.0	2.4
19.2	10.6	7.4	6.4	4.3	6.3		8.2	8.1
6.6	4.2	3.7	2.3	1.2	1.6	% Profit Before Taxes/Total Assets	3.4	3.2
1.3	1.0	.9	.5	-.7	-.3		.2	.2
1.9	.4	.2	.3	1.5	1.0		.4	.4
.3	.2	.2	.2	.3	.3	Sales/Net Fixed Assets	.2	.2
.2	.1	.1	.1	.1	.1		.1	.1
1.0	.3	.2	.2	.3	.5		.3	.3
.3	.2	.1	.1	.2	.2	Sales/Total Assets	.2	.2
.2	.1	.1	.1	.1	.1		.1	.1
6.6	10.7	11.5	8.7	4.1	5.6		10.6	11.0
(118) 14.0	(433) 17.4	(511) 19.4	(137) 17.7	(19) 10.3	(17) 16.9	% Depr., Dep., Amort./Sales	(1839) 17.3	(1719) 17.9
20.1	26.2	27.0	27.4	27.7	22.8		25.0	26.4
4.5	2.7	1.5	1.5				4.0	2.4
(10) 11.2	(39) 5.6	(34) 4.8	(14) 6.2			% Officers', Directors' Owners' Comp/Sales	(173) 7.1	(143) 6.0
36.3	12.8	15.6	10.4				13.2	13.5
47967M	**271187M**	**692927M**	**1160465M**	**493886M**	**1994014M**	Net Sales ($)	**5826073M**	**3923703M**
46486M	**593727M**	**2636289M**	**3246147M**	**1403424M**	**3849091M**	Total Assets ($)	**16954725M**	**11508371M**

M = $ thousand MM = $ million

See Pages 9 through 22 for Explanation of Ratios and Data

Comparative Historical Data / Current Data Sorted by Sales

4/1/11-3/31/12 ALL	4/1/12-3/31/13 ALL	4/1/13-3/31/14 ALL	Type of Statement	0-1MM	1-3MM	3-5MM	5-10MM	10-25MM	25MM & OVER
78	61	68	Unqualified	18	15	10	7	9	9
86	61	46	Reviewed	21	7	9	3	3	3
229	191	163	Compiled	100	40	12	6	3	2
1039	927	688	Tax Returns	603	73	4	3	2	3
630	561	483	Other	326	97	19	10	18	13
				79 (4/1-9/30/13)			1,369 (10/1/13-3/31/14)		
2062	1801	1448	**NUMBER OF STATEMENTS**	1068	232	54	29	35	30
%	%	%	**ASSETS**	%	%	%	%	%	%
6.1	6.3	6.1	Cash & Equivalents	4.9	7.9	14.4	9.8	11.1	9.0
1.8	1.8	1.7	Trade Receivables (net)	.6	2.0	4.0	11.5	6.4	17.5
1.3	1.5	1.0	Inventory	.4	2.2	1.1	5.0	5.8	5.5
1.7	1.8	1.9	All Other Current	1.6	2.6	3.5	2.7	4.6	2.9
10.8	11.4	10.7	Total Current	7.5	14.7	23.1	29.1	28.0	34.9
79.7	79.3	80.1	Fixed Assets (net)	84.7	73.9	63.6	51.0	62.1	44.0
2.4	2.1	2.7	Intangibles (net)	2.3	3.2	4.3	4.0	4.4	6.5
7.1	7.2	6.5	All Other Non-Current	5.6	8.2	8.9	15.9	5.6	14.6
100.0	100.0	100.0	Total	100.0	100.0	100.0	100.0	100.0	100.0
			LIABILITIES						
3.8	3.6	3.1	Notes Payable-Short Term	2.7	3.8	4.0	4.4	3.8	4.9
4.6	4.4	4.1	Cur. Mat.-L.T.D.	4.2	3.9	4.4	2.9	2.2	2.2
1.1	1.2	1.4	Trade Payables	.5	2.2	1.6	10.1	3.9	14.7
.0	.0	.0	Income Taxes Payable	.0	.0	.2	1.1	.0	.0
5.2	5.2	5.4	All Other Current	4.8	5.5	13.6	6.0	8.7	7.6
14.6	14.4	13.9	Total Current	12.3	15.3	23.8	24.5	18.6	29.4
62.8	60.8	62.4	Long-Term Debt	62.9	69.8	53.9	32.9	53.2	39.9
.1	.0	.1	Deferred Taxes	.0	.0	.0	.4	.1	.8
4.8	5.0	6.0	All Other Non-Current	5.1	9.0	11.4	6.3	3.8	4.3
17.7	19.8	17.7	Net Worth	19.7	5.8	11.0	35.8	24.2	25.6
100.0	100.0	100.0	Total Liabilties & Net Worth	100.0	100.0	100.0	100.0	100.0	100.0
			INCOME DATA						
100.0	100.0	100.0	Net Sales	100.0	100.0	100.0	100.0	100.0	100.0
			Gross Profit						
52.7	52.2	53.0	Operating Expenses	49.1	57.1	69.6	70.5	75.9	88.9
47.3	47.8	47.0	Operating Profit	50.9	42.9	30.4	29.5	24.1	11.1
24.9	23.2	21.5	All Other Expenses (net)	23.9	17.1	14.6	5.8	15.0	6.8
22.4	24.6	25.4	Profit Before Taxes	27.0	25.8	15.7	23.7	9.1	4.3
			RATIOS						
2.1	2.3	2.2		1.9	3.0	2.2	3.6	3.5	2.2
.6	.7	.6	Current	.5	.9	1.0	1.3	1.2	1.5
.2	.2	.2		.1	.3	.2	.5	.6	1.0
1.5	1.7	1.6		1.5	2.1	1.4	3.2	1.8	1.6
(2059) .5	(1800) .5	(1447) .4	Quick	(1067) .4	.6	.7	.5	.7	.9
.1	.1	.1		.1	.1	.2	.2	.2	.5
0 UND	0 UND	0 UND		0 UND	0 UND	0 UND	0 UND	0 UND	8 44.3
0 UND	0 UND	0 UND	Sales/Receivables	0 UND	0 UND	2 229.2	5 78.4	6 58.8	19 18.9
0 UND	0 999.8	1 261.4		0 UND	5 78.5	14 26.0	23 16.1	28 13.0	49 7.4
			Cost of Sales/Inventory						
			Cost of Sales/Payables						
7.1	6.5	6.7		8.1	3.2	5.6	3.2	3.4	8.5
-13.1	-15.0	-12.4	Sales/Working Capital	-8.1	-39.0	NM	123.0	20.7	24.8
-2.6	-2.7	-2.3		-2.0	-3.4	-1.7	-2.9	-16.4	NM
7.8	8.1	7.0		7.2	5.6	6.9	11.3	5.3	15.4
(753) 4.0	(704) 4.2	(623) 4.1	EBIT/Interest	(401) 4.4	(126) 3.9	(32) 3.1	(22) 3.7	(18) 1.8	(24) 4.2
1.9	2.2	1.8		2.2	1.7	1.0	1.3	-1.2	1.8
3.1	2.9	2.8		3.2	2.6				
(88) 1.9	(62) 1.6	(56) 1.8	Net Profit + Depr., Dep., Amort./Cur. Mat. L/T/D	(22) 1.5	(19) 1.8				
1.0	.9	.9		.7	1.5				
1.8	1.7	1.7		1.9	1.8	1.0	.8	.7	.3
4.3	4.0	4.2	Fixed/Worth	4.4	4.3	2.8	1.6	2.2	1.5
44.4	34.0	55.8		41.0	-10.5	7.2	14.7	37.5	NM
1.4	1.2	1.2		1.2	1.3	.9	.5	.9	1.3
4.1	3.6	4.0	Debt/Worth	4.0	4.7	2.9	1.7	2.0	2.7
56.7	46.7	82.9		46.9	-13.3	51.4	20.7	36.5	-16.4
32.4	34.9	31.4		31.2	29.3	33.0	71.4	23.7	68.9
(1598) 14.2	(1398) 14.7	(1102) 14.3	% Profit Before Taxes/Tangible Net Worth	(832) 14.5	(154) 14.2	(42) 9.2	(24) 16.5	(28) 9.5	(22) 29.6
3.4	4.4	4.0		4.1	4.2	.7	4.7	-.1	6.6
8.1	8.5	8.5		8.1	10.3	10.1	19.0	8.2	12.9
3.5	3.9	3.7	% Profit Before Taxes/Total Assets	3.6	5.1	2.4	4.8	2.2	5.4
.5	.9	.8		.8	1.5	.4	.6	-2.3	1.8
.4	.4	.4		.3	.7	5.5	11.3	6.1	58.6
.2	.2	.2	Sales/Net Fixed Assets	.2	.2	.3	1.9	.5	2.9
.1	.1	.1		.1	.2	.1	.3	.2	.9
.3	.3	.3		.2	.4	1.3	2.0	1.5	3.7
.2	.2	.2	Sales/Total Assets	.1	.2	.3	.4	.3	1.1
.1	.1	.1		.1	.1	.1	.2	.2	.6
10.8	10.6	10.3		12.7	7.4	2.4	1.6	2.2	.5
(1805) 17.9	(1554) 17.8	(1235) 18.1	% Depr., Dep., Amort./Sales	(906) 19.4	(201) 15.7	(46) 10.9	(27) 4.4	(31) 12.4	(24) 3.3
25.9	25.7	26.3		27.4	25.3	22.4	14.5	20.7	6.3
3.3	2.1	2.7		2.7	3.9				
(141) 5.9	(111) 5.7	(100) 5.8	% Officers', Directors' Owners' Comp/Sales	(50) 6.6	(28) 6.7				
11.2	11.8	12.7		15.2	12.7				
4692733M	5082382M	4660446M	Net Sales ($)	356916M	396884M	209243M	212602M	564418M	2920383M
14097724M	12893817M	11775164M	Total Assets ($)	2603258M	2187783M	1333367M	697976M	2336914M	2615866M

M = $ thousand MM = $ million

See Pages 9 through 22 for Explanation of Ratios and Data

Current Data Sorted by Assets / Comparative Historical Data

Type of Statement	0-500M	500M-2MM	2-10MM	10-50MM	50-100MM	100-250MM	4/1/09-3/31/10 ALL	4/1/10-3/31/11 ALL
Unqualified	2	2	6	9	2	3	46	38
Reviewed		7	14	7	1	3	40	33
Compiled	16	15	23	5			96	86
Tax Returns	125	92	35	6	2	1	363	304
Other	75	81	79	42	9	6	289	306
		51 (4/1-9/30/13)		617 (10/1/13-3/31/14)				
NUMBER OF STATEMENTS	218	197	157	69	14	13	834	767
ASSETS	%	%	%	%	%	%	%	%
Cash & Equivalents	43.0	20.6	16.8	14.9	29.2	22.2	20.0	21.1
Trade Receivables (net)	5.4	6.7	7.1	9.2	4.3	4.6	6.0	6.0
Inventory	.8	4.0	.8	1.9	4.3	2.6	2.7	2.0
All Other Current	5.6	5.1	5.1	7.6	.7	9.2	5.3	6.0
Total Current	54.8	36.4	29.8	33.5	38.5	38.6	34.0	35.1
Fixed Assets (net)	26.3	41.7	49.5	36.2	44.4	24.8	45.7	45.0
Intangibles (net)	5.0	5.8	6.2	6.4	3.0	3.6	6.2	6.6
All Other Non-Current	13.8	16.2	14.5	23.9	14.1	33.1	14.1	13.4
Total	100.0	100.0	100.0	100.0	100.0	100.0	100.0	100.0
LIABILITIES								
Notes Payable-Short Term	18.0	7.0	5.7	6.5	2.0	7.5	15.9	13.7
Cur. Mat.-L.T.D.	2.8	2.8	2.9	2.8	2.9	1.5	4.5	4.0
Trade Payables	6.4	4.9	4.5	6.0	1.6	4.4	4.3	4.0
Income Taxes Payable	.2	.0	.1	.1	.0	.2	.1	.1
All Other Current	25.3	15.3	11.1	11.8	12.0	10.2	15.5	17.1
Total Current	52.7	29.9	24.1	27.2	18.4	23.8	40.3	38.8
Long-Term Debt	21.3	33.6	36.5	24.8	44.0	20.1	36.7	38.1
Deferred Taxes	.0	.0	.1	.0	.2	.0	.0	.0
All Other Non-Current	12.1	7.4	10.1	4.9	4.6	2.6	8.2	11.9
Net Worth	13.9	29.1	29.2	43.1	32.7	53.5	14.7	11.2
Total Liabilities & Net Worth	100.0	100.0	100.0	100.0	100.0	100.0	100.0	100.0
INCOME DATA								
Net Sales	100.0	100.0	100.0	100.0	100.0	100.0	100.0	100.0
Gross Profit								
Operating Expenses	83.3	76.3	73.3	77.6	78.3	85.1	79.9	80.0
Operating Profit	16.7	23.7	26.7	22.4	21.7	14.9	20.1	20.0
All Other Expenses (net)	2.7	7.0	8.8	6.1	10.1	3.7	10.5	9.6
Profit Before Taxes	14.1	16.7	17.9	16.3	11.6	11.2	9.7	10.4
RATIOS								
Current	4.4	3.1	3.2	2.9	4.4	3.5	2.8	2.9
	1.4	1.2	1.2	1.3	2.5	1.3	1.1	1.2
	.5	.3	.4	.7	1.1	.9	.3	.4
Quick	4.1	2.7	2.7	2.2	4.4	3.0	2.1	2.3
	1.2	.9	1.0	.9	2.1	.9	(832) .7	.8
	.4	.3	.3	.3	.8	.3	.2	.2
Sales/Receivables	0 UND	0 UND	0 UND	0 UND	0 UND	1 365.4	0 UND	0 UND
	0 UND	0 UND	0 999.8	5 69.0	5 69.3	7 48.7	0 UND	0 UND
	0 958.5	5 80.8	10 37.8	33 11.1	26 14.0	24 15.4	9 41.6	7 52.3
Cost of Sales/Inventory								
Cost of Sales/Payables								
Sales/Working Capital	13.1	8.2	6.0	4.0	3.4	3.6	7.9	8.0
	65.5	75.0	33.1	23.5	7.1	6.3	177.3	105.6
	-27.9	-8.2	-7.3	-13.4	NM	NM	-6.1	-8.5
EBIT/Interest	51.7	20.4	27.6	48.6			9.0	9.7
	(106) 12.3	(108) 5.7	(100) 7.1	(52) 7.5			(471) 2.6	(428) 3.3
	3.0	2.2	3.0	3.0			-.6	.4
Net Profit + Depr., Dep., Amort./Cur. Mat. L/T/D							2.6	2.9
							(42) 1.3	(29) 1.7
							.2	.5
Fixed/Worth	.0	.2	.4	.1	.0	.1	.3	.3
	.5	1.3	1.6	.9	1.4	.1	2.0	2.2
	-7.5	5.6	12.4	3.7	4.8	1.4	-21.4	-12.0
Debt/Worth	.3	.6	.7	.6	.6	.2	.8	.8
	1.7	2.4	2.4	1.5	2.0	.6	3.4	3.5
	-4.9	11.7	14.2	5.1	6.2	4.8	-12.4	-12.4
% Profit Before Taxes/Tangible Net Worth	280.1	99.4	65.1	62.2	70.3	56.1	50.5	70.5
	(149) 100.0	(160) 36.9	(123) 26.6	(60) 20.0	(12) 28.2	(12) 12.9	(589) 14.8	(531) 20.6
	20.7	10.9	7.3	5.2	10.3	4.9	.9	2.0
% Profit Before Taxes/Total Assets	96.2	31.6	19.8	16.7	11.9	21.2	12.6	18.6
	36.9	9.6	9.6	6.5	6.5	8.8	3.4	4.6
	6.2	2.1	2.5	2.0	-.5	.7	-2.0	-.8
Sales/Net Fixed Assets	999.8	75.5	31.6	43.4	UND	80.1	51.6	52.1
	73.0	15.4	3.7	8.0	8.7	7.9	6.9	8.1
	16.6	.3	.2	.3	.3	.8	.3	.3
Sales/Total Assets	16.6	4.5	3.2	2.3	2.3	2.0	4.8	5.3
	6.8	1.3	.8	.7	1.0	1.3	1.1	1.4
	2.4	.2	.2	.2	.2	.2	.2	.2
% Depr., Dep., Amort./Sales	.3	.5	1.0	.7	2.4		1.0	.8
	(93) 1.2	(137) 1.7	(112) 4.0	(56) 1.7	(10) 3.5		(621) 4.3	(526) 3.0
	3.1	14.4	16.8	9.0	20.6		16.4	14.8
% Officers', Directors' Owners' Comp/Sales	2.8	1.6	2.1	2.9			2.3	2.2
	(92) 6.4	(55) 3.9	(44) 4.3	(11) 3.4			(221) 6.1	(226) 5.2
	12.6	12.0	8.5	7.1			12.9	13.3
Net Sales ($)	410891M	721116M	1714198M	2114676M	2108628M	3008315M	10899980M	10089862M
Total Assets ($)	44330M	217330M	692695M	1511294M	1034237M	2220443M	8329032M	6026779M

M = $ thousand MM = $ million

See Pages 9 through 22 for Explanation of Ratios and Data

Comparative Historical Data				Current Data Sorted by Sales					
			Type of Statement						
38	37	24	Unqualified	1	1	1	3	10	8
41	25	32	Reviewed	3	5	4	6	6	8
77	85	59	Compiled	21	15	5	5	12	1
332	281	261	Tax Returns	143	55	24	21	12	6
339	299	292	Other	88	65	23	42	31	43
4/1/11-3/31/12 ALL	4/1/12-3/31/13 ALL	4/1/13-3/31/14 ALL			51 (4/1-9/30/13)		617 (10/1/13-3/31/14)		
				0-1MM	1-3MM	3-5MM	5-10MM	10-25MM	25MM & OVER
827	727	668	**NUMBER OF STATEMENTS**	256	141	57	77	71	66
%	%	%	**ASSETS**	%	%	%	%	%	%
22.8	27.1	26.7	Cash & Equivalents	22.4	24.8	38.7	33.3	29.0	26.5
6.8	6.6	6.5	Trade Receivables (net)	3.7	5.9	8.1	8.3	9.3	12.5
2.2	1.9	1.9	Inventory	1.6	2.9	1.3	2.0	1.7	2.1
5.2	5.9	5.5	All Other Current	4.3	6.5	2.5	4.0	10.5	7.4
37.0	41.4	40.6	Total Current	31.9	40.1	50.6	47.7	50.4	48.4
42.0	37.7	37.7	Fixed Assets (net)	53.6	36.4	21.3	26.2	21.9	23.3
6.5	5.9	5.6	Intangibles (net)	2.3	7.2	6.3	4.2	9.8	11.4
14.5	15.0	16.1	All Other Non-Current	12.2	16.3	21.9	21.9	17.9	16.9
100.0	100.0	100.0	Total	100.0	100.0	100.0	100.0	100.0	100.0
			LIABILITIES						
14.5	11.4	10.1	Notes Payable-Short Term	10.8	14.4	9.0	6.6	7.9	5.7
3.5	3.7	2.8	Cur. Mat.-L.T.D.	3.0	2.6	3.8	3.2	1.9	1.6
5.3	5.2	5.3	Trade Payables	2.8	5.1	5.0	7.6	9.1	9.1
.1	.1	.1	Income Taxes Payable	.0	.3	.0	.1	.0	.1
18.8	21.5	17.0	All Other Current	14.3	21.3	15.7	18.1	18.8	16.8
42.1	41.9	35.4	Total Current	31.1	43.6	33.5	35.6	37.6	33.2
34.6	31.2	29.3	Long-Term Debt	38.1	34.4	17.2	18.9	14.4	23.2
.1	.1	.0	Deferred Taxes	.0	.0	.0	.0	.2	.0
13.1	9.7	9.2	All Other Non-Current	7.4	8.8	14.6	7.6	13.6	9.1
10.1	17.1	26.1	Net Worth	23.4	13.2	34.7	38.0	34.3	34.5
100.0	100.0	100.0	Total Liabilties & Net Worth	100.0	100.0	100.0	100.0	100.0	100.0
			INCOME DATA						
100.0	100.0	100.0	Net Sales	100.0	100.0	100.0	100.0	100.0	100.0
			Gross Profit						
81.2	80.9	78.2	Operating Expenses	63.9	81.2	84.2	91.7	92.1	91.5
18.8	19.1	21.8	Operating Profit	36.1	18.8	15.8	8.3	7.9	8.5
8.5	7.0	5.9	All Other Expenses (net)	12.6	3.6	.9	.9	.4	.9
10.3	12.2	15.9	Profit Before Taxes	23.5	15.2	14.9	7.4	7.4	7.6
			RATIOS						
2.9	3.5	3.5		3.5	3.1	4.6	3.4	3.8	2.6
1.2	1.3	1.3	Current	1.0	1.1	1.8	1.7	1.6	1.5
.3	.5	.5		.3	.5	.7	1.0	.9	1.0
2.3	2.9	3.0		3.3	2.7	4.5	3.1	3.2	2.2
.8	1.0	1.0	Quick	.7	.7	1.4	1.5	1.2	1.2
.2	.3	.3		.2	.2	.5	.7	.6	.6
0 UND	0 UND	0 UND		0 UND	0 UND	0 UND	0 UND	0 999.8	0 947.6
0 UND	0 UND	0 UND	Sales/Receivables	0 UND	0 UND	0 UND	1 256.4	3 113.6	5 77.2
7 55.6	8 46.6	6 59.5		0 UND	9 40.5	7 50.5	6 64.7	12 30.8	24 15.2
			Cost of Sales/Inventory						
			Cost of Sales/Payables						
8.9	6.3	8.1		6.2	8.5	9.3	6.8	12.9	8.5
109.0	64.8	43.8	Sales/Working Capital	UND	141.1	22.6	37.9	33.1	31.4
-8.0	-12.1	-12.0		-2.8	-10.8	-36.8	813.6	-138.0	UND
12.0	30.0	32.0		17.9	14.3	70.4	82.3	97.4	68.2
(447) 4.3	(394) 7.1	(383) 8.0	EBIT/Interest	(107) 5.0	(92) 5.4	(33) 11.8	(48) 8.5	(52) 15.1	(51) 13.9
1.0	2.2	2.6		2.5	1.3	4.3	5.1	3.9	3.5
4.9	5.9	8.9							
(30) 1.0	(16) 1.7	(20) 2.6	Net Profit + Depr., Dep., Amort./Cur. Mat. L/T/D						
.3	.4	.9							
.2	.2	.1		.1	.1	.0	.1	.1	.1
1.7	1.3	1.1	Fixed/Worth	1.8	1.6	.3	.5	.5	.7
-16.4	-283.2	8.0		10.9	-7.0	3.4	2.8	2.2	2.7
.8	.6	.5		.5	.7	.4	.3	.5	.6
3.3	2.6	2.0	Debt/Worth	2.6	3.1	1.4	.9	1.1	1.7
-13.8	-18.8	37.3		37.7	-9.1	NM	9.2	5.2	5.9
66.8	109.3	105.9		94.6	138.6	145.9	125.1	100.9	100.5
(581) 21.6	(529) 29.9	(516) 36.9	% Profit Before Taxes/Tangible Net Worth	(201) 22.5	(98) 43.1	(43) 73.4	(62) 34.1	(59) 56.0	(53) 56.1
1.3	6.5	10.9		5.7	5.0	23.2	9.7	27.6	21.6
19.6	37.7	40.2		24.8	44.0	74.9	45.6	43.8	40.6
5.1	9.7	12.5	% Profit Before Taxes/Total Assets	7.0	10.8	26.8	14.8	18.3	19.0
-.3	1.8	2.7		1.5	1.9	8.6	4.6	6.9	7.4
77.6	112.8	115.2		55.7	118.1	276.0	148.6	115.8	112.9
12.1	21.0	20.9	Sales/Net Fixed Assets	.7	24.7	61.4	39.4	44.7	36.8
.4	.6	.6		.2	1.3	9.8	8.1	13.8	15.9
5.2	5.9	6.8		2.5	7.3	9.4	15.7	10.3	7.9
1.7	2.0	2.1	Sales/Total Assets	.3	2.1	3.4	4.6	4.9	3.2
.2	.3	.3		.1	.6	1.5	1.5	1.9	1.7
.8	.6	.6		2.7	.5	.2	.3	.3	.5
(547) 2.9	(475) 1.8	(414) 1.9	% Depr., Dep., Amort./Sales	(152) 13.6	(83) 1.7	(32) .8	(52) 1.0	(53) .8	(42) .9
15.5	13.5	13.1		21.8	7.5	2.0	3.1	1.7	1.7
2.3	2.6	2.4		7.9	2.6	1.7	1.5	1.5	1.3
(236) 4.8	(202) 5.6	(208) 5.1	% Officers', Directors' Owners' Comp/Sales	(55) 11.8	(57) 4.6	(23) 3.4	(34) 3.1	(22) 3.0	(17) 3.0
10.5	10.7	11.6		19.6	10.3	6.5	6.0	5.7	7.9
10189475M	10778414M	10077824M	Net Sales ($)	94218M	244126M	220942M	554739M	1162909M	7800890M
7292826M	6968998M	5720329M	Total Assets ($)	344507M	381922M	228535M	594429M	842180M	3328756M

M = $ thousand MM = $ million

See Pages 9 through 22 for Explanation of Ratios and Data

	Current Data Sorted by Assets						Comparative Historical Data	
Type of Statement								
Unqualified	2	5	12	12	3	3	63	43
Reviewed	1	4	10	7	1		20	13
Compiled	6	13	12	2			42	32
Tax Returns	72	65	39	8			234	218
Other	38	51	48	21	4	1	189	207
	37 (4/1-9/30/13)			403 (10/1/13-3/31/14)			4/1/09-3/31/10	4/1/10-3/31/11
	0-500M	500M-2MM	2-10MM	10-50MM	50-100MM	100-250MM	ALL	ALL
NUMBER OF STATEMENTS	119	138	121	50	8	4	548	513
ASSETS	%	%	%	%	%	%	%	%
Cash & Equivalents	34.0	22.0	14.4	12.0			17.9	18.3
Trade Receivables (net)	5.6	10.3	6.7	9.3			7.0	7.0
Inventory	1.0	1.3	2.2	1.8			2.8	3.4
All Other Current	4.7	4.5	5.2	6.1			3.0	3.0
Total Current	45.2	38.1	28.5	29.2			30.7	31.7
Fixed Assets (net)	28.2	43.7	51.5	48.2			50.6	51.1
Intangibles (net)	9.1	5.0	6.2	7.7			4.1	3.1
All Other Non-Current	17.5	13.1	13.7	14.9			14.5	14.0
Total	100.0	100.0	100.0	100.0			100.0	100.0
LIABILITIES								
Notes Payable-Short Term	8.8	8.2	6.5	2.4			8.9	9.0
Cur. Mat.-L.T.D.	2.0	1.6	1.8	1.6			3.2	3.2
Trade Payables	7.5	3.3	2.5	3.9			4.5	3.5
Income Taxes Payable	.0	.0	.0	.4			.1	.1
All Other Current	26.1	14.9	11.2	13.1			20.3	17.7
Total Current	44.5	28.1	22.0	21.4			37.0	33.5
Long-Term Debt	28.2	33.5	41.1	41.8			41.5	43.8
Deferred Taxes	.0	.0	.1	.0			.1	.0
All Other Non-Current	12.1	7.2	6.5	3.4			3.1	4.3
Net Worth	15.2	31.3	30.3	33.4			18.3	18.3
Total Liabilties & Net Worth	100.0	100.0	100.0	100.0			100.0	100.0
INCOME DATA								
Net Sales	100.0	100.0	100.0	100.0			100.0	100.0
Gross Profit								
Operating Expenses	86.0	71.6	74.1	70.7			76.7	75.1
Operating Profit	14.0	28.4	25.9	29.3			23.3	24.9
All Other Expenses (net)	4.8	11.1	11.8	13.0			14.0	13.1
Profit Before Taxes	9.2	17.3	14.2	16.2			9.3	11.8
RATIOS								
	4.0	4.6	3.7	4.3			2.0	2.9
Current	1.1	1.6	1.3	1.6			.8	.9
	.5	.5	.5	.6			.2	.2
	3.6	3.4	2.8	3.3			1.7	2.1
Quick	(118) 1.0	1.2	(120) 1.0	1.0			.6	(512) .7
	.3	.2	.2	.4			.1	.2
	0 UND	0 UND	0 UND	0 UND			0 UND	0 UND
Sales/Receivables	0 UND	0 UND	0 UND	2 163.1			0 UND	0 UND
	5 75.0	18 19.9	12 31.3	21 17.2			14 25.6	14 26.2
Cost of Sales/Inventory								
Cost of Sales/Payables								
	13.3	4.2	3.4	2.9			8.5	6.4
Sales/Working Capital	83.0	21.6	15.2	10.7			-29.4	-50.3
	-15.5	-9.7	-12.3	-9.3			-3.3	-4.2
	53.8	46.9	15.2	13.8			10.7	13.7
EBIT/Interest	(54) 17.0	(64) 8.4	(67) 3.9	(24) 4.3			(256) 3.3	(232) 3.2
	2.6	3.0	.2	2.6			.9	1.2
							13.2	14.6
Net Profit + Depr., Dep., Amort./Cur. Mat. L/T/D							(23) 3.1	(16) 4.2
							1.3	2.7
	.0	.0	.4	.2			.2	.2
Fixed/Worth	.5	1.0	2.3	1.8			2.3	2.3
	9.5	16.6	49.2	98.6			275.7	36.6
	.5	.4	.8	.9			1.0	.9
Debt/Worth	2.8	2.5	2.8	2.3			4.3	4.0
	UND	-68.3	105.2	NM			-39.7	-194.1
	369.4	93.2	53.5	53.6			47.0	59.9
% Profit Before Taxes/Tangible Net Worth	(90) 73.9	(101) 33.5	(95) 14.3	(38) 15.8			(394) 15.1	(383) 17.4
	9.0	16.1	1.4	.6			.2	2.1
	61.7	26.6	12.4	8.9			12.2	13.9
% Profit Before Taxes/Total Assets	14.1	10.3	3.8	3.5			3.2	3.9
	.9	1.8	.1	.5			-.8	.0
	UND	193.6	14.7	25.7			54.5	39.1
Sales/Net Fixed Assets	63.7	6.2	.9	.6			1.2	1.8
	8.9	.2	.2	.2			.2	.2
	8.6	2.5	1.0	.9			2.1	2.2
Sales/Total Assets	3.9	.8	.4	.3			.5	.6
	1.1	.2	.1	.1			.1	.1
	.9	1.5	1.4	1.9			1.8	1.7
% Depr., Dep., Amort./Sales	(46) 2.0	(82) 10.7	(85) 8.5	(41) 5.0			(391) 9.6	(330) 9.7
	15.5	22.5	21.9	20.6			19.4	19.9
	4.7	4.3	2.4				3.1	3.2
% Officers', Directors' Owners' Comp/Sales	(55) 10.5	(27) 7.6	(26) 6.1				(102) 7.0	(99) 6.3
	17.3	17.8	13.4				14.2	12.3
Net Sales ($)	107901M	247782M	497271M	873226M	101131M	835413M	5422831M	4027960M
Total Assets ($)	27300M	146443M	554270M	1041657M	499989M	615871M	4254321M	3714879M

M = $ thousand MM = $ million

See Pages 9 through 22 for Explanation of Ratios and Data

Comparative Historical Data / Current Data Sorted by Sales

4/1/11-3/31/12 ALL	4/1/12-3/31/13 ALL	4/1/13-3/31/14 ALL		0-1MM	1-3MM	3-5MM	5-10MM	10-25MM	25MM & OVER
			Type of Statement						
74	46	37	Unqualified	6	13	2	9	4	3
25	16	23	Reviewed	3	6	4	4	2	4
49	32	33	Compiled	15	11	4	1	2	
276	180	184	Tax Returns	118	47	8	7	4	
257	179	163	Other	62	44	18	18	10	11
					37 (4/1-9/30/13)		403 (10/1/13-3/31/14)		
681	453	440	**NUMBER OF STATEMENTS**	204	121	36	39	22	18
%	%	%	**ASSETS**	%	%	%	%	%	%
17.7	19.4	21.8	Cash & Equivalents	21.1	19.9	25.8	21.0	34.5	19.2
6.6	6.7	7.8	Trade Receivables (net)	3.4	8.8	15.5	8.5	11.8	30.3
2.8	1.2	1.5	Inventory	.9	2.3	3.0	.6	2.3	1.5
3.0	3.3	5.2	All Other Current	3.9	5.3	7.7	5.0	1.9	17.5
30.1	30.7	36.3	Total Current	29.3	36.2	51.9	35.1	50.5	68.5
52.7	50.7	42.2	Fixed Assets (net)	53.5	36.3	23.2	44.6	20.6	13.4
3.4	5.2	6.7	Intangibles (net)	4.1	10.6	6.1	10.5	5.3	5.1
13.8	13.5	14.8	All Other Non-Current	13.1	16.9	18.7	9.8	23.6	13.0
100.0	100.0	100.0	Total	100.0	100.0	100.0	100.0	100.0	100.0
			LIABILITIES						
5.4	8.4	7.0	Notes Payable-Short Term	7.6	4.9	10.9	6.9	10.6	3.8
3.2	2.8	1.8	Cur. Mat.-L.T.D.	2.1	1.6	.9	1.9	.8	2.5
3.7	3.9	4.2	Trade Payables	2.7	4.3	5.7	4.4	9.9	10.2
.1	.1	.1	Income Taxes Payable	.1	.0	.0	.0	.0	1.0
20.9	16.6	16.6	All Other Current	14.7	18.7	17.8	12.6	21.1	25.6
33.3	31.7	29.8	Total Current	27.1	29.5	35.4	25.8	42.4	43.1
45.2	40.1	35.1	Long-Term Debt	43.9	30.2	30.4	30.3	15.5	12.5
.1	.0	.0	Deferred Taxes	.0	.1	.0	.1	.0	.0
4.4	10.5	7.9	All Other Non-Current	9.0	9.1	3.7	5.2	5.2	5.0
17.0	17.6	27.2	Net Worth	19.9	31.1	30.6	38.6	36.8	39.4
100.0	100.0	100.0	Total Liabilties & Net Worth	100.0	100.0	100.0	100.0	100.0	100.0
			INCOME DATA						
100.0	100.0	100.0	Net Sales	100.0	100.0	100.0	100.0	100.0	100.0
			Gross Profit						
75.3	76.0	76.0	Operating Expenses	69.8	79.3	81.2	82.4	85.3	87.7
24.7	24.0	24.0	Operating Profit	30.2	20.7	18.8	17.6	14.7	12.3
13.9	11.7	9.9	All Other Expenses (net)	15.2	6.8	3.1	5.8	2.7	.4
10.8	12.3	14.2	Profit Before Taxes	15.0	13.8	15.6	11.8	12.0	11.9
			RATIOS						
2.5	3.4	4.1		3.9	4.8	5.6	3.5	4.1	2.6
1.0	1.1	1.3	Current	1.1	1.8	1.9	1.4	1.4	1.6
.2	.3	.5		.3	.6	1.0	.6	.8	1.0
2.0	2.8	3.2		2.9	3.4	4.3	3.2	3.1	1.7
(680) .7	(451) .9	(438) 1.0	Quick	(203) .8	1.4	1.5	(38) 1.3	1.1	1.1
.2	.2	.3		.2	.4	.4	.4	.6	.7
0 UND	0 UND	0 UND		0 UND	0 UND	0 UND	0 UND	0 UND	17 21.5
0 UND	0 UND	0 UND	Sales/Receivables	0 UND	1 410.0	4 84.7	3 132.1	7 54.5	26 13.9
12 30.5	7 50.2	11 31.8		0 UND	12 30.4	20 18.5	13 27.6	30 12.1	36 10.1
			Cost of Sales/Inventory						
			Cost of Sales/Payables						
5.3	5.4	4.7		5.2	4.0	3.3	5.4	4.4	8.4
UND	124.3	34.6	Sales/Working Capital	80.7	28.3	12.6	34.6	21.2	18.6
-4.0	-5.5	-12.7		-5.0	-24.9	-999.8	-16.2	-24.6	-731.1
11.6	16.7	30.0		19.4	32.7	97.5	47.8	128.4	52.5
(301) 3.1	(230) 4.8	(218) 5.7	EBIT/Interest	(74) 3.9	(68) 9.0	(18) 7.3	(32) 5.5	(14) 9.5	(12) 12.8
.8	1.6	2.0		1.2	2.8	2.4	1.6	2.2	5.5
5.2	6.8	11.0							
(27) 1.9	(13) 2.6	(12) 4.5	Net Profit + Depr., Dep., Amort./Cur. Mat. L/T/D						
.1	1.2	2.0							
.3	.2	.0		.0	.0	.0	.5	.1	.1
2.5	2.2	1.2	Fixed/Worth	2.4	.9	.4	2.1	.5	.2
-159.7	UND	12.7		UND	5.1	19.9	59.0	2.3	.7
.8	.8	.6		1.0	.4	.4	.7	.3	.8
3.7	3.3	2.6	Debt/Worth	3.7	1.7	3.4	2.1	2.2	1.5
-24.2	-48.2	490.8		-32.2	13.7	UND	88.7	17.5	4.4
50.7	65.4	100.0		73.3	97.1	288.0	57.8	223.5	114.6
(490) 12.6	(331) 21.7	(335) 28.6	% Profit Before Taxes/Tangible Net Worth	(148) 19.2	(94) 30.4	(27) 101.8	(30) 19.1	(20) 45.7	(16) 53.0
.4	2.4	4.6		1.4	8.2	36.4	3.5	8.9	22.9
12.2	16.0	24.1		15.0	35.9	60.6	26.9	39.7	28.3
3.0	4.5	7.5	% Profit Before Taxes/Total Assets	3.2	10.6	15.5	7.7	6.9	18.9
-.8	.0	1.1		.0	2.1	5.1	2.0	1.8	8.7
42.6	57.3	134.9		131.2	167.1	273.6	39.6	174.2	197.6
1.1	2.1	6.5	Sales/Net Fixed Assets	.6	14.7	33.1	6.2	39.7	39.0
.2	.2	.2		.2	.6	6.2	.5	3.6	22.0
1.8	2.4	3.2		1.3	4.7	5.2	3.3	6.5	5.5
.4	.6	.8	Sales/Total Assets	.2	1.2	2.0	1.5	1.8	3.4
.1	.2	.2		.1	.3	.7	.4	.5	1.5
1.9	1.8	1.3		9.7	.9	.6	1.9	.2	.4
(462) 12.3	(299) 10.0	(261) 6.9	% Depr., Dep., Amort./Sales	(120) 17.9	(67) 2.6	(19) 1.4	(23) 3.6	(16) 1.9	(16) .5
23.2	21.3	19.5		25.8	13.6	4.0	6.7	4.9	2.3
3.5	3.4	4.2		6.5	5.0		1.9		
(113) 8.8	(88) 8.3	(114) 8.0	% Officers', Directors' Owners' Comp/Sales	(47) 11.0	(38) 10.5		(16) 2.9		
15.5	14.8	16.0		19.0	16.0		6.7		
4406599M	4022746M	2662724M	Net Sales ($)	76993M	224388M	139195M	263106M	340130M	1618912M
4869329M	2853801M	2885530M	Total Assets ($)	313448M	502034M	221160M	530343M	571046M	747499M

M = $ thousand MM = $ million

See Pages 9 through 22 for Explanation of Ratios and Data

	Current Data Sorted by Assets						Comparative Historical Data	
Type of Statement								
Unqualified		1	9	13	2	2	20	22
Reviewed	1		13	4		1	17	20
Compiled	3	9	12	2			37	36
Tax Returns	30	82	50	4	1		108	119
Other	26	39	70	32	7	2	123	136
	30 (4/1-9/30/13)			385 (10/1/13-3/31/14)			4/1/09-3/31/10	4/1/10-3/31/11
	0-500M	**500M-2MM**	**2-10MM**	**10-50MM**	**50-100MM**	**100-250MM**	**ALL**	**ALL**
NUMBER OF STATEMENTS	60	131	154	55	10	5	305	333
ASSETS	%	%	%	%	%	%	%	%
Cash & Equivalents	31.0	5.7	9.1	8.2	2.4		12.2	11.3
Trade Receivables (net)	5.6	4.2	6.9	3.2	4.1		4.3	5.7
Inventory	2.6	.5	.6	1.8	1.1		1.6	1.3
All Other Current	7.7	3.4	4.5	1.8	5.8		3.7	4.8
Total Current	46.9	13.8	21.0	14.9	13.4		21.7	23.1
Fixed Assets (net)	41.8	75.2	67.1	68.6	56.9		65.0	62.3
Intangibles (net)	3.0	1.6	2.8	4.9	5.5		3.2	3.1
All Other Non-Current	8.3	9.4	9.1	11.5	24.2		10.0	11.5
Total	100.0	100.0	100.0	100.0	100.0		100.0	100.0
LIABILITIES								
Notes Payable-Short Term	17.1	6.0	5.1	.7	1.0		7.3	9.7
Cur. Mat.-L.T.D.	1.9	1.6	2.0	2.7	3.0		4.7	3.9
Trade Payables	9.0	1.2	3.0	3.1	2.7		2.3	5.4
Income Taxes Payable	1.7	.0	.0	.0	.0		.0	.0
All Other Current	17.7	9.2	8.4	6.5	6.6		10.0	8.9
Total Current	47.5	18.0	18.5	13.0	13.3		24.4	27.8
Long-Term Debt	27.2	65.5	50.2	42.1	39.9		48.3	50.2
Deferred Taxes	.0	.0	.2	.7	.0		.1	.1
All Other Non-Current	8.7	8.1	5.8	6.9	1.1		5.1	7.8
Net Worth	16.6	8.5	25.3	37.4	45.7		22.2	14.1
Total Liabilties & Net Worth	100.0	100.0	100.0	100.0	100.0		100.0	100.0
INCOME DATA								
Net Sales	100.0	100.0	100.0	100.0	100.0		100.0	100.0
Gross Profit								
Operating Expenses	78.3	59.1	60.8	64.2	61.6		65.7	63.8
Operating Profit	21.7	40.9	39.2	35.8	38.4		34.3	36.2
All Other Expenses (net)	7.6	22.0	20.1	13.6	11.7		18.9	19.5
Profit Before Taxes	14.1	18.9	19.1	22.2	26.7		15.4	16.6
RATIOS								
	7.6	2.5	2.8	3.2	1.6		2.7	2.4
Current	1.0	.7	.8	1.0	.5		.9	.9
	.4	.2	.2	.3	.2		.2	.3
	5.8	2.0	2.1	3.2	1.0		2.2	1.8
Quick	.8	.5	.6	.8	.2		(304) .7	.6
	.3	.2	.2	.2	.0		.2	.1
	0 UND	0 UND	0 UND	0 UND	0 UND		0 UND	0 UND
Sales/Receivables	0 UND	0 UND	0 UND	2 218.5	4 88.8		0 UND	0 UND
	0 UND	0 UND	18 19.8	19 19.4	36 10.2		8 44.6	11 32.2
Cost of Sales/Inventory								
Cost of Sales/Payables								
	10.3	6.3	3.2	5.0	8.6		5.5	7.0
Sales/Working Capital	UND	-20.2	-52.4	114.4	-6.2		-79.7	-59.8
	-11.1	-3.5	-2.5	-2.6	-2.4		-3.4	-3.9
	30.5	9.6	14.8	30.6			9.3	14.0
EBIT/Interest	(23) 6.5	(52) 4.1	(70) 4.8	(29) 3.8			(135) 4.2	(137) 4.2
	-.3	2.0	2.6	1.7			1.7	1.5
							3.5	4.2
Net Profit + Depr., Dep., Amort./Cur. Mat. L/T/D							(15) 2.4	(15) 2.4
							.6	.7
	.1	1.8	1.3	1.0	.4		1.0	.9
Fixed/Worth	1.6	5.0	4.2	2.1	1.8		3.6	3.4
	-39.2	-22.5	19.9	7.7	2.5		15.6	70.3
	.6	1.6	1.4	.6	.5		1.0	1.2
Debt/Worth	5.2	6.0	4.5	2.1	1.5		3.6	4.1
	-5.7	-15.9	25.7	6.9	5.0		19.2	UND
	289.8	29.6	37.0	28.6	29.8		43.7	37.2
% Profit Before Taxes/Tangible Net Worth	(40) 34.7	(91) 13.9	(122) 14.8	(48) 9.2	16.9		(247) 14.7	(250) 13.9
	3.8	4.2	4.0	-.1	.8		1.9	1.8
	55.5	8.1	9.2	8.7	10.7		10.9	8.9
% Profit Before Taxes/Total Assets	14.2	3.5	3.9	3.4	5.4		3.4	3.5
	-.2	.5	.5	-.1	.5		.0	.2
	348.8	.7	2.3	1.3	14.4		10.3	15.0
Sales/Net Fixed Assets	24.7	.2	.2	.2	.3		.2	.3
	.3	.1	.1	.1	.1		.1	.1
	8.9	.4	.5	.6	.4		1.0	.9
Sales/Total Assets	3.1	.2	.2	.2	.2		.2	.2
	.3	.1	.1	.1	.1		.1	.1
	1.0	9.3	6.4	7.1			4.2	4.4
% Depr., Dep., Amort./Sales	(31) 5.8	(110) 16.7	(123) 18.5	(44) 15.7			(245) 15.6	(259) 14.2
	16.7	23.0	25.6	23.0			24.5	22.4
	3.4	7.5	2.0				4.1	3.2
% Officers', Directors' Owners' Comp/Sales	(15) 7.9	(12) 17.3	(15) 6.3				(49) 9.8	(52) 8.6
	16.6	24.2	10.2				19.6	18.1
Net Sales ($)	67676M	65640M	990235M	607114M	288129M	95466M	1654231M	1624055M
Total Assets ($)	15568M	154434M	714863M	1230076M	711042M	740185M	2863515M	3248009M

M = $ thousand MM = $ million

See Pages 9 through 22 for Explanation of Ratios and Data

Comparative Historical Data | **Current Data Sorted by Sales**

			Type of Statement						
15	36	27	Unqualified	4	4	4	7	5	3
16	15	19	Reviewed	7	2	4	1	4	1
32	30	26	Compiled	16	8	1	1		
142	143	167	Tax Returns	139	16	4	4	2	2
161	190	176	Other	78	49	12	15	10	12
4/1/11-3/31/12 ALL	4/1/12-3/31/13 ALL	4/1/13-3/31/14 ALL			30 (4/1-9/30/13)		385 (10/1/13-3/31/14)		
				0-1MM	1-3MM	3-5MM	5-10MM	10-25MM	25MM & OVER
366	414	415	NUMBER OF STATEMENTS	244	79	25	28	21	18
%	%	%	ASSETS	%	%	%	%	%	%
11.4	10.7	10.9	Cash & Equivalents	8.0	12.6	21.1	12.3	15.8	20.4
6.6	6.6	5.2	Trade Receivables (net)	1.4	6.7	12.6	14.2	10.5	21.0
1.4	1.4	1.1	Inventory	.7	.8	.0	.9	3.7	5.0
3.7	2.9	4.3	All Other Current	3.9	4.8	2.2	5.2	7.0	4.8
23.2	21.6	21.5	Total Current	14.0	25.0	35.9	32.5	37.1	51.3
62.3	62.5	65.8	Fixed Assets (net)	76.9	65.0	41.8	41.1	36.2	24.5
3.8	3.6	2.8	Intangibles (net)	1.9	3.5	7.0	2.4	3.3	5.6
10.7	12.2	10.0	All Other Non-Current	7.2	6.5	15.3	24.0	23.4	18.7
100.0	100.0	100.0	Total	100.0	100.0	100.0	100.0	100.0	100.0
			LIABILITIES						
8.0	5.2	6.4	Notes Payable-Short Term	6.2	5.6	9.0	7.7	8.7	4.1
4.2	3.6	2.0	Cur. Mat.-L.T.D.	1.9	2.2	2.5	1.4	1.2	2.6
5.0	3.4	3.3	Trade Payables	1.5	4.9	2.5	5.2	6.3	14.5
.1	.0	.3	Income Taxes Payable	.1	.8	.0	.2	.0	.1
8.6	9.8	9.6	All Other Current	7.9	12.6	8.2	10.8	11.5	18.0
25.9	22.1	21.5	Total Current	17.6	26.1	22.1	25.3	27.8	39.3
46.7	48.4	50.2	Long-Term Debt	61.0	47.0	28.4	26.8	23.7	16.4
.2	.2	.2	Deferred Taxes	.0	.0	1.3	.0	1.7	.0
5.9	6.7	6.9	All Other Non-Current	6.3	9.3	13.4	6.7	.9	2.6
21.4	22.6	21.2	Net Worth	15.1	17.6	34.8	41.1	45.9	41.7
100.0	100.0	100.0	Total Liabilties & Net Worth	100.0	100.0	100.0	100.0	100.0	100.0
			INCOME DATA						
100.0	100.0	100.0	Net Sales	100.0	100.0	100.0	100.0	100.0	100.0
			Gross Profit						
64.8	62.0	63.2	Operating Expenses	55.6	67.5	80.0	74.8	78.8	88.5
35.2	38.0	36.8	Operating Profit	44.4	32.5	20.0	25.2	21.2	11.5
17.5	17.5	17.7	All Other Expenses (net)	24.5	13.4	4.7	4.5	2.7	1.3
17.7	20.5	19.1	Profit Before Taxes	20.0	19.1	15.3	20.7	18.5	10.2
			RATIOS						
2.5	2.8	2.9		2.9	2.5	3.6	5.6	3.8	2.4
.9	.9	.9	Current	.7	.8	1.2	1.5	.9	1.5
.3	.3	.3		.2	.3	.3	.6	.6	1.0
1.7	2.1	2.2		2.2	1.9	2.8	4.1	2.8	1.8
.7	.7	.7	Quick	.5	.7	1.2	1.0	.8	1.2
.2	.2	.2		.1	.1	.3	.2	.4	.6
0 UND	**0** UND	**0** UND		**0** UND	**0** UND	**0** UND	**0** UND	**0** 920.6	**3** 121.6
0 UND	**0** UND	**0** UND	Sales/Receivables	**0** UND	**0** UND	**1** 315.9	**5** 68.6	**16** 23.3	**31** 11.9
11 33.9	**10** 37.7	**8** 44.5		**0** UND	**14** 26.2	**35** 10.5	**47** 7.7	**39** 9.3	**59** 6.2
			Cost of Sales/Inventory						
			Cost of Sales/Payables						
5.8	6.4	5.6		5.1	7.7	6.6	2.5	3.1	5.1
-68.0	-92.1	-57.7	Sales/Working Capital	-17.5	-32.8	49.8	14.0	-80.0	21.6
-4.6	-3.5	-3.2		-2.4	-2.9	-4.1	-16.1	-10.1	NM
15.3	13.3	14.8		9.7	9.2	22.3	21.4	118.1	117.9
(167) 5.0	(184) 4.4	(185) 4.6	EBIT/Interest	(81) 4.4	(41) 3.7	(17) 6.9	(17) 7.4	(16) 9.0	(13) 10.2
1.9	2.1	2.3		2.2	1.6	2.5	2.8	2.0	3.3
5.7	4.4	7.8							
(20) 2.1	(19) 1.8	(17) 4.2	Net Profit + Depr., Dep., Amort./Cur. Mat. L/T/D						
.6	1.2	1.6							
.9	1.0	1.2		1.7	1.4	.1	.1	.1	.2
2.6	3.1	3.6	Fixed/Worth	4.7	4.0	1.6	1.1	.4	.4
30.9	38.7	22.9		85.7	-30.4	9.6	4.6	2.2	2.0
.9	1.0	1.1		1.7	1.2	.6	.2	.3	.5
3.0	4.1	4.3	Debt/Worth	5.4	4.8	1.8	.8	1.5	1.3
41.4	118.2	78.1		-150.4	-32.5	11.3	5.2	6.2	6.6
41.0	48.5	37.7		28.6	70.9	87.0	39.0	35.1	62.9
(280) 15.1	(319) 15.6	(316) 14.8	% Profit Before Taxes/Tangible Net Worth	(179) 12.9	(59) 11.8	(21) 18.2	(23) 14.8	(18) 22.5	(16) 38.2
2.4	3.0	3.7		1.8	5.0	3.5	3.7	4.8	6.5
13.4	12.6	10.5		7.8	15.9	20.6	19.4	20.7	31.2
3.9	3.8	4.3	% Profit Before Taxes/Total Assets	2.9	5.2	5.9	8.1	8.7	10.6
.6	.9	.5		.3	.4	1.4	1.7	2.7	2.0
9.9	9.9	4.9		.4	10.1	49.9	50.5	41.0	62.2
.3	.3	.3	Sales/Net Fixed Assets	.2	.3	15.2	4.4	7.8	32.5
.1	.1	.1		.1	.2	.3	.3	.5	5.9
1.5	.9	.7		.3	.9	4.7	2.2	2.6	5.2
.2	.2	.2	Sales/Total Assets	.2	.3	.9	.6	1.2	2.2
.1	.1	.1		.1	.1	.2	.2	.2	.7
4.3	4.2	6.9		12.4	3.9	.5	1.2	.9	.7
(277) 14.1	(323) 15.9	(320) 16.7	% Depr., Dep., Amort./Sales	(197) 18.7	(58) 15.9	(18) 2.0	(18) 8.9	(17) 2.4	(12) 1.7
22.8	22.9	24.0		25.6	23.3	15.5	14.2	15.7	4.9
2.4	3.6	3.4		7.3	4.0				
(41) 5.5	(47) 10.3	(50) 9.1	% Officers', Directors' Owners' Comp/Sales	(17) 16.9	(15) 9.5				
14.8	15.0	17.0		20.4	16.6				
2239113M	2277312M	2114260M	Net Sales ($)	80505M	129664M	91520M	206734M	326489M	1279348M
3508920M	4088801M	3566168M	Total Assets ($)	501502M	625799M	232531M	733007M	695044M	778285M

M = $ thousand MM = $ million

See Pages 9 through 22 for Explanation of Ratios and Data

	Current Data Sorted by Assets						Comparative Historical Data	
Type of Statement								
Unqualified	4	4	19	25	14	14	97	101
Reviewed	3	12	31	19	5	2	48	53
Compiled	8	32	46	14	1	3	95	95
Tax Returns	114	274	213	41	1	2	817	784
Other	93	142	198	105	26	14	581	654
	71 (4/1-9/30/13)			1,408 (10/1/13-3/31/14)			4/1/09-3/31/10	4/1/10-3/31/11
	0-500M	500M-2MM	2-10MM	10-50MM	50-100MM	100-250MM	ALL	ALL
NUMBER OF STATEMENTS	222	464	507	204	47	35	1638	1687
ASSETS	%	%	%	%	%	%	%	%
Cash & Equivalents	29.0	8.2	8.1	8.5	11.6	10.0	9.3	11.4
Trade Receivables (net)	5.7	3.5	4.1	5.3	8.6	4.2	4.7	4.7
Inventory	3.2	6.4	8.1	8.4	3.7	7.6	12.5	8.5
All Other Current	4.0	3.4	3.0	4.5	7.3	11.0	2.8	3.6
Total Current	41.9	21.6	23.3	26.8	31.1	32.8	29.3	28.1
Fixed Assets (net)	40.8	64.6	62.0	52.6	38.0	41.2	55.0	57.2
Intangibles (net)	3.9	2.7	2.8	3.3	5.1	6.1	2.3	2.3
All Other Non-Current	13.4	11.2	11.9	17.3	25.9	19.8	13.4	12.4
Total	100.0	100.0	100.0	100.0	100.0	100.0	100.0	100.0
LIABILITIES								
Notes Payable-Short Term	15.2	8.4	6.1	7.0	8.0	5.3	11.4	9.3
Cur. Mat.-L.T.D.	3.0	3.0	2.5	2.9	2.5	4.6	4.0	3.3
Trade Payables	5.0	2.2	2.5	2.4	4.7	4.5	2.8	2.2
Income Taxes Payable	.9	.0	.0	.1	.0	.7	.1	.0
All Other Current	30.9	10.6	7.4	8.5	8.2	8.7	11.2	9.8
Total Current	55.0	24.2	18.5	20.9	23.5	23.7	29.4	24.7
Long-Term Debt	27.6	48.2	51.9	39.0	43.1	41.5	48.2	49.2
Deferred Taxes	.0	.0	.0	.2	.1	.5	.1	.1
All Other Non-Current	9.1	4.5	5.9	4.6	6.3	3.9	5.1	5.2
Net Worth	8.2	23.1	23.6	35.4	27.0	30.4	17.1	20.8
Total Liabilties & Net Worth	100.0	100.0	100.0	100.0	100.0	100.0	100.0	100.0
INCOME DATA								
Net Sales	100.0	100.0	100.0	100.0	100.0	100.0	100.0	100.0
Gross Profit								
Operating Expenses	77.8	63.9	63.4	69.1	73.5	76.7	69.4	67.1
Operating Profit	22.2	36.1	36.6	30.9	26.5	23.3	30.6	32.9
All Other Expenses (net)	6.9	18.0	19.2	13.7	11.2	8.8	20.1	19.6
Profit Before Taxes	15.3	18.1	17.4	17.2	15.3	14.5	10.5	13.3
RATIOS								
Current	3.2	2.6	3.1	2.6	4.4	2.3	2.5	3.1
	1.1	.8	1.1	1.3	1.5	1.3	.9	1.0
	.2	.2	.3	.5	1.0	.6	.2	.2
Quick	2.8	1.7	1.8	2.1	3.7	1.4	1.3	1.7
	.7	.4	.6	.7	1.0	.5	(1635) .3	(1685) .4
	.2	.1	.2	.2	.4	.2	.1	.1
Sales/Receivables	0 UND	0 UND	0 UND	0 UND	0 UND	1 406.8	0 UND	0 UND
	0 UND	0 UND	0 UND	1 508.6	9 39.7	16 22.8	0 UND	0 UND
	0 UND	0 UND	6 57.8	21 17.4	63 5.8	37 9.9	5 69.6	4 84.0
Cost of Sales/Inventory								
Cost of Sales/Payables								
Sales/Working Capital	9.5	6.3	2.8	3.2	2.0	2.0	3.8	3.5
	157.8	-25.7	73.2	17.0	7.5	15.3	-50.6	-166.7
	-9.3	-2.6	-3.4	-5.5	-74.4	-6.6	-2.8	-3.3
EBIT/Interest	27.6	10.2	13.1	10.8	15.3	8.3	7.2	9.4
	(96) 7.5	(200) 4.0	(226) 3.9	(115) 3.9	(31) 6.1	(28) 2.9	(671) 2.6	(683) 3.5
	1.2	1.2	1.7	1.8	2.7	1.2	.6	1.2
Net Profit + Depr., Dep., Amort./Cur. Mat. L/T/D			4.8	4.9			6.6	5.2
			(17) 3.2	(15) 2.6			(45) 2.4	(39) 2.1
			1.1	1.1			.8	.5
Fixed/Worth	.0	.7	.7	.3	.0	.1	.3	.4
	.9	3.2	3.5	1.7	1.1	1.2	2.8	2.7
	7.9	19.1	31.6	6.8	5.1	6.4	27.1	24.6
Debt/Worth	.4	1.2	1.3	.8	.6	1.0	1.3	1.0
	2.1	3.6	4.3	2.3	2.0	3.0	4.9	3.9
	-19.2	49.0	56.3	9.4	7.6	14.2	942.6	63.4
% Profit Before Taxes/Tangible Net Worth	115.3	36.8	46.6	34.8	26.0	29.3	36.4	39.1
	(166) 28.9	(362) 14.7	(397) 16.1	(178) 11.5	(40) 9.2	(29) 11.3	(1244) 9.6	(1316) 12.0
	4.7	2.7	2.5	2.0	1.1	2.4	-.7	.7
% Profit Before Taxes/Total Assets	52.1	8.7	7.0	7.5	9.6	6.0	7.0	9.2
	10.2	3.2	2.9	3.0	3.1	2.9	1.7	2.7
	.0	.1	.5	.4	.4	.2	-.9	-.2
Sales/Net Fixed Assets	UND	9.2	5.6	9.5	96.0	30.9	25.2	22.5
	20.5	.2	.2	.4	3.1	1.5	.4	.3
	.6	.1	.1	.1	.3	.4	.1	.1
Sales/Total Assets	7.9	.6	.4	.6	.8	.5	.7	.8
	2.3	.2	.2	.2	.3	.4	.2	.2
	.4	.1	.1	.1	.1	.2	.1	.1
% Depr., Dep., Amort./Sales	1.2	7.4	3.4	1.5	.6	.7	2.8	3.6
	(110) 5.1	(330) 18.2	(362) 17.1	(138) 9.1	(29) 3.0	(20) 7.4	(1094) 13.9	(1130) 14.6
	17.7	26.9	27.2	23.3	14.5	24.3	23.4	24.0
% Officers', Directors' Owners' Comp/Sales	4.6	3.1	1.8	.9			2.1	2.2
	(48) 12.2	(54) 8.2	(59) 3.9	(20) 3.5			(218) 5.1	(236) 5.5
	22.6	16.2	8.6	6.0			12.6	13.8
Net Sales ($)	190116M	441023M	1454893M	3129800M	3509199M	3836340M	9677855M	11293104M
Total Assets ($)	52348M	551393M	2298571M	4512309M	3392573M	5801179M	15751710M	14869047M

M = $ thousand MM = $ million

See Pages 9 through 22 for Explanation of Ratios and Data

Comparative Historical Data | **Current Data Sorted by Sales**

4/1/11-3/31/12 ALL	4/1/12-3/31/13 ALL	4/1/13-3/31/14 ALL		0-1MM	1-3MM	3-5MM	5-10MM	10-25MM	25MM & OVER
			Type of Statement						
89	83	80	Unqualified	11	15	3	5	14	32
53	58	72	Reviewed	20	13	8	6	13	12
109	106	104	Compiled	56	21	7	5	10	5
912	713	645	Tax Returns	495	88	25	21	10	6
628	547	578	Other	289	134	43	35	36	41
				71 (4/1-9/30/13)			1,408 (10/1/13-3/31/14)		
1791	1507	1479	**NUMBER OF STATEMENTS**	871	271	86	72	83	96
%	%	%	**ASSETS**	%	%	%	%	%	%
9.7	11.3	11.5	Cash & Equivalents	8.0	15.7	20.6	16.8	15.5	15.6
4.0	4.4	4.5	Trade Receivables (net)	1.6	5.2	8.8	11.4	9.6	14.8
7.9	7.9	6.7	Inventory	3.5	9.5	11.3	15.8	12.5	12.4
3.2	3.8	3.8	All Other Current	2.1	5.1	9.6	3.0	6.0	9.0
24.9	27.4	26.5	Total Current	15.2	35.5	50.3	47.0	43.5	51.8
59.9	57.3	57.1	Fixed Assets (net)	72.0	43.4	29.8	31.2	31.5	25.9
2.6	2.9	3.2	Intangibles (net)	2.1	4.8	2.1	2.1	6.8	6.4
12.6	12.4	13.3	All Other Non-Current	10.6	16.3	17.8	19.7	18.2	16.0
100.0	100.0	100.0	Total	100.0	100.0	100.0	100.0	100.0	100.0
			LIABILITIES						
8.2	9.9	8.3	Notes Payable-Short Term	7.4	8.7	10.2	12.3	11.8	7.7
3.4	3.0	2.8	Cur. Mat.-L.T.D.	3.0	2.6	1.1	2.3	2.2	4.4
1.9	2.7	2.9	Trade Payables	.9	4.0	5.9	5.8	7.0	9.5
.0	.0	.2	Income Taxes Payable	.2	.1	.0	.0	.2	.3
9.3	9.7	12.1	All Other Current	10.0	18.9	13.2	10.0	13.0	12.7
23.0	25.3	26.4	Total Current	21.5	34.4	30.4	30.4	34.2	34.5
49.3	45.4	44.8	Long-Term Debt	53.8	36.6	27.9	29.7	26.0	29.0
.0	.0	.0	Deferred Taxes	.0	.0	.0	.0	.5	.2
5.4	6.3	5.7	All Other Non-Current	5.1	8.1	2.3	7.4	7.3	5.2
22.3	23.0	23.1	Net Worth	19.6	21.0	39.3	32.5	32.0	31.0
100.0	100.0	100.0	Total Liabilties & Net Worth	100.0	100.0	100.0	100.0	100.0	100.0
			INCOME DATA						
100.0	100.0	100.0	Net Sales	100.0	100.0	100.0	100.0	100.0	100.0
			Gross Profit						
65.2	65.9	67.1	Operating Expenses	58.5	74.0	80.8	78.4	85.7	89.1
34.8	34.1	32.9	Operating Profit	41.5	26.0	19.2	21.6	14.3	10.9
20.8	17.8	15.7	All Other Expenses (net)	22.3	9.4	3.9	3.7	5.5	2.6
14.0	16.3	17.2	Profit Before Taxes	19.2	16.5	15.3	17.9	8.9	8.3
			RATIOS						
2.7	2.9	2.9		2.5	3.5	4.8	5.2	3.3	2.3
.9	1.0	1.1	Current	.7	1.2	1.9	1.6	1.5	1.5
.2	.3	.3		.1	.4	1.0	.9	.9	1.1
1.6	1.7	2.0		1.8	2.3	3.6	2.3	1.6	1.6
(1790) .5	(1504) .5	.6	Quick	.4	.6	1.0	1.1	.7	.9
.1	.1	.1		.1	.2	.3	.5	.3	.3
0 UND	0 UND	0 UND		0 UND	0 UND	0 UND	0 UND	0 UND	2 154.1
0 UND	0 UND	0 UND	Sales/Receivables	0 UND	0 UND	0 UND	5 73.1	3 121.3	19 19.4
3 128.3	4 85.3	5 68.5		0 UND	7 52.2	13 28.0	45 8.2	25 14.8	45 8.1
			Cost of Sales/Inventory						
			Cost of Sales/Payables						
4.6	4.3	4.0		5.2	2.6	2.6	2.6	4.1	4.5
-57.1	UND	100.0	Sales/Working Capital	-18.4	40.7	9.6	12.3	18.0	17.8
-3.0	-3.3	-3.9		-2.2	-6.5	UND	-53.4	-34.8	93.7
10.0	12.3	13.5		7.3	15.1	32.5	26.4	28.1	19.1
(707) 3.4	(653) 4.2	(696) 4.1	EBIT/Interest	(280) 3.6	(167) 4.2	(62) 6.3	(50) 6.3	(61) 7.0	(76) 4.8
1.1	1.5	1.6		1.5	1.3	1.4	2.1	2.0	2.4
5.3	4.0	4.9			4.1			29.3	5.8
(46) 2.6	(40) 1.8	(49) 2.9	Net Profit + Depr., Dep., Amort./Cur. Mat. L/T/D		(10) 3.7			(10) 2.3	(14) 2.8
.9	.8	1.1			.5			.7	1.0
.6	.4	.3		1.3	.1	.0	.1	.1	.1
3.0	2.7	2.4	Fixed/Worth	3.8	1.2	.3	.5	.8	.6
18.1	17.8	14.6		34.4	9.6	2.4	2.3	6.4	2.3
1.2	1.0	1.0		1.2	.7	.4	.6	.6	.9
3.9	3.6	3.3	Debt/Worth	4.0	3.7	1.3	1.9	3.1	1.9
45.0	49.7	36.9		65.0	116.4	6.0	9.8	34.2	5.1
33.6	44.5	44.5		31.8	59.6	89.8	65.0	121.8	55.3
(1401) 11.5	(1184) 15.2	(1172) 15.0	% Profit Before Taxes/Tangible Net Worth	(678) 11.0	(206) 18.6	(73) 22.6	(62) 24.7	(70) 27.0	(83) 27.1
.5	2.8	2.5		1.4	3.3	6.7	4.3	5.7	10.4
7.6	9.6	9.6		6.7	15.8	24.2	26.0	16.1	16.0
2.5	3.1	3.5	% Profit Before Taxes/Total Assets	2.6	4.2	8.5	6.5	5.3	7.3
-.2	.4	.3		.0	.6	1.2	2.0	.4	1.7
13.8	24.0	21.0		.5	90.6	86.4	118.2	61.8	91.1
.3	.3	.3	Sales/Net Fixed Assets	.2	3.2	18.1	10.7	16.3	21.0
.1	.1	.1		.1	.2	1.0	.8	1.2	2.5
.6	.9	.9		.2	2.2	2.7	2.4	3.6	3.2
.2	.2	.2	Sales/Total Assets	.1	.4	.9	1.1	1.3	1.4
.1	.1	.1		.1	.1	.3	.2	.3	.5
5.0	3.8	2.8		13.0	1.2	.3	.3	.5	.3
(1244) 16.0	(993) 14.9	(989) 14.9	% Depr., Dep., Amort./Sales	(622) 20.0	(151) 6.3	(52) 1.0	(38) 1.3	(57) 1.5	(69) 1.0
25.1	23.3	25.0		29.3	18.9	4.7	5.0	5.8	3.1
1.9	3.3	2.7		4.8	3.5	2.3	2.1	1.1	.3
(195) 6.3	(187) 6.5	(188) 6.0	% Officers', Directors' Owners' Comp/Sales	(70) 15.4	(48) 7.0	(24) 4.6	(17) 3.0	(17) 1.8	(12) .9
14.2	14.8	15.9		22.7	11.5	7.8	5.2	4.5	10.9
9039784M	8991268M	12561371M	Net Sales ($)	287521M	477452M	334633M	503326M	1298679M	9659760M
14978075M	14045115M	16608373M	Total Assets ($)	2148015M	2267882M	899368M	1510907M	2570724M	7211477M

M = $ thousand MM = $ million

See Pages 9 through 22 for Explanation of Ratios and Data

Current Data Sorted by Assets							Comparative Historical Data	
						Type of Statement		
		2	19	6	2	Unqualified	26	24
	3	14	14		1	Reviewed	17	22
2	6	8				Compiled	21	15
9	9	11	3			Tax Returns	31	19
2	19	15	12	4	5	Other	42	45
24 (4/1-9/30/13)		142 (10/1/13-3/31/14)					4/1/09-3/31/10 ALL	4/1/10-3/31/11 ALL
0-500M	500M-2MM	2-10MM	10-50MM	50-100MM	100-250MM			
13	37	50	48	10	8	**NUMBER OF STATEMENTS**	137	125
%	%	%	%	%	%	**ASSETS**	%	%
13.1	11.3	9.6	5.7	3.2		Cash & Equivalents	10.9	9.2
13.0	7.7	7.4	4.6	3.2		Trade Receivables (net)	7.9	7.0
16.1	5.3	7.4	10.7	17.5		Inventory	12.5	12.5
1.2	1.7	3.4	2.7	10.3		All Other Current	4.7	4.8
43.3	26.1	27.8	23.8	34.2		Total Current	36.0	33.4
48.0	67.3	61.8	70.2	51.4		Fixed Assets (net)	53.2	55.3
.3	5.4	6.1	1.9	2.0		Intangibles (net)	2.2	1.9
8.4	1.3	4.2	4.1	12.3		All Other Non-Current	8.6	9.3
100.0	100.0	100.0	100.0	100.0		Total	100.0	100.0
						LIABILITIES		
18.4	9.6	13.1	20.7	9.4		Notes Payable-Short Term	27.4	22.8
4.1	8.3	2.4	7.2	13.6		Cur. Mat.-L.T.D.	7.2	8.5
9.4	7.0	5.2	2.4	1.4		Trade Payables	5.2	3.1
.0	.0	.0	.1	.0		Income Taxes Payable	.2	.3
24.2	5.4	7.3	2.3	3.6		All Other Current	9.8	7.8
56.1	30.4	27.9	32.6	28.1		Total Current	49.7	42.4
41.2	36.3	47.9	44.3	44.1		Long-Term Debt	28.9	26.9
.0	.1	.6	1.3	1.6		Deferred Taxes	.5	.6
9.2	10.3	4.0	2.2	2.1		All Other Non-Current	2.7	4.0
-6.5	23.0	19.6	19.6	24.1		Net Worth	18.1	26.1
100.0	100.0	100.0	100.0	100.0		Total Liabilities & Net Worth	100.0	100.0
						INCOME DATA		
100.0	100.0	100.0	100.0	100.0		Net Sales	100.0	100.0
						Gross Profit		
100.1	89.3	93.3	94.2	92.5		Operating Expenses	89.0	85.6
-.1	10.7	6.7	5.8	7.5		Operating Profit	11.0	14.4
-.1	1.1	1.5	2.5	1.3		All Other Expenses (net)	3.3	3.7
.0	9.7	5.2	3.3	6.2		Profit Before Taxes	7.7	10.8
						RATIOS		
1.2	3.3	2.9	2.4	2.0			1.5	1.9
.8	1.0	1.4	1.2	1.4		Current	.8	1.1
.4	.5	.5	.3	1.1			.2	.3
1.2	2.5	2.5	1.8	1.1			.9	1.4
.3	.6	1.0	.8	.5		Quick	.3	.4
.1	.4	.2	.2	.1			.1	.1
0 UND	**0** UND	**1** 344.6	**9** 42.8	**7** 53.9			**3** 107.1	**2** 167.6
2 234.5	**6** 61.4	**9** 39.7	**19** 19.3	**20** 18.0		Sales/Receivables	**13** 28.3	**11** 33.3
40 9.2	**36** 10.1	**30** 12.1	**36** 10.2	**31** 11.7			**29** 12.4	**32** 11.3
						Cost of Sales/Inventory		
						Cost of Sales/Payables		
38.5	11.7	6.8	7.7	2.3			10.7	7.2
-175.9	54.7	35.6	68.1	15.5		Sales/Working Capital	-19.7	40.8
-6.1	-5.7	-9.0	-2.7	NM			-2.2	-2.0
10.0	8.7	3.5	2.6				5.8	4.8
(11) 1.4	(31) 2.9	(43) 1.7	(47) 1.4			EBIT/Interest	(120) 1.7	(108) 2.3
-3.8	1.5	1.0	.8				1.1	1.4
							6.5	10.7
						Net Profit + Depr., Dep., Amort./Cur. Mat. L/T/D	(14) 2.8	(10) 1.6
							.8	.1
1.1	1.7	1.3	2.8	.2			.7	.6
5.1	3.3	5.2	4.9	1.6		Fixed/Worth	2.6	2.0
-2.4	-66.0	28.6	9.7	9.6			8.6	7.7
2.8	1.6	2.4	3.3	1.8			1.9	1.6
15.6	3.9	5.0	5.6	3.7		Debt/Worth	4.3	3.8
-9.6	-77.7	53.9	11.0	21.1			15.6	12.5
	70.6	62.8	27.1	31.8			39.6	47.4
	(27) 21.5	(39) 13.6	(46) 6.8	15.9		% Profit Before Taxes/Tangible Net Worth	(117) 15.4	(111) 19.7
	10.3	3.1	-6.4	8.4			2.1	7.8
17.7	14.1	11.3	4.1	4.0			7.6	8.3
.9	5.1	2.1	1.2	2.2		% Profit Before Taxes/Total Assets	2.7	4.1
-8.5	.9	.0	-1.0	1.4			.2	.9
133.5	4.0	6.4	1.7	36.6			6.5	7.4
2.9	1.3	1.1	.7	1.3		Sales/Net Fixed Assets	1.5	1.3
1.0	.6	.6	.6	.5			.8	.6
3.6	1.7	1.6	.8	.9			1.2	1.0
2.0	1.1	.6	.6	.6		Sales/Total Assets	.7	.7
.7	.5	.4	.4	.4			.5	.5
	14.7	17.0	16.2				7.9	10.0
	(29) 20.7	(40) 31.3	(40) 31.9			% Depr., Dep., Amort./Sales	(94) 22.7	(86) 25.3
	30.7	47.9	42.4				38.4	37.4
	3.4	2.1	.9				1.5	1.3
	(11) 7.8	(22) 3.8	(16) 1.4			% Officers', Directors' Owners' Comp/Sales	(40) 2.9	(34) 3.2
	10.7	6.9	2.4				7.2	5.8
7862M	57088M	307979M	941375M	455639M	831555M	Net Sales ($)	2135919M	2359232M
3066M	42321M	253502M	1111356M	688144M	1502156M	Total Assets ($)	2693886M	2627599M

M = $ thousand MM = $ million

See Pages 9 through 22 for Explanation of Ratios and Data

Comparative Historical Data / Current Data Sorted by Sales

4/1/11-3/31/12 ALL	4/1/12-3/31/13 ALL	4/1/13-3/31/14 ALL	Type of Statement	0-1MM	1-3MM	3-5MM	5-10MM	10-25MM	25MM & OVER
38	33	29	Unqualified			1	8	9	11
21	21	32	Reviewed	1	7	3	8	11	2
24	14	16	Compiled	6	8			2	
41	24	32	Tax Returns	14	8	2	5	2	1
71	54	57	Other	15	10	6	10	5	11
				24 (4/1-9/30/13)		142 (10/1/13-3/31/14)			
195	146	166	NUMBER OF STATEMENTS	36	33	12	31	29	25
%	%	%	ASSETS	%	%	%	%	%	%
12.3	10.8	8.5	Cash & Equivalents	9.2	12.6	8.3	8.2	7.3	3.5
5.4	5.5	6.8	Trade Receivables (net)	6.0	4.7	12.9	7.6	4.0	10.2
7.3	6.2	9.9	Inventory	8.1	5.9	19.2	8.4	7.7	17.7
2.6	2.9	3.1	All Other Current	1.8	.6	3.5	1.8	6.8	5.3
27.5	25.3	28.3	Total Current	25.2	23.8	43.9	26.0	25.8	36.7
59.6	63.7	63.6	Fixed Assets (net)	70.4	66.1	44.5	62.3	69.1	55.3
5.3	3.9	3.8	Intangibles (net)	1.0	6.0	6.4	6.9	2.9	1.2
7.6	7.0	4.3	All Other Non-Current	3.5	4.1	5.2	4.9	2.3	6.7
100.0	100.0	100.0	Total	100.0	100.0	100.0	100.0	100.0	100.0
			LIABILITIES						
16.7	15.4	15.2	Notes Payable-Short Term	12.5	11.2	14.9	16.9	20.0	16.8
5.6	4.2	6.0	Cur. Mat.-L.T.D.	5.3	7.5	3.0	1.4	7.7	10.5
3.0	3.6	4.8	Trade Payables	2.3	7.7	6.3	5.8	1.9	6.1
.5	.3	.0	Income Taxes Payable	.0	.0	.0	.1	.0	.1
10.6	4.7	6.4	All Other Current	11.6	3.8	6.4	5.8	5.5	3.8
36.3	28.2	32.4	Total Current	31.8	30.1	30.6	30.0	35.1	37.2
37.7	42.8	43.2	Long-Term Debt	45.0	47.1	34.0	48.1	38.7	39.4
.6	1.1	.7	Deferred Taxes	.0	.5	.5	1.5	1.1	.6
6.7	5.7	5.2	All Other Non-Current	6.7	8.3	10.4	4.1	.8	2.9
18.7	22.2	18.4	Net Worth	16.5	14.0	24.5	16.4	24.3	19.9
100.0	100.0	100.0	Total Liabilties & Net Worth	100.0	100.0	100.0	100.0	100.0	100.0
			INCOME DATA						
100.0	100.0	100.0	Net Sales	100.0	100.0	100.0	100.0	100.0	100.0
			Gross Profit						
89.7	93.0	93.0	Operating Expenses	85.9	96.6	98.1	96.3	93.2	91.8
10.3	7.0	7.0	Operating Profit	14.1	3.4	1.9	3.7	6.8	8.2
3.0	.4	1.6	All Other Expenses (net)	2.7	1.3	-1.8	.7	2.6	2.3
7.3	6.6	5.3	Profit Before Taxes	11.5	2.1	3.7	3.0	4.2	5.8
			RATIOS						
2.6	4.1	2.5		1.5	3.4	2.4	3.6	2.3	2.1
1.2	1.3	1.2	Current	1.1	.8	1.8	1.3	1.1	1.4
.3	.5	.4		.4	.4	1.0	.8	.2	.3
2.4	3.7	2.1		1.5	2.4	2.2	2.8	2.0	1.2
.8	1.0	.7	Quick	.7	.5	.8	1.0	.5	.5
.2	.3	.2		.2	.2	.5	.4	.1	.2
0 UND	4 101.4	2 155.6		0 UND	0 UND	3 141.7	6 61.4	6 62.2	10 35.5
8 46.4	11 32.8	13 28.0	Sales/Receivables	0 UND	7 50.1	31 11.9	14 26.5	17 21.3	21 17.4
23 15.8	28 13.1	32 11.4		35 10.5	26 13.8	72 5.1	26 14.1	38 9.6	33 11.1
			Cost of Sales/Inventory						
			Cost of Sales/Payables						
6.8	5.2	7.7		12.9	7.6	1.9	8.2	8.7	4.2
48.6	19.0	47.6	Sales/Working Capital	75.9	-175.9	11.1	34.0	58.7	28.9
-4.1	-7.5	-5.8		-3.0	-3.8	NM	-31.5	-2.7	-5.7
4.5	3.8	3.9		9.0	4.3	4.8	2.9	2.6	5.6
(165) 2.2	(133) 1.9	(149) 1.8	EBIT/Interest	(30) 2.9	(32) 1.7	(10) 1.5	(26) 1.6	(27) 1.6	(24) 2.2
1.3	1.1	1.0		1.0	.1	.7	.5	1.1	1.5
8.3			Net Profit + Depr., Dep.,						
(11) 4.3			Amort./Cur. Mat. L/T/D						
1.1									
1.1	1.8	1.8		1.6	2.3	.3	3.2	2.0	.3
4.0	4.2	4.4	Fixed/Worth	3.1	7.3	2.7	5.7	4.1	3.6
10.3	9.6	11.3		NM	NM	NM	14.8	8.4	8.4
2.2	2.6	2.7		1.9	2.4	2.4	3.2	2.5	3.5
5.5	4.9	5.4	Debt/Worth	4.1	7.7	5.1	5.6	4.2	6.3
14.0	11.9	15.4		NM	NM	NM	17.1	9.8	10.8
44.3	39.4	47.3	% Profit Before Taxes/Tangible	57.9	88.0		59.1	18.6	56.4
(164) 22.4	(129) 18.0	(139) 13.4	Net Worth	(27) 18.5	(25) 13.6		(26) 14.9	(27) 6.7	24.2
9.5	5.5	3.1		4.2	.9		-6.4	2.6	8.2
9.7	7.3	6.8	% Profit Before Taxes/Total	8.9	7.1	22.9	12.8	4.0	5.6
4.1	2.9	2.2	Assets	3.0	2.0	2.0	2.8	1.5	2.2
.8	.5	.1		-.1	-4.2	.3	-.9	-.2	1.4
5.5	3.1	4.6		1.9	2.8	14.0	6.7	1.9	23.4
1.2	1.1	1.1	Sales/Net Fixed Assets	.7	1.2	4.5	1.3	.7	1.5
.6	.6	.6		.3	.6	.9	.7	.6	.7
1.3	1.2	1.4		1.1	1.3	2.2	2.1	.9	1.5
.7	.6	.7	Sales/Total Assets	.5	.9	.7	.7	.6	.7
.5	.5	.4		.2	.4	.5	.5	.4	.5
12.2	17.2	14.9		16.5	20.0		10.0	19.8	
(142) 27.2	(111) 30.4	(120) 29.0	% Depr., Dep., Amort./Sales	(30) 25.9	(26) 31.4		(24) 34.4	(24) 30.9	
38.0	40.3	40.3		42.4	58.1		45.6	39.8	
1.6	1.3	1.4	% Officers', Directors'		2.4		1.7	.8	
(60) 3.5	(47) 3.2	(55) 2.9	Owners' Comp/Sales		(17) 6.0		(11) 2.2	(12) 1.2	
5.9	5.9	6.7			10.3		4.2	3.3	
2439707M	2826414M	2601498M	Net Sales ($)	16668M	67543M	46894M	231042M	441421M	1797930M
3163791M	3600528M	3600545M	Total Assets ($)	44096M	107019M	61352M	327178M	744468M	2316432M

M = $ thousand MM = $ million

See Pages 9 through 22 for Explanation of Ratios and Data

Current Data Sorted by Assets							Comparative Historical Data	
		1	10	6	4	**Type of Statement** Unqualified	27	22
		2	17	2	2	Reviewed	24	23
1		5	1			Compiled	27	13
7	6	3				Tax Returns	18	14
1	3	6	12	4	1	Other	38	31
22 (4/1-9/30/13)		72 (10/1/13-3/31/14)					4/1/09-3/31/10 ALL	4/1/10-3/31/11 ALL
0-500M	500M-2MM	2-10MM	10-50MM	50-100MM	100-250MM			
9	9	17	40	12	7	NUMBER OF STATEMENTS	134	103
%	%	%	%	%	%	**ASSETS**	%	%
		5.3	4.3	6.0		Cash & Equivalents	6.0	5.4
		9.7	10.4	11.5		Trade Receivables (net)	9.0	9.6
		7.7	9.3	.1		Inventory	4.6	5.0
		2.4	5.0	8.4		All Other Current	4.7	6.4
		25.2	29.0	26.0		Total Current	24.4	26.4
		58.6	54.3	55.8		Fixed Assets (net)	53.3	52.8
		5.5	1.8	.1		Intangibles (net)	1.0	1.4
		10.6	15.0	18.1		All Other Non-Current	21.3	19.3
		100.0	100.0	100.0		Total	100.0	100.0
						LIABILITIES		
		6.3	11.7	.0		Notes Payable-Short Term	10.8	12.1
		6.5	9.4	8.2		Cur. Mat.-L.T.D.	9.8	10.1
		5.5	1.3	6.1		Trade Payables	2.8	2.4
		.0	.0	.0		Income Taxes Payable	.2	.1
		3.1	3.3	7.2		All Other Current	7.1	6.4
		21.4	25.8	21.4		Total Current	30.8	31.1
		50.2	50.0	58.5		Long-Term Debt	54.9	49.6
		1.7	2.0	1.6		Deferred Taxes	.9	1.2
		14.4	3.7	2.2		All Other Non-Current	5.3	5.5
		12.4	18.5	16.3		Net Worth	8.2	12.7
		100.0	100.0	100.0		Total Liabilties & Net Worth	100.0	100.0
						INCOME DATA		
		100.0	100.0	100.0		Net Sales	100.0	100.0
						Gross Profit		
		91.8	87.3	82.2		Operating Expenses	86.9	84.7
		8.2	12.7	17.8		Operating Profit	13.1	15.3
		5.1	5.2	8.4		All Other Expenses (net)	10.6	9.4
		3.0	7.4	9.5		Profit Before Taxes	2.5	5.9
						RATIOS		
		5.1	4.2	22.9			2.6	3.0
		1.0	1.3	1.6		Current	1.0	1.0
		.3	.3	.2			.3	.2
		3.2	2.2	7.4			1.5	2.0
		.5	.8	1.2		Quick	.5	.4
		.2	.2	.2			.2	.1
		3 108.5	**6** 56.2	**1** 324.9			**4** 88.2	**3** 109.0
		15 23.8	**20** 18.0	**24** 15.0		Sales/Receivables	**15** 24.8	**20** 17.8
		34 10.7	**61** 6.0	**55** 6.6			**38** 9.7	**51** 7.2
						Cost of Sales/Inventory		
						Cost of Sales/Payables		
		5.9	3.7	1.2			4.2	3.5
		204.8	14.6	6.6		Sales/Working Capital	NM	-84.1
		-2.6	-1.7	-1.3			-2.4	-1.8
		3.0	2.6	3.3			2.5	2.9
		(15) 1.4	(37) 1.8	(11) 2.0		EBIT/Interest	(99) 1.4	(79) 1.7
		.7	1.3	1.6			1.0	1.0
							1.0	
						Net Profit + Depr., Dep., Amort./Cur. Mat. L/T/D	(10) .8	
							-.1	
		2.3	.1	.9			1.4	.7
		26.1	4.0	3.6		Fixed/Worth	5.8	3.8
		-4.7	8.1	6.9			86.3	20.0
		4.1	4.1	4.2			3.9	3.6
		25.6	7.0	6.3		Debt/Worth	10.2	7.6
		-8.7	9.5	9.2			600.3	46.4
		129.2	26.6	33.5			22.5	35.0
		(11) 43.1	(38) 14.1	18.8		% Profit Before Taxes/Tangible Net Worth	(102) 11.9	(83) 13.7
		6.1	7.4	9.1			1.9	4.2
		5.6	3.6	5.0			3.4	4.4
		1.7	1.9	2.3		% Profit Before Taxes/Total Assets	1.2	1.9
		-.9	1.0	1.6			.1	.1
		24.1	14.7	4.6			12.2	11.4
		.8	.6	.5		Sales/Net Fixed Assets	.8	.9
		.3	.4	.4			.5	.5
		.8	.5	.5			.6	.6
		.6	.4	.4		Sales/Total Assets	.4	.4
		.2	.2	.2			.3	.2
		26.3	16.4				6.3	6.0
		(15) 47.3	(26) 56.1			% Depr., Dep., Amort./Sales	(86) 36.9	(63) 30.3
		59.6	73.9				70.6	57.2
							2.3	2.6
						% Officers', Directors' Owners' Comp/Sales	(39) 3.4	(30) 4.5
							5.7	7.8
5693M	19470M	134957M	450749M	287037M	440647M	Net Sales ($)	1732376M	1759416M
2881M	9940M	90589M	1054628M	811999M	1021093M	Total Assets ($)	3529629M	3581762M

M = $ thousand MM = $ million

See Pages 9 through 22 for Explanation of Ratios and Data

Comparative Historical Data				Current Data Sorted by Sales					
			Type of Statement						
24	28	21	Unqualified			1	3	8	9
29	19	23	Reviewed			5	6	12	
13	13	7	Compiled	2	4		1		
17	13	16	Tax Returns	12	3			1	
42	29	27	Other		10	2	5	6	4
4/1/11-3/31/12 ALL	4/1/12-3/31/13 ALL	4/1/13-3/31/14 ALL		22 (4/1-9/30/13)			72 (10/1/13-3/31/14)		
				0-1MM	1-3MM	3-5MM	5-10MM	10-25MM	25MM & OVER
125	102	94	**NUMBER OF STATEMENTS**	14	17	8	15	27	13
%	%	%	**ASSETS**	%	%	%	%	%	%
6.3	5.4	8.1	Cash & Equivalents	16.4	8.6		6.8	8.0	2.7
7.5	5.8	10.7	Trade Receivables (net)	4.5	10.7		7.4	10.5	26.7
7.4	5.7	6.2	Inventory	.0	3.5		8.3	12.1	4.7
8.5	6.9	5.0	All Other Current	1.6	1.0		4.2	3.5	16.7
29.7	23.7	29.9	Total Current	22.5	23.7		26.7	34.0	50.7
51.3	58.5	54.1	Fixed Assets (net)	64.0	48.6		49.4	56.8	47.1
2.2	1.9	1.9	Intangibles (net)	2.5	4.8		1.2	.8	.8
16.9	15.9	14.1	All Other Non-Current	11.0	22.9		22.7	8.4	1.4
100.0	100.0	100.0	Total	100.0	100.0		100.0	100.0	100.0
			LIABILITIES						
13.1	13.8	11.9	Notes Payable-Short Term	27.9	1.2		5.9	12.5	18.3
8.5	7.6	8.4	Cur. Mat.-L.T.D.	12.3	8.8		9.8	7.4	2.9
3.1	2.3	2.8	Trade Payables	.2	1.4		1.0	4.5	7.0
.2	.1	.1	Income Taxes Payable	.1	.2		.1	.0	.0
4.0	4.8	6.4	All Other Current	20.0	6.2		1.2	2.1	9.6
28.9	28.6	29.4	Total Current	60.5	17.7		18.0	26.5	37.8
49.9	52.0	46.2	Long-Term Debt	42.0	51.2		55.8	45.6	27.2
1.1	1.1	1.7	Deferred Taxes	.0	1.1		1.4	3.3	1.5
4.8	2.9	5.4	All Other Non-Current	3.1	8.7		9.1	2.4	7.0
15.3	15.4	17.2	Net Worth	-5.6	21.3		15.6	22.3	26.5
100.0	100.0	100.0	Total Liabilities & Net Worth	100.0	100.0		100.0	100.0	100.0
			INCOME DATA						
100.0	100.0	100.0	Net Sales	100.0	100.0		100.0	100.0	100.0
			Gross Profit						
82.2	86.3	86.5	Operating Expenses	88.8	81.3		87.1	88.1	83.7
17.8	13.7	13.5	Operating Profit	11.2	18.7		12.9	11.9	16.3
8.5	6.6	4.4	All Other Expenses (net)	.9	6.3		5.9	4.5	3.6
9.4	7.1	9.1	Profit Before Taxes	10.3	12.4		7.0	7.4	12.7
			RATIOS						
3.9	2.8	4.8		9.2	2.9		7.2	4.8	4.7
1.2	1.1	1.2	Current	.3	.9		1.8	1.9	1.3
.4	.3	.3		.1	.3		.6	.3	.6
2.1	1.8	2.8		5.3	2.6		2.7	4.1	1.4
.6	.6	.8	Quick	.3	.5		1.2	1.2	.7
.2	.1	.2		.1	.2		.4	.2	.1
3 107.2	0 999.8	3 110.2		0 UND	4 103.4		7 48.7	6 57.5	1 248.2
12 31.6	11 33.6	16 22.6	Sales/Receivables	4 98.3	14 25.7		26 14.2	19 18.8	23 15.6
33 11.0	30 12.0	41 8.8		43 8.4	34 10.6		62 5.9	38 9.6	79 4.6
			Cost of Sales/Inventory						
			Cost of Sales/Payables						
3.9	3.9	3.9		2.2	10.1		3.7	3.2	.7
16.7	121.9	18.1	Sales/Working Capital	-1.4	-6.4		8.6	8.9	15.4
-3.3	-2.7	-1.6		-.7	-3.0		-2.8	-3.4	NM
3.5	3.3	3.6		3.2	20.7		3.4	2.6	11.4
(107) 1.9	(90) 1.7	(84) 2.0	EBIT/Interest	(10) 1.3	(13) 1.2		(14) 1.6	2.2	4.1
1.4	1.3	1.3		.0	.7		1.3	1.4	1.8
12.6									
(10) 1.2			Net Profit + Depr., Dep., Amort./Cur. Mat. L/T/D						
.1									
.3	.9	.6		1.8	.4		.1	.1	.7
3.3	3.4	3.1	Fixed/Worth	25.8	3.4		5.8	2.6	1.3
9.9	11.1	10.2		-.7	-5.7		9.1	6.8	2.7
3.4	3.0	2.6		1.2	.9		5.5	2.7	2.0
6.3	6.5	6.0	Debt/Worth	26.8	8.5		7.2	5.1	4.0
20.0	17.2	11.7		-6.0	-7.8		9.5	7.9	9.0
39.7	30.8	33.5			134.6		19.0	22.8	37.9
(108) 16.3	(88) 14.1	(80) 17.1	% Profit Before Taxes/Tangible Net Worth		(11) 30.5		(13) 11.7	11.3	25.3
8.0	5.9	8.7			2.7		6.0	8.8	15.1
5.9	4.4	5.5		8.6	21.4		2.8	4.5	9.4
2.5	1.8	2.3	% Profit Before Taxes/Total Assets	1.7	1.8		1.7	2.5	4.2
1.2	.9	1.0		-1.7	-.6		.7	1.6	2.3
18.3	6.7	11.7		2.1	10.1		31.1	33.2	42.2
.8	.7	.7	Sales/Net Fixed Assets	.6	.9		.6	.6	2.2
.5	.4	.4		.3	.5		.4	.4	.6
.6	.7	.6		.6	1.4		.5	.6	1.1
.4	.4	.4	Sales/Total Assets	.4	.4		.3	.4	.5
.2	.3	.3		.2	.2		.2	.3	.4
7.0	14.4	7.7		41.3	12.5		18.5	1.0	
(79) 36.2	(65) 33.5	(61) 31.7	% Depr., Dep., Amort./Sales	(10) 59.4	(13) 47.3		(12) 61.5	(12) 13.8	
64.2	63.1	64.8		75.0	58.9		76.6	29.8	
1.3	2.3	1.8							
(35) 3.5	(24) 5.0	(22) 5.7	% Officers', Directors' Owners' Comp/Sales						
8.5	9.4	9.8							
2448676M	1754886M	1338553M	Net Sales ($)	4739M	32930M	32805M	109490M	448766M	709823M
4579177M	3636528M	2991130M	Total Assets ($)	19493M	115528M	109949M	379298M	1193021M	1173841M

M = $ thousand MM = $ million

See Pages 9 through 22 for Explanation of Ratios and Data

Current Data Sorted by Assets | **Comparative Historical Data**

						Type of Statement		
	1	4	12	18	12	Unqualified	45	56
	1	22	49	5	1	Reviewed	62	75
	2	13	2	1		Compiled	47	41
12	18	10	5			Tax Returns	33	30
8	14	35	52	18	18	Other	117	133
44 (4/1-9/30/13)		289 (10/1/13-3/31/14)					4/1/09-3/31/10 ALL	4/1/10-3/31/11 ALL
0-500M	500M-2MM	2-10MM	10-50MM	50-100MM	100-250MM			
20	36	84	120	42	31	NUMBER OF STATEMENTS	304	335
%	%	%	%	%	%	ASSETS	%	%
22.2	11.1	10.1	8.5	5.6	4.1	Cash & Equivalents	7.7	8.7
5.7	11.0	6.9	9.7	10.5	12.7	Trade Receivables (net)	10.5	10.5
2.8	3.9	9.7	9.3	5.2	4.2	Inventory	9.1	7.1
.8	3.9	3.2	3.0	3.3	2.1	All Other Current	4.5	4.5
31.5	29.9	29.9	30.5	24.5	23.1	Total Current	31.7	30.9
59.1	65.5	59.5	56.1	62.1	61.7	Fixed Assets (net)	57.6	55.8
.0	.5	1.7	3.1	2.5	1.6	Intangibles (net)	1.7	2.3
9.4	4.2	8.9	10.2	10.9	13.6	All Other Non-Current	9.0	11.0
100.0	100.0	100.0	100.0	100.0	100.0	Total	100.0	100.0
						LIABILITIES		
11.7	5.6	8.4	9.7	6.6	8.6	Notes Payable-Short Term	12.4	11.2
11.8	9.0	10.5	10.9	11.5	11.9	Cur. Mat.-L.T.D.	12.0	11.0
2.4	4.6	4.8	3.6	3.4	2.5	Trade Payables	5.0	4.4
.1	.0	.0	.4	.1	.9	Income Taxes Payable	.2	.1
11.2	2.9	6.9	6.2	3.0	4.6	All Other Current	9.0	7.6
37.2	22.1	30.6	30.8	24.6	28.5	Total Current	38.5	34.5
59.8	48.0	39.7	32.8	41.9	42.6	Long-Term Debt	35.6	34.7
.0	.0	.4	1.4	2.8	3.3	Deferred Taxes	1.9	1.8
27.0	12.9	5.1	2.0	2.6	3.0	All Other Non-Current	4.9	3.2
-24.1	17.0	24.1	33.0	28.2	22.6	Net Worth	19.0	25.9
100.0	100.0	100.0	100.0	100.0	100.0	Total Liabilties & Net Worth	100.0	100.0
						INCOME DATA		
100.0	100.0	100.0	100.0	100.0	100.0	Net Sales	100.0	100.0
						Gross Profit		
92.6	78.5	84.9	87.5	89.0	80.9	Operating Expenses	90.7	86.3
7.4	21.5	15.1	12.5	11.0	19.1	Operating Profit	9.3	13.7
4.3	3.8	2.3	1.7	4.5	6.1	All Other Expenses (net)	5.1	4.4
3.1	17.7	12.9	10.8	6.4	13.1	Profit Before Taxes	4.2	9.4
						RATIOS		
3.4	3.9	1.5	1.5	1.3	1.1		1.6	1.7
.9	1.5	.8	1.0	1.1	.8	Current	.9	1.0
.1	.3	.4	.5	.7	.5		.4	.4
3.2	3.3	1.0	1.1	1.0	.8		1.1	1.3
.9	1.0	.5	.5	.6	.5	Quick	.5	.5
.1	.2	.2	.3	.3	.3		.2	.2
0 UND	**0** UND	**0** UND	**8** 43.4	**18** 20.3	**29** 12.4		**4** 99.3	**1** 271.3
0 UND	**2** 213.3	**7** 54.2	**27** 13.7	**26** 14.2	**37** 9.8	Sales/Receivables	**27** 13.7	**26** 13.8
11 32.7	**31** 11.6	**32** 11.3	**45** 8.1	**43** 8.5	**60** 6.1		**42** 8.6	**45** 8.1
						Cost of Sales/Inventory		
						Cost of Sales/Payables		
18.0	3.3	11.4	12.5	15.3	24.0		8.3	7.2
UND	17.7	-16.6	719.3	134.6	-14.8	Sales/Working Capital	-59.5	-117.0
-2.9	-5.8	-2.7	-5.1	-11.0	-5.0		-3.9	-4.6
16.7	11.2	5.2	6.0	4.4	5.8		3.1	5.3
(14) 1.9	(31) 2.3	(72) 2.6	(111) 3.4	(39) 2.7	(26) 3.9	EBIT/Interest	(265) 1.5	(290) 2.2
.0	-2.0	1.3	2.2	2.0	2.5		.3	1.2
			2.4				2.9	2.4
			(39) 1.4			Net Profit + Depr., Dep., Amort./Cur. Mat. L/T/D	(59) 1.3	(55) 1.2
			1.0				.9	1.0
.7	.9	1.1	1.1	1.3	1.8		1.2	1.0
3.4	3.5	2.7	2.4	2.8	2.5	Fixed/Worth	2.3	2.0
NM	-7.6	8.9	3.7	5.0	4.1		11.7	6.3
1.6	.6	1.2	1.3	1.6	1.9		1.4	1.2
4.9	3.8	3.8	2.7	4.2	3.6	Debt/Worth	3.6	2.9
-5.3	-9.9	16.8	5.0	5.4	8.0		26.5	13.4
95.2	58.0	47.8	27.4	29.6	28.9		25.4	30.7
(14) 25.2	(24) 29.0	(68) 21.5	(114) 19.1	(40) 16.1	(30) 20.9	% Profit Before Taxes/Tangible Net Worth	(244) 9.6	(274) 14.4
-31.6	11.2	6.7	11.2	6.9	17.9		.1	5.1
39.4	20.7	10.8	7.5	5.9	7.3		5.9	8.9
6.2	7.4	4.3	4.8	3.7	4.0	% Profit Before Taxes/Total Assets	1.7	3.4
-5.2	-.6	1.0	2.8	2.3	2.9		-2.0	.6
28.6	2.3	4.7	5.2	2.7	2.3		4.9	5.5
3.3	1.6	.9	1.6	1.4	.7	Sales/Net Fixed Assets	1.4	1.6
.5	.7	.5	.6	.6	.5		.7	.7
2.9	1.4	1.5	2.0	1.2	.7		1.5	1.5
1.9	1.0	.6	.8	.7	.5	Sales/Total Assets	.8	.9
.4	.5	.3	.4	.5	.3		.4	.4
8.1	8.9	7.2	4.5	4.5			5.6	6.1
(14) 50.8	(27) 23.8	(71) 29.4	(105) 14.3	(24) 8.8		% Depr., Dep., Amort./Sales	(232) 20.6	(241) 16.9
97.7	43.7	60.7	39.7	19.9			38.8	35.5
		1.5	.8				1.4	1.6
		(22) 4.0	(20) 2.8			% Officers', Directors' Owners' Comp/Sales	(56) 2.6	(49) 3.4
		8.4	5.3				8.0	7.3
6800M	55949M	501584M	3888386M	2819365M	3494984M	Net Sales ($)	6466322M	8225728M
3232M	40540M	434866M	2924955M	3167291M	5595039M	Total Assets ($)	8297885M	9892467M

M = $ thousand MM = $ million

See Pages 9 through 22 for Explanation of Ratios and Data

Comparative Historical Data				Current Data Sorted by Sales					
			Type of Statement						
51	51	47	Unqualified	3	1		4	6	33
77	73	78	Reviewed		8	12	12	23	23
31	30	18	Compiled	4	7	2	2	1	2
29	29	45	Tax Returns	21	12	3	4	4	1
131	143	145	Other	18	25	11	22	16	53
4/1/11-3/31/12 ALL	4/1/12-3/31/13 ALL	4/1/13-3/31/14 ALL		44 (4/1-9/30/13)			289 (10/1/13-3/31/14)		
				0-1MM	1-3MM	3-5MM	5-10MM	10-25MM	25MM & OVER
319	326	333	**NUMBER OF STATEMENTS**	46	53	28	44	50	112
%	%	%	**ASSETS**	%	%	%	%	%	%
10.2	10.1	9.2	Cash & Equivalents	13.5	10.1	9.9	9.7	6.0	8.1
10.7	10.5	9.3	Trade Receivables (net)	7.6	5.5	8.7	10.8	11.5	10.3
8.1	6.7	7.4	Inventory	2.4	4.1	.6	8.5	7.8	12.3
4.1	4.1	2.9	All Other Current	1.0	3.7	3.5	1.9	4.2	3.1
33.2	31.4	28.9	Total Current	24.6	23.4	22.6	30.9	29.5	33.8
54.2	59.0	59.4	Fixed Assets (net)	68.0	66.9	58.6	57.1	53.5	56.2
2.0	1.5	2.1	Intangibles (net)	.8	1.1	4.2	1.9	2.5	2.4
10.6	8.1	9.6	All Other Non-Current	6.6	8.5	14.6	10.0	14.6	7.7
100.0	100.0	100.0	Total	100.0	100.0	100.0	100.0	100.0	100.0
			LIABILITIES						
9.0	7.9	8.5	Notes Payable-Short Term	6.1	5.5	7.2	10.5	10.1	9.8
11.6	10.9	10.8	Cur. Mat.-L.T.D.	10.8	9.8	14.5	11.0	10.3	10.5
4.9	4.1	3.8	Trade Payables	1.6	3.5	2.1	5.0	3.7	4.8
.2	.3	.3	Income Taxes Payable	.1	.0	.9	.0	.3	.4
6.3	6.0	5.8	All Other Current	7.5	7.5	4.6	4.2	4.0	6.0
32.1	29.2	29.2	Total Current	26.1	26.4	29.3	30.8	28.3	31.5
40.8	38.3	39.9	Long-Term Debt	56.7	40.2	31.5	41.4	36.3	35.9
1.8	1.4	1.3	Deferred Taxes	.0	.4	.5	.6	1.0	2.8
4.4	6.0	5.6	All Other Non-Current	14.1	6.4	4.1	8.4	2.6	2.5
20.8	25.1	24.0	Net Worth	3.1	26.7	34.7	18.8	31.8	27.3
100.0	100.0	100.0	Total Liabilities & Net Worth	100.0	100.0	100.0	100.0	100.0	100.0
			INCOME DATA						
100.0	100.0	100.0	Net Sales	100.0	100.0	100.0	100.0	100.0	100.0
			Gross Profit						
85.5	84.6	85.7	Operating Expenses	76.4	81.1	82.0	84.4	87.2	92.6
14.5	15.4	14.3	Operating Profit	23.6	18.9	18.0	15.6	12.8	7.4
4.1	3.9	3.0	All Other Expenses (net)	5.9	3.2	1.6	4.9	2.1	1.7
10.5	11.5	11.3	Profit Before Taxes	17.7	15.7	16.5	10.6	10.6	5.7
			RATIOS						
1.8 / 1.0 / .4	1.8 / 1.1 / .5	1.5 / .9 / .4	Current	2.8 / .9 / .2	1.9 / .7 / .2	1.4 / .7 / .3	1.8 / .8 / .3	1.6 / 1.0 / .5	1.3 / 1.1 / .7
1.4 / .5 / .2	1.4 / .6 / .3	1.1 / .5 / .2	Quick	2.8 / .5 / .1	1.3 / .4 / .1	1.3 / .7 / .3	1.4 / .4 / .2	1.0 / .5 / .2	1.0 / .5 / .3
6 62.0 / 24 14.9 / 44 8.3	1 260.9 / 23 16.2 / 46 8.0	2 178.5 / 22 16.9 / 40 9.2	Sales/Receivables	0 UND / 0 UND / 25 14.8	0 UND / 1 319.0 / 30 12.1	0 UND / 26 14.1 / 49 7.5	16 22.8 / 34 10.7 / 47 7.8	12 31.2 / 28 12.9 / 41 9.0	12 30.3 / 24 15.0 / 39 9.4
			Cost of Sales/Inventory						
			Cost of Sales/Payables						
6.2 / 97.4 / -5.2	7.5 / 71.7 / -5.7	11.6 / -101.2 / -4.3	Sales/Working Capital	4.0 / -27.7 / -2.0	6.5 / -9.8 / -2.1	7.6 / -11.0 / -2.7	5.9 / -32.7 / -2.4	8.9 / 286.9 / -6.3	17.3 / 131.8 / -12.6
5.9 / (282) 2.7 / 1.3	5.5 / (286) 3.0 / 1.6	5.8 / (293) 2.8 / 1.9	EBIT/Interest	7.3 / (34) 2.2 / .3	7.8 / (48) 2.7 / 1.7	12.2 / (24) 2.2 / 1.0	5.7 / (39) 2.8 / 1.9	6.6 / (44) 3.3 / 1.8	4.9 / (104) 3.0 / 2.3
3.0 / (58) 1.3 / 1.0	2.3 / (57) 1.4 / .9	2.4 / (61) 1.4 / .9	Net Profit + Depr., Dep., Amort./Cur. Mat. L/T/D				2.6 / (10) 1.3 / .6	1.5 / (10) 1.2 / .8	2.4 / (32) 1.4 / 1.1
1.0 / 2.1 / 5.8	1.0 / 2.4 / 6.0	1.2 / 2.6 / 5.2	Fixed/Worth	1.1 / 3.7 / UND	1.2 / 2.2 / 11.1	.5 / 2.3 / 4.3	1.1 / 3.0 / 4.3	.9 / 1.6 / 4.0	1.5 / 2.6 / 4.5
1.5 / 3.2 / 11.5	1.3 / 3.3 / 8.3	1.4 / 3.2 / 8.0	Debt/Worth	1.4 / 3.9 / -10.1	.9 / 2.2 / 21.9	.8 / 2.6 / 8.7	1.4 / 2.9 / 7.8	.9 / 3.2 / 8.6	1.8 / 3.3 / 5.4
37.5 / (266) 19.0 / 8.2	39.0 / (280) 21.5 / 8.7	34.8 / (290) 20.3 / 10.7	% Profit Before Taxes/Tangible Net Worth	54.2 / (34) 23.4 / -2.6	47.2 / (43) 21.0 / 9.8	49.0 / (26) 23.3 / 8.2	26.7 / (37) 17.8 / 12.3	31.7 / (45) 22.0 / 11.2	29.4 / (105) 19.5 / 10.5
10.8 / 4.6 / .8	9.2 / 4.6 / 1.9	8.9 / 4.7 / 2.2	% Profit Before Taxes/Total Assets	16.9 / 6.8 / -3.5	9.9 / 4.3 / 1.7	8.8 / 3.8 / .5	9.0 / 4.0 / 2.4	10.7 / 5.8 / 2.1	6.7 / 4.4 / 2.9
6.5 / 1.4 / .6	5.4 / 1.2 / .6	4.6 / 1.3 / .5	Sales/Net Fixed Assets	2.1 / .6 / .3	1.8 / .7 / .4	3.6 / .9 / .5	7.9 / .8 / .4	7.3 / 2.0 / .7	5.9 / 2.1 / .8
1.7 / .8 / .4	1.6 / .8 / .4	1.6 / .7 / .4	Sales/Total Assets	1.3 / .4 / .3	1.0 / .5 / .3	1.0 / .5 / .3	1.1 / .5 / .3	1.7 / .8 / .5	2.3 / 1.2 / .6
4.7 / (233) 17.0 / 35.9	5.0 / (241) 17.2 / 37.0	4.6 / (248) 16.9 / 47.4	% Depr., Dep., Amort./Sales	17.3 / (33) 43.3 / 68.6	28.0 / (41) 50.5 / 72.8	8.2 / (24) 34.0 / 61.8	4.6 / (41) 24.1 / 43.7	4.4 / (39) 13.4 / 29.4	2.2 / (70) 5.0 / 9.2
2.0 / (45) 4.6 / 15.7	1.3 / (41) 4.6 / 9.1	1.4 / (56) 3.6 / 6.4	% Officers', Directors' Owners' Comp/Sales		3.8 / (14) 5.5 / 8.5		2.6 / (15) 4.9 / 8.5	1.2 / (10) 2.2 / 4.6	
8403877M	8641096M	10767068M	Net Sales ($)	20519M	95692M	109954M	324420M	799550M	9416933M
9072229M	10144197M	12165923M	Total Assets ($)	56639M	243791M	374044M	1002007M	1432641M	9056801M

M = $ thousand MM = $ million

See Pages 9 through 22 for Explanation of Ratios and Data

Current Data Sorted by Assets / Comparative Historical Data

0-500M	500M-2MM	2-10MM	10-50MM	50-100MM	100-250MM		4/1/09-3/31/10 ALL	4/1/10-3/31/11 ALL
						Type of Statement		
		1	1			Unqualified	14	8
	1	2	2			Reviewed	14	13
1	1	4				Compiled	10	13
5	6	3	1			Tax Returns	25	20
1	8	10	6	3		Other	27	22
	5 (4/1-9/30/13)		51 (10/1/13-3/31/14)					
7	16	20	10	3		**NUMBER OF STATEMENTS**	90	76
%	%	%	%	%	%	**ASSETS**	%	%
	15.2	7.6	4.2		DATA NOT AVAILABLE	Cash & Equivalents	9.1	7.2
	5.6	12.9	1.6			Trade Receivables (net)	10.6	10.7
	17.9	24.3	19.3			Inventory	15.6	15.7
	3.3	1.9	9.2			All Other Current	3.4	2.3
	42.1	46.6	34.2			Total Current	38.7	35.9
	45.1	40.7	30.6			Fixed Assets (net)	44.6	46.6
	6.2	5.0	13.6			Intangibles (net)	4.8	6.8
	6.6	7.8	21.6			All Other Non-Current	12.0	10.7
	100.0	100.0	100.0			Total	100.0	100.0
						LIABILITIES		
	17.8	22.8	24.6			Notes Payable-Short Term	14.9	19.6
	4.2	7.3	3.9			Cur. Mat.-L.T.D.	7.5	8.2
	5.2	8.4	4.8			Trade Payables	7.3	9.1
	.6	.8	.0			Income Taxes Payable	.3	.3
	6.6	13.3	4.4			All Other Current	10.2	11.5
	34.5	52.7	37.6			Total Current	40.2	48.7
	18.8	22.2	31.5			Long-Term Debt	37.9	33.8
	.0	.3	.0			Deferred Taxes	.6	.4
	6.3	3.2	12.1			All Other Non-Current	13.9	9.8
	40.4	21.6	18.9			Net Worth	7.5	7.3
	100.0	100.0	100.0			Total Liabilities & Net Worth	100.0	100.0
						INCOME DATA		
	100.0	100.0	100.0			Net Sales	100.0	100.0
						Gross Profit		
	86.1	88.2	89.6			Operating Expenses	88.8	90.2
	13.9	11.8	10.4			Operating Profit	11.2	9.8
	2.0	4.5	2.7			All Other Expenses (net)	6.5	4.6
	11.8	7.3	7.8			Profit Before Taxes	4.6	5.1
						RATIOS		
	2.7	2.3	1.5				2.1	1.4
	1.3	.7	1.1			Current	1.1	.8
	.3	.2	.3				.4	.2
	1.7	.9	1.2				1.2	.9
	.3	.2	.1			Quick	.5	.3
	.1	.0	.0				.2	.1
	0 UND	0 UND	0 789.1				0 UND	0 UND
	0 UND	0 999.8	2 205.6			Sales/Receivables	11 33.0	4 87.4
	4 87.8	43 8.5	10 35.4				33 11.2	35 10.3
						Cost of Sales/Inventory		
						Cost of Sales/Payables		
	6.5	6.0	7.2				7.1	9.6
	14.6	-16.1	57.3			Sales/Working Capital	118.9	-22.7
	-15.6	-4.0	-5.9				-7.4	-4.4
	19.2	8.8	4.6				4.9	5.8
	(13) 4.9	(17) 4.2	2.9			EBIT/Interest	(73) 2.6	(66) 3.3
	1.8	1.9	2.6				1.1	1.0
							2.6	
						Net Profit + Depr., Dep., Amort./Cur. Mat. L/T/D	(10) 1.8	
							.6	
	.4	.7	.2				.6	.9
	1.0	2.3	2.1			Fixed/Worth	3.0	4.0
	3.5	-50.8	-1.4				-4.7	-3.6
	.8	1.2	4.6				1.1	1.5
	1.6	3.7	9.0			Debt/Worth	4.7	5.4
	2.8	-58.4	-3.3				-11.8	-10.1
	88.9	89.7					49.9	57.8
	(14) 55.2	(14) 18.7				% Profit Before Taxes/Tangible Net Worth	(64) 16.9	(46) 26.8
	13.7	7.3					2.3	5.6
	36.3	17.5	7.3				10.6	12.8
	16.4	5.6	4.3			% Profit Before Taxes/Total Assets	4.1	5.4
	4.6	1.6	3.5				.3	.4
	15.6	29.3	23.3				13.8	11.5
	7.9	10.3	15.3			Sales/Net Fixed Assets	4.9	3.9
	1.9	2.9	2.4				1.9	2.0
	3.4	3.3	1.6				2.8	2.3
	1.8	2.1	1.3			Sales/Total Assets	1.8	1.6
	1.2	1.6	.4				.8	.8
		1.4					2.2	4.4
		(14) 9.9				% Depr., Dep., Amort./Sales	(72) 8.1	(52) 10.3
		31.3					22.3	22.9
							3.1	2.6
						% Officers', Directors' Owners' Comp/Sales	(38) 5.5	(23) 5.1
							10.1	9.9
5666M	38379M	207113M	321216M	265917M		Net Sales ($)	1209335M	1151641M
1765M	16171M	85420M	315358M	180755M		Total Assets ($)	1289414M	1036857M

M = $ thousand MM = $ million

See Pages 9 through 22 for Explanation of Ratios and Data

Comparative Historical Data / Current Data Sorted by Sales

Type of Statement									
Unqualified	9	7	2					1	1
Reviewed	12	11	5		1	1	1	1	1
Compiled	13	11	6	1	2			3	
Tax Returns	27	18	15	6	5		1	3	
Other	29	28	28	5	3	2	7	4	7
	4/1/11-3/31/12 ALL	4/1/12-3/31/13 ALL	4/1/13-3/31/14 ALL		5 (4/1-9/30/13)		51 (10/1/13-3/31/14)		
				0-1MM	1-3MM	3-5MM	5-10MM	10-25MM	25MM & OVER
NUMBER OF STATEMENTS	90	75	56	12	11	3	9	12	9
ASSETS	%	%	%	%	%	%	%	%	%
Cash & Equivalents	10.4	14.4	9.4	8.4	11.1			11.0	
Trade Receivables (net)	9.8	10.9	6.8	2.4	.9			18.3	
Inventory	16.7	15.8	19.2	3.9	25.0			13.8	
All Other Current	3.3	4.0	5.1	10.2	2.6			9.8	
Total Current	40.1	45.0	40.5	25.0	39.6			52.9	
Fixed Assets (net)	41.0	37.9	42.9	63.6	43.1			27.3	
Intangibles (net)	7.7	7.3	6.6	3.8	6.0			7.2	
All Other Non-Current	11.2	9.8	10.0	7.6	11.3			12.6	
Total	100.0	100.0	100.0	100.0	100.0			100.0	
LIABILITIES									
Notes Payable-Short Term	21.9	20.9	18.9	4.6	22.4			17.0	
Cur. Mat.-L.T.D.	5.5	5.7	6.7	9.2	6.6			6.5	
Trade Payables	5.3	7.5	7.1	6.5	4.3			7.3	
Income Taxes Payable	.4	.9	.5	.0	.9			1.2	
All Other Current	11.9	8.5	8.0	4.1	5.9			16.8	
Total Current	45.0	43.6	41.2	24.4	40.0			48.9	
Long-Term Debt	20.7	21.9	30.7	61.2	21.7			20.2	
Deferred Taxes	.4	.5	.1	.0	.0			.4	
All Other Non-Current	13.2	6.6	6.9	10.0	4.0			2.8	
Net Worth	20.6	27.5	21.2	4.5	34.4			27.7	
Total Liabilties & Net Worth	100.0	100.0	100.0	100.0	100.0			100.0	
INCOME DATA									
Net Sales	100.0	100.0	100.0	100.0	100.0			100.0	
Gross Profit									
Operating Expenses	89.7	90.6	87.2	64.0	99.6			95.7	
Operating Profit	10.3	9.4	12.8	36.0	.4			4.3	
All Other Expenses (net)	2.4	1.3	3.0	7.8	-.2			.3	
Profit Before Taxes	8.0	8.2	9.8	28.2	.6			4.0	
RATIOS									
Current	2.1	2.5	2.2	3.7	1.7			2.3	
	1.0	1.3	.9	.7	1.2			1.3	
	.3	.3	.2	.1	.2			.3	
Quick	1.3	1.7	1.0	2.0	.7			2.0	
	.6	.4	.2	.2	.2			.7	
	.1	.1	.0	.1	.1			.1	
Sales/Receivables	0 UND	0 UND	0 UND	0 UND	0 UND			0 UND	
	1 285.3	5 69.0	0 999.8	0 UND	0 UND			13 27.2	
	27 13.4	34 10.8	9 39.2	3 136.1	3 108.3			55 6.6	
Cost of Sales/Inventory									
Cost of Sales/Payables									
Sales/Working Capital	7.5	5.1	6.5	2.3	7.7			4.9	
	-549.7	18.7	-546.0	-51.1	108.3			18.9	
	-4.5	-11.5	-4.6	-2.5	-17.7			-6.0	
EBIT/Interest	5.8	10.6	8.2		15.8			7.5	
	(75) 2.5	(64) 3.7	(49) 3.0		3.0			(11) 4.2	
	1.2	2.2	1.9		1.3			2.1	
Net Profit + Depr., Dep., Amort./Cur. Mat. L/T/D									
Fixed/Worth	.5	.2	.5	.8	.4			.2	
	2.9	1.5	2.7	3.9	1.2			.6	
	-2.4	48.1	8.5	-51.6	2.8			5.8	
Debt/Worth	1.2	.8	1.4	.8	1.2			1.0	
	4.9	2.9	3.6	3.3	1.7			5.6	
	-8.6	102.7	29.1	-57.4	2.6			14.4	
% Profit Before Taxes/Tangible Net Worth	55.7	127.0	96.4		72.3			55.8	
	(58) 22.6	(58) 31.5	(43) 28.7		(10) 34.4			(10) 17.6	
	7.4	15.3	12.7		4.9			11.9	
% Profit Before Taxes/Total Assets	18.0	18.4	22.8	22.8	27.9			9.1	
	5.7	9.1	6.0	7.1	4.6			5.4	
	.8	3.4	3.4	5.0	1.2			2.0	
Sales/Net Fixed Assets	19.4	21.9	22.2	8.6	22.8			54.2	
	5.4	8.4	9.0	1.8	6.5			23.5	
	2.2	2.7	2.4	.3	2.1			2.8	
Sales/Total Assets	2.4	2.5	2.6	1.8	2.4			3.4	
	1.7	1.8	1.8	.7	1.8			2.1	
	.9	1.2	1.2	.2	1.4			1.5	
% Depr., Dep., Amort./Sales	3.9	3.3	2.2	6.6					
	(56) 11.0	(44) 11.7	(35) 14.7	(10) 15.4					
	29.6	26.2	31.2	28.6					
% Officers', Directors' Owners' Comp/Sales	1.7	1.7	1.6						
	(33) 3.3	(31) 5.2	(17) 5.3						
	10.7	8.9	8.5						
Net Sales ($)	1504989M	1341395M	838291M	5892M	22610M	13406M	60088M	171309M	564986M
Total Assets ($)	1219686M	1101273M	599469M	11777M	11525M	6478M	69737M	147457M	352495M

M = $ thousand MM = $ million

See Pages 9 through 22 for Explanation of Ratios and Data

Current Data Sorted by Assets							Comparative Historical Data	
0-500M	500M-2MM	2-10MM	10-50MM	50-100MM	100-250MM	**Type of Statement**	4/1/09-3/31/10 ALL	4/1/10-3/31/11 ALL
			1	1	1	Unqualified	8	7
1	1	5	1			Reviewed	12	11
	3	5	1			Compiled	6	6
1	3	6				Tax Returns	20	15
4	10	10	11		2	Other	29	35
	10 (4/1-9/30/13)		57 (10/1/13-3/31/14)					
6	17	26	14	1	3	**NUMBER OF STATEMENTS**	75	74
%	%	%	%	%	%	**ASSETS**	%	%
	9.8	5.3	7.5			Cash & Equivalents	8.2	10.6
	23.6	23.4	34.5			Trade Receivables (net)	20.8	19.0
	9.4	6.7	7.3			Inventory	9.8	9.7
	1.9	4.9	5.5			All Other Current	2.2	3.6
	44.7	40.2	54.7			Total Current	41.0	43.0
	43.1	51.4	35.7			Fixed Assets (net)	44.9	39.8
	4.1	4.9	6.8			Intangibles (net)	5.8	5.8
	8.2	3.4	2.8			All Other Non-Current	8.3	11.4
	100.0	100.0	100.0			Total	100.0	100.0
						LIABILITIES		
	10.4	5.1	10.2			Notes Payable-Short Term	7.9	9.3
	10.5	10.9	9.7			Cur. Mat.-L.T.D.	8.7	8.4
	11.9	15.0	14.0			Trade Payables	8.9	7.6
	.0	.2	2.4			Income Taxes Payable	.3	.4
	4.5	4.1	7.2			All Other Current	7.7	8.1
	37.4	35.3	43.5			Total Current	33.6	33.9
	30.8	34.9	13.4			Long-Term Debt	32.8	26.7
	.0	.5	2.0			Deferred Taxes	.7	.8
	2.2	3.3	2.2			All Other Non-Current	6.5	8.2
	29.6	26.0	38.9			Net Worth	26.4	30.5
	100.0	100.0	100.0			Total Liabilties & Net Worth	100.0	100.0
						INCOME DATA		
	100.0	100.0	100.0			Net Sales	100.0	100.0
						Gross Profit		
	92.0	92.6	92.2			Operating Expenses	88.4	90.6
	8.0	7.4	7.8			Operating Profit	11.6	9.4
	1.4	4.9	1.2			All Other Expenses (net)	4.0	3.5
	6.6	2.5	6.6			Profit Before Taxes	7.6	5.9
						RATIOS		
	3.0	1.8	1.6				1.9	2.2
	1.6	1.1	1.2			Current	1.2	1.2
	.6	.7	1.0				.9	.7
	2.1	1.5	1.2				1.6	1.6
	(16) 1.5	.8	.9			Quick	.9	.9
	.4	.3	.7				.5	.4
	4 85.2	0 UND	74 4.9				7 52.7	0 UND
	34 10.7	57 6.4	87 4.2			Sales/Receivables	46 8.0	37 9.9
	64 5.7	94 3.9	114 3.2				64 5.7	64 5.7
						Cost of Sales/Inventory		
						Cost of Sales/Payables		
	5.4	13.5	6.9				8.6	8.4
	17.7	51.0	15.8			Sales/Working Capital	37.7	57.1
	-10.5	-9.6	NM				-27.4	-17.3
	4.6	26.8	10.1				8.0	13.8
	(15) 3.3	(24) 2.0	(13) 6.1			EBIT/Interest	(66) 4.1	(66) 3.9
	-.8	-1.4	2.1				1.1	.8
							3.7	7.7
						Net Profit + Depr., Dep., Amort./Cur. Mat. L/T/D	(11) 1.9	(15) 1.2
							1.2	.6
	.3	1.1	.9				.6	.5
	1.6	2.0	1.2			Fixed/Worth	1.7	1.3
	NM	7.5	1.4				-99.1	14.0
	.5	1.1	1.2				.9	.8
	2.6	3.1	2.1			Debt/Worth	2.6	2.3
	NM	11.1	3.1				-159.5	25.8
	83.0	38.1	34.0				69.3	57.4
	(13) 17.5	(21) 7.2	(13) 26.5			% Profit Before Taxes/Tangible Net Worth	(56) 24.2	(60) 21.3
	-11.6	-6.9	14.9				6.7	.4
	25.5	14.7	11.4				18.8	20.1
	8.1	2.1	8.4			% Profit Before Taxes/Total Assets	6.8	6.4
	-7.6	-3.3	3.5				.3	-.3
	15.1	5.6	9.2				12.3	14.2
	8.4	3.9	4.0			Sales/Net Fixed Assets	4.9	6.3
	2.9	1.7	2.9				2.2	2.3
	3.4	2.7	1.5				2.6	2.7
	2.4	1.8	1.4			Sales/Total Assets	1.8	1.6
	1.4	.9	1.1				.9	.9
	2.0	4.9	5.4				2.3	3.1
	(12) 4.7	(21) 10.2	(13) 5.9			% Depr., Dep., Amort./Sales	(55) 6.2	(50) 7.4
	7.8	17.7	12.8				17.6	15.1
		1.3					3.0	2.5
		(11) 3.7				% Officers', Directors' Owners' Comp/Sales	(21) 5.7	(26) 5.6
		6.8					17.0	13.9
4840M	48860M	227566M	371976M	62280M	312400M	Net Sales ($)	1234311M	1267885M
1527M	20288M	127852M	286132M	77373M	379138M	Total Assets ($)	1231979M	1228176M

M = $ thousand MM = $ million

See Pages 9 through 22 for Explanation of Ratios and Data

Comparative Historical Data				Current Data Sorted by Sales					
			Type of Statement						
7	7	3	Unqualified				1	1	1
6	8	8	Reviewed	1	3	1	1	2	
5	10	9	Compiled		3	2	2	2	
15	16	10	Tax Returns	2	2	1	2	3	
27	27	37	Other	3	7	5	5	8	9
4/1/11-3/31/12 ALL	**4/1/12-3/31/13 ALL**	**4/1/13-3/31/14 ALL**			**10 (4/1-9/30/13)**			**57 (10/1/13-3/31/14)**	
				0-1MM	**1-3MM**	**3-5MM**	**5-10MM**	**10-25MM**	**25MM & OVER**
60	68	67	**NUMBER OF STATEMENTS**	6	15	9	11	16	10
%	%	%	**ASSETS**	%	%	%	%	%	%
10.2	10.9	9.8	Cash & Equivalents		6.3		9.4	4.9	9.0
22.7	26.9	25.4	Trade Receivables (net)		16.1		26.7	32.5	31.4
7.4	9.8	7.3	Inventory		9.7		6.6	6.7	10.3
4.5	3.2	3.7	All Other Current		.2		10.9	4.7	2.3
44.8	50.8	46.2	Total Current		32.4		53.6	48.8	53.0
41.9	37.0	42.2	Fixed Assets (net)		58.1		37.3	47.5	22.0
4.8	4.1	5.5	Intangibles (net)		7.2		4.3	1.3	16.8
8.5	8.1	6.1	All Other Non-Current		2.3		4.8	2.5	8.2
100.0	100.0	100.0	Total		100.0		100.0	100.0	100.0
			LIABILITIES						
8.7	8.7	11.0	Notes Payable-Short Term		14.6		11.2	12.5	5.9
7.7	6.0	9.3	Cur. Mat.-L.T.D.		12.0		11.5	10.9	6.6
8.2	11.6	13.2	Trade Payables		12.6		14.0	12.3	21.3
.5	.4	.6	Income Taxes Payable		.0		.4	1.9	.4
15.2	12.0	5.4	All Other Current		3.5		8.1	4.6	8.4
40.3	38.8	39.4	Total Current		42.7		45.3	42.2	42.6
24.5	25.6	26.9	Long-Term Debt		46.2		26.3	25.2	12.7
.8	.9	.8	Deferred Taxes		.0		3.0	.6	1.5
2.3	6.5	3.7	All Other Non-Current		7.1		2.2	1.5	5.8
32.1	28.2	29.1	Net Worth		4.1		23.3	30.5	37.3
100.0	100.0	100.0	Total Liabilties & Net Worth		100.0		100.0	100.0	100.0
			INCOME DATA						
100.0	100.0	100.0	Net Sales		100.0		100.0	100.0	100.0
			Gross Profit						
87.6	94.2	91.5	Operating Expenses		94.0		95.6	87.5	94.2
12.4	5.8	8.5	Operating Profit		6.0		4.4	12.5	5.8
2.9	.7	2.9	All Other Expenses (net)		2.2		1.1	4.6	1.4
9.5	5.1	5.6	Profit Before Taxes		3.8		3.2	7.9	4.4
			RATIOS						
2.7	2.7	2.0			2.4		2.2	1.7	1.8
1.4	1.5	1.2	Current		.7		1.3	1.2	1.2
1.0	1.0	.7			.2		.7	1.0	1.0
2.3	2.1	1.6			1.9		1.5	1.6	1.2
1.0	1.2	(66) 1.0	Quick		(14) .5		1.0	.9	1.0
.7	.6	.6			.2		.7	.6	.8
0 UND	**19** 19.0	**8** 43.0			**0** UND		**0** UND	**29** 12.5	**51** 7.2
49 7.5	**50** 7.3	**59** 6.2	Sales/Receivables		**19** 19.2		**83** 4.4	**79** 4.6	**62** 5.9
73 5.0	**73** 5.0	**87** 4.2			**59** 6.2		**104** 3.5	**96** 3.8	**91** 4.0
			Cost of Sales/Inventory						
			Cost of Sales/Payables						
5.0	5.3	6.2			8.9		5.1	8.2	9.0
12.3	13.6	19.7	Sales/Working Capital		-17.6		18.0	15.5	18.8
UND	324.7	-17.6			-5.6		-11.2	769.4	NM
20.8	14.2	8.7			4.5		32.4	11.2	
(51) 6.8	(55) 4.6	(58) 3.3	EBIT/Interest		(12) 1.8		4.5	4.4	
1.9	1.6	.9			-1.3		-3.6	1.3	
2.7	6.6	3.2							
(10) 1.5	(16) 1.9	(15) 1.8	Net Profit + Depr., Dep., Amort./Cur. Mat. L/T/D						
1.0	1.4	.8							
.6	.3	.7			3.1		.2	1.1	.5
1.2	1.1	1.3	Fixed/Worth		7.8		1.2	1.3	1.1
3.7	4.8	6.4			-2.0		-3.5	1.9	NM
.5	.7	1.1			4.3		.7	1.2	1.6
1.7	1.3	2.3	Debt/Worth		10.9		2.6	2.1	2.3
6.0	5.7	10.2			-4.0		-9.1	6.4	NM
63.3	44.8	43.2						39.8	
(54) 27.9	(56) 17.3	(54) 22.2	% Profit Before Taxes/Tangible Net Worth					(15) 33.0	
6.4	3.2	1.8						7.2	
23.7	19.6	19.8			22.1		21.7	17.3	11.1
7.9	7.3	8.1	% Profit Before Taxes/Total Assets		8.1		8.1	9.1	6.0
.8	1.0	.3			-12.9		-2.9	.9	3.8
9.2	20.3	11.3			8.4		36.8	4.6	22.6
4.6	6.1	4.5	Sales/Net Fixed Assets		2.3		9.2	3.6	7.0
2.5	3.7	2.4			1.3		1.7	2.6	4.0
2.8	2.6	2.8			8.2		2.9	2.3	2.3
1.7	1.9	1.6	Sales/Total Assets		1.5		2.3	1.6	1.4
1.0	1.3	1.1			.8		.8	1.3	1.2
3.2	2.6	4.2						5.8	
(46) 6.9	(48) 6.3	(49) 6.9	% Depr., Dep., Amort./Sales					(15) 8.6	
15.1	10.3	13.0						15.5	
1.4	2.6	1.9							
(20) 2.9	(24) 5.3	(21) 4.0	% Officers', Directors' Owners' Comp/Sales						
9.5	7.3	7.1							
882757M	906006M	1027922M	Net Sales ($)	3885M	25768M	34041M	76107M	276895M	611226M
736052M	581743M	892310M	Total Assets ($)	13508M	19297M	19032M	83687M	273070M	483716M

M = $ thousand MM = $ million

See Pages 9 through 22 for Explanation of Ratios and Data

Current Data Sorted by Assets							Comparative Historical Data	
						Type of Statement		
		1		1	1	Unqualified	4	4
	2	5	1			Reviewed	13	14
1	4	8				Compiled	16	14
15	12	7				Tax Returns	19	24
6	15	8	6	4	1	Other	30	25
	9 (4/1-9/30/13)		89 (10/1/13-3/31/14)				4/1/09-3/31/10 ALL	4/1/10-3/31/11 ALL
0-500M	**500M-2MM**	**2-10MM**	**10-50MM**	**50-100MM**	**100-250MM**			
22	33	29	7	5	2	**NUMBER OF STATEMENTS**	82	81
%	%	%	%	%	%	**ASSETS**	%	%
32.4	17.8	8.2				Cash & Equivalents	9.9	11.0
12.4	12.3	15.4				Trade Receivables (net)	12.4	12.7
3.9	7.4	9.5				Inventory	14.2	7.4
1.1	.6	1.3				All Other Current	2.4	2.7
49.7	38.1	34.5				Total Current	38.8	33.8
42.3	48.0	49.6				Fixed Assets (net)	47.9	53.6
1.4	4.5	4.5				Intangibles (net)	6.5	5.2
6.7	9.4	11.4				All Other Non-Current	6.8	7.4
100.0	100.0	100.0				Total	100.0	100.0
						LIABILITIES		
13.5	6.5	6.4				Notes Payable-Short Term	15.2	15.8
6.0	3.1	7.3				Cur. Mat.-L.T.D.	6.2	9.5
9.1	4.8	6.6				Trade Payables	6.5	7.0
.0	.5	.0				Income Taxes Payable	.1	.1
18.9	11.3	6.6				All Other Current	5.8	6.5
47.5	26.1	26.8				Total Current	34.0	38.9
36.2	25.8	28.3				Long-Term Debt	34.3	31.4
.0	.1	1.4				Deferred Taxes	.5	.6
10.4	4.3	15.5				All Other Non-Current	11.5	12.2
5.9	43.7	28.0				Net Worth	19.8	16.9
100.0	100.0	100.0				Total Liabilties & Net Worth	100.0	100.0
						INCOME DATA		
100.0	100.0	100.0				Net Sales	100.0	100.0
						Gross Profit		
84.9	89.3	86.1				Operating Expenses	89.7	96.0
15.1	10.7	13.9				Operating Profit	10.3	4.0
.5	1.5	2.2				All Other Expenses (net)	5.9	3.0
14.6	9.1	11.7				Profit Before Taxes	4.4	1.0
						RATIOS		
2.4	4.1	1.9					2.4	2.5
1.1	1.6	.9				Current	1.0	1.1
.5	.6	.4					.6	.4
2.4	3.1	1.4					1.5	1.9
1.0	1.3	.5				Quick	.6	.6
.4	.2	.2					.2	.2
0 UND	0 UND	0 UND					0 UND	0 UND
0 UND	2 242.0	18 19.9				Sales/Receivables	17 21.1	16 22.8
23 16.1	31 11.8	32 11.4					40 9.1	41 8.9
						Cost of Sales/Inventory		
						Cost of Sales/Payables		
12.0	5.2	7.1					4.9	7.3
399.6	20.9	-94.3				Sales/Working Capital	268.5	85.0
-10.6	-10.4	-10.9					-8.9	-6.4
35.5	18.2	23.5					4.3	5.4
(16) 16.8	(28) 4.9	(28) 7.1				EBIT/Interest	(65) 1.7	(72) 2.2
7.2	1.5	1.4					-.7	-.1
							2.6	5.5
						Net Profit + Depr., Dep., Amort./Cur. Mat. L/T/D	(11) 1.9	(11) 2.4
							1.2	1.1
.4	.4	.6					.7	.8
1.6	1.2	1.7				Fixed/Worth	2.3	2.3
NM	3.7	7.6					UND	-7.8
.3	.2	1.3					1.4	1.4
4.3	1.1	2.8				Debt/Worth	4.6	4.0
-8.0	7.4	8.6					-42.1	-8.7
409.5	82.4	73.6					39.4	40.1
(15) 52.3	(27) 34.6	(25) 32.6				% Profit Before Taxes/Tangible Net Worth	(61) 12.3	(55) 14.5
19.3	8.8	.1					-6.8	2.7
70.2	29.6	18.4					15.1	12.0
35.5	10.4	8.5				% Profit Before Taxes/Total Assets	3.0	3.2
24.0	2.6	.9					-3.7	-3.1
29.0	16.3	10.0					13.7	8.8
16.0	4.2	4.1				Sales/Net Fixed Assets	3.9	3.1
5.5	2.2	1.5					1.7	1.4
7.8	3.2	2.4					2.3	2.6
5.0	2.4	1.3				Sales/Total Assets	1.4	1.6
2.1	1.4	.8					.7	1.0
	3.5	4.7					5.0	6.0
	(22) 7.1	(21) 7.9				% Depr., Dep., Amort./Sales	(61) 11.7	(63) 11.9
	14.8	12.5					17.9	18.9
5.6	3.3	2.7					3.1	4.1
(12) 7.0	(19) 5.0	(12) 3.7				% Officers', Directors' Owners' Comp/Sales	(29) 5.1	(33) 5.5
11.9	7.2	5.5					9.9	6.7
27465M	90147M	185177M	236842M	441170M	434001M	Net Sales ($)	872902M	708460M
5694M	37287M	119445M	136823M	352159M	377734M	Total Assets ($)	1126218M	554125M

M = $ thousand MM = $ million

See Pages 9 through 22 for Explanation of Ratios and Data

Comparative Historical Data | **Current Data Sorted by Sales**

4/1/11-3/31/12 ALL	4/1/12-3/31/13 ALL	4/1/13-3/31/14 ALL	Type of Statement	0-1MM	1-3MM	3-5MM	5-10MM	10-25MM	25MM & OVER
8	4	3	Unqualified					1	2
4	11	8	Reviewed		2	2	3		1
17	11	13	Compiled	1	5	4	2	1	
34	28	34	Tax Returns	7	15	6	5	1	
35	41	40	Other	6	14	6	1	2	11
				9 (4/1-9/30/13)		89 (10/1/13-3/31/14)			
98	95	98	NUMBER OF STATEMENTS	14	36	18	11	5	14
%	%	%	**ASSETS**	%	%	%	%	%	%
12.8	15.4	16.1	Cash & Equivalents	30.9	15.9	13.1	16.6		6.7
12.0	9.6	13.8	Trade Receivables (net)	6.6	13.9	14.8	17.1		15.3
8.6	6.7	9.1	Inventory	3.8	4.6	17.9	4.3		20.5
4.1	1.7	1.1	All Other Current	.1	1.4	1.4	.5		2.1
37.4	33.4	40.2	Total Current	41.5	35.8	47.2	38.4		44.6
45.0	50.0	44.1	Fixed Assets (net)	51.1	46.9	41.8	53.6		27.5
8.8	5.2	4.5	Intangibles (net)	2.1	4.3	1.3	4.3		8.7
8.9	11.4	11.2	All Other Non-Current	5.3	13.0	9.6	3.6		19.2
100.0	100.0	100.0	Total	100.0	100.0	100.0	100.0		100.0
			LIABILITIES						
10.6	11.9	11.0	Notes Payable-Short Term	18.7	6.5	4.9	6.0		27.4
7.2	5.0	4.8	Cur. Mat.-L.T.D.	3.5	4.0	9.5	4.1		2.0
9.2	7.0	6.9	Trade Payables	7.1	3.1	9.5	13.3		8.6
.0	.1	.2	Income Taxes Payable	.0	.0	.8	.0		.1
6.2	9.5	11.4	All Other Current	14.5	11.1	14.5	6.2		7.3
33.2	33.5	34.3	Total Current	43.8	24.7	39.1	29.7		45.4
27.8	32.2	29.5	Long-Term Debt	49.5	26.4	25.8	28.0		28.2
.2	.4	.5	Deferred Taxes	.0	.1	.9	1.5		.6
11.6	17.0	9.5	All Other Non-Current	.5	13.5	9.2	9.5		10.3
27.2	16.9	26.1	Net Worth	6.1	35.3	25.0	31.3		15.5
100.0	100.0	100.0	Total Liabilties & Net Worth	100.0	100.0	100.0	100.0		100.0
			INCOME DATA						
100.0	100.0	100.0	Net Sales	100.0	100.0	100.0	100.0		100.0
			Gross Profit						
92.0	89.3	88.1	Operating Expenses	74.4	87.7	88.9	93.9		93.8
8.0	10.7	11.9	Operating Profit	25.6	12.3	11.1	6.1		6.2
3.4	2.8	1.6	All Other Expenses (net)	2.5	1.8	.9	.3		2.3
4.6	7.9	10.3	Profit Before Taxes	23.0	10.5	10.2	5.8		3.9
			RATIOS						
3.1	2.6	3.0		2.5	4.6	2.6	3.1		3.2
1.2	.9	1.1	Current	.9	1.3	1.3	1.1		.8
.5	.4	.5		.2	.4	.5	.9		.4
2.3	2.2	2.3		2.5	3.3	1.7	3.1		1.1
.7	.8	.7	Quick	.8	1.1	.6	1.1		.4
.2	.2	.2		.2	.2	.2	.5		.1
0 UND	0 UND	0 UND		0 UND	0 UND	0 UND	2 191.5		0 UND
15 24.9	8 47.1	13 28.2	Sales/Receivables	0 UND	10 35.7	14 26.9	17 21.4		23 15.8
33 10.9	25 14.4	31 11.9		30 12.0	25 14.8	28 13.1	32 11.5		51 7.2
			Cost of Sales/Inventory						
			Cost of Sales/Payables						
8.4	12.0	9.4		7.5	5.3	4.8	32.7		8.1
59.0	-85.9	160.6	Sales/Working Capital	-60.0	35.7	102.3	70.4		-27.2
-8.8	-7.3	-9.7		-4.3	-8.9	-15.5	-14.6		-4.5
9.1	13.7	22.1		22.8	29.7	46.9	24.3		6.8
(83) 3.3	(80) 4.4	(85) 6.8	EBIT/Interest	(10) 7.9	(31) 7.9	(16) 13.9	(10) 7.1		(13) 2.5
.9	1.2	2.2		2.4	3.2	2.6	1.2		2.1
6.5									
(10) 1.6			Net Profit + Depr., Dep., Amort./Cur. Mat. L/T/D						
.8									
.7	.9	.5		.4	.4	.1	1.2		.5
1.8	2.4	1.6	Fixed/Worth	1.9	2.1	.8	1.7		2.0
-24.0	-12.0	7.5		-2.2	9.6	3.1	4.2		-27.3
.7	1.1	.7		.3	.4	.5	1.4		1.9
2.4	2.8	2.4	Debt/Worth	2.9	2.7	1.2	2.3		4.6
-13.6	-21.7	12.0		-3.4	14.0	6.3	9.0		-114.8
48.8	80.9	74.8			82.7	74.7	120.7		41.8
(71) 17.4	(69) 29.4	(77) 35.1	% Profit Before Taxes/Tangible Net Worth		(29) 35.1	(15) 47.4	(10) 42.8		(10) 33.2
3.6	7.7	11.1			17.8	12.9	.8		15.2
17.7	21.7	31.7		53.5	30.7	35.8	29.7		8.5
3.7	9.9	10.4	% Profit Before Taxes/Total Assets	20.1	15.2	16.7	8.5		5.5
-.8	1.9	3.3		-.1	6.8	1.7	.6		3.3
14.8	15.3	16.8		22.9	16.5	17.9	16.6		22.5
5.0	4.7	5.9	Sales/Net Fixed Assets	5.3	4.2	12.2	5.4		7.7
2.2	1.5	2.6		1.2	2.0	3.4	2.0		5.2
2.6	3.0	3.5		6.4	3.6	4.2	6.1		2.1
1.7	1.9	2.0	Sales/Total Assets	1.9	1.4	2.6	2.6		1.7
1.1	.9	1.2		.7	1.1	1.2	1.5		.9
4.3	3.6	3.4			5.1	1.8			
(64) 9.4	(61) 7.9	(58) 6.8	% Depr., Dep., Amort./Sales		(25) 8.3	(10) 4.0			
19.3	15.1	11.5			14.8	7.5			
2.7	3.9	3.4			3.6	3.3			
(41) 5.0	(45) 6.6	(44) 5.2	% Officers', Directors' Owners' Comp/Sales		(19) 5.7	(11) 3.7			
6.9	11.9	7.6			8.0	6.6			
1551990M	2535562M	1414802M	Net Sales ($)	7485M	69181M	68051M	83549M	63696M	1122840M
1257662M	1190488M	1029142M	Total Assets ($)	8054M	56422M	35415M	37462M	30166M	861623M

M = $ thousand MM = $ million

See Pages 9 through 22 for Explanation of Ratios and Data

Current Data Sorted by Assets							Comparative Historical Data	
			6		3	**Type of Statement** Unqualified	11	13
	3	5	4	1		Reviewed	12	11
6	7	7				Compiled	22	19
7	12	10			2	Tax Returns	44	46
5	21	20	4	3		Other	41	51
	13 (4/1-9/30/13)		113 (10/1/13-3/31/14)				**4/1/09-3/31/10 ALL**	**4/1/10-3/31/11 ALL**
0-500M	**500M-2MM**	**2-10MM**	**10-50MM**	**50-100MM**	**100-250MM**			
18	43	42	14	4	5	**NUMBER OF STATEMENTS**	130	140
%	%	%	%	%	%	**ASSETS**	%	%
13.1	15.2	7.8	5.2			Cash & Equivalents	8.8	8.7
12.8	7.3	9.0	21.1			Trade Receivables (net)	6.6	9.7
19.2	10.0	12.5	22.2			Inventory	10.0	10.1
3.1	1.1	1.6	3.4			All Other Current	3.0	2.6
48.2	33.6	30.9	51.9			Total Current	28.5	31.1
47.8	56.2	62.0	24.8			Fixed Assets (net)	60.4	59.4
1.7	3.0	2.9	6.8			Intangibles (net)	3.3	4.1
2.3	7.2	4.2	16.5			All Other Non-Current	7.8	5.4
100.0	100.0	100.0	100.0			Total	100.0	100.0
						LIABILITIES		
13.5	11.8	20.1	22.0			Notes Payable-Short Term	12.4	12.3
17.9	7.9	4.7	2.1			Cur. Mat.-L.T.D.	8.1	8.8
10.8	5.8	9.5	5.8			Trade Payables	4.5	6.0
.0	1.1	.0	.0			Income Taxes Payable	.1	.2
12.1	6.3	4.5	7.0			All Other Current	6.0	7.8
54.4	32.9	38.8	36.9			Total Current	31.1	35.1
71.3	33.4	28.9	23.3			Long-Term Debt	44.3	44.6
1.1	.5	.3	.2			Deferred Taxes	.5	.6
27.3	6.5	4.6	5.1			All Other Non-Current	11.3	11.0
-54.0	26.7	27.3	34.5			Net Worth	12.8	8.7
100.0	100.0	100.0	100.0			Total Liabilties & Net Worth	100.0	100.0
						INCOME DATA		
100.0	100.0	100.0	100.0			Net Sales	100.0	100.0
						Gross Profit		
91.2	85.7	81.4	82.6			Operating Expenses	88.5	86.4
8.8	14.3	18.6	17.4			Operating Profit	11.5	13.6
2.6	1.7	5.0	1.4			All Other Expenses (net)	6.9	6.4
6.2	12.6	13.6	16.1			Profit Before Taxes	4.6	7.2
						RATIOS		
2.0	3.7	3.0	1.8				2.1	2.1
1.2	1.1	1.1	1.4			Current	.8	.9
.5	.3	.4	.7				.3	.4
1.4	2.1	2.5	.9				1.1	1.3
.5	.5	.6	.6			Quick	.5	.6
.1	.1	.2	.3				.2	.2
0 UND	**0** UND	**0** UND	**0** UND				**0** UND	**0** UND
8 47.9	**7** 50.8	**19** 19.2	**10** 35.9			Sales/Receivables	**12** 29.3	**12** 29.3
34 10.8	**23** 16.2	**27** 13.4	**76** 4.8				**36** 10.1	**38** 9.6
						Cost of Sales/Inventory		
						Cost of Sales/Payables		
11.3	6.5	6.7	2.7				9.5	6.6
31.4	100.6	103.3	13.8			Sales/Working Capital	-32.5	-78.7
-14.3	-5.1	-4.4	-7.8				-4.7	-7.0
3.4	17.9	11.5	15.3				3.5	4.5
(17) 2.4	(37) 5.1	(31) 4.9	(13) 7.3			EBIT/Interest	(106) 1.0	(118) 2.8
-.6	1.3	1.9	2.8				-.9	.6
							4.6	
						Net Profit + Depr., Dep., Amort./Cur. Mat. L/T/D	(15) 1.6	
							1.0	
1.5	1.2	1.1	.1				1.2	1.2
-2.0	3.4	2.1	.2			Fixed/Worth	2.9	3.3
-.5	10.9	3.5	1.8				-7.5	-4.0
4.6	1.3	1.2	1.3				1.2	1.3
-6.6	4.7	1.7	1.7			Debt/Worth	2.9	4.2
-1.9	27.0	3.6	5.5				-12.7	-6.1
	76.6	40.7	36.3				30.2	41.7
	(35) 38.5	(36) 24.9	(13) 30.6			% Profit Before Taxes/Tangible Net Worth	(91) 7.1	(91) 13.7
	13.1	12.4	8.1				-4.8	2.6
18.7	23.0	13.6	13.2				7.9	10.6
8.9	10.5	8.9	9.1			% Profit Before Taxes/Total Assets	.4	4.5
-11.2	1.7	2.3	3.0				-5.0	-1.5
14.9	7.3	7.8	211.8				5.4	5.9
7.5	3.0	1.9	22.6			Sales/Net Fixed Assets	2.3	3.1
4.5	1.0	.4	5.0				.6	1.0
4.9	2.8	2.1	2.3				2.2	2.5
3.1	1.6	1.2	1.2			Sales/Total Assets	1.3	1.5
2.0	.7	.3	.4				.4	.6
	7.8	6.5					8.9	5.8
	(29) 12.4	(30) 13.2				% Depr., Dep., Amort./Sales	(104) 16.2	(100) 11.2
	27.1	25.7					28.7	21.9
	2.7						2.9	2.6
	(19) 4.8					% Officers', Directors' Owners' Comp/Sales	(51) 5.8	(41) 7.5
	7.8						11.5	12.5
17516M	**93335M**	**268497M**	**552705M**	**236515M**	**1343759M**	Net Sales ($)	**1148233M**	**3702456M**
5026M	**49041M**	**190801M**	**418078M**	**290992M**	**908224M**	Total Assets ($)	**1309845M**	**2707227M**

M = $ thousand MM = $ million

See Pages 9 through 22 for Explanation of Ratios and Data

Comparative Historical Data				Current Data Sorted by Sales					
			Type of Statement						
14	6	9	Unqualified				1	2	6
12	10	13	Reviewed	1	2	1	2	3	4
27	18	20	Compiled	4	8	4	3	1	
54	42	31	Tax Returns	12	7	4	4	2	2
58	47	53	Other	19	14	6	3	7	4
4/1/11-3/31/12 ALL	**4/1/12-3/31/13 ALL**	**4/1/13-3/31/14 ALL**		**13 (4/1-9/30/13)**			**113 (10/1/13-3/31/14)**		
165	123	126	**NUMBER OF STATEMENTS**	**0-1MM** 36	**1-3MM** 31	**3-5MM** 15	**5-10MM** 13	**10-25MM** 15	**25MM & OVER** 16
%	%	%	**ASSETS**	%	%	%	%	%	%
9.1	11.2	10.3	Cash & Equivalents	9.9	11.6	16.4	12.4	7.0	4.4
8.9	9.0	10.5	Trade Receivables (net)	2.1	11.3	7.0	13.7	28.0	11.8
12.1	11.1	13.8	Inventory	10.5	9.5	10.6	17.9	21.1	22.6
1.7	2.8	1.8	All Other Current	2.1	.5	1.9	1.2	3.2	2.5
31.7	34.2	36.4	Total Current	24.6	32.8	36.0	45.3	59.3	41.4
54.0	51.7	53.1	Fixed Assets (net)	69.2	57.8	57.2	37.7	29.4	38.6
4.4	4.4	3.4	Intangibles (net)	2.6	2.1	4.6	2.2	2.0	8.9
10.0	9.7	7.1	All Other Non-Current	3.6	7.3	2.2	14.9	9.3	11.1
100.0	100.0	100.0	Total	100.0	100.0	100.0	100.0	100.0	100.0
			LIABILITIES						
11.0	10.5	15.4	Notes Payable-Short Term	10.6	22.5	18.7	7.6	19.0	12.4
6.0	7.2	7.7	Cur. Mat.-L.T.D.	10.1	6.5	9.0	9.2	3.6	6.4
7.0	6.1	8.8	Trade Payables	6.3	4.7	6.1	5.4	21.4	15.9
.1	.3	.4	Income Taxes Payable	.0	1.1	.1	1.1	.1	.3
9.6	8.0	6.5	All Other Current	6.7	4.7	7.0	5.9	8.9	7.5
33.7	32.1	39.0	Total Current	33.7	39.6	40.9	29.2	53.0	42.6
39.0	38.8	36.6	Long-Term Debt	51.7	33.1	39.0	38.8	12.8	27.4
.6	.5	.7	Deferred Taxes	.3	.9	.0	.9	.0	2.2
11.5	8.6	8.9	All Other Non-Current	8.7	15.3	8.3	1.5	6.4	6.0
15.2	20.0	14.9	Net Worth	5.5	11.1	11.9	29.6	27.8	21.8
100.0	100.0	100.0	Total Liabilities & Net Worth	100.0	100.0	100.0	100.0	100.0	100.0
			INCOME DATA						
100.0	100.0	100.0	Net Sales	100.0	100.0	100.0	100.0	100.0	100.0
			Gross Profit						
83.6	86.0	85.2	Operating Expenses	70.7	93.4	85.8	87.9	91.0	93.3
16.4	14.0	14.8	Operating Profit	29.3	6.6	14.2	12.1	9.0	6.7
7.8	4.4	3.0	All Other Expenses (net)	7.8	.5	1.1	.6	1.8	2.0
8.6	9.6	11.8	Profit Before Taxes	21.5	6.1	13.1	11.4	7.2	4.6
			RATIOS						
2.4	2.3	2.8		2.8	2.0	4.5	3.1	2.0	3.2
1.1	1.2	1.1	Current	.8	1.1	1.1	1.1	1.6	1.2
.4	.5	.4		.2	.3	.4	.9	1.0	.6
1.6	1.5	1.6		1.8	1.5	4.0	2.6	1.5	.9
.6	.7	.6	Quick	.4	.5	.7	.8	.6	.6
.2	.2	.2		.1	.2	.0	.4	.4	.2
0 UND	0 UND	0 UND		0 UND	2 217.0	0 UND	0 UND	15 23.9	0 UND
8 46.4	12 29.8	13 28.4	Sales/Receivables	0 UND	18 20.3	9 40.9	24 15.1	31 11.7	25 14.8
30 12.3	27 13.3	33 11.0		5 66.8	33 11.0	27 13.6	42 8.6	52 7.0	52 7.0
			Cost of Sales/Inventory						
			Cost of Sales/Payables						
7.4	8.0	6.6		6.6	11.7	7.4	6.0	3.5	3.5
66.7	51.5	57.3	Sales/Working Capital	-32.9	100.6	46.7	67.9	19.9	17.1
-8.7	-8.3	-5.9		-2.5	-6.1	-4.1	-58.1	-377.9	-7.3
8.5	10.7	11.2		5.1	6.9	12.8	34.0	14.4	28.5
(122) 2.8	(99) 4.9	(107) 4.3	EBIT/Interest	(23) 2.6	(30) 3.1	(14) 5.1	8.5	(12) 6.1	(15) 6.9
.9	2.0	1.8		-.4	1.0	1.9	4.2	1.9	1.9
			Net Profit + Depr., Dep., Amort./Cur. Mat. L/T/D						
.7	.7	1.0		1.6	1.2	1.6	.6	.2	.2
2.3	1.8	2.2	Fixed/Worth	3.5	2.2	3.4	1.5	.4	1.2
-4.9	12.9	16.9		NM	-10.5	-2.3	3.4	2.4	NM
.9	1.0	1.3		1.6	1.3	1.8	1.3	.9	.9
3.1	2.2	2.8	Debt/Worth	5.2	4.6	3.4	2.1	1.4	2.1
-9.9	20.0	38.0		NM	-19.4	-6.5	9.0	2.6	NM
31.4	49.4	42.7		43.0	40.8	91.9	84.3	39.7	34.2
(116) 14.7	(96) 23.7	(97) 25.7	% Profit Before Taxes/Tangible Net Worth	(27) 20.7	(23) 24.9	(10) 29.0	(12) 40.8	(13) 30.9	(12) 13.2
3.1	12.2	9.4		2.6	1.0	13.8	22.0	16.5	9.1
11.1	17.4	16.2		14.8	15.5	23.0	29.2	18.8	9.1
3.8	7.4	8.3	% Profit Before Taxes/Total Assets	5.4	8.9	13.4	14.3	10.7	5.1
.0	2.7	1.9		.0	.4	3.1	8.2	2.6	1.5
11.6	11.3	12.4		4.5	7.7	16.6	16.9	59.7	36.6
3.5	3.6	3.4	Sales/Net Fixed Assets	.8	3.5	3.6	7.2	13.7	9.3
.5	1.7	1.0		.1	2.0	1.4	2.5	4.1	1.5
2.3	2.7	2.6		1.1	2.8	2.7	2.7	2.6	2.7
1.4	1.5	1.5	Sales/Total Assets	.4	2.0	1.9	1.8	2.1	1.2
.3	1.0	.7		.1	1.5	1.1	1.2	.7	.8
4.9	4.8	5.1		8.9	5.2	7.6			
(102) 12.2	(77) 10.7	(75) 10.6	% Depr., Dep., Amort./Sales	(21) 22.9	(22) 11.7	(12) 10.8			
21.6	18.9	22.9		62.0	19.3	15.8			
2.2	2.5	2.4			3.0				
(50) 5.7	(50) 6.4	(38) 4.9	% Officers', Directors' Owners' Comp/Sales		(20) 5.3				
10.5	10.2	7.9			7.6				
3277524M	3048407M	2512327M	Net Sales ($)	18187M	61798M	62468M	92703M	258213M	2018958M
2610006M	2307023M	1862162M	Total Assets ($)	58316M	43895M	48000M	88772M	232456M	1390723M

M = $ thousand MM = $ million

See Pages 9 through 22 for Explanation of Ratios and Data

Current Data Sorted by Assets							Comparative Historical Data	
						Type of Statement		
	1	11	6	6	7	Unqualified	15	22
	2	1	12	1		Reviewed	19	18
1	2	6	2			Compiled	16	14
15	19	9				Tax Returns	49	49
13	15	16	16	7	5	Other	63	55
15 (4/1-9/30/13)		158 (10/1/13-3/31/14)					4/1/09-3/31/10	4/1/10-3/31/11
0-500M	**500M-2MM**	**2-10MM**	**10-50MM**	**50-100MM**	**100-250MM**		**ALL**	**ALL**
29	39	43	36	14	12	**NUMBER OF STATEMENTS**	162	158
%	%	%	%	%	%	**ASSETS**	%	%
26.5	12.5	12.8	8.2	5.0	6.6	Cash & Equivalents	9.9	10.8
5.2	9.7	8.2	11.1	10.1	2.8	Trade Receivables (net)	10.1	11.4
1.5	.1	5.4	6.6	.4	1.3	Inventory	2.4	3.9
2.4	2.0	2.2	6.7	1.1	.2	All Other Current	3.5	3.3
35.6	24.4	28.6	32.7	16.7	10.7	Total Current	25.9	29.4
53.0	60.6	59.1	57.5	69.5	85.7	Fixed Assets (net)	60.8	58.2
6.4	5.1	3.2	2.3	1.7	1.1	Intangibles (net)	2.1	1.0
5.0	10.0	9.0	7.4	12.1	2.5	All Other Non-Current	11.2	11.4
100.0	100.0	100.0	100.0	100.0	100.0	Total	100.0	100.0
						LIABILITIES		
11.4	3.5	3.6	5.2	5.7	3.9	Notes Payable-Short Term	7.4	5.7
7.0	6.1	7.6	6.6	4.3	9.7	Cur. Mat.-L.T.D.	10.2	8.8
1.2	1.8	5.7	6.9	8.2	.9	Trade Payables	5.7	5.2
.0	.0	.0	.5	.0	.0	Income Taxes Payable	.0	.1
9.5	15.1	6.9	7.7	3.4	3.4	All Other Current	8.6	9.4
29.1	26.5	23.8	26.9	21.6	18.0	Total Current	32.0	29.3
36.2	54.2	37.7	31.2	40.1	40.3	Long-Term Debt	51.8	47.5
.0	.0	.3	1.3	2.7	.7	Deferred Taxes	.8	.4
2.5	8.5	3.8	1.6	2.4	1.2	All Other Non-Current	5.2	5.0
32.2	10.9	34.4	38.9	33.1	39.8	Net Worth	10.2	17.9
100.0	100.0	100.0	100.0	100.0	100.0	Total Liabilties & Net Worth	100.0	100.0
						INCOME DATA		
100.0	100.0	100.0	100.0	100.0	100.0	Net Sales	100.0	100.0
						Gross Profit		
71.3	64.4	68.9	77.1	80.1	65.8	Operating Expenses	74.2	75.1
28.7	35.6	31.1	22.9	19.9	34.2	Operating Profit	25.8	24.9
8.2	14.7	5.6	6.9	5.4	8.7	All Other Expenses (net)	10.1	9.1
20.5	20.9	25.6	16.0	14.5	25.5	Profit Before Taxes	15.7	15.8
						RATIOS		
4.6	3.9	2.1	1.7	1.6	1.6		1.7	2.5
2.0	.8	1.1	1.1	1.1	1.2	Current	.8	1.1
.3	.2	.3	.7	.3	.3		.3	.4
3.0	3.2	1.9	1.2	1.6	1.3		1.5	2.0
1.9	.7	.9	.6	1.0	.9	Quick	.5	.8
.3	.2	.2	.3	.3	.3		.2	.2
0 UND	0 UND	0 UND	1 436.9	12 29.6	10 36.0		0 UND	0 UND
0 UND	0 999.8	0 999.8	31 11.9	42 8.6	18 20.1	Sales/Receivables	10 35.7	22 16.7
5 80.0	51 7.1	42 8.6	51 7.2	96 3.8	42 8.6		52 7.0	51 7.1
						Cost of Sales/Inventory		
						Cost of Sales/Payables		
2.5	6.3	4.5	8.9	7.1	5.5		8.0	5.1
36.9	-19.5	55.8	87.9	32.3	28.7	Sales/Working Capital	-16.5	36.2
-2.9	-2.2	-3.2	-5.4	-1.9	-5.1		-3.2	-5.3
35.2	9.0	22.8	21.1	3.8	9.4		6.8	10.3
(16) 5.1	(19) 4.6	(34) 8.6	(30) 5.3	(10) 2.4	(10) 7.9	EBIT/Interest	(126) 2.9	(124) 3.9
2.1	1.6	4.3	2.4	1.3	2.2		1.1	1.0
							10.6	5.8
						Net Profit + Depr., Dep., Amort./Cur. Mat. L/T/D	(16) 3.1	(15) 1.9
							1.0	.7
.6	1.5	.7	.7	.9	1.8		1.0	.8
1.2	5.3	1.9	1.5	2.3	2.2	Fixed/Worth	2.4	1.8
-42.6	-2.9	6.0	3.6	6.1	3.2		UND	10.7
.2	1.4	.8	.7	1.1	1.2		1.0	.8
.8	9.1	3.5	2.4	2.9	1.6	Debt/Worth	3.4	2.2
-44.3	-7.0	6.9	4.5	11.2	2.5		-51.0	22.5
103.5	56.6	75.6	36.4	30.5	24.1		47.5	51.9
(21) 32.9	(25) 20.3	(40) 26.6	(35) 21.9	(13) 16.0	20.5	% Profit Before Taxes/Tangible Net Worth	(120) 12.4	(122) 16.4
7.0	.5	9.1	11.3	1.7	8.6		1.9	5.5
45.8	19.4	19.7	11.9	6.4	11.8		15.6	17.9
13.9	4.8	8.2	5.9	2.9	6.2	% Profit Before Taxes/Total Assets	5.4	5.9
.9	.1	3.5	2.3	.5	3.0		.4	-.1
12.4	4.8	4.8	5.0	.9	.4		3.2	3.8
2.5	.8	.6	1.6	.4	.3	Sales/Net Fixed Assets	1.1	1.3
.5	.2	.2	.2	.1	.2		.5	.4
3.2	1.7	1.2	1.3	.4	.4		1.5	1.4
.8	.3	.4	.9	.2	.2	Sales/Total Assets	.6	.7
.3	.1	.2	.2	.1	.2		.3	.3
6.0	14.1	10.3	3.1	8.1			8.2	8.4
(17) 15.9	(28) 24.1	(37) 29.0	(33) 8.2	(11) 27.2		% Depr., Dep., Amort./Sales	(125) 21.7	(124) 20.2
51.3	37.9	42.1	26.4	37.2			39.5	43.9
							2.6	1.2
						% Officers', Directors' Owners' Comp/Sales	(33) 4.0	(24) 3.3
							9.5	4.7
12148M	38802M	194595M	946923M	281402M	557848M	Net Sales ($)	1581112M	1759274M
7282M	44270M	206696M	921711M	1012978M	2066826M	Total Assets ($)	2747322M	2955014M

M = $ thousand MM = $ million

See Pages 9 through 22 for Explanation of Ratios and Data

Comparative Historical Data				Current Data Sorted by Sales					
			Type of Statement						
24	28	31	Unqualified	3	5	3	4	4	12
22	16	16	Reviewed	1	2	4		5	4
14	24	11	Compiled	5	2		1	2	1
68	52	43	Tax Returns	28	12	2	1		
93	63	72	Other	25	13	7	4	12	11
4/1/11-3/31/12 ALL	4/1/12-3/31/13 ALL	4/1/13-3/31/14 ALL		15 (4/1-9/30/13)			158 (10/1/13-3/31/14)		
				0-1MM	1-3MM	3-5MM	5-10MM	10-25MM	25MM & OVER
221	183	173	**NUMBER OF STATEMENTS**	62	34	16	10	23	28
%	%	%	**ASSETS**	%	%	%	%	%	%
10.3	14.4	13.0	Cash & Equivalents	14.3	16.8	15.0	4.9	9.3	10.4
9.1	8.2	8.4	Trade Receivables (net)	5.5	5.7	4.4	8.8	13.8	15.9
3.0	3.0	3.1	Inventory	1.0	.1	4.5	11.2	5.8	5.6
2.3	2.4	2.9	All Other Current	2.2	.0	2.6	.1	6.3	6.3
24.8	27.9	27.5	Total Current	23.1	22.6	26.6	24.9	35.2	38.2
61.3	59.2	60.8	Fixed Assets (net)	63.9	65.1	60.1	65.1	50.0	56.3
3.5	2.1	3.7	Intangibles (net)	5.3	4.0	1.1	6.5	2.0	1.8
10.4	10.8	8.0	All Other Non-Current	7.7	8.3	12.2	3.5	12.8	3.8
100.0	100.0	100.0	Total	100.0	100.0	100.0	100.0	100.0	100.0
			LIABILITIES						
7.2	5.7	5.4	Notes Payable-Short Term	6.8	1.7	3.8	7.6	6.8	5.8
9.0	8.6	6.8	Cur. Mat.-L.T.D.	7.0	5.5	10.8	4.8	4.8	8.3
3.4	5.8	4.2	Trade Payables	.9	2.8	1.8	3.7	8.9	11.0
.1	.0	.1	Income Taxes Payable	.0	.0	.9	.0	.0	.1
11.3	7.4	8.8	All Other Current	7.0	14.6	13.1	2.8	5.8	7.9
31.0	27.6	25.3	Total Current	21.7	24.6	30.4	18.9	26.2	33.2
45.0	41.8	40.2	Long-Term Debt	46.8	47.5	37.9	38.8	31.0	25.8
.5	.5	.6	Deferred Taxes	.0	.0	1.7	2.1	1.5	1.1
5.7	8.5	3.9	All Other Non-Current	2.9	9.5	1.3	6.8	1.0	2.3
17.8	21.6	29.9	Net Worth	28.6	18.4	28.8	33.4	40.3	37.7
100.0	100.0	100.0	Total Liabilities & Net Worth	100.0	100.0	100.0	100.0	100.0	100.0
			INCOME DATA						
100.0	100.0	100.0	Net Sales	100.0	100.0	100.0	100.0	100.0	100.0
			Gross Profit						
75.8	72.5	70.7	Operating Expenses	58.8	71.6	74.3	76.0	81.2	83.3
24.2	27.5	29.3	Operating Profit	41.2	28.4	25.7	24.0	18.8	16.7
8.0	6.8	8.5	All Other Expenses (net)	14.5	7.7	6.7	7.4	2.8	2.5
16.3	20.7	20.8	Profit Before Taxes	26.6	20.7	19.0	16.6	16.1	14.2
			RATIOS						
2.0	2.6	2.1		3.4	2.8	1.4	1.9	2.3	1.7
1.0	1.1	1.1	Current	1.0	1.0	.6	1.1	1.6	1.2
.4	.4	.3		.1	.2	.4	.3	1.1	.8
1.7	2.2	1.9		2.6	2.8	1.2	1.3	1.6	1.3
.8	.9	.8	Quick	.8	.9	.4	.5	1.1	.9
.3	.3	.3		.1	.2	.2	.2	.6	.5
0 UND	0 UND	0 UND		0 UND	0 UND	0 UND	14 26.1	2 185.0	18 20.6
13 28.4	7 54.7	11 33.4	Sales/Receivables	0 UND	0 UND	2 149.3	35 10.3	28 12.9	39 9.3
45 8.2	36 10.1	47 7.8		47 7.8	23 16.1	29 12.8	62 5.9	51 7.1	54 6.8
			Cost of Sales/Inventory						
			Cost of Sales/Payables						
6.5	4.7	5.6		2.4	9.4	7.2	6.0	2.9	7.7
462.1	50.2	80.5	Sales/Working Capital	UND	-42.9	-10.3	192.0	8.9	16.4
-3.8	-4.7	-3.2		-1.5	-4.3	-1.0	-3.5	95.2	-100.4
12.5	9.9	14.4		14.4	17.2	49.5		25.3	8.7
(167) 4.3	(137) 4.4	(119) 5.6	EBIT/Interest	(31) 5.2	(24) 6.6	(12) 4.3		(20) 8.1	(24) 5.3
1.5	2.0	2.2		2.5	1.0	2.5		2.4	2.1
15.1	6.8	11.9							
(21) 4.1	(18) 2.2	(15) 3.2	Net Profit + Depr., Dep., Amort./Cur. Mat. L/T/D						
1.8	.9	1.9							
1.0	.7	.9		1.0	1.3	.5	1.2	.5	.8
2.2	1.8	2.2	Fixed/Worth	3.3	4.0	2.7	2.6	1.3	1.9
8.6	5.0	7.2		NM	NM	15.0	NM	3.2	2.5
.9	.6	.7		.5	.9	1.4	1.3	.7	1.0
2.1	1.8	2.6	Debt/Worth	3.5	4.2	4.4	7.1	1.6	1.9
11.8	8.4	11.4		NM	NM	14.6	NM	4.3	3.4
40.6	44.0	44.2		54.3	96.4	77.8		38.9	30.2
(179) 18.4	(152) 19.5	(146) 22.7	% Profit Before Taxes/Tangible Net Worth	(47) 22.7	(26) 19.2	(15) 23.3		24.3	(27) 21.9
3.9	3.8	7.1		5.4	2.2	11.3		12.2	14.9
15.6	18.1	16.7		19.5	28.8	27.7	12.1	13.3	12.0
6.2	7.5	6.5	% Profit Before Taxes/Total Assets	5.3	7.2	5.5	6.8	10.9	6.5
.6	1.7	2.2		1.1	-.5	2.5	2.7	2.7	2.8
2.8	5.7	4.7		1.5	6.7	6.8	7.6	5.2	10.0
1.1	.8	.7	Sales/Net Fixed Assets	.4	1.3	.4	.5	2.1	1.4
.4	.3	.2		.2	.2	.2	.1	.4	.4
1.3	1.6	1.3		.5	2.8	1.9	1.3	1.6	1.5
.5	.5	.4	Sales/Total Assets	.3	.5	.2	.4	1.0	.8
.2	.2	.2		.1	.2	.1	.1	.2	.4
9.4	8.3	7.5		16.0	15.4	7.3		5.1	2.5
(163) 21.3	(134) 21.4	(135) 21.5	% Depr., Dep., Amort./Sales	(46) 31.9	(24) 26.9	(14) 18.6		(20) 7.5	(23) 8.1
38.7	35.6	38.4		47.5	40.2	34.8		28.4	16.5
2.3	1.1	2.6							
(35) 3.6	(19) 3.1	(26) 5.7	% Officers', Directors' Owners' Comp/Sales						
6.6	11.3	10.9							
2543562M	2207122M	2031718M	Net Sales ($)	21071M	54900M	58233M	71989M	378101M	1447424M
4884056M	3806714M	4259763M	Total Assets ($)	75123M	160004M	343493M	284995M	1124144M	2272004M

M = $ thousand MM = $ million

See Pages 9 through 22 for Explanation of Ratios and Data

Current Data Sorted by Assets | **Comparative Historical Data**

0-500M	500M-2MM	2-10MM	10-50MM	50-100MM	100-250MM	Type of Statement	4/1/09-3/31/10 ALL	4/1/10-3/31/11 ALL
	1	6	11	7	15	Unqualified	57	73
2	5	30	39	5	1	Reviewed	98	90
2	13	21	11			Compiled	59	47
12	23	10				Tax Returns	42	67
8	30	50	46	26	22	Other	141	149
56 (4/1-9/30/13)			340 (10/1/13-3/31/14)					
24	72	117	107	38	38	NUMBER OF STATEMENTS	397	426
%	%	%	%	%	%	**ASSETS**	%	%
20.7	13.2	9.7	6.1	5.2	5.0	Cash & Equivalents	8.6	9.1
8.8	12.6	13.8	15.1	10.0	9.8	Trade Receivables (net)	13.3	14.1
9.8	7.2	10.4	13.0	14.8	8.3	Inventory	11.2	10.8
7.6	2.3	1.7	2.3	1.3	3.4	All Other Current	3.0	3.1
46.9	35.3	35.5	36.5	31.3	26.5	Total Current	36.0	37.0
43.3	52.8	54.9	53.8	52.4	61.2	Fixed Assets (net)	54.7	52.8
2.0	3.5	2.1	2.7	5.7	4.9	Intangibles (net)	3.0	2.7
7.8	8.3	7.6	7.1	10.6	7.5	All Other Non-Current	6.3	7.5
100.0	100.0	100.0	100.0	100.0	100.0	Total	100.0	100.0
						LIABILITIES		
9.5	6.8	8.5	10.8	9.8	8.9	Notes Payable-Short Term	9.7	9.1
10.1	9.8	9.1	8.2	6.1	4.6	Cur. Mat.-L.T.D.	9.8	8.5
4.0	4.3	5.2	5.0	5.0	3.9	Trade Payables	4.8	5.7
.6	.3	.4	.2	.7	.4	Income Taxes Payable	.3	.3
19.0	5.8	5.5	4.9	3.0	4.4	All Other Current	5.5	6.0
43.2	27.1	28.7	29.2	24.6	22.2	Total Current	30.0	29.6
42.5	32.1	26.4	30.6	36.9	36.6	Long-Term Debt	30.6	28.8
.9	.6	1.4	1.4	1.3	3.6	Deferred Taxes	1.1	1.3
10.4	6.9	5.2	4.3	4.5	2.7	All Other Non-Current	4.6	4.7
3.1	33.3	38.3	34.4	32.7	34.9	Net Worth	33.7	35.6
100.0	100.0	100.0	100.0	100.0	100.0	Total Liabilities & Net Worth	100.0	100.0
						INCOME DATA		
100.0	100.0	100.0	100.0	100.0	100.0	Net Sales	100.0	100.0
						Gross Profit		
85.7	78.0	84.7	88.8	85.2	92.1	Operating Expenses	91.4	89.4
14.3	22.0	15.3	11.2	14.8	7.9	Operating Profit	8.6	10.6
3.8	3.0	2.5	1.7	4.1	3.4	All Other Expenses (net)	4.6	3.2
10.5	19.0	12.8	9.5	10.7	4.5	Profit Before Taxes	4.0	7.4
						RATIOS		
6.4	2.7	2.3	1.8	2.2	2.2		2.2	2.4
1.0	1.2	1.1	1.3	1.3	1.2	Current	1.2	1.3
.5	.5	.6	.8	.8	1.0		.6	.6
3.2	2.2	1.7	1.4	1.5	1.6		1.5	1.7
.7	.9	.7	.7	.6	.9	Quick	(396) .7	(425) .7
.2	.4	.3	.4	.3	.4		.3	.4
0 UND	0 UND	19 19.3	34 10.7	34 10.7	41 8.8		21 17.5	22 17.0
0 UND	19 18.9	38 9.7	55 6.6	56 6.5	60 6.1	Sales/Receivables	41 8.8	45 8.0
15 24.7	50 7.3	66 5.5	74 4.9	62 5.9	68 5.4		64 5.7	69 5.3
						Cost of Sales/Inventory		
						Cost of Sales/Payables		
3.2	5.6	5.0	5.3	4.3	4.3		5.0	4.6
NM	23.0	64.7	13.8	18.3	12.2	Sales/Working Capital	24.4	16.6
-10.3	-5.1	-4.8	-12.5	-11.4	170.7		-6.6	-7.7
12.0	20.7	13.0	9.5	5.5	5.5		4.5	5.7
(15) 2.3	(60) 6.0	(107) 4.0	(103) 4.2	(37) 2.9	(37) 2.6	EBIT/Interest	(353) 1.6	(389) 2.2
-2.8	1.3	1.9	2.1	1.9	.7		-.4	.7
		3.7	2.3				2.8	3.0
		(21) 1.8	(30) 1.7			Net Profit + Depr., Dep., Amort./Cur. Mat. L/T/D	(100) 1.2	(84) 1.6
		1.3	1.0				.5	.9
.3	.7	.7	.9	.8	1.0		.8	.7
2.5	1.6	1.7	1.7	2.1	2.0	Fixed/Worth	1.8	1.5
UND	10.1	3.1	3.0	4.6	3.6		4.5	3.3
1.1	.6	.9	1.2	1.4	1.1		.9	.9
5.0	2.0	1.9	1.9	2.4	2.7	Debt/Worth	2.1	1.7
UND	55.5	3.6	4.1	4.6	6.2		5.7	4.8
149.7	56.2	35.5	40.3	33.2	19.5		24.6	26.4
(18) 20.7	(55) 18.8	(106) 18.9	(97) 24.2	(35) 14.8	(37) 11.4	% Profit Before Taxes/Tangible Net Worth	(348) 6.7	(381) 9.2
-35.8	.6	6.1	9.6	6.6	-1.0		-11.2	-.3
28.5	21.3	14.4	11.4	7.5	6.3		8.5	9.1
6.3	8.2	6.7	7.1	4.8	3.5	% Profit Before Taxes/Total Assets	1.4	2.7
-4.1	.3	1.6	3.0	2.0	-.5		-4.7	-1.3
72.7	5.6	4.7	3.9	6.0	1.9		4.9	5.9
7.4	1.5	1.6	1.4	1.2	1.0	Sales/Net Fixed Assets	1.4	1.6
.9	.5	.8	.8	.6	.6		.7	.8
5.2	1.7	1.3	1.2	.9	.9		1.4	1.4
1.3	.8	.9	.8	.6	.6	Sales/Total Assets	.8	.8
.4	.3	.4	.6	.5	.4		.5	.5
3.2	8.1	6.4	9.9	6.0			6.8	7.1
(17) 15.0	(58) 20.8	(97) 11.9	(89) 14.4	(26) 13.7		% Depr., Dep., Amort./Sales	(317) 14.4	(337) 14.8
42.4	47.6	33.0	21.3	22.8			30.3	28.1
	2.4	2.1	.9				2.2	1.8
	(24) 4.9	(26) 3.8	(17) 2.6			% Officers', Directors' Owners' Comp/Sales	(86) 4.2	(89) 4.1
	10.6	6.5	4.3				7.4	7.2
15456M	116247M	641619M	2372723M	2178102M	4535043M	Net Sales ($)	8742446M	9404533M
5896M	88291M	601509M	2607484M	2810104M	6124197M	Total Assets ($)	10872783M	10785786M

M = $ thousand MM = $ million

See Pages 9 through 22 for Explanation of Ratios and Data

Comparative Historical Data | **Current Data Sorted by Sales**

						Type of Statement												
	64		47		40	Unqualified		3		1		1		3		7		25
	87		75		82	Reviewed		6		7		10		13		25		21
	58		52		47	Compiled		10		12		7		10		6		2
	50		40		45	Tax Returns		23		15		2		2		2		1
	161		184		182	Other		26		28		11		25		35		57
	4/1/11-3/31/12		4/1/12-3/31/13		4/1/13-3/31/14			56 (4/1-9/30/13)						340 (10/1/13-3/31/14)				
	ALL		ALL		ALL			0-1MM		1-3MM		3-5MM		5-10MM		10-25MM		25MM & OVER
	420		398		396	NUMBER OF STATEMENTS		68		63		31		53		75		106
	%		%		%	ASSETS		%		%		%		%		%		%
	10.0		9.8		9.1	Cash & Equivalents		10.7		16.4		10.7		8.8		5.9		5.8
	15.5		13.7		12.9	Trade Receivables (net)		4.9		12.3		11.9		16.3		15.5		15.0
	11.5		10.2		10.7	Inventory		4.5		5.5		14.0		10.3		16.7		12.8
	2.5		2.8		2.4	All Other Current		3.8		2.0		2.3		3.1		.9		2.6
	39.4		36.5		35.2	Total Current		23.9		36.2		38.9		38.5		39.0		36.2
	50.5		54.3		53.9	Fixed Assets (net)		62.9		50.5		50.7		56.1		51.3		51.7
	2.5		3.5		3.1	Intangibles (net)		3.6		2.3		2.1		2.5		2.6		4.2
	7.6		5.6		7.9	All Other Non-Current		9.6		11.0		8.3		2.9		7.0		7.9
	100.0		100.0		100.0	Total		100.0		100.0		100.0		100.0		100.0		100.0
						LIABILITIES												
	9.9		10.2		9.0	Notes Payable-Short Term		8.8		3.9		9.4		9.3		10.2		11.2
	9.2		8.5		8.3	Cur. Mat.-L.T.D.		9.9		10.8		11.0		8.1		8.5		5.1
	6.2		5.2		4.8	Trade Payables		1.9		2.3		5.0		5.9		6.9		5.9
	.3		.2		.4	Income Taxes Payable		.2		.5		.6		.1		.4		.5
	6.7		7.0		5.9	All Other Current		4.4		11.3		5.1		5.7		3.6		5.6
	32.4		31.1		28.4	Total Current		25.4		28.9		31.1		29.0		29.6		28.2
	27.4		31.5		31.5	Long-Term Debt		34.7		34.7		26.6		29.4		32.8		29.2
	1.5		1.3		1.4	Deferred Taxes		.8		1.0		1.2		1.7		1.4		2.0
	4.1		4.3		5.3	All Other Non-Current		5.2		9.0		3.6		3.6		3.6		5.7
	34.6		31.8		33.4	Net Worth		34.0		26.4		37.5		36.4		32.7		34.9
	100.0		100.0		100.0	Total Liabilties & Net Worth		100.0		100.0		100.0		100.0		100.0		100.0
						INCOME DATA												
	100.0		100.0		100.0	Net Sales		100.0		100.0		100.0		100.0		100.0		100.0
						Gross Profit												
	88.2		87.8		85.4	Operating Expenses		69.3		87.1		88.2		88.9		88.0		90.3
	11.8		12.2		14.6	Operating Profit		30.7		12.9		11.8		11.1		12.0		9.7
	2.3		2.4		2.7	All Other Expenses (net)		6.0		2.6		.2		1.5		1.6		2.7
	9.5		9.8		11.9	Profit Before Taxes		24.7		10.3		11.6		9.6		10.4		7.0
						RATIOS												
	2.3		2.4		2.2			2.6		2.7		2.1		2.8		1.8		2.2
	1.3		1.3		1.2	Current		.7		1.0		1.3		1.5		1.2		1.3
	.6		.7		.6			.3		.5		.6		.8		.9		1.0
	1.6		1.6		1.6			1.8		2.2		1.6		1.7		1.4		1.5
	.8		.8		.7	Quick		.5		.8		.6		.9		.7		.9
	.4		.4		.4			.1		.3		.4		.3		.5		.4
19	19.1	19	19.6	15	24.4		0	UND	0	UND	28	13.2	28	12.9	32	11.4	41	8.8
46	7.9	46	8.0	45	8.2	Sales/Receivables	0	UND	32	11.4	36	10.1	47	7.7	49	7.4	57	6.4
72	5.1	66	5.5	65	5.6		39	9.4	58	6.3	49	7.4	68	5.4	74	4.9	69	5.3
						Cost of Sales/Inventory												
						Cost of Sales/Payables												
	4.5		5.3		5.0			5.3		5.3		4.4		5.0		5.6		4.7
	17.0		16.5		19.6	Sales/Working Capital		-11.1		UND		14.2		7.9		16.9		11.4
	-8.6		-9.4		-8.6			-2.1		-4.5		-8.6		-17.8		-32.3		-131.8
	8.3		9.0		9.9			18.9		9.9		8.7		15.4		9.2		7.9
(379)	3.1	(359)	3.4	(359)	3.5	EBIT/Interest	(52)	4.7	(52)	3.4	(29)	3.6	(50)	3.4	(74)	4.2	(102)	3.1
	1.4		1.6		1.9			1.5		.7		2.4		1.6		2.2		1.9
	3.7		4.6		2.9					5.8				4.1		2.4		4.9
(102)	1.9	(76)	2.3	(67)	1.8	Net Profit + Depr., Dep., Amort./Cur. Mat. L/T/D			(10)	1.9			(12)	1.5	(17)	1.8	(18)	2.4
	1.0		1.1		1.2					.7				1.3		1.3		1.7
	.6		.7		.8			.9		.6		.5		.8		.8		.8
	1.4		1.7		1.8	Fixed/Worth		1.8		1.9		1.6		2.4		1.7		1.7
	2.9		4.1		3.7			8.8		UND		2.8		4.7		2.9		3.4
	.9		.9		1.0			.5		.8		1.1		.8		1.3		1.1
	1.7		2.0		2.1	Debt/Worth		1.7		2.6		1.8		2.1		1.9		2.0
	3.9		5.2		4.8			10.8		UND		3.3		5.0		3.1		4.5
	36.5		37.2		36.6			28.8		50.5		38.7		47.9		36.8		30.3
(377)	15.0	(344)	18.4	(348)	18.5	% Profit Before Taxes/Tangible Net Worth	(56)	12.0	(48)	18.1	(30)	23.8	(47)	25.0	(69)	25.7	(98)	14.6
	4.5		4.5		5.5			.3		-.6		12.1		7.9		11.5		6.0
	12.6		11.5		13.0			16.0		17.1		12.0		14.0		12.3		10.1
	5.2		5.9		6.2	% Profit Before Taxes/Total Assets		6.6		6.8		7.2		6.7		7.0		4.7
	.8		1.3		1.5			.5		-2.2		3.4		2.3		3.3		1.6
	7.2		5.0		4.9			1.7		6.5		5.7		4.6		5.8		7.6
	1.9		1.5		1.4	Sales/Net Fixed Assets		.5		1.7		2.0		1.6		1.6		1.4
	.8		.8		.7			.3		.8		1.2		.9		1.0		.8
	1.5		1.5		1.3			.6		1.5		1.7		1.6		1.3		1.3
	.9		.9		.8	Sales/Total Assets		.3		.9		1.0		.9		.9		.8
	.5		.5		.5			.2		.4		.6		.6		.6		.5
	5.2		6.2		7.6			16.2		10.0		7.2		6.7		8.9		2.9
(324)	12.3	(304)	15.4	(296)	13.7	% Depr., Dep., Amort./Sales	(57)	35.1	(46)	19.2	(25)	11.9	(48)	13.2	(62)	12.9	(58)	9.9
	24.1		25.6		29.0			59.3		55.2		16.5		23.3		19.9		15.8
	1.8		2.2		1.9					2.0		2.1		2.4				.6
(100)	3.6	(93)	4.0	(75)	3.5	% Officers', Directors' Owners' Comp/Sales			(16)	4.6	(11)	3.2	(16)	5.3			(14)	1.2
	6.7		6.3		7.1					7.9		6.4		8.6				2.9
	9162167M		10002523M		9859190M	Net Sales ($)		30317M		112962M		123357M		375806M		1187261M		8029487M
	11186115M		11617453M		12237481M	Total Assets ($)		92059M		196046M		148828M		489831M		1598628M		9712089M

M = $ thousand MM = $ million

See Pages 9 through 22 for Explanation of Ratios and Data

Current Data Sorted by Assets							Comparative Historical Data	
						Type of Statement		
		3	5	5	4	Unqualified	18	14
1	1	5	3	2		Reviewed	9	19
2	4	4	3			Compiled	17	21
4	9	7				Tax Returns	22	31
8	5	15	7	4	3	Other	44	40
14 (4/1-9/30/13)			90 (10/1/13-3/31/14)				4/1/09-3/31/10 ALL	4/1/10-3/31/11 ALL
0-500M	**500M-2MM**	**2-10MM**	**10-50MM**	**50-100MM**	**100-250MM**			
15	19	34	18	11	7	**NUMBER OF STATEMENTS**	110	125
%	%	%	%	%	%	**ASSETS**	%	%
28.1	20.5	8.4	6.2	4.4		Cash & Equivalents	11.1	11.9
8.4	19.7	14.4	13.1	18.5		Trade Receivables (net)	14.5	14.2
4.6	4.2	6.0	6.4	6.8		Inventory	7.4	7.0
9.0	.0	3.8	3.4	7.0		All Other Current	8.4	6.9
50.1	44.4	32.6	29.1	36.7		Total Current	41.4	40.0
47.0	39.6	51.0	47.5	46.1		Fixed Assets (net)	41.5	43.4
.0	7.0	1.4	2.9	5.1		Intangibles (net)	2.0	2.9
2.9	8.9	15.1	20.5	12.2		All Other Non-Current	15.1	13.7
100.0	100.0	100.0	100.0	100.0		Total	100.0	100.0
						LIABILITIES		
27.9	6.9	6.3	5.7	4.9		Notes Payable-Short Term	10.4	15.8
3.4	12.6	9.2	11.2	11.7		Cur. Mat.-L.T.D.	9.3	8.4
3.3	6.9	6.9	4.9	5.0		Trade Payables	6.9	7.4
.0	.0	.1	.0	.2		Income Taxes Payable	.2	.1
11.3	5.9	8.1	5.3	10.3		All Other Current	12.9	9.8
45.8	32.4	30.6	27.1	32.1		Total Current	39.6	41.5
18.6	22.9	32.9	39.1	41.1		Long-Term Debt	30.3	30.0
.0	.0	.6	.4	1.5		Deferred Taxes	.5	.4
8.6	11.0	10.4	2.1	6.8		All Other Non-Current	6.4	5.7
26.9	33.7	25.4	31.3	18.4		Net Worth	23.3	22.4
100.0	100.0	100.0	100.0	100.0		Total Liabilties & Net Worth	100.0	100.0
						INCOME DATA		
100.0	100.0	100.0	100.0	100.0		Net Sales	100.0	100.0
						Gross Profit		
77.3	86.6	83.5	89.6	86.2		Operating Expenses	84.8	80.4
22.7	13.4	16.5	10.4	13.8		Operating Profit	15.2	19.6
2.2	3.4	7.4	6.0	7.0		All Other Expenses (net)	6.6	5.6
20.5	10.1	9.1	4.4	6.8		Profit Before Taxes	8.6	14.0
						RATIOS		
2.9	5.0	1.8	2.4	1.8			2.4	2.4
1.1	1.4	1.1	1.3	1.4		Current	1.2	1.0
.4	.8	.4	.7	.3			.5	.4
1.3	3.1	1.4	1.9	1.4			1.8	1.5
1.0	1.4	.7	.8	.6		Quick	.7	.5
.3	.8	.3	.3	.3			.2	.2
0 UND	**16** 22.7	**4** 95.4	**26** 14.2	**19** 18.8			**0** UND	**0** UND
14 25.3	**32** 11.5	**29** 12.6	**44** 8.3	**30** 12.3		Sales/Receivables	**19** 19.2	**21** 17.5
36 10.2	**54** 6.7	**42** 8.7	**70** 5.2	**60** 6.1			**52** 7.1	**51** 7.1
						Cost of Sales/Inventory		
						Cost of Sales/Payables		
3.0	4.8	6.9	4.1	1.6			2.7	5.2
45.7	8.3	51.0	27.4	13.0		Sales/Working Capital	17.4	-281.0
-8.4	-11.2	-5.5	-9.9	-1.5			-5.6	-4.5
	17.3	8.6	3.9	3.2			7.1	9.5
	(14) 3.3	(31) 3.0	(16) 1.8	2.3		EBIT/Interest	(91) 2.3	(92) 2.8
	1.7	1.2	1.1	1.8			1.0	1.2
						Net Profit + Depr., Dep., Amort./Cur. Mat. L/T/D		
.0	.1	1.0	.6	.9			.2	.3
1.7	2.0	1.8	1.4	3.0		Fixed/Worth	1.8	1.7
3.8	-2.4	6.4	5.0	6.8			7.4	7.4
.7	.5	1.1	1.1	2.0			1.5	1.0
2.2	3.5	3.3	3.5	6.2		Debt/Worth	3.8	3.3
146.0	-7.0	10.7	7.3	6.4			26.3	26.2
112.2	81.3	37.1	36.6				42.8	51.3
(12) 39.8	(13) 19.4	(28) 18.0	(17) 21.3			% Profit Before Taxes/Tangible Net Worth	(87) 16.9	(100) 19.7
9.8	4.1	5.8	4.2				2.6	9.5
46.6	14.0	11.1	5.9	5.2			12.1	15.5
13.3	4.4	3.9	2.7	3.2		% Profit Before Taxes/Total Assets	4.5	5.1
6.3	3.6	.7	.7	2.1			.0	.2
999.8	28.8	5.3	12.6	8.6			37.6	20.6
2.9	3.7	1.1	1.8	2.0		Sales/Net Fixed Assets	2.6	2.3
1.8	.8	.4	.5	.5			.8	.7
2.2	2.7	1.8	1.3	.9			1.7	2.0
1.5	1.0	.6	.6	.5		Sales/Total Assets	.7	.8
1.1	.6	.3	.3	.3			.4	.4
	1.8	5.7	2.0				2.4	2.9
	(14) 12.2	(29) 23.7	(15) 18.0			% Depr., Dep., Amort./Sales	(70) 14.6	(83) 16.5
	69.1	57.9	72.4				62.3	54.5
		2.9					4.2	1.8
		(11) 5.4				% Officers', Directors' Owners' Comp/Sales	(19) 5.3	(24) 7.0
		11.8					11.8	11.4
13225M	**39919M**	**230641M**	**339589M**	**514538M**	**497725M**	Net Sales ($)	**1612105M**	**1231676M**
3471M	**23068M**	**171614M**	**408775M**	**793710M**	**1036609M**	Total Assets ($)	**2952130M**	**1430599M**

M = $ thousand MM = $ million

See Pages 9 through 22 for Explanation of Ratios and Data

Comparative Historical Data | **Current Data Sorted by Sales**

4/1/11-3/31/12 ALL	4/1/12-3/31/13 ALL	4/1/13-3/31/14 ALL	Type of Statement	0-1MM	1-3MM	3-5MM	5-10MM	10-25MM	25MM & OVER
14	11	17	Unqualified		2	1	3	2	9
16	12	12	Reviewed	1	2	2	3	2	2
27	17	13	Compiled	5	3	1	1	1	2
38	35	20	Tax Returns	11	6		2	1	
37	51	42	Other	11	5	6	4	7	9
				14 (4/1-9/30/13)			90 (10/1/13-3/31/14)		
132	126	104	**NUMBER OF STATEMENTS**	28	18	10	13	13	22
%	%	%	**ASSETS**	%	%	%	%	%	%
9.5	10.3	12.2	Cash & Equivalents	13.8	20.3	17.8	10.5	6.3	5.6
15.0	13.7	14.0	Trade Receivables (net)	9.4	12.0	5.0	16.8	33.6	12.5
6.5	4.7	5.6	Inventory	1.4	4.6	1.3	7.4	10.8	9.5
5.5	5.3	5.7	All Other Current	6.6	.2	2.4	3.1	2.1	14.1
36.6	34.0	37.5	Total Current	31.2	37.0	26.5	37.8	52.8	41.8
48.8	51.3	44.3	Fixed Assets (net)	54.6	43.5	58.7	48.5	27.3	32.8
3.3	1.9	3.0	Intangibles (net)	3.6	2.9	.8	.2	1.3	5.7
11.3	12.7	15.2	All Other Non-Current	10.6	16.6	14.0	13.5	18.5	19.7
100.0	100.0	100.0	Total	100.0	100.0	100.0	100.0	100.0	100.0
			LIABILITIES						
11.0	7.4	8.9	Notes Payable-Short Term	16.9	3.7	14.8	5.8	8.5	2.4
9.6	8.2	9.6	Cur. Mat.-L.T.D.	10.3	6.3	10.6	16.2	3.5	10.7
6.1	5.2	5.5	Trade Payables	3.0	5.3	.4	8.5	6.7	8.6
.4	.2	.1	Income Taxes Payable	.0	.0	.0	.0	.3	.2
8.4	7.1	7.8	All Other Current	3.6	4.3	18.0	6.2	17.5	6.3
35.5	28.0	31.9	Total Current	33.9	19.7	43.8	36.7	36.5	28.3
29.3	38.6	32.0	Long-Term Debt	28.8	43.8	26.3	30.3	19.8	37.2
.2	.2	.4	Deferred Taxes	.0	.0	.0	.4	1.7	.8
7.2	7.7	8.6	All Other Non-Current	4.8	16.5	4.8	13.6	5.4	7.4
27.8	25.5	27.1	Net Worth	32.5	19.9	25.0	19.0	36.6	26.3
100.0	100.0	100.0	Total Liabilities & Net Worth	100.0	100.0	100.0	100.0	100.0	100.0
			INCOME DATA						
100.0	100.0	100.0	Net Sales	100.0	100.0	100.0	100.0	100.0	100.0
			Gross Profit						
79.2	78.7	84.4	Operating Expenses	72.4	88.1	87.8	90.5	87.6	89.6
20.8	21.3	15.6	Operating Profit	27.6	11.9	12.2	9.5	12.4	10.4
4.6	4.4	5.8	All Other Expenses (net)	7.9	5.7	6.0	3.4	5.8	4.4
16.2	16.9	9.8	Profit Before Taxes	19.8	6.2	6.3	6.1	6.6	5.9
			RATIOS						
2.0	3.1	2.3		2.3	3.7	1.7	1.7	2.8	1.8
1.0	1.2	1.3	Current	.9	1.8	.8	1.3	2.0	1.5
.4	.4	.6		.3	.7	.1	.6	1.1	.8
1.4	2.2	1.7		1.2	3.1	1.5	1.6	2.2	1.1
.6	.8	.8	Quick	.6	1.7	.5	.7	1.4	.7
.2	.3	.3		.2	.7	.1	.3	.8	.3
0 UND	0 UND	10 35.6		0 UND	5 79.8	0 UND	23 16.1	12 31.6	24 15.3
21 17.3	21 17.7	30 12.3	Sales/Receivables	14 26.0	25 14.8	24 15.4	44 8.3	37 9.8	33 11.2
47 7.8	60 6.1	51 7.2		52 7.0	43 8.4	51 7.2	74 4.9	81 4.5	43 8.5
			Cost of Sales/Inventory						
			Cost of Sales/Payables						
7.1	5.7	4.6		2.1	3.9	21.4	6.4	3.4	3.8
NM	30.2	16.8	Sales/Working Capital	UND	9.8	-21.8	14.5	7.0	12.3
-4.0	-5.9	-9.7		-3.9	-7.3	-1.6	-7.4	86.8	-16.9
9.8	9.7	7.7		6.8	10.7		6.4	9.6	7.9
(105) 3.2	(102) 3.7	(86) 2.3	EBIT/Interest	(17) 3.4	(16) 2.2		1.9	(12) 3.2	(21) 3.2
1.7	1.9	1.5		1.6	1.1		1.1	1.6	1.8
8.6	14.7	10.9							
(17) 4.0	(14) 4.3	(14) 1.9	Net Profit + Depr., Dep., Amort./Cur. Mat. L/T/D						
1.5	.8	.7							
.5	.6	.5		.6	.1	1.0	.9	.3	.1
1.7	2.0	1.6	Fixed/Worth	1.8	2.8	2.0	2.1	.7	1.2
8.5	14.0	5.3		8.9	-16.9	NM	4.1	1.1	5.2
.9	1.0	1.2		.8	1.0	1.4	2.1	.8	1.8
2.9	3.2	3.5	Debt/Worth	2.0	7.4	3.9	3.5	2.6	4.4
12.4	18.8	10.1		10.4	-14.1	NM	6.0	4.2	7.3
57.4	49.3	47.6		51.0	37.8		77.7	43.8	46.7
(108) 23.8	(101) 20.2	(86) 19.4	% Profit Before Taxes/Tangible Net Worth	(23) 13.7	(11) 30.3		(12) 26.6	(12) 15.0	(20) 21.8
7.5	9.2	6.3		5.5	6.8		3.6	4.3	13.3
14.7	15.6	12.3		13.8	8.6	11.0	13.5	13.3	8.2
6.1	7.4	4.1	% Profit Before Taxes/Total Assets	5.7	4.0	1.8	3.6	4.7	4.5
1.5	2.3	1.3		1.3	1.5	-.2	.6	1.0	2.1
12.1	10.6	17.0		3.5	32.3	12.0	7.4	19.6	23.7
2.0	1.9	2.2	Sales/Net Fixed Assets	1.1	1.7	1.6	3.7	8.8	6.6
.7	.6	.8		.4	.5	.7	.8	2.7	1.8
1.9	1.9	1.8		1.3	2.3	4.2	2.2	3.2	1.8
.8	.7	.8	Sales/Total Assets	.6	.6	.6	.9	1.8	.9
.4	.4	.3		.2	.3	.4	.5	.2	.5
2.6	4.8	2.6		14.6	6.6		2.9	1.6	1.8
(96) 13.3	(89) 17.9	(75) 15.6	% Depr., Dep., Amort./Sales	(21) 27.1	(11) 47.1		(12) 15.3	(11) 2.0	(13) 3.2
37.3	52.2	51.7		69.9	60.2		26.9	5.3	10.7
2.2	2.6	2.8							
(34) 5.8	(26) 6.0	(27) 5.4	% Officers', Directors' Owners' Comp/Sales						
11.3	11.5	11.8							
2098727M	1537125M	1635637M	Net Sales ($)	11350M	28105M	42107M	98375M	174658M	1281042M
2160236M	2340057M	2437247M	Total Assets ($)	41240M	77524M	89096M	120859M	458956M	1649572M

M = $ thousand MM = $ million

See Pages 9 through 22 for Explanation of Ratios and Data

Current Data Sorted by Assets							Comparative Historical Data	
						Type of Statement		
	2	11	27	19	9	Unqualified	74	69
3	14	37	36	4		Reviewed	85	95
9	20	33	4		2	Compiled	69	81
34	62	43	3			Tax Returns	114	108
19	60	121	67	17	23	Other	220	207
	79 (4/1-9/30/13)		600 (10/1/13-3/31/14)				4/1/09-3/31/10	4/1/10-3/31/11
0-500M	500M-2MM	2-10MM	10-50MM	50-100MM	100-250MM		ALL	ALL
65	158	245	137	40	34	**NUMBER OF STATEMENTS**	562	560
%	%	%	%	%	%	**ASSETS**	%	%
20.3	12.2	8.7	8.1	6.9	2.7	Cash & Equivalents	9.2	9.2
8.8	14.3	12.8	15.1	13.6	20.6	Trade Receivables (net)	14.1	15.0
3.0	4.9	7.2	10.2	7.7	5.0	Inventory	6.9	6.0
1.8	2.6	3.0	2.8	4.2	5.5	All Other Current	4.5	4.6
33.9	33.9	31.7	36.2	32.3	33.8	Total Current	34.7	34.8
55.9	54.5	59.4	47.5	56.1	38.3	Fixed Assets (net)	53.2	52.7
.4	3.7	2.7	3.3	2.0	8.1	Intangibles (net)	2.3	3.3
9.9	7.9	6.2	13.0	9.6	19.8	All Other Non-Current	9.8	9.2
100.0	100.0	100.0	100.0	100.0	100.0	Total	100.0	100.0
						LIABILITIES		
13.2	7.5	6.4	10.7	7.8	8.9	Notes Payable-Short Term	10.8	9.8
14.2	7.2	7.2	6.7	6.5	3.9	Cur. Mat.-L.T.D.	10.3	10.1
3.5	7.1	5.4	5.1	4.1	3.7	Trade Payables	5.3	5.9
.1	.1	.1	.2	.1	.2	Income Taxes Payable	.1	.3
13.4	7.4	6.6	5.6	4.7	4.1	All Other Current	7.7	7.8
44.5	29.3	25.7	28.4	23.2	20.8	Total Current	34.2	34.0
46.8	45.2	35.9	29.2	43.2	45.5	Long-Term Debt	32.3	32.6
.3	.2	.5	1.5	.3	3.8	Deferred Taxes	.6	.8
11.9	4.5	4.2	5.2	3.5	3.2	All Other Non-Current	5.8	7.4
-3.5	20.8	33.7	35.7	29.7	26.6	Net Worth	27.2	25.2
100.0	100.0	100.0	100.0	100.0	100.0	Total Liabilties & Net Worth	100.0	100.0
						INCOME DATA		
100.0	100.0	100.0	100.0	100.0	100.0	Net Sales	100.0	100.0
						Gross Profit		
73.1	73.9	74.8	82.0	80.2	71.1	Operating Expenses	82.6	83.2
26.9	26.1	25.2	18.0	19.8	28.9	Operating Profit	17.4	16.8
2.4	8.2	8.3	5.3	7.6	11.0	All Other Expenses (net)	6.8	5.3
24.5	17.9	17.0	12.6	12.1	17.9	Profit Before Taxes	10.6	11.5
						RATIOS		
2.7	2.7	2.5	2.0	2.2	5.4		2.2	2.3
.7	1.3	1.1	1.3	1.2	1.5	Current	1.1	1.1
.2	.5	.4	.7	.6	1.1		.5	.5
2.7	2.0	1.7	1.5	1.4	3.2		1.5	1.7
.5	(157) 1.0	.7	.8	.6	1.0	Quick	.7	.7
.2	.3	.2	.4	.4	.6		.3	.3
0 UND	0 UND	0 UND	20 18.3	17 21.8	10 35.5		0 UND	1 490.2
0 UND	16 22.7	17 21.4	46 7.9	50 7.3	65 5.6	Sales/Receivables	27 13.3	31 11.8
7 51.2	41 8.8	54 6.7	73 5.0	72 5.1	130 2.8		55 6.7	59 6.2
						Cost of Sales/Inventory		
						Cost of Sales/Payables		
12.2	6.5	4.5	3.6	3.7	1.0		5.5	5.2
-41.4	36.8	40.2	15.6	35.9	7.7	Sales/Working Capital	40.9	49.4
-3.7	-6.4	-5.3	-9.9	-5.7	74.5		-6.3	-6.6
23.0	15.2	10.7	13.0	8.2	7.1		6.0	8.4
(46) 8.4	(108) 4.6	(184) 4.9	(117) 4.7	(32) 3.0	(25) 3.4	EBIT/Interest	(454) 2.2	(483) 3.2
1.7	1.2	2.0	2.2	1.2	2.2		.5	1.1
	3.9	3.8	5.6				4.0	5.0
	(10) 2.1	(44) 1.8	(39) 1.8			Net Profit + Depr., Dep., Amort./Cur. Mat. L/T/D	(76) 1.6	(87) 2.1
	1.1	1.1	1.1				1.0	1.0
.6	.6	.7	.3	.6	.0		.7	.8
2.9	2.1	1.8	1.5	2.0	2.3	Fixed/Worth	1.8	1.8
-2.8	-17.8	6.8	2.7	3.9	4.1		9.5	9.6
.7	.8	.9	1.0	1.2	2.7		.9	.9
3.2	3.3	2.2	1.9	2.8	4.3	Debt/Worth	2.6	2.3
-4.7	-25.2	8.0	4.2	9.2	10.5		15.9	14.8
184.4	72.5	46.1	39.7	36.7	46.1		40.0	40.8
(45) 54.4	(112) 22.9	(214) 20.7	(129) 18.2	(37) 15.3	(31) 17.9	% Profit Before Taxes/Tangible Net Worth	(456) 16.4	(450) 18.2
24.8	2.8	5.6	5.3	4.4	10.6		1.8	2.6
53.4	29.8	12.0	11.9	9.4	7.5		13.6	14.1
21.5	7.7	5.6	5.9	4.0	3.8	% Profit Before Taxes/Total Assets	3.4	4.9
4.0	.4	1.5	1.9	.2	1.7		-1.0	.1
14.6	9.6	5.6	8.4	2.9	61.5		6.3	6.0
2.7	2.5	1.3	1.9	.8	1.6	Sales/Net Fixed Assets	1.8	2.2
1.2	.5	.2	.8	.4	.7		.7	.8
4.1	2.4	1.6	1.4	.7	.6		1.5	1.8
1.9	.9	.7	.7	.4	.3	Sales/Total Assets	.8	.9
.8	.3	.2	.3	.2	.1		.4	.4
4.9	6.3	6.1	4.3	9.8	.9		5.3	6.5
(39) 9.9	(111) 16.3	(204) 14.8	(113) 10.0	(27) 18.2	(13) 3.2	% Depr., Dep., Amort./Sales	(446) 16.6	(449) 15.1
25.4	35.4	24.2	21.0	35.8	13.5		35.5	35.2
4.4	4.2	2.0	.7				2.2	1.9
(14) 5.9	(43) 6.3	(48) 3.9	(21) 2.2			% Officers', Directors' Owners' Comp/Sales	(114) 4.5	(122) 4.9
15.6	14.4	9.1	4.5				10.2	9.6
48692M	283319M	1154939M	2940987M	1377955M	2353758M	Net Sales ($)	10671039M	7744054M
16820M	179584M	1170834M	3243939M	2741052M	5410376M	Total Assets ($)	10084459M	8810970M

M = $ thousand MM = $ million

See Pages 9 through 22 for Explanation of Ratios and Data

Comparative Historical Data | **Current Data Sorted by Sales**

4/1/11-3/31/12 ALL	4/1/12-3/31/13 ALL	4/1/13-3/31/14 ALL	Type of Statement	0-1MM	1-3MM	3-5MM	5-10MM	10-25MM	25MM & OVER
75	55	68	Unqualified	3	5	2	10	23	25
85	79	94	Reviewed	8	19	9	22	20	16
92	80	68	Compiled	25	18	9	8	6	2
145	119	142	Tax Returns	85	30	9	11	9	
271	274	307	Other	79	70	31	34	40	53
				79 (4/1-9/30/13)			600 (10/1/13-3/31/14)		
668	607	679	**NUMBER OF STATEMENTS**	200	142	58	85	98	96
%	%	%	**ASSETS**	%	%	%	%	%	%
10.9	10.4	10.1	Cash & Equivalents	10.6	12.4	6.9	11.3	9.5	6.9
13.3	13.3	13.7	Trade Receivables (net)	5.4	12.8	15.7	20.7	20.3	18.0
5.5	7.2	6.8	Inventory	.9	4.5	11.9	7.4	11.6	13.9
3.8	3.9	2.9	All Other Current	1.7	4.6	3.4	2.2	4.2	2.2
33.4	34.8	33.5	Total Current	18.7	34.2	37.8	41.6	45.6	41.0
54.1	50.9	54.3	Fixed Assets (net)	70.3	54.3	49.5	44.7	42.9	43.8
3.6	3.7	3.1	Intangibles (net)	1.6	3.5	4.6	3.6	2.8	4.4
8.9	10.6	9.2	All Other Non-Current	9.3	7.9	8.2	10.2	8.7	10.9
100.0	100.0	100.0	Total	100.0	100.0	100.0	100.0	100.0	100.0
			LIABILITIES						
9.3	9.4	8.4	Notes Payable-Short Term	6.4	7.7	12.5	7.9	8.7	11.1
7.6	7.5	7.6	Cur. Mat.-L.T.D.	9.4	8.0	6.8	8.1	5.8	5.0
5.0	6.0	5.4	Trade Payables	1.6	5.0	8.5	8.1	7.9	7.2
.2	.2	.1	Income Taxes Payable	.0	.1	.1	.1	.3	.1
6.8	7.1	7.0	All Other Current	6.6	8.8	5.6	6.0	6.8	7.0
28.9	30.2	28.5	Total Current	24.0	29.5	33.5	30.3	29.6	30.4
37.1	36.0	38.7	Long-Term Debt	51.7	42.2	33.1	28.2	29.2	28.3
.8	.9	.8	Deferred Taxes	.1	.3	.5	1.3	.8	2.3
6.1	5.8	5.1	All Other Non-Current	6.5	3.5	5.5	6.4	5.0	3.4
27.2	27.1	27.0	Net Worth	17.6	24.5	27.4	33.8	35.4	35.5
100.0	100.0	100.0	Total Liabilties & Net Worth	100.0	100.0	100.0	100.0	100.0	100.0
			INCOME DATA						
100.0	100.0	100.0	Net Sales	100.0	100.0	100.0	100.0	100.0	100.0
			Gross Profit						
76.1	77.9	76.0	Operating Expenses	58.6	77.9	78.9	88.5	86.4	86.1
23.9	22.1	24.0	Operating Profit	41.4	22.1	21.1	11.5	13.6	13.9
8.0	6.2	7.2	All Other Expenses (net)	13.8	5.9	5.4	3.3	4.3	2.9
15.9	15.9	16.8	Profit Before Taxes	27.6	16.1	15.7	8.3	9.3	11.0
			RATIOS						
2.6	2.5	2.5		2.4	3.3	2.5	2.5	3.1	1.7
1.2	1.2	1.2	Current	.7	1.2	1.4	1.4	1.4	1.3
.5	.6	.5		.1	.5	.7	.8	.9	.9
1.9	1.7	1.8		1.9	2.5	1.8	1.8	1.8	1.3
(667) .8	(606) .8	(678) .8	Quick	.5	.8	(57) .9	.9	.9	.9
.3	.3	.3		.1	.2	.3	.5	.4	.5
0 UND	**0** UND	**0** UND		**0** UND	**0** UND	**8** 45.0	**17** 21.2	**21** 17.3	**24** 15.0
26 14.2	**24** 15.4	**24** 15.5	Sales/Receivables	**0** UND	**14** 26.7	**32** 11.3	**40** 9.2	**45** 8.1	**51** 7.2
54 6.8	**54** 6.8	**60** 6.1		**10** 35.3	**55** 6.6	**66** 5.5	**68** 5.4	**74** 4.9	**66** 5.5
			Cost of Sales/Inventory						
			Cost of Sales/Payables						
4.5	4.5	4.9		4.0	4.7	4.6	5.1	3.4	6.3
22.4	24.0	27.7	Sales/Working Capital	-10.8	43.9	19.9	17.0	13.3	12.7
-6.3	-6.6	-6.5		-2.2	-5.1	-29.0	-18.0	-39.0	-93.0
11.2	11.8	12.0		13.9	8.3	19.9	8.7	13.9	16.9
(517) 4.2	(473) 4.2	(512) 4.7	EBIT/Interest	(114) 5.3	(100) 3.1	(52) 6.0	(72) 3.7	(87) 4.8	(87) 4.9
1.6	1.7	1.9		1.9	1.1	2.9	1.7	1.8	2.5
4.1	3.5	3.8		2.7	2.8		3.9	6.9	17.2
(92) 2.2	(78) 1.8	(105) 1.7	Net Profit + Depr., Dep., Amort./Cur. Mat. L/T/D	(18) 2.0	(19) 1.4		(15) 1.7	(26) 1.6	(20) 2.4
1.4	1.3	1.1		1.1	.4		1.0	1.0	1.5
.7	.5	.6		1.3	.6	.4	.3	.3	.3
1.8	1.7	1.9	Fixed/Worth	3.5	1.9	1.4	1.4	1.3	1.5
6.0	6.4	6.5		68.3	10.1	3.3	3.7	2.8	3.4
.9	.8	.9		1.0	.7	.8	.9	1.0	1.0
2.3	2.3	2.3	Debt/Worth	3.5	2.3	1.8	2.3	2.1	2.3
9.8	10.9	10.0		71.9	51.5	7.2	7.7	5.6	4.8
45.1	47.2	47.7		45.5	62.3	68.0	47.9	47.4	46.0
(549) 19.0	(494) 20.8	(568) 22.0	% Profit Before Taxes/Tangible Net Worth	(155) 23.6	(110) 16.4	(49) 24.6	(73) 22.0	(92) 17.3	(89) 27.5
6.3	6.9	6.2		6.2	1.8	10.7	5.2	5.0	11.6
15.1	16.7	15.8		16.5	19.4	27.8	13.0	12.4	13.1
5.9	6.3	6.3	% Profit Before Taxes/Total Assets	5.4	6.0	8.8	6.7	4.9	7.3
1.3	1.5	1.5		1.1	.3	3.4	1.3	1.4	3.0
7.0	7.7	7.8		1.8	7.9	14.9	12.6	18.2	17.8
1.7	2.0	1.8	Sales/Net Fixed Assets	.4	2.0	3.6	3.6	2.8	2.5
.5	.6	.5		.1	.5	.9	1.2	1.2	.9
1.8	1.8	1.7		.7	1.9	2.3	2.2	1.8	1.6
.8	.8	.7	Sales/Total Assets	.3	.8	1.2	1.2	1.1	1.0
.3	.3	.2		.1	.3	.4	.5	.4	.5
6.4	6.8	5.6		11.5	6.1	1.8	4.9	4.2	1.7
(507) 15.4	(440) 14.0	(507) 13.5	% Depr., Dep., Amort./Sales	(152) 21.8	(106) 15.6	(46) 7.9	(65) 9.7	(74) 10.0	(64) 6.8
28.9	29.0	27.0		37.4	40.6	19.9	20.0	19.8	11.6
2.1	2.1	2.3		6.0	4.6	2.3	2.2	1.1	.6
(140) 4.7	(121) 5.9	(132) 4.6	% Officers', Directors' Owners' Comp/Sales	(20) 12.6	(36) 6.7	(16) 3.9	(25) 3.5	(25) 2.9	(10) .8
9.8	10.7	9.4		23.4	16.4	8.6	6.0	4.4	1.8
9052068M	8529896M	8159650M	Net Sales ($)	90046M	257116M	229138M	618720M	1478051M	5486579M
11438913M	11180138M	12762605M	Total Assets ($)	431083M	596213M	400407M	1382428M	3174593M	6777881M

M = $ thousand MM = $ million

See Pages 9 through 22 for Explanation of Ratios and Data

Current Data Sorted by Assets							Comparative Historical Data	
Type of Statement								
Unqualified		4	6	8		3	22	22
Reviewed		1		1			1	7
Compiled	1		2				4	4
Tax Returns	2	2	2				17	17
Other	6	8	8	4	1	2	24	24
		4 (4/1-9/30/13)		57 (10/1/13-3/31/14)			4/1/09-3/31/10	4/1/10-3/31/11
	0-500M	500M-2MM	2-10MM	10-50MM	50-100MM	100-250MM	ALL	ALL
NUMBER OF STATEMENTS	9	15	18	13	1	5	68	74
ASSETS	%	%	%	%	%	%	%	%
Cash & Equivalents		13.9	9.2	23.3			14.4	21.2
Trade Receivables (net)		12.5	5.4	9.8			8.2	8.1
Inventory		1.1	1.8	7.7			2.1	3.6
All Other Current		2.2	6.0	8.7			8.4	7.8
Total Current		29.8	22.3	49.5			33.1	40.7
Fixed Assets (net)		46.2	59.0	22.5			39.6	39.0
Intangibles (net)		16.9	6.6	19.6			11.9	9.7
All Other Non-Current		7.1	12.1	8.4			15.3	10.6
Total		100.0	100.0	100.0			100.0	100.0
LIABILITIES								
Notes Payable-Short Term		2.1	2.1	1.7			7.5	5.9
Cur. Mat.-L.T.D.		3.0	2.4	2.3			11.6	5.2
Trade Payables		7.3	3.4	5.2			4.9	5.9
Income Taxes Payable		.0	.2	.3			.1	.3
All Other Current		8.9	18.9	18.5			11.9	13.2
Total Current		21.2	26.9	27.9			36.0	30.5
Long-Term Debt		31.6	36.0	23.6			35.9	29.1
Deferred Taxes		.0	.0	.2			.3	.4
All Other Non-Current		8.3	8.5	6.1			6.5	4.2
Net Worth		38.9	28.5	42.2			21.3	35.7
Total Liabilities & Net Worth		100.0	100.0	100.0			100.0	100.0
INCOME DATA								
Net Sales		100.0	100.0	100.0			100.0	100.0
Gross Profit								
Operating Expenses		59.4	52.3	72.1			74.6	70.2
Operating Profit		40.6	47.7	27.9			25.4	29.8
All Other Expenses (net)		17.1	14.4	4.3			14.1	9.7
Profit Before Taxes		23.5	33.2	23.6			11.3	20.1
RATIOS								
Current		4.4	2.9	9.4			2.9	4.0
		1.9	.8	1.5			1.0	1.2
		.3	.3	1.0			.5	.5
Quick		4.2	2.3	6.7			1.4	2.4
		1.2	.6	1.1			.6	.7
		.3	.1	.7			.2	.1
Sales/Receivables		**0** UND	**0** UND	**5** 66.4			**0** UND	**0** UND
		14 25.9	**0** UND	**32** 11.5			**5** 68.1	**5** 76.0
		46 7.9	**31** 11.7	**38** 9.5			**29** 12.7	**33** 11.2
Cost of Sales/Inventory								
Cost of Sales/Payables								
Sales/Working Capital		5.0	3.5	2.6			6.4	3.5
		11.1	-41.0	8.1			208.0	30.1
		-3.0	-3.1	NM			-4.8	-4.9
EBIT/Interest			32.4				16.3	23.9
			(10) 4.9				(44) 4.1	(40) 7.2
			2.9				1.0	3.0
Net Profit + Depr., Dep., Amort./Cur. Mat. L/T/D							8.9	
							(10) 1.1	
							.5	
Fixed/Worth		.0	1.2	.2			.5	.1
		2.1	3.4	.5			2.7	1.4
		4.9	9.0	-.3			-1.6	9.3
Debt/Worth		.9	1.7	.4			1.2	.5
		1.9	4.7	2.0			5.9	2.5
		21.3	11.9	-4.8			-8.7	-87.2
% Profit Before Taxes/Tangible Net Worth		68.4	64.2				57.2	71.8
		(12) 18.9	(15) 17.6				(43) 18.1	(55) 25.2
		8.7	11.6				.2	12.6
% Profit Before Taxes/Total Assets		18.7	11.7	23.8			14.9	25.0
		13.8	6.7	10.6			3.7	8.5
		3.2	3.7	4.0			-2.1	3.4
Sales/Net Fixed Assets		UND	16.4	32.0			33.8	114.5
		11.1	.3	11.3			4.9	5.3
		.2	.1	5.1			.3	.4
Sales/Total Assets		2.6	.9	2.0			1.8	1.5
		.3	.2	1.2			.7	.7
		.1	.1	.4			.2	.3
% Depr., Dep., Amort./Sales			2.0	.7			1.5	1.0
			(16) 7.3	(10) 1.2			(52) 3.9	(51) 3.8
			20.5	4.9			16.3	12.7
% Officers', Directors' Owners' Comp/Sales							2.1	
							(11) 8.8	
							16.8	
Net Sales ($)	3567M	15916M	113008M	361884M	17120M	442372M	2484571M	2229393M
Total Assets ($)	2316M	20976M	94266M	290576M	57575M	747282M	1551292M	1097087M

M = $ thousand MM = $ million

See Pages 9 through 22 for Explanation of Ratios and Data

Comparative Historical Data				Current Data Sorted by Sales					
			Type of Statement						
31	24	21	Unqualified	2	5	2	1	6	5
3	2	2	Reviewed	1					1
5	6	3	Compiled	2		1			
24	14	6	Tax Returns	5	1				
28	37	29	Other	18	3	2	1	1	4
4/1/11-3/31/12	4/1/12-3/31/13	4/1/13-3/31/14		4 (4/1-9/30/13)			57 (10/1/13-3/31/14)		
ALL	ALL	ALL		0-1MM	1-3MM	3-5MM	5-10MM	10-25MM	25MM & OVER
91	83	61	NUMBER OF STATEMENTS	28	9	5	2	7	10
%	%	%	**ASSETS**	%	%	%	%	%	%
14.4	10.5	15.4	Cash & Equivalents	10.2					19.2
5.7	7.2	7.4	Trade Receivables (net)	1.0					11.0
6.2	3.5	2.5	Inventory	.0					1.1
7.7	5.5	4.9	All Other Current	1.5					9.9
33.9	26.6	30.2	Total Current	12.6					41.2
40.7	46.2	38.5	Fixed Assets (net)	58.3					12.6
10.5	15.9	19.0	Intangibles (net)	16.8					33.2
14.9	11.2	12.4	All Other Non-Current	12.3					13.0
100.0	100.0	100.0	Total	100.0					100.0
			LIABILITIES						
6.7	7.6	2.9	Notes Payable-Short Term	3.0					1.1
6.6	2.9	3.0	Cur. Mat.-L.T.D.	4.1					1.9
4.1	3.4	5.6	Trade Payables	3.7					8.1
.1	.0	.1	Income Taxes Payable	.0					.1
9.5	18.6	13.7	All Other Current	4.9					31.7
26.9	32.5	25.3	Total Current	15.7					42.9
39.2	37.3	31.5	Long-Term Debt	43.4					19.7
.7	.9	.8	Deferred Taxes	.0					3.4
5.3	7.4	8.4	All Other Non-Current	7.3					10.7
27.9	21.9	34.0	Net Worth	33.6					23.3
100.0	100.0	100.0	Total Liabilties & Net Worth	100.0					100.0
			INCOME DATA						
100.0	100.0	100.0	Net Sales	100.0					100.0
			Gross Profit						
65.3	70.1	63.7	Operating Expenses	51.9					78.0
34.7	29.9	36.3	Operating Profit	48.1					22.0
12.5	11.5	11.7	All Other Expenses (net)	16.8					8.3
22.2	18.5	24.6	Profit Before Taxes	31.3					13.7
			RATIOS						
3.7	2.2	3.0		3.1					1.3
1.1	1.0	1.2	Current	1.1					.9
.5	.3	.6		.2					.6
2.5	1.3	2.3		3.0					1.1
.7	.7	1.0	Quick	1.0					.8
.2	.2	.3		.2					.3
0 UND	**0** UND	**0** UND		**0** UND					**12** 31.6
3 109.8	**5** 69.8	**12** 29.8	Sales/Receivables	**0** UND					**26** 13.8
31 11.7	**33** 11.0	**35** 10.5		**5** 76.8					**38** 9.5
			Cost of Sales/Inventory						
			Cost of Sales/Payables						
2.6	9.1	4.4		3.4					20.2
22.9	-237.4	28.2	Sales/Working Capital	323.6					NM
-4.6	-3.0	-6.5		-3.1					-8.2
21.8	20.0	27.7		6.8					
(48) 4.6	(50) 4.7	(33) 5.2	EBIT/Interest	(11) 4.5					
1.8	2.0	2.3		2.2					
			Net Profit + Depr., Dep., Amort./Cur. Mat. L/T/D						
.1	.5	.1		.0					.3
1.4	2.7	2.1	Fixed/Worth	2.4					-1.8
67.9	36.8	NM		6.6					-.2
1.0	1.7	.8		.6					2.8
5.3	3.4	2.8	Debt/Worth	2.6					-4.8
-32.9	-18.4	-5.3		-5.8					-1.3
85.9	81.9	73.5		52.7					
(66) 22.6	(59) 29.8	(42) 19.0	% Profit Before Taxes/Tangible Net Worth	(20) 18.0					
7.5	10.3	11.1		10.0					
17.6	12.1	18.6		13.7					22.9
6.1	4.3	7.5	% Profit Before Taxes/Total Assets	5.9					4.5
1.7	1.7	3.2		3.2					1.2
50.8	30.7	56.4		UND					39.7
3.1	3.0	11.1	Sales/Net Fixed Assets	.3					25.3
.3	.2	.2		.1					12.6
1.2	1.6	2.0		.7					3.3
.5	.5	.5	Sales/Total Assets	.2					2.0
.2	.2	.1		.1					.4
1.3	1.3	1.1		12.1					
(67) 4.6	(64) 6.1	(39) 3.4	% Depr., Dep., Amort./Sales	(16) 19.5					
17.5	17.7	21.5		28.3					
			% Officers', Directors' Owners' Comp/Sales						
2555362M	1470377M	953867M	Net Sales ($)	11431M	16976M	18871M	16948M	120589M	769052M
2424270M	2133826M	1212991M	Total Assets ($)	55997M	167688M	54840M	9836M	157710M	766920M

M = $ thousand MM = $ million

See Pages 9 through 22 for Explanation of Ratios and Data

PROFESSIONAL, SCIENTIFIC, AND TECHNICAL SERVICES

Current Data Sorted by Assets							Comparative Historical Data	
						Type of Statement		
6	6	19	25	10	16	Unqualified	115	109
6	18	79	61	10	5	Reviewed	209	222
56	74	80	34	1		Compiled	275	263
346	227	103	11	2	1	Tax Returns	654	643
285	301	313	139	49	21	Other	938	962
123 (4/1-9/30/13)			2,181 (10/1/13-3/31/14)				4/1/09-3/31/10 ALL	4/1/10-3/31/11 ALL
0-500M	500M-2MM	2-10MM	10-50MM	50-100MM	100-250MM			
699	626	594	270	72	43	NUMBER OF STATEMENTS	2191	2199
%	%	%	%	%	%	**ASSETS**	%	%
42.6	36.9	30.0	28.4	36.9	34.8	Cash & Equivalents	33.4	34.2
6.4	11.1	21.3	24.9	12.3	16.0	Trade Receivables (net)	16.1	15.4
.3	.6	1.3	2.7	.5	.5	Inventory	1.3	1.0
10.7	13.4	16.0	12.3	12.5	11.9	All Other Current	12.0	13.7
60.0	62.0	68.7	68.2	62.3	63.1	Total Current	62.7	64.3
19.7	19.6	16.0	16.3	23.5	22.3	Fixed Assets (net)	21.0	19.1
3.5	3.8	1.7	3.4	2.7	6.1	Intangibles (net)	2.8	2.5
16.8	14.6	13.5	12.1	11.5	8.5	All Other Non-Current	13.5	14.2
100.0	100.0	100.0	100.0	100.0	100.0	Total	100.0	100.0
						LIABILITIES		
44.0	17.9	14.4	7.5	5.5	4.9	Notes Payable-Short Term	26.0	26.0
5.0	3.0	2.2	2.0	2.3	1.8	Cur. Mat.-L.T.D.	4.4	4.1
3.1	3.2	4.3	3.9	2.2	2.3	Trade Payables	2.9	3.1
.4	.2	.8	.8	.4	.6	Income Taxes Payable	.6	.5
40.2	28.1	25.1	20.0	23.8	17.4	All Other Current	30.6	32.5
92.8	52.4	46.8	34.3	34.2	26.9	Total Current	64.4	66.3
17.3	14.2	11.5	8.9	8.7	10.6	Long-Term Debt	14.6	12.3
.0	.1	.3	.5	.1	.0	Deferred Taxes	.2	.2
5.9	6.8	5.2	7.7	4.9	7.3	All Other Non-Current	6.9	6.4
-16.0	26.6	36.2	48.6	52.1	55.2	Net Worth	13.9	14.7
100.0	100.0	100.0	100.0	100.0	100.0	Total Liabilties & Net Worth	100.0	100.0
						INCOME DATA		
100.0	100.0	100.0	100.0	100.0	100.0	Net Sales	100.0	100.0
						Gross Profit		
84.5	80.6	79.6	76.5	70.7	66.1	Operating Expenses	80.7	81.1
15.5	19.4	20.4	23.5	29.3	33.9	Operating Profit	19.3	18.9
.9	2.0	1.8	1.5	2.5	1.5	All Other Expenses (net)	1.5	1.6
14.6	17.5	18.6	22.0	26.8	32.4	Profit Before Taxes	17.7	17.4
						RATIOS		
2.1	3.0	3.6	5.6	7.0	7.2		2.9	3.0
.9	1.2	1.6	2.3	1.8	3.1	Current	1.2	1.2
.3	.7	1.0	1.1	1.0	1.3		.6	.6
1.6	2.4	2.8	4.1	5.2	5.9		2.3	2.3
(698) .7	(625) 1.0	1.1	1.7	1.6	2.9	Quick	(2187) 1.0	(2192) 1.0
.2	.4	.6	.9	.7	1.1		.4	.3
0 UND	0 UND	0 UND	0 UND	0 UND	0 UND		0 UND	0 UND
0 UND	0 UND	4 92.8	12 29.2	4 100.8	5 75.2	Sales/Receivables	0 UND	0 UND
0 UND	4 81.9	58 6.3	78 4.7	15 24.6	46 7.9		24 15.1	18 20.2
						Cost of Sales/Inventory		
						Cost of Sales/Payables		
35.5	10.2	4.9	4.1	6.3	4.7		8.0	8.0
-191.0	53.4	15.8	8.3	13.1	7.2	Sales/Working Capital	51.2	54.0
-17.8	-28.5	-183.9	46.7	NM	27.3		-29.2	-28.8
71.0	95.6	177.1	296.8	367.4	504.7		118.6	124.0
(472) 17.1	(439) 14.2	(482) 22.5	(222) 67.1	(58) 102.9	(38) 281.9	EBIT/Interest	(1715) 17.9	(1730) 17.9
1.8	1.5	3.3	5.1	20.1	50.6		1.8	2.2
	1.9	7.0	16.7	109.3			7.5	7.2
	(19) 1.6	(53) 2.0	(40) 2.1	(11) 5.6		Net Profit + Depr., Dep., Amort./Cur. Mat. L/T/D	(136) 1.8	(144) 2.0
	.4	.6	.2	1.2			.6	.8
.0	.0	.1	.1	.2	.2		.1	.1
.7	.5	.2	.3	.5	.4	Fixed/Worth	.6	.4
-.9	12.9	1.3	.8	.8	.6		-24.3	16.1
.7	.7	.6	.3	.3	.2		.6	.6
8.4	3.0	1.6	1.0	.9	.5	Debt/Worth	3.0	2.5
-3.1	-137.5	9.6	3.8	2.7	1.8		-17.0	-36.2
650.8	337.7	236.0	243.3	288.9	269.8		340.1	335.1
(407) 176.7	(467) 105.5	(513) 90.4	(248) 89.3	(69) 200.1	(40) 170.5	% Profit Before Taxes/Tangible Net Worth	(1541) 118.2	(1605) 111.0
31.0	17.0	12.4	16.3	62.8	101.6		17.7	19.1
204.8	112.1	97.3	125.9	171.3	154.7		129.0	131.9
51.9	24.7	23.2	30.3	130.9	109.8	% Profit Before Taxes/Total Assets	31.0	31.1
2.6	2.4	2.8	3.5	8.4	32.9		1.8	3.1
943.7	310.9	139.4	56.2	26.4	21.3		158.6	170.9
125.7	66.2	48.5	29.3	19.7	17.7	Sales/Net Fixed Assets	43.3	49.0
36.3	20.3	22.3	15.2	11.9	11.4		17.8	19.4
19.2	8.1	4.8	4.3	5.3	3.8		8.9	8.8
9.5	4.2	2.8	2.7	3.8	3.0	Sales/Total Assets	4.2	4.3
4.8	2.0	1.7	1.6	2.2	2.2		2.2	2.4
.2	.3	.4	.6	.9	.8		.4	.4
(270) .6	(328) .7	(401) .8	(227) 1.1	(60) 1.3	(27) 1.3	% Depr., Dep., Amort./Sales	(1354) .9	(1313) .9
1.1	1.4	1.4	1.5	2.0	2.0		1.6	1.6
11.2	8.3	7.6	5.1	3.3			9.6	9.7
(381) 20.0	(313) 20.6	(236) 20.7	(96) 16.6	(20) 12.8		% Officers', Directors' Owners' Comp/Sales	(1038) 22.0	(1032) 22.2
32.4	32.9	34.3	30.1	37.6			34.1	34.5
1812013M	3764422M	11073726M	18559042M	18033675M	20389466M	Net Sales ($)	82554282M	71199502M
155847M	673151M	2803995M	5753506M	4751860M	6551100M	Total Assets ($)	19999008M	18856727M

M = $ thousand MM = $ million

See Pages 9 through 22 for Explanation of Ratios and Data

	Comparative Historical Data				Current Data Sorted by Sales					
Type of Statement										
Unqualified	109	95	82		5	5	2	5	11	54
Reviewed	237	163	179			2	3	16	56	102
Compiled	313	221	245		21	41	29	54	66	34
Tax Returns	751	691	690		165	233	90	114	67	21
Other	1102	1057	1108		121	215	131	204	196	241
	4/1/11-3/31/12 ALL	4/1/12-3/31/13 ALL	4/1/13-3/31/14 ALL		123 (4/1-9/30/13)			2,181 (10/1/13-3/31/14)		
					0-1MM	1-3MM	3-5MM	5-10MM	10-25MM	25MM & OVER
NUMBER OF STATEMENTS	2512	2227	2304		312	496	255	393	396	452
ASSETS	%	%	%		%	%	%	%	%	%
Cash & Equivalents	34.2	34.9	35.8		37.0	42.1	33.7	33.3	33.7	33.3
Trade Receivables (net)	14.3	14.3	14.1		7.3	8.8	11.0	16.1	20.5	18.9
Inventory	1.3	1.1	1.0		.2	.3	.7	1.7	1.4	1.2
All Other Current	14.4	12.7	13.1		8.2	12.7	18.1	15.1	14.3	11.1
Total Current	64.1	63.0	63.9		52.7	63.9	63.5	66.3	69.9	64.5
Fixed Assets (net)	19.4	19.6	18.5		30.2	15.5	16.5	14.7	15.3	20.9
Intangibles (net)	2.9	2.7	3.1		2.8	3.9	3.6	3.6	1.9	3.0
All Other Non-Current	13.6	14.7	14.5		14.3	16.8	16.5	15.4	12.9	11.6
Total	100.0	100.0	100.0		100.0	100.0	100.0	100.0	100.0	100.0
LIABILITIES										
Notes Payable-Short Term	24.9	23.0	23.1		33.0	30.9	25.7	28.9	14.2	8.9
Cur. Mat.-L.T.D.	3.5	3.1	3.3		3.0	3.5	2.0	5.0	2.8	2.7
Trade Payables	3.1	3.4	3.5		3.1	2.5	3.7	4.4	4.3	3.4
Income Taxes Payable	.4	.4	.5		.2	.3	.8	.5	.7	.6
All Other Current	32.0	31.8	29.7		27.5	35.5	33.0	30.4	30.1	22.0
Total Current	63.8	61.7	60.0		66.7	72.8	65.2	69.2	52.0	37.6
Long-Term Debt	13.8	14.6	13.5		30.6	11.8	14.7	9.7	10.0	9.5
Deferred Taxes	.2	.2	.1		.0	.0	.2	.2	.3	.3
All Other Non-Current	6.6	6.2	6.2		6.0	7.2	5.3	6.3	5.5	6.1
Net Worth	15.5	17.3	20.1		-3.4	8.3	14.6	14.6	32.2	46.5
Total Liabilties & Net Worth	100.0	100.0	100.0		100.0	100.0	100.0	100.0	100.0	100.0
INCOME DATA										
Net Sales	100.0	100.0	100.0		100.0	100.0	100.0	100.0	100.0	100.0
Gross Profit										
Operating Expenses	81.0	80.0	80.5		76.4	83.8	83.0	83.0	81.2	75.3
Operating Profit	19.0	20.0	19.5		23.6	16.2	17.0	17.0	18.8	24.7
All Other Expenses (net)	1.6	1.7	1.5		5.5	.8	.6	.7	.5	1.9
Profit Before Taxes	17.4	18.4	18.0		18.1	15.4	16.4	16.3	18.3	22.8
RATIOS										
	3.3	3.2	3.4		2.3	2.2	3.3	3.5	3.6	5.5
Current	1.3	1.2	1.3		1.0	1.0	1.2	1.3	1.6	2.1
	.7	.7	.7		.4	.5	.6	.7	1.0	1.0
	2.5	2.5	2.7		2.1	1.7	2.4	2.5	2.7	4.2
Quick	(2509) 1.0	(2224) 1.0	(2302) 1.0		.8	(494) .8	.8	1.0	1.2	1.7
	.3	.4	.4		.3	.3	.2	.3	.6	.8
	0 UND	0 UND	0 UND		0 UND	0 UND	0 UND	0 UND	0 UND	0 UND
Sales/Receivables	0 UND	0 UND	0 UND		0 UND	0 UND	0 UND	0 UND	2 178.2	4 83.9
	17 21.8	17 22.1	14 25.8		0 UND	0 999.8	4 88.9	24 15.4	47 7.7	42 8.7
Cost of Sales/Inventory										
Cost of Sales/Payables										
	7.8	8.1	7.8		10.6	12.8	9.1	9.0	6.1	6.1
Sales/Working Capital	49.4	45.3	40.8		-251.5	215.9	67.7	43.1	19.8	16.9
	-30.4	-30.0	-33.5		-7.4	-18.7	-26.5	-33.9	-330.8	396.4
	131.6	125.2	138.5		31.0	70.7	80.8	122.2	276.7	352.6
EBIT/Interest	(1877) 18.5	(1684) 22.8	(1711) 22.5		(183) 7.4	(343) 15.4	(183) 17.5	(307) 22.9	(322) 31.5	(373) 87.7
	2.1	3.0	2.6		1.6	1.9	2.0	2.0	2.8	6.2
	7.0	11.4	7.8					5.5	6.1	18.1
Net Profit + Depr., Dep., Amort./Cur. Mat. L/T/D	(143) 2.0	(109) 2.4	(138) 2.0					(19) 2.0	(31) 1.6	(76) 2.8
	.7	.9	.6					.0	.0	.9
	.1	.1	.1		.0	.0	.0	.0	.1	.2
Fixed/Worth	.4	.4	.4		1.1	.4	.3	.3	.3	.4
	10.2	6.9	4.8		-14.1	-4.1	8.9	UND	1.6	1.1
	.6	.6	.5		.9	.7	.5	.6	.6	.3
Debt/Worth	2.5	2.5	2.1		5.9	4.6	3.0	2.5	1.6	1.0
	-29.5	-74.7	814.6		-4.9	-6.4	-56.0	-27.9	14.2	3.7
	328.2	341.5	332.9		226.9	355.4	383.1	362.9	335.4	314.8
% Profit Before Taxes/Tangible Net Worth	(1833) 106.7	(1657) 124.2	(1744) 115.3		(205) 55.9	(329) 90.5	(186) 122.8	(284) 136.1	(332) 100.7	(408) 155.7
	18.5	25.5	18.3		11.3	18.5	26.0	26.6	13.8	26.1
	128.8	135.1	134.9		74.2	107.7	132.5	139.7	126.8	168.1
% Profit Before Taxes/Total Assets	28.5	36.9	32.0		14.8	28.5	29.3	37.6	27.6	82.3
	2.2	4.1	2.9		1.7	2.7	2.4	3.0	2.1	5.1
	211.2	208.4	250.9		692.8	999.8	356.9	430.2	188.1	55.5
Sales/Net Fixed Assets	53.5	53.7	55.5		48.7	92.7	81.2	102.9	56.0	27.9
	20.5	19.9	21.2		3.5	25.4	34.4	33.0	26.6	17.0
	9.0	8.5	8.8		5.9	9.6	10.5	10.5	8.8	6.6
Sales/Total Assets	4.3	4.1	4.2		2.5	4.7	4.8	5.0	4.0	4.2
	2.2	2.2	2.2		.7	2.2	2.1	2.4	2.3	2.8
	.4	.3	.4		.6	.2	.3	.2	.4	.6
% Depr., Dep., Amort./Sales	(1444) .8	(1319) .8	(1313) .8		(134) 2.1	(210) .6	(125) .6	(205) .5	(269) .7	(370) 1.1
	1.5	1.4	1.4		14.8	1.1	1.0	1.1	1.3	1.5
	9.5	8.4	9.5		12.1	10.3	10.0	5.7	7.6	7.4
% Officers', Directors' Owners' Comp/Sales	(1186) 20.4	(1037) 18.9	(1055) 19.7		(143) 19.9	(260) 20.5	(122) 18.7	(200) 17.5	(179) 21.5	(151) 19.6
	34.1	31.9	33.0		30.8	32.7	33.1	30.0	37.6	35.1
Net Sales ($)	73874927M	67904917M	73632344M		164955M	923343M	1004724M	2827229M	6327418M	62384675M
Total Assets ($)	20455781M	18240133M	20689459M		170398M	372331M	374571M	957879M	2172233M	16642047M

M = $ thousand MM = $ million

See Pages 9 through 22 for Explanation of Ratios and Data

Current Data Sorted by Assets							Comparative Historical Data	
						Type of Statement		
	2	1	3	2	2	Unqualified	10	8
	1	1	1			Reviewed	4	5
2	4	2	2			Compiled	11	9
14	10	4			1	Tax Returns	33	24
12	8	10	5		2	Other	43	47
	6 (4/1-9/30/13)		83 (10/1/13-3/31/14)				**4/1/09-3/31/10 ALL**	**4/1/10-3/31/11 ALL**
0-500M	**500M-2MM**	**2-10MM**	**10-50MM**	**50-100MM**	**100-250MM**			
28	25	18	11	2	5	**NUMBER OF STATEMENTS**	101	93
%	%	%	%	%	%	**ASSETS**	%	%
50.7	38.4	29.0	23.8			Cash & Equivalents	34.0	33.9
3.6	10.9	18.5	22.2			Trade Receivables (net)	10.1	9.3
.0	.0	.0	.1			Inventory	.7	.9
1.7	4.2	27.0	7.9			All Other Current	7.6	9.7
55.9	53.5	74.5	53.9			Total Current	52.4	53.8
20.0	21.4	4.5	17.1			Fixed Assets (net)	23.4	18.6
6.3	7.0	.9	16.2			Intangibles (net)	10.5	11.2
17.8	18.1	20.0	12.8			All Other Non-Current	13.7	16.4
100.0	100.0	100.0	100.0			Total	100.0	100.0
						LIABILITIES		
19.4	4.3	7.2	4.4			Notes Payable-Short Term	12.6	16.1
1.6	1.1	.8	1.2			Cur. Mat.-L.T.D.	1.6	2.8
3.0	3.8	8.3	10.1			Trade Payables	14.6	8.2
.0	.2	.0	.8			Income Taxes Payable	.2	.1
29.6	23.4	30.1	26.6			All Other Current	23.7	23.4
53.6	32.7	46.4	43.1			Total Current	52.7	50.7
21.8	20.4	12.7	11.3			Long-Term Debt	14.3	13.1
.0	.0	.0	.3			Deferred Taxes	.2	.2
3.4	4.8	5.1	1.9			All Other Non-Current	7.7	10.2
21.2	42.0	35.8	43.4			Net Worth	25.1	25.7
100.0	100.0	100.0	100.0			Total Liabilties & Net Worth	100.0	100.0
						INCOME DATA		
100.0	100.0	100.0	100.0			Net Sales	100.0	100.0
						Gross Profit		
84.0	82.4	89.6	90.6			Operating Expenses	92.1	89.1
16.0	17.6	10.4	9.4			Operating Profit	7.9	10.9
.1	1.0	-.5	.1			All Other Expenses (net)	.9	1.6
15.9	16.7	10.8	9.3			Profit Before Taxes	7.0	9.3
						RATIOS		
2.5	8.3	3.6	2.2				2.3	2.1
1.2	2.4	1.6	1.2			Current	1.1	1.2
.5	1.0	1.0	1.0				.6	.7
2.5	8.3	2.4	1.3				2.0	2.0
1.2	2.2	1.2	1.1			Quick	1.0	1.0
.5	1.0	.4	1.0				.4	.4
0 UND	0 UND	0 UND	4 99.4				0 UND	0 UND
0 UND	0 UND	4 103.0	22 16.7			Sales/Receivables	1 279.8	2 211.6
0 UND	9 39.4	38 9.6	49 7.5				24 15.0	17 22.1
						Cost of Sales/Inventory		
						Cost of Sales/Payables		
20.4	6.6	3.0	16.2				9.7	10.4
UND	11.4	7.5	33.1			Sales/Working Capital	114.5	48.8
-27.4	NM	29.0	971.0				-20.8	-18.0
60.8	144.5	108.4					26.5	32.4
(16) 9.0	(15) 21.1	(12) 37.0				EBIT/Interest	(71) 10.5	(68) 6.9
-1.4	3.2	8.2					.4	.3
								11.6
						Net Profit + Depr., Dep., Amort./Cur. Mat. L/T/D		(10) 6.4
								2.1
.1	.1	.0	.3				.2	.1
.6	.5	.1	.5			Fixed/Worth	.9	.6
-1.1	1.6	NM	16.1				-4.9	-6.9
.4	.3	.4	.9				.6	.7
3.1	1.2	1.6	2.0			Debt/Worth	2.0	2.4
-3.1	13.4	NM	33.1				-22.7	-12.1
999.8	147.4	75.1					168.3	147.9
(19) 174.9	(21) 56.0	(14) 30.1				% Profit Before Taxes/Tangible Net Worth	(73) 71.0	(65) 51.3
57.9	10.0	11.3					12.4	9.0
229.2	72.9	23.7	32.0				50.8	39.1
46.6	27.5	11.5	20.0			% Profit Before Taxes/Total Assets	16.2	11.5
-13.6	2.4	3.6	4.5				.4	-.3
918.6	155.3	84.2	55.5				53.5	76.4
55.3	30.3	52.6	16.7			Sales/Net Fixed Assets	24.0	30.2
25.2	8.1	38.2	10.2				10.6	11.7
14.5	5.0	3.1	3.8				5.9	4.6
9.3	2.2	1.3	2.4			Sales/Total Assets	2.7	2.7
4.3	1.2	.4	2.1				1.5	1.4
.4	.5						.9	.6
(14) 1.1	(19) 1.4					% Depr., Dep., Amort./Sales	(68) 1.6	(62) 1.7
1.8	3.4						3.2	2.5
6.8	4.5						4.7	3.7
(12) 12.6	(10) 12.4					% Officers', Directors' Owners' Comp/Sales	(41) 9.3	(31) 6.8
26.6	19.4						26.7	27.5
42065M	85788M	132897M	1950283M	190935M	1990188M	Net Sales ($)	897930M	977044M
5004M	29683M	78216M	221499M	110648M	731962M	Total Assets ($)	464161M	533688M

M = $ thousand MM = $ million

See Pages 9 through 22 for Explanation of Ratios and Data

Comparative Historical Data				Current Data Sorted by Sales					
			Type of Statement						
7	4	10	Unqualified		1			3	6
3	2	3	Reviewed			1		2	
14	9	10	Compiled	2	2		3	1	2
42	31	29	Tax Returns	12	7	4	5		1
45	40	37	Other	8	12	5	3	3	6
4/1/11-3/31/12 ALL	4/1/12-3/31/13 ALL	4/1/13-3/31/14 ALL		6 (4/1-9/30/13)		83 (10/1/13-3/31/14)			
				0-1MM	1-3MM	3-5MM	5-10MM	10-25MM	25MM & OVER
111	86	89	NUMBER OF STATEMENTS	22	22	10	11	9	15
%	%	%	**ASSETS**	%	%	%	%	%	%
34.8	36.8	37.0	Cash & Equivalents	31.5	49.3	51.3	43.5		14.5
14.1	11.9	12.5	Trade Receivables (net)	4.4	15.0	4.2	13.8		21.2
.2	.0	.1	Inventory	.0	.0	.0	.0		.6
7.0	7.3	8.6	All Other Current	9.8	5.1	.3	12.2		12.5
56.1	55.9	58.2	Total Current	45.8	69.5	55.8	69.6		48.8
19.7	18.1	16.5	Fixed Assets (net)	21.7	14.0	11.6	19.7		17.8
12.5	9.6	7.9	Intangibles (net)	7.5	8.1	.9	.8		18.9
11.7	16.4	17.4	All Other Non-Current	24.9	8.4	31.7	10.0		14.5
100.0	100.0	100.0	Total	100.0	100.0	100.0	100.0		100.0
			LIABILITIES						
9.5	7.1	10.6	Notes Payable-Short Term	14.8	17.3	3.4	3.4		5.6
1.7	1.2	1.2	Cur. Mat.-L.T.D.	.9	2.3	.8	.4		1.6
11.2	6.9	5.3	Trade Payables	2.6	5.6	3.7	2.1		9.4
.0	.1	.2	Income Taxes Payable	.0	.0	.0	.0		.5
23.8	27.1	26.0	All Other Current	27.5	21.4	46.0	16.1		20.5
46.3	42.4	43.3	Total Current	45.9	46.7	53.8	22.1		37.5
17.6	14.6	17.6	Long-Term Debt	32.9	18.8	8.2	11.6		10.8
.3	.2	.1	Deferred Taxes	.0	.0	.0	.0		.7
9.9	18.0	4.6	All Other Non-Current	7.4	1.7	.3	2.2		7.3
25.9	24.7	34.4	Net Worth	13.8	32.8	37.6	64.2		43.6
100.0	100.0	100.0	Total Liabilties & Net Worth	100.0	100.0	100.0	100.0		100.0
			INCOME DATA						
100.0	100.0	100.0	Net Sales	100.0	100.0	100.0	100.0		100.0
			Gross Profit						
90.0	86.6	85.8	Operating Expenses	80.3	85.4	82.3	90.8		91.9
10.0	13.4	14.2	Operating Profit	19.7	14.6	17.7	9.2		8.1
2.4	1.4	.3	All Other Expenses (net)	1.7	-.4	.0	-1.0		1.2
7.7	12.1	13.9	Profit Before Taxes	18.0	15.1	17.7	10.2		7.0
			RATIOS						
3.3	3.0	3.2		10.4	4.2	2.7	13.6		2.2
1.6	1.5	1.5	Current	1.1	1.5	1.4	3.1		1.4
.8	.9	1.0		.4	.9	.9	2.3		1.1
3.1	2.7	3.1		10.4	4.1	2.7	5.1		1.3
1.3	1.3	1.3	Quick	.9	1.5	1.3	2.5		1.1
.6	.6	.7		.3	.8	.9	1.3		.8
0 UND	0 UND	0 UND		0 UND	0 UND	0 UND	0 UND		7 52.5
1 334.0	0 UND	0 UND	Sales/Receivables	0 UND	0 UND	0 UND	0 UND		32 11.5
26 14.3	17 21.7	29 12.4		0 UND	8 47.0	2 212.8	29 12.7		49 7.5
			Cost of Sales/Inventory						
			Cost of Sales/Payables						
6.8	7.7	8.5		10.5	6.3	11.6	3.9		10.1
20.7	25.1	26.6	Sales/Working Capital	61.8	14.1	75.2	7.5		32.0
-24.6	-71.5	-542.7		-16.8	-61.7	-768.4	11.4		299.3
27.7	94.2	121.8		12.9	132.8				138.8
(70) 7.4	(52) 15.4	(54) 19.3	EBIT/Interest	(14) 5.1	(13) 54.0				(11) 43.6
-.8	3.0	4.2		-.2	1.9				8.3
5.2									
(10) 3.0			Net Profit + Depr., Dep., Amort./Cur. Mat. L/T/D						
-5.9									
.1	.1	.1		.1	.1	.0	.1		.4
.4	.6	.4	Fixed/Worth	1.1	.4	.1	.3		.5
70.2	-4.0	5.4		-.4	5.8	.6	.6		16.1
.5	.5	.4		.5	.6	.2	.2		.9
2.3	3.5	1.7	Debt/Worth	6.1	7.6	1.1	.4		2.0
-7.4	-13.8	27.9		-2.6	35.8	14.4	.9		33.1
116.0	241.9	202.4		437.0	547.5		89.9		180.1
(78) 40.0	(59) 100.8	(69) 64.2	% Profit Before Taxes/Tangible Net Worth	(13) 28.8	(18) 195.5		(10) 53.1		(12) 52.5
4.8	31.3	19.0		5.1	3.6		26.8		24.7
31.1	67.5	75.8		46.2	169.6	146.2	71.0		32.0
11.0	24.3	20.0	% Profit Before Taxes/Total Assets	9.9	23.2	52.5	24.9		20.0
-.1	4.4	4.2		-7.1	.0	20.4	10.1		8.6
137.4	143.7	117.3		290.1	132.0	651.0	101.1		51.8
29.1	34.8	40.0	Sales/Net Fixed Assets	44.6	37.7	188.6	53.7		23.2
10.6	13.2	14.6		7.3	26.9	38.9	7.2		12.9
4.6	4.7	6.9		9.9	8.4	10.1	5.5		4.9
2.5	3.0	2.9	Sales/Total Assets	2.8	2.4	6.3	3.3		3.0
1.5	1.4	1.4		.8	1.1	2.2	1.5		2.3
.4	.3	.6		1.1	.4				.6
(71) 1.2	(52) 1.1	(53) 1.2	% Depr., Dep., Amort./Sales	(11) 1.9	(12) .9				(12) 1.0
2.6	2.0	1.9		6.0	1.5				2.0
4.7	4.2	4.9			5.0				
(44) 7.3	(35) 9.1	(32) 9.5	% Officers', Directors' Owners' Comp/Sales		(11) 11.9				
13.7	13.1	18.6			20.8				
1153620M	1327444M	4392156M	Net Sales ($)	13573M	38644M	40392M	71866M	151596M	4076085M
675309M	766218M	1177012M	Total Assets ($)	12662M	29474M	9635M	34344M	108176M	982721M

M = $ thousand MM = $ million

See Pages 9 through 22 for Explanation of Ratios and Data

Current Data Sorted by Assets							Comparative Historical Data	
						Type of Statement		
		4	3	1		Unqualified	5	5
	2	2	1		1	Reviewed	1	1
1		3				Compiled	2	3
7	5	2				Tax Returns	7	6
3	6	9	11	1		Other	13	25
	7 (4/1-9/30/13)		55 (10/1/13-3/31/14)				4/1/09-3/31/10	4/1/10-3/31/11
0-500M	500M-2MM	2-10MM	10-50MM	50-100MM	100-250MM		ALL	ALL
11	13	20	15	2	1	NUMBER OF STATEMENTS	28	40
%	%	%	%	%	%	**ASSETS**	%	%
64.1	22.7	25.3	29.7			Cash & Equivalents	33.1	26.8
15.2	28.9	29.6	18.9			Trade Receivables (net)	19.5	24.1
.0	.1	1.6	.7			Inventory	.1	2.8
7.7	5.4	8.3	13.8			All Other Current	13.6	6.3
86.9	57.1	64.9	63.1			Total Current	66.3	60.0
10.5	28.7	19.8	18.7			Fixed Assets (net)	14.3	20.7
.0	7.8	4.1	13.6			Intangibles (net)	10.2	11.1
2.6	6.5	11.2	4.6			All Other Non-Current	9.2	8.2
100.0	100.0	100.0	100.0			Total	100.0	100.0
						LIABILITIES		
7.0	13.8	16.7	1.4			Notes Payable-Short Term	17.5	14.0
.0	.1	1.1	3.2			Cur. Mat.-L.T.D.	3.1	2.9
10.8	2.8	10.7	6.3			Trade Payables	4.8	2.7
.1	.0	1.5	1.2			Income Taxes Payable	.0	.3
22.3	8.5	7.7	18.3			All Other Current	15.3	15.6
40.1	25.2	37.7	30.4			Total Current	40.7	35.5
6.6	20.4	12.0	12.3			Long-Term Debt	12.3	12.9
.0	.0	.0	.0			Deferred Taxes	.3	.6
5.6	3.7	4.2	4.7			All Other Non-Current	7.6	8.3
47.7	50.8	46.1	52.6			Net Worth	39.1	42.7
100.0	100.0	100.0	100.0			Total Liabilities & Net Worth	100.0	100.0
						INCOME DATA		
100.0	100.0	100.0	100.0			Net Sales	100.0	100.0
						Gross Profit		
86.5	87.6	88.6	76.8			Operating Expenses	80.4	85.5
13.5	12.4	11.4	23.2			Operating Profit	19.6	14.5
.1	.5	.1	2.6			All Other Expenses (net)	1.3	.8
13.5	11.9	11.3	20.5			Profit Before Taxes	18.3	13.7
						RATIOS		
5.9	8.2	4.5	5.8				2.8	5.4
3.1	4.3	1.9	1.9			Current	1.6	2.3
1.6	.5	1.0	1.3				.8	1.2
5.9	7.7	4.5	5.7				2.5	4.6
3.1	4.2	1.7	1.4			Quick	1.0	2.1
1.6	.3	.8	1.1				.5	.6
0 UND	**0** UND	**0** UND	**0** UND				**0** UND	**0** UND
0 UND	**4** 84.0	**16** 22.3	**40** 9.1			Sales/Receivables	**0** UND	**34** 10.8
36 10.0	**65** 5.6	**78** 4.7	**54** 6.8				**49** 7.5	**59** 6.2
						Cost of Sales/Inventory		
						Cost of Sales/Payables		
2.1	5.7	4.7	3.9				6.5	5.5
11.9	9.7	8.4	9.2			Sales/Working Capital	12.7	9.4
80.4	-524.2	NM	19.0				-20.1	121.9
	33.0	54.9	537.3				170.6	42.1
	(11) 11.4	(15) 15.4	(13) 193.1			EBIT/Interest	(21) 38.4	(31) 8.3
	1.2	2.3	18.6				3.4	1.5
						Net Profit + Depr., Dep., Amort./Cur. Mat. L/T/D		
.0	.0	.1	.1				.0	.1
.1	.2	.3	.4			Fixed/Worth	.2	.4
.9	3.0	1.6	2.5				3.9	NM
.2	.1	.4	.2				.5	.5
1.0	1.2	1.4	1.7			Debt/Worth	1.2	1.0
4.8	6.9	9.7	5.3				30.4	NM
863.1	204.3	149.5	173.6				245.1	125.0
(10) 131.3	(12) 62.5	(18) 30.5	(12) 87.1			% Profit Before Taxes/Tangible Net Worth	(22) 80.9	(30) 69.5
9.4	17.5	5.2	15.3				38.9	15.7
486.6	108.1	39.5	76.3				68.9	47.7
64.7	18.3	7.3	23.5			% Profit Before Taxes/Total Assets	37.1	16.7
5.6	3.9	1.3	7.0				6.3	1.9
UND	UND	101.0	92.2				284.7	97.8
174.5	57.6	31.9	22.4			Sales/Net Fixed Assets	59.2	27.9
10.6	6.9	6.3	9.4				13.2	10.8
18.0	8.2	4.1	4.1				4.7	4.9
6.1	4.5	1.9	2.2			Sales/Total Assets	3.0	2.5
1.4	2.0	.9	1.4				1.6	1.1
		.3	.4				.4	.4
		(15) .8	(12) 1.6			% Depr., Dep., Amort./Sales	(16) 1.7	(27) 1.2
		2.2	2.5				2.8	2.9
								11.0
						% Officers', Directors' Owners' Comp/Sales		(10) 19.8
								23.7
16131M	72114M	254559M	913093M	191911M	202869M	Net Sales ($)	937527M	1037540M
2247M	14062M	108469M	315544M	131114M	112308M	Total Assets ($)	376407M	703529M

M = $ thousand MM = $ million

See Pages 9 through 22 for Explanation of Ratios and Data

Comparative Historical Data				Current Data Sorted by Sales					
4	7	8	**Type of Statement** Unqualified			1	2	1	4
4	7	6	Reviewed				2	2	2
6	4	4	Compiled	1				2	1
6	16	14	Tax Returns	7	2	2	2	1	
26	22	30	Other	3	6	1	2	9	9
4/1/11-3/31/12 ALL	4/1/12-3/31/13 ALL	4/1/13-3/31/14 ALL		7 (4/1-9/30/13)		55 (10/1/13-3/31/14)			
				0-1MM	1-3MM	3-5MM	5-10MM	10-25MM	25MM & OVER
46	56	62	**NUMBER OF STATEMENTS**	11	8	4	8	15	16
%	%	%	**ASSETS**	%	%	%	%	%	%
26.4	32.0	32.5	Cash & Equivalents	57.9				19.2	31.1
31.8	25.5	23.7	Trade Receivables (net)	24.3				37.5	23.2
1.2	1.2	.7	Inventory	.0				.4	.7
8.1	5.0	10.0	All Other Current	.1				12.3	17.2
67.5	63.7	66.8	Total Current	82.2				69.4	72.1
17.5	19.8	20.1	Fixed Assets (net)	16.2				11.6	15.4
6.4	7.6	6.4	Intangibles (net)	.0				7.4	7.5
8.6	9.0	6.7	All Other Non-Current	1.5				11.6	5.1
100.0	100.0	100.0	Total	100.0				100.0	100.0
			LIABILITIES						
13.2	13.3	10.0	Notes Payable-Short Term	9.4				22.8	5.2
2.3	1.7	2.3	Cur. Mat.-L.T.D.	.0				1.6	6.9
3.3	3.6	7.7	Trade Payables	1.3				11.8	7.1
.4	.1	.8	Income Taxes Payable	.1				.2	.9
18.3	20.2	13.2	All Other Current	26.2				8.8	16.3
37.3	38.8	34.0	Total Current	37.1				45.2	36.5
9.6	11.2	12.4	Long-Term Debt	7.2				8.8	4.9
.5	.3	.0	Deferred Taxes	.0				.0	.0
8.1	9.3	4.3	All Other Non-Current	5.7				6.6	.2
44.5	40.4	49.3	Net Worth	50.0				39.5	58.4
100.0	100.0	100.0	Total Liabilties & Net Worth	100.0				100.0	100.0
			INCOME DATA						
100.0	100.0	100.0	Net Sales	100.0				100.0	100.0
			Gross Profit						
84.8	88.3	85.3	Operating Expenses	85.7				86.9	82.2
15.2	11.7	14.7	Operating Profit	14.3				13.1	17.8
1.7	1.7	.8	All Other Expenses (net)	.4				.3	1.8
13.5	10.0	13.9	Profit Before Taxes	13.9				12.7	15.9
			RATIOS						
3.7	5.4	5.7		5.3				5.8	8.1
2.2	1.8	2.0	Current	2.1				1.9	1.9
1.6	.9	1.0		1.3				.9	1.3
2.9	5.1	5.2		5.2				5.8	5.0
1.8	1.7	1.9	Quick	2.1				1.9	1.5
1.1	.8	.8		1.3				.3	1.1
0 UND	0 UND	0 UND		0 UND				0 UND	0 UND
36 10.1	15 24.5	16 22.3	Sales/Receivables	0 UND				42 8.7	37 9.8
85 4.3	64 5.7	55 6.6		40 9.1				79 4.6	54 6.8
			Cost of Sales/Inventory						
			Cost of Sales/Payables						
4.0	5.8	4.5		1.2				4.7	4.4
7.5	12.4	9.4	Sales/Working Capital	10.1				9.5	8.2
25.1	-117.9	169.8		80.4				-82.0	17.9
170.3	49.8	97.8						154.7	537.3
(33) 12.5	(42) 9.5	(43) 24.6	EBIT/Interest					(13) 33.0	(13) 41.2
3.3	-2.2	3.4						3.6	17.5
			Net Profit + Depr., Dep., Amort./Cur. Mat. L/T/D						
.0	.1	.0		.0				.1	.1
.2	.3	.3	Fixed/Worth	.1				.4	.2
.8	2.3	1.2		1.0				1.5	.5
.5	.4	.3		.3				.3	.1
1.2	1.5	1.2	Debt/Worth	1.0				1.9	1.1
4.1	6.6	5.0		1.2				14.6	2.6
143.3	146.7	184.0		274.4				144.5	187.3
(40) 49.4	(49) 46.1	(55) 63.8	% Profit Before Taxes/Tangible Net Worth	(10) 22.5				(12) 76.2	(14) 127.9
7.3	2.8	8.0		9.4				6.9	11.6
47.4	51.2	66.0		88.9				52.4	129.2
14.7	11.4	18.8	% Profit Before Taxes/Total Assets	19.3				23.3	39.5
3.3	.5	2.5		5.6				2.5	4.0
204.7	142.7	185.9		UND				199.6	86.3
30.6	41.0	36.3	Sales/Net Fixed Assets	141.5				57.6	23.4
12.5	14.7	8.7		3.1				16.0	11.1
4.2	5.0	4.9		6.8				4.8	4.5
2.7	2.9	2.6	Sales/Total Assets	1.4				2.5	2.6
1.6	2.0	1.3		.4				1.6	1.8
.6	.5	.5						.2	.5
(31) 1.4	(39) .8	(41) 1.1	% Depr., Dep., Amort./Sales					(10) .8	(14) 1.3
2.7	2.7	2.3						2.1	2.4
6.1	3.0	5.1							
(11) 21.7	(20) 8.6	(26) 11.1	% Officers', Directors' Owners' Comp/Sales						
26.8	23.6	22.4							
814300M	1183394M	1650677M	Net Sales ($)	6046M	14884M	15645M	53614M	253233M	1307255M
383452M	637818M	683744M	Total Assets ($)	5537M	23981M	10433M	22499M	112940M	508354M

M = $ thousand MM = $ million

See Pages 9 through 22 for Explanation of Ratios and Data

Current Data Sorted by Assets							Comparative Historical Data	
		1	2		1	Type of Statement Unqualified	37	23
	2	1	1			Reviewed	9	7
14	22	24	2	1	1	Compiled	81	88
115	70	18		3	1	Tax Returns	225	222
121	123	163	50	7	7	Other	480	499
	163 (4/1-9/30/13)		587 (10/1/13-3/31/14)				4/1/09-3/31/10	4/1/10-3/31/11
0-500M	500M-2MM	2-10MM	10-50MM	50-100MM	100-250MM		ALL	ALL
250	217	207	55	11	10	NUMBER OF STATEMENTS	832	839
%	%	%	%	%	%	ASSETS	%	%
30.0	14.7	15.1	16.4	27.4	12.9	Cash & Equivalents	17.4	17.7
17.0	27.4	37.0	39.4	24.9	24.2	Trade Receivables (net)	31.7	30.2
1.1	3.0	4.8	4.7	6.7	2.3	Inventory	3.3	3.5
3.3	4.1	7.8	7.9	5.1	6.7	All Other Current	5.3	7.2
51.4	49.2	64.7	68.4	64.1	46.0	Total Current	57.7	58.5
21.5	20.4	14.9	11.4	8.1	9.6	Fixed Assets (net)	18.4	18.2
14.9	19.0	11.8	7.8	10.2	29.9	Intangibles (net)	12.1	12.2
12.2	11.4	8.6	12.4	17.7	14.5	All Other Non-Current	11.8	11.1
100.0	100.0	100.0	100.0	100.0	100.0	Total	100.0	100.0
						LIABILITIES		
32.3	11.5	8.6	5.8	22.5	5.3	Notes Payable-Short Term	18.2	19.1
3.2	3.6	2.3	2.3	1.3	3.5	Cur. Mat.-L.T.D.	5.1	3.6
4.1	2.1	2.3	4.3	1.0	3.2	Trade Payables	3.8	3.4
.3	.2	.1	.3	.0	.0	Income Taxes Payable	.2	.3
25.8	12.6	15.6	14.0	12.1	10.6	All Other Current	19.2	18.8
65.8	30.0	29.0	26.8	36.9	22.6	Total Current	46.5	45.3
19.1	22.4	14.3	10.5	5.0	20.6	Long-Term Debt	17.0	18.6
.0	.4	.1	.0	.0	.2	Deferred Taxes	.3	.2
5.9	6.5	8.1	9.0	15.9	13.3	All Other Non-Current	6.2	7.2
9.2	40.7	48.5	53.7	42.3	43.4	Net Worth	29.9	28.8
100.0	100.0	100.0	100.0	100.0	100.0	Total Liabilties & Net Worth	100.0	100.0
						INCOME DATA		
100.0	100.0	100.0	100.0	100.0	100.0	Net Sales	100.0	100.0
						Gross Profit		
83.4	83.1	83.5	80.2	79.2	74.4	Operating Expenses	84.1	83.4
16.6	16.9	16.5	19.8	20.8	25.6	Operating Profit	15.9	16.6
1.0	3.5	2.7	1.8	.5	1.3	All Other Expenses (net)	2.7	2.6
15.6	13.4	13.8	18.0	20.3	24.3	Profit Before Taxes	13.3	13.9
						RATIOS		
2.8	4.4	4.7	6.4	4.7	3.7		3.8	4.0
.9	1.7	2.4	2.7	1.9	1.5	Current	1.6	1.7
.3	.7	1.5	1.6	1.2	.8		.8	.9
2.6	3.7	3.7	4.7	3.2	3.3		3.2	3.1
.9	1.4	1.7	2.4	1.2	1.2	Quick	1.3	(838) 1.4
.3	.6	1.0	1.2	1.1	.7		.6	.7
0 UND	0 UND	34 10.6	41 8.9	0 UND	31 11.7		0 UND	0 UND
0 UND	35 10.4	51 7.2	61 6.0	28 13.0	49 7.5	Sales/Receivables	41 8.9	41 8.9
20 17.9	65 5.6	76 4.8	83 4.4	53 6.9	74 4.9		68 5.3	69 5.3
						Cost of Sales/Inventory		
						Cost of Sales/Payables		
13.3	5.6	4.4	3.4	6.6	5.4		5.6	5.2
-244.4	16.3	7.6	5.7	12.0	8.8	Sales/Working Capital	15.5	12.5
-17.7	-37.0	15.8	9.2	52.0	-30.9		-45.7	-102.7
68.1	31.9	75.0	138.4				33.7	46.0
(162) 10.9	(172) 7.6	(173) 16.0	(44) 58.4			EBIT/Interest	(657) 9.6	(662) 10.5
1.7	3.1	4.1	7.8				2.0	2.3
		6.4					8.1	6.8
		(11) 2.4				Net Profit + Depr., Dep., Amort./Cur. Mat. L/T/D	(34) 3.2	(40) 3.2
		1.2					.7	1.3
.0	.1	.1	.1	.1	.2		.1	.1
.6	.4	.2	.2	.3	.5	Fixed/Worth	.3	.3
-2.6	7.9	1.2	.6	.8	-.1		4.3	4.3
.6	.5	.5	.3	.3	.3		.5	.5
4.4	2.1	1.2	.8	1.4	2.0	Debt/Worth	1.9	1.9
-2.8	-14.2	6.2	3.6	9.2	-2.3		UND	-90.0
423.2	120.1	114.8	139.4				151.6	152.9
(153) 144.3	(160) 34.2	(177) 57.4	(50) 79.6			% Profit Before Taxes/Tangible Net Worth	(629) 57.5	(622) 63.7
41.0	9.7	11.3	15.6				8.8	10.0
160.6	34.0	51.7	55.7	133.7	91.4		68.0	64.2
49.6	12.0	17.4	31.1	66.6	64.3	% Profit Before Taxes/Total Assets	18.7	20.3
5.0	2.4	3.8	4.2	4.8	13.2		2.0	2.6
UND	208.3	64.8	55.8	814.9	37.8		120.5	110.8
71.3	35.6	32.3	28.7	35.1	22.9	Sales/Net Fixed Assets	31.4	33.3
23.6	13.9	16.9	15.4	18.8	18.9		15.1	16.1
11.5	4.0	3.3	2.8	9.6	3.5		5.0	4.7
6.4	2.5	2.4	2.1	2.8	2.0	Sales/Total Assets	3.0	2.9
3.3	1.4	1.8	1.7	2.2	1.2		1.9	1.9
.6	.9	.8	.9				.9	.9
(104) 1.1	(129) 1.3	(156) 1.4	(41) 1.3			% Depr., Dep., Amort./Sales	(511) 1.6	(524) 1.5
2.2	4.6	2.2	1.8				2.8	2.5
12.5	12.0	16.6	5.6				10.9	13.1
(156) 20.8	(108) 19.4	(96) 23.2	(24) 19.5			% Officers', Directors' Owners' Comp/Sales	(406) 21.9	(438) 21.8
30.3	29.4	30.9	30.0				31.7	31.1
366912M	722274M	2373776M	2481248M	4939713M	3245287M	Net Sales ($)	18739443M	18540903M
47907M	222990M	943020M	1121138M	827301M	1531025M	Total Assets ($)	6881308M	6524767M

M = $ thousand MM = $ million

See Pages 9 through 22 for Explanation of Ratios and Data

Comparative Historical Data				Current Data Sorted by Sales					
			Type of Statement						
18	8	4	Unqualified					2	2
8	7	4	Reviewed	1			2	1	
97	52	64	Compiled	17	11	12	11	9	4
242	221	207	Tax Returns	91	59	25	17	10	5
535	500	471	Other	83	107	52	67	95	67
					163 (4/1-9/30/13)			587 (10/1/13-3/31/14)	
4/1/11-3/31/12 ALL	4/1/12-3/31/13 ALL	4/1/13-3/31/14 ALL		0-1MM	1-3MM	3-5MM	5-10MM	10-25MM	25MM & OVER
900	788	750	**NUMBER OF STATEMENTS**	192	177	89	97	117	78
%	%	%	**ASSETS**	%	%	%	%	%	%
18.9	21.5	20.2	Cash & Equivalents	20.5	21.3	21.0	19.9	19.2	17.7
29.2	27.5	27.4	Trade Receivables (net)	13.2	26.5	31.5	35.2	35.4	37.9
3.1	3.4	3.0	Inventory	.9	2.7	3.0	4.7	4.9	4.2
6.1	5.5	5.2	All Other Current	2.8	3.7	5.1	5.3	8.9	9.0
57.3	57.9	55.8	Total Current	37.3	54.2	60.6	65.1	68.4	68.8
19.1	16.9	18.3	Fixed Assets (net)	33.4	15.3	12.8	11.6	12.8	10.4
13.1	14.1	14.8	Intangibles (net)	16.3	19.8	13.0	13.8	10.1	10.2
10.5	11.2	11.1	All Other Non-Current	12.9	10.7	13.7	9.5	8.7	10.5
100.0	100.0	100.0	Total	100.0	100.0	100.0	100.0	100.0	100.0
			LIABILITIES						
18.9	18.1	17.3	Notes Payable-Short Term	18.9	28.6	15.0	11.1	10.9	7.4
3.6	3.2	3.0	Cur. Mat.-L.T.D.	4.6	2.3	2.8	2.7	2.4	2.3
3.1	2.5	3.0	Trade Payables	2.2	4.2	1.7	1.8	3.8	4.1
.3	.3	.2	Income Taxes Payable	.4	.1	.1	.1	.2	.2
17.5	18.1	17.9	All Other Current	12.8	16.7	26.7	20.5	19.4	17.6
43.3	42.2	41.4	Total Current	38.9	51.9	46.3	36.2	36.6	31.7
18.7	17.5	17.9	Long-Term Debt	29.4	20.1	13.7	10.7	11.0	8.9
.2	.1	.1	Deferred Taxes	.0	.4	.1	.0	.2	.0
8.3	8.3	7.2	All Other Non-Current	7.4	5.4	8.4	8.2	7.0	8.2
29.6	31.9	33.4	Net Worth	24.3	22.2	31.6	44.9	45.2	51.2
100.0	100.0	100.0	Total Liabilties & Net Worth	100.0	100.0	100.0	100.0	100.0	100.0
			INCOME DATA						
100.0	100.0	100.0	Net Sales	100.0	100.0	100.0	100.0	100.0	100.0
			Gross Profit						
83.7	82.7	82.9	Operating Expenses	73.3	86.4	90.9	86.7	84.7	82.3
16.3	17.3	17.1	Operating Profit	26.7	13.6	9.1	13.3	15.3	17.7
2.6	2.8	2.3	All Other Expenses (net)	5.4	1.1	1.1	1.3	1.3	1.2
13.7	14.4	14.8	Profit Before Taxes	21.3	12.5	8.0	12.0	14.0	16.5
			RATIOS						
4.0	4.1	4.1		2.8	4.2	4.5	4.8	4.7	4.4
1.7	1.9	1.8	Current	1.0	1.2	1.9	2.5	2.3	2.2
.9	.9	.8		.3	.6	.7	1.2	1.3	1.3
3.5	3.5	3.5		2.7	3.7	4.1	4.0	3.5	3.6
(899) 1.4	1.5	1.4	Quick	.8	1.1	1.6	2.0	1.6	1.9
.7	.7	.6		.3	.4	.6	1.0	1.0	1.0
0 UND	**0** UND	**0** UND		**0** UND	**0** UND	**0** UND	**3** 143.4	**28** 13.1	**31** 11.7
38 9.7	**35** 10.5	**33** 11.1	Sales/Receivables	**0** UND	**19** 19.4	**44** 8.3	**47** 7.8	**47** 7.7	**51** 7.2
65 5.6	**64** 5.7	**60** 6.1		**24** 15.1	**56** 6.5	**74** 4.9	**74** 4.9	**61** 6.0	**73** 5.0
			Cost of Sales/Inventory						
			Cost of Sales/Payables						
5.8	5.5	5.7		9.8	7.0	4.8	5.1	5.0	4.4
14.4	14.9	14.1	Sales/Working Capital	-358.3	57.1	15.4	7.7	8.7	7.4
-63.5	-70.5	-48.5		-10.3	-31.7	-52.2	57.5	19.5	22.7
44.9	56.7	64.6		29.5	54.9	45.9	61.7	101.7	143.3
(720) 12.6	(609) 14.7	(566) 13.2	EBIT/Interest	(111) 8.0	(136) 10.1	(75) 10.6	(80) 13.2	(99) 18.4	(65) 42.8
2.9	3.0	3.3		3.0	3.1	2.4	3.1	4.6	6.8
3.9	8.8	6.1							
(39) 2.1	(31) 2.8	(29) 2.4	Net Profit + Depr., Dep., Amort./Cur. Mat. L/T/D						
.5	.9	1.0							
.1	.1	.1		.0	.0	.1	.1	.1	.1
.3	.3	.3	Fixed/Worth	1.2	.3	.4	.2	.2	.2
12.1	6.7	5.0		UND	-2.1	9.9	1.0	1.0	.6
.5	.4	.5		.7	.4	.5	.4	.5	.3
2.2	1.8	1.8	Debt/Worth	4.8	3.6	2.3	1.2	1.3	.9
-15.8	-11.0	-54.1		-4.1	-3.2	NM	5.5	5.7	3.1
154.4	192.0	169.9		306.2	206.4	114.1	140.2	133.8	144.6
(656) 65.2	(573) 67.5	(556) 70.7	% Profit Before Taxes/Tangible Net Worth	(127) 98.6	(111) 70.4	(67) 24.3	(81) 68.5	(101) 74.1	(69) 91.1
16.2	14.6	13.9		19.6	17.9	2.5	11.4	16.1	6.1
61.1	79.3	70.0		111.7	73.3	32.7	53.7	62.7	74.6
20.3	24.7	23.5	% Profit Before Taxes/Total Assets	24.1	25.6	7.0	18.0	26.8	37.1
3.8	4.0	3.9		4.6	5.8	1.5	2.6	5.3	3.8
105.6	152.1	188.9		444.5	999.8	176.8	119.7	65.7	71.6
34.0	38.7	37.8	Sales/Net Fixed Assets	32.1	62.6	45.7	47.5	31.8	29.6
16.1	19.1	17.9		4.6	20.4	26.7	25.9	19.1	18.6
5.1	5.2	5.4		6.1	7.0	7.3	4.6	4.1	3.5
3.0	3.0	2.9	Sales/Total Assets	2.4	3.5	3.0	3.2	2.8	2.7
1.9	1.9	1.9		.9	2.1	2.0	2.0	2.2	1.9
.9	.8	.7		1.3	.6	.7	.6	.9	.7
(566) 1.4	(458) 1.3	(442) 1.3	% Depr., Dep., Amort./Sales	(95) 4.6	(88) 1.2	(53) 1.1	(63) 1.0	(89) 1.4	(54) 1.3
2.5	2.2	2.3		19.6	2.0	1.7	1.5	2.0	1.7
12.1	14.7	12.6		12.5	10.6	17.6	18.5	14.5	9.3
(463) 22.3	(426) 22.1	(389) 21.0	% Officers', Directors' Owners' Comp/Sales	(96) 17.0	(110) 19.8	(43) 23.0	(52) 28.7	(53) 21.4	(35) 21.2
30.9	30.6	30.1		24.7	30.6	30.9	34.2	29.2	30.6
17245273M	**12072661M**	**14129210M**	Net Sales ($)	**93384M**	**331783M**	**348215M**	**691578M**	**1762202M**	**10902048M**
7400842M	**5070759M**	**4693381M**	Total Assets ($)	**93496M**	**184705M**	**144776M**	**272718M**	**636905M**	**3360781M**

M = $ thousand MM = $ million

See Pages 9 through 22 for Explanation of Ratios and Data

Current Data Sorted by Assets | **Comparative Historical Data**

0-500M	500M-2MM	2-10MM	10-50MM	50-100MM	100-250MM		4/1/09-3/31/10 ALL	4/1/10-3/31/11 ALL
	5 (4/1-9/30/13)		20 (10/1/13-3/31/14)			**Type of Statement**		
					1	Unqualified	3	2
						Reviewed		1
1						Compiled		1
6	2					Tax Returns	9	5
4	6	3	1		1	Other	9	11
11	8	3	1		2	**NUMBER OF STATEMENTS**	21	20
%	%	%	%	%	%	**ASSETS**	%	%
19.3				DATA NOT AVAILABLE		Cash & Equivalents	13.5	17.0
14.4						Trade Receivables (net)	20.2	25.6
5.3						Inventory	2.2	.0
4.7						All Other Current	5.0	5.5
43.7						Total Current	40.9	48.1
25.1						Fixed Assets (net)	27.2	9.4
8.5						Intangibles (net)	22.3	37.5
22.6						All Other Non-Current	9.4	4.9
100.0						Total	100.0	100.0
						LIABILITIES		
4.4						Notes Payable-Short Term	42.5	15.1
9.2						Cur. Mat.-L.T.D.	1.9	2.2
10.1						Trade Payables	10.3	10.6
.0						Income Taxes Payable	.3	1.1
16.7						All Other Current	25.6	6.4
40.3						Total Current	80.5	35.4
16.1						Long-Term Debt	19.6	19.3
.0						Deferred Taxes	.6	.7
18.5						All Other Non-Current	12.6	9.2
25.1						Net Worth	-13.2	35.4
100.0						Total Liabilties & Net Worth	100.0	100.0
						INCOME DATA		
100.0						Net Sales	100.0	100.0
						Gross Profit		
86.9						Operating Expenses	83.9	81.0
13.1						Operating Profit	16.1	19.0
.4						All Other Expenses (net)	.8	.2
12.6						Profit Before Taxes	15.3	18.8
						RATIOS		
3.4							2.6	8.4
.9						Current	1.4	2.2
.2							.2	.5
3.7							2.1	6.7
(10) 1.0						Quick	1.0	2.1
.1							.1	.4
0 UND							0 UND	0 UND
0 UND						Sales/Receivables	22 16.4	18 20.9
0 UND							61 6.0	89 4.1
						Cost of Sales/Inventory		
						Cost of Sales/Payables		
50.2							9.8	5.0
-490.0						Sales/Working Capital	43.7	14.7
-21.8							-9.1	-36.2
							22.6	67.2
						EBIT/Interest	(19) 5.8	(18) 9.9
							3.0	2.4
						Net Profit + Depr., Dep., Amort./Cur. Mat. L/T/D		
.0							.4	.0
.8						Fixed/Worth	7.3	.2
13.0							-.1	-.3
.1							1.2	1.1
40.8						Debt/Worth	26.9	3.9
-4.0							-1.7	-1.5
							370.6	220.9
						% Profit Before Taxes/Tangible Net Worth	(11) 137.8	(11) 103.8
							28.7	37.0
188.7							85.9	72.9
20.8						% Profit Before Taxes/Total Assets	37.8	28.6
-31.4							10.8	13.9
144.2							58.1	UND
75.3						Sales/Net Fixed Assets	12.7	65.5
9.7							8.6	19.7
17.9							8.2	4.7
6.0						Sales/Total Assets	2.8	2.9
2.6							1.2	1.3
							1.3	
						% Depr., Dep., Amort./Sales	(14) 3.1	
							7.9	
							10.0	
						% Officers', Directors' Owners' Comp/Sales	(10) 19.2	
							22.6	
13057M	17376M	64287M	10879M		280178M	Net Sales ($)	674465M	614460M
1632M	8774M	18366M	11378M		344291M	Total Assets ($)	557173M	602679M

M = $ thousand MM = $ million

See Pages 9 through 22 for Explanation of Ratios and Data

Comparative Historical Data | **Current Data Sorted by Sales**

	4/1/11-3/31/12 ALL	4/1/12-3/31/13 ALL	4/1/13-3/31/14 ALL	0-1MM	1-3MM	3-5MM	5-10MM	10-25MM	25MM & OVER
Type of Statement									
Unqualified	3	3	1						1
Reviewed	1								
Compiled	1		1				1		
Tax Returns	9	8	8	5	3				
Other	7	19	15	5	2	2	2	1	3
				5 (4/1-9/30/13)		20 (10/1/13-3/31/14)			
NUMBER OF STATEMENTS	21	30	25	10	5	2	3	1	4
ASSETS	%	%	%	%	%	%	%	%	%
Cash & Equivalents	17.2	22.9	18.8	25.2					
Trade Receivables (net)	23.3	19.4	13.8	15.9					
Inventory	.0	.3	2.6	.0					
All Other Current	9.4	6.2	9.4	7.1					
Total Current	49.9	48.8	44.6	48.2					
Fixed Assets (net)	17.8	16.6	18.2	17.2					
Intangibles (net)	18.2	18.4	20.1	10.8					
All Other Non-Current	14.0	16.2	17.1	23.8					
Total	100.0	100.0	100.0	100.0					
LIABILITIES									
Notes Payable-Short Term	15.8	15.8	7.0	7.3					
Cur. Mat.-L.T.D.	2.7	2.1	5.1	9.1					
Trade Payables	3.3	8.9	6.0	11.0					
Income Taxes Payable	.2	1.8	.3	.0					
All Other Current	25.7	10.0	18.4	8.1					
Total Current	47.7	38.6	36.8	35.5					
Long-Term Debt	28.0	24.8	19.7	3.8					
Deferred Taxes	.7	.6	.0	.0					
All Other Non-Current	11.2	2.6	9.6	20.3					
Net Worth	12.3	33.4	33.9	40.4					
Total Liabilties & Net Worth	100.0	100.0	100.0	100.0					
INCOME DATA									
Net Sales	100.0	100.0	100.0	100.0					
Gross Profit									
Operating Expenses	82.1	77.8	86.3	79.5					
Operating Profit	17.9	22.2	13.7	20.5					
All Other Expenses (net)	1.9	1.8	1.4	1.1					
Profit Before Taxes	16.0	20.4	12.3	19.4					
RATIOS									
Current	2.4	3.9	3.4	4.6					
	1.5	1.7	1.4	1.0					
	1.1	.5	.3	.6					
Quick	1.9	3.2	2.2	3.7					
	1.3	1.3	(24) 1.1	1.0					
	.6	.4	.3	.5					
Sales/Receivables	0 UND	0 UND	0 UND	0 UND					
	4 83.9	20 18.4	0 UND	0 UND					
	79 4.6	57 6.4	49 7.5	0 UND					
Cost of Sales/Inventory									
Cost of Sales/Payables									
Sales/Working Capital	5.1	6.3	7.1	15.7					
	13.9	17.2	62.0	NM					
	UND	-37.6	-10.2	-8.1					
EBIT/Interest	34.9	23.5	21.0						
	(13) 10.6	(22) 12.6	(17) 11.7						
	1.9	4.1	2.6						
Net Profit + Depr., Dep., Amort./Cur. Mat. L/T/D									
Fixed/Worth	.0	.0	.1	.1					
	.2	.3	.5	.4					
	NM	-2.3	UND	1.5					
Debt/Worth	1.0	.4	.5	.1					
	2.1	1.8	4.8	1.1					
	-2.9	-5.2	-5.0	NM					
% Profit Before Taxes/Tangible Net Worth	133.6	136.9	550.0						
	(14) 53.4	(20) 63.2	(17) 68.4						
	35.7	18.5	40.0						
% Profit Before Taxes/Total Assets	61.8	81.5	37.4	171.9					
	18.0	22.6	17.0	26.7					
	7.5	6.8	-.2	2.2					
Sales/Net Fixed Assets	552.4	598.3	80.1	76.9					
	74.4	74.9	37.7	33.3					
	6.7	12.0	9.2	11.5					
Sales/Total Assets	4.6	4.5	5.1	8.5					
	2.0	2.6	2.8	2.8					
	.6	.5	1.2	1.5					
% Depr., Dep., Amort./Sales	.3	.6	.6						
	(10) 5.4	(12) 1.6	(13) 2.0						
	8.2	7.3	4.0						
% Officers', Directors' Owners' Comp/Sales		5.6							
		(12) 13.1							
		21.6							
Net Sales ($)	568126M	1002218M	385777M	4106M	8162M	7348M	18228M	10879M	337054M
Total Assets ($)	639700M	657344M	384441M	2090M	4994M	1284M	4794M	11378M	359901M

M = $ thousand MM = $ million

See Pages 9 through 22 for Explanation of Ratios and Data

Current Data Sorted by Assets							Comparative Historical Data	
						Type of Statement		
	2	5	3	1	1	Unqualified	8	10
		1	5	1		Reviewed	7	4
	1	1	2			Compiled	2	4
3	4		1			Tax Returns	13	10
12	3	16	8	2	4	Other	17	28
	3 (4/1-9/30/13)		73 (10/1/13-3/31/14)				4/1/09-3/31/10 ALL	4/1/10-3/31/11 ALL
0-500M	500M-2MM	2-10MM	10-50MM	50-100MM	100-250MM			
15	10	23	19	4	5	**NUMBER OF STATEMENTS**	47	56
%	%	%	%	%	%	**ASSETS**	%	%
54.0	52.1	45.1	31.8			Cash & Equivalents	33.9	34.3
4.6	4.4	19.4	7.6			Trade Receivables (net)	7.8	15.3
.0	.0	.0	.1			Inventory	.4	.4
6.4	24.1	19.1	34.1			All Other Current	23.8	20.8
65.0	80.6	83.6	73.6			Total Current	65.9	70.8
22.4	4.5	4.6	5.8			Fixed Assets (net)	13.4	8.3
8.8	10.5	4.7	6.1			Intangibles (net)	5.7	8.1
3.7	4.4	7.1	14.5			All Other Non-Current	14.9	12.9
100.0	100.0	100.0	100.0			Total	100.0	100.0
						LIABILITIES		
32.7	5.3	9.3	10.4			Notes Payable-Short Term	14.7	10.4
4.9	.4	1.4	1.3			Cur. Mat.-L.T.D.	1.8	.7
7.4	.9	8.7	1.5			Trade Payables	3.7	2.2
.4	9.9	.1	.0			Income Taxes Payable	2.6	.6
18.7	47.1	59.7	63.5			All Other Current	45.8	57.0
64.1	63.5	79.3	76.7			Total Current	68.6	70.9
24.6	7.2	5.0	5.4			Long-Term Debt	8.6	7.6
.0	.0	.1	.0			Deferred Taxes	.1	.1
22.1	1.0	1.2	13.2			All Other Non-Current	15.8	6.1
-10.9	28.3	14.2	4.7			Net Worth	6.9	15.3
100.0	100.0	100.0	100.0			Total Liabilties & Net Worth	100.0	100.0
						INCOME DATA		
100.0	100.0	100.0	100.0			Net Sales	100.0	100.0
						Gross Profit		
85.6	82.0	94.7	92.0			Operating Expenses	93.5	94.8
14.4	18.0	5.3	8.0			Operating Profit	6.5	5.2
1.5	-.3	.3	1.9			All Other Expenses (net)	1.4	.5
12.9	18.3	5.1	6.1			Profit Before Taxes	5.1	4.7
						RATIOS		
5.1	5.7	1.2	1.0				1.8	1.5
3.8	1.0	1.0	1.0			Current	1.0	1.0
.6	.9	.9	.9				1.0	.9
5.1	4.4	1.0	1.0				1.7	1.3
3.3	.9	.8	.5			Quick	1.0	.9
.4	.4	.4	.0				.1	.2
0 UND	0 UND	0 999.8	4 100.3				0 UND	0 UND
0 UND	0 UND	3 115.7	6 60.0			Sales/Receivables	1 325.4	7 50.7
1 405.3	2 230.4	28 13.1	20 18.0				11 32.9	34 10.7
						Cost of Sales/Inventory		
						Cost of Sales/Payables		
6.1	7.8	14.9	14.6				8.8	10.8
67.5	514.0	140.2	999.8			Sales/Working Capital	47.4	131.5
-45.2	-6.3	-39.1	-11.2				-16.5	-16.5
		161.8	85.8				15.0	28.7
		(16) 25.8	(15) 16.3			EBIT/Interest	(32) 5.8	(33) 3.1
		5.2	1.3				-1.7	-.1
						Net Profit + Depr., Dep., Amort./Cur. Mat. L/T/D		
.0	.0	.1	.3				.0	.0
.2	.2	.2	.7			Fixed/Worth	.8	.5
-.6	-6.0	1.2	-1.1				-.8	-2.1
.2	.3	3.3	20.4				2.3	1.8
3.2	57.4	13.1	58.1			Debt/Worth	23.1	12.1
-2.8	-19.8	-17.0	-55.5				-30.4	-21.0
		193.2	180.9				205.5	90.1
		(16) 60.7	(13) 64.4			% Profit Before Taxes/Tangible Net Worth	(32) 42.7	(37) 27.3
		25.8	9.2				12.8	7.2
207.9	35.1	16.8	4.0				16.6	10.0
38.9	9.4	7.4	1.9			% Profit Before Taxes/Total Assets	5.3	4.7
9.3	3.7	1.5	.8				.2	.1
UND	UND	691.8	72.6				303.0	885.2
130.0	33.0	155.2	30.2			Sales/Net Fixed Assets	30.9	45.5
30.8	19.0	30.9	12.4				8.5	13.4
27.7	7.3	13.6	.8				9.5	5.9
23.2	1.5	3.1	.3			Sales/Total Assets	1.4	.9
3.0	.3	.5	.2				.3	.3
		.0	.9				.5	.3
		(10) .4	(15) 1.5			% Depr., Dep., Amort./Sales	(24) 1.4	(36) 1.4
		1.4	3.2				2.8	2.9
							2.1	3.5
						% Officers', Directors' Owners' Comp/Sales	(13) 8.2	(12) 7.7
							12.7	14.5
69811M	115541M	755009M	998456M	112096M	979073M	Net Sales ($)	4541762M	5719627M
2838M	13713M	98319M	486068M	280639M	619814M	Total Assets ($)	1920120M	1793793M

M = $ thousand MM = $ million

See Pages 9 through 22 for Explanation of Ratios and Data

Comparative Historical Data				Current Data Sorted by Sales					
			Type of Statement						
14	16	12	Unqualified		2		2	2	6
6	8	7	Reviewed		2	1	1	2	1
4	2	4	Compiled		1		2	1	
10	16	8	Tax Returns	4	1	2	1		
39	44	45	Other	10	5	5	5	8	12
4/1/11-3/31/12 ALL	4/1/12-3/31/13 ALL	4/1/13-3/31/14 ALL		3 (4/1-9/30/13)			73 (10/1/13-3/31/14)		
				0-1MM	1-3MM	3-5MM	5-10MM	10-25MM	25MM & OVER
73	86	76	**NUMBER OF STATEMENTS**	14	11	8	11	13	19
%	%	%	**ASSETS**	%	%	%	%	%	%
37.4	42.6	41.5	Cash & Equivalents	60.9	62.3		34.6	28.5	25.2
12.8	11.0	13.6	Trade Receivables (net)	.0	5.7		6.1	33.7	23.6
.3	.0	.0	Inventory	.0	.0		.2	.1	.0
15.0	15.8	21.2	All Other Current	11.5	15.0		41.3	16.4	26.2
65.5	69.4	76.4	Total Current	72.4	83.0		82.2	78.7	75.1
9.9	7.1	8.5	Fixed Assets (net)	20.8	5.3		3.3	6.2	8.4
13.8	7.6	7.2	Intangibles (net)	4.7	8.1		8.0	6.7	8.3
10.8	15.9	8.0	All Other Non-Current	2.1	3.7		6.5	8.5	8.2
100.0	100.0	100.0	Total	100.0	100.0		100.0	100.0	100.0
			LIABILITIES						
9.5	6.7	14.2	Notes Payable-Short Term	22.9	22.1		8.1	16.5	11.3
2.8	.9	2.0	Cur. Mat.-L.T.D.	.4	3.6		3.4	1.2	2.7
9.6	4.6	4.8	Trade Payables	1.4	6.7		3.9	11.7	2.5
1.4	.1	1.4	Income Taxes Payable	7.5	.0		.0	.0	.2
45.8	56.2	49.6	All Other Current	39.4	52.5		62.2	46.5	47.1
69.1	68.5	72.0	Total Current	71.6	84.8		77.6	75.8	63.7
11.7	6.7	10.8	Long-Term Debt	4.5	34.7		1.1	7.1	13.7
.0	.3	.1	Deferred Taxes	.0	.0		.0	.3	.2
4.0	7.0	8.8	All Other Non-Current	9.5	1.2		19.1	.1	6.2
15.1	17.4	8.2	Net Worth	14.4	-20.7		2.2	16.7	16.2
100.0	100.0	100.0	Total Liabilties & Net Worth	100.0	100.0		100.0	100.0	100.0
			INCOME DATA						
100.0	100.0	100.0	Net Sales	100.0	100.0		100.0	100.0	100.0
			Gross Profit						
91.5	91.0	88.6	Operating Expenses	77.1	88.6		89.7	96.5	90.0
8.5	9.0	11.4	Operating Profit	22.9	11.4		10.3	3.5	10.0
1.0	1.0	1.2	All Other Expenses (net)	1.6	.6		1.5	1.0	1.7
7.5	8.0	10.2	Profit Before Taxes	21.3	10.9		8.7	2.6	8.4
			RATIOS						
1.5	1.9	1.5		4.5	1.3		1.2	1.3	1.5
1.0	1.0	1.0	Current	1.0	1.0		1.0	1.0	1.2
.8	.9	.9		.9	.6		1.0	.9	.9
1.2	1.6	1.4		4.0	1.0		1.0	1.2	1.4
.9	1.0	1.0	Quick	1.0	.8		.4	1.0	.7
.3	.4	.3		.8	.3		.0	.3	.3
0 UND	0 UND	0 UND		0 UND	0 UND		0 UND	9 40.3	0 804.7
2 178.1	3 108.0	3 119.0	Sales/Receivables	0 UND	3 115.7		17 21.7	30 12.0	2 179.2
29 12.6	23 16.1	23 16.1		0 UND	7 51.2		26 13.9	45 8.1	56 6.5
			Cost of Sales/Inventory						
			Cost of Sales/Payables						
17.1	9.7	8.8		6.1	8.3		6.3	12.8	20.9
578.6	46.2	84.1	Sales/Working Capital	25.2	-45.2		14.6	-180.4	140.2
-15.3	-11.9	-23.9		-6.3	-21.6		-124.9	-16.6	-150.4
49.3	32.0	85.7					177.6	7.7	105.6
(40) 8.7	(46) 11.5	(50) 15.7	EBIT/Interest				(10) 69.3	(10) 2.3	(14) 12.1
2.1	1.6	2.6					11.9	-.1	4.4
			Net Profit + Depr., Dep., Amort./Cur. Mat. L/T/D						
.0	.0	.1		.0	.0		.2	.1	.0
.5	.6	.3	Fixed/Worth	.5	.6		.3	.7	.2
-.6	-.4	-2.9		-.6	-.1		1.0	NM	1.1
2.3	1.7	3.4		.2	18.6		4.3	2.0	3.3
33.9	14.4	33.4	Debt/Worth	NM	-82.4		34.3	18.0	6.2
-9.1	-18.2	-18.1		-6.9	-2.8		58.1	NM	-7.9
170.3	139.9	161.0						294.7	111.0
(46) 70.3	(57) 60.0	(49) 64.4	% Profit Before Taxes/Tangible Net Worth					(10) 17.3	(14) 48.9
32.1	15.6	25.9						-4.0	29.7
21.5	18.7	19.8		40.0	59.0		25.1	7.1	16.4
4.3	4.1	5.1	% Profit Before Taxes/Total Assets	5.7	20.0		4.0	3.2	9.7
1.7	.7	1.5		1.3	1.2		.8	.3	5.0
UND	650.7	551.9		UND	UND		88.6	168.3	999.8
65.4	68.9	65.8	Sales/Net Fixed Assets	25.6	75.5		30.9	30.2	155.2
16.4	21.1	20.7		12.1	25.7		17.4	12.0	41.4
9.9	6.4	11.3		4.2	24.0		3.0	6.0	33.9
2.2	1.2	1.2	Sales/Total Assets	.4	1.4		.9	1.3	13.6
.3	.3	.2		.2	.5		.2	.4	.9
.3	.2	.5							.0
(43) 1.5	(48) 1.0	(41) 1.5	% Depr., Dep., Amort./Sales						(11) .8
2.9	2.2	2.8							3.4
4.5	5.7	3.5							
(15) 13.7	(19) 9.4	(13) 8.6	% Officers', Directors' Owners' Comp/Sales						
22.3	20.0	14.0							
6475343M	7203052M	3029986M	Net Sales ($)	7650M	21169M	31677M	87098M	208979M	2673413M
1444058M	1657186M	1501391M	Total Assets ($)	16716M	34370M	90133M	211528M	295714M	852930M

M = $ thousand MM = $ million

See Pages 9 through 22 for Explanation of Ratios and Data

Current Data Sorted by Assets							Comparative Historical Data	
						Type of Statement		
	2	3	8	1		Unqualified	18	23
1	1	6	2			Reviewed	11	6
5	3	2				Compiled	7	9
35	16	4	2			Tax Returns	63	48
38	33	16	11		4	Other	82	89
	17 (4/1-9/30/13)		176 (10/1/13-3/31/14)				**4/1/09-3/31/10 ALL**	**4/1/10-3/31/11 ALL**
0-500M	**500M-2MM**	**2-10MM**	**10-50MM**	**50-100MM**	**100-250MM**			
79	55	31	23	1	4	**NUMBER OF STATEMENTS**	181	175
%	%	%	%	%	%	**ASSETS**	%	%
35.9	17.1	16.4	22.3			Cash & Equivalents	23.9	23.1
15.2	27.4	32.0	28.9			Trade Receivables (net)	21.8	22.1
.0	2.9	1.6	.6			Inventory	1.4	1.7
3.2	4.5	5.9	17.7			All Other Current	6.2	8.6
54.4	51.9	56.0	69.5			Total Current	53.2	55.5
17.0	23.1	19.1	8.8			Fixed Assets (net)	19.1	17.0
12.4	9.8	9.6	14.9			Intangibles (net)	12.3	13.2
16.2	15.2	15.4	6.8			All Other Non-Current	15.4	14.2
100.0	100.0	100.0	100.0			Total	100.0	100.0
						LIABILITIES		
22.0	14.4	3.7	6.8			Notes Payable-Short Term	12.9	19.1
2.6	4.1	1.3	1.8			Cur. Mat.-L.T.D.	4.9	2.5
8.9	3.9	5.1	11.5			Trade Payables	6.2	5.8
.0	.0	.0	.4			Income Taxes Payable	.3	.4
25.5	14.2	22.4	25.4			All Other Current	25.0	28.1
59.0	36.5	32.4	45.9			Total Current	49.3	55.9
13.9	16.6	15.0	10.3			Long-Term Debt	21.2	16.9
.0	.0	.0	.8			Deferred Taxes	.2	.4
13.3	9.1	5.6	20.0			All Other Non-Current	16.4	7.8
13.8	37.7	47.0	23.1			Net Worth	12.9	19.0
100.0	100.0	100.0	100.0			Total Liabilties & Net Worth	100.0	100.0
						INCOME DATA		
100.0	100.0	100.0	100.0			Net Sales	100.0	100.0
						Gross Profit		
84.0	85.9	83.6	79.8			Operating Expenses	87.9	87.2
16.0	14.1	16.4	20.2			Operating Profit	12.1	12.8
.3	.7	2.7	1.5			All Other Expenses (net)	1.3	1.2
15.7	13.4	13.7	18.6			Profit Before Taxes	10.8	11.7
						RATIOS		
4.9	3.2	3.8	2.2				3.2	2.5
1.0	1.5	1.7	1.5			Current	1.2	1.2
.5	.8	1.2	1.0				.6	.6
4.8	3.2	3.7	1.9				2.8	2.1
1.0	(54) 1.3	1.6	1.0			Quick	1.0	1.0
.4	.7	1.1	.8				.4	.4
0 UND	0 UND	0 999.8	17 20.9				0 UND	0 UND
0 UND	34 10.7	46 7.9	48 7.6			Sales/Receivables	13 27.1	8 47.1
16 22.5	53 6.9	64 5.7	73 5.0				54 6.7	51 7.1
						Cost of Sales/Inventory		
						Cost of Sales/Payables		
10.0	5.6	5.5	2.3				6.2	7.6
745.0	18.1	9.8	12.1			Sales/Working Capital	38.5	34.8
-24.8	-70.7	64.7	53.3				-16.1	-20.2
33.3	38.9	43.9	44.6				22.6	28.6
(42) 11.0	(45) 11.0	(23) 11.2	(19) 4.2			EBIT/Interest	(122) 5.6	(124) 7.3
7.2	2.1	5.1	.3				1.2	1.8
							4.2	14.8
						Net Profit + Depr., Dep., Amort./Cur. Mat. L/T/D	(12) 3.1	(15) 6.6
							1.1	2.3
.0	.1	.1	.0				.1	.1
.4	.5	.2	.5			Fixed/Worth	.7	.5
-2.1	4.9	1.6	2.0				UND	-2.5
.5	.6	.5	1.1				.7	.8
2.1	2.4	1.5	6.4			Debt/Worth	4.6	4.8
-5.5	27.0	5.3	57.8				-9.4	-4.3
313.0	249.4	77.1	164.2				122.5	125.3
(48) 103.6	(44) 88.0	(28) 38.5	(18) 49.0			% Profit Before Taxes/Tangible Net Worth	(129) 49.2	(111) 55.1
44.3	22.0	10.0	13.4				13.6	21.4
122.4	68.0	20.9	20.6				38.8	47.6
38.7	19.6	13.3	9.8			% Profit Before Taxes/Total Assets	11.7	13.3
11.4	6.6	4.6	.0				.6	3.2
999.8	125.1	94.8	122.7				86.6	177.0
80.2	32.0	57.4	41.9			Sales/Net Fixed Assets	23.5	37.7
29.2	9.1	5.0	12.9				9.8	11.7
9.9	5.2	3.8	2.7				5.0	5.3
5.6	2.5	2.2	1.4			Sales/Total Assets	2.5	3.0
3.0	1.4	.7	.3				1.1	1.5
.6	.5	.3	.8				.9	.7
(32) 1.2	(35) 1.2	(20) .9	(17) 1.4			% Depr., Dep., Amort./Sales	(102) 1.4	(101) 1.4
2.2	5.3	3.7	2.9				2.8	3.1
10.5	4.2	2.7					8.9	4.7
(43) 17.9	(23) 11.6	(12) 15.2				% Officers', Directors' Owners' Comp/Sales	(66) 17.8	(71) 9.8
28.0	21.5	31.4					30.5	25.2
82025M	180846M	557319M	954864M	53898M	2405744M	Net Sales ($)	6112608M	7431157M
14930M	57009M	138736M	546848M	83781M	692474M	Total Assets ($)	2678154M	2411204M

M = $ thousand MM = $ million

See Pages 9 through 22 for Explanation of Ratios and Data

Comparative Historical Data				Current Data Sorted by Sales					
			Type of Statement						
16	14	14	Unqualified		1		1	5	7
4	3	10	Reviewed		3	1	1	5	
7	6	10	Compiled	4	4		1	1	
53	55	57	Tax Returns	28	15	10	3	1	
99	92	102	Other	31	29	11	10	7	14
					17 (4/1-9/30/13)		176 (10/1/13-3/31/14)		
4/1/11-3/31/12 ALL	4/1/12-3/31/13 ALL	4/1/13-3/31/14 ALL		0-1MM	1-3MM	3-5MM	5-10MM	10-25MM	25MM & OVER
179	170	193	**NUMBER OF STATEMENTS**	63	52	22	16	19	21
%	%	%	**ASSETS**	%	%	%	%	%	%
27.2	27.2	25.4	Cash & Equivalents	27.8	33.1	17.8	19.0	16.5	19.8
22.6	23.2	23.3	Trade Receivables (net)	13.7	18.4	25.8	42.6	35.9	35.5
1.0	.9	1.1	Inventory	.0	1.3	3.8	2.9	.6	.6
6.5	6.0	5.7	All Other Current	4.4	3.1	6.1	7.7	12.8	7.7
57.3	57.2	55.5	Total Current	45.9	55.8	53.5	72.2	65.8	63.7
16.2	17.8	17.9	Fixed Assets (net)	26.0	16.5	18.3	6.5	11.7	10.6
13.3	12.1	12.1	Intangibles (net)	12.9	11.5	7.5	9.6	10.0	19.9
13.3	12.9	14.5	All Other Non-Current	15.3	16.2	20.7	11.7	12.6	5.8
100.0	100.0	100.0	Total	100.0	100.0	100.0	100.0	100.0	100.0
			LIABILITIES						
15.6	12.8	14.9	Notes Payable-Short Term	15.8	20.6	16.1	9.1	5.8	9.4
2.4	2.9	2.7	Cur. Mat.-L.T.D.	2.1	4.0	1.8	1.9	3.5	2.3
7.1	8.0	7.0	Trade Payables	9.4	2.0	4.6	9.6	6.8	13.5
.6	.9	.1	Income Taxes Payable	.0	.0	.0	.0	.0	.4
21.4	20.8	21.6	All Other Current	21.8	19.1	20.9	20.8	26.0	24.5
47.1	45.5	46.3	Total Current	49.1	45.6	43.4	41.4	42.2	50.2
16.6	15.8	14.3	Long-Term Debt	14.8	19.9	12.5	11.5	4.8	11.9
.2	.1	.1	Deferred Taxes	.0	.0	.0	.0	.0	.9
13.6	6.4	11.7	All Other Non-Current	13.6	10.1	13.2	2.3	9.7	17.0
22.5	32.2	27.6	Net Worth	22.6	24.4	30.9	44.7	43.4	20.0
100.0	100.0	100.0	Total Liabilties & Net Worth	100.0	100.0	100.0	100.0	100.0	100.0
			INCOME DATA						
100.0	100.0	100.0	Net Sales	100.0	100.0	100.0	100.0	100.0	100.0
			Gross Profit						
84.1	85.3	84.3	Operating Expenses	81.5	83.0	84.5	83.8	89.6	91.5
15.9	14.7	15.7	Operating Profit	18.5	17.0	15.5	16.2	10.4	8.5
1.3	1.6	1.0	All Other Expenses (net)	1.2	1.1	.3	.2	.8	1.5
14.6	13.2	14.7	Profit Before Taxes	17.3	16.0	15.2	16.0	9.6	6.9
			RATIOS						
3.6	3.2	3.8		6.3	4.8	2.5	4.4	2.5	2.4
1.4	1.5	1.5	Current	1.6	1.5	1.1	1.6	1.8	1.2
.7	.8	.8		.4	.7	.7	1.2	1.4	1.0
3.4	2.7	3.2		5.2	3.6	2.3	4.3	2.2	2.3
(178) 1.2	1.4	(192) 1.3	Quick	1.5	1.4	.9	1.4	(18) 1.6	1.0
.5	.7	.6		.3	.7	.5	1.1	1.2	.8
0 UND	**0** UND	**0** UND		**0** UND	**0** UND	**0** UND	**17** 22.1	**23** 15.9	**40** 9.2
6 56.8	**17** 21.2	**19** 19.4	Sales/Receivables	**0** UND	**5** 72.3	**26** 14.3	**36** 10.1	**54** 6.8	**52** 7.0
51 7.2	**49** 7.4	**53** 6.9		**28** 13.0	**41** 8.9	**51** 7.2	**68** 5.4	**72** 5.1	**73** 5.0
			Cost of Sales/Inventory						
			Cost of Sales/Payables						
7.1	7.8	6.7		8.0	5.7	9.5	6.1	5.4	6.9
28.6	21.9	21.1	Sales/Working Capital	23.3	23.9	259.6	10.9	8.8	21.6
-34.1	-45.0	-55.5		-17.0	-40.6	-39.0	40.5	14.4	-120.5
51.7	29.8	33.6		17.0	55.7	34.1	87.8	71.2	22.3
(122) 12.4	(123) 10.3	(133) 10.4	EBIT/Interest	(29) 8.8	(43) 11.0	(19) 11.0	(10) 10.6	(15) 14.5	(17) 2.7
4.0	3.6	2.5		3.0	4.0	3.4	2.6	4.2	-5.5
6.5									
(12) 4.7			Net Profit + Depr., Dep., Amort./Cur. Mat. L/T/D						
1.6									
.0	.1	.1		.0	.1	.1	.0	.1	.2
.5	.4	.5	Fixed/Worth	.4	.5	.8	.1	.2	.6
-1.4	8.4	13.9		4.5	-2.3	3.8	1.0	2.2	-.6
.5	.6	.5		.5	.5	.6	.3	.5	1.2
3.3	2.2	2.5	Debt/Worth	1.3	3.0	6.0	1.4	1.7	6.5
-5.1	-51.9	-13.7		-5.6	-6.2	NM	6.4	21.5	-5.1
168.2	190.5	214.1		163.0	318.3	512.0	285.7	76.6	203.2
(117) 77.1	(127) 80.0	(140) 70.2	% Profit Before Taxes/Tangible Net Worth	(46) 70.0	(33) 89.5	(17) 128.5	(14) 56.3	(16) 49.0	(14) 96.2
31.8	20.4	20.5		14.6	35.9	16.1	16.3	10.5	13.4
73.7	64.1	66.0		103.3	53.0	114.2	152.3	21.4	31.3
27.1	20.3	19.4	% Profit Before Taxes/Total Assets	25.0	26.0	21.1	24.7	12.1	8.4
6.5	4.1	5.4		5.4	7.3	7.4	7.3	3.3	-1.9
473.1	214.0	222.6		306.5	658.0	343.8	169.6	80.8	106.0
51.7	40.2	46.1	Sales/Net Fixed Assets	42.7	45.9	32.2	92.1	57.4	40.6
19.2	14.0	13.5		6.5	12.7	10.4	47.3	20.4	12.0
6.1	5.6	6.1		6.0	6.9	5.9	7.2	3.8	4.7
3.5	3.1	3.2	Sales/Total Assets	3.4	3.4	3.9	4.0	2.2	2.7
1.5	1.5	1.5		1.4	1.5	2.5	1.9	1.4	1.4
.6	.6	.6		.8	.6	.6		.5	.6
(92) 1.2	(91) 1.2	(105) 1.1	% Depr., Dep., Amort./Sales	(27) 1.9	(24) 1.4	(16) 1.0		(15) .9	(14) .9
2.8	3.0	2.4		4.1	2.9	1.9		3.6	1.6
5.6	6.2	7.2		10.5	5.3	3.4			
(73) 12.5	(72) 12.9	(80) 16.5	% Officers', Directors' Owners' Comp/Sales	(31) 18.5	(23) 16.0	(10) 10.5			
20.5	22.1	27.6		28.2	19.6	28.2			
7434064M	4135699M	4234696M	Net Sales ($)	32612M	96841M	86804M	114132M	265308M	3638999M
1710155M	1377314M	1533778M	Total Assets ($)	35237M	75064M	54797M	55923M	205622M	1107135M

M = $ thousand MM = $ million

See Pages 9 through 22 for Explanation of Ratios and Data

Current Data Sorted by Assets							Comparative Historical Data	
						Type of Statement		
	1	9	13	2	6	Unqualified	42	41
	9	55	19	4		Reviewed	112	129
13	21	22	2	1		Compiled	99	91
65	34	17				Tax Returns	127	129
36	53	76	28	6	3	Other	222	212
35 (4/1-9/30/13)		460 (10/1/13-3/31/14)					4/1/09-3/31/10 ALL	4/1/10-3/31/11 ALL
0-500M	500M-2MM	2-10MM	10-50MM	50-100MM	100-250MM			
114	118	179	62	13	9	**NUMBER OF STATEMENTS**	602	602
%	%	%	%	%	%	**ASSETS**	%	%
32.6	22.9	11.5	14.0	13.5		Cash & Equivalents	16.4	17.2
12.1	34.1	52.3	50.7	36.8		Trade Receivables (net)	40.5	39.3
.3	1.8	2.3	2.3	1.3		Inventory	1.5	1.7
4.0	3.1	6.3	10.4	13.9		All Other Current	6.7	7.9
49.0	61.9	72.4	77.4	65.4		Total Current	65.2	66.1
31.5	25.5	15.8	10.6	12.4		Fixed Assets (net)	21.5	20.8
3.7	2.2	4.3	3.0	7.4		Intangibles (net)	3.1	3.3
15.9	10.4	7.5	9.1	14.8		All Other Non-Current	10.2	9.8
100.0	100.0	100.0	100.0	100.0		Total	100.0	100.0
						LIABILITIES		
40.9	13.1	6.7	4.9	4.1		Notes Payable-Short Term	18.8	16.0
3.9	3.0	1.9	2.2	2.1		Cur. Mat.-L.T.D.	3.4	2.9
6.9	13.3	16.4	18.5	11.2		Trade Payables	14.5	14.9
.6	.2	2.0	2.2	2.4		Income Taxes Payable	1.9	1.8
25.7	18.8	15.7	22.0	27.6		All Other Current	19.5	20.4
78.0	48.4	42.7	49.8	47.4		Total Current	58.2	55.9
22.0	12.4	9.5	6.9	4.1		Long-Term Debt	11.1	10.8
.0	.2	1.1	2.0	.4		Deferred Taxes	1.0	.8
19.0	4.9	6.4	6.9	5.1		All Other Non-Current	5.9	8.3
-19.0	34.1	40.3	34.4	43.1		Net Worth	23.7	24.2
100.0	100.0	100.0	100.0	100.0		Total Liabilties & Net Worth	100.0	100.0
						INCOME DATA		
100.0	100.0	100.0	100.0	100.0		Net Sales	100.0	100.0
						Gross Profit		
92.7	89.1	90.8	94.6	94.5		Operating Expenses	97.2	94.7
7.3	10.9	9.2	5.4	5.5		Operating Profit	2.8	5.3
1.2	2.5	1.9	.5	.8		All Other Expenses (net)	1.7	1.5
6.1	8.4	7.3	4.9	4.6		Profit Before Taxes	1.1	3.8
						RATIOS		
2.1	4.2	2.9	2.2	1.8			2.4	2.6
.8	1.4	1.7	1.6	1.4		Current	1.4	1.4
.2	.9	1.2	1.2	1.1			.9	1.0
2.1	3.4	2.5	2.0	1.5			2.2	2.2
.8	1.4	1.5	1.4	1.0		Quick	(601) 1.2	1.2
.2	.7	1.0	1.0	.6			.7	.8
0 UND	**0** UND	**58** 6.3	**64** 5.7	**51** 7.2			**0** UND	**0** UND
0 UND	**39** 9.4	**79** 4.6	**85** 4.3	**64** 5.7		Sales/Receivables	**63** 5.8	**60** 6.0
1 260.5	**76** 4.8	**107** 3.4	**118** 3.1	**111** 3.3			**102** 3.6	**91** 4.0
						Cost of Sales/Inventory		
						Cost of Sales/Payables		
32.4	6.4	4.4	4.5	4.9			5.6	5.7
-89.1	23.6	8.0	8.2	8.5		Sales/Working Capital	13.7	12.8
-11.7	-44.8	34.5	21.6	38.6			-54.0	-234.2
34.8	61.8	64.9	57.3	44.9			19.4	21.3
(82) 6.2	(94) 11.2	(145) 15.8	(55) 15.1	(11) 15.7		EBIT/Interest	(473) 2.3	(463) 5.3
1.0	1.0	4.4	2.5	2.0			-8.6	-1.9
		15.1	6.3				5.9	5.5
		(31) 3.5	(26) 3.4			Net Profit + Depr., Dep., Amort./Cur. Mat. L/T/D	(123) 1.6	(105) 2.5
		1.1	1.8				-1.1	.5
.1	.2	.1	.1	.3			.1	.2
1.2	.4	.3	.2	.3		Fixed/Worth	.4	.4
-.7	3.4	.7	.6	.5			2.4	1.4
.6	.4	.6	.9	1.1			.7	.7
10.6	1.4	1.4	2.0	1.7		Debt/Worth	1.9	1.9
-2.5	13.0	3.5	3.7	3.1			7.3	7.0
285.2	72.0	60.7	44.7	48.6			47.6	52.0
(65) 82.8	(94) 34.9	(163) 25.0	(60) 24.3	20.7		% Profit Before Taxes/Tangible Net Worth	(496) 11.2	(494) 16.7
22.0	5.2	8.5	11.2	4.9			-20.6	-4.9
73.7	31.9	21.8	14.5	19.2			17.6	21.7
23.4	11.1	8.7	8.9	4.1		% Profit Before Taxes/Total Assets	2.4	5.2
.0	.1	2.0	1.2	1.7			-11.8	-3.4
277.3	53.6	55.3	56.5	23.4			54.6	54.7
36.4	29.9	23.5	27.1	17.1		Sales/Net Fixed Assets	23.4	23.4
19.4	12.2	15.0	16.0	8.7			10.9	11.3
17.0	5.0	2.9	2.7	2.0			4.3	3.9
7.4	3.1	2.3	2.0	1.7		Sales/Total Assets	2.6	2.6
3.9	1.9	1.8	1.6	1.3			1.7	1.8
.4	.7	.8	.9	1.4			.7	.8
(56) 1.1	(79) 1.2	(140) 1.2	(56) 1.2	(12) 1.8		% Depr., Dep., Amort./Sales	(453) 1.5	(442) 1.5
1.9	2.1	1.8	1.9	2.2			2.5	2.4
7.8	5.4	3.4	2.2				6.4	4.5
(82) 10.5	(56) 9.7	(60) 7.0	(14) 7.6			% Officers', Directors' Owners' Comp/Sales	(249) 12.4	(249) 9.6
18.4	16.0	10.8	14.6				19.5	17.9
226675M	520402M	1957023M	2897168M	2777385M	3765682M	Net Sales ($)	9757855M	10780629M
25295M	133065M	860133M	1385042M	1010592M	1480138M	Total Assets ($)	4513410M	5240868M

M = $ thousand MM = $ million

See Pages 9 through 22 for Explanation of Ratios and Data

Comparative Historical Data / Current Data Sorted by Sales

4/1/11-3/31/12 ALL	4/1/12-3/31/13 ALL	4/1/13-3/31/14 ALL	Type of Statement	0-1MM	1-3MM	3-5MM	5-10MM	10-25MM	25MM & OVER
36	24	31	Unqualified				2	9	20
114	90	87	Reviewed		1	5	20	44	17
95	65	59	Compiled	5	16	8	15	12	3
146	116	116	Tax Returns	37	35	18	20	5	1
205	188	202	Other	20	40	28	36	44	34
				35 (4/1-9/30/13)			460 (10/1/13-3/31/14)		
596	483	495	NUMBER OF STATEMENTS	62	92	59	93	114	75
%	%	%	**ASSETS**	%	%	%	%	%	%
17.4	18.4	19.7	Cash & Equivalents	15.6	32.0	19.2	17.4	17.0	15.0
40.3	38.0	37.8	Trade Receivables (net)	10.9	22.9	41.4	44.6	51.2	46.7
1.9	1.4	1.7	Inventory	.0	1.5	1.3	2.6	1.9	2.2
6.0	5.6	5.8	All Other Current	4.9	3.2	2.6	5.0	7.6	10.7
65.6	63.4	64.9	Total Current	31.4	59.7	64.5	69.6	77.6	74.6
20.8	21.1	20.8	Fixed Assets (net)	51.1	24.8	17.5	16.5	12.9	11.2
3.2	4.0	3.6	Intangibles (net)	1.2	4.7	6.7	3.7	1.9	4.4
10.3	11.5	10.6	All Other Non-Current	16.3	10.8	11.3	10.2	7.6	9.9
100.0	100.0	100.0	Total	100.0	100.0	100.0	100.0	100.0	100.0
			LIABILITIES						
16.0	19.3	16.0	Notes Payable-Short Term	31.5	20.9	21.3	10.8	10.5	7.6
2.8	2.8	2.7	Cur. Mat.-L.T.D.	3.5	2.3	2.8	3.1	2.1	2.7
14.5	13.8	13.6	Trade Payables	5.4	11.4	13.9	12.3	19.3	15.6
1.4	1.4	1.3	Income Taxes Payable	.0	.3	1.4	.7	2.8	1.8
16.1	18.0	20.1	All Other Current	15.0	17.0	19.0	17.8	23.0	27.3
50.8	55.2	53.6	Total Current	55.4	51.9	58.4	44.7	57.7	54.9
13.2	13.8	12.5	Long-Term Debt	39.1	16.0	8.9	7.4	5.1	7.0
.7	.5	.7	Deferred Taxes	.0	.1	.0	1.0	1.2	1.5
9.6	8.1	9.0	All Other Non-Current	16.7	6.0	9.8	13.6	4.7	6.1
25.7	22.4	24.3	Net Worth	-11.0	26.0	22.9	33.3	31.3	30.5
100.0	100.0	100.0	Total Liabilties & Net Worth	100.0	100.0	100.0	100.0	100.0	100.0
			INCOME DATA						
100.0	100.0	100.0	Net Sales	100.0	100.0	100.0	100.0	100.0	100.0
			Gross Profit						
92.9	92.6	91.5	Operating Expenses	73.8	93.8	94.4	92.6	95.1	94.2
7.1	7.4	8.5	Operating Profit	26.2	6.2	5.6	7.4	4.9	5.8
1.2	1.7	1.7	All Other Expenses (net)	10.1	.6	.2	.4	.2	.9
5.9	5.7	6.8	Profit Before Taxes	16.1	5.6	5.4	7.0	4.7	4.9
			RATIOS						
2.7	2.5	2.6		1.3	8.9	2.7	3.9	2.4	2.0
1.5	1.4	1.4	Current	.7	1.4	1.4	2.0	1.6	1.4
1.0	.9	.9		.1	.6	.9	1.1	1.2	1.2
2.5	2.3	2.3		1.2	8.0	2.7	3.3	2.0	1.8
1.3	1.3	1.3	Quick	.5	1.4	1.2	1.7	1.4	1.1
.8	.7	.7		.1	.4	.7	1.1	1.0	.8
0 UND	0 UND	0 UND		0 UND	0 UND	0 UND	32 11.5	50 7.3	55 6.6
61 6.0	61 6.0	59 6.2	Sales/Receivables	0 UND	0 UND	51 7.1	68 5.4	79 4.6	74 4.9
96 3.8	89 4.1	91 4.0		5 69.2	60 6.1	101 3.6	104 3.5	104 3.5	101 3.6
			Cost of Sales/Inventory						
			Cost of Sales/Payables						
5.6	6.0	5.8		71.0	5.8	6.2	4.5	5.5	5.4
12.3	16.5	15.5	Sales/Working Capital	-18.3	42.0	19.9	9.5	10.0	9.4
802.3	-98.1	-109.7		-4.8	-27.4	-97.3	93.2	39.0	27.2
29.3	49.0	55.0		31.1	59.0	30.2	75.6	84.2	44.9
(468) 7.6	(367) 9.6	(395) 13.0	EBIT/Interest	(37) 5.2	(67) 11.0	(50) 5.8	(76) 18.4	(98) 17.1	(67) 15.1
1.1	1.3	2.4		1.8	1.9	.9	2.7	4.5	5.0
10.3	10.2	9.0						27.2	5.0
(88) 2.8	(72) 3.0	(77) 2.6	Net Profit + Depr., Dep., Amort./Cur. Mat. L/T/D					(26) 4.3	(35) 2.6
.7	1.0	1.1						1.8	1.1
.1	.1	.1		.2	.1	.1	.1	.1	.2
.4	.4	.3	Fixed/Worth	2.5	.5	.3	.3	.3	.3
1.4	2.1	1.9		UND	-4.5	5.7	.9	.6	.6
.6	.6	.6		1.0	.2	.6	.4	.9	1.0
1.7	2.0	1.9	Debt/Worth	9.5	1.4	2.1	1.2	1.6	2.1
7.2	18.5	9.9		-5.4	-6.2	-10.5	4.9	3.5	3.7
58.6	63.5	71.5		234.8	77.7	81.9	69.8	65.2	46.2
(488) 19.6	(378) 21.0	(403) 28.7	% Profit Before Taxes/Tangible Net Worth	(43) 32.8	(63) 41.9	(44) 42.2	(80) 32.8	(102) 24.0	(71) 25.0
2.9	3.2	8.6		5.3	9.3	3.7	10.9	7.5	11.1
22.9	29.1	29.6		44.6	41.8	37.2	30.8	21.7	15.4
8.0	7.6	9.5	% Profit Before Taxes/Total Assets	8.2	16.6	8.2	11.1	6.8	8.9
.5	.4	1.1		1.0	.5	-1.7	1.2	2.1	2.1
55.0	71.3	63.5		42.6	75.5	92.3	59.2	58.4	53.0
25.8	30.7	27.1	Sales/Net Fixed Assets	12.0	31.2	32.6	28.5	26.2	25.7
12.1	12.8	15.0		.2	17.7	16.4	15.0	17.1	13.7
4.3	4.6	4.7		6.0	6.6	7.6	3.9	3.7	2.9
2.6	2.7	2.7	Sales/Total Assets	2.4	3.6	3.2	2.7	2.5	2.1
1.7	1.9	1.9		.2	2.5	2.1	2.0	1.9	1.6
.7	.7	.6		1.8	.6	.6	.7	.6	.9
(444) 1.4	(342) 1.3	(350) 1.2	% Depr., Dep., Amort./Sales	(36) 7.2	(47) 1.2	(40) .9	(67) 1.2	(93) 1.1	(67) 1.2
2.2	2.1	1.9		19.6	2.1	1.7	1.7	1.6	1.9
6.5	5.7	5.4		7.9	6.4	5.6	5.0	2.4	6.6
(235) 11.4	(190) 11.3	(215) 9.5	% Officers', Directors' Owners' Comp/Sales	(26) 10.3	(57) 10.9	(37) 9.6	(43) 8.6	(36) 5.4	(16) 9.8
17.9	17.9	15.4		19.9	15.9	16.4	14.2	11.7	15.9
10878412M	8471426M	12144335M	Net Sales ($)	30063M	171613M	234686M	665602M	1723932M	9318439M
4494282M	4025404M	4894265M	Total Assets ($)	51040M	59631M	81863M	268215M	699318M	3734198M

M = $ thousand MM = $ million

See Pages 9 through 22 for Explanation of Ratios and Data

Current Data Sorted by Assets							Comparative Historical Data	
						Type of Statement		
		2	2	1		Unqualified	6	11
	6	14	2	1		Reviewed	33	33
2	8	7				Compiled	19	16
27	15	3				Tax Returns	61	52
12	19	14	1			Other	72	64
	10 (4/1-9/30/13)		126 (10/1/13-3/31/14)				4/1/09-3/31/10 ALL	4/1/10-3/31/11 ALL
0-500M	500M-2MM	2-10MM	10-50MM	50-100MM	100-250MM			
41	48	40	5	2		**NUMBER OF STATEMENTS**	191	176
%	%	%	%	%	%	**ASSETS**	%	%
20.4	12.8	10.1			DATA NOT AVAILABLE	Cash & Equivalents	14.1	15.6
19.2	37.2	37.8				Trade Receivables (net)	30.0	29.5
3.5	6.2	4.7				Inventory	6.1	7.0
1.4	4.8	4.2				All Other Current	4.0	4.3
44.5	61.0	56.8				Total Current	54.3	56.4
38.6	29.8	31.3				Fixed Assets (net)	33.2	30.6
3.0	1.6	4.9				Intangibles (net)	3.2	3.0
13.9	7.6	7.0				All Other Non-Current	9.3	10.0
100.0	100.0	100.0				Total	100.0	100.0
						LIABILITIES		
11.2	11.2	7.8				Notes Payable-Short Term	16.1	16.1
1.9	5.2	4.4				Cur. Mat.-L.T.D.	6.5	4.8
6.9	15.8	10.5				Trade Payables	13.1	12.1
.0	.6	1.9				Income Taxes Payable	.8	.6
13.1	7.2	8.5				All Other Current	16.4	11.0
33.0	39.9	33.1				Total Current	52.8	44.6
41.8	19.2	20.6				Long-Term Debt	20.5	20.9
.0	.0	.8				Deferred Taxes	.3	.1
15.2	4.4	2.9				All Other Non-Current	7.0	6.8
9.9	36.4	42.5				Net Worth	19.4	27.7
100.0	100.0	100.0				Total Liabilties & Net Worth	100.0	100.0
						INCOME DATA		
100.0	100.0	100.0				Net Sales	100.0	100.0
						Gross Profit		
91.9	95.1	91.5				Operating Expenses	96.3	93.0
8.1	4.9	8.5				Operating Profit	3.7	7.0
.8	1.4	2.1				All Other Expenses (net)	1.8	2.2
7.4	3.5	6.4				Profit Before Taxes	1.9	4.8
						RATIOS		
5.2	2.6	2.7					2.4	3.3
1.5	1.6	1.9				Current	1.5	1.6
.5	1.0	1.2					.7	.8
5.0	2.1	2.3					1.9	2.4
1.4	1.4	1.3				Quick	1.1	1.1
.4	.6	1.0					.5	.5
0 UND	**16** 23.0	**32** 11.5					**8** 45.7	**9** 42.3
4 90.6	**33** 11.2	**51** 7.1				Sales/Receivables	**39** 9.4	**32** 11.4
27 13.5	**87** 4.2	**74** 4.9					**69** 5.3	**59** 6.2
						Cost of Sales/Inventory		
						Cost of Sales/Payables		
11.7	9.7	5.8					6.5	6.4
33.8	14.5	9.5				Sales/Working Capital	18.1	18.9
-49.6	NM	35.1					-25.7	-43.8
22.0	15.1	25.2					8.4	12.9
(36) 10.4	(41) 2.7	(37) 7.6				EBIT/Interest	(154) 2.1	(144) 4.2
1.6	-3.5	2.4					-1.1	-.8
		8.0					3.4	6.6
		(12) 2.7				Net Profit + Depr., Dep., Amort./Cur. Mat. L/T/D	(28) 1.4	(16) 1.0
		1.6					-.3	.2
.4	.2	.3					.3	.3
1.4	.9	.7				Fixed/Worth	.8	.9
-2.1	3.1	1.2					86.7	33.5
.6	.7	.6					.8	.6
3.6	1.6	1.5				Debt/Worth	2.1	1.9
-5.9	7.8	2.6					UND	80.8
179.8	59.1	61.7					52.0	71.8
(26) 75.0	(41) 27.3	(36) 27.5				% Profit Before Taxes/Tangible Net Worth	(144) 15.0	(135) 18.4
29.6	1.4	8.7					-4.0	-1.6
54.6	24.3	28.1					16.6	22.2
17.3	7.4	8.5				% Profit Before Taxes/Total Assets	4.1	4.8
.8	-7.1	2.1					-4.7	-3.5
40.1	31.7	23.6					28.9	36.0
18.4	18.4	10.2				Sales/Net Fixed Assets	11.5	14.7
6.3	5.9	4.8					5.2	6.4
7.6	4.3	3.0					4.1	4.1
4.4	3.1	2.3				Sales/Total Assets	2.6	2.9
2.9	2.3	1.9					1.6	1.8
.9	1.1	1.1					1.5	1.2
(22) 2.8	(30) 2.8	(37) 1.8				% Depr., Dep., Amort./Sales	(140) 2.9	(124) 2.7
6.1	4.4	3.3					4.8	5.1
5.2	3.6	1.8					3.9	2.5
(28) 7.7	(25) 5.9	(18) 3.2				% Officers', Directors' Owners' Comp/Sales	(88) 6.8	(85) 5.5
11.5	10.3	9.9					11.5	9.3
48075M	175441M	450032M	189512M	145958M		Net Sales ($)	1427877M	2616312M
9841M	51907M	174058M	111512M	107420M		Total Assets ($)	716433M	1193809M

M = $ thousand MM = $ million

See Pages 9 through 22 for Explanation of Ratios and Data

Comparative Historical Data				Current Data Sorted by Sales					
			Type of Statement						
10	4	5	Unqualified					2	3
21	26	23	Reviewed		2	5	5	8	3
19	11	17	Compiled	3	4	3	6	1	
53	56	45	Tax Returns	16	16	8	2	3	
58	50	46	Other	7	14	10	8	4	3
4/1/11-3/31/12 ALL	4/1/12-3/31/13 ALL	4/1/13-3/31/14 ALL		10 (4/1-9/30/13)			126 (10/1/13-3/31/14)		
				0-1MM	1-3MM	3-5MM	5-10MM	10-25MM	25MM & OVER
161	147	136	**NUMBER OF STATEMENTS**	26	36	26	21	18	9
%	%	%	**ASSETS**	%	%	%	%	%	%
14.8	14.6	14.0	Cash & Equivalents	14.8	15.4	15.0	11.8	13.9	
26.5	28.8	31.4	Trade Receivables (net)	24.5	22.0	41.6	35.5	36.1	
6.3	4.5	4.8	Inventory	1.9	6.1	5.9	5.1	5.8	
4.5	6.1	3.5	All Other Current	2.2	1.2	6.4	3.1	7.1	
52.0	53.9	53.6	Total Current	43.4	44.7	68.8	55.6	62.9	
35.0	35.1	33.7	Fixed Assets (net)	43.6	41.1	18.9	33.6	25.2	
2.8	2.5	3.5	Intangibles (net)	4.9	1.7	1.8	4.4	3.9	
10.2	8.5	9.2	All Other Non-Current	8.1	12.5	10.6	6.4	8.0	
100.0	100.0	100.0	Total	100.0	100.0	100.0	100.0	100.0	
			LIABILITIES						
15.4	11.7	9.8	Notes Payable-Short Term	7.5	14.5	10.4	8.2	8.0	
5.7	8.0	4.0	Cur. Mat.-L.T.D.	1.1	2.8	5.4	7.5	4.2	
11.9	11.8	11.4	Trade Payables	4.9	12.3	16.7	10.1	11.3	
.1	.6	.8	Income Taxes Payable	.0	.0	1.1	1.4	2.4	
12.7	11.3	9.4	All Other Current	8.0	11.0	11.6	6.4	9.7	
45.8	43.5	35.4	Total Current	21.6	40.7	45.2	33.6	35.7	
28.2	24.9	26.4	Long-Term Debt	43.4	35.6	14.3	22.7	12.0	
.2	.4	.3	Deferred Taxes	.0	.1	.2	1.2	.3	
5.6	4.8	7.6	All Other Non-Current	18.8	6.4	3.1	4.1	3.7	
20.2	26.5	30.3	Net Worth	16.2	17.2	37.2	38.5	48.4	
100.0	100.0	100.0	Total Liabilties & Net Worth	100.0	100.0	100.0	100.0	100.0	
			INCOME DATA						
100.0	100.0	100.0	Net Sales	100.0	100.0	100.0	100.0	100.0	
			Gross Profit						
93.1	92.5	93.2	Operating Expenses	86.8	93.5	97.9	92.2	95.3	
6.9	7.5	6.8	Operating Profit	13.2	6.5	2.1	7.8	4.7	
2.0	.8	1.4	All Other Expenses (net)	4.4	1.0	.1	1.5	.3	
4.8	6.7	5.4	Profit Before Taxes	8.8	5.5	2.0	6.3	4.4	
			RATIOS						
2.6	2.9	3.0		5.6	2.6	2.0	4.3	2.3	
1.4	1.4	1.6	Current	1.7	1.4	1.5	1.7	1.9	
.8	.8	1.0		.8	.5	1.2	1.2	1.1	
2.2	2.2	2.6		5.3	2.4	1.7	3.6	2.1	
1.1	1.1	1.3	Quick	1.6	1.1	1.3	1.2	1.2	
.4	.5	.8		.4	.4	.8	1.0	1.0	
4 88.3	**1** 665.9	**6** 56.2		**0** UND	**0** UND	**10** 38.1	**30** 12.3	**24** 15.3	
29 12.7	**31** 11.9	**32** 11.4	Sales/Receivables	**14** 26.2	**18** 19.8	**45** 8.2	**46** 7.9	**43** 8.5	
54 6.8	**59** 6.2	**65** 5.6		**37** 9.8	**46** 8.0	**94** 3.9	**66** 5.5	**60** 6.1	
			Cost of Sales/Inventory						
			Cost of Sales/Payables						
6.9	7.3	8.5		7.9	10.4	10.0	5.1	8.3	
24.7	23.3	15.2	Sales/Working Capital	28.2	24.7	14.4	14.2	10.1	
-32.7	-40.8	-375.4		-15.4	-28.4	60.0	28.7	40.9	
12.5	19.4	18.2		18.7	17.0	26.7	18.8	17.4	
(132) 4.7	(123) 6.8	(121) 6.2	EBIT/Interest	(19) 7.0	(32) 4.8	(24) 7.1	(20) 7.2	(17) 7.1	
1.4	1.7	1.5		-1.9	.9	-3.5	2.5	2.6	
6.0	5.0	7.1							
(17) 3.8	(19) 1.8	(18) 2.2	Net Profit + Depr., Dep., Amort./Cur. Mat. L/T/D						
2.0	.2	.7							
.4	.4	.3		.3	.6	.2	.4	.4	
1.0	1.1	.9	Fixed/Worth	1.2	2.0	.6	1.0	.6	
5.1	7.2	13.3		-6.6	-2.9	1.5	1.6	.9	
.8	.7	.6		.3	.7	1.2	.6	.6	
2.1	2.1	2.0	Debt/Worth	3.1	3.2	1.7	1.9	1.4	
15.8	15.8	25.5		-14.3	-8.0	7.5	5.7	2.4	
89.0	92.4	82.8		107.6	263.0	65.4	57.1	51.4	
(131) 24.0	(120) 35.3	(108) 34.0	% Profit Before Taxes/Tangible Net Worth	(18) 51.7	(24) 57.9	(23) 19.7	(18) 27.5	20.6	
4.8	7.5	8.4		17.1	3.0	.0	14.5	8.1	
21.6	29.9	31.8		44.1	40.3	21.1	26.2	26.6	
8.5	10.9	11.0	% Profit Before Taxes/Total Assets	20.6	11.0	4.2	12.6	10.1	
1.1	2.8	1.6		-.9	.0	-5.7	2.9	1.7	
30.4	31.2	28.2		21.8	30.3	48.2	22.0	32.8	
12.3	13.4	14.3	Sales/Net Fixed Assets	6.6	11.7	25.3	10.2	13.4	
5.1	5.6	5.1		3.9	4.4	14.7	4.5	6.1	
4.4	4.7	4.5		4.2	5.5	6.0	3.7	4.2	
2.9	3.1	3.0	Sales/Total Assets	2.8	3.3	3.7	2.5	2.7	
1.7	1.9	2.1		1.4	2.3	2.5	1.8	2.2	
1.2	1.4	1.2		2.4	1.4	.9	1.0	1.1	
(113) 2.8	(106) 2.6	(96) 2.6	% Depr., Dep., Amort./Sales	(15) 7.2	(20) 3.0	(17) 1.6	(19) 2.8	(17) 1.7	
4.7	4.7	4.2		20.4	5.3	2.8	4.0	3.1	
3.0	3.4	3.6		4.8	5.4	3.9			
(90) 5.6	(75) 5.3	(72) 6.0	% Officers', Directors' Owners' Comp/Sales	(15) 7.1	(20) 6.5	(18) 5.9			
9.0	11.7	10.6		17.6	10.3	11.9			
1680301M	**1884565M**	**1009018M**	Net Sales ($)	**13677M**	**70248M**	**99145M**	**151440M**	**259309M**	**415199M**
841974M	**538392M**	**454738M**	Total Assets ($)	**12955M**	**27788M**	**29169M**	**62776M**	**91514M**	**230536M**

M = $ thousand MM = $ million

See Pages 9 through 22 for Explanation of Ratios and Data

Current Data Sorted by Assets / Comparative Historical Data

Type of Statement	0-500M	500M-2MM	2-10MM	10-50MM	50-100MM	100-250MM	4/1/09-3/31/10 ALL	4/1/10-3/31/11 ALL
Unqualified		8	55	95	23	13	222	243
Reviewed	4	31	183	76	3	3	353	337
Compiled	20	69	118	16		2	219	248
Tax Returns	148	126	71	8	1		286	315
Other	62	164	265	167	26	22	634	709
	183 (4/1-9/30/13)			1,596 (10/1/13-3/31/14)				
NUMBER OF STATEMENTS	234	398	692	362	53	40	1714	1852
ASSETS	%	%	%	%	%	%	%	%
Cash & Equivalents	32.3	16.3	14.3	12.8	12.1	10.2	15.8	16.6
Trade Receivables (net)	17.7	41.4	47.7	45.1	40.5	35.6	41.8	41.9
Inventory	2.2	3.8	4.3	4.2	2.9	4.0	4.0	3.8
All Other Current	4.5	3.8	6.5	9.9	12.3	11.1	7.2	6.8
Total Current	56.7	65.3	72.9	72.0	67.9	60.9	68.7	69.2
Fixed Assets (net)	27.6	22.8	16.5	13.4	13.3	12.9	18.6	18.3
Intangibles (net)	3.6	3.8	2.9	6.2	10.8	20.1	4.6	4.1
All Other Non-Current	12.1	8.1	7.7	8.4	8.0	6.1	8.1	8.4
Total	100.0	100.0	100.0	100.0	100.0	100.0	100.0	100.0
LIABILITIES								
Notes Payable-Short Term	30.3	12.1	7.6	6.7	4.7	6.5	15.2	13.1
Cur. Mat.-L.T.D.	6.3	3.1	2.1	4.0	2.7	2.4	3.8	3.2
Trade Payables	9.3	10.1	11.3	10.9	11.9	9.6	10.0	10.8
Income Taxes Payable	.1	.3	1.7	3.2	2.6	2.9	1.7	1.7
All Other Current	24.4	11.9	14.9	17.6	21.3	24.5	16.2	16.0
Total Current	70.5	37.6	37.6	42.4	43.3	45.8	47.0	45.0
Long-Term Debt	18.5	16.1	9.8	8.4	10.9	14.9	12.6	11.4
Deferred Taxes	.0	.2	.8	1.0	.9	.9	.9	1.0
All Other Non-Current	12.1	5.0	4.5	4.9	6.2	6.8	6.2	5.2
Net Worth	-1.2	41.1	47.3	43.3	38.7	31.6	33.4	37.5
Total Liabilties & Net Worth	100.0	100.0	100.0	100.0	100.0	100.0	100.0	100.0
INCOME DATA								
Net Sales	100.0	100.0	100.0	100.0	100.0	100.0	100.0	100.0
Gross Profit								
Operating Expenses	91.2	88.9	92.1	94.0	93.3	93.2	95.0	93.7
Operating Profit	8.8	11.1	7.9	6.0	6.7	6.8	5.0	6.3
All Other Expenses (net)	1.4	2.4	1.4	.6	1.9	1.3	1.3	1.4
Profit Before Taxes	7.3	8.7	6.5	5.4	4.7	5.5	3.7	4.8
RATIOS								
Current	3.2	4.0	3.5	2.6	2.2	2.0	3.0	3.1
	1.2	1.9	2.0	1.8	1.5	1.5	1.8	1.8
	.3	1.0	1.4	1.3	1.2	1.1	1.1	1.2
Quick	2.9	3.5	3.1	2.1	1.7	1.7	2.6	2.7
	(233) 1.0	1.7	1.7	1.5	1.2	1.1	(1711) 1.4	1.5
	.3	.8	1.1	1.0	.9	.8	.9	.9
Sales/Receivables	**0** UND	**11** 32.9	**46** 8.0	**54** 6.8	**58** 6.3	**65** 5.6	**33** 11.0	**35** 10.6
	0 UND	**52** 7.0	**68** 5.4	**74** 4.9	**74** 4.9	**73** 5.0	**62** 5.9	**66** 5.6
	23 16.1	**85** 4.3	**96** 3.8	**99** 3.7	**101** 3.6	**87** 4.2	**93** 3.9	**94** 3.9
Cost of Sales/Inventory								
Cost of Sales/Payables								
Sales/Working Capital	14.5	5.0	4.2	4.4	4.7	4.7	5.0	4.6
	99.2	10.2	7.1	6.8	8.6	10.0	9.2	8.8
	-21.9	446.4	14.5	15.7	19.7	49.1	43.2	40.0
EBIT/Interest	32.5	38.1	68.4	48.6	31.8	38.0	24.8	30.7
	(159) 9.3	(297) 9.9	(562) 14.5	(309) 15.3	(45) 13.0	(38) 12.2	(1403) 5.5	(1483) 7.4
	.2	2.1	3.6	5.3	3.6	3.1	.2	1.3
Net Profit + Depr., Dep., Amort./Cur. Mat. L/T/D		8.3	8.0	5.7	6.3	5.1	6.4	9.3
		(23) 2.5	(129) 3.2	(130) 3.3	(27) 2.7	(12) 2.6	(342) 2.5	(380) 2.5
		-.1	1.1	1.9	1.5	1.7	.8	.8
Fixed/Worth	.1	.1	.1	.1	.1	.3	.1	.1
	1.0	.3	.2	.2	.4	.7	.3	.3
	-1.9	1.9	.6	.6	1.0	-.3	1.2	1.0
Debt/Worth	.5	.4	.4	.7	1.3	1.3	.6	.6
	3.7	1.2	1.1	1.3	2.4	3.0	1.5	1.4
	-5.1	4.6	2.8	3.1	4.7	-6.7	5.6	4.2
% Profit Before Taxes/Tangible Net Worth	166.5	77.4	52.2	42.4	50.1	55.3	50.4	53.1
	(156) 72.9	(347) 33.6	(654) 24.9	(341) 23.1	(45) 21.9	(26) 24.5	(1442) 20.0	(1635) 21.7
	18.3	7.7	7.3	11.8	8.1	15.1	.9	3.3
% Profit Before Taxes/Total Assets	73.0	34.2	23.6	16.7	13.5	10.9	21.3	21.5
	28.2	13.9	10.7	8.5	5.7	6.2	7.0	7.9
	1.0	1.8	2.9	3.7	2.4	3.0	-1.0	.8
Sales/Net Fixed Assets	353.2	88.2	68.1	52.1	37.6	37.1	67.0	65.8
	47.9	26.7	28.2	24.7	18.6	19.0	25.7	26.4
	16.1	10.7	11.3	12.4	8.9	8.6	11.0	11.3
Sales/Total Assets	16.5	4.3	3.3	2.7	2.4	2.2	3.7	3.7
	7.1	2.9	2.4	2.1	1.9	1.6	2.6	2.4
	3.3	1.9	1.8	1.6	1.5	1.1	1.8	1.8
% Depr., Dep., Amort./Sales	.7	.6	.6	.6	1.0	1.2	.7	.7
	(113) 1.3	(261) 1.5	(552) 1.2	(325) 1.2	(47) 1.8	(26) 1.7	(1327) 1.5	(1406) 1.4
	2.7	3.0	2.1	1.9	2.8	2.6	2.6	2.6
% Officers', Directors' Owners' Comp/Sales	7.1	3.8	2.3	2.0			4.2	3.4
	(146) 12.8	(168) 6.7	(182) 4.5	(53) 3.6			(551) 8.9	(567) 7.2
	19.6	11.6	9.4	10.6			15.4	13.3
Net Sales ($)	**520890M**	**1624204M**	**8871911M**	**17782179M**	**7122703M**	**11523065M**	**45127541M**	**46965845M**
Total Assets ($)	**53264M**	**479447M**	**3424742M**	**8045736M**	**3589075M**	**6537299M**	**19972985M**	**20998610M**

M = $ thousand MM = $ million

See Pages 9 through 22 for Explanation of Ratios and Data

Comparative Historical Data / Current Data Sorted by Sales

4/1/11-3/31/12 ALL	4/1/12-3/31/13 ALL	4/1/13-3/31/14 ALL		0-1MM	1-3MM	3-5MM	5-10MM	10-25MM	25MM & OVER
			Type of Statement						
227	196	194	Unqualified	2	2	4	13	42	131
345	301	300	Reviewed	1	14	23	66	116	80
253	194	225	Compiled	11	27	40	80	48	19
368	341	354	Tax Returns	89	104	54	70	30	7
737	744	706	Other	48	97	65	130	165	201
				183 (4/1-9/30/13)			1,596 (10/1/13-3/31/14)		
1930	1776	1779	**NUMBER OF STATEMENTS**	151	244	186	359	401	438
%	%	%	**ASSETS**	%	%	%	%	%	%
17.0	17.6	16.7	Cash & Equivalents	16.2	21.0	21.0	18.6	15.3	12.2
41.5	40.8	41.4	Trade Receivables (net)	14.6	33.5	40.8	44.0	47.0	47.8
4.0	3.6	3.8	Inventory	2.0	3.6	3.8	4.7	3.9	3.8
6.7	6.8	6.6	All Other Current	3.7	3.8	4.5	5.2	7.7	10.1
69.2	68.8	68.5	Total Current	36.5	61.9	70.2	72.5	74.0	74.0
18.4	19.0	18.6	Fixed Assets (net)	49.2	22.7	19.1	15.8	14.5	11.6
4.3	3.6	4.5	Intangibles (net)	3.9	4.2	2.8	4.0	3.3	7.0
8.1	8.5	8.5	All Other Non-Current	10.4	11.1	8.0	7.7	8.2	7.4
100.0	100.0	100.0	Total	100.0	100.0	100.0	100.0	100.0	100.0
			LIABILITIES						
14.3	12.1	11.3	Notes Payable-Short Term	18.6	19.7	12.9	10.4	8.3	7.0
2.8	3.1	3.3	Cur. Mat.-L.T.D.	4.6	4.3	3.1	2.5	2.5	3.7
10.3	10.0	10.7	Trade Payables	7.9	8.8	9.2	11.3	11.2	12.4
1.6	1.4	1.5	Income Taxes Payable	.1	.3	.7	1.4	1.8	2.9
15.6	16.1	16.4	All Other Current	11.5	15.9	14.4	14.9	17.1	19.9
44.6	42.7	43.3	Total Current	42.6	49.0	40.3	40.5	41.0	46.0
13.2	13.9	12.2	Long-Term Debt	33.1	18.1	12.3	8.6	8.5	8.0
.9	.7	.6	Deferred Taxes	.1	.3	.1	.7	1.0	.8
6.0	5.4	5.8	All Other Non-Current	5.6	8.9	6.9	5.2	5.1	4.8
35.3	37.4	38.1	Net Worth	18.7	23.6	40.5	45.0	44.5	40.5
100.0	100.0	100.0	Total Liabilties & Net Worth	100.0	100.0	100.0	100.0	100.0	100.0
			INCOME DATA						
100.0	100.0	100.0	Net Sales	100.0	100.0	100.0	100.0	100.0	100.0
			Gross Profit						
92.7	91.4	91.7	Operating Expenses	69.9	93.2	93.5	93.9	93.8	93.9
7.3	8.6	8.3	Operating Profit	30.1	6.8	6.5	6.1	6.2	6.1
1.4	1.7	1.5	All Other Expenses (net)	11.8	1.0	.1	.5	.2	.8
5.9	6.8	6.8	Profit Before Taxes	18.4	5.8	6.3	5.6	6.0	5.3
			RATIOS						
3.1	3.4	3.2		2.6	4.4	4.6	3.8	3.1	2.4
1.8	1.9	1.8	Current	1.0	1.9	2.2	2.0	2.0	1.7
1.2	1.2	1.2		.3	.8	1.3	1.3	1.3	1.2
2.7	2.8	2.8		1.9	4.0	4.4	3.4	2.6	2.0
1.5	1.5	(1778) 1.5	Quick	.8	(243) 1.7	1.9	1.7	1.7	1.3
.9	.9	.9		.3	.7	1.1	1.1	1.1	1.0
32 11.4	**30** 12.2	**32** 11.4		**0** UND	**0** UND	**24** 15.5	**35** 10.4	**46** 8.0	**52** 7.0
63 5.8	**61** 6.0	**62** 5.9	Sales/Receivables	**0** UND	**47** 7.8	**61** 6.0	**60** 6.1	**65** 5.6	**70** 5.2
91 4.0	**89** 4.1	**91** 4.0		**35** 10.4	**89** 4.1	**99** 3.7	**91** 4.0	**94** 3.9	**91** 4.0
			Cost of Sales/Inventory						
			Cost of Sales/Payables						
4.8	4.7	4.7		6.7	4.8	4.1	4.5	4.6	5.2
8.8	8.6	8.8	Sales/Working Capital	-191.0	14.5	7.9	7.5	7.7	8.3
31.7	28.8	31.4		-4.5	-41.7	24.9	21.3	15.5	19.4
37.5	43.3	47.3		19.3	27.5	53.5	43.3	68.1	55.2
(1558) 10.0	(1355) 11.2	(1410) 12.9	EBIT/Interest	(79) 6.3	(176) 5.9	(146) 11.6	(290) 11.2	(339) 16.2	(380) 15.8
2.0	2.5	3.2		2.0	-.1	1.9	2.7	4.1	5.8
10.6	9.2	6.4			19.2	7.4	7.2	7.1	5.8
(341) 3.3	(306) 3.3	(322) 3.2	Net Profit + Depr., Dep., Amort./Cur. Mat. L/T/D		(10) 2.3	(21) 2.7	(47) 2.6	(92) 3.3	(150) 3.3
1.4	1.3	1.6			-1.2	.0	1.3	1.5	1.8
.1	.1	.1		.3	.1	.1	.1	.1	.1
.3	.3	.3	Fixed/Worth	2.3	.5	.3	.2	.2	.3
1.0	1.0	1.0		25.4	5.2	.9	.7	.6	.7
.6	.5	.5		.8	.4	.3	.4	.5	.8
1.4	1.3	1.3	Debt/Worth	3.4	1.4	.9	1.1	1.1	1.5
4.4	4.1	3.9		43.0	40.1	3.5	3.1	2.6	3.7
58.6	61.4	60.4		92.6	92.1	67.4	56.0	56.4	47.7
(1662) 25.2	(1559) 26.9	(1569) 28.3	% Profit Before Taxes/Tangible Net Worth	(118) 37.9	(186) 31.6	(164) 31.5	(328) 27.6	(378) 24.9	(395) 26.9
7.1	7.9	9.5		12.1	2.6	6.5	5.4	8.1	13.0
23.8	28.2	26.7		34.3	39.8	32.1	25.7	26.4	17.8
9.9	10.6	11.0	% Profit Before Taxes/Total Assets	9.5	13.1	15.8	12.2	10.5	9.5
1.8	2.1	3.0		1.7	-1.0	1.5	2.3	3.1	4.5
78.8	73.7	72.2		33.9	115.7	70.1	91.6	75.6	56.2
28.4	27.7	27.6	Sales/Net Fixed Assets	7.9	28.9	27.2	30.2	30.1	28.6
12.1	11.5	11.7		.2	11.8	11.0	12.4	14.1	14.4
3.9	3.7	3.7		3.4	6.0	4.3	3.9	3.6	3.2
2.5	2.5	2.5	Sales/Total Assets	1.5	2.8	2.7	2.7	2.5	2.4
1.8	1.8	1.8		.2	1.9	1.8	1.9	1.9	1.8
.7	.6	.6		1.8	.7	.6	.6	.6	.5
(1421) 1.3	(1321) 1.3	(1324) 1.3	% Depr., Dep., Amort./Sales	(98) 7.9	(134) 1.5	(138) 1.2	(251) 1.3	(320) 1.2	(383) 1.1
2.4	2.2	2.2		18.3	2.9	2.2	2.1	1.9	1.8
3.5	3.5	3.3		8.5	5.8	4.0	3.2	2.0	1.4
(611) 7.4	(549) 7.4	(556) 6.8	% Officers', Directors' Owners' Comp/Sales	(47) 18.1	(130) 10.0	(94) 6.3	(121) 6.2	(109) 4.1	(55) 3.5
13.7	13.3	12.9		28.7	17.2	10.7	11.2	9.1	9.5
47186737M	**53112551M**	**47444952M**	Net Sales ($)	**69268M**	**485591M**	**746101M**	**2587489M**	**6429109M**	**37127394M**
22780803M	**21677851M**	**22129563M**	Total Assets ($)	**124172M**	**256754M**	**341123M**	**1142904M**	**2823251M**	**17441359M**

M = $ thousand MM = $ million

See Pages 9 through 22 for Explanation of Ratios and Data

Current Data Sorted by Assets							Comparative Historical Data	
						Type of Statement		
			1	1		Unqualified	9	7
	1	2	1			Reviewed	7	5
2	7	5				Compiled	7	7
19	6	4		1	1	Tax Returns	26	27
7	9	7	3	1	1	Other	23	30
	8 (4/1-9/30/13)			71 (10/1/13-3/31/14)			4/1/09-3/31/10 ALL	4/1/10-3/31/11 ALL
0-500M	500M-2MM	2-10MM	10-50MM	50-100MM	100-250MM			
28	23	18	5	3	2	**NUMBER OF STATEMENTS**	72	76
%	%	%	%	%	%	**ASSETS**	%	%
20.9	18.7	6.4				Cash & Equivalents	14.9	13.8
11.0	36.5	45.2				Trade Receivables (net)	28.8	32.8
.9	.6	2.0				Inventory	1.7	2.2
2.1	9.1	3.1				All Other Current	5.4	6.2
34.9	64.9	56.8				Total Current	50.8	55.1
41.8	22.8	24.6				Fixed Assets (net)	24.2	25.4
8.2	.1	6.8				Intangibles (net)	8.6	4.8
15.0	12.2	11.9				All Other Non-Current	16.4	14.8
100.0	100.0	100.0				Total	100.0	100.0
						LIABILITIES		
28.9	7.7	8.2				Notes Payable-Short Term	25.8	14.4
15.0	2.5	3.4				Cur. Mat.-L.T.D.	7.8	6.3
5.5	4.9	4.7				Trade Payables	8.0	6.0
.1	.5	.0				Income Taxes Payable	.3	1.2
21.5	11.8	7.3				All Other Current	11.4	19.2
71.0	27.4	23.6				Total Current	53.2	47.0
61.6	20.4	21.3				Long-Term Debt	26.8	32.4
2.0	2.1	.0				Deferred Taxes	1.0	1.1
12.2	3.4	1.8				All Other Non-Current	15.5	11.8
-46.8	46.9	53.2				Net Worth	3.5	7.6
100.0	100.0	100.0				Total Liabilities & Net Worth	100.0	100.0
						INCOME DATA		
100.0	100.0	100.0				Net Sales	100.0	100.0
						Gross Profit		
96.3	90.3	88.4				Operating Expenses	96.2	96.7
3.7	9.7	11.6				Operating Profit	3.8	3.3
2.2	.4	.9				All Other Expenses (net)	2.4	1.2
1.6	9.2	10.7				Profit Before Taxes	1.4	2.1
						RATIOS		
3.1	8.7	3.4					4.1	2.4
.5	3.3	2.3				Current	1.3	1.4
.1	.8	1.9					.7	.6
2.6	8.7	2.8					3.3	2.3
.5	3.3	2.3				Quick	1.1	1.0
.1	.8	1.6					.5	.5
0 UND	**0** UND	**53** 6.9					**0** UND	**0** UND
0 UND	**54** 6.7	**79** 4.6				Sales/Receivables	**49** 7.4	**48** 7.6
0 UND	**91** 4.0	**107** 3.4					**93** 3.9	**89** 4.1
						Cost of Sales/Inventory		
						Cost of Sales/Payables		
19.8	3.8	4.0					5.0	5.6
-89.0	6.6	7.0				Sales/Working Capital	30.1	34.7
-6.8	-35.2	11.4					-16.9	-15.9
9.2	82.0	47.5					10.1	7.2
(24) 3.1	(18) 21.2	(17) 15.6				EBIT/Interest	(60) 3.3	(66) 1.9
1.7	2.2	2.1					-4.8	-2.0
								18.4
						Net Profit + Depr., Dep., Amort./Cur. Mat. L/T/D		(10) 2.7
								1.8
.5	.1	.1					.1	.2
8.9	.3	.6				Fixed/Worth	.8	1.0
-.6	.8	.9					-.6	-1.7
2.5	.2	.5					.5	.6
29.8	.8	.9				Debt/Worth	3.0	3.1
-1.6	3.6	2.8					-2.8	-4.5
203.9	109.5	73.0					48.5	80.8
(16) 44.3	(19) 50.2	29.1				% Profit Before Taxes/Tangible Net Worth	(44) 9.1	(50) 11.5
2.7	14.8	11.3					-17.7	-7.6
18.6	58.6	30.2					18.3	18.1
10.7	20.1	14.9				% Profit Before Taxes/Total Assets	2.6	3.4
.7	3.3	3.7					-22.9	-8.5
46.6	58.7	34.2					47.3	41.3
16.3	26.0	7.9				Sales/Net Fixed Assets	17.7	13.7
7.1	6.9	4.4					8.6	7.4
6.7	3.2	2.7					4.2	4.2
4.8	2.5	2.0				Sales/Total Assets	2.5	2.5
2.0	1.9	1.4					1.3	1.5
2.0	.7	1.3					1.0	1.3
(18) 3.8	(14) 1.8	(14) 2.7				% Depr., Dep., Amort./Sales	(54) 2.7	(47) 2.1
5.1	5.2	4.4					4.0	4.8
8.4	4.1						5.9	6.7
(20) 12.2	(11) 6.1					% Officers', Directors' Owners' Comp/Sales	(35) 12.6	(35) 14.9
20.8	19.9						19.6	24.4
27927M	75885M	171233M	106551M	279055M	1216440M	Net Sales ($)	1052927M	933394M
6188M	26139M	85141M	79669M	209898M	333944M	Total Assets ($)	938693M	738636M

M = $ thousand MM = $ million

See Pages 9 through 22 for Explanation of Ratios and Data

Comparative Historical Data | **Current Data Sorted by Sales**

4/1/11-3/31/12 ALL	4/1/12-3/31/13 ALL	4/1/13-3/31/14 ALL		0-1MM	1-3MM	3-5MM	5-10MM	10-25MM	25MM & OVER
			Type of Statement						
5	2	2	Unqualified					1	1
10	8	4	Reviewed		1			2	1
10	9	14	Compiled	3	3	2	5	1	
19	32	31	Tax Returns	10	11	5	2	1	2
31	36	28	Other	6	7	4	5	3	3
				8 (4/1-9/30/13)			71 (10/1/13-3/31/14)		
75	87	79	**NUMBER OF STATEMENTS**	19	22	11	12	8	7
%	%	%	**ASSETS**	%	%	%	%	%	%
13.3	19.7	15.7	Cash & Equivalents	14.4	20.1	12.7	20.4		
38.3	27.3	28.0	Trade Receivables (net)	9.4	32.0	38.6	27.3		
4.6	2.3	1.1	Inventory	.0	1.3	1.3	1.8		
4.7	6.7	5.7	All Other Current	9.3	1.6	5.3	3.6		
60.8	55.9	50.5	Total Current	33.1	55.0	57.9	53.0		
17.7	23.1	29.2	Fixed Assets (net)	42.7	28.8	27.7	28.5		
8.9	7.2	7.6	Intangibles (net)	3.9	7.1	4.1	3.1		
12.4	13.8	12.7	All Other Non-Current	20.2	9.0	10.2	15.4		
100.0	100.0	100.0	Total	100.0	100.0	100.0	100.0		
			LIABILITIES						
18.1	19.0	15.6	Notes Payable-Short Term	36.9	9.9	2.9	8.9		
4.6	5.9	7.3	Cur. Mat.-L.T.D.	10.4	8.7	6.6	4.5		
6.3	6.6	4.9	Trade Payables	6.7	4.3	4.8	2.9		
1.1	.3	.2	Income Taxes Payable	.2	.4	.0	.3		
15.2	14.1	14.4	All Other Current	34.7	7.5	3.6	7.5		
45.4	45.9	42.4	Total Current	88.9	30.8	17.9	24.1		
20.8	26.2	33.7	Long-Term Debt	53.0	41.4	33.6	20.3		
2.2	1.2	1.8	Deferred Taxes	2.9	1.5	1.3	.0		
5.6	9.2	8.9	All Other Non-Current	13.0	6.7	2.4	1.6		
26.0	17.6	13.1	Net Worth	-57.7	19.6	44.8	54.0		
100.0	100.0	100.0	Total Liabilities & Net Worth	100.0	100.0	100.0	100.0		
			INCOME DATA						
100.0	100.0	100.0	Net Sales	100.0	100.0	100.0	100.0		
			Gross Profit						
94.5	88.8	90.6	Operating Expenses	95.8	94.1	87.9	86.8		
5.5	11.2	9.4	Operating Profit	4.2	5.9	12.1	13.2		
1.0	1.3	1.0	All Other Expenses (net)	2.5	1.0	1.1	.2		
4.5	9.8	8.4	Profit Before Taxes	1.7	4.9	11.0	13.0		
			RATIOS						
4.4	5.4	3.8		1.9	3.4	9.0	4.5		
1.6	2.0	2.1	Current	.3	2.4	5.5	3.1		
.9	.7	.6		.1	.7	2.1	1.5		
3.4	3.8	3.3		1.9	3.4	8.9	4.3		
1.3	1.6	2.0	Quick	.3	2.4	5.5	2.3		
.6	.5	.5		.1	.7	1.0	1.4		
31 11.6	0 UND	0 UND		0 UND	0 UND	39 9.4	0 UND		
68 5.4	46 7.9	46 7.9	Sales/Receivables	0 UND	49 7.4	65 5.6	43 8.4		
99 3.7	78 4.7	85 4.3		13 28.3	87 4.2	101 3.6	91 4.0		
			Cost of Sales/Inventory						
			Cost of Sales/Payables						
4.5	4.2	4.2		48.2	4.2	3.9	3.9		
10.2	7.9	10.4	Sales/Working Capital	-8.3	9.3	5.3	9.2		
-43.7	-30.9	-35.2		-2.9	-96.7	9.9	17.7		
15.4	29.0	30.7		5.5	25.7		61.2		
(63) 3.1	(71) 6.9	(67) 7.4	EBIT/Interest	(14) 2.5	(20) 3.9		(11) 21.2		
-1.3	2.7	2.2		1.0	1.2		4.6		
10.1	20.5								
(15) 2.8	(10) 13.0		Net Profit + Depr., Dep., Amort./Cur. Mat. L/T/D						
1.1	2.7								
.1	.1	.2		.6	.2	.1	.1		
.4	.6	.6	Fixed/Worth	10.4	.6	.6	.5		
-1.6	4.6	11.3		-.5	-10.7	.9	1.1		
.5	.3	.7		2.9	.8	.2	.4		
2.2	1.3	2.4	Debt/Worth	38.9	2.6	.7	.7		
-7.7	268.0	-15.5		-1.6	-14.6	2.6	1.5		
59.8	93.3	92.2		55.0	150.8	104.0	121.8		
(54) 28.3	(66) 42.0	(59) 37.6	% Profit Before Taxes/Tangible Net Worth	(11) 23.6	(16) 46.2	(10) 47.6	(11) 51.1		
.6	13.4	12.7		-33.3	4.7	17.4	21.7		
24.4	39.2	30.7		11.0	38.5	30.7	75.2		
7.5	15.1	12.7	% Profit Before Taxes/Total Assets	3.3	12.6	25.8	27.4		
-2.4	5.1	3.3		-8.5	-.7	7.6	10.1		
50.2	48.7	48.9		32.3	57.6	47.9	42.4		
23.9	19.0	18.9	Sales/Net Fixed Assets	7.7	21.5	23.5	20.1		
10.2	7.2	6.0		2.0	7.2	5.7	5.6		
3.5	4.5	4.7		6.1	6.0	3.2	5.1		
2.3	2.4	2.5	Sales/Total Assets	2.0	2.8	2.8	2.4		
1.5	1.6	1.4		1.0	2.2	1.7	1.7		
1.4	1.3	1.1		1.8	.9		1.1		
(48) 2.4	(57) 2.7	(50) 2.7	% Depr., Dep., Amort./Sales	(13) 3.9	(15) 3.6		(10) 2.6		
4.0	4.5	4.6		8.0	4.7		4.4		
5.3	4.7	4.9		8.7	5.9				
(35) 11.7	(47) 9.9	(42) 8.5	% Officers', Directors' Owners' Comp/Sales	(12) 14.7	(14) 11.7				
21.3	18.2	17.8		29.7	20.3				
1885149M	667246M	1877091M	Net Sales ($)	9197M	42331M	44097M	86473M	145565M	1549428M
663622M	408913M	740979M	Total Assets ($)	6044M	16067M	22645M	36861M	83277M	576085M

M = $ thousand MM = $ million

See Pages 9 through 22 for Explanation of Ratios and Data

Current Data Sorted by Assets							Comparative Historical Data	
						Type of Statement		
1	1		10	5	2	Unqualified	35	27
1	2	11	5	1		Reviewed	33	36
3	13	12	4			Compiled	22	28
14	28	9				Tax Returns	43	53
17	29	45	29	4	6	Other	97	97
44 (4/1-9/30/13)		208 (10/1/13-3/31/14)					4/1/09-3/31/10 ALL	4/1/10-3/31/11 ALL
0-500M	500M-2MM	2-10MM	10-50MM	50-100MM	100-250MM			
36	73	77	48	10	8	NUMBER OF STATEMENTS	230	241
%	%	%	%	%	%	**ASSETS**	%	%
23.0	15.3	16.0	10.9	19.5		Cash & Equivalents	13.6	12.4
23.0	24.6	31.1	27.5	29.1		Trade Receivables (net)	29.6	30.1
2.1	3.7	2.9	2.2	4.3		Inventory	3.2	3.9
3.9	3.3	3.4	4.3	4.1		All Other Current	4.6	3.5
52.1	47.1	53.4	45.0	56.9		Total Current	51.0	49.8
36.1	39.9	31.2	34.7	21.6		Fixed Assets (net)	34.2	34.2
2.9	3.9	8.7	14.6	16.4		Intangibles (net)	7.3	6.6
8.8	9.1	6.7	5.7	5.1		All Other Non-Current	7.5	9.4
100.0	100.0	100.0	100.0	100.0		Total	100.0	100.0
						LIABILITIES		
7.4	10.2	5.3	4.8	1.8		Notes Payable-Short Term	9.5	10.0
3.6	3.2	2.9	4.5	2.7		Cur. Mat.-L.T.D.	5.2	5.5
6.5	7.7	5.9	6.1	7.8		Trade Payables	6.9	8.0
.0	.2	.3	.2	.2		Income Taxes Payable	.3	.4
12.4	11.6	8.9	13.2	16.3		All Other Current	11.4	11.1
29.9	32.9	23.2	28.9	28.8		Total Current	33.4	35.1
21.0	23.5	14.7	11.3	14.3		Long-Term Debt	18.4	18.6
.0	.3	.7	2.0	1.0		Deferred Taxes	.7	.9
26.1	9.1	3.5	2.4	3.6		All Other Non-Current	5.1	7.8
23.0	34.2	57.8	55.4	52.4		Net Worth	42.4	37.7
100.0	100.0	100.0	100.0	100.0		Total Liabilties & Net Worth	100.0	100.0
						INCOME DATA		
100.0	100.0	100.0	100.0	100.0		Net Sales	100.0	100.0
						Gross Profit		
84.5	91.5	89.1	91.2	84.4		Operating Expenses	90.9	91.2
15.5	8.5	10.9	8.8	15.6		Operating Profit	9.1	8.8
2.6	2.2	.8	2.0	.8		All Other Expenses (net)	2.1	2.0
12.8	6.3	10.2	6.9	14.8		Profit Before Taxes	7.0	6.8
						RATIOS		
10.8	4.6	3.9	3.0	4.6			3.2	3.0
2.7	1.7	2.5	1.4	1.7		Current	1.8	1.8
.9	.8	1.5	.9	1.3			1.0	1.0
9.0	3.6	3.5	2.3	3.8			2.8	2.7
2.7	1.3	2.0	1.3	1.5		Quick	1.5	1.6
.7	.7	1.3	.8	.8			.8	.8
0 UND	**6** 61.5	**39** 9.3	**47** 7.7	**58** 6.3			**38** 9.7	**34** 10.6
25 14.6	**42** 8.7	**56** 6.5	**64** 5.7	**69** 5.3		Sales/Receivables	**55** 6.6	**55** 6.6
48 7.6	**61** 6.0	**72** 5.1	**74** 4.9	**76** 4.8			**73** 5.0	**73** 5.0
						Cost of Sales/Inventory		
						Cost of Sales/Payables		
4.9	5.4	3.8	5.6	3.4			5.2	5.5
11.2	17.9	6.2	12.7	8.8		Sales/Working Capital	11.4	11.4
-79.9	-52.0	14.0	-41.4	13.8			-194.0	NM
17.9	17.0	31.9	22.2	833.9			17.9	18.9
(24) 8.1	(61) 5.6	(61) 9.7	(41) 5.5	18.5		EBIT/Interest	(191) 5.2	(205) 6.5
1.8	1.1	3.7	1.9	6.3			1.0	1.8
		6.4	8.6				7.1	7.4
		(12) 2.2	(24) 3.8			Net Profit + Depr., Dep., Amort./Cur. Mat. L/T/D	(52) 2.8	(66) 2.6
		2.1	1.6				1.3	1.1
.2	.4	.2	.4	.2			.4	.4
.7	1.2	.6	.8	.7		Fixed/Worth	.9	1.0
NM	16.8	1.2	2.4	4.9			2.8	4.5
.2	.5	.3	.4	.9			.5	.5
1.3	1.7	.8	.9	1.5		Debt/Worth	1.2	1.3
NM	16.6	1.6	4.1	9.5			6.7	9.1
148.3	53.8	56.3	51.8	111.5			66.1	58.7
(27) 96.4	(59) 19.7	(73) 27.2	(43) 24.9	35.3		% Profit Before Taxes/Tangible Net Worth	(193) 22.8	(200) 27.0
25.1	3.8	6.5	10.4	8.7			6.5	7.4
75.9	25.4	20.5	19.6	29.2			21.1	24.4
26.0	8.0	12.9	6.9	8.2		% Profit Before Taxes/Total Assets	7.5	9.5
2.7	.1	3.1	1.4	3.7			.3	2.3
26.2	15.4	26.3	11.2	11.7			13.5	16.8
15.2	8.0	7.5	5.1	6.7		Sales/Net Fixed Assets	5.9	6.6
4.6	3.4	3.6	3.3	4.2			3.4	3.5
4.6	3.3	2.4	2.2	1.6			2.8	2.9
3.2	2.3	1.8	1.7	1.3		Sales/Total Assets	1.9	2.0
2.2	1.5	1.2	.9	1.0			1.1	1.2
1.6	2.2	1.6	3.4				2.1	2.0
(23) 3.7	(57) 3.6	(61) 3.8	(42) 4.3			% Depr., Dep., Amort./Sales	(179) 3.8	(190) 3.8
11.1	6.6	6.4	6.3				6.0	6.2
5.2	3.0	2.2					2.9	2.9
(13) 9.5	(37) 7.0	(30) 3.8				% Officers', Directors' Owners' Comp/Sales	(63) 6.2	(90) 6.1
10.7	10.7	6.8					11.0	9.9
39598M	**223902M**	**634522M**	**1814960M**	**1009445M**	**1334397M**	Net Sales ($)	**4398189M**	**4863611M**
10925M	**84055M**	**321202M**	**1124626M**	**704610M**	**1386740M**	Total Assets ($)	**3275100M**	**3518265M**

M = $ thousand MM = $ million

See Pages 9 through 22 for Explanation of Ratios and Data

Comparative Historical Data / Current Data Sorted by Sales

4/1/11-3/31/12 ALL	4/1/12-3/31/13 ALL	4/1/13-3/31/14 ALL	Type of Statement	0-1MM	1-3MM	3-5MM	5-10MM	10-25MM	25MM & OVER
24	18	19	Unqualified	1	2		1	3	12
30	24	20	Reviewed	2	1	4	5	4	4
30	23	32	Compiled		7	6	11	4	4
63	42	51	Tax Returns	9	24	6	9	3	
93	99	130	Other	19	25	16	21	19	30
				44 (4/1-9/30/13)			208 (10/1/13-3/31/14)		
240	206	252	NUMBER OF STATEMENTS	31	59	32	47	33	50
%	%	%	**ASSETS**	%	%	%	%	%	%
15.0	14.1	15.6	Cash & Equivalents	17.7	16.6	14.1	17.7	15.9	12.1
27.8	28.3	26.9	Trade Receivables (net)	16.1	25.7	27.3	28.9	28.1	32.2
2.7	4.3	2.9	Inventory	1.2	3.7	3.5	3.2	2.5	2.7
4.1	3.5	3.8	All Other Current	4.8	2.5	4.7	1.9	5.0	4.9
49.6	50.2	49.2	Total Current	39.8	48.5	49.6	51.7	51.5	51.9
36.0	33.8	34.5	Fixed Assets (net)	41.9	39.4	35.0	35.4	26.5	28.2
6.0	8.8	8.6	Intangibles (net)	4.8	4.7	6.8	7.8	14.3	13.5
8.4	7.3	7.7	All Other Non-Current	13.6	7.4	8.7	5.1	7.6	6.4
100.0	100.0	100.0	Total	100.0	100.0	100.0	100.0	100.0	100.0
			LIABILITIES						
7.5	8.0	6.6	Notes Payable-Short Term	5.4	10.9	6.9	6.1	4.1	4.2
6.2	4.0	3.3	Cur. Mat.-L.T.D.	3.3	2.8	3.2	4.6	1.5	4.2
6.3	7.1	6.6	Trade Payables	3.9	7.7	7.7	6.0	6.1	7.0
.4	.3	.2	Income Taxes Payable	.0	.0	.4	.4	.2	.3
10.9	10.9	11.3	All Other Current	3.9	15.1	7.8	8.7	10.2	16.7
31.3	30.4	28.0	Total Current	16.5	36.5	26.0	25.8	22.1	32.5
21.4	18.6	17.7	Long-Term Debt	35.6	19.8	15.6	15.9	9.0	13.0
.7	.7	.9	Deferred Taxes	.0	.2	.9	.9	.5	2.4
8.8	6.4	8.4	All Other Non-Current	3.6	22.4	3.5	5.8	1.8	4.9
37.7	43.8	45.0	Net Worth	44.3	21.2	53.9	51.6	66.7	47.2
100.0	100.0	100.0	Total Liabilties & Net Worth	100.0	100.0	100.0	100.0	100.0	100.0
			INCOME DATA						
100.0	100.0	100.0	Net Sales	100.0	100.0	100.0	100.0	100.0	100.0
			Gross Profit						
88.9	87.2	89.4	Operating Expenses	73.9	91.6	92.1	92.7	92.4	89.7
11.1	12.8	10.6	Operating Profit	26.1	8.4	7.9	7.3	7.6	10.3
1.9	2.2	1.7	All Other Expenses (net)	6.4	1.8	.6	.7	.9	1.0
9.2	10.6	8.8	Profit Before Taxes	19.7	6.5	7.4	6.6	6.7	9.3
			RATIOS						
3.5	3.8	4.0		11.0	5.0	4.2	3.7	3.5	2.5
1.9	2.0	2.0	Current	2.9	1.6	2.6	2.1	2.5	1.8
1.0	1.0	1.0		.8	.9	1.3	1.3	1.1	1.0
3.4	3.1	3.4		9.1	3.7	3.3	3.6	3.0	2.2
1.5	1.6	1.7	Quick	2.0	1.6	1.8	1.9	1.7	1.4
.9	.8	.9		.5	.7	1.0	1.2	.9	.8
32 11.3	**31** 11.9	**29** 12.5		**0** UND	**13** 29.1	**30** 12.3	**35** 10.4	**46** 8.0	**45** 8.1
53 6.9	**49** 7.5	**52** 7.0	Sales/Receivables	**27** 13.5	**49** 7.5	**50** 7.3	**51** 7.2	**61** 6.0	**65** 5.6
72 5.1	**65** 5.6	**69** 5.3		**46** 7.9	**61** 6.0	**73** 5.0	**66** 5.5	**76** 4.8	**74** 4.9
			Cost of Sales/Inventory						
			Cost of Sales/Payables						
4.9	5.6	4.7		3.3	5.6	3.7	5.5	4.2	5.9
9.4	11.1	9.5	Sales/Working Capital	10.0	17.2	7.6	8.9	5.7	8.7
336.1	999.8	107.2		-51.0	-37.7	25.3	30.5	NM	126.5
29.2	30.8	21.5		13.8	18.1	29.1	17.4	51.8	39.0
(198) 8.2	(168) 8.5	(205) 6.9	EBIT/Interest	(19) 6.4	(48) 7.0	(26) 9.7	(38) 5.0	(28) 12.2	(46) 7.6
2.7	2.8	2.2		1.8	.9	3.2	1.5	2.4	3.6
12.3	7.9	7.8					3.7		13.6
(50) 2.6	(38) 3.2	(52) 3.8	Net Profit + Depr., Dep., Amort./Cur. Mat. L/T/D				(12) 2.2		(26) 5.7
1.1	1.5	1.7					1.3		2.1
.4	.3	.3		.1	.5	.2	.5	.2	.3
.9	.9	.8	Fixed/Worth	1.1	1.4	.8	.7	.5	1.0
3.3	2.2	2.6		24.2	-2.0	1.5	1.6	1.0	4.4
.5	.4	.4		.1	.5	.3	.3	.4	.6
1.3	1.4	1.1	Debt/Worth	1.4	1.7	.6	1.2	.6	1.6
7.0	4.7	4.5		24.1	-37.8	2.7	3.6	1.7	9.8
70.8	60.6	61.5		134.1	54.2	51.3	53.6	54.3	72.1
(198) 27.9	(178) 31.3	(218) 27.6	% Profit Before Taxes/Tangible Net Worth	(26) 77.7	(44) 23.6	(29) 22.8	(43) 14.0	30.1	(43) 29.9
13.2	12.0	8.2		17.6	3.0	4.7	4.6	4.4	16.1
26.6	30.3	23.7		44.3	27.7	21.9	18.7	24.8	20.9
12.4	10.3	10.1	% Profit Before Taxes/Total Assets	12.8	11.7	10.5	8.3	12.9	7.9
3.4	3.6	2.2		.9	-.5	1.7	1.3	2.2	4.5
17.8	19.2	17.3		27.8	20.4	13.3	13.6	33.2	12.0
7.0	7.8	6.9	Sales/Net Fixed Assets	4.6	7.6	6.5	8.0	11.5	5.8
3.6	4.2	3.7		.8	3.5	3.0	4.0	5.0	4.2
3.1	3.3	2.9		2.4	3.4	2.7	3.2	3.0	2.5
2.1	2.2	1.9	Sales/Total Assets	1.6	2.3	2.0	2.1	1.8	1.7
1.2	1.3	1.3		.2	1.4	1.3	1.6	1.0	1.1
1.8	1.8	2.0		3.5	1.6	2.1	2.1	1.5	2.2
(195) 3.8	(151) 3.7	(197) 4.0	% Depr., Dep., Amort./Sales	(23) 7.3	(42) 4.2	(25) 2.8	(38) 3.8	(25) 4.0	(44) 4.0
5.9	6.0	6.3		22.2	6.6	5.1	6.5	5.0	5.8
3.4	2.9	2.2			5.1		1.9		
(94) 6.0	(75) 5.4	(89) 5.6	% Officers', Directors' Owners' Comp/Sales		(29) 7.7		(25) 3.5		
9.1	9.0	9.8			12.1		7.2		
4605802M	5088085M	5056824M	Net Sales ($)	16096M	114673M	126692M	334977M	515355M	3949031M
2971321M	3053745M	3632158M	Total Assets ($)	20783M	93014M	83827M	180794M	380666M	2873074M

M = $ thousand MM = $ million

See Pages 9 through 22 for Explanation of Ratios and Data

Current Data Sorted by Assets							Comparative Historical Data	
						Type of Statement		
		1	2			Unqualified	1	3
1	2	8	4			Reviewed	8	6
	7	3	1			Compiled	10	8
23	15	7				Tax Returns	28	27
15	14	16	7			Other	38	44
11 (4/1-9/30/13)		115 (10/1/13-3/31/14)					4/1/09-3/31/10 ALL	4/1/10-3/31/11 ALL
0-500M	500M-2MM	2-10MM	10-50MM	50-100MM	100-250MM			
39	38	35	14			NUMBER OF STATEMENTS	85	88
%	%	%	%	%	%	**ASSETS**	%	%
39.4	17.5	18.3	6.9	D	D	Cash & Equivalents	22.1	14.6
16.4	28.0	27.3	37.2	A	A	Trade Receivables (net)	25.4	29.6
6.0	20.4	20.2	13.7	T	T	Inventory	14.1	18.1
5.6	5.4	7.2	4.9	A	A	All Other Current	6.3	4.4
67.4	71.4	73.1	62.6			Total Current	67.9	66.7
24.5	18.7	19.1	20.6	N	N	Fixed Assets (net)	22.1	19.9
1.5	4.9	2.9	8.5	O	O	Intangibles (net)	3.1	2.7
6.3	5.1	4.9	8.3	T	T	All Other Non-Current	6.9	10.8
100.0	100.0	100.0	100.0			Total	100.0	100.0
				A	A	**LIABILITIES**		
13.5	12.6	9.8	9.7	V	V	Notes Payable-Short Term	19.4	26.8
1.9	1.4	2.9	4.9	A	A	Cur. Mat.-L.T.D.	2.0	1.9
11.1	12.9	12.5	15.5	I	I	Trade Payables	22.7	13.9
.0	.3	.1	.5	L	L	Income Taxes Payable	1.5	.2
29.4	19.4	21.5	19.4	A	A	All Other Current	24.6	23.6
56.0	46.6	46.7	50.0	B	B	Total Current	70.3	66.4
26.3	17.1	7.2	16.0	L	L	Long-Term Debt	14.4	14.4
.0	.2	.7	.5	E	E	Deferred Taxes	.3	.1
6.1	13.6	6.2	2.6			All Other Non-Current	4.0	7.7
11.5	22.5	39.2	30.8			Net Worth	11.2	11.5
100.0	100.0	100.0	100.0			Total Liabilties & Net Worth	100.0	100.0
						INCOME DATA		
100.0	100.0	100.0	100.0			Net Sales	100.0	100.0
						Gross Profit		
91.3	95.9	88.1	91.4			Operating Expenses	98.4	92.8
8.7	4.1	11.9	8.6			Operating Profit	1.6	7.2
.9	2.8	2.1	.5			All Other Expenses (net)	1.6	1.5
7.8	1.2	9.8	8.1			Profit Before Taxes	.0	5.7
						RATIOS		
2.3	3.0	2.8	1.8				2.4	2.4
1.5	1.6	1.6	1.5			Current	1.2	1.4
1.0	.9	1.2	1.0				.7	.9
2.3	1.3	2.5	1.5				1.6	1.5
(38) 1.2	.8	1.0	1.0			Quick	.8	1.0
.5	.5	.5	.4				.4	.3
0 UND	8 44.9	10 35.8	29 12.8				0 UND	4 92.6
0 UND	35 10.5	24 15.0	46 8.0			Sales/Receivables	24 15.1	31 11.7
36 10.0	59 6.2	57 6.4	66 5.5				47 7.8	66 5.5
						Cost of Sales/Inventory		
						Cost of Sales/Payables		
10.7	5.0	4.9	9.8				8.2	8.1
27.6	9.5	11.3	13.5			Sales/Working Capital	46.7	18.4
-198.3	-58.3	32.3	NM				-15.6	-35.1
13.0	18.6	123.8	15.7				21.5	19.6
(15) 5.0	(27) 3.5	(21) 19.9	(13) 4.7			EBIT/Interest	(64) 1.7	(66) 5.2
-1.3	-1.9	6.8	2.8				-1.5	1.3
							8.5	
						Net Profit + Depr., Dep., Amort./Cur. Mat. L/T/D	(10) 1.7	
							.1	
.1	.1	.0	.3				.1	.1
.5	.7	.3	.9			Fixed/Worth	.6	.5
-3.3	-58.6	.9	NM				NM	10.0
.6	1.2	.5	1.0				.7	.8
2.7	3.4	1.6	2.4			Debt/Worth	2.8	3.2
-4.7	-134.2	7.7	NM				-13.2	92.1
200.0	99.6	88.2	61.1				93.0	114.4
(27) 70.8	(27) 45.9	(32) 30.6	(11) 30.8			% Profit Before Taxes/Tangible Net Worth	(61) 33.8	(67) 30.5
19.2	-3.5	19.8	10.1				-6.2	5.7
51.9	16.0	21.1	18.0				26.3	22.3
23.1	6.2	15.0	10.7			% Profit Before Taxes/Total Assets	2.4	9.8
-1.7	-3.3	5.7	5.6				-11.2	1.3
182.5	62.7	89.5	80.5				217.2	88.9
45.6	22.0	29.7	28.2			Sales/Net Fixed Assets	26.7	27.7
10.8	12.7	10.2	6.7				9.6	10.7
9.7	4.1	3.2	3.4				5.4	4.2
4.9	2.8	2.7	2.4			Sales/Total Assets	3.3	3.0
2.5	1.7	1.6	2.2				2.0	1.8
.2	.4	.2	.7				.4	.4
(17) .7	(23) .7	(22) .8	(12) 1.3			% Depr., Dep., Amort./Sales	(53) .9	(56) .9
2.3	1.7	1.6	2.3				3.0	2.3
5.4	3.5	2.5					3.5	4.1
(20) 8.4	(17) 6.5	(16) 4.6				% Officers', Directors' Owners' Comp/Sales	(44) 7.1	(37) 6.3
19.1	10.1	7.8					13.7	8.5
39308M	111799M	386802M	611280M			Net Sales ($)	2882128M	652176M
8218M	40025M	142367M	230145M			Total Assets ($)	566116M	233752M

M = $ thousand MM = $ million

See Pages 9 through 22 for Explanation of Ratios and Data

Comparative Historical Data | **Current Data Sorted by Sales**

4/1/11-3/31/12 ALL	4/1/12-3/31/13 ALL	4/1/13-3/31/14 ALL	**Type of Statement**	0-1MM	1-3MM	3-5MM	5-10MM	10-25MM	25MM & OVER
10	3	3	Unqualified					1	2
15	9	15	Reviewed	1	1	2	1	4	6
10	7	11	Compiled	1	4	2	1	2	1
50	51	45	Tax Returns	18	16	5	5	1	
55	58	52	Other	12	13	3	12	6	6
				11 (4/1-9/30/13)			115 (10/1/13-3/31/14)		
140	128	126	**NUMBER OF STATEMENTS**	32	34	12	19	14	15
%	%	%	**ASSETS**	%	%	%	%	%	%
15.2	17.9	23.3	Cash & Equivalents	29.4	28.3	22.6	19.7	19.5	7.9
32.4	25.9	25.2	Trade Receivables (net)	13.2	23.7	36.9	34.8	20.5	37.3
17.6	17.1	15.1	Inventory	7.0	16.2	13.0	19.9	24.8	16.8
3.7	4.3	5.9	All Other Current	6.1	7.3	13.5	.4	3.5	5.6
68.9	65.3	69.6	Total Current	55.7	75.5	86.1	74.8	68.2	67.7
17.6	19.9	20.8	Fixed Assets (net)	33.0	17.6	10.9	13.7	19.6	20.0
3.3	2.7	3.7	Intangibles (net)	2.4	4.0	.0	6.0	1.6	8.0
10.2	12.1	5.8	All Other Non-Current	8.6	2.9	3.0	5.5	10.6	4.4
100.0	100.0	100.0	Total	100.0	100.0	100.0	100.0	100.0	100.0
			LIABILITIES						
18.1	16.9	11.8	Notes Payable-Short Term	9.7	13.7	13.7	12.4	12.2	9.0
1.8	1.8	2.4	Cur. Mat.-L.T.D.	4.7	1.4	.1	1.0	1.0	4.6
15.3	19.5	12.5	Trade Payables	11.0	10.1	11.2	18.3	11.5	16.0
.3	.3	.2	Income Taxes Payable	.0	.0	.9	.0	.0	.5
25.4	20.2	23.1	All Other Current	25.7	23.5	24.8	21.7	18.6	21.2
60.8	58.8	49.9	Total Current	51.0	48.7	50.8	53.4	43.3	51.3
12.1	13.7	17.1	Long-Term Debt	36.6	14.6	.2	9.1	5.8	15.2
.1	.5	.3	Deferred Taxes	.0	.0	.8	1.3	.0	.5
16.1	18.6	8.0	All Other Non-Current	4.9	15.2	7.7	8.4	3.3	2.4
10.8	8.4	24.6	Net Worth	7.4	21.4	40.6	27.8	47.5	30.6
100.0	100.0	100.0	Total Liabilities & Net Worth	100.0	100.0	100.0	100.0	100.0	100.0
			INCOME DATA						
100.0	100.0	100.0	Net Sales	100.0	100.0	100.0	100.0	100.0	100.0
			Gross Profit						
95.5	94.2	91.8	Operating Expenses	85.8	95.7	92.0	92.9	91.4	95.0
4.5	5.8	8.2	Operating Profit	14.2	4.3	8.0	7.1	8.6	5.0
1.3	2.3	1.8	All Other Expenses (net)	5.8	.7	-.3	.4	.1	.5
3.3	3.6	6.4	Profit Before Taxes	8.4	3.6	8.3	6.7	8.5	4.5
			RATIOS						
2.3	2.2	2.5		2.6	2.5	7.3	1.8	2.7	1.9
1.3	1.4	1.5	Current	1.6	1.6	2.8	1.4	1.6	1.5
.8	.8	1.0		.4	1.1	.9	1.1	1.2	1.1
1.6	1.7	1.9		2.3	1.5	5.2	1.5	2.5	1.5
1.0	.8	(125) 1.0	Quick	(31) .9	1.0	1.8	.9	.7	1.0
.4	.3	.5		.3	.6	.5	.7	.6	.4
6 61.1	0 UND	1 308.1		0 UND	0 UND	0 UND	18 20.5	11 32.8	20 18.5
27 13.7	23 15.7	25 14.6	Sales/Receivables	0 UND	32 11.3	30 12.1	30 12.0	22 16.4	41 9.0
61 6.0	51 7.2	53 6.9		38 9.7	52 7.0	63 5.8	63 5.8	46 7.9	63 5.8
			Cost of Sales/Inventory						
			Cost of Sales/Payables						
7.0	6.8	6.4		6.3	5.1	3.3	9.0	5.7	9.7
20.8	25.6	15.4	Sales/Working Capital	27.1	10.3	16.1	17.3	9.6	14.3
-34.0	-38.8	303.6		-4.1	177.0	-38.6	108.3	36.8	30.2
21.4	20.5	25.5		5.0	18.9		34.4		19.2
(105) 4.6	(89) 6.0	(76) 7.7	EBIT/Interest	(11) -.3	(22) 5.1		(14) 8.7		(14) 6.0
1.3	1.9	2.0		-4.3	-1.7		3.2		2.9
7.1									
(10) 1.8			Net Profit + Depr., Dep., Amort./Cur. Mat. L/T/D						
-.6									
.1	.1	.1		.2	.1	.0	.1	.1	.2
.4	.4	.5	Fixed/Worth	1.4	.4	.3	.4	.3	.8
3.8	-8.4	4.0		-1.2	9.6	NM	1.0	.8	6.4
1.0	1.0	.8		.5	1.2	.2	1.0	.5	1.0
3.3	3.7	2.7	Debt/Worth	2.7	3.6	2.0	5.1	.9	2.2
114.1	-13.3	62.0		-5.1	-134.2	NM	8.3	2.7	7.7
139.5	71.2	98.8		144.8	97.2		161.8	50.4	55.8
(108) 34.0	(89) 32.6	(97) 43.3	% Profit Before Taxes/Tangible Net Worth	(21) 33.3	(25) 44.4		(17) 98.1	(13) 24.3	(12) 27.7
4.3	10.8	13.9		13.5	-1.4		40.5	20.4	10.3
27.7	23.1	28.2		49.2	24.2	55.7	39.1	23.7	17.1
6.2	10.2	13.5	% Profit Before Taxes/Total Assets	8.8	10.9	17.2	17.4	14.7	7.9
.0	.5	2.9		-10.3	-3.3	3.4	5.7	7.7	5.6
139.9	98.8	92.2		109.6	111.7	702.2	224.4	128.7	84.4
39.6	35.4	29.3	Sales/Net Fixed Assets	29.2	22.0	61.5	35.3	25.1	37.3
16.1	15.2	10.5		2.4	11.0	21.5	13.9	10.3	7.0
5.6	4.8	4.8		8.6	4.5	5.8	4.8	3.2	4.2
3.5	3.1	2.9	Sales/Total Assets	2.5	2.9	2.9	3.4	2.8	2.5
2.2	1.9	2.0		.9	2.0	1.6	2.7	2.1	2.3
.3	.4	.4		.5	.3		.3		.4
(92) .7	(78) .7	(74) .8	% Depr., Dep., Amort./Sales	(13) 2.8	(20) .7		(12) .6		(13) 1.2
1.6	1.2	1.8		4.6	1.3		1.5		2.2
4.0	4.0	3.0		5.1	5.5				
(65) 8.0	(63) 6.4	(59) 5.7	% Officers', Directors' Owners' Comp/Sales	(11) 8.9	(18) 7.2				
12.5	11.5	9.7		19.4	10.9				
7974069M	1987022M	1149189M	Net Sales ($)	15778M	67892M	47052M	128580M	200114M	689773M
667466M	527124M	420755M	Total Assets ($)	14430M	30065M	20509M	41108M	77302M	237341M

M = $ thousand MM = $ million

See Pages 9 through 22 for Explanation of Ratios and Data

Current Data Sorted by Assets | **Comparative Historical Data**

Type of Statement								
Unqualified			3	7		2	13	15
Reviewed		3	8	3			21	21
Compiled	2	5	6				19	13
Tax Returns	15	8	7				36	26
Other	21	30	12	9	2		54	54
	18 (4/1-9/30/13)			125 (10/1/13-3/31/14)			4/1/09-3/31/10	4/1/10-3/31/11
	0-500M	500M-2MM	2-10MM	10-50MM	50-100MM	100-250MM	ALL	ALL
NUMBER OF STATEMENTS	38	46	36	19	2	2	143	129
ASSETS	%	%	%	%	%	%	%	%
Cash & Equivalents	29.0	23.7	11.9	14.1			18.8	15.8
Trade Receivables (net)	31.8	32.6	37.6	29.8			28.9	29.1
Inventory	6.7	5.6	6.8	8.3			6.6	8.5
All Other Current	3.4	2.7	3.8	4.4			3.5	3.2
Total Current	70.9	64.6	60.1	56.6			57.8	56.6
Fixed Assets (net)	18.2	25.8	26.6	16.1			30.3	29.8
Intangibles (net)	2.9	3.9	5.2	19.2			4.2	6.8
All Other Non-Current	8.0	5.7	8.2	8.2			7.7	6.8
Total	100.0	100.0	100.0	100.0			100.0	100.0
LIABILITIES								
Notes Payable-Short Term	37.4	10.2	8.1	2.9			23.7	17.2
Cur. Mat.-L.T.D.	10.3	2.8	2.6	3.0			4.4	4.1
Trade Payables	19.2	11.3	13.4	13.6			12.2	11.4
Income Taxes Payable	.5	1.4	.3	.1			.3	.3
All Other Current	21.0	11.6	12.7	10.3			13.0	11.2
Total Current	88.4	37.3	37.0	29.8			53.5	44.2
Long-Term Debt	17.1	19.8	16.8	19.0			15.0	16.7
Deferred Taxes	.0	.1	.0	.1			.2	.2
All Other Non-Current	16.9	20.4	8.6	32.1			8.7	12.7
Net Worth	-22.4	22.4	37.5	19.0			22.6	26.2
Total Liabilities & Net Worth	100.0	100.0	100.0	100.0			100.0	100.0
INCOME DATA								
Net Sales	100.0	100.0	100.0	100.0			100.0	100.0
Gross Profit								
Operating Expenses	92.6	96.7	90.0	88.5			96.1	92.7
Operating Profit	7.4	3.3	10.0	11.5			3.9	7.3
All Other Expenses (net)	1.0	1.2	2.4	4.8			1.1	2.3
Profit Before Taxes	6.4	2.1	7.5	6.7			2.8	5.1
RATIOS								
Current	3.0	4.4	2.4	2.7			2.8	3.3
	1.4	2.0	1.6	1.8			1.4	1.4
	.5	1.1	1.1	1.4			.9	.9
Quick	2.5	4.1	2.1	2.3			2.2	2.9
	1.0	1.9	1.2	1.4			1.2	1.1
	.3	.8	.8	.9			.6	.6
Sales/Receivables	0 UND	17 21.6	31 11.8	42 8.6			18 20.2	22 16.5
	24 15.5	43 8.4	43 8.4	48 7.6			38 9.5	43 8.4
	51 7.1	66 5.5	70 5.2	79 4.6			60 6.0	66 5.5
Cost of Sales/Inventory								
Cost of Sales/Payables								
Sales/Working Capital	9.5	4.9	6.1	4.6			6.0	6.0
	47.1	10.9	12.6	6.4			15.3	14.3
	-10.4	NM	49.6	17.1			-58.2	-66.6
EBIT/Interest	45.3	25.3	39.8	22.2			11.0	17.8
	(26) 9.8	(33) 2.7	(30) 10.5	(16) 5.1			(120) 2.8	(110) 3.7
	.8	-.6	1.9	.9			-1.1	1.0
Net Profit + Depr., Dep., Amort./Cur. Mat. L/T/D							4.7	5.1
							(24) 2.0	(15) 1.8
							.3	.3
Fixed/Worth	.0	.2	.2	.2			.3	.3
	.2	1.0	.5	.7			.7	.8
	-1.7	-6.9	1.6	-.7			4.7	7.0
Debt/Worth	.9	.5	.7	.9			.6	.5
	32.5	3.5	1.3	1.3			2.0	1.7
	-3.2	-13.6	2.8	-4.9			19.8	162.1
% Profit Before Taxes/Tangible Net Worth	306.9	83.6	70.8	51.5			45.2	70.6
	(20) 108.0	(29) 27.0	(32) 31.2	(11) 25.3			(114) 12.1	(98) 19.6
	41.1	5.0	8.7	6.8			-.3	2.6
% Profit Before Taxes/Total Assets	81.8	21.0	25.8	15.2			15.3	21.1
	23.5	5.2	9.4	5.0			4.5	6.1
	-.1	-2.1	3.1	-2.6			-4.5	-.4
Sales/Net Fixed Assets	UND	44.5	39.8	202.0			38.4	38.7
	71.5	21.3	19.8	15.4			12.7	14.0
	26.2	7.2	4.4	2.9			5.5	4.0
Sales/Total Assets	10.5	4.5	4.0	2.5			4.2	3.7
	4.9	2.6	2.7	1.8			2.6	2.4
	2.9	2.0	1.9	1.1			1.9	1.4
% Depr., Dep., Amort./Sales	.3	.6	1.0	.2			.9	1.0
	(13) .8	(28) 1.9	(29) 2.0	(15) 2.7			(113) 2.2	(95) 2.5
	1.5	3.0	3.7	5.3			4.5	4.5
% Officers', Directors' Owners' Comp/Sales	7.7	4.4	3.4				5.3	3.1
	(18) 10.8	(23) 7.9	(13) 6.1				(65) 10.1	(54) 6.9
	13.0	13.3	11.5				19.0	11.7
Net Sales ($)	46857M	165335M	453749M	774930M	285993M	454438M	1373045M	2066632M
Total Assets ($)	8106M	52528M	167872M	457793M	123401M	256484M	732035M	1353247M

M = $ thousand MM = $ million

See Pages 9 through 22 for Explanation of Ratios and Data

Comparative Historical Data				Current Data Sorted by Sales					
			Type of Statement						
11	16	12	Unqualified		1			3	8
24	17	14	Reviewed		1	2	6	2	3
23	16	13	Compiled		3	2	3	4	1
36	36	30	Tax Returns	7	12	4	5	1	1
56	55	74	Other	20	17	12	8	7	10
4/1/11-3/31/12 ALL	4/1/12-3/31/13 ALL	4/1/13-3/31/14 ALL		18 (4/1-9/30/13)		125 (10/1/13-3/31/14)			
				0-1MM	1-3MM	3-5MM	5-10MM	10-25MM	25MM & OVER
150	140	143	**NUMBER OF STATEMENTS**	27	34	20	22	17	23
%	%	%	**ASSETS**	%	%	%	%	%	%
17.0	18.7	20.3	Cash & Equivalents	26.3	24.2	20.1	19.6	11.6	14.8
30.8	30.2	33.3	Trade Receivables (net)	26.6	27.7	37.1	40.9	33.0	39.0
8.7	6.7	7.0	Inventory	4.3	8.8	4.4	3.3	10.1	11.0
5.0	2.6	3.3	All Other Current	3.1	2.5	1.7	3.8	5.3	4.3
61.5	58.2	63.9	Total Current	60.3	63.2	63.4	67.7	60.1	69.1
25.0	26.0	22.1	Fixed Assets (net)	30.0	23.0	25.6	20.2	21.8	10.8
4.4	5.6	6.8	Intangibles (net)	3.5	3.0	4.7	5.6	9.1	17.3
9.1	10.2	7.2	All Other Non-Current	6.2	10.8	6.3	6.6	9.0	2.8
100.0	100.0	100.0	Total	100.0	100.0	100.0	100.0	100.0	100.0
			LIABILITIES						
12.4	15.1	15.8	Notes Payable-Short Term	29.1	27.7	6.1	11.1	6.2	2.9
5.1	5.7	4.7	Cur. Mat.-L.T.D.	13.1	3.0	2.7	3.3	2.4	2.0
12.0	11.8	14.4	Trade Payables	6.0	19.0	14.4	14.5	11.9	19.2
.3	.5	.7	Income Taxes Payable	.3	1.1	.5	1.6	.2	.1
12.3	13.2	14.2	All Other Current	20.8	8.6	20.5	7.5	18.0	12.9
42.1	46.3	49.8	Total Current	69.3	59.3	44.1	38.1	38.7	37.2
14.5	17.2	17.9	Long-Term Debt	14.7	33.5	10.3	10.6	14.1	15.1
.4	.2	.2	Deferred Taxes	.0	.0	.1	.0	.0	.8
10.7	8.3	17.7	All Other Non-Current	29.0	4.7	27.6	10.2	13.6	25.3
32.4	28.1	14.4	Net Worth	-13.1	2.5	17.8	41.2	33.6	21.6
100.0	100.0	100.0	Total Liabilties & Net Worth	100.0	100.0	100.0	100.0	100.0	100.0
			INCOME DATA						
100.0	100.0	100.0	Net Sales	100.0	100.0	100.0	100.0	100.0	100.0
			Gross Profit						
91.1	91.8	92.8	Operating Expenses	90.1	93.0	95.2	91.6	95.7	92.6
8.9	8.2	7.2	Operating Profit	9.9	7.0	4.8	8.4	4.3	7.4
1.3	1.5	1.9	All Other Expenses (net)	4.4	2.7	.3	.5	.8	1.5
7.5	6.7	5.3	Profit Before Taxes	5.5	4.3	4.5	8.0	3.5	5.8
			RATIOS						
3.4	3.1	3.0		5.0	2.4	3.7	4.0	2.2	2.8
1.6	1.7	1.6	Current	1.9	1.4	1.9	1.9	1.6	1.8
1.0	.9	1.0		.5	.7	1.0	1.1	1.2	1.5
3.1	2.8	2.4		5.0	2.0	2.5	4.0	1.9	2.0
1.3	1.3	1.3	Quick	1.6	.9	1.8	1.4	1.1	1.4
.7	.7	.8		.4	.5	.8	.9	.9	1.0
11 32.5	13 27.1	20 18.1		0 UND	0 UND	22 16.5	36 10.1	28 13.2	43 8.5
42 8.7	42 8.6	43 8.5	Sales/Receivables	24 15.3	26 13.9	45 8.2	46 8.0	43 8.5	51 7.1
61 6.0	62 5.9	64 5.7		54 6.8	68 5.4	68 5.4	74 4.9	62 5.9	72 5.1
			Cost of Sales/Inventory						
			Cost of Sales/Payables						
6.5	5.9	6.1		4.9	7.4	7.6	5.1	10.2	5.6
13.0	14.4	12.7	Sales/Working Capital	19.9	36.1	13.7	10.2	13.1	7.2
UND	-76.1	UND		-5.8	-15.0	NM	NM	33.2	12.8
19.3	18.7	31.6		49.8	10.3	34.6	39.2	15.0	41.4
(115) 6.4	(108) 5.7	(109) 6.2	EBIT/Interest	(16) 9.2	(26) 3.3	(14) 13.1	(19) 9.9	(13) 5.8	(21) 9.5
2.0	1.2	1.1		1.1	-21.5	1.8	3.7	.6	1.4
6.2	3.2	7.8							
(29) 2.8	(28) 2.1	(16) 4.3	Net Profit + Depr., Dep., Amort./Cur. Mat. L/T/D						
1.2	.8	1.4							
.2	.2	.1		.0	.0	.5	.1	.2	.2
.6	.7	.6	Fixed/Worth	1.4	.6	NM	.5	.4	.5
2.1	10.3	-7.9		-1.0	NM	-1.6	1.3	NM	-2.6
.4	.5	.8		.8	.9	.5	.6	.7	.9
1.3	1.6	2.2	Debt/Worth	9.4	3.7	NM	1.4	1.3	1.6
7.5	32.8	-8.1		-2.1	-6.1	-8.1	4.8	NM	-9.0
79.0	68.9	90.3		156.3	177.8	55.1	168.0	61.1	69.1
(123) 27.7	(107) 31.2	(95) 38.8	% Profit Before Taxes/Tangible Net Worth	(15) 37.8	(22) 42.6	(10) 40.6	(19) 38.8	(13) 22.1	(16) 56.1
6.6	7.5	7.8		7.7	-1.3	12.2	9.6	3.4	26.7
26.0	30.6	28.9		29.6	47.2	26.0	38.7	17.2	23.1
9.3	10.1	9.4	% Profit Before Taxes/Total Assets	4.8	7.5	13.8	9.2	7.7	10.9
1.9	1.0	.5		-3.6	-6.2	3.7	2.5	-.9	1.0
49.0	58.4	146.4		530.0	581.4	39.4	91.1	52.6	186.9
18.6	18.1	27.9	Sales/Net Fixed Assets	26.6	37.5	18.5	22.1	25.2	36.9
6.1	5.6	7.7		2.0	12.5	7.8	7.1	5.2	11.8
4.5	4.0	4.5		4.7	7.1	5.2	4.7	4.0	3.0
2.7	2.5	2.7	Sales/Total Assets	2.5	3.1	3.2	2.8	3.0	2.1
1.8	1.7	1.9		1.3	2.0	2.5	1.9	1.9	1.7
1.0	.7	.6		.7	.5	.2	1.1	1.1	.2
(110) 1.7	(101) 2.1	(88) 1.6	% Depr., Dep., Amort./Sales	(10) 1.8	(18) 1.7	(14) 1.8	(15) 2.5	(12) 2.0	(19) 1.1
3.6	4.1	3.1		22.1	2.8	3.3	3.8	4.6	2.7
4.2	4.3	4.3			7.7	4.3	3.4		
(62) 7.1	(66) 8.3	(56) 8.3	% Officers', Directors' Owners' Comp/Sales		(19) 10.5	(12) 5.3	(13) 6.0		
12.2	12.7	12.4			13.3	11.0	12.0		
2295101M	2145555M	2181302M	Net Sales ($)	14152M	63569M	78675M	158563M	262383M	1603960M
1076354M	1006788M	1066184M	Total Assets ($)	12460M	47127M	23608M	67391M	131447M	784151M

M = $ thousand MM = $ million

See Pages 9 through 22 for Explanation of Ratios and Data

	Current Data Sorted by Assets						Comparative Historical Data	
Type of Statement								
Unqualified				3			1	2
Reviewed		3	4				5	7
Compiled		2	3					1
Tax Returns	4	6	3				3	
Other	1	5	5	8	1		4	7
		3 (4/1-9/30/13)		45 (10/1/13-3/31/14)			4/1/09-3/31/10 ALL	4/1/10-3/31/11 ALL
	0-500M	500M-2MM	2-10MM	10-50MM	50-100MM	100-250MM		
NUMBER OF STATEMENTS	5	16	15	11	1		13	17
ASSETS	%	%	%	%	%	%	%	%
Cash & Equivalents		18.3	15.3	10.0		DATA NOT AVAILABLE	8.6	8.9
Trade Receivables (net)		37.2	34.3	38.5			33.1	34.9
Inventory		2.7	16.9	10.4			16.6	19.5
All Other Current		3.3	1.2	2.4			8.7	6.0
Total Current		61.5	67.7	61.3			67.0	69.2
Fixed Assets (net)		26.4	20.9	20.0			21.5	14.8
Intangibles (net)		4.0	2.5	15.3			7.0	9.0
All Other Non-Current		8.2	8.8	3.3			4.5	7.1
Total		100.0	100.0	100.0			100.0	100.0
LIABILITIES								
Notes Payable-Short Term		11.7	10.2	5.5			21.4	12.9
Cur. Mat.-L.T.D.		2.2	.8	5.0			2.2	4.2
Trade Payables		12.1	16.5	11.2			17.8	14.8
Income Taxes Payable		.1	1.0	.3			.2	.9
All Other Current		11.0	16.3	10.3			9.8	10.9
Total Current		37.1	44.8	32.3			51.4	43.7
Long-Term Debt		18.9	12.6	14.6			13.7	10.1
Deferred Taxes		.0	.0	1.7			1.0	.0
All Other Non-Current		.1	.5	9.5			10.9	5.3
Net Worth		43.9	42.1	41.8			23.0	40.8
Total Liabilities & Net Worth		100.0	100.0	100.0			100.0	100.0
INCOME DATA								
Net Sales		100.0	100.0	100.0			100.0	100.0
Gross Profit								
Operating Expenses		86.9	93.3	87.9			99.8	93.2
Operating Profit		13.1	6.7	12.1			.2	6.8
All Other Expenses (net)		4.0	-.4	1.7			1.0	2.3
Profit Before Taxes		9.1	7.0	10.4			-.8	4.5
RATIOS								
Current		2.8	2.7	7.0			1.7	2.6
		1.7	1.4	3.1			1.2	1.4
		.9	1.2	.8			.9	1.1
Quick		2.7	2.2	3.0			1.1	2.0
		1.6	1.2	1.7			.8	1.0
		.7	.8	.8			.4	.6
Sales/Receivables		**0** 768.2	**26** 14.2	**31** 11.8			**19** 19.7	**21** 17.0
		47 7.8	**47** 7.7	**57** 6.4			**46** 8.0	**48** 7.6
		56 6.5	**70** 5.2	**101** 3.6			**57** 6.4	**62** 5.9
Cost of Sales/Inventory								
Cost of Sales/Payables								
Sales/Working Capital		7.7	5.7	3.7			7.9	7.6
		11.3	13.6	4.7			27.0	12.9
		NM	21.6	-12.9			-62.4	33.0
EBIT/Interest		117.0	21.0	187.8			8.9	32.1
		(12) 7.5	(11) 11.6	(10) 6.5			4.2	(14) 5.1
		-3.2	5.1	2.8			-1.0	1.6
Net Profit + Depr., Dep., Amort./Cur. Mat. L/T/D								
Fixed/Worth		.2	.1	.0			.3	.1
		.5	.4	5.1			1.1	.4
		2.0	2.1	-3.1			NM	1.2
Debt/Worth		.8	.8	.5			1.5	1.0
		1.6	2.0	7.2			4.7	1.7
		3.6	5.1	-9.5			NM	4.2
% Profit Before Taxes/Tangible Net Worth		54.5	51.2				79.0	53.9
		(15) 17.9	(14) 17.0				(10) 25.6	(16) 20.9
		-17.6	8.5				-110.6	9.6
% Profit Before Taxes/Total Assets		33.4	29.5	26.4			17.2	14.3
		8.7	7.1	19.0			4.5	8.0
		-3.3	2.6	5.4			-13.1	1.8
Sales/Net Fixed Assets		53.3	58.0	153.8			72.1	85.7
		19.0	30.9	6.2			27.0	25.7
		8.6	5.4	4.7			11.0	14.4
Sales/Total Assets		4.0	2.9	2.3			4.4	3.4
		3.4	2.4	1.4			3.7	2.9
		2.3	1.6	1.4			2.5	1.8
% Depr., Dep., Amort./Sales		.3	.5				.9	.6
		(13) 1.0	(12) .7				(10) 1.2	(11) 1.4
		3.9	1.3				3.1	3.7
% Officers', Directors' Owners' Comp/Sales			3.2					
			(10) 6.9					
			7.3					
Net Sales ($)	2427M	65377M	178944M	373627M	62153M		378779M	277733M
Total Assets ($)	353M	19226M	76553M	225932M	87074M		129582M	159880M

M = $ thousand MM = $ million

See Pages 9 through 22 for Explanation of Ratios and Data

Comparative Historical Data				Current Data Sorted by Sales					
			Type of Statement						
1	2	3	Unqualified						3
7	7	7	Reviewed			2	2	3	
6	4	5	Compiled	1	1		1	2	
7	8	13	Tax Returns	4	2		4	3	
15	15	20	Other	1	1	5	3	2	8
4/1/11-3/31/12 ALL	**4/1/12-3/31/13 ALL**	**4/1/13-3/31/14 ALL**		**3 (4/1-9/30/13)**			**45 (10/1/13-3/31/14)**		
				0-1MM	**1-3MM**	**3-5MM**	**5-10MM**	**10-25MM**	**25MM & OVER**
36	36	48	**NUMBER OF STATEMENTS**	6	4	7	10	10	11
%	%	%	**ASSETS**	%	%	%	%	%	%
18.1	18.1	18.0	Cash & Equivalents				16.9	15.3	11.1
23.6	27.2	33.4	Trade Receivables (net)				36.8	44.0	32.4
15.8	17.4	8.5	Inventory				17.4	14.6	7.4
4.2	4.4	2.0	All Other Current				2.1	1.1	2.1
61.6	67.1	62.0	Total Current				73.1	74.9	53.0
24.0	16.9	23.8	Fixed Assets (net)				14.8	14.3	20.2
7.2	4.2	7.4	Intangibles (net)				6.3	3.6	22.9
7.3	11.7	6.9	All Other Non-Current				5.8	7.2	3.9
100.0	100.0	100.0	Total				100.0	100.0	100.0
			LIABILITIES						
9.1	9.5	15.4	Notes Payable-Short Term				13.7	14.9	2.6
5.0	4.4	2.8	Cur. Mat.-L.T.D.				.7	1.0	5.0
11.0	11.1	11.9	Trade Payables				10.2	21.3	12.0
.0	.4	.4	Income Taxes Payable				.2	1.4	.3
22.1	19.8	13.3	All Other Current				15.4	17.0	10.7
47.1	45.3	43.8	Total Current				40.3	55.7	30.5
15.9	17.4	20.5	Long-Term Debt				8.7	7.0	18.4
.4	.8	.4	Deferred Taxes				.0	.0	1.7
19.3	12.9	2.8	All Other Non-Current				.0	.7	11.5
17.5	23.5	32.5	Net Worth				51.0	36.6	37.9
100.0	100.0	100.0	Total Liabilties & Net Worth				100.0	100.0	100.0
			INCOME DATA						
100.0	100.0	100.0	Net Sales				100.0	100.0	100.0
			Gross Profit						
91.4	91.8	88.8	Operating Expenses				88.9	93.3	90.6
8.6	8.2	11.2	Operating Profit				11.1	6.7	9.4
2.2	1.7	1.8	All Other Expenses (net)				-.5	.1	2.2
6.3	6.5	9.5	Profit Before Taxes				11.6	6.6	7.2
			RATIOS						
3.0	2.9	3.2					2.9	2.1	4.6
1.6	1.6	1.6	Current				1.7	1.2	1.8
1.0	1.0	.9					1.2	.9	.8
2.3	2.4	2.6					2.2	1.6	2.7
(35) 1.0	1.0	1.3	Quick				1.2	1.1	1.8
.6	.5	.8					1.0	.8	.8
0 UND	**26** 13.9	**6** 59.0					**5** 77.2	**38** 9.7	**31** 11.8
30 12.1	**41** 8.8	**48** 7.6	Sales/Receivables				**51** 7.2	**49** 7.5	**57** 6.4
57 6.4	**60** 6.1	**69** 5.3					**68** 5.4	**83** 4.4	**96** 3.8
			Cost of Sales/Inventory						
			Cost of Sales/Payables						
4.0	4.3	5.9					5.0	7.9	3.8
12.1	9.6	12.6	Sales/Working Capital				9.3	16.5	9.5
-141.4	NM	-50.8					56.5	-42.0	-12.9
8.3	19.1	69.6							
(27) 3.4	(31) 5.7	(38) 9.7	EBIT/Interest						
.3	2.1	2.6							
		16.7							
		(10) 2.5	Net Profit + Depr., Dep., Amort./Cur. Mat. L/T/D						
		1.0							
.2	.1	.1					.1	.0	.1
.7	.3	.9	Fixed/Worth				.2	.7	17.6
3.9	2.3	5.0					1.5	1.5	-2.5
.9	1.1	.8					.5	.7	1.7
3.4	2.6	2.6	Debt/Worth				1.2	2.6	45.9
NM	22.8	17.4					4.5	5.4	-6.2
68.3	52.5	85.6							
(27) 23.8	(30) 21.7	(40) 34.6	% Profit Before Taxes/Tangible Net Worth						
13.3	11.1	11.9							
19.3	17.3	31.8					46.9	27.9	20.6
8.9	8.6	12.5	% Profit Before Taxes/Total Assets				25.2	6.9	7.6
1.7	2.0	2.8					10.6	1.7	4.3
68.6	61.5	57.7					86.6	182.6	79.2
25.5	33.6	20.1	Sales/Net Fixed Assets				49.0	49.9	6.2
5.2	9.7	5.6					25.1	6.4	4.7
3.5	3.9	3.7					5.6	3.3	2.7
2.3	2.2	2.6	Sales/Total Assets				3.1	2.6	1.4
1.3	1.4	1.5					1.6	1.7	1.3
1.1	.3	.5							
(25) 2.0	(23) 1.0	(36) 1.1	% Depr., Dep., Amort./Sales						
4.4	3.8	5.3							
1.8		3.9							
(15) 7.6		(20) 6.9	% Officers', Directors' Owners' Comp/Sales						
23.7		10.9							
526237M	**486744M**	**682528M**	Net Sales ($)	**1409M**	**7989M**	**28197M**	**72660M**	**143615M**	**428658M**
297993M	**276335M**	**409138M**	Total Assets ($)	**2727M**	**2764M**	**9861M**	**28567M**	**63450M**	**301769M**

M = $ thousand MM = $ million

See Pages 9 through 22 for Explanation of Ratios and Data

Current Data Sorted by Assets | **Comparative Historical Data**

0-500M	500M-2MM	2-10MM	10-50MM	50-100MM	100-250MM	Type of Statement	4/1/09-3/31/10 ALL	4/1/10-3/31/11 ALL
1	5	21	36	11	17	Unqualified	126	118
1	10	42	14	2		Reviewed	73	76
3	24	32	6			Compiled	64	55
57	71	26	2			Tax Returns	101	102
33	77	142	82	24	28	Other	338	341
73 (4/1-9/30/13)		694 (10/1/13-3/31/14)						
95	187	263	140	37	45	NUMBER OF STATEMENTS	702	692
%	%	%	%	%	%	**ASSETS**	%	%
39.3	26.3	21.7	22.4	17.0	18.8	Cash & Equivalents	23.4	22.0
17.7	40.8	44.3	34.1	28.3	21.2	Trade Receivables (net)	38.4	39.9
.9	.7	1.2	1.7	3.3	2.4	Inventory	1.8	2.3
5.1	3.9	4.2	6.2	8.2	6.6	All Other Current	6.0	4.5
62.9	71.7	71.5	64.5	56.9	49.1	Total Current	69.6	68.8
20.1	14.7	13.2	8.5	7.1	8.7	Fixed Assets (net)	11.9	12.5
5.5	3.3	6.3	17.6	27.8	35.8	Intangibles (net)	9.8	9.2
11.5	10.3	9.0	9.4	8.2	6.5	All Other Non-Current	8.7	9.5
100.0	100.0	100.0	100.0	100.0	100.0	Total	100.0	100.0
						LIABILITIES		
38.1	9.5	7.7	6.5	3.8	.6	Notes Payable-Short Term	14.1	11.8
6.6	2.1	1.8	2.5	1.1	1.8	Cur. Mat.-L.T.D.	3.2	2.1
9.4	12.9	11.4	10.2	9.2	8.1	Trade Payables	11.9	11.0
.5	.8	.3	.6	.2	.4	Income Taxes Payable	.6	.4
22.3	16.0	22.6	27.2	27.5	22.1	All Other Current	24.3	23.0
76.9	41.2	43.9	47.1	41.9	32.9	Total Current	54.1	48.3
19.4	14.0	11.2	11.8	12.8	25.1	Long-Term Debt	9.5	9.0
.0	.2	.3	.3	1.7	1.8	Deferred Taxes	.4	.4
8.3	6.6	8.1	9.5	5.0	6.7	All Other Non-Current	10.9	10.9
-4.6	38.0	36.5	31.3	38.6	33.4	Net Worth	25.1	31.4
100.0	100.0	100.0	100.0	100.0	100.0	Total Liabilties & Net Worth	100.0	100.0
						INCOME DATA		
100.0	100.0	100.0	100.0	100.0	100.0	Net Sales	100.0	100.0
						Gross Profit		
91.5	88.6	91.8	93.5	94.2	94.9	Operating Expenses	93.5	91.4
8.5	11.4	8.2	6.5	5.8	5.1	Operating Profit	6.5	8.6
1.0	1.7	1.0	1.5	.6	4.2	All Other Expenses (net)	1.2	1.3
7.5	9.7	7.3	5.1	5.2	.8	Profit Before Taxes	5.3	7.4
						RATIOS		
3.3	4.7	3.1	2.1	1.8	2.2		2.8	3.0
1.1	1.9	1.8	1.3	1.5	1.4	Current	1.6	1.6
.5	1.1	1.2	.9	1.1	.9		1.0	1.0
3.2	4.4	2.9	2.1	1.5	1.7		2.5	2.7
1.1	1.7	1.6	1.1	1.0	1.0	Quick	(701) 1.4	1.4
.3	1.0	1.0	.7	.8	.8		.8	.9
0 UND	**13** 29.1	**38** 9.7	**40** 9.2	**45** 8.2	**40** 9.1		**29** 12.7	**33** 10.9
0 UND	**38** 9.5	**55** 6.6	**52** 7.0	**69** 5.3	**59** 6.2	Sales/Receivables	**52** 7.0	**55** 6.7
27 13.3	**60** 6.1	**74** 4.9	**74** 4.9	**85** 4.3	**70** 5.2		**75** 4.9	**76** 4.8
						Cost of Sales/Inventory		
						Cost of Sales/Payables		
17.1	6.5	5.5	5.2	4.2	6.4		5.4	5.1
289.5	14.1	10.3	15.1	11.0	15.0	Sales/Working Capital	13.8	11.4
-26.6	73.2	40.7	-64.2	39.1	-103.8		-174.0	395.3
41.4	53.5	125.5	73.2	48.0	12.9		27.2	53.2
(60) 8.4	(123) 13.0	(192) 23.4	(103) 17.7	(27) 3.5	(36) 2.3	EBIT/Interest	(495) 7.4	(496) 14.1
.8	3.8	3.3	2.9	1.2	-2.6		.7	3.0
		21.8	22.0		5.2	Net Profit + Depr., Dep.,	14.1	19.1
		(24) 3.5	(30) 6.0		(16) 2.3	Amort./Cur. Mat. L/T/D	(72) 3.4	(65) 3.6
		1.2	.4		-2.5		.5	1.9
.1	.0	.1	.1	.1	.1		.1	.1
.7	.1	.2	.3	.4	-11.5	Fixed/Worth	.3	.2
-.6	.9	1.2	-69.9	-.2	-.2		6.0	1.9
.6	.4	.6	.9	1.3	.8		.7	.7
8.3	1.3	1.4	3.1	2.9	-35.1	Debt/Worth	2.0	1.9
-2.9	8.5	6.5	-40.0	-4.3	-1.8		182.1	14.9
335.2	135.0	83.7	61.0	63.9	31.2	% Profit Before Taxes/Tangible	78.5	83.9
(61) 98.8	(164) 59.3	(216) 43.2	(102) 33.4	(24) 13.5	(22) 15.9	Net Worth	(530) 30.5	(550) 40.1
47.5	18.7	18.3	15.3	5.4	-17.1		9.8	14.1
95.6	43.6	33.8	19.0	12.7	11.0	% Profit Before Taxes/Total	24.4	29.9
34.1	19.7	14.7	9.6	3.4	3.1	Assets	10.0	13.6
4.6	6.2	4.0	1.5	.5	-5.2		.9	3.0
999.8	793.0	105.5	92.9	59.6	37.2		145.4	152.6
121.7	86.7	44.0	38.9	29.4	16.3	Sales/Net Fixed Assets	44.1	44.4
28.3	24.9	16.7	16.7	16.4	9.3		16.6	16.7
20.8	5.7	3.9	3.0	1.9	2.4		4.3	4.2
8.7	3.9	2.8	1.9	1.2	.9	Sales/Total Assets	2.8	2.6
4.6	2.7	1.9	1.2	.8	.7		1.6	1.5
.2	.2	.4	.5	.4	.5		.4	.3
(46) .9	(95) .5	(177) 1.0	(89) 1.2	(19) 1.2	(28) 2.1	% Depr., Dep., Amort./Sales	(409) 1.0	(410) .9
2.7	1.4	2.1	2.2	2.9	4.3		2.2	2.2
3.8	1.5	2.0	1.3			% Officers', Directors'	2.7	2.6
(60) 6.7	(77) 5.5	(61) 4.1	(10) 4.0			Owners' Comp/Sales	(191) 6.0	(168) 6.9
13.4	10.8	7.3	11.5				11.9	13.8
241158M	998477M	3494402M	6436732M	3729525M	9792142M	Net Sales ($)	17538981M	18634430M
23213M	220745M	1178083M	3100938M	2616005M	6939497M	Total Assets ($)	11756229M	11618559M

M = $ thousand MM = $ million

See Pages 9 through 22 for Explanation of Ratios and Data

Comparative Historical Data | Current Data Sorted by Sales

Type of Statement	4/1/11-3/31/12 ALL	4/1/12-3/31/13 ALL	4/1/13-3/31/14 ALL	0-1MM	1-3MM	3-5MM	5-10MM	10-25MM	25MM & OVER
Unqualified	114	106	91		2	3	5	15	66
Reviewed	79	66	69		2	6	20	22	19
Compiled	61	43	65	4	8	4	22	23	4
Tax Returns	142	134	156	16	42	42	41	14	1
Other	369	373	386	15	53	30	70	105	113
					73 (4/1-9/30/13)		694 (10/1/13-3/31/14)		
NUMBER OF STATEMENTS	765	722	767	35	107	85	158	179	203
ASSETS	%	%	%	%	%	%	%	%	%
Cash & Equivalents	23.9	24.0	24.7	14.0	32.0	30.4	26.0	25.3	19.0
Trade Receivables (net)	37.9	37.0	36.2	10.8	29.0	28.5	43.0	41.7	37.4
Inventory	2.1	2.1	1.3	.0	1.2	.4	.9	1.1	2.5
All Other Current	4.2	5.0	5.0	2.0	6.4	3.9	3.1	5.4	6.2
Total Current	68.2	68.2	67.2	26.8	68.5	63.2	73.0	73.5	65.0
Fixed Assets (net)	12.9	11.8	13.0	45.4	13.9	17.9	11.2	10.3	8.8
Intangibles (net)	9.4	11.6	10.3	15.0	6.2	5.0	6.7	6.9	19.7
All Other Non-Current	9.5	8.5	9.5	12.8	11.3	13.9	9.2	9.4	6.4
Total	100.0	100.0	100.0	100.0	100.0	100.0	100.0	100.0	100.0
LIABILITIES									
Notes Payable-Short Term	11.3	10.9	11.1	32.3	17.6	13.0	11.2	7.4	6.3
Cur. Mat.-L.T.D.	2.6	3.2	2.6	2.4	2.1	6.3	1.7	2.7	1.8
Trade Payables	10.8	10.7	11.0	3.6	10.4	10.0	12.8	10.6	12.0
Income Taxes Payable	.4	.2	.5	.6	.5	.6	.6	.4	.5
All Other Current	21.8	22.5	22.0	16.3	17.2	15.5	23.4	24.1	25.3
Total Current	47.0	47.5	47.2	55.1	47.9	45.4	49.7	45.3	45.9
Long-Term Debt	11.0	10.2	13.9	33.4	16.7	15.6	9.3	9.4	15.9
Deferred Taxes	.4	.5	.4	.0	.1	.3	.3	.2	.8
All Other Non-Current	11.7	9.3	7.8	7.5	12.2	9.1	7.0	7.3	6.1
Net Worth	29.9	32.5	30.7	4.0	23.1	29.7	33.7	37.8	31.3
Total Liabilties & Net Worth	100.0	100.0	100.0	100.0	100.0	100.0	100.0	100.0	100.0
INCOME DATA									
Net Sales	100.0	100.0	100.0	100.0	100.0	100.0	100.0	100.0	100.0
Gross Profit									
Operating Expenses	91.2	92.2	91.6	63.1	89.6	91.9	94.8	91.7	94.8
Operating Profit	8.8	7.8	8.4	36.9	10.4	8.1	5.2	8.3	5.2
All Other Expenses (net)	1.1	1.3	1.4	12.0	.9	1.3	.2	.7	1.6
Profit Before Taxes	7.6	6.5	7.0	24.8	9.6	6.8	5.1	7.6	3.7
RATIOS									
	3.4	3.1	3.1	2.3	7.7	6.9	2.6	3.0	2.1
Current	1.6	1.6	1.6	.9	2.1	1.9	1.6	1.8	1.4
	1.0	1.0	1.0	.2	1.0	.9	1.1	1.1	1.0
	3.0	2.8	2.8	2.3	6.6	6.8	2.5	2.9	1.9
Quick	1.5	1.4	1.4	.7	1.9	1.8	1.5	1.7	1.1
	.9	.9	.9	.2	.9	.8	1.0	.9	.8
	25 14.7	26 14.1	27 13.4	0 UND	0 UND	0 UND	35 10.5	34 10.8	40 9.2
Sales/Receivables	49 7.5	49 7.4	47 7.7	0 UND	29 12.7	28 12.9	51 7.1	53 6.9	55 6.6
	73 5.0	69 5.3	69 5.3	28 12.9	51 7.2	63 5.8	73 5.0	68 5.4	73 5.0
Cost of Sales/Inventory									
Cost of Sales/Payables									
	5.5	5.8	6.1	20.0	5.4	5.4	6.0	6.5	6.4
Sales/Working Capital	12.7	12.6	14.1	-54.3	12.4	19.4	15.3	10.9	15.0
	201.6	147.2	195.3	-3.4	365.0	-134.8	59.5	68.0	171.1
	49.9	55.4	72.6	25.1	37.5	31.0	53.5	156.3	71.2
EBIT/Interest	(532) 11.3	(512) 12.6	(541) 13.4	(18) 6.8	(62) 9.5	(60) 9.3	(113) 13.9	(131) 30.4	(157) 11.9
	2.8	2.5	2.5	2.7	2.3	.9	2.9	5.5	1.7
	19.1	18.3	18.1					22.5	17.0
Net Profit + Depr., Dep., Amort./Cur. Mat. L/T/D	(79) 3.9	(78) 4.2	(83) 4.1					(19) 4.1	(47) 5.1
	1.4	.7	.4					.4	.3
	.1	.1	.1	.5	.0	.0	.1	.1	.1
Fixed/Worth	.3	.3	.3	4.0	.2	.4	.3	.2	.3
	3.4	3.9	4.2	-5.3	21.2	2.3	.8	1.0	-1.3
	.6	.7	.7	1.9	.4	.5	.7	.5	1.0
Debt/Worth	1.7	2.1	2.0	10.5	2.7	1.5	1.6	1.3	3.1
	23.7	327.7	34.4	-4.0	-106.1	10.3	7.5	6.7	-13.1
	85.9	93.4	96.4	172.3	131.2	134.4	93.6	98.8	68.6
% Profit Before Taxes/Tangible Net Worth	(593) 41.0	(546) 46.7	(589) 45.2	(24) 44.1	(79) 59.5	(67) 62.1	(132) 37.3	(148) 51.6	(139) 32.0
	13.1	16.9	16.9	8.6	26.4	15.9	14.0	22.1	13.4
	34.1	36.5	32.7	71.3	49.0	44.5	35.2	36.4	18.9
% Profit Before Taxes/Total Assets	13.1	14.0	13.5	13.9	16.9	17.0	12.1	18.6	9.5
	3.4	3.5	2.7	2.5	5.0	.7	2.0	5.5	1.4
	185.9	169.1	187.1	144.7	999.8	600.8	195.8	136.5	91.2
Sales/Net Fixed Assets	46.2	47.4	47.2	12.6	95.9	49.0	49.9	48.3	39.7
	16.7	18.0	17.8	.2	32.1	14.2	22.2	21.9	15.9
	4.7	4.8	4.5	3.3	5.8	6.9	4.6	4.6	3.6
Sales/Total Assets	2.8	2.8	3.0	.8	3.7	3.4	3.4	3.1	2.4
	1.5	1.5	1.6	.1	2.1	1.9	2.3	1.9	1.2
	.3	.3	.3	2.5	.2	.2	.3	.3	.4
% Depr., Dep., Amort./Sales	(449) 1.0	(391) .9	(454) .9	(21) 9.5	(44) .7	(45) 1.1	(95) .9	(115) .8	(134) .9
	2.2	2.0	2.2	26.1	1.8	3.5	2.0	1.7	2.2
	2.3	2.3	2.6	8.3	3.5	4.1	1.4	1.6	.6
% Officers', Directors' Owners' Comp/Sales	(219) 5.2	(213) 5.2	(211) 5.1	(11) 15.0	(55) 7.6	(39) 6.4	(53) 3.7	(39) 4.1	(14) 1.7
	11.9	10.7	10.4	27.3	12.3	12.4	7.3	6.2	4.7
Net Sales ($)	20069493M	21033368M	24692436M	12424M	218779M	333290M	1134757M	2825169M	20168017M
Total Assets ($)	12323285M	13188372M	14078481M	27621M	178888M	137255M	510340M	1423084M	11801293M

M = $ thousand MM = $ million

See Pages 9 through 22 for Explanation of Ratios and Data

Current Data Sorted by Assets							Comparative Historical Data	
						Type of Statement		
	2	31	56	20	17	Unqualified	161	166
2	23	64	28			Reviewed	102	123
7	28	26	5	1	3	Compiled	53	61
37	53	41	4			Tax Returns	91	88
29	85	203	114	25	23	Other	368	381
100 (4/1-9/30/13)		827 (10/1/13-3/31/14)					4/1/09-3/31/10 ALL	4/1/10-3/31/11 ALL
0-500M	500M-2MM	2-10MM	10-50MM	50-100MM	100-250MM			
75	191	365	207	46	43	**NUMBER OF STATEMENTS**	775	819
%	%	%	%	%	%	**ASSETS**	%	%
41.0	26.1	19.8	17.4	15.5	11.0	Cash & Equivalents	17.8	17.6
23.6	41.4	46.1	44.9	31.6	24.9	Trade Receivables (net)	44.8	45.3
4.5	3.2	4.0	4.0	2.8	3.4	Inventory	4.8	4.6
2.5	2.3	4.8	6.3	8.8	7.3	All Other Current	5.2	5.5
71.5	73.1	74.6	72.6	58.7	46.6	Total Current	72.7	73.0
12.9	14.3	11.4	9.1	7.1	8.4	Fixed Assets (net)	11.1	10.4
4.7	4.1	5.3	12.1	27.3	36.5	Intangibles (net)	8.9	8.9
10.9	8.5	8.7	6.2	6.9	8.5	All Other Non-Current	7.4	7.8
100.0	100.0	100.0	100.0	100.0	100.0	Total	100.0	100.0
						LIABILITIES		
30.1	11.7	8.6	6.1	4.6	3.7	Notes Payable-Short Term	14.4	12.5
7.4	2.0	1.4	1.5	2.8	1.9	Cur. Mat.-L.T.D.	3.0	2.3
15.0	16.4	17.3	19.8	12.6	14.3	Trade Payables	17.5	16.9
.3	.2	.4	.4	.5	.5	Income Taxes Payable	.5	.6
24.6	14.5	17.0	20.0	21.6	12.8	All Other Current	19.1	21.1
77.4	44.8	44.7	47.8	42.1	33.1	Total Current	54.5	53.4
14.9	11.7	7.3	5.3	18.0	19.6	Long-Term Debt	10.8	9.3
.0	.5	.3	.3	1.0	2.2	Deferred Taxes	.4	.3
16.5	5.8	8.6	6.8	9.3	11.1	All Other Non-Current	6.2	7.5
-8.9	37.1	39.1	39.8	29.6	34.0	Net Worth	28.1	29.5
100.0	100.0	100.0	100.0	100.0	100.0	Total Liabilities & Net Worth	100.0	100.0
						INCOME DATA		
100.0	100.0	100.0	100.0	100.0	100.0	Net Sales	100.0	100.0
						Gross Profit		
93.1	90.4	93.0	94.5	94.9	92.9	Operating Expenses	94.3	94.2
6.9	9.6	7.0	5.5	5.1	7.1	Operating Profit	5.7	5.8
.6	2.1	1.1	.5	2.7	2.2	All Other Expenses (net)	1.3	.7
6.3	7.5	5.9	4.9	2.4	4.9	Profit Before Taxes	4.4	5.1
						RATIOS		
3.3	4.6	3.1	2.2	2.2	2.1		2.2	2.4
1.3	1.7	1.7	1.4	1.3	1.6	Current	1.4	1.5
.6	1.1	1.2	1.1	1.0	.9		1.0	1.1
3.4	4.2	2.9	1.9	2.0	1.6		1.9	2.2
(74) 1.2	1.5	1.5	1.2	1.0	1.0	Quick	1.3	1.3
.5	1.0	1.0	.9	.7	.7		.8	.8
0 UND	**18** 20.2	**35** 10.4	**42** 8.6	**45** 8.1	**49** 7.5		**35** 10.4	**37** 9.9
4 84.9	**36** 10.2	**50** 7.3	**57** 6.4	**60** 6.1	**63** 5.8	Sales/Receivables	**55** 6.7	**57** 6.4
29 12.8	**54** 6.7	**68** 5.4	**76** 4.8	**89** 4.1	**76** 4.8		**73** 5.0	**74** 4.9
						Cost of Sales/Inventory		
						Cost of Sales/Payables		
13.4	6.6	5.6	5.9	5.4	5.0		6.7	6.6
55.2	15.1	11.2	12.8	15.8	9.7	Sales/Working Capital	14.4	14.1
-39.7	67.2	38.5	61.2	-403.5	-50.1		793.9	95.7
40.7	48.4	83.1	57.2	18.7	9.2		32.6	37.4
(47) 6.1	(134) 10.0	(252) 18.5	(151) 13.2	(39) 3.9	(36) 1.4	EBIT/Interest	(604) 7.6	(643) 11.3
-1.0	2.6	4.0	2.4	-.2	-.7		1.1	2.4
		31.4	22.4	8.0			15.6	21.6
		(28) 3.8	(32) 4.5	(13) 3.8		Net Profit + Depr., Dep., Amort./Cur. Mat. L/T/D	(103) 3.4	(112) 5.0
		1.6	1.1	.2			.6	1.8
.0	.0	.0	.1	.2	.2		.1	.1
.2	.2	.1	.2	1.0	-.5	Fixed/Worth	.3	.2
-1.7	1.7	.6	1.1	-.2	-.1		2.8	1.4
.3	.4	.5	.9	1.1	1.6		.9	.8
6.7	1.8	1.5	2.5	12.1	-8.3	Debt/Worth	2.4	2.3
-3.2	11.6	4.8	7.0	-4.4	-2.1		38.4	12.4
208.9	98.6	71.3	77.0	72.1	73.8		64.5	73.8
(42) 63.7	(156) 44.2	(320) 39.1	(179) 32.4	(26) 28.7	(19) 34.0	% Profit Before Taxes/Tangible Net Worth	(602) 30.1	(654) 38.9
18.4	15.2	14.1	10.2	8.5	11.6		8.0	13.3
66.0	38.6	29.0	19.9	14.6	10.5		21.8	24.3
23.8	16.6	13.7	10.0	4.9	4.2	% Profit Before Taxes/Total Assets	8.0	10.9
-1.3	4.6	4.1	1.7	.5	-3.1		.3	2.6
UND	368.9	230.4	198.5	65.0	107.1		157.9	187.1
153.1	81.1	73.5	58.1	30.6	39.0	Sales/Net Fixed Assets	58.0	66.2
47.8	28.3	22.9	20.9	14.2	12.0		20.9	22.9
14.8	6.5	4.4	3.7	2.2	2.2		4.3	4.4
7.2	4.4	3.2	2.7	1.7	1.2	Sales/Total Assets	3.0	3.1
4.2	2.8	2.0	1.7	.9	.8		1.9	1.8
.2	.3	.3	.2	.5	.4		.3	.3
(32) .4	(110) .7	(235) .7	(148) .7	(33) 1.7	(21) .7	% Depr., Dep., Amort./Sales	(490) .7	(544) .7
1.2	2.1	1.7	1.4	3.0	3.7		1.6	1.7
5.0	2.6	1.5	.5				2.4	2.9
(43) 7.2	(68) 4.1	(87) 3.3	(25) 1.2			% Officers', Directors' Owners' Comp/Sales	(186) 5.2	(173) 5.4
11.9	8.5	6.0	2.4				10.9	10.8
186701M	1045380M	5833293M	11368046M	5994182M	11404398M	Net Sales ($)	27717292M	32220806M
18179M	225550M	1775935M	4356224M	3298284M	6952963M	Total Assets ($)	14067052M	15261793M

M = $ thousand MM = $ million

See Pages 9 through 22 for Explanation of Ratios and Data

Comparative Historical Data | **Current Data Sorted by Sales**

4/1/11-3/31/12 ALL	4/1/12-3/31/13 ALL	4/1/13-3/31/14 ALL		0-1MM	1-3MM	3-5MM	5-10MM	10-25MM	25MM & OVER
			Type of Statement						
150	129	126	Unqualified		1	2	9	31	83
113	102	117	Reviewed	1	4	5	27	37	43
60	67	70	Compiled	2	14	13	13	19	9
130	144	135	Tax Returns	24	25	23	33	24	6
432	476	479	Other	16	40	39	75	135	174
				100 (4/1-9/30/13)		827 (10/1/13-3/31/14)			
885	918	927	**NUMBER OF STATEMENTS**	43	84	82	157	246	315
%	%	%	**ASSETS**	%	%	%	%	%	%
19.9	21.4	21.6	Cash & Equivalents	22.6	32.3	29.6	25.1	21.2	15.2
43.3	41.8	41.3	Trade Receivables (net)	13.6	28.2	36.9	40.6	47.0	45.7
4.3	4.9	3.8	Inventory	3.5	4.4	1.9	5.1	3.5	3.8
4.7	5.1	4.7	All Other Current	1.1	1.4	3.3	2.9	5.3	7.0
72.3	73.2	71.5	Total Current	40.8	66.2	71.7	73.7	77.1	71.7
11.3	12.0	11.2	Fixed Assets (net)	42.7	17.0	10.2	9.9	9.3	7.9
8.8	7.7	9.0	Intangibles (net)	7.0	6.3	8.6	5.4	6.5	14.0
7.6	7.1	8.2	All Other Non-Current	9.5	10.5	9.5	10.9	7.1	6.5
100.0	100.0	100.0	Total	100.0	100.0	100.0	100.0	100.0	100.0
			LIABILITIES						
11.0	11.4	10.0	Notes Payable-Short Term	11.5	17.4	16.3	10.5	7.7	7.7
2.2	2.3	2.1	Cur. Mat.-L.T.D.	3.4	6.1	1.7	1.7	1.4	1.7
18.3	18.5	17.1	Trade Payables	7.9	14.0	12.0	14.7	16.9	21.9
.5	.4	.4	Income Taxes Payable	.0	.5	.1	.5	.4	.4
20.5	18.0	17.8	All Other Current	24.9	13.4	13.6	17.2	18.8	18.7
52.5	50.6	47.4	Total Current	47.7	51.5	43.8	44.6	45.1	50.4
9.4	9.9	9.5	Long-Term Debt	44.4	14.1	7.2	6.9	5.4	8.4
.4	.3	.5	Deferred Taxes	.0	.0	.1	.8	.4	.6
5.9	6.6	8.4	All Other Non-Current	1.9	17.7	9.2	9.7	5.6	8.2
31.9	32.5	34.2	Net Worth	6.0	16.6	39.7	38.0	43.4	32.3
100.0	100.0	100.0	Total Liabilities & Net Worth	100.0	100.0	100.0	100.0	100.0	100.0
			INCOME DATA						
100.0	100.0	100.0	Net Sales	100.0	100.0	100.0	100.0	100.0	100.0
			Gross Profit						
93.1	93.5	92.9	Operating Expenses	68.9	92.3	93.4	94.3	93.8	94.8
6.9	6.5	7.1	Operating Profit	31.1	7.7	6.6	5.7	6.2	5.2
.9	1.2	1.3	All Other Expenses (net)	13.6	1.3	.7	.2	.4	1.0
6.0	5.3	5.8	Profit Before Taxes	17.5	6.4	5.9	5.5	5.8	4.2
			RATIOS						
2.6	2.5	2.9		3.3	5.0	5.1	3.9	3.1	2.1
1.5	1.5	1.6	Current	1.2	2.1	2.0	1.7	1.7	1.4
1.0	1.1	1.1		.3	.8	1.1	1.0	1.2	1.1
2.3	2.2	2.5		2.1	4.8	4.7	3.4	2.8	1.7
1.3	1.3	(926) 1.4	Quick	1.1	1.6	1.8	(156) 1.5	1.5	1.2
.8	.8	.9		.3	.8	1.0	.9	1.0	.9
33 11.0	**29** 12.6	**30** 12.2		**0** UND	**0** 771.1	**22** 16.4	**21** 17.0	**36** 10.0	**42** 8.7
51 7.1	**49** 7.4	**47** 7.7	Sales/Receivables	**0** UND	**28** 12.9	**40** 9.1	**42** 8.7	**50** 7.3	**56** 6.5
70 5.2	**68** 5.4	**68** 5.4		**30** 12.3	**49** 7.4	**64** 5.7	**65** 5.6	**68** 5.4	**74** 4.9
			Cost of Sales/Inventory						
			Cost of Sales/Payables						
6.5	6.7	6.0		5.6	4.9	5.4	5.8	5.8	7.1
13.2	14.1	13.4	Sales/Working Capital	29.5	14.5	9.7	14.6	11.7	14.0
155.2	119.7	70.3		-5.4	NM	42.1	79.0	43.8	68.9
48.2	48.3	57.0		13.1	21.9	64.0	79.2	86.5	40.3
(639) 11.1	(680) 11.1	(659) 12.1	EBIT/Interest	(18) 3.1	(52) 6.5	(54) 11.9	(112) 10.4	(179) 18.7	(244) 9.9
3.1	1.8	2.4		-.4	1.9	2.9	1.5	4.6	2.1
15.9	16.8	14.7						14.1	25.0
(92) 5.1	(94) 4.2	(86) 3.3	Net Profit + Depr., Dep., Amort./Cur. Mat. L/T/D					(26) 3.0	(49) 3.7
1.7	1.4	.8						.4	1.0
.0	.0	.0		.0	.0	.0	.0	.0	.1
.2	.2	.2	Fixed/Worth	2.4	.3	.2	.2	.1	.2
1.7	1.7	1.4		9.5	5.2	1.8	1.1	.5	2.4
.7	.7	.6		.6	.3	.3	.5	.5	1.1
2.0	2.1	2.1	Debt/Worth	4.8	2.5	2.2	1.7	1.5	2.9
12.9	11.6	12.3		-13.8	-10.6	24.1	9.8	4.3	20.1
83.0	77.3	80.6		66.9	119.8	71.6	90.4	77.8	76.8
(703) 42.2	(743) 37.7	(742) 39.2	% Profit Before Taxes/Tangible Net Worth	(31) 13.9	(59) 39.6	(64) 47.8	(127) 40.0	(214) 40.4	(247) 37.3
14.9	13.8	13.9		4.9	18.4	14.1	9.1	17.4	16.3
28.2	26.9	28.1		26.0	34.0	39.6	37.1	30.1	19.6
12.3	11.5	11.5	% Profit Before Taxes/Total Assets	5.6	15.3	14.0	13.3	16.0	9.5
3.2	2.2	2.8		.4	3.4	3.0	1.5	5.6	1.9
220.3	214.4	223.3		UND	212.5	190.9	312.5	239.6	197.1
68.7	63.5	71.5	Sales/Net Fixed Assets	16.7	49.6	71.7	78.9	80.4	63.5
22.0	22.1	22.9		.2	15.5	28.4	31.3	25.7	21.6
4.6	4.7	4.7		3.5	5.9	5.4	5.6	4.9	4.1
3.2	3.2	3.2	Sales/Total Assets	1.2	3.4	3.6	3.6	3.3	2.9
1.9	2.0	1.9		.1	1.5	1.8	2.5	2.2	1.8
.3	.2	.3		1.8	.5	.4	.3	.2	.2
(542) .7	(575) .6	(579) .7	% Depr., Dep., Amort./Sales	(26) 17.1	(40) 1.2	(44) .9	(95) .7	(158) .6	(216) .6
1.7	1.5	1.7		25.5	3.2	1.7	1.4	1.5	1.4
2.8	2.1	1.8		6.2	4.4	3.7	2.1	1.3	.5
(223) 6.3	(214) 5.1	(226) 4.0	% Officers', Directors' Owners' Comp/Sales	(13) 9.7	(34) 5.9	(33) 6.7	(56) 3.6	(57) 2.6	(33) 1.1
11.7	10.9	7.8		27.7	8.7	8.8	7.1	4.8	3.8
30861684M	**36317336M**	**35832000M**	Net Sales ($)	**18244M**	**176176M**	**336451M**	**1153875M**	**3953229M**	**30194025M**
13953493M	**15763602M**	**16627135M**	Total Assets ($)	**41398M**	**79924M**	**168767M**	**461386M**	**1611403M**	**14264257M**

M = $ thousand MM = $ million

See Pages 9 through 22 for Explanation of Ratios and Data

Current Data Sorted by Assets							Comparative Historical Data	
						Type of Statement		
		1	3	1	2	Unqualified	4	12
	1		1			Reviewed	1	3
1		4	1		1	Compiled	3	
1	5	2				Tax Returns	3	3
3	7	6	5	3	1	Other	10	13
	4 (4/1-9/30/13)		45 (10/1/13-3/31/14)				**4/1/09-3/31/10 ALL**	**4/1/10-3/31/11 ALL**
0-500M	**500M-2MM**	**2-10MM**	**10-50MM**	**50-100MM**	**100-250MM**			
5	13	13	10	4	4	**NUMBER OF STATEMENTS**	21	31
%	%	%	%	%	%	**ASSETS**	%	%
	21.2	8.2	17.6			Cash & Equivalents	17.1	15.5
	46.8	30.9	49.3			Trade Receivables (net)	36.0	36.3
	2.8	.9	1.1			Inventory	3.0	4.3
	3.2	5.8	8.2			All Other Current	3.5	10.5
	74.0	45.8	76.2			Total Current	59.6	66.7
	13.3	21.5	12.2			Fixed Assets (net)	26.6	12.2
	7.4	24.2	6.6			Intangibles (net)	6.0	10.8
	5.3	8.5	4.9			All Other Non-Current	7.9	10.3
	100.0	100.0	100.0			Total	100.0	100.0
						LIABILITIES		
	14.8	8.2	10.7			Notes Payable-Short Term	8.4	8.1
	3.6	2.3	1.6			Cur. Mat.-L.T.D.	7.5	2.8
	9.6	14.8	21.6			Trade Payables	19.3	15.3
	2.0	.0	.5			Income Taxes Payable	.2	.3
	12.2	16.0	12.1			All Other Current	15.5	21.4
	42.2	41.3	46.5			Total Current	50.9	47.9
	9.6	24.3	5.7			Long-Term Debt	16.6	8.6
	.0	.5	.1			Deferred Taxes	.7	.4
	4.8	6.5	4.3			All Other Non-Current	3.8	12.1
	43.5	27.4	43.5			Net Worth	28.0	31.1
	100.0	100.0	100.0			Total Liabilities & Net Worth	100.0	100.0
						INCOME DATA		
	100.0	100.0	100.0			Net Sales	100.0	100.0
	49.4	56.4	36.7			Gross Profit	45.4	47.4
	44.3	51.5	30.5			Operating Expenses	35.7	39.6
	5.1	4.9	6.2			Operating Profit	9.7	7.8
	.1	.3	.6			All Other Expenses (net)	2.5	3.4
	5.0	4.6	5.6			Profit Before Taxes	7.2	4.5
						RATIOS		
	2.6	3.2	3.9				2.1	1.9
	1.6	1.6	1.5			Current	1.3	1.3
	1.1	.5	1.1				.7	.8
	2.6	2.8	3.9				1.8	1.6
	1.6	.7	1.2			Quick	1.0	1.1
	1.0	.4	.8				.6	.5
	1 506.9	**17** 21.8	**38** 9.6				**16** 22.5	**23** 15.8
	43 8.4	**46** 8.0	**63** 5.8			Sales/Receivables	**41** 9.0	**52** 7.0
	56 6.5	**72** 5.1	**78** 4.7				**74** 4.9	**81** 4.5
	0 UND	**0** UND	**0** UND				**0** UND	**0** UND
	0 UND	**0** UND	**0** UND			Cost of Sales/Inventory	**0** UND	**0** 999.8
	1 511.8	**0** UND	**2** 182.2				**8** 43.9	**9** 40.8
	0 UND	**20** 18.6	**22** 16.5				**14** 25.3	**19** 19.6
	13 27.8	**56** 6.5	**30** 12.1			Cost of Sales/Payables	**42** 8.7	**41** 8.9
	27 13.3	**76** 4.8	**42** 8.7				**115** 3.2	**128** 2.8
	7.7	7.4	5.3				8.8	6.7
	14.9	19.4	11.7			Sales/Working Capital	21.7	20.3
	49.5	-11.6	NM				-18.2	-14.7
	79.1	46.2					22.8	100.6
	(10) 19.6	(11) 6.6				EBIT/Interest	(18) 4.1	(24) 7.5
	1.0	3.0					1.0	1.7
						Net Profit + Depr., Dep., Amort./Cur. Mat. L/T/D		
	.0	.2	.1				.2	.1
	.1	3.9	.1			Fixed/Worth	1.2	.3
	.7	-.4	1.4				UND	45.8
	.7	.7	.3				1.0	1.0
	1.5	4.4	2.6			Debt/Worth	6.0	2.5
	7.8	-3.2	4.5				UND	52.6
	131.7						181.0	70.2
	(12) 49.9					% Profit Before Taxes/Tangible Net Worth	(17) 76.9	(24) 31.8
	11.7						33.2	7.2
	46.3	18.3	27.8				48.9	20.4
	18.7	8.1	12.8			% Profit Before Taxes/Total Assets	12.0	6.8
	3.3	5.8	5.9				2.4	.8
	900.8	64.2	135.5				100.6	147.2
	75.5	17.2	92.1			Sales/Net Fixed Assets	22.5	63.0
	24.9	8.5	19.1				8.2	20.7
	7.0	3.8	4.1				4.2	3.6
	5.0	2.9	3.2			Sales/Total Assets	2.9	2.3
	4.0	1.3	2.1				1.9	.9
		.3					.7	.3
		(10) .9				% Depr., Dep., Amort./Sales	(14) 2.7	(19) .6
		4.9					5.4	1.9
						% Officers', Directors' Owners' Comp/Sales		
3574M	**84105M**	**173209M**	**607572M**	**398006M**	**1591150M**	Net Sales ($)	**675775M**	**1582728M**
779M	**15863M**	**63032M**	**203216M**	**232247M**	**653617M**	Total Assets ($)	**490627M**	**1224585M**

M = $ thousand MM = $ million

See Pages 9 through 22 for Explanation of Ratios and Data

Comparative Historical Data				Current Data Sorted by Sales					
			Type of Statement						
9	8	7	Unqualified				1		6
4	1	2	Reviewed				1		1
1	3	7	Compiled	1			2	2	2
11	4	8	Tax Returns	1		1	4	2	
11	19	25	Other	1	4	2	5	5	8
4/1/11-3/31/12 ALL	4/1/12-3/31/13 ALL	4/1/13-3/31/14 ALL		4 (4/1-9/30/13)			45 (10/1/13-3/31/14)		
				0-1MM	1-3MM	3-5MM	5-10MM	10-25MM	25MM & OVER
36	35	49	**NUMBER OF STATEMENTS**	3	4	3	13	9	17
%	%	%	**ASSETS**	%	%	%	%	%	%
18.1	20.5	17.5	Cash & Equivalents				14.3		21.6
47.0	39.5	37.7	Trade Receivables (net)				44.3		43.4
4.1	1.9	1.3	Inventory				.0		.7
6.1	5.5	5.2	All Other Current				1.4		6.9
75.4	67.4	61.7	Total Current				60.1		72.6
11.5	11.5	17.8	Fixed Assets (net)				14.1		13.6
6.2	13.3	14.7	Intangibles (net)				14.8		7.8
7.0	7.9	5.9	All Other Non-Current				11.0		6.0
100.0	100.0	100.0	Total				100.0		100.0
			LIABILITIES						
6.7	11.4	20.9	Notes Payable-Short Term				4.5		7.6
3.2	3.0	2.7	Cur. Mat.-L.T.D.				5.3		1.6
19.4	17.0	13.3	Trade Payables				11.8		15.6
.1	.2	.9	Income Taxes Payable				2.0		1.0
26.7	18.5	28.5	All Other Current				17.4		16.4
56.0	50.1	66.3	Total Current				40.9		42.2
10.7	9.8	17.2	Long-Term Debt				18.5		14.1
.2	.3	.4	Deferred Taxes				.5		.8
6.6	5.5	10.6	All Other Non-Current				6.6		4.1
26.5	34.4	5.4	Net Worth				33.4		38.8
100.0	100.0	100.0	Total Liabilities & Net Worth				100.0		100.0
			INCOME DATA						
100.0	100.0	100.0	Net Sales				100.0		100.0
46.9	41.7	47.0	Gross Profit				47.5		34.0
40.4	37.3	42.1	Operating Expenses				43.2		28.4
6.5	4.4	4.8	Operating Profit				4.3		5.5
.6	.6	.7	All Other Expenses (net)				.1		.9
5.9	3.8	4.2	Profit Before Taxes				4.2		4.6
			RATIOS						
2.6	2.2	2.6					2.4		3.1
1.5	1.5	1.5	Current				1.6		1.7
1.1	.9	.7					.8		1.2
2.0	2.2	2.5					2.4		3.0
1.4	1.4	1.2	Quick				1.4		1.5
.9	.6	.5					.8		1.1
38 9.6	36 10.0	21 17.4					22 16.9		34 10.7
52 7.0	50 7.3	43 8.4	Sales/Receivables				48 7.6		47 7.7
65 5.6	68 5.4	64 5.7					68 5.4		72 5.1
0 UND	0 UND	0 UND					0 UND		0 UND
0 UND	0 UND	0 UND	Cost of Sales/Inventory				0 UND		0 UND
4 93.7	1 374.9	0 UND					0 UND		0 UND
9 40.3	19 19.6	11 33.5					8 45.1		16 22.6
23 15.8	29 12.8	22 16.3	Cost of Sales/Payables				23 15.8		23 16.1
46 8.0	57 6.4	46 7.9					51 7.1		38 9.5
7.9	6.9	7.7					7.7		5.1
14.4	11.9	19.4	Sales/Working Capital				14.9		9.8
130.3	-56.1	-32.1					-213.4		28.2
42.8	23.2	33.3					60.0		33.3
(29) 17.3	(26) 10.0	(40) 10.2	EBIT/Interest				(12) 13.7		(12) 14.0
2.4	4.0	3.1					2.4		4.7
	28.7								
	(10) 4.1		Net Profit + Depr., Dep., Amort./Cur. Mat. L/T/D						
	1.9								
.1	.1	.1					.0		.1
.2	.2	.4	Fixed/Worth				.4		.2
4.2	1.3	NM					NM		2.2
.9	1.1	1.1					1.0		.7
1.7	2.9	2.7	Debt/Worth				2.5		2.6
12.7	20.8	-4.3					-4.3		5.1
105.3	66.2	72.3							49.6
(29) 52.0	(28) 35.8	(35) 32.4	% Profit Before Taxes/Tangible Net Worth						(15) 32.4
32.1	12.1	16.6							17.8
30.3	22.3	26.3					26.9		20.4
21.6	7.2	8.9	% Profit Before Taxes/Total Assets				7.7		11.9
6.4	3.6	5.4					2.9		5.8
127.2	108.3	139.4					233.8		144.0
62.7	48.5	54.7	Sales/Net Fixed Assets				57.2		75.7
37.5	16.1	12.0					14.8		8.9
5.5	4.4	5.2					5.2		4.0
3.7	2.9	3.4	Sales/Total Assets				4.1		2.9
2.5	1.8	2.4					2.3		2.2
.4	.5	.3							.1
(28) .7	(24) 1.2	(31) 1.0	% Depr., Dep., Amort./Sales						(13) .3
1.6	3.5	3.3							3.0
5.1		3.6							
(13) 7.3		(10) 6.3	% Officers', Directors' Owners' Comp/Sales						
17.1		10.3							
1521490M	2031343M	2857616M	Net Sales ($)	1331M	6991M	13781M	97628M	142546M	2595339M
576650M	976617M	1168754M	Total Assets ($)	230M	2289M	6231M	33782M	96147M	1030075M

M = $ thousand MM = $ million

See Pages 9 through 22 for Explanation of Ratios and Data

	Current Data Sorted by Assets						Comparative Historical Data	
Type of Statement								
Unqualified	1	1	14	16	8	9	81	71
Reviewed		8	31	7			68	78
Compiled	4	23	17	3			47	45
Tax Returns	74	70	34	3			128	170
Other	30	77	116	41	11	5	294	301
		42 (4/1-9/30/13)		561 (10/1/13-3/31/14)			4/1/09-3/31/10 ALL	4/1/10-3/31/11 ALL
	0-500M	500M-2MM	2-10MM	10-50MM	50-100MM	100-250MM		
NUMBER OF STATEMENTS	109	179	212	70	19	14	618	665
ASSETS	%	%	%	%	%	%	%	%
Cash & Equivalents	39.8	20.1	17.5	20.2	9.5	18.6	16.9	19.6
Trade Receivables (net)	20.0	43.1	48.9	35.2	33.7	32.2	42.1	41.3
Inventory	1.9	6.4	3.8	3.2	5.4	2.2	4.2	3.2
All Other Current	.9	2.8	2.9	5.7	6.6	10.7	4.3	4.6
Total Current	62.6	72.5	73.0	64.4	55.3	63.8	67.5	68.7
Fixed Assets (net)	18.2	12.6	11.8	17.4	9.9	5.4	15.0	14.9
Intangibles (net)	6.4	7.3	6.3	10.7	30.0	24.8	8.8	7.9
All Other Non-Current	12.7	7.7	8.9	7.5	4.9	6.0	8.7	8.5
Total	100.0	100.0	100.0	100.0	100.0	100.0	100.0	100.0
LIABILITIES								
Notes Payable-Short Term	36.9	13.5	11.2	4.7	9.3	5.6	14.8	13.8
Cur. Mat.-L.T.D.	4.1	2.0	2.1	2.7	2.3	1.6	4.1	2.8
Trade Payables	11.2	12.6	18.1	14.5	13.7	25.2	15.7	15.2
Income Taxes Payable	.3	.1	.3	.4	.3	.0	.2	.4
All Other Current	18.0	14.4	17.0	20.7	18.2	21.6	18.4	19.1
Total Current	70.5	42.6	48.7	43.0	43.8	54.1	53.3	51.1
Long-Term Debt	15.4	12.4	7.4	11.6	16.8	26.1	16.1	13.0
Deferred Taxes	.0	.2	.2	.4	1.2	1.1	.2	.3
All Other Non-Current	11.0	7.8	7.4	9.1	7.5	6.5	11.1	9.5
Net Worth	3.0	37.0	36.3	35.9	30.8	12.1	19.3	26.1
Total Liabilties & Net Worth	100.0	100.0	100.0	100.0	100.0	100.0	100.0	100.0
INCOME DATA								
Net Sales	100.0	100.0	100.0	100.0	100.0	100.0	100.0	100.0
Gross Profit								
Operating Expenses	90.5	92.6	92.4	93.3	95.1	98.2	94.4	91.7
Operating Profit	9.5	7.4	7.6	6.7	4.9	1.8	5.6	8.3
All Other Expenses (net)	1.1	.9	1.4	.9	3.5	2.7	1.4	1.4
Profit Before Taxes	8.4	6.5	6.3	5.8	1.4	-.9	4.2	6.9
RATIOS								
Current	3.0	4.5	2.9	2.4	1.5	2.1	2.7	2.8
	1.4	1.9	1.7	1.5	1.0	1.1	1.5	1.4
	.4	1.1	1.1	1.0	1.0	.9	.9	1.0
Quick	2.8	3.6	2.6	2.4	1.2	1.7	2.3	2.4
	1.3	1.6	1.4	1.3	.9	1.0	1.2	(664) 1.3
	.4	.9	.9	.8	.6	.7	.7	.8
Sales/Receivables	0 UND	16 23.4	36 10.0	40 9.2	59 6.2	51 7.2	26 14.1	17 21.7
	0 999.8	39 9.3	51 7.2	54 6.7	70 5.2	64 5.7	49 7.5	47 7.8
	25 14.8	59 6.2	69 5.3	78 4.7	74 4.9	79 4.6	70 5.2	68 5.3
Cost of Sales/Inventory								
Cost of Sales/Payables								
Sales/Working Capital	13.5	6.2	6.3	4.0	7.8	4.8	7.1	7.1
	55.3	13.0	11.7	12.0	305.3	37.2	16.2	16.9
	-17.0	75.6	87.3	NM	-130.9	-24.5	-98.8	-256.5
EBIT/Interest	36.0	44.2	59.6	55.0	32.7	150.5	24.4	42.0
	(65) 9.5	(134) 11.0	(153) 14.6	(53) 10.2	(17) 2.9	(11) 5.0	(487) 5.3	(507) 7.5
	1.3	2.5	4.3	1.2	1.3	-3.1	1.0	1.8
Net Profit + Depr., Dep., Amort./Cur. Mat. L/T/D			11.3	20.8			14.4	10.7
			(13) 3.0	(11) 3.0			(42) 3.8	(63) 2.8
			1.7	1.3			1.4	.9
Fixed/Worth	.0	.0	.0	.1	.0	.1	.1	.1
	.2	.2	.1	.5	1.2	7.1	.3	.3
	5.7	1.1	.9	2.1	-.1	.0	37.3	5.3
Debt/Worth	.7	.4	.6	.7	1.8	1.3	.7	.6
	2.2	1.4	1.6	2.4	6.1	72.3	2.7	2.3
	-4.8	6.4	6.3	10.7	-2.1	-2.7	-70.9	45.6
% Profit Before Taxes/Tangible Net Worth	163.3	95.5	74.4	88.7	35.8		77.7	91.4
	(77) 79.5	(144) 51.5	(182) 41.1	(59) 38.9	(10) 27.1		(461) 33.4	(506) 51.0
	20.7	17.1	18.6	7.5	8.7		7.4	19.8
% Profit Before Taxes/Total Assets	73.0	39.6	26.7	22.7	6.4	6.8	24.3	34.3
	27.5	16.4	14.3	9.9	3.0	.7	8.4	13.2
	2.1	3.9	4.2	.6	1.1	-8.0	.5	3.2
Sales/Net Fixed Assets	UND	646.3	288.5	80.5	142.0	305.0	172.4	183.0
	340.3	81.8	81.4	23.1	45.1	35.5	52.2	58.3
	23.6	21.4	22.2	6.4	15.2	9.8	15.9	18.6
Sales/Total Assets	11.1	5.8	4.6	3.0	2.9	2.7	4.9	5.3
	6.9	4.0	3.4	1.8	1.5	1.8	3.2	3.3
	3.8	2.7	2.2	1.1	1.0	.8	1.9	2.2
% Depr., Dep., Amort./Sales	.3	.2	.2	.5	.4		.3	.3
	(43) 1.2	(90) .6	(138) .6	(57) 1.5	(13) 2.2		(387) .8	(402) .9
	2.4	1.7	1.6	3.3	4.2		2.5	2.3
% Officers', Directors' Owners' Comp/Sales	4.1	2.1	1.9	.9			2.2	2.8
	(62) 7.3	(80) 4.6	(66) 2.8	(15) 3.1			(201) 5.6	(246) 6.0
	14.9	9.8	5.7	7.5			10.2	10.7
Net Sales ($)	184518M	905348M	3217029M	2987972M	2468182M	4337488M	14904573M	17327406M
Total Assets ($)	23855M	205994M	953394M	1453356M	1369737M	2389341M	7623524M	7531513M

M = $ thousand MM = $ million

See Pages 9 through 22 for Explanation of Ratios and Data

Comparative Historical Data / Current Data Sorted by Sales

			Type of Statement						
67	61	49	Unqualified	1			4	15	29
77	62	46	Reviewed		2	3	12	24	5
59	46	47	Compiled	4	6	9	16	9	3
182	188	181	Tax Returns	34	51	35	32	24	5
344	305	280	Other	23	38	33	49	71	66
4/1/11-3/31/12 ALL	4/1/12-3/31/13 ALL	4/1/13-3/31/14 ALL		42 (4/1-9/30/13)			561 (10/1/13-3/31/14)		
				0-1MM	1-3MM	3-5MM	5-10MM	10-25MM	25MM & OVER
729	662	603	NUMBER OF STATEMENTS	62	97	80	113	143	108
%	%	%	**ASSETS**	%	%	%	%	%	%
20.5	21.5	22.4	Cash & Equivalents	29.7	29.6	23.5	19.5	19.2	18.1
41.6	39.2	39.5	Trade Receivables (net)	16.5	26.7	38.0	46.5	47.8	47.0
3.5	3.9	4.2	Inventory	2.8	3.7	6.2	4.2	5.2	2.5
3.9	3.4	3.2	All Other Current	.2	2.8	1.7	2.6	3.1	7.0
69.5	67.9	69.2	Total Current	49.2	62.7	69.4	72.8	75.2	74.6
14.5	14.9	13.6	Fixed Assets (net)	28.6	17.0	14.5	10.2	10.8	8.8
6.8	7.4	8.3	Intangibles (net)	11.9	10.3	5.0	7.8	5.4	11.1
9.2	9.8	8.9	All Other Non-Current	10.4	10.0	11.1	9.2	8.5	5.5
100.0	100.0	100.0	Total	100.0	100.0	100.0	100.0	100.0	100.0
			LIABILITIES						
12.0	11.7	15.6	Notes Payable-Short Term	29.7	22.1	12.8	12.8	13.8	9.0
2.7	3.1	2.5	Cur. Mat.-L.T.D.	3.4	3.0	2.3	3.3	1.5	2.1
15.1	14.9	14.8	Trade Payables	8.1	12.0	8.8	14.6	19.0	20.3
.3	.2	.3	Income Taxes Payable	.0	.3	.0	.3	.4	.4
16.6	17.4	17.0	All Other Current	17.3	15.2	16.0	17.6	16.8	18.8
46.6	47.2	50.2	Total Current	58.5	52.7	39.9	48.6	51.5	50.7
12.9	12.3	11.5	Long-Term Debt	23.7	17.0	11.5	6.3	6.8	11.4
.3	.3	.2	Deferred Taxes	.0	.0	.4	.2	.2	.5
10.1	8.6	8.3	All Other Non-Current	8.1	13.2	9.2	5.4	8.1	6.9
30.0	31.6	29.7	Net Worth	9.5	17.0	39.0	39.6	33.4	30.6
100.0	100.0	100.0	Total Liabilties & Net Worth	100.0	100.0	100.0	100.0	100.0	100.0
			INCOME DATA						
100.0	100.0	100.0	Net Sales	100.0	100.0	100.0	100.0	100.0	100.0
			Gross Profit						
91.4	91.9	92.4	Operating Expenses	83.7	91.9	92.8	94.0	93.7	94.4
8.6	8.1	7.6	Operating Profit	16.3	8.1	7.2	6.0	6.3	5.6
1.1	1.4	1.2	All Other Expenses (net)	6.5	.2	.8	.3	.7	1.1
7.5	6.8	6.3	Profit Before Taxes	9.7	7.9	6.4	5.7	5.6	4.5
			RATIOS						
3.2	3.4	3.1		2.5	4.1	4.8	3.0	2.9	2.3
1.7	1.6	1.6	Current	.9	1.6	2.0	1.7	1.6	1.4
1.0	1.0	1.0		.3	.9	1.1	1.0	1.1	1.0
3.1	3.2	2.7		2.5	3.8	4.1	2.9	2.6	2.2
(661) 1.4	1.4	1.4	Quick	.8	1.5	1.8	1.6	1.4	1.2
.9	.9	.8		.2	.7	.8	.9	.9	.9
23 16.1	**18** 20.3	**19** 18.8		**0** UND	**0** UND	**11** 32.4	**29** 12.5	**32** 11.5	**42** 8.7
47 7.7	**46** 8.0	**43** 8.5	Sales/Receivables	**0** UND	**24** 15.0	**39** 9.3	**45** 8.2	**49** 7.4	**57** 6.4
69 5.3	**68** 5.4	**63** 5.8		**33** 10.9	**45** 8.1	**62** 5.9	**65** 5.6	**64** 5.7	**70** 5.2
			Cost of Sales/Inventory						
			Cost of Sales/Payables						
6.2	6.3	6.9		8.3	7.6	5.3	6.9	7.0	6.0
14.4	14.4	15.3	Sales/Working Capital	-58.0	24.5	10.5	16.2	13.7	13.9
239.5	535.6	-226.4		-5.7	-77.9	101.6	578.8	75.0	303.0
40.3	47.9	48.0		17.1	33.0	51.0	31.5	64.3	81.8
(533) 10.0	(467) 11.0	(433) 11.1	EBIT/Interest	(28) 4.1	(72) 10.8	(57) 9.6	(82) 7.4	(110) 22.9	(84) 15.3
2.3	1.9	2.3		-.1	2.5	2.5	2.1	5.5	2.0
10.0	8.5	10.3						9.5	15.3
(57) 4.2	(59) 3.4	(33) 2.9	Net Profit + Depr., Dep., Amort./Cur. Mat. L/T/D					(11) 6.8	(14) 2.7
1.9	.7	1.3						3.0	1.2
.0	.0	.0		.0	.0	.0	.0	.0	.0
.2	.2	.2	Fixed/Worth	.3	.2	.2	.2	.2	.3
2.7	1.3	1.9		5.5	3.1	2.1	2.0	.8	2.6
.6	.6	.6		.8	.6	.3	.5	.6	.7
1.9	1.6	1.8	Debt/Worth	2.6	2.0	1.4	1.5	1.5	2.8
22.7	8.8	10.3		-4.0	-21.9	7.1	9.2	4.8	25.1
95.7	89.4	90.7		115.5	148.7	83.2	100.3	81.9	77.3
(572) 50.4	(534) 42.2	(480) 46.3	% Profit Before Taxes/Tangible Net Worth	(41) 36.7	(71) 57.8	(64) 49.6	(94) 43.2	(125) 46.2	(85) 39.8
17.7	13.8	15.5		4.0	11.4	11.4	17.1	21.5	12.4
39.1	36.9	33.3		38.5	49.4	40.7	31.9	28.7	23.9
16.6	14.4	14.6	% Profit Before Taxes/Total Assets	10.3	22.0	16.1	12.4	16.3	9.9
3.7	2.8	3.5		-.1	3.2	4.1	3.2	4.8	3.2
317.7	342.4	431.8		UND	883.3	766.5	706.8	281.9	250.5
65.3	66.1	72.7	Sales/Net Fixed Assets	41.9	55.7	56.0	103.9	73.8	62.2
19.1	17.8	19.2		2.9	19.2	18.0	25.3	21.4	22.2
5.0	5.1	5.4		5.9	7.3	5.7	6.1	5.1	4.5
3.3	3.4	3.5	Sales/Total Assets	3.2	3.5	3.6	3.9	3.8	3.0
2.2	2.1	2.1		.7	2.2	2.4	2.6	2.4	1.8
.3	.2	.3		1.4	.4	.2	.3	.3	.3
(425) .9	(377) .8	(348) .8	% Depr., Dep., Amort./Sales	(25) 7.0	(49) 1.1	(41) .6	(58) .8	(98) .5	(77) .7
2.2	2.5	2.2		21.9	2.1	1.5	1.6	2.0	2.1
2.4	1.9	2.1		4.0	4.2	2.6	2.0	1.5	.7
(240) 5.3	(219) 4.4	(227) 4.3	% Officers', Directors' Owners' Comp/Sales	(22) 11.2	(49) 7.1	(42) 4.7	(49) 3.8	(42) 2.7	(23) 1.3
9.9	9.6	9.3		19.6	12.8	9.1	7.4	5.8	3.6
17407148M	**13445396M**	**14100537M**	Net Sales ($)	**30500M**	**191324M**	**323080M**	**821697M**	**2332498M**	**10401438M**
7353858M	**7313979M**	**6395677M**	Total Assets ($)	**39505M**	**83805M**	**118540M**	**302876M**	**966131M**	**4884820M**

M = $ thousand MM = $ million

See Pages 9 through 22 for Explanation of Ratios and Data

Current Data Sorted by Assets							Comparative Historical Data	
						Type of Statement		
1	6	42	41	10	13	Unqualified	130	129
3	21	40	15	2	1	Reviewed	78	73
10	21	28	4			Compiled	61	66
68	52	22	4		1	Tax Returns	137	139
49	86	136	78	17	18	Other	310	351
83 (4/1-9/30/13)			706 (10/1/13-3/31/14)				4/1/09-3/31/10 ALL	4/1/10-3/31/11 ALL
0-500M	500M-2MM	2-10MM	10-50MM	50-100MM	100-250MM			
131	186	268	142	29	33	**NUMBER OF STATEMENTS**	716	758
%	%	%	%	%	%	**ASSETS**	%	%
40.3	27.4	19.6	16.9	14.6	18.4	Cash & Equivalents	20.4	20.0
16.7	30.2	41.7	37.0	26.5	19.5	Trade Receivables (net)	34.8	35.3
1.3	.9	1.3	1.4	3.0	2.7	Inventory	2.2	1.9
4.1	5.8	6.9	7.3	7.2	11.1	All Other Current	7.0	6.8
62.4	64.3	69.5	62.6	51.3	51.7	Total Current	64.4	64.0
17.7	14.6	12.2	14.1	9.3	13.9	Fixed Assets (net)	16.5	15.7
6.3	6.0	5.3	11.7	25.8	28.6	Intangibles (net)	6.5	7.1
13.6	15.1	13.0	11.5	13.7	5.7	All Other Non-Current	12.6	13.1
100.0	100.0	100.0	100.0	100.0	100.0	Total	100.0	100.0
						LIABILITIES		
31.5	14.0	7.8	7.2	8.6	4.0	Notes Payable-Short Term	14.1	14.3
3.1	1.9	1.9	2.6	2.0	3.0	Cur. Mat.-L.T.D.	3.4	2.8
11.3	8.8	11.4	12.3	7.9	4.6	Trade Payables	10.5	11.4
.2	.2	1.0	.6	.2	1.3	Income Taxes Payable	.4	.6
30.1	23.5	18.0	17.5	13.7	25.7	All Other Current	20.0	21.4
76.2	48.4	40.1	40.2	32.4	38.6	Total Current	48.4	50.5
19.7	11.4	9.6	14.0	24.4	26.1	Long-Term Debt	12.0	11.8
.1	.3	.2	.6	.6	1.8	Deferred Taxes	.5	.4
9.6	7.3	6.9	11.2	6.6	10.2	All Other Non-Current	8.1	8.1
-5.7	32.7	43.2	34.1	36.0	23.3	Net Worth	31.0	29.2
100.0	100.0	100.0	100.0	100.0	100.0	Total Liabilties & Net Worth	100.0	100.0
						INCOME DATA		
100.0	100.0	100.0	100.0	100.0	100.0	Net Sales	100.0	100.0
						Gross Profit		
84.6	86.1	89.3	90.7	85.1	92.4	Operating Expenses	90.2	90.0
15.4	13.9	10.7	9.3	14.9	7.6	Operating Profit	9.8	10.0
1.5	1.8	1.4	2.2	2.4	2.1	All Other Expenses (net)	1.8	1.6
14.0	12.2	9.3	7.1	12.5	5.4	Profit Before Taxes	8.0	8.5
						RATIOS		
4.3	4.7	3.3	2.5	2.8	2.2		2.8	2.9
1.2	1.7	1.8	1.6	1.5	1.5	Current	1.5	1.6
.4	.8	1.2	1.1	1.1	.9		.9	.9
4.3	4.1	3.0	2.3	2.4	1.9		2.4	2.5
1.1	1.5	1.5	1.3	1.2	1.1	Quick	1.3	(757) 1.3
.3	.8	1.0	.9	.8	.5		.7	.7
0 UND	0 UND	27 13.3	28 12.9	27 13.3	35 10.4		8 47.1	8 44.6
0 UND	25 14.7	53 6.9	61 6.0	52 7.0	51 7.2	Sales/Receivables	42 8.6	45 8.2
21 17.8	50 7.3	74 4.9	79 4.6	81 4.5	68 5.4		67 5.5	72 5.1
						Cost of Sales/Inventory		
						Cost of Sales/Payables		
11.1	5.8	5.1	4.7	3.8	4.0		5.8	5.8
159.0	16.2	9.9	9.7	13.3	8.8	Sales/Working Capital	14.5	14.9
-15.1	-25.1	37.3	66.8	51.1	-58.0		-125.4	-94.5
73.1	74.2	80.0	54.5	16.1	28.5		31.0	43.5
(68) 17.7	(120) 12.8	(181) 16.3	(109) 9.5	(26) 3.8	(28) 6.8	EBIT/Interest	(515) 8.4	(533) 10.0
3.8	3.3	3.6	2.9	1.0	1.9		1.4	2.1
		26.4	12.9		38.8		8.3	9.9
		(18) 3.9	(29) 3.5		(11) 4.9	Net Profit + Depr., Dep., Amort./Cur. Mat. L/T/D	(73) 2.5	(74) 2.8
		2.7	.9		1.9		.4	1.3
.0	.0	.0	.1	.1	.2		.1	.1
.2	.2	.1	.3	.3	2.7	Fixed/Worth	.3	.3
-2.9	3.4	.7	2.3	-.5	-.1		2.8	2.9
.4	.4	.5	1.0	.6	1.7		.6	.6
3.9	1.3	1.3	2.3	1.9	28.6	Debt/Worth	1.9	2.0
-2.7	17.7	4.5	22.2	-4.3	-2.4		16.0	21.1
578.6	94.8	88.8	68.6	31.5	59.9		80.8	94.1
(79) 119.8	(148) 44.3	(236) 44.6	(114) 38.3	(20) 19.5	(18) 30.2	% Profit Before Taxes/Tangible Net Worth	(568) 33.7	(597) 38.3
37.2	14.6	15.6	6.1	3.3	11.5		9.1	10.7
154.9	46.2	34.5	24.5	11.2	14.1		31.9	32.0
51.0	19.4	17.9	10.4	5.3	6.6	% Profit Before Taxes/Total Assets	10.4	12.4
11.4	3.5	3.9	1.4	.6	2.6		1.2	1.9
UND	339.5	244.3	90.6	166.4	38.4		137.0	148.0
125.0	68.4	71.2	35.7	64.7	22.0	Sales/Net Fixed Assets	43.0	49.3
22.7	22.3	24.4	10.6	8.9	10.1		15.0	15.5
14.3	5.8	4.1	3.0	2.4	1.7		4.7	4.6
6.5	3.6	2.8	2.0	1.4	1.3	Sales/Total Assets	2.8	2.9
2.7	1.7	1.8	1.2	.7	.6		1.5	1.6
.3	.4	.3	.5	.5	1.1		.5	.4
(55) .9	(99) .8	(174) .6	(102) 1.1	(17) 2.3	(23) 1.9	% Depr., Dep., Amort./Sales	(467) 1.0	(476) 1.0
1.9	2.0	1.7	2.3	4.3	2.7		2.4	2.3
6.3	3.9	2.9	1.4				3.7	3.1
(65) 12.2	(70) 9.0	(40) 6.7	(15) 3.7			% Officers', Directors' Owners' Comp/Sales	(191) 10.2	(189) 6.8
20.8	15.3	15.7	14.6				17.3	16.3
271444M	811177M	3850497M	6675160M	4398367M	7138342M	Net Sales ($)	20531091M	20173293M
26888M	206752M	1294951M	3219791M	2025233M	5348169M	Total Assets ($)	10385864M	10065959M

M = $ thousand MM = $ million

See Pages 9 through 22 for Explanation of Ratios and Data

Comparative Historical Data | **Current Data Sorted by Sales**

			Type of Statement						
131	97	113	Unqualified	3	2	1	13	31	63
73	73	82	Reviewed	3	4	5	22	36	12
82	50	63	Compiled	4	15	12	11	18	3
185	153	147	Tax Returns	50	39	15	26	10	7
397	379	384	Other	47	48	40	51	100	98
4/1/11-3/31/12 ALL	**4/1/12-3/31/13 ALL**	**4/1/13-3/31/14 ALL**		**83 (4/1-9/30/13)**			**706 (10/1/13-3/31/14)**		
				0-1MM	**1-3MM**	**3-5MM**	**5-10MM**	**10-25MM**	**25MM & OVER**
868	752	789	**NUMBER OF STATEMENTS**	107	108	73	123	195	183
%	%	%	**ASSETS**	%	%	%	%	%	%
22.0	23.6	24.2	Cash & Equivalents	27.1	32.4	27.9	26.1	21.8	17.3
33.9	33.7	32.5	Trade Receivables (net)	11.4	21.0	29.0	37.8	43.7	37.5
1.7	1.2	1.4	Inventory	.7	.8	1.2	1.5	1.5	1.9
6.4	6.3	6.4	All Other Current	5.3	6.3	3.6	5.6	6.8	8.5
64.0	64.8	64.5	Total Current	44.5	60.5	61.7	71.0	73.8	65.2
13.9	14.0	14.0	Fixed Assets (net)	26.8	13.3	13.2	13.5	9.0	12.9
7.1	7.8	8.5	Intangibles (net)	9.9	5.9	6.4	4.5	7.6	13.7
15.0	13.4	13.0	All Other Non-Current	18.8	20.2	18.8	11.0	9.6	8.2
100.0	100.0	100.0	Total	100.0	100.0	100.0	100.0	100.0	100.0
			LIABILITIES						
13.7	12.4	13.0	Notes Payable-Short Term	11.3	18.7	25.5	13.9	10.9	7.1
3.2	2.1	2.3	Cur. Mat.-L.T.D.	3.4	1.6	2.3	2.5	1.7	2.5
10.4	11.3	10.5	Trade Payables	5.4	11.6	8.1	9.5	12.5	12.4
.6	.4	.6	Income Taxes Payable	.3	.4	.1	.9	.7	.8
20.4	18.9	21.4	All Other Current	28.0	17.8	22.4	20.5	21.0	20.3
48.3	45.2	47.7	Total Current	48.4	50.1	58.4	47.3	46.7	43.1
12.1	12.4	13.7	Long-Term Debt	31.3	10.9	13.7	8.2	7.9	15.0
.3	.3	.3	Deferred Taxes	.0	.2	.2	.4	.2	.8
7.2	9.4	8.3	All Other Non-Current	8.1	9.5	8.7	8.2	5.9	10.3
32.2	32.7	29.9	Net Worth	12.2	29.3	19.0	35.9	39.3	30.7
100.0	100.0	100.0	Total Liabilties & Net Worth	100.0	100.0	100.0	100.0	100.0	100.0
			INCOME DATA						
100.0	100.0	100.0	Net Sales	100.0	100.0	100.0	100.0	100.0	100.0
			Gross Profit						
87.7	88.9	88.0	Operating Expenses	76.6	81.5	90.9	90.7	90.6	92.6
12.3	11.1	12.0	Operating Profit	23.4	18.5	9.1	9.3	9.4	7.4
1.6	1.7	1.7	All Other Expenses (net)	5.4	2.6	1.0	.2	1.2	.9
10.8	9.3	10.3	Profit Before Taxes	18.0	15.9	8.0	9.1	8.2	6.5
			RATIOS						
3.1	3.4	3.2		7.2	4.5	4.2	4.1	3.1	2.4
1.6	1.7	1.7	Current	1.6	1.5	1.6	1.8	1.7	1.5
.9	1.0	1.0		.4	.7	.6	1.0	1.2	1.1
2.8	3.0	2.9		7.0	3.6	3.9	3.7	2.8	2.2
(867) 1.3	1.4	1.4	Quick	1.2	1.2	1.3	1.6	1.6	1.2
.7	.8	.8		.3	.5	.5	.9	.9	.9
0 UND	**1** 306.0	**2** 151.7		**0** UND	**0** UND	**0** UND	**6** 58.9	**27** 13.4	**30** 12.1
39 9.3	**41** 9.0	**38** 9.5	Sales/Receivables	**0** UND	**7** 50.5	**28** 13.1	**40** 9.2	**52** 7.0	**54** 6.8
68 5.4	**66** 5.5	**68** 5.4		**35** 10.5	**47** 7.8	**62** 5.9	**63** 5.8	**78** 4.7	**70** 5.2
			Cost of Sales/Inventory						
			Cost of Sales/Payables						
5.8	5.8	5.5		3.4	4.0	7.0	5.1	5.5	6.6
14.8	14.5	13.4	Sales/Working Capital	18.7	16.4	28.7	13.0	11.3	13.0
-112.1	482.7	-134.8		-6.6	-26.0	-14.6	255.8	31.7	70.0
59.2	57.6	62.8		14.9	67.0	69.6	123.5	79.6	61.0
(597) 15.0	(495) 11.0	(532) 12.9	EBIT/Interest	(49) 6.2	(62) 18.5	(53) 9.3	(87) 17.7	(134) 13.8	(147) 12.3
2.2	2.5	2.8		.7	6.4	1.5	4.7	3.0	2.6
9.9	7.3	17.8						26.4	18.6
(89) 2.7	(64) 3.1	(71) 3.8	Net Profit + Depr., Dep., Amort./Cur. Mat. L/T/D					(14) 4.5	(47) 4.0
.6	1.3	1.2						2.2	1.4
.0	.0	.0		.0	.0	.0	.0	.0	.1
.2	.2	.2	Fixed/Worth	.3	.1	.2	.1	.1	.5
1.5	1.4	2.1		-3.7	1.3	-6.8	1.9	.5	44.0
.4	.5	.6		.4	.3	.5	.3	.6	1.0
1.6	1.7	1.7	Debt/Worth	2.3	1.3	2.6	1.4	1.4	2.7
16.4	10.5	28.2		-4.3	28.5	-15.8	7.0	5.9	-53.1
108.9	93.8	94.2		128.5	158.1	100.0	97.4	92.3	83.4
(694) 50.3	(601) 44.3	(615) 42.5	% Profit Before Taxes/Tangible Net Worth	(72) 31.8	(88) 56.7	(50) 60.7	(99) 46.1	(169) 41.7	(137) 41.2
14.4	13.9	14.5		5.9	17.8	19.8	19.3	15.3	12.8
44.4	36.9	39.6		52.2	80.5	53.4	42.7	34.1	25.6
15.6	14.0	16.8	% Profit Before Taxes/Total Assets	12.8	30.4	15.5	19.7	17.0	10.4
3.1	3.4	3.2		.6	7.1	1.2	5.4	2.4	3.1
287.6	289.7	266.4		UND	UND	268.9	398.4	323.4	87.5
64.4	59.9	62.5	Sales/Net Fixed Assets	20.6	88.7	68.5	82.7	85.7	35.7
20.2	20.0	19.3		2.5	24.1	23.5	29.2	31.7	17.2
4.9	5.0	4.7		3.7	6.3	5.6	6.0	4.4	4.0
3.0	3.1	2.8	Sales/Total Assets	1.5	2.9	3.6	3.6	2.9	2.6
1.7	1.7	1.6		.3	1.3	2.2	2.0	1.9	1.6
.4	.3	.4		.9	.5	.4	.2	.2	.5
(515) .8	(457) .9	(470) .8	% Depr., Dep., Amort./Sales	(51) 2.5	(47) .9	(43) .8	(73) .6	(123) .6	(133) .9
2.1	2.0	2.0		6.0	2.0	1.8	2.0	1.3	2.1
3.2	5.0	3.5		7.5	8.0	3.5	1.6	2.8	.9
(227) 8.2	(185) 10.6	(194) 9.2	% Officers', Directors' Owners' Comp/Sales	(36) 14.5	(50) 12.4	(27) 7.2	(36) 5.2	(30) 5.1	(15) 2.9
17.5	20.0	16.9		30.0	19.2	13.4	13.7	15.6	5.3
26990789M	18264268M	23144987M	Net Sales ($)	48121M	203516M	282141M	918529M	3180328M	18512352M
12737179M	9002182M	12121784M	Total Assets ($)	100980M	168984M	111532M	600586M	1843836M	9295866M

M = $ thousand MM = $ million

See Pages 9 through 22 for Explanation of Ratios and Data

Current Data Sorted by Assets							Comparative Historical Data	
						Type of Statement		
	3	4	9	3	1	Unqualified	30	24
	1	4	4			Reviewed	23	24
1	6	4	1			Compiled	14	14
10	8	3				Tax Returns	15	19
8	19	16	11	4	3	Other	65	70
	17 (4/1-9/30/13)		106 (10/1/13-3/31/14)				4/1/09-3/31/10 ALL	4/1/10-3/31/11 ALL
0-500M	500M-2MM	2-10MM	10-50MM	50-100MM	100-250MM			
19	37	31	25	7	4	NUMBER OF STATEMENTS	147	151
%	%	%	%	%	%	**ASSETS**	%	%
43.3	26.7	19.2	16.2			Cash & Equivalents	22.3	20.1
26.1	33.2	47.5	31.4			Trade Receivables (net)	33.9	41.4
.0	.1	.0	.9			Inventory	.5	1.3
6.0	6.8	2.6	8.6			All Other Current	5.3	7.4
75.4	66.7	69.3	57.1			Total Current	62.1	70.2
14.9	10.9	11.9	8.7			Fixed Assets (net)	15.3	11.2
3.7	9.1	6.9	24.6			Intangibles (net)	10.0	9.7
6.0	13.3	11.9	9.6			All Other Non-Current	12.6	8.9
100.0	100.0	100.0	100.0			Total	100.0	100.0
						LIABILITIES		
30.7	12.2	11.0	8.8			Notes Payable-Short Term	16.9	19.7
4.8	2.9	.9	1.5			Cur. Mat.-L.T.D.	3.5	1.4
3.1	8.2	6.5	7.8			Trade Payables	10.2	8.0
.0	.1	3.9	1.2			Income Taxes Payable	.6	.4
29.5	19.7	19.4	25.3			All Other Current	25.3	25.7
68.1	43.2	41.8	44.8			Total Current	56.6	55.3
6.7	33.2	4.0	6.9			Long-Term Debt	13.5	8.4
.0	.0	.0	1.4			Deferred Taxes	.5	.4
12.5	5.5	9.3	5.6			All Other Non-Current	5.4	8.1
12.7	18.1	44.9	41.3			Net Worth	24.0	27.7
100.0	100.0	100.0	100.0			Total Liabilties & Net Worth	100.0	100.0
						INCOME DATA		
100.0	100.0	100.0	100.0			Net Sales	100.0	100.0
						Gross Profit		
92.3	92.6	92.7	92.0			Operating Expenses	94.8	94.8
7.7	7.4	7.3	8.0			Operating Profit	5.2	5.2
.1	1.4	1.9	2.2			All Other Expenses (net)	1.5	.8
7.5	6.0	5.4	5.8			Profit Before Taxes	3.7	4.5
						RATIOS		
13.3	2.7	5.1	1.9				2.5	4.0
1.4	1.8	2.1	1.3			Current	1.3	1.4
.6	1.0	1.1	1.0				.9	1.0
13.3	2.5	4.9	1.6				2.4	3.4
1.3	1.3	2.0	1.1			Quick	1.2	(150) 1.3
.6	.9	1.1	.8				.8	.9
0 UND	**0** 999.8	**26** 14.0	**17** 20.9				**9** 39.0	**8** 45.5
0 UND	**26** 14.1	**41** 9.0	**46** 8.0			Sales/Receivables	**35** 10.6	**40** 9.1
35 10.3	**38** 9.7	**73** 5.0	**94** 3.9				**53** 6.9	**60** 6.1
						Cost of Sales/Inventory		
						Cost of Sales/Payables		
13.8	9.3	7.1	5.3				8.7	7.9
69.0	19.6	11.7	30.9			Sales/Working Capital	22.5	16.7
-41.0	NM	58.5	298.0				-141.8	-211.3
47.8	31.6	42.8	144.2				14.9	33.0
(12) 16.3	(23) 13.3	(17) 11.1	(22) 9.0			EBIT/Interest	(106) 4.1	(110) 10.5
3.7	5.6	5.3	4.9				-.1	2.2
							8.5	19.7
						Net Profit + Depr., Dep., Amort./Cur. Mat. L/T/D	(12) 2.1	(13) 2.8
							-.4	1.5
.0	.0	.0	.1				.0	.0
.8	.1	.1	.3			Fixed/Worth	.3	.1
-.2	5.0	.6	NM				7.1	2.0
.1	.7	.3	1.7				.6	.6
1.4	2.1	1.0	4.0			Debt/Worth	1.7	2.2
-4.9	76.4	4.1	NM				-808.2	-20.0
257.5	134.0	55.0	67.4				74.0	83.0
(13) 69.0	(30) 45.8	(28) 34.3	(19) 23.8			% Profit Before Taxes/Tangible Net Worth	(110) 28.9	(112) 26.5
-.4	9.7	15.1	6.8				4.5	8.5
82.1	33.4	30.1	14.7				26.0	23.6
45.5	12.4	13.9	7.1			% Profit Before Taxes/Total Assets	7.0	9.4
7.1	4.9	4.1	4.2				-1.2	2.2
UND	999.8	542.4	299.5				364.0	999.8
400.0	226.7	148.6	83.8			Sales/Net Fixed Assets	62.5	133.4
45.6	48.7	29.0	30.5				15.3	33.1
20.7	9.4	7.0	6.2				6.5	6.2
8.1	5.5	4.1	2.3			Sales/Total Assets	3.7	4.2
4.8	2.8	2.1	1.1				1.8	2.2
	.1	.1	.1				.3	.1
	(17) .3	(16) .4	(18) .4			% Depr., Dep., Amort./Sales	(89) .7	(85) .7
	1.1	3.0	.9				1.9	1.5
	2.0						2.9	1.7
	(16) 4.5					% Officers', Directors' Owners' Comp/Sales	(40) 5.4	(40) 4.8
	12.0						14.9	10.3
53711M	**505545M**	**714234M**	**2793247M**	**1774193M**	**792758M**	Net Sales ($)	**6068615M**	**5576264M**
4102M	**43991M**	**144629M**	**571062M**	**503247M**	**779231M**	Total Assets ($)	**2234487M**	**1679920M**

M = $ thousand MM = $ million

See Pages 9 through 22 for Explanation of Ratios and Data

Comparative Historical Data				Current Data Sorted by Sales					
			Type of Statement						
26	20	20	Unqualified			1	5	3	11
19	12	9	Reviewed				2	2	5
21	22	12	Compiled		1	4	2	3	2
24	16	21	Tax Returns	4	8	2	2	3	
60	69	61	Other	4	8	4	9	14	22
4/1/11-3/31/12 ALL	**4/1/12-3/31/13 ALL**	**4/1/13-3/31/14 ALL**		**17 (4/1-9/30/13)**			**106 (10/1/13-3/31/14)**		
				0-1MM	**1-3MM**	**3-5MM**	**5-10MM**	**10-25MM**	**25MM & OVER**
150	139	123	**NUMBER OF STATEMENTS**	8	17	11	22	25	40
%	%	%	**ASSETS**	%	%	%	%	%	%
21.5	18.5	25.1	Cash & Equivalents		35.6	17.9	20.3	33.2	19.6
39.6	44.6	35.3	Trade Receivables (net)		31.6	34.5	38.6	37.0	40.7
.5	.7	.4	Inventory		.0	.0	.3	.0	.9
8.0	6.8	6.3	All Other Current		2.9	9.7	3.6	4.7	8.1
69.6	70.7	67.1	Total Current		70.1	62.2	62.8	74.9	69.4
11.6	10.8	10.9	Fixed Assets (net)		10.7	9.3	15.4	3.4	6.1
9.8	7.6	11.6	Intangibles (net)		11.2	7.8	4.4	16.8	14.2
9.0	10.9	10.4	All Other Non-Current		8.0	20.7	17.4	5.0	10.2
100.0	100.0	100.0	Total		100.0	100.0	100.0	100.0	100.0
			LIABILITIES						
17.7	16.5	14.1	Notes Payable-Short Term		12.5	11.5	15.9	5.3	13.6
2.1	1.8	2.4	Cur. Mat.-L.T.D.		5.8	1.1	4.8	.2	1.5
11.5	8.2	6.5	Trade Payables		4.4	7.5	6.7	9.4	6.5
.8	.6	1.3	Income Taxes Payable		.0	.0	.1	4.3	1.2
27.4	27.7	24.1	All Other Current		20.5	6.9	19.4	16.6	33.1
59.5	54.8	48.3	Total Current		43.2	27.0	46.9	35.8	55.9
8.6	9.9	14.0	Long-Term Debt		13.2	11.1	41.3	1.0	5.1
.2	.4	.4	Deferred Taxes		.0	.0	.9	.0	.6
9.3	10.6	7.6	All Other Non-Current		14.7	9.0	7.1	9.4	4.5
22.3	24.3	29.7	Net Worth		28.8	52.9	3.7	53.8	33.8
100.0	100.0	100.0	Total Liabilities & Net Worth		100.0	100.0	100.0	100.0	100.0
			INCOME DATA						
100.0	100.0	100.0	Net Sales		100.0	100.0	100.0	100.0	100.0
			Gross Profit						
96.2	93.4	93.2	Operating Expenses		96.0	90.2	95.1	95.1	94.6
3.8	6.6	6.8	Operating Profit		4.0	9.8	4.9	4.9	5.4
.9	1.5	1.4	All Other Expenses (net)		.5	4.6	.5	.2	1.6
2.9	5.1	5.4	Profit Before Taxes		3.5	5.2	4.4	4.7	3.8
			RATIOS						
2.4	2.9	2.9			9.2	9.1	2.3	8.8	1.9
1.3	1.4	1.5	Current		1.4	2.7	1.3	2.1	1.3
.9	1.0	1.0			.7	.8	1.0	1.8	1.0
2.2	2.5	2.6			9.2	5.0	2.3	8.5	1.5
1.2	1.2	1.3	Quick		1.3	1.3	1.2	2.0	1.1
.7	.8	.9			.7	.7	1.0	1.4	.7
8 48.4	**15** 24.8	**2** 237.5			**0** UND	**13** 27.3	**26** 14.1	**1** 331.0	**8** 43.5
35 10.3	**39** 9.4	**33** 10.9	Sales/Receivables		**20** 18.5	**39** 9.3	**33** 10.9	**40** 9.1	**34** 10.8
57 6.4	**58** 6.3	**52** 7.0			**37** 9.8	**79** 4.6	**45** 8.1	**78** 4.7	**60** 6.1
			Cost of Sales/Inventory						
			Cost of Sales/Payables						
9.3	8.7	8.5			10.0	4.1	11.9	5.3	12.0
27.0	20.8	23.3	Sales/Working Capital		33.5	12.1	24.2	10.0	43.4
-81.0	537.5	242.7			-108.0	-34.4	NM	21.4	NM
36.9	39.7	39.6			47.8		28.0	50.7	88.1
(115) 9.2	(109) 7.5	(84) 11.4	EBIT/Interest		(12) 11.7		(16) 6.1	(12) 8.6	(35) 15.1
2.1	1.5	4.9			.3		2.6	1.2	5.6
	36.8	26.2							
	(14) 5.9	(13) 10.0	Net Profit + Depr., Dep., Amort./Cur. Mat. L/T/D						
	-.5	2.5							
.0	.0	.0			.0	.0	.1	.0	.1
.3	.2	.2	Fixed/Worth		.2	.0	.2	.1	.2
-3.7	1.3	2.5			-.2	.4	2.1	.4	1.0
.8	.7	.6			.2	.4	.5	.2	1.4
3.0	2.0	2.2	Debt/Worth		4.6	.9	2.1	.9	3.1
-10.3	27.9	33.2			-3.8	2.4	136.1	5.0	16.3
78.4	69.7	75.1			300.0	76.5	60.9	75.5	78.3
(105) 28.2	(107) 36.6	(98) 39.9	% Profit Before Taxes/Tangible Net Worth		(11) 27.6	(10) 33.3	(19) 28.1	(20) 49.4	(32) 55.9
10.9	7.7	9.7			-8.1	-11.7	6.3	16.8	17.8
20.6	31.5	32.8			45.7	30.1	31.0	39.5	21.8
8.7	9.9	9.9	% Profit Before Taxes/Total Assets		23.9	25.6	6.5	16.3	8.5
1.1	1.5	4.6			-7.3	.1	1.7	4.9	4.8
405.5	478.5	656.3			UND	413.9	398.9	620.0	855.3
110.9	99.1	174.1	Sales/Net Fixed Assets		346.5	121.7	162.3	141.1	241.8
29.8	38.8	32.7			35.7	29.0	10.5	46.0	42.2
6.9	6.9	8.1			8.5	5.3	7.6	6.5	10.0
4.2	4.2	4.5	Sales/Total Assets		6.4	2.6	5.5	4.2	5.5
2.2	2.3	2.0			2.7	1.8	2.2	1.3	2.2
.1	.2	.1					.4		.1
(95) .4	(87) .4	(65) .5	% Depr., Dep., Amort./Sales				(13) 1.1		(29) .2
1.6	1.4	1.2					3.4		.6
1.9	1.1	2.1							
(40) 5.3	(35) 2.7	(35) 7.0	% Officers', Directors' Owners' Comp/Sales						
17.1	8.6	12.3							
7464343M	**6824333M**	**6633688M**	Net Sales ($)	**4158M**	**30932M**	**44894M**	**166803M**	**398192M**	**5988709M**
2200536M	**2110916M**	**2046262M**	Total Assets ($)	**8598M**	**8840M**	**22519M**	**163153M**	**236854M**	**1606298M**

M = $ thousand MM = $ million

See Pages 9 through 22 for Explanation of Ratios and Data

Current Data Sorted by Assets							Comparative Historical Data	
						Type of Statement		
		6	9	5	4	Unqualified	24	23
	3	15	10		1	Reviewed	21	22
2	6	14	3			Compiled	23	25
16	22	11	2	1		Tax Returns	29	21
16	28	53	22	2	5	Other	76	108
20 (4/1-9/30/13)			236 (10/1/13-3/31/14)				4/1/09-3/31/10	4/1/10-3/31/11
0-500M	500M-2MM	2-10MM	10-50MM	50-100MM	100-250MM		ALL	ALL
34	59	99	46	8	10	**NUMBER OF STATEMENTS**	173	199
%	%	%	%	%	%	**ASSETS**	%	%
33.9	22.3	18.7	18.4		28.9	Cash & Equivalents	20.0	20.4
22.8	39.0	40.1	45.2		26.6	Trade Receivables (net)	32.2	33.0
1.6	2.8	3.9	3.4		6.7	Inventory	5.5	4.2
1.4	5.9	3.7	5.1		6.6	All Other Current	5.3	7.1
59.7	70.0	66.5	72.0		68.8	Total Current	63.0	64.7
14.9	15.1	15.0	10.3		7.2	Fixed Assets (net)	14.7	14.8
5.4	4.4	5.8	11.8		22.0	Intangibles (net)	10.5	10.6
20.0	10.5	12.7	5.8		2.0	All Other Non-Current	11.8	9.9
100.0	100.0	100.0	100.0		100.0	Total	100.0	100.0
						LIABILITIES		
24.6	14.5	6.5	6.0		3.4	Notes Payable-Short Term	11.6	14.6
2.4	4.1	2.2	3.9		3.0	Cur. Mat.-L.T.D.	2.9	4.1
15.4	16.5	15.5	20.2		13.2	Trade Payables	14.8	13.1
.0	.0	.7	.8		.5	Income Taxes Payable	.4	.3
37.7	18.6	17.7	21.4		25.8	All Other Current	19.7	21.3
80.1	53.7	42.7	52.2		45.9	Total Current	49.4	53.5
13.2	15.6	8.5	12.1		14.0	Long-Term Debt	11.0	13.4
.0	.0	.2	.4		1.4	Deferred Taxes	.3	.2
17.5	15.1	9.5	9.9		4.7	All Other Non-Current	8.6	8.5
-10.6	15.6	39.2	25.4		34.0	Net Worth	30.7	24.4
100.0	100.0	100.0	100.0		100.0	Total Liabilities & Net Worth	100.0	100.0
						INCOME DATA		
100.0	100.0	100.0	100.0		100.0	Net Sales	100.0	100.0
						Gross Profit		
90.7	92.8	90.6	93.6		92.3	Operating Expenses	92.6	90.1
9.3	7.2	9.4	6.4		7.7	Operating Profit	7.4	9.9
2.8	.0	.8	1.1		2.9	All Other Expenses (net)	1.3	1.4
6.4	7.2	8.6	5.3		4.8	Profit Before Taxes	6.1	8.5
						RATIOS		
1.8	2.6	2.9	1.9		2.3		2.5	2.8
.7	1.5	1.6	1.5		1.6	Current	1.3	1.4
.4	.8	1.0	1.1		.7		.9	1.0
1.8	2.4	2.8	1.9		2.2		1.9	2.2
.7	1.4	1.5	1.3		1.3	Quick	1.2	1.2
.4	.7	.8	.9		.6		.7	.7
0 UND	13 28.3	23 15.8	53 6.9		36 10.0		18 20.1	16 23.5
0 UND	34 10.7	49 7.4	70 5.2		51 7.2	Sales/Receivables	43 8.5	42 8.6
44 8.3	63 5.8	73 5.0	91 4.0		99 3.7		68 5.3	65 5.6
						Cost of Sales/Inventory		
						Cost of Sales/Payables		
41.6	10.2	6.5	6.1		2.3		7.7	6.9
-64.6	18.9	12.6	11.6		7.3	Sales/Working Capital	19.6	16.6
-12.1	-64.3	60.6	51.1		-9.5		-57.7	-367.9
39.0	35.6	78.3	62.0				24.7	30.5
(19) 7.6	(42) 7.0	(66) 18.5	(36) 6.9			EBIT/Interest	(134) 3.7	(147) 7.5
.9	-.3	5.7	2.1				.7	2.0
			8.2			Net Profit + Depr., Dep.,	4.3	21.8
			(13) 2.2			Amort./Cur. Mat. L/T/D	(15) 1.5	(18) 8.2
			.7				.7	2.8
.0	.1	.1	.2		.1		.1	.1
.9	.3	.2	.4		.3	Fixed/Worth	.5	.4
UND	-3.0	2.0	-5.3		-.1		-2.5	-9.1
1.2	.6	.5	1.4		.8		.8	.9
8.8	2.4	1.3	5.4		2.3	Debt/Worth	3.4	2.4
-4.3	-8.0	7.0	-35.9		-2.4		-12.2	-12.6
617.4	109.8	88.4	119.2			% Profit Before Taxes/Tangible	108.2	135.6
(21) 116.2	(39) 61.0	(84) 44.6	(33) 46.3			Net Worth	(122) 39.1	(144) 51.4
17.7	9.7	12.2	7.7				4.7	11.6
90.3	48.8	37.7	19.1		12.2	% Profit Before Taxes/Total	25.9	41.5
41.1	14.2	16.8	10.8		5.9	Assets	7.5	11.0
-1.8	-.6	3.9	1.0		-2.4		.2	2.5
UND	266.0	141.0	82.6		62.8		111.6	104.1
115.4	85.7	44.5	34.3		25.3	Sales/Net Fixed Assets	35.2	37.3
19.8	19.8	13.7	15.2		10.2		12.8	15.3
11.3	6.1	4.1	3.1		2.1		4.6	4.5
5.3	4.0	2.9	2.2		1.2	Sales/Total Assets	2.7	2.8
3.6	2.8	2.1	1.5		.7		1.7	1.7
.5	.3	.4	.5				.6	.5
(12) 1.0	(26) 1.0	(66) .9	(38) .9			% Depr., Dep., Amort./Sales	(109) 1.4	(121) 1.0
2.6	2.0	1.9	1.9				2.2	2.3
4.6	3.1	2.5	2.3			% Officers', Directors'	2.9	2.5
(18) 6.7	(29) 5.7	(28) 4.1	(11) 3.9			Owners' Comp/Sales	(60) 6.5	(57) 6.3
16.5	11.7	6.3	5.6				15.3	11.7
67406M	376418M	1506884M	2354546M	1015671M	2105661M	Net Sales ($)	6096471M	5756488M
10098M	68343M	467518M	999414M	578510M	1560426M	Total Assets ($)	3131834M	3088800M

M = $ thousand MM = $ million

See Pages 9 through 22 for Explanation of Ratios and Data

Comparative Historical Data				Current Data Sorted by Sales					
			Type of Statement						
33	30	24	Unqualified				3	3	18
32	20	29	Reviewed			2	6	10	11
29	27	25	Compiled		3	4	7	7	4
33	38	52	Tax Returns	5	20	3	13	7	4
110	118	126	Other	9	16	12	22	36	31
4/1/11-3/31/12 ALL	4/1/12-3/31/13 ALL	4/1/13-3/31/14 ALL		20 (4/1-9/30/13)		236 (10/1/13-3/31/14)			
				0-1MM	1-3MM	3-5MM	5-10MM	10-25MM	25MM & OVER
237	233	256	**NUMBER OF STATEMENTS**	14	39	21	51	63	68
%	%	%	**ASSETS**	%	%	%	%	%	%
20.4	18.9	21.6	Cash & Equivalents	26.1	20.6	23.4	19.3	26.1	18.3
33.0	36.1	37.3	Trade Receivables (net)	13.0	35.2	31.1	37.2	44.5	38.7
3.3	4.1	3.4	Inventory	2.4	2.2	1.0	4.7	1.3	5.9
8.1	6.1	4.5	All Other Current	2.2	5.9	4.5	3.7	2.7	6.7
64.7	65.2	66.8	Total Current	43.8	63.9	60.0	64.9	74.6	69.5
16.3	14.3	13.6	Fixed Assets (net)	39.4	10.8	15.2	16.7	9.7	10.8
9.9	9.7	8.3	Intangibles (net)	1.3	5.6	8.9	6.6	7.3	13.4
9.1	10.8	11.3	All Other Non-Current	15.5	19.7	15.9	11.8	8.4	6.3
100.0	100.0	100.0	Total	100.0	100.0	100.0	100.0	100.0	100.0
			LIABILITIES						
10.5	13.3	10.5	Notes Payable-Short Term	12.6	15.7	21.4	11.8	5.9	6.9
2.6	3.1	3.0	Cur. Mat.-L.T.D.	3.6	2.5	1.9	4.0	2.0	3.7
12.7	14.5	16.2	Trade Payables	11.0	19.5	12.6	15.6	18.0	15.4
.6	.1	.5	Income Taxes Payable	.0	.0	.0	.0	1.6	.3
22.2	22.2	21.8	All Other Current	59.0	15.3	15.9	21.9	16.2	24.8
48.7	53.2	52.0	Total Current	86.2	53.0	51.8	53.3	43.7	51.1
13.8	14.1	12.2	Long-Term Debt	40.2	8.5	11.8	15.0	5.1	13.3
.3	.2	.3	Deferred Taxes	.0	.0	.0	.2	.3	.7
8.7	9.5	11.8	All Other Non-Current	6.1	15.3	31.3	9.7	8.0	9.9
28.5	23.0	23.7	Net Worth	-32.2	23.2	5.1	21.9	42.9	25.0
100.0	100.0	100.0	Total Liabilties & Net Worth	100.0	100.0	100.0	100.0	100.0	100.0
			INCOME DATA						
100.0	100.0	100.0	Net Sales	100.0	100.0	100.0	100.0	100.0	100.0
			Gross Profit						
89.8	90.6	91.6	Operating Expenses	77.4	92.0	93.0	93.3	91.3	92.9
10.2	9.4	8.4	Operating Profit	22.6	8.0	7.0	6.7	8.7	7.1
1.8	1.1	1.1	All Other Expenses (net)	9.1	.2	.1	.1	.5	1.4
8.4	8.3	7.3	Profit Before Taxes	13.5	7.8	6.9	6.6	8.2	5.7
			RATIOS						
2.5	2.4	2.4		1.4	2.4	2.4	2.1	3.3	2.3
1.4	1.4	1.5	Current	.7	1.4	1.2	1.3	2.0	1.4
.9	.9	.9		.4	.7	.5	.9	1.2	1.0
2.1	2.1	2.3		1.0	2.3	2.4	1.8	3.2	2.1
(232) 1.1	1.1	1.3	Quick	.5	1.3	.9	1.2	1.9	1.2
.7	.7	.7		.3	.6	.5	.7	1.2	.7
12 29.5	19 19.4	21 17.1		0 UND	0 UND	3 111.2	24 14.9	26 13.8	35 10.5
46 8.0	43 8.4	49 7.5	Sales/Receivables	0 UND	44 8.3	34 10.7	49 7.5	51 7.2	53 6.9
69 5.3	66 5.5	73 5.0		51 7.2	74 4.9	52 7.0	87 4.2	73 5.0	74 4.9
			Cost of Sales/Inventory						
			Cost of Sales/Payables						
7.1	7.6	7.0		33.8	7.6	7.6	7.7	6.0	6.8
17.4	17.9	16.1	Sales/Working Capital	-140.7	12.8	25.7	24.0	9.2	15.4
-69.3	-39.8	-82.9		-3.4	-28.7	-15.4	-74.3	27.0	NM
36.7	39.4	54.6			32.9	13.8	55.5	194.0	70.0
(168) 8.6	(161) 12.0	(177) 10.2	EBIT/Interest		(27) 7.6	(14) 4.4	(38) 12.7	(41) 27.1	(53) 9.8
2.2	3.6	2.1			1.4	-3.0	1.2	7.1	2.2
8.0	8.9	8.2							5.6
(26) 3.7	(29) 3.6	(25) 2.2	Net Profit + Depr., Dep., Amort./Cur. Mat. L/T/D						(16) 2.2
1.2	2.0	.8							1.0
.1	.1	.1		.0	.0	.0	.1	.1	.2
.5	.5	.4	Fixed/Worth	3.6	.1	.4	.4	.2	.6
UND	-4.2	UND		-5.7	1.6	NM	4.3	1.1	-.3
.7	.7	.7		3.8	.6	1.1	.8	.4	.9
3.3	3.4	2.7	Debt/Worth	UND	2.7	6.1	1.9	1.1	5.4
-258.5	-16.0	-26.2		-3.4	-5.0	-18.3	-265.9	5.7	-7.2
116.3	108.6	105.9			120.7	153.2	88.3	98.0	106.3
(177) 51.3	(164) 44.5	(185) 50.3	% Profit Before Taxes/Tangible Net Worth		(26) 58.6	(15) 34.2	(38) 40.2	(54) 60.8	(45) 50.3
15.1	9.6	12.2			11.6	5.6	6.4	24.7	10.0
31.6	37.0	39.2		37.2	63.0	49.0	29.2	45.8	23.9
12.8	12.7	14.0	% Profit Before Taxes/Total Assets	6.8	15.0	8.6	9.4	23.6	10.0
2.7	3.0	2.3		-23.2	1.5	1.4	2.0	10.0	3.1
160.8	196.8	221.5		UND	UND	883.1	128.6	121.6	149.7
38.3	43.8	47.9	Sales/Net Fixed Assets	5.7	93.1	69.7	43.1	44.5	46.9
14.7	16.4	16.7		.5	33.3	11.0	13.5	18.2	16.5
4.5	4.7	4.6		5.5	5.3	4.7	4.9	4.6	3.9
2.7	3.0	3.0	Sales/Total Assets	2.1	4.0	2.8	2.8	3.3	2.7
1.8	1.9	2.0		.2	2.7	2.0	1.9	2.2	1.6
.5	.3	.5			.4		.7	.4	.5
(154) 1.1	(151) .9	(151) 1.0	% Depr., Dep., Amort./Sales		(16) 1.0		(30) 1.3	(43) .9	(49) 1.0
2.1	1.9	2.1			2.4		2.5	1.9	2.0
3.3	3.0	2.7			5.4		3.3	2.3	2.1
(68) 5.3	(57) 4.8	(86) 5.1	% Officers', Directors' Owners' Comp/Sales		(23) 7.7		(17) 5.2	(23) 3.8	(13) 2.8
10.6	11.1	9.4			17.5		8.4	4.7	5.6
6109105M	7547380M	7426586M	Net Sales ($)	5767M	80724M	85172M	361842M	1023496M	5869585M
3397934M	3551688M	3684309M	Total Assets ($)	8541M	27108M	34718M	176410M	401582M	3035950M

M = $ thousand MM = $ million

See Pages 9 through 22 for Explanation of Ratios and Data

	Current Data Sorted by Assets						Comparative Historical Data	
Type of Statement								
Unqualified		2	11	16	5	9	32	30
Reviewed	4	2	8	12	1		18	19
Compiled	1	7	8				14	17
Tax Returns	4	4	6				12	14
Other	9	14	31	32	10	7	59	67
	25 (4/1-9/30/13)		178 (10/1/13-3/31/14)				4/1/09-3/31/10	4/1/10-3/31/11
	0-500M	500M-2MM	2-10MM	10-50MM	50-100MM	100-250MM	ALL	ALL
NUMBER OF STATEMENTS	18	29	64	60	16	16	135	147
ASSETS	%	%	%	%	%	%	%	%
Cash & Equivalents	33.6	16.8	15.0	18.5	11.9	10.6	11.8	12.5
Trade Receivables (net)	38.8	45.2	42.8	35.6	26.1	31.1	41.4	43.3
Inventory	4.5	6.8	4.1	2.8	4.3	6.9	4.7	3.4
All Other Current	1.3	1.1	4.5	6.2	4.4	2.9	5.8	8.0
Total Current	78.2	69.9	66.5	63.0	46.8	51.5	63.6	67.2
Fixed Assets (net)	7.6	11.4	18.0	21.1	21.5	13.0	17.7	17.1
Intangibles (net)	6.6	6.8	6.0	9.9	25.5	29.0	7.2	8.2
All Other Non-Current	7.6	12.0	9.5	5.9	6.3	6.5	11.5	7.5
Total	100.0	100.0	100.0	100.0	100.0	100.0	100.0	100.0
LIABILITIES								
Notes Payable-Short Term	23.8	18.0	12.3	7.3	5.3	7.7	16.1	15.5
Cur. Mat.-L.T.D.	1.1	4.0	3.8	3.2	5.6	1.6	4.1	2.7
Trade Payables	22.8	20.9	18.3	19.4	15.0	13.4	18.4	18.0
Income Taxes Payable	.3	.1	.1	.3	.2	.2	.4	.3
All Other Current	40.1	9.2	11.5	17.9	12.5	15.1	12.3	15.4
Total Current	88.1	52.2	46.0	48.0	38.7	37.9	51.3	51.9
Long-Term Debt	7.3	13.6	10.6	11.9	18.2	25.1	7.4	9.9
Deferred Taxes	.0	.0	.3	.5	2.5	.7	.4	.5
All Other Non-Current	.5	14.6	9.9	3.6	7.7	4.9	5.0	7.1
Net Worth	4.2	19.6	33.2	35.9	33.0	31.5	36.0	30.6
Total Liabilties & Net Worth	100.0	100.0	100.0	100.0	100.0	100.0	100.0	100.0
INCOME DATA								
Net Sales	100.0	100.0	100.0	100.0	100.0	100.0	100.0	100.0
Gross Profit								
Operating Expenses	91.7	94.8	93.9	93.9	92.8	87.5	95.9	92.7
Operating Profit	8.3	5.2	6.1	6.1	7.2	12.5	4.1	7.3
All Other Expenses (net)	.0	.3	.4	.7	.9	2.0	.8	1.0
Profit Before Taxes	8.3	4.9	5.7	5.4	6.2	10.5	3.3	6.4
RATIOS								
Current	4.5	2.9	3.0	1.7	1.9	2.1	2.1	2.2
	1.2	1.5	1.4	1.3	1.1	1.4	1.2	1.4
	.5	1.0	.9	1.0	.9	1.0	.9	1.0
Quick	2.8	2.7	2.6	1.6	1.8	1.7	1.8	2.0
	1.2	1.4	1.2	1.2	.8	1.2	1.0	1.1
	.5	1.0	.7	.9	.6	.7	.7	.7
Sales/Receivables	0 UND	11 33.2	30 12.2	32 11.4	34 10.7	34 10.7	29 12.8	32 11.4
	20 18.2	27 13.4	45 8.1	44 8.3	46 8.0	44 8.3	45 8.1	47 7.8
	31 11.8	44 8.3	72 5.1	70 5.2	64 5.7	66 5.5	63 5.8	66 5.5
Cost of Sales/Inventory								
Cost of Sales/Payables								
Sales/Working Capital	17.9	13.0	7.2	7.2	9.9	7.2	9.1	6.9
	56.5	34.2	20.9	20.0	72.9	20.1	33.9	16.5
	-16.5	NM	-249.7	-214.4	-57.5	NM	-42.3	-144.0
EBIT/Interest		41.5	27.7	109.8	12.2	14.5	16.0	30.6
		(23) 13.0	(54) 8.8	(51) 8.9	(13) 3.9	(14) 5.1	(112) 4.5	(117) 6.9
		1.7	2.0	1.6	.2	2.2	.5	2.6
Net Profit + Depr., Dep., Amort./Cur. Mat. L/T/D				10.9			6.0	20.8
				(20) 3.8			(26) 2.3	(26) 4.2
				1.4			.7	1.6
Fixed/Worth	.0	.0	.1	.2	.8	.2	.1	.1
	.0	.3	.3	1.1	3.5	3.8	.3	.5
	.3	-1.3	1.4	3.4	-.1	-.2	1.8	6.0
Debt/Worth	.3	.7	.6	1.3	1.4	1.8	.7	.8
	3.7	2.8	2.6	2.6	9.1	41.2	2.3	2.4
	-3.3	-9.3	6.2	20.9	-3.6	-2.3	7.3	30.8
% Profit Before Taxes/Tangible Net Worth	181.1	101.8	77.9	73.3	29.6		55.9	69.7
	(12) 93.0	(19) 46.1	(52) 24.1	(48) 38.1	(10) 14.5		(113) 20.2	(114) 29.6
	69.4	25.9	11.8	9.5	-6.2		2.7	11.6
% Profit Before Taxes/Total Assets	91.1	29.3	20.7	21.5	14.1	11.5	16.8	28.6
	46.3	21.1	8.8	9.0	5.7	8.8	5.9	10.2
	2.2	2.0	2.3	1.9	-.4	5.2	.0	2.2
Sales/Net Fixed Assets	UND	999.8	154.0	81.9	74.0	93.9	124.4	143.0
	UND	138.1	33.5	29.3	24.5	25.8	39.4	32.8
	122.7	25.0	15.9	5.3	4.1	16.7	13.8	13.9
Sales/Total Assets	13.6	10.1	4.6	3.4	2.7	2.9	5.0	4.9
	7.9	6.3	3.1	2.3	1.8	1.5	3.3	3.2
	4.5	3.9	2.0	1.6	1.1	.8	2.0	1.7
% Depr., Dep., Amort./Sales		.1	.2	.5	.6	.6	.4	.4
		(13) .5	(50) .9	(49) 1.0	(10) 1.3	(10) 1.0	(88) 1.0	(109) .8
		1.6	2.2	3.4	3.2	2.2	2.5	2.6
% Officers', Directors' Owners' Comp/Sales			1.5				2.3	1.5
			(11) 3.5				(27) 3.4	(39) 2.5
			4.3				6.9	7.3
Net Sales ($)	43263M	227756M	1089755M	4342573M	2321598M	6488510M	8503553M	11037564M
Total Assets ($)	4074M	32354M	317028M	1345412M	1063120M	2955105M	3036446M	3989416M

M = $ thousand MM = $ million

See Pages 9 through 22 for Explanation of Ratios and Data

Comparative Historical Data			Type of Statement	Current Data Sorted by Sales					
32	44	43	Unqualified			1	6	4	32
19	27	27	Reviewed	1	4	1	3	3	15
12	17	16	Compiled	1	5	3	3	3	1
8	10	14	Tax Returns	2	3	1	3	5	
68	92	103	Other	4	7	2	14	24	52
4/1/11-3/31/12 ALL	4/1/12-3/31/13 ALL	4/1/13-3/31/14 ALL		25 (4/1-9/30/13)			178 (10/1/13-3/31/14)		
				0-1MM	1-3MM	3-5MM	5-10MM	10-25MM	25MM & OVER
139	190	203	NUMBER OF STATEMENTS	8	19	8	29	39	100
%	%	%	**ASSETS**	%	%	%	%	%	%
13.1	14.1	17.3	Cash & Equivalents		24.3		15.3	20.5	14.8
41.0	39.0	38.4	Trade Receivables (net)		35.5		44.1	37.7	38.9
2.5	2.8	4.4	Inventory		4.2		4.5	4.3	3.6
7.4	4.5	4.1	All Other Current		5.3		2.9	2.8	5.1
63.9	60.3	64.3	Total Current		69.2		66.9	65.2	62.4
19.5	21.7	16.9	Fixed Assets (net)		17.2		13.0	17.5	17.8
6.9	8.4	10.7	Intangibles (net)		7.0		5.9	8.1	14.2
9.6	9.7	8.1	All Other Non-Current		6.6		14.1	9.3	5.5
100.0	100.0	100.0	Total		100.0		100.0	100.0	100.0
			LIABILITIES						
12.4	10.5	11.7	Notes Payable-Short Term		24.0		14.3	17.0	7.9
2.7	2.4	3.4	Cur. Mat.-L.T.D.		2.5		3.2	2.6	3.3
15.8	16.7	18.8	Trade Payables		18.8		12.5	21.5	20.4
.7	.4	.2	Income Taxes Payable		.3		.2	.2	.2
17.1	15.2	15.9	All Other Current		19.8		7.4	10.3	16.2
48.7	45.1	50.0	Total Current		65.4		37.6	51.5	47.9
14.3	15.1	12.9	Long-Term Debt		14.2		7.4	13.8	13.8
.7	.4	.5	Deferred Taxes		.0		.0	.5	.8
7.4	12.9	7.3	All Other Non-Current		5.4		7.6	7.6	8.3
29.0	26.6	29.3	Net Worth		15.0		47.3	26.5	29.2
100.0	100.0	100.0	Total Liabilties & Net Worth		100.0		100.0	100.0	100.0
			INCOME DATA						
100.0	100.0	100.0	Net Sales		100.0		100.0	100.0	100.0
			Gross Profit						
92.4	91.4	93.2	Operating Expenses		88.0		95.0	94.9	93.7
7.6	8.6	6.8	Operating Profit		12.0		5.0	5.1	6.3
.9	1.2	.6	All Other Expenses (net)		.2		-.1	.4	.9
6.7	7.4	6.2	Profit Before Taxes		11.8		5.2	4.8	5.3
			RATIOS						
2.6	2.3	2.3			2.9		4.4	2.3	1.9
1.4	1.4	1.3	Current		1.3		1.9	1.3	1.2
1.0	.9	1.0			.5		1.2	.9	1.0
2.4	2.0	2.0			2.3		3.0	1.9	1.6
1.1	1.2	1.2	Quick		1.3		1.7	1.1	1.1
.7	.8	.8			.3		1.1	.9	.7
30 12.1	25 14.4	25 14.5			0 UND		28 13.0	26 14.0	33 10.9
45 8.2	42 8.7	40 9.1	Sales/Receivables		19 19.2		40 9.1	40 9.1	45 8.2
70 5.2	59 6.2	66 5.5			38 9.5		65 5.6	74 4.9	65 5.6
			Cost of Sales/Inventory						
			Cost of Sales/Payables						
7.4	7.4	8.2			5.5		4.7	8.9	9.0
19.1	23.8	26.4	Sales/Working Capital		39.3		16.0	25.5	29.1
-215.6	-110.4	-170.3			-14.5		53.6	-85.9	-214.4
30.1	37.1	29.5					42.8	21.0	33.9
(107) 8.5	(152) 7.8	(159) 8.5	EBIT/Interest				(26) 14.7	(33) 5.8	(85) 6.2
3.0	1.8	1.9					3.7	.5	2.0
7.9	21.7	10.4							10.8
(27) 3.0	(34) 3.7	(36) 3.8	Net Profit + Depr., Dep., Amort./Cur. Mat. L/T/D						(29) 3.3
1.4	2.0	1.4							1.3
.1	.1	.1			.0		.0	.1	.2
.5	.6	.5	Fixed/Worth		.1		.2	.6	1.2
5.6	5.1	7.4			2.2		.5	-57.4	-4.9
.7	.7	.8			.5		.5	1.4	1.3
3.1	2.9	3.1	Debt/Worth		3.7		.8	3.1	4.5
33.0	318.8	-134.5			-5.8		2.5	-111.8	-88.6
69.2	88.5	81.2			100.9		81.2	99.5	68.7
(107) 32.3	(145) 33.9	(150) 31.5	% Profit Before Taxes/Tangible Net Worth		(13) 77.3		(25) 23.3	(29) 30.7	(71) 30.0
12.3	14.6	13.7			19.4		12.8	11.6	10.4
29.4	28.9	23.3			78.0		25.1	26.2	19.6
10.7	11.3	10.4	% Profit Before Taxes/Total Assets		25.1		11.6	7.8	9.6
2.8	2.0	2.2			2.2		2.2	1.1	2.8
139.1	114.1	164.0			UND		430.8	100.8	101.5
28.1	32.0	48.6	Sales/Net Fixed Assets		130.9		82.6	32.4	35.7
9.2	8.1	11.6			10.6		23.1	8.7	9.4
4.6	4.9	5.4			10.6		6.7	5.3	5.1
2.8	3.1	2.9	Sales/Total Assets		4.9		3.4	2.9	2.7
1.7	1.7	1.6			.6		2.3	1.7	1.7
.3	.6	.3					.2	.4	.3
(99) 1.1	(135) 1.1	(133) .9	% Depr., Dep., Amort./Sales				(16) .8	(29) 1.4	(76) .9
3.2	2.6	2.5					1.9	3.0	2.1
1.7	1.7	1.5							
(26) 4.1	(35) 4.7	(30) 2.9	% Officers', Directors' Owners' Comp/Sales						
15.1	14.5	5.7							
9491162M	12960643M	14513455M	Net Sales ($)	4210M	36329M	34172M	202774M	613170M	13622800M
3587026M	5281499M	5717093M	Total Assets ($)	6433M	41699M	12566M	74564M	244846M	5336985M

M = $ thousand MM = $ million

See Pages 9 through 22 for Explanation of Ratios and Data

Current Data Sorted by Assets							Comparative Historical Data	
						Type of Statement		
	2	9	28	8	5	Unqualified	90	87
	7	19	14		1	Reviewed	50	65
4	10	10	5			Compiled	42	40
28	24	9			1	Tax Returns	74	73
25	51	62	27	10	12	Other	187	208
	42 (4/1-9/30/13)		329 (10/1/13-3/31/14)				4/1/09-3/31/10 ALL	4/1/10-3/31/11 ALL
0-500M	500M-2MM	2-10MM	10-50MM	50-100MM	100-250MM			
57	94	109	74	18	19	NUMBER OF STATEMENTS	443	473
%	%	%	%	%	%	**ASSETS**	%	%
32.0	31.3	19.5	19.0	10.5	13.1	Cash & Equivalents	18.6	18.8
17.8	29.5	45.7	40.8	34.4	25.8	Trade Receivables (net)	39.5	42.7
3.7	3.2	1.7	4.1	3.7	.6	Inventory	2.7	2.5
7.1	3.4	6.5	7.3	7.5	3.6	All Other Current	7.3	6.5
60.5	67.3	73.4	71.3	56.1	43.2	Total Current	68.1	70.4
14.2	18.2	13.6	8.3	18.6	8.8	Fixed Assets (net)	15.3	13.6
9.1	3.2	4.0	10.1	16.8	36.6	Intangibles (net)	6.9	6.5
16.1	11.3	9.0	10.3	8.5	11.4	All Other Non-Current	9.7	9.4
100.0	100.0	100.0	100.0	100.0	100.0	Total	100.0	100.0
						LIABILITIES		
21.8	11.1	9.4	8.6	5.1	2.1	Notes Payable-Short Term	16.2	14.7
1.4	2.6	1.7	2.3	4.7	3.4	Cur. Mat.-L.T.D.	3.3	2.5
13.6	7.1	11.7	13.3	13.0	6.6	Trade Payables	12.8	14.1
.2	.1	.2	.8	.7	1.0	Income Taxes Payable	.9	.6
42.5	19.9	16.6	19.6	20.9	19.8	All Other Current	22.7	19.1
79.6	40.8	39.6	44.7	44.4	32.8	Total Current	55.9	51.0
15.5	13.5	8.0	10.8	13.9	23.7	Long-Term Debt	10.2	9.6
.0	.3	.1	.2	.5	3.0	Deferred Taxes	.3	.4
17.3	6.3	9.2	8.4	12.0	14.0	All Other Non-Current	7.4	5.8
-12.4	39.0	43.1	35.9	29.2	26.6	Net Worth	26.3	33.1
100.0	100.0	100.0	100.0	100.0	100.0	Total Liabilties & Net Worth	100.0	100.0
						INCOME DATA		
100.0	100.0	100.0	100.0	100.0	100.0	Net Sales	100.0	100.0
						Gross Profit		
88.8	86.1	88.6	91.3	86.8	81.8	Operating Expenses	92.1	90.9
11.2	13.9	11.4	8.7	13.2	18.2	Operating Profit	7.9	9.1
1.5	1.8	1.9	2.3	2.1	8.2	All Other Expenses (net)	2.0	1.4
9.7	12.0	9.5	6.4	11.0	10.0	Profit Before Taxes	5.9	7.7
						RATIOS		
3.2	3.7	4.1	2.7	1.9	2.5		2.5	3.1
1.2	1.8	1.9	1.6	1.3	1.5	Current	1.4	1.6
.4	.7	1.3	1.1	.9	.7		1.0	1.0
3.2	3.7	3.5	2.5	1.5	2.0		2.1	2.8
(56) 1.0	1.6	1.9	1.4	1.0	1.5	Quick	1.2	1.4
.3	.7	1.1	.9	.6	.6		.7	.8
0 UND	**0** UND	**38** 9.6	**38** 9.5	**40** 9.1	**43** 8.4		**21** 17.7	**25** 14.7
0 UND	**31** 11.9	**55** 6.6	**59** 6.2	**54** 6.7	**65** 5.6	Sales/Receivables	**51** 7.1	**52** 7.0
26 13.8	**55** 6.6	**78** 4.7	**79** 4.6	**78** 4.7	**85** 4.3		**78** 4.7	**79** 4.6
						Cost of Sales/Inventory		
						Cost of Sales/Payables		
11.5	6.0	4.7	4.2	5.1	4.3		6.2	5.6
105.9	13.1	8.7	9.9	15.4	8.7	Sales/Working Capital	14.7	12.1
-18.0	-72.4	28.5	40.0	NM	-9.8		-140.7	99.0
30.0	70.8	59.3	48.7	40.5	18.6		42.4	46.4
(33) 8.8	(60) 11.1	(73) 13.6	(56) 7.0	(16) 3.5	(15) 4.9	EBIT/Interest	(335) 8.0	(333) 13.7
-.6	4.2	3.7	1.5	1.3	1.7		1.6	2.8
			17.1				17.6	17.0
			(13) 4.3			Net Profit + Depr., Dep., Amort./Cur. Mat. L/T/D	(60) 2.6	(59) 3.8
			.2				.9	.9
.0	.0	.0	.1	.4	.1		.1	.0
.2	.1	.2	.2	.8	1.7	Fixed/Worth	.3	.2
-.4	1.0	1.2	.8	-.4	.0		2.0	1.3
.4	.4	.4	.6	.9	1.0		.7	.5
9.2	1.4	1.5	1.8	8.3	4.1	Debt/Worth	2.1	1.6
-2.3	4.7	4.1	7.8	-3.7	-1.7		22.5	12.1
266.1	118.8	89.9	59.4	108.3	34.6		71.3	88.9
(32) 77.9	(78) 50.3	(98) 37.2	(63) 32.4	(11) 21.4	(10) 24.2	% Profit Before Taxes/Tangible Net Worth	(345) 32.7	(384) 39.4
24.9	13.9	17.0	10.3	2.1	10.5		8.3	13.7
92.8	52.9	38.0	20.5	13.3	13.1		25.7	29.9
20.6	23.7	14.1	10.1	5.7	5.0	% Profit Before Taxes/Total Assets	9.8	12.4
2.8	5.5	5.0	.6	1.4	2.8		.8	3.1
UND	UND	217.3	136.9	72.1	69.9		143.9	179.4
172.1	77.4	53.2	60.6	17.9	37.2	Sales/Net Fixed Assets	43.8	54.2
40.4	16.1	16.0	21.9	4.5	8.0		16.6	17.6
12.8	5.3	4.0	3.4	2.7	1.6		4.4	4.4
5.4	3.4	2.9	2.2	1.8	1.0	Sales/Total Assets	3.0	2.9
3.0	2.3	1.9	1.2	.7	.4		1.7	1.8
.2	.3	.3	.3	.8			.4	.3
(19) .5	(46) 1.1	(73) .8	(59) .9	(13) 2.2		% Depr., Dep., Amort./Sales	(287) .9	(310) .8
1.7	2.3	1.8	1.8	6.2			2.1	2.0
4.2	3.0	1.8	.4				2.3	3.5
(25) 8.6	(39) 6.2	(21) 3.0	(10) 3.1			% Officers', Directors' Owners' Comp/Sales	(119) 5.0	(122) 6.9
22.9	11.0	9.6	5.3				9.8	14.4
111471M	492941M	1438704M	3708978M	2389804M	4038719M	Net Sales ($)	13614314M	14657336M
13311M	105982M	491883M	1533550M	1237935M	3097257M	Total Assets ($)	6757700M	7033760M

M = $ thousand MM = $ million

See Pages 9 through 22 for Explanation of Ratios and Data

Comparative Historical Data / Current Data Sorted by Sales

4/1/11-3/31/12 ALL	4/1/12-3/31/13 ALL	4/1/13-3/31/14 ALL	Type of Statement	0-1MM	1-3MM	3-5MM	5-10MM	10-25MM	25MM & OVER
56	54	52	Unqualified		4	1	3	15	29
55	38	41	Reviewed		2	3	5	14	17
38	27	29	Compiled	5	6	3	6	5	4
65	65	62	Tax Returns	19	14	7	10	9	3
199	169	187	Other	16	34	19	36	37	45
				42 (4/1-9/30/13)			329 (10/1/13-3/31/14)		
413	353	371	NUMBER OF STATEMENTS	40	60	33	60	80	98
%	%	%	**ASSETS**	%	%	%	%	%	%
20.5	24.3	23.5	Cash & Equivalents	27.1	26.2	29.8	28.1	24.5	14.8
38.6	37.0	34.7	Trade Receivables (net)	9.4	23.5	33.0	41.0	43.7	41.5
1.3	2.6	2.9	Inventory	5.3	2.3	5.3	1.3	.5	4.4
6.8	6.2	5.9	All Other Current	4.5	6.1	1.9	6.5	6.4	6.9
67.1	70.1	67.1	Total Current	46.2	58.1	70.0	76.8	75.2	67.5
15.1	12.9	13.8	Fixed Assets (net)	26.9	19.8	13.2	12.1	10.0	9.1
8.0	6.7	8.1	Intangibles (net)	6.2	5.0	7.3	2.8	6.7	15.4
9.8	10.3	11.0	All Other Non-Current	20.5	17.2	9.4	8.2	8.2	7.9
100.0	100.0	100.0	Total	100.0	100.0	100.0	100.0	100.0	100.0
			LIABILITIES						
14.2	10.5	11.0	Notes Payable-Short Term	4.0	14.2	13.9	13.1	12.8	8.1
2.8	2.2	2.2	Cur. Mat.-L.T.D.	1.1	3.4	2.1	2.0	2.1	2.2
11.4	11.6	10.9	Trade Payables	11.5	10.0	5.2	8.7	11.8	13.9
.9	.4	.4	Income Taxes Payable	.1	.1	.5	.2	.2	.9
19.8	19.7	22.4	All Other Current	22.3	30.7	21.2	19.2	19.8	21.9
49.1	44.4	47.0	Total Current	39.1	58.4	43.0	43.2	46.7	47.0
10.5	11.4	12.2	Long-Term Debt	24.4	19.5	11.1	5.8	5.6	12.4
.4	.2	.3	Deferred Taxes	.0	.1	.1	.4	.3	.7
6.3	8.1	9.9	All Other Non-Current	22.2	8.3	4.2	9.2	9.5	8.7
33.7	36.0	30.6	Net Worth	14.3	13.7	41.6	41.4	37.8	31.2
100.0	100.0	100.0	Total Liabilties & Net Worth	100.0	100.0	100.0	100.0	100.0	100.0
			INCOME DATA						
100.0	100.0	100.0	Net Sales	100.0	100.0	100.0	100.0	100.0	100.0
			Gross Profit						
87.8	90.6	88.1	Operating Expenses	74.5	85.1	91.9	91.4	88.6	91.8
12.2	9.4	11.9	Operating Profit	25.5	14.9	8.1	8.6	11.4	8.2
2.0	1.3	2.2	All Other Expenses (net)	6.8	1.9	.6	.5	1.4	2.8
10.2	8.1	9.7	Profit Before Taxes	18.7	13.0	7.4	8.0	10.0	5.4
			RATIOS						
3.3	3.6	3.2	Current	3.4	3.9	4.0	4.3	2.7	2.4
1.5	1.9	1.6		1.2	1.5	2.9	2.4	1.7	1.4
1.0	1.2	1.0		.3	.6	1.1	1.2	1.3	1.1
2.9	3.0	3.0	Quick	3.2	3.6	3.8	4.1	2.6	2.1
1.4	1.6	(370) 1.4		1.0	1.2	1.8	2.1	(79) 1.6	1.3
.7	1.0	.7		.1	.4	.9	1.0	1.1	.8
14 26.0	11 32.0	8 44.6	Sales/Receivables	0 UND	0 UND	0 UND	26 14.0	33 11.1	40 9.2
50 7.3	48 7.6	45 8.1		0 UND	22 16.3	46 8.0	51 7.2	51 7.2	58 6.3
74 4.9	73 5.0	70 5.2		35 10.4	45 8.1	69 5.3	79 4.6	72 5.1	78 4.7
			Cost of Sales/Inventory						
			Cost of Sales/Payables						
5.7	4.8	5.7	Sales/Working Capital	7.3	6.4	4.3	4.4	5.5	6.7
13.1	9.7	12.2		76.8	16.9	9.5	8.2	11.4	11.7
-547.7	50.4	564.1		-5.4	-11.8	397.0	28.7	31.5	81.9
45.1	66.1	50.4	EBIT/Interest	11.1	48.9	46.1	95.9	59.3	39.9
(295) 14.4	(241) 13.8	(253) 9.8		(18) 3.9	(41) 8.8	(20) 6.6	(40) 16.2	(53) 19.7	(81) 5.9
3.1	3.2	2.5		-.2	2.2	2.0	4.8	3.9	1.2
7.2	9.7	15.0	Net Profit + Depr., Dep., Amort./Cur. Mat. L/T/D						17.9
(40) 2.9	(35) 3.6	(31) 2.8							(20) 6.5
.8	-.8	.9							1.1
.0	.0	.0	Fixed/Worth	.0	.0	.0	.0	.0	.1
.2	.2	.2		.1	.3	.1	.1	.2	.3
1.9	1.1	1.8		NM	-8.1	1.1	.8	.8	NM
.6	.5	.5	Debt/Worth	.3	.4	.3	.4	.6	.9
1.8	1.4	1.6		3.0	1.5	.7	1.4	1.5	2.6
12.0	9.3	14.5		-5.9	-5.3	6.4	4.4	5.9	NM
87.1	92.0	104.6	% Profit Before Taxes/Tangible Net Worth	175.0	101.8	74.5	120.1	92.5	73.5
(326) 43.3	(296) 40.2	(292) 39.3		(28) 69.4	(42) 33.4	(26) 42.1	(53) 44.6	(69) 37.6	(74) 36.4
12.5	12.0	14.4		16.6	6.8	5.9	18.4	16.1	14.2
34.7	35.8	35.7	% Profit Before Taxes/Total Assets	39.3	33.5	49.3	48.2	39.5	23.1
14.8	14.2	13.3		11.1	17.1	15.0	20.2	13.5	8.9
3.3	3.5	3.1		.9	3.4	3.0	5.7	6.0	2.2
243.9	269.4	278.4	Sales/Net Fixed Assets	UND	406.5	635.7	306.4	293.8	137.8
54.1	71.4	61.7		93.2	41.7	106.9	69.3	69.5	50.5
19.7	22.3	18.1		1.2	11.0	19.8	16.3	23.4	21.9
4.4	4.7	4.6	Sales/Total Assets	3.7	5.3	5.2	5.2	5.3	4.0
2.8	3.0	2.9		.9	3.4	3.3	3.0	3.4	2.5
1.6	1.7	1.7		.2	1.7	2.3	2.5	1.9	1.7
.3	.3	.3	% Depr., Dep., Amort./Sales	.5	.4	.2	.3	.2	.3
(249) 1.1	(210) .9	(216) 1.0		(18) 11.4	(31) 1.8	(14) .7	(37) .9	(51) .7	(65) 1.0
2.3	2.0	2.1		16.3	3.2	1.6	1.8	1.5	1.8
3.3	3.9	2.7	% Officers', Directors' Owners' Comp/Sales		5.8	2.3	3.1	2.0	1.1
(106) 6.9	(93) 8.6	(97) 5.6			(20) 11.4	(17) 3.9	(17) 8.9	(20) 3.0	(14) 2.7
12.0	17.8	13.1			20.7	8.3	16.3	6.7	5.3
12563034M	10437824M	12180617M	Net Sales ($)	15747M	118956M	128475M	430610M	1293469M	10193360M
5137569M	5396415M	6479918M	Total Assets ($)	36237M	171527M	56772M	160331M	847416M	5207635M

M = $ thousand MM = $ million

See Pages 9 through 22 for Explanation of Ratios and Data

Current Data Sorted by Assets							Comparative Historical Data	
						Type of Statement		
	2	5	10	1	2	Unqualified	20	28
	4	20	8			Reviewed	28	42
4	8	9	1			Compiled	15	23
14	15	4				Tax Returns	24	33
6	24	27	16		1	Other	57	55
	15 (4/1-9/30/13)		166 (10/1/13-3/31/14)				4/1/09-3/31/10 ALL	4/1/10-3/31/11 ALL
0-500M	**500M-2MM**	**2-10MM**	**10-50MM**	**50-100MM**	**100-250MM**			
24	53	65	35	1	3	**NUMBER OF STATEMENTS**	144	181
%	%	%	%	%	%	**ASSETS**	%	%
32.8	15.1	11.7	12.7			Cash & Equivalents	15.0	14.4
26.4	41.4	49.8	43.3			Trade Receivables (net)	44.2	43.0
.4	1.6	2.3	4.7			Inventory	2.0	2.1
6.8	3.5	6.3	7.2			All Other Current	5.6	5.8
66.4	61.6	70.1	67.8			Total Current	66.8	65.4
17.8	29.3	16.8	19.5			Fixed Assets (net)	19.2	20.8
2.9	3.1	5.5	8.0			Intangibles (net)	4.8	5.1
12.9	6.0	7.5	4.7			All Other Non-Current	9.2	8.7
100.0	100.0	100.0	100.0			Total	100.0	100.0
						LIABILITIES		
15.8	10.2	7.0	3.8			Notes Payable-Short Term	11.0	14.4
5.7	3.2	3.6	3.2			Cur. Mat.-L.T.D.	3.8	6.9
18.2	11.0	12.8	14.0			Trade Payables	11.5	14.4
.0	1.2	.3	.1			Income Taxes Payable	.9	.5
11.4	11.5	12.0	13.2			All Other Current	12.5	13.6
51.1	37.1	35.7	34.2			Total Current	39.7	49.8
31.3	21.9	11.2	12.4			Long-Term Debt	13.4	12.9
.0	.4	.7	1.4			Deferred Taxes	.7	1.0
7.7	6.7	3.1	5.2			All Other Non-Current	3.5	4.3
10.0	33.9	49.3	46.8			Net Worth	42.6	32.0
100.0	100.0	100.0	100.0			Total Liabilties & Net Worth	100.0	100.0
						INCOME DATA		
100.0	100.0	100.0	100.0			Net Sales	100.0	100.0
						Gross Profit		
93.5	85.3	93.8	91.9			Operating Expenses	94.5	92.4
6.5	14.7	6.2	8.1			Operating Profit	5.5	7.6
1.1	4.5	.8	.2			All Other Expenses (net)	.7	1.0
5.4	10.3	5.4	7.9			Profit Before Taxes	4.8	6.6
						RATIOS		
2.6	4.7	3.5	3.1				2.8	2.5
1.3	1.8	2.1	1.9			Current	1.8	1.6
.7	1.1	1.5	1.4				1.1	1.1
2.0	4.5	3.4	2.4				2.6	2.2
1.1	1.6	1.7	1.8			Quick	1.5	1.4
.6	1.0	1.2	1.1				1.0	.9
0 UND	23 16.1	58 6.3	57 6.4				35 10.5	36 10.2
12 31.5	62 5.9	76 4.8	89 4.1			Sales/Receivables	63 5.8	66 5.5
45 8.1	83 4.4	99 3.7	126 2.9				91 4.0	93 3.9
						Cost of Sales/Inventory		
						Cost of Sales/Payables		
12.8	4.4	4.3	3.1				5.0	5.4
48.7	12.1	6.7	5.2			Sales/Working Capital	8.8	10.2
-61.8	268.0	11.3	18.9				51.0	103.5
40.6	13.3	41.9	39.7				34.5	30.0
(19) 11.2	(36) 5.3	(55) 7.2	(32) 10.1			EBIT/Interest	(115) 8.3	(150) 7.9
1.3	-.6	1.7	6.4				1.2	1.7
		11.7	9.0				10.1	6.2
		(15) 2.1	(14) 4.6			Net Profit + Depr., Dep., Amort./Cur. Mat. L/T/D	(20) 3.1	(35) 2.9
		.1	1.6				.8	1.3
.0	.1	.1	.1				.1	.1
.5	.5	.3	.6			Fixed/Worth	.4	.3
-.7	5.6	.8	1.1				1.3	1.3
.6	.5	.5	.7				.5	.7
4.2	1.8	1.0	1.3			Debt/Worth	1.1	1.5
-3.1	8.9	2.1	3.5				4.0	4.1
204.3	72.6	45.5	46.2				47.3	62.3
(16) 76.6	(44) 38.6	(60) 17.0	(31) 23.8			% Profit Before Taxes/Tangible Net Worth	(126) 20.1	(154) 29.7
-15.8	4.6	2.6	11.4				3.5	7.9
90.5	26.2	22.6	17.3				23.8	27.5
26.8	8.7	8.9	9.6			% Profit Before Taxes/Total Assets	9.2	11.4
-1.8	-1.2	1.3	4.6				.2	3.0
969.6	135.3	32.7	39.5				56.5	52.2
90.9	21.1	21.7	12.9			Sales/Net Fixed Assets	20.8	26.1
29.6	5.5	7.4	4.5				8.8	9.5
10.7	3.8	3.0	2.3				3.7	3.6
6.9	2.4	2.3	1.5			Sales/Total Assets	2.6	2.5
2.8	1.2	1.7	1.4				1.7	1.8
.4	.3	.8	.9				.7	.9
(10) .9	(31) 1.2	(57) 1.7	(30) 1.8			% Depr., Dep., Amort./Sales	(119) 1.4	(135) 1.6
3.4	5.2	3.0	3.3				3.4	3.2
5.3	2.8	1.9					4.3	2.7
(14) 8.0	(24) 5.4	(25) 3.2				% Officers', Directors' Owners' Comp/Sales	(54) 7.9	(69) 5.2
11.1	8.6	9.8					13.7	12.2
50083M	157645M	692865M	1418000M	134936M	256464M	Net Sales ($)	2081202M	3721799M
6163M	60862M	296369M	811969M	81681M	356794M	Total Assets ($)	939104M	1845876M

M = $ thousand MM = $ million

See Pages 9 through 22 for Explanation of Ratios and Data

Comparative Historical Data				Current Data Sorted by Sales					
			Type of Statement						
26	21	20	Unqualified		1	1	2	4	12
39	39	32	Reviewed	1	3	2	7	16	3
26	17	22	Compiled	4	3	2	10	2	1
28	39	33	Tax Returns	9	11	6	6	1	
82	53	74	Other	5	14	8	18	17	12
				15 (4/1-9/30/13)			166 (10/1/13-3/31/14)		
4/1/11-3/31/12 ALL	4/1/12-3/31/13 ALL	4/1/13-3/31/14 ALL		0-1MM	1-3MM	3-5MM	5-10MM	10-25MM	25MM & OVER
201	169	181	**NUMBER OF STATEMENTS**	19	32	19	43	40	28
%	%	%	**ASSETS**	%	%	%	%	%	%
14.9	14.6	15.5	Cash & Equivalents	12.7	23.3	17.9	17.7	10.1	11.3
43.3	42.1	42.3	Trade Receivables (net)	24.2	33.6	53.5	42.4	53.7	40.8
3.2	3.0	2.3	Inventory	.1	1.5	2.8	2.3	1.9	4.9
6.1	6.1	5.8	All Other Current	4.8	7.4	1.6	2.4	9.7	6.9
67.5	65.7	65.9	Total Current	41.8	65.8	75.8	64.8	75.3	64.0
18.6	20.6	21.1	Fixed Assets (net)	40.6	24.9	13.9	20.8	15.5	17.2
5.6	4.8	5.8	Intangibles (net)	2.8	2.7	4.7	6.3	4.6	13.5
8.3	8.9	7.1	All Other Non-Current	14.8	6.7	5.6	8.2	4.6	5.4
100.0	100.0	100.0	Total	100.0	100.0	100.0	100.0	100.0	100.0
			LIABILITIES						
10.3	11.3	8.4	Notes Payable-Short Term	5.8	15.7	9.7	7.5	7.7	3.4
3.8	3.9	3.7	Cur. Mat.-L.T.D.	2.4	4.7	3.5	4.5	2.8	3.3
13.1	14.3	13.0	Trade Payables	12.4	13.5	13.8	11.8	12.6	15.1
.8	.5	.5	Income Taxes Payable	.0	1.2	.1	.6	.4	.1
12.2	12.2	11.9	All Other Current	9.2	10.3	11.9	11.9	15.2	11.2
40.2	42.3	37.5	Total Current	29.7	45.4	39.0	36.4	38.6	33.1
13.1	13.4	17.6	Long-Term Debt	44.7	24.3	14.6	13.6	6.9	15.2
.9	1.1	.6	Deferred Taxes	.0	.6	.2	.3	1.0	1.5
4.5	5.9	5.3	All Other Non-Current	8.4	10.8	4.6	2.3	3.2	4.9
41.3	37.3	38.9	Net Worth	17.3	18.9	41.7	47.5	50.2	45.3
100.0	100.0	100.0	Total Liabilities & Net Worth	100.0	100.0	100.0	100.0	100.0	100.0
			INCOME DATA						
100.0	100.0	100.0	Net Sales	100.0	100.0	100.0	100.0	100.0	100.0
			Gross Profit						
92.4	94.6	90.9	Operating Expenses	70.5	91.7	93.7	95.7	92.4	92.7
7.6	5.4	9.1	Operating Profit	29.5	8.3	6.3	4.3	7.6	7.3
1.1	.3	1.9	All Other Expenses (net)	10.0	1.4	2.2	.7	.4	.6
6.5	5.1	7.2	Profit Before Taxes	19.5	7.0	4.2	3.6	7.2	6.7
			RATIOS						
3.4	2.9	3.3		6.7	3.4	2.9	3.5	3.3	2.5
1.9	1.8	1.9	Current	1.6	1.6	1.9	1.9	1.9	1.9
1.3	1.1	1.2		.5	.7	1.4	1.2	1.4	1.4
3.2	2.6	3.0		6.4	2.9	2.8	3.4	3.2	2.2
1.6	1.5	1.6	Quick	1.5	1.4	1.7	1.6	1.7	1.6
1.0	.9	1.0		.5	.6	1.2	1.0	1.1	1.0
39 9.3	39 9.3	43 8.4		0 UND	12 31.6	51 7.2	42 8.6	62 5.9	53 6.9
68 5.4	63 5.8	69 5.3	Sales/Receivables	32 11.4	48 7.6	68 5.4	68 5.4	74 4.9	81 4.5
96 3.8	89 4.1	91 4.0		73 5.0	72 5.1	99 3.7	99 3.7	99 3.7	99 3.7
			Cost of Sales/Inventory						
			Cost of Sales/Payables						
4.7	4.8	4.4		3.2	4.3	4.3	4.5	3.9	4.5
8.5	9.1	8.8	Sales/Working Capital	13.5	13.1	11.0	8.4	6.9	6.1
20.4	75.4	28.7		-15.9	-40.0	16.9	59.6	18.1	11.7
32.3	29.8	34.0		20.1	12.8	158.2	32.5	59.5	39.7
(167) 8.8	(142) 7.1	(146) 7.4	EBIT/Interest	(12) 6.8	(24) 5.3	(16) 7.0	(32) 6.0	(34) 19.3	9.7
2.4	1.8	1.7		2.0	-4.1	-.3	-1.3	3.8	6.1
11.3	5.7	11.0							10.0
(39) 3.8	(28) 3.0	(32) 3.3	Net Profit + Depr., Dep., Amort./Cur. Mat. L/T/D						(12) 5.2
1.1	1.2	1.5							2.2
.1	.1	.1		.0	.1	.1	.1	.1	.2
.4	.5	.4	Fixed/Worth	2.7	.6	.3	.4	.2	.6
1.0	1.5	1.6		-1.4	93.0	.5	1.4	.8	3.5
.5	.6	.6		1.0	.7	.6	.4	.5	.8
1.2	1.2	1.3	Debt/Worth	3.6	3.2	1.6	.9	1.1	1.5
3.3	5.0	6.1		-3.9	NM	3.5	2.3	2.1	16.1
53.8	50.2	57.5		64.4	98.5	73.9	49.7	50.8	50.1
(177) 27.4	(140) 17.8	(152) 26.0	% Profit Before Taxes/Tangible Net Worth	(13) 26.9	(24) 45.6	(18) 34.7	(37) 14.3	(38) 27.6	(22) 33.4
11.5	5.4	3.8		.4	-1.6	-7.6	2.1	8.3	16.0
24.3	25.5	24.7		24.8	33.0	21.0	20.4	26.6	22.8
11.4	7.5	9.2	% Profit Before Taxes/Total Assets	8.0	10.0	12.6	7.2	11.4	9.3
3.9	1.1	1.1		1.6	-4.3	-2.9	.5	4.0	4.7
62.4	46.5	66.6		UND	144.0	74.9	79.4	49.7	36.4
23.9	18.4	21.7	Sales/Net Fixed Assets	8.1	26.1	24.5	22.7	26.3	14.0
9.5	7.0	7.0		.4	6.4	13.4	6.4	10.0	6.7
3.4	3.4	3.3		3.2	3.9	4.1	3.9	3.2	2.6
2.3	2.3	2.3	Sales/Total Assets	.6	2.5	3.4	2.5	2.3	1.7
1.7	1.6	1.5		.1	1.9	1.9	1.6	1.5	1.5
.7	.8	.7			.6	.4	.6	.7	.8
(155) 1.2	(138) 1.6	(130) 1.7	% Depr., Dep., Amort./Sales		(19) 1.2	(11) 1.0	(35) 1.4	(34) 1.1	(23) 1.8
2.6	2.9	3.3			3.2	2.8	3.8	2.2	2.9
2.4	3.2	2.8			2.9	3.4	2.2	1.1	
(71) 5.6	(59) 6.9	(67) 5.4	% Officers', Directors' Owners' Comp/Sales		(15) 5.4	(10) 6.4	(21) 5.4	(12) 3.2	
11.5	12.2	9.4			8.8	8.5	10.0	9.2	
3313801M	2654281M	2709993M	Net Sales ($)	8520M	58203M	77528M	297474M	650915M	1617353M
1781304M	1369182M	1613838M	Total Assets ($)	12821M	25390M	32618M	138488M	339736M	1064785M

M = $ thousand MM = $ million

See Pages 9 through 22 for Explanation of Ratios and Data

	Current Data Sorted by Assets						Comparative Historical Data	
Type of Statement								
Unqualified		2	21	7	2	7	52	60
Reviewed		5	18	7			32	33
Compiled	5	9	12	3			14	15
Tax Returns	18	16	8	1			28	27
Other	15	30	74	24	5	4	112	148
	27 (4/1-9/30/13)		266 (10/1/13-3/31/14)				4/1/09-3/31/10	4/1/10-3/31/11
	0-500M	500M-2MM	2-10MM	10-50MM	50-100MM	100-250MM	ALL	ALL
NUMBER OF STATEMENTS	38	62	133	42	7	11	238	283
ASSETS	%	%	%	%	%	%	%	%
Cash & Equivalents	37.1	22.2	16.2	13.9		14.0	17.7	17.7
Trade Receivables (net)	21.1	36.5	41.6	43.6		28.2	42.1	39.6
Inventory	3.0	4.9	3.5	2.2		.2	2.9	2.3
All Other Current	1.2	2.8	5.6	7.8		7.4	5.6	6.9
Total Current	62.4	66.3	67.0	67.5		49.7	68.2	66.5
Fixed Assets (net)	20.9	18.8	18.2	18.1		12.6	16.4	16.9
Intangibles (net)	3.0	4.1	5.0	5.8		27.2	7.2	8.7
All Other Non-Current	13.7	10.8	9.8	8.6		10.5	8.1	8.0
Total	100.0	100.0	100.0	100.0		100.0	100.0	100.0
LIABILITIES								
Notes Payable-Short Term	34.6	12.8	10.4	8.4		1.6	10.7	10.6
Cur. Mat.-L.T.D.	5.3	2.0	2.5	2.8		1.5	3.1	2.6
Trade Payables	9.7	9.7	13.3	16.4		10.4	12.6	10.9
Income Taxes Payable	.0	.0	.5	1.5		1.1	.6	.7
All Other Current	11.1	19.5	17.7	19.0		14.2	19.0	18.4
Total Current	60.7	44.0	44.4	48.1		28.8	46.0	43.2
Long-Term Debt	31.7	13.5	9.6	8.0		25.6	14.4	10.8
Deferred Taxes	.0	.0	.4	.4		2.5	.6	.7
All Other Non-Current	12.6	3.2	6.2	6.7		22.7	7.0	4.6
Net Worth	-5.0	39.3	39.5	36.9		20.3	32.0	40.7
Total Liabilities & Net Worth	100.0	100.0	100.0	100.0		100.0	100.0	100.0
INCOME DATA								
Net Sales	100.0	100.0	100.0	100.0		100.0	100.0	100.0
Gross Profit								
Operating Expenses	87.3	88.0	91.3	94.3		91.2	92.8	91.1
Operating Profit	12.7	12.0	8.7	5.7		8.8	7.2	8.9
All Other Expenses (net)	1.2	2.9	1.5	2.6		5.4	1.6	1.7
Profit Before Taxes	11.4	9.2	7.3	3.2		3.5	5.6	7.3
RATIOS								
Current	2.4	3.8	3.2	2.2		2.9	3.1	3.1
	1.7	1.7	1.9	1.4		2.0	1.6	1.6
	.4	1.0	1.0	1.0		1.1	1.1	1.1
Quick	2.4	3.5	2.9	2.2		2.0	2.7	2.8
	1.6	1.5	1.6	1.1		1.4	1.4	1.4
	.4	.7	.8	.7		.9	.9	.8
Sales/Receivables	0 UND	0 UND	31 11.9	39 9.3		57 6.4	30 12.1	27 13.4
	0 UND	35 10.3	49 7.4	57 6.4		65 5.6	54 6.7	55 6.6
	38 9.7	58 6.3	69 5.3	89 4.1		85 4.3	75 4.9	78 4.7
Cost of Sales/Inventory								
Cost of Sales/Payables								
Sales/Working Capital	10.7	5.8	5.2	5.9		2.6	5.3	5.0
	31.8	12.8	10.5	15.7		8.2	13.0	9.5
	-36.0	-299.0	402.4	999.8		40.9	79.3	87.0
EBIT/Interest	33.4	43.2	76.3	21.2			38.3	42.7
	(23) 13.9	(41) 21.6	(97) 13.3	(34) 8.2			(175) 8.0	(208) 12.8
	1.5	2.3	2.1	.6			1.5	2.2
Net Profit + Depr., Dep., Amort./Cur. Mat. L/T/D			12.5				19.6	17.5
			(15) 4.9				(34) 2.3	(39) 3.3
			.8				1.2	1.4
Fixed/Worth	.1	.0	.0	.1		.1	.1	.1
	.3	.1	.1	.3		1.8	.4	.3
	NM	1.7	1.4	1.6		-.1	2.2	1.6
Debt/Worth	.7	.3	.5	.8		1.9	.7	.5
	2.6	1.4	1.3	1.9		11.1	2.3	1.9
	-3.4	4.5	4.5	5.0		-1.7	12.5	7.3
% Profit Before Taxes/Tangible Net Worth	305.7	106.8	81.0	46.7			77.9	77.3
	(25) 110.5	(53) 44.8	(115) 41.4	(36) 20.3			(195) 36.6	(239) 38.0
	25.1	8.6	9.7	2.7			8.5	8.6
% Profit Before Taxes/Total Assets	116.7	47.7	33.6	17.2		10.0	26.6	29.3
	60.3	20.9	14.1	5.9		5.4	10.0	10.1
	6.7	2.3	2.8	.9		1.5	1.6	1.8
Sales/Net Fixed Assets	580.4	333.4	162.9	129.2		113.0	125.9	114.0
	52.9	88.9	53.4	42.0		74.7	38.7	40.5
	27.3	15.4	9.7	11.0		3.2	11.6	12.8
Sales/Total Assets	11.0	6.3	3.9	3.5		3.2	4.5	3.9
	6.2	3.7	2.9	2.4		1.0	2.9	2.6
	3.6	2.0	2.1	1.5		.4	1.6	1.5
% Depr., Dep., Amort./Sales	.4	.3	.3	.2			.4	.4
	(18) .8	(33) 1.1	(89) .8	(37) 1.0			(164) 1.0	(183) 1.3
	1.5	3.1	2.1	2.7			2.2	2.4
% Officers', Directors' Owners' Comp/Sales	5.4	2.9	2.1				2.3	2.4
	(17) 9.2	(22) 4.9	(29) 3.2				(54) 4.8	(56) 4.2
	16.2	13.6	5.6				11.2	12.1
Net Sales ($)	72107M	303746M	2035635M	2363666M	710547M	2465504M	8004503M	10416688M
Total Assets ($)	9221M	68270M	634875M	896592M	505617M	1808592M	3769377M	5233833M

M = $ thousand MM = $ million

See Pages 9 through 22 for Explanation of Ratios and Data

Comparative Historical Data | **Current Data Sorted by Sales**

4/1/11-3/31/12 ALL	4/1/12-3/31/13 ALL	4/1/13-3/31/14 ALL		0-1MM	1-3MM	3-5MM	5-10MM	10-25MM	25MM & OVER
			Type of Statement						
45	52	39	Unqualified	1	5	1	3	10	19
27	37	30	Reviewed		1	4	4	13	8
14	16	29	Compiled	4	4	3	8	7	3
29	42	43	Tax Returns	9	11	10	7	6	
151	140	152	Other	13	16	16	27	42	38
				27 (4/1-9/30/13)			266 (10/1/13-3/31/14)		
266	287	293	**NUMBER OF STATEMENTS**	27	37	34	49	78	68
%	%	%	**ASSETS**	%	%	%	%	%	%
18.3	19.8	20.1	Cash & Equivalents	17.9	31.4	25.2	18.1	18.4	15.5
42.6	41.2	37.3	Trade Receivables (net)	11.9	24.1	33.2	40.3	48.4	41.9
3.2	2.9	3.3	Inventory	2.5	3.1	5.2	4.1	4.5	1.1
4.8	5.6	4.7	All Other Current	.5	3.4	1.5	4.4	4.9	8.7
68.9	69.4	65.5	Total Current	32.9	62.0	65.0	67.0	76.2	67.1
15.7	14.9	18.5	Fixed Assets (net)	47.2	24.2	18.0	19.1	12.6	10.7
6.3	5.9	5.7	Intangibles (net)	7.8	1.9	2.8	4.5	3.9	11.2
9.1	9.8	10.4	All Other Non-Current	12.2	11.9	14.2	9.5	7.4	11.0
100.0	100.0	100.0	Total	100.0	100.0	100.0	100.0	100.0	100.0
			LIABILITIES						
12.5	13.2	13.3	Notes Payable-Short Term	22.1	15.5	20.7	10.1	13.2	7.3
2.6	1.6	2.8	Cur. Mat.-L.T.D.	4.9	3.4	1.4	1.9	3.6	2.1
12.1	13.9	12.4	Trade Payables	7.2	8.5	8.2	10.4	14.7	17.6
.5	.5	.5	Income Taxes Payable	.0	.0	.0	.1	.9	.9
18.6	19.0	17.1	All Other Current	8.7	9.0	18.7	21.8	18.4	19.2
46.3	48.2	46.1	Total Current	43.0	36.5	49.1	44.2	50.8	47.1
12.0	9.9	13.8	Long-Term Debt	48.5	20.5	12.5	7.7	8.2	8.0
.4	.3	.3	Deferred Taxes	.0	.4	.1	.2	.2	.7
7.6	6.6	7.1	All Other Non-Current	15.1	7.1	5.7	8.4	3.8	7.5
33.6	34.9	32.7	Net Worth	-6.6	35.6	32.7	39.5	37.0	36.7
100.0	100.0	100.0	Total Liabilties & Net Worth	100.0	100.0	100.0	100.0	100.0	100.0
			INCOME DATA						
100.0	100.0	100.0	Net Sales	100.0	100.0	100.0	100.0	100.0	100.0
			Gross Profit						
91.8	91.7	90.5	Operating Expenses	72.4	88.4	92.8	92.2	92.2	94.4
8.2	8.3	9.5	Operating Profit	27.6	11.6	7.2	7.8	7.8	5.6
1.9	.8	2.1	All Other Expenses (net)	8.0	3.8	1.9	1.0	.7	1.2
6.3	7.5	7.5	Profit Before Taxes	19.6	7.8	5.3	6.7	7.1	4.5
			RATIOS						
3.1	3.2	3.1		1.8	7.4	4.0	3.2	2.7	2.3
1.7	1.6	1.7	Current	.8	2.4	1.6	2.0	1.7	1.4
1.1	1.1	1.0		.2	1.5	.8	.9	1.2	1.0
3.0	2.9	2.6		1.7	6.6	3.7	2.8	2.5	2.1
1.5	1.4	1.4	Quick	.7	2.2	1.4	1.8	1.5	1.2
.9	.9	.8		.1	.8	.8	.7	.9	.7
24 15.1	**24** 15.2	**18** 20.0		**0** UND	**0** UND	**0** UND	**35** 10.5	**34** 10.7	**32** 11.5
53 6.9	**49** 7.4	**45** 8.2	Sales/Receivables	**0** UND	**19** 19.6	**41** 9.0	**46** 8.0	**54** 6.8	**59** 6.2
74 4.9	**74** 4.9	**69** 5.3		**37** 9.8	**52** 7.0	**72** 5.1	**72** 5.1	**66** 5.5	**81** 4.5
			Cost of Sales/Inventory						
			Cost of Sales/Payables						
5.1	5.9	5.8		7.6	3.4	6.1	4.7	7.1	6.5
12.8	14.9	12.8	Sales/Working Capital	-37.6	8.3	24.9	7.6	12.6	17.3
163.0	121.4	UND		-4.2	34.3	-41.9	-168.2	51.4	423.4
58.1	84.2	45.6		38.0	21.0	48.1	72.9	104.4	34.4
(193) 10.3	(214) 13.1	(211) 13.3	EBIT/Interest	(15) 9.4	(24) 7.9	(25) 11.4	(32) 23.8	(60) 19.4	(55) 9.7
1.6	3.8	1.5		1.0	2.0	1.5	.4	2.4	.7
18.9	19.4	10.0						38.5	7.5
(22) 2.4	(39) 3.7	(25) 3.3	Net Profit + Depr., Dep., Amort./Cur. Mat. L/T/D					(12) 4.8	(11) 3.3
1.3	1.6	1.0						.4	1.4
.1	.1	.0		.3	.1	.0	.0	.0	.1
.2	.2	.2	Fixed/Worth	4.9	.2	.3	.1	.2	.3
1.5	1.1	1.8		-1.6	1.2	1.5	1.1	1.2	1.7
.6	.5	.6		2.2	.3	.7	.4	.5	.8
1.7	1.7	1.5	Debt/Worth	71.1	1.2	1.3	1.1	1.4	2.2
9.8	6.7	6.7		-2.4	2.5	5.5	2.8	5.7	19.0
81.1	87.0	89.5		160.0	85.1	114.7	77.8	102.5	63.6
(213) 38.3	(240) 41.3	(241) 41.4	% Profit Before Taxes/Tangible Net Worth	(15) 14.3	(34) 25.1	(28) 21.0	(42) 43.2	(67) 54.6	(55) 39.2
10.7	14.0	7.6		2.8	2.6	4.3	19.2	15.9	5.2
33.8	32.1	37.0		75.5	38.0	60.1	44.9	47.7	18.4
12.8	13.9	13.1	% Profit Before Taxes/Total Assets	6.0	9.2	15.5	20.6	20.2	8.6
2.4	3.2	2.0		.4	1.2	.4	3.2	4.8	1.4
179.1	183.9	164.7		46.0	157.8	999.8	120.9	187.7	162.4
53.0	51.6	54.4	Sales/Net Fixed Assets	6.8	51.6	67.5	54.4	77.0	60.4
15.9	15.3	11.0		.4	4.5	14.6	9.4	20.7	15.6
4.7	4.7	4.7		3.8	4.9	6.9	3.7	5.3	4.0
3.0	3.1	3.0	Sales/Total Assets	1.2	2.7	3.8	2.7	3.4	3.0
1.6	2.0	1.8		.2	1.0	2.0	2.1	2.4	1.4
.3	.4	.3		1.3	.5	.3	.3	.2	.2
(163) .7	(184) .8	(189) .8	% Depr., Dep., Amort./Sales	(15) 20.8	(22) 1.8	(13) .8	(30) .8	(57) .7	(52) .7
2.1	2.2	2.1		28.2	12.3	2.0	2.3	1.9	1.9
2.3	2.3	2.7			3.3	5.2	4.2	2.1	
(62) 4.6	(70) 5.3	(72) 5.0	% Officers', Directors' Owners' Comp/Sales		(12) 8.4	(12) 7.1	(15) 5.1	(22) 2.8	
9.8	10.0	10.5			15.3	13.5	9.9	6.2	
7588477M	**10078355M**	**7951205M**	Net Sales ($)	**9892M**	**68816M**	**136329M**	**363175M**	**1332831M**	**6040162M**
3495690M	**3718564M**	**3923167M**	Total Assets ($)	**21772M**	**68210M**	**49719M**	**154906M**	**467080M**	**3161480M**

M = $ thousand MM = $ million

See Pages 9 through 22 for Explanation of Ratios and Data

Current Data Sorted by Assets							Comparative Historical Data	
						Type of Statement		
	2	4	5		1	Unqualified	11	6
		4	2	1		Reviewed	1	2
		1	1			Compiled	3	1
2	3	1	1			Tax Returns	1	2
2	5	8	5	2	4	Other	10	15
	9 (4/1-9/30/13)		45 (10/1/13-3/31/14)				4/1/09-3/31/10 ALL	4/1/10-3/31/11 ALL
0-500M	500M-2MM	2-10MM	10-50MM	50-100MM	100-250MM			
4	10	18	14	3	5	**NUMBER OF STATEMENTS**	26	26
%	%	%	%	%	%	**ASSETS**	%	%
	15.3	29.9	22.6			Cash & Equivalents	16.7	18.5
	45.2	28.0	20.5			Trade Receivables (net)	19.8	18.0
	4.0	2.4	5.3			Inventory	1.9	4.2
	4.2	6.7	5.1			All Other Current	6.8	7.1
	68.6	67.0	53.5			Total Current	45.2	47.8
	22.1	17.2	33.1			Fixed Assets (net)	25.1	33.1
	2.2	1.8	5.6			Intangibles (net)	16.1	9.9
	7.1	14.0	7.8			All Other Non-Current	13.5	9.2
	100.0	100.0	100.0			Total	100.0	100.0
						LIABILITIES		
	6.6	4.5	5.8			Notes Payable-Short Term	15.9	7.8
	1.6	15.1	4.4			Cur. Mat.-L.T.D.	.7	1.6
	22.4	14.5	6.4			Trade Payables	8.4	8.6
	.0	1.0	.4			Income Taxes Payable	.3	.1
	38.7	26.8	13.3			All Other Current	13.0	14.5
	69.3	61.9	30.3			Total Current	38.2	32.5
	3.6	4.9	16.3			Long-Term Debt	11.7	21.0
	.8	.0	.2			Deferred Taxes	.8	.9
	3.9	.4	10.0			All Other Non-Current	4.0	6.3
	22.4	32.8	43.3			Net Worth	45.2	39.3
	100.0	100.0	100.0			Total Liabilities & Net Worth	100.0	100.0
						INCOME DATA		
	100.0	100.0	100.0			Net Sales	100.0	100.0
						Gross Profit		
	99.6	87.1	91.8			Operating Expenses	90.2	96.7
	.4	12.9	8.2			Operating Profit	9.8	3.3
	1.2	-.1	.2			All Other Expenses (net)	2.5	2.2
	-.8	13.0	8.0			Profit Before Taxes	7.3	1.1
						RATIOS		
	6.8	8.4	4.4				2.5	2.9
	2.4	1.4	2.2			Current	1.6	1.4
	.6	.7	1.2				1.0	.9
	6.1	7.2	3.7				2.3	2.4
	2.1	1.3	1.5			Quick	1.3	1.3
	.5	.6	.8				.7	.7
	29 12.7	20 18.0	41 8.9				16 23.1	23 16.2
	59 6.2	34 10.6	54 6.7			Sales/Receivables	54 6.7	49 7.5
	73 5.0	64 5.7	65 5.6				71 5.1	63 5.8
						Cost of Sales/Inventory		
						Cost of Sales/Payables		
	6.2	4.4	3.4				4.9	5.0
	NM	21.4	6.5			Sales/Working Capital	13.4	12.7
	-5.1	-10.0	21.8				NM	-37.2
		196.6	28.2				39.3	30.5
		(13) 26.7	(12) 9.5			EBIT/Interest	(20) 7.6	(18) 2.1
		2.3	1.6				1.6	-2.9
						Net Profit + Depr., Dep., Amort./Cur. Mat. L/T/D		
	.1	.1	.4				.2	.2
	.5	.5	.9			Fixed/Worth	.5	1.2
	NM	NM	NM				1.4	41.9
	.2	.1	.5				.6	.5
	1.1	2.0	1.3			Debt/Worth	1.0	3.0
	-3.4	NM	NM				3.6	124.6
		101.4	65.7				68.2	35.2
		(14) 56.1	(11) 20.9			% Profit Before Taxes/Tangible Net Worth	(23) 23.5	(21) 12.9
		2.8	2.2				-.3	-21.4
	25.1	58.3	25.2				20.8	15.6
	4.7	17.7	10.3			% Profit Before Taxes/Total Assets	5.2	2.3
	-1.8	.7	1.0				-.2	-4.9
	69.7	107.9	16.5				29.9	24.8
	25.1	32.9	6.2			Sales/Net Fixed Assets	13.3	6.2
	5.6	8.1	1.9				2.5	1.9
	4.1	3.5	2.1				1.7	2.2
	2.9	2.6	1.1			Sales/Total Assets	1.3	1.3
	2.4	2.0	1.0				.7	.7
		.3	2.0				1.3	2.0
		(13) .9	3.1			% Depr., Dep., Amort./Sales	(20) 2.7	(17) 5.1
		3.4	6.6				3.9	10.4
						% Officers', Directors' Owners' Comp/Sales		
7490M	34537M	251087M	401833M	223120M	789871M	Net Sales ($)	1106825M	529984M
934M	11627M	102816M	312986M	229075M	744162M	Total Assets ($)	1393361M	738630M

M = $ thousand MM = $ million

See Pages 9 through 22 for Explanation of Ratios and Data

Comparative Historical Data | **Current Data Sorted by Sales**

4/1/11-3/31/12 ALL	4/1/12-3/31/13 ALL	4/1/13-3/31/14 ALL		0-1MM	1-3MM	3-5MM	5-10MM	10-25MM	25MM & OVER
			Type of Statement						
6	13	12	Unqualified		1	1	2	4	4
4	5	7	Reviewed					4	3
3	4	2	Compiled					2	
6	2	7	Tax Returns	1	3		1	2	
26	39	26	Other	1	3	1	7	4	10
				9 (4/1-9/30/13)			45 (10/1/13-3/31/14)		
45	63	54	**NUMBER OF STATEMENTS**	2	7	2	10	16	17
%	%	%	**ASSETS**	%	%	%	%	%	%
24.0	21.8	27.4	Cash & Equivalents				35.3	22.8	24.5
20.9	25.3	25.8	Trade Receivables (net)				15.2	27.7	22.5
4.9	6.4	3.5	Inventory				2.2	1.7	5.7
6.3	5.6	5.6	All Other Current				8.9	5.5	5.8
56.1	59.1	62.3	Total Current				61.5	57.8	58.6
25.1	22.9	24.2	Fixed Assets (net)				24.3	32.5	22.6
7.9	5.5	3.9	Intangibles (net)				1.4	1.2	9.0
10.9	12.6	9.6	All Other Non-Current				12.8	8.6	9.7
100.0	100.0	100.0	Total				100.0	100.0	100.0
			LIABILITIES						
9.7	4.9	5.6	Notes Payable-Short Term				12.0	3.9	3.4
1.3	2.3	6.8	Cur. Mat.-L.T.D.				5.0	14.3	4.2
9.8	12.5	11.4	Trade Payables				7.9	10.4	9.8
.3	.7	.4	Income Taxes Payable				.0	.4	1.0
13.3	19.5	26.3	All Other Current				22.8	17.1	18.1
34.4	39.9	50.5	Total Current				47.8	46.1	36.4
17.1	12.0	9.1	Long-Term Debt				2.0	10.8	15.8
.8	.4	.2	Deferred Taxes				.0	.0	.1
7.1	10.0	7.4	All Other Non-Current				.1	.3	20.7
40.6	37.6	32.8	Net Worth				50.2	42.7	27.0
100.0	100.0	100.0	Total Liabilities & Net Worth				100.0	100.0	100.0
			INCOME DATA						
100.0	100.0	100.0	Net Sales				100.0	100.0	100.0
			Gross Profit						
90.0	96.4	93.4	Operating Expenses				86.8	91.6	92.7
10.0	3.6	6.6	Operating Profit				13.2	8.4	7.3
.9	2.1	.7	All Other Expenses (net)				2.2	.0	1.8
9.0	1.4	5.9	Profit Before Taxes				11.0	8.4	5.5
			RATIOS						
4.6	3.5	6.7					10.7	10.4	3.1
1.6	1.6	1.7	Current				2.8	2.5	1.2
.9	.9	.9					.5	1.0	1.0
3.7	3.4	5.9					8.8	9.6	2.9
1.4	1.5	1.3	Quick				2.2	1.8	1.0
.6	.5	.6					.4	1.0	.8
20 18.0	**27** 13.3	**23** 16.2					**0** UND	**24** 15.5	**38** 9.7
41 9.0	**48** 7.6	**50** 7.3	Sales/Receivables				**1** 471.0	**50** 7.3	**54** 6.8
69 5.3	**59** 6.2	**72** 5.1					**48** 7.6	**78** 4.7	**76** 4.8
			Cost of Sales/Inventory						
			Cost of Sales/Payables						
4.4	3.6	4.1					4.9	2.7	4.2
11.2	9.1	10.1	Sales/Working Capital				39.1	6.0	17.8
-79.7	-31.4	-40.9					-2.0	NM	NM
66.4	25.4	50.7						156.4	38.4
(30) 13.1	(40) 3.5	(41) 5.0	EBIT/Interest					(14) 7.5	(14) 8.2
1.4	.0	1.6						2.3	.0
		8.3							
		(10) 2.4	Net Profit + Depr., Dep., Amort./Cur. Mat. L/T/D						
		2.2							
.2	.2	.2					.2	.3	.4
.6	.5	.6	Fixed/Worth				.5	.6	1.0
5.4	1.7	2.0					NM	1.3	-1.6
.5	.5	.3					.1	.3	1.3
1.2	1.2	1.6	Debt/Worth				.4	.5	2.1
UND	3.5	NM					NM	6.9	-12.2
86.4	34.5	64.6						62.6	68.5
(34) 19.1	(52) 10.3	(41) 22.0	% Profit Before Taxes/Tangible Net Worth					(14) 10.8	(12) 42.0
3.4	-1.0	1.8						.7	-5.8
35.3	16.5	25.7					55.2	23.3	25.7
10.9	4.2	6.6	% Profit Before Taxes/Total Assets				13.5	8.8	6.8
.8	-8.1	-1.5					-.9	.8	-6.2
38.4	36.0	54.0					151.3	37.5	18.4
7.9	14.6	10.1	Sales/Net Fixed Assets				28.6	7.5	9.7
4.4	4.6	5.1					8.6	2.2	4.3
2.8	2.5	3.2					4.1	3.2	2.2
1.5	1.6	2.0	Sales/Total Assets				2.8	2.1	1.3
.9	.8	1.1					1.2	1.1	.9
1.7	1.1	.9						.8	1.5
(29) 3.1	(44) 2.4	(40) 2.9	% Depr., Dep., Amort./Sales					(14) 3.0	(16) 3.1
4.7	4.4	5.2						5.0	6.1
1.4									
(12) 6.1			% Officers', Directors' Owners' Comp/Sales						
9.0									
1749119M	**3587476M**	**1707938M**	Net Sales ($)	**684M**	**14536M**	**8354M**	**72400M**	**240890M**	**1371074M**
1308968M	**2371780M**	**1401600M**	Total Assets ($)	**525M**	**5628M**	**2640M**	**49542M**	**236062M**	**1107203M**

M = $ thousand MM = $ million

See Pages 9 through 22 for Explanation of Ratios and Data

Current Data Sorted by Assets							Comparative Historical Data	
						Type of Statement		
	2	12	27	7	14	Unqualified	92	74
		8	1			Reviewed	21	25
2	3	5			2	Compiled	8	12
6	4	4				Tax Returns	20	23
9	13	19	29	3	8	Other	101	115
44 (4/1-9/30/13)			134 (10/1/13-3/31/14)				4/1/09-3/31/10	4/1/10-3/31/11
0-500M	500M-2MM	2-10MM	10-50MM	50-100MM	100-250MM		ALL	ALL
17	22	48	57	10	24	**NUMBER OF STATEMENTS**	242	249
%	%	%	%	%	%	**ASSETS**	%	%
37.4	24.4	16.3	24.0	10.7	20.3	Cash & Equivalents	21.5	20.4
16.1	27.4	37.4	18.4	20.9	19.0	Trade Receivables (net)	27.6	29.5
1.0	6.7	4.6	2.4	4.7	3.1	Inventory	5.3	4.9
.2	4.8	5.7	9.3	4.3	4.7	All Other Current	6.5	6.7
54.6	63.2	63.9	54.2	40.6	47.2	Total Current	60.8	61.5
30.7	24.5	21.7	25.6	21.8	25.7	Fixed Assets (net)	22.8	21.8
2.0	1.8	3.6	6.4	26.7	12.7	Intangibles (net)	5.1	6.2
12.6	10.5	10.7	13.9	10.9	14.5	All Other Non-Current	11.3	10.6
100.0	100.0	100.0	100.0	100.0	100.0	Total	100.0	100.0
						LIABILITIES		
38.0	9.0	8.1	4.0	3.3	.4	Notes Payable-Short Term	5.7	7.1
.4	1.2	4.5	1.7	2.6	2.2	Cur. Mat.-L.T.D.	1.8	1.6
17.0	7.4	9.1	7.8	10.0	6.8	Trade Payables	10.6	9.4
.5	.2	.2	.8	.1	.6	Income Taxes Payable	.5	.4
22.3	11.4	17.4	17.3	12.2	15.5	All Other Current	16.8	16.8
78.1	29.1	39.3	31.7	28.2	25.5	Total Current	35.4	35.3
7.7	13.2	8.7	12.1	18.4	16.1	Long-Term Debt	10.3	11.1
.0	.0	.4	.3	1.6	1.0	Deferred Taxes	.4	.7
20.2	25.7	5.2	5.8	6.8	12.4	All Other Non-Current	6.3	6.0
-6.1	32.0	46.4	50.1	45.0	45.0	Net Worth	47.6	46.9
100.0	100.0	100.0	100.0	100.0	100.0	Total Liabilties & Net Worth	100.0	100.0
						INCOME DATA		
100.0	100.0	100.0	100.0	100.0	100.0	Net Sales	100.0	100.0
						Gross Profit		
92.4	94.1	93.9	94.6	98.6	98.1	Operating Expenses	93.0	91.5
7.6	5.9	6.1	5.4	1.4	1.9	Operating Profit	7.0	8.5
.9	1.1	-.1	1.3	2.7	.9	All Other Expenses (net)	1.2	.7
6.7	4.8	6.1	4.1	-1.3	1.0	Profit Before Taxes	5.8	7.8
						RATIOS		
6.5	4.2	3.9	3.5	1.9	3.9		3.5	3.3
.5	2.3	1.7	1.7	1.2	2.3	Current	1.9	1.8
.4	1.3	1.0	1.0	1.0	1.4		1.2	1.2
6.5	3.6	2.7	3.0	1.6	2.5		2.9	2.8
.5	2.0	1.4	1.3	.9	1.8	Quick	1.5	1.5
.4	.8	.9	.7	.7	.8		.9	.8
0 UND	**0** UND	**38** 9.7	**25** 14.6	**42** 8.6	**48** 7.6		**28** 13.2	**26** 14.1
0 UND	**18** 20.6	**53** 6.9	**46** 8.0	**52** 7.0	**58** 6.3	Sales/Receivables	**48** 7.7	**51** 7.2
24 15.1	**53** 6.9	**85** 4.3	**65** 5.6	**72** 5.1	**76** 4.8		**68** 5.3	**75** 4.8
						Cost of Sales/Inventory		
						Cost of Sales/Payables		
11.7	5.2	3.9	2.4	4.7	2.0		3.2	3.3
-31.0	7.7	8.1	7.1	28.5	4.8	Sales/Working Capital	7.6	7.3
-7.3	115.8	141.5	NM	101.9	17.7		24.7	26.6
29.9	25.6	27.0	56.4		6.5		38.4	51.7
(10) 2.8	(15) 6.2	(38) 12.6	(44) 7.1		(15) 2.7	EBIT/Interest	(168) 8.8	(176) 8.3
-8.3	-40.2	3.3	-3.0		-.3		1.4	1.3
							9.4	34.5
						Net Profit + Depr., Dep., Amort./Cur. Mat. L/T/D	(34) 3.5	(43) 7.8
							1.4	2.9
.4	.1	.1	.1	.7	.2		.1	.1
3.2	.3	.3	.4	1.7	.6	Fixed/Worth	.4	.3
-1.0	3.9	1.2	1.1	-.4	3.7		1.1	1.3
1.0	.2	.4	.4	1.1	.4		.4	.5
5.0	1.1	1.1	.9	3.1	1.0	Debt/Worth	1.0	1.1
-3.3	10.1	4.0	2.2	-6.5	7.3		2.8	3.9
205.6	66.9	38.9	27.6		22.4		51.0	53.7
(12) 31.8	(18) 33.7	(46) 18.1	(48) 9.9		(19) 9.8	% Profit Before Taxes/Tangible Net Worth	(216) 14.7	(221) 20.9
17.4	-8.8	-1.0	-.5		-4.6		.7	3.8
70.6	36.2	20.4	13.2	4.5	9.8		19.7	26.1
12.3	10.9	7.0	4.1	.9	2.6	% Profit Before Taxes/Total Assets	7.0	8.6
-7.6	-7.4	-1.5	-1.2	-.8	-3.0		.2	.6
113.1	91.3	53.4	30.5	20.1	17.0		44.6	57.4
22.9	30.9	14.9	7.7	6.9	6.7	Sales/Net Fixed Assets	14.6	19.0
14.2	9.1	6.6	2.2	3.3	2.0		3.5	4.0
10.3	5.0	3.0	2.1	1.6	1.3		2.8	3.2
6.1	3.3	2.0	1.1	1.4	.8	Sales/Total Assets	1.7	1.8
3.9	2.2	1.2	.7	.9	.5		1.0	.9
	.8	.8	.8		1.8		1.0	.9
	(13) 2.0	(37) 1.8	(50) 2.5		(17) 3.8	% Depr., Dep., Amort./Sales	(187) 2.6	(178) 2.1
	12.3	4.3	5.8		7.7		5.9	4.6
							3.9	1.8
						% Officers', Directors' Owners' Comp/Sales	(33) 8.6	(34) 6.6
							12.9	14.8
32464M	76399M	560256M	1859893M	885982M	4264467M	Net Sales ($)	9982321M	10609510M
4276M	23667M	253114M	1361514M	723910M	3894399M	Total Assets ($)	7387910M	7575469M

M = $ thousand MM = $ million

See Pages 9 through 22 for Explanation of Ratios and Data

Comparative Historical Data

Current Data Sorted by Sales

4/1/11-3/31/12 ALL	4/1/12-3/31/13 ALL	4/1/13-3/31/14 ALL	Type of Statement	0-1MM	1-3MM	3-5MM	5-10MM	10-25MM	25MM & OVER
72	64	62	Unqualified	1	2	3	7	12	37
15	8	9	Reviewed		2	1	1	4	1
10	9	12	Compiled	3		1	1	2	2
25	19	14	Tax Returns	3	4	3	2	2	
109	91	81	Other	2	15	6	12	17	29
				44 (4/1-9/30/13)		134 (10/1/13-3/31/14)			
231	191	178	**NUMBER OF STATEMENTS**	9	23	14	26	37	69
%	%	%	**ASSETS**	%	%	%	%	%	%
21.7	21.4	22.0	Cash & Equivalents		18.4	26.7	21.1	18.4	21.7
25.8	23.8	24.6	Trade Receivables (net)		26.1	22.1	20.1	32.2	24.0
4.7	4.2	3.6	Inventory		2.2	4.8	3.0	5.1	3.5
6.2	6.0	6.0	All Other Current		3.0	.9	6.4	8.2	7.2
58.3	55.4	56.3	Total Current		49.6	54.5	50.6	63.9	56.4
23.0	25.3	24.7	Fixed Assets (net)		28.1	28.7	33.9	20.2	20.2
7.3	6.4	6.6	Intangibles (net)		3.2	4.6	2.5	6.1	10.9
11.4	12.9	12.4	All Other Non-Current		19.1	12.2	12.9	9.8	12.6
100.0	100.0	100.0	Total		100.0	100.0	100.0	100.0	100.0
			LIABILITIES						
7.5	7.2	8.4	Notes Payable-Short Term		19.0	6.5	10.2	7.4	3.6
1.7	2.4	2.4	Cur. Mat.-L.T.D.		1.0	1.0	2.9	4.9	1.8
10.6	9.0	9.0	Trade Payables		17.7	3.2	5.0	10.1	9.2
.4	.4	.5	Income Taxes Payable		.0	.4	.1	.1	.9
21.3	17.8	16.6	All Other Current		13.7	11.7	12.1	18.4	18.8
41.7	36.7	36.8	Total Current		51.4	22.8	30.3	40.9	34.2
13.4	15.6	11.8	Long-Term Debt		11.6	9.1	16.4	9.8	11.4
.4	.6	.4	Deferred Taxes		.0	.2	.4	.2	.8
7.8	7.4	10.4	All Other Non-Current		24.5	15.4	7.5	4.0	7.9
36.7	39.7	40.5	Net Worth		12.5	52.4	45.3	45.1	45.7
100.0	100.0	100.0	Total Liabilties & Net Worth		100.0	100.0	100.0	100.0	100.0
			INCOME DATA						
100.0	100.0	100.0	Net Sales		100.0	100.0	100.0	100.0	100.0
			Gross Profit						
94.5	92.9	94.8	Operating Expenses		91.4	93.6	92.8	96.8	96.3
5.5	7.1	5.2	Operating Profit		8.6	6.4	7.2	3.2	3.7
1.3	1.9	.9	All Other Expenses (net)		2.5	.8	-.3	.4	.8
4.1	5.2	4.3	Profit Before Taxes		6.1	5.6	7.5	2.8	2.9
			RATIOS						
3.0	3.3	3.8	Current		3.8	8.1	3.9	3.9	3.1
1.7	1.9	1.8			1.8	2.9	1.4	1.8	1.6
1.1	1.0	1.0			.4	.9	1.0	1.0	1.1
2.5	2.8	2.8	Quick		2.4	7.9	2.8	2.8	2.5
1.3	1.5	1.4			1.7	2.8	1.3	1.5	1.3
.7	.8	.7			.4	.8	.9	.8	.8
21 17.1	**22** 16.9	**21** 17.3	Sales/Receivables		**0** UND	**13** 29.1	**17** 22.1	**31** 11.7	**40** 9.2
46 8.0	**44** 8.3	**46** 7.9			**32** 11.5	**26** 14.2	**42** 8.7	**52** 7.0	**49** 7.4
70 5.2	**63** 5.8	**65** 5.6			**69** 5.3	**64** 5.7	**62** 5.9	**87** 4.2	**65** 5.6
			Cost of Sales/Inventory						
			Cost of Sales/Payables						
3.8	3.9	3.6	Sales/Working Capital		4.0	1.7	4.8	3.4	3.9
8.6	9.4	8.2			11.4	12.8	7.7	6.0	8.8
68.0	238.9	NM			-7.4	-47.9	-766.6	302.7	62.4
27.6	40.2	26.7	EBIT/Interest		12.8	45.8	30.6	47.2	39.9
(162) 6.3	(136) 9.9	(131) 6.8			(13) -.4	(10) 5.1	(25) 8.5	(28) 17.3	(51) 6.1
.7	1.5	-1.1			-6.2	-18.3	.4	1.8	-.3
12.1	10.3	11.3	Net Profit + Depr., Dep., Amort./Cur. Mat. L/T/D						26.4
(38) 3.5	(24) 4.8	(19) 4.0							(12) 5.6
1.5	1.8	1.9							3.2
.1	.1	.1	Fixed/Worth		.2	.1	.2	.1	.1
.4	.4	.6			.7	.5	.8	.3	.6
1.9	1.5	2.4			201.9	1.4	1.9	2.2	2.1
.5	.5	.4	Debt/Worth		.4	.1	.4	.4	.5
1.2	1.3	1.1			1.1	.4	1.2	1.1	1.2
4.7	3.2	5.0			208.3	4.3	5.0	4.8	3.9
47.2	49.5	37.3	% Profit Before Taxes/Tangible Net Worth		76.8	27.2	112.6	30.9	28.1
(189) 14.3	(165) 20.0	(149) 14.9			(18) 39.1	(12) 5.9	(25) 17.9	(31) 12.2	(56) 13.6
1.8	3.0	-1.6			.0	-7.9	-1.0	2.6	-1.7
16.4	21.6	15.8	% Profit Before Taxes/Total Assets		23.1	21.5	27.9	14.0	13.0
4.9	7.9	4.7			2.1	6.3	4.7	4.6	5.0
-.7	.7	-1.8			-11.9	-5.2	-1.1	-2.5	-1.2
50.2	51.4	43.8	Sales/Net Fixed Assets		89.5	60.8	44.8	31.8	43.3
15.0	15.5	12.2			21.9	9.8	10.9	15.3	12.0
3.3	3.4	4.3			7.4	2.3	2.4	6.2	3.8
2.8	3.0	3.1	Sales/Total Assets		4.8	5.3	3.6	2.9	2.5
1.6	1.8	1.6			3.1	2.3	1.6	2.0	1.4
.9	.9	1.0			1.0	.5	.8	1.0	1.0
1.1	.9	.8	% Depr., Dep., Amort./Sales		.6		1.3	.8	.9
(176) 2.5	(137) 2.1	(133) 2.2			(14) 1.6		(20) 2.5	(30) 1.6	(54) 2.5
5.7	6.0	5.8			12.5		8.3	3.3	5.4
3.7	2.5	3.3	% Officers', Directors' Owners' Comp/Sales						
(35) 6.0	(37) 8.0	(20) 5.6							
10.1	17.6	16.6							
10790863M	8851620M	7679461M	Net Sales ($)	4932M	46931M	58292M	185094M	595419M	6788793M
8465097M	6857380M	6260880M	Total Assets ($)	4805M	65943M	64912M	203835M	528234M	5393151M

M = $ thousand MM = $ million

See Pages 9 through 22 for Explanation of Ratios and Data

Current Data Sorted by Assets							Comparative Historical Data	
						Type of Statement		
	2	3	14		5	Unqualified	35	29
		1				Reviewed	5	3
1	1			1		Compiled	6	6
2	3	1				Tax Returns	4	3
2	6	4	7	2	3	Other	18	27
	27 (4/1-9/30/13)		31 (10/1/13-3/31/14)				4/1/09-3/31/10	4/1/10-3/31/11
0-500M	500M-2MM	2-10MM	10-50MM	50-100MM	100-250MM		ALL	ALL
5	12	9	21	3	8	**NUMBER OF STATEMENTS**	68	68
%	%	%	%	%	%	**ASSETS**	%	%
	31.4		29.4			Cash & Equivalents	23.0	26.9
	28.2		28.3			Trade Receivables (net)	30.0	25.6
	.0		1.3			Inventory	1.0	.9
	3.3		5.7			All Other Current	6.6	6.6
	62.9		64.7			Total Current	60.6	60.1
	20.4		13.4			Fixed Assets (net)	18.8	19.8
	6.6		3.2			Intangibles (net)	6.8	3.8
	10.1		18.8			All Other Non-Current	13.7	16.3
	100.0		100.0			Total	100.0	100.0
						LIABILITIES		
	11.3		3.8			Notes Payable-Short Term	10.6	6.4
	.6		.8			Cur. Mat.-L.T.D.	1.9	1.6
	6.4		11.4			Trade Payables	10.1	6.7
	1.5		.1			Income Taxes Payable	.1	.2
	19.4		19.9			All Other Current	16.8	19.5
	39.2		36.0			Total Current	39.5	34.5
	17.2		5.9			Long-Term Debt	10.2	13.7
	.0		.1			Deferred Taxes	.1	.2
	11.3		5.0			All Other Non-Current	5.9	6.8
	32.3		53.0			Net Worth	44.4	44.8
	100.0		100.0			Total Liabilties & Net Worth	100.0	100.0
						INCOME DATA		
	100.0		100.0			Net Sales	100.0	100.0
						Gross Profit		
	87.5		95.5			Operating Expenses	99.2	95.5
	12.5		4.5			Operating Profit	.8	4.5
	3.3		-.7			All Other Expenses (net)	.9	1.6
	9.2		5.2			Profit Before Taxes	-.1	2.9
						RATIOS		
	2.5		2.5				2.9	3.5
	1.9		1.6			Current	1.7	2.1
	.9		1.3				1.1	1.3
	2.4		2.1				2.6	3.0
	1.5		1.4			Quick	1.5	1.7
	.9		1.1				.7	1.0
	0 UND		**1** 254.4				**6** 63.5	**14** 26.5
	47 7.8		**42** 8.6			Sales/Receivables	**53** 6.8	**52** 7.0
	85 4.3		**81** 4.5				**84** 4.3	**74** 5.0
						Cost of Sales/Inventory		
						Cost of Sales/Payables		
	5.4		4.0				3.4	2.9
	13.3		11.8			Sales/Working Capital	10.1	7.1
	NM		101.9				73.3	29.4
			30.9				25.1	61.9
			(12) 11.1			EBIT/Interest	(45) 6.0	(44) 8.6
			3.5				-3.8	-.1
						Net Profit + Depr., Dep., Amort./Cur. Mat. L/T/D		
	.0		.0				.1	.1
	.5		.1			Fixed/Worth	.3	.3
	NM		.6				1.6	1.0
	.8		.5				.5	.3
	4.4		1.1			Debt/Worth	1.3	1.1
	NM		1.9				4.7	3.7
			39.3				34.6	36.4
			15.1			% Profit Before Taxes/Tangible Net Worth	(59) 7.6	(60) 15.1
			5.9				-5.0	2.1
	31.3		19.5				12.9	16.6
	3.7		6.6			% Profit Before Taxes/Total Assets	2.4	5.9
	-5.1		3.2				-4.5	-.6
	UND		999.8				75.7	69.6
	242.9		63.9			Sales/Net Fixed Assets	24.7	19.0
	22.7		4.5				4.5	4.4
	6.9		4.2				3.4	2.9
	3.1		2.2			Sales/Total Assets	2.1	1.7
	.8		1.0				.9	.7
			.4				.9	.7
			(17) 1.2			% Depr., Dep., Amort./Sales	(48) 1.8	(54) 1.5
			3.4				3.6	3.4
							6.6	3.7
						% Officers', Directors' Owners' Comp/Sales	(16) 15.3	(14) 17.5
							20.9	31.1
12471M	45908M	58779M	3934954M	507188M	1413002M	Net Sales ($)	6259637M	7717288M
1122M	13109M	38442M	557002M	196116M	1375172M	Total Assets ($)	2423251M	3529552M

M = $ thousand MM = $ million

See Pages 9 through 22 for Explanation of Ratios and Data

Comparative Historical Data				Current Data Sorted by Sales					
			Type of Statement						
33	30	24	Unqualified		1	1	2	7	13
5	5	1	Reviewed				1		
4	6	3	Compiled	1		1			1
4	4	6	Tax Returns	3	1			2	
25	32	24	Other	4	3	1	2	3	11
4/1/11-3/31/12 ALL	**4/1/12-3/31/13 ALL**	**4/1/13-3/31/14 ALL**		**27 (4/1-9/30/13)**			**31 (10/1/13-3/31/14)**		
				0-1MM	**1-3MM**	**3-5MM**	**5-10MM**	**10-25MM**	**25MM & OVER**
71	77	58	**NUMBER OF STATEMENTS**	8	5	3	5	12	25
%	%	%	**ASSETS**	%	%	%	%	%	%
27.5	27.2	30.6	Cash & Equivalents					44.3	25.1
28.1	26.5	22.1	Trade Receivables (net)					14.7	28.4
1.2	1.8	2.7	Inventory					4.3	2.7
4.6	5.2	5.0	All Other Current					4.6	5.0
61.4	60.7	60.3	Total Current					67.9	61.2
16.4	19.9	20.3	Fixed Assets (net)					18.0	16.2
4.5	4.9	4.1	Intangibles (net)					1.9	5.1
17.7	14.6	15.3	All Other Non-Current					12.2	17.4
100.0	100.0	100.0	Total					100.0	100.0
			LIABILITIES						
4.4	4.1	9.4	Notes Payable-Short Term					28.3	2.8
.6	.8	1.0	Cur. Mat.-L.T.D.					.2	1.6
7.5	6.4	9.6	Trade Payables					8.5	10.1
.1	.2	.3	Income Taxes Payable					.0	.1
18.6	20.6	20.8	All Other Current					11.8	24.4
31.2	32.1	41.2	Total Current					48.8	38.9
6.8	9.8	13.9	Long-Term Debt					5.0	8.9
.2	.3	.2	Deferred Taxes					.3	.3
7.1	6.3	13.9	All Other Non-Current					2.8	10.3
54.6	51.5	30.8	Net Worth					43.1	41.6
100.0	100.0	100.0	Total Liabilities & Net Worth					100.0	100.0
			INCOME DATA						
100.0	100.0	100.0	Net Sales					100.0	100.0
			Gross Profit						
89.7	95.1	94.9	Operating Expenses					96.0	97.3
10.3	4.9	5.1	Operating Profit					4.0	2.7
1.1	2.4	1.7	All Other Expenses (net)					-.8	.9
9.1	2.5	3.4	Profit Before Taxes					4.9	1.8
			RATIOS						
3.5	3.7	3.6						4.6	2.5
2.1	2.1	1.7	Current					1.5	1.5
1.3	1.2	1.0						1.1	1.1
3.4	2.9	2.6						4.2	1.9
1.6	(76) 1.9	1.4	Quick					1.5	1.3
1.0	.9	1.0						1.0	.9
5 78.9	**8** 48.3	**1** 317.5						**0** UND	**12** 31.2
47 7.7	**43** 8.5	**33** 11.2	Sales/Receivables					**30** 12.3	**43** 8.4
74 4.9	**73** 5.0	**64** 5.7						**69** 5.3	**64** 5.7
			Cost of Sales/Inventory						
			Cost of Sales/Payables						
2.9	2.4	3.0						2.9	4.9
8.4	5.9	10.8	Sales/Working Capital					4.9	20.4
39.3	70.1	NM						180.3	NM
75.5	73.5	29.9							61.3
(36) 29.2	(52) 11.7	(33) 5.8	EBIT/Interest						(16) 14.2
.2	1.1	-13.1							-3.6
			Net Profit + Depr., Dep., Amort./Cur. Mat. L/T/D						
.0	.0	.0						.1	.0
.1	.2	.2	Fixed/Worth					.5	.2
.6	.8	.9						1.0	.6
.3	.3	.5						.2	.5
.6	.7	1.2	Debt/Worth					.5	1.3
2.3	2.2	7.0						2.1	3.3
47.7	40.9	37.0						26.4	68.6
(65) 19.8	(68) 11.2	(48) 12.0	% Profit Before Taxes/Tangible Net Worth					(11) 4.8	(23) 15.1
6.1	-.4	2.4						-.5	7.4
25.9	19.3	17.0						19.7	19.5
9.8	5.6	4.2	% Profit Before Taxes/Total Assets					2.1	5.8
2.3	-.9	-.9						-.7	.0
105.3	136.6	473.4						283.9	571.5
36.0	21.3	22.8	Sales/Net Fixed Assets					21.4	41.3
5.1	3.2	3.9						4.2	5.3
3.6	3.1	3.5						7.6	4.2
1.8	1.8	1.7	Sales/Total Assets					1.7	2.2
1.0	.6	.7						.7	.8
.6	.4	.7							.5
(54) 1.0	(55) 1.2	(39) 2.3	% Depr., Dep., Amort./Sales						(17) 2.1
3.1	5.4	4.1							3.9
	4.0								
	(16) 9.6		% Officers', Directors' Owners' Comp/Sales						
	20.5								
7701664M	5992559M	5972302M	Net Sales ($)	2429M	10148M	11707M	29788M	157865M	5760365M
3583548M	2765893M	2180963M	Total Assets ($)	5415M	9831M	8743M	19537M	135938M	2001499M

M = $ thousand MM = $ million

See Pages 9 through 22 for Explanation of Ratios and Data

Current Data Sorted by Assets							Comparative Historical Data	
						Type of Statement		
1	1	6	10	2	11	Unqualified	29	26
1	4	26	14	1		Reviewed	67	70
7	14	29	2			Compiled	61	60
39	25	19	4	1		Tax Returns	96	107
27	44	65	32	5	6	Other	195	209
40 (4/1-9/30/13)		356 (10/1/13-3/31/14)					4/1/09-3/31/10 ALL	4/1/10-3/31/11 ALL
0-500M	500M-2MM	2-10MM	10-50MM	50-100MM	100-250MM			
75	88	145	62	9	17	**NUMBER OF STATEMENTS**	448	472
%	%	%	%	%	%	**ASSETS**	%	%
30.4	23.1	21.9	22.3		14.3	Cash & Equivalents	18.9	21.9
21.4	44.3	44.2	41.1		21.8	Trade Receivables (net)	40.7	39.8
1.4	2.5	2.2	5.3		.2	Inventory	3.3	2.7
1.4	1.3	4.6	6.2		5.2	All Other Current	5.0	4.9
54.6	71.2	73.0	74.8		41.5	Total Current	67.9	69.2
24.6	16.9	12.3	7.9		5.4	Fixed Assets (net)	15.7	15.0
4.8	2.7	5.6	9.2		49.1	Intangibles (net)	5.9	6.7
15.9	9.3	9.1	8.0		4.0	All Other Non-Current	10.6	9.0
100.0	100.0	100.0	100.0		100.0	Total	100.0	100.0
						LIABILITIES		
26.1	10.5	5.9	2.6		.5	Notes Payable-Short Term	17.2	13.9
3.6	2.4	1.8	1.8		3.1	Cur. Mat.-L.T.D.	3.1	2.9
24.0	22.9	33.6	36.5		18.5	Trade Payables	27.5	26.6
.0	.0	.2	.2		2.5	Income Taxes Payable	.2	.2
22.4	14.2	18.6	23.0		15.5	All Other Current	22.9	22.3
76.2	50.1	60.2	64.2		40.2	Total Current	70.9	65.8
23.1	13.6	7.0	7.6		12.4	Long-Term Debt	10.8	11.7
.0	.0	.2	.1		4.8	Deferred Taxes	.2	.2
16.8	7.4	4.3	8.4		12.2	All Other Non-Current	7.9	8.6
-16.1	28.9	28.3	19.6		30.4	Net Worth	10.2	13.6
100.0	100.0	100.0	100.0		100.0	Total Liabilties & Net Worth	100.0	100.0
						INCOME DATA		
100.0	100.0	100.0	100.0		100.0	Net Sales	100.0	100.0
						Gross Profit		
91.4	88.6	93.2	95.8		94.5	Operating Expenses	96.3	93.4
8.6	11.4	6.8	4.2		5.5	Operating Profit	3.7	6.6
1.4	2.3	.7	.5		2.5	All Other Expenses (net)	1.1	1.3
7.2	9.2	6.1	3.7		3.0	Profit Before Taxes	2.6	5.3
						RATIOS		
2.4	3.4	1.7	1.6		1.4		1.7	2.1
.9	1.4	1.2	1.1		1.0	Current	1.1	1.1
.4	1.0	1.0	.9		.7		.7	.8
2.4	3.2	1.6	1.2		1.2		1.5	1.8
.8	1.4	1.1	1.0		.9	Quick	(447) .9	1.0
.4	.9	.8	.8		.7		.6	.7
0 UND	16 23.0	34 10.7	38 9.7		44 8.3		24 15.4	21 17.7
0 UND	38 9.5	47 7.7	51 7.1		70 5.2	Sales/Receivables	46 7.9	45 8.0
27 13.4	61 6.0	68 5.4	96 3.8		107 3.4		76 4.8	68 5.4
						Cost of Sales/Inventory		
						Cost of Sales/Payables		
28.5	7.0	7.9	8.2		8.6		10.1	8.9
-213.1	20.0	22.1	45.4		-87.7	Sales/Working Capital	65.2	39.1
-15.1	-193.9	-211.6	-53.2		-12.9		-18.6	-27.1
21.6	81.4	88.5	70.5		22.8		20.9	38.7
(51) 7.8	(61) 20.8	(96) 17.1	(47) 22.5		(15) 2.1	EBIT/Interest	(336) 3.7	(328) 8.0
.5	3.5	3.1	4.9		.2		-2.4	1.2
		11.1	9.1				9.1	14.1
		(11) 1.6	(11) 3.1			Net Profit + Depr., Dep., Amort./Cur. Mat. L/T/D	(37) 2.1	(50) 4.3
		.8	1.5				.5	2.1
.1	.0	.1	.2		.6		.2	.1
2.3	.2	.3	.5		-.4	Fixed/Worth	.7	.6
-.4	2.2	3.0	NM		-.1		-1.1	-1.8
1.0	.7	1.1	2.4		4.7		1.3	1.1
10.2	2.4	2.5	9.9		-3.4	Debt/Worth	5.6	5.9
-2.7	28.9	32.1	NM		-1.6		-6.5	-8.4
188.4	130.3	76.9	116.3				99.7	112.1
(43) 84.0	(67) 51.7	(113) 37.2	(47) 39.6			% Profit Before Taxes/Tangible Net Worth	(296) 31.1	(323) 43.3
7.9	8.6	14.6	9.8				.7	7.2
69.8	58.7	19.5	13.7		8.2		22.1	26.6
21.7	14.4	10.4	4.2		2.4	% Profit Before Taxes/Total Assets	5.1	8.8
.0	3.2	3.3	1.4		-2.1		-4.3	.6
373.4	272.0	153.5	127.2		36.0		99.6	120.3
59.0	77.6	56.6	47.1		23.3	Sales/Net Fixed Assets	37.5	40.6
21.3	22.0	19.1	18.5		16.7		16.1	18.4
12.4	5.7	4.4	3.8		1.8		5.1	5.3
7.1	4.1	3.5	2.3		1.0	Sales/Total Assets	3.4	3.3
4.0	2.6	2.2	1.2		.8		1.8	1.9
.3	.4	.3	.2				.5	.4
(32) 1.0	(52) .6	(102) .7	(55) .7			% Depr., Dep., Amort./Sales	(306) 1.1	(318) 1.0
1.9	1.0	1.3	1.9				2.1	2.1
6.1	3.7	2.2	.8				3.2	3.8
(44) 9.4	(41) 5.9	(48) 3.6	(19) 1.2			% Officers', Directors' Owners' Comp/Sales	(182) 5.8	(193) 6.7
14.7	10.6	9.7	2.5				11.1	12.3
133673M	445595M	2364122M	3327887M	1433009M	3292345M	Net Sales ($)	8527079M	8093203M
16282M	100030M	707970M	1295344M	656954M	2753934M	Total Assets ($)	4271237M	4028991M

M = $ thousand MM = $ million

See Pages 9 through 22 for Explanation of Ratios and Data

Comparative Historical Data | **Current Data Sorted by Sales**

Comparative Historical Data				Current Data Sorted by Sales					
			Type of Statement						
33	26	31	Unqualified			2	2	6	23
63	42	46	Reviewed	1		2	6	20	17
63	56	52	Compiled	5	9	5	10	15	8
130	89	88	Tax Returns	21	19	18	13	11	6
183	215	179	Other	13	26	19	27	51	43
4/1/11-3/31/12 ALL	**4/1/12-3/31/13 ALL**	**4/1/13-3/31/14 ALL**		**40 (4/1-9/30/13)**		**356 (10/1/13-3/31/14)**			
				0-1MM	**1-3MM**	**3-5MM**	**5-10MM**	**10-25MM**	**25MM & OVER**
472	428	396	**NUMBER OF STATEMENTS**	40	54	44	58	103	97
%	%	%	**ASSETS**	%	%	%	%	%	%
20.7	23.1	23.5	Cash & Equivalents	20.4	27.4	24.9	23.8	23.9	21.3
38.3	38.0	38.4	Trade Receivables (net)	14.9	33.8	40.9	40.6	46.2	39.7
2.1	2.4	2.5	Inventory	.4	1.4	2.2	2.5	3.7	3.0
4.5	4.5	3.5	All Other Current	1.4	.9	.7	3.5	4.9	5.7
65.6	67.8	67.9	Total Current	37.2	63.4	68.7	70.4	78.7	69.7
16.0	13.7	14.5	Fixed Assets (net)	42.0	16.9	16.8	11.6	9.8	7.5
6.9	8.2	7.6	Intangibles (net)	3.0	7.1	3.5	6.6	4.5	15.5
11.5	10.2	10.0	All Other Non-Current	17.8	12.6	11.0	11.4	7.0	7.3
100.0	100.0	100.0	Total	100.0	100.0	100.0	100.0	100.0	100.0
			LIABILITIES						
15.4	13.5	9.9	Notes Payable-Short Term	19.0	18.3	19.7	8.5	5.5	2.4
2.1	2.2	2.3	Cur. Mat.-L.T.D.	2.5	2.9	3.8	2.5	2.0	1.6
24.4	26.2	29.5	Trade Payables	22.3	20.0	15.5	24.6	37.1	39.0
.3	.3	.2	Income Taxes Payable	.1	.0	.0	.2	.1	.7
20.4	19.4	18.9	All Other Current	20.0	16.5	18.7	16.4	20.8	19.5
62.6	61.6	60.9	Total Current	63.9	57.7	57.7	52.1	65.5	63.1
12.5	10.4	11.9	Long-Term Debt	36.1	15.3	10.8	10.5	6.2	7.6
.3	.2	.3	Deferred Taxes	.0	.0	.1	.0	.3	.9
6.6	5.6	8.4	All Other Non-Current	17.5	11.4	12.5	4.1	4.3	8.2
18.0	22.2	18.5	Net Worth	-17.4	15.5	18.8	33.3	23.8	20.2
100.0	100.0	100.0	Total Liabilities & Net Worth	100.0	100.0	100.0	100.0	100.0	100.0
			INCOME DATA						
100.0	100.0	100.0	Net Sales	100.0	100.0	100.0	100.0	100.0	100.0
			Gross Profit						
93.5	92.0	92.4	Operating Expenses	78.3	94.0	90.6	92.0	94.4	96.3
6.5	8.0	7.6	Operating Profit	21.7	6.0	9.4	8.0	5.6	3.7
1.2	1.1	1.2	All Other Expenses (net)	7.8	-.1	1.2	.0	.5	.6
5.2	6.9	6.4	Profit Before Taxes	13.8	6.2	8.2	8.0	5.0	3.1
			RATIOS						
1.7	1.8	2.0		2.3	4.0	3.8	2.0	1.6	1.5
1.1	1.2	1.2	Current	.7	1.3	1.2	1.4	1.2	1.1
.8	.8	.9		.3	.7	.8	1.0	1.0	.9
1.5	1.7	1.7		2.3	3.9	3.7	1.9	1.5	1.1
1.0	1.1	1.1	Quick	.7	1.1	1.2	1.3	1.1	.9
.7	.7	.7		.2	.7	.8	1.0	.8	.8
21 17.6	**18** 20.2	**20** 18.3		**0** UND	**0** UND	**22** 16.7	**19** 18.8	**36** 10.1	**31** 11.8
46 8.0	**46** 7.9	**42** 8.6	Sales/Receivables	**0** UND	**30** 12.0	**41** 8.9	**38** 9.7	**48** 7.6	**49** 7.4
72 5.1	**72** 5.1	**66** 5.5		**27** 13.5	**66** 5.5	**63** 5.8	**66** 5.5	**74** 4.9	**70** 5.2
			Cost of Sales/Inventory						
			Cost of Sales/Payables						
10.9	10.2	8.6		8.3	7.4	8.6	7.6	8.1	11.6
46.6	37.5	35.1	Sales/Working Capital	-54.4	37.2	33.6	23.1	19.6	53.7
-33.5	-35.5	-43.9		-6.8	-36.2	-36.2	-827.2	-227.1	-40.5
41.3	60.9	48.0		16.9	13.6	37.4	137.9	85.3	45.9
(335) 9.7	(293) 14.2	(277) 13.0	EBIT/Interest	(21) 7.8	(37) 4.6	(33) 13.8	(39) 36.5	(75) 20.8	(72) 11.4
1.6	2.1	2.4		-2.5	.5	3.7	10.8	3.9	1.3
9.1	6.8	9.0						10.5	9.5
(41) 3.7	(38) 2.6	(32) 2.5	Net Profit + Depr., Dep., Amort./Cur. Mat. L/T/D					(12) 1.7	(14) 3.5
1.4	1.6	1.4						1.0	1.5
.1	.1	.1		.2	.0	.1	.1	.1	.2
.5	.4	.5	Fixed/Worth	2.4	.5	.7	.1	.4	.7
12.9	4.5	-5.4		-1.6	-.7	-3.8	.8	-191.0	-.9
1.1	1.1	1.1		1.0	.3	.7	.6	1.4	2.6
4.3	4.4	4.7	Debt/Worth	5.3	2.7	4.0	2.2	4.0	10.5
-41.8	-57.2	-17.2		-3.6	-4.7	-11.4	9.4	-999.8	-7.9
95.3	111.6	104.3		100.5	101.7	128.0	147.8	90.7	96.4
(348) 44.2	(317) 44.8	(279) 42.3	% Profit Before Taxes/Tangible Net Worth	(26) 9.2	(37) 49.7	(28) 57.8	(49) 58.9	(77) 37.2	(62) 29.8
11.4	12.5	11.7		-1.0	.1	11.7	23.7	16.1	9.0
24.6	31.8	26.9		51.9	64.4	59.7	42.3	19.6	13.7
8.8	10.9	9.8	% Profit Before Taxes/Total Assets	4.6	14.3	14.5	14.3	10.4	3.9
1.1	1.7	1.9		-.6	.7	4.5	7.4	3.0	.9
139.4	218.2	163.9		103.6	240.2	398.9	276.7	134.3	168.1
42.4	52.6	50.7	Sales/Net Fixed Assets	17.4	68.4	39.8	70.7	49.6	47.9
17.2	18.0	20.8		.3	23.8	18.0	35.9	20.9	22.7
5.2	5.2	5.3		7.0	7.4	7.4	6.0	4.6	4.5
3.3	3.3	3.6	Sales/Total Assets	2.6	4.2	4.4	4.0	3.5	3.1
1.9	2.0	2.1		.2	2.4	3.1	2.3	2.2	1.8
.5	.4	.3		1.6	.3	.4	.3	.3	.2
(321) .9	(267) .9	(252) .7	% Depr., Dep., Amort./Sales	(18) 6.4	(25) .6	(26) .6	(38) .6	(76) .7	(69) .5
2.0	1.8	1.5		21.6	1.6	1.1	1.3	1.4	1.2
3.0	2.6	2.6		7.9	6.4	4.5	3.9	2.1	.7
(181) 6.3	(154) 5.7	(152) 5.6	% Officers', Directors' Owners' Comp/Sales	(12) 10.9	(30) 9.9	(28) 6.8	(24) 7.6	(36) 3.2	(22) 1.2
12.4	11.1	11.2		19.7	15.8	11.6	12.1	6.4	2.3
10237648M	**10181537M**	**10996631M**	Net Sales ($)	**16632M**	**103444M**	**167751M**	**413082M**	**1620397M**	**8675325M**
5252834M	**5445019M**	**5530514M**	Total Assets ($)	**25877M**	**35790M**	**49981M**	**138523M**	**680323M**	**4600020M**

M = $ thousand MM = $ million

See Pages 9 through 22 for Explanation of Ratios and Data

Current Data Sorted by Assets							Comparative Historical Data	
						Type of Statement		
	2	6	4			Unqualified	19	11
	2	4	1	1		Reviewed	9	10
1	3					Compiled	14	12
8	3	2				Tax Returns	13	8
8	11	12	5	1	2	Other	22	36
	13 (4/1-9/30/13)		63 (10/1/13-3/31/14)				4/1/09-3/31/10	4/1/10-3/31/11
0-500M	**500M-2MM**	**2-10MM**	**10-50MM**	**50-100MM**	**100-250MM**		**ALL**	**ALL**
17	21	24	10	2	2	**NUMBER OF STATEMENTS**	77	77
%	%	%	%	%	%	**ASSETS**	%	%
45.0	26.6	19.8	8.6			Cash & Equivalents	23.9	19.9
17.5	32.2	39.1	39.8			Trade Receivables (net)	39.0	37.6
.1	.9	1.9	.8			Inventory	2.9	1.6
3.5	6.3	3.7	12.8			All Other Current	3.5	3.4
66.0	66.0	64.5	62.0			Total Current	69.2	62.5
11.9	16.1	20.8	18.5			Fixed Assets (net)	14.6	17.0
1.2	6.3	5.7	13.4			Intangibles (net)	5.4	9.0
20.8	11.6	9.1	6.1			All Other Non-Current	10.7	11.4
100.0	100.0	100.0	100.0			Total	100.0	100.0
						LIABILITIES		
28.0	14.4	7.4	9.4			Notes Payable-Short Term	12.7	12.3
.5	.5	1.8	4.1			Cur. Mat.-L.T.D.	3.0	2.8
18.3	14.6	18.6	11.4			Trade Payables	12.3	10.7
.0	.1	.0	1.9			Income Taxes Payable	.7	.8
17.8	30.5	17.8	24.9			All Other Current	22.0	16.3
64.6	60.0	45.6	51.7			Total Current	50.8	43.0
8.3	7.9	14.4	14.1			Long-Term Debt	11.5	13.4
.0	.0	.5	.0			Deferred Taxes	.7	.6
6.1	2.6	23.9	15.0			All Other Non-Current	9.3	9.1
21.0	29.5	15.5	19.1			Net Worth	27.7	33.9
100.0	100.0	100.0	100.0			Total Liabilties & Net Worth	100.0	100.0
						INCOME DATA		
100.0	100.0	100.0	100.0			Net Sales	100.0	100.0
						Gross Profit		
91.0	88.4	95.1	86.6			Operating Expenses	93.0	92.5
9.0	11.6	4.9	13.4			Operating Profit	7.0	7.5
1.9	.2	2.5	1.6			All Other Expenses (net)	1.7	.6
7.1	11.5	2.3	11.9			Profit Before Taxes	5.4	6.9
						RATIOS		
6.7	3.4	3.0	1.5				2.7	2.7
.8	1.4	1.8	1.1			Current	1.4	1.5
.5	.6	.9	.7				.8	.9
6.7	3.2	2.6	1.4				2.3	2.6
.8	1.4	1.4	.9			Quick	1.3	1.5
.4	.6	.8	.4				.8	.7
0 UND	1 643.9	25 14.4	30 12.2				25 14.5	13 27.7
0 UND	30 12.2	44 8.3	72 5.1			Sales/Receivables	45 8.1	52 7.0
16 23.2	65 5.6	57 6.4	107 3.4				68 5.4	70 5.2
						Cost of Sales/Inventory		
						Cost of Sales/Payables		
14.8	6.8	5.9	6.5				6.1	5.5
-174.9	23.1	10.9	19.5			Sales/Working Capital	21.6	14.3
-29.9	-21.4	-62.6	-12.6				-47.1	-94.3
142.0	71.6	38.4	30.4				23.9	29.8
(11) 32.0	(14) 20.4	(17) 11.3	9.1			EBIT/Interest	(58) 7.2	(58) 7.0
1.4	1.0	-1.1	1.8				1.1	1.9
							14.8	
						Net Profit + Depr., Dep., Amort./Cur. Mat. L/T/D	(13) 2.7	
							.9	
.0	.0	.1	.2				.1	.1
.4	.2	.9	1.2			Fixed/Worth	.4	.5
-.4	2.3	-5.8	-.3				-8.0	13.7
.4	.5	.7	2.3				.9	.6
1.9	1.5	2.3	4.5			Debt/Worth	2.3	1.7
-4.8	11.8	-21.8	-3.6				-30.9	NM
263.8	241.0	43.8					87.2	94.7
(11) 91.6	(17) 75.1	(16) 16.8				% Profit Before Taxes/Tangible Net Worth	(56) 25.7	(58) 30.4
5.3	-11.1	-5.2					3.5	4.0
98.9	52.6	21.0	21.6				32.2	29.8
50.4	35.2	4.7	9.7			% Profit Before Taxes/Total Assets	7.7	9.6
7.2	-.1	-2.8	2.6				-.1	.7
UND	862.3	65.8	58.8				112.6	204.5
202.7	47.3	32.2	25.2			Sales/Net Fixed Assets	36.0	41.7
86.5	23.7	12.7	14.8				19.3	17.2
20.4	6.9	4.2	2.7				4.9	4.7
10.7	3.5	2.8	2.3			Sales/Total Assets	3.3	2.7
6.4	2.1	1.8	.8				2.2	1.6
		.8	.6				.4	.7
		(18) 1.6	1.0			% Depr., Dep., Amort./Sales	(60) 1.0	(46) 1.2
		2.3	2.6				1.6	1.8
							6.0	6.5
						% Officers', Directors' Owners' Comp/Sales	(28) 10.5	(31) 12.0
							16.1	16.5
49277M	166384M	336154M	465918M	216560M	321941M	Net Sales ($)	1891481M	2918938M
4437M	23156M	118994M	217663M	121936M	305790M	Total Assets ($)	1041493M	1028158M

M = $ thousand MM = $ million

See Pages 9 through 22 for Explanation of Ratios and Data

Comparative Historical Data				Current Data Sorted by Sales					
			Type of Statement						
15	12	12	Unqualified		2	1	2	3	4
11	11	8	Reviewed		1		1	4	2
8	7	4	Compiled		1		3		
14	19	13	Tax Returns	1	6	1	3	2	
38	46	39	Other	3	10	4	7	8	7
				13 (4/1-9/30/13)			63 (10/1/13-3/31/14)		
4/1/11-3/31/12 ALL	4/1/12-3/31/13 ALL	4/1/13-3/31/14 ALL		0-1MM	1-3MM	3-5MM	5-10MM	10-25MM	25MM & OVER
86	95	76	NUMBER OF STATEMENTS	4	20	6	16	17	13
%	%	%	**ASSETS**	%	%	%	%	%	%
27.5	24.2	25.2	Cash & Equivalents		23.9		26.5	24.3	13.0
32.3	33.6	31.9	Trade Receivables (net)		21.8		37.6	37.9	37.8
2.1	1.1	1.4	Inventory		.0		1.4	1.5	3.9
5.0	5.5	5.6	All Other Current		6.9		6.8	5.8	5.3
66.9	64.4	64.2	Total Current		52.7		72.3	69.5	60.1
14.6	18.9	16.5	Fixed Assets (net)		24.7		13.5	13.7	11.0
8.9	5.0	7.5	Intangibles (net)		.2		7.7	6.5	21.8
9.6	11.8	11.7	All Other Non-Current		22.4		6.5	10.3	7.2
100.0	100.0	100.0	Total		100.0		100.0	100.0	100.0
			LIABILITIES						
14.0	13.8	13.9	Notes Payable-Short Term		22.3		16.1	6.6	5.9
2.1	2.6	1.6	Cur. Mat.-L.T.D.		.9		.5	2.2	4.5
13.3	13.8	16.1	Trade Payables		10.8		30.2	11.5	21.0
.4	.3	.3	Income Taxes Payable		.0		.1	.0	1.8
21.6	20.8	22.2	All Other Current		15.0		26.7	31.6	23.9
51.4	51.3	54.0	Total Current		48.9		73.6	51.9	57.0
11.4	14.5	11.6	Long-Term Debt		18.4		8.5	10.3	11.2
.1	.5	.2	Deferred Taxes		.0		.0	.7	.0
8.8	9.9	12.0	All Other Non-Current		2.2		21.8	15.3	13.4
28.2	23.7	22.2	Net Worth		30.5		-3.9	21.8	18.3
100.0	100.0	100.0	Total Liabilties & Net Worth		100.0		100.0	100.0	100.0
			INCOME DATA						
100.0	100.0	100.0	Net Sales		100.0		100.0	100.0	100.0
			Gross Profit						
92.9	88.4	91.4	Operating Expenses		91.2		96.7	90.8	94.7
7.1	11.6	8.6	Operating Profit		8.8		3.3	9.2	5.3
1.5	2.4	1.8	All Other Expenses (net)		3.1		.8	1.7	2.3
5.6	9.2	6.9	Profit Before Taxes		5.6		2.5	7.5	3.0
			RATIOS						
3.4	3.1	2.9			3.3		1.5	2.8	1.9
1.7	1.4	1.4	Current		.9		1.1	2.1	1.1
.9	.8	.7			.5		.6	1.1	.6
3.4	2.8	2.6			2.8		1.5	2.7	1.7
1.5	1.4	1.2	Quick		.9		1.1	1.4	.8
.7	.7	.6			.3		.5	.9	.4
1 347.5	**8** 45.1	**2** 213.2			**0** UND		**4** 102.1	**30** 12.1	**31** 11.7
39 9.4	**38** 9.5	**36** 10.1	Sales/Receivables		**7** 53.7		**38** 9.6	**47** 7.7	**64** 5.7
65 5.6	**60** 6.1	**65** 5.6			**38** 9.5		**79** 4.6	**65** 5.6	**72** 5.1
			Cost of Sales/Inventory						
			Cost of Sales/Payables						
6.2	5.6	7.2			9.1		10.3	6.2	7.4
15.0	15.2	17.4	Sales/Working Capital		-124.8		124.3	8.2	38.1
-79.8	-26.6	-26.7			-14.6		-21.9	169.6	-10.9
27.6	48.4	42.8			82.3		39.4	40.3	34.3
(62) 10.1	(62) 13.9	(56) 11.2	EBIT/Interest		(15) 15.0		(13) 10.5	(11) 17.7	(12) 1.9
2.8	2.2	1.0			.8		1.1	1.0	-.2
	2.4	20.4							
	(13) 1.4	(14) 3.3	Net Profit + Depr., Dep., Amort./Cur. Mat. L/T/D						
	.7	.9							
.1	.1	.1			.0		.0	.1	.2
.3	.4	.4	Fixed/Worth		.5		1.4	.4	21.6
NM	14.3	-4.4			3.9		-1.7	-6.2	-.2
.6	.5	.7			.5		2.4	.5	2.1
2.1	2.7	2.6	Debt/Worth		1.4		31.0	1.6	45.4
-9.2	99.5	-13.5			6.4		-3.0	-34.6	-2.1
96.9	102.2	182.9			88.3			63.2	
(62) 19.6	(73) 45.4	(53) 50.9	% Profit Before Taxes/Tangible Net Worth		(16) 46.6			(12) 31.9	
1.0	8.1	1.2			-3.7			8.2	
30.8	42.8	50.0			60.5		24.8	25.0	20.9
10.6	11.9	13.3	% Profit Before Taxes/Total Assets		35.7		9.8	14.2	6.6
.0	1.8	-.2			-1.1		-4.3	-.7	-3.4
175.9	150.4	222.2			643.4		735.2	73.7	75.3
39.3	45.4	45.9	Sales/Net Fixed Assets		56.2		51.5	34.0	28.9
19.4	14.8	20.0			19.3		30.6	14.8	17.9
5.6	5.1	7.0			10.1		9.8	4.0	4.4
3.1	3.0	3.3	Sales/Total Assets		4.3		3.8	2.9	2.5
2.1	1.6	2.0			1.5		2.7	2.2	1.9
.6	.4	.5			.4			.7	.7
(56) .8	(63) 1.2	(47) 1.4	% Depr., Dep., Amort./Sales		(10) 1.0			(13) 1.1	(12) 1.6
1.5	1.9	2.3			5.0			2.2	2.6
6.2	4.5	6.0							
(37) 11.6	(42) 7.5	(18) 9.5	% Officers', Directors' Owners' Comp/Sales						
22.6	12.7	16.6							
1671867M	1658499M	1556234M	Net Sales ($)	2317M	45682M	22372M	112858M	269839M	1103166M
896626M	791327M	791976M	Total Assets ($)	1943M	31072M	6621M	39154M	104621M	608565M

M = $ thousand MM = $ million

See Pages 9 through 22 for Explanation of Ratios and Data

Current Data Sorted by Assets							Comparative Historical Data	
						Type of Statement		
		1			2	Unqualified	6	7
	1	2	1			Reviewed	2	2
		2				Compiled	2	1
4	1	3	1			Tax Returns	8	3
2	5	5	5		2	Other	16	16
	1 (4/1-9/30/13)		36 (10/1/13-3/31/14)				4/1/09-3/31/10 ALL	4/1/10-3/31/11 ALL
0-500M	500M-2MM	2-10MM	10-50MM	50-100MM	100-250MM			
6	7	13	7		4	NUMBER OF STATEMENTS	34	29
%	%	%	%	%	%	**ASSETS**	%	%
		26.5		DATA NOT AVAILABLE		Cash & Equivalents	12.9	20.8
		39.0				Trade Receivables (net)	32.2	32.3
		1.3				Inventory	2.4	2.5
		.9				All Other Current	1.8	2.9
		67.8				Total Current	49.4	58.5
		7.9				Fixed Assets (net)	21.4	15.4
		5.9				Intangibles (net)	17.4	18.4
		18.4				All Other Non-Current	11.8	7.7
		100.0				Total	100.0	100.0
						LIABILITIES		
		1.3				Notes Payable-Short Term	17.2	15.4
		1.1				Cur. Mat.-L.T.D.	2.2	1.6
		31.4				Trade Payables	16.3	20.3
		.1				Income Taxes Payable	2.7	.1
		35.2				All Other Current	14.9	26.5
		69.1				Total Current	53.2	63.9
		7.6				Long-Term Debt	18.5	10.8
		.0				Deferred Taxes	.8	.2
		4.9				All Other Non-Current	7.0	3.4
		18.4				Net Worth	20.5	21.7
		100.0				Total Liabilties & Net Worth	100.0	100.0
						INCOME DATA		
		100.0				Net Sales	100.0	100.0
						Gross Profit		
		93.4				Operating Expenses	99.3	94.0
		6.6				Operating Profit	.7	6.0
		.9				All Other Expenses (net)	1.9	1.2
		5.7				Profit Before Taxes	-1.1	4.8
						RATIOS		
		1.7					1.5	1.9
		.9				Current	1.1	1.1
		.8					.7	.6
		1.6					1.4	1.5
		.9				Quick	.9	1.0
		.8					.6	.6
		24 15.1					**12** 31.0	**12** 30.2
		65 5.6				Sales/Receivables	**52** 7.0	**46** 8.0
		87 4.2					**77** 4.8	**85** 4.3
						Cost of Sales/Inventory		
						Cost of Sales/Payables		
		19.6					9.2	7.2
		-77.3				Sales/Working Capital	323.3	50.6
		-11.1					-14.2	-15.8
							4.6	21.8
						EBIT/Interest	(26) -.5	(21) 2.6
							-7.7	-4.8
						Net Profit + Depr., Dep., Amort./Cur. Mat. L/T/D		
		.1					.4	.2
		1.7				Fixed/Worth	2.3	.5
		-.8					-1.0	-12.6
		1.9					1.2	1.7
		12.1				Debt/Worth	15.4	4.4
		-16.5					-4.2	-11.5
							66.1	188.0
						% Profit Before Taxes/Tangible Net Worth	(20) 1.2	(19) 36.9
							-102.5	-12.2
		30.2					9.5	33.7
		25.3				% Profit Before Taxes/Total Assets	-.9	7.7
		.2					-13.7	-.5
		114.0					87.5	121.9
		61.8				Sales/Net Fixed Assets	21.6	29.3
		33.3					7.6	9.2
		5.1					4.7	4.1
		2.5				Sales/Total Assets	2.3	2.3
		1.8					1.3	1.5
		.3					1.7	.6
		(10) .5				% Depr., Dep., Amort./Sales	(18) 2.4	(18) 2.0
		1.7					4.3	5.3
							4.0	
						% Officers', Directors' Owners' Comp/Sales	(13) 7.4	
							9.3	
17353M	38444M	210819M	365092M		1139936M	Net Sales ($)	994235M	1365000M
1317M	6918M	71249M	184443M		693882M	Total Assets ($)	736528M	697137M

M = $ thousand MM = $ million

See Pages 9 through 22 for Explanation of Ratios and Data

Comparative Historical Data				Current Data Sorted by Sales					
			Type of Statement						
4	8	3	Unqualified				1		2
3	3	4	Reviewed				1	2	1
3	1	2	Compiled					1	1
6	8	9	Tax Returns	1	2	2	2	1	1
16	10	19	Other		2	3	5	4	5
4/1/11-3/31/12 ALL	**4/1/12-3/31/13 ALL**	**4/1/13-3/31/14 ALL**		**1 (4/1-9/30/13)**			**36 (10/1/13-3/31/14)**		
				0-1MM	**1-3MM**	**3-5MM**	**5-10MM**	**10-25MM**	**25MM & OVER**
32	30	37	**NUMBER OF STATEMENTS**	1	4	5	9	8	10
%	%	%	**ASSETS**	%	%	%	%	%	%
21.7	31.6	26.8	Cash & Equivalents						31.8
29.5	31.1	33.8	Trade Receivables (net)						34.0
2.4	4.4	2.5	Inventory						1.4
2.9	1.5	3.2	All Other Current						3.6
56.6	68.5	66.4	Total Current						70.7
16.0	12.2	9.1	Fixed Assets (net)						5.6
13.8	9.5	11.1	Intangibles (net)						15.6
13.6	9.8	13.4	All Other Non-Current						8.1
100.0	100.0	100.0	Total						100.0
			LIABILITIES						
10.1	24.4	17.2	Notes Payable-Short Term						.0
1.1	1.0	1.5	Cur. Mat.-L.T.D.						1.0
16.9	22.8	24.4	Trade Payables						35.8
.1	.1	.0	Income Taxes Payable						.0
24.7	17.2	19.4	All Other Current						20.7
52.9	65.4	62.6	Total Current						57.5
9.1	6.5	5.8	Long-Term Debt						7.0
.8	.6	.5	Deferred Taxes						1.4
9.3	6.9	8.4	All Other Non-Current						15.0
27.9	20.6	22.7	Net Worth						19.1
100.0	100.0	100.0	Total Liabilties & Net Worth						100.0
			INCOME DATA						
100.0	100.0	100.0	Net Sales						100.0
			Gross Profit						
93.3	92.6	92.5	Operating Expenses						96.6
6.7	7.4	7.5	Operating Profit						3.4
1.1	1.4	.6	All Other Expenses (net)						1.0
5.7	6.0	6.9	Profit Before Taxes						2.4
			RATIOS						
1.9	2.7	2.8							1.9
1.3	1.4	1.3	Current						1.2
.8	1.0	.8							.9
1.7	2.4	2.4							1.5
1.0	1.2	1.1	Quick						1.1
.7	1.0	.8							.9
15 24.3	**11** 34.4	**4** 81.2							**12** 29.9
33 11.0	**51** 7.2	**34** 10.7	Sales/Receivables						**42** 8.6
87 4.2	**76** 4.8	**68** 5.4							**76** 4.8
			Cost of Sales/Inventory						
			Cost of Sales/Payables						
10.6	4.5	5.3							5.3
29.4	17.5	51.5	Sales/Working Capital						31.8
-25.8	NM	-16.1							-68.7
74.0	159.6	77.2							
(24) 8.2	(21) 9.0	(18) 4.1	EBIT/Interest						
.7	-2.9	-.5							
			Net Profit + Depr., Dep., Amort./Cur. Mat. L/T/D						
.1	.1	.1							.6
.6	.2	.3	Fixed/Worth						1.8
26.5	1.2	NM							-.5
1.2	.7	.8							10.4
2.4	1.8	3.8	Debt/Worth						86.0
NM	NM	-16.5							-12.6
107.9	143.7	119.7							
(24) 59.0	(23) 52.7	(27) 71.3	% Profit Before Taxes/Tangible Net Worth						
12.9	8.1	10.8							
42.0	36.8	31.4							18.5
13.9	13.5	12.7	% Profit Before Taxes/Total Assets						7.7
-.2	-.2	-.2							-.5
164.3	150.9	189.5							225.9
56.2	33.8	81.1	Sales/Net Fixed Assets						128.4
11.0	16.0	21.4							15.0
5.2	4.5	6.3							4.9
2.5	2.8	3.4	Sales/Total Assets						3.4
1.5	1.2	1.3							1.0
.3	.2	.2							
(16) .6	(20) .4	(20) .4	% Depr., Dep., Amort./Sales						
3.0	1.9	1.3							
2.7		3.5							
(10) 7.0		(13) 9.2	% Officers', Directors' Owners' Comp/Sales						
12.4		22.0							
1535626M	**2415382M**	**1771644M**	Net Sales ($)	**72M**	**7824M**	**21019M**	**69604M**	**118534M**	**1554591M**
804544M	**1027241M**	**957809M**	Total Assets ($)	**187M**	**1205M**	**26569M**	**34746M**	**73924M**	**821178M**

M = $ thousand MM = $ million

See Pages 9 through 22 for Explanation of Ratios and Data

Current Data Sorted by Assets							Comparative Historical Data	
						Type of Statement		
		2	2		3	Unqualified	9	13
		5	4			Reviewed	13	9
	2	4	2			Compiled	12	8
11	9	5				Tax Returns	14	8
4	7	17	2	1	5	Other	24	31
	5 (4/1-9/30/13)		80 (10/1/13-3/31/14)				4/1/09-3/31/10 ALL	4/1/10-3/31/11 ALL
0-500M	**500M-2MM**	**2-10MM**	**10-50MM**	**50-100MM**	**100-250MM**			
15	18	33	10	1	8	**NUMBER OF STATEMENTS**	72	69
%	%	%	%	%	%	**ASSETS**	%	%
25.0	21.2	12.1	10.2			Cash & Equivalents	12.3	12.3
11.4	16.6	23.3	14.2			Trade Receivables (net)	21.9	21.4
2.7	2.5	7.4	6.0			Inventory	7.3	6.6
4.7	1.3	2.7	2.8			All Other Current	5.5	5.8
43.8	41.6	45.5	33.1			Total Current	47.0	46.0
44.4	46.2	40.6	43.5			Fixed Assets (net)	39.0	34.1
4.4	3.6	4.9	8.3			Intangibles (net)	6.4	10.4
7.5	8.6	8.9	15.1			All Other Non-Current	7.6	9.6
100.0	100.0	100.0	100.0			Total	100.0	100.0
						LIABILITIES		
8.6	2.4	10.2	.0			Notes Payable-Short Term	10.2	7.5
11.8	6.5	2.8	3.6			Cur. Mat.-L.T.D.	4.9	4.5
7.9	8.5	11.9	3.5			Trade Payables	12.6	11.9
.0	.2	.1	.4			Income Taxes Payable	.0	.1
13.5	16.9	11.4	13.8			All Other Current	14.0	12.2
41.8	34.5	36.5	21.3			Total Current	41.7	36.2
36.1	46.5	19.1	26.0			Long-Term Debt	41.3	34.4
.0	.0	.1	.0			Deferred Taxes	.3	.3
42.2	4.6	6.0	9.5			All Other Non-Current	4.3	9.1
-20.1	14.4	38.2	43.2			Net Worth	12.5	20.0
100.0	100.0	100.0	100.0			Total Liabilties & Net Worth	100.0	100.0
						INCOME DATA		
100.0	100.0	100.0	100.0			Net Sales	100.0	100.0
						Gross Profit		
84.4	81.0	85.0	85.9			Operating Expenses	91.5	90.7
15.6	19.0	15.0	14.1			Operating Profit	8.5	9.3
1.1	8.3	2.8	5.5			All Other Expenses (net)	4.3	3.6
14.5	10.7	12.3	8.6			Profit Before Taxes	4.1	5.7
						RATIOS		
1.6	2.6	2.4	2.9				2.0	2.2
.8	1.3	.9	1.9			Current	1.1	1.3
.4	.8	.7	1.1				.9	.8
1.3	2.6	2.2	2.6				1.6	1.5
.6	1.2	.8	1.5			Quick	(71) .9	1.0
.3	.7	.3	.8				.4	.5
0 UND	**0** UND	**15** 25.1	**29** 12.7				**17** 20.9	**20** 18.3
0 UND	**23** 15.8	**42** 8.7	**49** 7.4			Sales/Receivables	**39** 9.3	**42** 8.6
22 16.7	**42** 8.7	**63** 5.8	**65** 5.6				**57** 6.4	**61** 6.0
						Cost of Sales/Inventory		
						Cost of Sales/Payables		
20.9	5.1	5.6	4.1				6.9	4.8
-999.8	28.3	-60.2	10.9			Sales/Working Capital	32.2	22.7
-19.1	-17.8	-9.9	NM				-45.7	-17.3
56.9	12.9	42.1					4.8	7.7
(12) 9.9	(12) 6.0	(31) 9.4				EBIT/Interest	(62) 1.8	(58) 2.0
.7	2.2	4.6					.2	.4
						Net Profit + Depr., Dep., Amort./Cur. Mat. L/T/D		
1.5	.7	.5	.5				.6	.3
-108.7	2.7	1.3	.9			Fixed/Worth	1.7	2.6
-.8	-1.0	2.7	NM				-14.6	-1.3
5.7	.7	1.0	.4				1.5	1.0
-127.3	2.0	2.1	2.0			Debt/Worth	5.0	3.5
-3.1	-5.4	7.7	NM				-16.4	-4.2
	42.1	80.1					46.6	39.7
	(11) 4.7	(28) 33.9				% Profit Before Taxes/Tangible Net Worth	(51) 10.8	(47) 18.4
	-13.6	13.9					-11.8	.7
78.8	25.0	18.1	14.4				10.1	16.0
36.9	10.5	10.2	8.3			% Profit Before Taxes/Total Assets	1.4	3.6
.5	.2	4.3	2.5				-2.7	-1.0
29.9	14.8	34.0	14.4				28.3	26.2
16.3	1.8	5.1	1.5			Sales/Net Fixed Assets	9.7	6.3
2.5	.6	.7	.8				1.0	1.1
6.0	2.5	2.9	1.7				2.7	2.4
4.0	1.1	1.4	.8			Sales/Total Assets	1.6	1.5
2.1	.5	.6	.5				.7	.6
	2.1	1.1					1.1	1.1
	(14) 6.4	(25) 2.9				% Depr., Dep., Amort./Sales	(59) 3.9	(58) 3.6
	20.0	12.4					14.4	13.0
5.9		2.1					3.2	4.3
(10) 8.6		(17) 4.4				% Officers', Directors' Owners' Comp/Sales	(28) 5.2	(19) 7.4
13.4		7.2					8.5	10.9
22230M	40309M	323063M	238620M	12850M	1118704M	Net Sales ($)	1846735M	1733658M
3818M	19935M	171988M	187128M	53524M	1174637M	Total Assets ($)	1220077M	1882220M

M = $ thousand MM = $ million

See Pages 9 through 22 for Explanation of Ratios and Data

Comparative Historical Data / Current Data Sorted by Sales

4/1/11-3/31/12 ALL	4/1/12-3/31/13 ALL	4/1/13-3/31/14 ALL	Type of Statement	0-1MM	1-3MM	3-5MM	5-10MM	10-25MM	25MM & OVER
8	4	7	Unqualified				2	1	4
14	9	9	Reviewed		1	1	3	3	1
10	9	8	Compiled	1	1	2	1	1	2
13	26	25	Tax Returns	9	8	3	2	2	1
44	33	36	Other	9	7	1	8	3	8
				5 (4/1-9/30/13)			80 (10/1/13-3/31/14)		
89	81	85	NUMBER OF STATEMENTS	19	17	7	16	10	16
%	%	%	**ASSETS**	%	%	%	%	%	%
16.0	15.9	15.8	Cash & Equivalents	11.5	18.5		13.4	21.9	13.0
23.7	20.9	17.5	Trade Receivables (net)	4.8	16.3		29.4	25.8	23.4
7.5	6.2	4.9	Inventory	2.0	1.1		7.7	6.1	8.9
3.8	2.2	3.4	All Other Current	1.7	3.4		1.2	2.0	7.1
51.0	45.3	41.5	Total Current	19.9	39.3		51.6	55.8	52.4
33.6	40.0	41.2	Fixed Assets (net)	66.1	48.6		33.4	28.8	18.0
6.2	5.7	8.5	Intangibles (net)	6.1	8.2		4.0	9.2	19.0
9.3	9.1	8.8	All Other Non-Current	7.9	3.9		11.0	6.1	10.6
100.0	100.0	100.0	Total	100.0	100.0		100.0	100.0	100.0
			LIABILITIES						
8.9	8.7	6.2	Notes Payable-Short Term	9.5	4.1		5.7	6.0	4.2
5.3	4.1	5.3	Cur. Mat.-L.T.D.	6.6	7.2		3.4	1.3	2.5
12.3	11.1	8.7	Trade Payables	2.9	7.1		18.3	13.1	7.9
.1	.0	.1	Income Taxes Payable	.0	.0		.5	.0	.2
12.7	11.5	13.0	All Other Current	4.7	14.8		17.3	10.1	19.9
39.4	35.6	33.4	Total Current	23.7	33.2		45.1	30.5	34.6
37.1	34.9	34.7	Long-Term Debt	43.7	51.5		16.9	17.1	39.1
.3	.3	.1	Deferred Taxes	.0	.0		.3	.0	.0
16.9	9.0	12.5	All Other Non-Current	24.3	13.4		9.1	1.4	8.6
6.2	20.2	19.4	Net Worth	8.2	1.8		28.6	51.0	17.7
100.0	100.0	100.0	Total Liabilties & Net Worth	100.0	100.0		100.0	100.0	100.0
			INCOME DATA						
100.0	100.0	100.0	Net Sales	100.0	100.0		100.0	100.0	100.0
			Gross Profit						
88.6	86.6	84.3	Operating Expenses	74.4	77.7		91.7	90.7	88.9
11.4	13.4	15.7	Operating Profit	25.6	22.3		8.3	9.3	11.1
3.8	2.7	4.7	All Other Expenses (net)	9.3	5.1		1.7	1.6	5.4
7.6	10.6	11.0	Profit Before Taxes	16.3	17.2		6.7	7.7	5.7
			RATIOS						
2.6	3.6	2.5	Current	1.7	2.3		2.5	4.5	2.2
1.4	1.5	1.3		.8	1.3		1.1	2.8	1.4
.8	.7	.7		.5	.7		.8	1.3	1.2
2.1	3.0	2.1	Quick	1.7	2.0		2.3	3.6	1.8
1.0	1.1	.9		.7	1.2		.8	2.6	1.3
.5	.4	.5		.4	.3		.6	.8	.7
18 19.8	24 15.1	0 UND	Sales/Receivables	0 UND	0 UND		39 9.4	19 19.7	27 13.7
38 9.7	35 10.5	28 12.9		0 UND	24 15.5		50 7.3	42 8.6	49 7.5
54 6.7	51 7.2	60 6.1		27 13.6	65 5.6		73 5.0	61 6.0	62 5.9
			Cost of Sales/Inventory						
			Cost of Sales/Payables						
5.9	4.9	8.2	Sales/Working Capital	11.1	4.3		5.7	4.2	6.6
18.0	18.2	24.2		-32.7	22.1		NM	16.2	14.0
-19.8	-15.9	-16.7		-8.3	-23.5		-11.8	NM	26.5
29.2	12.7	29.0	EBIT/Interest	10.2	13.5		43.8		46.8
(67) 4.0	(65) 5.9	(70) 7.2		(13) 1.9	(14) 6.5		7.2		(13) 14.6
1.1	2.0	2.3		.9	4.0		3.4		.2
10.4		21.6	Net Profit + Depr., Dep., Amort./Cur. Mat. L/T/D						
(13) 3.1		(10) 6.3							
1.3		1.4							
.2	.4	.6	Fixed/Worth	1.6	1.5		.7	.1	.1
1.5	1.6	1.7		5.3	-108.7		1.6	.8	.5
-3.7	-5.1	-8.3		-7.9	-.9		NM	1.5	-.4
.6	.5	1.2	Debt/Worth	.8	1.3		1.2	.4	1.5
3.0	2.3	3.2		5.7	-127.3		2.7	.9	3.0
-7.2	-6.8	-13.2		-11.1	-2.9		NM	5.2	-1.7
63.6	53.7	89.2	% Profit Before Taxes/Tangible Net Worth	24.5			46.2		132.8
(63) 26.2	(58) 24.0	(57) 24.5		(11) 4.7			(12) 22.1		(11) 32.6
9.3	8.6	7.0		-3.2			11.8		17.5
25.9	21.8	21.2	% Profit Before Taxes/Total Assets	27.2	30.5		12.4	21.9	30.4
9.1	9.3	10.0		4.6	7.8		8.4	12.1	10.4
.5	2.9	2.0		-.9	1.1		2.8	6.3	2.1
44.0	35.4	19.9	Sales/Net Fixed Assets	2.5	17.2		38.6	41.3	26.0
10.3	5.6	3.8		1.1	3.6		6.8	8.9	13.2
1.5	1.2	1.0		.4	.6		1.8	1.6	3.2
3.3	3.8	2.8	Sales/Total Assets	1.9	3.7		2.8	3.2	2.9
1.7	1.5	1.3		.7	1.3		1.7	2.6	1.4
.9	.7	.6		.2	.4		.8	.8	.7
.8	1.0	1.4	% Depr., Dep., Amort./Sales	1.9	1.6		1.0		1.0
(64) 4.0	(61) 3.3	(63) 2.9		(15) 3.7	(13) 5.6		(12) 3.7		(11) 1.9
13.0	10.9	13.2		17.8	23.5		6.1		2.7
3.2	2.5	3.8	% Officers', Directors' Owners' Comp/Sales						
(36) 5.6	(38) 4.6	(32) 5.7							
10.6	8.5	9.0							
1718604M	864234M	1755776M	Net Sales ($)	9741M	29233M	26801M	119370M	147714M	1422917M
1205510M	816709M	1611030M	Total Assets ($)	21834M	49029M	19057M	99499M	122149M	1299462M

M = $ thousand MM = $ million

See Pages 9 through 22 for Explanation of Ratios and Data

Current Data Sorted by Assets							Comparative Historical Data	
						Type of Statement		
	1	2	7	3	1	Unqualified	12	14
	1	12	2			Reviewed	28	25
1	3	5	2			Compiled	14	11
6	6	6				Tax Returns	19	14
	10	19	13	1	1	Other	51	44
	19 (4/1-9/30/13)		83 (10/1/13-3/31/14)				4/1/09-3/31/10	4/1/10-3/31/11
0-500M	**500M-2MM**	**2-10MM**	**10-50MM**	**50-100MM**	**100-250MM**		**ALL**	**ALL**
7	21	44	24	4	2	**NUMBER OF STATEMENTS**	124	108
%	%	%	%	%	%	**ASSETS**	%	%
	28.5	19.3	17.0			Cash & Equivalents	16.3	14.2
	20.1	31.1	25.0			Trade Receivables (net)	31.6	30.9
	3.2	3.0	5.7			Inventory	3.6	3.3
	1.0	2.8	5.5			All Other Current	4.7	3.8
	52.7	56.1	53.1			Total Current	56.2	52.2
	22.7	31.8	21.2			Fixed Assets (net)	24.8	26.0
	9.2	4.6	17.9			Intangibles (net)	12.4	14.0
	15.3	7.4	7.8			All Other Non-Current	6.5	7.7
	100.0	100.0	100.0			Total	100.0	100.0
						LIABILITIES		
	12.7	4.2	5.3			Notes Payable-Short Term	7.0	6.9
	4.5	4.1	4.7			Cur. Mat.-L.T.D.	7.8	4.2
	19.3	15.6	17.3			Trade Payables	15.3	17.8
	.3	.3	.1			Income Taxes Payable	.3	.1
	18.2	22.0	30.8			All Other Current	17.7	18.7
	55.0	46.2	58.1			Total Current	48.1	47.8
	19.9	17.7	15.7			Long-Term Debt	22.0	24.0
	.0	.4	.9			Deferred Taxes	.3	.5
	12.4	4.8	4.8			All Other Non-Current	9.3	9.7
	12.7	30.9	20.4			Net Worth	20.4	18.0
	100.0	100.0	100.0			Total Liabilties & Net Worth	100.0	100.0
						INCOME DATA		
	100.0	100.0	100.0			Net Sales	100.0	100.0
						Gross Profit		
	92.0	91.6	96.3			Operating Expenses	95.0	93.5
	8.0	8.4	3.7			Operating Profit	5.0	6.5
	.6	2.1	.9			All Other Expenses (net)	1.8	2.4
	7.4	6.3	2.8			Profit Before Taxes	3.2	4.1
						RATIOS		
	2.2	1.8	1.4				1.9	1.7
	1.2	1.1	1.0			Current	1.3	1.1
	.6	.8	.8				.9	.7
	2.2	1.6	1.1				1.6	1.5
	1.0	1.0	.9			Quick	1.0	.9
	.5	.7	.6				.7	.6
	2 147.4	**14** 26.0	**29** 12.4				**28** 13.2	**22** 17.0
	12 31.6	**41** 8.8	**43** 8.4			Sales/Receivables	**45** 8.1	**46** 8.0
	34 10.8	**62** 5.9	**55** 6.6				**69** 5.3	**65** 5.6
						Cost of Sales/Inventory		
						Cost of Sales/Payables		
	22.1	8.0	13.3				7.4	10.0
	73.9	53.7	215.8			Sales/Working Capital	34.5	65.2
	-13.2	-46.1	-16.0				-43.6	-15.6
	33.6	46.6	32.2				12.2	10.0
	(14) 6.3	(33) 12.6	(22) 6.3			EBIT/Interest	(108) 3.2	(89) 2.2
	-2.0	3.3	2.6				.9	.1
		10.0	5.5				3.5	5.2
		(10) 3.8	(11) 3.7			Net Profit + Depr., Dep., Amort./Cur. Mat. L/T/D	(23) 1.4	(17) 2.3
		1.2	.7				.3	1.3
	.2	.4	.7				.3	.4
	.9	1.5	2.0			Fixed/Worth	1.4	2.3
	-1.9	2.9	-2.3				-1.9	-1.1
	.5	1.3	2.5				1.2	1.5
	2.5	2.9	6.6			Debt/Worth	3.6	4.8
	-4.9	8.1	-11.3				-6.7	-4.8
	188.8	69.6	132.4				70.8	63.7
	(13) 60.0	(38) 35.2	(17) 56.3			% Profit Before Taxes/Tangible Net Worth	(84) 24.9	(71) 21.0
	.7	11.1	23.9				1.6	.6
	47.7	19.1	16.8				15.9	11.8
	11.9	7.6	8.7			% Profit Before Taxes/Total Assets	5.2	5.4
	-6.9	2.3	3.0				-2.0	-.2
	555.7	29.5	29.4				33.4	28.5
	59.2	12.1	11.4			Sales/Net Fixed Assets	12.6	14.3
	13.3	5.4	5.7				6.1	6.4
	8.4	3.4	2.8				3.3	3.5
	6.7	2.4	2.1			Sales/Total Assets	2.4	2.3
	2.3	1.8	1.2				1.5	1.4
	1.8	.6	1.3				1.2	1.2
	(11) 3.0	(40) 1.9	(22) 2.0			% Depr., Dep., Amort./Sales	(94) 2.8	(85) 2.3
	6.9	4.7	5.4				5.2	4.6
		2.0					1.9	2.2
		(15) 2.8				% Officers', Directors' Owners' Comp/Sales	(44) 4.9	(32) 5.4
		9.0					9.3	9.1
9514M	147976M	705315M	1187770M	246971M	562234M	Net Sales ($)	3411150M	3175894M
1311M	22511M	250039M	579191M	257519M	374339M	Total Assets ($)	2114650M	1997676M

M = $ thousand MM = $ million

See Pages 9 through 22 for Explanation of Ratios and Data

Comparative Historical Data / Current Data Sorted by Sales

Type of Statement	4/1/11-3/31/12 ALL	4/1/12-3/31/13 ALL	4/1/13-3/31/14 ALL	0-1MM	1-3MM	3-5MM	5-10MM	10-25MM	25MM & OVER
				19 (4/1-9/30/13)			83 (10/1/13-3/31/14)		
Unqualified	13	15	14				1	3	10
Reviewed	21	16	15		1		3	7	4
Compiled	16	15	11	2			3	4	2
Tax Returns	30	19	18	4	6	1	3	4	
Other	54	58	44	2	1	4	9	10	18
NUMBER OF STATEMENTS	134	123	102	8	8	5	19	28	34
ASSETS	%	%	%	%	%	%	%	%	%
Cash & Equivalents	16.5	14.9	19.3				35.5	18.2	16.8
Trade Receivables (net)	27.9	29.4	27.3				27.1	32.0	26.1
Inventory	2.4	3.0	3.9				4.8	2.3	6.9
All Other Current	3.2	3.1	3.0				2.0	1.9	5.2
Total Current	50.0	50.4	53.5				69.4	54.5	54.9
Fixed Assets (net)	24.7	24.2	25.3				16.7	24.9	21.9
Intangibles (net)	14.0	16.2	12.2				4.9	9.9	17.5
All Other Non-Current	11.2	9.1	9.0				9.0	10.8	5.7
Total	100.0	100.0	100.0				100.0	100.0	100.0
LIABILITIES									
Notes Payable-Short Term	10.6	8.7	8.4				4.3	6.7	5.0
Cur. Mat.-L.T.D.	7.2	4.2	4.7				5.2	4.3	4.7
Trade Payables	16.5	19.1	18.5				10.8	24.3	17.1
Income Taxes Payable	.1	.1	.2				.1	.7	.1
All Other Current	19.2	20.4	24.1				38.3	14.6	28.5
Total Current	53.6	52.5	56.0				58.7	50.6	55.4
Long-Term Debt	21.6	21.1	18.9				15.7	10.9	20.8
Deferred Taxes	.3	.5	.6				.0	.8	1.2
All Other Non-Current	15.0	13.4	7.2				3.2	9.1	5.7
Net Worth	9.6	12.5	17.3				22.5	28.6	16.8
Total Liabilties & Net Worth	100.0	100.0	100.0				100.0	100.0	100.0
INCOME DATA									
Net Sales	100.0	100.0	100.0				100.0	100.0	100.0
Gross Profit									
Operating Expenses	93.2	91.6	94.2				96.4	94.7	96.8
Operating Profit	6.8	8.4	5.8				3.6	5.3	3.2
All Other Expenses (net)	1.6	2.3	1.6				-.9	.8	1.2
Profit Before Taxes	5.2	6.1	4.2				4.5	4.4	2.0
RATIOS									
Current	2.0	1.7	1.6				2.0	1.5	1.4
	1.1	1.0	1.0				1.5	1.0	1.0
	.6	.7	.8				1.2	.8	.8
Quick	1.7	1.5	1.3				2.0	1.5	1.1
	.9	.9	.9				1.4	.8	.9
	.5	.6	.6				1.0	.7	.6
Sales/Receivables	**13** 28.0	**17** 21.7	**13** 29.0				**6** 56.2	**15** 24.5	**21** 17.3
	36 10.1	**42** 8.6	**35** 10.4				**24** 15.4	**50** 7.3	**40** 9.1
	62 5.9	**63** 5.8	**58** 6.3				**55** 6.6	**61** 6.0	**61** 6.0
Cost of Sales/Inventory									
Cost of Sales/Payables									
Sales/Working Capital	8.4	11.4	13.2				6.7	23.1	16.9
	144.4	132.5	75.6				25.8	399.5	441.4
	-10.6	-15.7	-18.6				65.7	-18.4	-21.3
EBIT/Interest	18.9	22.3	28.5				340.0	26.6	20.7
	(109) 5.3	(100) 5.1	(79) 6.5				(11) 72.0	(24) 10.6	(32) 5.3
	1.4	1.5	.8				2.3	1.2	.2
Net Profit + Depr., Dep., Amort./Cur. Mat. L/T/D	5.3	13.5	5.5						5.5
	(25) 1.8	(26) 2.9	(24) 2.1						(15) 2.0
	1.2	1.0	.8						.7
Fixed/Worth	.3	.4	.4				.1	.3	.8
	1.5	2.2	1.7				.4	1.6	2.9
	-1.3	-.9	-3.8				2.1	NM	-.7
Debt/Worth	1.2	1.5	1.5				.5	1.3	3.3
	8.6	5.6	4.5				1.9	3.0	7.6
	-4.0	-4.6	-7.3				15.8	NM	-5.7
% Profit Before Taxes/Tangible Net Worth	67.7	80.1	93.4				99.5	81.2	132.4
	(80) 27.7	(78) 37.3	(71) 38.1				(16) 50.4	(21) 37.0	(21) 48.6
	6.3	10.4	19.1				7.9	9.5	25.8
% Profit Before Taxes/Total Assets	19.3	17.2	19.0				36.6	23.0	16.6
	7.0	7.0	7.6				8.0	9.1	7.7
	.2	1.4	.1				-.2	.8	-.5
Sales/Net Fixed Assets	88.6	60.3	49.4				76.1	77.9	34.6
	18.2	17.1	15.2				26.9	13.2	12.4
	6.9	7.5	6.4				12.6	4.7	7.7
Sales/Total Assets	4.5	3.9	4.0				8.0	3.5	3.9
	2.6	2.4	2.4				3.1	2.4	2.3
	1.7	1.4	1.6				2.1	1.7	1.5
% Depr., Dep., Amort./Sales	.9	.8	1.0				.7	.5	1.1
	(101) 2.2	(100) 1.9	(79) 2.0				(14) 2.6	(24) 1.9	(28) 1.9
	4.1	4.8	5.3				4.5	5.3	5.2
% Officers', Directors' Owners' Comp/Sales	2.3	1.9	2.1					1.9	
	(55) 5.6	(35) 3.8	(30) 5.6					(10) 2.8	
	9.0	11.4	9.3					7.8	
Net Sales ($)	2663054M	3064585M	2859780M	3214M	13678M	20508M	132085M	458604M	2231691M
Total Assets ($)	1465957M	1677939M	1484910M	12503M	15279M	6219M	43422M	231900M	1175587M

M = $ thousand MM = $ million

See Pages 9 through 22 for Explanation of Ratios and Data

Current Data Sorted by Assets							Comparative Historical Data	
						Type of Statement		
			2	1	3	Unqualified	14	8
	1	3	5			Reviewed	15	13
		4				Compiled	2	3
4	3	2	1			Tax Returns	7	8
2	4	9	6	2	2	Other	32	22
8 (4/1-9/30/13)			46 (10/1/13-3/31/14)				4/1/09-3/31/10	4/1/10-3/31/11
0-500M	500M-2MM	2-10MM	10-50MM	50-100MM	100-250MM		ALL	ALL
6	8	18	14	3	5	NUMBER OF STATEMENTS	70	54
%	%	%	%	%	%	**ASSETS**	%	%
		22.7	18.2			Cash & Equivalents	13.5	14.4
		41.4	34.4			Trade Receivables (net)	35.0	32.8
		10.2	10.5			Inventory	8.4	8.2
		2.2	4.7			All Other Current	5.0	6.7
		76.6	67.8			Total Current	61.8	62.0
		16.8	19.3			Fixed Assets (net)	21.6	17.8
		2.5	2.1			Intangibles (net)	12.7	12.8
		4.1	10.8			All Other Non-Current	3.8	7.4
		100.0	100.0			Total	100.0	100.0
						LIABILITIES		
		9.7	5.1			Notes Payable-Short Term	12.4	14.3
		2.0	7.8			Cur. Mat.-L.T.D.	6.9	9.5
		26.1	19.9			Trade Payables	20.2	18.4
		.2	.1			Income Taxes Payable	.3	.1
		13.5	11.8			All Other Current	19.9	19.8
		51.4	44.7			Total Current	59.7	62.1
		6.4	4.9			Long-Term Debt	16.1	15.9
		.5	2.0			Deferred Taxes	.7	.6
		8.9	3.3			All Other Non-Current	5.5	6.8
		32.7	45.0			Net Worth	18.0	14.7
		100.0	100.0			Total Liabilties & Net Worth	100.0	100.0
						INCOME DATA		
		100.0	100.0			Net Sales	100.0	100.0
						Gross Profit		
		90.5	96.4			Operating Expenses	94.8	93.7
		9.5	3.6			Operating Profit	5.2	6.3
		.7	1.4			All Other Expenses (net)	1.9	2.1
		8.7	2.1			Profit Before Taxes	3.4	4.2
						RATIOS		
		2.1	3.3				2.3	1.9
		1.5	1.5			Current	1.2	1.3
		1.1	1.0				.8	.9
		2.1	2.1				1.7	1.6
		1.2	1.3			Quick	.9	1.0
		.9	.8				.5	.5
		22 16.9	**31** 11.9				**24** 15.3	**22** 16.8
		47 7.8	**61** 6.0			Sales/Receivables	**42** 8.6	**40** 9.2
		70 5.2	**94** 3.9				**63** 5.8	**56** 6.5
						Cost of Sales/Inventory		
						Cost of Sales/Payables		
		8.5	4.2				7.0	7.4
		12.9	12.4			Sales/Working Capital	31.8	26.5
		NM	NM				-27.1	-22.5
		51.9	41.3				13.5	12.9
		(13) 20.6	(11) 8.7			EBIT/Interest	(62) 2.6	(48) 4.9
		4.9	6.1				.6	2.0
							2.2	
						Net Profit + Depr., Dep., Amort./Cur. Mat. L/T/D	(11) .3	
							-.4	
		.0	.1				.2	.1
		.1	.4			Fixed/Worth	1.2	.6
		1.3	1.5				-1.0	-3.7
		1.1	.4				1.1	.7
		2.3	1.5			Debt/Worth	3.4	2.6
		5.3	29.0				-4.6	-44.5
		118.8	48.8				64.9	77.0
		(17) 44.2	(12) 24.8			% Profit Before Taxes/Tangible Net Worth	(48) 17.4	(39) 26.2
		14.3	8.6				2.9	11.8
		25.5	12.4				12.9	17.0
		11.5	7.9			% Profit Before Taxes/Total Assets	3.6	8.2
		3.1	1.8				-.7	2.4
		359.7	58.8				82.9	99.1
		96.5	16.9			Sales/Net Fixed Assets	23.2	29.9
		13.0	3.3				7.3	10.1
		4.3	2.6				4.2	4.6
		3.3	1.5			Sales/Total Assets	2.6	2.6
		2.2	1.3				1.7	1.6
		.2	.7				.6	.3
		(12) .6	(12) 2.3			% Depr., Dep., Amort./Sales	(56) 1.4	(41) 1.2
		3.4	5.0				3.9	3.2
		2.3					1.0	2.7
		(11) 3.2				% Officers', Directors' Owners' Comp/Sales	(19) 4.8	(12) 5.9
		6.5					10.2	13.4
6716M	39377M	277334M	589042M	212531M	1044379M	Net Sales ($)	2470391M	1313010M
2033M	10579M	87900M	311936M	227099M	828156M	Total Assets ($)	1216555M	811422M

M = $ thousand MM = $ million

See Pages 9 through 22 for Explanation of Ratios and Data

Comparative Historical Data / Current Data Sorted by Sales

4/1/11-3/31/12 ALL	4/1/12-3/31/13 ALL	4/1/13-3/31/14 ALL		0-1MM	1-3MM	3-5MM	5-10MM	10-25MM	25MM & OVER
			Type of Statement						
12	8	6	Unqualified						6
7	11	9	Reviewed			1	1	5	2
3	7	4	Compiled				2	1	1
13	15	10	Tax Returns	3	1	3	1	1	1
23	28	25	Other	2	2	1	5	4	11
				8 (4/1-9/30/13)		46 (10/1/13-3/31/14)			
58	69	54	**NUMBER OF STATEMENTS**	5	3	5	9	11	21
%	%	%	**ASSETS**	%	%	%	%	%	%
12.8	14.8	15.2	Cash & Equivalents					29.0	12.4
32.7	32.0	37.2	Trade Receivables (net)					32.8	41.8
6.0	9.4	9.0	Inventory					11.2	11.3
5.5	4.3	3.1	All Other Current					3.1	3.4
57.0	60.5	64.6	Total Current					76.1	68.8
19.3	21.1	19.0	Fixed Assets (net)					17.4	11.7
14.7	7.3	9.1	Intangibles (net)					1.5	15.7
9.0	11.1	7.3	All Other Non-Current					5.1	3.7
100.0	100.0	100.0	Total					100.0	100.0
			LIABILITIES						
12.2	9.6	10.3	Notes Payable-Short Term					5.7	10.3
2.7	11.7	3.4	Cur. Mat.-L.T.D.					2.0	5.9
17.9	18.6	20.2	Trade Payables					25.8	21.0
.2	.0	.2	Income Taxes Payable					.1	.1
14.4	16.5	14.7	All Other Current					9.5	18.6
47.4	56.4	48.8	Total Current					43.1	55.8
16.0	14.2	10.3	Long-Term Debt					4.8	11.2
.7	.6	1.5	Deferred Taxes					1.5	2.5
5.0	5.4	5.9	All Other Non-Current					7.1	6.4
30.9	23.5	33.5	Net Worth					43.5	24.1
100.0	100.0	100.0	Total Liabilities & Net Worth					100.0	100.0
			INCOME DATA						
100.0	100.0	100.0	Net Sales					100.0	100.0
			Gross Profit						
89.2	92.7	93.9	Operating Expenses					93.9	100.8
10.8	7.3	6.1	Operating Profit					6.1	-.8
2.3	1.2	1.7	All Other Expenses (net)					.1	1.1
8.5	6.2	4.4	Profit Before Taxes					6.0	-2.0
			RATIOS						
2.1	2.6	1.8	Current					4.5	1.5
1.2	1.3	1.4						1.7	1.3
.8	1.0	1.0						1.5	1.0
1.7	1.9	1.5	Quick					4.2	1.4
1.0	1.0	1.1						1.4	1.0
.6	.6	.7						1.0	.8
31 11.6	**13** 28.2	**31** 11.7	Sales/Receivables					**22** 16.4	**35** 10.4
49 7.5	**40** 9.1	**53** 6.9						**38** 9.6	**69** 5.3
68 5.4	**61** 6.0	**87** 4.2						**85** 4.3	**104** 3.5
			Cost of Sales/Inventory						
			Cost of Sales/Payables						
6.8	7.5	8.0	Sales/Working Capital					5.3	9.4
28.5	20.9	24.7						8.1	25.9
-30.1	NM	-619.5						9.6	NM
14.8	26.7	32.6	EBIT/Interest						42.4
(44) 3.9	(51) 5.6	(40) 8.1							(18) 2.7
2.2	2.0	1.4							-4.1
			Net Profit + Depr., Dep., Amort./Cur. Mat. L/T/D						
.2	.1	.1	Fixed/Worth					.1	.1
.8	.5	.5						.4	1.4
NM	4.1	29.9						.5	-1.0
.9	.5	.8	Debt/Worth					.8	1.9
3.8	2.4	2.2						1.8	7.8
-17.7	36.8	NM						3.3	-10.1
38.0	69.8	77.7	% Profit Before Taxes/Tangible Net Worth					75.8	130.4
(42) 20.5	(53) 27.3	(41) 32.5						30.2	(13) 32.5
7.7	7.4	10.3						16.8	9.8
13.4	23.0	21.7	% Profit Before Taxes/Total Assets					24.9	13.8
6.2	9.3	6.7						8.5	3.7
2.4	1.5	.9						3.6	-10.7
75.9	91.8	106.8	Sales/Net Fixed Assets					285.8	99.4
19.9	34.6	23.5						55.2	30.9
6.5	8.3	8.0						7.7	13.2
3.0	4.6	3.9	Sales/Total Assets					4.2	3.7
2.1	3.0	2.3						2.7	2.1
1.1	1.9	1.4						1.4	1.3
.7	.6	.5	% Depr., Dep., Amort./Sales						.6
(45) 1.4	(48) 1.1	(37) 1.6							(13) 1.6
3.1	2.8	4.1							2.6
3.9	2.1	2.4	% Officers', Directors' Owners' Comp/Sales						
(14) 6.8	(26) 4.4	(21) 4.9							
15.6	8.4	7.3							
1925369M	3422621M	2169379M	Net Sales ($)	2746M	5733M	20407M	68753M	185097M	1886643M
1244386M	1205425M	1467703M	Total Assets ($)	6834M	1127M	35169M	26531M	96365M	1301677M

M = $ thousand MM = $ million

See Pages 9 through 22 for Explanation of Ratios and Data

Current Data Sorted by Assets							Comparative Historical Data	
						Type of Statement		
1		2	5	4	3	Unqualified	21	25
	1	8	5			Reviewed	17	19
1	11	3	2		1	Compiled	13	17
18	10	6				Tax Returns	33	29
8	18	33	19	5	5	Other	71	89
	20 (4/1-9/30/13)		149 (10/1/13-3/31/14)				4/1/09-3/31/10	4/1/10-3/31/11
0-500M	500M-2MM	2-10MM	10-50MM	50-100MM	100-250MM		ALL	ALL
28	40	52	31	9	9	**NUMBER OF STATEMENTS**	155	179
%	%	%	%	%	%	**ASSETS**	%	%
32.6	19.6	21.0	9.2			Cash & Equivalents	19.8	17.3
18.8	37.4	42.9	30.1			Trade Receivables (net)	33.6	30.6
2.9	10.2	8.2	13.3			Inventory	7.1	12.8
.5	1.8	3.2	3.6			All Other Current	5.6	3.9
54.9	68.9	75.4	56.2			Total Current	66.1	64.6
28.9	16.2	11.8	16.5			Fixed Assets (net)	15.7	14.8
1.5	5.2	3.1	18.4			Intangibles (net)	10.2	10.9
14.7	9.6	9.7	8.9			All Other Non-Current	8.0	9.6
100.0	100.0	100.0	100.0			Total	100.0	100.0
						LIABILITIES		
19.9	14.4	10.2	9.9			Notes Payable-Short Term	14.2	15.1
6.2	1.3	1.9	2.4			Cur. Mat.-L.T.D.	4.4	2.3
6.7	18.9	27.1	12.0			Trade Payables	20.6	17.6
.4	.2	.3	.1			Income Taxes Payable	.4	.8
22.8	14.3	18.9	13.0			All Other Current	19.1	16.2
56.0	49.1	58.5	37.4			Total Current	58.7	52.1
17.2	14.3	12.0	15.7			Long-Term Debt	14.9	12.1
.0	.0	.2	.4			Deferred Taxes	.4	.3
6.8	14.0	6.8	9.1			All Other Non-Current	6.7	5.2
19.8	22.6	22.5	37.5			Net Worth	19.3	30.3
100.0	100.0	100.0	100.0			Total Liabilties & Net Worth	100.0	100.0
						INCOME DATA		
100.0	100.0	100.0	100.0			Net Sales	100.0	100.0
						Gross Profit		
92.8	93.0	92.9	90.2			Operating Expenses	95.8	91.8
7.2	7.0	7.1	9.8			Operating Profit	4.2	8.2
2.1	2.8	.6	3.1			All Other Expenses (net)	2.0	1.6
5.1	4.2	6.5	6.7			Profit Before Taxes	2.2	6.6
						RATIOS		
3.9	3.7	2.2	2.5				2.1	2.5
1.1	1.4	1.3	1.5			Current	1.2	1.3
.3	.9	1.0	1.1				.8	.9
3.1	2.5	2.0	1.5				1.8	1.8
.9	1.1	1.1	1.2			Quick	1.0	1.0
.3	.7	.7	.6				.5	.5
0 UND	**12** 30.1	**26** 13.8	**31** 11.9				**23** 15.6	**22** 16.7
0 UND	**31** 11.8	**55** 6.6	**46** 8.0			Sales/Receivables	**41** 8.8	**40** 9.1
27 13.6	**50** 7.3	**81** 4.5	**68** 5.4				**62** 5.9	**61** 6.0
						Cost of Sales/Inventory		
						Cost of Sales/Payables		
10.6	6.8	7.0	6.1				6.5	7.3
NM	22.1	17.7	10.3			Sales/Working Capital	24.8	19.2
-8.2	-133.5	-115.0	63.2				-27.6	-61.7
17.0	29.5	29.2	16.2				12.1	13.5
(15) 2.9	(29) 7.5	(36) 7.5	(26) 5.1			EBIT/Interest	(132) 2.6	(132) 4.8
-2.3	.4	2.7	1.2				.6	1.4
							6.5	7.6
						Net Profit + Depr., Dep., Amort./Cur. Mat. L/T/D	(21) 1.7	(21) 1.9
							.8	1.3
.0	.0	.1	.2				.1	.1
.6	.4	.3	.8			Fixed/Worth	.8	.3
-9.0	-20.9	2.5	-1.1				-1.3	30.1
.5	1.2	.8	1.2				1.1	.8
2.8	4.0	3.5	2.6			Debt/Worth	4.2	2.8
-8.4	-7.0	22.0	-6.9				-6.6	296.0
199.7	71.3	96.0	57.3				52.7	73.9
(18) 88.6	(26) 27.8	(42) 40.3	(19) 13.7			% Profit Before Taxes/Tangible Net Worth	(102) 12.4	(135) 28.7
-3.7	6.6	18.3	.8				-4.3	9.5
49.8	26.3	28.2	11.9				16.8	20.3
16.8	8.0	11.2	6.3			% Profit Before Taxes/Total Assets	3.2	7.9
-4.4	.2	3.6	.9				-3.3	1.9
829.1	596.1	302.0	68.3				120.4	169.6
49.0	107.0	49.5	18.8			Sales/Net Fixed Assets	30.7	48.4
16.5	12.2	19.4	12.1				12.2	13.5
14.0	6.8	3.8	3.1				4.6	4.4
5.4	3.8	3.0	1.6			Sales/Total Assets	2.5	2.6
2.4	2.0	2.3	1.2				1.6	1.5
.8	.5	.3	.5				.6	.4
(13) 1.6	(23) 1.0	(35) .5	(25) 1.5			% Depr., Dep., Amort./Sales	(112) 1.4	(122) 1.1
3.9	3.8	1.9	3.8				3.3	3.2
4.2	3.1	1.2					2.6	2.6
(12) 10.4	(20) 6.2	(15) 3.1				% Officers', Directors' Owners' Comp/Sales	(63) 5.5	(59) 5.1
21.1	10.8	6.5					11.6	9.8
47405M	209674M	1006637M	1153157M	1428464M	1203422M	Net Sales ($)	4213893M	5303910M
7419M	46000M	268457M	619732M	580208M	1452777M	Total Assets ($)	2271723M	2989774M

M = $ thousand MM = $ million

See Pages 9 through 22 for Explanation of Ratios and Data

Comparative Historical Data				Current Data Sorted by Sales					
			Type of Statement						
17	8	15	Unqualified	2				1	12
18	11	14	Reviewed	1			1	8	4
20	21	18	Compiled		6	2	4	5	1
31	35	34	Tax Returns	10	9	5	6	4	
82	69	88	Other	4	8	9	13	24	30
				20 (4/1-9/30/13)			149 (10/1/13-3/31/14)		
4/1/11-3/31/12 ALL	**4/1/12-3/31/13 ALL**	**4/1/13-3/31/14 ALL**		**0-1MM**	**1-3MM**	**3-5MM**	**5-10MM**	**10-25MM**	**25MM & OVER**
168	144	169	**NUMBER OF STATEMENTS**	17	23	16	24	42	47
%	%	%	**ASSETS**	%	%	%	%	%	%
17.0	17.0	19.2	Cash & Equivalents	24.2	23.0	25.1	28.3	16.2	11.6
31.8	31.4	34.3	Trade Receivables (net)	12.7	25.0	34.7	36.0	45.9	35.2
8.6	10.6	8.3	Inventory	.7	10.9	7.5	10.2	6.2	10.9
4.2	3.3	2.7	All Other Current	1.3	.9	2.4	1.1	2.5	5.2
61.6	62.4	64.5	Total Current	38.8	59.8	69.6	75.6	70.8	62.9
17.4	15.5	16.2	Fixed Assets (net)	46.8	22.0	9.9	10.9	11.2	11.8
13.9	12.0	9.2	Intangibles (net)	2.7	7.5	3.4	5.0	7.7	17.9
7.2	10.0	10.1	All Other Non-Current	11.6	10.7	17.2	8.6	10.3	7.4
100.0	100.0	100.0	Total	100.0	100.0	100.0	100.0	100.0	100.0
			LIABILITIES						
13.9	17.0	12.6	Notes Payable-Short Term	9.1	24.3	12.6	11.5	9.2	11.7
2.8	1.8	2.6	Cur. Mat.-L.T.D.	2.8	1.3	8.2	1.4	1.9	2.5
18.5	17.5	18.1	Trade Payables	3.2	10.2	10.4	20.7	29.1	18.9
.2	.5	.3	Income Taxes Payable	.2	.0	.6	.0	.5	.2
15.6	17.6	16.6	All Other Current	17.7	22.3	13.0	15.9	12.6	18.7
51.0	54.4	50.2	Total Current	33.0	58.0	44.8	49.5	53.3	52.1
16.7	14.2	14.9	Long-Term Debt	35.4	15.1	10.5	8.0	12.4	14.8
.4	.1	.2	Deferred Taxes	.0	.0	.0	.1	.0	.8
8.0	8.5	10.2	All Other Non-Current	3.3	7.9	17.9	14.6	3.7	14.8
24.0	22.8	24.3	Net Worth	27.9	18.9	26.7	27.9	30.7	17.4
100.0	100.0	100.0	Total Liabilties & Net Worth	100.0	100.0	100.0	100.0	100.0	100.0
			INCOME DATA						
100.0	100.0	100.0	Net Sales	100.0	100.0	100.0	100.0	100.0	100.0
			Gross Profit						
90.8	91.9	92.2	Operating Expenses	79.9	94.1	93.7	93.1	93.2	93.9
9.2	8.1	7.8	Operating Profit	20.1	5.9	6.3	6.9	6.8	6.1
1.7	2.8	2.2	All Other Expenses (net)	10.6	.8	.7	-.1	1.1	2.3
7.4	5.3	5.6	Profit Before Taxes	9.5	5.1	5.6	7.0	5.7	3.8
			RATIOS						
2.1	2.5	2.4		7.8	3.7	4.3	4.5	2.6	1.6
1.4	1.3	1.3	Current	1.7	1.0	1.8	2.0	1.3	1.2
.7	.8	.9		.4	.4	1.1	.9	1.0	1.0
1.8	2.0	1.8		4.6	1.8	4.2	3.4	1.9	1.2
1.0	1.0	1.1	Quick	.9	.8	1.8	1.4	1.1	1.0
.6	.4	.6		.3	.4	.6	.9	.8	.6
14 25.5	**7** 50.2	**17** 21.2		**0** UND	**0** UND	**3** 124.1	**14** 25.6	**35** 10.4	**34** 10.8
38 9.5	**35** 10.4	**39** 9.3	Sales/Receivables	**0** UND	**26** 14.2	**42** 8.6	**23** 16.0	**56** 6.5	**48** 7.6
61 6.0	**51** 7.1	**63** 5.8		**24** 15.3	**52** 7.0	**68** 5.4	**45** 8.1	**79** 4.6	**79** 4.6
			Cost of Sales/Inventory						
			Cost of Sales/Payables						
8.2	8.2	7.0		4.7	9.5	6.8	6.2	6.5	9.2
18.2	24.2	19.5	Sales/Working Capital	70.5	80.5	14.4	16.0	17.7	19.5
-37.9	-22.5	-79.3		-7.8	-9.1	37.8	NM	-149.9	-99.3
18.6	21.6	17.2			17.0		62.0	23.1	9.9
(124) 4.6	(100) 4.8	(122) 5.0	EBIT/Interest		(17) 1.6		(18) 26.6	(31) 6.3	(41) 4.2
1.5	1.8	1.2			-3.5		8.7	2.0	1.3
16.3	4.9	4.4							
(13) 4.4	(10) 2.9	(13) 1.9	Net Profit + Depr., Dep., Amort./Cur. Mat. L/T/D						
1.8	1.6	1.1							
.1	.1	.1		.1	.1	.0	.1	.1	.3
.6	.5	.5	Fixed/Worth	1.2	.8	.1	.2	.4	1.9
-1.0	-1.4	-2.3		NM	-1.2	.6	-1.9	2.3	-.3
1.0	1.0	1.2		.4	1.2	.8	.5	1.0	1.9
4.0	5.3	4.3	Debt/Worth	2.1	5.6	1.6	4.6	2.7	9.4
-5.1	-4.9	-7.7		-10.6	-4.4	54.7	-7.1	12.7	-3.8
62.4	85.4	88.6		100.0	254.5	51.5	97.6	84.6	76.5
(110) 26.5	(93) 28.5	(113) 30.9	% Profit Before Taxes/Tangible Net Worth	(11) 14.8	(15) 90.6	(13) 33.3	(14) 58.4	(34) 22.6	(26) 16.6
5.9	10.4	7.4		-1.4	3.7	23.0	31.5	8.5	.4
20.6	22.2	24.5		39.0	28.3	20.8	45.3	21.2	15.0
7.6	8.1	7.8	% Profit Before Taxes/Total Assets	2.5	3.1	15.1	14.2	7.0	6.9
1.9	1.8	.6		-2.1	-6.2	1.7	7.4	2.1	.3
149.4	186.9	189.1		UND	213.3	UND	479.6	174.1	94.1
39.0	44.6	38.8	Sales/Net Fixed Assets	6.6	31.7	130.7	166.1	37.1	28.3
11.8	13.9	13.0		.3	11.9	31.2	25.4	15.7	12.3
4.1	4.9	4.5		4.9	6.4	4.6	7.8	3.8	3.2
2.9	2.9	2.9	Sales/Total Assets	1.5	3.4	3.4	4.3	2.8	2.4
1.8	1.9	1.8		.2	1.8	2.2	2.4	2.1	1.2
.5	.3	.4		1.7	.8		.2	.4	.4
(105) 1.2	(88) 1.0	(110) 1.2	% Depr., Dep., Amort./Sales	(10) 5.3	(13) 1.6		(11) .5	(31) .7	(38) 1.5
2.8	2.3	2.8		23.4	4.5		1.5	2.0	3.4
2.2	2.8	1.9			5.1		1.2	2.3	
(64) 5.2	(57) 4.5	(52) 4.7	% Officers', Directors' Owners' Comp/Sales		(14) 11.0		(12) 3.0	(10) 3.8	
9.2	9.9	10.8			19.6		6.0	6.8	
4861573M	3402810M	5048759M	Net Sales ($)	8323M	44025M	58077M	168915M	697098M	4072321M
2723531M	1976133M	2974593M	Total Assets ($)	19353M	44755M	20334M	46205M	301313M	2542633M

M = $ thousand MM = $ million

See Pages 9 through 22 for Explanation of Ratios and Data

Current Data Sorted by Assets							Comparative Historical Data	
						Type of Statement		
	2	5	6	2	5	Unqualified	25	22
1	5	6	1			Reviewed	14	17
1	4	7	1			Compiled	16	18
9	6	3				Tax Returns	17	16
6	20	16	8	2	5	Other	66	62
	26 (4/1-9/30/13)		95 (10/1/13-3/31/14)				4/1/09-3/31/10	4/1/10-3/31/11
0-500M	500M-2MM	2-10MM	10-50MM	50-100MM	100-250MM		ALL	ALL
17	37	37	16	4	10	**NUMBER OF STATEMENTS**	138	135
%	%	%	%	%	%	**ASSETS**	%	%
30.1	12.4	15.6	16.2		17.9	Cash & Equivalents	16.7	17.4
32.7	45.6	44.6	29.8		16.7	Trade Receivables (net)	37.6	40.5
3.4	1.6	.4	1.9		.0	Inventory	2.3	2.3
5.3	3.5	5.6	7.7		5.0	All Other Current	5.9	5.2
71.4	63.1	66.2	55.7		39.6	Total Current	62.5	65.5
12.0	23.5	16.3	14.2		9.0	Fixed Assets (net)	19.2	16.0
9.3	6.2	5.8	19.5		44.8	Intangibles (net)	8.7	8.6
7.3	7.3	11.7	10.7		6.6	All Other Non-Current	9.6	9.9
100.0	100.0	100.0	100.0		100.0	Total	100.0	100.0
						LIABILITIES		
13.8	17.4	9.3	4.0		1.1	Notes Payable-Short Term	12.4	16.2
.4	2.5	1.8	.9		1.6	Cur. Mat.-L.T.D.	6.5	2.5
16.5	13.4	8.8	6.7		3.7	Trade Payables	14.6	15.0
.2	.1	.2	.3		.9	Income Taxes Payable	.2	.4
29.7	19.6	32.1	16.8		19.2	All Other Current	19.3	22.0
60.6	53.0	52.2	28.8		26.5	Total Current	53.0	56.1
14.4	16.8	8.5	13.2		19.9	Long-Term Debt	16.3	11.5
.1	.0	.2	2.4		3.4	Deferred Taxes	.5	.6
8.8	4.7	9.1	13.2		3.7	All Other Non-Current	7.9	10.8
16.2	25.5	30.0	42.4		46.5	Net Worth	22.3	21.0
100.0	100.0	100.0	100.0		100.0	Total Liabilties & Net Worth	100.0	100.0
						INCOME DATA		
100.0	100.0	100.0	100.0		100.0	Net Sales	100.0	100.0
						Gross Profit		
96.9	93.0	90.3	83.0		84.8	Operating Expenses	93.7	92.0
3.1	7.0	9.7	17.0		15.2	Operating Profit	6.3	8.0
2.0	2.1	.0	1.8		1.8	All Other Expenses (net)	2.6	2.3
1.1	4.9	9.7	15.3		13.4	Profit Before Taxes	3.7	5.7
						RATIOS		
2.9	3.0	2.6	3.8		1.5		2.3	2.7
1.7	1.6	1.5	2.0		1.2	Current	1.4	1.3
.6	.6	.9	1.2		.9		1.0	.9
2.9	2.7	2.2	3.7		1.4		2.1	2.4
1.5	1.5	1.2	1.6		1.0	Quick	1.2	1.1
.6	.5	.9	1.2		.7		.8	.7
0 UND	**25** 14.4	**43** 8.4	**52** 7.0		**40** 9.1		**30** 12.0	**25** 14.8
0 UND	**50** 7.3	**65** 5.6	**78** 4.7		**62** 5.9	Sales/Receivables	**50** 7.3	**54** 6.7
61 6.0	**69** 5.3	**94** 3.9	**91** 4.0		**87** 4.2		**77** 4.7	**76** 4.8
						Cost of Sales/Inventory		
						Cost of Sales/Payables		
10.9	6.7	6.3	2.4		7.9		6.0	6.3
17.4	13.6	10.1	6.9		24.0	Sales/Working Capital	18.3	24.9
-19.0	-14.1	-76.8	18.1		-30.1		-195.5	-35.1
41.0	16.0	129.7	118.3				19.5	29.8
(11) 6.6	(27) 7.6	(29) 21.2	(12) 10.9			EBIT/Interest	(103) 5.4	(105) 7.0
1.5	1.3	6.5	4.2				.9	1.3
							8.6	13.3
						Net Profit + Depr., Dep., Amort./Cur. Mat. L/T/D	(21) 4.4	(13) 7.4
							2.1	3.6
.1	.0	.1	.2		.7		.1	.1
.2	.4	.5	.6		NM	Fixed/Worth	.5	.5
-.3	-1.6	2.4	-4.6		-.1		4.1	4.3
.4	.4	.8	.6		2.1		.8	.8
2.1	1.5	2.3	2.8		NM	Debt/Worth	2.7	2.9
-3.0	-7.1	8.3	-28.5		-1.9		36.7	107.7
64.3	106.8	159.2	106.4				64.3	86.7
(11) 17.7	(27) 31.6	(32) 81.0	(11) 31.9			% Profit Before Taxes/Tangible Net Worth	(106) 21.6	(103) 39.8
6.1	5.7	28.1	8.8				2.1	10.0
32.0	34.6	45.9	17.1		14.0		19.5	19.4
11.1	14.3	15.8	9.5		8.0	% Profit Before Taxes/Total Assets	6.7	7.8
-.7	1.3	5.3	4.3		1.8		-1.1	.7
245.5	296.6	82.5	24.5		36.7		70.8	97.3
120.3	33.3	32.0	12.6		29.1	Sales/Net Fixed Assets	27.0	38.6
36.9	8.4	11.8	7.8		7.6		9.8	13.5
8.1	4.6	3.2	2.0		1.2		4.0	4.6
6.3	3.7	2.6	1.3		1.1	Sales/Total Assets	2.5	2.7
3.5	1.7	1.6	.8		.7		1.6	1.8
.3	.6	.6	1.2				.7	.6
(12) 1.2	(20) 2.0	(29) 1.4	(15) 2.4			% Depr., Dep., Amort./Sales	(100) 1.5	(90) 1.0
1.7	3.0	2.4	6.2				2.6	1.8
4.6							3.3	2.3
(11) 9.3						% Officers', Directors' Owners' Comp/Sales	(33) 8.2	(38) 4.4
21.3							16.3	8.9
25120M	149592M	505225M	502191M	482946M	1729678M	Net Sales ($)	3765111M	4142290M
4760M	44648M	197903M	345768M	250488M	1735655M	Total Assets ($)	2314504M	2349560M

M = $ thousand MM = $ million

See Pages 9 through 22 for Explanation of Ratios and Data

Comparative Historical Data / Current Data Sorted by Sales

4/1/11-3/31/12 ALL	4/1/12-3/31/13 ALL	4/1/13-3/31/14 ALL	Type of Statement	0-1MM	1-3MM	3-5MM	5-10MM	10-25MM	25MM & OVER
26	9	20	Unqualified		1		3	4	12
17	10	13	Reviewed		3	1	4	5	
16	9	13	Compiled	1	3	1	3	4	1
31	12	18	Tax Returns	5	7	1	3	2	
70	63	57	Other	2	15	7	11	9	13
				26 (4/1-9/30/13)			95 (10/1/13-3/31/14)		
160	103	121	**NUMBER OF STATEMENTS**	8	29	10	24	24	26
%	%	%	**ASSETS**	%	%	%	%	%	%
19.6	19.3	17.5	Cash & Equivalents		19.2	15.6	11.2	15.7	21.4
37.4	40.7	38.3	Trade Receivables (net)		36.1	41.4	54.1	42.2	30.2
2.1	1.6	1.3	Inventory		1.8	2.7	.0	1.8	.2
5.4	6.1	5.4	All Other Current		2.5	4.6	5.9	6.7	7.4
64.5	67.7	62.5	Total Current		59.6	64.3	71.1	66.4	59.2
15.4	13.9	17.0	Fixed Assets (net)		22.6	19.5	16.1	11.4	10.9
10.9	9.9	11.5	Intangibles (net)		9.3	3.8	7.6	9.4	23.7
9.2	8.5	9.0	All Other Non-Current		8.5	12.4	5.1	12.7	6.2
100.0	100.0	100.0	Total		100.0	100.0	100.0	100.0	100.0
			LIABILITIES						
11.2	11.3	10.7	Notes Payable-Short Term		16.6	10.5	15.1	6.4	3.0
2.8	1.8	1.6	Cur. Mat.-L.T.D.		1.5	3.3	1.2	2.1	1.3
12.6	15.2	10.6	Trade Payables		15.2	7.4	13.1	10.3	6.9
.9	.2	.3	Income Taxes Payable		.2	.0	.1	.3	.6
22.2	20.0	24.8	All Other Current		20.3	20.1	20.1	37.4	24.1
49.6	48.5	48.0	Total Current		53.8	41.3	49.6	56.6	35.9
12.0	10.0	13.2	Long-Term Debt		24.8	3.5	11.2	7.0	10.7
.6	.7	.7	Deferred Taxes		.0	.0	.4	.8	2.2
8.0	13.3	7.6	All Other Non-Current		6.5	23.6	8.1	7.6	4.7
29.8	27.5	30.5	Net Worth		14.8	31.6	30.7	28.0	46.6
100.0	100.0	100.0	Total Liabilties & Net Worth		100.0	100.0	100.0	100.0	100.0
			INCOME DATA						
100.0	100.0	100.0	Net Sales		100.0	100.0	100.0	100.0	100.0
			Gross Profit						
94.1	90.4	90.6	Operating Expenses		92.4	83.0	90.4	92.6	88.2
5.9	9.6	9.4	Operating Profit		7.6	17.0	9.6	7.4	11.8
1.6	1.9	1.4	All Other Expenses (net)		1.5	3.0	.4	-.3	1.6
4.3	7.6	8.0	Profit Before Taxes		6.1	14.0	9.2	7.6	10.2
			RATIOS						
2.6	2.9	2.7			3.5	10.9	2.5	2.5	2.0
1.3	1.5	1.6	Current		1.7	2.7	1.7	1.3	1.5
1.0	1.1	.9			.5	.7	1.1	.9	1.1
2.5	2.8	2.3			3.4	10.9	2.5	1.9	1.7
1.1	1.3	1.3	Quick		1.7	1.7	1.5	1.1	1.4
.7	.8	.7			.4	.7	1.0	.7	.9
25 14.6	34 10.7	32 11.5			0 UND	31 11.8	50 7.3	38 9.5	48 7.6
51 7.2	52 7.0	58 6.3	Sales/Receivables		45 8.2	62 5.9	64 5.7	64 5.7	62 5.9
76 4.8	78 4.7	78 4.7			68 5.4	118 3.1	85 4.3	74 4.9	85 4.3
			Cost of Sales/Inventory						
			Cost of Sales/Payables						
6.5	6.4	6.5			5.4	2.3	6.5	7.2	6.6
20.4	16.2	11.4	Sales/Working Capital		15.9	8.0	10.9	35.9	9.7
-114.5	125.5	-30.2			-15.4	-14.1	242.5	-53.8	44.4
35.8	48.1	42.4			9.3		93.7	85.5	81.7
(124) 7.5	(74) 10.7	(90) 11.6	EBIT/Interest		(20) 3.4		(18) 10.7	(19) 20.3	(22) 14.5
1.3	1.4	2.0			1.4		3.1	11.9	4.0
16.6		11.5							
(22) 3.1		(13) 8.1	Net Profit + Depr., Dep., Amort./Cur. Mat. L/T/D						
1.6		2.0							
.1	.1	.1			.0	.0	.1	.1	.1
.4	.4	.5	Fixed/Worth		.3	.6	.5	.5	.6
4.4	21.7	-5.5			-1.1	-1.4	-.7	3.7	-2.9
.6	1.0	.6			.6	.4	.5	.8	.8
2.4	2.2	2.3	Debt/Worth		2.4	1.0	1.9	3.9	2.3
41.7	-34.6	-43.5			-2.7	-5.9	-11.7	15.7	-15.8
94.0	135.0	110.5			62.4		158.4	282.5	73.5
(122) 31.8	(75) 52.6	(90) 40.3	% Profit Before Taxes/Tangible Net Worth		(20) 31.8		(17) 78.3	(22) 89.2	(18) 29.8
6.3	9.7	14.8			4.7		23.3	40.8	16.7
22.4	32.1	26.6			21.3	72.0	53.6	35.0	17.7
8.9	12.6	13.4	% Profit Before Taxes/Total Assets		10.6	16.4	19.4	15.6	10.4
1.1	1.5	3.3			.6	4.5	5.6	4.6	3.8
131.9	84.5	104.4			502.5	308.8	130.9	85.9	42.6
43.4	38.3	30.8	Sales/Net Fixed Assets		63.6	20.4	33.9	33.0	24.3
14.0	15.8	11.6			8.8	2.3	12.1	16.8	9.1
4.3	4.4	4.1			5.6	4.7	4.4	3.7	2.7
2.6	3.1	2.7	Sales/Total Assets		3.5	1.7	3.7	2.6	1.3
1.8	1.9	1.4			1.6	1.0	2.2	1.7	1.0
.5	.5	.8			.5		.4	.6	.9
(103) 1.2	(69) 1.1	(82) 1.4	% Depr., Dep., Amort./Sales		(18) 1.7		(19) 1.4	(19) 1.2	(17) 1.4
2.4	2.1	2.7			2.4		3.0	2.3	3.2
3.9	4.3	2.2			3.1				
(55) 7.3	(33) 6.1	(32) 4.3	% Officers', Directors' Owners' Comp/Sales		(11) 4.0				
15.5	10.0	9.2			8.3				
4659157M	2506687M	3394752M	Net Sales ($)	4588M	56906M	39698M	164460M	425548M	2703552M
2821465M	1496802M	2579222M	Total Assets ($)	5511M	31685M	40311M	65944M	193882M	2241889M

M = $ thousand MM = $ million

See Pages 9 through 22 for Explanation of Ratios and Data

Current Data Sorted by Assets							Comparative Historical Data	
						Type of Statement		
			2	1		Unqualified	4	4
	1					Reviewed	3	1
1	1	1				Compiled	8	6
11	4	1	1			Tax Returns	21	17
5	5	3	2			Other	14	21
6 (4/1-9/30/13)			33 (10/1/13-3/31/14)				4/1/09-3/31/10	4/1/10-3/31/11
0-500M	**500M-2MM**	**2-10MM**	**10-50MM**	**50-100MM**	**100-250MM**		**ALL**	**ALL**
17	11	5	5	1		**NUMBER OF STATEMENTS**	50	49
%	%	%	%	%	%	**ASSETS**	%	%
38.9	14.5				DATA NOT AVAILABLE	Cash & Equivalents	17.9	19.3
1.7	27.5					Trade Receivables (net)	5.3	11.6
2.8	3.4					Inventory	7.3	4.7
.1	4.6					All Other Current	3.1	3.4
43.5	50.1					Total Current	33.5	38.9
45.4	34.1					Fixed Assets (net)	38.9	39.1
3.7	4.9					Intangibles (net)	16.6	13.2
7.4	10.9					All Other Non-Current	11.1	8.7
100.0	100.0					Total	100.0	100.0
						LIABILITIES		
28.7	6.7					Notes Payable-Short Term	24.0	14.9
10.5	3.4					Cur. Mat.-L.T.D.	4.6	3.3
5.4	11.2					Trade Payables	11.0	10.5
.0	1.1					Income Taxes Payable	.1	.1
20.9	7.1					All Other Current	15.9	13.5
65.4	29.5					Total Current	55.7	42.3
20.5	24.3					Long-Term Debt	33.2	29.2
.0	.0					Deferred Taxes	.2	.3
35.7	15.6					All Other Non-Current	9.2	7.5
-21.6	30.7					Net Worth	1.8	20.8
100.0	100.0					Total Liabilities & Net Worth	100.0	100.0
						INCOME DATA		
100.0	100.0					Net Sales	100.0	100.0
						Gross Profit		
95.6	96.0					Operating Expenses	96.9	92.5
4.4	4.0					Operating Profit	3.1	7.5
1.1	2.1					All Other Expenses (net)	3.0	1.9
3.3	1.9					Profit Before Taxes	.1	5.6
						RATIOS		
2.3	2.7						2.1	2.3
.8	1.4					Current	.6	1.2
.3	1.2						.3	.4
2.3	1.7						1.3	2.1
.8	1.4					Quick	.4	.7
.2	.7						.2	.2
0 UND	**2** 156.8						**0** UND	**0** UND
0 UND	**49** 7.5					Sales/Receivables	**1** 364.3	**4** 90.5
1 306.8	**89** 4.1						**8** 44.9	**21** 17.5
						Cost of Sales/Inventory		
						Cost of Sales/Payables		
12.0	2.2						13.1	10.2
-307.0	21.1					Sales/Working Capital	-32.9	56.6
-7.8	28.5						-7.3	-10.7
9.3	11.5						4.4	8.6
(12) 3.1	2.3					EBIT/Interest	(38) .0	(41) 3.5
.3	-.4						-4.0	1.3
						Net Profit + Depr., Dep., Amort./Cur. Mat. L/T/D		
1.4	.8						.7	.8
3.9	1.2					Fixed/Worth	NM	2.3
-.5	3.7						-.6	-1.0
2.0	1.4						.9	.8
3.3	3.1					Debt/Worth	NM	3.3
-2.0	7.1						-2.1	-3.8
							121.0	75.4
						% Profit Before Taxes/Tangible Net Worth	(25) 8.9	(32) 26.1
							-9.4	6.3
31.8	24.9						12.8	14.9
11.0	3.6					% Profit Before Taxes/Total Assets	-1.1	7.9
-8.0	-.9						-15.5	1.9
42.1	16.7						20.2	19.4
19.1	10.1					Sales/Net Fixed Assets	12.4	7.6
4.7	5.1						5.9	4.4
11.9	3.9						6.2	3.7
7.0	2.6					Sales/Total Assets	3.1	2.3
2.0	1.6						1.7	1.4
.8	1.8						1.6	3.1
(11) 1.4	(10) 3.7					% Depr., Dep., Amort./Sales	(37) 3.0	(31) 4.1
3.0	7.4						5.8	6.6
4.1							3.5	2.2
(10) 8.8						% Officers', Directors' Owners' Comp/Sales	(25) 8.7	(20) 6.6
16.5							18.4	15.7
23417M	**37423M**	**69520M**	**444071M**	**85108M**		Net Sales ($)	**1105905M**	**1621031M**
3260M	**14154M**	**27523M**	**119970M**	**91494M**		Total Assets ($)	**550991M**	**699591M**

M = $ thousand MM = $ million

See Pages 9 through 22 for Explanation of Ratios and Data

Comparative Historical Data / Current Data Sorted by Sales

			Type of Statement						
2	2	3	Unqualified						3
6	7	1	Reviewed				1		
6	7	3	Compiled	1		1		1	
27	11	17	Tax Returns	7	5	1	2	1	1
16	17	15	Other	4	5	1	2		3
4/1/11-3/31/12 ALL	4/1/12-3/31/13 ALL	4/1/13-3/31/14 ALL		6 (4/1-9/30/13)		33 (10/1/13-3/31/14)			
				0-1MM	1-3MM	3-5MM	5-10MM	10-25MM	25MM & OVER
57	44	39	NUMBER OF STATEMENTS	12	10	3	5	2	7
%	%	%	**ASSETS**	%	%	%	%	%	%
20.9	28.3	26.6	Cash & Equivalents	35.0	23.5				
13.2	11.5	11.4	Trade Receivables (net)	4.1	10.7				
7.3	5.4	3.5	Inventory	5.0	.5				
1.4	2.6	1.9	All Other Current	2.2	2.1				
42.7	47.8	43.4	Total Current	46.2	36.8				
30.1	31.9	37.6	Fixed Assets (net)	43.9	37.1				
13.8	7.9	7.6	Intangibles (net)	.3	6.4				
13.4	12.5	11.3	All Other Non-Current	9.6	19.7				
100.0	100.0	100.0	Total	100.0	100.0				
			LIABILITIES						
13.2	9.7	15.0	Notes Payable-Short Term	23.1	26.6				
3.7	4.4	6.8	Cur. Mat.-L.T.D.	10.2	7.4				
9.7	8.3	7.3	Trade Payables	7.5	1.6				
.1	.1	1.3	Income Taxes Payable	.0	.0				
21.8	6.5	16.2	All Other Current	6.4	24.8				
48.5	29.0	46.6	Total Current	47.2	60.4				
22.7	20.3	24.1	Long-Term Debt	20.1	12.6				
.4	.5	.6	Deferred Taxes	.0	.0				
16.8	8.6	21.5	All Other Non-Current	52.5	6.5				
11.7	41.6	7.2	Net Worth	-19.8	20.5				
100.0	100.0	100.0	Total Liabilties & Net Worth	100.0	100.0				
			INCOME DATA						
100.0	100.0	100.0	Net Sales	100.0	100.0				
			Gross Profit						
96.8	89.8	95.1	Operating Expenses	96.6	94.6				
3.2	10.2	4.9	Operating Profit	3.4	5.4				
1.7	1.8	1.7	All Other Expenses (net)	2.5	1.3				
1.5	8.4	3.2	Profit Before Taxes	.9	4.0				
			RATIOS						
2.4	3.9	2.5		4.5	1.3				
1.2	1.5	1.2	Current	2.2	.8				
.5	.7	.5		.7	.1				
1.9	3.0	1.9		2.9	1.3				
1.0	1.3	1.0	Quick	1.5	.6				
.4	.5	.4		.4	.1				
0 UND	0 UND	0 UND		0 UND	0 UND				
5 72.3	1 353.0	1 286.4	Sales/Receivables	0 UND	0 UND				
26 14.1	33 10.9	20 18.0		6 59.6	12 30.9				
			Cost of Sales/Inventory						
			Cost of Sales/Payables						
10.9	4.4	8.1		2.1	25.2				
123.7	16.3	75.0	Sales/Working Capital	12.0	-188.4				
-10.1	-21.2	-17.9		-82.4	-7.9				
8.2	10.5	11.3							
(43) 2.1	(31) 3.0	(32) 2.6	EBIT/Interest						
-3.0	1.5	-.3							
			Net Profit + Depr., Dep., Amort./Cur. Mat. L/T/D						
.7	.2	.6		.7	.2				
3.2	.7	1.9	Fixed/Worth	2.5	1.9				
-.4	3.3	-.7		-.4	-3.9				
.8	.5	.7		1.6	.9				
5.7	1.4	2.7	Debt/Worth	2.6	2.6				
-2.0	9.8	-2.6		-1.9	-6.1				
40.8	85.1	56.9							
(33) 14.9	(36) 20.6	(25) 20.3	% Profit Before Taxes/Tangible Net Worth						
-.2	3.6	.6							
15.5	23.0	27.8		32.6	27.7				
4.8	6.3	8.3	% Profit Before Taxes/Total Assets	9.6	13.6				
-17.4	1.3	-.9		-5.3	-1.4				
23.4	24.0	28.4		26.7	43.9				
13.8	10.1	10.8	Sales/Net Fixed Assets	7.7	13.6				
6.7	5.2	5.1		2.2	5.8				
4.3	3.5	6.4		8.4	11.6				
3.2	2.4	2.9	Sales/Total Assets	2.0	6.3				
1.6	1.4	1.6		.7	1.7				
.9	2.7	1.2							
(39) 2.8	(27) 4.6	(30) 2.8	% Depr., Dep., Amort./Sales						
6.9	8.6	4.5							
2.4	2.7	3.1							
(30) 5.3	(21) 7.9	(19) 6.5	% Officers', Directors' Owners' Comp/Sales						
9.4	19.7	15.7							
1573383M	341108M	659539M	Net Sales ($)	5313M	22373M	13551M	28414M	30552M	559336M
611707M	197448M	256401M	Total Assets ($)	3860M	8477M	4047M	8737M	12156M	219124M

M = $ thousand MM = $ million

See Pages 9 through 22 for Explanation of Ratios and Data

Current Data Sorted by Assets							Comparative Historical Data	
						Type of Statement		
				1		Unqualified	1	2
	1	3				Reviewed	6	7
2	3					Compiled	2	2
5	2	1				Tax Returns	8	3
3	4	4	1			Other	10	17
	5 (4/1-9/30/13)		25 (10/1/13-3/31/14)				4/1/09-3/31/10	4/1/10-3/31/11
0-500M	**500M-2MM**	**2-10MM**	**10-50MM**	**50-100MM**	**100-250MM**		**ALL**	**ALL**
10	10	8	1	1		**NUMBER OF STATEMENTS**	27	31
%	%	%	%	%	%	**ASSETS**	%	%
25.6	16.8				DATA NOT AVAILABLE	Cash & Equivalents	12.1	7.2
17.4	28.5					Trade Receivables (net)	18.4	24.1
1.9	6.3					Inventory	5.6	3.9
.5	8.8					All Other Current	7.0	7.2
45.4	60.5					Total Current	43.1	42.4
49.0	16.4					Fixed Assets (net)	41.3	43.2
1.1	6.4					Intangibles (net)	7.3	5.5
4.3	16.8					All Other Non-Current	8.3	8.9
100.0	100.0					Total	100.0	100.0
						LIABILITIES		
10.4	7.1					Notes Payable-Short Term	13.3	22.6
2.6	.8					Cur. Mat.-L.T.D.	7.0	8.5
10.6	25.7					Trade Payables	12.1	16.5
.0	.0					Income Taxes Payable	.1	.3
16.9	17.1					All Other Current	26.5	18.4
40.5	50.7					Total Current	58.9	66.2
36.5	20.1					Long-Term Debt	29.9	19.3
.0	.0					Deferred Taxes	.9	.7
1.8	15.3					All Other Non-Current	7.3	4.6
21.1	13.9					Net Worth	3.0	9.3
100.0	100.0					Total Liabilties & Net Worth	100.0	100.0
						INCOME DATA		
100.0	100.0					Net Sales	100.0	100.0
						Gross Profit		
93.5	93.0					Operating Expenses	95.3	90.0
6.5	7.0					Operating Profit	4.7	10.0
.4	.4					All Other Expenses (net)	3.2	2.0
6.1	6.6					Profit Before Taxes	1.5	8.1
						RATIOS		
3.4	3.1						1.5	2.5
1.2	1.5					Current	.9	1.1
.6	.6						.4	.6
3.4	2.8						1.0	2.1
1.0	.6					Quick	.7	.8
.6	.3						.2	.3
0 UND	**0** UND						**2** 222.7	**2** 196.0
17 22.0	**22** 16.6					Sales/Receivables	**23** 15.9	**41** 9.0
34 10.6	**64** 5.7						**61** 6.0	**62** 5.9
						Cost of Sales/Inventory		
						Cost of Sales/Payables		
14.5	7.1						9.7	7.6
UND	20.6					Sales/Working Capital	-75.0	23.3
-64.3	-20.6						-11.7	-15.0
							3.5	12.1
						EBIT/Interest	(22) 1.0	(25) 4.6
							-.5	.3
						Net Profit + Depr., Dep., Amort./Cur. Mat. L/T/D		
.6	.1						.9	.6
1.0	5.7					Fixed/Worth	5.4	1.6
-1.0	-.3						-2.1	UND
.2	.7						1.3	1.0
.9	13.2					Debt/Worth	7.9	4.3
-3.2	-3.9						-6.5	UND
							36.0	57.2
						% Profit Before Taxes/Tangible Net Worth	(18) 7.7	(24) 39.7
							-25.5	-36.0
72.8	61.0						8.0	26.6
28.1	31.8					% Profit Before Taxes/Total Assets	.0	10.7
2.1	-16.9						-7.4	-.8
44.5	79.6						19.3	17.7
10.5	42.6					Sales/Net Fixed Assets	12.0	8.9
6.0	10.1						3.1	2.1
8.8	4.7						5.8	3.8
4.8	3.3					Sales/Total Assets	1.9	2.5
2.7	2.5						1.2	.9
							3.3	2.2
						% Depr., Dep., Amort./Sales	(19) 4.6	(25) 2.9
							6.1	7.0
							4.5	2.4
						% Officers', Directors' Owners' Comp/Sales	(12) 6.4	(12) 4.7
							18.7	9.9
9514M	**42419M**	**123578M**	**32750M**	**85108M**		Net Sales ($)	**196316M**	**261483M**
1624M	**11121M**	**46844M**	**24181M**	**91493M**		Total Assets ($)	**127408M**	**181007M**

M = $ thousand MM = $ million

See Pages 9 through 22 for Explanation of Ratios and Data

Comparative Historical Data				Current Data Sorted by Sales					
			Type of Statement						
1	1	1	Unqualified						1
7	4	4	Reviewed		1		1	1	1
3	5	5	Compiled	1	2	2			
8	7	8	Tax Returns	4	3	1			
18	12	12	Other	2	2	1	3	3	1
				5 (4/1-9/30/13)			25 (10/1/13-3/31/14)		
4/1/11-3/31/12 ALL	4/1/12-3/31/13 ALL	4/1/13-3/31/14 ALL		0-1MM	1-3MM	3-5MM	5-10MM	10-25MM	25MM & OVER
37	29	30	**NUMBER OF STATEMENTS**	7	8	4	4	4	3
%	%	%	**ASSETS**	%	%	%	%	%	%
13.1	11.4	16.3	Cash & Equivalents						
21.0	24.4	21.0	Trade Receivables (net)						
5.4	6.6	6.1	Inventory						
8.5	4.5	3.4	All Other Current						
48.0	46.8	46.8	Total Current						
37.1	36.9	35.0	Fixed Assets (net)						
3.0	7.4	6.4	Intangibles (net)						
11.9	8.8	11.7	All Other Non-Current						
100.0	100.0	100.0	Total						
			LIABILITIES						
10.4	9.3	9.3	Notes Payable-Short Term						
5.1	5.6	3.4	Cur. Mat.-L.T.D.						
11.2	10.4	14.5	Trade Payables						
.3	.2	.4	Income Taxes Payable						
12.0	14.1	15.5	All Other Current						
39.0	39.7	43.2	Total Current						
28.7	36.7	26.0	Long-Term Debt						
1.5	.7	.2	Deferred Taxes						
11.4	3.9	8.9	All Other Non-Current						
19.5	19.0	21.7	Net Worth						
100.0	100.0	100.0	Total Liabilities & Net Worth						
			INCOME DATA						
100.0	100.0	100.0	Net Sales						
			Gross Profit						
96.3	92.6	89.7	Operating Expenses						
3.7	7.4	10.3	Operating Profit						
.8	3.1	3.7	All Other Expenses (net)						
2.9	4.3	6.7	Profit Before Taxes						
			RATIOS						
2.4	2.2	2.9							
1.2	1.0	1.2	Current						
.6	.6	.5							
2.2	1.4	2.5							
.7	.7	.9	Quick						
.3	.4	.4							
6 64.8	2 180.0	0 UND							
29 12.4	13 27.1	21 17.1	Sales/Receivables						
59 6.2	72 5.1	48 7.6							
			Cost of Sales/Inventory						
			Cost of Sales/Payables						
5.5	10.5	7.1							
17.1	148.0	40.2	Sales/Working Capital						
-20.8	-25.2	-17.8							
12.1	7.5	26.1							
(33) 3.4	(24) 5.0	(25) 4.7	EBIT/Interest						
1.3	.8	.2							
			Net Profit + Depr., Dep., Amort./Cur. Mat. L/T/D						
.5	.7	.4							
1.5	4.4	1.3	Fixed/Worth						
NM	-2.6	-1.0							
.7	1.1	.7							
3.0	7.9	3.8	Debt/Worth						
NM	-5.6	-4.8							
53.4	50.4	115.8							
(28) 29.9	(19) 26.9	(21) 40.2	% Profit Before Taxes/Tangible Net Worth						
4.9	-1.1	17.6							
23.5	18.0	47.1							
9.3	5.7	16.0	% Profit Before Taxes/Total Assets						
.5	-.8	-.1							
18.4	24.7	38.6							
10.2	11.2	14.5	Sales/Net Fixed Assets						
2.9	3.7	7.7							
3.6	5.5	6.0							
2.6	3.4	3.3	Sales/Total Assets						
1.3	.8	2.2							
1.5	1.7	1.6							
(27) 2.2	(23) 2.6	(24) 2.3	% Depr., Dep., Amort./Sales						
5.9	5.8	4.2							
3.6	4.8	6.2							
(18) 8.6	(13) 9.3	(13) 10.5	% Officers', Directors' Owners' Comp/Sales						
16.4	13.0	12.0							
333229M	312882M	293369M	Net Sales ($)	2679M	16443M	17181M	28347M	55170M	173549M
206743M	214260M	175263M	Total Assets ($)	3315M	4208M	5292M	15547M	22042M	124859M

M = $ thousand MM = $ million

See Pages 9 through 22 for Explanation of Ratios and Data

Current Data Sorted by Assets							Comparative Historical Data	
						Type of Statement		
	2	4		2	1	Unqualified	8	7
1		6	3			Reviewed	13	12
52	33	10	1		1	Compiled	74	84
207	109	14			1	Tax Returns	280	251
103	81	24	7	3	1	Other	132	164
	25 (4/1-9/30/13)		641 (10/1/13-3/31/14)				4/1/09-3/31/10	4/1/10-3/31/11
0-500M	**500M-2MM**	**2-10MM**	**10-50MM**	**50-100MM**	**100-250MM**		**ALL**	**ALL**
363	225	58	11	5	4	**NUMBER OF STATEMENTS**	507	518
%	%	%	%	%	%	**ASSETS**	%	%
31.9	17.3	12.8	23.7			Cash & Equivalents	18.4	20.7
3.3	3.3	4.4	17.3			Trade Receivables (net)	4.6	4.4
12.5	4.7	5.0	11.1			Inventory	8.4	8.6
2.7	1.8	1.3	5.1			All Other Current	1.6	2.3
50.5	27.0	23.7	57.2			Total Current	33.1	36.1
31.3	45.4	60.6	26.6			Fixed Assets (net)	40.5	39.7
10.9	19.1	7.2	11.9			Intangibles (net)	16.4	14.3
7.4	8.4	8.5	4.4			All Other Non-Current	10.0	9.9
100.0	100.0	100.0	100.0			Total	100.0	100.0
						LIABILITIES		
12.9	5.0	1.1	5.3			Notes Payable-Short Term	12.2	11.2
6.0	4.1	4.6	3.2			Cur. Mat.-L.T.D.	5.8	6.0
8.2	3.6	5.1	12.7			Trade Payables	8.2	10.6
.3	.5	.1	.0			Income Taxes Payable	.0	.1
22.2	9.2	5.4	13.5			All Other Current	16.0	13.8
49.7	22.4	16.3	34.7			Total Current	42.1	41.7
39.9	52.0	46.0	22.6			Long-Term Debt	45.4	44.3
.0	.1	.1	.0			Deferred Taxes	.1	.1
10.5	6.2	3.2	2.4			All Other Non-Current	4.5	11.9
-.1	19.3	34.4	40.3			Net Worth	7.9	2.0
100.0	100.0	100.0	100.0			Total Liabilties & Net Worth	100.0	100.0
						INCOME DATA		
100.0	100.0	100.0	100.0			Net Sales	100.0	100.0
						Gross Profit		
92.2	82.2	78.2	94.0			Operating Expenses	90.4	89.7
7.8	17.8	21.8	6.0			Operating Profit	9.6	10.3
.9	5.8	9.1	4.8			All Other Expenses (net)	3.4	2.9
6.9	11.9	12.7	1.1			Profit Before Taxes	6.2	7.4
						RATIOS		
4.4	4.1	2.7	2.1				2.5	3.1
1.4	1.4	1.2	1.6			Current	.9	1.0
.6	.5	.7	1.3				.4	.4
2.9	3.0	2.2	1.9				1.8	2.2
.9	1.2	1.0	1.3			Quick	(506) .5	(517) .6
.3	.3	.6	.5				.2	.2
0 UND	0 UND	0 UND	2 204.8				0 UND	0 UND
0 UND	0 UND	1 502.1	10 35.1			Sales/Receivables	0 UND	0 UND
1 287.3	3 116.5	7 52.5	36 10.0				3 108.7	3 106.4
						Cost of Sales/Inventory		
						Cost of Sales/Payables		
16.8	11.1	7.0	8.9				20.4	17.6
74.8	50.1	74.1	15.5			Sales/Working Capital	-202.0	999.8
-37.8	-27.3	-21.7	114.7				-15.1	-15.8
27.8	18.4	16.9	49.8				12.2	16.8
(258) 7.9	(178) 6.6	(38) 5.9	(10) 6.1			EBIT/Interest	(391) 3.6	(404) 4.1
1.2	1.9	2.8	2.4				.9	1.3
							7.0	5.4
						Net Profit + Depr., Dep., Amort./Cur. Mat. L/T/D	(19) 4.8	(14) 1.5
							1.1	.8
.2	1.0	.9	.2				.7	.7
2.3	8.8	3.1	.7			Fixed/Worth	15.1	4.2
-.9	-.6	9.7	4.1				-.8	-.8
.7	1.1	.8	.8				1.2	1.0
6.7	10.6	2.7	2.3			Debt/Worth	69.0	12.5
-2.8	-2.8	10.9	11.2				-2.7	-3.0
224.3	173.0	79.2	192.2				201.1	180.8
(203) 87.6	(129) 63.4	(47) 35.8	(10) 31.2			% Profit Before Taxes/Tangible Net Worth	(265) 61.4	(292) 61.4
25.3	25.7	12.9	16.2				13.1	13.8
71.6	38.6	27.9	20.5				46.5	41.6
26.8	14.2	7.7	8.8			% Profit Before Taxes/Total Assets	13.6	14.2
3.6	4.0	3.7	3.4				.0	1.9
130.1	27.0	8.7	31.4				45.3	52.6
30.4	9.0	2.5	16.4			Sales/Net Fixed Assets	15.6	15.7
12.0	1.9	.2	4.3				4.6	4.4
11.6	3.9	3.0	3.4				7.6	7.8
6.9	2.2	1.2	2.7			Sales/Total Assets	3.8	3.8
3.9	1.3	.2	2.0				1.8	1.8
.7	1.6	1.8					1.1	1.1
(201) 1.6	(147) 3.1	(51) 3.5				% Depr., Dep., Amort./Sales	(347) 2.5	(323) 2.4
3.3	7.0	14.8					4.9	4.6
5.8	5.2	4.2					5.8	5.4
(255) 9.5	(105) 7.1	(17) 7.1				% Officers', Directors' Owners' Comp/Sales	(321) 9.6	(336) 8.4
13.4	10.2	9.2					14.0	14.0
557639M	644648M	453136M	2539877M	556320M	2162874M	Net Sales ($)	7263151M	3612776M
79586M	229359M	250483M	184055M	361620M	684290M	Total Assets ($)	1510029M	1116320M

M = $ thousand MM = $ million

See Pages 9 through 22 for Explanation of Ratios and Data

Comparative Historical Data				Current Data Sorted by Sales					
			Type of Statement						
8	8	9	Unqualified		2		2	1	4
16	11	10	Reviewed		1	1	3	2	3
88	75	97	Compiled	22	44	16	10	3	2
317	330	331	Tax Returns	119	168	24	13	5	2
217	220	219	Other	56	95	28	19	8	13
4/1/11-3/31/12 ALL	**4/1/12-3/31/13 ALL**	**4/1/13-3/31/14 ALL**		25 (4/1-9/30/13)			641 (10/1/13-3/31/14)		
				0-1MM	**1-3MM**	**3-5MM**	**5-10MM**	**10-25MM**	**25MM & OVER**
646	644	666	**NUMBER OF STATEMENTS**	197	310	69	47	19	24
%	%	%	**ASSETS**	%	%	%	%	%	%
21.6	25.9	24.9	Cash & Equivalents	20.8	26.9	24.0	33.1	28.0	16.3
4.8	4.1	3.6	Trade Receivables (net)	2.3	3.5	4.8	4.2	4.3	12.3
9.4	8.4	9.2	Inventory	7.5	10.3	11.0	5.9	5.8	12.9
1.7	1.5	2.3	All Other Current	2.2	1.5	4.1	3.0	5.4	3.9
37.5	39.9	40.0	Total Current	33.0	42.1	43.8	46.2	43.5	45.5
38.5	37.0	38.5	Fixed Assets (net)	49.9	33.2	30.4	41.2	42.1	28.4
13.9	12.9	13.7	Intangibles (net)	10.9	16.6	13.5	6.2	5.8	22.5
10.0	10.2	7.7	All Other Non-Current	6.2	8.1	12.3	6.5	8.7	3.7
100.0	100.0	100.0	Total	100.0	100.0	100.0	100.0	100.0	100.0
			LIABILITIES						
10.2	10.9	9.0	Notes Payable-Short Term	8.4	10.0	7.7	9.6	3.9	7.2
5.6	4.9	5.2	Cur. Mat.-L.T.D.	4.7	5.3	5.6	4.0	10.3	3.7
8.6	6.8	6.4	Trade Payables	4.5	6.7	9.6	5.4	5.7	12.5
.1	.1	.4	Income Taxes Payable	.4	.4	.2	.6	.0	.0
12.7	12.4	15.9	All Other Current	16.8	15.9	11.8	24.8	8.0	9.6
37.1	35.1	36.9	Total Current	34.8	38.4	34.9	44.3	28.0	33.0
44.1	41.0	44.2	Long-Term Debt	59.2	42.4	26.1	32.6	34.7	26.5
.0	.0	.0	Deferred Taxes	.0	.0	.0	.2	.2	.0
6.5	8.9	8.1	All Other Non-Current	9.7	6.4	11.6	7.7	17.1	2.5
12.3	15.0	10.7	Net Worth	-3.7	12.8	27.4	15.1	20.0	38.0
100.0	100.0	100.0	Total Liabilties & Net Worth	100.0	100.0	100.0	100.0	100.0	100.0
			INCOME DATA						
100.0	100.0	100.0	Net Sales	100.0	100.0	100.0	100.0	100.0	100.0
			Gross Profit						
88.7	87.1	87.7	Operating Expenses	79.1	90.8	92.0	92.2	91.7	92.9
11.3	12.9	12.3	Operating Profit	20.9	9.2	8.0	7.8	8.3	7.1
3.7	2.8	3.4	All Other Expenses (net)	9.1	1.1	.3	.3	.7	3.0
7.6	10.1	9.0	Profit Before Taxes	11.9	8.1	7.7	7.5	7.6	4.1
			RATIOS						
3.2	3.3	4.0		4.2	3.8	3.8	4.8	4.4	2.1
1.2	1.3	1.4	Current	1.1	1.6	1.4	1.6	1.4	1.3
.5	.5	.6		.4	.6	.8	.7	1.0	1.0
2.3	2.6	2.8		2.6	2.9	2.4	4.5	3.8	1.6
(644) .8	.9	1.0	Quick	.8	1.1	1.1	1.4	1.2	.7
.3	.3	.3		.2	.3	.3	.7	.7	.4
0 UND	0 UND	0 UND		0 UND	0 UND	0 UND	0 UND	0 UND	1 451.3
0 UND	0 UND	0 UND	Sales/Receivables	0 UND	0 UND	0 UND	0 UND	2 188.0	5 79.0
3 105.1	2 158.3	2 154.5		0 UND	2 152.9	5 77.3	2 150.3	5 78.8	24 15.3
			Cost of Sales/Inventory						
			Cost of Sales/Payables						
17.0	15.2	14.1		12.7	14.9	14.0	17.9	17.7	13.4
116.4	78.7	62.7	Sales/Working Capital	137.3	53.7	64.3	50.1	36.7	30.4
-21.6	-24.5	-34.1		-9.4	-43.9	-89.0	-36.6	-574.4	-276.6
18.0	25.5	23.2		10.6	22.0	54.0	51.4	50.7	46.3
(495) 5.3	(473) 8.0	(492) 6.6	EBIT/Interest	(122) 3.0	(237) 6.7	(58) 14.6	(36) 12.8	(18) 15.1	(21) 5.5
1.7	2.4	1.8		.7	2.4	3.2	2.7	3.6	2.5
9.7	7.0	9.8							
(19) 1.6	(18) 2.4	(23) 5.4	Net Profit + Depr., Dep., Amort./Cur. Mat. L/T/D						
.7	1.4	1.8							
.5	.4	.5		.9	.4	.3	.4	.8	.5
3.3	2.7	3.3	Fixed/Worth	7.2	3.1	1.3	1.0	1.3	1.2
-1.8	-2.0	-1.2		-1.2	-.6	-6.5	-5.8	9.9	-3.6
.9	.9	.8		1.5	.7	.4	.6	.8	.7
6.9	5.4	6.7	Debt/Worth	18.0	7.1	3.2	2.7	1.7	2.5
-3.9	-4.4	-3.4		-2.8	-2.6	-11.3	-16.5	27.0	-6.8
162.4	200.3	169.5		90.0	176.0	226.9	223.3	224.4	93.1
(404) 62.4	(394) 78.9	(394) 62.3	% Profit Before Taxes/Tangible Net Worth	(107) 45.9	(176) 85.8	(47) 63.4	(32) 97.0	(15) 93.1	(17) 37.0
20.3	28.3	19.5		9.5	25.6	36.4	32.7	13.2	17.3
48.3	59.5	49.1		33.2	56.2	57.7	92.5	121.9	33.7
17.6	20.3	18.3	% Profit Before Taxes/Total Assets	7.2	22.9	29.4	38.1	32.8	8.9
3.3	5.4	3.8		.0	7.7	7.0	8.1	7.8	1.6
67.7	79.8	59.0		30.4	76.3	91.1	45.7	47.6	22.2
17.4	20.2	16.8	Sales/Net Fixed Assets	7.2	24.2	23.6	23.6	12.3	11.6
4.9	6.0	5.6		1.0	8.3	9.1	8.6	5.6	7.1
7.8	8.3	8.3		5.8	8.8	10.6	10.6	15.9	4.8
3.9	4.5	4.1	Sales/Total Assets	2.3	4.8	4.0	6.2	4.9	2.9
1.9	1.9	2.0		.6	2.5	2.3	3.4	2.4	1.9
1.3	1.0	1.0		2.2	.8	.5	.9	1.2	1.3
(385) 2.5	(382) 2.1	(413) 2.4	% Depr., Dep., Amort./Sales	(130) 5.4	(172) 1.8	(48) 1.5	(30) 1.5	(17) 1.8	(16) 2.2
5.2	4.4	4.9		17.2	3.4	3.0	2.6	3.0	3.0
5.7	5.8	5.5		6.7	5.7	3.8	3.4		
(387) 9.1	(398) 8.9	(382) 8.6	% Officers', Directors' Owners' Comp/Sales	(93) 9.9	(215) 8.3	(34) 6.7	(25) 5.9		
14.1	13.3	12.7		14.5	12.7	10.0	11.5		
5160350M	8433006M	6914494M	Net Sales ($)	113418M	542442M	255384M	334627M	245308M	5423315M
1458852M	1631447M	1789393M	Total Assets ($)	123092M	176552M	81129M	89696M	77281M	1241643M

M = $ thousand MM = $ million

See Pages 9 through 22 for Explanation of Ratios and Data

Current Data Sorted by Assets							Comparative Historical Data	
						Type of Statement		
3	6	36	40	8	5	Unqualified	119	109
	10	54	14	1		Reviewed	103	104
17	27	36	4			Compiled	128	96
192	121	64	7			Tax Returns	334	346
103	158	176	47	16	7	Other	373	517
96 (4/1-9/30/13)			1,056 (10/1/13-3/31/14)				4/1/09-3/31/10	4/1/10-3/31/11
0-500M	500M-2MM	2-10MM	10-50MM	50-100MM	100-250MM		ALL	ALL
315	322	366	112	25	12	**NUMBER OF STATEMENTS**	1057	1172
%	%	%	%	%	%	**ASSETS**	%	%
40.7	17.9	15.8	15.7	12.1	11.4	Cash & Equivalents	20.6	20.3
15.5	30.2	39.2	30.3	27.5	16.3	Trade Receivables (net)	27.3	29.6
3.6	6.0	5.0	3.7	4.1	1.2	Inventory	5.5	5.0
2.9	3.7	4.0	6.2	5.2	7.0	All Other Current	4.4	4.0
62.7	57.7	64.0	56.0	48.9	36.0	Total Current	57.8	59.0
19.9	25.4	21.4	17.6	21.4	31.1	Fixed Assets (net)	24.4	23.6
3.9	4.3	6.1	14.8	22.1	21.9	Intangibles (net)	6.1	6.2
13.5	12.5	8.5	11.7	7.6	11.0	All Other Non-Current	11.7	11.2
100.0	100.0	100.0	100.0	100.0	100.0	Total	100.0	100.0
						LIABILITIES		
31.3	10.9	8.9	6.2	6.3	3.0	Notes Payable-Short Term	16.1	13.7
4.8	4.1	2.1	2.7	3.5	1.1	Cur. Mat.-L.T.D.	3.8	3.2
10.4	10.8	12.1	10.7	9.3	8.0	Trade Payables	10.6	11.0
.1	.1	.4	.4	.8	.9	Income Taxes Payable	.2	.3
22.5	13.4	17.2	12.8	8.5	7.5	All Other Current	16.1	15.5
69.0	39.2	40.7	32.8	28.5	20.5	Total Current	46.7	43.6
16.7	21.7	14.2	11.1	15.5	39.7	Long-Term Debt	17.1	16.9
.0	.0	.2	.4	.7	2.3	Deferred Taxes	.2	.2
10.8	8.1	5.4	5.4	6.3	5.7	All Other Non-Current	7.2	9.8
3.4	31.0	39.5	50.2	48.9	31.7	Net Worth	28.8	29.5
100.0	100.0	100.0	100.0	100.0	100.0	Total Liabilties & Net Worth	100.0	100.0
						INCOME DATA		
100.0	100.0	100.0	100.0	100.0	100.0	Net Sales	100.0	100.0
						Gross Profit		
88.2	88.8	90.5	92.4	87.0	90.0	Operating Expenses	91.8	91.1
11.8	11.2	9.5	7.6	13.0	10.0	Operating Profit	8.2	8.9
.6	3.0	1.8	.6	5.0	2.6	All Other Expenses (net)	1.8	2.0
11.3	8.2	7.7	6.9	8.0	7.4	Profit Before Taxes	6.4	6.9
						RATIOS		
4.0	3.4	3.5	3.0	2.8	2.7		3.3	3.5
1.3	1.6	1.7	1.9	1.7	1.8	Current	1.5	1.6
.5	.9	1.0	1.2	.9	1.3		.8	.9
3.7	2.8	2.8	2.6	1.9	1.8		2.7	3.1
1.1	1.2	1.4	1.5	1.5	1.3	Quick	1.2	1.3
.4	.5	.8	.9	.5	.9		.6	.6
0 UND	0 UND	28 12.9	31 11.6	28 13.2	46 8.0		0 UND	0 UND
0 UND	27 13.5	54 6.8	51 7.2	57 6.4	53 6.9	Sales/Receivables	31 11.9	34 10.8
18 20.2	54 6.8	73 5.0	72 5.1	96 3.8	61 6.0		58 6.3	60 6.0
						Cost of Sales/Inventory		
						Cost of Sales/Payables		
11.0	6.7	5.3	4.1	2.6	4.3		6.8	6.1
65.2	18.7	10.6	9.1	8.9	8.4	Sales/Working Capital	22.8	18.3
-24.9	-46.4	152.1	28.3	-156.2	15.5		-40.2	-63.9
37.0	30.3	49.3	43.8	10.8	17.0		25.0	27.7
(177) 9.5	(231) 5.5	(284) 9.4	(92) 10.0	(17) 3.5	(10) 5.0	EBIT/Interest	(800) 5.3	(850) 6.1
2.1	1.3	2.6	2.2	.7	1.0		.7	1.2
		15.5	4.5				6.8	8.6
		(26) 6.0	(22) 2.8			Net Profit + Depr., Dep., Amort./Cur. Mat. L/T/D	(77) 2.7	(86) 3.0
		2.4	1.4				.8	1.2
.0	.1	.1	.1	.1	.5		.1	.1
.4	.5	.4	.5	1.6	1.0	Fixed/Worth	.6	.5
-22.5	25.4	1.6	1.7	-2.6	NM		6.3	4.8
.4	.6	.5	.5	.5	.7		.6	.5
3.7	2.0	1.5	1.3	1.4	1.3	Debt/Worth	1.9	2.0
-4.9	493.7	6.5	5.1	-8.8	NM		64.7	26.2
295.8	100.5	76.5	50.1	31.4			81.5	91.0
(208) 91.5	(246) 36.9	(313) 38.2	(95) 28.5	(17) 10.2		% Profit Before Taxes/Tangible Net Worth	(817) 32.6	(908) 36.6
31.1	7.2	8.5	4.8	1.1			4.8	6.3
97.6	32.4	29.5	19.2	11.0	13.5		31.0	33.6
32.4	11.1	12.6	8.8	3.2	5.1	% Profit Before Taxes/Total Assets	9.5	12.2
7.8	1.1	2.4	1.7	-.8	1.6		-.1	.8
UND	199.3	95.5	71.2	84.9	26.1		120.7	143.6
82.2	32.9	26.7	21.9	22.3	4.8	Sales/Net Fixed Assets	28.1	28.5
19.7	8.1	6.7	6.1	3.0	1.8		7.8	7.3
12.2	5.1	3.5	2.7	1.6	1.6		5.1	5.0
6.5	3.1	2.5	1.6	.9	1.0	Sales/Total Assets	2.9	2.9
3.4	1.8	1.6	1.0	.6	.4		1.5	1.6
.4	.5	.5	.7	.6			.5	.5
(120) 1.4	(178) 1.8	(260) 1.5	(84) 1.8	(17) 3.1		% Depr., Dep., Amort./Sales	(716) 1.5	(763) 1.5
3.5	5.0	3.9	3.7	6.3			3.9	3.8
4.2	3.2	2.3	1.4				3.4	3.1
(170) 9.1	(148) 5.8	(121) 4.1	(20) 3.5			% Officers', Directors' Owners' Comp/Sales	(455) 7.2	(457) 7.0
17.0	10.5	7.4	12.5				14.7	13.2
517990M	1288798M	4409767M	4261369M	2505245M	1879675M	Net Sales ($)	14078423M	19614452M
68295M	354792M	1648355M	2190846M	1827026M	1816114M	Total Assets ($)	8524632M	9922402M

M = $ thousand MM = $ million

See Pages 9 through 22 for Explanation of Ratios and Data

Comparative Historical Data				Current Data Sorted by Sales					
			Type of Statement						
127	89	98	Unqualified	3	5	6	16	31	37
118	87	79	Reviewed	1	2	7	15	38	16
137	117	84	Compiled	11	21	12	22	12	6
422	400	384	Tax Returns	102	134	64	45	36	3
540	574	507	Other	80	98	76	92	97	64
4/1/11-3/31/12 ALL	**4/1/12-3/31/13 ALL**	**4/1/13-3/31/14 ALL**		**96 (4/1-9/30/13)**			**1,056 (10/1/13-3/31/14)**		
				0-1MM	**1-3MM**	**3-5MM**	**5-10MM**	**10-25MM**	**25MM & OVER**
1344	1267	1152	**NUMBER OF STATEMENTS**	197	260	165	190	214	126
%	%	%	**ASSETS**	%	%	%	%	%	%
21.4	22.4	23.1	Cash & Equivalents	29.0	28.1	23.5	21.3	18.6	13.1
28.5	27.0	28.8	Trade Receivables (net)	11.8	21.3	31.7	33.5	40.1	41.1
5.2	5.4	4.7	Inventory	1.7	6.3	5.8	5.5	5.0	2.8
3.9	4.2	3.9	All Other Current	3.5	3.0	2.1	4.3	4.6	7.0
59.0	58.9	60.5	Total Current	46.0	58.6	63.2	64.6	68.4	63.9
22.9	22.0	21.9	Fixed Assets (net)	36.8	21.6	21.3	18.3	15.9	15.3
6.6	6.6	6.3	Intangibles (net)	4.4	4.3	5.9	7.1	5.9	13.7
11.5	12.5	11.3	All Other Non-Current	12.7	15.5	9.6	10.1	9.8	7.0
100.0	100.0	100.0	Total	100.0	100.0	100.0	100.0	100.0	100.0
			LIABILITIES						
15.5	13.5	15.2	Notes Payable-Short Term	20.1	18.4	17.3	14.6	10.2	7.5
3.3	3.0	3.5	Cur. Mat.-L.T.D.	2.4	5.0	4.5	2.7	3.0	2.7
11.2	11.2	11.1	Trade Payables	5.2	10.8	12.7	12.7	11.7	15.2
.3	.3	.2	Income Taxes Payable	.1	.1	.1	.3	.1	.8
17.4	14.3	16.9	All Other Current	23.3	15.3	17.0	15.0	16.1	14.0
47.7	42.2	46.8	Total Current	51.0	49.7	51.5	45.2	41.1	40.3
18.0	17.7	17.0	Long-Term Debt	23.6	22.1	16.8	13.3	9.4	14.6
.3	.4	.2	Deferred Taxes	.0	.0	.1	.2	.1	.6
10.8	8.9	7.7	All Other Non-Current	8.9	9.4	9.7	6.8	5.4	4.4
23.2	30.9	28.4	Net Worth	16.5	18.7	21.8	34.5	44.0	40.1
100.0	100.0	100.0	Total Liabilties & Net Worth	100.0	100.0	100.0	100.0	100.0	100.0
			INCOME DATA						
100.0	100.0	100.0	Net Sales	100.0	100.0	100.0	100.0	100.0	100.0
			Gross Profit						
90.0	89.1	89.5	Operating Expenses	77.1	90.7	92.2	91.9	92.7	93.7
10.0	10.9	10.5	Operating Profit	22.9	9.3	7.8	8.1	7.3	6.3
2.0	1.8	1.7	All Other Expenses (net)	6.7	.9	1.0	.3	.4	1.2
8.0	9.0	8.8	Profit Before Taxes	16.1	8.4	6.8	7.8	6.9	5.0
			RATIOS						
3.2	3.8	3.5		4.4	3.5	3.6	3.5	3.5	2.5
1.5	1.6	1.6	Current	1.2	1.5	1.7	1.7	1.8	1.8
.8	.8	.9		.3	.7	.9	1.0	1.1	1.2
2.7	3.2	3.0		4.0	3.0	3.3	3.0	2.9	2.1
(1343) 1.2	1.3	1.3	Quick	1.0	1.1	1.4	1.2	1.6	1.4
.6	.6	.6		.3	.5	.6	.7	.9	1.0
0 UND	**0** UND	**0** UND		**0** UND	**0** UND	**0** UND	**13** 28.0	**24** 15.1	**37** 9.9
32 11.3	**29** 12.4	**32** 11.5	Sales/Receivables	**0** UND	**10** 35.1	**31** 11.8	**41** 8.9	**50** 7.3	**55** 6.6
58 6.3	**57** 6.4	**61** 6.0		**28** 12.9	**41** 8.8	**65** 5.6	**68** 5.4	**66** 5.5	**72** 5.1
			Cost of Sales/Inventory						
			Cost of Sales/Payables						
6.7	6.3	6.3		8.2	6.7	6.8	5.1	6.1	6.0
20.5	18.5	17.1	Sales/Working Capital	57.5	26.9	15.4	15.6	12.1	11.4
-55.8	-53.2	-65.0		-8.4	-21.1	-117.6	-283.6	61.8	34.1
29.5	29.0	37.4		23.3	33.1	30.3	48.4	53.3	41.9
(952) 7.3	(869) 7.9	(811) 8.5	EBIT/Interest	(78) 5.2	(194) 6.4	(127) 6.0	(150) 8.3	(154) 15.6	(108) 9.6
1.5	1.7	1.8		1.5	1.4	1.4	2.0	3.2	2.0
6.0	13.7	8.2						15.0	4.4
(92) 2.5	(76) 3.8	(58) 3.2	Net Profit + Depr., Dep., Amort./Cur. Mat. L/T/D					(24) 5.7	(23) 2.7
1.3	1.4	1.6						2.7	1.7
.1	.1	.1		.0	.0	.1	.1	.1	.1
.5	.4	.5	Fixed/Worth	.6	.6	.5	.6	.3	.5
6.5	3.8	4.2		10.3	UND	-6.0	6.2	1.2	2.0
.6	.5	.5		.4	.6	.4	.5	.5	.7
2.1	1.8	1.7	Debt/Worth	2.5	2.6	1.7	1.6	1.3	1.9
269.5	23.1	56.0		UND	-10.8	-24.9	27.8	3.8	9.9
97.2	100.8	100.0		124.9	143.1	100.3	107.5	85.3	59.2
(1023) 43.6	(996) 43.4	(888) 40.7	% Profit Before Taxes/Tangible Net Worth	(148) 38.9	(184) 50.3	(118) 41.2	(151) 45.7	(186) 41.5	(101) 31.9
10.4	12.8	10.2		6.9	13.5	9.1	7.3	16.7	7.1
36.5	37.4	38.1		50.5	51.4	37.4	39.5	34.3	21.3
12.7	13.4	13.7	% Profit Before Taxes/Total Assets	12.1	17.7	12.4	12.4	15.1	9.5
1.6	2.7	2.5		.8	2.9	2.4	2.7	4.5	1.4
128.9	161.6	209.9		UND	307.4	199.3	141.9	175.5	97.5
31.1	33.8	34.2	Sales/Net Fixed Assets	18.9	38.4	36.9	33.2	41.1	33.1
8.5	9.3	9.4		.8	11.8	11.2	10.7	11.4	12.0
5.1	5.2	5.3		5.5	6.7	6.5	4.6	4.5	4.2
3.0	2.9	3.0	Sales/Total Assets	1.9	3.7	3.6	2.7	3.0	2.4
1.7	1.6	1.7		.4	2.0	2.2	1.8	2.0	1.3
.5	.5	.5		1.8	.6	.6	.4	.4	.4
(814) 1.4	(730) 1.5	(663) 1.6	% Depr., Dep., Amort./Sales	(88) 10.3	(131) 1.8	(89) 1.7	(115) 1.4	(150) 1.2	(90) .9
3.7	3.6	3.9		21.6	4.1	3.4	3.2	2.7	2.6
2.9	2.8	3.2		7.9	4.2	3.3	2.6	1.5	1.4
(518) 6.1	(483) 6.1	(462) 5.8	% Officers', Directors' Owners' Comp/Sales	(69) 12.9	(136) 7.9	(83) 5.4	(88) 4.2	(66) 3.5	(20) 5.4
11.6	12.8	12.1		22.2	14.1	8.7	6.7	6.8	13.0
20070212M	**17365726M**	**14862844M**	Net Sales ($)	**85892M**	**492667M**	**634699M**	**1388425M**	**3378038M**	**8883123M**
9668764M	**7843921M**	**7905428M**	Total Assets ($)	**161463M**	**229203M**	**342305M**	**738314M**	**1586945M**	**4847198M**

M = $ thousand MM = $ million

See Pages 9 through 22 for Explanation of Ratios and Data

MANAGEMENT OF COMPANIES AND ENTERPRISES

MANAGEMENT OF COMPANIES AND ENTERPRISES

Current Data Sorted by Assets							Comparative Historical Data	
						Type of Statement		
3	2	11	30	14	18	Unqualified	89	88
	2	14	16	5	4	Reviewed	62	50
7	13	22	6	1	1	Compiled	92	93
38	57	56	12	1	1	Tax Returns	259	248
19	52	76	58	20	19	Other	253	270
57 (4/1-9/30/13)			521 (10/1/13-3/31/14)				4/1/09-3/31/10	4/1/10-3/31/11
0-500M	500M-2MM	2-10MM	10-50MM	50-100MM	100-250MM		ALL	ALL
67	126	179	122	41	43	NUMBER OF STATEMENTS	755	749
%	%	%	%	%	%	**ASSETS**	%	%
30.5	10.2	9.2	12.7	8.8	9.2	Cash & Equivalents	9.1	8.8
8.0	6.7	9.7	13.2	14.7	14.6	Trade Receivables (net)	7.7	8.8
1.2	3.1	7.3	9.9	9.6	10.4	Inventory	4.5	4.8
4.2	3.7	2.9	3.5	6.7	4.4	All Other Current	3.3	3.4
43.9	23.7	29.1	39.2	39.8	38.7	Total Current	24.7	25.8
32.1	59.5	52.5	37.5	33.8	32.5	Fixed Assets (net)	56.7	56.4
4.4	4.0	5.9	11.4	12.0	15.0	Intangibles (net)	4.7	4.7
19.6	12.7	12.4	11.9	14.4	13.9	All Other Non-Current	13.9	13.0
100.0	100.0	100.0	100.0	100.0	100.0	Total	100.0	100.0
						LIABILITIES		
10.6	5.4	3.9	6.1	5.0	7.4	Notes Payable-Short Term	6.8	5.9
2.4	3.1	3.2	5.2	3.2	3.8	Cur. Mat.-L.T.D.	4.5	4.1
5.0	6.4	7.0	6.9	9.1	10.3	Trade Payables	4.4	4.1
.1	.7	.1	.3	.1	.0	Income Taxes Payable	.3	.1
23.2	7.0	9.3	8.2	11.8	9.5	All Other Current	10.0	8.7
41.3	22.7	23.5	26.7	29.2	31.1	Total Current	26.0	22.9
17.5	42.2	41.9	22.0	26.4	31.8	Long-Term Debt	42.6	41.6
.0	.1	.1	.5	.5	1.4	Deferred Taxes	.3	.3
7.1	8.3	8.2	6.8	4.8	3.8	All Other Non-Current	6.3	6.3
34.1	26.7	26.3	44.0	39.1	31.9	Net Worth	24.8	28.9
100.0	100.0	100.0	100.0	100.0	100.0	Total Liabilties & Net Worth	100.0	100.0
						INCOME DATA		
100.0	100.0	100.0	100.0	100.0	100.0	Net Sales	100.0	100.0
						Gross Profit		
72.3	63.5	67.8	78.4	85.2	85.9	Operating Expenses	66.6	64.9
27.7	36.5	32.2	21.6	14.8	14.1	Operating Profit	33.4	35.1
4.6	13.6	11.6	4.2	5.3	7.5	All Other Expenses (net)	15.6	14.2
23.1	22.9	20.6	17.4	9.5	6.6	Profit Before Taxes	17.8	20.8
						RATIOS		
5.3	4.1	2.7	2.5	2.5	1.8		2.0	2.1
2.1	1.2	1.1	1.4	1.3	1.2	Current	.9	1.0
.8	.2	.4	.9	.8	.9		.3	.3
4.8	2.7	1.6	1.9	1.6	1.3		1.4	1.5
2.0	.8	.7	1.0	.8	.7	Quick	.6	.7
.5	.2	.2	.4	.4	.4		.2	.2
0 UND	**0** UND	**0** UND	**0** UND	**7** 50.8	**3** 109.7		**0** UND	**0** UND
0 UND	**0** UND	**1** 668.2	**24** 14.9	**33** 11.1	**34** 10.8	Sales/Receivables	**0** 999.8	**0** UND
5 78.0	**13** 27.8	**31** 11.9	**50** 7.3	**57** 6.4	**58** 6.3		**29** 12.5	**36** 10.0
						Cost of Sales/Inventory		
						Cost of Sales/Payables		
6.7	6.3	5.5	3.9	3.8	6.0		8.0	6.2
16.5	150.8	76.8	14.0	15.6	13.6	Sales/Working Capital	-71.0	173.0
-62.8	-3.6	-4.3	-71.0	-12.3	-50.7		-3.3	-4.2
37.5	9.7	13.4	16.1	6.5	7.3		8.4	12.2
(25) 6.6	(70) 3.7	(118) 4.3	(101) 4.5	(31) 3.1	(37) 3.1	EBIT/Interest	(415) 3.5	(424) 4.6
3.2	1.9	1.7	1.2	.7	-.2		1.3	1.9
			8.3	3.9			4.3	4.5
			(28) 3.8	(10) 3.0		Net Profit + Depr., Dep., Amort./Cur. Mat. L/T/D	(88) 1.8	(90) 2.1
			1.1	2.4			.8	1.1
.0	.8	.5	.3	.1	.7		.7	.6
.5	2.5	2.4	1.1	1.6	1.8	Fixed/Worth	2.6	2.2
3.1	12.0	15.6	2.5	NM	39.6		21.8	8.5
.1	.7	1.1	.6	.7	1.4		1.0	.9
.8	3.3	3.1	1.5	2.4	6.5	Debt/Worth	3.4	2.5
UND	73.2	34.8	5.8	NM	47.3		40.4	12.9
155.9	66.7	43.1	30.7	27.8	45.4		38.6	39.3
(51) 65.4	(101) 22.0	(139) 18.0	(104) 10.3	(31) 6.8	(34) 25.4	% Profit Before Taxes/Tangible Net Worth	(593) 14.8	(617) 16.7
9.3	6.8	7.0	.9	-.4	3.8		3.1	3.9
72.6	13.8	12.0	11.8	11.1	8.6		9.3	11.2
17.0	5.7	5.7	4.3	3.8	4.2	% Profit Before Taxes/Total Assets	4.2	5.1
3.2	.6	1.1	.4	-.2	-.5		.3	1.0
UND	17.6	14.6	19.5	25.2	20.3		10.0	10.9
30.7	.4	.7	4.8	3.5	3.9	Sales/Net Fixed Assets	.5	.6
3.6	.2	.2	.4	.7	1.4		.2	.2
6.8	2.3	1.9	2.1	1.9	1.6		1.3	1.4
2.2	.3	.4	.9	.8	1.0	Sales/Total Assets	.3	.3
.5	.1	.1	.2	.2	.3		.1	.1
.7	3.6	2.0	1.0	.8	.6		3.4	3.2
(31) 7.9	(97) 16.6	(137) 10.3	(108) 2.9	(34) 3.5	(28) 3.8	% Depr., Dep., Amort./Sales	(620) 13.3	(610) 12.9
18.6	24.2	21.2	11.1	9.8	11.0		21.6	21.4
6.2	4.8	1.3	.9				2.1	1.7
(17) 12.4	(20) 8.9	(35) 3.9	(17) 3.9			% Officers', Directors' Owners' Comp/Sales	(95) 5.2	(99) 4.6
26.8	15.9	7.8	10.9				13.4	15.3
38818M	**170390M**	**1193247M**	**4804054M**	**3533608M**	**9136900M**	Net Sales ($)	**13073172M**	**15284663M**
14450M	**139081M**	**823069M**	**2814219M**	**2872797M**	**7102219M**	Total Assets ($)	**12414948M**	**13417041M**

M = $ thousand **MM = $ million**

See Pages 9 through 22 for Explanation of Ratios and Data

Comparative Historical Data | **Current Data Sorted by Sales**

			Type of Statement						
94	80	78	Unqualified	4	7	4	9	11	43
46	53	41	Reviewed	4	3		4	11	19
73	58	50	Compiled	25	10	6	3	4	2
266	219	165	Tax Returns	101	24	9	15	10	6
265	263	244	Other	82	46	18	13	32	53
					57 (4/1-9/30/13)			521 (10/1/13-3/31/14)	
4/1/11-3/31/12 ALL	4/1/12-3/31/13 ALL	4/1/13-3/31/14 ALL		0-1MM	1-3MM	3-5MM	5-10MM	10-25MM	25MM & OVER
744	673	578	NUMBER OF STATEMENTS	216	90	37	44	68	123
%	%	%	ASSETS	%	%	%	%	%	%
10.0	10.2	12.6	Cash & Equivalents	11.8	14.2	12.4	12.3	13.3	12.5
8.0	10.1	10.3	Trade Receivables (net)	2.0	9.2	10.3	13.4	16.8	21.0
5.2	5.1	6.6	Inventory	.5	4.5	6.4	11.5	14.3	13.0
3.4	3.4	3.7	All Other Current	2.9	4.2	1.9	4.8	5.1	4.3
26.5	28.8	33.3	Total Current	17.3	32.1	31.0	42.1	49.5	50.8
53.8	51.9	45.7	Fixed Assets (net)	66.6	42.6	42.0	33.9	24.3	28.4
6.0	5.7	7.6	Intangibles (net)	2.8	6.2	10.1	12.1	12.7	11.9
13.6	13.5	13.5	All Other Non-Current	13.4	19.2	16.9	11.9	13.5	8.9
100.0	100.0	100.0	Total	100.0	100.0	100.0	100.0	100.0	100.0
			LIABILITIES						
5.1	5.4	5.8	Notes Payable-Short Term	5.0	5.3	2.8	6.0	6.7	8.1
4.6	3.5	3.5	Cur. Mat.-L.T.D.	3.2	2.7	3.5	3.4	2.9	5.2
4.8	4.9	7.0	Trade Payables	1.3	4.4	7.0	21.7	9.9	12.0
.2	.1	.3	Income Taxes Payable	.5	.0	.0	.1	.3	.3
8.4	9.9	10.4	All Other Current	9.4	8.7	6.8	12.8	12.7	12.3
23.1	23.7	27.0	Total Current	19.3	21.2	20.0	44.0	32.5	37.9
41.4	37.4	33.1	Long-Term Debt	45.9	29.7	30.6	32.2	21.5	20.6
.3	.2	.3	Deferred Taxes	.0	.0	.1	.4	.1	1.2
7.4	7.7	7.2	All Other Non-Current	5.1	12.7	9.0	6.9	9.3	5.4
27.9	30.9	32.3	Net Worth	29.7	36.5	40.3	16.5	36.6	34.9
100.0	100.0	100.0	Total Liabilties & Net Worth	100.0	100.0	100.0	100.0	100.0	100.0
			INCOME DATA						
100.0	100.0	100.0	Net Sales	100.0	100.0	100.0	100.0	100.0	100.0
			Gross Profit						
67.7	67.7	72.2	Operating Expenses	53.5	68.5	74.5	89.7	84.9	93.8
32.3	32.3	27.8	Operating Profit	46.5	31.5	25.5	10.3	15.1	6.2
13.4	11.4	8.9	All Other Expenses (net)	17.9	6.6	3.0	3.6	3.4	1.5
18.8	20.9	18.9	Profit Before Taxes	28.6	24.9	22.5	6.7	11.7	4.7
			RATIOS						
2.1	2.5	2.9		3.8	7.4	3.7	2.2	3.0	2.0
1.0	1.2	1.2	Current	.9	1.5	1.5	1.2	1.5	1.3
.3	.5	.5		.2	.5	.5	.5	1.0	1.0
1.6	1.8	2.2		2.6	5.4	3.2	1.4	2.0	1.6
.6	(672) .8	.8	Quick	.7	1.0	.8	.7	.8	.9
.2	.2	.3		.2	.3	.3	.2	.4	.6
0 UND	0 UND	0 UND		0 UND	0 UND	0 UND	0 UND	6 60.7	10 34.9
0 999.8	1 296.5	3 105.5	Sales/Receivables	0 UND	4 89.5	5 68.4	22 16.5	25 14.8	36 10.2
34 10.8	36 10.0	37 9.8		0 UND	26 14.3	21 17.5	65 5.6	45 8.1	58 6.3
			Cost of Sales/Inventory						
			Cost of Sales/Payables						
6.7	5.4	5.1		4.3	4.1	6.5	5.3	4.0	6.0
UND	41.4	29.6	Sales/Working Capital	-154.8	34.0	113.7	16.5	12.4	16.2
-4.3	-6.5	-8.5		-2.6	-6.6	-9.9	-7.8	NM	136.5
11.2	15.3	11.5		8.2	14.8	10.6	9.9	22.8	12.6
(455) 4.3	(413) 5.3	(382) 4.3	EBIT/Interest	(98) 4.4	(54) 4.5	(26) 3.9	(37) 1.7	(54) 3.8	(113) 4.5
1.6	2.4	1.6		2.6	1.7	1.6	-1.1	1.4	1.4
5.1	6.7	6.8							7.7
(82) 2.5	(72) 2.8	(54) 3.1	Net Profit + Depr., Dep., Amort./Cur. Mat. L/T/D						(36) 3.4
1.3	1.2	1.1							1.6
.6	.4	.3		.8	.2	.0	.2	.1	.4
2.2	2.0	1.6	Fixed/Worth	2.7	1.3	1.5	1.6	.7	1.2
38.4	9.9	9.1		9.9	83.7	-33.4	NM	9.3	6.0
.9	.8	.7		.6	.4	.5	1.2	.7	1.2
2.8	2.4	2.3	Debt/Worth	2.5	1.6	1.5	3.3	2.0	2.5
176.2	15.8	17.1		12.7	UND	-14.3	-13.4	22.0	11.5
44.1	48.8	47.5		39.0	47.7	110.0	36.1	75.8	45.8
(563) 17.7	(541) 20.7	(460) 18.2	% Profit Before Taxes/Tangible Net Worth	(180) 16.3	(69) 16.6	(25) 26.7	(31) 15.5	(53) 23.2	(102) 23.3
4.0	6.6	3.7		5.2	3.5	4.5	-2.2	3.2	3.0
11.9	13.4	13.4		10.3	13.8	22.2	10.0	16.0	15.0
4.8	6.0	5.6	% Profit Before Taxes/Total Assets	4.9	7.2	9.9	2.4	7.7	5.1
.8	1.5	.7		1.1	1.5	.7	-1.3	1.0	.6
12.6	16.2	25.9		1.8	34.7	652.5	28.7	48.6	29.0
1.1	1.3	3.3	Sales/Net Fixed Assets	.2	1.8	7.5	7.9	9.6	10.4
.2	.2	.2		.1	.3	.6	.6	3.2	3.4
1.6	1.8	2.2		.4	2.4	3.7	2.9	3.1	3.1
.4	.3	.6	Sales/Total Assets	.2	.4	1.1	1.3	1.7	1.8
.2	.1	.2		.1	.2	.3	.2	.8	1.0
2.7	1.9	1.6		13.4	2.0	2.2	1.2	.8	.6
(597) 10.1	(520) 9.2	(435) 6.7	% Depr., Dep., Amort./Sales	(157) 20.4	(63) 8.1	(22) 4.0	(35) 2.2	(55) 2.0	(103) 1.9
21.2	20.1	19.5		25.5	18.0	21.0	10.0	4.3	4.3
2.2	2.0	1.8		5.6	4.9	4.1	1.0	.9	.3
(104) 5.1	(92) 5.2	(93) 6.0	% Officers', Directors' Owners' Comp/Sales	(20) 9.9	(17) 9.2	(13) 8.2	(16) 2.8	(15) 2.3	(12) .9
19.4	11.7	13.8		23.8	19.9	19.4	13.7	4.9	5.8
14401527M	16055526M	18877017M	Net Sales ($)	75145M	163062M	147799M	313370M	1079192M	17098449M
14889959M	13391986M	13765835M	Total Assets ($)	423569M	748271M	394698M	1014764M	1694765M	9489768M

M = $ thousand MM = $ million

See Pages 9 through 22 for Explanation of Ratios and Data

Current Data Sorted by Assets							Comparative Historical Data	
						Type of Statement		
1			2	1	3	Unqualified	4	3
		1			1	Reviewed	5	5
1	1	2	2	2		Compiled	2	3
2	4	4	1			Tax Returns	5	2
2	4	3	10	1	2	Other	11	15
	7 (4/1-9/30/13)		43 (10/1/13-3/31/14)				4/1/09-3/31/10 ALL	4/1/10-3/31/11 ALL
0-500M	**500M-2MM**	**2-10MM**	**10-50MM**	**50-100MM**	**100-250MM**			
6	9	10	15	4	6	**NUMBER OF STATEMENTS**	27	28
%	%	%	%	%	%	**ASSETS**	%	%
		11.0	14.1			Cash & Equivalents	11.2	8.8
		9.6	13.9			Trade Receivables (net)	13.6	12.1
		.1	5.9			Inventory	5.9	6.1
		6.1	14.3			All Other Current	11.6	10.3
		26.7.	48.2			Total Current	42.2	37.2
		45.9	24.0			Fixed Assets (net)	32.2	37.5
		2.0	14.2			Intangibles (net)	11.4	8.0
		25.4	13.7			All Other Non-Current	14.1	17.3
		100.0	100.0			Total	100.0	100.0
						LIABILITIES		
		6.6	9.4			Notes Payable-Short Term	5.8	8.7
		1.0	2.2			Cur. Mat.-L.T.D.	4.5	4.8
		1.9	5.4			Trade Payables	7.9	11.9
		.0	.0			Income Taxes Payable	.3	.2
		14.9	14.9			All Other Current	19.1	28.1
		24.5	31.9			Total Current	37.6	53.6
		21.9	20.2			Long-Term Debt	29.1	28.9
		.0	.1			Deferred Taxes	.0	.5
		15.4	5.9			All Other Non-Current	10.4	5.3
		38.3	42.0			Net Worth	22.9	11.7
		100.0	100.0			Total Liabilties & Net Worth	100.0	100.0
						INCOME DATA		
		100.0	100.0			Net Sales	100.0	100.0
						Gross Profit		
		74.1	91.4			Operating Expenses	83.2	77.0
		25.9	8.6			Operating Profit	16.8	23.0
		7.4	3.1			All Other Expenses (net)	8.6	9.2
		18.5	5.5			Profit Before Taxes	8.2	13.8
						RATIOS		
		3.4	2.3				2.0	1.5
		1.1	1.3			Current	1.3	.8
		.4	.8				.4	.2
		3.4	1.3				1.4	1.0
		.9	.8			Quick	.5	.4
		.2	.5				.2	.1
		0 UND	**0** UND				**0** UND	**0** UND
		0 UND	**27** 13.5			Sales/Receivables	**21** 17.3	**10** 37.6
		33 11.2	**76** 4.8				**39** 9.4	**52** 7.0
						Cost of Sales/Inventory		
						Cost of Sales/Payables		
		4.5	1.2				5.5	8.6
		NM	21.6			Sales/Working Capital	50.1	-10.0
		-2.0	-16.1				-5.1	-3.2
							6.7	22.4
						EBIT/Interest	(19) 2.6	(23) 6.0
							.5	1.0
						Net Profit + Depr., Dep., Amort./Cur. Mat. L/T/D		
		.2	.0				.1	.5
		1.8	.8			Fixed/Worth	1.6	1.8
		NM	1.8				-341.3	-1.8
		.3	.6				1.5	1.2
		1.3	1.8			Debt/Worth	2.7	3.3
		NM	6.5				-20.5	-5.4
			22.5				26.8	52.9
			(12) 5.6			% Profit Before Taxes/Tangible Net Worth	(19) 9.4	(18) 31.3
			-.2				-1.8	1.9
		45.4	8.7				12.8	15.9
		3.8	1.3			% Profit Before Taxes/Total Assets	1.5	7.5
		-2.6	-1.0				-.7	.2
		25.1	42.9				88.3	17.7
		5.3	7.9			Sales/Net Fixed Assets	7.1	6.5
		.1	2.0				.7	.6
		2.0	1.6				1.9	1.8
		.6	.9			Sales/Total Assets	1.0	1.0
		.1	.1				.4	.3
			1.4				1.0	1.5
			(14) 4.2			% Depr., Dep., Amort./Sales	(21) 2.8	(22) 3.0
			7.1				12.0	16.9
						% Officers', Directors' Owners' Comp/Sales		
9388M	**25945M**	**44335M**	**296327M**	**412939M**	**1231866M**	Net Sales ($)	**835525M**	**1161552M**
1378M	**11551M**	**47733M**	**312337M**	**298583M**	**993019M**	Total Assets ($)	**834727M**	**947444M**

M = $ thousand **MM = $ million**

See Pages 9 through 22 for Explanation of Ratios and Data

Comparative Historical Data | **Current Data Sorted by Sales**

			Type of Statement						
7	12	7	Unqualified			1		1	5
3	5	2	Reviewed			1			1
9	3	8	Compiled	1	2		2		3
4	7	11	Tax Returns	4	3	2	1	1	
13	17	22	Other	3	6	1	2	5	5
4/1/11-3/31/12 ALL	4/1/12-3/31/13 ALL	4/1/13-3/31/14 ALL			7 (4/1-9/30/13)		43 (10/1/13-3/31/14)		
				0-1MM	1-3MM	3-5MM	5-10MM	10-25MM	25MM & OVER
36	44	50	NUMBER OF STATEMENTS	8	11	5	5	7	14
%	%	%	ASSETS	%	%	%	%	%	%
18.7	17.0	17.7	Cash & Equivalents		16.5				15.8
14.9	15.9	15.0	Trade Receivables (net)		11.0				21.4
3.4	6.0	5.8	Inventory		5.2				12.0
12.4	8.1	9.6	All Other Current		5.0				4.1
49.5	47.1	48.2	Total Current		37.6				53.3
28.1	34.4	28.4	Fixed Assets (net)		31.6				27.1
11.7	6.9	5.4	Intangibles (net)		10.6				5.4
10.8	11.6	18.1	All Other Non-Current		20.2				14.2
100.0	100.0	100.0	Total		100.0				100.0
			LIABILITIES						
12.8	10.1	9.7	Notes Payable-Short Term		7.7				5.5
5.2	4.3	2.8	Cur. Mat.-L.T.D.		2.3				2.9
8.3	9.6	6.6	Trade Payables		2.6				10.1
.4	.4	.2	Income Taxes Payable		.0				.6
15.6	13.0	13.8	All Other Current		23.8				8.8
42.3	37.4	33.0	Total Current		36.4				27.9
28.1	25.6	19.5	Long-Term Debt		20.2				16.3
.4	.1	.4	Deferred Taxes		.0				.6
4.5	10.3	9.4	All Other Non-Current		23.5				7.2
24.7	26.6	37.7	Net Worth		19.9				48.0
100.0	100.0	100.0	Total Liabilties & Net Worth		100.0				100.0
			INCOME DATA						
100.0	100.0	100.0	Net Sales		100.0				100.0
			Gross Profit						
85.9	83.0	85.2	Operating Expenses		89.1				92.1
14.1	17.0	14.8	Operating Profit		10.9				7.9
7.4	5.1	4.1	All Other Expenses (net)		3.5				.1
6.7	11.9	10.6	Profit Before Taxes		7.4				7.8
			RATIOS						
1.5	1.9	3.6			2.3				4.2
1.2	1.2	1.5	Current		.9				1.7
.7	.8	.8			.4				1.2
1.1	1.4	1.8			1.0				3.9
.8	.8	.9	Quick		.8				1.2
.5	.4	.5			.3				.7
0 UND	0 UND	0 UND			0 UND				39 9.4
20 17.9	9 38.6	21 17.0	Sales/Receivables		3 109.9				53 6.9
48 7.6	48 7.6	62 5.9			59 6.2				74 4.9
			Cost of Sales/Inventory						
			Cost of Sales/Payables						
6.5	5.5	4.2			5.7				4.8
57.5	19.7	10.7	Sales/Working Capital		-24.8				6.1
-7.8	-24.9	-18.5			-6.1				21.4
22.2	11.1	21.7							18.3
(30) 6.9	(28) 5.4	(29) 2.9	EBIT/Interest						(11) 4.3
1.7	2.0	-3.5							-3.3
			Net Profit + Depr., Dep., Amort./Cur. Mat. L/T/D						
.1	.2	.0			.0				.2
1.3	.9	.5	Fixed/Worth		1.5				.5
24.6	17.4	2.6			-4.6				1.6
1.4	.8	.5			.6				.6
3.6	2.6	1.4	Debt/Worth		999.8				1.2
NM	17.2	NM			-3.2				1.6
106.4	35.4	34.6							27.8
(27) 37.0	(34) 21.4	(38) 18.7	% Profit Before Taxes/Tangible Net Worth						(13) 11.7
5.7	9.4	-2.6							-6.9
19.2	19.4	17.1			16.8				10.5
7.2	6.2	2.6	% Profit Before Taxes/Total Assets		.2				4.8
1.0	1.8	-3.6			-6.7				-1.6
27.9	50.0	67.3			25.1				30.6
11.5	9.6	9.3	Sales/Net Fixed Assets		8.2				7.9
4.0	1.3	2.0			.2				3.5
3.9	2.5	2.2			3.0				2.0
1.7	1.4	1.2	Sales/Total Assets		.7				1.6
.8	.3	.3			.1				1.3
1.3	1.1	1.0							1.4
(28) 2.5	(32) 2.1	(33) 2.0	% Depr., Dep., Amort./Sales						(13) 2.6
4.1	8.4	5.5							5.1
			% Officers', Directors' Owners' Comp/Sales						
1832510M	2794786M	2020800M	Net Sales ($)	2597M	19248M	19064M	30486M	113450M	1835955M
1352119M	1503332M	1664601M	Total Assets ($)	12794M	112988M	20822M	31615M	162270M	1324112M

M = $ thousand MM = $ million

See Pages 9 through 22 for Explanation of Ratios and Data

ADMINISTRATIVE AND SUPPORT AND WASTE MANAGEMENT AND REMEDIATION SERVICES

ADMINISTRATIVE AND SUPPORT AND WASTE MANAGEMENT AND REMEDIATION SERVICES

Current Data Sorted by Assets							Comparative Historical Data	
						Type of Statement		
2	1	9	9	2	6	Unqualified	47	52
2	7	10	7	1		Reviewed	40	29
9	12	6	2	1		Compiled	16	19
34	25	14	1			Tax Returns	67	84
36	22	38	19	9	7	Other	142	157
	39 (4/1-9/30/13)		252 (10/1/13-3/31/14)				4/1/09-3/31/10 ALL	4/1/10-3/31/11 ALL
0-500M	500M-2MM	2-10MM	10-50MM	50-100MM	100-250MM			
83	67	77	38	13	13	**NUMBER OF STATEMENTS**	312	341
%	%	%	%	%	%	**ASSETS**	%	%
40.2	24.7	22.2	13.9	13.9	9.3	Cash & Equivalents	20.1	19.9
10.8	17.2	28.4	28.0	15.7	11.1	Trade Receivables (net)	22.8	21.5
.6	1.2	1.6	6.1	4.1	1.2	Inventory	2.5	1.9
5.9	7.5	4.2	4.2	12.9	2.2	All Other Current	6.7	8.8
57.4	50.6	56.4	52.2	46.5	23.7	Total Current	52.2	52.1
19.8	24.9	24.1	31.9	22.3	37.5	Fixed Assets (net)	24.5	25.3
1.2	3.1	6.0	8.4	16.8	24.7	Intangibles (net)	9.6	5.9
21.6	21.4	13.5	7.5	14.4	14.1	All Other Non-Current	13.7	16.7
100.0	100.0	100.0	100.0	100.0	100.0	Total	100.0	100.0
						LIABILITIES		
20.5	12.8	4.5	6.2	2.0	.0	Notes Payable-Short Term	12.2	6.7
2.4	4.3	2.0	2.8	2.0	1.6	Cur. Mat.-L.T.D.	3.0	3.3
6.7	9.3	10.6	9.4	9.7	5.1	Trade Payables	10.8	9.8
.0	.0	.2	.2	1.8	.0	Income Taxes Payable	.5	.3
35.6	13.7	20.0	19.3	20.1	11.6	All Other Current	19.1	22.0
65.1	40.1	37.3	37.9	35.6	18.2	Total Current	45.5	42.0
10.4	13.4	15.8	24.6	16.0	40.5	Long-Term Debt	22.8	18.8
.0	.1	.3	.5	.7	1.4	Deferred Taxes	.2	.2
12.7	5.3	6.0	5.4	4.2	7.5	All Other Non-Current	9.4	9.7
11.7	41.1	40.6	31.6	43.4	32.4	Net Worth	22.0	29.3
100.0	100.0	100.0	100.0	100.0	100.0	Total Liabilties & Net Worth	100.0	100.0
						INCOME DATA		
100.0	100.0	100.0	100.0	100.0	100.0	Net Sales	100.0	100.0
						Gross Profit		
87.8	87.4	87.4	91.2	96.8	91.3	Operating Expenses	90.2	87.4
12.2	12.6	12.6	8.8	3.2	8.7	Operating Profit	9.8	12.6
.9	2.5	3.3	3.2	1.4	4.3	All Other Expenses (net)	2.9	2.9
11.3	10.1	9.3	5.6	1.9	4.4	Profit Before Taxes	6.9	9.7
						RATIOS		
5.5	5.8	3.5	2.0	2.0	3.0		2.7	3.0
1.2	1.6	1.8	1.4	1.2	1.9	Current	1.4	1.5
.4	.5	1.0	1.0	.9	1.0		.7	.8
4.7	4.9	3.1	1.5	1.9	2.7		2.3	2.2
1.2	1.0	1.5	1.1	.9	1.8	Quick	1.1	1.1
.3	.2	.9	.7	.6	.8		.4	.5
0 UND	0 UND	1 324.7	5 74.1	8 48.0	16 23.5		0 UND	0 UND
0 UND	10 35.3	34 10.6	39 9.3	35 10.5	36 10.2	Sales/Receivables	19 19.1	13 27.1
5 72.6	32 11.5	62 5.9	68 5.4	53 6.9	54 6.8		54 6.8	50 7.3
						Cost of Sales/Inventory		
						Cost of Sales/Payables		
10.9	5.9	4.3	7.2	3.8	3.6		6.3	6.2
95.5	19.3	13.2	13.6	29.7	6.0	Sales/Working Capital	22.9	19.2
-16.4	-9.7	165.4	-855.7	-17.3	NM		-49.3	-35.7
34.9	90.0	24.5	16.3	35.5	4.6		26.0	27.6
(33) 9.6	(43) 6.1	(52) 8.9	(28) 4.0	(10) 3.5	2.2	EBIT/Interest	(228) 6.7	(223) 7.0
2.4	1.2	2.7	1.6	-4.3	1.2		1.1	1.6
							7.5	15.1
						Net Profit + Depr., Dep., Amort./Cur. Mat. L/T/D	(32) 2.5	(29) 4.6
							1.0	2.1
.0	.1	.0	.2	.2	1.0		.1	.1
.3	.3	.3	.8	1.3	3.9	Fixed/Worth	.7	.5
5.5	3.2	2.7	4.9	4.0	-1.3		26.7	7.5
.3	.2	.5	1.0	.7	.7		.7	.6
2.1	1.0	1.9	2.5	1.8	6.1	Debt/Worth	2.8	2.0
-7.4	6.4	12.4	112.7	56.4	-5.1		-41.7	-144.5
192.5	73.4	77.7	43.2	159.3			74.7	88.7
(56) 54.6	(56) 32.3	(68) 34.1	(30) 21.6	(11) 28.1		% Profit Before Taxes/Tangible Net Worth	(229) 40.0	(252) 24.6
7.1	5.1	7.2	1.0	-5.5			8.7	6.0
82.2	44.3	28.1	14.7	20.3	5.1		26.1	28.5
19.5	15.4	6.0	5.3	5.1	2.1	% Profit Before Taxes/Total Assets	9.3	8.4
.0	.9	2.0	.0	-.2	.2		.1	.9
UND	96.3	130.5	64.7	35.6	16.7		112.8	137.8
127.2	32.5	28.1	12.3	15.4	6.1	Sales/Net Fixed Assets	26.0	22.7
13.6	8.0	5.2	2.5	3.9	.6		6.1	5.0
10.9	4.5	4.3	3.1	1.9	1.9		4.5	5.0
5.4	2.9	2.3	2.0	1.2	.9	Sales/Total Assets	2.5	2.3
2.8	1.2	.7	.9	.4	.4		1.2	1.0
.6	.4	.3	.7	1.2	2.9		.5	.6
(27) 1.3	(45) 1.2	(60) 1.5	(31) 2.5	(10) 2.4	(10) 6.0	% Depr., Dep., Amort./Sales	(210) 1.8	(232) 2.1
3.6	3.3	5.6	6.2	5.5	11.4		4.1	5.4
7.7	2.8	.9					3.9	3.4
(27) 12.6	(24) 6.7	(15) 2.6				% Officers', Directors' Owners' Comp/Sales	(79) 7.9	(75) 8.9
17.0	12.8	11.7					20.1	18.0
132515M	217963M	1207764M	1947150M	1154359M	1748035M	Net Sales ($)	10977076M	8068743M
17901M	70897M	394903M	834782M	962270M	1977306M	Total Assets ($)	5183679M	5572062M

M = $ thousand MM = $ million

See Pages 9 through 22 for Explanation of Ratios and Data

Comparative Historical Data				Current Data Sorted by Sales					
			Type of Statement						
47	45	29	Unqualified	2	2	2	3	5	15
34	32	27	Reviewed	4	2	5	3	5	8
23	30	30	Compiled	7	9	3	5	2	4
84	70	74	Tax Returns	32	18	3	5	2	2
148	134	131	Other	25	29	12	8	2	2
						8	21	13	35
4/1/11-3/31/12 ALL	4/1/12-3/31/13 ALL	4/1/13-3/31/14 ALL		39 (4/1-9/30/13)		252 (10/1/13-3/31/14)			
				0-1MM	1-3MM	3-5MM	5-10MM	10-25MM	25MM & OVER
336	311	291	**NUMBER OF STATEMENTS**	70	60	30	40	27	64
%	%	%	**ASSETS**	%	%	%	%	%	%
24.1	22.5	25.9	Cash & Equivalents	28.0	28.2	39.4	23.1	27.9	15.8
22.1	18.3	19.4	Trade Receivables (net)	10.1	11.2	15.3	26.7	24.9	32.2
1.6	1.5	1.9	Inventory	.5	.6	2.0	.3	1.9	5.6
6.9	7.0	5.7	All Other Current	7.0	3.4	8.1	8.7	5.9	3.5
54.6	49.3	52.9	Total Current	45.6	43.4	64.9	58.7	60.7	57.2
22.2	26.4	24.6	Fixed Assets (net)	30.8	29.1	17.6	20.5	17.7	22.4
7.5	7.5	5.6	Intangibles (net)	.2	4.3	2.8	4.1	10.9	12.7
15.6	16.9	16.9	All Other Non-Current	23.5	23.3	14.7	16.6	10.7	7.7
100.0	100.0	100.0	Total	100.0	100.0	100.0	100.0	100.0	100.0
			LIABILITIES						
9.1	8.0	10.9	Notes Payable-Short Term	15.1	13.9	12.8	11.3	4.5	4.9
3.4	3.1	2.7	Cur. Mat.-L.T.D.	2.3	3.8	3.3	2.4	1.4	2.6
9.9	7.5	8.8	Trade Payables	5.7	5.5	11.6	7.9	10.4	13.6
.4	.2	.1	Income Taxes Payable	.0	.0	.2	.0	.1	.5
19.9	25.2	22.5	All Other Current	32.0	19.5	13.1	21.5	17.3	22.3
42.7	44.0	45.0	Total Current	55.2	42.7	41.0	43.2	33.7	43.9
14.9	18.0	16.0	Long-Term Debt	21.5	14.8	7.3	13.6	10.6	18.9
.1	.2	.3	Deferred Taxes	.0	.0	.2	.2	.6	.7
8.2	8.4	7.7	All Other Non-Current	12.1	8.5	5.0	5.6	3.9	6.2
34.1	29.2	31.1	Net Worth	11.2	34.0	46.6	37.4	51.2	30.3
100.0	100.0	100.0	Total Liabilities & Net Worth	100.0	100.0	100.0	100.0	100.0	100.0
			INCOME DATA						
100.0	100.0	100.0	Net Sales	100.0	100.0	100.0	100.0	100.0	100.0
			Gross Profit						
88.4	87.6	88.6	Operating Expenses	79.0	90.3	89.9	93.2	89.1	93.9
11.6	12.4	11.4	Operating Profit	21.0	9.7	10.1	6.8	10.9	6.1
2.3	2.6	2.4	All Other Expenses (net)	6.1	2.4	-.3	.7	.3	1.4
9.3	9.7	9.0	Profit Before Taxes	14.9	7.3	10.3	6.1	10.7	4.7
			RATIOS						
2.8	3.2	3.6		6.3	5.8	4.7	3.5	4.6	2.1
1.4	1.3	1.5	Current	1.4	1.2	1.7	1.9	1.8	1.2
.7	.7	.8		.2	.4	.9	.9	1.3	1.0
2.5	2.4	3.2		4.4	5.8	4.2	3.1	4.5	1.8
1.2	1.1	1.2	Quick	1.2	1.0	1.3	1.6	1.5	1.1
.4	.5	.5		.2	.3	.8	.7	.8	.7
0 UND	0 UND	0 UND		0 UND	0 UND	0 UND	0 865.6	0 999.8	11 32.1
14 26.9	11 33.6	11 32.2	Sales/Receivables	0 UND	0 UND	16 22.5	16 23.2	34 10.6	41 9.0
53 6.9	52 7.0	46 8.0		28 13.2	14 25.5	34 10.7	62 5.9	47 7.7	63 5.8
			Cost of Sales/Inventory						
			Cost of Sales/Payables						
6.1	5.9	5.9		3.7	10.8	6.8	5.1	4.9	7.6
21.8	31.4	22.5	Sales/Working Capital	23.0	97.0	18.2	11.1	12.9	35.4
-41.4	-20.9	-38.8		-7.7	-8.3	-650.3	-76.4	37.9	-567.4
23.8	22.3	25.5		12.0	33.5	29.1	104.5	29.2	15.0
(215) 8.0	(204) 4.4	(179) 6.1	EBIT/Interest	(28) 3.2	(37) 7.3	(16) 6.7	(29) 13.6	(17) 9.8	(52) 4.8
2.0	.8	1.8		1.3	.2	-.5	3.3	3.3	1.6
7.7	11.9	59.1							
(36) 3.4	(38) 2.9	(15) 3.1	Net Profit + Depr., Dep., Amort./Cur. Mat. L/T/D						
1.7	1.8	2.4							
.0	.1	.0		.0	.1	.0	.1	.0	.2
.4	.7	.4	Fixed/Worth	.3	.6	.3	.3	.2	.7
3.3	5.1	4.5		8.0	7.2	1.3	2.4	1.6	5.8
.6	.6	.5		.5	.2	.2	.4	.5	1.2
1.8	2.2	1.9	Debt/Worth	2.4	1.9	1.4	1.0	.8	3.7
28.2	62.6	44.6		-18.5	UND	3.7	35.6	3.6	NM
92.4	100.0	84.8		65.9	121.5	150.5	75.9	93.6	77.0
(264) 30.2	(244) 28.7	(229) 31.2	% Profit Before Taxes/Tangible Net Worth	(51) 21.5	(46) 38.3	(26) 42.5	(34) 32.5	(24) 40.4	(48) 28.6
8.0	1.8	5.5		4.1	4.6	-1.4	8.1	18.6	7.0
27.6	26.7	31.6		33.0	51.1	78.6	31.0	27.4	18.4
9.7	6.9	9.8	% Profit Before Taxes/Total Assets	5.7	13.8	12.0	14.1	14.3	5.4
1.8	.0	1.0		.0	.0	-.9	3.7	5.7	.9
282.0	192.3	193.6		UND	126.9	136.5	99.5	193.6	117.8
29.2	22.3	29.0	Sales/Net Fixed Assets	26.9	25.5	49.9	35.2	48.8	23.4
6.4	4.8	6.4		1.4	6.6	13.7	10.2	7.6	6.1
4.8	4.6	5.1		4.7	6.0	10.1	4.8	4.5	5.2
2.5	2.3	2.6	Sales/Total Assets	1.5	3.6	3.5	2.6	2.4	2.5
1.0	1.0	1.1		.3	1.2	2.0	1.3	1.1	1.4
.6	.7	.5		1.7	.8	.6	.4	.3	.4
(202) 1.9	(201) 2.4	(183) 1.6	% Depr., Dep., Amort./Sales	(27) 6.8	(33) 1.8	(20) .8	(33) 1.6	(21) 1.4	(49) 1.4
4.0	6.0	5.3		20.5	4.8	3.2	3.3	4.6	3.9
2.5	3.2	2.6		6.4	5.3	2.4	3.3		.5
(103) 7.4	(76) 6.8	(76) 7.6	% Officers', Directors' Owners' Comp/Sales	(19) 11.7	(20) 8.8	(12) 6.0	(10) 10.2		(11) .9
15.3	15.3	14.1		21.1	15.8	12.9	12.6		3.9
10167093M	7715686M	6407786M	Net Sales ($)	35623M	106178M	124046M	294904M	409776M	5437259M
4704802M	4849959M	4258059M	Total Assets ($)	80669M	92667M	56071M	279956M	281990M	3466706M

M = $ thousand MM = $ million

See Pages 9 through 22 for Explanation of Ratios and Data

Current Data Sorted by Assets							Comparative Historical Data	
						Type of Statement		
		5	12	3	4	Unqualified	30	31
	3	7				Reviewed	19	15
		4	1			Compiled	7	5
8	5	7				Tax Returns	16	17
3	8	32	19	2	1	Other	47	45
	19 (4/1-9/30/13)		105 (10/1/13-3/31/14)				4/1/09-3/31/10	4/1/10-3/31/11
0-500M	500M-2MM	2-10MM	10-50MM	50-100MM	100-250MM		ALL	ALL
11	16	55	32	5	5	NUMBER OF STATEMENTS	119	113
%	%	%	%	%	%	**ASSETS**	%	%
25.8	19.4	19.3	16.8			Cash & Equivalents	17.2	16.1
22.0	37.3	42.2	35.6			Trade Receivables (net)	36.3	41.7
.9	1.1	3.0	1.0			Inventory	2.6	2.4
2.1	2.2	2.8	7.1			All Other Current	5.5	8.1
50.8	60.1	67.2	60.5			Total Current	61.6	68.4
30.9	28.2	17.4	21.7			Fixed Assets (net)	25.8	22.1
1.0	7.5	7.2	7.3			Intangibles (net)	4.9	3.4
17.3	4.3	8.2	10.5			All Other Non-Current	7.7	6.1
100.0	100.0	100.0	100.0			Total	100.0	100.0
						LIABILITIES		
10.2	7.1	8.2	6.6			Notes Payable-Short Term	9.9	10.7
3.4	2.0	3.0	2.5			Cur. Mat.-L.T.D.	3.9	2.8
6.8	8.2	12.0	10.4			Trade Payables	10.3	14.1
.0	.9	.2	.3			Income Taxes Payable	.3	.5
10.7	24.4	16.7	21.9			All Other Current	16.1	17.3
31.1	42.5	40.1	41.7			Total Current	40.5	45.4
46.2	20.2	11.9	7.7			Long-Term Debt	18.6	14.0
.0	.0	.2	.7			Deferred Taxes	.2	.9
13.9	5.9	3.1	7.9			All Other Non-Current	4.7	6.0
8.6	31.4	44.7	42.1			Net Worth	36.0	33.7
100.0	100.0	100.0	100.0			Total Liabilties & Net Worth	100.0	100.0
						INCOME DATA		
100.0	100.0	100.0	100.0			Net Sales	100.0	100.0
						Gross Profit		
93.3	88.2	92.8	95.7			Operating Expenses	90.5	91.8
6.7	11.8	7.2	4.3			Operating Profit	9.5	8.2
.0	6.1	.8	.3			All Other Expenses (net)	2.6	1.5
6.7	5.7	6.4	4.0			Profit Before Taxes	6.9	6.7
						RATIOS		
6.5	2.2	2.9	2.2				2.6	2.7
4.1	1.6	1.7	1.4			Current	1.5	1.7
.6	.9	1.1	1.0				1.0	1.2
6.5	2.1	2.5	2.0				2.4	2.4
3.3	1.4	1.5	1.2			Quick	1.3	1.3
.4	.9	1.0	.8				.9	1.0
0 UND	**0** UND	**30** 12.3	**31** 11.8				**20** 18.5	**31** 12.0
10 36.5	**46** 7.9	**43** 8.4	**46** 7.9			Sales/Receivables	**43** 8.5	**44** 8.4
21 17.7	**73** 5.0	**57** 6.4	**62** 5.9				**62** 5.9	**63** 5.8
						Cost of Sales/Inventory		
						Cost of Sales/Payables		
8.1	9.4	6.5	6.3				6.8	5.8
100.4	12.0	12.6	17.2			Sales/Working Capital	14.1	10.4
-110.1	-64.8	67.9	NM				964.0	42.8
	26.4	54.7	93.0				31.8	22.7
	(11) 6.2	(44) 9.9	(25) 20.4			EBIT/Interest	(94) 6.9	(84) 8.3
	.8	2.4	2.0				1.2	1.6
							6.2	9.2
						Net Profit + Depr., Dep., Amort./Cur. Mat. L/T/D	(15) 2.0	(19) 2.8
							.3	1.6
.3	.1	.1	.2				.1	.1
9.0	.8	.3	.4			Fixed/Worth	.4	.3
-.3	44.9	1.4	2.0				2.6	1.7
.6	.5	.5	.5				.7	.7
18.3	3.5	1.2	1.5			Debt/Worth	1.9	1.7
-3.4	51.0	4.6	7.0				4.8	4.7
	52.5	69.2	48.9				60.1	79.3
	(13) 32.6	(47) 35.2	(27) 24.3			% Profit Before Taxes/Tangible Net Worth	(102) 29.4	(100) 35.6
	1.8	11.4	6.6				5.8	13.3
71.8	25.6	30.0	21.2				23.2	26.0
36.7	5.5	14.9	8.6			% Profit Before Taxes/Total Assets	10.0	13.6
15.6	.3	1.3	2.2				.5	3.8
229.6	97.4	117.0	127.6				138.2	127.2
55.1	18.8	47.4	39.2			Sales/Net Fixed Assets	27.4	41.4
9.3	2.4	12.2	5.3				4.5	5.6
25.7	4.4	4.8	4.3				4.7	5.0
6.2	3.0	3.3	2.9			Sales/Total Assets	2.8	3.4
4.4	.8	1.7	1.3				1.4	1.6
	.3	.3	.3				.4	.5
	(13) .8	(40) .6	(26) 1.4			% Depr., Dep., Amort./Sales	(82) 1.8	(82) 1.3
	4.8	2.2	3.5				3.1	3.6
							1.1	1.5
						% Officers', Directors' Owners' Comp/Sales	(24) 3.2	(24) 4.9
							5.4	7.3
37456M	62118M	916944M	2308124M	506385M	961497M	Net Sales ($)	4394957M	4606991M
2773M	19511M	262606M	662149M	409847M	786540M	Total Assets ($)	2053514M	1948687M

M = $ thousand MM = $ million

See Pages 9 through 22 for Explanation of Ratios and Data

Comparative Historical Data				Current Data Sorted by Sales					
			Type of Statement						
34	28	24	Unqualified		1		2	4	17
20	13	10	Reviewed			2	2	4	2
7	8	5	Compiled			1	2	1	1
19	18	20	Tax Returns	5	4	2	6	3	
61	54	65	Other	4	5	2	11	16	27
4/1/11-3/31/12 ALL	**4/1/12-3/31/13 ALL**	**4/1/13-3/31/14 ALL**		**19 (4/1-9/30/13)**			**105 (10/1/13-3/31/14)**		
				0-1MM	**1-3MM**	**3-5MM**	**5-10MM**	**10-25MM**	**25MM & OVER**
141	121	124	**NUMBER OF STATEMENTS**	9	10	7	23	28	47
%	%	%	**ASSETS**	%	%	%	%	%	%
15.8	18.8	18.1	Cash & Equivalents		16.2		20.4	20.4	15.9
39.9	33.3	36.4	Trade Receivables (net)		26.1		37.1	35.2	42.8
2.7	1.9	2.0	Inventory		1.9		5.3	.4	1.4
6.3	4.8	3.8	All Other Current		.2		3.3	6.1	4.3
64.7	58.8	60.3	Total Current		44.4		66.1	62.2	64.4
23.6	24.1	21.8	Fixed Assets (net)		32.8		17.2	25.1	15.4
3.8	6.3	8.8	Intangibles (net)		13.5		5.9	1.2	12.9
7.9	10.7	9.1	All Other Non-Current		9.3		10.9	11.5	7.4
100.0	100.0	100.0	Total		100.0		100.0	100.0	100.0
			LIABILITIES						
10.7	8.5	7.5	Notes Payable-Short Term		6.1		10.0	6.1	7.4
4.2	3.8	3.0	Cur. Mat.-L.T.D.		3.1		1.4	3.6	3.7
13.8	9.2	10.4	Trade Payables		2.5		10.9	10.6	13.6
.2	.2	.3	Income Taxes Payable		.0		.3	.0	.3
14.1	17.5	17.8	All Other Current		18.2		11.4	16.2	20.6
43.0	39.3	39.0	Total Current		29.9		34.0	36.5	45.6
12.8	18.1	16.8	Long-Term Debt		31.3		13.6	8.9	12.0
.4	.2	.3	Deferred Taxes		.0		.0	.7	.5
3.0	5.1	6.9	All Other Non-Current		3.6		9.6	4.7	8.3
40.8	37.4	37.0	Net Worth		35.2		42.8	49.1	33.7
100.0	100.0	100.0	Total Liabilties & Net Worth		100.0		100.0	100.0	100.0
			INCOME DATA						
100.0	100.0	100.0	Net Sales		100.0		100.0	100.0	100.0
			Gross Profit						
90.1	90.6	93.5	Operating Expenses		90.7		93.0	93.5	96.5
9.9	9.4	6.5	Operating Profit		9.3		7.0	6.5	3.5
1.0	.9	1.6	All Other Expenses (net)		.7		.6	.2	1.6
8.9	8.5	4.9	Profit Before Taxes		8.6		6.4	6.3	1.9
			RATIOS						
2.8	3.2	2.6			7.0		5.0	3.2	2.2
1.7	1.7	1.5	Current		3.6		2.0	1.6	1.3
1.2	1.2	1.0			.2		1.0	1.0	1.1
2.7	2.6	2.2			7.0		4.9	3.1	2.1
1.3	1.5	1.4	Quick		3.2		1.7	1.4	1.2
1.0	1.0	.9			.2		.9	1.0	.9
25 14.8	**9** 39.7	**24** 15.4			**13** 27.7		**29** 12.4	**25** 14.6	**34** 10.7
46 8.0	**40** 9.1	**44** 8.3	Sales/Receivables		**31** 11.7		**46** 7.9	**43** 8.5	**46** 8.0
62 5.9	**56** 6.5	**62** 5.9			**94** 3.9		**62** 5.9	**65** 5.6	**61** 6.0
			Cost of Sales/Inventory						
			Cost of Sales/Payables						
6.1	5.7	7.1			5.5		4.2	6.8	10.2
13.4	13.4	13.4	Sales/Working Capital		54.6		9.2	13.0	19.3
56.5	63.7	170.9			-4.2		55.5	NM	103.4
46.9	41.8	46.6					47.0	95.2	56.2
(107) 12.3	(88) 12.3	(94) 9.9	EBIT/Interest				(20) 10.4	(22) 9.0	(37) 9.8
3.7	3.6	2.1					2.9	.9	1.8
25.4	33.4	18.1							6.8
(21) 6.1	(12) 4.0	(17) 2.8	Net Profit + Depr., Dep., Amort./Cur. Mat. L/T/D						(11) 2.8
2.2	1.3	1.9							2.0
.1	.1	.1			.4		.0	.1	.1
.3	.4	.5	Fixed/Worth		1.1		.4	.4	.4
1.0	1.8	25.8			-3.3		5.4	1.2	-41.1
.6	.6	.5			.2		.2	.4	.8
1.7	1.4	1.7	Debt/Worth		.9		.7	1.2	2.4
4.0	3.9	51.4			-5.4		17.7	2.4	-120.5
68.1	69.3	64.2					45.6	68.0	66.3
(127) 31.3	(99) 31.5	(97) 32.9	% Profit Before Taxes/Tangible Net Worth				(18) 31.4	27.9	(35) 39.0
8.0	6.8	7.2					5.5	1.4	10.7
24.9	34.6	24.9			36.9		27.1	31.6	22.0
13.0	13.7	9.3	% Profit Before Taxes/Total Assets		16.8		17.6	9.8	7.9
3.1	3.8	1.3			-8.2		1.3	1.2	1.6
151.5	132.6	114.9			116.3		117.0	117.1	128.6
40.4	34.2	36.2	Sales/Net Fixed Assets		9.5		31.0	25.5	47.4
5.7	7.4	6.7			1.0		15.6	6.7	14.5
5.1	5.7	4.6			5.5		4.2	4.9	5.1
3.2	3.2	3.1	Sales/Total Assets		1.8		2.9	3.3	3.8
1.4	1.2	1.3			.7		1.7	1.4	1.8
.4	.4	.3					.2	.4	.3
(106) 1.0	(80) 1.2	(94) 1.0	% Depr., Dep., Amort./Sales				(16) 1.1	(22) .9	(38) .9
3.8	3.3	2.8					2.8	3.5	2.2
.8	2.0	1.4							
(23) 2.6	(21) 4.0	(20) 2.9	% Officers', Directors' Owners' Comp/Sales						
7.1	7.8	12.2							
4460830M	4350593M	4792524M	Net Sales ($)	3767M	20185M	28103M	167021M	455774M	4117674M
1877346M	2187216M	2143426M	Total Assets ($)	6378M	26221M	12153M	69273M	250328M	1779073M

M = $ thousand MM = $ million

See Pages 9 through 22 for Explanation of Ratios and Data

	Current Data Sorted by Assets						Comparative Historical Data	
Type of Statement								
Unqualified		1	9	15	3	2	45	42
Reviewed	2	9	29	13			61	43
Compiled	6	23	17	1			43	44
Tax Returns	50	21	9			1	50	75
Other	18	49	67	29	4	4	155	211
		47 (4/1-9/30/13)		335 (10/1/13-3/31/14)			4/1/09-3/31/10 ALL	4/1/10-3/31/11 ALL
	0-500M	500M-2MM	2-10MM	10-50MM	50-100MM	100-250MM		
NUMBER OF STATEMENTS	76	103	131	58	7	7	354	415
ASSETS	%	%	%	%	%	%	%	%
Cash & Equivalents	48.4	17.4	11.3	10.4			14.4	15.8
Trade Receivables (net)	24.7	56.8	65.7	60.5			51.5	53.1
Inventory	.0	.1	.1	.3			.6	.3
All Other Current	2.2	2.1	4.1	5.6			6.8	7.1
Total Current	75.4	76.4	81.1	76.8			73.2	76.3
Fixed Assets (net)	7.2	8.8	7.3	6.3			10.0	9.4
Intangibles (net)	5.8	4.2	4.2	9.7			5.5	5.0
All Other Non-Current	11.6	10.6	7.4	7.1			11.3	9.3
Total	100.0	100.0	100.0	100.0			100.0	100.0
LIABILITIES								
Notes Payable-Short Term	24.0	19.9	20.1	18.5			20.3	22.0
Cur. Mat.-L.T.D.	3.1	1.4	1.8	2.2			3.1	2.6
Trade Payables	12.1	5.2	7.6	8.5			7.4	8.5
Income Taxes Payable	.0	.4	.2	.1			.5	.6
All Other Current	39.4	19.2	15.5	18.1			22.7	23.0
Total Current	78.6	46.1	45.2	47.4			54.0	56.8
Long-Term Debt	13.0	5.4	5.2	15.3			9.1	8.3
Deferred Taxes	.0	.1	.3	.4			.2	.1
All Other Non-Current	10.5	4.7	3.9	3.4			5.8	9.8
Net Worth	-2.1	43.6	45.3	33.6			30.9	25.0
Total Liabilties & Net Worth	100.0	100.0	100.0	100.0			100.0	100.0
INCOME DATA								
Net Sales	100.0	100.0	100.0	100.0			100.0	100.0
Gross Profit								
Operating Expenses	95.4	94.5	94.9	96.4			98.5	96.1
Operating Profit	4.6	5.5	5.1	3.6			1.5	3.9
All Other Expenses (net)	.4	.6	.2	1.0			.9	1.0
Profit Before Taxes	4.2	4.9	4.8	2.6			.7	2.9
RATIOS								
Current	3.7	3.8	3.8	2.5			2.8	2.7
	1.0	1.7	1.7	1.5			1.5	1.6
	.7	1.0	1.3	1.1			1.0	1.0
Quick	3.0	3.8	3.7	2.3			2.5	2.4
	(75) 1.0	1.6	1.6	1.4			1.4	1.4
	.7	1.0	1.2	1.0			.9	.9
Sales/Receivables	0 UND	26 13.8	36 10.1	45 8.1			27 13.7	21 17.7
	1 711.1	37 9.8	46 8.0	54 6.7			43 8.4	42 8.8
	30 12.3	51 7.1	58 6.3	70 5.2			63 5.8	61 6.0
Cost of Sales/Inventory								
Cost of Sales/Payables								
Sales/Working Capital	18.4	9.5	9.3	8.4			9.4	10.0
	999.8	19.1	13.9	19.3			18.4	18.5
	-32.0	-999.8	32.4	35.5			NM	574.0
EBIT/Interest	65.5	91.2	50.0	36.7			14.4	26.7
	(42) 13.2	(82) 14.3	(112) 18.7	(53) 8.9			(283) 2.9	(331) 6.5
	2.5	2.8	4.0	2.3			-2.2	1.9
Net Profit + Depr., Dep., Amort./Cur. Mat. L/T/D			57.9	5.8			10.4	15.8
			(14) 23.2	(16) 2.4			(34) 2.4	(25) 2.3
			8.2	-.1			.0	.7
Fixed/Worth	.0	.0	.0	.1			.0	.0
	.0	.1	.1	.3			.2	.1
	UND	.6	.2	1.4			1.1	1.1
Debt/Worth	.7	.4	.5	.8			.6	.7
	35.4	1.3	1.3	3.3			1.8	1.9
	-5.0	5.5	3.2	19.6			11.1	14.7
% Profit Before Taxes/Tangible Net Worth	200.0	73.7	77.1	49.1			57.4	78.2
	(49) 100.0	(88) 37.5	(124) 41.9	(45) 34.2			(288) 15.1	(332) 34.0
	13.7	17.8	17.7	16.4			-4.2	9.0
% Profit Before Taxes/Total Assets	75.7	31.1	31.1	21.4			16.3	25.6
	14.3	14.5	16.9	10.5			5.1	11.6
	.0	3.3	6.6	3.6			-5.7	1.6
Sales/Net Fixed Assets	UND	999.8	584.6	200.6			438.7	490.5
	UND	332.3	230.1	116.9			124.8	158.5
	93.8	78.3	72.9	48.9			37.8	55.6
Sales/Total Assets	28.6	8.2	6.9	5.5			6.7	7.6
	14.6	6.0	5.4	4.3			4.7	5.3
	5.8	4.3	4.2	2.8			3.0	3.5
% Depr., Dep., Amort./Sales	.1	.0	.1	.1			.1	.1
	(20) .4	(59) .1	(96) .2	(50) .3			(248) .4	(257) .3
	1.1	.4	.3	.8			.7	.7
% Officers', Directors' Owners' Comp/Sales	1.9	1.4	.6	.7			1.5	1.5
	(25) 5.7	(42) 2.6	(40) 1.5	(10) 3.1			(105) 2.8	(125) 3.7
	12.6	5.6	2.7	12.0			7.2	8.0
Net Sales ($)	355941M	837069M	3761842M	4358886M	1154709M	2690628M	13266747M	15099783M
Total Assets ($)	17478M	119429M	614485M	1018007M	470498M	1196972M	3059295M	3560467M

M = $ thousand MM = $ million

See Pages 9 through 22 for Explanation of Ratios and Data

Comparative Historical Data / Current Data Sorted by Sales

			Type of Statement						
41	36	30	Unqualified		1	1		6	22
46	54	53	Reviewed	1	2	3	4	10	33
49	39	47	Compiled		4	10	13	12	8
79	64	81	Tax Returns	13	12	15	21	16	4
221	202	171	Other	7	15	7	29	52	61
4/1/11-3/31/12 ALL	4/1/12-3/31/13 ALL	4/1/13-3/31/14 ALL		47 (4/1-9/30/13)			335 (10/1/13-3/31/14)		
				0-1MM	1-3MM	3-5MM	5-10MM	10-25MM	25MM & OVER
436	395	382	NUMBER OF STATEMENTS	21	34	36	67	96	128
%	%	%	ASSETS	%	%	%	%	%	%
17.5	16.9	20.2	Cash & Equivalents	29.8	30.7	33.1	25.0	18.0	11.5
55.2	53.9	53.4	Trade Receivables (net)	23.2	39.9	38.6	50.2	59.6	63.1
.4	.1	.1	Inventory	.0	.0	.1	.1	.1	.3
5.3	5.0	3.5	All Other Current	1.5	1.6	3.3	1.6	3.3	5.5
78.4	75.9	77.2	Total Current	54.5	72.2	75.0	76.9	80.9	80.2
6.5	8.5	7.4	Fixed Assets (net)	17.4	12.5	10.1	6.1	5.6	5.8
6.6	5.6	6.4	Intangibles (net)	12.7	2.5	6.7	4.9	6.0	7.4
8.5	10.0	9.0	All Other Non-Current	15.2	12.9	8.3	12.1	7.5	6.5
100.0	100.0	100.0	Total	100.0	100.0	100.0	100.0	100.0	100.0
			LIABILITIES						
21.4	20.8	20.3	Notes Payable-Short Term	11.8	23.7	23.7	22.1	19.1	19.8
2.2	2.0	2.4	Cur. Mat.-L.T.D.	.9	2.6	1.3	3.6	1.9	2.5
8.1	8.5	7.9	Trade Payables	8.3	3.8	9.9	7.0	7.7	9.0
.3	.5	.2	Income Taxes Payable	.0	1.1	.0	.1	.1	.2
20.9	19.2	21.7	All Other Current	30.4	38.5	16.0	20.6	19.4	19.5
52.9	51.1	52.5	Total Current	51.5	69.7	50.9	53.5	48.3	51.1
9.5	7.8	8.7	Long-Term Debt	11.2	27.1	7.2	3.0	5.2	9.5
.1	.1	.2	Deferred Taxes	.0	.4	.0	.0	.5	.2
8.5	7.9	5.5	All Other Non-Current	10.1	18.1	3.7	4.5	4.3	3.4
29.0	33.1	33.1	Net Worth	27.2	-15.2	38.2	39.1	41.8	35.8
100.0	100.0	100.0	Total Liabilties & Net Worth	100.0	100.0	100.0	100.0	100.0	100.0
			INCOME DATA						
100.0	100.0	100.0	Net Sales	100.0	100.0	100.0	100.0	100.0	100.0
			Gross Profit						
95.5	94.7	95.1	Operating Expenses	85.8	93.0	94.1	94.8	96.7	96.4
4.5	5.3	4.9	Operating Profit	14.2	7.0	5.9	5.2	3.3	3.6
.4	.5	.5	All Other Expenses (net)	2.6	.6	.5	.2	.2	.7
4.1	4.8	4.4	Profit Before Taxes	11.6	6.3	5.4	5.1	3.1	3.0
			RATIOS						
3.0	3.0	3.3		5.6	6.1	3.8	3.9	3.5	2.7
1.6	1.6	1.6	Current	1.0	1.6	1.3	1.6	1.6	1.5
1.1	1.1	1.0		.3	.7	.9	1.0	1.2	1.2
2.8	2.8	3.3		4.6	6.1	3.8	4.0	3.3	2.5
1.5	1.4	(381) 1.5	Quick	1.0	1.6	1.0	(66) 1.5	1.5	1.4
1.0	1.0	1.0		.3	.6	.9	1.0	1.1	1.1
26 14.3	**26** 14.3	**26** 14.1		**0** UND	**0** UND	**0** 830.5	**3** 109.9	**29** 12.8	**36** 10.1
43 8.5	**41** 9.0	**41** 8.8	Sales/Receivables	**20** 18.4	**32** 11.3	**31** 11.9	**38** 9.6	**41** 8.9	**48** 7.6
60 6.1	**55** 6.6	**56** 6.5		**53** 6.9	**60** 6.1	**50** 7.3	**51** 7.2	**54** 6.7	**61** 6.0
			Cost of Sales/Inventory						
			Cost of Sales/Payables						
9.1	9.4	9.6		5.9	9.7	6.8	10.1	9.6	9.9
18.1	19.9	20.2	Sales/Working Capital	927.0	40.9	63.4	32.4	19.1	19.6
114.8	120.6	544.7		-13.2	-17.7	-164.0	UND	60.5	37.8
34.6	39.7	49.9			39.3	57.9	108.2	84.5	38.6
(337) 9.7	(320) 10.6	(303) 11.3	EBIT/Interest		(26) 12.7	(24) 5.4	(54) 19.1	(79) 11.5	(114) 11.5
2.4	2.8	2.9			3.1	-1.9	3.0	3.6	2.8
42.9	34.8	41.8						52.5	18.9
(27) 16.6	(34) 7.8	(43) 7.8	Net Profit + Depr., Dep., Amort./Cur. Mat. L/T/D					(12) 14.2	(27) 5.8
3.0	3.6	1.1						.7	1.1
.0	.0	.0		.0	.0	.0	.0	.0	.1
.1	.1	.1	Fixed/Worth	.2	.1	.0	.1	.1	.1
.5	.5	.6		UND	-60.3	.5	.2	.4	.6
.6	.7	.5		.3	.5	.4	.3	.5	.8
1.8	1.8	1.9	Debt/Worth	2.8	2.1	2.4	1.6	1.8	2.3
14.5	7.0	17.0		-4.0	-3.6	31.9	16.8	5.5	9.5
70.4	82.5	85.4		377.8	176.4	103.9	103.3	83.3	56.1
(355) 36.4	(334) 39.0	(312) 39.7	% Profit Before Taxes/Tangible Net Worth	(14) 66.7	(23) 54.9	(30) 27.4	(57) 40.6	(83) 37.3	(105) 36.1
10.9	16.5	17.5		9.4	33.0	-4.2	24.5	11.8	19.1
27.4	30.2	31.1		73.7	63.9	35.0	36.9	31.6	23.5
13.4	13.7	14.1	% Profit Before Taxes/Total Assets	10.8	20.0	8.5	17.7	11.7	12.6
2.8	4.6	3.2		-6.2	10.8	.1	2.9	3.3	4.0
827.7	653.5	999.8		UND	999.8	UND	UND	968.6	318.8
210.9	192.3	232.3	Sales/Net Fixed Assets	994.0	189.9	490.5	479.5	254.8	138.9
83.0	68.0	68.9		4.8	50.7	61.2	122.1	93.1	59.7
7.7	7.9	8.0		7.4	9.1	10.6	9.8	8.2	7.1
5.3	5.6	5.5	Sales/Total Assets	3.2	5.7	5.2	6.2	5.9	5.1
3.6	3.6	4.0		.5	3.7	4.1	4.2	4.4	3.8
.1	.1	.1			.1	.1	.1	.1	.1
(248) .2	(253) .2	(235) .2	% Depr., Dep., Amort./Sales		(17) .3	(16) .4	(30) .1	(65) .2	(101) .2
.5	.4	.5			1.1	1.2	.3	.3	.5
1.9	1.4	1.1			1.2	3.1	1.4	.7	.5
(129) 4.1	(121) 3.1	(118) 2.5	% Officers', Directors' Owners' Comp/Sales		(10) 5.2	(16) 5.0	(27) 2.2	(36) 1.4	(22) 1.7
8.1	5.6	5.7			9.2	7.9	5.2	3.0	4.0
16693831M	13425125M	13159075M	Net Sales ($)	8940M	72758M	145887M	477466M	1535884M	10918140M
3564384M	3113486M	3436869M	Total Assets ($)	4195M	19965M	31824M	105374M	327616M	2947895M

M = $ thousand MM = $ million

See Pages 9 through 22 for Explanation of Ratios and Data

Current Data Sorted by Assets							Comparative Historical Data	
						Type of Statement		
	1	9	28	7	3	Unqualified	55	57
1	13	35	11			Reviewed	67	46
10	31	26	3		1	Compiled	43	58
21	21	3				Tax Returns	36	44
16	35	68	48	9	7	Other	178	199
	25 (4/1-9/30/13)		382 (10/1/13-3/31/14)				4/1/09-3/31/10 ALL	4/1/10-3/31/11 ALL
0-500M	**500M-2MM**	**2-10MM**	**10-50MM**	**50-100MM**	**100-250MM**			
48	101	141	90	16	11	**NUMBER OF STATEMENTS**	379	404
%	%	%	%	%	%	**ASSETS**	%	%
25.8	19.4	10.7	10.4	10.8	7.8	Cash & Equivalents	14.0	12.5
34.3	50.6	63.2	60.2	44.5	39.1	Trade Receivables (net)	52.5	55.1
.0	.2	.4	.1	1.6	.0	Inventory	.1	.2
6.2	4.2	5.0	6.5	2.2	7.0	All Other Current	7.6	7.7
66.3	74.5	79.3	77.2	59.2	54.0	Total Current	74.2	75.5
12.6	12.1	7.7	5.7	3.0	5.5	Fixed Assets (net)	8.4	8.1
2.1	3.9	4.2	8.5	29.0	35.9	Intangibles (net)	6.6	6.5
19.0	9.6	8.7	8.6	8.9	4.7	All Other Non-Current	10.8	9.9
100.0	100.0	100.0	100.0	100.0	100.0	Total	100.0	100.0
						LIABILITIES		
21.1	18.4	19.1	16.9	5.3	8.8	Notes Payable-Short Term	19.4	21.4
3.8	1.3	1.3	1.5	2.1	7.6	Cur. Mat.-L.T.D.	2.8	3.2
14.7	6.1	7.4	9.1	6.3	4.9	Trade Payables	7.6	7.1
.5	.2	.2	.3	.2	.2	Income Taxes Payable	.4	.5
20.3	16.3	18.9	21.9	20.5	19.0	All Other Current	22.0	23.2
60.4	42.3	46.9	49.7	34.4	40.4	Total Current	52.1	55.4
11.3	9.8	3.5	6.4	18.6	13.4	Long-Term Debt	7.1	8.5
.0	.0	.0	.2	.3	1.8	Deferred Taxes	.2	.2
14.0	3.2	4.1	6.3	5.7	7.9	All Other Non-Current	8.6	8.5
14.3	44.6	45.6	37.4	40.9	36.5	Net Worth	32.0	27.5
100.0	100.0	100.0	100.0	100.0	100.0	Total Liabilities & Net Worth	100.0	100.0
						INCOME DATA		
100.0	100.0	100.0	100.0	100.0	100.0	Net Sales	100.0	100.0
						Gross Profit		
96.1	94.8	96.7	96.3	95.0	97.0	Operating Expenses	98.6	96.2
3.9	5.2	3.3	3.7	5.0	3.0	Operating Profit	1.4	3.8
.1	.8	.1	.4	.7	1.4	All Other Expenses (net)	.6	.8
3.8	4.4	3.2	3.3	4.2	1.6	Profit Before Taxes	.8	3.0
						RATIOS		
3.3	5.4	2.8	2.2	2.5	1.9		2.5	2.5
1.3	2.0	1.7	1.5	2.1	1.4	Current	1.5	1.5
.6	1.2	1.2	1.2	1.5	1.2		1.0	1.0
3.3	5.0	2.8	2.0	2.3	1.8		2.3	2.3
1.3	1.9	1.6	1.4	2.0	1.4	Quick	1.4	1.3
.4	1.2	1.2	1.1	1.4	1.1		.9	.9
0 UND	23 15.8	31 11.8	34 10.7	53 6.9	40 9.1		26 14.1	27 13.4
6 61.7	34 10.6	41 8.9	48 7.6	56 6.5	51 7.2	Sales/Receivables	42 8.7	40 9.2
32 11.5	50 7.3	58 6.3	61 6.0	69 5.3	59 6.2		56 6.5	57 6.4
						Cost of Sales/Inventory		
						Cost of Sales/Payables		
17.6	8.5	10.7	10.5	8.1	11.2		10.2	9.9
93.1	16.2	17.2	19.7	11.4	13.9	Sales/Working Capital	20.8	22.0
-53.3	33.5	38.2	47.4	20.0	46.5		209.4	291.8
26.0	49.3	32.6	44.1	22.6			15.6	26.2
(31) 8.7	(83) 10.3	(120) 13.9	(83) 14.4	(14) 7.4		EBIT/Interest	(321) 3.3	(336) 7.0
1.2	2.9	3.4	7.6	1.2			-2.1	2.0
		80.6	75.8				13.0	41.8
		(12) 7.9	(20) 15.2			Net Profit + Depr., Dep., Amort./Cur. Mat. L/T/D	(45) 3.2	(45) 4.9
		5.5	5.2				-.3	1.5
.0	.0	.0	.1	.0	.8		.0	.0
.1	.1	.1	.1	.3	-1.2	Fixed/Worth	.2	.2
1.4	.4	.3	.3	-.1	-.1		1.1	1.1
.6	.3	.5	.8	.8	2.5		.6	.8
2.0	1.1	1.1	2.1	6.9	-27.2	Debt/Worth	1.8	2.3
170.5	3.3	3.5	4.8	-2.5	-3.3		9.3	14.3
114.6	65.7	69.2	58.5				51.9	85.7
(37) 41.6	(93) 36.0	(132) 35.9	(81) 35.2			% Profit Before Taxes/Tangible Net Worth	(308) 15.3	(324) 39.5
8.0	9.7	14.8	22.8				-2.9	14.5
27.2	35.4	25.7	18.9	16.9	6.2		15.2	25.7
14.0	12.7	11.9	11.5	8.3	3.5	% Profit Before Taxes/Total Assets	3.7	11.3
1.0	4.6	5.0	6.5	2.0	-4.1		-4.6	2.5
UND	813.6	459.6	282.0	273.0	228.2		353.1	470.2
490.0	169.5	171.7	164.5	164.4	71.0	Sales/Net Fixed Assets	135.3	146.9
69.9	51.6	58.2	84.3	55.4	36.6		48.8	61.1
16.5	7.6	6.7	6.2	3.8	4.2		6.9	7.3
9.3	5.8	5.4	4.8	2.6	2.7	Sales/Total Assets	4.9	5.1
4.5	4.2	4.3	3.7	1.9	1.8		3.6	3.6
.1	.1	.1	.1				.1	.1
(16) .2	(63) .3	(111) .2	(71) .2			% Depr., Dep., Amort./Sales	(272) .3	(274) .2
.5	.5	.4	.4				.6	.6
1.9	1.2	1.1	.3				1.1	1.3
(18) 4.7	(35) 2.4	(42) 2.1	(13) .4			% Officers', Directors' Owners' Comp/Sales	(131) 2.5	(124) 2.9
8.6	4.0	3.9	1.5				4.9	4.9
160399M	895467M	3543795M	9906729M	2845170M	6046469M	Net Sales ($)	29333582M	24368330M
13185M	124070M	615666M	1898358M	1028113M	1907031M	Total Assets ($)	6046474M	5624884M

M = $ thousand MM = $ million

See Pages 9 through 22 for Explanation of Ratios and Data

Comparative Historical Data

Current Data Sorted by Sales

4/1/11-3/31/12 ALL	4/1/12-3/31/13 ALL	4/1/13-3/31/14 ALL	Type of Statement	0-1MM	1-3MM	3-5MM	5-10MM	10-25MM	25MM & OVER
63	34	48	Unqualified		1		1	3	43
55	56	60	Reviewed	1	2	4	4	16	33
64	59	71	Compiled	5	3	8	22	22	11
31	42	45	Tax Returns	4	11	8	12	9	1
191	188	183	Other	6	13	9	21	47	87
				25 (4/1-9/30/13)			382 (10/1/13-3/31/14)		
404	379	407	NUMBER OF STATEMENTS	16	30	29	60	97	175
%	%	%	ASSETS	%	%	%	%	%	%
12.2	14.1	14.5	Cash & Equivalents	22.8	19.9	17.5	18.4	14.4	11.1
58.6	56.0	54.6	Trade Receivables (net)	33.0	40.1	49.1	50.0	59.2	59.0
.4	.3	.3	Inventory	.0	.2	1.7	.0	.1	.3
5.2	5.1	5.2	All Other Current	3.6	6.4	5.3	5.5	4.8	5.3
76.4	75.5	74.6	Total Current	59.4	66.5	73.6	74.0	78.5	75.6
8.0	8.0	8.7	Fixed Assets (net)	26.9	14.8	9.7	10.1	8.7	5.3
6.8	5.8	6.7	Intangibles (net)	.4	1.5	5.9	5.1	3.8	10.4
8.8	10.8	10.0	All Other Non-Current	13.2	17.1	10.8	10.7	8.9	8.7
100.0	100.0	100.0	Total	100.0	100.0	100.0	100.0	100.0	100.0
			LIABILITIES						
19.7	20.0	17.8	Notes Payable-Short Term	10.5	21.6	18.8	18.5	23.0	14.6
2.4	1.1	1.8	Cur. Mat.-L.T.D.	1.3	8.8	2.3	.4	.9	1.6
6.7	7.4	8.2	Trade Payables	2.9	10.7	18.8	5.6	7.6	7.8
.3	.3	.3	Income Taxes Payable	.1	.8	.1	.2	.2	.2
21.2	22.3	19.1	All Other Current	11.6	19.0	20.5	15.3	14.9	23.3
50.2	51.1	47.3	Total Current	26.2	60.9	60.6	40.1	46.6	47.5
7.6	6.6	7.5	Long-Term Debt	21.7	13.8	7.9	5.7	6.0	6.5
.2	.1	.1	Deferred Taxes	.0	.0	.0	.0	.1	.2
5.7	5.3	5.7	All Other Non-Current	1.0	15.1	2.5	6.4	3.8	5.9
36.2	37.0	39.4	Net Worth	51.1	10.2	29.1	47.8	43.6	39.9
100.0	100.0	100.0	Total Liabilities & Net Worth	100.0	100.0	100.0	100.0	100.0	100.0
			INCOME DATA						
100.0	100.0	100.0	Net Sales	100.0	100.0	100.0	100.0	100.0	100.0
			Gross Profit						
96.5	95.2	96.0	Operating Expenses	82.8	97.3	95.4	96.2	97.1	96.5
3.5	4.8	4.0	Operating Profit	17.2	2.7	4.6	3.8	2.9	3.5
.6	.6	.4	All Other Expenses (net)	3.1	.3	.6	-.3	.3	.5
2.9	4.2	3.6	Profit Before Taxes	14.1	2.4	4.1	4.1	2.7	3.1
			RATIOS						
2.7	2.4	3.0		6.1	4.3	2.4	6.1	3.2	2.2
1.7	1.6	1.7	Current	2.0	1.5	1.5	2.3	1.7	1.6
1.1	1.2	1.2		.9	.8	1.0	1.3	1.2	1.2
2.5	2.3	2.8		6.1	4.2	2.2	5.4	3.1	2.1
1.6	1.5	1.6	Quick	2.0	1.4	1.4	2.0	1.6	1.5
1.1	1.0	1.1		.8	.5	.7	1.2	1.2	1.1
28 12.9	25 14.7	26 14.0		0 UND	0 UND	16 22.4	23 15.6	27 13.5	32 11.4
42 8.6	38 9.6	40 9.1	Sales/Receivables	0 UND	30 12.0	36 10.2	34 10.6	39 9.3	46 7.9
57 6.4	58 6.3	56 6.5		107 3.4	55 6.6	62 5.9	45 8.1	54 6.7	57 6.4
			Cost of Sales/Inventory						
			Cost of Sales/Payables						
9.7	10.5	10.0		3.9	10.2	9.5	7.4	10.9	11.3
17.9	20.2	18.5	Sales/Working Capital	8.4	23.6	25.7	14.0	18.5	18.7
74.6	73.6	59.5		NM	-51.3	NM	58.5	45.3	47.3
29.8	27.2	36.8			25.0	37.8	64.4	28.7	38.4
(321) 7.8	(294) 10.1	(340) 12.6	EBIT/Interest		(25) 4.0	(21) 12.2	(49) 18.4	(84) 8.5	(154) 14.7
2.7	3.0	3.5			.8	3.6	4.6	2.2	6.6
40.9	21.9	73.5						10.8	105.8
(35) 4.6	(43) 6.8	(41) 8.7	Net Profit + Depr., Dep., Amort./Cur. Mat. L/T/D					(11) 6.7	(28) 22.4
1.3	1.9	4.3						1.5	5.2
.0	.0	.0		.0	.0	.0	.0	.0	.1
.1	.1	.1	Fixed/Worth	.1	.2	.1	.1	.1	.1
.6	.5	.5		2.3	4.2	.5	.2	.3	.4
.7	.7	.6		.1	.7	.5	.2	.6	.7
1.6	1.6	1.5	Debt/Worth	1.3	2.2	1.8	.9	1.3	1.8
7.6	5.9	4.7		3.0	NM	22.3	3.2	4.0	5.4
68.7	68.8	66.6		57.1	88.7	70.5	69.2	67.2	64.6
(338) 34.9	(324) 35.6	(356) 34.8	% Profit Before Taxes/Tangible Net Worth	(15) 22.3	(23) 18.3	(23) 35.0	(56) 34.4	(91) 36.0	(148) 35.8
11.8	16.0	14.8		11.2	3.2	8.5	11.9	6.2	19.9
24.3	24.1	24.9		34.3	18.9	25.7	32.6	26.4	22.4
12.5	13.1	11.7	% Profit Before Taxes/Total Assets	8.9	9.9	15.0	11.8	10.9	11.5
3.5	4.1	4.9		2.8	2.1	3.2	5.0	3.0	6.2
488.7	567.8	458.1		UND	UND	800.8	425.8	500.9	312.9
166.0	193.1	174.0	Sales/Net Fixed Assets	154.2	376.2	115.6	170.0	169.6	175.7
67.3	69.8	58.9		1.3	28.0	39.1	59.0	50.9	81.7
7.2	7.6	7.3		3.4	9.1	10.0	8.3	7.4	6.9
5.2	5.5	5.4	Sales/Total Assets	1.9	4.8	4.4	5.6	5.7	5.2
3.8	4.0	3.9		.7	3.4	3.3	4.2	4.5	3.9
.1	.1	.1			.2	.2	.1	.1	.1
(269) .2	(259) .2	(273) .2	% Depr., Dep., Amort./Sales		(10) .3	(17) .3	(40) .2	(65) .3	(132) .2
.5	.4	.4			.9	.7	.4	.4	.4
1.2	.9	1.0			2.8		1.7	1.0	.4
(118) 2.3	(104) 2.3	(110) 2.1	% Officers', Directors' Owners' Comp/Sales		(11) 5.1		(20) 3.1	(35) 1.8	(33) 1.1
4.1	4.7	4.2			11.6		5.7	3.3	2.3
20459886M	18444734M	23398029M	Net Sales ($)	9108M	62105M	116257M	428095M	1542403M	21240061M
4797703M	4640857M	5586423M	Total Assets ($)	8216M	18584M	39947M	100569M	295494M	5123613M

M = $ thousand MM = $ million

See Pages 9 through 22 for Explanation of Ratios and Data

Current Data Sorted by Assets							Comparative Historical Data	
2	7	8	7	3	1	**Type of Statement** Unqualified	19	16
	1	5				Reviewed	7	11
2	1	3				Compiled	7	4
3	2	4				Tax Returns	6	11
6	10	26	14	3		Other	32	36
11 (4/1-9/30/13)			97 (10/1/13-3/31/14)				4/1/09-3/31/10 ALL	4/1/10-3/31/11 ALL
0-500M	500M-2MM	2-10MM	10-50MM	50-100MM	100-250MM			
13	21	46	21	6	1	NUMBER OF STATEMENTS	71	78
%	%	%	%	%	%	**ASSETS**	%	%
47.2	23.1	21.9	24.2			Cash & Equivalents	31.8	23.2
18.1	42.3	47.1	28.8			Trade Receivables (net)	26.4	35.2
.0	.0	.0	.0			Inventory	.1	.1
8.3	4.5	7.4	12.0			All Other Current	14.7	11.3
73.5	70.0	76.5	64.9			Total Current	73.0	69.8
11.3	9.6	5.4	9.8			Fixed Assets (net)	9.3	9.9
1.0	3.1	5.9	14.8			Intangibles (net)	8.9	10.4
14.3	17.4	12.3	10.5			All Other Non-Current	8.8	9.9
100.0	100.0	100.0	100.0			Total	100.0	100.0
						LIABILITIES		
13.0	11.0	10.0	6.0			Notes Payable-Short Term	9.5	10.6
.9	1.0	1.0	1.8			Cur. Mat.-L.T.D.	1.2	1.5
18.5	12.5	8.2	5.6			Trade Payables	4.2	6.1
.0	.0	1.3	.1			Income Taxes Payable	1.8	.7
22.2	20.8	43.1	37.9			All Other Current	42.8	32.9
54.7	45.3	63.5	51.3			Total Current	59.5	51.8
10.9	3.3	2.8	5.9			Long-Term Debt	9.0	10.7
.0	.0	.1	.4			Deferred Taxes	.3	.2
10.9	11.8	9.1	10.5			All Other Non-Current	3.1	5.6
23.5	39.6	24.5	32.0			Net Worth	28.0	31.7
100.0	100.0	100.0	100.0			Total Liabilities & Net Worth	100.0	100.0
						INCOME DATA		
100.0	100.0	100.0	100.0			Net Sales	100.0	100.0
						Gross Profit		
97.4	94.8	95.8	93.8			Operating Expenses	97.1	95.5
2.6	5.2	4.2	6.2			Operating Profit	2.9	4.5
.4	.2	.1	1.1			All Other Expenses (net)	1.9	.8
2.2	5.0	4.1	5.1			Profit Before Taxes	1.0	3.7
						RATIOS		
3.6	2.5	2.2	1.6				2.1	2.5
1.6	1.4	1.5	1.2			Current	1.2	1.4
.9	1.1	1.0	1.0				.9	1.0
3.6	2.5	2.2	1.2				1.8	2.2
1.4	1.2	1.4	1.0			Quick	1.0	1.3
.9	.8	.9	.7				.6	.8
0 UND	**2** 184.2	**6** 56.5	**2** 176.8				**0** UND	**1** 255.3
0 999.8	**11** 33.9	**31** 11.7	**13** 28.9			Sales/Receivables	**5** 67.8	**22** 16.7
6 64.9	**45** 8.2	**45** 8.2	**41** 8.9				**42** 8.7	**53** 6.9
						Cost of Sales/Inventory		
						Cost of Sales/Payables		
20.0	9.1	10.5	12.1				11.4	11.2
225.7	103.6	37.5	46.7			Sales/Working Capital	115.1	31.4
NM	999.8	NM	999.8				-497.4	NM
	132.6	81.1	40.5				27.7	30.1
	(12) 30.2	(32) 20.3	(16) 9.1			EBIT/Interest	(46) 3.7	(53) 9.8
	3.4	3.9	-.1				.5	2.8
							12.7	5.6
						Net Profit + Depr., Dep., Amort./Cur. Mat. L/T/D	(11) 3.5	(12) 1.8
							.8	.8
.0	.0	.0	.1				.0	.0
.0	.0	.1	.3			Fixed/Worth	.2	.2
.4	.2	.4	1.0				.9	1.4
.6	.5	1.0	1.5				1.2	.9
1.2	2.4	2.7	2.9			Debt/Worth	3.3	2.9
NM	5.2	7.6	10.2				14.3	22.3
134.2	84.3	116.2	110.2				64.2	107.4
(10) 71.4	(20) 63.0	(42) 48.5	(18) 34.4			% Profit Before Taxes/Tangible Net Worth	(59) 20.4	(64) 41.5
16.1	32.9	21.0	-8.0				.6	13.9
58.6	35.9	29.4	18.6				16.7	26.8
42.4	16.6	13.6	7.8			% Profit Before Taxes/Total Assets	2.7	10.5
.5	6.9	6.3	-2.6				-.7	2.7
UND	UND	999.8	727.8				999.8	977.7
UND	999.8	391.3	300.5			Sales/Net Fixed Assets	419.6	239.7
46.1	88.3	114.2	31.5				66.6	45.8
49.4	30.0	16.5	17.9				23.6	16.1
23.7	9.2	5.9	4.6			Sales/Total Assets	9.8	5.4
7.5	3.6	4.3	2.1				4.1	3.3
		.0	.0				.1	.1
		(28) .1	(15) .4			% Depr., Dep., Amort./Sales	(37) .2	(45) .2
		.2	.9				1.1	.5
							.8	1.3
						% Officers', Directors' Owners' Comp/Sales	(16) 1.6	(16) 2.9
							5.8	7.3
107448M	358820M	2572083M	3675747M	735485M	91924M	Net Sales ($)	7891491M	6389591M
3429M	22511M	225979M	477129M	425647M	176319M	Total Assets ($)	1327616M	1426389M

M = $ thousand MM = $ million

See Pages 9 through 22 for Explanation of Ratios and Data

Comparative Historical Data | **Current Data Sorted by Sales**

4/1/11-3/31/12 ALL	4/1/12-3/31/13 ALL	4/1/13-3/31/14 ALL	Type of Statement	0-1MM	1-3MM	3-5MM	5-10MM	10-25MM	25MM & OVER
11	24	28	Unqualified		1	1	1	5	20
9	14	6	Reviewed				1	1	4
4	4	6	Compiled				2	2	2
12	10	9	Tax Returns	1		2	2	4	
60	49	59	Other	2	6	1	5	11	34
				11 (4/1-9/30/13)			97 (10/1/13-3/31/14)		
96	101	108	NUMBER OF STATEMENTS	3	7	4	11	23	60
%	%	%	**ASSETS**	%	%	%	%	%	%
25.5	25.3	25.9	Cash & Equivalents				41.3	20.7	24.8
38.4	31.1	36.8	Trade Receivables (net)				36.5	45.3	35.0
.0	.0	.0	Inventory				.0	.0	.0
10.3	14.5	8.5	All Other Current				6.1	4.6	11.6
74.2	70.9	71.2	Total Current				83.9	70.6	71.3
7.6	11.2	7.5	Fixed Assets (net)				2.3	5.3	5.7
8.8	9.2	7.8	Intangibles (net)				1.5	6.1	10.2
9.4	8.6	13.4	All Other Non-Current				12.3	18.0	12.7
100.0	100.0	100.0	Total				100.0	100.0	100.0
			LIABILITIES						
19.4	9.7	9.2	Notes Payable-Short Term				12.7	11.6	6.3
1.6	1.1	1.1	Cur. Mat.-L.T.D.				.0	.3	1.3
5.7	5.8	9.3	Trade Payables				8.3	8.3	9.3
.4	.6	.6	Income Taxes Payable				.6	.9	.6
40.1	35.9	36.4	All Other Current				23.9	53.0	37.4
67.2	53.2	56.6	Total Current				45.5	74.2	54.9
7.1	6.6	5.3	Long-Term Debt				2.0	4.5	4.5
.4	.5	.3	Deferred Taxes				.0	.0	.6
12.1	9.0	9.8	All Other Non-Current				6.0	12.4	7.1
13.1	30.6	28.0	Net Worth				46.5	9.0	32.9
100.0	100.0	100.0	Total Liabilities & Net Worth				100.0	100.0	100.0
			INCOME DATA						
100.0	100.0	100.0	Net Sales				100.0	100.0	100.0
			Gross Profit						
98.2	94.8	95.7	Operating Expenses				91.3	94.8	98.6
1.8	5.2	4.3	Operating Profit				8.7	5.2	1.4
.3	1.4	.6	All Other Expenses (net)				.0	.2	.7
1.5	3.8	3.7	Profit Before Taxes				8.7	5.0	.8
			RATIOS						
2.1	2.1	2.1					4.6	2.2	1.7
1.2	1.3	1.3	Current				2.1	1.5	1.2
.9	1.0	1.0					1.1	1.0	1.0
1.9	1.9	2.0					4.6	2.2	1.4
1.1	1.1	1.2	Quick				2.1	1.3	1.1
.6	.6	.8					1.1	.9	.8
3 142.8	1 419.0	3 136.8					0 999.8	11 33.9	2 234.3
24 15.2	10 37.2	14 27.0	Sales/Receivables				35 10.3	32 11.3	9 42.0
43 8.4	42 8.7	42 8.6					48 7.6	44 8.3	42 8.7
			Cost of Sales/Inventory						
			Cost of Sales/Payables						
12.5	13.9	12.6					6.5	9.0	18.7
120.7	52.2	45.5	Sales/Working Capital				11.6	27.1	82.0
-163.9	NM	999.8					752.8	-260.8	999.8
62.9	47.0	74.3						59.5	47.8
(70) 8.8	(69) 12.0	(70) 11.8	EBIT/Interest					(13) 13.4	(39) 10.6
1.0	2.8	1.4						1.7	.3
	43.4	33.5							
	(13) 2.5	(10) 8.2	Net Profit + Depr., Dep., Amort./Cur. Mat. L/T/D						
	.9	1.1							
.0	.0	.0					.0	.0	.0
.4	.2	.1	Fixed/Worth				.0	.1	.1
-4.8	3.1	.6					.1	.4	.8
1.1	.9	1.0					.2	1.1	1.1
7.6	3.1	2.8	Debt/Worth				1.3	3.0	2.9
-11.5	56.2	11.6					4.8	11.6	13.0
96.2	94.6	104.8					136.7	116.9	95.6
(63) 36.6	(79) 40.5	(93) 50.5	% Profit Before Taxes/Tangible Net Worth				42.8	(20) 60.1	(52) 48.5
6.2	14.7	19.1					13.1	30.0	16.7
21.7	24.8	30.4					42.4	36.0	25.4
8.1	10.6	12.0	% Profit Before Taxes/Total Assets				18.7	15.7	9.6
.4	3.8	2.6					2.0	5.5	2.1
999.8	999.8	999.8					UND	UND	999.8
236.5	194.4	377.1	Sales/Net Fixed Assets				402.9	316.5	485.2
76.0	52.3	93.9					104.9	106.7	102.0
21.5	23.5	20.6					30.6	6.2	24.7
6.1	6.9	5.9	Sales/Total Assets				4.6	4.8	10.7
4.3	4.0	3.7					2.1	4.0	4.6
.1	.1	.0						.0	.0
(48) .1	(60) .2	(59) .1	% Depr., Dep., Amort./Sales					(10) .1	(38) .1
.4	.8	.3						.3	.3
.8	1.1	2.0							
(26) 2.2	(21) 2.3	(18) 3.6	% Officers', Directors' Owners' Comp/Sales						
6.0	6.8	7.3							
10507880M	10236184M	7541507M	Net Sales ($)	2400M	13660M	14424M	81032M	377584M	7052407M
1371239M	1578897M	1331014M	Total Assets ($)	984M	15343M	2281M	29015M	158669M	1124722M

M = $ thousand MM = $ million

See Pages 9 through 22 for Explanation of Ratios and Data

Current Data Sorted by Assets							Comparative Historical Data	
						Type of Statement		
		1	3	1	1	Unqualified	7	9
	2	1	2			Reviewed	2	
	2	2	1			Compiled	2	1
						Tax Returns	2	3
1	2	7	1	4		Other	15	22
	6 (4/1-9/30/13)		25 (10/1/13-3/31/14)				4/1/09-3/31/10	4/1/10-3/31/11
0-500M	500M-2MM	2-10MM	10-50MM	50-100MM	100-250MM		ALL	ALL
1	6	11	7	5	1	**NUMBER OF STATEMENTS**	28	35
%	%	%	%	%	%	**ASSETS**	%	%
		20.3				Cash & Equivalents	9.7	12.7
		34.5				Trade Receivables (net)	41.9	36.0
		.0				Inventory	.4	3.1
		2.6				All Other Current	8.4	8.9
		57.4				Total Current	60.4	60.6
		21.4				Fixed Assets (net)	22.7	20.5
		14.7				Intangibles (net)	8.9	14.5
		6.6				All Other Non-Current	7.9	4.4
		100.0				Total	100.0	100.0
						LIABILITIES		
		8.6				Notes Payable-Short Term	24.0	9.9
		4.9				Cur. Mat.-L.T.D.	6.3	3.8
		8.4				Trade Payables	11.1	9.6
		3.9				Income Taxes Payable	.6	.5
		16.0				All Other Current	26.1	20.6
		41.8				Total Current	68.1	44.3
		19.2				Long-Term Debt	14.4	14.4
		.0				Deferred Taxes	.4	.3
		1.8				All Other Non-Current	5.5	8.1
		37.2				Net Worth	11.6	32.8
		100.0				Total Liabilties & Net Worth	100.0	100.0
						INCOME DATA		
		100.0				Net Sales	100.0	100.0
						Gross Profit		
		90.2				Operating Expenses	96.3	94.7
		9.8				Operating Profit	3.7	5.3
		4.5				All Other Expenses (net)	1.4	2.0
		5.3				Profit Before Taxes	2.3	3.3
						RATIOS		
		2.4					2.4	2.8
		1.5				Current	1.4	1.7
		1.1					.4	1.2
		2.4					2.2	2.4
		1.2				Quick	1.2	1.5
		1.1					.3	.8
		17 21.5					**35** 10.4	**26** 14.0
		43 8.4				Sales/Receivables	**45** 8.1	**45** 8.1
		54 6.8					**60** 6.1	**64** 5.7
						Cost of Sales/Inventory		
						Cost of Sales/Payables		
		11.1					10.9	6.3
		16.0				Sales/Working Capital	19.1	12.4
		102.0					-18.4	56.4
		42.4					20.2	12.8
		(10) 23.7				EBIT/Interest	(25) 1.9	(31) 6.4
		-9.2					-.8	-1.9
						Net Profit + Depr., Dep., Amort./Cur. Mat. L/T/D		
		.3					.3	.3
		.7				Fixed/Worth	.9	.9
		-2.8					-1.3	-6.1
		.7					.5	.8
		4.0				Debt/Worth	3.7	2.8
		-20.8					-2.6	-20.6
							51.4	96.1
						% Profit Before Taxes/Tangible Net Worth	(17) 40.7	(25) 43.9
							1.2	4.1
		25.3					20.0	30.3
		11.2				% Profit Before Taxes/Total Assets	4.4	12.0
		-.4					-10.8	-4.4
		48.7					47.6	32.7
		35.3				Sales/Net Fixed Assets	21.1	15.5
		15.1					10.9	11.1
		5.4					5.1	4.3
		4.2				Sales/Total Assets	3.4	2.4
		1.7					2.1	1.7
							1.1	1.2
						% Depr., Dep., Amort./Sales	(19) 2.0	(28) 2.2
							3.0	3.1
						% Officers', Directors' Owners' Comp/Sales		
1525M	42000M	180487M	400476M	719651M	569668M	Net Sales ($)	2441258M	3035183M
106M	7176M	55638M	166600M	316189M	210598M	Total Assets ($)	909557M	1329773M

M = $ thousand MM = $ million

See Pages 9 through 22 for Explanation of Ratios and Data

Comparative Historical Data / Current Data Sorted by Sales

			Type of Statement						
5	4	6	Unqualified					2	4
4	2	5	Reviewed			2		1	2
2	2	5	Compiled				1	3	1
2	2		Tax Returns						
24	24	15	Other	1	1	1	1	5	6
				6 (4/1-9/30/13)			25 (10/1/13-3/31/14)		
4/1/11-3/31/12 ALL	4/1/12-3/31/13 ALL	4/1/13-3/31/14 ALL		0-1MM	1-3MM	3-5MM	5-10MM	10-25MM	25MM & OVER
37	34	31	NUMBER OF STATEMENTS	1	1	3	2	11	13
%	%	%	ASSETS	%	%	%	%	%	%
12.4	12.9	17.5	Cash & Equivalents					24.7	7.1
36.2	34.3	37.4	Trade Receivables (net)					29.8	49.3
.1	.8	.0	Inventory					.0	.1
5.3	4.6	4.8	All Other Current					2.8	4.6
54.0	52.6	59.8	Total Current					57.3	61.1
22.4	22.1	20.5	Fixed Assets (net)					10.7	19.8
14.8	21.1	15.2	Intangibles (net)					25.9	14.0
8.8	4.2	4.5	All Other Non-Current					6.2	5.0
100.0	100.0	100.0	Total					100.0	100.0
			LIABILITIES						
8.5	7.1	16.5	Notes Payable-Short Term					8.4	17.0
3.2	3.7	4.1	Cur. Mat.-L.T.D.					3.0	5.6
10.5	12.6	10.8	Trade Payables					7.7	13.8
.5	.3	1.5	Income Taxes Payable					4.0	.1
21.0	19.3	17.7	All Other Current					15.1	18.0
43.8	43.0	50.6	Total Current					38.2	54.4
16.5	19.6	15.4	Long-Term Debt					8.4	15.5
.3	.1	.2	Deferred Taxes					.0	.2
14.4	4.0	3.1	All Other Non-Current					1.8	4.8
24.9	33.4	30.8	Net Worth					51.5	25.0
100.0	100.0	100.0	Total Liabilties & Net Worth					100.0	100.0
			INCOME DATA						
100.0	100.0	100.0	Net Sales					100.0	100.0
			Gross Profit						
97.2	91.9	95.9	Operating Expenses					97.0	99.0
2.8	8.1	4.1	Operating Profit					3.0	1.0
1.5	1.6	3.2	All Other Expenses (net)					3.1	3.6
1.4	6.4	.9	Profit Before Taxes					-.1	-2.6
			RATIOS						
2.4	1.9	2.2						3.1	1.8
1.2	1.3	1.1	Current					1.7	1.0
.8	1.0	.9						1.1	.8
2.0	1.8	1.8						2.8	1.6
1.1	1.2	1.1	Quick					1.7	.9
.6	.7	.8						1.1	.8
21 17.4	**24** 15.3	**17** 21.5						**17** 21.5	**55** 6.6
43 8.4	**46** 7.9	**51** 7.1	Sales/Receivables					**43** 8.4	**66** 5.5
57 6.4	**58** 6.3	**66** 5.5						**54** 6.8	**74** 4.9
			Cost of Sales/Inventory						
			Cost of Sales/Payables						
10.0	11.4	14.3						11.1	12.4
43.2	29.7	63.7	Sales/Working Capital					16.0	-113.2
-54.1	UND	-36.3						102.0	-22.1
17.8	30.9	23.9							11.8
(31) 5.0	(27) 8.0	(29) 6.0	EBIT/Interest						4.7
-2.6	.4	-6.6							-7.1
			Net Profit + Depr., Dep., Amort./Cur. Mat. L/T/D						
.4	.3	.3						.2	1.3
1.2	1.5	2.5	Fixed/Worth					.5	7.7
-2.3	-2.0	-10.4						-2.8	-3.6
1.0	.9	.8						.5	3.5
2.9	6.1	14.0	Debt/Worth					1.8	41.8
-13.9	-10.2	-28.4						-20.8	-25.7
127.1	188.2	294.2							
(25) 50.9	(22) 50.6	(20) 58.7	% Profit Before Taxes/Tangible Net Worth						
-16.1	28.7	17.6							
35.0	24.5	16.5						25.3	16.4
8.5	13.9	7.0	% Profit Before Taxes/Total Assets					9.9	7.0
-7.4	.6	-23.6						-.4	-23.9
39.7	44.7	54.0						169.0	35.4
22.0	23.1	25.5	Sales/Net Fixed Assets					38.1	19.4
9.0	9.2	12.2						18.5	10.3
5.3	4.2	5.3						5.9	3.4
3.3	2.9	3.4	Sales/Total Assets					4.2	2.7
2.1	1.8	2.0						1.7	2.2
1.4	.8	1.1							1.2
(28) 2.1	(22) 1.5	(23) 1.6	% Depr., Dep., Amort./Sales						(10) 1.9
2.8	2.7	3.1							3.0
			% Officers', Directors' Owners' Comp/Sales						
1470253M	2244319M	1913807M	Net Sales ($)	552M	1525M	12366M	15529M	172548M	1711287M
712612M	1093590M	756307M	Total Assets ($)	2231M	106M	2681M	2594M	67276M	681419M

M = $ thousand MM = $ million

See Pages 9 through 22 for Explanation of Ratios and Data

Current Data Sorted by Assets							Comparative Historical Data	
			2		1	**Type of Statement** Unqualified	12	8
	2	11				Reviewed	9	8
3	2	1				Compiled	10	8
11	3	4	1			Tax Returns	15	24
3	9	9	2	1		Other	26	39
	7 (4/1-9/30/13)		58 (10/1/13-3/31/14)				4/1/09-3/31/10 ALL	4/1/10-3/31/11 ALL
0-500M	500M-2MM	2-10MM	10-50MM	50-100MM	100-250MM			
17	16	25	5	1	1	NUMBER OF STATEMENTS	72	87
%	%	%	%	%	%	**ASSETS**	%	%
28.5	20.4	7.3				Cash & Equivalents	13.3	16.8
24.2	26.3	37.1				Trade Receivables (net)	31.0	24.2
4.9	4.8	7.4				Inventory	8.6	5.8
2.0	3.1	2.2				All Other Current	1.8	5.4
59.6	54.6	54.0				Total Current	54.7	52.3
22.5	30.1	33.0				Fixed Assets (net)	27.1	27.9
11.6	5.8	6.0				Intangibles (net)	10.9	8.1
6.2	9.6	6.9				All Other Non-Current	7.3	11.7
100.0	100.0	100.0				Total	100.0	100.0
						LIABILITIES		
11.4	3.7	10.0				Notes Payable-Short Term	13.3	14.2
5.7	1.5	4.3				Cur. Mat.-L.T.D.	5.3	4.6
17.5	16.6	11.4				Trade Payables	15.8	14.9
.1	.0	.2				Income Taxes Payable	1.2	.1
14.3	15.3	14.7				All Other Current	14.5	14.5
49.0	37.0	40.6				Total Current	50.1	48.3
18.8	27.6	19.9				Long-Term Debt	19.5	22.9
.0	.1	1.2				Deferred Taxes	.7	.3
12.2	3.6	3.7				All Other Non-Current	7.3	12.3
20.0	31.7	34.6				Net Worth	22.5	16.2
100.0	100.0	100.0				Total Liabilties & Net Worth	100.0	100.0
						INCOME DATA		
100.0	100.0	100.0				Net Sales	100.0	100.0
						Gross Profit		
91.6	91.8	96.9				Operating Expenses	98.3	95.0
8.4	8.2	3.1				Operating Profit	1.7	5.0
2.9	1.5	.1				All Other Expenses (net)	1.1	1.5
5.5	6.6	2.9				Profit Before Taxes	.6	3.5
						RATIOS		
3.0	1.9	2.1					2.0	2.5
1.4	1.4	1.2				Current	1.4	1.1
.9	1.0	1.0					.7	.7
2.7	1.6	1.8					1.6	1.4
1.0	1.3	1.1				Quick	.9	.8
.8	.6	.8					.5	.5
1 293.3	**1** 321.9	**24** 15.2					**21** 17.6	**8** 48.3
8 46.2	**20** 18.4	**39** 9.3				Sales/Receivables	**40** 9.2	**33** 11.0
31 11.7	**47** 7.8	**51** 7.1					**66** 5.5	**50** 7.3
						Cost of Sales/Inventory		
						Cost of Sales/Payables		
10.1	12.4	8.8					9.4	8.7
45.2	32.5	19.4				Sales/Working Capital	24.0	64.6
-531.7	NM	NM					-15.7	-16.4
21.4	66.0	14.5					8.7	17.7
(13) 4.7	(11) 14.1	(22) 5.7				EBIT/Interest	(61) 2.3	(72) 4.1
1.3	-.8	2.4					-.6	1.0
							3.2	5.7
						Net Profit + Depr., Dep., Amort./Cur. Mat. L/T/D	(17) 1.9	(13) 2.5
							.7	.9
.2	.1	.5					.4	.5
26.0	.9	1.0				Fixed/Worth	1.6	1.9
-.8	-14.8	2.5					-2.1	-.8
.4	.8	1.2					1.1	1.0
42.3	2.3	2.0				Debt/Worth	2.8	6.7
-3.0	-21.3	6.4					-6.5	-4.6
168.2	74.2	42.5					42.4	65.3
(10) 118.0	(11) 41.0	(21) 22.1				% Profit Before Taxes/Tangible Net Worth	(45) 15.1	(53) 36.7
69.5	-15.9	12.4					-15.0	3.3
43.1	31.0	12.0					15.4	23.4
27.7	15.7	7.2				% Profit Before Taxes/Total Assets	2.2	9.8
1.9	-2.0	3.2					-8.2	.3
395.3	87.4	29.9					30.0	37.5
21.5	19.6	9.8				Sales/Net Fixed Assets	14.7	15.7
11.2	2.1	3.8					5.4	6.4
10.7	4.8	4.9					4.3	5.0
5.1	3.8	2.9				Sales/Total Assets	2.8	2.8
2.9	1.1	1.7					2.1	1.7
.6		1.3					1.1	1.0
(10) 1.4		(20) 2.4				% Depr., Dep., Amort./Sales	(55) 2.7	(62) 2.8
3.1		5.8					5.4	5.5
6.0							3.6	2.8
(12) 12.4						% Officers', Directors' Owners' Comp/Sales	(25) 8.8	(36) 7.6
14.6							14.8	16.5
17666M	84952M	329202M	191699M	298681M	217838M	Net Sales ($)	1262133M	1841372M
3813M	18837M	88940M	157831M	99045M	114829M	Total Assets ($)	859549M	796731M

M = $ thousand MM = $ million

See Pages 9 through 22 for Explanation of Ratios and Data

Comparative Historical Data				Current Data Sorted by Sales					
			Type of Statement						
9	3	3	Unqualified					1	2
6	9	13	Reviewed		1	1	4	5	2
5	6	6	Compiled	1	2	1	2		
30	25	19	Tax Returns	6	4	3	1	3	2
29	33	24	Other	6	4	4	4	4	2
4/1/11-3/31/12	4/1/12-3/31/13	4/1/13-3/31/14		7 (4/1-9/30/13)			58 (10/1/13-3/31/14)		
ALL	ALL	ALL		0-1MM	1-3MM	3-5MM	5-10MM	10-25MM	25MM & OVER
79	76	65	**NUMBER OF STATEMENTS**	13	11	9	11	13	8
%	%	%	**ASSETS**	%	%	%	%	%	%
15.3	18.9	16.4	Cash & Equivalents	29.5	14.7		14.8	4.9	
25.4	26.4	30.4	Trade Receivables (net)	10.3	28.1		27.5	53.0	
7.3	8.0	6.2	Inventory	4.2	3.3		14.3	5.3	
2.2	1.9	2.6	All Other Current	1.9	3.7		1.1	4.2	
50.2	55.1	55.7	Total Current	46.0	49.8		57.6	67.5	
31.5	26.6	28.2	Fixed Assets (net)	28.9	32.6		31.0	17.0	
7.8	11.0	8.8	Intangibles (net)	11.0	11.9		3.3	9.6	
10.5	7.2	7.4	All Other Non-Current	14.1	5.7		8.0	5.9	
100.0	100.0	100.0	Total	100.0	100.0		100.0	100.0	
			LIABILITIES						
15.7	11.0	8.6	Notes Payable-Short Term	4.1	13.9		5.8	14.8	
5.2	4.0	3.8	Cur. Mat.-L.T.D.	5.0	4.6		6.4	1.7	
10.6	13.5	14.2	Trade Payables	14.1	15.9		12.8	12.9	
.2	.2	.1	Income Taxes Payable	.0	.1		.0	.3	
17.3	12.3	14.1	All Other Current	12.6	10.0		19.9	18.3	
49.1	40.9	40.8	Total Current	35.8	44.4		45.0	48.0	
23.6	21.4	20.8	Long-Term Debt	25.8	28.8		19.9	13.5	
.4	.4	1.1	Deferred Taxes	.0	.0		1.4	2.7	
4.5	9.2	6.4	All Other Non-Current	5.9	16.2		2.8	5.2	
22.4	28.0	30.9	Net Worth	32.4	10.5		30.9	30.6	
100.0	100.0	100.0	Total Liabilties & Net Worth	100.0	100.0		100.0	100.0	
			INCOME DATA						
100.0	100.0	100.0	Net Sales	100.0	100.0		100.0	100.0	
			Gross Profit						
93.9	91.7	94.1	Operating Expenses	92.6	92.6		95.6	96.4	
6.1	8.3	5.9	Operating Profit	7.4	7.4		4.4	3.6	
2.6	1.4	1.4	All Other Expenses (net)	4.5	1.3		.3	.8	
3.5	6.8	4.5	Profit Before Taxes	2.8	6.1		4.1	2.9	
			RATIOS						
2.3	3.8	2.1		4.0	1.5		1.7	2.6	
1.1	1.5	1.4	Current	1.9	1.0		1.2	1.7	
.8	.9	1.0		.8	.6		1.0	.9	
2.0	3.1	1.7		3.9	1.4		1.1	2.3	
.9	1.1	1.1	Quick	1.3	.8		1.0	1.2	
.5	.7	.7		.8	.5		.7	.8	
16 23.1	3 105.7	9 42.9		0 UND	9 39.6		26 13.9	23 15.7	
31 11.8	23 15.8	33 11.1	Sales/Receivables	1 330.5	28 12.9		39 9.4	49 7.5	
51 7.1	47 7.8	51 7.2		8 44.8	39 9.3		48 7.6	65 5.6	
			Cost of Sales/Inventory						
			Cost of Sales/Payables						
7.0	8.3	9.3		9.2	16.7		13.3	7.9	
61.3	19.7	23.8	Sales/Working Capital	22.9	999.8		23.8	11.4	
-25.0	-46.9	-999.8		UND	-17.7		127.0	-68.0	
11.8	12.9	27.4					4.9	42.1	
(65) 3.9	(62) 4.1	(53) 5.6	EBIT/Interest				(10) 3.0	(11) 11.7	
1.2	1.3	.4					-5.3	4.9	
4.1	3.1	13.0							
(13) 1.1	(11) 1.2	(15) 2.0	Net Profit + Depr., Dep., Amort./Cur. Mat. L/T/D						
.9	.6	1.3							
.4	.2	.4		.2	1.0		.4	.2	
1.3	.8	1.1	Fixed/Worth	2.5	-14.5		1.0	.8	
UND	6.5	-15.2		-11.9	-.3		1.9	NM	
1.0	.7	.9		.4	.9		1.4	1.3	
2.5	1.9	2.4	Debt/Worth	3.6	-19.3		2.4	6.0	
UND	NM	-26.5		-26.5	-2.7		3.3	NM	
72.5	91.2	86.7					44.1	126.5	
(60) 33.5	(57) 29.4	(47) 30.1	% Profit Before Taxes/Tangible Net Worth				(10) 14.7	(10) 38.5	
1.6	10.2	15.7					-19.6	14.1	
30.7	28.4	27.6		43.1	31.7		7.8	24.7	
7.6	12.4	7.8	% Profit Before Taxes/Total Assets	17.9	11.0		3.0	7.2	
.3	4.0	.8		-1.6	-.2		-11.0	4.4	
39.4	59.2	62.6		159.3	74.0		26.1	67.8	
11.6	17.8	13.9	Sales/Net Fixed Assets	10.8	11.6		6.8	35.3	
4.9	6.4	5.2		3.3	1.7		4.2	20.4	
5.4	4.6	5.4		6.8	7.0		4.0	7.3	
2.7	3.2	3.3	Sales/Total Assets	3.0	3.4		2.7	3.9	
1.7	1.7	1.9		1.1	.9		1.8	3.1	
1.3	1.1	1.0							
(54) 4.2	(46) 3.1	(43) 2.2	% Depr., Dep., Amort./Sales						
6.7	5.3	5.0							
4.3	3.4	4.0							
(40) 6.9	(31) 5.3	(28) 8.1	% Officers', Directors' Owners' Comp/Sales						
12.4	10.5	14.6							
1237062M	796157M	1140038M	Net Sales ($)	6694M	18400M	33258M	69128M	218046M	794512M
918423M	383829M	483295M	Total Assets ($)	5204M	9752M	12299M	27763M	98561M	329716M

M = $ thousand MM = $ million

See Pages 9 through 22 for Explanation of Ratios and Data

	Current Data Sorted by Assets						Comparative Historical Data	
Type of Statement								
Unqualified	1	5	13	11	6	4	72	75
Reviewed		7	7	4			25	21
Compiled	3	3	9	1			26	21
Tax Returns	6	7	3		1		28	28
Other	4	16	22	20	5	5	77	91
	18 (4/1-9/30/13)		145 (10/1/13-3/31/14)				4/1/09-3/31/10 ALL	4/1/10-3/31/11 ALL
	0-500M	500M-2MM	2-10MM	10-50MM	50-100MM	100-250MM		
NUMBER OF STATEMENTS	14	38	54	36	12	9	228	236
ASSETS	%	%	%	%	%	%	%	%
Cash & Equivalents	38.6	32.1	27.7	20.1	8.3		26.0	26.2
Trade Receivables (net)	11.4	31.6	24.1	24.3	22.5		24.6	23.8
Inventory	3.2	5.3	.0	.1	.0		1.4	1.3
All Other Current	.6	4.3	6.0	10.4	13.7		10.4	8.2
Total Current	53.7	73.4	57.8	55.0	44.5		62.4	59.7
Fixed Assets (net)	32.3	11.5	22.2	15.4	2.6		18.0	18.0
Intangibles (net)	4.7	3.5	9.9	17.0	47.2		11.0	12.4
All Other Non-Current	9.3	11.6	10.1	12.6	5.7		8.6	10.0
Total	100.0	100.0	100.0	100.0	100.0		100.0	100.0
LIABILITIES								
Notes Payable-Short Term	39.8	10.2	6.6	6.7	7.3		9.2	12.3
Cur. Mat.-L.T.D.	7.9	3.0	3.0	3.7	5.5		4.2	4.1
Trade Payables	9.9	12.5	12.6	6.4	1.0		10.5	9.0
Income Taxes Payable	.0	.1	.5	.2	.0		.3	.2
All Other Current	38.9	16.7	17.0	18.7	4.6		19.4	17.2
Total Current	96.5	42.5	39.7	35.7	18.4		43.4	42.8
Long-Term Debt	20.7	13.6	12.2	13.4	30.1		16.4	16.3
Deferred Taxes	.0	.0	.3	1.0	1.8		.5	.3
All Other Non-Current	9.0	5.3	12.5	4.1	9.7		6.9	5.8
Net Worth	-26.2	38.7	35.2	45.9	40.0		32.7	34.8
Total Liabilties & Net Worth	100.0	100.0	100.0	100.0	100.0		100.0	100.0
INCOME DATA								
Net Sales	100.0	100.0	100.0	100.0	100.0		100.0	100.0
Gross Profit								
Operating Expenses	83.1	88.8	92.6	88.5	76.7		90.4	90.0
Operating Profit	16.9	11.2	7.4	11.5	23.3		9.6	10.0
All Other Expenses (net)	1.1	-.1	1.2	.9	5.9		1.4	2.3
Profit Before Taxes	15.8	11.3	6.2	10.7	17.4		8.2	7.7
RATIOS								
Current	3.0	3.1	2.3	2.7	2.6		2.8	2.8
	.6	1.7	1.4	1.7	1.7		1.4	1.5
	.2	1.3	.8	1.0	1.4		1.0	1.0
Quick	2.9	3.0	2.0	2.6	2.3		2.2	2.3
	.6	1.6	1.2	1.4	1.5		1.2	1.3
	.2	1.0	.6	.8	.5		.7	.8
Sales/Receivables	**0** UND	**3** 107.6	**14** 26.3	**23** 15.7	**8** 44.5		**8** 46.7	**8** 44.1
	0 UND	**22** 16.5	**27** 13.7	**41** 8.8	**28** 12.9		**27** 13.6	**26** 13.8
	13 28.6	**40** 9.1	**41** 9.0	**59** 6.2	**126** 2.9		**45** 8.2	**43** 8.5
Cost of Sales/Inventory								
Cost of Sales/Payables								
Sales/Working Capital	16.0	6.0	8.5	4.5	1.0		7.0	7.2
	-14.9	12.3	33.9	10.3	7.8		19.7	18.1
	-5.8	66.0	-21.3	NM	17.3		653.0	-192.5
EBIT/Interest	54.9	40.6	34.6	22.0	10.1		36.6	31.3
	(11) 7.8	(26) 12.3	(40) 11.2	(30) 11.5	2.3		(174) 7.9	(183) 5.6
	.5	.8	3.4	2.4	1.2		1.9	1.5
Net Profit + Depr., Dep., Amort./Cur. Mat. L/T/D							4.8	6.4
							(30) 2.7	(29) 2.4
							.6	.7
Fixed/Worth	.0	.0	.2	.2	.1		.2	.2
	UND	.3	.5	.6	-.2		.5	.5
	-.6	.6	1.7	1.9	-.1		2.8	5.6
Debt/Worth	.5	.8	.8	.8	1.4		.7	.7
	UND	1.2	1.9	1.8	-1.8		2.3	2.3
	-1.8	2.5	4.7	14.7	-1.4		13.3	31.5
% Profit Before Taxes/Tangible Net Worth		113.2	94.9	92.1			89.4	107.0
		(36) 54.5	(48) 45.6	(29) 39.2			(183) 49.5	(182) 45.2
		3.9	13.8	6.1			22.7	13.5
% Profit Before Taxes/Total Assets	211.0	62.9	39.8	22.0	19.7		34.1	35.1
	36.7	22.9	15.5	12.9	6.0		15.4	12.7
	-.7	2.9	1.8	2.3	.9		3.8	2.3
Sales/Net Fixed Assets	UND	343.7	54.3	37.9	145.1		62.4	61.9
	29.1	53.1	24.0	22.7	45.2		25.3	27.2
	16.8	25.5	11.3	8.8	20.2		11.6	13.7
Sales/Total Assets	15.6	5.6	4.4	2.6	.9		4.7	4.5
	6.0	4.1	2.8	1.6	.7		3.1	3.3
	4.1	2.5	2.0	.8	.5		1.5	1.6
% Depr., Dep., Amort./Sales		.5	1.0	1.1			.8	.8
		(19) .8	(44) 1.9	(30) 2.0			(156) 1.7	(169) 1.8
		2.0	3.4	3.0			2.8	2.7
% Officers', Directors' Owners' Comp/Sales		4.4	2.2				2.5	2.9
		(13) 6.4	(14) 4.4				(51) 4.6	(53) 4.9
		18.9	7.4				9.8	10.1
Net Sales ($)	**28475M**	**185608M**	**848166M**	**1279046M**	**552261M**	**1650297M**	**6969291M**	**8278977M**
Total Assets ($)	**3594M**	**41614M**	**267285M**	**759331M**	**812929M**	**1582596M**	**4048188M**	**3928459M**

M = $ thousand MM = $ million

See Pages 9 through 22 for Explanation of Ratios and Data

Comparative Historical Data				Current Data Sorted by Sales					
			Type of Statement						
72	41	40	Unqualified	1		1	6	11	21
23	18	18	Reviewed		1	2	7	6	2
26	26	16	Compiled	2	3	2	2	6	1
25	28	17	Tax Returns	3	7	1	4	1	1
91	76	72	Other	3	7	5	9	26	22
4/1/11-3/31/12	**4/1/12-3/31/13**	**4/1/13-3/31/14**		**18 (4/1-9/30/13)**			**145 (10/1/13-3/31/14)**		
ALL	**ALL**	**ALL**		**0-1MM**	**1-3MM**	**3-5MM**	**5-10MM**	**10-25MM**	**25MM & OVER**
237	189	163	**NUMBER OF STATEMENTS**	9	18	11	28	50	47
%	%	%	**ASSETS**	%	%	%	%	%	%
24.7	24.5	25.7	Cash & Equivalents		34.0	23.4	35.9	21.7	20.0
23.6	22.5	24.8	Trade Receivables (net)		21.5	33.5	23.4	27.6	26.1
1.1	1.2	1.5	Inventory		5.9	.0	.1	.0	.1
9.6	7.5	6.4	All Other Current		.4	7.1	7.2	8.6	6.9
58.9	55.6	58.4	Total Current		61.8	64.1	66.5	58.0	53.1
16.8	17.8	16.8	Fixed Assets (net)		17.6	16.1	16.6	17.7	11.4
12.3	11.8	14.2	Intangibles (net)		8.3	10.1	7.1	14.1	24.4
11.9	14.8	10.6	All Other Non-Current		12.4	9.7	9.8	10.2	11.1
100.0	100.0	100.0	Total		100.0	100.0	100.0	100.0	100.0
			LIABILITIES						
14.8	9.3	10.6	Notes Payable-Short Term		14.4	7.2	7.9	10.6	4.7
3.8	3.4	3.7	Cur. Mat.-L.T.D.		4.8	.9	7.5	2.8	2.9
9.6	9.0	9.8	Trade Payables		7.5	15.4	10.7	11.0	8.4
.1	.3	.2	Income Taxes Payable		.0	.0	.2	.5	.2
17.7	19.6	17.7	All Other Current		27.0	17.1	22.5	15.1	14.1
45.9	41.6	42.0	Total Current		53.7	40.7	48.7	40.0	30.4
14.8	14.4	15.1	Long-Term Debt		8.8	13.0	26.9	7.6	16.5
.3	.3	.5	Deferred Taxes		.0	.0	.0	.6	1.1
8.2	10.1	8.1	All Other Non-Current		10.9	2.1	7.8	10.5	6.2
30.7	33.7	34.3	Net Worth		26.5	44.3	16.5	41.3	45.8
100.0	100.0	100.0	Total Liabilities & Net Worth		100.0	100.0	100.0	100.0	100.0
			INCOME DATA						
100.0	100.0	100.0	Net Sales		100.0	100.0	100.0	100.0	100.0
			Gross Profit						
88.7	88.7	88.3	Operating Expenses		85.8	95.0	88.7	89.4	88.8
11.3	11.3	11.7	Operating Profit		14.2	5.0	11.3	10.6	11.2
2.1	3.0	1.3	All Other Expenses (net)		.5	-.5	.5	.5	2.9
9.2	8.3	10.3	Profit Before Taxes		13.7	5.4	10.7	10.1	8.4
			RATIOS						
2.7	2.3	2.4			11.9	2.4	1.9	2.7	2.4
1.5	1.4	1.7	Current		2.3	1.8	1.5	1.4	1.7
.9	.8	1.0			.6	1.3	.9	.9	1.3
2.4	2.1	2.3			11.8	2.4	1.9	2.2	2.2
1.2	1.1	1.4	Quick		2.3	1.5	1.3	1.1	1.5
.7	.7	.8			.4	.8	.7	.6	1.1
9 40.4	6 57.0	10 37.2			0 UND	22 16.8	5 71.5	15 24.3	21 17.5
26 14.2	24 14.9	29 12.6	Sales/Receivables		0 UND	28 13.1	20 18.7	29 12.5	35 10.4
42 8.6	43 8.5	47 7.8			43 8.5	43 8.5	36 10.1	54 6.7	52 7.0
			Cost of Sales/Inventory						
			Cost of Sales/Payables						
6.6	7.5	5.9			4.5	7.4	10.0	4.7	5.7
17.7	20.1	14.2	Sales/Working Capital		16.2	9.4	19.4	23.8	10.4
-100.5	-41.0	-417.1			-13.0	37.1	-142.8	-67.6	25.3
33.3	25.9	25.8			31.2		59.9	26.5	18.2
(188) 8.1	(145) 7.3	(127) 9.5	EBIT/Interest		(13) 8.8		(22) 13.3	(39) 11.7	(39) 5.1
1.8	2.4	1.9			-1.2		5.1	3.4	1.2
13.8	21.1	15.4							
(23) 4.2	(29) 3.9	(18) 3.9	Net Profit + Depr., Dep., Amort./Cur. Mat. L/T/D						
1.7	1.9	1.1							
.1	.1	.1			.0	.1	.1	.2	.2
.5	.4	.4	Fixed/Worth		.3	.4	.4	.5	.5
5.3	2.3	1.9			-.9	.9	NM	1.2	-.4
.6	.7	.8			.2	.7	.9	.8	.9
2.1	1.9	1.9	Debt/Worth		2.3	1.8	2.0	2.0	1.9
18.8	10.9	9.7			-3.1	6.4	NM	4.7	-4.3
92.6	111.0	107.5			157.9	108.1	220.3	92.6	94.8
(183) 45.8	(152) 50.2	(130) 49.5	% Profit Before Taxes/Tangible Net Worth		(12) 90.9	(10) 59.2	(21) 75.1	(44) 47.8	(35) 42.5
16.6	15.2	12.4			18.9	14.0	9.8	18.1	7.0
33.2	31.1	37.1			63.4	40.7	50.6	24.9	23.6
12.2	12.7	15.3	% Profit Before Taxes/Total Assets		36.3	21.8	24.0	15.5	9.1
3.1	2.4	2.0			-3.1	1.1	4.2	3.9	1.2
69.3	61.8	82.0			429.6	82.9	175.1	46.1	50.7
31.3	26.0	29.7	Sales/Net Fixed Assets		72.7	34.9	46.1	23.4	29.6
14.1	14.7	16.3			23.0	18.7	22.6	10.4	12.0
4.4	4.0	4.6			5.9	4.9	5.6	4.0	3.3
2.9	2.7	2.6	Sales/Total Assets		3.2	3.5	4.1	2.4	2.1
1.5	1.4	1.3			1.9	2.2	2.2	1.5	.8
.7	.7	.8					.4	.9	1.3
(163) 1.5	(138) 1.5	(108) 1.8	% Depr., Dep., Amort./Sales				(17) 1.3	(43) 1.8	(30) 1.9
2.8	2.8	3.0					3.4	3.4	2.8
2.8	3.5	3.5							
(59) 6.0	(47) 8.2	(37) 6.5	% Officers', Directors' Owners' Comp/Sales						
10.9	13.8	10.6							
7359716M	4166517M	4543853M	Net Sales ($)	4783M	31388M	41933M	196745M	786329M	3482675M
3904135M	2952418M	3467349M	Total Assets ($)	12318M	11506M	15266M	78471M	530924M	2818864M

M = $ thousand MM = $ million

See Pages 9 through 22 for Explanation of Ratios and Data

Current Data Sorted by Assets							Comparative Historical Data	
						Type of Statement		
2	5	21	22	11	14	Unqualified	115	100
1	4	25	12	1		Reviewed	102	76
18	13	15	2	1		Compiled	93	77
68	51	20				Tax Returns	174	139
32	54	75	48	11	15	Other	359	318
74 (4/1-9/30/13)			467 (10/1/13-3/31/14)				4/1/09-3/31/10 ALL	4/1/10-3/31/11 ALL
0-500M	500M-2MM	2-10MM	10-50MM	50-100MM	100-250MM			
121	127	156	84	24	29	**NUMBER OF STATEMENTS**	843	710
%	%	%	%	%	%	**ASSETS**	%	%
31.4	18.4	16.3	17.0	12.8	9.6	Cash & Equivalents	18.2	20.3
13.1	25.0	31.4	33.5	24.5	24.1	Trade Receivables (net)	28.2	26.7
8.1	5.7	5.7	6.1	7.0	2.1	Inventory	7.2	6.8
3.0	2.3	8.2	6.8	6.6	11.9	All Other Current	6.1	5.5
55.5	51.4	61.6	63.3	51.0	47.8	Total Current	59.7	59.3
22.6	32.0	24.3	17.5	16.5	14.2	Fixed Assets (net)	24.1	23.4
6.3	5.2	4.6	10.2	27.0	30.7	Intangibles (net)	7.7	8.5
15.7	11.4	9.5	9.1	5.5	7.3	All Other Non-Current	8.6	8.9
100.0	100.0	100.0	100.0	100.0	100.0	Total	100.0	100.0
						LIABILITIES		
21.8	8.1	8.9	6.1	9.7	4.9	Notes Payable-Short Term	12.1	9.6
4.6	3.1	3.9	2.2	3.4	2.0	Cur. Mat.-L.T.D.	4.0	3.7
14.9	9.9	13.0	11.0	14.2	7.4	Trade Payables	11.9	13.1
.6	.3	.4	.1	.4	.4	Income Taxes Payable	.5	.5
33.6	20.7	16.5	21.7	12.0	21.1	All Other Current	19.5	19.5
75.5	42.1	42.6	41.2	39.7	35.8	Total Current	47.9	46.4
22.7	26.2	14.4	12.2	15.4	20.6	Long-Term Debt	17.7	17.2
.0	.2	.4	.6	2.2	2.2	Deferred Taxes	.3	.4
16.3	5.1	6.1	6.2	5.9	6.3	All Other Non-Current	8.3	8.4
-14.5	26.4	36.5	39.9	36.7	35.1	Net Worth	25.7	27.5
100.0	100.0	100.0	100.0	100.0	100.0	Total Liabilities & Net Worth	100.0	100.0
						INCOME DATA		
100.0	100.0	100.0	100.0	100.0	100.0	Net Sales	100.0	100.0
						Gross Profit		
90.7	87.7	85.6	90.5	92.7	94.8	Operating Expenses	91.6	89.7
9.3	12.3	14.4	9.5	7.3	5.2	Operating Profit	8.4	10.3
1.4	3.5	3.8	1.8	3.8	2.6	All Other Expenses (net)	2.9	2.8
7.9	8.9	10.6	7.7	3.5	2.6	Profit Before Taxes	5.4	7.5
						RATIOS		
4.1	2.8	3.4	3.1	1.5	1.8		2.8	2.8
1.0	1.5	1.6	1.5	1.1	1.3	Current	1.4	1.5
.4	.6	1.0	1.0	.9	1.1		.9	.9
2.5	2.4	2.7	2.8	1.3	1.5		2.1	2.3
.9	1.2	1.3	1.1	.9	1.0	Quick	(842) 1.1	1.1
.3	.4	.6	.8	.5	.7		.5	.6
0 UND	**0** UND	**14** 27.0	**31** 11.6	**28** 13.2	**35** 10.5		**8** 46.1	**6** 62.0
0 UND	**19** 19.4	**38** 9.5	**51** 7.1	**56** 6.5	**57** 6.4	Sales/Receivables	**36** 10.2	**31** 11.6
12 30.9	**42** 8.6	**54** 6.7	**74** 4.9	**87** 4.2	**81** 4.5		**60** 6.1	**58** 6.3
						Cost of Sales/Inventory		
						Cost of Sales/Payables		
14.3	8.5	4.6	4.4	6.6	6.6		5.7	6.6
999.8	23.1	12.7	14.2	31.3	15.6	Sales/Working Capital	15.8	16.3
-11.6	-14.1	UND	-910.9	-39.0	96.0		-54.6	-55.7
29.7	24.5	43.7	37.0	10.6	14.2		16.4	24.4
(66) 9.6	(92) 5.3	(109) 12.1	(64) 6.6	(19) 2.6	(27) 2.7	EBIT/Interest	(637) 3.9	(515) 5.3
1.4	.8	2.4	1.2	.6	.7		.5	1.5
		5.6	5.3				8.3	10.6
		(15) 3.4	(15) 3.5			Net Profit + Depr., Dep., Amort./Cur. Mat. L/T/D	(79) 2.8	(71) 3.8
		1.7	2.2				.9	1.2
.0	.1	.1	.1	.3	.3		.1	.1
.6	.8	.4	.5	1.2	1.7	Fixed/Worth	.7	.7
-.9	13.4	2.6	3.1	-31.4	-1.2		11.4	16.6
.6	.7	.5	.9	2.0	2.3		.8	.7
16.1	2.3	1.5	2.5	9.9	6.9	Debt/Worth	2.5	2.5
-2.9	33.5	6.5	11.5	-64.0	-3.4		378.0	-935.8
144.3	97.0	70.0	68.4	51.7	43.2		64.1	77.5
(70) 69.9	(98) 31.1	(130) 28.5	(69) 32.6	(17) 27.2	(18) 19.3	% Profit Before Taxes/Tangible Net Worth	(640) 22.9	(532) 35.2
25.6	6.4	6.1	5.9	4.9	2.1		2.7	8.4
54.8	24.4	24.1	17.5	6.6	6.8		20.6	24.2
22.9	7.6	10.6	7.0	3.0	2.6	% Profit Before Taxes/Total Assets	6.1	9.0
.0	.3	1.5	1.5	.0	-.6		-.5	1.2
UND	133.0	80.0	49.2	49.5	29.4		75.0	87.9
63.1	21.7	27.5	19.1	20.7	17.9	Sales/Net Fixed Assets	23.8	22.6
15.5	3.2	4.9	8.7	6.6	9.6		6.4	7.2
10.9	5.1	3.8	2.9	2.0	1.8		4.1	4.2
5.7	2.8	2.5	2.1	1.3	1.2	Sales/Total Assets	2.5	2.4
2.6	1.4	1.1	1.1	.6	.7		1.2	1.3
.4	.3	.4	.5	1.3	.6		.6	.7
(52) 1.0	(82) 2.0	(123) 1.4	(69) 1.5	(15) 3.5	(15) 2.9	% Depr., Dep., Amort./Sales	(574) 1.7	(486) 1.6
2.6	8.9	3.4	3.4	6.7	4.6		4.6	4.3
4.2	2.9	1.0					2.4	2.7
(52) 8.2	(52) 5.6	(32) 3.4				% Officers', Directors' Owners' Comp/Sales	(236) 4.9	(194) 5.2
20.0	8.6	6.1					11.1	10.5
213579M	521719M	1957712M	4705317M	2272291M	9036206M	Net Sales ($)	23152596M	22770488M
26438M	139044M	724741M	1838558M	1635648M	4739258M	Total Assets ($)	12929000M	11841992M

M = $ thousand MM = $ million

See Pages 9 through 22 for Explanation of Ratios and Data

Comparative Historical Data / Current Data Sorted by Sales

4/1/11-3/31/12 ALL	4/1/12-3/31/13 ALL	4/1/13-3/31/14 ALL	Type of Statement	0-1MM	1-3MM	3-5MM	5-10MM	10-25MM	25MM & OVER
90	61	75	Unqualified	3	5	4	4	15	44
55	51	43	Reviewed	1	4	1	7	20	10
68	52	49	Compiled	11	11	11	9	7	
148	132	139	Tax Returns	58	36	13	21	11	
284	262	235	Other	37	25	26	38	43	66
				74 (4/1-9/30/13)			467 (10/1/13-3/31/14)		
645	558	541	NUMBER OF STATEMENTS	110	81	55	79	96	120
%	%	%	**ASSETS**	%	%	%	%	%	%
21.0	20.3	19.7	Cash & Equivalents	20.4	20.3	26.0	21.9	21.8	12.8
26.0	26.3	25.4	Trade Receivables (net)	8.0	16.6	23.0	32.9	38.7	32.9
6.5	6.3	6.1	Inventory	4.7	6.2	8.1	5.1	7.7	5.9
5.8	4.6	5.6	All Other Current	1.8	6.2	4.7	5.3	5.9	8.9
59.2	57.5	56.9	Total Current	34.9	49.3	61.8	65.2	74.2	60.5
22.7	24.6	23.8	Fixed Assets (net)	44.2	27.8	22.5	19.2	13.4	14.2
8.0	7.7	8.4	Intangibles (net)	6.5	6.7	5.9	4.9	3.8	18.4
10.1	10.2	11.0	All Other Non-Current	14.3	16.2	9.9	10.7	8.6	6.9
100.0	100.0	100.0	Total	100.0	100.0	100.0	100.0	100.0	100.0
			LIABILITIES						
9.1	9.9	11.0	Notes Payable-Short Term	15.1	6.7	20.4	11.6	8.9	7.0
3.2	3.5	3.5	Cur. Mat.-L.T.D.	3.2	5.8	3.9	3.1	3.2	2.5
14.0	13.1	12.1	Trade Payables	9.6	12.1	10.4	10.8	15.4	13.5
.2	.4	.4	Income Taxes Payable	.6	.0	.5	.4	.1	.5
18.6	19.1	22.2	All Other Current	26.9	27.6	15.3	17.1	20.4	22.1
45.1	46.0	49.1	Total Current	55.5	52.3	50.5	43.0	47.9	45.5
18.2	18.7	19.1	Long-Term Debt	38.0	23.6	14.4	15.1	6.7	13.3
.3	.3	.5	Deferred Taxes	.2	.1	.1	.4	.3	1.2
9.1	9.5	8.2	All Other Non-Current	17.0	5.9	6.2	6.7	5.2	5.8
27.3	25.4	23.2	Net Worth	-10.6	18.1	28.8	34.7	39.9	34.1
100.0	100.0	100.0	Total Liabilties & Net Worth	100.0	100.0	100.0	100.0	100.0	100.0
			INCOME DATA						
100.0	100.0	100.0	Net Sales	100.0	100.0	100.0	100.0	100.0	100.0
			Gross Profit						
90.3	88.5	88.8	Operating Expenses	73.7	89.2	93.1	93.5	93.6	93.5
9.7	11.5	11.2	Operating Profit	26.3	10.8	6.9	6.5	6.4	6.5
2.3	3.1	2.8	All Other Expenses (net)	9.2	1.5	.4	1.2	.7	1.8
7.4	8.4	8.4	Profit Before Taxes	17.2	9.3	6.5	5.3	5.7	4.7
			RATIOS						
2.8	2.5	2.8		4.6	4.2	3.5	3.1	2.8	1.8
1.5	1.3	1.4	Current	.9	1.3	1.4	1.8	1.7	1.3
.9	.8	.8		.2	.6	.6	1.0	1.1	1.0
2.3	2.0	2.4		2.8	2.1	3.0	2.7	2.6	1.5
1.1	1.1	1.1	Quick	.7	.8	1.2	1.5	1.4	1.0
.6	.5	.5		.2	.4	.4	.7	.9	.7
2 170.8	0 776.2	0 UND		0 UND	0 UND	0 UND	12 30.8	23 15.6	31 11.8
32 11.3	31 11.9	27 13.7	Sales/Receivables	0 UND	9 39.7	20 18.0	40 9.2	43 8.4	49 7.4
54 6.7	54 6.7	54 6.8		8 46.4	28 12.9	42 8.7	59 6.2	62 5.9	70 5.2
			Cost of Sales/Inventory						
			Cost of Sales/Payables						
6.5	6.9	6.8		4.3	8.6	7.1	7.7	6.4	7.2
18.3	23.6	22.2	Sales/Working Capital	-149.8	47.3	25.2	16.7	13.1	17.3
-67.9	-43.6	-38.4		-3.5	-15.2	-38.7	-224.9	101.7	NM
28.8	25.8	32.2		10.3	29.0	21.4	48.9	48.6	33.5
(465) 6.9	(402) 7.5	(377) 7.1	EBIT/Interest	(49) 4.0	(55) 9.5	(39) 4.9	(59) 9.5	(73) 12.1	(102) 6.0
2.1	2.0	1.3		.2	2.4	-.3	.6	1.8	1.3
10.1	14.1	7.9						4.6	13.1
(63) 3.8	(46) 3.4	(49) 4.0	Net Profit + Depr., Dep., Amort./Cur. Mat. L/T/D					(12) 3.4	(25) 4.6
1.4	1.0	2.1						.8	3.3
.1	.1	.1		.3	.1	.1	.1	.1	.2
.6	.7	.6	Fixed/Worth	3.8	.9	.4	.3	.2	.7
5.0	9.9	32.7		-1.9	-5.8	29.5	2.6	.8	-31.4
.7	.8	.7		.9	.7	.3	.4	.6	1.4
2.2	2.5	2.7	Debt/Worth	14.3	3.2	2.3	1.5	1.3	4.2
57.6	-132.2	-33.8		-3.4	-7.0	182.1	12.2	3.8	-28.8
82.4	84.7	85.1		91.5	157.9	96.5	76.9	70.2	73.7
(491) 33.0	(415) 35.5	(402) 34.7	% Profit Before Taxes/Tangible Net Worth	(66) 29.3	(55) 63.2	(42) 35.3	(67) 27.9	(84) 30.2	(88) 35.6
8.2	9.3	6.3		4.1	18.9	2.9	.7	6.2	15.6
27.5	26.6	26.7		23.5	33.9	35.6	29.0	28.1	18.4
10.3	10.0	8.8	% Profit Before Taxes/Total Assets	5.6	14.5	13.2	11.3	10.9	6.0
1.6	1.6	.7		.0	3.1	-1.2	.2	1.5	.8
114.6	121.7	107.2		87.5	293.6	111.0	138.5	143.2	49.8
28.3	28.5	26.1	Sales/Net Fixed Assets	5.6	25.4	48.2	39.4	42.7	24.2
7.8	7.5	7.4		.2	7.0	11.5	11.2	16.5	10.9
4.9	5.3	4.7		3.0	6.4	7.3	5.3	5.2	3.5
2.6	2.7	2.7	Sales/Total Assets	1.1	3.2	3.9	3.4	3.3	2.2
1.5	1.3	1.2		.2	1.8	2.1	1.5	1.8	1.3
.6	.5	.4		2.2	.4	.7	.3	.3	.3
(434) 1.5	(363) 1.5	(356) 1.5	% Depr., Dep., Amort./Sales	(67) 13.1	(37) 1.3	(36) 1.6	(57) .9	(72) .9	(87) 1.4
3.4	4.5	4.0		19.2	5.1	3.2	2.5	2.2	3.4
2.7	2.0	2.2		6.0	4.0	2.7	2.1	1.0	
(178) 5.0	(180) 4.1	(146) 5.7	% Officers', Directors' Owners' Comp/Sales	(24) 13.3	(40) 6.6	(21) 3.9	(28) 6.8	(25) 2.9	
11.6	8.1	12.2		29.7	12.5	12.3	9.2	4.3	
19331232M	12744933M	18706824M	Net Sales ($)	46037M	150758M	213460M	573813M	1587284M	16135472M
9253439M	8083478M	9103687M	Total Assets ($)	114743M	111000M	93183M	359446M	759285M	7666030M

M = $ thousand MM = $ million

See Pages 9 through 22 for Explanation of Ratios and Data

Current Data Sorted by Assets							Comparative Historical Data	
	2	5	9	3	4	**Type of Statement** Unqualified	14	18
1	3	2	3	1		Reviewed	10	21
	6	2	2			Compiled	23	15
7	7	3				Tax Returns	23	39
6	14	16	15		1	Other	59	54
	26 (4/1-9/30/13)		86 (10/1/13-3/31/14)				4/1/09-3/31/10 ALL	4/1/10-3/31/11 ALL
0-500M	**500M-2MM**	**2-10MM**	**10-50MM**	**50-100MM**	**100-250MM**			
14	32	28	29	4	5	**NUMBER OF STATEMENTS**	129	147
%	%	%	%	%	%	**ASSETS**	%	%
38.9	40.3	41.6	38.4			Cash & Equivalents	37.1	37.8
10.7	14.9	18.1	11.8			Trade Receivables (net)	15.5	16.8
1.4	.7	.3	1.9			Inventory	.4	.6
6.0	4.4	14.2	12.7			All Other Current	8.8	9.5
56.9	60.3	74.2	64.8			Total Current	61.8	64.7
15.3	19.1	10.3	7.5			Fixed Assets (net)	14.1	12.6
16.6	6.9	4.1	15.9			Intangibles (net)	10.3	9.2
11.2	13.7	11.4	11.9			All Other Non-Current	13.8	13.6
100.0	100.0	100.0	100.0			Total	100.0	100.0
						LIABILITIES		
13.2	10.4	5.9	.7			Notes Payable-Short Term	8.8	8.8
3.0	2.8	2.0	.6			Cur. Mat.-L.T.D.	1.9	2.6
10.8	14.7	16.7	14.2			Trade Payables	17.3	18.3
.1	.1	.3	.7			Income Taxes Payable	.2	.3
15.6	17.1	31.0	42.8			All Other Current	37.1	32.5
42.8	45.2	55.9	59.1			Total Current	65.3	62.4
11.2	12.5	10.5	4.4			Long-Term Debt	14.8	8.3
.4	.0	.0	.7			Deferred Taxes	.1	.3
6.9	14.7	9.6	5.5			All Other Non-Current	8.4	12.6
38.7	27.5	24.1	30.3			Net Worth	11.4	16.3
100.0	100.0	100.0	100.0			Total Liabilties & Net Worth	100.0	100.0
						INCOME DATA		
100.0	100.0	100.0	100.0			Net Sales	100.0	100.0
						Gross Profit		
96.2	94.0	92.3	95.9			Operating Expenses	96.3	95.5
3.8	6.0	7.7	4.1			Operating Profit	3.7	4.5
1.4	.8	-.6	.3			All Other Expenses (net)	.9	-.1
2.5	5.2	8.3	3.8			Profit Before Taxes	2.8	4.6
						RATIOS		
4.9	2.7	1.8	1.7				1.6	2.0
2.1	1.5	1.3	1.2			Current	1.0	1.2
.7	.6	1.0	.7				.6	.7
4.9	2.7	1.3	1.5				1.5	1.7
1.3	1.4	1.0	1.0			Quick	.8	1.0
.5	.5	.7	.6				.4	.6
0 UND	0 UND	2 166.4	1 306.6				0 999.8	0 999.8
0 UND	3 145.4	19 19.3	11 33.5			Sales/Receivables	6 64.8	4 81.2
7 53.2	15 23.8	41 8.9	28 13.1				25 14.7	31 11.7
						Cost of Sales/Inventory		
						Cost of Sales/Payables		
20.0	11.4	7.7	7.6				10.4	11.6
308.1	75.6	66.6	87.3			Sales/Working Capital	-947.2	65.5
-92.0	-46.0	NM	-19.7				-12.0	-22.0
	25.7	78.9	22.4				21.6	33.4
	(18) 3.0	(10) 12.0	(10) 5.2			EBIT/Interest	(75) 3.7	(76) 8.5
	.7	4.4	-10.9				-.4	1.9
								30.5
						Net Profit + Depr., Dep., Amort./Cur. Mat. L/T/D		(13) 11.0
								2.4
.0	.0	.1	.1				.1	.1
.2	.5	.2	.4			Fixed/Worth	.7	.4
NM	NM	1.7	-.5				-1.6	-33.3
.2	.6	1.0	1.2				1.1	1.1
1.5	2.6	2.5	3.7			Debt/Worth	6.5	4.3
-7.2	-24.9	38.9	-21.5				-7.0	-47.3
	107.2	127.7	97.4				58.6	82.5
	(23) 30.6	(23) 48.4	(21) 42.5			% Profit Before Taxes/Tangible Net Worth	(87) 17.6	(106) 33.7
	6.1	15.1	16.2				3.7	13.4
49.6	31.0	16.1	16.3				12.4	21.6
9.9	6.1	11.0	8.3			% Profit Before Taxes/Total Assets	4.6	8.9
1.6	.0	3.6	2.0				-.6	2.7
UND	999.8	293.9	180.8				240.2	277.0
407.2	150.6	55.0	92.7			Sales/Net Fixed Assets	48.6	73.7
154.5	27.8	15.7	25.6				14.9	22.3
46.0	14.0	4.9	3.6				6.7	7.4
9.3	4.8	2.3	2.7			Sales/Total Assets	2.6	3.1
3.6	2.4	.9	1.3				1.4	1.6
	.1	.1	.2				.3	.2
	(17) .9	(23) .6	(19) .3			% Depr., Dep., Amort./Sales	(90) .7	(97) .7
	3.0	1.2	.9				2.4	1.7
	1.3						1.6	1.0
	(15) 3.2					% Officers', Directors' Owners' Comp/Sales	(43) 3.3	(52) 2.5
	4.5						6.7	6.5
99351M	461056M	779385M	2525480M	943834M	769251M	Net Sales ($)	14477811M	3958779M
3911M	35388M	121399M	645290M	294005M	626202M	Total Assets ($)	1936846M	1646473M

M = $ thousand MM = $ million

See Pages 9 through 22 for Explanation of Ratios and Data

Comparative Historical Data / Current Data Sorted by Sales

4/1/11-3/31/12 ALL	4/1/12-3/31/13 ALL	4/1/13-3/31/14 ALL	Type of Statement	0-1MM	1-3MM	3-5MM	5-10MM	10-25MM	25MM & OVER
22	14	23	Unqualified		1	4	1		17
12	8	10	Reviewed		1		5		4
16	12	10	Compiled	2		1	1	1	5
41	22	17	Tax Returns	2	6	1	3	3	2
56	46	52	Other	3	10	3	8	10	18
				26 (4/1-9/30/13)			86 (10/1/13-3/31/14)		
147	102	112	**NUMBER OF STATEMENTS**	7	18	9	18	14	46
%	%	%	**ASSETS**	%	%	%	%	%	%
35.6	33.6	39.2	Cash & Equivalents		50.3		31.4	54.2	37.9
16.4	18.8	14.5	Trade Receivables (net)		13.7		20.1	7.7	14.5
.3	.5	.9	Inventory		.0		3.0	.0	.5
9.5	8.2	9.4	All Other Current		1.9		12.9	12.5	11.0
61.8	61.2	63.9	Total Current		66.0		67.3	74.4	64.0
13.4	11.4	13.0	Fixed Assets (net)		10.0		15.0	7.2	9.3
7.3	10.1	10.9	Intangibles (net)		8.7		7.3	4.5	15.5
17.6	17.4	12.1	All Other Non-Current		15.4		10.3	13.9	11.2
100.0	100.0	100.0	Total		100.0		100.0	100.0	100.0
			LIABILITIES						
6.8	7.9	6.3	Notes Payable-Short Term		12.7		7.8	4.2	1.8
1.9	.8	1.9	Cur. Mat.-L.T.D.		1.2		4.0	1.8	1.0
16.6	13.4	15.4	Trade Payables		13.6		14.7	21.3	17.6
.4	.5	.4	Income Taxes Payable		.2		.2	.2	.7
33.9	29.2	27.1	All Other Current		24.4		26.4	24.3	32.6
59.5	51.8	51.2	Total Current		52.1		53.1	51.7	53.7
8.9	8.1	10.1	Long-Term Debt		8.9		13.0	7.5	6.3
.2	.1	.3	Deferred Taxes		.0		.1	.0	.7
15.6	5.6	9.4	All Other Non-Current		.4		22.5	10.3	5.9
15.8	34.5	29.0	Net Worth		38.7		11.4	30.6	33.5
100.0	100.0	100.0	Total Liabilties & Net Worth		100.0		100.0	100.0	100.0
			INCOME DATA						
100.0	100.0	100.0	Net Sales		100.0		100.0	100.0	100.0
			Gross Profit						
96.3	95.3	93.9	Operating Expenses		88.5		94.8	95.9	95.7
3.7	4.7	6.1	Operating Profit		11.5		5.2	4.1	4.3
.6	.5	.4	All Other Expenses (net)		-.3		.2	.1	.3
3.1	4.3	5.7	Profit Before Taxes		11.8		5.0	4.1	4.0
			RATIOS						
1.9	1.8	2.3	Current		3.7		2.5	3.0	1.8
1.1	1.2	1.3			1.0		1.6	1.6	1.2
.7	.8	.8			.5		.9	1.0	.9
1.7	1.6	2.0	Quick		3.7		2.3	2.2	1.6
.9	1.1	1.0			1.0		.9	1.2	1.0
.5	.6	.6			.5		.5	.7	.7
0 999.8	1 629.2	0 928.9	Sales/Receivables		0 UND		3 142.4	0 UND	1 305.4
5 66.6	7 50.8	8 46.4			15 25.0		17 21.8	0 739.1	9 42.1
23 16.1	38 9.7	25 14.5			43 8.5		27 13.5	4 93.0	24 15.1
			Cost of Sales/Inventory						
			Cost of Sales/Payables						
15.9	14.4	9.9	Sales/Working Capital		4.0		9.6	22.2	12.0
145.0	65.8	88.5			636.5		38.3	157.8	98.2
-34.7	-36.0	-64.5			-6.9		-23.5	NM	-158.4
30.0	33.0	46.4	EBIT/Interest						63.0
(76) 7.3	(50) 8.8	(50) 8.2							(22) 14.3
2.2	2.0	2.0							2.5
12.3			Net Profit + Depr., Dep., Amort./Cur. Mat. L/T/D						
(13) 3.0									
1.1									
.1	.1	.0	Fixed/Worth		.0		.1	.0	.1
.3	.3	.3			.1		.4	.2	.4
-6.5	1.5	4.4			8.3		NM	.5	3.0
.9	.8	.9	Debt/Worth		.5		.6	.8	1.2
3.3	2.2	2.8			4.8		1.6	2.5	2.7
-21.9	17.5	-44.1			-756.8		NM	-19.0	NM
108.5	100.0	110.3	% Profit Before Taxes/Tangible Net Worth		103.4		101.1	170.1	120.4
(103) 31.7	(83) 41.0	(82) 34.3			(13) 21.2		(14) 41.9	(10) 50.6	(35) 38.4
11.5	12.4	12.9			9.8		6.9	11.7	13.4
23.1	24.4	21.8	% Profit Before Taxes/Total Assets		49.6		29.7	34.7	17.9
7.8	9.2	9.4			10.1		13.4	12.5	9.7
2.0	3.1	3.1			1.9		4.9	3.3	3.4
388.8	317.7	460.5	Sales/Net Fixed Assets		552.2		244.4	UND	387.9
93.7	93.3	93.0			68.8		46.4	361.0	106.4
26.3	20.2	18.6			11.9		17.8	85.0	20.9
11.5	7.7	8.2	Sales/Total Assets		4.3		11.2	16.8	11.0
4.5	3.4	2.8			1.8		3.9	8.1	3.4
2.1	1.8	1.7			.8		2.2	2.4	2.0
.1	.2	.2	% Depr., Dep., Amort./Sales		.5		.4		.1
(97) .5	(73) .5	(70) .6			(10) .9		(14) .9		(30) .3
1.3	1.4	1.1			1.4		1.3		.8
1.2	.8	.7	% Officers', Directors' Owners' Comp/Sales						
(48) 3.0	(32) 2.2	(34) 1.9							
6.7	6.3	4.3							
7298450M	6066798M	5578357M	Net Sales ($)	3998M	35398M	36565M	134805M	209546M	5158045M
1918108M	1834008M	1726195M	Total Assets ($)	4595M	35500M	32909M	59859M	57124M	1536208M

M = $ thousand MM = $ million

See Pages 9 through 22 for Explanation of Ratios and Data

Current Data Sorted by Assets							Comparative Historical Data	
						Type of Statement		
	2	1	2	2		Unqualified	13	12
	3	1	1			Reviewed	7	4
	2					Compiled	10	4
3	3	2	2			Tax Returns	17	11
6	2	7	6	3	2	Other	19	25
	9 (4/1-9/30/13)		41 (10/1/13-3/31/14)				4/1/09-3/31/10 ALL	4/1/10-3/31/11 ALL
0-500M	500M-2MM	2-10MM	10-50MM	50-100MM	100-250MM			
9	12	11	11	5	2	**NUMBER OF STATEMENTS**	66	56
%	%	%	%	%	%	**ASSETS**	%	%
	51.4	23.4	31.7			Cash & Equivalents	28.0	29.9
	7.8	5.6	15.6			Trade Receivables (net)	7.6	10.0
	1.3	.9	1.3			Inventory	.5	.6
	8.1	3.9	8.0			All Other Current	6.3	10.3
	68.6	33.8	56.5			Total Current	42.4	50.8
	8.2	49.9	24.8			Fixed Assets (net)	36.1	31.4
	7.0	2.3	1.5			Intangibles (net)	3.5	4.8
	16.2	14.0	17.2			All Other Non-Current	18.0	13.0
	100.0	100.0	100.0			Total	100.0	100.0
						LIABILITIES		
	9.2	5.4	.6			Notes Payable-Short Term	5.2	5.5
	.4	2.3	2.2			Cur. Mat.-L.T.D.	6.6	4.2
	3.3	7.7	19.3			Trade Payables	8.0	11.7
	.4	.0	.0			Income Taxes Payable	.2	.1
	55.0	24.7	34.8			All Other Current	30.8	29.9
	68.3	40.0	56.9			Total Current	50.8	51.5
	6.8	20.8	10.3			Long-Term Debt	24.0	21.0
	.0	.0	1.2			Deferred Taxes	.2	.2
	7.4	8.5	6.9			All Other Non-Current	9.2	12.1
	17.4	30.6	24.6			Net Worth	15.9	15.1
	100.0	100.0	100.0			Total Liabilties & Net Worth	100.0	100.0
						INCOME DATA		
	100.0	100.0	100.0			Net Sales	100.0	100.0
						Gross Profit		
	96.9	94.1	92.8			Operating Expenses	96.2	95.8
	3.1	5.9	7.2			Operating Profit	3.8	4.2
	.2	2.4	.5			All Other Expenses (net)	1.3	.1
	3.0	3.6	6.7			Profit Before Taxes	2.6	4.1
						RATIOS		
	1.3	1.8	1.2				1.4	2.1
	1.0	1.4	1.0			Current	.8	1.1
	.8	.6	.7				.4	.7
	1.1	1.8	1.2				1.1	1.4
	.8	1.1	.7			Quick	.6	.9
	.6	.5	.6				.3	.4
	0 UND	1 706.5	0 UND				0 UND	0 999.8
	1 727.2	8 47.3	13 27.8			Sales/Receivables	2 156.2	5 69.2
	4 82.6	21 17.8	36 10.1				10 37.0	17 21.6
						Cost of Sales/Inventory		
						Cost of Sales/Payables		
	27.3	20.5	7.7				29.5	12.6
	-197.2	40.2	-567.0			Sales/Working Capital	-40.5	90.8
	-39.7	-2.0	-15.8				-6.6	-12.7
							9.7	24.0
						EBIT/Interest	(34) 1.7	(35) 3.5
							.4	1.4
						Net Profit + Depr., Dep., Amort./Cur. Mat. L/T/D		
	.1	.5	.0				.3	.2
	.4	1.3	.6			Fixed/Worth	2.1	1.4
	-.9	5.8	2.7				-6.4	UND
	2.1	.9	2.0				1.2	1.2
	14.1	4.4	4.5			Debt/Worth	5.1	4.6
	-26.5	16.0	6.4				-11.5	UND
		27.2	57.1				86.4	82.3
		(10) 12.4	(10) 34.4			% Profit Before Taxes/Tangible Net Worth	(44) 24.4	(43) 28.6
		-27.1	16.9				9.2	9.4
	19.3	14.2	17.9				13.4	15.0
	7.4	1.2	8.0			% Profit Before Taxes/Total Assets	5.3	6.8
	1.6	-2.5	4.0				.1	1.8
	334.3	35.5	598.3				57.0	90.2
	113.8	2.1	41.3			Sales/Net Fixed Assets	17.0	24.9
	38.8	.9	4.0				2.6	2.9
	6.2	1.7	3.8				4.2	4.5
	4.5	1.1	1.6			Sales/Total Assets	2.0	2.3
	3.2	.7	1.0				1.4	1.1
			.1				.6	.4
			(10) 1.1			% Depr., Dep., Amort./Sales	(53) 2.4	(46) 1.4
			5.2				8.2	6.0
							.7	.9
						% Officers', Directors' Owners' Comp/Sales	(19) 1.7	(18) 2.5
							4.0	6.8
14993M	89104M	77470M	457675M	503970M	577838M	Net Sales ($)	3984628M	2227949M
2672M	14997M	45346M	196256M	366250M	379958M	Total Assets ($)	2030493M	1375844M

M = $ thousand MM = $ million

See Pages 9 through 22 for Explanation of Ratios and Data

Comparative Historical Data				Current Data Sorted by Sales					
			Type of Statement						
9	5	7	Unqualified		2		1		4
3	3	5	Reviewed			1	3	1	
3		2	Compiled		1			1	
16	13	10	Tax Returns		5	1		1	3
22	26	26	Other	3	3	5	3	5	7
4/1/11-3/31/12 ALL	4/1/12-3/31/13 ALL	4/1/13-3/31/14 ALL			9 (4/1-9/30/13)		41 (10/1/13-3/31/14)		
				0-1MM	1-3MM	3-5MM	5-10MM	10-25MM	25MM & OVER
53	47	50	**NUMBER OF STATEMENTS**	3	11	7	7	8	14
%	%	%	**ASSETS**	%	%	%	%	%	%
32.0	28.2	33.4	Cash & Equivalents		27.2				32.3
10.6	9.8	9.9	Trade Receivables (net)		6.8				17.8
1.4	1.1	.9	Inventory		.7				1.3
9.8	12.8	9.3	All Other Current		11.1				14.9
53.8	51.9	53.4	Total Current		45.8				66.3
29.5	26.7	25.1	Fixed Assets (net)		27.7				15.6
3.4	7.2	4.0	Intangibles (net)		7.3				.3
13.3	14.1	17.4	All Other Non-Current		19.3				17.8
100.0	100.0	100.0	Total		100.0				100.0
			LIABILITIES						
10.5	4.1	4.7	Notes Payable-Short Term		12.8				1.5
4.7	3.6	2.6	Cur. Mat.-L.T.D.		4.1				.6
10.8	12.5	9.8	Trade Payables		13.8				15.6
.1	.2	.1	Income Taxes Payable		.0				.0
30.9	36.0	42.8	All Other Current		64.6				43.1
57.0	56.5	60.0	Total Current		95.3				61.0
23.8	26.9	10.1	Long-Term Debt		8.9				9.3
.2	.3	.3	Deferred Taxes		.0				.0
8.2	6.5	6.4	All Other Non-Current		4.1				5.3
10.9	9.8	23.3	Net Worth		-8.3				24.5
100.0	100.0	100.0	Total Liabilties & Net Worth		100.0				100.0
			INCOME DATA						
100.0	100.0	100.0	Net Sales		100.0				100.0
			Gross Profit						
95.7	91.0	93.8	Operating Expenses		97.5				94.2
4.3	9.0	6.2	Operating Profit		2.5				5.8
2.4	1.7	1.8	All Other Expenses (net)		1.6				-.1
1.9	7.3	4.4	Profit Before Taxes		.9				6.0
			RATIOS						
1.9	1.9	1.5			.8				1.4
1.3	1.2	1.0	Current		.3				1.2
.6	.6	.6			.2				.9
1.5	1.6	1.3			.6				1.3
.9	.8	.8	Quick		.2				.9
.3	.3	.4			.1				.5
0 UND	0 UND	0 UND			0 UND				0 UND
4 97.5	3 137.8	2 217.3	Sales/Receivables		1 706.5				5 67.9
24 15.2	13 29.0	14 26.8			6 57.4				34 10.8
			Cost of Sales/Inventory						
			Cost of Sales/Payables						
7.7	8.3	14.0			-19.9				6.0
47.9	62.4	-197.2	Sales/Working Capital		-9.1				134.9
-11.3	-13.1	-8.5			-4.2				-26.8
12.4	33.2	17.7							
(38) 3.6	(28) 4.0	(23) 3.7	EBIT/Interest						
1.3	.9	1.0							
			Net Profit + Depr., Dep., Amort./Cur. Mat. L/T/D						
.2	.1	.0			.6				.0
1.7	2.7	.7	Fixed/Worth		16.4				.7
NM	-1.7	NM			-.2				NM
1.2	1.2	1.3			10.4				1.5
4.0	6.2	4.0	Debt/Worth		55.9				2.6
-143.7	-11.8	NM			-2.5				NM
74.6	69.3	49.0							55.9
(39) 30.2	(30) 35.9	(38) 20.3	% Profit Before Taxes/Tangible Net Worth						(11) 35.1
5.7	7.4	5.7							12.6
15.6	21.4	16.0			3.2				17.9
4.1	8.2	5.1	% Profit Before Taxes/Total Assets		.1				7.8
.3	2.0	1.4			-3.0				3.4
127.9	330.7	277.3			210.0				296.6
33.0	32.7	44.2	Sales/Net Fixed Assets		47.0				53.2
3.4	4.7	4.0			5.1				14.4
4.6	5.1	4.6			4.7				4.9
2.6	2.7	2.3	Sales/Total Assets		3.1				2.5
1.3	1.4	1.1			.9				1.2
.3	.2	.2							.1
(44) 1.3	(31) 1.4	(33) .9	% Depr., Dep., Amort./Sales						(11) .9
7.0	6.2	6.0							1.3
.9	.7	2.1							
(18) 2.5	(12) 3.4	(11) 5.5	% Officers', Directors' Owners' Comp/Sales						
4.7	10.2	6.5							
2477551M	2376696M	1721050M	Net Sales ($)	1877M	21050M	27249M	50319M	126050M	1494505M
1422562M	1174832M	1005479M	Total Assets ($)	976M	13171M	17436M	19454M	106896M	847546M

M = $ thousand MM = $ million

See Pages 9 through 22 for Explanation of Ratios and Data

Current Data Sorted by Assets | **Comparative Historical Data**

0-500M	500M-2MM	2-10MM	10-50MM	50-100MM	100-250MM	Type of Statement	4/1/09-3/31/10 ALL	4/1/10-3/31/11 ALL
		5	11		6	Unqualified	13	10
1	1	3	1			Reviewed	4	2
	2	1				Compiled	2	3
	4	3				Tax Returns	5	4
3	3	13	6	8	4	Other	21	26
9 (4/1-9/30/13)		66 (10/1/13-3/31/14)						
4	10	25	18	8	10	NUMBER OF STATEMENTS	45	45
%	%	%	%	%	%	ASSETS	%	%
	53.9	38.8	23.7		29.7	Cash & Equivalents	27.7	26.8
	6.8	13.8	17.1		9.2	Trade Receivables (net)	16.9	17.4
	17.1	5.9	9.5		1.1	Inventory	1.5	2.3
	10.2	7.7	4.7		4.6	All Other Current	11.6	8.7
	88.0	66.3	55.0		44.6	Total Current	57.7	55.1
	3.4	16.9	22.3		13.1	Fixed Assets (net)	22.4	20.9
	6.0	4.1	7.1		18.4	Intangibles (net)	8.5	11.1
	2.6	12.8	15.6		23.8	All Other Non-Current	11.2	12.9
	100.0	100.0	100.0		100.0	Total	100.0	100.0
						LIABILITIES		
	11.0	5.3	3.1		4.3	Notes Payable-Short Term	5.7	7.5
	7.4	1.9	3.0		1.0	Cur. Mat.-L.T.D.	.8	1.7
	13.2	16.9	12.7		22.1	Trade Payables	14.7	12.6
	.0	.2	2.5		.9	Income Taxes Payable	1.6	1.3
	43.4	29.5	25.4		29.3	All Other Current	19.6	21.1
	74.9	53.7	46.7		57.6	Total Current	42.3	44.2
	2.6	7.8	36.7		7.6	Long-Term Debt	9.4	14.3
	.0	.4	2.1		1.0	Deferred Taxes	.3	.7
	1.6	3.7	4.5		2.3	All Other Non-Current	14.2	6.7
	20.9	34.4	10.0		31.5	Net Worth	34.0	34.1
	100.0	100.0	100.0		100.0	Total Liabilities & Net Worth	100.0	100.0
						INCOME DATA		
	100.0	100.0	100.0		100.0	Net Sales	100.0	100.0
						Gross Profit		
	92.9	96.7	94.1		97.1	Operating Expenses	93.4	95.9
	7.1	3.3	5.9		2.9	Operating Profit	6.6	4.1
	.5	1.5	.9		-1.0	All Other Expenses (net)	2.8	.1
	6.6	1.8	5.0		4.0	Profit Before Taxes	3.8	4.0
						RATIOS		
	1.5	1.7	2.2		1.3		2.9	2.9
	1.1	1.2	1.4		.8	Current	1.4	1.3
	1.0	.8	.8		.5		.7	.8
	1.2	1.4	1.6		1.1		2.8	2.1
	.9	.9	1.1		.6	Quick	1.0	1.0
	.3	.6	.6		.4		.5	.7
	0 UND	2 203.6	9 40.7		8 45.8		5 72.8	5 77.8
	0 UND	11 34.4	18 20.4		13 28.0	Sales/Receivables	21 17.1	19 19.1
	0 766.2	30 12.1	53 6.9		31 11.9		44 8.4	40 9.1
						Cost of Sales/Inventory		
						Cost of Sales/Payables		
	16.2	8.8	4.1		225.0		2.1	4.1
	303.3	33.5	8.7		-16.8	Sales/Working Capital	12.5	35.0
	-248.2	-28.7	-75.6		-2.3		-23.5	-14.5
		46.0	29.2				25.0	42.5
		(18) 22.7	(13) 7.4			EBIT/Interest	(26) 3.8	(26) 8.3
		3.4	-3.4				-.3	.5
						Net Profit + Depr., Dep., Amort./Cur. Mat. L/T/D		
	.0	.0	.0		.2		.2	.2
	.0	.5	.7		3.7	Fixed/Worth	.5	.9
	.8	4.4	NM		-.6		NM	13.8
	2.0	.9	.9		.9		.8	.7
	5.4	1.8	1.6		16.1	Debt/Worth	1.2	1.8
	NM	51.6	NM		-3.7		NM	589.1
		47.7	66.1				32.0	95.1
		(20) 18.1	(14) 19.0			% Profit Before Taxes/Tangible Net Worth	(34) 13.2	(36) 25.4
		8.3	3.5				-.7	12.6
	78.1	12.1	16.6		9.1		11.1	15.2
	19.4	7.4	7.3		4.0	% Profit Before Taxes/Total Assets	6.9	6.8
	3.9	2.2	-1.5		1.5		-1.6	1.6
	UND	341.0	138.3		158.7		64.8	62.2
	UND	34.0	16.8		6.2	Sales/Net Fixed Assets	13.1	19.4
	123.5	6.7	3.1		4.2		4.1	3.3
	17.6	4.5	3.7		2.3		3.3	3.5
	5.6	2.6	1.1		.8	Sales/Total Assets	1.2	1.3
	2.0	1.4	.6		.6		.7	.8
		.1	1.3				.3	1.1
		(17) .5	(12) 2.6			% Depr., Dep., Amort./Sales	(28) 1.9	(28) 1.9
		5.0	8.5				3.5	5.1
		2.1						
		(10) 5.5				% Officers', Directors' Owners' Comp/Sales		
		8.7						
31116M	137530M	474111M	678562M	866448M	2917912M	Net Sales ($)	2016808M	1535348M
1137M	9280M	131724M	368568M	588291M	1495879M	Total Assets ($)	1765936M	1438098M

M = $ thousand MM = $ million

See Pages 9 through 22 for Explanation of Ratios and Data

Comparative Historical Data				Current Data Sorted by Sales					
			Type of Statement						
14	15	22	Unqualified			1	2	8	11
4	4	6	Reviewed	1		1		1	3
3	2	3	Compiled				2		1
4	6	7	Tax Returns		2	1	1	3	
30	33	37	Other	1	4	3	5	7	17
				9 (4/1-9/30/13)			66 (10/1/13-3/31/14)		
4/1/11-3/31/12 ALL	**4/1/12-3/31/13 ALL**	**4/1/13-3/31/14 ALL**		**0-1MM**	**1-3MM**	**3-5MM**	**5-10MM**	**10-25MM**	**25MM & OVER**
55	60	75	**NUMBER OF STATEMENTS**	2	6	6	10	19	32
%	%	%	**ASSETS**	%	%	%	%	%	%
27.5	32.2	35.5	Cash & Equivalents				28.8	35.4	30.8
15.6	14.1	12.5	Trade Receivables (net)				12.9	15.2	14.3
3.3	9.0	7.8	Inventory				8.0	12.1	8.5
5.7	5.1	8.6	All Other Current				14.4	5.0	6.4
52.1	60.5	64.3	Total Current				64.0	67.7	60.0
22.7	16.2	14.8	Fixed Assets (net)				19.5	15.2	13.0
9.7	8.5	7.9	Intangibles (net)				9.3	5.9	9.4
15.5	14.8	12.9	All Other Non-Current				7.2	11.1	17.5
100.0	100.0	100.0	Total				100.0	100.0	100.0
			LIABILITIES						
12.1	6.2	5.0	Notes Payable-Short Term				5.8	5.9	4.5
3.5	.7	2.5	Cur. Mat.-L.T.D.				9.2	1.4	1.6
15.2	20.6	14.5	Trade Payables				9.9	13.7	19.6
.9	.6	.8	Income Taxes Payable				.0	2.4	.4
23.0	34.5	31.7	All Other Current				18.4	30.2	30.6
54.6	62.6	54.5	Total Current				43.4	53.7	56.7
9.9	9.1	14.6	Long-Term Debt				9.5	5.9	19.8
.4	.8	.8	Deferred Taxes				2.4	.8	.7
13.7	6.7	4.1	All Other Non-Current				3.4	4.0	5.4
21.3	20.9	25.9	Net Worth				41.4	35.6	17.5
100.0	100.0	100.0	Total Liabilities & Net Worth				100.0	100.0	100.0
			INCOME DATA						
100.0	100.0	100.0	Net Sales				100.0	100.0	100.0
			Gross Profit						
93.1	94.2	94.9	Operating Expenses				95.3	93.1	96.9
6.9	5.8	5.1	Operating Profit				4.7	6.9	3.1
.6	-.2	.6	All Other Expenses (net)				.9	1.1	-.2
6.4	6.0	4.5	Profit Before Taxes				3.8	5.8	3.3
			RATIOS						
2.0	2.2	1.8	Current				2.2	2.0	1.8
1.0	1.3	1.2					1.8	1.4	1.1
.6	.8	.8					1.3	.9	.7
1.6	1.6	1.5	Quick				2.0	1.5	1.5
1.0	.9	.9					1.1	.9	.7
.5	.5	.5					.8	.4	.5
6 65.2	**0** UND	**1** 255.8	Sales/Receivables				**0** UND	**5** 66.5	**7** 49.4
15 24.9	**10** 37.7	**10** 36.2					**19** 18.9	**14** 25.9	**11** 33.4
46 8.0	**33** 11.0	**29** 12.8					**56** 6.5	**51** 7.1	**28** 13.2
			Cost of Sales/Inventory						
			Cost of Sales/Payables						
5.7	9.1	6.9	Sales/Working Capital				4.6	4.1	10.5
999.8	52.7	35.6					9.0	18.7	740.9
-19.0	-13.0	-29.2					40.4	-29.2	-16.3
27.6	65.9	42.9	EBIT/Interest					173.8	65.4
(34) 7.1	(33) 20.5	(46) 12.1						(12) 27.0	(17) 15.8
1.7	5.6	2.9						2.8	2.8
			Net Profit + Depr., Dep., Amort./Cur. Mat. L/T/D						
.3	.1	.0	Fixed/Worth				.0	.0	.1
1.0	.6	.5					.3	.3	.5
-7.3	4.9	6.4					2.7	1.7	-.7
1.0	.9	.9	Debt/Worth				.9	.7	.8
2.3	2.8	2.1					1.8	1.8	2.9
-43.8	317.6	72.2					14.1	-999.8	-9.3
90.4	129.5	83.3	% Profit Before Taxes/Tangible Net Worth				178.9	45.3	91.2
(39) 28.8	(50) 41.9	(58) 22.2					34.9	(14) 18.7	(23) 27.7
6.3	19.1	9.5					-9.3	9.2	9.8
22.3	26.0	15.4	% Profit Before Taxes/Total Assets				33.2	18.2	14.9
5.7	8.6	7.4					9.3	7.9	8.0
1.0	2.6	2.4					-3.5	3.9	3.3
63.6	290.7	341.2	Sales/Net Fixed Assets				UND	567.5	340.4
16.6	36.5	43.5					42.3	34.0	46.5
3.2	4.6	4.7					4.5	4.6	4.7
4.5	6.9	4.0	Sales/Total Assets				4.7	2.9	6.1
1.4	2.3	1.8					1.8	1.8	2.3
.8	.9	.8					.6	1.0	.8
1.3	.3	.2	% Depr., Dep., Amort./Sales					.1	.1
(32) 2.1	(39) 1.9	(45) 1.3						(13) 2.3	(24) 1.3
7.9	3.3	4.1						3.8	2.7
		1.0	% Officers', Directors' Owners' Comp/Sales						
		(16) 3.7							
		7.1							
1803253M	4025359M	5105679M	Net Sales ($)	1432M	10670M	22478M	69163M	327724M	4674212M
1577314M	2091577M	2594879M	Total Assets ($)	2500M	101341M	14007M	64250M	210576M	2202205M

M = $ thousand MM = $ million

See Pages 9 through 22 for Explanation of Ratios and Data

Current Data Sorted by Assets							Comparative Historical Data	
						Type of Statement		
	2	4	8	3	2	Unqualified	30	17
	2	6	7			Reviewed	25	21
	3	12			1	Compiled	17	17
3	5	2				Tax Returns	16	26
6	16	19	13	1	3	Other	52	60
8 (4/1-9/30/13)			110 (10/1/13-3/31/14)				4/1/09-3/31/10	4/1/10-3/31/11
0-500M	500M-2MM	2-10MM	10-50MM	50-100MM	100-250MM		ALL	ALL
9	28	43	28	4	6	**NUMBER OF STATEMENTS**	140	141
%	%	%	%	%	%	**ASSETS**	%	%
	13.2	10.7	6.8			Cash & Equivalents	14.0	14.6
	42.2	58.1	59.4			Trade Receivables (net)	49.3	45.9
	.8	.5	2.6			Inventory	1.3	1.4
	1.2	6.5	6.5			All Other Current	6.0	5.1
	57.4	75.8	75.2			Total Current	70.6	67.1
	29.5	11.1	6.0			Fixed Assets (net)	14.0	17.3
	4.4	4.6	8.9			Intangibles (net)	5.5	7.3
	8.7	8.5	9.8			All Other Non-Current	9.9	8.3
	100.0	100.0	100.0			Total	100.0	100.0
						LIABILITIES		
	13.7	15.2	12.2			Notes Payable-Short Term	18.8	18.7
	1.6	2.8	1.2			Cur. Mat.-L.T.D.	2.9	2.7
	6.9	10.2	12.6			Trade Payables	7.7	7.4
	.0	.2	.2			Income Taxes Payable	.6	.3
	21.2	22.6	21.9			All Other Current	21.2	21.3
	43.4	51.0	48.1			Total Current	51.2	50.3
	18.8	4.8	7.6			Long-Term Debt	12.0	12.3
	.0	.2	.2			Deferred Taxes	.1	.0
	8.2	9.2	9.5			All Other Non-Current	7.6	7.9
	29.7	34.8	34.6			Net Worth	29.1	29.5
	100.0	100.0	100.0			Total Liabilities & Net Worth	100.0	100.0
						INCOME DATA		
	100.0	100.0	100.0			Net Sales	100.0	100.0
						Gross Profit		
	91.4	96.5	95.8			Operating Expenses	95.8	94.8
	8.6	3.5	4.2			Operating Profit	4.2	5.2
	3.2	.2	.2			All Other Expenses (net)	.7	.9
	5.4	3.3	3.9			Profit Before Taxes	3.5	4.2
						RATIOS		
	3.3	1.9	2.5				2.1	2.7
	1.5	1.4	1.6			Current	1.5	1.4
	.8	1.1	1.2				1.0	1.0
	3.3	1.8	2.4				2.1	2.5
	1.4	1.2	1.2			Quick	1.3	1.3
	.8	1.1	1.0				.8	.8
	17 22.0	**35** 10.5	**47** 7.8				**34** 10.7	**31** 11.9
	31 11.7	**43** 8.4	**55** 6.6			Sales/Receivables	**41** 8.9	**42** 8.7
	45 8.1	**55** 6.6	**72** 5.1				**54** 6.7	**54** 6.8
						Cost of Sales/Inventory		
						Cost of Sales/Payables		
	10.9	10.6	9.5				10.6	10.1
	38.0	21.7	15.5			Sales/Working Capital	23.1	22.6
	-25.9	73.1	29.1				UND	NM
	32.1	32.0	26.0				17.0	29.6
	(25) 9.3	(36) 11.0	(25) 12.1			EBIT/Interest	(126) 5.5	(117) 8.9
	.9	3.7	2.7				2.2	2.1
							6.7	11.2
						Net Profit + Depr., Dep., Amort./Cur. Mat. L/T/D	(37) 2.9	(24) 5.5
							.9	2.6
	.2	.1	.0				.1	.1
	.9	.2	.3			Fixed/Worth	.3	.3
	30.6	.8	.6				2.0	2.2
	.6	1.0	1.1				.9	.8
	1.9	1.9	2.8			Debt/Worth	1.9	1.8
	32.3	3.4	7.5				10.6	17.0
	124.5	75.2	95.4				79.2	81.7
	(22) 48.9	(39) 38.9	(23) 41.8			% Profit Before Taxes/Tangible Net Worth	(113) 32.6	(114) 34.7
	1.1	17.8	18.2				11.1	18.2
	36.3	23.6	20.4				22.0	25.9
	15.5	12.0	10.2			% Profit Before Taxes/Total Assets	10.1	12.5
	.4	3.0	2.2				3.2	4.1
	91.3	188.3	249.7				140.0	119.9
	22.3	60.6	95.2			Sales/Net Fixed Assets	59.1	50.0
	6.6	25.0	45.4				22.9	16.9
	7.5	6.1	5.2				5.9	6.2
	4.2	4.8	3.9			Sales/Total Assets	4.4	4.1
	2.8	3.7	3.1				3.4	3.1
	.4	.4	.2				.3	.4
	(20) .7	(38) .6	(18) .6			% Depr., Dep., Amort./Sales	(102) .7	(104) .7
	2.1	1.1	1.3				1.4	1.7
		1.5					1.6	1.9
		(15) 1.6				% Officers', Directors' Owners' Comp/Sales	(40) 3.8	(45) 4.3
		3.0					8.2	7.9
26479M	181338M	879690M	2391455M	1191543M	2593053M	Net Sales ($)	9659551M	6630587M
2749M	34771M	184885M	618644M	308462M	775936M	Total Assets ($)	2195757M	2234734M

M = $ thousand MM = $ million

See Pages 9 through 22 for Explanation of Ratios and Data

Comparative Historical Data

Current Data Sorted by Sales

4/1/11-3/31/12 ALL	4/1/12-3/31/13 ALL	4/1/13-3/31/14 ALL	Type of Statement	0-1MM	1-3MM	3-5MM	5-10MM	10-25MM	25MM & OVER
				8 (4/1-9/30/13)			110 (10/1/13-3/31/14)		
16	11	19	Unqualified		1		1		17
20	18	15	Reviewed			1	3	4	7
29	10	16	Compiled	1	1	1	2	8	3
23	12	10	Tax Returns		1	3	3	3	
52	50	58	Other	6	3	3	11	12	23
140	101	118	NUMBER OF STATEMENTS	7	6	8	20	27	50
%	%	%	ASSETS	%	%	%	%	%	%
13.1	14.5	12.7	Cash & Equivalents				23.8	9.6	7.1
46.0	50.5	51.7	Trade Receivables (net)				42.4	56.5	63.3
1.1	1.2	1.1	Inventory				.9	.6	1.6
4.1	4.0	4.9	All Other Current				5.3	4.6	6.6
64.3	70.2	70.4	Total Current				72.4	71.3	78.5
18.5	14.1	14.3	Fixed Assets (net)				15.7	12.1	6.8
9.4	8.1	5.8	Intangibles (net)				4.7	7.0	5.8
7.9	7.6	9.5	All Other Non-Current				7.1	9.5	8.8
100.0	100.0	100.0	Total				100.0	100.0	100.0
			LIABILITIES						
21.2	13.1	12.0	Notes Payable-Short Term				8.7	18.0	11.6
3.7	2.3	2.1	Cur. Mat.-L.T.D.				1.6	2.9	1.9
7.3	8.8	9.3	Trade Payables				12.3	8.6	10.5
.4	.3	.1	Income Taxes Payable				.0	.0	.3
15.7	19.2	23.8	All Other Current				20.6	21.2	26.2
48.2	43.6	47.4	Total Current				43.2	50.8	50.6
11.7	9.8	11.5	Long-Term Debt				7.6	5.3	10.2
.2	.0	.3	Deferred Taxes				.3	.0	.5
10.7	8.1	11.1	All Other Non-Current				17.5	8.4	10.6
29.2	38.5	29.8	Net Worth				31.4	35.4	28.1
100.0	100.0	100.0	Total Liabilties & Net Worth				100.0	100.0	100.0
			INCOME DATA						
100.0	100.0	100.0	Net Sales				100.0	100.0	100.0
			Gross Profit						
95.0	94.7	94.8	Operating Expenses				97.1	95.8	96.1
5.0	5.3	5.2	Operating Profit				2.9	4.2	3.9
1.1	1.1	1.2	All Other Expenses (net)				-.2	.6	1.0
3.9	4.1	3.9	Profit Before Taxes				3.1	3.5	2.9
			RATIOS						
2.5	2.6	2.6	Current				3.8	2.0	2.3
1.5	1.6	1.6					1.8	1.5	1.6
1.1	1.2	1.1					1.1	1.1	1.3
2.3	2.4	2.4	Quick				3.2	1.8	2.1
1.3	1.4	1.3					1.7	1.2	1.4
.9	1.0	1.0					.9	1.0	1.1
27 13.4	29 12.5	31 11.7	Sales/Receivables				15 24.3	31 11.7	43 8.4
41 8.8	41 8.9	44 8.3					39 9.4	38 9.6	52 7.0
52 7.0	58 6.3	57 6.4					54 6.8	49 7.4	69 5.3
			Cost of Sales/Inventory						
			Cost of Sales/Payables						
10.1	9.5	10.2	Sales/Working Capital				9.5	11.8	10.1
22.8	19.4	18.2					17.3	28.7	17.0
93.8	58.6	77.1					76.1	167.4	30.6
21.9	33.3	30.8	EBIT/Interest				30.7	49.6	28.6
(117) 5.9	(87) 12.6	(102) 10.4					(15) 9.3	(24) 10.2	(46) 12.2
1.8	4.8	1.9					-.1	1.0	3.3
19.1	33.3	19.5	Net Profit + Depr., Dep., Amort./Cur. Mat. L/T/D						20.5
(22) 10.6	(12) 5.4	(18) 4.6							(12) 6.9
.4	2.4	1.3							2.0
.2	.1	.1	Fixed/Worth				.2	.1	.1
.6	.3	.3					.4	.3	.2
2.4	1.0	2.8					2.8	1.0	.9
.8	.8	1.0	Debt/Worth				.7	1.0	1.2
2.0	2.3	2.2					2.4	1.4	2.4
11.2	9.3	12.1					10.9	5.8	7.1
85.0	91.5	87.9	% Profit Before Taxes/Tangible Net Worth				156.1	112.1	83.1
(113) 38.7	(83) 50.0	(94) 41.8					(16) 37.2	(23) 50.4	(40) 39.4
11.5	22.4	14.8					-7.4	4.2	17.9
24.5	32.2	26.9	% Profit Before Taxes/Total Assets				33.0	26.9	22.0
8.1	14.5	11.6					14.3	8.5	10.9
2.4	5.9	1.5					-3.7	.3	2.0
104.6	192.9	202.1	Sales/Net Fixed Assets				193.7	225.2	207.2
33.9	63.1	61.7					40.6	64.1	78.0
13.3	22.5	22.9					22.1	29.2	56.1
6.0	6.1	6.0	Sales/Total Assets				7.6	6.5	5.5
4.2	4.5	4.3					4.2	5.7	4.6
3.0	3.2	3.2					3.2	3.8	3.4
.4	.2	.3	% Depr., Dep., Amort./Sales				.5	.4	.2
(100) .9	(70) .4	(83) .6					(14) .7	(23) .6	(33) .4
1.7	1.0	1.2					2.1	1.1	.7
1.4	1.6	1.2	% Officers', Directors' Owners' Comp/Sales					1.1	
(48) 3.0	(35) 2.7	(27) 2.1						(10) 1.5	
5.0	5.8	4.8						2.8	
6544599M	7712927M	7263558M	Net Sales ($)	2954M	11748M	32668M	154219M	444607M	6617362M
2178529M	2036310M	1925447M	Total Assets ($)	4677M	7893M	7805M	45044M	92577M	1767451M

M = $ thousand MM = $ million

See Pages 9 through 22 for Explanation of Ratios and Data

Current Data Sorted by Assets | Comparative Historical Data

0-500M	500M-2MM	2-10MM	10-50MM	50-100MM	100-250MM	Type of Statement	4/1/09-3/31/10 ALL	4/1/10-3/31/11 ALL
		5	10	4	5	Unqualified	44	38
	5	23	12			Reviewed	43	54
2	9	7	1			Compiled	28	27
13	16	12			1	Tax Returns	42	41
7	31	30	22	3	9	Other	93	104
	32 (4/1-9/30/13)		195 (10/1/13-3/31/14)					
22	61	77	45	7	15	NUMBER OF STATEMENTS	250	264
%	%	%	%	%	%	**ASSETS**	%	%
21.8	14.4	14.9	9.7		2.7	Cash & Equivalents	10.6	10.7
32.0	38.5	38.9	27.5		8.2	Trade Receivables (net)	30.9	31.3
11.5	10.4	10.0	10.3		4.4	Inventory	10.1	10.8
5.9	2.3	4.4	5.7		1.7	All Other Current	4.6	5.8
71.2	65.6	68.3	53.2		17.0	Total Current	56.2	58.7
17.0	19.9	14.1	11.4		7.7	Fixed Assets (net)	18.3	15.7
6.8	8.5	7.6	26.0		63.3	Intangibles (net)	15.9	15.6
5.1	6.0	10.1	9.3		12.0	All Other Non-Current	9.6	10.0
100.0	100.0	100.0	100.0		100.0	Total	100.0	100.0
						LIABILITIES		
13.4	14.0	12.9	6.7		1.9	Notes Payable-Short Term	12.7	13.9
4.5	2.5	2.8	2.6		.8	Cur. Mat.-L.T.D.	4.3	4.6
16.2	15.9	17.9	14.6		5.8	Trade Payables	15.7	15.6
.4	.4	.2	.4		.0	Income Taxes Payable	.3	.7
20.3	12.6	16.4	22.4		7.3	All Other Current	18.7	20.0
54.9	45.4	50.2	46.6		15.8	Total Current	51.7	54.8
14.0	21.0	13.6	35.6		48.4	Long-Term Debt	26.3	24.9
.0	.0	.3	.3		.3	Deferred Taxes	.1	.3
6.4	9.1	7.5	6.3		8.6	All Other Non-Current	9.4	9.9
24.7	24.4	28.4	11.2		27.0	Net Worth	12.5	10.1
100.0	100.0	100.0	100.0		100.0	Total Liabilties & Net Worth	100.0	100.0
						INCOME DATA		
100.0	100.0	100.0	100.0		100.0	Net Sales	100.0	100.0
						Gross Profit		
94.2	93.0	92.6	95.6		99.2	Operating Expenses	95.6	95.2
5.8	7.0	7.4	4.4		.8	Operating Profit	4.4	4.8
.3	1.7	.5	1.5		10.7	All Other Expenses (net)	2.2	1.9
5.5	5.3	6.8	2.9		-9.9	Profit Before Taxes	2.2	2.9
						RATIOS		
3.4	2.5	2.3	1.8		1.3		2.0	1.9
1.5	1.4	1.6	1.2		.6	Current	1.2	1.2
.9	1.0	1.0	.6		.2		.7	.8
2.2	2.2	1.9	1.2		1.0		1.4	1.4
1.1	1.0	1.2	.8		.4	Quick	.9	.8
.4	.7	.7	.4		.1		.5	.4
0 UND	31 11.6	36 10.0	26 13.8		8 46.0		23 16.2	23 15.6
29 12.8	47 7.7	50 7.3	44 8.3		15 25.0	Sales/Receivables	38 9.7	41 8.9
47 7.8	66 5.5	78 4.7	68 5.4		58 6.3		58 6.3	60 6.1
						Cost of Sales/Inventory		
						Cost of Sales/Payables		
5.9	7.3	6.5	8.3		20.0		8.4	7.8
18.9	21.1	10.7	22.4		-16.6	Sales/Working Capital	29.3	26.2
-43.1	-142.6	126.4	-8.5		-4.2		-20.1	-20.5
20.5	25.4	44.5	38.3		7.8		12.5	16.6
(14) 6.5	(51) 8.5	(69) 12.1	(42) 9.1		(12) -1.3	EBIT/Interest	(225) 3.0	(224) 3.2
-.1	1.8	4.7	2.8		-1.8		.7	.8
		6.5				Net Profit + Depr., Dep.,	7.4	5.3
		(12) 2.6				Amort./Cur. Mat. L/T/D	(34) 2.5	(43) 2.7
		1.2					1.5	1.1
.2	.3	.1	.2		.3		.2	.2
.6	.6	.3	.9		-.3	Fixed/Worth	1.0	.9
-2.3	-5.0	1.8	-.3		.0		-.6	-.6
.5	1.0	1.1	1.5		1.6		1.2	1.3
4.0	2.7	2.2	7.4		-1.6	Debt/Worth	4.2	7.9
-10.6	-30.9	15.1	-2.1		-1.1		-3.8	-3.6
189.5	87.9	75.2	63.8			% Profit Before Taxes/Tangible	56.6	62.4
(15) 56.0	(45) 31.9	(61) 34.5	(26) 42.0			Net Worth	(156) 27.1	(162) 20.9
13.0	4.3	18.4	17.7				4.3	4.0
33.8	25.7	19.7	15.4		10.0	% Profit Before Taxes/Total	16.7	16.0
15.6	11.1	10.8	7.9		-3.1	Assets	5.1	5.3
-.5	2.3	5.3	3.7		-16.0		-2.4	-.5
145.8	57.8	109.5	38.4		47.1		53.5	72.0
38.8	28.5	27.3	18.9		26.6	Sales/Net Fixed Assets	22.8	25.0
12.5	12.6	15.0	12.2		4.8		10.5	12.9
5.1	4.2	3.4	2.7		.6		3.8	3.5
3.6	2.9	2.5	1.9		.5	Sales/Total Assets	2.5	2.5
3.1	1.9	1.8	1.4		.3		1.6	1.5
	.6	.5	.8				.8	.7
	(37) 1.1	(54) 1.1	(33) 1.9			% Depr., Dep., Amort./Sales	(173) 1.6	(183) 1.5
	1.8	2.3	3.2				3.1	2.6
	3.6	2.3				% Officers', Directors'	3.0	2.9
	(27) 6.1	(31) 4.5				Owners' Comp/Sales	(98) 4.6	(83) 4.6
	10.0	8.6					10.4	8.9
28303M	234580M	965672M	1853022M	1268435M	2816184M	Net Sales ($)	5177143M	7124041M
6110M	74317M	371356M	965930M	536319M	2494625M	Total Assets ($)	3036239M	4266530M

M = $ thousand MM = $ million

See Pages 9 through 22 for Explanation of Ratios and Data

Comparative Historical Data / Current Data Sorted by Sales

	Comparative Historical Data								Current Data Sorted by Sales											
						Type of Statement														
	39		26		24	Unqualified								2		6		16		
	63		48		40	Reviewed				2		3		10		12		13		
	28		15		19	Compiled		1		2		3		9		4				
	47		29		42	Tax Returns		11		13		7		8		2		1		
	102		114		102	Other		4		14		16		18		19		31		
	4/1/11-3/31/12 ALL		4/1/12-3/31/13 ALL		4/1/13-3/31/14 ALL				32 (4/1-9/30/13)				195 (10/1/13-3/31/14)							
								0-1MM		1-3MM		3-5MM		5-10MM		10-25MM		25MM & OVER		
	279		232		227	**NUMBER OF STATEMENTS**		16		31		29		47		43		61		
	%		%		%	**ASSETS**		%		%		%		%		%		%		
	12.0		12.4		13.3	Cash & Equivalents		18.4		12.5		17.6		15.4		13.6		8.7		
	32.2		32.1		33.3	Trade Receivables (net)		17.0		39.5		36.6		37.9		35.3		27.7		
	9.9		9.8		9.9	Inventory		9.7		10.5		12.3		7.6		12.2		8.6		
	4.7		5.5		4.4	All Other Current		7.3		2.2		1.9		2.2		6.1		6.4		
	58.8		59.8		60.9	Total Current		52.4		64.6		68.5		63.1		67.3		51.3		
	14.2		14.0		14.8	Fixed Assets (net)		31.2		19.9		14.8		14.3		11.5		10.7		
	18.5		16.4		15.9	Intangibles (net)		5.6		11.8		9.6		9.0		12.7		31.4		
	8.5		9.7		8.4	All Other Non-Current		10.8		3.6		7.2		13.5		8.5		6.6		
	100.0		100.0		100.0	Total		100.0		100.0		100.0		100.0		100.0		100.0		
						LIABILITIES														
	13.5		11.9		10.9	Notes Payable-Short Term		13.4		13.5		21.3		9.0		13.5		3.6		
	3.1		2.9		2.7	Cur. Mat.-L.T.D.		3.9		3.4		3.2		2.2		2.1		2.5		
	14.4		14.4		15.4	Trade Payables		3.7		18.5		12.8		20.0		16.1		13.9		
	.3		.6		.3	Income Taxes Payable		.5		.0		.0		.6		.4		.3		
	16.4		18.0		16.7	All Other Current		13.0		13.0		15.5		12.7		20.3		20.6		
	47.8		47.8		45.9	Total Current		34.5		48.4		52.8		44.5		52.3		40.9		
	25.8		24.0		24.5	Long-Term Debt		31.7		17.1		16.6		11.9		14.9		46.4		
	.3		.3		.2	Deferred Taxes		.0		.0		.0		.1		.4		.4		
	7.3		8.5		7.6	All Other Non-Current		2.6		10.7		2.4		11.1		8.6		6.4		
	18.9		19.4		21.9	Net Worth		31.2		23.8		28.2		32.3		23.8		6.0		
	100.0		100.0		100.0	Total Liabilties & Net Worth		100.0		100.0		100.0		100.0		100.0		100.0		
						INCOME DATA														
	100.0		100.0		100.0	Net Sales		100.0		100.0		100.0		100.0		100.0		100.0		
						Gross Profit														
	93.8		94.0		93.8	Operating Expenses		86.2		93.4		92.7		93.6		94.9		96.0		
	6.2		6.0		6.2	Operating Profit		13.8		6.6		7.3		6.4		5.1		4.0		
	2.7		1.8		1.8	All Other Expenses (net)		6.8		.5		.5		.6		1.2		3.1		
	3.4		4.2		4.4	Profit Before Taxes		7.0		6.1		6.8		5.7		3.9		.9		
						RATIOS														
	2.3		2.1		2.2			3.9		2.6		3.1		2.2		1.9		1.9		
	1.3		1.3		1.3	Current		1.4		1.3		1.4		1.5		1.3		1.1		
	.8		.8		.9			.6		.9		1.0		1.0		.9		.6		
	1.6		1.5		1.9			2.4		2.1		2.2		2.0		1.6		1.2		
	.9		1.0		1.0	Quick		.9		1.1		1.0		1.2		1.0		.9		
	.5		.5		.6			.3		.7		.7		.7		.6		.4		
23	15.9	27	13.6	27	13.6		0	UND	30	12.0	33	10.9	33	11.1	34	10.7	24	15.5		
42	8.7	42	8.6	45	8.2	Sales/Receivables	23	15.7	52	7.0	47	7.7	45	8.2	46	7.9	43	8.5		
63	5.8	63	5.8	66	5.5		37	9.8	83	4.4	65	5.6	63	5.8	78	4.7	59	6.2		
						Cost of Sales/Inventory														
						Cost of Sales/Payables														
	7.2		7.9		7.2			5.5		5.3		6.7		7.2		7.4		8.7		
	20.5		22.1		18.4	Sales/Working Capital		20.6		15.7		20.3		18.4		13.2		42.9		
	-20.8		-33.9		-43.6			-6.9		-43.6		195.3		290.0		-66.7		-12.7		
	16.8		24.0		28.4					27.5		27.0		54.1		18.9		30.4		
(239)	4.7	(205)	5.0	(195)	8.5	EBIT/Interest			(27)	7.8	(26)	8.5	(41)	14.1	(40)	10.7	(54)	6.5		
	1.1		1.2		2.5					1.8		2.0		3.5		2.5		1.6		
	10.5		6.0		7.7													14.3		
(45)	3.8	(33)	3.0	(26)	2.6	Net Profit + Depr., Dep., Amort./Cur. Mat. L/T/D											(11)	3.1		
	1.4		1.8		1.3													1.3		
	.2		.2		.2			.2		.4		.2		.1		.2		.2		
	.7		.8		.6	Fixed/Worth		.5		1.9		.5		.4		.3		-5.8		
	-.4		-.5		-1.0			NM		-.6		NM		1.2		-4.6		-.2		
	1.1		1.2		1.1			.3		1.0		1.0		.9		1.1		2.3		
	3.7		5.0		3.5	Debt/Worth		4.0		3.9		2.3		2.2		3.1		-13.3		
	-3.2		-3.7		-6.0			NM		-11.1		-26.6		5.0		-9.1		-1.6		
	71.5		76.2		75.3			52.0		138.0		84.0		75.3		87.5		64.9		
(178)	32.6	(147)	29.9	(151)	34.6	% Profit Before Taxes/Tangible Net Worth	(12)	14.5	(21)	58.5	(21)	31.9	(39)	32.5	(31)	34.6	(27)	48.6		
	8.5		10.0		13.0			2.1		8.3		10.8		10.1		17.9		21.2		
	20.0		18.5		21.2			13.7		27.5		27.4		22.0		17.5		22.4		
	7.2		6.9		10.0	% Profit Before Taxes/Total Assets		4.9		14.6		11.1		11.2		9.8		7.4		
	.3		.6		3.6			.2		2.2		3.5		4.8		4.6		1.2		
	76.4		70.6		59.4			38.2		72.9		53.8		66.6		92.7		59.2		
	27.0		26.2		26.3	Sales/Net Fixed Assets		12.9		34.8		24.0		31.8		25.9		25.8		
	13.7		13.9		13.0			6.2		4.8		15.3		15.3		13.3		12.6		
	3.8		3.6		3.5			3.3		4.3		4.0		3.8		3.2		3.3		
	2.5		2.5		2.5	Sales/Total Assets		2.4		2.7		2.9		2.5		2.4		2.0		
	1.5		1.5		1.5			.5		1.4		2.1		1.8		1.8		.9		
	.6		.7		.7					.9		.6		.5		.8		.6		
(169)	1.4	(149)	1.3	(139)	1.4	% Depr., Dep., Amort./Sales			(16)	1.4	(15)	1.4	(29)	1.0	(34)	1.5	(37)	1.5		
	2.4		2.8		2.5					3.1		2.1		1.8		2.4		2.6		
	2.6		3.1		2.8					3.6		3.8		2.3		2.2				
(91)	4.4	(74)	5.5	(75)	5.6	% Officers', Directors' Owners' Comp/Sales			(12)	9.8	(16)	4.9	(19)	6.4	(13)	2.9				
	7.3		11.8		10.0					12.3		9.0		7.9		12.2				
	7685994M		7333820M		7166196M	Net Sales ($)		8575M		60117M		114956M		345774M		672358M		5964416M		
	5277644M		4226540M		4448657M	Total Assets ($)		8916M		36353M		49874M		196852M		391367M		3765295M		

M = $ thousand MM = $ million

See Pages 9 through 22 for Explanation of Ratios and Data

Current Data Sorted by Assets / **Comparative Historical Data**

0-500M	500M-2MM	2-10MM	10-50MM	50-100MM	100-250MM		4/1/09-3/31/10 ALL	4/1/10-3/31/11 ALL
						Type of Statement		
		2	1			Unqualified	4	5
		5	1			Reviewed	9	10
1	6	4	1			Compiled	11	9
10	14	3	1			Tax Returns	25	27
6	11	14	7	1	2	Other	43	33
	6 (4/1-9/30/13)		84 (10/1/13-3/31/14)					
17	31	28	11	1	2	**NUMBER OF STATEMENTS**	92	84
%	%	%	%	%	%	**ASSETS**	%	%
34.6	14.0	22.8	17.7			Cash & Equivalents	16.5	20.4
11.2	22.2	21.5	14.6			Trade Receivables (net)	17.6	17.2
1.3	4.2	7.0	10.3			Inventory	3.6	3.9
.6	.4	2.8	1.9			All Other Current	6.2	4.8
47.8	40.8	54.1	44.5			Total Current	43.8	46.2
40.3	33.5	26.4	30.2			Fixed Assets (net)	29.8	30.6
9.5	10.4	9.0	21.0			Intangibles (net)	16.9	14.3
2.3	15.3	10.5	4.3			All Other Non-Current	9.5	8.9
100.0	100.0	100.0	100.0			Total	100.0	100.0
						LIABILITIES		
7.2	8.8	4.6	6.3			Notes Payable-Short Term	9.5	14.3
5.5	3.5	3.5	2.7			Cur. Mat.-L.T.D.	5.6	5.7
4.0	9.3	11.8	10.8			Trade Payables	8.0	9.5
.0	.0	.1	.0			Income Taxes Payable	.3	.1
22.9	13.9	17.2	19.7			All Other Current	18.7	19.9
39.5	35.4	37.2	39.5			Total Current	42.1	49.6
54.6	46.9	10.3	15.4			Long-Term Debt	36.8	23.3
.0	.0	.0	.0			Deferred Taxes	.0	.1
7.1	1.4	1.7	1.1			All Other Non-Current	4.9	6.4
-1.1	16.3	50.7	44.0			Net Worth	16.2	20.7
100.0	100.0	100.0	100.0			Total Liabilties & Net Worth	100.0	100.0
						INCOME DATA		
100.0	100.0	100.0	100.0			Net Sales	100.0	100.0
						Gross Profit		
88.7	90.5	85.3	86.7			Operating Expenses	89.9	92.9
11.3	9.5	14.7	13.3			Operating Profit	10.1	7.1
.6	1.8	1.0	4.2			All Other Expenses (net)	2.1	1.8
10.7	7.7	13.6	9.1			Profit Before Taxes	8.1	5.2
						RATIOS		
11.4	2.2	2.5	2.9				2.5	2.0
3.2	1.3	1.7	1.0			Current	1.2	1.0
.4	.6	.8	.6				.6	.6
10.6	2.0	2.2	2.3				2.2	1.8
3.2	1.0	1.4	.6			Quick	1.0	.7
.3	.5	.7	.5				.5	.4
0 UND	0 UND	16 22.5	10 35.8				0 UND	3 120.0
0 UND	19 19.6	22 16.7	19 18.9			Sales/Receivables	19 19.7	19 19.3
20 18.3	26 14.0	30 12.3	27 13.4				32 11.6	31 11.6
						Cost of Sales/Inventory		
						Cost of Sales/Payables		
7.5	19.9	8.9	6.8				10.0	12.7
30.8	62.9	14.3	132.2			Sales/Working Capital	64.9	-226.7
-12.9	-25.5	-33.5	-11.6				-18.0	-12.0
67.4	23.4	74.0					19.0	17.8
(13) 11.0	(28) 6.6	(25) 25.0				EBIT/Interest	(78) 5.5	(74) 4.4
.6	1.4	3.9					1.5	.6
							17.6	6.6
						Net Profit + Depr., Dep., Amort./Cur. Mat. L/T/D	(15) 7.6	(15) 2.5
							.4	1.7
.0	.1	.2	.3				.4	.5
1.1	2.4	.4	.5			Fixed/Worth	2.5	1.8
-.9	23.0	2.3	5.6				-1.5	-2.6
.4	1.1	.4	.4				1.0	1.0
4.3	2.7	.9	2.3			Debt/Worth	7.5	3.6
-2.0	23.6	3.5	14.4				-5.2	-7.1
	187.0	97.0					72.3	95.0
	(26) 51.3	(25) 46.7				% Profit Before Taxes/Tangible Net Worth	(52) 31.4	(54) 23.2
	8.7	19.1					13.9	.3
83.7	48.6	41.4	24.0				24.1	29.8
39.7	14.9	17.9	19.6			% Profit Before Taxes/Total Assets	12.0	9.0
7.7	2.4	7.4	2.7				2.6	-.4
148.1	124.9	68.4	69.0				37.9	29.8
26.5	12.7	16.6	11.1			Sales/Net Fixed Assets	14.6	14.8
8.4	6.4	9.8	3.9				7.7	7.0
10.3	5.9	4.4	2.8				4.4	4.5
4.7	4.5	3.1	2.4			Sales/Total Assets	2.9	3.0
3.1	2.5	1.8	1.6				1.7	1.9
	.7	.9	.6				1.5	1.5
	(23) 1.6	(18) 2.1	2.4			% Depr., Dep., Amort./Sales	(58) 2.9	(57) 2.6
	3.0	4.0	3.0				5.1	4.0
	2.8						3.1	2.8
	(17) 5.5					% Officers', Directors' Owners' Comp/Sales	(53) 5.1	(47) 5.2
	9.9						8.4	9.3
17599M	163869M	371922M	693674M	113379M	519830M	Net Sales ($)	1246452M	1509083M
3083M	36223M	130061M	323803M	62110M	260937M	Total Assets ($)	523619M	615979M

M = $ thousand MM = $ million

See Pages 9 through 22 for Explanation of Ratios and Data

Comparative Historical Data				Current Data Sorted by Sales					
			Type of Statement						
6	3	3	Unqualified		1			1	1
10	11	6	Reviewed					4	2
14	8	12	Compiled		3	1	3	4	1
24	38	28	Tax Returns	12	4	4	3	5	
47	36	41	Other	6	6	4	6	7	12
					6 (4/1-9/30/13)		84 (10/1/13-3/31/14)		
4/1/11-3/31/12 ALL	4/1/12-3/31/13 ALL	4/1/13-3/31/14 ALL		0-1MM	1-3MM	3-5MM	5-10MM	10-25MM	25MM & OVER
101	96	90	**NUMBER OF STATEMENTS**	18	14	9	12	21	16
%	%	%	**ASSETS**	%	%	%	%	%	%
19.0	21.4	21.7	Cash & Equivalents	22.1	23.5		21.8	22.4	23.8
18.6	16.8	18.7	Trade Receivables (net)	6.7	15.0		32.7	27.8	18.4
2.7	2.7	5.2	Inventory	1.0	2.0		9.0	7.3	8.6
2.8	2.8	1.6	All Other Current	.6	.4		3.0	2.2	2.4
43.1	43.7	47.2	Total Current	30.5	40.9		66.6	59.7	53.3
33.3	32.6	31.8	Fixed Assets (net)	55.5	36.4		17.2	16.4	22.9
14.9	13.3	11.4	Intangibles (net)	12.8	10.6		1.5	12.2	18.4
8.7	10.4	9.6	All Other Non-Current	1.2	12.1		14.7	11.7	5.4
100.0	100.0	100.0	Total	100.0	100.0		100.0	100.0	100.0
			LIABILITIES						
10.3	8.1	6.6	Notes Payable-Short Term	7.4	7.1		6.6	6.8	4.3
5.2	5.4	3.8	Cur. Mat.-L.T.D.	6.4	1.7		4.3	3.2	2.7
8.1	8.2	9.2	Trade Payables	2.4	5.0		12.6	18.5	9.2
.1	.4	.0	Income Taxes Payable	.0	.0		.0	.0	.0
15.7	13.4	17.7	All Other Current	5.1	24.1		32.1	14.4	26.9
39.4	35.4	37.3	Total Current	21.3	38.0		55.5	42.9	43.1
27.7	34.1	32.2	Long-Term Debt	63.0	29.4		16.7	9.3	10.4
.1	.1	.0	Deferred Taxes	.0	.0		.0	.0	.0
11.2	9.1	2.8	All Other Non-Current	6.9	.3		2.6	1.4	2.4
21.7	21.3	27.7	Net Worth	8.9	32.4		25.1	46.5	44.1
100.0	100.0	100.0	Total Liabilties & Net Worth	100.0	100.0		100.0	100.0	100.0
			INCOME DATA						
100.0	100.0	100.0	Net Sales	100.0	100.0		100.0	100.0	100.0
			Gross Profit						
90.1	91.4	88.1	Operating Expenses	75.4	90.4		91.4	90.5	92.2
9.9	8.6	11.9	Operating Profit	24.6	9.6		8.6	9.5	7.8
2.1	1.4	1.6	All Other Expenses (net)	4.5	2.8		.2	.5	-.1
7.7	7.2	10.4	Profit Before Taxes	20.1	6.9		8.5	9.0	7.9
			RATIOS						
2.5	2.7	3.2	Current	11.4	5.3		2.0	2.5	2.8
1.1	1.2	1.3		.9	1.2		1.6	1.7	1.2
.6	.7	.6		.2	.5		.9	.8	.6
2.3	2.4	2.4	Quick	10.1	5.0		1.9	2.3	2.2
.9	1.1	1.2		.8	1.1		1.1	1.5	1.0
.5	.5	.5		.2	.5		.6	.8	.5
0 UND	**0** UND	**1** 535.4	Sales/Receivables	**0** UND	**3** 139.3		**17** 21.8	**17** 21.2	**17** 21.3
17 21.3	**14** 26.2	**19** 19.0		**0** UND	**19** 19.5		**30** 12.1	**22** 16.8	**22** 16.7
28 13.0	**26** 14.3	**27** 13.7		**0** UND	**26** 14.0		**36** 10.2	**33** 11.2	**29** 12.5
			Cost of Sales/Inventory						
			Cost of Sales/Payables						
9.6	15.6	10.5	Sales/Working Capital	13.9	7.5		12.0	9.0	7.3
145.5	45.2	35.2		NM	163.8		29.7	13.8	21.5
-27.4	-36.0	-17.9		-6.5	-10.2		-332.4	-70.1	-13.3
17.0	35.5	37.6	EBIT/Interest	17.5	26.3		184.7	104.1	51.3
(84) 7.5	(80) 9.9	(77) 11.6		(13) 11.0	(11) 4.5		21.6	(19) 25.0	(13) 20.8
2.4	2.7	2.3		.5	1.1		.6	6.2	4.3
9.4	14.4		Net Profit + Depr., Dep., Amort./Cur. Mat. L/T/D						
(10) 5.3	(21) 5.8								
1.4	2.1								
.4	.4	.2	Fixed/Worth	.4	.1		.1	.1	.2
1.7	1.6	.9		3.6	2.5		.2	.3	.5
-2.3	-5.5	14.8		-1.7	10.0		NM	3.1	2.3
.8	.9	.7	Debt/Worth	.9	.4		.8	.6	.8
3.3	3.2	1.9		4.7	2.6		1.5	1.0	1.7
-6.1	-10.3	28.0		-2.1	11.2		NM	9.2	11.7
82.8	95.1	99.3	% Profit Before Taxes/Tangible Net Worth	238.9	90.5			110.8	67.5
(69) 23.4	(65) 46.6	(71) 60.1		(10) 53.4	(12) 27.1			(19) 92.5	(13) 61.1
8.5	19.9	18.4		29.9	5.0			40.0	19.0
31.5	35.0	48.1	% Profit Before Taxes/Total Assets	51.5	35.6		51.1	53.2	29.3
10.3	17.2	19.3		22.5	11.0		10.8	27.6	20.5
2.6	4.1	3.2		3.6	.9		.0	11.3	9.8
38.9	36.6	72.3	Sales/Net Fixed Assets	38.5	80.5		270.0	133.9	43.5
18.8	16.0	15.6		8.4	7.6		62.8	28.7	13.4
6.0	8.3	6.6		3.1	3.4		16.3	13.6	6.2
5.5	5.7	5.0	Sales/Total Assets	7.2	3.9		6.9	5.6	2.9
3.2	3.7	3.2		3.4	2.8		4.7	3.8	2.4
1.9	2.3	2.1		1.0	1.6		3.2	2.6	1.7
.8	1.2	.9	% Depr., Dep., Amort./Sales	2.9				.5	.9
(63) 2.2	(71) 1.8	(62) 2.3		(10) 5.1				(13) 1.7	(15) 2.4
3.9	3.2	3.9		19.2				3.9	3.2
3.8	2.5	2.9	% Officers', Directors' Owners' Comp/Sales						
(45) 6.4	(50) 5.1	(35) 5.5							
9.3	8.3	13.7							
2922295M	**2160939M**	**1880273M**	Net Sales ($)	**9360M**	**29931M**	**35695M**	**89186M**	**305030M**	**1411071M**
771913M	**819432M**	**816217M**	Total Assets ($)	**9213M**	**32015M**	**9994M**	**23273M**	**93173M**	**648549M**

M = $ thousand MM = $ million

See Pages 9 through 22 for Explanation of Ratios and Data

Current Data Sorted by Assets							Comparative Historical Data	
						Type of Statement		
	1	7	13	6	1	Unqualified	36	34
2	10	34	8			Reviewed	55	55
8	13	14	2			Compiled	29	40
36	27	9				Tax Returns	77	56
23	44	43	13	6	4	Other	119	126
	47 (4/1-9/30/13)		277 (10/1/13-3/31/14)				4/1/09-3/31/10	4/1/10-3/31/11
0-500M	500M-2MM	2-10MM	10-50MM	50-100MM	100-250MM		ALL	ALL
69	95	107	36	12	5	**NUMBER OF STATEMENTS**	316	311
%	%	%	%	%	%	**ASSETS**	%	%
26.9	14.5	15.9	10.1	8.6		Cash & Equivalents	13.3	14.0
24.8	39.2	43.6	42.8	38.8		Trade Receivables (net)	38.0	40.0
3.2	3.3	2.0	.6	.4		Inventory	3.0	2.3
3.7	3.7	3.6	8.1	6.0		All Other Current	5.0	4.3
58.5	60.7	65.2	61.7	53.8		Total Current	59.4	60.6
25.1	22.4	18.7	14.4	13.4		Fixed Assets (net)	20.2	19.1
7.7	8.4	6.9	12.4	25.3		Intangibles (net)	10.9	9.9
8.7	8.5	9.3	11.5	7.6		All Other Non-Current	9.5	10.4
100.0	100.0	100.0	100.0	100.0		Total	100.0	100.0
						LIABILITIES		
35.3	9.9	11.6	10.8	4.1		Notes Payable-Short Term	14.6	12.9
10.9	2.9	2.5	3.6	2.7		Cur. Mat.-L.T.D.	5.9	4.9
8.3	12.0	13.4	9.1	9.9		Trade Payables	12.7	12.8
.1	.7	.2	.1	.1		Income Taxes Payable	.5	.3
14.3	14.8	17.2	22.0	18.4		All Other Current	16.2	16.9
68.9	40.2	45.0	45.6	35.2		Total Current	49.8	47.8
31.7	19.6	11.8	9.2	17.9		Long-Term Debt	17.8	18.1
.0	.1	.4	.0	2.7		Deferred Taxes	.3	.2
7.1	7.5	4.4	9.6	10.4		All Other Non-Current	8.4	6.9
-7.8	32.6	38.5	35.5	33.7		Net Worth	23.7	27.0
100.0	100.0	100.0	100.0	100.0		Total Liabilties & Net Worth	100.0	100.0
						INCOME DATA		
100.0	100.0	100.0	100.0	100.0		Net Sales	100.0	100.0
						Gross Profit		
93.6	93.0	95.3	93.9	96.9		Operating Expenses	95.2	94.3
6.4	7.0	4.7	6.1	3.1		Operating Profit	4.8	5.7
.7	1.2	.5	.6	1.4		All Other Expenses (net)	.7	.8
5.7	5.8	4.3	5.5	1.6		Profit Before Taxes	4.0	4.9
						RATIOS		
3.4	3.2	2.4	1.8	1.8			2.0	2.3
1.0	1.5	1.5	1.4	1.4		Current	1.2	1.4
.5	.9	1.0	1.0	1.1			.9	1.0
2.4	2.7	2.2	1.6	1.7			1.8	2.1
(68) .9	1.4	1.3	1.1	1.2		Quick	1.1	1.2
.5	.8	1.0	.9	1.0			.7	.8
0 UND	**15** 24.4	**28** 13.2	**26** 14.2	**47** 7.7			**18** 20.2	**20** 18.3
2 214.0	**31** 11.7	**38** 9.5	**41** 9.0	**54** 6.8		Sales/Receivables	**31** 11.7	**33** 11.2
33 11.2	**41** 8.9	**51** 7.2	**56** 6.5	**63** 5.8			**49** 7.5	**53** 6.9
						Cost of Sales/Inventory		
						Cost of Sales/Payables		
12.1	9.7	8.9	12.0	9.9			13.5	11.2
UND	24.5	20.1	19.9	19.8		Sales/Working Capital	42.3	32.3
-26.5	-193.8	-999.8	331.6	52.9			-67.6	-163.3
35.7	37.0	37.3	20.0	104.8			22.5	27.6
(50) 7.3	(83) 8.3	(86) 8.2	(28) 7.5	2.0		EBIT/Interest	(282) 7.2	(270) 6.9
1.4	2.8	2.4	2.6	.4			1.9	2.5
		8.0					11.8	8.1
		(19) 2.8				Net Profit + Depr., Dep., Amort./Cur. Mat. L/T/D	(51) 3.7	(47) 3.1
		1.1					1.2	1.7
.0	.2	.2	.2	.3			.2	.2
3.7	.8	.4	.4	17.5		Fixed/Worth	.8	.6
-.9	9.3	1.6	1.4	-.4			20.8	4.4
.8	.7	.7	1.3	1.1			1.2	.9
-112.3	2.3	1.6	3.9	32.4		Debt/Worth	3.2	2.7
-3.0	-156.4	4.4	15.9	-4.4			-72.2	22.9
188.3	97.2	70.3	89.6				103.7	100.0
(34) 63.1	(71) 39.6	(92) 37.5	(29) 49.1			% Profit Before Taxes/Tangible Net Worth	(234) 46.0	(247) 46.4
26.7	15.8	14.1	22.3				10.4	15.0
67.9	31.3	26.3	17.6	13.7			28.6	29.6
22.1	15.7	13.2	9.2	3.3		% Profit Before Taxes/Total Assets	11.7	13.4
3.2	4.5	2.4	3.8	-2.6			3.5	3.8
714.8	131.2	67.0	98.3	78.0			90.7	91.3
55.7	29.6	31.7	41.0	25.8		Sales/Net Fixed Assets	38.4	36.7
15.9	12.3	17.2	16.5	14.7			15.5	15.9
12.7	7.3	5.3	5.2	3.4			6.8	6.4
6.0	4.7	4.3	3.9	2.5		Sales/Total Assets	4.6	4.2
3.3	2.9	2.6	2.7	1.8			2.8	2.8
.3	.4	.4	.3				.5	.5
(35) .6	(61) .9	(93) .7	(32) .7			% Depr., Dep., Amort./Sales	(218) .9	(229) .9
3.4	1.7	1.3	1.5				2.0	1.8
3.1	1.9	1.3					2.6	1.9
(37) 7.3	(45) 3.5	(41) 2.4				% Officers', Directors' Owners' Comp/Sales	(137) 5.0	(125) 4.2
10.7	5.1	4.9					7.4	6.8
145559M	552670M	2053685M	3204719M	2582171M	2071167M	Net Sales ($)	12577136M	11203189M
16510M	102635M	501188M	781712M	971666M	762288M	Total Assets ($)	3010756M	3145691M

M = $ thousand MM = $ million

See Pages 9 through 22 for Explanation of Ratios and Data

Comparative Historical Data | **Current Data Sorted by Sales**

Type of Statement	4/1/11-3/31/12 ALL	4/1/12-3/31/13 ALL	4/1/13-3/31/14 ALL	0-1MM	1-3MM	3-5MM	5-10MM	10-25MM	25MM & OVER
Unqualified	33	22	28	1			2	6	19
Reviewed	57	49	54		2	3	6	20	23
Compiled	32	26	37	5	7	4	9	8	4
Tax Returns	104	76	72	15	21	13	15	8	
Other	137	129	133	12	18	21	22	30	30
				47 (4/1-9/30/13)			277 (10/1/13-3/31/14)		
NUMBER OF STATEMENTS	363	302	324	33	48	41	54	72	76
ASSETS	%	%	%	%	%	%	%	%	%
Cash & Equivalents	14.4	17.4	16.8	12.8	23.4	17.7	21.6	16.7	10.5
Trade Receivables (net)	36.0	38.4	37.8	26.2	27.9	36.4	33.6	44.6	46.5
Inventory	2.3	2.7	2.4	2.3	5.7	2.5	3.1	1.6	.6
All Other Current	4.3	3.0	4.3	2.3	4.5	3.1	4.9	3.5	6.2
Total Current	57.0	61.5	61.4	43.5	61.5	59.6	63.3	66.4	63.9
Fixed Assets (net)	23.1	20.1	20.4	43.0	16.6	26.3	20.1	15.9	14.5
Intangibles (net)	10.7	9.2	9.1	7.1	13.0	7.8	5.9	7.8	11.8
All Other Non-Current	9.2	9.2	9.1	6.3	8.8	6.4	10.7	9.8	9.9
Total	100.0	100.0	100.0	100.0	100.0	100.0	100.0	100.0	100.0
LIABILITIES									
Notes Payable-Short Term	14.6	13.5	15.6	24.5	28.4	13.1	14.0	11.8	10.0
Cur. Mat.-L.T.D.	3.1	3.1	4.5	6.1	5.2	4.3	8.2	2.5	2.8
Trade Payables	11.7	11.1	11.2	7.3	10.1	9.5	9.5	13.4	13.5
Income Taxes Payable	.3	.1	.3	.0	.5	.1	.2	.7	.2
All Other Current	14.8	18.2	16.5	8.5	15.0	11.4	16.2	19.3	21.2
Total Current	44.5	46.1	48.1	46.4	59.2	38.3	48.1	47.6	47.7
Long-Term Debt	20.5	19.8	18.4	43.5	24.5	24.2	15.7	11.4	8.8
Deferred Taxes	.3	.2	.3	.0	.0	.1	.5	.1	.6
All Other Non-Current	5.9	6.0	6.8	.5	9.4	10.4	4.6	4.8	9.5
Net Worth	28.9	28.0	26.4	9.4	6.9	27.0	31.1	36.0	33.4
Total Liabilties & Net Worth	100.0	100.0	100.0	100.0	100.0	100.0	100.0	100.0	100.0
INCOME DATA									
Net Sales	100.0	100.0	100.0	100.0	100.0	100.0	100.0	100.0	100.0
Gross Profit									
Operating Expenses	93.3	93.9	94.2	86.7	95.8	92.6	94.7	95.6	95.5
Operating Profit	6.7	6.1	5.8	13.3	4.2	7.4	5.3	4.4	4.5
All Other Expenses (net)	1.2	.4	.8	3.8	.5	1.2	.0	.1	.7
Profit Before Taxes	5.5	5.8	5.0	9.5	3.8	6.3	5.3	4.3	3.8
RATIOS									
Current	2.5 1.4 .9	2.4 1.4 1.0	2.4 1.4 .9	2.8 1.1 .5	5.6 1.6 .7	3.2 1.8 1.0	2.8 1.3 .8	2.2 1.4 1.0	1.8 1.3 1.0
Quick	2.2 1.2 .8	2.3 1.3 .8	2.2 (323) 1.2 .8	2.6 1.1 .4	4.3 (47) 1.6 .6	2.8 1.4 .9	2.4 1.1 .7	2.1 1.3 1.0	1.7 1.2 .9
Sales/Receivables	15 24.4 31 11.9 48 7.6	17 21.2 35 10.5 53 6.9	16 22.2 33 11.1 51 7.2	0 UND 6 65.5 43 8.5	0 UND 28 13.0 54 6.8	15 24.0 33 11.2 46 7.9	0 UND 31 11.8 42 8.6	24 15.4 33 10.9 49 7.4	29 12.6 38 9.5 54 6.8
Cost of Sales/Inventory									
Cost of Sales/Payables									
Sales/Working Capital	10.9 33.3 -90.3	10.6 25.8 -432.7	10.1 25.0 -113.9	8.0 89.0 -25.0	7.0 17.0 -43.6	8.2 19.6 UND	9.3 30.2 -74.0	11.2 21.4 -649.1	14.6 27.5 251.3
EBIT/Interest	32.5 (307) 8.2 2.4	33.8 (255) 8.3 2.9	32.7 (264) 8.2 2.3	12.1 (19) 3.6 2.1	19.3 (41) 5.7 -.8	38.4 (33) 12.7 4.4	51.1 (45) 8.1 2.5	55.6 (61) 8.7 3.2	43.1 (65) 8.9 2.2
Net Profit + Depr., Dep., Amort./Cur. Mat. L/T/D	6.8 (42) 3.7 1.6	9.8 (34) 3.4 1.5	13.7 (41) 3.1 1.2					24.0 (13) 3.1 .9	32.1 (18) 5.1 2.0
Fixed/Worth	.2 .8 6.1	.2 .6 7.2	.2 .6 18.7	.0 2.4 -2.9	.1 .9 -7.0	.2 .9 -5.1	.2 .6 NM	.2 .4 1.7	.2 .5 2.2
Debt/Worth	.9 2.4 31.6	.7 2.6 54.7	.8 2.5 -40.8	.7 5.6 -3.5	.9 2.9 -7.4	.5 3.2 -21.2	.6 1.8 NM	.7 1.8 4.4	1.1 3.4 50.7
% Profit Before Taxes/Tangible Net Worth	104.5 (284) 44.2 18.8	74.2 (231) 38.5 12.6	93.4 (236) 41.9 18.1	80.8 (18) 29.1 13.9	80.3 (31) 28.5 6.7	117.2 (28) 47.8 21.4	179.8 (41) 51.4 12.7	83.9 (60) 45.7 22.3	80.2 (58) 43.2 21.2
% Profit Before Taxes/Total Assets	34.6 13.0 3.3	27.5 12.9 3.3	29.6 14.2 3.3	35.6 7.8 1.3	29.0 14.2 -5.8	34.3 21.6 10.8	39.8 18.9 4.9	26.8 13.7 4.0	25.4 9.9 2.2
Sales/Net Fixed Assets	102.4 33.9 12.1	113.7 38.4 17.2	101.7 35.9 14.7	UND 11.6 1.6	227.7 42.4 11.8	154.2 21.6 10.6	117.7 44.0 20.3	90.8 47.1 20.7	96.3 39.7 22.4
Sales/Total Assets	6.7 4.2 2.6	6.9 4.5 2.7	6.3 4.4 2.8	4.5 2.8 .9	6.3 4.2 2.6	6.2 4.3 2.9	9.7 5.6 3.1	6.3 4.5 2.9	6.2 4.4 3.0
% Depr., Dep., Amort./Sales	.4 (273) 1.0 2.1	.4 (219) 1.0 1.8	.4 (231) .7 1.6	2.3 (18) 6.2 21.5	.2 (24) .8 1.8	.6 (23) 1.5 2.2	.3 (41) .7 1.5	.3 (62) .6 1.1	.3 (63) .7 1.2
% Officers', Directors' Owners' Comp/Sales	2.2 (159) 4.4 8.1	2.0 (137) 3.7 7.1	1.8 (130) 3.6 6.9	6.5 (12) 12.1 15.0	3.6 (26) 7.3 9.8	2.0 (18) 2.6 4.2	1.8 (29) 3.1 5.9	1.4 (28) 2.9 4.1	.6 (17) 1.4 2.6
Net Sales ($)	11143622M	10913059M	10609971M	15715M	88167M	157750M	407143M	1182751M	8758445M
Total Assets ($)	2812848M	2539962M	3135999M	17532M	28468M	40344M	111994M	318043M	2619618M

M = $ thousand MM = $ million

See Pages 9 through 22 for Explanation of Ratios and Data

Current Data Sorted by Assets							Comparative Historical Data	
						Type of Statement		
	1	12	8	3	2	Unqualified	26	27
2	13	40	11			Reviewed	72	86
12	19	15			1	Compiled	76	82
131	81	19	1	1	7	Tax Returns	193	226
53	90	68	18	3	2	Other	184	194
38 (4/1-9/30/13)			575 (10/1/13-3/31/14)				4/1/09-3/31/10	4/1/10-3/31/11
0-500M	**500M-2MM**	**2-10MM**	**10-50MM**	**50-100MM**	**100-250MM**		**ALL**	**ALL**
198	204	154	38	7	12	**NUMBER OF STATEMENTS**	551	615
%	%	%	%	%	%	**ASSETS**	%	%
19.7	12.1	9.9	8.3		20.4	Cash & Equivalents	12.6	11.6
14.6	25.3	32.2	26.1		21.0	Trade Receivables (net)	22.8	24.5
5.4	4.5	6.8	6.3		7.2	Inventory	6.5	5.6
3.2	1.8	4.2	5.5		7.2	All Other Current	3.5	4.2
42.8	43.7	53.1	46.3		55.8	Total Current	45.4	45.9
45.1	41.7	35.0	37.0		37.0	Fixed Assets (net)	41.2	39.5
3.9	5.2	5.0	6.4		6.3	Intangibles (net)	4.4	6.0
8.1	9.4	6.9	10.3		.9	All Other Non-Current	9.0	8.6
100.0	100.0	100.0	100.0		100.0	Total	100.0	100.0
						LIABILITIES		
20.2	10.4	8.9	4.2		6.8	Notes Payable-Short Term	15.2	15.5
7.3	5.3	6.0	6.6		.3	Cur. Mat.-L.T.D.	6.6	6.4
10.8	11.3	13.1	9.4		4.2	Trade Payables	10.1	10.6
.2	.2	.1	.3		.6	Income Taxes Payable	.2	.2
17.0	6.3	8.0	8.8		7.8	All Other Current	10.9	10.4
55.5	33.6	36.1	29.4		19.7	Total Current	43.0	43.0
46.0	32.5	19.5	19.1		30.5	Long-Term Debt	31.7	29.9
.0	.2	1.0	.4		.0	Deferred Taxes	.3	.3
7.8	3.8	2.6	5.9		10.8	All Other Non-Current	6.1	7.7
-9.5	30.0	40.9	45.2		39.0	Net Worth	18.8	19.1
100.0	100.0	100.0	100.0		100.0	Total Liabilties & Net Worth	100.0	100.0
						INCOME DATA		
100.0	100.0	100.0	100.0		100.0	Net Sales	100.0	100.0
						Gross Profit		
93.5	92.5	94.7	94.0		93.9	Operating Expenses	95.0	94.3
6.5	7.5	5.3	6.0		6.1	Operating Profit	5.0	5.7
1.3	1.2	.8	.3		.4	All Other Expenses (net)	2.0	1.8
5.2	6.3	4.5	5.7		5.6	Profit Before Taxes	3.0	3.9
						RATIOS		
2.6	2.7	2.1	2.3		9.5		2.2	2.2
.9	1.4	1.4	1.5		3.6	Current	1.2	1.2
.4	.7	1.0	.9		1.9		.7	.7
2.3	2.2	1.8	1.8		8.1		1.8	1.9
.8	1.2	1.1	1.1		2.7	Quick	.9	(613) .9
.2	.5	.8	.6		1.8		.4	.5
0 UND	**5** 67.0	**26** 13.9	**34** 10.7		**0** UND		**6** 61.2	**5** 69.2
4 83.3	**27** 13.3	**44** 8.3	**47** 7.8		**26** 14.0	Sales/Receivables	**27** 13.7	**28** 12.9
23 15.8	**46** 7.9	**64** 5.7	**61** 6.0		**49** 7.5		**50** 7.4	**52** 7.1
						Cost of Sales/Inventory		
						Cost of Sales/Payables		
19.0	9.2	7.6	5.9		3.8		10.2	9.9
-231.3	29.5	15.8	12.2		10.7	Sales/Working Capital	36.8	38.4
-15.0	-25.3	131.4	-132.9		17.2		-24.6	-23.3
16.3	19.2	12.4	40.9		29.4		11.3	11.2
(164) 5.1	(179) 6.8	(144) 5.8	(35) 7.4		11.6	EBIT/Interest	(487) 2.9	(552) 4.1
.6	2.0	2.1	1.9		2.0		.3	1.0
	4.9	4.3	3.3				4.4	5.1
	(12) 2.1	(36) 2.4	(10) 1.6			Net Profit + Depr., Dep., Amort./Cur. Mat. L/T/D	(76) 1.8	(63) 2.0
	1.0	1.7	.6				.7	.5
.7	.6	.5	.3		.3		.6	.5
3.6	1.4	1.0	1.0		.8	Fixed/Worth	1.5	1.5
-2.0	8.8	2.1	2.1		NM		172.0	-14.3
1.3	.9	.8	.6		.6		.8	.8
12.2	2.2	1.7	1.5		1.1	Debt/Worth	2.8	3.1
-3.4	26.0	4.3	2.9		NM		-639.0	-18.0
179.8	88.8	50.4	42.0				65.7	63.0
(118) 62.2	(162) 38.3	(143) 22.4	(35) 19.5			% Profit Before Taxes/Tangible Net Worth	(413) 20.9	(439) 25.3
9.3	13.7	6.5	2.3				.0	3.0
41.0	27.9	15.2	14.4		37.1		22.4	20.4
17.1	12.2	8.0	7.9		7.8	% Profit Before Taxes/Total Assets	6.1	7.9
-1.0	2.8	2.6	2.4		1.4		-2.4	.0
40.9	20.0	13.0	10.8		15.3		18.5	20.1
13.1	9.2	7.4	5.8		10.9	Sales/Net Fixed Assets	8.6	9.4
5.9	4.1	4.6	3.2		6.1		4.3	4.3
8.4	4.4	3.1	2.5		3.7		4.3	4.4
5.1	3.0	2.4	2.0		3.1	Sales/Total Assets	2.8	2.7
3.0	2.1	1.4	1.6		2.1		1.9	1.8
1.3	1.6	1.7	2.0				2.1	2.0
(131) 3.1	(148) 3.3	(140) 2.9	(36) 5.0			% Depr., Dep., Amort./Sales	(427) 3.9	(472) 3.7
7.8	5.9	4.8	6.9				6.1	6.1
4.5	2.7	1.6	.5				2.6	2.8
(128) 6.8	(116) 4.6	(66) 2.6	(10) 1.2			% Officers', Directors' Owners' Comp/Sales	(285) 5.3	(329) 5.4
11.9	7.4	3.5	2.2				8.8	9.3
250038M	**751928M**	**1650240M**	**1611869M**	**1197109M**	**8366134M**	Net Sales ($)	**8577746M**	**10050545M**
45985M	**223941M**	**673716M**	**792338M**	**492827M**	**2140967M**	Total Assets ($)	**3099988M**	**3258990M**

M = $ thousand MM = $ million

See Pages 9 through 22 for Explanation of Ratios and Data

Comparative Historical Data / Current Data Sorted by Sales

4/1/11-3/31/12 ALL	4/1/12-3/31/13 ALL	4/1/13-3/31/14 ALL		0-1MM	1-3MM	3-5MM	5-10MM	10-25MM	25MM & OVER
			Type of Statement						
26	21	26	Unqualified		2	4	2	7	11
83	70	66	Reviewed	2	5	12	19	22	6
83	53	47	Compiled	10	15	12	3	5	2
224	217	240	Tax Returns	71	89	38	25	7	10
226	227	234	Other	39	66	33	33	42	21
					38 (4/1-9/30/13)		575 (10/1/13-3/31/14)		
642	588	613	**NUMBER OF STATEMENTS**	122	177	99	82	83	50
%	%	%	**ASSETS**	%	%	%	%	%	%
12.6	14.4	13.9	Cash & Equivalents	15.0	17.3	13.6	8.9	10.5	13.6
24.8	24.1	23.6	Trade Receivables (net)	10.2	18.9	25.8	35.2	35.0	31.1
5.1	5.0	5.5	Inventory	4.9	5.8	4.9	5.5	6.4	5.0
4.4	3.5	3.2	All Other Current	3.7	1.9	2.2	2.5	5.2	6.2
46.9	47.0	46.2	Total Current	33.8	43.9	46.6	52.2	57.1	55.9
37.0	37.5	40.8	Fixed Assets (net)	52.7	42.3	37.8	37.9	28.9	36.1
6.0	5.7	4.9	Intangibles (net)	5.1	4.6	5.0	3.5	7.0	3.8
10.2	9.8	8.2	All Other Non-Current	8.3	9.2	10.7	6.5	7.0	4.2
100.0	100.0	100.0	Total	100.0	100.0	100.0	100.0	100.0	100.0
			LIABILITIES						
13.3	15.3	12.7	Notes Payable-Short Term	16.6	15.0	12.1	11.1	9.1	5.2
6.7	5.4	6.1	Cur. Mat.-L.T.D.	6.3	5.4	6.6	7.1	6.4	4.3
12.9	11.1	11.3	Trade Payables	9.5	9.5	10.4	15.7	14.9	10.7
.3	.3	.2	Income Taxes Payable	.3	.3	.1	.1	.1	.2
11.2	10.3	10.5	All Other Current	19.0	8.0	7.8	6.9	9.9	10.5
44.5	42.3	40.7	Total Current	51.7	38.3	36.9	40.8	40.4	30.8
28.0	30.0	32.7	Long-Term Debt	48.2	35.8	34.4	22.7	16.9	23.1
.5	.2	.3	Deferred Taxes	.1	.0	.7	1.0	.4	.1
5.9	6.8	5.0	All Other Non-Current	8.0	5.5	4.2	2.8	3.3	4.4
21.1	20.7	21.2	Net Worth	-8.0	20.4	23.8	32.6	39.0	41.5
100.0	100.0	100.0	Total Liabilties & Net Worth	100.0	100.0	100.0	100.0	100.0	100.0
			INCOME DATA						
100.0	100.0	100.0	Net Sales	100.0	100.0	100.0	100.0	100.0	100.0
			Gross Profit						
94.7	93.8	93.5	Operating Expenses	88.4	93.8	95.1	96.5	94.8	95.2
5.3	6.2	6.5	Operating Profit	11.6	6.2	4.9	3.5	5.2	4.8
1.1	1.0	1.0	All Other Expenses (net)	3.9	.5	.2	.1	.6	.2
4.2	5.1	5.4	Profit Before Taxes	7.8	5.7	4.7	3.4	4.7	4.7
			RATIOS						
2.3	2.6	2.6		2.2	3.3	2.5	1.9	1.9	3.3
1.3	1.3	1.3	Current	.8	1.5	1.4	1.3	1.4	1.8
.6	.7	.7		.4	.5	.7	.9	1.1	1.1
1.9	2.2	2.1		1.9	3.1	2.2	1.8	1.6	2.7
1.0	1.0	1.1	Quick	.7	1.2	1.2	1.1	1.1	1.5
.4	.5	.5		.2	.4	.5	.8	.8	.9
8 44.6	**3** 123.1	**2** 146.6		**0** UND	**0** UND	**4** 96.3	**22** 16.6	**26** 14.3	**29** 12.8
27 13.3	**26** 13.8	**27** 13.7	Sales/Receivables	**1** 466.5	**16** 22.4	**31** 11.6	**38** 9.6	**38** 9.6	**43** 8.5
47 7.8	**50** 7.3	**49** 7.4		**28** 13.2	**36** 10.0	**53** 6.9	**60** 6.1	**55** 6.6	**55** 6.6
			Cost of Sales/Inventory						
			Cost of Sales/Payables						
10.7	10.1	10.4		19.4	9.6	8.6	9.5	10.5	5.8
39.3	31.0	30.9	Sales/Working Capital	-64.4	52.6	28.4	22.6	18.9	13.3
-21.6	-30.0	-28.6		-8.8	-19.5	-57.2	-72.0	158.7	41.8
12.9	15.6	17.2		12.1	16.4	17.7	19.6	16.9	30.7
(571) 4.8	(524) 5.4	(541) 6.3	EBIT/Interest	(93) 3.7	(151) 5.3	(93) 4.9	(77) 7.4	(78) 7.1	(49) 12.5
1.3	1.3	1.8		.1	1.5	1.9	1.9	3.2	2.9
6.0	5.8	4.4				3.8	5.9	4.5	7.0
(70) 2.3	(54) 2.3	(62) 2.4	Net Profit + Depr., Dep., Amort./Cur. Mat. L/T/D			(13) 2.3	(11) 2.4	(21) 2.6	(10) 1.8
.7	1.3	1.4				1.3	2.0	1.6	1.1
.5	.5	.6		1.0	.6	.6	.6	.4	.4
1.2	1.4	1.5	Fixed/Worth	3.2	1.6	1.3	1.1	1.0	.8
-69.4	22.0	12.7		-5.8	-37.3	6.3	3.2	2.1	2.3
.8	.8	.9		1.9	.7	.8	.9	.9	.7
2.6	2.6	2.4	Debt/Worth	8.8	2.4	2.3	1.9	1.8	1.6
-34.7	-68.4	42.6		-3.8	-80.0	24.3	7.9	4.6	3.5
61.9	65.4	77.3		112.5	97.0	75.6	67.9	52.0	49.1
(467) 23.0	(436) 27.1	(474) 32.9	% Profit Before Taxes/Tangible Net Worth	(76) 40.0	(130) 37.4	(80) 33.8	(69) 24.8	(73) 31.7	(46) 19.3
5.5	6.9	8.4		.6	13.7	11.6	5.4	12.3	8.3
20.6	23.3	25.7		30.6	31.7	30.1	20.9	17.2	22.0
7.9	8.3	10.1	% Profit Before Taxes/Total Assets	6.7	14.5	9.8	10.6	9.5	8.4
.6	1.1	2.1		-2.9	2.9	2.2	1.5	4.9	4.0
23.9	23.3	21.9		13.6	26.6	21.2	22.3	20.5	15.3
10.0	9.9	9.4	Sales/Net Fixed Assets	5.9	11.1	10.3	9.3	10.3	8.2
5.1	5.0	4.7		2.2	4.3	5.6	5.9	6.7	5.0
5.0	4.6	4.9		5.1	6.1	5.3	4.4	4.2	3.2
3.0	2.9	3.0	Sales/Total Assets	2.8	3.4	3.1	3.1	2.9	2.7
2.0	2.0	2.0		1.0	2.2	2.1	2.3	2.0	2.1
1.7	1.8	1.7		2.3	1.7	1.2	1.4	1.6	1.6
(459) 3.3	(419) 3.1	(463) 3.1	% Depr., Dep., Amort./Sales	(81) 5.8	(128) 3.3	(74) 2.8	(70) 3.0	(72) 2.5	(38) 3.1
5.3	5.4	6.0		12.3	6.3	4.1	4.4	4.3	6.2
2.7	2.6	2.6		5.6	3.6	2.6	2.3	.9	.9
(330) 4.7	(300) 4.7	(326) 4.7	% Officers', Directors' Owners' Comp/Sales	(60) 9.2	(115) 5.6	(60) 4.6	(39) 2.9	(37) 1.8	(15) 2.2
8.2	8.4	8.1		13.5	7.9	7.6	4.8	3.1	8.8
11976732M	**9510096M**	**13827318M**	Net Sales ($)	**61780M**	**342204M**	**395896M**	**575980M**	**1283519M**	**11167939M**
3054973M	**3661864M**	**4369774M**	Total Assets ($)	**47723M**	**151911M**	**160178M**	**209608M**	**532678M**	**3267676M**

M = $ thousand MM = $ million

See Pages 9 through 22 for Explanation of Ratios and Data

Current Data Sorted by Assets							Comparative Historical Data	
						Type of Statement		
		1	1		1	Unqualified	2	2
	1	2				Reviewed	7	2
2	3	1				Compiled	9	8
17	12	1				Tax Returns	28	18
6	15	6	1	4	1	Other	24	30
	5 (4/1-9/30/13)		70 (10/1/13-3/31/14)				**4/1/09-3/31/10 ALL**	**4/1/10-3/31/11 ALL**
0-500M	**500M-2MM**	**2-10MM**	**10-50MM**	**50-100MM**	**100-250MM**			
25	31	11	2	4	2	**NUMBER OF STATEMENTS**	70	60
%	%	%	%	%	%	**ASSETS**	%	%
15.2	12.4	9.9				Cash & Equivalents	16.0	14.4
13.7	24.6	31.2				Trade Receivables (net)	25.1	26.5
2.6	5.7	10.7				Inventory	4.6	2.6
1.7	1.6	1.7				All Other Current	3.8	2.2
33.1	44.3	53.6				Total Current	49.5	45.7
32.5	34.2	33.2				Fixed Assets (net)	28.0	30.6
20.9	6.4	5.2				Intangibles (net)	11.9	10.7
13.4	15.1	8.0				All Other Non-Current	10.6	13.0
100.0	100.0	100.0				Total	100.0	100.0
						LIABILITIES		
13.5	9.7	4.4				Notes Payable-Short Term	22.6	9.8
9.0	3.6	5.5				Cur. Mat.-L.T.D.	4.6	4.0
3.9	13.8	11.7				Trade Payables	9.0	8.0
.0	.0	.1				Income Taxes Payable	.0	.2
11.6	6.6	10.3				All Other Current	10.3	8.9
38.0	33.8	32.0				Total Current	46.5	31.0
56.3	24.8	21.9				Long-Term Debt	31.7	24.8
.4	.4	.3				Deferred Taxes	.1	.0
2.0	8.7	6.4				All Other Non-Current	6.2	9.1
3.2	32.3	39.4				Net Worth	15.5	35.0
100.0	100.0	100.0				Total Liabilties & Net Worth	100.0	100.0
						INCOME DATA		
100.0	100.0	100.0				Net Sales	100.0	100.0
						Gross Profit		
93.8	89.8	89.0				Operating Expenses	94.3	92.5
6.2	10.2	11.0				Operating Profit	5.7	7.5
.9	2.8	2.7				All Other Expenses (net)	1.0	.9
5.3	7.4	8.2				Profit Before Taxes	4.7	6.6
						RATIOS		
2.6	3.7	2.9					3.2	4.9
.7	1.6	1.5				Current	1.5	1.7
.2	.6	1.2					.7	.8
2.2	2.9	2.1					2.9	4.1
.7	1.3	1.4				Quick	(69) 1.2	1.6
.2	.4	1.0					.6	.7
0 UND	5 66.7	36 10.2					3 118.2	3 125.1
1 262.6	33 11.2	73 5.0				Sales/Receivables	24 15.0	30 12.1
31 11.7	64 5.7	111 3.3					48 7.6	57 6.4
						Cost of Sales/Inventory		
						Cost of Sales/Payables		
12.7	6.7	3.6					9.1	8.4
-53.7	17.9	8.4				Sales/Working Capital	25.0	19.3
-17.8	-10.9	35.5					-21.5	-104.3
10.5	37.7	29.7					19.6	31.0
(23) 5.3	(27) 10.6	6.5				EBIT/Interest	(66) 4.6	(54) 8.8
1.3	4.0	1.2					1.1	1.6
						Net Profit + Depr., Dep., Amort./Cur. Mat. L/T/D		
1.0	.3	.4					.3	.3
-31.0	.8	.7				Fixed/Worth	.9	.8
-.3	7.3	2.3					-1.6	-12.7
1.9	.9	.8					.8	.7
-15.0	1.2	1.5				Debt/Worth	1.6	1.6
-2.1	10.9	5.2					-4.6	-33.9
206.5	56.8						111.4	91.7
(11) 86.5	(26) 38.2					% Profit Before Taxes/Tangible Net Worth	(49) 30.8	(44) 36.2
33.9	16.7						8.4	3.3
54.0	21.1	15.5					27.1	42.3
23.9	11.7	10.0				% Profit Before Taxes/Total Assets	9.3	11.4
1.5	2.7	.1					-1.2	2.3
76.6	30.8	23.2					56.6	43.3
24.4	11.5	7.1				Sales/Net Fixed Assets	16.7	13.3
9.5	5.2	3.4					8.2	7.1
7.0	3.8	2.4					5.5	4.7
4.8	2.9	2.1				Sales/Total Assets	3.5	3.3
2.7	2.1	1.3					2.3	2.3
1.9	1.0						.9	1.5
(14) 3.1	(19) 1.9					% Depr., Dep., Amort./Sales	(38) 2.6	(36) 2.9
5.1	3.7						5.2	4.5
3.0	3.0						3.1	2.0
(16) 6.7	(18) 6.1					% Officers', Directors' Owners' Comp/Sales	(46) 6.4	(30) 5.4
12.1	11.0						9.4	10.0
32512M	94928M	120377M	397991M	796273M	187716M	Net Sales ($)	260805M	554482M
5652M	34945M	64722M	54270M	271121M	299642M	Total Assets ($)	103130M	231950M

M = $ thousand MM = $ million

See Pages 9 through 22 for Explanation of Ratios and Data

Comparative Historical Data				Current Data Sorted by Sales					
			Type of Statement						
5	1	3	Unqualified					1	2
5	2	3	Reviewed			1		2	
7	7	6	Compiled	1	1	3	1		
24	14	30	Tax Returns	11	12	5	2		
28	30	33	Other	6	9	4	4	4	6
4/1/11-3/31/12 ALL	4/1/12-3/31/13 ALL	4/1/13-3/31/14 ALL		5 (4/1-9/30/13)			70 (10/1/13-3/31/14)		
				0-1MM	1-3MM	3-5MM	5-10MM	10-25MM	25MM & OVER
69	54	75	**NUMBER OF STATEMENTS**	18	22	13	7	7	8
%	%	%	**ASSETS**	%	%	%	%	%	%
16.5	17.3	13.9	Cash & Equivalents	6.7	16.4	16.9			
22.5	23.6	21.3	Trade Receivables (net)	8.1	24.6	20.8			
5.2	3.9	5.2	Inventory	3.5	1.6	8.8			
3.5	2.3	2.3	All Other Current	.9	2.8	.9			
47.7	47.1	42.7	Total Current	19.2	45.4	47.3			
38.5	30.4	31.7	Fixed Assets (net)	43.9	29.0	33.4			
4.2	6.4	12.9	Intangibles (net)	15.4	16.3	5.9			
9.6	16.1	12.6	All Other Non-Current	21.5	9.3	13.4			
100.0	100.0	100.0	Total	100.0	100.0	100.0			
			LIABILITIES						
12.1	6.6	9.2	Notes Payable-Short Term	9.0	13.3	8.5			
8.0	5.4	5.4	Cur. Mat.-L.T.D.	7.7	7.6	2.7			
9.8	6.6	9.4	Trade Payables	5.1	8.6	8.0			
.1	.2	.1	Income Taxes Payable	.0	.0	.0			
11.1	20.3	9.9	All Other Current	4.1	12.8	8.5			
41.1	39.1	34.0	Total Current	25.9	42.3	27.6			
36.2	24.1	33.2	Long-Term Debt	58.6	34.4	26.6			
.3	.6	.7	Deferred Taxes	.6	.0	1.0			
10.3	9.4	6.0	All Other Non-Current	2.8	4.5	12.5			
12.1	26.8	26.0	Net Worth	12.0	18.9	32.3			
100.0	100.0	100.0	Total Liabilties & Net Worth	100.0	100.0	100.0			
			INCOME DATA						
100.0	100.0	100.0	Net Sales	100.0	100.0	100.0			
			Gross Profit						
92.7	88.3	91.2	Operating Expenses	79.9	95.9	94.1			
7.3	11.7	8.8	Operating Profit	20.1	4.1	5.9			
1.3	2.8	2.4	All Other Expenses (net)	5.9	.6	.3			
5.9	8.9	6.4	Profit Before Taxes	14.3	3.6	5.7			
			RATIOS						
2.4	3.1	2.6		2.6	4.0	3.7			
1.2	1.6	1.5	Current	.7	.9	2.1			
.8	.6	.6		.2	.4	.9			
2.3	2.9	2.1		1.6	3.4	2.9			
(68) 1.0	1.1	1.2	Quick	.7	.9	1.6			
.6	.6	.4		.2	.2	.7			
2 177.0	**3** 130.4	**1** 270.0		**0** UND	**0** UND	**0** UND			
21 17.7	**24** 15.0	**24** 14.9	Sales/Receivables	**10** 36.0	**26** 14.1	**19** 19.3			
46 8.0	**49** 7.5	**52** 7.0		**35** 10.4	**54** 6.8	**45** 8.2			
			Cost of Sales/Inventory						
			Cost of Sales/Payables						
10.0	8.2	8.3		10.1	9.2	6.7			
35.3	25.5	19.6	Sales/Working Capital	-45.8	NM	9.0			
-40.0	-24.0	-22.6		-8.6	-10.4	NM			
21.6	29.7	33.7		8.5	42.3	26.0			
(60) 5.1	(47) 6.7	(68) 8.7	EBIT/Interest	(15) 4.5	(19) 7.2	10.6			
1.4	.6	3.6		1.3	2.2	4.0			
5.5									
(10) 2.2			Net Profit + Depr., Dep., Amort./Cur. Mat. L/T/D						
1.3									
.4	.2	.3		1.2	.4	.3			
1.5	.6	1.3	Fixed/Worth	49.2	1.5	.8			
-2.5	UND	-5.2		-.7	-1.1	2.3			
.8	.6	.9		1.7	.8	.8			
2.3	1.8	2.0	Debt/Worth	NM	2.0	1.5			
-6.9	UND	-7.4		-2.4	-2.3	6.1			
75.3	71.3	85.8			87.3	89.0			
(48) 39.9	(41) 33.8	(52) 40.2	% Profit Before Taxes/Tangible Net Worth		(15) 38.3	(12) 39.1			
5.3	10.4	19.6			25.7	13.5			
32.7	26.4	31.9		29.9	39.4	51.0			
10.9	12.4	15.5	% Profit Before Taxes/Total Assets	12.2	17.1	17.8			
1.1	.0	2.3		.9	.4	4.2			
26.6	46.0	33.7		59.4	55.5	39.9			
11.9	14.9	14.0	Sales/Net Fixed Assets	9.5	19.3	26.8			
6.1	5.6	6.2		2.5	8.5	6.1			
5.3	4.4	4.7		3.6	5.6	4.3			
3.4	2.6	2.9	Sales/Total Assets	1.6	3.8	3.6			
2.5	1.7	2.1		.5	2.6	2.8			
1.5	.9	1.1		3.2	1.0	.4			
(48) 2.6	(29) 2.4	(48) 2.4	% Depr., Dep., Amort./Sales	(12) 5.2	(11) 1.9	(10) 1.5			
3.7	4.0	4.1		15.7	3.6	2.8			
3.1	5.0	3.4			3.2				
(34) 6.3	(19) 6.9	(36) 6.3	% Officers', Directors' Owners' Comp/Sales		(17) 6.0				
10.3	8.8	11.7			10.8				
1122035M	764306M	1629797M	Net Sales ($)	8525M	40696M	53356M	48795M	96445M	1381980M
373058M	412140M	730352M	Total Assets ($)	11660M	11565M	14533M	20602M	46959M	625033M

M = $ thousand MM = $ million

See Pages 9 through 22 for Explanation of Ratios and Data

Current Data Sorted by Assets							Comparative Historical Data	
						Type of Statement		
1		3	2			Unqualified	9	7
	4	9	4			Reviewed	28	29
1	7	5				Compiled	16	10
29	22	9				Tax Returns	38	50
10	27	19	5	2	2	Other	43	39
	15 (4/1-9/30/13)		146 (10/1/13-3/31/14)				4/1/09-3/31/10 ALL	4/1/10-3/31/11 ALL
0-500M	500M-2MM	2-10MM	10-50MM	50-100MM	100-250MM			
41	60	45	11	2	2	**NUMBER OF STATEMENTS**	134	135
%	%	%	%	%	%	**ASSETS**	%	%
19.6	14.8	7.7	14.2			Cash & Equivalents	14.3	18.4
19.3	27.6	38.5	47.6			Trade Receivables (net)	33.0	29.7
7.6	6.4	7.6	4.6			Inventory	7.2	6.8
1.1	2.0	4.1	2.8			All Other Current	4.2	3.3
47.6	50.8	57.8	69.2			Total Current	58.7	58.1
30.1	32.3	24.1	23.4			Fixed Assets (net)	25.6	26.3
12.6	7.1	8.0	4.0			Intangibles (net)	6.0	4.4
9.7	9.8	10.0	3.4			All Other Non-Current	9.6	11.1
100.0	100.0	100.0	100.0			Total	100.0	100.0
						LIABILITIES		
21.9	10.4	9.7	9.8			Notes Payable-Short Term	13.4	14.4
4.2	4.1	2.7	3.4			Cur. Mat.-L.T.D.	4.2	3.7
7.7	9.9	13.0	19.3			Trade Payables	12.1	13.1
.0	.1	.6	.8			Income Taxes Payable	.3	.3
22.0	10.3	12.2	13.4			All Other Current	13.1	14.9
55.8	34.8	38.2	46.8			Total Current	43.0	46.5
43.3	26.2	16.7	11.9			Long-Term Debt	22.1	23.3
.0	.0	.3	.0			Deferred Taxes	.3	.1
7.0	5.5	2.5	4.0			All Other Non-Current	8.0	8.1
-6.1	33.4	42.3	37.3			Net Worth	26.6	21.9
100.0	100.0	100.0	100.0			Total Liabilties & Net Worth	100.0	100.0
						INCOME DATA		
100.0	100.0	100.0	100.0			Net Sales	100.0	100.0
						Gross Profit		
92.4	86.4	88.8	93.3			Operating Expenses	92.7	92.0
7.6	13.6	11.2	6.7			Operating Profit	7.3	8.0
1.7	3.5	2.3	.9			All Other Expenses (net)	1.1	2.0
5.9	10.1	8.9	5.8			Profit Before Taxes	6.1	6.0
						RATIOS		
4.1	3.0	2.4	1.8				2.9	2.5
1.3	1.5	1.5	1.4			Current	1.6	1.4
.2	1.0	1.2	1.0				.9	.8
3.7	2.6	2.0	1.6				2.5	2.2
1.2	1.4	1.2	1.2			Quick	1.3	1.2
.1	.8	.8	.9				.7	.6
0 UND	2 205.2	31 11.9	48 7.6				9 41.7	5 71.3
0 UND	30 12.2	51 7.2	60 6.1			Sales/Receivables	37 10.0	33 11.0
24 14.9	53 6.9	81 4.5	96 3.8				66 5.5	55 6.6
						Cost of Sales/Inventory		
						Cost of Sales/Payables		
15.3	6.6	6.5	7.0				6.9	7.9
55.3	16.3	14.4	16.2			Sales/Working Capital	14.8	23.4
-8.8	779.6	34.7	-203.1				-244.0	-33.5
20.7	40.4	43.9	71.3				18.7	26.7
(29) 3.9	(47) 8.4	(36) 11.0	(10) 9.7			EBIT/Interest	(113) 5.6	(113) 4.7
2.1	3.0	2.4	3.0				1.4	1.4
		12.0					7.7	6.3
		(11) 5.0				Net Profit + Depr., Dep., Amort./Cur. Mat. L/T/D	(21) 2.5	(11) 2.4
		1.3					.5	1.1
.5	.3	.1	.2				.2	.1
22.8	1.1	.6	.7			Fixed/Worth	.7	.7
-.4	11.4	1.8	1.5				5.8	5.7
.7	.7	.8	1.0				.7	.9
UND	2.6	1.6	1.6			Debt/Worth	2.0	2.4
-2.6	39.0	3.9	8.8				48.2	24.8
165.6	105.2	59.8					87.7	88.2
(22) 91.1	(47) 49.7	(40) 25.7				% Profit Before Taxes/Tangible Net Worth	(104) 36.8	(104) 22.9
34.3	16.8	9.2					5.4	5.4
46.6	36.2	18.2	24.3				27.9	25.5
13.3	12.1	10.2	14.8			% Profit Before Taxes/Total Assets	11.7	8.6
5.8	3.9	1.4	3.1				.8	1.0
103.1	58.1	83.3	83.4				72.3	79.2
25.1	18.8	15.2	16.7			Sales/Net Fixed Assets	22.1	26.1
7.1	5.8	5.3	5.0				8.7	9.3
7.0	4.7	3.9	4.3				5.2	5.2
4.7	3.0	2.5	2.7			Sales/Total Assets	3.1	2.9
3.0	1.8	1.2	1.7				1.9	2.1
.9	.7	.9	.3				.8	.7
(18) 3.1	(42) 2.0	(32) 1.8	(10) 1.7			% Depr., Dep., Amort./Sales	(87) 1.6	(94) 1.5
12.0	6.3	5.8	2.2				4.0	3.5
4.1	2.7	1.5					3.4	3.2
(24) 7.2	(30) 5.4	(13) 4.3				% Officers', Directors' Owners' Comp/Sales	(68) 6.8	(62) 6.7
14.9	8.8	6.5					11.0	12.7
43773M	213968M	545384M	621625M	273890M	336603M	Net Sales ($)	3193842M	1274605M
9101M	64426M	214501M	255112M	130336M	247948M	Total Assets ($)	906469M	524569M

M = $ thousand MM = $ million

See Pages 9 through 22 for Explanation of Ratios and Data

Comparative Historical Data				Current Data Sorted by Sales					
			Type of Statement						
10	7	6	Unqualified	1		1		2	2
28	25	17	Reviewed		3	2	3	6	3
13	18	13	Compiled	1	5	2	1	4	
54	50	60	Tax Returns	24	15	11	7	3	
59	59	65	Other	10	16	8	10	8	13
					15 (4/1-9/30/13)			146 (10/1/13-3/31/14)	
4/1/11-3/31/12 ALL	**4/1/12-3/31/13 ALL**	**4/1/13-3/31/14 ALL**		**0-1MM**	**1-3MM**	**3-5MM**	**5-10MM**	**10-25MM**	**25MM & OVER**
164	159	161	**NUMBER OF STATEMENTS**	36	39	24	21	23	18
%	%	%	**ASSETS**	%	%	%	%	%	%
16.5	15.2	13.9	Cash & Equivalents	14.0	16.7	15.4	11.7	9.6	13.1
31.6	28.9	29.8	Trade Receivables (net)	11.3	28.0	28.6	41.7	39.8	45.8
8.5	8.7	6.9	Inventory	4.5	8.8	7.7	6.5	8.3	5.3
3.3	3.7	2.4	All Other Current	.7	3.4	2.9	1.9	2.9	2.5
59.9	56.6	53.0	Total Current	30.6	56.9	54.5	61.8	60.7	66.8
23.5	25.8	29.2	Fixed Assets (net)	45.9	23.1	25.7	22.1	26.7	25.2
5.8	6.7	8.4	Intangibles (net)	12.4	10.7	8.1	7.3	3.5	3.5
10.8	10.9	9.4	All Other Non-Current	11.1	9.2	11.7	8.8	9.1	4.6
100.0	100.0	100.0	Total	100.0	100.0	100.0	100.0	100.0	100.0
			LIABILITIES						
9.2	13.3	12.9	Notes Payable-Short Term	18.0	15.0	10.8	8.5	11.2	8.4
2.6	4.0	3.7	Cur. Mat.-L.T.D.	4.2	2.7	2.5	3.0	7.5	2.8
13.5	11.7	11.0	Trade Payables	6.3	6.0	12.2	17.9	14.0	17.4
.3	.2	.2	Income Taxes Payable	.0	.0	1.0	.2	.1	.6
15.1	19.8	13.9	All Other Current	20.4	8.7	11.0	15.1	13.9	14.8
40.7	49.0	41.8	Total Current	48.9	32.4	37.4	44.8	46.5	44.1
25.0	19.2	26.7	Long-Term Debt	52.8	28.1	14.7	19.1	17.7	7.5
.3	.1	.1	Deferred Taxes	.0	.0	.1	.1	.4	.0
10.6	7.5	4.9	All Other Non-Current	8.0	4.9	5.5	1.6	3.5	3.6
23.5	24.1	26.5	Net Worth	-9.8	34.6	42.2	34.3	31.9	44.8
100.0	100.0	100.0	Total Liabilties & Net Worth	100.0	100.0	100.0	100.0	100.0	100.0
			INCOME DATA						
100.0	100.0	100.0	Net Sales	100.0	100.0	100.0	100.0	100.0	100.0
			Gross Profit						
92.4	90.4	89.2	Operating Expenses	75.6	89.0	95.3	95.7	95.7	92.7
7.6	9.6	10.8	Operating Profit	24.4	11.0	4.7	4.3	4.3	7.3
1.1	1.5	2.5	All Other Expenses (net)	11.0	-.5	-.3	.1	.6	.7
6.5	8.1	8.4	Profit Before Taxes	13.4	11.5	5.0	4.3	3.8	6.6
			RATIOS						
3.0	2.7	2.9		3.3	3.9	2.1	1.6	2.2	1.8
1.6	1.5	1.5	Current	1.2	2.7	1.5	1.2	1.4	1.5
1.0	.9	.9		.1	1.0	1.2	1.0	.9	1.2
2.5	2.1	2.4		3.3	3.9	1.9	1.5	1.4	1.6
1.4	1.3	1.2	Quick	1.0	2.2	1.3	1.0	1.2	1.3
.7	.6	.7		.1	.8	.7	.8	.7	1.0
9 42.2	2 155.2	2 181.7		0 UND	0 UND	3 121.1	28 13.0	17 21.0	34 10.7
35 10.5	33 11.0	31 11.6	Sales/Receivables	0 UND	27 13.3	30 12.0	40 9.2	52 7.0	56 6.5
59 6.2	58 6.3	61 6.0		29 12.6	56 6.5	56 6.5	72 5.1	76 4.8	66 5.5
			Cost of Sales/Inventory						
			Cost of Sales/Payables						
7.5	6.2	7.6		14.5	5.9	11.8	8.8	7.9	7.3
15.4	15.5	19.8	Sales/Working Capital	80.8	11.2	27.0	38.6	19.8	14.7
625.9	-101.5	-101.4		-6.9	-108.6	48.8	NM	-97.7	37.4
28.5	26.6	36.6		6.5	32.9	56.4	62.4	12.6	68.2
(141) 8.2	(130) 8.3	(126) 9.1	EBIT/Interest	(18) 3.2	(32) 9.6	(20) 19.4	(17) 9.3	(22) 7.6	(17) 21.1
2.5	2.3	2.7		2.0	2.5	3.6	2.1	1.5	7.5
11.9	11.4	10.6							
(17) 6.1	(14) 3.8	(19) 2.9	Net Profit + Depr., Dep., Amort./Cur. Mat. L/T/D						
2.2	2.9	1.3							
.1	.2	.3		1.8	.1	.3	.3	.1	.3
.6	.7	1.1	Fixed/Worth	UND	1.1	.7	.8	.6	.7
5.6	4.1	19.0		-.7	-3.7	1.1	9.0	2.0	1.1
.7	.7	.8		1.9	.5	.7	1.2	.9	.7
1.9	1.9	2.5	Debt/Worth	UND	1.2	2.0	2.6	2.0	1.3
20.3	11.6	UND		-3.9	-11.8	4.7	58.0	6.7	2.5
87.0	76.8	102.2		93.5	105.2	155.2	134.1	60.8	71.4
(128) 41.3	(125) 28.7	(122) 41.8	% Profit Before Taxes/Tangible Net Worth	(19) 49.7	(27) 70.2	(22) 54.2	(17) 38.4	(20) 31.2	(17) 38.1
11.5	14.5	15.8		18.3	9.9	17.5	7.5	12.7	18.6
34.1	24.6	30.6		20.1	41.7	40.0	21.3	19.4	24.8
12.1	11.1	11.6	% Profit Before Taxes/Total Assets	7.7	18.0	15.5	7.4	9.3	17.4
2.6	3.9	4.0		2.7	5.4	4.4	1.4	3.1	9.6
80.3	53.7	60.5		37.3	60.2	64.1	63.0	112.2	61.2
24.3	17.3	17.8	Sales/Net Fixed Assets	8.2	21.3	25.0	26.2	21.5	16.1
8.4	7.0	5.7		.4	7.7	7.3	6.6	8.9	4.9
5.0	4.5	4.7		5.4	4.8	5.3	4.7	4.6	4.8
3.2	2.8	3.1	Sales/Total Assets	2.0	2.9	3.2	3.5	3.7	3.0
2.0	1.7	1.7		.3	2.0	2.2	1.8	2.5	1.6
.7	.7	.9		6.5	.7	.5	.4	.8	.4
(108) 1.3	(100) 1.7	(104) 1.9	% Depr., Dep., Amort./Sales	(20) 15.5	(21) 1.7	(18) 1.7	(12) 1.2	(18) 1.4	(15) 1.1
3.0	3.9	5.5		21.6	3.9	4.7	6.4	2.5	2.1
3.0	3.1	2.7			3.7	2.8			
(74) 5.3	(77) 5.9	(69) 5.2	% Officers', Directors' Owners' Comp/Sales		(26) 6.7	(15) 4.9			
8.7	10.7	9.1			9.3	8.6			
2067445M	2117049M	2035243M	Net Sales ($)	14716M	71546M	94654M	155578M	343901M	1354848M
772458M	934089M	921424M	Total Assets ($)	22877M	43357M	37944M	58392M	142235M	616619M

M = $ thousand MM = $ million

See Pages 9 through 22 for Explanation of Ratios and Data

Current Data Sorted by Assets							Comparative Historical Data	
						Type of Statement		
		2	2	2	2	Unqualified	9	8
	1	9	11			Reviewed	9	20
1	5	5	1		1	Compiled	12	14
3	22	7			1	Tax Returns	16	26
5	11	23	21	3	2	Other	42	45
25 (4/1-9/30/13)		115 (10/1/13-3/31/14)					4/1/09-3/31/10	4/1/10-3/31/11
0-500M	500M-2MM	2-10MM	10-50MM	50-100MM	100-250MM		ALL	ALL
9	39	46	35	5	6	**NUMBER OF STATEMENTS**	88	113
%	%	%	%	%	%	**ASSETS**	%	%
	20.2	9.6	4.7			Cash & Equivalents	9.4	11.9
	25.4	31.8	26.9			Trade Receivables (net)	25.0	29.4
	13.4	16.2	18.4			Inventory	13.4	12.6
	2.3	2.6	1.6			All Other Current	2.5	2.6
	61.4	60.2	51.7			Total Current	50.4	56.5
	26.1	27.5	35.2			Fixed Assets (net)	34.2	27.1
	7.3	7.6	8.1			Intangibles (net)	8.0	8.8
	5.1	4.8	4.9			All Other Non-Current	7.4	7.6
	100.0	100.0	100.0			Total	100.0	100.0
						LIABILITIES		
	3.8	8.0	10.9			Notes Payable-Short Term	15.4	11.9
	.9	2.0	3.8			Cur. Mat.-L.T.D.	4.1	2.4
	19.0	19.4	19.3			Trade Payables	16.6	18.0
	.2	.4	.9			Income Taxes Payable	.1	.1
	20.5	7.2	5.6			All Other Current	15.6	11.1
	44.5	37.0	40.5			Total Current	51.8	43.6
	17.6	14.5	19.1			Long-Term Debt	27.0	19.4
	.0	.2	1.0			Deferred Taxes	.1	.2
	4.4	3.8	4.7			All Other Non-Current	7.5	11.5
	33.5	44.4	34.6			Net Worth	13.7	25.3
	100.0	100.0	100.0			Total Liabilties & Net Worth	100.0	100.0
						INCOME DATA		
	100.0	100.0	100.0			Net Sales	100.0	100.0
						Gross Profit		
	87.6	92.2	94.4			Operating Expenses	91.8	93.2
	12.4	7.8	5.6			Operating Profit	8.2	6.8
	2.6	1.4	.9			All Other Expenses (net)	3.5	2.1
	9.8	6.4	4.7			Profit Before Taxes	4.8	4.8
						RATIOS		
	2.6	3.0	1.7				2.2	2.7
	1.5	1.7	1.1			Current	1.3	1.4
	1.0	1.2	1.0				.8	.9
	1.8	1.9	1.0				1.5	1.8
	1.0	1.2	.8			Quick	.8	.9
	.6	.8	.5				.5	.5
	3 131.0	25 14.4	32 11.4				24 15.0	23 16.1
	29 12.6	36 10.2	43 8.5			Sales/Receivables	36 10.1	37 9.9
	43 8.5	50 7.3	58 6.3				51 7.1	55 6.6
						Cost of Sales/Inventory		
						Cost of Sales/Payables		
	8.1	6.3	9.4				7.7	7.1
	18.3	13.5	31.4			Sales/Working Capital	20.3	19.3
	-218.4	38.3	-133.0				-19.5	-52.8
	21.3	32.4	24.0				7.9	16.1
	(26) 6.3	(37) 8.3	(34) 6.5			EBIT/Interest	(69) 2.8	(96) 5.7
	1.1	3.2	2.3				.8	1.8
							9.1	13.1
						Net Profit + Depr., Dep., Amort./Cur. Mat. L/T/D	(14) 4.8	(21) 3.5
							1.2	1.1
	.1	.1	.7				.5	.2
	.8	.6	1.5			Fixed/Worth	1.4	.9
	4.4	1.1	3.4				NM	3.1
	.4	.7	1.3				.9	.9
	3.1	1.2	3.0			Debt/Worth	3.6	2.2
	11.2	3.4	5.5				-48.4	13.3
	82.8	81.5	39.7				62.7	78.7
	(30) 44.4	(43) 27.1	(31) 27.2			% Profit Before Taxes/Tangible Net Worth	(65) 23.2	(87) 26.9
	10.7	8.6	15.1				3.8	8.3
	28.6	20.7	15.9				16.3	19.0
	9.2	10.1	7.9			% Profit Before Taxes/Total Assets	8.0	8.1
	4.2	2.9	3.3				.2	1.9
	90.7	182.7	14.1				21.4	44.8
	21.3	14.1	6.6			Sales/Net Fixed Assets	8.8	15.4
	6.4	4.7	3.4				4.1	5.4
	4.3	4.4	2.7				4.1	4.0
	3.0	2.8	1.9			Sales/Total Assets	2.4	2.7
	1.8	1.9	1.2				1.4	1.7
	.7	.5	1.3				1.3	.9
	(23) 2.3	(39) 1.5	(32) 2.4			% Depr., Dep., Amort./Sales	(70) 2.8	(88) 1.7
	5.6	4.4	3.5				6.2	4.0
	3.0	1.5					2.3	2.1
	(25) 4.7	(16) 2.2				% Officers', Directors' Owners' Comp/Sales	(28) 5.4	(38) 3.8
	10.5	5.7					11.7	6.6
14091M	148419M	764141M	1735070M	864392M	2274620M	Net Sales ($)	1998033M	2343381M
3081M	45206M	254001M	810685M	335535M	878665M	Total Assets ($)	825213M	1058281M

M = $ thousand MM = $ million

See Pages 9 through 22 for Explanation of Ratios and Data

Comparative Historical Data				Current Data Sorted by Sales					
			Type of Statement						
12	12	8	Unqualified					2	6
21	23	21	Reviewed		1		1	6	13
14	12	13	Compiled		2	2	4	2	3
28	33	33	Tax Returns	9	7	7	5	4	1
36	52	65	Other	3	4	7	8	15	28
4/1/11-3/31/12 ALL	**4/1/12-3/31/13 ALL**	**4/1/13-3/31/14 ALL**			**25 (4/1-9/30/13)**			**115 (10/1/13-3/31/14)**	
				0-1MM	**1-3MM**	**3-5MM**	**5-10MM**	**10-25MM**	**25MM & OVER**
111	132	140	**NUMBER OF STATEMENTS**	12	14	16	18	29	51
%	%	%	**ASSETS**	%	%	%	%	%	%
10.6	8.6	12.6	Cash & Equivalents	21.1	24.0	14.9	14.8	13.3	5.6
27.0	29.3	28.1	Trade Receivables (net)	7.9	27.8	21.2	34.5	33.7	29.7
15.8	16.5	16.4	Inventory	1.8	14.3	13.3	15.5	15.6	22.0
3.8	2.3	2.1	All Other Current	.4	.4	5.7	1.0	3.8	1.3
57.2	56.7	59.2	Total Current	31.3	66.4	55.2	65.8	66.4	58.7
26.7	25.9	27.7	Fixed Assets (net)	56.3	15.6	29.5	25.7	20.0	28.8
9.4	8.7	8.1	Intangibles (net)	10.3	11.8	6.8	3.1	10.8	7.2
6.7	8.8	5.0	All Other Non-Current	2.2	6.2	8.5	5.3	2.8	5.4
100.0	100.0	100.0	Total	100.0	100.0	100.0	100.0	100.0	100.0
			LIABILITIES						
15.3	12.9	7.8	Notes Payable-Short Term	.7	6.5	4.6	3.5	6.0	13.4
2.9	3.6	2.0	Cur. Mat.-L.T.D.	1.4	.2	1.0	1.3	1.2	3.5
15.6	17.0	18.6	Trade Payables	.9	10.1	21.5	24.9	21.6	20.3
.1	.2	.5	Income Taxes Payable	.0	.5	.0	1.0	.0	.8
12.9	9.1	10.4	All Other Current	17.3	11.8	10.1	15.2	9.9	7.1
46.7	42.9	39.3	Total Current	20.3	29.1	37.2	46.0	38.8	45.1
19.4	18.0	16.7	Long-Term Debt	43.9	13.0	12.8	13.3	11.3	16.8
.3	.1	.4	Deferred Taxes	.0	.0	.0	.0	.1	1.1
4.8	7.2	5.9	All Other Non-Current	5.6	8.1	7.2	3.0	5.3	6.4
28.8	31.8	37.7	Net Worth	30.1	49.9	42.8	37.7	44.5	30.6
100.0	100.0	100.0	Total Liabilties & Net Worth	100.0	100.0	100.0	100.0	100.0	100.0
			INCOME DATA						
100.0	100.0	100.0	Net Sales	100.0	100.0	100.0	100.0	100.0	100.0
			Gross Profit						
89.3	94.2	91.7	Operating Expenses	62.9	92.0	93.2	95.0	96.4	94.1
10.7	5.8	8.3	Operating Profit	37.1	8.0	6.8	5.0	3.6	5.9
2.9	1.5	1.7	All Other Expenses (net)	13.5	.3	.7	.3	.1	1.0
7.8	4.3	6.6	Profit Before Taxes	23.6	7.6	6.1	4.8	3.4	4.9
			RATIOS						
2.8	2.5	2.6		13.0	3.7	6.5	2.6	3.1	1.6
1.4	1.4	1.5	Current	1.6	2.3	1.6	1.6	1.8	1.2
.9	1.0	1.1		.2	1.5	1.1	1.0	1.4	1.0
2.1	2.0	1.7		13.0	3.0	2.6	1.8	2.0	1.0
.9	.9	1.0	Quick	1.4	1.7	1.0	1.3	1.3	.8
.5	.5	.6		.2	1.2	.7	.7	.9	.5
14 26.1	**30** 12.1	**25** 14.8		**0** UND	**26** 14.3	**9** 38.8	**26** 14.3	**29** 12.5	**30** 12.1
37 9.8	**39** 9.3	**38** 9.7	Sales/Receivables	**0** UND	**33** 10.9	**27** 13.7	**36** 10.2	**40** 9.2	**41** 8.8
53 6.9	**54** 6.7	**50** 7.3		**0** UND	**43** 8.4	**43** 8.4	**58** 6.3	**52** 7.0	**57** 6.4
			Cost of Sales/Inventory						
			Cost of Sales/Payables						
7.4	7.8	6.9		1.9	4.6	8.0	7.7	6.0	11.9
18.1	17.4	15.5	Sales/Working Capital	38.4	9.9	20.7	15.1	8.9	22.4
-86.3	-106.5	151.4		-2.1	17.5	143.8	-200.5	31.9	-164.5
28.6	16.3	19.8				8.9	54.4	41.7	20.5
(88) 5.9	(106) 4.8	(109) 6.5	EBIT/Interest			(10) -.1	(15) 13.0	(23) 4.6	(49) 7.0
1.8	1.3	1.9				-5.1	3.6	.4	2.6
9.2	8.5	5.9							5.5
(18) 3.7	(20) 4.7	(19) 3.4	Net Profit + Depr., Dep., Amort./Cur. Mat. L/T/D						(12) 3.3
2.3	.7	2.4							2.0
.3	.2	.1		.1	.0	.4	.1	.1	.4
1.1	.8	.8	Fixed/Worth	3.1	.2	.8	.7	.4	1.3
4.0	4.9	2.8		NM	1.4	2.3	3.1	.9	3.4
.7	.7	.7		.3	.4	.2	.5	.7	1.8
2.3	2.3	2.2	Debt/Worth	3.6	1.4	1.6	2.6	1.2	3.4
14.5	258.2	7.0		-10.7	5.7	14.7	5.0	2.8	6.7
70.2	53.4	72.3			61.7	93.6	93.7	46.1	69.3
(87) 28.8	(100) 18.6	(118) 28.3	% Profit Before Taxes/Tangible Net Worth		(12) 28.7	(13) 12.2	(16) 57.9	(25) 21.4	(44) 32.5
12.7	7.3	11.0			-5.1	-52.6	10.1	3.6	19.4
17.8	13.7	20.2		17.2	35.6	37.3	27.1	18.6	18.2
8.3	6.8	8.0	% Profit Before Taxes/Total Assets	9.0	13.1	4.6	13.1	5.6	8.6
2.3	1.3	2.9		1.7	1.4	-7.2	5.7	.2	3.9
55.2	54.6	82.0		26.6	UND	83.2	92.0	201.4	40.3
17.1	12.5	12.7	Sales/Net Fixed Assets	.6	48.7	11.6	25.5	25.7	10.6
5.5	5.8	5.1		.1	9.3	5.8	5.1	4.7	5.1
4.0	4.2	3.7		1.2	3.9	4.5	4.3	4.9	3.4
2.7	2.5	2.6	Sales/Total Assets	.4	2.6	2.6	3.2	2.8	2.6
1.7	1.8	1.7		.1	2.0	2.0	2.3	1.8	1.8
.9	1.0	.8				.8	.5	.2	.9
(87) 2.1	(97) 2.1	(108) 1.9	% Depr., Dep., Amort./Sales			(12) 1.7	(15) 1.2	(23) 1.8	(46) 1.6
5.5	4.4	3.7				3.8	4.4	3.0	3.3
1.7	1.6	2.0					3.4	1.5	1.4
(34) 4.2	(53) 4.1	(55) 3.8	% Officers', Directors' Owners' Comp/Sales				(12) 5.1	(11) 2.1	(11) 2.1
6.2	6.7	7.2					8.5	6.8	6.2
2515277M	**3953421M**	**5800733M**	Net Sales ($)	**5310M**	**27177M**	**60974M**	**115880M**	**459851M**	**5131541M**
1156916M	**1936771M**	**2327173M**	Total Assets ($)	**19069M**	**10253M**	**30783M**	**41182M**	**216026M**	**2009860M**

M = $ thousand MM = $ million

See Pages 9 through 22 for Explanation of Ratios and Data

Current Data Sorted by Assets							Comparative Historical Data	
						Type of Statement		
		3	2	2	1	Unqualified	5	4
	2	3	3			Reviewed	4	5
1	2	4				Compiled	1	2
4	5	3				Tax Returns	2	8
3	2	14	9	1	1	Other	15	12
	5 (4/1-9/30/13)		60 (10/1/13-3/31/14)				4/1/09-3/31/10	4/1/10-3/31/11
0-500M	500M-2MM	2-10MM	10-50MM	50-100MM	100-250MM		ALL	ALL
8	11	27	14	3	2	**NUMBER OF STATEMENTS**	27	31
%	%	%	%	%	%	**ASSETS**	%	%
	27.3	19.2	11.1			Cash & Equivalents	15.3	23.5
	27.0	31.3	24.6			Trade Receivables (net)	29.5	23.2
	.4	4.1	12.7			Inventory	5.6	8.6
	8.0	4.5	9.0			All Other Current	8.2	5.4
	62.7	59.1	57.5			Total Current	58.5	60.7
	21.9	22.7	19.4			Fixed Assets (net)	20.8	23.8
	3.6	10.8	11.8			Intangibles (net)	14.1	6.4
	11.8	7.4	11.3			All Other Non-Current	6.6	9.1
	100.0	100.0	100.0			Total	100.0	100.0
						LIABILITIES		
	7.4	7.0	7.5			Notes Payable-Short Term	10.9	22.1
	2.1	2.3	1.7			Cur. Mat.-L.T.D.	2.0	4.6
	17.1	12.0	10.1			Trade Payables	15.0	10.5
	.0	.4	.3			Income Taxes Payable	.0	.1
	21.4	35.0	18.4			All Other Current	25.8	39.0
	48.0	56.8	37.9			Total Current	53.7	76.2
	16.5	16.5	13.1			Long-Term Debt	37.8	21.8
	.0	.0	.0			Deferred Taxes	.3	.1
	15.6	8.5	12.3			All Other Non-Current	10.8	6.1
	19.9	18.2	36.6			Net Worth	-2.6	-4.3
	100.0	100.0	100.0			Total Liabilties & Net Worth	100.0	100.0
						INCOME DATA		
	100.0	100.0	100.0			Net Sales	100.0	100.0
						Gross Profit		
	88.4	88.5	93.2			Operating Expenses	96.2	91.1
	11.6	11.5	6.8			Operating Profit	3.8	8.9
	1.9	3.0	1.4			All Other Expenses (net)	2.1	1.4
	9.6	8.5	5.5			Profit Before Taxes	1.7	7.5
						RATIOS		
	4.8	2.0	3.3				2.8	2.1
	2.7	1.4	1.3			Current	1.3	1.3
	.8	.7	.9				.7	.7
	4.8	1.9	2.0				2.0	1.5
	1.5	1.1	.7			Quick	1.1	.9
	.8	.5	.5				.4	.4
	1 321.9	17 21.0	21 17.5				15 24.9	1 260.3
	16 22.3	36 10.2	45 8.1			Sales/Receivables	24 15.2	26 14.1
	52 7.0	58 6.3	78 4.7				54 6.8	67 5.4
						Cost of Sales/Inventory		
						Cost of Sales/Payables		
	6.9	11.9	3.6				11.5	7.9
	12.1	28.1	19.0			Sales/Working Capital	25.2	33.7
	-25.5	-13.2	-200.0				-122.6	-23.3
		31.6	26.9				7.6	28.7
		(17) 16.9	(12) 4.2			EBIT/Interest	(23) 2.4	(28) 4.6
		5.2	1.2				1.7	1.5
						Net Profit + Depr., Dep., Amort./Cur. Mat. L/T/D		
	.0	.2	.2				.7	.2
	9.7	1.6	.6			Fixed/Worth	-504.0	1.0
	-.2	-4.9	NM				-.5	73.6
	.4	1.3	1.0				1.8	1.1
	18.6	4.5	2.0			Debt/Worth	-999.8	8.0
	-10.9	-13.6	NM				-3.4	-22.0
		109.0	27.2				52.3	89.5
		(18) 67.4	(11) 18.0			% Profit Before Taxes/Tangible Net Worth	(13) 19.5	(22) 44.9
		33.6	7.1				7.0	21.9
	42.8	20.9	9.8				15.1	24.3
	31.2	15.3	6.7			% Profit Before Taxes/Total Assets	8.5	12.8
	6.8	5.8	1.1				2.8	3.0
	199.5	78.7	49.0				139.6	133.0
	74.4	19.7	19.8			Sales/Net Fixed Assets	35.0	45.6
	10.3	6.9	5.8				8.5	4.6
	5.3	4.3	2.6				4.6	5.2
	4.0	3.0	1.5			Sales/Total Assets	3.6	2.6
	2.8	1.9	1.0				1.4	1.4
		.4					.4	.5
		(17) .7				% Depr., Dep., Amort./Sales	(18) 1.8	(24) 1.6
		2.9					3.8	4.2
								2.8
						% Officers', Directors' Owners' Comp/Sales		(14) 5.9
								12.7
21415M	62281M	409255M	530660M	798786M	283699M	Net Sales ($)	701193M	564598M
1679M	14513M	129459M	321582M	207487M	356506M	Total Assets ($)	545870M	399607M

M = $ thousand MM = $ million

See Pages 9 through 22 for Explanation of Ratios and Data

Comparative Historical Data				Current Data Sorted by Sales					
			Type of Statement						
3	6	8	Unqualified				2	2	4
3	8	8	Reviewed			1	1	2	4
7	5	7	Compiled			1	4		2
5	4	12	Tax Returns	4	4		4		
18	16	30	Other	1	1	5	3	12	8
4/1/11-3/31/12	**4/1/12-3/31/13**	**4/1/13-3/31/14**		**5 (4/1-9/30/13)**			**60 (10/1/13-3/31/14)**		
ALL	**ALL**	**ALL**		**0-1MM**	**1-3MM**	**3-5MM**	**5-10MM**	**10-25MM**	**25MM & OVER**
36	39	65	**NUMBER OF STATEMENTS**	5	5	7	14	16	18
%	%	%	**ASSETS**	%	%	%	%	%	%
20.9	21.9	21.2	Cash & Equivalents				27.2	17.7	17.8
32.5	31.1	24.8	Trade Receivables (net)				22.1	38.7	21.5
5.2	2.4	4.5	Inventory				5.5	6.6	6.0
2.4	5.0	6.6	All Other Current				5.8	3.9	9.6
61.0	60.4	57.0	Total Current				60.6	66.9	54.9
17.7	25.2	22.3	Fixed Assets (net)				16.8	14.2	20.7
11.0	5.8	10.7	Intangibles (net)				9.0	11.2	14.0
10.3	8.6	10.0	All Other Non-Current				13.6	7.7	10.4
100.0	100.0	100.0	Total				100.0	100.0	100.0
			LIABILITIES						
19.3	10.7	8.7	Notes Payable-Short Term				5.9	11.7	4.3
1.3	1.9	2.1	Cur. Mat.-L.T.D.				2.9	2.1	1.8
15.1	15.9	13.3	Trade Payables				14.4	15.1	10.7
.3	.0	.3	Income Taxes Payable				.7	.0	.4
21.8	20.6	26.1	All Other Current				34.5	28.7	23.6
57.8	49.0	50.4	Total Current				58.5	57.6	40.8
12.3	15.4	15.1	Long-Term Debt				5.5	12.7	15.6
.3	.1	.1	Deferred Taxes				.0	.0	.2
13.4	6.1	14.7	All Other Non-Current				13.8	10.8	10.4
16.3	29.4	19.7	Net Worth				22.2	18.8	33.1
100.0	100.0	100.0	Total Liabilties & Net Worth				100.0	100.0	100.0
			INCOME DATA						
100.0	100.0	100.0	Net Sales				100.0	100.0	100.0
			Gross Profit						
94.2	89.6	91.1	Operating Expenses				91.2	95.8	93.8
5.8	10.4	8.9	Operating Profit				8.8	4.2	6.2
.6	2.7	2.1	All Other Expenses (net)				.8	1.0	.8
5.2	7.7	6.8	Profit Before Taxes				8.0	3.2	5.4
			RATIOS						
2.8	1.9	2.2					4.0	2.0	2.4
1.2	1.2	1.4	Current				1.6	1.4	1.2
.8	.8	.7					.6	.7	1.0
2.6	1.7	2.0					3.9	1.9	1.6
1.0	1.1	1.1	Quick				1.3	1.3	.8
.6	.7	.5					.3	.5	.6
8 47.9	**13** 29.1	**7** 54.3					**15** 24.2	**25** 14.8	**8** 45.8
30 12.0	**39** 9.4	**28** 12.9	Sales/Receivables				**24** 15.4	**51** 7.1	**26** 13.8
73 5.0	**73** 5.0	**51** 7.2					**38** 9.6	**85** 4.3	**47** 7.8
			Cost of Sales/Inventory						
			Cost of Sales/Payables						
6.4	8.6	9.4					7.5	8.3	8.4
36.9	25.5	32.4	Sales/Working Capital				20.2	16.6	24.1
-33.8	-30.5	-28.2					-26.1	-9.8	-281.9
18.5	23.3	30.9						27.2	32.3
(27) 4.8	(29) 8.2	(43) 8.1	EBIT/Interest					(12) 6.8	(15) 8.1
1.1	2.4	2.4						2.2	2.4
			Net Profit + Depr., Dep., Amort./Cur. Mat. L/T/D						
.1	.2	.2					.1	.1	.1
1.0	.7	1.5	Fixed/Worth				.9	1.8	.6
-.7	-14.1	-1.8					NM	-.4	NM
.9	1.2	1.2					.6	1.8	.8
4.2	2.6	3.7	Debt/Worth				1.8	5.2	1.9
-5.6	-64.6	-11.0					NM	-5.8	-4.5
79.6	95.9	97.8					97.8	99.4	76.2
(25) 39.3	(28) 56.4	(43) 49.3	% Profit Before Taxes/Tangible Net Worth				(11) 54.7	(11) 49.3	(13) 18.0
16.9	17.9	9.7					34.1	20.0	6.8
21.1	27.2	20.9					29.3	17.3	17.7
5.8	15.6	11.5	% Profit Before Taxes/Total Assets				20.0	12.3	6.7
1.8	3.0	2.8					9.9	1.8	2.4
149.9	92.3	102.8					266.9	152.4	58.8
49.2	29.5	26.8	Sales/Net Fixed Assets				50.7	43.3	22.4
12.1	5.7	7.4					6.7	9.6	9.3
5.0	4.2	4.9					4.5	4.2	5.1
3.5	3.1	2.9	Sales/Total Assets				3.9	2.4	2.6
1.5	1.8	1.5					2.4	1.7	1.2
.4	.5	.4					.3		.3
(24) 1.1	(30) 2.0	(39) 1.4	% Depr., Dep., Amort./Sales				(10) .5		(12) 1.4
3.1	4.5	4.3					2.5		3.0
1.5	2.4	1.7							
(14) 3.8	(15) 6.5	(19) 4.2	% Officers', Directors' Owners' Comp/Sales						
20.8	12.4	14.2							
664982M	**799464M**	**2106096M**	Net Sales ($)	**2078M**	**10268M**	**27371M**	**107941M**	**277301M**	**1681137M**
418991M	**375782M**	**1031226M**	Total Assets ($)	**6968M**	**2225M**	**10388M**	**63380M**	**132085M**	**816180M**

M = $ thousand MM = $ million

See Pages 9 through 22 for Explanation of Ratios and Data

Current Data Sorted by Assets							Comparative Historical Data	
						Type of Statement		
		12	17	5	1	Unqualified	30	37
1	3	22	8			Reviewed	29	41
5	12	15				Compiled	29	35
16	18	13	1			Tax Returns	65	48
18	19	34	19	4	5	Other	102	111
35 (4/1-9/30/13)			213 (10/1/13-3/31/14)				4/1/09-3/31/10	4/1/10-3/31/11
0-500M	**500M-2MM**	**2-10MM**	**10-50MM**	**50-100MM**	**100-250MM**		**ALL**	**ALL**
40	52	96	45	9	6	**NUMBER OF STATEMENTS**	255	272
%	%	%	%	%	%	**ASSETS**	%	%
39.0	19.0	15.6	12.4			Cash & Equivalents	16.1	16.9
16.4	19.1	31.2	24.7			Trade Receivables (net)	23.8	29.2
4.0	8.4	10.1	12.0			Inventory	8.1	7.2
5.8	8.0	3.5	5.5			All Other Current	4.5	6.0
65.1	54.6	60.5	54.7			Total Current	52.5	59.3
19.8	31.9	32.0	25.5			Fixed Assets (net)	28.5	24.9
4.1	3.7	2.2	10.3			Intangibles (net)	9.6	7.3
11.1	9.9	5.3	9.4			All Other Non-Current	9.4	8.5
100.0	100.0	100.0	100.0			Total	100.0	100.0
						LIABILITIES		
10.9	10.1	7.7	6.9			Notes Payable-Short Term	14.1	12.7
6.0	2.9	2.3	2.9			Cur. Mat.-L.T.D.	3.6	3.9
10.3	9.9	14.9	10.7			Trade Payables	11.1	12.8
.0	.2	.3	.2			Income Taxes Payable	.4	.4
30.8	8.6	11.5	16.3			All Other Current	15.8	22.2
58.0	31.7	36.7	36.9			Total Current	44.9	52.0
10.0	24.1	18.3	15.6			Long-Term Debt	20.3	18.1
.0	.3	.3	.2			Deferred Taxes	.4	.4
8.2	5.6	3.6	5.5			All Other Non-Current	8.1	7.5
23.9	38.2	41.1	41.8			Net Worth	26.3	22.0
100.0	100.0	100.0	100.0			Total Liabilties & Net Worth	100.0	100.0
						INCOME DATA		
100.0	100.0	100.0	100.0			Net Sales	100.0	100.0
						Gross Profit		
93.8	84.5	88.0	94.0			Operating Expenses	92.2	91.9
6.2	15.5	12.0	6.0			Operating Profit	7.8	8.1
.4	4.3	3.4	1.7			All Other Expenses (net)	2.1	1.9
5.8	11.2	8.6	4.4			Profit Before Taxes	5.7	6.2
						RATIOS		
4.8	4.2	3.3	2.7				2.6	2.7
1.5	1.7	1.6	1.4			Current	1.3	1.4
.6	1.0	1.1	1.0				.8	.9
4.7	2.5	2.7	1.7				2.0	2.2
1.5	1.3	1.2	1.0			Quick	.9	1.1
.4	.6	.7	.7				.4	.6
0 UND	**0** UND	**6** 60.5	**15** 24.2				**3** 119.5	**8** 48.1
0 UND	**5** 74.9	**39** 9.3	**36** 10.0			Sales/Receivables	**27** 13.7	**35** 10.3
20 18.7	**36** 10.2	**65** 5.6	**68** 5.4				**48** 7.5	**56** 6.6
						Cost of Sales/Inventory		
						Cost of Sales/Payables		
18.6	4.6	6.3	6.4				8.8	7.4
79.5	13.0	11.4	16.1			Sales/Working Capital	27.9	20.7
-53.7	NM	76.8	544.4				-22.1	-61.9
39.6	52.7	34.5	45.7				18.1	18.8
(21) 5.8	(38) 7.6	(66) 9.4	(39) 5.7			EBIT/Interest	(198) 3.7	(203) 5.1
1.0	2.5	3.2	1.8				.4	1.0
		26.0				Net Profit + Depr., Dep.,	11.1	8.1
		(13) 8.2				Amort./Cur. Mat. L/T/D	(29) 3.2	(40) 4.2
		2.9					1.7	.9
.0	.1	.1	.2				.2	.2
.5	.6	.4	.8			Fixed/Worth	.9	.8
7.3	2.5	1.6	1.8				-6.0	5.0
.6	.5	.7	1.0				.8	.7
3.2	1.5	1.7	1.7			Debt/Worth	3.2	2.0
NM	7.6	4.9	5.8				-8.8	24.6
333.5	96.5	59.5	61.1			% Profit Before Taxes/Tangible	60.0	69.7
(30) 103.4	(45) 30.5	(92) 29.8	(39) 22.4			Net Worth	(181) 23.3	(211) 31.9
23.1	1.6	13.6	7.2				2.5	9.5
85.8	31.8	21.5	18.1			% Profit Before Taxes/Total	20.3	29.1
24.8	13.1	10.1	8.5			Assets	6.4	9.2
1.6	.6	3.2	1.3				-1.7	.8
UND	142.1	112.1	72.8				74.6	79.4
70.3	12.5	19.3	16.9			Sales/Net Fixed Assets	15.1	20.8
19.1	4.3	2.2	3.6				5.2	6.4
15.4	4.3	3.9	3.2				4.7	4.9
5.5	2.9	2.4	1.7			Sales/Total Assets	2.4	3.0
3.1	.7	1.1	1.0				1.1	1.5
.5	.9	.4	.7				.5	.5
(20) 1.5	(32) 2.9	(75) 2.4	(40) 2.1			% Depr., Dep., Amort./Sales	(176) 2.3	(196) 1.5
2.8	11.1	6.7	4.2				5.0	4.6
2.7	1.6	1.6				% Officers', Directors'	2.5	3.0
(21) 7.1	(16) 3.6	(30) 3.2				Owners' Comp/Sales	(85) 5.1	(76) 6.5
16.8	8.4	6.7					9.8	13.2
87614M	185656M	1179150M	3174062M	1008759M	1188512M	Net Sales ($)	7192441M	7330894M
8167M	57176M	446083M	1011204M	613220M	854319M	Total Assets ($)	3655078M	3446741M

M = $ thousand MM = $ million

See Pages 9 through 22 for Explanation of Ratios and Data

Comparative Historical Data				Current Data Sorted by Sales					
			Type of Statement						
43	25	35	Unqualified		2		4	10	19
37	27	34	Reviewed	1	3	3	7	12	8
47	23	32	Compiled	5	8	5	7	5	2
51	44	48	Tax Returns	18	14	3	5	7	1
134	99	99	Other	19	13	10	13	19	25
4/1/11-3/31/12 ALL	4/1/12-3/31/13 ALL	4/1/13-3/31/14 ALL		35 (4/1-9/30/13)			213 (10/1/13-3/31/14)		
				0-1MM	1-3MM	3-5MM	5-10MM	10-25MM	25MM & OVER
312	218	248	**NUMBER OF STATEMENTS**	43	40	21	36	53	55
%	%	%	**ASSETS**	%	%	%	%	%	%
22.2	17.8	19.2	Cash & Equivalents	20.1	25.9	25.2	20.9	17.9	11.7
26.0	25.0	24.6	Trade Receivables (net)	8.6	14.5	21.6	31.2	31.8	34.2
7.1	7.0	8.5	Inventory	2.3	10.4	10.6	8.6	9.5	10.3
4.3	6.0	5.5	All Other Current	7.8	3.2	4.0	3.6	6.7	6.3
59.6	55.7	57.9	Total Current	38.7	54.0	61.5	64.3	65.9	62.5
25.5	26.8	28.0	Fixed Assets (net)	51.5	26.4	27.0	29.6	20.1	17.9
4.9	6.5	6.1	Intangibles (net)	2.4	5.4	5.8	2.0	5.0	13.6
10.0	11.0	7.9	All Other Non-Current	7.4	14.3	5.9	4.2	9.0	6.0
100.0	100.0	100.0	Total	100.0	100.0	100.0	100.0	100.0	100.0
			LIABILITIES						
11.6	11.5	8.3	Notes Payable-Short Term	5.0	11.1	11.6	8.7	6.8	8.7
2.4	2.4	3.1	Cur. Mat.-L.T.D.	5.2	2.8	4.0	2.6	2.1	2.7
11.1	10.8	11.8	Trade Payables	6.3	7.8	13.7	9.8	15.8	15.7
.3	.1	.2	Income Taxes Payable	.0	.3	.0	.1	.5	.2
15.8	14.7	15.4	All Other Current	19.5	13.5	9.3	15.0	13.7	17.6
41.2	39.5	38.8	Total Current	35.9	35.5	38.7	36.2	39.0	45.0
16.2	18.4	18.7	Long-Term Debt	34.9	22.8	12.6	15.4	10.4	15.6
.3	.3	.2	Deferred Taxes	.0	.3	.0	.7	.2	.2
9.6	9.9	5.6	All Other Non-Current	5.9	8.0	7.1	2.4	3.0	7.4
32.8	31.9	36.7	Net Worth	23.3	33.4	41.6	45.3	47.4	31.8
100.0	100.0	100.0	Total Liabilities & Net Worth	100.0	100.0	100.0	100.0	100.0	100.0
			INCOME DATA						
100.0	100.0	100.0	Net Sales	100.0	100.0	100.0	100.0	100.0	100.0
			Gross Profit						
90.9	89.8	89.7	Operating Expenses	73.4	89.5	95.9	92.3	92.5	95.7
9.1	10.2	10.3	Operating Profit	26.6	10.5	4.1	7.7	7.5	4.3
1.5	2.2	2.8	All Other Expenses (net)	12.1	1.6	.6	-.2	.6	1.1
7.6	8.0	7.5	Profit Before Taxes	14.5	8.9	3.5	7.9	6.9	3.1
			RATIOS						
3.4	2.7	3.3		5.9	5.0	3.3	3.3	2.9	2.0
1.7	1.5	1.5	Current	1.2	1.9	1.5	1.7	1.6	1.3
.9	.9	1.0		.4	1.1	.9	1.2	1.1	1.1
2.8	2.2	2.2		5.3	3.3	2.3	3.2	1.9	1.8
1.3	(217) 1.2	1.2	Quick	.9	1.5	1.3	1.4	1.2	1.0
.7	.5	.6		.3	.6	.6	.9	.8	.7
2 157.6	2 186.5	1 496.3		0 UND	0 UND	0 UND	8 45.0	12 30.4	21 17.3
27 13.5	31 11.7	27 13.4	Sales/Receivables	0 UND	4 96.5	29 12.5	43 8.4	30 12.3	42 8.7
52 7.0	58 6.3	56 6.5		4 86.0	47 7.7	56 6.5	96 3.8	55 6.6	65 5.6
			Cost of Sales/Inventory						
			Cost of Sales/Payables						
6.2	7.0	6.4		5.6	4.8	4.9	4.4	7.5	8.6
13.7	18.8	16.2	Sales/Working Capital	44.0	19.1	10.9	8.6	14.9	18.5
-137.8	-55.7	195.5		-6.2	141.3	-142.4	33.6	109.5	88.9
24.5	30.6	33.0		7.8	38.7	18.6	56.8	53.9	23.7
(227) 6.6	(165) 6.5	(176) 7.2	EBIT/Interest	(16) 2.4	(32) 7.7	(14) 8.1	(28) 7.6	(41) 18.6	(45) 5.9
2.1	1.5	2.5		-.5	2.4	-5.4	2.8	3.3	1.2
8.3	39.1	19.9							20.3
(35) 3.6	(19) 8.2	(29) 6.3	Net Profit + Depr., Dep., Amort./Cur. Mat. L/T/D						(17) 4.4
2.1	2.7	1.9							.4
.1	.1	.1		.2	.2	.0	.1	.0	.1
.6	.7	.6	Fixed/Worth	2.1	.5	.8	.5	.2	.6
2.4	3.9	2.6		8.7	4.8	2.0	1.6	1.5	6.4
.5	.6	.7		1.1	.3	.5	.7	.6	1.1
1.7	1.9	1.8	Debt/Worth	3.4	1.6	1.6	1.5	1.2	2.5
7.8	10.5	7.7		20.3	9.2	8.0	2.3	4.0	19.6
78.2	64.9	68.4		54.6	184.5	100.3	54.4	66.0	71.6
(258) 29.2	(175) 32.9	(212) 30.8	% Profit Before Taxes/Tangible Net Worth	(34) 21.1	(33) 33.0	(18) 31.3	(35) 24.0	(50) 41.1	(42) 37.9
11.0	9.1	10.7		.8	11.8	-.2	8.6	17.0	13.8
29.0	28.6	26.5		14.5	40.3	35.4	22.6	30.7	20.5
12.4	11.0	10.5	% Profit Before Taxes/Total Assets	2.8	14.2	8.7	11.4	15.0	10.4
2.5	1.7	1.8		-1.2	6.0	-1.5	2.5	6.1	1.6
113.2	119.6	114.4		54.0	136.5	151.1	58.1	226.5	80.8
25.2	20.4	20.8	Sales/Net Fixed Assets	2.7	19.1	19.6	9.8	35.7	26.6
6.5	4.8	3.9		.2	5.3	5.9	5.9	6.0	9.2
5.2	4.8	4.5		3.0	5.8	4.7	3.4	5.0	4.8
3.1	2.7	2.5	Sales/Total Assets	.3	3.0	3.5	2.4	2.9	2.9
1.5	1.2	1.2		.1	1.5	1.1	1.2	1.6	1.6
.6	.5	.6		1.7	1.0	.5	1.1	.3	.5
(197) 1.3	(147) 2.0	(177) 2.2	% Depr., Dep., Amort./Sales	(30) 14.8	(24) 2.7	(14) 2.7	(25) 2.3	(39) .9	(45) .9
4.3	5.1	6.2		25.1	8.1	7.8	4.4	4.2	3.0
2.5	2.7	1.8		6.0	1.9		2.4	1.4	
(95) 5.8	(59) 5.1	(73) 4.4	% Officers', Directors' Owners' Comp/Sales	(11) 13.5	(17) 4.4		(17) 3.5	(19) 3.5	
12.0	11.7	9.1		23.6	11.3		6.6	7.0	
6829927M	6463945M	6823753M	Net Sales ($)	18770M	73313M	84482M	266422M	877387M	5503379M
2955891M	2442610M	2990169M	Total Assets ($)	61927M	60233M	74065M	190673M	477689M	2125582M

M = $ thousand MM = $ million

See Pages 9 through 22 for Explanation of Ratios and Data

Current Data Sorted by Assets							Comparative Historical Data	
	1	2	15	5	5	**Type of Statement** Unqualified	37	29
1	8	21	11	2		Reviewed	43	36
3	8	14	3			Compiled	50	46
21	24	16	2			Tax Returns	72	49
5	19	26	33	10	9	Other	94	98
39 (4/1-9/30/13)			225 (10/1/13-3/31/14)				**4/1/09-3/31/10**	**4/1/10-3/31/11**
0-500M	**500M-2MM**	**2-10MM**	**10-50MM**	**50-100MM**	**100-250MM**		**ALL**	**ALL**
30	60	79	64	17	14	**NUMBER OF STATEMENTS**	296	258
%	%	%	%	%	%	**ASSETS**	%	%
20.0	11.1	8.5	10.3	7.6	3.5	Cash & Equivalents	11.8	11.7
19.2	20.4	15.5	15.9	10.0	7.9	Trade Receivables (net)	17.0	19.3
1.1	1.1	1.9	1.1	1.2	1.4	Inventory	1.4	1.2
.4	4.0	3.8	2.8	3.6	2.8	All Other Current	3.2	3.9
40.8	36.6	29.6	30.1	22.5	15.6	Total Current	33.4	36.1
40.8	47.1	54.2	55.7	42.4	55.1	Fixed Assets (net)	49.4	46.3
3.0	4.7	7.7	8.6	22.3	23.7	Intangibles (net)	8.9	9.3
15.5	11.5	8.6	5.7	12.8	5.6	All Other Non-Current	8.3	8.3
100.0	100.0	100.0	100.0	100.0	100.0	Total	100.0	100.0
						LIABILITIES		
41.9	6.6	4.2	3.7	1.6	1.8	Notes Payable-Short Term	5.0	8.2
9.2	5.2	8.8	7.2	5.9	4.1	Cur. Mat.-L.T.D.	7.5	6.8
16.3	12.0	8.5	9.3	6.0	5.2	Trade Payables	9.7	10.3
.0	.1	.2	.0	.1	.0	Income Taxes Payable	.3	.3
15.8	8.6	6.8	7.8	5.7	4.9	All Other Current	11.4	9.1
83.1	32.4	28.5	28.0	19.4	16.1	Total Current	33.9	34.7
57.2	45.5	35.3	37.0	32.5	41.0	Long-Term Debt	37.5	29.8
.0	.2	.4	.5	.9	4.4	Deferred Taxes	.8	1.2
23.4	16.0	5.8	6.3	6.4	10.4	All Other Non-Current	8.0	8.8
-63.5	5.9	30.1	28.2	40.9	28.0	Net Worth	19.8	25.5
100.0	100.0	100.0	100.0	100.0	100.0	Total Liabilties & Net Worth	100.0	100.0
						INCOME DATA		
100.0	100.0	100.0	100.0	100.0	100.0	Net Sales	100.0	100.0
						Gross Profit		
90.8	92.0	91.3	93.5	91.4	91.9	Operating Expenses	93.1	91.5
9.2	8.0	8.7	6.5	8.6	8.1	Operating Profit	6.9	8.5
3.1	2.2	1.7	1.5	2.3	3.2	All Other Expenses (net)	2.3	1.8
6.1	5.7	7.1	5.0	6.3	4.9	Profit Before Taxes	4.6	6.6
						RATIOS		
2.1	2.7	1.6	1.9	1.9	1.2		2.0	1.9
.8	1.3	1.0	1.1	.9	1.0	Current	1.0	1.0
.2	.5	.5	.6	.5	.6		.6	.6
1.7	2.4	1.4	1.8	1.6	.9		1.7	1.7
.8	1.0	.8	.9	.7	.7	Quick	(295) .8	.9
.2	.4	.3	.5	.4	.5		.5	.5
0 UND	**6** 64.3	**18** 20.5	**27** 13.5	**28** 13.0	**23** 15.9		**17** 21.6	**19** 18.7
5 71.4	**28** 13.0	**28** 13.2	**36** 10.0	**33** 10.9	**32** 11.5	Sales/Receivables	**31** 11.6	**32** 11.5
24 15.1	**43** 8.4	**38** 9.7	**43** 8.4	**46** 7.9	**43** 8.5		**45** 8.2	**45** 8.0
						Cost of Sales/Inventory		
						Cost of Sales/Payables		
19.1	9.9	12.8	8.2	7.9	33.2		11.2	10.0
-75.6	51.2	320.7	55.9	-68.5	544.0	Sales/Working Capital	UND	174.5
-7.7	-15.3	-10.9	-10.8	-6.9	-16.5		-14.3	-17.9
13.0	10.2	11.9	8.4	13.6	11.7		7.5	10.6
(21) 2.6	(52) 3.6	(75) 4.6	(62) 3.9	6.0	3.8	EBIT/Interest	(272) 3.2	(239) 4.6
.7	.0	1.4	1.7	2.2	1.4		1.1	1.9
		3.2	2.2				3.4	2.3
		(16) 1.9	(21) 1.6			Net Profit + Depr., Dep., Amort./Cur. Mat. L/T/D	(57) 1.9	(63) 1.8
		1.5	1.3				1.4	1.2
.7	1.0	1.1	1.5	1.2	3.2		1.1	.9
UND	5.1	2.1	2.6	3.3	8.5	Fixed/Worth	2.8	2.1
-.5	-2.3	32.8	10.7	8.9	-10.2		-7.2	-43.0
1.9	1.4	1.1	1.4	2.2	3.9		1.4	1.1
-24.0	11.2	2.8	3.3	3.9	11.5	Debt/Worth	3.3	3.0
-1.6	-4.8	61.2	17.4	13.2	-15.1		-12.2	-83.9
999.8	143.4	62.8	43.5	64.1			50.2	61.4
(14) 153.3	(35) 31.0	(62) 27.9	(53) 27.6	(14) 24.2		% Profit Before Taxes/Tangible Net Worth	(212) 25.7	(189) 30.0
54.8	13.0	8.4	7.3	21.6			6.4	12.3
40.4	19.5	15.9	12.3	11.3	7.2		13.6	18.6
27.1	7.9	7.0	5.3	6.0	4.0	% Profit Before Taxes/Total Assets	6.3	7.6
1.3	-.8	1.2	2.1	2.4	.4		.4	1.5
46.9	16.4	7.2	3.6	4.4	2.4		8.1	10.3
10.9	5.8	3.4	2.3	2.5	1.7	Sales/Net Fixed Assets	3.8	4.0
4.9	3.5	1.9	1.7	1.4	1.1		1.9	2.0
7.1	4.0	2.4	1.8	1.2	1.3		2.8	3.0
4.1	2.6	1.7	1.3	.9	.8	Sales/Total Assets	1.7	1.7
2.5	1.3	1.2	1.0	.6	.7		1.1	1.1
1.4	2.3	3.6	5.5	4.7			4.5	3.5
(19) 4.0	(45) 4.8	(76) 6.9	(62) 8.0	7.9		% Depr., Dep., Amort./Sales	(250) 7.6	(216) 6.4
9.8	8.3	11.6	10.9	11.5			10.8	10.1
3.8	2.4	1.5	.8				2.3	2.6
(11) 6.0	(33) 4.2	(33) 2.7	(15) 2.4			% Officers', Directors' Owners' Comp/Sales	(110) 4.5	(82) 4.5
13.5	6.0	4.2	5.1				6.9	7.3
36965M	187315M	754620M	2090206M	1148404M	2044360M	Net Sales ($)	5933994M	4514085M
7482M	68415M	395904M	1372936M	1251870M	2278895M	Total Assets ($)	4131736M	3724377M

M = $ thousand MM = $ million

See Pages 9 through 22 for Explanation of Ratios and Data

Comparative Historical Data				Current Data Sorted by Sales					
			Type of Statement						
26	35	28	Unqualified			1	2	9	16
43	40	43	Reviewed	3	2	2	11	19	6
39	28	28	Compiled	2	9	4	6	6	1
79	48	63	Tax Returns	11	24	13	11	4	
102	104	102	Other	7	12	13	7	26	37
4/1/11-3/31/12 ALL	4/1/12-3/31/13 ALL	4/1/13-3/31/14 ALL		39 (4/1-9/30/13)			225 (10/1/13-3/31/14)		
				0-1MM	1-3MM	3-5MM	5-10MM	10-25MM	25MM & OVER
289	255	264	**NUMBER OF STATEMENTS**	23	47	33	37	64	60
%	%	%	**ASSETS**	%	%	%	%	%	%
11.6	10.6	10.5	Cash & Equivalents	7.7	14.2	14.4	10.1	10.0	7.3
19.0	19.0	16.4	Trade Receivables (net)	14.8	13.4	19.4	19.4	18.8	13.2
1.6	1.0	1.4	Inventory	1.4	.1	.8	2.6	1.7	1.5
3.4	3.6	3.2	All Other Current	3.8	3.3	1.1	2.7	4.4	2.9
35.6	34.2	31.4	Total Current	27.7	31.1	35.7	34.8	34.9	24.9
47.2	46.6	50.7	Fixed Assets (net)	58.0	49.7	52.8	44.5	51.7	50.3
8.9	9.0	8.5	Intangibles (net)	3.2	4.5	2.3	10.6	7.6	16.6
8.2	10.2	9.4	All Other Non-Current	11.1	14.7	9.3	10.1	5.8	8.2
100.0	100.0	100.0	Total	100.0	100.0	100.0	100.0	100.0	100.0
			LIABILITIES						
7.8	7.3	8.6	Notes Payable-Short Term	48.9	4.9	6.8	7.3	4.0	2.8
8.0	7.5	7.2	Cur. Mat.-L.T.D.	10.3	6.9	4.0	8.6	7.2	7.1
11.4	11.1	10.0	Trade Payables	3.7	10.0	14.5	12.5	10.7	7.7
.2	.1	.1	Income Taxes Payable	.0	.1	.1	.2	.1	.1
8.7	11.1	8.3	All Other Current	16.7	7.6	6.2	7.7	8.7	6.6
36.0	37.2	34.2	Total Current	79.7	29.6	31.7	36.3	30.6	24.3
36.1	34.9	40.7	Long-Term Debt	60.9	55.0	40.8	37.3	30.3	34.7
.6	.9	.6	Deferred Taxes	.3	.0	.3	.5	.4	1.6
11.4	14.2	10.5	All Other Non-Current	25.5	19.2	7.5	6.9	4.8	7.9
16.0	12.8	14.1	Net Worth	-66.2	-3.8	19.8	19.1	33.8	31.6
100.0	100.0	100.0	Total Liabilties & Net Worth	100.0	100.0	100.0	100.0	100.0	100.0
			INCOME DATA						
100.0	100.0	100.0	Net Sales	100.0	100.0	100.0	100.0	100.0	100.0
			Gross Profit						
92.8	92.6	92.0	Operating Expenses	75.7	93.8	92.6	93.7	93.0	94.2
7.2	7.4	8.0	Operating Profit	24.3	6.2	7.4	6.3	7.0	5.8
1.6	2.5	2.1	All Other Expenses (net)	7.3	3.2	.9	1.1	.6	1.9
5.6	4.9	6.0	Profit Before Taxes	16.9	3.0	6.5	5.1	6.4	3.9
			RATIOS						
1.8	1.8	1.9		1.9	2.4	5.5	2.0	1.7	1.6
1.0	1.0	1.1	Current	.4	.9	1.3	1.1	1.3	.9
.6	.6	.5		.1	.4	.5	.5	.6	.6
1.5	1.6	1.7		1.2	2.2	5.0	1.8	1.6	1.2
.8	.9	.8	Quick	.3	.8	1.0	.9	1.0	.7
.5	.5	.4		.1	.3	.4	.5	.5	.5
13 27.3	**17** 21.2	**17** 21.2		**0** UND	**0** UND	**7** 54.6	**16** 22.4	**23** 16.0	**24** 15.0
28 12.9	**31** 11.6	**29** 12.6	Sales/Receivables	**1** 712.0	**19** 19.0	**29** 12.8	**28** 13.0	**33** 10.9	**34** 10.6
42 8.6	**45** 8.2	**41** 8.9		**28** 13.2	**38** 9.7	**38** 9.5	**45** 8.2	**42** 8.7	**43** 8.4
			Cost of Sales/Inventory						
			Cost of Sales/Payables						
14.7	13.4	11.8		27.9	11.9	11.0	9.5	9.7	13.0
-999.8	-999.8	264.8	Sales/Working Capital	-9.3	-243.3	48.9	320.7	36.2	-422.2
-13.0	-12.4	-10.9		-2.7	-10.3	-17.7	-13.4	-16.6	-12.2
10.2	9.7	11.2		4.6	6.0	17.7	8.6	12.2	11.4
(261) 4.3	(227) 3.1	(241) 3.9	EBIT/Interest	(11) 3.0	(43) 2.4	(29) 4.8	3.1	(62) 5.5	(59) 4.3
1.3	.6	1.4		.5	-.6	2.6	1.3	1.6	1.8
6.0	2.3	2.8						2.1	3.4
(43) 2.4	(46) 1.6	(54) 1.9	Net Profit + Depr., Dep., Amort./Cur. Mat. L/T/D					(19) 1.6	(21) 1.9
1.2	1.3	1.3						1.5	1.3
.9	1.1	1.2		1.2	1.0	1.1	1.4	.9	1.6
2.5	2.8	3.3	Fixed/Worth	-5.2	5.9	3.1	3.5	1.8	3.4
-16.3	-13.3	-10.8		-.5	-1.9	NM	-2.5	10.5	15.5
1.3	1.4	1.3		1.3	1.2	1.0	1.7	1.1	2.0
3.6	4.3	4.4	Debt/Worth	-7.4	12.6	4.2	5.1	2.5	4.0
-26.5	-17.5	-17.2		-1.6	-3.6	NM	-6.0	17.8	23.9
70.8	64.0	72.8		265.4	143.4	156.9	74.2	43.9	59.7
(207) 31.9	(181) 24.5	(186) 30.2	% Profit Before Taxes/Tangible Net Worth	(10) 46.8	(27) 26.5	(25) 61.5	(25) 33.2	(53) 25.7	(46) 25.4
16.9	5.5	10.5		14.2	5.5	15.3	8.4	8.3	14.7
19.4	13.6	16.5		35.5	21.7	27.5	15.7	13.6	11.4
9.1	5.4	6.9	% Profit Before Taxes/Total Assets	11.2	5.2	13.3	4.4	6.4	5.2
1.3	-.5	1.6		2.2	-3.4	5.5	.7	1.9	2.1
12.3	10.5	7.4		6.6	12.9	10.0	13.0	7.6	3.8
4.8	4.2	3.5	Sales/Net Fixed Assets	3.9	5.4	4.5	4.8	3.3	2.4
2.3	2.0	1.9		.8	2.2	2.4	2.5	2.0	1.7
3.6	3.0	2.8		3.3	3.6	4.4	3.6	2.2	1.7
2.1	1.7	1.7	Sales/Total Assets	1.3	2.2	2.2	1.9	1.7	1.3
1.3	1.0	1.0		.7	1.1	1.7	1.3	1.2	.9
3.7	3.9	3.6		3.4	4.8	2.7	3.3	3.3	4.8
(226) 6.7	(199) 6.9	(221) 7.0	% Depr., Dep., Amort./Sales	(16) 8.3	(35) 7.9	(26) 6.8	(35) 4.5	(62) 6.5	(47) 7.9
10.1	10.6	10.3		20.9	13.3	10.2	8.6	9.8	10.3
2.2	1.8	2.1			3.3	2.4	1.4	1.5	
(110) 4.2	(87) 4.1	(95) 3.5	% Officers', Directors' Owners' Comp/Sales		(25) 5.0	(18) 2.9	(17) 2.8	(24) 2.8	
6.7	6.1	5.1			9.0	4.4	5.9	4.5	
6715103M	6055821M	6261870M	Net Sales ($)	10979M	88992M	130380M	260321M	1058903M	4712295M
4126424M	5389744M	5375502M	Total Assets ($)	20142M	67762M	59841M	174470M	912921M	4140366M

M = $ thousand MM = $ million

See Pages 9 through 22 for Explanation of Ratios and Data

Current Data Sorted by Assets							Comparative Historical Data	
						Type of Statement		
		1	1	1		Unqualified	3	
		4	4			Reviewed	4	2
1	1	1				Compiled	7	7
4	5	3				Tax Returns	10	12
	3	3	6		1	Other	26	10
	2 (4/1-9/30/13)		37 (10/1/13-3/31/14)				4/1/09-3/31/10 ALL	4/1/10-3/31/11 ALL
0-500M	500M-2MM	2-10MM	10-50MM	50-100MM	100-250MM			
5	9	12	11	1	1	**NUMBER OF STATEMENTS**	50	31
%	%	%	%	%	%	**ASSETS**	%	%
		6.0	8.8			Cash & Equivalents	7.3	11.7
		22.0	30.3			Trade Receivables (net)	16.2	20.3
		1.7	4.3			Inventory	3.3	1.1
		1.0	.5			All Other Current	3.4	2.3
		30.7	43.8			Total Current	30.2	35.4
		57.8	41.8			Fixed Assets (net)	52.3	53.2
		5.2	6.9			Intangibles (net)	6.9	3.8
		6.4	7.5			All Other Non-Current	10.6	7.7
		100.0	100.0			Total	100.0	100.0
						LIABILITIES		
		1.9	4.5			Notes Payable-Short Term	6.5	5.4
		9.6	4.3			Cur. Mat.-L.T.D.	9.6	10.2
		12.2	13.0			Trade Payables	10.6	14.3
		.0	.3			Income Taxes Payable	.0	.0
		10.1	6.4			All Other Current	10.9	9.6
		33.7	28.5			Total Current	37.7	39.5
		36.2	20.7			Long-Term Debt	41.5	36.1
		.0	1.2			Deferred Taxes	.8	.5
		3.9	1.2			All Other Non-Current	2.5	9.4
		26.2	48.4			Net Worth	17.5	14.5
		100.0	100.0			Total Liabilties & Net Worth	100.0	100.0
						INCOME DATA		
		100.0	100.0			Net Sales	100.0	100.0
						Gross Profit		
		92.2	96.0			Operating Expenses	91.3	86.8
		7.8	4.0			Operating Profit	8.7	13.2
		1.5	1.0			All Other Expenses (net)	2.3	2.9
		6.3	3.1			Profit Before Taxes	6.4	10.3
						RATIOS		
		1.4	2.2				1.5	1.7
		1.0	1.4			Current	.8	.8
		.6	1.2				.4	.5
		1.4	2.0				1.1	1.7
		.9	1.3			Quick	.6	.8
		.5	1.1				.3	.3
		20 18.3	**29** 12.4				**7** 52.2	**13** 27.2
		38 9.7	**40** 9.1			Sales/Receivables	**31** 11.8	**33** 11.0
		47 7.8	**43** 8.4				**51** 7.1	**47** 7.7
						Cost of Sales/Inventory		
						Cost of Sales/Payables		
		22.5	9.5				19.8	10.9
		NM	21.3			Sales/Working Capital	-37.4	-30.2
		-11.9	37.3				-8.3	-7.1
		4.6	42.7				8.0	20.0
		(10) 3.4	(10) 10.0			EBIT/Interest	(46) 2.5	(28) 5.4
		1.0	1.0				1.1	2.0
						Net Profit + Depr., Dep., Amort./Cur. Mat. L/T/D		
		1.4	.5				1.1	.7
		2.8	1.1			Fixed/Worth	2.5	2.7
		18.1	1.7				-16.0	19.7
		1.5	.7				1.6	.8
		4.9	1.5			Debt/Worth	4.0	2.6
		22.9	3.7				-29.7	30.5
		193.2	42.5				53.1	62.7
		38.9	20.1			% Profit Before Taxes/Tangible Net Worth	(35) 29.2	(24) 21.0
		8.4	3.1				9.7	12.8
		11.9	13.4				20.6	20.8
		6.5	8.0			% Profit Before Taxes/Total Assets	7.3	6.9
		2.2	1.1				.4	2.8
		4.6	28.2				9.4	10.2
		3.2	3.2			Sales/Net Fixed Assets	3.8	4.4
		1.3	2.3				1.6	1.4
		2.3	4.4				2.9	3.3
		2.0	1.7			Sales/Total Assets	1.7	1.8
		1.0	1.5				1.0	.8
		5.6					2.6	2.7
		(10) 7.6				% Depr., Dep., Amort./Sales	(40) 7.4	(26) 8.9
		14.2					12.6	13.0
							2.1	3.0
						% Officers', Directors' Owners' Comp/Sales	(20) 3.4	(16) 4.2
							6.5	6.5
3670M	25587M	185953M	564250M	97812M	268805M	Net Sales ($)	616788M	448252M
1838M	9086M	52013M	176535M	86426M	211045M	Total Assets ($)	461201M	342906M

M = $ thousand MM = $ million

See Pages 9 through 22 for Explanation of Ratios and Data

Comparative Historical Data				Current Data Sorted by Sales					
			Type of Statement						
1		3	Unqualified				1		2
4	8	8	Reviewed				2	3	3
8	5	3	Compiled		2	1			
7	9	12	Tax Returns	5	5	1	1		
12	23	13	Other			5	2	3	3
4/1/11-3/31/12 ALL	4/1/12-3/31/13 ALL	4/1/13-3/31/14 ALL			2 (4/1-9/30/13)			37 (10/1/13-3/31/14)	
				0-1MM	1-3MM	3-5MM	5-10MM	10-25MM	25MM & OVER
32	45	39	**NUMBER OF STATEMENTS**	5	7	7	6	6	8
%	%	%	**ASSETS**	%	%	%	%	%	%
5.2	9.6	12.3	Cash & Equivalents						
22.8	25.3	23.6	Trade Receivables (net)						
1.7	2.4	2.4	Inventory						
2.3	2.6	1.1	All Other Current						
32.1	39.9	39.3	Total Current						
52.4	45.6	48.5	Fixed Assets (net)						
7.1	4.2	5.9	Intangibles (net)						
8.4	10.3	6.3	All Other Non-Current						
100.0	100.0	100.0	Total						
			LIABILITIES						
5.7	5.5	5.4	Notes Payable-Short Term						
9.5	6.8	6.6	Cur. Mat.-L.T.D.						
12.4	13.4	10.2	Trade Payables						
.0	.0	.1	Income Taxes Payable						
13.2	9.6	9.7	All Other Current						
40.8	35.4	32.0	Total Current						
35.1	20.7	33.0	Long-Term Debt						
.5	.0	.4	Deferred Taxes						
3.4	9.4	3.5	All Other Non-Current						
20.1	34.5	31.1	Net Worth						
100.0	100.0	100.0	Total Liabilties & Net Worth						
			INCOME DATA						
100.0	100.0	100.0	Net Sales						
			Gross Profit						
92.3	91.2	90.3	Operating Expenses						
7.7	8.8	9.7	Operating Profit						
2.6	1.0	2.5	All Other Expenses (net)						
5.1	7.8	7.2	Profit Before Taxes						
			RATIOS						
1.6	2.2	2.1							
.7	1.2	1.3	Current						
.5	.6	.8							
1.1	2.0	2.0							
.6	1.1	1.2	Quick						
.4	.5	.6							
2 217.0	**20** 17.9	**19** 18.8							
29 12.4	**37** 9.9	**36** 10.2	Sales/Receivables						
42 8.6	**51** 7.2	**43** 8.4							
			Cost of Sales/Inventory						
			Cost of Sales/Payables						
32.7	10.7	9.5							
-23.1	36.3	37.3	Sales/Working Capital						
-9.5	-16.2	-29.0							
11.7	25.7	15.1							
(29) 3.4	(38) 5.6	(33) 4.4	EBIT/Interest						
.4	1.1	1.4							
			Net Profit + Depr., Dep., Amort./Cur. Mat. L/T/D						
1.3	.6	.7							
4.3	1.5	1.7	Fixed/Worth						
95.5	7.3	4.9							
1.7	.7	.8							
5.2	1.8	2.0	Debt/Worth						
267.5	9.9	13.9							
104.9	78.9	61.3							
(25) 33.2	(39) 30.4	(34) 26.3	% Profit Before Taxes/Tangible Net Worth						
-5.4	7.6	6.4							
20.5	21.1	13.4							
5.6	11.4	7.3	% Profit Before Taxes/Total Assets						
-2.4	.4	1.7							
9.7	23.7	11.3							
3.9	4.3	4.6	Sales/Net Fixed Assets						
2.2	2.2	2.4							
4.0	4.2	3.1							
2.2	2.1	1.9	Sales/Total Assets						
1.3	1.3	1.3							
2.5	1.7	2.7							
(28) 8.1	(34) 5.5	(30) 6.7	% Depr., Dep., Amort./Sales						
12.8	9.3	10.7							
2.1	3.4	1.9							
(14) 3.5	(14) 4.7	(12) 2.7	% Officers', Directors' Owners' Comp/Sales						
5.7	7.6	6.0							
618033M	852775M	1146077M	Net Sales ($)	2100M	16019M	27550M	45353M	103988M	951067M
218051M	403891M	536943M	Total Assets ($)	6198M	9223M	11045M	36449M	66925M	407103M

M = $ thousand MM = $ million

See Pages 9 through 22 for Explanation of Ratios and Data

Current Data Sorted by Assets							Comparative Historical Data	
						Type of Statement		
		2	10		1	Unqualified	8	17
	2	6	7			Reviewed	14	16
		1	1			Compiled	8	5
1	2	3				Tax Returns	5	5
1	2	5	9	4	1	Other	23	28
7 (4/1-9/30/13)			51 (10/1/13-3/31/14)				4/1/09-3/31/10	4/1/10-3/31/11
0-500M	**500M-2MM**	**2-10MM**	**10-50MM**	**50-100MM**	**100-250MM**		**ALL**	**ALL**
2	6	17	27	4	2	**NUMBER OF STATEMENTS**	58	71
%	%	%	%	%	%	**ASSETS**	%	%
		12.3	17.8			Cash & Equivalents	8.2	9.3
		33.1	20.5			Trade Receivables (net)	25.2	28.7
		2.0	2.7			Inventory	1.7	2.6
		1.7	3.8			All Other Current	5.1	3.3
		49.2	44.8			Total Current	40.2	43.9
		37.1	37.1			Fixed Assets (net)	39.6	40.7
		5.9	8.6			Intangibles (net)	11.1	8.9
		7.8	9.5			All Other Non-Current	9.1	6.6
		100.0	100.0			Total	100.0	100.0
						LIABILITIES		
		4.8	4.4			Notes Payable-Short Term	7.5	2.8
		4.3	4.2			Cur. Mat.-L.T.D.	8.3	6.5
		17.0	8.8			Trade Payables	13.1	14.6
		.8	.1			Income Taxes Payable	.2	.1
		11.8	7.8			All Other Current	11.0	8.0
		38.6	25.3			Total Current	40.1	32.0
		16.7	15.4			Long-Term Debt	22.7	20.9
		.3	.8			Deferred Taxes	.9	1.0
		4.4	4.2			All Other Non-Current	4.7	3.5
		40.0	54.2			Net Worth	31.7	42.7
		100.0	100.0			Total Liabilties & Net Worth	100.0	100.0
						INCOME DATA		
		100.0	100.0			Net Sales	100.0	100.0
						Gross Profit		
		94.0	89.7			Operating Expenses	96.5	92.6
		6.0	10.3			Operating Profit	3.5	7.4
		.4	2.2			All Other Expenses (net)	1.4	1.0
		5.6	8.1			Profit Before Taxes	2.1	6.5
						RATIOS		
		1.8	4.7				1.8	1.8
		1.4	2.1			Current	1.2	1.4
		1.0	1.0				.7	1.0
		1.7	4.2				1.4	1.7
		1.2	1.6			Quick	1.0	1.2
		.9	.9				.6	.8
		29 12.6	**32** 11.4				**36** 10.1	**32** 11.3
		53 6.9	**42** 8.6			Sales/Receivables	**47** 7.7	**48** 7.6
		65 5.6	**74** 4.9				**62** 5.9	**68** 5.3
						Cost of Sales/Inventory		
						Cost of Sales/Payables		
		10.1	3.6				8.6	8.8
		16.2	6.1			Sales/Working Capital	31.5	20.8
		NM	89.3				-25.9	128.3
		21.0	28.5				11.1	18.4
		(14) 7.9	(23) 14.7			EBIT/Interest	(55) 3.6	(65) 6.4
		2.6	6.5				-.3	3.4
							4.4	6.9
						Net Profit + Depr., Dep., Amort./Cur. Mat. L/T/D	(17) 1.2	(18) 1.9
							.9	1.5
		.5	.5				.7	.6
		1.0	.7			Fixed/Worth	1.1	1.2
		1.6	1.7				3.5	2.9
		1.0	.6				1.0	1.0
		1.5	1.0			Debt/Worth	1.8	1.7
		4.2	2.4				18.7	3.4
		65.3	65.6				36.2	62.2
		(16) 30.9	20.4			% Profit Before Taxes/Tangible Net Worth	(45) 14.8	(66) 33.1
		8.9	7.4				-7.9	14.9
		20.9	14.1				14.3	19.8
		9.2	10.6			% Profit Before Taxes/Total Assets	6.0	10.2
		3.4	4.1				-3.2	4.5
		13.9	13.8				14.3	10.2
		7.0	3.3			Sales/Net Fixed Assets	5.0	5.6
		2.9	2.0				2.5	2.3
		2.7	2.3				2.5	2.7
		2.3	1.3			Sales/Total Assets	1.6	1.9
		1.7	.9				1.2	1.2
		2.2	3.5				3.9	2.1
		(15) 3.7	(24) 4.8			% Depr., Dep., Amort./Sales	(45) 5.3	(61) 4.1
		6.5	7.4				9.1	6.0
								1.4
						% Officers', Directors' Owners' Comp/Sales		(19) 3.2
								4.3
4932M	18340M	200972M	954900M	347787M	422687M	Net Sales ($)	1491693M	3659995M
469M	7307M	76762M	613509M	294191M	366572M	Total Assets ($)	1129551M	2401453M

M = $ thousand MM = $ million

See Pages 9 through 22 for Explanation of Ratios and Data

Comparative Historical Data

Current Data Sorted by Sales

						Type of Statement								
	13		8		13	Unqualified			1	1		3		8
	15		12		15	Reviewed		1	2	1		7		4
	9		4		2	Compiled						2		
	6		7		6	Tax Returns	2		2	1		1		
	22		25		22	Other			3	6		2		11
	4/1/11-3/31/12 ALL		4/1/12-3/31/13 ALL		4/1/13-3/31/14 ALL		7 (4/1-9/30/13)			51 (10/1/13-3/31/14)				
							0-1MM	1-3MM	3-5MM	5-10MM		10-25MM		25MM & OVER
	65		56		58	NUMBER OF STATEMENTS	2	1	8	9		15		23
	%		%		%	ASSETS	%	%	%	%		%		%
	10.6		13.4		14.2	Cash & Equivalents						11.6		16.6
	28.1		34.9		24.5	Trade Receivables (net)						32.2		23.0
	1.7		1.6		2.7	Inventory						3.5		2.9
	4.7		2.8		3.3	All Other Current						3.0		4.4
	45.0		52.7		44.7	Total Current						50.4		46.9
	38.3		29.2		35.6	Fixed Assets (net)						32.0		36.1
	10.0		9.1		9.6	Intangibles (net)						13.2		9.2
	6.7		9.1		10.1	All Other Non-Current						4.4		7.9
	100.0		100.0		100.0	Total						100.0		100.0
						LIABILITIES								
	5.4		6.6		3.7	Notes Payable-Short Term						2.9		3.0
	3.6		5.2		5.2	Cur. Mat.-L.T.D.						5.3		4.9
	11.3		14.4		11.7	Trade Payables						15.6		11.4
	.7		.3		.3	Income Taxes Payable						.0		.1
	12.5		12.4		8.9	All Other Current						8.6		11.7
	33.4		38.9		29.8	Total Current						32.4		31.1
	25.9		15.2		23.0	Long-Term Debt						11.9		17.8
	.9		.5		.8	Deferred Taxes						.0		1.8
	3.5		2.3		4.2	All Other Non-Current						1.7		3.1
	36.2		43.1		42.3	Net Worth						54.0		46.2
	100.0		100.0		100.0	Total Liabilties & Net Worth						100.0		100.0
						INCOME DATA								
	100.0		100.0		100.0	Net Sales						100.0		100.0
						Gross Profit								
	93.1		92.3		91.7	Operating Expenses						93.6		94.4
	6.9		7.7		8.3	Operating Profit						6.4		5.6
	2.0		.9		2.4	All Other Expenses (net)						4.8		1.9
	4.8		6.8		5.9	Profit Before Taxes						1.6		3.7
						RATIOS								
	2.1		2.4		3.2							2.5		2.6
	1.5		1.5		1.7	Current						1.6		1.1
	.9		.9		1.0							1.2		.9
	1.8		2.3		2.5							2.0		2.1
	1.3		1.4		1.4	Quick						1.4		1.0
	.8		.9		.9							1.1		.8
32	11.4	41	8.9	32	11.5						32	11.5	38	9.7
49	7.4	57	6.4	43	8.5	Sales/Receivables					63	5.8	42	8.7
69	5.3	65	5.6	69	5.3						78	4.7	69	5.3
						Cost of Sales/Inventory								
						Cost of Sales/Payables								
	7.6		7.1		5.8							3.5		5.8
	12.3		14.4		10.4	Sales/Working Capital						10.9		33.8
	-74.8		-90.6		-667.1							38.0		-156.1
	19.1		33.2		20.7							21.0		18.9
(56)	3.9	(50)	13.4	(48)	8.3	EBIT/Interest					(14)	12.5	(21)	8.5
	1.8		2.6		3.0							4.2		3.2
	5.3				33.7									
(13)	1.5			(12)	3.3	Net Profit + Depr., Dep., Amort./Cur. Mat. L/T/D								
	1.1				1.7									
	.4		.2		.5							.5		.5
	1.1		.7		.7	Fixed/Worth						.6		.7
	4.5		1.5		1.8							1.3		2.0
	.8		.8		.6							.6		.7
	1.9		1.5		1.3	Debt/Worth						1.3		1.3
	7.8		4.2		3.7							2.1		4.3
	50.0		73.7		65.8							47.0		72.4
(54)	19.3	(50)	27.8	(55)	28.2	% Profit Before Taxes/Tangible Net Worth					(14)	17.1		28.2
	8.0		11.6		7.4							7.0		6.4
	17.9		26.8		17.9							12.9		14.2
	6.3		14.6		8.7	% Profit Before Taxes/Total Assets						8.0		8.0
	2.2		4.5		2.8							4.0		2.9
	21.0		21.7		15.2							17.8		14.3
	6.6		6.8		4.4	Sales/Net Fixed Assets						3.8		3.5
	2.7		3.2		2.4							2.2		2.8
	2.9		3.1		2.5							2.6		2.9
	2.1		2.0		1.6	Sales/Total Assets						1.6		1.4
	1.2		1.3		1.1							.9		1.1
	1.9		1.0		2.5							2.2		3.1
(57)	4.2	(41)	2.9	(48)	4.8	% Depr., Dep., Amort./Sales						4.0	(21)	4.7
	7.0		5.5		6.9							7.0		6.2
	2.2		2.0		2.9									
(12)	3.5	(15)	5.7	(11)	5.6	% Officers', Directors' Owners' Comp/Sales								
	6.6		10.0		8.8									
	2094130M		1508760M		1949618M	Net Sales ($)	1151M	1498M	31607M	61974M		249204M		1604184M
	1584460M		1004056M		1358810M	Total Assets ($)	866M	834M	43093M	58272M		180654M		1075091M

M = $ thousand MM = $ million

See Pages 9 through 22 for Explanation of Ratios and Data

Current Data Sorted by Assets							Comparative Historical Data	
		3	8	4	4	**Type of Statement** Unqualified	31	22
	2	10	4			Reviewed	19	17
1	2	9	1			Compiled	13	13
1	2					Tax Returns	11	5
	6	4	4	4	3	Other	35	37
	10 (4/1-9/30/13)		62 (10/1/13-3/31/14)				4/1/09-3/31/10 ALL	4/1/10-3/31/11 ALL
0-500M	500M-2MM	2-10MM	10-50MM	50-100MM	100-250MM			
2	12	26	17	8	7	**NUMBER OF STATEMENTS**	109	94
%	%	%	%	%	%	**ASSETS**	%	%
	17.2	16.2	10.7			Cash & Equivalents	13.1	10.3
	26.2	14.8	11.6			Trade Receivables (net)	14.5	16.1
	1.0	.2	1.5			Inventory	1.4	1.6
	10.2	1.7	4.1			All Other Current	4.6	2.8
	54.5	32.9	27.8			Total Current	33.5	30.9
	35.6	40.8	52.2			Fixed Assets (net)	50.3	53.6
	5.6	5.6	9.5			Intangibles (net)	5.2	6.0
	4.3	20.7	10.5			All Other Non-Current	10.9	9.5
	100.0	100.0	100.0			Total	100.0	100.0
						LIABILITIES		
	6.0	2.7	4.3			Notes Payable-Short Term	5.5	4.2
	3.9	6.3	5.1			Cur. Mat.-L.T.D.	4.7	7.2
	12.6	6.6	5.9			Trade Payables	9.8	7.9
	.0	.0	.0			Income Taxes Payable	.1	.1
	29.2	9.0	12.8			All Other Current	12.0	9.4
	51.7	24.5	28.1			Total Current	32.1	28.9
	19.7	27.5	24.4			Long-Term Debt	29.0	24.6
	.0	.0	.3			Deferred Taxes	.8	.5
	2.4	12.0	12.3			All Other Non-Current	8.8	9.1
	26.2	35.9	34.9			Net Worth	29.3	37.0
	100.0	100.0	100.0			Total Liabilties & Net Worth	100.0	100.0
						INCOME DATA		
	100.0	100.0	100.0			Net Sales	100.0	100.0
						Gross Profit		
	89.1	85.8	87.7			Operating Expenses	91.2	89.4
	10.9	14.2	12.3			Operating Profit	8.8	10.6
	-.2	2.4	4.4			All Other Expenses (net)	3.1	2.6
	11.2	11.8	7.9			Profit Before Taxes	5.6	7.9
						RATIOS		
	4.5	3.1	1.6				2.8	2.2
	1.8	1.4	1.0			Current	1.3	1.1
	.5	.6	.6				.6	.5
	4.1	3.1	1.4				2.3	2.0
	1.0	1.3	.9			Quick	1.1	.9
	.5	.6	.5				.5	.5
	0 UND	**18** 19.9	**30** 12.3				**24** 15.4	**25** 14.4
	26 14.1	**33** 11.1	**37** 9.8			Sales/Receivables	**37** 10.0	**39** 9.3
	50 7.3	**45** 8.1	**54** 6.8				**50** 7.3	**54** 6.8
						Cost of Sales/Inventory		
						Cost of Sales/Payables		
	7.9	8.7	6.2				5.5	6.0
	44.5	19.1	999.8			Sales/Working Capital	24.3	69.2
	-11.4	-10.6	-11.5				-13.6	-7.2
		26.8	9.0				9.2	10.2
		(24) 9.3	2.2			EBIT/Interest	(91) 3.2	(81) 4.2
		1.6	-.3				.8	1.2
							3.4	3.5
						Net Profit + Depr., Dep., Amort./Cur. Mat. L/T/D	(30) 2.0	(28) 1.7
							1.4	1.3
	.3	.6	1.1				.8	.8
	1.1	1.3	1.5			Fixed/Worth	1.8	1.9
	1.7	NM	NM				8.8	7.2
	.4	.6	.8				.7	.8
	.7	1.5	1.5			Debt/Worth	2.1	1.9
	5.3	NM	NM				19.0	9.2
	145.6	94.0	35.9				38.6	42.5
	(10) 41.7	(20) 46.7	(13) 12.7			% Profit Before Taxes/Tangible Net Worth	(90) 15.8	(81) 21.8
	6.9	24.3	-10.9				-.1	5.0
	63.0	30.4	12.1				13.6	14.0
	21.8	15.6	2.7			% Profit Before Taxes/Total Assets	4.6	6.3
	1.6	1.7	-3.5				-.6	.4
	70.6	7.9	3.7				6.7	5.2
	16.6	3.8	2.2			Sales/Net Fixed Assets	2.2	2.0
	2.0	1.6	.8				1.0	.9
	3.8	2.4	1.4				2.4	2.1
	2.9	1.5	.7			Sales/Total Assets	1.2	1.1
	.9	.9	.5				.6	.5
		4.2	6.3				4.3	4.7
		(23) 6.2	(16) 11.0			% Depr., Dep., Amort./Sales	(92) 7.8	(88) 8.4
		12.0	15.8				14.0	15.1
							1.9	1.7
						% Officers', Directors' Owners' Comp/Sales	(30) 3.3	(22) 3.4
							5.0	4.1
1777M	48310M	219725M	410040M	587100M	545268M	Net Sales ($)	2108479M	1583555M
485M	15394M	133611M	420432M	519961M	900584M	Total Assets ($)	2675820M	1719610M

M = $ thousand MM = $ million

See Pages 9 through 22 for Explanation of Ratios and Data

Comparative Historical Data				Current Data Sorted by Sales					
			Type of Statement						
16	18	19	Unqualified			1	3	3	12
17	17	16	Reviewed			2	5	8	1
7	9	13	Compiled	1	3	1	5	3	
10	4	3	Tax Returns	2	1				
27	35	21	Other	1	5	3	1	3	8
4/1/11-3/31/12 ALL	4/1/12-3/31/13 ALL	4/1/13-3/31/14 ALL		10 (4/1-9/30/13)			62 (10/1/13-3/31/14)		
				0-1MM	1-3MM	3-5MM	5-10MM	10-25MM	25MM & OVER
77	83	72	**NUMBER OF STATEMENTS**	4	9	7	14	17	21
%	%	%	**ASSETS**	%	%	%	%	%	%
15.4	11.3	12.7	Cash & Equivalents				16.7	14.0	8.3
16.4	14.0	15.9	Trade Receivables (net)				18.4	17.0	12.0
2.6	2.2	1.0	Inventory				.2	1.4	1.5
3.4	1.8	3.8	All Other Current				3.0	3.2	2.3
37.8	29.2	33.3	Total Current				38.3	35.6	24.1
45.7	51.5	45.0	Fixed Assets (net)				40.2	45.4	49.5
6.5	6.9	7.5	Intangibles (net)				1.8	6.8	15.1
10.1	12.4	14.2	All Other Non-Current				19.7	12.2	11.3
100.0	100.0	100.0	Total				100.0	100.0	100.0
			LIABILITIES						
4.9	2.9	4.6	Notes Payable-Short Term				1.7	1.7	4.4
5.7	5.6	4.9	Cur. Mat.-L.T.D.				5.2	6.3	4.0
9.1	8.2	7.4	Trade Payables				11.1	7.0	7.4
.0	.0	.0	Income Taxes Payable				.0	.0	.0
7.7	7.4	14.0	All Other Current				12.4	7.1	10.6
27.5	24.0	30.8	Total Current				30.4	22.1	26.4
21.8	23.2	24.6	Long-Term Debt				25.8	23.4	26.9
.7	.5	.3	Deferred Taxes				.0	.0	1.0
9.6	12.7	9.5	All Other Non-Current				14.5	7.9	11.6
40.4	39.5	34.7	Net Worth				29.4	46.6	34.1
100.0	100.0	100.0	Total Liabilties & Net Worth				100.0	100.0	100.0
			INCOME DATA						
100.0	100.0	100.0	Net Sales				100.0	100.0	100.0
			Gross Profit						
88.9	88.8	89.1	Operating Expenses				89.5	90.5	95.6
11.1	11.2	10.9	Operating Profit				10.5	9.5	4.4
2.5	2.0	2.1	All Other Expenses (net)				1.2	.5	3.5
8.6	9.2	8.8	Profit Before Taxes				9.3	9.0	.8
			RATIOS						
2.7	2.2	2.3					2.7	2.4	1.4
1.3	1.1	1.2	Current				1.2	1.4	.8
.8	.7	.6					.5	1.0	.6
2.2	2.1	2.1					2.6	2.1	1.2
1.1	1.0	1.0	Quick				1.1	1.2	.7
.6	.6	.5					.5	.9	.5
24 15.4	22 16.7	23 15.7					24 15.1	18 19.8	31 11.8
34 10.8	36 10.0	34 10.8	Sales/Receivables				41 8.8	30 12.0	36 10.2
49 7.5	57 6.4	48 7.6					46 7.9	48 7.6	48 7.6
			Cost of Sales/Inventory						
			Cost of Sales/Payables						
6.1	7.7	10.0					4.5	10.1	18.6
24.0	32.6	49.8	Sales/Working Capital				49.0	23.9	-24.4
-15.6	-21.8	-11.6					-3.8	NM	-10.1
26.8	10.0	16.4					16.5	31.3	6.9
(67) 6.0	(73) 3.8	(64) 6.0	EBIT/Interest				8.6	(15) 9.2	2.7
2.6	-.1	.8					.4	-1.1	.3
14.0	14.9	5.1							
(15) 2.8	(16) 2.0	(14) 1.8	Net Profit + Depr., Dep., Amort./Cur. Mat. L/T/D						
1.5	.8	.7							
.7	.8	.7					.5	.6	1.3
1.3	1.6	1.5	Fixed/Worth				1.2	1.2	2.8
3.1	4.4	6.1					NM	1.7	NM
.5	.7	.6					.6	.7	1.2
1.7	1.8	1.6	Debt/Worth				2.7	1.2	3.5
4.8	5.2	6.6					NM	1.7	NM
44.9	58.4	58.4					66.0	75.0	19.5
(66) 21.2	(72) 19.3	(58) 22.1	% Profit Before Taxes/Tangible Net Worth				(11) 35.7	(15) 31.0	(16) 6.3
6.9	1.9	1.1					-1.8	-6.7	-20.1
18.4	17.9	23.0					23.4	40.8	3.9
7.2	4.8	5.5	% Profit Before Taxes/Total Assets				7.0	13.4	1.6
1.0	-.3	-.6					1.1	-2.0	-2.2
7.6	5.1	7.0					15.6	6.7	3.6
2.7	2.0	2.8	Sales/Net Fixed Assets				2.8	4.1	1.7
1.4	.8	1.1					1.3	1.9	1.0
2.4	1.8	2.4					1.8	2.8	1.5
1.1	.8	1.2	Sales/Total Assets				1.3	1.6	1.0
.7	.4	.6					.7	.6	.5
3.4	4.0	4.5					4.1	4.5	4.9
(62) 7.2	(74) 7.8	(60) 7.6	% Depr., Dep., Amort./Sales				(13) 6.2	(16) 6.5	(18) 8.5
12.9	14.6	14.0					11.0	17.5	13.0
1.8	1.9	1.0							
(17) 3.2	(20) 3.2	(13) 2.2	% Officers', Directors' Owners' Comp/Sales						
4.5	4.6	3.5							
1885343M	1717690M	1812220M	Net Sales ($)	3145M	16501M	31900M	97256M	243021M	1420397M
2169838M	2075376M	1990467M	Total Assets ($)	5968M	15463M	43528M	97455M	262525M	1565528M

M = $ thousand MM = $ million

See Pages 9 through 22 for Explanation of Ratios and Data

Current Data Sorted by Assets | **Comparative Historical Data**

0-500M	500M-2MM	2-10MM	10-50MM	50-100MM	100-250MM	Type of Statement	4/1/09-3/31/10 ALL	4/1/10-3/31/11 ALL
		1	3	2	2	Unqualified	10	6
	3	4	1			Reviewed	5	2
	3	3				Compiled	5	6
4	6	5				Tax Returns	7	12
3	4	11	4	4	1	Other	16	18
	10 (4/1-9/30/13)		54 (10/1/13-3/31/14)					
7	16	24	8	6	3	NUMBER OF STATEMENTS	43	44
%	%	%	%	%	%	ASSETS	%	%
	18.1	6.6				Cash & Equivalents	10.0	11.2
	20.7	18.1				Trade Receivables (net)	16.0	16.5
	.7	1.6				Inventory	2.2	2.2
	1.2	3.6				All Other Current	2.8	5.5
	40.7	29.8				Total Current	31.1	35.3
	36.6	52.8				Fixed Assets (net)	54.6	49.0
	6.3	3.8				Intangibles (net)	6.2	4.0
	16.4	13.6				All Other Non-Current	8.1	11.7
	100.0	100.0				Total	100.0	100.0
						LIABILITIES		
	7.2	7.4				Notes Payable-Short Term	4.8	5.8
	7.1	5.1				Cur. Mat.-L.T.D.	5.0	5.9
	13.9	8.2				Trade Payables	10.7	9.6
	.7	.0				Income Taxes Payable	.1	.1
	8.8	10.1				All Other Current	10.2	10.5
	37.8	30.8				Total Current	30.8	31.9
	33.7	31.3				Long-Term Debt	27.7	27.1
	.3	.5				Deferred Taxes	1.3	.0
	3.9	8.3				All Other Non-Current	9.4	11.2
	24.3	29.1				Net Worth	30.8	29.8
	100.0	100.0				Total Liabilties & Net Worth	100.0	100.0
						INCOME DATA		
	100.0	100.0				Net Sales	100.0	100.0
						Gross Profit		
	88.5	89.9				Operating Expenses	90.3	88.0
	11.5	10.1				Operating Profit	9.7	12.0
	2.1	2.8				All Other Expenses (net)	3.7	3.5
	9.3	7.3				Profit Before Taxes	6.0	8.5
						RATIOS		
	2.4	1.9				Current	2.3	2.0
	.9	.9					1.3	1.3
	.2	.5					.8	1.0
	2.3	1.4				Quick	1.6	1.6
	.9	.7					1.1	1.1
	.2	.4					.5	.7
	0 UND	21 17.0				Sales/Receivables	26 14.2	22 16.5
	2 238.7	38 9.7					37 10.0	32 11.3
	45 8.2	54 6.8					60 6.1	42 8.7
						Cost of Sales/Inventory		
						Cost of Sales/Payables		
	10.6	6.9				Sales/Working Capital	11.3	8.6
	-363.3	-60.0					26.2	32.1
	-8.5	-9.9					-26.7	-303.9
	38.0	22.5				EBIT/Interest	12.0	17.8
	(13) 6.2	(23) 4.5					(38) 1.4	(39) 4.8
	.8	.2					-.9	1.5
						Net Profit + Depr., Dep., Amort./Cur. Mat. L/T/D		
	.3	.7				Fixed/Worth	.8	.8
	1.4	2.0					1.5	1.6
	NM	6.3					10.3	11.7
	1.0	1.3				Debt/Worth	.7	1.0
	5.1	2.5					2.5	2.1
	NM	8.3					13.1	14.9
	113.3	60.6				% Profit Before Taxes/Tangible Net Worth	54.0	57.9
	(12) 23.7	(19) 8.9					(33) 11.8	(35) 29.9
	19.5	-6.2					-3.9	5.0
	19.8	14.8				% Profit Before Taxes/Total Assets	17.4	20.3
	8.5	4.6					1.9	6.4
	-1.5	-2.5					-4.8	1.5
	46.8	7.6				Sales/Net Fixed Assets	3.9	11.2
	10.2	2.9					2.3	2.9
	5.4	1.5					1.2	1.3
	5.7	2.6				Sales/Total Assets	1.9	2.7
	3.1	1.7					1.2	1.3
	2.1	.8					.8	.9
		3.4				% Depr., Dep., Amort./Sales	4.6	3.3
		(21) 6.9					(33) 7.1	(33) 6.0
		14.2					13.1	10.9
						% Officers', Directors' Owners' Comp/Sales		2.1
								(13) 3.9
								5.6
12065M	73332M	172217M	350715M	450362M	217581M	Net Sales ($)	1176923M	866797M
2009M	20920M	107194M	282291M	443827M	359978M	Total Assets ($)	1165373M	751386M

M = $ thousand MM = $ million

See Pages 9 through 22 for Explanation of Ratios and Data

Comparative Historical Data				Current Data Sorted by Sales					
			Type of Statement						
10	8	8	Unqualified		1		2	1	4
8	13	8	Reviewed		2	2	3		1
8	5	6	Compiled	3		2		1	
17	11	15	Tax Returns	2	2	2	7	2	
25	35	27	Other	4	3	2	5	5	8
4/1/11-3/31/12 ALL	4/1/12-3/31/13 ALL	4/1/13-3/31/14 ALL		10 (4/1-9/30/13)			54 (10/1/13-3/31/14)		
				0-1MM	1-3MM	3-5MM	5-10MM	10-25MM	25MM & OVER
68	72	64	**NUMBER OF STATEMENTS**	9	8	8	17	9	13
%	%	%	**ASSETS**	%	%	%	%	%	%
12.7	11.2	10.8	Cash & Equivalents				13.6		8.1
21.8	21.5	17.9	Trade Receivables (net)				20.7		15.7
2.3	3.5	1.6	Inventory				.3		1.4
3.8	3.8	3.1	All Other Current				1.2		2.7
40.5	40.0	33.5	Total Current				35.9		27.9
44.6	47.4	47.8	Fixed Assets (net)				41.6		54.0
8.6	5.5	5.6	Intangibles (net)				1.7		10.5
6.3	7.2	13.2	All Other Non-Current				20.8		7.5
100.0	100.0	100.0	Total				100.0		100.0
			LIABILITIES						
5.7	5.6	8.0	Notes Payable-Short Term				11.1		5.2
5.3	4.9	6.2	Cur. Mat.-L.T.D.				3.5		6.3
11.7	11.3	9.0	Trade Payables				12.1		7.6
.0	.2	.2	Income Taxes Payable				.0		.1
9.3	10.5	8.3	All Other Current				2.6		9.5
32.1	32.4	31.7	Total Current				29.4		28.8
29.7	25.4	36.3	Long-Term Debt				35.0		39.9
.3	.5	.5	Deferred Taxes				.0		.0
10.3	7.9	9.2	All Other Non-Current				3.6		1.5
27.6	33.8	22.3	Net Worth				32.0		29.9
100.0	100.0	100.0	Total Liabilties & Net Worth				100.0		100.0
			INCOME DATA						
100.0	100.0	100.0	Net Sales				100.0		100.0
			Gross Profit						
90.3	90.0	91.8	Operating Expenses				92.6		93.1
9.7	10.0	8.2	Operating Profit				7.4		6.9
1.5	1.4	2.2	All Other Expenses (net)				.1		2.6
8.2	8.6	6.0	Profit Before Taxes				7.3		4.3
			RATIOS						
2.7	2.4	2.1					3.0		1.5
1.4	1.2	.9	Current				.9		.9
.9	.8	.5					.5		.6
2.5	2.0	1.6					3.0		1.2
1.2	1.0	.8	Quick				.8		.8
.7	.6	.5					.5		.5
21 17.6	22 16.5	8 44.3					0 UND		34 10.7
42 8.7	41 8.8	33 11.0	Sales/Receivables				28 13.0		41 9.0
51 7.1	55 6.6	52 7.0					51 7.1		60 6.1
			Cost of Sales/Inventory						
			Cost of Sales/Payables						
8.7	7.6	7.4					13.7		10.5
25.8	26.7	-100.5	Sales/Working Capital				-104.4		-66.6
-45.1	-24.6	-10.1					-10.6		-10.4
16.9	14.8	13.1					18.0		9.3
(65) 6.9	(68) 6.8	(58) 4.3	EBIT/Interest				(15) 7.5		2.0
1.8	1.7	.2					1.0		.3
	2.5	4.5							
	(13) 1.9	(11) .9	Net Profit + Depr., Dep., Amort./Cur. Mat. L/T/D						
	.9	-.3							
.6	.8	.9					.6		1.2
1.7	1.6	2.3	Fixed/Worth				.8		1.4
9.5	6.1	-9.2					4.0		NM
.7	.7	1.3					1.4		1.3
2.2	1.9	3.1	Debt/Worth				3.2		2.4
13.7	7.0	-18.8					11.5		NM
75.4	66.9	60.6					106.4		42.3
(55) 37.0	(57) 28.9	(47) 20.7	% Profit Before Taxes/Tangible Net Worth				(15) 50.5		(10) 22.6
12.4	6.3	3.0					9.1		-2.0
23.6	20.9	14.9					31.9		10.9
9.4	11.6	6.4	% Profit Before Taxes/Total Assets				14.1		4.6
2.1	2.5	-2.3					.3		-2.4
8.3	10.0	12.6					50.5		2.7
4.3	4.0	3.8	Sales/Net Fixed Assets				7.7		1.9
2.0	1.9	1.8					1.9		1.9
2.8	2.5	3.0					5.3		1.4
1.8	1.8	1.7	Sales/Total Assets				2.7		1.2
1.1	1.2	1.0					1.4		1.0
2.0	2.4	3.1					4.1		4.2
(55) 5.8	(55) 5.2	(48) 6.7	% Depr., Dep., Amort./Sales				(11) 6.4		(10) 5.6
10.0	7.9	10.9					20.8		8.6
2.2	1.5	2.0							
(21) 3.0	(27) 3.2	(15) 3.7	% Officers', Directors' Owners' Comp/Sales						
4.5	3.9	5.8							
1361571M	1230297M	1276272M	Net Sales ($)	4516M	18016M	30748M	115430M	152344M	955218M
1083536M	909327M	1216219M	Total Assets ($)	10979M	26453M	18265M	198031M	85084M	877407M

M = $ thousand MM = $ million

See Pages 9 through 22 for Explanation of Ratios and Data

Current Data Sorted by Assets							Comparative Historical Data	
						Type of Statement		
	1	4	7	2	4	Unqualified	21	25
4	8	30	4			Reviewed	34	35
1	7	6				Compiled	11	15
3	5	5	1			Tax Returns	18	16
3	15	23	12	5	8	Other	38	39
22 (4/1-9/30/13)		136 (10/1/13-3/31/14)					4/1/09-3/31/10 ALL	4/1/10-3/31/11 ALL
0-500M	500M-2MM	2-10MM	10-50MM	50-100MM	100-250MM			
11	36	68	24	7	12	**NUMBER OF STATEMENTS**	122	130
%	%	%	%	%	%	**ASSETS**	%	%
22.8	10.0	11.4	8.4		5.2	Cash & Equivalents	11.5	11.6
30.4	43.7	43.7	34.8		27.6	Trade Receivables (net)	37.0	37.8
.0	1.1	3.2	1.4		1.0	Inventory	2.8	3.1
5.6	4.9	3.7	8.7		4.4	All Other Current	5.3	7.7
58.8	59.7	61.9	53.3		38.2	Total Current	56.7	60.3
31.7	25.3	25.6	28.3		22.9	Fixed Assets (net)	30.0	25.6
.4	4.3	4.6	6.6		34.1	Intangibles (net)	4.8	6.4
9.1	10.7	7.8	11.8		4.9	All Other Non-Current	8.6	7.7
100.0	100.0	100.0	100.0		100.0	Total	100.0	100.0
						LIABILITIES		
7.3	10.7	9.0	5.1		4.5	Notes Payable-Short Term	11.7	9.5
1.1	2.6	5.8	3.6		3.1	Cur. Mat.-L.T.D.	6.2	7.4
15.0	9.9	12.1	17.2		10.8	Trade Payables	14.1	15.0
.0	.2	.4	.5		1.8	Income Taxes Payable	.6	.2
33.4	12.4	11.1	11.8		10.4	All Other Current	9.7	11.6
56.7	35.8	38.5	38.1		30.6	Total Current	42.2	43.7
8.5	14.1	16.2	15.4		26.8	Long-Term Debt	21.7	17.8
.0	.1	.6	.8		3.8	Deferred Taxes	.9	.6
7.4	1.6	2.3	1.8		2.9	All Other Non-Current	5.7	6.2
27.3	48.3	42.5	43.8		35.9	Net Worth	29.4	31.6
100.0	100.0	100.0	100.0		100.0	Total Liabilities & Net Worth	100.0	100.0
						INCOME DATA		
100.0	100.0	100.0	100.0		100.0	Net Sales	100.0	100.0
						Gross Profit		
95.0	90.5	94.4	93.9		97.3	Operating Expenses	95.9	94.8
5.0	9.5	5.6	6.1		2.7	Operating Profit	4.1	5.2
.0	-.1	.3	-.4		2.9	All Other Expenses (net)	1.1	.9
5.0	9.6	5.3	6.5		-.2	Profit Before Taxes	3.0	4.2
						RATIOS		
15.0	3.1	2.9	1.9		1.7		2.5	2.2
1.6	2.0	1.6	1.6		1.3	Current	1.5	1.5
.7	1.2	1.2	1.1		.9		1.1	1.1
15.0	2.9	2.3	1.6		1.3		2.2	2.0
1.3	1.9	1.5	1.2		1.0	Quick	1.3	1.2
.6	.9	1.0	1.0		.8		.8	.8
0 UND	**30** 12.2	**51** 7.1	**56** 6.5		**66** 5.5		**35** 10.3	**41** 8.9
23 16.0	**62** 5.9	**76** 4.8	**72** 5.1		**81** 4.5	Sales/Receivables	**60** 6.1	**67** 5.5
48 7.6	**81** 4.5	**96** 3.8	**89** 4.1		**94** 3.9		**85** 4.3	**83** 4.4
						Cost of Sales/Inventory		
						Cost of Sales/Payables		
6.9	6.7	4.7	6.4		9.0		6.3	6.0
15.1	11.8	10.8	9.8		15.5	Sales/Working Capital	13.4	11.3
-20.7	41.4	35.9	34.7		NM		84.8	76.2
	44.3	29.3	26.8		3.8		10.5	15.6
	(30) 11.1	(60) 7.5	9.8		1.7	EBIT/Interest	(107) 3.2	(117) 5.3
	4.0	3.5	6.0		-1.2		-.6	1.6
		5.2					5.1	6.3
		(10) 3.7				Net Profit + Depr., Dep., Amort./Cur. Mat. L/T/D	(32) 2.1	(23) 2.6
		1.8					.5	1.2
.2	.2	.2	.3		2.5		.3	.2
.7	.5	.6	.6		-2.3	Fixed/Worth	.7	.8
2.9	.9	1.3	1.7		-.2		3.2	3.4
.1	.4	.5	.9		3.7		.7	.8
1.4	1.1	1.8	1.2		-7.8	Debt/Worth	1.6	2.1
5.0	2.5	3.4	3.3		-2.9		6.5	9.2
	94.0	48.9	44.0				47.6	47.6
	(33) 48.4	(63) 28.0	(23) 17.0			% Profit Before Taxes/Tangible Net Worth	(98) 19.3	(107) 25.7
	12.2	10.1	6.5				-4.9	10.4
29.1	38.1	17.5	14.1		7.2		18.0	17.7
3.3	15.0	9.3	7.7		2.1	% Profit Before Taxes/Total Assets	5.8	7.6
.0	2.7	3.4	2.1		-4.7		-2.6	1.8
44.0	49.5	24.0	16.3		15.1		28.1	35.0
26.3	17.7	11.4	5.8		6.7	Sales/Net Fixed Assets	9.6	12.1
7.3	6.2	4.7	3.4		3.6		3.9	5.0
11.6	3.6	2.7	2.0		1.7		3.2	2.9
4.1	2.4	2.1	1.7		1.1	Sales/Total Assets	2.1	2.1
2.3	1.9	1.5	1.5		.9		1.5	1.5
	.6	1.0	.7				1.4	1.1
	(24) 1.9	(61) 2.3	(23) 3.0			% Depr., Dep., Amort./Sales	(103) 2.9	(104) 2.1
	3.3	4.3	6.0				5.8	4.1
	2.8	1.1					2.8	1.5
	(19) 5.3	(28) 2.2				% Officers', Directors' Owners' Comp/Sales	(51) 5.8	(59) 3.0
	8.2	5.1					10.1	6.2
22605M	135407M	748216M	841776M	560999M	2632118M	Net Sales ($)	2213531M	3957630M
3196M	44099M	341203M	451927M	422282M	2103757M	Total Assets ($)	1684133M	2402559M

M = $ thousand MM = $ million

See Pages 9 through 22 for Explanation of Ratios and Data

Comparative Historical Data / Current Data Sorted by Sales

4/1/11-3/31/12 ALL	4/1/12-3/31/13 ALL	4/1/13-3/31/14 ALL	Type of Statement	0-1MM	1-3MM	3-5MM	5-10MM	10-25MM	25MM & OVER
28	17	18	Unqualified				1	5	12
40	39	46	Reviewed	1	4	6	15	17	3
11	9	14	Compiled		6	3	5		
18	7	14	Tax Returns	1	4	1	4	4	
45	52	66	Other	5	8	7	13	15	18
					22 (4/1-9/30/13)		136 (10/1/13-3/31/14)		
142	124	158	NUMBER OF STATEMENTS	7	22	17	38	41	33
%	%	%	**ASSETS**	%	%	%	%	%	%
11.7	10.4	11.0	Cash & Equivalents		11.2	7.7	15.6	9.9	7.9
42.9	39.1	39.3	Trade Receivables (net)		38.1	43.3	39.1	46.5	33.8
2.2	2.5	2.0	Inventory		.7	.7	4.2	1.9	1.7
4.2	5.8	4.9	All Other Current		4.0	2.7	2.6	4.9	7.4
61.0	57.7	57.2	Total Current		53.9	54.4	61.5	63.3	50.8
26.0	25.7	25.8	Fixed Assets (net)		26.4	29.3	23.6	23.0	24.4
5.5	7.1	8.0	Intangibles (net)		5.2	6.9	3.7	6.7	18.7
7.5	9.6	8.9	All Other Non-Current		14.4	9.4	11.2	7.0	6.0
100.0	100.0	100.0	Total		100.0	100.0	100.0	100.0	100.0
			LIABILITIES						
9.0	8.8	8.1	Notes Payable-Short Term		9.7	7.2	7.1	11.2	4.7
4.1	3.4	4.0	Cur. Mat.-L.T.D.		2.5	4.2	2.9	6.6	3.6
12.9	13.5	12.4	Trade Payables		11.5	9.9	10.7	15.2	14.3
.4	.6	.4	Income Taxes Payable		.0	.1	.1	.9	.8
11.1	8.5	12.8	All Other Current		10.2	11.3	10.8	10.2	12.0
37.6	34.8	37.7	Total Current		33.9	32.7	31.7	44.1	35.4
17.9	16.5	15.5	Long-Term Debt		13.5	25.1	14.0	11.9	18.4
.7	1.1	.8	Deferred Taxes		.0	1.1	.2	.5	2.4
4.9	3.5	3.0	All Other Non-Current		6.2	2.4	2.0	2.2	4.0
39.0	44.2	43.0	Net Worth		46.4	38.7	52.2	41.3	39.8
100.0	100.0	100.0	Total Liabilties & Net Worth		100.0	100.0	100.0	100.0	100.0
			INCOME DATA						
100.0	100.0	100.0	Net Sales		100.0	100.0	100.0	100.0	100.0
			Gross Profit						
93.4	94.0	94.0	Operating Expenses		93.8	93.0	96.3	94.0	96.0
6.6	6.0	6.0	Operating Profit		6.2	7.0	3.7	6.0	4.0
.8	.3	.3	All Other Expenses (net)		-.9	.4	-.1	.3	1.3
5.8	5.6	5.6	Profit Before Taxes		7.1	6.6	3.8	5.7	2.6
			RATIOS						
2.5	2.4	2.6			3.7	2.5	4.0	2.2	2.0
1.5	1.7	1.6	Current		1.9	2.0	1.9	1.5	1.4
1.2	1.1	1.2			1.1	1.1	1.2	1.2	1.1
2.3	2.1	2.3			3.7	2.3	3.4	2.0	1.5
1.4	1.4	1.4	Quick		1.8	1.9	1.8	1.4	1.1
1.0	.9	1.0			.7	1.0	.9	1.1	.9
45 8.2	**44** 8.3	**48** 7.6			**21** 17.1	**64** 5.7	**46** 8.0	**58** 6.3	**55** 6.6
69 5.3	**66** 5.5	**69** 5.3	Sales/Receivables		**50** 7.3	**76** 4.8	**64** 5.7	**74** 4.9	**74** 4.9
96 3.8	**94** 3.9	**91** 4.0			**85** 4.3	**99** 3.7	**87** 4.2	**101** 3.6	**89** 4.1
			Cost of Sales/Inventory						
			Cost of Sales/Payables						
5.5	5.6	5.3			7.2	4.8	4.1	6.9	6.7
10.3	11.5	10.8	Sales/Working Capital		12.4	8.5	9.8	14.1	12.5
33.4	35.6	38.9			162.9	NM	26.3	26.3	47.1
26.7	25.1	27.0			31.6	11.9	44.7	20.7	16.0
(128) 8.3	(112) 5.6	(135) 7.4	EBIT/Interest		(17) 13.6	6.4	(33) 11.8	(34) 7.5	5.9
2.2	1.4	2.4			-4.6	3.8	3.1	4.5	1.3
6.1	8.9	5.2							3.8
(30) 2.8	(29) 2.7	(27) 3.1	Net Profit + Depr., Dep., Amort./Cur. Mat. L/T/D						(10) 2.1
.8	1.8	1.3							.0
.3	.2	.3			.2	.3	.1	.2	.5
.6	.6	.6	Fixed/Worth		.5	.6	.5	.6	1.2
1.9	2.3	1.7			2.4	25.2	.9	1.2	-2.3
.6	.4	.6			.2	.8	.3	.7	1.0
1.7	1.5	1.6	Debt/Worth		1.2	1.9	1.0	1.6	2.7
5.6	4.6	3.6			4.3	28.3	3.3	2.5	-7.8
56.1	55.1	54.2			117.7	53.9	46.8	51.2	50.9
(124) 24.8	(108) 24.0	(137) 25.5	% Profit Before Taxes/Tangible Net Worth		(19) 43.0	(14) 19.8	(37) 19.0	(38) 27.7	(23) 25.9
8.7	2.5	6.6			.0	11.3	3.4	14.3	5.5
24.6	17.1	17.7			40.9	16.7	18.6	17.2	13.9
9.4	8.5	8.4	% Profit Before Taxes/Total Assets		12.6	6.5	9.5	9.2	5.9
2.5	1.2	1.8			-.9	2.0	1.6	3.9	.6
31.8	31.9	26.8			34.2	19.9	29.3	32.3	17.7
11.0	10.0	10.9	Sales/Net Fixed Assets		16.8	8.3	13.5	11.0	7.6
4.7	4.5	4.6			4.3	4.3	4.4	6.7	3.9
3.3	2.8	2.8			3.3	2.4	3.1	3.3	2.1
2.1	1.9	2.0	Sales/Total Assets		2.3	2.1	1.9	2.5	1.7
1.4	1.4	1.5			1.6	1.2	1.4	1.8	1.1
1.2	1.0	1.0			.6	1.7	1.2	.7	1.2
(109) 2.9	(98) 2.5	(126) 2.3	% Depr., Dep., Amort./Sales		(18) 2.1	(13) 3.7	(29) 3.1	(37) 1.7	(26) 3.4
4.2	4.9	4.4			4.3	7.9	4.4	3.2	5.4
2.1	1.7	1.3			4.1		1.4	.9	
(53) 4.3	(50) 3.9	(58) 3.7	% Officers', Directors' Owners' Comp/Sales		(13) 6.1		(13) 2.9	(19) 1.6	
7.5	8.4	6.9			10.3		5.1	2.9	
3693904M	3200744M	4941121M	Net Sales ($)	2497M	41408M	60330M	273704M	661605M	3901577M
2548224M	2165044M	3366464M	Total Assets ($)	2358M	19724M	49909M	194664M	337891M	2761918M

M = $ thousand MM = $ million

See Pages 9 through 22 for Explanation of Ratios and Data

	Current Data Sorted by Assets						Comparative Historical Data	
Type of Statement								
Unqualified			2	8		1	14	19
Reviewed	1	2	9	10	1		21	20
Compiled	1	1	6	2		1	16	21
Tax Returns	5	5	4	1			13	7
Other	3	8	14	9	1	2	31	30
		13 (4/1-9/30/13)		84 (10/1/13-3/31/14)			4/1/09-3/31/10	4/1/10-3/31/11
	0-500M	500M-2MM	2-10MM	10-50MM	50-100MM	100-250MM	ALL	ALL
NUMBER OF STATEMENTS	10	16	35	30	2	4	95	97
ASSETS	%	%	%	%	%	%	%	%
Cash & Equivalents	31.1	10.1	12.8	8.7			10.3	12.5
Trade Receivables (net)	32.5	20.9	22.2	19.5			18.1	19.0
Inventory	5.0	5.2	9.4	10.7			8.4	8.2
All Other Current	1.9	2.6	2.4	2.5			4.0	4.1
Total Current	70.6	38.9	46.8	41.3			40.8	43.8
Fixed Assets (net)	28.7	46.6	43.8	44.4			47.6	41.3
Intangibles (net)	.1	2.1	2.5	3.2			3.7	7.5
All Other Non-Current	.7	12.4	6.9	11.1			8.0	7.4
Total	100.0	100.0	100.0	100.0			100.0	100.0
LIABILITIES								
Notes Payable-Short Term	36.2	11.8	8.3	6.1			7.6	8.2
Cur. Mat.-L.T.D.	10.6	6.1	6.4	6.6			6.0	4.7
Trade Payables	10.9	16.1	14.3	11.7			11.8	9.8
Income Taxes Payable	.0	.4	.0	.3			.2	.1
All Other Current	26.2	15.7	6.7	9.6			9.8	7.6
Total Current	84.0	50.1	35.7	34.3			35.4	30.5
Long-Term Debt	32.4	36.8	22.7	26.6			29.1	20.7
Deferred Taxes	.0	.1	.6	.3			.2	.5
All Other Non-Current	1.6	3.7	3.1	8.2			7.2	6.2
Net Worth	-17.9	9.4	37.9	30.6			28.0	42.1
Total Liabilities & Net Worth	100.0	100.0	100.0	100.0			100.0	100.0
INCOME DATA								
Net Sales	100.0	100.0	100.0	100.0			100.0	100.0
Gross Profit								
Operating Expenses	97.8	95.9	94.2	95.9			95.3	88.6
Operating Profit	2.2	4.1	5.8	4.1			4.7	11.4
All Other Expenses (net)	-2.1	2.0	3.3	1.1			2.1	3.7
Profit Before Taxes	4.3	2.2	2.5	2.9			2.6	7.7
RATIOS								
Current	2.7	1.5	2.5	2.2			1.8	2.6
	1.0	.9	1.1	1.4			1.1	1.5
	.6	.3	.7	.7			.7	.7
Quick	2.6	1.3	2.3	1.5			1.3	1.8
	1.0	.7	.8	.9			.8	.8
	.5	.3	.4	.7			.4	.5
Sales/Receivables	**0** UND	**0** UND	**12** 30.2	**29** 12.8			**19** 19.0	**14** 26.3
	26 14.2	**14** 25.7	**32** 11.4	**38** 9.7			**36** 10.1	**33** 10.9
	36 10.0	**29** 12.4	**40** 9.2	**49** 7.5			**47** 7.8	**49** 7.4
Cost of Sales/Inventory								
Cost of Sales/Payables								
Sales/Working Capital	13.6	25.7	7.3	6.8			11.2	8.4
	669.3	-60.9	76.0	21.5			84.9	33.3
	-34.7	-14.4	-14.4	-14.3			-14.3	-17.3
EBIT/Interest		17.4	16.8	7.9			7.3	17.6
		(13) 9.0	(32) 5.0	4.0			(90) 2.6	(80) 6.4
		.3	.3	.8			-.2	2.4
Net Profit + Depr., Dep., Amort./Cur. Mat. L/T/D							7.1	10.5
							(18) 2.0	(27) 1.9
							1.2	1.2
Fixed/Worth	.0	.4	.5	.7			.7	.5
	.6	1.6	1.5	1.7			1.7	1.5
	-.3	NM	3.9	4.6			4.1	4.4
Debt/Worth	.7	1.5	.6	.9			1.0	.6
	13.9	4.2	2.0	2.0			2.2	1.8
	-2.0	NM	5.5	10.0			5.5	6.2
% Profit Before Taxes/Tangible Net Worth		145.1	52.0	53.7			33.3	80.7
		(12) 35.4	(31) 13.1	(27) 16.3			(82) 15.2	(82) 28.7
		-25.2	5.3	-.2			1.3	10.1
% Profit Before Taxes/Total Assets	63.7	37.1	19.3	7.8			9.7	26.7
	31.2	19.3	3.8	5.0			4.1	12.0
	-12.8	-3.6	-.2	-.9			-1.8	3.6
Sales/Net Fixed Assets	UND	50.9	14.5	6.9			10.9	19.0
	22.2	18.4	6.5	5.0			3.6	5.8
	9.6	3.5	2.7	1.7			2.0	2.2
Sales/Total Assets	7.3	7.4	4.3	2.7			3.0	3.4
	4.7	5.9	2.3	1.4			1.6	1.9
	3.7	2.7	1.2	.9			1.1	1.2
% Depr., Dep., Amort./Sales		1.5	.7	1.6			2.2	1.7
		(11) 3.4	(32) 4.0	(29) 3.6			(81) 4.8	(83) 3.3
		5.0	8.4	7.6			8.5	7.4
% Officers', Directors' Owners' Comp/Sales			.8				.7	1.0
			(15) 1.4				(26) 2.6	(23) 2.6
			3.8				4.8	5.4
Net Sales ($)	17556M	126183M	434894M	1294158M	318221M	1228794M	2297197M	2541930M
Total Assets ($)	2803M	16735M	165798M	716057M	139291M	590985M	1209899M	1473549M

M = $ thousand MM = $ million

See Pages 9 through 22 for Explanation of Ratios and Data

Comparative Historical Data | Current Data Sorted by Sales

4/1/11-3/31/12 ALL	4/1/12-3/31/13 ALL	4/1/13-3/31/14 ALL	Type of Statement	0-1MM	1-3MM	3-5MM	5-10MM	10-25MM	25MM & OVER
12	12	11	Unqualified				2	3	6
18	22	23	Reviewed	2	2		2	6	11
15	11	11	Compiled		1	3	2	2	3
14	22	15	Tax Returns	4	3	3	4		1
43	40	37	Other	2	4	4	6	9	12
				13 (4/1-9/30/13)			84 (10/1/13-3/31/14)		
102	107	97	NUMBER OF STATEMENTS	8	10	10	16	20	33
%	%	%	**ASSETS**	%	%	%	%	%	%
16.3	11.6	12.5	Cash & Equivalents		11.7	31.3	9.8	11.8	6.6
20.8	21.1	22.3	Trade Receivables (net)		32.8	7.8	21.4	28.6	23.7
10.1	10.4	9.3	Inventory		9.0	3.4	6.5	9.1	14.5
3.3	4.1	2.4	All Other Current		3.2	1.2	2.0	1.2	3.6
50.6	47.3	46.5	Total Current		56.8	43.7	39.6	50.8	48.4
37.5	40.1	42.2	Fixed Assets (net)		38.2	47.5	44.7	37.5	38.9
5.4	4.0	3.0	Intangibles (net)		2.1	.8	2.8	1.0	5.5
6.5	8.6	8.4	All Other Non-Current		3.0	8.0	12.9	10.7	7.2
100.0	100.0	100.0	Total		100.0	100.0	100.0	100.0	100.0
			LIABILITIES						
7.1	7.1	11.0	Notes Payable-Short Term		37.3	2.5	13.4	7.7	8.7
4.9	5.0	6.6	Cur. Mat.-L.T.D.		20.8	6.3	5.3	4.5	5.5
12.8	15.4	13.4	Trade Payables		10.5	5.2	15.0	22.7	12.1
.2	.1	.2	Income Taxes Payable		.0	.3	.0	.1	.3
7.4	10.6	10.9	All Other Current		14.3	18.0	7.0	9.5	11.7
32.4	38.2	42.0	Total Current		82.9	32.3	40.7	44.5	38.3
24.0	25.1	26.5	Long-Term Debt		39.5	35.7	43.3	13.1	18.2
.3	.5	.3	Deferred Taxes		.0	.1	.4	1.1	.1
6.5	5.8	4.6	All Other Non-Current		6.4	6.2	3.0	4.1	4.7
36.8	30.5	26.5	Net Worth		-28.8	25.8	12.6	37.2	38.8
100.0	100.0	100.0	Total Liabilties & Net Worth		100.0	100.0	100.0	100.0	100.0
			INCOME DATA						
100.0	100.0	100.0	Net Sales		100.0	100.0	100.0	100.0	100.0
			Gross Profit						
89.3	91.6	95.6	Operating Expenses		99.6	95.0	96.3	94.8	97.9
10.7	8.4	4.4	Operating Profit		.4	5.0	3.7	5.2	2.1
2.3	2.0	1.7	All Other Expenses (net)		-1.1	.8	1.3	.2	.8
8.3	6.4	2.7	Profit Before Taxes		1.5	4.2	2.4	5.0	1.4
			RATIOS						
2.3	2.1	2.2			2.0	2.8	2.3	2.4	2.1
1.6	1.3	1.2	Current		1.0	1.3	.9	1.0	1.4
1.0	.7	.7			.4	.3	.6	.7	1.0
1.8	1.7	1.6			1.5	2.3	2.2	2.1	1.3
1.1	.9	.9	Quick		.9	1.1	.8	.8	.9
.7	.4	.5			.3	.2	.4	.6	.6
15 24.4	10 35.9	14 25.7			21 17.3	0 UND	15 24.4	26 13.9	23 15.9
29 12.6	26 13.9	32 11.4	Sales/Receivables		31 11.9	4 91.7	30 12.0	36 10.1	36 10.0
41 9.0	42 8.6	43 8.5			49 7.5	23 15.7	43 8.5	52 7.0	45 8.2
			Cost of Sales/Inventory						
			Cost of Sales/Payables						
7.3	9.5	8.3			12.7	6.8	9.1	8.7	6.8
16.0	29.5	35.9	Sales/Working Capital		NM	26.1	-42.0	NM	20.8
212.2	-21.6	-15.9			-5.6	-15.0	-13.6	-9.5	639.0
17.5	14.4	16.1			32.9	19.3	18.6	16.0	13.6
(83) 5.6	(92) 4.9	(89) 5.4	EBIT/Interest		9.0	10.0	2.2	(18) 8.0	5.3
1.5	1.2	.7			1.5	-4.9	.0	3.5	.5
8.0	8.2	19.6							
(17) 3.2	(22) 3.4	(12) 3.5	Net Profit + Depr., Dep., Amort./Cur. Mat. L/T/D						
1.6	1.3	1.3							
.4	.5	.4			.6	.5	.2	.3	.5
1.3	1.4	1.4	Fixed/Worth		1.6	2.9	1.9	1.3	.9
3.2	9.2	4.4			-.3	NM	-33.7	4.6	2.5
.7	.8	.8			1.2	.7	1.7	.7	.7
1.8	2.0	2.0	Debt/Worth		NM	7.1	3.6	2.1	1.4
6.6	19.2	10.0			-2.0	NM	-91.3	10.0	3.5
63.5	55.5	55.3					90.9	56.4	19.7
(85) 32.5	(85) 25.3	(82) 14.8	% Profit Before Taxes/Tangible Net Worth				(11) 14.0	31.7	(30) 9.2
9.8	8.6	-.2					-6.3	16.2	-.3
24.3	17.0	18.2			48.6	46.2	21.2	18.8	7.9
10.8	8.7	5.5	% Profit Before Taxes/Total Assets		19.2	11.6	4.1	9.0	5.2
2.4	1.0	-.4			-1.8	-10.1	-2.7	4.1	-1.0
24.2	22.2	23.7			23.7	20.8	36.1	39.9	16.2
6.8	7.2	6.8	Sales/Net Fixed Assets		9.0	9.7	6.7	6.5	7.1
2.9	3.4	2.7			2.9	.8	1.4	3.4	4.7
4.1	4.1	4.4			5.8	6.2	5.7	4.5	3.8
2.3	2.4	2.6	Sales/Total Assets		3.8	2.5	2.2	2.6	2.8
1.1	1.5	1.2			.8	.7	1.0	1.4	1.4
1.1	1.2	1.4					2.5	1.2	.5
(85) 2.7	(93) 3.2	(81) 3.5	% Depr., Dep., Amort./Sales				(13) 7.1	(19) 3.3	(30) 1.8
5.2	5.7	7.2					11.9	7.2	3.7
.7	1.2	1.0							
(20) 2.3	(21) 2.7	(29) 2.1	% Officers', Directors' Owners' Comp/Sales						
5.7	7.9	4.9							
4561673M	3233823M	3419806M	Net Sales ($)	4104M	20706M	37723M	117921M	336302M	2903050M
1978731M	1533185M	1631669M	Total Assets ($)	8769M	15066M	34179M	73565M	180756M	1319334M

M = $ thousand MM = $ million

See Pages 9 through 22 for Explanation of Ratios and Data

Current Data Sorted by Assets							Comparative Historical Data	
						Type of Statement		
			1		2	Unqualified		2
	1	3				Reviewed	3	5
1	2	1				Compiled	2	1
5	3	2				Tax Returns	8	9
3	4	4	1		1	Other	6	7
	2 (4/1-9/30/13)		32 (10/1/13-3/31/14)				4/1/09-3/31/10 ALL	4/1/10-3/31/11 ALL
0-500M	500M-2MM	2-10MM	10-50MM	50-100MM	100-250MM			
9	10	10	2		3	**NUMBER OF STATEMENTS**	19	24
%	%	%	%	%	%	**ASSETS**	%	%
	13.2	11.0				Cash & Equivalents	18.0	14.9
	15.0	19.5				Trade Receivables (net)	18.7	19.2
	2.2	7.0				Inventory	5.8	2.4
	.0	.4				All Other Current	1.9	3.4
	30.4	37.9				Total Current	44.5	40.0
	43.6	49.6				Fixed Assets (net)	43.6	43.5
	14.6	4.2				Intangibles (net)	6.5	11.4
	11.4	8.2				All Other Non-Current	5.5	5.0
	100.0	100.0				Total	100.0	100.0
						LIABILITIES		
	2.7	6.0				Notes Payable-Short Term	12.3	9.8
	4.4	7.0				Cur. Mat.-L.T.D.	5.7	8.3
	4.3	9.3				Trade Payables	14.4	6.8
	.0	.0				Income Taxes Payable	.0	.3
	10.1	2.7				All Other Current	8.2	9.1
	21.5	24.9				Total Current	40.6	34.3
	43.1	20.4				Long-Term Debt	35.1	30.4
	.0	1.6				Deferred Taxes	.0	.0
	1.3	1.7				All Other Non-Current	10.4	5.9
	34.1	51.4				Net Worth	14.0	29.4
	100.0	100.0				Total Liabilties & Net Worth	100.0	100.0
						INCOME DATA		
	100.0	100.0				Net Sales	100.0	100.0
						Gross Profit		
	90.7	89.4				Operating Expenses	97.8	91.0
	9.3	10.6				Operating Profit	2.2	9.0
	1.1	.0				All Other Expenses (net)	1.4	1.1
	8.2	10.6				Profit Before Taxes	.8	8.0
						RATIOS		
	3.5	4.2					3.4	2.8
	2.0	1.7				Current	1.2	1.2
	.8	.8					.6	.4
	3.1	4.2					1.8	2.0
	2.0	1.5				Quick	1.1	1.0
	.8	.6					.5	.3
	0 UND	0 UND					3 120.8	0 UND
	26 13.8	36 10.1				Sales/Receivables	19 19.3	24 15.3
	41 8.8	63 5.8					43 8.5	46 7.9
						Cost of Sales/Inventory		
						Cost of Sales/Payables		
	11.0	6.1					10.3	8.0
	16.2	19.3				Sales/Working Capital	53.1	96.0
	-95.0	-38.5					-12.0	-10.3
	13.0	20.6					3.9	17.5
	7.1	10.1				EBIT/Interest	(18) .7	(22) 6.1
	1.1	7.3					-4.5	1.6
						Net Profit + Depr., Dep., Amort./Cur. Mat. L/T/D		
	.8	.8					.9	.8
	3.2	1.1				Fixed/Worth	2.3	3.2
	-2.5	1.6					-5.4	-2.0
	.8	.5					1.1	.8
	4.2	1.1				Debt/Worth	3.5	3.5
	-5.4	1.8					-13.8	-4.6
		74.2					36.7	141.6
		36.6				% Profit Before Taxes/Tangible Net Worth	(13) 10.7	(15) 58.0
		21.4					-22.5	12.9
	21.5	32.8					11.9	32.8
	15.4	11.0				% Profit Before Taxes/Total Assets	-.6	16.8
	.1	8.1					-10.2	2.8
	7.9	6.2					14.5	13.2
	4.2	4.5				Sales/Net Fixed Assets	5.6	5.9
	3.0	2.1					2.9	2.4
	2.6	2.4					3.0	3.4
	2.1	1.8				Sales/Total Assets	2.4	2.2
	1.6	1.5					1.6	1.3
		2.2					2.7	2.9
		4.2				% Depr., Dep., Amort./Sales	(17) 10.4	(17) 9.0
		8.7					16.0	17.2
								3.6
						% Officers', Directors' Owners' Comp/Sales		(12) 5.5
								8.7
8657M	25747M	95359M	58072M		759081M	Net Sales ($)	234291M	315276M
2786M	11931M	46469M	27827M		574043M	Total Assets ($)	93051M	226010M

DATA NOT AVAILABLE

M = $ thousand MM = $ million

See Pages 9 through 22 for Explanation of Ratios and Data

Comparative Historical Data / Current Data Sorted by Sales

4/1/11-3/31/12 ALL	4/1/12-3/31/13 ALL	4/1/13-3/31/14 ALL	Type of Statement	0-1MM	1-3MM	3-5MM	5-10MM	10-25MM	25MM & OVER
2		3	Unqualified						3
6	3	4	Reviewed			1	1	2	
6	3	4	Compiled		2		2		
13	7	10	Tax Returns	3	5	1	1		
11	8	13	Other	3	3	1	3	2	1
					2 (4/1-9/30/13)		32 (10/1/13-3/31/14)		
38	21	34	NUMBER OF STATEMENTS	6	10	3	7	4	4
%	%	%	**ASSETS**	%	%	%	%	%	%
13.4	18.1	13.6	Cash & Equivalents		13.5				
22.5	20.1	16.1	Trade Receivables (net)		15.4				
2.0	1.7	3.6	Inventory		.6				
2.1	2.3	.4	All Other Current		.3				
39.9	42.2	33.8	Total Current		29.8				
41.0	43.5	48.6	Fixed Assets (net)		53.6				
13.0	7.6	9.4	Intangibles (net)		8.2				
6.1	6.7	8.2	All Other Non-Current		8.5				
100.0	100.0	100.0	Total		100.0				
			LIABILITIES						
14.9	7.5	5.2	Notes Payable-Short Term		3.4				
10.0	4.4	7.5	Cur. Mat.-L.T.D.		4.4				
10.1	7.6	10.1	Trade Payables		13.1				
.0	.1	.0	Income Taxes Payable		.0				
8.8	6.9	5.6	All Other Current		4.6				
43.9	26.6	28.4	Total Current		25.5				
42.0	35.8	32.8	Long-Term Debt		42.8				
.7	1.2	.7	Deferred Taxes		.0				
10.1	4.6	10.0	All Other Non-Current		6.9				
3.2	31.9	28.0	Net Worth		24.8				
100.0	100.0	100.0	Total Liabilties & Net Worth		100.0				
			INCOME DATA						
100.0	100.0	100.0	Net Sales		100.0				
			Gross Profit						
91.0	90.4	92.9	Operating Expenses		87.9				
9.0	9.6	7.1	Operating Profit		12.1				
3.6	1.3	1.0	All Other Expenses (net)		1.1				
5.4	8.3	6.0	Profit Before Taxes		11.0				
			RATIOS						
2.6	4.0	2.9			3.3				
1.3	1.8	1.7	Current		2.1				
.5	.9	.6			1.1				
2.5	3.8	2.6			3.3				
1.1	1.5	1.5	Quick		2.0				
.5	.7	.5			1.1				
10 37.9	9 38.9	0 UND			0 UND				
36 10.2	38 9.7	26 13.8	Sales/Receivables		24 15.3				
51 7.1	59 6.2	43 8.5			37 9.8				
			Cost of Sales/Inventory						
			Cost of Sales/Payables						
6.6	6.7	6.9			14.3				
22.8	16.1	16.2	Sales/Working Capital		16.2				
-18.1	NM	-25.6			NM				
18.6	20.1	14.5			29.3				
(34) 4.4	(19) 6.4	(33) 7.4	EBIT/Interest		8.5				
1.1	2.4	1.1			1.1				
			Net Profit + Depr., Dep., Amort./Cur. Mat. L/T/D						
.5	.7	.9			.9				
2.1	1.2	1.5	Fixed/Worth		3.2				
-2.0	-8.9	37.2			-2.8				
.8	.9	.8			1.1				
4.5	2.4	1.7	Debt/Worth		4.2				
-3.8	-12.0	42.3			-5.6				
62.3	58.6	42.8							
(24) 31.7	(15) 30.4	(27) 26.7	% Profit Before Taxes/Tangible Net Worth						
8.9	23.6	.3							
16.3	38.4	22.9			32.6				
7.9	12.7	10.2	% Profit Before Taxes/Total Assets		18.9				
1.4	5.2	.0			.3				
16.9	12.0	6.7			12.5				
6.0	5.9	4.2	Sales/Net Fixed Assets		4.4				
3.6	3.9	2.7			2.5				
3.3	3.5	2.8			3.2				
2.4	2.5	2.0	Sales/Total Assets		2.2				
1.7	1.7	1.4			1.6				
2.1	2.3	3.4							
(27) 6.3	(14) 4.4	(28) 6.3	% Depr., Dep., Amort./Sales						
9.3	8.0	12.6							
1.9	3.8	2.2							
(14) 3.8	(11) 10.3	(13) 4.6	% Officers', Directors' Owners' Comp/Sales						
8.1	18.8	7.9							
582891M	719551M	946916M	Net Sales ($)	3381M	16603M	11079M	46644M	71232M	797977M
446755M	512225M	663056M	Total Assets ($)	2347M	8115M	4571M	24177M	34279M	589567M

M = $ thousand MM = $ million

See Pages 9 through 22 for Explanation of Ratios and Data

Current Data Sorted by Assets							Comparative Historical Data	
			5	3	1	Type of Statement Unqualified	16	20
	2	14	8			Reviewed	25	27
2	5	7	1			Compiled	22	12
17	11	9				Tax Returns	23	28
5	13	10	7	5	3	Other	39	41
10 (4/1-9/30/13)			118 (10/1/13-3/31/14)				4/1/09-3/31/10	4/1/10-3/31/11
0-500M	500M-2MM	2-10MM	10-50MM	50-100MM	100-250MM		ALL	ALL
24	31	40	21	8	4	NUMBER OF STATEMENTS	125	128
%	%	%	%	%	%	ASSETS	%	%
22.0	14.8	10.2	5.2			Cash & Equivalents	12.0	13.5
17.7	15.3	29.6	22.8			Trade Receivables (net)	24.2	22.6
7.0	2.5	2.0	6.5			Inventory	4.2	3.8
3.8	2.8	1.9	1.0			All Other Current	4.1	2.6
50.4	35.4	43.7	35.4			Total Current	44.5	42.5
36.0	53.7	44.6	47.6			Fixed Assets (net)	41.0	39.9
4.1	3.4	7.1	9.0			Intangibles (net)	6.8	8.2
9.4	7.4	4.6	8.0			All Other Non-Current	7.8	9.4
100.0	100.0	100.0	100.0			Total	100.0	100.0
						LIABILITIES		
5.0	8.7	2.6	4.5			Notes Payable-Short Term	9.3	8.4
5.8	6.6	10.5	4.3			Cur. Mat.-L.T.D.	6.9	6.4
8.2	7.6	13.3	12.3			Trade Payables	12.5	10.6
.0	.1	.1	.0			Income Taxes Payable	.3	.4
5.4	3.3	7.5	3.2			All Other Current	5.8	11.0
24.4	26.3	33.9	24.3			Total Current	34.7	36.7
35.0	33.0	26.3	23.9			Long-Term Debt	24.4	28.5
.0	.0	.1	.5			Deferred Taxes	.8	.2
3.0	10.4	4.8	4.6			All Other Non-Current	8.2	7.6
37.5	30.4	34.8	46.7			Net Worth	31.9	27.0
100.0	100.0	100.0	100.0			Total Liabilties & Net Worth	100.0	100.0
						INCOME DATA		
100.0	100.0	100.0	100.0			Net Sales	100.0	100.0
						Gross Profit		
89.6	90.2	93.2	90.0			Operating Expenses	94.2	92.9
10.4	9.8	6.8	10.0			Operating Profit	5.8	7.1
3.1	2.8	1.6	1.6			All Other Expenses (net)	1.8	2.0
7.3	7.0	5.2	8.4			Profit Before Taxes	4.0	5.0
						RATIOS		
9.2	6.8	2.4	2.1				2.4	2.4
2.7	1.3	1.5	1.6			Current	1.3	1.3
1.5	.6	1.0	1.1				.8	.8
4.2	5.8	2.1	1.7				2.0	2.1
2.1	1.3	1.5	1.1			Quick	1.0	1.1
1.2	.6	.9	.8				.6	.6
0 UND	**0** UND	**27** 13.5	**32** 11.4				**25** 14.6	**13** 29.1
0 UND	**18** 20.5	**45** 8.2	**41** 9.0			Sales/Receivables	**41** 9.0	**39** 9.3
34 10.6	**33** 11.0	**54** 6.7	**58** 6.3				**67** 5.4	**52** 7.0
						Cost of Sales/Inventory		
						Cost of Sales/Payables		
6.7	6.6	8.6	10.5				7.4	7.5
16.6	124.3	18.1	13.7			Sales/Working Capital	24.6	31.3
97.4	-11.1	-255.5	149.0				-24.6	-28.7
7.7	19.9	17.9	16.0				8.5	9.0
(16) 3.2	(24) 4.7	(39) 5.1	(19) 4.8			EBIT/Interest	(112) 2.9	(113) 3.7
.2	-.5	1.4	3.1				1.0	1.1
							4.7	3.0
						Net Profit + Depr., Dep., Amort./Cur. Mat. L/T/D	(24) 2.0	(20) 2.3
							1.4	1.2
.2	.5	.6	.9				.5	.6
1.4	2.0	1.7	1.1			Fixed/Worth	1.8	1.6
23.2	-69.5	5.5	2.7				11.1	9.8
.3	.4	.5	.5				.8	.8
2.0	2.1	2.5	1.4			Debt/Worth	2.7	2.5
66.8	-114.9	13.7	3.1				20.1	226.7
71.6	61.1	72.3	20.8				49.6	66.3
(19) 19.1	(23) 39.2	(33) 28.2	(18) 11.1			% Profit Before Taxes/Tangible Net Worth	(99) 20.8	(99) 19.3
2.7	10.4	7.2	8.6				3.9	3.2
32.9	27.3	23.8	11.4				15.0	18.9
12.5	14.1	9.3	4.6			% Profit Before Taxes/Total Assets	5.3	7.0
-1.1	1.9	1.1	2.7				.0	.6
45.1	17.2	12.7	10.6				15.2	15.2
16.1	5.5	5.2	4.5			Sales/Net Fixed Assets	4.5	6.4
6.2	1.6	3.0	1.2				2.4	3.0
7.4	4.5	3.1	2.6				2.7	3.4
4.4	2.8	2.2	1.9			Sales/Total Assets	1.8	2.1
2.3	1.2	1.6	.8				1.2	1.2
1.0	1.9	3.2	1.6				2.0	2.4
(12) 3.0	(20) 5.0	(34) 5.1	(19) 3.3			% Depr., Dep., Amort./Sales	(108) 5.4	(106) 5.9
13.3	13.2	8.7	7.0				10.1	10.6
7.2	1.1	1.2					2.1	3.1
(11) 8.6	(11) 2.9	(19) 2.8				% Officers', Directors' Owners' Comp/Sales	(40) 4.3	(46) 5.6
17.7	6.0	6.6					8.3	9.0
35474M	98123M	418200M	847685M	614066M	778877M	Net Sales ($)	1591795M	1900693M
6781M	31621M	174500M	477643M	474740M	665319M	Total Assets ($)	1239734M	1411344M

M = $ thousand MM = $ million

See Pages 9 through 22 for Explanation of Ratios and Data

Comparative Historical Data				Current Data Sorted by Sales					
			Type of Statement						
18	14	9	Unqualified				1	3	5
28	13	24	Reviewed	1	2	1	6	9	5
14	16	15	Compiled	3	1	4	4	2	1
25	17	37	Tax Returns	9	13	6	6	3	
45	55	43	Other	4	9	6	8	3	13
4/1/11-3/31/12 ALL	**4/1/12-3/31/13 ALL**	**4/1/13-3/31/14 ALL**		**10 (4/1-9/30/13)**			**118 (10/1/13-3/31/14)**		
				0-1MM	**1-3MM**	**3-5MM**	**5-10MM**	**10-25MM**	**25MM & OVER**
130	115	128	**NUMBER OF STATEMENTS**	17	25	17	25	20	24
%	%	%	**ASSETS**	%	%	%	%	%	%
12.9	11.7	12.3	Cash & Equivalents	18.9	13.1	10.8	14.3	13.4	4.8
23.8	23.1	21.9	Trade Receivables (net)	3.5	20.9	13.9	28.9	28.5	28.7
3.8	3.3	4.3	Inventory	2.0	5.4	5.0	1.9	2.5	8.4
1.9	3.5	2.4	All Other Current	5.0	.2	5.1	2.7	.9	1.7
42.4	41.5	40.9	Total Current	29.4	39.6	34.8	47.8	45.2	43.6
41.1	39.6	45.2	Fixed Assets (net)	57.5	48.9	46.7	42.4	42.4	36.9
7.1	7.3	6.8	Intangibles (net)	4.2	3.9	9.2	5.3	7.7	10.9
9.3	11.5	7.1	All Other Non-Current	9.0	7.6	9.3	4.5	4.7	8.5
100.0	100.0	100.0	Total	100.0	100.0	100.0	100.0	100.0	100.0
			LIABILITIES						
5.5	6.4	4.8	Notes Payable-Short Term	11.4	3.6	6.8	1.9	2.8	4.3
6.0	4.8	7.1	Cur. Mat.-L.T.D.	5.5	6.2	8.6	10.8	6.7	4.5
10.0	10.1	10.3	Trade Payables	1.2	11.6	6.6	10.7	11.5	16.7
.2	.1	.1	Income Taxes Payable	.0	.0	.1	.1	.1	.0
8.3	7.7	5.1	All Other Current	2.1	3.7	3.8	6.9	8.0	5.6
29.8	29.1	27.4	Total Current	20.1	25.2	25.9	30.5	29.2	31.2
23.8	22.4	29.2	Long-Term Debt	45.8	25.2	46.6	22.3	24.1	20.8
.4	.4	.2	Deferred Taxes	.0	.0	.0	.2	.0	1.1
5.7	4.6	5.8	All Other Non-Current	2.6	8.1	3.0	11.1	2.7	4.5
40.3	43.5	37.4	Net Worth	31.5	41.5	24.4	36.0	44.0	42.3
100.0	100.0	100.0	Total Liabilties & Net Worth	100.0	100.0	100.0	100.0	100.0	100.0
			INCOME DATA						
100.0	100.0	100.0	Net Sales	100.0	100.0	100.0	100.0	100.0	100.0
			Gross Profit						
94.3	92.3	91.0	Operating Expenses	77.3	97.0	88.9	91.8	92.3	94.2
5.7	7.7	9.0	Operating Profit	22.7	3.0	11.1	8.2	7.7	5.8
.5	.8	2.2	All Other Expenses (net)	8.4	.9	1.3	1.8	1.4	.7
5.2	6.9	6.8	Profit Before Taxes	14.3	2.1	9.9	6.4	6.3	5.1
			RATIOS						
2.6	3.2	3.0		8.8	4.7	2.6	5.4	2.6	2.3
1.4	1.6	1.6	Current	1.7	1.9	1.3	1.8	1.6	1.5
1.0	.9	1.0		.7	.6	.9	1.1	1.0	1.0
2.1	2.5	2.5		7.3	3.6	1.6	4.3	2.6	1.7
1.2	1.3	1.5	Quick	1.6	1.8	1.1	1.6	1.5	1.2
.8	.7	.8		.7	.5	.7	1.1	.8	.8
21 17.5	20 18.4	10 35.3		0 UND	0 UND	0 UND	22 16.7	29 12.6	32 11.4
39 9.3	37 9.9	33 11.0	Sales/Receivables	0 UND	21 17.1	26 13.8	47 7.7	41 9.0	45 8.2
61 6.0	54 6.7	49 7.4		21 17.0	38 9.7	36 10.0	60 6.1	49 7.5	70 5.2
			Cost of Sales/Inventory						
			Cost of Sales/Payables						
7.1	6.7	7.1		3.5	10.3	8.8	5.0	10.7	6.2
18.1	17.4	17.9	Sales/Working Capital	21.4	24.3	27.8	10.3	18.5	17.9
-463.9	-60.9	-215.8		-14.5	-16.2	-221.6	120.5	NM	NM
15.8	13.9	17.7		6.0	15.1	21.7	14.0	22.7	28.8
(115) 4.6	(97) 3.5	(109) 4.8	EBIT/Interest	(12) 3.4	(17) 1.1	8.0	(21) 5.1	(18) 5.6	6.2
1.2	1.6	1.4		-1.2	-1.0	2.2	1.4	1.3	3.9
5.0	3.4	3.8							
(16) 2.3	(13) 1.9	(22) 1.8	Net Profit + Depr., Dep., Amort./Cur. Mat. L/T/D						
1.5	.9	1.0							
.6	.4	.6		.8	.5	.5	.4	.6	.7
1.1	1.2	1.5	Fixed/Worth	2.9	1.8	1.7	1.5	1.3	1.1
3.6	5.4	9.4		59.0	NM	-36.3	4.2	2.1	8.1
.5	.4	.5		.6	.3	.8	.3	.6	.6
1.5	1.3	2.0	Debt/Worth	2.6	1.9	2.3	1.3	1.6	1.9
9.5	11.5	17.3		66.3	NM	-59.9	10.2	3.6	15.3
54.1	53.2	52.5		68.8	52.4	88.8	45.1	118.8	28.0
(104) 23.9	(94) 17.7	(103) 20.4	% Profit Before Taxes/Tangible Net Worth	(14) 15.2	(19) 27.1	(12) 49.8	(22) 15.7	(17) 25.1	(19) 16.5
2.2	2.7	8.1		2.0	8.1	10.5	.1	9.4	9.5
21.1	17.6	20.5		14.4	24.6	25.2	21.9	27.2	14.4
9.6	4.6	9.0	% Profit Before Taxes/Total Assets	9.4	14.1	18.0	7.1	9.3	5.4
.6	1.0	1.5		.7	-2.9	5.0	1.3	2.3	1.9
14.6	13.2	16.4		16.1	31.1	12.8	18.0	13.5	16.8
5.1	5.1	5.8	Sales/Net Fixed Assets	1.9	7.4	8.3	5.2	7.2	5.3
2.7	2.5	2.8		.3	3.1	3.2	2.2	3.3	2.9
3.0	3.1	3.9		4.1	4.9	4.4	3.2	4.3	3.0
2.0	2.0	2.2	Sales/Total Assets	.7	3.4	2.2	2.1	2.3	1.9
1.2	1.0	1.3		.2	2.0	1.8	1.4	1.6	1.3
2.9	2.1	1.8		4.2	1.0	.7	2.1	2.4	1.6
(107) 5.1	(88) 4.6	(96) 4.5	% Depr., Dep., Amort./Sales	(12) 13.4	(14) 4.3	(11) 4.4	(21) 5.3	(15) 4.0	(23) 3.3
9.2	8.1	9.0		16.7	10.6	8.7	9.3	7.4	6.7
2.3	3.0	1.3			2.6	1.6			
(39) 5.4	(37) 5.1	(42) 3.1	% Officers', Directors' Owners' Comp/Sales		(13) 7.5	(10) 2.1			
9.2	10.3	8.7			10.3	7.9			
2482460M	2099389M	2792425M	Net Sales ($)	6971M	43184M	68813M	192177M	322742M	2158538M
1655502M	1782908M	1830604M	Total Assets ($)	10493M	16727M	69794M	173788M	194977M	1364825M

M = $ thousand MM = $ million

See Pages 9 through 22 for Explanation of Ratios and Data

EDUCATIONAL SERVICES

Current Data Sorted by Assets							Comparative Historical Data	
						Type of Statement		
55	116	375	657	254	208	Unqualified	1303	1412
2	14	60	30	2		Reviewed	73	88
6	15	27	3		1	Compiled	58	57
23	35	29	4			Tax Returns	75	85
47	64	111	127	31	22	Other	341	356
	2,132 (4/1-9/30/13)		186 (10/1/13-3/31/14)				4/1/09-3/31/10	4/1/10-3/31/11
0-500M	500M-2MM	2-10MM	10-50MM	50-100MM	100-250MM		ALL	ALL
133	244	602	821	287	231	**NUMBER OF STATEMENTS**	1850	1998
%	%	%	%	%	%	**ASSETS**	%	%
40.5	36.3	23.8	20.1	21.4	19.8	Cash & Equivalents	21.5	21.6
12.0	10.9	7.9	5.2	5.1	4.3	Trade Receivables (net)	6.3	6.4
.0	.1	.1	.1	.1	.1	Inventory	.2	.2
4.2	3.9	2.8	2.6	2.5	4.4	All Other Current	2.8	3.1
56.8	51.1	34.6	28.0	29.1	28.7	Total Current	30.7	31.4
27.8	39.8	57.2	61.0	60.8	60.8	Fixed Assets (net)	59.0	56.8
2.9	1.4	.8	.9	.6	1.0	Intangibles (net)	.9	.9
12.5	7.7	7.4	10.1	9.6	9.5	All Other Non-Current	9.5	10.9
100.0	100.0	100.0	100.0	100.0	100.0	Total	100.0	100.0
						LIABILITIES		
8.1	3.7	1.8	1.2	1.0	.8	Notes Payable-Short Term	2.8	2.6
1.6	3.2	3.2	2.1	2.6	2.5	Cur. Mat.-L.T.D.	2.3	2.0
13.4	5.5	3.5	2.0	2.2	1.8	Trade Payables	3.3	3.3
.1	.0	.1	.0	.0	.0	Income Taxes Payable	.1	.1
35.4	14.9	9.7	7.9	7.0	6.9	All Other Current	10.7	11.5
58.6	27.3	18.3	13.3	12.8	12.0	Total Current	19.2	19.5
13.1	18.5	30.7	31.2	34.7	37.3	Long-Term Debt	31.4	30.7
.0	.1	.0	.0	.0	.0	Deferred Taxes	.0	.0
13.9	6.6	5.8	5.6	5.9	5.0	All Other Non-Current	5.6	5.1
14.5	47.6	45.3	49.8	46.5	45.7	Net Worth	43.8	44.6
100.0	100.0	100.0	100.0	100.0	100.0	Total Liabilities & Net Worth	100.0	100.0
						INCOME DATA		
100.0	100.0	100.0	100.0	100.0	100.0	Net Sales	100.0	100.0
						Gross Profit		
96.3	94.6	92.7	94.7	94.5	93.6	Operating Expenses	95.9	94.6
3.7	5.4	7.3	5.3	5.5	6.4	Operating Profit	4.1	5.4
1.1	1.1	2.5	1.0	1.1	2.1	All Other Expenses (net)	4.4	1.8
2.6	4.3	4.8	4.2	4.4	4.3	Profit Before Taxes	-.3	3.5
						RATIOS		
4.0	5.6	4.7	4.8	4.4	4.5		3.9	4.0
1.3	2.4	2.3	2.2	2.2	2.3	Current	1.8	1.9
.5	1.1	1.1	1.2	1.3	1.4		.9	1.0
3.7	5.3	4.5	4.4	4.2	3.8		3.5	3.6
1.1	2.3	2.1	2.0	2.1	1.9	Quick	(1849) 1.6	1.6
.5	.9	1.0	1.0	1.1	1.2		.8	.8
0 UND	0 UND	1 321.1	2 190.3	2 195.0	2 220.9		1 339.4	1 277.2
1 325.0	4 96.2	7 55.9	9 40.7	11 34.2	10 36.9	Sales/Receivables	7 54.6	8 43.6
11 33.4	19 19.0	24 15.3	30 12.3	39 9.3	49 7.5		24 15.5	28 13.0
						Cost of Sales/Inventory		
						Cost of Sales/Payables		
10.1	4.5	3.2	2.5	2.3	1.9		3.2	3.2
41.5	9.6	7.7	5.5	4.3	4.2	Sales/Working Capital	9.0	8.3
-25.3	144.4	59.2	32.5	17.1	13.6		-163.3	-318.0
12.1	14.7	6.4	5.7	4.4	4.0		3.7	5.0
(43) 2.1	(126) 3.5	(430) 2.2	(689) 2.3	(256) 2.2	(210) 1.8	EBIT/Interest	(1447) 1.2	(1573) 2.0
-9.0	1.2	.6	.9	.8	.8		-.7	.6
							10.2	4.1
						Net Profit + Depr., Dep., Amort./Cur. Mat. L/T/D	(17) 2.7	(13) 2.1
							1.8	.9
.1	.2	.6	.8	.8	.9		.7	.7
.4	.6	1.2	1.2	1.3	1.4	Fixed/Worth	1.2	1.2
4.0	2.0	2.8	2.2	2.3	2.6		2.5	2.4
.3	.3	.4	.4	.5	.5		.4	.4
1.3	.8	1.1	.9	1.1	1.2	Debt/Worth	1.1	1.0
-8.0	3.0	3.0	2.3	2.5	2.9		2.6	2.7
97.8	35.5	18.4	10.3	8.1	7.7		11.8	12.3
(98) 26.8	(217) 13.7	(560) 5.7	(796) 3.8	(275) 3.4	(220) 3.1	% Profit Before Taxes/Tangible Net Worth	(1726) 1.5	(1865) 4.0
.8	-1.4	-.9	-.4	-1.1	-.7		-6.5	-1.6
30.3	16.8	7.2	4.5	3.8	3.5		5.0	5.6
8.4	5.7	2.7	1.8	1.6	1.3	% Profit Before Taxes/Total Assets	.6	1.8
-15.2	-.9	-.7	-.3	-.6	-.4		-3.3	-.8
247.5	38.7	4.0	1.3	1.1	1.1		2.6	2.7
30.3	8.5	1.2	.8	.8	.8	Sales/Net Fixed Assets	1.0	1.0
11.0	1.9	.7	.6	.5	.6		.6	.6
8.1	3.8	1.5	.8	.7	.7		1.3	1.3
4.7	2.1	.8	.5	.5	.5	Sales/Total Assets	.6	.6
3.3	1.1	.5	.4	.3	.3		.4	.4
.5	1.0	2.5	4.0	4.1	3.9		2.6	2.9
(71) 1.0	(177) 2.3	(504) 4.4	(720) 5.9	(252) 6.3	(198) 5.3	% Depr., Dep., Amort./Sales	(1565) 4.7	(1689) 5.0
2.1	3.9	6.3	7.8	8.7	6.9		7.1	7.4
3.2	2.9	2.7	3.0	3.9	2.3		3.7	3.7
(26) 5.2	(37) 6.7	(51) 4.2	(61) 5.5	(19) 5.6	(23) 5.2	% Officers', Directors' Owners' Comp/Sales	(216) 7.1	(190) 6.5
9.5	10.6	11.8	9.9	9.6	8.5		14.4	12.4
196990M	825070M	3779761M	15366709M	14932216M	22215978M	Net Sales ($)	36506660M	37832362M
33366M	286216M	3148112M	20289866M	20331133M	36045501M	Total Assets ($)	51921585M	57042299M

M = $ thousand MM = $ million

See Pages 9 through 22 for Explanation of Ratios and Data

Comparative Historical Data				Current Data Sorted by Sales					
			Type of Statement						
1416	1620	1665	Unqualified	26	187	197	308	437	510
88	91	108	Reviewed	13	39	20	26	10	
70	60	52	Compiled	5	22	13	9	2	1
113	101	91	Tax Returns	38	36	10	3	4	
344	384	402	Other	45	86	54	83	77	57
4/1/11-3/31/12 ALL	4/1/12-3/31/13 ALL	4/1/13-3/31/14 ALL		2,132 (4/1-9/30/13)			186 (10/1/13-3/31/14)		
				0-1MM	1-3MM	3-5MM	5-10MM	10-25MM	25MM & OVER
2031	2256	2318	**NUMBER OF STATEMENTS**	127	370	294	429	530	568
%	%	%	**ASSETS**	%	%	%	%	%	%
22.6	23.9	24.1	Cash & Equivalents	21.4	27.2	26.2	22.7	22.9	23.7
6.6	6.3	6.8	Trade Receivables (net)	6.4	7.0	7.4	6.1	6.1	7.5
.3	.2	.1	Inventory	.0	.0	.1	.1	.1	.1
2.6	3.0	3.0	All Other Current	2.0	2.4	2.1	2.2	2.6	5.2
32.1	33.4	34.0	Total Current	29.9	36.7	35.9	31.1	31.6	36.5
57.4	56.3	55.9	Fixed Assets (net)	56.1	54.8	54.5	57.8	55.5	56.1
1.1	1.0	1.0	Intangibles (net)	2.9	1.2	.9	1.1	.5	.9
9.4	9.2	9.1	All Other Non-Current	11.0	7.3	8.8	10.0	12.4	6.4
100.0	100.0	100.0	Total	100.0	100.0	100.0	100.0	100.0	100.0
			LIABILITIES						
2.4	2.0	2.0	Notes Payable-Short Term	4.5	3.5	2.3	1.4	1.1	1.4
2.2	2.1	2.5	Cur. Mat.-L.T.D.	2.6	3.3	2.5	2.2	1.9	2.9
3.0	3.0	3.4	Trade Payables	4.9	5.0	3.4	2.7	2.9	3.2
.1	.0	.1	Income Taxes Payable	.0	.1	.0	.0	.1	.1
11.3	9.8	10.5	All Other Current	17.4	14.1	11.8	10.3	8.1	8.3
19.0	16.9	18.5	Total Current	29.3	25.9	20.0	16.6	14.1	15.9
31.0	29.3	29.7	Long-Term Debt	36.1	27.1	26.8	28.1	26.6	35.7
.0	.0	.0	Deferred Taxes	.0	.1	.0	.0	.0	.0
6.9	6.5	6.2	All Other Non-Current	9.8	6.5	6.3	5.8	5.7	6.0
43.1	47.2	45.6	Net Worth	24.8	40.4	46.9	49.5	53.5	42.4
100.0	100.0	100.0	Total Liabilities & Net Worth	100.0	100.0	100.0	100.0	100.0	100.0
			INCOME DATA						
100.0	100.0	100.0	Net Sales	100.0	100.0	100.0	100.0	100.0	100.0
			Gross Profit						
93.7	94.6	94.1	Operating Expenses	85.7	93.3	94.0	94.8	95.3	95.0
6.3	5.4	5.9	Operating Profit	14.3	6.7	6.0	5.2	4.7	5.0
1.6	2.7	1.5	All Other Expenses (net)	6.4	2.2	1.6	1.0	.0	1.8
4.7	2.8	4.3	Profit Before Taxes	8.0	4.5	4.4	4.2	4.7	3.1
			RATIOS						
4.4	4.9	4.6		5.1	5.1	4.6	4.6	5.2	4.1
2.1	2.3	2.2	Current	1.5	2.1	2.3	2.1	2.4	2.2
1.0	1.2	1.1		.4	.9	1.0	1.2	1.3	1.3
4.0	4.5	4.3		4.7	4.8	4.4	4.3	4.8	3.7
1.8	2.0	2.0	Quick	1.3	2.0	2.2	2.0	2.2	1.9
.9	1.0	1.0		.3	.7	1.0	1.0	1.1	1.1
1 407.4	0 743.7	1 339.0		0 UND	0 UND	1 311.5	1 248.9	3 132.4	1 369.6
8 45.7	7 55.2	8 47.9	Sales/Receivables	0 UND	4 96.3	7 49.0	8 47.8	11 34.4	10 37.8
30 12.3	26 14.0	27 13.4		16 23.5	17 20.9	25 14.7	24 15.1	30 12.2	36 10.0
			Cost of Sales/Inventory						
			Cost of Sales/Payables						
3.0	2.7	2.8		4.4	3.6	3.1	2.6	2.3	2.8
7.9	6.5	6.7	Sales/Working Capital	24.0	11.8	7.0	6.6	5.1	5.8
621.7	43.3	42.1		-7.1	-35.8	125.5	40.8	21.7	18.8
6.3	4.5	5.8		5.5	6.0	8.5	6.9	6.3	4.3
(1600) 2.2	(1733) 1.8	(1754) 2.2	EBIT/Interest	(63) 1.8	(245) 1.9	(203) 2.4	(332) 2.3	(427) 2.9	(484) 1.9
.8	.1	.8		.6	.6	.8	.6	1.1	.7
13.1	14.5	19.4							
(20) 5.6	(15) 5.3	(17) 5.4	Net Profit + Depr., Dep., Amort./Cur. Mat. L/T/D						
.9	2.0	2.1							
.7	.6	.6		.4	.4	.5	.7	.7	.8
1.3	1.2	1.2	Fixed/Worth	1.6	1.2	1.1	1.1	1.0	1.4
2.6	2.4	2.4		7.7	3.2	2.4	2.3	1.8	2.4
.4	.4	.4		.5	.4	.4	.4	.4	.6
1.1	1.0	1.0	Debt/Worth	1.7	1.1	1.1	.9	.8	1.2
3.0	2.6	2.7		21.0	3.8	2.8	2.5	1.9	3.0
15.5	13.5	13.3		29.8	23.8	19.6	11.3	9.7	10.5
(1882) 6.1	(2106) 3.5	(2166) 4.7	% Profit Before Taxes/Tangible Net Worth	(101) 5.1	(327) 8.0	(275) 6.6	(412) 4.6	(512) 3.4	(539) 4.5
-.6	-3.0	-.6		-2.1	-.3	-.2	-.7	.2	-2.0
6.9	5.8	6.0		8.9	9.8	8.1	5.5	4.7	4.6
2.7	1.5	2.2	% Profit Before Taxes/Total Assets	2.4	2.9	2.9	2.1	2.0	1.7
-.4	-1.6	-.5		-1.7	-1.0	-.4	-.6	.0	-.9
2.9	2.8	3.2		19.2	13.0	7.8	2.2	1.5	2.3
1.0	1.0	1.0	Sales/Net Fixed Assets	1.3	1.4	1.1	.9	.9	1.0
.6	.6	.6		.4	.7	.7	.6	.6	.7
1.3	1.3	1.4		2.9	2.7	1.6	1.1	.8	1.2
.6	.6	.6	Sales/Total Assets	.8	.9	.7	.6	.5	.7
.4	.4	.4		.3	.5	.5	.4	.4	.5
2.7	3.0	3.0		1.6	2.0	2.6	3.4	3.7	3.1
(1754) 4.8	(1889) 5.0	(1922) 5.0	% Depr., Dep., Amort./Sales	(82) 4.7	(290) 4.2	(246) 4.8	(382) 5.5	(476) 5.9	(446) 4.5
7.1	7.4	7.2		14.0	6.4	6.7	7.7	7.8	6.3
3.2	3.3	3.0		5.2	2.7	2.0	3.8	3.7	2.8
(213) 6.1	(270) 6.5	(217) 5.4	% Officers', Directors' Owners' Comp/Sales	(22) 8.0	(44) 4.8	(23) 2.7	(22) 6.7	(37) 5.7	(69) 5.6
12.4	12.1	9.9		13.1	9.9	6.7	21.9	10.7	8.7
37380914M	57456732M	57316724M	Net Sales ($)	80269M	731696M	1176251M	3117703M	8477372M	43733433M
57576767M	77339127M	80134194M	Total Assets ($)	248002M	1090051M	1882725M	5969410M	17893830M	53050176M

M = $ thousand MM = $ million

See Pages 9 through 22 for Explanation of Ratios and Data

Current Data Sorted by Assets / Comparative Historical Data

0-500M	500M-2MM	2-10MM	10-50MM	50-100MM	100-250MM	Type of Statement	4/1/09-3/31/10 ALL	4/1/10-3/31/11 ALL
	3	9	18	8	9	Unqualified	48	60
						Reviewed	4	
				1		Compiled		2
		2				Tax Returns	1	2
		5	4	4	2	Other	13	16
	53 (4/1-9/30/13)		12 (10/1/13-3/31/14)				4/1/09-3/31/10 ALL	4/1/10-3/31/11 ALL
0-500M	500M-2MM	2-10MM	10-50MM	50-100MM	100-250MM			
	3	16	22	13	11	NUMBER OF STATEMENTS	66	80
%	%	%	%	%	%	**ASSETS**	%	%
DATA NOT AVAILABLE								
		30.3	14.1	29.4	12.8	Cash & Equivalents	21.4	24.4
		14.9	10.0	9.3	9.0	Trade Receivables (net)	9.1	13.7
		1.5	.4	.8	.6	Inventory	.8	.9
		.2	2.2	2.7	1.3	All Other Current	4.4	1.8
		46.9	26.7	42.2	23.7	Total Current	35.7	40.8
		39.2	50.6	47.5	67.7	Fixed Assets (net)	46.4	44.0
		1.2	1.0	1.0	.0	Intangibles (net)	3.3	2.3
		12.6	21.6	9.3	8.6	All Other Non-Current	14.6	12.9
		100.0	100.0	100.0	100.0	Total	100.0	100.0
						LIABILITIES		
		3.0	1.0	3.4	.0	Notes Payable-Short Term	1.2	2.5
		3.6	2.0	1.5	2.6	Cur. Mat.-L.T.D.	2.8	1.8
		4.5	3.0	3.1	3.4	Trade Payables	6.1	4.5
		.1	.3	.0	.1	Income Taxes Payable	.1	.2
		14.2	8.2	17.6	8.0	All Other Current	12.2	12.1
		25.3	14.5	25.7	14.1	Total Current	22.4	21.0
		25.6	20.1	13.2	18.0	Long-Term Debt	20.9	19.6
		.5	.2	.0	.0	Deferred Taxes	.2	.4
		15.7	5.2	3.8	6.5	All Other Non-Current	4.8	5.8
		32.9	60.0	57.4	61.5	Net Worth	51.7	53.2
		100.0	100.0	100.0	100.0	Total Liabilties & Net Worth	100.0	100.0
						INCOME DATA		
		100.0	100.0	100.0	100.0	Net Sales	100.0	100.0
						Gross Profit		
		88.7	93.4	96.0	95.6	Operating Expenses	94.3	90.4
		11.3	6.6	4.0	4.4	Operating Profit	5.7	9.6
		2.7	2.7	.6	.6	All Other Expenses (net)	2.6	-.5
		8.5	3.9	3.3	3.8	Profit Before Taxes	3.1	10.1
						RATIOS		
		3.4	3.6	4.5	3.3		2.7	4.3
		1.8	2.1	2.0	2.0	Current	1.7	2.2
		.6	1.3	1.3	1.3		1.2	1.3
		3.3	3.0	4.1	3.1		2.4	4.1
		1.8	1.7	2.0	1.9	Quick	1.5	2.1
		.5	1.2	1.0	1.3		.9	1.2
		4 89.1	**8** 45.9	**7** 51.8	**32** 11.4		**10** 37.2	**10** 35.2
		24 14.9	**19** 19.3	**19** 19.7	**51** 7.2	Sales/Receivables	**23** 15.8	**28** 12.8
		57 6.4	**66** 5.5	**70** 5.2	**72** 5.1		**45** 8.1	**53** 6.9
						Cost of Sales/Inventory		
						Cost of Sales/Payables		
		4.6	2.9	2.3	3.5		3.3	2.9
		6.9	6.9	6.1	5.4	Sales/Working Capital	7.8	6.2
		-12.0	13.2	12.6	7.0		36.9	14.3
			13.4	8.0			27.4	34.3
			(19) 3.3	(12) 4.1		EBIT/Interest	(55) 3.2	(58) 8.2
			.1	1.6			.1	3.4
						Net Profit + Depr., Dep., Amort./Cur. Mat. L/T/D		
		.2	.6	.6	.9		.7	.5
		.8	.7	.9	1.2	Fixed/Worth	.9	.8
		4.2	1.3	2.2	1.5		1.3	1.2
		.5	.3	.3	.1		.5	.3
		.9	.7	.6	.7	Debt/Worth	.8	.8
		3.3	1.7	3.4	1.2		1.5	2.4
		36.7	9.7	15.0	13.0		39.0	39.2
		(14) 1.6	3.4	3.3	4.5	% Profit Before Taxes/Tangible Net Worth	(64) 7.1	(77) 12.9
		-15.9	-3.0	.6	-5.3		-1.0	4.4
		12.1	5.8	5.1	7.4		16.0	15.5
		1.1	1.5	2.2	2.1	% Profit Before Taxes/Total Assets	3.5	6.9
		-18.0	-1.7	.3	-1.9		-.9	2.4
		30.1	2.2	4.9	1.0		6.1	7.9
		6.1	1.1	1.7	.6	Sales/Net Fixed Assets	1.2	1.6
		1.0	.7	1.1	.5		.8	.9
		2.5	.9	1.3	.7		2.0	1.7
		1.2	.6	.9	.4	Sales/Total Assets	.7	.8
		.8	.4	.6	.3		.5	.5
		1.1	2.5	2.9			2.3	2.2
		(14) 3.5	(20) 5.1	(12) 4.2		% Depr., Dep., Amort./Sales	(60) 3.7	(71) 3.9
		7.7	6.4	5.6			6.3	6.1
						% Officers', Directors' Owners' Comp/Sales		
	8296M	130518M	497567M	982171M	1311691M	Net Sales ($)	2874920M	2818110M
	3711M	77689M	712017M	932493M	2018076M	Total Assets ($)	3683554M	3920339M

M = $ thousand MM = $ million

See Pages 9 through 22 for Explanation of Ratios and Data

Comparative Historical Data | **Current Data Sorted by Sales**

4/1/11-3/31/12 ALL	4/1/12-3/31/13 ALL	4/1/13-3/31/14 ALL		0-1MM	1-3MM	3-5MM	5-10MM	10-25MM	25MM & OVER
			Type of Statement						
38	47	47	Unqualified	1	2	4	9	7	24
			Reviewed						
		1	Compiled						1
1	1	2	Tax Returns	1			1		
14	14	15	Other	1		1	2	4	7
				53 (4/1-9/30/13)			12 (10/1/13-3/31/14)		
53	62	65	**NUMBER OF STATEMENTS**	3	2	5	12	11	32
%	%	%	**ASSETS**	%	%	%	%	%	%
19.7	20.3	21.7	Cash & Equivalents				25.8	17.3	22.1
11.8	8.9	11.8	Trade Receivables (net)				7.8	15.4	11.4
.6	.6	.8	Inventory				1.2	1.0	.7
2.7	1.7	1.6	All Other Current				1.0	3.7	1.5
34.9	31.5	35.9	Total Current				35.8	37.4	35.8
47.7	45.0	49.2	Fixed Assets (net)				39.1	39.5	55.3
3.5	1.7	.9	Intangibles (net)				2.0	.6	.6
13.8	21.9	14.1	All Other Non-Current				23.1	22.5	8.3
100.0	100.0	100.0	Total				100.0	100.0	100.0
			LIABILITIES						
.8	.9	1.8	Notes Payable-Short Term				3.6	1.1	1.7
2.2	1.6	2.4	Cur. Mat.-L.T.D.				1.2	4.8	1.9
4.8	2.6	3.5	Trade Payables				3.2	3.9	3.4
.1	.3	.1	Income Taxes Payable				.0	.3	.1
10.6	9.9	12.4	All Other Current				8.1	12.0	14.8
18.5	15.2	20.1	Total Current				16.1	22.1	21.9
20.3	18.6	18.9	Long-Term Debt				16.1	22.8	15.4
.5	.2	.2	Deferred Taxes				.0	.3	.0
3.9	4.6	7.9	All Other Non-Current				1.4	14.5	9.6
56.8	61.3	53.0	Net Worth				66.4	40.3	53.2
100.0	100.0	100.0	Total Liabilties & Net Worth				100.0	100.0	100.0
			INCOME DATA						
100.0	100.0	100.0	Net Sales				100.0	100.0	100.0
			Gross Profit						
89.2	93.6	92.9	Operating Expenses				93.9	93.5	96.7
10.8	6.4	7.1	Operating Profit				6.1	6.5	3.3
1.2	.3	1.7	All Other Expenses (net)				4.6	-.6	.3
9.6	6.1	5.4	Profit Before Taxes				1.6	7.1	3.1
			RATIOS						
3.6	5.0	3.4					6.4	3.1	3.3
2.2	2.4	2.0	Current				3.0	1.9	2.0
1.1	1.5	1.3					1.4	1.3	1.3
3.3	4.6	3.0					5.3	1.9	3.1
1.7	2.2	1.9	Quick				2.6	1.3	1.9
1.0	1.2	1.1					1.4	.7	1.3
8 47.4	**8** 47.1	**8** 44.8					**6** 63.2	**5** 68.2	**11** 33.6
24 15.3	**28** 13.2	**32** 11.4	Sales/Receivables				**25** 14.7	**21** 17.1	**44** 8.3
63 5.8	**56** 6.5	**63** 5.8					**57** 6.4	**74** 4.9	**70** 5.2
			Cost of Sales/Inventory						
			Cost of Sales/Payables						
2.4	2.3	3.7					2.6	5.7	3.9
6.7	4.7	6.0	Sales/Working Capital				4.6	7.1	6.0
39.4	13.3	16.7					22.2	11.8	14.7
31.9	13.6	12.3							8.5
(43) 6.5	(45) 3.9	(48) 3.4	EBIT/Interest						(27) 3.6
3.0	1.3	.8							.9
			Net Profit + Depr., Dep., Amort./Cur. Mat. L/T/D						
.6	.5	.6					.2	.3	.8
.8	.8	.9	Fixed/Worth				.6	.7	1.0
1.4	1.2	1.5					1.0	1.7	1.5
.3	.3	.4					.1	.4	.3
.7	.6	.7	Debt/Worth				.5	.5	.8
1.5	1.3	1.3					.9	1.6	1.8
38.0	16.4	17.6					8.8	9.6	13.0
9.0	6.1	(63) 3.5	% Profit Before Taxes/Tangible Net Worth				-2.2	(10) 2.2	(31) 4.5
1.5	-.1	-2.6					-5.5	-2.5	-1.6
10.3	8.4	7.8					8.2	8.2	6.3
4.8	3.5	2.1	% Profit Before Taxes/Total Assets				-.8	2.2	2.0
.8	-.1	-1.4					-3.6	-.6	-1.0
6.7	5.5	5.8					26.2	19.8	3.3
1.2	1.2	1.3	Sales/Net Fixed Assets				1.9	1.4	1.2
.7	.7	.7					.7	.7	.8
1.4	1.0	1.6					1.7	1.9	1.3
.7	.6	.7	Sales/Total Assets				.8	.6	.8
.5	.4	.4					.3	.4	.6
2.1	2.6	2.5						1.1	3.3
(51) 4.3	(56) 4.2	(57) 4.6	% Depr., Dep., Amort./Sales					(10) 3.5	(29) 4.6
6.4	6.5	7.6						5.2	7.3
			% Officers', Directors' Owners' Comp/Sales						
2917713M	2528496M	2930243M	Net Sales ($)	2083M	5287M	18466M	82242M	199976M	2622189M
3341499M	4033555M	3743986M	Total Assets ($)	10291M	2381M	42616M	161765M	314811M	3212122M

M = $ thousand MM = $ million

See Pages 9 through 22 for Explanation of Ratios and Data

Current Data Sorted by Assets							Comparative Historical Data	
						Type of Statement		
2		41	144	149	197	Unqualified	616	646
			1		1	Reviewed	6	2
		1	1		1	Compiled	3	3
1	1	4	1		1	Tax Returns	4	14
7	6	13	35	21	38	Other	112	112
576 (4/1-9/30/13)			90 (10/1/13-3/31/14)				4/1/09-3/31/10	4/1/10-3/31/11
0-500M	**500M-2MM**	**2-10MM**	**10-50MM**	**50-100MM**	**100-250MM**		**ALL**	**ALL**
10	7	59	182	170	238	**NUMBER OF STATEMENTS**	741	777
%	%	%	%	%	%	**ASSETS**	%	%
35.3		23.1	16.7	12.5	15.0	Cash & Equivalents	16.0	16.8
8.1		8.3	6.4	3.8	3.7	Trade Receivables (net)	5.7	5.3
.0		.9	.8	.2	.3	Inventory	.5	.6
.2		3.5	3.1	3.1	2.1	All Other Current	3.1	3.1
43.6		35.9	27.0	19.5	21.1	Total Current	25.3	25.7
37.1		52.2	54.8	53.1	50.6	Fixed Assets (net)	51.9	51.2
.4		1.8	1.2	1.3	1.6	Intangibles (net)	1.7	1.3
18.4		10.1	16.9	26.1	26.7	All Other Non-Current	21.0	21.8
100.0		100.0	100.0	100.0	100.0	Total	100.0	100.0
						LIABILITIES		
1.4		1.8	2.3	1.7	.9	Notes Payable-Short Term	1.7	2.1
.1		2.8	2.7	2.1	1.3	Cur. Mat.-L.T.D.	1.8	1.8
1.3		5.3	3.3	2.6	2.3	Trade Payables	3.2	3.1
.0		.2	.1	.0	.0	Income Taxes Payable	.0	.1
19.7		11.0	7.5	4.5	4.8	All Other Current	7.5	6.8
22.5		21.1	15.8	10.9	9.4	Total Current	14.2	13.9
11.0		25.0	28.8	27.6	24.9	Long-Term Debt	27.2	27.5
.0		.1	.0	.1	.0	Deferred Taxes	.1	.1
16.0		12.0	4.6	4.2	4.8	All Other Non-Current	4.8	5.2
50.4		41.7	50.8	57.2	60.9	Net Worth	53.7	53.3
100.0		100.0	100.0	100.0	100.0	Total Liabilties & Net Worth	100.0	100.0
						INCOME DATA		
100.0		100.0	100.0	100.0	100.0	Net Sales	100.0	100.0
						Gross Profit		
87.1		92.0	92.4	94.6	93.6	Operating Expenses	93.9	91.3
12.9		8.0	7.6	5.4	6.4	Operating Profit	6.1	8.7
3.1		2.4	2.4	-.5	-1.4	All Other Expenses (net)	9.5	.8
9.8		5.7	5.2	6.0	7.8	Profit Before Taxes	-3.4	7.9
						RATIOS		
6.1		4.0	3.7	3.7	3.9		3.5	3.8
1.2		1.8	1.8	1.9	2.0	Current	1.7	1.7
.9		.9	.9	.8	1.1		.9	.9
6.1		3.4	3.4	3.0	3.6		2.9	3.1
1.2		1.3	1.4	1.5	1.7	Quick	1.4	1.4
.8		.8	.7	.6	.9		.7	.7
0 UND		**2** 159.5	**7** 49.9	**9** 40.1	**8** 45.4		**6** 57.1	**7** 54.5
0 UND		**13** 27.7	**18** 20.2	**17** 21.6	**17** 20.9	Sales/Receivables	**16** 22.8	**15** 23.8
31 11.9		**29** 12.7	**36** 10.1	**29** 12.4	**35** 10.4		**35** 10.4	**31** 11.6
						Cost of Sales/Inventory		
						Cost of Sales/Payables		
6.3		4.2	2.5	3.1	2.2		3.2	3.0
67.9		12.0	10.6	7.0	6.0	Sales/Working Capital	8.8	7.4
UND		-89.2	-30.1	-35.7	45.1		-103.7	-104.6
		9.2	6.9	6.8	10.3		3.7	7.6
		(44) 2.6	(139) 2.8	(156) 3.0	(209) 4.2	EBIT/Interest	(612) .6	(652) 3.8
		.8	.8	1.4	1.4		-3.6	1.6
							16.5	22.2
						Net Profit + Depr., Dep., Amort./Cur. Mat. L/T/D	(37) 6.6	(29) 12.4
							2.8	3.3
.0		.5	.7	.6	.6		.7	.6
.7		1.2	1.0	1.0	.8	Fixed/Worth	.9	.9
3.0		2.2	1.9	1.3	1.1		1.5	1.4
.1		.4	.4	.4	.3		.4	.4
.8		.9	.9	.7	.6	Debt/Worth	.8	.7
5.2		2.0	1.8	1.1	.9		1.5	1.4
		23.3	13.3	8.6	7.8		7.2	12.0
		(54) 7.8	(171) 5.0	(164) 3.6	(229) 4.7	% Profit Before Taxes/Tangible Net Worth	(715) -1.1	(749) 6.0
		.0	-.1	.5	.7		-10.1	1.8
49.5		12.6	5.7	4.7	5.0		4.1	6.6
12.1		3.3	2.6	1.9	2.7	% Profit Before Taxes/Total Assets	-.7	3.3
3.5		-1.0	-.3	.3	.3		-5.8	.7
121.3		7.2	2.2	1.2	1.0		1.5	1.5
16.6		1.7	1.0	.9	.8	Sales/Net Fixed Assets	.9	.9
.8		.9	.6	.7	.6		.6	.7
6.1		1.9	.8	.6	.5		.7	.7
4.0		1.0	.6	.5	.4	Sales/Total Assets	.5	.5
.6		.6	.4	.4	.3		.3	.3
		2.1	3.7	5.0	5.2		4.3	4.3
		(51) 3.5	(175) 5.2	(166) 6.6	(218) 6.5	% Depr., Dep., Amort./Sales	(679) 6.0	(714) 5.9
		5.5	7.8	7.8	8.4		7.8	8.2
					3.0		3.6	5.4
					(19) 10.0	% Officers', Directors' Owners' Comp/Sales	(93) 10.3	(74) 10.3
					14.8		19.7	21.0
7410M	**21329M**	**454946M**	**3634393M**	**7151946M**	**17981485M**	Net Sales ($)	**31617495M**	**32583743M**
2354M	**8942M**	**329156M**	**5000365M**	**12957646M**	**38381402M**	Total Assets ($)	**59939574M**	**63935007M**

M = $ thousand MM = $ million

See Pages 9 through 22 for Explanation of Ratios and Data

Comparative Historical Data | **Current Data Sorted by Sales**

4/1/11-3/31/12 ALL	4/1/12-3/31/13 ALL	4/1/13-3/31/14 ALL	Type of Statement	0-1MM	1-3MM	3-5MM	5-10MM	10-25MM	25MM & OVER
542	629	533	Unqualified	3	19	24	43	105	339
6	2	2	Reviewed			1			1
3	1	3	Compiled		1	1			1
13	5	8	Tax Returns		3		1	3	1
115	120	120	Other	6	9	10	10	22	63
					576 (4/1-9/30/13)		90 (10/1/13-3/31/14)		
679	757	666	**NUMBER OF STATEMENTS**	9	32	36	54	130	405
%	%	%	**ASSETS**	%	%	%	%	%	%
16.9	16.4	16.0	Cash & Equivalents		22.9	18.7	13.6	13.8	16.1
6.1	5.2	5.0	Trade Receivables (net)		4.2	5.6	7.4	5.2	4.7
.5	.4	.5	Inventory		.3	.6	.9	.5	.4
2.3	2.7	2.7	All Other Current		2.5	2.2	2.7	2.7	2.8
25.8	24.7	24.2	Total Current		29.9	27.1	24.7	22.2	24.0
50.7	48.9	52.1	Fixed Assets (net)		54.9	64.8	55.3	52.4	50.3
1.9	1.9	1.6	Intangibles (net)		1.2	.4	3.2	1.1	1.7
21.6	24.5	22.1	All Other Non-Current		14.0	7.7	16.8	24.4	24.0
100.0	100.0	100.0	Total		100.0	100.0	100.0	100.0	100.0
			LIABILITIES						
1.6	2.2	1.8	Notes Payable-Short Term		2.3	4.8	2.3	2.5	1.2
1.8	1.9	2.0	Cur. Mat.-L.T.D.		3.4	1.5	5.3	2.1	1.5
3.3	2.8	2.9	Trade Payables		1.4	1.4	2.7	3.0	3.2
.1	.1	.1	Income Taxes Payable		.0	.0	.1	.1	.1
7.5	6.9	6.4	All Other Current		8.8	3.7	9.4	6.5	5.7
14.3	13.8	13.1	Total Current		16.0	11.4	19.7	14.1	11.6
28.5	25.2	26.4	Long-Term Debt		37.0	34.9	28.7	29.2	23.6
.1	.1	.1	Deferred Taxes		.1	.0	.1	.0	.1
4.6	5.1	5.4	All Other Non-Current		3.4	6.2	5.9	3.8	5.8
52.6	55.8	55.0	Net Worth		43.6	47.4	45.6	52.8	58.9
100.0	100.0	100.0	Total Liabilties & Net Worth		100.0	100.0	100.0	100.0	100.0
			INCOME DATA						
100.0	100.0	100.0	Net Sales		100.0	100.0	100.0	100.0	100.0
			Gross Profit						
89.8	93.9	93.3	Operating Expenses		84.7	86.7	89.3	95.3	94.8
10.2	6.1	6.7	Operating Profit		15.3	13.3	10.7	4.7	5.2
1.2	4.7	.2	All Other Expenses (net)		10.1	4.1	4.3	-.4	-1.4
9.0	1.4	6.5	Profit Before Taxes		5.3	9.2	6.4	5.0	6.6
			RATIOS						
3.5	3.5	3.7			10.3	6.0	4.3	2.9	3.7
1.6	1.7	1.9	Current		1.2	3.4	1.4	1.5	2.1
.9	.9	1.0			.6	1.1	.6	.8	1.1
3.3	3.2	3.3			10.1	5.2	3.0	2.8	3.3
1.4	1.5	1.5	Quick		1.1	2.9	1.1	1.2	1.7
.7	.7	.7			.2	1.0	.4	.6	.9
6 57.0	6 62.7	7 51.1			0 UND	0 UND	5 79.5	8 46.6	9 39.5
16 23.5	15 24.0	17 21.5	Sales/Receivables		9 40.7	7 51.2	16 23.1	19 19.1	18 20.3
31 11.7	32 11.3	33 11.2			29 12.7	31 11.9	35 10.3	34 10.7	31 11.7
			Cost of Sales/Inventory						
			Cost of Sales/Payables						
3.0	3.0	2.8			1.1	1.5	3.5	3.5	2.8
9.9	8.1	7.7	Sales/Working Capital		9.2	4.8	11.1	14.5	6.5
-76.6	-76.4	-222.6			-11.2	313.1	-13.1	-19.0	49.8
10.8	5.6	8.1			4.1	6.9	7.9	6.3	9.8
(547) 4.4	(608) 1.8	(557) 3.3	EBIT/Interest		(16) 1.8	(25) 2.9	(38) 2.1	(106) 2.8	(366) 3.6
1.9	-.5	1.2			.7	.7	-.5	.9	1.4
14.0	16.7	15.2							15.9
(38) 6.0	(31) 4.9	(23) 3.9	Net Profit + Depr., Dep., Amort./Cur. Mat. L/T/D						(17) 4.6
1.6	1.0	2.2							2.0
.6	.5	.6			.4	.7	.6	.6	.6
.9	.8	.9	Fixed/Worth		1.2	1.3	1.2	1.0	.8
1.5	1.3	1.5			2.8	2.9	2.1	1.8	1.2
.4	.3	.4			.4	.2	.4	.4	.4
.8	.6	.7	Debt/Worth		1.2	.9	1.0	.7	.6
1.6	1.4	1.3			5.1	3.3	2.2	1.6	1.0
17.7	7.5	10.3			25.6	22.5	13.2	11.7	9.1
(638) 7.9	(719) 1.9	(633) 4.8	% Profit Before Taxes/Tangible Net Worth		(30) 3.1	(32) 5.5	(47) 3.5	(121) 4.5	(395) 4.8
2.3	-2.5	.5			-1.6	-4.7	-.7	.4	1.0
8.2	3.8	5.3			6.8	9.2	4.2	5.1	5.2
4.2	.8	2.6	% Profit Before Taxes/Total Assets		.8	2.7	1.6	2.6	2.8
.9	-1.6	.1			-.9	-1.5	-1.2	.0	.6
1.8	1.6	1.4			2.7	1.5	3.4	1.5	1.4
1.0	.9	.9	Sales/Net Fixed Assets		.7	.7	1.0	.9	.9
.7	.6	.7			.3	.3	.6	.6	.7
.8	.7	.7			1.0	.9	1.1	.7	.7
.5	.5	.5	Sales/Total Assets		.3	.5	.5	.4	.5
.4	.3	.3			.2	.2	.3	.3	.4
3.8	4.2	4.4			2.1	3.5	3.4	4.1	4.7
(627) 5.4	(699) 6.1	(618) 6.0	% Depr., Dep., Amort./Sales		(23) 7.5	(32) 8.1	(50) 5.4	(127) 5.8	(384) 6.0
7.5	8.2	7.9			12.1	12.4	11.1	7.7	7.6
4.0	4.4	3.9							4.4
(59) 9.5	(57) 10.1	(46) 8.9	% Officers', Directors' Owners' Comp/Sales						(30) 9.5
16.8	15.9	15.8							16.5
31291525M	33016672M	29251509M	Net Sales ($)	4039M	60546M	146407M	410028M	2274766M	26355723M
53192790M	66107115M	56679865M	Total Assets ($)	25465M	344912M	433490M	1309760M	6341188M	48225050M

M = $ thousand MM = $ million

See Pages 9 through 22 for Explanation of Ratios and Data

Current Data Sorted by Assets							Comparative Historical Data	
						Type of Statement		
3		2	9	2	2	Unqualified	22	32
1		6		1		Reviewed	1	4
	1	2	1			Compiled	3	
	1	2				Tax Returns	10	11
5	3	7	2	1	3	Other	23	27
	16 (4/1-9/30/13)		38 (10/1/13-3/31/14)				4/1/09-3/31/10 ALL	4/1/10-3/31/11 ALL
0-500M	500M-2MM	2-10MM	10-50MM	50-100MM	100-250MM			
9	5	19	12	4	5	**NUMBER OF STATEMENTS**	59	74
%	%	%	%	%	%	**ASSETS**	%	%
		19.5	30.3			Cash & Equivalents	21.3	24.2
		25.0	8.6			Trade Receivables (net)	18.1	19.8
		2.1	2.3			Inventory	1.2	1.3
		6.2	2.4			All Other Current	7.5	3.7
		52.8	43.6			Total Current	48.1	49.1
		27.4	43.8			Fixed Assets (net)	31.8	28.9
		10.7	3.1			Intangibles (net)	10.0	7.7
		9.1	9.5			All Other Non-Current	10.1	14.2
		100.0	100.0			Total	100.0	100.0
						LIABILITIES		
		8.6	.5			Notes Payable-Short Term	6.5	3.4
		2.0	2.4			Cur. Mat.-L.T.D.	2.9	1.5
		9.3	4.6			Trade Payables	7.1	8.2
		.3	.0			Income Taxes Payable	.3	.2
		13.0	26.0			All Other Current	20.8	15.9
		33.3	33.5			Total Current	37.5	29.2
		19.1	21.4			Long-Term Debt	18.2	13.5
		.2	.0			Deferred Taxes	.3	.2
		11.3	2.0			All Other Non-Current	9.1	17.9
		36.1	43.1			Net Worth	34.9	39.1
		100.0	100.0			Total Liabilties & Net Worth	100.0	100.0
						INCOME DATA		
		100.0	100.0			Net Sales	100.0	100.0
						Gross Profit		
		88.0	90.0			Operating Expenses	93.2	93.7
		12.0	10.0			Operating Profit	6.8	6.3
		3.1	.5			All Other Expenses (net)	2.0	1.3
		8.9	9.6			Profit Before Taxes	4.8	5.1
						RATIOS		
		3.1	3.8				3.6	4.7
		1.3	1.6			Current	1.6	1.8
		1.0	.8				.6	.8
		2.8	3.8				3.1	4.5
		1.2	1.6			Quick	1.3	1.6
		.7	.7				.4	.7
		16 22.3	2 197.8				2 174.3	1 287.3
		39 9.4	19 19.7			Sales/Receivables	27 13.4	23 15.6
		58 6.3	25 14.5				49 7.5	51 7.2
						Cost of Sales/Inventory		
						Cost of Sales/Payables		
		4.3	2.5				5.0	4.7
		19.0	12.7			Sales/Working Capital	10.7	14.8
		999.8	NM				-10.2	-95.9
		25.3					13.4	48.7
		(13) 5.6				EBIT/Interest	(40) 3.8	(44) 7.0
		2.1					-.3	.2
						Net Profit + Depr., Dep., Amort./Cur. Mat. L/T/D		
		.1	.3				.4	.1
		.5	.7			Fixed/Worth	1.0	.6
		3.3	2.8				-4.6	4.8
		.8	.7				.4	.4
		1.6	1.3			Debt/Worth	1.4	1.2
		6.5	2.3				-14.2	8.7
		64.4	57.7				44.3	73.6
		(16) 11.2	(11) 12.5			% Profit Before Taxes/Tangible Net Worth	(43) 10.8	(61) 21.2
		2.2	-1.1				1.7	.3
		18.7	25.0				18.1	20.0
		8.0	6.2			% Profit Before Taxes/Total Assets	4.7	6.9
		1.6	-.6				-.9	-.9
		78.5	13.4				35.3	53.7
		25.8	4.6			Sales/Net Fixed Assets	12.3	10.9
		3.3	1.1				2.3	2.8
		3.2	2.3				3.6	2.8
		1.6	1.2			Sales/Total Assets	1.9	1.8
		1.0	.7				.8	1.0
			.5				1.1	.8
			3.3			% Depr., Dep., Amort./Sales	(39) 2.0	(52) 2.1
			6.6				4.6	4.6
							4.8	3.0
						% Officers', Directors' Owners' Comp/Sales	(14) 8.6	(14) 7.3
							12.7	14.4
40681M	15052M	191481M	380903M	539051M	1027597M	Net Sales ($)	1458802M	2205115M
1945M	4587M	93292M	223272M	264892M	992860M	Total Assets ($)	1122320M	1333001M

M = $ thousand MM = $ million

See Pages 9 through 22 for Explanation of Ratios and Data

Comparative Historical Data | Current Data Sorted by Sales

			Type of Statement						
21	23	18	Unqualified	2		1	3	4	8
8	6	8	Reviewed		1	2		3	2
2	5	4	Compiled		1		2	1	
3	1	3	Tax Returns	2					1
39	23	21	Other	3	4	2	4	2	6
4/1/11-3/31/12 ALL	**4/1/12-3/31/13 ALL**	**4/1/13-3/31/14 ALL**		**16 (4/1-9/30/13)**			**38 (10/1/13-3/31/14)**		
				0-1MM	**1-3MM**	**3-5MM**	**5-10MM**	**10-25MM**	**25MM & OVER**
73	58	54	**NUMBER OF STATEMENTS**	7	6	5	9	10	17
%	%	%	**ASSETS**	%	%	%	%	%	%
22.3	23.0	24.1	Cash & Equivalents					24.6	22.1
21.2	22.6	20.9	Trade Receivables (net)					24.9	19.0
2.2	2.4	2.5	Inventory					.2	3.9
6.1	4.5	4.3	All Other Current					2.7	4.8
51.8	52.5	51.9	Total Current					52.4	49.8
32.4	24.9	22.5	Fixed Assets (net)					38.9	12.9
6.7	11.2	15.2	Intangibles (net)					.2	25.8
9.1	11.4	10.4	All Other Non-Current					8.5	11.5
100.0	100.0	100.0	Total					100.0	100.0
			LIABILITIES						
5.2	5.1	12.0	Notes Payable-Short Term					5.9	.6
2.9	3.2	3.8	Cur. Mat.-L.T.D.					3.1	1.7
6.2	8.3	12.7	Trade Payables					4.7	18.3
.2	1.5	.7	Income Taxes Payable					.6	1.6
19.1	20.7	22.3	All Other Current					9.9	40.8
33.5	38.8	51.5	Total Current					24.1	63.0
18.6	18.3	20.3	Long-Term Debt					24.0	22.7
.4	.4	.3	Deferred Taxes					.3	.6
8.7	8.3	15.8	All Other Non-Current					6.2	3.9
38.7	34.2	12.1	Net Worth					45.4	9.8
100.0	100.0	100.0	Total Liabilties & Net Worth					100.0	100.0
			INCOME DATA						
100.0	100.0	100.0	Net Sales					100.0	100.0
			Gross Profit						
89.2	93.4	89.7	Operating Expenses					95.8	87.4
10.8	6.6	10.3	Operating Profit					4.2	12.6
2.7	1.3	1.8	All Other Expenses (net)					.3	1.3
8.1	5.3	8.5	Profit Before Taxes					3.9	11.3
			RATIOS						
6.2	2.9	2.8						3.3	2.1
1.8	1.6	1.3	Current					2.4	1.3
1.0	.9	.7						1.2	.7
5.8	2.6	2.2						3.1	1.8
1.7	1.3	1.0	Quick					2.3	.8
.7	.8	.6						1.1	.6
5 73.8	**9** 39.2	**5** 69.8						**0** UND	**9** 39.6
30 12.3	**31** 11.6	**30** 12.2	Sales/Receivables					**32** 11.4	**38** 9.7
57 6.4	**57** 6.4	**53** 6.9						**63** 5.8	**59** 6.2
			Cost of Sales/Inventory						
			Cost of Sales/Payables						
3.3	5.1	5.3						2.4	9.5
10.3	12.0	21.1	Sales/Working Capital					8.7	14.9
-159.2	-71.6	-15.2						100.4	-11.9
35.9	52.1	28.9							205.1
(48) 7.0	(40) 4.1	(37) 4.6	EBIT/Interest						(13) 3.7
2.4	.2	1.0							1.6
			Net Profit + Depr., Dep., Amort./Cur. Mat. L/T/D						
.1	.1	.1						.1	.1
.7	.7	.9	Fixed/Worth					.6	.7
2.2	2.3	-.4						3.1	-.9
.5	.7	.9						.8	1.3
1.5	1.7	2.5	Debt/Worth					.9	3.4
4.6	7.0	-3.5						2.9	-1.6
66.1	116.7	62.8						43.9	66.5
(64) 20.2	(49) 17.6	(36) 16.0	% Profit Before Taxes/Tangible Net Worth					11.9	(10) 36.8
4.3	2.5	2.2						-2.0	5.5
22.2	19.3	25.3						10.9	25.5
8.8	6.8	6.8	% Profit Before Taxes/Total Assets					5.4	7.0
2.1	-.1	1.4						-.9	4.4
44.0	81.0	109.2						35.2	158.8
11.6	14.1	24.2	Sales/Net Fixed Assets					6.0	20.9
2.7	4.1	7.4						1.8	12.2
2.9	2.9	3.5						2.5	3.0
2.0	1.7	1.9	Sales/Total Assets					1.3	2.3
.9	1.0	1.0						.9	1.2
.7	.8	.7							.4
(44) 2.5	(37) 2.7	(31) 2.1	% Depr., Dep., Amort./Sales						(12) .8
5.1	4.6	4.6							3.4
			% Officers', Directors' Owners' Comp/Sales						
1576924M	1893817M	2194765M	Net Sales ($)	3428M	12432M	20221M	70296M	152078M	1936310M
1060652M	1415912M	1580848M	Total Assets ($)	5173M	11103M	11374M	48990M	112207M	1392001M

M = $ thousand MM = $ million

See Pages 9 through 22 for Explanation of Ratios and Data

Current Data Sorted by Assets | **Comparative Historical Data**

0-500M	500M-2MM	2-10MM	10-50MM	50-100MM	100-250MM		4/1/09-3/31/10 ALL	4/1/10-3/31/11 ALL
8 (4/1-9/30/13)		29 (10/1/13-3/31/14)				**Type of Statement**		
1	4	7	2	1	1	Unqualified	5	12
		1				Reviewed		
	1					Compiled	1	2
1	2	2				Tax Returns	2	1
1	2	5	5		1	Other	13	11
3	9	15	7	1	2	**NUMBER OF STATEMENTS**	21	26
%	%	%	%	%	%	**ASSETS**	%	%
		18.8				Cash & Equivalents	21.0	16.3
		20.9				Trade Receivables (net)	16.8	17.6
		2.1				Inventory	4.2	3.3
		3.2				All Other Current	3.8	5.5
		45.0				Total Current	45.8	42.7
		36.1				Fixed Assets (net)	40.9	32.1
		4.7				Intangibles (net)	2.3	8.4
		14.1				All Other Non-Current	11.0	16.8
		100.0				Total	100.0	100.0
						LIABILITIES		
		2.1				Notes Payable-Short Term	5.3	6.9
		3.0				Cur. Mat.-L.T.D.	.9	1.6
		3.4				Trade Payables	3.2	3.4
		.0				Income Taxes Payable	.1	.2
		25.4				All Other Current	25.0	21.2
		33.8				Total Current	34.5	33.2
		30.1				Long-Term Debt	13.7	16.5
		.2				Deferred Taxes	.4	.4
		14.4				All Other Non-Current	15.7	10.7
		21.5				Net Worth	35.7	39.1
		100.0				Total Liabilities & Net Worth	100.0	100.0
						INCOME DATA		
		100.0				Net Sales	100.0	100.0
						Gross Profit		
		91.5				Operating Expenses	94.9	84.2
		8.5				Operating Profit	5.1	15.8
		4.4				All Other Expenses (net)	.9	.1
		4.1				Profit Before Taxes	4.2	15.7
						RATIOS		
		2.5					2.1	3.4
		1.4				Current	1.3	1.4
		.9					.8	.9
		2.3					2.0	1.9
		1.3				Quick	.9	1.2
		.8					.8	.7
		9 40.2					5 66.5	0 UND
		79 4.6				Sales/Receivables	25 14.7	25 14.5
		118 3.1					152 2.4	90 4.1
						Cost of Sales/Inventory		
						Cost of Sales/Payables		
		3.0					3.1	5.9
		7.1				Sales/Working Capital	31.0	9.7
		-17.8					-15.5	-23.1
		12.9					78.7	49.0
		(13) 5.8				EBIT/Interest	(18) 19.9	(20) 10.9
		-5.7					2.4	2.8
						Net Profit + Depr., Dep., Amort./Cur. Mat. L/T/D		
		.6					.4	.4
		1.0				Fixed/Worth	.8	.6
		1.7					1.9	1.7
		1.0					.9	.8
		2.5				Debt/Worth	1.3	1.6
		5.4					2.9	2.9
		37.3					59.1	81.0
		(13) 6.0				% Profit Before Taxes/Tangible Net Worth	(18) 28.6	(24) 52.5
		-15.1					1.3	16.6
		6.6					23.3	30.8
		2.8				% Profit Before Taxes/Total Assets	10.6	20.5
		-3.4					-3.7	3.7
		6.8					8.9	11.8
		2.9				Sales/Net Fixed Assets	3.2	6.7
		2.4					1.7	2.4
		1.6					1.6	1.9
		1.1				Sales/Total Assets	1.1	1.3
		.8					.6	.9
		1.9					1.7	1.8
		2.8				% Depr., Dep., Amort./Sales	(18) 3.4	(22) 3.5
		5.9					7.6	5.4
						% Officers', Directors' Owners' Comp/Sales		
1948M	16925M	96181M	269996M	95770M	206584M	Net Sales ($)	893209M	1162906M
701M	13943M	59806M	244071M	55103M	257106M	Total Assets ($)	777305M	673976M

M = $ thousand MM = $ million

See Pages 9 through 22 for Explanation of Ratios and Data

Comparative Historical Data				Current Data Sorted by Sales					
			Type of Statement						
16	11	16	Unqualified	1	6	1	3	3	2
		1	Reviewed						1
1	2	1	Compiled		1				
2	5	5	Tax Returns	2	2	1			
11	16	14	Other	1	5	1		1	6
				8 (4/1-9/30/13)		29 (10/1/13-3/31/14)			
4/1/11-3/31/12 ALL	4/1/12-3/31/13 ALL	4/1/13-3/31/14 ALL		0-1MM	1-3MM	3-5MM	5-10MM	10-25MM	25MM & OVER
30	34	37	**NUMBER OF STATEMENTS**	4	14	3	3	4	9
%	%	%	**ASSETS**	%	%	%	%	%	%
26.0	25.7	16.5	Cash & Equivalents		16.0				
19.5	13.5	24.5	Trade Receivables (net)		28.9				
3.3	3.3	2.4	Inventory		2.1				
4.1	6.6	3.5	All Other Current		.1				
52.9	49.1	46.9	Total Current		47.1				
27.3	31.9	31.8	Fixed Assets (net)		32.0				
5.1	5.0	8.3	Intangibles (net)		7.6				
14.6	13.9	13.0	All Other Non-Current		13.3				
100.0	100.0	100.0	Total		100.0				
			LIABILITIES						
2.7	1.6	1.6	Notes Payable-Short Term		1.4				
2.4	2.2	2.6	Cur. Mat.-L.T.D.		3.2				
3.4	2.7	3.9	Trade Payables		3.0				
.1	.2	.1	Income Taxes Payable		.1				
22.1	16.6	25.5	All Other Current		21.9				
30.7	23.3	33.6	Total Current		29.6				
14.1	11.3	20.1	Long-Term Debt		21.2				
.2	.2	.3	Deferred Taxes		.0				
10.0	10.2	10.8	All Other Non-Current		11.8				
45.0	54.9	35.1	Net Worth		37.3				
100.0	100.0	100.0	Total Liabilties & Net Worth		100.0				
			INCOME DATA						
100.0	100.0	100.0	Net Sales		100.0				
			Gross Profit						
87.8	91.1	93.3	Operating Expenses		91.5				
12.2	8.9	6.7	Operating Profit		8.5				
.6	.4	2.2	All Other Expenses (net)		.6				
11.6	8.5	4.5	Profit Before Taxes		7.9				
			RATIOS						
3.5	8.3	2.5			2.5				
1.9	2.0	1.4	Current		1.7				
1.1	1.3	.9			.9				
3.5	3.3	2.3			2.4				
1.4	1.8	1.3	Quick		1.6				
1.0	1.0	.8			.9				
10 36.7	4 86.3	9 40.1			32 11.5				
35 10.4	18 20.7	69 5.3	Sales/Receivables		99 3.7				
118 3.1	74 4.9	111 3.3			122 3.0				
			Cost of Sales/Inventory						
			Cost of Sales/Payables						
2.7	3.0	3.7			2.0				
5.3	6.2	8.5	Sales/Working Capital		7.1				
20.5	12.6	-46.2			-46.9				
67.2	21.1	16.4			21.0				
(24) 15.6	(26) 7.3	(31) 6.4	EBIT/Interest		(13) 7.3				
2.9	.9	1.1			2.7				
			Net Profit + Depr., Dep., Amort./Cur. Mat. L/T/D						
.3	.3	.4			.4				
.5	.7	1.0	Fixed/Worth		1.2				
1.3	1.1	2.3			2.3				
.9	.4	1.0			1.2				
1.1	.9	2.1	Debt/Worth		2.6				
2.2	1.7	5.2			5.1				
84.3	45.3	61.8			84.0				
(29) 32.6	(32) 21.4	(34) 17.7	% Profit Before Taxes/Tangible Net Worth		42.6				
9.7	1.9	-.8			4.0				
25.6	22.9	13.9			21.7				
12.7	10.7	5.4	% Profit Before Taxes/Total Assets		7.5				
4.1	1.0	-.4			.5				
13.7	9.7	9.5			10.4				
6.5	4.5	4.9	Sales/Net Fixed Assets		3.8				
3.0	2.7	2.8			2.3				
1.6	1.9	1.7			1.6				
1.1	1.3	1.1	Sales/Total Assets		1.1				
.7	.9	.8			.6				
2.3	2.1	1.9			1.7				
(25) 3.3	(32) 3.5	(34) 3.3	% Depr., Dep., Amort./Sales		(13) 2.4				
5.5	4.5	5.9			5.8				
			% Officers', Directors' Owners' Comp/Sales						
703633M	676144M	687404M	Net Sales ($)	2172M	27817M	9287M	21325M	59814M	566989M
447293M	382187M	630730M	Total Assets ($)	2945M	26725M	8240M	38337M	51438M	503045M

M = $ thousand MM = $ million

See Pages 9 through 22 for Explanation of Ratios and Data

Current Data Sorted by Assets / Comparative Historical Data

0-500M	500M-2MM	2-10MM	10-50MM	50-100MM	100-250MM		4/1/09-3/31/10 ALL	4/1/10-3/31/11 ALL
						Type of Statement		
2	6	23	15	2	8	Unqualified	65	63
	1	1	3			Reviewed	1	2
	2	2				Compiled	9	6
4	4	3				Tax Returns	11	9
6	13	21	10	3	3	Other	51	59
	59 (4/1-9/30/13)		73 (10/1/13-3/31/14)					
12	26	50	28	5	11	**NUMBER OF STATEMENTS**	137	139
%	%	%	%	%	%	**ASSETS**	%	%
23.1	24.4	23.5	23.8		9.7	Cash & Equivalents	20.8	22.2
27.4	21.8	21.7	17.8		8.9	Trade Receivables (net)	17.9	19.3
1.5	3.7	2.4	1.3		.9	Inventory	1.7	1.7
.8	3.8	2.1	2.6		3.7	All Other Current	4.1	4.0
52.8	53.8	49.6	45.6		23.2	Total Current	44.4	47.2
35.8	41.1	40.6	40.1		34.0	Fixed Assets (net)	34.8	35.4
4.9	.6	2.2	5.6		17.4	Intangibles (net)	9.2	7.8
6.6	4.6	7.6	8.8		25.4	All Other Non-Current	11.5	9.7
100.0	100.0	100.0	100.0		100.0	Total	100.0	100.0
						LIABILITIES		
13.3	2.7	1.6	.7		2.6	Notes Payable-Short Term	3.1	4.5
9.8	2.3	2.9	1.3		2.0	Cur. Mat.-L.T.D.	3.7	2.5
7.6	3.3	4.0	4.8		3.9	Trade Payables	6.9	8.2
.0	.0	.1	.5		.0	Income Taxes Payable	.5	.2
39.1	10.9	22.1	15.6		11.3	All Other Current	20.3	25.5
69.8	19.2	30.8	23.0		19.8	Total Current	34.6	40.9
36.7	21.7	15.3	17.8		17.2	Long-Term Debt	16.1	16.7
.0	.0	.3	.6		2.7	Deferred Taxes	.2	.3
8.0	9.9	6.9	11.0		1.2	All Other Non-Current	7.6	6.7
-14.6	49.1	46.7	47.6		59.1	Net Worth	41.4	35.5
100.0	100.0	100.0	100.0		100.0	Total Liabilties & Net Worth	100.0	100.0
						INCOME DATA		
100.0	100.0	100.0	100.0		100.0	Net Sales	100.0	100.0
						Gross Profit		
93.5	84.2	89.0	96.0		89.1	Operating Expenses	88.4	89.0
6.5	15.8	11.0	4.0		10.9	Operating Profit	11.6	11.0
2.9	5.2	1.5	2.0		-.4	All Other Expenses (net)	2.2	1.6
3.6	10.6	9.4	2.0		11.3	Profit Before Taxes	9.4	9.4
						RATIOS		
3.8	9.3	2.3	4.0		2.0		2.1	2.5
.9	3.2	1.5	1.9		1.6	Current	1.3	1.3
.3	1.3	1.2	1.1		1.1		.9	.9
3.8	7.9	2.1	3.6		1.7		1.9	2.1
.8	3.0	1.4	1.7		1.3	Quick	(136) 1.2	1.1
.3	1.2	1.1	1.0		.8		.7	.7
1 617.6	**0** UND	**4** 83.4	**25** 14.5		**32** 11.3		**8** 43.2	**7** 51.4
14 25.5	**35** 10.4	**32** 11.3	**35** 10.3		**50** 7.3	Sales/Receivables	**28** 13.2	**30** 12.1
32 11.4	**85** 4.3	**94** 3.9	**94** 3.9		**51** 7.2		**68** 5.3	**85** 4.3
						Cost of Sales/Inventory		
						Cost of Sales/Payables		
6.8	2.8	4.4	2.1		3.7		4.7	4.9
NM	4.0	9.8	6.0		9.3	Sales/Working Capital	11.5	18.1
-10.5	11.5	29.4	29.9		36.9		-100.2	-32.1
	18.2	60.6	26.1				23.9	42.0
	(15) 6.6	(38) 12.1	(26) 5.5			EBIT/Interest	(100) 7.3	(111) 11.1
	-2.0	1.0	2.2				2.0	3.1
							17.1	27.1
						Net Profit + Depr., Dep., Amort./Cur. Mat. L/T/D	(22) 5.4	(16) 8.6
							2.8	3.1
.2	.3	.4	.5		.5		.4	.4
NM	.7	.8	1.1		1.0	Fixed/Worth	.8	.9
-.7	2.3	1.5	1.6		1.5		2.1	1.9
1.1	.2	.6	.6		.3		.7	.8
NM	1.2	1.3	1.1		1.2	Debt/Worth	1.6	1.5
-3.6	2.3	1.9	3.5		2.6		4.1	3.8
	59.0	59.8	29.5				55.7	68.5
	(24) 17.2	(48) 15.2	(27) 15.8			% Profit Before Taxes/Tangible Net Worth	(118) 19.4	(118) 32.7
	5.8	.5	4.4				5.1	8.2
57.1	23.1	17.2	8.4		9.0		17.7	22.1
14.6	8.1	6.8	5.3		1.9	% Profit Before Taxes/Total Assets	7.3	11.0
-5.3	3.5	.3	.6		-.4		1.8	3.9
47.3	12.6	11.6	7.1		5.9		15.1	14.1
26.2	5.7	4.1	3.2		4.8	Sales/Net Fixed Assets	5.4	5.2
6.2	1.7	1.7	1.5		1.0		1.8	1.9
6.8	2.0	1.9	1.5		1.0		1.9	2.2
5.1	1.6	1.3	1.0		.7	Sales/Total Assets	1.3	1.3
1.5	.8	.8	.7		.3		.7	.8
	1.2	1.7	2.6				1.5	2.0
	(16) 2.1	(47) 2.7	(27) 3.4			% Depr., Dep., Amort./Sales	(119) 3.0	(108) 3.4
	4.6	5.4	4.9				5.3	5.3
							4.2	4.4
						% Officers', Directors' Owners' Comp/Sales	(16) 10.4	(22) 10.9
							25.0	21.0
14624M	56132M	372968M	686758M	344556M	1560245M	Net Sales ($)	4543889M	5677882M
3719M	32740M	268794M	597937M	300532M	1757249M	Total Assets ($)	3058990M	3449402M

M = $ thousand MM = $ million

See Pages 9 through 22 for Explanation of Ratios and Data

Comparative Historical Data				Current Data Sorted by Sales					
			Type of Statement						
70	59	56	Unqualified	1	10	5	12	12	16
2	3	5	Reviewed			1	1	2	1
7	4	4	Compiled		3			1	
21	15	11	Tax Returns	6	4		1		
60	58	56	Other	7	12	6	12	11	8
4/1/11-3/31/12 ALL	**4/1/12-3/31/13 ALL**	**4/1/13-3/31/14 ALL**		**59 (4/1-9/30/13)**			**73 (10/1/13-3/31/14)**		
				0-1MM	**1-3MM**	**3-5MM**	**5-10MM**	**10-25MM**	**25MM & OVER**
160	139	132	**NUMBER OF STATEMENTS**	14	29	12	26	26	25
%	%	%	**ASSETS**	%	%	%	%	%	%
21.2	25.4	22.1	Cash & Equivalents	21.9	23.0	26.0	26.4	26.7	10.0
19.8	20.2	19.9	Trade Receivables (net)	11.5	23.7	16.6	20.6	24.0	16.6
2.0	2.4	2.2	Inventory	4.2	1.9	.7	1.5	3.9	1.1
3.5	3.1	2.5	All Other Current	2.5	2.7	3.0	2.1	.9	3.9
46.5	51.1	46.7	Total Current	40.1	51.4	46.4	50.6	55.6	31.6
35.0	31.9	38.5	Fixed Assets (net)	56.3	40.0	44.1	34.5	35.0	32.1
9.5	8.4	6.3	Intangibles (net)	.9	2.3	1.4	6.1	1.9	21.0
8.9	8.6	8.5	All Other Non-Current	2.6	6.3	8.1	8.8	7.5	15.3
100.0	100.0	100.0	Total	100.0	100.0	100.0	100.0	100.0	100.0
			LIABILITIES						
3.6	3.5	2.7	Notes Payable-Short Term	.1	7.7	1.6	1.6	1.7	1.3
2.0	2.6	3.0	Cur. Mat.-L.T.D.	1.1	5.9	5.8	.9	2.6	1.9
5.5	5.4	4.3	Trade Payables	.9	4.8	3.2	3.7	6.9	3.9
.5	.4	.2	Income Taxes Payable	.0	.0	.1	.2	.3	.3
25.0	19.5	18.9	All Other Current	23.2	17.6	12.9	22.8	21.2	14.7
36.7	31.4	29.1	Total Current	25.4	36.0	23.6	29.2	32.8	22.1
16.1	17.0	19.0	Long-Term Debt	35.9	26.9	20.3	9.6	13.8	15.2
.4	.5	.5	Deferred Taxes	.0	.0	.2	.3	.7	1.5
9.8	5.7	7.8	All Other Non-Current	10.7	8.1	8.6	5.5	8.3	7.3
36.9	45.4	43.5	Net Worth	28.1	29.0	47.3	55.4	44.4	53.9
100.0	100.0	100.0	Total Liabilties & Net Worth	100.0	100.0	100.0	100.0	100.0	100.0
			INCOME DATA						
100.0	100.0	100.0	Net Sales	100.0	100.0	100.0	100.0	100.0	100.0
			Gross Profit						
90.9	91.6	90.1	Operating Expenses	76.1	92.3	91.1	86.7	96.9	91.4
9.1	8.4	9.9	Operating Profit	23.9	7.7	8.9	13.3	3.1	8.6
1.2	1.1	2.3	All Other Expenses (net)	12.9	2.0	.8	.3	.1	2.0
7.9	7.2	7.5	Profit Before Taxes	10.9	5.7	8.1	13.0	3.0	6.6
			RATIOS						
2.8	3.3	3.3		62.9	4.5	3.0	2.6	3.1	2.4
1.5	1.5	1.6	Current	2.7	1.7	2.0	1.8	1.5	1.5
.9	1.1	1.2		.6	.9	1.4	1.1	1.2	1.1
2.2	2.9	3.2		30.1	3.8	2.8	2.6	3.0	2.2
1.4	1.3	1.4	Quick	2.7	1.6	1.9	1.5	1.5	1.1
.8	.9	1.0		.4	.5	1.2	1.0	1.2	.8
5 78.8	**8** 46.4	**7** 49.7		**0** UND	**2** 189.7	**17** 21.5	**5** 67.1	**15** 23.9	**29** 12.8
30 12.3	**31** 11.8	**33** 10.9	Sales/Receivables	**0** UND	**29** 12.4	**32** 11.3	**40** 9.1	**38** 9.6	**40** 9.2
69 5.3	**78** 4.7	**79** 4.6		**73** 5.0	**89** 4.1	**69** 5.3	**101** 3.6	**83** 4.4	**52** 7.0
			Cost of Sales/Inventory						
			Cost of Sales/Payables						
4.4	4.0	3.3		1.2	3.2	4.0	2.9	2.5	5.5
11.8	9.4	9.3	Sales/Working Capital	3.8	12.2	7.4	5.9	7.9	12.3
-82.3	57.9	32.9		-25.1	NM	16.1	34.4	19.4	72.7
36.3	26.0	36.0			11.7		148.4	45.7	37.5
(113) 6.9	(102) 5.7	(98) 6.4	EBIT/Interest		(19) 2.9		(19) 17.4	(23) 4.7	(23) 7.9
2.5	1.0	1.1			.7		3.1	1.4	.9
11.5	4.2	5.5							
(25) 5.4	(21) 2.7	(18) 2.6	Net Profit + Depr., Dep., Amort./Cur. Mat. L/T/D						
1.6	1.3	.7							
.4	.3	.4		.3	.3	.4	.4	.5	.4
.9	.8	.8	Fixed/Worth	4.5	.8	1.1	.6	.7	1.0
3.7	1.6	1.9		-4.7	2.4	2.0	1.1	1.4	2.8
.6	.6	.6		.1	.4	.8	.6	.6	1.0
1.9	1.3	1.3	Debt/Worth	3.7	1.2	1.3	1.0	1.2	1.3
6.2	3.8	2.7		-6.7	1.8	1.7	1.8	4.0	3.6
71.1	52.0	48.8			53.4	68.4	66.3	43.8	40.0
(132) 28.4	(128) 14.1	(118) 14.2	% Profit Before Taxes/Tangible Net Worth		(24) 8.7	22.7	(25) 16.1	16.1	(22) 17.7
6.7	.2	2.0			-1.5	-4.3	5.5	.7	5.5
24.9	19.3	14.8		9.0	23.1	22.0	21.4	11.6	10.0
7.7	4.9	6.8	% Profit Before Taxes/Total Assets	5.8	5.2	11.3	8.5	5.4	5.4
1.9	.0	.4		-10.6	.1	-3.2	2.8	.4	.3
18.9	20.0	12.7		14.5	26.2	9.1	13.3	8.2	12.7
7.1	5.5	4.6	Sales/Net Fixed Assets	1.3	8.5	4.1	4.2	4.9	5.1
2.1	2.0	1.6		.3	2.0	1.7	1.4	2.3	1.8
2.5	2.3	1.9		1.0	3.3	1.8	1.8	2.2	2.4
1.5	1.2	1.1	Sales/Total Assets	.5	1.7	1.6	1.1	1.3	.8
.9	.8	.7		.2	.9	.8	.8	1.0	.7
1.5	1.6	1.7			1.3	1.8	1.8	2.2	1.7
(133) 2.8	(107) 3.1	(102) 3.1	% Depr., Dep., Amort./Sales		(21) 2.8	(10) 2.4	(23) 2.8	(24) 3.1	(17) 3.8
4.9	5.0	5.1			8.0	5.7	4.6	4.8	4.8
3.4	3.2	5.0							
(28) 10.3	(19) 5.9	(19) 10.6	% Officers', Directors' Owners' Comp/Sales						
17.8	14.6	22.7							
3532884M	**3272241M**	**3035283M**	Net Sales ($)	**6933M**	**54252M**	**45383M**	**188987M**	**399825M**	**2339903M**
2644310M	**3005424M**	**2960971M**	Total Assets ($)	**19913M**	**46337M**	**39381M**	**309864M**	**341041M**	**2204435M**

M = $ thousand MM = $ million

See Pages 9 through 22 for Explanation of Ratios and Data

Current Data Sorted by Assets							Comparative Historical Data	
						Type of Statement		
2	2	12	12	4	3	Unqualified	28	30
			1			Reviewed	1	1
1						Compiled	2	2
4	4					Tax Returns	10	11
9	2	3	3	1		Other	15	18
34 (4/1-9/30/13)			29 (10/1/13-3/31/14)				4/1/09-3/31/10	4/1/10-3/31/11
0-500M	500M-2MM	2-10MM	10-50MM	50-100MM	100-250MM		ALL	ALL
16	8	15	16	5	3	**NUMBER OF STATEMENTS**	56	62
%	%	%	%	%	%	**ASSETS**	%	%
37.5		14.4	24.3			Cash & Equivalents	22.2	19.7
4.2		8.6	4.4			Trade Receivables (net)	8.4	9.4
2.7		.1	1.0			Inventory	2.8	.5
5.3		1.5	.9			All Other Current	2.5	.6
49.7		24.7	30.5			Total Current	36.0	30.1
34.1		68.3	58.9			Fixed Assets (net)	42.6	49.8
5.6		.2	.6			Intangibles (net)	2.1	1.8
10.5		6.7	10.0			All Other Non-Current	19.2	18.2
100.0		100.0	100.0			Total	100.0	100.0
						LIABILITIES		
4.4		3.0	.2			Notes Payable-Short Term	5.4	1.7
1.5		8.4	1.0			Cur. Mat.-L.T.D.	1.1	1.6
1.6		2.5	2.4			Trade Payables	6.0	2.5
.0		.0	.2			Income Taxes Payable	.9	1.9
19.0		3.8	4.9			All Other Current	12.7	12.5
26.5		17.7	8.5			Total Current	26.0	20.2
15.7		18.6	16.8			Long-Term Debt	16.9	34.8
.0		.0	.0			Deferred Taxes	.0	.0
6.2		3.6	4.0			All Other Non-Current	4.9	1.9
51.5		60.0	70.7			Net Worth	52.2	43.1
100.0		100.0	100.0			Total Liabilties & Net Worth	100.0	100.0
						INCOME DATA		
100.0		100.0	100.0			Net Sales	100.0	100.0
						Gross Profit		
90.3		100.1	100.7			Operating Expenses	94.7	92.9
9.7		-.1	-.7			Operating Profit	5.3	7.1
.0		-.6	1.4			All Other Expenses (net)	1.3	2.3
9.7		.5	-2.1			Profit Before Taxes	4.0	4.8
						RATIOS		
5.4		17.4	19.1				6.7	4.0
2.3		1.7	4.3			Current	1.3	1.5
.6		.6	1.6				.9	.5
5.1		14.1	19.1				5.3	3.6
1.4		1.6	3.4			Quick	1.1	1.4
.5		.6	.9				.5	.4
0 UND		**3** 131.7	**6** 62.6				**0** UND	**0** UND
0 UND		**19** 19.6	**26** 14.0			Sales/Receivables	**4** 93.3	**4** 90.1
0 UND		**52** 7.0	**60** 6.1				**31** 11.9	**37** 9.9
						Cost of Sales/Inventory		
						Cost of Sales/Payables		
7.3		3.9	1.1				5.0	5.4
33.3		24.2	2.8			Sales/Working Capital	28.7	37.2
-23.2		-14.4	9.3				-96.9	-13.9
		4.8	14.2				14.0	21.6
		(10) -.6	(12) 1.7			EBIT/Interest	(35) 3.9	(42) 5.7
		-9.7	-1.9				-.4	.6
						Net Profit + Depr., Dep., Amort./Cur. Mat. L/T/D		
.2		.9	.5				.3	.3
.7		1.3	.9			Fixed/Worth	.8	1.1
8.0		1.8	1.4				1.7	2.3
.2		.3	.1				.2	.3
1.1		.7	.4			Debt/Worth	.6	.9
7.4		1.3	1.2				2.3	2.6
131.6		11.9	3.3				47.5	37.6
(15) 31.0		-1.0	.9			% Profit Before Taxes/Tangible Net Worth	(52) 10.0	(57) 12.6
-3.7		-4.8	-4.7				-5.4	-3.0
57.7		5.8	2.1				21.9	18.4
12.6		-.7	.6			% Profit Before Taxes/Total Assets	5.6	4.8
-.1		-3.3	-3.2				-3.0	-2.0
65.1		1.8	1.2				21.7	15.5
13.7		1.1	.7			Sales/Net Fixed Assets	5.8	2.2
8.2		.3	.5				1.2	.9
5.9		.9	.8				3.3	2.7
3.9		.8	.5			Sales/Total Assets	1.4	1.0
2.7		.3	.3				.7	.5
		4.8	4.1				1.5	1.7
		(12) 5.6	7.0			% Depr., Dep., Amort./Sales	(43) 3.0	(43) 4.0
		14.0	9.8				5.1	6.4
								3.7
						% Officers', Directors' Owners' Comp/Sales		(11) 4.3
								16.3
11134M	8666M	61837M	247397M	170763M	386674M	Net Sales ($)	517202M	655601M
3023M	7803M	92661M	399609M	344194M	429615M	Total Assets ($)	497496M	670891M

M = $ thousand MM = $ million

See Pages 9 through 22 for Explanation of Ratios and Data

Comparative Historical Data				Current Data Sorted by Sales					
			Type of Statement						
40	37	35	Unqualified	2	6	6	9	3	9
3	2	1	Reviewed				1		
3	1	1	Compiled	1					
17	12	8	Tax Returns	7	1				
24	15	18	Other	8	4	1	2	2	1
4/1/11-3/31/12	**4/1/12-3/31/13**	**4/1/13-3/31/14**		**34 (4/1-9/30/13)**			**29 (10/1/13-3/31/14)**		
ALL	**ALL**	**ALL**		**0-1MM**	**1-3MM**	**3-5MM**	**5-10MM**	**10-25MM**	**25MM & OVER**
87	67	63	**NUMBER OF STATEMENTS**	18	11	7	12	5	10
%	%	%	**ASSETS**	%	%	%	%	%	%
19.3	22.4	23.2	Cash & Equivalents	26.7	19.5		20.4		23.2
5.6	5.6	5.0	Trade Receivables (net)	2.9	4.8		10.4		1.8
1.0	1.8	1.4	Inventory	1.4	3.8		.7		.4
2.4	2.8	2.2	All Other Current	3.2	2.5		2.7		1.2
28.2	32.6	31.7	Total Current	34.1	30.6		34.2		26.7
52.3	54.5	55.6	Fixed Assets (net)	52.6	59.6		52.2		58.0
2.4	2.6	2.5	Intangibles (net)	5.0	2.8		.2		2.4
17.0	10.4	10.1	All Other Non-Current	8.1	7.0		13.4		12.9
100.0	100.0	100.0	Total	100.0	100.0		100.0		100.0
			LIABILITIES						
4.2	4.3	2.6	Notes Payable-Short Term	4.2	1.9		.8		2.6
2.5	2.2	3.2	Cur. Mat.-L.T.D.	3.0	6.9		4.4		1.2
3.9	3.6	2.1	Trade Payables	1.1	1.4		1.9		4.4
1.3	.0	.1	Income Taxes Payable	.0	.0		.0		.4
11.7	14.5	10.8	All Other Current	18.7	8.5		6.7		8.6
23.6	24.6	18.8	Total Current	27.0	18.7		13.8		17.2
23.7	22.8	24.9	Long-Term Debt	42.3	12.2		15.1		26.5
.0	.0	.0	Deferred Taxes	.0	.0		.0		.0
10.5	7.1	4.2	All Other Non-Current	5.5	.9		2.9		9.1
42.2	45.7	52.1	Net Worth	25.1	68.2		68.1		47.2
100.0	100.0	100.0	Total Liabilities & Net Worth	100.0	100.0		100.0		100.0
			INCOME DATA						
100.0	100.0	100.0	Net Sales	100.0	100.0		100.0		100.0
			Gross Profit						
92.6	93.3	96.4	Operating Expenses	91.6	96.4		98.1		96.3
7.4	6.7	3.6	Operating Profit	8.4	3.6		1.9		3.7
2.9	2.9	1.0	All Other Expenses (net)	2.7	1.5		-.2		-.5
4.5	3.8	2.6	Profit Before Taxes	5.7	2.1		2.2		4.2
			RATIOS						
3.3	4.6	7.4		5.3	6.4		15.1		6.7
1.2	1.7	1.8	Current	1.5	1.5		2.9		1.1
.6	.7	.7		.4	.7		1.3		.5
2.7	3.8	7.4		4.8	6.4		12.1		4.8
1.1	1.5	1.6	Quick	.9	1.5		2.4		1.0
.5	.6	.6		.3	.5		.9		.3
0 UND	**0** UND	**0** UND		**0** UND	**0** UND		**7** 53.4		**2** 200.4
3 110.3	**5** 77.7	**6** 61.8	Sales/Receivables	**0** UND	**3** 131.7		**49** 7.5		**6** 60.4
16 23.5	**17** 21.6	**43** 8.5		**0** UND	**33** 11.1		**54** 6.7		**12** 29.7
			Cost of Sales/Inventory						
			Cost of Sales/Payables						
6.1	4.1	2.9		9.6	7.6		2.5		2.8
49.4	14.4	11.4	Sales/Working Capital	58.4	24.2		3.9		NM
-11.5	-38.8	-14.9		-10.8	-14.4		33.1		-5.7
24.3	11.8	9.5							
(62) 5.0	(47) 2.2	(40) 2.8	EBIT/Interest						
.7	-1.4	-1.0							
			Net Profit + Depr., Dep., Amort./Cur. Mat. L/T/D						
.5	.7	.6		.5	.3		.6		.8
1.0	1.1	1.0	Fixed/Worth	1.7	1.1		.8		1.3
2.1	2.1	1.8		14.9	1.7		1.2		2.0
.4	.3	.2		.5	.2		.1		.5
1.0	.9	.7	Debt/Worth	1.7	.3		.4		1.3
3.7	1.8	1.5		22.7	1.2		1.1		1.9
30.5	34.8	25.8		94.7	64.4		19.7		12.2
(76) 6.9	(61) 7.3	(60) 2.3	% Profit Before Taxes/Tangible Net Worth	(15) 26.5	-1.4		.5		4.2
-2.1	-3.2	-5.3		-8.4	-5.8		-4.7		1.2
16.6	12.8	7.7		26.3	61.2		6.1		5.5
2.7	5.1	1.6	% Profit Before Taxes/Total Assets	4.2	-.7		.4		2.3
-1.5	-2.4	-3.0		-3.1	-3.8		-3.2		.8
9.0	6.3	8.6		31.7	13.6		3.9		2.4
1.5	1.6	1.1	Sales/Net Fixed Assets	6.6	1.2		1.1		1.0
.6	.8	.5		.7	.3		.5		.7
2.3	2.2	2.4		4.6	3.7		.9		1.1
.9	.9	.8	Sales/Total Assets	2.3	.9		.8		.7
.4	.5	.3		.7	.3		.3		.4
2.4	2.5	3.4		.7			3.7		
(69) 4.9	(53) 4.4	(51) 5.4	% Depr., Dep., Amort./Sales	(12) 3.5			(10) 5.1		
7.9	6.7	10.2		22.9			9.2		
6.0	6.2								
(13) 10.8	(12) 9.4		% Officers', Directors' Owners' Comp/Sales						
13.1	25.5								
971910M	**814598M**	**886471M**	Net Sales ($)	**8680M**	**17477M**	**27400M**	**81297M**	**76321M**	**675296M**
1183695M	**856092M**	**1276905M**	Total Assets ($)	**13146M**	**34739M**	**66154M**	**171808M**	**163309M**	**827749M**

M = $ thousand MM = $ million

See Pages 9 through 22 for Explanation of Ratios and Data

Current Data Sorted by Assets							Comparative Historical Data	
						Type of Statement		
		2	3	1		Unqualified	3	3
1			2			Reviewed		2
3	3	1				Compiled	1	4
23	3	3				Tax Returns	6	12
10	9	8	3			Other	9	18
	15 (4/1-9/30/13)		60 (10/1/13-3/31/14)				**4/1/09-3/31/10 ALL**	**4/1/10-3/31/11 ALL**
0-500M	**500M-2MM**	**2-10MM**	**10-50MM**	**50-100MM**	**100-250MM**			
37	15	14	8	1		**NUMBER OF STATEMENTS**	19	39
%	%	%	%	%	%	**ASSETS**	%	%
34.0	21.2	15.4			D	Cash & Equivalents	18.6	22.2
3.7	9.1	9.9			A	Trade Receivables (net)	8.5	6.6
4.5	.5	9.1			T	Inventory	5.6	4.5
2.5	9.2	2.0			A	All Other Current	1.1	2.2
44.7	40.1	36.4				Total Current	33.8	35.5
34.3	44.3	51.4			N	Fixed Assets (net)	33.2	47.1
7.7	5.6	8.6			O	Intangibles (net)	9.9	5.4
13.3	10.0	3.5			T	All Other Non-Current	23.1	12.1
100.0	100.0	100.0				Total	100.0	100.0
					A	**LIABILITIES**		
13.5	4.4	4.8			V	Notes Payable-Short Term	5.4	9.3
.9	1.1	1.9			A	Cur. Mat.-L.T.D.	2.6	2.7
3.5	3.5	6.1			I	Trade Payables	3.9	6.8
.6	.0	.0			L	Income Taxes Payable	.1	1.8
13.8	15.9	7.1			A	All Other Current	15.1	16.3
32.1	25.0	20.0			B	Total Current	27.1	36.8
25.7	28.3	30.0			L	Long-Term Debt	30.7	31.4
.0	.0	.0			E	Deferred Taxes	.0	.0
10.7	3.3	13.9				All Other Non-Current	5.5	14.9
31.3	43.4	36.2				Net Worth	36.7	16.9
100.0	100.0	100.0				Total Liabilties & Net Worth	100.0	100.0
						INCOME DATA		
100.0	100.0	100.0				Net Sales	100.0	100.0
						Gross Profit		
94.3	88.1	82.6				Operating Expenses	89.5	87.2
5.7	11.9	17.4				Operating Profit	10.5	12.8
.4	1.7	4.7				All Other Expenses (net)	6.1	4.8
5.2	10.2	12.7				Profit Before Taxes	4.4	8.0
						RATIOS		
8.8	24.0	5.2					6.8	3.8
1.8	1.7	2.3				Current	.9	1.5
.8	.6	1.0					.2	.2
8.3	10.3	3.8					4.6	3.2
1.7	1.7	1.7				Quick	.7	1.2
.4	.5	.4					.1	.2
0 UND	**0** UND	**0** UND					**0** UND	**0** UND
0 UND	**0** UND	**3** 138.6				Sales/Receivables	**0** 999.8	**1** 501.1
0 UND	**6** 66.1	**34** 10.6					**34** 10.7	**18** 20.5
						Cost of Sales/Inventory		
						Cost of Sales/Payables		
7.7	5.8	4.1					4.9	5.2
33.0	14.0	11.2				Sales/Working Capital	-37.3	51.1
-86.5	-11.3	NM					-6.5	-4.2
32.5		87.8					6.7	4.9
(23) 11.0		(10) 6.3				EBIT/Interest	(11) 2.8	(24) 1.8
.3		3.0					.0	-2.3
						Net Profit + Depr., Dep., Amort./Cur. Mat. L/T/D		
.2	.1	.6					.2	.4
.9	.7	2.5				Fixed/Worth	.9	2.4
-2.0	4.3	NM					-4.4	-12.5
.2	.4	.7					.2	.8
.8	1.2	3.8				Debt/Worth	2.8	3.9
-4.5	8.0	NM					-7.9	-16.5
78.4	97.2	62.7					48.5	93.2
(26) 40.5	(13) 49.7	(11) 35.0				% Profit Before Taxes/Tangible Net Worth	(14) 15.8	(28) 13.2
9.8	20.8	9.0					-5.3	-3.0
44.9	42.6	23.1					20.3	11.9
24.0	15.4	7.8				% Profit Before Taxes/Total Assets	3.8	6.3
.6	3.7	3.8					-4.8	-2.0
114.2	85.9	97.6					32.7	22.0
20.3	25.0	1.9				Sales/Net Fixed Assets	16.1	6.2
6.0	.9	.5					2.0	.6
6.3	3.8	2.9					3.3	3.4
3.5	2.2	1.1				Sales/Total Assets	1.9	2.0
2.5	.8	.4					.9	.5
.7							1.4	1.9
(26) 1.6						% Depr., Dep., Amort./Sales	(16) 2.8	(28) 4.9
4.3							5.7	15.8
8.1								
(24) 12.4						% Officers', Directors' Owners' Comp/Sales		
16.9								
35585M	**40176M**	**108816M**	**107919M**	**170042M**		Net Sales ($)	**88558M**	**149843M**
8141M	**16339M**	**64437M**	**123236M**	**50562M**		Total Assets ($)	**78410M**	**168585M**

M = $ thousand MM = $ million

See Pages 9 through 22 for Explanation of Ratios and Data

Comparative Historical Data | **Current Data Sorted by Sales**

4/1/11-3/31/12 ALL	4/1/12-3/31/13 ALL	4/1/13-3/31/14 ALL	Type of Statement	0-1MM	1-3MM	3-5MM	5-10MM	10-25MM	25MM & OVER
3	2	6	Unqualified		1		1	1	3
2	3	3	Reviewed		1			2	
5	4	7	Compiled	3	3		1		
19	18	29	Tax Returns	18	8	2			1
18	22	30	Other	8	12	2	6	2	
				15 (4/1-9/30/13)		60 (10/1/13-3/31/14)			
47	49	75	NUMBER OF STATEMENTS	29	25	4	8	5	4
%	%	%	ASSETS	%	%	%	%	%	%
22.4	24.5	25.9	Cash & Equivalents	30.4	23.2				
7.7	6.7	6.1	Trade Receivables (net)	1.4	6.0				
2.7	4.3	4.8	Inventory	3.5	2.0				
4.9	2.6	3.6	All Other Current	2.7	5.8				
37.8	38.0	40.4	Total Current	38.0	37.1				
47.3	49.2	42.2	Fixed Assets (net)	42.3	48.1				
2.3	2.6	7.6	Intangibles (net)	8.2	5.2				
12.6	10.1	9.8	All Other Non-Current	11.4	9.6				
100.0	100.0	100.0	Total	100.0	100.0				
			LIABILITIES						
7.7	10.0	8.6	Notes Payable-Short Term	11.2	2.7				
4.7	1.8	1.5	Cur. Mat.-L.T.D.	1.1	1.3				
3.2	4.7	4.2	Trade Payables	2.6	3.1				
1.5	.0	.3	Income Taxes Payable	.7	.0				
17.6	15.1	13.5	All Other Current	14.3	11.9				
34.8	31.6	28.0	Total Current	29.9	18.9				
33.5	31.5	27.6	Long-Term Debt	39.6	21.6				
.0	.0	.0	Deferred Taxes	.0	.0				
10.8	17.4	9.4	All Other Non-Current	12.2	5.4				
20.9	19.5	34.9	Net Worth	18.1	54.0				
100.0	100.0	100.0	Total Liabilties & Net Worth	100.0	100.0				
			INCOME DATA						
100.0	100.0	100.0	Net Sales	100.0	100.0				
			Gross Profit						
88.2	85.4	91.0	Operating Expenses	91.5	90.4				
11.8	14.6	9.0	Operating Profit	8.5	9.6				
3.5	5.1	1.6	All Other Expenses (net)	2.5	1.0				
8.3	9.5	7.4	Profit Before Taxes	6.0	8.6				
			RATIOS						
4.0	4.0	6.1		11.0	7.1				
1.1	1.7	1.8	Current	1.8	2.0				
.5	.5	.7		.8	.7				
3.2	3.9	5.9		8.4	7.1				
.9	1.1	1.6	Quick	1.7	1.9				
.2	.4	.4		.6	.4				
0 UND	0 UND	0 UND		0 UND	0 UND				
0 UND	0 UND	0 UND	Sales/Receivables	0 UND	0 UND				
13 28.1	14 26.1	6 66.1		0 UND	1 260.8				
			Cost of Sales/Inventory						
			Cost of Sales/Payables						
6.1	6.3	5.8		5.6	6.4				
59.5	21.4	24.9	Sales/Working Capital	29.6	20.8				
-8.5	-16.7	-49.8		-86.5	-36.7				
15.6	36.2	34.2		24.3	35.2				
(25) 3.8	(30) 5.0	(50) 7.5	EBIT/Interest	(18) 4.8	(14) 12.0				
.8	.3	2.3		-.1	3.1				
			Net Profit + Depr., Dep., Amort./Cur. Mat. L/T/D						
.3	.3	.2		.4	.2				
1.7	6.5	1.1	Fixed/Worth	2.3	.8				
-14.7	-4.7	53.2		-1.4	2.9				
.8	.7	.3		.4	.2				
2.5	7.4	1.7	Debt/Worth	7.4	.6				
-19.7	-8.8	-49.7		-3.8	5.5				
62.7	115.7	76.9		77.1	98.5				
(33) 27.1	(34) 35.2	(56) 43.9	% Profit Before Taxes/Tangible Net Worth	(19) 54.6	(22) 35.4				
9.3	5.8	12.2		.0	12.4				
26.8	24.0	36.4		44.2	32.9				
5.0	11.4	15.4	% Profit Before Taxes/Total Assets	13.0	14.8				
1.1	1.2	1.7		-1.7	3.7				
44.0	44.3	83.1		83.1	52.3				
5.7	6.6	8.9	Sales/Net Fixed Assets	10.4	5.4				
.8	.8	1.9		4.2	.9				
3.8	4.5	4.0		4.9	3.7				
1.6	1.9	2.5	Sales/Total Assets	2.9	2.2				
.5	.7	1.3		1.8	.9				
1.5	.9	.8		.8	.7				
(30) 3.6	(34) 2.1	(49) 2.6	% Depr., Dep., Amort./Sales	(20) 2.8	(15) 2.6				
10.0	6.7	7.3		7.5	9.4				
2.5	3.9	5.9		7.4					
(21) 6.8	(22) 7.2	(33) 9.7	% Officers', Directors' Owners' Comp/Sales	(18) 12.4					
10.4	11.3	14.7		15.5					
123715M	142967M	462538M	Net Sales ($)	14019M	46453M	13880M	54278M	73656M	260252M
85382M	101357M	262715M	Total Assets ($)	13339M	42458M	11332M	28385M	85351M	81850M

M = $ thousand MM = $ million

See Pages 9 through 22 for Explanation of Ratios and Data

Current Data Sorted by Assets | **Comparative Historical Data**

0-500M	500M-2MM	2-10MM	10-50MM	50-100MM	100-250MM		4/1/09-3/31/10 ALL	4/1/10-3/31/11 ALL
						Type of Statement		
4	14	33	38	7	6	Unqualified	105	120
1		8	2			Reviewed	7	13
2	4	3	1			Compiled	7	14
21	11	5			1	Tax Returns	26	41
25	27	32	18	3	2	Other	75	75
143 (4/1-9/30/13)			125 (10/1/13-3/31/14)					
53	56	81	59	10	9	**NUMBER OF STATEMENTS**	220	263
%	%	%	%	%	%	**ASSETS**	%	%
35.7	26.4	21.0	16.8	12.0		Cash & Equivalents	22.9	23.2
10.8	13.7	11.7	11.6	3.5		Trade Receivables (net)	13.0	11.7
2.8	2.3	2.6	1.6	.1		Inventory	1.4	2.5
3.9	2.6	3.4	4.3	8.7		All Other Current	4.0	3.7
53.2	45.0	38.7	34.2	24.3		Total Current	41.3	41.1
28.5	42.0	45.9	48.0	52.9		Fixed Assets (net)	44.2	44.1
7.7	4.5	4.3	3.8	5.9		Intangibles (net)	5.5	5.3
10.6	8.6	11.1	13.9	17.0		All Other Non-Current	9.0	9.5
100.0	100.0	100.0	100.0	100.0		Total	100.0	100.0
						LIABILITIES		
12.8	7.8	3.1	2.9	1.5		Notes Payable-Short Term	6.9	5.0
2.4	1.5	1.9	2.2	1.3		Cur. Mat.-L.T.D.	2.5	2.9
7.5	6.7	3.8	4.4	1.9		Trade Payables	5.1	6.0
.1	.0	.1	.6	.0		Income Taxes Payable	.1	.1
16.5	15.6	14.0	10.9	5.6		All Other Current	15.8	10.9
39.3	31.6	22.9	21.1	10.3		Total Current	30.3	24.9
19.6	18.4	21.1	21.1	24.3		Long-Term Debt	22.3	25.9
.0	.0	.0	.0	.7		Deferred Taxes	.1	.1
22.6	13.3	7.6	7.4	5.5		All Other Non-Current	10.3	12.9
18.5	36.6	48.4	50.4	59.3		Net Worth	37.0	36.2
100.0	100.0	100.0	100.0	100.0		Total Liabilties & Net Worth	100.0	100.0
						INCOME DATA		
100.0	100.0	100.0	100.0	100.0		Net Sales	100.0	100.0
						Gross Profit		
92.3	93.4	91.0	94.9	93.1		Operating Expenses	93.0	91.0
7.7	6.6	9.0	5.1	6.9		Operating Profit	7.0	9.0
2.8	2.9	2.1	.7	2.8		All Other Expenses (net)	4.2	2.9
4.8	3.7	6.9	4.4	4.1		Profit Before Taxes	2.8	6.1
						RATIOS		
14.0	6.6	6.0	5.0	5.2			3.9	4.8
2.4	1.8	1.9	2.2	1.9		Current	1.7	2.0
.6	.6	1.1	1.2	1.3			.8	1.0
12.3	5.9	4.8	4.4	4.4			3.6	3.9
1.5	1.2	1.7	1.5	1.5		Quick	1.4	1.7
.5	.4	.8	.8	.6			.6	.7
0 UND	0 UND	1 245.2	4 90.8	6 65.7			1 636.2	0 UND
0 UND	5 80.9	19 18.9	27 13.3	21 17.0		Sales/Receivables	13 27.9	8 43.9
3 129.8	26 13.9	39 9.4	54 6.7	32 11.5			38 9.6	36 10.1
						Cost of Sales/Inventory		
						Cost of Sales/Payables		
8.4	4.4	2.8	2.9	2.2			4.5	4.0
19.8	17.3	9.7	6.6	7.3		Sales/Working Capital	12.7	10.0
-31.6	-25.0	311.7	23.3	NM			-21.1	-239.9
13.0	17.9	18.2	4.8				10.1	10.5
(27) 5.0	(28) 4.1	(60) 4.5	(44) 2.0			EBIT/Interest	(137) 2.5	(173) 2.9
-1.5	1.2	1.3	.9				.4	.5
								7.7
						Net Profit + Depr., Dep., Amort./Cur. Mat. L/T/D		(12) 2.5
								.8
.0	.2	.4	.4	.4			.4	.4
.9	1.2	1.0	1.0	1.1		Fixed/Worth	1.1	1.3
NM	3.9	1.8	1.7	2.1			2.9	3.5
.2	.4	.3	.3	.2			.5	.4
1.9	1.4	.9	.8	.6		Debt/Worth	1.3	1.3
-12.7	4.4	3.9	1.7	1.7			4.8	5.9
115.7	77.7	32.0	13.3				32.5	37.5
(38) 30.8	(48) 12.6	(71) 6.7	(54) 4.6			% Profit Before Taxes/Tangible Net Worth	(189) 7.3	(221) 11.9
6.9	-8.9	.2	-.4				-3.4	-.3
29.3	24.4	9.7	5.5	6.0			15.0	14.7
8.3	5.4	3.2	2.1	.5		% Profit Before Taxes/Total Assets	3.3	5.0
-1.3	-6.6	.1	-.4	-1.6			-1.5	-.3
999.8	36.5	18.8	7.5	4.9			21.9	24.9
32.1	6.1	2.8	1.4	.8		Sales/Net Fixed Assets	4.3	4.6
6.5	1.9	.8	.7	.4			.9	.9
8.2	3.7	2.1	1.3	.9			3.1	3.2
3.8	2.1	1.1	.7	.5		Sales/Total Assets	1.4	1.5
2.3	1.0	.5	.5	.3			.6	.6
.5	.8	1.2	2.7				1.5	1.4
(24) 1.8	(38) 2.6	(67) 3.4	(50) 5.0			% Depr., Dep., Amort./Sales	(161) 3.0	(199) 2.9
4.1	4.2	6.6	7.1				6.1	5.7
3.8	3.8						3.2	3.9
(25) 6.8	(11) 5.7					% Officers', Directors' Owners' Comp/Sales	(38) 6.3	(56) 6.5
14.6	18.8						11.2	11.1
51499M	201853M	482516M	1222426M	405609M	1817761M	Net Sales ($)	3624860M	5221849M
11020M	66800M	376158M	1243792M	664870M	1407749M	Total Assets ($)	3651425M	3359854M

M = $ thousand MM = $ million

See Pages 9 through 22 for Explanation of Ratios and Data

Comparative Historical Data				Current Data Sorted by Sales					
			Type of Statement						
125	98	102	Unqualified	5	16	15	21	26	19
11	12	11	Reviewed	1	2	3	2	3	
17	13	10	Compiled	5	1	2		2	
59	51	38	Tax Returns	18	10	4	3	2	1
74	96	107	Other	29	25	15	12	17	9
4/1/11-3/31/12 ALL	4/1/12-3/31/13 ALL	4/1/13-3/31/14 ALL		143 (4/1-9/30/13)			125 (10/1/13-3/31/14)		
				0-1MM	1-3MM	3-5MM	5-10MM	10-25MM	25MM & OVER
286	270	268	**NUMBER OF STATEMENTS**	58	54	39	38	50	29
%	%	%	**ASSETS**	%	%	%	%	%	%
27.8	28.3	24.3	Cash & Equivalents	25.1	26.4	27.2	23.0	17.7	27.7
10.6	10.0	11.4	Trade Receivables (net)	6.6	12.1	12.7	8.8	16.0	13.1
2.3	1.6	2.2	Inventory	1.3	1.1	5.3	.7	3.8	.8
2.8	3.2	3.7	All Other Current	2.5	4.0	2.3	3.7	1.9	10.5
43.5	43.1	41.5	Total Current	35.6	43.6	47.5	36.2	39.3	52.0
44.2	39.5	42.1	Fixed Assets (net)	48.6	41.0	36.7	43.3	43.8	33.6
3.9	6.2	4.9	Intangibles (net)	7.7	3.4	3.4	4.1	5.7	4.0
8.4	11.1	11.5	All Other Non-Current	8.1	12.0	12.4	16.4	11.2	10.3
100.0	100.0	100.0	Total	100.0	100.0	100.0	100.0	100.0	100.0
			LIABILITIES						
4.6	6.0	5.8	Notes Payable-Short Term	5.5	4.9	10.4	7.4	3.8	3.4
3.2	2.6	2.0	Cur. Mat.-L.T.D.	1.6	2.3	1.2	2.9	2.3	1.7
5.4	5.2	5.4	Trade Payables	5.7	3.4	4.0	3.8	8.3	7.5
.1	.0	.2	Income Taxes Payable	.0	.1	.0	.0	.8	.1
10.7	14.9	13.7	All Other Current	11.5	11.7	11.8	14.4	15.6	20.0
24.1	28.8	27.1	Total Current	24.2	22.5	27.5	28.4	30.7	32.8
20.2	21.2	20.3	Long-Term Debt	23.7	23.9	14.9	20.3	18.7	16.6
.1	.4	.1	Deferred Taxes	.0	.0	.0	.0	.0	.5
9.8	10.0	11.5	All Other Non-Current	19.9	11.6	4.9	13.4	8.6	6.3
45.8	39.6	41.1	Net Worth	32.3	42.0	52.7	37.8	42.0	43.8
100.0	100.0	100.0	Total Liabilties & Net Worth	100.0	100.0	100.0	100.0	100.0	100.0
			INCOME DATA						
100.0	100.0	100.0	Net Sales	100.0	100.0	100.0	100.0	100.0	100.0
			Gross Profit						
90.3	91.3	92.5	Operating Expenses	89.4	91.5	95.3	89.9	97.4	91.5
9.7	8.7	7.5	Operating Profit	10.6	8.5	4.7	10.1	2.6	8.5
3.3	3.1	2.2	All Other Expenses (net)	4.7	3.0	.8	1.1	.7	1.1
6.4	5.6	5.4	Profit Before Taxes	5.9	5.4	3.9	9.0	1.9	7.4
			RATIOS						
5.8	6.4	6.7		12.1	11.0	9.0	3.7	2.8	5.2
2.2	2.1	2.0	Current	2.4	3.3	3.5	1.4	1.5	1.6
.9	.9	.8		.6	.7	1.0	.8	1.1	1.0
5.3	6.0	5.0		10.8	9.0	8.2	3.0	2.7	4.4
2.0	1.6	1.5	Quick	1.6	2.8	2.6	1.4	1.4	1.4
.7	.6	.6		.5	.6	.7	.7	.8	.6
0 UND	**0** UND	**0** UND		**0** UND	**0** UND	**2** 157.0	**3** 141.3	**7** 55.5	**5** 73.6
6 62.6	**6** 65.1	**11** 32.0	Sales/Receivables	**0** UND	**2** 150.9	**17** 21.6	**13** 29.1	**31** 11.7	**21** 17.5
32 11.5	**30** 12.0	**38** 9.5		**18** 19.9	**33** 11.2	**42** 8.6	**25** 14.4	**53** 6.9	**45** 8.1
			Cost of Sales/Inventory						
			Cost of Sales/Payables						
3.9	3.8	3.4		5.2	3.3	2.5	3.5	4.3	3.0
12.1	11.7	10.8	Sales/Working Capital	19.9	8.8	6.4	17.6	13.5	9.2
-112.8	-46.3	-57.7		-27.7	-93.8	402.6	-17.9	41.6	NM
9.5	8.8	13.8		8.0	14.5	20.0	40.0	9.2	25.1
(190) 3.3	(164) 3.1	(173) 3.2	EBIT/Interest	(32) 1.6	(27) 4.5	(30) 5.3	(27) 5.5	(34) 2.7	(23) 2.2
1.2	1.1	1.1		-.5	.5	1.5	2.2	1.2	-2.9
			Net Profit + Depr., Dep., Amort./Cur. Mat. L/T/D						
.3	.3	.4		.4	.1	.2	.6	.6	.2
1.0	.9	1.0	Fixed/Worth	1.3	1.0	.5	1.0	1.0	.7
2.6	2.6	2.4		4.5	2.2	2.1	3.5	1.5	1.6
.3	.3	.3		.2	.3	.1	.4	.5	.3
1.0	1.3	1.0	Debt/Worth	1.4	1.1	.5	1.0	.9	1.1
3.1	5.2	4.5		12.1	5.3	2.6	10.2	3.5	2.3
49.2	48.0	32.9		46.7	28.9	21.5	51.4	23.3	15.1
(250) 13.2	(230) 7.7	(228) 8.4	% Profit Before Taxes/Tangible Net Worth	(47) 11.0	(48) 10.6	(34) 5.4	(30) 13.5	(44) 5.0	(25) 6.3
1.0	.1	.2		.0	-5.6	-1.9	6.2	.7	-.6
19.7	18.6	12.5		22.1	18.1	8.9	18.5	8.5	5.7
5.3	4.6	3.3	% Profit Before Taxes/Total Assets	4.2	5.3	3.1	5.6	2.2	3.0
.3	.0	-.7		-2.0	-2.2	-1.4	1.0	.1	-2.2
24.8	38.0	30.3		47.9	72.6	33.3	15.3	22.5	24.2
3.8	5.2	4.1	Sales/Net Fixed Assets	3.7	6.3	4.2	2.3	2.4	5.4
1.1	1.0	1.1		.7	1.3	1.7	.7	1.2	1.1
3.2	3.7	2.9		3.0	3.8	2.3	2.7	2.5	2.6
1.3	1.4	1.4	Sales/Total Assets	1.4	1.6	1.6	1.3	1.2	1.4
.6	.6	.6		.5	.7	.7	.5	.6	.6
1.4	1.0	1.4		2.0	1.3	1.0	1.3	2.1	1.2
(214) 3.3	(190) 3.2	(195) 3.5	% Depr., Dep., Amort./Sales	(31) 4.3	(34) 3.9	(30) 2.4	(34) 3.5	(42) 4.0	(24) 2.7
5.3	5.8	6.3		10.7	7.4	4.3	6.9	6.2	6.0
4.3	3.4	3.0		4.9	2.6				
(56) 7.5	(58) 8.8	(49) 5.7	% Officers', Directors' Owners' Comp/Sales	(16) 7.0	(15) 5.7				
11.8	14.0	12.9		15.5	12.2				
2935852M	2869784M	4181664M	Net Sales ($)	31311M	90431M	154257M	279323M	762733M	2863609M
2776223M	3286627M	3770389M	Total Assets ($)	71166M	119320M	178897M	500447M	823985M	2076574M

M = $ thousand MM = $ million

See Pages 9 through 22 for Explanation of Ratios and Data

Current Data Sorted by Assets							Comparative Historical Data	
						Type of Statement		
3	13	37	58	25	23	Unqualified	224	232
	2	3	1			Reviewed	22	17
1	4	4				Compiled	14	10
6	7	3	1	1		Tax Returns	25	28
12	21	26	15	2	5	Other	68	87
157 (4/1-9/30/13)			116 (10/1/13-3/31/14)				4/1/09-3/31/10 ALL	4/1/10-3/31/11 ALL
0-500M	500M-2MM	2-10MM	10-50MM	50-100MM	100-250MM			
22	47	73	75	28	28	**NUMBER OF STATEMENTS**	353	374
%	%	%	%	%	%	**ASSETS**	%	%
37.0	33.1	28.8	25.1	19.9	28.5	Cash & Equivalents	24.5	26.2
7.1	17.0	20.9	12.4	8.0	7.6	Trade Receivables (net)	13.0	13.4
1.5	2.7	.8	2.2	.2	.2	Inventory	2.1	1.9
8.7	2.8	2.8	2.2	4.5	3.4	All Other Current	3.7	3.7
54.2	55.6	53.3	41.8	32.6	39.7	Total Current	43.3	45.2
24.6	29.5	33.6	39.1	38.6	31.2	Fixed Assets (net)	40.3	36.4
4.9	4.7	3.6	7.1	5.5	8.7	Intangibles (net)	4.3	3.8
16.2	10.1	9.4	12.0	23.3	20.3	All Other Non-Current	12.1	14.5
100.0	100.0	100.0	100.0	100.0	100.0	Total	100.0	100.0
						LIABILITIES		
16.9	8.3	3.2	1.3	.9	1.0	Notes Payable-Short Term	8.0	5.1
.2	2.7	1.4	2.0	1.8	1.7	Cur. Mat.-L.T.D.	3.9	2.6
4.9	11.3	4.9	5.6	4.6	2.6	Trade Payables	6.0	7.0
.1	.1	.1	.1	.0	.0	Income Taxes Payable	.2	.0
18.3	24.8	10.0	12.6	11.3	11.0	All Other Current	14.9	15.1
40.5	47.1	19.7	21.6	18.6	16.4	Total Current	33.0	29.8
7.4	13.8	13.6	25.4	39.1	31.0	Long-Term Debt	22.1	20.6
.0	.0	.6	.1	.0	.7	Deferred Taxes	.0	.1
10.3	5.0	7.1	5.5	4.2	5.1	All Other Non-Current	6.7	7.1
41.8	34.1	59.1	47.3	38.0	46.7	Net Worth	38.1	42.4
100.0	100.0	100.0	100.0	100.0	100.0	Total Liabilties & Net Worth	100.0	100.0
						INCOME DATA		
100.0	100.0	100.0	100.0	100.0	100.0	Net Sales	100.0	100.0
						Gross Profit		
93.0	89.5	91.4	95.6	85.1	83.0	Operating Expenses	94.8	93.0
7.0	10.5	8.6	4.4	14.9	17.0	Operating Profit	5.2	7.0
.8	3.6	3.0	1.7	5.3	10.1	All Other Expenses (net)	4.2	1.7
6.2	6.9	5.6	2.7	9.7	6.9	Profit Before Taxes	1.0	5.3
						RATIOS		
5.9	4.7	6.7	4.2	5.2	3.8		4.1	4.3
1.2	1.2	2.7	2.2	1.5	2.0	Current	1.8	1.9
.4	.6	1.6	1.1	.9	.9		1.0	1.1
5.6	4.3	6.3	4.0	5.2	3.2		3.5	3.9
1.2	1.0	2.6	1.8	1.4	1.7	Quick	(373) 1.5	1.7
.3	.6	1.4	.9	.6	.6		.7	.8
0 UND	**2** 234.8	**7** 56.0	**12** 29.4	**4** 89.0	**8** 46.9		**1** 333.9	**3** 107.6
0 UND	**15** 24.3	**30** 12.3	**27** 13.7	**23** 16.1	**32** 11.4	Sales/Receivables	**16** 22.4	**19** 19.3
3 132.8	**31** 11.6	**55** 6.6	**63** 5.8	**50** 7.3	**78** 4.7		**44** 8.3	**50** 7.2
						Cost of Sales/Inventory		
						Cost of Sales/Payables		
10.3	7.1	2.2	1.9	2.2	1.1		3.1	3.0
100.2	92.8	5.0	3.9	7.6	4.6	Sales/Working Capital	8.6	7.2
-51.0	-10.3	18.3	74.7	-95.1	-75.4		-82.7	92.8
41.2	180.6	32.7	6.7	10.5	70.8		10.5	15.0
(13) 9.5	(21) 3.7	(44) 4.8	(50) 1.9	(19) 2.8	(17) 2.4	EBIT/Interest	(263) 2.2	(257) 3.0
3.7	-.6	.2	-.7	.8	.7		-.4	1.1
							7.6	7.8
						Net Profit + Depr., Dep., Amort./Cur. Mat. L/T/D	(13) 3.6	(14) 3.7
							1.6	1.2
.1	.1	.1	.2	.1	.2		.2	.2
.3	.9	.5	.8	1.1	1.2	Fixed/Worth	1.0	.8
1.1	2.2	1.4	2.5	11.9	6.0		2.1	1.7
.3	.2	.2	.3	.4	.3		.4	.4
.7	1.5	.7	1.0	1.4	1.3	Debt/Worth	1.3	1.0
3.5	34.7	1.7	5.7	NM	10.5		3.5	3.5
122.3	80.7	28.5	14.9	19.6	11.3		17.5	23.0
(19) 65.5	(36) 19.0	(70) 6.8	(66) 2.8	(21) 7.9	(23) 2.8	% Profit Before Taxes/Tangible Net Worth	(305) 4.0	(334) 7.9
15.4	.8	-1.1	-2.8	.9	-.4		-5.3	.3
64.5	38.5	16.3	4.6	6.9	6.4		8.7	10.2
26.8	7.1	4.3	1.6	2.6	1.4	% Profit Before Taxes/Total Assets	1.3	3.1
-2.0	-1.8	-.6	-1.6	-.8	.1		-2.9	-.3
UND	140.5	89.9	17.4	13.3	8.2		30.2	25.3
47.3	36.2	16.7	3.0	2.5	1.5	Sales/Net Fixed Assets	3.3	4.2
8.6	4.9	1.2	.7	.5	.9		.9	.9
9.0	4.2	2.6	1.6	1.4	1.0		2.3	2.2
5.3	2.5	1.5	.9	.6	.5	Sales/Total Assets	1.1	1.0
3.2	1.4	.6	.4	.1	.1		.5	.5
	.7	.8	1.6	1.2	1.7		1.3	1.0
	(29) 1.3	(51) 1.9	(66) 3.7	(24) 3.7	(23) 3.1	% Depr., Dep., Amort./Sales	(274) 3.4	(291) 3.0
	5.5	5.7	6.9	7.7	6.3		5.6	6.1
			2.7				4.1	2.9
			(10) 8.8			% Officers', Directors' Owners' Comp/Sales	(51) 8.2	(45) 6.6
			13.8				12.7	12.9
57370M	178910M	556184M	1753320M	1657812M	2264605M	Net Sales ($)	8060336M	9800108M
5592M	55729M	341617M	1810185M	1923177M	4470956M	Total Assets ($)	8871953M	11780799M

M = $ thousand MM = $ million

See Pages 9 through 22 for Explanation of Ratios and Data

Comparative Historical Data / Current Data Sorted by Sales

			Type of Statement						
222	179	159	Unqualified	5	16	16	29	40	53
22	12	6	Reviewed	1		1	1	2	1
4	6	9	Compiled	2	2	2	1	2	
24	28	18	Tax Returns	5	5	5	2	1	
91	95	81	Other	9	18	11	16	18	9
					157 (4/1-9/30/13)			116 (10/1/13-3/31/14)	
4/1/11-3/31/12 ALL	4/1/12-3/31/13 ALL	4/1/13-3/31/14 ALL		0-1MM	1-3MM	3-5MM	5-10MM	10-25MM	25MM & OVER
363	320	273	NUMBER OF STATEMENTS	22	41	35	49	63	63
%	%	%	ASSETS	%	%	%	%	%	%
27.2	27.5	28.2	Cash & Equivalents	22.5	29.8	33.5	32.1	26.1	25.4
12.8	12.3	14.1	Trade Receivables (net)	7.1	6.4	10.5	17.3	19.7	15.4
1.8	1.7	1.5	Inventory	1.3	1.2	1.8	1.9	1.4	1.2
3.4	3.9	3.3	All Other Current	4.7	5.1	1.6	2.2	1.8	5.1
45.2	45.4	47.1	Total Current	35.6	42.4	47.5	53.6	48.9	47.1
37.6	36.0	34.0	Fixed Assets (net)	53.4	38.8	31.0	27.9	33.5	30.8
3.9	4.5	5.6	Intangibles (net)	.5	3.8	7.9	3.0	3.6	11.3
13.3	14.1	13.4	All Other Non-Current	10.5	15.0	13.6	15.5	14.0	10.8
100.0	100.0	100.0	Total	100.0	100.0	100.0	100.0	100.0	100.0
			LIABILITIES						
5.4	3.7	4.2	Notes Payable-Short Term	10.1	8.0	7.0	1.6	1.8	2.5
2.0	2.3	1.8	Cur. Mat.-L.T.D.	1.3	1.0	1.5	1.0	2.7	2.4
6.3	5.1	5.9	Trade Payables	1.8	4.3	3.9	4.5	9.6	7.1
.0	.1	.1	Income Taxes Payable	.1	.0	.0	.2	.2	.0
13.2	12.6	14.2	All Other Current	5.8	15.9	16.1	13.1	11.4	18.5
26.9	23.9	26.2	Total Current	19.1	29.2	28.5	20.4	25.6	30.5
21.2	20.1	20.8	Long-Term Debt	35.5	18.2	11.9	24.0	19.6	20.9
.1	.1	.3	Deferred Taxes	.0	.0	.9	.0	.2	.4
6.1	5.8	6.1	All Other Non-Current	7.3	5.2	3.5	7.2	6.4	6.4
45.8	50.1	46.7	Net Worth	38.1	47.4	55.2	48.5	48.2	41.8
100.0	100.0	100.0	Total Liabilties & Net Worth	100.0	100.0	100.0	100.0	100.0	100.0
			INCOME DATA						
100.0	100.0	100.0	Net Sales	100.0	100.0	100.0	100.0	100.0	100.0
			Gross Profit						
92.3	93.1	90.8	Operating Expenses	75.8	90.7	93.0	87.0	94.0	94.8
7.7	6.9	9.2	Operating Profit	24.2	9.3	7.0	13.0	6.0	5.2
1.9	2.9	3.5	All Other Expenses (net)	16.3	4.0	-.9	6.9	.8	1.3
5.8	4.0	5.6	Profit Before Taxes	7.9	5.3	7.9	6.2	5.2	3.9
			RATIOS						
5.0	6.5	4.9		7.4	5.9	7.6	7.1	4.8	3.2
2.1	2.2	2.0	Current	2.2	2.2	2.6	2.3	2.0	1.7
1.0	1.1	1.0		.4	.7	.9	1.2	1.3	1.0
4.4	5.8	4.6		7.4	5.6	6.9	6.2	4.1	2.9
1.8	2.0	1.8	Quick	2.1	1.9	1.5	2.2	1.7	1.5
.9	.9	.8		.3	.6	.9	.9	1.1	.6
1 252.3	0 873.2	3 106.1		0 UND	0 UND	0 999.8	4 89.0	14 25.5	16 22.6
16 22.4	17 21.2	23 16.2	Sales/Receivables	0 UND	4 101.4	17 21.7	30 12.3	32 11.4	33 11.1
46 8.0	41 8.8	51 7.2		23 16.1	21 17.8	36 10.0	52 7.0	68 5.4	64 5.7
			Cost of Sales/Inventory						
			Cost of Sales/Payables						
2.5	2.5	2.5		2.1	2.5	2.5	1.5	2.3	3.3
7.1	6.7	8.1	Sales/Working Capital	34.9	9.5	13.1	3.8	6.9	9.3
101.0	109.9	UND		-6.7	-42.9	-54.8	24.6	74.7	-123.5
10.9	8.1	16.2		7.0	29.0	149.9	20.1	36.8	9.5
(253) 3.3	(206) 2.0	(164) 3.5	EBIT/Interest	(11) 3.1	(15) 2.4	(20) 5.6	(23) 2.2	(46) 4.1	(49) 2.3
1.1	-.5	.0		-1.2	.2	-.9	-.9	1.6	-.4
9.0	6.4	13.4							7.2
(13) 4.0	(16) 2.4	(16) 2.5	Net Profit + Depr., Dep., Amort./Cur. Mat. L/T/D						(10) 2.4
1.3	1.0	1.4							1.0
.2	.1	.1		.0	.1	.1	.1	.1	.2
.8	.8	.8	Fixed/Worth	1.2	1.0	.7	.6	.7	1.0
2.0	1.6	2.0		UND	2.0	1.4	1.8	2.0	2.5
.3	.3	.3		.2	.2	.1	.2	.4	.3
.9	.8	1.0	Debt/Worth	.9	.8	.7	.8	.9	1.3
3.4	2.3	5.0		-146.4	3.0	2.2	7.1	3.7	6.6
20.6	16.6	30.9		60.4	34.1	65.7	17.9	28.9	19.2
(322) 6.5	(281) 4.4	(235) 7.5	% Profit Before Taxes/Tangible Net Worth	(16) 12.3	(34) 4.8	(31) 18.2	(43) 3.1	(60) 7.6	(51) 4.8
.2	-2.9	-.8		2.1	-11.1	1.7	-1.0	-1.3	-.8
9.5	8.4	11.8		25.5	16.6	36.8	8.9	9.8	8.3
3.1	1.8	2.5	% Profit Before Taxes/Total Assets	3.3	3.9	7.0	1.4	2.4	2.4
-.1	-2.2	-.8		-1.0	-5.7	.8	-1.0	-.7	-.9
31.6	40.6	46.2		UND	90.1	182.6	68.5	24.2	18.8
4.0	4.6	8.0	Sales/Net Fixed Assets	1.9	10.9	16.7	11.1	7.0	5.4
.8	.9	1.1		.2	.6	1.2	.8	1.1	2.2
2.2	2.4	2.4		2.2	3.3	3.2	2.1	2.5	1.8
1.0	1.0	1.3	Sales/Total Assets	.4	1.5	1.9	.8	1.0	1.3
.4	.5	.5		.1	.4	.7	.1	.5	.7
1.1	1.2	1.0		5.7	1.1	.7	.7	.9	1.4
(299) 2.7	(243) 3.1	(200) 2.7	% Depr., Dep., Amort./Sales	(12) 21.8	(22) 5.6	(22) 2.0	(36) 2.3	(57) 2.6	(51) 2.4
5.8	6.4	6.2		27.3	12.1	5.6	9.7	5.6	3.9
3.3	2.1	2.2							
(49) 8.3	(45) 8.2	(38) 4.6	% Officers', Directors' Owners' Comp/Sales						
13.8	16.1	10.1							
8640953M	8332479M	6468201M	Net Sales ($)	10640M	72965M	137887M	354329M	996460M	4895920M
11329186M	10746034M	8607256M	Total Assets ($)	33784M	153540M	184005M	1462645M	1656764M	5116518M

M = $ thousand MM = $ million

See Pages 9 through 22 for Explanation of Ratios and Data

HEALTH CARE AND SOCIAL ASSISTANCE

Current Data Sorted by Assets | **Comparative Historical Data**

0-500M	500M-2MM	2-10MM	10-50MM	50-100MM	100-250MM	Type of Statement	4/1/09-3/31/10 ALL	4/1/10-3/31/11 ALL
3	14	45	86	36	23	Unqualified	222	247
6	26	76	26	3		Reviewed	162	140
310	243	149	20	3		Compiled	698	667
840	464	169	19	4	4	Tax Returns	1634	1520
551	560	373	148	23	21	Other	1356	1521
	339 (4/1-9/30/13)		3,906 (10/1/13-3/31/14)					
1710	1307	812	299	69	48	NUMBER OF STATEMENTS	4072	4095
%	%	%	%	%	%	**ASSETS**	%	%
42.4	28.9	17.8	14.3	14.0	16.2	Cash & Equivalents	27.5	28.2
3.1	6.8	15.7	23.2	17.4	13.8	Trade Receivables (net)	9.5	9.7
1.3	1.1	1.1	1.2	.8	.6	Inventory	1.0	1.1
3.3	3.9	3.8	3.5	5.7	4.5	All Other Current	4.2	3.7
50.1	40.6	38.4	42.1	37.9	35.1	Total Current	42.2	42.8
30.8	40.2	44.4	42.5	31.3	35.2	Fixed Assets (net)	41.1	40.2
4.8	4.7	5.5	5.5	18.6	17.0	Intangibles (net)	4.5	4.7
14.3	14.4	11.8	9.9	12.1	12.7	All Other Non-Current	12.3	12.4
100.0	100.0	100.0	100.0	100.0	100.0	Total	100.0	100.0
						LIABILITIES		
30.5	15.7	7.4	3.8	3.5	10.5	Notes Payable-Short Term	18.5	18.9
6.3	5.6	6.0	4.5	3.8	5.1	Cur. Mat.-L.T.D.	7.9	7.0
3.0	3.3	4.7	6.4	6.1	4.9	Trade Payables	3.2	3.4
.2	.1	.4	.7	1.4	.2	Income Taxes Payable	.4	.3
34.5	22.1	17.0	16.7	17.9	12.1	All Other Current	27.3	26.5
74.5	46.9	35.5	32.1	32.8	32.8	Total Current	57.2	56.1
23.8	30.7	31.5	27.3	21.9	26.8	Long-Term Debt	32.6	30.1
.0	.1	.4	.3	.4	.6	Deferred Taxes	.1	.2
8.8	4.5	3.3	4.2	7.3	8.2	All Other Non-Current	4.8	5.6
-7.1	17.8	29.3	36.1	37.7	31.6	Net Worth	5.2	8.0
100.0	100.0	100.0	100.0	100.0	100.0	Total Liabilities & Net Worth	100.0	100.0
						INCOME DATA		
100.0	100.0	100.0	100.0	100.0	100.0	Net Sales	100.0	100.0
						Gross Profit		
88.2	84.7	81.0	86.9	92.7	93.6	Operating Expenses	87.8	87.1
11.8	15.3	19.0	13.1	7.3	6.4	Operating Profit	12.2	12.9
.2	2.7	5.3	3.8	1.6	2.9	All Other Expenses (net)	2.6	2.5
11.6	12.6	13.6	9.3	5.8	3.5	Profit Before Taxes	9.6	10.4
						RATIOS		
2.4	2.6	2.3	2.5	2.0	2.4		2.1	2.3
.9	.9	1.1	1.2	1.3	1.5	Current	.9	.9
.3	.3	.5	.8	.8	.9		.3	.3
2.2	2.2	2.1	2.2	1.7	2.1		1.8	2.0
(1705) .8	(1306) .8	1.0	(298) 1.1	1.1	1.2	Quick	(4065) .8	(4089) .8
.2	.3	.3	.7	.6	.8		.2	.3
0 UND	0 UND	0 UND	8 44.9	14 25.4	8 44.7		0 UND	0 UND
0 UND	0 UND	0 UND	32 11.4	33 11.2	33 10.9	Sales/Receivables	0 UND	0 UND
0 UND	0 UND	32 11.3	50 7.3	43 8.4	45 8.1		2 174.0	5 80.0
						Cost of Sales/Inventory		
						Cost of Sales/Payables		
34.5	18.6	11.7	8.0	9.9	9.0		24.7	19.3
-244.6	-242.4	80.1	24.6	25.9	18.6	Sales/Working Capital	-207.7	-337.5
-24.0	-20.9	-20.9	-40.1	-42.0	-66.3		-20.9	-21.6
47.0	50.3	48.4	31.7	17.4	8.7		22.7	27.9
(1049) 9.8	(992) 9.5	(611) 7.6	(233) 7.9	(59) 3.9	(43) 2.4	EBIT/Interest	(3073) 5.4	(3014) 6.3
1.3	1.6	1.8	1.7	.8	-.1		1.0	1.1
5.9	6.9	8.2	4.1	3.8			4.4	4.8
(21) 2.9	(31) 1.7	(76) 1.5	(49) 1.5	(24) 1.5		Net Profit + Depr., Dep., Amort./Cur. Mat. L/T/D	(245) 1.8	(194) 1.8
1.0	.7	.7	.8	.4			.8	1.0
.1	.4	.4	.5	.5	.7		.5	.4
1.2	2.3	1.7	1.3	1.3	1.5	Fixed/Worth	2.7	2.3
-1.7	-4.9	18.4	4.9	-27.8	-.4		-3.4	-4.3
.7	.8	.8	.8	1.1	.7		1.1	.9
8.0	4.6	2.9	2.5	2.6	2.1	Debt/Worth	6.8	5.4
-3.4	-8.2	54.6	9.7	-46.9	-2.7		-6.6	-7.4
500.1	213.7	149.2	66.3	68.4	26.9		225.1	222.2
(1012) 133.3	(854) 75.6	(626) 44.2	(255) 24.6	(50) 17.2	(33) 11.7	% Profit Before Taxes/Tangible Net Worth	(2549) 59.3	(2671) 60.4
33.7	18.0	10.1	2.4	1.3	-.2		9.7	10.4
135.0	66.5	38.2	19.3	10.5	18.6		58.4	64.4
42.0	20.2	8.6	6.2	4.7	3.8	% Profit Before Taxes/Total Assets	12.0	13.9
2.2	1.6	1.5	.4	-.6	-1.8		.3	.4
427.0	73.3	32.3	18.0	30.4	26.1		82.3	86.3
66.2	23.5	12.9	6.8	10.5	8.3	Sales/Net Fixed Assets	22.3	22.9
19.2	6.8	2.4	1.8	4.1	3.2		7.8	7.6
21.3	11.2	6.2	3.7	3.5	2.8		13.5	13.1
11.3	5.4	3.1	2.1	1.9	1.7	Sales/Total Assets	6.4	5.8
5.5	2.3	1.0	1.0	.9	1.0		2.6	2.6
.4	.7	1.2	1.5	1.4	.8		.8	.8
(818) .9	(837) 1.7	(667) 2.3	(271) 2.6	(61) 2.2	(27) 1.9	% Depr., Dep., Amort./Sales	(2860) 1.8	(2739) 1.7
1.8	4.2	7.6	5.5	3.5	3.6		3.7	3.7
12.6	8.8	8.1	7.8	8.7	11.6		12.3	12.5
(1103) 21.7	(644) 18.9	(282) 20.5	(64) 19.4	(14) 27.9	(11) 17.8	% Officers', Directors' Owners' Comp/Sales	(2193) 23.8	(2130) 23.0
32.4	30.8	32.9	31.7	32.6	33.8		34.0	33.0
5372941M	10552359M	14988778M	16308319M	13776992M	20604061M	Net Sales ($)	97386418M	90946410M
367917M	1360712M	3636277M	6375043M	4928443M	7569599M	Total Assets ($)	22074414M	23196586M

M = $ thousand MM = $ million

See Pages 9 through 22 for Explanation of Ratios and Data

Comparative Historical Data / Current Data Sorted by Sales

4/1/11-3/31/12 ALL	4/1/12-3/31/13 ALL	4/1/13-3/31/14 ALL	Type of Statement	0-1MM	1-3MM	3-5MM	5-10MM	10-25MM	25MM & OVER
244	202	207	Unqualified	4	11	10	18	41	123
170	128	137	Reviewed	5	8	8	20	43	53
775	645	725	Compiled	123	159	104	125	148	66
2038	1684	1500	Tax Returns	412	441	202	210	163	72
1760	1740	1676	Other	268	370	202	253	295	288
				339 (4/1-9/30/13)			3,906 (10/1/13-3/31/14)		
4987	4399	4245	NUMBER OF STATEMENTS	812	989	526	626	690	602
%	%	%	ASSETS	%	%	%	%	%	%
30.9	30.6	30.8	Cash & Equivalents	27.4	33.4	35.9	34.4	30.1	23.7
8.1	8.1	8.4	Trade Receivables (net)	2.9	5.0	6.2	7.9	13.0	18.6
1.0	1.1	1.2	Inventory	1.0	1.0	1.5	1.1	1.4	1.2
3.9	3.6	3.6	All Other Current	2.2	3.9	3.4	3.8	4.1	4.7
43.9	43.4	44.0	Total Current	33.5	43.3	46.9	47.2	48.5	48.2
38.6	39.0	37.2	Fixed Assets (net)	50.2	34.8	31.4	35.6	34.7	33.2
4.8	4.9	5.3	Intangibles (net)	4.0	5.1	6.7	5.0	5.4	6.6
12.7	12.7	13.5	All Other Non-Current	12.3	16.8	15.0	12.3	11.4	12.0
100.0	100.0	100.0	Total	100.0	100.0	100.0	100.0	100.0	100.0
			LIABILITIES						
19.4	18.3	19.0	Notes Payable-Short Term	20.2	23.4	21.3	18.9	16.9	10.6
7.0	6.7	5.9	Cur. Mat.-L.T.D.	4.5	5.3	6.3	7.2	6.6	6.0
3.4	3.7	3.7	Trade Payables	2.0	2.3	3.8	4.5	4.9	6.3
.3	.3	.3	Income Taxes Payable	.1	.2	.1	.1	.4	.7
27.2	24.9	25.6	All Other Current	18.3	21.9	26.1	26.8	33.7	30.2
57.2	53.9	54.4	Total Current	45.0	53.1	57.6	57.6	62.5	53.8
29.0	29.9	27.6	Long-Term Debt	39.4	26.8	30.1	24.4	22.5	20.2
.1	.1	.1	Deferred Taxes	.0	.0	.0	.2	.2	.5
6.3	6.2	6.1	All Other Non-Current	6.3	7.7	5.9	7.4	3.8	4.7
7.4	9.8	11.7	Net Worth	9.3	12.4	6.4	10.4	11.0	20.8
100.0	100.0	100.0	Total Liabilties & Net Worth	100.0	100.0	100.0	100.0	100.0	100.0
			INCOME DATA						
100.0	100.0	100.0	Net Sales	100.0	100.0	100.0	100.0	100.0	100.0
			Gross Profit						
86.7	85.1	85.8	Operating Expenses	71.3	84.9	87.7	89.6	92.4	93.7
13.3	14.9	14.2	Operating Profit	28.7	15.1	12.3	10.4	7.6	6.3
2.5	2.8	2.3	All Other Expenses (net)	9.0	1.9	.4	.2	-.3	.3
10.8	12.1	11.9	Profit Before Taxes	19.7	13.2	11.8	10.2	7.9	5.9
			RATIOS						
2.2	2.4	2.4		2.5	3.5	2.6	2.5	2.1	1.9
.9	1.0	1.0	Current	.8	1.0	1.0	1.0	1.0	1.1
.3	.3	.4		.2	.3	.4	.4	.4	.6
1.9	2.2	2.2		2.2	3.0	2.3	2.2	1.9	1.7
(4985) .8	(4396) .8	(4238) .9	Quick	(811) .7	(986) .9	(525) 1.0	(625) .9	(689) .9	.9
.3	.3	.3		.2	.3	.4	.3	.3	.5
0 UND	0 UND	0 UND		0 UND	0 UND	0 UND	0 UND	0 UND	0 UND
0 UND	0 UND	0 UND	Sales/Receivables	0 UND	0 UND	0 UND	0 UND	0 UND	13 27.8
0 UND	0 999.8	1 715.8		0 UND	0 UND	0 UND	0 UND	26 13.9	38 9.6
			Cost of Sales/Inventory						
			Cost of Sales/Payables						
21.3	18.1	18.1		14.0	17.2	22.4	24.3	20.8	15.2
-349.5	-999.8	-999.8	Sales/Working Capital	-69.5	999.8	902.7	-568.8	NM	281.1
-23.3	-22.3	-23.4		-6.5	-18.1	-26.6	-32.5	-33.4	-41.1
29.9	39.0	45.1		22.5	45.7	50.5	56.3	54.3	40.2
(3511) 6.8	(3016) 7.7	(2987) 8.9	EBIT/Interest	(369) 5.7	(661) 9.9	(394) 9.6	(498) 11.3	(569) 8.5	(496) 6.9
1.2	1.2	1.5		2.1	2.3	1.4	1.6	1.0	1.0
4.4	4.9	5.5			2.9	5.4	13.1	6.3	4.1
(247) 1.9	(224) 1.9	(209) 1.7	Net Profit + Depr., Dep., Amort./Cur. Mat. L/T/D		(15) 1.6	(11) 2.3	(24) 2.2	(50) 1.9	(107) 1.5
1.0	.8	.8			.6	-.8	1.1	.8	.7
.3	.3	.3		.2	.2	.2	.3	.4	.4
2.1	1.9	1.6	Fixed/Worth	2.3	1.4	1.4	1.7	1.4	1.4
-3.8	-6.1	-6.3		83.3	-4.0	-1.8	-3.5	-6.5	-22.8
.9	.8	.8		.7	.5	.7	.9	.8	1.0
5.7	4.6	4.2	Debt/Worth	3.4	4.4	5.0	6.1	4.3	3.5
-6.6	-8.0	-7.8		-17.8	-6.2	-4.7	-6.6	-7.4	-18.0
245.6	248.7	255.0		140.2	264.1	348.9	386.4	250.3	152.5
(3206) 71.5	(2913) 70.6	(2830) 72.4	% Profit Before Taxes/Tangible Net Worth	(583) 39.2	(645) 100.0	(328) 108.0	(395) 94.9	(449) 65.7	(430) 34.1
13.7	13.5	13.6		10.0	34.5	31.6	17.6	10.3	2.9
70.8	77.2	78.7		63.4	102.6	106.7	91.6	65.8	37.5
15.4	16.2	18.3	% Profit Before Taxes/Total Assets	10.9	32.7	29.4	23.7	13.6	8.5
.7	.8	1.4		1.6	4.5	3.0	1.3	.2	-.1
124.2	114.3	119.4		102.3	137.3	203.6	97.6	123.9	75.5
27.3	24.2	26.3	Sales/Net Fixed Assets	8.2	27.4	37.1	33.8	32.4	22.9
8.4	7.4	7.9		.2	8.7	13.2	13.6	12.6	9.3
14.5	13.2	13.2		6.6	11.5	15.1	16.8	17.6	12.4
6.7	6.0	5.9	Sales/Total Assets	2.3	5.6	7.7	8.6	8.0	5.3
2.8	2.4	2.5		.2	2.7	3.6	4.1	3.8	2.7
.7	.7	.7		1.6	.5	.5	.6	.7	.8
(3145) 1.7	(2810) 1.6	(2681) 1.6	% Depr., Dep., Amort./Sales	(459) 10.3	(573) 1.2	(274) 1.5	(400) 1.3	(507) 1.4	(468) 1.6
3.7	3.7	3.6		21.1	3.3	3.3	2.7	2.5	2.6
11.4	10.9	10.6		13.1	10.8	10.1	8.1	11.0	8.6
(2673) 21.9	(2200) 20.6	(2118) 20.6	% Officers', Directors' Owners' Comp/Sales	(301) 20.2	(608) 18.3	(290) 20.0	(344) 20.5	(356) 24.5	(219) 22.8
32.2	32.1	31.9		30.4	29.3	33.2	31.0	35.9	34.1
108650402M	90631247M	81603450M	Net Sales ($)	429993M	1823599M	2053657M	4478079M	10705361M	62112761M
25140183M	24479378M	24237991M	Total Assets ($)	729368M	1221260M	696143M	1153292M	2659663M	17778265M

M = $ thousand MM = $ million

See Pages 9 through 22 for Explanation of Ratios and Data

Current Data Sorted by Assets							Comparative Historical Data	
						Type of Statement		
1	1	4	4	2		Unqualified	9	18
		1	1			Reviewed	4	5
6	6	4				Compiled	19	15
33	10	9				Tax Returns	27	24
17	18	16	4	2	2	Other	29	35
	18 (4/1-9/30/13)		123 (10/1/13-3/31/14)				4/1/09-3/31/10	4/1/10-3/31/11
0-500M	500M-2MM	2-10MM	10-50MM	50-100MM	100-250MM		ALL	ALL
57	35	34	9	4	2	NUMBER OF STATEMENTS	88	97
%	%	%	%	%	%	**ASSETS**	%	%
55.1	28.9	15.6				Cash & Equivalents	19.2	24.2
1.6	10.0	17.4				Trade Receivables (net)	14.8	15.7
.9	2.7	1.3				Inventory	.4	1.3
1.7	5.7	6.5				All Other Current	3.8	4.9
59.3	47.3	40.8				Total Current	38.3	46.1
23.4	25.2	47.1				Fixed Assets (net)	40.0	35.4
3.7	11.6	1.9				Intangibles (net)	6.6	6.0
13.7	15.8	10.2				All Other Non-Current	15.0	12.5
100.0	100.0	100.0				Total	100.0	100.0
						LIABILITIES		
23.9	23.2	5.9				Notes Payable-Short Term	17.0	17.9
6.1	3.0	4.7				Cur. Mat.-L.T.D.	11.7	4.8
.9	6.6	3.7				Trade Payables	6.4	4.9
.1	.0	.0				Income Taxes Payable	.1	.7
44.9	15.0	36.8				All Other Current	24.9	22.4
75.9	47.9	51.2				Total Current	60.1	50.6
22.8	28.3	28.3				Long-Term Debt	29.6	25.1
.0	.0	.5				Deferred Taxes	.3	.3
4.1	2.4	1.6				All Other Non-Current	4.3	5.6
-2.8	21.4	18.5				Net Worth	5.7	18.3
100.0	100.0	100.0				Total Liabilties & Net Worth	100.0	100.0
						INCOME DATA		
100.0	100.0	100.0				Net Sales	100.0	100.0
						Gross Profit		
84.7	82.9	84.1				Operating Expenses	86.8	87.8
15.3	17.1	15.9				Operating Profit	13.2	12.2
1.5	.7	5.9				All Other Expenses (net)	3.7	2.3
13.8	16.4	10.0				Profit Before Taxes	9.5	9.9
						RATIOS		
4.1	11.6	2.4					2.2	3.4
1.2	1.7	1.0				Current	.9	1.4
.4	.7	.3					.4	.5
4.1	10.8	1.7					1.8	2.9
1.1	1.7	.8				Quick	.8	1.0
.4	.5	.2					.3	.4
0 UND	0 UND	0 UND					0 UND	0 UND
0 UND	0 UND	9 39.6				Sales/Receivables	1 428.1	1 276.4
0 UND	3 106.4	32 11.4					42 8.6	38 9.5
						Cost of Sales/Inventory		
						Cost of Sales/Payables		
17.8	11.7	11.3					11.3	6.2
151.2	36.4	NM				Sales/Working Capital	-302.2	57.3
-41.9	-31.2	-5.5					-13.1	-32.1
82.9	95.7	20.6					16.7	44.0
(40) 29.2	(25) 16.3	(21) 4.8				EBIT/Interest	(68) 3.0	(70) 4.7
4.2	1.4	1.9					-.1	1.0
						Net Profit + Depr., Dep., Amort./Cur. Mat. L/T/D		
.0	.3	.3					.5	.3
.4	1.7	1.2				Fixed/Worth	1.4	1.3
NM	-9.0	6.9					-2.7	-4.9
.2	.4	.6					1.0	.4
2.3	3.7	3.0				Debt/Worth	3.7	2.2
-3.1	-635.0	7.7					-5.7	-7.5
528.3	216.8	55.2					120.4	177.7
(38) 165.7	(25) 117.9	(31) 19.7				% Profit Before Taxes/Tangible Net Worth	(60) 26.6	(66) 25.8
51.3	40.8	9.0					-.2	3.2
183.7	62.5	18.4					50.8	60.5
71.1	30.2	6.1				% Profit Before Taxes/Total Assets	6.8	11.3
10.2	2.4	1.5					-1.7	.1
UND	113.5	77.6					47.7	93.2
87.2	27.4	13.2				Sales/Net Fixed Assets	18.9	20.8
26.3	10.5	.7					3.7	4.0
25.4	6.9	6.2					10.2	9.5
13.3	3.8	2.6				Sales/Total Assets	3.3	3.4
6.0	1.5	.6					1.4	1.5
.3	.7	1.7					.9	.8
(25) .9	(23) 1.1	(21) 2.9				% Depr., Dep., Amort./Sales	(66) 2.2	(64) 2.0
1.5	2.3	18.2					4.9	3.8
10.7	7.3						10.4	8.0
(39) 18.1	(16) 13.5					% Officers', Directors' Owners' Comp/Sales	(32) 16.0	(37) 22.5
29.9	21.0						31.2	32.7
133500M	206813M	508916M	168954M	504637M	436700M	Net Sales ($)	1436445M	2602003M
9661M	34778M	149833M	166359M	283371M	353100M	Total Assets ($)	737601M	1152021M

M = $ thousand MM = $ million

See Pages 9 through 22 for Explanation of Ratios and Data

Comparative Historical Data / Current Data Sorted by Sales

4/1/11-3/31/12 ALL	4/1/12-3/31/13 ALL	4/1/13-3/31/14 ALL	Type of Statement	0-1MM	1-3MM	3-5MM	5-10MM	10-25MM	25MM & OVER
17	14	12	Unqualified	1			1	5	5
3	1	2	Reviewed					1	1
23	12	16	Compiled	2	5	2	1	5	1
58	45	52	Tax Returns	22	12	7	7	1	3
55	43	59	Other	11	12	6	11	11	8
				18 (4/1-9/30/13)			123 (10/1/13-3/31/14)		
156	115	141	NUMBER OF STATEMENTS	36	29	15	20	23	18
%	%	%	**ASSETS**	%	%	%	%	%	%
32.0	32.1	36.1	Cash & Equivalents	40.9	50.4	32.2	34.6	18.4	30.7
10.0	8.8	8.5	Trade Receivables (net)	5.1	4.0	.0	5.9	22.0	15.5
.7	.7	1.3	Inventory	.2	.0	.3	4.2	3.9	.4
3.8	5.9	4.0	All Other Current	1.4	3.3	3.8	3.1	7.2	7.1
46.5	47.5	49.9	Total Current	47.7	57.7	36.2	47.7	51.5	53.7
32.4	28.7	31.6	Fixed Assets (net)	36.3	22.6	30.2	32.8	32.6	35.5
9.2	9.2	5.5	Intangibles (net)	5.8	2.5	14.7	5.4	5.0	2.4
12.0	14.5	13.0	All Other Non-Current	10.2	17.2	18.9	14.1	10.9	8.4
100.0	100.0	100.0	Total	100.0	100.0	100.0	100.0	100.0	100.0
			LIABILITIES						
19.8	24.0	17.1	Notes Payable-Short Term	14.4	20.8	10.6	23.9	11.1	22.1
3.6	5.3	4.6	Cur. Mat.-L.T.D.	5.2	5.3	5.8	5.0	3.4	2.7
4.6	4.1	3.7	Trade Payables	2.3	4.8	.0	3.5	3.8	8.2
.8	.4	.1	Income Taxes Payable	.0	.0	.5	.0	.0	.6
20.3	32.9	32.1	All Other Current	19.2	43.8	35.2	23.8	46.8	26.7
49.2	66.7	57.7	Total Current	41.0	74.6	52.1	56.2	65.2	60.3
16.3	18.8	24.9	Long-Term Debt	33.9	17.2	33.5	29.2	19.8	14.0
.0	.2	.1	Deferred Taxes	.0	.0	.0	.0	.0	.9
6.7	7.7	2.7	All Other Non-Current	5.5	3.9	.6	1.6	.8	.3
27.8	6.7	14.6	Net Worth	19.5	4.4	13.9	13.0	14.2	24.5
100.0	100.0	100.0	Total Liabilties & Net Worth	100.0	100.0	100.0	100.0	100.0	100.0
			INCOME DATA						
100.0	100.0	100.0	Net Sales	100.0	100.0	100.0	100.0	100.0	100.0
			Gross Profit						
87.8	85.5	85.4	Operating Expenses	73.5	79.1	88.4	90.7	96.5	97.0
12.2	14.5	14.6	Operating Profit	26.5	20.9	11.6	9.3	3.5	3.0
2.5	2.2	2.4	All Other Expenses (net)	6.5	2.4	.2	.0	1.1	-.1
9.7	12.3	12.2	Profit Before Taxes	20.0	18.5	11.4	9.3	2.4	3.1
			RATIOS						
3.1	2.6	3.2		6.5	9.4	3.2	1.8	4.6	1.7
1.2	1.3	1.3	Current	1.3	1.6	1.8	.8	1.4	1.3
.5	.3	.5		.4	.5	.4	.5	1.0	.9
2.9	2.4	2.8		6.5	7.7	2.9	1.6	2.7	1.5
.9	.9	1.2	Quick	1.1	1.5	1.1	.8	1.3	1.1
.4	.2	.5		.4	.5	.2	.3	.8	.8
0 UND	0 UND	0 UND		0 UND	0 UND	0 UND	0 UND	10 36.6	0 UND
0 UND	0 UND	0 UND	Sales/Receivables	0 UND	0 UND	0 UND	0 UND	26 13.9	16 23.1
26 13.8	20 18.3	15 24.7		0 UND	0 UND	0 UND	1 277.1	45 8.1	32 11.4
			Cost of Sales/Inventory						
			Cost of Sales/Payables						
10.4	12.8	12.6		11.9	12.7	14.6	35.5	6.1	10.9
169.2	197.2	42.2	Sales/Working Capital	95.8	36.1	41.2	-331.8	30.9	31.2
-23.0	-13.1	-37.6		-19.0	-50.6	-22.2	-31.0	-999.8	-64.4
31.2	66.3	70.8		75.9	203.5	121.7	27.9	5.6	20.1
(95) 8.0	(77) 9.6	(99) 9.3	EBIT/Interest	(16) 29.6	(21) 42.8	(13) 42.5	(18) 8.6	(16) 2.7	(15) 6.8
.7	1.7	1.7		3.5	4.4	9.1	1.6	.1	1.2
			Net Profit + Depr., Dep., Amort./Cur. Mat. L/T/D						
.1	.1	.2		.0	.2	.1	.6	.2	.3
1.0	1.0	.9	Fixed/Worth	.8	.3	1.2	1.6	1.2	1.0
54.8	-11.1	8.8		32.2	1.1	10.0	-2.7	2.5	1.6
.5	.7	.5		.1	.2	.6	1.2	.3	.6
2.0	2.9	2.1	Debt/Worth	2.7	1.1	2.5	12.0	.9	2.3
-25.0	-4.4	UND		UND	NM	-28.8	-3.0	5.5	6.7
138.8	292.6	192.5		335.3	217.5	837.5	352.2	20.6	63.8
(113) 39.3	(78) 126.0	(108) 62.0	% Profit Before Taxes/Tangible Net Worth	(28) 86.8	(22) 118.6	(11) 183.7	(13) 78.4	(18) 8.9	(16) 17.9
1.5	11.2	11.5		17.8	51.3	40.1	44.2	-1.6	.5
58.9	99.1	89.1		159.7	176.5	113.4	93.9	22.6	19.4
11.7	26.0	18.5	% Profit Before Taxes/Total Assets	21.8	44.1	46.0	29.8	5.7	5.2
-.1	1.5	2.1		1.9	14.5	1.9	3.2	-.7	.0
254.0	156.1	168.0		UND	146.3	999.8	230.5	84.5	260.6
27.7	36.1	27.4	Sales/Net Fixed Assets	29.5	37.2	26.4	47.1	15.4	15.3
7.4	9.1	6.6		1.2	24.2	5.5	10.4	2.5	2.2
11.3	13.4	12.5		10.9	15.9	15.5	23.4	4.3	7.9
4.7	5.7	5.0	Sales/Total Assets	3.9	5.7	7.6	8.6	2.6	5.6
1.5	2.2	1.8		.3	3.7	3.4	4.8	1.5	1.3
.8	.4	.8		1.2	.3		.3	1.1	1.7
(91) 2.1	(68) 1.0	(82) 1.6	% Depr., Dep., Amort./Sales	(19) 4.8	(17) .5		(10) 1.3	(15) 2.5	(12) 2.7
4.3	3.6	3.5		21.5	1.0		2.5	3.5	4.1
9.6	9.4	8.4		14.7	9.3	7.5	6.4		
(63) 17.3	(57) 17.2	(64) 15.6	% Officers', Directors' Owners' Comp/Sales	(15) 22.2	(17) 15.1	(10) 12.1	(13) 9.1		
33.9	31.6	26.0		29.5	19.9	26.4	30.7		
4257141M	2369894M	1959520M	Net Sales ($)	20077M	54700M	57650M	139521M	337673M	1349899M
1432879M	1014716M	997102M	Total Assets ($)	33854M	11824M	17609M	24858M	191027M	717930M

M = $ thousand MM = $ million

See Pages 9 through 22 for Explanation of Ratios and Data

Current Data Sorted by Assets / Comparative Historical Data

0-500M	500M-2MM	2-10MM	10-50MM	50-100MM	100-250MM	Type of Statement	4/1/09-3/31/10 ALL	4/1/10-3/31/11 ALL
3	4	3	4	3	3	Unqualified	27	24
3	2	4	3			Reviewed	7	14
153	107	14		3		Compiled	226	235
853	332	29	2	1	4	Tax Returns	792	832
428	258	32	12	4	4	Other	330	481
89 (4/1-9/30/13)			2,179 (10/1/13-3/31/14)				4/1/09-3/31/10	4/1/10-3/31/11
0-500M	500M-2MM	2-10MM	10-50MM	50-100MM	100-250MM		ALL	ALL
1440	703	82	21	11	11	NUMBER OF STATEMENTS	1382	1586
%	%	%	%	%	%	**ASSETS**	%	%
29.7	16.1	12.2	23.9	17.3	20.5	Cash & Equivalents	22.0	23.0
2.2	2.3	9.0	6.7	7.1	4.6	Trade Receivables (net)	4.0	4.4
.3	.2	1.2	.2	1.8	1.2	Inventory	.4	.5
2.2	1.8	2.6	1.4	1.9	1.8	All Other Current	2.9	3.1
34.4	20.4	25.0	32.1	28.1	28.2	Total Current	29.3	30.9
38.3	40.3	52.9	28.6	24.9	25.4	Fixed Assets (net)	42.8	41.8
15.2	26.5	13.6	28.8	41.3	43.6	Intangibles (net)	17.0	16.6
12.0	12.8	8.5	10.5	5.7	2.8	All Other Non-Current	10.8	10.7
100.0	100.0	100.0	100.0	100.0	100.0	Total	100.0	100.0
						LIABILITIES		
17.9	7.1	5.0	2.1	4.1	.8	Notes Payable-Short Term	13.8	13.5
7.2	5.0	3.0	7.6	7.0	3.1	Cur. Mat.-L.T.D.	8.2	7.5
2.4	.9	2.9	4.1	4.4	3.7	Trade Payables	1.8	2.1
.1	.0	.5	.0	.0	.1	Income Taxes Payable	.1	.1
19.9	6.4	10.5	8.3	18.4	10.2	All Other Current	19.0	15.2
47.5	19.4	21.8	22.1	33.9	17.9	Total Current	43.0	38.4
54.2	58.0	48.0	20.4	46.0	21.9	Long-Term Debt	49.1	49.0
.0	.0	.0	.6	.7	2.2	Deferred Taxes	.1	.1
7.6	3.7	4.3	3.6	8.6	2.8	All Other Non-Current	6.2	8.9
-9.3	18.8	25.9	53.3	10.8	55.2	Net Worth	1.5	3.6
100.0	100.0	100.0	100.0	100.0	100.0	Total Liabilties & Net Worth	100.0	100.0
						INCOME DATA		
100.0	100.0	100.0	100.0	100.0	100.0	Net Sales	100.0	100.0
						Gross Profit		
88.0	81.4	77.6	87.4	98.2	91.5	Operating Expenses	87.1	85.4
12.0	18.6	22.4	12.6	1.8	8.5	Operating Profit	12.9	14.6
1.5	4.1	9.0	-.1	4.5	3.2	All Other Expenses (net)	2.7	2.9
10.6	14.5	13.4	12.8	-2.8	5.3	Profit Before Taxes	10.2	11.6
						RATIOS		
3.0	3.8	2.6	3.1	1.3	2.9		2.3	2.9
.9	1.1	1.2	1.1	1.0	1.1	Current	.8	1.0
.3	.3	.5	.7	.6	.7		.2	.3
2.8	3.4	2.3	3.1	1.0	2.6		2.0	2.5
(1439) .8	1.0	1.0	1.0	.8	.8	Quick	(1381) .6	(1583) .8
.2	.2	.4	.6	.4	.4		.2	.2
0 UND	0 UND	0 UND	0 UND	0 UND	0 UND		0 UND	0 UND
0 UND	0 UND	0 UND	5 67.0	20 18.1	19 19.3	Sales/Receivables	0 UND	0 UND
0 UND	0 UND	23 16.0	30 12.0	37 9.9	31 11.7		0 UND	0 UND
						Cost of Sales/Inventory		
						Cost of Sales/Payables		
25.5	13.6	12.8	17.6	53.3	28.6		25.8	19.3
-404.5	272.5	40.3	533.5	-827.0	69.4	Sales/Working Capital	-111.7	-855.8
-18.1	-16.5	-37.6	-28.0	-12.9	-22.7		-14.9	-17.0
20.8	16.4	20.9	16.7	24.0			15.6	18.6
(1027) 7.0	(583) 5.5	(59) 5.0	(15) 5.5	.5		EBIT/Interest	(1107) 4.4	(1240) 5.7
2.0	1.9	2.5	3.1	-.5			1.3	1.5
							7.9	7.4
						Net Profit + Depr., Dep., Amort./Cur. Mat. L/T/D	(30) 2.5	(42) 1.6
							1.0	.6
.5	1.1	1.1	.2	-5.0	.5		.9	.9
20.5	485.0	4.1	2.3	-.4	1.9	Fixed/Worth	UND	42.5
-.7	-.8	-25.2	-1.9	-.2	-.2		-.9	-.8
1.1	2.1	1.3	.5	-23.1	.3		1.6	1.5
-16.6	-21.0	7.2	3.0	-2.2	1.5	Debt/Worth	-24.0	-137.8
-2.1	-2.2	-16.3	-2.7	-1.8	-1.5		-2.4	-2.5
418.2	221.9	107.6	87.3				283.5	296.9
(670) 139.1	(326) 77.8	(58) 50.8	(14) 35.8			% Profit Before Taxes/Tangible Net Worth	(660) 96.3	(783) 108.6
38.9	26.7	8.4	13.4				24.2	30.9
87.0	41.0	23.8	28.1	14.4	92.9		61.0	71.5
33.3	18.2	8.0	10.9	-1.8	-.7	% Profit Before Taxes/Total Assets	19.7	24.6
4.9	3.8	2.5	3.2	-9.4	-3.2		1.4	2.6
77.7	23.0	9.6	86.5	15.8	32.3		36.5	38.9
20.1	8.1	4.8	12.3	10.4	7.8	Sales/Net Fixed Assets	13.1	13.2
8.2	3.0	.9	3.2	5.1	6.5		5.5	5.3
10.2	3.2	3.0	3.2	10.9	7.7		7.8	7.8
5.4	2.0	1.7	1.9	1.8	1.8	Sales/Total Assets	4.0	3.7
2.8	1.2	.3	1.1	.8	1.1		2.1	1.9
1.0	2.1	2.0	1.3				1.3	1.3
(765) 2.5	(432) 4.7	(61) 4.0	(13) 4.7			% Depr., Dep., Amort./Sales	(910) 2.9	(1000) 2.8
5.3	9.3	16.3	6.4				5.8	6.1
11.6	8.6	4.2					10.6	10.1
(1018) 18.2	(458) 13.9	(26) 14.0				% Officers', Directors' Owners' Comp/Sales	(965) 17.7	(1067) 16.6
25.2	19.6	22.4					26.4	25.5
1845362M	1578889M	780537M	3628458M	5217325M	7285506M	Net Sales ($)	19358930M	23196089M
330755M	634546M	283635M	489083M	879461M	1812986M	Total Assets ($)	5245972M	5441375M

M = $ thousand MM = $ million

See Pages 9 through 22 for Explanation of Ratios and Data

Comparative Historical Data				Current Data Sorted by Sales					
			Type of Statement						
22	25	20	Unqualified	2	5	1		3	9
11	10	12	Reviewed	1	2	2		4	3
291	254	277	Compiled	90	133	35	9	6	4
1338	1129	1221	Tax Returns	580	524	63	37	8	9
654	656	738	Other	272	332	64	41	16	13
4/1/11-3/31/12	4/1/12-3/31/13	4/1/13-3/31/14		89 (4/1-9/30/13)			2,179 (10/1/13-3/31/14)		
ALL	ALL	ALL		0-1MM	1-3MM	3-5MM	5-10MM	10-25MM	25MM & OVER
2316	2074	2268	**NUMBER OF STATEMENTS**	945	996	165	87	37	38
%	%	%	**ASSETS**	%	%	%	%	%	%
24.4	25.2	24.7	Cash & Equivalents	22.7	26.7	24.7	25.0	15.7	26.2
3.4	3.2	2.6	Trade Receivables (net)	1.5	2.6	3.9	6.0	11.0	6.7
.4	.4	.3	Inventory	.2	.4	.4	.3	2.1	1.3
2.6	2.5	2.1	All Other Current	1.8	2.2	1.7	2.0	5.9	1.8
30.8	31.4	29.6	Total Current	26.2	32.0	30.7	33.3	34.7	36.0
40.4	40.1	39.2	Fixed Assets (net)	42.0	36.7	39.5	44.1	39.2	26.2
17.8	17.6	19.1	Intangibles (net)	19.6	18.6	19.9	11.7	16.0	31.9
11.0	10.9	12.1	All Other Non-Current	12.2	12.7	9.9	10.9	10.1	5.9
100.0	100.0	100.0	Total	100.0	100.0	100.0	100.0	100.0	100.0
			LIABILITIES						
14.3	14.7	13.8	Notes Payable-Short Term	14.4	14.2	10.9	15.6	7.6	2.0
7.7	7.0	6.4	Cur. Mat.-L.T.D.	6.1	6.4	7.5	7.6	5.0	6.3
1.8	1.5	2.0	Trade Payables	1.3	2.4	1.8	3.0	5.1	4.2
.1	.1	.1	Income Taxes Payable	.0	.1	.0	.0	.8	.0
15.4	15.8	15.2	All Other Current	16.1	13.8	14.9	21.9	11.1	19.5
39.3	39.0	37.4	Total Current	37.9	36.8	35.1	48.1	29.6	32.2
52.1	55.5	54.7	Long-Term Debt	62.5	50.9	52.5	38.6	33.6	26.4
.0	.0	.1	Deferred Taxes	.0	.1	.0	.0	.0	1.2
10.1	6.7	6.2	All Other Non-Current	6.5	6.2	6.1	4.4	9.3	3.6
-1.5	-1.2	1.7	Net Worth	-6.9	6.0	6.3	8.9	27.6	36.7
100.0	100.0	100.0	Total Liabilities & Net Worth	100.0	100.0	100.0	100.0	100.0	100.0
			INCOME DATA						
100.0	100.0	100.0	Net Sales	100.0	100.0	100.0	100.0	100.0	100.0
			Gross Profit						
86.2	85.5	85.6	Operating Expenses	83.8	86.4	86.1	89.9	92.2	92.4
13.8	14.5	14.4	Operating Profit	16.2	13.6	13.9	10.1	7.8	7.6
2.8	2.8	2.6	All Other Expenses (net)	4.4	1.5	.9	.5	.6	2.0
11.1	11.7	11.8	Profit Before Taxes	11.8	12.2	12.9	9.6	7.2	5.7
			RATIOS						
3.2	3.1	3.1		3.1	3.5	3.3	1.9	1.9	2.4
1.0	1.0	1.0	Current	.9	1.0	1.0	.8	1.1	1.0
.3	.3	.3		.2	.3	.3	.2	.8	.7
2.9	2.9	2.9		2.9	3.1	3.0	1.8	1.6	2.1
(2315) .9	(2071) .9	(2267) .9	Quick	(944) .7	1.0	1.0	.8	.9	1.0
.2	.2	.2		.2	.3	.3	.2	.6	.5
0 UND	0 UND	0 UND		0 UND	0 UND	0 UND	0 UND	0 UND	0 UND
0 UND	0 UND	0 UND	Sales/Receivables	0 UND	0 UND	0 UND	0 UND	13 28.9	0 746.5
0 UND	0 UND	0 UND		0 UND	0 UND	0 UND	1 725.4	29 12.4	31 11.7
			Cost of Sales/Inventory						
			Cost of Sales/Payables						
18.2	19.1	20.4		19.0	19.9	25.5	24.6	26.7	30.8
UND	UND	UND	Sales/Working Capital	-207.0	521.8	615.4	-121.3	710.1	529.9
-17.9	-18.1	-18.2		-9.9	-23.5	-35.4	-25.2	-75.1	-26.8
19.0	18.4	19.5		10.7	26.1	28.9	44.1	23.5	65.0
(1817) 5.2	(1601) 5.5	(1704) 6.2	EBIT/Interest	(657) 4.1	(779) 8.5	(134) 12.2	(73) 8.3	(31) 5.2	(30) 2.1
1.6	1.8	1.9		1.5	2.7	1.9	1.3	2.4	.1
5.2	4.3								
(42) 1.8	(24) 1.7		Net Profit + Depr., Dep., Amort./Cur. Mat. L/T/D						
.7	.4								
.8	.7	.7		.8	.6	.7	1.0	1.2	.6
54.8	22.9	20.8	Fixed/Worth	UND	11.5	4.9	7.9	4.5	UND
-.7	-.7	-.7		-.5	-.8	-1.2	-1.4	-2.9	-.4
1.6	1.4	1.3		1.8	1.1	1.1	1.8	1.5	.5
-25.8	-56.5	-24.3	Debt/Worth	-9.6	-41.3	48.4	21.8	10.6	UND
-2.1	-2.1	-2.2		-1.9	-2.3	-2.7	-3.7	-6.1	-2.1
302.0	310.1	323.2		241.9	360.9	494.0	322.2	246.8	432.6
(1103) 105.1	(1011) 104.2	(1076) 104.1	% Profit Before Taxes/Tangible Net Worth	(418) 66.9	(480) 120.0	(86) 202.1	(47) 127.8	(25) 60.0	(20) 86.7
31.7	31.1	32.4		19.9	48.8	58.2	45.1	8.6	22.6
68.0	69.0	66.0		46.4	83.8	100.8	76.4	26.4	81.9
23.5	25.1	24.2	% Profit Before Taxes/Total Assets	15.9	33.8	36.2	27.6	10.0	10.2
3.7	3.7	3.9		2.6	7.6	4.1	1.4	3.8	-2.3
44.9	45.6	45.0		33.0	56.2	60.2	44.0	21.5	85.0
14.0	13.3	14.3	Sales/Net Fixed Assets	10.1	16.6	16.7	18.8	11.7	14.9
5.5	5.4	5.6		3.2	7.4	7.9	8.6	6.8	6.4
7.8	7.3	7.3		5.2	8.4	10.1	11.8	7.6	9.1
3.7	3.6	3.6	Sales/Total Assets	2.5	4.3	5.4	6.3	3.8	2.4
2.0	1.8	1.9		1.3	2.4	3.1	3.3	2.1	1.3
1.4	1.1	1.3		1.9	1.0	1.1	.9	1.5	.9
(1370) 3.1	(1215) 2.8	(1278) 3.2	% Depr., Dep., Amort./Sales	(529) 5.4	(551) 2.5	(91) 2.6	(63) 1.8	(28) 2.1	(16) 2.9
6.3	6.0	6.8		10.8	5.1	4.5	3.2	3.6	6.6
10.3	10.5	10.4		11.6	9.7	7.9	11.6	3.1	7.4
(1533) 16.7	(1388) 16.5	(1513) 16.6	% Officers', Directors' Owners' Comp/Sales	(590) 18.1	(727) 15.5	(109) 16.7	(60) 18.7	(14) 15.8	(13) 18.5
24.6	24.3	23.7		23.9	22.5	29.2	31.1	31.9	22.5
13617511M	14801659M	20336077M	Net Sales ($)	579378M	1688819M	630874M	576336M	572520M	16288150M
4989526M	5147448M	4430466M	Total Assets ($)	367678M	497578M	170306M	132680M	221771M	3040453M

M = $ thousand MM = $ million

See Pages 9 through 22 for Explanation of Ratios and Data

Current Data Sorted by Assets							Comparative Historical Data	
						Type of Statement		
		1			1	Unqualified	3	5
		1				Reviewed		
6	2					Compiled	20	22
76	15	2			1	Tax Returns	79	92
45	17	3	2			Other	51	71
6 (4/1-9/30/13)			166 (10/1/13-3/31/14)				4/1/09-3/31/10 ALL	4/1/10-3/31/11 ALL
0-500M	500M-2MM	2-10MM	10-50MM	50-100MM	100-250MM			
127	34	7	2		2	**NUMBER OF STATEMENTS**	153	190
%	%	%	%	%	%	**ASSETS**	%	%
34.1	20.7			DATA NOT AVAILABLE		Cash & Equivalents	27.7	24.9
2.5	2.4					Trade Receivables (net)	11.0	7.1
1.3	.0					Inventory	.2	1.1
1.4	3.9					All Other Current	2.6	1.9
39.2	27.0					Total Current	41.6	35.1
39.8	45.4					Fixed Assets (net)	37.9	39.0
7.4	9.0					Intangibles (net)	8.1	10.3
13.6	18.6					All Other Non-Current	12.3	15.7
100.0	100.0					Total	100.0	100.0
						LIABILITIES		
25.8	11.0					Notes Payable-Short Term	18.6	18.1
3.2	1.9					Cur. Mat.-L.T.D.	3.8	5.0
1.5	.2					Trade Payables	1.9	1.4
.9	.0					Income Taxes Payable	.1	.3
14.8	14.2					All Other Current	12.9	13.8
46.3	27.3					Total Current	37.3	38.7
26.2	32.0					Long-Term Debt	33.2	28.8
.0	.0					Deferred Taxes	.3	.0
6.0	3.4					All Other Non-Current	2.7	13.9
21.4	37.2					Net Worth	26.5	18.6
100.0	100.0					Total Liabilties & Net Worth	100.0	100.0
						INCOME DATA		
100.0	100.0					Net Sales	100.0	100.0
						Gross Profit		
84.8	72.9					Operating Expenses	81.1	84.1
15.2	27.1					Operating Profit	18.9	15.9
.6	6.8					All Other Expenses (net)	2.2	1.9
14.6	20.3					Profit Before Taxes	16.7	14.1
						RATIOS		
4.0	4.9						4.0	3.2
1.3	1.4					Current	1.3	.8
.4	.1						.4	.3
3.9	3.9						4.0	3.2
1.3	1.2					Quick	1.2	.8
.3	.1						.3	.2
0 UND	0 UND						0 UND	0 UND
0 UND	0 UND					Sales/Receivables	0 UND	0 UND
0 UND	0 UND						0 UND	0 UND
						Cost of Sales/Inventory		
						Cost of Sales/Payables		
16.7	6.8						12.1	19.4
228.0	81.3					Sales/Working Capital	68.2	-126.0
-24.9	-5.5						-23.9	-15.5
33.5	26.8						38.6	34.0
(75) 9.5	(18) 6.4					EBIT/Interest	(101) 12.0	(123) 9.0
4.0	2.0						3.5	4.0
						Net Profit + Depr., Dep., Amort./Cur. Mat. L/T/D		
.4	.3						.3	.4
1.2	1.4					Fixed/Worth	1.1	1.5
UND	-18.1						UND	-5.1
.3	.3						.3	.4
2.1	1.7					Debt/Worth	2.5	2.8
-17.3	-21.1						-165.1	-4.3
542.0	92.7						415.3	289.8
(92) 178.2	(25) 34.7					% Profit Before Taxes/Tangible Net Worth	(114) 99.8	(129) 91.9
57.7	14.0						40.5	27.6
146.6	45.1						99.3	80.9
55.8	18.5					% Profit Before Taxes/Total Assets	43.3	36.8
21.1	2.6						12.1	6.0
78.3	17.1						59.9	51.2
19.3	7.7					Sales/Net Fixed Assets	15.2	15.9
6.6	.8						6.2	6.0
10.9	2.5						7.4	7.2
6.2	1.5					Sales/Total Assets	3.9	3.8
2.7	.5						2.0	1.8
.9	1.2						.8	.8
(64) 2.1	(23) 4.3					% Depr., Dep., Amort./Sales	(89) 2.0	(106) 1.8
3.3	10.1						3.9	3.5
7.5	6.1						8.6	9.3
(101) 12.6	(16) 11.7					% Officers', Directors' Owners' Comp/Sales	(93) 15.6	(123) 13.7
20.6	14.7						25.7	20.4
86387M	60557M	90611M	28292M		464002M	Net Sales ($)	1760090M	2056374M
15689M	31871M	27820M	55716M		273954M	Total Assets ($)	421249M	686287M

M = $ thousand MM = $ million

See Pages 9 through 22 for Explanation of Ratios and Data

Comparative Historical Data				Current Data Sorted by Sales					
			Type of Statement						
	1	2	Unqualified			1			1
1	1	1	Reviewed					1	
18	16	8	Compiled	6	2				
97	95	94	Tax Returns	71	12	6	3		2
65	64	67	Other	47	13	3	1	3	
				6 (4/1-9/30/13)			166 (10/1/13-3/31/14)		
4/1/11-3/31/12 ALL	4/1/12-3/31/13 ALL	4/1/13-3/31/14 ALL		0-1MM	1-3MM	3-5MM	5-10MM	10-25MM	25MM & OVER
181	176	172	**NUMBER OF STATEMENTS**	124	27	10	4	4	3
%	%	%	**ASSETS**	%	%	%	%	%	%
27.9	27.5	30.7	Cash & Equivalents	30.2	31.1	32.1			
7.2	6.4	4.2	Trade Receivables (net)	2.7	2.5	4.6			
1.1	1.0	1.3	Inventory	1.0	1.4	.1			
2.0	3.0	1.9	All Other Current	1.2	4.5	4.9			
38.2	38.0	38.2	Total Current	35.1	39.6	41.7			
34.7	37.1	39.8	Fixed Assets (net)	43.2	34.0	35.1			
11.8	10.0	7.5	Intangibles (net)	8.0	8.1	.9			
15.4	15.0	14.6	All Other Non-Current	13.7	18.4	22.4			
100.0	100.0	100.0	Total	100.0	100.0	100.0			
			LIABILITIES						
17.7	20.9	21.4	Notes Payable-Short Term	20.5	36.0	15.2			
5.6	6.0	2.8	Cur. Mat.-L.T.D.	3.1	2.6	.8			
2.8	.7	1.7	Trade Payables	1.4	1.3	.1			
.0	.0	.7	Income Taxes Payable	.1	3.7	.0			
9.8	11.5	14.3	All Other Current	12.6	10.3	41.6			
36.0	39.2	40.9	Total Current	37.8	53.9	57.6			
40.4	29.2	26.7	Long-Term Debt	31.1	14.8	23.1			
.1	.0	.2	Deferred Taxes	.0	.0	.0			
9.9	7.0	5.9	All Other Non-Current	5.6	4.8	6.8			
13.6	24.6	26.4	Net Worth	25.6	26.5	12.5			
100.0	100.0	100.0	Total Liabilties & Net Worth	100.0	100.0	100.0			
			INCOME DATA						
100.0	100.0	100.0	Net Sales	100.0	100.0	100.0			
			Gross Profit						
82.0	81.9	82.2	Operating Expenses	81.3	84.9	84.7			
18.0	18.1	17.8	Operating Profit	18.7	15.1	15.3			
3.9	2.0	1.9	All Other Expenses (net)	2.6	.7	-1.3			
14.1	16.1	16.0	Profit Before Taxes	16.1	14.4	16.6			
			RATIOS						
4.1	3.7	4.2		4.1	5.6	2.9			
1.3	1.3	1.4	Current	1.3	1.4	1.4			
.4	.3	.4		.3	.5	.4			
3.9	3.3	4.0		4.0	5.4	1.9			
1.2	1.2	1.3	Quick	1.1	1.3	1.0			
.3	.2	.3		.2	.5	.4			
0 UND	0 UND	0 UND		0 UND	0 UND	0 UND			
0 UND	0 UND	0 UND	Sales/Receivables	0 UND	0 UND	0 UND			
0 UND	0 UND	0 UND		0 UND	0 UND	0 UND			
			Cost of Sales/Inventory						
			Cost of Sales/Payables						
12.3	13.1	13.3		14.0	16.7	13.1			
103.1	107.8	83.0	Sales/Working Capital	157.0	86.7	187.4			
-22.1	-17.2	-21.8		-17.3	-40.7	-13.0			
26.0	43.9	32.3		27.3	43.4				
(116) 7.6	(112) 11.5	(101) 9.9	EBIT/Interest	(71) 8.1	(16) 20.5				
2.1	3.1	3.7		3.5	3.1				
			Net Profit + Depr., Dep., Amort./Cur. Mat. L/T/D						
.2	.1	.3		.5	.3	.3			
1.5	1.0	1.2	Fixed/Worth	1.3	.9	1.1			
-3.3	UND	UND		UND	-8.5	-5.6			
.6	.4	.3		.4	.1	.8			
4.8	2.3	1.9	Debt/Worth	2.1	.8	1.7			
-4.0	-6.6	-41.8		-25.3	-15.5	-10.7			
381.4	533.3	381.2		399.8	305.3				
(117) 102.5	(123) 114.0	(126) 132.7	% Profit Before Taxes/Tangible Net Worth	(90) 145.2	(20) 82.4				
29.0	54.5	31.3		37.6	23.4				
92.9	112.7	115.5		109.7	175.8	119.1			
33.3	52.3	39.4	% Profit Before Taxes/Total Assets	39.1	47.6	45.6			
7.5	11.9	11.4		10.8	16.7	1.6			
95.4	65.3	55.0		52.1	57.5	37.1			
19.3	15.9	16.0	Sales/Net Fixed Assets	14.6	20.4	18.9			
8.7	6.9	5.5		3.6	10.2	5.5			
7.4	9.1	9.6		9.1	12.1	6.7			
4.5	4.4	4.3	Sales/Total Assets	4.1	6.4	3.4			
1.9	2.0	1.8		1.7	2.1	2.0			
1.1	.9	1.0		1.1	1.0				
(85) 2.7	(92) 2.0	(94) 2.1	% Depr., Dep., Amort./Sales	(65) 2.6	(14) 1.2				
5.1	4.3	4.3		5.8	2.0				
10.6	9.4	7.4		7.8	6.3				
(112) 16.4	(120) 13.8	(123) 12.6	% Officers', Directors' Owners' Comp/Sales	(89) 13.2	(20) 10.5				
22.9	22.1	18.9		20.6	16.0				
242854M	**2706596M**	**729849M**	Net Sales ($)	**57511M**	**41560M**	**38371M**	**27484M**	**66454M**	**498469M**
112205M	**493627M**	**405050M**	Total Assets ($)	**28061M**	**12447M**	**13613M**	**11744M**	**62444M**	**276741M**

M = $ thousand MM = $ million

See Pages 9 through 22 for Explanation of Ratios and Data

Current Data Sorted by Assets							Comparative Historical Data	
						Type of Statement		
			2		1	Unqualified	4	2
2	3	10	3	1		Reviewed	18	15
21	20	4				Compiled	45	65
129	46	10	1		2	Tax Returns	148	127
58	35	21	6	1		Other	85	89
19 (4/1-9/30/13)			357 (10/1/13-3/31/14)				4/1/09-3/31/10 ALL	4/1/10-3/31/11 ALL
0-500M	**500M-2MM**	**2-10MM**	**10-50MM**	**50-100MM**	**100-250MM**			
210	104	45	12	2	3	**NUMBER OF STATEMENTS**	300	298
%	%	%	%	%	%	**ASSETS**	%	%
25.7	21.7	12.1	14.0			Cash & Equivalents	21.5	21.6
4.0	7.0	17.5	10.8			Trade Receivables (net)	9.2	9.6
14.8	8.8	7.6	7.9			Inventory	12.5	11.0
1.8	2.4	2.4	4.4			All Other Current	1.6	2.2
46.3	39.9	39.5	37.2			Total Current	44.8	44.4
39.3	42.7	43.9	45.3			Fixed Assets (net)	36.7	36.9
6.0	6.8	10.3	7.7			Intangibles (net)	10.5	9.3
8.4	10.5	6.3	9.8			All Other Non-Current	8.0	9.5
100.0	100.0	100.0	100.0			Total	100.0	100.0
						LIABILITIES		
18.7	11.5	2.9	4.9			Notes Payable-Short Term	10.5	9.5
13.5	7.7	7.4	4.1			Cur. Mat.-L.T.D.	9.1	7.5
5.6	4.1	6.7	14.3			Trade Payables	5.8	5.1
.0	.1	.0	.0			Income Taxes Payable	.1	.1
19.3	12.8	14.4	13.0			All Other Current	16.3	14.3
57.1	36.2	31.4	36.3			Total Current	41.8	36.6
40.6	42.8	31.5	30.0			Long-Term Debt	38.6	37.9
.0	.1	.5	.0			Deferred Taxes	.1	.1
9.6	6.9	4.3	2.2			All Other Non-Current	6.2	5.1
-7.2	14.0	32.3	31.5			Net Worth	13.4	20.3
100.0	100.0	100.0	100.0			Total Liabilties & Net Worth	100.0	100.0
						INCOME DATA		
100.0	100.0	100.0	100.0			Net Sales	100.0	100.0
						Gross Profit		
90.6	87.5	86.4	88.2			Operating Expenses	87.8	88.7
9.4	12.5	13.6	11.8			Operating Profit	12.2	11.3
.9	2.5	5.7	5.7			All Other Expenses (net)	2.7	1.8
8.5	10.1	7.9	6.0			Profit Before Taxes	9.5	9.5
						RATIOS		
3.3	2.3	2.2	2.0				3.2	3.6
1.1	1.2	1.2	.9			Current	1.3	1.4
.4	.6	.7	.7				.6	.7
2.1	1.6	1.5	1.8				2.1	2.6
(209) .7	.7	.9	.7			Quick	(299) .8	(296) .9
.1	.3	.4	.4				.3	.4
0 UND	0 UND	0 UND	2 201.1				0 UND	0 UND
0 UND	0 UND	18 20.4	15 24.8			Sales/Receivables	0 UND	0 UND
0 UND	10 37.3	33 11.1	24 15.4				15 24.8	14 25.6
						Cost of Sales/Inventory		
						Cost of Sales/Payables		
14.9	15.2	12.9	11.4				15.3	12.9
301.1	142.1	57.2	-61.5			Sales/Working Capital	75.6	58.6
-24.4	-30.8	-29.1	-17.8				-30.6	-35.7
27.3	25.6	28.4	24.8				21.1	24.4
(146) 7.5	(91) 8.6	(34) 7.4	(11) 10.8			EBIT/Interest	(233) 5.5	(243) 7.2
1.5	2.2	-1.0	6.2				1.5	1.4
							2.5	5.9
						Net Profit + Depr., Dep., Amort./Cur. Mat. L/T/D	(13) 1.6	(11) 3.8
							.8	1.4
.4	.6	.8	.6				.5	.4
3.2	4.2	2.8	1.7			Fixed/Worth	2.5	2.0
-1.2	-2.5	NM	-70.6				-1.4	-3.4
.8	1.0	1.2	1.0				1.1	.8
9.2	4.4	4.7	2.7			Debt/Worth	4.9	3.6
-2.9	-5.2	NM	-84.5				-3.8	-6.3
325.4	124.6	99.3					172.5	190.7
(124) 79.4	(67) 51.3	(34) 30.6				% Profit Before Taxes/Tangible Net Worth	(187) 70.1	(199) 62.8
19.3	11.0	7.5					14.0	15.8
78.6	37.8	28.3	16.8				55.3	50.2
27.9	13.9	6.1	10.4			% Profit Before Taxes/Total Assets	18.5	16.7
1.8	2.2	-.6	5.7				1.9	1.1
74.0	41.2	18.5	11.8				51.1	50.5
21.5	14.5	8.6	5.9			Sales/Net Fixed Assets	17.8	18.2
8.2	5.5	4.2	3.9				6.5	6.9
12.0	8.2	6.0	3.7				8.3	8.3
6.5	4.3	3.5	2.8			Sales/Total Assets	4.5	4.4
3.3	2.2	1.2	1.7				2.7	2.3
.9	.8	2.0	2.2				1.3	1.2
(125) 2.1	(73) 2.4	(39) 3.7	(11) 3.2			% Depr., Dep., Amort./Sales	(196) 2.5	(184) 2.2
5.0	5.3	7.0	3.7				4.3	4.3
8.9	6.0	7.5					8.1	8.1
(138) 13.6	(65) 13.9	(22) 13.8				% Officers', Directors' Owners' Comp/Sales	(183) 13.6	(174) 14.6
19.5	24.4	19.5					23.0	24.9
332603M	497562M	774381M	620630M	126554M	2846949M	Net Sales ($)	3185274M	3178082M
45790M	95590M	209904M	264991M	125740M	535690M	Total Assets ($)	1150549M	960793M

M = $ thousand MM = $ million

See Pages 9 through 22 for Explanation of Ratios and Data

Comparative Historical Data / Current Data Sorted by Sales

4/1/11-3/31/12 ALL	4/1/12-3/31/13 ALL	4/1/13-3/31/14 ALL		0-1MM	1-3MM	3-5MM	5-10MM	10-25MM	25MM & OVER
				19 (4/1-9/30/13)			357 (10/1/13-3/31/14)		
			Type of Statement						
4	5	3	Unqualified						3
13	12	19	Reviewed	2	3	1	2	5	6
57	50	45	Compiled	3	16	9	11	4	2
224	189	188	Tax Returns	87	55	22	13	7	4
93	124	121	Other	36	33	9	13	15	15
391	380	376	**NUMBER OF STATEMENTS**	128	107	41	39	31	30
%	%	%	**ASSETS**	%	%	%	%	%	%
19.9	23.2	22.4	Cash & Equivalents	20.1	23.9	28.1	28.3	19.8	13.5
8.5	7.5	6.7	Trade Receivables (net)	4.6	4.8	5.5	8.2	11.5	17.4
12.5	12.3	12.1	Inventory	14.6	12.9	8.1	10.0	7.2	11.9
2.5	1.9	2.1	All Other Current	1.5	1.4	1.2	3.6	5.4	3.0
43.4	44.9	43.3	Total Current	40.9	43.1	42.8	50.1	43.9	45.8
36.0	35.7	40.9	Fixed Assets (net)	46.5	38.4	41.0	34.8	39.9	34.6
11.2	9.0	7.2	Intangibles (net)	5.9	6.9	7.5	6.4	10.0	11.2
9.4	10.4	8.7	All Other Non-Current	6.8	11.7	8.7	8.7	6.2	8.4
100.0	100.0	100.0	Total	100.0	100.0	100.0	100.0	100.0	100.0
			LIABILITIES						
10.5	11.5	14.1	Notes Payable-Short Term	15.7	15.1	23.8	9.0	6.8	4.7
6.8	9.5	10.7	Cur. Mat.-L.T.D.	10.4	8.3	23.3	9.9	10.6	5.1
4.5	6.3	5.5	Trade Payables	5.1	5.4	4.9	5.4	4.2	10.3
.1	.1	.1	Income Taxes Payable	.0	.1	.0	.0	.0	.2
20.0	16.6	16.6	All Other Current	15.3	13.9	17.4	25.8	14.4	20.4
41.9	44.0	47.0	Total Current	46.6	42.8	69.3	50.1	36.0	40.6
33.7	43.4	39.6	Long-Term Debt	41.8	45.6	40.2	29.9	38.4	21.8
.0	.1	.1	Deferred Taxes	.0	.1	.0	.0	.0	.7
6.6	6.9	7.9	All Other Non-Current	7.1	12.8	5.3	1.8	11.6	1.6
17.7	5.6	5.4	Net Worth	4.5	-1.2	-14.8	18.2	14.0	35.2
100.0	100.0	100.0	Total Liabilties & Net Worth	100.0	100.0	100.0	100.0	100.0	100.0
			INCOME DATA						
100.0	100.0	100.0	Net Sales	100.0	100.0	100.0	100.0	100.0	100.0
			Gross Profit						
89.9	87.9	89.1	Operating Expenses	82.0	93.1	91.8	90.7	95.8	92.6
10.1	12.1	10.9	Operating Profit	18.0	6.9	8.2	9.3	4.2	7.4
1.6	2.0	2.1	All Other Expenses (net)	5.4	.3	.1	-.6	1.3	1.9
8.5	10.1	8.8	Profit Before Taxes	12.7	6.6	8.2	10.0	2.9	5.5
			RATIOS						
2.8	3.5	2.5		3.6	3.2	2.0	1.7	3.6	1.7
1.3	1.4	1.2	Current	1.2	1.3	.8	1.1	1.2	.9
.6	.6	.5		.3	.7	.2	.8	.4	.8
1.8	2.3	1.7		2.2	1.7	1.3	1.7	2.0	1.4
.8	(378) .9	(375) .7	Quick	.7	.8	.5	(38) .7	.9	.7
.3	.3	.2		.1	.2	.2	.4	.3	.3
0 UND	0 UND	0 UND		0 UND	0 UND	0 UND	0 UND	0 UND	3 112.3
0 UND	0 UND	0 UND	Sales/Receivables	0 UND	0 UND	0 UND	0 UND	0 UND	16 22.3
13 28.9	11 34.0	9 41.8		0 UND	0 UND	4 100.8	14 25.9	19 19.7	34 10.8
			Cost of Sales/Inventory						
			Cost of Sales/Payables						
14.1	13.9	14.4		9.9	15.0	16.6	36.8	15.0	20.6
60.8	58.8	172.6	Sales/Working Capital	117.3	81.2	-121.6	205.5	98.7	-86.5
-30.2	-32.9	-28.7		-11.5	-43.7	-19.4	-32.2	-32.2	-26.9
24.8	31.4	24.9		23.0	18.9	31.8	58.8	21.5	21.1
(294) 6.3	(289) 8.1	(286) 7.6	EBIT/Interest	(81) 6.4	(82) 8.0	(35) 15.0	(31) 13.2	5.5	(26) 6.2
1.2	1.6	1.7		1.5	2.5	2.2	-.2	.4	2.9
4.0		3.3							
(15) 2.5		(17) 1.9	Net Profit + Depr., Dep., Amort./Cur. Mat. L/T/D						
.9		1.2							
.4	.4	.5		.5	.4	.6	.4	.6	.6
1.8	2.0	3.0	Fixed/Worth	2.7	5.2	14.5	2.5	3.3	1.4
-2.2	-2.3	-2.1		-2.1	-1.5	-1.0	-4.4	-2.4	NM
.7	.9	1.0		.8	.9	1.4	1.1	.7	1.2
3.8	4.6	5.9	Debt/Worth	5.4	22.5	789.0	3.9	4.2	2.2
-4.5	-4.5	-4.3		-4.0	-3.4	-2.9	-8.4	-5.9	NM
131.5	243.8	176.3		183.8	149.0	476.9	514.9	102.6	69.8
(247) 57.1	(252) 86.6	(236) 56.7	% Profit Before Taxes/Tangible Net Worth	(82) 58.9	(63) 65.0	(21) 84.4	(26) 77.8	(21) 16.2	(23) 33.3
14.6	26.5	12.2		18.3	24.0	-6.1	19.8	-3.0	10.3
44.0	63.9	59.1		63.2	48.9	118.9	99.5	35.1	23.8
14.0	20.7	17.1	% Profit Before Taxes/Total Assets	18.2	21.0	31.5	27.5	9.8	7.5
.9	2.7	1.6		1.5	3.5	1.1	.0	-1.5	3.6
40.1	59.1	47.6		42.3	50.3	59.6	108.8	41.6	31.3
17.5	19.6	15.4	Sales/Net Fixed Assets	8.8	16.0	19.9	28.3	18.3	13.1
7.6	8.2	6.7		2.6	8.5	11.9	9.5	10.6	5.6
7.4	8.9	9.4		6.9	9.4	12.7	13.2	11.0	6.8
4.3	4.9	5.0	Sales/Total Assets	3.1	5.3	7.4	8.5	6.1	3.6
2.7	2.7	2.6		1.7	3.0	4.4	4.4	4.3	2.3
1.3	1.1	1.1		1.1	1.2	.5	.6	1.4	1.6
(250) 2.6	(220) 2.2	(251) 2.5	% Depr., Dep., Amort./Sales	(84) 3.8	(66) 2.5	(26) 2.0	(27) 1.3	(24) 2.2	(24) 2.7
4.5	3.9	5.2		10.4	4.6	3.3	4.3	3.6	3.6
8.6	7.9	8.0		9.0	7.3	7.3	6.7	15.6	6.6
(241) 13.7	(228) 13.1	(229) 13.6	% Officers', Directors' Owners' Comp/Sales	(68) 13.4	(77) 11.7	(20) 14.2	(33) 16.9	(20) 20.1	(11) 11.4
23.9	23.8	20.2		17.6	19.3	21.2	29.1	31.0	14.2
4525875M	2872785M	5198679M	Net Sales ($)	70915M	195157M	159236M	266717M	434049M	4072605M
855314M	662482M	1277705M	Total Assets ($)	57500M	60585M	26220M	55170M	80398M	997832M

M = $ thousand MM = $ million

See Pages 9 through 22 for Explanation of Ratios and Data

Current Data Sorted by Assets / Comparative Historical Data

0-500M	500M-2MM	2-10MM	10-50MM	50-100MM	100-250MM		4/1/09-3/31/10 ALL	4/1/10-3/31/11 ALL
						Type of Statement		
1	5	15	6	1		Unqualified	17	23
	1	1				Reviewed	10	2
		2				Compiled	6	13
19	2	3				Tax Returns	22	25
7	12	6	4	2	2	Other	20	21
29 (4/1-9/30/13)			60 (10/1/13-3/31/14)					
27	20	27	10	3	2	**NUMBER OF STATEMENTS**	75	84
%	%	%	%	%	%	**ASSETS**	%	%
43.5	22.0	18.1	26.9			Cash & Equivalents	25.1	29.5
8.2	26.7	25.2	18.0			Trade Receivables (net)	20.7	21.0
1.9	.3	.2	.0			Inventory	.2	.1
.4	4.2	6.4	2.1			All Other Current	5.0	3.7
54.0	53.2	49.9	46.9			Total Current	51.0	54.2
23.5	23.6	39.4	43.8			Fixed Assets (net)	34.6	30.3
2.8	4.7	2.2	.9			Intangibles (net)	5.0	2.3
19.6	18.4	8.5	8.3			All Other Non-Current	9.4	13.2
100.0	100.0	100.0	100.0			Total	100.0	100.0
						LIABILITIES		
16.2	9.0	3.7	.0			Notes Payable-Short Term	7.4	14.8
4.4	1.7	.9	1.5			Cur. Mat.-L.T.D.	2.0	1.6
2.5	4.5	4.3	5.3			Trade Payables	6.8	3.8
.0	.0	2.6	.0			Income Taxes Payable	.9	.9
19.5	6.6	12.4	9.6			All Other Current	17.3	18.5
42.6	21.7	23.9	16.4			Total Current	34.4	39.7
9.8	17.5	20.5	23.0			Long-Term Debt	24.5	16.8
.0	.0	.2	.0			Deferred Taxes	.0	.0
9.4	14.2	3.4	1.5			All Other Non-Current	6.5	7.2
38.3	46.5	52.0	59.0			Net Worth	34.6	36.2
100.0	100.0	100.0	100.0			Total Liabilties & Net Worth	100.0	100.0
						INCOME DATA		
100.0	100.0	100.0	100.0			Net Sales	100.0	100.0
						Gross Profit		
88.3	81.2	94.2	96.8			Operating Expenses	91.5	92.3
11.7	18.8	5.8	3.2			Operating Profit	8.5	7.7
.0	3.3	1.1	.0			All Other Expenses (net)	2.4	.4
11.7	15.5	4.7	3.2			Profit Before Taxes	6.1	7.3
						RATIOS		
6.3	15.9	3.4	3.8				3.9	4.7
1.3	3.8	2.5	2.9			Current	1.9	2.2
.6	1.1	1.8	2.0				.9	1.2
6.3	15.8	3.2	3.7				3.8	3.9
1.3	3.3	1.9	2.8			Quick	1.8	2.1
.5	1.0	1.5	2.0				.8	1.1
0 UND	0 UND	17 22.1	24 15.2				0 UND	0 UND
0 UND	33 11.0	47 7.8	33 10.9			Sales/Receivables	20 18.7	18 20.0
0 UND	85 4.3	66 5.5	50 7.3				48 7.6	46 8.0
						Cost of Sales/Inventory		
						Cost of Sales/Payables		
23.9	3.0	5.0	3.1				9.7	6.6
111.6	8.5	7.4	5.3			Sales/Working Capital	22.6	13.1
-41.5	153.7	13.4	16.6				-87.6	82.6
57.3		25.4					16.0	39.0
(15) 26.3		(24) 4.2				EBIT/Interest	(49) 2.9	(55) 8.8
3.2		.2					-.5	2.8
						Net Profit + Depr., Dep., Amort./Cur. Mat. L/T/D		
.0	.0	.3	.6				.3	.1
.4	.3	.7	.8			Fixed/Worth	.7	.4
8.0	3.3	1.4	1.1				6.8	1.3
.2	.4	.4	.4				.3	.3
1.0	1.5	.7	.8			Debt/Worth	1.2	.8
UND	4.1	1.2	1.1				7.9	3.2
504.1	65.8	46.1	12.1				97.5	80.3
(21) 154.0	(18) 45.3	(26) 10.0	7.0			% Profit Before Taxes/Tangible Net Worth	(60) 23.2	(71) 26.7
41.8	-2.0	-1.1	3.1				.5	4.8
157.1	39.3	20.8	7.9				46.2	54.6
82.5	16.3	5.1	3.8			% Profit Before Taxes/Total Assets	5.1	11.4
11.5	-.1	-1.1	1.4				-.2	2.6
399.8	UND	26.4	5.8				71.9	153.2
67.5	99.4	6.0	3.8			Sales/Net Fixed Assets	20.4	24.4
31.7	4.4	3.3	2.2				4.4	4.0
16.2	4.2	2.9	2.4				6.6	8.1
8.6	1.6	1.9	1.6			Sales/Total Assets	3.5	3.7
5.1	.8	1.5	1.2				1.8	1.5
.3	.6	.7	1.1				.7	.7
(15) .6	(11) 1.0	(25) 1.7	2.6			% Depr., Dep., Amort./Sales	(64) 1.3	(56) 2.0
1.0	7.5	3.0	3.8				3.0	3.4
5.4							4.6	4.0
(21) 13.3						% Officers', Directors' Owners' Comp/Sales	(27) 10.2	(35) 7.7
25.2							15.0	16.6
51651M	62177M	402661M	358657M	244666M	370516M	Net Sales ($)	970002M	964673M
5796M	23969M	134314M	230950M	172462M	368342M	Total Assets ($)	500884M	716131M

M = $ thousand MM = $ million

See Pages 9 through 22 for Explanation of Ratios and Data

Comparative Historical Data / Current Data Sorted by Sales

			Type of Statement						
37	25	28	Unqualified		5		9	7	7
1		2	Reviewed	1				1	
8	7	2	Compiled					1	1
33	21	24	Tax Returns	6	8	7	2		1
25	36	33	Other	5	12	3	5	2	6
4/1/11-3/31/12 ALL	4/1/12-3/31/13 ALL	4/1/13-3/31/14 ALL		29 (4/1-9/30/13)			60 (10/1/13-3/31/14)		
				0-1MM	1-3MM	3-5MM	5-10MM	10-25MM	25MM & OVER
104	89	89	NUMBER OF STATEMENTS	12	25	10	16	11	15
%	%	%	ASSETS	%	%	%	%	%	%
29.2	31.2	27.4	Cash & Equivalents	27.5	33.1	32.0	25.8	20.9	21.1
19.5	17.5	19.2	Trade Receivables (net)	2.9	13.5	31.8	23.2	32.7	18.9
.1	.2	.7	Inventory	.0	2.4	.1	.0	.1	.0
5.0	3.8	3.4	All Other Current	.1	.7	3.4	8.4	5.7	3.4
53.8	52.8	50.7	Total Current	30.6	49.8	67.3	57.4	59.5	43.5
32.1	34.7	30.4	Fixed Assets (net)	27.4	31.7	12.2	33.6	31.9	38.4
5.6	4.2	4.6	Intangibles (net)	6.5	3.7	1.7	2.7	2.2	10.6
8.6	8.3	14.3	All Other Non-Current	35.6	14.8	18.9	6.2	6.5	7.5
100.0	100.0	100.0	Total	100.0	100.0	100.0	100.0	100.0	100.0
			LIABILITIES						
7.7	17.1	8.1	Notes Payable-Short Term	13.7	11.3	10.0	7.3	5.2	.0
6.2	1.4	2.3	Cur. Mat.-L.T.D.	.3	5.1	2.7	.9	1.0	1.5
3.7	3.1	3.9	Trade Payables	.8	2.1	7.9	3.7	6.7	4.6
.5	.8	.8	Income Taxes Payable	.0	.0	.0	1.0	3.2	1.4
27.3	21.9	12.8	All Other Current	11.7	11.8	17.8	10.8	13.7	13.2
45.5	44.2	27.8	Total Current	26.6	30.2	38.4	23.6	29.9	20.7
22.4	18.7	17.3	Long-Term Debt	33.5	13.8	3.3	19.3	10.8	21.9
.3	.1	.1	Deferred Taxes	.0	.0	.0	.0	.0	.5
8.9	5.4	7.9	All Other Non-Current	22.2	10.4	3.9	3.8	2.1	3.6
22.9	31.6	46.9	Net Worth	17.7	45.6	54.3	53.3	57.3	53.2
100.0	100.0	100.0	Total Liabilties & Net Worth	100.0	100.0	100.0	100.0	100.0	100.0
			INCOME DATA						
100.0	100.0	100.0	Net Sales	100.0	100.0	100.0	100.0	100.0	100.0
			Gross Profit						
95.2	91.0	89.7	Operating Expenses	77.6	86.8	84.7	95.7	97.9	95.0
4.8	9.0	10.3	Operating Profit	22.4	13.2	15.3	4.3	2.1	5.0
2.0	1.1	1.1	All Other Expenses (net)	4.1	.6	2.1	.5	.2	.3
2.8	7.9	9.2	Profit Before Taxes	18.3	12.6	13.2	3.8	1.9	4.7
			RATIOS						
3.4	3.5	5.7		10.6	9.9	9.9	6.3	3.4	3.6
1.8	2.0	2.3	Current	1.1	3.0	2.1	2.5	2.9	2.3
.9	1.2	1.1		.3	1.0	1.2	1.8	1.1	1.5
3.3	3.2	4.8		10.6	9.6	9.9	5.6	3.2	3.5
1.6	1.6	2.0	Quick	.9	2.4	2.0	2.0	1.9	2.3
.7	1.0	1.0		.3	.9	.9	1.4	1.1	1.4
0 UND	0 UND	0 UND		0 UND	0 UND	0 UND	11 33.7	22 16.8	25 14.6
15 24.0	10 37.4	27 13.6	Sales/Receivables	0 UND	0 UND	31 11.9	51 7.2	47 7.8	37 9.9
40 9.1	38 9.5	54 6.8		0 UND	37 9.8	72 5.1	69 5.3	51 7.1	49 7.4
			Cost of Sales/Inventory						
			Cost of Sales/Payables						
6.1	7.7	5.0		13.5	3.6	6.5	3.4	5.0	4.0
20.1	22.0	10.5	Sales/Working Capital	NM	24.7	8.6	6.7	8.6	7.8
-202.6	111.4	152.6		-31.4	NM	NM	20.7	76.2	13.5
21.1	27.6	26.9			21.8		65.8		12.4
(72) 4.3	(62) 5.6	(62) 5.9	EBIT/Interest		(12) 3.9		6.0		(13) 5.9
1.1	1.1	1.6			1.0		1.6		2.1
			Net Profit + Depr., Dep., Amort./Cur. Mat. L/T/D						
.1	.2	.1		.0	.0	.0	.3	.1	.6
.7	.7	.7	Fixed/Worth	2.0	.5	.2	.8	.7	.9
2.9	2.1	1.4		UND	4.9	1.2	1.3	1.2	1.8
.5	.4	.4		.7	.3	.3	.4	.4	.4
1.4	.9	.8	Debt/Worth	30.9	.7	.6	1.2	.6	1.0
6.7	3.6	4.0		UND	UND	8.3	1.8	.8	2.0
51.2	92.2	74.4			135.0		46.5	23.7	21.0
(85) 15.1	(74) 19.0	(78) 24.8	% Profit Before Taxes/Tangible Net Worth		(20) 49.7		21.9	2.6	(13) 11.2
.7	1.5	1.9			3.3		.5	-7.3	4.8
28.1	60.8	46.9		132.9	82.4	105.1	27.0	14.5	10.7
6.1	8.9	10.9	% Profit Before Taxes/Total Assets	22.0	29.9	33.1	9.3	1.5	5.4
-.5	.5	.9		5.3	1.8	5.8	.2	-3.7	3.1
173.1	75.3	200.5		UND	397.2	UND	27.5	46.6	15.6
23.2	17.1	17.3	Sales/Net Fixed Assets	337.5	61.2	110.4	5.8	26.4	4.6
4.0	3.9	4.3		5.4	6.4	29.6	3.4	2.2	2.9
7.0	8.3	6.4		8.5	9.8	9.2	4.0	4.2	3.0
3.6	3.1	2.5	Sales/Total Assets	2.8	4.1	5.6	2.0	2.8	1.7
1.6	1.7	1.4		.7	1.3	1.8	1.5	1.7	1.2
.6	.7	.6			.2		1.1	.6	1.5
(76) 1.8	(65) 1.8	(65) 1.3	% Depr., Dep., Amort./Sales		(16) 1.3		(15) 1.4	.8	(13) 2.3
3.2	3.3	3.0			3.5		3.0	2.5	3.5
4.0	6.5	3.6			5.6				
(36) 10.7	(29) 11.5	(32) 9.5	% Officers', Directors' Owners' Comp/Sales		(13) 14.9				
23.9	25.3	22.8			28.1				
1444742M	1593022M	1490328M	Net Sales ($)	5750M	40102M	40171M	117722M	179043M	1107540M
804193M	597105M	935833M	Total Assets ($)	4816M	22241M	13501M	113216M	70246M	711813M

M = $ thousand MM = $ million

See Pages 9 through 22 for Explanation of Ratios and Data

Current Data Sorted by Assets							Comparative Historical Data	
						Type of Statement		
	2	4	9	2		Unqualified	18	19
	5	5	1			Reviewed	22	14
9	8	4	3			Compiled	36	33
83	32	10			1	Tax Returns	96	90
47	29	14	10	2		Other	81	94
	24 (4/1-9/30/13)		256 (10/1/13-3/31/14)				4/1/09-3/31/10	4/1/10-3/31/11
0-500M	**500M-2MM**	**2-10MM**	**10-50MM**	**50-100MM**	**100-250MM**		**ALL**	**ALL**
139	76	37	23	4	1	**NUMBER OF STATEMENTS**	253	250
%	%	%	%	%	%	**ASSETS**	%	%
44.2	16.5	12.8	14.2			Cash & Equivalents	24.8	26.8
6.5	24.9	32.6	38.1			Trade Receivables (net)	18.6	18.3
.0	.5	.3	.5			Inventory	.4	.3
1.9	.6	1.3	2.5			All Other Current	3.8	4.7
52.6	42.6	47.1	55.3			Total Current	47.6	50.2
31.2	40.4	32.5	33.3			Fixed Assets (net)	32.4	30.2
5.3	6.1	7.8	5.7			Intangibles (net)	7.1	7.5
10.9	11.0	12.6	5.7			All Other Non-Current	12.8	12.2
100.0	100.0	100.0	100.0			Total	100.0	100.0
						LIABILITIES		
23.1	12.8	9.2	4.0			Notes Payable-Short Term	18.3	17.2
5.4	1.6	2.2	1.9			Cur. Mat.-L.T.D.	6.8	4.7
1.7	3.0	2.7	6.6			Trade Payables	4.0	4.1
.2	.2	.0	.1			Income Taxes Payable	.1	.1
16.8	12.0	11.4	15.6			All Other Current	16.8	16.9
47.2	29.6	25.5	28.3			Total Current	46.0	42.9
23.3	26.0	25.0	17.9			Long-Term Debt	28.3	20.3
.0	.0	.1	.0			Deferred Taxes	.1	.4
9.0	4.6	4.4	3.4			All Other Non-Current	6.1	7.0
20.6	39.7	45.0	50.4			Net Worth	19.5	29.4
100.0	100.0	100.0	100.0			Total Liabilties & Net Worth	100.0	100.0
						INCOME DATA		
100.0	100.0	100.0	100.0			Net Sales	100.0	100.0
						Gross Profit		
88.5	79.5	86.8	93.7			Operating Expenses	87.0	89.8
11.5	20.5	13.2	6.3			Operating Profit	13.0	10.2
.9	6.0	3.6	1.9			All Other Expenses (net)	2.1	1.0
10.6	14.5	9.6	4.5			Profit Before Taxes	10.9	9.2
						RATIOS		
5.7	3.9	4.4	3.9				4.1	3.9
1.7	1.4	2.2	2.6			Current	1.3	1.5
.4	.5	.9	1.1				.5	.7
5.7	3.9	4.2	3.9				3.8	3.6
(138) 1.6	1.3	2.0	2.6			Quick	1.2	(249) 1.4
.4	.5	.8	1.0				.4	.6
0 UND	**0** UND	**0** UND	**38** 9.5				**0** UND	**0** UND
0 UND	**2** 231.0	**46** 7.9	**61** 6.0			Sales/Receivables	**0** UND	**0** UND
0 UND	**42** 8.6	**66** 5.5	**74** 4.9				**44** 8.3	**40** 9.1
						Cost of Sales/Inventory		
						Cost of Sales/Payables		
13.2	7.5	6.0	3.4				9.3	9.8
61.5	33.1	11.5	6.4			Sales/Working Capital	38.9	27.4
-39.3	-31.2	-98.7	54.4				-26.1	-52.0
45.5	86.9	40.3	24.3				21.7	26.2
(79) 11.5	(49) 12.6	(27) 17.8	(20) 7.1			EBIT/Interest	(189) 7.1	(186) 7.7
3.9	2.8	5.6	1.4				1.8	1.9
							10.6	19.1
						Net Profit + Depr., Dep., Amort./Cur. Mat. L/T/D	(16) 3.7	(24) 3.6
							1.7	1.6
.1	.1	.1	.1				.1	.2
.8	1.1	.6	.8			Fixed/Worth	.8	.7
-7.5	5.0	8.2	1.5				17.0	4.3
.2	.6	.4	.5				.6	.4
2.0	2.0	.8	.9			Debt/Worth	2.2	1.6
-7.0	6.5	12.2	3.3				-14.9	85.3
255.6	100.0	81.3	35.3				210.2	200.1
(96) 98.6	(63) 40.0	(32) 41.3	(21) 12.3			% Profit Before Taxes/Tangible Net Worth	(185) 66.7	(190) 62.3
23.8	11.1	11.3	1.2				16.0	10.4
123.7	37.5	32.1	16.3				72.8	56.9
43.5	13.6	11.5	6.1			% Profit Before Taxes/Total Assets	22.5	21.1
11.1	2.8	4.5	.9				3.2	3.1
177.4	69.0	76.4	104.2				88.9	94.2
40.1	15.5	15.9	14.3			Sales/Net Fixed Assets	22.5	27.5
17.0	2.1	3.0	1.9				8.0	10.2
13.0	6.0	4.4	3.3				7.9	8.5
8.3	2.6	2.2	2.0			Sales/Total Assets	4.0	4.2
4.5	1.4	1.0	1.0				2.2	2.1
.4	.8	.6	.4				.6	.6
(76) .6	(57) 1.5	(31) 1.6	(20) 2.7			% Depr., Dep., Amort./Sales	(173) 1.5	(173) 1.4
1.6	7.7	3.0	4.0				2.9	2.7
7.4	2.9	1.8					6.8	5.8
(88) 11.4	(33) 5.1	(16) 3.5				% Officers', Directors' Owners' Comp/Sales	(108) 11.9	(109) 13.6
18.1	8.2	7.3					20.1	20.1
193797M	268457M	457886M	871546M	717403M	460972M	Net Sales ($)	6328356M	5314787M
25281M	80023M	162850M	424921M	263358M	169402M	Total Assets ($)	1180297M	1893239M

M = $ thousand MM = $ million

See Pages 9 through 22 for Explanation of Ratios and Data

Comparative Historical Data				Current Data Sorted by Sales					
			Type of Statement						
27	21	17	Unqualified		2	3	3	2	7
10	9	11	Reviewed		1	1	3	3	3
34	22	24	Compiled	1	10	4	2	5	2
119	105	126	Tax Returns	63	35	16	7	4	1
94	104	102	Other	22	41	7	12	9	11
4/1/11-3/31/12 ALL	4/1/12-3/31/13 ALL	4/1/13-3/31/14 ALL			24 (4/1-9/30/13)		256 (10/1/13-3/31/14)		
				0-1MM	1-3MM	3-5MM	5-10MM	10-25MM	25MM & OVER
284	261	280	**NUMBER OF STATEMENTS**	86	89	31	27	23	24
%	%	%	**ASSETS**	%	%	%	%	%	%
24.4	27.1	29.5	Cash & Equivalents	29.2	41.4	30.8	15.9	17.6	11.7
18.7	19.2	18.1	Trade Receivables (net)	5.6	9.5	25.7	28.1	47.0	46.0
.9	.5	.2	Inventory	.1	.4	.0	.4	.2	.4
3.8	4.3	1.5	All Other Current	2.2	.8	.5	.9	2.7	2.5
47.8	51.1	49.3	Total Current	37.0	52.1	57.1	45.3	67.5	60.6
32.5	31.9	33.8	Fixed Assets (net)	47.8	29.1	25.5	37.2	22.1	19.5
8.3	6.9	6.2	Intangibles (net)	4.2	7.3	8.8	2.0	4.2	12.8
11.4	10.1	10.6	All Other Non-Current	10.9	11.5	8.6	15.5	6.2	7.1
100.0	100.0	100.0	Total	100.0	100.0	100.0	100.0	100.0	100.0
			LIABILITIES						
18.7	17.3	18.0	Notes Payable-Short Term	21.1	17.7	10.3	14.8	16.1	23.6
4.5	2.6	3.7	Cur. Mat.-L.T.D.	4.0	4.9	2.9	1.6	2.0	3.4
3.8	3.3	2.6	Trade Payables	.4	2.8	2.8	2.3	6.7	6.1
.4	.0	.2	Income Taxes Payable	.3	.0	.6	.0	.0	.1
15.6	14.4	14.7	All Other Current	13.6	14.5	16.2	9.5	15.9	21.8
43.1	37.6	39.1	Total Current	39.2	39.9	32.7	28.3	40.7	55.1
23.5	21.6	23.9	Long-Term Debt	37.5	20.9	14.3	17.8	11.6	17.1
.1	.1	.0	Deferred Taxes	.0	.0	.0	.0	.2	.0
7.8	6.9	6.7	All Other Non-Current	10.3	4.8	8.2	4.3	3.6	4.0
25.6	33.8	30.4	Net Worth	13.1	34.5	44.8	49.5	43.8	23.9
100.0	100.0	100.0	Total Liabilities & Net Worth	100.0	100.0	100.0	100.0	100.0	100.0
			INCOME DATA						
100.0	100.0	100.0	Net Sales	100.0	100.0	100.0	100.0	100.0	100.0
			Gross Profit						
88.3	86.1	86.4	Operating Expenses	77.0	88.5	89.1	93.7	91.9	95.5
11.7	13.9	13.6	Operating Profit	23.0	11.5	10.9	6.3	8.1	4.5
2.4	2.1	2.8	All Other Expenses (net)	7.8	.7	-.2	.7	.5	.7
9.3	11.8	10.8	Profit Before Taxes	15.2	10.9	11.1	5.6	7.6	3.7
			RATIOS						
3.7	5.1	4.6		3.3	5.8	6.0	4.2	4.6	3.1
1.6	2.0	1.8	Current	.8	2.0	1.8	2.3	2.0	1.4
.5	.8	.6		.2	.6	1.3	.8	1.1	1.0
3.6	4.3	4.5		3.4	5.6	5.7	4.0	4.3	3.1
1.3	1.8	(279) 1.7	Quick	(85) .8	2.0	1.8	2.3	1.9	1.4
.4	.7	.6		.2	.6	1.2	.7	1.1	.9
0 UND	0 UND	0 UND		0 UND	0 UND	0 UND	0 UND	0 UND	36 10.2
0 UND	0 UND	0 UND	Sales/Receivables	0 UND	0 UND	6 64.7	33 10.9	46 7.9	62 5.9
40 9.2	38 9.7	38 9.6		0 UND	14 26.6	53 6.9	43 8.4	68 5.4	73 5.0
			Cost of Sales/Inventory						
			Cost of Sales/Payables						
8.3	8.0	7.8		14.5	7.7	7.2	8.7	5.8	6.2
36.3	22.9	37.9	Sales/Working Capital	-196.3	29.7	24.0	25.5	11.5	14.8
-27.9	-71.5	-43.1		-11.2	-58.0	156.8	-59.3	139.0	205.4
28.7	32.8	43.3		20.7	34.9	113.2	96.1	48.3	29.8
(193) 7.6	(176) 9.6	(180) 11.2	EBIT/Interest	(45) 7.5	(50) 10.8	(23) 34.7	(22) 15.0	(18) 33.4	(22) 9.2
2.0	1.8	3.3		2.9	3.6	7.9	.7	6.6	3.3
24.5	18.7								
(13) 2.6	(12) 4.0		Net Profit + Depr., Dep., Amort./Cur. Mat. L/T/D						
1.7	2.1								
.1	.1	.1		.3	.1	.0	.2	.1	.0
.8	.7	.9	Fixed/Worth	2.6	.5	.7	.7	.4	1.1
12.8	5.0	10.2		-28.2	UND	1.8	2.5	1.1	-5.5
.4	.4	.4		.7	.2	.5	.4	.4	.6
2.2	1.6	1.8	Debt/Worth	3.1	1.0	1.5	.7	.8	3.0
439.0	25.7	56.9		-10.0	-42.3	9.0	2.3	3.8	-11.3
128.9	166.0	146.6		171.4	160.3	274.7	84.7	76.3	78.2
(215) 49.3	(205) 46.7	(213) 50.2	% Profit Before Taxes/Tangible Net Worth	(60) 37.6	(66) 74.4	(27) 97.2	(24) 30.4	(19) 39.5	(17) 33.0
11.1	12.8	13.0		15.1	15.4	11.2	.3	11.5	11.8
53.4	66.2	67.6		80.3	88.1	109.0	58.2	34.8	20.7
16.5	21.6	20.5	% Profit Before Taxes/Total Assets	15.1	32.2	20.5	15.6	16.1	9.4
2.4	3.8	5.3		3.4	10.3	8.5	.1	5.4	4.1
91.5	147.2	117.8		82.3	131.2	141.5	138.8	107.2	244.3
23.7	23.5	26.8	Sales/Net Fixed Assets	16.0	35.0	30.0	20.0	41.3	30.5
6.5	6.4	8.5		.4	13.0	14.4	2.0	10.8	14.3
7.2	7.6	8.7		10.6	10.0	10.0	6.8	6.6	4.3
3.9	4.4	4.5	Sales/Total Assets	3.6	6.4	6.0	4.5	4.5	3.1
1.9	2.1	2.0		.3	2.8	2.2	1.9	2.0	2.0
.7	.5	.5		.6	.5	.4	.7	.4	.1
(193) 1.7	(169) 1.3	(184) 1.2	% Depr., Dep., Amort./Sales	(58) 2.8	(49) .8	(22) .9	(19) 1.5	(19) .8	(17) 1.6
3.2	2.8	3.2		16.4	1.7	1.6	2.6	1.9	3.2
7.1	4.8	4.4		8.9	6.5	3.3	2.7	1.7	
(132) 11.2	(126) 8.9	(142) 9.0	% Officers', Directors' Owners' Comp/Sales	(46) 15.1	(51) 9.5	(17) 5.5	(10) 3.8	(12) 2.6	
19.7	15.6	15.3		19.3	14.1	8.8	5.3	7.4	
6002827M	6440209M	2970061M	Net Sales ($)	42665M	147562M	122871M	188728M	359120M	2109115M
1860753M	1474412M	1125835M	Total Assets ($)	39591M	52162M	49878M	90577M	125671M	767956M

M = $ thousand MM = $ million

See Pages 9 through 22 for Explanation of Ratios and Data

Current Data Sorted by Assets							Comparative Historical Data	
						Type of Statement		
						Unqualified		
		1				Reviewed		
2	2	1				Compiled	13	5
18	3	1				Tax Returns	39	28
15	5	1	1			Other	9	15
2 (4/1-9/30/13)			48 (10/1/13-3/31/14)				4/1/09-3/31/10 ALL	4/1/10-3/31/11 ALL
0-500M	500M-2MM	2-10MM	10-50MM	50-100MM	100-250MM			
35	10	4	1			**NUMBER OF STATEMENTS**	61	48
%	%	%	%	%	%	**ASSETS**	%	%
37.7	13.0			DATA NOT AVAILABLE	DATA NOT AVAILABLE	Cash & Equivalents	25.9	26.6
1.8	3.1					Trade Receivables (net)	4.0	7.7
.9	.0					Inventory	1.4	.8
4.5	1.0					All Other Current	4.6	2.9
45.0	17.0					Total Current	36.0	38.1
42.6	52.5					Fixed Assets (net)	32.3	30.4
4.5	15.5					Intangibles (net)	13.7	16.8
7.9	15.0					All Other Non-Current	18.0	14.7
100.0	100.0					Total	100.0	100.0
						LIABILITIES		
18.1	9.9					Notes Payable-Short Term	25.5	26.1
5.9	4.2					Cur. Mat.-L.T.D.	6.2	5.6
6.4	.0					Trade Payables	4.0	3.3
.0	.0					Income Taxes Payable	.0	.7
26.0	8.7					All Other Current	23.2	22.1
56.3	22.9					Total Current	58.9	57.7
23.8	47.7					Long-Term Debt	45.7	34.3
.0	.0					Deferred Taxes	.0	.0
9.1	12.0					All Other Non-Current	4.0	5.4
10.9	17.5					Net Worth	-8.5	2.6
100.0	100.0					Total Liabilities & Net Worth	100.0	100.0
						INCOME DATA		
100.0	100.0					Net Sales	100.0	100.0
						Gross Profit		
87.8	80.1					Operating Expenses	88.9	88.8
12.2	19.9					Operating Profit	11.1	11.2
1.0	4.0					All Other Expenses (net)	2.9	1.0
11.2	15.9					Profit Before Taxes	8.1	10.2
						RATIOS		
7.9	3.0						5.7	1.8
.8	1.5					Current	.6	.7
.3	.1						.1	.2
2.5	2.8						5.1	1.6
.8	1.3					Quick	.6	.6
.3	.1						.1	.1
0 UND	0 UND						0 UND	0 UND
0 UND	0 UND					Sales/Receivables	0 UND	0 UND
0 UND	0 UND						0 UND	0 UND
						Cost of Sales/Inventory		
						Cost of Sales/Payables		
24.4	11.8						37.3	23.3
-162.1	24.0					Sales/Working Capital	-46.3	-92.2
-19.9	-20.3						-13.5	-16.7
13.6							14.4	16.9
(24) 6.1						EBIT/Interest	(44) 3.4	(29) 4.3
1.0							-.5	1.0
						Net Profit + Depr., Dep., Amort./Cur. Mat. L/T/D		
.4	1.9						.4	.4
11.2	NM					Fixed/Worth	-40.5	2.6
-1.8	-2.7						-.4	-.7
1.0	5.6						.8	.6
23.3	NM					Debt/Worth	-7.8	17.8
-4.2	-5.1						-2.1	-2.0
478.6							169.2	342.6
(19) 92.2						% Profit Before Taxes/Tangible Net Worth	(27) 83.9	(27) 127.3
12.5							18.6	54.6
90.7	51.0						76.7	77.3
38.7	12.4					% Profit Before Taxes/Total Assets	31.4	32.3
-.8	.7						-.9	3.9
75.6	18.0						70.9	89.4
15.7	8.0					Sales/Net Fixed Assets	25.8	20.5
10.1	.8						13.5	11.8
12.6	4.8						10.5	10.0
7.8	2.3					Sales/Total Assets	5.3	5.2
4.9	.6						2.9	3.3
.8							.9	.8
(21) 1.2						% Depr., Dep., Amort./Sales	(39) 1.9	(27) 1.5
2.5							3.8	3.3
12.3							11.6	10.8
(22) 17.7						% Officers', Directors' Owners' Comp/Sales	(49) 19.3	(36) 17.7
26.2							30.8	27.3
66471M	23522M	16896M	35683M			Net Sales ($)	110355M	113758M
7512M	10066M	12720M	17989M			Total Assets ($)	24946M	27125M

M = $ thousand MM = $ million

See Pages 9 through 22 for Explanation of Ratios and Data

Comparative Historical Data / Current Data Sorted by Sales

4/1/11-3/31/12 ALL	4/1/12-3/31/13 ALL	4/1/13-3/31/14 ALL	Type of Statement	0-1MM	1-3MM	3-5MM	5-10MM	10-25MM	25MM & OVER
			Unqualified						
	1	1	Reviewed			1			
4	2	5	Compiled	2		1	1	1	
41	18	22	Tax Returns	10	8	2	2		
26	24	22	Other	11	6	2	2		1
				2 (4/1-9/30/13)		48 (10/1/13-3/31/14)			
71	45	50	**NUMBER OF STATEMENTS**	23	14	6	5	1	1
%	%	%	**ASSETS**	%	%	%	%	%	%
26.8	30.6	29.4	Cash & Equivalents	26.1	38.9				
4.9	4.7	4.4	Trade Receivables (net)	2.8	1.8				
2.0	1.4	.6	Inventory	.3	1.7				
2.4	2.1	3.5	All Other Current	4.8	.0				
36.0	38.7	37.9	Total Current	34.0	42.4				
36.6	39.1	46.0	Fixed Assets (net)	53.1	37.8				
10.3	7.1	6.8	Intangibles (net)	6.5	11.9				
17.1	15.0	9.3	All Other Non-Current	6.4	7.9				
100.0	100.0	100.0	Total	100.0	100.0				
			LIABILITIES						
22.6	30.1	14.7	Notes Payable-Short Term	8.5	22.6				
8.1	7.4	5.1	Cur. Mat.-L.T.D.	2.9	5.0				
.9	1.4	4.6	Trade Payables	7.2	.0				
.0	.0	.0	Income Taxes Payable	.0	.0				
20.6	12.3	20.5	All Other Current	24.1	20.7				
52.2	51.3	45.0	Total Current	42.7	48.4				
40.8	33.5	30.9	Long-Term Debt	29.6	22.8				
.0	.0	.0	Deferred Taxes	.0	.0				
8.2	12.1	9.2	All Other Non-Current	5.6	16.7				
-1.1	3.1	14.9	Net Worth	22.2	12.1				
100.0	100.0	100.0	Total Liabilties & Net Worth	100.0	100.0				
			INCOME DATA						
100.0	100.0	100.0	Net Sales	100.0	100.0				
			Gross Profit						
86.0	85.3	84.6	Operating Expenses	73.9	95.4				
14.0	14.7	15.4	Operating Profit	26.1	4.6				
2.1	.8	2.2	All Other Expenses (net)	4.4	.2				
11.9	13.9	13.3	Profit Before Taxes	21.8	4.3				
			RATIOS						
2.3	3.2	5.4	Current	7.8	8.4				
.9	.8	1.0		1.4	1.0				
.3	.4	.4		.4	.3				
2.1	3.2	2.5	Quick	4.6	3.8				
(70) .7	.7	.8		.8	1.0				
.2	.4	.3		.2	.3				
0 UND	0 UND	0 UND	Sales/Receivables	0 UND	0 UND				
0 UND	0 UND	0 UND		0 UND	0 UND				
0 UND	0 UND	0 UND		0 UND	0 UND				
			Cost of Sales/Inventory						
			Cost of Sales/Payables						
32.1	15.5	20.4	Sales/Working Capital	15.8	20.4				
-174.2	-103.1	-726.7		41.4	NM				
-24.9	-21.5	-22.1		-18.9	-21.2				
28.9	37.5	13.9	EBIT/Interest	11.0					
(54) 8.6	(40) 10.4	(36) 6.3		(17) 6.5					
1.1	1.8	1.2		3.3					
			Net Profit + Depr., Dep., Amort./Cur. Mat. L/T/D						
.6	.6	.7	Fixed/Worth	.4	.2				
13.5	1.5	9.3		2.2	UND				
-1.0	-3.4	-2.7		-7.1	-.9				
1.0	.8	1.3	Debt/Worth	.2	6.0				
22.1	10.2	20.0		3.0	UND				
-3.4	-3.4	-5.1		-9.3	-3.9				
340.0	310.1	418.0	% Profit Before Taxes/Tangible Net Worth	426.1					
(39) 122.2	(24) 103.5	(29) 84.7		(15) 84.7					
58.3	82.3	43.3		47.6					
68.8	103.5	64.8	% Profit Before Taxes/Total Assets	60.7	61.7				
22.2	47.5	20.7		22.7	15.2				
.5	8.5	-.3		4.3	-3.4				
91.1	52.7	55.9	Sales/Net Fixed Assets	49.3	85.4				
28.1	18.8	13.9		6.6	15.2				
11.9	8.0	5.9		.8	12.7				
12.8	11.8	10.0	Sales/Total Assets	8.5	10.7				
6.1	6.6	5.9		2.6	7.5				
2.9	3.2	2.2		.8	5.4				
.6	1.1	.9	% Depr., Dep., Amort./Sales	.9					
(41) 1.4	(22) 2.0	(30) 1.4		(13) 4.8					
2.9	3.1	4.9		15.8					
11.0	7.9	10.1	% Officers', Directors' Owners' Comp/Sales	11.3					
(50) 17.8	(28) 14.5	(28) 17.7		(14) 17.0					
28.1	22.7	25.0		25.0					
1660149M	151890M	142572M	Net Sales ($)	12447M	25689M	22944M	33877M	11932M	35683M
140487M	42991M	48287M	Total Assets ($)	11714M	4171M	8191M	3669M	2553M	17989M

M = $ thousand MM = $ million

See Pages 9 through 22 for Explanation of Ratios and Data

Current Data Sorted by Assets | **Comparative Historical Data**

0-500M	500M-2MM	2-10MM	10-50MM	50-100MM	100-250MM		4/1/09-3/31/10 ALL	4/1/10-3/31/11 ALL
						Type of Statement		
2	4	6	10	1	4	Unqualified	53	44
		4	1			Reviewed	23	15
11	7	10	2			Compiled	38	30
87	27	7	1			Tax Returns	124	117
47	36	14	14	1	4	Other	92	117
26 (4/1-9/30/13)			274 (10/1/13-3/31/14)					
147	74	41	28	2	8	**NUMBER OF STATEMENTS**	330	323
%	%	%	%	%	%	**ASSETS**	%	%
39.3	23.5	14.1	9.5			Cash & Equivalents	21.4	23.8
6.0	14.0	33.0	22.9			Trade Receivables (net)	16.5	14.9
2.8	1.8	2.4	1.6			Inventory	3.2	3.2
3.6	3.1	4.0	4.0			All Other Current	4.3	4.1
51.7	42.3	53.4	38.0			Total Current	45.3	45.9
27.6	40.0	34.8	42.6			Fixed Assets (net)	36.7	33.3
4.0	7.8	5.6	7.1			Intangibles (net)	5.8	7.4
16.6	10.0	6.2	12.2			All Other Non-Current	12.2	13.4
100.0	100.0	100.0	100.0			Total	100.0	100.0
						LIABILITIES		
23.6	10.2	7.0	4.6			Notes Payable-Short Term	14.9	16.0
5.0	3.5	5.0	4.6			Cur. Mat.-L.T.D.	6.1	6.0
3.9	8.8	8.7	6.3			Trade Payables	5.7	5.0
.7	.1	.0	.1			Income Taxes Payable	.1	.3
25.8	15.2	15.0	15.0			All Other Current	19.9	22.0
59.1	37.8	35.7	30.7			Total Current	46.8	49.3
24.7	27.7	21.2	17.1			Long-Term Debt	30.8	27.4
.0	.2	.3	.4			Deferred Taxes	.1	.1
11.8	6.8	4.0	5.3			All Other Non-Current	8.4	7.8
4.3	27.6	38.7	46.5			Net Worth	13.8	15.4
100.0	100.0	100.0	100.0			Total Liabilties & Net Worth	100.0	100.0
						INCOME DATA		
100.0	100.0	100.0	100.0			Net Sales	100.0	100.0
						Gross Profit		
88.0	86.1	85.2	88.0			Operating Expenses	89.9	87.7
12.0	13.9	14.8	12.0			Operating Profit	10.1	12.3
.6	3.0	3.2	1.8			All Other Expenses (net)	2.1	1.3
11.4	10.9	11.7	10.2			Profit Before Taxes	8.1	11.0
						RATIOS		
3.9	5.0	2.8	2.7				2.5	3.4
1.1	1.5	1.5	1.5			Current	1.3	1.3
.5	.6	.9	1.0				.5	.5
3.4	4.6	2.4	2.2				2.2	2.7
(146) .9	1.3	1.3	1.1			Quick	1.0	(322) 1.1
.4	.5	.7	.8				.3	.3
0 UND	0 UND	0 UND	7 50.9				0 UND	0 UND
0 UND	0 UND	32 11.4	36 10.2			Sales/Receivables	2 228.3	0 UND
0 UND	23 15.7	69 5.3	58 6.3				36 10.1	39 9.4
						Cost of Sales/Inventory		
						Cost of Sales/Payables		
18.2	9.8	5.5	5.5				9.8	8.7
209.9	32.4	19.1	12.0			Sales/Working Capital	50.3	54.4
-32.5	-22.7	-61.2	281.7				-23.7	-24.6
64.3	30.5	43.7	67.0				22.4	20.9
(77) 12.7	(55) 6.0	(29) 7.7	(27) 8.6			EBIT/Interest	(249) 6.0	(222) 5.9
2.0	1.4	2.0	2.2				1.2	1.4
							23.6	
						Net Profit + Depr., Dep., Amort./Cur. Mat. L/T/D	(12) 3.5	
							.7	
.1	.3	.2	.7				.3	.3
.6	1.8	1.2	1.0			Fixed/Worth	1.3	1.0
-3.2	-3.5	3.7	2.0				-45.0	-23.0
.4	.5	.6	.4				.7	.5
2.7	2.5	1.3	.9			Debt/Worth	2.7	1.9
-3.6	-5.8	16.3	4.5				-19.7	-11.6
366.8	101.8	146.3	83.0				124.2	131.0
(100) 121.9	(52) 40.0	(34) 24.0	(25) 12.2			% Profit Before Taxes/Tangible Net Worth	(237) 40.3	(231) 42.2
50.4	13.2	1.9	2.9				6.8	8.0
134.1	37.3	22.1	32.5				44.9	60.3
42.7	13.4	7.9	8.2			% Profit Before Taxes/Total Assets	12.7	14.7
6.3	2.0	-.2	1.2				.8	1.5
458.5	46.7	65.5	10.5				65.4	78.2
45.0	13.8	14.1	4.9			Sales/Net Fixed Assets	15.3	17.2
18.3	2.4	2.2	1.5				4.2	4.9
15.2	6.2	4.9	2.9				7.7	7.1
7.6	2.7	2.6	1.8			Sales/Total Assets	3.8	3.4
4.1	1.6	1.0	.9				1.8	1.6
.5	.7	.7	2.1				.8	.8
(76) .9	(47) 2.0	(31) 1.7	(27) 3.0			% Depr., Dep., Amort./Sales	(244) 2.1	(211) 2.1
2.2	5.5	4.8	5.1				4.3	4.4
9.4	4.9	.8					5.9	5.5
(80) 16.6	(33) 9.0	(12) 2.4				% Officers', Directors' Owners' Comp/Sales	(147) 11.9	(128) 11.3
23.0	17.3	14.2					22.9	25.0
282907M	322747M	519153M	1483275M	288804M	2799928M	Net Sales ($)	8996080M	6265935M
27915M	76814M	184479M	629679M	141321M	1352843M	Total Assets ($)	2716232M	2558353M

M = $ thousand MM = $ million

See Pages 9 through 22 for Explanation of Ratios and Data

Comparative Historical Data				Current Data Sorted by Sales					
			Type of Statement						
29	23	27	Unqualified	3	2	3	5	3	11
11	7	5	Reviewed	1				2	2
29	29	30	Compiled	5	6	5	3	9	2
128	144	122	Tax Returns	54	41	11	10	5	1
139	135	116	Other	24	32	15	15	13	17
				26 (4/1-9/30/13)			274 (10/1/13-3/31/14)		
4/1/11-3/31/12 ALL	**4/1/12-3/31/13 ALL**	**4/1/13-3/31/14 ALL**		**0-1MM**	**1-3MM**	**3-5MM**	**5-10MM**	**10-25MM**	**25MM & OVER**
336	338	300	**NUMBER OF STATEMENTS**	87	81	34	33	32	33
%	%	%	**ASSETS**	%	%	%	%	%	%
25.2	26.8	28.3	Cash & Equivalents	32.3	30.7	33.2	32.0	16.0	14.7
14.8	14.4	13.9	Trade Receivables (net)	4.3	7.6	17.1	21.4	28.2	30.0
2.8	3.5	2.4	Inventory	2.0	3.8	1.3	.6	2.8	2.2
3.7	4.9	3.6	All Other Current	3.1	3.7	2.5	4.9	3.8	4.5
46.6	49.6	48.2	Total Current	41.8	45.8	54.1	58.9	50.9	51.4
31.7	28.3	32.7	Fixed Assets (net)	40.5	32.3	22.9	25.8	35.7	26.8
6.3	8.8	6.0	Intangibles (net)	4.2	4.7	10.3	3.0	6.3	12.5
15.5	13.2	13.1	All Other Non-Current	13.6	17.1	12.7	12.3	7.1	9.3
100.0	100.0	100.0	Total	100.0	100.0	100.0	100.0	100.0	100.0
			LIABILITIES						
19.1	18.9	15.6	Notes Payable-Short Term	19.8	17.7	15.2	16.6	8.9	5.5
4.8	4.6	4.8	Cur. Mat.-L.T.D.	3.3	7.4	2.4	3.3	3.8	7.1
4.8	7.1	6.0	Trade Payables	3.5	3.3	7.2	8.4	12.9	9.0
.1	.1	.4	Income Taxes Payable	.8	.5	.0	.0	.0	.3
21.1	21.1	20.6	All Other Current	22.8	12.9	26.3	26.6	24.4	17.8
49.9	51.7	47.4	Total Current	50.3	41.7	51.1	54.9	50.1	39.7
23.8	20.8	25.0	Long-Term Debt	34.2	27.6	15.9	13.3	16.7	23.8
.1	.1	.2	Deferred Taxes	.0	.1	.6	.1	.1	.8
9.2	8.2	8.8	All Other Non-Current	11.7	10.0	9.5	4.8	4.3	6.0
17.0	19.1	18.5	Net Worth	3.7	20.6	22.8	26.8	28.8	29.6
100.0	100.0	100.0	Total Liabilties & Net Worth	100.0	100.0	100.0	100.0	100.0	100.0
			INCOME DATA						
100.0	100.0	100.0	Net Sales	100.0	100.0	100.0	100.0	100.0	100.0
			Gross Profit						
87.4	88.1	87.3	Operating Expenses	81.3	88.0	88.5	92.4	94.5	87.6
12.6	11.9	12.7	Operating Profit	18.7	12.0	11.5	7.6	5.5	12.4
2.2	1.2	1.7	All Other Expenses (net)	4.0	.4	.5	1.6	-.6	1.8
10.4	10.8	11.1	Profit Before Taxes	14.6	11.5	11.0	6.0	6.1	10.6
			RATIOS						
3.0	3.6	3.5		4.3	4.7	5.4	2.8	2.4	2.5
1.4	1.3	1.3	Current	.9	1.7	1.5	1.3	1.3	1.4
.6	.6	.6		.3	.7	.5	.7	.7	.9
2.6	2.6	3.2		3.8	4.2	5.1	2.3	2.1	2.1
1.1	1.0	(299) 1.1	Quick	(86) .9	1.6	1.2	1.2	1.2	1.0
.4	.4	.5		.3	.4	.4	.7	.6	.7
0 UND	**0** UND	**0** UND		**0** UND	**0** UND	**0** UND	**0** UND	**0** UND	**17** 22.1
0 UND	**0** UND	**0** UND	Sales/Receivables	**0** UND	**0** UND	**1** 292.6	**5** 68.7	**22** 16.5	**41** 9.0
31 11.7	**31** 11.6	**29** 12.7		**0** UND	**0** UND	**32** 11.3	**53** 6.9	**46** 7.9	**52** 7.0
			Cost of Sales/Inventory						
			Cost of Sales/Payables						
9.2	10.2	11.0		11.3	14.1	10.1	5.5	11.3	9.8
59.9	47.1	53.7	Sales/Working Capital	-116.0	32.3	28.1	65.3	73.1	24.4
-23.1	-26.2	-34.5		-11.6	-47.9	-35.8	-72.8	-94.9	-78.5
27.3	32.5	44.4		14.1	68.6	74.4	15.3	48.9	81.7
(236) 6.9	(220) 8.8	(198) 7.7	EBIT/Interest	(41) 4.5	(56) 10.3	(21) 11.1	(20) 6.7	(28) 10.8	(32) 18.5
1.7	2.2	1.9		2.0	1.3	2.4	2.5	.5	2.1
3.9		6.5							
(11) 1.4		(15) 5.0	Net Profit + Depr., Dep., Amort./Cur. Mat. L/T/D						
-.2		1.5							
.2	.1	.2		.1	.2	.2	.1	.5	.5
.9	.9	1.0	Fixed/Worth	1.5	.8	1.0	.8	1.1	.9
-24.7	-28.0	-15.5		-2.1	UND	-1.3	3.4	2.4	-3.4
.5	.6	.5		.5	.3	.5	.5	.6	.6
2.0	2.1	1.9	Debt/Worth	3.0	2.3	2.2	1.5	1.5	1.7
-15.6	-9.4	-9.7		-3.4	-10.7	-9.0	9.0	63.6	-17.2
131.0	221.6	189.3		228.9	168.5	295.8	105.6	199.0	153.6
(240) 48.5	(238) 63.9	(214) 66.3	% Profit Before Taxes/Tangible Net Worth	(56) 66.6	(58) 76.2	(24) 123.5	(27) 19.4	(26) 30.6	(23) 77.4
11.1	11.0	12.1		11.3	16.3	19.8	1.7	-15.5	19.2
53.6	80.7	76.6		106.4	81.2	135.7	47.2	69.3	53.8
14.8	22.4	20.2	% Profit Before Taxes/Total Assets	19.7	33.4	28.9	12.3	9.2	19.0
2.4	2.7	2.4		1.7	4.6	3.8	.7	-3.2	5.0
102.3	172.1	124.5		303.0	126.0	183.6	171.0	106.6	42.4
21.9	28.1	24.5	Sales/Net Fixed Assets	21.5	25.0	39.0	40.6	15.3	11.0
5.9	9.0	4.8		2.0	7.2	18.4	7.3	9.8	5.3
8.0	9.0	8.7		8.7	9.7	8.6	14.7	8.9	5.6
3.6	4.1	4.2	Sales/Total Assets	3.1	4.6	5.7	4.7	4.9	2.9
1.8	2.0	1.9		1.0	2.4	2.2	1.5	2.1	1.8
.7	.6	.7		.9	.7	.5	.6	.5	1.1
(212) 1.8	(190) 1.6	(187) 1.7	% Depr., Dep., Amort./Sales	(45) 3.4	(45) 1.0	(20) 1.4	(21) 2.0	(30) 1.1	(26) 2.4
4.0	3.4	3.8		13.9	2.1	4.6	5.3	2.4	4.1
6.6	7.6	6.9		11.3	6.5	6.6	8.1	1.5	
(147) 13.0	(148) 12.4	(131) 13.3	% Officers', Directors' Owners' Comp/Sales	(38) 17.9	(44) 10.6	(19) 11.0	(12) 16.1	(13) 5.4	
27.8	20.8	22.3		25.3	17.5	20.3	28.4	23.9	
5182951M	5793352M	5696814M	Net Sales ($)	39237M	140260M	124902M	236292M	471387M	4684736M
2348050M	2212616M	2413051M	Total Assets ($)	49976M	54934M	36188M	172595M	157372M	1941986M

M = $ thousand MM = $ million

See Pages 9 through 22 for Explanation of Ratios and Data

Current Data Sorted by Assets / Comparative Historical Data

						Type of Statement		
2	3	3	9			Unqualified	33	33
		1				Reviewed	1	1
	1	1				Compiled		1
3		1				Tax Returns	4	2
3	2	1	1		1	Other	17	14
18 (4/1-9/30/13)			14 (10/1/13-3/31/14)				4/1/09-3/31/10	4/1/10-3/31/11
0-500M	**500M-2MM**	**2-10MM**	**10-50MM**	**50-100MM**	**100-250MM**		**ALL**	**ALL**
8	6	7	10		1	**NUMBER OF STATEMENTS**	55	51
%	%	%	%	%	%	**ASSETS**	%	%
			19.1	DATA NOT AVAILABLE		Cash & Equivalents	18.2	22.8
			8.6			Trade Receivables (net)	11.0	12.1
			2.2			Inventory	1.5	1.5
			3.4			All Other Current	2.3	2.4
			33.3			Total Current	33.0	38.9
			45.6			Fixed Assets (net)	49.8	43.2
			.2			Intangibles (net)	4.5	2.0
			20.9			All Other Non-Current	12.7	16.0
			100.0			Total	100.0	100.0
						LIABILITIES		
			.9			Notes Payable-Short Term	1.9	4.9
			.7			Cur. Mat.-L.T.D.	1.8	2.0
			2.5			Trade Payables	4.6	4.7
			.0			Income Taxes Payable	.1	.0
			5.1			All Other Current	5.6	8.3
			9.1			Total Current	14.0	19.8
			14.8			Long-Term Debt	26.2	15.9
			.0			Deferred Taxes	.0	.1
			.4			All Other Non-Current	3.7	2.1
			75.7			Net Worth	56.0	62.1
			100.0			Total Liabilties & Net Worth	100.0	100.0
						INCOME DATA		
			100.0			Net Sales	100.0	100.0
						Gross Profit		
			100.4			Operating Expenses	92.3	90.4
			-.4			Operating Profit	7.7	9.6
			-2.3			All Other Expenses (net)	2.1	.7
			1.9			Profit Before Taxes	5.7	8.9
						RATIOS		
			6.6				4.5	5.1
			4.0			Current	2.5	2.4
			2.4				1.2	1.2
			5.1				3.7	4.7
			2.9			Quick	2.2	2.1
			1.8				.9	.8
			19 19.5				5 71.5	8 44.1
			33 11.2			Sales/Receivables	22 16.6	27 13.6
			51 7.2				38 9.6	41 8.8
						Cost of Sales/Inventory		
						Cost of Sales/Payables		
			3.0				3.4	3.3
			4.5			Sales/Working Capital	6.5	6.6
			8.5				33.7	34.4
							14.5	21.2
						EBIT/Interest	(41) 2.7	(34) 6.5
							.2	1.6
						Net Profit + Depr., Dep., Amort./Cur. Mat. L/T/D		
			.3				.4	.3
			.6			Fixed/Worth	1.0	.7
			1.0				2.4	1.3
			.1				.2	.1
			.3			Debt/Worth	.7	.4
			.7				2.2	1.4
			8.7				13.8	19.4
			4.6			% Profit Before Taxes/Tangible Net Worth	(48) 6.6	(46) 9.0
			2.3				-5.9	2.7
			6.3				10.0	12.3
			4.1			% Profit Before Taxes/Total Assets	3.5	6.7
			1.9				-3.1	1.9
			3.6				5.8	6.2
			1.8			Sales/Net Fixed Assets	2.5	2.8
			1.2				1.4	1.9
			1.3				1.7	1.7
			.9			Sales/Total Assets	1.2	1.1
			.6				.7	.7
			2.4				1.9	1.9
			3.4			% Depr., Dep., Amort./Sales	(45) 2.9	(46) 2.9
			5.1				4.6	4.3
						% Officers', Directors' Owners' Comp/Sales		
7480M	16949M	52745M	261685M		96721M	Net Sales ($)	1099743M	923497M
905M	6122M	41023M	277491M		109264M	Total Assets ($)	1024244M	1060838M

M = $ thousand MM = $ million

See Pages 9 through 22 for Explanation of Ratios and Data

Comparative Historical Data				Current Data Sorted by Sales					
			Type of Statement						
28	23	17	Unqualified	2	2		2	7	4
2		1	Reviewed		1				
2		2	Compiled	1			1		
1		4	Tax Returns	2	1			1	
15	13	8	Other	3	3			1	1
				18 (4/1-9/30/13)			14 (10/1/13-3/31/14)		
4/1/11-3/31/12 ALL	4/1/12-3/31/13 ALL	4/1/13-3/31/14 ALL		0-1MM	1-3MM	3-5MM	5-10MM	10-25MM	25MM & OVER
48	36	32	**NUMBER OF STATEMENTS**	8	7		3	9	5
%	%	%	**ASSETS**	%	%	%	%	%	%
24.4	31.1	26.2	Cash & Equivalents			DATA NOT AVAILABLE			
11.3	11.7	9.0	Trade Receivables (net)						
1.3	1.4	1.8	Inventory						
1.7	2.6	8.0	All Other Current						
38.6	46.8	45.0	Total Current						
44.2	42.3	43.2	Fixed Assets (net)						
2.9	.1	3.3	Intangibles (net)						
14.2	10.8	8.4	All Other Non-Current						
100.0	100.0	100.0	Total						
			LIABILITIES						
3.1	3.9	4.2	Notes Payable-Short Term						
2.9	1.2	.8	Cur. Mat.-L.T.D.						
3.8	5.2	3.9	Trade Payables						
.0	.0	.2	Income Taxes Payable						
10.4	8.7	14.9	All Other Current						
20.2	19.0	24.0	Total Current						
23.8	14.2	14.3	Long-Term Debt						
.1	.1	.0	Deferred Taxes						
2.2	.3	1.4	All Other Non-Current						
53.8	66.4	60.3	Net Worth						
100.0	100.0	100.0	Total Liabilties & Net Worth						
			INCOME DATA						
100.0	100.0	100.0	Net Sales						
			Gross Profit						
92.2	91.8	92.5	Operating Expenses						
7.8	8.2	7.5	Operating Profit						
.9	.4	.0	All Other Expenses (net)						
6.9	7.8	7.5	Profit Before Taxes						
			RATIOS						
5.9	7.0	6.1							
2.7	3.8	2.9	Current						
1.0	2.3	1.0							
5.0	6.7	5.2							
2.5	3.4	2.5	Quick						
1.0	2.1	.8							
1 729.3	**2** 173.0	**0** UND							
19 19.4	**24** 15.4	**15** 24.1	Sales/Receivables						
39 9.3	**38** 9.6	**34** 10.8							
			Cost of Sales/Inventory						
			Cost of Sales/Payables						
2.8	2.5	3.3							
6.2	4.5	7.7	Sales/Working Capital						
198.3	11.6	UND							
18.1	24.0	15.3							
(39) 7.3	(27) 6.0	(21) 7.3	EBIT/Interest						
-2.0	2.0	3.4							
			Net Profit + Depr., Dep., Amort./Cur. Mat. L/T/D						
.3	.3	.4							
.7	.6	.8	Fixed/Worth						
1.2	1.1	1.8							
.1	.1	.2							
.5	.3	.5	Debt/Worth						
1.5	.8	1.5							
19.7	21.8	34.0							
(42) 10.0	(34) 8.0	(31) 8.7	% Profit Before Taxes/Tangible Net Worth						
1.6	.9	2.7							
13.7	16.1	12.6							
7.5	7.1	5.5	% Profit Before Taxes/Total Assets						
.9	1.2	.9							
10.2	6.4	9.7							
2.7	2.3	2.6	Sales/Net Fixed Assets						
1.7	1.4	1.8							
2.0	1.7	5.4							
1.3	1.0	1.3	Sales/Total Assets						
.7	.8	.9							
1.5	2.0	1.9							
(43) 3.4	(29) 3.6	(25) 3.2	% Depr., Dep., Amort./Sales						
4.7	4.6	3.8							
			% Officers', Directors' Owners' Comp/Sales						
990586M	462921M	435580M	Net Sales ($)	4181M	12617M		25172M	140930M	252680M
936591M	447252M	434805M	Total Assets ($)	2193M	11241M		18617M	176113M	226641M

M = $ thousand MM = $ million

See Pages 9 through 22 for Explanation of Ratios and Data

Current Data Sorted by Assets							Comparative Historical Data	
						Type of Statement		
2	8	46	49	6	2	Unqualified	91	124
		3	2			Reviewed		2
	4	3				Compiled	3	4
8	6	4	1		1	Tax Returns	12	16
6	12	25	19	2	1	Other	33	49
138 (4/1-9/30/13)			72 (10/1/13-3/31/14)				4/1/09-3/31/10	4/1/10-3/31/11
0-500M	**500M-2MM**	**2-10MM**	**10-50MM**	**50-100MM**	**100-250MM**		**ALL**	**ALL**
16	30	81	71	8	4	**NUMBER OF STATEMENTS**	139	195
%	%	%	%	%	%	**ASSETS**	%	%
32.1	28.6	21.3	22.0			Cash & Equivalents	22.1	22.4
6.1	19.0	21.6	13.9			Trade Receivables (net)	20.4	18.7
3.4	.1	.1	.3			Inventory	.1	.2
7.2	8.3	3.0	2.6			All Other Current	5.3	4.1
48.8	56.0	46.0	38.9			Total Current	47.9	45.4
23.0	35.8	43.1	50.7			Fixed Assets (net)	40.4	44.2
12.2	1.3	1.5	2.0			Intangibles (net)	4.4	3.0
16.0	6.9	9.4	8.4			All Other Non-Current	7.3	7.5
100.0	100.0	100.0	100.0			Total	100.0	100.0
						LIABILITIES		
61.4	7.2	2.7	1.4			Notes Payable-Short Term	5.6	4.5
5.5	.8	2.0	2.4			Cur. Mat.-L.T.D.	3.1	2.8
4.0	5.9	7.5	4.7			Trade Payables	7.1	7.2
.0	.7	.0	.1			Income Taxes Payable	.1	.1
36.3	13.6	11.9	9.1			All Other Current	16.0	15.1
107.3	28.2	24.2	17.7			Total Current	32.0	29.6
17.4	20.5	18.8	26.1			Long-Term Debt	21.0	21.0
.9	.0	.1	.2			Deferred Taxes	.0	.0
.6	4.5	4.0	6.8			All Other Non-Current	3.0	3.4
-26.2	46.7	52.9	49.2			Net Worth	44.1	45.9
100.0	100.0	100.0	100.0			Total Liabilties & Net Worth	100.0	100.0
						INCOME DATA		
100.0	100.0	100.0	100.0			Net Sales	100.0	100.0
						Gross Profit		
88.5	92.6	95.2	95.3			Operating Expenses	95.9	93.9
11.5	7.4	4.8	4.7			Operating Profit	4.1	6.1
.4	1.5	.2	1.2			All Other Expenses (net)	.4	2.0
11.1	5.9	4.6	3.5			Profit Before Taxes	3.7	4.1
						RATIOS		
2.2	5.0	3.7	3.6				2.8	2.9
1.0	2.1	2.1	2.2			Current	1.9	1.9
.2	1.0	1.1	1.4				1.2	1.2
2.2	4.3	3.1	3.4				2.6	2.8
.5	2.0	2.0	2.0			Quick	1.7	1.7
.1	.9	1.1	1.2				1.0	1.0
0 UND	**0** UND	**18** 20.4	**17** 21.5				**14** 25.9	**12** 31.2
0 UND	**12** 29.8	**33** 11.1	**32** 11.3			Sales/Receivables	**30** 12.0	**30** 12.0
0 UND	**33** 11.1	**50** 7.3	**48** 7.6				**46** 7.9	**48** 7.6
						Cost of Sales/Inventory		
						Cost of Sales/Payables		
34.4	4.3	5.0	4.0				5.8	5.6
NM	11.8	9.3	7.2			Sales/Working Capital	10.9	10.2
-17.2	-819.1	47.6	16.0				39.1	46.6
17.0	46.3	9.2	11.8				8.3	9.9
(11) 8.0	(22) 5.6	(57) 2.1	(62) 3.3			EBIT/Interest	(107) 3.4	(157) 3.1
4.5	-1.8	-1.2	.6				1.0	1.3
								22.7
						Net Profit + Depr., Dep., Amort./Cur. Mat. L/T/D		(10) 5.7
								2.4
.2	.1	.3	.6				.4	.5
.5	.6	.8	1.0			Fixed/Worth	1.0	.9
NM	4.5	1.5	1.5				1.9	2.0
.4	.3	.3	.4				.5	.5
2.1	.8	.8	.8			Debt/Worth	1.1	1.0
-4.6	10.0	1.8	1.8				2.9	2.4
420.0	50.7	18.0	9.1				21.4	19.4
(11) 91.6	(27) 23.8	(77) 3.7	(69) 3.4			% Profit Before Taxes/Tangible Net Worth	(123) 6.6	(177) 5.9
20.2	-3.5	-4.3	-1.1				-.3	.5
77.0	24.7	7.0	6.9				9.7	10.4
20.0	7.2	2.6	2.1			% Profit Before Taxes/Total Assets	3.1	2.8
8.4	-1.8	-1.7	-.7				-.2	.1
193.3	59.4	14.2	5.0				25.5	12.6
49.1	16.5	4.6	2.5			Sales/Net Fixed Assets	4.3	3.9
25.2	4.8	2.0	1.4				2.2	2.1
12.4	5.1	3.0	1.7				3.9	3.1
7.3	3.4	1.9	1.2			Sales/Total Assets	1.8	1.8
3.8	1.7	1.0	.8				1.2	1.1
.5	.7	.9	1.7				.9	1.3
(11) .9	(23) 1.2	(77) 1.7	(67) 2.8			% Depr., Dep., Amort./Sales	(122) 1.8	(174) 2.1
1.3	2.1	2.9	3.8				2.5	3.3
3.5							5.9	2.1
(10) 8.9						% Officers', Directors' Owners' Comp/Sales	(24) 11.6	(26) 6.1
14.5							25.0	11.6
35311M	**115024M**	**895084M**	**2232254M**	**607053M**	**2155020M**	Net Sales ($)	**2296461M**	**3730706M**
4004M	**34324M**	**440001M**	**1512208M**	**555947M**	**477986M**	Total Assets ($)	**1333839M**	**2212061M**

M = $ thousand MM = $ million

See Pages 9 through 22 for Explanation of Ratios and Data

Comparative Historical Data | **Current Data Sorted by Sales**

4/1/11-3/31/12 ALL	4/1/12-3/31/13 ALL	4/1/13-3/31/14 ALL	Type of Statement	0-1MM	1-3MM	3-5MM	5-10MM	10-25MM	25MM & OVER
128	124	113	Unqualified	2	9	10	20	35	37
4	2	5	Reviewed		1		1	1	2
8	3	7	Compiled		3	1	2	1	
16	17	20	Tax Returns	7	2	2	7	1	1
42	50	65	Other	4	8	6	10	25	12
				138 (4/1-9/30/13)			72 (10/1/13-3/31/14)		
198	196	210	NUMBER OF STATEMENTS	13	23	19	40	63	52
%	%	%	**ASSETS**	%	%	%	%	%	%
22.9	21.9	23.2	Cash & Equivalents	22.6	29.2	24.1	17.9	24.7	22.4
17.9	17.3	16.8	Trade Receivables (net)	.4	9.0	16.5	19.2	20.1	18.7
.2	.2	.4	Inventory	4.0	.2	.0	.0	.2	.2
2.7	3.0	4.0	All Other Current	13.9	6.2	2.8	2.4	3.2	3.1
43.7	42.4	44.3	Total Current	40.8	44.6	43.4	39.5	48.2	44.4
45.3	46.9	42.6	Fixed Assets (net)	45.4	39.9	45.2	46.6	43.2	38.3
2.6	3.0	4.2	Intangibles (net)	8.3	3.9	.2	3.8	1.1	8.9
8.4	7.8	8.9	All Other Non-Current	5.5	11.6	11.2	10.1	7.5	8.4
100.0	100.0	100.0	Total	100.0	100.0	100.0	100.0	100.0	100.0
			LIABILITIES						
4.9	4.6	7.3	Notes Payable-Short Term	65.7	3.7	3.8	6.7	2.2	2.1
1.8	2.8	2.7	Cur. Mat.-L.T.D.	3.0	.9	3.0	2.3	2.3	4.0
6.1	5.7	5.8	Trade Payables	1.2	4.5	5.4	5.3	6.8	6.9
.0	.1	.1	Income Taxes Payable	.0	.0	1.1	.0	.0	.2
13.8	13.6	12.9	All Other Current	11.3	7.4	30.1	10.3	12.0	12.8
26.6	26.7	28.9	Total Current	81.2	16.5	43.4	24.6	23.3	26.0
23.7	24.8	22.1	Long-Term Debt	28.8	19.0	23.8	24.9	22.6	18.2
.1	.1	.2	Deferred Taxes	.0	.7	.0	.0	.1	.2
4.1	4.4	5.1	All Other Non-Current	.8	4.9	3.1	.7	9.7	4.7
45.6	44.0	43.8	Net Worth	-10.8	59.0	29.7	49.8	44.3	50.8
100.0	100.0	100.0	Total Liabilities & Net Worth	100.0	100.0	100.0	100.0	100.0	100.0
			INCOME DATA						
100.0	100.0	100.0	Net Sales	100.0	100.0	100.0	100.0	100.0	100.0
			Gross Profit						
95.4	94.3	93.9	Operating Expenses	79.5	86.1	98.6	94.6	96.4	95.5
4.6	5.7	6.1	Operating Profit	20.5	13.9	1.4	5.4	3.6	4.5
1.5	1.8	.8	All Other Expenses (net)	5.9	1.7	.0	.2	.1	.8
3.2	3.9	5.3	Profit Before Taxes	14.6	12.2	1.4	5.2	3.5	3.7
			RATIOS						
3.5	3.4	3.6		5.0	9.0	11.5	2.7	4.0	2.4
2.1	2.0	2.1	Current	.8	3.4	1.4	2.0	2.5	1.9
1.4	1.2	1.1		.1	1.2	.8	1.1	1.4	1.2
3.3	3.2	3.3		3.2	8.9	11.5	2.7	3.7	2.3
1.9	1.8	1.9	Quick	.7	2.9	1.2	1.5	2.5	1.7
1.2	1.1	1.1		.1	1.1	.8	1.1	1.2	1.2
9 40.8	12 30.9	10 36.1		0 UND	0 UND	2 219.1	8 43.3	19 18.9	16 22.2
28 13.2	27 18.3	28 13.1	Sales/Receivables	0 UND	19 18.8	22 16.8	31 11.7	34 10.8	36 10.2
49 7.5	46 8.0	46 8.0		0 UND	33 11.1	47 7.7	47 7.8	50 7.3	51 7.1
			Cost of Sales/Inventory						
			Cost of Sales/Payables						
4.9	4.9	4.6		4.9	3.2	2.9	6.5	3.8	5.7
7.6	9.7	9.9	Sales/Working Capital	-25.1	7.1	11.7	12.6	8.1	11.0
23.5	53.2	61.6		-5.2	59.5	-97.1	104.3	29.1	30.2
11.2	10.2	10.6			56.3	9.8	6.9	13.4	8.3
(165) 2.9	(167) 3.1	(163) 3.6	EBIT/Interest		(16) 8.6	(17) 4.5	(30) 1.7	(50) 3.7	(44) 3.2
.7	.6	.5			2.1	-.4	-.8	.3	1.4
31.8	12.5								
(10) 4.6	(12) 2.6		Net Profit + Depr., Dep., Amort./Cur. Mat. L/T/D						
1.3	.9								
.5	.6	.4		.1	.1	.4	.4	.5	.5
.9	.9	.9	Fixed/Worth	1.2	.7	.9	1.1	.8	.9
1.8	1.6	1.9		22.0	1.5	2.4	2.0	1.5	1.3
.4	.4	.4		.4	.2	.2	.4	.3	.5
.9	.8	.9	Debt/Worth	1.2	.7	.6	1.1	.9	.9
2.0	1.9	2.3		NM	1.5	3.0	2.8	1.9	2.0
16.8	15.0	19.0		84.2	54.9	31.7	28.2	16.2	9.2
(181) 6.1	(177) 5.5	(191) 5.3	% Profit Before Taxes/Tangible Net Worth	(10) 13.3	(22) 20.8	(17) 1.9	(37) 3.6	(59) 4.7	(46) 4.1
-.5	-.4	-1.1		-8.2	6.5	-4.0	-2.7	-3.0	-1.0
9.0	7.6	10.1		31.9	42.0	9.6	17.2	8.9	6.9
3.3	2.5	2.9	% Profit Before Taxes/Total Assets	4.9	11.9	.2	1.7	3.1	2.6
-.7	-.4	-.7		-2.1	2.9	-2.3	-.9	-1.5	-.3
11.1	10.3	18.8		UND	39.1	29.1	24.6	9.5	17.3
3.5	3.4	4.4	Sales/Net Fixed Assets	10.4	9.4	3.2	4.9	3.7	4.0
1.7	1.9	1.9		.3	1.2	1.0	1.7	2.0	2.1
2.5	3.0	3.3		5.1	4.6	5.6	3.3	2.6	2.9
1.6	1.6	1.7	Sales/Total Assets	1.0	2.1	1.6	1.8	1.7	1.7
1.0	1.0	1.0		.3	.7	.6	1.0	1.0	1.1
1.2	1.3	1.0			.7	1.2	.9	1.1	1.0
(174) 2.3	(178) 2.3	(189) 2.0	% Depr., Dep., Amort./Sales		(19) 1.3	(16) 2.6	(36) 1.6	(60) 2.0	(50) 2.0
3.4	3.5	3.4			4.7	5.1	2.7	3.1	3.1
7.6	1.9	3.9							
(22) 10.8	(29) 5.1	(26) 7.8	% Officers', Directors' Owners' Comp/Sales						
27.0	12.8	18.0							
3766175M	3941649M	6039746M	Net Sales ($)	6355M	51644M	76110M	285680M	1011931M	4608026M
2403718M	2721791M	3024470M	Total Assets ($)	11606M	59551M	70195M	195507M	727313M	1960298M

M = $ thousand MM = $ million

See Pages 9 through 22 for Explanation of Ratios and Data

Current Data Sorted by Assets | Comparative Historical Data

0-500M	500M-2MM	2-10MM	10-50MM	50-100MM	100-250MM	Type of Statement	4/1/09-3/31/10 ALL	4/1/10-3/31/11 ALL
	1	2	6	1	1	Unqualified	11	9
		1	1			Reviewed	7	3
1	2	2			1	Compiled	2	8
	3	2				Tax Returns	8	9
1	10	6	3		1	Other	41	35
	5 (4/1-9/30/13)		40 (10/1/13-3/31/14)					
2	16	13	10	1	3	NUMBER OF STATEMENTS	69	64
%	%	%	%	%	%	**ASSETS**	%	%
	11.8	18.8	11.5			Cash & Equivalents	13.0	13.6
	24.7	21.5	21.2			Trade Receivables (net)	25.9	22.4
	1.8	1.4	3.0			Inventory	2.6	1.5
	2.0	7.2	6.4			All Other Current	6.0	5.7
	40.3	48.9	42.1			Total Current	47.5	43.2
	43.9	24.8	31.3			Fixed Assets (net)	34.2	38.5
	7.6	7.8	20.1			Intangibles (net)	8.8	9.2
	8.2	18.5	6.5			All Other Non-Current	9.5	9.1
	100.0	100.0	100.0			Total	100.0	100.0
						LIABILITIES		
	25.1	1.7	1.4			Notes Payable-Short Term	1.5	11.2
	8.8	5.5	4.1			Cur. Mat.-L.T.D.	7.2	8.9
	12.0	3.3	4.3			Trade Payables	11.4	6.8
	.0	1.9	2.3			Income Taxes Payable	.3	.3
	10.6	11.4	15.6			All Other Current	22.8	17.7
	56.4	23.9	27.8			Total Current	43.1	45.0
	38.0	21.3	10.2			Long-Term Debt	21.1	21.7
	.0	.0	.6			Deferred Taxes	.1	.0
	1.8	4.1	12.8			All Other Non-Current	8.9	8.6
	3.8	50.6	48.7			Net Worth	26.8	24.6
	100.0	100.0	100.0			Total Liabilities & Net Worth	100.0	100.0
						INCOME DATA		
	100.0	100.0	100.0			Net Sales	100.0	100.0
						Gross Profit		
	89.5	67.6	87.1			Operating Expenses	88.4	86.1
	10.5	32.4	12.9			Operating Profit	11.6	13.9
	3.3	3.5	.7			All Other Expenses (net)	2.7	1.5
	7.1	28.9	12.3			Profit Before Taxes	9.0	12.4
						RATIOS		
	1.5	3.4	3.5				3.5	2.7
	1.0	2.6	1.5			Current	1.8	1.6
	.5	1.4	1.0				.7	.6
	1.3	3.4	2.6				3.1	2.4
	.8	2.2	1.1			Quick	1.5	1.2
	.5	1.3	.7				.5	.4
	0 UND	**0** UND	**33** 11.2				**10** 35.1	**1** 307.0
	41 8.8	**40** 9.2	**46** 7.9			Sales/Receivables	**51** 7.2	**46** 7.9
	61 6.0	**45** 8.2	**51** 7.1				**69** 5.3	**65** 5.7
						Cost of Sales/Inventory		
						Cost of Sales/Payables		
	12.2	4.5	6.2				4.9	5.4
	NM	8.7	10.0			Sales/Working Capital	8.7	20.3
	-9.9	25.7	-468.6				-35.3	-11.9
	15.2	191.9					35.4	16.2
	(14) 5.6	(12) 11.0				EBIT/Interest	(50) 8.8	(55) 6.7
	1.4	3.6					1.2	1.5
							47.0	
						Net Profit + Depr., Dep., Amort./Cur. Mat. L/T/D	(13) 9.3	
							1.0	
	1.3	.1	.6				.4	.4
	NM	.5	1.2			Fixed/Worth	1.0	1.6
	-.8	1.1	NM				-6.0	-4.3
	1.5	.3	.8				.5	.5
	NM	.8	2.0			Debt/Worth	1.8	2.9
	-3.3	8.1	NM				-6.6	-6.3
		120.1					96.9	167.6
		(11) 89.9				% Profit Before Taxes/Tangible Net Worth	(49) 30.3	(46) 57.1
		27.7					6.0	6.7
	43.2	77.9	38.3				31.0	38.2
	21.9	37.7	12.5			% Profit Before Taxes/Total Assets	10.0	10.7
	3.8	10.2	5.0				.9	1.2
	10.9	140.8	10.1				19.4	13.3
	8.1	15.5	7.4			Sales/Net Fixed Assets	8.8	5.6
	3.2	3.4	4.0				3.7	3.6
	4.0	3.2	2.6				3.5	3.7
	2.5	1.7	1.6			Sales/Total Assets	2.0	2.0
	1.8	1.0	.9				1.3	1.3
	3.0	.7					1.3	1.8
	(14) 3.7	(10) 1.7				% Depr., Dep., Amort./Sales	(61) 2.4	(55) 3.0
	5.2	4.9					3.8	4.7
							4.4	2.9
						% Officers', Directors' Owners' Comp/Sales	(17) 8.0	(12) 7.3
							33.2	32.0
4739M	49761M	93272M	398356M	101320M	434104M	Net Sales ($)	1384215M	1451181M
834M	19138M	54843M	240758M	89701M	397301M	Total Assets ($)	923818M	1067345M

M = $ thousand MM = $ million

See Pages 9 through 22 for Explanation of Ratios and Data

Comparative Historical Data				Current Data Sorted by Sales					
			Type of Statement						
14	9	11	Unqualified		2		1	1	7
3	2	2	Reviewed				1	1	
5	5	6	Compiled			2	3		1
15	9	5	Tax Returns	1	1	2	1		
45	40	21	Other		7	4	5	1	4
4/1/11-3/31/12 ALL	**4/1/12-3/31/13 ALL**	**4/1/13-3/31/14 ALL**		**5 (4/1-9/30/13)**			**40 (10/1/13-3/31/14)**		
				0-1MM	**1-3MM**	**3-5MM**	**5-10MM**	**10-25MM**	**25MM & OVER**
82	65	45	**NUMBER OF STATEMENTS**	1	10	8	11	3	12
%	%	%	**ASSETS**	%	%	%	%	%	%
16.2	16.0	13.0	Cash & Equivalents		10.6		17.9		7.6
23.4	24.2	23.0	Trade Receivables (net)		32.3		12.1		21.7
1.9	1.9	1.9	Inventory		2.3		1.8		2.7
3.4	2.5	4.3	All Other Current		.0		7.8		5.4
45.0	44.6	42.1	Total Current		45.2		39.6		37.4
35.7	28.3	32.5	Fixed Assets (net)		37.2		32.1		30.4
9.5	14.2	13.1	Intangibles (net)		7.6		6.8		24.6
9.8	12.9	12.3	All Other Non-Current		10.0		21.5		7.5
100.0	100.0	100.0	Total		100.0		100.0		100.0
			LIABILITIES						
5.7	5.6	11.1	Notes Payable-Short Term		28.5		5.4		.9
6.7	4.7	5.7	Cur. Mat.-L.T.D.		7.4		5.1		3.3
6.7	7.1	6.5	Trade Payables		13.8		2.9		3.9
.3	.4	1.1	Income Taxes Payable		.0		.1		1.9
18.5	16.7	11.0	All Other Current		8.2		14.5		13.7
37.9	34.5	35.4	Total Current		57.9		28.0		23.8
21.0	20.1	23.8	Long-Term Debt		37.5		18.2		15.6
.0	.1	.1	Deferred Taxes		.0		.0		.5
4.6	4.4	11.8	All Other Non-Current		7.1		4.9		23.7
36.4	41.0	28.9	Net Worth		-2.5		48.9		36.4
100.0	100.0	100.0	Total Liabilties & Net Worth		100.0		100.0		100.0
			INCOME DATA						
100.0	100.0	100.0	Net Sales		100.0		100.0		100.0
			Gross Profit						
86.5	79.6	82.5	Operating Expenses		93.2		71.6		84.9
13.5	20.4	17.5	Operating Profit		6.8		28.4		15.1
1.5	2.8	2.9	All Other Expenses (net)		4.1		1.1		2.3
12.0	17.5	14.6	Profit Before Taxes		2.7		27.2		12.8
			RATIOS						
3.3	3.4	3.0			2.1		3.5		3.1
1.7	1.7	1.5	Current		1.2		2.6		2.4
.8	.9	.9			.5		.5		1.0
2.7	2.9	2.7			2.0		3.5		2.7
1.5	1.6	1.4	Quick		1.1		2.2		1.8
.7	.7	.7			.5		.5		.8
0 UND	**0** UND	**28** 13.0			**36** 10.0		**0** UND		**34** 10.6
44 8.3	**49** 7.4	**42** 8.6	Sales/Receivables		**52** 7.0		**31** 11.7		**48** 7.6
63 5.8	**69** 5.3	**55** 6.6			**68** 5.4		**51** 7.2		**56** 6.5
			Cost of Sales/Inventory						
			Cost of Sales/Payables						
5.9	4.7	6.9			5.0		7.7		6.3
12.1	12.1	11.6	Sales/Working Capital		NM		9.5		8.2
-45.2	-44.5	-49.8			-4.6		-17.3		NM
29.7	44.6	31.7			9.3				26.8
(67) 9.2	(49) 15.5	(41) 7.6	EBIT/Interest		1.8				8.0
2.4	3.4	2.7			-6.4				3.2
			Net Profit + Depr., Dep., Amort./Cur. Mat. L/T/D						
.4	.3	.6			1.1		.1		.7
.8	.6	1.4	Fixed/Worth		-1.0		.6		10.4
-18.2	4.5	-1.1			-.6		-6.8		-1.1
.4	.5	.8			1.6		.2		1.1
1.5	1.1	4.9	Debt/Worth		-6.9		.8		34.2
-48.3	17.3	-5.1			-2.9		-10.6		-3.2
121.2	112.4	119.3							
(60) 52.4	(50) 51.2	(28) 51.5	% Profit Before Taxes/Tangible Net Worth						
16.0	18.2	13.7							
35.5	35.1	41.5			20.8		80.3		35.8
11.4	16.7	17.9	% Profit Before Taxes/Total Assets		6.8		38.3		12.5
2.7	3.8	5.3			-25.5		17.9		8.6
28.7	30.7	17.9			28.5		34.4		8.6
6.7	9.1	7.9	Sales/Net Fixed Assets		5.4		14.2		6.1
3.4	4.5	3.5			2.6		3.4		4.6
4.6	3.6	2.8			2.6		4.0		2.5
2.0	1.7	1.9	Sales/Total Assets		1.8		1.8		1.4
1.2	.9	1.2			1.0		.9		1.2
1.2	1.3	1.7							
(69) 2.1	(51) 2.6	(36) 3.3	% Depr., Dep., Amort./Sales						
4.0	4.2	5.0							
6.3	1.3								
(14) 8.7	(10) 7.0		% Officers', Directors' Owners' Comp/Sales						
23.9	18.3								
1699715M	**1201251M**	**1081552M**	Net Sales ($)	**212M**	**18954M**	**29225M**	**77181M**	**53584M**	**902396M**
1201739M	**942195M**	**802575M**	Total Assets ($)	**1869M**	**17211M**	**10766M**	**50300M**	**36025M**	**686404M**

M = $ thousand MM = $ million

See Pages 9 through 22 for Explanation of Ratios and Data

	Current Data Sorted by Assets						Comparative Historical Data	
Type of Statement								
Unqualified		2	20	13	2	4	30	36
Reviewed		4	15	4		1	23	30
Compiled	12	19	20	2			44	37
Tax Returns	23	28	25	5			81	67
Other	16	45	72	24	2	4	127	146
	25 (4/1-9/30/13)		337 (10/1/13-3/31/14)					
	0-500M	500M-2MM	2-10MM	10-50MM	50-100MM	100-250MM	4/1/09-3/31/10 ALL	4/1/10-3/31/11 ALL
NUMBER OF STATEMENTS	51	98	152	48	4	9	305	316
ASSETS	%	%	%	%	%	%	%	%
Cash & Equivalents	34.8	29.6	16.0	14.9			17.3	19.8
Trade Receivables (net)	11.2	13.1	23.4	21.8			16.0	15.6
Inventory	.8	3.0	3.1	2.3			2.3	2.9
All Other Current	5.6	2.7	1.8	3.1			2.7	2.9
Total Current	52.5	48.4	44.3	42.1			38.4	41.2
Fixed Assets (net)	28.5	35.2	44.9	41.0			45.6	45.7
Intangibles (net)	7.2	8.9	6.6	10.4			8.3	7.7
All Other Non-Current	11.8	7.5	4.2	6.5			7.7	5.4
Total	100.0	100.0	100.0	100.0			100.0	100.0
LIABILITIES								
Notes Payable-Short Term	26.4	5.3	4.3	2.1			13.3	10.0
Cur. Mat.-L.T.D.	9.3	8.2	5.7	5.1			7.4	9.2
Trade Payables	6.7	7.9	6.0	7.4			5.2	5.3
Income Taxes Payable	.0	.0	.0	.5			.4	.4
All Other Current	33.3	12.1	8.9	10.0			14.0	14.2
Total Current	75.7	33.5	25.0	25.1			40.4	39.0
Long-Term Debt	27.9	33.9	28.4	34.0			35.7	36.7
Deferred Taxes	.0	.0	.0	.1			.1	.1
All Other Non-Current	13.1	2.3	1.8	2.1			4.4	5.2
Net Worth	-16.7	30.3	44.9	38.8			19.4	19.1
Total Liabilties & Net Worth	100.0	100.0	100.0	100.0			100.0	100.0
INCOME DATA								
Net Sales	100.0	100.0	100.0	100.0			100.0	100.0
Gross Profit								
Operating Expenses	82.4	79.3	74.5	79.3			80.1	80.1
Operating Profit	17.6	20.7	25.5	20.7			19.9	19.9
All Other Expenses (net)	.3	1.7	2.9	2.7			3.4	2.8
Profit Before Taxes	17.3	19.1	22.6	18.0			16.5	17.1
RATIOS								
Current	5.8	4.5	3.6	2.9			2.8	2.9
	1.1	1.9	1.8	1.7			1.5	1.5
	.4	1.0	1.0	1.1			.5	.6
Quick	4.9	4.0	3.3	2.5			2.4	2.6
	.8	1.7	1.5	1.4			1.1	1.2
	.3	.8	.9	1.0			.4	.5
Sales/Receivables	**0** UND	**0** UND	**2** 148.6	**23** 16.0			**0** UND	**0** UND
	0 UND	**0** UND	**35** 10.4	**42** 8.6			**24** 15.2	**26** 13.8
	0 UND	**31** 11.8	**56** 6.5	**60** 6.1			**47** 7.7	**46** 7.9
Cost of Sales/Inventory								
Cost of Sales/Payables								
Sales/Working Capital	25.5	9.0	5.9	4.0			7.8	7.7
	416.0	20.4	12.9	9.4			29.2	24.7
	-19.6	-806.4	935.7	109.2			-25.6	-28.5
EBIT/Interest	76.4	165.5	99.7	56.2			39.8	42.8
	(33) 9.1	(81) 36.2	(126) 24.8	(40) 20.8			(261) 11.0	(270) 13.0
	1.3	7.7	6.9	5.6			2.7	3.1
Net Profit + Depr., Dep., Amort./Cur. Mat. L/T/D			36.2				6.6	10.9
			(14) 18.9				(19) 2.3	(22) 4.3
			4.5				1.4	1.5
Fixed/Worth	.0	.4	.5	.4			.5	.6
	.9	1.0	1.0	1.0			1.6	1.7
	-1.0	-14.0	3.9	15.5			13.5	-9.4
Debt/Worth	.5	.5	.5	.5			.7	.7
	13.7	1.4	1.4	1.3			2.6	2.5
	-2.0	-45.4	5.4	18.2			64.1	-10.9
% Profit Before Taxes/Tangible Net Worth	984.9	258.5	191.6	99.3			183.3	188.4
	(28) 214.6	(72) 121.8	(133) 91.3	(39) 62.0			(234) 79.2	(226) 91.3
	32.9	27.9	35.7	7.7			20.0	33.1
% Profit Before Taxes/Total Assets	279.5	117.7	80.6	45.2			69.1	67.3
	103.4	50.4	36.0	15.6			24.6	29.0
	7.5	14.0	9.6	4.0			4.7	6.1
Sales/Net Fixed Assets	UND	40.9	11.9	9.9			24.5	18.6
	87.6	11.2	5.4	5.3			6.6	6.2
	21.9	5.5	1.9	1.7			2.6	2.9
Sales/Total Assets	22.9	5.4	3.0	2.5			5.1	4.3
	10.8	3.7	2.1	1.4			2.2	2.4
	5.6	2.4	1.1	.8			1.2	1.4
% Depr., Dep., Amort./Sales	.6	1.3	2.5	2.5			2.2	2.5
	(21) .9	(77) 2.5	(136) 4.4	(42) 3.6			(248) 3.8	(261) 4.4
	2.1	5.0	7.3	7.7			7.5	7.7
% Officers', Directors' Owners' Comp/Sales	6.8	3.9	4.2				5.8	4.3
	(18) 17.9	(16) 14.1	(10) 11.3				(80) 14.6	(60) 13.2
	35.8	23.8	25.0				33.0	31.3
Net Sales ($)	146452M	490720M	1594322M	1985089M	380628M	1130414M	4286828M	3845529M
Total Assets ($)	11845M	115714M	717798M	1121329M	310038M	1335284M	2908497M	2423440M

M = $ thousand MM = $ million

See Pages 9 through 22 for Explanation of Ratios and Data

Comparative Historical Data				Current Data Sorted by Sales					
			Type of Statement						
41	34	41	Unqualified		2	3	10	8	18
20	27	24	Reviewed			4	5	12	3
54	42	53	Compiled	6	12	16	10	9	
117	82	81	Tax Returns	14	17	19	18	9	4
176	148	163	Other	9	24	25	41	38	26
4/1/11-3/31/12 ALL	4/1/12-3/31/13 ALL	4/1/13-3/31/14 ALL		25 (4/1-9/30/13)			337 (10/1/13-3/31/14)		
				0-1MM	1-3MM	3-5MM	5-10MM	10-25MM	25MM & OVER
408	333	362	**NUMBER OF STATEMENTS**	29	55	67	84	76	51
%	%	%	**ASSETS**	%	%	%	%	%	%
20.1	19.4	21.9	Cash & Equivalents	15.9	21.6	25.0	24.1	24.8	13.5
14.3	17.4	18.3	Trade Receivables (net)	9.8	13.0	12.9	20.1	24.5	24.0
2.6	2.7	2.6	Inventory	.0	1.7	2.9	3.7	3.1	2.2
3.1	2.9	2.7	All Other Current	2.1	1.3	4.2	2.2	2.7	3.7
40.2	42.5	45.5	Total Current	27.8	37.7	44.9	50.0	55.1	43.4
45.1	41.9	38.9	Fixed Assets (net)	56.6	44.8	40.1	37.2	32.9	32.7
8.0	10.0	8.8	Intangibles (net)	3.8	9.2	9.2	9.4	6.1	14.1
6.7	5.6	6.7	All Other Non-Current	11.8	8.4	5.8	3.3	5.9	9.9
100.0	100.0	100.0	Total	100.0	100.0	100.0	100.0	100.0	100.0
			LIABILITIES						
8.1	8.1	7.3	Notes Payable-Short Term	7.4	13.9	9.4	7.4	3.6	2.4
8.7	8.6	6.8	Cur. Mat.-L.T.D.	1.8	12.0	9.7	5.4	5.2	4.9
5.4	6.1	6.8	Trade Payables	3.0	8.8	6.5	6.0	6.7	8.9
.1	.1	.1	Income Taxes Payable	.0	.0	.0	.0	.1	.4
12.9	12.9	13.3	All Other Current	15.8	12.6	10.5	14.8	14.9	11.3
35.1	35.9	34.2	Total Current	28.0	47.3	36.2	33.6	30.4	27.8
36.7	36.9	30.6	Long-Term Debt	51.1	37.0	32.3	29.6	16.6	32.0
.0	.0	.0	Deferred Taxes	.0	.0	.0	.0	.0	.1
4.2	4.2	3.8	All Other Non-Current	5.6	11.1	1.6	1.5	1.7	4.7
24.0	23.0	31.4	Net Worth	15.3	4.6	29.9	35.3	51.3	35.3
100.0	100.0	100.0	Total Liabilties & Net Worth	100.0	100.0	100.0	100.0	100.0	100.0
			INCOME DATA						
100.0	100.0	100.0	Net Sales	100.0	100.0	100.0	100.0	100.0	100.0
			Gross Profit						
77.5	78.2	77.8	Operating Expenses	53.8	87.9	81.2	77.4	75.7	79.7
22.5	21.8	22.2	Operating Profit	46.2	12.1	18.8	22.6	24.3	20.3
3.0	2.2	2.1	All Other Expenses (net)	15.9	3.5	.9	.7	-.2	.5
19.4	19.5	20.1	Profit Before Taxes	30.4	8.7	17.9	21.9	24.5	19.8
			RATIOS						
3.3	3.2	3.7		16.3	2.9	4.4	3.8	4.3	2.5
1.5	1.5	1.7	Current	.9	1.1	1.5	2.3	2.1	1.5
.6	.7	.9		.2	.4	.8	1.2	1.2	1.0
2.8	2.6	3.3		16.3	2.8	3.9	3.6	3.4	2.1
1.2	1.3	1.5	Quick	.9	1.1	1.4	1.8	1.7	1.4
.5	.6	.8		.2	.4	.6	1.1	1.1	.8
0 UND	**0** UND	**0** UND		**0** UND	**0** UND	**0** UND	**0** UND	**0** UND	**26** 13.9
19 19.3	**27** 13.6	**26** 14.3	Sales/Receivables	**0** UND	**0** UND	**0** UND	**32** 11.5	**34** 10.8	**42** 8.7
45 8.2	**45** 8.1	**46** 7.9		**0** UND	**38** 9.5	**41** 8.8	**49** 7.5	**52** 7.0	**54** 6.8
			Cost of Sales/Inventory						
			Cost of Sales/Payables						
7.3	7.7	7.5		3.3	11.3	7.3	5.7	6.4	7.6
31.2	26.5	18.4	Sales/Working Capital	-20.9	38.8	25.6	13.7	12.7	13.5
-31.3	-35.6	-111.6		-4.1	-9.4	-53.2	46.7	51.9	-993.6
64.7	64.2	85.2			43.1	75.3	100.6	207.6	77.7
(329) 11.9	(272) 17.3	(293) 21.9	EBIT/Interest		(40) 5.0	(62) 21.7	(71) 22.2	(62) 48.9	(49) 21.9
3.3	3.7	6.1			.7	5.6	8.3	17.1	5.0
16.4	23.7	33.5							34.6
(26) 5.1	(31) 4.5	(32) 8.5	Net Profit + Depr., Dep., Amort./Cur. Mat. L/T/D						(16) 8.9
2.1	1.4	2.3							.9
.5	.6	.4		.1	.5	.6	.4	.4	.5
1.6	1.4	1.0	Fixed/Worth	3.0	2.5	1.2	.8	.7	1.3
-8.4	-38.9	15.7		NM	-2.8	-41.2	3.7	1.5	995.9
.6	.5	.5		.7	.7	.5	.4	.4	.8
2.0	2.0	1.7	Debt/Worth	13.1	5.6	2.0	1.0	.9	2.1
-13.7	-82.2	26.4		-8.5	-4.9	-59.4	6.4	2.5	999.8
212.6	222.5	207.3		144.2	211.6	275.0	191.6	201.7	282.0
(289) 98.4	(246) 92.9	(280) 97.4	% Profit Before Taxes/Tangible Net Worth	(21) 28.6	(31) 38.2	(50) 117.1	(69) 99.2	(70) 113.7	(39) 89.4
40.2	28.0	31.3		12.8	.0	18.4	48.9	51.0	43.1
89.0	93.7	89.7		20.4	97.6	115.6	101.3	106.5	63.2
29.4	32.2	35.7	% Profit Before Taxes/Total Assets	11.0	17.5	40.9	45.2	53.1	31.2
6.3	4.5	9.0		3.2	-.4	10.6	14.5	19.9	7.3
22.5	22.6	24.7		UND	52.3	38.7	28.8	20.9	16.0
7.0	7.4	8.3	Sales/Net Fixed Assets	1.0	7.0	8.8	7.7	11.0	7.1
2.8	2.8	3.3		.2	1.5	3.9	3.5	5.8	3.1
5.2	5.1	4.4		2.8	5.9	5.3	4.4	4.3	3.4
2.4	2.4	2.6	Sales/Total Assets	.5	2.7	2.7	2.8	2.8	2.1
1.3	1.2	1.3		.2	1.1	1.7	1.3	1.8	1.1
1.9	1.8	1.9		9.6	2.0	1.4	2.0	1.7	1.9
(317) 3.6	(271) 3.7	(288) 3.5	% Depr., Dep., Amort./Sales	(19) 17.1	(39) 3.8	(54) 3.7	(68) 3.9	(64) 2.9	(44) 2.8
7.4	6.6	6.0		21.6	13.1	5.5	5.6	4.0	4.2
4.5	4.5	4.2				9.1	3.8	3.6	
(77) 12.2	(54) 12.8	(51) 14.0	% Officers', Directors' Owners' Comp/Sales			(10) 14.4	(15) 8.2	(12) 16.4	
27.9	28.5	28.1				31.4	27.2	26.9	
4892343M	5949435M	5727625M	Net Sales ($)	15326M	108866M	264450M	601294M	1098356M	3639333M
3170818M	3653866M	3612008M	Total Assets ($)	47947M	99907M	169610M	303872M	478615M	2512057M

M = $ thousand MM = $ million

See Pages 9 through 22 for Explanation of Ratios and Data

Current Data Sorted by Assets							Comparative Historical Data	
						Type of Statement		
1	5	23	44	12	3	Unqualified	110	102
1	4	7	4			Reviewed	19	16
10	10	4	1			Compiled	29	18
21	19	9	1		1	Tax Returns	59	57
11	27	59	32	10	7	Other	119	126
85 (4/1-9/30/13)			241 (10/1/13-3/31/14)				4/1/09-3/31/10 ALL	4/1/10-3/31/11 ALL
0-500M	500M-2MM	2-10MM	10-50MM	50-100MM	100-250MM			
44	65	102	82	22	11	NUMBER OF STATEMENTS	336	319
%	%	%	%	%	%	**ASSETS**	%	%
42.8	21.9	15.9	16.4	13.7	9.3	Cash & Equivalents	20.1	17.9
6.5	18.7	16.3	18.2	9.8	8.5	Trade Receivables (net)	18.4	16.2
.9	2.3	1.6	1.2	.9	1.7	Inventory	1.9	2.0
3.7	4.9	4.6	4.0	4.2	3.8	All Other Current	4.7	4.6
53.8	47.8	38.5	39.8	28.7	23.3	Total Current	45.1	40.7
26.8	35.9	44.5	45.2	42.6	41.0	Fixed Assets (net)	40.6	44.1
4.1	7.1	7.9	6.1	12.5	13.9	Intangibles (net)	4.8	5.6
15.3	9.3	9.1	8.9	16.2	21.9	All Other Non-Current	9.5	9.6
100.0	100.0	100.0	100.0	100.0	100.0	Total	100.0	100.0
						LIABILITIES		
36.5	11.0	3.1	3.4	.2	.0	Notes Payable-Short Term	6.2	5.8
8.5	3.1	5.2	2.7	2.2	2.1	Cur. Mat.-L.T.D.	4.9	4.8
2.9	7.7	6.5	6.0	5.6	5.8	Trade Payables	6.8	7.2
.0	.0	.1	.1	.1	.6	Income Taxes Payable	.1	.2
26.2	12.1	10.2	10.0	8.2	3.7	All Other Current	13.5	11.3
74.1	33.9	25.1	22.1	16.2	12.2	Total Current	31.5	29.3
26.0	20.8	25.3	22.1	26.5	40.4	Long-Term Debt	27.6	28.6
.0	.0	.1	.2	.2	.0	Deferred Taxes	.3	.3
8.3	11.3	6.7	3.6	2.0	3.0	All Other Non-Current	5.5	8.4
-8.4	33.9	42.9	52.0	55.2	44.4	Net Worth	35.1	33.4
100.0	100.0	100.0	100.0	100.0	100.0	Total Liabilties & Net Worth	100.0	100.0
						INCOME DATA		
100.0	100.0	100.0	100.0	100.0	100.0	Net Sales	100.0	100.0
						Gross Profit		
90.6	83.4	84.8	93.6	91.6	92.6	Operating Expenses	87.8	89.4
9.4	16.6	15.2	6.4	8.4	7.4	Operating Profit	12.2	10.6
.0	1.8	3.1	.3	2.4	3.6	All Other Expenses (net)	2.6	1.9
9.4	14.8	12.2	6.1	6.0	3.8	Profit Before Taxes	9.6	8.7
						RATIOS		
3.2	3.2	3.5	3.1	2.4	3.2		3.5	3.2
1.0	1.7	1.8	1.9	1.7	1.9	Current	1.7	1.7
.5	.7	.8	1.2	1.1	1.3		.9	1.0
2.5	3.0	2.6	2.8	2.2	2.3		3.1	2.6
.8	1.3	1.5	1.7	1.4	1.3	Quick	(335) 1.4	(318) 1.5
.4	.5	.8	1.1	.9	1.1		.7	.8
0 UND	**0** UND	**1** 489.2	**23** 16.2	**19** 19.6	**3** 137.4		**0** UND	**0** UND
0 UND	**7** 54.0	**26** 13.8	**41** 8.8	**31** 11.7	**30** 12.1	Sales/Receivables	**28** 12.9	**29** 12.7
0 UND	**35** 10.5	**47** 7.7	**60** 6.1	**54** 6.8	**41** 8.8		**50** 7.3	**49** 7.4
						Cost of Sales/Inventory		
						Cost of Sales/Payables		
24.1	8.7	5.7	4.8	5.0	4.3		5.8	6.5
-389.8	20.4	13.7	8.0	11.7	14.7	Sales/Working Capital	16.5	15.4
-21.0	-33.4	-71.2	31.1	72.7	177.9		-87.3	-818.9
34.5	102.2	43.3	18.2	28.7			28.5	23.3
(27) 5.6	(50) 16.1	(77) 9.3	(70) 4.2	(20) 4.1		EBIT/Interest	(257) 6.0	(247) 5.5
.2	4.3	2.2	.4	1.0			1.3	1.6
							12.9	4.1
						Net Profit + Depr., Dep., Amort./Cur. Mat. L/T/D	(27) 5.2	(22) 1.8
							1.1	1.1
.0	.2	.4	.6	.5	.5		.4	.6
1.5	.9	1.0	1.0	1.0	1.2	Fixed/Worth	1.0	1.1
-.7	5.1	2.8	1.7	3.1	-1.7		3.7	4.0
.7	.6	.5	.4	.4	.5		.6	.6
21.9	1.4	1.1	1.0	.9	1.1	Debt/Worth	1.4	1.3
-2.5	25.9	4.9	2.2	3.5	-4.9		7.1	6.2
908.3	243.4	81.7	37.1	17.2			100.8	78.6
(24) 205.7	(53) 98.3	(91) 21.1	(79) 8.1	(19) 9.9		% Profit Before Taxes/Tangible Net Worth	(277) 24.3	(270) 19.7
37.7	41.7	3.2	-3.8	.9			3.4	5.5
144.3	77.1	29.5	14.3	8.6	7.9		37.0	28.4
24.7	29.4	8.8	3.4	4.2	4.9	% Profit Before Taxes/Total Assets	9.3	7.7
-1.8	2.9	.5	-2.5	.2	1.2		.3	1.2
999.8	74.7	14.1	5.2	6.7	4.8		17.4	15.5
93.3	13.0	4.7	2.8	2.1	2.7	Sales/Net Fixed Assets	6.3	4.8
22.2	6.7	2.4	1.8	1.1	1.8		2.4	2.2
16.8	5.2	2.7	1.8	1.4	2.0		3.9	3.5
8.1	3.5	1.9	1.4	.9	1.0	Sales/Total Assets	1.9	1.8
4.2	2.3	.9	.9	.5	.5		1.1	1.0
.4	.5	1.5	2.1	2.7			1.6	1.6
(18) 1.1	(51) 2.1	(88) 2.8	(78) 3.2	(20) 4.1		% Depr., Dep., Amort./Sales	(271) 3.0	(270) 2.8
2.9	4.3	6.2	4.5	5.2			5.5	4.9
6.5	5.7	5.8					3.2	3.2
(19) 11.6	(18) 17.4	(13) 6.6				% Officers', Directors' Owners' Comp/Sales	(60) 9.8	(55) 7.2
24.9	24.6	16.7					20.8	17.4
88000M	305314M	1136230M	2736280M	1870078M	4146288M	Net Sales ($)	7138527M	6803997M
9594M	74168M	544995M	1872718M	1539716M	1597482M	Total Assets ($)	3979168M	4663866M

M = $ thousand MM = $ million

See Pages 9 through 22 for Explanation of Ratios and Data

Comparative Historical Data | Current Data Sorted by Sales

			Type of Statement						
95	64	88	Unqualified		2	6	9	34	37
15	16	16	Reviewed		3	3	2	5	3
28	27	25	Compiled	3	9	5	6	2	
78	53	51	Tax Returns	9	20	8	6	4	2
131	132	146	Other	14	15	14	35	28	40
4/1/11-3/31/12 ALL	4/1/12-3/31/13 ALL	4/1/13-3/31/14 ALL		85 (4/1-9/30/13)			241 (10/1/13-3/31/14)		
				0-1MM	1-3MM	3-5MM	5-10MM	10-25MM	25MM & OVER
347	292	326	NUMBER OF STATEMENTS	26	49	36	60	73	82
%	%	%	ASSETS	%	%	%	%	%	%
21.3	20.1	20.5	Cash & Equivalents	14.3	32.1	20.2	22.6	18.2	16.1
16.6	16.3	15.2	Trade Receivables (net)	3.6	10.8	18.5	15.0	18.0	17.7
1.3	1.0	1.5	Inventory	2.5	.8	1.5	2.3	1.3	1.3
4.2	3.8	4.3	All Other Current	6.0	3.7	3.4	5.5	3.3	4.7
43.4	41.2	41.5	Total Current	26.4	47.5	43.5	45.4	40.9	39.8
41.6	44.1	40.3	Fixed Assets (net)	47.0	36.2	42.4	35.3	42.6	41.5
5.5	6.6	7.3	Intangibles (net)	5.8	6.2	6.6	9.6	7.7	6.8
9.5	8.1	10.8	All Other Non-Current	20.9	10.1	7.6	9.8	8.9	12.0
100.0	100.0	100.0	Total	100.0	100.0	100.0	100.0	100.0	100.0
			LIABILITIES						
7.5	11.5	9.0	Notes Payable-Short Term	28.7	18.8	6.7	7.9	3.8	3.2
4.9	6.9	4.3	Cur. Mat.-L.T.D.	9.4	6.9	4.4	4.2	2.8	2.4
5.6	6.1	6.1	Trade Payables	3.8	4.8	4.8	6.1	6.6	7.5
.1	.2	.1	Income Taxes Payable	.0	.0	.1	.0	.0	.2
12.9	11.5	12.4	All Other Current	15.3	12.0	14.3	12.2	12.2	11.0
31.1	36.1	31.7	Total Current	57.2	42.5	30.3	30.5	25.4	24.3
29.2	29.5	24.3	Long-Term Debt	48.5	26.6	21.0	19.0	19.1	25.1
.2	.2	.1	Deferred Taxes	.0	.0	.0	.0	.2	.1
7.4	7.1	6.6	All Other Non-Current	1.2	10.3	6.4	7.9	8.7	3.4
32.1	27.1	37.3	Net Worth	-6.9	20.6	42.4	42.6	46.6	47.0
100.0	100.0	100.0	Total Liabilities & Net Worth	100.0	100.0	100.0	100.0	100.0	100.0
			INCOME DATA						
100.0	100.0	100.0	Net Sales	100.0	100.0	100.0	100.0	100.0	100.0
			Gross Profit						
87.4	88.3	88.2	Operating Expenses	81.8	85.4	87.8	85.4	88.9	93.6
12.6	11.7	11.8	Operating Profit	18.2	14.6	12.2	14.6	11.1	6.4
1.9	2.2	1.7	All Other Expenses (net)	9.4	1.3	1.5	.7	.9	1.0
10.7	9.5	10.1	Profit Before Taxes	8.8	13.3	10.7	13.9	10.2	5.4
			RATIOS						
3.4	3.1	3.2		1.8	4.6	3.9	3.5	3.0	2.6
1.9	1.5	1.7	Current	.7	1.8	1.8	2.1	1.8	1.7
1.0	.8	.9		.1	.5	.8	1.0	1.2	1.2
3.0	2.7	2.6		1.3	4.6	3.3	2.7	2.5	2.3
1.7	1.3	1.5	Quick	.5	1.0	1.6	1.5	1.5	1.5
.7	.7	.7		.1	.5	.7	.8	1.0	1.1
0 UND	0 UND	0 UND		0 UND	0 UND	0 UND	0 UND	18 20.3	19 19.7
26 13.9	25 14.5	24 15.4	Sales/Receivables	0 UND	0 UND	28 12.9	19 18.8	34 10.7	35 10.4
50 7.3	51 7.1	47 7.8		1 465.8	21 17.2	53 6.9	37 9.8	57 6.4	52 7.0
			Cost of Sales/Inventory						
			Cost of Sales/Payables						
5.6	6.3	6.3		26.2	8.3	6.8	6.7	6.0	5.5
11.8	18.3	16.1	Sales/Working Capital	-17.0	55.0	14.6	15.1	10.0	13.3
-274.2	-54.5	-95.6		-2.6	-17.0	-105.0	NM	116.5	66.5
22.4	29.3	35.3		11.9	47.3	71.0	65.4	54.1	10.1
(271) 6.0	(238) 7.0	(253) 6.4	EBIT/Interest	(15) 3.0	(34) 5.6	(28) 16.4	(44) 22.7	(61) 7.3	(71) 3.7
2.0	1.4	1.6		-3.1	1.7	3.8	3.1	.7	1.4
10.0	14.5	9.7							14.3
(24) 3.2	(18) 6.5	(22) 3.6	Net Profit + Depr., Dep., Amort./Cur. Mat. L/T/D						(10) 3.5
1.8	3.9	2.2							2.6
.4	.5	.4		.1	.1	.4	.4	.4	.5
1.0	1.2	1.0	Fixed/Worth	3.5	1.5	1.1	.8	.9	1.0
2.9	3.8	3.1		-1.6	UND	2.5	3.1	1.6	2.0
.5	.6	.5		2.0	.6	.5	.4	.4	.5
1.2	1.6	1.2	Debt/Worth	9.2	4.7	1.0	1.1	1.0	1.1
5.9	9.7	5.8		-3.1	-95.4	6.9	5.9	2.2	3.4
90.2	98.5	102.6		125.5	338.2	158.4	152.9	90.9	21.9
(288) 30.1	(235) 24.2	(273) 21.4	% Profit Before Taxes/Tangible Net Worth	(14) 21.3	(36) 101.8	(31) 54.6	(51) 49.4	(69) 15.2	(72) 8.8
8.0	3.9	1.6		2.9	29.3	2.6	7.8	-2.5	1.1
34.3	35.5	34.2		55.1	97.7	51.2	50.8	27.3	9.5
11.9	9.8	8.2	% Profit Before Taxes/Total Assets	3.9	21.6	19.6	17.7	5.4	3.8
1.4	.4	.3		-8.0	2.3	-.3	2.9	-2.0	.5
22.7	18.7	24.2		402.8	258.3	25.6	26.5	12.5	9.1
5.2	4.5	5.6	Sales/Net Fixed Assets	4.6	27.7	6.8	8.1	3.9	3.8
2.2	2.1	2.4		.3	3.2	2.3	4.4	2.1	2.0
3.9	3.6	3.7		3.0	8.0	3.9	5.3	2.7	2.8
2.0	1.9	2.0	Sales/Total Assets	1.5	3.8	2.9	2.5	1.6	1.4
1.1	1.1	1.0		.2	1.5	.9	1.6	.9	1.0
1.6	1.6	1.5		2.8	.5	2.1	1.0	1.7	1.7
(281) 3.0	(241) 3.0	(263) 2.9	% Depr., Dep., Amort./Sales	(15) 8.5	(32) 1.6	(29) 3.6	(47) 2.8	(67) 2.7	(73) 2.7
5.5	5.8	4.8		23.0	12.2	5.7	4.3	4.2	4.2
2.6	3.1	5.8			5.6		6.1	5.4	
(64) 6.8	(57) 6.7	(59) 8.4	% Officers', Directors' Owners' Comp/Sales		(17) 11.6		(15) 7.1	(10) 7.7	
15.7	18.2	23.4			25.7		28.6	27.4	
6297217M	6691019M	10282190M	Net Sales ($)	14900M	98035M	141748M	432744M	1258525M	8336238M
3967693M	3955542M	5638673M	Total Assets ($)	36127M	67421M	101242M	215490M	1111167M	4107226M

M = $ thousand MM = $ million

See Pages 9 through 22 for Explanation of Ratios and Data

Current Data Sorted by Assets							Comparative Historical Data	
						Type of Statement		
		8	12	9	7	Unqualified	50	32
	1	7	4			Reviewed	25	19
15	10	7	4			Compiled	24	43
18	13	16				Tax Returns	51	49
16	28	34	18	15	6	Other	124	106
	28 (4/1-9/30/13)		220 (10/1/13-3/31/14)				4/1/09-3/31/10 ALL	4/1/10-3/31/11 ALL
0-500M	500M-2MM	2-10MM	10-50MM	50-100MM	100-250MM			
49	52	72	38	24	13	**NUMBER OF STATEMENTS**	274	249
%	%	%	%	%	%	**ASSETS**	%	%
33.4	20.6	18.2	15.0	10.9	5.8	Cash & Equivalents	16.7	18.7
10.2	20.5	27.5	28.1	15.9	17.0	Trade Receivables (net)	23.9	22.0
1.3	2.2	2.3	2.5	2.2	5.9	Inventory	2.2	2.4
3.3	1.5	3.1	6.4	4.9	2.9	All Other Current	3.0	4.0
48.2	44.8	51.1	52.0	34.0	31.6	Total Current	45.8	47.1
35.5	39.7	36.4	35.2	18.9	27.4	Fixed Assets (net)	36.6	36.2
4.0	4.7	7.5	6.7	38.2	23.0	Intangibles (net)	8.7	8.5
12.3	10.7	4.9	6.1	8.9	18.0	All Other Non-Current	9.0	8.2
100.0	100.0	100.0	100.0	100.0	100.0	Total	100.0	100.0
						LIABILITIES		
8.1	13.9	5.7	4.0	.7	3.1	Notes Payable-Short Term	7.3	10.5
12.1	6.4	5.1	5.2	6.9	1.8	Cur. Mat.-L.T.D.	7.7	9.2
6.3	5.6	7.4	6.8	5.6	9.4	Trade Payables	8.5	7.8
.0	.1	.3	1.2	.1	.1	Income Taxes Payable	.6	.5
30.6	10.3	12.4	10.3	8.1	9.2	All Other Current	17.5	19.2
57.1	36.3	30.9	27.6	21.4	23.6	Total Current	41.5	47.2
23.6	35.8	18.7	19.0	44.2	20.2	Long-Term Debt	26.1	26.7
.0	.6	.2	.2	1.1	1.5	Deferred Taxes	.3	.4
14.7	9.7	3.0	3.5	2.7	12.7	All Other Non-Current	8.0	6.2
4.6	17.6	47.2	49.7	30.5	42.0	Net Worth	24.0	19.5
100.0	100.0	100.0	100.0	100.0	100.0	Total Liabilties & Net Worth	100.0	100.0
						INCOME DATA		
100.0	100.0	100.0	100.0	100.0	100.0	Net Sales	100.0	100.0
						Gross Profit		
84.0	82.0	85.5	91.2	90.5	93.3	Operating Expenses	88.4	89.6
16.0	18.0	14.5	8.8	9.5	6.7	Operating Profit	11.6	10.4
.9	4.3	2.4	1.7	3.3	2.2	All Other Expenses (net)	1.7	2.0
15.1	13.6	12.2	7.0	6.2	4.6	Profit Before Taxes	9.9	8.3
						RATIOS		
3.0	3.3	3.3	3.2	2.3	2.1		2.6	2.4
.9	1.1	1.8	2.2	1.7	1.2	Current	1.5	1.4
.4	.4	.8	1.4	1.1	1.0		.9	.7
3.0	3.3	3.0	2.8	1.6	1.7		2.2	2.0
.8	.9	(71) 1.6	1.9	1.3	1.0	Quick	1.2	1.1
.3	.3	.7	1.2	1.0	.8		.7	.5
0 UND	0 UND	2 183.7	29 12.8	41 9.0	43 8.5		13 29.1	0 UND
0 UND	0 UND	35 10.4	50 7.3	52 7.0	50 7.3	Sales/Receivables	39 9.4	33 10.9
1 340.7	30 12.0	56 6.5	76 4.8	72 5.1	54 6.8		61 6.0	56 6.5
						Cost of Sales/Inventory		
						Cost of Sales/Payables		
25.2	8.2	5.3	4.0	6.3	6.8		7.0	7.7
-432.0	106.1	14.4	6.7	12.3	30.7	Sales/Working Capital	17.6	27.6
-22.7	-17.0	-32.0	24.6	90.8	NM		-60.9	-28.4
35.0	26.5	65.5	24.0	19.1	83.7		28.3	26.5
(27) 10.6	(36) 3.6	(57) 15.1	(30) 6.0	(21) 5.4	(12) 5.3	EBIT/Interest	(227) 6.8	(201) 4.5
3.9	1.5	3.1	3.3	-.5	-.3		2.3	1.2
		8.6				Net Profit + Depr., Dep.,	9.9	5.0
		(11) 5.3				Amort./Cur. Mat. L/T/D	(46) 2.4	(41) 2.5
		2.5					1.3	1.0
.2	.2	.2	.4	.4	.5		.4	.5
.8	2.8	.7	.6	-9.8	.7	Fixed/Worth	1.1	1.3
-9.8	-5.9	3.9	2.0	-.2	-1.0		8.2	11.3
.5	.9	.4	.5	.4	.6		.6	.7
1.5	4.2	1.0	1.1	-34.7	1.0	Debt/Worth	1.8	2.6
-3.6	-13.9	6.4	2.4	-1.5	-3.3		31.2	52.8
865.0	140.0	113.7	35.8	44.1		% Profit Before Taxes/Tangible	101.3	110.0
(33) 145.8	(38) 34.6	(62) 41.4	(36) 23.5	(11) 16.1		Net Worth	(213) 39.2	(190) 37.0
45.3	11.3	7.9	9.4	7.2			10.4	4.4
254.0	43.6	39.8	16.0	22.7	20.3	% Profit Before Taxes/Total	35.5	34.9
47.0	10.2	18.6	9.6	7.3	6.7	Assets	12.7	11.2
5.5	2.3	3.6	5.1	-5.0	-3.2		2.9	1.0
231.0	75.2	31.0	16.8	10.6	7.5		24.7	26.3
56.8	17.8	10.0	6.4	6.6	4.1	Sales/Net Fixed Assets	7.5	9.6
10.9	4.4	3.6	2.6	4.5	3.3		3.2	3.5
24.0	6.8	3.6	2.2	1.5	1.8		3.9	5.0
8.1	3.5	2.4	1.7	1.3	1.1	Sales/Total Assets	2.2	2.5
3.3	1.5	1.7	1.2	.7	.7		1.3	1.5
.6	1.1	1.2	1.7	3.4			1.9	1.7
(24) 1.8	(31) 2.4	(55) 3.4	(37) 3.6	(17) 6.1		% Depr., Dep., Amort./Sales	(212) 3.8	(191) 3.6
5.8	5.9	6.2	6.4	9.1			6.3	6.3
5.9	5.3	3.0				% Officers', Directors'	2.8	3.4
(18) 8.9	(15) 8.0	(30) 8.8				Owners' Comp/Sales	(65) 8.5	(69) 8.2
17.5	21.3	17.7					16.7	17.6
131842M	256577M	978329M	1540388M	2137144M	2847152M	Net Sales ($)	8613558M	7664890M
11296M	53634M	348090M	848361M	1783143M	2324706M	Total Assets ($)	6193601M	4652708M

M = $ thousand MM = $ million

See Pages 9 through 22 for Explanation of Ratios and Data

Comparative Historical Data				Current Data Sorted by Sales					
			Type of Statement						
36	26	36	Unqualified				2	7	27
26	19	12	Reviewed		1		2	8	1
37	27	36	Compiled	11	5	5	2	8	5
60	45	47	Tax Returns	9	10	5	12	8	3
132	125	117	Other	9	21	10	21	19	37
4/1/11-3/31/12 ALL	**4/1/12-3/31/13 ALL**	**4/1/13-3/31/14 ALL**		**28 (4/1-9/30/13)**			**220 (10/1/13-3/31/14)**		
				0-1MM	**1-3MM**	**3-5MM**	**5-10MM**	**10-25MM**	**25MM & OVER**
291	242	248	**NUMBER OF STATEMENTS**	29	37	20	39	50	73
%	%	%	**ASSETS**	%	%	%	%	%	%
19.5	20.2	19.9	Cash & Equivalents	26.3	20.0	28.5	23.0	21.0	12.4
19.5	20.1	21.1	Trade Receivables (net)	7.2	19.4	5.9	25.0	30.2	23.2
2.0	2.6	2.3	Inventory	.0	1.0	5.4	1.7	3.0	2.8
3.8	4.0	3.5	All Other Current	1.8	1.4	1.8	5.7	1.8	5.5
44.7	46.9	46.7	Total Current	35.3	41.7	41.5	55.4	56.1	44.0
36.4	34.0	34.6	Fixed Assets (net)	52.7	39.2	39.9	26.7	37.3	25.9
9.1	9.0	9.9	Intangibles (net)	5.1	4.1	8.4	9.6	3.2	19.9
9.8	10.2	8.9	All Other Non-Current	6.8	15.0	10.2	8.3	3.4	10.2
100.0	100.0	100.0	Total	100.0	100.0	100.0	100.0	100.0	100.0
			LIABILITIES						
12.3	8.6	7.0	Notes Payable-Short Term	5.3	12.7	4.0	14.5	4.3	3.5
7.3	7.3	6.8	Cur. Mat.-L.T.D.	11.4	6.7	9.6	5.8	5.8	5.4
8.2	6.2	6.7	Trade Payables	1.8	5.7	2.0	11.6	6.1	8.0
.3	.2	.3	Income Taxes Payable	.0	.0	.4	.3	.1	.7
14.1	11.8	14.7	All Other Current	18.5	7.7	13.6	19.5	21.3	9.9
42.2	34.1	35.4	Total Current	37.0	32.7	29.5	51.7	37.6	27.5
22.7	24.9	25.9	Long-Term Debt	36.7	28.3	9.9	33.9	18.6	25.3
.4	.5	.4	Deferred Taxes	.0	.0	.0	.8	.2	.8
8.1	5.2	7.3	All Other Non-Current	10.8	14.7	3.1	8.4	3.1	5.5
26.6	35.3	31.1	Net Worth	15.5	24.3	57.5	5.3	40.5	40.8
100.0	100.0	100.0	Total Liabilties & Net Worth	100.0	100.0	100.0	100.0	100.0	100.0
			INCOME DATA						
100.0	100.0	100.0	Net Sales	100.0	100.0	100.0	100.0	100.0	100.0
			Gross Profit						
88.2	86.5	86.2	Operating Expenses	73.3	79.9	79.5	95.3	86.0	91.8
11.8	13.5	13.8	Operating Profit	26.7	20.1	20.5	4.7	14.0	8.2
2.1	2.7	2.5	All Other Expenses (net)	11.6	1.4	-.3	.6	1.2	2.1
9.7	10.8	11.3	Profit Before Taxes	15.1	18.7	20.8	4.1	12.8	6.2
			RATIOS						
2.7	3.1	3.0		2.8	3.8	4.6	2.5	3.6	2.5
1.4	1.7	1.6	Current	.8	1.4	1.1	1.3	2.4	1.9
.6	.8	.7		.2	.4	.6	.6	.9	1.1
2.3	2.7	2.8		2.8	3.4	4.5	2.4	3.5	2.0
1.2	1.4	(247) 1.4	Quick	.5	1.2	.8	1.0	(49) 2.1	1.4
.6	.6	.6		.1	.4	.4	.5	.8	.9
0 UND	**0** UND	**0** UND		**0** UND	**0** UND	**0** UND	**0** UND	**16** 22.4	**32** 11.5
32 11.3	**35** 10.3	**30** 12.2	Sales/Receivables	**0** UND	**0** UND	**0** UND	**20** 18.5	**34** 10.6	**49** 7.4
54 6.8	**54** 6.8	**53** 6.9		**0** UND	**47** 7.7	**6** 64.4	**52** 7.0	**65** 5.6	**65** 5.6
			Cost of Sales/Inventory						
			Cost of Sales/Payables						
7.4	6.4	6.3		8.4	11.1	7.5	11.7	4.6	5.1
24.4	16.1	21.9	Sales/Working Capital	-33.2	69.2	NM	65.0	8.2	12.3
-24.1	-45.3	-31.4		-3.6	-16.8	-50.5	-20.3	-124.8	57.5
23.9	25.8	37.1		35.3	41.4	58.2	21.2	70.9	33.3
(242) 5.2	(200) 6.3	(183) 7.2	EBIT/Interest	(12) 9.7	(26) 7.6	(11) 28.8	(35) 5.8	(37) 11.2	(62) 6.4
.9	1.1	2.2		.4	3.5	3.8	1.0	3.1	1.9
7.8	6.7	9.6							11.1
(32) 3.2	(27) 2.3	(30) 4.2	Net Profit + Depr., Dep., Amort./Cur. Mat. L/T/D						(16) 2.7
1.3	.8	2.1							1.5
.4	.3	.3		.1	.2	.1	.3	.2	.4
1.1	.8	.9	Fixed/Worth	2.4	2.0	.7	1.4	.7	.7
11.0	3.9	30.6		7.3	-3.7	2.7	-1.8	2.9	-1.2
.6	.5	.5		.5	.3	.2	1.1	.4	.5
2.0	1.5	1.6	Debt/Worth	2.4	3.0	.9	8.8	1.2	1.1
-679.0	9.3	345.0		40.0	-7.4	3.2	-10.6	2.7	-7.0
81.3	97.4	125.3		216.4	187.0	391.5	73.2	98.4	48.6
(218) 39.9	(192) 39.5	(187) 36.7	% Profit Before Taxes/Tangible Net Worth	(24) 43.4	(23) 85.5	111.6	(25) 29.1	(44) 32.7	(51) 23.7
5.3	7.8	10.2		12.1	33.3	24.9	-16.5	12.2	8.7
33.9	35.3	40.7		55.0	68.3	118.8	27.2	42.3	24.4
10.4	11.7	13.9	% Profit Before Taxes/Total Assets	6.1	22.9	47.1	13.0	16.8	9.7
.0	2.0	2.9		.5	8.5	5.3	-3.0	3.2	1.7
32.1	31.0	47.0		91.7	61.9	106.5	98.9	36.1	12.9
9.0	8.4	10.5	Sales/Net Fixed Assets	4.7	13.6	37.4	22.8	11.4	7.5
3.4	3.6	4.3		.2	4.3	3.8	6.5	3.9	4.5
4.7	4.5	4.8		4.9	6.8	9.1	7.1	3.7	2.3
2.4	2.1	2.3	Sales/Total Assets	1.6	3.3	4.1	3.5	2.6	1.7
1.3	1.2	1.3		.1	1.3	1.9	1.9	1.8	1.1
1.7	1.6	1.5		2.4	1.0	1.0	1.2	.7	1.7
(215) 3.5	(172) 3.2	(171) 3.4	% Depr., Dep., Amort./Sales	(17) 12.5	(21) 2.3	(13) 3.5	(19) 4.1	(42) 2.9	(59) 3.3
7.6	7.1	6.2		21.0	5.7	5.9	6.1	5.5	6.4
3.7	4.6	4.2			5.0		6.8	2.5	1.9
(84) 7.3	(69) 9.4	(73) 8.4	% Officers', Directors' Owners' Comp/Sales		(14) 7.7		(15) 10.4	(23) 4.9	(10) 13.4
17.5	17.1	18.3			11.1		21.8	16.3	21.0
7401431M	**8060583M**	**7891432M**	Net Sales ($)	**13145M**	**74607M**	**77780M**	**281495M**	**756289M**	**6688116M**
5577072M	**5179617M**	**5369230M**	Total Assets ($)	**17914M**	**34601M**	**23520M**	**98305M**	**337964M**	**4856926M**

M = $ thousand MM = $ million

See Pages 9 through 22 for Explanation of Ratios and Data

Current Data Sorted by Assets | **Comparative Historical Data**

0-500M	500M-2MM	2-10MM	10-50MM	50-100MM	100-250MM		4/1/09-3/31/10 ALL	4/1/10-3/31/11 ALL
						Type of Statement		
		6	7	2	2	Unqualified	18	28
1	4	13	9			Reviewed	23	21
2	16	8	1			Compiled	35	42
16	18	15	1			Tax Returns	39	50
7	34	48	22	4	6	Other	122	127
19 (4/1-9/30/13)		223 (10/1/13-3/31/14)						
26	72	90	40	6	8	**NUMBER OF STATEMENTS**	237	268
%	%	%	%	%	%	**ASSETS**	%	%
37.6	22.9	13.9	8.5			Cash & Equivalents	14.9	14.9
5.8	14.0	22.2	18.7			Trade Receivables (net)	16.8	14.8
.5	.5	1.1	.3			Inventory	.6	.3
.6	2.6	4.0	4.2			All Other Current	3.6	4.6
44.5	40.0	41.2	31.6			Total Current	35.8	34.7
33.1	43.4	43.9	41.7			Fixed Assets (net)	49.8	47.8
12.7	7.3	7.6	14.9			Intangibles (net)	7.1	7.4
9.6	9.3	7.3	11.7			All Other Non-Current	7.3	10.2
100.0	100.0	100.0	100.0			Total	100.0	100.0
						LIABILITIES		
75.3	19.2	6.5	2.4			Notes Payable-Short Term	9.9	9.2
8.2	8.8	7.0	7.8			Cur. Mat.-L.T.D.	12.5	13.0
45.6	3.7	5.2	4.6			Trade Payables	7.0	4.7
.0	.3	.1	.4			Income Taxes Payable	.3	.2
44.8	15.5	11.0	10.4			All Other Current	11.7	12.0
173.8	47.5	29.9	25.6			Total Current	41.5	39.1
8.2	32.5	29.0	30.1			Long-Term Debt	36.5	37.4
.0	.0	.1	.9			Deferred Taxes	.1	.1
2.9	8.5	5.9	6.9			All Other Non-Current	4.7	6.8
-84.9	11.4	35.2	36.4			Net Worth	17.2	16.6
100.0	100.0	100.0	100.0			Total Liabilties & Net Worth	100.0	100.0
						INCOME DATA		
100.0	100.0	100.0	100.0			Net Sales	100.0	100.0
						Gross Profit		
91.9	85.2	83.7	84.5			Operating Expenses	87.6	85.3
8.1	14.8	16.3	15.5			Operating Profit	12.4	14.7
.8	3.0	1.4	.6			All Other Expenses (net)	2.5	2.1
7.3	11.8	14.9	15.0			Profit Before Taxes	9.9	12.6
						RATIOS		
1.8	2.9	3.1	2.0				1.9	2.4
.5	1.2	1.4	1.4			Current	1.0	1.1
.1	.4	.7	.6				.4	.4
1.8	2.5	2.6	1.8				1.8	2.0
.5	1.1	1.3	1.2			Quick	.8	1.0
.1	.3	.6	.6				.3	.3
0 UND	0 UND	0 UND	5 66.8				0 UND	0 UND
0 UND	0 UND	34 10.7	36 10.0			Sales/Receivables	26 14.0	24 15.3
0 UND	43 8.5	57 6.4	49 7.5				46 7.9	42 8.8
						Cost of Sales/Inventory		
						Cost of Sales/Payables		
228.4	10.5	6.9	9.3				12.2	11.1
-24.3	83.2	21.1	20.2			Sales/Working Capital	-327.6	63.1
-8.0	-18.7	-33.8	-17.0				-10.6	-14.5
57.9	38.5	66.6	17.5				14.7	23.4
(17) 8.2	(63) 4.5	(80) 20.6	(36) 9.7			EBIT/Interest	(208) 4.6	(233) 6.4
-1.8	-.3	5.7	4.0				1.2	2.0
		16.2					3.2	6.6
		(14) 5.7				Net Profit + Depr., Dep., Amort./Cur. Mat. L/T/D	(15) 2.0	(16) 2.2
		1.9					1.0	1.4
.4	.3	.5	.7				1.0	.8
-6.4	1.3	1.3	2.2			Fixed/Worth	2.6	2.1
-.2	-2.2	3.0	7.0				-6.8	-3.9
1.2	.5	.7	1.2				1.1	.8
-7.5	2.8	1.7	2.6			Debt/Worth	3.7	2.9
-1.3	-3.9	5.8	9.9				-8.6	-8.8
999.8	196.0	163.5	130.9				115.2	129.1
(10) 261.4	(48) 60.4	(75) 49.5	(33) 55.0			% Profit Before Taxes/Tangible Net Worth	(166) 53.9	(188) 56.2
47.2	9.8	14.3	14.4				15.6	18.8
227.9	51.6	52.2	35.1				42.2	43.8
27.6	13.5	17.4	20.3			% Profit Before Taxes/Total Assets	14.0	18.5
-23.4	.1	4.6	5.4				1.6	1.7
999.8	28.0	11.9	7.6				10.8	12.0
93.5	7.5	4.8	5.0			Sales/Net Fixed Assets	4.6	5.2
8.2	3.0	2.9	2.9				2.3	2.7
46.3	5.0	3.1	2.8				3.7	3.8
8.3	2.4	2.0	1.7			Sales/Total Assets	2.0	2.2
4.7	1.4	1.3	1.1				1.2	1.3
.3	2.9	3.2	3.8				3.8	3.8
(15) .9	(50) 7.7	(76) 5.6	(38) 5.4			% Depr., Dep., Amort./Sales	(202) 6.9	(215) 6.7
1.9	13.9	8.4	7.2				12.5	13.8
	4.9	6.6	20.3				5.0	4.1
	(13) 8.2	(21) 16.4	(11) 25.5			% Officers', Directors' Owners' Comp/Sales	(56) 13.7	(67) 9.8
	16.9	28.4	32.3				23.5	22.5
120887M	496187M	1025689M	1644153M	383018M	1051630M	Net Sales ($)	4073446M	4450823M
5878M	86885M	400829M	871722M	473827M	1262736M	Total Assets ($)	2150317M	2216101M

M = $ thousand MM = $ million

See Pages 9 through 22 for Explanation of Ratios and Data

Comparative Historical Data | Current Data Sorted by Sales

4/1/11-3/31/12 ALL	4/1/12-3/31/13 ALL	4/1/13-3/31/14 ALL	Type of Statement	0-1MM	1-3MM	3-5MM	5-10MM	10-25MM	25MM & OVER
19	21	17	Unqualified		1		3	4	9
28	16	27	Reviewed		4	3	5	8	7
32	31	27	Compiled	5	9	1	9	3	
51	56	50	Tax Returns	10	13	12	9	4	2
135	121	121	Other	5	19	11	27	28	31
				19 (4/1-9/30/13)			223 (10/1/13-3/31/14)		
265	245	242	NUMBER OF STATEMENTS	20	46	27	53	47	49
%	%	%	ASSETS	%	%	%	%	%	%
17.5	16.7	17.8	Cash & Equivalents	8.5	18.3	28.1	20.4	14.6	15.6
17.2	19.9	16.8	Trade Receivables (net)	2.0	16.4	9.3	24.4	21.3	14.8
.4	.9	.7	Inventory	.6	.2	.3	2.1	.2	.4
2.9	3.7	3.2	All Other Current	6.3	3.6	.3	3.0	2.2	4.5
37.9	41.3	38.5	Total Current	17.4	38.5	38.0	49.8	38.2	35.3
46.9	41.9	41.6	Fixed Assets (net)	70.0	45.6	44.2	33.7	39.7	35.1
7.0	8.6	10.6	Intangibles (net)	9.7	7.5	10.9	8.1	9.0	18.2
8.2	8.3	9.3	All Other Non-Current	2.9	8.3	6.9	8.5	13.1	11.4
100.0	100.0	100.0	Total	100.0	100.0	100.0	100.0	100.0	100.0
			LIABILITIES						
11.0	14.4	16.8	Notes Payable-Short Term	26.5	7.0	41.1	16.5	15.5	10.1
13.5	10.8	7.9	Cur. Mat.-L.T.D.	14.1	7.6	6.9	7.1	7.1	7.6
6.4	7.8	8.9	Trade Payables	27.5	11.3	11.8	7.1	3.7	4.7
.3	.1	.2	Income Taxes Payable	.0	.0	.0	.4	.2	.4
13.5	12.3	15.5	All Other Current	13.9	6.4	25.5	13.1	16.4	20.8
44.6	45.4	49.3	Total Current	82.0	32.4	85.3	44.1	43.0	43.7
34.4	30.4	28.0	Long-Term Debt	44.0	29.3	31.0	28.5	18.6	27.2
.1	.0	.2	Deferred Taxes	.0	.0	.0	.1	.1	.8
5.3	9.9	6.3	All Other Non-Current	11.0	8.8	2.1	8.8	2.2	5.7
15.5	14.2	16.2	Net Worth	-37.0	29.5	-18.4	18.6	36.1	22.7
100.0	100.0	100.0	Total Liabilties & Net Worth	100.0	100.0	100.0	100.0	100.0	100.0
			INCOME DATA						
100.0	100.0	100.0	Net Sales	100.0	100.0	100.0	100.0	100.0	100.0
			Gross Profit						
87.5	85.4	85.2	Operating Expenses	82.6	86.9	84.8	86.7	80.0	88.2
12.5	14.6	14.8	Operating Profit	17.4	13.1	15.2	13.3	20.0	11.8
1.9	1.7	1.8	All Other Expenses (net)	9.6	1.3	1.3	.5	2.0	.7
10.6	12.9	13.0	Profit Before Taxes	7.7	11.8	13.9	12.8	18.0	11.1
			RATIOS						
2.2	2.4	2.5		1.1	3.2	4.1	3.6	2.7	2.0
1.1	1.2	1.3	Current	.2	1.5	.9	1.5	1.3	1.4
.5	.5	.5		.0	.7	.3	.9	.5	.6
2.1	2.2	2.3		.7	3.2	4.1	3.2	2.7	1.7
1.0	1.0	1.2	Quick	.1	1.5	.9	1.5	1.2	1.2
.4	.4	.4		.0	.6	.2	.7	.5	.6
0 UND	0 UND	0 UND		0 UND	0 UND	0 UND	0 UND	0 UND	0 UND
24 15.0	29 12.7	27 13.7	Sales/Receivables	0 UND	0 UND	0 UND	35 10.3	33 11.0	34 10.6
46 8.0	54 6.8	47 7.7		0 UND	55 6.6	29 12.5	63 5.8	45 8.1	46 7.9
			Cost of Sales/Inventory						
			Cost of Sales/Payables						
10.2	8.7	8.7		NM	4.9	12.6	6.3	9.6	8.7
79.3	79.5	47.4	Sales/Working Capital	-4.5	41.3	-176.3	21.8	49.0	27.0
-13.5	-20.3	-18.8		-1.4	-22.6	-16.0	-94.1	-20.0	-31.2
22.7	34.7	46.0		7.7	45.7	38.5	65.8	88.5	19.8
(225) 8.2	(215) 9.9	(209) 9.5	EBIT/Interest	(15) 1.4	(40) 5.4	(23) 6.5	(48) 17.6	(40) 34.3	(43) 9.6
2.1	2.1	2.1		-4.4	1.1	-.3	4.8	6.4	1.1
3.2	10.6	9.3							
(15) 1.7	(14) 1.4	(24) 3.3	Net Profit + Depr., Dep., Amort./Cur. Mat. L/T/D						
1.2	.7	1.1							
.7	.6	.6		3.0	.5	.6	.3	.5	.8
1.5	1.8	1.5	Fixed/Worth	-5.3	1.2	2.0	1.1	1.2	2.4
-81.8	-4.1	NM		-.9	4.0	-14.5	4.2	4.7	NM
.8	.9	.8		2.2	.2	.6	.8	.5	1.8
2.0	2.4	2.2	Debt/Worth	-7.5	1.4	3.0	2.0	1.6	5.1
-22.3	-6.0	-12.0		-2.1	8.6	-4.5	-17.2	6.0	-6.2
104.6	160.8	163.5			92.3	277.9	141.9	317.5	140.6
(192) 48.9	(166) 69.0	(175) 55.0	% Profit Before Taxes/Tangible Net Worth		(36) 35.7	(19) 79.8	(39) 55.8	(41) 69.1	(34) 60.2
11.4	18.0	13.0			7.4	13.8	29.2	18.2	9.6
39.9	47.3	46.6		22.9	41.7	66.7	48.8	86.1	30.7
16.0	20.0	15.8	% Profit Before Taxes/Total Assets	2.5	13.5	15.1	14.0	33.1	15.3
1.9	3.4	2.8		-14.6	1.0	-4.1	5.4	6.6	1.7
17.9	24.1	22.9		5.0	12.3	36.5	32.2	49.3	10.1
5.1	5.4	5.5	Sales/Net Fixed Assets	1.0	5.1	6.0	7.4	6.3	5.7
2.8	3.3	3.0		.3	2.5	2.5	4.0	3.7	3.9
4.1	4.0	4.0		2.9	2.7	6.4	4.2	5.2	4.1
2.3	2.2	2.1	Sales/Total Assets	.8	1.7	2.4	2.4	2.5	2.3
1.3	1.3	1.2		.2	1.1	1.4	1.6	1.6	1.1
2.7	2.3	2.8		2.7	2.9	2.8	1.3	2.8	3.1
(208) 5.6	(190) 5.2	(189) 5.5	% Depr., Dep., Amort./Sales	(19) 16.4	(33) 6.9	(21) 5.6	(43) 4.9	(36) 5.7	(37) 5.3
10.4	9.0	8.7		33.5	12.3	8.6	7.0	7.2	6.5
6.0	3.6	6.5					6.5	2.3	24.0
(64) 14.0	(57) 9.6	(55) 19.4	% Officers', Directors' Owners' Comp/Sales				(15) 15.0	(10) 11.0	(14) 28.3
30.0	25.4	29.6					27.1	29.0	33.1
4517450M	3869321M	4721564M	Net Sales ($)	12550M	89273M	100141M	387758M	782426M	3349416M
1955941M	2069655M	3101877M	Total Assets ($)	22378M	57878M	69726M	208883M	434526M	2308486M

M = $ thousand MM = $ million

See Pages 9 through 22 for Explanation of Ratios and Data

Current Data Sorted by Assets							Comparative Historical Data	
						Type of Statement		
4	9	22	44	9	9	Unqualified	128	147
1	5	10	8			Reviewed	36	28
6	20	19	3		1	Compiled	40	58
57	42	16	2			Tax Returns	83	107
58	72	73	47	12	13	Other	216	256
90 (4/1-9/30/13)		472 (10/1/13-3/31/14)					4/1/09-3/31/10 ALL	4/1/10-3/31/11 ALL
0-500M	**500M-2MM**	**2-10MM**	**10-50MM**	**50-100MM**	**100-250MM**			
126	148	140	104	21	23	**NUMBER OF STATEMENTS**	503	596
%	%	%	%	%	%	**ASSETS**	%	%
31.4	19.3	15.8	19.2	14.1	6.6	Cash & Equivalents	21.5	20.8
22.3	34.6	40.2	31.4	17.3	23.4	Trade Receivables (net)	34.0	29.2
1.4	1.5	2.9	2.0	1.3	1.3	Inventory	1.1	1.7
3.3	5.1	4.4	3.0	4.0	2.1	All Other Current	3.4	3.9
58.4	60.5	63.3	55.6	36.6	33.4	Total Current	60.0	55.6
19.5	19.3	19.4	23.1	25.3	15.6	Fixed Assets (net)	18.9	21.5
10.3	9.7	6.4	7.9	25.6	45.5	Intangibles (net)	9.1	10.6
11.8	10.5	10.9	13.4	12.4	5.5	All Other Non-Current	12.0	12.4
100.0	100.0	100.0	100.0	100.0	100.0	Total	100.0	100.0
						LIABILITIES		
17.8	9.9	8.9	5.1	1.5	1.7	Notes Payable-Short Term	10.0	10.4
2.6	2.2	3.6	2.7	4.0	2.5	Cur. Mat.-L.T.D.	2.9	4.5
7.1	6.9	9.1	8.9	8.3	4.1	Trade Payables	8.6	8.4
.0	.2	.0	.2	.0	.1	Income Taxes Payable	.3	.2
29.8	18.7	13.8	14.0	13.6	12.4	All Other Current	21.2	18.0
57.3	37.8	35.4	30.8	27.5	20.9	Total Current	43.0	41.4
19.9	18.8	13.5	15.1	18.3	34.4	Long-Term Debt	13.7	16.1
.0	.1	.3	.1	.5	2.9	Deferred Taxes	.7	.3
14.1	11.5	5.0	8.2	3.2	10.0	All Other Non-Current	6.6	8.2
8.8	31.7	45.8	45.9	50.4	31.7	Net Worth	36.0	34.0
100.0	100.0	100.0	100.0	100.0	100.0	Total Liabilties & Net Worth	100.0	100.0
						INCOME DATA		
100.0	100.0	100.0	100.0	100.0	100.0	Net Sales	100.0	100.0
						Gross Profit		
93.0	90.5	92.1	94.8	97.6	95.1	Operating Expenses	93.2	91.8
7.0	9.5	7.9	5.2	2.4	4.9	Operating Profit	6.8	8.2
.3	2.5	1.0	.1	.7	2.6	All Other Expenses (net)	1.0	1.2
6.7	7.0	6.8	5.1	1.7	2.2	Profit Before Taxes	5.8	7.1
						RATIOS		
3.6	3.5	3.7	3.0	2.0	1.7		3.3	3.1
1.7	1.8	2.0	1.9	1.4	1.4	Current	1.8	1.7
.5	.9	1.1	1.2	1.0	1.1		1.0	1.0
3.5	3.3	3.4	2.9	1.7	1.6		3.1	2.8
(125) 1.5	1.5	1.8	1.7	1.2	1.3	Quick	1.6	1.5
.4	.8	1.0	1.0	.9	.9		.9	.8
0 UND	**6** 62.9	**32** 11.3	**39** 9.4	**34** 10.6	**42** 8.7		**19** 18.9	**10** 35.0
0 UND	**32** 11.4	**49** 7.4	**47** 7.8	**41** 9.0	**49** 7.4	Sales/Receivables	**38** 9.5	**37** 9.8
25 14.7	**51** 7.2	**68** 5.4	**64** 5.7	**56** 6.5	**64** 5.7		**56** 6.5	**55** 6.6
						Cost of Sales/Inventory		
						Cost of Sales/Payables		
12.2	7.1	4.7	4.2	6.4	10.6		6.3	6.2
55.4	17.2	9.7	10.2	19.9	17.9	Sales/Working Capital	15.4	15.4
-39.0	-132.6	42.1	24.4	95.6	49.2		-999.8	-936.2
45.9	54.2	50.7	28.8	9.1	5.0		26.7	37.4
(70) 12.8	(109) 7.8	(105) 9.8	(89) 10.5	(20) 4.7	2.2	EBIT/Interest	(362) 7.1	(443) 9.6
2.5	1.2	3.1	2.0	1.8	.4		1.7	2.9
		21.6	7.5				23.0	12.5
		(11) 11.2	(12) 3.1			Net Profit + Depr., Dep., Amort./Cur. Mat. L/T/D	(39) 3.7	(41) 3.0
		.5	1.4				1.8	1.6
.0	.1	.1	.2	.4	.8		.1	.1
.4	.5	.3	.4	1.0	-.2	Fixed/Worth	.4	.5
UND	UND	1.3	1.1	3.5	-.1		2.7	4.5
.5	.5	.4	.4	.8	2.6		.4	.5
2.1	1.8	1.1	1.0	2.9	-2.4	Debt/Worth	1.4	1.5
-3.8	-25.7	4.5	2.9	NM	-1.7		12.8	21.3
241.0	89.5	75.4	37.1	28.5			91.7	94.9
(84) 111.1	(109) 30.4	(121) 26.2	(89) 12.6	(16) 10.7		% Profit Before Taxes/Tangible Net Worth	(398) 29.7	(461) 34.3
17.9	5.7	7.2	5.0	2.2			5.9	8.8
110.8	39.8	24.7	15.2	7.1	8.5		33.6	35.3
35.5	9.2	10.9	6.4	3.0	3.3	% Profit Before Taxes/Total Assets	11.4	12.4
3.0	1.0	2.7	1.7	1.1	-1.7		2.2	3.5
999.8	149.7	137.2	52.4	36.2	84.1		159.4	135.9
107.3	65.0	38.6	10.2	5.8	24.0	Sales/Net Fixed Assets	44.3	31.7
41.6	13.6	7.5	3.5	2.8	7.4		11.2	7.2
15.2	5.7	3.9	2.8	1.6	2.0		5.5	5.0
7.9	3.8	2.6	1.8	1.1	1.3	Sales/Total Assets	3.2	2.9
4.1	2.1	1.6	1.2	.9	1.0		1.7	1.5
.3	.3	.4	.9	1.5	.6		.4	.5
(52) .5	(88) .8	(102) .9	(92) 1.5	(17) 2.8	(11) 1.0	% Depr., Dep., Amort./Sales	(350) 1.0	(402) 1.2
1.5	1.7	2.3	2.6	5.8	1.8		2.2	2.4
3.5	2.0	1.8	.8				2.3	2.6
(55) 8.6	(45) 4.6	(42) 4.2	(11) 3.7			% Officers', Directors' Owners' Comp/Sales	(125) 5.0	(155) 4.8
14.2	7.8	7.8	13.5				10.2	8.8
263006M	**664003M**	**1744547M**	**4464932M**	**2124121M**	**5709127M**	Net Sales ($)	**12583706M**	**16392439M**
28158M	**162958M**	**626011M**	**2184902M**	**1605918M**	**3694020M**	Total Assets ($)	**6372925M**	**8834946M**

M = $ thousand **MM = $ million**

See Pages 9 through 22 for Explanation of Ratios and Data

Comparative Historical Data | Current Data Sorted by Sales

			Type of Statement						
135	109	97	Unqualified	6	2	3	13	27	46
37	23	24	Reviewed		2	3	2	8	9
65	51	49	Compiled	3	9	10	13	10	4
146	116	117	Tax Returns	33	32	21	18	9	4
276	304	275	Other	30	55	40	46	39	65
4/1/11-3/31/12 ALL	4/1/12-3/31/13 ALL	4/1/13-3/31/14 ALL			90 (4/1-9/30/13)		472 (10/1/13-3/31/14)		
				0-1MM	1-3MM	3-5MM	5-10MM	10-25MM	25MM & OVER
659	603	562	NUMBER OF STATEMENTS	72	100	77	92	93	128
%	%	%	ASSETS	%	%	%	%	%	%
21.8	21.7	20.4	Cash & Equivalents	24.5	22.6	21.0	20.2	22.4	14.8
32.1	32.1	31.6	Trade Receivables (net)	16.7	30.2	29.0	34.8	38.7	35.1
1.5	1.8	1.9	Inventory	.8	1.4	2.3	3.3	1.8	1.8
2.8	3.8	4.0	All Other Current	1.5	4.1	9.7	3.7	2.5	2.9
58.2	59.3	57.8	Total Current	43.5	58.3	62.0	62.1	65.4	54.5
18.0	18.2	20.1	Fixed Assets (net)	35.8	16.9	17.1	19.6	16.7	18.4
9.7	10.2	10.8	Intangibles (net)	9.5	11.8	9.2	7.3	6.2	17.3
14.1	12.3	11.3	All Other Non-Current	11.2	13.0	11.7	11.0	11.7	9.7
100.0	100.0	100.0	Total	100.0	100.0	100.0	100.0	100.0	100.0
			LIABILITIES						
9.6	12.0	9.9	Notes Payable-Short Term	7.4	14.0	12.2	12.3	9.0	5.4
3.2	3.3	2.8	Cur. Mat.-L.T.D.	2.6	2.4	3.5	2.6	2.5	3.3
9.1	7.9	7.8	Trade Payables	2.9	5.5	11.6	6.6	9.0	10.2
.3	.1	.1	Income Taxes Payable	.0	.1	.2	.0	.0	.2
19.0	16.1	18.6	All Other Current	28.3	20.8	15.6	18.5	15.1	15.9
41.1	39.5	39.2	Total Current	41.2	42.7	43.1	40.0	35.6	35.0
16.4	14.7	17.7	Long-Term Debt	30.2	24.1	14.7	11.9	8.2	18.4
.4	.4	.3	Deferred Taxes	.0	.2	.0	.1	.3	.7
8.4	7.3	9.5	All Other Non-Current	12.5	11.2	15.5	7.0	3.3	9.1
33.7	38.1	33.4	Net Worth	16.1	21.8	26.6	41.0	52.6	36.8
100.0	100.0	100.0	Total Liabilties & Net Worth	100.0	100.0	100.0	100.0	100.0	100.0
			INCOME DATA						
100.0	100.0	100.0	Net Sales	100.0	100.0	100.0	100.0	100.0	100.0
			Gross Profit						
93.2	92.9	92.7	Operating Expenses	83.7	92.9	92.1	94.5	94.5	95.4
6.8	7.1	7.3	Operating Profit	16.3	7.1	7.9	5.5	5.5	4.6
1.2	.9	1.1	All Other Expenses (net)	5.7	.6	.4	.5	-.4	1.1
5.6	6.2	6.2	Profit Before Taxes	10.6	6.5	7.5	5.0	5.9	3.6
			RATIOS						
3.5	3.7	3.4		3.7	4.3	3.4	3.5	3.9	2.1
1.7	1.9	1.8	Current	1.9	2.0	1.8	1.9	2.1	1.5
1.0	1.1	1.0		.5	.7	.9	1.1	1.3	1.1
3.3	3.4	3.1		3.7	4.0	2.9	3.2	3.7	2.1
(658) 1.6	(602) 1.7	(561) 1.6	Quick	1.7	1.6	(76) 1.4	1.7	2.0	1.4
.9	.9	.8		.5	.6	.7	.9	1.2	1.0
12 30.2	**14** 25.6	**11** 33.5		**0** UND	**0** UND	**0** 853.1	**18** 20.0	**29** 12.7	**36** 10.0
38 9.7	**40** 9.1	**38** 9.7	Sales/Receivables	**0** UND	**22** 16.4	**34** 10.8	**37** 9.8	**42** 8.7	**47** 7.7
56 6.5	**59** 6.2	**59** 6.2		**38** 9.7	**60** 6.1	**52** 7.0	**52** 7.0	**63** 5.8	**63** 5.8
			Cost of Sales/Inventory						
			Cost of Sales/Payables						
6.7	5.8	6.4		6.7	6.0	5.5	6.2	5.1	8.0
15.8	12.7	15.7	Sales/Working Capital	17.6	20.3	16.8	14.2	9.9	17.2
-385.1	127.3	999.8		-32.1	-37.8	-170.5	338.1	30.8	53.0
32.1	42.9	44.2		23.7	14.9	60.1	57.7	64.6	27.6
(441) 8.3	(410) 9.0	(416) 8.6	EBIT/Interest	(32) 5.5	(67) 4.5	(61) 15.6	(65) 13.9	(76) 14.0	(115) 5.8
1.4	2.0	1.9		-4.7	1.0	3.0	2.7	4.4	1.4
5.5	6.9	7.9							6.9
(53) 1.7	(39) 2.4	(37) 3.2	Net Profit + Depr., Dep., Amort./Cur. Mat. L/T/D						(25) 3.0
.8	.5	.6							.8
.1	.1	.1		.0	.0	.1	.1	.1	.2
.4	.3	.4	Fixed/Worth	.7	.5	.4	.4	.3	.6
3.6	1.7	4.3		5.1	NM	4.4	9.3	.7	-1.4
.4	.4	.5		.5	.5	.5	.4	.3	.7
1.3	1.3	1.6	Debt/Worth	1.4	2.1	2.1	1.1	.9	1.9
81.0	8.2	78.1		UND	-3.7	NM	24.0	2.7	-8.6
73.4	75.7	88.4		73.2	176.9	93.6	101.8	69.6	57.8
(505) 27.5	(482) 25.0	(427) 26.2	% Profit Before Taxes/Tangible Net Worth	(54) 20.5	(68) 57.3	(58) 47.4	(71) 31.1	(85) 23.5	(91) 13.1
5.5	6.1	6.4		3.9	9.8	10.1	5.5	7.3	4.0
29.4	33.1	30.9		36.3	47.3	46.4	43.4	27.2	13.0
9.8	9.6	9.6	% Profit Before Taxes/Total Assets	4.9	13.0	18.6	13.3	10.0	5.3
.6	1.9	1.8		.4	2.2	5.5	2.3	2.9	1.2
194.4	176.6	146.6		556.4	243.9	206.0	116.8	181.0	80.6
48.1	44.0	46.5	Sales/Net Fixed Assets	48.2	69.8	54.1	60.4	40.0	23.8
10.7	9.6	9.0		1.0	25.1	13.1	13.7	7.0	5.3
5.5	5.0	5.6		8.7	6.8	7.5	6.0	5.2	3.7
3.1	2.7	2.9	Sales/Total Assets	2.5	3.5	3.9	3.8	2.9	2.1
1.6	1.5	1.6		.4	2.0	2.0	2.2	1.6	1.4
.3	.4	.4		1.1	.3	.3	.3	.3	.6
(428) .9	(382) 1.1	(362) 1.1	% Depr., Dep., Amort./Sales	(36) 4.1	(50) .7	(47) .7	(62) .8	(68) .9	(99) 1.4
2.2	2.2	2.3		17.3	1.8	1.9	1.6	2.2	2.1
2.7	2.2	2.1		7.5	3.0	1.9	2.3	1.4	.5
(192) 5.2	(160) 4.3	(155) 5.2	% Officers', Directors' Owners' Comp/Sales	(19) 13.0	(38) 7.4	(32) 4.5	(28) 4.3	(26) 3.0	(12) 1.8
10.3	8.5	10.5		18.9	12.5	8.5	6.7	9.4	6.7
15040145M	15238247M	14969736M	Net Sales ($)	37131M	196409M	301648M	668041M	1510577M	12255930M
8545739M	9362923M	8301967M	Total Assets ($)	44015M	106788M	113618M	278249M	832034M	6927263M

M = $ thousand MM = $ million

See Pages 9 through 22 for Explanation of Ratios and Data

Current Data Sorted by Assets							Comparative Historical Data	
						Type of Statement		
	1	12	7	4	1	Unqualified	20	27
	2	12	4		1	Reviewed	11	14
1	4	17	1	1		Compiled	13	16
7	14	13				Tax Returns	24	25
9	16	28	8		1	Other	41	47
	25 (4/1-9/30/13)		139 (10/1/13-3/31/14)				4/1/09-3/31/10 ALL	4/1/10-3/31/11 ALL
0-500M	**500M-2MM**	**2-10MM**	**10-50MM**	**50-100MM**	**100-250MM**			
17	37	82	20	5	3	**NUMBER OF STATEMENTS**	109	129
%	%	%	%	%	%	**ASSETS**	%	%
30.7	19.6	12.8	10.5			Cash & Equivalents	16.1	18.0
11.5	26.2	32.3	30.3			Trade Receivables (net)	26.3	23.9
.7	.0	.9	.8			Inventory	.8	1.0
4.6	2.3	1.6	2.6			All Other Current	5.3	3.6
47.5	48.0	47.6	44.2			Total Current	48.5	46.5
41.1	35.8	40.9	45.9			Fixed Assets (net)	37.9	39.2
2.2	3.8	3.9	3.4			Intangibles (net)	6.8	3.4
9.2	12.3	7.6	6.5			All Other Non-Current	6.8	10.9
100.0	100.0	100.0	100.0			Total	100.0	100.0
						LIABILITIES		
10.4	13.3	6.3	8.9			Notes Payable-Short Term	9.6	6.2
11.1	4.2	5.3	3.8			Cur. Mat.-L.T.D.	5.8	5.8
4.1	4.1	4.6	6.6			Trade Payables	4.5	7.1
.1	.0	.2	.2			Income Taxes Payable	.5	.4
24.8	11.3	7.2	6.9			All Other Current	11.3	10.6
50.5	33.0	23.6	26.4			Total Current	31.5	30.1
64.4	30.1	24.1	21.7			Long-Term Debt	28.3	21.5
.0	.0	.4	.2			Deferred Taxes	.6	.6
11.7	17.8	4.6	.6			All Other Non-Current	4.3	3.3
-26.5	19.1	47.2	51.1			Net Worth	35.3	44.5
100.0	100.0	100.0	100.0			Total Liabilties & Net Worth	100.0	100.0
						INCOME DATA		
100.0	100.0	100.0	100.0			Net Sales	100.0	100.0
						Gross Profit		
89.8	92.0	94.8	95.4			Operating Expenses	91.2	91.6
10.2	8.0	5.2	4.6			Operating Profit	8.8	8.4
.2	1.0	.3	.3			All Other Expenses (net)	1.6	1.7
10.0	7.0	4.9	4.3			Profit Before Taxes	7.3	6.7
						RATIOS		
8.3	5.4	5.0	3.6				3.8	3.7
2.2	1.9	2.3	2.5			Current	1.7	1.8
.3	1.0	1.2	1.5				.9	1.0
8.3	5.3	4.4	3.4				3.3	3.4
2.0	1.9	2.2	2.4			Quick	1.4	1.5
.2	1.0	1.2	1.4				.8	.8
0 UND	**0** UND	**33** 11.1	**51** 7.1				**0** UND	**0** UND
0 UND	**23** 15.6	**54** 6.7	**65** 5.6			Sales/Receivables	**41** 8.9	**43** 8.5
0 UND	**66** 5.5	**81** 4.5	**87** 4.2				**66** 5.5	**69** 5.3
						Cost of Sales/Inventory		
						Cost of Sales/Payables		
15.1	5.3	3.8	3.4				5.8	4.7
24.0	18.7	9.1	7.0			Sales/Working Capital	16.0	14.5
-22.5	NM	44.2	12.1				-65.7	629.4
16.6	28.0	12.3	10.5				17.0	15.5
(13) 5.7	(30) 6.3	(79) 2.5	(18) 2.3			EBIT/Interest	(93) 5.6	(103) 5.6
1.3	1.4	.5	.9				2.9	1.7
							4.7	2.6
						Net Profit + Depr., Dep., Amort./Cur. Mat. L/T/D	(24) 2.8	(25) 1.6
							1.9	1.1
.5	.4	.5	.6				.5	.5
1.2	1.0	.9	.9			Fixed/Worth	1.1	1.0
-1.3	94.9	2.1	1.6				5.1	2.9
.6	.5	.5	.2				.4	.3
2.4	1.8	1.0	1.1			Debt/Worth	1.9	1.2
-2.6	183.4	2.7	3.1				7.7	4.6
232.2	87.6	31.4	14.9				68.6	48.2
(12) 77.8	(29) 26.8	(77) 6.9	(19) 7.6			% Profit Before Taxes/Tangible Net Worth	(87) 33.8	(114) 19.4
28.5	2.8	-4.1	.0				9.4	3.6
108.3	33.4	15.4	8.8				27.0	19.5
25.7	10.6	3.4	2.7			% Profit Before Taxes/Total Assets	11.5	7.8
5.1	.8	-1.7	.2				3.2	.5
438.2	25.1	12.8	8.1				13.8	15.0
29.0	11.4	5.8	3.8			Sales/Net Fixed Assets	7.3	6.3
3.9	4.6	2.8	2.0				4.3	3.1
12.6	5.3	2.8	2.4				3.5	3.6
6.8	3.3	2.0	1.4			Sales/Total Assets	2.2	2.1
2.5	1.8	1.2	1.0				1.6	1.1
	2.8	3.0	2.4				2.1	2.6
	(24) 5.0	(70) 4.2	4.3			% Depr., Dep., Amort./Sales	(90) 3.5	(108) 4.3
	7.7	6.4	6.4				5.6	6.5
	2.1	1.4					1.9	2.1
	(12) 4.8	(29) 2.1				% Officers', Directors' Owners' Comp/Sales	(33) 4.0	(29) 3.4
	9.8	5.7					7.8	5.1
34651M	144466M	894541M	778277M	382136M	866348M	Net Sales ($)	7892524M	2478212M
4714M	40237M	420230M	449526M	315597M	641174M	Total Assets ($)	2343736M	1452786M

M = $ thousand MM = $ million

See Pages 9 through 22 for Explanation of Ratios and Data

Comparative Historical Data | Current Data Sorted by Sales

4/1/11-3/31/12 ALL	4/1/12-3/31/13 ALL	4/1/13-3/31/14 ALL	Type of Statement	0-1MM	1-3MM	3-5MM	5-10MM	10-25MM	25MM & OVER
21	24	25	Unqualified	2	1		5	6	11
13	12	19	Reviewed	1	2	1		11	4
22	25	24	Compiled	2	1	2	8	10	1
25	30	34	Tax Returns	3	11	6	11	3	
59	57	62	Other	6	13	10	9	17	7
				25 (4/1-9/30/13)			139 (10/1/13-3/31/14)		
140	148	164	NUMBER OF STATEMENTS	14	28	19	33	47	23
%	%	%	ASSETS	%	%	%	%	%	%
16.0	17.0	15.7	Cash & Equivalents	14.2	23.4	14.8	17.6	14.1	8.7
25.6	25.7	28.4	Trade Receivables (net)	6.4	23.5	26.8	27.6	36.2	34.3
1.4	1.1	.8	Inventory	1.0	.3	.6	1.0	.6	1.7
2.6	3.6	2.2	All Other Current	5.2	.6	3.4	2.6	1.3	2.7
45.6	47.5	47.1	Total Current	26.7	47.8	45.6	48.8	52.3	47.3
41.5	39.4	40.7	Fixed Assets (net)	54.6	43.4	37.3	36.4	38.3	42.9
4.2	4.3	3.6	Intangibles (net)	2.2	1.4	3.8	6.5	3.1	3.8
8.6	8.7	8.6	All Other Non-Current	16.5	7.5	13.4	8.3	6.3	6.0
100.0	100.0	100.0	Total	100.0	100.0	100.0	100.0	100.0	100.0
			LIABILITIES						
10.1	7.9	8.6	Notes Payable-Short Term	.7	9.2	9.2	5.6	13.6	6.2
5.5	6.0	5.5	Cur. Mat.-L.T.D.	5.1	2.1	3.4	8.8	6.5	5.0
6.2	6.4	4.6	Trade Payables	5.2	2.3	3.2	3.0	6.8	6.4
.3	.2	.1	Income Taxes Payable	.0	.0	.1	.0	.3	.1
9.8	8.1	10.2	All Other Current	16.7	9.4	7.4	7.4	12.0	10.2
31.9	28.5	29.1	Total Current	27.7	23.1	23.4	24.7	39.1	27.7
25.7	28.2	29.5	Long-Term Debt	53.7	30.8	32.0	35.5	18.5	24.9
.4	.3	.2	Deferred Taxes	.0	.0	.2	.0	.6	.1
7.0	4.8	7.8	All Other Non-Current	1.6	8.5	25.9	9.8	3.6	1.6
35.0	38.1	33.4	Net Worth	17.0	37.6	18.6	30.0	38.2	45.7
100.0	100.0	100.0	Total Liabilties & Net Worth	100.0	100.0	100.0	100.0	100.0	100.0
			INCOME DATA						
100.0	100.0	100.0	Net Sales	100.0	100.0	100.0	100.0	100.0	100.0
			Gross Profit						
90.2	90.3	93.4	Operating Expenses	77.2	92.1	95.7	97.0	95.6	93.3
9.8	9.7	6.6	Operating Profit	22.8	7.9	4.3	3.0	4.4	6.7
1.8	.9	.5	All Other Expenses (net)	2.7	.8	.8	-.6	.2	.8
7.9	8.9	6.1	Profit Before Taxes	20.1	7.2	3.5	3.6	4.2	5.9
			RATIOS						
4.3	4.9	5.0		8.4	15.1	4.2	5.9	2.7	3.2
1.9	2.1	2.3	Current	3.7	4.5	1.9	2.8	1.6	2.4
1.0	.9	1.1		.5	1.7	1.0	1.4	1.1	1.3
3.7	4.1	4.6		8.2	15.1	3.7	4.5	2.6	3.0
1.7	1.8	2.2	Quick	3.1	4.3	1.9	2.2	1.6	2.1
.8	.8	1.1		.4	1.7	1.0	1.4	1.0	1.1
0 UND	**0** UND	**0** UND		**0** UND	**0** UND	**0** UND	**0** UND	**33** 11.0	**54** 6.8
46 7.9	**43** 8.4	**50** 7.3	Sales/Receivables	**24** 15.2	**0** UND	**38** 9.6	**47** 7.7	**52** 7.0	**65** 5.6
81 4.5	**73** 5.0	**74** 4.9		**85** 4.3	**78** 4.7	**60** 6.1	**76** 4.8	**72** 5.1	**89** 4.1
			Cost of Sales/Inventory						
			Cost of Sales/Payables						
4.0	4.0	4.2		1.6	3.7	9.3	4.2	5.0	3.2
10.9	11.1	11.3	Sales/Working Capital	10.6	12.9	19.9	9.0	11.9	7.7
271.8	-150.1	65.2		-11.9	25.5	-375.0	68.0	85.4	14.7
15.8	17.7	16.3		17.1	34.5	8.1	12.4	22.1	14.5
(115) 4.7	(130) 5.6	(147) 3.6	EBIT/Interest	(10) 4.9	(23) 8.3	(16) 1.4	(31) 4.4	(46) 2.7	(21) 3.5
1.4	1.0	.7		.9	1.9	-.2	-2.4	.6	1.4
2.8	4.6	5.2							
(21) 1.6	(22) 2.4	(17) 2.0	Net Profit + Depr., Dep., Amort./Cur. Mat. L/T/D						
1.2	1.6	.6							
.5	.4	.5		.4	.3	.4	.5	.5	.7
1.2	1.0	1.0	Fixed/Worth	1.1	.8	1.4	1.3	1.0	1.1
3.3	2.1	2.9		2.8	1.9	165.0	7.1	2.1	1.7
.5	.4	.5		.1	.4	.6	.4	.5	.7
1.6	1.2	1.3	Debt/Worth	.8	.9	2.2	1.9	1.2	1.2
5.2	4.1	5.6		2.7	5.5	316.0	19.9	4.0	3.5
60.7	48.1	47.6		33.4	120.2	65.7	93.1	34.7	22.5
(121) 24.6	(131) 16.9	(145) 10.6	% Profit Before Taxes/Tangible Net Worth	(12) 2.6	(26) 24.8	(15) 5.9	(26) 6.5	(44) 9.1	(22) 9.1
3.5	2.1	.0		.4	6.5	-6.5	-13.4	-3.2	3.8
22.0	22.0	20.4		22.7	27.5	28.7	32.8	18.0	9.4
7.7	8.8	5.3	% Profit Before Taxes/Total Assets	6.2	9.8	1.1	4.3	5.5	2.7
.9	.8	-.3		.3	3.6	-3.9	-3.4	-1.6	1.7
13.3	14.8	14.3		6.3	15.8	29.2	23.1	13.9	8.0
5.9	6.4	6.7	Sales/Net Fixed Assets	1.8	6.1	11.4	6.9	8.1	5.3
2.2	2.6	2.9		.2	2.1	4.1	3.3	4.4	2.1
3.1	3.3	3.6		1.2	4.4	5.7	5.2	3.3	2.4
1.9	2.0	2.2	Sales/Total Assets	.6	2.4	2.2	2.5	2.4	1.7
1.0	1.1	1.3		.2	.7	1.5	1.6	1.8	1.0
2.4	2.4	3.0		7.6	4.9	2.4	1.8	2.5	2.7
(108) 3.9	(117) 4.8	(126) 4.4	% Depr., Dep., Amort./Sales	(10) 14.2	(16) 7.0	(12) 3.7	(27) 3.9	(41) 4.0	(20) 3.7
6.2	6.5	6.7		34.8	9.0	7.2	6.1	6.0	5.6
2.8	1.4	1.5					1.8	1.3	
(40) 4.7	(37) 3.2	(51) 3.4	% Officers', Directors' Owners' Comp/Sales				(13) 4.1	(15) 1.8	
7.5	7.8	7.3					7.7	5.5	
2669958M	3172235M	3100419M	Net Sales ($)	7827M	48851M	77187M	239349M	776842M	1950363M
1896193M	1879964M	1871478M	Total Assets ($)	20144M	37933M	39570M	106690M	354449M	1312692M

M = $ thousand MM = $ million

See Pages 9 through 22 for Explanation of Ratios and Data

Current Data Sorted by Assets							Comparative Historical Data	
						Type of Statement		
		7	22	2	6	Unqualified	38	33
			1			Reviewed	1	1
						Compiled		1
		1				Tax Returns		3
1		2	5	4	1	Other	13	13
	21 (4/1-9/30/13)		31 (10/1/13-3/31/14)				4/1/09-3/31/10	4/1/10-3/31/11
0-500M	500M-2MM	2-10MM	10-50MM	50-100MM	100-250MM		ALL	ALL
1		10	28	6	7	**NUMBER OF STATEMENTS**	52	51
%	%	%	%	%	%	**ASSETS**	%	%
	DATA NOT AVAILABLE	33.6	25.9			Cash & Equivalents	15.8	18.6
		18.4	17.4			Trade Receivables (net)	20.8	17.7
		5.9	3.4			Inventory	6.7	9.8
		2.0	2.4			All Other Current	2.1	1.6
		60.0	49.0			Total Current	45.3	47.7
		31.7	36.8			Fixed Assets (net)	39.2	38.4
		.0	1.5			Intangibles (net)	1.8	1.4
		8.3	12.7			All Other Non-Current	13.7	12.6
		100.0	100.0			Total	100.0	100.0
						LIABILITIES		
		.0	.5			Notes Payable-Short Term	2.1	3.3
		2.4	1.0			Cur. Mat.-L.T.D.	1.5	2.4
		10.0	6.5			Trade Payables	10.0	12.2
		.0	.2			Income Taxes Payable	.1	.0
		4.8	9.6			All Other Current	9.3	8.4
		17.2	17.7			Total Current	23.1	26.3
		7.5	9.9			Long-Term Debt	17.0	17.0
		.3	.0			Deferred Taxes	.0	.0
		.6	4.2			All Other Non-Current	2.5	1.9
		74.3	68.2			Net Worth	57.3	54.8
		100.0	100.0			Total Liabilties & Net Worth	100.0	100.0
						INCOME DATA		
		100.0	100.0			Net Sales	100.0	100.0
						Gross Profit		
		99.6	94.9			Operating Expenses	94.5	92.0
		.4	5.1			Operating Profit	5.5	8.0
		-.5	-1.6			All Other Expenses (net)	-.1	.2
		.9	6.7			Profit Before Taxes	5.6	7.8
						RATIOS		
		9.8	6.1				3.7	4.4
		3.5	3.5			Current	2.1	2.5
		1.7	1.6				1.4	1.6
		8.8	5.1				3.3	3.6
		3.2	3.1			Quick	1.5	1.9
		1.3	1.3				.9	1.0
		27 13.3	38 9.6				34 10.7	34 10.8
		35 10.5	45 8.1			Sales/Receivables	42 8.7	42 8.7
		47 7.7	53 6.9				51 7.1	48 7.5
						Cost of Sales/Inventory		
						Cost of Sales/Payables		
		2.5	2.3				4.0	2.9
		5.7	4.4			Sales/Working Capital	7.0	6.2
		18.8	11.1				16.7	13.5
			58.3				31.6	65.4
			(21) 15.6			EBIT/Interest	(42) 14.7	(37) 12.3
			5.0				4.1	5.3
						Net Profit + Depr., Dep., Amort./Cur. Mat. L/T/D		
		.1	.3				.5	.4
		.4	.5			Fixed/Worth	.6	.6
		.9	.8				.9	1.2
		.1	.2				.3	.3
		.2	.3			Debt/Worth	.6	.6
		1.2	.7				1.3	1.1
		12.5	16.2				18.4	24.5
		-.9	(27) 8.6			% Profit Before Taxes/Tangible Net Worth	(50) 12.2	(48) 10.2
		-6.0	2.9				4.3	6.5
		10.1	11.3				10.0	12.6
		-.5	8.1			% Profit Before Taxes/Total Assets	7.7	7.0
		-4.0	2.4				1.3	4.0
		17.3	7.8				8.2	9.8
		5.7	3.1			Sales/Net Fixed Assets	3.5	3.2
		3.4	2.0				2.3	2.4
		2.9	1.5				2.2	1.9
		1.8	1.1			Sales/Total Assets	1.5	1.4
		1.2	1.0				1.0	1.0
			1.8				1.9	2.1
			(27) 2.6			% Depr., Dep., Amort./Sales	(49) 2.8	(46) 3.0
			3.8				3.3	4.1
						% Officers', Directors' Owners' Comp/Sales		
1482M		154439M	882744M	334144M	1081042M	Net Sales ($)	3010679M	2447852M
415M		72925M	721034M	450545M	1140540M	Total Assets ($)	1996571M	1827449M

M = $ thousand MM = $ million

See Pages 9 through 22 for Explanation of Ratios and Data

Comparative Historical Data | **Current Data Sorted by Sales**

4/1/11-3/31/12 ALL	4/1/12-3/31/13 ALL	4/1/13-3/31/14 ALL	Type of Statement	0-1MM	1-3MM	3-5MM	5-10MM	10-25MM	25MM & OVER
41	41	37	Unqualified				3	8	26
1	1	1	Reviewed					1	
1			Compiled						
1		1	Tax Returns						
14	16	13	Other		1		1	4	8
					21 (4/1-9/30/13)		31 (10/1/13-3/31/14)		
58	58	52	NUMBER OF STATEMENTS		1		4	13	34
%	%	%	**ASSETS**	%	%	%	%	%	%
18.5	19.7	24.5	Cash & Equivalents	DATA NOT AVAILABLE		DATA NOT AVAILABLE		25.1	23.3
19.6	17.7	16.3	Trade Receivables (net)					16.6	16.4
6.8	5.1	4.7	Inventory					3.0	5.8
3.9	3.5	2.2	All Other Current					2.6	1.9
48.7	45.9	47.7	Total Current					47.3	47.5
35.2	32.7	31.7	Fixed Assets (net)					39.6	26.5
3.1	4.3	4.7	Intangibles (net)					.1	6.9
13.1	17.0	16.0	All Other Non-Current					13.0	19.0
100.0	100.0	100.0	Total					100.0	100.0
			LIABILITIES						
1.6	.6	.4	Notes Payable-Short Term					.2	.4
1.8	1.6	1.3	Cur. Mat.-L.T.D.					.8	1.0
12.6	8.4	6.9	Trade Payables					5.7	7.4
.0	.2	.1	Income Taxes Payable					.0	.2
7.4	9.1	8.2	All Other Current					5.7	10.2
23.4	19.8	17.0	Total Current					12.4	19.3
10.6	17.2	11.0	Long-Term Debt					7.6	9.3
.4	.5	.3	Deferred Taxes					.0	.4
3.8	2.9	2.8	All Other Non-Current					1.5	3.7
61.8	59.6	68.8	Net Worth					78.5	67.4
100.0	100.0	100.0	Total Liabilities & Net Worth					100.0	100.0
			INCOME DATA						
100.0	100.0	100.0	Net Sales					100.0	100.0
			Gross Profit						
95.3	93.9	94.8	Operating Expenses					96.9	93.4
4.7	6.1	5.2	Operating Profit					3.1	6.6
-.4	-.6	-1.6	All Other Expenses (net)					-1.2	-1.9
5.1	6.8	6.8	Profit Before Taxes					4.2	8.5
			RATIOS						
4.5	4.3	4.6						8.5	4.4
2.6	2.6	2.9	Current					3.5	2.5
1.6	1.4	1.8						2.5	1.7
3.4	3.6	4.4						7.6	4.1
2.0	1.9	2.7	Quick					3.2	2.2
1.2	1.0	1.4						2.1	1.2
36 10.2	**33** 11.0	**35** 10.3						**35** 10.5	**38** 9.5
44 8.3	**41** 8.9	**45** 8.1	Sales/Receivables					**39** 9.3	**47** 7.7
58 6.3	**56** 6.5	**52** 7.0						**52** 7.0	**52** 7.0
			Cost of Sales/Inventory						
			Cost of Sales/Payables						
3.0	2.8	2.8						2.7	2.8
5.3	5.9	4.9	Sales/Working Capital					4.9	5.0
11.6	13.7	8.0						11.8	7.6
33.5	33.1	56.7							59.1
(45) 8.7	(45) 12.3	(35) 12.5	EBIT/Interest						(24) 13.6
3.1	5.6	4.0							5.9
			Net Profit + Depr., Dep., Amort./Cur. Mat. L/T/D						
.4	.3	.3						.3	.2
.5	.5	.5	Fixed/Worth					.4	.5
1.1	1.0	.8						1.0	.7
.3	.3	.2						.1	.2
.5	.5	.4	Debt/Worth					.2	.4
1.2	1.1	1.0						.6	1.1
12.9	17.2	18.3						15.7	19.9
(54) 8.1	(55) 10.0	(51) 8.9	% Profit Before Taxes/Tangible Net Worth					6.5	(33) 11.9
2.3	3.8	1.8						-.9	3.7
10.4	10.9	13.9						12.6	14.9
5.6	5.9	6.2	% Profit Before Taxes/Total Assets					4.0	9.0
1.8	2.8	1.8						-.8	2.8
10.0	10.8	8.6						7.5	13.0
4.0	3.8	3.8	Sales/Net Fixed Assets					3.2	4.1
2.3	2.2	2.5						2.1	2.8
2.0	1.6	1.6						1.8	1.3
1.3	1.2	1.1	Sales/Total Assets					1.2	1.1
1.0	.9	.9						1.0	.9
1.9	2.1	1.9						1.9	1.8
(55) 2.7	(50) 3.2	(44) 2.7	% Depr., Dep., Amort./Sales					2.3	(27) 2.6
4.3	4.1	3.8						3.6	3.8
			% Officers', Directors' Owners' Comp/Sales						
2716036M	3421436M	2453851M	Net Sales ($)		1482M		30017M	226960M	2195392M
2141288M	3064583M	2385459M	Total Assets ($)		415M		30543M	185753M	2168748M

M = $ thousand MM = $ million

See Pages 9 through 22 for Explanation of Ratios and Data

Current Data Sorted by Assets							Comparative Historical Data	
						Type of Statement		
	2	13	21	7	7	Unqualified	98	88
1	3	4	4			Reviewed	15	13
6	3	13				Compiled	30	21
15	4	6				Tax Returns	46	30
10	24	26	26	5	9	Other	109	120
38 (4/1-9/30/13)		171 (10/1/13-3/31/14)					**4/1/09-3/31/10**	**4/1/10-3/31/11**
0-500M	**500M-2MM**	**2-10MM**	**10-50MM**	**50-100MM**	**100-250MM**		**ALL**	**ALL**
32	36	62	51	12	16	**NUMBER OF STATEMENTS**	298	272
%	%	%	%	%	%	**ASSETS**	%	%
37.7	20.1	16.8	16.3	6.7	15.0	Cash & Equivalents	19.4	20.6
9.0	21.7	28.7	25.0	18.8	27.2	Trade Receivables (net)	22.3	22.5
5.9	1.4	2.0	.9	6.1	1.8	Inventory	3.5	3.4
1.5	3.5	5.1	5.6	5.8	5.3	All Other Current	4.1	4.8
54.1	46.6	52.6	47.8	37.4	49.3	Total Current	49.3	51.3
39.7	42.8	34.0	28.9	21.7	19.4	Fixed Assets (net)	33.7	31.2
.8	4.9	6.1	14.7	30.3	20.5	Intangibles (net)	7.3	6.1
5.4	5.7	7.3	8.7	10.5	10.8	All Other Non-Current	9.8	11.4
100.0	100.0	100.0	100.0	100.0	100.0	Total	100.0	100.0
						LIABILITIES		
22.1	8.6	5.3	3.1	5.2	7.6	Notes Payable-Short Term	7.8	8.3
2.4	6.2	3.9	2.1	3.0	7.8	Cur. Mat.-L.T.D.	4.0	4.8
7.1	5.1	9.4	8.6	7.6	8.2	Trade Payables	8.5	7.9
.0	.1	.3	.1	.0	.1	Income Taxes Payable	.1	.1
20.8	18.3	11.9	15.3	11.1	22.0	All Other Current	13.5	16.4
52.3	38.3	30.9	29.3	27.0	45.7	Total Current	34.0	37.5
37.3	26.1	17.7	24.2	24.0	33.1	Long-Term Debt	21.7	21.2
.0	.0	.3	1.0	1.2	.3	Deferred Taxes	.3	.2
4.6	8.4	6.9	6.7	8.9	7.0	All Other Non-Current	7.5	10.2
5.8	27.2	44.3	38.9	38.9	13.9	Net Worth	36.5	31.0
100.0	100.0	100.0	100.0	100.0	100.0	Total Liabilities & Net Worth	100.0	100.0
						INCOME DATA		
100.0	100.0	100.0	100.0	100.0	100.0	Net Sales	100.0	100.0
						Gross Profit		
89.4	86.6	89.7	93.0	93.7	100.0	Operating Expenses	90.8	90.7
10.6	13.4	10.3	7.0	6.3	.0	Operating Profit	9.2	9.3
2.6	2.8	2.7	2.0	2.9	1.3	All Other Expenses (net)	2.8	2.2
7.9	10.6	7.6	5.0	3.4	-1.4	Profit Before Taxes	6.5	7.1
						RATIOS		
3.9	3.5	3.6	2.8	2.1	1.7		2.9	3.0
1.5	1.3	1.7	1.6	1.4	1.1	Current	1.6	1.6
.4	.6	1.0	1.0	.9	.9		1.0	.9
3.8	3.4	3.5	2.2	1.3	1.4		2.3	2.4
1.1	1.1	1.5	1.4	1.0	1.0	Quick	1.4	1.3
.2	.5	.8	.8	.9	.8		.8	.6
0 UND	**0** UND	**2** 169.0	**33** 11.0	**41** 8.9	**18** 20.4		**3** 105.3	**2** 219.0
0 UND	**5** 68.0	**36** 10.1	**50** 7.3	**58** 6.3	**49** 7.4	Sales/Receivables	**33** 11.0	**33** 10.9
0 UND	**43** 8.4	**70** 5.2	**74** 4.9	**118** 3.1	**63** 5.8		**54** 6.8	**53** 6.9
						Cost of Sales/Inventory		
						Cost of Sales/Payables		
37.1	13.3	5.5	5.3	5.2	7.7		6.1	5.9
224.3	52.7	11.9	8.0	11.4	19.5	Sales/Working Capital	14.4	14.7
-18.0	-13.8	-241.5	-206.5	NM	-77.0		680.1	-143.4
18.6	33.0	54.3	19.0	8.8	8.7		21.2	18.9
(18) 2.3	(23) 5.5	(46) 8.2	(37) 2.8	(10) 2.6	1.7	EBIT/Interest	(219) 5.2	(202) 4.8
.0	.7	1.4	-.3	-.9	-1.3		1.4	1.5
							10.1	5.9
						Net Profit + Depr., Dep., Amort./Cur. Mat. L/T/D	(29) 2.6	(30) 3.2
							1.6	1.7
.3	.4	.2	.2	.6	1.0		.2	.2
1.0	1.2	.7	1.1	1.4	-4.2	Fixed/Worth	.9	.8
-3.4	-28.9	2.0	-16.6	-.5	-.6		3.3	4.8
.5	.7	.5	.7	1.6	2.7		.6	.7
1.7	2.6	1.2	1.6	2.5	-53.3	Debt/Worth	1.6	1.6
-4.3	-64.4	5.7	-62.4	-3.7	-4.0		6.2	10.6
489.1	87.0	88.6	21.2				64.6	69.4
(21) 51.6	(25) 19.4	(54) 18.9	(38) 6.2			% Profit Before Taxes/Tangible Net Worth	(251) 14.4	(220) 18.3
23.3	7.8	1.6	-.3				2.1	4.3
81.5	52.2	29.2	11.8	9.9	11.1		21.5	20.0
22.8	6.9	7.8	1.8	4.3	.0	% Profit Before Taxes/Total Assets	6.4	6.9
.7	2.2	.2	-1.3	-1.4	-7.8		.3	.6
145.6	70.3	40.0	28.0	14.8	33.3		42.9	57.0
37.8	14.0	10.4	8.4	8.0	20.9	Sales/Net Fixed Assets	10.4	12.9
10.9	3.8	4.7	2.3	2.6	3.0		3.0	3.2
25.9	5.6	3.8	2.3	1.3	2.7		4.1	4.3
9.0	4.2	2.3	1.4	.8	2.0	Sales/Total Assets	2.1	2.2
4.5	1.8	1.3	.9	.7	1.1		1.1	1.2
.9	.6	1.0	1.3	1.7	1.0		1.1	1.0
(18) 1.9	(22) 1.7	(52) 2.0	(46) 2.8	(10) 3.8	(12) 2.4	% Depr., Dep., Amort./Sales	(230) 2.3	(207) 2.3
3.6	6.0	5.4	6.8	5.2	3.2		4.1	4.4
4.4							4.2	3.7
(13) 20.0						% Officers', Directors' Owners' Comp/Sales	(60) 7.9	(48) 10.3
25.2							16.7	24.3
85702M	**162091M**	**817406M**	**2198715M**	**868984M**	**5715823M**	Net Sales ($)	**12693628M**	**13357263M**
6497M	**41071M**	**322770M**	**1216848M**	**883548M**	**2728026M**	Total Assets ($)	**6726600M**	**6273289M**

M = $ thousand MM = $ million

See Pages 9 through 22 for Explanation of Ratios and Data

Comparative Historical Data | **Current Data Sorted by Sales**

Type of Statement									
Unqualified	80	58	50		1	3	5	8	33
Reviewed	12	8	12		2	2		7	1
Compiled	18	25	22	4	3	4	7	3	1
Tax Returns	53	33	25	5	8	5	4	3	
Other	103	109	100	6	17	10	16	20	31
	4/1/11-3/31/12 ALL	4/1/12-3/31/13 ALL	4/1/13-3/31/14 ALL	38 (4/1-9/30/13)		171 (10/1/13-3/31/14)			
				0-1MM	1-3MM	3-5MM	5-10MM	10-25MM	25MM & OVER
NUMBER OF STATEMENTS	266	233	209	15	31	24	32	41	66
ASSETS	%	%	%	%	%	%	%	%	%
Cash & Equivalents	23.4	25.4	19.7	20.4	21.8	25.0	21.1	20.5	15.5
Trade Receivables (net)	21.0	23.3	22.9	9.2	12.4	14.6	29.1	22.3	31.3
Inventory	2.5	2.8	2.5	3.6	3.9	.5	3.4	1.7	2.3
All Other Current	4.8	3.1	4.4	.9	7.1	3.0	2.3	4.6	5.4
Total Current	51.7	54.6	49.5	34.1	45.2	43.1	55.8	49.2	54.5
Fixed Assets (net)	31.2	27.2	33.3	60.0	42.4	41.6	32.5	30.2	22.2
Intangibles (net)	6.3	8.3	9.7	.9	2.4	4.9	6.6	13.9	15.6
All Other Non-Current	10.8	9.8	7.5	4.9	10.0	10.4	5.1	6.6	7.6
Total	100.0	100.0	100.0	100.0	100.0	100.0	100.0	100.0	100.0
LIABILITIES									
Notes Payable-Short Term	9.1	8.4	8.1	19.9	11.6	10.3	7.3	5.0	5.2
Cur. Mat.-L.T.D.	4.4	4.1	3.9	1.5	4.1	3.9	4.5	5.4	3.0
Trade Payables	7.4	7.6	7.9	11.1	4.5	4.0	7.2	10.0	9.2
Income Taxes Payable	.1	.1	.2	.0	.0	.0	.5	.4	.0
All Other Current	15.9	12.6	15.9	5.2	18.9	16.7	15.2	13.2	18.8
Total Current	36.9	32.7	35.9	37.7	39.1	34.9	34.8	33.9	36.3
Long-Term Debt	22.0	20.5	25.3	61.2	34.2	20.6	13.6	22.0	22.4
Deferred Taxes	.2	.3	.4	.0	.0	.0	.5	.7	.6
All Other Non-Current	7.2	5.5	6.9	9.3	4.0	7.2	7.8	7.9	6.5
Net Worth	33.7	40.9	31.5	-8.2	22.7	37.3	43.4	35.5	34.3
Total Liabilities & Net Worth	100.0	100.0	100.0	100.0	100.0	100.0	100.0	100.0	100.0
INCOME DATA									
Net Sales	100.0	100.0	100.0	100.0	100.0	100.0	100.0	100.0	100.0
Gross Profit									
Operating Expenses	90.6	90.4	90.9	76.4	84.8	89.4	91.1	94.2	95.6
Operating Profit	9.4	9.6	9.1	23.6	15.2	10.6	8.9	5.8	4.4
All Other Expenses (net)	2.3	1.5	2.4	10.8	4.8	2.8	.2	1.5	1.1
Profit Before Taxes	7.1	8.2	6.6	12.9	10.4	7.8	8.8	4.3	3.4
RATIOS									
Current	3.8	4.2	3.0	3.7	5.6	3.6	3.3	2.7	2.5
	1.7	1.9	1.5	.9	1.4	1.9	2.0	1.5	1.5
	1.0	1.1	.8	.1	.4	.7	1.0	.9	1.0
Quick	3.2	3.6	2.6	1.7	3.9	3.5	2.8	2.3	2.0
	1.4	1.6	1.3	.9	.7	1.9	1.7	1.4	1.3
	.8	.9	.7	.1	.1	.7	.9	.8	.9
Sales/Receivables	0 UND	0 UND	0 UND	0 UND	0 UND	0 UND	4 82.7	11 31.8	34 10.8
	27 13.7	34 10.8	34 10.7	0 UND	0 UND	0 UND	40 9.2	35 10.3	48 7.6
	53 6.9	54 6.7	59 6.2	12 30.2	28 13.1	34 10.6	70 5.2	59 6.2	66 5.5
Cost of Sales/Inventory									
Cost of Sales/Payables									
Sales/Working Capital	6.0	5.4	6.6	6.9	5.1	9.9	6.1	6.4	6.6
	18.4	12.5	17.9	-76.1	64.6	86.6	11.1	16.1	14.0
	601.0	141.3	-52.8	-3.6	-17.5	-28.3	NM	-100.3	NM
EBIT/Interest	23.7	35.2	21.0		8.5	17.0	81.8	55.2	15.0
	(192) 7.1	(161) 5.1	(150) 4.8		(20) 4.1	(17) 2.1	(26) 6.1	(33) 6.0	(49) 2.9
	1.7	1.1	.2		.3	-.5	-2.0	1.3	-.6
Net Profit + Depr., Dep., Amort./Cur. Mat. L/T/D	11.7	15.3	6.2						6.4
	(22) 2.7	(22) 2.0	(22) 2.3						(13) 2.0
	1.5	.9	.6						.7
Fixed/Worth	.2	.1	.3	.4	.2	.5	.1	.3	.2
	.7	.6	1.1	3.7	1.2	1.0	.5	1.7	1.0
	4.3	2.5	-40.4	-92.3	-2.7	NM	2.2	NM	-2.0
Debt/Worth	.5	.3	.7	1.0	.5	.4	.5	1.0	.7
	1.5	1.1	1.8	3.8	2.0	1.3	1.0	1.8	2.0
	13.1	6.0	-64.9	-65.9	-4.5	NM	5.8	NM	-10.4
% Profit Before Taxes/Tangible Net Worth	94.4	73.7	75.5	104.5	36.5	98.9	127.3	122.4	41.0
	(212) 24.3	(190) 23.7	(153) 16.1	(10) 28.3	(21) 11.9	(18) 33.2	(26) 39.2	(31) 18.3	(47) 7.0
	5.4	1.7	1.8	13.7	-1.6	-2.6	2.2	1.9	.1
% Profit Before Taxes/Total Assets	32.5	35.6	24.3	39.7	21.0	28.5	57.7	27.6	14.6
	9.0	9.6	5.9	7.1	4.1	4.0	18.4	8.5	2.8
	1.2	.1	-.8	2.8	-.8	-1.4	-2.2	.8	-1.8
Sales/Net Fixed Assets	59.5	71.1	39.2	30.7	65.9	83.7	68.1	33.2	33.6
	13.6	16.8	12.3	2.2	16.1	17.3	10.8	9.1	13.3
	3.4	4.5	4.3	.1	4.4	4.6	5.0	3.9	5.2
Sales/Total Assets	4.9	5.2	4.4	7.7	8.8	6.2	5.3	4.3	3.2
	2.4	2.5	2.2	1.8	4.1	3.8	2.7	1.7	2.0
	1.3	1.3	1.2	.1	.8	1.1	1.8	1.0	1.2
% Depr., Dep., Amort./Sales	1.0	.8	1.1	2.0	1.5	.6	1.1	1.0	1.0
	(205) 2.2	(169) 2.1	(160) 2.5	(10) 14.8	(23) 3.4	(16) 1.8	(22) 2.0	(34) 2.9	(55) 2.1
	4.7	4.0	5.5	25.8	6.6	6.8	4.0	6.0	3.5
% Officers', Directors' Owners' Comp/Sales	4.1	3.3	3.5						
	(54) 7.8	(50) 8.5	(30) 7.0						
	17.4	19.9	16.4						
Net Sales ($)	8043358M	8852713M	9848721M	7404M	58974M	90532M	251503M	700044M	8740264M
Total Assets ($)	3915852M	4118505M	5198760M	22764M	89782M	63777M	109171M	489557M	4423709M

M = $ thousand MM = $ million

See Pages 9 through 22 for Explanation of Ratios and Data

Current Data Sorted by Assets							Comparative Historical Data	
						Type of Statement		
2	1	19	67	65	65	Unqualified	284	320
	3	4	5			Reviewed	13	23
2	4	11	2	3	3	Compiled	21	21
8	3	2	2			Tax Returns	13	18
2	13	40	66	45	46	Other	237	251
199 (4/1-9/30/13)			284 (10/1/13-3/31/14)				4/1/09-3/31/10	4/1/10-3/31/11
0-500M	500M-2MM	2-10MM	10-50MM	50-100MM	100-250MM		ALL	ALL
14	24	76	142	113	114	**NUMBER OF STATEMENTS**	568	633
%	%	%	%	%	%	**ASSETS**	%	%
30.2	24.8	14.2	11.8	11.6	13.5	Cash & Equivalents	14.4	14.8
4.3	18.1	21.0	19.5	14.9	12.6	Trade Receivables (net)	17.6	17.6
4.4	1.9	4.1	2.5	1.9	1.7	Inventory	2.2	2.2
2.1	1.3	2.6	3.5	3.7	3.9	All Other Current	3.5	3.3
41.0	46.1	41.8	37.4	32.1	31.7	Total Current	37.6	37.9
39.2	36.6	45.4	49.8	45.2	43.2	Fixed Assets (net)	44.7	45.1
.4	3.8	5.2	2.4	1.8	3.9	Intangibles (net)	2.6	3.1
18.9	13.5	7.5	10.4	20.9	21.2	All Other Non-Current	15.1	13.8
100.0	100.0	100.0	100.0	100.0	100.0	Total	100.0	100.0
						LIABILITIES		
10.1	8.3	4.6	2.0	2.6	.9	Notes Payable-Short Term	3.1	3.7
1.4	4.2	3.7	4.3	3.0	1.9	Cur. Mat.-L.T.D.	3.9	3.6
2.8	7.0	9.4	7.5	6.3	5.6	Trade Payables	6.0	6.8
.0	.3	.0	.1	.0	.1	Income Taxes Payable	.0	.1
11.0	29.9	11.9	10.4	10.4	7.5	All Other Current	11.7	11.3
25.4	49.6	29.5	24.3	22.3	16.0	Total Current	24.7	25.5
23.8	16.1	33.0	37.5	26.1	25.9	Long-Term Debt	29.3	29.2
.1	.8	.0	.0	.1	.0	Deferred Taxes	.1	.1
3.3	.5	3.1	3.5	4.9	4.6	All Other Non-Current	5.1	5.5
47.2	33.0	34.4	34.7	46.6	53.6	Net Worth	40.8	39.7
100.0	100.0	100.0	100.0	100.0	100.0	Total Liabilties & Net Worth	100.0	100.0
						INCOME DATA		
100.0	100.0	100.0	100.0	100.0	100.0	Net Sales	100.0	100.0
						Gross Profit		
87.7	95.2	81.0	90.3	96.2	95.5	Operating Expenses	93.3	91.9
12.3	4.8	19.0	9.7	3.8	4.5	Operating Profit	6.7	8.1
-.6	.1	6.5	2.3	.0	.1	All Other Expenses (net)	1.5	1.4
13.0	4.7	12.5	7.4	3.8	4.4	Profit Before Taxes	5.2	6.7
						RATIOS		
3.7	2.7	3.0	2.5	2.2	3.0		3.0	2.8
2.0	1.2	1.5	1.7	1.6	2.0	Current	1.9	1.8
1.0	.4	1.0	1.2	1.2	1.3		1.3	1.2
2.8	2.4	2.7	2.2	1.8	2.4		2.4	2.5
2.0	1.1	1.2	1.4	1.3	1.6	Quick	1.6	1.5
.5	.4	.8	1.0	1.0	1.1		1.1	.9
0 UND	**0** UND	**0** 955.9	**36** 10.0	**41** 8.9	**40** 9.1		**36** 10.2	**34** 10.8
0 UND	**22** 16.7	**33** 11.1	**48** 7.6	**47** 7.7	**47** 7.8	Sales/Receivables	**45** 8.1	**44** 8.4
0 UND	**43** 8.5	**51** 7.2	**60** 6.1	**58** 6.3	**57** 6.4		**55** 6.7	**55** 6.7
						Cost of Sales/Inventory		
						Cost of Sales/Payables		
16.2	10.1	6.4	4.9	5.7	3.3		4.7	5.0
60.8	131.7	12.2	9.7	10.0	7.2	Sales/Working Capital	8.6	9.5
NM	-9.2	NM	31.8	32.4	17.5		24.0	37.4
	54.7	47.1	13.0	6.7	7.3		8.3	11.5
	(12) 16.0	(58) 6.6	(125) 3.2	(103) 3.1	(107) 3.3	EBIT/Interest	(517) 2.9	(569) 3.6
	-1.0	1.0	1.2	.8	1.6		.9	1.4
			4.2	5.2			5.6	5.2
			(15) 3.1	(12) 2.2		Net Profit + Depr., Dep., Amort./Cur. Mat. L/T/D	(23) 2.9	(36) 2.8
			2.2	.8			1.6	.9
.6	.5	.6	.7	.7	.6		.7	.6
.7	.9	.8	1.2	1.0	.8	Fixed/Worth	1.0	1.0
1.5	3.3	7.1	3.7	1.5	1.3		2.0	2.1
.2	.4	.4	.5	.6	.5		.6	.5
.7	1.4	1.1	1.3	1.1	.9	Debt/Worth	1.1	1.1
3.5	NM	15.3	5.3	2.3	1.6		2.9	3.4
721.5	63.2	90.6	49.7	14.3	11.2		17.2	29.2
(12) 69.8	(18) 41.0	(62) 19.3	(120) 8.9	(110) 4.7	(109) 5.8	% Profit Before Taxes/Tangible Net Worth	(500) 6.6	(551) 8.1
12.0	3.7	2.7	.6	-.4	1.9		.0	1.6
188.1	35.2	24.1	11.7	5.8	6.3		9.0	10.8
22.7	11.9	7.8	3.8	2.3	3.4	% Profit Before Taxes/Total Assets	3.1	4.3
.3	-5.0	.0	.3	-.2	1.2		-.5	.5
62.6	99.4	13.1	4.3	3.4	2.7		4.7	5.3
29.0	11.7	4.8	2.4	2.4	2.1	Sales/Net Fixed Assets	2.6	2.8
3.9	4.1	1.1	1.6	1.7	1.5		1.8	1.8
12.4	7.0	2.9	1.7	1.4	1.0		1.7	1.8
6.1	3.1	2.0	1.1	1.1	.9	Sales/Total Assets	1.2	1.2
2.6	2.1	.5	.8	.8	.7		.8	.8
.4	1.2	2.6	3.3	3.8	4.7		3.3	2.9
(10) 1.4	(15) 3.2	(66) 3.9	(138) 5.1	(108) 4.7	(81) 5.7	% Depr., Dep., Amort./Sales	(481) 4.7	(558) 4.5
4.5	7.1	16.3	6.8	6.7	7.0		6.1	6.3
					6.8		6.2	7.9
					(12) 15.5	% Officers', Directors' Owners' Comp/Sales	(66) 13.8	(65) 15.3
					38.5		36.5	39.8
28373M	**170750M**	**902912M**	**5646137M**	**9537652M**	**17790225M**	Net Sales ($)	**39889287M**	**43915672M**
3360M	**27880M**	**419023M**	**3634312M**	**8075992M**	**18871635M**	Total Assets ($)	**36954669M**	**38810551M**

M = $ thousand MM = $ million

See Pages 9 through 22 for Explanation of Ratios and Data

Comparative Historical Data | **Current Data Sorted by Sales**

Type of Statement									
Unqualified	309	249	219	4	8	1	5	38	163
Reviewed	14	10	12		2	5		3	3
Compiled	35	20	25	5	4	3	3	3	2
Tax Returns	19	23	15	1	5	2	3	3	7
Other	262	219	212	5	12	11	14	34	136
	4/1/11-3/31/12 ALL	4/1/12-3/31/13 ALL	4/1/13-3/31/14 ALL	199 (4/1-9/30/13)			284 (10/1/13-3/31/14)		
				0-1MM	1-3MM	3-5MM	5-10MM	10-25MM	25MM & OVER
NUMBER OF STATEMENTS	639	521	483	15	31	22	25	81	309
ASSETS	%	%	%	%	%	%	%	%	%
Cash & Equivalents	15.6	15.0	13.7	13.0	12.6	19.5	18.9	15.0	12.7
Trade Receivables (net)	15.4	15.7	16.5	4.8	5.1	13.2	18.8	20.3	17.3
Inventory	2.4	2.5	2.4	.1	2.5	2.2	3.0	3.6	2.2
All Other Current	2.9	3.2	3.4	6.5	1.3	.3	.9	3.8	3.7
Total Current	36.2	36.3	36.0	24.4	21.5	35.2	41.6	42.7	35.9
Fixed Assets (net)	45.2	45.9	45.5	61.5	64.3	43.9	37.7	45.9	43.5
Intangibles (net)	2.7	2.7	3.1	.4	2.3	5.4	9.9	2.2	2.8
All Other Non-Current	15.9	15.1	15.3	13.3	11.9	15.5	10.8	9.2	17.7
Total	100.0	100.0	100.0	100.0	100.0	100.0	100.0	100.0	100.0
LIABILITIES									
Notes Payable-Short Term	3.6	3.2	2.8	5.4	2.6	3.7	8.4	2.9	2.2
Cur. Mat.-L.T.D.	3.3	2.9	3.2	4.9	3.6	3.9	4.5	3.9	2.8
Trade Payables	6.1	6.4	6.9	2.4	2.6	4.2	10.7	8.4	7.1
Income Taxes Payable	.1	.0	.1	.0	.0	.3	.0	.0	.1
All Other Current	12.3	11.3	10.9	7.1	13.3	11.2	14.2	13.3	10.0
Total Current	25.5	23.8	24.0	19.7	22.1	23.2	37.7	28.5	22.1
Long-Term Debt	29.3	28.8	29.9	55.4	36.3	40.8	27.0	32.0	27.0
Deferred Taxes	.1	.1	.1	.1	.0	.0	.9	.1	.0
All Other Non-Current	3.9	5.4	3.9	4.4	1.6	1.7	1.2	4.1	4.4
Net Worth	41.3	42.0	42.2	20.2	40.0	34.3	33.2	35.3	46.5
Total Liabilties & Net Worth	100.0	100.0	100.0	100.0	100.0	100.0	100.0	100.0	100.0
INCOME DATA									
Net Sales	100.0	100.0	100.0	100.0	100.0	100.0	100.0	100.0	100.0
Gross Profit									
Operating Expenses	92.4	90.6	91.6	79.2	73.2	77.9	87.5	92.3	95.2
Operating Profit	7.6	9.4	8.4	20.8	26.8	22.1	12.5	7.7	4.8
All Other Expenses (net)	1.6	2.9	1.7	14.5	9.2	7.0	.0	.7	.3
Profit Before Taxes	6.0	6.5	6.7	6.3	17.6	15.1	12.5	6.9	4.5
RATIOS									
	2.8	3.0	2.6	2.3	3.0	4.7	2.0	3.2	2.5
Current	1.8	1.8	1.7	1.1	1.2	2.5	1.3	1.7	1.7
	1.1	1.1	1.2	.2	.6	1.1	.6	1.3	1.2
	2.5	2.6	2.2	2.3	2.3	4.4	1.8	2.5	2.1
Quick	1.5	1.5	1.4	.6	1.0	2.4	1.2	1.4	1.4
	.9	.9	1.0	.1	.4	1.0	.5	1.0	1.0
	33 11.2	**31** 11.7	**33** 10.9	**0** UND	**0** UND	**0** UND	**4** 95.8	**33** 10.9	**40** 9.1
Sales/Receivables	**45** 8.2	**45** 8.1	**45** 8.1	**0** UND	**0** UND	**27** 13.3	**27** 13.4	**46** 8.0	**48** 7.6
	54 6.7	**54** 6.7	**56** 6.5	**54** 6.7	**33** 10.9	**53** 6.9	**49** 7.5	**62** 5.9	**58** 6.3
Cost of Sales/Inventory									
Cost of Sales/Payables									
	4.8	4.4	5.2	5.0	6.1	5.5	9.4	4.9	4.9
Sales/Working Capital	9.0	8.7	10.3	21.4	162.4	12.6	46.6	8.1	9.6
	63.7	50.0	41.5	-3.2	-6.2	NM	-22.3	30.9	24.3
	10.7	11.3	11.0		14.4	34.1	140.8	17.6	9.4
EBIT/Interest	(563) 3.5	(452) 3.6	(414) 3.6		(17) 4.8	(13) 6.5	(21) 13.5	(69) 4.2	(286) 3.3
	.8	.8	1.1		-1.0	-1.2	1.5	.7	1.2
	7.9	9.3	5.7						5.7
Net Profit + Depr., Dep., Amort./Cur. Mat. L/T/D	(32) 2.9	(27) 2.8	(35) 2.9						(23) 3.1
	1.6	1.8	1.6						1.8
	.6	.6	.6	1.2	.8	.4	.6	.6	.6
Fixed/Worth	1.0	1.0	.9	3.5	1.0	.7	.9	1.0	.9
	2.2	2.4	2.1	-9.2	6.5	14.4	2.3	2.5	1.6
	.5	.5	.5	.7	.3	.3	.8	.4	.5
Debt/Worth	1.1	1.1	1.1	3.1	1.3	.7	1.2	1.1	1.1
	3.2	3.3	3.1	-10.3	5.9	NM	6.0	4.0	2.3
	26.7	33.9	26.7	35.1	53.8	179.4	116.2	26.5	16.3
% Profit Before Taxes/Tangible Net Worth	(560) 7.6	(468) 8.3	(431) 7.6	(11) 2.8	(26) 18.5	(17) 45.5	(20) 48.0	(72) 7.6	(285) 6.4
	.6	.9	.6	-10.0	1.9	-1.0	13.7	-.4	.7
	9.3	11.0	9.9	4.0	14.2	52.4	28.9	11.2	8.7
% Profit Before Taxes/Total Assets	3.4	3.6	3.6	.4	6.7	10.6	9.6	3.4	3.4
	-.4	-.1	.1	-1.2	-1.1	-1.8	3.0	-.6	.4
	5.2	4.9	4.7	4.2	5.5	20.1	16.6	6.8	3.7
Sales/Net Fixed Assets	2.5	2.6	2.5	.5	.5	5.1	7.6	3.1	2.4
	1.6	1.6	1.6	.1	.2	.7	2.9	1.7	1.8
	1.8	1.8	1.8	1.2	2.0	3.2	4.3	2.3	1.4
Sales/Total Assets	1.1	1.1	1.1	.2	.3	1.8	2.1	1.2	1.1
	.8	.8	.8	.1	.2	.4	1.1	.9	.8
	3.0	3.1	3.5	5.2	5.6	2.1	2.9	2.5	3.7
% Depr., Dep., Amort./Sales	(565) 4.6	(454) 4.6	(418) 5.0	(12) 27.7	(26) 18.0	(19) 6.2	(17) 3.8	(78) 4.3	(266) 4.9
	6.6	6.7	6.9	38.6	26.9	18.3	8.3	6.3	6.4
	5.0	5.3	9.5						9.1
% Officers', Directors' Owners' Comp/Sales	(68) 23.9	(64) 18.1	(44) 19.4						(26) 16.5
	39.1	38.7	38.5						37.8
Net Sales ($)	41837397M	32894220M	34076049M	7414M	59861M	81945M	189350M	1400711M	32336768M
Total Assets ($)	38948192M	30958953M	31032202M	38902M	227384M	212601M	228689M	1263005M	29061621M

M = $ thousand MM = $ million

See Pages 9 through 22 for Explanation of Ratios and Data

Current Data Sorted by Assets | **Comparative Historical Data**

0-500M	500M-2MM	2-10MM	10-50MM	50-100MM	100-250MM	Type of Statement	4/1/09-3/31/10 ALL	4/1/10-3/31/11 ALL
	4	6	38	35	37	Unqualified	207	231
						Reviewed		
						Compiled		
						Tax Returns		
		8	12	15	22	Other	116	134
	134 (4/1-9/30/13)		43 (10/1/13-3/31/14)					
0-500M	500M-2MM	2-10MM	10-50MM	50-100MM	100-250MM		4/1/09-3/31/10 ALL	4/1/10-3/31/11 ALL
	4	14	50	50	59	**NUMBER OF STATEMENTS**	323	365
%	%	%	%	%	%	**ASSETS**	%	%
DATA NOT AVAILABLE		14.0	15.0	13.5	12.5	Cash & Equivalents	11.0	12.9
		26.4	14.9	14.4	13.3	Trade Receivables (net)	14.7	15.1
		5.7	2.0	2.3	1.6	Inventory	2.1	2.0
		2.0	3.7	3.9	1.7	All Other Current	2.9	3.7
		48.1	35.5	34.1	29.2	Total Current	30.7	33.7
		45.1	49.0	45.5	46.0	Fixed Assets (net)	47.1	46.5
		.3	.4	.9	.8	Intangibles (net)	.8	.8
		6.5	15.1	19.5	24.0	All Other Non-Current	21.4	19.0
		100.0	100.0	100.0	100.0	Total	100.0	100.0
						LIABILITIES		
		1.8	.8	.7	.5	Notes Payable-Short Term	.5	.8
		3.4	3.3	2.2	2.0	Cur. Mat.-L.T.D.	2.2	2.4
		14.3	6.5	6.3	5.7	Trade Payables	5.9	6.7
		.0	.0	.0	.0	Income Taxes Payable	.0	.0
		12.3	9.2	11.9	8.3	All Other Current	9.6	11.1
		31.8	19.8	21.1	16.6	Total Current	18.2	21.0
		21.1	26.6	24.3	27.3	Long-Term Debt	26.2	28.7
		.0	.0	.0	.0	Deferred Taxes	.0	.0
		5.4	1.9	6.1	7.0	All Other Non-Current	6.1	7.1
		41.8	51.7	48.6	49.1	Net Worth	49.5	43.2
		100.0	100.0	100.0	100.0	Total Liabilties & Net Worth	100.0	100.0
						INCOME DATA		
		100.0	100.0	100.0	100.0	Net Sales	100.0	100.0
						Gross Profit		
		100.8	100.1	98.4	98.4	Operating Expenses	97.5	97.3
		-.8	-.1	1.6	1.6	Operating Profit	2.5	2.7
		-.7	-.6	-2.5	-1.0	All Other Expenses (net)	.8	.8
		-.1	.6	4.1	2.6	Profit Before Taxes	1.6	1.8
						RATIOS		
		2.6	3.4	2.5	2.8		2.5	2.8
		1.4	2.1	1.8	2.0	Current	1.8	1.8
		.9	1.5	1.2	1.2		1.3	1.2
		2.2	2.6	2.1	2.5		2.1	2.3
		1.1	1.7	1.4	1.5	Quick	1.5	1.5
		.9	1.0	.9	1.0		1.0	.9
		21 17.5	**37** 9.9	**37** 9.9	**40** 9.2		**38** 9.6	**38** 9.6
		37 9.9	**51** 7.1	**46** 8.0	**46** 8.0	Sales/Receivables	**46** 7.9	**46** 8.0
		59 6.2	**59** 6.2	**58** 6.3	**58** 6.3		**54** 6.7	**54** 6.8
						Cost of Sales/Inventory		
						Cost of Sales/Payables		
		6.4	3.5	4.0	3.9		5.5	4.6
		16.1	6.6	8.5	8.5	Sales/Working Capital	9.1	9.0
		-67.5	11.9	24.7	22.9		21.2	29.1
		12.0	4.9	9.8	7.0		4.9	5.1
		(13) 1.8	(46) 1.0	(47) 3.8	(55) 1.9	EBIT/Interest	(308) 2.6	(340) 2.5
		-3.7	-1.7	2.4	.0		.4	.7
						Net Profit + Depr., Dep., Amort./Cur. Mat. L/T/D		
		.6	.6	.7	.6		.7	.7
		1.5	.8	.9	.8	Fixed/Worth	1.0	1.0
		2.4	1.3	1.2	1.5		1.4	1.5
		.4	.5	.5	.5		.6	.6
		1.4	.7	1.0	.9	Debt/Worth	.9	1.1
		4.2	1.5	1.9	1.8		1.7	2.0
		34.7	8.8	11.4	8.3		9.2	9.6
		(13) 10.1	(48) .6	(49) 6.3	(58) 3.3	% Profit Before Taxes/Tangible Net Worth	(317) 3.6	(344) 4.4
		-7.4	-6.6	2.1	-1.9		-.9	-1.2
		12.3	5.3	6.1	5.0		4.8	4.6
		1.9	.1	3.0	1.8	% Profit Before Taxes/Total Assets	1.8	2.1
		-5.2	-4.2	1.3	-1.3		-.6	-.6
		9.7	2.9	3.2	2.7		3.1	3.4
		5.9	2.2	2.2	2.0	Sales/Net Fixed Assets	2.3	2.4
		1.9	1.6	1.8	1.6		1.7	1.8
		2.9	1.4	1.4	1.2		1.4	1.5
		2.2	1.0	1.1	.9	Sales/Total Assets	1.0	1.1
		1.2	.8	.8	.8		.8	.9
		1.5	4.0	4.1	4.9		4.0	3.8
		2.5	(48) 5.3	5.0	(43) 5.5	% Depr., Dep., Amort./Sales	(274) 5.0	(324) 4.8
		4.6	6.5	6.2	6.7		6.0	6.0
							10.1	
						% Officers', Directors' Owners' Comp/Sales	(10) 21.1	
							41.6	
	9766M	187809M	1617685M	4092227M	9457711M	Net Sales ($)	33447591M	36209025M
	5312M	83261M	1536611M	3550794M	9658312M	Total Assets ($)	31586656M	33016109M

M = $ thousand MM = $ million

See Pages 9 through 22 for Explanation of Ratios and Data

Comparative Historical Data | **Current Data Sorted by Sales**

			Type of Statement						
114	103	120	Unqualified	1	3		2	20	94
1	1		Reviewed						
			Compiled						
			Tax Returns						
41	44	57	Other			1	3	9	44
4/1/11-3/31/12 ALL	4/1/12-3/31/13 ALL	4/1/13-3/31/14 ALL		134 (4/1-9/30/13)			43 (10/1/13-3/31/14)		
				0-1MM	1-3MM	3-5MM	5-10MM	10-25MM	25MM & OVER
156	148	177	NUMBER OF STATEMENTS	1	3	1	5	29	138
%	%	%	ASSETS	%	%	%	%	%	%
12.9	14.3	14.2	Cash & Equivalents					10.8	14.0
14.9	13.8	15.1	Trade Receivables (net)					17.6	14.6
2.4	2.0	2.2	Inventory					2.4	2.0
3.4	2.5	2.9	All Other Current					4.2	2.8
33.6	32.6	34.5	Total Current					35.0	33.3
45.7	47.2	46.0	Fixed Assets (net)					49.8	45.8
.7	.7	.7	Intangibles (net)					.4	.8
20.0	19.4	18.8	All Other Non-Current					14.9	20.1
100.0	100.0	100.0	Total					100.0	100.0
			LIABILITIES						
1.0	.7	.7	Notes Payable-Short Term					.5	.7
2.0	2.1	2.5	Cur. Mat.-L.T.D.					4.3	2.2
6.2	6.2	6.8	Trade Payables					6.9	6.8
.0	.1	.0	Income Taxes Payable					.0	.0
8.8	9.5	10.0	All Other Current					9.4	10.0
18.0	18.6	20.0	Total Current					21.1	19.7
26.7	25.6	25.4	Long-Term Debt					29.6	25.0
.1	.0	.0	Deferred Taxes					.0	.0
7.3	7.3	5.1	All Other Non-Current					3.6	5.6
47.9	48.5	49.4	Net Worth					45.7	49.7
100.0	100.0	100.0	Total Liabilties & Net Worth					100.0	100.0
			INCOME DATA						
100.0	100.0	100.0	Net Sales					100.0	100.0
			Gross Profit						
97.1	97.2	99.0	Operating Expenses					100.9	98.5
2.9	2.8	1.0	Operating Profit					-.9	1.5
.6	.2	-1.3	All Other Expenses (net)					-.1	-1.7
2.3	2.6	2.3	Profit Before Taxes					-.8	3.1
			RATIOS						
3.1	3.1	2.7						2.7	2.8
2.0	1.8	1.9	Current					2.0	1.9
1.3	1.2	1.3						1.4	1.2
2.6	2.7	2.3						2.2	2.3
1.6	1.5	1.5	Quick					1.5	1.5
1.0	1.0	1.0						.9	1.0
35 10.3	35 10.5	38 9.7						37 9.9	39 9.4
44 8.3	43 8.5	46 7.9	Sales/Receivables					51 7.1	46 7.9
53 6.9	56 6.5	58 6.3						65 5.6	58 6.3
			Cost of Sales/Inventory						
			Cost of Sales/Payables						
3.8	3.8	4.0						4.8	3.8
8.4	8.9	7.3	Sales/Working Capital					7.1	8.3
20.6	27.2	19.7						11.4	21.9
6.1	7.8	7.8						6.1	8.1
(143) 2.5	(137) 3.0	(163) 2.9	EBIT/Interest					(27) .9	(129) 3.5
.8	.5	-.1						-4.3	.6
			Net Profit + Depr., Dep., Amort./Cur. Mat. L/T/D						
.7	.6	.6						.6	.6
1.0	.9	.8	Fixed/Worth					1.0	.8
1.3	1.4	1.4						2.6	1.3
.6	.5	.5						.4	.5
1.0	.9	.9	Debt/Worth					.9	.8
1.9	1.9	1.8						3.5	1.8
10.3	10.1	10.9						10.1	11.0
(147) 4.0	(139) 4.6	(172) 4.0	% Profit Before Taxes/Tangible Net Worth					(27) .1	(135) 4.3
-.7	-.6	-2.1						-7.8	-.8
5.0	5.5	5.7						5.4	5.8
1.8	2.2	2.2	% Profit Before Taxes/Total Assets					.1	2.4
-.6	-.9	-1.5						-4.9	-.6
3.3	3.2	3.2						4.6	3.0
2.2	2.2	2.2	Sales/Net Fixed Assets					2.0	2.2
1.6	1.6	1.7						1.1	1.8
1.5	1.4	1.3						1.8	1.3
1.0	1.0	1.0	Sales/Total Assets					.9	1.0
.8	.8	.8						.6	.8
3.7	3.9	3.9						2.8	4.1
(145) 5.1	(139) 5.3	(158) 5.2	% Depr., Dep., Amort./Sales					(28) 5.3	(121) 5.3
6.2	6.5	6.4						7.7	6.3
		8.8							8.6
		(11) 10.4	% Officers', Directors' Owners' Comp/Sales						(10) 10.3
		38.3							24.3
13387312M	13978517M	15365198M	Net Sales ($)	410M	4493M	3896M	36369M	528370M	14791660M
13026712M	12747777M	14834290M	Total Assets ($)	750M	8947M	3403M	16775M	611934M	14192481M

M = $ thousand MM = $ million

See Pages 9 through 22 for Explanation of Ratios and Data

Current Data Sorted by Assets							Comparative Historical Data	
						Type of Statement		
	2	15	29	6	6	Unqualified	46	49
		3	1			Reviewed	5	11
	1	2				Compiled	2	3
	2	1				Tax Returns	5	9
1	1	7	12	2	2	Other	27	22
54 (4/1-9/30/13)			39 (10/1/13-3/31/14)				4/1/09-3/31/10 ALL	4/1/10-3/31/11 ALL
0-500M	500M-2MM	2-10MM	10-50MM	50-100MM	100-250MM			
1	6	28	42	8	8	**NUMBER OF STATEMENTS**	85	94
%	%	%	%	%	%	**ASSETS**	%	%
		16.5	17.2			Cash & Equivalents	17.9	21.1
		26.2	17.8			Trade Receivables (net)	18.9	14.9
		1.3	.3			Inventory	.5	.3
		5.8	3.8			All Other Current	4.0	3.5
		49.8	39.1			Total Current	41.3	39.8
		37.0	48.5			Fixed Assets (net)	42.6	40.3
		3.1	2.7			Intangibles (net)	5.3	4.2
		10.1	9.6			All Other Non-Current	10.8	15.8
		100.0	100.0			Total	100.0	100.0
						LIABILITIES		
		5.9	2.0			Notes Payable-Short Term	12.6	8.6
		2.2	1.8			Cur. Mat.-L.T.D.	3.7	2.5
		9.1	4.3			Trade Payables	8.6	5.9
		.1	.1			Income Taxes Payable	.1	.1
		10.5	9.6			All Other Current	13.5	25.5
		27.8	17.9			Total Current	38.4	42.7
		13.3	30.2			Long-Term Debt	27.7	22.9
		.0	.0			Deferred Taxes	.0	.0
		13.6	2.7			All Other Non-Current	4.5	7.0
		45.2	49.2			Net Worth	29.4	27.3
		100.0	100.0			Total Liabilities & Net Worth	100.0	100.0
						INCOME DATA		
		100.0	100.0			Net Sales	100.0	100.0
						Gross Profit		
		96.3	93.6			Operating Expenses	93.6	91.6
		3.7	6.4			Operating Profit	6.4	8.4
		-.2	.8			All Other Expenses (net)	2.4	1.6
		4.0	5.6			Profit Before Taxes	4.0	6.8
						RATIOS		
		3.2	3.4				2.8	3.0
		2.2	2.2			Current	1.8	1.8
		1.3	1.6				1.0	.7
		2.8	2.8				2.5	2.8
		1.5	1.9			Quick	1.6	1.6
		1.0	1.2				.8	.6
		19 19.6	**18** 20.0				**18** 20.0	**7** 48.8
		37 9.9	**38** 9.5			Sales/Receivables	**37** 9.8	**28** 13.0
		56 6.5	**51** 7.1				**55** 6.7	**41** 9.0
						Cost of Sales/Inventory		
						Cost of Sales/Payables		
		5.1	4.6				4.6	5.7
		10.5	7.1			Sales/Working Capital	11.4	13.0
		28.3	16.2				-365.2	-42.0
		12.6	10.1				8.8	14.6
		(22) 3.4	(37) 2.0			EBIT/Interest	(71) 3.1	(77) 6.4
		2.0	1.0				.4	1.6
							16.2	39.9
						Net Profit + Depr., Dep., Amort./Cur. Mat. L/T/D	(10) 3.1	(11) 16.3
							.2	2.8
		.3	.7				.7	.5
		.9	1.0			Fixed/Worth	1.1	1.0
		2.3	1.4				3.1	2.0
		.6	.6				.6	.6
		.9	1.0			Debt/Worth	1.3	1.1
		3.0	1.7				6.5	4.7
		57.4	20.7				28.3	43.5
		(23) 7.7	(39) 4.3			% Profit Before Taxes/Tangible Net Worth	(68) 6.6	(78) 11.0
		.7	.4				-1.7	1.4
		16.4	10.9				12.4	25.9
		6.7	3.4			% Profit Before Taxes/Total Assets	4.1	7.5
		.6	.4				-1.3	.6
		37.9	5.8				10.0	17.7
		9.4	2.6			Sales/Net Fixed Assets	3.5	4.3
		2.2	1.7				2.2	2.6
		3.9	1.8				2.7	3.3
		1.9	1.5			Sales/Total Assets	1.8	2.0
		1.2	1.0				1.1	1.3
		.6	1.7				1.5	1.1
		(26) 1.6	(40) 2.6			% Depr., Dep., Amort./Sales	(79) 2.4	(81) 2.0
		2.7	3.5				3.6	3.5
								.7
						% Officers', Directors' Owners' Comp/Sales		(10) 2.5
								26.0
932M	14535M	373202M	1497781M	899270M	658517M	Net Sales ($)	2603123M	2701356M
52M	8409M	156672M	905621M	574028M	997317M	Total Assets ($)	1937680M	1578541M

M = $ thousand MM = $ million

See Pages 9 through 22 for Explanation of Ratios and Data

Comparative Historical Data				Current Data Sorted by Sales					
			Type of Statement						
46	34	58	Unqualified		1	3	6	16	32
1	4	4	Reviewed				1	1	2
5		3	Compiled		1			1	1
3	3	3	Tax Returns	2			1		
22	31	25	Other	1	3	1	1	6	13
4/1/11-3/31/12 ALL	4/1/12-3/31/13 ALL	4/1/13-3/31/14 ALL			54 (4/1-9/30/13)		39 (10/1/13-3/31/14)		
				0-1MM	1-3MM	3-5MM	5-10MM	10-25MM	25MM & OVER
77	72	93	**NUMBER OF STATEMENTS**	3	5	4	9	24	48
%	%	%	**ASSETS**	%	%	%	%	%	%
20.0	19.7	16.3	Cash & Equivalents					15.3	15.6
17.1	20.2	20.1	Trade Receivables (net)					24.8	21.3
.4	.1	.6	Inventory					.3	1.0
5.0	4.6	3.9	All Other Current					3.5	3.4
42.6	44.6	40.9	Total Current					43.8	41.3
38.2	42.0	42.2	Fixed Assets (net)					42.5	38.4
2.9	1.9	5.6	Intangibles (net)					.6	8.8
16.4	11.5	11.3	All Other Non-Current					13.1	11.5
100.0	100.0	100.0	Total					100.0	100.0
			LIABILITIES						
9.6	1.1	3.6	Notes Payable-Short Term					1.4	4.8
4.2	1.8	2.1	Cur. Mat.-L.T.D.					2.4	1.8
5.4	5.7	6.0	Trade Payables					6.4	6.4
.0	.0	.1	Income Taxes Payable					.1	.2
12.4	13.4	14.9	All Other Current					8.9	10.7
31.6	22.1	26.8	Total Current					19.1	23.9
18.0	24.1	23.3	Long-Term Debt					24.5	21.9
.0	.0	.1	Deferred Taxes					.0	.1
8.7	5.9	8.1	All Other Non-Current					10.2	4.0
41.7	47.9	41.8	Net Worth					46.2	50.1
100.0	100.0	100.0	Total Liabilties & Net Worth					100.0	100.0
			INCOME DATA						
100.0	100.0	100.0	Net Sales					100.0	100.0
			Gross Profit						
94.4	90.9	94.2	Operating Expenses					95.0	95.1
5.6	9.1	5.8	Operating Profit					5.0	4.9
-.3	3.4	.6	All Other Expenses (net)					.2	.1
5.8	5.7	5.2	Profit Before Taxes					4.9	4.8
			RATIOS						
3.3	3.1	2.9						3.5	2.7
2.0	1.9	1.9	Current					2.5	1.8
1.3	1.6	1.3						1.5	1.3
3.1	2.9	2.7						3.1	2.2
1.8	1.8	1.6	Quick					2.4	1.5
1.1	1.3	1.1						1.2	1.2
13 29.0	**16** 23.4	**18** 20.4						**22** 16.6	**26** 14.2
30 12.0	**34** 10.7	**38** 9.5	Sales/Receivables					**38** 9.6	**41** 8.8
49 7.4	**46** 7.9	**53** 6.9						**57** 6.4	**53** 6.9
			Cost of Sales/Inventory						
			Cost of Sales/Payables						
4.9	5.3	4.7						3.7	5.8
10.8	10.1	9.8	Sales/Working Capital					7.9	12.1
27.6	17.1	29.6						25.7	24.0
14.2	37.7	10.2						6.1	13.9
(60) 6.0	(58) 6.5	(76) 3.1	EBIT/Interest					(18) 3.1	(44) 4.3
1.5	.9	1.1						1.2	1.2
		24.3							
		(10) 7.0	Net Profit + Depr., Dep., Amort./Cur. Mat. L/T/D						
		1.5							
.4	.4	.6						.6	.6
.7	.8	1.0	Fixed/Worth					.8	.9
1.1	1.3	2.3						3.0	1.3
.3	.4	.6						.6	.6
.7	.8	1.0	Debt/Worth					.9	1.0
2.1	2.2	3.4						3.0	2.1
24.4	44.2	23.7						17.6	29.8
(69) 11.2	(67) 10.8	(79) 6.1	% Profit Before Taxes/Tangible Net Worth					(21) 3.3	(42) 14.7
3.9	-1.0	.7						1.4	3.0
12.5	15.7	11.4						16.1	11.2
6.1	4.7	3.7	% Profit Before Taxes/Total Assets					3.4	7.3
.9	-.7	.3						.8	.5
16.9	16.6	10.5						13.8	9.6
4.6	3.7	3.3	Sales/Net Fixed Assets					2.6	3.9
2.1	2.0	2.1						1.8	2.5
2.6	3.1	2.5						3.1	2.6
1.6	1.6	1.5	Sales/Total Assets					1.5	1.6
1.1	1.0	.9						.8	1.0
1.3	1.1	1.3						1.1	1.3
(63) 2.3	(64) 2.4	(87) 2.5	% Depr., Dep., Amort./Sales					(23) 2.4	(47) 2.4
3.4	3.9	3.9						3.2	3.8
			% Officers', Directors' Owners' Comp/Sales						
2639664M	2790255M	3444237M	Net Sales ($)	1499M	8856M	16066M	69833M	404952M	2943031M
1597150M	1751639M	2642099M	Total Assets ($)	3071M	21444M	18957M	49038M	303933M	2245656M

M = $ thousand MM = $ million

See Pages 9 through 22 for Explanation of Ratios and Data

Current Data Sorted by Assets							Comparative Historical Data	
						Type of Statement		
		8	17	11	9	Unqualified	68	58
		1	1			Reviewed	12	5
	1	3	2			Compiled	8	5
1			1		1	Tax Returns	8	13
1	6	27	20	9	10	Other	75	58
33 (4/1-9/30/13)		96 (10/1/13-3/31/14)					4/1/09-3/31/10	4/1/10-3/31/11
0-500M	**500M-2MM**	**2-10MM**	**10-50MM**	**50-100MM**	**100-250MM**		**ALL**	**ALL**
2	7	39	41	20	20	**NUMBER OF STATEMENTS**	171	139
%	%	%	%	%	%	**ASSETS**	%	%
		15.3	13.8	12.7	14.7	Cash & Equivalents	15.3	16.8
		35.1	21.0	12.7	13.5	Trade Receivables (net)	19.0	19.9
		1.5	2.0	1.3	1.7	Inventory	1.9	2.2
		1.5	2.1	1.4	2.0	All Other Current	5.4	2.6
		53.5	39.0	28.2	31.8	Total Current	41.5	41.5
		30.2	38.4	47.0	35.3	Fixed Assets (net)	40.6	40.9
		7.3	7.9	2.7	14.2	Intangibles (net)	5.2	5.5
		9.0	14.6	22.2	18.7	All Other Non-Current	12.7	11.9
		100.0	100.0	100.0	100.0	Total	100.0	100.0
						LIABILITIES		
		4.3	4.4	.7	.6	Notes Payable-Short Term	3.2	12.1
		3.2	3.3	3.6	3.5	Cur. Mat.-L.T.D.	3.3	4.1
		12.6	9.4	4.8	5.9	Trade Payables	7.3	7.5
		.0	.0	.0	.0	Income Taxes Payable	.2	.1
		14.3	8.7	7.5	10.3	All Other Current	18.0	14.9
		34.3	25.9	16.6	20.2	Total Current	32.0	38.6
		25.5	25.9	40.3	29.5	Long-Term Debt	30.3	27.0
		.1	.0	.0	.0	Deferred Taxes	.1	.2
		5.7	1.6	5.8	6.3	All Other Non-Current	3.8	5.1
		34.4	46.6	37.3	44.0	Net Worth	33.8	28.9
		100.0	100.0	100.0	100.0	Total Liabilties & Net Worth	100.0	100.0
						INCOME DATA		
		100.0	100.0	100.0	100.0	Net Sales	100.0	100.0
						Gross Profit		
		89.1	86.6	85.0	94.7	Operating Expenses	88.9	89.6
		10.9	13.4	15.0	5.3	Operating Profit	11.1	10.4
		3.5	2.2	4.7	.5	All Other Expenses (net)	3.3	1.3
		7.4	11.2	10.3	4.9	Profit Before Taxes	7.8	9.0
						RATIOS		
		2.7	3.1	2.5	2.3		2.7	2.5
		1.8	1.8	1.3	1.6	Current	1.7	1.6
		1.0	1.1	1.0	1.2		1.0	.8
		2.3	2.8	2.3	2.2		2.3	2.4
		1.5	1.7	1.2	1.4	Quick	1.4	1.5
		.9	1.0	.9	1.0		.8	.7
		28 13.1	**33** 10.9	**42** 8.6	**38** 9.7		**8** 48.5	**7** 51.4
		44 8.3	**51** 7.2	**49** 7.4	**57** 6.4	Sales/Receivables	**38** 9.5	**39** 9.4
		68 5.4	**61** 6.0	**69** 5.3	**63** 5.8		**55** 6.7	**53** 6.8
						Cost of Sales/Inventory		
						Cost of Sales/Payables		
		8.5	5.1	5.0	3.5		6.4	6.1
		15.8	11.2	17.3	9.9	Sales/Working Capital	13.4	14.3
		-999.8	60.4	251.3	19.1		155.5	-50.4
		30.7	65.7	16.3	14.6		19.6	20.8
		(34) 10.7	(35) 11.9	(18) 7.0	(19) 6.1	EBIT/Interest	(128) 3.4	(116) 6.8
		1.8	3.5	2.8	2.8		1.0	1.4
							4.3	
						Net Profit + Depr., Dep., Amort./Cur. Mat. L/T/D	(14) 2.5	
							-.9	
		.3	.5	.5	.4		.4	.5
		1.0	.7	1.2	1.3	Fixed/Worth	.9	1.3
		33.2	4.7	2.9	NM		10.1	10.5
		.9	.4	.6	.4		.5	.5
		1.8	1.6	2.5	2.5	Debt/Worth	1.5	1.7
		183.2	7.4	4.4	NM		14.8	26.9
		113.2	135.4	58.1	30.5		82.4	112.8
		(30) 50.2	(35) 19.4	(19) 20.7	(15) 16.2	% Profit Before Taxes/Tangible Net Worth	(138) 21.8	(109) 28.9
		9.3	6.7	3.5	8.7		.9	6.4
		35.5	23.5	15.8	10.2		24.0	33.5
		18.5	9.9	9.0	6.4	% Profit Before Taxes/Total Assets	6.7	8.7
		1.8	2.8	1.8	2.4		.0	2.1
		48.5	15.2	4.6	3.7		21.4	17.5
		14.9	5.0	1.7	2.9	Sales/Net Fixed Assets	4.7	5.7
		8.0	1.7	1.2	1.7		1.6	2.0
		3.8	2.7	1.2	1.2		3.1	3.2
		3.1	1.3	.9	1.0	Sales/Total Assets	1.5	1.8
		1.7	.7	.6	.5		.8	1.0
		.7	1.3	2.6	2.6		1.2	1.5
		(33) 1.5	(39) 2.8	(19) 4.8	(19) 4.3	% Depr., Dep., Amort./Sales	(155) 2.7	(120) 3.2
		4.1	6.1	8.6	5.1		5.5	5.5
							5.0	3.8
						% Officers', Directors' Owners' Comp/Sales	(29) 11.4	(28) 10.0
							28.4	30.8
13965M	**33342M**	**632065M**	**1862363M**	**1472655M**	**2777624M**	Net Sales ($)	**8339835M**	**6989521M**
587M	**8280M**	**194753M**	**1081327M**	**1452352M**	**3033840M**	Total Assets ($)	**6187651M**	**5399983M**

M = $ thousand MM = $ million

See Pages 9 through 22 for Explanation of Ratios and Data

Comparative Historical Data				Current Data Sorted by Sales					
			Type of Statement						
49	35	45	Unqualified		2	2	4	8	29
2	2	2	Reviewed					1	1
8	9	6	Compiled			2		3	1
10	7	3	Tax Returns		1	1			1
54	56	73	Other	1	1	4	12	19	36
4/1/11-3/31/12 ALL	4/1/12-3/31/13 ALL	4/1/13-3/31/14 ALL		33 (4/1-9/30/13)			96 (10/1/13-3/31/14)		
				0-1MM	1-3MM	3-5MM	5-10MM	10-25MM	25MM & OVER
123	109	129	**NUMBER OF STATEMENTS**	1	4	9	16	31	68
%	%	%	**ASSETS**	%	%	%	%	%	%
17.5	15.2	16.0	Cash & Equivalents				24.5	15.8	14.1
19.3	21.8	23.7	Trade Receivables (net)				34.3	31.1	20.2
2.3	1.9	1.9	Inventory				1.7	.7	2.3
1.6	2.6	1.7	All Other Current				1.5	1.0	2.2
40.7	41.5	43.2	Total Current				62.0	48.6	38.9
41.5	42.3	35.2	Fixed Assets (net)				21.7	26.1	38.3
6.2	7.4	7.7	Intangibles (net)				4.3	10.6	8.2
11.5	8.9	13.9	All Other Non-Current				11.9	14.8	14.7
100.0	100.0	100.0	Total				100.0	100.0	100.0
			LIABILITIES						
11.3	6.8	3.7	Notes Payable-Short Term				2.1	4.0	3.4
4.8	3.9	3.2	Cur. Mat.-L.T.D.				.5	3.5	3.5
7.1	7.5	10.0	Trade Payables				17.3	10.5	9.0
.0	.0	.0	Income Taxes Payable				.0	.0	.0
15.7	10.8	11.8	All Other Current				18.5	10.9	10.6
39.0	29.1	28.7	Total Current				38.4	28.9	26.5
28.7	31.6	28.1	Long-Term Debt				16.5	21.9	29.7
.1	.1	.0	Deferred Taxes				.2	.0	.0
3.6	5.6	4.4	All Other Non-Current				4.9	1.7	4.8
28.5	33.7	38.8	Net Worth				39.9	47.5	39.0
100.0	100.0	100.0	Total Liabilities & Net Worth				100.0	100.0	100.0
			INCOME DATA						
100.0	100.0	100.0	Net Sales				100.0	100.0	100.0
			Gross Profit						
89.9	86.2	89.1	Operating Expenses				92.0	86.2	91.2
10.1	13.8	10.9	Operating Profit				8.0	13.8	8.8
1.1	2.8	2.6	All Other Expenses (net)				.7	2.3	.5
9.1	11.0	8.3	Profit Before Taxes				7.4	11.5	8.3
			RATIOS						
3.2	3.8	2.9					4.1	4.0	2.5
1.7	2.0	1.7	Current				2.0	2.1	1.6
.9	1.0	1.0					1.1	1.1	1.1
3.0	3.6	2.6					4.1	3.9	2.3
1.5	1.6	1.5	Quick				1.9	2.0	1.4
.8	.9	1.0					1.0	1.1	1.0
15 24.4	**21** 17.3	**34** 10.7					**28** 13.0	**41** 9.0	**36** 10.0
43 8.4	**43** 8.4	**49** 7.5	Sales/Receivables				**43** 8.5	**51** 7.2	**50** 7.3
55 6.6	**57** 6.4	**64** 5.7					**72** 5.1	**70** 5.2	**59** 6.2
			Cost of Sales/Inventory						
			Cost of Sales/Payables						
5.3	4.7	6.0					7.9	3.9	6.5
13.4	11.6	12.9	Sales/Working Capital				11.5	10.9	13.0
-125.4	447.9	101.7					92.9	43.1	56.5
17.9	24.7	25.4					34.0	45.9	22.3
(103) 5.6	(92) 6.0	(113) 9.0	EBIT/Interest				(11) 1.9	(28) 12.6	(65) 7.9
1.2	2.0	2.6					.0	3.4	3.1
		21.4							24.3
		(16) 3.5	Net Profit + Depr., Dep., Amort./Cur. Mat. L/T/D						(13) 4.0
		1.9							2.1
.5	.5	.4					.1	.3	.5
1.1	1.3	1.0	Fixed/Worth				.4	.6	1.2
15.8	32.3	6.9					1.6	5.3	9.8
.5	.6	.5					.4	.4	.6
1.7	1.8	2.0	Debt/Worth				1.4	1.5	2.2
27.0	104.0	15.0					5.2	8.2	19.9
98.5	100.1	91.8					89.8	126.5	105.7
(97) 21.9	(84) 54.8	(106) 25.3	% Profit Before Taxes/Tangible Net Worth				(15) 34.6	(25) 44.8	(55) 24.9
2.9	6.1	6.3					-.1	10.0	8.9
30.2	31.9	24.0					36.2	35.5	18.1
8.2	9.7	9.1	% Profit Before Taxes/Total Assets				10.9	20.4	8.9
.7	1.5	1.9					-.6	3.0	3.7
15.9	13.9	23.5					101.9	57.0	9.3
3.5	4.9	5.4	Sales/Net Fixed Assets				42.8	14.9	3.4
1.9	1.5	1.8					8.7	2.1	1.7
3.0	3.1	3.0					3.8	3.6	2.7
1.6	1.6	1.5	Sales/Total Assets				3.2	2.0	1.2
.8	.8	.9					1.5	.8	.9
1.7	1.5	1.3						1.0	1.6
(107) 3.9	(94) 3.1	(114) 3.1	% Depr., Dep., Amort./Sales					(27) 2.4	(67) 3.3
6.1	5.7	5.3						4.5	5.0
8.6	3.8	6.7							
(22) 22.6	(16) 10.6	(12) 13.1	% Officers', Directors' Owners' Comp/Sales						
40.6	30.6	30.1							
4533864M	5208990M	6792014M	Net Sales ($)	907M	6560M	35426M	120690M	480143M	6148288M
4361686M	3925481M	5771139M	Total Assets ($)	7867M	49838M	88144M	88448M	439715M	5097127M

M = $ thousand MM = $ million

See Pages 9 through 22 for Explanation of Ratios and Data

Current Data Sorted by Assets							Comparative Historical Data	
						Type of Statement		
1	37	122	131	43	43	Unqualified	513	487
1	24	93	29	1	1	Reviewed	174	158
4	33	68	13	1	2	Compiled	117	121
29	25	27	5		1	Tax Returns	149	145
28	132	333	162	36	38	Other	685	822
345 (4/1-9/30/13)		1,118 (10/1/13-3/31/14)					4/1/09-3/31/10	4/1/10-3/31/11
0-500M	500M-2MM	2-10MM	10-50MM	50-100MM	100-250MM		ALL	ALL
63	251	643	340	81	85	**NUMBER OF STATEMENTS**	1638	1733
%	%	%	%	%	%	**ASSETS**	%	%
32.4	13.0	11.4	11.3	8.2	12.1	Cash & Equivalents	12.2	13.2
25.0	36.0	25.2	14.7	13.5	14.1	Trade Receivables (net)	20.2	19.9
.3	.7	.3	.3	.2	.3	Inventory	.3	.3
3.6	4.0	3.4	2.8	3.1	3.6	All Other Current	3.5	3.7
61.2	53.7	40.2	29.0	25.0	30.1	Total Current	36.1	37.2
28.5	32.4	41.8	50.5	52.9	48.3	Fixed Assets (net)	46.2	46.2
1.2	2.9	6.3	8.2	6.8	7.1	Intangibles (net)	5.3	4.8
9.1	11.0	11.7	12.3	15.4	14.4	All Other Non-Current	12.4	11.9
100.0	100.0	100.0	100.0	100.0	100.0	Total	100.0	100.0
						LIABILITIES		
9.1	6.2	3.5	2.7	2.4	2.4	Notes Payable-Short Term	3.8	4.4
1.1	3.8	3.2	3.7	2.2	3.1	Cur. Mat.-L.T.D.	3.7	3.6
15.0	17.3	11.0	5.6	5.8	5.2	Trade Payables	9.5	9.9
.0	.0	.1	.1	.0	.0	Income Taxes Payable	.0	.1
55.7	38.4	17.9	10.4	11.1	10.1	All Other Current	17.9	16.9
81.0	65.8	35.7	22.5	21.5	20.7	Total Current	34.9	35.1
16.3	26.0	39.0	45.0	46.3	45.0	Long-Term Debt	41.4	40.7
.0	.2	.1	.1	.0	.1	Deferred Taxes	.1	.1
10.1	7.0	5.6	7.3	12.5	10.0	All Other Non-Current	7.8	8.1
-7.4	1.0	19.7	25.1	19.7	24.2	Net Worth	15.8	16.1
100.0	100.0	100.0	100.0	100.0	100.0	Total Liabilties & Net Worth	100.0	100.0
						INCOME DATA		
100.0	100.0	100.0	100.0	100.0	100.0	Net Sales	100.0	100.0
						Gross Profit		
91.7	90.4	85.4	89.9	91.3	93.6	Operating Expenses	87.7	87.6
8.3	9.6	14.6	10.1	8.7	6.4	Operating Profit	12.3	12.4
.8	2.5	5.3	3.7	3.3	1.8	All Other Expenses (net)	5.1	5.0
7.5	7.1	9.3	6.4	5.3	4.6	Profit Before Taxes	7.2	7.4
						RATIOS		
2.9	2.0	2.3	2.5	2.1	2.5		2.1	2.2
1.2	1.1	1.4	1.5	1.3	1.5	Current	1.2	1.3
.4	.6	.7	.9	.8	1.0		.7	.7
2.9	1.8	2.2	2.2	1.9	2.2		2.0	2.0
1.2	1.0	1.2	1.3	1.2	1.3	Quick	1.1	1.1
.4	.5	.6	.8	.7	.8		.6	.6
0 UND	8 44.9	23 16.0	24 15.5	29 12.7	28 13.2		11 32.2	11 34.5
5 74.0	30 12.1	39 9.4	36 10.1	40 9.2	39 9.4	Sales/Receivables	32 11.3	32 11.5
26 14.3	44 8.3	54 6.8	49 7.5	49 7.4	49 7.4		44 8.3	44 8.3
						Cost of Sales/Inventory		
						Cost of Sales/Payables		
15.5	14.1	8.0	5.8	6.1	4.3		8.9	8.4
96.7	132.1	23.5	14.8	26.1	13.1	Sales/Working Capital	34.2	28.7
-11.5	-11.8	-15.3	-40.5	-23.4	NM		-19.5	-21.3
34.1	25.5	16.0	8.9	4.6	4.4		9.5	11.0
(30) 3.5	(154) 3.5	(467) 4.2	(289) 3.7	(73) 2.7	(80) 2.8	EBIT/Interest	(1268) 3.1	(1339) 3.1
-.8	-1.6	1.4	1.5	1.3	1.4		1.3	1.3
		4.3	6.6	36.3	4.0		7.3	6.7
		(30) 2.8	(30) 3.7	(10) 1.8	(10) 1.2	Net Profit + Depr., Dep., Amort./Cur. Mat. L/T/D	(118) 3.6	(124) 3.3
		1.7	2.1	-.7	-.2		1.6	1.5
.2	.3	.4	.9	1.2	1.3		.7	.7
1.0	1.1	2.1	3.3	5.1	3.0	Fixed/Worth	3.0	2.7
-.9	-2.5	-9.4	-16.9	-10.5	84.7		-8.9	-13.4
.4	.7	1.0	1.0	1.8	1.5		1.3	1.2
3.3	3.4	3.7	4.2	6.9	4.9	Debt/Worth	4.9	4.1
-2.9	-5.9	-13.0	-22.2	-19.6	123.3		-13.0	-17.5
202.8	82.7	62.4	43.6	51.2	38.8		74.8	71.0
(41) 80.0	(169) 33.6	(451) 29.7	(243) 11.8	(57) 10.0	(67) 14.0	% Profit Before Taxes/Tangible Net Worth	(1128) 28.7	(1206) 26.0
2.5	9.5	9.3	2.2	5.0	2.4		6.1	6.7
65.7	28.6	15.9	10.4	6.2	7.4		16.7	18.0
16.5	11.8	7.1	4.3	3.4	3.3	% Profit Before Taxes/Total Assets	5.9	6.0
-1.9	-1.4	1.5	.8	.6	.8		.6	.9
85.8	52.1	25.0	4.9	3.1	4.2		19.6	17.6
43.9	18.6	5.3	1.8	1.4	1.6	Sales/Net Fixed Assets	3.1	3.0
12.9	5.6	1.4	.9	.7	.9		1.1	1.0
10.7	5.5	3.1	1.6	1.5	1.6		3.3	3.4
6.6	4.0	1.7	.9	.6	.8	Sales/Total Assets	1.4	1.4
3.7	2.3	.9	.5	.4	.5		.7	.6
.3	.4	.9	2.0	2.4	2.2		1.2	1.2
(42) .7	(216) 1.0	(590) 2.2	(327) 4.0	(77) 4.5	(74) 4.1	% Depr., Dep., Amort./Sales	(1482) 2.9	(1554) 3.1
1.7	2.4	4.7	6.9	9.6	6.6		5.9	6.2
1.6	2.0	1.6	2.3				1.7	1.7
(17) 4.8	(29) 4.4	(65) 3.4	(35) 4.8			% Officers', Directors' Owners' Comp/Sales	(217) 3.9	(247) 4.2
12.9	7.7	9.1	8.0				7.8	7.8
94305M	1202172M	5896284M	9708183M	6554586M	14894967M	Net Sales ($)	36304439M	37746672M
14852M	310508M	3255532M	7307763M	5853394M	12344854M	Total Assets ($)	30224820M	31360308M

M = $ thousand MM = $ million

See Pages 9 through 22 for Explanation of Ratios and Data

Comparative Historical Data / Current Data Sorted by Sales

Type of Statement									
Unqualified	386	347	377	16	22	20	69	129	121
Reviewed	171	130	149	13	10	13	40	58	15
Compiled	147	123	121	14	19	18	37	25	8
Tax Returns	155	106	87	28	30	10	13	3	8
Other	772	802	729	58	86	55	212	189	129
	4/1/11-3/31/12 ALL	4/1/12-3/31/13 ALL	4/1/13-3/31/14 ALL		345 (4/1-9/30/13)			1,118 (10/1/13-3/31/14)	
				0-1MM	1-3MM	3-5MM	5-10MM	10-25MM	25MM & OVER
NUMBER OF STATEMENTS	1631	1508	1463	129	167	116	371	404	276
ASSETS	%	%	%	%	%	%	%	%	%
Cash & Equivalents	13.2	12.1	12.4	8.3	16.3	13.4	12.3	12.6	11.4
Trade Receivables (net)	20.7	22.9	23.3	4.4	13.9	25.3	28.1	28.4	23.1
Inventory	.3	.3	.3	.0	.4	.6	.3	.3	.4
All Other Current	3.4	3.5	3.4	4.7	3.3	3.6	3.1	3.2	3.3
Total Current	37.6	38.8	39.4	17.3	33.9	42.8	43.8	44.6	38.2
Fixed Assets (net)	44.9	43.6	42.6	65.2	53.2	42.4	36.5	38.4	40.4
Intangibles (net)	5.9	5.3	6.0	7.3	3.9	5.1	6.3	5.2	7.8
All Other Non-Current	11.6	12.2	12.0	10.2	8.9	9.7	13.5	11.8	13.7
Total	100.0	100.0	100.0	100.0	100.0	100.0	100.0	100.0	100.0
LIABILITIES									
Notes Payable-Short Term	4.1	4.2	3.9	2.0	5.3	7.3	3.2	3.4	4.2
Cur. Mat.-L.T.D.	3.8	3.4	3.2	5.3	2.2	2.0	3.4	3.3	3.1
Trade Payables	9.4	10.5	10.4	3.3	8.1	11.6	12.2	12.5	8.9
Income Taxes Payable	.0	.1	.1	.0	.1	.0	.1	.1	.1
All Other Current	18.5	20.3	20.5	12.2	24.4	38.5	23.2	17.1	15.7
Total Current	35.7	38.6	38.1	22.9	40.0	59.4	42.2	36.4	32.0
Long-Term Debt	38.9	38.5	37.9	69.0	49.8	31.2	34.9	28.6	36.8
Deferred Taxes	.1	.0	.1	.0	.0	.5	.1	.0	.1
All Other Non-Current	7.5	7.9	7.1	6.9	5.8	7.5	6.5	7.0	8.5
Net Worth	17.8	15.0	16.8	1.3	4.3	1.4	16.3	28.0	22.6
Total Liabilities & Net Worth	100.0	100.0	100.0	100.0	100.0	100.0	100.0	100.0	100.0
INCOME DATA									
Net Sales	100.0	100.0	100.0	100.0	100.0	100.0	100.0	100.0	100.0
Gross Profit									
Operating Expenses	88.2	88.1	88.4	50.6	81.1	93.7	92.8	93.8	94.4
Operating Profit	11.8	11.9	11.6	49.4	18.9	6.3	7.2	6.2	5.6
All Other Expenses (net)	4.8	4.7	3.9	21.0	7.4	2.9	1.9	1.3	.9
Profit Before Taxes	6.9	7.2	7.7	28.4	11.5	3.4	5.3	4.9	4.7
RATIOS									
	2.3	2.3	2.3	2.3	2.4	2.2	2.4	2.5	2.1
Current	1.3	1.3	1.4	.6	1.2	1.1	1.4	1.6	1.3
	.7	.7	.7	.2	.4	.6	.7	1.0	.9
	2.1	2.0	2.1	1.7	2.0	2.0	2.3	2.2	1.9
Quick	(1630) 1.1	1.1	1.2	.5	.9	1.0	1.3	1.4	1.2
	.6	.6	.6	.1	.4	.6	.6	.9	.8
	12 30.9	15 24.6	19 18.8	0 UND	0 UND	16 23.2	27 13.3	31 11.6	32 11.3
Sales/Receivables	31 11.7	33 10.9	36 10.1	0 UND	5 74.0	30 12.1	38 9.5	41 9.0	42 8.7
	45 8.2	48 7.6	50 7.3	0 UND	32 11.5	50 7.3	51 7.1	53 6.9	51 7.1
Cost of Sales/Inventory									
Cost of Sales/Payables									
	8.2	8.5	8.0	10.2	9.0	10.7	7.7	7.0	8.0
Sales/Working Capital	29.1	30.5	25.0	-10.9	42.8	61.2	21.5	15.9	25.1
	-19.1	-20.0	-20.5	-2.0	-8.8	-13.0	-22.1	-302.8	-35.7
	12.5	11.5	11.9	9.8	5.9	4.9	14.4	20.2	9.7
EBIT/Interest	(1272) 3.4	(1126) 3.3	(1093) 3.6	(51) 4.6	(100) 1.9	(81) 1.6	(279) 3.7	(326) 4.7	(256) 3.4
	1.4	1.1	1.3	2.4	.0	-.8	1.2	1.7	1.8
	7.9	5.1	5.5				4.0	6.2	8.0
Net Profit + Depr., Dep., Amort./Cur. Mat. L/T/D	(101) 3.8	(85) 2.8	(85) 2.8				(16) 2.4	(20) 3.5	(40) 2.4
	1.8	1.2	1.4				1.7	2.1	.7
	.6	.6	.6	2.2	.6	.6	.3	.5	.8
Fixed/Worth	2.5	2.6	2.3	23.8	4.8	3.0	1.6	1.3	2.6
	-8.8	-7.5	-8.5	-2.6	-2.9	-2.7	-9.4	43.5	NM
	1.1	1.1	.9	2.9	.8	1.3	.7	.8	1.4
Debt/Worth	4.0	4.4	4.0	30.2	7.1	6.5	3.4	2.4	4.2
	-14.9	-12.7	-14.0	-3.9	-4.7	-6.5	-15.2	123.6	-123.1
	76.6	70.9	59.7	65.2	79.0	67.1	51.1	63.4	57.9
% Profit Before Taxes/Tangible Net Worth	(1120) 29.5	(1036) 26.4	(1028) 24.5	(69) 35.1	(108) 29.1	(74) 23.8	(265) 24.0	(306) 25.4	(206) 18.3
	7.0	5.7	5.4	16.3	3.9	2.7	6.7	4.7	5.8
	17.9	17.2	15.4	12.2	18.1	15.2	18.1	18.9	11.5
% Profit Before Taxes/Total Assets	6.2	5.6	6.2	5.0	4.9	3.9	7.4	7.4	5.0
	1.0	.6	.8	1.7	-.8	-1.7	.6	1.3	1.8
	20.6	23.1	23.0	1.2	19.1	36.3	35.9	25.1	16.1
Sales/Net Fixed Assets	3.6	3.9	4.1	.2	2.3	10.5	9.0	4.8	3.6
	1.1	1.1	1.2	.2	.5	1.4	2.0	1.8	1.5
	3.4	3.6	3.4	.5	2.9	4.9	3.6	3.5	2.9
Sales/Total Assets	1.5	1.5	1.6	.2	1.0	2.3	2.0	1.8	1.6
	.7	.7	.7	.1	.4	.9	1.1	.9	.8
	1.1	.9	.9	10.8	1.2	.5	.6	.9	1.1
% Depr., Dep., Amort./Sales	(1472) 2.7	(1351) 2.5	(1326) 2.5	(107) 21.2	(146) 4.4	(99) 1.7	(333) 1.7	(384) 2.3	(257) 2.4
	6.0	5.8	5.5	29.7	12.2	4.6	4.0	4.3	4.1
	1.8	1.6	2.0	4.1	1.1	2.2	1.4	1.9	1.5
% Officers', Directors' Owners' Comp/Sales	(202) 4.3	(177) 4.2	(159) 4.0	(14) 7.2	(20) 2.5	(13) 3.3	(34) 2.5	(50) 4.9	(28) 4.4
	8.9	8.5	8.2	19.0	4.8	9.5	5.0	11.5	5.8
Net Sales ($)	41973015M	39079556M	38350497M	76467M	321940M	472618M	2761850M	6145600M	28572022M
Total Assets ($)	31874926M	29143347M	29086903M	437160M	704335M	401342M	2386116M	5808977M	19348973M

M = $ thousand MM = $ million

See Pages 9 through 22 for Explanation of Ratios and Data

	Current Data Sorted by Assets						Comparative Historical Data	
Type of Statement								
Unqualified	1	11	44	39	12	7	108	126
Reviewed		1	1				2	3
Compiled		1					3	4
Tax Returns	6	6	5	1			4	10
Other	2	3	26	15	2		53	40
		121 (4/1-9/30/13)		62 (10/1/13-3/31/14)			4/1/09-3/31/10 ALL	4/1/10-3/31/11 ALL
	0-500M	500M-2MM	2-10MM	10-50MM	50-100MM	100-250MM		
NUMBER OF STATEMENTS	9	22	76	55	14	7	170	183
ASSETS	%	%	%	%	%	%	%	%
Cash & Equivalents		15.4	17.5	15.8	12.5		16.1	17.3
Trade Receivables (net)		24.8	15.2	13.3	17.5		20.4	18.0
Inventory		.3	.2	.7	.4		.2	.2
All Other Current		4.0	1.6	3.2	4.2		4.0	2.8
Total Current		44.5	34.5	33.0	34.6		40.7	38.3
Fixed Assets (net)		40.5	52.7	55.4	44.5		48.1	48.3
Intangibles (net)		7.6	2.0	1.2	6.1		1.9	3.4
All Other Non-Current		7.5	10.8	10.4	14.9		9.2	9.9
Total		100.0	100.0	100.0	100.0		100.0	100.0
LIABILITIES								
Notes Payable-Short Term		3.6	2.2	2.3	4.3		4.3	3.3
Cur. Mat.-L.T.D.		3.8	2.9	2.7	2.1		3.2	3.3
Trade Payables		6.5	4.4	3.9	5.3		6.4	7.1
Income Taxes Payable		.0	.0	.0	.2		.1	.2
All Other Current		12.9	13.3	11.1	16.1		13.3	13.1
Total Current		26.7	22.9	20.0	28.0		27.3	27.1
Long-Term Debt		23.9	27.4	31.5	27.3		30.0	32.5
Deferred Taxes		.3	.2	.0	.2		.1	.1
All Other Non-Current		10.0	1.9	3.4	6.0		4.0	4.2
Net Worth		39.0	47.7	45.1	38.5		38.7	36.0
Total Liabilties & Net Worth		100.0	100.0	100.0	100.0		100.0	100.0
INCOME DATA								
Net Sales		100.0	100.0	100.0	100.0		100.0	100.0
Gross Profit								
Operating Expenses		87.1	95.8	96.3	96.6		94.5	93.3
Operating Profit		12.9	4.2	3.7	3.4		5.5	6.7
All Other Expenses (net)		4.3	1.2	1.0	2.7		2.8	2.5
Profit Before Taxes		8.5	3.0	2.7	.7		2.7	4.1
RATIOS								
		2.7	2.7	2.5	1.6		2.7	2.5
Current		2.2	1.4	1.7	1.1		1.4	1.5
		.9	.9	1.1	.8		1.0	.9
		2.6	2.7	2.1	1.6		2.6	2.4
Quick		1.6	1.3	1.5	1.1		1.3	1.4
		.7	.8	.9	.7		.8	.9
		0 UND	**17** 21.8	**25** 14.8	**32** 11.3		**20** 18.4	**23** 16.1
Sales/Receivables		**25** 14.4	**27** 13.5	**36** 10.2	**39** 9.4		**34** 10.6	**32** 11.4
		47 7.7	**35** 10.3	**42** 8.6	**47** 7.7		**51** 7.2	**41** 8.8
Cost of Sales/Inventory								
Cost of Sales/Payables								
		6.3	8.0	6.5	10.3		6.5	5.9
Sales/Working Capital		10.9	22.5	15.4	66.8		17.2	17.1
		-757.5	-53.1	90.2	-33.8		-401.7	-97.3
		12.6	6.6	3.9	3.7		5.2	5.5
EBIT/Interest		(18) 2.9	(63) 2.8	(50) 2.1	(13) 2.3		(140) 2.3	(156) 2.9
		.6	.8	1.0	.4		.8	1.6
								2.0
Net Profit + Depr., Dep., Amort./Cur. Mat. L/T/D								(12) 1.2
								.3
		.5	.7	.8	.9		.7	.7
Fixed/Worth		.9	1.2	1.2	1.2		1.2	1.3
		2.9	2.1	2.3	2.3		2.7	2.5
		.9	.5	.6	1.1		.7	.6
Debt/Worth		1.7	1.1	1.3	1.7		1.5	1.6
		6.1	2.5	2.4	4.9		4.3	4.5
		36.4	14.4	12.0	10.2		21.2	19.4
% Profit Before Taxes/Tangible Net Worth		(20) 11.0	(73) 4.8	(54) 3.8	(12) 3.5		(161) 8.3	(171) 10.1
		.0	-1.8	.2	-1.3		.7	3.4
		13.6	7.1	5.8	4.2		7.8	7.0
% Profit Before Taxes/Total Assets		3.9	2.8	2.0	1.2		2.6	3.2
		.0	-1.3	.1	-.5		-.2	.8
		24.6	7.4	4.1	6.6		7.9	6.1
Sales/Net Fixed Assets		10.7	3.1	2.4	3.4		3.4	3.1
		1.1	1.8	1.5	2.8		2.0	1.8
		4.7	2.6	1.7	2.1		2.5	2.2
Sales/Total Assets		2.9	1.6	1.3	1.4		1.7	1.5
		.8	.9	1.0	1.2		1.2	1.1
		1.3	1.4	2.0	1.4		1.6	1.7
% Depr., Dep., Amort./Sales		(19) 2.3	(72) 2.4	(53) 2.8	2.1		(156) 2.4	(173) 2.4
		6.3	3.9	3.9	3.2		3.4	3.6
			1.2				1.2	1.5
% Officers', Directors' Owners' Comp/Sales			(11) 2.3				(23) 2.7	(26) 3.9
			5.4				4.6	8.1
Net Sales ($)	14230M	94240M	762523M	1549895M	1523102M	1023559M	5064276M	5308052M
Total Assets ($)	2386M	30581M	424975M	1144499M	996837M	1021483M	3487884M	4073645M

M = $ thousand MM = $ million

See Pages 9 through 22 for Explanation of Ratios and Data

Comparative Historical Data				Current Data Sorted by Sales					
			Type of Statement						
134	98	114	Unqualified	4	6	10	24	34	36
4	4	2	Reviewed				2		
4	3	1	Compiled			1			
7	7	18	Tax Returns	6	4	1	4	3	
59	37	48	Other	2	5	3	8	22	8
4/1/11-3/31/12 ALL	**4/1/12-3/31/13 ALL**	**4/1/13-3/31/14 ALL**		**121 (4/1-9/30/13)**			**62 (10/1/13-3/31/14)**		
				0-1MM	**1-3MM**	**3-5MM**	**5-10MM**	**10-25MM**	**25MM & OVER**
208	149	183	**NUMBER OF STATEMENTS**	12	15	15	38	59	44
%	%	%	**ASSETS**	%	%	%	%	%	%
18.4	18.8	16.6	Cash & Equivalents	13.1	29.7	15.5	15.5	17.4	13.3
16.2	15.0	16.6	Trade Receivables (net)	12.5	12.0	20.5	12.5	18.0	19.6
.2	.4	.4	Inventory	.2	.1	.0	.7	.3	.4
4.6	2.5	2.5	All Other Current	5.8	1.3	1.3	2.8	1.9	3.1
39.4	36.8	36.1	Total Current	31.5	43.0	37.4	31.6	37.6	36.3
49.1	52.0	50.2	Fixed Assets (net)	59.2	51.0	53.5	49.4	50.1	47.2
2.7	2.4	2.7	Intangibles (net)	.3	.3	.3	3.3	3.7	3.0
8.9	8.7	11.0	All Other Non-Current	9.0	5.6	8.8	15.6	8.5	13.5
100.0	100.0	100.0	Total	100.0	100.0	100.0	100.0	100.0	100.0
			LIABILITIES						
3.3	4.0	3.0	Notes Payable-Short Term	.0	3.9	3.0	2.4	2.0	5.3
3.0	2.5	2.8	Cur. Mat.-L.T.D.	1.7	2.6	2.1	3.0	3.3	2.6
5.4	4.6	5.3	Trade Payables	8.0	4.2	5.2	4.1	4.7	6.7
.2	.0	.0	Income Taxes Payable	.0	.0	.0	.0	.1	.1
14.3	16.4	13.5	All Other Current	11.2	19.6	7.8	10.1	14.4	15.7
26.2	27.5	24.6	Total Current	20.8	30.3	18.0	19.6	24.5	30.3
30.0	30.4	28.3	Long-Term Debt	37.1	30.7	26.0	25.8	30.3	25.4
.1	.1	.1	Deferred Taxes	.0	.2	.0	.2	.2	.1
3.4	6.5	4.0	All Other Non-Current	6.7	3.5	2.4	3.7	2.9	5.8
40.3	35.5	42.9	Net Worth	35.3	35.3	53.6	50.6	42.1	38.4
100.0	100.0	100.0	Total Liabilties & Net Worth	100.0	100.0	100.0	100.0	100.0	100.0
			INCOME DATA						
100.0	100.0	100.0	Net Sales	100.0	100.0	100.0	100.0	100.0	100.0
			Gross Profit						
94.1	94.4	95.0	Operating Expenses	68.6	100.8	93.3	95.6	96.8	98.1
5.9	5.6	5.0	Operating Profit	31.4	-.8	6.7	4.4	3.2	1.9
1.7	2.3	1.6	All Other Expenses (net)	11.4	2.8	.4	1.8	.4	.3
4.1	3.4	3.4	Profit Before Taxes	19.9	-3.5	6.3	2.6	2.8	1.6
			RATIOS						
2.7	3.0	2.3		5.3	2.7	3.3	4.1	2.2	1.8
1.8	1.5	1.4	Current	1.4	1.4	2.3	1.4	1.6	1.1
1.0	1.0	.9		.5	1.1	.9	.9	1.0	.9
2.3	2.5	2.2		2.8	2.7	3.2	3.6	2.0	1.7
1.5	1.4	1.4	Quick	.8	1.4	2.2	1.3	1.5	1.0
.9	.9	.8		.5	1.1	.9	.7	1.0	.8
17 21.6	14 25.2	18 20.8		0 UND	0 UND	17 21.1	13 27.7	24 15.4	33 10.9
31 11.7	30 12.2	31 11.6	Sales/Receivables	0 UND	18 19.9	28 13.2	21 17.8	34 10.7	39 9.4
38 9.6	40 9.1	39 9.4		30 12.3	33 11.0	39 9.4	32 11.4	39 9.4	47 7.8
			Cost of Sales/Inventory						
			Cost of Sales/Payables						
5.8	5.4	7.5		1.2	6.8	8.9	5.4	8.0	11.8
13.4	14.8	23.2	Sales/Working Capital	NM	100.0	12.4	19.6	15.5	78.1
193.8	-221.1	-50.9		-10.4	204.4	-51.8	-103.2	-423.5	-41.5
6.4	6.9	5.0				11.3	4.5	6.0	3.9
(173) 2.9	(127) 2.4	(155) 2.5	EBIT/Interest			(13) 2.7	(33) 2.1	(50) 3.1	(43) 2.3
1.3	1.1	.8				.7	.8	.8	.9
4.1		3.6							
(21) 2.7		(12) 2.6	Net Profit + Depr., Dep., Amort./Cur. Mat. L/T/D						
1.3		1.3							
.7	.7	.7		1.2	.4	.5	.6	.7	.9
1.2	1.1	1.2	Fixed/Worth	2.1	.9	1.0	1.0	1.5	1.3
2.7	2.6	2.3		12.0	4.6	1.8	1.9	2.5	2.3
.6	.5	.6		.8	.4	.4	.4	.6	1.0
1.5	1.3	1.4	Debt/Worth	2.2	1.4	1.0	.8	1.6	2.0
3.4	3.1	2.9		11.7	4.6	1.7	2.9	2.7	3.6
21.2	13.1	15.2		12.7	52.7	24.5	7.3	18.0	13.0
(187) 7.9	(135) 5.4	(173) 4.8	% Profit Before Taxes/Tangible Net Worth	(11) 10.7	(13) 10.9	9.4	(36) 3.6	(55) 4.2	(43) 5.2
2.3	.3	-.5		2.9	-26.5	-2.0	.5	-1.0	-.4
10.1	5.7	6.3		5.4	19.8	13.6	4.6	7.2	4.4
3.3	2.3	2.3	% Profit Before Taxes/Total Assets	3.2	2.9	3.8	2.3	1.8	1.9
.5	.0	-.3		.2	-14.8	-.7	.0	-.3	-.2
7.1	5.4	8.1		12.6	35.9	13.0	9.6	7.5	5.5
3.0	2.7	3.1	Sales/Net Fixed Assets	.2	8.6	2.2	2.7	3.2	3.4
1.7	1.4	1.7		.1	1.8	.9	1.6	1.8	2.6
2.5	2.1	2.5		.8	7.5	3.6	2.4	2.7	2.3
1.5	1.4	1.5	Sales/Total Assets	.2	3.0	1.4	1.2	1.8	1.7
1.0	.8	1.0		.1	.7	.8	.9	1.2	1.3
1.5	1.7	1.6		6.0	.5	1.5	2.1	1.4	1.5
(192) 2.6	(141) 3.0	(173) 2.4	% Depr., Dep., Amort./Sales	(10) 18.3	(13) 2.2	(14) 2.6	(34) 2.9	(58) 2.2	2.2
3.8	4.2	3.8		38.4	4.0	4.2	3.8	3.6	3.0
1.8	1.5	1.7							
(17) 2.7	(13) 4.7	(24) 4.3	% Officers', Directors' Owners' Comp/Sales						
5.2	8.2	7.9							
5510782M	3572548M	4967549M	Net Sales ($)	6875M	31482M	54566M	278616M	945365M	3650645M
4191193M	2478876M	3620761M	Total Assets ($)	28804M	28965M	45416M	339622M	895564M	2282390M

M = $ thousand MM = $ million

See Pages 9 through 22 for Explanation of Ratios and Data

Current Data Sorted by Assets | **Comparative Historical Data**

	0-500M	500M-2MM	2-10MM	10-50MM	50-100MM	100-250MM	4/1/09-3/31/10 ALL	4/1/10-3/31/11 ALL
Type of Statement								
Unqualified	1	15	53	58	6	1	150	161
Reviewed		1	3	2			2	3
Compiled	3	3	1	1			4	8
Tax Returns	7	4	1	3			12	13
Other	3	7	30	27	10	1	87	83
	149 (4/1-9/30/13)			92 (10/1/13-3/31/14)				
NUMBER OF STATEMENTS	14	30	88	91	16	2	255	268
ASSETS	%	%	%	%	%	%	%	%
Cash & Equivalents	32.4	28.9	20.8	14.0	12.0		15.7	18.8
Trade Receivables (net)	26.8	18.2	18.4	13.6	13.5		15.7	15.8
Inventory	.0	.1	.1	.5	.0		.1	.1
All Other Current	1.4	3.6	2.6	2.4	1.9		2.7	3.0
Total Current	60.6	50.9	41.9	30.6	27.4		34.3	37.7
Fixed Assets (net)	33.4	40.6	50.1	55.8	39.4		53.2	51.5
Intangibles (net)	.2	1.9	.9	1.6	19.8		1.9	1.6
All Other Non-Current	5.8	6.6	7.1	12.1	13.4		10.6	9.2
Total	100.0	100.0	100.0	100.0	100.0		100.0	100.0
LIABILITIES								
Notes Payable-Short Term	5.9	3.4	3.4	2.6	2.4		2.8	2.6
Cur. Mat.-L.T.D.	3.7	2.1	2.1	2.7	4.0		5.1	2.8
Trade Payables	9.9	4.0	4.4	4.2	5.8		5.1	5.1
Income Taxes Payable	1.8	.0	.0	.0	.1		.1	.1
All Other Current	48.3	12.9	10.9	9.2	8.2		13.3	12.4
Total Current	69.5	22.4	20.7	18.6	20.4		26.4	23.0
Long-Term Debt	24.4	25.0	26.7	29.3	49.5		31.3	29.4
Deferred Taxes	.0	.0	.1	.0	.4		.0	.1
All Other Non-Current	11.5	9.6	5.2	5.3	2.6		5.9	4.5
Net Worth	-5.6	43.1	47.2	46.8	27.0		36.4	43.0
Total Liabilties & Net Worth	100.0	100.0	100.0	100.0	100.0		100.0	100.0
INCOME DATA								
Net Sales	100.0	100.0	100.0	100.0	100.0		100.0	100.0
Gross Profit								
Operating Expenses	93.4	92.8	91.4	96.6	94.3		95.3	95.4
Operating Profit	6.6	7.2	8.6	3.4	5.7		4.7	4.6
All Other Expenses (net)	4.6	1.2	2.3	.6	1.9		2.5	1.3
Profit Before Taxes	1.9	6.0	6.3	2.8	3.7		2.2	3.3
RATIOS								
Current	17.3	5.9	4.2	3.1	2.0		2.8	2.9
	2.3	2.8	2.4	1.9	1.5		1.6	1.7
	.5	1.3	1.3	1.0	.9		1.0	1.1
Quick	17.3	5.8	3.9	2.8	1.8		2.5	2.7
	2.3	2.5	2.2	1.6	1.4		1.4	1.6
	.4	.9	1.2	.9	.8		.8	1.0
Sales/Receivables	**0** UND	**1** 560.8	**20** 18.7	**21** 17.4	**39** 9.4		**13** 27.8	**13** 28.7
	10 37.1	**14** 26.6	**31** 11.7	**32** 11.3	**46** 8.0		**33** 10.9	**34** 10.9
	34 10.6	**42** 8.6	**45** 8.1	**49** 7.5	**59** 6.2		**50** 7.3	**47** 7.7
Cost of Sales/Inventory								
Cost of Sales/Payables								
Sales/Working Capital	7.2	4.7	4.5	4.8	5.0		6.6	5.7
	13.3	10.3	8.5	12.0	10.4		15.0	11.3
	-8.0	282.5	28.5	373.5	NM		999.8	56.2
EBIT/Interest		6.1	10.3	6.0	5.0		5.1	7.6
		(16) 2.3	(73) 2.1	(82) 1.4	(14) 1.4		(205) 1.8	(231) 2.4
		-.2	-1.2	-.9	.3		.2	1.0
Net Profit + Depr., Dep., Amort./Cur. Mat. L/T/D								
Fixed/Worth	.1	.1	.6	.7	1.0		.8	.7
	.9	.7	1.1	1.1	2.4		1.4	1.2
	-.9	4.2	2.1	2.2	-.8		2.9	2.4
Debt/Worth	.3	.2	.4	.4	.9		.7	.6
	1.0	1.1	.9	1.0	4.4		1.4	1.2
	-3.0	10.8	2.4	1.9	-2.8		3.9	2.7
% Profit Before Taxes/Tangible Net Worth	115.8	54.8	19.9	9.4	12.2		18.8	20.2
	(10) 45.2	(25) 5.6	(81) 5.5	(82) 2.2	(11) .7		(228) 6.7	(249) 7.1
	-38.9	-6.9	-2.4	-3.2	-9.1		-1.3	.5
% Profit Before Taxes/Total Assets	72.4	44.0	11.7	5.2	4.3		6.6	8.3
	7.7	4.9	2.5	1.6	1.8		2.0	2.7
	-21.6	-2.4	-1.9	-2.0	-1.7		-.9	.0
Sales/Net Fixed Assets	UND	52.9	7.9	3.3	3.9		6.0	6.2
	25.9	11.0	3.0	2.1	2.4		2.6	2.7
	2.8	1.6	1.6	1.3	1.9		1.5	1.4
Sales/Total Assets	9.5	3.9	2.6	1.9	1.4		2.2	2.2
	4.6	2.5	1.6	1.2	1.0		1.4	1.4
	1.3	1.1	1.0	.8	.5		.9	.8
% Depr., Dep., Amort./Sales		.8	1.3	2.1	2.3		1.7	1.7
		(21) 1.5	(83) 2.4	(88) 3.0	3.0		(232) 2.8	(243) 2.7
		4.3	3.9	4.3	4.9		4.3	4.2
% Officers', Directors' Owners' Comp/Sales			2.0				3.9	2.3
			(12) 4.5				(27) 8.1	(33) 6.9
			6.8				11.3	10.4
Net Sales ($)	**12673M**	**104270M**	**855942M**	**2401715M**	**1281685M**	**144246M**	**4977347M**	**5560151M**
Total Assets ($)	**3110M**	**34905M**	**465943M**	**1866050M**	**1182973M**	**265764M**	**4375838M**	**4932760M**

M = $ thousand MM = $ million

See Pages 9 through 22 for Explanation of Ratios and Data

Comparative Historical Data				Current Data Sorted by Sales					
			Type of Statement						
174	151	134	Unqualified	7	12	13	27	43	32
7	3	6	Reviewed				4	1	1
15	5	8	Compiled	3	3		1		1
11	12	15	Tax Returns	4	4	1	2	2	2
64	72	78	Other	7	5	5	15	20	26
4/1/11-3/31/12	**4/1/12-3/31/13**	**4/1/13-3/31/14**		**149 (4/1-9/30/13)**			**92 (10/1/13-3/31/14)**		
ALL	**ALL**	**ALL**		**0-1MM**	**1-3MM**	**3-5MM**	**5-10MM**	**10-25MM**	**25MM & OVER**
271	243	241	**NUMBER OF STATEMENTS**	21	24	19	49	66	62
%	%	%	**ASSETS**	%	%	%	%	%	%
16.0	17.0	19.2	Cash & Equivalents	20.9	25.9	31.6	19.8	18.5	12.6
15.6	13.5	16.7	Trade Receivables (net)	16.7	8.1	16.4	18.2	16.7	18.9
.1	.4	.2	Inventory	.0	.0	.2	.1	.2	.6
3.1	4.0	2.5	All Other Current	1.1	3.8	1.1	2.6	2.5	3.0
34.7	34.9	38.7	Total Current	38.7	37.7	49.3	40.8	37.9	35.1
56.1	54.2	49.3	Fixed Assets (net)	55.0	55.6	43.7	48.7	49.4	47.1
1.1	2.0	2.5	Intangibles (net)	.9	.2	1.5	1.1	2.7	5.3
8.1	8.9	9.4	All Other Non-Current	5.4	6.5	5.5	9.4	10.1	12.5
100.0	100.0	100.0	Total	100.0	100.0	100.0	100.0	100.0	100.0
			LIABILITIES						
2.7	3.4	3.2	Notes Payable-Short Term	6.0	5.3	1.5	2.6	2.0	3.7
2.6	2.8	2.6	Cur. Mat.-L.T.D.	3.7	1.8	1.6	1.9	2.1	3.8
5.6	5.1	4.7	Trade Payables	6.7	2.6	2.6	3.7	4.9	6.0
.1	.0	.1	Income Taxes Payable	.0	1.0	.0	.0	.0	.0
12.8	12.5	12.4	All Other Current	28.6	9.7	9.3	11.6	10.0	12.2
23.8	23.8	23.0	Total Current	45.0	20.4	15.1	19.8	19.0	25.7
34.1	29.6	29.1	Long-Term Debt	31.6	38.2	25.5	22.5	28.9	31.2
.1	.1	.1	Deferred Taxes	.0	.0	.0	.1	.0	.2
5.8	5.9	5.9	All Other Non-Current	2.1	8.6	13.2	1.7	7.0	6.2
36.3	40.6	41.9	Net Worth	21.3	32.7	46.2	55.9	45.1	36.7
100.0	100.0	100.0	Total Liabilties & Net Worth	100.0	100.0	100.0	100.0	100.0	100.0
			INCOME DATA						
100.0	100.0	100.0	Net Sales	100.0	100.0	100.0	100.0	100.0	100.0
			Gross Profit						
95.1	93.8	93.8	Operating Expenses	71.0	92.6	95.4	97.3	97.3	95.1
4.9	6.2	6.2	Operating Profit	29.0	7.4	4.6	2.7	2.7	4.9
2.3	2.0	1.6	All Other Expenses (net)	14.8	1.6	1.2	-.5	.2	.4
2.7	4.1	4.6	Profit Before Taxes	14.2	5.8	3.4	3.1	2.6	4.5
			RATIOS						
3.0	3.2	3.8		6.6	8.3	5.6	4.0	3.4	2.2
1.6	1.7	2.0	Current	2.2	3.0	3.9	2.6	2.0	1.5
1.0	1.0	1.1		.4	1.4	1.6	1.2	1.2	.9
2.7	2.9	3.4		6.6	8.3	5.6	3.9	3.0	1.9
1.5	1.5	1.8	Quick	1.5	2.6	3.7	2.1	2.0	1.4
1.0	.9	1.0		.3	1.1	1.4	1.2	1.1	.9
13 27.7	**12** 29.8	**16** 22.2		**0** UND	**0** UND	**19** 19.2	**24** 15.1	**21** 17.2	**27** 13.4
31 11.8	**29** 12.5	**31** 11.6	Sales/Receivables	**5** 72.8	**13** 27.2	**31** 11.9	**32** 11.4	**32** 11.4	**39** 9.4
47 7.7	**42** 8.6	**48** 7.6		**29** 12.8	**26** 14.1	**42** 8.6	**53** 6.9	**53** 6.9	**50** 7.3
			Cost of Sales/Inventory						
			Cost of Sales/Payables						
5.4	5.0	4.9		3.2	4.6	4.3	4.1	5.2	8.0
13.1	13.3	10.2	Sales/Working Capital	9.6	9.5	5.1	7.9	10.3	16.3
507.4	999.8	58.6		-4.1	30.7	26.9	30.5	44.5	-119.4
6.3	5.3	6.7		12.2	7.8	6.0	6.6	7.8	7.4
(229) 2.5	(200) 2.3	(196) 2.0	EBIT/Interest	(12) 3.0	(17) 1.7	(12) -.1	(40) 1.8	(58) 2.2	(57) 2.0
.4	.1	-.5		-2.5	.0	-1.6	-1.9	-.3	.0
		9.5							
		(10) 1.5	Net Profit + Depr., Dep., Amort./Cur. Mat. L/T/D						
		-1.8							
.8	.7	.6		.4	.7	.2	.6	.6	.8
1.4	1.3	1.1	Fixed/Worth	2.1	1.2	.7	.9	1.2	1.3
2.9	2.8	2.3		14.0	10.1	2.2	1.2	2.2	2.9
.6	.5	.4		.3	.4	.3	.3	.5	.6
1.4	1.2	1.0	Debt/Worth	1.4	1.1	.7	.7	1.1	1.3
3.6	3.3	3.1		17.6	12.7	2.4	1.4	2.6	3.9
20.1	17.4	18.1		58.6	45.3	22.2	9.3	17.3	17.1
(242) 6.3	(215) 5.1	(211) 4.2	% Profit Before Taxes/Tangible Net Worth	(18) 5.8	(19) 9.9	(16) 2.4	(46) 3.4	(59) 3.9	(53) 5.3
-2.6	-1.2	-3.6		-6.3	-6.4	-6.8	-2.5	-1.1	-3.3
8.1	7.5	8.1		8.5	18.1	16.7	6.1	6.6	8.8
2.6	2.3	2.4	% Profit Before Taxes/Total Assets	1.3	2.9	2.4	2.5	1.6	2.6
-1.6	-1.3	-2.0		-8.3	-2.3	-3.3	-1.5	-1.8	-1.7
5.3	5.9	7.1		84.1	23.2	25.0	6.7	6.7	6.1
2.3	2.3	2.7	Sales/Net Fixed Assets	1.3	2.1	4.4	2.4	2.5	3.0
1.2	1.3	1.5		.2	.9	1.3	1.1	1.6	2.1
2.2	2.1	2.5		2.4	3.6	2.7	2.3	2.4	2.2
1.3	1.3	1.4	Sales/Total Assets	.6	1.5	1.7	1.3	1.5	1.6
.8	.8	.9		.1	.7	1.1	.7	.9	1.1
1.7	1.7	1.7		4.1	1.4	1.1	1.2	1.8	1.8
(254) 2.8	(219) 2.9	(219) 2.9	% Depr., Dep., Amort./Sales	(16) 10.7	(18) 3.2	(16) 3.0	(45) 3.4	(63) 2.6	(61) 2.6
4.7	4.8	4.3		24.1	5.9	3.8	5.5	3.7	3.2
1.5	2.5	1.8							
(31) 6.0	(26) 6.6	(31) 5.6	% Officers', Directors' Owners' Comp/Sales						
10.9	12.3	10.4							
5258711M	**4356730M**	**4800531M**	Net Sales ($)	**10813M**	**49173M**	**75860M**	**358440M**	**1092598M**	**3213647M**
4677595M	**3670025M**	**3818745M**	Total Assets ($)	**47292M**	**45557M**	**60005M**	**363083M**	**1018019M**	**2284789M**

M = $ thousand MM = $ million

See Pages 9 through 22 for Explanation of Ratios and Data

	Current Data Sorted by Assets						Comparative Historical Data	
Type of Statement								
Unqualified	1	17	34	89	54	64	234	245
Reviewed	1	5	9	7			32	36
Compiled	6	6	5	1	1	2	24	23
Tax Returns	29	10	11	1			31	36
Other	17	30	34	55	45	24	174	197
	153 (4/1-9/30/13)			405 (10/1/13-3/31/14)			4/1/09-3/31/10	4/1/10-3/31/11
	0-500M	500M-2MM	2-10MM	10-50MM	50-100MM	100-250MM	ALL	ALL
NUMBER OF STATEMENTS	54	68	93	153	100	90	495	537
ASSETS	%	%	%	%	%	%	%	%
Cash & Equivalents	39.8	13.1	12.4	12.0	12.1	12.4	10.9	10.8
Trade Receivables (net)	7.2	14.1	11.2	4.5	3.0	3.1	9.5	7.9
Inventory	.7	.1	.8	.2	.1	.1	.2	.5
All Other Current	2.2	3.6	1.9	1.8	1.5	1.2	3.0	2.1
Total Current	49.9	30.9	26.2	18.5	16.6	16.9	23.7	21.3
Fixed Assets (net)	30.2	48.8	62.7	62.1	62.4	60.8	57.9	61.9
Intangibles (net)	7.6	6.9	3.7	3.5	1.9	2.0	3.0	2.9
All Other Non-Current	12.4	13.4	7.4	15.8	19.1	20.3	15.5	13.9
Total	100.0	100.0	100.0	100.0	100.0	100.0	100.0	100.0
LIABILITIES								
Notes Payable-Short Term	16.0	3.7	2.7	1.9	.4	.4	4.2	2.3
Cur. Mat.-L.T.D.	2.1	2.1	3.3	3.1	1.6	1.6	4.0	3.3
Trade Payables	18.6	5.9	5.1	2.7	1.7	2.2	4.9	4.4
Income Taxes Payable	.0	.0	.0	.0	.0	.0	.1	.1
All Other Current	36.8	21.2	12.1	10.5	7.3	4.8	12.8	12.8
Total Current	73.4	32.9	23.3	18.2	11.0	9.0	26.0	23.0
Long-Term Debt	23.1	42.6	57.3	40.7	48.0	42.0	49.5	52.9
Deferred Taxes	.0	.0	.1	.1	.1	.1	.5	.2
All Other Non-Current	9.5	5.9	4.3	16.0	29.6	38.4	18.1	16.7
Net Worth	-6.1	18.6	15.0	24.9	11.2	10.4	6.0	7.2
Total Liabilities & Net Worth	100.0	100.0	100.0	100.0	100.0	100.0	100.0	100.0
INCOME DATA								
Net Sales	100.0	100.0	100.0	100.0	100.0	100.0	100.0	100.0
Gross Profit								
Operating Expenses	90.7	87.3	83.6	93.4	95.0	93.0	91.9	90.2
Operating Profit	9.3	12.7	16.4	6.6	5.0	7.0	8.1	9.8
All Other Expenses (net)	2.5	3.6	9.4	1.2	1.2	4.7	5.9	7.0
Profit Before Taxes	6.8	9.0	7.0	5.4	3.8	2.3	2.2	2.8
RATIOS								
Current	1.7	1.8	2.1	3.3	3.4	3.4	2.5	2.4
	.8	.9	1.1	1.4	1.6	1.7	1.3	1.2
	.3	.4	.4	.7	.8	1.0	.6	.6
Quick	1.8	1.6	1.9	2.8	2.9	3.4	2.0	2.1
	(52) .8	.7	.9	1.3	1.4	1.6	1.1	1.0
	.3	.3	.3	.6	.7	.8	.5	.5
Sales/Receivables	**0** UND	**0** UND	**0** UND	**6** 65.8	**14** 26.7	**12** 30.2	**5** 74.0	**4** 99.1
	0 UND	**5** 80.1	**4** 84.9	**23** 16.0	**23** 15.8	**21** 17.2	**19** 18.9	**16** 22.8
	5 70.8	**27** 13.6	**32** 11.4	**34** 10.7	**35** 10.3	**30** 12.1	**34** 10.7	**32** 11.6
Cost of Sales/Inventory								
Cost of Sales/Payables								
Sales/Working Capital	26.5	16.7	7.4	3.7	2.6	2.0	6.1	5.9
	-148.9	-485.6	65.5	13.9	9.5	6.5	31.7	41.5
	-11.2	-13.1	-9.1	-19.7	-33.5	-195.3	-11.7	-11.7
EBIT/Interest	29.6	33.1	3.7	5.6	3.1	3.6	3.9	3.8
	(25) 7.0	(37) 8.3	(68) 1.8	(134) 2.3	(93) 1.8	(81) 2.0	(383) 1.5	(438) 1.6
	1.0	1.5	.7	.9	.9	.9	.5	.7
Net Profit + Depr., Dep., Amort./Cur. Mat. L/T/D							6.3	5.2
							(12) 2.7	(18) 2.3
							.8	.6
Fixed/Worth	.1	.5	.9	1.0	2.0	2.2	1.4	1.7
	1.6	2.0	6.4	2.4	6.2	5.1	5.7	7.2
	-.4	-2.6	-6.4	-24.8	-5.4	-9.1	-5.0	-5.2
Debt/Worth	.9	.7	1.1	.8	2.4	3.0	1.7	1.9
	13.1	3.7	9.0	3.1	8.2	6.2	8.0	9.7
	-2.5	-9.9	-8.0	-34.1	-9.7	-15.1	-7.5	-7.5
% Profit Before Taxes/Tangible Net Worth	237.8	78.0	32.5	17.6	17.6	16.0	36.8	35.3
	(30) 74.6	(46) 35.8	(56) 9.5	(113) 7.2	(64) 8.0	(58) 9.4	(302) 11.0	(324) 11.2
	3.6	6.2	-.4	2.2	2.6	2.6	-1.8	1.7
% Profit Before Taxes/Total Assets	70.9	25.6	8.1	5.6	3.3	3.2	7.8	5.8
	37.2	7.9	3.2	2.8	1.6	1.3	1.7	1.7
	-1.1	1.5	-.4	.0	-.4	-.6	-1.5	-1.0
Sales/Net Fixed Assets	259.2	33.8	4.4	1.3	.8	.7	3.7	2.4
	73.8	5.8	.8	.8	.5	.4	.8	.6
	10.7	.9	.4	.5	.4	.3	.4	.3
Sales/Total Assets	11.4	4.1	1.6	.7	.5	.4	1.5	1.2
	7.1	1.9	.7	.5	.3	.3	.5	.5
	4.0	.7	.3	.4	.3	.2	.3	.2
% Depr., Dep., Amort./Sales	.4	1.1	2.7	5.0	8.8	8.7	2.8	4.0
	(28) 1.0	(54) 3.3	(87) 6.4	(150) 8.0	(99) 11.3	(89) 13.8	(466) 7.2	(499) 9.2
	3.3	8.4	17.5	11.4	14.1	17.0	13.0	14.9
% Officers', Directors' Owners' Comp/Sales	4.3		2.1	3.9			2.6	2.4
	(11) 7.2		(11) 3.3	(12) 6.8			(54) 5.3	(69) 4.9
	23.9		9.1	19.3			11.9	9.6
Net Sales ($)	78354M	182902M	610206M	2222992M	3001427M	5179379M	8994926M	9725456M
Total Assets ($)	10715M	82258M	517129M	3938455M	7176284M	13720951M	17805355M	21219813M

M = $ thousand MM = $ million

See Pages 9 through 22 for Explanation of Ratios and Data

Comparative Historical Data				Current Data Sorted by Sales					
			Type of Statement						
233	191	259	Unqualified	8	17	16	27	110	81
28	30	22	Reviewed	4	6	4	7		1
30	14	21	Compiled		10	3	2	4	2
46	46	51	Tax Returns	27	18	6			
200	200	205	Other	22	23	18	29	67	46
4/1/11-3/31/12 ALL	**4/1/12-3/31/13 ALL**	**4/1/13-3/31/14 ALL**		**153 (4/1-9/30/13)**			**405 (10/1/13-3/31/14)**		
				0-1MM	**1-3MM**	**3-5MM**	**5-10MM**	**10-25MM**	**25MM & OVER**
537	481	558	**NUMBER OF STATEMENTS**	61	74	47	65	181	130
%	%	%	**ASSETS**	%	%	%	%	%	%
11.6	14.0	15.0	Cash & Equivalents	19.3	21.6	17.4	12.5	12.4	13.1
7.0	7.5	6.5	Trade Receivables (net)	2.5	6.7	6.8	12.8	6.3	5.5
.3	.3	.3	Inventory	.0	.1	.9	1.0	.2	.2
2.5	1.9	1.9	All Other Current	.9	2.4	2.4	1.9	2.0	1.9
21.4	23.6	23.8	Total Current	22.7	30.8	27.4	28.2	20.9	20.6
60.8	59.5	57.3	Fixed Assets (net)	60.1	54.6	51.9	54.9	59.6	57.5
3.6	2.6	3.8	Intangibles (net)	4.7	4.5	9.4	4.2	2.7	2.4
14.3	14.3	15.1	All Other Non-Current	12.4	10.1	11.3	12.6	16.9	19.4
100.0	100.0	100.0	Total	100.0	100.0	100.0	100.0	100.0	100.0
			LIABILITIES						
3.5	1.9	3.1	Notes Payable-Short Term	7.7	9.3	3.1	2.6	.7	1.1
4.2	3.5	2.4	Cur. Mat.-L.T.D.	2.8	2.7	2.4	2.7	2.2	2.2
4.4	5.5	4.8	Trade Payables	9.6	6.5	3.9	5.7	3.4	3.2
.0	.1	.0	Income Taxes Payable	.0	.0	.0	.0	.0	.0
12.3	12.7	13.1	All Other Current	19.0	16.8	20.8	16.1	9.1	9.6
24.3	23.7	23.4	Total Current	39.1	35.2	30.1	27.2	15.4	16.1
49.2	48.5	43.5	Long-Term Debt	49.4	55.0	42.9	40.1	38.7	42.9
.1	.1	.1	Deferred Taxes	.0	.0	.0	.0	.1	.2
17.8	19.2	18.3	All Other Non-Current	4.9	6.0	11.7	10.7	25.6	27.4
8.7	8.6	14.7	Net Worth	6.5	3.7	15.3	21.9	20.1	13.4
100.0	100.0	100.0	Total Liabilties & Net Worth	100.0	100.0	100.0	100.0	100.0	100.0
			INCOME DATA						
100.0	100.0	100.0	Net Sales	100.0	100.0	100.0	100.0	100.0	100.0
			Gross Profit						
89.6	88.3	91.0	Operating Expenses	77.1	87.2	92.0	92.7	94.0	94.3
10.4	11.7	9.0	Operating Profit	22.9	12.8	8.0	7.3	6.0	5.7
6.8	6.3	3.6	All Other Expenses (net)	14.0	4.0	4.1	1.5	1.9	1.5
3.6	5.4	5.4	Profit Before Taxes	9.0	8.8	3.9	5.7	4.1	4.2
			RATIOS						
2.0	2.3	2.7		1.5	1.9	2.3	2.4	3.6	2.7
1.1	1.3	1.3	Current	.4	.9	1.0	1.3	1.5	1.6
.5	.5	.7		.1	.4	.4	.7	.8	1.0
1.9	2.1	2.5		1.5	1.6	2.1	2.4	3.5	2.5
(534) 1.0	1.1	(556) 1.1	Quick	(60) .4	.8	.9	1.3	(180) 1.3	1.4
.4	.4	.5		.1	.3	.4	.6	.7	.9
3 136.8	**2** 178.2	**2** 164.0		**0** UND	**0** UND	**0** 999.8	**4** 103.7	**14** 26.9	**16** 22.7
16 23.5	**13** 27.2	**16** 22.3	Sales/Receivables	**0** UND	**2** 163.8	**2** 152.0	**18** 20.1	**25** 14.6	**25** 14.5
33 11.2	**31** 11.9	**30** 12.0		**3** 140.5	**7** 51.5	**9** 40.0	**38** 9.5	**37** 9.8	**34** 10.7
			Cost of Sales/Inventory						
			Cost of Sales/Payables						
6.7	6.6	4.7		22.6	15.4	7.7	5.5	2.8	3.0
65.6	33.3	24.5	Sales/Working Capital	-13.0	-129.5	-999.8	19.9	10.3	10.7
-10.5	-10.0	-17.0		-1.5	-14.7	-9.9	-19.8	-27.2	NM
4.2	5.3	5.0		2.8	28.3	7.1	4.3	4.7	4.0
(431) 1.8	(359) 2.0	(438) 2.1	EBIT/Interest	(19) 1.4	(55) 3.2	(35) 1.8	(52) 2.4	(154) 2.1	(123) 2.1
.6	.7	.9		.7	1.4	.2	.9	.7	1.1
4.0	7.1	15.2							
(11) 1.7	(13) 3.9	(13) 4.3	Net Profit + Depr., Dep., Amort./Cur. Mat. L/T/D						
.2	1.6	3.4							
1.4	1.3	1.2		1.0	.5	.8	.7	1.2	1.8
5.7	4.5	3.7	Fixed/Worth	4.6	5.6	8.9	6.2	2.9	3.5
-5.0	-5.1	-7.5		-4.9	-4.0	-3.3	-4.5	-11.9	-109.1
1.6	1.3	1.3		1.0	.9	1.3	.7	1.2	2.0
8.0	6.0	5.2	Debt/Worth	9.0	7.3	39.2	6.8	4.2	4.8
-7.7	-7.5	-10.1		-5.7	-3.5	-5.5	-7.6	-14.6	-146.1
37.2	37.5	28.7		47.7	53.2	180.5	36.3	17.4	22.1
(331) 11.4	(308) 11.5	(367) 9.7	% Profit Before Taxes/Tangible Net Worth	(36) 5.3	(44) 26.3	(26) 28.6	(42) 7.4	(122) 8.1	(97) 9.4
.3	1.4	2.5		-2.8	6.9	1.4	-.1	2.8	3.1
6.9	8.2	6.4		8.9	30.8	26.1	7.1	5.0	4.2
1.8	2.5	2.4	% Profit Before Taxes/Total Assets	1.3	7.4	2.1	3.3	2.0	1.9
-1.2	-.6	-.4		-1.3	1.2	-1.5	-.3	-.4	.1
2.4	3.6	2.6		33.1	84.5	16.6	3.8	1.3	1.2
.7	.7	.8	Sales/Net Fixed Assets	.7	3.9	3.0	.9	.7	.7
.4	.4	.4		.2	.7	.4	.5	.4	.5
1.2	1.4	1.2		2.8	5.2	4.0	1.5	.7	.7
.5	.5	.5	Sales/Total Assets	.5	1.5	.6	.6	.4	.4
.3	.3	.3		.1	.6	.3	.3	.3	.3
4.0	3.8	4.6		2.6	1.5	1.8	3.0	5.7	6.2
(497) 8.8	(429) 9.1	(507) 8.7	% Depr., Dep., Amort./Sales	(45) 15.0	(56) 5.8	(39) 6.5	(61) 6.1	(178) 10.0	(128) 9.3
14.6	14.6	13.7		31.1	9.2	12.0	11.5	13.9	13.7
2.5	3.4	3.5				2.8		3.9	
(59) 5.8	(49) 7.0	(49) 7.2	% Officers', Directors' Owners' Comp/Sales			(14) 4.4		(12) 13.2	
12.4	17.6	19.1				9.6		29.5	
9970572M	**8741911M**	**11275260M**	Net Sales ($)	**29126M**	**129974M**	**186348M**	**462664M**	**3048800M**	**7418348M**
22473858M	**17705606M**	**25445792M**	Total Assets ($)	**100576M**	**167212M**	**363464M**	**1252331M**	**9178042M**	**14384167M**

M = $ thousand MM = $ million

See Pages 9 through 22 for Explanation of Ratios and Data

Current Data Sorted by Assets							Comparative Historical Data	
						Type of Statement		
1	1	22	22	3	7	Unqualified	61	53
		5	2			Reviewed	10	19
4	9	8				Compiled	16	18
15	11	8	3		2	Tax Returns	44	38
21	21	40	27	4	2	Other	53	72
52 (4/1-9/30/13)		186 (10/1/13-3/31/14)					4/1/09-3/31/10	4/1/10-3/31/11
0-500M	500M-2MM	2-10MM	10-50MM	50-100MM	100-250MM		ALL	ALL
41	42	83	54	7	11	**NUMBER OF STATEMENTS**	184	200
%	%	%	%	%	%	**ASSETS**	%	%
29.6	16.5	13.1	6.7		13.5	Cash & Equivalents	15.1	16.4
10.0	11.4	4.5	4.3		12.5	Trade Receivables (net)	6.4	7.4
.0	.1	.1	.1		.2	Inventory	.2	.3
3.8	1.6	3.9	.8		1.7	All Other Current	3.1	2.6
43.5	29.6	21.6	11.8		28.0	Total Current	24.7	26.7
39.1	45.4	62.5	63.7		47.1	Fixed Assets (net)	59.3	60.5
7.7	5.0	5.6	5.8		2.2	Intangibles (net)	2.7	4.2
9.7	20.1	10.3	18.7		22.7	All Other Non-Current	13.3	8.6
100.0	100.0	100.0	100.0		100.0	Total	100.0	100.0
						LIABILITIES		
22.6	3.6	.6	1.1		.0	Notes Payable-Short Term	4.0	4.1
2.0	2.0	4.7	1.8		2.3	Cur. Mat.-L.T.D.	4.1	4.9
8.4	5.6	2.8	2.3		7.1	Trade Payables	7.3	5.9
.0	.1	.1	.1		.0	Income Taxes Payable	.0	.4
45.6	21.6	8.7	7.2		8.0	All Other Current	18.6	15.7
78.6	32.9	16.8	12.4		17.5	Total Current	34.0	31.0
16.2	45.7	65.6	59.0		38.4	Long-Term Debt	51.6	55.1
.0	.0	.0	.0		.0	Deferred Taxes	.0	.0
18.0	5.3	9.2	10.3		17.3	All Other Non-Current	9.0	9.4
-12.8	16.1	8.4	18.3		26.7	Net Worth	5.4	4.5
100.0	100.0	100.0	100.0		100.0	Total Liabilities & Net Worth	100.0	100.0
						INCOME DATA		
100.0	100.0	100.0	100.0		100.0	Net Sales	100.0	100.0
						Gross Profit		
89.9	88.6	84.7	84.2		86.2	Operating Expenses	87.3	88.5
10.1	11.4	15.3	15.8		13.8	Operating Profit	12.7	11.5
.4	4.5	8.1	10.6		1.4	All Other Expenses (net)	9.9	7.7
9.7	7.0	7.2	5.3		12.5	Profit Before Taxes	2.8	3.8
						RATIOS		
2.9	2.7	3.0	1.9		5.3		2.2	2.5
1.0	1.2	1.4	1.1		1.3	Current	1.0	1.2
.2	.5	.5	.3		.8		.4	.5
2.9	2.6	2.5	1.9		5.2		1.7	2.3
.8	.9	1.2	1.1		1.0	Quick	.8	(199) 1.1
.2	.5	.4	.3		.6		.2	.4
0 UND	**0** UND	**0** UND	**1** 248.3		**2** 201.7		**0** UND	**0** UND
0 UND	**2** 162.0	**3** 108.0	**16** 22.2		**26** 13.8	Sales/Receivables	**4** 89.7	**4** 91.0
6 56.7	**16** 23.4	**14** 25.7	**31** 11.8		**34** 10.6		**20** 18.2	**23** 15.7
						Cost of Sales/Inventory		
						Cost of Sales/Payables		
19.6	7.9	6.4	6.4		2.2		9.0	7.2
806.5	177.5	23.9	45.3		24.2	Sales/Working Capital	NM	63.3
-9.2	-13.9	-11.2	-9.9		-23.8		-6.8	-10.0
47.4	7.7	4.2	4.5				6.7	4.7
(16) 18.9	(25) 2.0	(71) 2.2	(41) 2.2			EBIT/Interest	(126) 1.8	(144) 2.0
7.9	1.3	.9	.7				1.0	.9
						Net Profit + Depr., Dep., Amort./Cur. Mat. L/T/D		
.1	.3	1.4	1.2		.4		1.1	1.1
.8	4.0	6.9	6.3		2.3	Fixed/Worth	7.7	11.4
-2.9	NM	-4.9	-6.3		-125.1		-4.3	-3.9
.6	.6	.8	1.5		.6		1.7	1.7
2.7	6.7	9.8	9.6		3.1	Debt/Worth	12.4	17.6
-2.6	NM	-6.6	-9.4		-137.6		-5.9	-5.9
196.4	116.0	55.2	18.5				68.9	68.9
(24) 90.7	(32) 47.1	(51) 11.2	(34) 8.4			% Profit Before Taxes/Tangible Net Worth	(106) 11.7	(113) 16.4
19.9	10.4	-.5	-.9				1.9	.9
77.8	18.5	10.1	5.1		9.4		8.1	9.6
39.8	11.2	5.0	1.7		4.0	% Profit Before Taxes/Total Assets	2.2	2.9
-.4	3.1	-.3	-.6		-.2		-.6	-1.0
171.9	33.2	2.6	1.2		2.4		8.7	11.9
19.8	7.1	.8	.7		.9	Sales/Net Fixed Assets	.9	.9
8.7	1.1	.5	.3		.4		.4	.4
9.4	4.0	1.0	.7		1.0		2.5	2.9
4.7	1.8	.6	.4		.4	Sales/Total Assets	.7	.7
3.5	.7	.4	.2		.3		.3	.4
.8	.8	3.4	4.1				2.6	2.6
(21) 1.4	(30) 3.1	(70) 6.7	(51) 8.3			% Depr., Dep., Amort./Sales	(159) 6.9	(175) 6.6
1.8	10.4	10.7	15.4				14.3	12.2
4.2							5.0	2.7
(14) 6.0						% Officers', Directors' Owners' Comp/Sales	(31) 6.5	(38) 5.9
9.5							11.4	11.0
46448M	89832M	415169M	748265M	172172M	2868857M	Net Sales ($)	2004492M	1877574M
9309M	42349M	419203M	1183635M	487688M	1545807M	Total Assets ($)	2843097M	2883463M

M = $ thousand MM = $ million

See Pages 9 through 22 for Explanation of Ratios and Data

Comparative Historical Data				Current Data Sorted by Sales					
			Type of Statement						
62	49	56	Unqualified	5	6	6	15	11	13
8	10	7	Reviewed	1	5		1		
15	14	21	Compiled	6	8	5	1	1	
30	25	39	Tax Returns	15	17	3	2		2
72	84	115	Other	12	53	18	8	15	9
4/1/11-3/31/12	4/1/12-3/31/13	4/1/13-3/31/14		52 (4/1-9/30/13)			186 (10/1/13-3/31/14)		
ALL	ALL	ALL		0-1MM	1-3MM	3-5MM	5-10MM	10-25MM	25MM & OVER
187	182	238	**NUMBER OF STATEMENTS**	39	89	32	27	27	24
%	%	%	**ASSETS**	%	%	%	%	%	%
13.9	12.7	14.9	Cash & Equivalents	19.8	14.5	13.9	10.0	17.3	13.1
7.3	6.4	7.0	Trade Receivables (net)	3.3	4.6	12.6	6.9	5.2	16.6
.1	.1	.1	Inventory	.1	.0	.1	.1	.2	.2
4.1	2.7	2.6	All Other Current	4.5	2.8	.9	1.0	3.4	1.5
25.3	22.0	24.6	Total Current	27.6	21.9	27.4	18.1	26.1	31.4
59.5	61.5	55.0	Fixed Assets (net)	50.3	60.1	55.6	60.0	48.4	44.6
4.7	4.2	5.7	Intangibles (net)	5.7	6.9	3.3	7.2	4.8	3.2
10.5	12.3	14.8	All Other Non-Current	16.4	11.2	13.6	14.7	20.7	20.9
100.0	100.0	100.0	Total	100.0	100.0	100.0	100.0	100.0	100.0
			LIABILITIES						
5.7	2.2	5.0	Notes Payable-Short Term	22.0	1.3	4.2	2.0	.4	.4
4.2	2.5	2.9	Cur. Mat.-L.T.D.	2.5	3.4	3.5	1.5	2.6	3.1
5.7	5.0	4.3	Trade Payables	4.2	2.9	7.9	3.2	3.8	6.6
.1	.0	.1	Income Taxes Payable	.0	.0	.2	.0	.0	.3
19.3	12.8	16.9	All Other Current	29.8	16.3	19.5	9.7	7.4	13.6
34.9	22.5	29.1	Total Current	58.5	23.9	35.2	16.4	14.1	24.0
52.2	52.2	50.1	Long-Term Debt	39.5	57.5	50.8	44.9	59.2	34.8
.0	.0	.0	Deferred Taxes	.0	.0	.0	.0	.0	.0
12.4	6.5	11.1	All Other Non-Current	14.2	7.3	6.4	16.3	18.7	12.3
.4	18.7	9.6	Net Worth	-12.2	11.3	7.6	22.4	8.0	28.9
100.0	100.0	100.0	Total Liabilties & Net Worth	100.0	100.0	100.0	100.0	100.0	100.0
			INCOME DATA						
100.0	100.0	100.0	Net Sales	100.0	100.0	100.0	100.0	100.0	100.0
			Gross Profit						
90.0	86.7	86.4	Operating Expenses	81.7	85.1	86.4	91.0	86.8	93.4
10.0	13.3	13.6	Operating Profit	18.3	14.9	13.6	9.0	13.2	6.6
6.7	7.5	6.2	All Other Expenses (net)	10.8	7.4	6.7	4.2	1.4	.9
3.3	5.8	7.4	Profit Before Taxes	7.5	7.5	6.8	4.9	11.7	5.7
			RATIOS						
2.0	2.7	2.6		5.1	2.6	3.0	2.2	2.9	2.7
1.0	1.0	1.3	Current	.7	1.3	1.0	1.1	1.6	1.3
.4	.4	.4		.2	.4	.5	.5	.7	.8
1.6	2.3	2.5		3.0	2.3	2.9	2.1	2.5	2.7
.7	.9	1.0	Quick	.6	1.2	.9	1.0	1.3	1.2
.3	.3	.4		.1	.3	.3	.4	.6	.8
0 UND	0 UND	0 UND		0 UND	0 UND	1 728.9	2 176.8	2 165.6	21 17.8
4 81.8	4 88.0	4 98.6	Sales/Receivables	0 UND	1 339.2	5 66.8	10 35.9	20 18.6	29 12.7
25 14.8	18 20.1	24 15.4		3 143.0	6 57.2	21 17.1	31 11.6	31 11.9	38 9.7
			Cost of Sales/Inventory						
			Cost of Sales/Payables						
9.8	7.7	7.1		5.4	8.8	7.5	6.6	3.9	6.6
577.3	483.4	53.0	Sales/Working Capital	-89.7	37.8	NM	317.2	11.7	29.9
-8.8	-11.3	-11.9		-2.2	-11.8	-11.0	-10.0	-22.3	-25.0
8.1	5.9	7.0		10.6	5.0	4.3	7.9	15.1	10.8
(139) 1.8	(123) 2.1	(168) 2.3	EBIT/Interest	(18) 1.4	(62) 2.0	(21) 2.5	(22) 2.3	(23) 3.2	(22) 3.7
.9	.8	1.0		.7	1.2	1.2	.3	1.4	1.1
			Net Profit + Depr., Dep., Amort./Cur. Mat. L/T/D						
1.2	1.0	.7		.1	1.1	1.2	.7	.5	.6
10.3	4.2	4.4	Fixed/Worth	2.1	20.1	6.1	2.0	1.6	1.8
-2.8	-10.6	-5.1		-3.6	-4.0	-3.9	16.5	-4.2	16.8
1.7	1.1	.8		.8	1.5	1.6	.7	.5	.7
13.3	5.7	6.1	Debt/Worth	11.9	22.9	9.2	2.5	1.6	2.3
-4.5	-14.4	-6.6		-3.9	-6.2	-5.7	20.9	-9.2	26.5
59.0	53.6	86.1		152.4	114.7	49.0	69.5	37.1	79.9
(105) 13.7	(121) 14.6	(153) 17.3	% Profit Before Taxes/Tangible Net Worth	(24) 28.1	(50) 36.0	(20) 12.9	(21) 11.2	(19) 9.8	(19) 11.2
1.1	1.9	4.1		.8	8.9	2.4	-1.2	2.1	2.8
14.6	15.4	13.9		42.5	13.5	10.2	7.7	14.2	15.7
2.2	4.3	4.9	% Profit Before Taxes/Total Assets	6.1	5.0	5.8	3.3	3.8	4.6
-1.3	-.3	-.1		-1.3	.6	1.0	-1.4	1.0	.5
14.7	7.1	10.4		128.0	8.9	18.2	2.6	7.8	11.8
1.0	.9	1.2	Sales/Net Fixed Assets	7.2	1.1	.9	.9	1.5	1.4
.4	.4	.5		.4	.5	.5	.5	.7	.8
3.3	3.1	3.1		4.1	2.9	4.2	1.1	1.6	3.2
.7	.6	.7	Sales/Total Assets	.8	.7	.6	.7	.7	.9
.3	.3	.4		.2	.4	.3	.4	.4	.4
2.8	2.4	2.1		1.7	1.8	2.6	2.6	2.2	1.0
(163) 6.0	(155) 6.7	(185) 6.4	% Depr., Dep., Amort./Sales	(22) 9.0	(69) 6.2	(24) 8.2	(26) 5.0	(24) 6.9	(20) 3.9
12.5	11.9	11.1		27.2	11.3	10.5	11.2	9.9	7.2
2.4	2.0	2.6			2.3				
(27) 5.0	(23) 4.5	(37) 5.6	% Officers', Directors' Owners' Comp/Sales		(18) 5.4				
8.0	7.2	8.9			8.3				
2493547M	1978978M	4340743M	Net Sales ($)	19140M	157622M	121542M	179855M	412913M	3449671M
3440617M	2666500M	3687991M	Total Assets ($)	62320M	327815M	243831M	333340M	773965M	1946720M

M = $ thousand MM = $ million

See Pages 9 through 22 for Explanation of Ratios and Data

Current Data Sorted by Assets							Comparative Historical Data	
						Type of Statement		
2	7	33	31	7	4	Unqualified	106	120
1	2	2				Reviewed	8	5
2	5	6				Compiled	8	8
7	3	3			1	Tax Returns	22	26
11	10	22	14	1	2	Other	60	62
91 (4/1-9/30/13)			85 (10/1/13-3/31/14)				4/1/09-3/31/10	4/1/10-3/31/11
0-500M	500M-2MM	2-10MM	10-50MM	50-100MM	100-250MM		ALL	ALL
23	27	66	45	8	7	NUMBER OF STATEMENTS	204	221
%	%	%	%	%	%	**ASSETS**	%	%
25.7	22.1	18.1	12.0			Cash & Equivalents	15.4	17.8
20.5	21.5	13.4	13.5			Trade Receivables (net)	16.3	13.9
.1	.2	.1	.0			Inventory	.4	.2
.9	2.3	1.0	1.7			All Other Current	3.1	3.5
47.1	46.1	32.6	27.3			Total Current	35.2	35.4
37.1	42.0	54.9	60.8			Fixed Assets (net)	50.8	50.3
3.4	1.8	3.8	2.6			Intangibles (net)	2.6	2.6
12.4	10.2	8.7	9.3			All Other Non-Current	11.4	11.7
100.0	100.0	100.0	100.0			Total	100.0	100.0
						LIABILITIES		
16.7	5.0	.6	2.7			Notes Payable-Short Term	6.1	4.6
.9	2.0	2.2	2.7			Cur. Mat.-L.T.D.	2.7	3.3
9.4	9.8	6.8	3.3			Trade Payables	5.4	6.8
.3	.0	.0	.0			Income Taxes Payable	.0	.0
20.7	10.3	8.2	9.1			All Other Current	13.1	15.4
48.1	27.1	17.9	17.9			Total Current	27.3	30.2
21.7	17.0	30.6	32.1			Long-Term Debt	34.7	31.2
.0	.0	.1	.6			Deferred Taxes	.1	.0
3.0	6.8	6.0	6.3			All Other Non-Current	6.5	8.4
27.2	49.1	45.4	43.1			Net Worth	31.3	30.2
100.0	100.0	100.0	100.0			Total Liabilties & Net Worth	100.0	100.0
						INCOME DATA		
100.0	100.0	100.0	100.0			Net Sales	100.0	100.0
						Gross Profit		
93.2	90.3	88.3	95.4			Operating Expenses	93.8	92.8
6.8	9.7	11.7	4.6			Operating Profit	6.2	7.2
1.4	2.6	2.4	1.3			All Other Expenses (net)	3.5	3.3
5.3	7.2	9.3	3.3			Profit Before Taxes	2.8	4.0
						RATIOS		
2.5	3.0	3.2	2.7				3.0	3.1
.9	1.7	1.6	1.8			Current	1.5	1.6
.5	.6	.8	1.2				.8	.8
2.5	2.7	3.2	2.6				2.7	2.9
.9	1.6	1.5	1.7			Quick	1.4	1.4
.5	.6	.8	1.0				.7	.6
0 UND	8 47.5	3 144.9	26 14.1				3 108.8	5 71.1
2 229.3	25 14.5	24 15.4	38 9.5			Sales/Receivables	29 12.7	27 13.6
28 13.0	38 9.6	39 9.3	57 6.4				48 7.6	42 8.7
						Cost of Sales/Inventory		
						Cost of Sales/Payables		
13.7	7.7	4.2	5.1				5.5	5.1
-999.8	18.4	11.5	11.1			Sales/Working Capital	21.1	15.6
-19.2	-28.3	-39.8	26.7				-43.1	-31.8
	11.2	6.5	4.1				6.1	5.8
	(19) 2.4	(51) 2.3	(39) 1.8			EBIT/Interest	(160) 2.1	(166) 2.1
	-2.1	1.2	.4				.6	.8
						Net Profit + Depr., Dep., Amort./Cur. Mat. L/T/D		
.3	.2	.7	.9				.6	.6
1.2	.7	1.1	1.7			Fixed/Worth	1.3	1.4
-9.8	2.2	5.1	3.3				6.4	4.5
.5	.5	.4	.5				.5	.6
1.5	.9	.8	1.5			Debt/Worth	1.5	1.5
-11.4	2.1	5.3	3.3				10.7	10.4
116.9	20.6	13.6	14.8				28.4	27.1
(17) 20.0	(24) 8.5	(55) 7.9	(40) 4.5			% Profit Before Taxes/Tangible Net Worth	(170) 8.0	(179) 8.5
-42.3	-8.3	.0	.1				-1.1	.8
48.0	12.4	8.5	4.4				9.3	8.6
14.5	3.9	4.0	1.6			% Profit Before Taxes/Total Assets	3.4	3.3
-1.5	-6.5	.6	-.4				-.7	-.2
232.2	26.1	4.6	2.6				9.0	9.5
25.2	7.4	2.2	1.4			Sales/Net Fixed Assets	2.8	2.7
8.9	2.2	.8	.7				1.1	1.0
9.9	4.1	2.0	1.4				2.6	2.5
6.5	2.6	1.1	.9			Sales/Total Assets	1.4	1.3
4.2	.8	.5	.4				.6	.6
.6	.7	1.9	2.6				1.8	1.6
(15) 1.0	(23) 2.9	(56) 3.2	(44) 3.7			% Depr., Dep., Amort./Sales	(180) 3.0	(195) 3.0
2.1	5.0	7.4	7.8				5.5	6.0
							4.1	2.1
						% Officers', Directors' Owners' Comp/Sales	(25) 6.4	(35) 6.3
							12.1	11.3
32479M	91669M	468377M	1036458M	479610M	1594085M	Net Sales ($)	3726694M	5141275M
5403M	34442M	336165M	973563M	538574M	1183288M	Total Assets ($)	3261640M	3736392M

M = $ thousand MM = $ million

See Pages 9 through 22 for Explanation of Ratios and Data

Comparative Historical Data				Current Data Sorted by Sales					
			Type of Statement						
125	92	84	Unqualified	6	4	10	18	24	22
4	6	5	Reviewed	1		2	1	1	
8	11	13	Compiled	4	5	2	2		
36	26	14	Tax Returns	6	4	1	1	1	1
80	59	60	Other	9	23	5	11	6	6
4/1/11-3/31/12 ALL	**4/1/12-3/31/13 ALL**	**4/1/13-3/31/14 ALL**		**91 (4/1-9/30/13)**			**85 (10/1/13-3/31/14)**		
				0-1MM	**1-3MM**	**3-5MM**	**5-10MM**	**10-25MM**	**25MM & OVER**
253	194	176	**NUMBER OF STATEMENTS**	26	36	20	33	32	29
%	%	%	**ASSETS**	%	%	%	%	%	%
18.0	17.8	17.8	Cash & Equivalents	13.4	17.9	22.1	21.8	18.1	14.0
13.8	12.6	15.6	Trade Receivables (net)	5.9	13.4	19.1	16.5	17.4	21.6
.3	.2	.1	Inventory	.0	.2	.0	.1	.0	.1
3.7	2.5	1.6	All Other Current	.7	.4	1.0	1.5	2.7	3.3
35.8	33.1	35.1	Total Current	20.0	31.9	42.3	39.9	38.2	38.9
50.2	50.4	51.9	Fixed Assets (net)	67.3	50.3	47.8	50.6	48.1	48.8
2.7	4.5	3.2	Intangibles (net)	3.3	5.9	2.2	.4	2.4	4.4
11.2	12.0	9.7	All Other Non-Current	9.5	11.8	7.7	9.1	11.2	7.9
100.0	100.0	100.0	Total	100.0	100.0	100.0	100.0	100.0	100.0
			LIABILITIES						
3.9	3.3	4.6	Notes Payable-Short Term	5.1	9.7	1.9	1.8	.8	7.3
3.0	3.0	2.2	Cur. Mat.-L.T.D.	2.1	1.6	1.9	1.7	3.3	2.3
5.0	6.3	6.4	Trade Payables	4.7	5.6	11.1	5.7	6.7	6.2
.0	.0	.1	Income Taxes Payable	.0	.2	.0	.0	.0	.1
15.7	10.7	10.3	All Other Current	8.2	12.0	9.6	8.7	10.4	12.5
27.6	23.3	23.6	Total Current	20.1	29.0	24.6	18.0	21.2	28.4
32.1	37.2	28.7	Long-Term Debt	38.6	29.7	32.7	19.3	20.6	35.2
.1	.2	.2	Deferred Taxes	1.0	.0	.0	.1	.0	.0
6.9	6.3	5.9	All Other Non-Current	2.3	8.6	8.2	4.5	7.0	4.8
33.3	33.0	41.6	Net Worth	37.9	32.6	34.5	58.1	51.1	31.6
100.0	100.0	100.0	Total Liabilties & Net Worth	100.0	100.0	100.0	100.0	100.0	100.0
			INCOME DATA						
100.0	100.0	100.0	Net Sales	100.0	100.0	100.0	100.0	100.0	100.0
			Gross Profit						
92.4	92.2	91.7	Operating Expenses	71.3	91.6	97.0	95.4	97.0	96.3
7.6	7.8	8.3	Operating Profit	28.7	8.4	3.0	4.6	3.0	3.7
3.4	3.2	1.9	All Other Expenses (net)	7.2	1.7	2.5	.8	.3	.1
4.2	4.6	6.4	Profit Before Taxes	21.4	6.8	.5	3.8	2.7	3.6
			RATIOS						
3.5	3.2	2.9		7.6	3.7	2.9	4.0	2.9	2.1
1.6	1.6	1.6	Current	.8	1.0	1.5	2.1	2.2	1.4
.7	.8	.8		.4	.5	.8	1.4	1.4	1.0
3.0	3.0	2.8		6.2	3.1	2.6	4.0	2.8	2.1
1.3	1.5	1.5	Quick	.8	1.0	1.5	2.0	2.0	1.4
.6	.7	.8		.4	.5	.8	1.2	1.3	.9
1 491.8	**2** 188.8	**5** 75.0		**0** UND	**0** UND	**6** 63.8	**24** 15.4	**25** 14.8	**25** 14.6
25 14.5	**26** 14.3	**27** 13.6	Sales/Receivables	**1** 286.6	**8** 43.7	**28** 13.0	**31** 11.6	**34** 10.8	**47** 7.8
40 9.2	**43** 8.4	**43** 8.4		**8** 43.9	**29** 12.4	**41** 9.0	**49** 7.4	**47** 7.7	**68** 5.4
			Cost of Sales/Inventory						
			Cost of Sales/Payables						
5.1	5.1	5.8		4.6	7.7	8.3	3.3	5.4	6.1
15.5	15.4	15.1	Sales/Working Capital	-103.2	672.1	17.1	9.8	8.8	16.6
-32.7	-42.0	-64.6		-4.5	-21.0	-28.8	30.7	17.2	-618.1
5.8	6.8	6.5		5.2	6.9	2.8	10.1	7.6	8.9
(189) 2.1	(136) 1.7	(133) 2.2	EBIT/Interest	(14) 2.2	(26) 2.1	(15) 1.7	(24) 2.1	(28) 2.9	(26) 2.1
.6	.3	1.0		1.2	.5	-1.2	-.8	1.8	1.1
3.1									
(15) 1.8			Net Profit + Depr., Dep., Amort./Cur. Mat. L/T/D						
.3									
.5	.5	.6		1.0	.5	.5	.5	.8	.9
1.3	1.1	1.2	Fixed/Worth	1.8	1.2	1.6	.8	1.0	2.2
3.4	4.4	3.7		5.0	-6.1	-6.5	1.6	1.8	6.2
.5	.3	.5		.6	.3	.4	.3	.5	1.1
1.5	1.3	1.1	Debt/Worth	1.2	1.2	1.7	.7	1.0	2.6
4.8	5.0	4.0		8.6	-7.7	-10.4	1.5	1.9	9.2
25.1	20.8	16.4		23.9	22.8	17.1	12.2	13.1	18.7
(214) 8.7	(163) 6.5	(149) 7.6	% Profit Before Taxes/Tangible Net Worth	(21) 9.7	(25) 8.9	(14) 5.7	5.8	(31) 6.0	(25) 7.6
-1.4	-2.8	.0		2.5	-8.0	-10.5	-2.0	.9	1.9
9.1	8.7	8.1		15.0	15.5	6.8	7.5	6.0	5.7
3.2	2.5	3.6	% Profit Before Taxes/Total Assets	4.7	5.1	1.3	3.1	3.1	3.5
-.7	-1.1	.0		.9	-.3	-5.5	-1.3	.4	.2
11.9	8.5	8.9		7.2	23.5	8.0	5.7	7.0	6.2
2.8	2.8	2.4	Sales/Net Fixed Assets	.5	4.3	3.6	2.1	2.6	2.7
.8	.9	1.1		.2	.6	1.2	1.4	1.4	1.5
2.6	2.5	2.7		2.5	5.8	3.5	2.5	2.2	2.4
1.4	1.2	1.3	Sales/Total Assets	.3	1.3	1.7	1.3	1.4	1.4
.5	.5	.6		.1	.4	.7	.6	.9	.8
1.6	1.7	1.7		2.1	.9	1.6	2.0	1.7	1.5
(210) 3.1	(170) 3.2	(152) 3.2	% Depr., Dep., Amort./Sales	(23) 10.7	(25) 4.1	(17) 3.3	(30) 3.0	(31) 2.7	(26) 3.2
8.1	7.0	6.6		18.7	9.3	6.2	4.9	3.8	4.7
2.9	2.8	3.7							
(31) 6.5	(37) 5.6	(26) 9.0	% Officers', Directors' Owners' Comp/Sales						
10.9	8.6	16.3							
4445557M	3016550M	3702678M	Net Sales ($)	14269M	70624M	74670M	241213M	513890M	2788012M
3592881M	2891147M	3071435M	Total Assets ($)	56495M	126233M	77700M	253991M	514947M	2042069M

M = $ thousand MM = $ million

See Pages 9 through 22 for Explanation of Ratios and Data

Current Data Sorted by Assets							Comparative Historical Data	
4	35	81	88	22	8	**Type of Statement** Unqualified	262	292
3			1			Reviewed	5	7
5	2	1	1			Compiled	3	4
7	7	5				Tax Returns	23	29
14	23	38	18	6	3	Other	94	105
268 (4/1-9/30/13)			104 (10/1/13-3/31/14)				4/1/09-3/31/10	4/1/10-3/31/11
0-500M	500M-2MM	2-10MM	10-50MM	50-100MM	100-250MM		ALL	ALL
33	67	125	108	28	11	**NUMBER OF STATEMENTS**	387	437
%	%	%	%	%	%	**ASSETS**	%	%
32.2	24.9	18.8	18.1	18.7	7.2	Cash & Equivalents	20.5	20.5
9.4	25.2	19.8	13.5	12.4	5.3	Trade Receivables (net)	15.1	16.9
.0	1.2	.1	.3	.1	.5	Inventory	.4	.5
8.6	3.3	2.9	2.2	2.4	3.0	All Other Current	3.5	3.6
50.3	54.7	41.5	34.1	33.6	16.0	Total Current	39.5	41.5
32.5	36.2	46.3	42.9	42.5	49.3	Fixed Assets (net)	47.7	44.3
5.1	2.4	1.5	3.2	2.0	.4	Intangibles (net)	.8	1.6
12.1	6.7	10.7	19.8	21.9	34.4	All Other Non-Current	12.0	12.6
100.0	100.0	100.0	100.0	100.0	100.0	Total	100.0	100.0
						LIABILITIES		
8.5	3.8	3.6	1.9	1.9	.5	Notes Payable-Short Term	4.3	3.8
4.9	1.2	1.6	1.6	1.8	.8	Cur. Mat.-L.T.D.	1.5	1.7
4.8	11.9	9.5	4.9	5.0	5.7	Trade Payables	7.8	8.2
.0	.0	.0	.0	.0	.0	Income Taxes Payable	.0	.0
21.0	10.3	12.7	8.8	7.4	2.0	All Other Current	10.4	11.0
39.2	27.2	27.4	17.2	16.1	9.1	Total Current	24.0	24.6
22.5	13.3	18.3	17.3	23.5	30.7	Long-Term Debt	20.5	20.2
.0	.0	.0	.0	.0	.0	Deferred Taxes	.0	.0
23.7	3.3	2.8	2.6	10.1	8.2	All Other Non-Current	4.6	3.8
14.6	56.2	51.4	62.9	50.3	52.1	Net Worth	50.9	51.3
100.0	100.0	100.0	100.0	100.0	100.0	Total Liabilities & Net Worth	100.0	100.0
						INCOME DATA		
100.0	100.0	100.0	100.0	100.0	100.0	Net Sales	100.0	100.0
						Gross Profit		
95.3	97.7	96.5	96.8	95.0	103.5	Operating Expenses	99.0	96.3
4.7	2.3	3.5	3.2	5.0	-3.5	Operating Profit	1.0	3.7
1.2	.9	1.3	-1.1	-.4	-.1	All Other Expenses (net)	1.6	.3
3.5	1.4	2.2	4.3	5.4	-3.4	Profit Before Taxes	-.6	3.4
						RATIOS		
7.0	4.5	2.9	3.7	3.0	2.6		3.7	3.7
1.1	2.4	1.6	2.1	2.0	1.7	Current	2.0	2.0
.4	1.2	1.0	1.2	1.6	1.3		1.0	1.1
4.3	4.0	2.7	3.4	2.9	2.2		3.5	3.2
.9	2.3	1.5	2.0	1.9	1.3	Quick	1.8	1.7
.3	1.2	1.0	1.1	1.4	.8		.9	1.0
0 UND	**4** 94.4	**6** 59.7	**21** 17.5	**28** 13.0	**10** 37.1		**6** 66.1	**7** 53.4
0 UND	**28** 12.9	**31** 11.9	**33** 10.9	**41** 8.8	**24** 15.1	Sales/Receivables	**26** 14.0	**30** 12.2
13 27.1	**43** 8.4	**53** 6.9	**51** 7.2	**60** 6.1	**39** 9.3		**44** 8.2	**50** 7.3
						Cost of Sales/Inventory		
						Cost of Sales/Payables		
8.1	5.9	6.3	3.1	3.2	5.7		4.5	4.5
248.0	9.6	12.6	8.7	5.9	20.1	Sales/Working Capital	10.5	10.5
-28.2	37.1	512.7	30.7	16.1	34.9		754.0	166.7
15.5	12.4	5.4	10.4	5.7			4.7	10.6
(14) 2.0	(44) 3.1	(89) 1.4	(87) 3.6	(22) 2.0		EBIT/Interest	(269) 1.2	(314) 2.7
-.4	-1.0	-3.1	.8	1.0			-3.0	.1
						Net Profit + Depr., Dep., Amort./Cur. Mat. L/T/D		
.0	.1	.4	.4	.4	.3		.5	.4
.6	.5	.9	.7	.9	.8	Fixed/Worth	.9	.8
-7.3	1.2	1.6	1.2	2.2	4.7		1.6	1.6
.1	.3	.3	.2	.4	.2		.3	.3
1.0	.7	.9	.5	.9	1.1	Debt/Worth	.7	.7
-3.6	1.9	2.0	1.2	2.4	4.8		1.9	2.0
29.4	18.6	8.1	8.8	13.9	5.1		8.6	13.3
(21) 3.3	(65) 5.1	(118) 1.6	(103) 2.5	(27) 3.2	(10) .6	% Profit Before Taxes/Tangible Net Worth	(365) .6	(409) 4.1
-17.5	-5.9	-4.3	-.6	-.3	-3.5		-5.9	-1.9
33.1	10.2	4.5	4.9	7.3	1.5		4.2	7.4
5.3	2.8	.7	1.5	1.4	-.3	% Profit Before Taxes/Total Assets	.3	2.1
-5.3	-4.3	-2.5	-.5	-.1	-3.5		-4.0	-1.2
361.6	62.5	13.2	6.0	3.6	7.1		10.2	14.1
32.5	15.1	3.5	2.3	2.2	.7	Sales/Net Fixed Assets	2.9	3.2
2.9	2.6	1.4	1.1	1.2	.5		1.1	1.3
10.2	4.0	2.8	1.6	1.3	1.0		2.9	2.9
4.2	2.2	1.6	1.0	1.0	.4	Sales/Total Assets	1.3	1.4
1.6	1.0	.7	.5	.5	.2		.7	.7
.3	.6	1.0	1.5	2.0	1.8		1.3	1.3
(19) 1.5	(54) 1.3	(114) 2.3	(100) 2.8	2.8	6.8	% Depr., Dep., Amort./Sales	(339) 2.3	(384) 2.4
4.0	2.7	4.4	4.7	4.6	9.6		4.5	4.4
4.5		.8					2.2	2.4
(11) 7.3		(11) 2.9				% Officers', Directors' Owners' Comp/Sales	(37) 6.2	(54) 4.6
18.4		6.2					12.3	14.0
33565M	278919M	1371375M	2825725M	1798726M	1443692M	Net Sales ($)	6406904M	7981294M
7310M	80218M	671515M	2289713M	1915129M	1547573M	Total Assets ($)	4908119M	6832681M

M = $ thousand MM = $ million

See Pages 9 through 22 for Explanation of Ratios and Data

Comparative Historical Data / Current Data Sorted by Sales

			Type of Statement						
287	214	238	Unqualified	12	25	35	33	69	64
7	5	4	Reviewed	2	1			1	
6	4	9	Compiled	4	3	1		1	
30	20	19	Tax Returns	9	5	2		3	
136	103	102	Other	17	22	12	12	19	20
				268 (4/1-9/30/13)			104 (10/1/13-3/31/14)		
4/1/11-3/31/12 ALL	**4/1/12-3/31/13 ALL**	**4/1/13-3/31/14 ALL**		**0-1MM**	**1-3MM**	**3-5MM**	**5-10MM**	**10-25MM**	**25MM & OVER**
466	346	372	**NUMBER OF STATEMENTS**	44	56	50	45	93	84
%	%	%	**ASSETS**	%	%	%	%	%	%
20.3	20.3	20.5	Cash & Equivalents	20.2	26.5	20.4	20.0	16.3	21.7
16.4	16.4	17.1	Trade Receivables (net)	5.2	14.6	20.5	16.6	22.2	17.4
.3	.2	.4	Inventory	.0	1.5	.0	.2	.1	.3
3.4	2.7	3.2	All Other Current	2.3	4.6	4.6	1.4	3.0	3.2
40.3	39.6	41.2	Total Current	27.7	47.2	45.5	38.1	41.7	42.7
43.9	45.1	42.1	Fixed Assets (net)	59.2	36.7	43.0	44.9	39.9	37.0
1.7	1.6	2.5	Intangibles (net)	5.4	2.2	1.3	1.8	2.5	2.1
14.0	13.8	14.3	All Other Non-Current	7.7	13.9	10.2	15.2	15.8	18.3
100.0	100.0	100.0	Total	100.0	100.0	100.0	100.0	100.0	100.0
			LIABILITIES						
4.6	4.4	3.4	Notes Payable-Short Term	3.4	3.6	5.0	2.0	3.9	2.3
1.5	1.9	1.8	Cur. Mat.-L.T.D.	3.0	2.3	.7	2.2	1.5	1.8
7.3	7.1	7.7	Trade Payables	2.3	6.8	5.6	8.5	7.9	11.8
.0	.0	.0	Income Taxes Payable	.0	.0	.0	.0	.0	.0
13.4	10.3	11.1	All Other Current	6.4	12.2	12.4	7.8	10.6	14.5
26.9	23.8	24.1	Total Current	15.1	25.0	23.7	20.5	24.0	30.5
17.0	19.3	18.3	Long-Term Debt	29.0	16.7	13.7	18.1	16.2	18.7
.0	.0	.0	Deferred Taxes	.0	.0	.0	.0	.0	.0
4.4	5.0	5.4	All Other Non-Current	13.2	6.2	2.9	2.3	3.9	5.6
51.8	51.9	52.3	Net Worth	42.7	52.1	59.7	59.1	56.0	45.3
100.0	100.0	100.0	Total Liabilties & Net Worth	100.0	100.0	100.0	100.0	100.0	100.0
			INCOME DATA						
100.0	100.0	100.0	Net Sales	100.0	100.0	100.0	100.0	100.0	100.0
			Gross Profit						
97.6	97.9	96.8	Operating Expenses	89.5	97.2	97.0	96.4	98.2	99.0
2.4	2.1	3.2	Operating Profit	10.5	2.8	3.0	3.6	1.8	1.0
.9	1.4	.3	All Other Expenses (net)	5.1	.5	.5	-.7	-1.2	-.2
1.6	.7	2.8	Profit Before Taxes	5.4	2.3	2.5	4.3	3.0	1.1
			RATIOS						
3.6	3.7	3.4	Current	6.3	6.3	5.4	3.8	3.0	2.3
2.0	1.9	1.9		2.0	2.3	2.3	2.2	1.8	1.7
1.0	1.0	1.1		.5	1.1	1.1	1.1	1.2	1.1
3.2	3.2	3.1	Quick	6.1	5.4	5.4	3.3	2.6	2.1
1.7	1.7	1.8		1.8	2.1	2.0	2.2	1.7	1.4
.9	1.0	1.0		.4	.9	1.0	1.1	1.1	.9
6 60.2	**7** 49.7	**8** 48.1	Sales/Receivables	**0** UND	**0** UND	**9** 42.2	**19** 19.4	**24** 15.4	**19** 18.8
29 12.7	**31** 11.8	**31** 11.9		**0** UND	**18** 20.1	**33** 11.1	**31** 11.9	**40** 9.1	**33** 10.9
45 8.1	**48** 7.6	**48** 7.6		**18** 20.7	**41** 8.8	**62** 5.9	**45** 8.2	**54** 6.7	**48** 7.6
			Cost of Sales/Inventory						
			Cost of Sales/Payables						
4.6	3.7	5.0	Sales/Working Capital	3.4	4.3	3.1	4.2	5.6	5.8
10.5	10.8	11.1		16.5	9.5	7.9	9.0	11.2	16.4
NM	240.0	95.2		-28.7	85.3	103.5	79.2	36.5	119.8
7.4	5.0	8.4	EBIT/Interest	5.4	8.5	4.6	28.1	9.9	7.0
(318) 2.3	(238) 1.0	(264) 2.2		(20) 1.3	(34) 2.5	(36) 1.2	(35) 4.3	(75) 3.4	(64) 1.9
-1.4	-3.7	-.4		.1	-3.1	-5.1	.0	-.1	.4
			Net Profit + Depr., Dep., Amort./Cur. Mat. L/T/D						
.4	.4	.3	Fixed/Worth	.3	.1	.2	.4	.4	.4
.8	.8	.8		1.1	.6	.7	.8	.8	.8
1.5	1.4	1.4		2.1	1.4	1.4	1.3	1.2	1.6
.3	.3	.3	Debt/Worth	.1	.2	.2	.2	.4	.4
.6	.6	.7		.6	.5	.6	.6	.7	1.2
1.8	2.0	2.0		3.4	1.8	1.3	1.5	1.5	2.9
10.9	6.9	11.0	% Profit Before Taxes/Tangible Net Worth	12.5	14.7	8.4	17.1	8.1	9.9
(430) 2.9	(321) .2	(344) 2.4		(36) 1.7	(49) 5.1	(49) .7	(42) 4.9	(90) 3.2	(78) 2.3
-4.4	-7.2	-3.3		-5.2	-3.8	-6.1	-1.6	-3.4	-1.5
6.0	4.4	6.2	% Profit Before Taxes/Total Assets	6.1	11.8	4.5	10.4	4.3	4.8
1.5	.3	1.3		1.3	3.0	.5	3.2	1.6	.6
-2.9	-3.9	-2.0		-4.2	-2.5	-3.5	-.6	-2.5	-.6
13.8	11.8	16.9	Sales/Net Fixed Assets	15.6	55.6	23.7	12.5	9.6	15.1
3.4	3.1	3.4		1.0	7.3	3.4	2.0	3.5	4.4
1.4	1.2	1.4		.3	1.2	1.4	1.1	1.8	2.2
2.9	2.5	2.8	Sales/Total Assets	1.8	3.6	2.3	2.2	2.7	3.0
1.4	1.3	1.4		.6	1.9	1.5	1.1	1.4	1.6
.7	.6	.6		.2	.5	.6	.5	.8	1.0
1.2	1.3	1.1	% Depr., Dep., Amort./Sales	3.4	.7	1.4	1.1	1.0	1.1
(400) 2.2	(299) 2.6	(326) 2.4		(30) 8.4	(44) 1.7	(41) 2.2	(44) 2.8	(86) 2.4	(81) 2.1
4.2	4.6	4.6		18.0	5.8	4.1	5.5	3.5	3.2
3.2	2.5	2.7	% Officers', Directors' Owners' Comp/Sales		3.1			.6	
(41) 6.0	(35) 4.8	(39) 4.5			(11) 4.4			(10) 2.6	
11.4	7.0	8.5			11.2			4.4	
8519693M	6886138M	7752002M	Net Sales ($)	20321M	115210M	198169M	339343M	1498333M	5580626M
6979174M	5818313M	6511458M	Total Assets ($)	55951M	195110M	239081M	384785M	1673166M	3963365M

M = $ thousand MM = $ million

See Pages 9 through 22 for Explanation of Ratios and Data

Current Data Sorted by Assets							Comparative Historical Data	
						Type of Statement		
6	12	84	54	19	6	Unqualified	144	167
3	2	3				Reviewed	6	6
2	4	3				Compiled	4	6
7	4	6				Tax Returns	10	17
10	12	30	23	5		Other	44	58
	206 (4/1-9/30/13)		89 (10/1/13-3/31/14)				4/1/09-3/31/10	4/1/10-3/31/11
0-500M	**500M-2MM**	**2-10MM**	**10-50MM**	**50-100MM**	**100-250MM**		**ALL**	**ALL**
28	34	126	77	24	6	**NUMBER OF STATEMENTS**	208	254
%	%	%	%	%	%	**ASSETS**	%	%
37.2	24.9	23.5	22.2	22.2		Cash & Equivalents	20.1	20.8
16.7	28.9	17.0	14.9	17.9		Trade Receivables (net)	18.3	18.2
.2	.6	.4	.6	.6		Inventory	.6	.5
1.9	3.6	4.9	2.7	5.5		All Other Current	4.4	3.8
56.0	58.0	45.8	40.4	46.3		Total Current	43.4	43.3
33.5	32.1	44.6	44.5	34.2		Fixed Assets (net)	44.9	43.5
4.2	4.3	2.5	2.1	5.0		Intangibles (net)	1.8	3.2
6.3	5.5	7.1	13.0	14.6		All Other Non-Current	9.9	10.0
100.0	100.0	100.0	100.0	100.0		Total	100.0	100.0
						LIABILITIES		
8.8	8.4	2.4	1.4	2.2		Notes Payable-Short Term	4.6	4.2
2.1	3.2	1.8	3.6	2.8		Cur. Mat.-L.T.D.	2.4	2.7
8.3	11.1	8.2	7.0	7.7		Trade Payables	5.9	6.5
.0	.0	.0	.0	.2		Income Taxes Payable	.0	.1
28.0	16.1	12.0	9.6	13.5		All Other Current	14.9	12.8
47.2	38.9	24.5	21.6	26.5		Total Current	27.7	26.4
14.1	14.5	21.6	18.1	24.4		Long-Term Debt	24.2	27.5
.0	.0	.1	.0	.0		Deferred Taxes	.0	.1
3.8	4.4	4.0	5.1	8.0		All Other Non-Current	5.6	3.6
34.8	42.2	49.8	55.2	41.1		Net Worth	42.5	42.5
100.0	100.0	100.0	100.0	100.0		Total Liabilities & Net Worth	100.0	100.0
						INCOME DATA		
100.0	100.0	100.0	100.0	100.0		Net Sales	100.0	100.0
						Gross Profit		
99.2	93.0	94.8	96.3	97.0		Operating Expenses	96.3	94.4
.8	7.0	5.2	3.7	3.0		Operating Profit	3.7	5.6
.1	2.0	1.2	-.5	-.1		All Other Expenses (net)	1.9	1.5
.8	5.0	4.0	4.2	3.1		Profit Before Taxes	1.9	4.1
						RATIOS		
9.5	6.1	3.7	4.4	4.0			3.6	3.5
1.2	1.8	2.1	2.1	1.9		Current	2.0	2.0
.9	.9	1.2	1.2	1.1			1.1	1.1
9.5	6.1	3.4	3.8	3.8			3.4	3.1
1.1	1.5	1.9	1.9	1.4		Quick	1.8	1.6
.8	.8	1.0	1.1	1.0			.9	.9
0 UND	**6** 59.2	**15** 24.8	**21** 17.2	**31** 11.7			**18** 20.8	**10** 37.9
9 41.1	**24** 15.4	**28** 13.1	**32** 11.3	**47** 7.7		Sales/Receivables	**31** 11.7	**29** 12.8
25 14.6	**41** 9.0	**43** 8.4	**48** 7.6	**58** 6.3			**47** 7.8	**46** 7.9
						Cost of Sales/Inventory		
						Cost of Sales/Payables		
17.8	5.4	4.9	3.3	2.9			4.6	5.0
45.0	19.0	9.4	7.4	6.8		Sales/Working Capital	8.9	11.0
-95.5	-62.5	41.8	33.8	76.2			74.6	218.4
8.3	30.6	12.5	15.2	11.4			7.1	13.3
(13) 1.5	(19) 1.6	(87) 2.8	(63) 5.1	(21) 3.3		EBIT/Interest	(170) 2.3	(201) 3.2
-2.7	-1.8	-.1	1.6	1.9			.3	.8
								3.3
						Net Profit + Depr., Dep., Amort./Cur. Mat. L/T/D		(10) 2.1
								.4
.1	.1	.4	.4	.5			.5	.4
.8	.7	.9	.9	1.1		Fixed/Worth	1.0	.9
3.5	3.8	1.5	1.7	2.3			2.1	2.2
.2	.4	.5	.3	.5			.5	.4
1.3	1.2	.8	.7	1.7		Debt/Worth	1.2	1.1
4.3	5.6	1.8	2.2	4.3			2.8	4.0
33.3	61.9	20.5	13.3	19.1			14.3	18.6
(23) 8.0	(32) 10.7	(117) 5.2	(75) 7.3	(21) 8.9		% Profit Before Taxes/Tangible Net Worth	(189) 5.6	(223) 6.6
-19.2	-4.8	-.4	1.4	2.1			-2.3	-.5
31.0	19.1	9.3	7.9	8.3			8.0	10.8
7.3	4.3	2.7	3.6	3.9		% Profit Before Taxes/Total Assets	2.6	3.6
-6.4	-2.1	-.3	.8	.6			-1.1	-.4
231.6	127.8	14.1	4.6	6.4			9.9	15.7
22.9	22.7	3.8	2.6	4.1		Sales/Net Fixed Assets	3.4	4.0
3.7	4.7	1.9	1.5	2.2			1.8	1.7
10.8	6.6	3.1	1.7	2.0			2.6	2.9
5.9	3.9	1.8	1.2	1.3		Sales/Total Assets	1.6	1.7
2.1	2.0	1.0	.7	.9			1.0	.9
.4	.5	.9	1.7	1.9			1.3	1.2
(19) 1.7	(25) 1.0	(109) 2.2	(75) 2.6	(23) 3.1		% Depr., Dep., Amort./Sales	(191) 2.4	(230) 2.4
2.8	2.7	3.8	3.8	4.1			3.9	4.0
5.1		1.6					1.2	2.3
(11) 6.6		(13) 2.6				% Officers', Directors' Owners' Comp/Sales	(29) 4.3	(30) 4.6
12.7		7.3					7.3	9.0
40906M	159514M	1267936M	2560445M	2609572M	757275M	Net Sales ($)	3688218M	4896281M
6979M	38707M	638823M	1816928M	1646513M	1110940M	Total Assets ($)	2402714M	3230895M

M = $ thousand MM = $ million

See Pages 9 through 22 for Explanation of Ratios and Data

Comparative Historical Data				Current Data Sorted by Sales					
			Type of Statement						
190	199	181	Unqualified	5	17	12	41	55	51
7	6	8	Reviewed	1	2	4		1	
5	2	9	Compiled	1	2		4	2	
11	9	17	Tax Returns	4	5	3	2	3	
65	73	80	Other	8	13	7	12	19	21
4/1/11-3/31/12	**4/1/12-3/31/13**	**4/1/13-3/31/14**		**206 (4/1-9/30/13)**			**89 (10/1/13-3/31/14)**		
ALL	**ALL**	**ALL**		**0-1MM**	**1-3MM**	**3-5MM**	**5-10MM**	**10-25MM**	**25MM & OVER**
278	289	295	**NUMBER OF STATEMENTS**	19	39	26	59	80	72
%	%	%	**ASSETS**	%	%	%	%	%	%
22.7	21.6	24.3	Cash & Equivalents	14.8	33.6	22.1	21.3	26.2	22.9
18.2	18.2	17.7	Trade Receivables (net)	9.3	17.8	20.8	15.5	16.6	21.7
.4	.6	.5	Inventory	.2	.1	.7	.8	.3	.5
3.7	3.7	3.9	All Other Current	.3	3.9	2.9	4.7	4.5	4.0
45.0	44.0	46.4	Total Current	24.7	55.4	46.5	42.3	47.6	49.1
41.5	42.5	41.4	Fixed Assets (net)	66.7	34.4	42.1	44.6	39.5	37.8
1.3	2.1	2.9	Intangibles (net)	.0	3.7	6.4	3.2	2.3	2.5
12.1	11.4	9.3	All Other Non-Current	8.6	6.5	5.0	9.9	10.6	10.6
100.0	100.0	100.0	Total	100.0	100.0	100.0	100.0	100.0	100.0
			LIABILITIES						
4.9	4.3	3.4	Notes Payable-Short Term	7.3	4.3	6.8	2.7	2.8	2.0
2.4	2.3	2.6	Cur. Mat.-L.T.D.	2.3	.9	2.8	1.6	2.9	3.9
7.1	7.0	8.1	Trade Payables	4.5	6.8	6.7	6.3	9.7	10.1
.1	.0	.0	Income Taxes Payable	.0	.0	.0	.0	.0	.1
14.4	17.9	13.3	All Other Current	3.9	21.1	10.6	10.6	14.0	14.1
28.8	31.5	27.5	Total Current	18.1	33.1	26.9	21.1	29.4	30.2
21.8	22.8	19.5	Long-Term Debt	36.4	20.9	16.2	17.1	18.6	18.4
.1	.1	.0	Deferred Taxes	.0	.0	.0	.0	.1	.0
2.5	6.1	5.0	All Other Non-Current	2.3	5.3	1.5	2.8	5.2	8.6
46.8	39.5	47.9	Net Worth	43.1	40.7	55.4	59.0	46.6	42.8
100.0	100.0	100.0	Total Liabilties & Net Worth	100.0	100.0	100.0	100.0	100.0	100.0
			INCOME DATA						
100.0	100.0	100.0	Net Sales	100.0	100.0	100.0	100.0	100.0	100.0
			Gross Profit						
97.1	97.1	95.7	Operating Expenses	78.7	96.1	97.2	94.9	98.0	97.4
2.9	2.9	4.3	Operating Profit	21.3	3.9	2.8	5.1	2.0	2.6
.8	1.5	.6	All Other Expenses (net)	9.2	.9	.0	-.1	.0	-.5
2.1	1.3	3.8	Profit Before Taxes	12.1	3.0	2.8	5.2	1.9	3.1
			RATIOS						
3.8	3.2	4.3		7.8	11.6	5.0	4.0	3.7	2.6
1.9	1.7	2.0	Current	1.2	3.2	2.3	2.1	2.1	1.7
1.1	1.0	1.1		.8	1.0	1.4	1.2	1.1	1.0
3.6	2.9	3.9		7.8	10.9	4.9	3.4	3.3	2.3
1.6	1.4	1.7	Quick	1.2	2.5	2.3	2.0	1.7	1.4
.9	.9	1.0		.6	.8	1.2	1.0	.9	1.0
12 29.6	14 26.5	14 26.2		0 UND	0 UND	17 20.9	14 26.2	15 24.8	24 15.1
30 12.0	31 11.9	29 12.4	Sales/Receivables	7 54.5	27 13.6	28 13.2	29 12.8	26 13.9	34 10.6
49 7.5	48 7.6	43 8.4		38 9.7	40 9.1	43 8.5	44 8.3	40 9.1	51 7.1
			Cost of Sales/Inventory						
			Cost of Sales/Payables						
4.4	5.1	4.4		3.6	4.7	4.5	4.5	4.8	3.8
11.3	12.9	11.1	Sales/Working Capital	41.5	17.5	7.7	9.7	9.2	14.8
204.7	438.7	118.3		-56.0	-495.0	32.0	41.1	159.8	117.5
8.3	10.6	12.3			17.9	20.6	17.5	9.3	13.2
(211) 2.6	(222) 2.1	(209) 3.3	EBIT/Interest		(18) 1.4	(22) 2.7	(41) 4.3	(59) 2.7	(60) 5.6
.1	-.9	1.0			-2.6	-.3	1.3	-1.0	2.1
			Net Profit + Depr., Dep., Amort./Cur. Mat. L/T/D						
.4	.4	.4		.8	.1	.4	.4	.3	.4
.8	1.0	.9	Fixed/Worth	3.2	.7	.8	.9	.9	.9
1.9	2.2	1.8		8.1	2.3	1.5	1.3	1.6	2.6
.3	.4	.4		.1	.4	.3	.4	.4	.5
1.0	1.1	1.0	Debt/Worth	3.5	.8	1.1	.7	.9	1.5
3.0	4.0	3.2		7.2	5.3	1.5	1.1	2.3	4.5
14.1	14.9	20.5		29.2	30.2	61.1	14.2	19.3	20.2
(254) 5.0	(251) 3.4	(274) 7.0	% Profit Before Taxes/Tangible Net Worth	(17) 7.1	(33) 11.8	(25) 4.1	(56) 5.0	(75) 5.4	(68) 9.0
-2.1	-4.0	.3		-.9	-5.4	-4.2	.4	-1.3	3.0
8.3	7.4	9.6		9.6	15.5	22.3	10.2	8.0	9.2
2.3	1.3	3.3	% Profit Before Taxes/Total Assets	2.0	5.2	3.1	3.2	2.2	3.9
-1.5	-3.1	.1		-.6	-1.9	-2.0	.3	-2.6	1.2
20.2	17.2	16.0		6.4	169.6	21.3	11.3	14.7	10.3
3.9	4.2	3.9	Sales/Net Fixed Assets	2.0	12.1	3.6	3.1	4.5	4.2
1.7	1.8	2.0		.1	1.9	1.5	1.7	2.2	2.5
3.2	3.1	3.2		2.1	6.7	4.7	2.6	3.4	2.6
1.7	1.7	1.6	Sales/Total Assets	1.1	2.6	1.9	1.5	2.1	1.5
.9	1.0	.9		.1	.7	.9	1.0	1.0	1.1
1.0	1.1	1.2		1.7	.5	.8	1.2	.9	1.4
(256) 2.4	(264) 2.2	(257) 2.3	% Depr., Dep., Amort./Sales	(15) 3.3	(27) 2.8	(22) 2.0	(52) 2.4	(73) 2.4	(68) 2.1
4.0	3.9	3.7		23.2	5.9	4.1	3.7	3.8	3.1
2.3	1.8	2.1			4.9			1.0	
(27) 3.8	(25) 2.5	(39) 4.4	% Officers', Directors' Owners' Comp/Sales		(10) 7.5			(10) 2.0	
7.9	4.6	12.7			10.8			19.5	
6497325M	6604083M	7395648M	Net Sales ($)	8517M	81359M	101085M	446063M	1246852M	5511772M
3912638M	4120857M	5258890M	Total Assets ($)	26165M	90832M	73029M	397177M	1023617M	3648070M

M = $ thousand MM = $ million

See Pages 9 through 22 for Explanation of Ratios and Data

Current Data Sorted by Assets							Comparative Historical Data	
						Type of Statement		
7	56	173	189	33	12	Unqualified	480	579
		2				Reviewed	8	12
4	4	2	1	1		Compiled	14	9
1	7	9				Tax Returns	28	23
18	25	69	48	10	3	Other	194	210
466 (4/1-9/30/13)			208 (10/1/13-3/31/14)				4/1/09-3/31/10	4/1/10-3/31/11
0-500M	500M-2MM	2-10MM	10-50MM	50-100MM	100-250MM		ALL	ALL
30	92	255	238	44	15	**NUMBER OF STATEMENTS**	724	833
%	%	%	%	%	%	**ASSETS**	%	%
30.4	26.0	21.5	17.5	18.8	20.5	Cash & Equivalents	20.7	21.0
27.3	23.4	17.2	14.2	11.6	9.5	Trade Receivables (net)	17.6	17.2
.6	.8	1.4	.8	.4	4.9	Inventory	1.4	1.3
4.4	5.5	2.9	2.9	2.5	5.2	All Other Current	4.8	4.3
62.8	55.6	43.0	35.4	33.3	40.2	Total Current	44.4	43.8
25.9	36.3	43.4	46.6	43.8	36.7	Fixed Assets (net)	42.2	42.6
2.5	2.3	1.8	1.4	1.5	6.8	Intangibles (net)	1.0	1.1
8.8	5.8	11.7	16.6	21.4	16.3	All Other Non-Current	12.3	12.6
100.0	100.0	100.0	100.0	100.0	100.0	Total	100.0	100.0
						LIABILITIES		
6.7	5.4	2.3	2.1	2.8	1.1	Notes Payable-Short Term	3.9	2.7
2.3	2.3	2.0	1.7	1.4	2.0	Cur. Mat.-L.T.D.	1.8	1.9
9.3	7.9	6.8	5.9	5.9	6.2	Trade Payables	6.5	6.5
1.0	.0	.4	.0	.0	.0	Income Taxes Payable	.1	.1
38.6	14.0	10.1	8.5	9.1	7.3	All Other Current	12.6	12.1
57.9	29.7	21.6	18.3	19.3	16.6	Total Current	24.9	23.3
9.3	20.8	17.9	19.8	24.3	23.7	Long-Term Debt	17.7	19.1
.0	.1	.0	.0	.8	.7	Deferred Taxes	.0	.0
18.6	1.0	2.8	5.0	7.6	3.8	All Other Non-Current	4.4	3.8
14.3	48.4	57.8	56.9	48.0	55.2	Net Worth	53.0	53.7
100.0	100.0	100.0	100.0	100.0	100.0	Total Liabilities & Net Worth	100.0	100.0
						INCOME DATA		
100.0	100.0	100.0	100.0	100.0	100.0	Net Sales	100.0	100.0
						Gross Profit		
96.1	98.9	96.4	95.9	97.8	95.7	Operating Expenses	97.9	96.7
3.9	1.1	3.6	4.1	2.2	4.3	Operating Profit	2.1	3.3
.4	.7	.5	-.6	.0	1.4	All Other Expenses (net)	1.4	.5
3.6	.4	3.2	4.7	2.3	2.9	Profit Before Taxes	.6	2.8
						RATIOS		
4.4	5.0	4.0	3.5	2.9	4.8		3.6	3.9
1.7	2.4	2.1	2.0	1.9	2.5	Current	1.9	2.1
1.0	1.2	1.3	1.2	1.1	.9		1.2	1.2
4.0	4.8	3.7	3.1	2.8	3.8		3.2	3.4
1.3	(91) 2.1	1.8	1.8	1.9	1.4	Quick	1.7	1.8
.7	.9	1.1	1.0	.9	.6		1.0	1.0
0 UND	8 47.5	11 34.6	17 21.9	16 23.0	0 UND		13 29.2	13 28.7
9 40.9	29 12.5	31 11.9	36 10.1	28 13.1	33 11.2	Sales/Receivables	31 11.6	33 11.1
45 8.2	48 7.6	49 7.5	51 7.2	56 6.5	52 7.0		49 7.4	51 7.2
						Cost of Sales/Inventory		
						Cost of Sales/Payables		
12.7	4.7	4.1	3.7	3.3	1.6		4.7	4.0
30.9	7.7	9.9	8.8	7.4	5.7	Sales/Working Capital	9.9	8.5
236.7	61.3	32.4	42.3	41.3	-33.5		44.3	33.7
27.9	6.5	10.4	16.8	6.7	6.4		6.7	10.3
(14) 7.4	(55) 1.3	(185) 2.3	(194) 3.1	(35) 1.7	(11) 1.8	EBIT/Interest	(516) 1.6	(612) 2.9
-.1	-2.9	-.5	.8	-.3	-.3		-1.6	.5
						Net Profit + Depr., Dep., Amort./Cur. Mat. L/T/D		
.1	.1	.3	.5	.4	.1		.4	.3
.7	.7	.8	.9	.9	.6	Fixed/Worth	.8	.8
UND	1.8	1.4	1.3	1.6	1.6		1.4	1.4
.3	.2	.3	.3	.5	.4		.3	.3
2.5	.8	.6	.6	1.2	.9	Debt/Worth	.8	.7
UND	2.1	1.6	1.2	2.5	1.7		1.8	1.7
100.0	15.6	12.6	10.6	10.8	9.4		14.9	13.2
(23) 20.5	(82) 1.6	(243) 3.5	(230) 4.2	(43) 2.2	(14) 1.9	% Profit Before Taxes/Tangible Net Worth	(694) 2.8	(805) 3.8
-9.3	-13.8	-3.2	-.3	-1.5	-9.2		-4.7	-1.9
28.5	7.4	6.5	6.5	6.1	6.0		7.0	7.1
12.5	1.1	2.0	2.4	1.1	1.4	% Profit Before Taxes/Total Assets	1.4	1.9
-2.7	-6.8	-1.5	-.2	-.9	-1.6		-3.0	-1.1
242.4	66.3	11.9	5.2	5.6	31.3		13.2	11.8
64.5	9.9	4.1	2.6	2.2	1.6	Sales/Net Fixed Assets	4.0	3.8
17.4	3.0	1.9	1.3	.8	.8		1.7	1.6
10.8	4.0	2.5	1.9	1.5	1.5		2.8	2.5
5.7	2.3	1.6	1.1	.9	.8	Sales/Total Assets	1.5	1.5
2.4	1.4	.9	.7	.5	.4		.8	.8
.4	.5	1.1	1.5	1.6	.9		1.1	1.1
(12) .9	(70) 1.4	(236) 2.0	(228) 2.7	(41) 3.5	(11) 2.9	% Depr., Dep., Amort./Sales	(625) 2.2	(744) 2.1
1.4	3.0	3.4	4.4	8.9	3.6		3.9	3.7
	4.1	2.1	2.8				2.5	2.4
	(12) 5.6	(20) 5.1	(16) 5.7			% Officers', Directors' Owners' Comp/Sales	(74) 6.1	(68) 4.6
	8.8	10.0	19.1				13.8	14.5
44623M	308403M	2629107M	6758570M	3581704M	2611577M	Net Sales ($)	15874106M	20043330M
7899M	109895M	1340084M	5301444M	3126879M	2224237M	Total Assets ($)	11473874M	13797065M

M = $ thousand MM = $ million

See Pages 9 through 22 for Explanation of Ratios and Data

Comparative Historical Data / Current Data Sorted by Sales

			Type of Statement						
556	473	470	Unqualified	12	63	27	100	138	130
7	4	2	Reviewed		2				
15	19	12	Compiled	2	1	3	3	2	1
30	24	17	Tax Returns	5	5	2	4	1	
192	183	173	Other	13	32	20	27	46	35
4/1/11-3/31/12 ALL	4/1/12-3/31/13 ALL	4/1/13-3/31/14 ALL		466 (4/1-9/30/13)			208 (10/1/13-3/31/14)		
				0-1MM	1-3MM	3-5MM	5-10MM	10-25MM	25MM & OVER
800	703	674	NUMBER OF STATEMENTS	32	103	52	134	187	166
%	%	%	**ASSETS**	%	%	%	%	%	%
21.4	22.3	20.9	Cash & Equivalents	18.8	23.4	22.9	24.1	18.7	19.1
16.5	15.7	16.9	Trade Receivables (net)	8.0	16.3	16.0	16.6	17.7	18.6
1.4	1.4	1.1	Inventory	.0	.6	.9	1.4	.9	1.7
3.6	3.4	3.3	All Other Current	1.3	3.8	3.9	3.6	3.5	2.8
42.9	42.8	42.2	Total Current	28.1	44.2	43.6	45.8	40.7	42.1
43.4	42.7	42.7	Fixed Assets (net)	59.4	43.3	39.5	40.6	45.2	38.8
.9	1.3	1.8	Intangibles (net)	.4	2.4	.0	2.8	1.3	2.2
12.8	13.2	13.3	All Other Non-Current	12.1	10.2	16.8	10.7	12.8	16.9
100.0	100.0	100.0	Total	100.0	100.0	100.0	100.0	100.0	100.0
			LIABILITIES						
3.8	3.8	2.8	Notes Payable-Short Term	2.7	4.7	2.9	2.3	2.4	2.7
2.0	1.8	1.9	Cur. Mat.-L.T.D.	2.2	2.4	1.0	1.8	1.9	2.0
6.8	6.3	6.7	Trade Payables	.8	5.7	6.6	5.9	7.2	8.6
.1	.0	.2	Income Taxes Payable	.0	.1	.6	.5	.0	.1
10.4	10.2	11.2	All Other Current	14.3	12.6	6.3	10.9	10.6	12.2
23.1	22.1	22.9	Total Current	20.0	25.4	17.5	21.4	22.1	25.6
19.5	18.8	19.1	Long-Term Debt	30.0	21.1	11.7	18.0	19.2	18.9
.0	.1	.1	Deferred Taxes	.0	.0	.0	.1	.0	.3
4.0	4.0	4.4	All Other Non-Current	5.8	1.9	7.0	2.7	3.1	7.5
53.4	55.1	53.5	Net Worth	44.2	51.6	63.8	57.8	55.5	47.6
100.0	100.0	100.0	Total Liabilties & Net Worth	100.0	100.0	100.0	100.0	100.0	100.0
			INCOME DATA						
100.0	100.0	100.0	Net Sales	100.0	100.0	100.0	100.0	100.0	100.0
			Gross Profit						
96.2	96.6	96.6	Operating Expenses	92.8	95.5	95.8	96.9	96.4	98.3
3.8	3.4	3.4	Operating Profit	7.2	4.5	4.2	3.1	3.6	1.7
.7	1.2	.1	All Other Expenses (net)	3.6	1.3	-.4	.2	-.7	-.4
3.2	2.3	3.3	Profit Before Taxes	3.6	3.3	4.6	2.9	4.3	2.1
			RATIOS						
4.1	4.5	4.0		3.8	6.8	7.7	4.3	3.6	2.8
2.1	2.2	2.0	Current	1.6	3.3	2.3	2.4	2.2	1.7
1.2	1.2	1.2		.7	1.2	1.4	1.4	1.2	1.1
3.6	3.9	3.6		3.3	6.2	6.9	3.8	3.4	2.5
1.8	1.9	(673) 1.8	Quick	1.5	2.8	2.0	(133) 2.1	1.8	1.5
1.0	1.0	1.0		.6	1.1	1.0	1.2	.9	.9
11 33.0	10 36.5	12 30.4		0 UND	9 42.7	6 57.4	9 38.7	19 18.9	15 23.6
31 11.7	29 12.7	32 11.4	Sales/Receivables	1 313.0	32 11.4	31 11.9	29 12.8	35 10.4	34 10.7
47 7.7	50 7.3	50 7.3		37 9.9	56 6.5	49 7.5	49 7.5	49 7.4	50 7.3
			Cost of Sales/Inventory						
			Cost of Sales/Payables						
3.9	3.7	4.1		4.4	3.2	3.8	3.7	4.2	5.7
8.7	8.1	9.6	Sales/Working Capital	18.2	5.9	8.0	8.9	8.9	14.0
37.6	40.0	39.7		NM	34.0	32.2	21.0	35.9	87.8
9.1	7.2	10.5		3.9	6.5	35.4	16.9	17.8	8.4
(583) 2.5	(502) 1.8	(494) 2.5	EBIT/Interest	(18) .9	(67) 1.0	(32) 1.7	(94) 3.4	(152) 3.1	(131) 2.6
.0	-1.1	-.3		-1.0	-1.4	-2.3	.5	-.2	.5
			Net Profit + Depr., Dep., Amort./Cur. Mat. L/T/D						
.4	.3	.4		.8	.2	.2	.4	.5	.4
.8	.8	.8	Fixed/Worth	1.4	.7	.5	.7	.8	.8
1.4	1.4	1.4		3.1	1.8	1.1	1.4	1.3	1.4
.3	.3	.3		.6	.2	.1	.3	.3	.5
.7	.6	.7	Debt/Worth	1.0	.5	.4	.5	.7	1.0
1.7	1.6	1.8		3.9	1.8	.8	1.4	1.5	2.1
13.2	9.8	12.5		21.2	12.7	10.7	13.8	12.6	11.5
(766) 4.3	(659) 2.5	(635) 3.8	% Profit Before Taxes/Tangible Net Worth	(29) 3.1	(92) 1.8	(50) 1.8	(127) 4.1	(180) 3.7	(157) 4.4
-1.3	-4.0	-2.2		-4.5	-5.7	-4.3	-1.3	-1.6	-.9
7.3	5.9	6.9		7.3	7.0	7.8	7.5	7.6	6.1
2.1	1.3	2.0	% Profit Before Taxes/Total Assets	.8	1.1	1.8	2.7	1.9	1.9
-1.0	-2.3	-1.3		-3.1	-3.1	-2.2	-.7	-1.0	-.6
11.8	13.1	11.9		14.4	23.1	25.9	12.3	6.8	10.5
3.6	3.6	3.6	Sales/Net Fixed Assets	.9	3.0	3.9	4.2	3.3	4.6
1.4	1.5	1.6		.3	.7	1.3	1.8	1.5	2.5
2.5	2.3	2.4		1.5	2.5	2.4	2.4	2.3	2.7
1.4	1.4	1.4	Sales/Total Assets	.8	1.1	1.2	1.5	1.4	1.6
.7	.7	.8		.3	.5	.5	.8	.8	1.1
1.1	1.2	1.2		2.5	1.3	1.2	1.0	1.4	1.0
(696) 2.2	(625) 2.3	(598) 2.3	% Depr., Dep., Amort./Sales	(22) 4.4	(77) 3.4	(42) 2.1	(127) 2.0	(173) 2.4	(157) 1.8
3.8	4.0	3.9		12.4	5.9	3.5	3.6	3.9	3.4
2.8	2.5	2.2			4.0		2.1	1.7	
(66) 6.0	(50) 6.2	(57) 5.6	% Officers', Directors' Owners' Comp/Sales		(16) 5.6		(12) 10.0	(13) 5.7	
12.4	11.8	11.0			8.8		24.8	13.2	
15734220M	15475438M	15933984M	Net Sales ($)	16915M	206031M	204377M	988279M	3009217M	11509165M
12353326M	12282380M	12110438M	Total Assets ($)	46022M	318622M	237900M	1103276M	3197591M	7207027M

M = $ thousand MM = $ million

See Pages 9 through 22 for Explanation of Ratios and Data

Current Data Sorted by Assets							Comparative Historical Data	
						Type of Statement		
	1	17	16	1		Unqualified	21	20
						Reviewed	1	
						Compiled	3	1
	1	1				Tax Returns		1
	1		7			Other	8	11
	36 (4/1-9/30/13)		9 (10/1/13-3/31/14)				4/1/09-3/31/10	4/1/10-3/31/11
0-500M	500M-2MM	2-10MM	10-50MM	50-100MM	100-250MM		ALL	ALL
	3	18	23	1		**NUMBER OF STATEMENTS**	33	33
%	%	%	%	%	%	**ASSETS**	%	%
DATA NOT AVAILABLE		14.8	23.7		DATA NOT AVAILABLE	Cash & Equivalents	21.6	22.3
		3.8	6.6			Trade Receivables (net)	5.9	10.4
		8.1	14.6			Inventory	14.4	10.6
		1.8	2.0			All Other Current	2.2	3.3
		28.5	46.9			Total Current	44.1	46.5
		61.6	44.6			Fixed Assets (net)	45.0	43.6
		.1	1.2			Intangibles (net)	.4	.1
		9.9	7.4			All Other Non-Current	10.4	9.9
		100.0	100.0			Total	100.0	100.0
						LIABILITIES		
		1.8	.9			Notes Payable-Short Term	2.8	2.3
		1.8	1.3			Cur. Mat.-L.T.D.	.9	2.9
		3.0	3.0			Trade Payables	6.1	6.4
		.0	.0			Income Taxes Payable	.0	.0
		4.3	3.6			All Other Current	3.7	4.1
		10.9	8.8			Total Current	13.5	15.7
		19.8	12.8			Long-Term Debt	9.8	9.1
		.0	.0			Deferred Taxes	.0	.0
		.3	1.2			All Other Non-Current	5.2	4.8
		69.1	77.2			Net Worth	71.5	70.4
		100.0	100.0			Total Liabilties & Net Worth	100.0	100.0
						INCOME DATA		
		100.0	100.0			Net Sales	100.0	100.0
						Gross Profit		
		97.0	87.2			Operating Expenses	91.7	92.0
		3.0	12.8			Operating Profit	8.3	8.0
		.9	5.6			All Other Expenses (net)	.4	.2
		2.1	7.2			Profit Before Taxes	7.9	7.7
						RATIOS		
		10.0	14.0				14.1	13.7
		3.4	8.5			Current	6.9	6.1
		1.0	3.8				1.8	1.8
		5.7	8.2				6.1	7.2
		2.4	4.9			Quick	3.5	3.0
		.7	2.3				1.3	1.3
		1 259.1	**2** 225.0				**0** 999.8	**0** 839.7
		4 98.3	**8** 47.3			Sales/Receivables	**3** 118.9	**7** 53.8
		14 25.9	**19** 19.4				**10** 37.2	**36** 10.0
						Cost of Sales/Inventory		
						Cost of Sales/Payables		
		6.7	1.8				5.0	3.5
		13.1	4.5			Sales/Working Capital	7.0	6.1
		NM	7.8				13.2	13.0
		13.2	165.1				21.6	49.1
		(12) 1.9	(12) 8.8			EBIT/Interest	(17) 6.1	(17) 6.0
		1.2	3.1				-4.0	2.4
						Net Profit + Depr., Dep., Amort./Cur. Mat. L/T/D		
		.5	.4				.3	.3
		.8	.6			Fixed/Worth	.6	.6
		1.5	.8				.9	.9
		.1	.1				.1	.1
		.3	.2			Debt/Worth	.3	.3
		.9	.5				.5	.8
		5.3	17.1				35.7	14.9
		2.8	9.4			% Profit Before Taxes/Tangible Net Worth	(32) 16.9	(32) 6.8
		.2	2.8				-1.9	-1.4
		4.2	11.5				22.8	10.6
		1.7	8.5			% Profit Before Taxes/Total Assets	11.4	6.2
		.0	2.3				-2.7	-.6
		8.5	7.6				14.9	20.7
		4.0	3.9			Sales/Net Fixed Assets	5.7	4.1
		.8	2.0				2.4	1.8
		4.0	2.8				3.8	3.4
		2.0	1.5			Sales/Total Assets	2.2	1.4
		.6	.7				1.3	1.0
		.9	.9				.7	.9
		2.2	(22) 1.6			% Depr., Dep., Amort./Sales	(28) 1.3	(29) 1.4
		5.4	3.7				2.1	3.4
						% Officers', Directors' Owners' Comp/Sales		
	16849M	338031M	725763M	111556M		Net Sales ($)	1705237M	792611M
	2502M	113141M	414905M	79365M		Total Assets ($)	449949M	364549M

M = $ thousand MM = $ million

See Pages 9 through 22 for Explanation of Ratios and Data

Comparative Historical Data | Current Data Sorted by Sales

4/1/11-3/31/12 ALL	4/1/12-3/31/13 ALL	4/1/13-3/31/14 ALL		0-1MM	1-3MM	3-5MM	5-10MM	10-25MM	25MM & OVER
					36 (4/1-9/30/13)			9 (10/1/13-3/31/14)	
			Type of Statement						
27	26	35	Unqualified		2	5	4	11	13
	1		Reviewed						
3			Compiled						
9	1	2	Tax Returns		1		1		
8	9	8	Other	1		1	2		4
47	37	45	**NUMBER OF STATEMENTS**	1	3	6	7	11	17
%	%	%	**ASSETS**	%	%	%	%	%	%
15.9	15.9	19.6	Cash & Equivalents					20.9	24.1
4.2	4.8	5.2	Trade Receivables (net)					8.7	3.7
13.3	8.3	11.2	Inventory					13.1	15.5
7.8	7.4	2.3	All Other Current					1.8	3.9
41.3	36.4	38.3	Total Current					44.5	47.2
42.9	47.7	53.0	Fixed Assets (net)					44.4	45.4
1.5	1.2	.6	Intangibles (net)					2.3	.1
14.3	14.7	8.1	All Other Non-Current					8.9	7.3
100.0	100.0	100.0	Total					100.0	100.0
			LIABILITIES						
1.9	1.3	1.2	Notes Payable-Short Term					1.1	.9
1.4	1.5	2.1	Cur. Mat.-L.T.D.					1.8	1.9
4.6	4.9	3.4	Trade Payables					4.1	2.4
.0	.0	.0	Income Taxes Payable					.0	.0
9.1	9.5	3.6	All Other Current					2.3	5.2
17.0	17.2	10.3	Total Current					9.2	10.3
9.8	16.2	17.3	Long-Term Debt					11.4	13.2
.0	.0	.0	Deferred Taxes					.0	.0
5.8	3.3	.7	All Other Non-Current					.6	1.3
67.4	63.3	71.6	Net Worth					78.8	75.1
100.0	100.0	100.0	Total Liabilties & Net Worth					100.0	100.0
			INCOME DATA						
100.0	100.0	100.0	Net Sales					100.0	100.0
			Gross Profit						
94.2	96.4	91.8	Operating Expenses					98.2	87.6
5.8	3.6	8.2	Operating Profit					1.8	12.4
1.0	1.7	3.3	All Other Expenses (net)					-2.3	8.7
4.8	1.8	4.9	Profit Before Taxes					4.1	3.7
			RATIOS						
11.6	7.8	11.1						10.2	15.0
4.3	4.5	6.9	Current					9.2	8.8
1.5	1.9	1.9						6.0	3.5
5.8	4.8	6.0						6.4	7.5
2.0	2.4	4.4	Quick					5.5	4.7
.4	.7	1.3						1.6	1.8
0 UND	0 UND	1 297.5						2 222.1	1 396.2
3 116.5	5 67.3	7 55.6	Sales/Receivables					3 112.1	4 93.5
18 20.5	18 20.2	15 23.8						19 19.4	8 45.5
			Cost of Sales/Inventory						
			Cost of Sales/Payables						
4.6	3.8	2.9						2.9	4.9
9.2	10.2	7.6	Sales/Working Capital					7.3	7.8
24.4	21.2	17.7						12.1	13.7
116.8	3.3	12.5							
(28) 6.3	(22) -.2	(27) 3.3	EBIT/Interest						
-1.4	-8.8	1.4							
			Net Profit + Depr., Dep., Amort./Cur. Mat. L/T/D						
.3	.3	.4						.4	.4
.5	.6	.7	Fixed/Worth					.5	.6
1.0	1.1	1.0						.7	.9
.1	.1	.1						.0	.1
.2	.4	.3	Debt/Worth					.2	.3
.6	.9	.7						.4	.6
10.7	17.5	15.9						15.5	18.5
(43) 2.4	(34) 1.7	5.1	% Profit Before Taxes/Tangible Net Worth					5.3	9.4
-4.8	-10.1	1.5						-11.7	1.7
8.2	10.0	10.0						10.0	12.4
1.2	.6	3.9	% Profit Before Taxes/Total Assets					3.9	7.7
-3.5	-8.4	.8						-1.8	1.3
21.0	11.7	7.8						8.9	8.4
6.1	3.2	4.1	Sales/Net Fixed Assets					4.3	7.6
2.0	1.5	1.5						2.1	4.1
3.4	4.1	3.3						3.6	4.7
1.9	2.1	1.7	Sales/Total Assets					2.1	2.9
.7	.8	.7						1.0	1.7
.6	.6	.9						.9	.7
(42) 1.5	(33) 1.8	(43) 1.4	% Depr., Dep., Amort./Sales					1.6	1.0
4.4	3.8	4.4						3.0	1.3
			% Officers', Directors' Owners' Comp/Sales						
1137223M	940880M	1192199M	Net Sales ($)	437M	6710M	26154M	59575M	197638M	901685M
568648M	462499M	609913M	Total Assets ($)	952M	9390M	53769M	75982M	123848M	345972M

M = $ thousand MM = $ million

See Pages 9 through 22 for Explanation of Ratios and Data

Current Data Sorted by Assets							Comparative Historical Data	
						Type of Statement		
3	6	13	11	2		Unqualified	23	27
1						Reviewed	1	1
1			1			Compiled	1	1
	1					Tax Returns		1
2	1	4	3			Other	9	8
42 (4/1-9/30/13)			7 (10/1/13-3/31/14)				**4/1/09-3/31/10**	**4/1/10-3/31/11**
0-500M	**500M-2MM**	**2-10MM**	**10-50MM**	**50-100MM**	**100-250MM**		**ALL**	**ALL**
7	8	17	15	2		**NUMBER OF STATEMENTS**	34	38
%	%	%	%	%	%	**ASSETS**	%	%
		25.2	14.2		DATA NOT AVAILABLE	Cash & Equivalents	16.9	17.8
		6.8	7.7			Trade Receivables (net)	8.9	7.7
		.4	.2			Inventory	.2	.3
		2.1	.7			All Other Current	3.1	2.6
		34.5	22.7			Total Current	29.1	28.4
		51.5	66.6			Fixed Assets (net)	56.6	62.0
		.0	.1			Intangibles (net)	.0	.7
		14.0	10.6			All Other Non-Current	14.2	8.9
		100.0	100.0			Total	100.0	100.0
						LIABILITIES		
		.8	.1			Notes Payable-Short Term	4.0	2.4
		.5	.4			Cur. Mat.-L.T.D.	1.1	.8
		2.3	6.2			Trade Payables	2.5	1.8
		.0	.0			Income Taxes Payable	.0	.0
		2.6	1.4			All Other Current	4.3	3.8
		6.3	8.1			Total Current	11.8	8.8
		12.9	18.8			Long-Term Debt	21.1	15.9
		.0	.0			Deferred Taxes	.0	.0
		.3	3.2			All Other Non-Current	1.2	3.1
		80.5	69.9			Net Worth	65.8	72.1
		100.0	100.0			Total Liabilities & Net Worth	100.0	100.0
						INCOME DATA		
		100.0	100.0			Net Sales	100.0	100.0
						Gross Profit		
		94.9	89.3			Operating Expenses	98.8	95.0
		5.1	10.7			Operating Profit	1.2	5.0
		-2.2	1.5			All Other Expenses (net)	2.2	-.1
		7.3	9.2			Profit Before Taxes	-1.0	5.1
						RATIOS		
		8.4	7.8				5.4	7.4
		5.8	4.2			Current	3.1	3.4
		2.4	2.9				1.4	1.7
		8.3	7.6				4.0	7.2
		4.8	4.2			Quick	2.3	2.9
		2.1	2.9				1.3	1.6
		0 UND	**4** 86.1				**2** 204.1	**8** 44.5
		18 19.9	**19** 19.4			Sales/Receivables	**22** 16.8	**20** 18.6
		36 10.2	**51** 7.1				**48** 7.6	**32** 11.4
						Cost of Sales/Inventory		
						Cost of Sales/Payables		
		2.3	2.5				3.2	2.7
		4.6	5.2			Sales/Working Capital	4.8	5.6
		8.5	10.2				14.2	10.5
							14.8	11.0
						EBIT/Interest	(23) 1.9	(24) 1.7
							-2.2	.6
						Net Profit + Depr., Dep., Amort./Cur. Mat. L/T/D		
		.3	.8				.5	.6
		.6	.9			Fixed/Worth	.9	.9
		1.1	1.9				1.3	1.3
		.1	.0				.2	.1
		.2	.2			Debt/Worth	.4	.2
		.4	1.5				1.2	.9
		13.2	9.6				6.9	13.3
		5.7	3.8			% Profit Before Taxes/Tangible Net Worth	-.6	2.1
		1.4	-.3				-7.7	-1.7
		10.7	5.7				4.0	10.4
		3.9	2.4			% Profit Before Taxes/Total Assets	-.4	1.5
		.9	-.3				-5.0	-.9
		4.1	1.1				3.0	2.3
		1.9	.8			Sales/Net Fixed Assets	1.3	.9
		.7	.3				.7	.7
		1.4	.9				1.2	1.1
		.6	.5			Sales/Total Assets	.8	.7
		.5	.2				.5	.5
		1.4	2.6				1.9	2.8
		(13) 3.1	(14) 4.9			% Depr., Dep., Amort./Sales	(29) 3.1	(35) 4.3
		6.0	10.3				5.7	6.3
						% Officers', Directors' Owners' Comp/Sales		
6356M	**11403M**	**69845M**	**183354M**	**60496M**		Net Sales ($)	**797560M**	**360305M**
2651M	**9814M**	**76074M**	**247768M**	**163321M**		Total Assets ($)	**684050M**	**567340M**

M = $ thousand MM = $ million

See Pages 9 through 22 for Explanation of Ratios and Data

Comparative Historical Data				Current Data Sorted by Sales					
			Type of Statement						
31	26	35	Unqualified	3	11	6	9	4	2
1	2	1	Reviewed	1					
1	3	2	Compiled	1					
1	1	1	Tax Returns	1				1	
7	7	10	Other	2	5	1	2		
4/1/11-3/31/12 ALL	4/1/12-3/31/13 ALL	4/1/13-3/31/14 ALL			42 (4/1-9/30/13)		7 (10/1/13-3/31/14)		
				0-1MM	1-3MM	3-5MM	5-10MM	10-25MM	25MM & OVER
41	39	49	**NUMBER OF STATEMENTS**	8	16	7	11	5	2
%	%	%	**ASSETS**	%	%	%	%	%	%
19.3	17.2	20.7	Cash & Equivalents		21.4		19.8		
9.2	6.0	7.6	Trade Receivables (net)		5.4		6.7		
.5	.9	1.4	Inventory		3.7		.1		
4.6	2.8	3.7	All Other Current		5.9		.7		
33.6	26.9	33.5	Total Current		36.3		27.3		
57.4	63.5	54.9	Fixed Assets (net)		54.6		54.9		
.6	.1	.4	Intangibles (net)		.9		.1		
8.4	9.4	11.2	All Other Non-Current		8.2		17.6		
100.0	100.0	100.0	Total		100.0		100.0		
			LIABILITIES						
2.3	.5	1.0	Notes Payable-Short Term		1.9		1.1		
.6	.7	.6	Cur. Mat.-L.T.D.		.4		.3		
3.7	2.4	4.0	Trade Payables		2.8		2.1		
.0	.0	.0	Income Taxes Payable		.0		.0		
3.8	3.2	3.4	All Other Current		4.0		2.9		
10.3	6.8	9.1	Total Current		9.1		6.4		
18.6	20.0	15.4	Long-Term Debt		13.8		13.1		
.0	.0	.0	Deferred Taxes		.0		.0		
4.7	1.5	1.3	All Other Non-Current		.8		4.8		
66.3	71.7	74.1	Net Worth		76.3		75.7		
100.0	100.0	100.0	Total Liabilties & Net Worth		100.0		100.0		
			INCOME DATA						
100.0	100.0	100.0	Net Sales		100.0		100.0		
			Gross Profit						
96.9	96.6	92.8	Operating Expenses		97.8		92.4		
3.1	3.4	7.2	Operating Profit		2.2		7.6		
-.4	.4	-.6	All Other Expenses (net)		-.4		-.1		
3.5	3.1	7.7	Profit Before Taxes		2.6		7.7		
			RATIOS						
6.2	6.8	6.9			8.7		6.3		
4.0	3.9	4.9	Current		5.6		3.0		
1.9	2.1	2.7			2.5		2.4		
5.3	6.1	6.8			8.5		6.3		
2.8	3.1	4.4	Quick		4.9		3.0		
1.7	1.6	2.3			2.3		1.9		
6 59.9	2 159.6	0 UND			0 UND		4 86.1		
20 18.7	14 26.2	22 16.3	Sales/Receivables		9 42.6		24 14.9		
41 8.8	34 10.8	38 9.7			27 13.3		33 11.1		
			Cost of Sales/Inventory						
			Cost of Sales/Payables						
2.9	3.0	2.6			3.4		4.0		
4.8	5.9	4.9	Sales/Working Capital		5.7		5.9		
9.0	11.2	10.1			10.9		10.2		
10.4	20.3	16.4							
(30) 1.9	(26) 2.7	(26) 3.9	EBIT/Interest						
-1.6	-1.5	1.2							
			Net Profit + Depr., Dep., Amort./Cur. Mat. L/T/D						
.6	.5	.5			.5		.3		
.9	.9	.8	Fixed/Worth		.7		.8		
1.3	1.6	1.0			1.0		.9		
.2	.1	.1			.0		.1		
.4	.3	.2	Debt/Worth		.2		.2		
1.1	.8	.5			.6		.5		
14.0	8.8	9.9			6.8		5.9		
1.5	4.2	4.6	% Profit Before Taxes/Tangible Net Worth		1.4		4.6		
-5.9	-3.5	-.1			-7.9		2.5		
8.4	7.4	7.5			6.5		5.1		
1.2	2.7	3.4	% Profit Before Taxes/Total Assets		.9		3.4		
-3.6	-1.9	-.1			-6.4		2.1		
3.4	4.2	4.3			5.3		4.4		
1.3	.9	1.4	Sales/Net Fixed Assets		2.3		.9		
.7	.6	.6			.8		.7		
1.7	1.7	1.6			1.9		1.5		
.8	.8	.8	Sales/Total Assets		1.2		.6		
.5	.4	.5			.6		.4		
2.2	2.2	1.9			1.1		2.3		
(39) 3.5	(37) 3.9	(42) 3.2	% Depr., Dep., Amort./Sales		(14) 2.0		(10) 4.1		
5.7	6.6	6.3			3.9		7.3		
			% Officers', Directors' Owners' Comp/Sales						
490580M	231905M	331454M	Net Sales ($)	5783M	29306M	28307M	79467M	82538M	106053M
798130M	369081M	499628M	Total Assets ($)	7868M	53967M	61546M	134159M	148360M	93728M

M = $ thousand MM = $ million

See Pages 9 through 22 for Explanation of Ratios and Data

Current Data Sorted by Assets							Comparative Historical Data	
						Type of Statement		
1	12	34	41	9	5	Unqualified	64	75
						Reviewed	1	2
2	2	2	1			Compiled		
	2	2				Tax Returns	2	3
	5	11	12	1		Other	32	36
	102 (4/1-9/30/13)		40 (10/1/13-3/31/14)				**4/1/09-3/31/10 ALL**	**4/1/10-3/31/11 ALL**
0-500M	**500M-2MM**	**2-10MM**	**10-50MM**	**50-100MM**	**100-250MM**			
3	21	49	54	10	5	**NUMBER OF STATEMENTS**	99	116
%	%	%	%	%	%	**ASSETS**	%	%
	16.9	11.1	12.5	21.4		Cash & Equivalents	11.1	15.6
	1.9	8.0	7.8	4.2		Trade Receivables (net)	9.0	10.1
	4.9	2.2	4.0	.7		Inventory	4.2	3.2
	4.0	6.3	3.3	8.2		All Other Current	4.8	3.5
	27.6	27.6	27.6	34.4		Total Current	29.1	32.4
	50.0	49.4	38.3	40.7		Fixed Assets (net)	45.6	43.3
	7.4	.4	1.2	.3		Intangibles (net)	.6	.9
	15.0	22.5	32.8	24.6		All Other Non-Current	24.6	23.3
	100.0	100.0	100.0	100.0		Total	100.0	100.0
						LIABILITIES		
	3.2	2.8	1.9	.9		Notes Payable-Short Term	3.2	2.2
	3.8	3.0	2.0	1.8		Cur. Mat.-L.T.D.	2.3	3.1
	3.1	3.6	2.7	2.3		Trade Payables	4.0	3.5
	.0	.0	.0	.0		Income Taxes Payable	.0	.0
	3.7	6.0	6.6	5.0		All Other Current	5.5	9.7
	13.8	15.4	13.2	10.0		Total Current	15.0	18.5
	32.1	28.2	28.9	42.6		Long-Term Debt	33.7	26.5
	.0	.0	.0	.0		Deferred Taxes	.0	.0
	2.3	2.8	3.5	11.8		All Other Non-Current	3.1	5.0
	51.8	53.6	54.4	35.5		Net Worth	48.2	50.0
	100.0	100.0	100.0	100.0		Total Liabilties & Net Worth	100.0	100.0
						INCOME DATA		
	100.0	100.0	100.0	100.0		Net Sales	100.0	100.0
						Gross Profit		
	92.8	93.2	90.4	87.3		Operating Expenses	90.2	89.6
	7.2	6.8	9.6	12.7		Operating Profit	9.8	10.4
	4.2	1.7	1.7	10.3		All Other Expenses (net)	5.9	2.8
	3.0	5.1	7.9	2.4		Profit Before Taxes	4.0	7.6
						RATIOS		
	5.9	4.5	5.4	8.0			4.2	5.2
	2.6	1.4	2.0	2.3		Current	2.2	2.1
	.6	.9	.9	1.6			1.1	1.0
	4.1	2.9	3.2	4.3			2.8	3.9
	2.2	1.0	1.1	1.5		Quick	1.3	1.6
	.3	.5	.6	1.1			.6	.6
	0 UND	**1** 316.5	**5** 71.2	**0** UND			**3** 123.8	**3** 117.7
	0 UND	**14** 25.7	**24** 15.3	**6** 57.5		Sales/Receivables	**21** 17.0	**23** 15.7
	5 67.4	**42** 8.6	**49** 7.5	**29** 12.5			**49** 7.4	**50** 7.3
						Cost of Sales/Inventory		
						Cost of Sales/Payables		
	2.2	3.0	2.0	1.0			1.9	1.8
	7.2	6.4	5.1	1.8		Sales/Working Capital	6.3	5.7
	-47.5	-63.5	-38.1	10.7			56.9	UND
	8.9	5.3	10.0				14.9	11.4
	(13) 1.8	(42) 2.1	(39) 1.8			EBIT/Interest	(62) 1.9	(88) 2.9
	-.4	.7	-1.3				.0	-.4
						Net Profit + Depr., Dep., Amort./Cur. Mat. L/T/D		
	.3	.3	.2	.2			.3	.3
	.8	.9	.6	1.4		Fixed/Worth	.9	.8
	2.8	2.1	1.6	3.7			2.1	1.6
	.3	.3	.2	.7			.3	.3
	.7	.7	.8	2.6		Debt/Worth	1.0	.9
	4.5	2.2	2.2	8.1			2.4	2.5
	21.2	10.0	11.0	16.7			9.7	15.1
	(18) 5.9	(48) 2.7	(52) 5.0	2.9		% Profit Before Taxes/Tangible Net Worth	(91) 3.4	(109) 6.1
	-6.1	-1.1	-2.0	-2.1			-1.6	-1.8
	13.0	3.6	5.4	3.1			5.8	8.4
	3.1	1.4	2.3	.4		% Profit Before Taxes/Total Assets	1.6	2.6
	-2.8	-.5	-.4	-1.1			-.8	-1.5
	7.3	2.9	5.0	6.9			4.4	5.2
	.7	1.7	1.7	1.7		Sales/Net Fixed Assets	1.4	1.8
	.3	.6	.7	.2			.6	.5
	1.0	1.3	.8	.8			.9	1.1
	.3	.5	.4	.3		Sales/Total Assets	.5	.5
	.2	.3	.2	.1			.2	.3
	2.3	2.0	1.3				1.4	1.0
	(15) 11.1	(45) 3.6	(47) 3.7			% Depr., Dep., Amort./Sales	(84) 3.6	(106) 3.1
	24.4	6.4	6.6				8.6	7.8
								3.9
						% Officers', Directors' Owners' Comp/Sales		(12) 6.6
								13.6
6051M	24874M	232466M	604900M	303980M	455848M	Net Sales ($)	1015670M	1003842M
912M	25674M	292390M	986592M	726266M	779721M	Total Assets ($)	1967712M	1993183M

M = $ thousand MM = $ million

See Pages 9 through 22 for Explanation of Ratios and Data

Comparative Historical Data				Current Data Sorted by Sales					
			Type of Statement						
90	78	102	Unqualified	13	21	16	27	17	8
1	1		Reviewed						
4	3	7	Compiled	5	2				
5	1	4	Tax Returns	2	2				
35	40	29	Other	6	4	3	8	4	4
4/1/11-3/31/12 ALL	4/1/12-3/31/13 ALL	4/1/13-3/31/14 ALL		102 (4/1-9/30/13)			40 (10/1/13-3/31/14)		
				0-1MM	1-3MM	3-5MM	5-10MM	10-25MM	25MM & OVER
135	123	142	**NUMBER OF STATEMENTS**	26	29	19	35	21	12
%	%	%	**ASSETS**	%	%	%	%	%	%
14.3	14.5	13.6	Cash & Equivalents	11.4	14.0	8.8	16.0	12.7	19.3
9.6	9.6	7.2	Trade Receivables (net)	2.3	1.7	12.3	5.9	12.1	17.9
3.7	3.4	3.0	Inventory	4.6	5.2	1.4	2.2	2.5	.4
3.5	4.2	4.9	All Other Current	1.0	8.1	6.9	3.0	4.5	8.6
31.2	31.7	28.7	Total Current	19.4	29.0	29.5	27.0	31.9	46.2
49.4	47.1	44.1	Fixed Assets (net)	56.5	40.7	37.8	43.3	46.3	33.6
.6	1.1	1.7	Intangibles (net)	3.9	.4	1.2	3.0	.3	.1
18.9	20.1	25.5	All Other Non-Current	20.2	29.9	31.4	26.6	21.6	20.1
100.0	100.0	100.0	Total	100.0	100.0	100.0	100.0	100.0	100.0
			LIABILITIES						
2.5	3.4	2.9	Notes Payable-Short Term	2.4	4.4	3.4	1.3	3.2	4.4
1.7	2.2	2.6	Cur. Mat.-L.T.D.	3.6	2.8	2.2	2.8	1.9	1.7
3.2	4.2	3.7	Trade Payables	1.0	5.1	4.2	3.7	4.2	4.8
.0	.0	.0	Income Taxes Payable	.0	.0	.0	.0	.0	.0
6.6	6.3	6.6	All Other Current	3.6	8.4	4.7	6.7	5.0	14.1
14.0	16.1	15.9	Total Current	10.6	20.6	14.6	14.5	14.3	24.9
33.1	31.5	29.9	Long-Term Debt	40.0	22.0	36.5	26.7	32.3	22.2
.0	.0	.0	Deferred Taxes	.0	.0	.0	.0	.0	.0
5.2	3.1	3.8	All Other Non-Current	1.9	4.2	2.4	2.5	4.0	12.7
47.7	49.4	50.3	Net Worth	47.6	53.1	46.5	56.2	49.4	40.2
100.0	100.0	100.0	Total Liabilties & Net Worth	100.0	100.0	100.0	100.0	100.0	100.0
			INCOME DATA						
100.0	100.0	100.0	Net Sales	100.0	100.0	100.0	100.0	100.0	100.0
			Gross Profit						
90.5	89.7	91.7	Operating Expenses	95.2	85.4	86.7	92.8	96.2	96.5
9.5	10.3	8.3	Operating Profit	4.8	14.6	13.3	7.2	3.8	3.5
3.2	3.8	2.4	All Other Expenses (net)	4.8	2.5	4.2	2.5	-.4	-.9
6.3	6.5	5.8	Profit Before Taxes	.1	12.1	9.0	4.7	4.2	4.3
			RATIOS						
5.4	5.1	5.3		5.3	8.2	5.3	5.7	5.5	2.8
2.6	2.1	2.0	Current	2.5	2.6	2.0	1.9	1.8	1.8
1.0	1.1	.9		.3	.6	1.1	.9	1.0	1.2
4.2	3.9	3.1		3.7	2.7	3.7	4.7	3.9	2.7
1.6	1.5	1.2	Quick	1.5	.9	1.1	1.3	1.3	1.3
.7	.7	.6		.3	.3	.7	.8	.8	1.0
2 197.0	**4** 82.8	**1** 617.5		**0** UND	**0** UND	**13** 27.4	**3** 131.7	**2** 185.2	**7** 56.0
20 18.7	**22** 16.4	**14** 25.6	Sales/Receivables	**0** UND	**4** 94.1	**43** 8.4	**17** 21.3	**20** 17.9	**28** 13.0
49 7.4	**46** 7.9	**45** 8.1		**21** 17.4	**32** 11.3	**94** 3.9	**45** 8.1	**38** 9.6	**51** 7.1
			Cost of Sales/Inventory						
			Cost of Sales/Payables						
1.9	1.8	2.0		1.3	1.5	1.1	2.5	2.7	3.7
5.6	5.9	5.7	Sales/Working Capital	5.5	4.0	3.1	5.7	12.6	10.5
-482.8	231.2	-78.9		-5.6	-14.9	55.7	-65.7	NM	43.9
11.2	13.2	7.9		3.4	9.9	8.2	10.8	7.5	16.0
(105) 2.9	(86) 2.8	(108) 2.0	EBIT/Interest	(17) 1.8	(24) 4.0	(17) 2.3	(23) 1.3	(16) 1.5	(11) 2.0
.3	.3	.4		.1	1.5	-3.5	-.7	-3.8	1.1
			Net Profit + Depr., Dep., Amort./Cur. Mat. L/T/D						
.5	.3	.3		.4	.2	.3	.2	.3	.1
1.0	.9	.8	Fixed/Worth	1.2	.7	.6	.8	1.4	1.0
2.6	2.2	2.4		5.2	1.4	1.8	1.3	2.7	3.1
.4	.4	.3		.4	.3	.6	.3	.2	.5
.9	.9	.8	Debt/Worth	.8	.6	1.5	.8	1.5	1.9
2.9	3.0	2.7		5.1	1.7	2.1	2.6	3.5	5.9
17.2	13.7	11.2		16.0	13.9	13.4	8.8	10.0	32.7
(126) 5.8	(117) 3.7	(135) 3.7	% Profit Before Taxes/Tangible Net Worth	(23) .4	(28) 4.4	2.8	(33) 3.6	(20) 3.8	4.9
-1.2	-.3	-1.9		-3.5	1.4	-1.9	-2.0	-3.6	.7
7.8	6.1	5.3		5.1	7.5	5.3	5.3	6.9	4.8
3.6	1.6	1.7	% Profit Before Taxes/Total Assets	.1	2.4	2.1	1.6	1.6	1.8
-.6	-.5	-.8		-2.6	.5	-1.2	-.6	-1.6	.3
5.6	5.5	5.0		1.5	7.2	11.2	4.9	5.5	8.7
1.2	1.5	1.6	Sales/Net Fixed Assets	.4	1.1	.7	1.9	2.7	4.3
.4	.5	.5		.2	.5	.4	1.1	1.1	1.5
1.1	1.2	1.0		.3	.5	.5	1.2	1.6	1.8
.5	.5	.4	Sales/Total Assets	.2	.3	.3	.6	1.3	1.2
.3	.3	.2		.1	.2	.2	.4	.4	.8
1.5	1.1	1.5		5.7	1.4	1.5	1.3	1.5	.7
(124) 3.6	(94) 2.9	(122) 3.7	% Depr., Dep., Amort./Sales	(22) 11.1	(26) 3.3	(15) 4.9	(30) 2.7	(18) 2.9	(11) 2.0
9.5	8.3	7.8		25.1	6.4	9.5	4.4	7.2	3.4
6.5		2.8							
(15) 14.2		(11) 11.6	% Officers', Directors' Owners' Comp/Sales						
31.2		21.0							
1389890M	1301570M	1628119M	Net Sales ($)	12380M	60604M	74433M	265260M	315414M	900028M
2518284M	2163866M	2811555M	Total Assets ($)	78534M	231854M	312731M	674864M	791349M	722223M

M = $ thousand MM = $ million

See Pages 9 through 22 for Explanation of Ratios and Data

Current Data Sorted by Assets							Comparative Historical Data	
						Type of Statement		
3	24	62	53	10	4	Unqualified	159	190
	2	1				Reviewed	3	4
	1	2	1			Compiled	8	4
2	5	3				Tax Returns	11	7
4	12	29	28	1	5	Other	80	77
	169 (4/1-9/30/13)		83 (10/1/13-3/31/14)				4/1/09-3/31/10	4/1/10-3/31/11
0-500M	**500M-2MM**	**2-10MM**	**10-50MM**	**50-100MM**	**100-250MM**		**ALL**	**ALL**
9	44	97	82	11	9	**NUMBER OF STATEMENTS**	261	282
%	%	%	%	%	%	**ASSETS**	%	%
	21.1	20.3	22.3	22.4		Cash & Equivalents	19.0	19.9
	25.7	22.7	16.0	19.7		Trade Receivables (net)	20.3	19.4
	2.5	2.1	2.4	3.5		Inventory	4.1	3.1
	2.9	3.2	3.3	.7		All Other Current	3.4	2.7
	52.1	48.4	44.0	46.2		Total Current	46.8	45.1
	33.0	43.3	42.1	45.0		Fixed Assets (net)	42.1	43.8
	5.1	1.3	1.3	4.2		Intangibles (net)	1.2	1.5
	9.8	7.0	12.6	4.6		All Other Non-Current	9.9	9.6
	100.0	100.0	100.0	100.0		Total	100.0	100.0
						LIABILITIES		
	6.3	2.7	.9	2.0		Notes Payable-Short Term	5.6	3.5
	2.3	1.8	1.4	1.8		Cur. Mat.-L.T.D.	2.2	2.1
	8.3	6.3	6.7	9.0		Trade Payables	7.8	6.7
	.0	.0	.2	.0		Income Taxes Payable	.1	.1
	12.3	12.2	10.8	11.0		All Other Current	13.0	11.9
	29.2	22.9	20.0	23.8		Total Current	28.7	24.3
	16.1	17.4	16.2	24.7		Long-Term Debt	17.4	19.0
	.0	.3	.0	.0		Deferred Taxes	.0	.0
	3.6	2.5	2.8	4.7		All Other Non-Current	3.7	3.7
	51.0	56.9	60.9	46.8		Net Worth	50.2	53.0
	100.0	100.0	100.0	100.0		Total Liabilties & Net Worth	100.0	100.0
						INCOME DATA		
	100.0	100.0	100.0	100.0		Net Sales	100.0	100.0
						Gross Profit		
	93.3	98.0	97.3	96.6		Operating Expenses	96.6	95.8
	6.7	2.0	2.7	3.4		Operating Profit	3.4	4.2
	.5	.0	-.2	-1.0		All Other Expenses (net)	1.0	.9
	6.3	2.0	2.9	4.4		Profit Before Taxes	2.4	3.3
						RATIOS		
	5.7	4.5	4.2	2.6			3.3	3.6
	2.4	2.7	2.6	1.6		Current	1.9	2.2
	1.1	1.3	1.7	1.4			1.2	1.4
	4.7	3.7	3.8	2.2			2.7	3.2
	2.0	2.4	2.3	1.5		Quick	1.5	1.8
	1.1	1.1	1.4	1.0			1.0	1.2
	26 14.0	23 16.0	14 25.2	13 28.3			14 26.2	15 24.0
	36 10.2	38 9.7	37 9.8	36 10.2		Sales/Receivables	31 11.6	33 11.0
	53 6.9	48 7.6	50 7.3	66 5.5			53 6.9	50 7.3
						Cost of Sales/Inventory		
						Cost of Sales/Payables		
	4.0	4.0	3.4	5.2			5.0	4.7
	9.1	7.7	6.4	8.1		Sales/Working Capital	11.6	8.7
	88.0	24.9	14.1	18.9			30.1	19.8
	38.9	5.5	14.3	11.1			13.2	10.3
	(30) 5.6	(76) 1.8	(65) 4.5	5.8		EBIT/Interest	(216) 3.5	(227) 4.1
	-.1	.0	1.0	4.1			-.5	1.0
						Net Profit + Depr., Dep., Amort./Cur. Mat. L/T/D		
	.2	.4	.3	.6			.4	.4
	.6	.9	.7	1.3		Fixed/Worth	.8	.9
	1.4	1.2	1.2	1.8			1.4	1.4
	.2	.3	.3	.9			.4	.4
	.9	.7	.5	1.2		Debt/Worth	.9	.8
	4.1	1.6	1.0	2.8			2.4	1.7
	24.1	11.4	11.5	18.7			17.9	16.9
	(39) 8.8	(95) 2.7	(80) 5.2	14.3		% Profit Before Taxes/Tangible Net Worth	(249) 6.6	(269) 7.2
	.0	-4.0	.1	5.0			-3.5	.2
	12.8	6.8	6.3	7.1			9.4	9.0
	5.5	1.6	3.9	4.7		% Profit Before Taxes/Total Assets	3.1	3.9
	-1.6	-1.4	.2	3.4			-2.2	.1
	42.2	14.0	6.3	9.9			16.5	10.8
	9.6	3.7	3.6	3.2		Sales/Net Fixed Assets	3.6	3.5
	3.1	2.1	1.8	1.4			2.0	1.8
	3.6	3.0	2.0	1.6			2.6	2.5
	2.6	1.7	1.3	1.2		Sales/Total Assets	1.6	1.6
	1.5	1.1	.9	1.0			1.1	1.0
	1.0	1.3	1.5	2.1			1.4	1.6
	(34) 2.5	(88) 2.5	(78) 2.6	3.0		% Depr., Dep., Amort./Sales	(228) 2.6	(254) 2.8
	5.0	3.8	3.8	3.9			4.0	4.0
							2.2	5.0
						% Officers', Directors' Owners' Comp/Sales	(34) 3.8	(26) 9.3
							8.8	19.3
18000M	138867M	1022761M	3125491M	1047868M	1871841M	Net Sales ($)	8433012M	8532590M
2260M	54432M	505036M	1841458M	741253M	1428667M	Total Assets ($)	4405106M	4727261M

M = $ thousand MM = $ million

See Pages 9 through 22 for Explanation of Ratios and Data

Comparative Historical Data				Current Data Sorted by Sales					
			Type of Statement						
192	150	156	Unqualified	4	22	13	27	41	49
6	5	3	Reviewed		1	1	1		
11	3	4	Compiled			1	3		
8	10	10	Tax Returns	2	3	1	2	2	
74	68	79	Other	3	11	4	16	22	23
4/1/11-3/31/12 ALL	4/1/12-3/31/13 ALL	4/1/13-3/31/14 ALL		169 (4/1-9/30/13)			83 (10/1/13-3/31/14)		
				0-1MM	1-3MM	3-5MM	5-10MM	10-25MM	25MM & OVER
291	236	252	**NUMBER OF STATEMENTS**	9	37	20	49	65	72
%	%	%	**ASSETS**	%	%	%	%	%	%
20.2	21.1	21.0	Cash & Equivalents		22.0	17.1	20.2	19.4	23.8
19.8	18.0	20.3	Trade Receivables (net)		17.1	21.7	22.2	20.4	21.5
3.2	3.6	2.4	Inventory		1.3	.7	1.9	2.0	3.9
3.1	2.6	3.6	All Other Current		3.2	4.6	2.8	3.8	2.2
46.3	45.3	47.3	Total Current		43.6	44.1	47.1	45.6	51.4
42.9	45.2	40.4	Fixed Assets (net)		44.6	45.5	40.4	41.0	37.2
1.8	1.7	2.0	Intangibles (net)		2.7	3.0	3.6	1.2	1.2
8.9	7.8	10.2	All Other Non-Current		9.1	7.4	8.9	12.2	10.2
100.0	100.0	100.0	Total		100.0	100.0	100.0	100.0	100.0
			LIABILITIES						
4.4	3.7	2.9	Notes Payable-Short Term		5.2	2.2	3.0	2.1	1.8
2.2	2.3	1.8	Cur. Mat.-L.T.D.		1.9	4.2	1.4	1.9	1.2
6.8	6.6	7.5	Trade Payables		3.5	7.2	6.6	6.6	10.0
.1	.0	.1	Income Taxes Payable		.0	.0	.0	.3	.0
13.3	10.8	11.9	All Other Current		9.5	10.2	11.4	11.3	13.4
26.8	23.4	24.1	Total Current		20.2	23.9	22.4	22.1	26.5
19.3	19.3	17.2	Long-Term Debt		18.4	25.8	15.1	16.5	14.7
.0	.0	.1	Deferred Taxes		.0	.0	.0	.5	.0
4.4	4.1	3.1	All Other Non-Current		2.6	1.2	3.9	3.5	3.1
49.5	53.1	55.4	Net Worth		58.7	49.2	58.6	57.4	55.7
100.0	100.0	100.0	Total Liabilities & Net Worth		100.0	100.0	100.0	100.0	100.0
			INCOME DATA						
100.0	100.0	100.0	Net Sales		100.0	100.0	100.0	100.0	100.0
			Gross Profit						
95.6	95.4	96.8	Operating Expenses		91.2	98.7	98.4	98.4	96.7
4.4	4.6	3.2	Operating Profit		8.8	1.3	1.6	1.6	3.3
.6	.8	-.1	All Other Expenses (net)		.1	.0	.2	-.3	-.5
3.8	3.8	3.2	Profit Before Taxes		8.7	1.3	1.4	1.8	3.8
			RATIOS						
3.6	4.0	4.3			6.9	5.4	4.8	3.5	3.6
2.2	2.3	2.4	Current		3.3	2.2	2.7	2.4	2.0
1.3	1.3	1.3			1.4	.9	1.2	1.2	1.4
3.2	3.5	3.8			5.7	5.0	4.3	3.0	3.0
1.8	2.0	2.2	Quick		3.3	2.1	2.4	2.1	1.7
1.0	1.1	1.1			1.2	.8	1.1	1.2	1.2
11 33.1	**11** 32.8	**21** 17.8			**12** 30.1	**26** 14.3	**24** 15.1	**24** 15.3	**11** 32.0
32 11.3	**31** 11.9	**37** 9.9	Sales/Receivables		**31** 11.6	**41** 8.9	**39** 9.4	**37** 9.9	**37** 9.9
48 7.6	**46** 8.0	**49** 7.4			**58** 6.3	**49** 7.4	**49** 7.4	**46** 8.0	**50** 7.3
			Cost of Sales/Inventory						
			Cost of Sales/Payables						
4.2	4.8	4.2			2.9	4.0	3.7	4.5	5.0
8.9	8.6	7.5	Sales/Working Capital		5.6	8.6	6.7	8.3	8.1
31.4	23.4	24.3			23.7	-101.9	37.2	44.9	18.2
9.8	11.4	12.8			43.6	10.1	11.4	12.1	14.3
(229) 3.9	(192) 3.7	(196) 3.5	EBIT/Interest		(29) 5.1	(14) 1.8	(40) 2.5	(51) 3.0	(57) 5.8
1.3	.9	.8			.0	-3.8	1.1	.6	1.6
			Net Profit + Depr., Dep., Amort./Cur. Mat. L/T/D						
.4	.5	.3			.1	.3	.4	.3	.3
.9	.9	.8	Fixed/Worth		.7	.9	.9	.7	.7
1.4	1.3	1.3			1.5	1.9	1.1	1.2	1.1
.4	.4	.3			.2	.3	.3	.3	.3
.8	.7	.7	Debt/Worth		.4	.8	.7	.6	.8
1.9	1.6	1.6			1.8	2.2	1.8	1.4	1.4
17.1	18.4	14.1			15.4	22.2	10.9	9.9	17.1
(272) 7.5	(223) 7.7	(240) 5.1	% Profit Before Taxes/Tangible Net Worth		(34) 7.5	(19) 2.6	(48) 4.6	(63) 2.8	(70) 7.9
.0	-.1	.0			-2.1	-12.4	-.5	-4.0	2.3
9.5	10.2	7.7			13.0	10.4	6.9	5.5	8.4
3.9	4.0	3.1	% Profit Before Taxes/Total Assets		3.3	.8	2.0	1.6	4.5
-.1	-.1	.0			-1.4	-6.4	-.3	-1.8	1.1
13.7	9.9	14.3			17.8	18.8	13.0	12.6	12.7
3.9	3.9	4.1	Sales/Net Fixed Assets		3.0	4.0	4.1	3.3	4.5
1.9	1.9	2.1			1.3	1.6	2.2	2.2	2.6
2.7	2.6	2.7			2.6	2.7	3.3	2.5	3.0
1.6	1.6	1.6	Sales/Total Assets		1.4	1.4	1.6	1.6	1.6
1.0	1.0	1.1			.7	1.2	1.1	1.1	1.2
1.4	1.6	1.4			2.5	1.3	1.2	1.4	1.2
(260) 2.7	(207) 2.7	(224) 2.7	% Depr., Dep., Amort./Sales		(30) 4.1	(17) 3.5	(42) 2.2	(60) 2.5	(69) 2.2
4.1	4.0	3.9			6.0	4.6	3.7	3.7	3.2
3.3	4.3	2.0							
(24) 9.7	(30) 8.9	(27) 6.4	% Officers', Directors' Owners' Comp/Sales						
29.6	21.2	16.6							
10714113M	7440014M	7224828M	Net Sales ($)	3966M	71961M	74381M	361095M	1073306M	5640119M
4730016M	4515609M	4573106M	Total Assets ($)	4480M	69280M	58840M	256626M	781427M	3402453M

M = $ thousand MM = $ million

See Pages 9 through 22 for Explanation of Ratios and Data

	Current Data Sorted by Assets						Comparative Historical Data	
Type of Statement								
Unqualified	2	15	38	29	2		92	96
Reviewed	2	4	10	2			27	10
Compiled	35	19	18	2			55	59
Tax Returns	165	69	32	1			201	236
Other	121	75	53	11	1	2	171	223
	127 (4/1-9/30/13)		581 (10/1/13-3/31/14)				4/1/09-3/31/10	4/1/10-3/31/11
	0-500M	500M-2MM	2-10MM	10-50MM	50-100MM	100-250MM	ALL	ALL
NUMBER OF STATEMENTS	325	182	151	45	3	2	546	624
ASSETS	%	%	%	%	%	%	%	%
Cash & Equivalents	36.0	15.3	12.3	14.5			20.9	22.3
Trade Receivables (net)	3.9	4.4	7.3	9.9			8.0	7.5
Inventory	.3	.1	.1	.0			.3	.3
All Other Current	2.1	4.0	1.7	3.9			2.5	2.7
Total Current	42.4	23.8	21.4	28.3			31.7	32.7
Fixed Assets (net)	34.4	59.5	70.5	55.0			50.8	49.8
Intangibles (net)	10.8	8.9	3.5	4.2			7.0	7.1
All Other Non-Current	12.4	7.8	4.7	12.6			10.5	10.5
Total	100.0	100.0	100.0	100.0			100.0	100.0
LIABILITIES								
Notes Payable-Short Term	11.2	3.7	1.5	6.1			6.2	7.7
Cur. Mat.-L.T.D.	4.1	2.8	2.4	2.1			5.3	2.7
Trade Payables	5.7	2.2	4.8	5.3			4.9	5.1
Income Taxes Payable	.2	.1	.0	.0			.0	.1
All Other Current	32.5	8.8	6.4	13.3			22.4	15.9
Total Current	53.7	17.5	15.2	26.8			38.8	31.5
Long-Term Debt	25.1	50.1	52.9	30.5			37.4	38.8
Deferred Taxes	.0	.0	.0	.1			.1	.1
All Other Non-Current	23.0	5.2	3.7	12.9			9.8	13.1
Net Worth	-1.8	27.3	28.2	29.8			14.0	16.5
Total Liabilties & Net Worth	100.0	100.0	100.0	100.0			100.0	100.0
INCOME DATA								
Net Sales	100.0	100.0	100.0	100.0			100.0	100.0
Gross Profit								
Operating Expenses	93.5	80.6	79.8	90.3			90.5	89.6
Operating Profit	6.5	19.4	20.2	9.7			9.5	10.4
All Other Expenses (net)	.6	9.1	10.9	5.2			4.4	4.4
Profit Before Taxes	5.9	10.3	9.3	4.5			5.1	6.0
RATIOS								
Current	4.1	3.0	2.9	3.0			2.8	3.8
	1.2	1.1	1.3	1.3			1.0	1.4
	.4	.3	.6	.6			.3	.5
Quick	3.8	2.4	2.5	2.8			2.5	3.2
	1.1	.9	1.2	1.2			1.0	1.3
	.3	.3	.4	.5			.3	.4
Sales/Receivables	0 UND	0 UND	0 UND	6 64.8			0 UND	0 UND
	0 UND	0 UND	0 999.8	16 22.7			0 UND	0 UND
	0 988.9	3 120.4	16 22.8	30 12.1			11 32.2	11 32.9
Cost of Sales/Inventory								
Cost of Sales/Payables								
Sales/Working Capital	19.0	10.8	9.5	6.2			14.4	11.4
	191.5	236.7	49.2	27.2			999.8	84.6
	-25.0	-11.7	-15.7	-20.4			-15.3	-25.0
EBIT/Interest	27.0	9.9	4.3	5.4			9.4	9.9
	(176) 6.3	(122) 3.1	(95) 2.2	(34) 2.5			(361) 2.7	(397) 3.1
	1.5	1.2	1.0	1.1			.7	1.0
Net Profit + Depr., Dep., Amort./Cur. Mat. L/T/D				8.3			8.6	11.7
				(11) 3.2			(18) 2.4	(18) 5.0
				1.1			1.3	1.8
Fixed/Worth	.3	.7	1.1	.7			.7	.5
	1.2	4.3	4.6	1.4			2.0	2.1
	-1.6	-24.6	82.1	5.1			-6.2	-16.0
Debt/Worth	.4	.9	1.0	.6			.7	.6
	3.0	5.4	4.9	1.6			3.5	3.1
	-3.4	-24.4	87.7	6.9			-8.7	-13.0
% Profit Before Taxes/Tangible Net Worth	183.9	94.1	42.4	23.5			73.8	84.3
	(205) 84.1	(128) 40.3	(119) 11.4	(40) 4.5			(366) 20.9	(433) 24.1
	24.4	8.9	1.2	-.6			1.4	4.5
% Profit Before Taxes/Total Assets	68.8	19.6	8.9	8.7			26.5	22.8
	31.2	6.2	2.8	2.6			5.9	6.4
	2.2	.6	.3	-.3			-.4	.4
Sales/Net Fixed Assets	89.9	14.8	2.7	7.5			28.1	30.2
	29.3	1.9	.9	2.1			8.2	8.7
	12.5	.7	.3	1.0			1.6	1.2
Sales/Total Assets	12.2	2.9	1.6	2.8			6.4	6.8
	7.1	1.3	.7	1.3			3.1	2.7
	4.2	.6	.3	.6			1.0	.9
% Depr., Dep., Amort./Sales	.6	1.6	1.8	1.4			1.0	1.1
	(201) 1.3	(138) 3.7	(130) 4.3	(44) 2.7			(412) 2.3	(459) 2.6
	2.3	6.4	12.6	4.5			4.7	5.1
% Officers', Directors' Owners' Comp/Sales	3.2	3.3	3.3				2.7	2.9
	(164) 6.1	(61) 6.2	(33) 5.3				(175) 5.5	(238) 5.2
	10.8	9.6	9.2				11.0	9.9
Net Sales ($)	404868M	357059M	1010799M	1744029M	238684M	1570036M	5317596M	5708220M
Total Assets ($)	62979M	199948M	618449M	799113M	223942M	211396M	2295982M	2184653M

M = $ thousand MM = $ million

See Pages 9 through 22 for Explanation of Ratios and Data

Comparative Historical Data / Current Data Sorted by Sales

4/1/11-3/31/12 ALL	4/1/12-3/31/13 ALL	4/1/13-3/31/14 ALL	Type of Statement	0-1MM	1-3MM	3-5MM	5-10MM	10-25MM	25MM & OVER
93	89	86	Unqualified	3	15	14	12	21	21
20	13	18	Reviewed	4	3	3	4	2	2
69	76	74	Compiled	28	35	4	4	1	2
294	372	267	Tax Returns	112	139	10	5		1
240	289	263	Other	101	113	12	19	9	9
				127 (4/1-9/30/13)			581 (10/1/13-3/31/14)		
716	839	708	NUMBER OF STATEMENTS	248	305	43	44	33	35
%	%	%	**ASSETS**	%	%	%	%	%	%
21.1	21.6	24.2	Cash & Equivalents	20.9	27.4	24.5	24.4	20.6	21.3
5.9	5.3	5.2	Trade Receivables (net)	3.2	2.7	14.3	8.6	13.4	17.3
.2	.2	.3	Inventory	.3	.1	.3	.0	.4	2.2
2.7	2.4	2.6	All Other Current	2.4	2.3	1.8	4.1	6.1	3.0
29.9	29.6	32.2	Total Current	26.8	32.5	40.8	37.1	40.5	43.8
51.8	51.6	49.8	Fixed Assets (net)	57.1	46.4	50.7	48.7	43.2	33.6
7.4	8.9	8.5	Intangibles (net)	7.6	10.8	2.5	5.0	4.8	9.6
10.9	9.9	9.5	All Other Non-Current	8.6	10.2	5.9	9.2	11.5	13.0
100.0	100.0	100.0	Total	100.0	100.0	100.0	100.0	100.0	100.0
			LIABILITIES						
8.0	7.1	6.8	Notes Payable-Short Term	9.2	6.3	4.1	3.2	.8	8.0
4.5	4.8	3.3	Cur. Mat.-L.T.D.	4.2	3.0	2.9	2.7	2.0	1.5
4.1	4.1	4.5	Trade Payables	2.8	4.4	2.3	6.6	11.6	12.0
.1	.1	.1	Income Taxes Payable	.2	.0	.2	.0	.0	.0
18.3	20.2	19.4	All Other Current	19.5	23.0	8.7	12.0	9.2	20.9
35.0	36.4	34.1	Total Current	35.8	36.6	18.2	24.5	23.7	42.4
38.2	42.7	37.8	Long-Term Debt	44.8	39.3	25.1	29.2	22.5	15.1
.1	.0	.0	Deferred Taxes	.0	.0	.1	.0	.0	.1
15.4	10.1	13.5	All Other Non-Current	13.8	16.2	3.4	5.2	6.3	18.5
11.4	10.8	14.5	Net Worth	5.6	7.9	53.2	41.1	47.5	23.9
100.0	100.0	100.0	Total Liabilties & Net Worth	100.0	100.0	100.0	100.0	100.0	100.0
			INCOME DATA						
100.0	100.0	100.0	Net Sales	100.0	100.0	100.0	100.0	100.0	100.0
			Gross Profit						
88.6	86.8	86.9	Operating Expenses	77.8	90.7	94.1	93.3	93.9	94.8
11.4	13.2	13.1	Operating Profit	22.2	9.3	5.9	6.7	6.1	5.2
4.9	5.9	5.3	All Other Expenses (net)	12.0	2.1	1.1	.9	1.2	.3
6.5	7.3	7.8	Profit Before Taxes	10.1	7.3	4.8	5.8	4.9	4.9
			RATIOS						
2.8	2.6	3.3		3.0	4.3	5.0	2.9	2.7	1.9
1.1	1.0	1.2	Current	.6	1.4	2.1	1.6	1.6	1.3
.3	.3	.4		.2	.5	1.0	.8	.9	.7
2.5	2.3	3.0		2.3	4.1	4.3	2.5	2.4	1.9
(713) .9	.9	1.1	Quick	.5	1.2	1.9	1.3	1.3	1.1
.3	.3	.3		.2	.4	1.0	.6	.7	.5
0 UND	**0** UND	**0** UND		**0** UND	**0** UND	**0** UND	**0** UND	**4** 86.1	**5** 80.5
0 UND	**0** UND	**0** UND	Sales/Receivables	**0** UND	**0** UND	**8** 44.1	**2** 146.7	**16** 22.7	**13** 27.5
7 53.3	**5** 69.2	**5** 66.5		**0** UND	**2** 231.3	**36** 10.2	**15** 24.3	**25** 14.7	**26** 13.9
			Cost of Sales/Inventory						
			Cost of Sales/Payables						
15.6	18.9	14.2		23.0	16.7	6.1	12.3	7.8	12.0
218.8	-999.8	119.0	Sales/Working Capital	-40.7	78.2	14.5	27.7	26.3	60.9
-21.2	-13.1	-19.3		-5.5	-43.9	-999.8	-52.3	-527.0	-36.5
13.0	10.1	13.4		9.1	13.6	15.9	22.7	14.9	20.4
(483) 3.5	(518) 2.8	(430) 3.4	EBIT/Interest	(108) 2.2	(211) 3.7	(31) 2.2	(35) 4.6	(21) 4.1	(24) 2.9
1.0	.9	1.2		.7	1.4	.6	1.7	1.6	-.4
6.8	12.9	7.7							
(23) 2.4	(15) 3.3	(26) 2.4	Net Profit + Depr., Dep., Amort./Cur. Mat. L/T/D						
.9	1.6	1.1							
.6	.6	.5		.7	.6	.2	.5	.3	.3
2.4	3.2	2.4	Fixed/Worth	8.6	3.0	1.1	1.0	.7	1.0
-6.5	-6.6	-13.2		-5.4	-3.8	1.6	1.9	2.2	3.1
.7	.7	.6		.8	.7	.2	.4	.4	.6
3.4	5.0	3.6	Debt/Worth	9.7	4.2	.7	1.0	1.1	1.6
-9.1	-7.5	-15.7		-6.5	-7.3	2.2	5.3	4.0	11.9
99.4	108.7	118.2		117.2	161.1	65.8	66.8	26.0	65.9
(478) 24.9	(548) 28.4	(496) 39.9	% Profit Before Taxes/Tangible Net Worth	(156) 46.2	(202) 59.2	(39) 12.4	(39) 27.7	(30) 5.6	(30) 4.6
4.0	4.4	4.3		8.3	8.9	-.3	3.3	1.6	-1.7
27.9	25.0	37.2		28.4	48.9	20.4	27.7	11.6	21.9
7.4	6.4	8.8	% Profit Before Taxes/Total Assets	4.7	15.0	7.8	7.6	4.1	2.0
.2	.0	.5		-.4	2.2	.6	1.5	.9	-.8
33.7	37.4	41.8		36.6	51.3	30.7	23.2	24.6	43.7
9.0	8.2	10.4	Sales/Net Fixed Assets	4.1	16.3	7.9	8.2	7.3	10.7
1.5	.9	1.1		.3	1.8	1.1	1.5	2.1	5.7
6.9	6.6	7.2		5.9	9.2	4.4	4.6	4.5	6.0
3.0	2.4	3.0	Sales/Total Assets	1.8	4.2	1.4	3.0	2.0	3.8
1.0	.7	.9		.2	1.3	.7	1.1	1.3	1.6
1.0	1.2	.9		1.5	.7	1.0	.6	.7	.4
(514) 2.4	(595) 2.7	(516) 2.3	% Depr., Dep., Amort./Sales	(168) 4.4	(216) 1.9	(37) 2.4	(35) 2.1	(30) 2.1	(30) 1.1
4.9	6.5	5.2		16.4	3.8	4.9	3.7	3.0	2.7
2.9	3.1	3.2		4.7	2.8	3.4	2.9		
(270) 5.3	(292) 5.7	(262) 6.1	% Officers', Directors' Owners' Comp/Sales	(88) 7.8	(138) 5.0	(15) 4.9	(12) 3.9		
9.6	8.6	9.7		13.3	8.5	9.0	6.7		
3567533M	4283114M	5325475M	Net Sales ($)	132358M	509310M	162236M	293980M	542273M	3685318M
2036134M	2064973M	2115827M	Total Assets ($)	244969M	321881M	147912M	174756M	374572M	851737M

M = $ thousand MM = $ million

See Pages 9 through 22 for Explanation of Ratios and Data

ARTS, ENTERTAINMENT, AND RECREATION

Current Data Sorted by Assets | **Comparative Historical Data**

0-500M	500M-2MM	2-10MM	10-50MM	50-100MM	100-250MM		4/1/09-3/31/10 ALL	4/1/10-3/31/11 ALL
						Type of Statement		
4	4	13	20	10	5	Unqualified	71	71
	1	3	2			Reviewed	5	7
	2	3				Compiled	18	12
5	7	4	1		2	Tax Returns	30	24
7	10	10	9	4	2	Other	42	49
71 (4/1-9/30/13)			57 (10/1/13-3/31/14)					
16	24	33	32	14	9	**NUMBER OF STATEMENTS**	166	163
%	%	%	%	%	%	**ASSETS**	%	%
49.7	27.1	11.8	26.5	13.9		Cash & Equivalents	16.0	16.7
3.3	2.3	4.2	3.4	6.4		Trade Receivables (net)	3.9	6.1
3.2	1.9	1.7	.3	.2		Inventory	1.7	2.1
5.9	6.3	2.2	4.7	1.5		All Other Current	4.2	5.1
62.0	37.5	19.9	34.9	21.9		Total Current	25.8	30.0
25.5	49.9	62.8	43.7	47.6		Fixed Assets (net)	51.0	47.5
1.1	2.2	2.5	.5	.4		Intangibles (net)	6.3	3.8
11.4	10.5	14.8	20.9	30.1		All Other Non-Current	16.9	18.7
100.0	100.0	100.0	100.0	100.0		Total	100.0	100.0
						LIABILITIES		
4.0	4.9	5.7	.8	.6		Notes Payable-Short Term	5.9	7.4
5.7	2.1	1.8	1.6	1.2		Cur. Mat.-L.T.D.	2.4	2.1
5.6	5.3	6.0	3.9	2.1		Trade Payables	6.4	9.1
.0	.0	.0	.1	.0		Income Taxes Payable	.1	.1
24.1	28.8	7.2	13.3	4.7		All Other Current	9.9	13.4
39.4	41.1	20.8	19.8	8.7		Total Current	24.7	32.1
8.3	23.3	29.5	16.5	15.9		Long-Term Debt	25.6	18.3
.0	.0	.0	.0	.0		Deferred Taxes	.0	.0
28.9	9.6	6.8	3.7	3.6		All Other Non-Current	7.9	8.4
23.4	26.0	42.9	60.1	71.8		Net Worth	41.8	41.1
100.0	100.0	100.0	100.0	100.0		Total Liabilties & Net Worth	100.0	100.0
						INCOME DATA		
100.0	100.0	100.0	100.0	100.0		Net Sales	100.0	100.0
						Gross Profit		
93.9	93.8	100.3	95.3	91.4		Operating Expenses	99.3	98.0
6.1	6.2	-.3	4.7	8.6		Operating Profit	.7	2.0
2.4	2.3	1.2	-.8	-1.3		All Other Expenses (net)	2.8	1.4
3.8	3.8	-1.5	5.5	9.9		Profit Before Taxes	-2.0	.6
						RATIOS		
10.3	2.3	2.1	3.5	13.0			2.5	2.4
2.5	1.1	.9	1.7	3.2		Current	1.0	1.1
.4	.5	.4	.9	.8			.6	.5
6.8	1.7	2.0	3.4	12.4			2.0	2.1
2.2	1.1	.8	1.3	2.1		Quick	(165) .8	(162) .8
.4	.3	.3	.7	.6			.3	.3
0 UND	**0** UND	**1** 695.6	**1** 449.0	**4** 84.7			**0** UND	**0** UND
0 UND	**0** UND	**5** 77.3	**5** 74.7	**42** 8.7		Sales/Receivables	**3** 106.4	**6** 65.8
8 46.6	**3** 115.7	**24** 15.5	**15** 23.9	**73** 5.0			**20** 18.2	**23** 15.7
						Cost of Sales/Inventory		
						Cost of Sales/Payables		
5.5	12.5	7.5	3.7	1.2			6.2	7.9
14.9	198.3	-46.3	9.4	3.9		Sales/Working Capital	228.2	88.1
-9.6	-10.7	-10.5	-33.2	-16.4			-12.9	-10.9
	27.9	9.6	12.8	4.5			4.7	9.4
	(14) 7.2	(27) 3.1	(23) 1.6	(10) 1.5		EBIT/Interest	(116) 1.0	(122) 1.6
	2.2	-.7	-2.8	-4.8			-4.5	-1.9
							18.1	
						Net Profit + Depr., Dep., Amort./Cur. Mat. L/T/D	(13) 4.5	
							1.5	
.0	.6	.8	.3	.3			.5	.4
.1	1.0	1.1	.7	.7		Fixed/Worth	1.1	1.0
.8	-12.6	3.3	1.3	1.1			5.9	5.8
.1	.3	.2	.2	.1			.2	.3
.5	1.3	.5	.5	.4		Debt/Worth	.8	.9
NM	-4.8	3.5	1.2	.8			5.5	6.2
148.2	51.7	11.0	18.0	16.6			10.0	20.7
(12) 32.4	(16) 6.2	(28) 1.6	(31) 2.4	.7		% Profit Before Taxes/Tangible Net Worth	(132) -.2	(137) 1.4
6.1	-8.1	-4.9	-1.9	-1.1			-10.2	-5.4
48.0	17.6	6.8	7.7	11.3			5.3	8.8
9.7	8.3	1.2	1.7	.5		% Profit Before Taxes/Total Assets	.0	.7
-3.0	-.1	-2.9	-.7	-.8			-6.5	-4.4
UND	20.9	8.9	8.9	2.4			7.7	11.9
86.5	5.3	1.5	2.1	.8		Sales/Net Fixed Assets	2.8	2.7
7.1	1.8	.5	.8	.4			.7	.9
7.0	4.5	1.9	1.5	.5			2.3	2.7
2.8	2.6	.8	.7	.4		Sales/Total Assets	1.0	1.3
2.4	1.1	.4	.4	.3			.4	.5
	1.9	1.8	2.9	1.8			2.2	1.8
	(17) 4.3	(28) 4.4	(27) 4.2	7.5		% Depr., Dep., Amort./Sales	(142) 4.1	(138) 4.1
	8.5	12.7	5.7	11.8			8.1	8.7
							2.9	3.7
						% Officers', Directors' Owners' Comp/Sales	(27) 4.4	(21) 7.9
							12.5	13.2
12346M	**70755M**	**240899M**	**871319M**	**389351M**	**4123883M**	Net Sales ($)	**2717815M**	**3865112M**
4342M	**25365M**	**173587M**	**680000M**	**887745M**	**1512480M**	Total Assets ($)	**4212677M**	**3250419M**

M = $ thousand MM = $ million

See Pages 9 through 22 for Explanation of Ratios and Data

Comparative Historical Data				Current Data Sorted by Sales					
			Type of Statement						
78	56	56	Unqualified	3	8	9	11	14	11
6	5	6	Reviewed	1		1	2	1	1
10	11	5	Compiled		2	1		2	
22	28	19	Tax Returns	7	4	3	1	1	3
45	45	42	Other	9	6	6	7	5	9
4/1/11-3/31/12 ALL	4/1/12-3/31/13 ALL	4/1/13-3/31/14 ALL		71 (4/1-9/30/13)			57 (10/1/13-3/31/14)		
				0-1MM	1-3MM	3-5MM	5-10MM	10-25MM	25MM & OVER
161	145	128	NUMBER OF STATEMENTS	20	20	20	21	23	24
%	%	%	**ASSETS**	%	%	%	%	%	%
16.5	21.5	23.7	Cash & Equivalents	39.2	14.1	15.4	28.7	20.8	24.1
4.5	4.9	3.6	Trade Receivables (net)	2.0	1.9	3.7	3.2	3.8	6.4
1.9	1.3	1.3	Inventory	3.6	.7	.8	1.6	.9	.5
4.3	3.8	4.1	All Other Current	9.2	1.7	3.1	2.5	4.3	3.8
27.1	31.5	32.7	Total Current	53.9	18.5	22.9	35.9	29.8	34.8
49.1	49.3	48.0	Fixed Assets (net)	40.2	69.6	51.8	41.8	51.8	35.2
3.7	3.6	2.2	Intangibles (net)	.4	3.1	.3	.1	3.7	4.9
20.1	15.7	17.2	All Other Non-Current	5.5	8.8	25.1	22.3	14.7	25.1
100.0	100.0	100.0	Total	100.0	100.0	100.0	100.0	100.0	100.0
			LIABILITIES						
5.0	5.2	3.2	Notes Payable-Short Term	3.3	5.3	7.4	1.6	1.4	1.0
1.7	2.2	2.2	Cur. Mat.-L.T.D.	3.2	4.3	1.2	.6	1.3	2.4
6.3	6.5	4.8	Trade Payables	3.8	3.7	4.2	6.7	2.7	7.6
.0	.0	.0	Income Taxes Payable	.0	.0	.0	.0	.0	.2
15.8	9.0	14.6	All Other Current	28.3	9.2	8.3	17.6	8.9	15.7
28.9	23.0	24.8	Total Current	38.7	22.6	21.0	26.6	14.3	26.8
20.2	24.9	20.4	Long-Term Debt	9.7	32.2	20.0	13.9	24.8	21.1
.0	.1	.0	Deferred Taxes	.0	.0	.0	.0	.0	.0
7.2	8.1	9.1	All Other Non-Current	15.2	10.2	11.5	9.2	3.6	6.2
43.7	44.0	45.7	Net Worth	36.4	35.0	47.5	50.3	57.3	45.9
100.0	100.0	100.0	Total Liabilities & Net Worth	100.0	100.0	100.0	100.0	100.0	100.0
			INCOME DATA						
100.0	100.0	100.0	Net Sales	100.0	100.0	100.0	100.0	100.0	100.0
			Gross Profit						
96.3	95.0	96.2	Operating Expenses	95.2	97.3	97.1	95.5	100.1	92.1
3.7	5.0	3.8	Operating Profit	4.8	2.7	2.9	4.5	-.1	7.9
1.0	2.1	.7	All Other Expenses (net)	2.9	3.4	-.1	.7	-.3	-1.7
2.7	2.9	3.1	Profit Before Taxes	1.9	-.6	3.0	3.7	.1	9.6
			RATIOS						
2.7	4.0	3.3		9.6	1.7	3.8	3.9	4.5	2.0
1.1	1.4	1.3	Current	1.7	.8	1.5	1.1	1.8	1.0
.5	.6	.6		.7	.2	.3	.6	.8	.7
2.1	3.2	2.8		3.3	1.6	3.8	3.7	3.5	1.9
.8	1.2	1.1	Quick	1.6	.7	1.3	.9	1.3	.8
.3	.4	.4		.7	.2	.2	.5	.5	.5
0 UND	**0** UND	**0** UND		**0** UND	**0** UND	**0** UND	**0** UND	**1** 464.9	**2** 160.9
4 81.3	**2** 241.3	**4** 93.0	Sales/Receivables	**0** UND	**6** 63.5	**1** 263.8	**3** 133.1	**5** 68.1	**8** 45.0
22 16.6	**17** 21.0	**17** 21.3		**5** 77.8	**16** 22.7	**10** 36.9	**11** 32.9	**39** 9.4	**30** 12.3
			Cost of Sales/Inventory						
			Cost of Sales/Payables						
5.4	5.4	5.5		5.2	18.3	4.3	5.0	2.3	10.2
59.5	22.9	34.3	Sales/Working Capital	10.6	-40.7	23.9	122.1	7.7	NM
-9.6	-17.4	-15.5		NM	-5.8	-15.7	-13.8	-46.3	-18.3
9.2	9.0	9.6			5.3	10.7	30.9	3.2	12.0
(119) 1.7	(96) 2.1	(83) 2.3	EBIT/Interest		(15) 2.0	(15) 5.4	(14) 5.1	(18) 1.4	(16) 2.0
-2.2	-3.9	-1.0			-4.1	2.0	-2.0	-1.0	-2.5
			Net Profit + Depr., Dep., Amort./Cur. Mat. L/T/D						
.5	.4	.3		.0	.8	.3	.2	.6	.2
1.0	1.0	.9	Fixed/Worth	.2	1.5	.9	.7	.9	.6
3.2	4.9	1.7		1.0	NM	4.3	1.1	1.4	1.5
.2	.2	.2		.1	.2	.2	.2	.2	.3
.8	.8	.7	Debt/Worth	.4	.7	.4	.6	.8	.8
5.0	10.5	3.1		29.0	NM	3.6	1.7	1.3	1.7
18.6	37.7	27.7		52.4	31.5	16.8	17.5	7.4	45.6
(134) 2.1	(117) 5.6	(109) 3.1	% Profit Before Taxes/Tangible Net Worth	(16) 3.9	(15) 1.1	(17) 5.7	(17) 1.8	(22) .7	(22) 19.7
-4.3	-3.1	-2.2		-2.6	-7.4	1.2	-3.4	-.8	-2.1
9.2	12.9	13.7		14.6	19.4	8.8	12.9	3.0	26.2
1.0	2.7	2.3	% Profit Before Taxes/Total Assets	2.6	1.3	3.5	3.6	.5	7.0
-3.8	-3.6	-1.9		-2.9	-3.9	-3.4	-1.9	-.4	-1.3
8.3	15.4	13.2		UND	5.1	10.7	24.8	4.3	14.5
1.8	2.7	2.6	Sales/Net Fixed Assets	19.2	.9	3.4	3.0	1.5	3.8
.6	.8	.8		.5	.3	.7	.8	.5	1.7
2.3	2.5	2.7		3.4	2.6	2.5	3.7	1.4	2.8
.8	1.0	1.0	Sales/Total Assets	1.5	.8	1.1	.7	.5	1.3
.3	.4	.4		.5	.3	.5	.5	.3	.7
2.1	1.9	2.3		3.6	4.3	2.1	1.1	2.5	1.9
(138) 4.0	(123) 4.2	(99) 4.5	% Depr., Dep., Amort./Sales	(10) 10.7	(15) 8.5	(17) 4.2	(16) 4.2	(22) 5.6	(19) 3.1
7.4	7.8	8.8		14.3	18.4	5.4	5.5	8.8	4.9
4.0	4.8	5.1							
(24) 7.0	(25) 8.0	(19) 8.1	% Officers', Directors' Owners' Comp/Sales						
16.5	14.9	13.6							
1892379M	**3704307M**	**5708553M**	Net Sales ($)	**12397M**	**31755M**	**77611M**	**150240M**	**394576M**	**5041974M**
3616536M	**2834505M**	**3283519M**	Total Assets ($)	**13169M**	**69923M**	**103644M**	**295787M**	**1092647M**	**1708349M**

M = $ thousand MM = $ million

See Pages 9 through 22 for Explanation of Ratios and Data

Current Data Sorted by Assets							Comparative Historical Data	
						Type of Statement		
1	4	6	4	2	1	Unqualified	22	21
	1					Reviewed	3	1
2						Compiled	2	6
2	2					Tax Returns	3	4
2	2	4	5		1	Other	12	17
27 (4/1-9/30/13)			12 (10/1/13-3/31/14)				4/1/09-3/31/10	4/1/10-3/31/11
0-500M	500M-2MM	2-10MM	10-50MM	50-100MM	100-250MM		ALL	ALL
7	9	10	9	2	2	**NUMBER OF STATEMENTS**	42	49
%	%	%	%	%	%	**ASSETS**	%	%
		31.5				Cash & Equivalents	17.4	20.8
		10.7				Trade Receivables (net)	8.3	4.8
		.6				Inventory	1.0	2.8
		11.9				All Other Current	4.4	4.6
		54.7				Total Current	31.1	33.0
		19.3				Fixed Assets (net)	30.0	33.1
		2.6				Intangibles (net)	5.5	1.6
		23.5				All Other Non-Current	33.5	32.3
		100.0				Total	100.0	100.0
						LIABILITIES		
		2.3				Notes Payable-Short Term	8.9	10.0
		.3				Cur. Mat.-L.T.D.	1.0	2.6
		2.5				Trade Payables	6.2	6.1
		.0				Income Taxes Payable	.0	.0
		19.3				All Other Current	6.8	5.8
		24.5				Total Current	23.0	24.5
		3.5				Long-Term Debt	22.5	19.9
		.0				Deferred Taxes	.3	.1
		6.0				All Other Non-Current	11.3	5.9
		66.0				Net Worth	42.9	49.6
		100.0				Total Liabilities & Net Worth	100.0	100.0
						INCOME DATA		
		100.0				Net Sales	100.0	100.0
						Gross Profit		
		94.3				Operating Expenses	97.8	96.7
		5.7				Operating Profit	2.2	3.3
		-3.4				All Other Expenses (net)	5.9	.8
		9.0				Profit Before Taxes	-3.7	2.5
						RATIOS		
		11.5					4.3	3.8
		5.4				Current	1.8	2.0
		1.2					.3	.7
		10.9					4.0	2.9
		4.1				Quick	1.3	1.0
		1.0					.1	.3
		0 UND					1 499.3	0 UND
		19 18.8				Sales/Receivables	10 36.5	6 64.4
		91 4.0					40 9.2	33 11.0
						Cost of Sales/Inventory		
						Cost of Sales/Payables		
		1.8					4.6	4.4
		3.5				Sales/Working Capital	24.1	13.3
		17.6					-4.9	-7.8
							3.3	8.3
						EBIT/Interest	(32) -2.9	(32) 1.4
							-25.7	-4.8
						Net Profit + Depr., Dep., Amort./Cur. Mat. L/T/D		
		.0					.1	.0
		.1				Fixed/Worth	.5	.4
		.5					1.3	1.3
		.2					.3	.2
		.4				Debt/Worth	.8	.7
		.9					3.0	2.1
							9.2	15.4
						% Profit Before Taxes/Tangible Net Worth	(36) -7.2	(45) 3.4
							-42.4	-7.2
		41.8					3.8	8.8
		9.7				% Profit Before Taxes/Total Assets	-4.3	2.2
		.8					-16.8	-4.7
		380.8					45.2	57.2
		18.6				Sales/Net Fixed Assets	9.1	7.2
		1.1					1.8	1.6
		2.2					2.2	1.8
		1.1				Sales/Total Assets	1.0	.9
		.5					.4	.4
							1.0	.8
						% Depr., Dep., Amort./Sales	(28) 1.9	(36) 2.2
							4.1	5.0
						% Officers', Directors' Owners' Comp/Sales		
15098M	17580M	61305M	732933M	84303M	35261M	Net Sales ($)	572572M	565531M
1668M	8932M	51857M	302138M	153148M	427873M	Total Assets ($)	958838M	1112079M

M = $ thousand MM = $ million

See Pages 9 through 22 for Explanation of Ratios and Data

Comparative Historical Data / Current Data Sorted by Sales

4/1/11-3/31/12 ALL	4/1/12-3/31/13 ALL	4/1/13-3/31/14 ALL	Type of Statement	0-1MM	1-3MM	3-5MM	5-10MM	10-25MM	25MM & OVER
17	29	18	Unqualified		5	3	2	6	2
	1	1	Reviewed		1				
4	1	2	Compiled	1	1				
4	3	4	Tax Returns	2	2				
19	12	14	Other	1	3	1	5	2	2
				27 (4/1-9/30/13)			12 (10/1/13-3/31/14)		
44	46	39	NUMBER OF STATEMENTS	4	12	4	7	8	4
%	%	%	**ASSETS**	%	%	%	%	%	%
26.0	32.7	24.5	Cash & Equivalents		26.9				
9.9	8.4	9.4	Trade Receivables (net)		14.1				
2.3	1.3	1.8	Inventory		5.5				
11.7	6.3	7.4	All Other Current		1.1				
50.0	48.6	43.2	Total Current		47.7				
19.4	17.1	20.8	Fixed Assets (net)		19.6				
1.7	1.6	2.4	Intangibles (net)		.7				
29.0	32.8	33.7	All Other Non-Current		32.1				
100.0	100.0	100.0	Total		100.0				
			LIABILITIES						
11.1	5.0	5.3	Notes Payable-Short Term		8.6				
1.4	.6	1.0	Cur. Mat.-L.T.D.		2.7				
6.2	3.5	9.8	Trade Payables		4.8				
.0	.0	.0	Income Taxes Payable		.0				
12.0	12.7	18.4	All Other Current		8.0				
30.6	21.8	34.4	Total Current		24.2				
11.9	14.6	10.2	Long-Term Debt		1.7				
.0	.0	.0	Deferred Taxes		.0				
6.3	13.9	8.0	All Other Non-Current		17.8				
51.2	49.8	47.4	Net Worth		56.3				
100.0	100.0	100.0	Total Liabilties & Net Worth		100.0				
			INCOME DATA						
100.0	100.0	100.0	Net Sales		100.0				
			Gross Profit						
94.0	97.6	97.9	Operating Expenses		100.9				
6.0	2.4	2.1	Operating Profit		-.9				
-1.2	1.9	-1.2	All Other Expenses (net)		-.7				
7.2	.4	3.3	Profit Before Taxes		-.3				
			RATIOS						
9.2	9.3	7.3			6.5				
3.0	3.4	2.5	Current		2.1				
.8	1.2	.7			.9				
6.6	8.2	6.3			6.5				
1.3	3.1	1.3	Quick		1.8				
.4	.8	.5			.5				
0 UND	**0** UND	**0** UND			**0** UND				
6 56.9	**15** 24.1	**13** 28.1	Sales/Receivables		**8** 46.5				
65 5.6	**46** 8.0	**52** 7.0			**57** 6.4				
			Cost of Sales/Inventory						
			Cost of Sales/Payables						
2.8	2.2	2.9			3.2				
6.5	4.8	8.3	Sales/Working Capital		8.3				
-46.8	59.8	-24.8			NM				
38.5	8.0	23.3			11.7				
(22) 5.7	(28) 2.1	(24) 1.6	EBIT/Interest		(10) 2.5				
1.4	-5.2	-2.4			-22.8				
			Net Profit + Depr., Dep., Amort./Cur. Mat. L/T/D						
.0	.0	.0			.0				
.1	.1	.1	Fixed/Worth		.2				
.7	1.3	.8			.7				
.2	.2	.2			.2				
.5	.5	.7	Debt/Worth		.8				
1.9	3.6	1.3			2.0				
39.2	9.4	23.5			28.2				
(38) 8.2	(40) -.9	(34) 3.7	% Profit Before Taxes/Tangible Net Worth		7.5				
.3	-7.4	-1.5			-1.6				
18.1	4.5	20.2			19.6				
5.1	-.3	1.7	% Profit Before Taxes/Total Assets		3.5				
.1	-4.5	-2.4			-1.7				
888.8	77.2	147.4			742.2				
20.9	25.4	24.9	Sales/Net Fixed Assets		48.8				
5.6	2.6	3.8			5.1				
2.9	2.0	2.8			4.9				
1.5	1.0	1.2	Sales/Total Assets		2.6				
.6	.4	.4			1.1				
.7	.5	.5							
(22) 2.5	(35) 1.4	(28) 2.2	% Depr., Dep., Amort./Sales						
4.3	4.6	5.9							
			% Officers', Directors' Owners' Comp/Sales						
393670M	655843M	946480M	Net Sales ($)	962M	22124M	15155M	52897M	126061M	729281M
855026M	1360014M	945616M	Total Assets ($)	1367M	17925M	33006M	86474M	572608M	234236M

M = $ thousand MM = $ million

See Pages 9 through 22 for Explanation of Ratios and Data

Current Data Sorted by Assets / Comparative Historical Data

0-500M	500M-2MM	2-10MM	10-50MM	50-100MM	100-250MM		4/1/09-3/31/10 ALL	4/1/10-3/31/11 ALL
						Type of Statement		
1		5	7	11	20	Unqualified	47	46
	1	1	3	2		Reviewed	7	8
1	2	3				Compiled	4	5
9	14	3				Tax Returns	19	22
3	9	12	8	7	19	Other	61	60
60 (4/1-9/30/13)			81 (10/1/13-3/31/14)					
14	26	24	18	20	39	**NUMBER OF STATEMENTS**	138	141
%	%	%	%	%	%	**ASSETS**	%	%
38.8	18.6	13.9	13.2	14.1	7.7	Cash & Equivalents	14.3	13.7
1.2	9.1	4.5	12.0	20.7	10.4	Trade Receivables (net)	8.4	7.1
1.5	3.4	1.9	3.5	1.1	.3	Inventory	1.2	1.2
2.5	4.2	4.9	3.9	4.1	6.0	All Other Current	5.0	5.2
44.1	35.4	25.2	32.6	40.0	24.4	Total Current	29.0	27.2
34.6	43.8	41.9	31.4	15.1	14.8	Fixed Assets (net)	32.1	30.3
5.8	6.5	13.7	23.0	25.5	30.5	Intangibles (net)	20.8	23.1
15.5	14.3	19.2	13.0	19.4	30.3	All Other Non-Current	18.1	19.3
100.0	100.0	100.0	100.0	100.0	100.0	Total	100.0	100.0
						LIABILITIES		
7.5	3.8	1.2	4.8	17.0	6.6	Notes Payable-Short Term	6.4	13.3
.9	.9	3.4	7.0	8.7	5.0	Cur. Mat.-L.T.D.	4.1	4.2
.5	8.4	7.3	7.4	7.6	6.8	Trade Payables	5.8	7.0
.0	.0	.3	.3	.0	.0	Income Taxes Payable	.1	.1
15.3	23.3	24.4	20.9	37.5	21.0	All Other Current	20.5	24.8
24.3	36.5	36.5	40.4	70.8	39.3	Total Current	36.8	49.4
32.9	31.3	21.3	35.2	61.9	61.4	Long-Term Debt	40.4	39.8
.0	.0	.2	.0	.5	.0	Deferred Taxes	.3	.4
15.6	23.8	23.4	16.4	26.0	33.6	All Other Non-Current	23.4	19.8
27.2	8.4	18.6	8.0	-59.3	-34.3	Net Worth	-.9	-9.4
100.0	100.0	100.0	100.0	100.0	100.0	Total Liabilities & Net Worth	100.0	100.0
						INCOME DATA		
100.0	100.0	100.0	100.0	100.0	100.0	Net Sales	100.0	100.0
						Gross Profit		
94.3	95.6	97.5	96.2	94.5	103.0	Operating Expenses	97.0	97.8
5.7	4.4	2.5	3.8	5.5	-3.0	Operating Profit	3.0	2.2
1.4	1.7	3.0	4.0	2.8	2.4	All Other Expenses (net)	4.8	4.5
4.3	2.7	-.5	-.2	2.7	-5.4	Profit Before Taxes	-1.8	-2.3
						RATIOS		
16.6	2.8	1.8	1.8	2.7	1.0		1.7	1.7
2.4	.9	.8	1.0	.6	.6	Current	.8	.7
.8	.7	.4	.3	.3	.4		.4	.4
16.6	2.2	1.6	1.5	2.2	.7		1.2	1.4
1.9	.9	.6	.6	.5	.5	Quick	.6	.5
.7	.5	.3	.2	.2	.3		.3	.2
0 UND	**0** UND	**1** 303.3	**7** 51.4	**13** 27.1	**18** 19.8		**6** 58.6	**4** 90.3
0 UND	**5** 68.3	**7** 50.7	**36** 10.2	**30** 12.0	**34** 10.8	Sales/Receivables	**18** 20.5	**16** 22.7
1 471.5	**29** 12.5	**29** 12.4	**104** 3.5	**96** 3.8	**65** 5.6		**42** 8.6	**40** 9.1
						Cost of Sales/Inventory		
						Cost of Sales/Payables		
5.6	13.0	8.6	6.8	6.2	-122.0		10.6	11.2
30.3	-95.0	-166.0	NM	-6.0	-8.8	Sales/Working Capital	-16.4	-14.2
-84.0	-12.8	-4.1	-2.3	-3.0	-3.3		-4.4	-3.6
38.9	14.4	8.5	7.8	7.5	2.3		2.9	2.7
(10) 9.3	(20) 3.6	(17) 2.8	(12) 1.6	(17) 1.0	(37) -.6	EBIT/Interest	(108) .4	(113) .3
-3.8	-2.1	-10.0	-.5	-1.8	-2.0		-1.9	-2.6
						Net Profit + Depr., Dep., Amort./Cur. Mat. L/T/D		
.1	1.0	.4	.3	.0	-1.1		.8	.7
.5	3.0	2.5	72.7	2.1	-.2	Fixed/Worth	19.0	18.6
UND	-1.6	-1.4	-.7	-.1	.0		-.3	-.2
.5	1.2	.8	1.3	.6	-3.4		1.6	1.4
1.5	6.5	2.4	87.8	-2.2	-2.5	Debt/Worth	-7.5	-6.1
UND	-3.8	-3.8	-2.6	-1.3	-1.5		-2.2	-2.0
112.8	230.9	36.8	108.5				26.8	24.9
(11) 55.4	(17) 14.7	(16) 7.8	(10) 9.0			% Profit Before Taxes/Tangible Net Worth	(64) 2.5	(64) 6.4
22.1	-8.0	-2.0	-22.2				-27.6	-9.5
36.0	17.5	6.8	8.0	17.4	5.9		6.4	5.9
18.1	.9	2.9	.7	1.8	-4.3	% Profit Before Taxes/Total Assets	-.5	-.6
-13.6	-8.8	-5.5	-10.2	-15.6	-10.6		-9.0	-9.9
183.1	20.9	8.6	42.6	171.8	43.5		28.4	24.5
16.6	6.3	5.0	6.1	42.4	11.8	Sales/Net Fixed Assets	5.7	6.6
3.6	2.4	1.4	.7	6.6	5.1		1.6	2.2
5.1	2.8	1.4	1.0	2.3	1.2		1.7	1.6
2.7	2.0	.8	.7	1.5	.9	Sales/Total Assets	.9	1.0
2.1	1.4	.3	.3	.8	.7		.5	.5
	1.2	1.6	.9	.4	1.4		1.7	1.6
	(20) 2.9	(21) 4.3	(15) 3.1	(13) 2.3	(15) 2.5	% Depr., Dep., Amort./Sales	(93) 3.7	(94) 3.3
	6.7	6.8	12.0	5.6	4.8		9.3	8.0
							5.0	4.8
						% Officers', Directors' Owners' Comp/Sales	(14) 6.6	(16) 7.1
							13.9	21.8
9218M	**70500M**	**126849M**	**447768M**	**2343404M**	**6325121M**	Net Sales ($)	**8089347M**	**8408501M**
3107M	**29646M**	**115874M**	**477340M**	**1469988M**	**6900534M**	Total Assets ($)	**9698000M**	**8872931M**

M = $ thousand MM = $ million

See Pages 9 through 22 for Explanation of Ratios and Data

Comparative Historical Data | Current Data Sorted by Sales

4/1/11-3/31/12 ALL	4/1/12-3/31/13 ALL	4/1/13-3/31/14 ALL	Type of Statement	0-1MM	1-3MM	3-5MM	5-10MM	10-25MM	25MM & OVER
53	43	44	Unqualified	1		1	6	4	32
7	9	7	Reviewed		2		1	2	2
9	6	6	Compiled	3	2	1			
35	25	26	Tax Returns	12	9	3	1	1	
76	66	58	Other	3	12	5	5	5	28
				60 (4/1-9/30/13)			81 (10/1/13-3/31/14)		
180	149	141	**NUMBER OF STATEMENTS**	19	25	10	13	12	62
%	%	%	**ASSETS**	%	%	%	%	%	%
15.3	14.5	15.5	Cash & Equivalents	30.1	11.7	22.4	16.6	19.7	10.3
9.3	8.3	9.9	Trade Receivables (net)	2.3	5.4	5.7	7.8	13.5	14.5
1.6	1.7	1.8	Inventory	1.5	2.5	2.6	1.8	1.0	1.6
4.2	4.1	4.6	All Other Current	1.1	6.7	2.9	.9	6.6	5.4
30.4	28.5	31.8	Total Current	35.0	26.4	33.5	27.2	40.9	31.8
28.1	31.7	28.9	Fixed Assets (net)	46.5	36.5	40.3	50.5	28.5	14.1
21.4	22.4	19.1	Intangibles (net)	4.3	18.4	6.5	14.3	15.6	27.7
20.1	17.4	20.2	All Other Non-Current	14.1	18.6	19.7	8.0	15.0	26.4
100.0	100.0	100.0	Total	100.0	100.0	100.0	100.0	100.0	100.0
			LIABILITIES						
15.8	9.4	6.5	Notes Payable-Short Term	6.8	3.6	.8	.5	3.9	10.3
5.9	8.4	4.3	Cur. Mat.-L.T.D.	1.5	1.2	4.2	9.8	1.2	6.0
6.6	5.2	6.7	Trade Payables	1.1	5.3	12.4	4.0	12.9	7.5
.2	.1	.1	Income Taxes Payable	.0	.0	.7	.2	.3	.0
27.9	26.4	23.8	All Other Current	12.2	16.3	21.5	23.4	24.3	30.7
56.4	49.5	41.4	Total Current	21.6	26.3	39.5	37.9	42.6	54.4
36.2	35.2	42.9	Long-Term Debt	37.1	31.9	16.7	16.3	20.4	63.3
.4	.2	.1	Deferred Taxes	.0	.0	.0	.3	.0	.2
30.1	27.2	25.0	All Other Non-Current	24.3	22.5	25.8	14.8	17.1	29.8
-23.0	-12.1	-9.5	Net Worth	16.9	19.2	18.0	30.7	20.0	-47.7
100.0	100.0	100.0	Total Liabilities & Net Worth	100.0	100.0	100.0	100.0	100.0	100.0
			INCOME DATA						
100.0	100.0	100.0	Net Sales	100.0	100.0	100.0	100.0	100.0	100.0
			Gross Profit						
95.7	97.4	97.8	Operating Expenses	92.7	97.4	99.5	89.8	97.9	100.9
4.3	2.6	2.2	Operating Profit	7.3	2.6	.5	10.2	2.1	-.9
4.3	4.0	2.5	All Other Expenses (net)	3.6	2.2	.5	3.7	4.3	2.1
.0	-1.3	-.3	Profit Before Taxes	3.7	.5	-.1	6.5	-2.2	-3.0
			RATIOS						
1.7	1.4	1.6		14.4	3.3	2.3	2.2	2.1	1.1
.8	.6	.8	Current	1.1	1.0	1.2	1.2	1.0	.6
.4	.3	.4		.5	.6	.4	.4	.6	.4
1.4	1.1	1.3		14.4	2.7	1.6	1.8	2.0	.7
(179) .6	.5	.6	Quick	.9	.9	1.1	1.2	.8	.5
.3	.2	.3		.5	.3	.4	.3	.5	.3
3 104.5	2 186.0	2 196.4		0 UND	0 UND	0 UND	5 79.5	10 37.2	16 22.4
12 29.3	17 21.7	19 19.7	Sales/Receivables	0 UND	4 98.1	1 271.9	10 35.9	14 25.6	32 11.3
33 11.0	38 9.6	51 7.2		7 49.8	31 11.9	26 14.1	57 6.4	114 3.2	68 5.4
			Cost of Sales/Inventory						
			Cost of Sales/Payables						
12.6	20.2	10.5		4.4	14.4	9.4	6.2	3.6	119.9
-27.7	-11.8	-24.4	Sales/Working Capital	311.0	-312.7	331.8	33.2	NM	-8.1
-3.6	-4.4	-4.7		-12.6	-11.4	-4.5	-5.3	-6.6	-3.2
3.6	5.0	7.2		15.3	7.7				2.8
(134) 1.0	(114) .9	(113) 1.0	EBIT/Interest	(14) 4.0	(21) .8				(56) -.2
-1.4	-3.3	-1.9		-3.8	-4.3				-2.1
			Net Profit + Depr., Dep., Amort./Cur. Mat. L/T/D						
.5	1.0	.7		.4	.7	.3	1.0	.2	1.8
10.3	-14.9	70.8	Fixed/Worth	1.7	3.8	1.4	3.6	36.5	-.2
-.2	-.1	-.1		UND	-.5	4.1	-2.6	-1.0	.0
1.2	2.2	1.7		.5	.9	.6	.8	1.5	-6.7
-8.9	-7.2	-7.6	Debt/Worth	2.0	9.3	2.0	3.2	44.1	-2.4
-1.9	-1.8	-2.0		UND	-3.0	10.5	-4.3	-5.9	-1.5
41.7	56.6	64.2		67.7	184.6				70.4
(83) 11.6	(69) 19.6	(67) 15.9	% Profit Before Taxes/Tangible Net Worth	(15) 49.7	(14) 16.2				(14) 22.7
-.2	-2.2	-4.3		6.0	-14.0				1.0
8.7	12.8	12.7		24.8	10.4	15.0	9.1	4.2	9.2
.7	.8	.4	% Profit Before Taxes/Total Assets	10.8	-2.0	12.3	3.9	-.5	-1.4
-8.1	-9.5	-9.4		-11.0	-11.2	-8.2	-2.1	-12.2	-11.9
47.2	39.6	42.4		66.4	17.3	13.7	11.0	32.7	67.8
8.6	10.3	8.7	Sales/Net Fixed Assets	3.9	5.3	6.7	3.5	5.9	17.3
2.8	2.3	2.9		1.3	2.9	2.0	.6	1.0	6.4
2.0	2.1	2.1		2.9	2.4	2.8	2.0	1.0	1.6
1.1	1.1	1.2	Sales/Total Assets	2.1	1.5	1.4	.8	.8	1.1
.6	.5	.7		.9	.6	1.2	.3	.4	.7
1.1	1.3	1.3		1.9	1.3		3.1	.9	.6
(113) 3.3	(107) 3.3	(93) 3.1	% Depr., Dep., Amort./Sales	(14) 6.1	(19) 3.2		(11) 5.6	(10) 3.1	(31) 1.9
7.1	8.6	6.4		13.4	6.9		17.3	11.3	3.4
4.6	4.5	3.0							
(29) 7.8	(25) 9.5	(21) 4.6	% Officers', Directors' Owners' Comp/Sales						
18.1	18.4	13.5							
9927990M	8971226M	9322860M	Net Sales ($)	10982M	49061M	37101M	92625M	174627M	8958464M
10650282M	8937040M	8996489M	Total Assets ($)	13410M	69083M	23544M	175544M	330056M	8384852M

M = $ thousand MM = $ million

See Pages 9 through 22 for Explanation of Ratios and Data

Current Data Sorted by Assets							Comparative Historical Data			
						Type of Statement				
		2	2	2	2	Unqualified		11		13
		1	1			Reviewed		2		2
						Compiled		2		1
2			1		1	Tax Returns		15		4
		4	3	2	3	Other		31		19
	2 (4/1-9/30/13)		24 (10/1/13-3/31/14)					4/1/09-3/31/10		4/1/10-3/31/11
0-500M	**500M-2MM**	**2-10MM**	**10-50MM**	**50-100MM**	**100-250MM**			**ALL**		**ALL**
2		7	7	4	6	**NUMBER OF STATEMENTS**		61		39
%	%	%	%	%	%	**ASSETS**		%		%
	DATA NOT AVAILABLE					Cash & Equivalents		13.5		16.8
						Trade Receivables (net)		6.5		7.0
						Inventory		2.8		3.8
						All Other Current		2.0		3.3
						Total Current		24.9		31.0
						Fixed Assets (net)		61.6		54.9
						Intangibles (net)		4.3		3.2
						All Other Non-Current		9.3		10.9
						Total		100.0		100.0
						LIABILITIES				
						Notes Payable-Short Term		6.9		5.3
						Cur. Mat.-L.T.D.		9.4		2.5
						Trade Payables		5.1		5.7
						Income Taxes Payable		.0		.1
						All Other Current		22.7		21.1
						Total Current		44.2		34.7
						Long-Term Debt		39.5		24.6
						Deferred Taxes		1.0		.9
						All Other Non-Current		6.5		9.4
						Net Worth		8.8		30.5
						Total Liabilties & Net Worth		100.0		100.0
						INCOME DATA				
						Net Sales		100.0		100.0
						Gross Profit				
						Operating Expenses		94.1		91.5
						Operating Profit		5.9		8.5
						All Other Expenses (net)		5.5		2.9
						Profit Before Taxes		.4		5.6
						RATIOS				
								2.0		2.9
						Current		.6		1.0
								.2		.4
								1.9		2.0
						Quick		.4		.8
								.1		.2
							1	423.6	**4**	101.3
						Sales/Receivables	**10**	36.4	**11**	32.3
							24	15.1	**26**	14.0
						Cost of Sales/Inventory				
						Cost of Sales/Payables				
								8.5		5.2
						Sales/Working Capital		-19.5		405.4
								-3.8		-6.5
								7.0		12.5
						EBIT/Interest	(47)	1.0	(28)	2.3
								-1.3		-2.9
						Net Profit + Depr., Dep., Amort./Cur. Mat. L/T/D				
								.8		.4
						Fixed/Worth		2.1		1.2
								-3.9		10.6
								.6		.3
						Debt/Worth		1.4		.9
								-5.4		9.8
								36.6		33.1
						% Profit Before Taxes/Tangible Net Worth	(43)	12.4	(31)	12.4
								-4.0		-9.7
								11.5		16.5
						% Profit Before Taxes/Total Assets		1.1		3.6
								-5.9		-7.6
								5.0		5.6
						Sales/Net Fixed Assets		2.1		1.9
								.7		1.0
								2.0		1.7
						Sales/Total Assets		1.0		1.2
								.5		.7
								3.4		3.0
						% Depr., Dep., Amort./Sales	(53)	7.0	(33)	5.0
								13.8		11.4
								1.8		
						% Officers', Directors' Owners' Comp/Sales	(10)	7.0		
								9.4		
1261M		**66165M**	**181597M**	**220044M**	**1164783M**	Net Sales ($)		**1715339M**		**1375738M**
817M		**35874M**	**212162M**	**313613M**	**886429M**	Total Assets ($)		**1862385M**		**1129113M**

M = $ thousand MM = $ million

See Pages 9 through 22 for Explanation of Ratios and Data

Comparative Historical Data				Current Data Sorted by Sales					
			Type of Statement						
13	9	8	Unqualified					3	5
1	2	2	Reviewed					2	
1	1		Compiled						
7	4	4	Tax Returns	1	1			1	1
12	12	12	Other		1	1	1	2	7
4/1/11-3/31/12	**4/1/12-3/31/13**	**4/1/13-3/31/14**			**2 (4/1-9/30/13)**			**24 (10/1/13-3/31/14)**	
ALL	**ALL**	**ALL**		**0-1MM**	**1-3MM**	**3-5MM**	**5-10MM**	**10-25MM**	**25MM & OVER**
34	28	26	**NUMBER OF STATEMENTS**	1	2	1	1	8	13
%	%	%	**ASSETS**	%	%	%	%	%	%
15.3	12.6	13.9	Cash & Equivalents						10.1
5.6	4.5	8.1	Trade Receivables (net)						4.9
2.2	1.2	1.7	Inventory						.9
1.8	1.6	.8	All Other Current						.9
25.0	20.0	24.4	Total Current						16.9
59.1	70.1	65.8	Fixed Assets (net)						74.1
6.6	2.2	2.2	Intangibles (net)						2.3
9.3	7.7	7.6	All Other Non-Current						6.7
100.0	100.0	100.0	Total						100.0
			LIABILITIES						
4.8	2.6	4.6	Notes Payable-Short Term						8.2
3.8	3.0	2.7	Cur. Mat.-L.T.D.						1.8
8.8	4.0	6.4	Trade Payables						4.8
.2	.0	.0	Income Taxes Payable						.0
37.9	35.4	15.5	All Other Current						15.1
55.6	45.0	29.2	Total Current						29.9
27.9	29.0	35.2	Long-Term Debt						40.7
1.4	1.8	1.3	Deferred Taxes						1.5
9.4	5.2	5.2	All Other Non-Current						6.6
5.6	19.0	29.0	Net Worth						21.4
100.0	100.0	100.0	Total Liabilties & Net Worth						100.0
			INCOME DATA						
100.0	100.0	100.0	Net Sales						100.0
			Gross Profit						
90.5	91.9	95.1	Operating Expenses						98.0
9.5	8.1	4.9	Operating Profit						2.0
3.7	3.5	.9	All Other Expenses (net)						.5
5.8	4.5	4.0	Profit Before Taxes						1.4
			RATIOS						
2.0	1.8	1.2							.8
.7	.6	.8	Current						.5
.3	.2	.4							.2
1.9	1.3	1.0							.7
.6	.5	.7	Quick						.4
.2	.0	.3							.2
0 UND	**1** 593.9	**4** 82.1							**1** 542.7
10 36.3	**10** 37.6	**10** 36.7	Sales/Receivables						**7** 51.0
25 14.8	**30** 12.2	**33** 11.1							**29** 12.5
			Cost of Sales/Inventory						
			Cost of Sales/Payables						
11.1	12.1	21.9							-31.5
-24.4	-14.2	-60.6	Sales/Working Capital						-9.3
-4.7	-4.6	-7.9							-5.5
13.4	26.6	19.9							10.0
(27) 2.5	(23) 2.4	(25) 1.8	EBIT/Interest						.5
-.9	.7	-1.1							-2.7
			Net Profit + Depr., Dep., Amort./Cur. Mat. L/T/D						
1.1	1.1	1.0							1.1
1.8	2.1	1.3	Fixed/Worth						1.3
-2.3	6.2	2.6							2.8
.6	.5	.5							.5
2.0	1.9	.8	Debt/Worth						.8
-3.3	16.1	2.3							2.3
27.5	20.8	19.7							20.9
(20) 12.2	(23) 12.9	(21) 2.2	% Profit Before Taxes/Tangible Net Worth						(11) .7
-4.3	-2.1	-1.1							-6.5
14.5	10.5	8.0							8.5
3.2	4.5	.6	% Profit Before Taxes/Total Assets						-.3
-3.8	-2.4	-1.7							-3.3
5.2	2.9	3.2							2.7
2.6	1.7	1.6	Sales/Net Fixed Assets						1.5
.8	.7	.8							.8
2.3	1.5	1.8							1.5
1.4	1.2	1.1	Sales/Total Assets						1.2
.6	.5	.6							.6
2.6	3.6	3.4							3.9
(29) 4.5	(25) 6.2	(22) 5.4	% Depr., Dep., Amort./Sales						(10) 5.9
10.1	10.5	7.9							10.4
			% Officers', Directors' Owners' Comp/Sales						
797605M	**967407M**	**1633850M**	Net Sales ($)	**142M**	**2689M**	**3379M**	**6834M**	**118449M**	**1502357M**
905753M	**1097756M**	**1448895M**	Total Assets ($)	**318M**	**3168M**	**2237M**	**5297M**	**178576M**	**1259299M**

M = $ thousand MM = $ million

See Pages 9 through 22 for Explanation of Ratios and Data

Current Data Sorted by Assets							Comparative Historical Data	
						Type of Statement		
3	5	7	16	7	4	Unqualified	61	39
		2	1			Reviewed	9	9
1	6	2			1	Compiled	15	8
11	8	5	1			Tax Returns	34	27
18	15	18	17	1	3	Other	43	46
	50 (4/1-9/30/13)		102 (10/1/13-3/31/14)				**4/1/09-3/31/10**	**4/1/10-3/31/11**
0-500M	**500M-2MM**	**2-10MM**	**10-50MM**	**50-100MM**	**100-250MM**		**ALL**	**ALL**
33	34	34	35	8	8	**NUMBER OF STATEMENTS**	162	129
%	%	%	%	%	%	**ASSETS**	%	%
43.1	15.3	18.4	12.7			Cash & Equivalents	16.1	15.4
4.4	8.9	8.3	6.7			Trade Receivables (net)	7.8	8.3
1.7	1.7	2.3	.2			Inventory	1.1	1.8
8.1	6.9	1.7	3.4			All Other Current	4.2	7.3
57.4	32.8	30.6	23.0			Total Current	29.2	32.8
28.3	53.1	42.4	54.9			Fixed Assets (net)	47.8	45.1
6.4	3.5	8.5	5.6			Intangibles (net)	8.9	7.6
7.8	10.5	18.5	16.6			All Other Non-Current	14.2	14.6
100.0	100.0	100.0	100.0			Total	100.0	100.0
						LIABILITIES		
21.6	9.0	4.2	3.7			Notes Payable-Short Term	4.7	7.9
.7	7.5	5.2	2.5			Cur. Mat.-L.T.D.	5.5	3.5
7.9	15.1	4.4	5.0			Trade Payables	6.6	5.9
.0	.1	.2	.0			Income Taxes Payable	.3	.6
24.2	8.2	11.6	17.2			All Other Current	14.1	14.0
54.3	39.8	25.6	28.4			Total Current	31.2	31.9
12.4	28.9	17.8	21.4			Long-Term Debt	29.7	19.8
.0	.0	.7	.0			Deferred Taxes	.3	.3
7.7	16.4	5.4	3.4			All Other Non-Current	10.2	13.3
25.6	14.8	50.6	46.8			Net Worth	28.6	34.7
100.0	100.0	100.0	100.0			Total Liabilties & Net Worth	100.0	100.0
						INCOME DATA		
100.0	100.0	100.0	100.0			Net Sales	100.0	100.0
						Gross Profit		
89.4	87.8	88.6	95.3			Operating Expenses	90.2	90.6
10.6	12.2	11.4	4.7			Operating Profit	9.8	9.4
1.3	6.0	5.2	2.2			All Other Expenses (net)	5.7	3.6
9.3	6.2	6.3	2.6			Profit Before Taxes	4.2	5.7
						RATIOS		
4.1	3.1	5.1	2.3				3.1	2.5
1.0	.9	1.3	.9			Current	1.1	1.0
.5	.3	.5	.6				.4	.5
3.6	2.9	4.4	1.7				2.7	1.8
1.0	.5	1.1	.8			Quick	.9	.8
.3	.2	.4	.4				.3	.3
0 UND	**0** UND	**0** UND	**5** 68.4				**0** UND	**0** UND
0 UND	**0** 999.8	**5** 81.1	**12** 30.4			Sales/Receivables	**9** 40.8	**5** 73.3
2 189.8	**10** 36.7	**33** 11.1	**39** 9.3				**23** 15.6	**21** 17.0
						Cost of Sales/Inventory		
						Cost of Sales/Payables		
15.3	6.7	7.3	5.5				5.6	6.9
-905.8	NM	26.5	-42.8			Sales/Working Capital	51.8	200.5
-15.4	-8.5	-12.9	-5.6				-9.7	-17.0
78.0	3.9	51.7	9.7				12.7	15.9
(15) 9.0	(26) 1.1	(18) 5.3	(17) 2.1			EBIT/Interest	(110) 2.2	(89) 3.6
-1.8	-3.0	.5	.8				-1.4	-.6
						Net Profit + Depr., Dep., Amort./Cur. Mat. L/T/D		
.0	.4	.1	.7				.7	.5
.7	1.6	.8	1.0			Fixed/Worth	1.6	1.4
-2.1	NM	2.9	4.0				-17.0	10.6
.2	.5	.3	.2				.4	.3
1.8	2.4	1.3	.6			Debt/Worth	2.1	1.6
-4.4	-7.8	5.3	12.6				-16.9	17.3
172.0	17.9	57.0	6.8				29.5	60.0
(23) 83.5	(25) 5.0	(30) 10.2	(27) 2.2			% Profit Before Taxes/Tangible Net Worth	(117) 6.3	(100) 8.4
12.9	-6.0	-2.4	-.1				-5.6	-2.3
87.4	6.9	16.6	3.3				9.8	19.4
33.7	.4	3.7	1.4			% Profit Before Taxes/Total Assets	2.1	3.6
-2.2	-5.4	-1.2	-1.2				-4.2	-1.7
818.4	34.2	55.9	2.0				22.1	38.9
49.0	3.4	7.6	.9			Sales/Net Fixed Assets	2.6	2.9
9.1	.6	.6	.4				.6	.6
14.1	5.4	2.2	1.0				2.6	3.4
5.5	1.3	1.0	.5			Sales/Total Assets	.8	1.0
3.0	.5	.4	.3				.3	.4
.3	3.3	1.8	6.1				1.9	1.3
(12) 1.3	(26) 4.8	(22) 4.9	(30) 9.2			% Depr., Dep., Amort./Sales	(119) 5.3	(99) 5.8
2.2	11.3	11.8	13.8				11.6	10.6
5.1							3.9	2.6
(13) 13.7						% Officers', Directors' Owners' Comp/Sales	(24) 6.9	(25) 5.5
19.7							11.2	11.3
41927M	**105856M**	**215591M**	**670055M**	**417181M**	**450992M**	Net Sales ($)	**4469713M**	**2629640M**
5971M	**40628M**	**161377M**	**810770M**	**566607M**	**1383530M**	Total Assets ($)	**5393117M**	**3057610M**

M = $ thousand MM = $ million

See Pages 9 through 22 for Explanation of Ratios and Data

Comparative Historical Data				Current Data Sorted by Sales					
			Type of Statement						
40	53	42	Unqualified	2	7	3	7	15	8
8	7	3	Reviewed				2		1
15	11	10	Compiled	3	2	1		3	1
29	28	25	Tax Returns	14	6	3	1	1	
73	61	72	Other	19	16	7	10	11	9
4/1/11-3/31/12 ALL	4/1/12-3/31/13 ALL	4/1/13-3/31/14 ALL		50 (4/1-9/30/13)			102 (10/1/13-3/31/14)		
				0-1MM	1-3MM	3-5MM	5-10MM	10-25MM	25MM & OVER
165	160	152	**NUMBER OF STATEMENTS**	38	31	14	20	30	19
%	%	%	**ASSETS**	%	%	%	%	%	%
20.5	21.7	22.4	Cash & Equivalents	20.8	28.0	13.0	29.4	19.5	21.0
7.2	6.7	6.6	Trade Receivables (net)	3.0	6.9	4.7	8.4	9.0	9.4
2.4	2.7	1.4	Inventory	.8	1.1	3.8	.1	2.6	.7
4.3	3.4	4.7	All Other Current	5.4	7.2	1.8	3.4	3.8	4.0
34.3	34.6	35.1	Total Current	29.9	43.2	23.3	41.3	34.9	35.0
49.0	47.9	44.4	Fixed Assets (net)	56.9	44.5	50.8	33.3	41.6	30.9
5.6	4.9	6.4	Intangibles (net)	6.7	.9	4.1	13.4	3.8	13.1
11.0	12.6	14.0	All Other Non-Current	6.4	11.4	21.8	12.0	19.7	21.1
100.0	100.0	100.0	Total	100.0	100.0	100.0	100.0	100.0	100.0
			LIABILITIES						
9.3	3.5	8.5	Notes Payable-Short Term	11.6	12.8	7.8	8.3	3.0	5.1
3.4	2.9	3.8	Cur. Mat.-L.T.D.	8.2	2.2	1.1	2.0	3.5	1.8
11.6	6.8	7.5	Trade Payables	1.9	7.2	10.2	17.9	8.1	5.5
.0	.2	.2	Income Taxes Payable	.0	.0	.2	.0	.2	.9
16.3	14.8	14.8	All Other Current	12.5	14.5	7.2	15.6	12.1	28.8
40.6	28.2	34.8	Total Current	34.1	36.7	26.4	43.8	26.9	42.1
22.8	24.8	22.2	Long-Term Debt	34.4	15.4	17.0	16.5	16.4	28.1
.2	.2	.1	Deferred Taxes	.0	.0	1.1	.0	.2	.0
9.5	11.8	7.8	All Other Non-Current	6.8	5.9	4.8	17.2	7.2	6.4
27.0	35.0	35.0	Net Worth	24.6	42.0	50.6	22.5	49.3	23.4
100.0	100.0	100.0	Total Liabilities & Net Worth	100.0	100.0	100.0	100.0	100.0	100.0
			INCOME DATA						
100.0	100.0	100.0	Net Sales	100.0	100.0	100.0	100.0	100.0	100.0
			Gross Profit						
87.4	89.0	90.4	Operating Expenses	78.1	93.1	98.2	89.8	96.1	96.2
12.6	11.0	9.6	Operating Profit	21.9	6.9	1.8	10.2	3.9	3.8
5.4	4.7	3.8	All Other Expenses (net)	9.9	2.6	1.4	3.6	-1.0	3.1
7.2	6.3	5.8	Profit Before Taxes	12.0	4.3	.4	6.6	4.8	.7
			RATIOS						
2.6	3.2	3.2		4.9	3.1	3.5	2.5	3.9	2.0
1.2	1.3	1.1	Current	.5	1.3	1.1	1.2	1.5	.8
.5	.6	.4		.2	.4	.5	.4	.9	.5
2.3	2.7	3.0		4.7	2.6	2.7	2.1	3.8	1.6
1.0	1.0	.9	Quick	.5	1.0	.6	1.1	1.1	.7
.3	.3	.3		.2	.2	.4	.3	.7	.4
0 UND	0 UND	0 UND		0 UND	0 UND	0 UND	0 812.8	1 491.9	11 33.4
5 73.7	7 54.2	4 82.9	Sales/Receivables	0 UND	3 119.3	6 64.3	4 84.5	10 37.6	27 13.3
27 13.7	27 13.4	24 14.9		2 157.1	14 26.0	32 11.5	54 6.7	26 14.2	60 6.1
			Cost of Sales/Inventory						
			Cost of Sales/Payables						
5.5	5.5	6.9		6.7	8.0	6.9	4.2	6.5	3.9
33.8	32.9	98.4	Sales/Working Capital	-40.4	119.3	NM	50.1	12.5	-31.5
-10.1	-10.9	-8.3		-2.4	-8.7	-12.0	-11.9	-30.2	-2.4
21.4	12.3	11.8		11.7	46.5	11.8	33.6	28.0	10.3
(110) 3.9	(103) 3.0	(89) 2.1	EBIT/Interest	(18) 1.8	(20) 1.5	(10) .4	(12) 3.1	(17) 5.1	(12) 2.1
.8	.2	.3		.7	-1.5	-9.5	-27.5	1.5	1.1
	12.4								
	(10) 1.2		Net Profit + Depr., Dep., Amort./Cur. Mat. L/T/D						
	-1.3								
.4	.4	.3		.5	.2	.5	.1	.3	.5
1.4	1.1	1.1	Fixed/Worth	2.9	.8	1.0	1.0	.8	3.1
5.3	4.7	8.8		-4.1	2.7	NM	NM	1.5	-.8
.4	.3	.3		.5	.2	.3	.2	.2	.6
2.0	1.7	1.4	Debt/Worth	3.2	.8	.5	1.6	.5	3.9
10.1	10.5	14.8		-5.9	4.5	NM	-11.7	3.9	-7.0
43.3	29.9	45.5		44.2	90.3	22.2	112.3	45.0	41.6
(135) 8.7	(127) 6.9	(118) 6.1	% Profit Before Taxes/Tangible Net Worth	(28) 11.4	(26) 4.6	(11) .4	(14) 3.8	(26) 3.3	(13) 5.9
-.5	-1.4	-.8		.8	-7.6	-4.0	-1.2	1.2	-.3
15.0	10.2	11.3		14.4	45.5	7.2	7.4	19.4	7.4
3.4	2.2	1.9	% Profit Before Taxes/Total Assets	3.1	1.8	-1.1	2.3	2.2	1.2
-.6	-2.0	-1.4		-.1	-3.4	-4.7	-3.5	-.2	-2.7
33.1	30.0	45.8		21.9	86.4	13.9	801.3	28.0	20.9
2.2	3.2	5.0	Sales/Net Fixed Assets	.7	8.5	2.5	8.2	2.0	3.1
.5	.5	.6		.2	1.2	.7	.5	.8	1.1
2.9	3.0	3.4		3.2	6.8	3.5	5.5	2.4	2.2
1.0	1.0	1.0	Sales/Total Assets	.6	1.9	.8	1.5	1.0	.8
.3	.3	.4		.2	.6	.4	.3	.4	.3
2.4	1.7	1.9		6.0	1.0	5.6	3.0	.9	1.0
(115) 6.3	(123) 5.3	(103) 6.8	% Depr., Dep., Amort./Sales	(21) 9.2	(21) 3.5	(10) 8.6	(12) 5.0	(24) 6.6	(15) 4.9
13.3	11.4	12.3		18.2	7.8	13.8	18.0	9.4	10.4
2.4	3.0	3.5		5.6					
(32) 5.5	(30) 7.0	(29) 7.7	% Officers', Directors' Owners' Comp/Sales	(12) 13.3					
9.2	13.9	15.6		16.6					
9300101M	3051718M	1901602M	Net Sales ($)	16965M	54097M	54478M	145764M	427810M	1202488M
3621897M	4103085M	2968883M	Total Assets ($)	40921M	92681M	77900M	294572M	661955M	1800854M

M = $ thousand MM = $ million

See Pages 9 through 22 for Explanation of Ratios and Data

Current Data Sorted by Assets							Comparative Historical Data	
						Type of Statement		
1		1	3		1	Unqualified	7	5
		2	1			Reviewed		1
	1		1			Compiled	3	4
3	3					Tax Returns	4	3
	1	5	4	1		Other	5	3
	4 (4/1-9/30/13)		24 (10/1/13-3/31/14)				4/1/09-3/31/10 ALL	4/1/10-3/31/11 ALL
0-500M	500M-2MM	2-10MM	10-50MM	50-100MM	100-250MM			
4	5	8	9	1	1	**NUMBER OF STATEMENTS**	19	16
%	%	%	%	%	%	**ASSETS**	%	%
						Cash & Equivalents	27.3	22.3
						Trade Receivables (net)	15.0	16.2
						Inventory	1.8	1.1
						All Other Current	6.3	10.7
						Total Current	50.5	50.3
						Fixed Assets (net)	22.7	22.8
						Intangibles (net)	10.9	10.7
						All Other Non-Current	15.8	16.1
						Total	100.0	100.0
						LIABILITIES		
						Notes Payable-Short Term	7.5	13.5
						Cur. Mat.-L.T.D.	5.3	22.0
						Trade Payables	11.6	12.4
						Income Taxes Payable	.2	.7
						All Other Current	13.0	25.8
						Total Current	37.6	74.5
						Long-Term Debt	10.3	47.2
						Deferred Taxes	.5	.7
						All Other Non-Current	8.7	7.2
						Net Worth	42.9	-29.6
						Total Liabilties & Net Worth	100.0	100.0
						INCOME DATA		
						Net Sales	100.0	100.0
						Gross Profit		
						Operating Expenses	98.4	92.7
						Operating Profit	1.6	7.3
						All Other Expenses (net)	3.8	.7
						Profit Before Taxes	-2.2	6.6
						RATIOS		
							2.6	1.7
						Current	1.6	1.0
							.6	.6
							2.2	1.2
						Quick	1.1	.7
							.5	.3
							0 UND	**0** UND
						Sales/Receivables	**14** 26.3	**13** 28.1
							37 9.9	**36** 10.0
						Cost of Sales/Inventory		
						Cost of Sales/Payables		
							4.6	21.0
						Sales/Working Capital	12.6	NM
							-33.1	-16.2
							45.9	37.6
						EBIT/Interest	(13) 3.3	(13) 7.1
							-.5	3.6
						Net Profit + Depr., Dep., Amort./Cur. Mat. L/T/D		
							.0	.4
						Fixed/Worth	.3	-2.3
							8.2	-.1
							.2	3.1
						Debt/Worth	1.4	-13.2
							38.8	-1.7
							364.2	
						% Profit Before Taxes/Tangible Net Worth	(16) 15.3	
							-3.2	
							41.8	66.5
						% Profit Before Taxes/Total Assets	3.5	19.5
							-7.0	2.4
							110.0	525.6
						Sales/Net Fixed Assets	44.1	22.0
							3.5	4.0
							6.9	7.8
						Sales/Total Assets	2.1	3.6
							.5	1.2
							.2	.8
						% Depr., Dep., Amort./Sales	(10) .7	(11) 1.2
							2.4	1.9
						% Officers', Directors' Owners' Comp/Sales		
5991M	28616M	84259M	386719M	234809M	139043M	Net Sales ($)	601414M	997202M
841M	4888M	37345M	182556M	58381M	241572M	Total Assets ($)	435431M	493086M

M = $ thousand MM = $ million

See Pages 9 through 22 for Explanation of Ratios and Data

Comparative Historical Data | Current Data Sorted by Sales

			Type of Statement						
5	5	6	Unqualified	1			1	2	2
3	3	3	Reviewed		1				2
3	2	2	Compiled		1				1
8	7	6	Tax Returns	1	1	3		1	
13	16	11	Other	1			1	4	5
4/1/11-3/31/12 ALL	4/1/12-3/31/13 ALL	4/1/13-3/31/14 ALL		4 (4/1-9/30/13)			24 (10/1/13-3/31/14)		
				0-1MM	1-3MM	3-5MM	5-10MM	10-25MM	25MM & OVER
32	33	28	NUMBER OF STATEMENTS	3	3	3	2	7	10
%	%	%	**ASSETS**	%	%	%	%	%	%
25.2	30.5	17.5	Cash & Equivalents						17.7
12.7	10.6	16.1	Trade Receivables (net)						19.1
4.7	3.8	8.3	Inventory						15.0
6.6	9.1	8.0	All Other Current						6.6
49.1	54.0	49.9	Total Current						58.4
24.5	17.2	20.7	Fixed Assets (net)						17.2
13.5	8.6	7.2	Intangibles (net)						12.8
12.9	20.2	22.2	All Other Non-Current						11.6
100.0	100.0	100.0	Total						100.0
			LIABILITIES						
11.7	4.1	12.0	Notes Payable-Short Term						4.8
1.5	3.0	2.2	Cur. Mat.-L.T.D.						3.2
9.3	7.2	9.2	Trade Payables						14.9
.2	.0	.1	Income Taxes Payable						.0
17.7	23.2	22.3	All Other Current						30.4
40.4	37.4	45.7	Total Current						53.2
17.9	16.4	14.3	Long-Term Debt						12.8
.3	1.8	.1	Deferred Taxes						.3
12.3	6.5	13.4	All Other Non-Current						12.3
29.1	37.9	26.4	Net Worth						21.4
100.0	100.0	100.0	Total Liabilties & Net Worth						100.0
			INCOME DATA						
100.0	100.0	100.0	Net Sales						100.0
			Gross Profit						
94.6	92.8	91.6	Operating Expenses						91.4
5.4	7.2	8.4	Operating Profit						8.6
-.2	1.8	1.4	All Other Expenses (net)						.5
5.6	5.4	7.1	Profit Before Taxes						8.1
			RATIOS						
3.7	4.7	2.0							2.9
1.4	1.3	1.1	Current						1.1
.8	.7	.5							.5
1.9	4.0	1.4							1.7
1.1	1.2	.8	Quick						.8
.7	.4	.4							.5
0 UND	1 333.5	0 UND							4 87.9
3 108.1	11 33.2	7 54.7	Sales/Receivables						20 18.7
25 14.6	22 16.3	24 15.3							34 10.8
			Cost of Sales/Inventory						
			Cost of Sales/Payables						
12.8	4.9	9.5							7.8
40.6	23.1	68.3	Sales/Working Capital						74.9
-25.2	-14.9	-39.8							-6.9
46.0	46.1	22.7							
(19) 13.8	(20) 12.8	(19) 6.9	EBIT/Interest						
.7	-.6	-.8							
			Net Profit + Depr., Dep., Amort./Cur. Mat. L/T/D						
.3	.0	.1							.0
1.2	.4	.6	Fixed/Worth						.5
-.6	-503.2	-2.7							-1.2
.5	.4	.6							.3
6.1	1.8	3.6	Debt/Worth						8.6
-4.6	-520.4	-7.2							-4.6
133.4	86.6	57.7							
(20) 51.9	(24) 42.5	(18) 40.9	% Profit Before Taxes/Tangible Net Worth						
5.1	3.4	.9							
32.4	38.3	33.5							33.9
11.6	8.8	8.1	% Profit Before Taxes/Total Assets						23.4
.2	-.9	-1.3							1.8
148.5	299.2	210.0							271.9
23.5	33.3	29.3	Sales/Net Fixed Assets						46.9
9.9	5.3	4.5							9.5
6.3	5.0	5.2							4.4
3.2	2.6	2.4	Sales/Total Assets						2.7
1.7	1.1	1.4							1.4
.2	.2	.3							
(20) .7	(19) 1.0	(17) 1.0	% Depr., Dep., Amort./Sales						
3.5	2.7	3.7							
			% Officers', Directors' Owners' Comp/Sales						
835995M	630183M	879437M	Net Sales ($)	920M	5308M	11983M	13849M	91571M	755806M
380315M	477263M	525583M	Total Assets ($)	5218M	4352M	1715M	4583M	63383M	446332M

M = $ thousand MM = $ million

See Pages 9 through 22 for Explanation of Ratios and Data

Current Data Sorted by Assets | **Comparative Historical Data**

	0-500M	500M-2MM	2-10MM	10-50MM	50-100MM	100-250MM	4/1/09-3/31/10 ALL	4/1/10-3/31/11 ALL
Type of Statement								
Unqualified	1		2	2			4	2
Reviewed			2		1			2
Compiled	1	1	1				1	
Tax Returns	3	1	1				2	2
Other		1	7	3	2	1	10	11
	6 (4/1-9/30/13)			24 (10/1/13-3/31/14)				
NUMBER OF STATEMENTS	5	3	13	5	3	1	17	17
ASSETS	%	%	%	%	%	%	%	%
Cash & Equivalents			16.2				23.0	25.7
Trade Receivables (net)			34.6				29.6	20.2
Inventory			6.8				.4	.3
All Other Current			5.2				2.6	4.5
Total Current			62.8				55.6	50.7
Fixed Assets (net)			20.3				11.6	16.7
Intangibles (net)			1.2				22.7	17.1
All Other Non-Current			15.8				10.1	15.8
Total			100.0				100.0	100.0
LIABILITIES								
Notes Payable-Short Term			12.9				10.8	13.5
Cur. Mat.-L.T.D.			.3				3.4	1.0
Trade Payables			25.6				18.0	24.7
Income Taxes Payable			.0				.1	.0
All Other Current			9.3				15.2	19.1
Total Current			48.0				47.5	58.3
Long-Term Debt			10.4				13.9	21.8
Deferred Taxes			.0				.5	.7
All Other Non-Current			13.9				15.4	9.0
Net Worth			27.7				22.7	10.4
Total Liabilties & Net Worth			100.0				100.0	100.0
INCOME DATA								
Net Sales			100.0				100.0	100.0
Gross Profit								
Operating Expenses			92.8				87.3	97.7
Operating Profit			7.2				12.7	2.3
All Other Expenses (net)			2.4				2.3	1.2
Profit Before Taxes			4.8				10.4	1.1
RATIOS								
Current			2.3				2.5	4.4
			1.6				1.3	.8
			1.0				.6	.6
Quick			1.8				2.1	3.5
			1.0				1.1	.8
			.7				.6	.4
Sales/Receivables			0 UND				2 167.3	0 UND
			33 10.9				57 6.4	33 10.9
			58 6.3				92 4.0	53 6.9
Cost of Sales/Inventory								
Cost of Sales/Payables								
Sales/Working Capital			7.7				8.9	12.3
			15.4				45.3	-23.4
			NM				-6.5	-11.4
EBIT/Interest			144.7				4.8	3.9
			13.6				(13) 1.5	(11) 1.0
			.1				-2.1	-9.0
Net Profit + Depr., Dep., Amort./Cur. Mat. L/T/D								
Fixed/Worth			.1				.1	.2
			.3				.8	1.6
			2.7				-.1	-.2
Debt/Worth			1.0				.7	.4
			2.1				13.1	28.7
			7.2				-2.1	-3.4
% Profit Before Taxes/Tangible Net Worth			73.9					100.7
			(11) 17.5					(10) 33.7
			-2.1					3.0
% Profit Before Taxes/Total Assets			39.5				27.8	17.9
			7.7				7.6	1.9
			.8				-3.2	-6.7
Sales/Net Fixed Assets			286.9				686.5	118.5
			45.9				84.2	53.0
			7.0				17.1	13.6
Sales/Total Assets			5.5				4.6	4.9
			3.3				2.1	3.2
			1.2				.9	1.3
% Depr., Dep., Amort./Sales								.4
								(11) 1.7
								4.6
% Officers', Directors' Owners' Comp/Sales								
Net Sales ($)	16046M	11947M	250862M	211456M	70037M	106884M	266625M	254743M
Total Assets ($)	1360M	3908M	67039M	125645M	198546M	120268M	141524M	346481M

M = $ thousand MM = $ million

See Pages 9 through 22 for Explanation of Ratios and Data

Comparative Historical Data				Current Data Sorted by Sales					
			Type of Statement						
2	1	5	Unqualified	1			1	2	1
3		3	Reviewed					2	1
2	1	3	Compiled	2				1	
2	5	5	Tax Returns	1	2			2	
10	14	14	Other	2	1			4	7
				6 (4/1-9/30/13)		24 (10/1/13-3/31/14)			
4/1/11-3/31/12 ALL	4/1/12-3/31/13 ALL	4/1/13-3/31/14 ALL		0-1MM	1-3MM	3-5MM	5-10MM	10-25MM	25MM & OVER
19	21	30	**NUMBER OF STATEMENTS**	6	3		1	11	9
%	%	%	**ASSETS**	%	%	%	%	%	%
30.5	30.5	26.9	Cash & Equivalents			DATA NOT AVAILABLE		39.5	
38.1	17.8	24.9	Trade Receivables (net)					18.3	
1.4	4.9	3.1	Inventory					7.3	
2.7	5.1	4.2	All Other Current					2.8	
72.7	58.3	59.0	Total Current					67.9	
14.4	20.3	12.8	Fixed Assets (net)					10.5	
6.6	12.2	15.1	Intangibles (net)					14.5	
6.3	9.3	13.1	All Other Non-Current					7.1	
100.0	100.0	100.0	Total					100.0	
			LIABILITIES						
1.1	10.8	9.9	Notes Payable-Short Term					9.2	
2.0	.4	1.8	Cur. Mat.-L.T.D.					2.8	
16.8	7.8	19.6	Trade Payables					22.1	
.7	.0	.0	Income Taxes Payable					.0	
13.8	28.8	14.8	All Other Current					15.8	
34.3	47.8	46.1	Total Current					50.0	
41.3	13.2	15.0	Long-Term Debt					11.8	
.6	.2	.4	Deferred Taxes					.0	
6.8	18.7	13.1	All Other Non-Current					19.5	
16.9	20.2	25.3	Net Worth					18.7	
100.0	100.0	100.0	Total Liabilties & Net Worth					100.0	
			INCOME DATA						
100.0	100.0	100.0	Net Sales					100.0	
			Gross Profit						
84.6	89.2	91.2	Operating Expenses					98.4	
15.4	10.8	8.8	Operating Profit					1.6	
1.4	2.1	4.5	All Other Expenses (net)					.5	
13.9	8.7	4.4	Profit Before Taxes					1.1	
			RATIOS						
6.8	5.2	2.0						2.2	
1.7	1.5	1.5	Current					1.5	
1.0	.6	.9						.9	
6.8	2.8	1.8						1.8	
1.7	1.0	1.1	Quick					1.0	
.9	.4	.8						.5	
3 140.5	**0** UND	**2** 185.8						**4** 85.5	
61 6.0	**8** 45.1	**40** 9.2	Sales/Receivables					**22** 16.3	
146 2.5	**47** 7.8	**72** 5.1						**89** 4.1	
			Cost of Sales/Inventory						
			Cost of Sales/Payables						
2.9	10.5	5.1						4.5	
32.0	53.3	13.2	Sales/Working Capital					15.4	
-265.0	-30.8	-536.7						-696.1	
	26.3	37.1							
	(12) 14.9	(25) 4.2	EBIT/Interest						
	5.9	-1.5							
			Net Profit + Depr., Dep., Amort./Cur. Mat. L/T/D						
.0	.0	.1						.2	
.2	.6	.3	Fixed/Worth					.3	
-8.0	NM	NM						-1.0	
.2	1.8	1.2						2.9	
2.5	10.8	4.4	Debt/Worth					6.6	
-13.3	-6.8	-10.0						-2.9	
197.7	250.5	115.3							
(12) 85.9	(12) 42.2	(20) 30.1	% Profit Before Taxes/Tangible Net Worth						
17.7	2.6	-1.8							
69.8	45.9	38.0						24.0	
39.0	15.6	5.8	% Profit Before Taxes/Total Assets					4.7	
5.7	2.2	-.4						-.4	
UND	999.8	394.3						407.2	
95.8	91.6	46.0	Sales/Net Fixed Assets					77.0	
16.1	8.4	13.3						20.4	
6.0	9.2	5.0						6.3	
2.4	4.2	2.4	Sales/Total Assets					2.7	
1.5	1.9	.6						.7	
	.1	.4							
	(10) .6	(16) 1.0	% Depr., Dep., Amort./Sales						
	2.0	1.8							
			% Officers', Directors' Owners' Comp/Sales						
238820M	**458345M**	**667232M**	Net Sales ($)	**2206M**	**5761M**		**9168M**	**168761M**	**481336M**
175009M	**346606M**	**516766M**	Total Assets ($)	**6726M**	**4576M**		**2603M**	**177803M**	**325058M**

M = $ thousand MM = $ million

See Pages 9 through 22 for Explanation of Ratios and Data

Current Data Sorted by Assets							Comparative Historical Data	
						Type of Statement		
1	2	20	36	14	15	Unqualified	120	123
		1			1	Reviewed	6	3
	3					Compiled	6	2
1	2	2				Tax Returns	9	5
3	5	13	22	6	7	Other	43	55
	85 (4/1-9/30/13)		69 (10/1/13-3/31/14)				4/1/09-3/31/10	4/1/10-3/31/11
0-500M	**500M-2MM**	**2-10MM**	**10-50MM**	**50-100MM**	**100-250MM**		**ALL**	**ALL**
5	12	36	58	20	23	**NUMBER OF STATEMENTS**	184	188
%	%	%	%	%	%	**ASSETS**	%	%
	12.8	13.1	10.9	13.2	5.1	Cash & Equivalents	12.0	11.5
	3.8	6.8	2.4	1.2	2.5	Trade Receivables (net)	4.3	4.0
	2.8	4.3	.8	.6	2.4	Inventory	3.9	3.1
	.6	.6	3.0	1.2	2.6	All Other Current	3.1	3.3
	20.1	24.9	17.1	16.2	12.6	Total Current	23.3	21.9
	67.4	60.1	53.9	57.1	51.3	Fixed Assets (net)	52.5	53.4
	.0	1.1	1.8	1.6	.7	Intangibles (net)	.3	.8
	12.5	13.8	27.2	25.2	35.4	All Other Non-Current	23.9	23.9
	100.0	100.0	100.0	100.0	100.0	Total	100.0	100.0
						LIABILITIES		
	1.6	3.2	.8	1.4	1.3	Notes Payable-Short Term	5.5	4.2
	1.7	.9	.7	.2	.6	Cur. Mat.-L.T.D.	1.0	1.1
	2.2	3.4	1.9	1.3	1.9	Trade Payables	3.6	3.2
	.0	.2	.2	.0	.0	Income Taxes Payable	.0	.1
	6.7	2.1	1.9	2.0	1.5	All Other Current	4.1	4.2
	12.2	9.7	5.6	4.9	5.3	Total Current	14.2	12.7
	22.2	10.9	9.5	15.6	11.2	Long-Term Debt	14.3	12.0
	.0	.0	.0	.0	.2	Deferred Taxes	.0	.0
	9.1	3.1	3.3	2.2	1.2	All Other Non-Current	3.9	3.4
	56.5	76.3	81.6	77.2	82.1	Net Worth	67.6	71.9
	100.0	100.0	100.0	100.0	100.0	Total Liabilties & Net Worth	100.0	100.0
						INCOME DATA		
	100.0	100.0	100.0	100.0	100.0	Net Sales	100.0	100.0
						Gross Profit		
	100.2	98.1	95.3	98.6	90.1	Operating Expenses	97.2	92.6
	-.2	1.9	4.7	1.4	9.9	Operating Profit	2.8	7.4
	1.5	1.4	1.0	-2.6	-2.7	All Other Expenses (net)	5.4	2.0
	-1.7	.5	3.7	4.0	12.7	Profit Before Taxes	-2.6	5.4
						RATIOS		
	5.2	7.1	9.5	6.1	6.4		7.2	6.8
	1.7	3.0	2.4	2.5	4.2	Current	2.2	2.7
	.9	1.2	1.1	1.2	1.9		1.0	1.1
	3.6	6.6	7.7	5.9	4.6		5.1	5.1
	1.1	2.5	2.2	1.9	3.4	Quick	1.5	1.7
	.8	1.1	.8	.8	1.6		.5	.6
	0 UND	**0** UND	**3** 141.8	**2** 180.7	**7** 55.2		**1** 725.5	**1** 421.8
	0 UND	**8** 45.0	**9** 38.9	**8** 44.5	**27** 13.7	Sales/Receivables	**11** 33.4	**8** 48.5
	23 16.0	**46** 8.0	**44** 8.3	**43** 8.5	**118** 3.1		**50** 7.3	**41** 8.8
						Cost of Sales/Inventory		
						Cost of Sales/Payables		
	5.1	1.8	1.5	1.4	1.5		1.8	1.8
	41.3	5.6	4.7	3.7	3.0	Sales/Working Capital	4.3	4.6
	-113.7	31.6	50.6	28.8	5.0		NM	83.2
		6.9	8.7	28.4	18.9		6.7	17.7
		(24) 1.8	(34) -.4	(18) .3	(14) 4.2	EBIT/Interest	(119) -.6	(123) 3.3
		-7.4	-14.7	-10.9	-.4		-7.5	-2.5
						Net Profit + Depr., Dep., Amort./Cur. Mat. L/T/D		
	.4	.5	.4	.5	.3		.4	.4
	1.2	.8	.7	.8	.6	Fixed/Worth	.8	.7
	3.2	1.2	.9	1.2	.9		1.1	1.1
	.1	.1	.0	.1	.0		.1	.1
	.8	.2	.1	.2	.1	Debt/Worth	.3	.2
	2.6	.6	.3	.7	.4		.8	.6
	10.1	9.0	4.3	5.1	6.7		7.8	7.8
	-.5	.9	(56) -.6	.6	2.9	% Profit Before Taxes/Tangible Net Worth	(178) -1.5	(184) 1.3
	-13.7	-5.1	-2.3	-1.9	-1.2		-5.3	-2.4
	7.6	6.2	3.0	4.7	5.0		5.2	5.1
	-.4	.8	-.5	.2	2.1	% Profit Before Taxes/Total Assets	-.9	.9
	-5.8	-4.4	-2.0	-1.6	-.9		-4.5	-2.1
	11.1	2.2	1.1	.6	.6		1.4	1.4
	.6	.7	.5	.3	.4	Sales/Net Fixed Assets	.6	.5
	.3	.2	.2	.2	.2		.3	.3
	1.3	1.0	.4	.2	.3		.5	.5
	.5	.5	.2	.2	.1	Sales/Total Assets	.3	.3
	.3	.2	.2	.1	.1		.2	.1
		4.2	7.3	7.2	7.2		4.4	4.0
		(32) 9.8	(49) 11.8	15.5	(22) 11.3	% Depr., Dep., Amort./Sales	(160) 9.5	(167) 9.6
		20.6	17.4	19.0	17.9		17.2	19.6
							2.9	1.7
						% Officers', Directors' Owners' Comp/Sales	(23) 6.0	(17) 4.3
							14.9	10.0
3798M	12140M	129763M	485124M	312589M	933630M	Net Sales ($)	2145985M	2414793M
1931M	13902M	204017M	1488164M	1357941M	3693201M	Total Assets ($)	7482266M	8347309M

M = $ thousand MM = $ million

See Pages 9 through 22 for Explanation of Ratios and Data

Comparative Historical Data				Current Data Sorted by Sales					
			Type of Statement						
119	89	88	Unqualified	5	18	10	27	21	7
3	1	2	Reviewed				1		1
4	2	3	Compiled	2	1				
5	2	5	Tax Returns	2	1	2			
67	61	56	Other	12	12	3	10	13	6
4/1/11-3/31/12	**4/1/12-3/31/13**	**4/1/13-3/31/14**		**85 (4/1-9/30/13)**			**69 (10/1/13-3/31/14)**		
ALL	**ALL**	**ALL**		**0-1MM**	**1-3MM**	**3-5MM**	**5-10MM**	**10-25MM**	**25MM & OVER**
198	155	154	**NUMBER OF STATEMENTS**	21	32	15	38	34	14
%	%	%	**ASSETS**	%	%	%	%	%	%
11.3	12.6	11.2	Cash & Equivalents	9.8	15.4	10.0	12.1	7.9	10.4
3.2	3.4	3.7	Trade Receivables (net)	2.8	3.8	3.8	4.7	3.1	3.1
3.5	2.1	2.0	Inventory	.8	1.3	1.6	3.1	1.3	4.8
3.0	2.9	2.2	All Other Current	3.5	2.3	.2	2.5	1.1	3.8
21.1	20.8	19.1	Total Current	17.0	22.7	15.6	22.4	13.5	22.1
53.3	54.5	56.4	Fixed Assets (net)	74.3	58.5	61.2	47.7	51.9	53.5
1.4	1.1	1.2	Intangibles (net)	.0	.1	1.4	1.7	1.8	2.9
24.3	23.6	23.3	All Other Non-Current	8.7	18.7	21.9	28.2	32.7	21.5
100.0	100.0	100.0	Total	100.0	100.0	100.0	100.0	100.0	100.0
			LIABILITIES						
2.0	2.6	1.8	Notes Payable-Short Term	1.6	2.1	.7	1.2	2.2	2.8
1.9	.8	.7	Cur. Mat.-L.T.D.	1.0	.5	1.3	.7	.5	.9
2.9	2.1	2.5	Trade Payables	1.5	2.7	2.0	2.6	2.1	4.3
.0	.1	.1	Income Taxes Payable	.3	.1	.4	.0	.2	.0
3.6	2.0	2.5	All Other Current	3.2	3.3	1.4	1.6	2.5	3.9
10.5	7.5	7.6	Total Current	7.7	8.7	5.8	6.1	7.4	11.9
13.1	11.4	11.9	Long-Term Debt	23.4	6.0	10.8	10.1	11.5	15.1
.0	.0	.0	Deferred Taxes	.0	.0	.0	.0	.0	.3
4.1	3.2	3.2	All Other Non-Current	.1	6.0	.3	4.0	2.9	2.3
72.3	77.8	77.3	Net Worth	68.8	79.3	83.1	79.7	78.1	70.3
100.0	100.0	100.0	Total Liabilities & Net Worth	100.0	100.0	100.0	100.0	100.0	100.0
			INCOME DATA						
100.0	100.0	100.0	Net Sales	100.0	100.0	100.0	100.0	100.0	100.0
			Gross Profit						
93.9	88.9	96.6	Operating Expenses	103.0	100.1	94.1	101.5	92.3	79.1
6.1	11.1	3.4	Operating Profit	-3.0	-.1	5.9	-1.5	7.7	20.9
3.2	2.9	.0	All Other Expenses (net)	3.2	1.8	-1.2	-1.7	-1.6	.4
2.9	8.1	3.4	Profit Before Taxes	-6.1	-1.9	7.1	.1	9.3	20.4
			RATIOS						
5.9	8.3	6.8		12.6	8.5	5.9	9.4	6.1	5.3
2.5	3.3	2.9	Current	1.6	3.3	2.4	3.4	3.6	1.9
1.2	1.4	1.1		.3	1.2	1.2	1.6	1.1	1.0
4.6	5.6	5.8		8.7	8.1	5.7	6.4	5.6	3.7
1.5	2.6	2.2	Quick	1.5	3.2	2.4	2.2	2.3	1.5
.6	.7	.8		.2	.9	.9	1.0	.9	.6
1 245.6	**1** 530.8	**1** 268.3		**0** UND	**0** UND	**0** UND	**4** 103.7	**2** 147.9	**3** 104.7
8 43.6	**6** 58.5	**11** 34.3	Sales/Receivables	**1** 344.0	**4** 86.5	**21** 17.2	**14** 25.4	**10** 35.5	**9** 38.6
39 9.4	**45** 8.1	**47** 7.8		**68** 5.4	**34** 10.8	**44** 8.3	**54** 6.8	**40** 9.1	**60** 6.1
			Cost of Sales/Inventory						
			Cost of Sales/Payables						
2.0	1.5	1.8		.9	1.4	2.9	1.7	1.8	2.8
4.8	3.7	4.7	Sales/Working Capital	13.3	3.4	9.1	2.6	5.1	4.8
49.7	28.0	39.1		-9.1	27.7	19.0	16.8	35.5	-204.8
7.3	13.1	10.7		2.1	9.0	13.0	4.2	26.0	17.2
(132) 1.9	(90) 3.8	(99) 1.6	EBIT/Interest	(14) -.5	(14) -10.6	(10) .5	(28) -.1	(22) 4.1	(11) 6.6
-3.6	-2.2	-9.3		-5.1	-28.9	-44.4	-9.0	-6.3	-.4
			Net Profit + Depr., Dep., Amort./Cur. Mat. L/T/D						
.4	.4	.4		.6	.4	.6	.3	.3	.6
.8	.8	.8	Fixed/Worth	1.0	.8	.8	.6	.7	.9
1.0	1.0	1.0		2.1	1.0	.9	1.0	.9	1.0
.1	.1	.0		.1	.0	.0	.1	.0	.1
.2	.2	.2	Debt/Worth	.2	.2	.1	.2	.2	.4
.6	.5	.5		1.1	.4	.3	.4	.6	.9
7.5	8.9	5.8		1.5	3.5	12.1	2.7	6.0	16.6
(190) .9	(152) 1.2	(152) .2	% Profit Before Taxes/Tangible Net Worth	-2.5	-1.0	1.9	(37) -1.3	(33) 1.5	8.3
-2.9	-2.3	-2.8		-11.1	-5.6	-1.9	-2.8	-1.1	3.3
4.8	6.6	4.1		.9	3.1	9.6	2.3	5.8	10.6
.6	.8	.2	% Profit Before Taxes/Total Assets	-1.3	-.9	1.8	-.7	1.1	5.1
-2.4	-2.2	-2.6		-5.7	-4.2	-1.5	-2.5	-1.0	2.1
1.6	1.3	1.3		.6	3.3	2.3	1.5	1.0	2.4
.5	.5	.5	Sales/Net Fixed Assets	.2	.5	.4	.5	.6	.6
.3	.3	.2		.1	.2	.2	.3	.3	.4
.5	.5	.5		.5	.5	1.1	.4	.4	1.0
.3	.3	.3	Sales/Total Assets	.2	.2	.3	.2	.3	.4
.2	.2	.1		.1	.1	.2	.1	.1	.2
4.7	4.6	5.8		6.1	4.9	3.6	7.0	5.0	4.3
(171) 10.2	(129) 9.3	(135) 11.8	% Depr., Dep., Amort./Sales	(17) 16.3	(21) 11.8	(14) 13.1	12.4	(33) 10.1	(12) 9.3
17.2	14.4	18.5		24.6	23.3	22.3	18.2	16.4	12.0
4.4	5.4								
(24) 6.7	(13) 7.3		% Officers', Directors' Owners' Comp/Sales						
13.8	27.7								
2492714M	**1771913M**	**1877044M**	Net Sales ($)	**10746M**	**66297M**	**59665M**	**279572M**	**535792M**	**924972M**
8517037M	**6237055M**	**6759156M**	Total Assets ($)	**68225M**	**323342M**	**227520M**	**1435849M**	**2613474M**	**2090746M**

M = $ thousand MM = $ million

See Pages 9 through 22 for Explanation of Ratios and Data

Current Data Sorted by Assets							Comparative Historical Data	
						Type of Statement		
		2	11	3	3	Unqualified	11	10
			1			Reviewed	1	1
						Compiled		
	1					Tax Returns		2
		2	2	3	1	Other	5	6
	12 (4/1-9/30/13)		17 (10/1/13-3/31/14)				4/1/09-3/31/10	4/1/10-3/31/11
0-500M	500M-2MM	2-10MM	10-50MM	50-100MM	100-250MM		ALL	ALL
	1	4	14	6	4	**NUMBER OF STATEMENTS**	17	19
%	%	%	%	%	%	**ASSETS**	%	%
D			18.9			Cash & Equivalents	20.2	11.7
A			1.8			Trade Receivables (net)	4.3	2.1
T			.6			Inventory	1.1	3.8
A			3.3			All Other Current	2.0	1.5
			24.7			Total Current	27.7	19.2
N			57.1			Fixed Assets (net)	52.6	52.6
O			.5			Intangibles (net)	.0	3.3
T			17.7			All Other Non-Current	19.7	25.0
			100.0			Total	100.0	100.0
A						**LIABILITIES**		
V			1.8			Notes Payable-Short Term	1.6	1.1
A			1.2			Cur. Mat.-L.T.D.	9.2	1.8
I			3.9			Trade Payables	2.2	2.1
L			.0			Income Taxes Payable	.0	.0
A			2.2			All Other Current	4.8	7.4
B			9.1			Total Current	17.9	12.3
L			18.7			Long-Term Debt	43.7	19.0
E			.0			Deferred Taxes	.0	.0
			3.5			All Other Non-Current	3.9	1.1
			68.7			Net Worth	34.6	67.6
			100.0			Total Liabilties & Net Worth	100.0	100.0
						INCOME DATA		
			100.0			Net Sales	100.0	100.0
						Gross Profit		
			90.5			Operating Expenses	94.8	82.3
			9.5			Operating Profit	5.2	17.7
			-1.4			All Other Expenses (net)	2.1	3.4
			10.9			Profit Before Taxes	3.0	14.3
						RATIOS		
			4.6				3.4	6.8
			2.0			Current	1.6	2.0
			1.2				.8	1.0
			3.0				3.3	5.9
			1.8			Quick	1.5	1.6
			.9				.8	.8
			1 441.2				2 218.8	2 229.0
			6 64.9			Sales/Receivables	9 40.9	7 55.4
			20 18.6				44 8.3	29 12.7
						Cost of Sales/Inventory		
						Cost of Sales/Payables		
			2.0				3.3	2.1
			6.1			Sales/Working Capital	8.1	7.5
			21.5				-35.2	71.0
			37.9				17.3	34.0
			(10) 7.9			EBIT/Interest	(12) 1.8	(14) 2.4
			-.2				-1.3	-.1
						Net Profit + Depr., Dep., Amort./Cur. Mat. L/T/D		
			.6				.0	.2
			.8			Fixed/Worth	.8	.9
			1.2				1.2	1.4
			.2				.1	.1
			.3			Debt/Worth	.3	.2
			1.3				1.4	1.3
			19.3				7.4	14.1
			10.3			% Profit Before Taxes/Tangible Net Worth	(16) 1.0	(17) 5.8
			1.5				-2.4	-.6
			8.6				6.3	6.9
			7.2			% Profit Before Taxes/Total Assets	.5	5.3
			1.3				-1.9	.3
			2.8				84.2	4.5
			.8			Sales/Net Fixed Assets	.5	.9
			.3				.3	.3
			.7				1.4	.9
			.6			Sales/Total Assets	.4	.5
			.3				.2	.3
			2.4				.7	2.0
			(12) 6.0			% Depr., Dep., Amort./Sales	(15) 9.6	(17) 5.4
			9.5				14.2	14.0
						% Officers', Directors' Owners' Comp/Sales		
	4371M	14027M	189975M	106807M	236496M	Net Sales ($)	222640M	311812M
	1033M	27858M	377366M	427428M	777801M	Total Assets ($)	664948M	887020M

M = $ thousand MM = $ million

See Pages 9 through 22 for Explanation of Ratios and Data

Comparative Historical Data				Current Data Sorted by Sales					
			Type of Statement						
18	17	19	Unqualified		1	2	3	10	3
1	2	1	Reviewed					1	
			Compiled						
	2	1	Tax Returns			1			
11	7	8	Other			1	2	3	2
4/1/11-3/31/12	4/1/12-3/31/13	4/1/13-3/31/14			12 (4/1-9/30/13)		17 (10/1/13-3/31/14)		
ALL	ALL	ALL		0-1MM	1-3MM	3-5MM	5-10MM	10-25MM	25MM & OVER
30	28	29	**NUMBER OF STATEMENTS**		1	4	5	14	5
%	%	%	**ASSETS**	%	%	%	%	%	%
13.4	13.3	16.5	Cash & Equivalents	DATA NOT AVAILABLE				17.3	
2.6	3.9	2.2	Trade Receivables (net)					2.6	
1.1	3.0	3.1	Inventory					.6	
3.1	3.7	4.2	All Other Current					3.4	
20.3	23.8	26.1	Total Current					23.9	
61.2	60.5	58.5	Fixed Assets (net)					57.8	
.2	.1	.3	Intangibles (net)					.6	
18.4	15.6	15.1	All Other Non-Current					17.8	
100.0	100.0	100.0	Total					100.0	
			LIABILITIES						
2.0	1.0	2.6	Notes Payable-Short Term					1.2	
2.6	4.7	1.2	Cur. Mat.-L.T.D.					1.0	
1.8	3.0	3.5	Trade Payables					4.0	
.0	.0	.0	Income Taxes Payable					.0	
4.1	3.4	2.5	All Other Current					3.0	
10.4	12.0	9.9	Total Current					9.2	
17.5	20.1	13.2	Long-Term Debt					13.8	
.0	.0	.0	Deferred Taxes					.0	
1.6	3.5	2.6	All Other Non-Current					2.2	
70.5	64.4	74.3	Net Worth					74.8	
100.0	100.0	100.0	Total Liabilties & Net Worth					100.0	
			INCOME DATA						
100.0	100.0	100.0	Net Sales					100.0	
			Gross Profit						
88.9	90.6	89.7	Operating Expenses					88.6	
11.1	9.4	10.3	Operating Profit					11.4	
3.9	.7	-.2	All Other Expenses (net)					1.0	
7.2	8.7	10.5	Profit Before Taxes					10.5	
			RATIOS						
6.4	5.8	4.3						3.0	
1.2	2.4	2.0	Current					1.9	
.8	1.0	1.1						1.1	
4.8	4.2	2.6						2.6	
1.0	1.0	1.5	Quick					1.4	
.6	.5	.8						.6	
0 UND	0 UND	2 242.3						1 256.4	
7 53.8	4 90.4	6 58.2	Sales/Receivables					10 36.3	
19 19.0	17 20.9	27 13.6						40 9.1	
			Cost of Sales/Inventory						
			Cost of Sales/Payables						
2.3	2.0	2.0						2.0	
23.2	6.2	4.9	Sales/Working Capital					7.2	
-22.4	NM	55.8						42.5	
7.4	16.4	30.0							
(23) 2.2	(20) 5.1	(20) 5.3	EBIT/Interest						
-2.6	.7	.6							
			Net Profit + Depr., Dep., Amort./Cur. Mat. L/T/D						
.6	.7	.5						.6	
.9	.9	.9	Fixed/Worth					.8	
1.1	1.3	1.1						1.0	
.1	.1	.2						.1	
.2	.4	.3	Debt/Worth					.2	
.6	1.0	.5						.8	
10.6	15.9	13.5						14.3	
(29) .8	(26) 4.1	5.3	% Profit Before Taxes/Tangible Net Worth					4.8	
-3.5	-2.4	.1						1.3	
9.1	14.4	8.4						8.4	
.8	3.5	4.8	% Profit Before Taxes/Total Assets					3.5	
-1.9	-1.5	.1						1.1	
1.7	1.8	1.7						1.6	
.5	.6	.6	Sales/Net Fixed Assets					.7	
.4	.3	.3						.3	
.6	.9	.7						.7	
.3	.4	.4	Sales/Total Assets					.4	
.3	.3	.2						.2	
6.8	3.0	2.4						2.4	
(27) 12.2	9.4	(25) 9.2	% Depr., Dep., Amort./Sales					(13) 8.1	
13.7	13.5	12.8						12.3	
			% Officers', Directors' Owners' Comp/Sales						
610824M	421433M	551676M	Net Sales ($)		1612M	15991M	33344M	227042M	273687M
1835716M	1270236M	1611486M	Total Assets ($)		9854M	26557M	104198M	650759M	820118M

M = $ thousand MM = $ million

See Pages 9 through 22 for Explanation of Ratios and Data

Current Data Sorted by Assets | **Comparative Historical Data**

0-500M	500M-2MM	2-10MM	10-50MM	50-100MM	100-250MM	Type of Statement	4/1/09-3/31/10 ALL	4/1/10-3/31/11 ALL
1			9		2	Unqualified	6	7
		6	8			Reviewed	14	16
1	1	5	4			Compiled	24	10
5	8	4	1			Tax Returns	25	23
4	11	10	8	2	2	Other	40	58
12 (4/1-9/30/13)		80 (10/1/13-3/31/14)						
11	20	25	30	2	4	NUMBER OF STATEMENTS	109	114
%	%	%	%	%	%	**ASSETS**	%	%
27.6	14.9	11.7	11.5			Cash & Equivalents	8.9	10.4
5.7	3.6	.6	1.8			Trade Receivables (net)	1.4	1.6
4.7	7.8	1.7	1.8			Inventory	4.6	1.6
4.0	3.2	1.4	.7			All Other Current	1.2	4.3
42.1	29.5	15.4	15.7			Total Current	16.1	17.9
38.9	43.3	66.2	76.5			Fixed Assets (net)	72.2	69.9
2.2	8.9	5.9	1.7			Intangibles (net)	2.0	3.3
16.8	18.3	12.5	6.1			All Other Non-Current	9.7	8.9
100.0	100.0	100.0	100.0			Total	100.0	100.0
						LIABILITIES		
6.4	3.4	3.2	1.8			Notes Payable-Short Term	5.9	6.4
5.3	2.9	4.3	3.6			Cur. Mat.-L.T.D.	6.7	5.1
4.2	6.2	2.9	3.1			Trade Payables	3.6	3.6
.1	.0	.1	.1			Income Taxes Payable	.1	.0
24.2	15.8	10.1	5.2			All Other Current	12.8	10.8
40.1	28.3	20.6	13.8			Total Current	29.1	25.8
18.0	40.8	37.2	42.2			Long-Term Debt	45.9	40.4
.0	.0	1.9	.4			Deferred Taxes	.8	1.0
64.9	5.5	3.4	6.5			All Other Non-Current	11.6	15.0
-23.0	25.4	36.9	37.1			Net Worth	12.6	17.8
100.0	100.0	100.0	100.0			Total Liabilties & Net Worth	100.0	100.0
						INCOME DATA		
100.0	100.0	100.0	100.0			Net Sales	100.0	100.0
						Gross Profit		
98.4	91.6	87.4	87.1			Operating Expenses	90.7	85.0
1.6	8.4	12.6	12.9			Operating Profit	9.3	15.0
1.9	2.3	3.0	4.8			All Other Expenses (net)	4.1	6.0
-.3	6.1	9.5	8.1			Profit Before Taxes	5.2	9.0
						RATIOS		
3.4	6.8	2.1	2.1				1.5	2.6
1.1	1.2	1.0	.9			Current	.6	.7
.2	.3	.3	.3				.2	.2
3.4	4.6	1.8	1.9				1.2	1.8
1.1	.6	.6	.6			Quick	.3	.4
.1	.2	.2	.2				.1	.1
0 UND	0 UND	0 UND	0 UND				0 UND	0 UND
0 UND	0 UND	1 307.9	2 183.1			Sales/Receivables	0 999.8	0 959.3
1 326.3	1 335.8	3 137.8	4 96.8				3 114.2	7 49.3
						Cost of Sales/Inventory		
						Cost of Sales/Payables		
22.8	8.3	7.7	8.1				24.0	12.6
251.5	NM	999.8	NM			Sales/Working Capital	-23.0	-28.4
-8.3	-9.5	-10.1	-5.4				-4.5	-4.9
	7.1	11.7	5.7				4.6	7.4
	(14) 1.8	(22) 4.7	(27) 3.1			EBIT/Interest	(88) 1.6	(94) 2.8
	.1	2.0	1.3				.2	1.0
							3.4	3.9
						Net Profit + Depr., Dep., Amort./Cur. Mat. L/T/D	(16) 2.3	(20) 2.4
							1.5	1.3
.6	.5	1.0	1.3				1.3	.9
1.6	1.5	2.5	2.9			Fixed/Worth	3.8	2.9
-1.7	-1.7	6.0	8.9				-10.0	23.8
.3	.2	.9	.5				.8	.7
6.3	3.1	2.7	2.2			Debt/Worth	3.7	2.7
-2.8	-4.9	6.2	13.7				-13.3	42.8
	50.0	48.8	32.3				40.7	54.9
	(13) 34.0	(22) 19.9	(27) 11.7			% Profit Before Taxes/Tangible Net Worth	(72) 13.3	(87) 21.2
	10.7	8.7	6.1				.8	2.5
6.0	18.4	16.3	8.9				8.3	15.2
-1.1	8.0	7.8	4.7			% Profit Before Taxes/Total Assets	1.9	5.6
-12.9	-1.5	1.5	1.1				-2.9	.3
35.9	15.5	3.1	1.5				3.5	3.8
12.0	4.7	1.2	.7			Sales/Net Fixed Assets	1.3	1.3
5.9	1.8	.6	.5				.5	.6
7.4	3.0	1.6	.9				2.1	1.6
2.4	1.8	.9	.6			Sales/Total Assets	.8	.9
1.5	.7	.5	.4				.4	.5
	2.8	4.7	5.8				5.4	5.9
	(14) 6.7	(24) 6.3	11.0			% Depr., Dep., Amort./Sales	(99) 10.0	(99) 9.0
	14.5	9.4	16.1				14.3	13.6
	2.0						3.8	1.7
	(10) 5.4					% Officers', Directors' Owners' Comp/Sales	(30) 5.5	(25) 4.8
	15.0						10.9	6.7
16324M	41186M	144942M	515645M	90409M	326185M	Net Sales ($)	1061394M	1209600M
2589M	22687M	142676M	734782M	159090M	565060M	Total Assets ($)	1720020M	1714907M

M = $ thousand MM = $ million

See Pages 9 through 22 for Explanation of Ratios and Data

Comparative Historical Data				Current Data Sorted by Sales					
			Type of Statement						
11	12	12	Unqualified		1		2	4	5
15	9	14	Reviewed		1		4	8	1
17	12	11	Compiled	1	1	3	3	2	1
23	22	18	Tax Returns	8	8	1	1		
48	44	37	Other	8	5	7	7	4	6
4/1/11-3/31/12 ALL	4/1/12-3/31/13 ALL	4/1/13-3/31/14 ALL		12 (4/1-9/30/13)			80 (10/1/13-3/31/14)		
				0-1MM	1-3MM	3-5MM	5-10MM	10-25MM	25MM & OVER
114	99	92	**NUMBER OF STATEMENTS**	17	16	11	17	18	13
%	%	%	**ASSETS**	%	%	%	%	%	%
13.2	15.0	14.1	Cash & Equivalents	15.8	15.6	13.0	14.3	11.8	13.8
1.5	2.1	2.3	Trade Receivables (net)	5.3	1.7	1.6	.9	2.4	1.4
2.4	2.5	3.3	Inventory	3.1	2.8	11.0	1.3	1.4	3.3
3.1	2.3	1.9	All Other Current	.7	6.0	2.4	.3	1.0	1.3
20.2	21.8	21.6	Total Current	24.9	26.1	28.0	16.8	16.7	19.8
67.6	63.9	60.5	Fixed Assets (net)	51.3	54.2	50.2	70.9	70.9	60.7
4.9	3.8	6.1	Intangibles (net)	6.7	10.8	3.0	1.6	3.0	12.2
7.3	10.4	11.8	All Other Non-Current	17.1	8.9	18.8	10.8	9.4	7.4
100.0	100.0	100.0	Total	100.0	100.0	100.0	100.0	100.0	100.0
			LIABILITIES						
6.1	5.1	3.0	Notes Payable-Short Term	6.5	2.8	3.9	1.4	.8	3.0
4.0	3.5	3.6	Cur. Mat.-L.T.D.	4.1	3.5	4.2	2.7	4.5	2.6
2.6	3.8	3.8	Trade Payables	2.7	4.7	5.6	2.5	4.3	3.4
.0	.0	.1	Income Taxes Payable	.0	.1	.0	.1	.2	.0
14.2	18.6	10.9	All Other Current	21.6	15.8	5.2	10.5	3.4	6.8
27.0	31.0	21.4	Total Current	34.9	26.8	18.8	17.2	13.2	15.8
42.2	27.3	35.9	Long-Term Debt	27.2	56.9	36.7	36.9	38.3	16.0
.4	.4	.7	Deferred Taxes	.0	.0	.0	1.7	1.8	.5
14.8	12.8	13.8	All Other Non-Current	44.0	4.9	4.5	4.0	7.3	15.1
15.5	28.5	28.2	Net Worth	-6.2	11.4	39.9	40.2	39.5	52.5
100.0	100.0	100.0	Total Liabilties & Net Worth	100.0	100.0	100.0	100.0	100.0	100.0
			INCOME DATA						
100.0	100.0	100.0	Net Sales	100.0	100.0	100.0	100.0	100.0	100.0
			Gross Profit						
90.0	88.6	88.9	Operating Expenses	89.1	92.8	89.9	88.7	87.1	85.5
10.0	11.4	11.1	Operating Profit	10.9	7.2	10.1	11.3	12.9	14.5
4.8	2.3	3.2	All Other Expenses (net)	5.4	4.5	1.1	2.5	3.6	1.2
5.2	9.0	7.9	Profit Before Taxes	5.5	2.7	9.0	8.8	9.3	13.3
			RATIOS						
1.8	3.2	3.0		3.9	4.1	7.1	2.3	2.1	3.9
.7	1.0	1.1	Current	.6	1.0	2.2	1.1	1.0	1.5
.2	.2	.3		.2	.2	.8	.3	.5	.6
1.4	2.8	2.5		3.1	1.2	4.8	2.2	1.9	3.4
.4	.6	.7	Quick	.3	.7	1.1	.9	.6	.8
.1	.2	.3		.1	.1	.4	.2	.4	.3
0 UND	0 UND	0 UND		0 UND	0 UND	0 UND	0 UND	0 UND	3 117.5
0 999.8	0 999.8	1 335.5	Sales/Receivables	0 UND	0 UND	0 999.8	1 307.9	2 198.8	4 83.3
3 112.6	4 94.5	4 101.3		0 UND	4 86.7	3 110.6	2 147.0	2 161.1	9 41.5
			Cost of Sales/Inventory						
			Cost of Sales/Payables						
13.3	5.5	8.7		12.9	9.1	6.3	12.2	8.1	3.3
-36.1	-370.5	157.1	Sales/Working Capital	-23.7	NM	12.8	163.3	NM	46.7
-4.9	-5.5	-8.7		-3.9	-4.7	-25.1	-8.5	-10.8	-14.0
5.7	10.0	10.3			4.7		15.8	10.6	
(97) 2.3	(76) 4.2	(71) 3.3	EBIT/Interest		(14) 1.6		(13) 3.3	5.1	
.7	.8	1.3			-.6		1.3	2.7	
5.1		5.7							
(13) 1.3		(14) 2.9	Net Profit + Depr., Dep., Amort./Cur. Mat. L/T/D						
-.1		1.3							
1.1	.8	.8		.7	1.0	.2	1.0	1.1	.7
3.6	2.4	2.3	Fixed/Worth	2.9	11.5	1.1	2.4	2.1	.9
-9.5	-271.9	15.4		-8.1	-1.7	7.7	8.1	5.6	3.4
.8	.3	.5		1.6	2.7	.2	.3	.6	.1
3.6	2.5	2.6	Debt/Worth	4.0	14.1	1.4	2.2	1.5	1.0
-10.7	-276.1	34.4		-11.8	-3.4	7.4	7.8	5.2	11.9
37.3	35.4	36.9		51.5			43.5	37.2	24.9
(81) 13.1	(74) 16.0	(73) 18.3	% Profit Before Taxes/Tangible Net Worth	(12) 22.3			(16) 10.0	(16) 17.9	(11) 11.7
-1.6	3.5	6.4		.2			5.8	11.4	4.5
13.7	15.1	13.9		6.6	15.9	18.6	18.2	12.3	16.7
3.4	6.4	5.7	% Profit Before Taxes/Total Assets	.9	4.1	10.7	4.8	6.9	8.3
-1.9	-.3	.9		-4.1	-3.7	2.6	.9	2.8	2.5
4.2	4.1	5.1		7.8	8.5	17.7	3.6	2.6	2.9
1.2	1.2	1.4	Sales/Net Fixed Assets	1.9	3.8	3.1	1.1	1.0	1.4
.5	.6	.6		.5	.8	.7	.5	.5	.9
2.2	1.8	1.8		2.2	3.0	2.8	1.6	1.6	1.3
.8	.8	.8	Sales/Total Assets	.7	1.3	1.3	.9	.7	.8
.5	.5	.5		.4	.5	.6	.4	.5	.6
5.3	4.7	4.2		2.4	2.7		5.7	5.0	3.1
(104) 10.1	(89) 7.6	(78) 7.5	% Depr., Dep., Amort./Sales	(15) 5.2	(13) 4.3		(14) 10.2	8.2	(11) 8.3
13.9	11.7	12.5		14.4	17.0		17.7	11.9	15.6
4.5	3.5	2.1							
(28) 6.1	(24) 6.9	(27) 5.9	% Officers', Directors' Owners' Comp/Sales						
9.3	10.2	9.7							
1249724M	1407856M	1134691M	Net Sales ($)	8649M	30824M	44660M	127918M	271606M	651034M
1981663M	2117867M	1626884M	Total Assets ($)	30437M	33563M	46504M	185269M	405895M	925216M

M = $ thousand MM = $ million

See Pages 9 through 22 for Explanation of Ratios and Data

Current Data Sorted by Assets							Comparative Historical Data	
						Type of Statement		
		1	4		5	Unqualified	13	13
1					1	Reviewed	2	6
1	2	3				Compiled	6	4
2	1	3				Tax Returns	8	6
4	2	5	3	5	7	Other	35	38
14 (4/1-9/30/13)			36 (10/1/13-3/31/14)				4/1/09-3/31/10	4/1/10-3/31/11
0-500M	500M-2MM	2-10MM	10-50MM	50-100MM	100-250MM		ALL	ALL
8	5	12	7	5	13	**NUMBER OF STATEMENTS**	64	67
%	%	%	%	%	%	**ASSETS**	%	%
		20.1			18.5	Cash & Equivalents	14.5	16.9
		.8			2.8	Trade Receivables (net)	2.7	3.5
		10.5			.6	Inventory	5.7	3.6
		4.2			1.1	All Other Current	4.8	1.6
		35.6			23.0	Total Current	27.6	25.6
		46.1			72.2	Fixed Assets (net)	61.7	60.5
		4.2			3.6	Intangibles (net)	4.5	7.3
		14.1			1.3	All Other Non-Current	6.3	6.6
		100.0			100.0	Total	100.0	100.0
						LIABILITIES		
		2.7			.0	Notes Payable-Short Term	5.4	6.2
		1.9			5.7	Cur. Mat.-L.T.D.	6.3	6.7
		8.6			2.3	Trade Payables	7.2	4.1
		.0			.0	Income Taxes Payable	.0	.0
		13.1			8.3	All Other Current	10.5	8.5
		26.4			16.2	Total Current	29.4	25.6
		19.4			31.4	Long-Term Debt	36.1	37.0
		.1			.0	Deferred Taxes	.1	.4
		21.9			.1	All Other Non-Current	4.3	12.2
		32.3			52.3	Net Worth	30.1	24.7
		100.0			100.0	Total Liabilties & Net Worth	100.0	100.0
						INCOME DATA		
		100.0			100.0	Net Sales	100.0	100.0
						Gross Profit		
		87.0			67.2	Operating Expenses	88.5	84.2
		13.0			32.8	Operating Profit	11.5	15.8
		4.9			3.0	All Other Expenses (net)	2.4	4.4
		8.1			29.8	Profit Before Taxes	9.0	11.4
						RATIOS		
		2.8			2.0		2.3	1.9
		1.5			1.5	Current	1.0	1.1
		.3			1.1		.4	.7
		2.6			1.7		1.6	1.7
		.2			1.4	Quick	.6	.9
		.1			.9		.1	.4
		0 UND			2 156.8		0 UND	0 UND
		0 999.8			4 88.2	Sales/Receivables	1 372.9	1 259.7
		1 526.8			7 51.3		5 74.8	5 73.7
						Cost of Sales/Inventory		
						Cost of Sales/Payables		
		6.5			10.2		8.4	9.7
		53.6			16.0	Sales/Working Capital	646.5	39.8
		-13.3			NM		-7.8	-16.6
		47.3			22.6		17.8	15.2
		(10) 6.2			(11) 19.9	EBIT/Interest	(58) 3.5	(60) 5.1
		.8			4.3		-.3	1.2
						Net Profit + Depr., Dep., Amort./Cur. Mat. L/T/D		
		.4			1.0		.8	.9
		2.0			1.3	Fixed/Worth	1.4	1.5
		NM			2.2		NM	-197.8
		.3			.5		.5	.6
		2.4			.9	Debt/Worth	1.0	1.3
		NM			1.9		NM	-246.9
					170.2		56.8	69.6
					58.4	% Profit Before Taxes/Tangible Net Worth	(48) 17.9	(50) 31.1
					28.7		.2	4.8
		27.4			50.2		23.1	24.3
		1.0			27.1	% Profit Before Taxes/Total Assets	4.9	11.5
		-1.1			17.8		-1.6	.8
		12.7			2.1		4.2	3.4
		2.8			1.3	Sales/Net Fixed Assets	2.1	1.7
		1.4			1.0		1.3	1.1
		3.6			1.4		2.0	1.5
		1.2			.9	Sales/Total Assets	1.3	1.0
		.9			.8		.8	.8
		4.1					5.6	6.7
		(11) 9.1				% Depr., Dep., Amort./Sales	(52) 7.6	(43) 9.5
		16.5					10.6	12.7
							2.3	2.3
						% Officers', Directors' Owners' Comp/Sales	(18) 4.4	(15) 5.2
							6.9	7.4
7855M	10051M	77556M	229666M	467885M	2581683M	Net Sales ($)	2556439M	3750231M
1589M	5155M	40712M	203100M	376711M	2305726M	Total Assets ($)	2501070M	3540487M

M = $ thousand MM = $ million

See Pages 9 through 22 for Explanation of Ratios and Data

Comparative Historical Data				Current Data Sorted by Sales					
			Type of Statement						
15	8	10	Unqualified				1		9
5	4	2	Reviewed		1				1
7	3	6	Compiled		4	2			
9	7	6	Tax Returns	3	2		1		
32	26	26	Other	4	2	1	3	2	14
4/1/11-3/31/12 ALL	4/1/12-3/31/13 ALL	4/1/13-3/31/14 ALL		14 (4/1-9/30/13)			36 (10/1/13-3/31/14)		
				0-1MM	1-3MM	3-5MM	5-10MM	10-25MM	25MM & OVER
68	48	50	**NUMBER OF STATEMENTS**	7	9	3	5	2	24
%	%	%	**ASSETS**	%	%	%	%	%	%
13.8	18.2	18.2	Cash & Equivalents						18.0
2.5	3.0	1.5	Trade Receivables (net)						2.7
4.2	2.5	4.2	Inventory						1.6
4.5	3.1	3.2	All Other Current						.9
25.0	26.7	27.2	Total Current						23.1
57.1	59.1	60.5	Fixed Assets (net)						69.8
8.6	4.7	5.9	Intangibles (net)						4.3
9.3	9.5	6.5	All Other Non-Current						2.9
100.0	100.0	100.0	Total						100.0
			LIABILITIES						
2.8	3.3	9.5	Notes Payable-Short Term						.0
6.5	5.1	4.1	Cur. Mat.-L.T.D.						6.0
6.4	5.3	5.0	Trade Payables						3.9
.0	.1	.0	Income Taxes Payable						.0
10.0	9.9	16.1	All Other Current						7.5
25.8	23.6	34.7	Total Current						17.4
33.5	32.8	24.4	Long-Term Debt						28.5
.0	.0	.0	Deferred Taxes						.0
8.0	11.4	12.8	All Other Non-Current						3.0
32.7	32.1	28.0	Net Worth						51.2
100.0	100.0	100.0	Total Liabilities & Net Worth						100.0
			INCOME DATA						
100.0	100.0	100.0	Net Sales						100.0
			Gross Profit						
81.9	82.6	82.3	Operating Expenses						72.8
18.1	17.4	17.7	Operating Profit						27.2
3.1	2.5	2.2	All Other Expenses (net)						2.3
15.1	14.9	15.6	Profit Before Taxes						24.8
			RATIOS						
1.8	2.4	2.0	Current						2.0
1.2	1.2	1.2							1.4
.5	.7	.6							.8
1.5	1.8	1.6	Quick						1.6
.7	1.0	.9							1.3
.2	.4	.4							.8
0 UND	0 UND	0 UND	Sales/Receivables						1 333.9
1 288.4	1 453.4	1 453.7							2 149.9
3 108.0	3 110.4	4 92.0							6 62.0
			Cost of Sales/Inventory						
			Cost of Sales/Payables						
9.1	8.0	11.7	Sales/Working Capital						9.3
68.5	30.6	81.4							18.4
-10.0	-17.1	-13.9							-37.1
16.8	21.3	25.6	EBIT/Interest						24.2
(62) 6.2	(41) 6.9	(40) 14.6							(20) 18.8
2.1	1.5	1.5							7.4
			Net Profit + Depr., Dep., Amort./Cur. Mat. L/T/D						
1.0	.7	.9	Fixed/Worth						1.0
1.7	1.4	1.7							1.3
17.5	15.8	6.8							2.4
.9	.6	.5	Debt/Worth						.5
1.9	1.4	1.7							.9
55.1	35.0	9.7							2.1
92.4	64.8	117.8	% Profit Before Taxes/Tangible Net Worth						141.6
(52) 44.1	(38) 32.8	(43) 53.5							55.9
10.7	14.1	11.9							23.0
28.0	32.6	31.9	% Profit Before Taxes/Total Assets						38.2
11.7	8.1	17.0							25.8
3.1	1.4	.0							12.3
4.1	6.9	6.2	Sales/Net Fixed Assets						2.1
1.7	2.0	2.1							1.4
1.1	1.0	1.3							1.1
1.3	1.8	2.9	Sales/Total Assets						1.4
1.0	1.1	1.3							1.0
.7	.7	.9							.9
5.8	4.4	3.8	% Depr., Dep., Amort./Sales						5.8
(47) 7.8	(27) 7.1	(35) 7.4							(13) 7.1
10.6	9.3	9.8							10.0
1.7			% Officers', Directors' Owners' Comp/Sales						
(11) 5.1									
11.5									
3556056M	3499498M	3374696M	Net Sales ($)	4453M	16226M	11875M	37353M	32263M	3272526M
3395083M	3253385M	2932993M	Total Assets ($)	6843M	11575M	9191M	23547M	7542M	2874295M

M = $ thousand MM = $ million

See Pages 9 through 22 for Explanation of Ratios and Data

Current Data Sorted by Assets / Comparative Historical Data

0-500M	500M-2MM	2-10MM	10-50MM	50-100MM	100-250MM	Type of Statement	4/1/09-3/31/10 ALL	4/1/10-3/31/11 ALL
		6	10	5	11	Unqualified	38	35
	1				1	Reviewed	2	3
		2	1			Compiled	8	4
6	2					Tax Returns	14	16
	5	7	6	6	8	Other	72	53
15 (4/1-9/30/13)			62 (10/1/13-3/31/14)					
6	8	15	17	11	20	NUMBER OF STATEMENTS	134	111
%	%	%	%	%	%	**ASSETS**	%	%
		25.2	21.4	16.8	19.2	Cash & Equivalents	19.0	17.5
		2.8	2.1	1.2	.9	Trade Receivables (net)	2.3	1.6
		2.0	.7	.6	.5	Inventory	.9	1.9
		1.6	1.2	1.5	.7	All Other Current	2.9	2.9
		31.6	25.3	20.2	21.3	Total Current	25.1	24.0
		60.2	62.8	75.2	71.5	Fixed Assets (net)	62.7	60.4
		4.0	5.7	3.0	1.9	Intangibles (net)	5.9	8.5
		4.2	6.2	1.6	5.3	All Other Non-Current	6.3	7.1
		100.0	100.0	100.0	100.0	Total	100.0	100.0
						LIABILITIES		
		.4	1.6	.4	.0	Notes Payable-Short Term	2.5	4.6
		30.1	4.0	3.0	6.3	Cur. Mat.-L.T.D.	9.0	12.1
		6.9	4.7	2.9	2.5	Trade Payables	3.7	4.3
		.0	.0	.0	.0	Income Taxes Payable	.1	.3
		24.9	15.0	10.7	8.0	All Other Current	10.9	9.4
		62.4	25.2	17.0	16.7	Total Current	26.2	30.6
		18.5	33.6	30.2	37.6	Long-Term Debt	34.2	32.8
		.0	.0	.0	.0	Deferred Taxes	.0	.0
		2.0	.8	1.4	.7	All Other Non-Current	7.1	10.6
		17.1	40.4	51.3	45.0	Net Worth	32.5	25.9
		100.0	100.0	100.0	100.0	Total Liabilties & Net Worth	100.0	100.0
						INCOME DATA		
		100.0	100.0	100.0	100.0	Net Sales	100.0	100.0
						Gross Profit		
		85.4	69.8	74.5	71.6	Operating Expenses	79.6	84.2
		14.6	30.2	25.5	28.4	Operating Profit	20.4	15.8
		1.2	2.2	2.2	4.0	All Other Expenses (net)	4.5	5.5
		13.4	28.1	23.3	24.4	Profit Before Taxes	15.9	10.3
						RATIOS		
		2.1	2.2	1.6	1.5		2.1	1.9
		.8	1.0	1.3	1.1	Current	1.1	1.2
		.5	.8	1.1	.7		.5	.6
		1.7	2.1	1.5	1.4		1.8	1.6
		.7	.9	1.2	1.0	Quick	(132) .9	(110) 1.0
		.4	.6	1.0	.7		.4	.5
		0 898.1	0 999.8	0 910.3	1 450.5		0 999.8	0 999.8
		2 179.0	1 322.1	2 148.1	3 121.4	Sales/Receivables	1 315.3	1 295.2
		5 73.0	3 110.0	4 88.0	5 79.0		3 120.5	4 95.3
						Cost of Sales/Inventory		
						Cost of Sales/Payables		
		12.1	18.0	15.1	20.3		12.0	11.1
		-27.7	-182.5	32.8	52.4	Sales/Working Capital	116.2	63.0
		-14.4	-23.0	50.2	-21.8		-15.0	-15.3
		36.6	16.1		21.2		31.0	14.3
		(11) 3.3	(12) 11.9		(17) 9.1	EBIT/Interest	(109) 5.8	(93) 4.2
		-.1	2.5		5.5		1.7	.7
						Net Profit + Depr., Dep., Amort./Cur. Mat. L/T/D		
		.9	.8	.9	1.1		1.0	1.0
		3.9	1.1	1.6	1.7	Fixed/Worth	1.9	2.0
		-6.1	NM	4.4	2.4		37.7	-5.8
		.4	.3	.3	.5		.5	.6
		3.3	.7	.9	1.4	Debt/Worth	1.5	1.9
		-17.3	NM	4.1	2.1		-139.1	-8.4
		220.6	153.5	119.7	80.7		96.1	71.0
		(11) 41.9	(13) 51.7	(10) 73.4	(19) 46.8	% Profit Before Taxes/Tangible Net Worth	(100) 45.7	(81) 35.6
		-15.3	12.4	30.3	23.0		16.9	10.6
		167.3	116.2	89.6	43.0		38.9	27.6
		9.3	29.8	17.4	18.0	% Profit Before Taxes/Total Assets	13.9	10.0
		-11.1	6.3	7.3	12.1		.5	-.7
		10.9	4.2	2.7	2.1		4.0	4.8
		3.6	2.5	1.3	1.3	Sales/Net Fixed Assets	1.7	1.8
		1.4	1.4	1.3	1.0		1.1	1.1
		5.6	2.5	2.1	1.2		2.1	2.3
		2.9	1.8	1.1	.9	Sales/Total Assets	1.1	1.1
		1.0	1.0	1.1	.8		.8	.7
		3.4	2.8	5.2			4.8	3.8
		4.6	(15) 6.2	6.5		% Depr., Dep., Amort./Sales	(103) 6.8	(92) 6.4
		9.9	8.3	8.5			9.8	9.1
							1.7	1.0
						% Officers', Directors' Owners' Comp/Sales	(19) 3.8	(14) 2.9
							5.2	5.8
20539M	22185M	284018M	616686M	1025341M	3301678M	Net Sales ($)	7792600M	6449335M
2187M	7847M	88003M	348076M	743427M	3112738M	Total Assets ($)	7413417M	6158384M

M = $ thousand MM = $ million

See Pages 9 through 22 for Explanation of Ratios and Data

Comparative Historical Data				Current Data Sorted by Sales					
			Type of Statement						
27	19	32	Unqualified				1	3	28
3	4	2	Reviewed		1				1
5	6	3	Compiled				2		1
20	17	8	Tax Returns		3	3	2		
56	44	32	Other	2	4	2	2	4	18
4/1/11-3/31/12	**4/1/12-3/31/13**	**4/1/13-3/31/14**			**15 (4/1-9/30/13)**		**62 (10/1/13-3/31/14)**		
ALL	**ALL**	**ALL**		**0-1MM**	**1-3MM**	**3-5MM**	**5-10MM**	**10-25MM**	**25MM & OVER**
111	90	77	**NUMBER OF STATEMENTS**	2	8	5	7	7	48
%	%	%	**ASSETS**	%	%	%	%	%	%
21.1	22.0	21.9	Cash & Equivalents						21.0
1.8	2.2	1.6	Trade Receivables (net)						1.9
2.2	2.3	1.2	Inventory						.8
2.6	3.5	1.7	All Other Current						1.0
27.7	30.0	26.3	Total Current						24.6
53.4	50.7	62.0	Fixed Assets (net)						68.6
9.9	13.0	6.0	Intangibles (net)						2.9
9.0	6.4	5.6	All Other Non-Current						3.9
100.0	100.0	100.0	Total						100.0
			LIABILITIES						
4.9	2.1	1.9	Notes Payable-Short Term						.7
9.7	7.8	9.9	Cur. Mat.-L.T.D.						4.9
5.0	4.9	6.6	Trade Payables						3.8
.2	.1	.1	Income Taxes Payable						.0
10.4	12.6	19.3	All Other Current						15.2
30.2	27.5	37.8	Total Current						24.6
32.5	37.7	29.1	Long-Term Debt						32.5
.1	.0	.0	Deferred Taxes						.0
9.3	7.7	1.7	All Other Non-Current						1.3
27.8	27.1	31.4	Net Worth						41.6
100.0	100.0	100.0	Total Liabilties & Net Worth						100.0
			INCOME DATA						
100.0	100.0	100.0	Net Sales						100.0
			Gross Profit						
87.1	85.4	78.8	Operating Expenses						72.2
12.9	14.6	21.2	Operating Profit						27.8
4.0	4.1	2.3	All Other Expenses (net)						2.7
8.9	10.5	18.9	Profit Before Taxes						25.1
			RATIOS						
2.1	2.8	1.9							1.6
1.2	1.2	1.1	Current						1.1
.6	.7	.7							.7
1.7	2.0	1.7							1.5
1.0	.9	1.0	Quick						1.0
.5	.6	.6							.7
0 UND	0 UND	0 999.8							1 613.0
1 332.1	1 330.3	1 278.9	Sales/Receivables						3 141.7
4 90.3	3 106.2	4 101.1							4 84.6
			Cost of Sales/Inventory						
			Cost of Sales/Payables						
10.4	14.5	16.9							19.7
60.2	99.6	69.1	Sales/Working Capital						58.2
-19.6	-17.6	-20.3							-25.7
10.4	17.6	16.2							16.7
(84) 4.0	(73) 6.4	(55) 5.9	EBIT/Interest						(36) 9.3
.6	2.0	2.5							2.9
			Net Profit + Depr., Dep., Amort./Cur. Mat. L/T/D						
.9	.8	.9							1.0
1.7	1.6	1.6	Fixed/Worth						1.6
-7.0	-3.6	7.1							4.0
.5	.4	.3							.4
1.5	1.4	1.3	Debt/Worth						1.1
-20.0	-10.4	7.1							4.0
66.0	87.7	117.2							125.7
(81) 39.4	(65) 33.2	(61) 46.8	% Profit Before Taxes/Tangible Net Worth						(41) 53.7
13.5	10.5	19.8							25.3
26.8	30.4	51.1							76.8
10.1	11.6	16.0	% Profit Before Taxes/Total Assets						22.8
-1.4	.8	7.3							11.6
10.6	20.5	7.4							4.0
2.4	3.7	2.4	Sales/Net Fixed Assets						1.6
1.2	1.4	1.3							1.3
2.7	3.7	3.1							2.3
1.3	1.4	1.3	Sales/Total Assets						1.1
.8	.9	.9							.9
2.9	2.2	2.9							3.9
(82) 5.7	(67) 5.1	(60) 5.4	% Depr., Dep., Amort./Sales						(36) 5.7
8.3	8.1	7.9							6.7
2.2									
(14) 3.0			% Officers', Directors' Owners' Comp/Sales						
4.8									
6084454M	4918051M	5270447M	Net Sales ($)	1463M	16635M	20864M	44611M	114890M	5071984M
5888286M	4234258M	4302278M	Total Assets ($)	2259M	18455M	13150M	36007M	54866M	4177541M

 M = $ thousand MM = $ million

See Pages 9 through 22 for Explanation of Ratios and Data

Current Data Sorted by Assets							Comparative Historical Data	
						Type of Statement		
			9	8	12	Unqualified	5	10
		1				Reviewed	2	2
	1		1			Compiled		
	1	3				Tax Returns	2	2
	2	10	11	3	7	Other	17	22
	16 (4/1-9/30/13)		53 (10/1/13-3/31/14)				**4/1/09-3/31/10**	**4/1/10-3/31/11**
0-500M	**500M-2MM**	**2-10MM**	**10-50MM**	**50-100MM**	**100-250MM**		**ALL**	**ALL**
	4	14	21	11	19	**NUMBER OF STATEMENTS**	26	36
%	%	%	%	%	%	**ASSETS**	%	%
DATA NOT AVAILABLE		20.9	15.0	15.2	16.0	Cash & Equivalents	24.4	20.9
		14.1	4.6	.8	2.3	Trade Receivables (net)	4.4	4.3
		6.5	2.0	.5	1.3	Inventory	3.9	1.2
		2.5	8.8	1.2	1.8	All Other Current	6.8	4.2
		43.9	30.4	17.7	21.3	Total Current	39.5	30.5
		37.4	47.2	79.8	75.2	Fixed Assets (net)	48.5	48.0
		12.3	13.2	.1	2.2	Intangibles (net)	6.7	15.5
		6.4	9.2	2.4	1.3	All Other Non-Current	5.2	5.9
		100.0	100.0	100.0	100.0	Total	100.0	100.0
						LIABILITIES		
		3.1	1.3	.0	3.0	Notes Payable-Short Term	4.4	2.3
		3.8	6.4	14.7	3.9	Cur. Mat.-L.T.D.	12.1	7.3
		14.1	3.7	3.6	3.3	Trade Payables	8.9	5.1
		.0	.0	.0	.0	Income Taxes Payable	1.0	.0
		7.1	18.4	13.4	9.7	All Other Current	13.6	11.2
		28.1	29.8	31.8	19.9	Total Current	40.1	26.0
		43.8	39.9	15.7	28.2	Long-Term Debt	32.6	29.9
		.0	.4	.0	.1	Deferred Taxes	.1	.6
		14.7	3.4	.0	4.0	All Other Non-Current	11.3	11.7
		13.5	26.5	52.5	47.8	Net Worth	15.9	31.8
		100.0	100.0	100.0	100.0	Total Liabilties & Net Worth	100.0	100.0
						INCOME DATA		
		100.0	100.0	100.0	100.0	Net Sales	100.0	100.0
						Gross Profit		
		84.7	72.5	69.4	71.9	Operating Expenses	95.2	84.5
		15.3	27.5	30.6	28.1	Operating Profit	4.8	15.5
		3.4	6.1	5.5	5.1	All Other Expenses (net)	4.6	4.6
		12.0	21.4	25.1	23.0	Profit Before Taxes	.2	10.9
						RATIOS		
		5.8	1.7	1.3	1.6		2.3	1.6
		1.6	1.1	.9	1.0	Current	1.1	.8
		1.0	.5	.6	.7		.7	.5
		5.3	1.7	1.2	1.4		2.1	1.6
		1.5	.9	.8	1.0	Quick	1.0	.7
		.6	.3	.5	.6		.4	.4
		1 582.1	0 945.3	1 327.2	1 362.3		0 UND	0 816.5
		12 30.0	7 53.5	2 167.7	3 110.6	Sales/Receivables	1 331.8	5 70.4
		37 9.8	28 13.1	4 101.7	7 54.7		22 16.9	35 10.5
						Cost of Sales/Inventory		
						Cost of Sales/Payables		
		6.1	9.5	29.7	12.4		11.1	13.9
		13.9	69.5	-122.8	217.4	Sales/Working Capital	42.0	-21.4
		NM	-14.3	-17.5	-13.8		-14.6	-9.5
		26.1	19.1		51.0		12.0	7.6
		5.1	(17) 5.1		(15) 11.8	EBIT/Interest	(23) 3.6	(32) 4.5
		1.5	1.5		3.2		-.3	.2
						Net Profit + Depr., Dep., Amort./Cur. Mat. L/T/D		
		.5	.9	.9	.9		1.0	1.2
		1.4	1.4	1.4	1.4	Fixed/Worth	3.0	2.6
		-1.4	-35.2	1.9	5.3		-4.7	NM
		1.5	.5	.1	.3		.5	1.2
		5.1	1.5	.5	.7	Debt/Worth	3.9	4.6
		-2.8	-46.3	1.2	4.7		-12.6	NM
			128.4	91.1	129.7		61.0	124.5
			(15) 20.9	(10) 42.5	(18) 36.0	% Profit Before Taxes/Tangible Net Worth	(18) 23.0	(27) 64.3
			5.3	25.1	13.5		1.7	-4.0
		48.6	51.0	54.7	41.6		14.9	25.6
		14.7	5.7	28.6	18.4	% Profit Before Taxes/Total Assets	4.7	9.4
		2.5	.9	11.8	10.6		-2.7	-.6
		18.6	6.6	2.3	1.5		8.8	6.3
		10.5	2.6	1.3	1.1	Sales/Net Fixed Assets	3.2	1.9
		3.7	1.5	.9	.9		1.3	1.0
		4.6	2.0	1.6	1.0		2.6	2.0
		2.7	1.2	1.0	.9	Sales/Total Assets	1.3	1.0
		1.0	.6	.8	.8		.7	.6
		2.1	3.3	5.8			3.0	3.7
		(10) 4.5	(20) 5.1	7.6		% Depr., Dep., Amort./Sales	(21) 5.5	(26) 9.0
		11.7	19.3	9.5			12.9	19.9
						% Officers', Directors' Owners' Comp/Sales		
	21674M	**193068M**	**935874M**	**960337M**	**3386251M**	Net Sales ($)	**860405M**	**1469393M**
	6114M	**60713M**	**566442M**	**813920M**	**3153405M**	Total Assets ($)	**908813M**	**1932743M**

M = $ thousand MM = $ million

See Pages 9 through 22 for Explanation of Ratios and Data

Comparative Historical Data				Current Data Sorted by Sales					
			Type of Statement						
18	17	29	Unqualified						29
1		1	Reviewed					1	
	1	2	Compiled	1				1	
3	7	4	Tax Returns				3	1	
35	37	33	Other		1	5	5	5	17
4/1/11-3/31/12 ALL	4/1/12-3/31/13 ALL	4/1/13-3/31/14 ALL		16 (4/1-9/30/13)			53 (10/1/13-3/31/14)		
				0-1MM	1-3MM	3-5MM	5-10MM	10-25MM	25MM & OVER
57	62	69	**NUMBER OF STATEMENTS**	1	1	5	8	8	46
%	%	%	**ASSETS**	%	%	%	%	%	%
20.2	17.8	16.0	Cash & Equivalents						17.2
4.6	5.8	5.4	Trade Receivables (net)						2.9
1.8	2.7	2.4	Inventory						1.6
4.2	4.3	4.3	All Other Current						2.7
30.8	30.7	28.2	Total Current						24.3
57.7	53.8	59.2	Fixed Assets (net)						67.9
3.7	4.8	7.8	Intangibles (net)						5.0
7.8	10.7	4.8	All Other Non-Current						2.8
100.0	100.0	100.0	Total						100.0
			LIABILITIES						
2.8	4.5	2.9	Notes Payable-Short Term						1.9
8.3	4.3	6.6	Cur. Mat.-L.T.D.						7.4
5.9	4.0	5.7	Trade Payables						5.2
.1	.0	.0	Income Taxes Payable						.0
11.6	14.8	12.0	All Other Current						12.1
28.6	27.7	27.2	Total Current						26.6
30.9	30.2	33.1	Long-Term Debt						31.6
.2	.2	.1	Deferred Taxes						.0
5.5	1.2	5.5	All Other Non-Current						3.5
34.8	40.7	34.0	Net Worth						38.3
100.0	100.0	100.0	Total Liabilties & Net Worth						100.0
			INCOME DATA						
100.0	100.0	100.0	Net Sales						100.0
			Gross Profit						
76.9	76.4	74.6	Operating Expenses						72.2
23.1	23.6	25.4	Operating Profit						27.8
5.5	4.2	5.1	All Other Expenses (net)						6.2
17.7	19.4	20.3	Profit Before Taxes						21.7
			RATIOS						
2.0	1.6	1.6							1.5
1.1	1.2	1.1	Current						1.1
.8	.8	.7							.6
1.5	1.4	1.5							1.3
.9	.8	.9	Quick						.9
.7	.5	.4							.5
1 305.2	0 834.5	1 580.6							1 586.0
4 99.2	4 92.5	3 110.6	Sales/Receivables						2 151.6
22 16.9	23 15.7	13 27.6							6 65.6
			Cost of Sales/Inventory						
			Cost of Sales/Payables						
10.2	10.9	11.1							15.7
69.9	54.6	69.5	Sales/Working Capital						154.7
-20.5	-21.2	-18.9							-15.8
25.8	31.5	29.1							33.2
(49) 7.4	(51) 7.7	(56) 7.4	EBIT/Interest						(34) 11.7
1.6	2.7	2.6							3.0
			Net Profit + Depr., Dep., Amort./Cur. Mat. L/T/D						
.7	.7	.9							.9
1.4	1.5	1.4	Fixed/Worth						1.5
4.1	5.1	6.5							5.5
.4	.5	.4							.4
1.2	1.4	1.4	Debt/Worth						.8
9.9	5.4	10.1							5.6
93.8	117.0	125.5							126.2
(45) 33.6	(52) 36.0	(55) 44.2	% Profit Before Taxes/Tangible Net Worth						(38) 42.5
8.8	14.7	14.2							13.5
37.9	41.4	44.3							54.8
16.6	18.2	18.4	% Profit Before Taxes/Total Assets						21.0
1.4	4.8	2.6							4.6
3.4	9.9	6.1							3.9
1.8	2.5	1.7	Sales/Net Fixed Assets						1.5
1.0	1.1	1.1							1.1
1.6	2.2	2.2							1.9
1.0	1.3	1.0	Sales/Total Assets						1.1
.7	.7	.8							.9
3.3	2.9	3.3							3.3
(36) 6.3	(40) 6.1	(50) 5.9	% Depr., Dep., Amort./Sales						(31) 5.6
10.0	11.1	9.7							9.0
			% Officers', Directors' Owners' Comp/Sales						
4651615M	4257601M	5497204M	Net Sales ($)	506M	2439M	19254M	53325M	107711M	5313969M
4719841M	3798347M	4600594M	Total Assets ($)	1819M	1158M	83628M	69042M	56234M	4388713M

M = $ thousand MM = $ million

See Pages 9 through 22 for Explanation of Ratios and Data

Current Data Sorted by Assets / Comparative Historical Data

0-500M	500M-2MM	2-10MM	10-50MM	50-100MM	100-250MM		4/1/09-3/31/10 ALL	4/1/10-3/31/11 ALL
						Type of Statement		
	3	87	112	8	3	Unqualified	257	263
3	12	60	21			Reviewed	112	99
10	38	49	8			Compiled	113	107
22	56	32	4	1		Tax Returns	130	138
17	40	131	67	6	4	Other	280	330
164 (4/1-9/30/13)			630 (10/1/13-3/31/14)					
52	149	359	212	15	7	**NUMBER OF STATEMENTS**	892	937
%	%	%	%	%	%	**ASSETS**	%	%
20.4	9.1	6.3	7.6	7.4		Cash & Equivalents	7.9	8.2
7.1	4.4	4.9	4.9	5.4		Trade Receivables (net)	4.3	4.4
7.2	3.7	2.1	1.3	.7		Inventory	2.3	2.4
2.0	1.1	.8	1.2	.9		All Other Current	1.3	1.8
36.6	18.2	14.1	15.0	14.4		Total Current	15.9	16.9
46.3	71.8	79.5	77.7	81.4		Fixed Assets (net)	76.1	75.1
4.5	2.2	1.9	1.4	1.5		Intangibles (net)	2.0	2.1
12.6	7.9	4.4	5.9	2.7		All Other Non-Current	6.0	5.9
100.0	100.0	100.0	100.0	100.0		Total	100.0	100.0
						LIABILITIES		
18.9	6.1	2.4	.9	.5		Notes Payable-Short Term	3.7	4.2
4.0	5.9	4.6	2.3	1.4		Cur. Mat.-L.T.D.	4.3	3.5
8.5	4.4	2.6	2.5	1.5		Trade Payables	3.6	3.1
.2	.1	.1	.1	.0		Income Taxes Payable	.1	.1
53.4	15.5	8.9	8.1	9.8		All Other Current	13.7	13.2
85.1	32.0	18.5	13.8	13.2		Total Current	25.5	24.2
42.3	48.9	43.5	23.3	21.1		Long-Term Debt	40.0	41.5
.0	.0	.1	.1	.8		Deferred Taxes	.1	.2
14.2	18.0	8.8	8.3	19.4		All Other Non-Current	10.3	11.6
-41.5	1.0	29.1	54.5	45.4		Net Worth	24.2	22.5
100.0	100.0	100.0	100.0	100.0		Total Liabilties & Net Worth	100.0	100.0
						INCOME DATA		
100.0	100.0	100.0	100.0	100.0		Net Sales	100.0	100.0
						Gross Profit		
96.0	96.7	97.6	100.8	98.2		Operating Expenses	99.8	99.0
4.0	3.3	2.4	-.8	1.8		Operating Profit	.2	1.0
1.8	4.3	2.9	-.7	-1.3		All Other Expenses (net)	3.3	3.1
2.3	-.9	-.5	-.1	3.1		Profit Before Taxes	-3.0	-2.1
						RATIOS		
2.6	1.8	1.6	2.1	1.6			1.7	1.7
.5	.7	.9	1.3	1.1		Current	.9	1.0
.2	.2	.4	.9	.9			.4	.5
2.2	1.3	1.3	1.6	1.1			1.4	1.4
.4	.4	.7	1.0	.9		Quick	(890) .7	(936) .7
.1	.1	.3	.6	.8			.2	.3
0 UND	**0** UND	**2** 183.0	**14** 25.3	**24** 15.0			**1** 391.6	**1** 351.7
0 UND	**0** 999.8	**23** 15.6	**27** 13.7	**36** 10.1		Sales/Receivables	**17** 21.1	**17** 21.0
3 135.8	**17** 22.0	**36** 10.1	**43** 8.4	**74** 4.9			**35** 10.4	**35** 10.3
						Cost of Sales/Inventory		
						Cost of Sales/Payables		
20.0	20.6	12.3	6.5	9.6			11.6	10.5
-22.1	-24.3	-95.8	17.4	26.1		Sales/Working Capital	-59.3	-127.3
-5.4	-4.7	-8.4	-23.9	-12.4			-6.9	-7.8
5.0	2.7	2.3	3.6	9.8			1.9	1.8
(27) 1.3	(129) 1.0	(315) .9	(183) 1.1	(12) 2.8		EBIT/Interest	(752) .5	(807) .5
-.3	-.5	-.1	-.9	.3			-1.2	-.9
		3.0	8.9				3.5	3.9
		(21) 1.8	(16) 4.9			Net Profit + Depr., Dep., Amort./Cur. Mat. L/T/D	(69) 1.5	(60) 1.8
		1.5	.8				.6	.6
.6	1.4	1.4	1.0	1.1			1.2	1.2
-15.9	4.7	2.8	1.3	1.3		Fixed/Worth	2.2	2.2
-.4	-7.1	10.8	2.1	2.3			28.6	13.4
.6	1.0	.7	.3	.3			.5	.6
-13.4	5.3	2.5	.7	.5		Debt/Worth	1.8	1.7
-1.9	-8.2	13.4	1.7	1.8			54.5	16.6
108.2	18.8	7.1	4.7	6.1			4.5	4.8
(22) 15.0	(100) .8	(284) -.3	(202) .5	(12) .5		% Profit Before Taxes/Tangible Net Worth	(688) -1.5	(734) -1.5
-.1	-12.4	-6.8	-3.0	-1.4			-10.9	-8.8
17.1	5.3	2.7	2.6	3.7			2.0	2.2
.9	.0	-.2	.3	1.0		% Profit Before Taxes/Total Assets	-1.2	-1.1
-6.4	-4.7	-2.7	-1.9	-1.1			-4.9	-4.5
57.7	2.6	1.2	.8	.6			1.3	1.3
7.5	1.3	.8	.5	.4		Sales/Net Fixed Assets	.7	.7
2.7	.7	.6	.4	.3			.5	.5
6.0	1.6	.9	.6	.4			.9	.9
3.3	1.0	.7	.4	.3		Sales/Total Assets	.6	.6
1.6	.6	.5	.4	.3			.4	.4
2.4	4.3	7.0	9.3	10.8			6.9	7.0
(31) 4.6	(135) 6.7	(334) 9.2	(196) 12.1	(14) 13.9		% Depr., Dep., Amort./Sales	(822) 10.3	(843) 10.2
8.6	10.4	11.9	15.3	17.5			13.9	13.6
3.7	1.7	2.9	2.3				2.8	3.3
(15) 6.7	(34) 3.5	(46) 6.1	(21) 3.9			% Officers', Directors' Owners' Comp/Sales	(139) 6.7	(161) 6.3
9.4	10.8	21.6	19.5				16.0	17.2
45970M	244025M	1304839M	2204267M	334386M	794993M	Net Sales ($)	4809586M	6111780M
12262M	183532M	1858060M	4401588M	942677M	1022053M	Total Assets ($)	8880453M	9818942M

M = $ thousand MM = $ million

See Pages 9 through 22 for Explanation of Ratios and Data

Comparative Historical Data / Current Data Sorted by Sales

4/1/11-3/31/12 ALL	4/1/12-3/31/13 ALL	4/1/13-3/31/14 ALL	Type of Statement	0-1MM	1-3MM	3-5MM	5-10MM	10-25MM	25MM & OVER
295	247	213	Unqualified		21	49	97	36	10
118	101	96	Reviewed	8	31	32	17	5	3
111	99	105	Compiled	26	57	11	9	2	
178	146	115	Tax Returns	54	48	8	1	3	1
367	323	265	Other	27	83	70	56	20	9
					164 (4/1-9/30/13)		630 (10/1/13-3/31/14)		
1069	916	794	NUMBER OF STATEMENTS	115	240	170	180	66	23
%	%	%	**ASSETS**	%	%	%	%	%	%
8.6	8.6	8.1	Cash & Equivalents	7.0	8.2	7.5	8.6	8.6	12.4
4.4	4.8	4.9	Trade Receivables (net)	2.9	4.2	5.5	5.8	5.0	11.1
2.8	3.1	2.5	Inventory	2.4	3.5	2.2	1.9	1.9	1.7
1.3	1.4	1.1	All Other Current	1.8	.6	.9	1.1	1.8	1.4
17.2	17.9	16.6	Total Current	14.1	16.5	16.1	17.3	17.2	26.6
75.3	74.8	75.4	Fixed Assets (net)	73.5	75.4	77.0	76.6	76.1	61.2
2.2	2.3	2.0	Intangibles (net)	2.7	3.3	.8	1.5	.8	3.3
5.3	5.0	6.0	All Other Non-Current	9.7	4.8	6.1	4.6	5.9	8.9
100.0	100.0	100.0	Total	100.0	100.0	100.0	100.0	100.0	100.0
			LIABILITIES						
4.6	4.5	3.7	Notes Payable-Short Term	11.4	3.9	2.0	1.5	.9	.5
4.4	3.8	4.1	Cur. Mat.-L.T.D.	3.6	6.2	4.1	2.8	2.0	2.3
3.7	3.9	3.3	Trade Payables	3.4	3.9	3.3	2.8	2.2	3.2
.1	.1	.1	Income Taxes Payable	.0	.2	.0	.1	.0	.0
13.5	12.2	12.9	All Other Current	23.7	15.0	8.5	8.6	9.8	13.3
26.2	24.5	24.1	Total Current	42.2	29.0	17.9	15.8	14.9	19.3
40.6	42.2	38.3	Long-Term Debt	52.7	46.6	39.1	25.7	23.3	17.3
.1	.0	.1	Deferred Taxes	.0	.0	.0	.1	.3	.0
10.7	10.8	11.1	All Other Non-Current	14.2	11.9	12.2	7.0	10.1	13.8
22.4	22.4	26.4	Net Worth	-9.1	12.4	30.8	51.4	51.4	49.5
100.0	100.0	100.0	Total Liabilties & Net Worth	100.0	100.0	100.0	100.0	100.0	100.0
			INCOME DATA						
100.0	100.0	100.0	Net Sales	100.0	100.0	100.0	100.0	100.0	100.0
			Gross Profit						
99.7	98.8	98.2	Operating Expenses	95.2	97.3	98.8	100.9	98.4	97.1
.3	1.2	1.8	Operating Profit	4.8	2.7	1.2	-.9	1.6	2.9
3.0	2.1	2.0	All Other Expenses (net)	7.1	3.5	1.5	-1.3	-1.3	.3
-2.7	-.9	-.2	Profit Before Taxes	-2.3	-.8	-.3	.4	3.0	2.6
			RATIOS						
1.8	1.9	1.8		1.4	1.7	1.6	2.1	1.6	2.1
1.0	1.1	1.0	Current	.5	.8	1.0	1.3	1.1	1.1
.4	.5	.5		.1	.3	.7	.8	.9	.8
1.4	1.6	1.5		.9	1.4	1.3	1.7	1.3	2.0
.8	(915) .8	.8	Quick	.2	.6	.8	1.1	.9	.9
.3	.3	.3		.1	.1	.5	.6	.6	.7
1 413.7	1 317.5	1 473.1		0 UND	0 UND	10 36.9	16 22.9	14 26.4	15 23.6
18 20.7	18 20.5	18 20.4	Sales/Receivables	0 UND	7 53.7	26 13.8	31 11.9	25 14.4	26 14.3
35 10.4	36 10.2	36 10.1		3 135.7	31 11.8	36 10.0	41 9.0	41 9.0	46 8.0
			Cost of Sales/Inventory						
			Cost of Sales/Payables						
9.9	8.9	10.9		36.5	15.1	12.6	6.6	7.8	6.4
999.8	160.0	357.6	Sales/Working Capital	-12.8	-26.1	222.5	17.8	29.4	115.9
-7.5	-9.5	-8.7		-3.1	-5.6	-9.0	-20.9	-28.7	-14.3
1.9	2.3	2.6		2.1	2.3	2.0	2.9	10.2	16.1
(923) .6	(790) .8	(672) 1.0	EBIT/Interest	(80) .9	(213) 1.0	(148) .6	(152) 1.2	(58) 2.4	(21) 2.9
-1.0	-.7	-.3		-.5	-.1	-.7	-.4	.0	.4
3.0	4.2	4.8				1.9	8.2		
(62) 1.9	(45) 2.0	(46) 2.0	Net Profit + Depr., Dep., Amort./Cur. Mat. L/T/D			(10) 1.1	(13) 2.2		
.8	1.0	1.2				.2	1.7		
1.2	1.2	1.2		1.6	1.5	1.2	1.0	1.0	.9
2.2	2.1	1.9	Fixed/Worth	5.8	3.9	2.1	1.3	1.2	1.3
72.0	77.1	9.6		-3.7	-13.0	8.3	2.2	1.9	1.7
.6	.5	.5		1.1	.9	.6	.3	.3	.5
1.8	1.7	1.6	Debt/Worth	9.1	3.6	2.0	.7	.5	.9
UND	-172.7	15.0		-5.1	-14.5	10.1	1.8	1.3	1.7
5.9	7.3	7.8		9.3	13.9	4.4	6.6	7.4	18.3
(802) -1.4	(684) .0	(626) .1	% Profit Before Taxes/Tangible Net Worth	(68) .0	(168) .2	(139) -1.2	(168) .5	(61) 1.7	(22) 2.9
-8.9	-6.0	-5.4		-7.7	-9.8	-7.1	-3.0	-1.7	-1.9
2.3	3.1	3.4		3.4	3.7	2.2	3.0	5.4	9.0
-1.0	-.2	.0	% Profit Before Taxes/Total Assets	.0	-.1	-.4	.5	.8	1.8
-4.7	-3.6	-2.7		-4.5	-3.8	-3.3	-1.9	-1.1	-.9
1.3	1.4	1.3		2.7	1.6	1.3	1.1	1.0	5.2
.7	.8	.8	Sales/Net Fixed Assets	.8	.9	.8	.7	.7	.9
.5	.5	.5		.4	.6	.5	.5	.5	.7
.9	1.0	1.0		1.2	1.2	.9	.8	.7	1.7
.6	.6	.6	Sales/Total Assets	.6	.7	.7	.6	.5	.7
.4	.4	.4		.3	.5	.4	.4	.4	.5
7.1	6.7	6.5		4.6	5.3	7.2	7.7	7.1	2.9
(955) 10.2	(814) 9.5	(713) 9.5	% Depr., Dep., Amort./Sales	(95) 8.5	(219) 8.6	(155) 9.4	(164) 10.7	(62) 10.9	(18) 7.3
13.5	13.0	12.9		14.0	12.0	12.5	13.2	14.1	11.8
3.4	3.7	2.7		4.0	2.4	3.3	2.3	1.1	
(170) 6.4	(134) 6.9	(119) 4.9	% Officers', Directors' Owners' Comp/Sales	(21) 7.3	(45) 3.7	(25) 6.0	(13) 4.1	(13) 3.3	
16.5	15.2	14.2		12.8	12.0	24.5	20.7	14.6	
6120802M	5301697M	4928480M	Net Sales ($)	63408M	464099M	677980M	1266593M	1003899M	1452501M
10792546M	9290581M	8420172M	Total Assets ($)	146173M	731838M	1349478M	2424219M	2028353M	1740111M

M = $ thousand MM = $ million

See Pages 9 through 22 for Explanation of Ratios and Data

Current Data Sorted by Assets							Comparative Historical Data	
		2	5	3	1	**Type of Statement** Unqualified	22	22
	1	3	8			Reviewed	12	10
1	2	1				Compiled	7	4
1	1	4				Tax Returns		5
1	2	6	3	3	3	Other	16	23
28 (4/1-9/30/13)			23 (10/1/13-3/31/14)				**4/1/09-3/31/10 ALL**	**4/1/10-3/31/11 ALL**
0-500M	**500M-2MM**	**2-10MM**	**10-50MM**	**50-100MM**	**100-250MM**			
3	6	16	16	6	4	**NUMBER OF STATEMENTS**	57	64
%	%	%	%	%	%	**ASSETS**	%	%
		18.1	14.3			Cash & Equivalents	8.8	10.7
		1.9	1.7			Trade Receivables (net)	1.4	1.4
		2.7	2.3			Inventory	1.7	3.2
		2.8	1.9			All Other Current	3.2	1.6
		25.5	20.2			Total Current	15.1	17.0
		67.0	64.6			Fixed Assets (net)	72.1	67.5
		1.9	2.9			Intangibles (net)	3.2	3.5
		5.7	12.3			All Other Non-Current	9.6	12.0
		100.0	100.0			Total	100.0	100.0
						LIABILITIES		
		2.9	.7			Notes Payable-Short Term	4.8	8.7
		4.3	2.5			Cur. Mat.-L.T.D.	4.5	4.5
		5.2	6.0			Trade Payables	4.3	5.8
		.6	.0			Income Taxes Payable	.2	.2
		11.8	9.6			All Other Current	13.6	13.9
		24.8	18.8			Total Current	27.4	33.1
		23.0	24.9			Long-Term Debt	20.6	29.4
		.9	1.0			Deferred Taxes	1.9	1.4
		5.7	17.6			All Other Non-Current	7.1	9.1
		45.6	37.6			Net Worth	42.9	27.1
		100.0	100.0			Total Liabilties & Net Worth	100.0	100.0
						INCOME DATA		
		100.0	100.0			Net Sales	100.0	100.0
						Gross Profit		
		92.6	88.7			Operating Expenses	92.1	93.2
		7.4	11.3			Operating Profit	7.9	6.8
		2.0	4.1			All Other Expenses (net)	3.0	4.1
		5.4	7.2			Profit Before Taxes	4.9	2.7
						RATIOS		
		2.2	1.5			Current	1.2	1.1
		.7	1.0				.6	.6
		.3	.7				.2	.3
		1.9	1.2			Quick	.8	.8
		.4	.8				.3	.4
		.1	.5				.1	.1
		0 UND	2 195.4			Sales/Receivables	0 915.5	0 994.6
		0 965.9	4 91.1				4 87.6	4 92.0
		3 136.4	8 48.2				8 44.0	7 50.4
						Cost of Sales/Inventory		
						Cost of Sales/Payables		
		9.8	10.9			Sales/Working Capital	50.1	313.9
		-22.2	-519.2				-11.0	-12.8
		-5.9	-25.5				-3.8	-5.4
		16.6	15.9			EBIT/Interest	11.2	7.1
		(14) 3.1	(15) 7.1				(54) 2.2	(54) 2.8
		1.1	1.0				.6	1.2
						Net Profit + Depr., Dep., Amort./Cur. Mat. L/T/D	9.1	4.3
							(19) 4.4	(13) 2.3
							2.0	.4
		1.0	1.0			Fixed/Worth	1.1	1.0
		1.7	1.8				1.7	1.8
		2.4	4.8				3.8	8.7
		.6	.9			Debt/Worth	.6	.6
		1.2	1.4				1.3	1.3
		3.1	4.8				4.3	11.0
		35.0	52.8			% Profit Before Taxes/Tangible Net Worth	22.1	24.6
		(14) 12.4	(15) 10.5				(47) 6.6	(51) 11.6
		2.6	3.5				-1.2	.3
		14.5	12.3			% Profit Before Taxes/Total Assets	9.3	11.9
		5.3	4.9				3.3	3.6
		.3	.3				-1.1	-2.3
		3.3	2.1			Sales/Net Fixed Assets	2.0	2.2
		1.5	1.0				1.2	1.2
		1.2	.7				.8	.9
		1.7	1.2			Sales/Total Assets	1.3	1.4
		1.3	.8				.9	.9
		.9	.5				.7	.5
		6.8	5.2			% Depr., Dep., Amort./Sales	6.7	6.4
		(15) 10.1	6.8				(53) 10.0	(56) 9.6
		12.4	13.9				13.4	12.8
						% Officers', Directors' Owners' Comp/Sales		
3757M	13197M	133715M	345328M	301702M	450431M	Net Sales ($)	1415453M	1346756M
1152M	7621M	93526M	354390M	422903M	564640M	Total Assets ($)	1895868M	1788306M

M = $ thousand MM = $ million

See Pages 9 through 22 for Explanation of Ratios and Data

Comparative Historical Data				Current Data Sorted by Sales					
			Type of Statement						
21	15	11	Unqualified				3	4	4
12	9	12	Reviewed		1	1	3	5	2
6	4	4	Compiled		1	2		1	
5	4	6	Tax Returns	1	3	1	1		
20	18	18	Other	3	1	2	3	3	6
				28 (4/1-9/30/13)			23 (10/1/13-3/31/14)		
4/1/11-3/31/12 ALL	**4/1/12-3/31/13 ALL**	**4/1/13-3/31/14 ALL**		**0-1MM**	**1-3MM**	**3-5MM**	**5-10MM**	**10-25MM**	**25MM & OVER**
64	50	51	**NUMBER OF STATEMENTS**	4	6	6	10	13	12
%	%	%	**ASSETS**	%	%	%	%	%	%
9.5	12.7	15.6	Cash & Equivalents				14.6	23.0	8.5
1.7	1.3	2.2	Trade Receivables (net)				.4	2.3	2.8
3.1	3.6	3.2	Inventory				1.0	3.6	2.2
3.1	1.7	4.5	All Other Current				4.5	1.5	1.7
17.4	19.3	25.4	Total Current				20.5	30.4	15.2
66.3	64.6	58.7	Fixed Assets (net)				63.5	60.8	56.3
3.9	4.4	6.6	Intangibles (net)				4.8	1.4	14.8
12.3	11.7	9.3	All Other Non-Current				11.1	7.3	13.7
100.0	100.0	100.0	Total				100.0	100.0	100.0
			LIABILITIES						
3.6	3.1	2.0	Notes Payable-Short Term				4.0	.0	2.7
3.6	3.9	3.2	Cur. Mat.-L.T.D.				1.7	2.4	1.2
5.0	4.6	5.9	Trade Payables				3.5	8.8	4.7
.1	.1	.2	Income Taxes Payable				.1	.7	.0
12.1	13.4	11.9	All Other Current				11.5	9.8	14.8
24.4	25.0	23.2	Total Current				20.8	21.7	23.5
34.6	34.3	22.4	Long-Term Debt				24.3	20.0	18.9
1.2	1.3	.7	Deferred Taxes				.5	1.5	.4
9.4	8.9	12.9	All Other Non-Current				11.3	13.8	12.1
30.3	30.5	40.9	Net Worth				43.1	43.0	45.1
100.0	100.0	100.0	Total Liabilties & Net Worth				100.0	100.0	100.0
			INCOME DATA						
100.0	100.0	100.0	Net Sales				100.0	100.0	100.0
			Gross Profit						
93.7	93.3	89.0	Operating Expenses				93.8	88.1	87.7
6.3	6.7	11.0	Operating Profit				6.2	11.9	12.3
3.4	2.7	2.7	All Other Expenses (net)				2.9	2.0	2.2
2.9	4.0	8.3	Profit Before Taxes				3.3	10.0	10.1
			RATIOS						
1.2	1.8	1.7					1.9	2.2	.9
.5	.6	.9	Current				.6	1.4	.6
.3	.3	.5					.3	.9	.4
.7	1.3	1.2					.9	2.0	.7
.3	.4	.6	Quick				.3	1.1	.4
.1	.1	.2					.1	.6	.3
0 999.8	1 699.4	0 999.8					0 999.8	0 UND	5 73.2
3 117.8	3 122.2	4 97.9	Sales/Receivables				1 294.1	2 152.9	8 48.6
9 39.0	7 53.0	9 39.1					4 85.3	9 42.6	16 22.6
			Cost of Sales/Inventory						
			Cost of Sales/Payables						
UND	9.4	12.5					8.0	7.2	-38.2
-9.5	-13.4	-34.8	Sales/Working Capital				-20.1	20.0	-9.1
-5.1	-4.7	-6.6					-4.9	-37.7	-6.2
6.2	4.8	17.3						28.4	137.8
(59) 2.5	(47) 1.7	(45) 4.1	EBIT/Interest					9.8	12.2
1.1	.3	1.1						2.9	1.3
6.2	3.7								
(17) 3.7	(12) 1.5		Net Profit + Depr., Dep., Amort./Cur. Mat. L/T/D						
2.1	-1.3								
1.1	1.1	1.0					1.3	.8	1.1
1.9	1.8	1.8	Fixed/Worth				2.1	1.3	1.5
11.3	7.9	5.3					10.1	2.2	4.7
.7	.9	.8					.7	.7	.8
1.3	1.4	1.3	Debt/Worth				1.8	1.2	1.0
15.7	8.2	5.1					21.6	2.4	4.8
27.1	25.3	44.3						58.1	45.8
(54) 10.6	(41) 8.0	(42) 15.1	% Profit Before Taxes/Tangible Net Worth					(12) 25.0	(10) 18.0
1.1	-3.0	3.8						7.9	2.6
9.2	6.2	14.5					8.6	23.2	13.4
4.4	1.9	6.3	% Profit Before Taxes/Total Assets				5.3	9.7	9.1
.3	-2.2	.5					.0	3.7	1.0
2.0	2.5	3.2					2.3	3.2	2.0
1.3	1.3	1.5	Sales/Net Fixed Assets				1.5	1.4	1.7
.8	.8	.9					1.3	.8	1.1
1.4	1.4	1.6					1.6	1.6	1.3
.9	.9	.9	Sales/Total Assets				1.0	1.0	.9
.5	.7	.5					.6	.7	.5
6.7	6.6	5.2					4.9	6.0	5.1
(54) 10.2	(46) 11.2	(46) 7.1	% Depr., Dep., Amort./Sales				8.9	(12) 6.9	(11) 5.4
13.8	13.9	11.9					12.8	9.8	10.5
2.1									
(10) 5.0			% Officers', Directors' Owners' Comp/Sales						
10.3									
1668383M	**1444318M**	**1248130M**	Net Sales ($)	**2753M**	**13074M**	**24781M**	**73783M**	**237841M**	**895898M**
2247687M	**1592452M**	**1444232M**	Total Assets ($)	**8356M**	**8982M**	**66062M**	**88097M**	**293275M**	**979460M**

M = $ thousand MM = $ million

See Pages 9 through 22 for Explanation of Ratios and Data

	Current Data Sorted by Assets						Comparative Historical Data	
Type of Statement								
Unqualified			2	2	1		9	7
Reviewed		1	9	7			33	20
Compiled	2	12	19	1	1		25	24
Tax Returns	8	22	15	2			39	41
Other	8	21	41	22	1	1	69	75
	25 (4/1-9/30/13)		173 (10/1/13-3/31/14)				**4/1/09-3/31/10 ALL**	**4/1/10-3/31/11 ALL**
	0-500M	**500M-2MM**	**2-10MM**	**10-50MM**	**50-100MM**	**100-250MM**		
NUMBER OF STATEMENTS	18	56	86	34	3	1	175	167
ASSETS	%	%	%	%	%	%	%	%
Cash & Equivalents	28.9	11.4	10.2	8.0			8.9	11.7
Trade Receivables (net)	12.2	5.8	4.7	3.2			5.2	6.7
Inventory	8.3	12.9	7.8	5.5			12.9	9.9
All Other Current	1.4	.9	2.1	.7			2.5	1.8
Total Current	50.8	30.9	24.8	17.4			29.4	30.1
Fixed Assets (net)	37.2	55.5	63.4	67.0			57.2	55.3
Intangibles (net)	7.5	6.3	4.8	7.8			5.5	5.7
All Other Non-Current	4.6	7.3	7.0	7.8			7.9	8.9
Total	100.0	100.0	100.0	100.0			100.0	100.0
LIABILITIES								
Notes Payable-Short Term	6.7	4.9	3.9	4.3			6.6	5.8
Cur. Mat.-L.T.D.	6.2	8.0	3.2	2.6			4.9	3.5
Trade Payables	8.6	3.0	1.7	1.8			3.4	3.1
Income Taxes Payable	.0	.0	.0	.0			.1	.0
All Other Current	29.5	17.1	11.8	3.7			11.2	12.2
Total Current	51.0	33.0	20.6	12.3			26.2	24.7
Long-Term Debt	69.4	58.5	53.3	59.9			51.4	49.9
Deferred Taxes	.0	.0	.3	.3			.2	.1
All Other Non-Current	7.9	7.7	3.4	4.7			15.4	13.4
Net Worth	-28.2	.9	22.4	22.9			6.8	11.9
Total Liabilities & Net Worth	100.0	100.0	100.0	100.0			100.0	100.0
INCOME DATA								
Net Sales	100.0	100.0	100.0	100.0			100.0	100.0
Gross Profit								
Operating Expenses	83.0	88.0	85.8	82.9			88.9	87.6
Operating Profit	17.0	12.0	14.2	17.1			11.1	12.4
All Other Expenses (net)	2.2	4.0	6.8	10.7			8.2	6.5
Profit Before Taxes	14.8	8.1	7.4	6.4			3.0	6.0
RATIOS								
Current	1.6	3.4	3.8	2.2			2.8	3.2
	1.1	1.4	1.5	1.2			1.2	1.4
	.6	.5	.9	.9			.5	.7
Quick	1.5	2.6	2.6	1.8			1.7	2.2
	.9	.7	.9	1.0			(174) .5	.9
	.4	.2	.3	.5			.2	.3
Sales/Receivables	**0** UND	**0** UND	**6** 61.5	**10** 38.4			**4** 83.2	**2** 225.8
	6 65.3	**8** 48.6	**18** 19.8	**19** 19.1			**16** 22.8	**13** 28.7
	23 15.7	**28** 13.1	**39** 9.4	**34** 10.7			**32** 11.3	**37** 9.7
Cost of Sales/Inventory								
Cost of Sales/Payables								
Sales/Working Capital	11.6	4.0	3.5	6.1			5.4	4.3
	UND	12.1	12.2	13.1			28.5	17.5
	-14.5	-12.1	-51.5	-92.5			-6.9	-12.5
EBIT/Interest	10.1	4.6	21.9	11.9			3.6	5.2
	(14) 5.2	(46) 2.6	(72) 3.8	(24) 2.5			(132) 1.5	(135) 2.3
	1.8	1.0	1.1	1.4			.5	.8
Net Profit + Depr., Dep., Amort./Cur. Mat. L/T/D			151.1					4.0
			(10) 4.3					(12) 2.4
			1.5					.6
Fixed/Worth	.6	1.0	1.1	2.1			1.2	.8
	2.0	16.1	2.0	4.9			4.8	2.9
	-.4	-1.3	-6.7	-11.6			-3.9	-4.9
Debt/Worth	.9	1.5	.9	1.5			.9	.8
	7.5	31.0	3.1	5.3			8.0	4.3
	-1.8	-2.6	-10.2	-20.4			-6.5	-6.4
% Profit Before Taxes/Tangible Net Worth	88.9	36.2	26.4	36.4			25.6	30.7
	(11) 66.2	(30) 12.4	(58) 12.1	(23) 18.4			(106) 6.5	(110) 10.9
	.0	-.4	1.7	9.0			-3.9	-.9
% Profit Before Taxes/Total Assets	48.6	16.5	10.2	6.8			6.2	9.6
	25.7	4.7	4.1	3.3			1.8	2.8
	2.8	.3	-.4	-.3			-2.0	-.8
Sales/Net Fixed Assets	173.5	8.7	1.8	1.4			3.1	5.7
	11.7	1.8	.8	.6			1.1	1.4
	3.1	.8	.4	.3			.5	.6
Sales/Total Assets	5.0	1.8	1.0	.7			1.2	1.4
	2.5	1.0	.6	.4			.7	.8
	1.4	.6	.3	.2			.4	.4
% Depr., Dep., Amort./Sales	1.1	1.9	4.6	5.8			3.8	3.1
	(12) 1.6	(44) 7.2	(80) 8.9	(32) 11.9			(148) 7.7	(136) 7.2
	7.3	12.0	16.2	22.2			14.9	12.5
% Officers', Directors' Owners' Comp/Sales		2.1	2.5				2.2	2.1
		(21) 4.1	(19) 4.5				(50) 5.2	(45) 6.5
		7.3	7.5				9.2	10.0
Net Sales ($)	13483M	78201M	262462M	243799M	98320M	74429M	764936M	994848M
Total Assets ($)	4854M	66787M	407512M	570469M	155490M	124655M	1255846M	1115751M

M = $ thousand MM = $ million

See Pages 9 through 22 for Explanation of Ratios and Data

Comparative Historical Data				Current Data Sorted by Sales					
			Type of Statement						
9	10	5	Unqualified				2	2	1
28	18	17	Reviewed		4	3	8	2	
39	26	35	Compiled	9	16	6	1	2	1
55	47	47	Tax Returns	23	19	2		3	
70	89	94	Other	23	35	18	14	2	2
4/1/11-3/31/12 ALL	**4/1/12-3/31/13 ALL**	**4/1/13-3/31/14 ALL**		**25 (4/1-9/30/13)**			**173 (10/1/13-3/31/14)**		
				0-1MM	**1-3MM**	**3-5MM**	**5-10MM**	**10-25MM**	**25MM & OVER**
201	190	198	**NUMBER OF STATEMENTS**	55	74	29	25	11	4
%	%	%	**ASSETS**	%	%	%	%	%	%
9.0	8.5	11.9	Cash & Equivalents	12.7	11.5	12.2	12.0	10.0	
6.4	5.6	5.4	Trade Receivables (net)	4.4	5.7	8.1	3.6	5.4	
11.9	9.7	8.9	Inventory	5.1	10.4	10.9	6.5	18.5	
1.4	2.1	1.4	All Other Current	2.6	1.0	.3	1.4	1.8	
28.7	25.9	27.6	Total Current	24.8	28.6	31.4	23.4	35.7	
56.6	60.7	59.1	Fixed Assets (net)	64.0	57.6	59.2	58.3	49.4	
7.3	5.7	6.3	Intangibles (net)	6.6	5.9	3.8	6.6	8.8	
7.4	7.7	7.0	All Other Non-Current	4.6	7.9	5.5	11.7	6.1	
100.0	100.0	100.0	Total	100.0	100.0	100.0	100.0	100.0	
			LIABILITIES						
7.6	6.1	4.4	Notes Payable-Short Term	3.2	5.4	2.8	3.2	12.6	
5.6	5.3	4.7	Cur. Mat.-L.T.D.	3.9	7.2	2.5	3.3	1.6	
3.8	3.1	2.7	Trade Payables	3.2	2.8	1.7	2.4	3.8	
.5	.3	.0	Income Taxes Payable	.0	.0	.0	.0	.0	
15.2	18.3	13.4	All Other Current	11.7	18.5	12.5	8.3	3.5	
32.7	33.1	25.3	Total Current	22.1	33.9	19.5	17.1	21.6	
47.2	52.4	57.8	Long-Term Debt	71.2	55.0	44.5	60.6	32.2	
.1	.3	.2	Deferred Taxes	.0	.0	.8	.0	1.2	
8.7	7.3	5.2	All Other Non-Current	5.0	6.6	2.8	4.0	6.8	
11.2	6.9	11.6	Net Worth	1.8	4.5	32.4	18.2	38.3	
100.0	100.0	100.0	Total Liabilities & Net Worth	100.0	100.0	100.0	100.0	100.0	
			INCOME DATA						
100.0	100.0	100.0	Net Sales	100.0	100.0	100.0	100.0	100.0	
			Gross Profit						
89.5	87.3	85.6	Operating Expenses	81.1	86.8	89.4	85.0	91.9	
10.5	12.7	14.4	Operating Profit	18.9	13.2	10.6	15.0	8.1	
7.2	7.3	6.2	All Other Expenses (net)	11.4	5.4	.9	5.2	2.0	
3.3	5.4	8.2	Profit Before Taxes	7.5	7.7	9.6	9.7	6.1	
			RATIOS						
2.7	2.4	3.3		3.0	3.6	4.9	2.1	7.2	
1.3	1.2	1.4	Current	1.2	1.3	1.7	1.2	1.7	
.5	.4	.9		.6	.5	1.0	.9	1.0	
1.7	1.7	2.5		1.8	2.6	4.8	1.9	5.9	
(200) .6	.6	.9	Quick	.9	.9	1.2	1.0	.7	
.2	.2	.3		.4	.2	.3	.6	.3	
4 88.1	**2** 155.3	**4** 93.3		**0** UND	**6** 64.1	**8** 44.3	**7** 55.6	**10** 37.5	
15 24.4	**12** 31.0	**13** 28.1	Sales/Receivables	**4** 92.5	**16** 23.1	**29** 12.5	**17** 21.1	**13** 28.5	
41 8.8	**27** 13.3	**35** 10.5		**35** 10.3	**37** 9.9	**40** 9.1	**31** 11.6	**25** 14.7	
			Cost of Sales/Inventory						
			Cost of Sales/Payables						
5.2	5.7	4.1		5.1	3.9	2.4	6.0	3.8	
23.7	25.7	13.3	Sales/Working Capital	32.3	12.2	8.0	44.1	8.4	
-6.6	-5.9	-32.4		-16.9	-9.9	224.6	-38.9	-999.8	
3.9	5.7	10.5		4.4	14.1	28.4	12.3	14.5	
(163) 1.8	(147) 2.0	(160) 2.9	EBIT/Interest	(39) 1.9	(61) 3.8	(25) 7.1	(20) 2.5	1.7	
.9	.6	1.2		.6	1.1	2.1	1.4	.6	
		9.1							
		(17) 2.6	Net Profit + Depr., Dep., Amort./Cur. Mat. L/T/D						
		1.8							
1.0	1.2	1.1		1.4	1.3	1.1	.8	.6	
3.6	5.5	3.9	Fixed/Worth	11.3	7.8	1.7	3.2	3.5	
-3.2	-3.3	-3.7		-5.9	-1.8	12.2	-2.0	20.7	
1.0	1.3	1.0		1.0	1.5	.8	.4	.6	
5.7	7.1	5.5	Debt/Worth	12.8	24.1	1.5	4.3	4.2	
-5.3	-5.9	-6.0		-6.9	-3.7	14.8	-4.7	57.6	
21.9	30.6	36.4		43.2	45.4	29.5	18.7		
(127) 7.1	(116) 10.3	(123) 14.9	% Profit Before Taxes/Tangible Net Worth	(34) 8.5	(41) 17.4	(23) 20.2	(15) 11.8		
.4	-2.2	1.2		-3.3	3.6	7.5	.5		
5.6	7.4	11.7		7.3	16.7	12.6	10.5	8.8	
1.2	3.0	4.7	% Profit Before Taxes/Total Assets	2.0	5.0	7.5	5.8	2.9	
-1.0	-.8	.0		-1.3	-1.0	2.0	.8	-.7	
3.3	4.5	2.9		2.6	4.7	3.2	1.9	7.3	
1.2	1.0	1.1	Sales/Net Fixed Assets	.6	1.1	1.0	1.2	1.5	
.5	.4	.5		.3	.6	.6	.7	1.4	
1.3	1.5	1.2		.9	1.6	1.3	1.0	1.2	
.7	.6	.7	Sales/Total Assets	.5	.8	.7	.6	1.0	
.3	.3	.4		.2	.4	.4	.4	.9	
3.4	2.7	3.7		4.8	2.6	4.5	4.1	2.4	
(177) 7.7	(157) 7.7	(172) 8.8	% Depr., Dep., Amort./Sales	(42) 11.9	(66) 8.9	(25) 6.6	10.3	(10) 4.8	
14.5	15.8	14.2		26.6	14.8	9.9	17.6	7.0	
2.1	3.0	2.2		2.2	1.6				
(58) 4.4	(42) 4.8	(50) 4.1	% Officers', Directors' Owners' Comp/Sales	(15) 5.3	(19) 2.9				
8.9	7.5	7.2		12.2	7.1				
1304784M	**712789M**	**770694M**	Net Sales ($)	**33076M**	**140739M**	**115247M**	**167826M**	**141057M**	**172749M**
1428625M	**1368874M**	**1329767M**	Total Assets ($)	**98668M**	**272701M**	**224003M**	**296783M**	**157467M**	**280145M**

M = $ thousand MM = $ million

See Pages 9 through 22 for Explanation of Ratios and Data

Current Data Sorted by Assets							Comparative Historical Data	
						Type of Statement		
		20	31	9	6	Unqualified	75	92
1	3	21	24			Reviewed	49	55
11	17	21	3			Compiled	65	55
85	52	26	2		2	Tax Returns	136	142
48	75	82	49	9	5	Other	193	229
60 (4/1-9/30/13)		542 (10/1/13-3/31/14)					**4/1/09-3/31/10**	**4/1/10-3/31/11**
0-500M	**500M-2MM**	**2-10MM**	**10-50MM**	**50-100MM**	**100-250MM**		**ALL**	**ALL**
145	147	170	109	18	13	**NUMBER OF STATEMENTS**	518	573
%	%	%	%	%	%	**ASSETS**	%	%
28.8	13.4	9.5	10.1	9.0	6.7	Cash & Equivalents	11.0	12.4
2.1	2.3	3.7	3.0	4.0	1.4	Trade Receivables (net)	3.2	3.0
2.9	1.6	.9	.5	.7	.6	Inventory	1.8	2.1
2.9	2.7	2.1	1.8	1.8	1.9	All Other Current	3.1	2.5
36.7	19.9	16.2	15.4	15.6	10.5	Total Current	19.0	20.0
45.2	65.6	72.9	73.7	71.4	59.8	Fixed Assets (net)	66.8	68.1
6.1	5.6	3.9	4.3	4.5	18.5	Intangibles (net)	5.8	4.5
12.0	8.8	7.0	6.6	8.5	11.3	All Other Non-Current	8.4	7.4
100.0	100.0	100.0	100.0	100.0	100.0	Total	100.0	100.0
						LIABILITIES		
19.5	3.7	2.3	.9	.5	.3	Notes Payable-Short Term	6.6	6.3
3.5	5.7	3.8	3.7	2.2	3.2	Cur. Mat.-L.T.D.	5.3	5.8
4.1	3.7	3.2	2.2	2.4	1.9	Trade Payables	4.1	5.0
.1	.0	.4	.1	.3	.0	Income Taxes Payable	.1	.2
38.7	9.8	11.6	8.0	4.8	14.4	All Other Current	10.0	11.6
65.9	23.0	21.3	15.0	10.2	19.8	Total Current	26.2	28.9
34.0	41.4	46.8	44.1	34.7	28.7	Long-Term Debt	42.4	46.2
.0	.0	.1	.0	.5	.7	Deferred Taxes	.1	.1
20.1	19.1	6.9	7.0	5.9	27.8	All Other Non-Current	11.4	11.6
-19.9	16.5	24.9	33.9	48.6	22.9	Net Worth	20.0	13.2
100.0	100.0	100.0	100.0	100.0	100.0	Total Liabilties & Net Worth	100.0	100.0
						INCOME DATA		
100.0	100.0	100.0	100.0	100.0	100.0	Net Sales	100.0	100.0
						Gross Profit		
93.0	85.9	85.2	87.3	90.1	92.6	Operating Expenses	91.5	91.4
7.0	14.1	14.8	12.7	9.9	7.4	Operating Profit	8.5	8.6
1.6	4.5	7.5	3.4	3.3	2.0	All Other Expenses (net)	4.3	4.3
5.4	9.6	7.3	9.3	6.6	5.4	Profit Before Taxes	4.2	4.3
						RATIOS		
4.1	2.5	1.9	2.4	2.9	.9		2.0	2.2
.9	.7	.8	1.0	1.0	.4	Current	.8	.8
.3	.2	.3	.6	.9	.2		.3	.3
3.4	2.0	1.6	1.9	2.8	.7		1.6	1.8
.7	.4	.6	.9	1.0	.3	Quick	(515) .6	(571) .6
.2	.1	.2	.5	.7	.1		.2	.2
0 UND	**0** UND	**0** UND	**1** 575.1	**7** 51.8	**0** UND		**0** UND	**0** UND
0 UND	**0** UND	**1** 405.6	**6** 59.4	**12** 30.3	**3** 109.9	Sales/Receivables	**1** 271.3	**1** 277.0
0 UND	**3** 125.6	**13** 28.8	**19** 19.2	**27** 13.3	**15** 24.2		**16** 23.2	**12** 30.1
						Cost of Sales/Inventory		
						Cost of Sales/Payables		
21.4	14.6	8.7	8.5	5.1	NM		13.1	11.7
-249.0	-25.6	-34.4	-142.0	264.6	-10.1	Sales/Working Capital	-55.4	-59.8
-12.7	-7.4	-6.6	-11.6	-64.4	-6.2		-6.8	-7.0
18.8	11.5	5.4	6.9	8.9	6.9		4.9	5.1
(88) 4.0	(121) 4.5	(133) 2.3	(98) 3.6	(16) 2.7	(12) 2.2	EBIT/Interest	(431) 1.8	(460) 2.0
.3	1.2	.6	1.7	1.3	-3.0		.3	.3
		4.4	4.1				4.9	5.3
		(14) 2.5	(18) 3.0			Net Profit + Depr., Dep., Amort./Cur. Mat. L/T/D	(39) 2.6	(53) 2.5
		1.1	1.8				.8	1.5
.4	1.1	1.4	1.3	1.2	1.7		1.2	1.2
2.3	3.8	3.9	2.4	1.7	48.1	Fixed/Worth	3.1	3.3
-1.6	-7.6	-41.9	7.3	2.3	-2.3		-24.6	-7.2
.5	1.0	1.0	.7	.7	1.1		.8	.8
6.7	3.7	3.5	2.0	1.2	55.4	Debt/Worth	3.0	3.2
-2.7	-10.8	-44.1	9.1	1.9	-5.1		-24.7	-10.4
199.8	114.9	41.1	29.8	16.7			56.6	61.5
(84) 72.1	(105) 34.2	(123) 12.8	(92) 11.5	(17) 7.2		% Profit Before Taxes/Tangible Net Worth	(372) 14.0	(392) 12.0
10.0	7.6	.9	2.8	3.2			-1.3	.0
52.7	30.6	9.3	10.8	8.2	7.3		12.2	13.7
17.1	8.3	4.1	4.3	3.3	2.2	% Profit Before Taxes/Total Assets	2.8	3.3
-.5	.6	-.7	1.4	1.1	-3.9		-2.7	-1.9
45.0	5.1	2.3	1.6	.9	2.0		4.7	4.4
10.7	2.3	.8	.9	.7	1.5	Sales/Net Fixed Assets	1.4	1.5
4.5	1.1	.4	.5	.5	.7		.7	.7
8.5	2.4	1.1	1.0	.7	1.2		2.1	2.5
4.0	1.5	.6	.6	.5	.8	Sales/Total Assets	1.0	1.0
2.4	.9	.4	.4	.4	.5		.5	.5
1.1	3.5	5.0	5.6	7.3			4.8	4.5
(95) 4.1	(116) 6.0	(154) 7.9	(103) 7.4	(16) 9.3		% Depr., Dep., Amort./Sales	(436) 7.6	(480) 7.2
7.5	10.4	14.0	11.6	10.9			11.4	11.1
4.7	3.4	2.3	.5				3.3	3.6
(60) 9.8	(42) 6.6	(37) 4.2	(13) 4.1			% Officers', Directors' Owners' Comp/Sales	(138) 6.3	(149) 6.2
15.1	12.7	6.0	7.3				12.2	12.9
140157M	245385M	830224M	2007790M	680163M	1661554M	Net Sales ($)	4890502M	6855852M
30830M	152496M	808886M	2289281M	1225483M	1909254M	Total Assets ($)	5961467M	6827826M

M = $ thousand MM = $ million

See Pages 9 through 22 for Explanation of Ratios and Data

Comparative Historical Data / Current Data Sorted by Sales

4/1/11-3/31/12 ALL	4/1/12-3/31/13 ALL	4/1/13-3/31/14 ALL	Type of Statement	0-1MM	1-3MM	3-5MM	5-10MM	10-25MM	25MM & OVER
93	64	66	Unqualified	2	9	12	12	13	18
59	49	49	Reviewed	2	7	9	13	16	2
71	71	52	Compiled	16	18	8	5	5	
173	188	167	Tax Returns	91	65	4	4		3
245	254	268	Other	58	98	29	23	33	27
				60 (4/1-9/30/13)		542 (10/1/13-3/31/14)			
641	626	602	NUMBER OF STATEMENTS	169	197	62	57	67	50
%	%	%	**ASSETS**	%	%	%	%	%	%
12.9	14.8	15.1	Cash & Equivalents	17.1	16.5	16.4	11.6	11.5	10.6
3.2	2.4	2.8	Trade Receivables (net)	1.3	2.4	2.8	2.3	4.8	7.4
1.5	1.5	1.5	Inventory	2.1	1.6	.7	1.1	.8	1.1
2.4	3.0	2.4	All Other Current	2.2	1.9	3.7	1.0	3.4	3.5
20.1	21.8	21.8	Total Current	22.7	22.3	23.5	16.0	20.6	22.6
66.9	64.3	64.3	Fixed Assets (net)	61.2	63.4	68.0	73.4	66.8	59.4
6.0	5.9	5.2	Intangibles (net)	6.4	4.7	2.0	2.4	6.1	9.7
7.1	8.0	8.7	All Other Non-Current	9.7	9.6	6.5	8.3	6.5	8.3
100.0	100.0	100.0	Total	100.0	100.0	100.0	100.0	100.0	100.0
			LIABILITIES						
5.7	5.5	6.5	Notes Payable-Short Term	15.5	4.3	2.6	.9	1.5	2.2
5.2	4.6	4.1	Cur. Mat.-L.T.D.	3.3	5.4	2.2	4.1	4.1	3.9
4.9	2.8	3.3	Trade Payables	2.0	4.3	2.9	3.3	3.1	4.5
.1	.1	.2	Income Taxes Payable	.0	.1	.0	.4	.7	.3
12.0	13.9	16.9	All Other Current	19.4	21.1	8.5	10.9	11.5	16.8
27.9	27.0	30.9	Total Current	40.2	35.2	16.2	19.6	20.9	27.7
44.3	41.2	41.2	Long-Term Debt	47.3	39.8	36.3	42.6	37.0	35.8
.0	.2	.1	Deferred Taxes	.0	.1	.0	.0	.0	.4
12.4	15.6	13.5	All Other Non-Current	15.1	18.2	7.9	5.0	4.0	18.2
15.4	16.1	14.4	Net Worth	-2.6	6.6	39.5	32.8	38.1	18.0
100.0	100.0	100.0	Total Liabilties & Net Worth	100.0	100.0	100.0	100.0	100.0	100.0
			INCOME DATA						
100.0	100.0	100.0	Net Sales	100.0	100.0	100.0	100.0	100.0	100.0
			Gross Profit						
89.8	88.1	87.9	Operating Expenses	86.8	87.0	89.8	88.9	87.9	91.8
10.2	11.9	12.1	Operating Profit	13.2	13.0	10.2	11.1	12.1	8.2
4.7	4.7	4.4	All Other Expenses (net)	8.0	3.5	3.0	2.9	1.7	2.4
5.5	7.2	7.7	Profit Before Taxes	5.2	9.5	7.1	8.2	10.4	5.9
			RATIOS						
2.2	2.6	2.3		3.0	2.6	2.5	2.0	1.9	1.6
.9	.9	.9	Current	.7	.8	1.0	.9	.9	.8
.3	.3	.3		.2	.3	.5	.5	.5	.5
1.9	2.2	2.0		2.6	2.0	2.1	1.8	1.5	1.4
.7	(625) .6	.7	Quick	.4	.7	.8	.7	.7	.7
.2	.2	.2		.1	.2	.4	.4	.3	.3
0 UND	0 UND	0 UND		0 UND	0 UND	0 UND	0 UND	0 999.8	3 128.0
1 655.8	0 UND	0 UND	Sales/Receivables	0 UND	0 UND	3 123.3	2 158.7	5 73.9	11 33.4
13 27.8	8 45.0	8 46.3		0 UND	3 117.2	16 22.2	13 28.4	18 20.2	23 15.9
			Cost of Sales/Inventory						
			Cost of Sales/Payables						
12.7	10.8	13.4		16.6	12.5	9.0	10.1	10.9	16.6
-118.3	-138.4	-62.1	Sales/Working Capital	-37.0	-62.2	NM	-88.9	-120.9	-39.5
-7.8	-8.8	-9.1		-4.1	-9.5	-20.2	-12.3	-10.2	-11.2
6.2	9.1	8.5		5.4	13.4	9.1	7.7	9.9	7.8
(519) 2.2	(492) 3.1	(468) 3.3	EBIT/Interest	(102) 2.1	(160) 3.9	(50) 2.9	(51) 3.1	(59) 4.0	(46) 3.5
.4	.8	1.1		-1.0	1.2	1.0	1.8	1.8	1.2
4.7	7.0	6.4			5.0				7.7
(46) 2.3	(45) 3.1	(43) 3.0	Net Profit + Depr., Dep., Amort./Cur. Mat. L/T/D		(11) 2.1				(12) 3.2
1.4	1.5	1.9			.9				1.6
1.2	1.1	1.1		1.1	1.0	.9	1.4	1.1	1.7
3.0	2.7	3.1	Fixed/Worth	6.2	3.0	2.1	2.7	2.0	3.0
-11.8	-22.6	-21.9		-4.2	-7.5	6.9	8.3	7.7	-3.8
.8	.7	.8		1.2	.9	.4	.9	.6	1.1
3.0	2.8	3.1	Debt/Worth	9.6	3.1	2.0	2.4	2.2	4.2
-13.1	-18.5	-15.2		-5.4	-8.5	17.9	8.3	8.6	-5.7
55.2	63.7	72.6		112.5	121.1	35.0	40.6	42.2	37.5
(455) 14.1	(447) 19.6	(428) 18.4	% Profit Before Taxes/Tangible Net Worth	(106) 23.6	(131) 28.3	(54) 10.5	(49) 13.9	(57) 20.2	(31) 9.2
-.4	.6	3.0		-1.2	6.9	.5	2.7	6.7	3.0
15.2	21.0	18.0		16.5	34.1	11.5	13.3	16.1	9.4
3.9	5.0	5.9	% Profit Before Taxes/Total Assets	3.8	9.3	4.3	5.8	8.3	4.4
-1.4	-.5	.4		-3.0	.9	.2	1.7	1.8	.2
4.9	6.2	6.6		11.6	8.3	4.7	2.7	2.6	4.4
1.5	1.9	1.7	Sales/Net Fixed Assets	2.7	2.6	1.1	1.0	1.2	1.6
.6	.7	.7		.5	.8	.6	.7	.8	.8
2.5	2.8	2.6		3.4	3.5	2.3	1.6	1.4	2.0
1.0	1.2	1.1	Sales/Total Assets	1.2	1.6	.8	.8	.9	.9
.5	.6	.6		.4	.6	.5	.6	.6	.6
4.0	3.8	4.0		3.3	3.5	4.2	5.3	4.3	4.3
(539) 7.2	(506) 6.5	(490) 6.9	% Depr., Dep., Amort./Sales	(118) 7.9	(161) 6.3	(54) 7.0	(55) 7.0	(63) 6.7	(39) 7.1
10.9	10.9	11.2		17.0	10.9	10.3	9.6	8.8	9.4
3.4	2.9	2.8		5.2	3.1	2.4	2.2	2.0	
(160) 6.6	(157) 5.4	(154) 6.1	% Officers', Directors' Owners' Comp/Sales	(48) 10.2	(60) 5.6	(19) 4.2	(11) 4.5	(13) 4.3	
10.6	10.8	11.6		17.4	10.5	11.8	6.9	7.6	
5644458M	5052862M	5565273M	Net Sales ($)	89317M	354728M	239196M	409088M	1072516M	3400428M
6726395M	6130505M	6416230M	Total Assets ($)	162262M	431768M	376926M	531590M	1489467M	3424217M

M = $ thousand MM = $ million

See Pages 9 through 22 for Explanation of Ratios and Data

Current Data Sorted by Assets							Comparative Historical Data	
			1			Unqualified	3	3
1	1	4				Reviewed	15	15
6	21	7				Compiled	49	52
20	21	8				Tax Returns	75	55
14	19	10	7	1		Other	37	53
33 (4/1-9/30/13)			108 (10/1/13-3/31/14)				4/1/09-3/31/10	4/1/10-3/31/11
0-500M	500M-2MM	2-10MM	10-50MM	50-100MM	100-250MM		ALL	ALL
41	62	29	8	1		NUMBER OF STATEMENTS	179	178

0-500M	500M-2MM	2-10MM	10-50MM	50-100MM	100-250MM	Type of Statement	4/1/09-3/31/10 ALL	4/1/10-3/31/11 ALL
%	%	%	%	%	%	**ASSETS**	%	%
17.3	11.7	8.2			DATA NOT AVAILABLE	Cash & Equivalents	12.2	12.5
1.6	.3	1.7				Trade Receivables (net)	.6	1.7
5.5	2.9	1.8				Inventory	4.6	3.5
1.5	1.3	.5				All Other Current	2.6	3.6
25.8	16.2	12.2				Total Current	20.0	21.2
45.8	68.3	67.0				Fixed Assets (net)	66.4	65.2
14.2	6.8	6.3				Intangibles (net)	4.1	5.4
14.3	8.7	14.4				All Other Non-Current	9.5	8.2
100.0	100.0	100.0				Total	100.0	100.0
						LIABILITIES		
13.5	6.7	3.5				Notes Payable-Short Term	4.9	9.2
2.4	6.6	6.4				Cur. Mat.-L.T.D.	5.7	6.4
7.1	5.1	2.1				Trade Payables	5.0	5.5
.0	.3	.0				Income Taxes Payable	.0	.1
26.7	20.1	15.2				All Other Current	17.4	14.0
49.7	38.9	27.2				Total Current	33.0	35.2
53.2	61.3	58.6				Long-Term Debt	59.7	58.4
.0	.0	.1				Deferred Taxes	.1	.1
47.5	15.4	2.4				All Other Non-Current	17.1	23.2
-50.3	-15.6	11.7				Net Worth	-9.9	-16.8
100.0	100.0	100.0				Total Liabilties & Net Worth	100.0	100.0
						INCOME DATA		
100.0	100.0	100.0				Net Sales	100.0	100.0
						Gross Profit		
101.0	90.4	93.4				Operating Expenses	96.3	94.4
-1.0	9.6	6.6				Operating Profit	3.7	5.6
.6	5.4	4.6				All Other Expenses (net)	3.9	4.9
-1.7	4.2	2.0				Profit Before Taxes	-.3	.8
						RATIOS		
1.2	1.1	1.6					1.3	1.5
.7	.6	.6				Current	.7	.7
.3	.2	.3					.3	.3
.9	1.0	1.4					.9	1.0
.5	(61) .3	.5				Quick	(178) .4	(177) .4
.1	.1	.2					.1	.1
0 UND	0 UND	0 UND					0 UND	0 UND
0 UND	0 UND	1 431.0				Sales/Receivables	0 UND	0 UND
1 654.9	1 700.5	10 35.6					1 435.2	1 443.2
						Cost of Sales/Inventory		
						Cost of Sales/Payables		
101.6	86.7	35.6					34.5	24.8
-48.0	-16.4	-17.7				Sales/Working Capital	-28.8	-33.5
-6.9	-3.6	-6.3					-7.5	-6.8
5.3	5.5	3.4					2.1	2.7
(29) .7	(52) 1.8	(27) 1.6				EBIT/Interest	(150) 1.0	(141) .9
-3.0	.4	.1					-.1	-.1
							3.1	2.5
						Net Profit + Depr., Dep., Amort./Cur. Mat. L/T/D	(13) 1.1	(16) 1.4
							.1	.3
.8	2.3	1.5					1.9	2.0
-1.1	-5.5	9.7				Fixed/Worth	22.1	32.7
-.3	-1.1	-6.8					-2.0	-1.5
1.4	2.2	1.2					2.1	2.1
-2.6	-8.1	11.1				Debt/Worth	32.0	39.0
-1.6	-2.5	-8.6					-3.5	-2.9
88.3	46.0	30.5					31.5	47.6
(15) 31.3	(26) 23.8	(17) 13.2				% Profit Before Taxes/Tangible Net Worth	(93) 6.0	(94) 13.6
-10.7	7.0	4.1					-13.1	-11.9
9.7	14.2	7.6					6.0	8.9
.0	2.8	2.6				% Profit Before Taxes/Total Assets	.0	.5
-14.6	-2.0	-4.8					-6.4	-7.2
20.7	3.4	2.6					5.8	5.6
8.4	1.9	1.6				Sales/Net Fixed Assets	1.9	1.9
4.4	.9	.6					1.0	1.0
5.0	2.1	1.3					2.6	2.5
3.2	1.3	.7				Sales/Total Assets	1.2	1.2
1.8	.8	.5					.8	.8
1.4	2.9	3.8					3.5	3.1
(31) 2.9	(54) 5.5	(27) 8.3				% Depr., Dep., Amort./Sales	(170) 6.4	(161) 5.8
4.9	9.6	13.6					10.2	9.6
3.1	3.7						2.7	3.2
(22) 7.9	(18) 6.1					% Officers', Directors' Owners' Comp/Sales	(78) 6.3	(65) 7.0
12.8	14.4						9.8	12.7
38360M	91847M	95330M	165066M	81263M		Net Sales ($)	576261M	464012M
11522M	64199M	120171M	190454M	65530M		Total Assets ($)	610333M	452489M

M = $ thousand MM = $ million

See Pages 9 through 22 for Explanation of Ratios and Data

Comparative Historical Data				Current Data Sorted by Sales					
			Type of Statement						
4	2	1	Unqualified					1	
12	8	6	Reviewed	1	3	1		1	
29	37	34	Compiled	15	17	1	1		
72	60	49	Tax Returns	19	21	6	3		
51	45	51	Other	13	23	8		4	3
4/1/11-3/31/12	**4/1/12-3/31/13**	**4/1/13-3/31/14**		**33 (4/1-9/30/13)**			**108 (10/1/13-3/31/14)**		
ALL	**ALL**	**ALL**		**0-1MM**	**1-3MM**	**3-5MM**	**5-10MM**	**10-25MM**	**25MM & OVER**
168	152	141	**NUMBER OF STATEMENTS**	48	64	16	4	6	3
%	%	%	**ASSETS**	%	%	%	%	%	%
12.3	13.2	12.4	Cash & Equivalents	8.7	13.9	16.6			
1.1	.8	1.0	Trade Receivables (net)	.9	.8	1.9			
4.3	3.9	3.4	Inventory	3.4	3.3	4.5			
2.9	2.6	1.2	All Other Current	.4	1.7	1.2			
20.5	20.5	17.9	Total Current	13.4	19.6	24.2			
64.1	64.6	62.2	Fixed Assets (net)	65.0	58.7	59.1			
5.7	5.4	8.5	Intangibles (net)	11.9	8.1	5.4			
9.7	9.4	11.4	All Other Non-Current	9.8	13.6	11.3			
100.0	100.0	100.0	Total	100.0	100.0	100.0			
			LIABILITIES						
5.9	4.7	8.0	Notes Payable-Short Term	4.8	11.2	2.9			
5.7	6.7	5.1	Cur. Mat.-L.T.D.	4.7	4.8	7.5			
4.9	5.5	4.9	Trade Payables	4.3	4.9	8.6			
.2	.4	.2	Income Taxes Payable	.0	.3	.0			
20.7	18.9	20.2	All Other Current	24.5	20.6	9.5			
37.4	36.3	38.3	Total Current	38.4	41.8	28.4			
48.1	50.3	57.9	Long-Term Debt	75.2	49.4	58.3			
.2	.2	.2	Deferred Taxes	.0	.1	.0			
28.5	21.2	21.4	All Other Non-Current	26.2	25.6	5.4			
-14.2	-7.9	-17.8	Net Worth	-39.8	-16.9	7.9			
100.0	100.0	100.0	Total Liabilties & Net Worth	100.0	100.0	100.0			
			INCOME DATA						
100.0	100.0	100.0	Net Sales	100.0	100.0	100.0			
			Gross Profit						
94.1	94.0	94.3	Operating Expenses	93.0	95.5	91.9			
5.9	6.0	5.7	Operating Profit	7.0	4.5	8.1			
4.8	4.1	3.6	All Other Expenses (net)	6.9	2.3	1.3			
1.1	1.9	2.1	Profit Before Taxes	.1	2.2	6.7			
			RATIOS						
1.6	1.4	1.1		1.0	1.4	1.2			
.7	.7	.6	Current	.4	.7	.9			
.2	.3	.2		.2	.3	.6			
1.1	1.1	.9		.6	1.2	1.0			
(167) .4	(150) .5	(140) .4	Quick	.2	(63) .6	.7			
.1	.1	.1		.0	.1	.4			
0 UND	0 UND	0 UND		0 UND	0 UND	0 UND			
0 UND	0 UND	0 UND	Sales/Receivables	0 UND	0 UND	0 917.8			
2 240.4	1 348.7	1 297.2		0 UND	1 288.3	2 232.0			
			Cost of Sales/Inventory						
			Cost of Sales/Payables						
24.8	28.6	98.5		512.5	29.4	69.6			
-25.9	-33.3	-21.8	Sales/Working Capital	-7.8	-43.4	-162.3			
-5.7	-6.7	-5.4		-3.3	-6.9	-17.9			
2.6	3.0	4.6		2.3	5.2	8.6			
(138) 1.0	(128) 1.3	(115) 1.6	EBIT/Interest	(39) 1.1	(52) 1.8	(14) 2.3			
-.2	.1	.0		-1.1	.0	.4			
3.0		3.1							
(13) 2.0		(10) 2.0	Net Profit + Depr., Dep., Amort./Cur. Mat. L/T/D						
.8		.2							
2.7	1.7	1.7		8.2	1.2	1.0			
-503.8	21.0	-12.6	Fixed/Worth	-3.1	-17.9	8.1			
-1.4	-1.7	-.9		-.6	-.8	-4.8			
2.8	2.2	1.6		11.3	1.0	.8			
-79.6	75.7	-14.0	Debt/Worth	-3.7	-11.9	10.4			
-3.3	-3.4	-2.4		-1.8	-2.4	-7.0			
29.8	56.3	48.2		93.3	36.5	141.5			
(82) 10.9	(79) 20.0	(64) 22.0	% Profit Before Taxes/Tangible Net Worth	(17) 27.4	(30) 19.9	(10) 48.2			
-5.8	-3.0	4.8		-15.9	3.4	6.0			
7.6	10.8	9.3		5.2	12.3	33.9			
.0	2.4	2.2	% Profit Before Taxes/Total Assets	1.1	3.0	4.6			
-5.7	-4.3	-3.5		-4.9	-6.7	-2.2			
4.9	5.8	7.7		7.6	10.7	9.2			
1.9	1.9	2.1	Sales/Net Fixed Assets	1.5	2.3	3.2			
.9	.8	1.0		.8	1.3	2.0			
2.5	3.0	2.6		1.9	3.5	4.0			
1.1	1.3	1.3	Sales/Total Assets	1.2	1.4	2.0			
.7	.7	.7		.6	.8	1.1			
3.3	2.9	2.8		3.1	2.3	3.5			
(154) 6.0	(129) 5.9	(120) 5.1	% Depr., Dep., Amort./Sales	(43) 4.9	(52) 3.8	(12) 5.4			
9.0	10.9	9.2		9.1	9.2	10.6			
2.6	2.1	2.7		4.6	3.0				
(71) 6.1	(63) 5.7	(53) 6.1	% Officers', Directors' Owners' Comp/Sales	(19) 12.8	(25) 5.7				
14.4	14.8	12.8		19.6	9.2				
546639M	**364197M**	**471866M**	Net Sales ($)	**27012M**	**108679M**	**59544M**	**24209M**	**121137M**	**131285M**
553437M	**371305M**	**451876M**	Total Assets ($)	**28741M**	**107388M**	**48701M**	**12851M**	**114075M**	**140120M**

Current Data Sorted by Assets							Comparative Historical Data	
						Type of Statement		
	3	15	14	5	5	Unqualified	48	55
	3	10	7			Reviewed	22	25
3	15	11	3			Compiled	37	48
49	40	27	1			Tax Returns	96	90
26	50	55	17	7	8	Other	125	128
63 (4/1-9/30/13)			311 (10/1/13-3/31/14)				4/1/09-3/31/10 ALL	4/1/10-3/31/11 ALL
0-500M	**500M-2MM**	**2-10MM**	**10-50MM**	**50-100MM**	**100-250MM**			
78	111	118	42	12	13	**NUMBER OF STATEMENTS**	328	346
%	%	%	%	%	%	**ASSETS**	%	%
30.1	15.4	11.4	12.3	6.0	19.8	Cash & Equivalents	15.0	15.9
2.6	5.8	4.5	3.9	3.3	3.1	Trade Receivables (net)	4.2	5.2
7.8	4.7	4.5	3.9	5.5	.7	Inventory	5.4	6.3
1.8	3.8	2.1	3.0	2.9	3.0	All Other Current	4.6	3.9
42.2	29.8	22.5	23.2	17.8	26.6	Total Current	29.1	31.3
38.2	57.1	62.0	57.1	55.6	55.5	Fixed Assets (net)	55.3	54.9
6.8	4.5	8.4	8.9	22.5	15.8	Intangibles (net)	7.3	5.2
12.6	8.7	7.1	10.9	4.1	2.0	All Other Non-Current	8.3	8.7
100.0	100.0	100.0	100.0	100.0	100.0	Total	100.0	100.0
						LIABILITIES		
15.9	8.1	2.1	2.7	1.5	1.1	Notes Payable-Short Term	10.6	9.4
2.1	3.8	3.0	3.6	3.1	2.4	Cur. Mat.-L.T.D.	3.6	3.5
6.3	5.7	4.4	8.6	5.9	5.0	Trade Payables	6.5	6.5
.0	.1	.1	.0	.0	.1	Income Taxes Payable	.5	.1
24.1	13.5	8.9	8.8	6.9	10.9	All Other Current	17.3	15.1
48.4	31.1	18.6	23.6	17.3	19.5	Total Current	38.4	34.5
31.8	35.3	35.6	25.8	27.9	39.3	Long-Term Debt	34.0	28.3
.0	.0	.2	.5	.9	.3	Deferred Taxes	.2	.4
15.9	8.4	8.6	8.8	9.0	15.3	All Other Non-Current	13.2	15.1
3.9	25.1	37.0	41.2	45.0	25.7	Net Worth	14.2	21.7
100.0	100.0	100.0	100.0	100.0	100.0	Total Liabilties & Net Worth	100.0	100.0
						INCOME DATA		
100.0	100.0	100.0	100.0	100.0	100.0	Net Sales	100.0	100.0
						Gross Profit		
91.8	82.4	89.5	88.8	87.9	80.2	Operating Expenses	92.4	91.6
8.2	17.6	10.5	11.2	12.1	19.8	Operating Profit	7.6	8.4
1.5	4.7	3.2	1.4	5.8	1.7	All Other Expenses (net)	4.3	3.7
6.6	13.0	7.3	9.8	6.3	18.1	Profit Before Taxes	3.3	4.7
						RATIOS		
4.7	2.2	3.4	1.8	1.9	3.2		2.6	2.8
1.0	.8	1.3	1.0	1.0	1.0	Current	1.0	1.2
.4	.3	.5	.6	.7	.7		.4	.4
4.7	1.5	2.3	1.7	1.0	3.0		1.9	2.2
.6	.5	.9	.7	.7	.9	Quick	.6	(343) .7
.2	.2	.3	.2	.2	.5		.2	.2
0 UND	0 UND	0 UND	2 165.3	1 373.3	0 UND		0 UND	0 UND
0 UND	0 UND	5 67.3	7 53.4	5 75.6	3 131.8	Sales/Receivables	1 607.4	2 234.4
0 UND	3 123.2	18 20.1	17 21.1	12 31.4	24 15.4		9 41.8	13 27.3
						Cost of Sales/Inventory		
						Cost of Sales/Payables		
16.9	12.2	5.7	8.3	16.2	3.4		8.3	7.8
UND	-92.6	27.3	NM	NM	119.4	Sales/Working Capital	722.7	67.2
-9.8	-7.2	-8.7	-11.4	-17.7	-10.8		-7.6	-9.2
17.0	19.8	8.2	16.9	5.1	20.3		7.0	8.4
(43) 3.4	(77) 5.2	(100) 2.9	(35) 4.5	(11) 3.1	(11) 10.2	EBIT/Interest	(253) 2.3	(246) 1.8
.0	1.1	1.4	1.3	.9	2.7		.3	-.1
							4.1	5.7
						Net Profit + Depr., Dep., Amort./Cur. Mat. L/T/D	(24) 2.9	(32) 2.6
							1.0	1.5
.4	.7	.9	1.0	1.2	.9		.8	.6
1.4	2.1	1.8	1.8	13.6	1.2	Fixed/Worth	1.9	1.5
-5.8	-25.0	10.2	7.0	-.8	2.2		-6.5	UND
.4	.7	.4	.4	.4	.2		.5	.4
4.8	2.9	1.6	2.1	25.9	.8	Debt/Worth	2.3	1.6
-4.6	-24.4	18.8	9.0	-4.6	1.7		-7.8	-43.5
228.5	92.2	39.7	34.5		43.8		36.6	47.6
(48) 66.6	(79) 37.2	(90) 10.0	(35) 16.1		(11) 16.4	% Profit Before Taxes/Tangible Net Worth	(226) 7.8	(255) 11.5
17.4	5.9	.5	5.5		1.1		-2.9	-2.5
36.8	32.8	12.3	11.0	11.9	24.2		13.1	16.5
14.5	8.4	4.1	6.2	5.7	9.6	% Profit Before Taxes/Total Assets	2.9	3.4
-2.3	1.2	.7	2.6	-.1	3.7		-3.8	-2.8
64.1	11.0	4.2	3.8	5.2	3.3		12.9	13.4
12.7	1.9	.9	1.5	2.1	1.1	Sales/Net Fixed Assets	2.5	2.5
5.9	.5	.5	.8	.9	.6		.9	.8
7.4	2.4	1.3	1.5	1.6	1.1		2.9	3.3
4.3	1.3	.7	.8	1.0	.8	Sales/Total Assets	1.3	1.2
2.3	.5	.4	.6	.5	.4		.6	.6
1.2	1.8	3.7	4.3	5.2			2.1	2.4
(45) 2.3	(73) 5.6	(98) 7.4	(39) 5.9	(10) 6.3		% Depr., Dep., Amort./Sales	(262) 5.3	(266) 6.2
5.1	10.7	11.8	10.8	10.9			10.6	11.2
5.5	3.1	2.0					2.4	3.5
(33) 8.8	(31) 6.1	(20) 4.5				% Officers', Directors' Owners' Comp/Sales	(94) 5.1	(104) 6.6
13.6	10.2	8.1					9.5	11.3
66664M	228829M	551687M	1430592M	814729M	1834398M	Net Sales ($)	4646323M	5009671M
15855M	123016M	541054M	996561M	783360M	2116834M	Total Assets ($)	3951271M	4783281M

M = $ thousand MM = $ million

See Pages 9 through 22 for Explanation of Ratios and Data

Comparative Historical Data				Current Data Sorted by Sales					
			Type of Statement						
50	35	42	Unqualified	3	7	4	6	6	16
22	22	20	Reviewed	1	4	3	6	4	2
50	42	32	Compiled	12	12	3	1	4	
134	144	117	Tax Returns	54	46	9	5	3	
167	147	163	Other	44	44	18	18	17	22
4/1/11-3/31/12	**4/1/12-3/31/13**	**4/1/13-3/31/14**			**63 (4/1-9/30/13)**			**311 (10/1/13-3/31/14)**	
ALL	**ALL**	**ALL**		**0-1MM**	**1-3MM**	**3-5MM**	**5-10MM**	**10-25MM**	**25MM & OVER**
423	390	374	**NUMBER OF STATEMENTS**	114	113	37	36	34	40
%	%	%	**ASSETS**	%	%	%	%	%	%
14.8	17.3	16.7	Cash & Equivalents	17.6	16.4	23.0	14.5	11.7	15.6
5.6	4.3	4.3	Trade Receivables (net)	1.3	5.1	3.9	9.3	6.4	5.0
5.3	4.8	5.1	Inventory	3.1	4.9	6.0	4.7	11.8	5.3
2.2	2.8	2.7	All Other Current	.8	4.5	1.3	2.7	3.7	3.9
28.1	29.3	28.8	Total Current	22.7	30.8	34.2	31.1	33.6	29.8
55.2	57.9	54.6	Fixed Assets (net)	61.8	55.2	50.8	50.8	42.0	50.4
7.0	5.5	7.7	Intangibles (net)	4.8	6.3	6.5	10.9	12.3	14.2
9.8	7.4	8.9	All Other Non-Current	10.7	7.8	8.5	7.2	12.1	5.7
100.0	100.0	100.0	Total	100.0	100.0	100.0	100.0	100.0	100.0
			LIABILITIES						
9.9	6.6	6.8	Notes Payable-Short Term	9.7	7.1	5.5	1.5	6.1	3.9
3.9	3.5	3.1	Cur. Mat.-L.T.D.	3.0	3.3	2.7	3.4	3.0	2.7
6.7	5.9	5.7	Trade Payables	3.2	6.2	5.0	5.5	9.8	8.9
.1	.1	.1	Income Taxes Payable	.1	.1	.2	.1	.0	.0
12.7	12.0	13.4	All Other Current	13.7	14.8	12.3	16.6	8.3	11.6
33.3	28.1	29.1	Total Current	29.7	31.4	25.8	27.1	27.2	27.1
32.5	32.8	33.5	Long-Term Debt	40.6	36.3	31.6	20.0	19.6	31.0
.3	.3	.2	Deferred Taxes	.0	.1	.0	.6	.0	.6
12.4	11.2	10.3	All Other Non-Current	10.6	10.8	12.2	7.2	7.6	11.9
21.4	27.7	26.9	Net Worth	19.1	21.3	30.4	45.2	45.5	29.4
100.0	100.0	100.0	Total Liabilties & Net Worth	100.0	100.0	100.0	100.0	100.0	100.0
			INCOME DATA						
100.0	100.0	100.0	Net Sales	100.0	100.0	100.0	100.0	100.0	100.0
			Gross Profit						
91.5	88.9	87.4	Operating Expenses	84.2	88.2	91.1	91.7	89.2	85.5
8.5	11.1	12.6	Operating Profit	15.8	11.8	8.9	8.3	10.8	14.5
3.5	3.3	3.1	All Other Expenses (net)	6.3	2.0	1.7	.0	1.5	2.6
5.0	7.8	9.5	Profit Before Taxes	9.5	9.7	7.2	8.3	9.3	11.9
			RATIOS						
2.3	3.1	2.5		3.5	2.4	4.6	3.6	2.4	2.2
1.0	1.1	1.0	Current	.8	1.1	1.1	1.2	1.4	1.0
.4	.5	.4		.3	.4	.5	.4	.8	.7
1.9	2.3	2.0		2.7	1.8	3.3	3.3	1.6	1.8
.7	(387) .8	.7	Quick	.5	.8	1.0	.7	.8	.7
.2	.3	.2		.2	.3	.3	.3	.2	.2
0 UND	**0** UND	**0** UND		**0** UND	**0** UND	**0** UND	**1** 517.9	**2** 149.7	**1** 575.4
1 404.8	**1** 651.0	**0** 776.0	Sales/Receivables	**0** UND	**0** 999.8	**1** 433.9	**7** 51.6	**9** 41.5	**5** 72.1
14 25.7	**10** 36.0	**10** 36.9		**0** UND	**12** 29.3	**11** 34.7	**24** 15.2	**25** 14.5	**14** 26.9
			Cost of Sales/Inventory						
			Cost of Sales/Payables						
9.7	8.9	9.3		12.7	9.2	5.7	7.9	8.1	10.2
322.0	69.9	668.8	Sales/Working Capital	-41.2	69.3	35.5	27.4	23.2	392.1
-9.2	-11.5	-9.5		-4.8	-10.6	-12.7	-10.2	-29.2	-13.7
9.7	13.8	12.3		7.2	12.1	8.7	39.2	17.8	18.3
(320) 2.2	(282) 3.4	(277) 3.7	EBIT/Interest	(70) 2.0	(90) 3.8	(27) 4.0	(28) 10.3	(31) 6.2	(31) 5.1
.3	1.0	1.1		-.2	1.4	1.3	1.5	2.1	2.7
3.3	4.3	9.4							
(28) 1.5	(24) 2.6	(19) 2.3	Net Profit + Depr., Dep., Amort./Cur. Mat. L/T/D						
1.1	1.1	1.4							
.8	.9	.8		.8	.8	.4	.6	.4	1.0
2.1	1.9	1.8	Fixed/Worth	2.5	1.8	1.6	1.5	1.1	2.4
-6.4	-24.7	-29.9		-718.0	-6.3	NM	NM	2.6	-2.8
.5	.4	.5		.4	.7	.3	.2	.5	.5
2.7	2.8	2.3	Debt/Worth	3.3	2.1	2.3	1.4	1.3	2.3
-8.2	-17.0	-26.1		-32.7	-9.7	NM	NM	7.6	-33.8
53.0	53.4	75.5		89.4	83.3	67.8	44.5	80.9	78.6
(291) 13.9	(281) 17.2	(270) 19.2	% Profit Before Taxes/Tangible Net Worth	(81) 18.4	(75) 28.9	(28) 16.4	(27) 12.4	(31) 19.3	(28) 22.3
-.9	2.1	5.1		-.5	6.4	3.3	5.1	9.9	7.9
17.4	18.3	22.6		21.2	29.1	30.4	25.1	18.3	16.8
4.2	6.1	6.6	% Profit Before Taxes/Total Assets	4.4	7.8	5.1	7.5	5.7	8.4
-1.7	.0	.6		-1.6	1.7	-1.2	2.7	1.8	4.5
11.3	9.9	10.8		10.8	11.6	22.3	11.6	11.8	8.8
2.3	2.1	2.4	Sales/Net Fixed Assets	1.3	2.4	2.6	2.5	3.1	2.5
.7	.6	.7		.4	.8	.8	1.0	1.1	1.0
3.2	2.8	2.7		3.4	2.8	2.5	2.5	2.3	2.1
1.2	1.1	1.1	Sales/Total Assets	.9	1.4	1.0	1.3	1.2	1.1
.5	.5	.5		.3	.6	.6	.7	.6	.7
2.8	2.9	2.9		1.9	2.8	2.9	3.1	1.4	3.9
(329) 6.3	(298) 6.4	(273) 6.0	% Depr., Dep., Amort./Sales	(76) 7.0	(77) 6.6	(31) 6.1	(29) 5.1	(29) 5.0	(31) 5.9
11.6	11.2	10.2		14.7	10.1	10.0	9.9	8.7	10.1
3.1	2.9	3.2		6.7	3.1				
(115) 6.3	(128) 6.1	(88) 6.3	% Officers', Directors' Owners' Comp/Sales	(31) 12.2	(34) 6.3				
9.2	11.4	11.6		15.7	9.1				
5317317M	**4428097M**	**4926899M**	Net Sales ($)	**55332M**	**201554M**	**143236M**	**247379M**	**550260M**	**3729138M**
4649174M	**4247002M**	**4576680M**	Total Assets ($)	**111485M**	**220252M**	**151927M**	**261075M**	**595122M**	**3236819M**

M = $ thousand MM = $ million

See Pages 9 through 22 for Explanation of Ratios and Data

ACCOMMODATION AND FOOD SERVICES

	Current Data Sorted by Assets						Comparative Historical Data	
Type of Statement								
Unqualified		1	20	37	12	8	115	107
Reviewed		7	43	31	3	2	124	102
Compiled	20	52	148	18			316	275
Tax Returns	117	288	403	30		1	1009	889
Other	46	149	344	143	15	18	683	718
	114 (4/1-9/30/13)			1,842 (10/1/13-3/31/14)			**4/1/09-3/31/10 ALL**	**4/1/10-3/31/11 ALL**
	0-500M	**500M-2MM**	**2-10MM**	**10-50MM**	**50-100MM**	**100-250MM**		
NUMBER OF STATEMENTS	183	497	958	259	30	29	2247	2091
ASSETS	%	%	%	%	%	%	%	%
Cash & Equivalents	32.5	9.1	6.6	6.9	10.6	7.7	8.4	8.5
Trade Receivables (net)	5.3	1.8	1.2	2.8	3.1	3.5	2.5	2.1
Inventory	1.9	1.0	.3	.7	1.7	.7	.8	.7
All Other Current	4.0	.9	1.4	2.6	1.3	1.4	1.8	1.6
Total Current	43.6	12.8	9.5	13.0	16.8	13.3	13.5	12.9
Fixed Assets (net)	40.2	76.4	81.4	76.1	66.7	72.6	74.9	75.9
Intangibles (net)	4.6	3.7	3.3	3.2	2.6	4.4	3.5	3.8
All Other Non-Current	11.6	7.1	5.8	7.7	13.9	9.6	8.0	7.5
Total	100.0	100.0	100.0	100.0	100.0	100.0	100.0	100.0
LIABILITIES								
Notes Payable-Short Term	5.2	2.4	1.4	1.1	.7	3.0	2.7	2.7
Cur. Mat.-L.T.D.	2.1	3.4	2.9	3.1	3.7	1.8	3.9	3.6
Trade Payables	6.6	2.6	1.7	2.8	3.1	3.3	3.1	2.4
Income Taxes Payable	.2	.0	.0	.2	.2	.0	.1	.1
All Other Current	31.5	10.8	6.7	9.2	10.0	10.6	11.2	10.3
Total Current	45.7	19.2	12.7	16.5	17.6	18.8	21.1	19.1
Long-Term Debt	31.5	65.3	72.5	58.1	54.0	50.7	66.5	65.9
Deferred Taxes	.0	.0	.0	.1	.6	.4	.0	.1
All Other Non-Current	24.2	5.7	5.2	7.4	8.2	9.5	6.8	6.8
Net Worth	-1.3	9.8	9.6	18.0	19.5	20.7	5.7	8.2
Total Liabilties & Net Worth	100.0	100.0	100.0	100.0	100.0	100.0	100.0	100.0
INCOME DATA								
Net Sales	100.0	100.0	100.0	100.0	100.0	100.0	100.0	100.0
Gross Profit								
Operating Expenses	90.6	83.4	80.5	85.4	85.8	91.2	88.4	86.1
Operating Profit	9.4	16.6	19.5	14.6	14.2	8.8	11.6	13.9
All Other Expenses (net)	2.3	8.0	10.4	7.4	4.8	5.1	12.4	11.2
Profit Before Taxes	7.1	8.6	9.1	7.2	9.4	3.7	-.8	2.7
RATIOS								
Current	4.5	2.0	2.0	1.7	1.6	1.3	1.7	1.9
	1.3	.7	.8	.8	.8	.9	.6	.7
	.5	.2	.3	.4	.3	.3	.2	.2
Quick	4.2	1.8	1.8	1.5	1.4	1.2	1.5	1.6
	(180) 1.2	(495) .6	(953) .7	.6	.8	.7	(2245) .5	(2086) .6
	.4	.2	.2	.3	.3	.2	.2	.2
Sales/Receivables	0 UND	0 UND	0 UND	3 145.6	5 75.3	5 68.9	0 UND	0 UND
	0 UND	0 UND	2 159.4	7 52.1	7 49.5	7 53.2	2 146.9	3 143.0
	2 172.2	6 65.5	7 52.2	11 32.2	12 30.3	14 25.8	8 45.7	8 46.1
Cost of Sales/Inventory								
Cost of Sales/Payables								
Sales/Working Capital	13.1	17.5	12.4	10.9	9.4	21.0	18.0	15.2
	66.7	-28.2	-45.6	-26.7	-40.8	-48.7	-22.4	-30.3
	-25.7	-5.5	-7.1	-8.6	-6.3	-4.9	-4.9	-5.8
EBIT/Interest	24.5	3.7	3.6	3.8	4.1	3.3	2.4	2.8
	(75) 4.6	(396) 2.1	(810) 2.1	(224) 2.0	(29) 2.1	(26) 1.8	(1555) 1.2	(1460) 1.5
	.0	1.1	1.1	.8	1.1	.8	.2	.6
Net Profit + Depr., Dep., Amort./Cur. Mat. L/T/D			4.1	5.3			2.4	4.0
			(15) 2.1	(23) 3.5			(73) 1.5	(74) 2.0
			1.2	1.1			.6	.7
Fixed/Worth	.2	2.2	3.3	1.8	1.5	1.6	2.7	2.5
	1.1	8.0	9.3	4.5	2.9	3.0	10.8	8.8
	-2.5	-7.8	-10.4	-41.1	-17.2	-16.8	-7.0	-8.2
Debt/Worth	.3	1.6	2.9	1.6	1.6	1.6	2.5	2.3
	2.1	9.1	9.7	4.4	3.8	4.0	13.0	10.5
	-3.2	-8.7	-12.7	-42.1	-17.4	-19.2	-8.5	-10.0
% Profit Before Taxes/Tangible Net Worth	116.0	46.1	59.2	34.5	40.3	18.9	26.6	37.7
	(117) 39.3	(313) 22.8	(607) 23.7	(189) 13.5	(21) 16.2	(21) 5.7	(1363) 4.9	(1314) 9.6
	7.9	4.7	6.2	2.7	.9	-3.4	-12.2	-5.2
% Profit Before Taxes/Total Assets	53.5	10.1	9.0	7.2	11.7	4.5	4.5	6.3
	13.2	4.1	3.9	2.8	4.4	1.7	.0	1.3
	-1.4	.2	.1	-.4	.4	-.7	-4.2	-2.5
Sales/Net Fixed Assets	119.7	1.4	.8	1.1	1.0	1.7	1.2	1.1
	13.2	.7	.5	.5	.8	.5	.5	.5
	4.3	.4	.4	.3	.5	.4	.3	.3
Sales/Total Assets	7.8	1.0	.6	.7	.8	.8	.8	.8
	4.2	.5	.4	.4	.5	.5	.4	.4
	1.6	.4	.3	.3	.3	.3	.3	.3
% Depr., Dep., Amort./Sales	1.1	5.2	7.0	6.5	6.1	6.4	6.9	6.6
	(121) 2.8	(426) 8.3	(840) 10.4	(236) 10.4	(27) 9.0	(19) 11.3	(1991) 11.2	(1827) 10.6
	5.5	12.8	15.1	14.8	11.9	13.6	16.8	15.9
% Officers', Directors' Owners' Comp/Sales	3.8	2.9	1.8	2.4			2.3	2.1
	(82) 6.3	(165) 5.1	(201) 3.7	(24) 3.3			(576) 4.4	(523) 4.2
	12.3	8.8	6.4	7.6			7.9	7.7
Net Sales ($)	**182950M**	**604063M**	**2459787M**	**3943598M**	**1770873M**	**4053475M**	**11528331M**	**11010263M**
Total Assets ($)	**44284M**	**622526M**	**4477415M**	**5232962M**	**2072876M**	**4573702M**	**19491656M**	**18957806M**

M = $ thousand MM = $ million

See Pages 9 through 22 for Explanation of Ratios and Data

Comparative Historical Data				Current Data Sorted by Sales					
			Type of Statement						
99	101	78	Unqualified		9	10	12	21	26
106	88	86	Reviewed	4	25	20	16	13	8
307	256	238	Compiled	77	119	22	11	9	
1090	995	839	Tax Returns	366	375	56	29	9	4
778	691	715	Other	169	265	103	79	51	48
4/1/11-3/31/12 ALL	4/1/12-3/31/13 ALL	4/1/13-3/31/14 ALL		114 (4/1-9/30/13)		1,842 (10/1/13-3/31/14)			
2380	2131	1956	**NUMBER OF STATEMENTS**	0-1MM 616	1-3MM 793	3-5MM 211	5-10MM 147	10-25MM 103	25MM & OVER 86
%	%	%	**ASSETS**	%	%	%	%	%	%
9.3	10.0	9.8	Cash & Equivalents	9.8	8.7	9.5	12.5	14.6	10.1
2.1	1.8	2.0	Trade Receivables (net)	1.2	1.5	2.2	3.8	4.7	5.2
.9	.7	.7	Inventory	.4	.4	1.2	1.2	2.1	1.8
1.7	1.6	1.7	All Other Current	1.2	1.4	1.3	3.1	3.4	3.4
14.0	14.1	14.2	Total Current	12.6	12.1	14.3	20.6	24.8	20.5
75.3	75.0	75.2	Fixed Assets (net)	77.1	78.9	75.4	64.0	60.1	65.1
3.4	3.5	3.5	Intangibles (net)	3.9	3.2	2.5	5.2	3.8	2.9
7.3	7.4	7.1	All Other Non-Current	6.4	5.8	7.7	10.2	11.2	11.4
100.0	100.0	100.0	Total	100.0	100.0	100.0	100.0	100.0	100.0
			LIABILITIES						
2.8	2.8	2.0	Notes Payable-Short Term	1.8	2.3	1.2	1.9	2.6	1.5
3.7	4.0	3.0	Cur. Mat.-L.T.D.	3.0	3.0	2.5	2.9	2.4	4.9
2.4	2.6	2.5	Trade Payables	1.7	2.2	2.6	4.1	6.4	4.9
.1	.1	.1	Income Taxes Payable	.0	.0	.1	.2	.0	.5
11.4	11.7	10.5	All Other Current	11.9	8.4	9.3	10.2	14.8	18.0
20.4	21.1	18.1	Total Current	18.5	15.9	15.7	19.3	26.3	29.7
65.2	63.5	64.3	Long-Term Debt	63.5	70.6	65.4	54.7	45.1	49.0
.1	.1	.0	Deferred Taxes	.0	.0	.0	.0	.3	.3
6.4	7.3	7.5	All Other Non-Current	9.4	5.7	7.0	7.8	8.4	10.3
7.9	8.1	10.1	Net Worth	8.6	7.8	11.9	18.2	19.9	10.6
100.0	100.0	100.0	Total Liabilties & Net Worth	100.0	100.0	100.0	100.0	100.0	100.0
			INCOME DATA						
100.0	100.0	100.0	Net Sales	100.0	100.0	100.0	100.0	100.0	100.0
			Gross Profit						
85.0	82.9	83.1	Operating Expenses	81.5	82.1	83.6	85.7	88.5	90.2
15.0	17.1	16.9	Operating Profit	18.5	17.9	16.4	14.3	11.5	9.8
10.3	9.7	8.5	All Other Expenses (net)	11.3	8.4	7.3	4.4	4.4	3.3
4.7	7.3	8.5	Profit Before Taxes	7.2	9.4	9.1	9.9	7.1	6.5
			RATIOS						
2.0	2.0	2.1		2.1	2.3	2.1	2.2	1.9	1.5
.7	.8	.8	Current	.6	.9	.9	1.2	1.0	.7
.2	.3	.3		.2	.3	.4	.5	.5	.3
1.7	1.7	1.8		1.9	2.0	1.8	1.7	1.6	1.2
(2371) .6	(2123) .7	(1946) .7	Quick	(610) .6	(789) .8	.7	.8	.8	.4
.2	.2	.2		.2	.2	.3	.3	.3	.2
0 UND	0 UND	0 UND		0 UND	0 UND	1 299.6	1 260.3	3 145.6	4 83.3
2 155.1	2 175.4	2 181.2	Sales/Receivables	0 UND	2 169.4	4 88.4	6 58.9	7 49.9	7 49.5
7 49.1	7 50.2	8 48.2		3 136.6	7 53.8	10 36.9	10 34.9	14 26.2	13 27.1
			Cost of Sales/Inventory						
			Cost of Sales/Payables						
13.4	12.8	12.8		15.2	12.8	12.5	11.4	14.4	17.2
-33.1	-45.8	-48.4	Sales/Working Capital	-26.1	-90.2	-52.3	52.6	290.1	-20.6
-6.0	-6.5	-7.3		-5.1	-8.2	-10.0	-11.6	-13.4	-6.0
3.0	3.6	3.8		3.2	3.8	4.0	6.1	5.4	3.4
(1800) 1.6	(1659) 2.0	(1560) 2.1	EBIT/Interest	(414) 1.7	(675) 2.1	(183) 2.5	(129) 2.5	(83) 2.8	(76) 1.6
.7	1.0	1.1		.9	1.2	1.2	1.0	1.2	.6
4.5	6.2	4.2						5.9	3.6
(96) 2.4	(62) 3.1	(51) 2.4	Net Profit + Depr., Dep., Amort./Cur. Mat. L/T/D					(13) 4.2	(16) 2.3
1.1	1.6	1.1						2.4	.5
2.3	2.4	2.2		2.2	3.0	2.3	1.3	.9	1.4
7.8	7.9	6.9	Fixed/Worth	6.9	9.3	7.6	4.8	2.5	3.1
-7.7	-8.3	-10.0		-15.5	-8.0	-10.2	-5.5	-12.0	-18.7
2.1	2.2	1.9		1.9	2.7	1.8	1.4	.9	1.3
8.8	9.1	7.7	Debt/Worth	7.2	9.7	7.5	5.8	2.8	4.1
-9.5	-10.3	-11.4		-13.2	-10.1	-11.2	-8.2	-14.1	-20.6
40.9	50.9	52.1		45.4	61.8	59.9	52.0	54.2	28.7
(1507) 12.9	(1356) 18.8	(1268) 21.2	% Profit Before Taxes/Tangible Net Worth	(408) 17.3	(493) 26.8	(138) 26.1	(95) 22.0	(72) 18.9	(62) 13.4
-.9	1.7	5.0		1.0	7.2	10.1	8.8	5.6	-.8
7.7	9.0	10.0		8.2	10.4	10.8	12.4	13.1	9.0
2.1	3.3	3.9	% Profit Before Taxes/Total Assets	2.2	4.4	5.0	5.3	5.5	2.4
-1.6	-.4	.0		-.8	.5	.3	.6	.9	-.8
1.2	1.2	1.2		.9	1.0	1.4	2.5	4.9	3.2
.6	.6	.6	Sales/Net Fixed Assets	.5	.6	.7	1.0	1.1	1.2
.4	.4	.4		.3	.4	.4	.6	.6	.6
.8	.8	.8		.6	.7	.9	1.2	1.7	1.4
.5	.5	.5	Sales/Total Assets	.4	.5	.5	.7	.9	.8
.3	.3	.3		.3	.3	.4	.5	.5	.5
6.4	5.8	5.8		6.3	6.3	6.0	4.0	3.3	5.1
(2049) 10.5	(1867) 9.3	(1669) 9.3	% Depr., Dep., Amort./Sales	(531) 9.9	(670) 9.8	(180) 9.0	(127) 7.9	(92) 7.0	(69) 7.0
15.8	13.8	14.0		15.6	14.2	14.1	12.2	10.5	11.0
2.0	2.1	2.2		3.4	1.9	1.8	1.9	.7	
(592) 4.0	(531) 3.8	(477) 4.4	% Officers', Directors' Owners' Comp/Sales	(189) 6.0	(201) 4.0	(46) 3.6	(17) 3.2	(18) 2.1	
7.2	7.3	8.0		9.4	6.6	6.2	8.7	3.9	
13948496M	14195101M	13014746M	Net Sales ($)	349052M	1395422M	796984M	1071949M	1600430M	7800909M
21819080M	20281865M	17023765M	Total Assets ($)	1031955M	3152585M	1596466M	1754035M	2302805M	7185919M

M = $ thousand MM = $ million

See Pages 9 through 22 for Explanation of Ratios and Data

Current Data Sorted by Assets							Comparative Historical Data	
						Type of Statement		
		1	3	7	7	Unqualified	24	28
					1	Reviewed	3	4
		2	1			Compiled	2	2
1			1			Tax Returns	4	2
	2	3	11	14	19	Other	46	57
22 (4/1-9/30/13)			51 (10/1/13-3/31/14)				**4/1/09-3/31/10 ALL**	**4/1/10-3/31/11 ALL**
0-500M	**500M-2MM**	**2-10MM**	**10-50MM**	**50-100MM**	**100-250MM**			
1	2	6	16	21	27	**NUMBER OF STATEMENTS**	79	93
%	%	%	%	%	%	**ASSETS**	%	%
			11.0	11.7	13.8	Cash & Equivalents	16.0	16.0
			1.5	1.4	1.1	Trade Receivables (net)	2.4	1.5
			.8	1.2	.6	Inventory	.7	1.2
			10.9	2.5	.9	All Other Current	2.9	1.9
			24.1	16.8	16.4	Total Current	22.1	20.6
			70.9	73.5	74.4	Fixed Assets (net)	68.0	70.8
			1.0	8.1	6.5	Intangibles (net)	3.9	4.0
			4.0	1.6	2.7	All Other Non-Current	6.1	4.6
			100.0	100.0	100.0	Total	100.0	100.0
						LIABILITIES		
			.3	.4	1.6	Notes Payable-Short Term	1.8	2.6
			3.9	6.1	8.0	Cur. Mat.-L.T.D.	17.3	6.4
			3.2	2.5	2.2	Trade Payables	3.3	2.5
			.0	.0	.0	Income Taxes Payable	.2	.1
			10.8	9.2	8.9	All Other Current	10.0	10.0
			18.3	18.2	20.7	Total Current	32.6	21.4
			34.4	42.6	46.4	Long-Term Debt	34.6	34.1
			.2	.0	.5	Deferred Taxes	.3	.4
			2.2	2.5	2.2	All Other Non-Current	9.1	7.3
			44.9	36.8	30.3	Net Worth	23.4	36.7
			100.0	100.0	100.0	Total Liabilties & Net Worth	100.0	100.0
						INCOME DATA		
			100.0	100.0	100.0	Net Sales	100.0	100.0
						Gross Profit		
			76.3	78.9	81.8	Operating Expenses	83.6	83.0
			23.7	21.1	18.2	Operating Profit	16.4	17.0
			4.2	3.0	5.6	All Other Expenses (net)	5.6	4.8
			19.4	18.2	12.6	Profit Before Taxes	10.8	12.2
						RATIOS		
			1.8	1.2	1.5		2.1	1.9
			1.1	.9	1.1	Current	1.1	1.1
			.7	.5	.8		.5	.6
			1.4	1.0	1.5		1.8	1.7
			.6	.9	1.0	Quick	(77) 1.0	1.0
			.3	.4	.6		.4	.4
			0 862.9	**1** 532.6	**2** 178.3		**1** 451.2	**1** 379.2
			2 222.7	**2** 174.5	**3** 107.2	Sales/Receivables	**2** 217.2	**2** 202.0
			5 72.2	**6** 62.9	**5** 77.4		**4** 91.7	**4** 94.2
						Cost of Sales/Inventory		
						Cost of Sales/Payables		
			11.6	42.2	17.7		11.4	10.3
			128.9	-156.1	60.2	Sales/Working Capital	83.4	59.5
			-23.4	-13.1	-26.1		-16.9	-14.5
			20.5	30.8	18.9		14.6	16.1
			(14) 7.1	(19) 4.8	(23) 5.4	EBIT/Interest	(67) 6.4	(82) 3.7
			1.6	1.9	1.1		1.0	.3
						Net Profit + Depr., Dep., Amort./Cur. Mat. L/T/D		
			1.0	1.0	1.4		1.0	1.1
			1.6	2.4	2.3	Fixed/Worth	1.8	1.9
			2.8	-11.0	5.4		-30.2	5.3
			.7	.3	.6		.5	.6
			1.5	1.8	2.0	Debt/Worth	1.7	1.4
			2.6	-13.7	6.7		-50.6	5.1
			76.4	84.4	84.7		70.3	72.5
			28.2	(15) 56.2	(22) 24.0	% Profit Before Taxes/Tangible Net Worth	(57) 39.5	(75) 32.8
			8.4	6.3	2.1		8.4	1.7
			21.7	32.8	23.4		28.6	29.0
			13.4	18.8	10.4	% Profit Before Taxes/Total Assets	9.4	8.3
			3.4	3.5	-.5		-1.6	-1.5
			2.0	2.2	1.8		2.8	2.4
			1.6	1.5	1.1	Sales/Net Fixed Assets	1.6	1.3
			1.0	1.1	.6		.9	.9
			1.5	1.7	1.0		1.7	1.4
			1.1	1.1	.8	Sales/Total Assets	1.0	.9
			.8	.8	.6		.7	.6
			5.0	5.3			4.9	5.5
			(15) 6.8	(19) 7.1		% Depr., Dep., Amort./Sales	(53) 6.6	(61) 7.2
			8.9	9.6			9.1	9.9
							2.5	
						% Officers', Directors' Owners' Comp/Sales	(11) 6.7	
							13.8	
1288M	**5291M**	**89130M**	**442755M**	**2081531M**	**4351680M**	Net Sales ($)	**6496012M**	**8126110M**
128M	**2295M**	**41655M**	**369522M**	**1579532M**	**4693448M**	Total Assets ($)	**6625493M**	**7751044M**

M = $ thousand MM = $ million

See Pages 9 through 22 for Explanation of Ratios and Data

Comparative Historical Data				Current Data Sorted by Sales					
			Type of Statement						
32	22	18	Unqualified					2	16
4	2	1	Reviewed						1
4	5	3	Compiled			1	1	1	
9	3	2	Tax Returns		2				
49	51	49	Other		3		1	5	40
4/1/11-3/31/12 ALL	4/1/12-3/31/13 ALL	4/1/13-3/31/14 ALL		22 (4/1-9/30/13)			51 (10/1/13-3/31/14)		
				0-1MM	1-3MM	3-5MM	5-10MM	10-25MM	25MM & OVER
98	83	73	**NUMBER OF STATEMENTS**		5	1	2	8	57
%	%	%	**ASSETS**	%	%	%	%	%	%
13.6	14.4	12.7	Cash & Equivalents	DATA NOT AVAILABLE					13.4
1.4	1.2	1.8	Trade Receivables (net)						1.4
.6	1.0	1.0	Inventory						.9
3.1	4.2	4.8	All Other Current						2.2
18.7	20.8	20.3	Total Current						17.8
71.5	69.1	71.3	Fixed Assets (net)						73.9
4.7	6.9	5.6	Intangibles (net)						6.2
5.2	3.2	2.8	All Other Non-Current						2.1
100.0	100.0	100.0	Total						100.0
			LIABILITIES						
1.8	.4	.9	Notes Payable-Short Term						.9
8.2	11.6	6.2	Cur. Mat.-L.T.D.						6.8
2.2	2.3	2.5	Trade Payables						2.7
.2	.0	.0	Income Taxes Payable						.0
7.5	10.1	10.8	All Other Current						9.2
19.9	24.4	20.4	Total Current						19.7
43.1	42.0	42.9	Long-Term Debt						42.4
.3	.2	.2	Deferred Taxes						.3
7.2	2.9	2.2	All Other Non-Current						2.4
29.6	30.4	34.3	Net Worth						35.3
100.0	100.0	100.0	Total Liabilties & Net Worth						100.0
			INCOME DATA						
100.0	100.0	100.0	Net Sales						100.0
			Gross Profit						
81.0	82.5	81.2	Operating Expenses						79.8
19.0	17.5	18.8	Operating Profit						20.2
6.7	4.7	4.1	All Other Expenses (net)						3.9
12.3	12.8	14.8	Profit Before Taxes						16.3
			RATIOS						
1.7	1.6	1.5							1.5
1.1	1.1	1.0	Current						1.0
.6	.8	.7							.7
1.5	1.4	1.3							1.4
(97) .8	.9	.8	Quick						.9
.4	.6	.5							.6
1 349.9	1 319.8	1 282.5							1 246.6
2 154.4	3 130.0	3 133.4	Sales/Receivables						3 126.0
4 93.4	5 74.7	5 73.6							5 73.2
			Cost of Sales/Inventory						
			Cost of Sales/Payables						
10.5	17.2	19.8							21.3
148.1	52.0	217.9	Sales/Working Capital						217.9
-13.3	-19.8	-21.4							-19.6
16.5	16.7	16.9							21.3
(82) 3.9	(71) 6.3	(63) 5.0	EBIT/Interest						(49) 6.2
1.1	1.5	1.4							1.9
3.2	5.3								
(10) 2.0	(10) 2.3		Net Profit + Depr., Dep., Amort./Cur. Mat. L/T/D						
.5	1.7								
1.3	1.2	1.1							1.3
2.8	2.7	2.3	Fixed/Worth						2.2
34.8	UND	7.4							7.0
.7	.6	.6							.6
2.6	2.5	2.0	Debt/Worth						1.9
42.8	UND	8.1							8.0
70.1	72.6	84.4							87.5
(76) 50.1	(63) 37.0	(59) 26.7	% Profit Before Taxes/Tangible Net Worth						(46) 44.2
4.2	5.6	5.5							5.7
25.9	26.7	24.4							27.1
9.4	11.5	11.7	% Profit Before Taxes/Total Assets						14.3
-1.0	.0	1.5							1.8
2.0	2.1	2.1							2.1
1.2	1.5	1.4	Sales/Net Fixed Assets						1.4
.7	1.0	1.0							1.0
1.4	1.5	1.6							1.6
.9	1.0	1.1	Sales/Total Assets						1.0
.6	.8	.8							.8
5.9	5.3	5.2							5.2
(74) 7.3	(60) 7.0	(50) 6.3	% Depr., Dep., Amort./Sales						(36) 6.7
10.2	8.5	9.0							8.9
2.9									
(14) 6.0			% Officers', Directors' Owners' Comp/Sales						
12.5									
7179641M	9320835M	6971675M	Net Sales ($)		10843M	4052M	14356M	123049M	6819375M
7739476M	7349910M	6686580M	Total Assets ($)		25259M	5881M	11176M	136514M	6507750M

M = $ thousand MM = $ million

See Pages 9 through 22 for Explanation of Ratios and Data

Current Data Sorted by Assets							Comparative Historical Data	
						Type of Statement		
	2	1	2		1	Unqualified		4
	1	1	2			Reviewed	5	4
2	6	6	1			Compiled	21	16
23	18	12	1		1	Tax Returns	47	49
1	3	11	2			Other	31	31
	6 (4/1-9/30/13)		91 (10/1/13-3/31/14)				4/1/09-3/31/10	4/1/10-3/31/11
0-500M	**500M-2MM**	**2-10MM**	**10-50MM**	**50-100MM**	**100-250MM**		**ALL**	**ALL**
26	30	31	8		2	**NUMBER OF STATEMENTS**	104	104
%	%	%	%	%	%	**ASSETS**	%	%
27.8	7.4	8.8		DATA NOT AVAILABLE		Cash & Equivalents	8.6	12.0
2.5	.7	1.3				Trade Receivables (net)	1.2	1.6
3.1	1.7	3.9				Inventory	3.8	3.1
1.5	1.1	2.7				All Other Current	1.1	2.0
34.8	10.9	16.8				Total Current	14.7	18.7
56.2	76.1	72.1				Fixed Assets (net)	72.1	64.2
4.6	8.3	6.8				Intangibles (net)	5.7	6.5
4.1	4.8	4.3				All Other Non-Current	7.5	10.6
100.0	100.0	100.0				Total	100.0	100.0
						LIABILITIES		
1.7	1.5	4.6				Notes Payable-Short Term	2.9	2.2
3.1	4.8	2.6				Cur. Mat.-L.T.D.	4.4	3.0
4.1	1.4	1.5				Trade Payables	1.5	1.5
.3	.0	.0				Income Taxes Payable	1.0	.1
15.0	2.9	6.5				All Other Current	8.4	11.5
24.1	10.6	15.1				Total Current	18.2	18.4
42.1	49.6	59.1				Long-Term Debt	63.0	55.4
.0	.1	.3				Deferred Taxes	.0	.0
16.3	9.0	8.7				All Other Non-Current	7.3	7.9
17.1	30.8	16.8				Net Worth	11.4	18.4
100.0	100.0	100.0				Total Liabilties & Net Worth	100.0	100.0
						INCOME DATA		
100.0	100.0	100.0				Net Sales	100.0	100.0
						Gross Profit		
89.0	82.8	79.8				Operating Expenses	79.7	83.5
11.0	17.2	20.2				Operating Profit	20.3	16.5
3.4	8.0	9.6				All Other Expenses (net)	10.1	8.5
7.7	9.2	10.6				Profit Before Taxes	10.1	8.1
						RATIOS		
8.5	6.7	3.0					2.6	3.0
1.8	1.7	1.4				Current	.8	1.2
.4	.2	.3					.3	.4
7.5	6.4	2.3					2.2	2.1
1.8	1.7	1.2				Quick	.6	.9
.3	.2	.2					.1	.2
0 UND	0 UND	0 UND					0 UND	0 UND
0 UND	0 UND	0 UND				Sales/Receivables	0 UND	0 UND
0 UND	0 UND	1 484.0					2 183.3	2 231.9
						Cost of Sales/Inventory		
						Cost of Sales/Payables		
11.6	7.6	5.8					9.3	11.1
33.3	22.4	26.9				Sales/Working Capital	-114.3	64.3
-24.9	-6.5	-6.8					-7.0	-10.8
8.7	7.3	5.5					5.7	5.5
(14) 3.6	(24) 1.3	(22) 2.6				EBIT/Interest	(66) 2.4	(69) 2.5
1.0	.9	1.7					1.2	1.0
						Net Profit + Depr., Dep., Amort./Cur. Mat. L/T/D		
.7	1.7	1.5					1.4	1.0
2.2	4.1	5.6				Fixed/Worth	6.4	4.8
-1.9	-111.3	-8.5					-3.7	-7.1
.3	.8	1.0					.9	.8
1.4	3.4	4.6				Debt/Worth	7.7	5.1
-4.6	-115.4	-12.1					-6.2	-11.0
69.2	46.5	57.2					67.4	48.5
(17) 54.1	(22) 11.1	(20) 15.8				% Profit Before Taxes/Tangible Net Worth	(66) 17.9	(67) 13.0
23.5	.3	4.5					3.6	2.6
33.4	7.6	9.9					13.5	13.6
13.5	1.1	4.6				% Profit Before Taxes/Total Assets	4.3	4.7
-.5	-.3	2.0					-.1	-1.0
16.4	1.9	1.1					2.3	3.2
2.8	.8	.8				Sales/Net Fixed Assets	.8	1.0
1.4	.3	.3					.4	.5
5.6	1.1	.9					1.3	1.2
2.1	.6	.5				Sales/Total Assets	.6	.7
1.0	.3	.3					.3	.4
1.8	4.8	7.2					5.2	5.2
(23) 4.9	(27) 14.7	(28) 11.7				% Depr., Dep., Amort./Sales	(87) 10.4	(88) 11.2
9.1	18.4	19.0					18.1	16.5
2.3	5.1						2.7	3.4
(15) 3.5	(10) 10.2					% Officers', Directors' Owners' Comp/Sales	(35) 5.8	(35) 6.3
8.8	14.7						10.8	8.6
12822M	29025M	76561M	52765M		205554M	Net Sales ($)	1183808M	454006M
6160M	35599M	133646M	132552M		225508M	Total Assets ($)	1033571M	702323M

M = $ thousand MM = $ million

See Pages 9 through 22 for Explanation of Ratios and Data

Comparative Historical Data				Current Data Sorted by Sales					
			Type of Statement						
6	6	6	Unqualified	1		1	2	1	1
5	3	4	Reviewed	1	1	1	1		
28	19	15	Compiled	5	7	2	1		
50	60	55	Tax Returns	36	12	5	1		1
44	26	17	Other	9	4	2	2		
4/1/11-3/31/12	4/1/12-3/31/13	4/1/13-3/31/14		6 (4/1-9/30/13)			91 (10/1/13-3/31/14)		
ALL	ALL	ALL		0-1MM	1-3MM	3-5MM	5-10MM	10-25MM	25MM & OVER
133	114	97	**NUMBER OF STATEMENTS**	52	24	11	7	1	2
%	%	%	**ASSETS**	%	%	%	%	%	%
9.3	11.9	13.0	Cash & Equivalents	15.4	11.3	11.6			
1.7	2.0	1.8	Trade Receivables (net)	1.3	1.8	1.5			
1.5	1.2	2.6	Inventory	1.2	2.4	11.9			
1.7	1.6	1.9	All Other Current	1.6	.5	1.7			
14.3	16.8	19.4	Total Current	19.5	15.9	26.7			
70.1	69.5	68.7	Fixed Assets (net)	72.8	69.0	60.8			
7.4	5.5	6.9	Intangibles (net)	4.2	11.4	8.4			
8.2	8.3	4.9	All Other Non-Current	3.4	3.7	4.2			
100.0	100.0	100.0	Total	100.0	100.0	100.0			
			LIABILITIES						
3.3	1.3	3.5	Notes Payable-Short Term	1.6	6.2	6.0			
3.3	4.8	3.3	Cur. Mat.-L.T.D.	4.2	2.6	1.9			
1.7	1.9	2.1	Trade Payables	2.2	1.8	3.0			
.1	.1	.1	Income Taxes Payable	.1	.0	.0			
11.6	12.4	8.3	All Other Current	9.9	4.7	3.7			
20.1	20.6	17.3	Total Current	18.0	15.4	14.7			
60.7	54.2	49.0	Long-Term Debt	57.1	47.7	31.8			
.1	.0	.1	Deferred Taxes	.0	.4	.1			
11.3	6.4	10.7	All Other Non-Current	10.9	4.8	21.6			
7.9	18.8	22.7	Net Worth	13.8	31.7	31.7			
100.0	100.0	100.0	Total Liabilties & Net Worth	100.0	100.0	100.0			
			INCOME DATA						
100.0	100.0	100.0	Net Sales	100.0	100.0	100.0			
			Gross Profit						
84.6	79.7	82.6	Operating Expenses	84.2	79.4	80.1			
15.4	20.3	17.4	Operating Profit	15.8	20.6	19.9			
9.7	8.8	7.5	All Other Expenses (net)	10.0	5.7	2.2			
5.7	11.5	9.8	Profit Before Taxes	5.8	14.9	17.7			
			RATIOS						
2.2	2.6	6.5		3.8	12.5	7.2			
.8	1.3	1.4	Current	.9	1.8	2.7			
.3	.3	.3		.2	.5	1.3			
1.7	2.1	4.1		3.0	10.7	6.2			
(131) .7	.8	1.2	Quick	.8	1.8	2.1			
.2	.2	.2		.1	.3	.3			
0 UND	0 UND	0 UND		0 UND	0 UND	0 UND			
0 UND	0 UND	0 UND	Sales/Receivables	0 UND	0 UND	0 UND			
2 149.2	0 886.4	0 731.5		0 UND	2 178.0	1 280.4			
			Cost of Sales/Inventory						
			Cost of Sales/Payables						
11.6	8.4	7.7		10.7	6.5	3.9			
-37.4	75.5	25.3	Sales/Working Capital	UND	18.5	8.7			
-5.4	-6.1	-7.3		-6.1	-11.8	23.5			
5.0	5.4	6.8		3.1	8.0	18.4			
(95) 1.7	(81) 2.1	(68) 2.4	EBIT/Interest	(34) 1.4	(16) 2.7	(10) 5.8			
.9	1.3	1.1		.9	1.4	3.2			
			Net Profit + Depr., Dep., Amort./Cur. Mat. L/T/D						
1.9	1.3	1.1		1.9	.9	1.1			
16.6	5.0	4.1	Fixed/Worth	9.1	2.5	2.4			
-3.0	-9.5	-7.5		-6.5	-8.1	-8.5			
1.6	1.0	.8		1.2	.2	.6			
21.4	5.4	3.4	Debt/Worth	9.8	2.7	1.9			
-4.7	-11.9	-11.0		-8.2	-14.9	-16.6			
84.1	75.5	62.9		67.2	47.9				
(76) 12.7	(79) 16.3	(67) 18.8	% Profit Before Taxes/Tangible Net Worth	(34) 22.5	(17) 17.0				
1.6	4.7	4.7		-2.8	5.9				
11.0	17.8	13.9		12.9	18.2	40.9			
2.7	4.1	5.3	% Profit Before Taxes/Total Assets	2.5	6.6	9.9			
-1.3	.5	.3		-.9	1.1	5.8			
1.9	2.2	2.6		2.4	2.6	3.6			
.8	.9	1.0	Sales/Net Fixed Assets	.8	1.0	1.5			
.4	.4	.4		.3	.4	.9			
1.1	1.3	1.4		1.7	1.4	1.9			
.6	.6	.7	Sales/Total Assets	.5	.8	1.0			
.3	.3	.3		.3	.3	.7			
4.8	4.9	3.1		4.7	4.5	.7			
(119) 11.8	(99) 9.1	(85) 9.3	% Depr., Dep., Amort./Sales	(45) 14.3	(22) 9.1	(10) 3.2			
18.5	17.4	17.2		18.6	12.5	10.9			
3.3	3.9	3.4		3.0					
(43) 6.2	(37) 8.5	(32) 7.1	% Officers', Directors' Owners' Comp/Sales	(19) 3.9					
10.6	13.0	11.2		13.6					
388276M	195630M	376727M	Net Sales ($)	24171M	38749M	43051M	52358M	12844M	205554M
582633M	323495M	533465M	Total Assets ($)	56289M	75851M	66088M	88961M	20768M	225508M

M = $ thousand MM = $ million

See Pages 9 through 22 for Explanation of Ratios and Data

Current Data Sorted by Assets | **Comparative Historical Data**

0-500M	500M-2MM	2-10MM	10-50MM	50-100MM	100-250MM	Type of Statement	4/1/09-3/31/10 ALL	4/1/10-3/31/11 ALL
	1	5	3			Unqualified	7	7
		5	1			Reviewed	9	7
	2	7	3			Compiled	7	6
5	8	1				Tax Returns	15	16
1	3	5	3		1	Other	14	12
	15 (4/1-9/30/13)		39 (10/1/13-3/31/14)					
6	14	23	10		1	NUMBER OF STATEMENTS	52	48
%	%	%	%	%	%	**ASSETS**	%	%
	15.4	15.8	14.2	DATA NOT AVAILABLE		Cash & Equivalents	9.7	6.3
	1.2	1.5	1.0			Trade Receivables (net)	1.7	1.8
	.4	.3	.8			Inventory	2.0	2.2
	.4	1.7	2.1			All Other Current	2.3	1.6
	17.4	19.4	18.1			Total Current	15.7	11.9
	70.4	62.2	59.5			Fixed Assets (net)	64.7	66.7
	7.4	9.3	2.8			Intangibles (net)	4.8	5.3
	4.8	9.2	19.7			All Other Non-Current	14.8	16.2
	100.0	100.0	100.0			Total	100.0	100.0
						LIABILITIES		
	2.2	.6	1.6			Notes Payable-Short Term	7.7	6.9
	1.5	1.0	2.3			Cur. Mat.-L.T.D.	4.3	5.3
	.8	1.0	1.2			Trade Payables	2.5	1.8
	.0	.6	.0			Income Taxes Payable	.0	.0
	13.2	11.2	5.7			All Other Current	7.1	19.1
	17.8	14.4	10.8			Total Current	21.5	33.0
	35.7	48.3	40.2			Long-Term Debt	34.2	41.7
	.0	.0	1.2			Deferred Taxes	.0	.0
	8.3	7.7	.3			All Other Non-Current	19.1	20.8
	38.2	29.6	47.4			Net Worth	25.1	4.5
	100.0	100.0	100.0			Total Liabilties & Net Worth	100.0	100.0
						INCOME DATA		
	100.0	100.0	100.0			Net Sales	100.0	100.0
						Gross Profit		
	81.6	85.8	87.7			Operating Expenses	91.9	90.8
	18.4	14.2	12.3			Operating Profit	8.1	9.2
	8.7	4.7	11.2			All Other Expenses (net)	3.6	3.7
	9.7	9.5	1.1			Profit Before Taxes	4.5	5.5
						RATIOS		
	4.0	5.2	3.8				1.6	1.0
	.7	1.7	1.2			Current	.5	.3
	.4	.9	.6				.1	.1
	4.0	5.2	3.4				1.2	.6
	.5	1.3	1.2			Quick	.3	.1
	.2	.4	.4				.1	.0
	0 UND	0 UND	0 UND				0 UND	0 UND
	0 UND	1 254.4	1 595.8			Sales/Receivables	0 UND	0 UND
	3 131.2	7 51.7	5 66.9				3 104.5	5 76.2
						Cost of Sales/Inventory		
						Cost of Sales/Payables		
	26.4	4.0	5.5				12.9	NM
	-20.2	13.3	17.5			Sales/Working Capital	-21.0	-13.6
	-8.8	-73.0	-16.9				-8.0	-4.0
		13.2					9.1	4.1
		(20) 5.0				EBIT/Interest	(39) 2.9	(39) 1.8
		1.3					1.2	.7
						Net Profit + Depr., Dep., Amort./Cur. Mat. L/T/D		
	1.2	.6	.8				1.1	1.5
	3.4	7.0	1.4			Fixed/Worth	2.6	5.4
	21.1	-3.0	-8.9				-12.8	-6.7
	.5	.6	.0				.8	1.0
	3.1	6.7	.7			Debt/Worth	2.9	8.7
	30.9	-5.3	-35.6				-15.1	-8.1
	38.3	49.3					25.2	29.7
	(12) 24.8	(15) 6.0				% Profit Before Taxes/Tangible Net Worth	(36) 10.8	(30) 5.9
	-3.6	.4					.0	-1.9
	16.7	11.4	12.9				12.4	5.0
	6.3	6.0	3.2			% Profit Before Taxes/Total Assets	3.0	2.3
	-3.6	.3	-1.6				-.6	-1.5
	2.4	2.4	4.2				4.3	3.5
	1.0	.9	.4			Sales/Net Fixed Assets	1.4	1.4
	.3	.6	.2				.7	.6
	1.7	1.0	1.1				1.4	1.8
	.5	.7	.3			Sales/Total Assets	.9	.8
	.3	.4	.2				.5	.5
	4.9	5.0					3.4	4.3
	(11) 8.7	(20) 6.9				% Depr., Dep., Amort./Sales	(47) 5.1	(42) 5.9
	20.4	9.8					7.9	9.1
							2.7	2.0
						% Officers', Directors' Owners' Comp/Sales	(20) 7.7	(16) 4.0
							12.5	8.9
2447M	17943M	108084M	119661M		65486M	Net Sales ($)	175470M	164136M
1242M	17196M	110984M	211540M		115329M	Total Assets ($)	206861M	198926M

M = $ thousand MM = $ million

See Pages 9 through 22 for Explanation of Ratios and Data

Comparative Historical Data				Current Data Sorted by Sales					
			Type of Statement						
10	6	9	Unqualified	1	1	2	3		2
3	5	6	Reviewed		2	1	2	1	
6	5	12	Compiled	2	7	1	1	1	
17	17	14	Tax Returns	10	3	1			
15	19	13	Other	2	5	3	1		2
4/1/11-3/31/12	4/1/12-3/31/13	4/1/13-3/31/14			15 (4/1-9/30/13)		39 (10/1/13-3/31/14)		
ALL	ALL	ALL		0-1MM	1-3MM	3-5MM	5-10MM	10-25MM	25MM & OVER
51	52	54	**NUMBER OF STATEMENTS**	15	18	8	7	2	4
%	%	%	**ASSETS**	%	%	%	%	%	%
13.4	17.7	15.3	Cash & Equivalents	13.5	11.0				
2.2	1.4	1.3	Trade Receivables (net)	1.3	.8				
.6	.6	.7	Inventory	.6	.9				
3.7	1.7	1.6	All Other Current	.5	2.2				
19.8	21.3	18.9	Total Current	15.9	14.9				
63.7	59.9	62.0	Fixed Assets (net)	73.3	63.9				
7.4	9.8	8.5	Intangibles (net)	4.0	12.6				
9.1	9.0	10.6	All Other Non-Current	6.8	8.6				
100.0	100.0	100.0	Total	100.0	100.0				
			LIABILITIES						
4.6	2.0	2.3	Notes Payable-Short Term	5.0	1.5				
4.0	2.6	1.8	Cur. Mat.-L.T.D.	2.9	1.0				
1.5	1.2	1.0	Trade Payables	.8	1.1				
.0	.0	.2	Income Taxes Payable	.0	.0				
13.1	11.2	26.9	All Other Current	32.7	34.5				
23.2	17.1	32.3	Total Current	41.3	38.1				
40.7	44.6	47.5	Long-Term Debt	68.7	47.1				
.0	.0	.2	Deferred Taxes	.0	.1				
8.3	5.2	8.1	All Other Non-Current	13.6	6.8				
27.8	33.1	11.8	Net Worth	-23.7	8.0				
100.0	100.0	100.0	Total Liabilties & Net Worth	100.0	100.0				
			INCOME DATA						
100.0	100.0	100.0	Net Sales	100.0	100.0				
			Gross Profit						
87.5	87.8	86.6	Operating Expenses	79.1	89.2				
12.5	12.2	13.4	Operating Profit	20.9	10.8				
4.1	3.4	6.9	All Other Expenses (net)	13.1	3.8				
8.3	8.8	6.6	Profit Before Taxes	7.8	7.0				
			RATIOS						
2.5	3.8	4.1		3.8	4.5				
.8	1.2	1.2	Current	1.0	1.6				
.2	.3	.4		.5	.2				
2.2	3.5	4.0		3.8	4.5				
.5	.9	.9	Quick	.6	1.5				
.2	.2	.3		.2	.2				
0 UND	0 UND	0 UND		0 UND	0 UND				
0 999.8	0 UND	0 999.8	Sales/Receivables	0 UND	1 271.6				
8 45.2	5 77.0	4 91.5		3 138.0	4 91.4				
			Cost of Sales/Inventory						
			Cost of Sales/Payables						
12.3	5.9	6.5		8.4	5.3				
-34.8	98.3	40.2	Sales/Working Capital	-24.8	36.0				
-6.3	-6.7	-8.8		-10.9	-6.7				
6.5	5.8	11.7			9.6				
(39) 2.6	(41) 2.6	(40) 4.3	EBIT/Interest		(15) 4.5				
1.2	.8	.1			1.4				
			Net Profit + Depr., Dep., Amort./Cur. Mat. L/T/D						
1.1	.7	.9		2.6	.9				
2.9	1.5	4.5	Fixed/Worth	14.3	2.3				
-4.0	-4.1	-3.1		-.5	-3.3				
.4	.3	.5		1.7	1.2				
3.0	1.1	4.5	Debt/Worth	14.1	3.1				
-6.1	-5.3	-5.3		-2.5	-4.4				
25.9	30.0	31.5		39.5	40.2				
(35) 10.5	(36) 9.7	(35) 4.2	% Profit Before Taxes/Tangible Net Worth	(10) 14.6	(12) 12.6				
.7	-.3	.0		-7.0	.6				
7.2	14.0	11.5		6.4	10.3				
3.8	5.1	3.2	% Profit Before Taxes/Total Assets	.0	4.4				
.6	.5	-3.5		-4.6	.2				
3.2	4.3	2.9		2.1	1.9				
1.3	1.3	1.0	Sales/Net Fixed Assets	.5	1.2				
.6	.7	.4		.2	.7				
1.4	1.6	1.3		.9	1.3				
.7	.8	.7	Sales/Total Assets	.4	.7				
.4	.4	.3		.2	.4				
3.7	4.0	4.8		4.9	4.6				
(44) 6.0	(39) 6.3	(44) 7.1	% Depr., Dep., Amort./Sales	11.8	(14) 6.7				
9.1	9.7	12.4		20.4	9.3				
3.1	2.8	2.5							
(15) 4.8	(17) 4.1	(13) 5.1	% Officers', Directors' Owners' Comp/Sales						
13.0	6.8	9.1							
232788M	246688M	313621M	Net Sales ($)	5800M	33434M	31179M	48420M	26436M	168352M
351539M	261874M	456291M	Total Assets ($)	23759M	60406M	54779M	141742M	27779M	147826M

M = $ thousand MM = $ million

See Pages 9 through 22 for Explanation of Ratios and Data

Current Data Sorted by Assets							Comparative Historical Data	
						Type of Statement		
	2		5			Unqualified	7	4
						Reviewed		1
	1	1		1		Compiled	3	2
4	3	3				Tax Returns	3	12
2	1	1	2			Other	2	3
	18 (4/1-9/30/13)		8 (10/1/13-3/31/14)				4/1/09-3/31/10	4/1/10-3/31/11
0-500M	**500M-2MM**	**2-10MM**	**10-50MM**	**50-100MM**	**100-250MM**		**ALL**	**ALL**
6	7	5	7	1		**NUMBER OF STATEMENTS**	15	22
%	%	%	%	%	%	**ASSETS**	%	%
					DATA NOT AVAILABLE	Cash & Equivalents	17.3	15.9
						Trade Receivables (net)	1.9	.7
						Inventory	.4	1.6
						All Other Current	.8	.5
						Total Current	20.5	18.7
						Fixed Assets (net)	65.4	71.1
						Intangibles (net)	3.1	3.2
						All Other Non-Current	11.0	7.0
						Total	100.0	100.0
						LIABILITIES		
						Notes Payable-Short Term	.9	3.3
						Cur. Mat.-L.T.D.	3.2	1.9
						Trade Payables	3.6	2.8
						Income Taxes Payable	.0	.0
						All Other Current	3.8	2.9
						Total Current	11.5	11.0
						Long-Term Debt	43.2	49.1
						Deferred Taxes	.0	.0
						All Other Non-Current	1.4	4.5
						Net Worth	43.9	35.4
						Total Liabilities & Net Worth	100.0	100.0
						INCOME DATA		
						Net Sales	100.0	100.0
						Gross Profit		
						Operating Expenses	95.3	84.4
						Operating Profit	4.7	15.6
						All Other Expenses (net)	8.7	10.4
						Profit Before Taxes	-4.0	5.2
						RATIOS		
							3.4	4.7
						Current	2.7	1.9
							.9	.6
							3.4	3.5
						Quick	2.0	1.4
							.7	.5
							0 UND	0 UND
						Sales/Receivables	0 UND	0 UND
							18 20.5	7 50.0
						Cost of Sales/Inventory		
						Cost of Sales/Payables		
							2.0	4.7
						Sales/Working Capital	12.9	11.8
							-316.0	-8.0
								6.5
						EBIT/Interest		(14) 1.9
								.2
						Net Profit + Depr., Dep., Amort./Cur. Mat. L/T/D		
							.9	.9
						Fixed/Worth	1.7	2.0
							6.1	NM
							.2	.4
						Debt/Worth	.8	1.2
							5.6	NM
							3.5	24.4
						% Profit Before Taxes/Tangible Net Worth	(12) -4.0	(17) 3.6
							-12.6	-2.3
							3.6	10.5
						% Profit Before Taxes/Total Assets	-2.0	2.0
							-8.9	-1.8
							1.2	.8
						Sales/Net Fixed Assets	.8	.4
							.2	.2
							.6	.7
						Sales/Total Assets	.3	.3
							.2	.2
							7.3	7.3
						% Depr., Dep., Amort./Sales	(11) 10.4	(16) 13.2
							17.9	20.2
						% Officers', Directors' Owners' Comp/Sales		
1532M	8138M	9766M	49108M	5015M		Net Sales ($)	45404M	41919M
1652M	9025M	20091M	143669M	99240M		Total Assets ($)	136878M	150366M

M = $ thousand MM = $ million

See Pages 9 through 22 for Explanation of Ratios and Data

Comparative Historical Data				Current Data Sorted by Sales					
			Type of Statement						
5	12	7	Unqualified		3	2	1		1
1	2		Reviewed						
4	3	3	Compiled	2			1		
10	10	10	Tax Returns	9			1		
10	10	6	Other	3	2	1	1		
4/1/11-3/31/12 ALL	**4/1/12-3/31/13 ALL**	**4/1/13-3/31/14 ALL**		**18 (4/1-9/30/13)**			**8 (10/1/13-3/31/14)**		
				0-1MM	**1-3MM**	**3-5MM**	**5-10MM**	**10-25MM**	**25MM & OVER**
30	37	26	**NUMBER OF STATEMENTS**	14	5	3	3		1
%	%	%	**ASSETS**	%	%	%	%	%	%
20.1	15.2	24.3	Cash & Equivalents	18.8				DATA NOT AVAILABLE	
.8	3.0	6.5	Trade Receivables (net)	7.4					
1.2	1.0	1.8	Inventory	.0					
.7	2.5	1.6	All Other Current	.5					
22.8	21.7	34.2	Total Current	26.7					
67.6	74.2	58.1	Fixed Assets (net)	66.6					
.9	.8	1.4	Intangibles (net)	2.1					
8.7	3.3	6.4	All Other Non-Current	4.5					
100.0	100.0	100.0	Total	100.0					
			LIABILITIES						
2.2	1.2	.5	Notes Payable-Short Term	.3					
1.6	2.1	1.8	Cur. Mat.-L.T.D.	1.3					
1.4	2.6	1.9	Trade Payables	.1					
.0	.0	.0	Income Taxes Payable	.0					
25.2	6.0	12.5	All Other Current	17.9					
30.4	11.9	16.7	Total Current	19.6					
51.6	53.1	34.8	Long-Term Debt	34.6					
.0	.0	.0	Deferred Taxes	.0					
3.4	2.5	3.3	All Other Non-Current	1.3					
14.7	32.5	45.3	Net Worth	44.4					
100.0	100.0	100.0	Total Liabilties & Net Worth	100.0					
			INCOME DATA						
100.0	100.0	100.0	Net Sales	100.0					
			Gross Profit						
86.2	74.6	80.4	Operating Expenses	82.6					
13.8	25.4	19.6	Operating Profit	17.4					
9.6	12.6	8.4	All Other Expenses (net)	9.1					
4.2	12.8	11.2	Profit Before Taxes	8.2					
			RATIOS						
5.4	7.2	9.8		38.3					
1.5	2.4	3.4	Current	2.9					
.2	.8	1.4		.8					
5.3	6.2	9.8		38.3					
1.1	1.8	3.3	Quick	2.9					
.2	.5	1.1		.6					
0 UND	0 UND	0 UND		0 UND					
0 UND	0 UND	0 UND	Sales/Receivables	0 UND					
5 75.7	20 18.7	19 19.2		76 4.8					
			Cost of Sales/Inventory						
			Cost of Sales/Payables						
3.2	2.2	.9		1.7					
17.8	4.8	2.7	Sales/Working Capital	5.3					
-2.9	-20.6	17.9		-11.8					
2.9	3.9	11.2							
(15) 1.7	(22) 2.2	(11) 5.8	EBIT/Interest						
.5	1.3	1.8							
			Net Profit + Depr., Dep., Amort./Cur. Mat. L/T/D						
1.8	1.2	.5		.7					
4.6	2.5	1.4	Fixed/Worth	1.5					
-50.2	7.6	3.3		3.3					
1.6	1.1	.5		.5					
4.1	2.1	1.0	Debt/Worth	1.0					
-64.8	7.9	3.0		3.0					
21.1	23.9	14.8		17.6					
(22) 11.7	(32) 10.9	(23) 8.3	% Profit Before Taxes/Tangible Net Worth	(13) 6.4					
-3.2	4.4	-.8		-11.3					
6.3	8.1	9.7		12.3					
1.2	4.1	2.8	% Profit Before Taxes/Total Assets	1.8					
-2.4	.6	-.7		-3.3					
3.0	.7	5.2		2.3					
.5	.3	.4	Sales/Net Fixed Assets	.3					
.3	.2	.2		.2					
.8	.5	.8		.5					
.3	.2	.2	Sales/Total Assets	.2					
.1	.1	.1		.2					
4.0	6.3	7.8							
(24) 9.3	(28) 11.2	(17) 16.7	% Depr., Dep., Amort./Sales						
19.2	19.2	22.8							
			% Officers', Directors' Owners' Comp/Sales						
47092M	125197M	73559M	Net Sales ($)	4231M	10149M	12897M	19936M		26346M
245739M	311389M	273677M	Total Assets ($)	16644M	41824M	73501M	131224M		10484M

M = $ thousand MM = $ million

See Pages 9 through 22 for Explanation of Ratios and Data

Current Data Sorted by Assets / Comparative Historical Data

	20 (4/1-9/30/13)		165 (10/1/13-3/31/14)				Comparative Historical Data	
Type of Statement								
Unqualified	2	1	5	9	1	2	12	13
Reviewed	1		9	1	1		10	22
Compiled	3	8	9	3	1	2	16	17
Tax Returns	27	16	13				30	33
Other	14	21	21	8	2	5	36	40
	0-500M	**500M-2MM**	**2-10MM**	**10-50MM**	**50-100MM**	**100-250MM**	**4/1/09-3/31/10 ALL**	**4/1/10-3/31/11 ALL**
NUMBER OF STATEMENTS	47	46	57	21	5	9	104	125
ASSETS	%	%	%	%	%	%	%	%
Cash & Equivalents	33.6	11.0	12.3	9.7			12.6	13.6
Trade Receivables (net)	3.2	18.1	17.4	24.3			20.3	22.9
Inventory	7.1	7.5	10.8	13.2			8.1	8.7
All Other Current	1.9	3.6	3.6	2.3			4.5	4.8
Total Current	45.7	40.2	44.1	49.5			45.5	50.1
Fixed Assets (net)	32.4	36.6	34.1	31.2			35.7	31.4
Intangibles (net)	13.1	7.1	10.9	11.4			7.9	8.2
All Other Non-Current	8.8	16.1	10.9	7.9			10.9	10.3
Total	100.0	100.0	100.0	100.0			100.0	100.0
LIABILITIES								
Notes Payable-Short Term	13.0	9.0	5.4	7.1			12.3	13.2
Cur. Mat.-L.T.D.	2.8	4.2	4.0	5.4			3.9	3.6
Trade Payables	7.7	18.1	13.9	15.2			14.5	16.5
Income Taxes Payable	.2	.3	.1	.0			.1	1.3
All Other Current	36.8	14.3	15.9	12.5			18.8	17.2
Total Current	60.4	45.9	39.3	40.2			49.6	51.8
Long-Term Debt	24.6	25.0	24.5	23.1			28.9	20.7
Deferred Taxes	.0	.0	.0	.7			.3	.1
All Other Non-Current	11.0	9.5	11.1	8.8			11.0	14.7
Net Worth	3.9	19.6	25.1	27.2			10.1	12.7
Total Liabilities & Net Worth	100.0	100.0	100.0	100.0			100.0	100.0
INCOME DATA								
Net Sales	100.0	100.0	100.0	100.0			100.0	100.0
Gross Profit								
Operating Expenses	92.9	92.4	94.7	91.9			92.8	95.7
Operating Profit	7.1	7.6	5.3	8.1			7.2	4.3
All Other Expenses (net)	.5	3.9	1.8	.7			2.4	1.7
Profit Before Taxes	6.6	3.7	3.5	7.4			4.7	2.7
RATIOS								
Current	2.9	1.4	1.8	2.0			1.8	2.0
	1.4	.9	1.0	1.1			1.1	1.2
	.4	.3	.5	.7			.6	.7
Quick	1.8	1.2	1.5	1.2			1.2	1.5
	1.1	.7	.7	.8			.8	(124) .8
	.2	.2	.3	.4			.4	.4
Sales/Receivables	0 UND	0 UND	0 999.8	8 44.7			0 999.8	0 UND
	0 UND	6 56.9	13 27.2	25 14.4			16 22.4	15 24.2
	0 999.8	17 22.1	30 12.3	35 10.3			32 11.5	30 12.0
Cost of Sales/Inventory								
Cost of Sales/Payables								
Sales/Working Capital	16.2	25.9	16.9	9.5			17.0	15.2
	80.3	-282.8	312.8	60.1			125.5	90.8
	-20.7	-13.6	-15.7	-19.1			-14.3	-20.5
EBIT/Interest	23.9	11.9	22.8	15.1			15.8	13.1
	(21) 7.8	(35) 4.8	(51) 5.1	(19) 4.4			(88) 3.7	(110) 4.6
	1.3	-.5	1.7	1.9			.5	.7
Net Profit + Depr., Dep., Amort./Cur. Mat. L/T/D							7.0	4.4
							(14) 2.8	(20) 3.2
							.3	.8
Fixed/Worth	.1	.4	.5	.4			.3	.5
	.8	2.0	2.2	2.4			2.6	1.6
	-1.2	-5.2	-2.5	8.4			-2.0	-2.0
Debt/Worth	.3	1.0	1.4	1.5			1.6	1.3
	1.4	3.6	4.0	2.9			7.0	5.9
	-2.4	-12.3	-10.1	26.2			-4.7	-5.5
% Profit Before Taxes/Tangible Net Worth	174.6	85.1	46.2	55.1			98.7	65.7
	(31) 71.9	(31) 26.8	(37) 24.7	(17) 22.3			(67) 40.9	(80) 20.1
	15.8	2.3	7.7	8.4			6.1	-3.9
% Profit Before Taxes/Total Assets	48.7	25.1	15.3	19.1			22.3	18.2
	18.6	5.6	5.6	4.7			6.9	6.9
	-1.1	-3.2	1.7	2.4			.3	-.7
Sales/Net Fixed Assets	129.2	50.6	41.4	27.3			36.4	71.1
	30.0	15.6	13.2	11.3			12.4	19.4
	7.0	5.7	4.1	4.2			4.5	6.2
Sales/Total Assets	8.1	6.8	5.0	4.5			5.9	6.3
	4.5	3.9	3.0	2.5			3.2	4.1
	2.3	1.9	1.5	1.4			2.0	2.2
% Depr., Dep., Amort./Sales	.5	1.0	.3	1.0			.8	.5
	(24) 1.0	(29) 2.4	(49) 1.3	(19) 1.7			(88) 1.8	(101) 1.6
	4.1	3.9	4.1	4.6			3.2	3.5
% Officers', Directors' Owners' Comp/Sales	2.1	1.8	1.4				1.8	1.2
	(21) 5.5	(20) 2.5	(16) 2.0				(33) 3.4	(51) 2.9
	7.0	4.9	4.8				7.6	9.2
Net Sales ($)	59321M	232125M	1054552M	1821954M	783366M	3209697M	3030712M	4451659M
Total Assets ($)	11070M	52195M	295467M	500356M	332612M	1651429M	1438213M	1117949M

M = $ thousand MM = $ million

See Pages 9 through 22 for Explanation of Ratios and Data

Comparative Historical Data				Current Data Sorted by Sales					
			Type of Statement						
19	20	20	Unqualified		3		2	2	13
21	12	12	Reviewed		1	1	1	4	5
25	15	26	Compiled	2	5		6	6	7
52	46	56	Tax Returns	19	14	11	7	5	
61	68	71	Other	11	14	5	11	12	18
4/1/11-3/31/12 ALL	4/1/12-3/31/13 ALL	4/1/13-3/31/14 ALL		20 (4/1-9/30/13)			165 (10/1/13-3/31/14)		
				0-1MM	1-3MM	3-5MM	5-10MM	10-25MM	25MM & OVER
178	161	185	**NUMBER OF STATEMENTS**	32	37	17	27	29	43
%	%	%	**ASSETS**	%	%	%	%	%	%
12.2	16.3	16.7	Cash & Equivalents	22.3	24.5	19.5	9.1	15.9	10.1
19.2	16.4	14.8	Trade Receivables (net)	1.4	4.7	13.4	19.6	18.7	28.6
8.3	10.0	9.3	Inventory	8.1	4.4	8.2	4.4	17.8	12.1
4.2	2.2	3.0	All Other Current	.3	8.3	.2	.7	3.0	3.0
43.8	44.9	43.8	Total Current	32.0	41.9	41.4	33.8	55.4	53.7
33.8	32.6	32.9	Fixed Assets (net)	40.7	39.0	37.8	40.5	20.0	23.7
9.7	11.6	11.9	Intangibles (net)	17.9	4.8	4.6	12.9	13.7	14.7
12.6	10.9	11.4	All Other Non-Current	9.4	14.3	16.3	12.7	10.9	7.9
100.0	100.0	100.0	Total	100.0	100.0	100.0	100.0	100.0	100.0
			LIABILITIES						
9.3	10.7	8.6	Notes Payable-Short Term	9.1	8.4	18.6	7.1	7.5	6.3
4.7	3.5	3.7	Cur. Mat.-L.T.D.	2.9	3.3	5.0	4.4	3.5	3.7
15.3	14.3	13.4	Trade Payables	4.7	9.9	15.1	17.5	17.3	16.9
.2	1.0	.2	Income Taxes Payable	.2	.1	.0	.6	.1	.1
15.8	17.0	20.3	All Other Current	37.3	20.0	12.9	21.9	14.2	14.1
45.3	46.5	46.2	Total Current	54.2	41.6	51.5	51.5	42.6	41.1
22.4	29.4	24.4	Long-Term Debt	32.3	30.1	27.6	23.3	17.4	17.6
.2	.1	.2	Deferred Taxes	.0	.0	.0	.0	.0	.9
10.3	17.0	10.6	All Other Non-Current	7.5	14.9	8.8	6.6	11.3	12.2
21.8	7.0	18.6	Net Worth	6.0	13.4	12.1	18.6	28.7	28.2
100.0	100.0	100.0	Total Liabilties & Net Worth	100.0	100.0	100.0	100.0	100.0	100.0
			INCOME DATA						
100.0	100.0	100.0	Net Sales	100.0	100.0	100.0	100.0	100.0	100.0
			Gross Profit						
95.1	92.4	93.4	Operating Expenses	80.1	95.4	96.3	98.4	94.8	96.6
4.9	7.6	6.6	Operating Profit	19.9	4.6	3.7	1.6	5.2	3.5
1.9	2.3	1.8	All Other Expenses (net)	5.8	2.0	.3	.3	1.1	.8
3.1	5.3	4.7	Profit Before Taxes	14.0	2.6	3.4	1.3	4.1	2.6
			RATIOS						
1.8	1.7	2.0		3.8	2.9	1.6	1.1	1.7	2.2
1.1	1.0	1.0	Current	1.0	1.1	1.0	.8	1.2	1.3
.4	.5	.5		.2	.5	.4	.3	.9	.7
1.2	1.4	1.5		1.8	1.8	1.3	1.1	1.3	1.6
.7	.7	.8	Quick	.3	1.1	.7	.6	.8	.9
.2	.3	.3		.1	.1	.3	.2	.5	.5
0 UND	**0** UND	**0** UND		**0** UND	**0** UND	**0** UND	**0** 999.8	**1** 279.5	**14** 26.5
8 48.3	**6** 63.5	**6** 60.1	Sales/Receivables	**0** UND	**0** UND	**1** 534.1	**9** 41.7	**13** 27.2	**30** 12.0
29 12.7	**26** 13.9	**26** 13.8		**0** UND	**4** 101.1	**20** 18.2	**42** 8.7	**26** 14.2	**37** 9.9
			Cost of Sales/Inventory						
			Cost of Sales/Payables						
19.1	20.2	17.8		12.9	14.3	36.2	88.2	16.9	11.4
136.7	710.7	209.7	Sales/Working Capital	330.3	223.0	312.8	-19.4	48.4	34.5
-17.5	-17.9	-15.5		-2.7	-13.2	-21.9	-8.3	-337.1	-31.2
14.9	24.3	17.1		27.0	9.7	12.3	12.9	19.5	30.1
(139) 4.0	(124) 6.9	(138) 5.1	EBIT/Interest	(13) 6.1	(23) 3.0	(13) 5.2	(23) 2.2	(26) 7.9	(40) 7.2
1.1	1.1	1.2		1.8	.2	.4	-10.9	2.9	1.6
7.0	6.2	4.1							3.9
(28) 2.4	(15) 1.8	(19) 2.1	Net Profit + Depr., Dep., Amort./Cur. Mat. L/T/D						(12) 2.1
1.4	.8	1.2							1.3
.4	.3	.4		.1	.2	.4	.9	.2	.3
1.6	2.0	1.8	Fixed/Worth	2.0	1.3	.8	3.2	.9	1.4
-6.0	-2.7	-2.8		-1.5	-26.5	NM	-1.7	-2.9	-2.8
1.2	1.2	1.0		.4	.7	.5	1.6	1.0	1.2
4.0	6.4	3.4	Debt/Worth	5.0	1.5	3.3	7.2	4.3	3.0
-18.1	-4.5	-6.4		-1.8	-39.2	NM	-4.4	-11.6	-8.2
69.7	111.5	78.8		93.2	79.1	226.0	157.3	86.0	52.9
(124) 25.7	(101) 46.4	(123) 32.6	% Profit Before Taxes/Tangible Net Worth	(20) 26.6	(27) 37.7	(13) 25.4	(16) 40.4	(17) 27.0	(30) 31.5
1.7	15.1	7.2		5.8	-6.4	9.4	9.9	8.9	6.0
22.6	32.5	23.9		30.2	36.5	48.7	11.4	23.7	19.9
8.3	11.1	6.6	% Profit Before Taxes/Total Assets	3.8	14.4	11.4	3.2	8.8	6.4
.2	2.1	.4		.1	-6.1	2.0	-8.6	2.6	2.0
76.1	72.0	52.2		98.7	49.5	50.8	23.5	55.4	95.9
15.2	20.6	17.2	Sales/Net Fixed Assets	10.5	16.0	13.1	10.7	26.2	19.4
5.0	5.4	5.1		2.9	4.3	5.0	3.3	15.5	5.9
6.0	6.2	5.9		4.3	5.9	7.6	5.9	6.0	5.4
3.9	3.7	3.2	Sales/Total Assets	2.1	3.0	5.0	3.6	4.0	3.7
2.0	2.1	1.8		.8	1.9	1.7	1.2	2.8	2.0
.6	.6	.6		2.6	.8	.6	1.8	.3	.3
(140) 1.7	(116) 1.5	(129) 1.7	% Depr., Dep., Amort./Sales	(16) 7.6	(24) 1.8	(11) 1.2	(18) 3.2	(25) 1.0	(35) 1.3
3.5	3.0	4.1		14.0	3.5	3.4	6.0	2.3	2.5
1.5	1.7	1.6			2.9	1.3			
(61) 3.7	(60) 3.5	(61) 2.8	% Officers', Directors' Owners' Comp/Sales		(14) 6.6	(13) 2.2			
7.9	5.6	6.0			7.0	4.8			
7092985M	**4737315M**	**7161015M**	Net Sales ($)	**15776M**	**66379M**	**65562M**	**190261M**	**490357M**	**6332680M**
2122532M	**2097340M**	**2843129M**	Total Assets ($)	**32770M**	**27953M**	**21300M**	**100523M**	**152668M**	**2507915M**

M = $ thousand MM = $ million

See Pages 9 through 22 for Explanation of Ratios and Data

Current Data Sorted by Assets | Comparative Historical Data

0-500M	500M-2MM	2-10MM	10-50MM	50-100MM	100-250MM	Type of Statement	4/1/09-3/31/10 ALL	4/1/10-3/31/11 ALL
	1					Unqualified	7	3
	1	4	2			Reviewed	13	12
5	5	7	2			Compiled	31	26
30	18	10	1	1		Tax Returns	70	62
11	14	16	3	1		Other	37	40
19 (4/1-9/30/13)			113 (10/1/13-3/31/14)					
46	39	37	8	2		NUMBER OF STATEMENTS	158	143
%	%	%	%	%	%	**ASSETS**	%	%
29.1	26.9	11.0			DATA NOT AVAILABLE	Cash & Equivalents	15.1	16.6
10.8	13.8	11.4				Trade Receivables (net)	8.5	14.0
5.8	5.7	2.0				Inventory	6.3	5.8
2.9	1.8	1.6				All Other Current	2.6	2.5
48.6	48.2	26.0				Total Current	32.5	38.9
31.7	32.1	58.1				Fixed Assets (net)	46.2	41.2
5.2	5.5	6.2				Intangibles (net)	8.8	7.5
14.5	14.2	9.7				All Other Non-Current	12.5	12.4
100.0	100.0	100.0				Total	100.0	100.0
						LIABILITIES		
10.9	4.9	4.2				Notes Payable-Short Term	9.3	6.9
5.0	3.1	1.7				Cur. Mat.-L.T.D.	5.0	5.2
8.2	15.0	7.7				Trade Payables	10.6	13.8
.0	.2	.3				Income Taxes Payable	.1	.2
35.0	20.7	18.4				All Other Current	29.9	22.3
59.1	43.9	32.4				Total Current	55.0	48.4
24.4	32.0	38.2				Long-Term Debt	33.0	30.8
.0	.0	.1				Deferred Taxes	.0	.0
9.5	8.6	11.4				All Other Non-Current	14.2	10.8
6.9	15.6	18.0				Net Worth	-2.2	10.1
100.0	100.0	100.0				Total Liabilities & Net Worth	100.0	100.0
						INCOME DATA		
100.0	100.0	100.0				Net Sales	100.0	100.0
						Gross Profit		
93.5	91.3	86.5				Operating Expenses	92.9	93.0
6.5	8.7	13.5				Operating Profit	7.1	7.0
.0	.9	4.0				All Other Expenses (net)	3.3	2.6
6.5	7.8	9.5				Profit Before Taxes	3.8	4.4
						RATIOS		
2.8	3.2	1.1					1.3	1.6
1.2	1.3	.7				Current	.6	.9
.3	.6	.2					.2	.3
2.5	2.4	.8					.9	1.4
.8	1.1	.4				Quick	.5	(142) .6
.2	.5	.2					.1	.2
0 UND	0 UND	0 UND					0 UND	0 UND
0 UND	3 117.2	4 104.0				Sales/Receivables	2 225.5	2 155.0
9 41.1	23 16.2	20 17.9					15 24.3	18 19.7
						Cost of Sales/Inventory		
						Cost of Sales/Payables		
12.4	11.2	91.8					60.1	21.0
98.2	96.0	-11.0				Sales/Working Capital	-35.6	-107.2
-12.6	-15.0	-4.9					-7.0	-10.3
33.7	29.8	22.7					8.5	13.4
(22) 11.0	(26) 7.4	(31) 5.3				EBIT/Interest	(115) 2.4	(100) 3.6
3.4	2.4	1.1					.1	.9
							4.5	5.6
						Net Profit + Depr., Dep., Amort./Cur. Mat. L/T/D	(16) 2.3	(12) 1.8
							1.3	1.1
.1	.1	1.5					.9	.5
.6	1.0	3.3				Fixed/Worth	3.5	2.4
-1.9	-6.3	-6.3					-3.4	-3.8
.4	.7	2.1					1.8	1.1
3.2	5.1	4.0				Debt/Worth	8.3	4.3
-2.9	-13.0	-7.9					-5.4	-5.2
106.0	108.9	98.9					92.2	79.0
(28) 73.7	(23) 32.9	(24) 44.1				% Profit Before Taxes/Tangible Net Worth	(95) 34.4	(94) 33.7
25.8	8.5	9.0					5.1	10.0
57.5	32.6	19.5					19.5	23.1
21.9	9.6	4.5				% Profit Before Taxes/Total Assets	3.9	7.1
-2.2	.5	.7					-2.3	.2
140.7	198.0	7.4					30.2	38.4
34.0	9.3	1.9				Sales/Net Fixed Assets	7.9	12.2
12.0	3.5	.9					2.5	3.7
9.7	4.7	2.1					6.3	6.7
6.5	3.1	1.0				Sales/Total Assets	2.8	3.7
3.3	1.6	.7					1.4	1.7
.5	1.2	1.1					1.5	1.1
(27) 1.3	(23) 1.9	(32) 3.6				% Depr., Dep., Amort./Sales	(130) 2.1	(122) 2.2
2.7	3.3	8.4					4.4	5.4
3.2	1.8	2.2					2.4	2.7
(23) 5.7	(16) 2.8	(15) 4.8				% Officers', Directors' Owners' Comp/Sales	(73) 4.8	(60) 4.4
10.0	5.4	12.0					8.7	7.4
60563M	137685M	263618M	361665M	1054967M		Net Sales ($)	3364442M	1763016M
9761M	42606M	158338M	127776M	161916M		Total Assets ($)	1120677M	615116M

M = $ thousand MM = $ million

See Pages 9 through 22 for Explanation of Ratios and Data

Comparative Historical Data				Current Data Sorted by Sales					
			Type of Statement						
4	4	1	Unqualified			1			
13	8	7	Reviewed				2	4	1
27	16	19	Compiled	3	9	1	5		1
58	80	60	Tax Returns	20	19	9	10	1	1
35	56	45	Other	8	16	7	6	3	5
4/1/11-3/31/12 ALL	4/1/12-3/31/13 ALL	4/1/13-3/31/14 ALL		19 (4/1-9/30/13)			113 (10/1/13-3/31/14)		
				0-1MM	1-3MM	3-5MM	5-10MM	10-25MM	25MM & OVER
137	164	132	**NUMBER OF STATEMENTS**	31	44	18	23	8	8
%	%	%	**ASSETS**	%	%	%	%	%	%
19.1	19.6	22.9	Cash & Equivalents	21.8	24.1	27.6	17.8		
12.0	9.7	12.4	Trade Receivables (net)	4.6	11.5	12.7	15.7		
3.9	5.3	4.6	Inventory	4.5	4.9	4.7	4.7		
4.0	3.0	2.1	All Other Current	4.2	2.0	.7	.9		
39.0	37.6	42.0	Total Current	35.1	42.4	45.8	39.0		
39.5	45.7	39.5	Fixed Assets (net)	45.4	37.1	40.6	40.5		
9.6	6.2	5.8	Intangibles (net)	4.3	5.8	1.7	10.4		
11.8	10.4	12.8	All Other Non-Current	15.2	14.7	11.8	10.0		
100.0	100.0	100.0	Total	100.0	100.0	100.0	100.0		
			LIABILITIES						
7.5	6.9	6.9	Notes Payable-Short Term	6.5	9.4	5.3	4.8		
3.2	3.0	3.3	Cur. Mat.-L.T.D.	4.6	3.4	2.7	2.9		
9.0	11.1	10.4	Trade Payables	5.0	13.8	7.1	10.9		
.2	.2	.2	Income Taxes Payable	.0	.0	.4	.1		
21.2	24.0	24.8	All Other Current	21.6	32.0	22.1	20.2		
41.2	45.2	45.6	Total Current	37.7	58.6	37.6	39.0		
30.8	35.4	32.2	Long-Term Debt	30.5	34.5	20.3	43.1		
.0	.0	.1	Deferred Taxes	.0	.0	.0	.0		
12.2	14.4	10.5	All Other Non-Current	13.2	10.9	4.5	9.7		
15.8	4.9	11.7	Net Worth	18.5	-4.0	37.5	8.1		
100.0	100.0	100.0	Total Liabilities & Net Worth	100.0	100.0	100.0	100.0		
			INCOME DATA						
100.0	100.0	100.0	Net Sales	100.0	100.0	100.0	100.0		
			Gross Profit						
91.9	91.2	91.0	Operating Expenses	82.2	94.8	89.3	93.0		
8.1	8.8	9.0	Operating Profit	17.8	5.2	10.7	7.0		
2.0	2.4	1.5	All Other Expenses (net)	5.2	.0	.4	.9		
6.0	6.4	7.6	Profit Before Taxes	12.5	5.3	10.3	6.2		
			RATIOS						
1.7 .8 .3	1.6 .8 .3	2.1 1.0 .4	Current	3.1 .9 .3	1.8 .9 .4	1.8 1.2 .6	2.4 .7 .3		
1.3 .5 .2	1.3 .6 .2	1.8 .7 .3	Quick	3.1 .6 .1	1.8 .7 .3	1.5 1.0 .4	2.4 .5 .2		
0 UND 3 141.8 17 21.7	0 UND 3 139.2 11 32.3	0 UND 3 138.1 17 21.3	Sales/Receivables	0 UND 0 UND 0 UND	0 UND 3 117.7 19 19.6	0 UND 0 UND 19 19.7	2 151.6 6 58.1 25 14.4		
			Cost of Sales/Inventory						
			Cost of Sales/Payables						
22.1 -45.3 -6.9	19.2 -57.8 -7.9	13.6 -362.3 -9.1	Sales/Working Capital	11.5 -86.2 -9.1	13.2 -134.9 -8.6	14.6 102.0 -7.6	27.1 -25.9 -3.9		
17.9 (98) 3.5 1.3	18.7 (112) 4.8 1.1	27.3 (88) 7.4 1.9	EBIT/Interest	10.1 (11) 3.7 1.1	33.6 (28) 10.1 1.1	53.0 (15) 10.3 3.3	19.3 (21) 5.6 2.1		
5.1 (11) 1.7 .7	9.3 (15) 3.1 1.0		Net Profit + Depr., Dep., Amort./Cur. Mat. L/T/D						
.5 3.2 -3.1	.6 3.0 -1.9	.2 1.7 -5.2	Fixed/Worth	.1 1.2 -5.5	.3 2.7 -1.3	.3 .9 3.1	.1 20.9 -2.2		
1.3 6.3 -6.6	1.3 5.7 -4.1	.9 3.9 -6.8	Debt/Worth	.4 8.5 -3.6	1.1 NM -3.4	.7 1.9 6.6	2.0 194.0 -4.2		
117.7 (90) 46.0 13.5	95.6 (100) 48.1 13.4	100.4 (81) 58.4 9.7	% Profit Before Taxes/Tangible Net Worth	100.0 (19) 64.9 15.3	99.5 (22) 61.7 16.3	108.0 (15) 64.3 6.0	114.2 (12) 31.4 9.8		
22.6 8.1 1.3	32.2 8.5 1.4	32.5 9.7 .8	% Profit Before Taxes/Total Assets	29.4 6.4 -1.6	42.1 11.4 -1.9	41.6 19.2 3.1	24.1 7.1 2.6		
33.8 11.7 3.0	46.4 9.8 2.5	82.0 12.6 2.4	Sales/Net Fixed Assets	64.0 7.8 .7	93.8 14.4 4.7	54.7 10.4 3.1	83.2 7.8 1.4		
5.3 3.0 1.4	5.5 3.0 1.2	6.7 3.2 1.2	Sales/Total Assets	5.2 2.3 .3	7.3 3.6 1.5	5.4 3.2 1.7	6.4 2.5 1.1		
1.1 (101) 2.0 4.8	.9 (121) 2.0 4.9	1.1 (91) 1.9 4.1	% Depr., Dep., Amort./Sales	1.5 (21) 3.3 10.0	.4 (28) 1.2 3.4	1.1 (13) 1.9 3.6	1.1 (16) 2.9 5.5		
2.2 (64) 3.7 7.6	2.3 (75) 4.6 6.9	2.8 (57) 4.7 8.7	% Officers', Directors' Owners' Comp/Sales		3.0 (20) 4.3 7.0	1.8 (12) 3.8 6.9	1.9 (11) 3.0 4.3		
1677835M	2528986M	1878498M	Net Sales ($)	15780M	82594M	70886M	169420M	120753M	1419065M
644259M	837271M	500397M	Total Assets ($)	23683M	43625M	34618M	92042M	67387M	239042M

M = $ thousand MM = $ million

See Pages 9 through 22 for Explanation of Ratios and Data

Current Data Sorted by Assets							Comparative Historical Data	
						Type of Statement		
		1				Unqualified	2	1
2	2					Reviewed	1	
17	11	7	1			Compiled	28	27
93	33	11				Tax Returns	118	129
39	34	14	2	1		Other	55	66
12 (4/1-9/30/13)			256 (10/1/13-3/31/14)				**4/1/09-3/31/10**	**4/1/10-3/31/11**
0-500M	**500M-2MM**	**2-10MM**	**10-50MM**	**50-100MM**	**100-250MM**		**ALL**	**ALL**
151	80	33	3	1		**NUMBER OF STATEMENTS**	204	223
%	%	%	%	%	%	**ASSETS**	%	%
18.4	13.1	12.2			D	Cash & Equivalents	16.4	15.4
1.0	1.2	2.4			A	Trade Receivables (net)	1.4	1.0
12.8	6.5	5.1			T	Inventory	7.6	8.8
1.9	2.5	5.0			A	All Other Current	2.5	1.9
34.2	23.3	24.7				Total Current	27.9	27.2
40.5	52.2	48.8			N	Fixed Assets (net)	46.9	51.6
13.8	13.1	15.7			O	Intangibles (net)	17.1	12.2
11.5	11.4	10.8			T	All Other Non-Current	8.1	9.1
100.0	100.0	100.0				Total	100.0	100.0
					A	**LIABILITIES**		
8.2	3.3	1.8			V	Notes Payable-Short Term	5.9	5.7
3.7	2.5	2.7			A	Cur. Mat.-L.T.D.	2.0	2.4
10.2	4.4	5.0			I	Trade Payables	5.9	6.1
.0	.0	.1			L	Income Taxes Payable	.1	.0
19.8	14.9	9.8			A	All Other Current	17.8	16.5
41.9	25.2	19.4			B	Total Current	31.7	30.8
20.9	27.9	30.4			L	Long-Term Debt	29.6	28.3
.0	.0	.0			E	Deferred Taxes	.1	.1
24.3	10.4	11.8				All Other Non-Current	20.9	21.9
12.8	36.5	38.4				Net Worth	17.7	19.0
100.0	100.0	100.0				Total Liabilties & Net Worth	100.0	100.0
						INCOME DATA		
100.0	100.0	100.0				Net Sales	100.0	100.0
61.4	64.0	65.7				Gross Profit	60.0	61.2
57.3	55.7	55.7				Operating Expenses	56.1	56.1
4.1	8.4	9.9				Operating Profit	4.0	5.1
.6	.5	1.9				All Other Expenses (net)	.9	.9
3.5	7.9	8.0				Profit Before Taxes	3.0	4.3
						RATIOS		
3.9	2.5	3.8					3.2	2.8
1.4	1.2	1.1				Current	1.0	1.2
.3	.5	.6					.4	.4
2.5	1.6	2.5					2.2	1.8
(149) .6	(79) .6	.6				Quick	(202) .5	(221) .6
.1	.2	.2					.1	.1
0 UND	**0** UND	**0** UND					**0** UND	**0** UND
0 UND	**0** UND	**0** UND				Sales/Receivables	**0** UND	**0** UND
0 UND	**0** 999.8	**7** 55.6					**0** UND	**0** UND
9 38.7	**11** 33.6	**11** 34.2					**7** 52.7	**9** 39.8
19 19.3	**19** 19.5	**22** 16.8				Cost of Sales/Inventory	**15** 24.5	**19** 19.5
30 12.3	**32** 11.3	**52** 7.0					**26** 14.2	**34** 10.8
0 UND	**0** UND	**2** 152.8					**0** UND	**0** UND
0 UND	**9** 39.7	**22** 16.8				Cost of Sales/Payables	**4** 90.2	**5** 74.0
19 19.5	**24** 14.9	**48** 7.6					**24** 15.0	**26** 14.3
21.0	12.3	7.9					19.0	21.8
79.2	146.7	45.3				Sales/Working Capital	UND	121.4
-20.7	-21.6	-19.4					-24.9	-19.4
13.0	19.6	40.6					8.7	13.6
(79) 3.5	(58) 6.2	(30) 5.3				EBIT/Interest	(140) 2.3	(138) 2.7
-.9	1.5	.8					.4	1.0
						Net Profit + Depr., Dep., Amort./Cur. Mat. L/T/D		
.4	.7	.6					.8	.8
1.8	1.5	2.3				Fixed/Worth	3.2	2.2
-1.9	-6.2	-46.1					-1.8	-3.2
.5	.5	.4					.8	.5
2.8	2.1	3.0				Debt/Worth	6.2	2.4
-3.7	-9.4	-9.1					-3.4	-4.6
113.6	103.0	57.7					97.8	87.7
(96) 38.8	(53) 42.9	(23) 24.5				% Profit Before Taxes/Tangible Net Worth	(127) 40.6	(151) 34.9
-1.5	16.9	4.6					3.1	.8
35.8	33.7	25.5					28.1	31.9
10.0	13.4	9.3				% Profit Before Taxes/Total Assets	7.7	8.3
-6.3	3.1	.1					-1.6	-1.6
49.0	10.9	7.1					27.1	25.1
14.5	4.8	3.8				Sales/Net Fixed Assets	8.6	6.4
5.5	2.3	1.9					3.4	2.5
8.2	3.4	2.3					5.8	6.1
4.0	2.3	1.4				Sales/Total Assets	3.1	3.2
2.4	1.5	1.1					1.6	1.6
1.1	1.2	2.6					1.6	1.2
(98) 2.0	(58) 2.8	(25) 3.7				% Depr., Dep., Amort./Sales	(162) 2.8	(170) 2.5
4.0	5.4	6.6					5.0	4.7
2.9	2.9	.5					2.4	2.3
(77) 5.8	(32) 4.3	(16) 2.7				% Officers', Directors' Owners' Comp/Sales	(104) 4.6	(98) 4.9
9.4	6.0	5.8					9.1	8.9
148113M	**214723M**	**193868M**	**1634234M**	**131427M**		Net Sales ($)	**2407176M**	**3761890M**
33275M	**78065M**	**120854M**	**77129M**	**68351M**		Total Assets ($)	**780191M**	**1119727M**

M = $ thousand MM = $ million

See Pages 9 through 22 for Explanation of Ratios and Data

Comparative Historical Data				Current Data Sorted by Sales					
			Type of Statement						
2		1	Unqualified					1	
4	1	4	Reviewed	2	1	1			
34	34	36	Compiled	9	11	7	8		1
154	150	137	Tax Returns	74	49	8	5	1	
93	83	90	Other	20	42	14	9	3	2
4/1/11-3/31/12 ALL	4/1/12-3/31/13 ALL	4/1/13-3/31/14 ALL		12 (4/1-9/30/13)		256 (10/1/13-3/31/14)			
				0-1MM	1-3MM	3-5MM	5-10MM	10-25MM	25MM & OVER
287	268	268	**NUMBER OF STATEMENTS**	105	103	30	22	5	3
%	%	%	**ASSETS**	%	%	%	%	%	%
15.4	17.1	16.1	Cash & Equivalents	15.4	17.0	17.9	9.9		
1.0	1.1	1.3	Trade Receivables (net)	1.2	1.4	.7	1.8		
8.8	8.6	9.9	Inventory	10.4	9.8	10.5	6.3		
3.1	2.3	2.5	All Other Current	1.6	3.1	3.5	2.1		
28.4	29.0	29.8	Total Current	28.6	31.2	32.6	20.1		
47.3	45.6	45.3	Fixed Assets (net)	43.9	45.5	41.8	56.7		
11.6	13.6	13.7	Intangibles (net)	15.5	12.6	14.3	10.2		
12.8	11.8	11.2	All Other Non-Current	11.9	10.6	11.1	13.0		
100.0	100.0	100.0	Total	100.0	100.0	100.0	100.0		
			LIABILITIES						
8.2	5.1	5.8	Notes Payable-Short Term	6.7	6.6	2.7	3.5		
3.4	2.3	3.2	Cur. Mat.-L.T.D.	4.3	2.0	5.5	1.6		
7.5	6.4	7.7	Trade Payables	8.7	6.5	9.0	5.8		
.1	.2	.0	Income Taxes Payable	.0	.0	.1	.1		
16.8	20.2	17.0	All Other Current	22.9	13.3	12.8	13.3		
36.0	34.3	33.8	Total Current	42.6	28.5	30.1	24.3		
29.3	27.4	24.4	Long-Term Debt	24.7	23.4	27.5	26.5		
.0	.0	.0	Deferred Taxes	.0	.0	.0	.0		
21.6	20.0	18.4	All Other Non-Current	28.4	14.5	3.6	12.9		
13.1	18.2	23.4	Net Worth	4.3	33.6	38.8	36.3		
100.0	100.0	100.0	Total Liabilties & Net Worth	100.0	100.0	100.0	100.0		
			INCOME DATA						
100.0	100.0	100.0	Net Sales	100.0	100.0	100.0	100.0		
62.5	62.9	62.8	Gross Profit	62.2	63.5	58.3	66.0		
57.3	58.2	56.7	Operating Expenses	59.2	56.0	50.1	56.5		
5.1	4.7	6.1	Operating Profit	3.0	7.5	8.2	9.5		
.6	.6	.7	All Other Expenses (net)	.9	.6	.6	1.0		
4.6	4.1	5.4	Profit Before Taxes	2.1	6.9	7.6	8.6		
			RATIOS						
2.8	3.5	3.4		3.6	3.6	2.5	1.7		
1.1	1.2	1.3	Current	1.3	1.8	1.1	1.0		
.4	.4	.4		.3	.6	.5	.4		
1.9	2.0	2.0		2.1	2.1	1.4	.9		
(286) .6	.6	(265) .6	Quick	(103) .5	1.1	(29) .5	.6		
.1	.1	.2		.1	.2	.2	.2		
0 UND	**0** UND	**0** UND		**0** UND	**0** UND	**0** UND	**0** UND		
0 UND	**0** UND	**0** UND	Sales/Receivables	**0** UND	**0** UND	**0** UND	**0** 999.8		
0 UND	**0** UND	**0** UND		**0** UND	**0** UND	**0** 999.8	**4** 95.7		
7 53.8	**8** 47.5	**10** 38.4		**10** 38.2	**11** 32.1	**5** 79.1	**13** 27.4		
15 23.8	**17** 22.1	**19** 19.1	Cost of Sales/Inventory	**19** 19.2	**20** 18.1	**12** 29.9	**24** 14.9		
30 12.3	**28** 12.9	**32** 11.3		**36** 10.1	**31** 11.9	**23** 15.7	**41** 8.8		
0 UND	**0** UND	**0** UND		**0** UND	**0** UND	**5** 76.9	**4** 96.4		
6 57.5	**4** 102.7	**5** 71.6	Cost of Sales/Payables	**0** UND	**2** 210.9	**10** 35.4	**20** 17.9		
31 11.6	**26** 14.2	**25** 14.6		**24** 15.4	**19** 19.5	**26** 13.9	**47** 7.8		
21.1	19.8	16.3		19.2	13.4	15.6	31.7		
148.2	104.9	98.0	Sales/Working Capital	130.4	54.2	190.2	NM		
-17.5	-18.1	-21.8		-7.2	-29.4	-47.2	-18.0		
15.9	14.0	14.9		7.1	15.1	35.3	59.4		
(194) 3.8	(157) 3.3	(170) 4.8	EBIT/Interest	(59) 2.0	(63) 5.3	(23) 9.7	(19) 8.8		
.2	-.2	.6		-3.0	1.3	1.1	1.2		
			Net Profit + Depr., Dep., Amort./Cur. Mat. L/T/D						
.6	.6	.6		.6	.6	.4	.8		
2.6	2.0	1.7	Fixed/Worth	3.3	1.4	.8	2.0		
-2.2	-3.2	-3.8		-1.6	-4.5	NM	NM		
.4	.4	.5		.7	.5	.4	.3		
5.2	2.6	2.6	Debt/Worth	4.8	1.8	1.3	2.1		
-3.8	-5.7	-5.3		-3.5	-8.8	-8.3	-77.5		
101.9	111.1	102.2		71.8	102.2	137.4	143.8		
(181) 41.7	(173) 44.9	(175) 38.8	% Profit Before Taxes/Tangible Net Worth	(61) 27.9	(71) 47.4	(21) 37.3	(16) 50.0		
7.2	4.9	7.6		-11.3	10.1	14.5	6.0		
34.0	34.5	32.5		20.9	40.3	44.1	72.5		
10.7	10.9	11.4	% Profit Before Taxes/Total Assets	4.7	14.0	13.4	15.4		
-2.3	-2.6	-1.1		-8.7	1.3	1.2	1.3		
21.8	24.8	24.8		29.4	26.0	57.7	10.1		
8.0	8.2	7.5	Sales/Net Fixed Assets	6.9	7.8	8.7	5.5		
3.0	3.7	3.3		3.0	4.0	2.7	2.3		
5.1	5.8	5.7		5.4	6.1	5.2	4.2		
3.1	3.1	2.9	Sales/Total Assets	2.6	3.2	2.9	2.8		
1.5	1.8	1.7		1.3	2.0	1.6	1.7		
1.2	.9	1.3		1.5	1.0	1.7	2.0		
(205) 2.7	(197) 2.2	(184) 2.6	% Depr., Dep., Amort./Sales	(74) 3.0	(72) 2.0	(16) 2.8	(18) 3.3		
5.6	4.3	4.8		5.8	4.0	4.9	5.2		
2.5	2.7	2.7		2.7	3.2	.8	2.7		
(129) 4.7	(110) 4.6	(127) 5.2	% Officers', Directors' Owners' Comp/Sales	(50) 5.6	(52) 5.4	(12) 1.9	(11) 4.8		
7.5	9.3	7.7		10.1	6.9	3.2	5.9		
1228379M	4174175M	2322365M	Net Sales ($)	54957M	174284M	112420M	156339M	65214M	1759151M
426034M	838431M	377674M	Total Assets ($)	32572M	70607M	51236M	70871M	17497M	134891M

M = $ thousand MM = $ million

See Pages 9 through 22 for Explanation of Ratios and Data

Current Data Sorted by Assets							Comparative Historical Data	
						Type of Statement		
6	8	15	44	15	25	Unqualified	135	130
21	24	53	29	4		Reviewed	172	156
155	144	106	25		1	Compiled	498	511
759	461	110	7	3	6	Tax Returns	1309	1271
336	392	286	144	31	29	Other	1073	1215
216 (4/1-9/30/13)			3,023 (10/1/13-3/31/14)				4/1/09-3/31/10	4/1/10-3/31/11
0-500M	500M-2MM	2-10MM	10-50MM	50-100MM	100-250MM		ALL	ALL
1277	1029	570	249	53	61	NUMBER OF STATEMENTS	3187	3283
%	%	%	%	%	%	**ASSETS**	%	%
23.3	16.5	13.6	11.2	6.9	8.5	Cash & Equivalents	14.7	14.8
1.5	2.0	1.9	2.5	1.3	2.0	Trade Receivables (net)	2.0	1.9
9.0	4.8	3.6	3.4	3.8	3.8	Inventory	6.2	6.1
2.7	2.6	2.2	2.2	1.8	4.5	All Other Current	2.8	2.9
36.4	25.9	21.3	19.2	13.9	18.7	Total Current	25.7	25.7
40.9	50.4	56.4	56.8	57.5	51.7	Fixed Assets (net)	52.8	51.5
11.4	11.5	12.0	16.5	22.1	23.6	Intangibles (net)	11.4	11.3
11.3	12.2	10.2	7.4	6.5	6.0	All Other Non-Current	10.2	11.5
100.0	100.0	100.0	100.0	100.0	100.0	Total	100.0	100.0
						LIABILITIES		
8.4	3.3	2.5	1.5	1.7	1.8	Notes Payable-Short Term	5.4	5.5
3.3	3.3	4.5	5.0	4.1	3.1	Cur. Mat.-L.T.D.	5.0	4.2
12.9	7.7	6.8	7.6	7.6	8.4	Trade Payables	9.7	10.1
.2	.1	.1	.1	.0	.0	Income Taxes Payable	.1	.1
29.9	16.1	13.4	13.2	11.9	14.6	All Other Current	21.5	19.6
54.7	30.6	27.3	27.3	25.3	27.9	Total Current	41.7	39.6
29.3	31.7	36.2	36.3	50.7	41.3	Long-Term Debt	36.3	34.6
.0	.0	.1	.2	.3	1.6	Deferred Taxes	.1	.1
20.4	12.3	7.1	7.5	16.3	10.7	All Other Non-Current	13.2	13.4
-4.4	25.5	29.3	28.7	7.3	18.5	Net Worth	8.7	12.2
100.0	100.0	100.0	100.0	100.0	100.0	Total Liabilties & Net Worth	100.0	100.0
						INCOME DATA		
100.0	100.0	100.0	100.0	100.0	100.0	Net Sales	100.0	100.0
59.1	61.2	60.3	61.9	58.2	60.5	Gross Profit	61.3	60.9
55.3	55.7	54.5	56.6	53.5	55.2	Operating Expenses	57.5	56.9
3.8	5.5	5.8	5.3	4.6	5.3	Operating Profit	3.8	4.0
.4	.8	1.0	1.5	2.3	2.0	All Other Expenses (net)	1.3	1.1
3.4	4.7	4.8	3.9	2.3	3.2	Profit Before Taxes	2.5	2.9
						RATIOS		
2.4	2.2	1.4	1.0	.8	.8		1.6	1.6
1.0	.9	.7	.7	.5	.5	Current	.7	.7
.4	.4	.3	.4	.3	.4		.3	.3
1.7	1.7	1.1	.8	.6	.5		1.0	1.1
(1267) .6	(1026) .6	(568) .5	.4	.3	(60) .3	Quick	(3160) .4	(3258) .4
.2	.2	.2	.2	.1	.2		.1	.1
0 UND	0 UND	0 UND	0 999.8	0 UND	0 999.8		0 UND	0 UND
0 UND	0 UND	0 999.8	1 297.1	1 253.8	2 153.8	Sales/Receivables	0 UND	0 UND
0 UND	1 565.7	2 188.9	5 78.1	4 97.5	5 76.0		1 276.1	1 289.7
4 101.6	6 63.2	6 58.3	8 47.9	6 57.7	7 53.9		6 64.4	6 60.5
8 44.0	10 37.5	9 38.5	11 32.2	12 31.7	11 33.8	Cost of Sales/Inventory	10 35.1	10 35.6
15 24.5	17 21.8	17 21.0	19 19.4	14 26.7	19 19.0		18 20.2	17 21.1
0 UND	0 UND	8 45.0	16 23.1	17 21.0	16 23.4		1 424.0	2 170.0
4 93.5	15 24.9	20 18.1	30 12.1	26 13.9	30 12.1	Cost of Sales/Payables	16 22.5	17 21.7
21 17.0	30 12.1	41 8.8	51 7.2	42 8.7	39 9.4		36 10.2	36 10.1
34.2	22.5	38.4	234.9	-66.7	-84.5		42.6	43.7
999.8	-215.2	-46.9	-28.7	-20.9	-22.2	Sales/Working Capital	-51.2	-60.6
-22.3	-17.3	-13.0	-13.1	-11.8	-12.6		-12.4	-13.4
19.2	19.8	15.2	9.9	6.5	10.8		9.1	10.3
(691) 5.0	(768) 5.4	(510) 5.8	(239) 4.8	(51) 2.1	(56) 3.7	EBIT/Interest	(2407) 2.8	(2459) 2.9
.5	1.1	1.7	1.7	.9	1.6		.4	.5
	10.9	8.1	4.1	3.8			4.9	5.8
	(30) 4.9	(44) 3.5	(69) 2.5	(22) 2.3		Net Profit + Depr., Dep., Amort./Cur. Mat. L/T/D	(218) 2.4	(181) 2.3
	2.5	1.9	1.3	1.6			1.2	1.4
.5	.8	1.2	1.6	2.7	2.0		1.0	.9
1.9	2.7	3.2	4.4	-8.8	-8.3	Fixed/Worth	4.3	3.7
-1.1	-3.8	-11.8	-4.6	-1.6	-1.0		-2.3	-2.4
.5	.6	1.0	1.1	2.6	1.7		1.0	.9
5.1	3.7	3.8	5.0	-11.3	-17.7	Debt/Worth	6.1	5.4
-2.7	-6.8	-19.9	-6.3	-3.4	-2.5		-4.3	-4.4
165.3	103.3	79.0	69.1	24.0	69.6		94.1	95.3
(737) 64.1	(679) 42.4	(401) 32.2	(163) 28.8	(21) 5.2	(28) 24.9	% Profit Before Taxes/Tangible Net Worth	(1924) 36.5	(1989) 35.1
21.3	14.7	9.8	10.3	-.6	7.0		7.2	7.6
50.9	30.2	20.1	15.8	7.5	13.3		23.9	24.8
18.1	13.5	9.1	7.8	3.8	5.1	% Profit Before Taxes/Total Assets	7.3	7.7
-.6	1.3	1.7	1.7	-.2	.8		-2.0	-1.1
63.3	16.6	9.0	6.5	6.7	7.8		17.6	18.7
19.9	6.8	4.5	3.7	2.9	4.2	Sales/Net Fixed Assets	6.7	6.9
8.2	3.3	2.0	2.4	1.9	2.7		3.0	3.1
10.4	4.6	3.4	2.7	2.4	2.7		5.7	5.7
6.4	3.0	2.2	2.1	1.8	1.9	Sales/Total Assets	3.2	3.2
4.0	1.9	1.2	1.4	1.2	1.4		1.8	1.9
.6	1.2	1.8	2.4	3.0	2.8		1.3	1.3
(899) 1.4	(828) 2.1	(505) 2.8	(240) 3.4	(49) 4.0	(22) 3.7	% Depr., Dep., Amort./Sales	(2652) 2.7	(2652) 2.6
2.6	3.5	4.2	4.5	5.4	4.5		4.5	4.3
2.4	2.0	1.3	1.2		2.2		2.0	1.8
(611) 4.4	(415) 3.4	(184) 2.5	(32) 2.2		(11) 4.4	% Officers', Directors' Owners' Comp/Sales	(1297) 4.0	(1340) 3.7
7.5	5.1	4.8	3.4		7.5		7.0	6.7
1830543M	3538773M	6509632M	13140844M	13308543M	28936271M	Net Sales ($)	56991284M	60039762M
290841M	1067460M	2533868M	5725803M	3879365M	9486847M	Total Assets ($)	25318175M	24590828M

M = $ thousand MM = $ million

See Pages 9 through 22 for Explanation of Ratios and Data

Comparative Historical Data / Current Data Sorted by Sales

			Type of Statement						
129	110	113	Unqualified	2	5	6	9	11	80
180	132	131	Reviewed	5	19	16	26	30	35
589	527	431	Compiled	71	170	60	57	50	23
1656	1446	1346	Tax Returns	346	662	186	106	30	16
1372	1191	1218	Other	153	393	176	152	139	205
					216 (4/1-9/30/13)		3,023 (10/1/13-3/31/14)		
4/1/11-3/31/12 ALL	4/1/12-3/31/13 ALL	4/1/13-3/31/14 ALL		0-1MM	1-3MM	3-5MM	5-10MM	10-25MM	25MM & OVER
3926	3406	3239	NUMBER OF STATEMENTS	577	1249	444	350	260	359
%	%	%	ASSETS	%	%	%	%	%	%
16.3	17.2	18.0	Cash & Equivalents	18.2	19.5	18.7	18.5	16.5	12.0
2.2	1.8	1.8	Trade Receivables (net)	1.2	1.5	2.0	3.0	2.2	2.3
6.4	6.4	6.1	Inventory	7.0	6.7	5.7	5.8	5.3	4.0
2.6	2.7	2.5	All Other Current	2.6	2.6	2.6	2.5	2.0	2.8
27.5	28.1	28.4	Total Current	28.9	30.1	29.0	29.9	26.1	21.1
50.3	49.8	48.3	Fixed Assets (net)	48.4	46.2	47.7	48.3	51.0	54.8
10.8	10.8	12.3	Intangibles (net)	12.8	11.2	11.8	10.6	12.7	17.6
11.4	11.3	10.9	All Other Non-Current	9.9	12.5	11.6	11.1	10.2	6.5
100.0	100.0	100.0	Total	100.0	100.0	100.0	100.0	100.0	100.0
			LIABILITIES						
5.6	5.5	5.0	Notes Payable-Short Term	10.2	4.9	4.3	2.0	3.6	1.7
4.3	3.8	3.7	Cur. Mat.-L.T.D.	2.9	3.3	3.2	4.6	5.4	4.7
11.0	9.9	9.6	Trade Payables	7.6	10.3	10.4	10.4	9.3	8.9
.1	.2	.1	Income Taxes Payable	.1	.1	.1	.1	.1	.1
21.5	21.3	20.8	All Other Current	26.6	22.5	20.0	16.6	14.9	14.6
42.6	40.7	39.1	Total Current	47.4	41.1	37.9	33.7	33.4	29.9
32.8	33.5	32.4	Long-Term Debt	31.9	33.9	27.2	29.7	31.4	37.5
.1	.1	.1	Deferred Taxes	.0	.0	.0	.0	.2	.4
14.8	15.5	14.2	All Other Non-Current	24.3	15.1	12.1	7.8	6.4	9.8
9.7	10.2	14.2	Net Worth	-3.5	9.9	22.7	28.8	28.6	22.4
100.0	100.0	100.0	Total Liabilties & Net Worth	100.0	100.0	100.0	100.0	100.0	100.0
			INCOME DATA						
100.0	100.0	100.0	Net Sales	100.0	100.0	100.0	100.0	100.0	100.0
60.3	60.1	60.2	Gross Profit	58.9	60.3	60.7	60.6	60.3	60.6
56.1	55.2	55.4	Operating Expenses	56.0	55.7	54.6	54.4	54.9	55.2
4.1	4.8	4.8	Operating Profit	2.9	4.6	6.1	6.2	5.4	5.4
.9	.9	.8	All Other Expenses (net)	.9	.7	.6	.7	.8	1.4
3.2	4.0	4.1	Profit Before Taxes	2.0	4.0	5.5	5.5	4.6	4.0
			RATIOS						
1.7	1.8	1.9		3.1	2.3	2.0	1.8	1.4	1.0
.8	.8	.8	Current	1.0	.9	.8	.9	.7	.6
.3	.4	.4		.3	.4	.4	.5	.4	.4
1.2	1.3	1.4		1.7	1.8	1.4	1.3	1.0	.8
(3903) .4	(3389) .5	(3223) .5	Quick	(573) .6	(1241) .6	(443) .5	(349) .6	(259) .5	(358) .4
.1	.2	.2		.1	.2	.2	.3	.3	.2
0 UND	0 UND	0 UND		0 UND	0 UND	0 UND	0 UND	0 UND	0 999.8
0 UND	0 UND	0 UND	Sales/Receivables	0 UND	0 UND	0 UND	0 999.8	0 999.8	1 301.2
1 303.3	1 401.5	1 361.9		0 UND	0 999.8	1 350.3	2 196.3	3 134.2	4 96.2
6 65.4	5 69.4	5 70.3		3 135.3	5 79.8	6 65.1	6 56.4	6 57.9	7 52.8
10 37.6	10 38.0	9 38.8	Cost of Sales/Inventory	9 40.9	9 41.0	9 38.6	10 36.8	9 39.1	10 34.8
16 22.3	17 22.1	16 22.7		17 21.7	15 24.2	16 22.7	17 21.1	16 22.9	17 22.1
0 UND	0 UND	0 UND		0 UND	0 UND	5 75.0	9 40.8	9 42.4	15 24.0
16 23.5	14 26.0	14 26.8	Cost of Sales/Payables	0 UND	10 37.0	16 23.5	20 18.4	21 17.5	27 13.5
34 10.7	33 11.1	31 11.8		13 28.7	29 12.7	30 12.3	38 9.7	42 8.7	44 8.3
38.4	36.9	32.9		28.4	28.8	29.9	28.4	42.6	-999.8
-67.4	-89.1	-104.5	Sales/Working Capital	519.0	-297.0	-90.9	-137.0	-53.5	-27.2
-15.3	-16.1	-16.6		-17.2	-17.4	-17.1	-17.4	-16.4	-13.4
10.8	14.0	16.9		8.5	18.0	22.3	20.1	18.5	12.6
(2852) 3.3	(2442) 4.2	(2315) 5.1	EBIT/Interest	(302) 2.3	(824) 4.8	(329) 6.8	(284) 6.9	(239) 6.3	(337) 5.2
.8	1.1	1.2		-.5	.7	1.5	1.9	2.5	1.8
5.1	5.6	5.4			5.8	12.2	13.7	5.4	4.0
(201) 2.3	(167) 2.6	(178) 2.8	Net Profit + Depr., Dep., Amort./Cur. Mat. L/T/D		(18) 3.8	(15) 5.1	(17) 4.3	(33) 2.9	(94) 2.5
1.4	1.4	1.6			1.3	1.3	1.8	1.7	1.6
.9	.8	.8		.7	.6	.7	.8	1.2	1.6
3.5	3.1	2.9	Fixed/Worth	3.7	2.4	2.6	2.3	3.1	5.7
-2.3	-2.6	-2.6		-1.2	-2.2	-4.2	-20.0	-4.9	-2.6
.9	.8	.7		.6	.5	.7	.7	1.0	1.4
5.5	4.9	4.3	Debt/Worth	7.1	4.6	3.4	2.7	4.1	8.3
-4.7	-4.6	-4.8		-2.6	-4.0	-7.9	-30.3	-8.5	-4.6
100.5	112.5	111.7		100.0	115.8	138.2	114.6	94.0	87.6
(2441) 36.7	(2121) 45.0	(2029) 43.7	% Profit Before Taxes/Tangible Net Worth	(323) 37.4	(771) 46.3	(300) 58.0	(251) 45.7	(173) 38.0	(211) 33.6
9.0	13.9	13.2		5.6	16.3	16.7	17.8	10.0	11.0
26.0	30.9	31.7		27.6	36.7	37.5	31.8	24.9	17.0
9.0	10.9	12.3	% Profit Before Taxes/Total Assets	7.5	13.9	16.2	14.8	12.5	8.0
-.2	.8	1.0		-5.0	.8	1.9	3.8	3.7	2.0
21.2	23.0	24.7		36.8	35.9	23.9	19.9	13.7	8.6
7.7	8.0	8.2	Sales/Net Fixed Assets	10.2	10.4	8.7	7.6	6.6	4.5
3.4	3.5	3.7		3.7	4.3	4.1	3.5	3.5	2.8
6.2	6.3	6.3		7.6	7.2	6.3	5.6	4.5	3.4
3.4	3.6	3.4	Sales/Total Assets	3.9	4.1	3.6	3.2	3.0	2.3
2.0	2.0	2.0		1.8	2.2	2.3	2.0	1.9	1.6
1.2	1.1	1.1		1.0	.9	1.0	1.2	1.7	2.2
(3122) 2.3	(2707) 2.1	(2543) 2.2	% Depr., Dep., Amort./Sales	(415) 2.1	(934) 1.8	(355) 1.8	(303) 2.2	(235) 2.6	(301) 3.2
3.9	3.6	3.7		4.1	3.3	2.9	3.6	3.8	4.4
2.1	2.1	2.0		3.1	2.2	2.0	1.2	1.2	1.3
(1586) 3.8	(1349) 3.8	(1260) 3.8	% Officers', Directors' Owners' Comp/Sales	(253) 5.6	(560) 3.8	(180) 3.6	(134) 2.4	(75) 2.6	(58) 2.5
6.5	6.4	6.4		9.4	5.9	5.9	3.9	4.8	5.3
77295435M	65266091M	67264606M	Net Sales ($)	360599M	2332736M	1686625M	2444544M	4229275M	56210827M
25722341M	22876941M	22984184M	Total Assets ($)	158184M	848068M	622564M	1012776M	1748212M	18594380M

M = $ thousand MM = $ million

See Pages 9 through 22 for Explanation of Ratios and Data

Current Data Sorted by Assets							Comparative Historical Data	
						Type of Statement		
5	5	18	31	14	20	Unqualified	118	74
4	17	47	43	4		Reviewed	112	110
179	289	312	64	2		Compiled	452	554
381	229	58	8	1	4	Tax Returns	591	548
217	237	245	137	42	34	Other	617	702
153 (4/1-9/30/13)			2,494 (10/1/13-3/31/14)				**4/1/09-3/31/10 ALL**	**4/1/10-3/31/11 ALL**
0-500M	**500M-2MM**	**2-10MM**	**10-50MM**	**50-100MM**	**100-250MM**			
786	777	680	283	63	58	**NUMBER OF STATEMENTS**	1890	1988
%	%	%	%	%	%	**ASSETS**	%	%
23.1	17.2	15.7	12.3	9.0	6.6	Cash & Equivalents	13.6	16.0
1.4	1.2	1.3	1.2	1.5	1.4	Trade Receivables (net)	1.6	1.6
6.2	3.3	2.4	2.1	1.4	1.8	Inventory	4.2	4.2
1.9	1.5	1.6	1.9	2.6	1.8	All Other Current	3.0	1.8
32.6	23.1	20.9	17.5	14.4	11.6	Total Current	22.4	23.6
41.4	49.6	48.0	50.6	51.3	53.8	Fixed Assets (net)	50.8	49.5
15.6	19.6	22.5	23.6	28.0	28.2	Intangibles (net)	18.0	18.0
10.4	7.7	8.6	8.2	6.2	6.5	All Other Non-Current	8.8	8.9
100.0	100.0	100.0	100.0	100.0	100.0	Total	100.0	100.0
						LIABILITIES		
4.5	1.8	1.4	1.7	.8	2.4	Notes Payable-Short Term	3.9	4.8
6.3	8.2	9.0	6.4	6.3	4.3	Cur. Mat.-L.T.D.	7.2	7.5
10.8	6.1	6.0	5.5	4.7	4.8	Trade Payables	7.5	8.1
.0	.0	.1	.0	.1	.1	Income Taxes Payable	.1	.1
29.4	15.0	11.0	11.0	9.6	8.7	All Other Current	17.6	15.6
50.9	31.1	27.5	24.7	21.6	20.2	Total Current	36.3	36.1
36.5	42.3	45.4	44.8	52.8	48.8	Long-Term Debt	47.2	41.6
.0	.0	.1	.4	.4	2.3	Deferred Taxes	.1	.1
17.3	6.7	5.7	6.2	6.1	11.5	All Other Non-Current	8.7	9.8
-4.7	19.8	21.4	24.0	19.0	17.2	Net Worth	7.8	12.3
100.0	100.0	100.0	100.0	100.0	100.0	Total Liabilities & Net Worth	100.0	100.0
						INCOME DATA		
100.0	100.0	100.0	100.0	100.0	100.0	Net Sales	100.0	100.0
60.0	62.4	62.6	62.8	63.1	60.3	Gross Profit	62.0	62.3
55.2	57.4	58.0	56.7	54.5	54.4	Operating Expenses	57.3	57.2
4.7	4.9	4.7	6.1	8.5	5.9	Operating Profit	4.7	5.1
.6	.9	.8	1.8	2.2	3.2	All Other Expenses (net)	1.1	1.1
4.2	4.0	3.9	4.2	6.3	2.6	Profit Before Taxes	3.6	4.0
						RATIOS		
2.2	1.7	1.2	1.2	.9	1.0		1.4	1.5
.8	.7	.7	.7	.5	.5	Current	.7	.7
.3	.3	.4	.4	.3	.4		.3	.3
1.6	1.3	1.1	1.0	.7	.6		1.0	1.2
(785) .6	(776) .5	(678) .5	.5	.4	.3	Quick	(1877) .4	(1984) .5
.2	.2	.2	.2	.2	.2		.1	.2
0 UND	0 UND	0 UND	0 UND	0 UND	0 UND		0 UND	0 UND
0 UND	0 UND	0 999.8	0 999.8	1 324.7	1 303.4	Sales/Receivables	0 UND	0 UND
0 UND	0 999.8	1 402.7	2 219.4	2 162.4	4 85.2		1 453.8	1 495.2
4 90.7	5 68.1	6 62.2	6 57.6	5 67.5	6 60.9		5 69.1	5 68.8
7 53.1	8 48.2	8 46.5	8 43.7	8 48.3	8 45.1	Cost of Sales/Inventory	9 42.3	8 43.6
10 35.0	11 34.5	10 36.6	11 34.3	10 36.9	12 30.0		12 31.5	11 32.0
0 UND	2 238.6	7 51.1	9 38.9	16 22.7	15 24.3		3 138.3	4 97.6
5 68.1	12 31.4	16 23.0	20 18.1	31 11.6	24 15.5	Cost of Sales/Payables	15 24.0	15 24.1
17 21.6	22 16.3	29 12.6	37 9.8	44 8.3	45 8.1		28 13.2	29 12.4
37.3	34.7	72.2	55.7	-138.9	NM		59.9	44.0
-159.4	-49.5	-41.3	-36.3	-18.5	-21.7	Sales/Working Capital	-44.5	-48.9
-20.2	-14.9	-15.8	-14.8	-12.0	-12.1		-14.7	-14.6
19.0	15.1	10.9	10.2	7.2	6.5		9.1	10.4
(531) 6.6	(666) 4.7	(643) 4.4	(271) 4.4	(62) 3.8	(55) 3.3	EBIT/Interest	(1622) 3.4	(1664) 3.8
1.1	1.5	1.8	2.1	2.0	1.2		1.2	1.3
5.2	4.7	6.7	4.1	3.1	4.3		3.9	5.2
(10) 2.9	(15) 1.9	(54) 2.6	(42) 2.3	(19) 2.3	(15) 1.9	Net Profit + Depr., Dep., Amort./Cur. Mat. L/T/D	(151) 2.1	(116) 2.5
1.1	1.1	1.2	1.6	1.6	1.5		1.1	1.3
.7	1.2	1.7	1.7	2.8	2.9		1.5	1.2
6.0	13.7	25.6	14.8	-5.4	-16.3	Fixed/Worth	22.5	11.9
-.8	-1.6	-1.4	-1.3	-1.4	-.6		-1.3	-1.5
1.0	1.3	1.9	1.4	2.4	2.8		1.8	1.3
64.7	18.3	47.2	23.8	-7.9	-23.3	Debt/Worth	42.1	22.7
-2.4	-3.3	-3.1	-3.2	-2.7	-1.9		-2.8	-3.2
217.1	114.1	87.9	74.3	106.0	53.9		130.6	118.1
(402) 81.2	(416) 47.5	(346) 40.7	(154) 34.8	(27) 40.7	(26) 29.4	% Profit Before Taxes/Tangible Net Worth	(978) 50.9	(1052) 46.7
29.1	16.1	15.4	14.5	24.9	8.9		16.9	14.6
58.4	26.7	18.2	13.6	13.9	10.5		23.6	25.6
23.7	11.5	8.2	7.8	7.7	5.8	% Profit Before Taxes/Total Assets	9.4	10.3
1.6	1.6	1.8	2.9	3.3	.5		1.0	1.3
53.2	16.2	10.7	7.9	5.6	6.6		14.4	15.6
16.8	7.7	6.8	4.6	2.8	3.0	Sales/Net Fixed Assets	6.4	7.1
6.9	3.7	3.5	2.6	2.0	2.0		3.4	3.6
9.4	4.9	4.0	2.9	2.2	2.1		5.0	5.3
5.8	3.1	2.7	2.2	1.5	1.5	Sales/Total Assets	3.0	3.1
3.3	2.0	1.8	1.5	1.2	1.0		1.8	1.8
.9	1.5	2.1	2.5	2.5	2.5		1.8	1.8
(547) 1.9	(639) 2.8	(598) 3.4	(267) 3.4	(59) 3.6	(30) 3.3	% Depr., Dep., Amort./Sales	(1591) 3.2	(1621) 3.2
3.5	4.6	5.0	4.6	4.6	4.6		4.9	4.8
2.0	1.4	.8	.5	.2			1.5	1.4
(318) 3.6	(280) 2.7	(215) 1.4	(60) 1.2	(10) 2.5		% Officers', Directors' Owners' Comp/Sales	(660) 3.1	(695) 3.0
6.7	4.8	2.5	1.8	14.8			5.6	5.1
1119015M	3056563M	9246074M	13523271M	8343919M	15452200M	Net Sales ($)	34025855M	34366617M
186693M	838930M	3165819M	5950422M	4480871M	9422431M	Total Assets ($)	16878193M	15838135M

M = $ thousand MM = $ million

See Pages 9 through 22 for Explanation of Ratios and Data

Comparative Historical Data / Current Data Sorted by Sales

Comparative Historical Data			Type of Statement	Current Data Sorted by Sales					
119	113	93	Unqualified	2	4	2	5	17	63
110	121	115	Reviewed		9	8	17	34	47
530	433	846	Compiled	67	207	126	186	189	71
617	668	681	Tax Returns	211	285	75	63	35	12
828	815	912	Other	131	212	97	113	144	215
4/1/11-3/31/12	4/1/12-3/31/13	4/1/13-3/31/14		153 (4/1-9/30/13)			2,494 (10/1/13-3/31/14)		
ALL	ALL	ALL		0-1MM	1-3MM	3-5MM	5-10MM	10-25MM	25MM & OVER
2204	2150	2647	**NUMBER OF STATEMENTS**	411	717	308	384	419	408
%	%	%	**ASSETS**	%	%	%	%	%	%
16.4	17.6	17.6	Cash & Equivalents	16.5	20.3	20.1	17.6	16.7	12.9
1.8	1.5	1.3	Trade Receivables (net)	1.4	1.0	1.1	1.2	1.2	1.9
3.9	4.0	3.7	Inventory	4.5	4.2	4.1	3.8	2.9	2.4
2.5	2.5	1.7	All Other Current	1.4	1.8	2.0	1.4	1.7	2.0
24.6	25.7	24.3	Total Current	23.8	27.3	27.3	23.9	22.5	19.3
49.0	47.6	47.0	Fixed Assets (net)	49.4	45.2	42.6	45.9	48.7	50.5
18.1	17.6	20.0	Intangibles (net)	17.5	16.8	21.9	21.7	22.3	22.7
8.3	9.1	8.7	All Other Non-Current	9.3	10.8	8.2	8.5	6.5	7.5
100.0	100.0	100.0	Total	100.0	100.0	100.0	100.0	100.0	100.0
			LIABILITIES						
3.6	2.7	2.5	Notes Payable-Short Term	4.2	2.5	2.6	2.2	1.5	2.0
7.4	6.2	7.5	Cur. Mat.-L.T.D.	5.7	6.2	8.1	10.4	9.4	6.5
7.7	7.5	7.3	Trade Payables	8.1	7.7	7.4	7.3	6.3	7.0
.1	.1	.0	Income Taxes Payable	.0	.0	.1	.0	.0	.1
17.3	16.7	17.5	All Other Current	23.5	21.4	18.9	14.2	12.4	12.1
36.1	33.2	34.9	Total Current	41.5	37.8	37.0	34.1	29.8	27.7
41.9	43.0	42.0	Long-Term Debt	41.9	37.7	43.1	43.4	45.0	44.5
.1	.1	.1	Deferred Taxes	.0	.0	.0	.0	.2	.6
10.1	10.0	9.6	All Other Non-Current	19.7	11.6	5.4	6.3	4.8	7.3
11.7	13.6	13.3	Net Worth	-3.1	13.0	14.4	16.2	20.1	20.0
100.0	100.0	100.0	Total Liabilities & Net Worth	100.0	100.0	100.0	100.0	100.0	100.0
			INCOME DATA						
100.0	100.0	100.0	Net Sales	100.0	100.0	100.0	100.0	100.0	100.0
61.4	60.8	61.7	Gross Profit	59.3	61.4	63.5	62.9	62.2	61.8
56.8	55.3	56.7	Operating Expenses	56.1	55.6	58.1	58.0	57.8	56.1
4.6	5.5	5.0	Operating Profit	3.2	5.8	5.5	4.9	4.5	5.8
.9	.9	1.0	All Other Expenses (net)	1.2	.9	.8	.9	.7	1.3
3.7	4.6	4.1	Profit Before Taxes	2.0	4.9	4.6	4.0	3.8	4.5
			RATIOS						
1.5	1.7	1.5		2.5	1.9	1.7	1.2	1.3	1.1
.7	.8	.7	Current	.8	.7	.8	.7	.7	.6
.3	.4	.3		.3	.3	.3	.3	.4	.4
1.1	1.3	1.2		1.7	1.5	1.3	1.0	1.1	.9
(2198) .5	(2145) .5	(2643) .5	Quick	(410) .5	(716) .6	.6	(383) .5	(418) .6	.5
.2	.2	.2		.2	.2	.2	.2	.3	.2
0 UND	0 UND	0 UND		0 UND	0 UND	0 UND	0 UND	0 UND	0 UND
0 UND	0 UND	0 UND	Sales/Receivables	0 UND	0 UND	0 UND	0 UND	0 999.8	0 776.7
1 380.0	1 581.5	1 562.1		0 UND	0 UND	0 999.8	1 564.6	1 387.7	2 183.2
5 72.2	5 77.3	5 70.1		4 90.6	4 82.5	5 67.6	6 58.5	6 63.5	6 62.5
8 45.6	8 47.4	8 47.9	Cost of Sales/Inventory	8 48.2	7 53.0	7 49.5	8 44.1	8 46.6	8 45.5
11 34.3	10 34.9	10 35.2		12 29.4	10 36.6	10 34.9	10 36.2	10 37.4	10 35.5
2 187.6	1 428.6	2 153.6		0 UND	0 UND	3 133.8	6 65.1	7 56.0	12 29.7
14 25.7	13 28.9	13 28.9	Cost of Sales/Payables	1 253.0	9 42.1	14 26.8	15 24.9	15 24.3	24 15.5
28 12.9	27 13.5	26 14.3		16 23.0	20 18.0	24 15.3	25 14.4	26 14.0	39 9.3
49.8	36.6	44.6		25.2	33.5	35.5	79.2	56.8	173.8
-51.6	-81.6	-52.9	Sales/Working Capital	-107.3	-67.6	-69.5	-44.5	-49.7	-29.8
-15.3	-17.6	-15.7		-11.6	-16.3	-16.7	-15.1	-19.6	-14.6
10.0	12.9	13.0		9.0	17.9	14.5	15.0	11.7	10.7
(1869) 3.8	(1767) 4.8	(2228) 4.7	EBIT/Interest	(287) 2.3	(536) 6.0	(267) 5.1	(350) 4.9	(397) 4.4	(391) 4.8
1.2	1.7	1.6		-1.0	1.4	1.6	1.8	2.2	2.0
4.6	4.4	4.7			7.2	3.4	2.5	5.8	4.3
(154) 2.1	(137) 2.3	(155) 2.2	Net Profit + Depr., Dep., Amort./Cur. Mat. L/T/D		(10) 3.8	(15) 1.9	(17) 1.4	(32) 2.5	(79) 2.3
1.3	1.6	1.4			1.1	.9	.9	1.6	1.6
1.2	1.1	1.2		1.0	.9	1.0	1.4	1.7	1.8
10.9	8.5	14.9	Fixed/Worth	14.3	6.0	21.3	-26.0	47.5	32.8
-1.4	-1.5	-1.3		-1.1	-1.5	-.9	-1.1	-1.3	-1.4
1.4	1.2	1.4		1.1	1.0	1.3	2.0	1.9	1.9
19.0	15.4	34.2	Debt/Worth	-66.3	12.1	61.2	-34.4	78.3	49.1
-3.1	-3.3	-2.9		-2.5	-3.3	-2.6	-2.7	-3.4	-3.1
127.2	122.5	126.4		103.6	162.1	138.5	116.2	110.8	101.3
(1201) 47.8	(1170) 51.3	(1371) 49.6	% Profit Before Taxes/Tangible Net Worth	(202) 47.8	(408) 57.5	(157) 57.6	(183) 41.6	(212) 44.6	(209) 45.1
14.4	18.5	17.7		8.3	21.8	19.2	16.1	19.3	18.9
25.3	28.7	27.7		35.2	38.5	35.3	23.0	19.7	16.2
9.7	11.9	10.8	% Profit Before Taxes/Total Assets	7.8	16.9	13.4	9.5	8.8	8.7
.7	2.7	1.9		-4.8	2.8	2.6	1.8	3.0	3.2
17.0	18.5	17.4		22.4	28.7	31.5	18.7	12.1	9.2
7.4	7.9	7.9	Sales/Net Fixed Assets	7.3	9.5	10.4	8.9	7.7	5.5
3.7	3.7	3.8		2.8	4.2	4.9	4.2	4.0	3.0
5.4	5.5	5.4		5.8	6.9	6.0	5.5	4.6	3.6
3.2	3.2	3.1	Sales/Total Assets	3.0	3.7	3.4	3.4	3.1	2.4
1.9	1.9	1.9		1.5	2.1	2.2	2.2	2.1	1.6
1.8	1.6	1.6		1.4	1.1	1.3	1.7	2.0	2.2
(1740) 3.0	(1762) 2.8	(2140) 2.8	% Depr., Dep., Amort./Sales	(284) 3.3	(543) 2.2	(233) 2.6	(327) 3.0	(390) 3.3	(363) 3.1
4.6	4.2	4.6		5.7	3.9	4.4	4.6	4.8	4.4
1.3	1.5	1.2		2.7	1.8	1.3	1.1	.8	.5
(778) 2.7	(744) 2.9	(888) 2.4	% Officers', Directors' Owners' Comp/Sales	(151) 5.1	(282) 3.1	(101) 2.1	(131) 1.6	(143) 1.3	(80) 1.2
5.2	5.1	4.7		7.9	5.4	3.7	3.1	2.2	2.3
39500269M	48947651M	50741042M	Net Sales ($)	256580M	1320125M	1179161M	2754162M	6657515M	38573499M
19045271M	21760072M	24045166M	Total Assets ($)	128656M	539498M	443879M	1047766M	2640623M	19244744M

M = $ thousand MM = $ million

See Pages 9 through 22 for Explanation of Ratios and Data

Current Data Sorted by Assets							Comparative Historical Data	
				2		**Type of Statement** Unqualified	7	5
1	1	4	4			Reviewed	16	11
6	9	4	2			Compiled	24	13
36	19	4				Tax Returns	52	44
26	34	18	9	2	1	Other	31	31
6 (4/1-9/30/13)		176 (10/1/13-3/31/14)					4/1/09-3/31/10 ALL	4/1/10-3/31/11 ALL
0-500M	500M-2MM	2-10MM	10-50MM	50-100MM	100-250MM			
69	63	30	15	4	1	**NUMBER OF STATEMENTS**	130	104
%	%	%	%	%	%	**ASSETS**	%	%
19.7	13.0	15.9	13.8			Cash & Equivalents	12.7	13.3
1.7	2.1	1.5	1.7			Trade Receivables (net)	3.2	2.9
5.7	2.5	2.6	3.5			Inventory	4.9	4.4
1.9	1.6	1.3	3.6			All Other Current	2.9	2.6
28.9	19.2	21.3	22.6			Total Current	23.6	23.1
51.0	48.8	46.3	39.2			Fixed Assets (net)	45.7	51.1
10.1	15.6	12.2	28.3			Intangibles (net)	20.1	15.1
9.9	16.4	20.2	10.0			All Other Non-Current	10.6	10.8
100.0	100.0	100.0	100.0			Total	100.0	100.0
						LIABILITIES		
6.2	1.9	5.0	.7			Notes Payable-Short Term	3.7	7.9
6.4	3.2	3.6	6.8			Cur. Mat.-L.T.D.	6.2	7.7
5.8	2.9	5.6	10.2			Trade Payables	4.8	8.8
.6	.0	.0	.1			Income Taxes Payable	.0	.1
28.9	15.8	15.8	11.1			All Other Current	10.2	15.0
47.9	23.8	30.0	28.9			Total Current	24.8	39.6
27.6	41.2	37.2	33.0			Long-Term Debt	41.4	47.8
.0	.0	.0	.2			Deferred Taxes	.0	.1
13.3	3.6	1.7	5.6			All Other Non-Current	13.4	20.5
11.3	31.4	31.0	32.2			Net Worth	20.4	-7.9
100.0	100.0	100.0	100.0			Total Liabilties & Net Worth	100.0	100.0
						INCOME DATA		
100.0	100.0	100.0	100.0			Net Sales	100.0	100.0
						Gross Profit		
92.5	89.5	88.7	91.8			Operating Expenses	94.4	94.7
7.5	10.5	11.3	8.2			Operating Profit	5.6	5.3
1.8	2.0	2.2	.4			All Other Expenses (net)	1.9	2.0
5.8	8.5	9.1	7.8			Profit Before Taxes	3.7	3.3
						RATIOS		
2.0	2.6	1.5	1.3				2.0	1.3
.8	.7	.8	.7			Current	.9	.6
.3	.3	.4	.4				.4	.3
1.2	1.7	1.3	1.1				1.2	1.0
.6	(62) .5	.6	.4			Quick	(128) .6	(103) .4
.2	.2	.2	.2				.2	.2
0 UND	0 UND	0 UND	0 999.8				0 UND	0 UND
0 UND	0 UND	1 546.1	2 227.1			Sales/Receivables	0 UND	0 UND
0 UND	1 388.5	4 90.2	3 107.1				1 366.1	3 108.6
						Cost of Sales/Inventory		
						Cost of Sales/Payables		
36.1	17.1	30.5	30.4				26.1	56.4
-89.8	-99.6	-48.1	-19.9			Sales/Working Capital	-153.3	-40.6
-10.7	-12.6	-16.2	-10.5				-18.9	-9.6
17.0	15.3	26.7	13.2				8.2	6.2
(41) 4.8	(47) 3.4	(22) 7.0	(14) 5.7			EBIT/Interest	(110) 3.1	(94) 2.1
2.2	1.6	2.5	4.4				.9	-.3
						Net Profit + Depr., Dep., Amort./Cur. Mat. L/T/D		
1.0	.9	.6	1.5				1.1	1.6
2.8	4.4	1.4	27.9			Fixed/Worth	10.1	UND
-2.7	-4.4	-16.3	-2.9				-1.3	-.9
.7	.9	.6	1.3				1.2	1.6
6.1	4.3	2.4	53.7			Debt/Worth	27.3	UND
-5.8	-6.9	-19.8	-5.3				-3.3	-2.5
159.9	86.6	52.5					105.9	97.6
(42) 58.5	(42) 48.8	(22) 20.8				% Profit Before Taxes/Tangible Net Worth	(70) 34.8	(52) 37.4
2.6	15.3	11.2					4.7	-1.0
49.2	23.1	17.8	19.0				21.9	17.3
21.2	10.4	9.6	11.9			% Profit Before Taxes/Total Assets	8.5	6.4
2.4	2.6	2.5	6.6				-.4	-3.4
21.3	10.0	9.3	9.3				14.5	12.5
7.3	4.1	5.9	4.7			Sales/Net Fixed Assets	5.4	6.3
3.5	2.1	2.8	2.3				2.8	3.3
6.0	2.9	3.0	2.2				3.7	4.4
3.1	1.6	1.8	1.6			Sales/Total Assets	2.1	2.4
2.1	1.1	1.1	1.4				1.2	1.5
1.4	2.6	2.5	2.5				2.5	2.4
(53) 3.2	(58) 4.1	(28) 3.3	(14) 5.6			% Depr., Dep., Amort./Sales	(104) 4.5	(83) 3.7
7.8	7.7	7.2	7.2				7.3	6.7
2.7	2.0						1.9	3.0
(35) 5.3	(25) 2.4					% Officers', Directors' Owners' Comp/Sales	(31) 5.1	(40) 6.8
7.3	6.7						9.4	10.7
66781M	128043M	335334M	435917M	472309M	172279M	Net Sales ($)	1243686M	1432167M
16879M	60417M	156689M	258957M	260269M	217911M	Total Assets ($)	565537M	827106M

M = $ thousand MM = $ million

See Pages 9 through 22 for Explanation of Ratios and Data

Comparative Historical Data				Current Data Sorted by Sales					
			Type of Statement						
1	1	3	Unqualified		1			1	1
33	12	9	Reviewed	1	1		2	3	2
14	24	21	Compiled	9	5	2	2	1	2
44	42	59	Tax Returns	28	19	3	8	1	
62	42	90	Other	34	23	9	2	12	10
4/1/11-3/31/12	**4/1/12-3/31/13**	**4/1/13-3/31/14**			**6 (4/1-9/30/13)**		**176 (10/1/13-3/31/14)**		
ALL	**ALL**	**ALL**		**0-1MM**	**1-3MM**	**3-5MM**	**5-10MM**	**10-25MM**	**25MM & OVER**
154	121	182	**NUMBER OF STATEMENTS**	72	49	14	14	18	15
%	%	%	**ASSETS**	%	%	%	%	%	%
10.7	9.9	16.0	Cash & Equivalents	14.1	15.2	21.6	21.7	16.5	16.3
2.8	2.2	2.1	Trade Receivables (net)	.7	3.6	.7	1.8	2.0	5.5
4.4	4.7	3.9	Inventory	2.8	4.5	3.2	7.9	3.0	5.3
3.3	2.4	1.8	All Other Current	2.7	.6	1.4	.4	2.0	3.5
21.1	19.2	23.8	Total Current	20.3	23.9	26.9	31.8	23.5	30.6
49.9	51.9	48.1	Fixed Assets (net)	56.5	42.8	39.3	38.9	40.4	51.7
23.2	15.4	14.2	Intangibles (net)	14.5	10.4	10.7	19.2	24.0	12.3
5.8	13.6	13.8	All Other Non-Current	8.6	22.9	23.0	10.0	12.1	5.5
100.0	100.0	100.0	Total	100.0	100.0	100.0	100.0	100.0	100.0
			LIABILITIES						
8.2	10.8	4.0	Notes Payable-Short Term	4.9	3.1	10.3	2.3	1.1	2.0
7.2	5.8	4.7	Cur. Mat.-L.T.D.	5.6	3.3	3.5	5.3	6.2	3.7
6.5	5.8	5.2	Trade Payables	3.0	4.1	4.3	11.2	6.8	12.5
.0	.1	.2	Income Taxes Payable	.6	.0	.0	.0	.0	.1
11.7	16.3	20.5	All Other Current	25.6	22.2	13.4	12.6	12.3	14.4
33.5	38.8	34.6	Total Current	39.7	32.7	31.4	31.5	26.5	32.7
43.1	39.2	34.1	Long-Term Debt	38.8	29.7	18.6	38.9	37.8	31.4
.0	.0	.1	Deferred Taxes	.0	.0	.0	.0	.3	.7
7.1	12.6	7.2	All Other Non-Current	14.2	1.3	3.9	2.5	5.0	3.5
16.2	9.4	24.0	Net Worth	7.4	36.3	46.1	27.1	30.5	31.7
100.0	100.0	100.0	Total Liabilties & Net Worth	100.0	100.0	100.0	100.0	100.0	100.0
			INCOME DATA						
100.0	100.0	100.0	Net Sales	100.0	100.0	100.0	100.0	100.0	100.0
			Gross Profit						
94.2	91.6	90.8	Operating Expenses	88.3	91.3	91.3	94.6	93.5	94.0
5.8	8.4	9.2	Operating Profit	11.7	8.7	8.7	5.4	6.5	6.0
1.8	1.8	1.8	All Other Expenses (net)	3.3	1.0	-.8	1.0	1.0	1.5
4.1	6.6	7.3	Profit Before Taxes	8.3	7.6	9.5	4.4	5.5	4.5
			RATIOS						
1.3	1.4	1.9		2.6	1.6	2.1	1.6	1.8	1.3
.6	.6	.8	Current	.6	.7	.8	.9	1.2	.8
.3	.2	.3		.3	.2	.3	.5	.4	.5
.9	1.0	1.3		1.7	1.0	1.9	1.2	1.4	1.0
(151) .4	.4	(181) .6	Quick	(71) .4	.6	.6	.7	.7	.6
.1	.1	.2		.1	.2	.0	.3	.3	.3
0 UND	0 UND	0 UND		0 UND	0 UND	0 UND	0 UND	0 UND	1 502.6
0 999.8	0 UND	0 UND	Sales/Receivables	0 UND	0 UND	0 UND	1 450.1	2 212.7	3 144.6
2 175.7	1 287.5	2 183.9		0 UND	3 140.2	0 881.8	3 132.4	5 69.1	20 18.3
			Cost of Sales/Inventory						
			Cost of Sales/Payables						
56.3	53.1	27.5		19.7	53.4	17.1	27.1	13.1	31.0
-30.7	-30.1	-87.8	Sales/Working Capital	-91.6	-53.6	-133.1	NM	70.9	-44.2
-11.5	-8.2	-11.3		-9.2	-6.0	-18.7	-27.4	-19.5	-10.7
9.7	12.8	15.4		8.9	20.8	69.5	24.5	10.5	14.8
(139) 3.4	(95) 5.0	(129) 5.4	EBIT/Interest	(47) 2.7	(28) 8.4	(13) 21.2	5.5	(14) 5.6	(13) 12.0
1.0	1.3	2.0		.2	2.0	9.0	2.8	2.8	1.2
3.4									
(10) 2.6			Net Profit + Depr., Dep., Amort./Cur. Mat. L/T/D						
.9									
1.7	1.0	1.0		1.5	.6	.2	1.0	1.2	1.2
16.8	5.4	3.4	Fixed/Worth	5.2	1.6	1.0	2.5	15.5	4.2
-1.0	-2.2	-3.8		-2.5	-8.2	9.5	NM	-1.1	-12.3
1.7	.9	.8		1.1	.6	.6	1.7	1.1	1.0
20.2	8.0	5.0	Debt/Worth	10.1	1.7	.8	5.9	30.2	5.0
-2.5	-4.7	-6.0		-3.5	-11.2	14.4	NM	-3.1	-23.0
113.6	96.5	92.7		74.3	110.4	169.9	231.1	129.2	37.7
(79) 52.9	(73) 44.5	(118) 47.1	% Profit Before Taxes/Tangible Net Worth	(40) 45.7	(34) 54.9	(12) 71.5	(11) 53.1	(11) 44.8	(10) 15.5
14.3	16.0	13.0		2.3	15.2	25.3	13.7	9.6	-.7
22.0	22.0	28.2		26.0	37.7	41.9	29.0	21.1	14.1
9.4	11.0	12.0	% Profit Before Taxes/Total Assets	7.8	16.8	31.7	8.4	12.0	4.8
.0	.5	2.4		-3.1	6.1	12.3	2.7	2.9	1.9
9.7	8.6	11.7		9.1	17.4	21.0	18.6	9.3	7.5
5.9	4.4	5.8	Sales/Net Fixed Assets	2.9	7.1	7.8	10.8	5.9	5.6
3.4	2.6	2.5		1.5	4.1	4.9	5.4	3.1	2.3
3.5	3.4	3.3		3.0	4.6	4.7	5.0	2.9	2.9
2.4	2.4	2.1	Sales/Total Assets	1.5	2.8	2.9	2.8	2.0	2.0
1.6	1.3	1.3		1.0	1.6	1.4	1.4	1.5	1.6
2.4	2.2	2.3		3.3	1.4		1.5	2.6	2.6
(128) 4.6	(95) 3.4	(156) 3.7	% Depr., Dep., Amort./Sales	(60) 6.9	(44) 2.7		3.8	(17) 3.9	(12) 3.3
6.9	6.3	7.5		11.0	3.8		7.7	5.0	6.7
2.7	1.6	2.1		2.2	2.3				
(46) 4.9	(36) 4.7	(66) 3.0	% Officers', Directors' Owners' Comp/Sales	(30) 3.4	(22) 5.6				
9.1	6.0	6.8		6.8	8.7				
2178461M	**1749925M**	**1610663M**	Net Sales ($)	**42818M**	**81287M**	**55460M**	**100947M**	**287665M**	**1042486M**
932563M	**909843M**	**971122M**	Total Assets ($)	**36580M**	**38028M**	**31084M**	**51040M**	**195392M**	**618998M**

M = $ thousand MM = $ million

See Pages 9 through 22 for Explanation of Ratios and Data

OTHER SERVICES (EXCEPT PUBLIC ADMINISTRATION)

Current Data Sorted by Assets							Comparative Historical Data	
						Type of Statement		
1	1	2		1	1	Unqualified	7	9
	3	7	3			Reviewed	16	20
23	20	15	1			Compiled	54	88
241	75	14	2	2	5	Tax Returns	282	289
113	64	22	11	2		Other	158	190
62 (4/1-9/30/13)			567 (10/1/13-3/31/14)				4/1/09-3/31/10	4/1/10-3/31/11
0-500M	**500M-2MM**	**2-10MM**	**10-50MM**	**50-100MM**	**100-250MM**		**ALL**	**ALL**
378	163	60	17	5	6	**NUMBER OF STATEMENTS**	517	596
%	%	%	%	%	%	**ASSETS**	%	%
27.0	13.7	14.2	6.2			Cash & Equivalents	15.8	17.8
8.4	10.8	10.8	10.4			Trade Receivables (net)	11.3	11.2
15.8	12.7	21.9	16.6			Inventory	18.0	16.4
4.3	2.1	1.7	1.5			All Other Current	3.2	3.2
55.4	39.3	48.7	34.7			Total Current	48.2	48.5
26.7	43.6	35.7	40.6			Fixed Assets (net)	35.0	34.3
6.8	7.5	6.6	9.0			Intangibles (net)	7.0	6.6
11.1	9.5	9.1	15.6			All Other Non-Current	9.9	10.6
100.0	100.0	100.0	100.0			Total	100.0	100.0
						LIABILITIES		
13.3	6.4	16.3	5.7			Notes Payable-Short Term	14.0	12.1
4.0	3.3	3.2	4.6			Cur. Mat.-L.T.D.	6.0	4.8
15.1	10.7	11.6	19.7			Trade Payables	15.4	14.9
.2	.0	.1	.2			Income Taxes Payable	.1	.2
21.1	10.8	15.0	24.2			All Other Current	17.9	15.3
53.7	31.3	46.2	54.6			Total Current	53.3	47.3
28.5	34.2	27.9	21.9			Long-Term Debt	35.2	29.8
.0	.1	.2	.1			Deferred Taxes	.1	.1
17.7	7.0	2.3	6.8			All Other Non-Current	9.2	12.6
.1	27.4	23.4	16.6			Net Worth	2.1	10.2
100.0	100.0	100.0	100.0			Total Liabilities & Net Worth	100.0	100.0
						INCOME DATA		
100.0	100.0	100.0	100.0			Net Sales	100.0	100.0
						Gross Profit		
95.5	90.2	90.8	94.2			Operating Expenses	94.5	93.5
4.5	9.8	9.2	5.8			Operating Profit	5.5	6.5
.5	2.9	4.5	3.5			All Other Expenses (net)	2.3	2.1
4.0	6.9	4.6	2.2			Profit Before Taxes	3.2	4.4
						RATIOS		
3.8	3.3	2.7	1.2				2.3	2.7
1.5	1.4	1.3	.9			Current	1.1	1.2
.7	.7	.8	.4				.5	.6
2.5	2.2	1.7	.8				1.3	1.7
(377) .8	1.0	.7	.3			Quick	(516) .5	(593) .7
.3	.3	.3	.1				.2	.2
0 UND	0 737.5	1 499.7	1 370.1				0 UND	0 UND
1 438.8	7 49.2	8 48.0	5 80.4			Sales/Receivables	4 91.0	4 86.5
7 51.7	17 21.0	26 13.8	23 16.1				15 24.9	16 23.4
						Cost of Sales/Inventory		
						Cost of Sales/Payables		
13.8	8.8	7.4	45.0				13.3	11.5
55.9	23.9	28.8	-44.2			Sales/Working Capital	126.7	75.7
-48.9	-30.6	-40.7	-24.0				-19.8	-25.3
16.0	16.6	16.0	25.1				9.7	10.3
(235) 5.3	(127) 3.7	(47) 2.8	(15) 3.9			EBIT/Interest	(392) 2.5	(424) 3.6
1.0	1.1	1.2	1.9				.6	1.1
		4.4					5.8	5.5
		(13) 2.3				Net Profit + Depr., Dep., Amort./Cur. Mat. L/T/D	(23) 1.4	(28) 2.7
		1.4					.7	1.0
.1	.5	.2	1.1				.4	.3
1.2	1.9	1.1	4.6			Fixed/Worth	2.6	1.7
-1.2	67.1	3.7	12.7				-1.4	-2.5
.7	.9	.9	3.0				1.1	.9
5.8	3.5	2.5	8.0			Debt/Worth	7.7	4.3
-3.4	80.6	47.4	23.9				-4.4	-5.8
210.4	63.7	34.0	145.7				100.0	90.9
(232) 78.8	(124) 30.4	(47) 14.5	(15) 40.7			% Profit Before Taxes/Tangible Net Worth	(308) 30.8	(393) 31.1
15.9	8.3	3.8	20.0				4.5	5.5
52.1	18.8	11.8	16.2				27.2	28.0
18.0	8.3	3.2	7.7			% Profit Before Taxes/Total Assets	7.5	9.6
.0	1.1	.7	2.7				-.4	.5
163.5	31.8	32.3	21.6				48.5	58.7
36.2	8.2	12.6	14.1			Sales/Net Fixed Assets	18.3	19.2
13.3	2.2	3.5	2.0				5.9	6.9
11.2	4.2	4.0	5.8				6.8	7.3
6.1	2.5	2.6	2.8			Sales/Total Assets	3.9	4.2
3.6	1.3	1.6	1.0				2.1	2.3
.6	.9	.8	.6				.8	.7
(218) 1.3	(124) 1.9	(46) 1.5	(15) 1.9			% Depr., Dep., Amort./Sales	(390) 1.7	(416) 1.5
2.9	3.9	3.0	2.5				3.0	2.9
4.4	1.9	.7					2.9	3.3
(233) 6.6	(90) 3.5	(26) 2.3				% Officers', Directors' Owners' Comp/Sales	(326) 5.2	(364) 5.7
9.6	5.8	5.7					9.1	8.7
448572M	428450M	1217774M	2145358M	1671400M	8836919M	Net Sales ($)	6205688M	8134657M
74853M	158708M	262351M	335975M	300844M	1025074M	Total Assets ($)	1686598M	2508894M

M = $ thousand MM = $ million

See Pages 9 through 22 for Explanation of Ratios and Data

Comparative Historical Data / Current Data Sorted by Sales

4/1/11-3/31/12 ALL	4/1/12-3/31/13 ALL	4/1/13-3/31/14 ALL	Type of Statement	0-1MM	1-3MM	3-5MM	5-10MM	10-25MM	25MM & OVER
5	8	6	Unqualified	1	1	1			3
17	13	13	Reviewed			3	2	5	3
89	66	59	Compiled	17	16	9	10	5	2
367	329	339	Tax Returns	156	137	17	13	5	11
210	199	212	Other	65	89	20	13	12	13
				62 (4/1-9/30/13)			567 (10/1/13-3/31/14)		
688	615	629	NUMBER OF STATEMENTS	239	243	50	38	27	32
%	%	%	**ASSETS**	%	%	%	%	%	%
18.3	18.6	21.7	Cash & Equivalents	21.9	23.7	17.1	20.9	19.7	15.9
11.0	10.2	9.4	Trade Receivables (net)	6.9	9.6	13.5	15.2	11.2	12.1
16.8	15.8	15.7	Inventory	13.8	15.1	17.2	19.0	20.4	24.2
2.7	2.4	3.3	All Other Current	3.9	3.3	4.0	1.4	2.6	1.1
48.7	47.0	50.1	Total Current	46.4	51.6	51.7	56.5	53.9	53.4
35.2	34.8	32.4	Fixed Assets (net)	35.7	29.8	35.4	29.5	28.3	30.1
5.5	6.8	7.0	Intangibles (net)	6.9	7.7	2.8	5.1	10.7	7.7
10.6	11.5	10.5	All Other Non-Current	11.1	10.9	10.1	8.9	7.1	8.8
100.0	100.0	100.0	Total	100.0	100.0	100.0	100.0	100.0	100.0
			LIABILITIES						
12.7	13.4	11.6	Notes Payable-Short Term	10.4	12.8	8.0	5.7	8.9	25.3
4.7	3.5	3.7	Cur. Mat.-L.T.D.	4.3	3.2	4.3	3.5	2.6	3.2
14.6	12.3	13.9	Trade Payables	12.3	12.7	19.3	15.3	19.1	20.1
.1	.1	.2	Income Taxes Payable	.2	.1	.2	.0	.2	.2
18.6	18.7	17.8	All Other Current	18.5	17.1	11.3	19.7	11.3	30.5
50.7	48.0	47.1	Total Current	45.7	46.0	43.1	44.3	42.1	79.3
32.7	32.2	30.5	Long-Term Debt	38.2	26.2	25.1	21.6	19.3	33.8
.1	.1	.0	Deferred Taxes	.0	.0	.2	.1	.3	.1
17.9	11.9	12.9	All Other Non-Current	20.7	10.2	7.9	2.7	2.6	4.2
-1.4	7.9	9.5	Net Worth	-4.6	17.6	23.8	31.3	35.7	-17.4
100.0	100.0	100.0	Total Liabilties & Net Worth	100.0	100.0	100.0	100.0	100.0	100.0
			INCOME DATA						
100.0	100.0	100.0	Net Sales	100.0	100.0	100.0	100.0	100.0	100.0
			Gross Profit						
93.0	91.9	93.6	Operating Expenses	90.9	94.2	96.4	96.8	98.9	96.5
7.0	8.1	6.4	Operating Profit	9.1	5.8	3.6	3.2	1.1	3.5
2.1	2.8	1.6	All Other Expenses (net)	3.3	.7	.1	.3	.0	1.4
4.9	5.3	4.8	Profit Before Taxes	5.8	5.2	3.5	2.8	1.1	2.1
			RATIOS						
2.6	3.2	3.4		4.1	3.6	2.7	2.5	2.0	1.2
1.3	1.3	1.4	Current	1.6	1.5	1.4	1.2	1.2	1.0
.6	.6	.7		.6	.7	.7	.9	1.0	.6
1.7	2.0	2.3		2.6	2.5	1.9	1.6	.9	1.0
(684) .7	(612) .8	(628) .8	Quick	(238) .8	.9	.9	.9	.6	.5
.2	.2	.3		.2	.3	.3	.5	.4	.2
0 UND	0 UND	0 UND		0 UND	0 UND	0 UND	1 282.1	1 299.3	1 306.5
3 118.4	2 168.3	2 175.5	Sales/Receivables	0 UND	4 89.1	7 52.4	10 38.2	8 46.8	5 66.8
13 27.3	14 26.7	12 31.3		5 67.0	13 28.9	18 20.4	30 12.3	19 19.1	25 14.4
			Cost of Sales/Inventory						
			Cost of Sales/Payables						
14.1	12.9	12.0		11.1	12.5	12.3	10.1	13.3	39.6
66.0	54.1	44.5	Sales/Working Capital	43.8	33.4	37.2	52.2	74.1	NM
-23.5	-22.5	-44.4		-38.5	-34.3	-56.2	-159.8	-999.8	-24.7
11.2	13.8	17.1		10.9	19.7	18.0	27.2	29.4	26.3
(486) 4.0	(431) 3.4	(434) 4.2	EBIT/Interest	(135) 4.0	(176) 4.5	(40) 3.4	(32) 6.2	(21) 3.1	(30) 4.2
1.3	1.1	1.2		.9	1.2	.8	1.9	1.5	1.9
6.4	6.1	4.7							
(29) 2.5	(25) 2.5	(26) 2.3	Net Profit + Depr., Dep., Amort./Cur. Mat. L/T/D						
1.2	1.3	1.1							
.4	.3	.3		.2	.2	.2	.2	.4	.4
1.8	1.6	1.4	Fixed/Worth	2.4	1.3	1.2	1.0	1.1	1.8
-2.2	-3.0	-4.8		-1.4	-2.7	-26.0	4.0	3.9	10.1
1.0	.8	.8		1.1	.6	.8	.7	1.5	1.7
4.6	4.0	4.4	Debt/Worth	10.1	3.5	2.3	2.1	2.8	5.7
-4.7	-6.5	-6.6		-2.9	-7.9	-35.5	NM	8.0	30.9
98.0	102.9	122.2		184.6	145.6	91.3	45.6	34.8	103.3
(448) 33.1	(421) 33.6	(427) 43.0	% Profit Before Taxes/Tangible Net Worth	(144) 44.3	(169) 54.9	(37) 47.2	(29) 22.5	(23) 13.5	(25) 41.8
10.2	7.8	8.7		7.9	13.7	3.3	6.8	.2	23.7
27.5	30.6	33.1		37.1	42.3	31.9	17.2	12.2	33.0
9.2	9.6	11.1	% Profit Before Taxes/Total Assets	9.8	15.0	15.9	9.2	3.9	9.7
1.1	.6	.8		-.9	1.7	.3	1.8	.7	2.6
64.8	71.8	89.9		132.8	89.8	47.8	91.6	39.8	101.3
18.2	21.4	21.1	Sales/Net Fixed Assets	20.4	24.5	19.6	19.5	18.2	18.6
6.8	6.3	7.3		4.8	8.6	8.1	8.4	8.1	7.3
7.8	7.4	7.8		8.8	7.9	8.4	7.5	5.2	7.9
4.3	4.2	4.3	Sales/Total Assets	4.0	4.4	4.7	4.0	4.0	4.2
2.3	2.1	2.3		1.6	2.6	2.7	2.4	2.9	2.2
.7	.7	.7		.9	.6	.5	.5	.7	.6
(472) 1.5	(414) 1.5	(409) 1.6	% Depr., Dep., Amort./Sales	(141) 2.3	(154) 1.5	(39) 1.1	(30) 1.0	(23) 1.2	(22) 1.7
3.1	3.4	3.2		5.3	2.9	2.0	2.2	1.8	2.3
3.0	3.1	3.1		5.4	3.1	2.3	1.2	.6	1.8
(395) 5.6	(352) 5.8	(359) 5.5	% Officers', Directors' Owners' Comp/Sales	(122) 8.0	(165) 4.9	(28) 3.2	(18) 2.9	(14) 1.3	(12) 3.3
8.6	9.3	9.0		11.3	8.6	5.5	4.0	2.5	9.3
8207939M	5635799M	14748473M	Net Sales ($)	134025M	410011M	195548M	256198M	433592M	13319099M
2321790M	1737566M	2157805M	Total Assets ($)	78679M	144462M	56236M	76797M	142139M	1659492M

M = $ thousand MM = $ million

See Pages 9 through 22 for Explanation of Ratios and Data

Current Data Sorted by Assets							Comparative Historical Data	
						Type of Statement		
			1			Unqualified	2	5
	1	1				Reviewed	3	2
1	6	2				Compiled	20	18
15	8	1				Tax Returns	23	26
11	8	1	2	1	1	Other	23	38
9 (4/1-9/30/13)		51 (10/1/13-3/31/14)					4/1/09-3/31/10 ALL	4/1/10-3/31/11 ALL
0-500M	**500M-2MM**	**2-10MM**	**10-50MM**	**50-100MM**	**100-250MM**			
27	23	5	3	1	1	**NUMBER OF STATEMENTS**	71	89
%	%	%	%	%	%	**ASSETS**	%	%
30.1	16.2					Cash & Equivalents	13.9	14.1
11.2	10.1					Trade Receivables (net)	14.8	15.1
13.1	26.2					Inventory	19.4	15.1
4.6	1.4					All Other Current	4.5	2.9
59.0	54.0					Total Current	52.6	47.2
21.3	33.0					Fixed Assets (net)	35.5	38.3
6.8	3.4					Intangibles (net)	6.8	6.9
12.9	9.7					All Other Non-Current	5.1	7.6
100.0	100.0					Total	100.0	100.0
						LIABILITIES		
14.2	6.6					Notes Payable-Short Term	12.5	10.4
1.2	5.5					Cur. Mat.-L.T.D.	2.6	4.0
14.0	17.9					Trade Payables	12.0	15.9
.1	.0					Income Taxes Payable	.2	.0
28.7	16.3					All Other Current	13.1	11.6
58.1	46.5					Total Current	40.4	41.9
34.9	22.9					Long-Term Debt	25.1	30.9
.0	.0					Deferred Taxes	.3	.0
16.8	6.8					All Other Non-Current	9.0	12.2
-9.8	23.9					Net Worth	25.2	15.1
100.0	100.0					Total Liabilities & Net Worth	100.0	100.0
						INCOME DATA		
100.0	100.0					Net Sales	100.0	100.0
						Gross Profit		
95.9	90.2					Operating Expenses	93.5	91.7
4.1	9.8					Operating Profit	6.5	8.3
.2	4.8					All Other Expenses (net)	2.2	4.0
3.9	4.9					Profit Before Taxes	4.3	4.2
						RATIOS		
2.3	2.1						3.1	2.3
1.7	1.7					Current	1.5	1.2
.7	1.2						.9	.6
2.1	1.7						2.5	1.5
1.0	.7					Quick	.8	.7
.3	.4						.3	.3
0 UND	0 UND						1 381.5	1 403.0
1 466.3	12 30.4					Sales/Receivables	14 26.2	9 39.3
11 33.7	20 18.7						37 9.8	22 16.7
						Cost of Sales/Inventory		
						Cost of Sales/Payables		
11.1	8.6						7.5	10.5
66.5	19.7					Sales/Working Capital	21.0	95.1
-46.9	41.0						-156.9	-24.4
11.9	11.9						6.1	12.2
(18) 2.5	(18) 4.7					EBIT/Interest	(58) 2.1	(64) 3.4
.1	-1.1						.6	.2
						Net Profit + Depr., Dep., Amort./Cur. Mat. L/T/D		
.2	.1						.3	.4
20.8	1.6					Fixed/Worth	1.3	1.7
-.4	5.8						12.5	-2.7
.8	1.3						.6	.9
-9.3	2.5					Debt/Worth	2.3	2.6
-3.1	12.6						-55.3	-4.6
230.5	98.3						60.7	54.0
(13) 66.1	(20) 21.1					% Profit Before Taxes/Tangible Net Worth	(53) 12.5	(62) 21.0
4.8	-1.7						-1.4	-5.8
33.5	34.4						15.0	24.9
5.5	6.2					% Profit Before Taxes/Total Assets	3.4	5.2
-7.7	-1.5						-1.1	-2.1
239.0	94.9						35.5	37.7
77.7	21.9					Sales/Net Fixed Assets	19.1	16.0
15.9	2.7						4.6	5.5
13.0	4.4						4.5	6.1
4.9	2.4					Sales/Total Assets	2.9	3.6
3.4	1.3						1.9	1.8
.3	.6						.7	.6
(13) .6	(15) 1.3					% Depr., Dep., Amort./Sales	(55) 1.9	(66) 1.5
1.2	6.0						3.0	2.8
4.0							2.1	2.6
(14) 7.6						% Officers', Directors' Owners' Comp/Sales	(35) 4.8	(46) 6.1
13.1							8.2	9.1
32119M	67317M	29817M	113639M	47130M	147438M	Net Sales ($)	1769501M	624669M
5264M	24047M	18853M	83769M	52611M	112604M	Total Assets ($)	602897M	307627M

M = $ thousand MM = $ million

See Pages 9 through 22 for Explanation of Ratios and Data

Comparative Historical Data / Current Data Sorted by Sales

	Comparative Historical Data			Current Data Sorted by Sales					
Type of Statement									
Unqualified	1	1	1						1
Reviewed	3	1	2	1			1		
Compiled	20	10	9	3	2		4		
Tax Returns	23	22	24	9	12	1	1	1	
Other	21	26	24	9	5	4	2		4
	4/1/11-3/31/12 ALL	**4/1/12-3/31/13 ALL**	**4/1/13-3/31/14 ALL**	**9 (4/1-9/30/13)**		**51 (10/1/13-3/31/14)**			
				0-1MM	**1-3MM**	**3-5MM**	**5-10MM**	**10-25MM**	**25MM & OVER**
NUMBER OF STATEMENTS	68	60	60	22	19	5	8	1	5
ASSETS	%	%	%	%	%	%	%	%	%
Cash & Equivalents	15.7	15.1	21.7	18.8	31.0				
Trade Receivables (net)	19.0	15.2	10.5	9.4	8.6				
Inventory	18.1	19.1	17.7	16.3	18.1				
All Other Current	1.1	2.7	3.7	6.2	.4				
Total Current	53.9	52.2	53.6	50.7	58.1				
Fixed Assets (net)	32.8	32.9	28.7	35.1	22.5				
Intangibles (net)	4.7	5.0	6.3	7.6	4.5				
All Other Non-Current	8.6	9.9	11.4	6.5	15.0				
Total	100.0	100.0	100.0	100.0	100.0				
LIABILITIES									
Notes Payable-Short Term	9.0	10.5	9.6	17.7	6.1				
Cur. Mat.-L.T.D.	3.2	3.3	3.4	2.3	4.4				
Trade Payables	16.4	17.7	14.0	11.4	12.6				
Income Taxes Payable	.1	.1	.3	.0	.1				
All Other Current	10.8	12.8	20.5	17.1	19.5				
Total Current	39.5	44.4	47.8	48.6	42.7				
Long-Term Debt	25.4	26.3	28.8	45.0	23.7				
Deferred Taxes	.3	.1	.8	.0	.0				
All Other Non-Current	14.1	16.1	11.9	17.2	7.4				
Net Worth	20.7	13.2	10.8	-10.8	26.2				
Total Liabilities & Net Worth	100.0	100.0	100.0	100.0	100.0				
INCOME DATA									
Net Sales	100.0	100.0	100.0	100.0	100.0				
Gross Profit									
Operating Expenses	90.5	92.3	92.3	88.1	96.9				
Operating Profit	9.5	7.7	7.7	11.9	3.1				
All Other Expenses (net)	3.4	1.8	2.6	6.4	-.3				
Profit Before Taxes	6.1	6.0	5.1	5.5	3.4				
RATIOS									
Current	2.5	2.6	2.1	2.6	2.1				
	1.4	1.4	1.7	1.4	1.7				
	.8	.7	.8	.4	1.3				
Quick	1.6	1.8	1.7	1.9	2.0				
	.9	.8	.7	.7	1.5				
	.4	.3	.4	.3	.4				
Sales/Receivables	2 200.0	1 260.9	0 UND	0 UND	0 UND				
	16 23.3	14 26.9	6 57.1	3 143.0	3 124.8				
	38 9.7	29 12.6	19 19.0	20 18.5	18 20.6				
Cost of Sales/Inventory									
Cost of Sales/Payables									
Sales/Working Capital	7.8	9.5	9.4	4.5	12.2				
	26.1	21.6	24.7	19.2	39.4				
	-28.6	-27.6	-47.2	-36.9	94.1				
EBIT/Interest	10.6	20.6	11.7	3.4	15.2				
	(53) 4.0	(49) 3.9	(45) 3.4	(15) 2.0	(13) 6.3				
	.3	1.1	.5	-1.0	-3.1				
Net Profit + Depr., Dep., Amort./Cur. Mat. L/T/D									
Fixed/Worth	.3	.3	.2	.0	.3				
	1.6	1.6	1.9	52.9	1.6				
	-2.8	-3.2	-1.4	-.4	3.1				
Debt/Worth	.9	.7	1.0	1.3	.7				
	2.9	3.3	6.2	NM	2.7				
	-5.0	-5.7	-4.8	-3.0	18.6				
% Profit Before Taxes/Tangible Net Worth	51.5	78.6	148.0	66.1	332.8				
	(48) 23.3	(41) 24.4	(42) 29.0	(11) 7.7	(16) 76.8				
	4.1	8.9	7.5	-4.6	-3.6				
% Profit Before Taxes/Total Assets	24.2	32.2	27.8	9.4	41.5				
	6.4	9.5	6.2	3.5	21.8				
	-.7	.6	-1.5	-2.2	-11.0				
Sales/Net Fixed Assets	61.4	61.4	141.4	181.6	231.3				
	18.6	22.1	32.2	26.4	46.0				
	4.2	7.6	5.7	5.7	12.9				
Sales/Total Assets	4.7	5.9	6.1	5.4	7.5				
	3.0	3.4	3.7	2.6	4.6				
	1.7	1.5	1.5	.9	2.3				
% Depr., Dep., Amort./Sales	.4	.6	.4	.8	.4				
	(43) 1.8	(40) 1.4	(38) 1.2	(11) 2.0	(12) .8				
	3.3	2.6	2.8	10.4	2.5				
% Officers', Directors' Owners' Comp/Sales	3.0	2.2	3.0		3.5				
	(29) 6.2	(20) 5.1	(24) 6.2		(10) 5.6				
	10.8	6.8	9.5		7.3				
Net Sales ($)	819893M	1376171M	437460M	11596M	35071M	20175M	51028M	11383M	308207M
Total Assets ($)	436975M	509628M	297148M	12302M	10624M	6460M	16110M	2668M	248984M

M = $ thousand MM = $ million

See Pages 9 through 22 for Explanation of Ratios and Data

Current Data Sorted by Assets							Comparative Historical Data	
						Type of Statement		
		1			1	Unqualified	8	6
	3	7	4			Reviewed	18	21
18	18	4			1	Compiled	43	51
82	65	17	2		3	Tax Returns	165	187
45	63	19	5	1	2	Other	105	121
43 (4/1-9/30/13)			318 (10/1/13-3/31/14)				4/1/09-3/31/10 ALL	4/1/10-3/31/11 ALL
0-500M	**500M-2MM**	**2-10MM**	**10-50MM**	**50-100MM**	**100-250MM**			
145	149	48	11	1	7	**NUMBER OF STATEMENTS**	339	386
%	%	%	%	%	%	**ASSETS**	%	%
25.4	22.3	14.7	16.5			Cash & Equivalents	19.2	20.1
13.4	14.4	14.5	15.2			Trade Receivables (net)	13.4	12.2
12.6	7.8	14.4	10.4			Inventory	9.5	9.7
2.4	4.1	1.9	2.4			All Other Current	3.1	3.6
53.8	48.6	45.4	44.4			Total Current	45.1	45.5
31.2	34.5	37.1	37.5			Fixed Assets (net)	36.0	37.9
4.6	6.9	8.4	14.7			Intangibles (net)	8.4	5.5
10.3	10.0	9.1	3.4			All Other Non-Current	10.5	11.1
100.0	100.0	100.0	100.0			Total	100.0	100.0
						LIABILITIES		
14.2	6.0	8.0	2.7			Notes Payable-Short Term	9.8	13.1
3.2	1.7	2.3	3.1			Cur. Mat.-L.T.D.	3.8	3.8
18.7	13.6	13.3	12.3			Trade Payables	15.9	14.6
.3	.2	.0	.0			Income Taxes Payable	.1	.2
22.9	12.4	9.5	6.2			All Other Current	16.9	15.5
59.3	33.9	33.2	24.2			Total Current	46.6	47.2
23.0	23.0	40.1	25.7			Long-Term Debt	31.8	27.7
.0	.2	.2	.4			Deferred Taxes	.2	.2
15.6	8.6	6.2	6.1			All Other Non-Current	9.0	16.7
2.1	34.3	20.4	43.6			Net Worth	12.6	8.2
100.0	100.0	100.0	100.0			Total Liabilties & Net Worth	100.0	100.0
						INCOME DATA		
100.0	100.0	100.0	100.0			Net Sales	100.0	100.0
						Gross Profit		
95.5	93.7	91.6	87.5			Operating Expenses	95.3	93.2
4.5	6.3	8.4	12.5			Operating Profit	4.7	6.8
.3	1.0	2.3	1.5			All Other Expenses (net)	2.0	1.8
4.2	5.3	6.1	11.0			Profit Before Taxes	2.7	5.0
						RATIOS		
3.1	2.7	2.2	2.6				2.0	2.2
1.3	1.5	1.5	1.8			Current	1.1	1.1
.4	.8	.9	.8				.6	.6
2.3	2.4	1.9	2.4				1.6	1.6
.9	(148) 1.2	.9	1.2			Quick	.7	(385) .7
.3	.5	.4	.5				.3	.4
0 UND	**3** 124.4	**6** 56.8	**16** 23.2				**1** 541.0	**0** UND
3 111.8	**9** 38.9	**15** 25.0	**19** 19.1			Sales/Receivables	**7** 49.1	**8** 47.6
12 31.7	**20** 18.3	**21** 17.3	**30** 12.2				**14** 25.7	**15** 24.8
						Cost of Sales/Inventory		
						Cost of Sales/Payables		
16.0	11.3	10.9	4.9				16.3	18.2
73.3	29.6	27.1	10.9			Sales/Working Capital	149.3	188.6
-24.2	-63.5	-68.4	-45.4				-26.8	-20.2
14.0	39.6	35.2					9.6	11.7
(97) 5.2	(107) 9.2	(41) 4.1				EBIT/Interest	(258) 3.0	(284) 3.7
1.1	1.8	1.3					.8	1.1
							6.6	5.2
						Net Profit + Depr., Dep., Amort./Cur. Mat. L/T/D	(27) 2.3	(23) 1.5
							1.2	.5
.3	.3	.6	.2				.5	.5
2.0	.9	2.2	1.5			Fixed/Worth	2.3	2.3
-1.8	8.2	UND	12.0				-2.4	-2.7
.7	.7	1.0	.4				1.0	1.1
4.5	1.7	5.0	2.6			Debt/Worth	5.4	5.7
-5.5	22.6	-49.5	14.5				-6.3	-6.5
176.2	88.0	65.8					106.1	89.2
(91) 55.6	(121) 38.2	(35) 27.4				% Profit Before Taxes/Tangible Net Worth	(229) 39.7	(252) 35.4
18.2	16.1	13.6					5.0	8.1
51.7	32.2	18.9	22.2				22.0	23.7
16.9	12.5	6.4	18.6			% Profit Before Taxes/Total Assets	7.7	8.4
2.2	3.0	1.5	8.6				-.5	.5
90.7	49.4	24.5	23.6				43.9	44.5
34.4	16.8	10.4	11.3			Sales/Net Fixed Assets	19.5	16.4
12.6	5.3	3.8	3.0				8.0	5.8
10.6	5.2	4.2	3.4				7.4	6.6
6.1	3.4	2.5	2.1			Sales/Total Assets	4.5	4.2
4.0	2.1	1.7	1.6				2.6	2.3
.4	.6	1.1	.9				.7	.6
(103) 1.0	(106) 1.1	(40) 1.8	(10) 1.5			% Depr., Dep., Amort./Sales	(264) 1.4	(277) 1.4
1.8	2.2	4.0	2.9				2.6	2.7
3.3	2.4	1.4					2.6	2.7
(93) 5.3	(94) 4.0	(20) 3.6				% Officers', Directors' Owners' Comp/Sales	(219) 4.8	(221) 5.0
8.7	6.3	5.0					7.7	7.5
221192M	574723M	526600M	399654M	52166M	6326219M	Net Sales ($)	6030364M	5217576M
33190M	153783M	191122M	172439M	76652M	1296484M	Total Assets ($)	1464296M	1224165M

M = $ thousand MM = $ million

See Pages 9 through 22 for Explanation of Ratios and Data

Comparative Historical Data | **Current Data Sorted by Sales**

4/1/11-3/31/12 ALL	4/1/12-3/31/13 ALL	4/1/13-3/31/14 ALL	Type of Statement	0-1MM	1-3MM	3-5MM	5-10MM	10-25MM	25MM & OVER
1	4	2	Unqualified					1	1
30	10	14	Reviewed		3	2	2	5	2
60	43	41	Compiled	9	15	6	7	3	1
244	204	169	Tax Returns	39	80	22	17	5	6
141	140	135	Other	23	42	25	24	14	7
				43 (4/1-9/30/13)		318 (10/1/13-3/31/14)			
476	401	361	**NUMBER OF STATEMENTS**	71	140	55	50	28	17
%	%	%	**ASSETS**	%	%	%	%	%	%
18.7	19.3	22.2	Cash & Equivalents	22.1	22.8	26.4	19.1	21.0	14.2
13.5	13.4	14.0	Trade Receivables (net)	8.4	14.1	12.9	19.2	19.9	15.5
9.6	9.9	11.0	Inventory	13.1	10.4	7.1	11.1	11.4	17.6
3.4	3.6	3.0	All Other Current	1.6	3.2	2.2	4.6	5.1	2.4
45.2	46.2	50.2	Total Current	45.2	50.5	48.7	54.0	57.5	49.6
35.3	34.7	33.2	Fixed Assets (net)	43.2	34.0	30.1	26.3	28.4	22.9
7.4	7.0	6.9	Intangibles (net)	3.8	4.4	10.7	8.0	8.2	23.0
12.1	12.1	9.7	All Other Non-Current	7.9	11.1	10.5	11.7	5.9	4.5
100.0	100.0	100.0	Total	100.0	100.0	100.0	100.0	100.0	100.0
			LIABILITIES						
14.2	11.4	9.4	Notes Payable-Short Term	15.5	7.7	8.3	5.3	15.8	3.5
3.4	4.9	2.4	Cur. Mat.-L.T.D.	2.0	3.0	2.7	1.8	1.8	2.3
15.6	15.5	15.6	Trade Payables	8.9	18.0	15.3	18.7	16.1	14.3
.1	.1	.2	Income Taxes Payable	.3	.2	.1	.4	.1	.2
15.1	19.9	15.9	All Other Current	13.2	19.2	17.0	14.8	9.9	9.7
48.3	51.9	43.5	Total Current	39.9	48.0	43.3	40.8	43.6	30.0
28.3	27.4	25.8	Long-Term Debt	31.8	26.5	16.7	23.3	26.2	31.0
.1	.1	.2	Deferred Taxes	.0	.0	.4	.3	.3	.6
13.4	13.7	10.9	All Other Non-Current	18.3	10.5	8.4	8.4	8.5	2.3
9.8	6.9	19.7	Net Worth	10.0	15.1	31.2	27.2	21.3	36.1
100.0	100.0	100.0	Total Liabilties & Net Worth	100.0	100.0	100.0	100.0	100.0	100.0
			INCOME DATA						
100.0	100.0	100.0	Net Sales	100.0	100.0	100.0	100.0	100.0	100.0
			Gross Profit						
93.8	93.6	93.9	Operating Expenses	90.0	94.8	94.6	95.2	96.4	93.1
6.2	6.4	6.1	Operating Profit	10.0	5.2	5.4	4.8	3.6	6.9
1.5	2.0	.9	All Other Expenses (net)	3.4	.7	-.1	-.3	-.1	.8
4.7	4.5	5.2	Profit Before Taxes	6.6	4.5	5.5	5.1	3.7	6.1
			RATIOS						
2.3	2.1	2.7		5.3	2.5	3.3	2.2	2.4	3.2
1.1	1.1	1.4	Current	1.6	1.3	1.5	1.4	1.6	1.8
.6	.5	.7		.4	.6	.5	.9	.9	1.0
1.7	1.5	2.3		3.4	2.2	2.5	1.9	2.2	2.4
(475) .7	(400) .7	(360) 1.0	Quick	1.2	(139) 1.0	1.2	.9	1.1	.9
.3	.3	.4		.2	.4	.4	.5	.5	.5
0 UND	0 UND	0 UND		0 UND	0 UND	2 159.5	5 67.2	10 35.5	12 31.4
8 44.0	8 48.5	8 43.2	Sales/Receivables	0 UND	8 44.3	8 43.4	11 33.4	16 23.1	18 20.5
16 22.3	16 23.0	17 21.5		11 33.8	16 23.1	13 28.0	24 15.1	23 16.1	31 11.6
			Cost of Sales/Inventory						
			Cost of Sales/Payables						
16.1	16.9	12.2		7.4	15.3	12.3	13.9	9.8	6.2
132.2	107.9	34.9	Sales/Working Capital	46.0	49.5	29.3	30.0	28.8	17.6
-28.2	-19.3	-36.1		-14.0	-25.5	-23.8	-91.7	-131.7	NM
14.2	19.8	29.7		8.3	17.2	49.5	39.9	116.8	200.7
(342) 4.9	(287) 4.5	(260) 6.1	EBIT/Interest	(44) 4.1	(100) 4.9	(39) 11.8	(39) 12.8	(24) 16.1	(14) 9.5
1.4	1.4	1.6		1.0	1.1	2.3	1.7	2.7	2.0
4.5	5.1	5.2							
(21) 2.7	(20) 2.3	(16) 3.1	Net Profit + Depr., Dep., Amort./Cur. Mat. L/T/D						
.7	.7	1.0							
.4	.5	.3		.5	.2	.2	.4	.3	.3
1.6	1.5	1.2	Fixed/Worth	4.5	1.2	.8	1.0	1.3	1.5
-4.7	-4.5	-9.7		-3.4	UND	18.8	-21.7	7.4	-.4
1.0	1.0	.7		1.0	.7	.5	.9	.8	.9
3.5	4.0	2.5	Debt/Worth	5.6	2.4	1.6	1.6	4.0	2.6
-6.8	-7.1	-21.4		-6.9	-28.2	999.8	-107.3	57.3	-3.3
86.2	90.8	114.4		114.9	126.7	114.3	121.6	80.2	83.6
(326) 36.5	(276) 37.2	(260) 43.9	% Profit Before Taxes/Tangible Net Worth	(45) 36.4	(103) 42.9	(42) 45.4	(37) 58.9	(22) 29.7	(11) 52.8
6.6	6.5	16.1		10.4	16.1	19.7	22.2	11.1	40.5
25.7	26.6	33.6		29.8	33.9	44.4	37.1	24.0	30.2
10.9	8.8	12.5	% Profit Before Taxes/Total Assets	9.8	11.2	21.3	13.6	9.0	16.1
.8	.7	2.6		.7	1.4	5.0	4.0	2.2	7.0
54.1	59.6	55.3		42.1	62.3	58.6	42.6	65.5	39.0
19.6	21.4	20.2	Sales/Net Fixed Assets	10.9	23.9	25.8	21.7	19.4	20.6
6.7	7.6	7.0		1.9	7.1	8.2	11.6	7.7	11.1
7.1	7.1	6.6		6.1	8.3	6.4	6.5	5.5	5.5
4.3	4.0	4.1	Sales/Total Assets	2.8	4.3	4.4	4.8	4.0	3.2
2.4	2.3	2.4		1.2	2.6	3.0	3.1	2.2	1.7
.7	.6	.6		1.0	.5	.4	.5	.9	.5
(332) 1.4	(285) 1.3	(262) 1.2	% Depr., Dep., Amort./Sales	(49) 2.7	(100) 1.0	(40) .9	(40) 1.0	(22) 1.2	(11) 1.1
2.9	2.4	2.3		7.7	2.2	1.7	1.8	2.0	2.3
2.4	2.7	2.8		5.2	3.1	2.4	1.3		
(271) 4.4	(233) 5.0	(211) 4.7	% Officers', Directors' Owners' Comp/Sales	(40) 8.4	(89) 4.4	(35) 4.2	(33) 2.7		
7.7	8.6	7.4		12.1	7.0	5.7	4.9		
6734324M	3522204M	8100554M	Net Sales ($)	42161M	269024M	221076M	347369M	426887M	6794037M
1409075M	1679889M	1923670M	Total Assets ($)	32346M	87809M	57676M	99715M	133982M	1512142M

M = $ thousand MM = $ million

See Pages 9 through 22 for Explanation of Ratios and Data

Current Data Sorted by Assets							Comparative Historical Data	
						Type of Statement		
		1				Unqualified	3	1
		1				Reviewed	2	3
1	2	1				Compiled	3	1
7	2	1				Tax Returns	16	12
3	2	1	1		1	Other	7	6
6 (4/1-9/30/13)		17 (10/1/13-3/31/14)					4/1/09-3/31/10 ALL	4/1/10-3/31/11 ALL
0-500M	500M-2MM	2-10MM	10-50MM	50-100MM	100-250MM			
11	6	4	1		1	NUMBER OF STATEMENTS	31	23
%	%	%	%	%	%	**ASSETS**	%	%
24.1				DATA NOT AVAILABLE		Cash & Equivalents	12.5	12.8
17.4						Trade Receivables (net)	26.3	21.5
13.8						Inventory	24.0	29.2
6.3						All Other Current	2.0	1.1
61.7						Total Current	64.8	64.7
31.2						Fixed Assets (net)	21.9	27.0
3.9						Intangibles (net)	3.1	2.2
3.2						All Other Non-Current	10.1	6.1
100.0						Total	100.0	100.0
						LIABILITIES		
17.2						Notes Payable-Short Term	10.5	16.4
4.1						Cur. Mat.-L.T.D.	7.6	2.2
17.2						Trade Payables	17.8	16.3
.0						Income Taxes Payable	.0	.3
8.3						All Other Current	9.0	10.7
46.8						Total Current	44.9	45.9
16.6						Long-Term Debt	25.5	20.5
.0						Deferred Taxes	.9	.3
20.6						All Other Non-Current	9.3	5.2
16.0						Net Worth	19.4	28.1
100.0						Total Liabilties & Net Worth	100.0	100.0
						INCOME DATA		
100.0						Net Sales	100.0	100.0
						Gross Profit		
90.0						Operating Expenses	95.9	94.3
10.0						Operating Profit	4.1	5.7
.4						All Other Expenses (net)	1.9	.9
9.6						Profit Before Taxes	2.2	4.8
						RATIOS		
2.8							2.8	3.4
1.5						Current	1.4	1.3
.7							.9	.8
2.2							2.0	1.8
1.0						Quick	.8	.8
.4							.4	.3
0 UND							**14** 25.5	**6** 59.0
8 44.1						Sales/Receivables	**18** 19.7	**18** 20.3
15 24.6							**31** 11.7	**28** 13.2
						Cost of Sales/Inventory		
						Cost of Sales/Payables		
6.2							10.3	8.7
30.0						Sales/Working Capital	18.3	34.8
-95.0							-40.5	-37.8
							3.8	14.4
						EBIT/Interest	(24) .3	(19) 4.9
							-3.5	.3
						Net Profit + Depr., Dep., Amort./Cur. Mat. L/T/D		
.2							.2	.2
1.5						Fixed/Worth	.9	.5
-2.8							-7.4	1.9
.5							.7	.6
3.4						Debt/Worth	2.8	2.3
-8.0							-40.7	7.7
							22.2	106.5
						% Profit Before Taxes/Tangible Net Worth	(22) 1.9	(21) 21.1
							-40.5	-.1
75.6							8.1	14.9
42.1						% Profit Before Taxes/Total Assets	.9	6.2
15.8							-10.2	-2.0
86.3							84.9	73.3
33.9						Sales/Net Fixed Assets	29.3	24.3
17.8							6.5	9.2
11.7							6.2	5.7
6.8						Sales/Total Assets	3.3	4.0
2.8							1.5	2.5
							.7	.5
						% Depr., Dep., Amort./Sales	(24) 1.1	(17) 1.3
							2.7	3.7
							2.0	2.4
						% Officers', Directors' Owners' Comp/Sales	(18) 4.1	(15) 4.0
							8.6	9.7
12497M	29665M	32704M	45218M		109902M	Net Sales ($)	2281002M	558171M
2010M	6927M	16489M	13446M		227214M	Total Assets ($)	346680M	94383M

M = $ thousand MM = $ million

See Pages 9 through 22 for Explanation of Ratios and Data

Comparative Historical Data | **Current Data Sorted by Sales**

4/1/11-3/31/12 ALL	4/1/12-3/31/13 ALL	4/1/13-3/31/14 ALL	Type of Statement	0-1MM	1-3MM	3-5MM	5-10MM	10-25MM	25MM & OVER
1	4		Unqualified						
2	2	1	Reviewed				1		
1	4	4	Compiled	1		2	1		
14	7	10	Tax Returns	4	3	1	1	1	
3	7	8	Other	1	3	1		1	2
				6 (4/1-9/30/13)			17 (10/1/13-3/31/14)		
21	24	23	NUMBER OF STATEMENTS	6	6	4	3	2	2
%	%	%	ASSETS	%	%	%	%	%	%
13.0	17.2	14.0	Cash & Equivalents						
27.3	18.7	17.4	Trade Receivables (net)						
13.6	23.1	20.2	Inventory						
1.7	.7	3.3	All Other Current						
55.6	59.7	55.0	Total Current						
29.7	23.4	32.9	Fixed Assets (net)						
3.6	8.7	6.0	Intangibles (net)						
11.2	8.3	6.0	All Other Non-Current						
100.0	100.0	100.0	Total						
			LIABILITIES						
15.6	14.1	14.8	Notes Payable-Short Term						
4.3	10.2	3.4	Cur. Mat.-L.T.D.						
21.9	15.3	15.1	Trade Payables						
1.5	.1	.0	Income Taxes Payable						
27.8	19.2	17.7	All Other Current						
71.1	58.9	50.9	Total Current						
25.6	49.9	21.4	Long-Term Debt						
.2	.6	.7	Deferred Taxes						
2.3	5.3	12.7	All Other Non-Current						
.7	-14.7	14.3	Net Worth						
100.0	100.0	100.0	Total Liabilties & Net Worth						
			INCOME DATA						
100.0	100.0	100.0	Net Sales						
			Gross Profit						
93.5	96.6	88.8	Operating Expenses						
6.5	3.4	11.2	Operating Profit						
1.5	1.5	1.8	All Other Expenses (net)						
5.0	1.9	9.5	Profit Before Taxes						
			RATIOS						
1.5	2.2	2.8							
1.0	1.4	1.6	Current						
.4	.8	1.0							
1.1	1.5	1.6							
.6	.8	.9	Quick						
.2	.4	.4							
13 27.4	**10** 35.0	**8** 44.1							
19 19.2	**17** 21.3	**16** 22.8	Sales/Receivables						
30 12.2	**24** 15.0	**20** 18.1							
			Cost of Sales/Inventory						
			Cost of Sales/Payables						
34.3	9.8	6.3							
999.8	39.0	19.5	Sales/Working Capital						
-10.6	-23.2	516.7							
5.1	5.1	17.0							
(16) 1.8	(17) 2.3	(19) 5.6	EBIT/Interest						
-3.9	-4.3	2.4							
			Net Profit + Depr., Dep., Amort./Cur. Mat. L/T/D						
.3	.2	.3							
1.9	.7	1.1	Fixed/Worth						
-2.1	-1.4	-2.8							
1.7	1.3	1.1							
4.0	3.5	2.4	Debt/Worth						
-6.5	-3.3	-8.0							
123.0	52.1	105.1							
(14) 30.8	(15) 34.7	(15) 41.0	% Profit Before Taxes/Tangible Net Worth						
-8.6	9.8	8.2							
30.8	19.5	59.6							
5.4	6.0	15.8	% Profit Before Taxes/Total Assets						
-12.8	-9.6	7.0							
96.6	78.7	60.1							
27.8	25.6	24.8	Sales/Net Fixed Assets						
5.4	6.0	7.6							
7.4	5.2	6.8							
5.1	3.9	4.2	Sales/Total Assets						
2.4	2.6	2.7							
.7	1.0	.7							
(17) 1.4	(15) 2.6	(15) 2.0	% Depr., Dep., Amort./Sales						
2.8	4.7	3.8							
2.3	1.7	2.2							
(13) 5.9	(11) 3.7	(11) 4.5	% Officers', Directors' Owners' Comp/Sales						
10.8	12.4	8.8							
127646M	247689M	229986M	Net Sales ($)	3108M	9579M	16458M	17244M	28477M	155120M
84619M	320935M	266086M	Total Assets ($)	1766M	1310M	7001M	5433M	9916M	240660M

M = $ thousand MM = $ million

See Pages 9 through 22 for Explanation of Ratios and Data

Current Data Sorted by Assets / Comparative Historical Data

0-500M	500M-2MM	2-10MM	10-50MM	50-100MM	100-250MM	Type of Statement	4/1/09-3/31/10 ALL	4/1/10-3/31/11 ALL
	1	1	1		1	Unqualified	2	4
	1	1	6			Reviewed	1	4
3	6	2	1	1		Compiled	6	9
45	21	7				Tax Returns	23	38
10	11	9	5	2	2	Other	22	38
	5 (4/1-9/30/13)		132 (10/1/13-3/31/14)					
58	40	20	13	3	3	NUMBER OF STATEMENTS	54	93
%	%	%	%	%	%	**ASSETS**	%	%
19.3	11.8	3.7	6.8			Cash & Equivalents	8.9	13.6
4.2	2.1	3.9	2.7			Trade Receivables (net)	3.1	4.7
17.5	5.7	4.8	6.9			Inventory	10.7	11.6
1.7	.9	.3	1.1			All Other Current	2.5	4.2
42.7	20.5	12.8	17.6			Total Current	25.3	34.0
26.3	63.6	68.8	52.9			Fixed Assets (net)	58.8	44.4
11.6	7.2	11.3	22.8			Intangibles (net)	12.0	13.9
19.4	8.6	7.1	6.6			All Other Non-Current	3.9	7.7
100.0	100.0	100.0	100.0			Total	100.0	100.0
						LIABILITIES		
11.5	.7	2.2	.9			Notes Payable-Short Term	4.6	3.0
2.2	3.1	3.3	3.1			Cur. Mat.-L.T.D.	4.0	3.9
13.8	6.1	3.7	6.7			Trade Payables	11.0	14.9
.0	.0	.1	.1			Income Taxes Payable	.0	.0
16.3	25.0	4.3	3.7			All Other Current	11.7	10.0
43.9	34.9	13.5	14.5			Total Current	31.3	31.9
30.6	60.8	61.2	53.4			Long-Term Debt	56.3	53.7
.0	.0	.2	.4			Deferred Taxes	.1	.2
4.8	7.1	3.6	5.0			All Other Non-Current	23.6	12.4
20.7	-2.8	21.5	26.7			Net Worth	-11.4	1.8
100.0	100.0	100.0	100.0			Total Liabilties & Net Worth	100.0	100.0
						INCOME DATA		
100.0	100.0	100.0	100.0			Net Sales	100.0	100.0
						Gross Profit		
93.2	80.8	75.6	92.4			Operating Expenses	91.4	91.0
6.8	19.2	24.4	7.6			Operating Profit	8.6	9.0
1.4	7.5	14.1	.0			All Other Expenses (net)	4.5	3.6
5.4	11.7	10.3	7.6			Profit Before Taxes	4.1	5.4
						RATIOS		
4.9	3.7	2.0	1.9				1.6	2.1
1.2	.8	.9	1.1			Current	.8	1.2
.5	.2	.3	.5				.3	.6
1.5	2.8	1.4	1.1				.9	1.6
.4	.4	.6	.3			Quick	.4	(92) .6
.0	.1	.2	.2				.2	.2
0 UND	0 UND	0 UND	1 261.0				0 UND	0 UND
0 UND	1 316.0	1 326.8	2 173.6			Sales/Receivables	0 759.3	1 244.0
1 247.7	3 106.1	9 41.4	5 73.4				4 85.9	7 53.4
						Cost of Sales/Inventory		
						Cost of Sales/Payables		
19.5	10.6	14.3	16.3				43.2	11.2
115.0	-114.1	-280.1	114.5			Sales/Working Capital	-44.4	75.7
-31.5	-8.5	-5.6	-19.4				-8.1	-17.7
29.3	5.9	12.6	15.0				5.3	6.9
(29) 10.0	(32) 3.2	(14) 4.7	(12) 4.1			EBIT/Interest	(42) 2.3	(66) 2.4
1.2	1.8	1.8	1.9				1.3	1.2
						Net Profit + Depr., Dep., Amort./Cur. Mat. L/T/D		
.0	1.6	2.4	1.5				1.2	.7
.9	6.8	8.8	4.3			Fixed/Worth	102.8	7.4
-3.3	-2.9	-23.2	-2.0				-1.9	-1.8
.6	2.5	2.0	1.2				2.6	2.6
3.8	8.8	8.9	4.3			Debt/Worth	-45.1	-66.2
-13.0	-4.2	-25.3	-5.3				-3.6	-2.8
215.6	84.4	36.7					56.8	90.1
(37) 113.0	(26) 43.0	(14) 22.5				% Profit Before Taxes/Tangible Net Worth	(26) 25.5	(45) 34.2
23.5	14.6	3.2					3.8	9.6
69.4	20.9	7.2	13.2				12.9	18.7
31.1	8.2	4.5	6.5			% Profit Before Taxes/Total Assets	6.4	6.9
4.0	2.0	.8	3.0				-1.0	-.2
785.1	10.7	2.9	10.9				9.1	45.3
72.9	1.5	1.2	3.1			Sales/Net Fixed Assets	2.5	5.3
16.5	.6	.2	.9				.8	1.4
9.3	2.8	1.5	2.2				3.7	3.3
6.3	1.0	.8	1.2			Sales/Total Assets	1.5	1.8
3.6	.4	.1	.8				.6	.9
.3	2.8	2.4	1.3				2.5	1.3
(26) 1.1	(28) 4.7	(16) 6.1	(12) 3.1			% Depr., Dep., Amort./Sales	(42) 3.8	(68) 3.1
3.4	13.0	11.4	5.5				13.4	6.8
.7	1.9						1.9	3.3
(25) 5.0	(11) 2.9					% Officers', Directors' Owners' Comp/Sales	(18) 4.1	(31) 4.2
7.7	12.4						8.4	7.2
56126M	94676M	123945M	413726M	76472M	639033M	Net Sales ($)	213435M	788649M
11086M	43754M	93912M	310314M	158069M	399986M	Total Assets ($)	165325M	573907M

M = $ thousand MM = $ million

See Pages 9 through 22 for Explanation of Ratios and Data

Comparative Historical Data / Current Data Sorted by Sales

4/1/11-3/31/12 ALL	4/1/12-3/31/13 ALL	4/1/13-3/31/14 ALL	Type of Statement	0-1MM	1-3MM	3-5MM	5-10MM	10-25MM	25MM & OVER
2	3	4	Unqualified					2	2
6	6	8	Reviewed		1		1	5	1
11	12	13	Compiled	6	1	3	2		1
53	48	73	Tax Returns	32	33	4	3	1	
34	51	39	Other	21	6	1	1	4	6
				5 (4/1-9/30/13)			132 (10/1/13-3/31/14)		
106	120	137	**NUMBER OF STATEMENTS**	59	41	8	7	12	10
%	%	%	**ASSETS**	%	%	%	%	%	%
15.0	16.8	13.1	Cash & Equivalents	14.4	11.4			13.9	4.1
3.2	4.9	3.5	Trade Receivables (net)	3.6	2.2			4.2	6.9
10.8	8.8	10.9	Inventory	8.0	15.9			8.6	14.3
2.8	3.3	1.3	All Other Current	.2	2.4			1.8	1.8
31.8	33.7	28.8	Total Current	26.3	32.0			28.5	27.1
47.0	47.9	46.6	Fixed Assets (net)	56.0	36.1			45.8	35.1
13.9	11.3	11.6	Intangibles (net)	7.5	13.5			18.1	30.5
7.3	7.0	13.0	All Other Non-Current	10.2	18.5			7.5	7.3
100.0	100.0	100.0	Total	100.0	100.0			100.0	100.0
			LIABILITIES						
6.1	6.6	6.0	Notes Payable-Short Term	7.0	6.8			3.3	4.8
3.8	3.8	2.7	Cur. Mat.-L.T.D.	2.5	2.7			3.1	3.3
10.5	10.2	9.0	Trade Payables	5.5	13.0			7.9	11.4
.2	.2	.0	Income Taxes Payable	.0	.0			.0	.2
9.5	8.8	15.5	All Other Current	15.6	13.2			8.0	6.7
30.2	29.5	33.2	Total Current	30.6	35.9			22.3	26.3
43.7	52.1	46.0	Long-Term Debt	50.2	42.5			36.8	42.1
.2	.1	.1	Deferred Taxes	.0	.0			.4	.3
15.4	16.2	5.3	All Other Non-Current	6.5	3.4			3.1	5.9
10.6	2.1	15.3	Net Worth	12.7	18.2			37.3	25.3
100.0	100.0	100.0	Total Liabilties & Net Worth	100.0	100.0			100.0	100.0
			INCOME DATA						
100.0	100.0	100.0	Net Sales	100.0	100.0			100.0	100.0
			Gross Profit						
90.3	86.8	86.5	Operating Expenses	79.3	92.2			92.7	94.1
9.7	13.2	13.5	Operating Profit	20.7	7.8			7.3	5.9
3.7	6.0	4.7	All Other Expenses (net)	10.8	.2			.3	-.1
6.0	7.2	8.8	Profit Before Taxes	9.8	7.6			7.0	6.0
			RATIOS						
3.4	2.6	2.8		3.9	4.0			2.4	1.2
1.1	1.2	1.0	Current	.8	1.4			1.5	.7
.6	.5	.4		.3	.5			.7	.5
1.6	1.5	1.5		2.9	1.0			1.5	.4
(105) .5	.7	.4	Quick	.7	.2			.8	.2
.2	.2	.1		.1	.0			.3	.2
0 UND	0 UND	0 UND		0 UND	0 UND			1 326.5	1 256.5
1 321.1	1 327.0	1 411.8	Sales/Receivables	0 UND	0 UND			3 145.5	2 173.4
3 106.7	4 87.3	3 106.4		3 131.0	2 241.6			5 69.8	10 35.8
			Cost of Sales/Inventory						
			Cost of Sales/Payables						
17.8	14.6	13.5		11.1	22.0			14.3	89.2
162.0	58.7	247.8	Sales/Working Capital	-128.0	140.1			52.2	-46.7
-14.8	-15.8	-13.8		-6.8	-35.1			-52.0	-15.9
9.3	7.0	11.6		6.8	26.3			15.0	
(79) 3.1	(83) 2.7	(92) 4.3	EBIT/Interest	(28) 1.9	(32) 7.3			5.4	
1.0	1.1	1.8		1.1	2.9			1.2	
		6.8							
		(10) 3.3	Net Profit + Depr., Dep., Amort./Cur. Mat. L/T/D						
		2.6							
.9	.7	.4		.5	.1			1.1	.6
5.6	9.9	3.5	Fixed/Worth	6.1	2.9			2.2	NM
-3.7	-1.7	-4.0		-14.4	-.6			NM	-.8
1.4	1.9	1.2		1.3	.7			.8	1.4
15.8	17.0	6.6	Debt/Worth	8.1	3.6			2.0	NM
-5.5	-3.2	-8.2		-15.4	-6.3			NM	-2.1
88.1	98.2	114.2		110.3	212.7				
(61) 34.5	(66) 39.4	(90) 43.0	% Profit Before Taxes/Tangible Net Worth	(40) 27.7	(26) 105.3				
9.1	13.8	16.1		10.2	33.6				
17.5	23.8	29.9		30.2	57.6			16.9	13.9
7.8	8.4	9.9	% Profit Before Taxes/Total Assets	3.7	19.5			7.7	11.2
.0	.8	2.7		.7	7.2			.1	6.8
34.6	58.8	66.5		42.9	166.7			27.4	25.4
4.8	6.3	8.0	Sales/Net Fixed Assets	1.8	28.4			3.1	8.2
1.3	.8	.9		.3	1.8			1.1	3.1
5.4	4.9	6.2		5.0	7.6			3.1	2.7
2.3	2.2	1.7	Sales/Total Assets	1.0	5.7			1.7	1.6
.9	.7	.8		.3	1.2			.8	1.0
1.5	1.6	1.3		2.3	.7			1.5	
(80) 2.8	(84) 3.9	(87) 3.3	% Depr., Dep., Amort./Sales	(36) 8.3	(22) 1.9			(10) 2.9	
7.4	7.1	8.4		17.1	4.7			5.4	
2.8	1.7	1.4		4.7	.6				
(41) 5.1	(43) 3.3	(44) 4.6	% Officers', Directors' Owners' Comp/Sales	(16) 5.8	(16) 1.3				
8.2	9.4	7.6		11.5	6.0				
788593M	781225M	1403978M	Net Sales ($)	27749M	69416M	30317M	49766M	227734M	998996M
545947M	650114M	1017121M	Total Assets ($)	54250M	33142M	102527M	30386M	183518M	613298M

M = $ thousand MM = $ million

See Pages 9 through 22 for Explanation of Ratios and Data

	Current Data Sorted by Assets						Comparative Historical Data	
Type of Statement								
Unqualified			1	1			5	7
Reviewed	1	1	7	4		1	16	16
Compiled	17	21	17	2			59	75
Tax Returns	59	72	24	2		1	170	171
Other	33	53	36	7	2		110	136
	18 (4/1-9/30/13)			344 (10/1/13-3/31/14)			4/1/09-3/31/10	4/1/10-3/31/11
	0-500M	500M-2MM	2-10MM	10-50MM	50-100MM	100-250MM	ALL	ALL
NUMBER OF STATEMENTS	110	147	85	16	2	2	360	405
ASSETS	%	%	%	%	%	%	%	%
Cash & Equivalents	23.7	7.2	6.4	10.3			10.7	11.7
Trade Receivables (net)	3.1	1.2	1.5	1.5			1.7	2.3
Inventory	3.3	2.0	1.5	1.2			3.8	4.1
All Other Current	3.3	1.6	1.1	2.3			2.9	2.6
Total Current	33.4	12.0	10.6	15.2			19.1	20.7
Fixed Assets (net)	47.9	75.5	75.7	76.7			63.3	61.0
Intangibles (net)	8.0	5.6	8.4	4.0			9.6	9.0
All Other Non-Current	10.7	6.9	5.3	4.1			8.0	9.3
Total	100.0	100.0	100.0	100.0			100.0	100.0
LIABILITIES								
Notes Payable-Short Term	10.2	3.7	1.3	3.8			4.9	6.4
Cur. Mat.-L.T.D.	5.5	4.7	4.4	4.8			5.4	4.4
Trade Payables	7.2	2.1	1.2	2.8			4.0	7.3
Income Taxes Payable	.2	.0	.0	.0			.1	.2
All Other Current	20.7	8.4	4.7	7.5			15.9	14.7
Total Current	43.8	18.9	11.6	18.9			30.3	32.9
Long-Term Debt	44.0	74.6	65.4	47.1			59.2	55.9
Deferred Taxes	.1	.0	.0	.0			.1	.1
All Other Non-Current	43.6	7.1	3.5	2.8			12.7	13.4
Net Worth	-31.4	-.7	19.5	31.2			-2.3	-2.3
Total Liabilties & Net Worth	100.0	100.0	100.0	100.0			100.0	100.0
INCOME DATA								
Net Sales	100.0	100.0	100.0	100.0			100.0	100.0
Gross Profit								
Operating Expenses	89.6	84.5	83.9	80.1			89.3	86.9
Operating Profit	10.4	15.5	16.1	19.9			10.7	13.1
All Other Expenses (net)	3.5	9.4	8.4	5.8			9.4	8.1
Profit Before Taxes	7.0	6.1	7.6	14.1			1.3	5.0
RATIOS								
	3.4	2.0	2.2	2.9			2.0	2.0
Current	.9	.6	.8	.6			.7	.7
	.3	.2	.3	.4			.2	.2
	2.3	1.6	1.8	2.6			1.2	1.4
Quick	(109) .7	.4	.7	.6			(359) .4	.4
	.3	.1	.2	.2			.1	.1
	0 UND	0 UND	0 UND	0 UND			0 UND	0 UND
Sales/Receivables	0 UND	0 UND	0 999.8	0 999.8			0 UND	0 UND
	1 704.4	1 335.0	1 286.9	3 136.6			1 271.2	1 269.7
Cost of Sales/Inventory								
Cost of Sales/Payables								
	22.0	21.0	10.9	10.6			25.5	26.8
Sales/Working Capital	-166.6	-17.4	-35.3	-43.4			-41.9	-43.3
	-9.0	-5.2	-8.4	-2.7			-5.1	-6.2
	11.2	5.8	4.5	116.1			4.7	6.4
EBIT/Interest	(64) 5.3	(115) 2.4	(71) 2.2	(12) 3.7			(238) 1.6	(273) 2.3
	.9	1.2	1.1	1.3			.6	1.2
							2.9	2.3
Net Profit + Depr., Dep., Amort./Cur. Mat. L/T/D							(21) 2.5	(18) 1.8
							1.7	1.2
	.8	2.6	2.5	1.3			2.0	1.5
Fixed/Worth	4.9	UND	5.4	4.8			28.5	13.4
	-.7	-3.8	-19.3	191.0			-1.9	-1.7
	.9	2.6	2.1	.8			2.3	1.8
Debt/Worth	UND	-66.0	5.0	4.7			120.3	21.5
	-2.1	-4.9	-20.7	233.2			-3.1	-3.2
	94.7	103.5	45.7	46.3			38.4	86.0
% Profit Before Taxes/Tangible Net Worth	(56) 31.5	(72) 36.0	(61) 17.6	(13) 16.4			(182) 16.1	(226) 29.2
	4.7	7.4	-.5	.1			-2.1	3.9
	36.4	12.0	10.3	10.0			9.6	15.4
% Profit Before Taxes/Total Assets	11.3	3.8	4.2	4.2			1.8	4.5
	-1.7	-.9	.0	-.7			-4.0	-.2
	42.0	1.8	1.3	2.9			8.2	9.3
Sales/Net Fixed Assets	7.3	.7	.6	.9			1.3	1.7
	1.4	.4	.4	.2			.5	.5
	7.5	1.1	.7	1.7			2.6	3.1
Sales/Total Assets	3.2	.5	.5	.7			.8	1.0
	.9	.3	.3	.2			.4	.4
	1.5	5.0	5.3	3.1			2.9	3.0
% Depr., Dep., Amort./Sales	(72) 4.2	(124) 12.2	(73) 11.1	(15) 4.0			(298) 8.0	(319) 7.8
	12.4	22.1	19.9	25.9			22.3	18.9
	3.7	2.2	1.9				2.7	2.8
% Officers', Directors' Owners' Comp/Sales	(46) 6.9	(43) 4.6	(16) 4.3				(124) 5.3	(132) 4.9
	12.7	9.2	10.2				9.2	9.3
Net Sales ($)	74820M	162399M	268121M	424575M	204318M	978057M	1001842M	5365202M
Total Assets ($)	25216M	163290M	349771M	335060M	144440M	349256M	1032971M	2221084M

M = $ thousand MM = $ million

See Pages 9 through 22 for Explanation of Ratios and Data

Comparative Historical Data				Current Data Sorted by Sales					
			Type of Statement						
6	5	2	Unqualified				1	1	
21	10	14	Reviewed	1	2	2		4	5
64	55	57	Compiled	32	19	1	5		
194	182	158	Tax Returns	108	37	7	4	1	1
122	137	131	Other	70	43	8	3	3	4
4/1/11-3/31/12	4/1/12-3/31/13	4/1/13-3/31/14		18 (4/1-9/30/13)			344 (10/1/13-3/31/14)		
ALL	ALL	ALL		0-1MM	1-3MM	3-5MM	5-10MM	10-25MM	25MM & OVER
407	389	362	**NUMBER OF STATEMENTS**	211	101	18	13	9	10
%	%	%	**ASSETS**	%	%	%	%	%	%
11.2	12.1	12.3	Cash & Equivalents	11.5	13.4	10.3	18.5		15.6
2.2	1.7	2.0	Trade Receivables (net)	1.1	2.4	2.2	4.8		10.0
3.5	3.1	2.2	Inventory	.8	4.0	4.1	7.4		2.2
2.1	1.5	2.0	All Other Current	2.1	2.2	.4	.9		4.7
19.0	18.3	18.6	Total Current	15.4	22.0	16.9	31.6		32.5
64.4	67.0	66.9	Fixed Assets (net)	71.1	61.4	68.4	53.0		53.2
8.1	6.7	7.1	Intangibles (net)	6.5	8.4	2.1	6.5		8.6
8.6	8.0	7.5	All Other Non-Current	6.9	8.1	12.6	8.9		5.7
100.0	100.0	100.0	Total	100.0	100.0	100.0	100.0		100.0
			LIABILITIES						
5.6	3.7	5.1	Notes Payable-Short Term	4.8	7.1	1.5	.8		4.7
6.1	3.8	4.9	Cur. Mat.-L.T.D.	4.3	6.1	4.1	5.6		2.7
3.1	2.8	3.5	Trade Payables	3.0	3.9	5.7	4.9		4.3
.1	.1	.1	Income Taxes Payable	.1	.0	.1	.0		.0
11.3	15.1	11.2	All Other Current	13.9	5.9	11.4	10.8		13.8
26.3	25.5	24.7	Total Current	26.1	23.1	22.8	22.1		25.5
61.4	59.8	61.4	Long-Term Debt	63.8	65.8	47.3	43.8		19.9
.0	.1	.0	Deferred Taxes	.0	.0	.0	.0		.7
11.1	13.2	17.1	All Other Non-Current	20.0	15.5	14.9	4.9		2.9
1.1	1.4	-3.3	Net Worth	-10.0	-4.5	15.0	29.2		51.0
100.0	100.0	100.0	Total Liabilities & Net Worth	100.0	100.0	100.0	100.0		100.0
			INCOME DATA						
100.0	100.0	100.0	Net Sales	100.0	100.0	100.0	100.0		100.0
			Gross Profit						
87.5	85.2	85.8	Operating Expenses	84.2	87.1	89.6	87.9		91.5
12.5	14.8	14.2	Operating Profit	15.8	12.9	10.4	12.1		8.5
9.9	9.7	7.1	All Other Expenses (net)	9.6	4.0	3.9	3.4		.6
2.6	5.2	7.1	Profit Before Taxes	6.2	8.9	6.5	8.7		8.0
			RATIOS						
2.3	2.1	2.5		2.3	2.9	1.6	3.7		3.6
.7	.7	.7	Current	.6	.9	.8	1.5		1.3
.2	.2	.3		.2	.4	.3	.3		.5
1.6	1.7	1.9		1.9	1.8	1.2	3.5		3.1
(406) .5	.5	(361) .6	Quick	(210) .5	.6	.6	.7		1.2
.1	.1	.2		.1	.2	.2	.2		.3
0 UND	0 UND	0 UND		0 UND	0 UND	0 UND	0 999.8		1 554.7
0 UND	0 UND	0 UND	Sales/Receivables	0 UND	0 UND	1 378.1	2 160.5		5 80.6
2 219.0	1 327.7	1 328.6		0 UND	1 311.0	2 161.8	4 98.1		16 22.9
			Cost of Sales/Inventory						
			Cost of Sales/Payables						
20.8	19.3	17.6		22.3	10.8	32.4	8.9		7.3
-36.6	-35.5	-35.5	Sales/Working Capital	-18.1	-58.8	-133.2	26.8		68.1
-5.5	-5.4	-6.3		-4.3	-9.5	-6.6	-8.2		-29.4
5.0	4.2	6.2		5.2	6.6	33.5	60.4		240.4
(289) 2.0	(252) 1.9	(266) 2.6	EBIT/Interest	(131) 2.0	(89) 3.4	(17) 3.1	(11) 3.9		21.1
.9	.7	1.2		.9	1.4	1.3	1.1		3.0
2.5									
(14) 1.8			Net Profit + Depr., Dep., Amort./Cur. Mat. L/T/D						
1.5									
1.8	1.6	1.7		2.6	1.6	.6	.2		.5
20.3	9.7	8.3	Fixed/Worth	UND	5.7	NM	2.8		1.1
-3.0	-3.4	-3.5		-2.6	-4.3	-5.3	15.3		6.3
2.1	1.9	1.8		2.7	1.4	.5	.7		.4
50.3	12.3	13.5	Debt/Worth	-86.8	7.8	NM	2.3		.9
-4.2	-4.5	-4.8		-4.0	-4.4	-7.4	NM		11.7
66.7	65.7	70.7		66.2	93.8		118.3		81.5
(214) 25.3	(218) 21.6	(206) 27.0	% Profit Before Taxes/Tangible Net Worth	(104) 18.6	(66) 39.5		(10) 34.0		33.8
1.0	2.9	4.3		.0	10.5		15.0		19.5
12.4	11.9	15.3		11.3	17.2	16.6	15.1		26.4
3.2	3.0	4.7	% Profit Before Taxes/Total Assets	2.7	8.0	9.1	7.4		18.2
-2.0	-1.7	-.5		-2.0	.9	.4	-.3		3.4
6.1	5.2	5.4		3.5	8.3	8.3	93.9		12.9
1.1	.9	.9	Sales/Net Fixed Assets	.6	1.6	2.2	2.1		4.0
.4	.4	.4		.3	.7	.7	1.1		2.8
2.6	2.2	2.3		1.2	3.3	3.1	4.2		4.4
.7	.7	.7	Sales/Total Assets	.5	1.0	1.9	1.5		2.3
.4	.3	.4		.3	.5	.6	.7		1.2
3.4	3.5	3.2		6.6	2.1	.8	2.5		
(324) 8.9	(315) 11.0	(287) 9.5	% Depr., Dep., Amort./Sales	(165) 14.9	(80) 5.4	(14) 8.5	(11) 3.9		
19.7	21.4	19.6		25.0	12.6	19.4	10.4		
3.9	3.4	2.7		3.5	3.7				
(125) 6.7	(124) 6.6	(108) 5.6	% Officers', Directors' Owners' Comp/Sales	(55) 6.9	(37) 6.3				
10.5	10.4	11.0		12.6	10.2				
2070498M	5914579M	2112290M	Net Sales ($)	96447M	167799M	72826M	91746M	128121M	1555351M
1480345M	1673029M	1367033M	Total Assets ($)	201289M	234691M	72039M	110268M	106994M	641752M

M = $ thousand MM = $ million

See Pages 9 through 22 for Explanation of Ratios and Data

Current Data Sorted by Assets							Comparative Historical Data	
						Type of Statement		
			2	1	1	Unqualified	3	1
1	1	6	1			Reviewed	7	6
2	4	7	2			Compiled	16	19
26	12	3	1			Tax Returns	68	57
17	14	12	4	1	1	Other	52	41
	15 (4/1-9/30/13)		104 (10/1/13-3/31/14)				4/1/09-3/31/10 ALL	4/1/10-3/31/11 ALL
0-500M	500M-2MM	2-10MM	10-50MM	50-100MM	100-250MM			
46	31	28	10	2	2	**NUMBER OF STATEMENTS**	146	124
%	%	%	%	%	%	**ASSETS**	%	%
33.9	15.9	12.7	5.6			Cash & Equivalents	15.2	14.5
11.3	20.7	14.4	15.4			Trade Receivables (net)	16.3	12.8
12.9	19.0	17.2	18.9			Inventory	16.3	18.5
1.6	2.3	3.1	1.4			All Other Current	2.0	2.1
59.7	57.9	47.5	41.3			Total Current	49.9	47.9
30.6	28.5	42.0	45.3			Fixed Assets (net)	33.8	35.2
1.0	5.7	2.5	9.0			Intangibles (net)	9.0	6.9
8.8	7.9	8.1	4.3			All Other Non-Current	7.4	10.1
100.0	100.0	100.0	100.0			Total	100.0	100.0
						LIABILITIES		
10.8	9.6	4.9	7.8			Notes Payable-Short Term	7.0	11.4
2.2	1.3	2.3	6.4			Cur. Mat.-L.T.D.	3.6	4.1
25.8	17.9	12.4	16.6			Trade Payables	20.1	19.1
.4	.2	.4	.0			Income Taxes Payable	.0	.1
18.4	11.2	6.5	7.4			All Other Current	22.3	11.6
57.5	40.2	26.5	38.2			Total Current	53.1	46.2
23.1	24.7	31.2	21.1			Long-Term Debt	32.1	28.7
.0	.0	.4	1.2			Deferred Taxes	.0	.0
21.4	8.5	4.9	2.7			All Other Non-Current	8.4	14.8
-2.0	26.7	37.0	36.7			Net Worth	6.5	10.3
100.0	100.0	100.0	100.0			Total Liabilties & Net Worth	100.0	100.0
						INCOME DATA		
100.0	100.0	100.0	100.0			Net Sales	100.0	100.0
						Gross Profit		
94.0	96.1	93.1	94.8			Operating Expenses	94.7	94.6
6.0	3.9	6.9	5.2			Operating Profit	5.3	5.4
-.1	.3	1.8	.6			All Other Expenses (net)	2.0	1.3
6.1	3.7	5.1	4.7			Profit Before Taxes	3.3	4.1
						RATIOS		
5.6	4.4	3.0	1.7				2.3	2.3
1.3	1.7	1.8	1.3			Current	1.1	1.2
.6	.7	1.1	.9				.6	.6
4.2	2.9	1.4	1.4				1.6	1.4
1.1	.8	1.0	.5			Quick	.6	.6
.4	.5	.5	.4				.2	.2
0 UND	3 126.2	5 76.4	13 27.1				1 628.0	0 989.8
1 260.0	17 20.9	11 34.7	24 15.2			Sales/Receivables	7 52.2	7 52.4
12 31.5	31 11.7	27 13.6	46 7.9				25 14.6	24 15.2
						Cost of Sales/Inventory		
						Cost of Sales/Payables		
8.7	6.0	5.2	14.5				10.6	10.5
40.8	18.7	11.0	27.7			Sales/Working Capital	64.5	52.0
-27.0	-15.9	113.5	-32.2				-15.3	-21.2
25.4	18.8	24.4	14.6				10.5	12.0
(26) 4.7	(24) 4.3	(26) 7.1	5.2			EBIT/Interest	(107) 2.8	(86) 4.6
2.8	1.3	2.6	1.2				.9	2.1
						Net Profit + Depr., Dep., Amort./Cur. Mat. L/T/D		
.2	.2	.5	1.0				.3	.4
.8	.7	1.1	1.5			Fixed/Worth	2.1	1.7
-11.3	-1.5	5.1	7.4				-1.3	-2.5
.3	.3	.7	1.1				.9	.9
2.5	3.2	1.6	2.5			Debt/Worth	4.5	4.2
-22.3	-26.2	7.1	16.0				-4.9	-6.7
100.6	71.2	38.5					85.5	71.9
(33) 61.0	(21) 26.7	(24) 23.7				% Profit Before Taxes/Tangible Net Worth	(91) 23.7	(81) 29.0
7.5	11.3	5.8					8.1	13.5
59.6	14.3	16.8	11.1				19.6	17.4
20.5	9.3	9.3	6.0			% Profit Before Taxes/Total Assets	5.3	9.3
1.9	1.1	2.5	.1				-.5	1.5
187.3	64.5	13.4	6.5				91.6	38.5
27.5	29.7	5.8	3.7			Sales/Net Fixed Assets	21.0	16.0
9.5	9.3	3.3	2.7				4.8	4.8
9.3	4.5	2.7	3.0				5.5	5.8
5.1	3.6	2.1	1.8			Sales/Total Assets	3.1	2.5
3.6	2.3	1.5	1.3				1.3	1.8
.4	.6	.9					.6	1.0
(21) 1.6	(21) 1.0	(25) 1.5				% Depr., Dep., Amort./Sales	(105) 1.9	(94) 1.7
2.2	2.3	3.4					3.9	3.4
4.6	2.4	1.3					2.2	2.8
(29) 7.1	(16) 4.6	(11) 3.2				% Officers', Directors' Owners' Comp/Sales	(67) 4.5	(57) 5.5
10.6	6.9	7.1					8.8	8.6
64342M	111941M	243361M	380851M	157058M	189923M	Net Sales ($)	1020588M	1344374M
11030M	32088M	107564M	176632M	153157M	273200M	Total Assets ($)	524975M	435874M

M = $ thousand MM = $ million

See Pages 9 through 22 for Explanation of Ratios and Data

Comparative Historical Data				Current Data Sorted by Sales					
			Type of Statement						
4	5	4	Unqualified					1	3
13	11	9	Reviewed	1		1	4	2	1
21	20	15	Compiled	2	1		5	5	2
73	64	42	Tax Returns	14	16	7	4	1	
52	59	49	Other	13	13	6	9	5	3
4/1/11-3/31/12	**4/1/12-3/31/13**	**4/1/13-3/31/14**		**15 (4/1-9/30/13)**		**104 (10/1/13-3/31/14)**			
ALL	**ALL**	**ALL**		**0-1MM**	**1-3MM**	**3-5MM**	**5-10MM**	**10-25MM**	**25MM & OVER**
163	159	119	**NUMBER OF STATEMENTS**	30	30	14	22	14	9
%	%	%	**ASSETS**	%	%	%	%	%	%
15.8	16.1	21.0	Cash & Equivalents	26.8	25.0	30.0	13.3	11.1	
15.4	15.4	14.7	Trade Receivables (net)	5.5	18.8	15.4	18.4	21.9	
18.9	15.7	15.9	Inventory	7.6	15.8	19.3	24.1	16.0	
2.8	1.7	2.1	All Other Current	1.9	.9	.9	5.9	.6	
52.8	48.8	53.6	Total Current	41.8	60.5	65.6	61.8	49.6	
31.8	35.4	33.4	Fixed Assets (net)	45.0	28.3	19.7	29.9	41.1	
5.7	7.8	5.1	Intangibles (net)	.6	5.6	5.2	1.4	5.3	
9.6	7.9	7.8	All Other Non-Current	12.6	5.7	9.4	6.9	4.0	
100.0	100.0	100.0	Total	100.0	100.0	100.0	100.0	100.0	
			LIABILITIES						
6.8	8.3	8.5	Notes Payable-Short Term	5.6	14.7	10.3	6.3	6.6	
2.3	2.8	2.4	Cur. Mat.-L.T.D.	2.0	1.5	2.4	1.6	5.4	
15.4	14.9	19.1	Trade Payables	28.6	16.0	21.8	15.4	11.2	
.1	.2	.3	Income Taxes Payable	.6	.1	.0	.2	.5	
14.2	10.8	12.5	All Other Current	16.9	9.6	20.1	9.0	10.5	
38.9	37.1	42.7	Total Current	53.7	41.9	54.8	32.6	34.3	
25.7	28.5	24.8	Long-Term Debt	41.4	14.7	28.1	20.8	19.6	
.2	.3	.4	Deferred Taxes	.0	.0	.0	.3	.3	
20.7	17.1	12.7	All Other Non-Current	29.3	6.8	4.5	10.5	2.3	
14.5	16.9	19.3	Net Worth	-24.4	36.6	12.6	35.8	43.5	
100.0	100.0	100.0	Total Liabilties & Net Worth	100.0	100.0	100.0	100.0	100.0	
			INCOME DATA						
100.0	100.0	100.0	Net Sales	100.0	100.0	100.0	100.0	100.0	
			Gross Profit						
94.1	91.0	94.2	Operating Expenses	91.7	93.3	97.6	97.0	95.8	
5.9	9.0	5.8	Operating Profit	8.3	6.7	2.4	3.0	4.2	
1.7	2.1	.6	All Other Expenses (net)	.7	.8	.8	.1	-.1	
4.2	6.9	5.2	Profit Before Taxes	7.6	5.9	1.7	2.9	4.3	
			RATIOS						
3.2	2.9	3.9		4.7	4.9	4.6	3.7	2.3	
1.6	1.6	1.5	Current	1.1	2.7	1.5	1.8	1.3	
.7	.8	.9		.4	.8	.9	1.3	1.0	
2.0	2.0	2.4		3.8	3.6	3.0	1.5	1.4	
.8	(158) 1.0	.9	Quick	.8	1.3	1.1	1.1	.8	
.3	.3	.5		.2	.5	.4	.7	.5	
0 955.0	**0** UND	**1** 293.2		**0** UND	**0** UND	**1** 608.7	**5** 74.7	**11** 34.0	
7 54.5	**8** 46.4	**10** 36.5	Sales/Receivables	**1** 269.4	**9** 42.2	**5** 79.1	**12** 29.9	**25** 14.5	
28 13.0	**26** 13.9	**28** 13.1		**11** 34.7	**36** 10.2	**30** 12.3	**29** 12.7	**49** 7.4	
			Cost of Sales/Inventory						
			Cost of Sales/Payables						
7.8	8.3	8.0		8.7	6.0	7.0	5.4	9.6	
23.8	20.7	17.9	Sales/Working Capital	117.8	11.3	28.7	14.3	26.7	
-32.3	-36.7	-161.5		-12.1	-27.0	NM	48.7	-311.5	
17.1	15.0	22.4		7.8	55.0	10.3	55.6	15.6	
(112) 3.7	(104) 3.9	(90) 4.6	EBIT/Interest	(14) 3.7	(24) 6.0	(10) 3.0	(20) 9.1	(13) 6.5	
1.6	1.5	2.4		2.4	2.8	1.3	1.0	2.1	
		3.4							
		(12) 1.7	Net Profit + Depr., Dep., Amort./Cur. Mat. L/T/D						
		1.4							
.2	.3	.2		.6	.2	.1	.2	.6	
1.2	1.2	1.0	Fixed/Worth	1.4	.8	.6	.6	1.1	
-8.9	-21.7	-48.9		-2.3	-49.5	-.7	7.1	2.9	
.8	.6	.5		.6	.3	.6	.5	.7	
3.8	2.6	2.5	Debt/Worth	4.7	2.6	6.3	1.8	1.7	
-10.6	-11.6	-97.5		-4.4	-350.7	-5.0	8.4	5.3	
63.6	54.0	80.9		86.6	97.9		38.1	91.4	
(115) 30.1	(116) 29.5	(88) 34.7	% Profit Before Taxes/Tangible Net Worth	(20) 52.3	(22) 51.4		(18) 23.1	(13) 26.8	
7.2	6.3	9.2		5.1	15.5		7.9	13.6	
19.8	22.6	23.1		42.0	61.4	18.2	13.8	19.7	
7.1	7.5	10.4	% Profit Before Taxes/Total Assets	15.4	12.2	5.9	8.9	11.5	
.7	.5	1.8		1.7	3.3	.9	.4	2.4	
58.2	42.0	44.3		43.3	68.4	145.1	43.5	13.0	
21.7	12.5	13.5	Sales/Net Fixed Assets	11.1	28.5	28.4	18.7	4.7	
5.7	3.8	4.5		2.8	10.1	9.0	5.4	3.1	
5.9	5.0	4.9		5.5	6.3	7.3	4.5	3.1	
3.2	2.9	3.3	Sales/Total Assets	3.5	4.1	4.8	3.7	2.2	
1.8	1.6	1.8		1.3	2.2	1.8	2.1	1.5	
.7	.8	.7		.4	.7		.9	1.0	
(117) 1.5	(115) 1.9	(79) 1.7	% Depr., Dep., Amort./Sales	(17) 1.8	(14) 1.3		(18) 1.2	(13) 1.8	
3.6	5.2	2.9		2.9	2.7		1.8	2.7	
1.9	2.7	2.8		6.4	2.9		1.4		
(76) 3.7	(72) 5.1	(58) 5.4	% Officers', Directors' Owners' Comp/Sales	(15) 9.4	(18) 4.8		(11) 2.6		
7.2	7.7	8.5		10.8	7.5		5.3		
1324392M	**1785706M**	**1147476M**	Net Sales ($)	**18222M**	**56362M**	**52288M**	**150065M**	**230778M**	**639761M**
795077M	**892147M**	**753671M**	Total Assets ($)	**10441M**	**21972M**	**16940M**	**53877M**	**110938M**	**539503M**

M = $ thousand MM = $ million

See Pages 9 through 22 for Explanation of Ratios and Data

Current Data Sorted by Assets							Comparative Historical Data	
						Type of Statement		
		1	1		1	Unqualified	7	4
		5				Reviewed	4	4
1	4	2				Compiled	5	5
4	3		1			Tax Returns	15	14
1	8	12	7	2	1	Other	20	17
5 (4/1-9/30/13)			49 (10/1/13-3/31/14)				4/1/09-3/31/10 ALL	4/1/10-3/31/11 ALL
0-500M	500M-2MM	2-10MM	10-50MM	50-100MM	100-250MM			
6	15	20	9	2	2	**NUMBER OF STATEMENTS**	51	44
%	%	%	%	%	%	**ASSETS**	%	%
	16.4	8.9				Cash & Equivalents	10.7	12.4
	28.5	44.2				Trade Receivables (net)	32.1	32.4
	17.4	16.0				Inventory	16.8	17.6
	3.5	6.6				All Other Current	4.2	3.0
	65.8	75.7				Total Current	63.8	65.4
	21.1	14.1				Fixed Assets (net)	21.2	19.4
	5.8	3.3				Intangibles (net)	10.8	6.4
	7.3	6.9				All Other Non-Current	4.2	8.7
	100.0	100.0				Total	100.0	100.0
						LIABILITIES		
	12.1	13.5				Notes Payable-Short Term	13.6	13.8
	2.5	1.7				Cur. Mat.-L.T.D.	6.2	3.0
	13.5	23.8				Trade Payables	19.9	13.7
	.0	.0				Income Taxes Payable	.4	.2
	22.9	14.2				All Other Current	18.4	12.3
	51.0	53.3				Total Current	58.4	43.0
	17.9	10.6				Long-Term Debt	31.5	15.9
	1.0	.1				Deferred Taxes	.5	.4
	6.4	7.2				All Other Non-Current	7.8	6.3
	23.8	28.8				Net Worth	1.8	34.4
	100.0	100.0				Total Liabilties & Net Worth	100.0	100.0
						INCOME DATA		
	100.0	100.0				Net Sales	100.0	100.0
						Gross Profit		
	90.1	95.7				Operating Expenses	95.5	93.5
	9.9	4.3				Operating Profit	4.5	6.5
	2.5	.1				All Other Expenses (net)	.8	1.2
	7.4	4.2				Profit Before Taxes	3.6	5.3
						RATIOS		
	4.4	2.3					1.6	2.6
	1.8	1.7				Current	1.2	1.7
	1.2	1.1					.9	1.1
	1.7	1.9					1.4	2.2
	1.2	1.0				Quick	.8	1.1
	1.0	.7					.5	.8
	10 36.2	**30** 12.2					**23** 15.6	**27** 13.4
	33 10.9	**50** 7.3				Sales/Receivables	**37** 10.0	**41** 9.0
	48 7.6	**61** 6.0					**58** 6.3	**58** 6.3
						Cost of Sales/Inventory		
						Cost of Sales/Payables		
	4.3	7.9					10.9	7.6
	14.1	12.7				Sales/Working Capital	38.3	12.0
	53.7	99.4					-53.4	36.1
	75.6	46.2					12.7	14.1
	(12) 7.2	(19) 13.0				EBIT/Interest	(46) 3.2	(37) 5.9
	4.9	5.4					.9	2.4
							3.2	
						Net Profit + Depr., Dep., Amort./Cur. Mat. L/T/D	(10) 1.3	
							.3	
	.1	.2					.4	.2
	.4	.5				Fixed/Worth	1.7	.7
	1.7	NM					-.6	2.4
	1.2	1.2					1.4	.8
	1.6	1.8				Debt/Worth	4.5	1.7
	3.5	-51.9					-2.9	10.3
	96.8	68.0					79.3	75.8
	(13) 32.9	(14) 32.8				% Profit Before Taxes/Tangible Net Worth	(30) 38.6	(36) 34.7
	14.3	18.1					7.5	14.8
	29.4	24.2					18.3	18.3
	15.2	9.9				% Profit Before Taxes/Total Assets	5.6	11.9
	2.5	6.1					-.5	2.5
	68.9	61.0					60.8	59.4
	32.6	29.6				Sales/Net Fixed Assets	25.6	24.1
	13.4	16.3					13.1	12.5
	6.0	4.1					4.5	4.1
	2.9	3.5				Sales/Total Assets	3.2	3.1
	1.8	2.5					2.1	2.2
	.3	.5					.9	.6
	(11) .8	(15) .7				% Depr., Dep., Amort./Sales	(39) 1.5	(32) 1.0
	1.4	1.2					2.5	1.8
							2.3	2.9
						% Officers', Directors' Owners' Comp/Sales	(20) 4.9	(15) 4.3
							9.3	11.0
6433M	84397M	336795M	375708M	172123M	337603M	Net Sales ($)	1132518M	862245M
1706M	20026M	102940M	156063M	146430M	288276M	Total Assets ($)	432341M	556497M

M = $ thousand MM = $ million

See Pages 9 through 22 for Explanation of Ratios and Data

Comparative Historical Data				Current Data Sorted by Sales					
			Type of Statement						
4	2	3	Unqualified						3
4	1	5	Reviewed					4	1
10	6	7	Compiled	2	1	1	1	2	
11	18	8	Tax Returns	3	2			3	
29	32	31	Other		3	3	9	7	9
4/1/11-3/31/12 ALL	**4/1/12-3/31/13 ALL**	**4/1/13-3/31/14 ALL**		**5 (4/1-9/30/13)**			**49 (10/1/13-3/31/14)**		
				0-1MM	**1-3MM**	**3-5MM**	**5-10MM**	**10-25MM**	**25MM & OVER**
58	59	54	**NUMBER OF STATEMENTS**	5	6	4	10	16	13
%	%	%	**ASSETS**	%	%	%	%	%	%
11.3	15.3	13.3	Cash & Equivalents				10.1	12.8	11.6
39.6	31.8	33.0	Trade Receivables (net)				30.0	39.8	36.4
19.6	16.8	18.1	Inventory				25.1	11.9	14.8
4.1	3.5	3.9	All Other Current				2.1	3.0	8.3
74.5	67.4	68.3	Total Current				67.3	67.6	71.1
12.9	18.3	17.0	Fixed Assets (net)				13.8	17.8	7.8
7.2	9.0	7.0	Intangibles (net)				7.6	3.3	15.2
5.4	5.4	7.8	All Other Non-Current				11.3	11.3	5.9
100.0	100.0	100.0	Total				100.0	100.0	100.0
			LIABILITIES						
15.1	12.6	11.5	Notes Payable-Short Term				12.8	8.4	8.3
3.2	2.0	2.1	Cur. Mat.-L.T.D.				1.2	2.7	1.2
20.6	18.2	19.7	Trade Payables				15.1	20.0	20.8
.1	.0	.1	Income Taxes Payable				.0	.0	.2
19.7	13.7	14.8	All Other Current				13.6	17.8	9.8
58.7	46.6	48.2	Total Current				42.7	48.9	40.4
12.3	13.2	13.0	Long-Term Debt				10.8	13.4	10.9
.3	.2	.7	Deferred Taxes				.0	.0	1.9
11.8	6.9	8.1	All Other Non-Current				11.2	3.4	9.1
16.9	33.1	30.0	Net Worth				35.3	34.3	37.8
100.0	100.0	100.0	Total Liabilties & Net Worth				100.0	100.0	100.0
			INCOME DATA						
100.0	100.0	100.0	Net Sales				100.0	100.0	100.0
			Gross Profit						
94.9	91.3	93.6	Operating Expenses				95.6	97.8	93.1
5.1	8.7	6.4	Operating Profit				4.4	2.2	6.9
1.0	1.0	1.1	All Other Expenses (net)				.1	.0	1.6
4.1	7.7	5.3	Profit Before Taxes				4.2	2.2	5.3
			RATIOS						
2.5	2.1	2.7					2.5	2.0	3.0
1.5	1.5	1.7	Current				1.9	1.6	1.7
1.0	1.0	1.2					1.2	1.1	1.1
1.7	1.5	1.8					1.9	1.6	2.2
.9	1.0	1.2	Quick				1.1	1.0	1.2
.6	.6	.7					.4	.7	.6
31 11.6	**24** 15.5	**25** 14.5					**14** 26.7	**30** 12.3	**36** 10.2
41 8.8	**41** 8.9	**41** 9.0	Sales/Receivables				**35** 10.3	**53** 6.9	**46** 7.9
55 6.6	**53** 6.9	**59** 6.2					**43** 8.4	**59** 6.2	**66** 5.5
			Cost of Sales/Inventory						
			Cost of Sales/Payables						
7.2	8.7	6.6					7.5	7.7	6.4
17.1	15.6	12.9	Sales/Working Capital				17.5	16.2	10.3
-107.3	868.0	71.4					33.0	210.9	NM
16.6	25.5	36.9						21.5	33.7
(52) 6.8	(44) 5.9	(42) 10.1	EBIT/Interest					(14) 12.3	(11) 4.9
1.4	3.1	4.9						5.6	-1.2
4.7	13.1								
(12) 2.0	(10) 3.3		Net Profit + Depr., Dep., Amort./Cur. Mat. L/T/D						
.1	2.3								
.2	.2	.1					.2	.2	.0
.6	.6	.4	Fixed/Worth				.4	.7	.2
NM	2.9	2.2					NM	1.5	NM
1.0	1.0	.8					1.2	.9	.6
2.7	2.4	1.6	Debt/Worth				1.6	1.6	2.6
-12.5	113.0	65.5					NM	22.7	-7.6
87.3	71.5	72.3						84.8	
(42) 40.1	(45) 38.3	(42) 32.5	% Profit Before Taxes/Tangible Net Worth					(14) 34.5	
19.2	15.6	12.6						18.2	
20.7	20.4	28.6					34.9	17.2	36.0
9.1	10.1	9.9	% Profit Before Taxes/Total Assets				9.0	10.4	24.2
.9	3.3	4.2					5.1	5.2	-4.4
70.9	79.0	64.0					61.6	57.9	336.6
28.9	27.8	28.8	Sales/Net Fixed Assets				38.8	22.9	44.7
15.5	13.2	13.3					20.4	11.0	15.4
4.1	4.3	4.2					6.0	5.3	3.9
3.3	3.0	2.9	Sales/Total Assets				3.5	2.8	3.0
2.4	2.4	2.0					2.7	2.1	1.5
.6	.6	.4						.5	
(43) 1.1	(40) 1.5	(36) .9	% Depr., Dep., Amort./Sales					(11) .9	
1.7	2.2	1.7						3.0	
2.2	2.0	1.6							
(20) 4.6	(27) 4.7	(12) 2.9	% Officers', Directors' Owners' Comp/Sales						
7.0	10.6	5.4							
1370543M	**1600274M**	**1313059M**	Net Sales ($)	**2425M**	**12694M**	**15778M**	**71857M**	**268673M**	**941632M**
613797M	**750544M**	**715441M**	Total Assets ($)	**2913M**	**4840M**	**7237M**	**21369M**	**109584M**	**569498M**

M = $ thousand MM = $ million

See Pages 9 through 22 for Explanation of Ratios and Data

	Current Data Sorted by Assets						Comparative Historical Data	
Type of Statement								
Unqualified			1	4			12	12
Reviewed	2	1	12	5			24	20
Compiled	3	6	2				26	14
Tax Returns	6	15	3				22	20
Other	3	15	13	4	5	3	45	50
	13 (4/1-9/30/13)			90 (10/1/13-3/31/14)			4/1/09-3/31/10 ALL	4/1/10-3/31/11 ALL
	0-500M	500M-2MM	2-10MM	10-50MM	50-100MM	100-250MM		
NUMBER OF STATEMENTS	14	37	31	13	5	3	129	116
ASSETS	%	%	%	%	%	%	%	%
Cash & Equivalents	25.7	14.4	13.3	14.4			13.0	12.0
Trade Receivables (net)	33.1	28.2	37.9	36.6			31.2	33.3
Inventory	10.6	13.3	15.1	14.4			17.4	17.1
All Other Current	.7	1.5	2.9	3.7			4.7	4.2
Total Current	70.1	57.3	69.2	69.1			66.2	66.6
Fixed Assets (net)	14.7	26.3	20.3	14.4			23.7	20.4
Intangibles (net)	4.9	9.0	7.3	11.1			4.0	6.7
All Other Non-Current	10.3	7.4	3.3	5.4			6.1	6.3
Total	100.0	100.0	100.0	100.0			100.0	100.0
LIABILITIES								
Notes Payable-Short Term	24.4	13.6	12.4	5.1			12.3	8.8
Cur. Mat.-L.T.D.	4.8	2.1	3.7	3.2			3.7	3.7
Trade Payables	22.4	12.0	13.0	15.1			11.9	12.0
Income Taxes Payable	1.5	.2	.1	.1			.5	.1
All Other Current	12.9	8.6	10.4	15.0			13.9	12.2
Total Current	66.0	36.4	39.7	38.5			42.3	36.7
Long-Term Debt	28.5	25.4	11.2	11.2			17.3	14.7
Deferred Taxes	.1	.0	1.0	.7			.5	.7
All Other Non-Current	3.9	5.9	10.3	5.7			3.4	9.3
Net Worth	1.5	32.2	37.8	44.0			36.5	38.6
Total Liabilities & Net Worth	100.0	100.0	100.0	100.0			100.0	100.0
INCOME DATA								
Net Sales	100.0	100.0	100.0	100.0			100.0	100.0
Gross Profit								
Operating Expenses	87.7	94.0	91.8	93.2			94.0	91.7
Operating Profit	12.3	6.0	8.2	6.8			6.0	8.3
All Other Expenses (net)	.7	.8	-.1	.8			1.5	1.0
Profit Before Taxes	11.7	5.2	8.3	5.9			4.5	7.3
RATIOS								
Current	4.0	3.1	4.1	2.5			3.1	3.5
	1.4	1.7	1.6	1.7			1.5	1.9
	.8	1.1	1.2	1.4			1.1	1.2
Quick	3.9	2.1	2.8	1.8			2.1	2.2
	1.1	1.3	1.2	1.2			1.0	1.4
	.6	.5	.9	1.0			.6	.7
Sales/Receivables	0 UND	5 78.4	34 10.6	41 8.8			29 12.8	29 12.6
	19 19.3	29 12.4	47 7.8	58 6.3			42 8.8	48 7.6
	45 8.1	49 7.4	66 5.5	79 4.6			58 6.3	68 5.4
Cost of Sales/Inventory								
Cost of Sales/Payables								
Sales/Working Capital	9.9	7.4	4.8	4.5			5.9	5.3
	42.5	14.3	8.4	7.6			11.7	8.7
	-41.7	219.3	40.1	12.1			67.0	26.1
EBIT/Interest		12.9	36.3	73.7			12.2	20.4
		(32) 5.2	(27) 12.9	14.5			(112) 4.1	(94) 5.3
		2.1	3.1	6.5			.9	1.7
Net Profit + Depr., Dep., Amort./Cur. Mat. L/T/D							3.6	11.8
							(27) 2.6	(24) 3.9
							1.2	1.2
Fixed/Worth	.0	.2	.1	.1			.2	.2
	.4	.8	.7	.4			.6	.4
	-.8	7.2	3.9	1.1			1.6	2.3
Debt/Worth	.3	.5	.7	.9			.7	.5
	2.8	2.9	1.5	1.4			2.1	1.8
	-4.0	22.7	8.9	3.1			4.7	7.6
% Profit Before Taxes/Tangible Net Worth		83.0	81.9	56.9			45.9	62.2
		(29) 23.9	(24) 33.1	(11) 33.2			(114) 22.0	(98) 26.7
		8.6	14.5	22.6			2.9	6.9
% Profit Before Taxes/Total Assets	102.8	19.7	32.0	17.9			17.3	22.2
	36.7	7.4	9.7	13.5			6.9	9.9
	5.3	2.2	5.6	9.5			.2	1.3
Sales/Net Fixed Assets	600.2	47.6	90.0	65.9			44.0	48.4
	37.2	20.9	17.1	18.3			14.9	17.3
	11.9	7.1	4.9	6.5			6.1	7.9
Sales/Total Assets	7.0	4.8	3.6	2.7			3.7	3.5
	3.9	3.1	2.7	2.0			2.4	2.2
	1.6	1.9	1.6	1.6			1.7	1.6
% Depr., Dep., Amort./Sales		.6	.4	.3			.8	.9
		(22) 1.1	(24) 1.4	(11) 1.0			(106) 1.8	(85) 1.8
		2.0	3.3	2.2			3.8	3.0
% Officers', Directors' Owners' Comp/Sales		2.9					3.1	2.4
		(23) 4.9					(49) 6.3	(45) 5.0
		11.7					9.7	7.4
Net Sales ($)	14023M	138649M	372352M	574963M	577479M	1339438M	2267479M	1998201M
Total Assets ($)	3405M	41102M	142133M	259455M	454256M	536243M	1175752M	1230546M

M = $ thousand MM = $ million

See Pages 9 through 22 for Explanation of Ratios and Data

Comparative Historical Data | Current Data Sorted by Sales

4/1/11-3/31/12 ALL	4/1/12-3/31/13 ALL	4/1/13-3/31/14 ALL	Type of Statement	0-1MM	1-3MM	3-5MM	5-10MM	10-25MM	25MM & OVER
7	5	5	Unqualified				1	2	2
22	19	20	Reviewed	1	2		2	9	6
18	19	11	Compiled	3	1	2	4	1	
35	26	24	Tax Returns	7	6	6	4	1	
50	46	43	Other	1	10	6	7	8	11
				13 (4/1-9/30/13)			90 (10/1/13-3/31/14)		
132	115	103	NUMBER OF STATEMENTS	12	19	14	18	21	19
%	%	%	**ASSETS**	%	%	%	%	%	%
14.4	9.6	14.9	Cash & Equivalents	25.0	18.9	10.7	16.4	11.2	10.1
32.0	32.8	31.8	Trade Receivables (net)	15.1	32.8	28.9	30.8	43.3	31.9
15.0	16.3	15.1	Inventory	12.4	11.6	14.8	14.8	14.4	21.7
2.7	3.1	2.0	All Other Current	.8	1.7	1.3	1.0	3.6	2.9
64.2	61.9	63.8	Total Current	53.3	65.0	55.8	63.1	72.4	66.5
20.4	23.2	20.9	Fixed Assets (net)	22.9	18.8	33.5	22.2	16.3	16.5
7.7	6.1	8.5	Intangibles (net)	13.1	9.4	5.4	8.6	6.2	9.5
7.7	8.8	6.7	All Other Non-Current	10.6	6.8	5.3	6.2	5.1	7.4
100.0	100.0	100.0	Total	100.0	100.0	100.0	100.0	100.0	100.0
			LIABILITIES						
12.9	10.7	14.6	Notes Payable-Short Term	7.6	27.6	8.1	10.7	14.5	14.9
3.0	3.4	3.1	Cur. Mat.-L.T.D.	3.6	3.2	2.0	3.1	3.8	2.9
12.9	15.0	14.2	Trade Payables	9.0	18.6	15.6	8.5	15.5	15.8
.3	.3	.3	Income Taxes Payable	.6	.7	.3	.1	.2	.1
12.8	11.4	10.4	All Other Current	12.8	6.3	6.9	14.3	9.1	13.3
42.0	40.9	42.6	Total Current	33.7	56.4	32.8	36.6	43.0	47.0
14.9	19.6	19.1	Long-Term Debt	23.9	30.6	26.2	18.5	7.0	13.5
.8	.5	.4	Deferred Taxes	.0	.1	.0	1.1	.5	.8
7.6	5.1	6.9	All Other Non-Current	7.1	6.0	4.4	12.8	5.2	6.0
34.7	33.9	30.9	Net Worth	35.4	6.9	36.6	31.0	44.4	32.7
100.0	100.0	100.0	Total Liabilities & Net Worth	100.0	100.0	100.0	100.0	100.0	100.0
			INCOME DATA						
100.0	100.0	100.0	Net Sales	100.0	100.0	100.0	100.0	100.0	100.0
			Gross Profit						
93.2	92.0	92.3	Operating Expenses	84.1	94.2	93.8	91.9	93.2	93.6
6.8	8.0	7.7	Operating Profit	15.9	5.8	6.2	8.1	6.8	6.4
1.1	1.9	.7	All Other Expenses (net)	1.0	.4	.3	.3	.6	1.4
5.7	6.1	7.1	Profit Before Taxes	14.8	5.4	5.9	7.8	6.2	4.9
			RATIOS						
2.7	2.6	3.0		4.0	3.9	2.8	4.2	3.2	2.2
1.6	1.6	1.6	Current	1.0	1.8	1.8	1.7	1.4	1.6
1.1	1.0	1.1		.6	.9	1.3	1.0	1.2	1.1
2.0	1.9	2.1		4.0	3.9	2.3	3.5	2.2	1.3
1.2	1.1	1.1	Quick	.7	1.4	1.5	1.2	1.2	.9
.7	.6	.7		.4	.3	.9	.8	1.0	.6
23 15.9	21 17.3	24 14.9		0 UND	8 44.7	25 14.8	8 48.2	37 9.8	41 9.0
45 8.1	41 9.0	41 9.0	Sales/Receivables	0 UND	29 12.4	33 10.9	39 9.3	47 7.8	55 6.6
62 5.9	60 6.1	61 6.0		29 12.6	51 7.2	63 5.8	49 7.4	65 5.6	65 5.6
			Cost of Sales/Inventory						
			Cost of Sales/Payables						
5.3	6.6	5.5		4.7	5.5	8.0	4.9	5.7	4.1
11.6	12.2	11.9	Sales/Working Capital	NM	10.5	14.0	10.2	12.5	10.5
62.7	484.0	66.4		-14.8	-50.9	32.2	NM	36.6	66.4
15.0	28.7	27.0			20.0	29.3	30.7	29.4	36.3
(111) 5.4	(96) 9.4	(87) 6.6	EBIT/Interest		(16) 4.8	7.6	(16) 8.7	(18) 9.2	(18) 11.5
2.0	2.5	3.1			1.4	1.3	3.5	3.1	3.4
6.0	7.2	7.7							
(22) 3.4	(16) 3.5	(18) 3.2	Net Profit + Depr., Dep., Amort./Cur. Mat. L/T/D						
1.3	1.8	1.1							
.1	.1	.2		.1	.0	.4	.2	.1	.2
.5	.4	.7	Fixed/Worth	.7	.7	1.2	.6	.4	.5
16.3	1.7	3.9		NM	-.6	2.7	NM	2.4	2.8
.6	.7	.8		.2	.4	.5	1.4	.6	1.4
1.8	1.7	2.2	Debt/Worth	2.2	2.2	2.3	2.9	1.2	2.4
NM	5.8	24.1		NM	-2.1	7.8	NM	6.9	8.9
60.7	61.8	76.8			47.7	78.0	131.0	74.0	57.0
(99) 30.1	(97) 29.5	(79) 31.8	% Profit Before Taxes/Tangible Net Worth		(11) 19.9	(12) 16.4	(14) 43.8	(17) 30.9	(16) 32.6
9.2	12.8	14.3			8.4	4.0	26.8	12.3	23.6
22.7	21.2	28.5		91.6	23.6	26.8	45.3	23.2	13.9
10.3	10.0	9.5	% Profit Before Taxes/Total Assets	20.0	9.3	7.2	10.5	10.4	10.4
2.8	3.5	4.1		2.4	.9	1.5	4.9	5.9	5.9
65.0	52.8	70.1		120.1	467.0	30.5	94.1	107.3	40.6
23.6	25.0	19.5	Sales/Net Fixed Assets	25.7	24.1	11.6	28.8	19.5	17.5
11.2	10.1	7.4		6.7	4.8	3.6	9.1	11.0	6.8
4.0	3.9	3.9		4.6	3.9	3.8	6.1	4.0	2.8
2.9	2.9	2.7	Sales/Total Assets	1.6	2.2	3.0	3.5	3.2	1.9
1.9	1.9	1.6		1.0	1.8	1.7	2.0	2.3	1.4
.8	.6	.5					.2	.5	.5
(90) 1.3	(86) 1.1	(68) 1.1	% Depr., Dep., Amort./Sales				(14) .9	(16) 1.2	(15) 1.0
2.5	2.4	2.5					2.6	2.2	2.2
3.0	2.2	3.0					2.2		
(56) 5.6	(40) 4.7	(42) 4.6	% Officers', Directors' Owners' Comp/Sales				(11) 4.3		
11.9	9.2	8.8					9.7		
2181687M	2741574M	3016904M	Net Sales ($)	6328M	36998M	53721M	123398M	329117M	2467342M
980201M	1340621M	1436594M	Total Assets ($)	4733M	16730M	24265M	49070M	126719M	1215077M

M = $ thousand MM = $ million

See Pages 9 through 22 for Explanation of Ratios and Data

Current Data Sorted by Assets							Comparative Historical Data	
						Type of Statement		
1	1	9	13	5	7	Unqualified	17	29
2	10	30	10			Reviewed	59	54
9	33	21	3			Compiled	62	55
58	58	31			3	Tax Returns	130	125
20	51	47	21	2	3	Other	110	127
61 (4/1-9/30/13)		387 (10/1/13-3/31/14)					4/1/09-3/31/10	4/1/10-3/31/11
0-500M	500M-2MM	2-10MM	10-50MM	50-100MM	100-250MM		ALL	ALL
90	153	138	47	7	13	NUMBER OF STATEMENTS	378	390
%	%	%	%	%	%	**ASSETS**	%	%
19.1	12.8	9.5	6.3		3.2	Cash & Equivalents	9.9	10.3
26.0	32.3	31.3	27.3		21.5	Trade Receivables (net)	26.8	29.6
10.6	14.9	19.8	18.5		24.2	Inventory	18.9	17.2
3.5	2.1	2.7	4.5		2.3	All Other Current	3.1	3.9
59.2	62.1	63.3	56.6		51.3	Total Current	58.7	61.1
28.9	28.3	25.9	27.7		27.7	Fixed Assets (net)	30.5	27.1
2.3	4.1	3.1	9.3		15.6	Intangibles (net)	4.1	5.6
9.6	5.5	7.8	6.4		5.4	All Other Non-Current	6.7	6.2
100.0	100.0	100.0	100.0		100.0	Total	100.0	100.0
						LIABILITIES		
16.1	11.3	11.2	9.4		21.6	Notes Payable-Short Term	10.9	12.1
4.7	3.0	2.9	3.5		2.9	Cur. Mat.-L.T.D.	4.6	4.5
13.6	13.6	12.7	13.2		10.3	Trade Payables	14.0	14.6
.1	.3	.2	.2		.1	Income Taxes Payable	.2	.3
13.9	9.3	9.6	12.9		6.7	All Other Current	10.8	11.0
48.6	37.5	36.7	39.2		41.5	Total Current	40.5	42.6
25.0	22.1	15.1	18.4		23.4	Long-Term Debt	23.8	21.3
.0	.2	.4	1.0		2.9	Deferred Taxes	.4	.5
12.4	4.2	3.3	3.4		6.8	All Other Non-Current	5.3	7.3
14.1	36.0	44.5	38.0		25.4	Net Worth	30.1	28.3
100.0	100.0	100.0	100.0		100.0	Total Liabilties & Net Worth	100.0	100.0
						INCOME DATA		
100.0	100.0	100.0	100.0		100.0	Net Sales	100.0	100.0
						Gross Profit		
93.9	91.4	93.2	92.9		94.8	Operating Expenses	95.2	93.5
6.1	8.6	6.8	7.1		5.2	Operating Profit	4.8	6.5
1.5	1.7	.9	1.6		.2	All Other Expenses (net)	1.5	1.7
4.5	6.9	5.9	5.5		5.0	Profit Before Taxes	3.4	4.8
						RATIOS		
3.1	2.8	3.2	2.1		2.1		2.8	2.6
1.4	1.8	1.8	1.5		1.6	Current	1.6	1.5
.6	1.0	1.2	1.2		1.0		1.0	1.1
2.5	2.3	2.2	1.3		1.4		1.9	1.8
1.0	1.3	1.1	.9		.8	Quick	(377) 1.0	(389) 1.1
.4	.7	.7	.5		.2		.5	.5
0 UND	**24** 15.3	**34** 10.8	**34** 10.6		**18** 19.9		**22** 16.8	**25** 14.6
18 20.4	**38** 9.5	**45** 8.2	**54** 6.7		**48** 7.6	Sales/Receivables	**39** 9.3	**44** 8.4
44 8.3	**55** 6.6	**62** 5.9	**69** 5.3		**61** 6.0		**56** 6.5	**60** 6.1
						Cost of Sales/Inventory		
						Cost of Sales/Payables		
9.7	6.0	5.3	6.6		6.5		5.8	5.7
24.7	12.0	9.7	13.1		11.8	Sales/Working Capital	13.6	13.4
-30.7	183.0	22.6	22.4		NM		-874.3	104.9
13.6	26.0	29.5	15.1		8.8		9.9	13.4
(66) 3.5	(127) 6.4	(121) 8.2	(44) 5.5		4.9	EBIT/Interest	(330) 2.5	(346) 4.7
.0	1.7	2.2	2.1		2.3		.0	1.1
	4.8	10.2	6.3				8.1	5.2
	(14) 1.9	(26) 3.4	(13) 4.2			Net Profit + Depr., Dep., Amort./Cur. Mat. L/T/D	(59) 2.2	(65) 2.1
	.6	1.6	2.0				1.1	1.2
.3	.2	.2	.3		.6		.3	.3
1.1	.7	.6	.8		2.2	Fixed/Worth	.8	.7
-6.4	3.7	1.1	1.7		-.8		4.2	3.5
1.0	.6	.5	1.0		2.0		.7	.8
2.8	1.6	1.3	2.6		5.4	Debt/Worth	2.1	2.2
-38.1	9.2	3.0	5.3		-4.6		16.1	11.6
79.0	90.9	50.8	52.3				40.4	58.8
(64) 40.6	(129) 41.3	(129) 22.2	(43) 35.7			% Profit Before Taxes/Tangible Net Worth	(309) 14.0	(315) 22.6
3.1	11.4	8.0	2.2				-1.1	4.5
31.9	29.6	17.4	13.4		10.5		16.4	18.9
11.9	12.2	9.4	8.5		7.0	% Profit Before Taxes/Total Assets	3.3	7.3
-1.0	2.3	2.5	1.4		3.4		-2.7	.4
60.1	39.6	30.1	21.8		16.3		32.8	38.2
24.4	16.0	12.1	12.8		5.4	Sales/Net Fixed Assets	12.6	13.8
8.7	5.9	5.3	3.2		2.8		4.7	5.3
6.3	4.0	3.2	2.7		1.9		3.6	3.6
4.2	2.8	2.3	1.8		1.5	Sales/Total Assets	2.4	2.4
2.7	1.9	1.6	1.1		1.1		1.6	1.5
.8	.5	.8	.8		.7		.9	.9
(49) 2.0	(106) 1.9	(113) 1.6	(46) 2.3		(10) 3.2	% Depr., Dep., Amort./Sales	(302) 2.0	(292) 1.9
4.1	3.8	3.2	4.7		5.7		4.2	4.3
5.1	3.0	1.6	.6				2.9	2.5
(57) 7.5	(81) 4.9	(69) 3.2	(10) 2.9			% Officers', Directors' Owners' Comp/Sales	(182) 5.5	(173) 5.3
13.6	7.7	5.3	5.8				9.0	8.9
110327M	538503M	1505490M	1848037M	531760M	4638543M	Net Sales ($)	5600415M	7933671M
22557M	180603M	636145M	963729M	425475M	2048545M	Total Assets ($)	2763258M	3403862M

M = $ thousand MM = $ million

See Pages 9 through 22 for Explanation of Ratios and Data

Comparative Historical Data | **Current Data Sorted by Sales**

4/1/11-3/31/12 ALL	4/1/12-3/31/13 ALL	4/1/13-3/31/14 ALL	Type of Statement	0-1MM	1-3MM	3-5MM	5-10MM	10-25MM	25MM & OVER
25	29	36	Unqualified		2	2	2	9	21
61	62	52	Reviewed	1	5	4	10	23	9
72	58	66	Compiled	9	15	13	19	8	2
158	142	150	Tax Returns	37	47	24	29	8	5
147	179	144	Other	19	28	20	30	27	20
				61 (4/1-9/30/13)			387 (10/1/13-3/31/14)		
463	470	448	NUMBER OF STATEMENTS	66	97	63	90	75	57
%	%	%	ASSETS	%	%	%	%	%	%
10.4	12.8	11.9	Cash & Equivalents	15.2	13.4	12.9	14.7	7.6	5.6
31.7	28.1	29.6	Trade Receivables (net)	21.0	25.1	30.9	37.0	33.1	29.7
18.1	18.2	16.4	Inventory	6.9	16.2	17.6	16.3	19.8	22.3
2.7	2.3	2.8	All Other Current	2.7	3.9	1.7	1.5	3.3	3.9
62.8	61.5	60.8	Total Current	45.8	58.6	63.1	69.6	63.8	61.5
26.3	27.0	27.6	Fixed Assets (net)	43.1	28.8	27.4	21.8	24.4	21.3
5.2	4.1	4.5	Intangibles (net)	4.5	4.6	2.4	2.5	3.9	10.9
5.7	7.4	7.1	All Other Non-Current	6.6	8.0	7.1	6.2	7.9	6.3
100.0	100.0	100.0	Total	100.0	100.0	100.0	100.0	100.0	100.0
			LIABILITIES						
12.5	10.6	12.3	Notes Payable-Short Term	15.1	12.7	13.5	9.5	11.6	12.3
4.1	3.3	3.4	Cur. Mat.-L.T.D.	3.8	3.4	3.5	3.4	3.1	3.1
14.5	13.1	13.1	Trade Payables	9.0	12.4	12.8	15.4	14.7	13.5
.3	.4	.3	Income Taxes Payable	.0	.1	.1	.6	.3	.4
12.1	11.6	10.7	All Other Current	13.6	7.8	11.3	9.8	11.0	12.2
43.4	39.1	39.7	Total Current	41.5	36.5	41.2	38.8	40.7	41.5
21.9	19.5	20.1	Long-Term Debt	27.4	25.0	21.0	17.6	11.8	17.0
.3	.4	.4	Deferred Taxes	.0	.1	.4	.5	.3	1.4
7.7	7.1	5.8	All Other Non-Current	14.1	5.9	2.2	3.3	6.3	2.8
26.7	33.9	34.1	Net Worth	17.0	32.5	35.2	39.8	40.9	37.2
100.0	100.0	100.0	Total Liabilties & Net Worth	100.0	100.0	100.0	100.0	100.0	100.0
			INCOME DATA						
100.0	100.0	100.0	Net Sales	100.0	100.0	100.0	100.0	100.0	100.0
			Gross Profit						
93.3	91.9	92.8	Operating Expenses	83.6	93.8	94.6	93.8	96.2	93.9
6.7	8.1	7.2	Operating Profit	16.4	6.2	5.4	6.2	3.8	6.1
1.4	1.0	1.3	All Other Expenses (net)	5.8	1.3	.1	.5	.2	.5
5.3	7.1	5.8	Profit Before Taxes	10.6	4.9	5.3	5.7	3.6	5.6
			RATIOS						
2.8	3.1	2.8		2.6	3.6	3.1	2.8	2.5	2.3
1.6	1.7	1.6	Current	1.1	1.8	1.9	1.9	1.6	1.5
1.1	1.1	1.1		.5	1.0	1.1	1.3	1.1	1.2
2.0	2.2	2.0		2.3	2.6	2.4	2.3	1.6	1.4
1.0	1.1	1.1	Quick	.8	1.1	1.3	1.3	.9	1.0
.6	.6	.6		.4	.5	.6	.8	.6	.5
25 14.4	**21** 17.4	**23** 16.2		**0** UND	**17** 21.7	**21** 17.2	**29** 12.6	**35** 10.3	**33** 11.2
42 8.7	**39** 9.3	**40** 9.1	Sales/Receivables	**19** 18.9	**33** 11.0	**40** 9.1	**41** 8.8	**47** 7.7	**44** 8.3
59 6.2	**56** 6.5	**59** 6.2		**54** 6.8	**51** 7.1	**59** 6.2	**60** 6.1	**64** 5.7	**62** 5.9
			Cost of Sales/Inventory						
			Cost of Sales/Payables						
6.1	5.8	5.9		6.5	5.3	5.9	5.8	6.0	6.4
12.3	11.4	12.3	Sales/Working Capital	356.5	12.7	12.5	10.1	11.8	13.1
117.9	57.9	74.8		-9.2	UND	40.9	20.6	30.7	24.8
17.1	24.2	20.7		6.7	21.5	25.5	26.6	28.9	18.4
(399) 5.1	(403) 7.3	(376) 6.1	EBIT/Interest	(38) 2.3	(82) 4.7	(54) 6.1	(80) 8.6	(68) 7.7	(54) 6.1
1.6	2.7	1.7		-1.5	1.0	1.8	2.6	1.6	3.7
7.4	8.8	7.4					8.8	9.7	6.5
(55) 2.2	(67) 3.7	(60) 3.0	Net Profit + Depr., Dep., Amort./Cur. Mat. L/T/D				(14) 1.9	(20) 3.4	(16) 3.9
1.4	1.8	1.6					.6	1.7	2.0
.2	.2	.3		.4	.3	.2	.2	.3	.2
.7	.7	.7	Fixed/Worth	1.9	1.0	.6	.5	.6	.7
3.4	2.5	2.8		UND	19.0	3.7	1.1	1.2	1.8
.8	.7	.7		.5	.7	.6	.6	.7	.9
2.1	1.7	1.8	Debt/Worth	3.4	1.9	1.3	1.3	1.5	2.5
12.4	7.0	7.6		-56.4	73.1	9.3	3.9	4.9	5.7
62.0	68.6	66.0		59.8	100.0	67.5	61.7	48.8	63.5
(371) 29.8	(396) 31.3	(377) 31.6	% Profit Before Taxes/Tangible Net Worth	(48) 27.7	(79) 35.0	(51) 41.3	(82) 29.8	(69) 20.6	(48) 40.2
6.6	12.2	8.7		5.3	5.5	10.0	8.9	2.9	20.0
23.2	25.5	20.6		21.4	23.9	31.2	25.1	16.6	14.8
9.2	11.1	10.2	% Profit Before Taxes/Total Assets	6.2	9.7	15.9	13.7	7.6	10.4
1.6	3.6	1.6		-1.4	-.3	3.3	3.4	1.3	5.1
44.2	39.6	39.1		40.1	37.0	36.5	50.3	30.8	36.7
16.5	14.4	15.3	Sales/Net Fixed Assets	12.1	13.4	16.3	19.5	16.6	15.8
6.5	5.7	5.6		1.7	4.8	7.1	9.0	5.3	5.3
3.6	3.7	3.8		4.1	4.7	4.2	4.1	3.5	3.4
2.7	2.6	2.7	Sales/Total Assets	2.4	2.4	3.0	3.1	2.5	2.0
1.7	1.6	1.6		.9	1.6	2.2	2.2	1.7	1.4
1.0	.9	.8		1.7	.6	.8	.6	.8	.4
(335) 1.9	(339) 1.8	(330) 1.9	% Depr., Dep., Amort./Sales	(38) 3.8	(59) 2.6	(46) 1.9	(68) 1.5	(69) 1.4	(50) 2.2
3.5	3.6	3.8		10.1	5.7	3.0	2.2	2.7	3.4
2.7	2.8	2.3		6.8	3.7	2.4	2.2	1.4	.5
(222) 4.7	(224) 5.4	(220) 4.9	% Officers', Directors' Owners' Comp/Sales	(30) 11.7	(55) 6.4	(34) 3.9	(53) 3.9	(35) 3.1	(13) 1.2
8.8	8.6	8.2		16.9	9.7	7.2	6.2	4.6	6.7
6439862M	8197498M	9172660M	Net Sales ($)	35147M	178554M	243630M	616814M	1157972M	6940543M
3089868M	3814361M	4277054M	Total Assets ($)	41249M	107229M	96395M	248829M	678102M	3105250M

M = $ thousand MM = $ million

See Pages 9 through 22 for Explanation of Ratios and Data

Current Data Sorted by Assets							Comparative Historical Data	
						Type of Statement		
	2	5	3	1		Unqualified	1	1
		2				Reviewed	12	11
		1				Compiled	7	4
5	1	1				Tax Returns	13	19
3	2	7	2	1		Other	22	23
3 (4/1-9/30/13)			33 (10/1/13-3/31/14)				4/1/09-3/31/10 ALL	4/1/10-3/31/11 ALL
0-500M	500M-2MM	2-10MM	10-50MM	50-100MM	100-250MM			
8	5	16	5	2		**NUMBER OF STATEMENTS**	55	58
%	%	%	%	%	%	**ASSETS**	%	%
		19.0			DATA NOT AVAILABLE	Cash & Equivalents	15.1	15.6
		25.8				Trade Receivables (net)	26.2	25.8
		8.8				Inventory	19.2	16.8
		7.4				All Other Current	5.8	2.7
		61.1				Total Current	66.3	60.9
		23.8				Fixed Assets (net)	22.4	24.7
		6.1				Intangibles (net)	3.5	4.5
		9.0				All Other Non-Current	7.8	9.9
		100.0				Total	100.0	100.0
						LIABILITIES		
		2.3				Notes Payable-Short Term	23.5	15.7
		7.4				Cur. Mat.-L.T.D.	10.1	4.3
		7.0				Trade Payables	18.0	16.0
		1.3				Income Taxes Payable	.2	.2
		18.8				All Other Current	18.0	21.9
		36.9				Total Current	69.8	58.1
		13.9				Long-Term Debt	18.6	18.3
		.8				Deferred Taxes	.6	.5
		4.7				All Other Non-Current	4.5	4.0
		43.7				Net Worth	6.5	19.1
		100.0				Total Liabilties & Net Worth	100.0	100.0
						INCOME DATA		
		100.0				Net Sales	100.0	100.0
						Gross Profit		
		96.5				Operating Expenses	95.8	93.4
		3.5				Operating Profit	4.2	6.6
		.4				All Other Expenses (net)	.8	1.1
		3.1				Profit Before Taxes	3.4	5.5
						RATIOS		
		2.2				Current	2.5	2.6
		1.4					1.6	1.5
		1.0					.9	1.0
		1.5				Quick	1.4	1.6
		.9					.9	.9
		.4					.4	.5
		6 63.6				Sales/Receivables	2 186.1	5 79.7
		25 14.4					34 10.9	30 12.2
		39 9.4					51 7.1	53 6.9
						Cost of Sales/Inventory		
						Cost of Sales/Payables		
		9.2				Sales/Working Capital	5.9	5.9
		18.2					13.6	18.2
		939.1					-48.1	NM
		16.7				EBIT/Interest	24.2	34.2
		(12) 7.1					(47) 6.4	(49) 7.2
		3.4					.4	2.9
						Net Profit + Depr., Dep., Amort./Cur. Mat. L/T/D		
		.0				Fixed/Worth	.1	.2
		.2					.5	.8
		1.9					2.4	NM
		.4				Debt/Worth	.7	.7
		2.1					2.3	2.2
		7.4					24.6	-248.1
		75.0				% Profit Before Taxes/Tangible Net Worth	70.3	63.8
		(14) 40.5					(44) 25.7	(43) 21.1
		13.4					10.0	6.6
		16.4				% Profit Before Taxes/Total Assets	20.7	22.0
		9.9					6.9	11.3
		2.0					.2	4.0
		308.8				Sales/Net Fixed Assets	66.0	47.1
		22.7					20.9	19.4
		5.3					9.4	7.5
		4.0				Sales/Total Assets	4.6	4.7
		2.3					3.3	3.0
		1.8					2.1	2.0
		.2				% Depr., Dep., Amort./Sales	.4	.9
		(12) 1.6					(40) 1.3	(39) 1.7
		3.2					2.1	2.7
						% Officers', Directors' Owners' Comp/Sales	2.6	2.9
							(26) 4.7	(26) 5.5
							8.4	6.8
19261M	10003M	268914M	438895M	792562M		Net Sales ($)	711707M	568593M
1326M	4715M	81197M	113329M	125179M		Total Assets ($)	280035M	234832M

M = $ thousand MM = $ million

See Pages 9 through 22 for Explanation of Ratios and Data

Comparative Historical Data / Current Data Sorted by Sales

Type of Statement	4/1/11-3/31/12 ALL	4/1/12-3/31/13 ALL	4/1/13-3/31/14 ALL	0-1MM	1-3MM	3-5MM	5-10MM	10-25MM	25MM & OVER
Unqualified	2		11	1	2			2	6
Reviewed	8	2	2					2	
Compiled	1	3	1					1	
Tax Returns	8	9	7	5			2		
Other	19	14	15	1	1	3	5	2	3
					3 (4/1-9/30/13)		33 (10/1/13-3/31/14)		
NUMBER OF STATEMENTS	38	28	36	7	3	3	7	7	9
	%	%	%	%	%	%	%	%	%
ASSETS									
Cash & Equivalents	15.1	16.7	18.1						
Trade Receivables (net)	22.1	15.5	20.6						
Inventory	17.9	15.4	15.7						
All Other Current	3.8	1.9	8.5						
Total Current	58.8	49.5	62.8						
Fixed Assets (net)	28.1	37.5	23.5						
Intangibles (net)	3.8	6.3	3.4						
All Other Non-Current	9.3	6.7	10.3						
Total	100.0	100.0	100.0						
LIABILITIES									
Notes Payable-Short Term	17.0	3.8	14.5						
Cur. Mat.-L.T.D.	3.0	5.3	5.3						
Trade Payables	17.8	7.6	6.5						
Income Taxes Payable	.3	.0	.6						
All Other Current	16.1	17.4	19.1						
Total Current	54.3	34.1	46.1						
Long-Term Debt	19.0	48.9	18.7						
Deferred Taxes	.6	.5	.4						
All Other Non-Current	8.8	6.6	5.7						
Net Worth	17.4	9.9	29.2						
Total Liabilties & Net Worth	100.0	100.0	100.0						
INCOME DATA									
Net Sales	100.0	100.0	100.0						
Gross Profit									
Operating Expenses	92.9	81.3	93.7						
Operating Profit	7.1	18.7	6.3						
All Other Expenses (net)	2.8	8.4	1.2						
Profit Before Taxes	4.3	10.3	5.1						
RATIOS									
	2.0	2.7	2.3						
Current	1.6	1.8	1.4						
	.6	1.0	.8						
	1.5	2.4	1.6						
Quick	.8	1.0	.8						
	.4	.4	.3						
	8 45.5	0 UND	0 UND						
Sales/Receivables	35 10.4	8 43.4	14 26.1						
	54 6.8	39 9.3	34 10.6						
Cost of Sales/Inventory									
Cost of Sales/Payables									
	5.4	7.2	7.3						
Sales/Working Capital	13.1	19.6	20.6						
	-26.1	UND	-95.2						
	10.3	24.0	17.3						
EBIT/Interest	(31) 4.1	(22) 5.5	(28) 5.3						
	1.6	3.2	1.9						
Net Profit + Depr., Dep., Amort./Cur. Mat. L/T/D									
	.1	.2	.0						
Fixed/Worth	.5	3.0	.3						
	3.2	36.9	1.9						
	.9	1.1	.8						
Debt/Worth	1.5	5.0	2.1						
	11.0	NM	58.3						
	37.4	97.6	75.2						
% Profit Before Taxes/Tangible Net Worth	(30) 11.8	(21) 31.4	(28) 41.5						
	3.1	18.2	12.3						
	13.2	16.6	19.4						
% Profit Before Taxes/Total Assets	4.8	11.6	9.2						
	.8	2.9	3.8						
	43.0	33.7	166.8						
Sales/Net Fixed Assets	20.0	11.6	34.5						
	6.6	3.9	8.6						
	3.8	6.2	8.0						
Sales/Total Assets	2.5	2.6	2.5						
	1.4	1.2	1.7						
	.6	1.0	.3						
% Depr., Dep., Amort./Sales	(28) 1.2	(21) 1.7	(25) 1.3						
	2.5	3.9	3.1						
	2.9		1.6						
% Officers', Directors' Owners' Comp/Sales	(14) 4.9		(11) 4.0						
	6.4		12.0						
Net Sales ($)	397403M	269777M	1529635M	2754M	4769M	12940M	48457M	105235M	1355480M
Total Assets ($)	204931M	156815M	325746M	3364M	2284M	8654M	17189M	65679M	228576M

M = $ thousand MM = $ million

See Pages 9 through 22 for Explanation of Ratios and Data

Current Data Sorted by Assets							Comparative Historical Data	
						Type of Statement		
		1	1			Unqualified	3	2
1		4	1			Reviewed	6	6
2	3	4	1			Compiled	13	9
26	11	2	1			Tax Returns	42	43
16	16	8	2			Other	22	33
12 (4/1-9/30/13)			88 (10/1/13-3/31/14)				4/1/09-3/31/10	4/1/10-3/31/11
0-500M	500M-2MM	2-10MM	10-50MM	50-100MM	100-250MM		ALL	ALL
45	30	19	6			**NUMBER OF STATEMENTS**	86	93
%	%	%	%	%	%	**ASSETS**	%	%
23.2	22.7	14.3		DATA NOT AVAILABLE	DATA NOT AVAILABLE	Cash & Equivalents	13.9	16.3
16.5	19.3	28.7				Trade Receivables (net)	20.6	20.2
16.7	15.3	16.7				Inventory	18.9	15.1
2.3	1.0	2.6				All Other Current	4.7	4.0
58.6	58.3	62.3				Total Current	58.1	55.5
22.4	27.1	30.8				Fixed Assets (net)	29.5	27.4
5.3	8.4	1.6				Intangibles (net)	4.8	7.6
13.7	6.2	5.3				All Other Non-Current	7.5	9.5
100.0	100.0	100.0				Total	100.0	100.0
						LIABILITIES		
28.5	10.3	9.5				Notes Payable-Short Term	13.4	9.8
5.5	2.1	4.6				Cur. Mat.-L.T.D.	6.1	3.8
9.5	9.3	14.5				Trade Payables	11.4	12.4
.2	.0	.1				Income Taxes Payable	.2	.1
23.7	8.7	14.7				All Other Current	13.7	10.6
67.4	30.4	43.4				Total Current	44.8	36.8
28.7	16.8	12.2				Long-Term Debt	27.8	16.8
.0	.0	1.1				Deferred Taxes	.1	.1
17.1	8.7	5.2				All Other Non-Current	5.8	11.9
-13.2	44.1	38.1				Net Worth	21.5	34.5
100.0	100.0	100.0				Total Liabilties & Net Worth	100.0	100.0
						INCOME DATA		
100.0	100.0	100.0				Net Sales	100.0	100.0
						Gross Profit		
91.0	91.8	94.0				Operating Expenses	92.4	93.9
9.0	8.2	6.0				Operating Profit	7.6	6.1
1.3	1.5	.4				All Other Expenses (net)	1.7	1.1
7.7	6.7	5.6				Profit Before Taxes	5.9	5.1
						RATIOS		
3.9	4.8	2.8					3.4	4.5
1.5	2.0	1.6				Current	1.5	1.7
.5	1.1	1.0					.7	.9
2.8	3.6	1.6					2.1	3.3
.8	1.3	.8				Quick	.8	1.0
.2	.5	.5					.3	.3
0 UND	0 UND	14 26.1					0 UND	0 UND
4 81.9	10 37.4	37 9.9				Sales/Receivables	22 16.5	15 23.6
22 16.4	51 7.1	46 7.9					46 7.9	47 7.7
						Cost of Sales/Inventory		
						Cost of Sales/Payables		
12.8	4.9	9.0					6.1	5.6
42.4	8.3	12.3				Sales/Working Capital	17.7	13.2
-18.2	56.4	93.0					-28.5	-74.8
16.3	107.8	132.3					19.3	18.5
(30) 4.2	(25) 16.1	(17) 6.5				EBIT/Interest	(67) 3.0	(73) 4.4
1.0	3.8	2.0					.4	1.4
						Net Profit + Depr., Dep., Amort./Cur. Mat. L/T/D		
.0	.1	.3					.2	.2
.6	.4	.6				Fixed/Worth	1.3	.7
-2.1	1.9	5.9					-2.1	3.8
.7	.3	.4					.7	.5
2.4	1.2	1.6				Debt/Worth	2.5	1.6
-5.1	15.5	36.1					-10.9	10.3
146.2	64.9	79.1					61.2	70.8
(29) 56.4	(24) 47.2	(16) 29.2				% Profit Before Taxes/Tangible Net Worth	(61) 22.3	(74) 25.7
21.1	12.5	13.7					-2.2	7.7
60.2	35.6	24.0					29.3	29.4
20.2	15.5	11.6				% Profit Before Taxes/Total Assets	8.3	9.3
3.1	5.7	4.5					-2.0	1.9
712.1	138.4	36.1					59.2	59.0
64.8	17.6	12.6				Sales/Net Fixed Assets	17.1	19.3
14.4	5.6	6.3					5.8	6.1
9.9	3.7	4.6					5.3	4.5
5.2	2.5	3.4				Sales/Total Assets	2.8	2.7
3.0	1.6	2.1					1.8	1.8
.8	.6	.5					.8	.5
(19) 1.4	(14) 2.0	(15) 1.5				% Depr., Dep., Amort./Sales	(59) 1.7	(65) 1.2
3.6	4.1	4.9					4.5	3.5
4.8	2.3						2.8	2.7
(31) 7.6	(18) 4.4					% Officers', Directors' Owners' Comp/Sales	(47) 5.1	(48) 6.1
11.9	11.8						9.2	9.3
50549M	104778M	256769M	1265823M			Net Sales ($)	834639M	1583453M
8565M	32686M	87141M	113696M			Total Assets ($)	349237M	294281M

M = $ thousand MM = $ million

See Pages 9 through 22 for Explanation of Ratios and Data

Comparative Historical Data / Current Data Sorted by Sales

4/1/11-3/31/12 ALL	4/1/12-3/31/13 ALL	4/1/13-3/31/14 ALL		0-1MM	1-3MM	3-5MM	5-10MM	10-25MM	25MM & OVER
			Type of Statement						
5	4	2	Unqualified					1	1
4	4	6	Reviewed	1			1	2	2
12	9	10	Compiled	1	4	3		1	1
48	46	40	Tax Returns	18	12	4	3	2	1
37	52	42	Other	9	15	5	6	7	
				12 (4/1-9/30/13)		88 (10/1/13-3/31/14)			
106	115	100	**NUMBER OF STATEMENTS**	29	31	12	10	13	5
%	%	%	**ASSETS**	%	%	%	%	%	%
20.3	18.4	20.5	Cash & Equivalents	18.7	26.2	19.0	14.4	20.4	
19.2	17.2	19.7	Trade Receivables (net)	11.3	25.3	18.3	20.3	23.5	
10.7	18.0	16.9	Inventory	21.7	7.5	26.5	20.5	17.3	
1.6	2.6	1.9	All Other Current	3.0	1.2	.8	.9	1.6	
51.9	56.1	59.1	Total Current	54.8	60.2	64.6	56.2	62.8	
29.4	26.3	25.7	Fixed Assets (net)	29.1	21.0	29.6	25.0	26.4	
8.8	6.8	5.7	Intangibles (net)	3.7	6.9	2.8	13.2	2.0	
9.9	10.7	9.5	All Other Non-Current	12.5	11.9	3.0	5.7	8.8	
100.0	100.0	100.0	Total	100.0	100.0	100.0	100.0	100.0	
			LIABILITIES						
15.4	19.4	20.7	Notes Payable-Short Term	22.1	24.4	15.9	9.2	9.9	
3.9	4.3	4.2	Cur. Mat.-L.T.D.	6.8	2.5	3.6	2.1	5.1	
9.2	12.7	10.8	Trade Payables	8.7	9.4	9.5	12.2	15.2	
.0	.1	.1	Income Taxes Payable	.3	.0	.0	.0	.1	
12.3	11.4	16.9	All Other Current	21.9	19.1	13.4	4.4	12.9	
40.8	48.0	52.7	Total Current	59.8	55.4	42.5	27.9	43.3	
29.6	24.1	20.7	Long-Term Debt	38.6	14.2	19.0	11.9	10.5	
.1	.1	.3	Deferred Taxes	.0	.0	.0	1.6	.3	
7.0	9.0	11.5	All Other Non-Current	30.2	4.1	1.8	6.1	4.5	
22.4	18.7	14.8	Net Worth	-28.7	26.2	36.8	52.4	41.5	
100.0	100.0	100.0	Total Liabilities & Net Worth	100.0	100.0	100.0	100.0	100.0	
			INCOME DATA						
100.0	100.0	100.0	Net Sales	100.0	100.0	100.0	100.0	100.0	
			Gross Profit						
92.3	90.2	92.0	Operating Expenses	86.8	93.7	97.5	94.3	92.0	
7.7	9.8	8.0	Operating Profit	13.2	6.3	2.5	5.7	8.0	
2.5	1.5	1.2	All Other Expenses (net)	3.7	-.2	.0	.8	.4	
5.3	8.4	6.8	Profit Before Taxes	9.5	6.5	2.5	4.9	7.5	
			RATIOS						
5.3	4.1	3.9		5.5	3.0	4.6	20.1	3.8	
1.4	1.8	1.6	Current	1.6	1.6	1.5	2.2	1.6	
.8	.8	.8		.6	.8	.8	1.1	1.0	
3.8	2.8	2.4		3.1	2.4	3.1	8.6	1.7	
(105) 1.2	1.0	1.1	Quick	.5	1.3	1.1	1.3	.8	
.5	.3	.3		.1	.6	.3	.4	.5	
0 UND	0 UND	0 UND		0 UND	0 UND	0 UND	0 UND	0 UND	
10 36.5	9 40.2	14 26.4	Sales/Receivables	4 95.0	16 23.3	9 41.8	37 9.8	14 26.1	
40 9.2	39 9.3	38 9.6		25 14.4	36 10.1	43 8.4	57 6.4	39 9.3	
			Cost of Sales/Inventory						
			Cost of Sales/Payables						
6.7	5.9	7.5		5.3	9.1	6.4	4.4	10.6	
21.9	21.9	18.9	Sales/Working Capital	13.0	21.5	41.7	8.1	22.6	
-96.4	-62.2	-71.7		-10.8	-56.4	NM	NM	NM	
10.9	36.1	36.0		14.8	47.7			99.4	
(76) 3.3	(90) 7.3	(78) 6.4	EBIT/Interest	(20) 3.1	(24) 10.1			(12) 10.5	
-1.7	2.3	1.8		1.3	1.5			2.9	
			Net Profit + Depr., Dep., Amort./Cur. Mat. L/T/D						
.1	.1	.1		.0	.1	.0	.1	.1	
.7	.6	.5	Fixed/Worth	.4	.5	.7	.5	.6	
UND	4.0	17.2		-1.7	2.2	2.0	21.1	3.3	
.5	.5	.4		.5	.4	.4	.1	.4	
2.3	2.1	1.9	Debt/Worth	4.8	1.8	2.6	2.3	1.4	
-19.0	-20.1	-32.3		-3.0	-17.7	9.8	30.4	21.3	
66.1	108.3	83.4		97.2	107.9	70.1		131.0	
(79) 15.7	(84) 50.5	(74) 41.8	% Profit Before Taxes/Tangible Net Worth	(18) 30.8	(22) 50.0	(10) 48.3		(11) 65.4	
-2.6	22.0	14.0		13.5	20.4	13.8		13.6	
24.2	43.7	40.5		45.2	45.9	31.5	28.5	57.8	
7.1	20.1	13.3	% Profit Before Taxes/Total Assets	10.6	17.6	9.8	15.9	18.4	
-4.6	4.7	4.2		.6	3.9	4.7	3.8	7.0	
82.3	108.6	126.7		UND	115.1	UND	69.1	57.6	
24.0	26.2	32.2	Sales/Net Fixed Assets	34.0	32.5	36.2	13.1	20.1	
6.4	8.7	7.6		6.5	11.2	4.4	6.8	12.5	
6.1	5.8	5.8		5.3	9.6	6.8	4.0	5.2	
3.6	3.4	3.5	Sales/Total Assets	2.9	3.8	3.5	3.2	4.4	
1.7	2.1	2.0		1.4	2.3	2.4	2.2	3.3	
.8	.4	.6		1.2	.6			.3	
(68) 2.1	(68) 1.2	(52) 1.5	% Depr., Dep., Amort./Sales	(14) 3.0	(13) 1.2			(10) 1.1	
4.4	2.8	3.9		7.3	3.8			1.9	
4.9	2.6	2.5		5.5	4.1				
(53) 7.7	(62) 5.6	(57) 5.9	% Officers', Directors' Owners' Comp/Sales	(17) 11.5	(21) 7.0				
12.4	8.2	11.6		21.8	11.5				
1124164M	528411M	1677919M	Net Sales ($)	12866M	57474M	46955M	71862M	210239M	1278523M
532508M	254887M	242088M	Total Assets ($)	7767M	22329M	20781M	34345M	60863M	96003M

M = $ thousand MM = $ million

See Pages 9 through 22 for Explanation of Ratios and Data

Current Data Sorted by Assets							Comparative Historical Data	
						Type of Statement		
		4	1	3		Unqualified	5	11
	1		1			Reviewed	5	6
4	5	4		1		Compiled	24	32
60	11	6	1		1	Tax Returns	102	89
31	27	11	3	1		Other	61	51
	14 (4/1-9/30/13)		162 (10/1/13-3/31/14)				4/1/09-3/31/10	4/1/10-3/31/11
0-500M	500M-2MM	2-10MM	10-50MM	50-100MM	100-250MM		ALL	ALL
95	44	25	6	5	1	NUMBER OF STATEMENTS	197	189
%	%	%	%	%	%	**ASSETS**	%	%
23.6	15.7	17.3				Cash & Equivalents	18.3	21.3
1.2	3.4	2.5				Trade Receivables (net)	3.7	4.0
11.5	6.3	9.2				Inventory	10.4	9.6
3.7	1.7	1.6				All Other Current	2.5	2.8
40.0	27.2	30.7				Total Current	34.9	37.6
40.3	56.3	39.2				Fixed Assets (net)	46.5	43.8
7.6	9.7	7.9				Intangibles (net)	10.3	7.8
12.2	6.8	22.2				All Other Non-Current	8.3	10.8
100.0	100.0	100.0				Total	100.0	100.0
						LIABILITIES		
17.5	5.5	1.9				Notes Payable-Short Term	8.8	8.2
5.5	2.4	2.5				Cur. Mat.-L.T.D.	3.9	4.3
7.1	4.6	6.3				Trade Payables	7.5	6.4
.0	.3	.6				Income Taxes Payable	.1	.1
28.1	17.6	15.4				All Other Current	25.6	24.9
58.3	30.4	26.7				Total Current	45.9	43.9
28.7	43.2	21.4				Long-Term Debt	30.8	32.8
.0	.0	.0				Deferred Taxes	.0	.0
15.1	5.2	6.5				All Other Non-Current	15.2	16.4
-2.1	21.2	45.4				Net Worth	8.1	6.9
100.0	100.0	100.0				Total Liabilties & Net Worth	100.0	100.0
						INCOME DATA		
100.0	100.0	100.0				Net Sales	100.0	100.0
						Gross Profit		
92.6	89.0	91.2				Operating Expenses	92.7	91.6
7.4	11.0	8.8				Operating Profit	7.3	8.4
1.0	5.2	.8				All Other Expenses (net)	2.0	2.9
6.4	5.9	8.0				Profit Before Taxes	5.3	5.5
						RATIOS		
2.3	1.7	2.0					2.0	2.6
1.1	1.0	1.1				Current	.9	1.1
.4	.4	.6					.3	.4
1.4	1.3	1.2					1.1	1.8
.6	.6	.6				Quick	(196) .4	.7
.2	.3	.4					.1	.2
0 UND	0 UND	0 UND					0 UND	0 UND
0 UND	0 UND	0 UND				Sales/Receivables	0 UND	0 UND
0 UND	1 716.5	0 750.2					0 UND	1 300.5
						Cost of Sales/Inventory		
						Cost of Sales/Payables		
27.6	29.1	11.7					21.6	18.2
601.8	NM	98.3				Sales/Working Capital	-195.5	225.0
-18.4	-14.5	-35.3					-14.5	-14.4
15.5	9.4	40.6					12.1	13.6
(64) 7.5	(34) 3.6	(21) 16.3				EBIT/Interest	(147) 4.3	(145) 3.9
.8	2.0	3.7					1.3	.9
								14.9
						Net Profit + Depr., Dep., Amort./Cur. Mat. L/T/D		(13) 4.9
								2.8
.4	1.1	.3					.6	.5
2.7	4.6	1.1				Fixed/Worth	3.1	3.2
-1.5	-3.6	3.0					-1.7	-2.0
.6	1.1	.4					.8	.7
5.3	6.3	1.6				Debt/Worth	5.0	5.2
-3.3	-7.2	4.0					-3.6	-3.8
200.0	57.5	61.2					92.7	98.8
(55) 61.9	(26) 23.3	(21) 24.6				% Profit Before Taxes/Tangible Net Worth	(123) 50.4	(112) 41.0
29.3	3.9	13.6					14.0	13.7
49.9	15.5	20.2					30.1	32.2
26.2	10.8	12.6				% Profit Before Taxes/Total Assets	11.3	9.4
.0	1.7	5.2					.5	.0
68.5	11.0	18.7					25.3	24.9
15.9	6.0	7.3				Sales/Net Fixed Assets	10.1	10.9
5.3	1.7	3.9					4.7	4.1
9.5	3.9	3.6					6.0	6.2
5.3	2.1	2.1				Sales/Total Assets	3.6	3.5
3.1	1.1	1.2					1.7	1.7
.7	1.0	.8					1.0	1.1
(60) 1.4	(33) 2.3	(18) 1.3				% Depr., Dep., Amort./Sales	(158) 1.8	(142) 2.4
2.7	5.1	2.4					3.5	4.1
4.4	2.8						2.3	2.9
(53) 7.0	(21) 4.6					% Officers', Directors' Owners' Comp/Sales	(86) 4.6	(89) 6.2
12.6	8.7						11.2	10.1
88924M	141655M	247378M	477604M	693223M	463020M	Net Sales ($)	2788639M	3440500M
15842M	48992M	96263M	141058M	345110M	117696M	Total Assets ($)	711407M	1053557M

M = $ thousand MM = $ million

See Pages 9 through 22 for Explanation of Ratios and Data

Comparative Historical Data / Current Data Sorted by Sales

4/1/11-3/31/12 ALL	4/1/12-3/31/13 ALL	4/1/13-3/31/14 ALL	Type of Statement	0-1MM	1-3MM	3-5MM	5-10MM	10-25MM	25MM & OVER
6	5	8	Unqualified	1				4	3
3	4	2	Reviewed					1	1
27	11	14	Compiled	4	2	2	3	2	1
110	100	79	Tax Returns	46	21	6	3	1	2
96	76	73	Other	25	23	7	9	6	3
				14 (4/1-9/30/13)		162 (10/1/13-3/31/14)			
242	196	176	NUMBER OF STATEMENTS	76	46	15	15	14	10
%	%	%	**ASSETS**	%	%	%	%	%	%
22.0	20.9	19.9	Cash & Equivalents	20.9	20.1	17.0	19.6	21.7	13.5
3.2	1.6	2.1	Trade Receivables (net)	1.1	3.0	1.0	3.0	2.8	3.9
10.6	9.8	9.4	Inventory	9.2	10.0	7.6	7.6	15.3	5.4
1.3	2.6	3.0	All Other Current	3.4	1.9	3.2	2.8	2.6	5.6
37.1	34.9	34.4	Total Current	34.6	35.1	28.8	33.0	42.4	28.4
46.2	44.2	44.9	Fixed Assets (net)	45.1	44.3	50.3	46.2	31.3	54.4
6.5	9.9	8.9	Intangibles (net)	6.2	10.7	13.3	8.8	12.0	10.6
10.3	10.9	11.8	All Other Non-Current	14.0	9.9	7.6	12.1	14.4	6.6
100.0	100.0	100.0	Total	100.0	100.0	100.0	100.0	100.0	100.0
			LIABILITIES						
10.9	10.0	11.2	Notes Payable-Short Term	12.9	16.4	6.6	6.8	1.3	1.0
3.0	11.8	4.3	Cur. Mat.-L.T.D.	4.2	6.1	2.1	2.2	2.0	7.1
5.9	3.7	6.4	Trade Payables	5.2	6.8	4.0	9.4	9.2	8.9
.1	.0	.2	Income Taxes Payable	.0	.0	.7	.6	.5	.0
22.7	23.2	22.9	All Other Current	27.3	18.3	19.9	25.2	18.9	16.8
42.5	48.7	44.9	Total Current	49.6	47.5	33.3	44.2	31.9	33.8
29.6	31.9	31.9	Long-Term Debt	31.1	37.4	46.0	16.6	12.5	41.9
.0	.0	.0	Deferred Taxes	.0	.0	.0	.0	.0	.2
18.3	13.3	11.2	All Other Non-Current	7.0	22.5	6.6	10.1	1.0	14.8
9.5	6.0	11.9	Net Worth	12.3	-7.4	14.1	29.2	54.6	9.3
100.0	100.0	100.0	Total Liabilties & Net Worth	100.0	100.0	100.0	100.0	100.0	100.0
			INCOME DATA						
100.0	100.0	100.0	Net Sales	100.0	100.0	100.0	100.0	100.0	100.0
			Gross Profit						
92.3	92.0	91.7	Operating Expenses	88.2	92.9	93.5	97.4	97.2	92.8
7.7	8.0	8.3	Operating Profit	11.8	7.1	6.5	2.6	2.8	7.2
1.9	1.9	2.1	All Other Expenses (net)	3.7	.8	2.2	-.4	1.0	1.8
5.8	6.1	6.2	Profit Before Taxes	8.1	6.3	4.3	2.9	1.8	5.4
			RATIOS						
2.4 1.0 .4	1.9 .9 .3	1.9 1.1 .5	Current	2.8 1.1 .4	1.7 1.0 .6	1.6 1.1 .4	1.6 .9 .6	2.2 1.1 .7	1.3 .6 .3
1.7 .6 .2	1.4 .5 .2	1.3 .6 .2	Quick	1.6 .6 .2	1.2 .6 .2	1.2 .7 .3	1.4 .5 .4	1.0 .6 .4	.9 .4 .1
0 UND 0 UND 0 UND	0 UND 0 UND 0 UND	0 UND 0 UND 0 UND	Sales/Receivables	0 UND 0 UND 0 UND	0 UND 0 UND 0 999.8	0 UND 0 UND 0 UND	0 UND 0 UND 1 582.2	0 UND 0 UND 3 142.3	0 UND 1 347.6 18 19.9
			Cost of Sales/Inventory						
			Cost of Sales/Payables						
19.0 UND -14.6	22.8 -233.1 -12.0	25.0 625.0 -16.6	Sales/Working Capital	22.3 611.5 -13.5	37.2 NM -21.8	35.4 601.8 -25.9	31.0 -130.0 -14.5	12.1 157.7 -35.8	14.2 -42.8 -9.3
19.9 (163) 5.2 1.2	14.3 (151) 4.4 1.2	15.5 (131) 5.3 1.3	EBIT/Interest	14.7 (46) 3.6 .5	15.1 (37) 8.0 3.0	10.8 (13) 3.8 1.6	26.3 (13) 2.9 -.5	42.7 (12) 16.4 7.6	9.3 3.8 .2
9.2 (10) 3.6 2.0			Net Profit + Depr., Dep., Amort./Cur. Mat. L/T/D						
.6 2.0 -2.9	.7 2.1 -1.9	.6 2.7 -2.4	Fixed/Worth	.3 1.9 -4.6	1.0 40.0 -.9	.9 36.0 -.5	.9 1.7 -2.3	.3 .9 1.5	1.5 4.3 -.9
.8 3.7 -5.6	.7 4.6 -3.6	.7 4.1 -4.8	Debt/Worth	.4 3.7 -5.0	1.0 63.7 -4.0	.6 55.1 -2.2	1.0 2.7 -6.9	.4 1.1 3.3	1.7 5.2 -2.5
102.1 (159) 53.5 13.6	105.6 (118) 45.7 13.1	87.0 (109) 40.0 13.6	% Profit Before Taxes/Tangible Net Worth	121.4 (46) 51.5 10.2	288.6 (25) 50.2 22.8		42.9 (11) 22.7 4.0	75.5 (13) 30.4 15.1	
34.4 13.6 1.4	44.2 12.0 .7	34.3 13.3 1.8	% Profit Before Taxes/Total Assets	43.7 13.3 -.8	34.7 16.0 5.5	15.5 12.4 1.8	17.1 2.6 .0	23.1 16.3 8.9	18.3 3.8 -3.7
28.7 9.4 3.8	29.9 9.5 4.2	29.5 9.4 3.7	Sales/Net Fixed Assets	39.1 10.7 3.1	55.7 12.4 3.5	13.4 7.6 4.9	12.9 7.3 5.2	22.2 17.4 7.0	7.3 4.0 2.5
7.0 3.5 1.7	6.3 3.6 1.9	6.3 3.6 1.9	Sales/Total Assets	6.6 3.5 1.9	8.4 4.5 1.6	6.2 3.8 2.4	4.2 3.7 2.0	5.7 3.6 2.5	4.1 2.1 1.3
1.0 (160) 1.9 4.0	.9 (129) 1.8 3.9	.8 (119) 1.7 3.3	% Depr., Dep., Amort./Sales	1.1 (48) 2.2 4.7	.5 (29) 1.3 2.5	.9 (11) 1.9 5.0	.6 (12) 1.0 1.6	.8 (12) 1.5 2.5	
2.8 (99) 5.6 10.0	3.9 (81) 6.6 12.9	3.4 (82) 6.1 11.8	% Officers', Directors' Owners' Comp/Sales	4.3 (34) 7.7 13.2	3.7 (31) 5.9 11.7				
3593751M	1493178M	2111804M	Net Sales ($)	36392M	80812M	56543M	111123M	228313M	1598621M
1162796M	740501M	764961M	Total Assets ($)	22358M	31165M	19822M	38644M	141368M	511604M

M = $ thousand MM = $ million

See Pages 9 through 22 for Explanation of Ratios and Data

	Current Data Sorted by Assets						Comparative Historical Data	
Type of Statement								
Unqualified		4	1	4	2		1	1
Reviewed							3	2
Compiled	3	3		1			4	1
Tax Returns	28	7	3			1	8	19
Other	16	17	4	1	2		10	20
	5 (4/1-9/30/13)			92 (10/1/13-3/31/14)			4/1/09-3/31/10	4/1/10-3/31/11
	0-500M	500M-2MM	2-10MM	10-50MM	50-100MM	100-250MM	ALL	ALL
NUMBER OF STATEMENTS	47	31	8	6	4	1	26	43
ASSETS	%	%	%	%	%	%	%	%
Cash & Equivalents	29.9	18.4					15.5	18.9
Trade Receivables (net)	3.1	3.5					4.0	7.3
Inventory	5.5	8.4					14.3	6.5
All Other Current	3.0	1.7					1.5	2.0
Total Current	41.4	32.0					35.2	34.7
Fixed Assets (net)	42.0	52.0					49.4	41.2
Intangibles (net)	11.3	4.2					10.5	13.4
All Other Non-Current	5.4	11.8					4.9	10.7
Total	100.0	100.0					100.0	100.0
LIABILITIES								
Notes Payable-Short Term	20.1	3.5					17.4	11.2
Cur. Mat.-L.T.D.	5.7	3.8					2.9	4.5
Trade Payables	6.1	2.9					6.4	3.9
Income Taxes Payable	.0	.4					.0	.0
All Other Current	28.4	16.3					18.2	17.8
Total Current	60.3	26.9					45.0	37.4
Long-Term Debt	17.5	16.9					31.2	31.3
Deferred Taxes	.0	.0					.0	.1
All Other Non-Current	15.6	24.7					20.1	14.6
Net Worth	6.5	31.5					3.7	16.6
Total Liabilties & Net Worth	100.0	100.0					100.0	100.0
INCOME DATA								
Net Sales	100.0	100.0					100.0	100.0
Gross Profit								
Operating Expenses	91.9	89.2					92.9	91.5
Operating Profit	8.1	10.8					7.1	8.5
All Other Expenses (net)	1.3	1.1					3.8	4.0
Profit Before Taxes	6.8	9.7					3.3	4.5
RATIOS								
Current	3.1	2.6					3.9	3.7
	.7	.8					1.5	1.2
	.3	.4					.3	.4
Quick	3.0	1.8					2.6	3.2
	.7	.7					.6	.9
	.2	.2					.1	.1
Sales/Receivables	0 UND	0 UND					0 UND	0 UND
	0 UND	0 UND					0 UND	0 UND
	0 UND	2 202.8					6 57.7	10 35.5
Cost of Sales/Inventory								
Cost of Sales/Payables								
Sales/Working Capital	14.4	10.6					7.7	11.4
	-47.7	-99.4					47.1	64.8
	-7.1	-11.6					-6.4	-8.0
EBIT/Interest	20.2	21.1					6.2	12.8
	(31) 5.5	(21) 4.8					(22) 2.4	(35) 3.7
	1.6	1.7					.1	.9
Net Profit + Depr., Dep., Amort./Cur. Mat. L/T/D								
Fixed/Worth	.3	.7					.5	.6
	3.8	1.5					10.9	1.4
	-1.7	-7.4					-1.4	-1.8
Debt/Worth	1.0	.6					.8	.7
	9.9	2.5					24.6	6.9
	-2.6	-15.4					-2.6	-6.0
% Profit Before Taxes/Tangible Net Worth	340.9	123.9					103.7	139.6
	(29) 91.4	(22) 42.1					(14) 42.0	(28) 40.7
	33.0	25.0					2.4	-.2
% Profit Before Taxes/Total Assets	52.5	34.2					18.4	42.2
	20.2	11.6					7.3	13.2
	3.8	3.0					-1.6	-.1
Sales/Net Fixed Assets	118.0	11.9					16.4	27.2
	8.5	4.3					9.8	7.6
	4.0	2.3					2.8	2.7
Sales/Total Assets	6.2	2.7					4.8	3.9
	3.8	2.3					2.7	2.2
	1.8	1.4					1.2	1.2
% Depr., Dep., Amort./Sales	1.2	2.1					2.4	2.1
	(31) 3.6	(23) 5.1					(21) 3.8	(32) 4.6
	6.3	7.5					9.3	10.4
% Officers', Directors' Owners' Comp/Sales	5.0	3.0					2.5	1.4
	(23) 9.6	(11) 5.5					(13) 4.7	(11) 7.2
	12.7	11.6					19.8	11.2
Net Sales ($)	43035M	75694M	84779M	173894M	293329M	878000M	1049139M	425261M
Total Assets ($)	10243M	32902M	40795M	131223M	264241M	128000M	568420M	505591M

M = $ thousand MM = $ million

See Pages 9 through 22 for Explanation of Ratios and Data

Comparative Historical Data				Current Data Sorted by Sales					
			Type of Statement						
4	4	11	Unqualified		2	1	1	5	2
1	2		Reviewed						
1	8	7	Compiled	4	2				1
19	32	39	Tax Returns	20	13		4	1	1
25	24	40	Other	13	17	3	3	1	3
				5 (4/1-9/30/13)		92 (10/1/13-3/31/14)			
4/1/11-3/31/12 ALL	4/1/12-3/31/13 ALL	4/1/13-3/31/14 ALL		0-1MM	1-3MM	3-5MM	5-10MM	10-25MM	25MM & OVER
50	70	97	**NUMBER OF STATEMENTS**	37	34	4	8	7	7
%	%	%	**ASSETS**	%	%	%	%	%	%
18.4	22.3	22.8	Cash & Equivalents	23.7	24.2				
.8	2.5	3.6	Trade Receivables (net)	4.4	1.4				
3.3	6.5	6.9	Inventory	5.1	8.8				
2.8	1.4	2.4	All Other Current	3.7	1.2				
25.3	32.6	35.8	Total Current	36.9	35.6				
48.2	46.4	44.7	Fixed Assets (net)	46.4	46.0				
19.0	14.0	11.6	Intangibles (net)	13.4	4.8				
7.6	7.0	7.8	All Other Non-Current	3.3	13.5				
100.0	100.0	100.0	Total	100.0	100.0				
			LIABILITIES						
5.8	8.7	11.4	Notes Payable-Short Term	20.9	7.5				
3.3	5.1	4.8	Cur. Mat.-L.T.D.	6.9	2.7				
6.2	5.9	5.4	Trade Payables	4.9	4.6				
.0	.3	.2	Income Taxes Payable	.0	.3				
17.1	27.2	21.5	All Other Current	21.6	28.0				
32.5	47.1	43.3	Total Current	54.3	43.1				
34.3	36.7	19.4	Long-Term Debt	23.8	11.6				
.0	.0	.1	Deferred Taxes	.0	.0				
20.6	12.5	18.6	All Other Non-Current	18.8	22.9				
12.6	3.6	18.5	Net Worth	3.0	22.4				
100.0	100.0	100.0	Total Liabilities & Net Worth	100.0	100.0				
			INCOME DATA						
100.0	100.0	100.0	Net Sales	100.0	100.0				
			Gross Profit						
94.1	91.3	90.4	Operating Expenses	92.9	88.0				
5.9	8.7	9.6	Operating Profit	7.1	12.0				
2.2	3.4	1.3	All Other Expenses (net)	1.7	.9				
3.7	5.4	8.3	Profit Before Taxes	5.4	11.1				
			RATIOS						
2.3	4.0	2.5		2.8	2.6				
1.1	.8	.8	Current	.8	.7				
.4	.4	.4		.4	.2				
1.9	2.1	1.9		2.5	1.7				
.7	.6	.7	Quick	.7	.6				
.2	.2	.2		.2	.2				
0 UND	0 UND	0 UND		0 UND	0 UND				
0 UND	0 UND	0 UND	Sales/Receivables	0 UND	0 UND				
0 999.8	1 625.9	2 175.1		0 UND	0 UND				
			Cost of Sales/Inventory						
			Cost of Sales/Payables						
12.0	17.2	13.2		11.5	16.9				
504.3	-86.1	-65.0	Sales/Working Capital	-51.4	-49.9				
-10.6	-8.1	-9.0		-4.9	-10.2				
11.0	15.3	19.8		18.7	22.9				
(35) 4.9	(53) 4.7	(69) 4.8	EBIT/Interest	(28) 2.2	(21) 8.8				
1.6	.4	1.6		-.6	3.0				
			Net Profit + Depr., Dep., Amort./Cur. Mat. L/T/D						
1.3	1.1	.6		.7	.4				
5.8	15.8	3.6	Fixed/Worth	4.9	2.6				
-1.1	-.9	-3.1		-2.2	-17.8				
1.6	1.2	1.0		1.3	1.0				
12.0	25.9	8.7	Debt/Worth	10.1	7.4				
-4.1	-3.2	-4.7		-2.5	-13.0				
184.1	122.7	169.8		340.9	188.6				
(29) 74.0	(37) 38.5	(61) 72.2	% Profit Before Taxes/Tangible Net Worth	(21) 80.7	(23) 79.3				
.9	9.9	24.7		33.8	25.6				
32.4	22.9	39.1		45.3	42.0				
8.1	10.0	12.0	% Profit Before Taxes/Total Assets	11.2	14.9				
-1.8	-.5	2.6		-2.4	5.4				
17.8	20.3	22.7		74.4	22.6				
5.9	5.7	6.0	Sales/Net Fixed Assets	5.4	6.5				
2.3	2.8	3.1		2.6	3.3				
4.0	4.2	4.4		5.2	4.7				
2.1	2.2	2.3	Sales/Total Assets	2.3	2.7				
1.0	1.3	1.5		1.5	1.8				
1.3	1.5	1.3		3.6	1.2				
(32) 3.5	(44) 3.1	(69) 3.9	% Depr., Dep., Amort./Sales	(24) 5.2	(27) 2.7				
12.0	9.1	7.7		10.2	6.3				
3.2	3.0	3.2		6.8	1.2				
(19) 5.7	(23) 5.0	(38) 7.1	% Officers', Directors' Owners' Comp/Sales	(21) 10.6	(10) 4.4				
12.2	9.6	12.0		13.5	8.3				
613681M	518112M	1548731M	Net Sales ($)	17563M	62304M	14802M	53150M	116694M	1284218M
704676M	358250M	607404M	Total Assets ($)	9195M	25312M	7229M	19828M	126039M	419801M

M = $ thousand MM = $ million

See Pages 9 through 22 for Explanation of Ratios and Data

Current Data Sorted by Assets							Comparative Historical Data	
						Type of Statement		
1				1	2	Unqualified	14	2
3	4	10	3			Reviewed	29	17
8	23	15	3	1	1	Compiled	77	69
56	80	20	2		2	Tax Returns	162	171
30	45	28	5	4	3	Other	80	89
	42 (4/1-9/30/13)		308 (10/1/13-3/31/14)				4/1/09-3/31/10	4/1/10-3/31/11
0-500M	**500M-2MM**	**2-10MM**	**10-50MM**	**50-100MM**	**100-250MM**		**ALL**	**ALL**
98	152	73	13	6	8	**NUMBER OF STATEMENTS**	362	348
%	%	%	%	%	%	**ASSETS**	%	%
22.0	11.5	8.7	12.3			Cash & Equivalents	11.8	14.0
19.7	13.1	9.0	3.9			Trade Receivables (net)	13.8	13.9
6.0	4.1	1.9	10.7			Inventory	4.7	5.3
1.0	2.9	4.2	4.7			All Other Current	2.2	2.4
48.6	31.6	23.8	31.6			Total Current	32.5	35.6
30.7	45.0	47.3	40.0			Fixed Assets (net)	42.2	41.8
13.1	9.9	9.5	6.0			Intangibles (net)	10.0	8.5
7.6	13.5	19.4	22.4			All Other Non-Current	15.3	14.2
100.0	100.0	100.0	100.0			Total	100.0	100.0
						LIABILITIES		
10.3	2.5	2.6	1.4			Notes Payable-Short Term	5.2	6.6
2.9	4.1	2.9	1.8			Cur. Mat.-L.T.D.	4.9	5.2
7.5	5.0	2.9	2.9			Trade Payables	5.7	5.4
.0	.0	.2	.4			Income Taxes Payable	.2	.1
20.9	12.7	10.2	7.1			All Other Current	7.7	14.5
41.7	24.4	18.7	13.7			Total Current	23.7	31.9
29.3	45.7	35.4	25.9			Long-Term Debt	39.9	39.6
.2	.0	.2	.1			Deferred Taxes	.1	.1
17.9	6.9	8.6	26.6			All Other Non-Current	10.9	12.7
10.9	23.0	37.1	33.8			Net Worth	25.4	15.6
100.0	100.0	100.0	100.0			Total Liabilties & Net Worth	100.0	100.0
						INCOME DATA		
100.0	100.0	100.0	100.0			Net Sales	100.0	100.0
						Gross Profit		
93.9	89.0	83.6	90.2			Operating Expenses	91.5	90.6
6.1	11.0	16.4	9.8			Operating Profit	8.5	9.4
.7	2.9	4.7	1.3			All Other Expenses (net)	2.6	3.0
5.3	8.1	11.7	8.5			Profit Before Taxes	6.0	6.4
						RATIOS		
4.7	3.5	3.7	6.0				3.9	4.2
2.0	1.5	1.3	2.9			Current	1.7	1.7
.7	.6	.6	1.0				.8	.7
3.8	2.6	3.4	3.4				3.2	3.2
1.7	1.1	1.1	.8			Quick	1.4	1.3
.6	.5	.5	.6				.6	.5
0 UND	**3** 128.7	**10** 36.5	**0** UND				**15** 24.3	**8** 43.4
21 17.8	**26** 14.2	**31** 11.8	**30** 12.3			Sales/Receivables	**29** 12.8	**25** 14.7
41 8.8	**38** 9.6	**46** 7.9	**42** 8.6				**44** 8.2	**43** 8.4
						Cost of Sales/Inventory		
						Cost of Sales/Payables		
6.2	6.0	5.2	1.9				5.8	5.9
17.9	21.8	23.5	7.7			Sales/Working Capital	15.7	18.2
-45.7	-12.9	-12.3	NM				-40.7	-34.5
12.5	8.2	15.5	5.2				7.1	8.6
(63) 3.2	(119) 3.6	(64) 4.4	(11) 2.6			EBIT/Interest	(299) 2.7	(277) 2.8
.3	1.5	1.8	1.4				1.3	1.3
	2.9	3.1					2.9	5.5
	(10) 1.9	(11) 1.7				Net Profit + Depr., Dep., Amort./Cur. Mat. L/T/D	(33) 1.2	(39) 2.8
	1.3	.9					.7	1.1
.4	.7	.8	.5				.6	.6
1.5	3.0	1.9	1.3			Fixed/Worth	1.9	2.1
-.5	-3.4	6.7	3.7				-6.4	-6.6
.4	1.1	.9	.8				.8	.9
1.4	4.4	2.1	2.4			Debt/Worth	3.4	3.6
-2.3	-9.2	16.6	5.4				-14.8	-11.0
97.9	58.1	41.4	27.3				43.8	47.5
(60) 18.4	(102) 25.1	(59) 23.6	(12) 14.9			% Profit Before Taxes/Tangible Net Worth	(253) 17.6	(241) 21.5
-.3	5.9	7.4	4.4				5.3	4.6
28.0	16.5	12.3	6.6				12.9	17.3
8.5	6.9	6.3	3.8			% Profit Before Taxes/Total Assets	5.4	6.3
-2.6	1.8	2.2	1.3				.7	.9
35.1	8.8	4.7	3.5				11.0	14.1
15.1	4.2	2.0	1.7			Sales/Net Fixed Assets	4.6	4.9
7.1	1.7	1.0	1.1				1.5	1.8
4.9	2.0	1.3	.9				2.4	3.0
3.3	1.3	.8	.6			Sales/Total Assets	1.4	1.6
2.1	.8	.5	.3				.7	.9
1.0	1.7	2.3	2.6				1.7	1.8
(74) 2.4	(135) 2.9	(62) 3.7	(11) 3.8			% Depr., Dep., Amort./Sales	(320) 3.4	(298) 3.0
4.4	5.7	6.1	6.5				6.2	5.2
5.6	7.7	5.1					6.2	5.6
(61) 11.1	(85) 10.5	(35) 7.7				% Officers', Directors' Owners' Comp/Sales	(214) 9.6	(208) 8.7
15.2	15.8	13.6					14.7	14.0
88498M	223583M	261653M	663923M	151239M	3109770M	Net Sales ($)	1767784M	2183384M
26683M	157904M	283206M	253439M	398093M	1242469M	Total Assets ($)	1591710M	1979947M

M = $ thousand MM = $ million

See Pages 9 through 22 for Explanation of Ratios and Data

Comparative Historical Data | **Current Data Sorted by Sales**

			Type of Statement						
12	5	4	Unqualified	1					3
24	15	20	Reviewed	1	7	3	6	3	
72	61	51	Compiled	9	26	5	7	3	1
187	167	160	Tax Returns	77	67	10	3		3
97	105	115	Other	47	41	10	9	4	4
4/1/11-3/31/12	4/1/12-3/31/13	4/1/13-3/31/14		42 (4/1-9/30/13)		308 (10/1/13-3/31/14)			
ALL	ALL	ALL		0-1MM	1-3MM	3-5MM	5-10MM	10-25MM	25MM & OVER
392	353	350	NUMBER OF STATEMENTS	135	141	28	25	10	11
%	%	%	**ASSETS**	%	%	%	%	%	%
12.6	12.1	13.7	Cash & Equivalents	14.7	13.8	12.8	11.4	6.0	13.6
13.9	13.5	13.8	Trade Receivables (net)	11.1	16.8	14.9	11.6	9.1	13.3
4.7	3.7	4.5	Inventory	4.4	4.1	4.0	3.5	8.9	10.2
2.6	3.1	2.8	All Other Current	1.3	2.7	2.6	9.1	5.2	6.2
33.9	32.3	34.8	Total Current	31.5	37.5	34.3	35.7	29.2	43.4
43.4	42.0	40.6	Fixed Assets (net)	45.9	37.1	39.8	36.9	33.1	36.2
8.9	10.1	10.5	Intangibles (net)	11.6	11.0	5.3	10.1	3.7	12.6
13.7	15.6	14.1	All Other Non-Current	11.0	14.4	20.6	17.4	34.0	7.9
100.0	100.0	100.0	Total	100.0	100.0	100.0	100.0	100.0	100.0
			LIABILITIES						
5.7	5.2	4.6	Notes Payable-Short Term	7.2	3.6	2.0	1.3	2.6	.2
3.5	2.7	3.3	Cur. Mat.-L.T.D.	2.6	4.3	2.8	2.7	3.1	.6
5.5	6.1	5.1	Trade Payables	4.3	6.1	5.0	6.1	2.2	3.5
.2	.2	.1	Income Taxes Payable	.0	.1	.3	.2	.1	.0
10.0	9.5	13.9	All Other Current	16.9	13.3	15.3	6.9	5.7	3.9
24.9	23.7	26.9	Total Current	31.0	27.4	25.4	17.3	13.7	8.2
39.5	42.8	37.2	Long-Term Debt	40.1	38.8	27.6	34.1	37.0	14.1
.4	.4	.2	Deferred Taxes	.0	.1	.4	.2	2.0	.1
10.4	9.8	12.0	All Other Non-Current	17.7	6.1	7.6	9.0	15.8	30.8
24.9	23.5	23.7	Net Worth	11.1	27.5	38.9	39.5	31.6	46.8
100.0	100.0	100.0	Total Liabilities & Net Worth	100.0	100.0	100.0	100.0	100.0	100.0
			INCOME DATA						
100.0	100.0	100.0	Net Sales	100.0	100.0	100.0	100.0	100.0	100.0
			Gross Profit						
90.2	89.3	89.2	Operating Expenses	85.3	92.2	91.5	89.7	88.6	91.3
9.8	10.7	10.8	Operating Profit	14.7	7.8	8.5	10.3	11.4	8.7
3.5	3.6	2.6	All Other Expenses (net)	5.8	.5	-.1	1.5	1.3	.7
6.4	7.1	8.2	Profit Before Taxes	8.9	7.3	8.6	8.8	10.1	8.0
			RATIOS						
4.4	3.2	4.2		4.9	3.4	4.6	3.5	4.8	10.4
1.8	1.6	1.7	Current	1.5	1.8	1.5	1.9	2.9	7.8
.7	.7	.7		.4	.8	.6	1.1	1.0	2.0
3.3	2.6	3.3		4.1	3.0	2.7	2.6	4.0	6.1
1.3	1.3	1.2	Quick	1.2	1.2	1.3	1.6	.8	2.0
.5	.5	.6		.3	.7	.5	.8	.3	.7
9 39.3	6 56.8	7 55.0		0 UND	15 23.9	16 23.2	19 19.0	0 UND	0 UND
25 14.5	26 14.1	25 14.4	Sales/Receivables	16 23.3	27 13.6	26 14.1	36 10.2	35 10.3	24 15.1
39 9.4	41 8.9	42 8.7		37 9.8	44 8.3	41 8.9	45 8.1	89 4.1	79 4.6
			Cost of Sales/Inventory						
			Cost of Sales/Payables						
6.1	6.3	5.4		5.4	5.9	5.8	4.0	1.9	1.0
16.5	20.8	18.6	Sales/Working Capital	26.8	18.9	20.5	8.6	5.1	5.7
-30.9	-22.4	-27.9		-9.1	-40.7	-12.3	111.2	NM	209.5
9.5	12.4	10.1		7.0	10.2	62.9	14.0		
(327) 3.0	(293) 3.5	(268) 3.7	EBIT/Interest	(86) 2.4	(118) 4.1	(23) 8.2	(23) 5.2		
1.2	1.4	1.4		.9	1.6	1.8	1.6		
5.7	6.2	3.9			3.6				
(40) 2.5	(28) 2.8	(28) 2.2	Net Profit + Depr., Dep., Amort./Cur. Mat. L/T/D		(12) 1.9				
1.2	1.7	1.1			1.4				
.5	.6	.6		.6	.5	.4	.6	.6	.1
2.2	2.1	1.8	Fixed/Worth	4.6	1.6	1.0	1.4	1.3	.8
-11.6	-4.0	-3.3		-1.2	-3.2	5.2	9.0	2.1	-1.7
.6	1.0	.7		.8	.6	.4	1.0	1.4	.2
2.9	3.6	2.7	Debt/Worth	7.2	2.8	1.5	1.7	3.4	1.3
-20.9	-9.9	-10.5		-3.7	-10.9	6.2	16.1	6.3	-5.3
43.1	58.3	55.4		68.6	60.6	38.0	59.1	36.6	
(275) 20.8	(239) 21.0	(243) 22.4	% Profit Before Taxes/Tangible Net Worth	(83) 17.3	(100) 27.9	(22) 27.0	(21) 19.4	20.5	
4.8	6.1	5.0		3.4	4.0	6.5	7.2	9.7	
15.3	17.0	17.3		13.5	20.4	19.4	15.9	7.0	29.6
5.3	5.9	6.6	% Profit Before Taxes/Total Assets	4.6	8.0	10.2	7.6	4.5	6.5
.9	1.1	1.3		-.2	2.2	2.2	1.3	.9	2.9
12.3	13.9	14.6		18.5	15.2	9.7	13.3	2.6	19.0
4.8	4.5	4.7	Sales/Net Fixed Assets	4.3	6.2	4.5	3.5	1.9	7.4
1.7	1.6	1.7		.9	2.7	2.1	1.5	1.6	1.2
3.0	2.6	2.6		2.5	3.1	2.2	1.7	1.1	5.4
1.5	1.4	1.4	Sales/Total Assets	1.2	1.8	1.4	.9	.7	.8
.8	.7	.8		.6	1.1	1.2	.7	.3	.3
1.9	1.5	1.7		1.9	1.3	2.0	1.7	2.4	
(340) 3.2	(301) 3.3	(293) 3.0	% Depr., Dep., Amort./Sales	(102) 4.4	(128) 2.7	(27) 2.5	(19) 3.4	2.9	
5.8	5.9	5.6		9.8	4.0	4.1	5.9	3.7	
5.6	5.2	6.2		5.5	6.6	5.4			
(240) 8.7	(220) 9.0	(187) 10.2	% Officers', Directors' Owners' Comp/Sales	(60) 11.3	(97) 10.3	(15) 8.8			
13.7	14.2	15.1		16.4	15.2	11.1			
2754793M	2191734M	4498666M	Net Sales ($)	79290M	249447M	102895M	164691M	164033M	3738310M
2332187M	1881712M	2361794M	Total Assets ($)	100992M	187455M	96650M	253253M	397214M	1326230M

M = $ thousand MM = $ million

See Pages 9 through 22 for Explanation of Ratios and Data

Current Data Sorted by Assets							Comparative Historical Data	
						Type of Statement		
	1		2	1		Unqualified	7	6
2		1	2	1		Reviewed	6	2
3	1	1				Compiled	10	8
8	7	3				Tax Returns	9	21
6	4	6	8	3		Other	21	25
10 (4/1-9/30/13)			50 (10/1/13-3/31/14)				**4/1/09-3/31/10 ALL**	**4/1/10-3/31/11 ALL**
0-500M	**500M-2MM**	**2-10MM**	**10-50MM**	**50-100MM**	**100-250MM**			
19	13	11	12	5		**NUMBER OF STATEMENTS**	53	62
%	%	%	%	%	%	**ASSETS**	%	%
26.4	14.2	8.6	9.1		DATA NOT AVAILABLE	Cash & Equivalents	9.4	8.2
13.3	8.6	11.1	10.2			Trade Receivables (net)	12.3	11.6
6.3	8.1	10.2	11.8			Inventory	7.5	12.5
1.3	4.4	2.8	4.9			All Other Current	1.9	2.2
47.3	35.3	32.7	36.0			Total Current	31.1	34.6
36.6	40.3	55.7	22.4			Fixed Assets (net)	39.1	34.1
8.9	3.6	1.5	3.3			Intangibles (net)	4.7	4.6
7.0	20.8	10.0	38.3			All Other Non-Current	25.1	26.7
100.0	100.0	100.0	100.0			Total	100.0	100.0
						LIABILITIES		
9.9	4.6	4.5	.3			Notes Payable-Short Term	4.5	4.0
5.3	3.3	.8	1.0			Cur. Mat.-L.T.D.	2.6	4.0
4.5	6.7	2.0	6.2			Trade Payables	3.4	2.6
.0	.0	.0	.0			Income Taxes Payable	.0	.0
40.4	11.0	7.8	7.8			All Other Current	16.9	19.1
60.2	25.6	15.0	15.2			Total Current	27.3	29.7
16.5	34.8	18.2	10.3			Long-Term Debt	21.3	25.0
.0	.0	.0	2.4			Deferred Taxes	.7	.6
4.5	11.7	9.6	23.6			All Other Non-Current	20.0	22.2
18.6	27.9	57.2	48.5			Net Worth	30.7	22.6
100.0	100.0	100.0	100.0			Total Liabilties & Net Worth	100.0	100.0
						INCOME DATA		
100.0	100.0	100.0	100.0			Net Sales	100.0	100.0
						Gross Profit		
83.4	86.5	83.0	86.0			Operating Expenses	90.3	92.2
16.6	13.5	17.0	14.0			Operating Profit	9.7	7.8
1.2	3.2	5.2	-.1			All Other Expenses (net)	2.1	.7
15.4	10.3	11.8	14.1			Profit Before Taxes	7.6	7.1
						RATIOS		
4.5	13.4	6.7	15.0				4.9	4.7
1.0	.8	2.3	4.6			Current	2.4	2.7
.7	.2	1.2	1.4				.7	.7
4.2	7.8	5.8	3.3				3.3	2.5
.8	.7	1.6	1.9			Quick	1.4	1.0
.2	.2	.9	.9				.6	.3
0 UND	**0** UND	**31** 11.9	**41** 9.0				**24** 15.1	**10** 36.1
18 19.9	**23** 15.9	**81** 4.5	**89** 4.1			Sales/Receivables	**59** 6.2	**40** 9.2
51 7.2	**58** 6.3	**135** 2.7	**166** 2.2				**133** 2.8	**85** 4.3
						Cost of Sales/Inventory		
						Cost of Sales/Payables		
5.3	3.3	2.1	.7				1.9	1.8
UND	-19.2	4.8	2.1			Sales/Working Capital	6.6	4.5
-12.2	-2.6	17.6	29.7				-5.6	-14.3
							5.7	8.0
						EBIT/Interest	(44) 3.3	(50) 2.4
							.9	.5
						Net Profit + Depr., Dep., Amort./Cur. Mat. L/T/D		
.2	.9	.5	.3				.6	.5
1.1	1.2	.9	.6			Fixed/Worth	1.2	1.0
-3.0	-2.0	1.6	1.4				6.1	4.1
.3	.7	.3	.3				.4	.8
2.6	3.6	1.0	.9			Debt/Worth	2.9	3.0
-4.8	-7.8	2.0	5.5				11.1	13.8
138.1		31.3	19.5				29.7	24.4
(12) 34.5		7.2	(11) 10.1			% Profit Before Taxes/Tangible Net Worth	(43) 13.1	(49) 11.0
5.0		1.2	2.7				1.1	3.8
79.5	11.6	10.5	9.1				11.4	7.7
21.6	5.5	3.5	3.7			% Profit Before Taxes/Total Assets	3.7	3.2
2.5	-.4	.9	2.3				.4	.1
61.1	34.1	1.8	4.2				3.9	4.5
5.8	2.7	.9	1.6			Sales/Net Fixed Assets	1.8	2.5
2.0	.6	.1	1.1				.8	1.0
4.3	1.7	.9	.5				1.1	1.5
1.9	.5	.3	.2			Sales/Total Assets	.5	.4
.5	.2	.1	.2				.3	.3
1.6			1.9				3.3	3.2
(13) 2.8			(10) 2.8			% Depr., Dep., Amort./Sales	(45) 4.7	(56) 4.1
11.7			5.5				8.3	7.4
							4.0	3.3
						% Officers', Directors' Owners' Comp/Sales	(12) 11.1	(11) 7.5
							16.5	22.8
7498M	**11074M**	**21085M**	**162636M**	**315630M**		Net Sales ($)	**305415M**	**288959M**
3661M	**13694M**	**43404M**	**293814M**	**285932M**		Total Assets ($)	**809576M**	**715980M**

M = $ thousand MM = $ million

See Pages 9 through 22 for Explanation of Ratios and Data

Comparative Historical Data / Current Data Sorted by Sales

4/1/11-3/31/12 ALL	4/1/12-3/31/13 ALL	4/1/13-3/31/14 ALL	Type of Statement	0-1MM	1-3MM	3-5MM	5-10MM	10-25MM	25MM & OVER
1	4	4	Unqualified	1			2	1	
3	2	6	Reviewed	1	1	1		2	1
7	5	5	Compiled	4	1				
15	15	18	Tax Returns	14	3	1			
23	18	27	Other	12	3	6	1	4	1
				10 (4/1-9/30/13)			50 (10/1/13-3/31/14)		
49	44	60	NUMBER OF STATEMENTS	32	8	8	3	7	2
%	%	%	ASSETS	%	%	%	%	%	%
8.1	10.6	15.4	Cash & Equivalents	20.3					
11.5	12.0	11.7	Trade Receivables (net)	10.5					
14.0	10.6	8.4	Inventory	8.2					
4.7	2.4	2.9	All Other Current	.6					
38.2	35.6	38.4	Total Current	39.7					
30.6	35.4	36.4	Fixed Assets (net)	45.5					
2.9	3.8	5.2	Intangibles (net)	5.4					
28.4	25.2	19.9	All Other Non-Current	9.3					
100.0	100.0	100.0	Total	100.0					
			LIABILITIES						
6.5	4.1	5.8	Notes Payable-Short Term	7.7					
5.1	2.6	2.8	Cur. Mat.-L.T.D.	2.9					
3.6	2.9	4.8	Trade Payables	5.2					
.3	.0	.0	Income Taxes Payable	.0					
16.8	19.6	18.4	All Other Current	29.8					
32.3	29.2	31.8	Total Current	45.5					
26.0	25.2	19.6	Long-Term Debt	19.7					
.0	.0	.5	Deferred Taxes	.0					
25.2	16.9	15.5	All Other Non-Current	7.5					
16.5	28.7	32.6	Net Worth	27.3					
100.0	100.0	100.0	Total Liabilties & Net Worth	100.0					
			INCOME DATA						
100.0	100.0	100.0	Net Sales	100.0					
			Gross Profit						
91.0	87.7	84.8	Operating Expenses	84.0					
9.0	12.3	15.2	Operating Profit	16.0					
1.4	2.7	2.0	All Other Expenses (net)	4.1					
7.6	9.6	13.2	Profit Before Taxes	11.9					
			RATIOS						
4.6	5.8	6.9		4.5					
2.5	2.7	2.1	Current	1.0					
.7	.7	.8		.7					
3.1	3.2	4.8		4.1					
1.2	1.4	1.1	Quick	.8					
.3	.4	.5		.2					
0 UND	**24** 14.9	**12** 30.9		**0** UND					
48 7.6	**51** 7.1	**46** 8.0	Sales/Receivables	**31** 11.6					
107 3.4	**122** 3.0	**122** 3.0		**83** 4.4					
			Cost of Sales/Inventory						
			Cost of Sales/Payables						
1.5	1.5	1.5		2.1					
5.0	4.0	5.5	Sales/Working Capital	UND					
-10.5	-36.8	-14.3		-8.7					
7.8	11.5	16.6		9.6					
(43) 2.7	(33) 4.5	(40) 5.3	EBIT/Interest	(17) 2.8					
1.1	1.7	1.9		.7					
			Net Profit + Depr., Dep., Amort./Cur. Mat. L/T/D						
.5	.4	.4		.5					
1.3	1.0	1.0	Fixed/Worth	1.1					
6.2	2.1	2.3		UND					
1.1	.4	.3		.3					
4.9	3.5	1.9	Debt/Worth	1.5					
30.4	10.4	UND		-7.3					
21.5	31.6	56.1		42.4					
(39) 8.3	(39) 12.9	(46) 9.5	% Profit Before Taxes/Tangible Net Worth	(22) 6.4					
.6	3.7	4.0		2.2					
9.3	9.3	12.2		18.7					
1.7	2.5	4.2	% Profit Before Taxes/Total Assets	3.4					
.1	.9	1.7		.3					
11.5	5.3	9.1		8.9					
2.4	1.7	2.1	Sales/Net Fixed Assets	1.8					
.9	.9	1.0		.4					
1.6	1.3	1.8		1.8					
.5	.5	.5	Sales/Total Assets	.5					
.2	.2	.2		.2					
2.0	2.1	2.0		1.8					
(43) 3.2	(34) 3.2	(44) 4.1	% Depr., Dep., Amort./Sales	(22) 5.6					
7.9	7.2	7.7		16.4					
5.1									
(13) 11.9			% Officers', Directors' Owners' Comp/Sales						
28.9									
139367M	139656M	517923M	Net Sales ($)	11148M	13618M	31308M	21698M	104855M	335296M
576474M	423048M	640505M	Total Assets ($)	36177M	18706M	108906M	87601M	304199M	84916M

M = $ thousand MM = $ million

See Pages 9 through 22 for Explanation of Ratios and Data

Current Data Sorted by Assets							Comparative Historical Data	
						Type of Statement		
						Unqualified	2	2
		2	1			Reviewed	7	7
2	1	4	1			Compiled	6	8
21	6	3				Tax Returns	35	36
6	8	9	2			Other	21	18
	3 (4/1-9/30/13)		63 (10/1/13-3/31/14)				4/1/09-3/31/10	4/1/10-3/31/11
0-500M	**500M-2MM**	**2-10MM**	**10-50MM**	**50-100MM**	**100-250MM**		**ALL**	**ALL**
29	15	18	4			**NUMBER OF STATEMENTS**	71	71
%	%	%	%	%	%	**ASSETS**	%	%
14.2	8.0	8.8		DATA NOT AVAILABLE	DATA NOT AVAILABLE	Cash & Equivalents	11.7	9.1
4.3	.6	5.9				Trade Receivables (net)	3.9	3.1
.4	.3	4.2				Inventory	1.7	2.5
.8	.0	3.6				All Other Current	3.9	2.4
19.8	8.9	22.5				Total Current	21.2	17.0
57.0	69.8	62.9				Fixed Assets (net)	61.0	61.4
16.1	13.8	7.9				Intangibles (net)	8.0	11.4
7.2	7.4	6.7				All Other Non-Current	9.7	10.2
100.0	100.0	100.0				Total	100.0	100.0
						LIABILITIES		
9.6	5.8	5.3				Notes Payable-Short Term	6.7	6.4
9.8	5.5	3.9				Cur. Mat.-L.T.D.	7.5	6.6
7.5	.2	5.8				Trade Payables	4.0	4.3
.2	.0	.0				Income Taxes Payable	.2	.2
12.2	1.2	5.5				All Other Current	6.1	11.4
39.3	12.7	20.6				Total Current	24.5	29.0
68.5	52.6	37.4				Long-Term Debt	60.2	57.5
.0	.0	.2				Deferred Taxes	.2	.1
17.0	5.6	7.3				All Other Non-Current	8.2	6.5
-24.6	29.1	34.6				Net Worth	6.9	6.8
100.0	100.0	100.0				Total Liabilties & Net Worth	100.0	100.0
						INCOME DATA		
100.0	100.0	100.0				Net Sales	100.0	100.0
						Gross Profit		
88.4	84.6	87.9				Operating Expenses	93.4	94.9
11.6	15.4	12.1				Operating Profit	6.6	5.1
2.8	6.1	2.4				All Other Expenses (net)	4.1	3.9
8.8	9.4	9.7				Profit Before Taxes	2.5	1.3
						RATIOS		
1.9	4.2	4.4					2.8	1.7
.4	.8	1.2				Current	.8	.4
.2	.2	.5					.2	.2
1.9	4.1	2.9					1.5	1.0
.3	.3	1.0				Quick	.4	.4
.1	.2	.2					.2	.2
0 UND	0 UND	0 UND					0 UND	0 UND
0 UND	0 UND	2 207.5				Sales/Receivables	0 UND	0 UND
0 UND	0 UND	15 24.8					7 51.8	2 217.3
						Cost of Sales/Inventory		
						Cost of Sales/Payables		
28.1	8.7	10.6					8.9	36.4
-30.0	-30.4	42.0				Sales/Working Capital	-71.0	-15.0
-5.0	-4.7	-16.6					-6.7	-5.7
10.8	8.6	11.7					4.6	6.2
(20) 4.3	(13) 2.6	(16) 5.7				EBIT/Interest	(53) 1.6	(54) 1.5
1.8	.7	1.6					.6	.0
						Net Profit + Depr., Dep., Amort./Cur. Mat. L/T/D		
.5	2.1	1.1					.8	1.1
2.1	7.6	2.9				Fixed/Worth	6.3	5.5
-3.5	-8.0	-19.0					-2.5	-2.0
.4	1.4	.8					.7	.9
3.4	6.9	2.8				Debt/Worth	8.5	5.5
-2.1	-9.2	-21.1					-4.2	-3.2
263.6	69.4	60.0					53.9	58.3
(19) 53.5	(11) 42.5	(13) 47.7				% Profit Before Taxes/Tangible Net Worth	(41) 19.6	(42) 12.0
26.4	-1.0	13.1					-7.2	-1.3
52.7	24.2	11.9					12.8	11.7
11.4	8.1	6.4				% Profit Before Taxes/Total Assets	3.6	1.0
4.7	-1.0	1.5					-3.3	-6.7
18.2	2.1	5.1					6.5	6.2
6.0	.7	1.9				Sales/Net Fixed Assets	2.4	2.2
1.3	.5	.9					1.1	1.2
4.4	1.0	2.1					2.2	2.1
1.9	.5	1.4				Sales/Total Assets	1.4	1.5
1.2	.4	.7					.7	.8
4.3		5.7					4.5	4.7
(20) 8.1		(16) 12.5				% Depr., Dep., Amort./Sales	(62) 8.0	(61) 13.4
24.5		16.4					15.8	19.3
4.4							2.6	2.0
(15) 7.9						% Officers', Directors' Owners' Comp/Sales	(29) 4.4	(34) 4.6
11.1							7.7	6.9
11278M	10531M	107133M	154794M			Net Sales ($)	572930M	303207M
5257M	14158M	71617M	117144M			Total Assets ($)	501316M	180341M

M = $ thousand MM = $ million

See Pages 9 through 22 for Explanation of Ratios and Data

Comparative Historical Data

Current Data Sorted by Sales

			Type of Statement						
3	2		Unqualified						
6	7	3	Reviewed			1	1	1	
17	5	8	Compiled	3	1	1	1	1	1
40	40	30	Tax Returns	27	3				
22	36	25	Other	13	2	5	1	3	1
				3 (4/1-9/30/13)			63 (10/1/13-3/31/14)		
4/1/11-3/31/12 ALL	4/1/12-3/31/13 ALL	4/1/13-3/31/14 ALL		0-1MM	1-3MM	3-5MM	5-10MM	10-25MM	25MM & OVER
88	90	66	NUMBER OF STATEMENTS	43	6	7	3	5	2
%	%	%	ASSETS	%	%	%	%	%	%
13.3	12.1	11.1	Cash & Equivalents	12.1					
1.9	3.8	3.7	Trade Receivables (net)	3.1					
1.9	2.3	1.6	Inventory	.4					
4.0	1.8	1.7	All Other Current	.5					
21.2	20.1	18.2	Total Current	16.1					
63.3	61.2	62.4	Fixed Assets (net)	63.3					
6.2	10.6	12.4	Intangibles (net)	15.7					
9.3	8.1	7.1	All Other Non-Current	5.0					
100.0	100.0	100.0	Total	100.0					
			LIABILITIES						
5.9	7.3	7.0	Notes Payable-Short Term	8.5					
5.2	5.7	7.0	Cur. Mat.-L.T.D.	7.8					
2.4	3.7	5.2	Trade Payables	5.1					
.1	.0	.1	Income Taxes Payable	.1					
12.6	10.3	7.4	All Other Current	9.0					
26.3	27.0	26.7	Total Current	30.6					
40.1	43.6	53.6	Long-Term Debt	63.6					
.1	.4	.1	Deferred Taxes	.0					
9.7	7.5	11.0	All Other Non-Current	14.1					
23.8	21.5	8.6	Net Worth	-8.2					
100.0	100.0	100.0	Total Liabilties & Net Worth	100.0					
			INCOME DATA						
100.0	100.0	100.0	Net Sales	100.0					
			Gross Profit						
86.9	87.4	86.7	Operating Expenses	86.8					
13.1	12.6	13.3	Operating Profit	13.2					
5.2	5.1	3.5	All Other Expenses (net)	4.2					
7.9	7.5	9.8	Profit Before Taxes	9.0					
			RATIOS						
2.2	2.7	2.6		2.7					
.9	.9	.9	Current	.5					
.4	.3	.2		.2					
1.6	1.9	1.9		2.6					
.5	.6	.4	Quick	.3					
.2	.2	.2		.2					
0 UND	0 UND	0 UND		0 UND					
0 UND	0 UND	0 UND	Sales/Receivables	0 UND					
2 220.5	3 106.6	3 123.1		0 UND					
			Cost of Sales/Inventory						
			Cost of Sales/Payables						
10.8	8.6	16.0		16.5					
-72.6	-72.9	-82.5	Sales/Working Capital	-30.0					
-8.0	-6.3	-8.4		-4.7					
7.1	7.3	11.5		10.2					
(66) 3.2	(72) 2.9	(53) 4.3	EBIT/Interest	(32) 3.1					
.9	1.3	1.7		1.5					
			Net Profit + Depr., Dep., Amort./Cur. Mat. L/T/D						
1.0	1.4	.9		.9					
2.5	3.8	3.1	Fixed/Worth	4.2					
-3.8	-8.2	-19.0		-5.9					
.6	1.1	.5		.8					
3.6	3.9	3.5	Debt/Worth	4.7					
-5.5	-10.8	-14.9		-4.4					
60.5	53.3	83.8		140.8					
(61) 23.7	(62) 23.3	(47) 42.5	% Profit Before Taxes/Tangible Net Worth	(29) 53.5					
6.5	7.7	15.1		15.0					
17.5	14.5	25.8		28.7					
6.7	6.1	7.8	% Profit Before Taxes/Total Assets	8.6					
-1.8	.3	2.2		1.8					
3.9	6.0	8.9		9.3					
1.9	2.1	2.1	Sales/Net Fixed Assets	2.0					
.9	.6	.8		.6					
2.0	1.9	2.2		2.6					
1.4	1.3	1.3	Sales/Total Assets	1.2					
.7	.5	.7		.5					
4.7	7.1	5.3		5.5					
(69) 10.6	(74) 12.2	(48) 10.9	% Depr., Dep., Amort./Sales	(27) 13.6					
18.1	20.0	18.7		25.6					
3.3	4.3	2.3		4.9					
(34) 5.1	(33) 6.6	(30) 5.3	% Officers', Directors' Owners' Comp/Sales	(18) 8.2					
11.7	9.8	9.2		11.4					
332132M	385905M	283736M	Net Sales ($)	18204M	9475M	27098M	20141M	79552M	129266M
257648M	286176M	208176M	Total Assets ($)	22109M	19094M	22611M	14414M	42762M	87186M

M = $ thousand MM = $ million

See Pages 9 through 22 for Explanation of Ratios and Data

Current Data Sorted by Assets							Comparative Historical Data	
						Type of Statement		
	1	1				Unqualified	12	8
	2	10	1			Reviewed	11	14
2	5	10				Compiled	31	15
24	19	3				Tax Returns	58	62
15	8	8	7			Other	39	56
	21 (4/1-9/30/13)		95 (10/1/13-3/31/14)				4/1/09-3/31/10	4/1/10-3/31/11
0-500M	500M-2MM	2-10MM	10-50MM	50-100MM	100-250MM		ALL	ALL
41	35	32	8			**NUMBER OF STATEMENTS**	151	155
%	%	%	%	%	%	**ASSETS**	%	%
18.9	9.5	11.2		DATA NOT AVAILABLE	DATA NOT AVAILABLE	Cash & Equivalents	10.3	10.3
3.7	7.4	15.0				Trade Receivables (net)	10.6	10.9
1.8	1.6	4.3				Inventory	3.1	2.9
.4	1.1	2.5				All Other Current	2.4	3.5
24.8	19.6	33.1				Total Current	26.4	27.6
51.9	56.2	46.9				Fixed Assets (net)	52.8	51.7
13.8	16.2	8.8				Intangibles (net)	11.0	10.7
9.5	8.0	11.3				All Other Non-Current	9.8	10.0
100.0	100.0	100.0				Total	100.0	100.0
						LIABILITIES		
13.0	5.6	5.5				Notes Payable-Short Term	8.4	7.7
8.2	7.0	6.9				Cur. Mat.-L.T.D.	8.8	7.8
2.1	4.0	7.4				Trade Payables	4.7	6.5
.5	.0	.1				Income Taxes Payable	.1	.1
24.4	9.2	8.2				All Other Current	15.2	12.8
48.4	25.8	28.1				Total Current	37.2	35.0
40.0	44.2	31.3				Long-Term Debt	43.6	42.8
.0	.0	.2				Deferred Taxes	.2	.2
27.6	11.0	5.6				All Other Non-Current	10.8	10.1
-16.0	19.0	34.8				Net Worth	8.2	11.9
100.0	100.0	100.0				Total Liabilities & Net Worth	100.0	100.0
						INCOME DATA		
100.0	100.0	100.0				Net Sales	100.0	100.0
						Gross Profit		
91.1	92.8	93.9				Operating Expenses	92.6	90.9
8.9	7.2	6.1				Operating Profit	7.4	9.1
1.0	2.6	1.3				All Other Expenses (net)	3.1	3.3
7.9	4.7	4.8				Profit Before Taxes	4.3	5.8
						RATIOS		
3.7	1.6	2.5					2.1	2.0
.7	.8	1.3				Current	.9	.9
.3	.4	.6					.4	.3
2.9	1.5	2.2					1.8	1.8
.7	.7	1.0				Quick	.7	.7
.2	.4	.4					.3	.3
0 UND	**0** UND	**7** 51.8					**0** UND	**0** UND
0 UND	**0** UND	**27** 13.7				Sales/Receivables	**10** 36.8	**10** 35.8
3 111.4	**20** 17.9	**43** 8.4					**29** 12.5	**30** 12.2
						Cost of Sales/Inventory		
						Cost of Sales/Payables		
36.2	24.6	8.0					15.9	18.7
-92.3	-53.7	31.0				Sales/Working Capital	-151.7	-75.7
-12.5	-16.0	-26.6					-11.9	-10.4
13.5	7.4	20.0					5.2	7.9
(29) 2.5	(31) 2.2	(31) 3.8				EBIT/Interest	(129) 2.3	(132) 2.7
.6	1.2	1.4					.7	1.3
							4.8	2.9
						Net Profit + Depr., Dep., Amort./Cur. Mat. L/T/D	(12) 1.2	(16) 1.2
							.9	.3
.9	1.3	.8					1.1	1.0
21.1	8.9	1.2				Fixed/Worth	3.8	6.1
-.7	-1.6	11.6					-1.6	-1.9
.4	1.7	.6					1.0	1.0
41.0	7.9	2.0				Debt/Worth	5.2	10.5
-2.4	-4.4	15.0					-3.5	-4.6
144.9	36.3	104.3					53.2	64.7
(22) 37.2	(20) 20.5	(25) 32.8				% Profit Before Taxes/Tangible Net Worth	(88) 20.5	(89) 25.9
7.6	3.7	4.1					-.1	8.4
39.5	13.0	18.9					17.0	18.4
13.2	4.7	9.9				% Profit Before Taxes/Total Assets	4.3	6.8
-.1	1.2	1.5					-1.2	2.0
30.2	13.6	7.4					9.5	11.0
6.9	5.0	5.1				Sales/Net Fixed Assets	5.2	5.3
2.1	2.2	2.9					2.2	2.3
8.0	3.3	2.4					3.8	3.6
4.2	2.4	2.1				Sales/Total Assets	1.9	2.1
1.6	.9	1.3					1.1	1.1
1.5	2.5	2.7					2.8	2.9
(27) 5.7	(25) 5.1	(30) 4.4				% Depr., Dep., Amort./Sales	(135) 4.8	(128) 4.8
10.3	9.4	6.8					8.6	9.5
5.1	2.8	2.6					2.5	3.0
(25) 8.9	(21) 4.7	(15) 4.4				% Officers', Directors' Owners' Comp/Sales	(77) 4.7	(76) 5.4
15.1	6.4	6.8					9.4	8.9
36914M	93903M	274727M	153415M			Net Sales ($)	979536M	986909M
9514M	39356M	135987M	138254M			Total Assets ($)	561249M	568218M

M = $ thousand MM = $ million

See Pages 9 through 22 for Explanation of Ratios and Data

Comparative Historical Data

Current Data Sorted by Sales

4/1/11-3/31/12 ALL	4/1/12-3/31/13 ALL	4/1/13-3/31/14 ALL	Type of Statement	0-1MM	1-3MM	3-5MM	5-10MM	10-25MM	25MM & OVER
5	8	2	Unqualified			1		1	
11	13	13	Reviewed			3	2	8	
21	25	17	Compiled	3	2	5	5	2	
94	56	46	Tax Returns	23	15	3	4	1	
44	40	38	Other	13	9	3	5	7	1
				21 (4/1-9/30/13)			95 (10/1/13-3/31/14)		
175	142	116	NUMBER OF STATEMENTS	39	26	15	16	19	1
%	%	%	**ASSETS**	%	%	%	%	%	%
12.2	12.8	13.5	Cash & Equivalents	13.3	18.4	11.4	11.5	10.3	
10.7	10.4	8.1	Trade Receivables (net)	2.2	5.3	13.7	11.3	16.7	
2.9	3.4	2.4	Inventory	1.2	1.3	3.6	2.1	5.6	
1.6	1.7	1.2	All Other Current	.3	.5	3.0	2.5	1.6	
27.4	28.3	25.2	Total Current	17.1	25.5	31.7	27.4	34.2	
49.8	46.7	52.1	Fixed Assets (net)	60.9	43.4	52.8	52.3	47.1	
13.3	12.6	12.4	Intangibles (net)	15.3	17.7	9.9	3.7	8.7	
9.5	12.4	10.3	All Other Non-Current	6.7	13.3	5.6	16.6	10.0	
100.0	100.0	100.0	Total	100.0	100.0	100.0	100.0	100.0	
			LIABILITIES						
7.3	6.3	7.9	Notes Payable-Short Term	11.0	5.7	5.0	12.5	3.4	
7.0	6.2	7.4	Cur. Mat.-L.T.D.	6.3	7.6	13.7	6.2	5.4	
6.4	5.7	4.4	Trade Payables	1.3	2.4	8.4	5.8	8.8	
.1	.1	.2	Income Taxes Payable	.1	.8	.1	.2	.1	
10.1	15.0	14.3	All Other Current	15.5	17.6	15.0	10.1	10.7	
30.9	33.4	34.2	Total Current	34.1	34.0	42.1	34.8	28.5	
40.8	37.1	37.8	Long-Term Debt	47.3	33.7	40.6	30.9	28.4	
.2	.3	.3	Deferred Taxes	.0	.5	.0	.3	.9	
12.1	9.7	14.8	All Other Non-Current	23.8	18.3	6.9	10.5	1.9	
16.0	19.6	12.9	Net Worth	-5.2	13.5	10.4	23.5	40.3	
100.0	100.0	100.0	Total Liabilties & Net Worth	100.0	100.0	100.0	100.0	100.0	
			INCOME DATA						
100.0	100.0	100.0	Net Sales	100.0	100.0	100.0	100.0	100.0	
			Gross Profit						
92.8	93.0	92.0	Operating Expenses	89.0	90.0	93.4	97.7	94.8	
7.2	7.0	8.0	Operating Profit	11.0	10.0	6.6	2.3	5.2	
2.6	1.4	1.9	All Other Expenses (net)	2.8	2.4	1.6	.8	.9	
4.7	5.6	6.1	Profit Before Taxes	8.2	7.6	5.1	1.5	4.3	
			RATIOS						
3.0	3.0	2.3		4.0	2.7	3.4	1.3	2.2	
1.0	1.3	.9	Current	.6	1.0	1.6	.9	1.3	
.4	.4	.4		.2	.5	.8	.5	.6	
2.5	2.4	2.2		2.3	2.4	2.2	1.1	2.1	
.8	1.0	.8	Quick	.5	1.0	.9	.7	.8	
.3	.3	.3		.1	.5	.4	.4	.5	
0 UND	0 UND	0 UND		0 UND	0 UND	6 66.3	0 UND	7 55.3	
7 56.1	6 63.5	3 122.4	Sales/Receivables	0 UND	0 UND	22 16.5	24 15.0	27 13.6	
27 13.3	28 12.9	25 14.7		2 226.7	11 34.6	35 10.4	38 9.5	39 9.3	
			Cost of Sales/Inventory						
			Cost of Sales/Payables						
17.1	11.8	18.6		30.0	23.2	7.6	52.0	8.5	
UND	57.8	-189.5	Sales/Working Capital	-31.2	UND	18.4	-288.0	35.2	
-15.0	-16.8	-16.0		-7.2	-24.3	-18.3	-23.1	-24.3	
7.7	11.7	11.1		3.8	43.3	9.0	14.1	20.6	
(142) 2.6	(120) 4.6	(99) 2.8	EBIT/Interest	(28) 1.4	(21) 7.4	(14) 2.4	1.4	6.0	
.8	1.1	1.2		.2	2.3	1.6	-.3	2.3	
3.6	5.7	3.5							
(15) 1.9	(16) 2.6	(13) 2.7	Net Profit + Depr., Dep., Amort./Cur. Mat. L/T/D						
1.5	1.3	.5							
.9	.7	.9		1.0	.5	1.2	.9	.7	
3.5	1.7	3.1	Fixed/Worth	35.0	2.1	6.9	1.4	1.1	
-2.8	-2.6	-3.2		-1.6	-1.0	-2.1	8.1	3.4	
.8	.5	.7		.4	.5	1.7	.5	.7	
5.0	2.6	4.0	Debt/Worth	41.0	3.3	12.0	2.6	1.1	
-4.6	-4.9	-6.5		-3.6	-2.6	-8.1	13.9	4.2	
72.6	79.9	70.6		101.8	67.6		63.0	54.1	
(112) 17.4	(95) 22.7	(75) 25.7	% Profit Before Taxes/Tangible Net Worth	(21) 18.9	(16) 30.8		(13) 19.9	(16) 23.3	
4.0	5.5	5.8		2.0	11.1		-22.4	6.0	
17.5	26.2	17.2		18.5	21.8	19.4	15.6	16.1	
5.8	8.5	7.9	% Profit Before Taxes/Total Assets	5.9	11.1	4.7	1.6	9.1	
.0	.8	1.0		.0	3.3	3.3	-6.7	2.6	
14.0	15.0	12.6		12.5	29.3	7.1	8.5	9.2	
6.0	6.0	5.1	Sales/Net Fixed Assets	3.4	10.1	3.9	6.4	5.3	
2.7	3.0	2.1		1.0	3.1	2.7	3.5	2.1	
4.5	3.9	3.9		4.4	5.1	2.9	4.2	3.0	
2.4	2.4	2.2	Sales/Total Assets	1.7	2.7	2.2	2.6	2.1	
1.3	1.3	1.2		.7	1.6	1.4	1.7	1.4	
2.4	2.0	2.5		5.2	1.6	2.7	2.3	3.1	
(133) 4.0	(113) 3.7	(90) 4.9	% Depr., Dep., Amort./Sales	(27) 9.5	(16) 2.4	(14) 5.0	(14) 3.5	(18) 4.7	
8.5	6.0	7.9		14.3	4.9	7.6	5.3	6.3	
2.7	2.9	3.4		5.7	3.5	2.6	2.1		
(99) 5.7	(82) 4.7	(63) 5.7	% Officers', Directors' Owners' Comp/Sales	(19) 8.9	(17) 6.4	(10) 4.6	(10) 4.5		
9.9	8.7	9.6		15.4	10.2	6.3	6.8		
2332932M	934784M	558959M	Net Sales ($)	19172M	44508M	63102M	103731M	273342M	55104M
608162M	573005M	323111M	Total Assets ($)	16949M	30429M	32889M	49136M	161133M	32575M

M = $ thousand MM = $ million

See Pages 9 through 22 for Explanation of Ratios and Data

Current Data Sorted by Assets / Comparative Historical Data

						Type of Statement		
		5	6			Unqualified	11	11
	2	6	6	1		Reviewed	14	19
1	1	2	2			Compiled	8	9
3	8	7				Tax Returns	9	9
	7	10	9		1	Other	33	27
12 (4/1-9/30/13)		65 (10/1/13-3/31/14)					4/1/09-3/31/10 ALL	4/1/10-3/31/11 ALL
0-500M	500M-2MM	2-10MM	10-50MM	50-100MM	100-250MM			
4	18	30	23	1	1	NUMBER OF STATEMENTS	75	75
%	%	%	%	%	%	ASSETS	%	%
	13.0	7.7	9.6			Cash & Equivalents	11.5	11.8
	17.8	17.0	16.9			Trade Receivables (net)	22.7	20.2
	15.7	18.6	12.2			Inventory	6.7	10.0
	.6	.6	2.9			All Other Current	2.8	2.5
	47.1	43.9	41.6			Total Current	43.7	44.5
	47.4	44.4	41.7			Fixed Assets (net)	45.3	41.5
	2.9	5.4	9.2			Intangibles (net)	6.0	6.1
	2.6	6.4	7.5			All Other Non-Current	5.0	7.9
	100.0	100.0	100.0			Total	100.0	100.0
						LIABILITIES		
	10.0	9.1	6.5			Notes Payable-Short Term	8.0	5.9
	4.2	4.1	8.8			Cur. Mat.-L.T.D.	4.9	4.0
	10.7	9.3	10.1			Trade Payables	8.6	10.1
	.0	.6	.1			Income Taxes Payable	.2	.2
	12.4	4.6	5.6			All Other Current	9.6	5.9
	37.4	27.8	31.1			Total Current	31.2	26.1
	26.3	32.8	20.2			Long-Term Debt	22.4	26.1
	.8	.0	.3			Deferred Taxes	.4	.5
	6.6	1.0	6.5			All Other Non-Current	4.9	5.4
	28.9	38.4	41.8			Net Worth	41.1	41.9
	100.0	100.0	100.0			Total Liabilties & Net Worth	100.0	100.0
						INCOME DATA		
	100.0	100.0	100.0			Net Sales	100.0	100.0
						Gross Profit		
	91.4	91.8	94.7			Operating Expenses	94.7	93.5
	8.6	8.2	5.3			Operating Profit	5.3	6.5
	3.1	3.4	1.7			All Other Expenses (net)	1.6	1.4
	5.5	4.7	3.6			Profit Before Taxes	3.8	5.1
						RATIOS		
	5.5	2.9	2.8				2.6	3.1
	2.4	1.8	1.4			Current	1.9	1.7
	.5	1.1	1.0				.9	1.1
	4.2	2.2	2.0				2.2	2.2
	.9	.9	1.1			Quick	1.2	1.2
	.2	.6	.4				.5	.8
	0 UND	**25** 14.4	**32** 11.5				**30** 12.0	**31** 12.0
	30 12.0	**32** 11.4	**36** 10.0			Sales/Receivables	**36** 10.2	**35** 10.4
	39 9.4	**46** 8.0	**41** 8.8				**42** 8.8	**41** 9.0
						Cost of Sales/Inventory		
						Cost of Sales/Payables		
	6.1	6.8	5.0				7.1	6.4
	8.7	10.8	18.3			Sales/Working Capital	12.2	10.9
	-9.3	45.8	84.9				-63.7	62.9
	9.3	15.3	13.2				12.8	16.0
	(15) 1.7	(28) 2.5	(22) 3.8			EBIT/Interest	(63) 3.8	(71) 6.7
	.2	1.6	.8				1.1	1.8
							9.3	6.3
						Net Profit + Depr., Dep., Amort./Cur. Mat. L/T/D	(15) 5.0	(12) 2.6
							1.0	.8
	.4	.5	.5				.7	.5
	1.2	1.5	1.1			Fixed/Worth	1.2	.9
	NM	5.0	22.4				2.6	2.9
	.9	.7	.4				.5	.5
	1.6	1.8	1.0			Debt/Worth	1.9	1.5
	NM	9.6	57.5				3.6	4.9
	49.1	34.9	30.1				38.5	41.0
	(14) 15.1	(25) 18.4	(18) 10.0			% Profit Before Taxes/Tangible Net Worth	(66) 21.4	(66) 14.7
	3.5	4.1	.6				5.2	4.7
	17.0	9.8	10.2				15.5	16.7
	3.2	4.0	4.4			% Profit Before Taxes/Total Assets	6.6	6.7
	-.9	1.2	-1.4				.5	.7
	13.9	9.2	6.9				7.7	9.6
	9.0	4.4	4.0			Sales/Net Fixed Assets	4.3	5.5
	2.0	2.1	2.7				2.6	2.9
	4.0	2.1	2.0				2.6	2.5
	2.5	1.7	1.7			Sales/Total Assets	1.8	1.8
	1.3	1.1	1.2				1.4	1.5
	1.8	1.9	2.1				2.5	2.3
	(16) 3.4	(28) 4.1	4.2			% Depr., Dep., Amort./Sales	(67) 4.4	(66) 4.4
	13.8	5.9	7.9				6.9	7.4
	2.8	1.9					1.7	2.9
	(11) 4.2	(13) 4.1				% Officers', Directors' Owners' Comp/Sales	(24) 3.7	(30) 3.9
	5.9	7.7					9.1	5.9
5742M	51481M	260595M	952197M	140319M	105702M	Net Sales ($)	1507996M	2021614M
1141M	22175M	165575M	589090M	79589M	101066M	Total Assets ($)	848317M	1192470M

M = $ thousand MM = $ million

See Pages 9 through 22 for Explanation of Ratios and Data

Comparative Historical Data				Current Data Sorted by Sales					
			Type of Statement						
9	7	11	Unqualified				4	2	5
21	15	15	Reviewed		1	2	2	5	5
13	5	6	Compiled	2			2	1	1
18	12	18	Tax Returns	2	5	6	3	2	
24	27	27	Other	2	5	2	4	5	9
4/1/11-3/31/12 ALL	**4/1/12-3/31/13 ALL**	**4/1/13-3/31/14 ALL**			**12 (4/1-9/30/13)**		**65 (10/1/13-3/31/14)**		
				0-1MM	**1-3MM**	**3-5MM**	**5-10MM**	**10-25MM**	**25MM & OVER**
85	66	77	**NUMBER OF STATEMENTS**	6	11	10	15	15	20
%	%	%	**ASSETS**	%	%	%	%	%	%
9.5	12.2	10.2	Cash & Equivalents		10.1	20.2	7.2	10.2	8.4
21.1	18.8	17.1	Trade Receivables (net)		16.3	19.0	18.4	17.9	19.4
14.5	14.0	15.8	Inventory		16.5	20.2	12.3	20.8	14.9
2.7	2.4	1.3	All Other Current		.9	.1	.9	.2	3.6
47.8	47.4	44.4	Total Current		43.8	59.5	38.8	49.0	46.3
39.6	43.8	42.8	Fixed Assets (net)		45.3	35.1	44.2	39.1	38.7
7.0	3.0	6.7	Intangibles (net)		4.0	3.1	7.7	5.9	8.2
5.7	5.8	6.1	All Other Non-Current		7.0	2.3	9.3	5.9	6.8
100.0	100.0	100.0	Total		100.0	100.0	100.0	100.0	100.0
			LIABILITIES						
11.3	11.1	8.6	Notes Payable-Short Term		14.6	9.7	3.6	10.2	9.0
5.8	4.3	6.2	Cur. Mat.-L.T.D.		11.1	2.7	5.1	4.0	8.7
10.4	8.4	10.1	Trade Payables		6.3	9.3	6.8	11.8	12.4
.3	.0	.3	Income Taxes Payable		.0	.0	1.1	.0	.1
7.5	7.8	8.0	All Other Current		14.4	9.1	5.6	4.5	6.3
35.3	31.6	33.1	Total Current		46.4	30.8	22.4	30.5	36.5
22.8	22.9	27.5	Long-Term Debt		40.7	21.6	27.5	28.5	14.3
.3	.4	.3	Deferred Taxes		.0	1.4	.0	.0	.5
7.6	5.6	4.3	All Other Non-Current		8.8	2.2	1.5	3.4	5.3
34.1	39.6	34.7	Net Worth		4.1	44.0	48.7	37.6	43.5
100.0	100.0	100.0	Total Liabilities & Net Worth		100.0	100.0	100.0	100.0	100.0
			INCOME DATA						
100.0	100.0	100.0	Net Sales		100.0	100.0	100.0	100.0	100.0
			Gross Profit						
93.8	93.8	92.6	Operating Expenses		96.5	94.2	95.4	95.0	94.7
6.2	6.2	7.4	Operating Profit		3.5	5.8	4.6	5.0	5.3
1.4	.5	2.5	All Other Expenses (net)		1.4	2.0	.4	2.4	1.2
4.8	5.8	4.9	Profit Before Taxes		2.1	3.8	4.1	2.6	4.1
			RATIOS						
2.6	3.0	3.1			5.0	5.9	2.3	3.8	2.8
1.7	1.8	1.8	Current		2.0	2.6	1.9	2.0	1.3
1.0	1.1	1.0			.6	1.1	1.2	.9	1.1
2.2	2.5	2.1			1.0	5.8	1.9	3.0	1.7
1.1	1.2	1.0	Quick		.8	2.4	1.0	1.0	1.1
.4	.6	.5			.3	.4	.6	.4	.5
28 13.2	**26** 13.8	**25** 14.4			**0** UND	**0** UND	**29** 12.5	**25** 14.4	**32** 11.4
33 11.1	**32** 11.4	**33** 11.2	Sales/Receivables		**29** 12.8	**30** 12.1	**32** 11.3	**36** 10.2	**37** 9.8
41 9.0	**41** 8.8	**41** 9.0			**39** 9.4	**36** 10.0	**53** 6.9	**42** 8.6	**44** 8.3
			Cost of Sales/Inventory						
			Cost of Sales/Payables						
7.1	5.5	7.0			7.8	4.3	7.4	4.7	6.3
12.8	11.5	12.2	Sales/Working Capital		9.6	7.6	14.1	7.9	19.2
-133.5	68.6	NM			-9.5	37.7	22.1	-34.0	34.7
10.6	20.6	10.9			9.3		13.2	18.5	13.2
(78) 3.8	(64) 7.4	(69) 2.8	EBIT/Interest		1.7		(14) 3.7	3.8	(18) 3.9
1.0	2.8	1.2			.2		1.2	1.7	.6
5.8	11.6	3.1							
(14) 2.6	(10) 3.0	(13) 2.4	Net Profit + Depr., Dep., Amort./Cur. Mat. L/T/D						
.6	2.3	1.1							
.4	.5	.5			.8	.1	.8	.5	.4
1.0	1.0	1.3	Fixed/Worth		11.2	.5	1.3	.7	.9
3.9	2.4	16.8			-1.8	3.0	2.0	-9.7	3.2
.6	.5	.7			1.1	.5	.7	.4	.4
2.1	1.3	1.6	Debt/Worth		13.2	1.4	1.1	1.0	1.1
6.5	3.9	39.5			-4.3	7.2	2.5	-30.4	9.0
54.4	43.0	33.1					33.2	24.9	26.9
(72) 17.1	(59) 27.2	(60) 17.8	% Profit Before Taxes/Tangible Net Worth				(14) 20.3	(11) 9.5	(17) 17.2
1.9	9.2	4.1					5.0	3.6	-.3
15.4	21.2	11.6			28.4	17.0	9.7	13.7	11.3
5.0	9.1	4.2	% Profit Before Taxes/Total Assets		3.9	4.8	5.8	4.4	3.8
-.2	4.2	.9			-2.7	2.4	1.2	.9	-1.0
12.9	11.2	10.6			12.9	44.3	5.3	16.3	7.0
6.0	5.4	4.7	Sales/Net Fixed Assets		8.8	13.1	4.4	4.3	4.8
3.4	2.5	2.3			2.1	5.2	2.3	2.4	2.8
3.0	2.8	2.5			4.5	3.6	2.1	2.2	2.1
2.0	1.9	1.8	Sales/Total Assets		2.6	2.7	1.7	1.7	1.7
1.6	1.4	1.3			1.3	1.7	1.0	1.4	1.3
1.9	2.3	2.0					2.4	1.7	2.0
(72) 3.9	(62) 3.8	(72) 3.9	% Depr., Dep., Amort./Sales				(14) 4.1	(14) 4.6	3.4
6.4	6.4	6.3					5.7	6.6	6.3
2.0	2.5	2.3							
(38) 3.6	(24) 4.3	(31) 4.2	% Officers', Directors' Owners' Comp/Sales						
7.1	7.3	6.1							
1845699M	**1437678M**	**1516036M**	Net Sales ($)	**3110M**	**25245M**	**43188M**	**114105M**	**206042M**	**1124346M**
936512M	**819982M**	**958636M**	Total Assets ($)	**15693M**	**10799M**	**21444M**	**74551M**	**127597M**	**708552M**

M = $ thousand MM = $ million

See Pages 9 through 22 for Explanation of Ratios and Data

Current Data Sorted by Assets							Comparative Historical Data	
						Type of Statement		
		1	3	1		Unqualified	5	5
		2	1			Reviewed	2	8
	1	3				Compiled	1	1
						Tax Returns		1
	2	5	5	1	1	Other	6	11
	4 (4/1-9/30/13)		22 (10/1/13-3/31/14)				4/1/09-3/31/10	4/1/10-3/31/11
0-500M	**500M-2MM**	**2-10MM**	**10-50MM**	**50-100MM**	**100-250MM**		**ALL**	**ALL**
	3	11	9	2	1	**NUMBER OF STATEMENTS**	14	26
%	%	%	%	%	%	**ASSETS**	%	%
DATA NOT AVAILABLE		9.2				Cash & Equivalents	11.9	8.6
		21.1				Trade Receivables (net)	19.6	23.2
		18.2				Inventory	11.8	9.7
		.5				All Other Current	1.8	1.4
		49.0				Total Current	45.0	42.9
		38.1				Fixed Assets (net)	39.1	41.9
		8.4				Intangibles (net)	6.5	7.3
		4.4				All Other Non-Current	9.4	7.9
		100.0				Total	100.0	100.0
						LIABILITIES		
		6.6				Notes Payable-Short Term	3.3	6.8
		4.7				Cur. Mat.-L.T.D.	11.4	10.0
		9.1				Trade Payables	8.7	11.9
		.1				Income Taxes Payable	.0	.1
		4.7				All Other Current	4.9	7.5
		25.2				Total Current	28.3	36.3
		17.0				Long-Term Debt	19.6	26.3
		.1				Deferred Taxes	.1	.1
		8.2				All Other Non-Current	4.0	4.9
		49.5				Net Worth	48.0	32.4
		100.0				Total Liabilties & Net Worth	100.0	100.0
						INCOME DATA		
		100.0				Net Sales	100.0	100.0
						Gross Profit		
		94.3				Operating Expenses	92.6	95.5
		5.7				Operating Profit	7.4	4.5
		1.6				All Other Expenses (net)	2.1	2.2
		4.2				Profit Before Taxes	5.3	2.3
						RATIOS		
		4.8					3.6	2.2
		1.4				Current	2.0	1.3
		1.0					1.1	.9
		3.6					2.5	1.3
		.9				Quick	1.5	1.0
		.6					.8	.6
		28 13.2					32 11.3	30 12.1
		39 9.4				Sales/Receivables	43 8.5	44 8.3
		45 8.1					52 7.1	64 5.7
						Cost of Sales/Inventory		
						Cost of Sales/Payables		
		4.9					6.1	6.8
		16.6				Sales/Working Capital	7.0	26.6
		-199.1					50.4	-38.6
		10.6					14.7	6.3
		(10) 4.6				EBIT/Interest	(13) 4.0	2.6
		1.6					1.3	1.2
						Net Profit + Depr., Dep., Amort./Cur. Mat. L/T/D		
		.4					.4	.9
		1.0				Fixed/Worth	1.1	1.4
		2.3					2.7	NM
		.3					.3	1.0
		1.9				Debt/Worth	1.0	2.1
		2.5					4.2	NM
		48.6					29.6	31.0
		(10) 22.0				% Profit Before Taxes/Tangible Net Worth	(12) 15.5	(20) 15.3
		1.6					4.7	3.5
		18.5					16.3	8.5
		5.2				% Profit Before Taxes/Total Assets	4.1	3.5
		1.5					.6	.9
		11.6					7.0	7.0
		5.5				Sales/Net Fixed Assets	3.1	5.1
		3.5					2.2	2.9
		3.3					2.3	2.2
		1.8				Sales/Total Assets	1.6	1.6
		1.0					1.0	1.2
							2.9	2.5
						% Depr., Dep., Amort./Sales	(13) 4.2	(25) 4.3
							7.0	6.1
						% Officers', Directors' Owners' Comp/Sales		
	13901M	139668M	410594M	110149M	147711M	Net Sales ($)	312641M	648620M
	3801M	69052M	244102M	132653M	107417M	Total Assets ($)	223406M	410072M

M = $ thousand MM = $ million

See Pages 9 through 22 for Explanation of Ratios and Data

Comparative Historical Data / Current Data Sorted by Sales

4/1/11-3/31/12 ALL	4/1/12-3/31/13 ALL	4/1/13-3/31/14 ALL	Type of Statement	0-1MM	1-3MM	3-5MM	5-10MM	10-25MM	25MM & OVER
				4 (4/1-9/30/13)		22 (10/1/13-3/31/14)			
8	5	5	Unqualified				1	2	2
6	2	3	Reviewed				2	1	
1	2	4	Compiled			1	1	1	1
3	3		Tax Returns						
12	8	14	Other			1	3	3	7
30	20	26	NUMBER OF STATEMENTS			2	7	7	10
%	%	%	ASSETS	%	%	%	%	%	%
6.7	10.6	7.6	Cash & Equivalents	D	D				7.9
18.7	21.3	24.2	Trade Receivables (net)	A	A				25.4
7.4	11.7	14.6	Inventory	T	T				14.2
7.3	1.0	.8	All Other Current	A	A				.9
40.1	44.5	47.2	Total Current						48.4
39.2	39.7	38.6	Fixed Assets (net)	N	N				36.9
12.5	10.0	10.6	Intangibles (net)	O	O				11.1
8.2	5.7	3.6	All Other Non-Current	T	T				3.6
100.0	100.0	100.0	Total						100.0
			LIABILITIES	A	A				
4.8	4.7	4.1	Notes Payable-Short Term	V	V				2.8
11.4	6.8	4.3	Cur. Mat.-L.T.D.	A	A				2.2
10.5	12.5	10.7	Trade Payables	I	I				9.1
.2	.1	.1	Income Taxes Payable	L	L				.1
9.5	5.2	5.1	All Other Current	A	A				6.5
36.3	29.4	24.2	Total Current	B	B				20.7
26.8	21.7	20.8	Long-Term Debt	L	L				19.0
.2	.0	.2	Deferred Taxes	E	E				.3
9.5	9.9	8.7	All Other Non-Current						3.3
27.3	39.1	46.0	Net Worth						56.6
100.0	100.0	100.0	Total Liabilties & Net Worth						100.0
			INCOME DATA						
100.0	100.0	100.0	Net Sales						100.0
			Gross Profit						
93.9	94.9	95.8	Operating Expenses						95.1
6.1	5.1	4.2	Operating Profit						4.9
3.5	1.6	1.5	All Other Expenses (net)						1.6
2.7	3.5	2.8	Profit Before Taxes						3.3
			RATIOS						
1.8	2.9	2.9							3.2
1.0	1.7	2.0	Current						2.3
.7	.7	1.1							1.7
1.1	2.4	2.4							2.4
.6	1.0	1.5	Quick						1.7
.4	.5	.7							1.4
27 13.5	32 11.5	33 11.1							24 15.4
38 9.6	41 9.0	39 9.4	Sales/Receivables						39 9.4
56 6.5	55 6.6	51 7.1							72 5.1
			Cost of Sales/Inventory						
			Cost of Sales/Payables						
13.8	6.0	5.2							4.9
UND	10.9	12.2	Sales/Working Capital						6.1
-14.6	-18.5	40.6							16.4
7.5	10.9	6.9							
(26) 3.0	(18) 5.1	(24) 3.5	EBIT/Interest						
.6	1.5	1.1							
			Net Profit + Depr., Dep., Amort./Cur. Mat. L/T/D						
1.0	.6	.5							.5
2.5	1.1	1.0	Fixed/Worth						.6
-2.9	8.5	2.7							4.0
1.0	.7	.5							.4
4.9	1.9	2.0	Debt/Worth						.9
-6.3	21.4	3.2							6.3
106.1	74.3	44.5							
(20) 19.9	(16) 15.0	(22) 6.8	% Profit Before Taxes/Tangible Net Worth						
-.1	4.4	2.6							
12.2	11.8	13.5							20.0
4.8	5.1	2.7	% Profit Before Taxes/Total Assets						2.5
-1.7	.5	.3							1.0
10.3	9.7	8.4							6.7
3.9	5.0	5.2	Sales/Net Fixed Assets						6.0
2.1	2.2	2.7							2.4
1.9	1.9	3.0							2.5
1.3	1.4	1.7	Sales/Total Assets						1.8
.9	1.1	1.2							1.2
3.2	1.8	2.5							2.2
(25) 4.3	(17) 3.4	(21) 3.4	% Depr., Dep., Amort./Sales						2.9
10.2	5.2	5.5							5.2
		2.4							
		(10) 4.5	% Officers', Directors' Owners' Comp/Sales						
		8.9							
539637M	543037M	822023M	Net Sales ($)			8570M	51306M	114169M	647978M
401396M	371618M	557025M	Total Assets ($)			2276M	34000M	76686M	444063M

M = $ thousand MM = $ million

See Pages 9 through 22 for Explanation of Ratios and Data

Current Data Sorted by Assets							Comparative Historical Data	
						Type of Statement		
2	1	1	1	2		Unqualified	11	7
	2	1				Reviewed	2	1
1	2	2				Compiled	5	5
39	12	1				Tax Returns	20	27
8	9	7	2			Other	20	36
	7 (4/1-9/30/13)		86 (10/1/13-3/31/14)				4/1/09-3/31/10	4/1/10-3/31/11
0-500M	500M-2MM	2-10MM	10-50MM	50-100MM	100-250MM		ALL	ALL
50	26	12	3	2		NUMBER OF STATEMENTS	58	76
%	%	%	%	%	%	**ASSETS**	%	%
31.8	15.3	9.4			DATA NOT AVAILABLE	Cash & Equivalents	18.1	18.5
1.3	2.9	2.0				Trade Receivables (net)	5.4	5.2
6.9	2.8	6.9				Inventory	3.3	3.1
3.7	.9	3.9				All Other Current	1.2	2.5
43.7	21.8	22.1				Total Current	28.0	29.3
41.5	65.0	55.6				Fixed Assets (net)	59.5	52.2
9.4	8.3	7.0				Intangibles (net)	2.0	9.3
5.4	4.9	15.2				All Other Non-Current	10.6	9.2
100.0	100.0	100.0				Total	100.0	100.0
						LIABILITIES		
10.0	4.4	2.9				Notes Payable-Short Term	12.4	8.2
7.0	1.4	2.2				Cur. Mat.-L.T.D.	4.2	2.7
2.8	.9	2.3				Trade Payables	6.2	1.6
.0	.3	.0				Income Taxes Payable	.9	.0
14.0	7.9	5.2				All Other Current	9.8	11.9
33.7	14.9	12.7				Total Current	33.5	24.4
27.5	37.7	38.1				Long-Term Debt	32.3	47.8
.0	.0	.0				Deferred Taxes	.1	.0
21.8	6.4	1.9				All Other Non-Current	5.0	8.2
16.9	41.0	47.3				Net Worth	29.1	19.6
100.0	100.0	100.0				Total Liabilties & Net Worth	100.0	100.0
						INCOME DATA		
100.0	100.0	100.0				Net Sales	100.0	100.0
						Gross Profit		
87.2	84.1	75.9				Operating Expenses	88.3	86.5
12.8	15.9	24.1				Operating Profit	11.7	13.5
1.8	6.9	8.4				All Other Expenses (net)	7.6	6.5
11.0	9.0	15.8				Profit Before Taxes	4.0	7.0
						RATIOS		
4.0	4.6	3.6					2.6	4.7
1.9	1.4	1.4				Current	1.3	1.6
.7	.4	.4					.3	.7
2.8	4.4	2.4					2.2	4.0
(49) 1.1	1.2	.4				Quick	1.1	1.1
.6	.3	.3					.3	.2
0 UND	0 UND	0 UND					0 UND	0 UND
0 UND	0 UND	2 205.9				Sales/Receivables	2 209.0	0 UND
0 UND	1 251.2	5 79.4					20 18.1	6 63.9
						Cost of Sales/Inventory		
						Cost of Sales/Payables		
12.9	11.0	8.1					7.2	7.8
27.6	44.4	NM				Sales/Working Capital	71.1	34.7
-49.4	-14.7	-13.9					-4.8	-19.7
19.1	5.7						9.6	7.2
(33) 6.8	(14) 3.1					EBIT/Interest	(39) 2.3	(51) 2.2
3.8	.8						.8	.8
						Net Profit + Depr., Dep., Amort./Cur. Mat. L/T/D		
.5	.8	.5					.6	.5
1.7	3.9	1.1				Fixed/Worth	1.5	2.3
-3.1	320.5	5.8					7.9	-4.0
.6	.2	.4					.5	.5
2.8	3.0	1.6				Debt/Worth	1.6	2.6
-4.5	329.9	4.8					21.7	-5.7
163.1	85.0	60.5					32.6	87.4
(32) 70.9	(21) 18.0	(11) 15.9				% Profit Before Taxes/Tangible Net Worth	(46) 10.3	(50) 15.1
43.1	-6.5	6.0					-1.0	.1
57.9	14.5	12.5					14.1	19.4
34.0	4.3	5.1				% Profit Before Taxes/Total Assets	2.1	3.9
11.7	-2.2	-.2					-1.8	-.5
37.7	7.1	6.5					10.1	23.9
13.5	1.5	1.3				Sales/Net Fixed Assets	1.4	4.1
4.9	.6	.4					.4	.8
6.7	2.1	2.1					3.2	3.6
4.4	.8	.5				Sales/Total Assets	.7	1.3
2.0	.5	.2					.3	.5
1.8	3.9						1.7	2.0
(32) 2.9	(19) 6.2					% Depr., Dep., Amort./Sales	(50) 4.0	(54) 4.7
4.7	11.0						8.6	7.9
4.4	4.2						3.1	4.5
(27) 7.9	(12) 7.2					% Officers', Directors' Owners' Comp/Sales	(19) 6.0	(32) 7.1
14.8	15.0						11.2	12.1
37298M	42830M	92888M	32708M	48717M		Net Sales ($)	533298M	210774M
10394M	25360M	58530M	78159M	139366M		Total Assets ($)	582657M	269803M

M = $ thousand MM = $ million

See Pages 9 through 22 for Explanation of Ratios and Data

Comparative Historical Data				Current Data Sorted by Sales					
			Type of Statement						
11	3	7	Unqualified	3		1	1	1	1
6	3	3	Reviewed	2				1	
10	5	5	Compiled	3	2				
45	41	52	Tax Returns	34	16	2			
47	58	26	Other	15	3	1	4	2	1
4/1/11-3/31/12	4/1/12-3/31/13	4/1/13-3/31/14		7 (4/1-9/30/13)		86 (10/1/13-3/31/14)			
ALL	ALL	ALL		0-1MM	1-3MM	3-5MM	5-10MM	10-25MM	25MM & OVER
119	110	93	**NUMBER OF STATEMENTS**	57	21	4	5	4	2
%	%	%	**ASSETS**	%	%	%	%	%	%
18.6	22.4	23.1	Cash & Equivalents	22.8	29.5				
5.8	3.1	1.9	Trade Receivables (net)	.7	2.3				
7.1	4.0	5.4	Inventory	4.8	6.4				
.6	3.3	2.8	All Other Current	2.6	4.8				
32.1	32.9	33.2	Total Current	30.9	43.0				
46.8	50.7	49.7	Fixed Assets (net)	54.5	41.4				
6.3	9.2	8.4	Intangibles (net)	9.3	8.6				
14.8	7.2	8.7	All Other Non-Current	5.4	7.0				
100.0	100.0	100.0	Total	100.0	100.0				
			LIABILITIES						
5.7	14.8	7.0	Notes Payable-Short Term	6.5	10.8				
5.0	3.1	4.5	Cur. Mat.-L.T.D.	5.4	4.0				
4.6	3.5	2.1	Trade Payables	2.0	1.9				
.2	.0	.1	Income Taxes Payable	.1	.0				
20.9	12.2	10.5	All Other Current	8.5	20.2				
36.4	33.6	24.1	Total Current	22.4	36.9				
38.4	36.3	30.9	Long-Term Debt	36.9	26.6				
.0	.0	.0	Deferred Taxes	.0	.0				
8.7	10.4	13.9	All Other Non-Current	16.4	14.7				
16.5	19.7	31.0	Net Worth	24.2	21.9				
100.0	100.0	100.0	Total Liabilties & Net Worth	100.0	100.0				
			INCOME DATA						
100.0	100.0	100.0	Net Sales	100.0	100.0				
			Gross Profit						
87.8	88.2	85.0	Operating Expenses	80.7	91.0				
12.2	11.8	15.0	Operating Profit	19.3	9.0				
4.8	3.4	4.0	All Other Expenses (net)	6.3	.3				
7.4	8.5	11.0	Profit Before Taxes	13.0	8.7				
			RATIOS						
3.5	6.6	4.0		4.6	2.7				
1.3	2.2	1.8	Current	1.6	1.6				
.3	.7	.6		.5	.4				
3.0	6.0	3.1		3.1	2.1				
1.0	1.6	(92) 1.1	Quick	(56) 1.1	.9				
.2	.3	.4		.5	.4				
0 UND	0 UND	0 UND		0 UND	0 UND				
0 UND	0 UND	0 UND	Sales/Receivables	0 UND	0 UND				
7 50.0	2 161.9	2 231.1		0 UND	2 182.9				
			Cost of Sales/Inventory						
			Cost of Sales/Payables						
12.0	10.0	11.0		11.0	16.7				
47.2	30.8	34.0	Sales/Working Capital	55.3	44.1				
-9.4	-34.2	-27.3		-22.0	-16.4				
11.6	18.8	19.9		18.4	8.8				
(88) 3.2	(66) 2.9	(58) 5.6	EBIT/Interest	(37) 5.2	(11) 4.0				
.8	-.3	2.1		2.1	2.1				
			Net Profit + Depr., Dep., Amort./Cur. Mat. L/T/D						
.4	.6	.5		.7	.5				
2.0	1.4	1.3	Fixed/Worth	3.5	1.2				
-6.4	-5.1	417.7		-10.0	-5.2				
.4	.2	.3		.7	.3				
4.1	1.6	2.1	Debt/Worth	4.0	2.2				
-7.8	-6.8	-37.3		-11.6	-8.2				
84.5	97.6	95.9		119.8	105.1				
(79) 15.2	(76) 46.4	(69) 44.2	% Profit Before Taxes/Tangible Net Worth	(39) 56.6	(15) 68.6				
2.2	5.0	7.4		12.2	18.0				
23.4	41.4	39.4		39.4	51.9				
5.4	12.7	14.0	% Profit Before Taxes/Total Assets	14.0	24.0				
-1.3	-.5	3.1		3.1	6.4				
31.5	24.4	16.7		15.5	25.9				
5.0	7.4	6.0	Sales/Net Fixed Assets	2.5	11.9				
.9	1.7	1.1		.7	3.9				
4.1	5.2	5.7		4.9	7.3				
1.6	2.7	2.0	Sales/Total Assets	1.5	4.3				
.6	.9	.6		.5	2.3				
1.4	1.6	1.9		2.5	1.8				
(77) 3.9	(67) 2.4	(64) 4.4	% Depr., Dep., Amort./Sales	(36) 5.4	(16) 3.2				
7.2	6.6	6.7		9.4	5.0				
3.6	4.5	4.2		5.1	2.2				
(50) 8.2	(43) 8.8	(41) 7.6	% Officers', Directors' Owners' Comp/Sales	(23) 8.7	(14) 5.5				
14.3	13.7	13.9		16.1	9.0				
1535662M	244702M	254441M	Net Sales ($)	28799M	30251M	15826M	37314M	55432M	86819M
975439M	160992M	311809M	Total Assets ($)	41419M	18106M	11881M	71020M	78291M	91092M

M = $ thousand MM = $ million

See Pages 9 through 22 for Explanation of Ratios and Data

Current Data Sorted by Assets							Comparative Historical Data	
						Type of Statement		
		3	4	3		Unqualified	20	17
	2	4	3			Reviewed	11	9
1	1	1	1			Compiled	9	5
4	3	5	2			Tax Returns	14	18
4	11	8	20	1	2	Other	33	27
9 (4/1-9/30/13)		74 (10/1/13-3/31/14)					4/1/09-3/31/10	4/1/10-3/31/11
0-500M	500M-2MM	2-10MM	10-50MM	50-100MM	100-250MM		ALL	ALL
9	17	21	30	4	2	**NUMBER OF STATEMENTS**	87	76
%	%	%	%	%	%	**ASSETS**	%	%
	19.0	18.9	16.7			Cash & Equivalents	13.3	14.7
	17.5	11.2	9.4			Trade Receivables (net)	12.7	9.9
	.0	.3	.2			Inventory	1.7	.7
	14.7	8.0	3.9			All Other Current	4.1	2.9
	51.2	38.4	30.2			Total Current	31.9	28.2
	38.3	39.9	56.5			Fixed Assets (net)	51.7	53.5
	2.8	4.0	2.1			Intangibles (net)	7.8	7.5
	7.7	17.7	11.3			All Other Non-Current	8.6	10.8
	100.0	100.0	100.0			Total	100.0	100.0
						LIABILITIES		
	8.8	2.7	3.5			Notes Payable-Short Term	8.4	4.5
	9.1	1.9	1.9			Cur. Mat.-L.T.D.	6.9	7.4
	7.3	5.7	7.7			Trade Payables	6.8	4.1
	.0	.1	.2			Income Taxes Payable	.1	.0
	9.9	24.1	12.3			All Other Current	15.2	10.6
	35.1	34.6	25.6			Total Current	37.4	26.7
	37.3	40.3	45.8			Long-Term Debt	43.5	46.0
	.0	.0	.1			Deferred Taxes	.3	.3
	1.2	7.0	.9			All Other Non-Current	5.5	6.1
	26.4	18.1	27.6			Net Worth	13.3	20.9
	100.0	100.0	100.0			Total Liabilties & Net Worth	100.0	100.0
						INCOME DATA		
	100.0	100.0	100.0			Net Sales	100.0	100.0
						Gross Profit		
	77.5	76.9	79.7			Operating Expenses	82.4	83.0
	22.5	23.1	20.3			Operating Profit	17.6	17.0
	9.0	6.6	6.6			All Other Expenses (net)	10.1	10.3
	13.6	16.4	13.6			Profit Before Taxes	7.5	6.7
						RATIOS		
	2.9	3.1	4.2				2.0	2.8
	1.5	1.2	1.4			Current	.9	1.1
	.8	.5	.8				.5	.6
	2.2	1.9	3.4				1.6	2.0
	1.3	1.0	1.1			Quick	.7	1.0
	.6	.4	.6				.4	.4
	0 UND	0 UND	0 UND				0 UND	0 UND
	0 999.8	4 91.2	8 45.1			Sales/Receivables	8 45.7	5 68.9
	38 9.7	20 18.3	21 17.4				37 10.0	29 12.5
						Cost of Sales/Inventory		
						Cost of Sales/Payables		
	4.7	4.6	4.7				12.5	7.5
	22.8	173.0	21.2			Sales/Working Capital	-166.7	41.9
	-18.6	-11.2	-24.1				-7.8	-10.1
	30.9	17.4	34.7				10.2	8.8
	(13) 11.3	(14) 10.5	(23) 6.8			EBIT/Interest	(58) 3.2	(54) 3.4
	5.8	4.6	2.8				1.4	1.5
							17.1	
						Net Profit + Depr., Dep., Amort./Cur. Mat. L/T/D	(10) 3.5	
							.1	
	.4	.4	.9				1.3	.8
	1.6	1.7	1.6			Fixed/Worth	4.0	3.2
	109.3	5.2	NM				-5.6	-44.8
	.7	1.4	1.2				1.7	1.4
	1.9	2.2	2.6			Debt/Worth	5.6	5.0
	112.1	22.7	NM				-9.2	-34.4
	79.0	69.5	33.7				104.7	51.7
	(14) 55.3	(17) 21.3	(23) 21.8			% Profit Before Taxes/Tangible Net Worth	(61) 31.1	(55) 25.9
	20.9	13.2	11.4				1.3	1.4
	36.5	13.7	16.0				13.4	12.7
	16.8	8.6	8.4			% Profit Before Taxes/Total Assets	4.1	4.1
	6.9	3.2	3.4				-.2	.1
	32.0	59.4	19.2				25.9	19.7
	8.8	2.6	.8			Sales/Net Fixed Assets	1.6	1.4
	.4	.5	.4				.3	.3
	4.3	2.8	2.9				3.7	3.4
	2.0	1.0	.5			Sales/Total Assets	1.2	.8
	.2	.2	.3				.2	.2
	.9	.6	1.5				.9	1.9
	(12) 1.9	(18) 1.2	(28) 5.7			% Depr., Dep., Amort./Sales	(74) 5.8	(65) 6.2
	9.6	8.7	13.9				13.0	14.4
							1.7	1.4
						% Officers', Directors' Owners' Comp/Sales	(21) 4.2	(15) 3.4
							11.3	12.3
14262M	44356M	198079M	1404818M	99456M	152296M	Net Sales ($)	2325808M	1446154M
1653M	18452M	92029M	650049M	273460M	374104M	Total Assets ($)	1955832M	1667018M

M = $ thousand MM = $ million

See Pages 9 through 22 for Explanation of Ratios and Data

Comparative Historical Data				Current Data Sorted by Sales					
			Type of Statement						
8	9	10	Unqualified			1	2	4	3
9	8	9	Reviewed			2	1	1	5
7	4	4	Compiled	1	1	2			
26	11	14	Tax Returns	5	5		2	1	1
38	50	46	Other	12	6	6	9	4	9
4/1/11-3/31/12 ALL	4/1/12-3/31/13 ALL	4/1/13-3/31/14 ALL		9 (4/1-9/30/13)			74 (10/1/13-3/31/14)		
				0-1MM	1-3MM	3-5MM	5-10MM	10-25MM	25MM & OVER
88	82	83	**NUMBER OF STATEMENTS**	18	12	11	14	10	18
%	%	%	**ASSETS**	%	%	%	%	%	%
14.3	15.1	20.4	Cash & Equivalents	15.1	22.7	19.7	24.2	24.6	19.5
13.3	11.8	10.7	Trade Receivables (net)	6.1	7.8	6.4	5.5	10.1	24.4
.9	.1	.2	Inventory	.1	.0	.0	.5	.0	.3
5.0	4.0	6.8	All Other Current	15.2	2.4	1.3	10.9	.9	4.8
33.5	31.1	38.2	Total Current	36.4	32.9	27.4	41.2	35.5	49.1
47.4	46.8	46.0	Fixed Assets (net)	49.7	51.1	56.2	47.7	50.5	29.0
5.1	5.2	2.5	Intangibles (net)	1.4	2.4	2.7	.4	7.3	2.4
14.0	17.0	13.3	All Other Non-Current	12.5	13.6	13.7	10.7	6.6	19.5
100.0	100.0	100.0	Total	100.0	100.0	100.0	100.0	100.0	100.0
			LIABILITIES						
5.1	6.6	4.2	Notes Payable-Short Term	.1	7.1	2.9	7.9	1.2	6.1
4.1	2.8	4.2	Cur. Mat.-L.T.D.	2.9	7.5	9.8	.9	3.2	3.0
6.0	6.8	6.8	Trade Payables	3.5	2.2	.9	7.6	9.4	14.7
.0	.1	.1	Income Taxes Payable	.0	.0	.0	.1	.0	.3
13.9	15.1	22.5	All Other Current	50.3	4.9	8.8	15.6	8.3	28.2
29.1	31.4	37.8	Total Current	56.9	21.7	22.4	32.0	22.0	52.3
47.7	45.0	41.4	Long-Term Debt	47.7	48.3	52.7	40.2	45.4	22.1
.1	.5	.1	Deferred Taxes	.0	.0	.0	.0	.0	.2
6.4	4.7	3.1	All Other Non-Current	3.8	4.2	1.0	5.5	1.6	2.1
16.7	18.5	17.6	Net Worth	-8.5	25.8	23.9	22.3	31.0	23.3
100.0	100.0	100.0	Total Liabilties & Net Worth	100.0	100.0	100.0	100.0	100.0	100.0
			INCOME DATA						
100.0	100.0	100.0	Net Sales	100.0	100.0	100.0	100.0	100.0	100.0
			Gross Profit						
79.4	79.4	80.3	Operating Expenses	63.2	84.0	83.1	80.7	76.8	94.7
20.6	20.6	19.7	Operating Profit	36.8	16.0	16.9	19.3	23.2	5.3
8.8	6.5	6.8	All Other Expenses (net)	15.2	7.2	6.1	5.3	5.1	.8
11.9	14.1	12.9	Profit Before Taxes	21.6	8.8	10.8	13.9	18.0	4.5
			RATIOS						
3.2	2.8	3.2		2.6	3.6	2.6	5.0	5.4	1.5
1.2	1.1	1.3	Current	.8	2.4	1.4	1.3	2.9	1.1
.6	.5	.6		.3	1.0	.6	.4	.8	.8
2.5	2.1	2.5		1.7	2.9	2.6	3.0	5.2	1.4
1.0	.9	1.1	Quick	.5	1.8	1.1	.8	2.8	1.1
.4	.5	.4		.1	1.0	.6	.1	.8	.6
0 UND	0 999.8	0 UND		0 UND	0 UND	0 UND	0 999.8	2 153.9	9 41.3
8 45.1	8 43.6	4 87.6	Sales/Receivables	0 UND	0 UND	0 UND	1 250.8	15 25.0	18 20.8
30 12.3	31 11.9	25 14.6		5 69.5	6 60.9	17 21.6	20 18.5	28 13.2	35 10.3
			Cost of Sales/Inventory						
			Cost of Sales/Payables						
7.4	5.8	5.1		1.1	5.1	9.0	3.0	1.7	19.5
52.8	125.3	46.4	Sales/Working Capital	-16.5	23.2	23.9	21.9	9.8	75.3
-14.9	-11.8	-14.0		-2.5	NM	-14.8	-10.9	-129.9	-22.5
15.3	8.8	24.4					14.8		32.2
(60) 5.1	(58) 4.7	(60) 7.9	EBIT/Interest				(11) 6.8		(16) 7.6
1.3	2.6	3.9					2.8		2.9
4.0	22.1	8.5							
(14) 2.5	(12) 3.5	(12) 3.3	Net Profit + Depr., Dep., Amort./Cur. Mat. L/T/D						
1.0	1.1	1.1							
.5	.4	.6		.4	.7	.4	.5	.6	.5
2.1	1.9	1.7	Fixed/Worth	1.8	2.0	2.2	1.5	1.0	1.3
-5.2	-23.1	13.3		21.2	6.8	-17.6	-18.4	-1.3	6.3
1.0	1.3	1.2		1.1	.9	.6	1.0	.4	1.8
3.0	3.3	2.8	Debt/Worth	2.5	4.1	2.8	1.6	1.3	3.4
-12.0	-18.9	155.9		NM	12.8	-25.6	-31.7	-2.5	13.0
50.4	53.8	62.9		56.5	76.2				75.8
(60) 24.9	(55) 28.5	(63) 23.5	% Profit Before Taxes/Tangible Net Worth	(14) 18.0	(10) 24.4				(15) 31.2
7.3	6.6	12.0		-1.9	3.5				17.8
13.2	15.8	17.6		14.6	31.3	41.4	18.4	19.2	17.3
6.9	9.1	10.2	% Profit Before Taxes/Total Assets	7.7	11.9	8.6	7.4	13.7	10.3
.9	2.3	2.5		-.6	1.1	2.7	2.4	7.5	4.0
42.1	32.9	34.5		111.9	17.8	26.6	50.9	37.6	88.9
4.0	2.9	2.6	Sales/Net Fixed Assets	.4	7.1	2.1	1.4	1.4	19.8
.4	.5	.4		.2	.3	.2	.5	.7	3.4
4.1	2.8	3.8		1.1	5.9	3.7	1.5	3.2	5.4
1.1	.9	1.0	Sales/Total Assets	.2	2.0	1.0	.6	.9	3.6
.3	.3	.3		.1	.2	.2	.4	.5	2.3
.8	.8	.8		3.4		1.3	.6		.4
(73) 3.8	(64) 4.8	(69) 3.6	% Depr., Dep., Amort./Sales	(10) 12.9		(10) 5.1	4.6		(17) .7
10.1	14.5	11.7		30.9		8.3	12.6		2.6
.9	1.3	1.9							
(27) 3.2	(16) 4.3	(22) 3.1	% Officers', Directors' Owners' Comp/Sales						
7.9	16.0	11.7							
1435694M	2398249M	1913267M	Net Sales ($)	7456M	25170M	40129M	101223M	160018M	1579271M
1328581M	1814759M	1409747M	Total Assets ($)	26836M	51248M	110441M	224677M	237789M	758756M

M = $ thousand MM = $ million

See Pages 9 through 22 for Explanation of Ratios and Data

Current Data Sorted by Assets							Comparative Historical Data	
						Type of Statement		
1	3	10	3	2	1	Unqualified	37	28
	3	7	2			Reviewed	34	21
7	9	5	1			Compiled	103	58
95	48	15	2			Tax Returns	280	210
52	46	33	12	4		Other	218	156
29 (4/1-9/30/13)		332 (10/1/13-3/31/14)					4/1/09-3/31/10 ALL	4/1/10-3/31/11 ALL
0-500M	500M-2MM	2-10MM	10-50MM	50-100MM	100-250MM			
155	109	70	20	6	1	**NUMBER OF STATEMENTS**	672	473
%	%	%	%	%	%	**ASSETS**	%	%
33.2	20.8	12.5	11.8			Cash & Equivalents	19.0	19.3
8.1	16.6	26.3	9.6			Trade Receivables (net)	15.8	14.0
5.3	4.8	5.2	8.0			Inventory	8.2	5.8
1.9	4.1	2.0	4.9			All Other Current	2.8	3.3
48.6	46.3	46.0	34.2			Total Current	45.9	42.4
33.1	33.0	37.0	43.4			Fixed Assets (net)	37.0	38.7
6.7	10.4	6.5	10.6			Intangibles (net)	5.8	7.8
11.6	10.3	10.5	11.7			All Other Non-Current	11.3	11.0
100.0	100.0	100.0	100.0			Total	100.0	100.0
						LIABILITIES		
17.0	11.0	4.7	4.6			Notes Payable-Short Term	12.1	8.9
5.0	3.0	3.1	4.7			Cur. Mat.-L.T.D.	4.6	4.7
6.7	9.4	13.9	7.4			Trade Payables	9.1	7.6
.0	.9	.7	.3			Income Taxes Payable	.2	.1
19.9	11.5	9.9	20.0			All Other Current	17.7	16.9
48.6	35.9	32.4	37.1			Total Current	43.6	38.3
22.3	26.7	29.4	14.8			Long-Term Debt	29.0	31.1
.0	.1	.4	.7			Deferred Taxes	.1	.1
23.3	6.9	5.2	5.9			All Other Non-Current	9.6	13.4
5.8	30.4	32.6	41.6			Net Worth	17.6	17.1
100.0	100.0	100.0	100.0			Total Liabilities & Net Worth	100.0	100.0
						INCOME DATA		
100.0	100.0	100.0	100.0			Net Sales	100.0	100.0
						Gross Profit		
92.3	89.8	87.7	93.8			Operating Expenses	91.7	89.7
7.7	10.2	12.3	6.2			Operating Profit	8.3	10.3
.8	1.7	2.3	1.3			All Other Expenses (net)	3.0	2.9
6.9	8.5	10.0	4.9			Profit Before Taxes	5.3	7.4
						RATIOS		
4.8	3.3	2.6	1.3				3.7	3.1
1.2	1.3	1.4	1.0			Current	1.3	1.3
.5	.8	.8	.6				.5	.6
3.7	2.7	2.2	1.1				2.7	2.4
1.0	1.0	1.0	.8			Quick	(671) 1.0	(471) 1.0
.3	.4	.3	.2				.3	.3
0 UND	0 UND	0 UND	1 666.0				0 UND	0 UND
0 UND	2 174.9	21 17.4	5 73.4			Sales/Receivables	5 77.0	0 999.8
1 330.2	30 12.3	49 7.5	40 9.2				37 9.9	31 11.8
						Cost of Sales/Inventory		
						Cost of Sales/Payables		
11.4	11.2	7.2	11.2				7.2	9.7
71.0	31.8	16.3	178.5			Sales/Working Capital	38.2	65.6
-20.1	-41.9	-20.2	-12.0				-17.0	-17.8
18.4	18.9	92.9	23.3				14.1	18.5
(80) 5.0	(84) 7.2	(53) 14.3	(16) 5.2			EBIT/Interest	(499) 3.0	(343) 4.5
1.0	2.1	1.9	.6				.4	1.4
							25.3	12.7
						Net Profit + Depr., Dep., Amort./Cur. Mat. L/T/D	(40) 2.3	(20) 3.3
							.7	1.5
.1	.2	.1	.5				.2	.2
1.5	1.1	1.1	1.2			Fixed/Worth	1.4	1.5
-2.3	128.5	4.0	5.2				-21.4	-6.6
.5	.8	.7	.7				.7	.8
3.6	3.1	1.8	3.4			Debt/Worth	3.1	2.7
-4.9	-144.1	7.6	5.5				-17.6	-12.6
168.4	173.1	73.5	60.4				71.2	96.9
(106) 67.5	(80) 70.1	(61) 29.0	(18) 25.9			% Profit Before Taxes/Tangible Net Worth	(485) 24.4	(330) 37.2
13.3	19.8	12.5	-1.3				2.6	6.1
48.6	36.0	23.8	21.2				22.6	35.1
17.6	14.4	9.6	7.5			% Profit Before Taxes/Total Assets	6.7	10.0
.0	2.7	2.9	-.3				-1.1	.8
190.0	67.7	82.0	20.5				59.9	55.8
25.8	15.2	6.9	3.3			Sales/Net Fixed Assets	12.8	12.9
8.8	5.0	2.1	1.5				3.2	3.1
9.7	4.3	3.5	2.5				4.4	5.1
5.0	2.7	2.2	1.3			Sales/Total Assets	2.5	2.7
2.9	1.5	1.0	.8				1.3	1.3
.7	.7	.6	.9				.8	.9
(75) 2.4	(67) 2.0	(49) 2.1	(18) 4.2			% Depr., Dep., Amort./Sales	(474) 2.6	(319) 2.9
4.7	4.7	9.2	7.8				7.1	7.2
3.9	2.4	1.0					3.0	2.7
(83) 7.8	(50) 3.9	(24) 1.9				% Officers', Directors' Owners' Comp/Sales	(285) 5.7	(212) 5.8
13.4	7.2	4.2					10.8	11.1
166946M	357364M	802998M	661601M	2054448M	157007M	Net Sales ($)	7583258M	6472785M
29560M	108959M	332252M	464656M	420150M	175172M	Total Assets ($)	3520629M	3500846M

M = $ thousand MM = $ million

See Pages 9 through 22 for Explanation of Ratios and Data

Comparative Historical Data | Current Data Sorted by Sales

4/1/11-3/31/12 ALL	4/1/12-3/31/13 ALL	4/1/13-3/31/14 ALL	Type of Statement	0-1MM	1-3MM	3-5MM	5-10MM	10-25MM	25MM & OVER
35	26	20	Unqualified	2	1	3	2	4	8
15	11	12	Reviewed		3	2	2	4	1
51	49	22	Compiled	7	6	2	4	1	2
224	178	160	Tax Returns	70	56	10	14	7	3
198	169	147	Other	43	36	21	17	18	12
					29 (4/1-9/30/13)		332 (10/1/13-3/31/14)		
523	433	361	NUMBER OF STATEMENTS	122	102	38	39	34	26
%	%	%	**ASSETS**	%	%	%	%	%	%
22.7	24.6	24.0	Cash & Equivalents	29.0	23.8	25.7	17.4	15.2	19.8
14.8	14.4	14.4	Trade Receivables (net)	5.1	11.5	20.1	27.5	30.0	20.3
4.8	5.4	5.2	Inventory	3.0	7.2	5.7	4.4	6.5	6.7
3.4	4.1	2.8	All Other Current	2.5	3.0	3.4	.6	3.4	4.7
45.7	48.6	46.3	Total Current	39.6	45.6	54.9	49.9	55.1	51.6
36.1	32.6	34.2	Fixed Assets (net)	41.3	35.0	24.2	30.4	28.7	24.7
5.2	7.1	8.4	Intangibles (net)	6.6	11.2	10.1	5.6	6.3	11.2
13.0	11.7	11.1	All Other Non-Current	12.6	8.2	10.8	14.0	9.9	12.5
100.0	100.0	100.0	Total	100.0	100.0	100.0	100.0	100.0	100.0
			LIABILITIES						
11.9	10.8	11.8	Notes Payable-Short Term	12.0	11.1	26.4	8.5	8.0	2.3
3.6	4.5	4.0	Cur. Mat.-L.T.D.	4.8	3.7	1.6	4.9	3.9	4.2
8.3	10.5	9.0	Trade Payables	3.1	10.2	8.2	15.0	16.8	13.6
.0	.1	.4	Income Taxes Payable	.0	.3	1.8	.1	.2	1.7
15.6	15.8	15.7	All Other Current	15.6	16.9	15.9	9.3	14.4	22.3
39.3	41.7	40.9	Total Current	35.5	42.2	54.0	37.7	43.3	44.2
25.3	28.4	24.8	Long-Term Debt	30.7	28.6	13.6	24.6	11.2	17.0
.1	.1	.2	Deferred Taxes	.0	.0	.4	.2	.5	1.1
12.0	11.0	13.6	All Other Non-Current	18.6	18.7	4.0	6.3	5.4	6.2
23.3	18.8	20.4	Net Worth	15.1	10.5	28.0	31.2	39.8	31.4
100.0	100.0	100.0	Total Liabilties & Net Worth	100.0	100.0	100.0	100.0	100.0	100.0
			INCOME DATA						
100.0	100.0	100.0	Net Sales	100.0	100.0	100.0	100.0	100.0	100.0
			Gross Profit						
90.4	91.2	90.8	Operating Expenses	87.7	92.6	90.9	93.3	90.5	94.3
9.6	8.8	9.2	Operating Profit	12.3	7.4	9.1	6.7	9.5	5.7
2.7	1.6	1.4	All Other Expenses (net)	3.1	.5	.5	.2	.8	.9
6.9	7.1	7.8	Profit Before Taxes	9.2	6.9	8.6	6.5	8.7	4.8
			RATIOS						
3.3	3.5	3.2		5.1	2.8	3.4	3.0	2.3	2.0
1.3	1.3	1.2	Current	1.6	1.1	1.3	1.4	1.2	1.2
.5	.6	.6		.5	.5	.8	1.0	.9	.8
2.6	2.8	2.5		4.4	1.8	2.3	2.4	2.1	1.6
1.1	(432) 1.1	1.0	Quick	1.1	.7	1.0	1.3	1.0	.9
.4	.3	.3		.3	.2	.4	.6	.4	.5
0 UND	0 UND	0 UND		0 UND	0 UND	0 UND	0 UND	2 190.8	2 155.9
1 277.2	1 497.0	0 UND	Sales/Receivables	0 UND	1 453.0	12 30.4	10 37.1	26 14.3	12 31.5
28 13.0	26 14.2	25 14.5		0 UND	20 18.4	36 10.1	56 6.5	69 5.3	43 8.4
			Cost of Sales/Inventory						
			Cost of Sales/Payables						
9.1	8.8	10.6		7.6	16.0	12.5	7.3	10.7	9.1
45.0	41.1	42.6	Sales/Working Capital	34.7	74.8	35.2	21.3	35.4	55.2
-24.3	-20.9	-23.7		-15.0	-20.4	-44.2	-999.8	-270.5	-23.9
14.7	22.9	31.5		14.0	15.2	73.3	43.8	262.5	80.2
(332) 4.1	(293) 5.0	(240) 6.5	EBIT/Interest	(67) 4.3	(66) 5.1	(26) 10.0	(30) 12.2	(29) 16.9	(22) 23.6
1.1	1.3	1.6		.7	2.6	1.1	2.6	4.0	1.3
7.3	13.1	36.7							
(18) 2.6	(19) 2.8	(12) 2.6	Net Profit + Depr., Dep., Amort./Cur. Mat. L/T/D						
.7	2.0	1.9							
.1	.1	.2		.2	.3	.1	.1	.1	.1
1.0	1.0	1.3	Fixed/Worth	1.5	2.1	.7	.8	.8	1.1
18.9	UND	UND		-7.1	-2.5	UND	4.0	4.4	4.3
.6	.7	.7		.5	1.0	.4	.7	.6	.9
1.9	2.6	2.7	Debt/Worth	3.3	4.8	1.6	1.5	1.9	3.4
UND	-35.8	-76.3		-9.0	-4.5	-28.3	8.9	6.4	14.1
104.0	104.8	134.2		128.8	172.8	225.3	81.1	119.1	83.0
(393) 35.6	(315) 47.3	(267) 51.7	% Profit Before Taxes/Tangible Net Worth	(84) 41.5	(70) 67.1	(28) 66.1	(33) 34.8	(31) 54.8	(21) 27.7
4.2	8.8	13.7		5.2	19.6	19.1	22.3	20.0	2.6
36.4	42.2	37.8		38.1	33.6	68.1	36.2	45.9	29.2
10.7	10.7	13.2	% Profit Before Taxes/Total Assets	9.9	14.4	21.4	13.9	17.4	8.1
.1	.9	2.1		-.7	2.9	1.0	3.6	5.6	1.5
71.3	103.6	95.6		77.8	77.7	279.2	100.6	98.2	279.8
15.2	19.2	17.0	Sales/Net Fixed Assets	10.4	18.1	45.1	28.4	12.2	27.7
4.3	5.3	5.5		2.3	6.7	10.5	6.1	4.9	5.5
6.0	5.5	5.7		5.3	6.6	6.3	5.4	4.3	4.3
3.0	3.1	3.3	Sales/Total Assets	2.5	3.8	4.1	3.6	3.1	2.8
1.3	1.5	1.6		1.0	2.1	3.0	1.9	1.7	1.9
.9	.7	.7		1.3	1.1	.3	.6	.7	.2
(316) 2.6	(253) 2.2	(212) 2.4	% Depr., Dep., Amort./Sales	(66) 3.3	(56) 2.8	(21) .7	(26) 1.3	(24) 2.1	(19) 1.2
6.0	5.3	5.7		9.6	5.3	3.3	3.3	4.4	5.1
2.8	2.8	2.4		3.8	2.4	3.6	1.7	.9	
(214) 5.3	(180) 6.0	(164) 4.7	% Officers', Directors' Owners' Comp/Sales	(53) 7.6	(54) 5.0	(21) 5.1	(16) 3.7	(14) 2.0	
11.0	12.3	10.3		13.6	9.8	8.9	8.9	3.6	
7644637M	5692677M	4200364M	Net Sales ($)	58247M	184929M	149071M	260533M	506133M	3041451M
3001560M	2312088M	1530749M	Total Assets ($)	57911M	95424M	71907M	107914M	273371M	924222M

M = $ thousand MM = $ million

See Pages 9 through 22 for Explanation of Ratios and Data

Current Data Sorted by Assets / Comparative Historical Data

0-500M	500M-2MM	2-10MM	10-50MM	50-100MM	100-250MM	Type of Statement	4/1/09-3/31/10 ALL	4/1/10-3/31/11 ALL
5	24	129	271	52	25	Unqualified	507	526
1	11	167	79	2	3	Reviewed	264	261
9	61	206	43	1		Compiled	291	329
3	7	7	1			Tax Returns	10	13
99	272	739	249	17	12	Other	1324	1537
861 (4/1-9/30/13)			1,634 (10/1/13-3/31/14)					
117	375	1248	643	72	40	NUMBER OF STATEMENTS	2396	2666
%	%	%	%	%	%	**ASSETS**	%	%
54.0	18.6	9.3	11.0	20.6	35.1	Cash & Equivalents	13.9	14.1
1.8	.8	.6	1.3	5.3	5.4	Trade Receivables (net)	1.4	1.2
.6	.7	.2	.2	.5	.3	Inventory	.3	.3
1.4	.9	.5	1.2	4.3	6.5	All Other Current	1.0	1.2
57.8	20.9	10.6	13.7	30.8	47.3	Total Current	16.7	16.8
35.1	74.5	85.8	78.1	47.9	27.6	Fixed Assets (net)	76.5	76.5
.5	.3	.2	.4	.2	.4	Intangibles (net)	.2	.3
6.6	4.3	3.4	7.8	21.1	24.7	All Other Non-Current	6.6	6.4
100.0	100.0	100.0	100.0	100.0	100.0	Total	100.0	100.0
						LIABILITIES		
2.1	2.4	1.1	1.2	1.6	.7	Notes Payable-Short Term	2.7	1.9
2.1	2.2	1.9	2.0	2.5	.3	Cur. Mat.-L.T.D.	2.0	2.0
2.3	.8	.5	.8	1.6	2.1	Trade Payables	1.1	1.1
.0	.0	.0	.0	.0	.0	Income Taxes Payable	.0	.0
10.8	3.4	1.6	2.5	7.8	13.1	All Other Current	3.5	3.7
17.4	8.8	5.1	6.5	13.5	16.1	Total Current	9.4	8.6
49.9	38.4	32.9	26.2	14.6	13.3	Long-Term Debt	33.8	32.8
.0	.0	.0	.0	.0	.0	Deferred Taxes	.0	.0
1.5	.8	.8	2.4	8.9	14.0	All Other Non-Current	2.0	2.1
31.2	52.0	61.3	64.8	63.0	56.6	Net Worth	54.9	56.4
100.0	100.0	100.0	100.0	100.0	100.0	Total Liabilties & Net Worth	100.0	100.0
						INCOME DATA		
100.0	100.0	100.0	100.0	100.0	100.0	Net Sales	100.0	100.0
						Gross Profit		
88.6	85.0	86.2	89.2	92.3	82.3	Operating Expenses	88.7	87.9
11.4	15.0	13.8	10.8	7.7	17.7	Operating Profit	11.3	12.1
3.2	7.0	6.1	3.7	3.0	3.5	All Other Expenses (net)	7.2	6.7
8.2	8.0	7.7	7.1	4.7	14.2	Profit Before Taxes	4.1	5.4
						RATIOS		
24.5	9.7	8.4	7.4	10.2	10.8		8.0	8.2
6.6	2.8	2.8	2.9	2.4	3.8	Current	2.6	2.6
1.9	1.1	1.0	1.2	1.2	1.6		.9	.9
24.5	9.5	8.1	7.0	9.2	10.4		7.4	7.5
6.0	2.6	2.6	2.6	2.0	3.2	Quick	2.3	2.3
1.6	.9	1.0	1.1	1.0	1.3		.8	.8
0 UND	0 UND	0 UND	0 UND	0 UND	0 UND		0 UND	0 UND
0 UND	0 UND	0 UND	0 UND	13 28.5	15 24.2	Sales/Receivables	0 UND	0 UND
0 UND	0 UND	0 UND	3 110.3	51 7.1	47 7.8		1 294.2	1 577.5
						Cost of Sales/Inventory		
						Cost of Sales/Payables		
2.5	3.4	3.4	2.7	.9	.4		3.2	3.0
5.9	9.1	7.6	6.1	3.5	1.2	Sales/Working Capital	9.2	8.6
34.8	127.0	185.5	37.6	28.9	6.3		-81.0	-95.7
5.5	3.7	3.7	5.0	13.2	16.4		3.1	3.2
(46) 2.8	(201) 2.0	(927) 1.9	(474) 2.1	(49) 3.7	(27) 4.8	EBIT/Interest	(1558) 1.4	(1732) 1.5
1.3	1.0	1.0	.7	1.9	1.8		.5	.6
						Net Profit + Depr., Dep., Amort./Cur. Mat. L/T/D		
.0	.9	1.1	.9	.3	.2		1.0	1.0
.2	1.5	1.4	1.2	.7	.3	Fixed/Worth	1.4	1.3
1.5	2.3	2.0	1.8	1.2	.6		2.1	2.0
.1	.3	.3	.2	.2	.3		.3	.3
.3	.8	.6	.5	.5	.6	Debt/Worth	.7	.6
3.9	1.8	1.2	1.1	1.3	1.9		1.5	1.4
39.9	12.4	7.3	7.3	6.6	10.2		6.2	6.5
(100) 11.5	(356) 3.6	(1239) 2.2	(637) 2.1	2.6	5.0	% Profit Before Taxes/Tangible Net Worth	(2333) 1.2	(2587) 1.6
-1.5	.0	-.1	-.4	.1	1.9		-2.1	-1.0
30.2	5.9	3.9	4.2	4.1	5.8		3.5	3.7
8.5	1.9	1.4	1.5	1.4	2.5	% Profit Before Taxes/Total Assets	.7	.9
-1.2	-.1	-.1	-.3	.1	.9		-1.2	-.7
UND	1.0	.5	.6	2.3	3.7		.7	.7
20.1	.5	.3	.3	.8	1.9	Sales/Net Fixed Assets	.4	.4
1.5	.2	.2	.2	.3	.9		.2	.2
3.9	.7	.4	.4	.4	.5		.5	.5
1.8	.4	.3	.3	.3	.3	Sales/Total Assets	.3	.3
.9	.2	.2	.2	.2	.2		.2	.2
1.3	3.1	5.5	6.0	1.6	1.6		4.5	4.1
(19) 2.4	(137) 6.6	(613) 9.2	(431) 9.0	(57) 4.4	(33) 2.4	% Depr., Dep., Amort./Sales	(1187) 8.1	(1346) 8.4
8.2	11.3	13.4	13.2	10.4	5.6		12.3	12.3
10.9	7.0	5.7	4.9	7.1			5.1	4.4
(17) 15.0	(59) 14.9	(134) 12.7	(65) 10.4	(10) 11.7		% Officers', Directors' Owners' Comp/Sales	(312) 12.8	(301) 12.2
27.2	24.4	25.0	21.9	19.6			24.7	22.7
77449M	300889M	2294277M	4886190M	1752097M	1813798M	Net Sales ($)	14053686M	13993502M
30442M	483520M	6275672M	12964615M	4884578M	6008451M	Total Assets ($)	33925080M	35798224M

M = $ thousand MM = $ million

See Pages 9 through 22 for Explanation of Ratios and Data

Comparative Historical Data | Current Data Sorted by Sales

4/1/11-3/31/12 ALL	4/1/12-3/31/13 ALL	4/1/13-3/31/14 ALL	Type of Statement	0-1MM	1-3MM	3-5MM	5-10MM	10-25MM	25MM & OVER
558	564	506	Unqualified	23	82	98	121	126	56
298	293	263	Reviewed	33	133	53	33	9	2
395	375	320	Compiled	142	136	26	16		
12	14	18	Tax Returns	10	4		2	2	
1789	1620	1388	Other	708	434	121	66	38	21
				861 (4/1-9/30/13)			1,634 (10/1/13-3/31/14)		
3052	2866	2495	NUMBER OF STATEMENTS	916	789	298	238	175	79
%	%	%	ASSETS	%	%	%	%	%	%
14.0	14.9	14.0	Cash & Equivalents	13.6	11.9	12.4	15.2	19.8	28.4
1.1	1.1	1.1	Trade Receivables (net)	.3	.7	1.2	2.1	2.7	7.6
.2	.2	.3	Inventory	.1	.3	.2	.7	.5	.5
.9	.9	1.0	All Other Current	.4	.6	.7	1.8	3.8	3.5
16.1	17.1	16.3	Total Current	14.4	13.5	14.5	19.8	26.8	40.0
78.0	76.9	77.7	Fixed Assets (net)	81.8	82.7	79.5	72.7	57.8	34.2
.3	.3	.3	Intangibles (net)	.3	.3	.2	.6	.4	.4
5.6	5.7	5.6	All Other Non-Current	3.5	3.6	5.9	6.8	15.1	25.4
100.0	100.0	100.0	Total	100.0	100.0	100.0	100.0	100.0	100.0
			LIABILITIES						
1.9	1.7	1.4	Notes Payable-Short Term	1.6	1.3	1.2	.9	1.4	1.7
1.9	2.1	2.0	Cur. Mat.-L.T.D.	1.7	2.2	2.3	2.2	1.8	.7
1.1	1.0	.8	Trade Payables	.4	.6	.8	1.3	1.8	3.5
.0	.0	.0	Income Taxes Payable	.0	.0	.1	.0	.0	.0
3.3	3.9	2.9	All Other Current	2.1	2.1	2.8	3.8	6.3	10.0
8.2	8.7	7.0	Total Current	5.9	6.2	7.0	8.2	11.3	15.9
32.9	33.0	31.9	Long-Term Debt	36.7	33.8	30.3	26.2	18.4	12.0
.0	.0	.0	Deferred Taxes	.0	.0	.0	.0	.0	.0
1.9	2.1	1.7	All Other Non-Current	.5	.9	1.4	3.0	6.3	9.8
57.1	56.2	59.3	Net Worth	56.9	59.1	61.3	62.6	64.0	62.3
100.0	100.0	100.0	Total Liabilties & Net Worth	100.0	100.0	100.0	100.0	100.0	100.0
			INCOME DATA						
100.0	100.0	100.0	Net Sales	100.0	100.0	100.0	100.0	100.0	100.0
			Gross Profit						
87.1	86.8	87.0	Operating Expenses	83.7	87.8	89.3	89.2	91.6	93.2
12.9	13.2	13.0	Operating Profit	16.3	12.2	10.7	10.8	8.4	6.8
6.9	6.4	5.3	All Other Expenses (net)	7.8	5.4	3.4	3.4	.8	-.2
6.0	6.8	7.6	Profit Before Taxes	8.6	6.8	7.3	7.5	7.5	7.1
			RATIOS						
7.9	7.6	8.6		11.0	8.5	7.8	7.5	7.7	4.8
2.7	2.7	2.9	Current	2.9	3.0	2.9	3.1	2.4	2.5
.9	1.0	1.1		.9	1.2	1.3	1.3	1.2	1.3
7.6	7.3	8.2		10.9	8.2	7.1	7.1	6.5	4.5
(3051) 2.5	2.6	2.7	Quick	2.7	2.9	2.7	2.9	2.0	2.1
.8	.9	1.0		.9	1.1	1.1	1.3	1.1	1.1
0 UND	0 UND	0 UND		0 UND	0 UND	0 UND	0 UND	0 UND	0 999.8
0 UND	0 UND	0 UND	Sales/Receivables	0 UND	0 UND	0 UND	0 999.8	2 221.1	13 27.8
1 572.9	0 881.6	0 999.8		0 UND	0 UND	2 215.6	6 63.9	19 19.7	47 7.7
			Cost of Sales/Inventory						
			Cost of Sales/Payables						
3.2	3.1	3.0		3.1	3.2	3.3	2.8	1.9	1.8
8.3	7.5	7.0	Sales/Working Capital	7.8	7.0	6.5	6.6	6.3	3.8
-144.9	197.2	73.4		-161.6	57.4	28.6	30.0	32.9	24.3
3.3	3.5	4.1		3.5	3.6	4.1	7.5	9.4	12.9
(2085) 1.6	(1992) 1.7	(1724) 2.0	EBIT/Interest	(533) 1.9	(597) 1.8	(225) 1.9	(191) 2.8	(125) 3.8	(53) 5.3
.8	.8	1.0		1.0	1.0	.9	.8	1.2	1.6
			Net Profit + Depr., Dep., Amort./Cur. Mat. L/T/D						
1.0	1.0	1.0		1.1	1.0	.9	.9	.4	.3
1.4	1.4	1.3	Fixed/Worth	1.4	1.4	1.3	1.2	1.0	.5
2.0	2.0	1.9		2.0	2.0	1.9	1.8	1.4	.9
.3	.3	.2		.2	.2	.2	.2	.2	.3
.6	.6	.6	Debt/Worth	.6	.6	.6	.6	.5	.5
1.4	1.4	1.3		1.3	1.4	1.2	1.3	1.1	1.1
6.8	7.9	8.2		7.5	7.2	8.5	9.7	11.6	10.2
(2974) 1.8	(2780) 2.5	(2444) 2.6	% Profit Before Taxes/Tangible Net Worth	(886) 2.0	(778) 2.1	(291) 2.9	(237) 4.8	(173) 4.2	5.1
-.7	-.4	-.1		-.1	-.1	-.4	-.5	.5	-1.1
3.7	4.1	4.5		4.2	3.9	4.9	6.1	6.5	6.1
1.1	1.4	1.5	% Profit Before Taxes/Total Assets	1.2	1.4	1.7	2.8	2.8	3.1
-.4	-.3	-.1		-.1	-.1	-.2	-.3	.3	-.9
.6	.7	.7		.4	.5	.7	.9	1.5	5.8
.3	.4	.4	Sales/Net Fixed Assets	.2	.3	.4	.5	.8	2.3
.2	.2	.2		.2	.2	.3	.4	.5	1.1
.5	.5	.5		.4	.5	.5	.6	.6	1.0
.3	.3	.3	Sales/Total Assets	.2	.3	.4	.4	.4	.6
.2	.2	.2		.1	.2	.2	.3	.3	.4
4.6	4.6	4.8		5.5	5.9	5.9	5.4	2.7	1.3
(1487) 8.5	(1467) 8.4	(1290) 8.5	% Depr., Dep., Amort./Sales	(273) 10.7	(397) 9.6	(218) 9.1	(180) 7.5	(151) 6.6	(71) 2.1
12.8	12.6	13.0		17.2	13.3	12.8	10.4	9.6	4.4
5.5	4.7	6.1		8.6	3.9	4.7	2.1	1.8	
(341) 12.5	(300) 10.9	(288) 13.1	% Officers', Directors' Owners' Comp/Sales	(137) 17.6	(77) 8.9	(29) 8.8	(21) 11.3	(18) 9.7	
23.7	21.3	24.1		27.1	17.4	20.5	19.0	18.9	
15142979M	13809143M	11124700M	Net Sales ($)	498851M	1386732M	1153885M	1678348M	2723810M	3683074M
37677505M	36968951M	30647278M	Total Assets ($)	2562631M	5606305M	3657786M	4861067M	7191398M	6768091M

M = $ thousand MM = $ million

See Pages 9 through 22 for Explanation of Ratios and Data

Current Data Sorted by Assets							Comparative Historical Data	
						Type of Statement		
1	4	15	18	9	9	Unqualified	52	66
						Reviewed	2	
	1	1			1	Compiled		
1	1	3				Tax Returns		1
3	1	13	7	2	2	Other	19	14
66 (4/1-9/30/13)			26 (10/1/13-3/31/14)				4/1/09-3/31/10 ALL	4/1/10-3/31/11 ALL
0-500M	500M-2MM	2-10MM	10-50MM	50-100MM	100-250MM			
5	7	32	25	11	12	**NUMBER OF STATEMENTS**	73	81
%	%	%	%	%	%	**ASSETS**	%	%
		37.0	31.6	42.4	30.8	Cash & Equivalents	32.6	27.0
		11.5	6.9	6.4	1.1	Trade Receivables (net)	8.4	9.8
		1.4	.2	.0	.0	Inventory	.7	.3
		1.9	4.7	.9	11.0	All Other Current	2.7	4.8
		51.8	43.5	49.8	42.9	Total Current	44.3	42.0
		26.1	19.5	16.5	4.4	Fixed Assets (net)	30.4	28.3
		1.0	.4	.2	.1	Intangibles (net)	.4	.5
		21.1	36.6	33.6	52.7	All Other Non-Current	24.9	29.3
		100.0	100.0	100.0	100.0	Total	100.0	100.0
						LIABILITIES		
		.3	.8	.3	.0	Notes Payable-Short Term	2.8	4.8
		1.3	1.8	.1	.3	Cur. Mat.-L.T.D.	.6	1.4
		1.8	3.3	4.2	.8	Trade Payables	3.9	6.2
		.0	.0	.0	.0	Income Taxes Payable	.1	.0
		10.4	7.0	5.7	3.9	All Other Current	10.7	7.6
		13.9	12.9	10.3	5.0	Total Current	18.2	20.0
		15.5	13.4	9.3	10.3	Long-Term Debt	15.5	17.1
		.0	.0	.0	.0	Deferred Taxes	.0	.0
		5.3	6.2	5.8	5.1	All Other Non-Current	2.8	3.1
		65.4	67.6	74.5	79.6	Net Worth	63.5	59.8
		100.0	100.0	100.0	100.0	Total Liabilties & Net Worth	100.0	100.0
						INCOME DATA		
		100.0	100.0	100.0	100.0	Net Sales	100.0	100.0
						Gross Profit		
		85.4	77.1	67.2	68.8	Operating Expenses	83.0	82.0
		14.6	22.9	32.8	31.2	Operating Profit	17.0	18.0
		3.3	6.5	4.0	2.5	All Other Expenses (net)	10.7	3.8
		11.3	16.4	28.8	28.7	Profit Before Taxes	6.3	14.2
						RATIOS		
		19.9	11.7	16.1	53.7		12.9	9.0
		5.1	5.3	8.8	6.5	Current	2.5	2.5
		1.9	2.5	2.0	1.6		1.3	1.2
		19.8	11.6	15.4	46.8		11.9	9.0
		4.1	4.5	3.0	4.8	Quick	2.3	2.3
		1.4	2.3	1.8	.2		1.1	1.1
	0	UND	0 UND	0 999.8	0 UND		0 UND	0 UND
	12	31.0	4 102.0	22 16.6	1 516.3	Sales/Receivables	8 44.0	22 16.5
	65	5.6	52 7.0	146 2.5	61 6.0		61 6.0	103 3.5
						Cost of Sales/Inventory		
						Cost of Sales/Payables		
		1.0	.5	.2	.1		.7	.8
		2.3	1.8	.4	.4	Sales/Working Capital	2.8	3.4
		7.3	4.6	5.3	11.3		13.6	12.7
		31.6	23.9				10.1	11.6
		(15) 3.6	(16) 3.4			EBIT/Interest	(31) 2.8	(42) 4.2
		-5.2	-.8				-1.2	1.0
						Net Profit + Depr., Dep., Amort./Cur. Mat. L/T/D		
		.0	.0	.0	.0		.0	.0
		.2	.1	.1	.0	Fixed/Worth	.3	.4
		.8	.6	.6	.1		.8	1.3
		.1	.1	.0	.1		.1	.1
		.4	.4	.2	.2	Debt/Worth	.5	.5
		1.3	1.1	.9	.3		1.5	1.7
		17.8	12.3	9.8	9.3	% Profit Before Taxes/Tangible	11.1	13.1
		(31) 5.1	3.9	7.5	(11) 5.3	Net Worth	(69) 2.5	(76) 4.6
		-1.8	-1.5	.6	-2.7		-2.6	-.1
		7.5	10.4	7.9	7.6	% Profit Before Taxes/Total	6.3	7.9
		1.7	3.3	3.4	3.3	Assets	1.2	1.9
		-2.0	-1.1	.2	-1.7		-2.0	-.9
		349.1	73.4	278.7	UND		55.2	66.0
		3.9	8.0	4.7	11.2	Sales/Net Fixed Assets	2.5	4.1
		.7	1.5	.1	1.2		.4	.5
		1.3	.7	.2	.2		.7	.8
		.4	.3	.1	.1	Sales/Total Assets	.3	.3
		.2	.1	.1	.1		.1	.1
		.7	.6				.5	.6
		(21) 1.7	(17) 1.3			% Depr., Dep., Amort./Sales	(58) 2.0	(60) 2.4
		4.2	6.1				7.7	10.4
						% Officers', Directors' Owners' Comp/Sales		
1812M	33039M	109862M	353643M	138446M	248620M	Net Sales ($)	1064506M	1086093M
877M	8582M	162784M	667661M	805132M	1872554M	Total Assets ($)	3154483M	3359153M

M = $ thousand MM = $ million

See Pages 9 through 22 for Explanation of Ratios and Data

Comparative Historical Data				Current Data Sorted by Sales					
			Type of Statement						
67	79	56	Unqualified	4	6	9	14	12	11
	1		Reviewed						
3	2	3	Compiled	1	1			1	
3	1	5	Tax Returns	1	3		1		
20	29	28	Other	8	8	3	6	2	1
4/1/11-3/31/12 ALL	4/1/12-3/31/13 ALL	4/1/13-3/31/14 ALL		66 (4/1-9/30/13)			26 (10/1/13-3/31/14)		
				0-1MM	1-3MM	3-5MM	5-10MM	10-25MM	25MM & OVER
93	112	92	**NUMBER OF STATEMENTS**	14	18	12	21	15	12
%	%	%	**ASSETS**	%	%	%	%	%	%
34.5	36.5	37.3	Cash & Equivalents	53.8	32.5	32.2	34.1	36.7	36.4
7.5	5.6	7.4	Trade Receivables (net)	.8	1.1	5.3	17.1	4.8	13.2
.3	.5	1.7	Inventory	.9	5.3	.8	1.8	.2	.1
2.8	2.8	4.0	All Other Current	.8	4.3	3.9	2.3	7.3	6.3
45.1	45.3	50.4	Total Current	56.2	43.3	42.2	55.3	49.0	56.1
26.6	19.7	19.5	Fixed Assets (net)	34.2	26.4	25.4	13.5	4.9	14.9
.6	.5	.9	Intangibles (net)	.4	2.9	.4	.2	1.2	.2
27.8	34.4	29.1	All Other Non-Current	9.2	27.4	32.0	31.0	44.9	28.8
100.0	100.0	100.0	Total	100.0	100.0	100.0	100.0	100.0	100.0
			LIABILITIES						
2.9	2.0	1.8	Notes Payable-Short Term	3.8	1.7	.0	.8	3.8	.7
.8	1.0	1.4	Cur. Mat.-L.T.D.	2.3	2.8	.8	.4	1.5	.4
5.0	2.3	2.8	Trade Payables	2.0	.3	1.8	2.5	2.4	9.8
.0	.0	.0	Income Taxes Payable	.0	.0	.0	.0	.0	.0
7.6	6.7	10.5	All Other Current	26.6	4.4	5.8	9.0	8.5	10.9
16.4	12.0	16.5	Total Current	34.6	9.2	8.5	12.7	16.2	21.7
19.6	16.9	15.6	Long-Term Debt	23.7	10.1	16.3	6.9	32.1	8.3
.0	.0	.0	Deferred Taxes	.0	.0	.0	.0	.0	.0
4.6	4.0	6.7	All Other Non-Current	8.8	4.0	1.4	9.4	10.8	3.6
59.4	67.2	61.2	Net Worth	32.9	76.7	73.9	71.1	40.9	66.4
100.0	100.0	100.0	Total Liabilities & Net Worth	100.0	100.0	100.0	100.0	100.0	100.0
			INCOME DATA						
100.0	100.0	100.0	Net Sales	100.0	100.0	100.0	100.0	100.0	100.0
			Gross Profit						
76.7	81.4	80.4	Operating Expenses	88.5	77.2	100.6	67.2	70.8	90.8
23.3	18.6	19.6	Operating Profit	11.5	22.8	-.6	32.8	29.2	9.2
6.3	7.3	3.7	All Other Expenses (net)	7.4	1.2	1.4	7.1	3.0	.6
17.0	11.2	15.9	Profit Before Taxes	4.1	21.7	-2.0	25.7	26.3	8.6
			RATIOS						
16.3	16.6	15.7		18.4	26.0	16.6	17.6	19.6	8.0
5.1	5.7	5.3	Current	7.0	6.8	4.6	5.9	4.7	2.9
1.7	2.0	2.2		1.2	2.0	3.1	2.3	2.0	1.4
16.0	14.6	14.3		18.1	25.9	16.6	15.0	15.4	7.4
4.4	5.0	4.5	Quick	7.0	4.0	4.2	5.1	2.5	2.6
1.3	1.7	1.8		1.2	1.2	2.7	2.2	1.0	.9
0 UND	0 UND	0 UND		0 UND	0 UND	0 UND	0 UND	0 UND	0 785.8
14 26.4	2 190.4	5 78.8	Sales/Receivables	0 UND	0 UND	23 15.7	31 11.8	22 16.6	19 19.6
43 8.4	36 10.1	53 6.9		3 139.7	10 35.9	99 3.7	81 4.5	64 5.7	62 5.9
			Cost of Sales/Inventory						
			Cost of Sales/Payables						
.7	.4	.5		.3	.5	1.1	.5	.2	1.3
1.9	1.6	1.9	Sales/Working Capital	1.8	1.4	2.4	2.1	.5	2.7
12.4	7.8	6.0		NM	44.1	4.1	10.0	8.4	13.3
11.4	20.3	30.7			35.7		63.8		
(47) 4.0	(46) 2.8	(48) 4.0	EBIT/Interest		(12) 4.4		(13) 17.3		
1.3	-5.5	-1.0			.9		2.1		
			Net Profit + Depr., Dep., Amort./Cur. Mat. L/T/D						
.0	.0	.0		.0	.0	.0	.0	.0	.0
.3	.1	.1	Fixed/Worth	.6	.3	.2	.1	.0	.1
1.1	.6	.6		4.4	.7	.6	.4	.3	.6
.1	.1	.1		.1	.1	.1	.1	.0	.1
.5	.2	.3	Debt/Worth	.8	.2	.3	.3	.3	.3
1.8	1.0	.9		NM	.6	.8	.6	1.4	1.6
14.6	8.9	12.6		6.3	21.0	6.4	17.7	11.1	12.6
(87) 7.3	(110) 2.5	(87) 5.3	% Profit Before Taxes/Tangible Net Worth	(11) 1.3	5.9	.8	8.4	(13) 7.1	10.2
1.1	-1.8	-1.4		-.9	.8	-3.8	.7	-1.5	-5.6
8.5	6.2	9.5		8.3	15.3	5.6	12.5	7.8	11.0
2.9	1.8	3.4	% Profit Before Taxes/Total Assets	.7	3.5	.6	4.6	6.1	4.0
.2	-1.1	-.9		-1.2	.7	-3.6	.5	.4	-5.2
55.8	245.4	143.1		UND	UND	71.1	104.6	401.2	80.7
5.4	13.1	8.1	Sales/Net Fixed Assets	5.5	3.5	4.1	8.2	59.9	12.2
.8	1.0	1.4		.2	.5	.4	1.8	4.1	3.0
.9	.8	1.1		.8	.4	1.7	1.7	.3	1.3
.2	.2	.3	Sales/Total Assets	.2	.2	.6	.5	.1	.7
.1	.1	.1		.1	.1	.1	.2	.1	.3
.8	.4	.5			.3		.2	.1	
(74) 2.8	(76) 1.4	(63) 1.3	% Depr., Dep., Amort./Sales		(11) 1.4		(18) .6	(11) 1.4	
6.5	5.4	3.8			4.5		1.3	2.2	
			% Officers', Directors' Owners' Comp/Sales						
1653023M	1208676M	885422M	Net Sales ($)	6668M	28838M	49877M	150325M	203287M	446427M
4032233M	3907891M	3517590M	Total Assets ($)	46170M	157954M	227039M	659870M	1420593M	1005964M

M = $ thousand MM = $ million

See Pages 9 through 22 for Explanation of Ratios and Data

Current Data Sorted by Assets

Comparative Historical Data

0-500M	500M-2MM	2-10MM	10-50MM	50-100MM	100-250MM		4/1/09-3/31/10 ALL	4/1/10-3/31/11 ALL
						Type of Statement		
	2	17	8	3	3	Unqualified	73	53
1						Reviewed	1	1
		1				Compiled		1
	2	1				Tax Returns	1	
1	4	7	4			Other	12	28
	40 (4/1-9/30/13)		14 (10/1/13-3/31/14)					
2	8	26	12	3	3	**NUMBER OF STATEMENTS**	87	83
%	%	%	%	%	%	**ASSETS**	%	%
		27.2	29.6			Cash & Equivalents	25.8	25.4
		21.9	10.2			Trade Receivables (net)	17.9	15.3
		.3	.6			Inventory	1.5	.8
		1.3	2.9			All Other Current	4.2	6.6
		50.6	43.3			Total Current	49.5	48.0
		33.6	37.2			Fixed Assets (net)	32.4	38.6
		1.4	.1			Intangibles (net)	.8	1.0
		14.4	19.4			All Other Non-Current	17.3	12.4
		100.0	100.0			Total	100.0	100.0
						LIABILITIES		
		1.9	.0			Notes Payable-Short Term	2.8	3.4
		2.0	.9			Cur. Mat.-L.T.D.	1.9	1.3
		7.3	4.1			Trade Payables	10.2	9.7
		.0	.0			Income Taxes Payable	.1	.2
		9.4	14.9			All Other Current	14.6	10.8
		20.7	19.8			Total Current	29.6	25.5
		11.5	12.1			Long-Term Debt	15.6	17.2
		.0	.0			Deferred Taxes	.0	.1
		4.7	2.0			All Other Non-Current	2.7	2.3
		63.2	66.1			Net Worth	52.1	54.9
		100.0	100.0			Total Liabilities & Net Worth	100.0	100.0
						INCOME DATA		
		100.0	100.0			Net Sales	100.0	100.0
						Gross Profit		
		100.2	97.9			Operating Expenses	94.9	92.9
		-.2	2.1			Operating Profit	5.1	7.1
		.4	-.5			All Other Expenses (net)	2.2	1.6
		-.6	2.6			Profit Before Taxes	2.8	5.6
						RATIOS		
		3.8	4.8				4.3	3.9
		2.7	3.3			Current	2.0	2.0
		1.6	1.1				1.3	1.1
		3.8	4.7				3.5	3.4
		2.6	2.7			Quick	1.8	1.7
		1.6	1.0				1.0	.9
		30 12.3	**9** 38.6				**4** 85.3	**4** 84.2
		45 8.2	**28** 13.0			Sales/Receivables	**35** 10.5	**28** 13.1
		54 6.7	**38** 9.5				**54** 6.8	**49** 7.4
						Cost of Sales/Inventory		
						Cost of Sales/Payables		
		3.4	2.7				3.1	3.9
		5.6	4.3			Sales/Working Capital	6.5	7.8
		9.5	140.9				29.7	55.0
		11.5					8.9	19.5
		(17) 3.4				EBIT/Interest	(60) 2.3	(58) 4.8
		-1.0					.5	2.0
						Net Profit + Depr., Dep., Amort./Cur. Mat. L/T/D		
		.1	.1				.1	.2
		.6	.5			Fixed/Worth	.5	.7
		1.0	.9				1.4	1.3
		.3	.2				.3	.3
		.7	.5			Debt/Worth	.7	.8
		1.0	.9				2.6	2.0
		17.6	7.4				13.7	18.2
		3.5	-2.0			% Profit Before Taxes/Tangible Net Worth	(84) 2.5	(81) 7.6
		-7.3	-8.4				-5.8	1.3
		8.8	5.3				7.6	8.2
		1.1	-1.2			% Profit Before Taxes/Total Assets	.9	3.8
		-3.6	-4.8				-2.8	.8
		23.9	37.0				58.1	22.6
		5.9	2.9			Sales/Net Fixed Assets	5.3	4.1
		2.2	1.6				2.3	2.0
		2.0	1.8				2.6	2.3
		1.7	1.1			Sales/Total Assets	1.4	1.5
		1.0	.7				.7	.8
		1.0	.8				.8	1.2
		(23) 2.1	2.4			% Depr., Dep., Amort./Sales	(76) 1.9	(70) 2.1
		4.1	4.8				3.3	3.6
							2.3	
						% Officers', Directors' Owners' Comp/Sales	(11) 4.8	
							7.6	
944M	43368M	287047M	374203M	417504M	462105M	Net Sales ($)	2756757M	1949190M
218M	11363M	149355M	264513M	152463M	521941M	Total Assets ($)	1827531M	1689121M

M = $ thousand MM = $ million

See Pages 9 through 22 for Explanation of Ratios and Data

Comparative Historical Data				Current Data Sorted by Sales					
			Type of Statement						
66	44	33	Unqualified	1	2	1	7	10	12
1	1	1	Reviewed	1					
		1	Compiled		1				
2	1	3	Tax Returns	1		2			
17	18	16	Other	1	2	2	3	6	2
4/1/11-3/31/12 ALL	4/1/12-3/31/13 ALL	4/1/13-3/31/14 ALL		40 (4/1-9/30/13)			14 (10/1/13-3/31/14)		
				0-1MM	1-3MM	3-5MM	5-10MM	10-25MM	25MM & OVER
86	64	54	**NUMBER OF STATEMENTS**	4	5	5	10	16	14
%	%	%	**ASSETS**	%	%	%	%	%	%
28.9	25.4	29.9	Cash & Equivalents				31.7	29.4	34.2
19.8	15.5	17.8	Trade Receivables (net)				26.4	14.5	17.0
1.3	.8	1.0	Inventory				.0	.5	2.7
4.8	3.2	2.6	All Other Current				1.3	2.8	4.9
54.8	45.0	51.3	Total Current				59.4	47.2	58.8
28.2	38.4	32.4	Fixed Assets (net)				27.3	41.1	22.0
.3	.7	.8	Intangibles (net)				1.9	1.1	.4
16.7	15.9	15.5	All Other Non-Current				11.4	10.7	18.9
100.0	100.0	100.0	Total				100.0	100.0	100.0
			LIABILITIES						
2.6	2.2	1.2	Notes Payable-Short Term				.8	1.7	.8
.8	.8	1.4	Cur. Mat.-L.T.D.				1.3	1.5	1.2
11.1	5.9	7.2	Trade Payables				6.3	6.8	6.3
.1	.1	.0	Income Taxes Payable				.0	.0	.0
12.2	10.7	14.1	All Other Current				16.0	8.8	21.8
26.8	19.8	23.9	Total Current				24.3	18.8	30.1
10.1	16.1	12.5	Long-Term Debt				10.6	16.7	7.6
.0	.0	.0	Deferred Taxes				.0	.0	.0
4.1	4.7	3.1	All Other Non-Current				8.1	1.5	1.1
59.0	59.4	60.5	Net Worth				56.9	63.0	61.2
100.0	100.0	100.0	Total Liabilties & Net Worth				100.0	100.0	100.0
			INCOME DATA						
100.0	100.0	100.0	Net Sales				100.0	100.0	100.0
			Gross Profit						
97.2	93.6	98.6	Operating Expenses				96.8	98.1	97.8
2.8	6.4	1.4	Operating Profit				3.2	1.9	2.2
-.4	1.7	.1	All Other Expenses (net)				-1.9	.4	-1.3
3.2	4.7	1.3	Profit Before Taxes				5.1	1.5	3.5
			RATIOS						
3.9	4.5	4.0					4.3	5.0	3.9
2.3	2.5	2.6	Current				2.7	2.8	1.9
1.3	1.5	1.4					1.6	1.2	1.4
3.3	3.8	3.9					4.3	4.3	3.8
1.9	2.4	2.5	Quick				2.7	2.6	1.5
1.2	1.4	1.4					1.6	1.2	1.1
7 52.0	7 51.4	11 33.5					19 19.2	24 15.1	6 65.9
36 10.1	27 13.3	34 10.8	Sales/Receivables				36 10.0	31 11.8	22 16.6
53 6.9	46 7.9	52 7.0					72 5.1	42 8.6	55 6.6
			Cost of Sales/Inventory						
			Cost of Sales/Payables						
3.6	3.3	3.3					3.0	4.0	2.9
7.1	7.0	5.9	Sales/Working Capital				4.6	6.6	7.4
19.0	15.5	14.5					13.1	32.7	21.8
9.7	7.0	12.5						15.4	
(57) 2.6	(47) 2.4	(33) 6.6	EBIT/Interest					(12) 4.8	
-3.3	-.9	.1						.0	
			Net Profit + Depr., Dep., Amort./Cur. Mat. L/T/D						
.1	.2	.1					.1	.1	.1
.4	.6	.5	Fixed/Worth				.4	.7	.3
.9	1.0	.9					.9	1.3	.7
.3	.2	.3					.4	.2	.4
.6	.7	.6	Debt/Worth				.8	.6	.6
1.2	1.7	1.0					1.2	.9	1.0
11.9	17.0	15.7					43.8	7.4	16.9
(84) 5.3	3.9	(53) 5.3	% Profit Before Taxes/Tangible Net Worth				13.2	1.8	9.5
-1.7	-1.9	-6.8					4.1	-9.6	-1.6
7.5	6.0	8.8					17.4	5.3	9.5
1.9	1.9	3.1	% Profit Before Taxes/Total Assets				6.7	.9	5.8
-.8	-1.4	-3.5					2.4	-3.0	-.9
82.0	24.0	36.3					73.6	15.0	55.6
5.5	3.0	5.6	Sales/Net Fixed Assets				8.9	4.0	18.6
2.3	1.7	2.1					2.1	1.7	4.8
2.5	2.0	2.1					2.0	2.0	3.1
1.4	1.2	1.5	Sales/Total Assets				1.8	1.5	1.7
.8	.6	.9					1.0	1.1	1.0
.5	1.2	.8						1.5	.4
(74) 1.8	(55) 2.5	(48) 1.7	% Depr., Dep., Amort./Sales					(15) 2.5	.9
3.3	4.4	4.4						4.9	2.0
			% Officers', Directors' Owners' Comp/Sales						
1943214M	2045480M	1585171M	Net Sales ($)	1657M	8997M	19537M	71415M	239613M	1243952M
1704176M	1481989M	1099853M	Total Assets ($)	3900M	12551M	15436M	51234M	172357M	844375M

M = $ thousand MM = $ million

See Pages 9 through 22 for Explanation of Ratios and Data

Current Data Sorted by Assets							Comparative Historical Data	
						Type of Statement		
1	3	10	15	5	5	Unqualified	32	41
1		1				Reviewed	1	
						Compiled		1
1	1	1				Tax Returns	2	2
1	3	5	2	1		Other	11	9
46 (4/1-9/30/13)			10 (10/1/13-3/31/14)				**4/1/09-3/31/10 ALL**	**4/1/10-3/31/11 ALL**
0-500M	**500M-2MM**	**2-10MM**	**10-50MM**	**50-100MM**	**100-250MM**			
4	7	17	17	6	5	**NUMBER OF STATEMENTS**	46	53
%	%	%	%	%	%	**ASSETS**	%	%
		26.5	26.7			Cash & Equivalents	27.5	27.3
		17.9	10.6			Trade Receivables (net)	17.1	14.9
		5.2	3.9			Inventory	2.3	4.9
		2.6	2.7			All Other Current	1.6	4.8
		52.1	43.9			Total Current	48.5	51.9
		32.5	22.5			Fixed Assets (net)	36.3	26.1
		.3	.6			Intangibles (net)	2.4	1.4
		15.2	33.0			All Other Non-Current	12.8	20.6
		100.0	100.0			Total	100.0	100.0
						LIABILITIES		
		3.7	.1			Notes Payable-Short Term	2.7	2.7
		.5	.5			Cur. Mat.-L.T.D.	1.3	.8
		4.4	5.2			Trade Payables	5.8	6.4
		.1	.0			Income Taxes Payable	.0	.0
		10.2	6.9			All Other Current	15.2	13.9
		18.9	12.7			Total Current	25.0	23.7
		9.8	2.6			Long-Term Debt	16.3	10.2
		.0	.0			Deferred Taxes	.0	.0
		.6	4.2			All Other Non-Current	4.1	3.5
		70.7	80.5			Net Worth	54.7	62.6
		100.0	100.0			Total Liabilties & Net Worth	100.0	100.0
						INCOME DATA		
		100.0	100.0			Net Sales	100.0	100.0
						Gross Profit		
		99.0	92.1			Operating Expenses	96.9	94.6
		1.0	7.9			Operating Profit	3.1	5.4
		-.8	-2.0			All Other Expenses (net)	1.8	-.6
		1.8	9.8			Profit Before Taxes	1.3	6.0
						RATIOS		
		8.9	7.5				8.5	7.3
		3.8	4.6			Current	2.5	2.8
		2.0	2.4				1.1	1.3
		8.9	6.4				5.7	5.6
		3.7	3.8			Quick	2.4	1.9
		1.7	2.2				1.0	1.0
		0 UND	**6** 57.5				**1** 287.6	**1** 305.1
		43 8.4	**37** 9.8			Sales/Receivables	**20** 17.9	**17** 21.2
		89 4.1	**126** 2.9				**59** 6.2	**53** 6.9
						Cost of Sales/Inventory		
						Cost of Sales/Payables		
		2.2	1.3				3.0	2.0
		3.9	2.4			Sales/Working Capital	6.1	5.8
		6.4	9.2				41.1	23.2
		13.4					5.0	12.4
		(10) 2.1				EBIT/Interest	(21) .7	(23) 1.5
		-5.8					-4.6	-.2
						Net Profit + Depr., Dep., Amort./Cur. Mat. L/T/D		
		.1	.0				.1	.0
		.5	.3			Fixed/Worth	.6	.2
		1.0	.4				1.9	.8
		.1	.1				.3	.1
		.3	.1			Debt/Worth	.7	.4
		.7	.5				2.6	1.3
		7.8	10.0				11.4	9.4
		1.3	4.4			% Profit Before Taxes/Tangible Net Worth	(45) 3.5	(51) 3.1
		-3.6	2.4				-13.9	-2.3
		5.3	9.0				5.9	4.5
		.7	3.7			% Profit Before Taxes/Total Assets	.3	1.3
		-3.0	1.9				-5.3	-1.0
		75.6	25.4				94.2	67.6
		4.5	9.9			Sales/Net Fixed Assets	4.7	9.1
		1.1	1.6				1.2	1.5
		1.6	1.7				2.6	2.4
		.8	.7			Sales/Total Assets	1.1	.9
		.3	.4				.5	.3
		1.4	.8				.4	.3
		(13) 2.8	(15) 1.1			% Depr., Dep., Amort./Sales	(36) 1.3	(41) 1.1
		7.9	4.4				3.7	3.3
						% Officers', Directors' Owners' Comp/Sales		
3413M	15704M	94198M	464552M	586986M	591256M	Net Sales ($)	661033M	1790694M
1297M	8296M	90979M	397205M	440710M	856911M	Total Assets ($)	752584M	1392840M

M = $ thousand MM = $ million

See Pages 9 through 22 for Explanation of Ratios and Data

Comparative Historical Data				Current Data Sorted by Sales					
			Type of Statement						
61	58	39	Unqualified	5	3	2	6	9	14
	1	2	Reviewed		1		1		
2			Compiled						
3	2	3	Tax Returns	1	1	1			
19	12	12	Other	2	5	2		2	1
4/1/11-3/31/12 ALL	**4/1/12-3/31/13 ALL**	**4/1/13-3/31/14 ALL**			**46 (4/1-9/30/13)**			**10 (10/1/13-3/31/14)**	
				0-1MM	**1-3MM**	**3-5MM**	**5-10MM**	**10-25MM**	**25MM & OVER**
85	73	56	**NUMBER OF STATEMENTS**	8	10	5	7	11	15
%	%	%	**ASSETS**	%	%	%	%	%	%
28.5	29.8	31.0	Cash & Equivalents		16.2			23.7	40.1
14.2	11.8	14.0	Trade Receivables (net)		18.9			20.6	10.6
4.1	1.4	2.8	Inventory		.3			.6	2.5
2.9	3.3	3.2	All Other Current		5.0			3.3	3.4
49.8	46.3	51.0	Total Current		40.4			48.2	56.5
25.8	26.9	25.1	Fixed Assets (net)		39.5			21.5	18.0
1.3	.3	.7	Intangibles (net)		2.0			.8	.5
23.2	26.5	23.2	All Other Non-Current		18.2			29.4	25.0
100.0	100.0	100.0	Total		100.0			100.0	100.0
			LIABILITIES						
2.7	2.3	2.3	Notes Payable-Short Term		.2			.8	.1
.8	1.0	.4	Cur. Mat.-L.T.D.		.2			.7	.5
5.4	6.0	9.3	Trade Payables		13.9			3.5	19.0
.0	.0	.0	Income Taxes Payable		.0			.0	.0
10.9	6.7	8.6	All Other Current		10.7			3.8	9.0
19.8	16.0	20.5	Total Current		25.0			8.8	28.5
11.0	9.4	9.3	Long-Term Debt		12.2			14.6	10.0
.0	.0	.0	Deferred Taxes		.0			.0	.0
5.4	5.7	4.9	All Other Non-Current		4.3			2.5	9.0
63.8	69.0	65.2	Net Worth		58.5			74.1	52.5
100.0	100.0	100.0	Total Liabilties & Net Worth		100.0			100.0	100.0
			INCOME DATA						
100.0	100.0	100.0	Net Sales		100.0			100.0	100.0
			Gross Profit						
92.0	92.9	92.9	Operating Expenses		95.8			84.9	90.6
8.0	7.1	7.1	Operating Profit		4.2			15.1	9.4
1.8	3.1	1.0	All Other Expenses (net)		-1.0			5.3	2.1
6.3	4.0	6.1	Profit Before Taxes		5.2			9.8	7.3
			RATIOS						
7.1	7.5	6.9			7.6			8.5	3.8
3.1	3.2	3.4	Current		2.8			6.3	2.1
1.5	1.6	1.8			1.1			3.7	1.1
6.5	6.6	6.5			6.2			8.4	3.8
2.0	3.0	2.9	Quick		2.6			5.3	1.4
1.0	1.3	1.3			1.1			2.8	.9
0 780.8	**0** UND	**2** 161.8			**0** UND			**14** 25.6	**2** 147.8
12 30.0	**15** 23.7	**30** 12.3	Sales/Receivables		**20** 18.3			**62** 5.9	**10** 36.0
65 5.6	**91** 4.0	**73** 5.0			**99** 3.7			**111** 3.3	**51** 7.2
			Cost of Sales/Inventory						
			Cost of Sales/Payables						
1.9	1.3	1.8			2.8			1.3	2.3
3.6	3.5	3.6	Sales/Working Capital		8.9			2.6	9.6
13.2	8.7	13.2			44.3			5.3	84.4
17.5	6.4	15.4							
(46) 2.0	(36) -1.6	(24) 3.0	EBIT/Interest						
.2	-19.0	-3.4							
			Net Profit + Depr., Dep., Amort./Cur. Mat. L/T/D						
.0	.0	.0			.2			.0	.0
.2	.2	.3	Fixed/Worth		.7			.3	.3
.7	.7	.7			1.3			.6	.4
.1	.1	.1			.1			.1	.4
.4	.3	.4	Debt/Worth		.6			.3	.7
1.2	.9	.9			4.0			.7	2.0
10.6	7.2	9.7						9.6	11.6
(83) 3.5	(71) .7	(53) 3.1	% Profit Before Taxes/Tangible Net Worth					(10) 5.1	(14) 7.6
-1.4	-5.6	.0						2.6	2.9
5.7	4.3	7.4			15.8			7.5	8.7
1.6	.3	2.1	% Profit Before Taxes/Total Assets		1.6			3.9	4.2
-1.3	-4.1	-.3			.5			1.9	1.1
62.5	43.7	85.7			69.2			104.7	98.0
8.9	4.5	8.1	Sales/Net Fixed Assets		2.5			6.1	14.7
1.3	1.2	1.6			.4			1.6	7.3
1.7	1.2	1.8			2.3			1.6	2.2
.7	.6	.8	Sales/Total Assets		1.1			.7	1.6
.3	.2	.4			.2			.4	.7
.4	.7	.5							.3
(71) 1.4	(54) 1.7	(46) 1.5	% Depr., Dep., Amort./Sales						(14) .9
4.0	3.8	4.7							1.5
			% Officers', Directors' Owners' Comp/Sales						
2906617M	1329811M	1756109M	Net Sales ($)	4400M	16434M	19216M	54768M	143996M	1517295M
3425443M	2380328M	1795398M	Total Assets ($)	44494M	38759M	29637M	54458M	471836M	1156214M

M = $ thousand MM = $ million

See Pages 9 through 22 for Explanation of Ratios and Data

Current Data Sorted by Assets							Comparative Historical Data	
						Type of Statement		
	2	7	6	1	3	Unqualified	15	20
		1	1			Reviewed		
						Compiled	2	
						Tax Returns		
	1	3	3	1	1	Other	9	8
20 (4/1-9/30/13)			10 (10/1/13-3/31/14)				4/1/09-3/31/10	4/1/10-3/31/11
0-500M	500M-2MM	2-10MM	10-50MM	50-100MM	100-250MM		ALL	ALL
	3	11	10	2	4	**NUMBER OF STATEMENTS**	26	28
%	%	%	%	%	%	**ASSETS**	%	%
DATA NOT AVAILABLE		13.5	13.0			Cash & Equivalents	17.8	31.5
		10.2	6.4			Trade Receivables (net)	14.7	11.4
		3.7	2.6			Inventory	.8	2.9
		1.5	1.8			All Other Current	5.6	5.7
		29.0	23.8			Total Current	38.9	51.5
		48.8	28.6			Fixed Assets (net)	50.5	39.5
		.0	1.9			Intangibles (net)	.1	.1
		22.2	45.8			All Other Non-Current	10.4	8.9
		100.0	100.0			Total	100.0	100.0
						LIABILITIES		
		3.7	.3			Notes Payable-Short Term	10.0	2.5
		5.1	1.7			Cur. Mat.-L.T.D.	2.2	1.0
		4.2	4.3			Trade Payables	5.1	4.5
		.0	.0			Income Taxes Payable	.7	.0
		3.5	2.6			All Other Current	9.3	28.2
		16.5	8.9			Total Current	27.3	36.2
		14.9	19.6			Long-Term Debt	24.5	18.9
		.0	.0			Deferred Taxes	.0	.0
		9.3	3.9			All Other Non-Current	2.3	2.2
		59.3	67.6			Net Worth	46.0	42.7
		100.0	100.0			Total Liabilties & Net Worth	100.0	100.0
						INCOME DATA		
		100.0	100.0			Net Sales	100.0	100.0
						Gross Profit		
		94.7	95.3			Operating Expenses	94.3	98.5
		5.3	4.7			Operating Profit	5.7	1.5
		.7	.7			All Other Expenses (net)	2.2	3.1
		4.6	4.1			Profit Before Taxes	3.4	-1.7
						RATIOS		
		7.6	15.0				5.9	8.9
		3.1	4.4			Current	2.4	2.8
		.9	1.6				1.1	1.2
		6.0	8.0				4.4	5.8
		1.1	4.4			Quick	1.4	1.9
		.7	1.3				1.0	.7
		13 28.4	0 UND				0 UND	4 88.1
		24 15.5	46 7.9			Sales/Receivables	22 17.0	18 20.1
		36 10.1	69 5.3				46 8.0	50 7.2
						Cost of Sales/Inventory		
						Cost of Sales/Payables		
		2.3	1.5				3.8	1.7
		6.8	4.0			Sales/Working Capital	10.9	5.6
		-119.0	13.6				288.8	60.6
		14.9					7.9	13.4
		(10) 2.9				EBIT/Interest	(17) 1.9	(17) 4.0
		-.9					-3.8	-.2
						Net Profit + Depr., Dep., Amort./Cur. Mat. L/T/D		
		.4	.1				.7	.1
		1.0	.3			Fixed/Worth	1.2	.6
		1.6	1.0				1.4	1.1
		.2	.1				.4	.1
		.8	.5			Debt/Worth	.8	.6
		1.2	.8				1.6	1.8
		11.2	16.3				15.3	15.2
		5.1	6.3			% Profit Before Taxes/Tangible Net Worth	(24) 5.1	(26) 3.2
		-5.4	-4.3				-2.7	-3.5
		6.3	10.7				7.1	5.8
		2.8	4.1			% Profit Before Taxes/Total Assets	1.4	1.3
		-2.4	-2.7				-3.0	-2.4
		11.6	22.5				28.9	39.8
		2.2	1.9			Sales/Net Fixed Assets	2.1	2.9
		1.2	1.3				.6	1.1
		1.7	.9				2.8	2.4
		1.2	.5			Sales/Total Assets	1.2	1.1
		.5	.2				.4	.5
			.6				1.0	1.3
			2.5			% Depr., Dep., Amort./Sales	(19) 1.7	(22) 2.7
			4.2				4.8	5.5
						% Officers', Directors' Owners' Comp/Sales		
	4073M	60084M	149485M	84440M	1848507M	Net Sales ($)	388592M	649745M
	2502M	46005M	225666M	116420M	739457M	Total Assets ($)	266704M	412875M

M = $ thousand MM = $ million

See Pages 9 through 22 for Explanation of Ratios and Data

Comparative Historical Data				Current Data Sorted by Sales					
			Type of Statement						
19	14	19	Unqualified	1	3	5	4	2	4
2	1	2	Reviewed			2			
			Compiled						
1	2		Tax Returns						
13	5	9	Other	1	2	2	1	1	2
4/1/11-3/31/12 ALL	**4/1/12-3/31/13 ALL**	**4/1/13-3/31/14 ALL**			**20 (4/1-9/30/13)**			**10 (10/1/13-3/31/14)**	
				0-1MM	**1-3MM**	**3-5MM**	**5-10MM**	**10-25MM**	**25MM & OVER**
35	22	30	**NUMBER OF STATEMENTS**	2	5	9	5	3	6
%	%	%	**ASSETS**	%	%	%	%	%	%
20.2	18.3	15.5	Cash & Equivalents						
7.8	11.9	12.9	Trade Receivables (net)						
2.9	4.7	4.6	Inventory						
4.5	3.5	2.2	All Other Current						
35.3	38.4	35.2	Total Current						
45.5	42.8	31.5	Fixed Assets (net)						
1.1	.2	.7	Intangibles (net)						
18.1	18.6	32.5	All Other Non-Current						
100.0	100.0	100.0	Total						
			LIABILITIES						
1.6	5.9	2.5	Notes Payable-Short Term						
1.4	1.0	2.5	Cur. Mat.-L.T.D.						
3.3	6.4	7.3	Trade Payables						
.0	.1	.0	Income Taxes Payable						
10.8	9.4	4.3	All Other Current						
17.2	22.8	16.5	Total Current						
17.3	20.3	16.0	Long-Term Debt						
.0	.0	.0	Deferred Taxes						
1.1	2.2	5.0	All Other Non-Current						
64.4	54.6	62.5	Net Worth						
100.0	100.0	100.0	Total Liabilities & Net Worth						
			INCOME DATA						
100.0	100.0	100.0	Net Sales						
			Gross Profit						
95.5	96.9	94.3	Operating Expenses						
4.5	3.1	5.7	Operating Profit						
1.5	1.7	.7	All Other Expenses (net)						
3.1	1.3	5.0	Profit Before Taxes						
			RATIOS						
7.2	4.1	9.7							
2.6	2.2	3.3	Current						
.9	.8	1.2							
6.2	3.6	6.8							
1.6	1.5	2.1	Quick						
.8	.6	.8							
0 UND	**12** 30.0	**9** 40.5							
10 35.8	**21** 17.2	**31** 11.7	Sales/Receivables						
53 6.9	**37** 9.9	**47** 7.7							
			Cost of Sales/Inventory						
			Cost of Sales/Payables						
2.6	4.5	2.0							
6.7	7.4	5.6	Sales/Working Capital						
-36.4	-80.5	34.3							
9.0	8.4	20.7							
(18) 3.2	(14) 1.9	(21) 4.3	EBIT/Interest						
.0	-.8	-.1							
			Net Profit + Depr., Dep., Amort./Cur. Mat. L/T/D						
.0	.1	.0							
.7	.8	.5	Fixed/Worth						
1.5	1.3	1.0							
.1	.3	.1							
.6	.6	.6	Debt/Worth						
.8	1.9	1.1							
16.1	10.3	16.3							
(34) .6	(21) 2.0	6.3	% Profit Before Taxes/Tangible Net Worth						
-1.9	-3.6	-1.7							
7.6	4.6	8.8							
.1	1.1	4.0	% Profit Before Taxes/Total Assets						
-1.2	-2.0	-1.1							
28.6	25.5	34.9							
1.4	3.5	3.7	Sales/Net Fixed Assets						
.7	1.1	1.3							
1.2	2.3	1.8							
.7	1.3	.8	Sales/Total Assets						
.4	.6	.3							
1.8	.9	.8							
(28) 2.9	(18) 1.7	(22) 1.7	% Depr., Dep., Amort./Sales						
6.0	2.3	3.8							
			% Officers', Directors' Owners' Comp/Sales						
495409M	203213M	2146589M	Net Sales ($)	798M	10441M	35915M	36906M	45635M	2016894M
476636M	217479M	1130050M	Total Assets ($)	4450M	26042M	239162M	132332M	29960M	698104M

M = $ thousand MM = $ million

See Pages 9 through 22 for Explanation of Ratios and Data

Current Data Sorted by Assets							Comparative Historical Data	
						Type of Statement		
	1	8	9	3	2	Unqualified	14	26
						Reviewed	1	
		1				Compiled		2
		2				Tax Returns	1	
3	3	7	1			Other	8	14
27 (4/1-9/30/13)			13 (10/1/13-3/31/14)				4/1/09-3/31/10	4/1/10-3/31/11
0-500M	500M-2MM	2-10MM	10-50MM	50-100MM	100-250MM		ALL	ALL
3	4	18	10	3	2	**NUMBER OF STATEMENTS**	24	42
%	%	%	%	%	%	**ASSETS**	%	%
		23.8	29.6			Cash & Equivalents	20.7	23.0
		4.9	9.5			Trade Receivables (net)	9.4	10.7
		2.3	3.5			Inventory	1.8	1.3
		4.4	6.0			All Other Current	3.6	3.7
		35.3	48.6			Total Current	35.4	38.7
		49.3	42.3			Fixed Assets (net)	40.1	38.8
		1.2	.2			Intangibles (net)	.1	.0
		14.2	8.9			All Other Non-Current	24.5	22.5
		100.0	100.0			Total	100.0	100.0
						LIABILITIES		
		2.9	.4			Notes Payable-Short Term	.8	1.0
		4.1	.6			Cur. Mat.-L.T.D.	1.5	.5
		3.8	3.7			Trade Payables	5.8	5.0
		.0	.0			Income Taxes Payable	.0	.0
		4.7	13.5			All Other Current	7.1	4.4
		15.6	18.2			Total Current	15.1	11.0
		18.0	13.1			Long-Term Debt	8.0	8.5
		.0	.0			Deferred Taxes	.0	.0
		5.2	1.0			All Other Non-Current	8.1	3.6
		61.3	67.7			Net Worth	68.8	76.9
		100.0	100.0			Total Liabilties & Net Worth	100.0	100.0
						INCOME DATA		
		100.0	100.0			Net Sales	100.0	100.0
						Gross Profit		
		92.4	93.6			Operating Expenses	96.8	94.9
		7.6	6.4			Operating Profit	3.2	5.1
		1.3	.2			All Other Expenses (net)	2.9	.2
		6.3	6.2			Profit Before Taxes	.3	4.9
						RATIOS		
		11.8	6.7				9.6	9.6
		3.3	3.8			Current	3.0	4.8
		1.3	1.7				1.7	1.6
		10.6	5.5				6.2	9.3
		2.8	2.9			Quick	2.7	4.0
		.5	.8				1.3	1.4
		0 UND	**17** 21.2				**0** UND	**5** 77.3
		11 33.9	**25** 14.5			Sales/Receivables	**7** 51.9	**25** 14.4
		19 19.5	**58** 6.3				**37** 9.7	**62** 5.9
						Cost of Sales/Inventory		
						Cost of Sales/Payables		
		1.9	1.2				2.5	2.0
		3.7	2.4			Sales/Working Capital	4.8	3.3
		UND	9.0				23.2	9.1
		11.3					17.1	17.3
		(13) 3.6				EBIT/Interest	(17) 1.0	(23) 3.3
		.1					-9.9	-.6
						Net Profit + Depr., Dep., Amort./Cur. Mat. L/T/D		
		.1	.1				.2	.1
		1.0	.7			Fixed/Worth	.6	.5
		1.7	.9				1.0	.8
		.2	.1				.1	.1
		.5	.4			Debt/Worth	.3	.2
		1.2	1.1				.8	.5
		26.2	9.3				4.6	8.8
		(17) 4.2	1.2			% Profit Before Taxes/Tangible Net Worth	(23) -.2	2.9
		-.1	-2.5				-4.3	-1.1
		10.9	7.6				4.5	7.7
		3.2	1.1			% Profit Before Taxes/Total Assets	-.7	2.1
		-.3	-.8				-3.5	-.9
		5.5	12.0				19.0	20.8
		2.1	1.4			Sales/Net Fixed Assets	3.2	3.2
		.5	.4				.9	.6
		1.1	1.1				2.1	1.4
		.5	.6			Sales/Total Assets	.8	.7
		.3	.2				.5	.4
		1.4	1.2				1.2	1.1
		(16) 2.6	3.8			% Depr., Dep., Amort./Sales	(20) 2.2	(38) 2.3
		8.1	7.6				4.3	5.0
						% Officers', Directors' Owners' Comp/Sales		
1776M	18065M	64815M	124694M	268771M	346386M	Net Sales ($)	762525M	945170M
534M	6491M	87584M	166015M	228220M	274482M	Total Assets ($)	861462M	1363738M

M = $ thousand MM = $ million

See Pages 9 through 22 for Explanation of Ratios and Data

Comparative Historical Data				Current Data Sorted by Sales					
			Type of Statement						
27	33	23	Unqualified	2	3	3	6	4	5
1			Reviewed						
1		1	Compiled			1			
2	2	2	Tax Returns	1	1				
8	11	14	Other	4	4	4	2		
				27 (4/1-9/30/13)			13 (10/1/13-3/31/14)		
4/1/11-3/31/12 ALL	**4/1/12-3/31/13 ALL**	**4/1/13-3/31/14 ALL**		**0-1MM**	**1-3MM**	**3-5MM**	**5-10MM**	**10-25MM**	**25MM & OVER**
39	46	40	**NUMBER OF STATEMENTS**	7	8	8	8	4	5
%	%	%	**ASSETS**	%	%	%	%	%	%
18.2	25.8	27.1	Cash & Equivalents						
14.7	15.5	12.3	Trade Receivables (net)						
1.6	.9	3.1	Inventory						
7.1	4.3	4.1	All Other Current						
41.6	46.5	46.6	Total Current						
32.8	32.4	38.6	Fixed Assets (net)						
.1	.1	.6	Intangibles (net)						
25.6	21.1	14.2	All Other Non-Current						
100.0	100.0	100.0	Total						
			LIABILITIES						
1.2	1.6	1.4	Notes Payable-Short Term						
.8	1.1	2.2	Cur. Mat.-L.T.D.						
11.7	8.5	7.5	Trade Payables						
.0	.1	.0	Income Taxes Payable						
5.0	5.5	8.3	All Other Current						
18.6	16.7	19.5	Total Current						
7.8	8.2	12.4	Long-Term Debt						
.0	.0	.0	Deferred Taxes						
6.7	5.6	6.2	All Other Non-Current						
66.9	69.5	61.9	Net Worth						
100.0	100.0	100.0	Total Liabilties & Net Worth						
			INCOME DATA						
100.0	100.0	100.0	Net Sales						
			Gross Profit						
95.5	91.2	95.4	Operating Expenses						
4.5	8.8	4.6	Operating Profit						
.4	.6	.2	All Other Expenses (net)						
4.1	8.2	4.4	Profit Before Taxes						
			RATIOS						
7.1	10.8	6.9							
3.6	3.9	3.3	Current						
1.2	1.6	1.4							
5.5	10.0	6.6							
3.3	3.6	2.9	Quick						
1.0	1.5	.9							
7 54.5	**6** 58.0	**3** 108.7							
30 12.3	**28** 13.0	**17** 22.0	Sales/Receivables						
73 5.0	**73** 5.0	**37** 9.9							
			Cost of Sales/Inventory						
			Cost of Sales/Payables						
1.9	1.7	1.9							
6.4	3.1	3.9	Sales/Working Capital						
19.2	9.6	10.3							
19.3	12.3	14.9							
(22) 4.0	(27) 2.9	(25) 3.9	EBIT/Interest						
-1.5	-4.1	.8							
			Net Profit + Depr., Dep., Amort./Cur. Mat. L/T/D						
.1	.1	.1							
.5	.3	.5	Fixed/Worth						
.9	.8	1.2							
.1	.1	.2							
.3	.3	.4	Debt/Worth						
1.1	1.0	1.2							
11.6	13.0	24.7							
(38) 2.0	1.6	(38) 3.9	% Profit Before Taxes/Tangible Net Worth						
-3.4	-1.2	-.1							
6.2	9.0	11.5							
1.1	1.3	2.1	% Profit Before Taxes/Total Assets						
-2.5	-.9	-.3							
19.1	20.6	16.6							
3.3	3.4	2.6	Sales/Net Fixed Assets						
1.1	.7	.7							
1.5	1.3	1.5							
.9	.8	.9	Sales/Total Assets						
.4	.3	.4							
1.1	.7	.8							
(35) 2.2	(37) 2.2	(36) 2.2	% Depr., Dep., Amort./Sales						
5.1	4.3	6.0							
			% Officers', Directors' Owners' Comp/Sales						
948346M	**1408267M**	**824507M**	Net Sales ($)	**5033M**	**14614M**	**30342M**	**62362M**	**71331M**	**640825M**
1208489M	**2118285M**	**763326M**	Total Assets ($)	**14476M**	**44234M**	**59556M**	**55014M**	**160318M**	**429728M**

M = $ thousand MM = $ million

See Pages 9 through 22 for Explanation of Ratios and Data

	Current Data Sorted by Assets						Comparative Historical Data	
Type of Statement								
Unqualified	9	33	108	105	13	13	347	333
Reviewed	1	3	4	2			8	3
Compiled	1	2	3	1			5	4
Tax Returns	4	4	2				8	11
Other	5	20	39	26	3	4	133	147
	267 (4/1-9/30/13)			138 (10/1/13-3/31/14)			4/1/09-3/31/10	4/1/10-3/31/11
	0-500M	500M-2MM	2-10MM	10-50MM	50-100MM	100-250MM	ALL	ALL
NUMBER OF STATEMENTS	20	62	156	134	16	17	501	498
ASSETS	%	%	%	%	%	%	%	%
Cash & Equivalents	43.7	31.2	24.5	20.7	26.8	27.3	22.3	24.5
Trade Receivables (net)	17.3	13.7	13.6	10.7	6.2	6.7	14.8	14.9
Inventory	.0	1.2	1.6	3.1	.3	.2	1.3	1.8
All Other Current	7.7	4.3	4.7	3.0	3.2	7.9	4.8	5.1
Total Current	68.6	50.4	44.3	37.6	36.5	42.1	43.3	46.3
Fixed Assets (net)	14.9	40.4	39.6	40.2	29.3	24.6	39.3	36.9
Intangibles (net)	2.6	1.0	.2	1.9	.9	.3	.6	.5
All Other Non-Current	13.9	8.2	15.9	20.3	33.3	33.0	16.8	16.2
Total	100.0	100.0	100.0	100.0	100.0	100.0	100.0	100.0
LIABILITIES								
Notes Payable-Short Term	8.0	2.0	2.7	1.0	.6	.3	2.7	2.9
Cur. Mat.-L.T.D.	.0	2.2	1.4	1.8	1.9	1.2	1.7	1.8
Trade Payables	15.2	6.7	7.2	3.8	8.3	4.4	6.2	7.0
Income Taxes Payable	.0	.0	.0	.0	.0	.0	.2	.0
All Other Current	24.6	11.6	10.0	6.4	3.4	13.8	10.5	10.7
Total Current	47.8	22.4	21.3	13.1	14.3	19.8	21.2	22.4
Long-Term Debt	9.7	15.3	14.2	20.2	21.9	15.3	18.5	16.1
Deferred Taxes	.0	.0	.0	.0	.0	.0	.0	.0
All Other Non-Current	1.5	3.0	3.6	5.0	3.1	5.8	4.0	4.3
Net Worth	41.0	59.3	60.9	61.8	60.7	59.2	56.3	57.2
Total Liabilties & Net Worth	100.0	100.0	100.0	100.0	100.0	100.0	100.0	100.0
INCOME DATA								
Net Sales	100.0	100.0	100.0	100.0	100.0	100.0	100.0	100.0
Gross Profit								
Operating Expenses	95.2	93.4	95.4	94.3	91.9	89.7	97.0	94.7
Operating Profit	4.8	6.6	4.6	5.7	8.1	10.3	3.0	5.3
All Other Expenses (net)	-.2	2.2	.2	.6	4.7	1.1	2.2	1.0
Profit Before Taxes	5.0	4.4	4.4	5.1	3.4	9.2	.8	4.3
RATIOS								
Current	8.0	7.5	5.4	6.0	7.1	5.6	4.8	5.7
	1.3	2.6	2.3	2.8	2.5	3.0	2.3	2.3
	.6	1.2	1.2	1.4	1.6	1.1	1.2	1.3
Quick	7.9	6.7	4.2	4.9	6.6	3.6	3.7	4.8
	1.3	2.4	1.8	2.3	2.4	2.0	1.9	1.9
	.5	1.2	1.0	1.1	1.5	1.0	1.0	1.0
Sales/Receivables	2 179.5	0 788.5	6 65.4	8 44.5	0 753.4	12 29.8	7 55.1	6 64.2
	15 25.0	17 20.9	22 16.7	25 14.4	41 9.0	34 10.8	27 13.4	25 14.5
	33 11.2	38 9.5	43 8.5	53 6.9	70 5.2	58 6.3	54 6.8	49 7.5
Cost of Sales/Inventory								
Cost of Sales/Payables								
Sales/Working Capital	4.1	2.5	2.4	1.8	1.1	.9	2.8	2.6
	49.0	7.8	6.5	6.1	1.7	3.3	7.2	6.7
	-16.8	77.5	41.2	22.1	11.8	195.0	30.8	22.7
EBIT/Interest		11.0	10.0	12.5	15.7	19.2	8.8	13.0
		(33) 3.0	(98) 3.0	(87) 3.7	(11) 7.9	(13) 1.0	(322) 2.3	(314) 3.1
		.1	.4	.6	1.6	-6.5	-1.1	.3
Net Profit + Depr., Dep., Amort./Cur. Mat. L/T/D								
Fixed/Worth	.0	.1	.2	.2	.2	.0	.2	.1
	.2	.6	.6	.6	.4	.3	.6	.6
	.7	1.2	1.1	1.1	1.1	.8	1.2	1.2
Debt/Worth	.1	.2	.2	.3	.2	.3	.3	.2
	.8	.4	.5	.5	.6	.7	.7	.6
	NM	1.2	1.3	1.5	2.0	.9	1.8	1.6
% Profit Before Taxes/Tangible Net Worth	47.6	25.0	15.1	9.7	6.8	11.0	11.7	14.1
	(15) 7.2	(59) 7.4	(154) 4.0	(131) 4.3	3.9	(16) 2.2	(483) 3.4	(477) 5.0
	-9.6	-.6	-4.0	-1.3	-.9	-.3	-4.5	-1.2
% Profit Before Taxes/Total Assets	23.1	12.8	9.3	6.9	5.8	6.1	6.0	7.7
	3.9	3.0	2.2	2.1	1.6	.7	1.2	2.5
	-7.2	-1.1	-1.9	-.7	-.3	-.4	-3.0	-.9
Sales/Net Fixed Assets	UND	57.0	26.0	7.7	8.8	32.6	20.5	30.2
	68.1	5.4	3.4	2.9	1.7	5.2	3.8	4.5
	24.1	1.3	.9	1.1	.7	1.2	1.3	1.3
Sales/Total Assets	7.1	3.2	2.1	1.5	1.2	1.3	2.2	2.2
	3.7	1.7	.9	.8	.5	.5	1.1	1.1
	1.7	.9	.5	.4	.2	.3	.5	.5
% Depr., Dep., Amort./Sales	.3	.6	.9	1.3	1.8	.9	.9	.8
	(12) .8	(45) 1.7	(140) 1.9	(119) 2.4	3.3	(16) 2.5	(431) 2.2	(420) 1.9
	1.6	2.7	5.3	4.4	5.1	4.1	4.4	4.2
% Officers', Directors' Owners' Comp/Sales							2.9	2.3
							(44) 5.5	(28) 10.2
							16.1	29.2
Net Sales ($)	20974M	200543M	1257693M	4168529M	1050491M	1925086M	10562276M	11523689M
Total Assets ($)	5482M	77549M	800949M	2978917M	1120080M	2474409M	9515603M	9883561M

M = $ thousand MM = $ million

See Pages 9 through 22 for Explanation of Ratios and Data

Comparative Historical Data				Current Data Sorted by Sales					
			Type of Statement						
358	294	281	Unqualified	15	56	33	53	61	63
5	7	10	Reviewed	2	3	1	1	1	2
4	7	7	Compiled	2	1	1		3	
23	16	10	Tax Returns	8		1	1		
153	120	97	Other	14	32	6	15	17	13
4/1/11-3/31/12	**4/1/12-3/31/13**	**4/1/13-3/31/14**		**267 (4/1-9/30/13)**			**138 (10/1/13-3/31/14)**		
ALL	**ALL**	**ALL**		**0-1MM**	**1-3MM**	**3-5MM**	**5-10MM**	**10-25MM**	**25MM & OVER**
543	444	405	**NUMBER OF STATEMENTS**	41	92	42	70	82	78
%	%	%	**ASSETS**	%	%	%	%	%	%
24.2	24.9	25.4	Cash & Equivalents	24.8	25.2	25.8	21.4	30.7	23.9
13.4	13.7	12.3	Trade Receivables (net)	6.3	10.9	12.1	12.7	15.6	13.1
2.0	2.2	1.8	Inventory	1.0	1.6	1.2	1.8	.6	4.3
4.2	4.2	4.3	All Other Current	4.0	3.4	4.8	3.8	6.5	3.5
43.9	45.0	43.8	Total Current	36.1	41.0	43.9	39.7	53.4	44.8
37.9	37.9	37.7	Fixed Assets (net)	47.0	40.8	44.1	38.2	30.8	32.2
.8	.7	1.0	Intangibles (net)	.7	.8	.8	.2	.5	2.9
17.4	16.4	17.5	All Other Non-Current	16.2	17.4	11.2	21.9	15.2	20.1
100.0	100.0	100.0	Total	100.0	100.0	100.0	100.0	100.0	100.0
			LIABILITIES						
2.7	3.0	2.1	Notes Payable-Short Term	2.5	2.2	2.0	1.6	2.5	1.7
1.8	1.3	1.6	Cur. Mat.-L.T.D.	2.2	2.1	1.5	1.4	1.0	1.5
5.8	6.5	6.3	Trade Payables	3.6	4.1	5.2	7.0	8.5	8.1
.0	.0	.0	Income Taxes Payable	.0	.0	.0	.0	.0	.0
10.7	9.7	9.7	All Other Current	12.2	7.0	7.8	7.7	10.5	13.5
20.9	20.5	19.7	Total Current	20.5	15.5	16.5	17.8	22.4	24.9
18.3	18.1	16.5	Long-Term Debt	21.9	20.3	14.1	15.8	12.0	15.7
.0	.0	.0	Deferred Taxes	.0	.0	.0	.1	.0	.0
4.0	3.8	3.9	All Other Non-Current	1.2	3.1	4.1	4.2	5.1	4.8
56.8	57.6	59.9	Net Worth	56.5	61.2	65.3	62.1	60.5	54.6
100.0	100.0	100.0	Total Liabilties & Net Worth	100.0	100.0	100.0	100.0	100.0	100.0
			INCOME DATA						
100.0	100.0	100.0	Net Sales	100.0	100.0	100.0	100.0	100.0	100.0
			Gross Profit						
93.6	96.4	94.4	Operating Expenses	85.2	92.5	95.4	95.7	98.5	95.2
6.4	3.6	5.6	Operating Profit	14.8	7.5	4.6	4.3	1.5	4.8
1.7	1.4	.8	All Other Expenses (net)	7.6	.5	.3	.6	-1.2	.2
4.7	2.2	4.8	Profit Before Taxes	7.3	6.9	4.3	3.6	2.7	4.6
			RATIOS						
5.4	6.0	6.1		11.4	10.4	6.2	4.5	5.7	3.7
2.2	2.6	2.6	Current	3.4	3.5	2.7	2.4	2.4	2.3
1.3	1.3	1.2		.4	1.3	1.2	1.2	1.5	1.2
4.3	5.0	4.8		10.3	8.8	4.8	3.6	4.5	3.1
1.8	2.2	2.1	Quick	1.9	2.9	2.5	1.9	2.2	1.9
1.0	1.1	1.1		.3	1.1	1.1	1.1	1.2	1.0
2 200.7	**3** 111.2	**5** 68.3		**0** UND	**2** 186.5	**4** 92.8	**7** 51.0	**12** 30.8	**8** 44.5
22 16.4	**23** 16.2	**22** 16.7	Sales/Receivables	**13** 28.3	**18** 20.1	**19** 19.1	**27** 13.3	**28** 13.0	**20** 18.4
50 7.3	**50** 7.3	**44** 8.3		**33** 11.0	**43** 8.4	**47** 7.7	**60** 6.1	**50** 7.3	**43** 8.5
			Cost of Sales/Inventory						
			Cost of Sales/Payables						
2.6	2.3	2.1		1.8	1.5	1.6	2.7	2.1	4.9
7.1	6.6	6.6	Sales/Working Capital	3.7	4.4	6.6	5.7	7.0	9.9
26.9	22.8	37.8		-5.2	16.0	51.1	26.4	24.9	52.7
9.9	10.3	11.2		20.6	9.7	5.1	14.6	10.8	22.3
(332) 2.4	(281) 2.4	(247) 3.1	EBIT/Interest	(17) 3.0	(62) 3.1	(26) 2.0	(40) 3.2	(45) 3.3	(57) 5.5
.2	-.6	.5		1.3	1.0	.2	-3.7	.1	.9
			Net Profit + Depr., Dep., Amort./Cur. Mat. L/T/D						
.1	.1	.1		.1	.1	.2	.1	.1	.2
.6	.6	.6	Fixed/Worth	.7	.6	.6	.5	.5	.6
1.2	1.2	1.1		1.3	1.1	1.2	1.1	.9	1.0
.3	.2	.2		.1	.2	.2	.2	.3	.3
.7	.6	.5	Debt/Worth	.4	.5	.4	.5	.5	.8
1.7	1.5	1.4		1.3	1.6	1.2	1.2	1.2	1.9
14.3	11.7	12.3		27.7	13.8	9.6	11.6	12.7	12.0
(528) 4.4	(428) 2.4	(391) 4.4	% Profit Before Taxes/Tangible Net Worth	(37) 3.3	(88) 4.0	(40) 2.5	2.3	(81) 4.9	(75) 5.0
-2.1	-4.1	-1.5		-2.1	-.4	-1.0	-3.0	-5.6	-.8
7.3	6.2	7.9		13.1	9.1	6.5	8.3	7.4	7.7
2.3	1.3	2.2	% Profit Before Taxes/Total Assets	2.0	2.5	1.5	1.3	3.3	2.9
-1.1	-2.2	-.9		-1.3	-.5	-.8	-1.4	-2.2	-.5
25.9	27.3	26.0		24.4	39.1	11.4	14.2	49.2	35.3
3.8	4.1	3.8	Sales/Net Fixed Assets	1.4	1.8	3.0	2.3	7.3	6.1
1.1	1.1	1.2		.3	.8	.7	1.1	2.1	2.8
2.1	2.1	2.1		1.4	1.1	2.5	1.8	3.4	2.9
1.0	.9	1.0	Sales/Total Assets	.7	.6	.8	.7	1.4	1.7
.5	.5	.5		.2	.4	.4	.5	.8	1.0
.9	.9	1.0		1.7	1.1	1.2	1.2	.7	.6
(454) 2.1	(374) 2.2	(348) 2.1	% Depr., Dep., Amort./Sales	(24) 2.7	(74) 2.9	(39) 2.6	(64) 2.3	(75) 1.8	(72) 1.7
5.1	4.6	4.3		18.7	6.5	6.0	5.4	3.0	2.7
2.1	1.7	1.1							.3
(40) 8.4	(32) 8.8	(22) 8.8	% Officers', Directors' Owners' Comp/Sales						(10) 3.7
11.8	21.8	25.7							16.8
10431236M	9881016M	8623316M	Net Sales ($)	24060M	177867M	165723M	507388M	1331961M	6416317M
12276070M	9360501M	7457386M	Total Assets ($)	77900M	439450M	379019M	859899M	1486466M	4214652M

Current Data Sorted by Assets							Comparative Historical Data	
						Type of Statement		
8	24	132	136	24	13	Unqualified	331	393
	3	9	6	1		Reviewed	21	24
5	14	10	1	1		Compiled	38	44
9	18	13				Tax Returns	40	58
24	36	74	64	11	3	Other	216	240
395 (4/1-9/30/13)			244 (10/1/13-3/31/14)				4/1/09-3/31/10	4/1/10-3/31/11
0-500M	**500M-2MM**	**2-10MM**	**10-50MM**	**50-100MM**	**100-250MM**		**ALL**	**ALL**
46	95	238	207	37	16	**NUMBER OF STATEMENTS**	646	759
%	%	%	%	%	%	**ASSETS**	%	%
51.6	27.9	21.5	21.6	21.0	15.7	Cash & Equivalents	21.5	20.4
11.8	11.4	9.3	7.0	3.4	3.5	Trade Receivables (net)	8.1	7.9
1.5	2.0	1.1	.9	.8	.1	Inventory	1.2	1.2
4.1	3.1	1.8	2.2	2.2	2.1	All Other Current	3.0	2.2
69.0	44.3	33.7	31.7	27.3	21.4	Total Current	33.8	31.6
24.3	48.4	49.8	47.9	59.6	43.4	Fixed Assets (net)	52.5	51.7
3.1	.2	.6	.8	1.5	4.9	Intangibles (net)	.6	.7
3.7	7.1	15.9	19.7	11.6	30.3	All Other Non-Current	13.1	15.9
100.0	100.0	100.0	100.0	100.0	100.0	Total	100.0	100.0
						LIABILITIES		
5.2	2.7	2.3	1.3	.8	.3	Notes Payable-Short Term	2.9	2.7
.7	2.1	1.2	1.8	2.1	1.5	Cur. Mat.-L.T.D.	2.2	1.7
12.8	5.0	4.7	3.1	2.3	3.0	Trade Payables	4.1	5.1
.0	.0	.0	.1	.0	.0	Income Taxes Payable	.1	.0
14.6	7.6	7.9	6.9	3.1	6.1	All Other Current	8.5	7.7
33.4	17.4	16.2	13.2	8.4	10.9	Total Current	17.8	17.2
18.8	26.8	18.1	18.2	23.8	24.3	Long-Term Debt	23.5	22.3
.0	.0	.0	.0	.0	.0	Deferred Taxes	.0	.0
1.3	5.9	3.5	4.5	4.7	2.7	All Other Non-Current	4.8	3.7
46.5	49.8	62.2	64.1	63.1	62.2	Net Worth	53.9	56.8
100.0	100.0	100.0	100.0	100.0	100.0	Total Liabilties & Net Worth	100.0	100.0
						INCOME DATA		
100.0	100.0	100.0	100.0	100.0	100.0	Net Sales	100.0	100.0
						Gross Profit		
95.1	90.0	95.7	94.4	92.7	84.5	Operating Expenses	96.5	94.8
4.9	10.0	4.3	5.6	7.3	15.5	Operating Profit	3.5	5.2
.5	4.7	.9	-.1	-.9	2.6	All Other Expenses (net)	2.7	1.8
4.4	5.4	3.4	5.7	8.1	12.9	Profit Before Taxes	.7	3.4
						RATIOS		
17.2	10.2	7.2	6.1	9.4	6.7		5.6	5.6
2.9	2.7	2.4	2.5	4.7	2.1	Current	2.3	2.5
1.3	1.2	1.2	1.3	1.1	.7		1.0	1.1
15.9	9.6	6.6	5.7	9.3	5.4		5.1	5.0
(45) 2.7	2.6	2.2	(206) 2.2	3.7	1.4	Quick	2.0	2.1
1.2	1.1	1.0	1.2	.9	.7		.8	.9
0 UND	**0** UND	**3** 123.4	**4** 87.5	**6** 60.4	**2** 158.4		**0** UND	**0** 999.8
2 210.7	**5** 77.9	**16** 22.7	**15** 25.1	**20** 18.6	**18** 20.6	Sales/Receivables	**9** 42.4	**10** 35.3
20 18.3	**32** 11.5	**41** 8.8	**35** 10.5	**37** 9.9	**58** 6.3		**36** 10.2	**35** 10.4
						Cost of Sales/Inventory		
						Cost of Sales/Payables		
2.3	2.8	2.5	2.1	.9	.8		2.4	2.7
9.5	6.6	5.5	5.8	2.9	5.1	Sales/Working Capital	6.4	6.3
UND	24.4	21.1	16.6	116.9	-256.7		436.0	114.9
5.3	7.8	6.9	12.7	12.6	19.5		4.3	5.6
(16) 1.8	(50) 1.8	(156) 2.4	(143) 3.3	(24) 2.7	(11) 5.2	EBIT/Interest	(422) 1.1	(503) 1.8
-1.3	-.1	-1.9	.1	-.5	2.4		-2.4	-.3
						Net Profit + Depr., Dep., Amort./Cur. Mat. L/T/D		
.0	.1	.3	.4	.8	.3		.4	.4
.3	.8	.8	.7	1.0	.7	Fixed/Worth	.9	.9
1.5	1.7	1.4	1.2	1.5	1.2		1.6	1.5
.1	.1	.2	.2	.2	.3		.2	.2
.5	.7	.5	.4	.5	.6	Debt/Worth	.6	.5
UND	1.9	1.0	1.0	.9	1.1		1.5	1.3
26.5	19.9	10.2	8.5	6.3	11.0		7.0	10.4
(36) 9.5	(86) 7.7	(232) 3.0	(199) 2.9	(35) 1.8	6.7	% Profit Before Taxes/Tangible Net Worth	(608) .8	(720) 2.3
-5.7	-3.3	-1.9	-1.1	-.4	1.8		-5.3	-2.2
17.7	11.7	5.8	5.5	4.5	6.0		4.1	5.3
6.0	3.3	2.0	1.8	1.4	2.4	% Profit Before Taxes/Total Assets	.3	1.4
-7.2	-2.5	-1.3	-.5	-.3	.5		-3.6	-1.6
653.0	39.7	8.2	3.8	1.1	2.4		5.9	5.5
37.5	2.6	1.5	1.3	.7	.6	Sales/Net Fixed Assets	1.2	1.3
3.3	.6	.6	.6	.3	.3		.6	.5
6.3	2.4	1.4	.9	.6	.4		1.2	1.2
2.3	1.2	.7	.5	.4	.2	Sales/Total Assets	.6	.6
1.3	.5	.4	.4	.2	.1		.3	.4
.5	1.6	1.4	1.9	4.4	3.9		2.0	2.0
(19) 2.4	(65) 3.8	(208) 3.9	(188) 4.5	(34) 7.3	(12) 8.1	% Depr., Dep., Amort./Sales	(510) 4.7	(602) 4.6
6.9	11.3	8.8	7.7	10.6	12.1		8.9	9.1
		5.2	1.4				2.6	1.9
		(14) 7.7	(16) 7.2			% Officers', Directors' Owners' Comp/Sales	(54) 7.0	(57) 5.9
		15.7	25.7				14.6	17.3
38212M	205089M	1209217M	3441357M	1180222M	756910M	Net Sales ($)	7539462M	8036057M
12592M	115639M	1212133M	4368840M	2742967M	2305402M	Total Assets ($)	11373463M	12459294M

M = $ thousand MM = $ million

See Pages 9 through 22 for Explanation of Ratios and Data

Comparative Historical Data

Current Data Sorted by Sales

						Type of Statement												
	445		414		337	Unqualified		17		50		49		85		85		51
	29		31		19	Reviewed		2		10		2		3		1		1
	38		38		31	Compiled		18		7		1		3		2		
	65		50		40	Tax Returns		22		15		1		1		1		
	270		209		212	Other		49		44		28		37		37		17
	4/1/11-3/31/12 ALL		4/1/12-3/31/13 ALL		4/1/13-3/31/14 ALL			395 (4/1-9/30/13)						244 (10/1/13-3/31/14)				
								0-1MM		1-3MM		3-5MM		5-10MM		10-25MM		25MM & OVER
	847		742		639	NUMBER OF STATEMENTS		108		126		81		129		126		69
	%		%		%	ASSETS		%		%		%		%		%		%
	21.7		22.2		24.5	Cash & Equivalents		27.5		22.0		24.6		24.9		25.2		22.1
	7.3		7.1		8.5	Trade Receivables (net)		4.0		8.5		9.6		8.8		9.7		12.0
	1.1		1.1		1.2	Inventory		.8		1.4		1.0		1.5		.6		1.8
	2.2		2.6		2.3	All Other Current		.6		2.7		1.9		2.5		2.6		3.6
	32.3		33.0		36.5	Total Current		32.9		34.5		37.0		37.7		38.2		39.5
	51.3		51.6		47.5	Fixed Assets (net)		59.3		49.6		45.1		43.3		42.8		44.9
	.5		.4		.9	Intangibles (net)		1.5		.4		1.2		1.0		.7		1.3
	15.8		15.0		15.0	All Other Non-Current		6.3		15.6		16.7		17.9		18.4		14.3
	100.0		100.0		100.0	Total		100.0		100.0		100.0		100.0		100.0		100.0
						LIABILITIES												
	2.2		1.8		2.1	Notes Payable-Short Term		1.8		3.7		1.6		2.1		1.5		1.2
	1.5		1.3		1.6	Cur. Mat.-L.T.D.		1.4		1.9		1.4		2.0		1.0		1.5
	4.1		4.4		4.7	Trade Payables		3.2		3.9		6.4		4.1		5.3		6.1
	.0		.0		.0	Income Taxes Payable		.0		.0		.0		.0		.1		.0
	8.0		7.1		7.7	All Other Current		3.8		9.7		5.4		7.6		8.2		12.3
	15.8		14.6		16.1	Total Current		10.3		19.1		14.9		15.8		16.1		21.2
	21.8		20.6		20.0	Long-Term Debt		29.8		22.8		19.3		15.3		15.5		17.0
	.0		.0		.0	Deferred Taxes		.0		.0		.0		.0		.0		.0
	3.7		4.4		4.1	All Other Non-Current		2.8		3.0		3.9		5.0		4.0		6.7
	58.7		60.5		59.9	Net Worth		57.0		55.1		61.9		63.9		64.3		55.2
	100.0		100.0		100.0	Total Liabilties & Net Worth		100.0		100.0		100.0		100.0		100.0		100.0
						INCOME DATA												
	100.0		100.0		100.0	Net Sales		100.0		100.0		100.0		100.0		100.0		100.0
						Gross Profit												
	94.6		94.0		93.9	Operating Expenses		86.8		95.4		96.6		95.8		95.2		93.4
	5.4		6.0		6.1	Operating Profit		13.2		4.6		3.4		4.2		4.8		6.6
	2.0		2.3		1.0	All Other Expenses (net)		6.2		.2		1.2		-.6		-.8		.6
	3.4		3.7		5.0	Profit Before Taxes		7.0		4.4		2.2		4.8		5.6		5.9
						RATIOS												
	5.9		6.2		7.2			14.5		7.5		7.0		6.4		6.7		4.5
	2.4		2.5		2.6	Current		4.0		2.2		2.5		2.4		2.9		2.3
	1.1		1.1		1.2			1.2		1.2		1.1		1.3		1.2		1.5
	5.3		5.5		6.6			13.7		7.0		6.8		6.4		6.5		4.2
	2.1	(741)	2.1	(637)	2.3	Quick		4.0	(125)	2.0		2.4	(128)	2.2		2.3		2.0
	.9		1.0		1.1			1.2		.9		.9		1.1		1.1		1.1
0	UND	0	834.0	2	209.5		0	UND	0	UND	4	93.2	3	122.8	5	67.3	10	38.1
10	36.1	10	37.4	13	27.8	Sales/Receivables	2	233.1	11	33.0	15	25.1	16	22.3	16	22.7	20	18.6
35	10.4	31	11.8	37	9.8		14	25.9	35	10.3	43	8.5	32	11.3	46	8.0	41	9.0
						Cost of Sales/Inventory												
						Cost of Sales/Payables												
	2.5		2.5		2.4			1.8		2.8		2.5		2.1		2.1		3.0
	6.3		6.5		5.8	Sales/Working Capital		3.9		6.6		5.2		6.0		5.7		6.3
	75.8		66.7		24.3			27.2		31.8		47.0		21.9		26.2		17.9
	5.1		8.0		9.0			4.2		10.1		4.8		8.2		13.7		21.2
(525)	1.5	(485)	2.2	(400)	2.6	EBIT/Interest	(52)	1.6	(80)	2.6	(53)	1.1	(85)	2.6	(80)	3.6	(50)	5.3
	-.9		-.3		-.2			.4		-.1		-4.0		-.9		-.1		1.5
						Net Profit + Depr., Dep., Amort./Cur. Mat. L/T/D												
	.3		.4		.3			.4		.3		.3		.3		.3		.4
	.9		.8		.8	Fixed/Worth		1.2		.8		.7		.7		.7		.8
	1.5		1.4		1.4			1.9		1.5		1.1		1.1		1.1		1.1
	.2		.2		.2			.1		.1		.2		.2		.2		.3
	.5		.5		.5	Debt/Worth		.6		.5		.5		.5		.4		.6
	1.3		1.1		1.1			1.5		1.2		1.0		1.2		1.0		1.0
	10.1		9.4		11.1			13.4		12.8		10.3		10.2		10.8		9.6
(802)	2.1	(716)	2.6	(604)	3.7	% Profit Before Taxes/Tangible Net Worth	(98)	4.3	(115)	2.8	(77)	2.1	(128)	3.7	(122)	3.6	(64)	4.7
	-3.2		-2.9		-1.7			-1.4		-2.4		-4.7		-2.6		-.3		.8
	5.6		6.1		6.4			7.0		6.9		6.0		5.9		7.0		5.9
	1.1		1.6		2.2	% Profit Before Taxes/Total Assets		2.4		2.2		.5		2.5		2.4		3.2
	-2.0		-1.7		-1.1			-1.2		-1.9		-2.7		-1.6		.1		.3
	5.8		4.6		8.8			6.8		11.3		11.2		7.5		10.2		9.5
	1.2		1.2		1.5	Sales/Net Fixed Assets		.6		1.3		1.5		1.8		1.9		1.6
	.5		.6		.6			.3		.6		.7		.8		.8		.9
	1.3		1.3		1.4			1.2		1.2		1.6		1.3		1.6		2.2
	.6		.6		.7	Sales/Total Assets		.4		.6		.6		.7		.8		.9
	.3		.4		.4			.2		.4		.4		.4		.5		.5
	1.9		2.0		1.8			3.7		1.7		2.0		1.8		1.5		1.5
(656)	5.0	(599)	4.6	(526)	4.5	% Depr., Dep., Amort./Sales	(67)	11.6	(100)	5.9	(65)	5.3	(117)	3.6	(114)	3.7	(63)	3.3
	8.9		8.2		8.6			19.8		9.4		9.4		7.0		6.5		7.3
	3.8		2.4		2.2					5.1				2.2				
(74)	8.7	(62)	5.6	(50)	6.3	% Officers', Directors' Owners' Comp/Sales			(16)	8.4			(10)	6.0				
	17.0		13.0		19.8					13.0				8.7				
	8946709M		9110063M		6831007M	Net Sales ($)		55071M		238469M		320009M		941347M		1909124M		3366987M
	13806925M		13288429M		10757573M	Total Assets ($)		200945M		482920M		770408M		1926799M		3358512M		4017989M

M = $ thousand MM = $ million

See Pages 9 through 22 for Explanation of Ratios and Data

	Current Data Sorted by Assets						Comparative Historical Data	
Type of Statement								
Unqualified	2	15	47	59	7	9	160	182
Reviewed	2	1	5				14	14
Compiled	3	5	4	1			14	9
Tax Returns	4	4	2				12	14
Other	16	21	28	8	4	2	103	115
	117 (4/1-9/30/13)			132 (10/1/13-3/31/14)			4/1/09-3/31/10	4/1/10-3/31/11
	0-500M	500M-2MM	2-10MM	10-50MM	50-100MM	100-250MM	ALL	ALL
NUMBER OF STATEMENTS	27	46	86	68	11	11	303	334
ASSETS	%	%	%	%	%	%	%	%
Cash & Equivalents	43.2	33.3	42.7	41.4	26.3	36.5	37.7	39.3
Trade Receivables (net)	19.8	9.7	7.9	9.6	9.9	5.9	12.8	10.7
Inventory	5.1	1.5	1.0	1.8	4.4	3.1	2.0	1.2
All Other Current	4.0	7.2	3.7	3.2	3.0	3.2	3.1	3.5
Total Current	72.0	51.7	55.3	56.1	43.5	48.7	55.6	54.6
Fixed Assets (net)	19.5	30.8	29.4	21.7	21.0	18.7	28.2	27.7
Intangibles (net)	.6	1.4	.8	2.7	.2	.7	1.4	1.9
All Other Non-Current	8.0	16.1	14.6	19.5	35.3	32.0	14.8	15.8
Total	100.0	100.0	100.0	100.0	100.0	100.0	100.0	100.0
LIABILITIES								
Notes Payable-Short Term	18.4	10.1	1.4	.8	2.6	2.1	4.1	3.8
Cur. Mat.-L.T.D.	.7	1.0	1.7	1.4	.3	.6	2.8	1.9
Trade Payables	18.6	5.5	7.1	7.5	9.2	6.6	10.9	8.1
Income Taxes Payable	.7	.0	.1	.1	.0	.0	.2	.1
All Other Current	31.9	12.3	15.8	15.2	11.0	15.0	16.0	15.2
Total Current	70.4	28.9	26.0	25.0	23.1	24.2	34.1	29.1
Long-Term Debt	7.5	14.9	9.7	9.1	4.5	8.6	12.7	13.3
Deferred Taxes	.0	.0	.1	.3	.6	.2	.1	.1
All Other Non-Current	19.0	12.4	8.6	16.0	12.8	13.6	9.7	9.8
Net Worth	3.2	43.8	55.7	49.6	59.0	53.5	43.5	47.8
Total Liabilties & Net Worth	100.0	100.0	100.0	100.0	100.0	100.0	100.0	100.0
INCOME DATA								
Net Sales	100.0	100.0	100.0	100.0	100.0	100.0	100.0	100.0
Gross Profit								
Operating Expenses	97.1	97.2	93.2	94.1	91.5	94.8	96.6	95.3
Operating Profit	2.9	2.8	6.8	5.9	8.5	5.2	3.4	4.7
All Other Expenses (net)	2.1	.5	-.3	-.9	-2.2	-2.9	2.0	.7
Profit Before Taxes	.7	2.4	7.1	6.9	10.7	8.1	1.4	3.9
RATIOS								
Current	5.1	4.6	5.0	4.6	2.9	6.9	5.6	6.7
	1.8	2.4	2.2	2.4	1.7	3.9	2.2	2.2
	1.0	1.1	1.3	1.4	1.3	1.1	1.1	1.1
Quick	5.1	3.5	4.9	4.4	2.6	6.0	5.1	5.9
	1.3	1.6	2.1	2.2	1.4	3.8	2.1	2.1
	.7	.7	1.0	1.0	1.0	.6	.9	.9
Sales/Receivables	**0** UND	**0** UND	**4** 91.1	**7** 52.1	**12** 31.6	**8** 47.1	**3** 114.5	**3** 115.8
	9 38.5	**8** 44.0	**12** 29.7	**22** 16.9	**14** 25.2	**15** 24.3	**15** 24.6	**14** 26.6
	25 14.7	**33** 11.1	**27** 13.7	**45** 8.1	**27** 13.5	**57** 6.4	**39** 9.3	**37** 9.9
Cost of Sales/Inventory								
Cost of Sales/Payables								
Sales/Working Capital	4.8	2.0	2.1	1.7	2.7	.9	2.0	1.9
	19.0	6.3	5.0	2.8	6.8	1.7	4.9	4.7
	-316.3	26.6	20.9	8.7	10.1	48.4	61.9	37.5
EBIT/Interest		4.1	9.8	23.2			9.2	12.2
		(21) 1.3	(40) 5.3	(27) 8.0			(145) 2.3	(146) 2.7
		-2.8	1.1	.1			-1.1	.4
Net Profit + Depr., Dep., Amort./Cur. Mat. L/T/D							19.0	16.0
							(17) 3.2	(17) 7.9
							.2	1.0
Fixed/Worth	.0	.0	.1	.1	.0	.1	.1	.1
	.0	.6	.3	.3	.2	.1	.4	.4
	3.1	1.1	1.0	.6	.7	1.2	1.3	1.1
Debt/Worth	.3	.3	.3	.4	.3	.3	.4	.3
	2.8	.9	.7	.8	.8	.6	.9	.8
	5.7	10.7	1.5	1.6	1.4	2.6	2.5	2.5
% Profit Before Taxes/Tangible Net Worth	20.4	8.0	17.9	18.0	13.6	18.4	15.1	16.6
	(22) -1.0	(40) 1.5	(85) 7.3	(65) 9.8	6.8	8.0	(274) 2.9	(303) 6.5
	-34.6	-12.8	-.4	1.9	3.9	3.6	-10.1	-1.9
% Profit Before Taxes/Total Assets	11.1	6.1	9.8	9.1	5.4	6.8	8.3	8.1
	-.6	.9	3.7	5.9	4.6	2.3	1.3	3.0
	-10.3	-5.9	-.2	.3	1.3	1.4	-5.4	-1.0
Sales/Net Fixed Assets	UND	154.4	50.6	17.2	22.6	17.9	32.1	45.5
	158.0	11.3	8.0	6.8	8.5	9.5	6.8	8.5
	11.7	1.5	1.5	2.8	1.4	3.1	1.9	1.6
Sales/Total Assets	7.0	1.9	1.9	1.3	2.2	.6	2.0	1.6
	3.3	1.1	1.1	.8	.7	.5	1.0	1.0
	2.0	.7	.5	.6	.6	.4	.6	.6
% Depr., Dep., Amort./Sales	.4	.8	1.0	1.5			1.1	1.2
	(10) 1.9	(32) 1.7	(61) 2.2	(57) 2.4			(241) 2.0	(244) 2.3
	2.6	4.3	4.1	4.4			3.9	4.2
% Officers', Directors' Owners' Comp/Sales							2.7	1.7
							(26) 6.0	(27) 8.2
							10.8	18.6
Net Sales ($)	23272M	84306M	550366M	1697516M	941176M	1338948M	6595203M	7318614M
Total Assets ($)	6170M	54250M	389155M	1538077M	779303M	1478848M	5254040M	6963737M

M = $ thousand MM = $ million

See Pages 9 through 22 for Explanation of Ratios and Data

Comparative Historical Data				Current Data Sorted by Sales					
			Type of Statement						
188	158	139	Unqualified	5	28	17	21	37	31
26	13	8	Reviewed	3	4		1		
18	8	13	Compiled	5	3	3	1	1	
16	15	10	Tax Returns	7	3				
106	93	79	Other	23	19	10	10	5	12
4/1/11-3/31/12 ALL	**4/1/12-3/31/13 ALL**	**4/1/13-3/31/14 ALL**		**117 (4/1-9/30/13)**			**132 (10/1/13-3/31/14)**		
				0-1MM	**1-3MM**	**3-5MM**	**5-10MM**	**10-25MM**	**25MM & OVER**
354	287	249	**NUMBER OF STATEMENTS**	43	57	30	33	43	43
%	%	%	**ASSETS**	%	%	%	%	%	%
40.3	42.1	39.7	Cash & Equivalents	38.4	33.6	39.8	48.9	48.0	33.5
10.2	7.2	10.0	Trade Receivables (net)	9.6	7.5	11.8	8.3	10.0	13.6
1.4	1.4	2.0	Inventory	2.1	2.4	.7	.5	1.2	4.2
3.5	3.7	4.2	All Other Current	5.8	3.3	4.4	1.7	3.6	6.1
55.5	54.4	55.8	Total Current	55.8	46.9	56.7	59.4	62.7	57.4
27.3	27.6	25.6	Fixed Assets (net)	29.8	36.9	27.8	20.0	17.6	17.3
1.7	.9	1.4	Intangibles (net)	1.4	1.1	.2	2.7	.3	2.7
15.5	17.1	17.2	All Other Non-Current	13.0	15.1	15.2	17.8	19.4	22.6
100.0	100.0	100.0	Total	100.0	100.0	100.0	100.0	100.0	100.0
			LIABILITIES						
5.0	4.2	4.8	Notes Payable-Short Term	12.4	2.4	2.1	10.1	.7	2.2
2.1	1.7	1.3	Cur. Mat.-L.T.D.	.6	1.3	3.1	1.4	.9	.8
7.7	6.8	8.2	Trade Payables	6.1	5.2	10.4	6.2	9.0	13.7
.4	.1	.1	Income Taxes Payable	.5	.0	.0	.2	.1	.1
15.2	15.1	16.5	All Other Current	20.1	13.2	17.3	18.3	14.6	17.0
30.3	27.8	30.9	Total Current	39.7	22.2	32.8	36.2	25.3	33.9
12.2	11.1	10.0	Long-Term Debt	15.6	16.6	9.0	4.1	4.4	6.4
.1	.1	.1	Deferred Taxes	.0	.0	.0	.0	.2	.6
9.8	12.0	12.8	All Other Non-Current	10.2	7.1	19.1	15.4	15.1	14.5
47.7	49.1	46.2	Net Worth	34.6	54.1	39.1	44.4	55.0	44.7
100.0	100.0	100.0	Total Liabilities & Net Worth	100.0	100.0	100.0	100.0	100.0	100.0
			INCOME DATA						
100.0	100.0	100.0	Net Sales	100.0	100.0	100.0	100.0	100.0	100.0
			Gross Profit						
95.6	94.9	94.6	Operating Expenses	92.9	92.7	93.6	97.0	96.7	95.6
4.4	5.1	5.4	Operating Profit	7.1	7.3	6.4	3.0	3.3	4.4
.9	.6	-.3	All Other Expenses (net)	2.7	1.3	-.9	-1.4	-2.3	-2.0
3.5	4.6	5.7	Profit Before Taxes	4.4	6.0	7.3	4.4	5.7	6.4
			RATIOS						
6.2	6.3	4.9		7.0	3.6	4.9	4.4	5.0	3.9
2.2	2.6	2.3	Current	2.7	2.3	2.2	2.0	2.8	1.7
1.1	1.2	1.2		1.1	1.0	1.4	1.1	1.6	1.2
6.1	6.0	4.5		7.0	2.9	4.8	4.4	4.9	3.8
2.0	2.2	1.9	Quick	1.8	1.4	2.2	1.9	2.7	1.4
1.0	1.0	.9		.7	.7	1.3	.8	1.3	.7
3 129.9	**2** 231.0	**4** 95.4		**0** UND	**0** UND	**9** 39.8	**3** 112.7	**9** 41.2	**10** 36.8
14 26.8	**11** 33.0	**13** 27.9	Sales/Receivables	**9** 39.5	**8** 43.0	**23** 16.1	**8** 43.9	**13** 28.2	**23** 16.0
41 9.0	**28** 13.0	**32** 11.5		**23** 15.7	**21** 17.1	**44** 8.3	**30** 12.1	**42** 8.7	**41** 8.8
			Cost of Sales/Inventory						
			Cost of Sales/Payables						
1.9	1.9	2.0		1.8	2.0	2.1	2.4	1.8	2.1
4.5	4.0	4.9	Sales/Working Capital	8.2	5.9	3.2	4.5	3.1	6.7
30.1	20.8	22.2		84.6	NM	19.0	NM	7.9	25.8
12.6	18.7	10.4		3.0	8.4	8.4	10.8	73.1	23.9
(174) 3.2	(128) 4.4	(103) 3.9	EBIT/Interest	(17) -.4	(28) 1.3	(14) 4.3	(13) 5.0	(13) 8.4	(18) 9.4
-.2	1.0	.1		-6.9	-.8	2.7	1.8	-3.8	4.7
10.7	6.4								
(19) 3.7	(14) .6		Net Profit + Depr., Dep., Amort./Cur. Mat. L/T/D						
.4	.1								
.1	.1	.1		.0	.1	.1	.1	.1	.1
.3	.4	.3	Fixed/Worth	.0	.6	.5	.3	.2	.2
1.3	1.1	1.0		1.3	1.4	1.1	.8	.4	.6
.3	.3	.3		.3	.2	.7	.4	.5	.4
.9	.8	.8	Debt/Worth	.8	.6	.9	.6	.8	1.0
2.1	2.0	2.4		5.2	1.9	1.6	2.9	1.1	4.6
15.8	17.1	16.8		5.9	15.9	19.7	15.6	20.5	21.0
(324) 4.5	(267) 6.6	(234) 6.4	% Profit Before Taxes/Tangible Net Worth	(39) .1	(53) 2.1	(28) 10.0	(31) 7.4	(42) 11.9	(41) 9.0
-3.3	-.4	-1.5		-16.8	-4.0	-.6	-3.3	.8	3.8
8.4	8.7	9.1		4.0	10.2	10.3	9.2	10.6	6.6
2.2	3.4	3.5	% Profit Before Taxes/Total Assets	.0	1.6	5.1	3.4	6.5	4.3
-1.9	-.5	-.7		-6.4	-1.7	.5	-1.4	.4	1.4
43.2	38.9	57.5		UND	54.6	47.4	94.6	20.4	25.4
9.7	7.5	10.1	Sales/Net Fixed Assets	19.9	2.4	6.1	18.2	10.2	10.7
1.6	1.8	2.1		1.2	1.0	1.6	3.0	4.2	5.0
1.9	1.7	2.0		3.1	1.5	1.9	2.4	1.7	2.1
1.0	.9	1.1	Sales/Total Assets	.9	.9	1.1	1.5	1.1	1.0
.6	.6	.6		.3	.4	.6	.7	.7	.6
1.1	1.0	1.0		1.2	1.4	.9	.7	1.1	.9
(272) 2.3	(217) 2.1	(178) 2.2	% Depr., Dep., Amort./Sales	(19) 2.5	(42) 3.0	(26) 1.5	(21) 2.4	(37) 1.7	(33) 2.1
4.3	3.9	4.2		17.4	5.5	2.8	3.5	2.7	4.6
2.6	2.9	2.6							
(27) 11.5	(18) 10.3	(17) 12.1	% Officers', Directors' Owners' Comp/Sales						
31.8	29.9	25.6							
5104552M	**3238969M**	**4635584M**	Net Sales ($)	**19383M**	**103890M**	**118950M**	**245676M**	**708321M**	**3439364M**
5475625M	**4173485M**	**4245803M**	Total Assets ($)	**47036M**	**217868M**	**135536M**	**261320M**	**738264M**	**2845779M**

M = $ thousand MM = $ million

See Pages 9 through 22 for Explanation of Ratios and Data

	Current Data Sorted by Assets						Comparative Historical Data	
Type of Statement								
Unqualified	1	8	49	56	11	7	146	167
Reviewed	1	2	3	2			4	8
Compiled		1	1	1			7	5
Tax Returns	1	3		1			10	13
Other	4	5	21	16	8	6	59	62
	112 (4/1-9/30/13)			96 (10/1/13-3/31/14)				
	0-500M	500M-2MM	2-10MM	10-50MM	50-100MM	100-250MM	4/1/09-3/31/10 ALL	4/1/10-3/31/11 ALL
NUMBER OF STATEMENTS	7	19	74	76	19	13	226	255
ASSETS	%	%	%	%	%	%	%	%
Cash & Equivalents		44.6	35.5	44.7	30.8	35.2	38.3	40.2
Trade Receivables (net)		9.1	10.9	6.9	8.7	2.9	9.8	8.5
Inventory		5.4	.3	1.3	.7	.2	1.6	1.1
All Other Current		2.7	5.0	2.6	7.1	1.8	3.2	4.6
Total Current		61.8	51.7	55.5	47.3	40.1	52.9	54.4
Fixed Assets (net)		28.6	26.8	22.3	17.1	14.0	28.9	25.2
Intangibles (net)		.0	2.1	.8	6.2	14.1	1.4	1.3
All Other Non-Current		9.5	19.4	21.4	29.3	31.8	16.9	19.1
Total		100.0	100.0	100.0	100.0	100.0	100.0	100.0
LIABILITIES								
Notes Payable-Short Term		4.0	.6	.7	.8	.0	2.8	1.8
Cur. Mat.-L.T.D.		.7	1.1	.6	.4	.8	1.5	1.0
Trade Payables		10.6	7.3	8.6	6.3	4.7	7.4	7.2
Income Taxes Payable		.0	.4	.5	.1	.0	.6	.4
All Other Current		10.7	19.2	12.8	16.7	15.2	14.6	15.6
Total Current		26.0	28.7	23.2	24.3	20.7	26.8	26.1
Long-Term Debt		10.0	11.1	8.6	7.8	12.6	15.6	12.6
Deferred Taxes		.0	.2	.0	.0	1.2	.3	.2
All Other Non-Current		5.4	9.5	9.9	10.3	8.0	11.3	11.5
Net Worth		58.6	50.4	58.2	57.5	57.4	46.1	49.6
Total Liabilities & Net Worth		100.0	100.0	100.0	100.0	100.0	100.0	100.0
INCOME DATA								
Net Sales		100.0	100.0	100.0	100.0	100.0	100.0	100.0
Gross Profit								
Operating Expenses		93.1	97.3	96.5	95.9	91.2	97.5	95.3
Operating Profit		6.9	2.7	3.5	4.1	8.8	2.5	4.7
All Other Expenses (net)		2.3	-1.0	-3.4	-2.9	-.1	1.9	-.4
Profit Before Taxes		4.6	3.7	6.9	7.0	8.9	.6	5.0
RATIOS								
Current		10.6	4.4	5.3	4.5	5.2	5.3	6.7
		3.5	2.0	3.2	1.6	1.7	2.2	2.1
		2.4	1.0	1.6	1.0	1.0	1.3	1.1
Quick		10.6	4.3	5.3	4.3	5.1	4.5	6.5
		2.8	1.7	2.9	1.0	1.5	1.9	1.8
		1.7	.9	1.5	.8	.9	1.1	1.0
Sales/Receivables		0 UND	3 142.3	7 53.4	4 84.4	0 UND	3 106.6	4 93.2
		6 62.8	18 19.9	15 23.6	15 24.4	20 18.6	14 26.2	14 26.7
		24 15.1	30 12.2	26 13.8	31 11.9	24 14.9	32 11.5	28 13.1
Cost of Sales/Inventory								
Cost of Sales/Payables								
Sales/Working Capital		1.3	2.4	1.1	2.0	2.8	1.8	1.6
		2.9	5.3	2.7	9.6	6.9	4.6	4.4
		7.8	66.7	7.4	-514.9	NM	20.1	30.9
EBIT/Interest			17.3	21.3			6.7	13.5
			(28) 2.5	(32) 6.2			(115) 2.1	(126) 3.4
			1.1	2.0			-1.7	1.2
Net Profit + Depr., Dep., Amort./Cur. Mat. L/T/D							9.7	
							(15) 2.7	
							1.1	
Fixed/Worth		.0	.1	.1	.0	.1	.2	.1
		.5	.3	.3	.4	.4	.5	.4
		1.0	1.0	.6	.8	.7	1.2	1.0
Debt/Worth		.1	.4	.3	.3	.4	.4	.4
		.5	.9	.6	.8	.9	1.0	.8
		.8	2.1	1.1	2.6	2.4	2.5	2.2
% Profit Before Taxes/Tangible Net Worth		10.7	14.7	13.5	24.8	11.9	11.4	13.4
		(18) 6.4	(69) 5.3	(75) 7.9	7.0	(11) 3.1	(210) .8	(241) 5.8
		-2.9	-.1	2.7	-.2	-8.8	-9.8	-.4
% Profit Before Taxes/Total Assets		7.3	6.8	7.9	9.0	10.8	5.0	7.0
		5.3	3.8	4.2	3.9	2.6	.3	2.8
		-1.4	.1	1.1	-.1	-3.7	-6.3	-.2
Sales/Net Fixed Assets		60.2	45.0	17.4	27.2	56.7	18.4	30.0
		3.5	6.8	5.4	12.3	10.0	5.0	5.6
		1.8	1.8	2.2	3.4	1.8	1.9	1.8
Sales/Total Assets		2.2	1.6	1.0	1.1	1.0	1.5	1.4
		1.1	1.0	.7	.7	.5	.9	.8
		.7	.5	.5	.6	.4	.5	.5
% Depr., Dep., Amort./Sales		1.0	1.1	1.2	.5		1.5	1.3
		(16) 1.9	(63) 1.9	(69) 2.2	(17) 2.2		(191) 2.5	(211) 2.5
		3.9	4.1	4.0	4.4		4.7	4.4
% Officers', Directors' Owners' Comp/Sales							3.3	2.1
							(17) 8.3	(15) 7.5
							29.9	23.1
Net Sales ($)	8612M	35715M	527579M	1886185M	1272605M	1785454M	7507235M	7250987M
Total Assets ($)	2127M	21936M	404025M	1719562M	1342444M	2053186M	7176157M	8047759M

M = $ thousand MM = $ million

See Pages 9 through 22 for Explanation of Ratios and Data

Comparative Historical Data | Current Data Sorted by Sales

4/1/11-3/31/12 ALL	4/1/12-3/31/13 ALL	4/1/13-3/31/14 ALL		0-1MM	1-3MM	3-5MM	5-10MM	10-25MM	25MM & OVER
			Type of Statement						
189	152	132	Unqualified	6	19	16	25	34	32
6	8	8	Reviewed	2	3	1		1	1
5	4	3	Compiled	1		1	1		
5	8	5	Tax Returns	2			2		1
61	46	60	Other	5	4	8	8	19	16
				112 (4/1-9/30/13)			96 (10/1/13-3/31/14)		
266	218	208	**NUMBER OF STATEMENTS**	16	26	26	36	54	50
%	%	%	**ASSETS**	%	%	%	%	%	%
39.4	42.1	39.5	Cash & Equivalents	39.3	33.3	38.3	41.7	42.0	39.1
8.3	8.7	8.3	Trade Receivables (net)	1.6	6.9	11.7	10.5	7.8	8.4
1.1	1.2	1.4	Inventory	.1	1.9	.4	2.8	.7	1.6
4.1	2.8	4.1	All Other Current	5.9	3.0	4.3	1.8	4.0	5.6
53.0	54.8	53.3	Total Current	46.9	45.2	54.7	56.8	54.5	54.8
25.6	24.5	23.6	Fixed Assets (net)	42.8	31.0	28.5	21.3	21.5	14.9
2.0	2.1	2.5	Intangibles (net)	.0	.1	3.0	.1	1.9	6.6
19.4	18.5	20.7	All Other Non-Current	10.3	23.7	13.9	21.8	22.0	23.6
100.0	100.0	100.0	Total	100.0	100.0	100.0	100.0	100.0	100.0
			LIABILITIES						
2.1	1.1	1.4	Notes Payable-Short Term	7.1	.3	3.0	.9	.6	.6
1.3	1.1	1.0	Cur. Mat.-L.T.D.	3.2	1.8	1.1	.5	.7	.6
7.2	5.8	7.6	Trade Payables	1.4	4.2	8.0	12.7	7.7	7.5
.5	.3	.4	Income Taxes Payable	.0	.0	1.2	.0	.8	.0
14.8	16.8	15.8	All Other Current	6.4	14.7	20.4	17.8	11.0	20.7
25.9	25.1	26.2	Total Current	18.1	21.0	33.7	31.8	20.8	29.4
11.0	10.8	10.9	Long-Term Debt	30.0	10.4	9.7	9.3	9.9	8.0
.2	.1	.2	Deferred Taxes	.1	.1	.0	.4	.0	.3
12.5	11.8	9.0	All Other Non-Current	1.7	6.2	11.0	7.1	9.5	12.5
50.4	52.3	53.7	Net Worth	50.1	62.3	45.6	51.5	59.8	49.7
100.0	100.0	100.0	Total Liabilties & Net Worth	100.0	100.0	100.0	100.0	100.0	100.0
			INCOME DATA						
100.0	100.0	100.0	Net Sales	100.0	100.0	100.0	100.0	100.0	100.0
			Gross Profit						
95.2	94.8	96.1	Operating Expenses	94.3	99.7	96.4	97.3	94.8	95.3
4.8	5.2	3.9	Operating Profit	5.7	.3	3.6	2.7	5.2	4.7
.5	.0	-1.6	All Other Expenses (net)	2.5	-1.2	-1.3	-2.4	-3.0	-1.4
4.3	5.2	5.5	Profit Before Taxes	3.2	1.6	4.9	5.1	8.1	6.2
			RATIOS						
6.2	6.3	5.2		13.9	7.1	4.7	4.4	5.4	4.9
2.3	2.8	2.4	Current	7.8	2.8	1.9	2.2	2.9	1.8
1.2	1.3	1.1		1.8	1.0	1.0	1.3	1.7	1.0
5.9	5.8	5.0		13.9	6.5	4.6	4.0	5.4	3.8
2.1	2.5	2.1	Quick	4.9	2.4	1.7	2.0	2.5	1.4
1.0	1.1	1.0		1.0	.8	1.0	1.2	1.6	.8
4 100.7	3 115.3	3 137.4		0 UND	2 235.8	5 67.0	3 120.4	7 50.3	2 158.8
11 33.0	12 31.7	15 24.1	Sales/Receivables	0 UND	15 24.3	17 21.2	15 23.9	17 22.1	16 22.7
27 13.6	29 12.7	27 13.5		8 45.3	27 13.7	40 9.2	30 12.0	26 14.2	27 13.4
			Cost of Sales/Inventory						
			Cost of Sales/Payables						
1.7	1.6	1.8		.9	1.9	1.8	2.4	1.7	2.0
4.3	3.9	4.4	Sales/Working Capital	2.3	3.0	4.1	5.9	3.3	7.0
19.7	14.9	28.5		22.4	205.9	NM	23.5	6.7	-411.7
11.4	15.1	19.7			19.3	41.6	20.9	21.3	69.1
(127) 4.4	(101) 4.4	(85) 5.0	EBIT/Interest		(12) 2.6	(10) 2.9	(14) 2.9	(24) 7.4	(19) 12.6
.6	.7	1.5			1.8	.9	-1.9	2.1	-.5
4.3	20.2								
(13) 1.9	(10) 3.7		Net Profit + Depr., Dep., Amort./Cur. Mat. L/T/D						
1.0	2.1								
.1	.1	.1		.2	.1	.1	.1	.0	.0
.4	.4	.3	Fixed/Worth	.7	.4	.4	.3	.2	.3
.9	.9	.8		1.6	.8	1.2	1.0	.6	.6
.4	.3	.3		.1	.2	.3	.5	.3	.5
.9	.8	.7	Debt/Worth	.3	.5	1.1	.6	.6	.9
1.8	1.7	1.5		1.1	1.1	3.0	1.8	1.2	2.4
15.4	14.8	14.0		11.1	6.9	14.8	12.0	14.3	24.8
(252) 6.9	(207) 6.2	(197) 6.7	% Profit Before Taxes/Tangible Net Worth	(14) 6.4	4.2	(24) 6.2	(34) 6.5	(52) 9.2	(47) 7.0
-1.8	-.9	.3		-1.1	-1.4	.3	-3.9	3.2	.1
8.0	7.9	8.1		10.1	5.0	6.8	6.5	8.5	9.6
3.8	3.7	4.0	% Profit Before Taxes/Total Assets	5.2	1.9	2.9	4.0	4.9	3.7
-.7	-.7	.1		-.6	-1.2	.2	-2.1	1.6	.1
24.7	22.8	34.4		13.4	28.3	26.2	59.1	27.5	40.3
5.0	6.7	6.1	Sales/Net Fixed Assets	2.3	2.9	5.7	8.6	6.0	11.9
1.7	2.0	2.1		.3	1.6	1.3	1.8	3.1	3.9
1.3	1.4	1.3		1.0	1.1	1.4	1.5	1.2	2.1
.8	.9	.8	Sales/Total Assets	.6	.7	.6	1.0	.9	.9
.5	.6	.6		.2	.4	.4	.6	.6	.7
1.3	1.3	1.0		1.0	1.6	1.4	.7	1.0	.7
(219) 2.4	(178) 2.2	(178) 2.1	% Depr., Dep., Amort./Sales	(14) 3.9	(22) 3.2	(23) 2.0	(33) 1.9	(47) 1.9	(39) 2.2
4.1	4.0	4.0		11.7	5.8	6.1	3.9	2.7	3.8
5.7	2.6	5.7							
(12) 14.7	(21) 7.2	(22) 14.5	% Officers', Directors' Owners' Comp/Sales						
32.2	16.8	23.6							
8667082M	5407989M	5516150M	Net Sales ($)	8639M	49605M	104000M	267882M	843869M	4242155M
8346493M	6516340M	5543280M	Total Assets ($)	26083M	89460M	203314M	356870M	1120845M	3746708M

M = $ thousand MM = $ million

See Pages 9 through 22 for Explanation of Ratios and Data

	Current Data Sorted by Assets						Comparative Historical Data	
Type of Statement								
Unqualified		8	15	18	6	3	60	67
Reviewed			2				3	2
Compiled				1			5	6
Tax Returns	2	2	1	1			7	5
Other	1	4	4	7	1	3	31	22
	53 (4/1-9/30/13)			26 (10/1/13-3/31/14)			4/1/09-3/31/10	4/1/10-3/31/11
	0-500M	500M-2MM	2-10MM	10-50MM	50-100MM	100-250MM	ALL	ALL
NUMBER OF STATEMENTS	3	14	22	27	7	6	106	102
ASSETS	%	%	%	%	%	%	%	%
Cash & Equivalents		62.2	35.0	48.6			48.2	45.7
Trade Receivables (net)		5.0	2.8	4.5			4.0	3.8
Inventory		.0	.0	.2			.2	.5
All Other Current		2.8	4.5	1.4			3.5	2.5
Total Current		69.9	42.3	54.7			55.9	52.5
Fixed Assets (net)		25.9	50.7	31.6			33.7	35.2
Intangibles (net)		.0	.0	2.5			.1	.4
All Other Non-Current		4.2	6.9	11.3			10.3	11.9
Total		100.0	100.0	100.0			100.0	100.0
LIABILITIES								
Notes Payable-Short Term		.1	.2	.0			1.9	.8
Cur. Mat.-L.T.D.		.8	1.6	.6			1.5	1.0
Trade Payables		2.7	1.0	2.1			2.5	3.2
Income Taxes Payable		.0	.0	.0			.0	.0
All Other Current		6.3	8.3	4.5			10.4	9.5
Total Current		9.8	11.1	7.2			16.3	14.5
Long-Term Debt		7.0	27.7	11.5			11.6	14.8
Deferred Taxes		.0	.0	.0			.0	.0
All Other Non-Current		.5	1.1	10.8			3.9	4.5
Net Worth		82.7	60.0	70.5			68.2	66.2
Total Liabilities & Net Worth		100.0	100.0	100.0			100.0	100.0
INCOME DATA								
Net Sales		100.0	100.0	100.0			100.0	100.0
Gross Profit								
Operating Expenses		97.6	91.6	95.6			95.0	94.3
Operating Profit		2.4	8.4	4.4			5.0	5.7
All Other Expenses (net)		2.5	1.0	-1.4			2.9	.4
Profit Before Taxes		.0	7.5	5.9			2.0	5.3
RATIOS								
Current		60.6	21.7	19.3			64.5	49.2
		15.5	5.2	9.0			6.8	5.5
		2.8	2.7	3.5			2.1	2.2
Quick		60.6	15.9	19.3			63.5	46.6
		15.5	4.4	8.0			6.1	5.0
		2.8	2.4	3.3			1.8	2.0
Sales/Receivables		0 UND	0 UND	0 UND			0 UND	0 UND
		0 UND	0 UND	16 23.2			1 299.4	3 118.7
		34 10.8	18 20.1	35 10.3			22 16.4	26 13.8
Cost of Sales/Inventory								
Cost of Sales/Payables								
Sales/Working Capital		1.0	1.7	1.0			1.3	1.0
		2.3	2.4	1.5			2.9	2.5
		3.9	4.9	2.9			7.8	6.4
EBIT/Interest			24.3	33.7			6.6	9.9
			(13) 1.2	(13) 3.4			(46) .5	(46) 1.4
			-.2	-.1			-4.0	-1.0
Net Profit + Depr., Dep., Amort./Cur. Mat. L/T/D								
Fixed/Worth		.0	.2	.0			.1	.0
		.1	.8	.5			.4	.5
		.7	2.2	.8			1.0	1.2
Debt/Worth		.0	.0	.1			.0	.0
		.1	.7	.2			.3	.3
		.6	1.9	.6			1.0	1.0
% Profit Before Taxes/Tangible Net Worth		12.9	17.7	12.4			12.9	9.6
		3.1	(21) 9.6	(26) 5.6			(102) .7	(97) 2.6
		-6.2	-8.7	-.9			-8.5	-5.1
% Profit Before Taxes/Total Assets		9.6	11.7	7.7			9.3	7.0
		2.9	5.2	1.8			.1	1.9
		-4.5	-3.2	-2.2			-6.0	-3.3
Sales/Net Fixed Assets		106.6	11.4	UND			28.2	45.0
		10.6	1.3	3.2			4.4	4.2
		2.3	.5	1.0			1.3	1.1
Sales/Total Assets		2.2	1.3	1.1			1.4	1.3
		1.0	.8	.6			.9	.7
		.6	.4	.4			.5	.4
% Depr., Dep., Amort./Sales		1.2	1.0	2.0			1.0	.7
		(11) 2.5	(21) 2.5	(15) 3.1			(80) 2.1	(79) 2.0
		4.7	6.5	6.3			4.4	4.4
% Officers', Directors' Owners' Comp/Sales							6.3	6.5
							(18) 16.1	(11) 12.8
							32.2	19.3
Net Sales ($)	2304M	20091M	96299M	557513M	370710M	594896M	2569269M	2301826M
Total Assets ($)	882M	15539M	102785M	749461M	516944M	881455M	2802757M	3508218M

M = $ thousand MM = $ million

See Pages 9 through 22 for Explanation of Ratios and Data

Comparative Historical Data				Current Data Sorted by Sales					
			Type of Statement						
73	51	50	Unqualified	6	8	3	13	9	11
3	4	2	Reviewed		2				
2	4	1	Compiled				1		
5	1	6	Tax Returns	4		1			1
35	30	20	Other	2	2	5	3	3	5
4/1/11-3/31/12	**4/1/12-3/31/13**	**4/1/13-3/31/14**		**53 (4/1-9/30/13)**			**26 (10/1/13-3/31/14)**		
ALL	**ALL**	**ALL**		**0-1MM**	**1-3MM**	**3-5MM**	**5-10MM**	**10-25MM**	**25MM & OVER**
118	90	79	**NUMBER OF STATEMENTS**	12	12	9	17	12	17
%	%	%	**ASSETS**	%	%	%	%	%	%
41.4	46.6	49.8	Cash & Equivalents	45.4	35.9		44.9	61.5	55.7
3.7	3.4	4.8	Trade Receivables (net)	1.6	5.2		2.7	5.1	10.5
.3	.1	.1	Inventory	.0	.0		.0	.1	.4
2.4	2.3	3.4	All Other Current	7.8	2.4		3.9	2.1	.8
47.9	52.3	58.1	Total Current	54.8	43.5		51.4	68.7	67.4
35.2	37.6	31.5	Fixed Assets (net)	44.2	51.6		34.9	18.7	17.7
.3	.3	.9	Intangibles (net)	.0	.0		3.8	.4	.1
16.7	9.9	9.5	All Other Non-Current	1.0	4.9		9.9	12.2	14.8
100.0	100.0	100.0	Total	100.0	100.0		100.0	100.0	100.0
			LIABILITIES						
.7	.7	.2	Notes Payable-Short Term	.1	.4		.0	.0	.5
1.4	1.4	.9	Cur. Mat.-L.T.D.	1.2	2.0		1.4	.1	.3
2.0	2.6	1.9	Trade Payables	3.3	.5		1.3	1.8	3.6
.0	.0	.0	Income Taxes Payable	.0	.0		.0	.0	.0
6.2	7.1	6.6	All Other Current	8.6	6.3		8.3	8.4	5.0
10.2	11.8	9.5	Total Current	13.2	9.1		10.9	10.2	9.5
12.1	14.3	13.1	Long-Term Debt	21.5	28.1		11.4	8.3	5.2
.1	.1	.0	Deferred Taxes	.0	.0		.0	.0	.0
6.0	7.3	5.0	All Other Non-Current	.5	.6		1.6	4.7	17.7
71.7	66.5	72.3	Net Worth	64.8	62.1		76.1	76.8	67.7
100.0	100.0	100.0	Total Liabilties & Net Worth	100.0	100.0		100.0	100.0	100.0
			INCOME DATA						
100.0	100.0	100.0	Net Sales	100.0	100.0		100.0	100.0	100.0
			Gross Profit						
91.7	94.9	92.7	Operating Expenses	89.5	100.3		94.9	92.7	93.9
8.3	5.1	7.3	Operating Profit	10.5	-.3		5.1	7.3	6.1
.8	1.7	-.1	All Other Expenses (net)	5.1	-1.2		-1.2	-1.0	-1.5
7.5	3.5	7.4	Profit Before Taxes	5.3	.9		6.3	8.2	7.6
			RATIOS						
29.0	22.2	45.4		50.2	28.0		39.7	253.2	127.5
7.5	4.8	9.9	Current	8.2	3.4		11.4	5.8	16.8
2.4	2.2	2.9		2.5	2.6		3.1	4.0	2.7
28.2	21.3	45.4		50.1	19.2		38.9	249.0	127.3
6.7	4.6	9.4	Quick	7.0	3.4		11.4	5.6	16.4
2.4	2.0	2.6		2.0	2.5		2.6	3.7	2.5
0 UND	**0** UND	**0** UND		**0** UND	**0** UND		**0** UND	**0** UND	**0** UND
0 UND	**0** 999.8	**1** 614.6	Sales/Receivables	**0** UND	**0** UND		**0** 999.8	**23** 16.2	**23** 15.9
27 13.7	**23** 16.2	**33** 11.1		**33** 11.2	**37** 9.9		**31** 11.7	**49** 7.5	**48** 7.6
			Cost of Sales/Inventory						
			Cost of Sales/Payables						
1.3	1.2	1.0		.9	2.4		.6	.7	.9
2.4	3.0	1.8	Sales/Working Capital	1.7	3.4		1.8	1.4	1.7
5.6	7.2	3.7		2.3	5.8		4.2	1.9	5.0
7.3	17.5	28.1					28.1		
(52) 2.6	(38) 3.8	(34) 2.8	EBIT/Interest				(10) 3.4		
.6	-.3	-.6					.5		
			Net Profit + Depr., Dep., Amort./Cur. Mat. L/T/D						
.0	.1	.0		.1	.1		.0	.0	.0
.5	.5	.3	Fixed/Worth	.6	.9		.5	.1	.2
1.1	1.0	.9		1.5	1.9		.9	.5	.6
.0	.0	.0		.1	.1		.1	.0	.0
.2	.3	.2	Debt/Worth	.6	.5		.2	.2	.1
.9	1.0	.7		1.3	1.6		.7	.6	1.2
10.0	10.3	13.8		11.6	15.7		10.7	13.5	14.0
(114) 4.7	(87) 2.9	(77) 6.5	% Profit Before Taxes/Tangible Net Worth	.4	(11) 6.3		1.7	8.7	(16) 5.7
-.9	-6.9	-3.0		-6.2	-6.0		-4.5	.7	-4.3
7.8	5.8	10.5		8.3	6.1		5.8	10.3	13.6
2.9	2.4	3.8	% Profit Before Taxes/Total Assets	.2	4.5		1.3	5.4	1.8
-1.0	-2.7	-2.2		-3.6	-2.8		-3.2	.4	-3.7
72.3	23.8	112.7		10.8	16.4		UND	UND	295.0
4.0	3.3	4.8	Sales/Net Fixed Assets	1.3	2.6		3.2	49.4	15.0
1.1	.9	1.1		.3	.5		.8	1.6	3.8
1.3	1.5	1.3		.9	1.9		1.3	1.1	1.5
.7	.7	.7	Sales/Total Assets	.5	1.0		.6	.6	1.1
.4	.4	.4		.2	.4		.2	.4	.6
.7	.6	1.0		1.9	.5		1.3		.6
(88) 2.1	(70) 1.8	(57) 2.3	% Depr., Dep., Amort./Sales	(10) 4.5	(11) 2.5		(11) 2.5		(14) 1.5
5.8	4.7	4.4		11.5	4.0		7.8		2.3
4.7	2.7	.3							
(17) 9.7	(13) 9.2	(13) 3.0	% Officers', Directors' Owners' Comp/Sales						
20.7	22.9	11.6							
2438894M	**1475001M**	**1641813M**	Net Sales ($)	**8018M**	**20791M**	**32577M**	**128461M**	**195548M**	**1256418M**
3008141M	**1711802M**	**2267066M**	Total Assets ($)	**18619M**	**32506M**	**53063M**	**345970M**	**392821M**	**1424087M**

M = $ thousand MM = $ million

See Pages 9 through 22 for Explanation of Ratios and Data

Current Data Sorted by Assets							Comparative Historical Data	
						Type of Statement		
23	43	52	42	10	5	Unqualified	174	198
3	4	4				Reviewed	11	19
4	2	8	1			Compiled	15	15
9	4	2	2			Tax Returns	16	18
57	42	42	18	5	1	Other	132	135
112 (4/1-9/30/13)			271 (10/1/13-3/31/14)				**4/1/09-3/31/10 ALL**	**4/1/10-3/31/11 ALL**
0-500M	**500M-2MM**	**2-10MM**	**10-50MM**	**50-100MM**	**100-250MM**			
96	95	108	63	15	6	**NUMBER OF STATEMENTS**	348	385
%	%	%	%	%	%	**ASSETS**	%	%
68.9	61.6	33.9	21.4	26.4		Cash & Equivalents	35.2	39.3
9.3	5.1	5.1	5.2	10.2		Trade Receivables (net)	9.0	8.0
.0	.4	1.4	.6	.6		Inventory	1.2	1.6
3.7	4.8	3.9	2.0	1.9		All Other Current	4.7	5.0
81.8	71.8	44.2	29.1	39.1		Total Current	50.0	53.8
7.8	17.5	42.9	52.6	31.9		Fixed Assets (net)	36.7	30.4
1.2	.4	1.9	2.3	5.0		Intangibles (net)	.9	.9
9.2	10.2	11.1	16.0	24.0		All Other Non-Current	12.4	14.8
100.0	100.0	100.0	100.0	100.0		Total	100.0	100.0
						LIABILITIES		
2.1	3.0	2.1	1.5	.5		Notes Payable-Short Term	4.7	3.5
6.5	4.5	2.9	1.2	1.0		Cur. Mat.-L.T.D.	2.8	2.2
7.8	5.1	4.8	3.3	2.2		Trade Payables	6.1	6.1
.6	.1	.1	.0	.3		Income Taxes Payable	.1	.1
14.1	10.5	10.1	11.5	13.8		All Other Current	12.2	11.4
31.0	23.2	20.1	17.5	17.7		Total Current	25.8	23.3
49.8	32.6	24.7	15.8	20.5		Long-Term Debt	25.7	25.8
.0	.0	.0	.1	.0		Deferred Taxes	.0	.0
3.8	4.9	5.0	7.8	2.2		All Other Non-Current	4.3	6.0
15.5	39.3	50.3	58.8	59.6		Net Worth	44.2	44.8
100.0	100.0	100.0	100.0	100.0		Total Liabilties & Net Worth	100.0	100.0
						INCOME DATA		
100.0	100.0	100.0	100.0	100.0		Net Sales	100.0	100.0
						Gross Profit		
86.9	88.3	87.3	94.2	93.1		Operating Expenses	91.8	90.8
13.1	11.7	12.7	5.8	6.9		Operating Profit	8.2	9.2
2.2	3.2	4.1	.3	3.3		All Other Expenses (net)	4.5	1.9
10.9	8.5	8.6	5.5	3.6		Profit Before Taxes	3.7	7.3
						RATIOS		
10.4	11.1	5.2	5.5	2.8			6.0	6.7
4.0	5.0	2.7	2.0	2.2		Current	2.4	3.0
2.3	1.7	1.1	1.0	1.2			1.2	1.3
10.4	10.9	5.0	4.8	2.8			5.7	6.5
3.9	4.6	2.3	1.6	1.7		Quick	(347) 2.1	2.3
1.9	1.7	.9	.7	.9			1.0	1.0
0 UND	0 999.8	2 198.0	2 237.8	4 83.5			1 473.4	2 233.3
5 78.8	5 67.7	7 52.2	17 21.0	17 21.6		Sales/Receivables	10 35.0	9 41.2
24 15.1	14 25.7	22 16.5	36 10.1	81 4.5			36 10.2	32 11.5
						Cost of Sales/Inventory		
						Cost of Sales/Payables		
1.4	1.3	1.9	1.9	1.7			2.1	1.9
3.4	2.4	4.2	5.1	7.0		Sales/Working Capital	4.9	4.9
7.7	6.0	37.8	-58.1	25.0			30.5	25.4
13.9	9.0	19.2	13.5	5.8			9.6	8.4
(39) 4.7	(44) 3.4	(70) 3.1	(42) 3.9	(10) 2.0		EBIT/Interest	(204) 2.7	(214) 2.5
2.2	-.1	1.1	1.3	-60.2			.2	.2
							45.8	
						Net Profit + Depr., Dep., Amort./Cur. Mat. L/T/D	(14) 8.1	
							2.1	
.0	.0	.1	.4	.0			.0	.0
.0	.0	.6	.9	.2		Fixed/Worth	.5	.3
.0	.6	1.6	1.3	1.1			1.3	1.2
.1	.1	.4	.2	.2			.2	.2
.7	.5	.9	.4	.6		Debt/Worth	.8	.6
-4.0	3.2	2.6	1.5	1.0			2.7	2.3
61.5	22.0	17.7	9.6	10.3			17.3	21.4
(68) 13.2	(80) 5.4	(103) 6.8	(59) 3.8	(14) .5		% Profit Before Taxes/Tangible Net Worth	(311) 4.2	(345) 6.6
-1.8	-4.7	.5	-.9	-1.3			-4.4	-.6
39.3	18.1	7.5	4.4	3.9			9.2	14.3
10.9	3.4	3.8	2.0	.3		% Profit Before Taxes/Total Assets	2.0	3.8
-1.5	-2.6	.3	-.9	-.4			-2.8	-.6
UND	UND	29.1	5.0	55.7			351.2	UND
UND	UND	2.5	.8	3.8		Sales/Net Fixed Assets	5.6	10.8
314.5	5.9	.6	.5	.6			.8	1.0
3.0	1.9	1.3	.7	.8			1.7	1.9
1.6	1.2	.7	.5	.5		Sales/Total Assets	.8	1.0
.8	.7	.4	.4	.2			.4	.5
.6	.3	1.2	2.0	1.6			1.2	1.0
(15) 1.0	(33) 1.5	(80) 4.9	(58) 6.3	(13) 4.4		% Depr., Dep., Amort./Sales	(220) 4.0	(220) 2.9
4.7	9.3	9.3	11.3	12.3			9.4	8.5
3.6	3.4	3.3					5.3	5.1
(17) 8.0	(14) 13.2	(13) 7.1				% Officers', Directors' Owners' Comp/Sales	(43) 8.1	(53) 11.3
22.5	26.9	16.4					23.1	24.1
41133M	136861M	486835M	980855M	666303M	255009M	Net Sales ($)	4896269M	5335122M
23974M	109636M	523901M	1431628M	957687M	744917M	Total Assets ($)	5458144M	6875674M

M = $ thousand MM = $ million

See Pages 9 through 22 for Explanation of Ratios and Data

Comparative Historical Data | Current Data Sorted by Sales

4/1/11-3/31/12 ALL	4/1/12-3/31/13 ALL	4/1/13-3/31/14 ALL	Type of Statement	0-1MM	1-3MM	3-5MM	5-10MM	10-25MM	25MM & OVER
219	232	175	Unqualified	35	46	24	32	25	13
26	18	11	Reviewed	6	2	1	1	1	
21	21	15	Compiled	7	5	1		2	
15	18	17	Tax Returns	13	2			1	1
185	210	165	Other	80	43	11	16	10	5
				112 (4/1-9/30/13)			271 (10/1/13-3/31/14)		
466	499	383	NUMBER OF STATEMENTS	141	98	37	49	39	19
%	%	%	ASSETS	%	%	%	%	%	%
41.4	46.6	46.9	Cash & Equivalents	59.7	50.2	34.1	35.6	25.4	34.1
7.6	6.0	6.3	Trade Receivables (net)	6.3	4.6	6.4	7.0	7.1	11.4
.7	.7	.6	Inventory	.0	.6	.2	1.3	1.6	2.3
3.5	3.5	3.6	All Other Current	3.1	5.2	3.4	2.4	2.5	5.1
53.2	56.7	57.5	Total Current	69.1	60.6	44.1	46.3	36.6	52.8
30.3	24.7	29.1	Fixed Assets (net)	20.7	28.1	28.2	41.7	47.1	28.3
1.5	1.5	1.5	Intangibles (net)	.9	1.4	3.9	.6	2.3	2.9
15.0	17.2	12.0	All Other Non-Current	9.4	9.9	23.7	11.5	14.1	16.0
100.0	100.0	100.0	Total	100.0	100.0	100.0	100.0	100.0	100.0
			LIABILITIES						
3.1	3.6	2.2	Notes Payable-Short Term	2.1	3.1	1.7	1.1	.9	5.0
2.0	3.3	3.8	Cur. Mat.-L.T.D.	4.1	6.4	2.2	1.8	1.6	1.7
5.8	5.1	5.3	Trade Payables	4.8	6.1	4.7	3.5	6.4	7.2
.1	.1	.2	Income Taxes Payable	.3	.3	.2	.0	.0	.6
14.6	16.4	11.6	All Other Current	11.1	11.1	12.4	12.5	10.9	14.9
25.7	28.5	23.1	Total Current	22.4	27.0	21.2	18.8	19.7	29.3
28.5	26.3	31.0	Long-Term Debt	39.5	35.9	33.9	16.7	13.3	10.0
.0	.0	.0	Deferred Taxes	.0	.0	.0	.0	.2	.0
3.4	4.4	5.0	All Other Non-Current	4.0	5.1	4.6	4.4	4.8	14.4
42.5	40.8	40.9	Net Worth	34.0	32.0	40.3	60.0	62.0	46.4
100.0	100.0	100.0	Total Liabilties & Net Worth	100.0	100.0	100.0	100.0	100.0	100.0
			INCOME DATA						
100.0	100.0	100.0	Net Sales	100.0	100.0	100.0	100.0	100.0	100.0
			Gross Profit						
90.1	91.9	88.9	Operating Expenses	83.3	89.9	88.7	94.1	97.5	94.3
9.9	8.1	11.1	Operating Profit	16.7	10.1	11.3	5.9	2.5	5.7
3.0	3.0	2.7	All Other Expenses (net)	5.1	1.5	3.3	1.4	-.1	-1.6
6.8	5.1	8.4	Profit Before Taxes	11.6	8.6	8.0	4.4	2.6	7.3
			RATIOS						
6.8	7.2	8.4		11.1	7.0	5.3	6.2	4.8	4.8
2.6	2.5	3.1	Current	4.5	3.3	2.4	2.7	1.8	2.2
1.1	1.2	1.3		2.1	1.2	1.1	1.1	1.0	1.2
6.3	6.2	7.5		10.9	6.5	5.1	5.7	4.0	4.8
2.3	2.3	2.8	Quick	4.1	2.7	1.9	2.1	1.6	1.8
.9	1.0	1.1		1.9	1.0	.9	1.0	.8	.7
1 419.9	0 UND	1 389.0		0 UND	1 330.7	3 143.7	3 104.5	3 128.5	9 41.1
7 51.2	4 90.4	7 52.4	Sales/Receivables	4 82.0	5 70.9	7 49.5	14 26.7	14 25.8	23 16.2
24 15.5	20 18.1	24 15.4		20 18.3	15 23.6	30 12.0	29 12.4	36 10.2	62 5.9
			Cost of Sales/Inventory						
			Cost of Sales/Payables						
1.8	1.9	1.6		1.1	1.6	2.3	2.2	2.0	1.9
5.3	5.4	3.4	Sales/Working Capital	2.5	3.1	4.6	3.8	8.6	7.0
34.5	27.3	16.8		6.9	25.4	54.3	28.4	-167.9	45.7
9.5	8.3	13.4		9.1	9.0	26.3	7.7	19.6	79.7
(223) 2.1	(244) 2.8	(210) 3.8	EBIT/Interest	(60) 3.7	(58) 3.4	(25) 4.0	(29) 3.5	(25) 2.7	(13) 6.5
.3	.3	1.1		1.3	1.0	1.7	1.1	.2	-23.9
5.5	7.1	9.8							
(11) 3.2	(11) 3.0	(13) 2.7	Net Profit + Depr., Dep., Amort./Cur. Mat. L/T/D						
.3	1.3	1.7							
.0	.0	.0		.0	.0	.0	.1	.2	.2
.2	.1	.2	Fixed/Worth	.0	.1	.3	.6	.9	.4
1.1	1.0	1.1		.7	1.3	1.2	1.2	1.1	1.1
.2	.2	.2		.1	.2	.2	.2	.2	.3
.7	.8	.6	Debt/Worth	.6	.8	.8	.6	.5	.7
2.9	3.3	3.0		5.5	7.6	3.7	1.6	1.5	1.4
21.8	20.7	18.5		29.9	14.0	17.7	12.7	10.1	19.0
(414) 6.6	(438) 5.8	(330) 6.1	% Profit Before Taxes/Tangible Net Worth	(116) 9.6	(81) 6.8	(31) 5.2	(47) 5.7	(38) 3.6	(17) 6.1
-1.7	-3.8	-1.0		-1.6	-1.1	.4	-2.0	-.3	2.9
12.5	12.2	13.1		23.4	12.1	10.1	7.6	7.6	13.4
3.4	3.3	3.7	% Profit Before Taxes/Total Assets	6.0	3.8	3.5	2.9	1.6	3.1
-1.1	-2.4	-.8		-1.2	-.6	.1	-1.8	-.1	1.7
UND	UND	UND		UND	UND	916.1	17.7	11.7	55.7
15.4	89.3	19.1	Sales/Net Fixed Assets	UND	96.5	8.0	1.9	.9	6.3
1.0	1.5	.9		3.9	1.0	1.0	.7	.6	1.6
1.9	1.8	1.7		1.7	1.9	1.7	1.5	1.1	3.6
1.0	1.0	.9	Sales/Total Assets	.9	1.1	.9	.8	.6	.9
.5	.6	.5		.4	.5	.4	.4	.4	.6
1.4	.9	1.1		1.5	.8	.6	1.5	2.0	.6
(250) 4.0	(227) 4.1	(205) 4.7	% Depr., Dep., Amort./Sales	(34) 8.0	(49) 4.5	(29) 2.2	(41) 5.0	(35) 6.5	(17) 2.2
9.3	9.1	9.6		19.0	7.1	6.1	8.6	11.1	5.8
3.2	2.9	3.4		3.8	2.5				
(55) 5.5	(50) 8.2	(51) 8.0	% Officers', Directors' Owners' Comp/Sales	(23) 8.6	(13) 13.2				
11.0	19.9	22.1		20.8	29.7				
4265548M	3471055M	2566996M	Net Sales ($)	58493M	178606M	141511M	342808M	662358M	1183220M
5093226M	4286543M	3791743M	Total Assets ($)	145547M	331421M	332758M	544779M	1353576M	1083662M

M = $ thousand MM = $ million

See Pages 9 through 22 for Explanation of Ratios and Data

Current Data Sorted by Assets							Comparative Historical Data	
						Type of Statement		
						Unqualified	12	14
		2				Reviewed	15	15
1	3	3		1		Compiled	14	13
3	1					Tax Returns	15	16
5	8	5	2			Other	40	42
	4 (4/1-9/30/13)		30 (10/1/13-3/31/14)				**4/1/09-3/31/10 ALL**	**4/1/10-3/31/11 ALL**
0-500M	**500M-2MM**	**2-10MM**	**10-50MM**	**50-100MM**	**100-250MM**			
9	12	10	2	1		**NUMBER OF STATEMENTS**	96	100
%	%	%	%	%	%	**ASSETS**	%	%
	12.9	10.4			DATA NOT AVAILABLE	Cash & Equivalents	13.4	17.5
	18.9	14.5				Trade Receivables (net)	16.0	15.4
	14.0	17.1				Inventory	10.7	11.2
	7.6	1.2				All Other Current	2.9	3.1
	53.5	43.2				Total Current	43.1	47.2
	39.9	43.8				Fixed Assets (net)	39.4	35.5
	.5	8.2				Intangibles (net)	6.8	4.6
	6.0	4.7				All Other Non-Current	10.7	12.6
	100.0	100.0				Total	100.0	100.0
						LIABILITIES		
	10.4	6.9				Notes Payable-Short Term	10.2	17.9
	4.5	2.3				Cur. Mat.-L.T.D.	3.2	3.0
	10.7	12.7				Trade Payables	7.0	11.2
	.4	.2				Income Taxes Payable	.2	.1
	15.6	11.5				All Other Current	6.6	8.4
	41.6	33.6				Total Current	27.2	40.7
	25.4	14.9				Long-Term Debt	32.3	26.9
	.0	.0				Deferred Taxes	.7	.2
	3.5	18.7				All Other Non-Current	5.2	5.0
	29.5	32.7				Net Worth	34.6	27.3
	100.0	100.0				Total Liabilties & Net Worth	100.0	100.0
						INCOME DATA		
	100.0	100.0				Net Sales	100.0	100.0
						Gross Profit		
	79.1	81.8				Operating Expenses	81.4	83.3
	20.9	18.2				Operating Profit	18.6	16.7
	3.5	2.9				All Other Expenses (net)	5.8	3.2
	17.5	15.3				Profit Before Taxes	12.9	13.5
						RATIOS		
	3.6	1.8					3.4	3.1
	.9	1.0				Current	1.8	1.4
	.5	.6					.8	.8
	2.5	1.3					2.6	2.4
	.4	.7				Quick	1.0	1.0
	.2	.4					.4	.4
	0 UND	0 UND					0 UND	0 UND
	3 132.8	17 22.0				Sales/Receivables	9 42.8	3 115.2
	46 7.9	41 8.9					47 7.8	40 9.2
						Cost of Sales/Inventory		
						Cost of Sales/Payables		
	5.5	15.2					4.6	6.6
	NM	NM				Sales/Working Capital	22.9	26.4
	-13.7	-3.7					-45.4	-34.0
							14.2	22.8
						EBIT/Interest	(69) 3.7	(65) 6.6
							.5	1.6
							5.3	
						Net Profit + Depr., Dep., Amort./Cur. Mat. L/T/D	(13) 1.4	
							.9	
	.2	1.0					.3	.2
	2.0	3.0				Fixed/Worth	.9	.7
	NM	-39.9					5.5	2.9
	.6	.9					.6	.4
	1.7	3.2				Debt/Worth	1.6	1.1
	NM	-153.9					8.9	6.4
							34.4	53.5
						% Profit Before Taxes/Tangible Net Worth	(77) 14.0	(82) 17.9
							.7	4.9
	23.7	18.0					19.0	28.3
	5.9	3.4				% Profit Before Taxes/Total Assets	4.5	7.5
	-2.4	.1					-1.0	2.0
	30.4	23.0					32.1	62.5
	9.0	10.8				Sales/Net Fixed Assets	5.8	10.9
	1.1	.8					.6	1.4
	3.2	5.0					3.2	4.5
	1.5	1.8				Sales/Total Assets	1.7	2.2
	.4	.7					.4	.6
							.9	.6
						% Depr., Dep., Amort./Sales	(72) 3.0	(71) 1.9
							8.2	7.0
							2.1	2.3
						% Officers', Directors' Owners' Comp/Sales	(18) 5.8	(31) 5.7
							9.0	19.4
11536M	**46681M**	**82023M**	**4220M**	**44697M**		Net Sales ($)	**2703065M**	**1980590M**
2249M	**15487M**	**40982M**	**42790M**	**74997M**		Total Assets ($)	**1588287M**	**1206599M**

M = $ thousand MM = $ million

See Pages 9 through 22 for Explanation of Ratios and Data

Comparative Historical Data				Current Data Sorted by Sales					
Type of Statement									
Unqualified	10	7						2	
Reviewed	9	4	2		2	1	2	2	1
Compiled	9	10	8	4					
Tax Returns	22	12	4	6	9	2	1	2	
Other	39	37	20						
					4 (4/1-9/30/13)		30 (10/1/13-3/31/14)		
	4/1/11-3/31/12 ALL	4/1/12-3/31/13 ALL	4/1/13-3/31/14 ALL	0-1MM	1-3MM	3-5MM	5-10MM	10-25MM	25MM & OVER
NUMBER OF STATEMENTS	89	70	34	10	11	3	3	6	1
ASSETS	%	%	%	%	%	%	%	%	%
Cash & Equivalents	17.8	18.8	17.5	24.3	15.5				
Trade Receivables (net)	13.6	13.3	13.3	2.9	14.4				
Inventory	12.1	11.0	12.6	7.0	11.4				
All Other Current	3.8	5.4	9.9	.0	24.2				
Total Current	47.4	48.6	53.4	34.2	65.5				
Fixed Assets (net)	39.1	34.7	37.8	57.3	30.1				
Intangibles (net)	3.3	4.7	5.0	7.9	.5				
All Other Non-Current	10.2	12.1	3.8	.6	3.9				
Total	100.0	100.0	100.0	100.0	100.0				
LIABILITIES									
Notes Payable-Short Term	10.8	11.2	26.9	6.2	10.4				
Cur. Mat.-L.T.D.	2.9	3.6	2.8	3.3	.3				
Trade Payables	11.2	13.1	8.7	1.4	4.2				
Income Taxes Payable	.3	.1	.2	.0	.5				
All Other Current	9.0	11.7	15.4	18.7	10.9				
Total Current	34.1	39.8	54.0	29.5	26.3				
Long-Term Debt	34.3	20.3	23.9	39.1	22.4				
Deferred Taxes	.1	.0	.0	.0	.0				
All Other Non-Current	7.2	14.5	9.8	18.5	2.1				
Net Worth	24.2	25.5	12.2	12.9	49.1				
Total Liabilties & Net Worth	100.0	100.0	100.0	100.0	100.0				
INCOME DATA									
Net Sales	100.0	100.0	100.0	100.0	100.0				
Gross Profit									
Operating Expenses	82.8	85.0	78.7	44.3	88.6				
Operating Profit	17.2	15.0	21.3	55.7	11.4				
All Other Expenses (net)	3.5	1.8	3.7	10.7	.8				
Profit Before Taxes	13.8	13.2	17.6	45.0	10.6				
RATIOS									
Current	4.0	3.1	3.5	3.7	9.0				
	1.8	1.2	1.2	1.6	2.6				
	.8	.7	.6	.3	.8				
Quick	3.4	2.4	2.5	3.7	2.4				
	1.1	.8	.6	1.3	.5				
	.4	.4	.3	.3	.2				
Sales/Receivables	0 UND	0 UND	0 UND	0 UND	0 UND				
	8 44.1	4 95.6	4 101.2	0 UND	2 147.1				
	42 8.7	37 9.8	39 9.4	28 12.9	54 6.8				
Cost of Sales/Inventory									
Cost of Sales/Payables									
Sales/Working Capital	4.7	6.4	5.5	4.5	.9				
	12.8	29.7	21.4	52.6	12.5				
	-35.1	-52.9	-20.5	-9.5	-20.3				
EBIT/Interest	15.5	19.5	7.9						
	(61) 3.5	(49) 3.5	(23) 3.8						
	.7	-.7	1.3						
Net Profit + Depr., Dep., Amort./Cur. Mat. L/T/D									
Fixed/Worth	.2	.1	.3	1.6	.1				
	1.1	.9	2.3	-4.8	.4				
	8.5	5.0	-2.6	-.9	1.2				
Debt/Worth	.5	.5	.7	.7	.4				
	1.6	1.4	2.6	-9.8	1.2				
	15.0	18.5	-10.6	-3.5	2.6				
% Profit Before Taxes/Tangible Net Worth	57.5	67.8	40.5		44.9				
	(73) 11.4	(55) 15.4	(23) 30.1		3.9				
	3.9	.3	2.3		-3.2				
% Profit Before Taxes/Total Assets	17.2	29.1	26.2	83.7	29.9				
	4.8	5.9	7.6	19.1	2.7				
	-.1	-2.2	.9	8.6	-2.0				
Sales/Net Fixed Assets	67.2	78.0	43.1	97.9	41.1				
	8.6	11.5	14.7	.5	13.0				
	.9	3.8	.9	.2	1.8				
Sales/Total Assets	3.7	5.5	5.0	15.6	2.9				
	1.5	2.7	1.6	.3	1.3				
	.3	.8	.5	.2	.6				
% Depr., Dep., Amort./Sales	.7	.7	.8						
	(64) 2.0	(37) 1.9	(19) 3.6						
	10.5	8.0	8.3						
% Officers', Directors' Owners' Comp/Sales	2.9	2.5							
	(27) 6.5	(20) 5.6							
	19.7	13.8							
Net Sales ($)	1610444M	725396M	189157M	4182M	21421M	11219M	20595M	87043M	44697M
Total Assets ($)	728019M	512183M	176505M	13422M	56979M	5928M	3907M	21272M	74997M

M = $ thousand MM = $ million

See Pages 9 through 22 for Explanation of Ratios and Data

PUBLIC ADMINISTRATION

Current Data Sorted by Assets							Comparative Historical Data	
						Type of Statement		
	6	28	104	38	67	Unqualified	103	109
		1				Reviewed		
		1				Compiled	5	2
		1				Tax Returns	5	1
1	3	5	9	2	2	Other	21	35
238 (4/1-9/30/13)			30 (10/1/13-3/31/14)				4/1/09-3/31/10	4/1/10-3/31/11
0-500M	500M-2MM	2-10MM	10-50MM	50-100MM	100-250MM		ALL	ALL
1	9	36	113	40	69	**NUMBER OF STATEMENTS**	134	147
%	%	%	%	%	%	**ASSETS**	%	%
		49.0	36.8	23.0	19.9	Cash & Equivalents	21.4	23.3
		9.6	6.8	9.6	5.4	Trade Receivables (net)	7.6	7.7
		.2	.4	.2	.3	Inventory	1.0	1.4
		9.0	6.3	3.5	4.2	All Other Current	3.8	3.3
		67.9	50.4	36.3	29.7	Total Current	33.8	35.7
		25.6	40.8	57.9	63.0	Fixed Assets (net)	55.6	53.1
		.1	.6	.3	.1	Intangibles (net)	.2	.5
		6.5	8.2	5.4	7.2	All Other Non-Current	10.4	10.7
		100.0	100.0	100.0	100.0	Total	100.0	100.0
						LIABILITIES		
		1.5	.7	.8	1.4	Notes Payable-Short Term	1.7	2.1
		1.5	1.4	1.8	1.8	Cur. Mat.-L.T.D.	2.2	2.9
		3.8	4.2	2.6	2.0	Trade Payables	4.0	3.5
		.1	.1	.0	1.1	Income Taxes Payable	.3	.5
		10.6	6.3	4.1	5.0	All Other Current	9.1	10.9
		17.3	12.7	9.3	11.2	Total Current	17.3	19.9
		11.8	24.2	26.4	24.4	Long-Term Debt	24.7	25.6
		.0	.0	.0	.0	Deferred Taxes	.1	.0
		.8	2.2	4.3	2.7	All Other Non-Current	4.0	4.3
		70.0	60.9	60.0	61.7	Net Worth	53.8	50.2
		100.0	100.0	100.0	100.0	Total Liabilties & Net Worth	100.0	100.0
						INCOME DATA		
		100.0	100.0	100.0	100.0	Net Sales	100.0	100.0
						Gross Profit		
		85.2	90.5	93.5	92.0	Operating Expenses	90.0	88.0
		14.8	9.5	6.5	8.0	Operating Profit	10.0	12.0
		6.4	5.9	1.6	3.6	All Other Expenses (net)	4.9	5.5
		8.5	3.6	4.9	4.4	Profit Before Taxes	5.2	6.5
						RATIOS		
		15.4	8.2	5.9	6.7		5.1	4.6
		5.3	4.5	3.8	4.1	Current	2.5	2.7
		2.4	2.8	2.6	2.5		1.1	1.2
		14.7	7.2	4.9	5.9		4.8	4.1
		4.6	4.0	3.7	3.6	Quick	2.1	2.2
		1.9	2.3	2.2	1.9		.9	1.1
		3 134.7	**6** 62.9	**17** 21.2	**8** 44.8		**5** 76.0	**1** 376.2
		15 23.9	**22** 16.8	**34** 10.8	**24** 15.1	Sales/Receivables	**23** 15.7	**20** 18.5
		35 10.3	**41** 8.9	**72** 5.1	**52** 7.0		**46** 7.9	**48** 7.5
						Cost of Sales/Inventory		
						Cost of Sales/Payables		
		1.2	1.3	1.2	1.2		1.8	1.9
		2.1	2.1	2.1	2.0	Sales/Working Capital	3.9	4.5
		5.4	5.4	4.0	3.8		99.6	18.9
		11.1	4.8	9.4	5.1		5.9	11.1
		(17) 2.1	(67) 1.9	(34) 2.0	(61) 2.2	EBIT/Interest	(101) 2.0	(106) 2.6
		-.6	-.1	-.7	.1		-1.1	.4
						Net Profit + Depr., Dep., Amort./Cur. Mat. L/T/D		
		.0	.0	.8	.8		.7	.5
		.0	.8	1.0	1.0	Fixed/Worth	1.0	1.0
		.9	1.4	1.6	1.2		1.5	1.6
		.1	.2	.2	.2		.3	.3
		.1	.5	.6	.4	Debt/Worth	.7	.6
		.9	1.2	1.1	.7		1.7	2.0
		16.5	11.4	6.9	3.7		8.6	9.4
		(33) 8.2	(107) 4.8	(39) 2.9	(66) 1.5	% Profit Before Taxes/Tangible Net Worth	(128) 2.1	(138) 2.5
		-.2	-.7	-2.1	-2.2		-3.1	-2.3
		11.5	6.5	3.9	2.5		4.2	4.8
		5.5	3.0	2.1	.9	% Profit Before Taxes/Total Assets	1.1	1.3
		-.3	-1.1	-1.2	-1.0		-1.4	-1.8
		UND	UND	1.2	.7		3.9	4.2
		UND	.8	.5	.5	Sales/Net Fixed Assets	.6	.7
		.8	.4	.3	.3		.3	.4
		2.0	1.6	.6	.4		1.0	1.3
		1.0	.4	.4	.3	Sales/Total Assets	.4	.4
		.4	.2	.2	.2		.2	.2
		7.1	7.0	8.8	8.0		5.0	4.5
		(15) 9.3	(56) 10.6	(31) 12.2	(44) 11.5	% Depr., Dep., Amort./Sales	(88) 8.9	(95) 8.4
		14.4	15.3	16.3	20.8		15.7	13.8
							3.0	1.2
						% Officers', Directors' Owners' Comp/Sales	(15) 8.9	(10) 7.7
							26.1	21.5
2099M	46595M	284444M	2882506M	2107347M	5679295M	Net Sales ($)	4631603M	5727994M
435M	13967M	195291M	2907136M	2861946M	10793561M	Total Assets ($)	7884151M	8907485M

M = $ thousand MM = $ million

See Pages 9 through 22 for Explanation of Ratios and Data

Comparative Historical Data				Current Data Sorted by Sales					
			Type of Statement						
164	187	243	Unqualified	2	14	20	33	68	106
		1	Reviewed	1					
1	1	1	Compiled			1			
	1	1	Tax Returns	1					
16	31	22	Other	1	6	2	5	5	3
				238 (4/1-9/30/13)			30 (10/1/13-3/31/14)		
4/1/11-3/31/12 ALL	**4/1/12-3/31/13 ALL**	**4/1/13-3/31/14 ALL**		**0-1MM**	**1-3MM**	**3-5MM**	**5-10MM**	**10-25MM**	**25MM & OVER**
181	220	268	**NUMBER OF STATEMENTS**	5	20	23	38	73	109
%	%	%	**ASSETS**	%	%	%	%	%	%
22.6	24.0	33.2	Cash & Equivalents		28.4	32.1	33.6	27.7	38.0
7.6	6.0	7.7	Trade Receivables (net)		2.0	5.7	3.6	6.8	11.2
.7	.3	.3	Inventory		.7	.4	.2	.2	.4
3.4	4.5	5.6	All Other Current		10.5	2.8	2.5	4.2	7.6
34.3	34.8	46.8	Total Current		41.5	41.0	39.9	38.9	57.3
56.0	56.5	45.7	Fixed Assets (net)		53.6	51.7	51.8	54.2	35.3
.4	.3	.4	Intangibles (net)		.8	1.2	.7	.2	.1
9.2	8.4	7.1	All Other Non-Current		4.1	6.0	7.6	6.7	7.4
100.0	100.0	100.0	Total		100.0	100.0	100.0	100.0	100.0
			LIABILITIES						
.9	.5	1.0	Notes Payable-Short Term		.6	.1	.5	1.1	1.3
2.4	1.6	1.7	Cur. Mat.-L.T.D.		2.1	1.5	1.9	2.1	1.2
3.3	3.2	3.4	Trade Payables		3.2	2.5	1.8	2.7	4.9
.0	.0	.3	Income Taxes Payable		.0	.0	.0	.1	.8
8.3	6.6	6.2	All Other Current		2.6	2.5	2.6	5.6	9.0
14.9	11.9	12.6	Total Current		8.5	6.5	6.7	11.5	17.3
27.6	22.6	22.6	Long-Term Debt		25.9	17.0	33.4	25.2	16.9
.0	.0	.0	Deferred Taxes		.1	.0	.0	.0	.0
2.5	2.9	2.5	All Other Non-Current		1.2	.4	1.6	1.4	4.2
55.0	62.6	62.3	Net Worth		64.2	76.1	58.3	61.9	61.6
100.0	100.0	100.0	Total Liabilties & Net Worth		100.0	100.0	100.0	100.0	100.0
			INCOME DATA						
100.0	100.0	100.0	Net Sales		100.0	100.0	100.0	100.0	100.0
			Gross Profit						
88.8	88.6	90.9	Operating Expenses		88.3	84.5	90.5	91.9	94.0
11.2	11.4	9.1	Operating Profit		11.7	15.5	9.5	8.1	6.0
4.7	5.1	4.6	All Other Expenses (net)		11.7	8.6	5.8	3.2	2.1
6.5	6.4	4.5	Profit Before Taxes		.0	7.0	3.8	4.9	4.0
			RATIOS						
5.1	6.8	8.1			12.0	12.2	8.8	8.0	6.5
3.1	3.7	4.3	Current		3.9	5.8	4.7	4.5	4.1
1.8	2.0	2.8			2.3	3.8	2.9	2.7	2.7
4.5	6.3	6.8			8.5	12.2	8.5	6.6	6.0
2.7	3.3	3.8	Quick		3.3	5.8	4.6	3.9	3.7
1.5	1.6	2.2			.6	3.0	2.6	2.2	2.2
9 39.5	**11** 31.8	**7** 54.0			**0** UND	**2** 236.4	**5** 67.3	**13** 27.7	**7** 50.2
28 13.1	**30** 12.1	**23** 16.0	Sales/Receivables		**3** 127.9	**28** 13.0	**20** 18.5	**34** 10.6	**22** 16.7
49 7.4	**47** 7.7	**47** 7.7			**26** 14.1	**54** 6.8	**43** 8.5	**55** 6.6	**40** 9.1
			Cost of Sales/Inventory						
			Cost of Sales/Payables						
1.5	1.3	1.3			1.0	1.0	1.2	1.0	1.7
2.7	2.3	2.1	Sales/Working Capital		2.1	1.7	1.8	1.8	2.8
5.7	5.8	4.8			5.7	2.7	4.0	4.7	4.9
8.2	8.2	6.3			1.4	3.0	7.5	8.2	5.9
(146) 2.6	(168) 3.0	(185) 2.1	EBIT/Interest		(11) -.1	(12) 1.1	(29) 2.1	(56) 2.1	(75) 2.4
.7	.8	-.1			-7.5	-4.7	.9	-.8	.0
			Net Profit + Depr., Dep., Amort./Cur. Mat. L/T/D						
.7	.7	.0			.0	.0	.3	.7	.0
1.0	1.0	.9	Fixed/Worth		.9	.8	1.0	.9	.7
1.5	1.3	1.3			3.2	1.4	1.5	1.3	1.1
.3	.2	.2			.1	.0	.2	.2	.2
.6	.5	.4	Debt/Worth		.2	.2	.5	.3	.4
1.3	1.0	1.1			2.7	.9	1.4	1.1	1.0
7.4	6.8	8.4			7.3	11.1	8.0	7.0	10.6
(169) 3.2	(212) 3.0	(254) 3.0	% Profit Before Taxes/Tangible Net Worth		(18) .2	1.4	(33) 4.1	(69) 2.4	(106) 3.9
-.4	-1.1	-1.6			-7.1	-2.6	-.6	-2.2	-1.3
4.7	4.1	5.9			5.6	8.7	5.1	4.5	6.4
1.6	1.6	2.0	% Profit Before Taxes/Total Assets		-.2	.7	1.7	2.0	2.5
-.6	-.7	-1.0			-1.7	-2.1	-1.4	-1.4	-.6
2.2	1.6	UND			UND	UND	4.0	10.6	UND
.6	.5	.7	Sales/Net Fixed Assets		.5	.5	.6	.5	1.3
.3	.3	.3			.2	.2	.3	.3	.6
.8	.7	1.4			1.0	.7	.7	.7	2.6
.4	.3	.4	Sales/Total Assets		.3	.3	.3	.3	.7
.2	.2	.2			.1	.2	.2	.2	.4
5.0	6.1	7.3			8.7	7.4	7.4	9.6	5.9
(134) 8.0	(150) 10.5	(147) 11.3	% Depr., Dep., Amort./Sales		(13) 14.0	(17) 11.6	(23) 10.2	(50) 12.4	(41) 8.3
14.5	17.2	16.2			19.0	23.7	15.8	17.7	11.7
3.3	2.4	2.5							
(13) 6.6	(11) 6.2	(17) 7.0	% Officers', Directors' Owners' Comp/Sales						
13.0	14.8	23.3							
6130670M	**7903130M**	**11002286M**	Net Sales ($)	**2293M**	**39239M**	**92839M**	**290653M**	**1215519M**	**9361743M**
11373182M	**13310991M**	**16772336M**	Total Assets ($)	**22142M**	**193856M**	**373649M**	**1097693M**	**4515031M**	**10569965M**

M = $ thousand MM = $ million

See Pages 9 through 22 for Explanation of Ratios and Data

Current Data Sorted by Assets							Comparative Historical Data	
						Type of Statement		
2	4	19	58	37	57	Unqualified	56	54
						Reviewed		1
		1	1			Compiled	1	1
						Tax Returns		
2	1	4	4	2	4	Other	6	8
177 (4/1-9/30/13)			19 (10/1/13-3/31/14)				4/1/09-3/31/10	4/1/10-3/31/11
0-500M	500M-2MM	2-10MM	10-50MM	50-100MM	100-250MM		ALL	ALL
4	5	24	63	39	61	NUMBER OF STATEMENTS	63	64
%	%	%	%	%	%	**ASSETS**	%	%
		36.5	24.3	17.3	15.3	Cash & Equivalents	22.3	14.9
		7.7	5.6	5.0	4.5	Trade Receivables (net)	4.9	5.2
		.4	.4	.2	.4	Inventory	.2	.3
		2.3	2.4	2.8	2.7	All Other Current	5.0	1.6
		46.8	32.7	25.3	22.9	Total Current	32.5	22.1
		38.9	60.2	68.7	69.9	Fixed Assets (net)	60.5	68.7
		.0	.2	.6	.4	Intangibles (net)	.5	.9
		14.3	6.8	5.4	6.9	All Other Non-Current	6.4	8.3
		100.0	100.0	100.0	100.0	Total	100.0	100.0
						LIABILITIES		
		.4	.6	.2	.2	Notes Payable-Short Term	.7	.7
		1.2	1.7	2.5	2.2	Cur. Mat.-L.T.D.	2.1	2.4
		2.4	3.2	1.5	1.2	Trade Payables	2.6	1.5
		.0	.0	.0	.0	Income Taxes Payable	.5	.0
		7.8	3.9	4.9	3.2	All Other Current	5.2	4.0
		11.7	9.4	9.1	6.7	Total Current	11.2	8.5
		18.4	24.1	34.2	36.3	Long-Term Debt	29.1	30.8
		.0	.0	.0	.0	Deferred Taxes	.0	.1
		5.8	3.9	5.7	5.4	All Other Non-Current	2.7	2.9
		64.0	62.6	51.0	51.6	Net Worth	57.1	57.7
		100.0	100.0	100.0	100.0	Total Liabilties & Net Worth	100.0	100.0
						INCOME DATA		
		100.0	100.0	100.0	100.0	Net Sales	100.0	100.0
						Gross Profit		
		87.0	89.4	85.4	84.8	Operating Expenses	89.0	87.9
		13.0	10.6	14.6	15.2	Operating Profit	11.0	12.1
		5.3	3.3	7.2	6.3	All Other Expenses (net)	3.4	5.0
		7.7	7.3	7.3	8.9	Profit Before Taxes	7.5	7.1
						RATIOS		
		11.8	6.3	4.3	6.8		4.7	4.2
		6.0	3.7	3.0	3.7	Current	2.5	2.7
		3.6	1.6	2.1	2.2		1.7	1.3
		11.8	6.0	4.2	5.7		4.6	3.9
		4.8	3.0	2.6	3.0	Quick	2.3	2.5
		2.9	1.5	1.8	1.8		1.5	1.2
		0 UND	9 42.4	20 18.0	26 14.3		10 36.6	11 33.8
		18 20.6	31 11.9	33 11.1	47 7.8	Sales/Receivables	28 13.1	32 11.4
		66 5.5	47 7.8	78 4.7	114 3.2		50 7.3	69 5.3
						Cost of Sales/Inventory		
						Cost of Sales/Payables		
		1.3	1.2	1.0	.8		1.6	1.7
		1.9	2.5	2.0	1.6	Sales/Working Capital	3.4	3.8
		4.3	4.2	3.8	2.6		6.5	10.0
		14.9	7.4	5.1	4.8		5.1	5.3
		(17) 5.2	(52) 3.3	(31) 2.7	(53) 2.3	EBIT/Interest	(52) 2.4	(54) 2.4
		1.9	.6	1.1	.7		.8	.9
						Net Profit + Depr., Dep., Amort./Cur. Mat. L/T/D		
		.0	.8	1.0	1.0		.9	.9
		.6	1.0	1.1	1.1	Fixed/Worth	1.1	1.3
		1.1	1.5	2.6	1.6		1.6	1.7
		.2	.2	.3	.3		.3	.3
		.4	.5	.5	.6	Debt/Worth	.7	.8
		.9	1.2	3.3	1.9		1.1	1.1
		19.1	6.8	6.0	4.9		7.6	8.8
		5.6	3.2	(35) 2.7	(58) 2.2	% Profit Before Taxes/Tangible Net Worth	(62) 1.9	(62) 2.6
		-.1	-1.6	-.1	-.4		-3.8	-.4
		8.9	4.9	3.9	2.9		4.8	4.3
		1.6	2.4	1.7	1.3	% Profit Before Taxes/Total Assets	1.0	1.5
		-.2	-.6	-.4	-.3		-.8	-.4
		UND	1.0	.6	.5		1.4	.8
		1.6	.4	.3	.3	Sales/Net Fixed Assets	.5	.3
		.8	.2	.2	.2		.3	.2
		1.2	.6	.4	.3		.8	.4
		.6	.3	.3	.2	Sales/Total Assets	.4	.2
		.4	.2	.2	.1		.2	.1
		3.1	7.0	5.8	8.7		4.5	7.0
		(13) 8.3	(50) 13.1	(37) 11.2	(56) 13.7	% Depr., Dep., Amort./Sales	(48) 8.8	(52) 14.2
		14.2	22.1	21.9	20.3		18.2	20.7
						% Officers', Directors' Owners' Comp/Sales		
2420M	6121M	138528M	1134113M	874375M	2426279M	Net Sales ($)	2310105M	1010607M
1212M	6806M	153403M	1632612M	2821301M	9814193M	Total Assets ($)	3308378M	3303039M

M = $ thousand MM = $ million

See Pages 9 through 22 for Explanation of Ratios and Data

Comparative Historical Data | **Current Data Sorted by Sales**

			Type of Statement						
113	133	177	Unqualified	7	19	14	26	50	61
	1		Reviewed		1	1			
		2	Compiled						
			Tax Returns						
10	13	17	Other	1	4	2	2	4	4
4/1/11-3/31/12 ALL	4/1/12-3/31/13 ALL	4/1/13-3/31/14 ALL		177 (4/1-9/30/13)			19 (10/1/13-3/31/14)		
				0-1MM	1-3MM	3-5MM	5-10MM	10-25MM	25MM & OVER
123	147	196	**NUMBER OF STATEMENTS**	8	24	17	28	54	65
%	%	%	**ASSETS**	%	%	%	%	%	%
19.9	23.2	22.6	Cash & Equivalents		24.2	20.2	20.8	19.0	25.3
6.8	7.3	5.4	Trade Receivables (net)		2.3	2.8	6.0	4.5	7.4
.3	.4	.4	Inventory		.1	.4	.2	.2	.6
3.1	3.7	3.1	All Other Current		4.6	1.2	2.2	2.4	3.5
30.1	34.7	31.5	Total Current		31.2	24.6	29.3	26.2	36.8
63.8	59.1	60.7	Fixed Assets (net)		59.9	58.5	63.3	68.3	55.3
.7	.5	.4	Intangibles (net)		.1	.0	.7	.2	.4
5.5	5.8	7.4	All Other Non-Current		8.7	16.8	6.7	5.4	7.5
100.0	100.0	100.0	Total		100.0	100.0	100.0	100.0	100.0
			LIABILITIES						
1.0	.3	.3	Notes Payable-Short Term		.9	.1	.0	.4	.3
2.4	2.4	2.2	Cur. Mat.-L.T.D.		2.8	1.7	2.3	1.9	2.0
2.3	2.5	2.2	Trade Payables		1.7	1.7	1.7	1.2	3.5
.0	.2	.0	Income Taxes Payable		.0	.0	.0	.0	.0
5.4	6.4	4.8	All Other Current		4.5	1.7	8.4	3.9	4.8
11.1	11.8	9.5	Total Current		9.9	5.2	12.4	7.4	10.6
28.2	25.7	28.9	Long-Term Debt		31.2	27.4	23.9	26.4	34.3
.0	.0	.0	Deferred Taxes		.0	.0	.0	.0	.0
4.0	3.2	4.9	All Other Non-Current		.9	6.9	4.5	2.8	8.0
56.6	59.3	56.6	Net Worth		58.0	60.5	59.2	63.4	47.1
100.0	100.0	100.0	Total Liabilities & Net Worth		100.0	100.0	100.0	100.0	100.0
			INCOME DATA						
100.0	100.0	100.0	Net Sales		100.0	100.0	100.0	100.0	100.0
			Gross Profit						
87.8	89.1	86.8	Operating Expenses		85.5	80.8	86.5	86.5	90.1
12.2	10.9	13.2	Operating Profit		14.5	19.2	13.5	13.5	9.9
4.3	4.3	5.1	All Other Expenses (net)		6.4	5.9	6.1	5.2	4.4
8.0	6.6	8.1	Profit Before Taxes		8.1	13.3	7.4	8.3	5.5
			RATIOS						
5.5	5.3	6.7			8.2	7.9	5.7	5.7	7.0
2.8	3.1	3.7	Current		3.5	5.0	3.0	3.7	3.8
1.4	1.8	2.2			1.8	2.6	1.2	2.5	2.2
5.0	4.9	6.0			8.2	7.1	4.4	4.9	6.8
2.5	2.7	3.1	Quick		3.3	4.7	2.6	3.5	3.0
1.4	1.6	1.8			1.6	2.3	1.2	2.3	1.8
16 22.9	22 16.7	16 23.3			0 UND	4 101.6	20 18.1	22 16.9	15 25.0
41 9.0	41 9.0	35 10.4	Sales/Receivables		24 15.2	24 15.3	38 9.7	45 8.1	30 12.3
96 3.8	94 3.9	79 4.6			47 7.7	58 6.3	79 4.6	81 4.5	72 5.1
			Cost of Sales/Inventory						
			Cost of Sales/Payables						
1.2	1.2	1.1			1.2	.8	1.6	1.0	1.3
2.3	2.3	1.9	Sales/Working Capital		2.0	2.3	2.5	1.8	2.3
7.0	4.5	3.7			5.5	3.1	13.2	2.6	4.0
9.1	7.0	6.4			7.2	7.8	11.0	6.5	4.8
(102) 3.2	(128) 2.6	(157) 3.0	EBIT/Interest		(21) 2.6	(12) 3.4	(25) 3.0	(44) 3.4	(50) 2.6
.8	.7	.8			.3	1.2	.5	1.3	.5
			Net Profit + Depr., Dep., Amort./Cur. Mat. L/T/D						
.9	.8	.8			.5	.7	.8	.9	.8
1.1	1.1	1.0	Fixed/Worth		1.0	1.1	1.2	1.0	1.0
1.6	1.4	1.5			1.5	1.8	1.5	1.3	1.8
.3	.3	.2			.2	.2	.3	.2	.3
.5	.6	.5	Debt/Worth		.4	.4	.5	.4	.6
1.1	1.1	1.3			1.0	2.3	1.2	.8	2.4
8.7	6.6	6.8			7.3	12.6	10.3	4.8	6.0
(115) 4.0	(144) 3.0	(188) 2.8	% Profit Before Taxes/Tangible Net Worth		(23) 2.4	4.1	4.6	(52) 2.2	(60) 2.4
-.2	-.1	-.6			-.9	1.0	.0	-.2	-1.9
5.4	3.8	4.0			4.7	5.4	4.7	3.3	4.1
2.4	1.7	1.7	% Profit Before Taxes/Total Assets		1.6	3.1	2.4	1.7	1.4
-.3	-.3	-.4			-.5	.5	-.1	-.2	-1.1
.8	1.2	.9			1.9	.7	.9	.5	1.4
.5	.5	.4	Sales/Net Fixed Assets		.3	.4	.3	.3	.5
.2	.2	.2			.2	.2	.2	.2	.3
.6	.6	.5			.6	.4	.6	.4	.8
.3	.3	.3	Sales/Total Assets		.2	.2	.2	.2	.4
.2	.2	.2			.1	.2	.1	.1	.2
7.1	6.3	7.1			9.2	10.1	7.7	8.8	4.5
(108) 12.9	(123) 11.1	(158) 12.1	% Depr., Dep., Amort./Sales		(17) 22.4	(13) 17.7	(26) 14.5	(50) 13.0	(48) 8.2
20.4	19.1	20.5			28.1	23.6	27.8	22.1	13.6
		3.0							
		(11) 16.5	% Officers', Directors' Owners' Comp/Sales						
		27.8							
3261881M	3331304M	4581836M	Net Sales ($)	3773M	49850M	68274M	213387M	899092M	3347460M
7033261M	9513178M	14429527M	Total Assets ($)	24456M	283970M	380458M	957995M	4883301M	7899347M

M = $ thousand MM = $ million

See Pages 9 through 22 for Explanation of Ratios and Data

Current Data Sorted by Assets / Comparative Historical Data

	0-500M	500M-2MM	2-10MM	10-50MM	50-100MM	100-250MM	4/1/09-3/31/10 ALL	4/1/10-3/31/11 ALL
Type of Statement								
Unqualified			7	14	6	8	16	15
Reviewed								
Compiled							1	
Tax Returns								1
Other				1	1	1	1	3
	35 (4/1-9/30/13)			3 (10/1/13-3/31/14)				
NUMBER OF STATEMENTS			7	15	7	9	18	19
	%	%	%	%	%	%	%	%
ASSETS								
Cash & Equivalents	DATA NOT AVAILABLE	DATA NOT AVAILABLE		39.5			29.5	29.4
Trade Receivables (net)				12.3			6.0	7.9
Inventory				.3			.2	.1
All Other Current				2.1			4.4	3.2
Total Current				54.2			40.1	40.7
Fixed Assets (net)				37.2			43.4	45.9
Intangibles (net)				.3			.9	.7
All Other Non-Current				8.3			15.7	12.7
Total				100.0			100.0	100.0
LIABILITIES								
Notes Payable-Short Term				.0			.4	1.2
Cur. Mat.-L.T.D.				1.1			1.6	1.3
Trade Payables				11.2			4.7	2.3
Income Taxes Payable				.0			.0	.0
All Other Current				7.2			12.0	16.2
Total Current				19.5			18.7	21.1
Long-Term Debt				14.6			15.3	22.7
Deferred Taxes				.0			.0	.0
All Other Non-Current				3.1			4.5	9.2
Net Worth				62.8			61.6	47.0
Total Liabilties & Net Worth				100.0			100.0	100.0
INCOME DATA								
Net Sales				100.0			100.0	100.0
Gross Profit								
Operating Expenses				86.1			95.1	83.2
Operating Profit				13.9			4.9	16.8
All Other Expenses (net)				3.8			2.5	6.7
Profit Before Taxes				10.2			2.4	10.1
RATIOS								
Current				12.1			5.3	5.9
				3.5			2.2	2.6
				1.9			1.1	1.2
Quick				12.1			4.5	5.0
				3.5			2.2	2.6
				1.7			1.0	1.2
Sales/Receivables				**15** 24.4			**0** UND	**0** UND
				35 10.4			**9** 42.0	**21** 17.8
				44 8.3			**36** 10.1	**38** 9.5
Cost of Sales/Inventory								
Cost of Sales/Payables								
Sales/Working Capital				1.9			2.3	2.4
				2.4			3.8	4.5
				5.6			NM	30.9
EBIT/Interest							5.8	25.8
							(12) .5	(13) 8.6
							-1.0	1.1
Net Profit + Depr., Dep., Amort./Cur. Mat. L/T/D								
Fixed/Worth				.0			.0	.0
				.5			.9	.8
				1.1			1.1	2.2
Debt/Worth				.4			.3	.3
				.5			.5	1.2
				1.2			1.1	3.7
% Profit Before Taxes/Tangible Net Worth				14.7			4.4	19.6
				2.4			(17) -.9	(18) 8.3
				.0			-15.7	2.1
% Profit Before Taxes/Total Assets				9.8			2.8	9.6
				1.5			-.7	4.8
				.0			-8.2	.7
Sales/Net Fixed Assets				UND			UND	UND
				2.2			1.6	1.7
				.3			.5	.2
Sales/Total Assets				3.1			1.4	3.6
				.9			.8	.6
				.2			.2	.2
% Depr., Dep., Amort./Sales							3.5	2.5
							(12) 4.1	(12) 8.4
							16.3	24.6
% Officers', Directors' Owners' Comp/Sales								
Net Sales ($)			91758M	409046M	219024M	531975M	726039M	865665M
Total Assets ($)			44245M	340771M	492461M	1526299M	1224953M	1143771M

M = $ thousand MM = $ million

See Pages 9 through 22 for Explanation of Ratios and Data

Comparative Historical Data				Current Data Sorted by Sales					
			Type of Statement						
13	31	35	Unqualified		3	2	4	10	16
1			Reviewed						
1			Compiled						
			Tax Returns						
11	6	3	Other				1		2
4/1/11-3/31/12 ALL	4/1/12-3/31/13 ALL	4/1/13-3/31/14 ALL			35 (4/1-9/30/13)		3 (10/1/13-3/31/14)		
				0-1MM	1-3MM	3-5MM	5-10MM	10-25MM	25MM & OVER
26	37	38	**NUMBER OF STATEMENTS**		3	2	5	10	18
%	%	%	**ASSETS**	%	%	%	%	%	%
17.8	19.5	29.3	Cash & Equivalents	DATA NOT AVAILABLE				23.5	34.7
5.7	9.1	9.6	Trade Receivables (net)					7.1	12.7
.1	.1	.3	Inventory					.3	.3
3.1	5.1	2.0	All Other Current					2.2	2.7
26.7	33.7	41.2	Total Current					33.1	50.3
57.3	55.7	45.8	Fixed Assets (net)					59.6	39.6
.7	.1	.6	Intangibles (net)					.2	1.0
15.3	10.5	12.4	All Other Non-Current					7.1	9.1
100.0	100.0	100.0	Total					100.0	100.0
			LIABILITIES						
1.4	1.5	.2	Notes Payable-Short Term					.1	.3
1.4	1.3	1.7	Cur. Mat.-L.T.D.					1.2	1.1
6.4	3.0	6.3	Trade Payables					3.8	9.9
.0	.0	.0	Income Taxes Payable					.0	.0
3.8	8.2	7.9	All Other Current					4.9	9.3
13.1	14.0	16.0	Total Current					10.0	20.6
32.6	20.2	24.3	Long-Term Debt					13.3	20.8
.0	.0	.2	Deferred Taxes					.0	.4
.8	3.9	3.7	All Other Non-Current					4.9	4.8
53.5	61.9	55.8	Net Worth					71.8	53.3
100.0	100.0	100.0	Total Liabilties & Net Worth					100.0	100.0
			INCOME DATA						
100.0	100.0	100.0	Net Sales					100.0	100.0
			Gross Profit						
81.7	93.0	89.9	Operating Expenses					95.2	94.5
18.3	7.0	10.1	Operating Profit					4.8	5.5
10.2	3.5	4.0	All Other Expenses (net)					2.0	1.1
8.2	3.5	6.0	Profit Before Taxes					2.8	4.3
			RATIOS						
6.5	6.0	7.3						7.6	4.7
2.8	3.1	3.3	Current					4.5	3.0
1.2	1.5	1.6						1.7	1.6
6.5	5.6	6.5						7.4	4.3
2.5	2.8	2.8	Quick					4.0	2.6
.9	1.3	1.5						1.5	1.4
0 UND	**15** 25.1	**9** 42.6						**5** 74.8	**9** 42.6
30 12.1	**27** 13.6	**26** 14.2	Sales/Receivables					**14** 25.7	**24** 15.4
43 8.5	**51** 7.2	**52** 7.0						**42** 8.7	**50** 7.3
			Cost of Sales/Inventory						
			Cost of Sales/Payables						
1.8	1.4	1.7						1.4	2.0
3.4	3.3	3.4	Sales/Working Capital					3.6	3.9
31.3	9.5	8.4						18.4	10.0
3.3	10.1	9.1							5.8
(17) 2.0	(25) 2.0	(27) 2.6	EBIT/Interest						(13) 1.6
1.2	-.1	-2.3							.2
			Net Profit + Depr., Dep., Amort./Cur. Mat. L/T/D						
.4	.2	.0						.4	.0
1.0	.9	.9	Fixed/Worth					.9	.9
1.5	1.4	1.4						1.1	1.5
.2	.2	.3						.1	.4
.7	.5	.6	Debt/Worth					.4	.6
4.2	1.3	1.3						.7	2.4
12.4	6.4	14.1						10.0	15.6
(25) 4.9	(36) 1.5	(37) 1.6	% Profit Before Taxes/Tangible Net Worth					2.1	.6
.3	-1.6	-4.6						-3.1	-7.6
5.2	4.3	6.5						7.7	6.5
1.8	1.1	1.0	% Profit Before Taxes/Total Assets					1.2	.5
-.4	-1.0	-1.8						-2.8	-2.0
4.9	7.7	UND						UND	UND
.5	.6	.8	Sales/Net Fixed Assets					.4	1.6
.2	.3	.3						.2	.6
.6	1.2	1.4						1.8	3.1
.2	.4	.4	Sales/Total Assets					.3	.8
.1	.2	.2						.2	.4
3.0	5.1	4.6							4.5
(18) 10.2	(27) 8.7	(26) 7.2	% Depr., Dep., Amort./Sales						(11) 5.6
21.3	12.2	16.6							7.1
			% Officers', Directors' Owners' Comp/Sales						
484725M	**1049686M**	**1251803M**	Net Sales ($)		**5630M**	**7126M**	**34025M**	**185100M**	**1019922M**
1259128M	**2432583M**	**2403776M**	Total Assets ($)		**25699M**	**45686M**	**68439M**	**668337M**	**1595615M**

 M = $ thousand MM = $ million

See Pages 9 through 22 for Explanation of Ratios and Data

Current Data Sorted by Assets							Comparative Historical Data	
						Type of Statement		
1	1	21	43	23	27	Unqualified	70	48
	1					Reviewed		
		2	2			Compiled	1	1
						Tax Returns		1
	1	4	5	3	3	Other	14	7
	128 (4/1-9/30/13)		9 (10/1/13-3/31/14)				4/1/09-3/31/10	4/1/10-3/31/11
0-500M	**500M-2MM**	**2-10MM**	**10-50MM**	**50-100MM**	**100-250MM**		**ALL**	**ALL**
1	3	27	50	26	30	**NUMBER OF STATEMENTS**	85	57
%	%	%	%	%	%	**ASSETS**	%	%
		34.8	30.9	21.9	13.3	Cash & Equivalents	22.9	16.8
		9.0	6.1	7.6	4.9	Trade Receivables (net)	8.3	8.2
		.1	.5	.6	.5	Inventory	1.0	1.1
		8.7	6.8	2.1	1.9	All Other Current	3.9	1.8
		52.5	44.3	32.1	20.5	Total Current	36.1	27.8
		43.6	49.1	61.8	70.6	Fixed Assets (net)	56.2	62.5
		.8	.1	.2	1.4	Intangibles (net)	.7	.5
		3.1	6.5	5.9	7.5	All Other Non-Current	7.0	9.1
		100.0	100.0	100.0	100.0	Total	100.0	100.0
						LIABILITIES		
		.0	.6	.0	.0	Notes Payable-Short Term	1.6	.2
		2.5	2.3	1.6	2.0	Cur. Mat.-L.T.D.	1.9	1.8
		3.2	3.0	2.9	1.4	Trade Payables	3.2	2.1
		.0	.0	.0	.0	Income Taxes Payable	.4	.1
		9.1	6.1	7.0	7.0	All Other Current	6.7	5.2
		14.8	12.0	11.4	10.5	Total Current	13.8	9.5
		19.0	26.4	23.3	20.5	Long-Term Debt	21.8	22.4
		.0	.1	.0	.0	Deferred Taxes	.0	.2
		5.1	4.3	4.9	2.6	All Other Non-Current	5.4	3.5
		61.1	57.3	60.4	66.5	Net Worth	59.1	64.5
		100.0	100.0	100.0	100.0	Total Liabilties & Net Worth	100.0	100.0
						INCOME DATA		
		100.0	100.0	100.0	100.0	Net Sales	100.0	100.0
						Gross Profit		
		85.4	88.8	88.4	94.2	Operating Expenses	92.4	92.2
		14.6	11.2	11.6	5.8	Operating Profit	7.6	7.8
		3.8	5.2	4.2	4.7	All Other Expenses (net)	1.8	2.1
		10.8	6.0	7.4	1.1	Profit Before Taxes	5.9	5.7
						RATIOS		
		9.9	7.4	7.1	5.0		6.8	7.9
		3.8	3.1	3.5	3.0	Current	2.6	3.4
		1.7	1.7	2.1	1.7		1.6	1.4
		9.2	6.5	6.2	5.0		6.5	7.1
		3.5	3.1	3.2	2.6	Quick	2.3	2.9
		1.0	1.1	2.1	1.5		1.3	1.2
		11 33.3	**9** 41.1	**19** 19.6	**19** 19.3		**8** 46.6	**14** 25.6
		28 13.2	**29** 12.8	**29** 12.8	**38** 9.6	Sales/Receivables	**25** 14.7	**34** 10.7
		38 9.6	**46** 8.0	**57** 6.4	**85** 4.3		**55** 6.7	**79** 4.6
						Cost of Sales/Inventory		
						Cost of Sales/Payables		
		1.5	1.2	1.1	1.2		1.3	1.3
		3.1	3.2	1.6	2.0	Sales/Working Capital	2.3	2.4
		12.2	7.1	5.0	3.7		10.3	12.4
		4.4	7.4	9.2	5.9		6.5	6.8
		(18) 2.5	(36) 3.4	(22) 3.5	(29) 2.0	EBIT/Interest	(72) 2.0	(50) 2.0
		.9	.4	.9	.0		-.2	-1.2
						Net Profit + Depr., Dep., Amort./Cur. Mat. L/T/D		
		.0	.0	.8	.9		.6	.7
		.7	.9	1.0	1.1	Fixed/Worth	1.0	1.0
		1.4	1.4	1.4	1.3		1.5	1.4
		.1	.2	.3	.1		.3	.2
		.5	.5	.5	.5	Debt/Worth	.7	.4
		1.1	1.0	1.3	.9		1.3	.9
		20.0	10.9	5.0	3.0		7.4	5.8
		(25) 3.0	(47) 4.8	(25) 2.5	(29) 1.2	% Profit Before Taxes/Tangible Net Worth	(83) 1.9	(56) 1.9
		-1.2	-1.3	.0	-1.7		-2.3	-1.9
		13.9	6.1	3.8	1.9		4.7	4.2
		2.3	2.3	2.3	.8	% Profit Before Taxes/Total Assets	.9	1.1
		-.5	-.8	.1	-.9		-1.4	-1.6
		UND	UND	.7	.5		1.8	1.1
		1.4	.5	.4	.3	Sales/Net Fixed Assets	.7	.4
		.4	.3	.3	.2		.3	.3
		1.9	1.5	.5	.3		.9	.6
		.7	.4	.3	.3	Sales/Total Assets	.4	.3
		.3	.2	.2	.2		.2	.2
		5.2	7.1	9.5	7.5		4.4	4.9
		(13) 9.5	(30) 13.0	(21) 10.9	(27) 13.7	% Depr., Dep., Amort./Sales	(51) 9.7	(41) 9.8
		19.1	18.8	14.9	20.2		13.1	14.6
						% Officers', Directors' Owners' Comp/Sales		
682M	4591M	225071M	1342165M	1120789M	1714104M	Net Sales ($)	3146493M	1498350M
421M	3831M	147403M	1407052M	1996858M	4780867M	Total Assets ($)	5146232M	3544996M

M = $ thousand MM = $ million

See Pages 9 through 22 for Explanation of Ratios and Data

Comparative Historical Data / Current Data Sorted by Sales

4/1/11-3/31/12 ALL	4/1/12-3/31/13 ALL	4/1/13-3/31/14 ALL	Type of Statement	0-1MM	1-3MM	3-5MM	5-10MM	10-25MM	25MM & OVER
55	97	116	Unqualified	4	10	11	11	30	50
		1	Reviewed		1				
1	3	4	Compiled	1	1		2		
1	1		Tax Returns						
7	10	16	Other	3	1	1	2	5	4
					128 (4/1-9/30/13)		9 (10/1/13-3/31/14)		
64	111	137	NUMBER OF STATEMENTS	8	13	12	15	35	54
%	%	%	ASSETS	%	%	%	%	%	%
16.4	29.6	26.3	Cash & Equivalents		24.2	20.3	19.8	25.6	30.8
6.3	9.4	6.7	Trade Receivables (net)		5.0	2.7	2.6	5.4	9.9
.9	.8	.4	Inventory		.0	.1	.1	.3	.8
2.7	4.2	5.2	All Other Current		2.7	10.2	.9	2.5	8.4
26.4	44.1	38.7	Total Current		31.8	33.3	23.4	33.9	49.9
62.0	48.2	55.0	Fixed Assets (net)		66.0	63.4	72.1	60.2	40.7
.6	.6	.5	Intangibles (net)		1.6	.2	.2	.1	.8
11.0	7.0	5.8	All Other Non-Current		.6	3.2	4.2	5.8	8.5
100.0	100.0	100.0	Total		100.0	100.0	100.0	100.0	100.0
			LIABILITIES						
.2	.6	.2	Notes Payable-Short Term		.1	.0	.0	.0	.6
2.0	2.2	2.1	Cur. Mat.-L.T.D.		3.5	2.8	3.4	2.0	1.6
2.1	3.7	2.7	Trade Payables		1.6	1.8	1.8	1.8	4.3
.0	.0	.0	Income Taxes Payable		.0	.0	.0	.0	.0
7.6	10.9	7.4	All Other Current		6.4	7.7	3.1	3.8	11.3
12.0	17.4	12.5	Total Current		11.6	12.4	8.3	7.6	17.8
30.5	18.9	22.5	Long-Term Debt		15.2	39.3	42.3	18.3	17.1
.1	.0	.0	Deferred Taxes		.0	.3	.0	.0	.0
2.2	2.3	4.0	All Other Non-Current		1.6	1.3	4.0	7.4	3.6
55.3	61.4	60.9	Net Worth		71.6	46.7	45.4	66.7	61.5
100.0	100.0	100.0	Total Liabilities & Net Worth		100.0	100.0	100.0	100.0	100.0
			INCOME DATA						
100.0	100.0	100.0	Net Sales		100.0	100.0	100.0	100.0	100.0
			Gross Profit						
85.4	89.6	88.9	Operating Expenses		84.2	79.5	81.4	95.8	92.7
14.6	10.4	11.1	Operating Profit		15.8	20.5	18.6	4.2	7.3
4.0	4.4	4.8	All Other Expenses (net)		6.6	2.3	12.6	1.5	4.4
10.6	6.0	6.4	Profit Before Taxes		9.2	18.1	6.0	2.7	2.9
			RATIOS						
6.2	7.1	7.0			4.5	5.1	6.9	8.4	6.8
3.2	3.5	3.2	Current		2.7	1.6	3.2	3.7	3.8
1.6	2.1	1.7			1.4	1.1	1.7	1.8	2.0
5.6	7.1	6.3			3.9	5.1	4.5	7.6	5.7
2.8	3.5	2.9	Quick		1.9	1.1	3.2	3.1	3.2
1.1	2.1	1.3			1.4	.7	1.7	1.5	1.8
14 25.9	**18** 20.6	**14** 26.2			**27** 13.4	**11** 32.9	**10** 37.0	**19** 19.7	**7** 49.8
33 11.0	**33** 11.1	**29** 12.5	Sales/Receivables		**32** 11.3	**21** 17.6	**38** 9.6	**29** 12.5	**26** 14.3
56 6.5	**57** 6.4	**48** 7.6			**61** 6.0	**37** 9.9	**47** 7.7	**54** 6.7	**51** 7.1
			Cost of Sales/Inventory						
			Cost of Sales/Payables						
1.5	1.1	1.2			1.5	1.3	.7	1.4	1.4
2.9	2.0	2.5	Sales/Working Capital		2.3	5.2	1.1	2.2	2.6
12.1	5.9	7.8			9.6	220.7	12.2	5.1	7.1
11.6	6.9	6.5					18.9	5.6	7.7
(54) 3.0	(89) 2.5	(106) 2.7	EBIT/Interest				(11) 3.3	(30) 1.9	(42) 2.7
.7	.8	.8					.9	.2	.0
			Net Profit + Depr., Dep., Amort./Cur. Mat. L/T/D						
.8	.0	.4			.6	.8	1.1	.6	.0
1.1	.9	1.0	Fixed/Worth		1.0	1.6	1.3	.9	.7
1.4	1.2	1.3			1.5	2.9	2.9	1.4	1.1
.3	.2	.2			.1	.5	.6	.2	.2
.5	.5	.5	Debt/Worth		.4	1.1	.9	.5	.4
1.0	1.2	1.0			.9	3.1	2.9	.8	1.1
8.4	8.2	7.5			19.7	23.9	5.9	4.9	7.1
(61) 4.1	(109) 3.3	(130) 2.5	% Profit Before Taxes/Tangible Net Worth		5.0	11.4	(13) 3.1	(34) 1.4	(51) 2.3
-.1	-.2	-.8			.2	1.7	.3	-1.4	-2.6
5.3	4.3	4.8			14.7	9.6	3.1	3.4	5.1
2.5	1.7	1.5	% Profit Before Taxes/Total Assets		3.8	5.5	1.5	.9	1.5
.0	-.1	-.5			.1	.6	-.5	-.7	-1.2
.8	UND	4.1			1.4	1.2	.5	2.0	UND
.5	.6	.5	Sales/Net Fixed Assets		.4	.4	.3	.4	1.2
.3	.3	.3			.2	.2	.2	.3	.4
.5	1.2	1.1			.8	.7	.3	.6	2.0
.3	.4	.3	Sales/Total Assets		.4	.3	.2	.3	.7
.2	.2	.2			.1	.2	.1	.2	.3
5.1	6.8	7.5			10.6		6.2	9.0	5.5
(50) 10.0	(73) 11.6	(93) 12.3	% Depr., Dep., Amort./Sales		(10) 16.9		(12) 15.0	(28) 12.7	(30) 10.4
15.5	18.2	18.5			26.1		19.3	15.1	14.7
			% Officers', Directors' Owners' Comp/Sales						
1751467M	**5438814M**	**4407402M**	Net Sales ($)	**6304M**	**23471M**	**45684M**	**105353M**	**620777M**	**3605813M**
4106077M	**6960886M**	**8336432M**	Total Assets ($)	**48167M**	**87701M**	**191562M**	**567873M**	**2182120M**	**5259009M**

M = $ thousand MM = $ million

See Pages 9 through 22 for Explanation of Ratios and Data

Current Data Sorted by Assets							Comparative Historical Data	
						Type of Statement		
1	12	40	90	49	57	Unqualified	196	200
1		3	1			Reviewed	7	2
		3	2			Compiled	9	4
		1				Tax Returns	2	
1	7	7	13	2	3	Other	65	38
	239 (4/1-9/30/13)		54 (10/1/13-3/31/14)				**4/1/09-3/31/10 ALL**	**4/1/10-3/31/11 ALL**
0-500M	**500M-2MM**	**2-10MM**	**10-50MM**	**50-100MM**	**100-250MM**			
3	19	54	106	51	60	**NUMBER OF STATEMENTS**	279	244
%	%	%	%	%	%	**ASSETS**	%	%
	60.4	39.1	37.4	26.6	18.3	Cash & Equivalents	28.3	30.0
	5.5	6.7	9.8	6.0	4.2	Trade Receivables (net)	8.2	8.0
	.0	2.0	.9	.2	.3	Inventory	.7	.5
	9.8	5.8	6.1	3.4	3.8	All Other Current	4.7	5.5
	75.7	53.6	54.2	36.3	26.6	Total Current	41.9	44.0
	13.7	36.1	40.7	59.5	66.0	Fixed Assets (net)	49.5	47.6
	.0	.6	.1	.0	.1	Intangibles (net)	.9	.4
	10.6	9.7	5.1	4.2	7.3	All Other Non-Current	7.8	8.0
	100.0	100.0	100.0	100.0	100.0	Total	100.0	100.0
						LIABILITIES		
	1.3	.5	.3	.1	.2	Notes Payable-Short Term	2.4	.9
	.3	1.5	1.5	2.1	1.8	Cur. Mat.-L.T.D.	2.0	1.8
	6.2	4.9	4.6	3.2	2.2	Trade Payables	4.0	4.8
	2.2	.0	.1	.0	.1	Income Taxes Payable	.3	.8
	13.0	10.0	8.3	4.2	2.9	All Other Current	7.3	8.2
	23.1	17.0	14.8	9.6	7.3	Total Current	16.0	16.4
	4.5	21.1	19.3	23.6	24.8	Long-Term Debt	23.7	22.9
	.0	.0	.0	.2	.0	Deferred Taxes	.0	.0
	9.2	4.3	5.4	3.9	3.6	All Other Non-Current	4.2	4.4
	63.3	57.6	60.4	62.8	64.4	Net Worth	56.0	56.2
	100.0	100.0	100.0	100.0	100.0	Total Liabilties & Net Worth	100.0	100.0
						INCOME DATA		
	100.0	100.0	100.0	100.0	100.0	Net Sales	100.0	100.0
						Gross Profit		
	98.6	90.8	88.0	90.1	91.3	Operating Expenses	92.4	90.6
	1.4	9.2	12.0	9.9	8.7	Operating Profit	7.6	9.4
	3.5	6.7	6.5	4.3	3.1	All Other Expenses (net)	3.8	2.8
	-2.0	2.4	5.5	5.6	5.6	Profit Before Taxes	3.8	6.6
						RATIOS		
	24.3	8.0	7.7	8.8	4.9	Current	7.4	6.4
	5.5	2.8	4.6	4.3	3.7		3.1	3.3
	1.9	1.7	2.3	1.9	2.6		1.6	1.7
	24.3	7.9	6.9	8.8	4.4	Quick	6.4	5.6
	3.6	2.5	3.9	3.9	3.4		2.9	(243) 3.1
	1.8	1.5	1.9	1.5	2.2		1.3	1.5
	0 UND	0 UND	10 36.2	15 23.7	13 27.1	Sales/Receivables	0 999.8	3 115.8
	2 212.3	7 56.0	21 17.4	36 10.0	32 11.5		19 19.2	25 14.3
	10 35.2	27 13.4	52 7.0	58 6.3	51 7.1		52 7.1	49 7.5
						Cost of Sales/Inventory		
						Cost of Sales/Payables		
	1.7	1.8	1.5	1.2	1.4	Sales/Working Capital	1.5	1.5
	3.7	4.4	2.8	1.8	1.9		2.8	3.2
	21.2	9.6	4.6	4.5	3.5		8.9	9.0
		21.6	9.5	5.9	6.6	EBIT/Interest	8.0	9.7
		(32) 2.3	(75) 3.9	(41) 1.7	(54) 2.5		(180) 2.2	(173) 2.4
		.7	.5	-.2	1.0		-.3	.6
						Net Profit + Depr., Dep., Amort./Cur. Mat. L/T/D		
	.0	.0	.0	.7	.8	Fixed/Worth	.2	.0
	.0	.5	.7	1.0	1.1		.9	.9
	.2	1.4	1.1	1.2	1.3		1.4	1.2
	.1	.3	.2	.2	.3	Debt/Worth	.2	.2
	.3	.6	.5	.3	.5		.6	.5
	1.2	1.6	.9	.7	.8		1.6	1.3
	4.4	11.1	10.2	6.6	6.0	% Profit Before Taxes/Tangible Net Worth	7.5	9.0
	(17) -.5	(51) 2.6	(102) 4.7	(49) 1.7	2.5		(267) 1.1	(234) 2.4
	-9.8	-1.9	-2.3	-.6	-.1		-3.2	-1.7
	4.3	8.0	7.0	4.3	3.5	% Profit Before Taxes/Total Assets	4.1	6.2
	-.5	1.4	3.3	.9	1.4		.8	1.5
	-8.6	-1.5	-1.2	-.6	-.1		-1.8	-.9
	UND	UND	UND	.9	.7	Sales/Net Fixed Assets	34.1	173.0
	UND	8.6	1.5	.4	.4		.8	.8
	40.1	.6	.4	.2	.3		.3	.3
	4.6	3.0	2.2	.5	.4	Sales/Total Assets	1.5	1.8
	1.9	1.0	.7	.3	.3		.5	.5
	1.0	.3	.3	.2	.2		.2	.2
		.8	4.6	9.0	6.1	% Depr., Dep., Amort./Sales	3.8	4.7
		(30) 7.2	(62) 8.9	(35) 13.0	(52) 10.6		(160) 8.2	(157) 9.7
		20.5	17.2	17.7	16.1		15.9	16.4
		1.6	3.7			% Officers', Directors' Owners' Comp/Sales	5.3	2.6
		(13) 3.4	(15) 10.4				(30) 8.9	(22) 5.8
		20.3	16.9				18.1	13.1
2033M	63048M	449778M	3272103M	1967548M	4324617M	Net Sales ($)	6180462M	6260311M
759M	22669M	274528M	2684034M	3547320M	10006378M	Total Assets ($)	11715031M	11560135M

M = $ thousand MM = $ million

See Pages 9 through 22 for Explanation of Ratios and Data

Comparative Historical Data / Current Data Sorted by Sales

4/1/11-3/31/12 ALL	4/1/12-3/31/13 ALL	4/1/13-3/31/14 ALL	Type of Statement	0-1MM	1-3MM	3-5MM	5-10MM	10-25MM	25MM & OVER
229	265	249	Unqualified	15	16	12	36	63	107
1		5	Reviewed	1		1		2	1
4	1	5	Compiled	1	2	2			
3	1	1	Tax Returns					1	
57	51	33	Other	5	6	2	3	12	5
				239 (4/1-9/30/13)			54 (10/1/13-3/31/14)		
294	318	293	NUMBER OF STATEMENTS	22	24	17	39	78	113
%	%	%	**ASSETS**	%	%	%	%	%	%
28.3	31.3	33.5	Cash & Equivalents	23.3	31.7	35.3	28.4	28.3	41.1
8.0	7.6	7.3	Trade Receivables (net)	.7	3.9	4.6	4.5	7.4	10.5
1.2	1.0	.8	Inventory	.0	.0	.4	.5	1.0	1.1
5.1	5.6	5.3	All Other Current	1.1	8.5	1.3	6.0	3.4	7.0
42.7	45.4	46.8	Total Current	25.0	44.2	41.7	39.4	40.1	59.7
48.6	48.0	46.3	Fixed Assets (net)	52.7	48.5	52.8	49.6	54.8	36.7
.7	.4	.2	Intangibles (net)	.1	.6	.1	.1	.2	.0
8.0	6.2	6.7	All Other Non-Current	22.2	6.7	5.5	10.9	4.9	3.6
100.0	100.0	100.0	Total	100.0	100.0	100.0	100.0	100.0	100.0
			LIABILITIES						
.9	1.2	.4	Notes Payable-Short Term	.4	.3	.3	.2	.7	.2
1.6	1.7	1.7	Cur. Mat.-L.T.D.	3.4	1.1	1.3	1.7	1.6	1.6
5.6	4.4	4.1	Trade Payables	.3	2.6	1.6	5.0	3.5	5.6
.4	.2	.2	Income Taxes Payable	.0	1.7	.0	.0	.0	.1
8.7	7.7	7.5	All Other Current	6.0	8.3	3.5	5.8	6.3	9.5
17.1	15.2	13.8	Total Current	10.1	14.1	6.6	12.8	12.2	16.9
21.9	19.7	20.3	Long-Term Debt	39.5	17.9	26.7	16.3	21.6	16.8
.0	.0	.0	Deferred Taxes	.0	.0	.0	.0	.0	.1
4.1	4.9	4.8	All Other Non-Current	.5	6.0	1.6	6.7	2.9	6.4
56.8	60.1	61.1	Net Worth	49.9	62.0	65.1	64.3	63.4	59.8
100.0	100.0	100.0	Total Liabilties & Net Worth	100.0	100.0	100.0	100.0	100.0	100.0
			INCOME DATA						
100.0	100.0	100.0	Net Sales	100.0	100.0	100.0	100.0	100.0	100.0
			Gross Profit						
90.7	90.9	90.3	Operating Expenses	81.2	94.5	94.7	84.7	91.1	92.0
9.3	9.1	9.7	Operating Profit	18.8	5.5	5.3	15.3	8.9	8.0
3.5	3.4	5.2	All Other Expenses (net)	18.4	5.3	4.7	6.8	4.3	2.8
5.8	5.7	4.5	Profit Before Taxes	.4	.2	.6	8.5	4.7	5.3
			RATIOS						
6.2	7.3	7.0		16.9	9.6	12.7	5.4	6.8	6.9
2.9	3.5	4.0	Current	2.8	3.9	4.0	3.3	3.7	4.4
1.5	1.8	2.2		1.4	2.0	1.5	2.1	2.2	2.5
5.4	6.8	6.3		16.2	9.6	12.7	4.7	6.4	5.9
2.6	3.2	3.4	Quick	2.8	2.5	3.9	3.0	3.3	3.9
1.4	1.5	1.9		1.4	1.5	1.5	1.6	1.9	1.9
6 58.0	**4** 102.6	**5** 70.3		**0** UND	**1** 548.8	**4** 84.5	**0** 999.8	**8** 46.4	**11** 33.2
25 14.6	**21** 17.1	**21** 17.7	Sales/Receivables	**0** UND	**9** 39.8	**27** 13.6	**17** 21.8	**26** 14.3	**25** 14.5
47 7.8	**47** 7.8	**46** 7.9		**13** 27.4	**26** 14.2	**76** 4.8	**54** 6.8	**46** 7.9	**46** 7.9
			Cost of Sales/Inventory						
			Cost of Sales/Payables						
1.6	1.5	1.5		.8	1.2	1.9	1.4	1.4	1.5
3.3	2.8	2.5	Sales/Working Capital	1.6	2.2	2.9	3.0	2.1	2.8
10.0	7.3	5.8		17.3	8.5	13.2	5.8	4.9	5.9
8.3	6.8	8.6			3.1	4.6	21.2	8.6	8.8
(207) 2.8	(229) 2.3	(209) 2.5	EBIT/Interest		(18) .3	(13) 2.3	(25) 8.0	(63) 2.7	(83) 2.8
.8	.7	.5			-.8	-.5	1.6	-.2	1.0
			Net Profit + Depr., Dep., Amort./Cur. Mat. L/T/D						
.1	.0	.0		.0	.0	.0	.1	.5	.0
.9	.9	.8	Fixed/Worth	1.0	.8	.9	.9	.9	.7
1.3	1.3	1.2		2.3	1.3	1.6	1.2	1.2	1.1
.3	.2	.2		.2	.3	.2	.2	.2	.2
.5	.5	.5	Debt/Worth	.8	.4	.6	.5	.4	.5
1.2	1.1	.9		7.9	1.0	1.0	.8	1.1	.9
10.0	10.1	8.1		4.0	4.4	7.1	12.2	7.1	9.5
(277) 3.0	(304) 3.2	(282) 2.6	% Profit Before Taxes/Tangible Net Worth	(20) -.2	(21) -.6	1.7	(38) 3.0	(77) 2.4	(109) 5.1
-.5	-.6	-1.5		-4.7	-3.6	-4.0	-1.0	-2.4	.1
5.2	5.2	5.2		1.6	2.9	4.1	7.4	4.7	6.5
1.9	1.8	1.7	% Profit Before Taxes/Total Assets	.0	-.8	.7	2.3	1.5	3.4
-.7	-.8	-1.1		-1.8	-2.7	-1.6	-.5	-1.4	.1
67.3	UND	UND		24.5	UND	UND	33.6	5.8	UND
.8	.8	.8	Sales/Net Fixed Assets	.3	.8	.8	1.0	.5	4.3
.3	.3	.3		.1	.2	.2	.3	.3	.5
1.4	1.4	1.5		.3	1.4	1.7	1.1	1.1	2.4
.5	.5	.5	Sales/Total Assets	.1	.5	.6	.5	.3	.9
.2	.2	.2		.1	.2	.2	.2	.2	.3
4.4	4.9	5.4		7.3	10.6	7.6	4.9	5.7	4.5
(192) 9.6	(204) 10.5	(184) 9.7	% Depr., Dep., Amort./Sales	(16) 28.1	(12) 16.5	(10) 17.5	(28) 11.9	(56) 9.5	(62) 7.7
17.2	16.6	16.5		38.9	21.4	24.1	15.3	16.0	13.8
2.3	3.9	2.1							2.2
(25) 7.4	(35) 7.6	(47) 8.5	% Officers', Directors' Owners' Comp/Sales						(28) 7.3
14.5	17.8	19.7							18.0
7253931M	8098744M	10079127M	Net Sales ($)	13248M	42370M	68687M	287198M	1287306M	8380318M
12669674M	14505087M	16535688M	Total Assets ($)	127125M	167466M	245445M	983242M	4134602M	10877808M

M = $ thousand MM = $ million

See Pages 9 through 22 for Explanation of Ratios and Data

Current Data Sorted by Assets							Comparative Historical Data	
						Type of Statement		
	11	28	16	1		Unqualified	38	48
	3	5				Reviewed	6	5
	1	4				Compiled	7	7
4	2	3				Tax Returns	8	8
4	9	10	2			Other	27	25
	70 (4/1-9/30/13)		33 (10/1/13-3/31/14)				4/1/09-3/31/10 ALL	4/1/10-3/31/11 ALL
0-500M	500M-2MM	2-10MM	10-50MM	50-100MM	100-250MM			
8	26	50	18	1		NUMBER OF STATEMENTS	86	93
%	%	%	%	%	%	**ASSETS**	%	%
	26.8	25.6	35.1		DATA NOT AVAILABLE	Cash & Equivalents	23.5	27.6
	1.5	8.0	8.9			Trade Receivables (net)	10.8	10.8
	.6	1.5	.6			Inventory	2.0	1.5
	.1	1.7	1.5			All Other Current	3.1	3.7
	29.0	36.8	46.1			Total Current	39.3	43.7
	66.0	60.2	43.7			Fixed Assets (net)	52.7	49.2
	.4	.3	6.3			Intangibles (net)	2.2	1.8
	4.6	2.7	3.8			All Other Non-Current	5.8	5.3
	100.0	100.0	100.0			Total	100.0	100.0
						LIABILITIES		
	.2	1.7	.0			Notes Payable-Short Term	3.5	4.1
	3.1	3.1	3.2			Cur. Mat.-L.T.D.	3.3	3.3
	.5	3.8	2.4			Trade Payables	4.0	4.1
	.0	.0	.0			Income Taxes Payable	.2	.1
	1.1	3.0	4.6			All Other Current	5.2	5.3
	4.9	11.7	10.1			Total Current	16.2	16.8
	29.0	29.1	29.2			Long-Term Debt	21.8	27.1
	.0	.2	.2			Deferred Taxes	.4	.4
	.2	1.9	6.6			All Other Non-Current	2.0	1.5
	65.9	57.1	53.9			Net Worth	59.6	54.2
	100.0	100.0	100.0			Total Liabilties & Net Worth	100.0	100.0
						INCOME DATA		
	100.0	100.0	100.0			Net Sales	100.0	100.0
						Gross Profit		
	82.5	91.2	96.8			Operating Expenses	92.0	94.3
	17.5	8.8	3.2			Operating Profit	8.0	5.7
	4.8	3.4	1.7			All Other Expenses (net)	2.2	2.5
	12.7	5.4	1.5			Profit Before Taxes	5.9	3.2
						RATIOS		
	16.4	6.2	9.3				6.6	9.4
	7.5	3.5	5.5			Current	3.5	3.7
	2.1	2.1	2.6				1.5	1.4
	13.5	5.8	9.3				6.4	9.1
	7.5	3.1	5.3			Quick	3.1	3.5
	2.1	1.8	2.5				1.3	1.2
	0 UND	**0** UND	**9** 42.5				**0** UND	**0** UND
	0 UND	**10** 35.8	**16** 22.6			Sales/Receivables	**5** 67.6	**8** 45.7
	20 18.1	**36** 10.2	**34** 10.7				**29** 12.7	**35** 10.4
						Cost of Sales/Inventory		
						Cost of Sales/Payables		
	1.0	1.5	1.3				1.9	1.6
	2.2	3.2	2.1			Sales/Working Capital	4.4	4.1
	10.3	7.9	4.0				10.4	10.8
	6.0	7.3	6.4				8.1	8.2
	(22) 3.7	(44) 3.6	(16) 3.0			EBIT/Interest	(60) 2.9	(69) 2.8
	1.4	.3	-.7				.7	.4
						Net Profit + Depr., Dep., Amort./Cur. Mat. L/T/D		
	.7	.6	.8				.5	.3
	1.0	1.1	1.0			Fixed/Worth	.9	.9
	1.9	1.9	1.8				1.7	1.5
	.1	.3	.3				.2	.2
	.4	.7	.8			Debt/Worth	.5	.6
	1.1	1.4	2.0				1.9	2.0
	12.7	14.2	10.9				17.4	17.5
	(25) 8.4	(48) 7.6	(16) 3.6			% Profit Before Taxes/Tangible Net Worth	(83) 5.6	(89) 5.8
	1.2	-1.8	-2.5				-.5	-5.1
	7.6	8.1	6.8				9.1	8.2
	4.1	4.3	3.2			% Profit Before Taxes/Total Assets	3.3	3.6
	1.0	-1.2	-1.7				-.4	-4.1
	1.4	2.0	5.4				10.6	17.9
	.5	.8	1.4			Sales/Net Fixed Assets	1.1	1.4
	.3	.3	.8				.4	.6
	.8	1.0	1.5				1.9	1.8
	.3	.5	.7			Sales/Total Assets	.7	.8
	.2	.3	.4				.3	.4
	9.1	5.3	4.2				3.9	3.3
	(18) 19.6	(39) 10.1	(16) 6.2			% Depr., Dep., Amort./Sales	(61) 8.5	(62) 7.2
	29.8	25.4	8.3				19.1	14.9
							2.5	1.2
						% Officers', Directors' Owners' Comp/Sales	(13) 4.4	(13) 3.4
							11.3	6.4
4987M	21753M	170912M	333863M	61589M		Net Sales ($)	1024833M	1296465M
1825M	35896M	202247M	362396M	85899M		Total Assets ($)	666735M	853510M

M = $ thousand MM = $ million

See Pages 9 through 22 for Explanation of Ratios and Data

Comparative Historical Data | Current Data Sorted by Sales

4/1/11-3/31/12 ALL	4/1/12-3/31/13 ALL	4/1/13-3/31/14 ALL	Type of Statement	0-1MM	1-3MM	3-5MM	5-10MM	10-25MM	25MM & OVER
70	76	56	Unqualified	14	10	12	6	11	3
11	9	8	Reviewed	5	1		2		
5	6	5	Compiled	3	1		1		
6	6	9	Tax Returns	6	1	1	1		
27	19	25	Other	14	8			2	1
				70 (4/1-9/30/13)			33 (10/1/13-3/31/14)		
119	116	103	NUMBER OF STATEMENTS	42	21	13	10	13	4
%	%	%	**ASSETS**	%	%	%	%	%	%
29.4	27.1	32.3	Cash & Equivalents	29.3	34.7	37.6	19.9	42.8	
8.4	6.6	5.8	Trade Receivables (net)	.9	2.6	3.9	20.4	15.9	
.5	1.2	1.4	Inventory	.3	2.2	.0	6.4	1.4	
1.8	3.6	1.2	All Other Current	.4	.4	.1	3.7	3.9	
40.1	38.5	40.8	Total Current	31.0	39.8	41.5	50.4	64.0	
55.8	56.9	54.7	Fixed Assets (net)	64.4	58.6	55.4	47.1	29.0	
1.0	.9	1.3	Intangibles (net)	.4	.0	.2	.0	3.7	
3.1	3.8	3.2	All Other Non-Current	4.1	1.5	2.9	2.5	3.2	
100.0	100.0	100.0	Total	100.0	100.0	100.0	100.0	100.0	
			LIABILITIES						
1.4	1.4	.9	Notes Payable-Short Term	.6	.0	.0	6.8	.0	
3.1	3.3	4.0	Cur. Mat.-L.T.D.	2.8	9.0	2.2	3.4	2.0	
2.7	2.3	2.4	Trade Payables	.4	.8	4.0	10.4	3.5	
.5	.1	.0	Income Taxes Payable	.0	.0	.0	.0	.0	
4.8	3.4	2.7	All Other Current	.4	2.6	3.4	4.2	6.1	
12.4	10.4	10.0	Total Current	4.2	12.4	9.7	24.8	11.7	
33.4	30.6	33.2	Long-Term Debt	27.4	57.9	31.8	28.3	17.8	
.2	.7	.1	Deferred Taxes	.2	.0	.0	.0	.2	
2.7	2.6	2.3	All Other Non-Current	.3	1.3	1.8	2.7	10.5	
51.2	55.8	54.3	Net Worth	67.9	28.4	56.7	44.3	59.8	
100.0	100.0	100.0	Total Liabilties & Net Worth	100.0	100.0	100.0	100.0	100.0	
			INCOME DATA						
100.0	100.0	100.0	Net Sales	100.0	100.0	100.0	100.0	100.0	
			Gross Profit						
92.4	92.1	90.2	Operating Expenses	85.3	91.3	91.7	97.2	95.2	
7.6	7.9	9.8	Operating Profit	14.7	8.7	8.3	2.8	4.8	
3.4	4.2	3.2	All Other Expenses (net)	5.2	.9	4.2	.7	2.6	
4.2	3.7	6.5	Profit Before Taxes	9.4	7.8	4.1	2.1	2.2	
			RATIOS						
9.9	12.9	11.6	Current	16.5	7.5	10.7	4.6	8.8	
4.5	5.5	4.8		6.9	3.4	5.7	2.2	6.7	
1.8	2.1	2.2		2.4	2.1	2.7	1.2	4.0	
9.9	10.8	10.2	Quick	13.8	7.5	10.7	4.5	8.8	
4.4	4.8	4.8		6.7	3.2	5.7	1.3	5.9	
1.7	1.7	2.1		2.3	2.1	2.7	.9	3.5	
0 UND	0 UND	0 UND	Sales/Receivables	0 UND	0 UND	4 102.2	3 135.8	14 26.0	
4 97.0	2 207.2	9 40.5		0 UND	1 245.7	14 25.5	13 27.7	20 18.1	
32 11.3	28 13.1	25 14.7		20 18.1	28 12.9	24 15.3	62 5.9	47 7.7	
			Cost of Sales/Inventory						
			Cost of Sales/Payables						
1.4	1.2	1.3	Sales/Working Capital	1.0	1.3	1.7	2.6	1.4	
2.3	2.3	2.5		1.9	3.2	2.4	10.1	2.1	
9.0	6.5	5.9		3.8	7.4	6.9	NM	3.8	
5.9	4.5	7.1	EBIT/Interest	4.6	7.9	10.4		6.7	
(93) 2.2	(86) 2.1	(86) 3.5		(33) 3.2	(17) 4.1	4.0		(11) 3.6	
-.1	.6	.9		1.0	-1.1	.4		2.1	
			Net Profit + Depr., Dep., Amort./Cur. Mat. L/T/D						
.6	.6	.6	Fixed/Worth	.8	.6	.6	.2	.0	
1.0	.9	1.0		1.0	1.1	1.0	1.0	.7	
1.6	1.5	1.7		1.9	1.9	1.6	2.4	1.3	
.3	.2	.2	Debt/Worth	.1	.3	.2	.6	.3	
.7	.5	.7		.4	.5	.4	1.6	.5	
1.6	1.4	1.3		1.1	2.0	1.1	2.5	1.2	
13.0	9.0	13.5	% Profit Before Taxes/Tangible Net Worth	10.3	13.8	14.4	74.3	15.9	
(114) 3.4	(112) 2.5	(96) 7.0		5.7	(17) 8.4	(12) 5.6	6.7	(12) 5.1	
-3.2	-2.2	-1.3		-1.2	-1.2	-2.1	-2.1	-6.3	
6.5	5.2	7.8	% Profit Before Taxes/Total Assets	6.3	9.9	10.1	16.0	7.5	
2.0	1.5	4.1		3.5	5.9	5.8	2.5	3.2	
-1.9	-1.4	-1.1		-1.1	-1.0	-1.2	-1.5	-1.5	
2.2	1.6	2.8	Sales/Net Fixed Assets	.6	2.1	2.0	57.7	UND	
1.0	.8	.9		.3	1.0	1.2	1.6	2.0	
.5	.4	.4		.3	.5	.6	1.1	1.3	
1.0	.9	1.1	Sales/Total Assets	.4	.9	1.3	2.7	2.0	
.5	.5	.5		.3	.5	.6	1.3	.8	
.3	.3	.3		.2	.4	.4	.8	.6	
5.2	5.8	5.8	% Depr., Dep., Amort./Sales	16.1	6.5	6.1			
(82) 9.5	(83) 11.0	(75) 9.5		(28) 25.5	(15) 8.9	(11) 8.0			
19.3	22.7	20.6		32.0	14.5	10.3			
		1.6	% Officers', Directors' Owners' Comp/Sales						
		(10) 2.9							
		5.7							
1016395M	898815M	593104M	Net Sales ($)	19526M	35365M	53782M	69229M	201999M	213203M
1381416M	1085106M	688263M	Total Assets ($)	72088M	65905M	84385M	61696M	237175M	167014M

M = $ thousand MM = $ million

See Pages 9 through 22 for Explanation of Ratios and Data

Current Data Sorted by Assets							Comparative Historical Data	
						Type of Statement		
	6	19	35	27	29	Unqualified	124	136
	1					Reviewed	2	1
						Compiled	2	
1						Tax Returns		
2		5	9	1	4	Other	28	22
	126 (4/1-9/30/13)		**13 (10/1/13-3/31/14)**				**4/1/09-3/31/10**	**4/1/10-3/31/11**
0-500M	**500M-2MM**	**2-10MM**	**10-50MM**	**50-100MM**	**100-250MM**		**ALL**	**ALL**
3	7	24	44	28	33	**NUMBER OF STATEMENTS**	156	159
%	%	%	%	%	%	**ASSETS**	%	%
		32.6	26.9	21.6	16.8	Cash & Equivalents	24.1	22.4
		9.5	12.4	11.1	7.5	Trade Receivables (net)	8.2	12.7
		.6	.4	.3	.2	Inventory	.8	.8
		3.5	4.0	3.0	2.1	All Other Current	3.1	4.0
		46.2	43.6	36.1	26.5	Total Current	36.2	39.9
		43.2	46.7	53.4	57.2	Fixed Assets (net)	51.0	50.3
		2.1	2.4	1.1	3.4	Intangibles (net)	.7	1.1
		8.4	7.4	9.4	12.9	All Other Non-Current	12.2	8.7
		100.0	100.0	100.0	100.0	Total	100.0	100.0
						LIABILITIES		
		.3	.8	.0	1.6	Notes Payable-Short Term	1.7	3.3
		3.2	2.0	2.1	2.1	Cur. Mat.-L.T.D.	2.7	2.7
		5.6	6.2	4.7	2.2	Trade Payables	5.2	5.1
		.0	.0	.1	.0	Income Taxes Payable	.0	.0
		11.1	11.6	10.4	6.8	All Other Current	9.7	11.2
		20.2	20.6	17.4	12.7	Total Current	19.2	22.4
		17.7	23.1	27.3	28.6	Long-Term Debt	25.4	23.8
		.6	.0	.0	.3	Deferred Taxes	.1	.0
		7.9	6.1	1.9	3.4	All Other Non-Current	5.1	6.4
		53.5	50.2	53.4	55.0	Net Worth	50.2	47.4
		100.0	100.0	100.0	100.0	Total Liabilties & Net Worth	100.0	100.0
						INCOME DATA		
		100.0	100.0	100.0	100.0	Net Sales	100.0	100.0
						Gross Profit		
		97.4	97.6	99.3	99.1	Operating Expenses	96.7	95.2
		2.6	2.4	.7	.9	Operating Profit	3.3	4.8
		.4	.9	-.8	.8	All Other Expenses (net)	2.5	.9
		2.2	1.5	1.5	.1	Profit Before Taxes	.8	3.9
						RATIOS		
		5.0	4.1	3.3	4.7		4.0	3.0
		2.5	2.3	2.3	2.2	Current	2.0	1.8
		1.3	1.1	1.3	1.4		1.3	1.1
		4.8	3.7	2.9	4.0		3.9	2.8
		1.8	1.8	2.2	1.8	Quick	1.8	1.5
		1.3	1.0	1.3	1.2		1.1	.9
		1 316.9	**4** 83.9	**13** 27.1	**8** 48.1		**2** 195.3	**4** 96.4
		8 47.0	**18** 20.0	**41** 8.8	**37** 9.8	Sales/Receivables	**14** 25.9	**22** 16.9
		24 15.4	**62** 5.9	**66** 5.5	**72** 5.1		**33** 11.2	**44** 8.4
						Cost of Sales/Inventory		
						Cost of Sales/Payables		
		3.9	2.8	3.1	2.9		3.4	4.7
		9.4	6.1	4.4	5.5	Sales/Working Capital	7.3	8.6
		23.9	35.7	31.1	11.7		26.6	76.8
		4.1	11.1	6.4	3.8		4.3	4.8
		(16) 1.3	(34) 3.6	(25) 1.6	(30) 1.7	EBIT/Interest	(112) 1.2	(113) 2.0
		-2.6	-1.2	.6	.5		-.7	.6
						Net Profit + Depr., Dep., Amort./Cur. Mat. L/T/D		
		.7	.2	.6	.9		.5	.3
		1.0	1.0	1.1	1.0	Fixed/Worth	1.0	1.1
		1.3	1.7	1.7	1.4		1.9	2.2
		.2	.4	.4	.4		.3	.4
		.7	.9	.9	.8	Debt/Worth	.8	1.1
		1.9	2.5	1.6	1.5		2.2	2.2
		18.3	14.3	6.0	4.4		7.6	11.5
		(23) 7.1	(42) 1.9	(27) 1.6	(32) 1.2	% Profit Before Taxes/Tangible Net Worth	(149) 1.7	(148) 3.8
		-3.5	-7.4	-.5	-1.6		-5.8	-1.8
		11.5	5.9	4.5	2.0		4.6	6.4
		2.0	-.2	.8	.7	% Profit Before Taxes/Total Assets	.8	2.0
		-2.6	-3.9	-.3	-.9		-2.8	-.8
		26.2	16.7	3.5	1.3		5.6	13.0
		4.4	2.0	1.0	.8	Sales/Net Fixed Assets	1.5	2.0
		1.2	.9	.8	.6		.8	.8
		3.1	1.6	1.0	.9		1.5	2.0
		1.7	.9	.6	.5	Sales/Total Assets	.8	1.0
		.8	.6	.3	.4		.5	.6
		1.0	2.3	2.0	4.2		2.0	1.6
		(19) 2.4	(36) 3.9	(24) 4.3	(27) 5.8	% Depr., Dep., Amort./Sales	(123) 3.3	(132) 3.0
		5.4	5.3	7.6	7.5		5.1	4.9
							2.3	3.2
						% Officers', Directors' Owners' Comp/Sales	(23) 7.3	(16) 6.5
							14.3	15.0
4140M	**37679M**	**238683M**	**1518118M**	**1617864M**	**3574064M**	Net Sales ($)	**6098055M**	**7325453M**
919M	**9945M**	**124697M**	**1128631M**	**1901014M**	**5409714M**	Total Assets ($)	**7529500M**	**8087131M**

M = $ thousand MM = $ million

See Pages 9 through 22 for Explanation of Ratios and Data

Comparative Historical Data | Current Data Sorted by Sales

4/1/11-3/31/12 ALL	4/1/12-3/31/13 ALL	4/1/13-3/31/14 ALL	Type of Statement	0-1MM	1-3MM	3-5MM	5-10MM	10-25MM	25MM & OVER
130	126	116	Unqualified		10	3	7	32	64
1	1	1	Reviewed	1					
	2		Compiled						
	2	1	Tax Returns			1			
20	13	21	Other	2		1	3	6	9
				126 (4/1-9/30/13)			13 (10/1/13-3/31/14)		
151	144	139	NUMBER OF STATEMENTS	3	10	5	10	38	73
%	%	%	ASSETS	%	%	%	%	%	%
21.5	25.2	25.1	Cash & Equivalents		20.5		33.1	26.4	23.1
10.9	9.9	10.8	Trade Receivables (net)		5.2		5.0	10.2	12.6
.7	.6	.4	Inventory		.0		.4	.3	.4
2.9	3.2	3.1	All Other Current		.7		3.5	2.3	4.0
36.0	38.9	39.4	Total Current		26.4		41.9	39.2	40.0
52.1	50.7	48.8	Fixed Assets (net)		59.3		50.7	44.6	50.0
2.4	1.9	2.2	Intangibles (net)		.0		.1	2.6	2.0
9.5	8.5	9.6	All Other Non-Current		14.4		7.4	13.5	8.0
100.0	100.0	100.0	Total		100.0		100.0	100.0	100.0
			LIABILITIES						
1.4	1.4	.7	Notes Payable-Short Term		.0		.5	.1	1.2
2.2	1.9	2.2	Cur. Mat.-L.T.D.		1.8		1.4	3.1	1.9
5.4	5.3	5.2	Trade Payables		1.0		7.2	4.8	5.4
.0	.0	.0	Income Taxes Payable		.0		.0	.0	.0
8.8	8.9	11.2	All Other Current		4.2		9.7	10.6	11.6
17.8	17.5	19.3	Total Current		7.0		18.7	18.7	20.2
22.7	25.0	22.9	Long-Term Debt		11.7		22.3	26.7	23.8
.2	.2	.2	Deferred Taxes		.0		.0	.4	.2
6.4	8.1	4.9	All Other Non-Current		6.4		1.6	8.4	3.8
53.0	49.2	52.8	Net Worth		74.8		57.4	45.8	52.1
100.0	100.0	100.0	Total Liabilties & Net Worth		100.0		100.0	100.0	100.0
			INCOME DATA						
100.0	100.0	100.0	Net Sales		100.0		100.0	100.0	100.0
			Gross Profit						
95.6	96.5	98.2	Operating Expenses		99.6		91.4	98.9	99.4
4.4	3.5	1.8	Operating Profit		.4		8.6	1.1	.6
.6	.5	.4	All Other Expenses (net)		-1.0		.0	1.1	.3
3.8	3.0	1.4	Profit Before Taxes		1.4		8.7	-.1	.3
			RATIOS						
4.2	4.4	4.2			11.1		4.3	4.3	4.0
1.9	2.3	2.2	Current		4.9		2.5	2.3	2.2
1.2	1.3	1.3			1.3		1.3	1.2	1.3
3.7	4.4	4.0			10.4		4.3	4.2	3.1
1.7	2.2	2.0	Quick		4.9		1.7	2.2	1.9
1.1	1.1	1.2			1.2		1.3	.9	1.2
3 120.1	4 93.6	6 58.7			2 174.9		1 712.4	8 43.0	7 52.6
17 21.1	18 20.6	20 18.5	Sales/Receivables		6 60.7		7 49.0	19 19.0	29 12.5
45 8.2	42 8.6	47 7.7			33 11.2		31 11.7	38 9.7	69 5.3
			Cost of Sales/Inventory						
			Cost of Sales/Payables						
3.7	2.9	3.5			1.5		3.2	3.7	3.4
7.9	6.5	6.1	Sales/Working Capital		7.1		6.2	7.3	5.5
24.4	18.9	20.2			16.7		20.4	NM	24.5
6.4	6.2	6.2						7.2	5.8
(113) 2.0	(108) 2.3	(108) 1.7	EBIT/Interest					(32) 1.0	(61) 1.9
.4	.5	-.1						-.6	.4
			Net Profit + Depr., Dep., Amort./Cur. Mat. L/T/D						
.6	.5	.6			.7		.4	.7	.7
1.0	1.0	1.0	Fixed/Worth		.9		.9	1.2	1.0
1.8	2.0	1.6			1.0		1.5	1.7	1.5
.3	.4	.4			.1		.3	.5	.4
.8	.8	.8	Debt/Worth		.2		.6	1.0	.9
2.0	2.2	1.9			.6		2.0	2.4	1.7
10.5	11.3	8.5			12.7		28.1	7.3	7.1
(144) 4.2	(135) 3.7	(133) 2.2	% Profit Before Taxes/Tangible Net Worth		-2.7		13.3	(35) .7	(70) 2.1
-2.3	-1.0	-3.2			-4.8		2.8	-6.4	-1.5
5.2	6.0	5.0			9.5		15.7	4.6	3.4
2.2	2.0	.8	% Profit Before Taxes/Total Assets		-1.1		5.8	.4	.8
-1.0	-1.2	-1.7			-4.2		.3	-2.9	-1.2
6.7	6.3	7.3			2.8		6.6	23.6	3.7
1.6	1.7	1.5	Sales/Net Fixed Assets		.9		3.0	2.1	1.2
.8	.7	.8			.4		1.3	.8	.8
1.6	1.8	1.6			1.0		2.4	1.8	1.5
.9	.8	.8	Sales/Total Assets		.7		1.3	.8	.8
.5	.5	.4			.3		.5	.4	.5
1.6	1.9	2.2						2.4	2.2
(121) 3.4	(117) 3.6	(113) 4.2	% Depr., Dep., Amort./Sales					(32) 4.1	(58) 4.4
5.8	6.6	7.0						7.7	6.4
3.2	1.6								
(12) 5.3	(13) 5.1		% Officers', Directors' Owners' Comp/Sales						
10.6	9.9								
6535657M	6167511M	6990548M	Net Sales ($)	1527M	20275M	20288M	77899M	637943M	6232616M
8234554M	7814508M	8574920M	Total Assets ($)	1924M	39244M	33402M	151418M	1027956M	7320976M

M = $ thousand MM = $ million

See Pages 9 through 22 for Explanation of Ratios and Data

Current Data Sorted by Assets							Comparative Historical Data	
						Type of Statement		
1	2	6	14	7	1	Unqualified	28	24
1						Reviewed	1	
						Compiled	1	1
						Tax Returns	2	1
	1	7	5		1	Other	6	8
	34 (4/1-9/30/13)		12 (10/1/13-3/31/14)				4/1/09-3/31/10	4/1/10-3/31/11
0-500M	500M-2MM	2-10MM	10-50MM	50-100MM	100-250MM		ALL	ALL
2	3	13	19	7	2	**NUMBER OF STATEMENTS**	38	34
%	%	%	%	%	%	**ASSETS**	%	%
		38.7	25.0			Cash & Equivalents	29.3	27.3
		19.8	18.3			Trade Receivables (net)	20.4	22.2
		.7	.7			Inventory	1.9	.3
		1.2	2.3			All Other Current	4.4	6.3
		60.4	46.3			Total Current	56.0	56.2
		19.1	32.8			Fixed Assets (net)	30.8	24.1
		1.2	.0			Intangibles (net)	2.1	.2
		19.2	20.9			All Other Non-Current	11.1	19.5
		100.0	100.0			Total	100.0	100.0
						LIABILITIES		
		2.2	1.2			Notes Payable-Short Term	4.6	2.7
		.8	1.4			Cur. Mat.-L.T.D.	2.2	.5
		4.5	9.5			Trade Payables	6.8	6.9
		.1	.0			Income Taxes Payable	.0	1.8
		12.8	12.3			All Other Current	13.2	22.9
		20.5	24.4			Total Current	26.8	34.8
		9.2	12.9			Long-Term Debt	8.5	10.2
		.5	.0			Deferred Taxes	.0	.0
		2.1	4.0			All Other Non-Current	7.6	7.7
		67.7	58.7			Net Worth	57.1	47.3
		100.0	100.0			Total Liabilties & Net Worth	100.0	100.0
						INCOME DATA		
		100.0	100.0			Net Sales	100.0	100.0
						Gross Profit		
		96.1	98.5			Operating Expenses	94.8	96.8
		3.9	1.5			Operating Profit	5.2	3.2
		-1.5	-2.0			All Other Expenses (net)	.9	-.6
		5.4	3.5			Profit Before Taxes	4.3	3.8
						RATIOS		
		13.1	6.6				5.1	3.8
		5.1	2.0			Current	2.1	1.6
		1.3	1.2				1.2	1.1
		13.1	6.1				4.2	3.3
		4.8	2.0			Quick	1.9	1.4
		1.2	.9				1.1	.9
		6 59.4	**6** 60.1				**2** 161.6	**7** 52.1
		35 10.4	**45** 8.2			Sales/Receivables	**23** 15.9	**34** 10.7
		54 6.7	**54** 6.8				**51** 7.2	**53** 6.9
						Cost of Sales/Inventory		
						Cost of Sales/Payables		
		2.5	2.8				3.2	3.7
		5.9	7.7			Sales/Working Capital	6.7	12.3
		45.0	26.0				23.5	40.1
			53.8				18.6	30.1
			(11) 6.5			EBIT/Interest	(16) 6.1	(14) 1.6
			2.9				-1.6	.2
						Net Profit + Depr., Dep., Amort./Cur. Mat. L/T/D		
		.0	.3				.1	.1
		.2	.6			Fixed/Worth	.5	.4
		.9	.9				1.1	.8
		.1	.1				.2	.4
		.3	.6			Debt/Worth	.6	1.0
		2.1	2.1				2.2	4.7
		14.6	14.7				19.8	30.1
		5.3	10.7			% Profit Before Taxes/Tangible Net Worth	(37) 7.0	(33) 4.7
		.9	.0				-3.6	-4.7
		9.2	9.5				11.2	14.0
		3.9	3.0			% Profit Before Taxes/Total Assets	3.4	.8
		.9	.0				-1.5	-1.3
		179.6	12.9				35.2	79.2
		34.9	2.7			Sales/Net Fixed Assets	9.6	23.1
		5.9	1.2				2.6	2.5
		4.1	2.9				3.2	4.0
		2.7	1.0			Sales/Total Assets	1.6	2.0
		1.1	.6				.9	.6
		.3	.5				.9	.4
		(10) .6	(13) 2.2			% Depr., Dep., Amort./Sales	(30) 1.9	(29) 1.1
		2.0	3.2				3.3	3.5
						% Officers', Directors' Owners' Comp/Sales		
3488M	11552M	144659M	1009712M	1154488M	229672M	Net Sales ($)	990210M	3503871M
839M	3924M	54933M	598317M	487557M	232219M	Total Assets ($)	788975M	1351328M

M = $ thousand MM = $ million

See Pages 9 through 22 for Explanation of Ratios and Data

Comparative Historical Data				Current Data Sorted by Sales					
			Type of Statement						
29	37	31	Unqualified		3	3	1	8	16
1	1	1	Reviewed		1				
	2		Compiled						
1	1		Tax Returns						
6	6	14	Other		1		4	5	4
					34 (4/1-9/30/13)			12 (10/1/13-3/31/14)	
4/1/11-3/31/12 ALL	**4/1/12-3/31/13 ALL**	**4/1/13-3/31/14 ALL**		**0-1MM**	**1-3MM**	**3-5MM**	**5-10MM**	**10-25MM**	**25MM & OVER**
37	47	46	**NUMBER OF STATEMENTS**		5	3	5	13	20
%	%	%	**ASSETS**	%	%	%	%	%	%
31.2	32.5	29.9	Cash & Equivalents	DATA NOT AVAILABLE				30.9	25.1
21.6	20.3	20.3	Trade Receivables (net)					14.7	25.0
.6	.5	.7	Inventory					.9	1.0
5.6	2.3	2.8	All Other Current					1.2	4.2
59.1	55.6	53.7	Total Current					47.6	55.3
29.3	30.5	27.9	Fixed Assets (net)					28.2	30.8
1.4	1.8	.4	Intangibles (net)					1.2	.1
10.3	12.2	18.0	All Other Non-Current					22.9	13.8
100.0	100.0	100.0	Total					100.0	100.0
			LIABILITIES						
3.0	2.0	1.2	Notes Payable-Short Term					2.3	1.1
2.5	.9	1.1	Cur. Mat.-L.T.D.					1.2	1.6
7.6	7.4	9.9	Trade Payables					4.2	12.0
.0	.0	.0	Income Taxes Payable					.1	.0
21.4	15.1	13.6	All Other Current					11.0	18.6
34.6	25.4	25.9	Total Current					18.8	33.3
12.9	10.7	12.3	Long-Term Debt					14.5	15.3
.0	.2	.2	Deferred Taxes					.5	.0
7.6	7.6	3.9	All Other Non-Current					2.7	4.8
44.9	56.1	57.6	Net Worth					63.5	46.7
100.0	100.0	100.0	Total Liabilities & Net Worth					100.0	100.0
			INCOME DATA						
100.0	100.0	100.0	Net Sales					100.0	100.0
			Gross Profit						
97.4	93.9	97.1	Operating Expenses					92.7	97.3
2.6	6.1	2.9	Operating Profit					7.3	2.7
.3	.1	-1.4	All Other Expenses (net)					-1.6	-.5
2.4	6.0	4.3	Profit Before Taxes					8.9	3.2
			RATIOS						
2.7	5.0	6.3						11.6	3.8
2.1	2.2	2.1	Current					2.2	2.0
1.2	1.4	1.3						1.1	1.1
2.4	4.7	6.0						11.5	3.6
1.4	1.8	1.9	Quick					2.2	1.7
1.1	1.2	1.0						1.0	.9
4 99.1	**14** 26.0	**6** 59.9						**0** UND	**7** 52.4
29 12.5	**41** 8.8	**39** 9.3	Sales/Receivables					**20** 18.4	**47** 7.8
62 5.9	**54** 6.8	**54** 6.8						**53** 6.9	**65** 5.6
			Cost of Sales/Inventory						
			Cost of Sales/Payables						
4.3	3.6	2.9						3.5	4.5
11.7	7.5	7.7	Sales/Working Capital					8.3	10.1
42.8	18.4	28.2						58.1	745.5
15.7	18.7	21.1							27.4
(21) 4.4	(31) 6.7	(22) 3.7	EBIT/Interest						(15) 4.8
1.7	2.8	1.6							1.4
			Net Profit + Depr., Dep., Amort./Cur. Mat. L/T/D						
.1	.1	.0						.0	.3
.5	.5	.4	Fixed/Worth					.3	.6
1.1	.9	.9						.9	1.1
.6	.2	.1						.1	.5
1.0	.7	.7	Debt/Worth					.6	.9
2.6	2.5	2.2						1.5	4.0
24.3	23.3	15.0						15.2	14.9
6.4	(46) 7.8	7.6	% Profit Before Taxes/Tangible Net Worth					10.7	5.7
.0	1.4	1.0						3.7	-.7
7.3	12.9	9.1						10.1	7.9
2.2	4.2	3.8	% Profit Before Taxes/Total Assets					7.9	2.8
.0	.5	.2						2.3	.0
72.8	64.0	108.5						104.5	69.5
21.7	5.3	7.0	Sales/Net Fixed Assets					11.5	5.1
2.3	2.2	2.4						1.4	2.5
3.8	3.0	3.4						4.1	3.4
2.0	1.5	1.8	Sales/Total Assets					1.9	1.8
1.2	1.0	.8						.7	1.0
.5	.5	.2							.1
(28) .9	(39) 2.0	(34) 2.0	% Depr., Dep., Amort./Sales						(15) 2.4
3.3	3.5	3.1							4.3
			% Officers', Directors' Owners' Comp/Sales						
2093004M	1875515M	2553571M	Net Sales ($)		8306M	11566M	35491M	223493M	2274715M
929964M	1234951M	1377789M	Total Assets ($)		7667M	22642M	38439M	219452M	1089589M

M = $ thousand MM = $ million

See Pages 9 through 22 for Explanation of Ratios and Data

Current Data Sorted by Assets | **Comparative Historical Data**

	0-500M	500M-2MM	2-10MM	10-50MM	50-100MM	100-250MM	4/1/09-3/31/10 ALL	4/1/10-3/31/11 ALL
Type of Statement								
Unqualified			16	30	19	21	61	63
Reviewed		1			1		7	3
Compiled		1	1	3			6	4
Tax Returns								1
Other			4	8	3	2	19	23
		83 (4/1-9/30/13)		27 (10/1/13-3/31/14)				
NUMBER OF STATEMENTS		2	21	41	23	23	93	94
ASSETS	%	%	%	%	%	%	%	%
Cash & Equivalents	DATA NOT AVAILABLE		22.3	13.6	11.1	16.9	12.9	13.8
Trade Receivables (net)			5.1	4.8	2.2	2.7	6.6	6.6
Inventory			.4	.8	.3	.4	1.5	1.9
All Other Current			.5	3.5	2.2	3.0	2.1	1.6
Total Current			28.3	22.6	15.7	23.1	23.1	23.9
Fixed Assets (net)			63.8	68.2	76.5	68.7	66.1	66.9
Intangibles (net)			1.0	.5	.5	.6	2.7	.7
All Other Non-Current			6.8	8.7	7.2	7.6	8.1	8.5
Total			100.0	100.0	100.0	100.0	100.0	100.0
LIABILITIES								
Notes Payable-Short Term			4.9	.6	.0	.0	2.6	1.4
Cur. Mat.-L.T.D.			2.3	2.8	2.1	1.1	4.6	3.1
Trade Payables			4.1	2.6	1.6	2.8	3.0	3.4
Income Taxes Payable			.0	.0	.0	.0	.0	.1
All Other Current			3.2	3.5	1.2	2.5	3.7	3.3
Total Current			14.5	9.5	5.0	6.4	13.9	11.2
Long-Term Debt			27.6	31.0	26.3	35.4	30.1	32.3
Deferred Taxes			.0	.0	.0	.0	.1	.2
All Other Non-Current			4.8	6.7	2.5	2.2	1.6	2.9
Net Worth			53.1	52.8	66.2	56.0	54.2	53.3
Total Liabilities & Net Worth			100.0	100.0	100.0	100.0	100.0	100.0
INCOME DATA								
Net Sales			100.0	100.0	100.0	100.0	100.0	100.0
Gross Profit								
Operating Expenses			89.0	84.4	84.7	83.5	85.2	87.9
Operating Profit			11.0	15.6	15.3	16.5	14.8	12.1
All Other Expenses (net)			6.7	10.8	5.8	3.1	7.3	5.7
Profit Before Taxes			4.4	4.7	9.5	13.4	7.4	6.4
RATIOS								
Current			7.3	5.0	5.3	8.4	4.9	4.9
			2.8	2.0	3.1	3.1	1.9	2.2
			1.3	1.3	1.5	1.2	.9	1.3
Quick			6.6	4.2	5.3	7.3	4.6	4.6
			2.8	1.7	2.4	2.3	1.7	1.9
			1.2	.8	1.5	1.1	.6	1.0
Sales/Receivables			**11** 34.2	**18** 20.0	**24** 15.3	**33** 11.1	**13** 27.7	**19** 18.7
			33 11.1	**41** 8.9	**36** 10.1	**49** 7.5	**33** 11.1	**35** 10.4
			43 8.5	**54** 6.7	**49** 7.5	**60** 6.1	**48** 7.6	**51** 7.2
Cost of Sales/Inventory								
Cost of Sales/Payables								
Sales/Working Capital			.9	1.3	1.1	.9	1.4	1.4
			3.6	3.4	2.1	2.4	6.0	3.9
			41.6	15.5	6.4	20.2	-14.3	15.7
EBIT/Interest			3.0	4.1	6.4	4.4	6.6	6.2
			(13) 1.8	(34) 2.7	(17) 4.3	(18) 2.6	(69) 2.6	(70) 2.3
			.3	1.1	1.4	.8	.8	1.2
Net Profit + Depr., Dep., Amort./Cur. Mat. L/T/D								
Fixed/Worth			.8	.9	.9	.9	.9	1.0
			1.2	1.1	1.1	1.2	1.2	1.3
			2.4	1.6	1.4	1.6	2.2	1.9
Debt/Worth			.2	.3	.2	.4	.3	.4
			1.0	.6	.5	.7	.8	.8
			1.7	1.6	.8	1.3	1.9	2.0
% Profit Before Taxes/Tangible Net Worth			6.0	7.4	5.6	6.3	7.8	6.9
			(19) .7	(39) 2.2	(22) 3.7	(22) 2.8	(83) 2.3	(88) 2.6
			-2.7	-1.9	-.6	-.5	-.5	-.1
% Profit Before Taxes/Total Assets			2.8	2.9	3.8	3.6	5.6	3.6
			.3	1.0	1.8	2.7	1.3	1.5
			-1.8	-1.2	-.5	-.3	-.3	-.2
Sales/Net Fixed Assets			1.1	.6	.4	.5	1.1	.9
			.4	.2	.2	.2	.3	.2
			.2	.2	.1	.1	.1	.1
Sales/Total Assets			.8	.3	.2	.3	.6	.5
			.3	.2	.2	.2	.2	.2
			.2	.1	.1	.1	.1	.1
% Depr., Dep., Amort./Sales			6.4	10.9	10.2	9.5	7.1	8.5
			(19) 17.1	(36) 16.5	(22) 20.7	(20) 15.7	(83) 18.2	(83) 16.7
			22.6	21.6	30.6	25.1	27.4	28.2
% Officers', Directors' Owners' Comp/Sales								1.1
								(12) 3.2
								6.3
Net Sales ($)		4540M	61735M	394979M	332307M	1030389M	1549335M	1656233M
Total Assets ($)		2697M	121624M	1073044M	1579531M	3347850M	3912737M	5155685M

M = $ thousand MM = $ million

See Pages 9 through 22 for Explanation of Ratios and Data

Comparative Historical Data				Current Data Sorted by Sales					
			Type of Statement						
77	101	86	Unqualified	6	14	12	19	22	13
2	3	2	Reviewed			1		1	
3	7	5	Compiled	1		1	1		2
2			Tax Returns						
14	19	17	Other	2	3	3	2	5	2
					83 (4/1-9/30/13)		27 (10/1/13-3/31/14)		
4/1/11-3/31/12 ALL	4/1/12-3/31/13 ALL	4/1/13-3/31/14 ALL		0-1MM	1-3MM	3-5MM	5-10MM	10-25MM	25MM & OVER
98	130	110	**NUMBER OF STATEMENTS**	9	17	17	22	28	17
%	%	%	**ASSETS**	%	%	%	%	%	%
14.5	13.5	15.4	Cash & Equivalents		18.7	10.1	17.9	14.9	16.6
4.5	3.7	4.3	Trade Receivables (net)		2.3	5.5	1.8	4.7	9.7
1.2	.5	.5	Inventory		.5	.2	.8	.4	.8
1.5	2.1	2.5	All Other Current		1.9	.5	2.4	1.9	7.1
21.7	19.8	22.7	Total Current		23.4	16.4	22.9	21.9	34.2
67.6	72.0	69.0	Fixed Assets (net)		64.7	76.9	69.7	70.8	58.6
.3	.6	.6	Intangibles (net)		1.3	.7	.7	.4	.4
10.4	7.6	7.7	All Other Non-Current		10.6	6.0	6.8	6.8	6.8
100.0	100.0	100.0	Total		100.0	100.0	100.0	100.0	100.0
			LIABILITIES						
.5	1.6	1.2	Notes Payable-Short Term		.0	1.2	.1	.0	.1
3.0	2.7	2.4	Cur. Mat.-L.T.D.		3.1	3.6	2.2	1.3	2.1
1.9	3.1	2.7	Trade Payables		1.4	1.0	2.2	3.5	6.6
.0	.0	.0	Income Taxes Payable		.0	.0	.0	.0	.0
3.1	6.0	2.7	All Other Current		1.2	1.9	3.2	3.3	4.7
8.6	13.4	9.0	Total Current		5.8	7.6	7.7	8.0	13.5
35.8	33.3	30.8	Long-Term Debt		45.2	23.0	35.2	26.9	21.5
.0	.0	.0	Deferred Taxes		.0	.0	.0	.0	.0
2.8	2.7	4.4	All Other Non-Current		2.5	6.1	3.4	7.6	3.1
52.9	50.5	55.7	Net Worth		46.5	63.3	53.6	57.6	61.9
100.0	100.0	100.0	Total Liabilties & Net Worth		100.0	100.0	100.0	100.0	100.0
			INCOME DATA						
100.0	100.0	100.0	Net Sales		100.0	100.0	100.0	100.0	100.0
			Gross Profit						
83.3	82.2	84.8	Operating Expenses		88.6	80.4	83.1	86.8	92.4
16.7	17.8	15.2	Operating Profit		11.4	19.6	16.9	13.2	7.6
8.0	9.1	7.4	All Other Expenses (net)		9.0	10.5	6.0	4.4	3.1
8.7	8.7	7.8	Profit Before Taxes		2.4	9.1	11.0	8.9	4.5
			RATIOS						
6.3	5.5	5.2			5.5	3.6	5.1	7.1	3.1
2.6	2.7	2.5	Current		3.8	1.5	2.5	3.4	2.4
1.5	1.4	1.3			1.3	.9	1.5	1.3	1.3
5.5	5.1	4.9			5.0	3.6	4.5	6.5	2.5
2.3	2.1	2.0	Quick		3.0	1.4	2.4	2.6	1.9
1.1	1.2	1.1			1.2	.6	1.5	1.2	1.0
15 24.1	**22** 16.9	**22** 16.3			**21** 17.0	**1** 335.8	**9** 39.2	**28** 13.1	**33** 11.1
36 10.0	**35** 10.5	**39** 9.4	Sales/Receivables		**34** 10.7	**38** 9.6	**40** 9.1	**48** 7.6	**47** 7.7
57 6.4	**49** 7.5	**54** 6.7			**44** 8.3	**62** 5.9	**52** 7.0	**65** 5.6	**56** 6.5
			Cost of Sales/Inventory						
			Cost of Sales/Payables						
1.3	1.1	1.2			.9	1.3	1.2	1.1	2.1
2.4	2.5	2.9	Sales/Working Capital		1.3	6.9	2.9	2.1	6.4
9.7	11.2	14.4			13.3	-19.4	5.0	16.8	18.5
6.1	5.2	4.3			3.4	4.0	5.3	4.4	7.9
(75) 2.7	(103) 2.5	(83) 2.6	EBIT/Interest		(14) 2.3	(13) 2.3	(16) 3.9	(20) 2.4	(16) 3.9
1.0	1.0	.8			.5	-1.5	1.1	1.0	.8
			Net Profit + Depr., Dep., Amort./Cur. Mat. L/T/D						
.9	1.0	.9			.9	.9	.9	.9	.6
1.2	1.2	1.1	Fixed/Worth		1.2	1.1	1.2	1.2	1.0
1.6	1.8	1.7			2.4	1.3	1.7	1.5	1.6
.3	.3	.3			.5	.2	.3	.2	.3
.6	.6	.6	Debt/Worth		1.1	.3	.6	.6	.5
1.2	1.5	1.6			2.4	1.5	1.6	1.3	1.1
7.5	6.6	6.2			9.8	4.4	7.8	6.0	7.0
(91) 3.1	(120) 3.3	(104) 2.1	% Profit Before Taxes/Tangible Net Worth		(15) 3.5	.9	(20) 3.1	(27) 2.0	4.5
-.2	-.2	-.7			-4.8	-2.3	-.8	-.4	-3.2
4.3	3.9	3.4			3.0	2.4	5.5	3.0	4.6
1.7	1.6	1.2	% Profit Before Taxes/Total Assets		1.4	.7	1.9	1.0	2.9
-.2	-.2	-.6			-2.1	-1.2	-.9	-.4	-.8
.7	.4	.6			.6	.3	.4	.5	2.2
.2	.2	.2	Sales/Net Fixed Assets		.3	.2	.2	.2	.8
.2	.1	.2			.2	.1	.2	.1	.4
.3	.3	.3			.3	.2	.2	.3	1.2
.2	.2	.2	Sales/Total Assets		.2	.2	.2	.2	.6
.1	.1	.1			.1	.1	.1	.1	.3
11.0	10.8	9.6			13.0	10.8	13.5	8.8	5.0
(87) 15.2	(118) 16.1	(98) 16.8	% Depr., Dep., Amort./Sales		(16) 17.4	(15) 17.4	(20) 18.9	(25) 16.7	(15) 9.6
22.5	25.1	24.4			24.8	25.4	27.7	25.1	13.4
	.7								
	(12) 4.8		% Officers', Directors' Owners' Comp/Sales						
	22.3								
1239821M	1586013M	1823950M	Net Sales ($)	5220M	33709M	66236M	161465M	438155M	1119165M
5157669M	6891229M	6124746M	Total Assets ($)	52180M	173545M	444409M	1048005M	2626616M	1779991M

M = $ thousand MM = $ million

See Pages 9 through 22 for Explanation of Ratios and Data

Current Data Sorted by Assets							Comparative Historical Data	
						Type of Statement		
	5	14	26	18	13	Unqualified	84	77
						Reviewed	1	2
	1	1				Compiled	2	1
1	1					Tax Returns	1	
		8	11	1	1	Other	21	39
	79 (4/1-9/30/13)		22 (10/1/13-3/31/14)				**4/1/09-3/31/10 ALL**	**4/1/10-3/31/11 ALL**
0-500M	**500M-2MM**	**2-10MM**	**10-50MM**	**50-100MM**	**100-250MM**			
1	7	23	37	19	14	**NUMBER OF STATEMENTS**	109	119
%	%	%	%	%	%	**ASSETS**	%	%
		10.0	17.5	18.8	9.9	Cash & Equivalents	15.7	15.3
		5.8	2.5	2.2	8.0	Trade Receivables (net)	6.1	4.2
		.7	1.4	.2	.3	Inventory	2.7	2.7
		3.5	1.5	1.9	1.5	All Other Current	3.4	2.8
		20.0	22.8	23.2	19.7	Total Current	27.9	25.0
		57.9	65.6	55.4	56.0	Fixed Assets (net)	52.7	54.0
		3.5	1.3	.0	.5	Intangibles (net)	1.2	1.7
		18.6	10.3	21.4	23.7	All Other Non-Current	18.2	19.3
		100.0	100.0	100.0	100.0	Total	100.0	100.0
						LIABILITIES		
		2.0	.3	.1	.2	Notes Payable-Short Term	2.4	3.8
		3.6	1.0	2.0	2.9	Cur. Mat.-L.T.D.	2.8	1.9
		4.9	1.2	1.4	1.1	Trade Payables	3.3	2.4
		.0	.0	.0	.0	Income Taxes Payable	.0	.0
		8.8	5.0	3.0	3.7	All Other Current	5.4	6.6
		19.3	7.6	6.4	7.9	Total Current	13.9	14.8
		37.0	26.3	23.1	35.8	Long-Term Debt	34.6	30.2
		.0	.0	.0	.0	Deferred Taxes	.3	.3
		4.1	2.6	3.0	7.3	All Other Non-Current	3.2	2.2
		39.5	63.5	67.4	49.0	Net Worth	48.0	52.5
		100.0	100.0	100.0	100.0	Total Liabilties & Net Worth	100.0	100.0
						INCOME DATA		
		100.0	100.0	100.0	100.0	Net Sales	100.0	100.0
						Gross Profit		
		90.6	98.9	98.7	97.5	Operating Expenses	94.1	90.2
		9.4	1.1	1.3	2.5	Operating Profit	5.9	9.8
		6.5	1.9	3.7	4.8	All Other Expenses (net)	4.8	5.2
		3.0	-.8	-2.4	-2.2	Profit Before Taxes	1.1	4.5
						RATIOS		
		3.0	9.3	10.7	6.2		5.2	4.9
		1.5	3.8	3.8	2.1	Current	2.3	2.1
		.3	1.8	1.9	.6		1.1	.9
		2.0	8.8	9.6	5.9		4.2	3.9
		1.1	3.3	3.7	1.5	Quick	1.5	1.5
		.3	1.5	1.8	.5		.7	.7
		2 175.4	**2** 217.7	**6** 62.4	**0** UND		**2** 157.9	**1** 422.3
		9 39.5	**5** 68.7	**15** 23.6	**38** 9.6	Sales/Receivables	**8** 44.6	**7** 54.6
		25 14.6	**14** 26.6	**29** 12.4	**60** 6.1		**32** 11.5	**26** 14.0
						Cost of Sales/Inventory		
						Cost of Sales/Payables		
		6.7	1.4	.8	1.3		1.6	2.1
		11.6	3.4	3.6	2.5	Sales/Working Capital	4.8	6.2
		-4.1	12.8	5.6	-6.6		43.2	-80.2
		5.3	2.4	2.1	1.7		6.7	7.8
		(14) 2.1	(30) -.8	(16) -1.0	(10) -.4	EBIT/Interest	(74) 1.3	(83) 3.3
		-3.3	-7.6	-6.8	-3.3		-.5	.6
						Net Profit + Depr., Dep., Amort./Cur. Mat. L/T/D		
		.6	.8	.5	.5		.5	.4
		1.1	1.0	.8	1.1	Fixed/Worth	1.0	1.0
		13.6	1.5	1.1	2.1		2.0	1.9
		.4	.2	.1	.3		.4	.2
		1.5	.4	.3	.9	Debt/Worth	.8	.7
		13.7	1.7	.9	5.0		2.4	2.2
		11.7	3.7	2.2	4.3		9.2	11.1
		(19) 2.5	(36) -.8	-1.0	-1.4	% Profit Before Taxes/Tangible Net Worth	(101) 1.5	(112) 4.1
		-17.3	-5.5	-5.1	-4.6		-3.9	-3.6
		5.4	2.0	1.7	.9		3.0	5.5
		1.3	-.5	-.4	-.4	% Profit Before Taxes/Total Assets	.3	1.9
		-2.5	-4.3	-4.1	-3.4		-2.0	-1.8
		4.9	1.3	1.5	1.1		3.0	2.8
		1.0	.8	.6	.4	Sales/Net Fixed Assets	.9	1.0
		.4	.3	.5	.2		.4	.4
		1.0	.9	.6	.3		.8	.9
		.4	.4	.3	.2	Sales/Total Assets	.4	.5
		.2	.2	.1	.1		.2	.2
		1.8	3.9	4.3	1.5		2.4	1.9
		(21) 6.7	(36) 7.7	(18) 9.4	(11) 16.8	% Depr., Dep., Amort./Sales	(92) 6.6	(104) 5.7
		10.7	17.1	13.6	21.9		13.0	12.6
							2.7	3.8
						% Officers', Directors' Owners' Comp/Sales	(12) 7.3	(12) 7.2
							18.8	16.9
171M	9475M	118461M	581408M	564435M	501385M	Net Sales ($)	1440944M	1576651M
238M	8771M	130600M	872450M	1392947M	2019676M	Total Assets ($)	3818664M	3203606M

M = $ thousand MM = $ million

See Pages 9 through 22 for Explanation of Ratios and Data

Comparative Historical Data / Current Data Sorted by Sales

4/1/11-3/31/12 ALL	4/1/12-3/31/13 ALL	4/1/13-3/31/14 ALL		0-1MM	1-3MM	3-5MM	5-10MM	10-25MM	25MM & OVER
			Type of Statement						
79	80	76	Unqualified	5	7	5	20	18	21
1	1		Reviewed						
1	6	2	Compiled		1	1			
2	2	2	Tax Returns	1	1				
33	28	21	Other	3	7	2	3	3	3
				79 (4/1-9/30/13)			22 (10/1/13-3/31/14)		
116	117	101	**NUMBER OF STATEMENTS**	9	16	8	23	21	24
%	%	%	**ASSETS**	%	%	%	%	%	%
17.2	17.1	15.7	Cash & Equivalents		12.3		17.1	11.2	18.9
3.5	4.2	3.9	Trade Receivables (net)		9.0		2.5	3.2	4.5
2.0	2.2	1.3	Inventory		3.6		.8	.3	.3
3.1	2.8	2.0	All Other Current		2.1		1.5	2.6	2.1
25.7	26.4	22.9	Total Current		26.9		21.9	17.2	25.9
52.8	54.9	59.3	Fixed Assets (net)		58.1		56.1	65.5	61.6
1.2	.8	1.3	Intangibles (net)		.3		1.9	.4	.0
20.3	17.9	16.4	All Other Non-Current		14.6		20.2	16.9	12.5
100.0	100.0	100.0	Total		100.0		100.0	100.0	100.0
			LIABILITIES						
1.5	2.4	.6	Notes Payable-Short Term		3.1		.4	.1	.1
1.9	1.8	2.5	Cur. Mat.-L.T.D.		6.9		1.5	1.3	2.1
1.6	1.3	2.2	Trade Payables		3.3		.9	1.9	3.0
.0	.0	.0	Income Taxes Payable		.0		.0	.0	.0
4.2	3.7	6.3	All Other Current		15.3		4.2	3.1	7.0
9.3	9.2	11.7	Total Current		28.6		7.0	6.4	12.3
29.6	28.8	29.3	Long-Term Debt		45.4		23.0	22.0	21.7
.0	.0	.0	Deferred Taxes		.0		.0	.0	.0
6.7	3.2	4.1	All Other Non-Current		1.9		3.6	6.5	2.5
54.4	58.8	55.0	Net Worth		24.2		66.4	65.1	63.6
100.0	100.0	100.0	Total Liabilties & Net Worth		100.0		100.0	100.0	100.0
			INCOME DATA						
100.0	100.0	100.0	Net Sales		100.0		100.0	100.0	100.0
			Gross Profit						
91.0	92.0	97.1	Operating Expenses		86.4		92.6	104.1	105.1
9.0	8.0	2.9	Operating Profit		13.6		7.4	-4.1	-5.1
5.1	3.9	4.1	All Other Expenses (net)		7.6		7.5	.3	-2.0
3.9	4.1	-1.2	Profit Before Taxes		5.9		-.1	-4.4	-3.1
			RATIOS						
5.8	8.5	6.6			7.6		9.7	4.8	4.5
3.2	3.7	2.7	Current		1.3		4.1	2.5	2.6
1.3	1.5	1.3			.3		1.7	1.8	1.3
5.1	7.0	5.5			6.8		9.2	4.2	4.4
2.4	2.9	2.5	Quick		1.0		3.7	2.5	2.2
1.0	1.0	1.0			.2		1.3	1.2	1.0
1 437.1	1 634.9	2 156.7			6 56.8		2 169.8	2 159.5	3 124.6
6 62.0	5 76.2	8 44.5	Sales/Receivables		10 35.4		9 40.0	5 68.7	9 42.2
25 14.5	24 15.3	29 12.6			43 8.4		30 12.1	24 15.0	34 10.8
			Cost of Sales/Inventory						
			Cost of Sales/Payables						
1.8	1.6	1.8			2.1		.9	2.8	3.2
4.2	3.3	4.5	Sales/Working Capital		14.8		2.1	7.1	8.0
18.0	8.5	19.0			-1.8		3.9	11.6	23.1
8.3	5.0	2.3			7.0		2.6	.6	1.9
(84) 2.8	(80) 1.4	(74) -.1	EBIT/Interest		(11) 2.2		(17) -1.2	(15) -1.3	(22) -2.9
-.5	-2.8	-5.5			-2.6		-12.9	-10.5	-5.3
			Net Profit + Depr., Dep., Amort./Cur. Mat. L/T/D						
.5	.6	.6			.2		.6	.6	.8
1.0	.9	1.0	Fixed/Worth		1.4		.8	1.0	.9
2.3	1.4	1.6			-6.5		1.3	1.4	1.2
.3	.2	.2			.5		.1	.1	.3
.5	.4	.6	Debt/Worth		3.1		.3	.4	.3
2.6	1.4	2.8			-8.4		1.3	1.0	1.4
9.1	7.1	4.7			6.7		5.4	3.6	2.7
(109) 3.0	(109) .0	(94) -.7	% Profit Before Taxes/Tangible Net Worth		(11) 3.9		.1	-1.8	-3.6
-2.6	-4.2	-5.6			-9.8		-6.1	-4.2	-5.8
4.9	4.0	1.9			2.7		1.7	1.5	1.8
1.5	.5	-.4	% Profit Before Taxes/Total Assets		1.5		.1	-1.2	-2.3
-1.8	-2.4	-4.1			-5.5		-4.8	-3.0	-4.4
2.9	1.8	1.6			109.7		1.1	1.3	1.9
.8	.8	.6	Sales/Net Fixed Assets		.6		.6	.5	1.2
.4	.4	.3			.3		.3	.3	.5
.7	.7	.8			.6		.5	1.0	1.1
.4	.4	.4	Sales/Total Assets		.3		.3	.4	.8
.2	.2	.2			.2		.1	.2	.4
3.0	2.9	3.4			3.2		4.3	3.8	2.5
(102) 6.6	(104) 6.3	(92) 8.1	% Depr., Dep., Amort./Sales		(12) 10.7		(22) 12.3	(20) 7.6	(22) 4.8
13.4	15.0	15.3			13.8		20.9	15.9	9.3
3.2	2.2								
(12) 5.3	(10) 6.0		% Officers', Directors' Owners' Comp/Sales						
13.8	15.2								
1774657M	1364710M	1775335M	Net Sales ($)	4599M	28871M	32890M	159496M	336255M	1213224M
3842390M	3605674M	4424682M	Total Assets ($)	24456M	188574M	175943M	792391M	1316509M	1926809M

M = $ thousand MM = $ million

See Pages 9 through 22 for Explanation of Ratios and Data

Current Data Sorted by Assets							Comparative Historical Data	
						Type of Statement		
1	6	15	18	3	4	Unqualified	57	54
						Reviewed	3	1
		1				Compiled	5	9
						Tax Returns	1	
	1	7	7	1	1	Other	25	25
49 (4/1-9/30/13)			16 (10/1/13-3/31/14)				4/1/09-3/31/10	4/1/10-3/31/11
0-500M	500M-2MM	2-10MM	10-50MM	50-100MM	100-250MM		ALL	ALL
1	7	23	25	4	5	NUMBER OF STATEMENTS	91	89
%	%	%	%	%	%	**ASSETS**	%	%
		21.3	31.2			Cash & Equivalents	19.7	23.1
		8.3	2.6			Trade Receivables (net)	14.9	10.2
		.4	3.9			Inventory	2.7	1.6
		2.4	5.4			All Other Current	3.5	5.0
		32.4	43.0			Total Current	40.9	39.9
		40.8	41.7			Fixed Assets (net)	33.1	38.6
		4.8	.5			Intangibles (net)	.3	.4
		22.0	14.9			All Other Non-Current	25.7	21.1
		100.0	100.0			Total	100.0	100.0
						LIABILITIES		
		1.5	.8			Notes Payable-Short Term	4.9	6.1
		3.2	2.9			Cur. Mat.-L.T.D.	4.8	3.0
		6.3	3.9			Trade Payables	4.0	3.2
		.1	.0			Income Taxes Payable	.0	.0
		12.1	8.2			All Other Current	9.6	6.7
		23.3	15.8			Total Current	23.3	19.0
		55.8	50.7			Long-Term Debt	33.9	28.9
		.0	.0			Deferred Taxes	.0	.0
		4.2	3.5			All Other Non-Current	4.1	6.7
		16.8	30.0			Net Worth	38.8	45.4
		100.0	100.0			Total Liabilties & Net Worth	100.0	100.0
						INCOME DATA		
		100.0	100.0			Net Sales	100.0	100.0
						Gross Profit		
		68.4	63.4			Operating Expenses	81.2	77.4
		31.6	36.6			Operating Profit	18.8	22.6
		23.2	21.1			All Other Expenses (net)	10.9	11.6
		8.4	15.5			Profit Before Taxes	7.9	11.0
						RATIOS		
		4.9	8.3				5.4	5.6
		1.3	3.0			Current	2.5	2.4
		.6	1.5				1.4	1.2
		4.2	8.2				4.6	4.6
		1.2	2.5			Quick	2.0	2.0
		.6	1.1				1.2	.8
		0 UND	**0** UND				**5** 66.8	**0** UND
		1 440.8	**4** 90.4			Sales/Receivables	**45** 8.2	**26** 13.8
		76 4.8	**30** 12.0				**123** 3.0	**69** 5.3
						Cost of Sales/Inventory		
						Cost of Sales/Payables		
		1.8	.8				.6	.7
		5.4	2.1			Sales/Working Capital	1.7	2.0
		-6.1	5.3				9.0	34.4
		4.0	21.1				7.5	9.6
		(12) 1.6	(15) 5.7			EBIT/Interest	(65) 2.4	(59) 1.9
		-.3	1.3				.6	.3
						Net Profit + Depr., Dep., Amort./Cur. Mat. L/T/D		
		.0	.1				.0	.0
		1.0	1.1			Fixed/Worth	.7	.9
		5.8	6.2				1.6	1.2
		.2	.3				.6	.4
		3.8	1.3			Debt/Worth	1.5	1.1
		45.9	NM				3.8	4.4
		37.1	23.9				8.4	16.7
		(18) 6.8	(19) 4.8			% Profit Before Taxes/Tangible Net Worth	(83) 2.1	(85) 3.1
		-2.6	-1.2				-2.6	-1.5
		8.0	11.4				4.1	8.2
		1.4	3.8			% Profit Before Taxes/Total Assets	.9	1.3
		-.6	-.4				-.9	-.8
		UND	75.2				43.2	44.4
		1.6	.5			Sales/Net Fixed Assets	2.5	1.8
		.3	.2				.4	.3
		.7	.7				.8	.6
		.4	.2			Sales/Total Assets	.2	.3
		.2	.1				.1	.1
		1.6	.7				.6	.6
		(11) 4.2	(16) 5.5			% Depr., Dep., Amort./Sales	(68) 2.9	(65) 2.7
		18.3	18.8				9.8	10.4
						% Officers', Directors' Owners' Comp/Sales		
2239M	8566M	50400M	232814M	53518M	191801M	Net Sales ($)	715852M	751325M
492M	7198M	113372M	651098M	279780M	882265M	Total Assets ($)	3089947M	2591769M

M = $ thousand MM = $ million

See Pages 9 through 22 for Explanation of Ratios and Data

Comparative Historical Data				Current Data Sorted by Sales					
			Type of Statement						
60	47	47	Unqualified	8	15	8	7	6	3
1	1		Reviewed						
8	1	1	Compiled				1		
1	1		Tax Returns						
20	17	17	Other	4	5	1	3	1	3
4/1/11-3/31/12	**4/1/12-3/31/13**	**4/1/13-3/31/14**		**49 (4/1-9/30/13)**			**16 (10/1/13-3/31/14)**		
ALL	**ALL**	**ALL**		**0-1MM**	**1-3MM**	**3-5MM**	**5-10MM**	**10-25MM**	**25MM & OVER**
90	67	65	**NUMBER OF STATEMENTS**	12	20	9	11	7	6
%	%	%	**ASSETS**	%	%	%	%	%	%
24.0	23.8	26.8	Cash & Equivalents	12.9	26.6		39.5		
8.4	13.6	6.5	Trade Receivables (net)	.9	9.9		.7		
2.7	.8	1.6	Inventory	.7	4.9		.0		
4.5	5.2	5.6	All Other Current	.1	4.5		6.2		
39.6	43.4	40.5	Total Current	14.5	45.9		46.4		
36.9	30.3	38.2	Fixed Assets (net)	59.3	40.8		33.1		
.3	3.2	3.3	Intangibles (net)	3.2	5.2		4.4		
23.3	23.1	18.0	All Other Non-Current	22.9	8.2		16.1		
100.0	100.0	100.0	Total	100.0	100.0		100.0		
			LIABILITIES						
2.6	2.8	2.3	Notes Payable-Short Term	.8	.3		.3		
3.5	3.2	4.0	Cur. Mat.-L.T.D.	9.3	1.7		4.6		
3.0	4.1	4.6	Trade Payables	.5	3.3		1.2		
.0	.0	.1	Income Taxes Payable	.3	.0		.0		
8.8	8.6	10.4	All Other Current	9.8	15.7		6.6		
17.9	18.6	21.3	Total Current	20.6	20.9		12.7		
46.7	35.0	64.2	Long-Term Debt	138.6	35.6		77.0		
.0	.0	.0	Deferred Taxes	.0	.0		.0		
6.3	7.4	7.9	All Other Non-Current	2.7	16.7		3.0		
29.2	39.1	6.5	Net Worth	-61.9	26.8		7.3		
100.0	100.0	100.0	Total Liabilties & Net Worth	100.0	100.0		100.0		
			INCOME DATA						
100.0	100.0	100.0	Net Sales	100.0	100.0		100.0		
			Gross Profit						
78.3	80.3	67.2	Operating Expenses	53.5	75.2		56.6		
21.7	19.7	32.8	Operating Profit	46.5	24.8		43.4		
13.6	8.0	20.6	All Other Expenses (net)	34.8	19.5		22.8		
8.1	11.7	12.3	Profit Before Taxes	11.7	5.4		20.6		
			RATIOS						
6.9	5.6	5.5		3.2	7.6		10.5		
2.6	2.9	2.0	Current	1.0	3.0		3.1		
1.2	.9	.7		.2	.9		.4		
6.3	4.6	5.3		3.1	7.2		10.5		
2.1	2.5	2.0	Quick	.9	2.5		3.1		
.8	.6	.6		.1	.7		.3		
0 UND	**0** UND	**0** UND		**0** UND	**0** UND		**0** UND		
16 23.0	**36** 10.2	**5** 80.0	Sales/Receivables	**3** 119.7	**4** 82.3		**0** 999.8		
72 5.1	**104** 3.5	**64** 5.7		**54** 6.7	**38** 9.7		**16** 23.3		
			Cost of Sales/Inventory						
			Cost of Sales/Payables						
.6	.6	1.0		1.8	1.1		.2		
2.3	3.3	3.3	Sales/Working Capital	NM	4.0		1.1		
16.1	-30.6	-7.0		-1.5	NM		-5.3		
9.9	11.2	7.6							
(54) 2.4	(41) 3.3	(32) 3.3	EBIT/Interest						
.2	.2	.9							
			Net Profit + Depr., Dep., Amort./Cur. Mat. L/T/D						
.0	.0	.0		.3	.0		.2		
.9	.4	1.0	Fixed/Worth	19.8	1.3		1.6		
1.8	1.2	6.8		-2.4	NM		-10.9		
.6	.6	.3		2.0	.1		1.3		
1.6	1.3	2.6	Debt/Worth	NM	1.0		6.5		
14.3	6.7	-49.9		-2.1	NM		-5.1		
10.4	9.8	21.0			22.7				
(72) 3.9	(57) 4.8	(47) 4.8	% Profit Before Taxes/Tangible Net Worth		(15) 1.2				
-.8	-2.6	-1.2			-2.9				
3.8	4.6	8.0		4.8	7.8		8.1		
1.1	1.7	1.9	% Profit Before Taxes/Total Assets	.9	.9		4.7		
-.5	-.9	-.4		-.8	-1.5		-.4		
53.5	41.9	144.3		1.1	174.7		3.3		
1.3	3.0	1.3	Sales/Net Fixed Assets	.2	1.4		1.2		
.3	.3	.3		.1	.3		.4		
.5	.5	.7		.3	.8		.5		
.2	.2	.3	Sales/Total Assets	.1	.3		.2		
.1	.1	.1		.1	.2		.2		
.9	.8	.5			.9				
(62) 4.8	(44) 2.5	(41) 2.5	% Depr., Dep., Amort./Sales		(11) 4.2				
17.0	10.4	16.1			18.3				
			% Officers', Directors' Owners' Comp/Sales						
799711M	484473M	539338M	Net Sales ($)	6356M	37037M	38233M	81808M	127389M	248515M
3191480M	2261877M	1934205M	Total Assets ($)	71016M	220276M	135002M	343604M	702872M	461435M

M = $ thousand MM = $ million

See Pages 9 through 22 for Explanation of Ratios and Data

Current Data Sorted by Assets							Comparative Historical Data	
						Type of Statement		
2	7	25	34	7	2	Unqualified	62	82
1		2				Reviewed	3	3
	1	2				Compiled	3	5
						Tax Returns	3	1
1	1	8	8	1	2	Other	33	29
	81 (4/1-9/30/13)		23 (10/1/13-3/31/14)				**4/1/09-3/31/10**	**4/1/10-3/31/11**
0-500M	**500M-2MM**	**2-10MM**	**10-50MM**	**50-100MM**	**100-250MM**		**ALL**	**ALL**
4	9	37	42	8	4	**NUMBER OF STATEMENTS**	104	120
%	%	%	%	%	%	**ASSETS**	%	%
		27.3	24.2			Cash & Equivalents	24.6	23.8
		9.6	6.3			Trade Receivables (net)	8.4	10.3
		2.5	.7			Inventory	.9	3.2
		8.5	4.6			All Other Current	4.4	7.0
		48.0	35.7			Total Current	38.3	44.3
		32.2	43.8			Fixed Assets (net)	42.0	36.3
		1.5	.9			Intangibles (net)	.4	.8
		18.3	19.7			All Other Non-Current	19.2	18.6
		100.0	100.0			Total	100.0	100.0
						LIABILITIES		
		6.8	1.0			Notes Payable-Short Term	3.4	1.6
		2.0	2.4			Cur. Mat.-L.T.D.	1.9	2.7
		4.2	3.7			Trade Payables	5.3	4.5
		.0	.0			Income Taxes Payable	.0	.0
		6.3	6.7			All Other Current	9.4	8.7
		19.3	13.8			Total Current	20.0	17.5
		33.7	39.2			Long-Term Debt	28.6	27.8
		.0	.0			Deferred Taxes	.0	.0
		2.1	4.9			All Other Non-Current	4.1	3.5
		44.9	42.1			Net Worth	47.3	51.2
		100.0	100.0			Total Liabilties & Net Worth	100.0	100.0
						INCOME DATA		
		100.0	100.0			Net Sales	100.0	100.0
						Gross Profit		
		84.1	81.8			Operating Expenses	86.1	85.3
		15.9	18.2			Operating Profit	13.9	14.7
		8.9	8.4			All Other Expenses (net)	11.2	7.2
		7.0	9.8			Profit Before Taxes	2.8	7.5
						RATIOS		
		7.6	5.1				4.9	7.7
		1.9	2.4			Current	2.0	2.5
		1.5	1.2				1.2	1.2
		3.9	4.4				4.7	5.4
		1.4	2.4			Quick	1.6	1.8
		.8	1.1				.8	.7
		0 UND	**1** 272.4				**0** UND	**0** 906.4
		8 45.3	**18** 20.8			Sales/Receivables	**9** 41.2	**13** 27.4
		45 8.2	**42** 8.6				**43** 8.5	**45** 8.0
						Cost of Sales/Inventory		
						Cost of Sales/Payables		
		.8	1.5				1.3	.9
		2.3	3.5			Sales/Working Capital	5.1	3.8
		8.8	17.9				23.7	22.8
		3.8	7.6				11.8	5.1
		(23) 2.2	(21) 2.2			EBIT/Interest	(54) 2.6	(69) 2.0
		-.4	-3.9				-.1	.5
						Net Profit + Depr., Dep., Amort./Cur. Mat. L/T/D		
		.0	.1				.1	.1
		.4	.8			Fixed/Worth	.8	.6
		1.5	2.1				1.5	1.4
		.5	.4				.4	.4
		1.0	1.1			Debt/Worth	.9	1.0
		2.0	2.3				2.7	1.9
		13.4	8.9				12.9	12.8
		(35) 4.4	(37) 1.9			% Profit Before Taxes/Tangible Net Worth	(98) 2.7	(118) 3.2
		-.5	-4.3				-4.2	-2.2
		4.3	4.7				4.7	6.6
		1.9	1.4			% Profit Before Taxes/Total Assets	.8	1.6
		-.8	-1.4				-1.6	-.8
		153.7	51.9				34.9	43.3
		4.9	1.1			Sales/Net Fixed Assets	2.2	2.6
		.6	.2				.2	.4
		.9	.9				1.4	1.4
		.4	.3			Sales/Total Assets	.3	.4
		.1	.1				.1	.1
		1.5	.7				.9	1.2
		(24) 3.5	(31) 6.4			% Depr., Dep., Amort./Sales	(82) 3.7	(92) 3.9
		9.0	18.5				16.0	14.3
							3.0	3.1
						% Officers', Directors' Owners' Comp/Sales	(17) 7.5	(10) 6.7
							17.8	28.1
2182M	**16138M**	**175183M**	**536033M**	**92819M**	**404058M**	Net Sales ($)	**1057916M**	**1591763M**
641M	**12172M**	**211836M**	**980310M**	**532975M**	**728899M**	Total Assets ($)	**2158283M**	**3060193M**

M = $ thousand MM = $ million

See Pages 9 through 22 for Explanation of Ratios and Data

Comparative Historical Data | **Current Data Sorted by Sales**

4/1/11-3/31/12 ALL	4/1/12-3/31/13 ALL	4/1/13-3/31/14 ALL	Type of Statement	0-1MM	1-3MM	3-5MM	5-10MM	10-25MM	25MM & OVER
107	94	77	Unqualified	14	15	10	12	19	7
2	3	3	Reviewed	3					
8	4	3	Compiled	2	1				
2	1		Tax Returns						
27	27	21	Other	6	4	3	1	2	5
				81 (4/1-9/30/13)			23 (10/1/13-3/31/14)		
146	129	104	NUMBER OF STATEMENTS	25	20	13	13	21	12
%	%	%	**ASSETS**	%	%	%	%	%	%
28.2	24.7	24.4	Cash & Equivalents	16.4	19.1	31.6	20.0	36.9	25.4
9.0	8.8	8.7	Trade Receivables (net)	9.5	3.6	6.0	11.3	7.7	17.8
1.9	.4	1.5	Inventory	1.1	4.8	.1	.1	.1	2.4
4.5	5.5	5.6	All Other Current	6.7	2.3	6.9	9.0	6.0	3.3
43.5	39.3	40.3	Total Current	33.6	29.8	44.6	40.3	50.7	48.9
35.4	40.0	37.9	Fixed Assets (net)	39.7	41.8	32.7	44.5	32.0	36.3
1.3	.8	1.0	Intangibles (net)	.4	.2	2.9	1.8	.9	.6
19.7	19.8	20.8	All Other Non-Current	26.2	28.1	19.8	13.4	16.5	14.2
100.0	100.0	100.0	Total	100.0	100.0	100.0	100.0	100.0	100.0
			LIABILITIES						
3.7	3.2	4.6	Notes Payable-Short Term	11.2	4.2	4.2	.7	1.0	2.3
1.8	2.4	2.2	Cur. Mat.-L.T.D.	1.8	3.2	2.8	2.3	2.3	.7
5.0	4.6	5.2	Trade Payables	2.9	2.8	5.5	5.0	6.8	11.3
.0	.0	.0	Income Taxes Payable	.0	.0	.0	.0	.0	.0
7.8	8.0	6.7	All Other Current	3.2	5.0	3.6	8.9	11.4	9.7
18.3	18.3	18.8	Total Current	19.2	15.2	16.2	16.9	21.5	24.1
27.7	27.4	33.8	Long-Term Debt	32.8	35.7	47.9	43.2	30.4	13.3
.0	.0	.0	Deferred Taxes	.0	.0	.0	.0	.0	.0
5.7	4.2	3.2	All Other Non-Current	1.8	3.2	.1	.8	9.0	1.6
48.3	50.1	44.2	Net Worth	46.2	45.9	35.8	39.1	39.1	61.0
100.0	100.0	100.0	Total Liabilties & Net Worth	100.0	100.0	100.0	100.0	100.0	100.0
			INCOME DATA						
100.0	100.0	100.0	Net Sales	100.0	100.0	100.0	100.0	100.0	100.0
			Gross Profit						
82.2	80.6	82.5	Operating Expenses	86.6	77.7	67.2	85.4	83.5	93.4
17.8	19.4	17.5	Operating Profit	13.4	22.3	32.8	14.6	16.5	6.6
8.2	9.3	8.8	All Other Expenses (net)	12.8	13.2	8.0	6.0	5.9	2.1
9.7	10.2	8.7	Profit Before Taxes	.6	9.0	24.8	8.7	10.6	4.5
			RATIOS						
6.5	5.8	4.9		6.2	3.0	11.5	10.2	3.8	6.2
2.7	2.2	2.2	Current	2.2	1.7	2.1	4.6	2.1	2.4
1.3	1.2	1.3		.7	1.2	1.3	1.8	1.2	1.2
5.3	5.0	4.3		5.3	2.4	8.9	5.9	3.5	6.2
2.4	1.9	1.6	Quick	1.6	1.4	1.6	3.3	2.0	1.5
1.1	.9	.9		.4	.6	.7	1.3	1.1	1.0
2 236.4	2 240.1	0 UND		0 UND	0 UND	0 UND	0 UND	3 110.0	9 41.0
18 20.4	19 19.2	16 22.2	Sales/Receivables	1 296.7	10 38.3	5 74.6	30 12.2	26 14.0	29 12.6
48 7.6	41 8.8	44 8.3		48 7.6	47 7.8	25 14.5	49 7.5	53 6.9	42 8.7
			Cost of Sales/Inventory						
			Cost of Sales/Payables						
1.2	1.2	1.2		.5	1.3	.8	1.1	1.9	3.2
3.2	3.0	3.0	Sales/Working Capital	2.2	4.5	2.1	2.1	3.8	5.5
14.3	37.7	15.9		-50.7	11.3	17.9	6.5	24.2	17.1
5.9	7.9	4.5		2.5	7.9			6.6	
(82) 2.4	(78) 2.8	(57) 2.1	EBIT/Interest	(14) 1.7	(10) 2.1			(12) 2.2	
.3	.6	-.7		-1.0	-.6			-4.2	
			Net Profit + Depr., Dep., Amort./Cur. Mat. L/T/D						
.0	.0	.1		.0	.3	.0	.6	.1	.1
.7	.7	.7	Fixed/Worth	.8	.7	.0	1.5	.7	.5
1.3	1.6	1.6		2.2	1.7	1.4	5.2	1.6	1.2
.3	.4	.5		.6	.5	.1	.6	.4	.2
.8	.9	1.1	Debt/Worth	1.4	1.0	2.1	1.1	.6	1.1
2.1	2.0	2.2		2.4	5.2	2.8	25.5	2.1	1.3
13.3	13.9	11.7		3.2	12.7	26.9	20.2	16.5	26.2
(135) 3.6	(125) 3.0	(96) 3.1	% Profit Before Taxes/Tangible Net Worth	(24) .0	3.9	(11) 13.4	(11) 1.9	(18) 4.0	3.9
-1.8	-1.6	-1.9		-2.9	-3.6	-.2	.2	-4.1	-2.8
6.0	6.8	4.7		1.7	3.6	18.5	5.7	13.5	14.3
1.8	1.5	1.7	% Profit Before Taxes/Total Assets	.0	2.0	4.7	1.8	2.6	1.9
-.6	-.7	-1.0		-2.2	-1.1	-.2	.3	-2.3	-1.4
108.1	118.7	86.0		UND	14.6	UND	6.7	63.9	79.5
3.8	2.0	1.9	Sales/Net Fixed Assets	.5	.8	80.1	1.0	4.0	6.6
.3	.2	.3		.2	.2	.1	.3	.9	1.1
1.5	1.4	1.1		.3	.4	.8	1.7	1.6	2.6
.4	.3	.3	Sales/Total Assets	.1	.1	.4	.4	.8	2.1
.1	.1	.1		.1	.1	.1	.2	.4	.4
1.4	1.3	1.1		1.9	1.6		1.4	.4	
(99) 4.9	(92) 5.7	(73) 4.7	% Depr., Dep., Amort./Sales	(14) 8.9	(17) 3.5		(10) 7.0	(17) 1.8	
13.8	18.5	15.9		33.2	14.7		17.7	7.0	
2.7	2.7								
(12) 6.3	(10) 8.5		% Officers', Directors' Owners' Comp/Sales						
22.2	21.9								
2599015M	2213260M	1226413M	Net Sales ($)	12185M	37652M	52338M	87892M	341295M	695051M
4870581M	3847281M	2466833M	Total Assets ($)	110059M	258664M	296578M	320532M	578657M	902343M

M = $ thousand MM = $ million

See Pages 9 through 22 for Explanation of Ratios and Data

CONSTRUCTION—PERCENTAGE OF COMPLETION BASIS OF ACCOUNTING*

Current Data Sorted by Revenue						Comparative Historical Data				
					Type of Statement					
	1		3	4	Unqualified	9	4	1	4	
	12	16		28	Reviewed	37	36	46	37	2
2	8	2		12	Compiled	65	52	30	19	1
15	31	4	2	52	Tax Returns	128	117	87	70	5
3	22	4	4	33	Other	93	62	53	40	3
14 (4/1-9/30/13)		115 (10/1/13-3/31/14)				**4/1/09-3/31/10**	**4/1/10-3/31/11**	**4/1/11-3/31/12**	**4/1/12-3/31/13**	**4/1 3/3**
0-1MM	**1-10MM**	**10-50MM**	**50 & OVER**	**ALL**		**ALL**	**ALL**	**ALL**	**ALL**	**A**
20	74	26	9	129	**NUMBER OF STATEMENTS**	332	271	217	170	1
%	%	%	%	%	**ASSETS**	%	%	%	%	
16.9	11.9	12.2		12.3	Cash & Equivalents	9.2	8.7	10.3	12.3	12
6.9	8.8	13.5		9.5	A/R - Progress Billings	6.9	6.2	9.9	10.8	9
.0	1.2	.0		.7	A/R - Current Retention	.5	1.8	1.7	1.8	
34.7	41.6	33.5		39.5	Inventory	50.9	49.9	44.9	40.1	39
1.1	3.3	3.8		2.9	Cost & Est. Earnings In Excess Billings	2.2	1.5	1.6	2.6	2
10.2	5.3	9.2		6.5	All Other Current	6.1	5.6	4.6	5.9	6
69.7	72.1	72.2		71.5	Total Current	75.7	73.7	73.0	73.5	71
26.6	13.7	8.1		14.1	Fixed Assets (net)	12.4	12.0	13.8	11.4	14
1.6	4.8	1.6		3.7	Joint Ventures & Investments	2.7	2.9	2.8	3.5	3
.5	1.9	.9		1.4	Intangibles (net)	.7	1.0	1.0	1.0	1
1.7	7.5	17.2		9.4	All Other Non-Current	8.4	10.4	9.4	10.7	9
100.0	100.0	100.0		100.0	Total	100.0	100.0	100.0	100.0	100
					LIABILITIES					
28.7	20.4	15.9		20.7	Notes Payable-Short Term	35.4	32.0	28.0	26.8	20
5.2	12.1	17.5		12.5	A/P - Trade	8.0	8.0	10.1	11.6	12
.2	.0	.0		.0	A/P - Retention	.2	.2	1.0	.6	
.0	1.7	3.7		1.8	Billings in Excess of Costs & Est. Earnings	2.0	1.5	2.3	2.6	1
.2	.9	.0		.6	Income Taxes Payable	.1	.1	.2	.1	
6.0	3.4	4.4		3.9	Cur. Mat.-L/T/D	2.9	4.3	4.8	5.3	3
10.0	9.6	6.1		9.5	All Other Current	8.9	9.4	8.8	11.4	9
50.3	48.1	47.7		49.0	Total Current	57.4	55.4	55.2	58.3	49
25.7	15.8	14.0		17.0	Long-Term Debt	17.4	16.8	14.4	14.3	17
.0	.0	.2		.1	Deferred Taxes	.1	.0	.0	.1	
6.3	9.8	10.6		9.3	All Other Non-Current	7.6	7.9	6.8	9.0	9
17.6	26.3	27.5		24.6	Net Worth	17.5	19.9	23.5	18.3	24
100.0	100.0	100.0		100.0	Total Liabilties & Net Worth	100.0	100.0	100.0	100.0	100
					INCOME DATA					
100.0	100.0	100.0		100.0	Contract Revenues	100.0	100.0	100.0	100.0	100
25.4	19.2	13.6		19.3	Gross Profit	18.3	17.8	18.5	17.0	19
23.2	15.0	10.4		15.3	Operating Expenses	16.4	15.7	16.1	14.3	15
2.2	4.3	3.2		4.0	Operating Profit	1.9	2.0	2.4	2.8	4
1.4	.7	.4		.7	All Other Expenses (net)	1.7	2.1	1.3	1.3	
.8	3.6	2.9		3.2	Profit Before Taxes	.2	-.1	1.0	1.5	3
					RATIOS					
7.2	3.1	2.1		3.0		2.6	2.4	2.3	2.2	3
1.4	1.7	1.5		1.5	Current	1.3	1.4	1.4	1.3	1
.7	1.1	1.2		1.1		.9	.9	1.0	.9	1
	1.2	1.1		1.1		1.2	1.5	1.7	1.3	1
	(60) .0	(23) .2		(100) .1	Receivables/Payables	(245) .1	(191) .3	(172) .5	(123) .1	(100)
	.0	.0		.0		.0	.0	.0	.0	
0 UND	0 UND	0 UND		0 UND		0 UND	0 UND	0 UND	0 UND	0 UN
0 UND	0 UND	2 190.6		0 UND	Revenues/Receivables	0 UND	0 UND	1 428.1	0 UND	0 UN
0 UND	11 34.2	23 15.7		11 33.8		8 43.3	14 26.1	27 13.4	19 19.5	11 33
0 UND	1 703.7	4 81.7		0 UND		0 UND	0 UND	0 UND	0 UND	0 UN
0 UND	14 26.0	21 17.8		14 25.8	Cost of Revenues/Payables	8 43.3	10 36.9	14 26.5	12 29.7	14 25
19 19.4	31 11.7	63 5.8		42 8.7		28 13.0	27 13.6	38 9.5	35 10.4	42 8
3.9	3.3	3.5		3.4		2.4	2.5	3.5	4.2	3
15.5	9.0	11.1		9.7	Revenues/Working Capital	9.8	8.7	9.3	12.3	9
-6.8	44.8	43.0		61.9		-43.5	-71.0	168.9	-27.6	61
15.3	10.8	21.5		15.5		8.8	6.9	9.0	10.0	15
(15) 1.0	(57) 3.5	(22) 9.6		(102) 4.6	EBIT/Interest	(270) 1.3	(210) 2.0	(168) 2.0	(132) 3.0	(102) 4
-4.2	1.0	2.3		1.0		-.8	-.1	.4	1.0	1
						3.5	25.3	5.5		
					Net Profit + Depr., Dep., Amort./Cur. Mat. L/T/D	(17) .5	(10) 13.1	(11) 1.1		
						-1.8	1.1	.1		
.0	.0	.0		.0		.0	.0	.0	.0	
.6	.4	.2		.3	Fixed/Worth	.2	.1	.2	.1	
UND	2.5	.6		1.2		3.4	1.9	1.4	1.2	1
1.1	.8	1.7		1.2		1.4	1.5	1.2	1.3	1
12.4	3.1	2.9		3.3	Debt/Worth	4.6	3.9	3.4	3.0	3
-9.2	20.8	6.0		18.3		44.9	34.1	16.7	64.8	1
200.4	74.6	55.2		68.3		38.2	41.5	34.7	49.1	68
(14) 13.1	(59) 19.8	(25) 21.6		(106) 19.6	% Profit Before Taxes/ Tangible Net Worth	(263) 7.8	(222) 10.5	(185) 8.0	(133) 17.3	(106) 1
-3.1	4.1	8.3		6.4		-7.9	-8.0	-2.4	.9	
9.9	13.3	12.3		12.4		8.1	9.1	8.1	11.5	1
.7	4.9	6.4		4.6	% Profit Before Taxes/ Total Assets	.7	1.8	2.0	3.8	
-6.0	.4	1.7		.3		-3.4	-2.6	-.9	-.4	
.5	.2	.1		.2		.3	.2	.2	.2	
(11) 1.3	(49) .5	(22) .3		(88) .5	% Depr., Dep., Amort./ Revenues	(197) .7	(170) .6	(144) .4	(105) .5	(88)
4.0	1.3	.7		1.0		1.6	1.3	1.4	.9	
2.8	1.0			1.3		1.7	1.7	1.2	1.6	
(12) 6.8	(39) 2.4			(62) 2.7	% Officers', Directors' Owners' Comp/Revenues	(164) 3.1	(131) 3.0	(107) 2.9	(79) 3.3	(62)
15.2	3.9			4.8		5.7	5.5	6.5	5.7	
10679M	**272053M**	**626978M**	**7912876M**	**8822586M**	Contract Revenues ($)	**79940276M**	**72988581M**	**89369896M**	**23210373M**	**88225**
11494M	**198548M**	**461915M**	**2357126M**	**3029083M**	Total Assets ($)	**53992673M**	**50223707M**	**68003233M**	**18562319M**	**30290**

M = $ thousand MM = $ million

See Pages 9 through 22 for Explanation of Ratios and Data

Current Data Sorted by Revenue / Comparative Historical Data

0-1MM	1-10MM	10-50MM	50 & OVER	ALL	Type of Statement	4/1/09-3/31/10 ALL	4/1/10-3/31/11 ALL	4/1/11-3/31/12 ALL	4/1/12-3/31/13 ALL	4/1/13-3/31/14 ALL
			1	1	Unqualified	2	4	3	1	1
		1		1	Reviewed	6	3	3	1	1
	3	2		5	Compiled	10	3	7	8	5
1		2		3	Tax Returns	6	9	4	6	3
	5	5		10	Other	15	8	13	11	10
0 (4/1-9/30/13)		20 (10/1/13-3/31/14)								
1	8	10	1	20	NUMBER OF STATEMENTS	39	27	30	27	20
%	%	%	%	%	**ASSETS**	%	%	%	%	%
		11.0		9.6	Cash & Equivalents	6.8	11.0	12.1	8.7	9.6
		.3		2.7	A/R - Progress Billings	4.7	9.7	12.4	16.1	2.7
		.0		.0	A/R - Current Retention	1.0	3.3	.4	.0	.0
		66.4		50.1	Inventory	53.6	30.2	38.5	30.3	50.1
		8.5		9.4	Cost & Est. Earnings In Excess Billings	.7	2.5	2.1	7.7	9.4
		1.6		7.4	All Other Current	8.5	8.1	6.4	10.4	7.4
		87.7		79.3	Total Current	75.3	65.0	72.0	73.2	79.3
		5.5		16.2	Fixed Assets (net)	15.5	18.7	20.5	21.7	16.2
		3.3		2.3	Joint Ventures & Investments	2.9	.5	.7	1.8	2.3
		1.0		.5	Intangibles (net)	.0	.0	.0	.1	.5
		2.4		1.7	All Other Non-Current	6.3	15.8	6.8	3.2	1.7
		100.0		100.0	Total	100.0	100.0	100.0	100.0	100.0
					LIABILITIES					
		36.8		33.8	Notes Payable-Short Term	20.0	18.1	18.0	33.6	33.8
		8.2		11.2	A/P - Trade	4.4	10.1	10.6	13.9	11.2
		.0		.0	A/P - Retention	.0	.3	.0	.0	.0
		1.0		3.3	Billings in Excess of Costs & Est. Earnings	.6	1.5	1.9	1.1	3.3
		.0		.0	Income Taxes Payable	.0	.0	.0	.0	.0
		.3		5.4	Cur. Mat.-L/T/D	5.0	2.0	4.8	4.9	5.4
		9.2		8.6	All Other Current	9.0	8.3	11.2	9.8	8.6
		55.5		62.3	Total Current	39.0	40.3	46.5	63.3	62.3
		7.1		10.4	Long-Term Debt	17.6	20.6	11.4	9.8	10.4
		.0		.0	Deferred Taxes	.2	.0	.3	.0	.0
		2.9		2.9	All Other Non-Current	12.5	12.5	5.3	8.8	2.9
		34.5		24.5	Net Worth	30.7	26.7	36.4	18.1	24.5
		100.0		100.0	Total Liabilties & Net Worth	100.0	100.0	100.0	100.0	100.0
					INCOME DATA					
		100.0		100.0	Contract Revenues	100.0	100.0	100.0	100.0	100.0
		10.9		11.6	Gross Profit	17.1	27.2	16.1	16.9	11.6
		9.0		9.4	Operating Expenses	19.3	22.8	12.5	14.3	9.4
		1.8		2.1	Operating Profit	-2.2	4.4	3.6	2.6	2.1
		.8		.7	All Other Expenses (net)	4.4	4.0	1.4	1.6	.7
		1.0		1.5	Profit Before Taxes	-6.6	.4	2.2	1.0	1.5
					RATIOS					
		2.3		2.2		4.3	3.9	2.5	2.4	2.2
		1.6		1.4	Current	1.7	1.4	1.5	1.4	1.4
		1.2		1.1		1.0	1.1	1.1	.9	1.1
				.2		2.0	1.6	1.1	2.3	.2
				(17) .0	Receivables/Payables	(35) .1	(25) .1	(27) .3	(24) .5	(17) .0
				.0		.0	.0	.0	.0	.0
		0 UND		0 UND		0 UND	0 UND	0 UND	0 UND	0 UND
		0 UND		0 UND	Revenues/Receivables	1 479.0	0 999.8	2 180.0	1 323.8	0 UND
		2 179.3		2 161.7		9 41.3	27 13.6	23 16.2	37 9.8	2 161.7
		12 29.8		3 107.1		0 797.0	1 411.9	5 69.3	5 68.0	3 107.1
		21 17.5		19 19.4	Cost of Revenues/Payables	12 30.9	17 21.4	18 19.8	19 19.7	19 19.4
		43 8.4		36 10.2		29 12.8	41 8.8	34 10.6	35 10.5	36 10.2
		2.3		2.8		.8	2.6	2.2	2.7	2.8
		5.2		6.0	Revenues/Working Capital	6.1	16.5	7.6	12.5	6.0
		9.8		17.8		50.0	493.5	33.3	-130.7	17.8
				9.0		2.2	5.2	5.2	12.4	9.0
				(13) 3.2	EBIT/Interest	(23) 1.1	(17) 2.1	(21) 1.7	(19) 4.5	(13) 3.2
				-.8		-3.1	1.3	.0	1.1	-.8
					Net Profit + Depr., Dep., Amort./Cur. Mat. L/T/D					
		.0		.0		.0	.0	.0	.0	.0
		.0		.1	Fixed/Worth	.2	.1	.3	.2	.1
		.3		.6		.8	1.1	1.4	1.3	.6
		1.0		1.2		1.1	1.8	.9	1.0	1.2
		3.0		3.3	Debt/Worth	2.4	4.1	1.7	2.6	3.3
		5.0		7.2		6.3	9.9	5.3	4.8	7.2
		60.0		51.6		9.0	34.7	20.5	27.1	51.6
		8.4		(18) 10.2	% Profit Before Taxes/ Tangible Net Worth	(33) -2.5	(24) 13.2	(27) 2.5	(25) 15.8	(18) 10.2
		-5.3		1.9		-22.8	.4	-4.5	4.0	1.9
		7.9		8.6		3.2	6.0	7.3	14.3	8.6
		2.3		3.0	% Profit Before Taxes/ Total Assets	-2.0	2.4	.7	4.3	3.0
		-2.8		.2		-8.1	.1	-1.9	1.2	.2
				.2		.2	.1	.3	.1	.2
				(10) .3	% Depr., Dep., Amort./ Revenues	(24) .5	(20) .4	(15) .8	(15) .3	(10) .3
				1.3		1.5	1.6	1.1	.7	1.3
						1.3				
					% Officers', Directors' Owners' Comp/Revenues	(10) 1.8				
						5.2				
810M	35978M	281652M	153245M	471685M	Contract Revenues ($)	514409M	621815M	2481577M	1273311M	471685M
664M	28722M	391956M	78271M	499613M	Total Assets ($)	1224331M	681761M	2581208M	596027M	499613M

M = $ thousand MM = $ million

See Pages 9 through 22 for Explanation of Ratios and Data

Current Data Sorted by Revenue						Comparative Historical Data				
					Type of Statement					
					Unqualified					
	2			2	Reviewed	3	3	6	2	2
	1	1		2	Compiled	6	7	5	1	2
4	4	1		9	Tax Returns	14	12	16	11	9
	7			7	Other	4	13	17	6	7
3 (4/1-9/30/13)		17 (10/1/13-3/31/14)				4/1/09-3/31/10	4/1/10-3/31/11	4/1/11-3/31/12	4/1/12-3/31/13	4/1/13-3/31/14
0-1MM	1-10MM	10-50MM	50 & OVER	ALL		ALL	ALL	ALL	ALL	ALL
4	14	2		20	**NUMBER OF STATEMENTS**	27	35	44	20	20
%	%	%	%	%	**ASSETS**	%	%	%	%	%
	17.4		D	17.4	Cash & Equivalents	24.1	18.0	21.0	13.9	17.4
	32.3		A	27.3	A/R - Progress Billings	12.5	21.2	25.6	27.0	27.3
	.0		T	.0	A/R - Current Retention	.0	5.2	.0	.3	.0
	.3		A	8.6	Inventory	11.6	10.8	8.7	7.2	8.6
	1.4			1.0	Cost & Est. Earnings In Excess Billings	1.7	5.7	5.4	.6	1.0
	1.4		N	1.1	All Other Current	2.4	3.2	3.2	4.3	1.1
	52.8		O	55.5	Total Current	52.3	64.2	63.8	53.3	55.5
	26.5		T	26.1	Fixed Assets (net)	33.8	24.9	25.3	34.8	26.1
	1.5			1.9	Joint Ventures & Investments	2.0	.0	.5	3.0	1.9
	6.2		A	4.3	Intangibles (net)	.0	3.1	2.8	1.2	4.3
	13.0		V	12.2	All Other Non-Current	11.8	7.8	7.6	7.7	12.2
	100.0		A	100.0	Total	100.0	100.0	100.0	100.0	100.0
			I		**LIABILITIES**					
	14.5		L	18.0	Notes Payable-Short Term	15.0	24.0	14.7	11.2	18.0
	28.5		A	23.0	A/P - Trade	17.9	14.0	22.1	27.4	23.0
	.0		B	.0	A/P - Retention	.0	.0	.0	.0	.0
	1.4		L	2.0	Billings in Excess of Costs & Est. Earnings	1.1	4.5	4.7	6.0	2.0
	.0		E	.0	Income Taxes Payable	.0	.1	.0	.0	.0
	2.9			2.9	Cur. Mat.-L/T/D	8.2	2.3	12.2	4.2	2.9
	8.4			8.4	All Other Current	18.2	16.4	18.9	12.3	8.4
	55.8			54.3	Total Current	60.4	61.3	72.5	61.1	54.3
	18.9			18.0	Long-Term Debt	27.1	9.5	12.8	43.4	18.0
	.0			.0	Deferred Taxes	.0	.3	.3	.0	.0
	8.9			8.7	All Other Non-Current	10.6	5.0	7.2	17.6	8.7
	16.4			19.0	Net Worth	1.8	23.9	7.2	-22.0	19.0
	100.0			100.0	Total Liabilties & Net Worth	100.0	100.0	100.0	100.0	100.0
					INCOME DATA					
	100.0			100.0	Contract Revenues	100.0	100.0	100.0	100.0	100.0
	23.7			24.4	Gross Profit	33.1	35.4	33.0	32.8	24.4
	21.1			22.2	Operating Expenses	28.2	30.5	31.5	29.3	22.2
	2.6			2.2	Operating Profit	4.8	5.0	1.6	3.5	2.2
	-.3			-.3	All Other Expenses (net)	.5	.4	.6	.2	-.3
	2.9			2.5	Profit Before Taxes	4.3	4.5	1.0	3.3	2.5
					RATIOS					
	1.3			1.7		4.0	2.5	1.6	1.5	1.7
	.9			.9	Current	.9	1.2	1.1	1.0	.9
	.6			.7		.5	.7	.8	.6	.7
	1.7			1.7		1.6	6.1	2.4	2.9	1.7
	(13) 1.0			(17) 1.0	Receivables/Payables	(20) .8	(27) 1.7	(38) 1.3	(14) 2.0	(17) 1.0
	.3			.0		.2	1.2	.7	.8	.0
	0 UND			0 UND		0 UND	0 862.8	2 190.2	0 UND	0 UND
	13 27.6			8 45.7	Revenues/Receivables	4 82.1	31 11.8	19 19.3	13 27.6	8 45.7
	38 9.5			40 9.2		14 25.3	50 7.3	48 7.6	45 8.2	40 9.2
	4 93.0			1 245.0		0 UND	0 UND	4 89.3	0 UND	1 245.0
	27 13.7			20 18.6	Cost of Revenues/Payables	9 40.1	20 18.5	25 14.6	16 22.7	20 18.6
	37 9.8			33 11.2		19 19.2	38 9.7	46 7.9	34 10.8	33 11.2
	46.9			18.9		5.5	6.6	15.3	24.9	18.9
	-58.4			-161.2	Revenues/Working Capital	-260.1	61.4	84.9	-360.9	-161.2
	-25.7			-23.5		-25.6	-25.8	-14.0	-14.4	-23.5
	8.7			8.4		37.0	27.6	16.2	8.7	8.4
	(11) 4.5			(16) 3.8	EBIT/Interest	(23) 14.0	(29) 7.1	(37) 4.3	(14) 2.5	(16) 3.8
	2.6			1.0		-.6	-3.1	-1.9	.5	1.0
					Net Profit + Depr., Dep., Amort./Cur. Mat. L/T/D					
	1.0			.3		.3	.1	.4	.6	.
	2.9			2.6	Fixed/Worth	1.5	.6	1.0	1.3	2.
	-1.0			NM		UND	3.8	-3.5	UND	NM
	1.8			2.1		.7	.5	1.3	2.2	2.
	10.1			5.5	Debt/Worth	5.6	2.6	3.9	4.4	5.
	-28.1			NM		UND	13.3	-23.6	UND	NM
				60.3		102.3	93.4	64.2	135.9	60.
				(15) 32.2	% Profit Before Taxes/ Tangible Net Worth	(21) 53.3	(28) 32.4	(30) 34.9	(15) 30.4	(15) 32.
				-15.7		2.1	-7.7	-5.9	-17.3	-15.
	20.1			20.4		44.3	25.3	20.9	48.5	20.
	6.8			6.3	% Profit Before Taxes/ Total Assets	20.0	8.6	8.7	3.3	6.
	2.4			-.5		-4.8	-4.8	-3.7	-4.8	-.
	.6			.6		.4	.6	.6	.5	.
	(10) .8			(15) .9	% Depr., Dep., Amort./ Revenues	(23) .9	(23) .9	(37) 1.0	(17) .9	(15) .
	1.4			1.3		2.2	2.0	1.7	1.8	1.
				1.8		3.5	2.8	2.8	1.5	1.
				(11) 3.7	% Officers', Directors' Owners' Comp/Revenues	(18) 5.1	(22) 4.9	(22) 4.9	(11) 3.3	(11) 3.
				4.7		7.8	8.7	7.8	6.1	4.
2501M	49186M	45734M		97421M	Contract Revenues ($)	86698M	4281227M	473958M	264907M	9742
1832M	13447M	13928M		29207M	Total Assets ($)	23180M	886693M	201690M	126684M	2920

M = $ thousand MM = $ million

See Pages 9 through 22 for Explanation of Ratios and Data

Current Data Sorted by Revenue						Comparative Historical Data				
					Type of Statement					
		4	5	9	Unqualified	19	8	11	5	9
	8	7	1	16	Reviewed	35	45	31	30	16
	1			1	Compiled	8	7	7	2	1
1	1	2		4	Tax Returns	6	11	6	5	4
	4		3	7	Other	20	34	31	25	7
7 (4/1-9/30/13)		30 (10/1/13-3/31/14)				4/1/09-3/31/10	4/1/10-3/31/11	4/1/11-3/31/12	4/1/12-3/31/13	4/1/13-3/31/14
0-1MM	1-10MM	10-50MM	50 & OVER	ALL		ALL	ALL	ALL	ALL	ALL
1	14	13	9	37	**NUMBER OF STATEMENTS**	88	105	86	67	37
%	%	%	%	%	**ASSETS**	%	%	%	%	%
	18.3	18.6		16.6	Cash & Equivalents	23.0	18.2	23.1	22.6	16.6
	46.3	40.5		45.4	A/R - Progress Billings	33.9	25.9	38.8	38.2	45.4
	.0	2.7		1.2	A/R - Current Retention	2.6	19.0	2.4	3.1	1.2
	1.2	.9		1.0	Inventory	2.4	3.0	2.3	2.1	1.0
	5.8	4.0		4.3	Cost & Est. Earnings In Excess Billings	4.1	6.1	7.0	7.3	4.3
	4.0	10.5		6.3	All Other Current	6.4	5.0	6.2	5.6	6.3
	75.6	77.1		74.8	Total Current	72.4	77.2	79.9	79.0	74.8
	15.1	15.5		16.2	Fixed Assets (net)	18.6	14.8	12.3	13.0	16.2
	1.7	1.0		1.2	Joint Ventures & Investments	.7	.4	.4	.4	1.2
	1.5	.3		2.1	Intangibles (net)	1.8	1.6	1.1	2.1	2.1
	6.3	6.1		5.7	All Other Non-Current	6.5	5.9	6.4	5.6	5.7
	100.0	100.0		100.0	Total	100.0	100.0	100.0	100.0	100.0
					LIABILITIES					
	8.7	4.1		5.6	Notes Payable-Short Term	5.3	4.1	5.2	4.5	5.6
	31.1	33.0		31.1	A/P - Trade	25.8	32.9	30.0	29.9	31.1
	1.0	1.7		1.2	A/P - Retention	1.2	2.0	1.3	1.3	1.2
	7.6	5.6		6.6	Billings in Excess of Costs & Est. Earnings	7.9	8.8	8.4	6.9	6.6
	.0	.0		.0	Income Taxes Payable	.5	.4	.2	.3	.0
	3.5	2.8		2.7	Cur. Mat.-L/T/D	2.3	2.3	1.9	2.1	2.7
	5.7	11.0		9.7	All Other Current	7.7	6.7	8.1	8.5	9.7
	57.7	58.2		57.0	Total Current	50.7	57.1	55.1	53.5	57.0
	12.4	8.4		9.8	Long-Term Debt	7.5	6.7	6.3	6.2	9.8
	.8	.0		.8	Deferred Taxes	.7	.5	.5	.4	.8
	5.6	5.7		5.3	All Other Non-Current	4.5	5.4	2.7	4.3	5.3
	23.4	27.6		27.2	Net Worth	36.5	30.2	35.5	35.5	27.2
	100.0	100.0		100.0	Total Liabilties & Net Worth	100.0	100.0	100.0	100.0	100.0
					INCOME DATA					
	100.0	100.0		100.0	Contract Revenues	100.0	100.0	100.0	100.0	100.0
	21.7	18.6		17.5	Gross Profit	19.2	16.4	16.4	15.7	17.5
	18.7	15.8		14.8	Operating Expenses	16.6	14.3	14.3	14.2	14.8
	3.0	2.9		2.8	Operating Profit	2.6	2.1	2.1	1.5	2.8
	.1	.3		-.1	All Other Expenses (net)	.5	.0	-.2	-.2	-.1
	2.9	2.6		2.9	Profit Before Taxes	2.2	2.1	2.3	1.7	2.9
					RATIOS					
	2.2	1.5		1.8		1.8	1.8	2.1	2.0	1.8
	1.6	1.3		1.3	Current	1.4	1.4	1.5	1.4	1.3
	.9	1.2		1.1		1.2	1.2	1.2	1.2	1.1
	2.3	3.2		2.8		2.3	2.0	2.5	2.8	2.8
	1.4	1.3		1.4	Receivables/Payables	(86) 1.4	(104) 1.3	(84) 1.3	1.3	1.4
	.9	1.1		1.1		1.0	.9	1.0	1.0	1.1
	35 10.4	**8** 46.3		**39** 9.4		**30** 12.1	**34** 10.9	**33** 10.9	**35** 10.5	**39** 9.4
	60 6.1	**54** 6.8		**57** 6.4	Revenues/Receivables	**50** 7.3	**55** 6.7	**51** 7.1	**58** 6.3	**57** 6.4
	76 4.8	**78** 4.7		**74** 4.9		**67** 5.4	**75** 4.9	**72** 5.1	**79** 4.6	**74** 4.9
	32 11.4	**14** 25.9		**29** 12.5		**18** 19.8	**26** 14.3	**26** 14.3	**23** 16.0	**29** 12.5
	51 7.2	**46** 7.9		**46** 7.9	Cost of Revenues/Payables	**39** 9.4	**44** 8.2	**42** 8.6	**49** 7.5	**46** 7.9
	59 6.2	**68** 5.4		**62** 5.9		**59** 6.2	**62** 5.9	**58** 6.3	**62** 5.9	**62** 5.9
	5.2	13.5		8.4		7.1	7.4	5.6	5.5	8.4
	12.6	17.8		17.8	Revenues/Working Capital	12.8	13.7	12.0	13.1	17.8
	-352.2	35.2		35.8		32.5	32.8	24.5	28.6	35.8
	19.3	35.0		33.8		67.8	31.8	59.6	31.6	33.8
	(13) 5.1	(12) 13.7		(34) 9.9	EBIT/Interest	(66) 6.3	(82) 4.5	(65) 11.2	(54) 10.9	(34) 9.9
	-2.1	4.6		2.1		-.4	-1.1	1.1	1.5	2.1
				18.3		6.1	7.9	12.8	7.1	18.3
				(10) 8.5	Net Profit + Depr., Dep., Amort./Cur. Mat. L/T/D	(17) 3.2	(27) 5.4	(15) 5.4	(21) 4.6	(10) 8.5
				3.8		.2	.3	-5.1	.4	3.8
	.1	.1		.1		.1	.1	.1	.1	.1
	.4	.3		.3	Fixed/Worth	.4	.3	.2	.3	.3
	-.8	.9		1.6		1.0	.8	.6	.7	1.6
	.9	1.2		1.1		.8	1.1	.8	1.0	1.1
	1.5	2.8		2.2	Debt/Worth	1.8	2.2	1.7	2.2	2.2
	-6.7	27.4		8.2		3.2	3.8	4.3	3.9	8.2
	61.7	61.1		57.6		49.9	35.4	44.5	32.8	57.6
	(10) 27.3	(12) 37.2		(31) 27.3	% Profit Before Taxes/ Tangible Net Worth	(82) 20.7	(96) 12.3	(78) 17.4	(62) 13.3	(31) 27.3
	11.1	13.7		13.0		.6	.1	4.7	3.2	13.0
	16.8	13.8		15.6		16.4	11.2	12.2	8.6	15.6
	6.0	6.2		5.9	% Profit Before Taxes/ Total Assets	5.3	3.3	5.7	3.8	5.9
	-2.6	2.5		1.0		-1.2	-1.8	.1	.7	1.0
	.5	.1		.1		.4	.3	.3	.3	.1
	(10) .8	.4		(33) .6	% Depr., Dep., Amort./ Revenues	(69) .8	(88) .7	(75) .7	(62) .5	(33) .6
	1.6	1.1		1.5		1.9	1.9	1.6	1.3	1.5
				.7		1.1	1.2	1.0	1.0	.7
				(11) 1.2	% Officers', Directors' Owners' Comp/Revenues	(36) 3.3	(45) 2.2	(33) 2.0	(23) 2.9	(11) 1.2
				3.8		6.9	3.8	4.0	8.5	3.8
874M	78580M	304312M	1160496M	1544262M	Contract Revenues ($)	10494772M	6377258M	7092504M	4899902M	1544262M
289M	29493M	137692M	601351M	768825M	Total Assets ($)	6040337M	3232821M	3164015M	2551722M	768825M

M = $ thousand MM = $ million

See Pages 9 through 22 for Explanation of Ratios and Data

Current Data Sorted by Revenue						Comparative Historical Data				
					Type of Statement					
1	3	16	19	39	Unqualified	66	50	41	39	
3	39	24	11	77	Reviewed	127	167	178	158	
1	6	4	3	14	Compiled	18	20	17	16	
2	10	4		16	Tax Returns	18	30	29	19	
1	18	13	10	42	Other	49	91	104	86	
34 (4/1-9/30/13)		154 (10/1/13-3/31/14)				**4/1/09-3/31/10**	**4/1/10-3/31/11**	**4/1/11-3/31/12**	**4/1/12-3/31/13**	**4/ 3/**
0-1MM	**1-10MM**	**10-50MM**	**50 & OVER**	**ALL**		**ALL**	**ALL**	**ALL**	**ALL**	
8	76	61	43	188	**NUMBER OF STATEMENTS**	278	358	369	318	
%	%	%	%	%	**ASSETS**	%	%	%	%	
	21.2	23.5	25.0	23.6	Cash & Equivalents	28.5	25.1	25.4	25.5	2
	39.3	41.0	45.0	40.5	A/R - Progress Billings	32.5	27.2	39.1	39.9	4
	1.7	3.3	3.3	2.5	A/R - Current Retention	3.0	14.9	4.3	3.7	
	2.1	2.8	2.0	2.2	Inventory	2.3	2.0	1.9	1.3	
	4.8	5.8	3.3	4.7	Cost & Est. Earnings In Excess Billings	3.7	5.0	5.5	5.3	
	5.9	4.3	7.0	5.5	All Other Current	6.6	5.0	5.8	5.1	
	75.0	80.7	85.5	78.9	Total Current	76.6	79.2	82.0	80.7	7
	15.2	11.6	8.5	13.3	Fixed Assets (net)	15.1	12.7	11.0	11.3	1
	1.2	.9	.9	1.0	Joint Ventures & Investments	1.2	1.1	.7	.8	
	.2	.1	1.8	.5	Intangibles (net)	1.1	.9	1.2	1.0	
	8.4	6.7	3.3	6.3	All Other Non-Current	6.1	6.0	5.1	6.2	
	100.0	100.0	100.0	100.0	Total	100.0	100.0	100.0	100.0	10
					LIABILITIES					
	7.7	3.6	.9	5.1	Notes Payable-Short Term	7.4	5.8	5.3	4.6	
	26.9	39.5	48.2	35.5	A/P - Trade	26.3	29.6	30.5	33.5	3
	1.0	2.3	2.7	1.8	A/P - Retention	2.1	2.6	3.0	3.0	
	7.2	8.9	9.7	8.3	Billings in Excess of Costs & Est. Earnings	6.9	8.5	8.1	8.6	
	.1	.0	.2	.1	Income Taxes Payable	.3	.4	.2	.3	
	1.7	1.0	.6	1.1	Cur. Mat.-L/T/D	2.0	2.1	2.2	1.4	
	5.9	6.3	10.6	7.1	All Other Current	9.4	7.2	8.0	6.0	
	50.6	61.5	72.9	59.0	Total Current	54.4	56.2	57.3	57.5	5
	7.5	5.4	3.1	5.8	Long-Term Debt	7.0	6.7	5.8	5.4	
	.5	.3	.6	.5	Deferred Taxes	.6	.3	.4	.3	
	3.9	1.5	.3	2.2	All Other Non-Current	2.9	4.5	3.9	3.6	
	37.5	31.2	23.1	32.6	Net Worth	35.1	32.2	32.7	33.3	3
	100.0	100.0	100.0	100.0	Total Liabilties & Net Worth	100.0	100.0	100.0	100.0	10
					INCOME DATA					
	100.0	100.0	100.0	100.0	Contract Revenues	100.0	100.0	100.0	100.0	10
	16.1	11.1	7.8	13.6	Gross Profit	17.4	15.8	14.4	14.7	1
	15.3	9.6	6.5	12.1	Operating Expenses	15.8	14.7	13.1	12.5	1
	.8	1.5	1.2	1.5	Operating Profit	1.6	1.1	1.3	2.2	
	.0	-.2	.2	.0	All Other Expenses (net)	.4	.2	.1	.0	
	.8	1.8	1.1	1.5	Profit Before Taxes	1.3	.9	1.2	2.2	
					RATIOS					
	2.5	1.6	1.4	1.9		2.1	2.0	2.0	1.8	
	1.5	1.3	1.2	1.3	Current	1.5	1.4	1.4	1.4	
	1.2	1.0	1.1	1.1		1.2	1.1	1.2	1.2	
	3.0	1.4	1.2	1.8		1.9	2.2	2.1	1.7	
	(74) 1.4	1.0	1.0	(185) 1.1	Receivables/Payables	(266) 1.3	(346) 1.3	(362) 1.3	(313) 1.2	(185)
	.9	.8	.9	.8		.9	.9	.9	.9	
	26 14.1	**36** 10.2	**49** 7.4	**32** 11.3		**23** 15.5	**33** 11.0	**31** 11.8	**33** 10.9	**32** 1
	45 8.2	**51** 7.1	**56** 6.5	**52** 7.0	Revenues/Receivables	**44** 8.3	**54** 6.8	**55** 6.6	**54** 6.7	**52**
	76 4.8	**65** 5.6	**70** 5.2	**69** 5.3		**64** 5.7	**76** 4.8	**76** 4.8	**72** 5.1	**69**
	17 21.5	**29** 12.6	**45** 8.2	**26** 14.3		**20** 18.4	**25** 14.6	**25** 14.7	**30** 12.1	**26** 1
	33 11.0	**51** 7.1	**62** 5.9	**46** 8.0	Cost of Revenues/Payables	**40** 9.0	**46** 7.9	**47** 7.8	**52** 7.0	**46**
	60 6.1	**76** 4.8	**74** 4.9	**72** 5.1		**58** 6.3	**70** 5.2	**69** 5.3	**72** 5.1	**72**
	6.2	9.9	12.8	7.4		6.5	6.2	6.5	7.1	
	10.9	16.2	21.1	15.3	Revenues/Working Capital	12.0	11.8	11.7	13.1	1
	31.7	441.5	54.6	48.4		27.8	30.4	26.9	26.9	4
	27.6	72.0	109.0	39.9		35.6	37.9	30.7	49.8	3
	(51) 5.2	(42) 8.0	(26) 15.2	(121) 6.8	EBIT/Interest	(202) 5.3	(266) 6.2	(261) 6.9	(210) 12.2	(121)
	-4.8	.7	2.1	-1.7		-4.9	-.5	.5	1.7	-
			14.3	9.4		13.0	8.3	7.4	14.8	
			(10) 8.2	(26) 5.8	Net Profit + Depr., Dep., Amort./Cur. Mat. L/T/D	(57) 4.6	(53) 2.7	(58) 2.7	(49) 6.7	(26)
			3.4	-2.1		.2	.8	-.1	2.2	-
	.1	.1	.1	.1		.1	.1	.1	.1	
	.3	.2	.2	.2	Fixed/Worth	.2	.2	.2	.1	
	.6	.5	.6	.6		.6	.5	.5	.4	
	.6	1.2	1.9	.8		.8	.9	1.0	.9	
	1.4	2.6	3.5	2.2	Debt/Worth	1.7	2.0	2.0	2.0	
	3.0	6.0	5.2	4.4		3.5	3.9	4.0	4.1	
	24.9	33.6	40.8	32.5		36.6	31.0	30.1	39.0	3
	(71) 7.9	(59) 14.0	(39) 19.1	(176) 13.3	% Profit Before Taxes/ Tangible Net Worth	(260) 11.9	(331) 12.0	(348) 10.1	(299) 15.6	(176) 1
	-8.7	.5	4.7	-1.6		-6.4	.3	.0	4.4	-
	10.7	11.3	7.8	10.3		13.7	9.2	10.3	11.8	1
	2.9	4.1	3.2	3.2	% Profit Before Taxes/ Total Assets	4.0	3.4	3.7	4.6	
	-5.2	-.1	.8	-1.6		-3.7	-.8	-.4	1.0	-
	.3	.2	.1	.2		.2	.3	.2	.2	
	(63) .5	(58) .3	(38) .2	(165) .4	% Depr., Dep., Amort./ Revenues	(231) .6	(303) .5	(315) .5	(269) .4	(165)
	1.7	.8	.5	1.1		1.7	1.2	1.1	1.0	
	2.1	.8		1.7		1.4	1.5	1.5	1.4	
	(26) 3.5	(15) 3.4		(51) 3.6	% Officers', Directors' Owners' Comp/Revenues	(133) 3.4	(154) 2.6	(134) 2.6	(115) 2.4	(51)
	5.0	4.7		6.8		6.7	5.3	4.9	4.9	
4026M	359539M	1422093M	20878176M	22663834M	Contract Revenues ($)	106919533M	57172335M	41182918M	42283108M	226638
2110M	154085M	596618M	10620148M	11372961M	Total Assets ($)	50228561M	38866333M	24930206M	25649089M	113729

M = $ thousand MM = $ million

See Pages 9 through 22 for Explanation of Ratios and Data

Current Data Sorted by Revenue | **Comparative Historical Data**

0-1MM	1-10MM	10-50MM	50 & OVER	ALL	Type of Statement	4/1/09-3/31/10 ALL	4/1/10-3/31/11 ALL	4/1/11-3/31/12 ALL	4/1/12-3/31/13 ALL	4/1/13-3/31/14 ALL
	2	4		6	Unqualified	14	11	9	6	6
	14	10		24	Reviewed	26	31	34	26	24
2	4		1	7	Compiled	12	9	6	7	7
2	3	1	1	7	Tax Returns	5	4	5	7	7
	5	2	2	9	Other	5	36	28	27	9
12 (4/1-9/30/13)		41 (10/1/13-3/31/14)								
4	28	17	4	53	NUMBER OF STATEMENTS	62	91	82	73	53
%	%	%	%	%	**ASSETS**	%	%	%	%	%
	15.5	15.0		13.7	Cash & Equivalents	17.8	17.8	18.2	17.3	13.7
	34.0	40.7		35.0	A/R - Progress Billings	29.2	20.3	30.1	30.6	35.0
	.7	.1		.4	A/R - Current Retention	.9	12.8	2.6	2.3	.4
	5.0	1.2		6.2	Inventory	4.3	2.9	2.7	4.4	6.2
	4.9	6.7		5.2	Cost & Est. Earnings In Excess Billings	4.0	5.7	7.0	5.7	5.2
	5.9	1.5		3.7	All Other Current	4.2	3.3	3.9	4.8	3.7
	66.0	65.2		64.2	Total Current	60.3	62.8	64.6	65.1	64.2
	26.6	26.6		29.1	Fixed Assets (net)	30.8	28.2	27.4	26.5	29.1
	.5	.0		.3	Joint Ventures & Investments	.4	.6	.3	.7	.3
	.5	.0		.3	Intangibles (net)	2.4	3.4	.6	.9	.3
	6.4	8.2		6.1	All Other Non-Current	6.1	5.0	7.1	6.8	6.1
	100.0	100.0		100.0	Total	100.0	100.0	100.0	100.0	100.0
					LIABILITIES					
	9.6	6.6		9.0	Notes Payable-Short Term	7.3	5.1	7.5	7.4	9.0
	14.4	21.9		16.5	A/P - Trade	16.4	20.9	18.1	16.7	16.5
	.1	.1		.1	A/P - Retention	.2	.5	.4	.4	.1
	2.2	5.4		3.3	Billings in Excess of Costs & Est. Earnings	3.1	5.0	4.6	3.9	3.3
	.3	.0		.1	Income Taxes Payable	.1	.3	.5	.1	.1
	2.4	3.3		5.7	Cur. Mat.-L/T/D	4.6	4.8	5.2	5.3	5.7
	6.4	3.3		5.4	All Other Current	6.5	4.0	4.9	6.3	5.4
	35.3	40.6		40.2	Total Current	38.2	40.5	41.3	40.1	40.2
	9.1	7.7		10.2	Long-Term Debt	15.0	12.9	11.2	13.4	10.2
	.9	1.7		1.0	Deferred Taxes	2.3	.9	1.0	1.0	1.0
	2.7	2.5		2.3	All Other Non-Current	3.3	3.7	2.9	4.1	2.3
	52.0	47.6		46.3	Net Worth	41.1	42.0	43.6	41.3	46.3
	100.0	100.0		100.0	Total Liabilties & Net Worth	100.0	100.0	100.0	100.0	100.0
					INCOME DATA					
	100.0	100.0		100.0	Contract Revenues	100.0	100.0	100.0	100.0	100.0
	25.9	18.7		26.0	Gross Profit	23.7	19.0	20.4	24.1	26.0
	22.6	14.8		21.9	Operating Expenses	22.5	18.0	18.9	21.3	21.9
	3.3	3.9		4.0	Operating Profit	1.2	1.1	1.5	2.7	4.0
	.2	-.1		.2	All Other Expenses (net)	.0	-.3	.0	-.4	.2
	3.1	4.1		3.9	Profit Before Taxes	1.2	1.4	1.5	3.1	3.9
					RATIOS					
	3.3	2.5		3.0		2.5	2.4	2.2	2.6	3.0
	1.9	1.5		1.6	Current	1.5	1.6	1.6	1.9	1.6
	1.2	1.3		1.2		1.1	1.2	1.2	1.3	1.2
	7.8	3.3		6.4		3.0	3.2	3.6	4.5	6.4
	3.2	2.2		(51) 2.3	Receivables/Payables	(60) 1.9	1.7	(81) 1.7	(70) 2.2	(51) 2.3
	1.4	1.4		1.4		1.2	1.0	1.1	1.3	1.4
	41 8.9	**49** 7.4		**41** 8.9		**29** 12.5	**38** 9.5	**36** 10.0	**33** 10.9	**41** 8.9
	63 5.8	**61** 6.0		**61** 6.0	Revenues/Receivables	**48** 7.6	**51** 7.1	**55** 6.6	**56** 6.5	**61** 6.0
	94 3.9	**85** 4.3		**73** 5.0		**72** 5.0	**67** 5.5	**74** 4.9	**74** 4.9	**73** 5.0
	11 33.3	**20** 18.0		**13** 28.9		**15** 23.8	**22** 16.8	**18** 20.2	**17** 21.6	**13** 28.9
	38 9.7	**39** 9.4		**35** 10.5	Cost of Revenues/Payables	**31** 11.8	**38** 9.6	**38** 9.6	**31** 11.8	**35** 10.5
	54 6.7	**68** 5.4		**53** 6.9		**60** 6.1	**52** 7.0	**55** 6.6	**53** 6.9	**53** 6.9
	3.5	4.4		4.0		5.3	6.1	5.7	5.2	4.0
	8.3	9.5		9.5	Revenues/Working Capital	10.9	10.9	9.9	9.8	9.5
	28.0	33.0		36.1		56.2	25.7	25.1	15.7	36.1
	19.4	22.5		22.6		10.2	12.4	12.0	31.4	22.6
	(25) 4.7	(13) 3.1		(44) 6.3	EBIT/Interest	(51) 2.6	(78) 3.2	(70) 5.9	(67) 6.6	(44) 6.3
	1.2	1.2		1.4		-3.0	-1.4	-2.9	2.3	1.4
						6.3	5.7	4.1	8.3	
					Net Profit + Depr., Dep., Amort./Cur. Mat. L/T/D	(18) 2.8	(22) 2.6	(13) 3.3	(17) 3.6	
						1.5	.5	-.1	2.3	
	.2	.3		.3		.3	.3	.3	.3	.3
	.5	.7		.7	Fixed/Worth	.6	.6	.6	.7	.7
	1.0	.8		1.0		1.4	1.2	1.2	1.3	1.0
	.3	.7		.4		.6	.6	.7	.5	.4
	.7	1.3		.9	Debt/Worth	1.1	1.5	1.4	1.1	.9
	2.2	1.9		2.6		2.9	3.1	2.6	2.6	2.6
	25.2	34.1		29.5		34.1	27.7	24.7	43.5	29.5
	(27) 9.0	11.1		(49) 12.8	% Profit Before Taxes/ Tangible Net Worth	(56) 8.8	(86) 9.8	(78) 10.3	(68) 17.4	(49) 12.8
	2.4	1.6		2.4		.6	-.4	-6.3	4.0	2.4
	13.0	15.7		15.7		14.2	9.9	11.1	17.7	15.7
	3.0	4.7		5.7	% Profit Before Taxes/ Total Assets	3.3	4.7	5.3	6.9	5.7
	.3	.6		.8		-1.7	-1.5	-3.5	1.3	.8
	1.4	1.9		1.5		2.1	1.2	1.7	1.2	1.5
	2.8	(16) 3.3		(48) 3.1	% Depr., Dep., Amort./ Revenues	(50) 3.6	(79) 3.0	(70) 3.3	(59) 2.8	(48) 3.1
	4.7	4.1		4.3		6.6	4.8	5.3	4.8	4.3
	2.5			1.3		1.3	1.4	1.5	1.2	1.3
	(10) 3.5			(20) 3.3	% Officers', Directors' Owners' Comp/Revenues	(25) 2.5	(40) 2.7	(29) 3.6	(33) 3.1	(20) 3.3
	4.9			4.8		5.9	4.9	6.6	5.7	4.8
1665M	147856M	403839M	6831915M	7385275M	Contract Revenues ($)	4498342M	9545546M	7157761M	7235448M	7385275M
289M	77311M	212511M	2370106M	2660217M	Total Assets ($)	3264021M	8374601M	3521766M	3677900M	2660217M

M = $ thousand MM = $ million

See Pages 9 through 22 for Explanation of Ratios and Data

Current Data Sorted by Revenue						Comparative Historical Data				
					Type of Statement					
		1	1	2	Unqualified	4	4	2	1	2
	2	1	1	4	Reviewed	17	11	12	8	4
	2	1		3	Compiled	16	11	5	6	3
15	3			18	Tax Returns	42	36	28	16	18
3	2	2		7	Other	33	27	15	16	7
2 (4/1-9/30/13)		32 (10/1/13-3/31/14)				4/1/09-3/31/10	4/1/10-3/31/11	4/1/11-3/31/12	4/1/12-3/31/13	4/1/13-3/31/14
0-1MM	1-10MM	10-50MM	50 & OVER	ALL		ALL	ALL	ALL	ALL	ALL
18	9	5	2	34	**NUMBER OF STATEMENTS**	112	89	62	47	34
%	%	%	%	%	**ASSETS**	%	%	%	%	%
12.5				8.1	Cash & Equivalents	4.4	3.7	6.1	7.2	8.1
1.6				1.0	A/R - Progress Billings	4.2	3.2	9.2	6.0	1.0
.0				.7	A/R - Current Retention	.2	.4	.7	.6	.7
19.3				24.3	Inventory	29.4	28.1	25.1	22.1	24.3
.0				.3	Cost & Est. Earnings In Excess Billings	.9	.5	.9	1.0	.3
4.1				9.0	All Other Current	7.6	5.3	8.0	3.8	9.0
37.5				43.4	Total Current	46.6	41.2	49.9	40.8	43.4
42.3				36.8	Fixed Assets (net)	39.4	45.2	30.0	43.9	36.8
.2				3.7	Joint Ventures & Investments	3.6	5.4	6.9	3.0	3.7
2.5				2.0	Intangibles (net)	1.8	.3	.3	.3	2.0
17.5				14.1	All Other Non-Current	8.7	7.9	12.9	12.1	14.1
100.0				100.0	Total	100.0	100.0	100.0	100.0	100.0
					LIABILITIES					
4.7				11.1	Notes Payable-Short Term	13.7	22.6	13.7	12.8	11.1
.8				2.2	A/P - Trade	2.9	2.1	5.1	4.7	2.2
.0				.0	A/P - Retention	.0	.0	1.2	.1	.0
.0				.9	Billings in Excess of Costs & Est. Earnings	.5	.6	.8	1.0	.9
.0				.0	Income Taxes Payable	.0	.0	.0	.0	.0
8.3				6.4	Cur. Mat.-L/T/D	7.5	2.1	2.1	2.7	6.4
4.9				4.9	All Other Current	4.9	3.9	4.0	6.2	4.9
18.7				25.6	Total Current	29.5	31.3	26.8	27.5	25.6
36.2				37.7	Long-Term Debt	37.0	42.0	31.6	35.0	37.7
.0				.3	Deferred Taxes	.3	.4	.0	.2	.3
4.7				4.9	All Other Non-Current	7.2	12.3	6.4	11.7	4.9
40.5				31.5	Net Worth	25.9	14.0	35.1	25.7	31.5
100.0				100.0	Total Liabilties & Net Worth	100.0	100.0	100.0	100.0	100.0
					INCOME DATA					
100.0				100.0	Contract Revenues	100.0	100.0	100.0	100.0	100.0
					Gross Profit					
74.3				78.7	Operating Expenses	85.0	79.6	85.5	82.4	78.7
25.7				21.3	Operating Profit	15.0	20.4	14.5	17.6	21.3
15.3				12.9	All Other Expenses (net)	17.1	20.5	10.8	10.3	12.9
10.5				8.4	Profit Before Taxes	-2.2	-.1	3.7	7.3	8.4
					RATIOS					
11.1				5.5		5.5	4.9	4.6	2.3	5.5
1.7				1.6	Current	1.4	1.5	1.8	1.4	1.6
.1				.5		.6	.5	.9	.4	.5
				UND		4.6	5.1	3.6	2.0	UND
				(22) .2	Receivables/Payables	(68) .5	(57) .2	(48) .1	(35) .0	(22) .2
				.0		.0	.0	.0	.0	.0
0 UND				0 UND		0 UND	0 UND	0 UND	0 UND	0 UND
0 UND				0 UND	Revenues/Receivables	0 UND	0 UND	0 UND	0 UND	0 UND
0 UND				7 51.2		8 48.5	5 77.3	33 11.2	5 72.5	7 51.2
					Cost of Revenues/Payables					
.4				1.1		.7	.7	.7	1.3	1.1
5.8				8.2	Revenues/Working Capital	5.3	4.2	4.2	14.8	8.2
-1.4				-4.5		-5.8	-5.6	-74.4	-6.9	-4.5
				3.2		4.1	5.4	7.4	13.6	3.2
				(20) 2.3	EBIT/Interest	(51) 1.5	(39) 1.4	(38) 1.5	(26) 2.7	(20) 2.3
				1.5		-.5	.8	-.7	.9	1.5
					Net Profit + Depr., Dep., Amort./Cur. Mat. L/T/D					
.0				.0		.0	.0	.0	.1	.
1.2				1.3	Fixed/Worth	1.1	1.9	.2	.7	1.
28.0				3.7		11.1	8.9	2.3	9.4	3.
.2				.8		1.2	1.7	.9	.9	.
1.7				3.5	Debt/Worth	3.4	4.9	2.0	2.8	3.
74.0				45.4		26.4	-210.9	4.5	133.9	45.
18.8				34.0		10.3	17.2	16.7	26.5	34.
(15) 6.7				(29) 6.7	% Profit Before Taxes/ Tangible Net Worth	(91) .0	(65) 4.2	(57) 3.3	(37) 11.4	(29) 6.
.2				1.7		-7.5	-7.1	-5.8	-1.5	1.
7.3				5.1		3.1	3.5	4.3	7.8	5.
2.6				2.5	% Profit Before Taxes/ Total Assets	.0	.3	1.4	2.2	2.
.0				.2		-2.7	-1.6	-1.2	.0	.
2.6				1.2		1.3	1.7	1.0	1.2	1.
(11) 10.5				(21) 10.5	% Depr., Dep., Amort./ Revenues	(68) 7.5	(58) 12.0	(38) 2.2	(31) 6.7	(21) 10.
18.9				21.8		19.9	18.8	10.8	19.7	21.
						.8	.4	.6	1.2	
					% Officers', Directors' Owners' Comp/Revenues	(24) 3.3	(15) 2.9	(15) 3.0	(10) 3.9	
						6.4	5.3	5.8	13.8	
5176M	39037M	133041M	156707M	333961M	Contract Revenues ($)	849933M	709997M	547570M	425748M	33396
36242M	177470M	529157M	99292M	842161M	Total Assets ($)	5824551M	5213510M	1754600M	1155795M	84216

M = $ thousand MM = $ million

See Pages 9 through 22 for Explanation of Ratios and Data

Current Data Sorted by Revenue | **Comparative Historical Data**

					Type of Statement					
2	6	20	10	38	Unqualified	47	44	41	32	38
1	14	13		28	Reviewed	37	43	47	30	28
	3	1		4	Compiled	8	5	4	2	4
	3		1	4	Tax Returns	9	8	6	7	4
1	2	7	11	21	Other	19	95	115	81	21
17 (4/1-9/30/13)		78 (10/1/13-3/31/14)				4/1/09-3/31/10	4/1/10-3/31/11	4/1/11-3/31/12	4/1/12-3/31/13	4/1/13-3/31/14
0-1MM	1-10MM	10-50MM	50 & OVER	ALL		ALL	ALL	ALL	ALL	ALL
4	28	41	22	95	NUMBER OF STATEMENTS	120	195	213	152	95
%	%	%	%	%	ASSETS	%	%	%	%	%
	16.6	16.1	15.4	15.6	Cash & Equivalents	17.9	20.3	18.1	19.1	15.6
	32.6	29.4	25.7	29.8	A/R - Progress Billings	27.4	15.6	29.9	29.7	29.8
	.2	1.5	.4	.8	A/R - Current Retention	2.1	13.9	3.0	2.6	.8
	1.9	2.5	4.2	2.7	Inventory	3.2	3.9	4.0	4.0	2.7
	3.4	5.5	5.2	4.7	Cost & Est. Earnings In Excess Billings	2.3	4.2	4.4	4.4	4.7
	3.7	2.8	7.1	4.0	All Other Current	4.2	4.2	3.3	2.5	4.0
	58.4	58.0	58.1	57.6	Total Current	57.1	62.1	62.8	62.3	57.6
	33.3	33.5	33.6	33.9	Fixed Assets (net)	34.0	30.8	29.2	29.1	33.9
	.5	3.4	1.7	2.0	Joint Ventures & Investments	.9	.4	.5	.5	2.0
	.3	.6	1.6	.8	Intangibles (net)	1.4	.9	1.2	1.3	.8
	7.5	4.5	5.0	5.8	All Other Non-Current	6.7	5.7	6.2	6.8	5.8
	100.0	100.0	100.0	100.0	Total	100.0	100.0	100.0	100.0	100.0
					LIABILITIES					
	13.7	1.9	2.0	6.0	Notes Payable-Short Term	5.6	3.6	5.6	5.8	6.0
	11.9	17.5	18.2	15.7	A/P - Trade	16.1	15.1	16.5	16.9	15.7
	.2	.8	.4	.5	A/P - Retention	.6	.5	.7	.6	.5
	3.2	5.6	4.5	4.4	Billings in Excess of Costs & Est. Earnings	3.9	4.2	4.5	4.2	4.4
	.1	.0	.0	.0	Income Taxes Payable	.2	.3	.2	.1	.0
	7.5	3.8	4.1	4.9	Cur. Mat.-L/T/D	5.1	4.1	3.7	4.0	4.9
	5.2	4.5	6.5	5.1	All Other Current	6.5	5.5	5.3	5.5	5.1
	41.8	34.0	35.7	36.6	Total Current	37.9	33.2	36.5	37.0	36.6
	12.3	15.6	17.1	14.7	Long-Term Debt	14.1	12.4	11.1	13.2	14.7
	1.7	.9	.5	1.0	Deferred Taxes	1.1	1.0	1.3	1.0	1.0
	1.2	1.2	1.4	1.3	All Other Non-Current	1.6	2.7	2.7	2.9	1.3
	42.9	48.2	45.2	46.4	Net Worth	45.4	50.7	48.3	45.8	46.4
	100.0	100.0	100.0	100.0	Total Liabilties & Net Worth	100.0	100.0	100.0	100.0	100.0
					INCOME DATA					
	100.0	100.0	100.0	100.0	Contract Revenues	100.0	100.0	100.0	100.0	100.0
	21.5	14.4	15.9	17.3	Gross Profit	21.3	18.6	15.4	16.1	17.3
	18.7	10.6	11.1	13.6	Operating Expenses	18.8	15.5	13.2	13.8	13.6
	2.8	3.8	4.8	3.7	Operating Profit	2.5	3.2	2.2	2.3	3.7
	-.5	.4	.3	.1	All Other Expenses (net)	.5	-.1	-.1	-.1	.1
	3.2	3.4	4.5	3.6	Profit Before Taxes	2.0	3.2	2.3	2.4	3.6
					RATIOS					
	2.6	2.2	2.0	2.1		2.2	2.8	2.4	2.6	2.1
	1.7	1.6	1.6	1.6	Current	1.6	1.8	1.7	1.6	1.6
	.9	1.3	1.2	1.2		1.1	1.4	1.3	1.3	1.2
	4.8	2.8	2.1	3.4		4.0	3.5	3.5	3.4	3.4
	(26) 2.9	1.9	(21) 1.4	(92) 2.0	Receivables/Payables	(117) 1.8	(193) 2.0	(212) 1.8	1.8	(92) 2.0
	1.8	1.2	1.1	1.3		1.3	1.2	1.3	1.3	1.3
	28 13.0	37 9.9	27 13.5	33 11.2		27 13.7	25 14.8	33 10.9	35 10.5	33 11.2
	50 7.3	62 5.9	45 8.1	58 6.3	Revenues/Receivables	45 8.1	47 7.8	51 7.2	52 7.0	58 6.3
	79 4.6	89 4.1	69 5.3	83 4.4		67 5.4	71 5.2	73 5.0	73 5.0	83 4.4
	7 52.3	17 21.4	20 18.7	16 23.2		13 29.1	13 28.2	14 25.6	17 21.8	16 23.2
	22 16.9	40 9.2	30 12.1	29 12.7	Cost of Revenues/Payables	27 13.4	25 14.7	32 11.5	33 11.2	29 12.7
	34 10.6	52 7.0	54 6.7	46 7.9		52 7.1	43 8.5	48 7.6	48 7.6	46 7.9
	5.7	5.6	5.3	5.7		6.0	4.8	5.2	5.4	5.7
	8.3	11.1	10.4	9.7	Revenues/Working Capital	12.1	8.3	9.1	9.6	9.7
	-48.6	19.3	28.0	27.4		32.4	15.0	16.6	18.2	27.4
	24.2	24.4	22.3	22.2		15.1	19.7	17.8	18.0	22.2
	(27) 6.5	(38) 3.1	(21) 7.4	(87) 5.0	EBIT/Interest	(108) 4.5	(173) 5.8	(190) 3.9	(138) 3.7	(87) 5.0
	1.1	1.3	1.3	1.1		-.8	1.5	.5	.7	1.1
	7.5			5.4		4.6	4.0	5.4	3.4	5.4
	(10) 2.1			(23) 1.8	Net Profit + Depr., Dep., Amort./Cur. Mat. L/T/D	(26) 2.1	(43) 2.5	(47) 2.4	(44) 1.7	(23) 1.8
	.7			1.0		.7	1.3	1.1	.9	1.0
	.4	.4	.5	.4		.4	.3	.4	.4	.4
	.7	.7	.8	.7	Fixed/Worth	.7	.7	.6	.6	.7
	1.1	1.2	1.5	1.3		1.4	1.0	.9	1.1	1.3
	.6	.5	.6	.6		.6	.5	.6	.6	.6
	.9	1.3	1.4	1.3	Debt/Worth	1.3	1.0	1.2	1.3	1.3
	2.5	2.2	3.1	2.5		2.5	2.0	1.9	2.3	2.5
	26.4	23.9	26.3	24.3		32.4	27.9	21.4	23.4	24.3
	(27) 12.6	9.6	14.6	(94) 11.7	% Profit Before Taxes/ Tangible Net Worth	(114) 12.0	(192) 11.1	(212) 9.3	(148) 9.9	(94) 11.7
	2.1	.9	2.4	1.3		-1.8	2.4	-.8	.2	1.3
	15.3	11.4	11.4	12.1		13.0	12.8	9.7	10.2	12.1
	5.9	3.7	4.9	4.6	% Profit Before Taxes/ Total Assets	5.7	5.5	4.2	3.8	4.6
	.6	.4	1.1	.3		-1.7	.9	-.3	.0	.3
	1.4	1.6	1.0	1.4		1.7	1.9	1.9	1.7	1.4
	(27) 2.3	(39) 2.6	(19) 2.9	(86) 2.5	% Depr., Dep., Amort./ Revenues	(108) 3.5	(177) 3.1	(186) 2.9	(135) 2.7	(86) 2.5
	3.7	4.2	3.3	4.0		5.5	4.7	4.3	4.1	4.0
	1.2	.5		.6		1.2	1.3	1.1	1.0	.6
	(15) 2.3	(10) .9		(30) 1.2	% Officers', Directors' Owners' Comp/Revenues	(62) 2.2	(74) 2.9	(73) 1.9	(60) 1.8	(30) 1.2
	4.7	1.6		2.6		5.9	4.8	3.4	3.6	2.6
1597M	160681M	1137509M	17186180M	18485967M	Contract Revenues ($)	24664202M	29688922M	25568948M	21037998M	18485967M
1440M	76423M	799202M	10088568M	10965633M	Total Assets ($)	22560228M	14849751M	14267143M	12562428M	10965633M

M = $ thousand MM = $ million

See Pages 9 through 22 for Explanation of Ratios and Data

Current Data Sorted by Revenue / Comparative Historical Data

	0-1MM	1-10MM	10-50MM	50 & OVER	ALL	4/1/09-3/31/10 ALL	4/1/10-3/31/11 ALL	4/1/11-3/31/12 ALL	4/1/12-3/31/13 ALL	4/1/ 3/31 AL
Type of Statement										
Unqualified		1	6	3	10	12	4	11	12	10
Reviewed		4	6		10	20	21	25	15	10
Compiled		2			2	2	3	5	5	2
Tax Returns	2	1			3	7	6	7	7	3
Other		4	2		6	14	34	34	21	6
	4 (4/1-9/30/13)		27 (10/1/13-3/31/14)							
NUMBER OF STATEMENTS	2	12	14	3	31	55	68	82	60	3
ASSETS	%	%	%	%	%	%	%	%	%	%
Cash & Equivalents		16.6	17.5		15.5	19.2	20.9	18.1	19.4	15.
A/R - Progress Billings		28.3	43.5		33.0	30.8	17.0	34.3	31.6	33.
A/R - Current Retention		.3	.0		.4	1.6	17.3	2.4	2.1	.
Inventory		1.9	5.2		3.6	1.8	2.0	2.3	5.3	3.
Cost & Est. Earnings In Excess Billings		2.8	5.7		4.3	3.3	4.4	5.4	6.3	4.
All Other Current		6.9	1.2		7.1	3.7	5.4	6.3	3.4	7.
Total Current		56.7	73.2		63.9	60.4	67.0	68.9	68.0	63
Fixed Assets (net)		31.6	20.3		27.0	32.6	24.5	21.1	21.9	27
Joint Ventures & Investments		.0	.2		.1	1.1	.0	.3	.5	
Intangibles (net)		.1	2.4		1.1	.8	1.2	1.8	1.9	1
All Other Non-Current		11.7	3.9		7.9	5.1	7.3	7.9	7.6	7
Total		100.0	100.0		100.0	100.0	100.0	100.0	100.0	100
LIABILITIES										
Notes Payable-Short Term		4.1	7.7		15.0	7.0	10.4	14.6	5.7	15
A/P - Trade		14.3	27.8		20.1	15.8	19.5	21.6	18.9	20
A/P - Retention		.3	.0		.1	.3	1.1	.8	.7	
Billings in Excess of Costs & Est. Earnings		4.5	8.5		7.1	4.7	6.8	6.5	7.6	7
Income Taxes Payable		.1	.0		.0	.2	.2	.7	.8	
Cur. Mat.-L/T/D		3.6	1.9		2.6	5.1	5.7	3.6	4.6	2
All Other Current		4.9	4.6		4.8	6.0	8.5	8.5	7.4	4
Total Current		31.8	50.5		49.6	39.1	52.2	56.3	45.7	49
Long-Term Debt		16.2	7.1		11.9	14.2	14.1	9.9	17.8	11
Deferred Taxes		1.1	1.2		1.0	.9	.8	.8	.6	
All Other Non-Current		2.1	7.1		8.6	4.6	5.7	8.8	4.4	8
Net Worth		48.9	34.1		28.9	41.0	27.1	24.2	31.5	2
Total Liabilties & Net Worth		100.0	100.0		100.0	100.0	100.0	100.0	100.0	10
INCOME DATA										
Contract Revenues		100.0	100.0		100.0	100.0	100.0	100.0	100.0	10
Gross Profit		23.5	14.3		22.4	26.9	19.9	19.0	18.2	2
Operating Expenses		16.4	13.3		19.3	22.7	16.8	16.6	15.8	1
Operating Profit		7.1	1.0		3.2	4.2	3.1	2.4	2.4	
All Other Expenses (net)		-1.0	.6		.2	.8	.3	-.1	-.1	
Profit Before Taxes		8.1	.4		2.9	3.4	2.8	2.5	2.6	
RATIOS										
Current		5.0 1.9 .8	1.6 1.4 1.3		2.1 1.4 1.0	2.2 1.6 1.1	2.6 1.5 1.2	2.0 1.5 1.2	2.5 1.8 1.2	
Receivables/Payables		4.5 (11) 1.5 1.2	2.3 1.7 1.1		2.7 (28) 1.5 1.1	5.3 (52) 2.2 1.2	4.0 (65) 1.6 1.0	3.9 (81) 1.8 1.1	3.0 (58) 1.8 1.2	 (28)
Revenues/Receivables		36 10.0 49 7.4 73 5.0	52 7.0 72 5.1 130 2.8		35 10.3 64 5.7 83 4.4	29 12.5 55 6.6 86 4.3	39 9.4 63 5.8 87 4.2	38 9.7 63 5.8 89 4.1	38 9.5 58 6.3 81 4.5	35 64 83
Cost of Revenues/Payables		17 21.0 26 14.1 58 6.3	35 10.5 58 6.3 74 4.9		22 16.9 41 8.8 63 5.8	7 54.4 29 12.6 52 7.0	20 18.5 38 9.5 63 5.8	22 16.4 38 9.6 68 5.4	20 17.9 35 10.3 53 6.9	22 41 63
Revenues/Working Capital		3.6 6.3 -25.4	5.5 8.6 17.0		5.1 8.6 -582.6	4.7 9.8 90.4	4.5 9.3 28.4	5.6 9.3 24.4	4.3 8.8 26.6	 -5
EBIT/Interest		44.2 (10) 5.7 1.4	13.7 (11) 3.6 -4.9		11.4 (26) 3.6 -.9	24.1 (52) 6.1 -.3	30.4 (63) 5.6 .4	21.8 (70) 5.7 1.1	22.1 (51) 7.7 1.1	 (26)
Net Profit + Depr., Dep., Amort./Cur. Mat. L/T/D						8.9 (13) 3.1 .3	18.9 (14) 4.2 .4	14.3 (20) 4.5 2.6	24.2 (16) 4.6 2.2	
Fixed/Worth		.3 .5 2.7	.1 .5 1.1		.3 .5 1.5	.3 .5 1.6	.3 .5 1.2	.2 .5 1.0	.3 .5 1.0	
Debt/Worth		.2 1.1 6.6	1.2 1.6 2.7		.9 1.6 4.1	.6 1.3 2.8	.9 1.7 4.1	.9 1.9 3.3	.6 1.8 5.2	
% Profit Before Taxes/ Tangible Net Worth		51.6 25.0 5.8	26.8 (13) 11.4 -1.4		38.0 (28) 16.4 2.8	35.0 (51) 16.3 .1	37.5 (61) 18.2 .6	29.2 (75) 13.8 -1.7	36.2 (54) 13.3 1.4	 (28)
% Profit Before Taxes/ Total Assets		29.0 11.4 2.5	7.6 4.1 -2.2		13.4 5.3 -1.8	16.8 5.3 -.6	12.7 4.6 -1.3	11.2 4.0 -.5	15.1 4.3 .1	
% Depr., Dep., Amort./ Revenues		2.6 (11) 3.4 4.8	.4 (13) 1.8 2.9		1.1 (28) 2.7 4.6	1.0 (48) 2.7 4.9	1.0 (56) 2.4 3.8	.8 (62) 2.2 3.7	.9 (48) 1.8 4.9	 (28)
% Officers', Directors' Owners' Comp/Revenues					1.5 (12) 2.4 6.4	1.7 (21) 4.7 6.2	1.8 (29) 2.8 4.8	1.9 (32) 3.0 4.4	1.5 (25) 2.3 4.6	 (12)
Contract Revenues ($)	1316M	64995M	245698M	719787M	1031796M	1846474M	12648638M	53985295M	50521469M	103
Total Assets ($)	596M	36462M	123822M	432541M	593421M	1677847M	8882264M	36646332M	25191789M	59

M = $ thousand MM = $ million

See Pages 9 through 22 for Explanation of Ratios and Data

Current Data Sorted by Revenue | **Comparative Historical Data**

0-1MM	1-10MM	10-50MM	50 & OVER	ALL		4/1/09-3/31/10 ALL	4/1/10-3/31/11 ALL	4/1/11-3/31/12 ALL	4/1/12-3/31/13 ALL	4/1/13-3/31/14 ALL
					Type of Statement					
		1	1	2	Unqualified	3	2	3	1	2
1	11	1	1	14	Reviewed	25	24	25	18	14
	4	1		5	Compiled	14	9	7	6	5
	9	1		10	Tax Returns	8	11	12	11	10
	1	1		2	Other	15	31	22	15	2
6 (4/1-9/30/13)		27 (10/1/13-3/31/14)								
1	25	5	2	33	**NUMBER OF STATEMENTS**	65	77	69	51	33
%	%	%	%	%	**ASSETS**	%	%	%	%	%
	15.4			13.7	Cash & Equivalents	12.7	9.7	14.6	17.8	13.7
	36.4			40.5	A/R - Progress Billings	38.5	27.5	38.4	40.6	40.5
	1.7			1.3	A/R - Current Retention	1.5	10.8	2.9	3.4	1.3
	2.9			2.3	Inventory	2.6	3.1	3.2	3.4	2.3
	2.3			3.1	Cost & Est. Earnings In Excess Billings	1.8	3.7	3.7	3.1	3.1
	5.2			7.0	All Other Current	4.9	4.3	5.6	3.6	7.0
	64.0			68.0	Total Current	62.0	59.0	68.4	71.9	68.0
	28.5			25.7	Fixed Assets (net)	27.5	32.0	23.0	21.4	25.7
	2.0			1.5	Joint Ventures & Investments	.1	.1	.5	1.9	1.5
	1.3			1.0	Intangibles (net)	2.5	1.5	3.1	.5	1.0
	4.3			3.7	All Other Non-Current	8.0	7.4	5.0	4.3	3.7
	100.0			100.0	Total	100.0	100.0	100.0	100.0	100.0
					LIABILITIES					
	7.5			9.6	Notes Payable-Short Term	12.0	14.9	15.4	16.0	9.6
	14.1			17.5	A/P - Trade	16.3	16.2	21.2	18.8	17.5
	.0			.0	A/P - Retention	.1	.2	.6	.4	.0
	1.9			3.5	Billings in Excess of Costs & Est. Earnings	3.1	3.3	3.1	3.8	3.5
	.2			.1	Income Taxes Payable	.5	.0	.2	.1	.1
	4.0			3.8	Cur. Mat.-L/T/D	4.4	5.5	3.6	2.9	3.8
	10.4			10.0	All Other Current	6.6	7.1	8.5	7.7	10.0
	38.1			44.6	Total Current	42.8	47.3	52.5	49.8	44.6
	15.2			13.3	Long-Term Debt	14.1	13.5	12.1	11.2	13.3
	.9			.8	Deferred Taxes	.7	1.3	.6	.2	.8
	1.6			2.4	All Other Non-Current	5.7	8.1	4.6	6.0	2.4
	44.3			38.8	Net Worth	36.7	29.8	30.2	32.7	38.8
	100.0			100.0	Total Liabilties & Net Worth	100.0	100.0	100.0	100.0	100.0
					INCOME DATA					
	100.0			100.0	Contract Revenues	100.0	100.0	100.0	100.0	100.0
	30.5			25.8	Gross Profit	25.0	23.2	20.9	22.6	25.8
	25.4			21.3	Operating Expenses	24.6	23.7	20.1	18.5	21.3
	5.1			4.5	Operating Profit	.4	-.5	.7	4.1	4.5
	-.6			-.6	All Other Expenses (net)	.3	1.0	.5	.3	-.6
	5.8			5.1	Profit Before Taxes	.1	-1.5	.2	3.8	5.1
					RATIOS					
	3.5			2.9		2.9	2.4	2.3	3.3	2.9
	1.9			1.7	Current	1.7	1.5	1.4	1.7	1.7
	1.2			1.1		1.0	1.0	1.0	1.2	1.1
	30.5			7.1		7.8	5.5	2.9	4.5	7.1
	(22) 3.8			(30) 2.6	Receivables/Payables	(64) 3.2	(72) 2.6	(64) 2.0	(48) 2.3	(30) 2.6
	1.8			1.5		1.8	1.6	1.2	1.6	1.5
	18 20.3			29 12.6		31 11.7	31 11.9	34 10.7	31 11.9	29 12.6
	61 6.0			63 5.8	Revenues/Receivables	60 6.1	54 6.8	64 5.7	65 5.6	63 5.8
	87 4.2			89 4.1		83 4.4	85 4.3	99 3.7	87 4.2	89 4.1
	0 UND			2 176.5		10 35.0	10 37.0	9 40.2	16 23.1	2 176.5
	14 26.7			20 17.9	Cost of Revenues/Payables	24 14.9	26 14.2	33 11.1	31 11.9	20 17.9
	47 7.7			47 7.7		48 7.6	49 7.5	62 5.9	46 8.0	47 7.7
	5.8			5.9		5.9	6.6	6.5	4.9	5.9
	9.2			10.7	Revenues/Working Capital	10.6	12.5	13.9	9.9	10.7
	41.7			65.4		237.7	-188.4	UND	24.2	65.4
	50.4			47.1		13.2	6.6	15.5	42.6	47.1
	(24) 10.5			(29) 9.3	EBIT/Interest	(57) 2.3	(72) 1.8	(65) 2.6	(45) 4.1	(29) 9.3
	3.2			2.7		-5.6	-4.7	-2.5	-1.2	2.7
						4.6	7.4			
					Net Profit + Depr., Dep., Amort./Cur. Mat. L/T/D	(16) 2.7	(14) 3.4			
						.6	1.2			
	.2			.2		.3	.4	.2	.1	.2
	.5			.7	Fixed/Worth	.6	1.0	.5	.4	.7
	2.5			2.5		1.3	2.2	2.1	.9	2.5
	.4			.5		.6	.6	.7	.5	.5
	1.2			1.6	Debt/Worth	1.3	1.8	1.6	1.0	1.6
	4.5			5.8		3.3	4.4	6.2	3.7	5.8
	67.8			50.1		37.1	28.3	29.3	40.9	50.1
	(22) 27.1			(29) 24.6	% Profit Before Taxes/ Tangible Net Worth	(57) 12.4	(64) 3.6	(57) 7.1	(45) 14.3	(29) 24.6
	7.4			6.5		-17.6	-9.4	-3.8	-4.5	6.5
	26.7			22.5		16.8	7.8	12.5	19.2	22.5
	9.9			9.6	% Profit Before Taxes/ Total Assets	4.0	2.0	2.2	8.2	9.6
	4.4			2.1		-8.5	-6.9	-3.0	-1.0	2.1
	1.0			.5		1.4	1.8	.8	.6	.5
	(22) 1.8			(28) 1.5	% Depr., Dep., Amort./ Revenues	(60) 2.8	(66) 2.5	(58) 2.3	(41) 1.9	(28) 1.5
	5.5			4.0		4.9	4.3	4.3	3.9	4.0
	1.9			1.6		1.9	1.9	1.9	2.1	1.6
	(15) 3.4			(18) 3.3	% Officers', Directors' Owners' Comp/Revenues	(38) 4.2	(39) 3.2	(36) 3.6	(29) 4.3	(18) 3.3
	6.3			6.3		8.4	7.7	8.6	7.6	6.3
30M	114671M	115122M	32366020M	32595843M	Contract Revenues ($)	24751762M	32191425M	26899826M	28748871M	32595843M
14M	43220M	39003M	10695490M	10777727M	Total Assets ($)	22364101M	12864213M	9595796M	12704539M	10777727M

M = $ thousand MM = $ million

See Pages 9 through 22 for Explanation of Ratios and Data

Current Data Sorted by Revenue						Comparative Historical Data				
					Type of Statement					
		1		1	Unqualified	6	3	3	1	1
1	4	5		10	Reviewed	15	23	15	17	10
1	2	1		4	Compiled	4	5	5	5	4
1	1	2		4	Tax Returns	3	1	2	3	4
	3	1	1	5	Other	8	18	16	5	5
2 (4/1-9/30/13)		22 (10/1/13-3/31/14)				4/1/09-3/31/10	4/1/10-3/31/11	4/1/11-3/31/12	4/1/12-3/31/13	4/1/13-3/31/14
0-1MM	1-10MM	10-50MM	50 & OVER	ALL		ALL	ALL	ALL	ALL	ALL
3	10	10	1	24	**NUMBER OF STATEMENTS**	36	50	41	31	24
%	%	%	%	%	**ASSETS**	%	%	%	%	%
	16.5	8.6		11.1	Cash & Equivalents	25.3	16.7	9.8	17.2	11.1
	37.8	49.0		44.8	A/R - Progress Billings	35.8	25.2	37.2	43.0	44.8
	.5	1.3		.7	A/R - Current Retention	2.7	19.6	7.0	2.7	.7
	2.8	13.5		7.9	Inventory	1.7	2.9	3.4	2.5	7.9
	2.3	1.5		2.1	Cost & Est. Earnings In Excess Billings	2.4	3.5	5.2	3.6	2.1
	9.9	4.9		6.2	All Other Current	4.6	3.4	9.0	8.5	6.2
	69.9	78.7		72.8	Total Current	72.5	71.4	71.6	77.4	72.8
	16.5	19.4		18.8	Fixed Assets (net)	19.4	18.2	18.2	15.5	18.8
	.0	.0		.0	Joint Ventures & Investments	.3	.2	.1	.0	.0
	.7	.3		.4	Intangibles (net)	.1	1.3	1.5	1.4	.4
	12.9	1.5		7.9	All Other Non-Current	7.7	9.0	8.7	5.7	7.9
	100.0	100.0		100.0	Total	100.0	100.0	100.0	100.0	100.0
					LIABILITIES					
	18.8	11.2		18.6	Notes Payable-Short Term	10.3	11.2	13.1	17.1	18.6
	12.7	24.0		16.9	A/P - Trade	11.4	14.9	17.5	16.9	16.9
	.0	.0		.0	A/P - Retention	1.0	.3	.8	.0	.0
	1.1	4.7		2.5	Billings in Excess of Costs & Est. Earnings	4.1	6.9	5.8	5.1	2.5
	.0	.6		.3	Income Taxes Payable	.0	.2	.0	.0	.3
	1.8	2.9		2.0	Cur. Mat.-L/T/D	3.0	2.1	3.8	2.3	2.0
	8.5	10.5		9.9	All Other Current	5.9	6.3	7.4	9.1	9.9
	42.9	53.8		50.1	Total Current	35.8	41.9	48.4	50.5	50.1
	9.1	9.8		14.5	Long-Term Debt	11.5	11.9	16.7	6.8	14.5
	.0	.2		.1	Deferred Taxes	1.1	.4	.3	.8	.
	.8	1.3		1.0	All Other Non-Current	3.8	11.1	5.9	.8	1.0
	47.2	34.9		34.3	Net Worth	47.7	34.7	28.6	41.1	34.3
	100.0	100.0		100.0	Total Liabilties & Net Worth	100.0	100.0	100.0	100.0	100.
					INCOME DATA					
	100.0	100.0		100.0	Contract Revenues	100.0	100.0	100.0	100.0	100.
	23.8	21.1		22.9	Gross Profit	26.2	17.8	15.7	23.6	22.
	22.5	17.3		20.4	Operating Expenses	22.9	18.9	16.5	17.5	20.
	1.3	3.8		2.5	Operating Profit	3.2	-1.1	-.9	6.2	2.
	.2	-.5		-.1	All Other Expenses (net)	.1	.1	.2	.5	-.
	1.2	4.3		2.6	Profit Before Taxes	3.1	-1.3	-1.0	5.7	2.
					RATIOS					
	4.0	1.8		1.9		4.1	2.5	2.0	2.2	1.
	1.7	1.4		1.7	Current	2.3	1.6	1.5	1.6	1.
	.7	1.2		1.2		1.4	1.3	1.1	1.2	1.
		4.3		7.1		6.6	5.7	4.1	5.1	7.
		2.7		(22) 3.0	Receivables/Payables	(34) 4.1	(48) 3.4	(40) 2.8	(30) 3.4	(22) 3
		1.2		1.5		1.7	2.5	1.6	1.9	1
	0 UND	**20** 17.9		**22** 16.6		**32** 11.6	**58** 6.2	**47** 7.7	**45** 8.2	**22** 16
	64 5.7	**72** 5.1		**68** 5.4	Revenues/Receivables	**57** 6.4	**85** 4.3	**74** 4.9	**68** 5.4	**68** 5
	68 5.4	**83** 4.4		**79** 4.6		**73** 5.0	**108** 3.4	**101** 3.6	**104** 3.5	**79** 4
	0 UND	**22** 16.8		**7** 51.4		**10** 38.1	**17** 21.5	**15** 24.1	**13** 27.1	**7** 51
	15 23.7	**27** 13.3		**25** 14.5	Cost of Revenues/Payables	**21** 17.5	**28** 12.8	**30** 12.2	**26** 14.3	**25** 14
	40 9.2	**36** 10.0		**36** 10.0		**26** 14.1	**46** 8.0	**58** 6.3	**43** 8.5	**36** 10
	3.2	9.4		7.1		3.8	4.3	5.2	7.0	7
	10.9	14.7		10.9	Revenues/Working Capital	5.8	7.2	8.0	11.8	10
	-12.6	19.7		22.0		13.6	15.7	34.0	29.9	22
		103.3		34.4		35.4	8.7	6.5	19.3	34
		23.0		(20) 7.1	EBIT/Interest	(28) 4.4	(42) 2.5	(39) 1.0	(27) 9.4	(20) 7
		3.8		1.5		1.1	-5.0	-13.2	4.3	1
							3.3			
					Net Profit + Depr., Dep., Amort./Cur. Mat. L/T/D		(12) 3.1			
							-.1			
	.1	.1		.1		.1	.1	.2	.2	
	.3	.5		.4	Fixed/Worth	.5	.4	.4	.3	
	1.0	1.5		1.0		.7	1.0	.9	.8	1
	.3	1.2		.9		.4	.7	.9	.7	
	1.2	1.8		1.5	Debt/Worth	.7	1.3	1.4	1.6	1
	3.9	3.7		3.4		1.8	2.2	3.6	3.2	3
		64.6		38.8		42.2	21.8	18.7	52.5	3
		15.8		(22) 15.6	% Profit Before Taxes/ Tangible Net Worth	(34) 12.4	(45) 5.5	(37) 4.6	(30) 29.2	(22) 1
		11.8		.2		.8	-11.1	-20.8	8.1	
	8.0	28.5		12.0		28.2	8.5	8.1	19.1	1
	4.3	4.5		4.5	% Profit Before Taxes/ Total Assets	5.0	1.9	.6	9.9	
	-.1	2.7		.0		.1	-8.7	-9.9	3.9	
				.6		.5	1.1	.9	.4	
				(20) .9	% Depr., Dep., Amort./ Revenues	(28) 1.6	(42) 1.6	(35) 1.6	(28) 1.0	(20)
				1.7		2.7	3.2	2.4	1.7	
				2.0		1.0	2.6	1.2	2.1	
				(13) 4.8	% Officers', Directors' Owners' Comp/Revenues	(19) 4.2	(18) 5.7	(18) 1.8	(15) 4.9	(13)
				9.5		13.5	8.8	4.0	9.5	
1868M	**56064M**	**208740M**	**187875M**	**454547M**	Contract Revenues ($)	**35222235M**	**8630796M**	**1621816M**	**398955M**	**454**
383M	**24497M**	**74154M**	**92013M**	**191047M**	Total Assets ($)	**21872885M**	**6164336M**	**1102333M**	**188751M**	**191**

M = $ thousand MM = $ million

See Pages 9 through 22 for Explanation of Ratios and Data

Current Data Sorted by Revenue | **Comparative Historical Data**

0-1MM	1-10MM	10-50MM	50 & OVER	ALL	Type of Statement	4/1/09-3/31/10 ALL	4/1/10-3/31/11 ALL	4/1/11-3/31/12 ALL	4/1/12-3/31/13 ALL	4/1/13-3/31/14 ALL
					Unqualified	1	1	2		
	6	4		10	Reviewed	12	15	18	15	10
	1			1	Compiled	3		1		1
1	3			4	Tax Returns	2	2	3	3	4
	4	1		5	Other	2	5	5	4	5
	6 (4/1-9/30/13)	14 (10/1/13-3/31/14)								
1	14	5		20	NUMBER OF STATEMENTS	20	23	29	22	20
%	%	%	%	%	**ASSETS**	%	%	%	%	%
	9.3		DATA NOT AVAILABLE	7.9	Cash & Equivalents	25.7	19.7	23.4	15.0	7.9
	56.8			57.8	A/R - Progress Billings	42.8	26.6	37.4	50.7	57.8
	1.3			1.0	A/R - Current Retention	3.1	19.4	2.8	2.2	1.0
	8.2			7.7	Inventory	3.2	6.6	4.3	4.7	7.7
	4.8			5.1	Cost & Est. Earnings In Excess Billings	4.3	4.0	5.1	5.3	5.1
	4.4			5.9	All Other Current	7.9	3.8	6.3	2.7	5.9
	84.7			85.4	Total Current	87.0	80.0	79.4	80.6	85.4
	9.3			9.3	Fixed Assets (net)	6.9	12.9	13.0	9.7	9.3
	.0			.0	Joint Ventures & Investments	1.2	1.4	.0	.0	.0
	4.6			3.3	Intangibles (net)	.2	.8	.6	6.1	3.3
	1.4			2.0	All Other Non-Current	4.7	4.8	7.0	3.7	2.0
	100.0			100.0	Total	100.0	100.0	100.0	100.0	100.0
					LIABILITIES					
	7.0			10.9	Notes Payable-Short Term	7.6	5.2	9.3	11.4	10.9
	23.6			24.5	A/P - Trade	13.3	14.8	12.9	15.4	24.5
	.0			.0	A/P - Retention	.1	.2	.1	.1	.0
	5.2			4.5	Billings in Excess of Costs & Est. Earnings	7.5	5.6	4.6	5.0	4.5
	.1			.1	Income Taxes Payable	.7	1.6	.7	.5	.1
	2.5			2.6	Cur. Mat.-L/T/D	1.1	3.5	1.0	1.5	2.6
	14.3			12.8	All Other Current	7.5	7.7	6.4	7.5	12.8
	52.7			55.4	Total Current	37.9	38.5	34.9	41.4	55.4
	13.9			11.2	Long-Term Debt	3.1	6.2	5.8	7.0	11.2
	.2			.1	Deferred Taxes	.2	.3	1.1	.2	.1
	6.5			4.9	All Other Non-Current	5.2	2.4	1.0	4.5	4.9
	26.7			28.5	Net Worth	53.6	52.5	57.2	46.9	28.5
	100.0			100.0	Total Liabilties & Net Worth	100.0	100.0	100.0	100.0	100.0
					INCOME DATA					
	100.0			100.0	Contract Revenues	100.0	100.0	100.0	100.0	100.0
	29.7			26.8	Gross Profit	30.0	28.9	32.9	30.5	26.8
	26.8			24.0	Operating Expenses	22.7	25.6	31.1	29.1	24.0
	2.9			2.8	Operating Profit	7.3	3.3	1.8	1.3	2.8
	.5			.4	All Other Expenses (net)	.1	.6	.1	.1	.4
	2.4			2.4	Profit Before Taxes	7.3	2.7	1.7	1.2	2.4
					RATIOS					
	4.0			3.6	Current	3.9	4.2	4.2	3.1	3.6
	2.0			1.8		2.2	2.3	3.1	2.4	1.8
	1.3			1.2		1.7	1.2	1.6	1.8	1.2
	5.8			4.8	Receivables/Payables	4.3	4.6	6.6	5.9	4.8
	(13) 2.6			(19) 2.5		3.5	3.4	(28) 3.4	(21) 3.7	(19) 2.5
	2.1			2.0		2.0	2.1	1.9	2.7	2.0
	54 6.7			57 6.4	Revenues/Receivables	31 11.7	62 5.9	41 8.8	61 6.0	57 6.4
	70 5.2			74 4.9		56 6.5	78 4.7	72 5.1	85 4.3	74 4.9
	83 4.4			87 4.2		74 4.9	89 4.1	104 3.5	104 3.5	87 4.2
	16 22.7			22 16.8	Cost of Revenues/Payables	17 21.4	16 22.2	13 28.9	17 21.0	22 16.8
	28 13.2			35 10.5		24 15.3	28 13.1	26 14.2	35 10.5	35 10.5
	45 8.2			53 6.9		28 13.2	40 9.1	49 7.5	46 7.9	53 6.9
	4.3			4.6	Revenues/Working Capital	4.2	4.0	2.9	3.7	4.6
	6.2			6.7		8.0	6.0	4.4	5.5	6.7
	NM			14.8		9.9	14.1	7.5	7.6	14.8
	26.3			19.5	EBIT/Interest	95.1	21.3	33.8	37.8	19.5
	5.2			5.4		(17) 25.2	(17) 1.7	(22) 3.1	(17) 4.9	5.4
	-.9			1.5		6.4	-11.6	-9.2	-2.0	1.5
					Net Profit + Depr., Dep., Amort./Cur. Mat. L/T/D					
	.1			.1	Fixed/Worth	.0	.1	.1	.1	.1
	.2			.2		.1	.2	.2	.1	.2
	NM			.9		.2	.5	.4	.4	.9
	.9			.9	Debt/Worth	.4	.3	.3	.4	.9
	1.3			1.5		1.0	.7	.7	.8	1.5
	NM			3.9		1.1	1.7	1.6	2.2	3.9
	52.6			36.6	% Profit Before Taxes/ Tangible Net Worth	69.7	41.7	18.7	36.0	36.6
	(11) 15.0			(16) 11.4		30.4	(22) 10.4	6.9	(20) 5.4	(16) 11.4
	-.1			6.4		11.4	-14.5	-12.4	.8	6.4
	28.2			14.0	% Profit Before Taxes/ Total Assets	28.9	15.1	10.6	11.6	14.0
	4.4			5.2		13.8	6.1	3.9	3.0	5.2
	-1.4			.5		5.8	-8.3	-5.2	-3.2	.5
				.5	% Depr., Dep., Amort./ Revenues	.4	.5	.7	.6	.5
				(13) .7		(16) .6	(20) 1.2	(24) 1.2	(18) .8	(13) .7
				.8		1.2	1.9	1.8	1.6	.8
	1.6			1.5	% Officers', Directors' Owners' Comp/Revenues	1.7	2.1	1.6	2.0	1.5
	(10) 3.3			(12) 2.6		(12) 5.0	(10) 3.5	(16) 3.5	(10) 2.7	(12) 2.6
	7.0			5.9		12.1	7.3	7.4	5.4	5.9
962M	81253M	96747M		178962M	Contract Revenues ($)	361448M	350593M	847155M	335624M	178962M
379M	26326M	38511M		65216M	Total Assets ($)	194199M	186308M	400310M	164551M	65216M

M = $ thousand MM = $ million

See Pages 9 through 22 for Explanation of Ratios and Data

Current Data Sorted by Revenue						Comparative Historical Data				
					Type of Statement					
		1		1	Unqualified	2	1	1		1
	9	8		17	Reviewed	27	31	37	31	17
1	4			5	Compiled	9	11	7	8	5
1	4			5	Tax Returns	7	9	11	7	5
	2			2	Other	11	15	23	9	2
1 (4/1-9/30/13)		29 (10/1/13-3/31/14)				4/1/09-3/31/10	4/1/10-3/31/11	4/1/11-3/31/12	4/1/12-3/31/13	4/1/1 3/31/
0-1MM	1-10MM	10-50MM	50 & OVER	ALL		ALL	ALL	ALL	ALL	ALL
2	19	9		30	**NUMBER OF STATEMENTS**	56	67	79	55	30
%	%	%	%	%	**ASSETS**	%	%	%	%	%
	10.9		D A T A N O T A V A I L A B L E	13.4	Cash & Equivalents	13.9	16.6	14.9	17.8	13.4
	47.9			49.5	A/R - Progress Billings	41.4	27.7	40.4	46.8	49.5
	.5			1.1	A/R - Current Retention	1.7	19.6	2.7	2.1	1.1
	6.9			5.8	Inventory	8.5	6.7	7.8	4.2	5.8
	4.5			4.3	Cost & Est. Earnings In Excess Billings	3.2	3.9	5.7	4.2	4.3
	4.3			3.7	All Other Current	3.5	4.0	4.2	4.7	3.7
	75.1			77.8	Total Current	72.2	78.5	75.7	79.8	77.8
	14.3			13.4	Fixed Assets (net)	20.7	15.8	18.3	16.0	13.4
	.0			.7	Joint Ventures & Investments	.1	.0	.2	.0	.7
	3.0			2.1	Intangibles (net)	1.7	.7	.5	.1	2.1
	7.6			6.0	All Other Non-Current	5.3	5.0	5.2	4.2	6.0
	100.0			100.0	Total	100.0	100.0	100.0	100.0	100.0
					LIABILITIES					
	7.7			7.8	Notes Payable-Short Term	10.1	14.0	10.4	10.0	7.8
	20.8			18.1	A/P - Trade	19.1	24.6	21.4	19.9	18.1
	.0			.0	A/P - Retention	.2	.0	.3	.0	.0
	4.5			4.5	Billings in Excess of Costs & Est. Earnings	4.0	5.6	5.4	5.9	4.5
	.0			.0	Income Taxes Payable	.1	.2	.1	.3	.0
	8.0			6.2	Cur. Mat.-L/T/D	3.0	7.2	3.4	3.2	6.2
	14.7			12.5	All Other Current	6.6	10.3	7.7	13.7	12.5
	55.7			49.1	Total Current	43.0	62.0	48.8	52.9	49.1
	14.1			10.8	Long-Term Debt	10.2	10.8	10.0	8.4	10.8
	.0			.0	Deferred Taxes	1.4	.4	.4	.2	.0
	2.6			4.4	All Other Non-Current	4.0	4.4	9.2	5.0	4.4
	27.6			35.7	Net Worth	41.5	22.5	31.5	33.5	35.7
	100.0			100.0	Total Liabilties & Net Worth	100.0	100.0	100.0	100.0	100.0
					INCOME DATA					
	100.0			100.0	Contract Revenues	100.0	100.0	100.0	100.0	100.0
	20.7			23.0	Gross Profit	26.9	25.7	26.1	25.6	23.0
	17.5			18.6	Operating Expenses	25.3	23.2	23.1	21.1	18.6
	3.2			4.4	Operating Profit	1.5	2.5	3.1	4.5	4.4
	.5			.2	All Other Expenses (net)	.0	.0	.3	.3	.2
	2.8			4.2	Profit Before Taxes	1.5	2.5	2.8	4.2	4.2
					RATIOS					
	2.7			3.1		2.4	2.9	2.7	2.6	3.1
	1.8			1.8	Current	1.7	1.7	1.7	1.7	1.8
	.9			1.2		1.3	1.1	1.1	1.3	1.2
	7.2			7.6		4.6	3.7	3.5	5.1	7.6
	(18) 2.3			(28) 3.4	Receivables/Payables	(55) 2.2	(64) 2.3	(73) 2.2	(53) 2.7	(28) 3.4
	1.7			1.9		1.4	1.7	1.5	2.0	1.9
	32 11.5			**36** 10.2		**33** 11.1	**30** 12.2	**38** 9.6	**35** 10.3	**36** 10.2
	60 6.1			**60** 6.1	Revenues/Receivables	**54** 6.7	**53** 6.9	**55** 6.6	**55** 6.6	**60** 6.1
	74 4.9			**74** 4.9		**77** 4.8	**83** 4.4	**73** 5.0	**70** 5.2	**74** 4.9
	6 56.7			**7** 51.3		**15** 25.0	**17** 21.3	**17** 21.4	**9** 41.1	**7** 51.3
	26 13.8			**22** 16.3	Cost of Revenues/Payables	**29** 12.6	**33** 11.1	**31** 11.6	**26** 14.0	**22** 16.3
	50 7.3			**39** 9.3		**52** 7.0	**50** 7.3	**49** 7.5	**43** 8.5	**39** 9.3
	7.1			6.8		7.1	6.1	6.0	6.0	6.8
	10.5			9.8	Revenues/Working Capital	11.5	12.6	11.9	9.6	9.8
	-34.3			21.5		20.5	32.7	31.2	30.3	21.5
	35.7			44.7		18.3	47.4	13.2	25.8	44.7
	(18) 7.4			(28) 15.3	EBIT/Interest	(48) 4.6	(62) 3.7	(69) 5.1	(45) 8.6	(28) 15.3
	2.5			3.1		-.7	-3.4	1.1	3.5	3.1
						10.3	2.4	4.0	9.5	
					Net Profit + Depr., Dep., Amort./Cur. Mat. L/T/D	(14) 2.4	(10) 1.1	(15) 2.3	(18) 4.2	
						.7	-5.5	1.0	1.5	
	.2			.1		.2	.1	.2	.1	.1
	.2			.2	Fixed/Worth	.4	.5	.4	.2	.2
	4.3			.7		1.2	.9	1.0	.8	.7
	.9			.8		.5	.6	.7	.7	.8
	1.4			1.1	Debt/Worth	1.6	1.5	1.8	1.3	1.1
	19.6			7.5		3.4	3.9	4.6	3.3	7.5
	48.2			73.7		37.6	34.0	45.2	58.7	73.7
	(15) 26.8			(26) 30.6	% Profit Before Taxes/ Tangible Net Worth	(53) 6.3	(56) 12.3	(70) 14.9	(50) 28.5	(26) 30.6
	10.9			10.7		-11.0	-3.7	3.4	10.7	10.7
	15.6			22.9		22.8	22.3	18.6	22.5	22.9
	7.6			12.9	% Profit Before Taxes/ Total Assets	3.5	5.3	4.1	10.8	12.9
	2.4			3.5		-5.6	-3.6	.5	3.6	3.5
	.4			.4		.6	.7	.7	.5	.4
	(16) .9			(25) .9	% Depr., Dep., Amort./ Revenues	(50) 1.6	(58) 1.3	(67) 1.1	(50) 1.0	(25) .9
	1.7			1.7		2.4	2.3	1.8	1.5	1.7
				2.1		1.9	2.5	2.4	2.3	2.1
				(13) 3.4	% Officers', Directors' Owners' Comp/Revenues	(37) 3.6	(39) 3.5	(40) 4.2	(27) 3.4	(13) 3.4
				4.6		5.2	6.2	6.4	6.4	4.6
1535M	118700M	194430M		314665M	Contract Revenues ($)	631640M	1261427M	4523350M	1009994M	31466
436M	39468M	55118M		95022M	Total Assets ($)	208200M	533265M	1853400M	435433M	9502

M = $ thousand MM = $ million

See Pages 9 through 22 for Explanation of Ratios and Data

Current Data Sorted by Revenue						Comparative Historical Data				
					Type of Statement					
	5	6	4	15	Unqualified	17	14	13	6	15
1	36	25	3	65	Reviewed	80	130	113	97	65
2	7	1	1	11	Compiled	29	28	30	19	11
4	10		1	15	Tax Returns	30	23	23	22	15
2	13	2	2	19	Other	35	63	66	58	19
22 (4/1-9/30/13)		103 (10/1/13-3/31/14)				4/1/09-3/31/10	4/1/10-3/31/11	4/1/11-3/31/12	4/1/12-3/31/13	4/1/13-3/31/14
0-1MM	1-10MM	10-50MM	50 & OVER	ALL		ALL	ALL	ALL	ALL	ALL
9	71	34	11	125	NUMBER OF STATEMENTS	191	258	245	202	125
%	%	%	%	%	**ASSETS**	%	%	%	%	%
	15.0	14.6	10.2	13.8	Cash & Equivalents	17.3	16.2	14.1	15.5	13.8
	43.5	48.0	47.7	45.1	A/R - Progress Billings	40.2	28.3	46.2	46.6	45.1
	.7	1.8	.9	.9	A/R - Current Retention	1.3	16.5	3.0	2.9	.9
	6.7	3.9	4.8	6.4	Inventory	5.8	6.0	5.7	4.9	6.4
	7.0	6.6	3.0	6.1	Cost & Est. Earnings In Excess Billings	4.8	6.3	6.7	6.7	6.1
	4.0	6.3	13.0	5.3	All Other Current	5.7	3.7	4.9	3.8	5.3
	76.9	81.1	79.6	77.7	Total Current	75.0	77.0	80.7	80.4	77.7
	15.0	14.0	9.1	15.1	Fixed Assets (net)	17.2	15.6	13.2	13.1	15.1
	.5	.3	1.1	.5	Joint Ventures & Investments	.7	.5	.3	.2	.5
	1.1	.1	2.4	.9	Intangibles (net)	.7	1.0	1.4	1.9	.9
	6.5	4.5	7.7	5.9	All Other Non-Current	6.4	5.8	4.3	4.3	5.9
	100.0	100.0	100.0	100.0	Total	100.0	100.0	100.0	100.0	100.0
					LIABILITIES					
	11.7	5.2	5.9	11.4	Notes Payable-Short Term	12.0	11.5	12.6	10.3	11.4
	18.5	20.8	21.8	18.8	A/P - Trade	17.5	18.7	19.8	19.3	18.8
	.0	.2	.1	.1	A/P - Retention	.1	.3	.1	.2	.1
	8.3	11.1	7.7	8.4	Billings in Excess of Costs & Est. Earnings	6.5	6.7	8.1	7.9	8.4
	.1	.1	.0	.1	Income Taxes Payable	.3	.7	.4	.3	.1
	2.8	1.6	2.7	2.4	Cur. Mat.-L/T/D	3.7	3.6	2.7	1.8	2.4
	7.1	7.4	17.8	7.8	All Other Current	8.9	8.4	7.1	8.4	7.8
	48.5	46.4	56.0	49.1	Total Current	48.9	50.0	50.8	48.4	49.1
	10.9	7.1	6.8	10.0	Long-Term Debt	11.0	8.1	6.1	6.7	10.0
	1.7	.2	.7	1.1	Deferred Taxes	.6	.5	.4	.4	1.1
	8.6	2.2	4.6	6.0	All Other Non-Current	4.6	4.1	2.4	2.5	6.0
	30.3	44.1	31.9	33.9	Net Worth	34.8	37.4	40.3	42.0	33.9
	100.0	100.0	100.0	100.0	Total Liabilties & Net Worth	100.0	100.0	100.0	100.0	100.0
					INCOME DATA					
	100.0	100.0	100.0	100.0	Contract Revenues	100.0	100.0	100.0	100.0	100.0
	24.8	19.1	21.3	24.6	Gross Profit	30.1	24.8	21.0	21.9	24.6
	22.3	14.7	16.9	21.2	Operating Expenses	28.3	23.9	18.6	18.8	21.2
	2.5	4.3	4.4	3.4	Operating Profit	1.8	.9	2.4	3.1	3.4
	.5	-.1	.5	.4	All Other Expenses (net)	.4	.2	.1	.2	.4
	2.0	4.4	3.9	3.0	Profit Before Taxes	1.4	.7	2.4	2.9	3.0
					RATIOS					
	2.3	2.2	1.6	2.2		2.6	2.5	2.3	2.3	2.2
	1.7	1.7	1.4	1.7	Current	1.7	1.6	1.7	1.6	1.7
	1.2	1.3	1.2	1.2		1.1	1.2	1.3	1.3	1.2
	5.6	5.8	5.2	5.6		4.7	4.4	4.6	4.6	5.6
	(67) 3.0	2.7	3.5	(121) 2.9	Receivables/Payables	(183) 2.7	(248) 2.6	(240) 2.8	(194) 2.7	(121) 2.9
	1.6	1.7	1.4	1.7		1.7	1.6	1.8	1.8	1.7
	39 9.3	**55** 6.6	**34** 10.7	**40** 9.2		**34** 10.7	**43** 8.6	**47** 7.8	**47** 7.8	**40** 9.2
	55 6.6	**65** 5.6	**74** 4.9	**61** 6.0	Revenues/Receivables	**49** 7.4	**60** 6.0	**68** 5.4	**69** 5.3	**61** 6.0
	74 4.9	**83** 4.4	**85** 4.3	**79** 4.6		**72** 5.0	**82** 4.5	**87** 4.2	**89** 4.1	**79** 4.6
	11 34.7	**16** 22.4	**11** 34.1	**12** 30.6		**11** 32.5	**16** 22.3	**17** 21.9	**17** 21.6	**12** 30.6
	24 15.3	**31** 11.6	**26** 14.0	**24** 15.3	Cost of Revenues/Payables	**25** 14.7	**27** 13.5	**30** 12.0	**28** 12.9	**24** 15.3
	42 8.7	**47** 7.8	**46** 8.0	**44** 8.3		**42** 8.8	**45** 8.2	**46** 8.0	**45** 8.2	**44** 8.3
	6.5	5.9	9.4	6.7		5.2	5.1	5.5	5.4	6.7
	10.4	9.3	16.6	10.5	Revenues/Working Capital	10.2	9.5	8.9	8.5	10.5
	24.1	13.0	21.2	22.2		48.5	27.9	19.3	16.7	22.2
	18.1	56.5	72.1	25.0		13.6	11.4	19.3	30.3	25.0
	(62) 7.3	(29) 18.8	(10) 8.3	(109) 9.0	EBIT/Interest	(165) 4.3	(211) 4.3	(203) 5.9	(175) 7.7	(109) 9.0
	1.4	7.4	1.9	1.9		-1.2	-2.4	1.6	1.2	1.9
	5.2			5.9		9.6	7.8	4.8	12.1	5.9
	(12) 3.6			(26) 4.2	Net Profit + Depr., Dep., Amort./Cur. Mat. L/T/D	(35) 2.9	(54) 2.0	(40) 2.6	(47) 4.0	(26) 4.2
	1.7			2.0		1.4	.8	1.0	1.5	2.0
	.1	.1	.1	.1		.1	.1	.1	.1	.1
	.3	.2	.3	.3	Fixed/Worth	.4	.3	.3	.2	.3
	1.0	.6	.8	.9		1.1	.8	.7	.5	.9
	.7	.7	1.5	.7		.7	.7	.8	.6	.7
	1.4	1.6	2.2	1.5	Debt/Worth	1.6	1.5	1.4	1.4	1.5
	5.3	2.9	5.2	4.5		4.4	3.8	3.2	2.8	4.5
	53.7	55.4	77.4	55.4		44.2	26.8	37.8	36.8	55.4
	(61) 20.9	(33) 26.4	19.6	(112) 21.0	% Profit Before Taxes/ Tangible Net Worth	(168) 18.2	(233) 8.9	(226) 14.8	(190) 17.3	(112) 21.0
	3.6	11.8	7.4	7.4		-1.9	-6.4	2.2	2.3	7.4
	20.1	19.8	36.6	19.4		17.2	11.4	14.4	15.6	19.4
	6.3	9.3	6.1	7.2	% Profit Before Taxes/ Total Assets	5.0	3.7	5.3	5.8	7.2
	.9	4.8	1.6	2.3		-2.4	-4.6	.8	.7	2.3
	.3	.3		.4		.5	.6	.4	.4	.4
	(61) .8	.7		(108) .8	% Depr., Dep., Amort./ Revenues	(164) 1.1	(225) 1.1	(214) .8	(169) .8	(108) .8
	1.4	1.2		1.4		2.0	1.8	1.4	1.4	1.4
	2.1			2.1		3.4	2.4	1.8	1.6	2.1
	(31) 4.1			(54) 3.7	% Officers', Directors' Owners' Comp/Revenues	(118) 5.4	(128) 4.5	(129) 3.3	(105) 3.2	(54) 3.7
	6.2			6.2		9.1	7.7	6.2	5.4	6.2
4914M	376898M	658642M	14151025M	15191479M	Contract Revenues ($)	26630772M	19686913M	18586706M	22762468M	15191479M
2325M	133136M	261426M	4428479M	4825366M	Total Assets ($)	10442463M	7456585M	7452267M	9397342M	4825366M

M = $ thousand MM = $ million

See Pages 9 through 22 for Explanation of Ratios and Data

Current Data Sorted by Revenue						Comparative Historical Data				
					Type of Statement					
	2	1	4	7	Unqualified	14	4	3	6	7
	26	29	4	59	Reviewed	81	122	118	99	59
1	10	1		12	Compiled	29	37	31	25	12
7	20	3	2	32	Tax Returns	44	51	45	39	32
5	10	13	4	32	Other	38	58	78	53	32
22 (4/1-9/30/13)		120 (10/1/13-3/31/14)				4/1/09-3/31/10	4/1/10-3/31/11	4/1/11-3/31/12	4/1/12-3/31/13	4/1/13-3/31/14
0-1MM	1-10MM	10-50MM	50 & OVER	ALL		ALL	ALL	ALL	ALL	ALL
13	68	47	14	142	**NUMBER OF STATEMENTS**	206	272	275	222	142
%	%	%	%	%	**ASSETS**	%	%	%	%	%
12.1	16.6	10.2	7.6	13.2	Cash & Equivalents	17.6	16.5	14.0	15.6	13.2
27.7	36.2	52.1	50.8	42.1	A/R - Progress Billings	37.5	25.3	43.0	41.3	42.1
.0	1.3	.7	.9	.9	A/R - Current Retention	1.4	17.4	3.0	3.1	.9
8.4	9.5	3.8	2.0	6.8	Inventory	8.7	7.6	7.9	7.7	6.8
1.8	4.8	6.2	7.9	5.3	Cost & Est. Earnings In Excess Billings	2.6	4.7	4.2	4.5	5.3
7.7	2.5	5.6	11.7	4.9	All Other Current	5.0	5.2	3.9	4.1	4.9
57.7	70.9	78.6	80.9	73.2	Total Current	72.8	76.6	76.0	76.3	73.2
24.9	17.5	14.1	15.4	16.9	Fixed Assets (net)	17.9	14.8	14.1	14.5	16.9
.0	.1	.7	.1	.3	Joint Ventures & Investments	.8	.1	.3	.3	.3
10.1	1.7	1.2	.4	2.2	Intangibles (net)	2.1	2.0	2.0	2.8	2.2
7.3	9.8	5.4	3.1	7.4	All Other Non-Current	6.5	6.4	7.5	6.2	7.4
100.0	100.0	100.0	100.0	100.0	Total	100.0	100.0	100.0	100.0	100.0
					LIABILITIES					
29.1	10.4	10.5	8.9	12.0	Notes Payable-Short Term	12.7	10.2	10.3	11.7	12.0
23.3	19.5	27.6	28.1	23.4	A/P - Trade	22.8	23.5	23.0	22.1	23.4
.0	.0	.2	.0	.1	A/P - Retention	.4	.7	.7	.7	.1
.2	4.9	9.8	8.6	6.5	Billings in Excess of Costs & Est. Earnings	5.1	6.7	6.4	7.0	6.5
.0	.1	.0	.1	.1	Income Taxes Payable	.2	.2	.1	.1	.1
26.0	3.4	3.0	3.1	5.3	Cur. Mat.-L/T/D	5.0	3.1	2.5	3.4	5.3
39.3	9.5	6.9	13.4	11.7	All Other Current	10.5	9.7	10.3	11.1	11.7
117.8	47.8	57.9	62.2	59.0	Total Current	56.7	54.2	53.4	56.0	59.0
86.2	17.2	7.4	17.9	20.3	Long-Term Debt	17.0	10.0	10.9	12.4	20.3
.2	.4	.2	.0	.3	Deferred Taxes	.4	.5	.2	.2	.3
.0	3.3	2.3	.9	2.4	All Other Non-Current	4.6	3.3	3.6	2.8	2.4
-104.3	31.2	32.3	19.1	18.0	Net Worth	21.3	32.1	31.9	28.6	18.0
100.0	100.0	100.0	100.0	100.0	Total Liabilities & Net Worth	100.0	100.0	100.0	100.0	100.0
					INCOME DATA					
100.0	100.0	100.0	100.0	100.0	Contract Revenues	100.0	100.0	100.0	100.0	100.0
54.1	30.2	17.9	20.3	27.3	Gross Profit	29.4	25.2	25.4	26.0	27.3
54.4	28.4	15.1	16.6	25.2	Operating Expenses	26.5	23.6	23.0	23.3	25.2
-.3	1.7	2.8	3.7	2.1	Operating Profit	2.9	1.7	2.4	2.8	2.1
.6	.4	.4	1.8	.5	All Other Expenses (net)	.5	.2	.2	.2	.5
-.9	1.3	2.5	1.9	1.5	Profit Before Taxes	2.4	1.5	2.2	2.6	1.5
					RATIOS					
2.5	2.8	1.7	1.5	2.3		2.3	2.2	2.3	2.4	2.3
1.0	1.5	1.3	1.4	1.4	Current	1.5	1.4	1.5	1.5	1.4
.7	1.1	1.2	1.2	1.1		1.0	1.1	1.2	1.1	1.1
UND	3.9	2.7	2.8	3.1		3.3	3.3	3.6	3.3	3.1
(12) 1.8	(63) 2.0	2.0	(13) 2.3	(135) 2.0	Receivables/Payables	(197) 1.9	(261) 1.9	(267) 2.2	(206) 2.2	(135) 2.0
.2	1.0	1.3	1.3	1.3		1.0	1.2	1.4	1.4	1.3
0 UND	**26** 13.8	**52** 7.0	**40** 9.2	**30** 12.1		**20** 18.6	**32** 11.4	**38** 9.6	**29** 12.5	**30** 12.1
20 18.1	**41** 8.9	**64** 5.7	**65** 5.6	**52** 7.0	Revenues/Receivables	**40** 9.0	**53** 6.9	**61** 6.0	**54** 6.8	**52** 7.0
31 11.6	**65** 5.6	**79** 4.6	**81** 4.5	**72** 5.1		**67** 5.4	**78** 4.7	**78** 4.7	**78** 4.7	**72** 5.1
0 UND	**14** 25.9	**27** 13.5	**24** 15.1	**18** 19.9		**18** 20.7	**19** 19.5	**19** 19.2	**18** 20.8	**18** 19.9
2 189.0	**24** 15.4	**38** 9.5	**36** 10.1	**32** 11.5	Cost of Revenues/Payables	**27** 13.3	**33** 11.1	**31** 11.7	**29** 12.6	**32** 11.5
55 6.6	**48** 7.6	**53** 6.9	**46** 7.9	**49** 7.4		**45** 8.1	**53** 6.9	**51** 7.1	**47** 7.7	**49** 7.4
21.9	7.1	9.2	10.5	8.4		6.8	6.7	6.7	6.8	8.4
UND	11.5	15.2	13.1	14.9	Revenues/Working Capital	15.3	12.4	12.1	13.0	14.9
-10.9	78.8	34.1	36.3	66.5		521.3	43.9	35.6	52.5	66.5
	17.8	34.9	39.6	24.6		15.2	20.5	27.6	34.1	24.6
	(58) 4.6	(42) 6.2	(10) 10.8	(117) 6.2	EBIT/Interest	(177) 5.4	(236) 4.6	(248) 6.5	(190) 6.5	(117) 6.2
	-.6	3.1	4.0	1.1		.8	-.5	1.0	1.6	1.1
	2.4	3.9		2.9		7.7	6.0	4.0	7.6	2.9
	(11) .5	(10) 1.1		(24) 1.1	Net Profit + Depr., Dep., Amort./Cur. Mat. L/T/D	(38) 2.6	(46) 2.1	(43) 2.6	(38) 3.4	(24) 1.1
	.0	.4		.3		-.1	-.4	.5	-.2	.3
.7	.1	.2	.2	.1		.1	.1	.1	.1	.1
-7.0	.3	.3	.3	.4	Fixed/Worth	.4	.3	.3	.3	.4
-.3	.9	.8	2.0	.9		2.6	1.2	1.0	1.2	.9
1.9	.8	1.3	1.6	1.2		.9	.8	.9	.9	1.2
-10.4	1.5	2.4	2.1	2.0	Debt/Worth	2.0	1.9	1.9	2.0	2.0
-1.9	5.1	3.9	5.7	7.0		10.5	5.8	4.5	5.5	7.0
	41.5	49.3	62.4	45.1		46.6	35.5	39.1	46.3	45.1
	(55) 11.5	(44) 20.6	(12) 31.0	(116) 18.3	% Profit Before Taxes/Tangible Net Worth	(162) 20.0	(232) 11.7	(243) 14.9	(190) 21.5	(116) 18.3
	-5.7	8.5	19.5	5.8		2.4	.5	2.6	4.1	5.8
7.8	15.7	14.8	19.7	15.9		17.6	13.2	14.9	16.6	15.9
.0	3.9	5.7	12.3	5.6	% Profit Before Taxes/Total Assets	6.5	4.4	5.4	5.9	5.6
-9.0	-2.7	1.5	5.1	.3		-.8	-1.6	.4	.3	.3
	.6	.5	.3	.5		.7	.6	.6	.5	.5
	(57) 1.0	(42) .8	(12) .5	(119) .9	% Depr., Dep., Amort./Revenues	(171) 1.1	(219) 1.0	(224) .9	(192) .8	(119) .9
	1.8	1.3	1.0	1.5		1.9	1.7	1.4	1.4	1.5
	2.9	1.2		2.0		2.8	2.0	1.5	1.6	2.
	(48) 5.4	(14) 1.6		(70) 4.7	% Officers', Directors' Owners' Comp/Revenues	(125) 5.0	(149) 3.6	(142) 3.0	(112) 3.7	(70) 4.
	8.7	4.2		8.6		8.2	6.4	5.3	6.1	8.
7237M	292897M	991959M	4778946M	6071039M	Contract Revenues ($)	58656308M	29407531M	26446235M	12003953M	607103
2378M	92218M	367349M	910120M	1372065M	Total Assets ($)	13672430M	9245807M	8884355M	3395737M	137206

M = $ thousand MM = $ million

See Pages 9 through 22 for Explanation of Ratios and Data

Current Data Sorted by Revenue						Comparative Historical Data				
					Type of Statement					
	1	1		2	Unqualified	8	4	4	1	2
1	4	8		13	Reviewed	25	39	29	24	13
	1		1	2	Compiled	7	12	10	8	2
4	3			7	Tax Returns	8	8	18	7	7
	3	1	1	5	Other	13	20	17	12	5
1 (4/1-9/30/13)		28 (10/1/13-3/31/14)				4/1/09-3/31/10	4/1/10-3/31/11	4/1/11-3/31/12	4/1/12-3/31/13	4/1/13-3/31/14
0-1MM	1-10MM	10-50MM	50 & OVER	ALL		ALL	ALL	ALL	ALL	ALL
5	12	10	2	29	**NUMBER OF STATEMENTS**	61	83	78	52	29
%	%	%	%	%	**ASSETS**	%	%	%	%	%
	15.5	7.8		15.4	Cash & Equivalents	17.6	13.1	12.8	14.0	15.4
	58.1	62.4		50.5	A/R - Progress Billings	47.5	35.6	51.9	48.8	50.5
	2.1	.6		1.9	A/R - Current Retention	1.4	18.8	3.8	3.5	1.9
	1.8	1.1		2.5	Inventory	4.9	2.8	5.2	3.2	2.5
	6.6	7.8		6.3	Cost & Est. Earnings In Excess Billings	2.2	5.1	5.1	5.2	6.3
	2.9	4.5		5.0	All Other Current	4.9	4.8	3.3	4.4	5.0
	86.9	84.2		81.7	Total Current	78.5	80.2	82.1	79.2	81.7
	11.0	6.3		11.9	Fixed Assets (net)	12.0	10.5	9.4	10.3	11.9
	.0	.1		.0	Joint Ventures & Investments	.3	.1	.1	.1	.0
	.1	5.1		1.8	Intangibles (net)	.7	1.6	1.7	2.1	1.8
	2.1	4.3		4.3	All Other Non-Current	8.5	7.6	6.8	8.4	4.3
	100.0	100.0		100.0	Total	100.0	100.0	100.0	100.0	100.0
					LIABILITIES					
	15.9	25.8		24.3	Notes Payable-Short Term	9.9	17.7	15.1	22.3	24.3
	16.4	13.8		13.9	A/P - Trade	16.6	13.1	15.4	18.7	13.9
	.0	.0		.0	A/P - Retention	.0	.2	.3	.3	.0
	6.6	5.8		5.6	Billings in Excess of Costs & Est. Earnings	6.8	5.0	6.5	6.1	5.6
	.0	.0		.0	Income Taxes Payable	.0	.3	.4	.1	.0
	2.4	1.7		2.5	Cur. Mat.-L/T/D	1.4	2.6	2.1	8.7	2.5
	9.0	9.6		13.6	All Other Current	10.8	9.5	8.5	7.9	13.6
	50.3	56.7		59.9	Total Current	45.6	48.3	48.4	64.2	59.9
	4.0	6.6		7.8	Long-Term Debt	5.5	8.0	5.7	5.6	7.8
	.7	.0		.3	Deferred Taxes	.5	.4	.3	.1	.3
	1.5	2.5		5.4	All Other Non-Current	8.8	6.3	5.7	3.9	5.4
	43.5	34.3		26.9	Net Worth	39.5	37.1	39.9	26.3	26.9
	100.0	100.0		100.0	Total Liabilities & Net Worth	100.0	100.0	100.0	100.0	100.0
					INCOME DATA					
	100.0	100.0		100.0	Contract Revenues	100.0	100.0	100.0	100.0	100.0
	17.3	18.9		21.5	Gross Profit	24.8	19.0	19.7	20.1	21.5
	16.4	13.3		18.1	Operating Expenses	23.4	18.8	18.6	18.1	18.1
	.9	5.6		3.5	Operating Profit	1.4	.3	1.1	2.0	3.5
	.2	.6		.3	All Other Expenses (net)	.3	.1	.1	.3	.3
	.7	5.0		3.2	Profit Before Taxes	1.1	.1	1.0	1.7	3.2
					RATIOS					
	2.7	2.0		2.4		3.6	3.2	2.8	2.3	2.4
	1.5	1.4		1.4	Current	2.0	1.8	1.8	1.5	1.4
	1.4	1.2		1.2		1.3	1.3	1.3	1.1	1.2
	11.9	7.1		7.1		9.6	8.4	6.5	6.1	7.1
	4.4	5.5		(26) 5.1	Receivables/Payables	(60) 4.8	(77) 4.5	(74) 4.0	(48) 3.6	(26) 5.1
	2.3	2.6		2.6		2.7	3.2	2.6	1.8	2.6
	54 6.8	63 5.8		51 7.2		44 8.3	60 6.1	55 6.6	47 7.7	51 7.2
	78 4.7	76 4.8		74 4.9	Revenues/Receivables	54 6.8	78 4.7	76 4.8	72 5.1	74 4.9
	107 3.4	91 4.0		99 3.7		69 5.3	101 3.6	94 3.9	87 4.2	99 3.7
	11 33.4	15 24.1		12 31.2		8 46.1	9 41.8	11 32.2	12 31.1	12 31.2
	21 17.6	17 21.5		19 19.7	Cost of Revenues/Payables	15 24.9	18 19.8	21 17.6	23 15.8	19 19.7
	27 13.5	33 11.2		31 11.8		28 13.1	30 12.1	35 10.5	41 9.0	31 11.8
	4.1	7.7		5.6		4.7	5.1	5.4	6.1	5.6
	10.8	14.2		14.1	Revenues/Working Capital	8.5	8.2	9.1	11.9	14.1
	20.6	32.5		22.1		18.6	15.9	18.8	31.1	22.1
	8.1	14.6		17.0		24.2	13.8	20.5	27.5	17.0
	(10) 4.0	8.2		(24) 5.3	EBIT/Interest	(49) 3.8	(76) 2.6	(68) 2.4	(46) 5.2	(24) 5.3
	-3.4	2.6		2.3		-6.7	-.5	-.5	2.3	2.3
								20.3		
					Net Profit + Depr., Dep., Amort./Cur. Mat. L/T/D			(12) 3.4		
								.8		
	.0	.1		.1		.1	.1	.1	.1	.1
	.2	.2		.2	Fixed/Worth	.1	.2	.2	.2	.2
	.8	1.2		1.1		.5	.4	.5	.6	1.1
	.7	1.6		.9		.4	.4	.7	.8	.9
	1.2	2.4		1.8	Debt/Worth	1.0	1.4	1.4	2.3	1.8
	3.1	8.7		5.1		2.5	2.8	3.7	5.2	5.1
	26.0			57.6		32.9	19.7	29.4	35.3	57.6
	11.1			(25) 21.2	% Profit Before Taxes/ Tangible Net Worth	(55) 16.1	(75) 5.2	(74) 8.3	(46) 16.5	(25) 21.2
	-5.1			1.0		-10.1	-2.9	-4.1	4.8	1.0
	10.6	22.0		19.9		16.9	7.0	11.1	10.3	19.9
	3.1	15.2		9.8	% Profit Before Taxes/ Total Assets	4.7	1.7	2.5	5.2	9.8
	-1.0	2.8		.5		-6.8	-1.5	-1.7	.8	.5
	.4	.2		.3		.5	.5	.4	.3	.3
	(10) .5	.5		(24) .6	% Depr., Dep., Amort./ Revenues	(51) .7	(66) .8	(67) .6	(44) .5	(24) .6
	.7	.7		.8		1.6	1.1	1.0	.8	.8
				2.4		2.0	1.9	1.7	2.2	2.4
				(15) 3.4	% Officers', Directors' Owners' Comp/Revenues	(30) 4.0	(44) 4.4	(53) 3.4	(33) 3.7	(15) 3.4
				8.0		11.1	7.4	6.4	7.1	8.0
2321M	75358M	188242M	693713M	959634M	Contract Revenues ($)	779420M	5314392M	4240723M	4508337M	959634M
1489M	29014M	63397M	131733M	225633M	Total Assets ($)	297755M	1804340M	1621460M	1325336M	225633M

M = $ thousand MM = $ million

See Pages 9 through 22 for Explanation of Ratios and Data

Current Data Sorted by Revenue | **Comparative Historical Data**

0-1MM	1-10MM	10-50MM	50 & OVER	ALL	Type of Statement	4/1/09-3/31/10 ALL	4/1/10-3/31/11 ALL	4/1/11-3/31/12 ALL	4/1/12-3/31/13 ALL	4/1/1 3/31/ ALL
					Unqualified	2	4			
	5	4		9	Reviewed	18	17	12	11	9
	3			3	Compiled	6	7	4	6	3
3	2			5	Tax Returns	5	3	9	8	5
1	2	1		4	Other	14	6	12	7	4
5 (4/1-9/30/13)		16 (10/1/13-3/31/14)								
4	12	5		21	**NUMBER OF STATEMENTS**	45	37	37	32	21
%	%	%	%	%	**ASSETS**	%	%	%	%	%
	12.1		DATA NOT AVAILABLE	19.0	Cash & Equivalents	17.2	17.3	15.2	24.6	19.0
	49.4			42.4	A/R - Progress Billings	44.4	34.5	41.0	32.4	42.4
	.1			.1	A/R - Current Retention	.3	9.8	.7	.9	.1
	1.8			2.1	Inventory	2.3	2.8	3.4	1.8	2.1
	4.4			3.7	Cost & Est. Earnings In Excess Billings	5.4	6.9	5.5	7.6	3.7
	6.3			4.0	All Other Current	5.2	3.5	3.1	3.3	4.0
	74.1			71.3	Total Current	74.8	74.8	68.9	70.6	71.3
	18.5			18.8	Fixed Assets (net)	16.1	15.9	17.2	19.8	18.8
	.0			.0	Joint Ventures & Investments	.6	.0	2.6	.0	.0
	.0			.0	Intangibles (net)	1.1	1.7	3.4	3.8	.0
	7.4			9.9	All Other Non-Current	7.4	7.6	7.9	5.9	9.9
	100.0			100.0	Total	100.0	100.0	100.0	100.0	100.0
					LIABILITIES					
	25.8			16.3	Notes Payable-Short Term	13.4	13.7	14.2	27.0	16.3
	12.7			9.6	A/P - Trade	13.4	12.2	13.2	11.7	9.6
	.0			.0	A/P - Retention	.0	.0	.0	.0	.0
	2.5			3.8	Billings in Excess of Costs & Est. Earnings	3.0	2.1	2.9	1.3	3.8
	.0			.0	Income Taxes Payable	.2	1.2	.7	.9	.0
	2.3			1.7	Cur. Mat.-L/T/D	2.2	1.9	1.7	1.8	1.7
	11.4			9.5	All Other Current	10.0	10.1	13.1	16.5	9.5
	54.8			40.9	Total Current	42.2	41.1	45.8	59.3	40.9
	8.7			8.5	Long-Term Debt	10.1	6.2	10.0	6.8	8.5
	.3			.2	Deferred Taxes	.6	1.5	.4	.5	.2
	5.5			4.0	All Other Non-Current	6.8	7.3	8.0	2.9	4.0
	30.7			46.4	Net Worth	40.4	44.0	35.8	30.5	46.4
	100.0			100.0	Total Liabilties & Net Worth	100.0	100.0	100.0	100.0	100.0
					INCOME DATA					
	100.0			100.0	Contract Revenues	100.0	100.0	100.0	100.0	100.0
	31.3			36.3	Gross Profit	28.6	30.1	32.5	32.5	36.3
	26.9			27.5	Operating Expenses	27.6	29.1	29.5	26.8	27.5
	4.4			8.8	Operating Profit	1.0	.9	3.0	5.7	8.8
	.2			-.4	All Other Expenses (net)	.1	-.1	-.1	.6	-.4
	4.2			9.2	Profit Before Taxes	.9	1.0	3.1	5.1	9.2
					RATIOS					
	2.4			2.9		3.2	3.6	3.0	2.7	2.9
	1.5			2.1	Current	2.0	2.0	2.0	2.0	2.1
	1.0			1.4		1.3	1.3	1.2	1.0	1.4
	UND			UND		9.4	7.8	6.4	7.2	UND
	5.7			(19) 6.6	Receivables/Payables	(43) 4.2	(36) 4.1	(33) 4.3	(28) 3.8	(19) 6.6
	2.2			3.5		1.9	2.5	2.1	1.9	3.5
	37 9.9			34 10.7		29 12.4	41 8.9	31 11.7	15 24.6	34 10.7
	53 6.9			48 7.6	Revenues/Receivables	56 6.6	62 5.9	49 7.4	49 7.5	48 7.6
	79 4.6			78 4.7		72 5.1	86 4.2	85 4.3	65 5.6	78 4.7
	0 UND			0 UND		8 43.8	11 31.9	8 44.2	6 62.4	0 UND
	10 37.3			7 53.9	Cost of Revenues/Payables	14 26.0	24 15.0	19 19.5	13 29.1	7 53.9
	34 10.6			30 12.2		37 9.7	34 10.6	29 12.8	30 12.2	30 12.2
	6.4			4.2		5.0	4.0	4.8	3.9	4.2
	10.7			8.2	Revenues/Working Capital	8.7	8.1	9.0	10.0	8.2
	NM			29.2		22.6	17.8	83.9	NM	29.2
	9.7			21.8		21.7	19.4	14.9	11.9	21.8
	(10) 5.5			(16) 6.5	EBIT/Interest	(38) 3.8	(31) 7.9	(29) 7.3	(22) 2.6	(16) 6.5
	1.7			4.0		-3.2	-2.5	3.3	-2.8	4.0
					Net Profit + Depr., Dep., Amort./Cur. Mat. L/T/D					
	.2			.1		.1	.1	.2	.1	.1
	.4			.3	Fixed/Worth	.3	.3	.4	.3	.3
	2.0			1.2		.8	.9	1.5	1.0	1.2
	.8			.3		.5	.4	.6	.6	.3
	1.3			1.0	Debt/Worth	1.0	1.3	1.2	1.0	1.0
	16.0			2.3		3.0	2.5	4.7	2.5	2.3
	73.8			73.6		26.0	31.9	28.9	46.2	73.6
	(11) 33.5			(20) 32.8	% Profit Before Taxes/ Tangible Net Worth	(39) 12.0	(34) 8.6	(32) 13.0	(28) 4.3	(20) 32.8
	5.9			7.3		-6.0	-14.2	3.8	-9.1	7.3
	18.9			30.3		14.5	13.1	17.2	19.2	30.3
	7.0			9.8	% Profit Before Taxes/ Total Assets	3.6	6.8	6.8	3.6	9.8
	1.2			2.8		-9.4	-6.1	1.0	-5.1	2.8
	.6			.6		.7	.7	.6	.6	.6
	(10) 1.3			(17) 1.1	% Depr., Dep., Amort./ Revenues	(37) 1.1	(31) 1.2	(28) 1.0	(26) 1.1	(17) 1.1
	2.4			2.5		2.0	2.3	2.2	2.7	2.5
				2.0		2.1	2.6	2.4	2.6	2.0
				(12) 5.6	% Officers', Directors' Owners' Comp/Revenues	(21) 3.5	(23) 4.0	(24) 5.7	(15) 5.0	(12) 5.6
				14.1		6.3	7.0	10.8	12.2	14.1
1064M	42184M	89486M		132734M	Contract Revenues ($)	282326M	235156M	7561829M	182979M	132734
667M	14722M	35967M		51356M	Total Assets ($)	104809M	90129M	7181411M	75674M	51356

M = $ thousand MM = $ million

See Pages 9 through 22 for Explanation of Ratios and Data

Current Data Sorted by Revenue / Comparative Historical Data

0-1MM	1-10MM	10-50MM	50 & OVER	ALL		4/1/09-3/31/10 ALL	4/1/10-3/31/11 ALL	4/1/11-3/31/12 ALL	4/1/12-3/31/13 ALL	4/1/13-3/31/14 ALL
					Type of Statement					
	3	7	1	11	Unqualified	19	19	10	13	11
	19	10		29	Reviewed	61	63	60	54	29
	9			9	Compiled	12	19	15	14	9
7	11	1	1	20	Tax Returns	18	22	15	13	20
1	10	7	1	19	Other	28	41	32	37	19
10 (4/1-9/30/13)		78 (10/1/13-3/31/14)								
8	52	25	3	88	**NUMBER OF STATEMENTS**	138	164	132	131	88
%	%	%	%	%	**ASSETS**	%	%	%	%	%
	14.3	15.1		16.3	Cash & Equivalents	11.3	12.1	9.5	12.6	16.3
	31.5	30.8		29.4	A/R - Progress Billings	24.8	23.6	35.1	31.4	29.4
	1.0	2.7		1.3	A/R - Current Retention	1.5	8.4	3.3	2.3	1.3
	2.3	1.9		2.0	Inventory	2.8	3.0	1.6	1.9	2.0
	2.6	6.2		3.5	Cost & Est. Earnings In Excess Billings	3.0	3.0	3.7	3.9	3.5
	7.3	7.1		7.4	All Other Current	4.1	5.2	5.5	6.9	7.4
	58.8	63.8		60.0	Total Current	47.5	55.3	58.8	59.0	60.0
	31.8	29.2		31.4	Fixed Assets (net)	45.0	35.2	33.1	31.9	31.4
	1.2	1.1		1.0	Joint Ventures & Investments	.8	1.1	.8	.5	1.0
	.8	2.3		1.1	Intangibles (net)	.9	1.6	.8	1.1	1.1
	7.4	3.7		6.5	All Other Non-Current	5.8	6.7	6.4	7.6	6.5
	100.0	100.0		100.0	Total	100.0	100.0	100.0	100.0	100.0
					LIABILITIES					
	13.4	3.9		11.4	Notes Payable-Short Term	8.6	12.2	10.0	11.6	11.4
	12.7	16.6		13.1	A/P - Trade	12.6	16.7	18.3	16.6	13.1
	.0	.2		.7	A/P - Retention	.1	.2	.5	.1	.7
	4.0	4.9		4.1	Billings in Excess of Costs & Est. Earnings	2.5	4.0	4.2	3.5	4.1
	.2	.1		.2	Income Taxes Payable	.0	.1	.1	.1	.2
	7.0	4.8		8.6	Cur. Mat.-L/T/D	8.9	6.8	7.1	4.8	8.6
	4.6	6.3		4.9	All Other Current	5.9	6.1	6.3	6.0	4.9
	41.9	36.8		43.0	Total Current	38.6	46.1	46.5	42.7	43.0
	19.9	11.8		17.6	Long-Term Debt	24.6	16.4	15.5	16.1	17.6
	1.4	2.4		1.5	Deferred Taxes	1.3	.7	1.0	.8	1.5
	15.0	1.4		10.4	All Other Non-Current	3.8	6.8	3.9	5.5	10.4
	21.7	47.7		27.5	Net Worth	31.6	30.0	33.1	34.9	27.5
	100.0	100.0		100.0	Total Liabilties & Net Worth	100.0	100.0	100.0	100.0	100.0
					INCOME DATA					
	100.0	100.0		100.0	Contract Revenues	100.0	100.0	100.0	100.0	100.0
	29.1	17.0		27.1	Gross Profit	31.9	26.2	23.0	25.3	27.1
	24.8	12.1		21.9	Operating Expenses	31.4	25.9	20.4	21.1	21.9
	4.3	4.9		5.2	Operating Profit	.6	.4	2.5	4.2	5.2
	.5	-.1		.3	All Other Expenses (net)	1.5	.2	.4	.3	.3
	3.8	5.0		4.9	Profit Before Taxes	-.9	.1	2.2	3.9	4.9
					RATIOS					
	3.1	2.9		3.0		2.1	2.0	1.9	2.7	3.0
	1.6	1.5		1.6	Current	1.3	1.4	1.3	1.5	1.6
	1.0	1.3		1.2		.8	.9	1.0	1.1	1.2
	8.4	3.6		6.5		7.2	4.7	4.1	4.8	6.5
	(44) 3.2	1.8		(77) 2.4	Receivables/Payables	(125) 2.7	(151) 2.4	(123) 2.3	(120) 2.4	(77) 2.4
	1.8	1.1		1.5		1.5	1.3	1.4	1.2	1.5
	21 17.7	**39** 9.3		**21** 17.7		**28** 13.2	**25** 14.6	**36** 10.1	**25** 14.4	**21** 17.7
	49 7.5	**66** 5.5		**49** 7.5	Revenues/Receivables	**49** 7.5	**55** 6.7	**64** 5.7	**59** 6.2	**49** 7.5
	70 5.2	**85** 4.3		**78** 4.7		**72** 5.1	**80** 4.6	**85** 4.3	**81** 4.5	**78** 4.7
	1 285.1	**15** 24.1		**2** 181.1		**5** 73.0	**11** 34.5	**15** 23.6	**11** 32.4	**2** 181.1
	16 23.2	**36** 10.2		**21** 17.7	Cost of Revenues/Payables	**24** 15.4	**28** 13.2	**31** 11.8	**26** 13.9	**21** 17.7
	33 11.0	**57** 6.4		**45** 8.1		**52** 7.0	**57** 6.4	**53** 6.9	**53** 6.9	**45** 8.1
	5.4	4.2		5.2		6.7	7.3	6.9	5.4	5.2
	12.5	8.3		11.1	Revenues/Working Capital	19.2	16.8	17.6	15.7	11.1
	522.7	22.1		42.7		-36.0	-32.5	NM	76.8	42.7
	20.1	20.2		19.8		4.3	7.1	12.4	20.1	19.8
	(51) 4.1	(23) 9.0		(84) 7.8	EBIT/Interest	(123) 1.2	(147) 2.1	(124) 3.2	(120) 5.9	(84) 7.8
	1.7	2.1		2.1		-3.4	-1.2	-.4	1.4	2.1
	3.6			7.5		2.9	2.6	3.7	5.4	7.5
	(10) 1.8			(16) 2.2	Net Profit + Depr., Dep., Amort./Cur. Mat. L/T/D	(34) 1.4	(30) 1.5	(25) 2.3	(26) 2.5	(16) 2.2
	.9			1.1		.7	-.2	1.5	1.3	1.1
	.5	.3		.4		.6	.5	.5	.4	.4
	1.0	.6		.9	Fixed/Worth	1.2	1.0	.8	.7	.9
	2.6	1.3		1.9		2.8	2.5	1.7	1.9	1.9
	.8	.5		.7		.8	.8	.9	.6	.7
	1.7	1.3		1.6	Debt/Worth	1.6	1.8	1.6	1.5	1.6
	9.1	1.9		4.8		4.6	6.3	3.7	4.0	4.8
	39.3	25.2		43.3		20.9	27.2	39.3	34.6	43.3
	(43) 20.2	17.2		(77) 20.0	% Profit Before Taxes/ Tangible Net Worth	(114) 3.2	(142) 8.1	(118) 11.2	(116) 16.2	(77) 20.0
	3.4	4.8		4.5		-19.8	-7.9	-4.0	2.6	4.5
	14.6	13.2		16.0		8.0	9.3	14.6	15.3	16.0
	5.8	7.1		7.2	% Profit Before Taxes/ Total Assets	.8	2.9	4.3	6.4	7.2
	.8	1.6		1.6		-11.4	-4.1	-1.9	1.2	1.6
	2.3	2.5		2.4		4.2	3.1	2.4	1.8	2.4
	(40) 4.1	(24) 3.5		(71) 3.8	% Depr., Dep., Amort./ Revenues	(118) 7.4	(145) 5.1	(119) 4.1	(115) 3.7	(71) 3.8
	6.9	4.2		5.6		11.7	7.7	6.9	5.7	5.6
	3.1	1.6		2.3		2.2	2.0	1.8	1.5	2.3
	(24) 5.3	(13) 3.0		(42) 4.5	% Officers', Directors' Owners' Comp/Revenues	(53) 4.8	(73) 4.0	(65) 3.7	(62) 3.1	(42) 4.5
	7.9	4.6		7.7		9.5	7.5	6.6	7.0	7.7
5211M	227612M	504278M	6541980M	7279081M	Contract Revenues ($)	4950012M	8150918M	7495841M	6905226M	7279081M
3419M	107884M	263575M	1343598M	1718476M	Total Assets ($)	4055686M	4808902M	3531624M	1991268M	1718476M

M = $ thousand MM = $ million

See Pages 9 through 22 for Explanation of Ratios and Data

Current Data Sorted by Revenue | **Comparative Historical Data**

0-1MM	1-10MM	10-50MM	50 & OVER	ALL		4/1/09-3/31/10 ALL	4/1/10-3/31/11 ALL	4/1/11-3/31/12 ALL	4/1/12-3/31/13 ALL	4/1/13-3/31/14 ALL
					Type of Statement					
		3	1	4	Unqualified	5	6	7	6	4
1	9	10	1	21	Reviewed	36	57	49	40	21
	5	1		6	Compiled	20	19	18	12	6
9	12		2	23	Tax Returns	33	28	21	26	23
	5	10	1	16	Other	29	43	32	39	16
11 (4/1-9/30/13)		59 (10/1/13-3/31/14)								
10	31	24	5	70	**NUMBER OF STATEMENTS**	123	153	127	123	70
%	%	%	%	%	**ASSETS**	%	%	%	%	%
38.7	18.9	19.3		22.5	Cash & Equivalents	14.8	13.9	16.1	17.4	22.5
5.3	29.5	43.8		31.3	A/R - Progress Billings	34.1	24.7	39.3	36.7	31.3
.0	.0	.1		.1	A/R - Current Retention	.8	13.5	1.3	.8	.1
.5	11.7	3.3		6.5	Inventory	9.2	6.4	7.6	7.8	6.5
.0	3.4	6.2		4.0	Cost & Est. Earnings In Excess Billings	2.9	4.5	4.5	4.4	4.0
.0	.6	2.6		1.2	All Other Current	2.9	3.1	2.4	2.9	1.2
44.5	64.1	75.3		65.6	Total Current	64.7	66.0	71.3	70.0	65.6
34.1	24.0	17.8		23.6	Fixed Assets (net)	21.2	23.2	20.5	20.4	23.6
3.3	.6	.2		.8	Joint Ventures & Investments	.5	.3	.2	.4	.8
.2	1.4	.9		.9	Intangibles (net)	2.9	3.3	2.0	2.5	.9
18.1	9.9	5.8		9.1	All Other Non-Current	10.7	7.1	5.9	6.7	9.1
100.0	100.0	100.0		100.0	Total	100.0	100.0	100.0	100.0	100.0
					LIABILITIES					
4.1	15.8	7.6		10.2	Notes Payable-Short Term	14.6	10.5	12.9	14.8	10.2
7.2	10.8	19.1		13.8	A/P - Trade	17.8	16.7	20.0	17.0	13.8
.0	.0	.0		.0	A/P - Retention	.1	.3	.3	.0	.0
3.3	1.9	7.6		4.3	Billings in Excess of Costs & Est. Earnings	2.4	4.6	5.3	3.5	4.3
.0	.1	.6		.2	Income Taxes Payable	.1	.2	.3	.2	.2
10.3	2.3	1.9		3.4	Cur. Mat.-L/T/D	5.3	5.6	3.8	6.3	3.4
7.0	5.9	5.8		7.6	All Other Current	8.8	7.4	14.2	7.8	7.6
32.0	36.7	42.5		39.6	Total Current	49.1	45.4	56.9	49.7	39.6
22.3	23.3	6.2		16.0	Long-Term Debt	23.8	16.3	13.8	13.7	16.0
.0	.9	1.0		.7	Deferred Taxes	.5	.4	.7	1.1	.7
20.5	4.2	1.7		5.4	All Other Non-Current	3.3	5.1	5.4	6.3	5.4
25.3	34.9	48.6		38.3	Net Worth	23.4	32.8	23.2	29.2	38.3
100.0	100.0	100.0		100.0	Total Liabilties & Net Worth	100.0	100.0	100.0	100.0	100.0
					INCOME DATA					
100.0	100.0	100.0		100.0	Contract Revenues	100.0	100.0	100.0	100.0	100.0
52.0	37.5	21.2		33.2	Gross Profit	33.9	28.4	28.9	28.3	33.2
45.6	33.0	17.2		28.8	Operating Expenses	29.5	25.5	24.5	22.7	28.8
6.4	4.5	4.1		4.4	Operating Profit	4.4	3.0	4.4	5.6	4.4
.5	.2	-.1		.1	All Other Expenses (net)	.7	.5	.9	.7	.1
5.9	4.3	4.2		4.3	Profit Before Taxes	3.7	2.5	3.5	4.9	4.3
					RATIOS					
3.5	5.1	2.3		4.5		2.5	2.6	2.5	3.1	4.5
1.1	2.2	1.7		1.8	Current	1.4	1.5	1.5	1.7	1.8
.7	1.4	1.3		1.2		.9	1.0	1.1	1.2	1.2
	16.6	5.6		13.4		5.8	5.4	5.7	5.2	13.4
	(26) 4.3	2.2		(58) 3.1	Receivables/Payables	(108) 2.4	(144) 2.6	(123) 2.4	(111) 2.6	(58) 3.1
	1.5	1.4		1.4		1.2	1.3	1.3	1.5	1.4
0 UND	18 20.4	27 13.3		13 28.8		14 25.4	24 14.9	30 12.1	19 19.0	13 28.8
0 UND	33 11.1	64 5.7		38 9.5	Revenues/Receivables	39 9.4	52 7.0	54 6.7	51 7.1	38 9.5
7 48.9	58 6.3	83 4.4		65 5.6		66 5.5	74 4.9	78 4.7	79 4.6	65 5.6
0 UND	0 954.0	10 37.2		0 UND		8 48.6	9 40.3	13 28.6	11 34.1	0 UND
0 UND	9 40.8	33 11.0		13 27.9	Cost of Revenues/Payables	22 16.5	23 15.8	24 15.3	23 15.9	13 27.9
0 UND	34 10.6	56 6.5		42 8.7		46 8.0	53 6.9	51 7.2	43 8.5	42 8.7
21.3	5.4	5.7		5.8		6.3	6.5	5.3	5.5	5.8
UND	7.6	7.6		8.9	Revenues/Working Capital	18.5	11.3	13.1	9.5	8.9
-50.9	37.3	14.2		44.6		-65.7	936.5	41.0	34.5	44.6
	38.2	42.5		33.3		20.2	15.3	17.2	27.5	33.3
	(27) 7.6	(21) 10.2		(61) 8.9	EBIT/Interest	(108) 5.6	(134) 4.1	(109) 4.9	(102) 7.7	(61) 8.9
	1.1	4.2		1.4		1.2	.8	1.1	2.7	1.4
				36.0		8.8	8.0	8.1	10.4	36.0
				(10) 6.7	Net Profit + Depr., Dep., Amort./Cur. Mat. L/T/D	(18) 3.4	(24) 2.1	(24) 3.3	(25) 4.5	(10) 6.7
				2.3		.3	.8	.9	2.1	2.3
.0	.1	.1		.1		.1	.2	.2	.2	.1
.5	.5	.2		.3	Fixed/Worth	.7	.5	.5	.4	.3
NM	2.2	.8		1.1		2.8	1.8	2.0	1.2	1.1
.4	.2	.5		.4		.8	.6	.6	.6	.4
8.3	1.3	1.2		1.3	Debt/Worth	2.3	1.8	2.4	1.4	1.3
-19.8	9.0	1.5		6.7		18.4	6.0	5.6	3.9	6.7
	53.0	37.3		53.4		73.8	51.5	57.8	64.5	53.4
	(25) 18.4	18.7		(60) 22.9	% Profit Before Taxes/ Tangible Net Worth	(99) 26.7	(129) 20.0	(103) 19.6	(103) 25.0	(60) 22.9
	-7.3	8.6		3.2		3.5	.4	4.8	10.3	3.2
49.6	33.1	15.4		28.3		25.6	16.7	17.9	26.5	28.3
18.9	13.2	9.9		10.3	% Profit Before Taxes/ Total Assets	10.0	5.6	7.3	11.0	10.3
-7.8	-.5	3.7		.8		.0	-.9	.3	3.0	.8
	.5	.7		.7		.7	.8	.8	.7	.7
	(23) 1.5	(21) 1.0		(51) 1.5	% Depr., Dep., Amort./ Revenues	(94) 1.6	(119) 1.8	(96) 1.8	(98) 1.6	(51) 1.5
	3.6	3.4		3.6		3.2	3.2	3.2	3.1	3.6
	2.1			1.6		2.6	2.5	2.7	2.4	1.6
	(16) 3.4			(33) 3.6	% Officers', Directors' Owners' Comp/Revenues	(76) 4.7	(70) 4.1	(57) 3.9	(54) 3.9	(33) 3.6
	4.7			6.7		8.5	7.4	6.3	6.9	6.7
4330M	127918M	419801M	943690M	1495739M	Contract Revenues ($)	926661M	5669988M	4525067M	7916775M	1495739M
1169M	46041M	204994M	281680M	533884M	Total Assets ($)	346370M	4781974M	2073772M	3489327M	533884M

M = $ thousand MM = $ million

See Pages 9 through 22 for Explanation of Ratios and Data

CONSTRUCTION FINANCIAL MANAGEMENT ASSOCIATION DATA

In the following section, we are unable to provide the 2014 CFMA reports due to scheduling. Please contact RMA directly to receive copies of the reports, studies@rmahq.org. eStatement Studies users will be able to access the reports starting on December 1, 2014. We apologize for the inconvenience.

About the Construction Financial Management Association (CFMA) Data
Web site: www.cfma.org

Once again, we are delighted to include excerpts from ***CFMA's 2014 Construction Industry Annual Financial Survey.*** CFMA is **The Source and Resource for Construction Financial Professionals** and has more than **7,000** members in **89** chapters throughout the U.S. and Canada.

The data presented are based on an online survey to which nearly 4,000 general members employed within U.S. and Canadian construction firms were invited to respond. Additionally, this data was augmented by several hundred firms outside of CFMA member ranks. The data submitted were compiled and analyzed by a third party vendor, in cooperation with CFMA, and was not engaged to and did not audit or review this information and, accordingly, does not express an opinion or any other form of assurance on it.

Fiscal year-end closing dates reflected in the CFMA survey range from 3/31/13 through 3/31/14. The CFMA data are most comparable to the RMA contractor data from 4/1/13 through 3/31/14 appearing in this edition.

The survey respondents were classified into four categories of construction based on the type of work performed. Classification was based on the level of contract volume reported for various NAICS codes. A contractor was included in a classification if at least one half of its annual contract revenue was attributable to that classification. CFMA categorized certain NAICS codes together. The classifications and NAICS codes included in each are as follows:

NAICS Codes

INDUSTRIAL AND NONRESIDENTIAL CONTRACTORS:
236210 Industrial Building Construction
236220 Commercial and Institutional Building Construction

HEAVY AND HIGHWAY CONTRACTORS:
237110 Water and Sewer Line and Related Structures Construction
237120 Oil and Gas Pipeline and Related Structures Construction
237130 Power and Communication Line and Related Structures Construction
237210 Land Subdivision
237310 Highway, Street, and Bridge Construction
237990 Other Heavy and Civil Engineering Construction

SPECIALTY TRADES CONTRACTORS:
238110 Poured Concrete Foundation and Structure Contractors
238120 Structural Steel and Precast Concrete Contractors
238130 Framing Contractors
238140 Masonry Contractors
238150 Glass and Glazing Contractors
238160 Roofing Contractors
238170 Siding Contractors
238190 Other Foundation, Structure, and Building Exterior Contractors
238210 Electrical Contractors
238220 Plumbing, Heating, and Air-Conditioning Contractors
238290 Other Building Equipment Contractors
238310 Drywall and Insulation Contractors
238320 Painting and Wall Covering Contractors
238330 Flooring Contractors
238340 Tile and Terrazzo Contractors
238350 Finish Carpentry Contractors
238390 Other Building Finishing Contractors
238910 Site Preparation Contractors
238990 All Other Specialty Trade Contractors
561621 Security Systems Services (except Locksmiths)
562910 Environmental Remediation Services

The CFMA financial data includes balance sheets, statements of earnings, and financial ratios. The balance sheets and statements of earnings represent a weighted average of all companies included in each classification. Percentages are presented for each dollar amount in the financial statements. Due to rounding, the totals may not agree to the sum of various accounts. Such variations are few and insignificant.

The financial ratios are calculated from the composite balance sheets and statements of earnings data. They are not averages of ratios for all companies included in the classification.

If you wish to purchase 2014 Financial Benchmarking reports ***(www.financialbenchmarker.com)*** or have questions regarding the data, contact Fern Oram, Director of Content Marketing & Communications; Construction Financial Management Association, 100 Village Blvd, Suite 200, Princeton, NJ 08540; Phone 609-452-8000; Fax 609-452-0474; E-mail foram@cfma.org.

Interpretation of the Construction Financial Management Association (CFMA) Data

CFMA's data should only be regarded as general information. It cannot be used to establish industry norms for a number of reasons, including the following:

(1) The financial statements used in the composite are not selected by any random or statistically reliable method. CFMA members voluntarily submitted their financial data. Note that contractors' statements have no upper asset/sales limit.
(2) Many companies provide varied services; CFMA includes a contractor in a classification if at least one-half (1/2) of its annual contract revenue was completed within that classification.
(3) Some of the NAICS group samples may be rather small in relation to the total number of firms in a given industry category. A relatively small sample can increase the chances that some of our composites do not fully represent an industry group.
(4) There is the chance that an extreme statement can be present in a sample, causing a disproportionate influence on the industry composite. This is particularly true in a relatively small sample.
(5) Companies within the same industry may differ in their method of operations, which in turn can directly influence their financial statements. Since such differences affect financial data included in our sample, our composite calculations could be significantly affected.
(6) Other considerations that can result in variation among different companies engaged in the same general line of business are: different labor markets; geographical location; different accounting methods; quality of service rendered; sources and methods of financing; and terms of sale.

The use of CFMA data may be helpful when considered with other methods of financial analysis. Nevertheless, RMA and CFMA do not recommend the use of CFMA's data to establish norms or parameters for a given industry or grouping, or the industry as a whole. Although CFMA believes that its data is accurate and representative within the confines of the aforementioned reasons, RMA and CFMA specifically make no representations regarding the accuracy of representativeness of the figures printed in this supplement of the RMA Annual Statement Studies.

PLEASE NOTE: If you wish to receive the 2014 CFMA data reports, please send your request to studies@rmahq.org. We apologize for any inconvenience.

TEXT—KEY WORD INDEX OF INDUSTRIES APPEARING IN THE STATEMENT STUDIES

TEXT—KEY WORD INDEX OF INDUSTRIES APPEARING IN THE STATEMENT STUDIES

STATEMENT STUDIES KEY WORD INDEX

A complete description of each industry category listed below begins on page 33.

A

Abrasive Product Manufacturing, 472-473, mfg
Adhesive Manufacturing, 414-415, mfg
Administration of Air and Water Resource and Solid Waste Management Programs, 1644-1645, pub admin
Administration of Education Programs, 1640-1641, pub admin
Administration of General Economic Programs, 1650-1651, pub admin
Administration of Housing Programs, 1646-1647, pub admin
Administration of Public Health Programs, 1642-1643, pub admin
Administration of Urban Planning and Community and Rural Development, 1648-1649, pub admin
Administrative Management and General Management Consulting Services, 1274-1275, prof serv
Advertising Agencies, 1294-1295, prof serv
Advertising Material Distribution Services, 1304-1305, prof serv
Agents and Managers for Artists, Athletes, Entertainers, and Other Public Figures, 1502-1503, ent
Air and Gas Compressor Manufacturing, 602-603, mfg
Air-Conditioning and Warm Air Heating Equipment and Commercial and Industrial Refrigeration Equipment Manufacturing, 584-585, mfg
Aircraft Engine and Engine Parts Manufacturing, 700-701, mfg
Aircraft Manufacturing, 698-699, mfg
All Other Amusement and Recreation Industries, 1526-1527, ent
All Other Automotive Repair and Maintenance, 1566-1567, other
All Other Basic Organic Chemical Manufacturing, 398-399, mfg
All Other Business Support Services, 1342-1343, Admin
All Other Consumer Goods Rental, 1220-1221, R/E
All Other Converted Paper Product Manufacturing, 376-377, mfg
All Other General Merchandise Stores, 992-993, rtl
All Other Grain Farming, 102-103, ag
All Other Health and Personal Care Stores, 962-963, rtl
All Other Home Furnishings Stores, 920-921, rtl
All Other Information Services, 1136-1137, info
All Other Insurance Related Activities, 1186-1187, fin
All Other Legal Services, 1240-1241, prof serv
All Other Miscellaneous Ambulatory Health Care Services, 1450-1451, HC
All Other Miscellaneous Chemical Product and Preparation Manufacturing, 426-427, mfg
All Other Miscellaneous Crop Farming, 124-125, ag
All Other Miscellaneous Electrical Equipment and Component Manufacturing, 676-677, mfg
All Other Miscellaneous Fabricated Metal Product Manufacturing, 556-557, mfg
All Other Miscellaneous Food Manufacturing, 298-299, mfg
All Other Miscellaneous General Purpose Machinery Manufacturing, 616-617, mfg
All Other Miscellaneous Manufacturing, 756-757, mfg
All Other Miscellaneous Nonmetallic Mineral Product Manufacturing, 476-477, mfg
All Other Miscellaneous Schools and Instruction, 1406-1407, edu
All Other Miscellaneous Store Retailers (except Tobacco Stores), 1010-1011, rtl
All Other Miscellaneous Textile Product Mills, 324-325, mfg
All Other Miscellaneous Waste Management Services, 1386-1387, Admin
All Other Miscellaneous Wood Product Manufacturing, 360-361, mfg
All Other Nondepository Credit Intermediation, 1146-1147, fin
All Other Outpatient Care Centers, 1438-1439, HC
All Other Personal Services, 1598-1599, other
All Other Petroleum and Coal Products Manufacturing, 392-393, mfg
All Other Plastics Product Manufacturing, 448-449, mfg
All Other Professional, Scientific, and Technical Services, 1316-1317, prof serv
All Other Publishers, 1106-1107, info
All Other Rubber Product Manufacturing, 456-457, mfg
All Other Specialty Food Stores, 950-951, rtl
All Other Specialty Trade Contractors, 246-247, cons-g
All Other Specialty Trade Contractors, 1672, cons-%
All Other Support Activities for Transportation, 1086-1087, trans
All Other Support Services, 1368-1369, Admin
All Other Telecommunications, 1130-1131, info
All Other Transit and Ground Passenger Transportation, 1060-1061, trans
All Other Transportation Equipment Manufacturing, 712-713, mfg
All Other Travel Arrangement and Reservation Services, 1348-1349, Admin
Aluminum Foundries (except Die-Casting), 500-501, mfg
Ambulance Services, 1446-1447, HC
Amusement and Theme Parks, 1508-1509, ent
Amusement Arcades, 1510-1511, ent
Analytical Laboratory Instrument Manufacturing, 654-655, mfg
Animal (except Poultry) Slaughtering, 270-271, mfg
Apparel Accessories and Other Apparel Manufacturing, 334-335, mfg
Apple Orchards, 110-111, ag
Appliance Repair and Maintenance, 1574-1575, other
Architectural Services, 1250-1251, prof serv
Art Dealers, 1004-1005, rtl
Asphalt Paving Mixture and Block Manufacturing, 388-389, mfg
Assisted Living Facilities for the Elderly, 1468-1469, HC
Audio and Video Equipment Manufacturing, 628-629, mfg
Automatic Environmental Control Manufacturing for Residential, Commercial, and Appliance Use, 646-647, mfg
Automobile and Other Motor Vehicle Merchant Wholesalers, 760-761, wsle
Automobile Manufacturing, 678-679, mfg
Automotive Body, Paint, and Interior Repair and Maintenance, 1558-1559, other
Automotive Glass Replacement Shops, 1560-1561, other
Automotive Oil Change and Lubrication Shops, 1562-1563, other
Automotive Parts and Accessories Stores, 912-913, rtl

B

Baked Goods Stores, 946-947, rtl
Ball and Roller Bearing Manufacturing, 550-551, mfg
Bare Printed Circuit Board Manufacturing, 630-631, mfg
Beauty Salons, 1578-1579, other
Beef Cattle Ranching and Farming, 126-12 ag
Beer and Ale Merchant Wholesalers, 880-8 wsle
Beer, Wine, and Liquor Stores, 952-953, rtl
Bituminous Coal and Lignite Surface Minin 160-161, mng
Blind and Shade Manufacturing, 732-733, r
Blood and Organ Banks, 1448-1449, HC
Boat Building, 708-709, mfg
Boat Dealers, 908-909, rtl
Bolt, Nut, Screw, Rivet, and Washer Manufacturing, 534-535, mfg
Book Publishers, 1104-1105, info
Book Stores, 988-989, rtl
Book, Periodical, and Newspaper Merchan Wholesalers, 886-887, wsle
Books Printing, 382-383, mfg
Bottled Water Manufacturing, 302-303, mfg
Bowling Centers, 1524-1525, ent
Breweries, 304-305, mfg
Brick, Stone, and Related Construction Material Merchant Wholesalers, 774-77 wsle
Broadwoven Fabric Mills, 310-311, mfg
Business Associations, 1616-1617, other
Business to Business Electronic Markets, 896-897, wsle

C

Cable and Other Subscription Programmin 1122-1123, info
Capacitor, Resistor, Coil, Transformer, and Other Inductor Manufacturing, 634-635, mfg
Car Washes, 1564-1565, other
Carpet and Rug Mills, 318-319, mfg
Carpet and Upholstery Cleaning Services, 1360-1361, Admin
Casino Hotels, 1532-1533, rest/lodg
Casinos (except Casino Hotels), 1512-151 ent
Caterers, 1542-1543, rest/lodg
Cattle Feedlots, 128-129, ag
Cemeteries and Crematories, 1584-1585, other
Charter Bus Industry, 1056-1057, trans
Cheese Manufacturing, 266-267, mfg
Chicken Egg Production, 134-135, ag
Child and Youth Services, 1472-1473, HC
Child Day Care Services, 1486-1487, HC
Civic and Social Organizations, 1614-1615, other
Claims Adjusting, 1182-1183, fin
Clay Building Material and Refractories Manufacturing, 458-459, mfg
Clothing Accessories Stores, 974-975, rtl
Coal and Other Mineral and Ore Merchant Wholesalers, 796-797, wsle
Coastal and Great Lakes Freight Transportation, 1034-1035, trans
Coffee and Tea Manufacturing, 288-289, m
Coin-Operated Laundries and Drycleaners, 1586-1587, other
Collection Agencies, 1340-1341, Admin
Colleges, Universities, and Professional Schools, 1394-1395, edu
Commercial Air, Rail, and Water Transportation Equipment Rental and Leasing, 1224-1225, R/E
Commercial and Industrial Machinery and Equipment (except Automotive and Electronic) Repair and Maintenance, 1572-1573, other
Commercial and Institutional Building Construction, 198-199, cons-g
Commercial and Institutional Building Construction, 1658, cons-%
Commercial Bakeries, 280-281, mfg
Commercial Photography, 1312-1313, prof serv
Commercial Printing (except Screen and Books), 378-379, mfg

STATEMENT STUDIES KEY WORD INDEX

A complete description of each industry category listed below begins on page 33.

ommercial Screen Printing, 380-381, mfg
ommercial, Industrial, and Institutional Electric Lighting Fixture Manufacturing, 660-661, mfg
ommodity Contracts Dealing, 1158-1159, fin
ommunity Food Services, 1478-1479, HC
omputer and Computer Peripheral Equipment and Software Merchant Wholesalers, 784-785, wsle
omputer and Office Machine Repair and Maintenance, 1568-1569, other
omputer Facilities Management Services, 1270-1271, prof serv
omputer Systems Design Services, 1268-1269, prof serv
omputer Terminal and Other Computer Peripheral Equipment Manufacturing, 620-621, mfg
oncrete Block and Brick Manufacturing, 466-467, mfg
oncrete Pipe Manufacturing, 468-469, mfg
onfectionery and Nut Stores, 948-949, rtl
onfectionery Manufacturing from Purchased Chocolate, 254-255, mfg
onfectionery Merchant Wholesalers, 858-859, wsle
onstruction and Mining (except Oil Well) Machinery and Equipment Merchant Wholesalers, 812-813, wsle
onstruction Machinery Manufacturing, 562-563, mfg
onstruction Sand and Gravel Mining, 166-167, mng
onstruction, Mining, and Forestry Machinery and Equipment Rental and Leasing, 1226-1227, R/E
onsumer Electronics and Appliances Rental, 1216-1217, R/E
onsumer Lending, 1142-1143, fin
ontinuing Care Retirement Communities, 1466-1467, HC
onvenience Stores, 940-941, rtl
onvention and Trade Show Organizers, 1366-1367, Admin
onveyor and Conveying Equipment Manufacturing, 604-605, mfg
ookie and Cracker Manufacturing, 282-283, mfg
opper Rolling, Drawing, Extruding, and Alloying, 488-489, mfg
orn Farming, 100-101, ag
orporate, Subsidiary, and Regional Managing Offices, 1322-1323, mgmt
orrugated and Solid Fiber Box Manufacturing, 364-365, mfg
osmetics, Beauty Supplies, and Perfume Stores, 956-957, rtl
osmetology and Barber Schools, 1398-1399, edu
otton Farming, 122-123, ag
otton Ginning, 146-147, ag
ouriers and Express Delivery Services, 1088-1089, trans
rude Petroleum and Natural Gas Extraction, 158-159, mng
rushed and Broken Limestone Mining and Quarrying, 162-163, mng
urrent-Carrying Wiring Device Manufacturing, 674-675, mfg
urtain and Linen Mills, 320-321, mfg
ustom Architectural Woodwork and Millwork Manufacturing, 724-725, mfg
ustom Compounding of Purchased Resins, 424-425, mfg
ustom Computer Programming Services, 1266-1267, prof serv
ut and Sew Apparel Contractors, 326-327, mfg
ut Stock, Resawing Lumber, and Planing, 350-351, mfg
ut Stone and Stone Product Manufacturing, 474-475, mfg
utting Tool and Machine Tool Accessory Manufacturing, 590-591, mfg

D

Dairy Cattle and Milk Production, 130-131, ag
Dairy Product (except Dried or Canned) Merchant Wholesalers, 854-855, wsle
Data Processing, Hosting, and Related Services, 1132-1133, info
Deep Sea Freight Transportation, 1032-1033, trans
Dental Equipment and Supplies Manufacturing, 738-739, mfg
Dental Laboratories, 742-743, mfg
Department Stores (except Discount Department Stores), 990-991, rtl
Diagnostic Imaging Centers, 1442-1443, HC
Direct Health and Medical Insurance Carriers, 1172-1173, fin
Direct Life Insurance Carriers, 1170-1171, fin
Direct Mail Advertising, 1302-1303, prof serv
Direct Property and Casualty Insurance Carriers, 1174-1175, fin
Direct Title Insurance Carriers, 1176-1177, fin
Doll, Toy, and Game Manufacturing, 748-749, mfg
Dried and Dehydrated Food Manufacturing, 262-263, mfg
Drilling Oil and Gas Wells, 168-169, mng
Drinking Places (Alcoholic Beverages), 1544-1545, rest/lodg
Drugs and Druggists' Sundries Merchant Wholesalers, 840-841, wsle
Drycleaning and Laundry Services (except Coin-Operated), 1588-1589, other
Drywall and Insulation Contractors, 232-233, cons-g
Drywall and Insulation Contractors, 1669, cons-%

E

Educational Support Services, 1408-1409, edu
Electric Power Distribution, 178-179, util
Electrical Apparatus and Equipment, Wiring Supplies, and Related Equipment Merchant Wholesalers, 798-799, wsle
Electrical Contractors and Other Wiring Installation Contractors, 226-227, cons-g
Electrical Contractors and Other Wiring Installation Contractors, 1667, cons-%
Electromedical and Electrotherapeutic Apparatus Manufacturing, 642-643, mfg
Electronic Computer Manufacturing, 618-619, mfg
Electronic Connector Manufacturing, 636-637, mfg
Electronic Shopping, 1012-1013, rtl
Electronics Stores, 924-925, rtl
Electroplating, Plating, Polishing, Anodizing, and Coloring, 540-541, mfg
Elementary and Secondary Schools, 1390-1391, edu
Employment Placement Agencies, 1330-1331, Admin
Engineering Services, 1254-1255, prof serv
Environment, Conservation and Wildlife Organizations, 1610-1611, other
Environmental Consulting Services, 1284-1285, prof serv
Ethyl Alcohol Manufacturing, 396-397, mfg
Executive and Legislative Offices, Combined, 1634-1635, pub admin
Executive Offices, 1628-1629, pub admin
Exterminating and Pest Control Services, 1354-1355, Admin

F

Fabric Coating Mills, 316-317, mfg
Fabricated Pipe and Pipe Fitting Manufacturing, 554-555, mfg
Fabricated Structural Metal Manufacturing, 512-513, mfg
Facilities Support Services, 1328-1329, Admin
Family Clothing Stores, 972-973, rtl
Family Planning Centers, 1430-1431, HC
Farm and Garden Machinery and Equipment Merchant Wholesalers, 814-815, wsle
Farm Machinery and Equipment Manufacturing, 558-559, mfg
Farm Management Services, 152-153, ag
Farm Product Warehousing and Storage, 1094-1095, trans
Farm Supplies Merchant Wholesalers, 884-885, wsle
Fertilizer (Mixing Only) Manufacturing, 404-405, mfg
Fiber, Yarn, and Thread Mills, 308-309, mfg
Financial Transactions Processing, Reserve, and Clearinghouse Activities, 1150-1151, fin
Fine Arts Schools, 1402-1403, edu
Finfish Fishing, 142-143, ag
Finish Carpentry Contractors, 240-241, cons-g
Fire Protection, 1638-1639, pub admin
Fish and Seafood Merchant Wholesalers, 860-861, wsle
Fitness and Recreational Sports Centers, 1522-1523, ent
Flat Glass Manufacturing, 460-461, mfg
Flavoring Syrup and Concentrate Manufacturing, 290-291, mfg
Floor Covering Stores, 918-919, rtl
Flooring Contractors, 236-237, cons-g
Florists, 994-995, rtl
Flour Milling, 252-253, mfg
Flower, Nursery Stock, and Florists' Supplies Merchant Wholesalers, 888-889, wsle
Fluid Milk Manufacturing, 264-265, mfg
Fluid Power Valve and Hose Fitting Manufacturing, 544-545, mfg
Folding Paperboard Box Manufacturing, 366-367, mfg
Food (Health) Supplement Stores, 960-961, rtl
Food Product Machinery Manufacturing, 568-569, mfg
Food Service Contractors, 1540-1541, rest/lodg
Footwear Manufacturing, 338-339, mfg
Footwear Merchant Wholesalers, 848-849, wsle
Framing Contractors, 216-217, cons-g
Freestanding Ambulatory Surgical and Emergency Centers, 1436-1437, HC
Freight Transportation Arrangement, 1082-1083, trans
Fresh Fruit and Vegetable Merchant Wholesalers, 864-865, wsle
Frozen Fruit, Juice, and Vegetable Manufacturing, 256-257, mfg
Frozen Specialty Food Manufacturing, 258-259, mfg
Fruit and Vegetable Canning, 260-261, mfg
Fruit and Vegetable Markets, 944-945, rtl
Fuel Dealers, 1018-1019, rtl
Full-Service Restaurants, 1546-1547, rest/lodg
Funeral Homes and Funeral Services, 1582-1583, other
Furniture Merchant Wholesalers, 768-769, wsle
Furniture Stores, 916-917, rtl

G

Gasket, Packing, and Sealing Device Manufacturing, 752-753, mfg
Gasoline Stations with Convenience Stores, 964-965, rtl
General Automotive Repair, 1554-1555, other
General Freight Trucking, Local, 1038-1039, trans
General Freight Trucking, Long-Distance, Less Than Truckload, 1042-1043, trans
General Freight Trucking, Long-Distance, Truckload, 1040-1041, trans
General Line Grocery Merchant Wholesalers, 850-851, wsle

STATEMENT STUDIES KEY WORD INDEX

A complete description of each industry category listed below begins on page 33.

General Medical and Surgical Hospitals, 1452-1453, HC
General Medical and Surgical Hospitals (Non-Profit), 1454-1455, HC
General Rental Centers, 1222-1223, R/E
General Warehousing and Storage, 1090-1091, trans
Gift, Novelty, and Souvenir Stores, 998-999, rtl
Glass and Glazing Contractors, 220-221, cons-g
Glass and Glazing Contractors, 1665, cons-%
Glass Product Manufacturing Made of Purchased Glass, 462-463, mfg
Golf Courses and Country Clubs, 1516-1517, ent
Grain and Field Bean Merchant Wholesalers, 868-869, wsle
Grantmaking Foundations, 1602-1603, other
Grape Vineyards, 112-113, ag
Graphic Design Services, 1262-1263, prof serv

H

Hardware Manufacturing, 524-525, mfg
Hardware Merchant Wholesalers, 804-805, wsle
Hardware Stores, 930-931, rtl
Hardwood Veneer and Plywood Manufacturing, 344-345, mfg
Hazardous Waste Treatment and Disposal, 1374-1375, Admin
Heating Equipment (except Warm Air Furnaces) Manufacturing, 582-583, mfg
Highway, Street, and Bridge Construction, 208-209, cons-g
Highway, Street, and Bridge Construction, 1661, cons-%
Hobby, Toy, and Game Stores, 984-985, rtl
Hog and Pig Farming, 132-133, ag
Home Centers, 926-927, rtl
Home Furnishing Merchant Wholesalers, 770-771, wsle
Home Health Care Services, 1444-1445, HC
Home Health Equipment Rental, 1218-1219, R/E
Horses and Other Equine Production, 136-137, ag
Hotels (except Casino Hotels) and Motels, 1530-1531, rest/lodg
Household Appliance Stores, 922-923, rtl
Household Appliances, Electric Housewares, and Consumer Electronics Merchant Wholesalers, 800-801, wsle
Human Resources Consulting Services, 1276-1277, prof serv
Human Rights Organizations, 1608-1609, other
Hydroelectric Power Generation, 174-175, util

I

Ice Cream and Frozen Dessert Manufacturing, 268-269, mfg
Industrial and Commercial Fan and Blower and Air Purification Equipment Manufacturing, 580-581, mfg
Industrial and Personal Service Paper Merchant Wholesalers, 838-839, wsle
Industrial Building Construction, 196-197, cons-g
Industrial Building Construction, 1657, cons-%
Industrial Launderers, 1592-1593, other
Industrial Machinery and Equipment Merchant Wholesalers, 816-817, wsle
Industrial Mold Manufacturing, 586-587, mfg
Industrial Process Furnace and Oven Manufacturing, 614-615, mfg
Industrial Supplies Merchant Wholesalers, 818-819, wsle
Industrial Truck, Tractor, Trailer, and Stacker Machinery Manufacturing, 608-609, mfg
Industrial Valve Manufacturing, 542-543, mfg
Inland Water Freight Transportation, 1036-1037, trans
Institutional Furniture Manufacturing, 720-721, mfg
Instrument Manufacturing for Measuring and Testing Electricity and Electrical Signals, 652-653, mfg
Instruments and Related Products Manufacturing for Measuring, Displaying, and Controlling Industrial Process Variables, 648-649, mfg
Insurance Agencies and Brokerages, 1180-1181, fin
Interior Design Services, 1260-1261, prof serv
Internet Publishing and Broadcasting and Web Search Portals, 1134-1135, info
Investment Advice, 1164-1165, fin
Investment Banking and Securities Dealing, 1154-1155, fin
Iron and Steel Forging, 502-503, mfg
Iron and Steel Mills and Ferroalloy Manufacturing, 478-479, mfg
Iron and Steel Pipe and Tube Manufacturing from Purchased Steel, 480-481, mfg
Iron Foundries, 494-495, mfg

J

Janitorial Services, 1356-1357, Admin
Jewelry and Silverware Manufacturing, 744-745, mfg
Jewelry Stores, 980-981, rtl
Jewelry, Watch, Precious Stone, and Precious Metal Merchant Wholesalers, 830-831, wsle
Junior Colleges, 1392-1393, edu

K

Kidney Dialysis Centers, 1434-1435, HC

L

Labor Unions and Similar Labor Organizations, 1620-1621, other
Laminated Plastics Plate, Sheet (except Packaging), and Shape Manufacturing, 438-439, mfg
Land Subdivision, 206-207, cons-g
Land Subdivision, 1660, cons-%
Landscape Architectural Services, 1252-1253, prof serv
Landscaping Services, 1358-1359, Admin
Lawn and Garden Tractor and Home Lawn and Garden Equipment Manufacturing, 560-561, mfg
Leather and Hide Tanning and Finishing, 336-337, mfg
Legislative Bodies, 1630-1631, pub admin
Lessors of Miniwarehouses and Self-Storage Units, 1198-1199, R/E
Lessors of Nonfinancial Intangible Assets (except Copyrighted Works), 1232-1233, R/E
Lessors of Nonresidential Buildings (except Miniwarehouses), 1196-1197, R/E
Lessors of Other Real Estate Property, 1200-1201, R/E
Lessors of Residential Buildings and Dwellings, 1194-1195, R/E
Limited-Service Restaurants, 1548-1549, rest/lodg
Limousine Service, 1052-1053, trans
Line-Haul Railroads, 1030-1031, trans
Linen Supply, 1590-1591, other
Logging, 140-141, ag
Lumber, Plywood, Millwork, and Wood Panel Merchant Wholesalers, 772-773, wsle

M

Machine Shops, 530-531, mfg
Machine Tool Manufacturing, 592-593, mfg
Mail-Order Houses, 1014-1015, rtl
Manufactured (Mobile) Home Dealers, 1006-1007, rtl
Manufactured Home (Mobile Home) Manufacturing, 356-357, mfg
Marinas, 1520-1521, ent
Marine Cargo Handling, 1072-1073, trans
Marketing Consulting Services, 1278-1279, prof serv
Marketing Research and Public Opinion Polling, 1308-1309, prof serv
Masonry Contractors, 218-219, cons-g
Materials Recovery Facilities, 1382-1383, Admin
Mattress Manufacturing, 730-731, mfg
Mayonnaise, Dressing, and Other Prepared Sauce Manufacturing, 292-293, mfg
Meat and Meat Product Merchant Wholesalers, 862-863, wsle
Meat Markets, 942-943, rtl
Meat Processed from Carcasses, 272-273, mfg
Mechanical Power Transmission Equipment Manufacturing, 598-599, mfg
Media Representatives, 1298-1299, prof s
Medical Laboratories, 1440-1441, HC
Medical, Dental, and Hospital Equipment and Supplies Merchant Wholesalers, 788-7 wsle
Medicinal and Botanical Manufacturing, 408-409, mfg
Men's and Boys' Cut and Sew Apparel Manufacturing, 328-329, mfg
Men's and Boys' Clothing and Furnishings Merchant Wholesalers, 844-845, wsle
Men's Clothing Stores, 968-969, rtl
Metal Coating, Engraving (except Jewelry and Silverware), and Allied Services to Manufacturers, 538-539, mfg
Metal Crown, Closure, and Other Metal Stamping (except Automotive), 506-50 mfg
Metal Heat Treating, 536-537, mfg
Metal Service Centers and Other Metal Merchant Wholesalers, 794-795, wsle
Metal Window and Door Manufacturing, 516-517, mfg
Mining Machinery and Equipment Manufacturing, 564-565, mfg
Miscellaneous Financial Investment Activit 1168-1169, fin
Miscellaneous Intermediation, 1160-1161,
Mortgage and Nonmortgage Loan Brokers 1148-1149, fin
Motion Picture and Video Production, 1110-1111, info
Motion Picture Theaters (except Drive-Ins) 1112-1113, info
Motor and Generator Manufacturing, 666-6 mfg
Motor Vehicle Body Manufacturing, 680-68 mfg
Motor Vehicle Electrical and Electronic Equipment Manufacturing, 688-689, m
Motor Vehicle Gasoline Engine and Engine Parts Manufacturing, 686-687, mfg
Motor Vehicle Metal Stamping, 694-695, m
Motor Vehicle Parts (Used) Merchant Wholesalers, 766-767, wsle
Motor Vehicle Seating and Interior Trim Manufacturing, 692-693, mfg
Motor Vehicle Supplies and New Parts Merchant Wholesalers, 762-763, wsle
Motor Vehicle Towing, 1078-1079, trans
Motor Vehicle Transmission and Power Tra Parts Manufacturing, 690-691, mfg
Motorcycle, ATV, and All Other Motor Vehi Dealers, 910-911, rtl
Motorcycle, Bicycle, and Parts Manufactur 710-711, mfg
Museums, 1504-1505, ent
Mushroom Production, 116-117, ag
Musical Groups and Artists, 1492-1493, e
Musical Instrument and Supplies Stores, 986-987, rtl
Musical Instrument Manufacturing, 754-75 mfg

N

Natural Gas Distribution, 180-181, util

STATEMENT STUDIES KEY WORD INDEX

A complete description of each industry category listed below begins on page 33.

Navigational Services to Shipping, 1074-1075, trans
New Car Dealers, 902-903, rtl
New Housing For-Sale Builders, 192-193, cons-g
New Housing For-Sale Builders, 1655, cons-%
New Multifamily Housing Construction (except For-Sale Builders), 190-191, cons-g
New Single-Family Housing Construction (except For-Sale Builders), 188-189, cons-g
New Single-Family Housing Construction (except For-Sale Builders), 1654, cons-%
Newspaper Publishers, 1100-1101, info
Nitrogenous Fertilizer Manufacturing, 402-403, mfg
Nonferrous Metal (except Copper and Aluminum) Rolling, Drawing, and Extruding, 490-491, mfg
Nonferrous Metal Die-Casting Foundries, 498-499, mfg
Nonresidential Property Managers, 1206-1207, R/E
Nonscheduled Chartered Passenger Air Transportation, 1026-1027, trans
Nonupholstered Wood Household Furniture Manufacturing, 718-719, mfg
Nonwoven Fabric Mills, 312-313, mfg
Nursery and Tree Production, 118-119, ag
Nursery, Garden Center, and Farm Supply Stores, 936-937, rtl
Nursing Care Facilities (Skilled Nursing Facilities), 1460-1461, HC

O

Office Administrative Services, 1326-1327, Admin
Office Equipment Merchant Wholesalers, 782-783, wsle
Office Furniture (except Wood) Manufacturing, 726-727, mfg
Office Machinery and Equipment Rental and Leasing, 1228-1229, R/E
Office Supplies and Stationery Stores, 996-997, rtl
Offices of All Other Miscellaneous Health Practitioners, 1428-1429, HC
Offices of Certified Public Accountants, 1242-1243, prof serv
Offices of Chiropractors, 1418-1419, HC
Offices of Dentists, 1416-1417, HC
Offices of Lawyers, 1236-1237, prof serv
Offices of Mental Health Practitioners (except Physicians), 1422-1423, HC
Offices of Optometrists, 1420-1421, HC
Offices of Other Holding Companies, 1320-1321, mgmt
Offices of Physical, Occupational and Speech Therapists, and Audiologists, 1424-1425, HC
Offices of Physicians (except Mental Health Specialists), 1412-1413, HC
Offices of Physicians, Mental Health Specialists, 1414-1415, HC
Offices of Podiatrists, 1426-1427, HC
Offices of Real Estate Agents and Brokers, 1202-1203, R/E
Oil and Gas Field Machinery and Equipment Manufacturing, 566-567, mfg
Oil and Gas Pipeline and Related Structures Construction, 202-203, cons-g
Open-End Investment Funds, 1188-1189, fin
Ophthalmic Goods Manufacturing, 740-741, mfg
Ophthalmic Goods Merchant Wholesalers, 790-791, wsle
Optical Goods Stores, 958-959, rtl
Optical Instrument and Lens Manufacturing, 576-577, mfg
Orange Groves, 108-109, ag
Ornamental and Architectural Metal Work Manufacturing, 520-521, mfg
Other Accounting Services, 1248-1249, prof serv
Other Activities Related to Credit Intermediation, 1152-1153, fin
Other Activities Related to Real Estate, 1208-1209, R/E
Other Aircraft Parts and Auxiliary Equipment Manufacturing, 702-703, mfg
Other Airport Operations, 1064-1065, trans
Other Aluminum Rolling, Drawing, and Extruding, 486-487, mfg
Other Animal Food Manufacturing, 250-251, mfg
Other Automotive Mechanical and Electrical Repair and Maintenance, 1556-1557, other
Other Basic Inorganic Chemical Manufacturing, 394-395, mfg
Other Building Equipment Contractors, 230-231, cons-g
Other Building Finishing Contractors, 242-243, cons-g
Other Building Material Dealers, 932-933, rtl
Other Business Service Centers (including Copy Shops), 1338-1339, Admin
Other Chemical and Allied Products Merchant Wholesalers, 874-875, wsle
Other Clothing Stores, 976-977, rtl
Other Commercial and Industrial Machinery and Equipment Rental and Leasing, 1230-1231, R/E
Other Commercial and Service Industry Machinery Manufacturing, 578-579, mfg
Other Commercial Equipment Merchant Wholesalers, 786-787, wsle
Other Communications Equipment Manufacturing, 626-627, mfg
Other Community Housing Services, 1482-1483, HC
Other Computer Related Services, 1272-1273, prof serv
Other Concrete Product Manufacturing, 470-471, mfg
Other Construction Material Merchant Wholesalers, 778-779, wsle
Other Crushed and Broken Stone Mining and Quarrying, 164-165, mng
Other Cut and Sew Apparel Manufacturing, 332-333, mfg
Other Direct Insurance (except Life, Health, and Medical) Carriers, 1178-1179, fin
Other Direct Selling Establishments, 1020-1021, rtl
Other Electric Power Generation, 176-177, util
Other Electronic and Precision Equipment Repair and Maintenance, 1570-1571, other
Other Electronic Component Manufacturing, 640-641, mfg
Other Electronic Parts and Equipment Merchant Wholesalers, 802-803, wsle
Other Fabricated Wire Product Manufacturing, 528-529, mfg
Other Farm Product Raw Material Merchant Wholesalers, 870-871, wsle
Other Financial Vehicles, 1190-1191, fin
Other Foundation, Structure, and Building Exterior Contractors, 224-225, cons-g
Other Gambling Industries, 1514-1515, ent
Other Gasoline Stations, 966-967, rtl
Other General Government Support, 1636-1637, pub admin
Other Grantmaking and Giving Services, 1606-1607, other
Other Grocery and Related Products Merchant Wholesalers, 866-867, wsle
Other Heavy and Civil Engineering Construction, 210-211, cons-g
Other Heavy and Civil Engineering Construction, 1662, cons-%
Other Individual and Family Services, 1476-1477, HC
Other Industrial Machinery Manufacturing, 574-575, mfg
Other Lighting Equipment Manufacturing, 662-663, mfg
Other Management Consulting Services, 1282-1283, prof serv
Other Measuring and Controlling Device Manufacturing, 656-657, mfg
Other Metal Container Manufacturing, 522-523, mfg
Other Metal Valve and Pipe Fitting Manufacturing, 548-549, mfg
Other Millwork (including Flooring), 352-353, mfg
Other Miscellaneous Durable Goods Merchant Wholesalers, 832-833, wsle
Other Miscellaneous Nondurable Goods Merchant Wholesalers, 894-895, wsle
Other Motion Picture and Video Industries, 1116-1117, info
Other Motor Vehicle Parts Manufacturing, 696-697, mfg
Other Nonhazardous Waste Treatment and Disposal, 1378-1379, Admin
Other Nonscheduled Air Transportation, 1028-1029, trans
Other Paperboard Container Manufacturing, 368-369, mfg
Other Personal and Household Goods Repair and Maintenance, 1576-1577, other
Other Personal Care Services, 1580-1581, other
Other Professional Equipment and Supplies Merchant Wholesalers, 792-793, wsle
Other Residential Care Facilities, 1470-1471, HC
Other Scientific and Technical Consulting Services, 1286-1287, prof serv
Other Services Related to Advertising, 1306-1307, prof serv
Other Services to Buildings and Dwellings, 1362-1363, Admin
Other Similar Organizations (except Business, Professional, Labor, and Political Organizations), 1622-1623, other
Other Snack Food Manufacturing, 286-287, mfg
Other Social Advocacy Organizations, 1612-1613, other
Other Specialized Design Services, 1264-1265, prof serv
Other Support Activities for Air Transportation, 1066-1067, trans
Other Support Activities for Road Transportation, 1080-1081, trans
Other Support Activities for Water Transportation, 1076-1077, trans
Other Technical and Trade Schools, 1400-1401, edu
Other Vegetable (except Potato) and Melon Farming, 106-107, ag
Other Warehousing and Storage, 1096-1097, trans
Other Waste Collection, 1372-1373, Admin
Outdoor Advertising, 1300-1301, prof serv
Outdoor Power Equipment Stores, 934-935, rtl
Outpatient Mental Health and Substance Abuse Centers, 1432-1433, HC
Overhead Traveling Crane, Hoist, and Monorail System Manufacturing, 606-607, mfg

P

Packaged Frozen Food Merchant Wholesalers, 852-853, wsle
Packaging and Labeling Services, 1364-1365, Admin
Packaging Machinery Manufacturing, 612-613, mfg
Packing and Crating, 1084-1085, trans
Paint and Coating Manufacturing, 412-413, mfg
Paint and Wallpaper Stores, 928-929, rtl
Paint, Varnish, and Supplies Merchant Wholesalers, 892-893, wsle

STATEMENT STUDIES KEY WORD INDEX

A complete description of each industry category listed below begins on page 33.

Painting and Wall Covering Contractors, 234-235, cons-g
Painting and Wall Covering Contractors, 1670, cons-%
Paper (except Newsprint) Mills, 362-363, mfg
Paper Bag and Coated and Treated Paper Manufacturing, 370-371, mfg
Parking Lots and Garages, 1596-1597, other
Passenger Car Leasing, 1212-1213, R/E
Passenger Car Rental, 1210-1211, R/E
Payroll Services, 1246-1247, prof serv
Periodical Publishers, 1102-1103, info
Perishable Prepared Food Manufacturing, 296-297, mfg
Pesticide and Other Agricultural Chemical Manufacturing, 406-407, mfg
Pet and Pet Supplies Stores, 1002-1003, rtl
Pet Care (except Veterinary) Services, 1594-1595, other
Petroleum and Petroleum Products Merchant Wholesalers (except Bulk Stations and Terminals), 878-879, wsle
Petroleum Bulk Stations and Terminals, 876-877, wsle
Petroleum Lubricating Oil and Grease Manufacturing, 390-391, mfg
Petroleum Refineries, 386-387, mfg
Pharmaceutical Preparation Manufacturing, 410-411, mfg
Pharmacies and Drug Stores, 954-955, rtl
Photographic Equipment and Supplies Merchant Wholesalers, 780-781, wsle
Photography Studios, Portrait, 1310-1311, prof serv
Piece Goods, Notions, and Other Dry Goods Merchant Wholesalers, 842-843, wsle
Plastics Bag and Pouch Manufacturing, 428-429, mfg
Plastics Bottle Manufacturing, 444-445, mfg
Plastics Material and Resin Manufacturing, 400-401, mfg
Plastics Materials and Basic Forms and Shapes Merchant Wholesalers, 872-873, wsle
Plastics Packaging Film and Sheet (including Laminated) Manufacturing, 430-431, mfg
Plastics Pipe and Pipe Fitting Manufacturing, 436-437, mfg
Plastics Plumbing Fixture Manufacturing, 446-447, mfg
Plate Work Manufacturing, 514-515, mfg
Plumbing and Heating Equipment and Supplies (Hydronics) Merchant Wholesalers, 806-807, wsle
Plumbing Fixture Fitting and Trim Manufacturing, 546-547, mfg
Plumbing, Heating, and Air-Conditioning Contractors, 228-229, cons-g
Plumbing, Heating, and Air-Conditioning Contractors, 1668, cons-%
Polish and Other Sanitation Good Manufacturing, 418-419, mfg
Polystyrene Foam Product Manufacturing, 440-441, mfg
Port and Harbor Operations, 1070-1071, trans
Portfolio Management, 1162-1163, fin
Postharvest Crop Activities (except Cotton Ginning), 150-151, ag
Potato Farming, 104-105, ag
Poultry and Poultry Product Merchant Wholesalers, 856-857, wsle
Poultry Processing, 274-275, mfg
Poured Concrete Foundation and Structure Contractors, 212-213, cons-g
Poured Concrete Foundation and Structure Contractors, 1663, cons-%
Powder Metallurgy Part Manufacturing, 504-505, mfg
Power and Communication Line and Related Structures Construction, 204-205, cons-g
Power, Distribution, and Specialty Transformer Manufacturing, 664-665, mfg
Precision Turned Product Manufacturing, 532-533, mfg
Prefabricated Metal Building and Component Manufacturing, 510-511, mfg
Prefabricated Wood Building Manufacturing, 358-359, mfg
Printed Circuit Assembly (Electronic Assembly) Manufacturing, 638-639, mfg
Printing and Writing Paper Merchant Wholesalers, 834-835, wsle
Printing Ink Manufacturing, 422-423, mfg
Printing Machinery and Equipment Manufacturing, 572-573, mfg
Private Households, 1624-1625, other
Process, Physical Distribution, and Logistics Consulting Services, 1280-1281, prof serv
Professional and Management Development Training, 1396-1397, edu
Professional Employer Organizations, 1334-1335, Admin
Professional Organizations, 1618-1619, other
Promoters of Performing Arts, Sports, and Similar Events with Facilities, 1498-1499, ent
Promoters of Performing Arts, Sports, and Similar Events without Facilities, 1500-1501, ent
Psychiatric and Substance Abuse Hospitals, 1456-1457, HC
Public Finance Activities, 1632-1633, pub admin
Public Relations Agencies, 1296-1297, prof serv
Pump and Pumping Equipment Manufacturing, 600-601, mfg

R

Racetracks, 1496-1497, ent
Radio and Television Broadcasting and Wireless Communications Equipment Manufacturing, 624-625, mfg
Radio Stations, 1118-1119, info
Railroad Rolling Stock Manufacturing, 704-705, mfg
Ready-Mix Concrete Manufacturing, 464-465, mfg
Real Estate Credit, 1144-1145, fin
Recreational and Vacation Camps (except Campgrounds), 1536-1537, rest/lodg
Recreational Vehicle Dealers, 906-907, rtl
Recyclable Material Merchant Wholesalers, 828-829, wsle
Refrigerated Warehousing and Storage, 1092-1093, trans
Refrigeration Equipment and Supplies Merchant Wholesalers, 810-811, wsle
Relay and Industrial Control Manufacturing, 670-671, mfg
Religious Organizations, 1600-1601, other
Remediation Services, 1380-1381, Admin
Research and Development in Biotechnology, 1288-1289, prof serv
Research and Development in the Physical, Engineering, and Life Sciences (except Biotechnology), 1290-1291, prof serv
Research and Development in the Social Sciences and Humanities, 1292-1293, prof serv
Residential Electric Lighting Fixture Manufacturing, 658-659, mfg
Residential Intellectual and Developmental Disability Facilities, 1462-1463, HC
Residential Mental Health and Substance Abuse Facilities, 1464-1465, HC
Residential Property Managers, 1204-1205, R/E
Residential Remodelers, 194-195, cons-g
Residential Remodelers, 1656, cons-%
Retail Bakeries, 278-279, mfg
Roasted Nuts and Peanut Butter Manufacturing, 284-285, mfg
Rolled Steel Shape Manufacturing, 482-483, mfg
Rolling Mill and Other Metalworking Machinery Manufacturing, 594-595, mfg
Roofing Contractors, 222-223, cons-g
Roofing Contractors, 1666, cons-%
Roofing, Siding, and Insulation Material Merchant Wholesalers, 776-777, wsle
Rooming and Boarding Houses, 1538-1539, rest/lodg
Rubber and Plastics Hoses and Belting Manufacturing, 452-453, mfg
Rubber Product Manufacturing for Mechanical Use, 454-455, mfg
RV (Recreational Vehicle) Parks and Campgrounds, 1534-1535, rest/lodg

S

Sales Financing, 1140-1141, fin
Sanitary Paper Product Manufacturing, 374-375, mfg
Saw Blade and Handtool Manufacturing, 508-509, mfg
Sawmill, Woodworking, and Paper Machinery Manufacturing, 570-571, mfg
Sawmills, 340-341, mfg
Scenic and Sightseeing Transportation, Water 1062-1063, trans
Scheduled Passenger Air Transportation, 1024-1025, trans
School and Employee Bus Transportation, 1054-1055, trans
Seafood Product Preparation and Packaging, 276-277, mfg
Search, Detection, Navigation, Guidance, Aeronautical, and Nautical System and Instrument Manufacturing, 644-645, mfg
Secondary Smelting, Refining, and Alloying o Nonferrous Metal (except Copper and Aluminum), 492-493, mfg
Securities Brokerage, 1156-1157, fin
Security Guards and Patrol Services, 1350-1351, Admin
Security Systems Services (except Locksmiths), 1352-1353, Admin
Semiconductor and Related Device Manufacturing, 632-633, mfg
Septic Tank and Related Services, 1384-1385, Admin
Service Establishment Equipment and Supplies Merchant Wholesalers, 820-821 wsle
Services for the Elderly and Persons with Disabilities, 1474-1475, HC
Sewage Treatment Facilities, 184-185, util
Sheet Metal Work Manufacturing, 518-519, mfg
Shellfish Fishing, 144-145, ag
Ship Building and Repairing, 706-707, mfg
Shoe Stores, 978-979, rtl
Showcase, Partition, Shelving, and Locker Manufacturing, 728-729, mfg
Sign Manufacturing, 750-751, mfg
Site Preparation Contractors, 244-245, cons
Site Preparation Contractors, 1671, cons-%
Skiing Facilities, 1518-1519, ent
Small Arms, Ordnance, and Ordnance Accessories Manufacturing, 552-553, mf
Snack and Nonalcoholic Beverage Bars, 1550-1551, rest/lodg
Soap and Other Detergent Manufacturing, 416-417, mfg
Soft Drink Manufacturing, 300-301, mfg
Software Publishers, 1108-1109, info
Soil Preparation, Planting, and Cultivating, 148-149, ag
Solid Waste Collection, 1370-1371, Admin
Solid Waste Landfill, 1376-1377, Admin
Soybean Farming, 96-97, ag
Special Die and Tool, Die Set, Jig, and Fixtu Manufacturing, 588-589, mfg
Special Needs Transportation, 1058-1059, trans
Specialized Freight (except Used Goods) Trucking, Local, 1046-1047, trans
Specialized Freight (except Used Goods) Trucking, Long-Distance, 1048-1049, tra
Specialty (except Psychiatric and Substanc Abuse) Hospitals, 1458-1459, HC

STATEMENT STUDIES KEY WORD INDEX

A complete description of each industry category listed below begins on page 33.

peed Changer, Industrial High-Speed Drive, and Gear Manufacturing, 596-597, mfg
pice and Extract Manufacturing, 294-295, mfg
porting and Athletic Goods Manufacturing, 746-747, mfg
porting and Recreational Goods and Supplies Merchant Wholesalers, 824-825, wsle
porting Goods Stores, 982-983, rtl
ports and Recreation Instruction, 1404-1405, edu
ports Teams and Clubs, 1494-1495, ent
pring Manufacturing, 526-527, mfg
tationery and Office Supplies Merchant Wholesalers, 836-837, wsle
tationery Product Manufacturing, 372-373, mfg
teel Foundries (except Investment), 496-497, mfg
teel Wire Drawing, 484-485, mfg
torage Battery Manufacturing, 672-673, mfg
tructural Steel and Precast Concrete Contractors, 214-215, cons-g
tructural Steel and Precast Concrete Contractors, 1664, cons-%
upermarkets and Other Grocery (except Convenience) Stores, 938-939, rtl
upport Activities for Animal Production, 154-155, ag
upport Activities for Oil and Gas Operations, 170-171, mng
upport Activities for Printing, 384-385, mfg
upport Activities for Rail Transportation, 1068-1069, trans
urgical and Medical Instrument Manufacturing, 734-735, mfg
urgical Appliance and Supplies Manufacturing, 736-737, mfg
urveying and Mapping (except Geophysical) Services, 1256-1257, prof serv
witchgear and Switchboard Apparatus Manufacturing, 668-669, mfg

T

ax Preparation Services, 1244-1245, prof serv
axi Service, 1050-1051, trans
elecommunications Resellers, 1128-1129, info
elemarketing Bureaus and Other Contact Centers, 1336-1337, Admin
elephone Apparatus Manufacturing, 622-623, mfg
eleproduction and Other Postproduction Services, 1114-1115, info
Television Broadcasting, 1120-1121, info
Temporary Help Services, 1332-1333, Admin
Temporary Shelters, 1480-1481, HC
Testing Laboratories, 1258-1259, prof serv
Textile and Fabric Finishing Mills, 314-315, mfg
Textile Bag and Canvas Mills, 322-323, mfg
Theater Companies and Dinner Theaters, 1490-1491, ent
Third Party Administration of Insurance and Pension Funds, 1184-1185, fin
Tile and Terrazzo Contractors, 238-239, cons-g
Timber Tract Operations, 138-139, ag
Tire and Tube Merchant Wholesalers, 764-765, wsle
Tire Dealers, 914-915, rtl
Tire Retreading, 450-451, mfg
Title Abstract and Settlement Offices, 1238-1239, prof serv
Tobacco and Tobacco Product Merchant Wholesalers, 890-891, wsle
Tobacco Farming, 120-121, ag
Tobacco Stores, 1008-1009, rtl
Toilet Preparation Manufacturing, 420-421, mfg
Totalizing Fluid Meter and Counting Device Manufacturing, 650-651, mfg
Tour Operators, 1346-1347, Admin
Toy and Hobby Goods and Supplies Merchant Wholesalers, 826-827, wsle
Transportation Equipment and Supplies (except Motor Vehicle) Merchant Wholesalers, 822-823, wsle
Travel Agencies, 1344-1345, Admin
Travel Trailer and Camper Manufacturing, 684-685, mfg
Tree Nut Farming, 114-115, ag
Truck Trailer Manufacturing, 682-683, mfg
Truck, Utility Trailer, and RV (Recreational Vehicle) Rental and Leasing, 1214-1215, R/E
Truss Manufacturing, 346-347, mfg
Trust, Fiduciary, and Custody Activities, 1166-1167, fin

U

Unlaminated Plastics Film and Sheet (except Packaging) Manufacturing, 432-433, mfg
Unlaminated Plastics Profile Shape Manufacturing, 434-435, mfg
Upholstered Household Furniture Manufacturing, 716-717, mfg
Urethane and Other Foam Product (except Polystyrene) Manufacturing, 442-443, mfg
Used Car Dealers, 904-905, rtl
Used Household and Office Goods Moving, 1044-1045, trans
Used Merchandise Stores, 1000-1001, rtl

V

Vending Machine Operators, 1016-1017, rtl
Veterinary Services, 1314-1315, prof serv
Vocational Rehabilitation Services, 1484-1485, HC
Voluntary Health Organizations, 1604-1605, other

W

Warm Air Heating and Air-Conditioning Equipment and Supplies Merchant Wholesalers, 808-809, wsle
Water and Sewer Line and Related Structures Construction, 200-201, cons-g
Water and Sewer Line and Related Structures Construction, 1659, cons-%
Water Supply and Irrigation Systems, 182-183, util
Welding and Soldering Equipment Manufacturing, 610-611, mfg
Wheat Farming, 98-99, ag
Wholesale Trade Agents and Brokers, 898-899, wsle
Wine and Distilled Alcoholic Beverage Merchant Wholesalers, 882-883, wsle
Wineries, 306-307, mfg
Wired Telecommunications Carriers, 1124-1125, info
Wireless Telecommunications Carriers (except Satellite), 1126-1127, info
Women's, Girls', and Infants' Cut and Sew Apparel Manufacturing, 330-331, mfg
Women's Clothing Stores, 970-971, rtl
Women's, Children's, and Infants' Clothing and Accessories Merchant Wholesalers, 846-847, wsle
Wood Container and Pallet Manufacturing, 354-355, mfg
Wood Kitchen Cabinet and Countertop Manufacturing, 714-715, mfg
Wood Office Furniture Manufacturing, 722-723, mfg
Wood Preservation, 342-343, mfg
Wood Window and Door Manufacturing, 348-349, mfg

Z

Zoos and Botanical Gardens, 1506-1507, ent

RMA'S CREDIT & LENDING DICTIONARY

A

sentee Owner: landlord who does not reside in his or her rental property.

stract of Title: condensed history of title to land and real property, consisting of ownership transfers and any conveyances or liens that may affect future ownership.

celeration Clause: provision in note or contract that allows holder to declare remaining balance due and payable immediately upon default in an obligation. Usual causes of default are failure to pay interest or principal installments in a timely manner, an adverse change in financing conditions, or failure to meet loan covenants.

ceptance: drawee's signed agreement to honor draft as presented, which consists of signature alone, but will frequently be evidenced by drawee writing word "accepted," date it is payable, and signature. Sometimes called Trade Acceptance or Banker's Acceptance, depending upon function of acceptor.

commodation: 1. lending or extending credit to borrower. 2. loan or commitment to lend money.

cord and Satisfaction: agreement between two or more persons or entities that satisfies or discharges obligation or settles claim or lawsuit. Generally involves disputed matter in which one party agrees to give and other party agrees to accept something in satisfaction different from, and usually less than, that originally asked for.

count: 1. statement showing balance along with detailed explanation covering debits and credits. 2. right of payment for goods sold or leased or for services rendered on open account basis. 3. summarized record of financial transaction. 4. customer.

countant: person in charge of and skilled in the recording of financial transactions and maintenance of financial records.

counting: 1. theory and system of classifying, recording, summarizing, and auditing books of firm. 2. art of analyzing, interpreting, and reporting financial position and operating results of business.

count Manager: 1. sometimes called Relationship Manager or Account Officer. 2. person responsible for overseeing all matters relating to a specific client or group of customers.

count Number: unique identification number used to designate specific customer.

counts Payable: short-term liability representing amounts due trade creditors.

counts Payable Department: section of business office responsible for processing open account balances and paying amounts owed for goods and services purchased.

counts Receivable: money due to a business by its customers for goods sold or services performed on open account (or credit). Usually refers to short-term receivables.

counts Receivable Aging Report: report by customer that lists age of accounts receivable generally by 30-day intervals from invoice or due date. See also Aging of Accounts Receivable.

counts Receivable Financing: form of secured lending in which borrowings are typically limited to percentage of receivables pledged as collateral.

crual Accounting: basis of accounting in which expenses are recorded when incurred and revenues are recognized when earned, regardless of when cash is actually paid or received.

crue: 1. something gained, added, or accumulated, such as profit from a business transaction. 2. right to sue has become exercisable.

crued Expenses: short-term liabilities that represent expenses for goods used but not yet paid.

crued Income: income earned but not yet collected.

crued Interest: interest accumulated since last interest payment due date.

crued Liabilities: expenses or obligations for goods or services incurred but not yet paid.

CH: see *Automated Clearinghouse.*

cid Test: ratio between company's most liquid assets (generally, cash and accounts receivable) and current liabilities that represents the degree to which current liabilities can be paid with those assets.

knowledgment: 1. declaration making known receipt of something done or to be done; confirmation of receipt of order or of terms of contract. 2. statement of notary or other competent officer certifying that signature on document was personally signed by individual whose signature is affixed to instrument.

quisition: merger or taking over of controlling interest of one business by another.

quisition and Development Loan: loan made for the purpose of purchasing a property and completing all on-site improvements such as street layout, utility installation, and community area grading necessary to bring the site to a buildable state.

quittal: 1. release from obligation or contract. 2. to have accusation of crime dismissed by some formal legal procedure.

tive Account: 1. customer who makes frequent purchases. 2. bank account in which regular deposits or withdrawals are made.

tivity Charge: service charge imposed for check or deposit activity or any other maintenance charge.

Act of God: event that could not be prevented by reasonable foresight, is caused exclusively by forces and violence of nature, and is uninfluenced by human power (storm, flood, earthquake, or lightning).

Additional Dating: means of extending credit beyond normal sales terms, granted to induce buyers to place orders in advance of season or for other special reasons. See also *Advance Dating and Dating.*

Adjudication: judgment rendered by court, primarily used in bankruptcy proceedings.

Adjustable Interest Rate: interest rate on loan that may be adjusted up or down at specific intervals. Index used in determining adjusted interest rate and potential frequency of adjustments must be stated in loan documents.

Adjustable Rate Mortgage: loan is pursuant to an agreement executed at the inception of the loan that permits creditor to adjust interest rate from time to time based on a specific interest rate index.

Adjuster: person who deals with insured party to settle amount of loss, claim, or debt.

Adjustment: 1. settlement of disputed account. 2. change or concession in price or terms. 3. determining amount one is to receive in settlement of claim. 4. in accounting, entry made to correct or compensate for error or difference in account.

Adjustment Bureau: organization that supervises debt extensions and compromise arrangements or oversees orderly liquidation of troubled businesses for benefit of creditors.

Advance: 1. payment made before it is due. 2. disbursement of loan proceeds.

Advance Dating: additional time granted customers to pay for goods received and to earn available discounts. See also Additional Dating and Dating.

Advancement of Costs: prepayment of necessary legal expenses. Such charges, set by law, may be for commencement of suit and vary in different courts and states. Some items for which prepaid costs may be requested are filing fees, process serving, premiums on court bonds, trial fees, posting security for costs, entering judgment, recording abstract of judgment, issue execution, and discovery actions after judgment.

Advertising Allowance: promotional discount in price or payment given customers who share expense of advertising supplier's product.

Affidavit: voluntary written statement of facts pertaining to a transaction or event, signed under oath and witnessed by an authorized person.

Affiliate: business entity connected with another through common ownership or management, usually responsible for payment of its own obligations.

After-Acquired Property: security interest by which secured creditor automatically obtains interest in assets that debtor acquires after lien had been filed.

Agency: legal relationship between two parties in which one is authorized to act for another.

Agent: person legally authorized to act for another.

Agent Bank: formal designation that applies to a bank responsible for negotiating, structuring, and overseeing a loan or commitment to a borrower in which more than one bank is involved. See also Lead Bank.

Aggregate Balances: combined total of two or more demand deposit accounts, money markets, or time certificates of deposit. Term can also be applied to credit facility totals.

Aging of Accounts Receivable: accounting record of customer's receivables showing how long receivables have remained unpaid beyond regular terms of sale. Used as basis for advancing credit.

Agreement: a contract involving an offer and an acceptance between two or more parties, governing the terms of the contract and binding on the parties to the agreement (e.g., a loan agreement, security agreement, or guaranty).

AKA: see *Also Known As.*

Alert Action: a series of information services provided by credit reporting agencies; provides subscribers with listing of specific accounts on which unfavorable payment condition has recently been reported.

Allegation: statement of party to action, setting out what he or she intends to prove or contend.

ALLL: see *Allowance for Loan and Lease Losses.*

Allocation: sub-limit within a total credit facility that is to be used for a specific purpose.

Allonge: paper attached to a negotiable instrument for additional endorsements or other terms and conditions.

Allowance: accounting provision used to set aside amounts for depreciation, returns, or bad debts.

Allowance for Bad Debts: contra account against which uncollectible receivables are charged. See also Bad Debt Reserve.

Allowance for Loan and Lease Losses (ALLL): contra account, generally found on asset side of balance sheet as deduction from total loans outstanding; amount is intended to cover future losses of loans currently in the financial institution's portfolio. The ALLL should be adjusted monthly, concurrently with the generation of current financial statements.

Also Known As (AKA): sometimes used to designate a fictitious trade style or name.

ALTA Policy: an extended coverage title insurance policy that protects the lender against losses resulting from any defects in the title or claims against the property. The policy's coverage includes encroachments, mechanic's liens, and other matters that a physical inspection or inquiry of the parties would disclose.

Altered Check: check on which original entries have been changed (date, payee, or amount); financial institutions generally refuse to honor or pay checks that have been altered.

Amend: to correct, add to, or alter legal document.

Amicus Curiae: friend of court; uninvolved third party who intervenes in lawsuit, with court's permission, to introduce information or arguments in respect to the issue or principle of law to be decided.

Amortization: 1. reduction of loan by periodic principal payments. 2. decline in the book value of an intangible asset over the period owned.

Amortization Tables: calculation charts showing amounts required periodically to discharge debts over various periods of time and at different interest rates.

Amortize: 1. to write off the value of an intangible asset over the period owned. 2. to reduce or pay off debt or obligation by making periodic payments of principal.

Annual Percentage Rate (APR): annual cost of credit expressed as percentage; creditors are required under Federal Truth in Lending Act to disclose true annual interest on consumer loans, as well as the total dollar cost and other terms of loan.

Annual Report: yearly report detailing a company's comparative financial and organizational conditions.

Annuity: series of fixed periodic payments made at regular intervals.

Antecedent Credit Information: historical record of significant business information concerning individuals who are involved in ownership or management of business enterprise.

Anticipation: bridge loan made to a municipal or government borrower to cover expenses until revenue or tax proceeds are collected.

Appeal: complaint made to higher court by either plaintiff or defendant for court's review, correction, or reversal of lower court's decision.

Appearance: coming into court formally as plaintiff or defendant in lawsuit.

Appraisal: opinion of current value of real or personal property based upon cost of replacement, market, income, or fair value analysis.

Appreciation: increase in value of asset over its cost due to economic and other conditions. Property that increases in value as result of improvements or additions is not considered to have appreciated.

Appropriation: sum of money designated for a special purpose only.

APR: See *Annual Percentage Rate.*

Arbitration: submission for settlement of disputed matter, by nonjudicial means, to one or more impartial or disinterested third persons selected by disputants.

Arm's Length: business transaction between two or more parties that is open, sincere, and without personal influence, favoritism, or close relations.

Arrangement: plan for corporate reorganization for rescheduling or extension of time for payment of unsecured debts, such as an arrangement under Chapter 11 or 13 of the U. S. Bankruptcy Code.

Arrears: total or partial debt amounts that remain unpaid and past due.

Articles of Agreement: any written statement or contract, terms to which all parties consent.

Articles of Incorporation: formal papers that set forth pertinent data for formation of corporation and are filed with appropriate state agency.

Assess: 1. to fix rate or amount. 2. to set value of real and personal property, as for tax purposes.

Assessed Value: in the case of real property, value set by government agency for purpose of levying taxes.

Asset: 1. anything owned having monetary value. 2. item listed on left-hand side of balance sheet representing cash, or property, real or personal, belonging to an individual or company and convertible to cash.

Assigned Account: 1. account receivable pledged by borrower to factor or lender as security. 2. past-due customer whose account has been placed with collection agency.

Assigned Risk: insurance plan that provides coverage for risks rejected by regular markets and in which all licensed insurers are made to participate by various state laws.

Assignee: person to whom some rights, authority, or property is assigned.

Assignment: 1. written contract for transfer of one's title, legal rights, or property from one person to another. 2. in some states, form used to transfer claim to agency that undertakes collection of account for benefit of assigning creditor.

Assignment for the Benefit of Creditors: A liquidation technique in which an insolvent debtor goes out of business and an assignee facilitates the transfer of the insolvent debtor's estate for administration and payment of debts. Property transferred to assignee places such assets beyond control of debtor or reach of creditors.

Assignment of Claim: claim assigned to third party for collection.

Assignor: 1. one who transfers claim, right, or property. 2. individual, partnership, or corporation making assignment.

Assumed Liability: acknowledgment of responsibility for payment of obliga[tion] by third party.

At Sight: words used in negotiable instrument directing that payment be m[ade] upon presentation or demand.

Attached Account: legally frozen account on which payments have been s[us]pended; release or disbursement of funds can be made only after court ord[er].

Attachment: 1. legal writ or process by which debtor's property (or any inte[rest] therein) is seized and placed in custody of law. 2. Supplemental data provi[ded] as clarifying information to a document.

Attorney-in-Fact: private attorney who has written authorization to act [for] another. This authority is given by an instrument called power of attorney.

Attorney of Record: lawyer whose name must appear in permanent court reco[rds] as person acting on behalf of party in legal matter.

Auction: public sale of property that is sold to highest bidder.

Audit: to examine a firm's records, accounts, or procedures for purpose of s[ub]stantiating or verifying individual transactions or to confirm if assets and [lia]bilities are properly accounted for, including income and expense items.

Audited Financial Statements: financial statements that have been examined [by] an independent certified public accountant to determine if the financial sta[te]ments present fairly the financial position, results of operations, and c[ash] flows in conformity with generally accepted accounting principles.

Auditor: person who deals with examination and verification of financial accou[nts] and with making financial reports.

Auditor's Report: part of complete set of financial statements that expla[ins] degree of responsibility that independent accountant assumed for express[ing] an opinion on management's financial statements and assurance that is p[ro]vided by said opinion.

Automated Cash Application: computerized procedures enabling payments to [be] quickly and automatically applied to accounts receivable.

Automated Clearinghouse (ACH): computer-based clearing and settlement fa[cil]ity for interchange of electronic debits and credits among financial insti[tu]tions. ACH entries can be substituted for checks in recurring payments s[uch] as mortgages or in direct deposit distribution of federal and corporate be[ne]fits payments. Federal Reserve Banks furnish data processing services [for] most ACHs, although some are privately operated. Final settlement, or settlement, of ACH transfers is made against reserve accounts at Fede[ral] Reserve Banks.

Available Balance: checking account balance that the customer actually may u[se]; that is, current balance less deposits not yet cleared through the account.

Average Collected Balances: average dollar amount on deposit in check[ing] accounts defined as the difference between ledger balance and deposit flo[at] or those deposits posted to the account but having not yet cleared the fin[an]cial institution upon which they are drawn. See also Uncollected Funds.

Average Collection Period: average number of days required to convert accou[nts] receivable to cash.

Average Daily Balance: average amount of money that depositor keeps [on] deposit when calculated on a daily basis.

B

Backdating: predating document prior to date on which it was drawn.

Backlog: amount of revenue expected to be realized from work to be perform[ed] on uncompleted contracts, including new contractual agreements on whi[ch] work has not begun.

Bad Check Laws: laws enacted in various states to encourage and facilitate law[ful] use of checks; statutes differ in various jurisdictions and are genera[lly] enforced according to state laws as well as local custom and usage.

Bad Debt: account receivable that proves uncollectible in normal course of bu[si]ness; full payment is doubtful.

Bad Debt Ratio: ratio of bad debt expense to sales, used as measure of quality [of] accounts receivable.

Bad Debt Reserve: reserve or provision for accounts receivables to be charg[ed] off company's books based on historical levels of bad debts or industry av[er]ages.

Balance: amount owed or unpaid on loan or credit transaction. Also called o[ut]standing or unpaid balance.

Balance Due: total amount owed after applying debits and credits of account.

Balance Sheet: A financial statement listing the assets, liabilities, and owne[rs'] equity of a business entity or individual as of a specific date.

Balloon Payment: lump-sum payment of principal and sometimes accrued inte[r]est, usually due at end of term of installment loan in which periodic insta[ll]ments of principal and interest did not fully amortize loan.

Bank: financial institution chartered by state or federal government to transa[ct] financial business that includes receiving deposits, lending money, exchan[g]ing currencies, providing safekeeping, and investing money.

Bank Draft: sight or demand draft (order to pay) drawn by a bank (drawer) on [its] account at another bank (drawee).

nker's Acceptance: draft or order to pay specified amount at specified time not to exceed 270 days, drawn on individuals, business firms, or financial institutions; draft becomes accepted when a financial institution formally acknowledges its obligation to honor such draft, usually by writing or stamping "Accepted" on face of instrument. When accepted in this manner, draft becomes liability of bank. See also *Draft* and *Time Draft*.

nk Overdraft: check presented for collection for which there are not sufficient funds on deposit to make normal payment. Financial institution may honor such check, considering payment as loan to depositor for which the institution will usually collect interest or service charge.

nkrupt: debtor who is unable to meet debt obligations as they become due or is insolvent and whose assets are administered for benefit of creditors.

nkruptcy: Legal action taken under the U.S. Bankruptcy Code by or against an insolvent debtor who is unable to meet obligations as they become due. The bankrupt, if given discharge, is released from further liability of most debts listed as of the date of the bankruptcy filing.

- *Voluntary Bankruptcy:* any individual, partnership, corporation, estate, trust, or governmental unit may be afforded protection of debtor under U.S. Bankruptcy Code by filing petition. Exceptions: railroads, insurance or banking corporations, building and loan associations.
- *Involuntary Bankruptcy:* involuntary petition can be filed in bankruptcy court by three or more creditors or, if there are fewer than 12 creditors, by any one creditor. Petitioning creditors' claims must aggregate at least $5,000 in excess of value of any collateral of debtor. Involuntary cases may be filed against individuals, partnerships, or corporations other than farmers and nonprofit corporations and may be instituted under either Chapter 7 or Chapter 11 of the U.S. Bankruptcy Code. Involuntary petition must allege one of two grounds for relief: either that the debtor is generally not paying debts as they become due, or that the non-bankruptcy custodian, other than one appointed to enforce lien on less than substantially all of debtor's property, was appointed for, or took possession of, substantially all of debtor's property within 120 days of filing.
- *Chapter 7 Cases:* liquidation proceedings, formerly referred to as "straight bankruptcy," wherein nonexempt assets of debtor are converted to cash and proceeds distributed pro rata among creditors.
- *Chapter 9 Cases:* reorganization proceedings wherein municipality that is insolvent or unable to meet debts as they mature effects plan to adjust such debts.
- *Chapter 11 Cases:* reorganization proceedings available to all business enterprises; may be instituted either by debtor or creditor(s). For plan to be confirmed by court under Chapter 11, each class of creditors, as set forth in such plan, must accept plan or each class must receive at least that which it would receive on liquidation. Class of creditors has accepted plan when majority in number and two-thirds in dollar amount of those creditors actually voting approve it.
- *Chapter 12 Cases:* reorganization proceedings for agricultural concerns and small family-owned farms having debts under $1.5 million.
- *Chapter 13 Cases:* reorganization cases that may be instituted only by individuals with regular income who owe unsecured debts of less than $100,000 and secured debts of less than $350,000, other than stockbroker or commodity broker. For plan to be confirmed, it must provide for submission to trustee of all or any portion of debtor's future earnings as necessary for execution of plan, payment in full of all priority claims, and equal treatment of each member of class of creditors. While consent of unsecured creditors is not required, value of what they receive under plan may not be less than if debtor were liquidated.

nkruptcy Judge: presiding judge of court in which bankruptcy cases are heard. (Formerly called Referee in Bankruptcy.) Duties of judge include supervising administrative details of bankrupt estates and ruling on all matters involving debtor-creditor problems.

sis: 1. number of days used in calculating interest earned in investment or interest payable on bank loan. Also called accrual base. 2. original cost of asset plus capital improvements from which any taxable gains (or losses) are determined after deducting depreciation expenses.

sis Point: 1/100th of a percent; 100 basis points equal 1%.

arer: negotiable item (check, note, bill, or draft) in which no payee is indicated or payee is shown as "cash" or "bearer." Item is payable to person in possession of it or to person who presents it for payment.

arer Paper: instrument that is made "payable to bearer." When negotiable instrument is endorsed in blank, it becomes bearer paper and can be transferred by delivery since it does not require endorsement.

neficiary: 1. person or organization named in will to inherit or receive property. 2. person or organization to whom insurance policy is payable. 3. person or organization for whose benefit trust is created.

d Bond: bond issued by surety on behalf of contractor that provides assurance to recipient of contractor's bid that if bid is accepted, contractor will execute contract and provide performance bond. Under bond, surety is obligated to pay recipient difference between contractor's bid and bid of next lowest responsible bidder if bid is accepted and contractor fails to execute contract or to provide performance bond.

Billing Cycle: number of days between payment due dates.

Bill of Costs: certified itemization of costs associated with lawsuit.

Bill of Lading: written instrument signed by common carrier or agent identifying freight and representing both receipt and contract for shipment. It must show name of consignee, description of goods, terms of carrier's contract, and directions for assigning to specific person at specific place. In form of negotiable instrument, it is evidence of holding title to goods being shipped.

Bill of Sale: written instrument evidencing transfer of title of specific personal property to buyer.

Binder: 1. written agreement that provides temporary legal protection pending issuance of final contract or policy. 2. temporary insurance contract; may be oral or written; also called cover note.

Blank Endorsement: endorser's writing on check, promissory note, or bill of exchange without indicating party to whom it is payable. Endorser merely signs his or her name, making the instrument "payable to bearer." Also called endorsement in blank.

Blanket Coverage: property coverage applicable to group of exposures (buildings, inventory, equipment, etc., combined or individually, at one or more locations), in single total amount of insurance; contrasts with Specific Coverage.

Blanket Mortgage: mortgage secured by two or more parcels of real property, frequently used by developers who acquire large tract of land for subdivision and resale to individual homeowners. Also called blanket trust deed.

Bond: contract issued by insurance or bonding company in support of principal's obligation to obligee. See also *Fidelity Bond* and *Surety Bond*.

Bonded Warehouse: federally approved warehouse under bond for strict observance of revenue laws; used for storing goods until duties are paid or property is otherwise released. Bonded warehouse assures owner of property that operators of warehouse are insured against loss by fraud and will keep proper inventory and accounting of goods in transit.

Bonding Company: company authorized to issue bid bonds, performance bonds, labor and materials bonds, or other types of surety bonds.

Book Value: 1. company's net worth calculated by adding total assets minus total liabilities. 2. value of asset (cost plus additions, less depreciation) shown on books or financial report of an entity.

Borrower's Certificate: A document required under a loan or other agreement to be submitted by the borrower or another designated party to certify the value of collateral and compliance with the terms of the agreement.

Bottom Line: (colloq.) final price, net profit, or end results.

Branch Banking: multioffice banking. Branch is any banking facility away from bank's main office that accepts deposits or makes loans. State laws strictly control opening of new banking offices by state-chartered banks, national banks, and thrift institutions.

Breach of Contract: failure to fulfill terms of contract, in part or whole.

Breach of Warranty: 1. failure to fully disclose information about condition of property or insured party. 2. failure to perform as promised.

Break-Even Analysis: A method of determining the number of units that must be sold at a given price to recover all fixed and variable costs.

Break-even Point: 1. point at which total sales are equal to total expenses. May be expressed in units or dollars. 2. amount received from sale that exactly equals amount of expense or cost.

Bridge Loan: loan that provides liquidity until defined event occurs that will generate cash, such as sale of noncurrent asset, replacement financing, or equity infusion.

Bulk Sales Acts: statutes designed to prevent defrauding of creditors through secret sale in bulk of merchant's goods. Most states require notice of proposed sale to all creditors.

Burden of Proof: 1. duty of producing sufficient evidence to prove position taken in lawsuit. 2. necessity of proving fact or facts as to truth of claim.

Business: 1. commercial, industrial, or mercantile activity engaged in by individual, partnership, corporation, or other form of organization for purpose of making, buying, or selling goods or services at profit. 2. occupation, profession, or trade.

Business Failure: 1. suspension of business resulting from insolvency or bankruptcy. 2. inability to fulfill normal business obligations.

Business Interruption Insurance: property insurance written to cover loss of profits and continuing expenses as result of shutdown by insured peril; exposure is classified as consequential loss. Also called earnings insurance.

Buyer's Market: market condition in which supply exceeds demand, which causes prices to decline.

Buy Out: to purchase at least a controlling percentage of a company's stock to take over its assets.

Bylaws: set of rules or regulations adopted to control internal affairs of organization.

C

C's of Credit: the "Five C's" of credit. A longstanding means of evaluating a customer by investigating Character, Collateral, Capacity, Conditions, and Capital.

Calendar Year: 12-month accounting period ending December 31.

Callable Loan: loan payable on demand.

Canceled Check: check that has been paid by a financial institution and on which the financial institution has imprinted evidence of payment so that it cannot be presented again.

Cancellation Clause: provision in contract or agreement allowing parties to rescind agreement under certain conditions.

Capacity: one of the "Five C's" of credit; a customer's ability to successfully absorb merchandise and to pay for the merchandise. Refers to customer's ability to produce sufficient cash so as to meet obligations when due.

Capital: 1. one of the "Five Cs" of credit; refers to financial resources the customer has at the time order is placed and those that he or she is likely to have when payment is due. 2. amount invested in business by owners or stockholders. 3. owner's equity in the business.

Cash: 1. money readily available for current expenditures; usually consists of cash on hand or money in a financial institution. 2. money equivalent, such as a check, paid at time of purchase. 3. any medium of exchange that the financial institution will accept at face value upon deposit.

Cash Basis Accounting: basis of accounting in which revenues and expenses are reported in the income statement when cash is received or paid out for the time period in which the revenues and expenses occur.

Cash Basis Loan: loan on which interest payments are recorded when collected from borrower. This is a loan in which the borrower has fallen behind on interest payments and is classified as a nonaccrual asset.

Cash Concentration and Disbursement (CCD): corporate electronic payment used in business-to-business and intracompany transfers of funds. Funds are cleared on overnight basis through nationwide automated clearinghouse network.

Cash Equivalents: accounting term for actual cash on hand and total of bank deposits.

Cash Flow: is based on an activity format, which classifies cash inflows and outflows in terms of operating, investing, and financing activities.

Cashier's Check: check drawn on financial institution's account, becoming direct obligation of the financial institution.

Cash Management Account: special type of deposit service that permits corporate customers to invest cash in demand deposit account until needed for operations.

Cash Surrender Value: in life insurance, amount payable under whole life policy when terminated by insured.

Casualty Insurance: coverage for automobile, liability, crime, boiler and machinery, health, bonds, aviation, workers' compensation, and other miscellaneous lines; contrasts with Property Insurance.

Certificate of Insurance: written statement issued by insurer indicating that insurance policy has been issued and showing details of coverage at time certificate was written; used as evidence of insurance.

Certified Check: depositor's check confirmed on its face as good by a financial institution and stamped "certified." It is then dated and signed by an authorized officer of the institution. Such check becomes an obligation of the financial institution, which guarantees that it is holding sufficient funds to cover payment of check on demand.

Certified Copy of Policy: document that provides evidence of insurance as of certain date; coverage may be terminated or changed after certification.

Certified Public Accountant (CPA): one who has been trained to do accounting and who has passed state test and received title of CPA; title certifies holder's qualification to practice accounting, audit, prepare reports, and analyze accounting information.

CGL: see *Comprehensive General Liability.*

Character: one of the "Five Cs" of credit; refers to evaluating qualities that would impel debtor to meet his or her obligations. Generally identified as customer's reputation, responsibility, integrity, and honesty.

Charge-Off: portion of principal balance of a loan or account receivable that an entity considers uncollectible; this amount may be partially or fully recovered in future. Also called a *Write-Off.*

Chart of Accounts: listing of all financial accounts or categories (usually numbered) into which business transactions are classified and recorded.

Chattel: item of tangible personal property, animate or inanimate, as distinguished from real property.

Chattel Mortgage: instrument of sale in which debtor transfers title in property to creditor as security for debt. Failure by debtor to comply with terms of contract may cause creditor's title in property to become absolute.

Check: order on a financial institution for payment of funds from depositor's account and payable on demand.

Claim: 1. action to recover payment, reimbursement, or compensation from entity legally liable for damage or injury.

Claimant: one who makes claim or asserts right.

Cleanup: period during which particular loan or entire borrowing has been p off; out-of-debt period required under line of credit.

Clearinghouse: association of financial institutions or security dealers create permit daily settlement and exchange of checks or delivery of stocks other items between members in local geographic area.

Closed-End Credit: consumer installment loan made for predetermined amo calling for periodic payments of principal and interest over specified perio term. Finance charge may be fixed or variable rate. Borrower does not h option of obtaining extra funds under original loan agreement. Contrasts w Open-End Credit.

Cloud on Title: outstanding claim or encumbrance on property that may im owner's title.

Cognovit Note: form of promissory note or statement that allows creditor, in c of default by debtor, to enter judgment without trial. (Not recognized ir jurisdictions.)

Collateral: 1. one of the "Five C's" of credit; refers to real or personal prop that may be available as security. 2. asset pledged by borrower in suppor loan. See also *Secured Loan.*

Collateral Note: form of promissory note given for loan, pledging real or p sonal property as security for payment of debt.

Collectible: account capable of being collected.

Collection Agency: professional business service employed as agent to co creditors' unpaid (past-due) accounts. Collection agency is usually comp sated by receiving agreed upon contingent percentage of amount collected

Collection Agency Report: report from collection agency that informs clien results of collection efforts, investigations, or recommendations.

Collection Charges: 1. fees charged by bank for collecting drafts, no coupons, or other instruments. 2. compensation paid to collection agency attorney for collecting delinquent accounts.

Collection Item: 1. term for item received for collection that is to be credite depositor's account after payment. Most financial institutions charge spe (collection) fees for handling such items. 2. past due account assigned collection.

Collection Period: number of days required for company's receivables to be lected and converted to cash.

Comaker: person who signs (and guarantees) note of another and by so do promises to pay in full. See also *Cosigner.*

Commensurate: describes deposit balances that are in acceptable proportio size of loan or commitment.

Commercial Debt: loan or obligation incurred for business purposes.

Commercial Law League of America (C.L.L.A.): national membership organ tion of commercial attorneys, commercial credit and collection agenc credit insurance companies, and law list publishers. Objectives include set standards for honorable dealings among members, improving the practic commercial law, and promoting uniformity of legislation affecting commer law.

Commercial Paper: short-term securities such as notes, drafts, bills of exchar and other negotiable paper that arise out of commercial activity and becc due on a definite maturity date.

Commercial Property: real estate used for business purposes or managed sc to produce income from rents and leases.

Commitment: agreement between a financial institution and borrower to m funds available under certain conditions for a specified period of time.

Commitment Fee: lender's charge for holding credit available, usually repla with interest when funds are advanced, as in revolving credit. In busin credit, a commitment fee is often charged for unused portion of line of cred

Commitment Letter: letter from lender stating willingness to advance funds named borrower, repayable at specified rate and time period, subject escape clause(s) allowing lender to rescind agreement in event of materi adverse changes in borrower's financial condition.

Committee Approval: credit is approved by several people acting as group.

Common Law: body of law that was originated, developed, and administered England.

Community Property: property shared by husband and wife, each having one-h interest in earnings of other; form of joint property ownership in some stat

Community Reinvestment Act of 1977 (CRA): federal law that requires mortg lenders to demonstrate their commitment to home mortgage financing in e nomically disadvantaged areas. Prohibits redlining or credit allocation ba on geographic region and requires lenders to file annual compliance sta ments.

Compensating Balance: demand deposit balance that must be maintained borrower to compensate financial institution for loan accommodations a other services.

Compound Interest: interest calculated by adding accumulated interest to date original principal. New balance becomes principal for additional interest c culations.

nprehensive General Liability (CGL): policy form providing automatic coverage for all insured's business operations; may include auto exposures; newer form of CGL is called commercial general liability.

cession: 1. granting of special privilege to digress from regular terms or previous conditions. 2. allowance or rebate from established price. 3. business enterprise operated under special permission.

ditional Sales Contract: contract for sale of goods under which possession is delivered to buyer but title retained by seller until goods are paid for in full or until other conditions are met. In most states, conditional sales contracts have been replaced by security agreements having substantially the same definition under Uniform Commercial Code.

ditions: one of the "Five C's" of credit; refers to general business environment and status of borrower's industry.

fession of Judgment Note: note in which (after maturity) debtor permits attorney to appear in court and have judgment entered if payment is not made as agreed. Acceptance of note varies by state. See also *Cognovit Note.*

firmation: 1. supplier's written acknowledgment that he or she has accepted buyer's order. 2. customer's written verification of order previously placed. 3. proof verifying agreement or existence of assets and liabilities or claims against assets and liabilities.

sent Judgment: judgment that debtor allows to be entered against him or her by motion filed with court.

sideration: 1. element in contract without which contract is not binding. Contract is generally not valid without consideration. 2. reason for contracting parties to enter into contract. Act, promise, price, or motive for which agreement is entered into. 3. value given in exchange for benefit that is to be derived from contract. 4. compensation. Exchange of consideration is usually mutual, each party giving something up to other.

sign: to send or forward goods to merchant, factor, or agent for sale with title retained by seller and with payment delayed, generally until sale is made.

signee: person or entity to which goods or property is consigned or shipped; ultimate recipient of shipment.

nsignment: arrangement under which consignor (seller) remains owner of property until such time as consignee (buyer) pays for goods; usually consignee pays consignor when goods are sold or holds proceeds of sale in trust for benefit of consignor.

nsignor: 1. one who delivers shipment or turns it over to carrier for transportation and delivery. 2. one who consigns goods to be sold without giving up title.

nsolidated Financial Statement: combined statement showing financial condition of parent corporation and its subsidiaries.

nsolidating Financial Statement: combined statement of subsidiary and parent companies that shows complete statement for each entity without netting intercompany transactions.

nstruction Loan: interim financing for development and construction of real property, generally converted to long-term financing upon completion of construction.

nsumer Credit: debt incurred for personal, family, or household use.

nsumer Credit Protection Act (Truth in Lending Act of 1968): law that requires most lenders and those who extend consumer credit to disclose true credit costs. Act provides for limits on garnishment of wages, prohibits excessive interest, and makes available contents of consumer credit reports.

nsumer Sale Disclosure Statement: form required to be provided by creditor to customer, disclosing finance charge details as required under Consumer Credit Protection Act.

ntingent Fee: fee to be paid only in event of specific occurrence, usually successful results. Arrangement, for example, in which collection agency will receive stated percentage of any amounts recovered or in which lawyer will receive payment only if successful in prosecuting lawsuit.

ntingent Liability: liability in which a person(s) or business(es) is indirectly responsible for obligations of a third party. Such indirect liability is usually established by guaranty or endorsement, and the liability holder may turn to guarantors or endorsers for satisfaction of debt. See also Endorsement and Guaranty.

ntra Account: account that partially or wholly offsets another account or balance.

ntract: agreement between two or more entities or legally competent persons that creates, modifies, or destroys legal arrangement.

ntrolled Disbursement: funds management technique in corporate cash management designed to maximize funds available for temporary investment in money market or for payment to trade creditors. Controls flow of checks through banking system to meet corporate investment and funds management requirements. Contrasts with delayed disbursement. See also *Federal Reserve Float* and *Treasury Workstation.*

ntroller: person in business organization responsible for finances, internal auditing, and accounting systems in use in company's operations.

nversion: process of consolidating or transferring data from one system to another.

Conveyance: 1. transfer of right, generally instrument transferring interest in real estate in form of deed. 2. transfer of property ownership (sometimes includes leases and mortgages) from one person or organization to another.

Copyright: intangible right granted to author or originator by federal government to solely and exclusively reproduce or publish specific literary, musical, or artistic work for certain number of years.

Corporate Reorganization: see *Bankruptcy.*

Corporate Veil: convention that corporate organization insulates organization's owners from liability for corporate activities.

Corporation: artificial person or legal entity organized under and treated by state laws, legally distinct from its shareholders and vested with capacity of continuous succession irrespective of changes in its ownership either in perpetuity or for limited term. It may be set up to contract, own, and discharge business within boundaries of powers granted it by its corporate charter.

Correspondent: organization or individual that carries on business relations or acts as agent with others in different cities or countries.

Cosigner: one of joint signers of loan documents. One who signs note of another as support for credit of the principal maker.

Cost of Funds: dollar cost of interest paid or accrued on funds acquired from various sources within bank and borrowed funds acquired from other financial institutions, including time deposits, advances at Federal Reserve discount window, federal funds purchased, and Eurodollar deposits. Financial institution may use internal cost of funds in pricing loans it makes.

Covenant: written agreement, convention, or promise between parties who pledge to do or not to do certain things or that stipulates truth of certain facts.

CPA: see *Certified Public Accountant.*

CRA: see *Community Reinvestment Act of 1977.*

Crash: sudden sharp decrease in business activity that can negatively affect stock market volumes and prices.

Credit: 1. privilege of buying goods and services, or for borrowing money in return for promise of future payment. 2. in bookkeeping, entry on ledger signifying cash payment, merchandise returned, or allowance to reduce debt. 3. accounting entry on right side of ledger sheet.

Credit Advisory Board (CAB): agency established by Financial Institutions Reform, Recovery, and Enforcement Act of 1989 "to monitor the credit standards and lending practices of insured depository institutions and the supervision of such standards and practices by the federal financial regulators" as well as to "ensure that insured depository institutions can meet the demands of a modern and globally competitive world." This board was granted permanent authorization by the Federal Deposit Insurance Corporation Improvement Act of 1991. Formerly known as Credit Standards Advisory Committee (CSAC).

Credit Analyst: person who evaluates the financial history and financial statements of credit applicants to assess creditworthiness. Analysts are trained to evaluate applicant's financial strength and to opine on the probability of full repayment, collateral adequacy, or whether a credit enhancement through a cosigner or guarantor is needed.

Credit Application: form completed by potential borrower and used by creditor to determine applicant's creditworthiness.

Credit Approval: decision to extend credit.

Credit Approval System: internal methods by which credit decisions are made.

Credit Bureau: agency that gathers information and provides its subscribers with credit reports on consumers.

Credit Checking: examining and analyzing creditworthiness of customer by contacting references, reviewing credit reports, etc.

Credit Department: department within a financial institution that performs operations and credit support functions for underwriting activities. May include maintenance of credit files, credit investigations, financial statement analysis and spreading, customers' accounts receivable audits, lender training, portfolio reporting, facilitation of credit meetings, etc.

Credit Enhancement: enhancement to creditworthiness of loans underlying asset-backed security or municipal bond, generally to get investment-grade rating from bond rating agency and to improve marketability of debt securities to investors. There are two general classifications of credit enhancements:

- third-party enhancement, in which third party pledges its own creditworthiness and guarantees repayment in form of standby letter of credit or commercial letter of credit issued by a financial institution, surety bond from insurance company, or special reserve fund managed by financial guaranty firm in exchange for fee.
- self-enhancement, which is generally done by issuer through over-collateralization—that is, pledging loans with book value greater than face value of bonds offered for sale.

Credit File: creditor's file that compiles information about customer, including correspondence, credit memorandums and analyses, credit ratings, a credit history, payment patterns, and credit inquiries.

Credit Granting: approval and extension of credit to a customer.

Credit Inquiry: request made by a financial institution or trade creditor concerning the responding bank's own customer.

Credit Insurance: life and health insurance issued in conjunction with borrowing by individuals; covers payments or unpaid balance when borrower is disabled or dies; in business, covers loss of receivables when debtor becomes insolvent.

Credit Interchange: exchange of credit information between individuals or groups.

Credit Interchange Bureau (CIB): 1. local bureaus offering members or subscribers credit reports usually based on recent ledger experiences. Generally refers to organized system of cooperating bureaus operated by regional credit associations. 2. credit agency that may limit its reporting to a particular trade.

Credit Investigation: inquiry made by a financial institution or trade creditor concerning subject that is not the responding financial institution's customer.

Credit Limit: maximum amount of credit made available to customer by specific creditor.

Credit Line: commitment by a financial institution to lend funds to a borrower up to a given amount over a specified future period under certain pre-established conditions. Normally reviewed annually.

Credit Management: function of planning, organizing, implementing, and supervising credit policies of a company.

Creditor: 1. one to whom debt is owed by another as a result of a financial transaction. 2. one who extends credit and to whom money is due.

Creditors' Committee: voluntary representative group of creditors that may examine affairs of insolvent debtor. Group will usually advise as to continuation of business, study accountant's and appraiser's reports, act as watchdog over operating business, make recommendations to appropriate groups or legal body so that creditors will realize largest settlement possible, and advise as to acceptability of settlement.

Creditors' Remedies: legal rights enabling creditors to collect delinquent debts owed them.

Credit Policy: company's written procedures for making credit decisions. Used to aid company in meeting its overall risk management objectives.

Credit Process Review: assessment of entire credit-granting process concerning specific financial institution loan portfolio(s).

Credit Rating: appraisal made by a financial institution or credit agency as to creditworthiness of a person or company. Such a report will include background on owners, estimate of financial strength and ability to pay when due, and company's payment record.

Credit Record: written history of how well a customer has handled debt repayment.

Credit Report: 1. report to aid management in reaching credit, sales, and financial decisions. 2. confidential report containing information obtained by mercantile agency that has investigated a company's background, credit history, financial strength, and payment record.

Credit Reporting Agency: company or trade interchange group that confidentially supplies subscribers or members with credit information and other relevant data as to a company's ability or likelihood to pay for goods and services purchased on credit.

Credit Research Foundation (CRF): education and research affiliate of National Association of Credit Management.

Credit Review: follow-up monitoring of loan or extension of credit by credit review officer or department, senior loan committee, auditor, or regulatory agency intended to determine whether loan was made in accordance with lender's written credit standards and policies and in compliance with banking regulations. Errors, omissions, concentrations, etc., if detected by credit review process, can then be corrected by lending officers, thus preventing deterioration in credit quality and possible loan losses. Also called loan review.

Credit Risk: 1. evaluation of a customer's ability or willingness to pay debts on time. 2. risk that a financial institution assumes when it makes an irrevocable payment on behalf of its customer against insufficient funds.

Credit Scoring: statistical model used to predict the creditworthiness of credit applicants. Credit scoring estimates repayment probability based on information in credit application and credit bureau report. The two main types of credit scoring are application scoring for new accounts and behavior scoring for accounts that have been activated and are carrying balances.

Credit Terms: stated and agreed on terms for debt repayment.

Credit Union: nonprofit cooperative financial organization chartered by state or federal government to provide financial services such as deposit and loan activities to a specific and limited group of people.

Creditworthy: term used to describe individual or entity deemed worthy of extension of credit.

CSAC: see *Credit Advisory Board.*

Current Assets: short-term assets of company, including cash, accounts receivable, temporary investments, and goods and materials in inventory.

Current Liabilities: short-term obligations due within one year, including current maturities of long-term debts.

Current Open Account: sale of goods or services for which customer does pay for each purchase but rather is required to settle in full periodicall within specified time period after each transaction.

Current Ratio: total of current assets divided by total current liabilities; use indication of a company's liquidity and ability to service current obligation

D

D&B: see *Dun & Bradstreet, Inc.*

Dating (Terms): extension of credit terms beyond normal terms becaus industry's seasonality or unusual circumstance.

Days Sales Outstanding (DSO): a calculation that expresses the average tim days that receivables are outstanding.

DBA: see *Doing Business As.*

DDA: see *Demand Deposit Account.*

Dealer Loan: see *Floor Plan.*

Debenture: unsecured, long-term indebtedness or corporate obligation.

Debit: entry on left side of accounting ledger.

Debit Card: magnetized plastic card that permits customers to withdraw c from automatic teller machines and make purchases with charges dedu from funds on deposit at a predesignated account.

Debt: 1. specified amount of money, goods, or services that is owed from on another, including not only obligation of debtor to pay but also right of cr tor to receive and enforce payment. 2. financial obligation of debtor.

Debtor: person or entity indebted to or owing money to another.

Debtor in Possession (DIP): In a Chapter 11 bankruptcy, a debtor may conti to maintain possession of its assets and use them in normal business op tions.

Debtor-in-Possession Financing: credit facilities extended to borrower wh reorganizing under Chapter 11 bankruptcy.

Debt Ratio: measure of firm's leverage position derived by dividing total debt equity.

Debt Service: total interest and scheduled principal payments on debt due wi given time frame.

Decision: judgment, decree, or verdict pronounced by court in determinatio case.

Declarations Page: policy form containing data regarding insured, policy te premium, type and amount of coverage, designation of forms and endo ments incorporated at time policy is issued, name of insurer, and counter nature of agent.

Deductible: portion of loss that is not insured; may be stated amount dedu from loss or percentage of loss or of value of property at time of loss.

Deduction: partial amount of payment that is withheld.

Deed: legal, written document used to transfer ownership of real property f one party to another.

Deed of Trust: legal document used in some states in lieu of mortgage. Titl real property passes from seller to trustee, who holds mortgaged prop until mortgage has been fully paid and then releases title to borrower. Tru is authorized to sell property if borrower defaults, paying amount of mortg loan to lender and any remaining balance to former owner.

Defalcation: misappropriation of funds held in trust for another.

Defamation: injury to person's or entity's character, reputation, or good nam false and malicious statements (includes both libel and slander).

Default: to fail to meet obligation or terms of loan agreement such as paymer principal or interest.

Default Charge: legally agreed upon charge or penalty added to account w payment of debt is late or another event of default occurs under a loan ag ment.

Defendant: person or entity defending or denying claim; party against which or charge has been filed in court of law. See also Plaintiff.

Defer: to postpone or delay action.

Deferred Payment Sale: selling on installment plan with payments delayec postponed until future date.

Deficiency Judgment: decree requiring debtor to pay amount remaining under defaulted contract after secured property has been liquidated.

Deficit: difference between receipts and expenses when expenses are greater.

Defraud: to deprive person of property by fraud, deceit, or artifice.

Defunct: business that has ceased to exist and is without assets; concern that failed.

Delayed Disbursement: practice in cash management whereby a firm pays v dors and other corporations by disbursing payments from a financial ins tion in a remote city. Also called remote disbursement. Contrasts with c trolled disbursement. See also Federal Reserve Float.

Delinquent: 1. past-due obligation; overdue and unpaid account. 2. to be arrears in payment of debts, loans, taxes. 3. to have failed in duty or respo bility.

and Deposit Account (DDA): funds on deposit in checking account that are payable by a financial institution upon demand of depositor. See also *Time Deposit.*

and Draft: written order directing that payment be made, on sight, to a third party.

and Letter: correspondence sent by creditor, collection agency, or lawyer to debtor requesting payment of obligation by specific date.

and Loan: loan with no fixed due date and payable on demand by maker of oan; loan that can be "called" by lender at any time.

urrage: charge that is fixed by contract and payable by recipient of goods for detaining freight car or ship longer than agreed in order to load or unload. Purpose is remuneration to owner of vessel for earnings he or she was mproperly caused to lose.

osit: 1. amount of money given as down payment for goods or as consideration for contract. 2. funds retained in customer's bank account.

reciation: decline in value of fixed assets, allocating purchase cost of an asset plus additions to value over its useful economic life as outlined by the Federal Tax Code.

vatives: broad family of financial instruments with characteristics of forward or option contracts.

ogatory Account Information: adverse information on customers who have not paid accounts with other creditors according to payment terms, as reported to a credit bureau.

ctors and Officers Liability Insurance: legal liability coverage for wrongful acts including breach of duty but not fraud or dishonesty. Often known as E & O, or Errors and Omissions Insurance.

ursement: full or partial advancement of funds.

harge: 1. to cancel or release obligation. 2. to release debtor from all or most debts in bankruptcy.

claimer Statement: notice disclaiming responsibility for accuracy, completeness, or timeliness of credit information. Most disclaimer statements urge recipients of the information not to rely unduly on it and stress the confidential nature of information being disclosed.

continued Operations: operations of a segment of a company, usually a subsidiary whose activities represent a separate line of business that, although still operating, is the subject of a formal plan of disposal approved by management.

count: 1. interest deducted from face amount of note at time loan is made. 2. trade term used for reduction of invoice amount when payment has been made within specified terms.

counted Note: 1. borrowing arrangement in which interest is deducted from face amount of note before proceeds are advanced (see also Note). 2. term used when customer endorses note received from another party and presents it to a financial institution to obtain funds.

honor: to fail to make payment of negotiable instrument on its due date.

intermediation: withdrawal of funds from interest-bearing deposit accounts when rates on competing financial instruments, such as money market mutual funds, stocks, and bonds, offer better returns.

missal: court order or judgment disposing action, suit, or motion without trial.

possess: legal action taken by landlord to put individual or business tenant out of his or her property.

solution of Corporation: termination of entity's existence by law, expiration of charter, loss of all members, or failure to meet statutory level of members.

tribution: one or more payments made to creditors who have approved claims filed in a bankruptcy proceeding, assignment for the benefit of creditors, or receivership.

tributor: business engaged in the distribution or marketing of manufacturer's goods to customers or dealers. See also Wholesaler.

idend: 1. periodic distribution of cash or property to shareholders of corporation as return on their investment.

ument: any written instrument that records letters with figures or marks that may be used as evidence.

umentary Evidence: any written record or inanimate object, as distinguished from oral evidence.

uments of Title: Include bill of lading, dock warrant, dock receipt, warehouse receipt, order for the delivery of goods, and any other document that in the regular course of business or financing is treated as adequately evidencing that the person in possession of it is entitled to receive, hold, and dispose of the document and the goods it covers. To be a document of title, a document must purport to be issued by, or addressed to, a bailee and purport to cover goods in the bailee's possession that are either identified or are fungible portions of an identified mass.

ng Business As (DBA): reference term placed before trade name under which business operates. Sometimes used as fictitious trade style acknowledging that name is not part of corporation title or registered trademark.

nestic Corporation: company doing business in state in which it is incorporated.

Dormant Account: inactive deposit account in which there have been no deposits or withdrawals for a long period of time.

Doubtful Assets: assets that have all weaknesses inherent in substandard assets with added characteristic that weaknesses make collection or liquidation in full, on basis of currently existing facts, conditions, and values, highly questionable and improbable. Possibility of loss is extremely high. Because of certain important and reasonably specific pending factors that may strengthen assets, classification as estimated loss is deferred until more exact status may be determined. Pending factors include proposed merger, acquisition, or liquidation procedures, capital injection, perfecting liens on additional collateral, and refinancing plans.

Downgrading: 1. lowering of assessment of customer's creditworthiness. 2. worsening the internally assigned credit quality rating of a loan or relationship in order to appropriately report risk.

Down Payment: up-front partial payment made to secure right to purchase goods.

Downstream Funding: funds borrowed by holding company for a subsidiary's use, generally to obtain more favorable rate; contrasts with Upstream Funding.

Draft: written order by one party (drawer) directing second party (drawee) to pay sum of money to third party (payee). See also *Banker's Acceptance, Letter of Credit, Sight Draft,* and *Time Draft.*

Drawee: person or entity that is expected to pay check or draft when instrument is presented for payment.

Drawer: party instructing drawee to pay someone else by writing or drawing check or draft. Also called maker or writer.

Drop Shipment: shipment of goods delivered directly from manufacturer to customer.

DSO: see *Days Sales Outstanding.*

Dual Banking: banking system in U.S., consisting of state banks, chartered and supervised by state banking departments, and national banks, chartered and regulated by Office of the Comptroller of the Currency.

Due Date: stated maturity date for debt obligation.

Due Diligence: 1. responsibility of an entity's directors and officers to act in a prudent manner in evaluating credit applications; in essence, using same degree of care that an ordinary person would use in making same analysis. 2. review that is made of a loan portfolio of a potential merger candidate by an acquiring institution.

Due Process of Law: law in its regular course of administration through courts as guaranteed by U.S. Constitution.

Dun: to repeatedly demand payment of debt; to be insistent in following debtor for payment.

Dun & Bradstreet, Inc. (D&B): international mercantile agency supplying information and credit ratings on all types of businesses.

Dun Letter: letter or notice sent by creditor requesting payment of past-due debt.

D-U-N-S Number: (Data Universal Numbering System) code developed by Dun & Bradstreet that identifies specific business name and location.

Durable Goods: goods that provide long-lasting qualities and continuing services.

Duress: unlawful constraint that forces person to do what he or she would not have done by choice.

Duty: 1. legal, moral, or ethical obligation. 2. tax collected on import or export of goods.

E

Earnest Money: money that one contracting party gives to another at the time of entering into the contract in order to bind the contract in good faith, and which will be forfeited if the purchaser fails to carry out the contract.

Earnings Report: 1. income statement showing a business's or individual's revenues and expenses for stated period of time.

Easement: right of owner of one parcel of land to use land of another for special purpose. Usually easement rights pass with land when it is sold.

Edge Act: banking legislation, passed in 1919, that allows national banks to conduct foreign lending operations through federal or state-chartered subsidiaries called Edge Act corporations. Such corporations can be chartered by other states and are allowed to own banks in foreign countries and to invest in foreign commercial and industrial firms.

EFT: see *Electronic Funds Transfer.*

Electronic Funds Transfer (EFT): computerized system enabling funds to be debited, credited, or transferred between financial institution accounts and vendors.

Embezzlement: fraudulent appropriation of one's property by person to whom it was entrusted.

Encumbrance: any right or interest in real or other property that diminishes the property's value and alters control of disposition.

Endorsement: 1. act of writing one's name on back of note, bill, check, or similar written instrument for payment of money; required on negotiable instrument to pass title properly to another. By signing such instrument, endorser becomes party to it and thereby liable, under certain conditions, for its payment. 2. change or addition to insurance policy, informally called rider.

Entrepreneur: person who plans, organizes, and runs operation of new business.

EOM Terms: Shipments during a month are invoiced in a single statement dated as of the last day of that month or the first day of the following month.

Equal Credit Opportunity Act of 1974: Federal Reserve Regulation B that prohibits creditors from discriminating against credit applicants on basis of age, race, color, religion, national origin, sex, marital status, age, or receipt of public assistance.

Equitable Subordination: principles in section 510 (c) of U.S. Bankruptcy Code that permit bankruptcy court to subordinate, for purposes of distribution, all or part of creditor's claim against debtor's estate to claims of another creditor of that debtor after court has determined that first creditor has engaged in some form of wrongful conduct that has improved position relative to other creditors.

Equity: value of ownership, calculated by subtracting total liabilities from total assets.

Escheat: right of state to claim property or money if there is no legal claim made to it.

Escrow Account: deposit account to which access is restricted or limited by terms of written agreement entered into by three parties, including a financial institution.

Estate: any right, title, or interest that a person may have in lands or other personal property.

Estimate: amount of labor, materials, and other costs that a contractor anticipates for a project, as summarized in contractor's bid proposal for project.

Event of Default: a breach of an agreement between parties to a contract; a violation of one or more of the loan covenants as set forth in either the loan agreement, commitment letter, or promissory note.

Evergreen Revolving Credit: commitment to lend money that remains in effect unless lender takes specific action to terminate agreement; agreement may provide that, in event of termination, any outstanding amount will convert to term loan.

Exchange Rate: value of one country's currency to that of another country at a particular point in time.

Exclusive Sales Agreement: contractual arrangement, generally between a retailer and a manufacturer or wholesaler, giving retailer exclusive rights for sale of articles or services within a defined geographic area or through a defined distribution channel.

Execute: to complete and give validity to a legal document by signing, sealing, and delivering it.

Exempt: 1. to release, discharge, or waive from a liability to which others in the same general class are subject. 2. property not available for seizure.

Exemption: 1. immunity from general burden, tax, or charge. 2. legal right of debtor to hold portion of property free from claims or judgments.

Expense: cost or outlay of money used in business operating cycle.

Export-Import Bank: also called Ex-Im Bank. Provides guarantees of working capital loans for U.S. exporters; guarantees the repayment of loans or makes loans to foreign purchasers of U.S. goods and services. Ex-Im Bank also provides credit insurance that protects U.S. exporters against the risks of nonpayment by foreign buyers for political or commercial reasons. Ex-Im Bank does not compete with commercial lenders, but assumes the risks they cannot accept.

F

Face Amount: indicated value of a financial instrument, as shown on its front.

Facility Fee: lender's charge for making a line of credit or other credit facility available to borrower (for example, a commitment fee).

Facsimile: exact copy of an original.

Factor: entity that purchases borrower's accounts receivable and may extend funds to borrower prior to collection of receivables.

Factoring: short-term financing from nonrecourse sale of accounts receivable to third party or factor. Factor assumes full risk of collection, including credit losses. Factoring is most common in the garment industry, but has been used in other industries as well. There are two basic types of factoring:

- discount factoring, in which factor pays discounted price for receivables before maturity date.
- maturity factoring, in which factor pays the client purchase price of factored accounts at maturity.

Fair Credit Billing Act of 1974 (FCBA): Federal Reserve Regulation Z details the provisions of this act by prescribing uniform methods of computing the cost of consumer credit, disclosure of credit terms, and procedures for resolving billing errors on certain kinds of credit accounts.

Fair Credit Reporting Act: federal legislation that regulates consumer credit reporting activities and gives consumer right to learn contents of his or her credit bureau file.

Fair Market Value: price that property would sell for between willing buyer willing seller, neither of whom is obligated to effect transaction.

Fannie Mae: see *Federal National Mortgage Association.*

FASB: see *Financial Accounting Standards Board.*

FFB: see *Federal Financing Bank.*

FCBA: see *Fair Credit Billing Act of 1974.*

FDIC: see *Federal Deposit Insurance Corporation.*

FDICIA: see *Federal Deposit Insurance Corporation Improvement Act of 1991.*

Federal Deposit Insurance Corporation (FDIC): 1. federal agency that insu bank accounts for up to $100,000 at both commercial banks and th through Bank Insurance Fund and Savings Association Fund. 2. fed regulator for state-chartered banks that are not members of Federal Rese System.

Federal Deposit Insurance Corporation Improvement Act of 1991 (FDICIA): islation that provides for recapitalization of Bank Insurance Fund and restr turing of financial services industry through:

- emphasis on more capital.
- government standards for lending, operations, and asset growth.
- quicker government seizure of struggling institutions.
- reduced liquidity options for all but the strongest banks.
- incentives for uninsured depositors to use only the largest and strong banks.
- sharply increased regulatory costs and fees.
- easier rules for acquiring banks and thrifts.

Federal Financial Institutions Examination Council (FFIEC): interagency gr of federal banking regulators formed in 1979 to maintain uniform standa for federal examination and supervision of federally insured depository in tutions, bank holding companies, and savings and loan holding compan Also runs schools for examiners employed by banks, thrifts, and credit un agencies. Council produces Uniform Bank Performance Report.

Federal Financing Bank (FFB): agency in U.S. Treasury established by Congr in 1973 to centralize borrowing by federal agencies. Instead of selling sec ties directly to financial markets, all but largest federal agencies raise cap by borrowing from U.S. Treasury through FFB. FFB makes loans at favora rates to agencies that do not have ready access to credit markets; its deb direct obligation of U.S. Treasury.

Federal Funds: unsecured advances of immediately available funds from exc balances in reserve accounts held at Federal Reserve Banks. Technica these funds are not borrowings but purchases of immediately available fun Banks advancing federal funds sell excess reserves; banks receiving fed funds buy excess reserves from selling banks. Federal funds sold are cr transactions on account of selling banks. See also *Federal Funds Rate.*

Federal Funds Rate: rate charged in interbank market for purchases of exc reserve balances. Rate of interest is key money market interest rate and c relates with rates on other short-term credit arrangements. Because the f eral funds rate re-prices with each transaction, it is the most sensitive money market rates and is watched carefully by the Federal Reserve Board.

Federal Home Loan Bank Board (FHLBB): federal agency established by Fed Home Loan Bank Act of 1932 to supervise reserve credit system, Fed Home Loan Bank System, for savings institutions. Board also acted as ch tering agency and primary regulator of federal savings and loan associati under Home Owners Loan Act of 1933. Financial Institutions Reform, Rec ery, and Enforcement Act of 1989 abolished board, transferring its powers examination and supervision of federally chartered savings institutions to r agency, Office of Thrift Supervision, bureau of U.S. Treasury Departme Regulatory oversight of district Home Loan Banks was transferred to the fi member Federal Housing Finance Board.

Federal Home Loan Bank System: system of 11 regional banks established Federal Home Loan Bank Act of 1932, acting as central credit system for s ings and loan institutions. District Home Loan Banks make short-term cre advances to savings institutions, much like Federal Reserve System acts lender of last resort to commercial banks. Each Home Loan Bank opera independently and has its own board of directors.

Federal Home Loan Mortgage Corporation (FHLMC): corporation authorized Congress in 1970 as secondary market conduit for residential mortgag Corporation purchases loans from mortgage originators and sells its o obligations and mortgage-backed bonds issued by Government Natic Mortgage Association to private investors, namely financial institution t funds, insurance companies, pension funds, and thrift institutions. Also ca Freddie Mac.

Federal Housing Administration (FHA): federal agency that insures resider mortgages. Created by National Housing Act of 1934, FHA is now part Department of Housing and Urban Development. Both FHA and Departmen Veterans Affairs have single-family mortgage programs to assist homebuy who are unable to obtain financing from conventional mortgage lend (banks, savings and loans, and other financial institutions).

Federal Housing Finance Board (FHFB): independent federal agency regulat credit advance activities of 11 Federal Home Loan Banks. This board, est ished by Financial Institutions Reform, Recovery, and Enforcement Act of 1989, has five members, including secretary of Housing and Urban Development, and four directors appointed by the President with Senate confirmation to serve seven-year terms. At least one director must represent the interests of community groups.

eral National Mortgage Association (FNMA): federally chartered, stockholder-owned corporation that purchases residential mortgages insured or guaranteed by federal agencies, as well as conventional mortgages, in secondary mortgage market. Corporation raises capital to support its operations through collection of insurance and commitment fees, issuance of stock, and sale of debentures and notes. Also called Fannie Mae.

eral Open Market Committee (FOMC): policy committee in Federal Reserve System that sets short-term monetary policy objectives for Fed. Committee is made up of seven governors of Federal Reserve Board, plus the presidents of six Federal Reserve Banks. President of Federal Reserve Bank of New York is permanent FOMC member. The other five slots are filled on rotating basis by presidents of other 11 Federal Reserve Banks. Committee carries out monetary objectives by instructing Open Market Desk at Federal Reserve Bank of New York to buy or sell government securities from special account, called open market account, at New York Fed.

eral Reserve Board (FRB): U.S.'s central bank responsible for conduct of monetary policy; also oversees state-chartered banks that are members of Federal Reserve System, bank holding companies, and Edge Act corporations.

eral Reserve Float: total amount of funds that Federal Reserve Banks, in their role as clearing agents, have credited to depositing institutions but have not charged to paying institutions.

eral Reserve System: central bank of U.S. created by Federal Reserve Act of 1913. System consists of Board of Governors, made up of seven members, and a network of 12 Federal Reserve Banks and 25 branches throughout U.S. Board of Governors is responsible for setting monetary policy and reserve requirements. Board and banks share responsibility for setting the discount rate, the interest rate that depository institutions are charged for borrowing from Federal Reserve Banks.

eral Trade Commission (FTC): federal regulatory agency that administers and enforces rules to prevent unfair business practices.

Simple: estate in which owner is entitled to entire property and has unconditional power over its disposition.

C: see *Federal Financial Institutions Examination Council.*

: see *Federal Housing Administration.*

BB: see *Federal Home Loan Bank Board.*

MC: see *Federal Home Loan Mortgage Corporation.*

itious Name: pretend name used by firm in business transactions. Company is usually required to register this name with local authorities, along with true names and addresses of company's owners.

lity Bond: contract issued by insurer to employer to cover loss caused by dishonest acts of employees; form of suretyship. Also called dishonesty insurance.

ciary: person or entity acting in capacity of trustee for another.

d Warehousing: method of using company's inventory to secure business loan. In leased and separate storage area of borrower's facility, goods act as security for loan and are released by custodian only upon lender's order.

: see *First-In First-Out.*

: 1. organized folder containing accumulation of information and items retained for preservation or reference. 2. to deposit legal document with proper authority.

Revision: routine gathering of credit information by credit grantor to update files on borrowers.

g Claims: 1. depositing of formal papers with proper public office and in manner and time frame prescribed by law in order to preserve creditor's rights. 2. method used to perfect security interest accomplished by recording in proper public office.

nce Charges: total costs to an individual or business of obtaining credit, including interest and any fees.

ncial Analysis: evaluation by credit analyst of customer's financial situation to determine whether customer has ability to meet his or her obligations as they become due. Factors such as general condition of customer's industry, organizational structure, available collateral or guarantors, and past financial performance are considered.

ncial Accounting Standards Board (FASB): independent board responsible for establishing and interpreting generally accepted accounting principles, formed in 1973 to succeed and continue activities of Accounting Principles Board.

ncial Institutions Reform, Recovery, and Enforcement Act of 1989 (FIRREA): act signed into law on August 9, 1989, to provide funding and regulatory structure necessary to close several hundred insolvent savings associations and liquidate their assets, to consolidate federal insurance of banks and savings associations under direction of the Federal Deposit Insurance Corporation, to provide regulatory agencies with sweeping new enforcement powers, and to increase substantially civil and criminal penalties for violations of federal banking statutes and regulations. Act substantially alters relationship between savings institutions and regulators and imposes new requirements that must be observed in day-to-day operations of institutions.

Financial Position: standing of company, combining assets and liabilities as entered on balance sheet.

Financial Statements: reports consisting of individual's or company's balance sheet, income statement, and statement of cash flows, footnotes, and any supplemental schedules.

Financing Statement: form required to be completed by creditor and filed with appropriate county and state authorities in order to perfect creditor's security interest in collateral and to give public notice of such interest.

FIRREA: see *Financial Institutions Reform, Recovery, and Enforcement Act of 1989.*

First Deed of Trust: first recorded deed of trust that acts as first lien on property it describes.

First-In First-Out (FIFO): method of valuing inventory in which the first goods received are the first goods used or sold. Using this method, costs of inventory used to determine cost of goods sold are related to costs that were incurred first.

First Mortgage: mortgage on property that is superior to any others by fact of having been filed first.

Fiscal: anything involving financial matters or issues.

Fiscal Agent: person or organization serving as another's financial agent or representative.

Fiscal Year: fixed accounting year used as basis for annual financial reporting by business or government.

Five C's of Credit: method of evaluating potential borrower's creditworthiness based on five criteria: Capacity, Capital, Character, Collateral, and Conditions.

Fixed Assets: property used in normal course of business that is of a long-term nature, such as land, machinery, fixtures, and equipment.

Fixed-Rate Loan: loan with interest rate that does not vary over term of loan.

Fixture: that which is permanently attached or affixed to real property.

Flagging an Account: temporarily identifying an account for specific purpose or reason; may involve suspending activity.

Float: uncollected funds represented by checks deposited in one bank but not yet cleared through bank on which they are drawn.

Floating Interest Rate: loan interest rate that changes whenever the stated index rate, or base rate, changes.

Floating Lien: loan or credit facility secured by inventory or receivables. This type of security agreement gives lender interest in assets acquired by borrower after agreement, as well as those owned when agreement was made. When agreement covers proceeds from sales, lender also has recourse against cash collected from the payment of receivables.

Floor Plan: loan made to dealer for purchase of inventory acquired for resale and secured by that inventory, such as automobiles or appliances.

FNMA: see *Federal National Mortgage Association.*

FOB: see *Free on Board.*

FOB Point: point at which responsibility for freight charges begins and title passes. See also *Free on Board.*

FOMC: see *Federal Open Market Committee.*

Forbearance: Temporarily giving up the right to enforce a valid claim, in return for a promise. It is sufficient consideration to make a promise binding (for example, protracted payment arrangements or interest rate reduction in exchange for additional collateral or guarantors).

Forced Sale: 1. court-ordered sale of property, usually without owner's approval. 2. voluntary sale of goods or property to raise cash or to reduce inventory.

Foreclosure: legal termination of all of debtor's rights in property secured by mortgage after debtor has defaulted on obligation supported by such mortgage.

Foreign Corporation: corporation established under laws of a state other than that in which it is doing business.

Foreign Exchange: conversion of money of one country into its equivalent in currency of another country.

Foreign Item: check drawn on any financial institution other than the financial institution where it is presented for payment. Also called transit item.

Foreign Judgment: judgment obtained in state or country other than the one where the debtor now lives, is doing business, or has assets.

Forfeiture: penalty resulting in automatic loss of cash, property, or rights for not complying with legal terms of agreement.

Forgery: false making or material altering of any writing with intent to defraud.

Form 8K: report disclosing significant events potentially affecting corporation's financial condition or market value of its shares, required by Securities and Exchange Commission. Report is filed within 30 days after event (pending merger, amendment to corporate charter, charge to earnings for credit losses) took place and summarizes information that any reasonable investor would want to know before buying or selling securities.

Form 10K: annual financial report filed with Securities and Exchange Commission. Issuers of registered securities are required to file 10K, as are corporations with 500 or more shareholders or assets of $2 million and exchange-listed corporations. Report, which becomes public information once filed, summarizes key financial information, including sources and uses of funds by type of business, net pretax operating income, provision for income taxes and credit losses, plus comparative financial statements for past two fiscal years. Summary of 10K report is included in annual report to stockholders.

Form 10Q: quarterly financial report filed by companies with listed securities and those corporations required to file annual 10K report with Securities and Exchange Commission. 10Q report, which does not have to be audited, summarizes key financial data on earnings and expenses and compares current financial information with data reported in same quarter of previous year.

Forwarding: referral or placement of out-of-town claims with attorney who then acts on behalf of creditor. In collection process, when authorized, agency may forward account to attorney for collection or suit.

Franchise: business agreement whereby one company allows another the right to conduct business under its name and/or distribute its products in exchange for royalties or another agreed upon method of payment.

Fraud: any act of deceit, omission, or commission used to deprive someone of right or property. Elements of fraud consist of intentional misrepresentation of fact, relied on by another to his or her detriment, that results in damages.

Fraudulent Conveyance: a transfer of property by a debtor, for the intent and purpose of defrauding creditors. Such property may be reached by the creditors through appropriate legal proceedings.

FRB: see *Federal Reserve Board.*

Freddie Mac: see *Federal Home Loan Mortgage Corporation.*

Free and Clear: 1. property with an unencumbered title. 2. title that is free of defects.

Free and Clear Delivery Receipt: delivery receipt signed by consignee completely absolving carrier from any claim for loss or damages.

Free Astray: freight shipment that has been lost. If it is carrier's fault and shipment is located, it is carrier's obligation to make delivery to original destination at no additional cost to shipper or consignee.

Free Demand Letter Service: pre-collection letter sent by collection agency to debtor, requesting that payment be made directly to creditor by given date. No charge is made for payments received within free demand period, but balances remaining unpaid are followed for collection by agency at its regular rates.

Free on Board (FOB): term identifying shipping point from which buyer assumes all responsibilities and costs for transportation.

Free Port: place where goods are imported or exported free of any duty.

Freight Forwarder: business that receives goods for transportation; services include consolidation of small freight shipments of less than carload, truckload, or container lots assembled for lower shipping rates.

Frozen Account: 1. account to which customer no longer has access. 2. account suspended by court order, violation of loan covenants, or checking account agreement, etc.

Frozen Assets: any assets that cannot be used by owner because of pending legal action.

FTC: see *Federal Trade Commission.*

Fund: cash or equivalents set aside for specific purpose.

Fund Accounting: fiscal and accounting entity with self-balancing set of accounts recording cash and other financial resources, together with all related liabilities and residual equities or balances, and changes therein, which are segregated for purpose of carrying on specific activities or obtaining certain objectives in accordance with special regulations, restrictions, or limitations.

Funded Debt: mortgages, bonds, debentures, notes, or other obligations with maturity of more than one year from statement date.

G

GAAP: see *Generally Accepted Accounting Principles.*

Garnishee: 1. person or entity that has possession of money or property belonging to defendant and is served with writ of garnishment to hold money or property for payment of defendant's debt to plaintiff. 2. one against whom garnishment has been served.

Garnishment: legal warning or procedure to one in possession of another's property not to allow owner access to such property as it will be used to satisfy judgment against owner.

General Contractor: contractor who enters into a contract with an owner for construction of a project and who takes full responsibility for its completion. Contractor may enter into subcontracts with various subcontractors for performance of specific parts or phases of project.

General Ledger: bookkeeping record comprising all assets, liabilities, proprietorship, revenue, and expense accounts. Entries for each account are posted, and balances are included for each entry.

Generally Accepted Accounting Principles (GAAP): conventions, rules, and p cedures that define accepted accounting practices, including broad guideli as well as detailed procedures. Financial Accounting Standards Board, independent self-regulatory organization, is responsible for promulga these principles.

General Obligation Debt: long-term debt or bond repaid from all otherwise u stricted revenues, sales taxes, property taxes, license fees, property sa rents, and so forth of municipality.

General Partner: participant in a business relationship who is personally lia without limitation, for all partnership debts.

Ginnie Mae: see *Government National Mortgage Association.*

GNMA: see *Government National Mortgage Association.*

Going Concern: assumes that a business entity has a reasonable expectatio continuing in business and generating a profit for an indefinite period of ti

Goods on Approval: goods offered by seller to buyer with option of exami goods for specific period of time before deciding to purchase them.

Goodwill: 1. intangible assets of business consisting of its good reputation, v able clientele, or desirable location that results in above normal ear power. 2. value or amount for which business could be sold above book v of its physical property and receivables.

Government National Mortgage Association (GNMA): corporation created Congress that administers mortgage-backed securities program that chan new sources of funds into residential mortgages through sale of securi Also called Ginnie Mae.

Grace Period: specified length of time beyond payment due date during w late fee will not be assessed.

Grantee: person to whom title in property is made.

Grantor: person who transfers title to property.

Gross Margin: gross profit as a percentage of sales.

Gross Profit: net sales less cost of sales.

Gross Sales: sales before returns and allowances; discounts are deducte arrive at net sales.

Guarantor: person who agrees by execution of a contract to repay the deb another if that person defaults.

Guaranty: separate agreement by which a party (or parties) other than de assumes responsibility for payment of obligation if principal debtor defa or is subsequently unable to perform under the terms of the obligation.

Guardian: person who is legally responsible for the care and management minor or individual who is not mentally or legally competent (or of such son's property).

H

Hard Goods: durable consumer goods, usually including such items as m appliances and furniture, with relatively long, useful lives.

Heavy Industry: industry involved in manufacturing basic products such as r als, machinery, or other equipment.

Hidden Assets: assets not easily identified and either intentionally not disclo or publicly reported at lower value than their true worth.

High Credit: largest amount of credit used by borrower during specified perio time.

Holder in Due Course: person who has taken negotiable instrument (chec note) for value, in good faith, and on assurance that it is complete and re lar, not overdue or dishonored, and has no defect in ownership on part of vious holder or endorser.

Holding Company: company organized to hold and control stock in other com nies.

Homestead Exemption: state's law allowing householder or head of famil exempt residence from attachment by creditors.

Housing and Urban Development, Department of: cabinet-level federal age founded in 1965, that promotes housing development in U.S. through di loans, mortgage insurance, and guaranties. It houses Federal Housing Adr istration and Government National Mortgage Association.

HUD: see *Housing and Urban Development, Department of.*

Hypothecate: to pledge or assign property owned by one entity as security or lateral for loan to second entity.

Hypothecation: 1. offer of stocks, bonds, or other assets owned by party o than borrower as collateral for loan, without transferring title. Borro retains possession but gives lender right to sell property in event of defaul borrower. 2. pledging of negotiable securities to collateralize broker's ma loan. If broker pledges same securities to bank as collateral for broker's l process is referred to as re-hypothecation.

I

Immunity: condition of being exempt from duty that others are generally requ to perform.

Import Letter of Credit: commercial letter of credit issued to finance impo goods.

ort Duty: government tax on imported items.
ound: to seize or take into legal custody, usually at order of court. Cash, documents, or records may be impounded.
tive Account: account that has shown little or no activity over a substantial period of time.
tive Files: 1. accounts on which collection activity has been completed or suspended (claims either collected or found to be uncollectible) and on which no further work is being done. Also called closed or dead files. 2. stored records available for reference.
rrears: amounts due but not yet paid.
me Property: real property acquired as investment and managed for profit.
me Statement: summary of revenue and expenses covering a specified period.
me Tax: tax levied by federal, state, or local governments on personal or business earnings.
rporation: formation of legal entity, with qualities of perpetual existence and succession.
mbrance: see *Encumbrance.*
btedness: total amount of money or liabilities owed.
efault: failing to abide by terms and conditions of note or loan agreement. This can include payments on interest or principal (or both) being past due.
mnity: 1. contract or assurance to reimburse another against anticipated loss, damage, or failure to fulfill obligation. 2. type of insurance that provides coverage for losses of this nature.
rect Liability: contingent liability such as a continuing guarantee.
vidual Signature: credit approved by one person on his or her own authority.
rsement: see *Endorsement.*
strial Consumer: purchaser who buys goods or services for business purposes.
iry: request for credit information on a bank's customer.
der Loans: loans to directors and officers of bank, which must be reported to bank regulators under Financial Institutions Reform Act of 1978. Banking laws require that loans to insiders be made at substantially the same rate and credit terms as loans to other borrowers.
lvency: 1. inability to meet debts as they become due in ordinary course of business. 2. financial condition in which assets are not sufficient to satisfy liabilities.
allment Sale: contract sale in which merchandise is purchased with down payment and balance is made in partial payments over agreed period of time.
rument: written formal or legal document.
ubstance Foreclosure Assets: loans for which borrower is perceived to have little or no equity in the asset or project and the financial institution can reasonably anticipate proceeds for repayment only from the operation or sale of collateral.
fficient Funds: see *Non-sufficient Funds.*
rable Interest: interest such that loss or damage inflicts economic loss.
rable Value: maximum possible loss to which property is exposed; actual amount depends on basis of calculation per insurance policy.
ngible Assets: nonmaterial assets of business that have no value in themselves but that represent value. Examples include trademarks, goodwill, patents, and copyrights.
rchange: confidential exchange of credit information between individuals and trade groups.
rchange Bureau: association organized to record and exchange or furnish confidential credit information about a member's payment experience and manner in which customers meet obligations.
rchange Group: trade membership group within specific industry that meets regularly to exchange credit experiences and other confidential information.
rchange Report: report usually obtained through credit interchange bureau showing recent credit experience as supplied by participating members.
r-creditor Agreement: document used when there is more than one lender involved in credit transaction to spell out each lender's rights and obligations.
rest: 1. legally allowed or agreed upon compensation to lender for use of borrowed money. 2. any right in property but less than title to it.
rest Bearing: term describing note or contract calling for payment of agreed interest.
rest Only: loan term during which no principal repayments are made.
rest Rate: cost of borrowing money expressed as an annualized percentage of the loan.
rnal Guidance Line of Credit: credit facility similar to a line of credit, but customer may or may not be advised of it; established for internal financial institution purposes, it provides financing for recurrent requests without referring each one to credit committee or other approval source.
rnational Consumer Credit Association: professional trade association of retail credit professionals. Association keeps members informed of latest developments in consumer credit and provides educational courses, seminars, textbooks, and other published material.
Intestate: dying without leaving valid will or any other specific instructions as to disposition of property.
Inventory: current assets of business that represent goods for sale, including raw materials, work in process, and finished goods.
Investigation: 1. gathering of credit information on a person or entity. 2. systematic research for information necessary for a business decision.
Investment: use of money for purpose of earning profit or return.
Investor: person or entity that puts money to use for capital appreciation or profit or to receive regular dividends.
Invoice: seller's descriptive, itemized billing for goods or services sold, showing date, terms, cost, purchase order number, method of shipment, and other identifying information.
Involuntary Bankruptcy: see *Bankruptcy.*
Itemized Statement: detailed listing of activity on account for particular period of time.

J

Jobber: see *Wholesaler.*
Joint Account: financial institution account shared or owned in name of two or more persons with full privileges available to each person.
Joint and Several: relative to liability, a term used when creditor has option of pursuing one or more signers of an agreement individually or all signers together.
Joint Tenancy with Rights of Survivorship: interest in property held by two or more persons that includes right of survivorship in which deceased person's interest passes to survivors. See also *Tenancy by Entirety.*
Joint Venture: business or undertaking entered into on one-time basis by two or more parties in which profits, losses, and control are shared.
Journal: account book of original entry in which all money receipts and expenses are chronologically recorded.
Judgment: court's determination of rights of parties to claim.
Judgment Creditor: one who has obtained judgment against debtor and can enforce it.
Judgment Debtor: one against whom judgment has been recovered but not satisfied.
Judgment Note: see *Cognovit Note.*
Judgment Lien: claim or encumbrance on property, allowed by law, usually against real estate of judgment debtor.
Judgment-Proof: term to describe judgment debtor from whom collection cannot be obtained or person who has no money or assets or has concealed or removed property subject to execution.
Judicial Sale: see *Forced Sale.*
Junior Mortgage: any mortgage filed after and subject to satisfaction of first mortgage.
Jurisdiction: 1. legal authority, power, capacity, and right of court to act. 2. geographic area within which court or government agency exercises power.

K

Keyperson Life Insurance: insurance policy written on owner or principal employee in which death benefits are payable to company.
Key Ratios: performance measures used to determine probable ability of business to operate profitably. Results are expressed in percentages that are then weighed against average percentages in each industry.

L

Landlord's Waiver: the relinquishment of a right(s) contained in a lease agreement by a lessor.
Last-In First-Out (LIFO): method of valuating inventory in which last goods received are the first ones sold. Using this method, inventory costs used to determine cost of goods sold are related to costs of inventory that were incurred last.
Late Charge: special legally agreed upon fee, charged by creditor, on any payment that is not made when due.
Lawful Money: legal tender for payment of all debts.
Law List: compiled publication of names and addresses of those in legal profession, often including court calendars, private investigators, and other information of interest to legal profession.
Lawsuit: suit, action, or cause instituted by one person against another in a court of law.
Lead Bank: financial institution that has the primary deposit or lending relationship in a multi-bank situation; usually in the context of shared credit and sometimes defined within an inter-creditor agreement. See also *Agent Bank.*
Leaseback: agreement by which one party sells property to another and, after completing sale, the first party rents it from second party.
Lease Contract: written agreement for which equipment or facilities can be obtained on rental payment basis for specified period of time.

Leased Department: section of department store not operated by store but by independent outside organization on contract or percentage-of-sales arrangement.

Leasehold: rights tenant holds in property as conferred by terms of lease.

Leasehold Improvement: permanent improvements made to rented property. Leasehold improvements are considered fixtures and depreciate over lease period.

Leasehold Interest: lessee's equity or ownership in leasehold improvements.

Lease-Purchase Agreement: contract providing for set amount of lease payments to be applied to purchase of property.

Ledger: in accounting, book of permanent records containing series of accounts to which debits and credits of transactions are posted from books of original entry.

Ledger Experience: trade experience reported by credit manager or interchange group. Such reports provide picture of account's paying habits, high credit, and terms of repayment.

Legal and Sovereign Risk: risk that government may intervene to affect bank's system or any participant of such system detrimentally.

Legal Composition: identification and description of lawful ownership or title to business entity.

Legal Entity: business organization that has capacity to make contract or agreement or assume obligation. Such organization may consist of individual proprietorship, partnership, corporation, or association.

Legal Right: natural right, right created by contract, and right created or recognized by law.

Legal Tender: any money that is recognized by law for payment of debt unless contract exists specifically calling for payment in another type of money.

Legal Title: document establishing right of ownership to property that is recognized and upheld by law.

Lender: one who extends funds to another with expectation of repayment with interest.

Lender's Loss Payable Endorsement: form attached to property insurance policies to cover lender's interest in what is insured; extends coverage to give lender protection beyond that in basic policy; language may be prescribed by banking industry, standard form prepared by insurance industry, or specified by lender. See also *Loss Payee Clause.*

Lessee: one to whom lease is given and therefore has right to use property in exchange for rental payments.

Lessor: owner who grants lease for use of property in return for rent.

Letter of Agreement: letter stating terms of agreement between addressor and addressee, usually prepared for signature by addressee as indication of acceptance of those terms as legally binding.

Letter of Credit: letter or document issued by bank on behalf of customer that is evidence of financial background of bank and ensures that payment will be made when proper documents confirm completion of related transaction. Such letters authorize drawing of sight or time drafts when certain terms and conditions are fulfilled. See also *Banker's Acceptance, Draft, Sight Draft, Standby Letter of Credit,* and *Time Draft.*

Letter of Intent: letter signifying intention to enter into formal agreement and usually setting forth general terms of such agreement.

Liable: duty or obligation enforceable by law.

Liabilities: indebtedness of an individual or entity.

Libel: written or published false and malicious statements about another that tend to defame or harm another's reputation.

LIBOR: see *London Interbank Offered Rate.*

Lien: legal right or encumbrance to secure payment performance on property pledged as collateral until the debt it secures is satisfied.

LIFO: see *Last-In First-Out.*

Limited Liability Company: legal entity that offers shareholders the same limitations on personal liability available to corporate shareholders. The owners of a limited liability company (LLC) have limited liability. They are not liable for the debts, liabilities, acts, or omissions of the company. Only their investment is at risk.

Limited Liability: legal exemption corporate stockholders or limited liability companies have from full financial responsibilities for debts of company.

Limited Partnership: partnership of one or more general partners who are personally, jointly, and separately responsible, with one or more special partners whose liabilities are limited to amount of investment.

Line of Credit: see *Credit Line.*

Liquid Assets: assets that can be readily converted into cash.

Liquidate: 1. to pay off or settle current obligation. 2. to sell off or convert assets into cash. 3. to dissolve business in order to raise cash for payment of debts.

Liquidation: process of dissolving a business, settling accounts, and paying off any claims or obligations; remaining cash is distributed to the owners of the business.

Liquidation Value: cash that can be realized from sale of assets in dissolving business, as distinct from its value as ongoing entity.

Liquidity: measure of quality and adequacy of current assets to meet cur obligations as they come due.

Liquidity Ratio: company's most liquid assets (generally cash and acco receivable) divided by current liabilities. Also called quick ratio.

List Price: generally advertised or posted price. Sometimes subject to trad cash discounts.

Litigation: lawsuit brought to court for purpose of enforcing a right.

LLC: see *Limited Liability Company.*

Loan: money advanced to a borrower with agreement of repayment usually interest within a specified period of time.

Loan Agreement: legal contract between a financial institution and a borro that governs the terms and conditions for the life of a loan. Elements usu include description of loan, representations, and warranties reaffirm known facts about the borrower such as legal structure, affirmative and n tive covenants, conditions that must be met before the loan is granted, d quent payment penalties, and statement of remedies that the financial ins tion may take in event of default.

Loan Participation: sharing of loan(s) by a group of financial institutions that together to make said loan(s), affording an opportunity to share the risk very large transaction. Arranged through correspondent banking network which smaller financial institutions buy a portion of an overall financing p age. Participations are a convenient way for smaller financial institution book loans that would otherwise exceed their legal lending limits. Also ca participation financing.

Loan Policy: principles that reflect a financial institution's credit culture, un writing procedures, and overall approach to lending.

Loans Past Due: loans with interest or principal payments that are contractu past due a certain number of days.

Loan-to-Value Ratio (LTV): relationship, expressed as percent, between princ amount of loan and appraised value of the asset securing financing.

Loan Value: amount of money that can be borrowed against real or pers property.

Lockbox: regional financial institution depository used by corporations to ob earlier receipt and collection of customer payments. Arrangement prov creditor with better control of accounts receivable and earlier availabilit cash balances. Many large financial institutions offer lockbox processing a cash management service to corporate customers. Lockboxes can be:

- retail, designed for remittance processing for consumer accounts.
- wholesale, in which payments from other entities are collected and sub ted through depository transfer check or electronic debit into a concen tion account for investment and disbursement as needed.

London Interbank Offered Rate (LIBOR): key rate index used in internati lending. LIBOR is the rate at which major financial institutions in London willing to lend Eurodollars to each other. This index is often used to detern interest rate charged to creditworthy borrowers.

Long-Arm Statutes: state statutes that allow state courts to exercise jurisdic over nonresident persons or property outside their state's borders.

Long-Term Capital Gain (Loss): gain or loss realized from sale or exchang capital asset held for longer than 12 months.

Long-Term Liabilities: all senior debt, including bonds, debentures, bank d mortgages, deferred portions of long term-debt, and capital lease obligati owed for longer than 12 months.

Loss: 1. circumstance in which expenses exceed revenues. 2. result if an ass sold for less than its depreciated book value.

Loss Assets: assets considered uncollectible and of such little value that t continuance as realizable assets is not warranted.

Loss Leader: deliberate sale of product or service at or below cost in orde attract new customers.

Loss Payee Clause: provision in insurance policy or added by endorsemen cover lender/mortgagee's interest in property loss settlement. Provision is as broad as lender's loss payable endorsement. Also called mortgagee cla and loss payable clause.

LTV: see *Loan-to-Value Ratio.*

Lump-sum Settlement: payment made in full with single, one-time payment.

M

Magnetic Ink Character Recognition (MICR): description of numbers and s bols that are printed in magnetic ink on documents for automated process Fully inscribed MICR line of information may include item's serial num routing and transit number, check digit, account number, process co number, and amount.

Mail-Fraud Statute: federal law against using mails to defraud creditors by n ing false financial statements. Prosecution under mail-fraud statute m prove beyond reasonable doubt that:

- statement is false.
- statement was made with intention it should be relied on.
- it was made for the purpose of securing money or property.

- statement was delivered by mail.
- money or property was obtained by means of false statement.

lgram: telegraphic message transmitted electronically by Western Union and delivered by U.S. Postal Service.

l Teller: employee of a financial institution who receives mail deposits, checks them for accuracy, and returns stamped receipts for deposits to customers.

ority Stockholder: person or entity that owns more than 50% of voting stock of a corporation, thereby having controlling interest.

er: one who signs or executes negotiable instrument.

practice: professional misconduct with negligence.

agement: persons responsible for administrating and carrying out policy of business or other organization.

agement Information System (MIS): established flow of information developed to keep managers informed of what is happening within their organization and to do it within a time frame that permits effective reaction when required. Efficient MIS helps managers make better decisions.

agement Report: statement in unaudited financial statements that says financials are representations of firm's management.

ifest: shipping document that lists freight's origin, contents, value, destination, carrier, and other pertinent information for use at terminals or custom house.

ufacturers Representative (Agent): independent, commissioned sales agent who represents several noncompeting manufacturers for sale of their products to related businesses within agreed, exclusive sales territory.

ginal Account: borderline credit risk that does not have sufficient operating capital and from which payment may be delayed.

kdown: price reduction of goods below normal selling price.

ket: 1. customer base for a company's goods or services. 2. securities exchange and its associated institutions.

ketability: ease and rapidity with which product, service, or other asset can be sold or converted to cash.

keting: 1. activities necessary to facilitate the sale of goods or services through planned research, manufacturing, promotion, advertising, and distribution. 2. business promotion devoted to getting the maximum purchases of products or services by consumers.

ket Value: price that goods or property would bring in current market of willing buyers and sellers.

kup: amount or percentage added to cost of goods to arrive at selling price.

urity Date: date when financial obligation, note, draft, bond, or instrument becomes due for payment.

chanic's Lien: enforceable claim, permitted by law in most states, securing payment to contractors, subcontractors, and suppliers of materials for work performed in constructing or repairing buildings. Lien attaches to real property, plus buildings and improvements situated on land, and remains in effect until workers have been paid in full or, in event of liquidation, gives contractor priority of lien ahead of other creditors.

dium of Exchange: money or commodity accepted in payment or settlement of debt.

morandum (Consignment) Sale: sale of goods for which seller is not paid until retailer has sold merchandise. Seller retains title to such goods until retailer has sold merchandise and payment is made to retailer.

rcantile Agency: organization that compiles credit and financial information and supplies subscribers or members with reports on applicants for credit; can also perform other functions such as collection of accounts or compiling of statistical trade information.

rchandise Shortage: goods purchased but not included in shipment.

rger: combining of two or more businesses to form a single organization.

zzanine Financing: 1. in corporate finance, leveraged buyout or restructuring financed through subordinated debt, such as preferred stock or convertible debentures. Transaction is financed by expanding equity, as opposed to debt. 2. second- or third-level financing of companies financed by venture capital. Senior to venture capital but junior to financial institution financing, it adds creditworthiness to firm. Generally used as intermediate-stage financing, preceding a company's initial public offering, it is considered less risky than start-up financing.

CR: see *Magnetic Ink Character Recognition.*

ddle-of-Month (M.O.M.) Billing Term: billing system in which all shipments are charged on one invoice issued twice a month. For first half of month, credit period runs to the 25th and, for the second half, to the tenth of the following month.

S: see *Management Information System.*

dified Accrual Accounting: basis of accounting in which expenditures are recognized when liability is incurred. Revenues are recognized when measurable and available. Exception is in debt service funds in which expenditures are recorded only when due.

O.M.: see *Middle-of-Month Billing Term.*

Money Judgment: court decision that adjudges payment of money rather than requiring act to be performed or property transferred.

Monitoring: service available through many credit reporting or interchange bureaus enabling subscribers to request that certain listed accounts be automatically monitored and reviewed and that updated reports be issued periodically.

Moratorium: 1. temporary extension or delay of normal period for payment of account. 2. Formal postponement during which debtor is permitted to delay payment of obligations.

Mortgage: debt instrument giving conditional ownership of asset to borrower, secured by the asset being financed. The instrument by which real estate is hypothecated as security for the repayment of a loan. Borrower gives lender a mortgage in exchange for the right to use property while mortgage is in effect and agrees to make regular payments of principal and interest. Mortgage lien is lender's security interest and is recorded in title documents in public land records. Lien is removed when debt is paid in full. Mortgage normally involves real estate and is considered long-term debt.

Mortgagee: lender who arranges mortgage financing, collects loan payments, and takes security interest in property financed.

Mortgagee Clause: provision in property policy, or added by endorsement, that extends protection, in limited manner, to mortgagee; not as broad as lender's loss payable endorsement.

Mortgagee Waiver: the relinquishment of right(s) contained in a mortgage by a mortgagee.

Mortgage Verification: request made by mortgagee to applicant's financial institution for information on applicant's accounts, as part of mortgagee's credit approval process.

Mortgagor: borrower in a mortgage contract who mortgages property in exchange for a loan.

Multinational Corporation: corporation whose operations are conducted on an international basis.

Multiple Signature Credit Approval: describes credit approval process in which credit is approved by two or more persons acting together.

Mutual Account Revision: routine exchange of credit information between two or more credit grantors that have extended credit to subject of inquiry.

N

NACM: see *National Association of Credit Management.*

National Association of Credit Management (NACM): national business organization of credit and financial professionals that promotes laws for sound credit, protects businesses against fraudulent debtors, improves the interchange of commercial credit information, develops credit practices, and provides education and certification programs for its members.

Negligence: failure to use reasonable care that an ordinarily prudent person would in like circumstances.

Negotiable: anything capable of being transferred by endorsement or delivery.

Negotiable Instrument: any written evidence of indebtedness, transferable by endorsement and delivery or by delivery only, that contains unconditional promise to pay specified sum on demand or at some fixed date.

Negotiate: to discuss, bargain, or work out plan of settlement, terms, or compromise in business transaction.

Net: amount left after necessary deductions have been made from gross amount.

Net Assets: sum of individual's or entity's total assets less total liabilities.

Net Earnings: total sales, less total operating, administrative, and overhead expenses, but before other expenses and income such as interest and dividends.

Net Income: amount of income remaining after deducting all expenses from total revenues.

Net Lease: agreement in which tenant assumes payment of other property expenses, such as taxes, maintenance, and insurance, in addition to rental payments.

Net Price: actual price paid after all discounts, allowances, and other authorized deductions have been taken.

Net Profit: income earned by business over specific period of time. Profit from transaction or sale, after deducting all costs, expenses, and miscellaneous reserves and adjustments from gross receipts.

Net Sales: total sales less returns, allowances, and discounts.

Net Working Capital: current assets less current liabilities; used as measure of a company's liquidity and indicates its ability to finance current operations.

Net Worth: total assets less total liabilities; reflects owners' net interest in company.

No Account: notation on rejected check when check writer does not have account at the financial institution on which check is drawn.

No Asset Case: insolvent or bankrupt estate with no assets available for payment of creditors' claims.

No Funds: notation on rejected check when check writer has account but not funds to cover check.

Nominal Balance: an account balance of less than $100.

Nominal Owner: person whose name appears on title to asset, but who has no interest in it.

Nonaccrual: loan on which a financial institution does not accrue interest; also known as a nonperforming loan.

Nonborrowing Account: banking relationship in which no extension of credit is involved.

Nonfinancial Information: facts used to evaluate a customer's creditworthiness; focuses on background and history rather than financial measures.

Nonpayment: failure or neglect to pay or discharge debt in accordance with terms of agreement.

Nonperforming Assets: total of earning assets listed as nonaccrual; formerly, earning assets acquired in foreclosure and through in-substance foreclosures.

Nonperforming Loans: amount of loans not meeting original terms of agreement, including renegotiated, restructured, and nonaccrual loans. Loans included in this total vary according to bank policy and regulation.

Nonprofit Corporation: organization specifically classified by the IRS as generally tax exempt and whose primary purpose for existence is to provide services of a charitable, fraternal, religious, social, or civic nature.

Nonrecource: inability of holder in due course to demand payment from endorser of debt instrument if party(ies) primarily liable fail to make payment.

Non-sufficient Funds (NSF): term used when collected demand deposit balances are less than the amount of the check being presented for payment and check is returned to payee's financial institution. See also Overdraft.

No Protest (N.P.): instructions given by one financial institution to another not to protest check or note when presented for payment. N.P. is usually stamped on instrument to avoid protest fee.

North American Industrial Classification System (NAICS): the Standard Industrial Classification (SIC) code is being replaced by the NAICS code. NAICS classifies establishments by their primary type of activity within a six-digit code. NAICS provides structural enhancements over SIC and identifies over 350 new industries. See also *SIC* and *Standard Industrial Classification.*

Notary Public: public officer authorized to administer oaths, attest and certify certain types of documents, and to take acknowledgements of conveyances.

Note: unconditional written promise by borrower to pay certain amount of money to lender on demand or at specified or determinable date. This instrument should meet all requirements of laws pertaining to negotiable instruments.

Notes Payable: liabilities represented by promissory notes, excluding trade debts, that are payable in future.

Notes Receivable: assets represented by promissory notes, excluding amounts due from customers for credit sales, to be collected in future.

Notice of Protest: formal statement that a certain bill of exchange, check, or promissory note was presented for payment or acceptance and that such payment or acceptance was not made. Such notice will also state that because instrument has been dishonored, maker, endorsers, or other parties to document will be held responsible for payment.

Novation: substitution of old contract for new one between same or different parties; substitution of new debtor or creditor for previous one, by mutual agreement.

NSF: see *Non-sufficient Funds.*

Nulla Bona: report made by sheriff when no assets are found within his or her jurisdiction on which to satisfy judgment against debtor.

O

Obligation: 1. law or duty binding parties to an agreement. 2. written promise to pay money or to do a specific thing.

Obligee: person or entity to which payment is due.

Obligor: person or entity required by contract to perform specific act.

Obsolescence: decline in perceived value of asset, frequently because of technological innovations, changes in an industry's processes, or changes required by law.

OCC: see *Office of the Comptroller of the Currency.*

Offer: proposal to make contract, usually presented by one party to another for acceptance.

Offering Basis: customer's loan requests considered individually on merits of each proposal.

Office of the Comptroller of the Currency (OCC): branch of the Treasury Department that regulates federally chartered banks.

Office of Thrift Supervision (OTS): branch of the Treasury Department that regulates state and federally chartered thrifts as well as those institutions in conservatorship.

Offset: amount allowed to be netted against another.

On Account: generally describes partial payment made toward settlement of unpaid balance.

On Account Payment: partial payment not intended as payment in full.

On Demand: debt instrument that is due and payable on presentation.

Open (Book) Account: credit extended without a formal written contract and resented on books and records of the seller as an unsecured account rec able for which payment is expected within a specified period after purchase

Open-End Credit: consumer line of credit that may be added to, up to pr credit limit, or paid down at any time. Customer has option of paying off standing balance, without penalty, or making several installment payme Contrasts with Closed-End Credit. Also called revolving credit or cha account credit.

Open Terms: selling on credit terms as opposed to having customer pay cash.

Operating Performance Ratios: financial measures designed to assist in eval tion of management performance.

Operating Statement: report of an individual's or entity's income and expen for a specified period of time. See also Income Statement.

Operational Risk: risk concerning computer network failure due to system o load or other disruptions; also includes potential losses from fraud, malici damage to data, and error.

Oral Contract: agreement that may or may not be written in whole or in par signed but is legally enforceable.

Order: informal bill of exchange or letter or request identifying person to be pa

Order for Relief: order issued by bankruptcy court judge upon filing of petition debtor or filing of petition by creditors.

Order to Order: agreement for payment to be made for prior shipment before r delivery will be made.

OREO: see *Other Real Estate Owned.*

Other Real Estate Owned: real property usually taken as collateral and sub quently acquired through foreclosure, or by obtaining a deed in lieu of fo closure, in satisfaction of the debts previously contracted. Real property merly used as banking premises, or real property sold in a "cove transaction" as defined by banking regulations.

OTS: see *Office of Thrift Supervision.*

Outlet Store: retail operation where manufacturers' production overruns, disc tinued merchandise, or irregular goods are sold at discount.

Out-of-Court Settlement: 1. settlement made by distressed debtor through di negotiations with creditors or through creditors' committee; acceptance such settlement is not obligatory to nonconsenting creditors. 2. agreem reached between opposing parties to settle pending lawsuit before matter been decided by court.

Out-of-Pocket Expense: business expenses for which individual pays.

Out-of-Trust: an event occurring in floor plan financing where a borrower s inventory securing the financial institution's loan and fails to promptly re the proceeds to the financial institution in accordance with the loan ag ment.

Outstanding: 1. amount of credit facility that is being used versus total amo made available. 2. unpaid or uncollected account.

Overdraft: negative account balance created when a check is paid when collec demand deposit balances are less than amount of check being presented payment. See also Non-sufficient Funds.

Overdue: debt obligation on which payments are past due.

Overhead: selling and administrative business costs as contrasted with costs goods sold.

Oversold: condition in which manufacturer or wholesaler finds itself after tak more orders than it can deliver within an agreed period of time.

Owed: debt that is due and payable.

Own: to have legal title to property.

Owner: person or entity that owns or has title to property.

Owner's Equity: mathematical difference between total assets and total liabili that represents shareholders' equity or an individual's net worth.

Ownership: exclusive rights that one has to property, to exclusion of all othe having complete title to property.

Owner's Risk: term used in transportation contracts to exempt carrier fr responsibility for loss or damage to goods.

P

Packing List: detailed listing of information on shipment's contents (enclosed inspection with package).

Paid Direct: payment made by debtor directly to original creditor instead o collection agency or attorney handling account for collection.

Paper Profit: unrealized income or gain on asset.

Paralegal: trained aide to attorney who handles various legal tasks.

Parent Company: an entity that holds controlling majority interest in subsidiari

Partial Payment: payment not in full for amount owed.

Participation: purchase or sale of a loan or credit facility among two or m financial institutions in which the acquiring institution(s) has no formal direct role in establishing the terms and conditions binding the borrower. P ticipants do not participate in the document negotiation between the origin ing financial institution and the borrower.

[...]nership: business arrangement in which two or more persons agree to engage, upon terms of mutual participation, in profits and losses.

[...]ty: person concerned or taking part in a transaction or proceeding.

[...] Due: payment or account that remains outstanding and unpaid after its agreed-upon payment or maturity date.

[...]: to satisfy, or make partial payments on, a debt obligation.

[...]able: obligation that is due now or in future.

[...]ables: liabilities owed to trade creditors for purchase of supplies. Also called accounts payable.

[...]ee: person or entity named on a negotiable instrument as the one to whom the obligation is due.

[...]er: party responsible for making payment as shown on check, note, or other type of negotiable instrument; also called maker or writer.

[...]ment: discharge, in whole or in part, of debt or performance of agreement.

[...]ment for Honor: payment of past-due obligation by someone else to save credit or reputation of person responsible for payment.

[...]off: receipt of payment in full on an obligation.

[...]alty: 1. legal fine, forfeiture, or payment imposed for defaulting or violating terms of contract. 2. interest charge imposed for late payments that is permissible by law and imposed with customer's prior agreement or knowledge of seller's terms of sale.

[...]centage Lease: lease of real property in which rental payments are based on percentage of retailer's sales.

[...]centage of Completion: method of accounting commonly used by contractors and developers in which costs are related to percentage of job completion.

[...]fection: with respect to security interests in personal property under Article 9 of the UCC, the action required to give the secured party rights in the collateral as against third parties with competing claims. In general, a security interest is not perfected until a properly executed financing statement has been recorded or the secured party is in the possession of the collateral, whichever applies as to that specific collateral type.

[...]formance: fulfillment of promise or agreement according to terms of contract or obligation.

[...]formance Bond: guaranty to project owner that the contractor will perform the work called for by the contract in accordance with the plans and specifications. Customarily issued by bonding and insurance companies, although financial institution letters of credit may be used.

[...]jury: willfully and knowingly giving false testimony under oath.

[...]son: individual (natural person) or incorporated enterprise (artificial person) having certain legal rights and responsibilities.

[...]sonal Check: check drawn by individual on his or her own bank account.

[...]sonality: legal term for personal property or possessions that are not real estate.

[...]sonally Liable: individual's responsibility for payment of obligation, generally used to refer to owner's or guarantor's responsibility.

[...]sonal Property: movable or chattel property of any kind.

[...]ition: written application, made in contradiction to motion. Also used in some states in place of complaint.

[...]tition in Bankruptcy: document filed in court to declare bankruptcy. Petition can be either voluntary (filed by debtor) or involuntary (filed by creditors), depending on bankruptcy chapter rules.

[...]tty Cash: cash on hand or in designated bank account that is available for small, miscellaneous purchases.

[...]ysical Inventory: inventory verification obtained by visual observation of items and itemization of quantities of goods on hand.

[...]ercing the Corporate Veil: legal action taken by creditor, when fraud or unjust enrichment may be involved, to hold principals of corporation (or other entities) liable for debts of corporation.

[...]aintiff: person or entity that initiates legal action against another.

[...]an of Arrangement: procedure in bankruptcy under Chapter 11 for debtor to restructure debts or rehabilitate by arriving at arrangement with creditors. See also Bankruptcy, Chapter 11 Cases.

[...]edge: promise of personal property as security for performance of act, payment of debt, or satisfaction of obligation.

[...]ints: 1. percentage fee charged to obtain a mortgage loan. 2. in shares of stock, one point equals $1.00.

[...]licy: 1. written statement by management that explains an organization's philosophy and approach to doing business. 2. written contract of insurance between insured and the insurance company.

[...]oling Accounts: arrangement by a debtor listing all his or her debts with a debt management or pro-rating service with the understanding that the service will receive, as its fee, a portion of debtor's payments to his or her creditors and proportionately distribute the balance of payments to each creditor on a scheduled basis. Activities of such services may be covered by individual state statutes.

[...]stdated Check: check written for payment, effective at future date.

[...]wer of Attorney: written document that authorizes one person to act as another's agent.

Preference: 1. right of a creditor to be paid before other creditors by virtue of having lien or collateral. 2. improperly paying or securing of one or more creditors, in whole or part, by an insolvent debtor to the exclusion of other creditors.

Preference Period: in bankruptcy, the 90-day period immediately preceding debtor entering into bankruptcy. If a creditor files new or additional liens against a debtor during this time, such claims may be disallowed by bankruptcy court.

Preferred Creditor: creditor whose account takes legal preference for payment over claims of others.

Prepaid Expenses: payment for goods or services not yet received.

Prepayment: payment of loan or debt before it actually becomes due.

Prime Contractor: contractor who enters into contract with the owner of the project for completion of all or portion of the project and takes full responsibility for its completion. See also *General Contractor.*

Prime Rate: an index or base rate published or publicly announced by a financial institution from time to time as the rate it is generally willing to give its most creditworthy customers.

Principal: 1. amount of money loaned or borrowed. 2. key decision maker or management of entity.

Priority: legal preferences that secured creditors have over general creditors in bankruptcy.

Priority Lien: lien recorded before other secured claims and payable ahead of other liens if liquidation of pledged collateral occurs. First mortgage has priority over second and third mortgages, known as junior liens. Secured creditor holding perfected security interest has priority over liens filed afterward.

Private Enterprise: business established to take economic risks for purpose of making profit.

Privilege: right that nature of debt gives to one debt holder over others.

Proceeds: actual amount of money given to or received from creditor after any deductions are made.

Profit: 1. amount of net income made by an entity in course of doing business. 2. increase in value of an asset over its depreciated book value at the time of sale.

Profit and Loss Statement (P & L): financial report of an individual's or entity's revenue and expenses for a given period of time. See also *Income Statement* and *Operating Statement.*

Pro Forma: projected financial statements.

Progress Payments: partial payments made on a long-term contract as it progresses. Required when a manufacturer or contractor cannot afford, or does not wish, to finance a project.

Projection: borrower's estimate of future performance over designated time period.

Promissory Note: written promise to make unconditional payment of specified amount on designated date, signed by maker.

Proof of Claim: creditor's formal document filed with court against estate of debtor if creditor is owed funds.

Proof of Loss: sworn statement filed by insured when making claim.

Property: something of value that is legally owned and in which person has exclusive and unrestricted right or interest.

Property Insurance: coverage that applies to loss caused by physical damage to property (buildings, contents, earnings, etc.) owned by insured.

Proposal: oral or written offer that, if accepted, constitutes a contract.

Proprietorship: single and exclusive ownership of a business by one person.

Pro Rata: share calculated in proportion to total amount.

Pro Rata Distribution: payment proportionate to uniform percentage of obligations to all creditors.

Protest: formal, written, notarized notice stating credit instrument has not been honored and that makers or endorsers will be held responsible for payment.

Prox.: see *Proximo.*

Proximo (Prox.): sales term used in invoices to mean next month after month of invoice. This term is sometimes used instead of EOM terms.

Proxy: written statement or power of attorney, authorizing an individual to act or speak for another.

Public Credit: debt incurred by government, federal and local, for a use that meet the needs of its citizens.

Purchase Money Lien: manufacturer's legal right to goods and products until the buyer makes payment. Under the Uniform Commercial Code, manufacturer's rights can take priority over lender's lien rights if both claim interest in same inventory. Lender may receive such priority if funds were provided to purchase asset, provided liens are filed within 20 days of borrower taking possession of collateral and noticing requirements have been met.

Purchase Money Mortgage: mortgage given by buyer to seller in lieu of cash, as partial payment on property.

Purchasing Power: value of money and its ability to buy goods and services in a given period.

Q

Qualified Acceptance: agreement to terms of contract only if certain conditions are meet. This constitutes counteroffer and rejection of original offer.

Qualified Endorsement: transfer of debt instrument to endorsee without recourse or liability to endorser.

Qualified Financial Statement: audit report issued by independent accountants that indicates restrictions on scope of audit performed, uncertainties, or disagreements with management.

Qualified Prospect: potential customer whose background and credit have been checked and approved.

Quantity Discount: price reduction extended to purchaser of a large volume of goods.

Quarterly Accounts Receivable Survey: index, compiled by Credit Research Foundation in affiliation with the National Association of Credit Management and published quarterly, that shows average days' sales outstanding for manufacturers and wholesalers.

Quick Assets: current assets that can be readily converted into cash (generally, accounts receivable).

Quick Assets Ratio: cash and cash equivalents plus trade receivables (net) divided by total current liabilities; used as measure of liquidity.

Quid Pro Quo: 1. giving of one valuable thing for another. 2. mutual consideration between parties to contract.

Quitclaim: to release or relinquish claim or title.

R

Rack Jobber: wholesale distributor who sells housewares and other convenience-type merchandise through retail stores and assumes responsibility for stocking and maintaining store's inventory.

Rate of Exchange: amount of one country's currency that can be bought with another country's currency at a particular point in time.

Rate of Interest: cost of borrowing money, usually expressed as annual percentage charge.

Rating: 1. assessment of borrower's financial strength and creditworthiness. 2. symbol used to denote borrower's creditworthiness.

Ratios: mathematical relationship between two or more things, used as indication of a company's financial strength relative to other companies of comparable size or in same industry.

Real Property: land and anything erected or growing on it or affixed to it.

Receivables: money due or collectible for goods sold, services performed, or money loaned. Also called accounts receivable.

Receivables Turnover: measurement of how effective a company is in collecting on its trade receivables.

Receiver: person appointed by the court to receive, take charge, and hold in trust a property in litigation or bankruptcy until a legal decision is made as to its disposition.

Receivership: 1. court action whereby money or property is placed under control, and administration of receiver is to be preserved for benefit of persons or creditors ultimately entitled to it. 2. procedure used to help a distressed debtor or to resolve a dispute.

Reclamation: 1. legal action by titleholder to recover property from another's possession. 2. process used to restore land to usable state.

Record: written account of act, transaction, or instrument drawn by proper legal authority that remains as permanent evidence.

Recourse: right of holder in due course to demand payment from anyone who endorsed instrument if original signer fails to pay.

Recovery: amount finally collected; amount of judgment.

Reference Check: contacting and interviewing business or professional associates of credit applicant to gain information about his or her creditworthiness.

References: names of trade suppliers or creditors provided by a customer to be used as a source of information about that customer.

Refer to Maker: term stamped by financial institution on a check to indicate its rejection.

Refinance: to reorganize existing debts by obtaining new debt that incorporates or pays off existing debts.

Register: book of factual public information, kept by a public official.

Regulation 9: regulation issued by the Comptroller of Currency allowing national banks to operate trust departments and act as fiduciaries. Under Regulation 9, a national bank is permitted to act as trustee, administrator, and registrar of stocks and bonds and engage in related activities, such as management of a collective investment fund, as long as these activities do not violate state legislation.

Regulation A: Federal Reserve Board regulation governing advances by Federal Reserve Banks to depository institutions at a Federal Reserve discount window. Credit advances are available to any bank or savings institution maintaining transaction accounts or non-personal time deposits. The Fed has two different programs for handling discount window borrowings:

- adjustment credit to meet temporary needs for funds when other sources not available.
- extended credit, designed to assist financial institutions with longer-t needs for funds. This includes seasonal credit privileges extended to sma financial institutions that do not have ready access to money market fu Federal Reserve Banks may also extend emergency credit to financial ins tions other than depository institutions in which failure to obtain cr would affect the economy adversely.

Regulation B: Federal Reserve regulation prohibiting discrimination against c sumer credit applicants and establishing guidelines for collecting and eval ing credit information. Regulation B prohibits creditors from discrimina on the basis of age, sex, race, color, religion, national origin, marital status receipt of public assistance. Regulation B also requires creditors to give v ten notification of rejection, statement of applicant's rights under Equal Cr Opportunity Act of 1974, and statement listing reasons for rejection, or ap cant has right to request reasons. If applicant is denied credit because adverse information in credit bureau report, applicant is entitled to rec copy of bureau report at no cost. Creditors who furnish credit informa when reporting information on married borrowers must report informatio name of each spouse.

Regulation C: Federal Reserve regulation implementing Home Mortgage Dis sure Act of 1975, requiring depository institutions to make annual disclos of location of certain residential loans to determine whether depository in tutions are meeting credit needs of their local communities. Specific exempted are institutions with assets of $10 million or less. Regulatio requires lenders of mortgages that are insured or guaranteed by a fed agency to disclose number and total dollar amount of mortgage loans or nated or purchased in recent calendar year, itemized by census tract wh property is located.

Regulation D: Federal Reserve regulation that sets uniform reserve requireme for depository financial institutions holding transaction accounts or non-p sonal time deposits. Reserves are maintained in form of vault cash or n interest-bearing balance at a Federal Reserve Bank or at a correspond bank.

Regulation E: Federal Reserve regulation that sets rules, liabilities, and pro dures for electronic funds transfers (EFT) and establishes consumer prot tions using EFT systems. This regulation prescribes rules for solicitation a issuance of EFT debit cards, governs consumer liability for unauthori transfers, and requires financial institutions to disclose annually terms a conditions of EFT services.

Regulation F: Federal Reserve regulation requiring state-chartered banks w 500 or more stockholders and at least $1 million in assets to file finan statements with the Board of Governors of the Federal Reserve System. general, these state-chartered member banks must file registration sta ments, periodic financial statements, proxy statements, and various other d closures of interest to investors. These regulations are substantially similar those issued by Securities and Exchange Commission.

Regulation G: Federal Reserve regulation governing credit secured by mar securities extended or arranged by parties other than banks or broker/deale It requires lenders to register credit extensions of $200,000, secured by m gin stock, or $500,000 in total credit, within 30 days after end of quarter.

Regulation H: Federal Reserve regulation defining membership requirements state-chartered banks that become members of the Federal Reserve Syste The regulation sets forth procedures as well as privileges and requireme for membership. The regulation also requires state-chartered banks acting securities transfer agents to register with board.

Regulation I: Federal Reserve regulation requiring each member bank joining t Federal Reserve System to purchase stock in its Federal Reserve Bank eq to 6% of its capital and surplus. Federal Reserve Bank stock, which pa interest semiannually, is nontransferable and cannot be used as collate When bank increases or decreases its capital base, it must adjust its own ship of Federal Reserve stock accordingly.

Regulation J: Federal Reserve regulation providing legal framework for collecti of checks and other cash items and net settlement of balances through Fe eral Reserve System. It specifies terms and conditions under which Fede Reserve Banks will receive checks for collection from depository institutio presentment to paying banks, and return of unpaid items. It is supplement by operating circulars issued by Federal Reserve Banks.

Regulation K: Federal Reserve regulation governing international banking ope tions by bank holding companies and foreign banks in the U.S. The regulati permits Edge Act corporations to engage in range of international banking a financial activities. It also permits U.S. banks to own up to 100% of no financial companies located outside the U.S. Regulation K also impos reserve requirements on Edge Act corporations, as specified in Regulation and limits interstate activities of foreign banks in the U.S.

Regulation L: Federal Reserve regulation prohibiting interlocking direct arrangements in member banks or bank holding companies. Manageme official of state member bank or bank holding company may not act simult neously as management official of another depository institution if both are not affiliated, are very large banks, or are located in same local area. Regulation L provides 10-year grandfather period for certain interlocks and allows some on exception basis, such as organizations owned by women or minority groups, newly chartered organizations, and in situations in which implementing regulation would endanger safety and soundness.

gulation M: Federal Reserve regulation implementing consumer leasing provisions of Truth in Lending Act of 1968. It covers leases on personal property for more than four months for family, personal, or household use. It requires leasing companies to disclose in writing the cost of lease, including security deposit and monthly payments, taxes, and other payments, and in case of an open-end lease, whether a balloon payment may be applied. It also requires written disclosure of terms of lease, including insurance, guaranties, responsibility for servicing property, and whether lessor has an option to buy property at lease termination.

gulation N: Federal Reserve regulation governing transactions among Federal Reserve Banks and transactions involving Federal Reserve Banks and foreign banks and governments. This regulation gives the board responsibility for approving in advance negotiations or agreements by Federal Reserve Banks and foreign banks, bankers, and governments. The Federal Reserve Bank may, under direction of the Federal Open Market Committee, undertake negotiations, agreements, or facilitate open market transactions. Reserve Banks must report quarterly to the Board of Governors on accounts they maintain with foreign banks.

gulation O: Federal Reserve regulation limiting amount of credit member banks may extend to their own executive officers. Regulation O also implements reporting requirements of Financial Institutions Regulatory and Interest Rate Control Act of 1978 and Garn-St. Germain Depository Institutions Act of 1982.

gulation P: Federal Reserve regulation that sets minimum standards for security devices, such as bank vaults and currency handling equipment, including automated teller machines. Member bank must appoint security officer to develop and administer program to deter thefts and file the annual compliance statement with its Federal Reserve Bank.

gulation Q: Federal Reserve regulation requiring depository institutions to state clearly terms for depositing and renewing time deposits and certificates of deposit and also any penalties for early withdrawal of savings accounts.

gulation R: Federal Reserve regulation prohibiting individuals who are engaged in securities underwriting, sale, and distribution from serving as directors, officers, or employees of member banks. Regulation R specifically exempts those involved in government securities trading and general obligations of states and municipalities.

gulation S: Federal Reserve regulation implementing section of Right to Financial Privacy Act of 1978 requiring government authorities to pay reasonable fees to financial institutions for financial records of individuals and small partnerships available to federal agencies in connection with government loan programs or Internal Revenue Service summons.

gulation T: Federal Reserve regulation governing credit extensions by securities brokers and dealers, including all members of national securities exchanges. Brokers/dealers may not extend credit to their customers unless such loans are secured by margin securities—securities listed and traded on national securities exchange, mutual funds, and over-the-counter stock designated by Securities and Exchange Commission as eligible for trading in national market system. Generally, brokers/dealers may not extend credit on margin securities in excess of percentage of current market value permitted by board.

egulation U: Federal Reserve regulation governing extensions of credit by banks for purchasing and carrying margin securities. Whenever lender makes loan secured by margin securities, bank must have customer execute purpose statement regardless of use of loan.

egulation V: Federal Reserve regulation dealing with financing of contractors, subcontractors, and others involved in national defense work. The regulation spells out the authority granted to Federal Reserve Banks under the Defense Production Act of 1950 to assist federal departments and agencies in making and administering loan guaranties to defense-related contractors and sets maximum interest rates, guaranty fees, and commitment fees.

egulation X: Federal Reserve regulation extending provisions of other securities-related regulations—Regulations G, T, and U—to foreign persons or organizations who obtain credit outside U.S. for purchase of U.S. Treasury securities.

egulation Y: Federal Reserve regulation governing banking and nonbanking activities of bank holding companies and divestiture of impermissible nonbank activities. Regulation Y spells out procedures for forming bank holding company and procedures to be followed by bank holding companies acquiring voting shares in bank or nonbank companies. Regulation Y also lists those nonbank activities that are deemed closely related to banking and therefore permissible for bank holding companies.

Regulation Z: Federal Reserve regulation implementing consumer credit protections in the Truth in Lending Act of 1968. Major areas of regulation require lenders to:

- give borrowers written disclosure on essential credit terms, including cost of credit expressed as finance charge and annual percentage rate.
- respond to consumer complaints of billing errors on certain credit accounts within specified period.
- identify credit transactions on periodic statements of open-end credit accounts.
- provide certain rights regarding credit cards.
- inform customers of right of rescission in certain mortgage-related loans within specified period.
- comply with special requirements when advertising credit.

Regulation AA: Federal Reserve regulation establishing procedures for handling consumer complaints about alleged unfair or deceptive practices by a state member bank.

Regulation BB: Federal Reserve regulation implementing Community Reinvestment Act of 1977 (CRA). Banks are required to make available to public a statement indicating communities served, type of credit the lender is prepared to extend, and public comments to its CRA statement.

Regulation CC: Federal Reserve regulation implementing Expedited Funds Availability Act of 1987, setting endorsement standards on checks collected by depository financial institutions. Endorsement standard is designed to facilitate identification of endorsing bank and prompt return of unpaid checks. The regulation specifies funds availability schedules that banks must comply with and procedures for returning dishonored checks.

Release: to discharge debt or give up claim against party from whom it is due by party to whom it is due.

Remedy: legal means by which right is enforced or violation of right is prevented or compensated.

Rent: periodic payments made by tenant to owner in return for leasing land, building space, or equipment.

Reorganization: 1. voluntary or court-ordered change in capital structure of corporation in which all assets of an old corporation are transferred to a newly formed corporation. 2. restructuring of business entity, whether in or out of bankruptcy.

Replevin: legal action taken to recover possession of property unlawfully taken.

Repossess: action taken by creditor in which he or she takes possession of goods purchased under credit agreement or pledged as collateral if debtor defaults on terms of contract.

Rescind: to void contract from its inception. Result is that parties are restored to relative positions before contract was made.

Rescission: agreement by parties to contract that effects cancellation of contract.

Reserve: in accounting, funds set aside for specific purpose.

Reserve for Bad Debts: valuation account established for accounts receivable that may prove uncollectible.

Residence: place where person legally lives part or full time.

Residual Value: the estimated recoverable amount of a depreciable asset as of the time of its removal from service.

Resolution Trust Corporation (RTC): federal agency established in 1989 to oversee the savings and loan bailout.

Restraint of Trade: any action, by agreement or by combination, that tends to eliminate competition, artificially sets up prices, or results in monopoly.

Restrictive Endorsement: endorsement on negotiable instrument that limits any further negotiability, for example, "for deposit only" written on back of check.

Restructured Loan: loan on which a bank, for economic or legal reasons related to debtor's financial difficulties, grants concession to debtor that would not be considered otherwise.

Retailer: company that sells its product directly to end-user.

Retained Earnings: cumulative earnings and losses of company that remain undistributed to shareholders.

Retentions: amounts withheld by customer from total billings until contractor has satisfactorily completed project.

Retroactive: 1. effective as of past date. 2. having reference to prior time.

Return: rate of profit or earnings on sales or investment.

Return Items/Returned Checks: checks, drafts, or notes returned unpaid to originating bank by drawee bank so that originator can correct any errors or irregularities and may present items for collection again.

Revenue: 1. income from sales, interest, or dividends. 2. income from investment or wages.

Reviewed Financial Statements: business financial statements that are reviewed by independent accountants through inquiries of management and performance of analytical procedures on financials to provide limited assurance that no material modifications are necessary for statements to conform to generally accepted accounting principles. Independent accountants do not express opinion on review statements.

Revolving Charge: credit type that allows borrower to become indebted up to an approved credit limit, with no fixed maturity date. Finance costs are assessed monthly on unpaid balance, and periodic payments are required.

Revolving Credit: commitment under which funds can be borrowed, repaid, and re-borrowed during life of credit. Such credits have stated maturity date at which time borrower may have option of converting outstanding balance into term loan. See also Evergreen Revolving Credit.

Rider: any schedule or amendment attached to a contract or document that becomes part of it.

Right of Rescission: consumer's right as prescribed by Truth in Lending Act of 1968 to rescind certain credit and mortgage contracts within three days without penalty.

Right of Setoff: right of financial institution to apply borrower's funds on deposit to debt owed to the financial institution in event that payment on the debt is not made as agreed.

Risk-Based Capital: level of capital that bank is required to maintain; level is determined by relating capital to risk by type of asset.

RMA: see *Risk Management Association.*

RMA General Figure Ranges: dollar amount ranges established by RMA to ensure accuracy and consistency when exchanging credit information. There are four ranges: low, 1-1.9; moderate, 2-3.9; medium, 4-6.9; and high, 7-9.9. Ranges can be applied to any figure category. Sample figure categories are: nominal = under $100; 3 figures = from $100 to $999; 4 figures = from $1,000 to $9,999; 5 figures = from $10,000 to $99,999;and 6 figures = from $100,000 to $999,999. Information is reported, using both range description and figure category; for example, "average balances are in medium 4-figure range."

Risk Management Association (RMA): association of lending, credit, and risk management professionals. Originally, RMA was founded to facilitate the exchange of credit information. Today, RMA works continuously to improve practices of the financial services industry and to provide members with networking opportunities, training, research publications, and seminars.

Robinson-Patman Act: federal legislation prohibiting firms engaged in interstate commerce from charging different buyers different prices for the same goods unless there is difference in costs or the price does not restrict competition.

R.O.G. Dating: payment term that uses date customer is in receipt of goods as effective sale date.

Royalty: compensation made to another for use of his or her work.

RTC: see *Resolution Trust Corporation.*

Rule of 72: method commonly used to approximate time required for sum of money to double at given rate of interest. Rule of 72 is computed by dividing interest rate by 72.

Rule of 78s: mathematical formula used in computing interest rebated when borrower pays off loan before maturity. Rule of 78s is applied mostly to consumer loans in which finance charges were computed using add-on interest or discounted interest method of interest calculation. Also called sum of digits method.

S

Sale: agreement or contract that transfers title of goods or property from one person or entity to another for consideration.

Sale and Lease Back: arrangement whereby company sells goods with intent to lease those same goods from buyer.

Sale on Approval: purchase of goods conditioned on buyer approval of goods or retention of them beyond reasonable time.

Salvage Value: estimated worth of a depreciated asset at the end of its useful life.

Satisfaction: paying debt in full.

Satisfaction of Judgment: legal evidence that recorded judgment has been paid or settled and entered in court records.

Satisfaction Piece: legal evidence that debt has been paid in full or settled and that liens on collateral have been released.

SBA: see *Small Business Administration.*

Schedule: listing by account name or number of total sales, current sales, monies owing or paid, chargebacks, or credits. Also called aging schedule or trial balance.

Scheduled Liability: 1. in property insurance, listing of property—items or locations—covered. 2. in dishonesty insurance (fidelity bonding), listing of persons or positions covered.

Scheduled Payment: partial payments made at dates specified in credit agreement.

Schedules: in bankruptcy, lists showing debtor's property—location, quantity, and money value; names and addresses of creditors and their class; or names and addresses of stockholders of each class.

Scrap Value: worth of asset that is going to be destroyed or used for its components.

Seasonal Loans: loans used to finance cyclical buildup of current (working capital) assets until those assets can be converted to cash.

Second Lien: lien that can be honored only after first lien is satisfied.

Second Mortgage: mortgage secured by equity in property but one that can enforce payment until claims of first mortgage are satisfied.

Secret Partner: partner in business whose interest in partnership is not pub known.

Secured Creditor: lender or other person whose claim is supported by taking lateral.

Secured Loan: loan supported by borrower's pledge of an asset such as m ketable securities, accounts receivable, inventories, real estate, equipme etc.

Secured Note: note that provides, upon default, certain pledged or mortga property that may be applied or sold in payment of debt.

Secured Party: 1. lender or other person to whom or in whose favor secu interest has been given. Includes person to whom accounts or chattel pa have been sold. 2. trustee or agent representing holders of obligations iss under indenture of trust, equipment trust agreement, or the like.

Securities: 1. documents that evidence debt or property pledged in fulfillment obligation. 2. evidence of indebtedness or right to participate in earnings a distribution of corporate, trust, and other property.

Security: guaranty or assets pledged that can be applied to loan or obligation.

Security Agreement: formally executed document that gives lender rights property pledged by borrower in support of debt.

Security Interest: right that lender or lienholder obtains to debtor's goods as e denced by security agreement.

Seller's Market: economic condition in which demand is greater than supply, a that typically causes prices to increase.

Sequestered Account: account that has been attached by court order with c bursements subject to court approval.

Service Business: firm that performs functions for its customers rather than s goods.

Setoff: 1. defendant's counterdemand against plaintiff. 2. right of parties to c tract to reduce debt owed to one party by netting it against amount owed other. See also *Right of Setoff.*

Settle: 1. to mutually reach agreement for adjustment or liquidation of debt. 2. negotiate payment of obligation or lawsuit for less than amount claimed.

Settlement: 1. adjustment or liquidation of accounts. 2. full and final payment debt. See also *Out-of-Court Settlement.*

Shared National Credit (SNC): any loan originally $20 million or more that shared at its inception by two or more financial institutions under a forr intercreditor or participation agreement or sold in part to one or more fina cial institutions with purchasing financial institution assuming its pro r share of credit risk.

Shareholder: person or entity that legally owns stock in a corporation.

Sheriff's Sale: court-ordered sale of property to satisfy judgment, mortgage, li or other outstanding debt against debtor.

Sherman Antitrust Act: federal legislation aimed at prevention of busine monopoly; act declares illegal every contract, combination, or conspiracy restraint of normal trade.

Short-Term Liabilities: current debts that are due within one year.

Short-Term Loan: current debt obligation that matures within one year, evidenc by promissory note that spells out terms of agreement.

SIC: see *Standard Industrial Classification.*

Sight Draft: draft payable on demand when presented to drawee. See also *Dr Letter of Credit,* and *Time Draft.*

Signal Action: notices that provide subscriber with list of accounts in which su scriber has interest and on which delinquent payments have been reported.

Signature Loan: unsecured loan backed only by borrower's signature on prom sory note. No collateral is taken by lender. This loan is generally offered individuals with good credit standing. Also called good faith loan or charac loan.

Signature Verification: examination of signature on negotiable instrument determine whether handwriting is genuine and whether person signing che is authorized to use account.

Simple Interest: interest calculated on outstanding principal amount of debt investment only.

Single Proprietorship: ownership of company by one person.

Skip Tracing: process used to obtain information to locate debtor's whereabou in order to collect payment on debts. Sources used include other credito friends, relatives, neighbors, directories, credit bureaus, court records, a other informants or references.

Slander: oral defamation of another's reputation.

Small Business Administration (SBA): federal agency whose function is advise and assist small businesses; provides loan guaranties for small bu nesses, minorities, and veterans plus financial assistance to small business that have suffered catastrophes.

SNC: see *Shared National Credit.*

Soft Goods: nondurable consumer goods such as clothing and linen, having short-term useful life.

ldier's and Sailor's Relief Act: federal act, also passed by various states, under which right to legally enforce an obligation against a person is suspended during the period that person is in military service or for period thereafter.

le Owner: one with title to proprietorship.

lvency: ability to pay one's debts in usual and ordinary course of business as they mature.

ecial Material: made-to-order material or work done to customer's specifications that has no value to seller if order is canceled.

ecial Mention Assets: as it relates to risk assessment of bank assets, assets that deserve management's close attention. If left uncorrected, these potential weaknesses may result in deterioration of repayment prospects for asset or in institution's credit position at some future date. Special mention assets are not adversely classified and do not expose institution to sufficient risk to warrant adverse classification.

ecific Coverage: property coverage on designated property or item. Contrasts with Blanket Coverage.

ecific Performance: court order directing party guilty of breach of contract to undertake complete performance of contractual obligation in instances in which damages would inadequately compensate injured party.

eculation: investment made with hope of achieving large financial gain.

eculator: one who makes risky investments for quick financial gain rather than long-term investment.

ale Check: negotiable draft that has been held too long to be honored for payment; time varies from state to state.

andard Industrial Classification (SIC): statistical classification standard underlying all establishment-based federal economic statistics classified by industry. SIC is used to promote comparability of establishment data describing various facets of the U.S. economy. Classification covers entire field of economic activities and defines industries in accordance with composition and structure of economy. It is revised periodically to reflect economy's changing industrial organization. See also *North American Industrial Classification System* and *NAICS*.

andby Letter of Credit: type of letter of credit issued by bank that may be drawn on by payee only if party that makes letter of credit (drawer) defaults or does not perform according to terms of specific contract or agreement. See also Letter of Credit.

atement: 1. itemized summary and accounting of charges, payments, and balance outstanding at close of billing period. 2. financial report.

atement of Cash Flows: financial statement that shows cash receipts and disbursements for given period.

atement of Changes in Owner's Equity: financial statement that reconciles changes in capital accounts (capital stock, paid in surplus, and retained earnings).

atute: written law.

atute of Frauds: law prohibiting filing of actions or suits against certain types of contracts unless the contracts are in writing.

atute of Limitations: law that sets time frame for bringing action against another. Time frame varies according to nature of claim and jurisdiction.

ay: act of arresting judicial proceeding by court order.

ipulation: agreement between opposing attorneys in lawsuit, usually required to be in writing.

ock: 1. merchandise or inventory on hand and available for sale. 2. certificate that indicates number of shares of ownership in corporation.

ock Power: document executed in form of power of attorney by which owner of stock authorizes another party to sell or transfer stock.

op Payment Order: instructions given by depositor to a financial institution to dishonor, or not make payment on, a certain check.

bchapter S: business concern chartered as corporation that is taxed as partnership. An S corporation has 35 or fewer shareholders and can use cash basis of accounting. Corporate gains (or losses) from operations are taxed to shareholders as individuals.

bcontract: contract between prime contractor and another contractor or supplier to perform specified work or to supply specified materials in accordance with plans and specifications for project.

bject: party on which credit information is requested.

blimit: specified, partial amount of credit facility that is designated for special use.

bordination: 1. signed agreement acknowledging that one's claim or interest is inferior to another's. 2. act of agreeing to take secondary position.

bpoena: process to demand person to appear in court and give testimony.

brogation: substitution of one creditor for another so that substituted creditor succeeds to rights, remedies, or proceeds of claim.

bsidiary: business entity owned or controlled by another organization.

bstandard Assets: as it relates to risk assessment of bank assets, assets that are inadequately protected by current sound worth and paying capacity of obligor or of collateral pledged, if any. Assets so classified must have well-defined weakness or weaknesses that jeopardize liquidation of debt. They are characterized by distinct possibility that bank will sustain some loss if deficiencies are not corrected.

Summons: formal notice served on defendant stating that action has been instituted against him or her and requiring defendant to appear in court to answer it.

Supplementary Proceedings: statutory action requiring judgment debtor to appear in court to discover property against which action can be taken by creditor to enforce collection of judgment.

Supplier: business that sells goods, materials, or services to customers. Also called vendor.

Surety: one who agrees to be primarily liable with another and to fulfill another's obligations under terms of agreement.

Surety Bond: guaranty that payment or performance of some specific act will be completed under penalty or forfeiture of bond usually issued by a bonding company.

Suretyship: undertaking by person or entity to pay obligation of obligee in favor of principal when obligee defaults; such undertaking by individual is known as personal suretyship and by insurance company as corporate suretyship.

Suspense File: group of accounts, records, or other items held temporarily until final disposition is determined.

Swap: A financial derivative contract between two parties to exchange fixed-rate interest payments for floating-rate interest payments, or floating-rate interest payments on different bases (e.g., prime rate versus LIBOR), calculated on specific floating indices by reference to a notional principal amount for a specified term.

Sweep Account: type of cash management tool in which, when prearranged amount of cash accumulates in account, amount is automatically invested.

Swindle: 1. to obtain money or property by deceitful misrepresentation. 2. to cheat or fraudulently induce individual to give up his or her property willingly.

Swing Loan: see *Bridge Loan*.

Syndicate: temporary association of persons or firms formed to carry out business venture or project of mutual interest.

Syndication: project financing whereby commercial or investment bankers agree to advance portion of funding. Syndicator acts as investment manager, collecting loan origination fee or commitment fee from borrower and arranging for sale to other banks in group. Typically, syndicator keeps only a small portion of total financing. A syndicated loan differs from loan participation because syndicate members are known at outset to borrower. Syndication also separates lead bank from group of financial institutions that ultimately fund obligation.

T

Takeover: acquisition, seizure, control, or management of one business by another.

Tangible Assets: assets that can be weighed, measured, or counted, including cash, property, machinery, and buildings.

Tax: payments imposed by legislative authority for support of government and its functions.

Taxable Income: portion of individual's or entity's income that is subject to taxation.

Tax Avoidance: act of using legal deductions, exemptions, and tax code provisions to reduce taxes payable.

Tax Evasion: failure to report taxable income to avoid proper payment of taxes.

Tax Foreclosure: legal seizure and sale of property by authorized public official to satisfy unpaid taxes.

Tax Levy: legislative action by which tax is imposed.

Tax Lien: statutory claim by state or municipality against property of person owing taxes. Property may be sold to satisfy obligation or judgment filed against it.

Tax Sale: sale of property seized by governmental taxing body for nonpayment of taxes.

Tenancy by Entirety: ownership in property by husband and wife in which each becomes whole owner of the entire estate upon the other's death. See also Joint Tenancy with Rights of Survivorship.

Tenancy in Common: two or more persons who hold title to land or other property in undivided ownership.

Tender: 1. unconditional offer of money or performance to satisfy claim. 2. offer to buy stock to take control of company.

Term Loan: fixed-term business loan with a maturity of more than one year and with defined periodic payments, providing borrower with working capital to acquire assets or inventory or to finance plant and equipment.

Terms: conditions and requirements as set forth in sales proposal, contract, or promissory note.

Terms of Sale: mutually agreed upon conditions for transfer of title or ownership of goods or property.

Testimony: written or oral evidence given in court under oath.

Third Party: one who is not directly related to action between two parties but who may be affected by its outcome.

Third-Party Claim: demand made by person who is not party to action for delivery or possession of personal property, title to which is claimed by third party.

Time Deposit: 1. interest-bearing funds deposited in a financial institution for a specified period of time, such as certificates of deposit and savings accounts. 2. under Regulation D, deposit in which depositor is not permitted to make withdrawals within six days after date of deposit unless deposit is subject to early withdrawal penalty.

Time Draft: draft payable on fixed date or certain number of days after sight or date of draft. See also *Banker's Acceptance, Draft, Letter of Credit,* and *Sight Draft.*

Title: document that evidences legal ownership and possession of property.

Title Company: business that as contracted researches specific property's history through real estate records and issues policy to purchaser or lienholder guaranteeing that there are no known defects in title.

Title Insurance: a guarantee by a title insurance company that it will indemnify the insured, in a specific amount, against losses resulting from defects in the title to a property. The insured may be the owner of the property, that person's heirs and devises, or the lender and future assignees.

Title Search: to review history of property's ownership and any judgments or liens filed against it.

Tolling the Statute: act of debtor to freeze statute of limitations that extends period for creditor to legally enforce payment of account. Individual state laws and statutes apply.

Tort: violation of legal duty that results in injury or damage to another.

Trade Acceptance: draft, accepted by buyer, sent with shipment of goods, requiring customer to pay amount involved at specific date and place.

Trade Credit: accounts payable; credit extended from one company to another.

Trade Debts: liabilities due from one business to another for purchase of supplies, inventory, etc.

Trade-in: property accepted by seller as partial down payment on purchase of new item.

Trade Information: confidential exchange of payment history and credit information among suppliers.

Trademark: distinctive identifying mark, word, or logo of product or service; protected when registered with U.S. Patent Office.

Trade Name: name used by a company to identify itself in the course of business. Also known as Trade Style or Fictitious Name.

Trade Payment Record: summary of performance of company in meeting terms of its credit obligations.

Trade References: names of suppliers or business creditors with whom credit information on customer can be exchanged.

Treasury Workstation: microcomputer-based information management system that allows corporate treasurer to automate daily balance reporting of collected balances, to invest idle funds in short-term money market, and to disburse funds to trade creditors. Overall aim is improvement in productivity and eventual integration of funds management and corporate accounting systems, such as order entry and invoicing.

Trial Balance: listing of all account balances from general ledger used in preparing financial statements.

Truck Jobber: wholesale merchant who sells and delivers products from truck inventory at time of sale. Also called *Wagon Distributor.*

Trust: right to real or personal property that is held by one for benefit of another.

Trust Company: business that acts as fiduciary and agent, handling trusts, estates, and guardianships for individuals and businesses.

Trustee: one who holds or is entrusted with management of property or funds for benefit of another.

Trustee in Bankruptcy: person appointed by court or elected by creditors to manage bankrupt property and carry out responsibilities of trust in proceedings.

Trust Receipt: trust agreement (in receipt form) between a financial institution and borrower. It is temporarily substituted for possessory collateral securing creditor's loan so that creditor may release instruments, documents, or other property without releasing title to property. Borrower agrees to keep property (collateral), as well as any funds received from its sale, separate and distinct from borrower's own property and subject to repossession by the financial institution in event that he or she fails to comply with conditions specified in trust agreement.

Truth in Lending Act of 1968: See *Regulation Z.*

Turnkey: something that is constructed, supplied, or installed and fully ready as intended.

U

UCC: see *Uniform Commercial Code.*

Ultra Vires: unauthorized acts taken by corporation beyond powers conferred on it by corporate charter.

Umbrella Policy: in liability insurance, policy that applies excess coverage to p mary or underlying contract; provides large limits and broad coverage or n cover only primary basis risks not otherwise insured.

Unaudited Financial Statement: financial statement or report based on figu that have not been verified by a qualified accountant.

Uncollected Funds: deposits not yet collected by a financial institution, such checks that have not yet cleared.

Uncollectible Accounts: receivables or debts not capable of being settled recovered.

Underwriter: 1. person who reviews application for insurance and deci whether or not to accept risk. 2. one who agrees to purchase entire issue bonds or securities at end of certain period.

Undue Influence: improper or illegal pressure used to wrongfully take advant of person or to influence his or her actions or decisions.

Unearned Discount: A term used to reflect a reduced price (from the face value an invoice) taken by a buyer without the consent of the seller.

Unearned Income: income received in advance of being earned.

Unencumbered Property: property that has no legal defects in its title; a prope free and clear of any liens or debts.

Unenforceable Claim: debt on which all collection efforts have failed.

Unfair Competition: any fraudulent or dishonest practice intended to harm unfairly attract competitor's customers.

Uniform Commercial Code (UCC): comprehensive set of statutes created to p vide uniformity in business laws in all states, as approved by National Con ence of Commissioners on Uniform State Laws. Statutes can vary from st to state.

Unit Banking: banking system in several states that prohibits branching or ope tion of more than one full-service banking office by state-chartered or natio banks. Limited branching laws encourage chartering of large numbers small, independently owned state banks and large multi-bank holding com nies that own numerous unit banks.

Unjust Enrichment: doctrine whereby one is not allowed to profit inequitably another's expense.

Unsatisfied Judgment: recorded judgment that has not been released or d charged.

Unsecured Creditor: one who grants credit without taking collateral in support it.

Unsecured Loan: loan made on strength of borrower's general financial con tion. Contrasts with Secured Loan.

Upstream Funding: funds borrowed by a subsidiary of a holding company holding company's use. Contrasts with Downstream Funding.

Usury: The rate of interest that exceeds the legal limit allowed to be charged the use of another's money. Legal limit of interest for different types of lo transactions is established by state law.

V

Valuable Consideration: see *Consideration.*

Valuation: 1. the estimated or determined worth of something. 2. process appraising or affixing value of something.

Value Received: phrase used in bill of exchange or promissory note to den that lawful consideration has been given.

Variable Interest Rate: interest rate that fluctuates with changes in an identif base rate or index.

Vendor: trade supplier or service provider.

Venture Capital: capital invested or available for investment in the ownership e ment of a new enterprise.

Verdict: formal decision of judge or jury on matter submitted in trial.

Verification: 1. affidavit or statement under oath swearing to truth or accuracy written document. 2. in accounting, confirmation of entries in books account.

Verification of Deposit (VOD): formal request by creditor to debtor's bank account balance information.

Vest: 1. to give immediate transfer of title to property. 2. to obtain absolute ow ership.

VOD: see *Verification of Deposit.*

Void: having no legal force.

Voidable Contract: contract that is nullified as to party who committed invalid a but not with respect to other party, unless he or she agrees to treat it as suc

Voluntary Bankruptcy: bankruptcy initiated by debtor petitioning court to declared bankrupt.

Voucher: 1. statement itemizing payment or receipt of money. 2. detachable p tion of check that describes purpose for which check was issued.

W

Wage Assignment: agreement by borrower that permits creditor to collect cert portion of borrower's wages from employer in the event of a default.

Wage Garnishment: court order requiring that percentage of debtor's earnings be withheld by employer and paid directly to creditor.

Waiver: intentional or voluntary relinquishing of known legal right.

Warehouse Loans: loans made against warehouse receipts that are evidence of collateral for material stored in public warehouse.

Warehouse Receipt: receipt issued by person engaged in business of storing goods for hire. It is document of title that gives evidence that person in possession of warehouse receipt is entitled to receive, hold, and dispose of document and goods it covers. Warehouse receipt in turn obligates warehouser to keep goods safely and to redeliver them upon surrender of receipt, properly endorsed, and payment of storage charges.

Wholesaler: company whose primary function is as intermediary between manufacturer of goods and retailer or other wholesalers.

Will: legal declaration by person making disposition of property, effective only after death.

Windfall Profit: large, unexpected return or income.

Wire Fate: instructions to financial institution requesting confirmation by wire that out-of-town check, sent for collection, has been paid.

Without Exception: see *Free and Clear.*

Without Prejudice: legal term used in offer, motion, or suit to indicate that parties' rights or privileges involved remain intact and to allow new suit to be brought on same cause of action.

Without Recourse: term used in endorsing negotiable instrument excluding endorser from responsibility should obligation not be paid.

With Prejudice: legal term used for dismissal of lawsuit that bars any future action and that, if prosecuted to final adjudication, would have been adverse to plaintiff.

With Recourse: endorsement of negotiable instrument on which endorser remains responsible should obligation not be paid.

Working Capital: 1. current assets less current liabilities, used as measure of firm's liquidity. 2. funds available to finance company's current operations.

Working Papers: information or schedules used by accountant in preparing financial reports.

Work in Process (WIP): goods in act of being manufactured, but not yet finished and ready for sale, representing a portion of inventory.

Workout: problem loan on which the financial institution is working closely with borrower for repayment, restructuring, or modification because of noncompliance with loan covenants.

Wrap-Around Mortgage: A second or junior mortgage with a face value of both the amount it secures and the balance due under the first mortgage. Covenant contained within second mortgage used to induce sellers of commercial properties to sell to buyer who has small down payment, normally when interest rates are high.

Writ of Execution: 1. writ issued by court ordering sheriff to attach debtor's property to enforce payment of judgment.

Write-down: partial reduction in book value of asset as result of obsolescence or depreciation.

Write-off: see *Charge-off.*

Writ of Attachment: court order directing sheriff to seize property of debtor held as security for satisfaction of judgment.

Y

Yield: rate of return on investment.

Z

Zero Balance Account: a checking account (subordinate account) used for disbursing or collecting funds in which no balances are maintained. At the end of the processing day, funds are transferred from a master account or concentration account to cover activity in the subordinate account.

Zoning Ordinance: municipal regulation dividing land into districts and prescribing structural, architectural, and nature of use of buildings within these districts.

NOTES

NOTES

NOTES

NOTES